BUN = blood urea nitrogen; ECG = electrocardiogram; PT = prothrombin time; PTT = partial thromboplastin time.

CECIL
Textbook
of Medicine

Associate Editors

Principles of Immunology and Inflammation
Diseases of Allergy and Clinical Immunology
Rheumatic Diseases

William P. Arend, MD
Scoville Professor of Medicine
Department of Medicine
Director, Rheumatology Clinical Programs
University of Colorado School of Medicine
Denver, Colorado

Hematologic Diseases
Oncology

James O. Armitage, MD
Dean, University of Nebraska College of Medicine
Joe Shapiro Professor of Internal Medicine
University of Nebraska Medical Center
Omaha, Nebraska

Respiratory Diseases
Critical Care Medicine

Jeffrey M. Drazen, MD
Professor of Medicine
Harvard Medical School
Editor-in-Chief, New England Journal of Medicine
Boston, Massachusetts

Metabolic Diseases
Nutritional Diseases
Endocrine Diseases
Women's Health
Diseases of Bone and Mineral Metabolism

Gordon N. Gill, MD
Professor of Medicine
Chair, Faculty of Basic Biomedical Sciences
University of California, San Diego
La Jolla, California

Neurology

Robert C. Griggs, MD
Chair, Department of Neurology
Professor of Neurology, Medicine, Pathology and
*   Laboratory Medicine, and Pediatrics*
Edward A. and Alma Vollersten Professor in
*   Neurophysiology*
University of Rochester School of Medicine and
*   Dentistry*
Rochester, New York

Gastrointestinal Diseases
Diseases of the Liver, Gallbladder, and Bile Ducts

Don W. Powell, MD
Professor of Internal Medicine
Professor of Physiology and Biophysics
Associate Dean for Research
University of Texas Medical Branch at Galveston
Galveston, Texas

Infectious Diseases
HIV and the Acquired Immunodeficiency Syndrome

W. Michael Scheld, MD
Professor of Internal Medicine
Clinical Professor of Neurosurgery
University of Virginia Health System
Charlottesville, Virginia

CECIL
Textbook
of Medicine

22nd Edition

VOLUME 2

EDITED BY

Lee Goldman, MD

Julius R. Krevans Distinguished Professor and Chair
Department of Medicine
Associate Dean for Clinical Affairs
University of California, San Francisco, School of Medicine
San Francisco, California

Dennis Ausiello, MD

Jackson Professor of Clinical Medicine
Harvard Medical School
Chief, Medical Service
Massachusetts General Hospital
Boston, Massachusetts

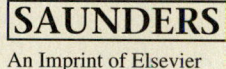
SAUNDERS
An Imprint of Elsevier

SAUNDERS
An Imprint of Elsevier

The Curtis Center
Independence Square West
Philadelphia, Pennsylvania 19106

Notice

Medicine is an ever-changing field. Standard safety precautions must be followed, but as new research
and clinical experience broaden our knowledge, changes in treatment and drug therapy become
necessary or appropriate. Readers are advised to check the product information currently provided by
the manufacturer of each drug to be administered to verify the recommended dose, the method and
duration of administration, and contraindications. It is the responsibility of the treating physician,
relying on experience and knowledge of the patient, to determine dosages and the best treatment for
each individual patient. Neither the Publisher nor the editors assume any responsibility for any injury
and/or damage to persons or property arising from this publication.

The Publisher

Library of Congress Cataloging-in-Publication Data

Cecil textbook of medicine / edited by Lee Goldman, Dennis Ausiello.—22nd ed.
    p. ; cm.
  Includes bibliographical references and index.
  ISBN 0–7216–9652–X
  1. Internal medicine.   I. Title: Textbook of medicine.   II. Cecil, Russell L. (Russell La Fayette),
1881–1965.   III. Goldman, Lee, MD.   IV. Ausiello, D. A.
  [DNLM: 1. Medicine. WB 100 C3888 2004]
RC46.C423 2004
616–dc21
                                                                2003042825

Executive Publisher, Global Medicine: Kim Murphy
Executive Director of Development: Lynne Gery
Publishing Services Manager: Frank Polizzano
Senior Project Manager: Robin E. Davis
Associate Developmental Editor: Joanie Milnes
Interior Design: Karen O'Keefe Owens

Printed in the United States of America.

Last digit is the print number: 9 8 7 6 5 4 3 2 1

Preface

The 22nd Edition of the *Cecil Textbook of Medicine* symbolizes a time of extraordinary advances in medicine and in the methods for the dissemination of information. This hardbound, published textbook and its associated electronic products incorporate the latest medical knowledge in formats that are designed to be appealing to physicians who prefer to access information in a variety of ways.

The contents of *Cecil* have remained true to the tradition of a comprehensive textbook of medicine that carefully explains the *why* (the underlying normal physiology and pathophysiology of disease, now at the cellular and molecular as well as the organ level) and the *how* (now frequently based on Grade A evidence from randomized controlled trials). Descriptions of physiology and pathophysiology include the latest genetic advances in a practical format that strives to be useful to the non-expert. Grade A evidence is now specifically highlighted in the text and referenced at the end of each chapter. The electronic version provides an immediate link to the cited reference and will be continuously updated to incorporate subsequent Grade A information.

The sections for each organ system begin with a chapter that summarizes an approach to patients with key symptoms, signs, or laboratory abnormalities associated with dysfunction of that organ system. As summarized in Table 1–1, the text specifically provides clear, concise information regarding how a physician should approach over 100 common symptoms, signs, and laboratory abnormalities, usually with a flow diagram and/or table for easy reference. In this way, *Cecil* remains a comprehensive text to guide diagnosis and therapy not only for patients with suspected or known diseases but also for patients who may have undiagnosed abnormalities that require an initial evaluation.

Perhaps the most obvious innovation of this edition is the full-color format. Color not only makes a text easier to read but also permits inclusion of hundreds of new figures, especially color photographs of patients with a wide range of physical findings.

Just as each edition brings new authors, it also reminds us of our gratitude to past editors and authors. Previous editors of the *Cecil Textbook of Medicine* include a short but remarkably distinguished group of leaders of American medicine: Russell Cecil, Paul Beeson, Walsh McDermott, James Wyngaarden, H. Lloyd Smith, Fred Plum, and J. Claude Bennett. As we welcome three new associate editors—William P. Arend, James O. Armitage, and W. Michael Scheld—we also express our appreciation to editors from the previous edition on whose foundation we have built. We specifically would like to thank Juha P. Kokko who served as consulting editor for the renal section for two editions, Gerald L. Mandell who served as consulting editor for infectious diseases for three editions, and Andrew I. Schafer who served as consulting editor for hematology and oncology for the 21st Edition. Our returning consulting editors for this edition—Jeffrey M. Drazen, Gordon N. Gill, Robert C. Griggs, and Don W. Powell—continue to make critical contributions to the selection of authors and the review of and approval of all manuscripts. The editors, however, are fully responsible for the book as well as the integration among chapters.

This edition includes new parts on Genetics, Immunology and Inflammation, and Clinical Pharmacology, as well as substantially expanded parts on Oncology and on Preventive and Environmental Medicine. Twenty-three chapters make their debuts in this edition: "Approach to the Patient: History and Physical Examination,"

"Common Clinical Sequelae of Aging," "Complementary and Alternative Medicine," "Principles of Genetics," "Single Gene and Chromosomal Disorders," "The Inherited Basis of Common Diseases," "The Innate and Adaptive Immune Systems," "Mechanisms of Immune-Mediated Tissue Injury," "Mechanisms of Inflammation and Tissue Repair," "Medical Aspects of Trauma and Burn Care," "Benign Prostatic Hyperplasia and Prostatitis," "Approach to the Patient with Jaundice or Abnormal Liver Tests," "Alcoholic and Nonalcoholic Steatohepatitis," "Hepatic Failure and Liver Transplantation," "The Peripheral Blood Smear," "Testicular Cancer," "Prostate Cancer," "Melanoma and Nonmelanoma Skin Cancers," "Chronobiology (Circadian Rhythms)," "Diagnostic Tests in Rheumatic Diseases," "Fibromyalgia," "Surgical Treatment of Joint Diseases," and "Prion Diseases." Of the other 455 chapters, 129 have new authors.

The tradition of *Cecil Textbook of Medicine* is that all chapters are written by distinguished experts in each field. We would also like to take this opportunity to thank several colleagues who assisted these individuals on specific chapters: Shao-Lee Lin ("Mechanisms of Inflammation and Tissue Repair"), Roy Kwak ("Applications and Limitation of Diagnostic Imaging"), Jacqueline M. Moline ("Principles of Occupational and Environmental Medicine"), George Juang ("Principles of Electrophysiology"), Michael Kilborn ("Antiarrhythmic Drugs"), James S. Zebrack ("ST-Elevation Acute Myocardial Infarction and Complications of Myocardial Infarction"), Tabo Sikaneta ("Cystic Kidney Diseases"), Jean A. Shafer ("The Peripheral Blood Smear"), Ivan Maillard ("Autoimmune and Intravascular Hemolytic Anemias"), Guillermo Garcia-Manero ("The Chronic Leukemias"), Miguel R. Arguedas ("Hepatic Tumors"), H. Shawn Hu ("Tumors of the Kidney, Bladder, Ureters, and Renal Pelvis"), Michael Ming ("Melanoma and Nonmelanoma Skin Cancers"), Timothy Quan and Insoo Kang ("Diagnostic Tests in Rheumatic Diseases"), W. Timothy Ballard ("Surgical Treatment of Joint Diseases"), Carolyn Calfee ("Infective Endocarditis"), John Ringman ("Diagnosis of Regional Cerebral Dysfunction"), Tomoko V. Nakawatase ("Alzheimer's Disease and Other Disorders of Cognition"), Andrea M. Vincent ("Amyotrophic Lateral Sclerosis and Other Motor Neuron Diseases"), and Gary Bellus and William Hahn ("Structure and Function of the Skin"). We are also most grateful for the editorial assistance in San Francisco of Vida Lynum and in Boston of Clinton Sours and Jane Newman; these individuals have shown extraordinary dedication and equanimity in managing the unending flow of manuscripts, disks, figures, and permissions. At Elsevier, Lynne Gery, Robin Davis, Karen O'Keefe Owens, and Pat Morrison have been critical to the planning and production process under the direction of Kimberly Murphy, to whom we are also most indebted. Many of the clinical photographs were supplied by Charles D. Forbes and William F. Jackson, authors of *Color Atlas and Text of Clinical Medicine*, Third Edition, published in 2003 by Elsevier Science Ltd. We thank them for graciously permitting us to include their pictures in our book. Finally, we would like to thank our families—Jill, Jeff, Daniel, and Robyn Goldman, and the Ausiello famiglia—for their understanding of the time and focus required to edit a book that attempts to sustain the tradition of our predecessors and to meet the needs of today's physician.

LEE GOLDMAN, MD
DENNIS AUSIELLO, MD

Features of the New Edition

- **Consistent internal chapter headings give quick access to the information you need.**

- **℞ Treatment boxes summarize therapeutic options.**

Respiratory Diseases

Table 89–2 • PRINCIPAL OCCUPATIONS ASSOCIATED WITH SILICON EXPOSURE

Abrasives workers	Silica flour workers
Foundry workers	Silica millers
Glass makers	Stone workers
Pottery workers	Surface mine drillers
Quarriers	Underground miners
Sandblasters	

Etiology

Crystalline silicon dioxide, the causal agent, is abundant and ubiquitous in the earth's crust and is used in a variety of industrial applications. Quartz is the most common form. Consequently, large numbers of workers, probably millions in the United States, are still exposed (Table 89–2).

Epidemiology

As for the other pneumoconioses, the risk of developing disease increases with the level and duration of exposure. Although the hazard posed by silica exposure has long been recognized and exposure standards have been promulgated, new cases continue to occur, even of acute silicosis, which has been recently reported in sandblasters, ground silica workers, and rock drillers.

Pathology

Like coal workers' pneumoconiosis, chronic silicosis occurs in a simple form and as progressive massive fibrosis. The earliest lesions are collections of dust-laden macrophages in the peribronchiolar and paraseptal or subpleural areas. The silicotic nodule has an acellular core composed of collagen surrounded by a cellular capsule with macrophages, lymphocytes, and fibroblasts. Silicotic nodules may also involve the hilar lymph nodes. Silicotic nodules coalesce to form the lesions of progressive massive fibrosis, masses of dense hyalinized connective tissue with little inflammation. Accelerated silicosis progresses rapidly to progressive massive fibrosis, whereas acute silicosis has a distinct pattern with few or no nodules and alveolar filling with proteinaceous material. Polarized light microscopy may show birefringent particles indicative of silica in the lungs of silica-exposed persons, including those with silicosis.

Clinical Manifestations

Chronic silicosis without progressive massive fibrosis is associated with little physiologic impairment. Cough and sputum production may reflect underlying bronchitis related to dust exposure or cigarette smoking. As in coal workers' pneumoconiosis, progressive massive fibrosis can be associated with significant impairment on lung function testing and clinically significant dyspnea. Both airflow obstruction and lung restriction may be present. Acute silicosis presents with rapidly progressive dyspnea. Persons with silicosis are at increased risk for mycobacterial infection (Chapter 341), and they may present with manifestations of infection such as fever and weight loss.

In chronic silicosis, the chest radiograph shows small nodules that tend to predominate in the upper lobes (Fig. 89–3). Calcification of the nodules is rare, as is so-called eggshell calcification of enlarged hilar nodes. In progressive massive fibrosis, the mass lesions are typically in the upper lobes and are often associated with compensatory hyperinflation of the lower lobes. Widespread consolidation is present on the chest radiograph in acute silicosis. Caplan's syndrome may also occur in silica-exposed workers, but it is rare.

Diagnosis

The diagnosis of chronic silicosis is made on the basis of characteristic radiographic findings and history of employment in a job associated with exposure to silica-containing dust. Before accepting a diagnosis of progressive massive fibrosis in a silica-exposed worker, other causes of lung masses should be considered, including, specifically, lung cancer and mycobacterial infection. Acute silicosis should be considered in heavily exposed individuals with a diffuse consolidating process. Unless the epidemiologic features of the case make the diagnosis of acute silicosis certain, lung biopsy may be indicated to establish the diagnosis and to exclude other diseases.

℞ Treatment

As in any chronic lung disease, supportive therapy, oxygen, and rehabilitation may be indicated. One report suggested possible short-term benefits of corticosteroid therapy, but steroid therapy cannot be recommended at present. Because of the increased risk of mycobacterial diseases, particularly *Mycobacterium tuberculosis*, all persons with silicosis should receive yearly tuberculin skin tests and evaluation for active tuberculosis if the test is positive. Isoniazid prophylaxis is recommended if the test is positive and active disease is not present. Some studies indicate that prolonged antituberculous therapy may be indicated in patients with silicosis and active tuberculosis (Chapter 341).

Prognosis

The prognosis of accelerated and acute silicosis is poor; both are associated with progressive loss of function, and acute silicosis may be rapidly fatal. Progressive massive fibrosis has a more variable course, which may also lead to progressive impairment and respiratory failure. Factors determining progression from chronic silicosis to progressive massive fibrosis are uncertain.

OTHER PNEUMOCONIOSES

Inhaling other minerals and metals may also cause pneumoconioses (see Table 89–1). Silicates other than asbestos have been linked to interstitial lung disease, including talc, kaolinite, mica, and vermiculite. Benign pneumoconioses are associated with inhaling forms of barium (baritosis) and tin (stannosis). Hard-metal disease occurs in workers exposed to cobalt in applications involving its use in alloys and abrasives. This diffuse interstitial disease, which can be associated with clinically significant impairment, should be considered in workers in foundries and in industries involving grinding of metals, gems, and other materials. Some workers exposed to man-made fibers develop small opacities, but a distinct pneumoconiosis has not yet been identified from exposure to these newer fibers. *Mixed-dust pneumoconiosis* is a nonspecific label often used for the presence of both rounded and irregular opacities on the chest radiograph of a worker with exposure to several types of dust. Typically, there is exposure to silica and to an additional mineral.

BERYLLIUM DISEASE

Beryllium disease is a granulomatous lung disease that results from inhaling beryllium, a rare metal now widely used in high-technology applications (Table 89–3). The typical cases currently observed present with gradual onset and are referred to as *chronic beryllium disease*; a more acute form was reported with past higher levels of exposure. When first recognized, the disease was found in workers who extracted and produced beryllium and in workers making fluorescent lamps containing a beryllium phosphor. Cases have been reported in bystanders not working directly with the metal and in persons

Table 89–3 • CURRENT INDUSTRIES USING BERYLLIUM

Aerospace	Nuclear reactors
Beryllium extraction, fabrication, smelting	Nuclear weapons
Ceramics	Plating
Dental alloys and prostheses	Telecommunications
Electronics	Tool and die
Foundries	

- **Clinical Manifestations boxes describe key signs and symptoms, aiding accurate diagnosis.**

- **Color-coded algorithms outline strategies for diagnosing and treating common complaints and diseases.**
  - **Blue boxes indicate diagnostic tests.**
  - **Green boxes indicate treatments.**
  - **Red boxes are used for all other steps.**

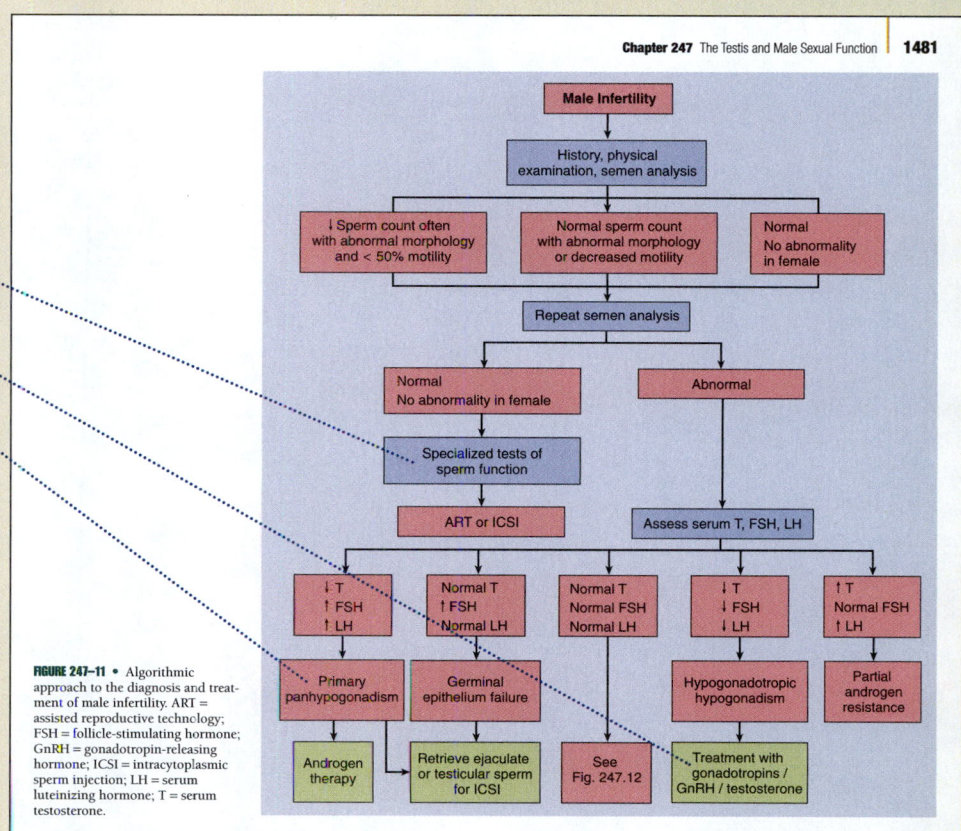

Male Infertility

History, physical examination, semen analysis

↓ Sperm count often with abnormal morphology and < 50% motility

Normal sperm count with abnormal morphology or decreased motility

Normal No abnormality in female

Repeat semen analysis

Normal No abnormality in female

Abnormal

Specialized tests of sperm function

ART or ICSI

Assess serum T, FSH, LH

↓ T ↑ FSH ↑ LH

Normal T ↑ FSH Normal LH

Normal T Normal FSH Normal LH

↓ T ↓ FSH ↓ LH

↑ T Normal FSH ↑ LH

Primary panhypogonadism

Germinal epithelium failure

Hypogonadotropic hypogonadism

Partial androgen resistance

Androgen therapy

Retrieve ejaculate or testicular sperm for ICSI

See Fig. 247.12

Treatment with gonadotropins / GnRH / testosterone

FIGURE 247–11 • Algorithmic approach to the diagnosis and treatment of male infertility. ART = assisted reproductive technology; FSH = follicle-stimulating hormone; GnRH = gonadotropin-releasing hormone; ICSI = intracytoplasmic sperm injection; LH = serum luteinizing hormone; T = serum testosterone.

Table 26–3 • DELIRIUM RISK FACTORS AND POTENTIAL INTERVENTIONS

RISK FACTOR	INTERVENTIONS
Cognitive impairment	Reality orientation program (reorienting techniques, communication) Therapeutic activities program
Sleep deprivation	Noise reduction strategies Scheduling of nighttime medications, procedures, and nursing activities to allow uninterrupted period of sleep
Immobilization	Early mobilization (e.g., ambulation or bedside exercises) Minimizing immobilizing equipment (e.g., bladder catheters)
Psychoactive medications	Restricted use of "as needed" sleep and psychoactive medications (e.g., sedative-hypnotics, narcotics, anticholinergic medications) Nonpharmacologic protocols for management of sleep and anxiety
Vision impairment	Provision of vision aids (e.g., magnifiers, special lighting) Provision of adaptive equipment (e.g., illuminated phone dials, large-print books)
Hearing impairment	Provision of amplifying devices Repair of hearing aids
Dehydration	Early recognition and volume repletion

it occurs. Preventive strategies should address important delirium risk factors and target patients at a moderate to high risk for delirium at baseline (Table 26–3). Randomized trials have shown that a geriatrics consultation or a multidisciplinary intervention aimed at the risk factors for delirium can reduce the incidence of delirium by 40%. On a larger scale, preventive efforts for delirium require system-wide changes to educate physicians and nurses to improve recognition and heighten awareness of the clinical implications, provide incentives to change practice patterns that lead to delirium (e.g., immobilization, use of sleep medications, bladder catheters, and physical restraints), and create systems that enhance high-quality geriatric care (e.g., geriatric expertise, case management, clinical pathways, and quality monitoring).

Future Directions

It is hoped that future research will elucidate the pathophysiology of delirium using neuroimaging modalities, neuropsychological testing, and laboratory markers; clarify the contribution of delirium to irreversible cognitive impairment; and improve the management of delirium.

1. Inouye SK, Bogardus ST, Charpentier PA, et al: A multicomponent intervention to prevent delirium in hospitalized older patients. N Engl J Med 1999;340: 669.
2. Marcantonio ER, Flacker JM, Wright RJ, Resnick NM: Reducing delirium after hip fracture: A randomized trial. J Am Geriatr Soc 2001;49:516.
3. Britton A, Russell R: Multidisciplinary team interventions for delirium in patients with chronic cognitive impairment. Cochrane Review. The Cochrane Library, Issue 4. Oxford, Update Software, 2003.

SUGGESTED READINGS
Carnes M, Howell T, Rosenberg M, et al: Physicians vary in approaches to the clinical management of delirium. J Am Geriatr Soc 2003;51:234–239. *This study documents the broad variability in pharmacologic management of delirium, in the absence of sound clinical evidence.*
Marcantonio ER, Simon SE, Bergmann MA, et al: Delirium symptoms in post-acute care: prevalent, persistent, and associated with poor functional recovery. J Am Geriatr Soc 2003;51:4–9. *This study reveals that delirium is a frequent complication of post-acute care that is associated with poor functional recovery.*
Roche V: Etiology and management of delirium. Am J Med Sci 2003;325:20–30. *An up-to-date review of literature on delirium.*

to have greater deleterious effects in patients with underlying cognitive impairment. The long-term detrimental effects most probably are related to the duration, severity, and underlying cause of the delirium and the vulnerability of the patient.

Prevention

The most effective intervention strategy to reduce delirium and its associated complications is primary prevention of delirium before

- **Highlighted Grade A Evidence references emphasize evidence-based treatments, to foster cost-effective, best practice in clinical medicine.**

- **Suggested Readings provide sources for further information.**

Contents

x | Contents

Part XXVI Eye, Ear, Nose, and Throat Diseases

Part XXVII Skin Diseases

Part XXVIII Reference Intervals and Laboratory Values

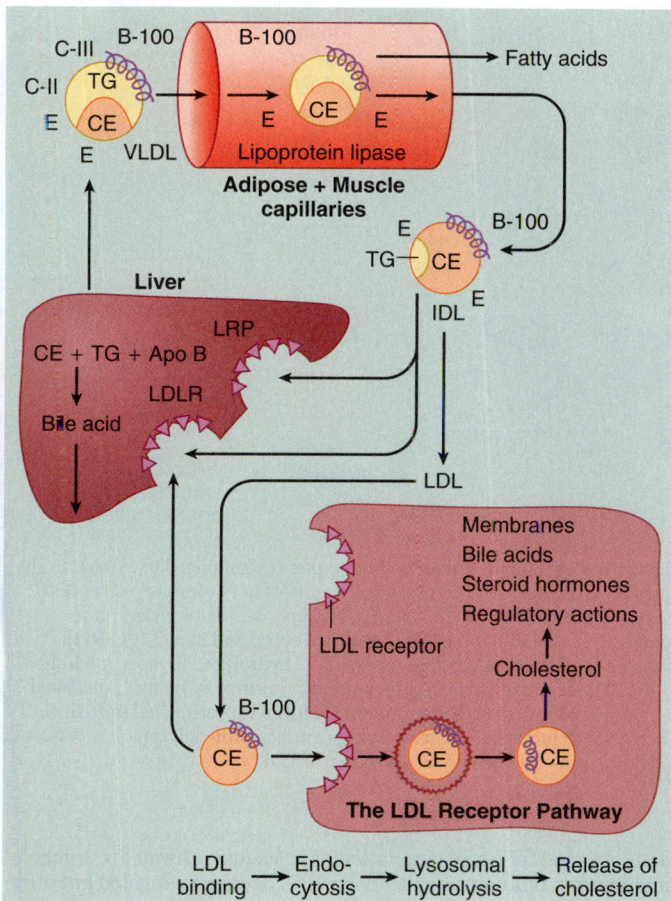

FIGURE 211–1 • Simplified scheme of metabolism of apo B–containing lipoproteins. In the liver, triglyceride (TG), cholesteryl esters (CE), and apolipoprotein B-100 (B-100) are packaged and released into plasma as very low density lipoproteins (VLDL). In capillary beds, lipoprotein lipase hydrolyzes TG to release free fatty acids. The TG-depleted particle is termed an intermediate-density lipoprotein (IDL). The particle is further metabolized to CE-rich low-density lipoprotein (LDL). A major fraction of IDL particles is removed from plasma by hepatic receptors, both by LDL receptors (LDLR) and LDL receptor-related protein (LRP). A portion of IDL is converted to LDL, which is then removed from plasma by LDLR on liver and peripheral cells. Uptake of LDL through the LDLR pathway leads to regulation of cholesterol synthesis and LDLR synthesis, as explained in the text. (Modified from Witztum JL: Current approaches to drug therapy for the hypercholesterolemic patient. Circulation 1989;80:1101–1114, with permission of the American Heart Association, Inc.)

is decreased. Each VLDL particle contains one molecule of apo B, yet under ordinary circumstances the rate of apo B synthesis is not rate limiting for VLDL secretion. Although enhanced triglyceride synthesis can lead to enhanced triglyceride output, the *number* of VLDL particles released is not necessarily increased. Instead, *larger* individual VLDL particles containing more triglyceride are released. Understanding the processes regulating VLDL assembly and release by the hepatocytes is necessary to understand the etiology of clinically important disorders, such as familial combined hyperlipidemia or hyperapobetalipoproteinemia, which are characterized by increased rates of secretion of VLDL particles from the liver. Other lipoprotein disorders (familial hypertriglyceridemia) are caused by hepatic secretion of a normal number of VLDL particles but ones that are enriched with triglycerides. The half-life of VLDL in plasma is about 1 hour or less.

The primary function of lipoprotein particles is to transport lipids from one site to another. Triglyceride-rich lipoproteins serve to transport endogenously synthesized triglyceride to adipose tissue for storage in the fed state or to muscle for utilization in the fasting state. The enzyme that catalyzes peripheral triglyceride uptake is lipoprotein lipase (LPL). This enzyme is synthesized in adipose tissue and skeletal muscle cells, secreted, and transported across the capillary endothelial cell, where it binds to glycoproteins on the endothelial luminal surface. When VLDL binds to LPL, the LPL is activated by apo C-II

present on the surface of the VLDL particle. This leads to triglyceride hydrolysis and release of fatty acids, which are then transported into the fat (or muscle) cell, where they are re-esterified with glycerol and stored as intracellular triglyceride. The vast majority of triglyceride in adipose tissue is acquired by this mechanism because essentially no lipogenesis occurs de novo from glucose in human adipose tissue. The activity of LPL in adipose tissue is increased in the fed state, effectively providing for triglyceride storage. Insulin is required to maintain adequate LPL levels in adipose tissue. It appears to do so by maintaining synthesis and release, but it does not acutely affect changes in LPL levels. This is in contrast to "hormone-sensitive lipase," an enzyme that hydrolyzes intracellular triglycerides, releasing fatty acids to plasma for uptake by the liver. Hormone-sensitive lipase is acutely inhibited by insulin, whereas glucagon increases its activity. Thus, after a meal, high insulin levels serve to promote storage of fatty acids in the adipocyte as triglyceride, whereas in the fasting state hydrolysis is promoted, providing fatty acids for uptake by muscle and liver.

As noted earlier, the action of LPL requires the cofactor, apo C-II. Shortly after VLDL enters into plasma, apo C-II is transferred to VLDL from a reservoir on circulating HDL. After hydrolysis of triglyceride in VLDL, the apo C-II is released and presumably picked up again by HDL. The importance of apo C-II is demonstrated by individuals with genetic deficiency of C-II, which leads to impaired LPL activity and massive hypertriglyceridemia. Other apolipoproteins, such as C-III, are also transferred between VLDL and HDL. In vitro, apo C-III can inhibit LPL-mediated hydrolysis, but its physiologic role in vivo is still unclear. Evidence from studies with transgenic mice supports the idea that increased plasma levels of apo C-III cause hypertriglyceridemia, directly or indirectly, by inhibiting LPL-mediated hydrolysis.

Hydrolysis of triglycerides in VLDL profoundly alters the structure of the VLDL, depleting the lipid content of the core. The excess surface components, including cholesterol, phospholipids, and the non-apo B apoproteins, are transferred to HDL. The triglyceride-depleted VLDL, with its associated loss of other lipids and apoproteins, now becomes an IDL, cholesterol-enriched and containing only apo B and apo E. Under normal conditions, this particle is rapidly removed from plasma by the liver through a complex interaction with several hepatic receptors, including the LDL receptor, which recognizes apo B and apo E, and with another receptor, termed the *remnant receptor,* which is specific for apo E. This latter receptor is thought to be the LDL-receptor-related protein (LRP). Whereas the majority of IDL particles are normally removed from plasma by this process in other species, in humans a significant fraction is converted into LDL. By the time the cholesterol-rich LDL has been formed, most of the triglyceride has been removed and apo B is now the sole apoprotein remaining from the original VLDL particle. Under normal circumstances, most of the cholesterol found in plasma is present in the form of LDL particles, and only minute amounts of IDL are present.

Apo E, which acts as a ligand for both the LDL receptor and the LRP, appears to be crucial for both the direct removal of IDL and conversion of IDL particles to LDL particles. Patients who either lack apo E or are homozygous for apo E isoforms that bind less efficiently to these receptors may have excess plasma accumulation of IDL particles (and chylomicron remnants) and are both hypercholesterolemic and hypertriglyceridemic, a condition known as *dysbetalipoproteinemia.*

Metabolism of LDL. Each LDL particle is derived from VLDL via IDL and contains one copy of apo B. All other apolipoproteins have now been removed, together with much of the phospholipid and triglyceride and some of the cholesterol. Although only a small percentage of VLDL particles ultimately end up as LDL particles, the bulk of plasma cholesterol is accounted for by LDL particles because of the relatively slow rate of clearance of LDL from plasma (half-life of 2 to 3 days). Because LDL particles contain only apo B, their efficient clearance can occur only by way of the LDL receptor pathway. In normal humans, approximately 75% of LDL particles are cleared by the LDL receptor pathway, and approximately two thirds of LDL particles are removed by the liver. Nobel Prize winners Brown and Goldstein elucidated the LDL receptor pathway, one of the major achievements of modern medical science. The rate of LDL removal through this pathway is the primary determinant of LDL levels. The LDL receptor, which binds apo B with high affinity and leads to internalization of the LDL particle, is found on virtually every mammalian cell. As shown in the right side of Figure 211–1, the LDL particle binds to the receptor on the surface of the cell, and subsequently the receptor and the bound LDL particle are internalized. LDL is then delivered to the lysosome, but the receptor recycles to the surface of the cell. Within the lysosome, the protein component, apo B, is degraded to amino acids or oligopeptides. The cholesteryl ester is hydrolyzed to free cholesterol, which can now leave the lysosome and is used by the cell for a variety of cellular processes, including new cell membrane synthesis, hormone synthesis (in adrenal, ovarian, or testicular cells), bile acid production (in hepatocytes), or for re-esterification to be stored as a cholesteryl-ester droplet. In addition, when sufficient cholesterol has been accumulated, downregulation of the LDL receptors is accomplished, as well as inhibition of the cell's own cholesterol synthetic pathway. Thus, this efficient regulatory pathway provides a cell with sufficient cholesterol for its physiologic needs, but it prevents the overaccumulation of cholesterol, which could be toxic. In particular, regulation of the *hepatic* LDL receptor pathway is a dominant mechanism for regulating plasma LDL levels in humans, and the ability to manipulate this pathway by therapeutic agents forms the basis of most of our current techniques to lower LDL levels.

It should also be appreciated that apo B-containing lipoproteins may be removed by the liver and other tissues by inefficient, low-affinity pathways as well. For example, in subjects with homozygous familial hypercholesterolemia, who have no functional LDL receptors, the fractional clearance of LDL is drastically reduced, but a new steady state is reached because of the nonspecific pathways for LDL removal. Greatly elevated plasma LDL levels occur, however, creating a very high risk for premature atherosclerosis. A scavenger pathway involving the macrophage system may also remove LDL particles by non-LDL receptor pathways, and in the artery wall this may play an important role in the genesis of the atherosclerotic lesion.

SYNTHESIS AND TRANSPORT OF EXOGENOUS (DIETARY) LIPIDS. After a triglyceride-rich meal, triglycerides and cholesterol are absorbed into the mucosal cells of the small intestine as free fatty acids and free cholesterol. There, they are re-esterified to triglyceride and cholesteryl esters and incorporated into the core of a nascent lipoprotein, the chylomicron. The surface coat of the chylomicron is composed of phospholipid and apo A-I, A-II, and A-IV. Apo B-48 is a crucial component of chylomicrons and is a product of the same gene that codes for the intact, full-length apo B-100. Apo B-48 is so named because it is identical to the first 48% (the amino terminal portion) of apo B-100. In humans, the intact, full-length apo B-100 is made only in the liver, whereas apo B-48 is made only in the intestine. Apo B-48 is transcribed from the apo B-100 gene, but the messenger RNA is first edited by a cytidine deaminase complex that leads to a site-specific C to U conversion that generates a stop codon. Thus, B-48 consists of the amino-terminal half of B-100. The domain of intact apo B-100 that binds to the LDL receptor is contained in the carboxy-terminal end. Because apo B-48 lacks this domain, it is unable to bind to LDL receptors. Thus, once the chylomicron has been secreted by the intestine, apo B-48 functions primarily as a structural component.

Triglycerides constitute more than 90% by weight of the chylomicron particle, and consequently the density of this lipoprotein is the lowest of any in plasma. When plasma is left overnight in the refrigerator, if chylomicrons are present, they will float to the top and appear as a layer of "cream" on top, which is the basis for the chylomicron test. In normal individuals, this test is always negative after an 8- to 12-hour fast, because chylomicrons have a short half-life in plasma. The presence of a positive chylomicron test in a 12-hour fasting sample is abnormal and indicative of marked delay in chylomicron clearance.

Chylomicrons are delivered to the plasma via the thoracic duct (Fig. 211–2). While in the lymph and after entering plasma, chylomicrons acquire apo C-II, C-III, and apo E by transfer. After having acquired sufficient apo C-II, which is absolutely required for LPL activity, the chylomicron can interact with LPL in a manner analogous to that of VLDL particles. After sufficient triglyceride hydrolysis has occurred, the remaining chylomicron particle, now termed a *remnant*, has a markedly reduced core volume, and its excess surface components, including apoproteins such as C-II, C-III, and some of the apo E, are transferred to HDL particles as described for the VLDL particles. The remnant particle is still relatively cholesteryl-ester-rich. In part, this cholesterol comes from dietary sources, but a significant amount is also transferred into the particle from HDL particles mediated by cholesterol ester transfer protein (CETP). In addition, because it is still a relatively large particle, it contains many copies of apo E on its surface, and it is believed that this represents the ligand that leads to rapid interaction with remnant receptors in the liver and effi-

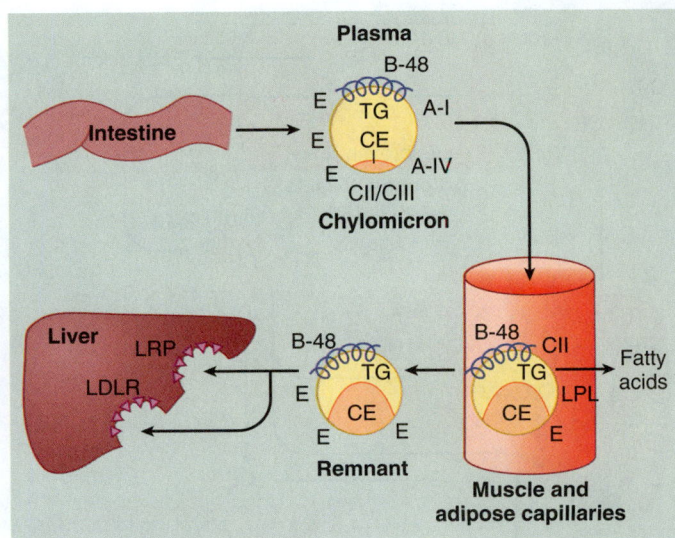

FIGURE 211–2 • Metabolism of chylomicrons (exogenous dietary fat). In the intestine, triglyceride (TG) and small amounts of cholesteryl esters (CE) are packaged with apo B-48, apo A-I, and apo A-IV and released into lymph. The chylomicron particle acquires apo E and apo C-II/C-III in lymph and plasma. In capillary beds, TG is hydrolyzed by lipoprotein lipase (LPL). The remnant particle is then removed primarily by liver, mediated by binding to low-density lipoprotein (LDL), receptor-related protein (LRP) and LDL receptors (LDLR) as well as to surface proteoglycans. Chylomicron remnants are not a source of LDL.

cient removal from the circulation. The exact pathway for uptake of chylomicron remnants by the liver is still being investigated but probably includes the LRP, the LDL receptor itself, and the cell-surface glycosaminoglycans that can also bind apo E. Apo E is central to the process of remnant removal, just as it is for IDL uptake. Individuals who either lack apo E or synthesize only apo E isoforms (E₂) that bind poorly to receptors can accumulate chylomicron remnants in plasma.

HDL-CONTAINING LIPOPROTEINS. When chylomicrons and VLDL particles are hydrolyzed by LPL to release fatty acids for peripheral use, their surface coat of unesterified cholesterol, phospholipid, and various apoproteins forms excess surface material that must be disposed of. HDL plays a principal role in this by acting as an acceptor, or "sink," for this excess surface material (Fig. 211–3). Nascent HDL particles are synthesized by the liver and the intestine and are composed primarily of phospholipid and two major structural proteins, apo A-I and A-II. HDL accepts the phospholipid (mainly lecithin) and unesterified cholesterol from the excess surface of triglyceride-rich lipoproteins as they are catabolized. An enzyme associated with HDL—lecithin-cholesterol acyl transferase (LCAT)—removes a fatty acid from lecithin and transfers it to cholesterol, producing cholesteryl ester and lysolecithin. The esterified cholesterol moves into the core of the HDL particle, making it possible to accept another free cholesterol molecule onto the surface of the HDL particle. In turn, the cholesteryl esters are then transported back to the liver (reverse cholesterol transport). In part, this occurs by direct uptake of HDL particles, but an important additional mechanism is a selective uptake of cholesteryl esters from HDL without uptake of the whole HDL particle. The receptor that mediates this is SR-B1, which has been cloned and identified on liver and certain steroidogenic cells. In addition, cholesteryl esters can be returned to the liver indirectly by transfer to other lipoproteins, such as VLDL, IDL, or LDL via CETP. The uptake of these cholesteryl-ester-enriched lipoproteins by the liver results in net removal from plasma of cholesteryl esters. This HDL/LCAT/CETP system plays a pivotal role in removing excess cellular cholesterol, facilitating its transfer back to the liver for excretion. The removal of excess cholesterol from arterial wall cells by such a mechanism could play a crucial role in minimizing cholesterol accumulation in the artery wall and thus inhibiting atherogenesis (Chapter 66). Thus, HDL may be viewed as playing a vital role in transporting excess cholesterol from extrahepatic tissues back to the liver, where it is excreted in the bile. In addition to its role in reverse cholesterol transport, HDL may also serve as the reservoir for apoproteins such as C-II, C-III, and E as they shuttle back and forth from triglyceride-rich lipoproteins while being catabolized.

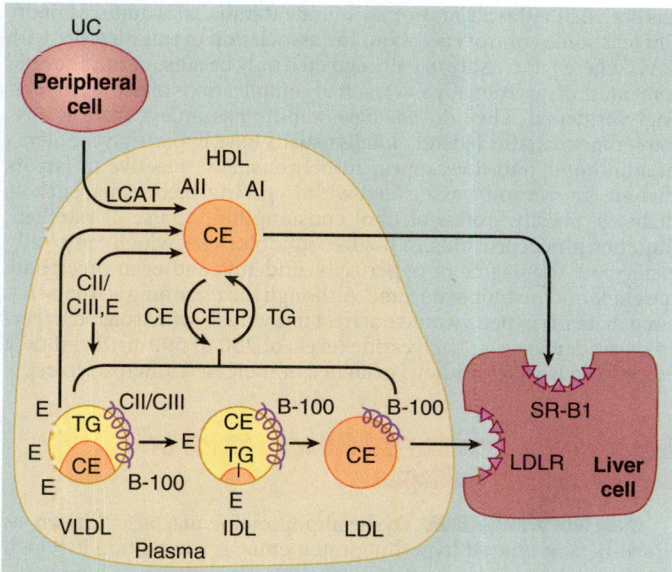

FIGURE 211-3 • Interactions of high-density lipoproteins (HDL) and apo B–containing lipoproteins. HDL has particles containing apo A-I and particles containing apo A-I, A-II. Nascent HDL, made primarily by liver and intestine, accepts unesterified cholesterol (UC) from very low density lipoproteins (VLDL) and from membranes of cells. The enzyme lecithin-cholesterol-acyltransferase (LCAT), which is associated with HDL, esterifies the cholesterol to form cholesteryl esters (CE), which then form the core of the HDL. The enzyme cholesterol ester transfer protein (CETP) transfers CE from HDL into apo B–containing lipoproteins in exchange for triglyceride (TG). HDL also serves as a "sink" for apoproteins C-II/C-III and E, which shuttle back and forth from the HDL to VLDL and intermediate-density lipoprotein (IDL). HDL also returns CE to the liver by binding to SR-B1, leading to selective delivery of CE into liver cells. LDL = low-density lipoprotein; LDLR = low-density lipoprotein receptor.

BILE ACID PRODUCTION. Nearly all cells of the body have the capacity to synthesize cholesterol de novo, but none has the ability to degrade it completely. However, hepatocytes have the capacity to convert cholesterol into bile acids, which can then be secreted into the bile along with free cholesterol and phospholipids. Nearly 95% of secreted bile acids are reabsorbed in the distal ileum and enter the enterohepatic circulation; that is, they are taken up by the liver and recycled. Cholesterol delivered to the liver in the form of chylomicrons or other lipoproteins could be recycled and secreted as VLDL or converted to bile acids for secretion into the bile.

DISORDERS OF LIPOPROTEIN METABOLISM

Disorders of lipoprotein metabolism can lead to hypercholesterolemia or hypertriglyceridemia or both. Although these disorders appear to be common in the general population, the molecular events responsible for them are only currently being elucidated. For purposes of organization, the hyperlipoproteinemias are grouped into disorders leading primarily to hypercholesterolemia (due to elevations of LDL levels) or to hypertriglyceridemia (due to elevations of VLDL or chylomicrons) or to combined elevations of both triglycerides and cholesterol. Several monogenic disorders have been defined that lead to each type of hyperlipidemia, but for many cases the cause is likely to be polygenic. These disorders affect plasma lipoprotein levels by overproduction of lipoproteins and/or decreased clearance.

Hyperlipoproteinemia Resulting Primarily in Hypercholesterolemia

FAMILIAL HYPERCHOLESTEROLEMIA AND FAMILIAL DEFECTIVE APOLIPOPROTEIN B.

Familial hypercholesterolemia (FH) is a common autosomal dominant disorder caused by the absence of or defective LDL receptors resulting in decreased capacity to remove plasma LDL. Familial defective apolipoprotein B is an autosomal dominant disorder in which the ligand-binding region of apo B is defective, also leading to delayed plasma LDL clearance. In both disorders, LDL-cholesterol levels are strikingly increased, frequently associated with characteristic xanthomas in the Achilles tendons, the patellar tendons, the extensor

tendons of the hands, and by the presence of xanthelasma. It is frequently associated with early coronary artery disease (CAD). In heterozygous FH, estimated to be present in 1 in 500 individuals, there is one abnormal allele for the LDL receptor. The abnormal allele may produce no receptors or produce abnormal LDL receptors that are largely nonfunctional. In the heterozygote, a 50% decrease exists in hepatic LDL receptor number, a corresponding decrease in LDL catabolism, and an approximately two-fold to three-fold increase in plasma LDL levels. In the rare homozygous FH patient (only 1 in 1 million people) almost no functional LDL receptors are found, and plasma LDL levels may be increased six-fold to ten-fold. In this situation, LDL can be removed from plasma only by low-affinity pathways. There is also a rare autosomal recessive hypercholesterolemia due not to a defect in the LDL receptor itself but to one in a cytosolic adaptor protein needed for normal LDL receptor function. In familial defective apolipoprotein B, the ligand-binding domain of apo B is defective because of a missense mutation at the codon for amino acid 3500. This mutation leads to impaired binding of LDL to the LDL receptor and clinical consequences similar to those seen in FH. It is likely that other mutations in apo B affecting its ability to bind to the LDL receptor also occur.

These disorders are characterized by greatly elevated concentrations of LDL cholesterol. If untreated, patients with FH have premature CAD, as well as other clinical manifestations of atherosclerosis (Chapter 66). Peripheral vascular disease and cerebral vascular disease are also increased, although not as much as CAD. Tendon xanthomas are seen only in FH and in patients with familial defective apo B. Bilateral, irregular, firm, and nodular thickenings in the Achilles tendons or extensor tendons of the hands or knees are usually present and can be so large as to interfere with normal functions, such as wearing shoes. Xanthelasma typically occurs in this setting, and corneal arcus is frequently seen as well, although this latter entity occurs in other lipoprotein disorders and can also be found in elderly, normolipidemic patients.

Plasma cholesterol levels in heterozygous FH exceed the upper 1% of levels seen in the general population and are generally in the range of 300 to 500 mg/dL. In rare patients, homozygous for FH, plasma cholesterol levels can exceed 800 to 1000 mg/dL. Triglyceride levels are usually normal but in 10% of subjects may be mildly elevated. Patients with defective remnant removal or with marked chylomicronemia may also have markedly elevated cholesterol levels, but they will have very high triglyceride levels as well. In addition, their plasma will appear turbid or creamy, in contrast to plasma in FH patients, which is always clear.

Because myocardial infarction can occur in men with heterozygous FH when they are in their early 40s, these subjects deserve vigorous therapy to lower LDL levels and to decrease other risk factors as well. Women with FH also have an accelerated risk for CAD, although the absolute risk is less than that of men and the CAD occurs at a later age. For both men and women, the risk of atherosclerosis is greatly accelerated by the presence of other risk factors, such as smoking, hypertension, diabetes, low HDL-cholesterol levels, and high Lp(a) levels. A diet low in saturated fat and cholesterol should be initiated in all affected individuals with this disorder, although frequently only modest reductions in LDL levels occur. Effective therapy can be achieved using HMG-CoA reductase inhibitors, a class of compounds termed *statins*, as first-line therapy because they effectively lower LDL-cholesterol levels by 20 to 45% and infrequently have side effects. When these statins are combined with a bile acid-binding resin, decreases of LDL levels by 50 to 60% or greater can frequently be achieved. In some individuals, triple therapy with a statin, a bile acid-binding resin, and niacin may be necessary to normalize LDL levels. Ezetimibe, an agent that inhibits intestinal cholesterol absorption, also shows great promise of providing additional cholesterol-lowering activity. It does not inhibit bile acid absorption. Unfortunately, subjects homozygous for FH usually do not respond to these measures, which work in large part by increasing the LDL receptor activity. For such individuals, heroic measures are required, such as repeated plasmapheresis or a more specialized procedure, termed *LDL apheresis,* in which apo B-containing lipoproteins are removed from blood as it passes extracorporeally through a column that binds apo B. In selected individuals, liver transplantation has been used. In the future, it is hoped that gene therapy may lead to correction of the primary genetic defect.

POLYGENIC HYPERCHOLESTEROLEMIA. Irrespective of one's definition of hypercholesterolemia, it is clear that a large number of individuals in the general population have elevated LDL-cholesterol levels (see Table

211–4). If one uses the conventional definition that the top 5% of the general population have hypercholesterolemia, then on average only 1 of 25 of such hypercholesterolemic individuals will have FH, and only 2 will have familial combined hyperlipidemia (described later). The large majority have hypercholesterolemia due to a complex interaction of multiple genetic factors and environmental factors, that is, polygenic hypercholesterolemia. The cause of the hypercholesterolemia is unknown, but it is likely due to the convergence of several subtle alterations that affect regulation of LDL levels. Differences may exist in dietary responsiveness to cholesterol and saturated fat, differences in regulation of cholesterol and/or bile acid biosynthesis, and/or differences in regulation of LDL receptor activity and in the secretion and intravascular catabolism of apo B-containing lipoproteins.

FAMILIAL HYPERALPHALIPOPROTEINEMIA. Occasionally, patients are seen who have mildly elevated total cholesterol levels due to elevated HDL-cholesterol. They usually have normal levels of LDL and VLDL. In these individuals, the elevated HDL-cholesterol level is genetic, and in some families it is inherited as an autosomal dominant trait. In other families, the cause appears to be polygenic. High HDL levels can also be seen with chronic alcoholism, in response to estrogen administration, and after exposure to chlorinated hydrocarbon pesticides. In some families, a genetic deficiency of CETP is associated with strikingly elevated HDL-cholesterol levels, especially in Japanese populations. Individuals with hyperalphalipoproteinemia do not have any unusual clinical features, and they have been reported to have slightly increased longevity because of a decreased incidence of CAD.

Hyperlipoproteinemias Resulting Primarily in Hypertriglyceridemia

LIPOPROTEIN LIPASE DEFICIENCY AND APO C-II DEFICIENCY. LPL deficiency is a rare autosomal recessive trait that is characterized by the absence of active LPL in all tissues, leading to massive hypertriglyceridemia from birth and the clinical consequences of eruptive xanthoma and episodes of pancreatitis. This same clinical syndrome may also occur with deficiency of apo C-II, an obligatory activator of LPL, although clinical manifestations tend to occur later in life.

In infants and young children with LPL deficiency, the hypertriglyceridemia results primarily from chylomicron accumulation, whereas impairment of VLDL triglyceride removal becomes more important in later life. Homozygosity for LPL deficiency or for apo C-II deficiency is necessary for this disorder to occur. Heterozygosity for LPL deficiency may lead to moderate hypertriglyceridemia and may be one factor in the etiology of familial combined hyperlipidemia. Infants with homozygous LPL deficiency have massive hypertriglyceridemia and grossly lipemic serum. They frequently fail to thrive and have severe abdominal pain and pancreatitis as a consequence of their marked hyperchylomicronemia. Eruptive xanthomas can occur on the extensor surfaces, notably on the elbows, knees, back, and buttocks, but can occur elsewhere, and when seen are pathognomonic for chylomicronemia. Hepatomegaly is frequent, as is splenomegaly, which occurs because of the accumulation of lipid-laden foam cells. LPL activity can be measured by assaying plasma after injection of heparin, which releases LPL into plasma. Apo C-II levels can be tested by immunoassay. The clinical manifestations will rapidly disappear with elimination of fat from the diet, which leads to elimination of the chylomicronemia. With effective fat restriction, plasma triglyceride levels can usually be maintained between 500 and 800 mg/dL or lower; and at this level, episodes of eruptive xanthoma, abdominal pain, and pancreatitis can usually be avoided. Substances that increase endogenous VLDL output, such as alcohol and glucocorticoids, must be avoided. With effective attention to diet, individuals can grow and easily reach adulthood without difficulty. There is no indication that any increased risk for atherosclerosis exists in this disorder.

FAMILIAL HYPERTRIGLYCERIDEMIA. Individuals with this condition have marked hypertriglyceridemia, normal to low LDL levels, and marked decreases in HDL-cholesterol levels. When studied in detail, the number of VLDL particles is relatively normal, but they are triglyceride enriched. LPL-related triglyceride removal and remnant removal appears to be normal. HDL cholesterol levels are low. However, HDL particle number is relatively normal, but the triglyceride content in the HDL, which is normally very low, is considerably increased at the expense of cholesterol. The underlying defect in this disorder is postulated to be enhanced hepatic triglyceride synthesis. This disorder

has been defined as an autosomal dominant trait that is quite common. There is some controversy about the association of this disorder with CAD. These patients are usually detected only because of routine lipid screening, or occasionally as a result of complications of marked hypertriglyceridemia. They do not have xanthomas unless there is chylomicronemia. Affected individuals usually have hypertriglyceridemia in adulthood, and they appear to be unusually sensitive to factors that are known to be associated with hypertriglyceridemia, such as diabetes, obesity, excess alcohol consumption, or use of estrogen, diuretics, glucocorticoids, or β-adrenergic blockers, which can greatly exaggerate the degree of hypertriglyceridemia and even precipitate the chylomicronemia syndrome. Although the reasoning is somewhat circular, many experts would not treat individuals with isolated hypertriglyceridemia (e.g., triglyceride levels of 250 to 500 mg/dL) if they come from families without evidence of increased atherosclerosis.

Hyperlipoproteinemias Resulting in Mixed or Combined Hyperlipidemia

DYSBETALIPOPROTEINEMIA. Dysbetalipoproteinemia, also known as broad-beta or type III hyperlipoproteinemia, is a condition in which there is abnormal accumulation of cholesterol-rich IDL-type particles, commonly termed β-VLDL. This disorder is due to interaction of (1) an autosomal recessive defect in apo E that leads to abnormal remnant catabolism and (2) an independent aggravating factor (e.g., hypothyroidism obesity, diabetes, pregnancy) or genetic factor (e.g., familial combined hyperlipidemia) leading to overproduction of apo B-containing lipoproteins. The combination of these two factors leads to accumulation of IDL-like particles (resulting from impaired VLDL catabolism) and remnants (resulting from impaired chylomicron metabolism) that lead to xanthomas, peripheral vascular disease, and CAD.

There are three major alleles for apo E, differing from each other by a single amino acid substitution at one or two sites. These are named E_2, E_3, and E_4. An individual can be homozygous for any of these alleles, or heterozygous for any combination. The apo E encoded by the E_2 allele has sharply reduced ability to bind to lipoprotein receptors. Individuals homozygous for this allele (i.e., E_2/E_2 homozygotes), who account for about 2% of the population, have a relative defect in IDL and remnant catabolism. This can lead to relative accumulation in plasma of cholesteryl-ester-rich IDL and chylomicron remnant particles (β-VLDL) and corresponding decrease in LDL levels because of defective conversion of VLDL to LDL (see Fig. 211–1). Yet in the absence of aggravating factors, total plasma cholesterol levels are actually low in such individuals and triglyceride levels are normal. In an estimated 1 in 100 individuals with E_2/E_2 homozygosity, however, there is also an associated condition leading to overproduction of VLDL. This combination results in the absolute accumulation of β-VLDL particles, which are atherogenic when present in excess. This is expressed as marked hypertriglyceridemia and hypercholesterolemia. Normally, VLDL particles have "pre-β" mobility on agarose gel electrophoresis, but the VLDL remnants in dysbetalipoproteinemia are much closer to LDL in composition and therefore have "β" mobility ("β-VLDL"), hence the designation *dysbetalipoproteinemia*. Because individuals who are homozygous for the E_2 allele have low levels of such qualitatively abnormal VLDLs present in plasma even when total lipids are normal (or even low), some experts use the term *dysbetalipoproteinemia* to refer to the condition of homozygosity for E_2, whereas the term *type III hyperlipoproteinemia* or *broad-beta syndrome* is reserved for those individuals with associated hyperlipidemia. The type III hyperlipoproteinemia phenotype can also be caused by total absence of apo E, which has been observed in rare families.

When overproduction of VLDL occurs, or when there is delayed clearance, marked hyperlipidemia appears, and this disorder may manifest as premature clinical atherosclerosis with peripheral vascular disease and/or CAD. The presence of hypothyroidism has been noted frequently in individuals with clinical symptoms. These patients frequently have highly characteristic planar xanthomas in the creases of the palms as well as tuberous or tuberoeruptive xanthomas on the elbows or knees that are virtually diagnostic for this disorder. Occasionally, these manifestations can be seen with obstructive liver disease. Although the apo E abnormality is present from birth, it is unusual to see hyperlipidemia in a male subject younger than 30 years of age or in a female subject before menopause. The presence of hypertriglyceridemia accompanied by unusual degrees of hypercholesterolemia when associated with palmar or tuberous xanthomas is highly suggestive of this disorder. Liver disease and hypothyroidism need to be excluded. Electrophoresis of a VLDL fraction of plasma will reveal particles of β mobility, rather than the typical pre-β mobility. The E_2 isoforms can be identified by isoelectric focusing in specialty laboratories, and genotyping is also available. The concentration of LDL is typically low even in hyperlipidemic patients, and a normal or elevated LDL level should make one consider an alternative diagnosis. HDL levels are normal or slightly decreased, depending on the degree of hypertriglyceridemia.

In many E_2/E_2 adults with clinical manifestations of hyperlipidemia, there is associated obesity, and weight reduction is of primary importance. In postmenopausal women, low-dose estrogen replacement frequently normalizes the abnormal lipoprotein profile and corrects the hyperlipidemia. All patients should be checked for mild degrees of hypothyroidism using sensitive thyroid-stimulating hormone assays; if hypothyroidism is present, treatment may frequently completely normalize the lipoprotein profile. Gemfibrozil is frequently effective in decreasing lipid levels in these individuals; high-dose nicotinic acid may also be useful. Use of an HMG-CoA reductase inhibitor has been found to be quite successful in reducing the hypercholesterolemia and, when combined with low-dose gemfibrozil, has frequently normalized triglyceride levels in severe cases.

FAMILIAL COMBINED HYPERLIPIDEMIA. Among patients with myocardial infarction, a significant number have an apparently dominantly inherited pattern of hyperlipoproteinemia that is expressed by a variable lipoprotein phenotype. Thus, individuals may have increased VLDL or LDL levels or both. Some first-degree relatives have elevated VLDL levels, some have elevated LDL, and some have both. This entity appears to be monogenic and inherited in an autosomal dominant manner and has been termed *familial combined hyperlipidemia* or *familial multiple lipoprotein-type hyperlipidemia*. The lipoprotein phenotype is not stable over time. A person can have VLDL elevations noted on one visit but marked increases in LDL, or both VLDL and LDL, at another visit. Although there remains much uncertainty about classification of this disorder, all clinicians seeing patients with premature CAD recognize the frequency of this pattern. A characteristic of this disorder is increased accumulation of small LDL particles, which are cholesterol depleted. Thus, patients may have a relatively normal "LDL cholesterol" level, yet the number of LDL particles is increased and therefore the LDL-apo B level is increased. Some investigators have termed this condition familial hyper*apo*betalipoproteinemia. Most evidence suggests that the underlying defect is increased hepatic secretion of VLDL. The VLDL particles appear to be smaller than normal, with less triglyceride per particle. Undoubtedly, this disorder represents several different genetic traits interacting with the basic defect-overproduction of VLDL. For example, overproduction of VLDL may become manifested primarily as elevations in VLDL levels if a relative or absolute defect in VLDL catabolism occurs in addition, as, for example, with relative deficiency in LPL activity. Recently, a number of cases of heterozygous LPL deficiency have been found in association with this phenotype. Conversely, in the face of appropriate VLDL and LDL catabolism, LDL may accumulate because of the increased rate of generation of LDL and/or functional disturbances in LDL catabolic mechanisms. These individuals also typically have low levels of HDL with decreases in both HDL-cholesterol and apo A-I.

This phenotype is associated with a clinical constellation that includes mild abdominal obesity, insulin resistance, mild hypertension, elevated VLDL levels, the presence of an excess number of small dense LDLs, and decreased HDL. This syndrome has been variously referred to as the *metabolic syndrome* or *insulin-resistance syndrome* or *syndrome X* (Chapter 242). This disorder is more typically seen in men and is associated with a strikingly high rate of premature CAD. The effect of other risk factors appears to be greatly exaggerated in these individuals, and a history of smoking is frequently found in those with early CAD. Patients do not have any characteristic xanthomas, and the diagnosis is made by a characteristic family history that is unusually positive for early CAD, by documentation of the variable lipoprotein phenotype, and, if possible, by lipoprotein phenotyping of first-degree relatives. Women may also be affected by this phenotype, although the clinical manifestations of CAD appear to be expressed later in life. Because this disorder is associated with a high risk of premature CAD, vigorous efforts should be made to lower lipoprotein levels of affected individuals. Nicotinic acid may be quite efficacious in some individuals in lowering VLDL and raising HDL levels. Other regimens include the use of an HMG-CoA reductase

inhibitor alone or in combination with niacin or fibrates, such as gemfibrozil, although use of these combinations poses a small but increased risk of myositis (see later). The use of gemfibrozil alone to lower VLDL levels often is highly effective but is almost always associated with significant rises in LDL.

OTHER FORMS OF HYPERTRIGLYCERIDEMIA. Mild hypertriglyceridemia is one of the most commonly encountered hyperlipidemias. Although many patients with hypertriglyceridemia fit into one of the categories noted earlier, there are many other patients with triglyceride levels of 400 to 2000 mg/dL who do not seem to fall into any of those categories. They may have a family history of hypertriglyceridemia or quite commonly have one of the secondary forms of hypertriglyceridemia, such as that due to excess alcohol use or diabetes mellitus. Frequently, treating the underlying cause will ameliorate the hypertriglyceridemia, but often a milder form remains, probably indicative of an underlying, as yet undefined genetic defect.

ACQUIRED DISORDERS OF LIPOPROTEIN METABOLISM

Many medical conditions are associated with mild or even severe hyperlipidemia in the absence of underlying genetic hyperlipoproteinemia. With underlying genetic hyperlipidemia, acquired disorders can lead to greatly exaggerated effects on lipoprotein levels. Table 211–3 lists disorders commonly associated with changes in lipoprotein levels.

DIABETES MELLITUS (Chapter 242). Persons with untreated type I (insulin-dependent) diabetes, as well as uncontrolled type II (non-insulin-dependent) diabetes, frequently have hypertriglyceridemia, low HDL levels, and associated small, dense LDL particles. These individuals appear to have low adipose tissue or muscle LPL activity, which leads to relative impairment in VLDL clearance. Although LDL levels are not absolutely elevated in these individuals as a rule, for the degree of hypertriglyceridemia, the LDL levels are higher than expected. This may be due in part to nonenzymatic glycosylation of the LDL particle caused by hyperglycemia as well as by downregulation of LDL receptors because of lack of insulin.

CHRONIC UREMIA AND DIALYSIS (Chapter 118). Many individuals with chronic uremia have elevated VLDL levels with associated hypertriglyceridemia and low HDL-cholesterol levels. This condition persists even after initiation of maintenance hemodialysis or peritoneal dialysis. These lipoprotein abnormalities are related to defects in LPL-mediated triglyceride removal and/or associated overproduction.

ALCOHOL AND OTHER DRUGS. Among the many associated factors that cause mild degrees of hypertriglyceridemia, alcohol consumption is probably the most common; it increases triglyceride levels in most individuals. This occurs because both fatty acid synthesis and VLDL output are stimulated, and LPL activity is inhibited. In individuals with normal baseline VLDL levels, this is not usually a problem, but in those in whom there is excess VLDL secretion or some other additional basis for impairment in VLDL clearance, marked hypertriglyceridemia ensues with alcohol use. Diuretic agents and β-adrenergic blocking agents are also frequently associated with mild increases in triglyceride levels in patients with no underlying abnormality in lipoprotein metabolism but with quite marked increases in those with underlying hypertriglyceridemia. In individuals with genetic hypertriglyceridemia or familial combined hyperlipidemia,

Table 211–3 • ACQUIRED DISORDERS OF LIPOPROTEIN METABOLISM

Hypercholesterolemia	Hypertriglyceridemia
Nephrotic syndrome	Diabetes mellitus
Hypothyroidism	Uremia
Dysgammaglobulinemia	Sepsis
Acute intermittent porphyria	Obesity
Obstructive liver disease	Systemic lupus erythematosus
Combined Hyperlipidemia	Dysgammaglobulinemia
Nephrotic syndrome	Glycogen storage disease, type I
Hypothyroidism	Lipodystrophy
Glucocorticoid excess/	**Drugs**
Cushing's disease	Alcohol
Diuretics	Estrogens
Uncontrolled diabetes	β-Adrenergic blocking agents
	Isotretinoin (13-*cis*-retinoic acid)

estrogen use may also lead to marked increases in VLDL levels. Hypertriglyceridemia occurs in 25% of people given isotretinoin (13-cis-retinoic acid) for cystic acne.

HYPOTHYROIDISM (Chapter 239). Thyroid hormone is crucial in many steps of lipoprotein metabolism. LDL receptor activity is particularly sensitive to thyroxine levels, and in hypothyroidism, LDL levels are elevated because of downregulation of LDL receptor number. In addition, LPL activity is low, leading to elevated VLDL levels and even, rarely, chylomicronemia, especially in subjects with dysbetalipoproteinemia.

NEPHROTIC SYNDROME (Chapter 119). With massive proteinuria and with hypoalbuminemia, a compensatory increase occurs in overall hepatic protein synthesis, and in particular there is a marked increase in VLDL output. An associated defect in VLDL catabolism is also seen, in part due to depressed LPL activity.

HYPERLIPOPROTEINEMIA AND ATHEROSCLEROSIS

The etiology of atherosclerosis is multifactorial; a more general discussion of its pathogenesis can be found in Chapter 66. However, the cause-and-effect relationship between hypercholesterolemia and atherosclerosis has been proved in a large number of animal model studies and by large randomized, double-blind clinical intervention trials. Reducing plasma LDL-cholesterol levels sharply reduces the risk of subsequent clinical CAD in both patients with preexisting CAD and those free of CAD at the beginning of the study. In studies extending over 5 to 7 years, rates of morbidity and mortality from new coronary events have been reduced by as much as 30 to 40%. A statistically significant decrease in *total* mortality was also seen in three large studies, the Scandinavian Simvastatin Survival Study, the West of Scotland Coronary Prevention Study, and the British Heart Protection Study. Angiographic studies have documented that intensive cholesterol-lowering regimens slow progression of coronary lesions: in some cases, there has even been significant regression of lesions. Plasma triglyceride levels also correlate very significantly with risk of CAD, but the interpretation of this correlation is less clear, because elevation of triglyceride levels is frequently associated with other factors that may be more immediately relevant to the increase in CAD risk.

CHYLOMICRONS AND VLDL. Almost no evidence exists that chylomicrons are proatherogenic, and they are probably too large to penetrate into the artery. VLDL may also be too large, but CAD risk correlates with hypertriglyceridemia almost as well as it does with hypercholesterolemia in the fasting state, and most of the triglycerides in plasma are carried in VLDL. This correlation may be explained by the frequent association of hypertriglyceridemia with obesity, low HDL levels, small, dense LDL, and diabetes mellitus. More likely is the possibility that the catabolic products of VLDL, the IDLs, are atherogenic. Indeed, in hyperlipidemic patients with dysbetalipoproteinemia, the lipoprotein that accumulates is a type of IDL, so-called β-VLDL. Such patients are at increased risk of atherosclerosis and its complications. Moreover, the lipoprotein class that accumulates in experimental animals fed a high-fat, high-cholesterol diet is predominantly the same sort of β-VLDL.

LDL. There is no doubt about the atherogenicity of LDL. Patients with FH have strikingly premature atherosclerosis. However, in addition to greatly increased LDL levels, they also have some increase in IDL levels. Yet patients with a mutation of apo B that reduces its affinity for the LDL receptor accumulate *only* LDL, and their risk of premature CAD at any given plasma cholesterol level appears to be just as great as that of patients with LDL receptor deficiency. Increasing evidence suggests that oxidative modification of LDL within the artery is important, if not obligatory, for mediating the atherogenicity of LDL. Much evidence has been obtained that oxidized LDL is formed in the artery wall. Products of oxidized LDL may contribute to atherogenesis by many mechanisms, including attracting monocytes to the lesion and facilitating their conversion into macrophages. In turn, macrophages express scavenger receptors that take up oxidized LDL, leading to foam cells and the fatty streak lesion. In addition, products of oxidized LDL are toxic, producing endothelial damage and initiating thrombosis. Treatment with antioxidants has been shown to slow the progress of atherosclerosis in several animal models, but large-scale clinical trials of natural antioxidants (vitamin E, vitamin C, and β-carotene) have been largely negative.

HDL. A wealth of epidemiologic evidence establishes that high plasma HDL levels are associated with a lower risk of CAD. Until recently, it was not certain whether the protective effect of a high HDL level was referable to a direct effect of the HDL or whether it repre-

sented a "marker" for some other factor. Studies in transgenic mice have now shown that increasing HDL reduces the susceptibility of these mice to atherosclerosis. It is widely believed that HDL protects against atherosclerosis by facilitating reverse cholesterol transport, that is, the ability of HDL to accept excess cholesterol from tissues and return it to the liver either directly or via other lipoproteins, but this has not been explicitly proved. It should be noted, however, that in individual cases, the dynamic activity of HDL in reverse cholesterol transport does not necessarily parallel its steady-state concentration in the plasma. Furthermore, the importance of a low HDL as a risk factor needs to be evaluated in relation to the accompanying level of LDL. For example, vegetarians have relatively low HDL levels but because their LDL levels are very low also, they are not at an increased risk.

Lp(a). An increased risk for CAD has been found in many populations in association with increased levels of Lp(a), in particular when elevated LDL levels are also present. However Lp(a) appears to be an independent risk factor. Lp(a) is an LDL particle to which an additional large protein, termed *apo (a)*, is attached via a disulfide bond. There are many different allelic forms of apo (a) protein, varying widely in molecular size and determined in large part by genetic factors. Apo (a) has high homology to plasminogen but lacks the catalytically active site. Speculation has centered on the possibility that it interferes with plasminogen binding to its receptors and thus inhibits plasmin formation and thrombolysis. Alternatively, Lp(a) may have increased binding to the extracellular matrix of the artery, leading to greater deposition of the associated LDL. To date, no therapy has been found to effectively lower elevated Lp(a) levels, although niacin may lower it modestly.

PRACTICAL MANAGEMENT OF HYPERLIPIDEMIA

Rx Treatment of Hypercholesterolemia

Irrespective of the cause of elevated LDL levels, patients are usually managed similarly. In almost all cases, lowering LDL levels is achieved first by dietary intervention[1,2] and then, if necessary, by adding drug therapy. Because the LDL receptor plays such an important role in regulating plasma LDL levels, therapy is aimed at achieving maximal expression of hepatic LDL receptor activity. Dietary cholesterol and saturated fat both lead to suppression of hepatic LDL receptor activity, and therefore reduction of these dietary components leads to upregulation of hepatic LDL receptors and lowered plasma cholesterol levels. Individuals heterozygous for FH are more restricted in their response, and generally even stringent diets lower their LDL levels by no more than 5 to 10% below baseline levels. However, all individuals should be instructed in these diets, because some are unusually responsive.

Regulation of hepatic LDL receptor activity also appears to underlie mechanisms by which many commonly used hyperlipidemic drugs affect plasma cholesterol levels. The hepatocyte is the primary site of cholesterol synthesis. The cholesterol made by this cell is either excreted into plasma in the form of VLDL or is converted into bile acids, which are released into the intestine in response to meals. Normally, more than 95% of bile acids are reabsorbed and transported to the liver through the enterohepatic circulation and recycled through the liver up to six or seven times per day. Bile acid-binding resins work by binding bile acids in the intestine and promoting their subsequent loss in the stool. This prevents reabsorption and results in depletion of hepatic bile acid pools. In response, the hepatocyte actually increases cholesterol (and triglyceride) synthesis, as well as compensatory bile acid synthesis to replete the depleted bile acid pool. Despite this enhanced cholesterol synthesis, it is not sufficient to compensate for depletion of some crucial intracellular sterol pool, and the hepatocyte responds by also increasing LDL receptor expression. In turn, this directly removes LDL particles (or their precursors) from circulation. In this way, a nonsystemic agent leads to enhanced removal of plasma LDL particles and lowered plasma cholesterol levels. Very likely the soluble dietary fibers, such as oat bran, also lower plasma cholesterol by binding bile acids in a similar manner. For many individuals, this degree of plasma cholesterol lowering is sufficient. In others, however, the enhanced cholesterol (and triglyceride) synthesis leads to enhanced VLDL synthesis and release and, in effect, negates in part the cholesterol-lowering effect. In fact, many patients develop a transient or even permanent increase of plasma triglycerides (VLDLs) in response to bile sequestrant therapy, even as LDL levels are lowered. This enhanced production of VLDL leads to generation of more LDL, which offsets in part the enhanced LDL removal, leading to suboptimal lowering of LDL levels. For this reason, a second agent, in combination with a bile sequestrant, is frequently used and leads to synergistic lowering of LDL levels. For example, nicotinic acid, which effectively inhibits release of lipoproteins from the liver, is quite effective when combined with a bile acid-binding resin. Even more effective is the use of an HMG-CoA reductase inhibitor. This class of drugs, which have been termed *statins,* directly inhibits cholesterol biosynthesis and as a result not only inhibits the production of new lipoproteins but also, by apparently depleting still further specific hepatic sterol pools, leads to maximal expression of hepatic LDL receptor activity. Because of their ease of administration and relatively low incidence of side effects, they are now widely used as the primary therapy to lower elevated LDL levels. This effect is greatly enhanced when used in combination with a bile acid-binding resin and can lower LDL levels by more than 50%. If these two drugs are combined with nicotinic acid as a third agent, LDL levels can be lowered by 70% or more.

WHOM TO TREAT. The definition of hypercholesterolemia has been undergoing marked changes in recent years because it has become clear that "ideal" or "optimal" cholesterol levels are quite different from "normal" levels, which have been arbitrarily defined as values below the 90th or 95th percentile of the bell-shaped curve of the general population. The expert panel of the National Cholesterol Education Program (NCEP) has revised its guidelines with respect to desirable blood cholesterol levels for the population as a whole. [3] Many experts have argued that any plasma cholesterol level above 160 to 180 mg/dL is above *ideal* values, such as those found in the Japanese, for example, who have a low incidence of CAD. Unfortunately, the vast majority of people in the United States have plasma cholesterol levels that are far above this ideal. For this reason, there is an intensive ongoing effort to educate the general public as to appropriate dietary guidelines to lower plasma cholesterol levels.

It should be appreciated that the NCEP cutoff points may be appropriate for the population as a whole, but assessment of appropriate cholesterol levels for any given patient must take into account the presence of other risk factors. Although many individuals with very high plasma cholesterol levels clearly are at increased risk for CAD (Chapter 68), most patients who develop CAD actually have total and LDL cholesterol levels that would place them in the borderline or, not infrequently, even below the borderline category. Thus, individuals with hypertension, [4] diabetes, [5,6] or peripheral vascular disease are clearly at increased risk at any given plasma cholesterol level and benefit from drug therapy. Individuals with low HDL levels (i.e., <40 mg/dL) are also at significantly increased risk. A strong family history of heart disease is highly predictive of those individuals who are at increased risk. Finally, for diabetic patients or patients who have existing CAD and, in particular, for those who have already undergone coronary artery bypass graft or other types of intervention, the goal of therapy is to reduce LDL cholesterol levels to values well below 100 mg/dL. Studies in experimental animals and data from clinical trials show that the greater the reduction in plasma cholesterol levels, the greater the clinical benefit achieved. For example, the recently completed Heart Protection Study enrolled more than 20,000 men and women, 40 to 80 years of age, who had evidence of CAD or occlusive diseases of noncoronary arteries, were treated hypertensives, or had diabetes. The only lipid criterion was a total cholesterol level greater than 135 mg/dL. The subjects were randomized to a statin or placebo. After a mean follow-up period of approximately 5 years, there was a 17% reduction in the rate of mortality from all vascular causes, and a 12% reduction in the rate of all-cause mortality. Major vascular events were decreased 24% and this effect was seen for all age groups, even those 75 years of age or older on entry. [7] Furthermore, the positive benefits were observed irrespective of baseline total or LDL cholesterol levels (e.g., persons with LDL cholesterol <100 mg/dL on entry benefited proportionally as much as those with LDL cholesterol >130 mg/dL).

The NCEP continues to develop the optimal protocol for screening and management of cholesterol levels in the general population. It is now recommended that all adults 20 years of age or older undergo a fasting lipoprotein profile (total cholesterol, LDL cholesterol, HDL cholesterol and triglyceride) once every 5 years. If a fasting sample cannot be obtained, only the total and HDL cholesterol values will be useful. In this situation, if total cholesterol is 200 mg/dL or greater or HDL is less than 40 mg/dL, then a subsequent fasting lipoprotein profile should be obtained. Because the relationship between LDL cholesterol and CAD risk is continuous, the newest NCEP guidelines base the classification of cholesterol levels on LDL values (Fig. 211–4).

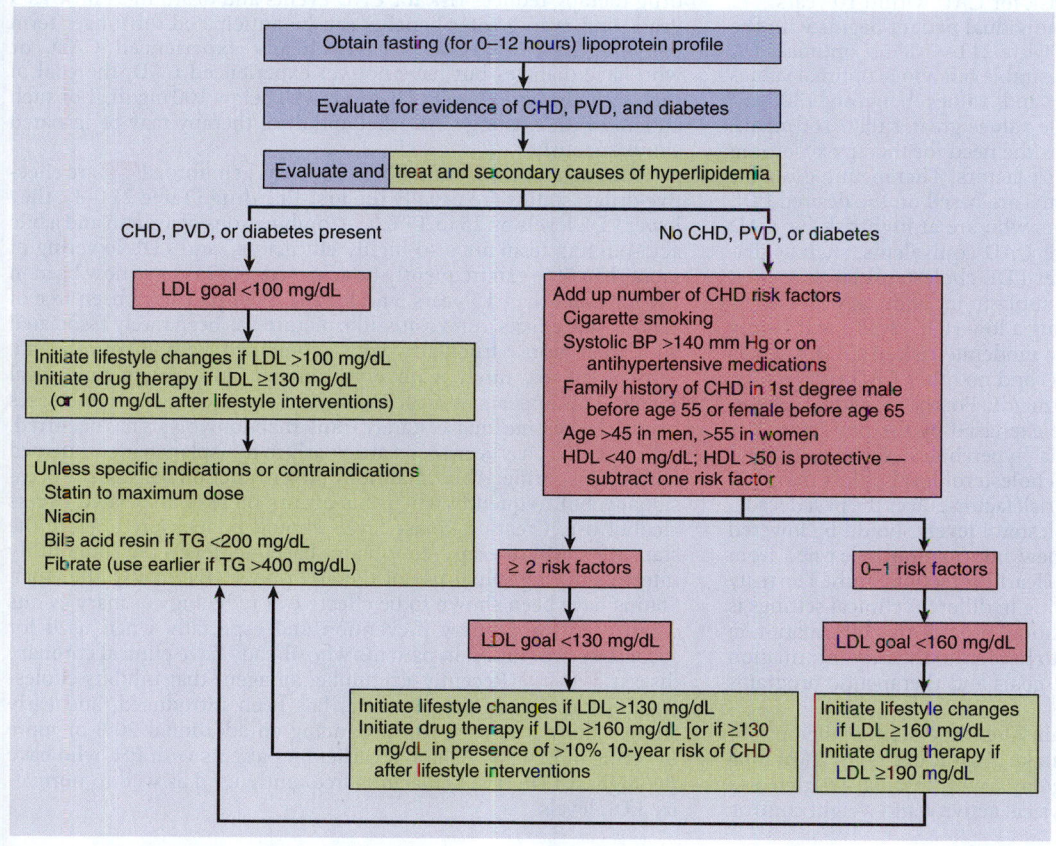

FIGURE 211–4 • Approach to lipid screening and treatment. BP = blood pressure; CHD = coronary heart disease; HDL = high-density lipoprotein; LDL = low-density lipoprotein; PVD = peripheral vascular disease; TG = triglycerides. (Based on recommendations of the Executive Summary of the Third Report of the National Cholesterol Education Program [NCEP] Expert Panel on detection, evaluation, and treatment of high blood cholesterol in adults [Adult Treatment Panel III]. JAMA 2001;285:2486-2497.)

Table 211–4 • PRIMARY LIPOPROTEIN DISORDERS AMENABLE TO TREATMENT BY DIET AND DRUGS

DISORDER	MECHANISMS	COMPLICATIONS	TREATMENT*
Familial or polygenic hypercholesterolemia	Diminished LDL receptor activity Defective apolipoprotein B that is poorly recognized by the LDL receptor	CAD; occasionally PVD, stroke	Diet Statin Bile acid–binding resin Nicotinic acid Fibrate if statin intolerance
Familial combined hyperlipidemia[†]	Increased hepatic secretion of apolipoprotein B–rich VLDL and conversion to LDL	CAD, PVD, stroke	Diet and weight loss Statin Nicotinic acid Fibrate[†]
Familial hypertriglyceridemia[§]	Decreased serum triglyceride removal resulting from decreased LPL activity Increased hepatic secretion of triglyceride-rich VLDL	Pancreatitis at triglyceride concentrations >2000 mg/dL; variable risk of CAD	Diet and weight loss Fibrate[†] Nicotinic acid n-3 fatty acids Oxandrolone
Remnant removal disease (familial dysbetalipoproteinemia)	Increased secretion of VLDL Impaired removal of remnant lipoproteins resulting from heterozygosity ($\varepsilon_2/\varepsilon_2$) or heterozygosity ($\varepsilon_2/\varepsilon_3$ or $\varepsilon_2/\varepsilon_4$) for apolipoprotein E ε_2	PVD, CAD, stroke	Diet, weight loss Fibrate[†] Nicotinic acid Statin
Familial hypoalphalipoproteinemia (low-HDL syndrome)[§]	Diminished apolipoprotein A-I formation, increased removal, increased CETP or hepatic lipase activity	CAD, PVD (may be associated with hypertriglyceridemia)	Exercise and weight loss Nicotinic acid Fibrate[†] Statin

* Treatments may be given alone or in combination; the primary treatment is listed first, followed by other treatments in decreasing order of importance.
[†] Diabetes mellitus can greatly exacerbate the condition. The hyperlipidemia of diabetes is mechanistically closest to familial combined hyperlipidemia.
[‡] Combined treatment with a fibrate and a statin can increase the risk of myopathy.
[§] This disorder is characterized by low concentrations of HDL cholesterol.
CAD = coronary artery disease; CETP = cholesterol ester transfer protein; HDL = high-density lipoprotein; LPL = lipoprotein lipase; PVD = peripheral vascular disease; VLDL = very low density lipoprotein.
From Knopp RH: Drug treatment of lipid disorders. N Engl J Med 1999;341:498–511.

It should be appreciated that the LDL value of 160 mg/dL, designated as high, is a value that represents the top 20th percentile of the U.S. adult population and corresponds to a value at which the risk for CAD rises sharply. Similarly, an HDL value of less than 40 mg/dL also represents an independent risk factor. Other factors that increase risk independent of the LDL cholesterol value include the presence of existing CAD, as it confers a high risk for CAD within 10 years.

The classification of risk of an individual patient begins with the LDL cholesterol level, as noted in Figure 211–4. Thus, optimal LDL values are well below 100 mg/dL, desirable but above optimal values are between 100 and 129 mg/dL, and values between 130 and 159 mg/dL are borderline high while values greater than 160 mg/dL are frankly high. One then addresses the need for therapy according to the presence of the associated risk factors. Therapeutic goals for the treatment of hypercholesterolemia are based on the desired LDL cholesterol levels. Thus, for patients who are at high risk for CAD because of already existing CAD, or CAD equivalents, such as diabetes, the goal of therapy is to lower LDL cholesterol levels to well below 100 mg/dL. This would also apply to individuals with two or more risk equivalents, such as having a low HDL level[8] and family history of CAD. Patients with more moderate risk of CAD, such as those with no family history of CAD and no other CAD risk factors, can have a target goal of less than 130 mg/dL. For the individual patient, considerable judgment needs to be exercised by the physician. For example, in an individual with familial hypercholesterolemia, it would seem prudent to strive for an LDL cholesterol level of less than 100 mg/dL, even in the absence of other risk factors. Over the past decade, the target levels to which LDL cholesterol levels should be lowered have been continually revised as new information is learned from clinical trials, as exemplified in the Heart Protection Study. The truly optimal degree of cholesterol lowering in different clinical settings is not yet known, but ongoing trials should provide this information in the coming years. Physicians need to be alert to the new information so as to provide optimal treatment goals and therapeutic programs for their patients.

Primary prevention of CAD remains the cornerstone of therapy.[1,2] This includes a diet with reduced intake of saturated fat (<7% of total calories) and cholesterol (<200 mg/day), with total fat restricted to 25 to 35% of calories, increased physical activity, and weight control.

This applies even to individuals with optimal or near-optimal cholesterol levels. Such therapeutic lifestyle changes are the foundation of primary prevention. Ordinarily, such lifestyle changes should be tried for 3 months or more before a decision is made with regard to the need for drug therapy. However, for individuals with higher risk because of increased LDL levels or the presence of other risk factors, drug therapy reduces risk for CAD events and death in as little as 5 years, and even greater benefits can be anticipated for longer term use. For individuals who have already experienced CAD, or who have diabetes but have not yet experienced CAD, the goal of therapy is always to lower LDL levels well below 100 mg/dL. For such patients with existing CAD, diet and drug therapy may be initiated simultaneously.

Although niacin[6,9] and fibrates such as gemfibrozil[8,10] are effective drugs, statins are usually the first-line drug (Table 211–4); they lower LDL levels by 25 to 45%.[3,7] Combinations of a statin and a bile acid-binding resin are also highly efficacious, and LDL lowering of more than 50% can frequently be achieved. Statins have now been in use for more than 15 years, and for the most part have been free of serious side effects. A myositis-like picture has been rarely associated with their use, particularly when combined with nicotinic acid, gemfibrozil, or, rarely, with erythromycin and certain antifungal agents. This appears as muscle pain and is associated with increases in muscle creatine kinase. Rarely, frank rhabdomyolysis has occurred. This side effect has been seen particularly in transplant patients treated with cyclosporine. Abnormalities in liver function tests occur occasionally, but frequently when this occurs there is associated excess alcohol use. Creatine kinase levels should be measured before the start of statin therapy to obtain baseline levels, at bimonthly intervals during initial use of therapy, and semiannually after that. Statins have been shown to be effective at reducing coronary events when used for primary prevention and especially when used for secondary prevention in patients who already have clinical coronary disease.[3–5,7,11,12] Recently, ezetimibe, an agent that inhibits cholesterol absorption in the intestine, has been introduced, and early studies show it is useful in producing an additional 20% or more lowering of LDL.[13] As noted earlier, in patients with FH, who have the highest LDL levels, niacin is frequently used as well to normalize LDL levels.

Rx Treatment of Mild Hypertriglyceridemia

The new NCEP guidelines have defined the normal triglyceride level as less 150 mg/dL; borderline high as 150 to 199 mg/dL; high as 200 to 499 mg/dL; and very high as 500 mg/dL or greater. As noted earlier, the link between triglycerides and CAD is complex and may be explained by associations between high triglyceride and low HDL levels and atherogenic forms of LDL. Nevertheless, recent meta-analysis studies suggest that elevated triglycerides may be an independent risk factor for CAD. Therefore, attention should be paid to elevated levels. Patients with milder degrees of hypertriglyceridemia should be treated initially with nonpharmacologic therapy. This should include weight reduction in overweight patients, increased physical activity, and low-fat diets. Alcohol should be restricted. Gemfibrozil lowers VLDL levels, but frequently there is an associated rise in LDL levels. Niacin has been used to both decrease VLDL and increase HDL. Many experts now use a statin as initial therapy for treating patients with familial combined hyperlipidemia. VLDL levels are lowered, HDL levels increase, and there is no increase in LDL levels. In some patients, a combination of a statin and niacin is used, and in others the combined use of gemfibrozil and a statin has been useful, but these combinations may increase slightly the risk of myositis.

RECOGNITION AND TREATMENT OF MARKED HYPERTRIGLYCERIDEMIA: THE CHYLOMICRONEMIA SYNDROME. Marked chylomicronemia with plasma triglyceride levels greater than 1000 mg/dL is associated with a combination of signs and symptoms that has been termed the *chylomicronemia syndrome*. Prompt and effective therapy is indicated to prevent severe medical complications, including pancreatitis. This syndrome occurs whenever there is excess accumulation of chylomicrons. Rarely, this occurs as a result of homozygous LPL deficiency, or apo C-II deficiency. More commonly, this may be due to a combination of an inherited defect in a factor involved in triglyceride clearance (e.g., heterozygosity for LPL deficiency) and an acquired exacerbating problem (see Table 211–3). Uncontrolled diabetic ketoacidosis is a common cause.

Plasma triglyceride levels may become exceedingly high, with values well in excess of 20,000 mg/dL. For reasons that are not understood, the clinical signs and symptoms do not necessarily correlate with the level of hypertriglyceridemia, and patients who have triglyceride levels as high as 20,000 mg/dL can be asymptomatic, whereas other individuals with triglyceride levels of 3000 mg/dL or lower may have abdominal pain and/or pancreatitis. Lipemia retinalis can often be observed, and eruptive xanthomas are also frequently seen. Patients may complain of paresthesias of the extremities, particularly on the dorsum of the hands and feet, and frequently have an erythematous flush on the face and chest. With marked hyperchylomicronemia, impairment of recent memory has been noted. Patients also may complain of symmetric arthralgia, although physical findings of joint involvement are not found. In diabetic patients, this syndrome may be associated with marked insulin resistance, marked hyperglycemia, and frequently marked diabetic ketoacidosis. Because of the marked hyperchylomicronemia, an increased proportion of the total blood volume is occupied by fat, and many routine laboratory tests will be invalid because fat is sampled as well as the water space. For example, hyponatremia is frequently seen in samples from hyperchylomicronemic subjects, but this is a "pseudo hyponatremia" that occurs because of inclusion of lipid in the aliquot of blood sampled, and lipid does not contain sodium. Simple removal of chylomicrons from plasma by a brief centrifugation step before laboratory tests can eliminate such artifacts. Frequently a false-negative finding for amylase occurs in lipemic plasma, apparently due to an inhibitor of amylase activity.

The diagnosis is made by the presence of chylomicrons in fasting plasma, which will always appear milky. Plasma will usually appear turbid when plasma triglycerides are greater than 350 mg/dL, because of the excess accumulation of VLDL, and will appear grossly lipemic when triglycerides are greater than 1000 mg/dL. With extreme degrees of hypertriglyceridemia, the whole blood takes on the appearance of cream of tomato soup, and plasma allowed to sit in a refrigerator overnight will develop a thick layer of chylomicrons on top. Because the major cause of hyperchylomicronemia is accumulation of dietary fat, the treatment is absolute elimination of fat from the diet until triglyceride levels have fallen to a safe level. With associated pancreatitis, patients usually receive nothing orally; and in this setting plasma triglyceride levels will usually fall by 50% every 2 to 3 days. When refeeding begins, fat (of all kinds) must be totally avoided initially and then replaced very gradually.

RARE DISORDERS OF LIPOPROTEIN METABOLISM

There are a number of inherited disorders of lipoprotein metabolism that are rare but that have taught us a great deal about lipoprotein function. Patients with hypobetalipoproteinemia have mutations in one or both apo B alleles that lead to truncated apo B proteins. Because of defective synthesis and/or enhanced intravascular catabolism, there are markedly reduced levels of apo B-containing lipoproteins in plasma. Heterozygotes may have LDL-cholesterol levels less than 50 mg/dL, and rare compound heterozygotes may have LDL-cholesterol levels less than 5 mg/dL. Usually these patients are asymptomatic and long lived. Patients with the rare autosomal recessive disorder of abetalipoproteinemia have a total inability to release apo B-48, and hence chylomicrons, from intestinal cells and apo B-100, and thus VLDL, from liver. As noted earlier, they have a normal apo B gene but lack MTP, which is required for assembly of lipoproteins. Because they cannot make chylomicrons, they malabsorb fat and fat-soluble vitamins. They manifest ataxia, neuropathy, and retinitis pigmentosa and are responsive to high doses of vitamin E. Patients with Tangier disease, a Mendelian recessive disorder, have virtually no HDL in plasma, yet their gene for apo A1 is perfectly normal. The defective gene codes for an ATP-binding cassette (ABCA1) transporter required for the removal of cholesterol from cells. This results in the accumulation of cholesteryl esters in phagocytic cells. Patients typically have enlarged, orange tonsils and develop corneal opacities and polyneuropathy. Despite the near absence of HDL, these homozygotes do not show an obvious increase in CAD risk, and this may be because their LDL cholesterol levels are usually very low. Therapy to lower their LDL levels may be indicated. Preliminary data suggest that heterozygotes are at increased risk, possibly because their LDL levels are higher.

Patients with mutations in cholesterol ester transfer protein (CETP) have also recently been described, particularly in Japanese populations. This condition is associated with cholesteryl ester enrichment of HDL and greatly elevated HDL-cholesterol values, frequently more than 100 mg/dL. Although not proven, it is generally believed that this mutation is associated with protection from CAD. In contrast, in patients with deficiency of lecithin cholesterol acyltransferase (LCAT), unesterified cholesterol accumulates in plasma and tissues, and patients may develop premature CAD. In addition, they have corneal opacities, hemolytic anemia, and early renal failure. Therapy consists of renal transplantation and fat-restricted diets. Two rare disorders leading to accumulation of abnormal sterols have also been described. Patients with cerebrotendinous xanthomatosis have defective bile acid synthesis with associated oversynthesis and accumulation of cholestanol and cholesterol in brain, tendons, and other tissues. They can have neurologic symptoms (including cerebellar ataxia and dementia), tendon xanthomas, atherosclerosis, and cataracts. Finally, patients may have large tendon xanthomas due to abnormal accumulation of plant sterols, chiefly β-sitosterol. Normally, plant sterols are not absorbed, but in patients with sitosterolemia, there is enhanced intestinal absorption and accumulation of β-sitosterol in plasma and tendons. Recently, mutations in two adjacent genes that encoded ATP binding cassette half-transporters, ABCG5 and ABCG8, which together play a putative role in sterol transport in the intestine and liver, have been discovered in patients with this disorder. Because these patients also hyperabsorb cholesterol, these proteins may be involved in general in intestinal sterol absorption. Treatment consists of diets low in plant sterols and cholesterol and the use of cholestyramine to promote gastrointestinal loss.

1. Knopp RH, Walden CE, Retzlaff BM, et al: Long-term cholesterol-lowering effects of 4 fat-restricted diets in hypercholesterolemic and combined hyperlipidemic men. JAMA 1997;278:1509–1515.
2. Knopp RH, Retzlaff B, Walden C, et al: One-year effects of increasingly fat-restricted, carbohydrate-enriched diets on lipoprotein levels in free-living subjects. Proc Soc Exp Biol Med 2002;225:191–199.
3. Executive Summary of the Third Report of the National Cholesterol Education Program (NCEP) Expert Panel on Detection, Evaluation, and Treatment of High Blood Cholesterol in Adults (Adult Treatment Panel III). JAMA 2001;285:2486–2497.
4. Sever PS, Dahlof B, Poulter NR, et al: Prevention of coronary and stroke events with atorvastatin in hypertensive patients who have average or lower-than-average cholesterol concentrations, in the Anglo-Scandinavian Cardiac Outcomes

Trial–Lipid Lowering Arm (ASCOT-LLA): A multicentre randomised controlled trial. Lancet 2003;361:1149–1158.

5. Collins R, Armitage J, Parish S, et al: MRC/BHF Heart Protection Study of cholesterol-lowering with simvastatin in 5963 people with diabetes: A randomised placebo-controlled trial. Lancet 2003;361:2005–2016.

6. Elam MB, Hunninghake DB, Davis KB, et al: Effect of niacin on lipid and lipoprotein levels and glycemic control in patients with diabetes and peripheral arterial disease: The ADMIT study: A randomized trial. Arterial Disease Multiple Intervention Trial. JAMA 2000;284:1263–1270.

7. Heart Protection Study Collaborative Group: MRC/BHF Heart Protection Study of antioxidant vitamin supplementation in 20,536 high-risk individuals: a randomised placebo-controlled trial. Lancet 2002;360:23–33.

8. Robins SJ, Collins D, Wittes JT, et al: Relation of gemfibrozil treatment and lipid levels with major coronary events: VA-HIT: A randomized controlled trial. JAMA 2001;285:1585–1591.

9. Canner PL, Berge KG, Wenger NK, et al: Fifteen year mortality in Coronary Drug Project patients: Long-term benefit with niacin. J Am Coll Cardiol 1986;8:1245–1255.

10. Rubins HB, Robins SJ, Collins D, et al: Gemfibrozil for the secondary prevention of coronary heart disease in men with low levels of high-density lipoprotein cholesterol. N Engl J Med 1999;341:410–418.

11. Randomised trial of cholesterol lowering in 4444 patients with coronary heart disease: The Scandinavian Simvastatin Survival Study (4S). Lancet 1994;344:1383–1389.

12. Schwartz GG, Olsson AG, Ezekowitz MD, et al: Effects of atorvastatin on early recurrent ischemic events in acute coronary syndromes: The MIRACL study: A randomized controlled trial. JAMA 2001;285:1711–1718.

13. Ballantyne CM, Houri J, Notarbartolo A, et al: Effect of ezetimibe coadministered with atorvastatin in 628 patients with primary hypercholesterolemia: a prospective, randomized, double-blind trial. Circulation 2003;107:2409–2415.

SUGGESTED READINGS

Glass CK, Witztum JL: Atherosclerosis: The road ahead. Cell 2001;104:503–516. *A look into future approaches to understanding and treating atherosclerosis.*

Libby P: Inflammation in atherosclerosis. Nature 2002;420:868–874. *Comprehensive review of modern concepts of the atherogenic process as an inflammatory disease.*

Steinberg D: Atherogenesis in perspective: Hypercholesterolemia and inflammation as partners in crime. Nat Med 2002;11:1211–1217. *Provides a conceptual framework to explain the interactive nature of the two major theories of atherogenesis. An understanding of these concepts provides a rational basis to approach therapy.*

Witztum JL, Steinberg D: The oxidative modification hypothesis of atherosclerosis: Does it hold for humans? Trends Cardiovasc Med 2001;11:93–102. *The appropriate clinical trials to test the importance of oxidation in the pathogenesis of atherosclerosis in humans remain to be performed.*

212 GALACTOSEMIA

Louis J. Elsas II

Definition

Classic galactosemia is an autosomal recessive trait characterized by neonatal jaundice, bleeding diathesis, feeding intolerance, lethargy, *Escherichia coli* sepsis, hypotension, and death if untreated. This clinical syndrome is caused by absent function of galactose-1-phosphate uridyl transferase (GALT) (E.C. 2.7.7.12) and results in the accumulation of galactose and galactose-1-phosphate in blood and excretion of excess galactose and galactitol in urine if lactose ingestion continues (Fig. 212–1). Impairment of two other enzymes can cause less severe elevation of blood galactose in this evolutionarily conserved galactose metabolic pathway. Deficiency of uridine diphosphate (UDP)-galactose-4-epimerase (GALE) increases erythrocyte galactose-1-p and galactose in the presence of normally functioning GALT. Benign and "generalized" neurologic dysfunctions are described in GALE deficiency. Galactosemia and excess urinary galactitol accumulate in galactokinase (GALK) deficiency. In the absence of galactose-1-phosphate accumulation, patients with GALK deficiency have neonatal and childhood cataracts without hepatocellular dysfunction. For all of these enzyme-deficient, inherited metabolic disorders, lactose (galactose)-restricted diets should be implemented during the first days of life.

Incidence and Prevalence

The incidence of GALT deficiency is defined from many newborn, population-based screening programs. The severe mutations in either homozygous or compound heterozygous genotypes have an incidence of about 1 in 35,000 newborns. However, less severe mutations that impair erythrocyte GALT activity to below 15% of normal and increase erythrocyte galactose-1-phosphate have an incidence of about 1 in 8000 newborns. GALK deficiency has an unknown incidence in the general population, probably less than 1 in 100,000. Within inbred isolates such as the Roma Gypsy, however, the prevalence is 1 in 1600, with the carrier rate as high as 5% in that population. GALE deficiency has an estimated prevalence of 1 in 23,000 in Japan, but the prevalence is unknown and less frequent in Europe and the United States.

Pathophysiology and Clinical Manifestations

The galactose metabolic pathway outlined in Figure 212–1 is evolutionarily conserved. In *E. coli* and *Saccharomyces cerevisiae*, the genes for these enzymes are regulated through *operons* and *regulons*. Although humans have maintained structural homology for the proteins, their genes are located on separate chromosomes (Table 212–1). The products of this pathway produce energy and CO_2 from glucose-1-phosphate and maintain the pools of UDP glucose and UDP galactose that are essential substrates for glycogen synthesis, post-translational production of glycoproteins, and the formation of glycolipids. In brief, this pathway is essential for cellular growth and differentiation. As can be seen in Figure 212–1, there are several pathways available to maintain homeostasis of UDP glucose and UDP galactose concentrations even when GALT

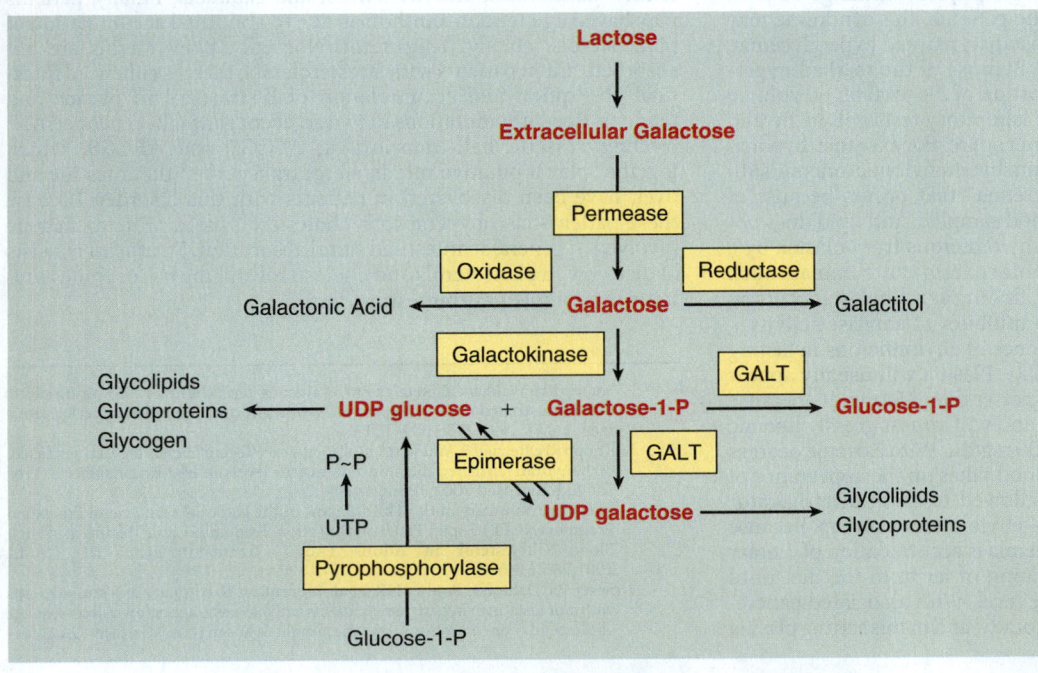

FIGURE 212–1 • Metabolic pathway for galactose conversion to glucose-1-P, UDP glucose, and UDP galactose. Trivial names for enzymes are boxed in black, and substrates and products of galactose metabolism are depicted in red. Three enzymes produce galactosemia when impaired in humans: GALT (galactose-1-phosphate uridyl transferase), GALE (UDP-galactose-4-epimerase), and GALK (galactokinase). Normally, end products of galactose metabolism include CO_2 production from glucose-1-P and the synthesis of glycogen, glycolipid, and glycoproteins. Alternate pathways for accumulated galactose are indicated and include the increased production of galactitol and galactonic acid. Galactonic acid is metabolized through the pentose pathway while galactitol accumulates in cells as an end product. UDP = uridine diphosphate; UTP = uridine triphosphate.

is impaired. Recent expression microarray experiments with GALT-deficient yeast and their revertants have defined the toxic effects of galactose-1-phosphate when accumulated to millimolar concentrations. Galactose-1-P inhibits glucose-1-phosphate pyrophosphorylase, thus decreasing the amount of UDP glucose and consequently UDP galactose that is available for important neonatal functions such as bilirubin conjugation, brain myelin formation, and the post-translational processing of many secreted proteins, such as follicle-stimulating hormone, and membrane receptors. This pleiotropic effect of accumulated intracellular galactose-1-phosphate is severe in GALT deficiency and may occur to a lesser degree in GALE deficiency. Its effects are recognized pathologically in the newborn as rising direct bilirubin (and kernicterus), hepatocellular failure, growth failure, and, if untreated, as severe neurologic deficits such as mental retardation, tremor, spasticity, and seizures. Approximately 10% of newborns with GALT deficiency have *E. coli* sepsis and die. Public health newborn screening programs have reduced but not eliminated this natural pathologic history. Lethal sepsis may result from reduced glycoprotein cell wall barriers to intestinal bacteria and from decreased cellular resistance secondary to reduced galactosyl and neuraminic acid residues on surface proteins.

If the infant with GALT deficiency is detected within a few days of life and galactose removed from the diet, there is rapid remission of hepatocellular damage and normalization of health. However, an enigmatic set of chronic problems occurs later in life, including verbal dyspraxia (56%), reduced IQ (46%), cataracts (10%), ovarian failure (up to 85% in females), ataxia and tremors (18%), and growth delay (before puberty). The pathobiology of these conditions is not known. Some could be embryologic in origin and related to "toxic" effects of accumulating galactose-1-P on glycoproteins in rapidly dividing embryologic cells. Intracellular accumulation of galactitol is known to cause cataracts and seizures by its osmotic effects in lens epithelium and neurons, respectively.

Cataracts without hepatic, ovarian, or central nervous system pathologic conditions are found in GALK deficiency. As compared to GALT deficiency, galactitol but not galactose-1-P is accumulated through the alternate aldose reductase pathway (see Fig. 212–1). The accumulation of galactitol in lens fibers produces an osmotic gradient, swelling of cells, loss of permeability, cell death, and scarring. This process also occurs in GALT deficiency and is progressive if galactose intake continues.

Deficiency of GALE has a bias of ascertainment with regard to clinical outcome, since most reported families have been identified for evaluation of pervasive mental delays. At a molecular level, some mutations such as V94M are found in more than one family, have been evaluated in vitro, and are presumed to cause disease in humans. Further molecular studies of heterozygous mutations in GALK, GALT, and GALE may reveal "sensitivity" genes for more common adult disorders such as ovarian failure, presenile dementia, liver failure, and early cataract formation. Some mutations in GALT and GALE have a "dominant negative" effect on the normal allele, and multiple heterozygous hits on this important glycobiologic pathway could have additive effects, producing organ pathology.

Diagnosis

Since GALT deficiency can be lethal yet is preventable in the neonatal period, population-based newborn screening is used to identify and urgently treat affected newborns. The GALT enzyme is measured in erythrocytes from dried blood on filter paper using enzyme-linked fluorometric methods. In classic galactosemia, there is no GALT activity, but variant galactosemia is also detected with approximately 5 to 25% activity. In hot, humid months, prevalence of these variant forms is greater because of the instability of mutant GALT dimeric proteins. State-based laboratories also use accumulation of galactose and galactose-1-P as part of the screening process.

A positive screening test should *immediately* be followed by retrieval of the newborn, removal of lactose from the diet, and a more quan-

Table 212–1 • DISORDERS OF GALACTOSE METABOLISM AND ASSOCIATED MUTATIONS

DEFICIENT ENZYME	CHROMOSOMAL LOCATION	SOME COMMON MUTATIONS	GEOGRAPHIC OR ETHNIC ORIGIN	CLINICAL SYMPTOMS* (UNTREATED)
GALT (galactose-1-phosphate-uridyl transferase)	9p13	Q188R	Northern Europe	Severe
		S135L	Africa	Moderate
		K285N	Southern Germany Croatia	Severe
		L195P	Europe	Severe
		Y209C	Asia	Severe
		F161S	Europe	Severe
		N314D	Panethnic	Benign
		5Kbdel	Ashkenazim	Severe
		IVS2 nt2a → g (167 more)	Hispanic	Moderate
GALK (galactokinase)	17q24	P28T	Roma Gypsies	Cataracts
		R68C	Europe	Cataracts
		T288M	Europe	Cataracts
		R256W	Japan	Cataracts
		A384P	Europe	Cataracts
		T344M	Japan	Cataracts
		G349S	Japan	Cataracts
		410delg	Japan	Cataracts
		509-510delgt (12 more)	Japan	Cataracts
GALE (UDP galactose-4-epimerase)	1p36	L183P	Pakistani Europe	Late childhood mental retardation
		N34S	Pakistani Europe	Late childhood mental retardation
		G90E	Asia	Mental retardation
		D103G	Asia	Mental retardation
		K257R	Africa	Benign
		V94M	British	Pervasive delays Hepatomegaly
		L313M	Asia	Benign
		D103G	British	Benign

*See text for description in more detail.
UDP = uridine diphosphate.

titative measurement of GALT activity and its isoforms by isoelectric focusing. Additional studies include quantitation of erythrocyte galactose-1-P, urinary galactitol, and molecular genotyping of GALT. All of the above are available through commercial laboratories on an emergency status. An additional study, the "breath test" quantitates total body oxidation of ^{13}C-galactose to $^{13}CO_2$ in the infant's breath. GALT enzyme activity below 5% of control, erythrocyte galactose-1-phosphate above 1.5 mg/dL, urinary galactitol above 78 mmoles/mole creatinine, and $^{13}CO_2$ in breath below 5% of administered ^{13}C-D-galactose indicate clinically significantly impaired GALT. This full set of diagnostic tests is recommended, confirms the diagnosis, and provides a basis for prognosis. For example, the S135L mutation, common in African Americans with GALT-deficient galactosemia, has no erythrocyte GALT activity, but total body oxidation of ^{13}C-galactose to $^{13}CO_2$ is normal and prognosis is good if the deficiency is detected and treated in the newborn period. By contrast, the Q188R mutation is common in people of Northern European descent and has absent erythrocyte GALT activity, but these patients have less than 5% of ^{13}C-galactose recovered as $^{13}CO_2$ during their breath test. If the Q188R mutation is either homozygous or associated with another "severe" mutant allele listed in Table 212–1, outcome for dyspraxic speech and for ovarian failure is increased 10-fold.

Population newborn screening may not be universal or timely and thus the diagnosis should be entertained in any infant with jaundice, progressive hepatocellular dysfunction, cataracts, or *E. coli* sepsis. Quantitation of erythrocyte galactose-1-P, urinary galactitol, GALT enzyme assay in erythrocytes, GALT molecular genotype, and galactose oxidation studies are available.* The differential diagnosis includes other causes for hepatocellular dysfunction, such as hepatitis, biliary obstruction, and other rare inborn errors such as Niemann-Pick disease, hereditary fructose intolerance, and tyrosinemia, type I.

The diagnosis of GALE deficiency is entertained when newborn screening results indicate elevated red blood cell galactose-1-P and galactose but normal erythrocyte GALT activity. Most newborns remain asymptomatic, but they may develop cataracts or mental retardation later in life. The diagnosis is made by finding reduced GALE activity in erythrocytes, cultured fibroblasts, or transformed lymphoblasts. Molecular analysis of the GALE gene is available on a research basis.

Deficiency of GALK will *not* be detected by most public health newborn screening programs and should be suspected in any patient with congenital or early-onset cataracts. Diagnosis is suspected on finding increased urinary galactitol and confirmed by finding reduced GALK (galactokinase) in peripheral erythrocytes. Molecular analysis of the GALK gene is available on a research basis. Molecular analysis of GALK is important when considering heterozygosity for GALK deficiency as a diagnosis for patients with later-onset cataracts and a positive family history. The enzyme analysis alone for GALK may not differentiate heterozygosity from homozygous normal, and further molecular analysis is recommended.

Rx Prevention and Treatment

Treatment of galactosemia is exclusion of galactose from the diet, which involves the elimination of milk and its products. The mainstay of the diet for an infant is the substitution of soy preparation for all milk products. Since endogenous galactose production continues, strict avoidance of all casein-derived proteins as well as lactose itself is necessary in the newborn. Some fruits and vegetables, such as watermelons and tomatoes, contain bioavailable galactosides and are avoided. Education of parents and older children about the galactose content of foods is important. Lists of the galactose content of foods are available that are useful in management. Calcium supplements are necessary, and approximately 500 to 1000 mg ionized calcium per day should be prescribed. Lactose must not be used as filler or as a medication by the pharmacy. For example, lactulose is used in managing the hyperammonemia of liver disease but contains gram quantities of free lactose and must be avoided in newborns with liver disease secondary to GALT deficiency. Speech evaluation is indicated at age 2 to 3 years, and speech therapy can prevent later "learning disabilities" if early intervention is provided. In females, estrogen creams and replacement therapy may be indicated when ovarian failure is present. Ophthalmologic evaluation for cataracts may be required periodically.

*Gene Tests/Gene Clinics. http://www.genetests.org Accessed May 8, 2003. *Updated, inclusive website for diagnostic laboratories and for clinical reviews of galactosemia.*

Determination of the galactose-1-phosphate content of erythrocytes and urinary galactitol is useful in monitoring adherence to the diet. Erythrocyte galactose-1-phosphate should be kept below 3.5 mg/dL (140 mmol/L). Concentrations above this level increase the odds ratios for developing dyspraxia and ovarian failure.

Primary prevention of galactosemia involves heterozygote detection and prenatal counseling of at-risk family members and parents of galactosemic children. Prenatal monitoring is available in the early second trimester by combined GALT enzyme analysis of cultured amniotic fluid cells or chorionic villous cells. Mutational analysis of DNA from these cells is the most sensitive and specific prenatal diagnostic method. To use mutational analysis, the genotype of the proband must be known. Late trimester analysis of galactitol in amniotic fluid is useful. As measured by gas chromatography/mass spectroscopy or high-pressure liquid chromatography, amniotic fluid from affected fetuses have a range of 5.9 to 10.6 µM galactitol, with normal being 0.23 to 1.6 µM. There is no evidence that restricting maternal lactose intake will influence the intracellular overproduction by affected fetal cells of either galactose-1-P or galactitol.

Prognosis

If a galactose-restricted diet is provided during the first 7 days and continued throughout life, the presenting hepatotoxic symptoms resolve quickly and prognosis is good. If the diagnosis of GALT-deficient galactosemia is not established within days of life, the infant treated only with intravenous antibiotics and partially restricted lactose intake demonstrates relapsing and episodic jaundice and bleeding from altered hemostasis. If treatment is delayed, complications such as mental and growth retardation are likely. Despite early and adequate therapy, the long-term outcome in older children and adults with "severe" galactosemia can include speech defects, poor growth, poor intellectual function, neurologic deficits (predominantly extrapyramidal findings with ataxia), and ovarian failure. Outcome and the "disease burden" can be predicted based on the level of GALT activity, GALT genotype, age at which successful therapeutic control was achieved, and compliance with galactose restrictions. The most accurate prognostic test for treated infants is the galactose-oxidation breath test. If total body oxidation of ^{13}C-D-galactose to $^{13}CO_2$ during the breath test is greater than 5% at 2 hours, outcome is good.

SUGGESTED READINGS

Elsas LJ: Prenatal diagnosis of galactose-1-phosphate uridyltransferase (GALT)-deficient galactosemia. Prenat Diagn 2001;21:302–303. *Comprehensive review of ethics, methodology, and outcome of prenatal diagnosis for GALT deficiency.*

Mutation database. http://www.emory.edu/PEDIATRICS/medgen/research/db.html Accessed November 1, 2002. *A website with updated listing of all mutations in the hGALT gene.*

OMIM-Online Mendelian Inheritance in Man. http://www3.ncbi.nlm.nih.gov/Omim/ Accessed May 8, 2003. *Updated history and molecular and clinical manifestations of these autosomal recessive disorders of galactose metabolism.*

213 GLYCOGEN STORAGE DISEASES

Harry L. Greene

Glycogen is the storage form of glucose and is present in varying amounts in virtually all cells, although the liver is the primary organ for storage and subsequent release of glucose into the circulation. Glycogen is synthesized primarily from dietary glucose. During periods of fasting, glycogen is hydrolyzed to release glucose; this highly regulated process helps maintain normal blood glucose concentrations. At least eight enzymes involved in glycogen synthesis and hydrolysis to glucose are utilized in this control.

Glycogen storage diseases are characterized by an abnormal tissue concentration (>70 mg/g of liver or >15 mg/g of muscle) and/or an abnormal structure of the glycogen molecule. During the past four decades, patients have been identified with deficient activity in virtually every enzyme important in the normal synthesis or degradation of glycogen. More recently, identification of numerous genetic mutations has led to more individualized treatments and specific molecular classifications. Clinical expression of the various types of glycogenoses can usually be traced to specific enzymatic defects in either the liver or the muscle.

Table 213–1 • CLASSIFICATION OF GLYCOGEN STORAGE DISEASES

TYPE	ENZYME AFFECTED	PRIMARY ORGAN INVOLVED	MANIFESTATIONS
O	Glycogen synthetase	Liver	Hypoglycemia, hyperketonia, FTT, early death
Ia	Glucose-6-phosphatase	Liver	Enlarged liver and kidney growth failure, fasting hypoglycemia, acidosis, thrombocyte dysfunction
Ib	Microsomal membrane G-6-P translocase	Liver	As in Ia: in addition, recurrent neutropenia, bacterial infections
Ic	Microsomal membrane P-transporter	Liver	As in Ia
II	Lysosomal acid glucosidase	Skeletal and cardiac muscle	*Infantile form:* early-onset, progressive muscle hypotonia, cardiac failure, death before 2 years of age *Juvenile form:* late-onset myopathy and variable cardiac involvement *Adult form:* limb-girdle muscular dystrophy–like feature
III	Amylo-1,6-glucosidase (debrancher enzyme)	Liver, skeletal muscle, heart	Fasting hypoglycemia, hepatomegaly in infancy; some have myopathic features, rarely clinical cardiac features
IV	Amylo-1,4-1,6-transglucosidase (brancher enzyme)	Liver, muscle	Hepatosplenomegaly, cirrhosis; may have late-onset myopathy
V	Muscle phosphorylase	Skeletal muscle	Exercise-induced muscular pain, cramps, and progressive weakness, sometimes with myoglobinuria: symptoms usually begin during adolescence or early adulthood
VI	Liver phosphorylase	Liver	Hepatomegaly, mild hypoglycemia, good prognosis
VII	Phosphofructokinase	Muscle, red blood cells	As in V; in addition, mild hemolytic anemia
Formerly VIb, VIII, or IX	Phosphorylase b kinase	Liver, leukocytes, (?) muscle	As in VI; X-linked inheritance
X	Cyclic AMP–dependent kinase	Liver, muscle	Hepatomegaly, mild hypoglycemia

AMP = adenosine monophosphate; FTT = failure to thrive.

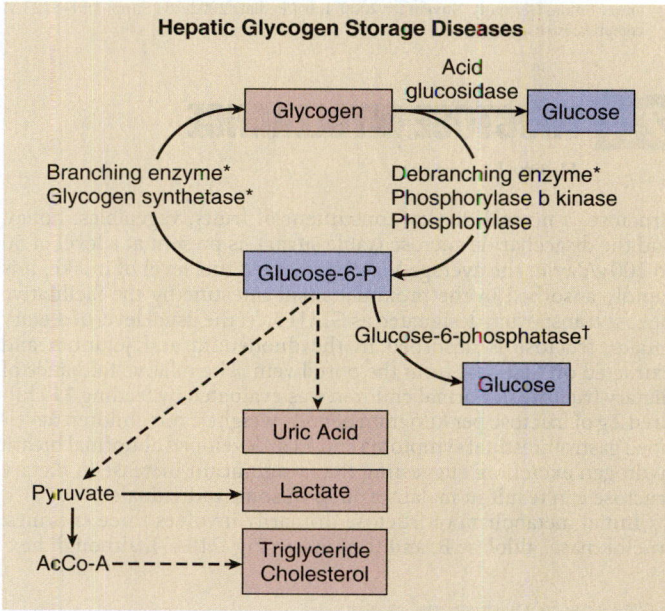

FIGURE 213–1 • Mechanism for abnormalities in lipid, purine, and carbohydrate metabolism in type I (glucose-6-phosphatase deficiency) glycogen storage disease. *Associated with hepatic cirrhosis. †Associated with elevated serum uric acid, lactate, and lipid levels and with hepatic adenoma. AcCo-A = acetyl coenzyme A.

Hepatic Forms of Glycogenesis

The various hepatic enzymatic deficiencies are expressed primarily as hypoglycemia and hepatomegaly, and three defects (in branching enzyme, glycogen synthetase, and debranching enzyme) result in the accumulation of abnormally structured glycogen and may cause progressive hepatic cirrhosis and associated splenomegaly. Conversely, the accumulation of normally structured glycogen, as seen with deficiency of phosphorylase, phosphorylase *b* kinase, acid α-glucosidase, or glucose-6-phosphatase, is not usually associated with hepatic fibrosis and splenomegaly. Figure 213–1 summarizes the general location of enzymatic defects resulting in the hepatic forms of glycogenesis. With the exception of lysosomal acid glucosidase deficiency, hypoglycemia is a common presenting feature. Clinical and biochemical expressions of the various types of glycogen storage diseases are sum-

marized in Table 213–1, and the more commonly diagnosed types are discussed in the following sections. Although medical treatment aimed at maintenance of normal blood glucose can be highly successful in the majority of patients, hepatic transplantation has proven beneficial in some.

GLUCOSE-6-PHOSPHATASE DEFICIENCY (TYPE I GLYCOGEN STORAGE DISEASE). The incidence of type I glycogen storage disease (GSD-I) is 1 in 100,000 to 1 in 300,000 live births. GSD-I has been subcategorized into types a, b, or c, with type a the most common. Although all three types have similar clinical features, type b (glucose 6-phosphate translocase deficiency) and type c (pyrophosphate/phosphate transporter deficiency) also have neutropenia and frequent bacterial infections. As noted in Figure 213–1, all other enzymatic defects directly affect the formation or degradation of glycogen, with the exception of glucose-6-phosphatase. Similarly, the clinical expression of this defect is distinctly different from that of the other forms of glycogenesis. For example, fasting-induced hypoglycemia may be extreme and associated with lactic acidosis, hyperlipidemia, and hyperuricemia. The mechanism for the striking abnormalities in lipid and purine metabolism results primarily from overproduction of substrate in response to a decline in blood glucose, as indicated in Figure 213–1. The documented reversal of these abnormalities by treatment that maintains the blood glucose level between 80 and 90 mg/dL supports this postulate. Therapeutic intervention aimed at maintenance of blood glucose concentrations within these physiologic ranges has resulted in favorable development of many patients with delivery of unaffected offspring.

Late Complications. As more patients have survived and developed into active, functioning adults, two subsequent, unexpected complications have become apparent: (1) single or multiple hepatic adenomas, developing between 16 and 22 years of age, and (2) progressive glomerulosclerosis with renal failure. Because adenomas may become malignant, annual monitoring by ultrasonography is recommended. Any rapidly expanding lesion should be considered potentially malignant and should undergo surgical biopsy because serum α-fetoprotein measurements have been an unreliable marker for malignant transformation. There has been some indication that the adenomas could be prevented or reduced in younger children by more stringent dietary control; however, this hypothesis has not been substantiated in older individuals.

Development of progressive glomerulosclerosis, proteinuria, hypertension, and renal failure usually occurs in older patients (>18 years) who are less well managed and exhibit recurrent hypoglycemic episodes, chronic hypertriglyceridemia, and lactic acidosis. The mechanism causing the renal lesion is not defined, although regulation of blood glucose within the normal range can reduce the risk of renal involvement as well as improve proteinuria.

DEBRANCHING ENZYME DEFICIENCY (TYPE III GSD). GSD-III has an incidence of about 1 in 100,000 live births. This disease most often affects only the liver but may affect muscle as well, although a single variant in North African Jews show both liver and muscle involvement with a prevalence of about 1 in 5400. Elevated serum creatine kinase concentrations indicate muscle involvement, but these concentrations may not become elevated until later childhood or adolescence. Hypoglycemia with fasting is less severe (usually 40 to 50 mg/dL) than in patients with GSD-I, although hepatic enlargement may be substantially greater. Serum aspartate aminotransferase and alanine aminotransaminase concentrations are commonly above 500 units/mL. Correspondingly, hepatic fibrosis of varying degrees is usually present during childhood and may be progressive. Adult patients may present with "cryptogenic cirrhosis."

Treating patients with GSD-III has not been advocated because the natural course of the disease has been thought to be benign. However, because growth retardation and cirrhosis may be serious complications, several patients have been treated with frequent feedings and raw cornstarch to maintain blood glucose levels between 75 and 100 mg/dL. Treated patients often show a significant reduction in serum transaminase levels and improvements in growth, and they may demonstrate improved muscle strength, although serum creatine kinase activities remain elevated. Identification of specific gene mutations should provide better prognostic predictions.

Clinical and laboratory features of the other, less common forms of hepatic glycogenesis are presented in Table 213–1.

Muscular Forms of Glycogen Storage

ACID α-GLUCOSIDASE DEFICIENCY (POMPE'S DISEASE, TYPE II GSD). In this condition, virtually all tissues have an increased glycogen content. However, presenting clinical manifestations of the illness are cardiac enlargement, myocardial failure, and generalized muscle hypotonia without apparent muscle wasting. The classic infantile form manifests during the first months of life, and few infants survive past the first year. The juvenile variant manifests in later infancy or early childhood and progresses more slowly, with death in the second or third decade. The adult type manifests as a slowly developing adult-onset myopathy. In each case, the diagnosis is dependent on finding deficient activity of acid α-1,4-glucosidase in muscle specimens or cultured fibroblasts. More recently, diagnosis is possible by identification of genetic mutations. No accepted treatment has proven benefit. However, twice weekly intravenous infusions of recombinant α-glucosidase have resulted in substantial improvement in three patients after several months of treatment. Chimerization in other tissues after liver transplantation in two patients with GSD-IV may also offer some encouragement for future treatment.

MYOPHOSPHORYLASE DEFICIENCY (TYPE V GSD, McARDLE'S DISEASE). Most patients with this condition are asymptomatic during early childhood and escape diagnosis until the second or third decade of life. A history of muscle pain and cramps after exercise, signs of myoglobinuria, and painful cramping on an ischemic exercise test are characteristic. The diagnosis is suggested by an elevation in serum muscle creatine kinase isoenzyme activity and by failure to elevate the serum lactate level with exercise. The diagnosis is established by documenting elevated muscle glycogen in the sarcolemmal regions and reduced muscle phosphorylase activity. Glucose or fructose ingestion before exercise is said to reduce the symptoms.

MUSCLE PHOSPHOFRUCTOKINASE DEFICIENCY (MUSCLE PHOSPHOGLYCERATE MUTASE DEFICIENCY, LACTATE DEHYDROGENASE-M SUBUNIT DEFICIENCY, TYPE VII GSD). These muscle glycogeneses are rare and clinically similar to myophosphorylase deficiency. Patients with phosphofructokinase deficiency may also show a mild hemolytic anemia. Diagnosis depends on muscle enzyme analysis or identification of the genetic mutations. Treatment is aimed at avoiding strenuous exercise.

Diagnosis and Prenatal Diagnosis of Glycogen Storage Disease

Diagnostic enzyme or genetic analysis of fibroblasts or hepatic or muscle tissue for most types of glycogen storage diseases can usually be performed at Duke Medical Center, Division of Genetics (Dr. Y.T. Chen).

1. Amalfitano A, Bengur AR, Morse RP, et al: Recombinant human acid α-glucosidase enzyme therapy for infantile glycogen storage disease type II: Results of a phase I/II clinical trial. Genet Med 2001;3:132–138.

SUGGESTED READINGS
Kannourakis G: Glycogen storage disease. Semin Hematol 2002;39:103–106. *Emphasizes approaches to the neutropenia and neutrophil dysfunction.*
Smit GPA, Fernandes J, Labrune P, et al: Glycogen storage disease types 1 and 2: Recent developments, management and outcome. Proceedings of an international symposium. Fulda, Germany, November 2000. Eur J Pediatr 2002;161 Suppl 1:S1–S123. *A comprehensive update.*

214 FRUCTOSE INTOLERANCE

Harry L. Greene

Fructose, a normal dietary constituent of fruits, vegetables, honey, and the disaccharide sucrose (table sugar), is present at a level of 50 to 100 g/day in the average Western diet. At this level of intake, it is rapidly absorbed in the proximal small intestine by the facilitative hexose transporter, designated as GLUT5. At the usual level of dietary intake, fructose is absorbed in the duodenum and jejunum and extracted on first pass from the portal vein. The relative tolerance of dietary fructose in normal children was evaluated by feeding 31 children 2 g of fructose per kilogram of body weight. Four children developed gastrointestinal symptoms and 71% developed abnormal breath hydrogen excretion, suggesting that a significant increase in dietary fructose can result in malabsorption in some individuals.

Initial metabolism of fructose primarily involves three enzymes: fructokinase, aldolase B, and triokinase (Fig. 214–1), although hex-

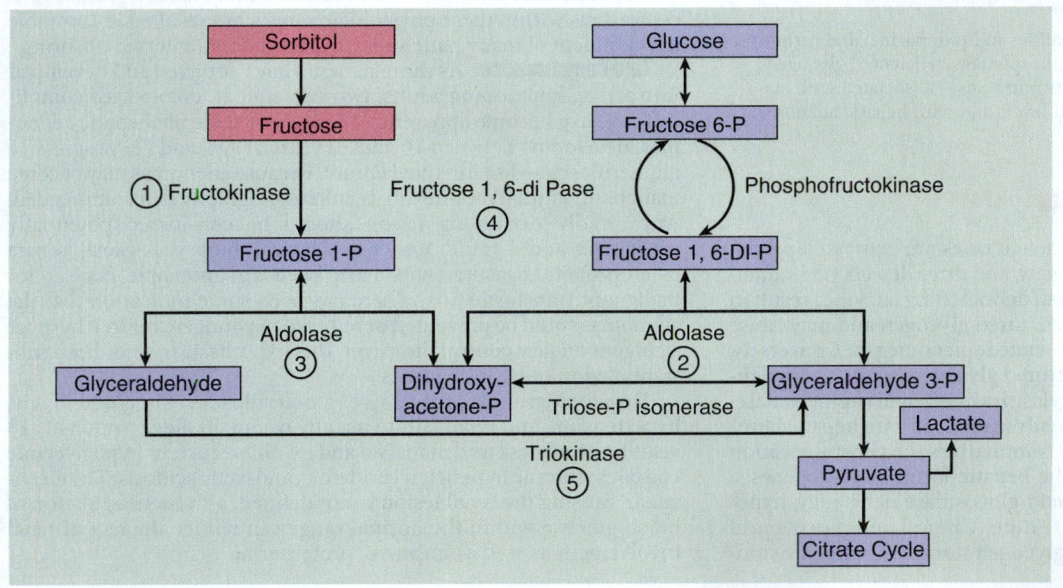

FIGURE 214–1 • The major pathway for fructose metabolism in the liver, showing the five defects discussed in the text. Aldolase deficiency consists primarily of defects in aldolase B (3). Aldolase A deficiency (2) is extremely rare and is expressed primarily during embryogenesis.

okinase phosphorylates some of the fructose. Five enzymatic defects involving fructose metabolism have been identified: (1) fructokinase deficiency, (2) aldolase A deficiency, (3) aldolase B deficiency, (4) fructose-1,6-bisphosphatase deficiency, and (5) D-glycerate kinase deficiency. The enzymatic defects in fructose metabolism are illustrated in Figure 214–1 and are discussed in the following sections.

FRUCTOKINASE DEFICIENCY

Fructokinase deficiency (essential fructosuria) is a rare (about 1 in 130,000 live births), asymptomatic, autosomal recessive condition caused by deficient activity of fructokinase, the first enzyme in fructose utilization. Because no pathologic condition results from this defect, the primary concern relates to the fact that fructose is a reducing sugar. Thus, a positive reaction with urinary Clinitest tablets may result in the erroneous suggestion of diabetes unless glucose oxidase level is determined with a dipstick.

ALDOLASE DEFICIENCY

Three aldolases (A, B, and C) are responsible for the conversion of fructose-1,6-diphosphate into glyceraldehyde-3-phosphate and dihydroxyacetone phosphate. Embryonic tissue produces aldolase A; adult liver, kidney, and intestine express aldolase B; and nervous tissue expresses aldolase C. Although all three aldolases are tetramers of identical 40-kD subunits, each is coded for different genes on different chromosomes: aldolase A on chromosome 16,16q22-q24, aldolase B on chromosome 9,9q13-q32, and aldolase C on chromosome 17,17cen-q21.

ALDOLASE A DEFICIENCY. Aldolase A deficiency may be detrimental because of its pivotal role in glycolysis. This is apparently of special relevance to the developing embryo, which expresses only aldolase A. Only a few patients with this deficit have been described, and not all symptoms are expressed to the same degree. Potential symptoms include mental retardation, short stature, hemolytic anemia, and abnormal facial appearance. Because aldolase B becomes normal at birth as aldolase A declines, newborns with hereditary fructose intolerance (HFI) do not show fructosuria, explaining why neonates with HFI are unaffected in utero.

ALDOLASE B DEFICIENCY (HEREDITARY FRUCTOSE INTOLERANCE). Aldolase B deficiency (prevalence, about 1 in 23,000 live births) is a potentially life-threatening autosomal recessive disorder that can be effectively treated by eliminating dietary fructose. This disorder is caused by deficiency of fructose-1-phosphate aldolase (aldolase B). Aldolase B is normally present in large amounts in the liver, intestine, and renal cortex; thus, excessive fructose intake by patients with HFI adversely affects each of these organs. Recent expression of the C134R mutation showed partial activity of the enzyme, explaining why gluconeogenesis/glycolysis is maintained in patients with HFI.

Symptoms become manifested only when patients ingest fructose or sorbitol-containing foods. Because lactose is the carbohydrate source in mammalian milk, infants do not develop symptoms until the introduction of dietary fruits or other fructose-containing foods or medication (e.g., fruits, fruit juices, medicinal syrups, sucrose-containing infant formulas, or sorbitol-sweeteners). The primary presentation is vomiting and other features of hypoglycemia within 20 to 30 minutes after fructose ingestion. These acute manifestations of hypoglycemia may not be apparent after lower chronic intakes. For example, fructose-containing infant formulas also contain glucose, which may prevent hypoglycemic symptoms. In these instances, failure to thrive, hepatomegaly, and cirrhosis may represent the dominant presenting features. Concomitant laboratory findings include an acute decrease in serum glucose and phosphate concentrations and an elevated uric acid concentration. With continued exposure to fructose, hyperbilirubinemia, lactic acidosis, hepatosplenomegaly, and liver failure develop in conjunction with renal tubular dysfunction (bicarbonaturia, aminoaciduria, phosphaturia). At this stage, fatty infiltration of liver, cellular necrosis, and mild bile duct proliferation with fibrosis occur. If exposure to fructose continues, progressive fibrosis, cirrhosis, and death from liver failure follow. The brain may also show diminished neurons.

The diagnosis is suggested by the presence of urinary reducing sugar detectable by Clinitest tablets and not by urinary dipstick, which measures glucose oxidase. Because similar clinical features may be present with galactosemia or tyrosinemia, diagnosis can be confirmed by genetic screen. An intravenous fructose tolerance test (0.2 to 0.3 g/kg in adults or 3 g/m² in children) after restriction of dietary fructose for several weeks has been used to confirm the illness, but this procedure may cause hypoglycemia and is no longer recommended.

There are many well described mutations of aldolase single base substitutions, nonsense codons, splicing defects, deletions, and base insertions. Regions of the enzyme where mutations have been observed recurrently are encoded by exons 5 and 9. The three most common mutations are found in these exons, making screening methods more feasible. Recent findings implicate the C-terminus in maintaining the overall stability of the enzyme tetramer.

In spite of recurrent bouts of hypoglycemia and substantial liver disease, restriction of dietary fructose usually results in almost complete recovery during a 3- to 5-week period, and affected adults have normal intelligence. Older children and adults are protected from large dietary intakes of fructose by an aversion to sweets, although small amounts taken chronically may result in isolated, often reversible, somatic growth retardation.

FRUCTOSE-1,6-BISPHOSPHATASE DEFICIENCY

This rare disorder was first described in 1970. Patients usually present before the age of 6 months with fasting-induced lactic acidosis, hypoglycemia, and hepatomegaly. The reaction to glycerol is similar to the reaction to fructose ingestion but is less severe than that of patients with HFI. The condition is caused by a defect of hepatic fructose-1,6-bisphosphatase, a gluconeogenic enzyme (see Fig. 214–1). Thus, when hepatic glycogen stores are depleted, fasting hypoglycemia develops. During fasting, urinary organic acids are similar to those of tyrosinemia type I but with an absence of succinyl acetate. In addition, starvation leads to increased excretion of glycerol.

The enzyme is a tetramer for identical 36 kD subunits. The diagnosis is suspected when, after 12 to 16 hours of fasting, the blood sugar concentration falls and is not restored when glucagon is administered, and acidosis (lactate) is present. Loading tests with fructose or glycerol may be dangerous, because they lead to hypoglycemia and lactic acidosis. Diagnosis is confirmed by measuring the amount of enzyme in the hepatic biopsy material. Treatment consists of avoiding fasting and restricting dietary fructose and glycerol.

D-GLYCERATE KINASE DEFICIENCY (D-GLYCERIC ACIDURIA)

This is a rare, clinically variable disorder resulting in either no symptoms or metabolic acidosis and failure to thrive and profound psychomotor retardation and seizures. The variable phenotypic expression has not been fully explained on the basis of the enzymatic defect, but all patients who show a substantial increase in D-glycerate excretion after fructose ingestion should avoid dietary fructose.

SUGGESTED READINGS

Cox TM: Iatrogenic deaths in hereditary fructose intolerance. Arch Dis Child 1993;69:413–415. *This paper illustrates the need to restrict intravenous sorbitol as well as fructose in patients with HFI.*

Esposito G, Vitagliano L, Santamaria R, et al: Structural and functional analysis of aldolase B mutants related to hereditary fructose intolerance. FEBS Lett 2002;531:152–156. *Overview of the genetic mutations and their functional implications.*

215 PRIMARY HYPEROXALURIA

Richard E. Hillman

Primary hyperoxaluria refers to two different peroxisomal enzyme deficiencies that are characterized by massive synthesis and urinary excretion of oxalic acid. Until recently, primary hyperoxaluria was considered a very rare disease. The ready availability of oxalate assays in the past few years, however, has led to the description of milder cases, mostly type II, which are either asymptomatic or present only with water deprivation. Oxalate is also deposited in the heart, the eye, the skin, and other organs, leading to a variety of clinical pictures. Of particular interest, oxalate has led to cardiac conduction system block. Particularly in type I disease, the clinical manifestations appear early in childhood with nephrolithiasis or nephrocalcinosis and lead to renal failure within the first decade of life. Both types are inherited as autosomal recessive traits and must be distinguished from secondary hyperoxalurias due to increased absorption of oxalate by the gut. These secondary causes include inflammatory bowel disease and fat malabsorption, which may tie up calcium and convert insoluble calcium oxalate to more absorbable salts. Although most adult patients with calcium oxalate nephrolithiasis excrete normal amounts of oxalate, it is now clear that hyperoxaluria must be considered in the differential diagnosis.

Primary hyperoxaluria type I (glycolic aciduria) is caused by a defect in the peroxisomal enzyme alanine:glyoxylate amino transferase. This enzyme normally converts glycolic acid to the amino acid glycine. In its absence, glycolic acid leaves the peroxisome and is converted to oxalic acid by lactic dehydrogenase. Both glycolic and oxalic acids are excreted in large amounts, usually more than 60 mg/ 1.73 m^2/24 hours. In most cases, this concentration exceeds the solubility of oxalic acid. This enzyme has been cloned, and multiple defects have been demonstrated.

Primary hyperoxaluria type II (glyceric aciduria) is due to a deficiency of D-glycerate dehydrogenase/glyoxylate reductase, a dual functional enzyme whose absence leads to the accumulation of both hydroxypyruvate and glyoxylate. The hydroxypyruvate is reduced in the cytoplasm to L-glyceric acid, and the glyoxylate, as in type I disease, is converted to oxylate by lactic dehydrogenase. Type II is a much milder disease than type I and may manifest only after dehydration. A review of 24 cases suggests the variability of the clinical presentation of this defect and that this diagnosis should be considered in any patient with urolithiasis or nephrocalcinosis. Like type I disease, it is inherited as an autosomal recessive trait.

Some patients with type I disease respond to large doses of pyridoxine (50 to 200 mg/day). This vitamin is the cofactor for the enzyme. It appears to act by stabilizing the remaining activity and is effective only in patients with some enzyme, in general the milder cases. Dilute urine should be maintained by high fluid intake, and some reports suggest that diuretics may help. Attempts to form more soluble salts of oxalate, particularly with magnesium orthophosphate and citrate, have met with some success. The only "cure" for this disease has been a combined renal and liver transplant. Renal transplants alone have failed, owing to the accumulation of oxalate produced in the liver. Therapeutic outcomes in type II patients are very variable. Pyridoxine has no effect. Other measures that maintain a dilute urine seem to be sufficient in the milder cases.

SUGGESTED READINGS

Kenper MJ, Conrad S, Muller-Wiefel DE: Primary hyperoxaluria type 2. Eur J Pediatr 1997;156:509–512. *A review of the variability and therapeutic approaches to type II disease.*

Pirulli D, Marangella M, Amoroso A: Primary hyperoxaluria: Genotype-phenotype correlation. J Nephrol 2003;16:297–309. *Homozygous genotypes were more frequent than expected and generally had a less severe form of the disease than compound heterozygotes.*

Santana A, Salido E, Torres A, Shapiro LJ: Primary hyperoxaluria type 1 in the Canary Islands: A conformational disease due to I244T mutation in the P11L-containing alanine:glyoxylate aminotransferase. Proc Natl Acad Sci U S A 2003;100:7277–7282. *This is the second most common mutation, and it may respond to therapies that minimize protein aggregation.*

216 DISORDERS OF PURINE AND PYRIMIDINE METABOLISM

Michael S. Hershfield
Beverly S. Mitchell

PURINE ENZYME DEFICIENCIES AND DISORDERS OF IMMUNE FUNCTION

ADENOSINE DEAMINASE DEFICIENCY

In its usual early-onset form, deficiency of adenosine deaminase (ADA) causes the syndrome of severe combined immunodeficiency disease (SCID), with profound depletion of T, B, and natural killer cells and absence of both cellular and humoral immune function. ADA deficiency accounts for 15% of all cases of SCID and about one third of those with autosomal recessive inheritance. Less complete ADA deficiency is associated with T-cell dysfunction and more variable loss of B-cell function, causing progressive immune dysfunction in adolescents or adults. A so-called "partial ADA deficiency,"

associated with no clinical manifestations, has been identified by screening erythrocyte ADA activity in populations and families of immunodeficient patients. ADA deficiency has been estimated to occur in 1 in 200,000 to 1 in 1 million births.

Etiology and Pathogenesis

More than 70 mutations leading to loss of ADA enzymatic activity have been identified in the 12-exon *ADA* gene located on chromosome 20q. About two thirds are single base changes within the coding region; the remainder are deletions and splicing mutations. Most patients possess two different mutant alleles. The ADA catalytic activity of cloned mutant alleles expressed in *Escherichia coli* correlates well with both clinical severity and the level of specific metabolic abnormalities in patient erythrocytes. Some mildly affected patients have shown mosaicism for the reversion of a mutant allele in lymphoid cells.

ADA catalyzes the irreversible deamination of adenosine to inosine and of 2′-deoxyadenosine to 2′-deoxyinosine (Fig. 216–1). In the absence of ADA activity, plasma levels of both ADA substrates are increased to 0.5 to 10 μmol/L; high levels of 2′-deoxyadenosine, but not adenosine, are excreted in the urine. Two pathognomonic metabolic abnormalities occur in erythrocytes of immunodeficient patients with ADA deficiency (but not in healthy individuals with "partial deficiency"): (1) a marked elevation (50- to more than 1000-fold) in the level of 2′-deoxyadenosine triphosphate (dATP) derived from 2′-deoxyadenosine, and (2) decreased activity of the enzyme S-adenosylhomocysteine hydrolase, due to its inactivation by 2′-deoxyadenosine.

Lymphocyte depletion and immunodeficiency appear to stem mainly from the preferential phosphorylation of 2′-deoxyadenosine and subsequent accumulation of dATP in immature thymocytes. Expansion of the dATP pool has several cytotoxic effects: (1) it inhibits the enzyme ribonucleotide reductase, thus blocking DNA replication; (2) dATP participates in a cytoplasmic complex with cytochrome c released from mitochondria and the protein Apoptosis Activating Factor I to initiate a caspase proteolytic cascade leading to cell death;

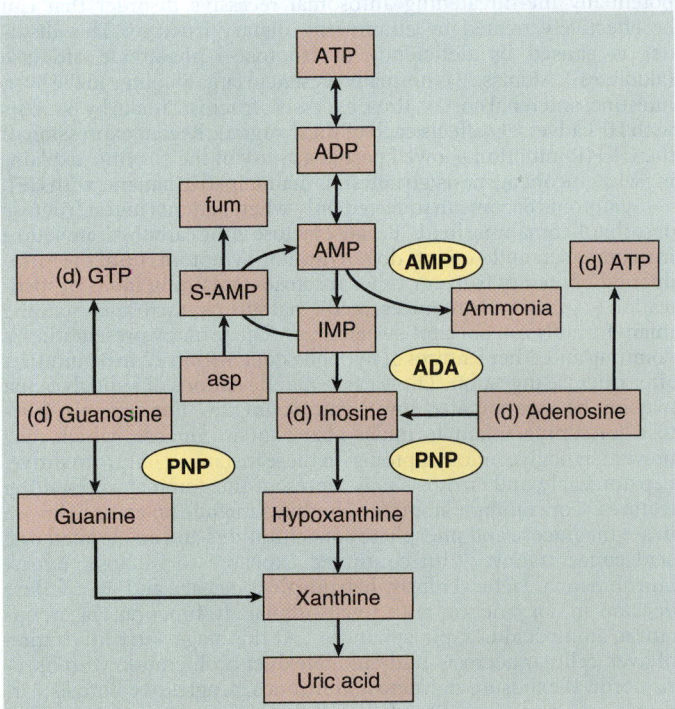

FIGURE 216–1 • Schema of purine metabolism demonstrating metabolic reactions catalyzed by adenosine deaminase (ADA), purine nucleoside phosphorylase (PNP), and adenosine monophosphate (AMP) deaminase (AMPD). ATP = adenosine triphosphate; ADP = adenosine diphosphate; S-AMP = succinyl adenosine monophosphate; asp = aspartate; fum = fumarate; IMP = inosine monophosphate; GTP = guanosine triphosphate.

and (3) dATP accumulation induces single-strand breaks in DNA. In addition to these effects of dATP, inactivation of S-adenosylhomocysteine hydrolase by 2′-deoxyadenosine causes the accumulation of S-adenosylhomocysteine, an inhibitor of S-adenosylmethionine-dependent transmethylation reactions. It has also been postulated that elevated levels of extracellular adenosine, acting through cell membrane adenosine receptors, may interfere with lymphocyte differentiation or function.

Clinical Manifestations

A case of ADA-deficient SCID is manifested in infants by failure to thrive and recurrent infections with ordinary pathogens and opportunistic organisms. *Pneumocystis carinii* and viral pneumonitis, persistent diarrhea, and candidiasis of the skin and gastrointestinal tract are common, as are cytomegalovirus, varicella virus, and adenovirus infections. Vaccination with live organisms may be fatal, and unirradiated blood products may cause fatal graft-versus-host disease; an increased incidence of B-cell lymphomas has been reported. Serum transaminase elevation or hepatitis, and diverse neurologic abnormalities in some cases, may be due to metabolic effects of ADA deficiency as well as to infection. Lymph nodes and tonsillar tissue are absent, and some infants show prominent costochondral junctions. Chest radiographs reveal the absence of a thymus and cupping and flaring of rib ends. Peripheral blood shows an absolute lymphopenia, often of less than 500/μL, with decreased numbers of T, B, and natural killer cells. Hypogammaglobulinemia and lack of specific antibody response to immunization and infection are found, and in vitro tests of lymphocyte function, including proliferative responses to mitogens and antigens, are absent or decreased. In older patients with less complete ADA deficiency, recurring respiratory infections are often the primary manifestation of combined immunodeficiency; chronic pulmonary insufficiency is often present by the time the diagnosis is made. Elevated serum IgE, asthma, and autoimmune cytopenias also occur due to immune dysregulation.

Diagnosis

The disorder should be considered in individuals of any age with recurrent infections associated with unexplained lymphopenia. The diagnosis is made by measuring ADA activity in the hemolysates of untransfused patients. Finding elevated dATP and decreased S-adenosylhomocysteine hydrolase activity in erythrocytes is confirmatory and may help gauge the degree of ADA deficiency. Prenatal diagnosis can be accomplished by assay of ADA activity in cultured amniotic or chorionic villi cells. In kindreds in which *ADA* gene mutations have been previously identified, the diagnosis can be made by DNA sequencing or restriction enzyme digestion. Because of the genetic diversity, however, mutation analysis is not an efficient method of diagnosis in cases in which genotype is unknown.

 Treatment

Specific antibiotic and antiviral treatment for infections is essential. In addition, patients should receive prophylaxis for *P. carinii* and fungal infections and should not receive live virus vaccines or unirradiated blood products. Most patients are also treated with intravenous immunoglobulin. Once the diagnosis is established, the patient is a candidate for either bone marrow transplantation or enzyme replacement therapy with polyethylene glycol (PEG)–conjugated bovine ADA (PEG-ADA, Adagen). Trials of gene therapy are in progress.

For SCID patients, the long-term survival rate after human leukocyte antigen (HLA)–identical sibling marrow transplantation is 70 to 90%, and this remains the treatment of choice if a donor is available. Transplanting T-cell–depleted marrow from HLA-haploidentical (usually a parent) or matched unrelated donors has been less successful, with long-term survival rates ranging from 28 to 67% at different transplant centers (ADA-deficient patients have generally fared worse than patients with SCID, owing to other genetic defects). Enzyme replacement by intramuscular injection

of PEG-ADA once or twice a week is used for patients who lack an HLA-identical donor and who are considered poor candidates for transplantation, or for whom the risks associated with transplantation are unacceptable. By maintaining high ADA activity in plasma, PEG-ADA eliminates circulating ADA substrates and corrects levels of their toxic metabolites in cells. Improvement in lymphocyte counts and function follows, usually within several weeks to a few months of initiating treatment. Although immune function is often only partly restored, the majority of patients have done well clinically. PEG-ADA is well tolerated, and the overall survival rate among more than 100 patients treated over the past 15 years is comparable to the best results reported with HLA-nonidentical transplantation. The major limitation to its long-term use is the potential for developing neutralizing antibody to PEG-ADA, which has occurred in about 10% of patients.

Experimental gene therapy has been used in about a dozen patients, who have been treated concomitantly with PEG-ADA. Most of these patients received repeated infusions of autologous T cells that had been transfected ex vivo with a retroviral vector containing human ADA cDNA. Three prenatally diagnosed neonates received transfected CD34+ umbilical cord stem cells shortly after birth. The vector was found to persist for several years in 1 to 10% of circulating T lymphocytes of some patients, a finding consistent with selection for ADA-expressing lymphocytes. The future success of gene therapy will depend on the development of improved vectors that more efficiently transduce stem cells, and the demonstration that concomitant treatment with PEG-ADA can safely be discontinued.

PURINE NUCLEOSIDE PHOSPHORYLASE DEFICIENCY

Encoded by a six-exon gene on chromosome 14q, purine nucleoside phosphorylase (PNP) catalyzes the reversible phosphorolytic cleavage of inosine and 2′-deoxyinosine (products of the ADA reaction), and of guanosine and 2′-deoxyguanosine, to their respective purine bases (hypoxanthine or guanine) plus ribose- or deoxyribose-1-PO_4 (see Fig. 216–1). PNP deficiency is diagnosed about one tenth as often as ADA deficiency but also causes T-cell depletion and cellular immune dysfunction. B-cell function may be normal but more often is depressed or hyperactive, and about one third of patients develop significant autoimmune disorders such as hemolytic anemia or thrombocytopenia. Various neurologic abnormalities (spasticity, ataxia, behavioral abnormalities, hypertonia, hypotonia) occur in more than 50% of patients and may be apparent before immunodeficiency is evident. The most severely affected patients have a SCID-like presentation as infants, but the disorder may manifest at any time in the first decade of life, often with disseminated varicella, or with other serious recurrent viral infections. T-lymphocyte counts and in vitro function are reduced, and a thymus gland is absent on chest radiography.

Absent or markedly reduced PNP activity in erythrocytes or blood mononuclear cells is diagnostic. Inability to produce hypoxanthine and guanine due to lack of PNP prevents the formation of uric acid. Thus, in the proper clinical setting (infections, neurologic abnormalities, autoimmunity, and T lymphopenia) a serum uric acid level of 1 mg/dL or less should raise suspicion of PNP deficiency. Serum and urinary levels of all four nucleoside substrates of PNP are increased. In erythrocytes, the level of guanosine triphosphate is decreased and 2′-deoxyguanosine triphosphate (dGTP), derived from 2′-deoxyguanosine, is elevated (but far less than dATP is increased in cases of ADA deficiency). Accumulation of dGTP in T-cell precursors, which may occur selectively in mitochondria because of a deoxyguanosine kinase in this organelle, is thought to inhibit ribonucleotide reductase and DNA replication, resulting in T-cell death. Treatment with red blood cell transfusions or infusions of deoxycytidine aimed at restoring DNA replication has not resulted in any consistent therapeutic response. Bone marrow transplantation has been curative, but outcome reported for fewer than a dozen patients suggests a high rate of failure. PEG-conjugated PNP and gene therapy are being investigated in mouse models, but the small number of patients with PNP deficiency makes clinical research on this disorder difficult.

Metabolic Diseases

OTHER INHERITED DISORDERS OF PURINE METABOLISM

LESCH-NYHAN SYNDROME

This is an X-linked disorder caused by the absence of the enzyme hypoxanthine phosphoribosyltransferase (HPRT). It is manifested in affected males as uric acid nephrolithiasis or gout, and a devastating neurologic disorder consisting of compulsive self-mutilation, choreoathetosis, spasticity, and often mental retardation. The syndrome occurs in about 1 in 100,000 births. Partial deficiency of HPRT also causes hyperuricemia and severe gout, but without severe neurologic deficits; this disorder accounts for less than 1% of patients with gout (Chapter 299).

Etiology and Pathogenesis

HPRT deficiency has been attributed to more than 200 different point mutations, splicing defects, and deletions. HPRT catalyzes the condensation of the purine bases hypoxanthine and guanine (the PNP reaction products) with ribose-5-PO$_4$ derived from phosphoribosylpyrophosphate to form the nucleotides inosine monophosphate (IMP) and guanosine monophosphate. In the absence of these "purine salvage" reactions, hypoxanthine and guanine can be catabolized only via xanthine oxidase to uric acid, causing hyperuricemia and markedly increased uric aciduria. Loss of HPRT also leads to increased intracellular phosphoribosylpyrophosphate and reduced formation of IMP and guanosine monophosphate, which activate the de novo synthesis of purine nucleotides, further increasing the generation of uric acid. In Lesch-Nyhan patients, hyperuricemia and increased uric acid excretion lead to the juvenile onset of uric acid stone formation and gouty arthritis.

The pathogenesis of the neurologic defects is not well understood but could involve guanine nucleotide deficiency in neurons that depend on the salvage pathway for purine nucleotide synthesis. Basal ganglia dopamine was decreased by 60 to 90% in three autopsied brains, and positron emission tomography has demonstrated a selective decrease in dopamine transporters of 50 to 70% in the caudate and putamen. Although anatomic studies of the brains of affected individuals have not revealed specific structural lesions, imaging studies have shown a significant reduction in caudate volume.

Clinical Manifestations

The Lesch-Nyhan syndrome is manifested during the first year of life by delayed motor development, followed by extrapyramidal signs leading to choreoathetosis and, at approximately 1 year of age, by pyramidal tract involvement with hyperreflexia, clonus, and scissoring of the legs. Compulsive self-destructive behavior (such as biting fingers, lips, and buccal mucosa, and self-inflicted head trauma) appears some time between early childhood and adolescence. This behavior pattern, which is unique to this disorder, necessitates restraints and in some cases edentulation. Patients are unable to walk, and mental and growth retardation occur in the majority. Uric acid crystalluria may first be noted as orange crystals in the diaper during the first weeks of life. If untreated, uricaciduria may lead to nephrolithiasis, obstructive uropathy, and azotemia. Hyperuricemia may attain levels of 18 mg/dL. Gout may develop later in the course of the disease but generally not before puberty. Death usually occurs in the second or third decade from infection or renal failure.

In patients with partial deficiency of HPRT, uric acid crystalluria and renal calculi develop in childhood, and gouty arthritis often begins before the age of 20 years. Neurologic manifestations may occur in 20% of these patients, including mental retardation, mild spastic quadriplegia, dysarthria, cerebellar ataxia, and seizures, but self-mutilation does not develop. Patients with partial HPRT deficiency may seek medical attention after passing a renal calculus or following an attack of gouty arthritis. Life expectancy is normal.

Diagnosis

The Lesch-Nyhan syndrome is strongly suggested by the self-mutilation and characteristic choreoathetosis; mental retardation of other origins is rarely accompanied by self-injury, especially in the presence of intact sensation. The presence of hyperuricemia supports the diagnosis. Definitive diagnosis is made by demonstrating a lack of HPRT enzymatic activity in red blood cells or other tissues. Female carriers cannot be definitively identified by assay of HPRT activity in peripheral blood cells but may be detected by analysis of DNA if the mutation in an affected male relative has been defined.

Partial deficiency of HPRT is manifested by the early onset of gouty arthritis or uric acid crystalluria or nephrolithiasis in male patients. In patients with normal renal function, uric acid overexcretion is marked. HPRT activity in red cells is usually in the range of 0.2 to 5% of normal, and occasionally as high as 30 to 50%, whereas patients with Lesch-Nyhan syndrome have less than 0.01% of control values.

 Treatment

Uric acid stone formation, tophi, and gouty arthritis can be controlled in patients with both the Lesch-Nyhan syndrome and partial deficiency of HPRT with allopurinol to inhibit xanthine oxidase activity. Xanthine renal stones may occur with this therapy. No effective pharmacologic treatment of the neurologic disorder has been developed. Neither bone marrow transplantation nor red blood cell transfusions have significantly ameliorated the neurologic disorder, which makes it unlikely that enzyme replacement therapy or hematopoietic stem cell gene transduction will play any role in treatment. Attempts at developing methods for direct delivery of HPRT cDNA to the central nervous system are under way.

MYOADENYLATE DEAMINASE DEFICIENCY AND MYOPATHY

Myoadenylate deaminase is the muscle-specific isoenzyme of adenosine monophosphate deaminase (AMPD). It is the product of one (AMPD1) of three distinct genes encoding AMPD isoenzymes. This enzyme, which catalyzes the deamination of adenosine monophosphate (AMP) to IMP plus ammonia (NH$_3$), is an integral part of the purine nucleotide cycle that appears to play a role in energy production in skeletal muscle (see Fig. 216–1). Deficiency of AMPD1 has been found in 2% of all muscle biopsies submitted for histologic examination. Inherited deficiency of myoadenylate deaminase is associated with exercise-related cramps and myalgias, but these symptoms are often mild and variable. An acquired deficiency of AMPD1 is associated with a number of primary muscle disorders.

Etiology and Pathogenesis

The 16-exon AMPD1 gene, located on chromosome 1p, is expressed predominantly in skeletal muscle, in which the AMPD1 protein has been shown to bind to myosin heavy chain. AMPD2 and AMPD3 are expressed in other tissues. AMPD1 transcripts normally undergo alternative splicing of the 12-base pair second exon, such that 0.6 to 2% of the mRNA in human skeletal muscle lacks exon 2 and encodes a catalytically active protein lacking four amino acids. A nonsense mutation within this second exon has been found at frequencies of 0.13 to 0.19 in the general population. Homozygosity for this nonsense mutation is responsible for the vast majority of cases of inherited myoadenylate deaminase deficiency. An acquired (secondary) AMPD1 deficiency, associated with decreased AMPD1 mRNA levels, occurs in a variety of muscle disorders and may be due to a pleiotropic regulatory defect in expression of multiple muscle genes.

During muscle contraction, the AMPD1-catalyzed generation of IMP and NH$_3$ from AMP increases markedly. Following exertion, AMP is regenerated with the production of fumarate, a citric acid cycle intermediate, by the next two enzymatic steps in the purine nucleotide cycle (see Fig. 216–1). Several mechanisms have been proposed by which these reactions might enhance regeneration of adenosine triphosphate. Patients with a complete functional deficiency of AMPD1 do not generate IMP, NH$_3$, or fumarate in skeletal muscle during exercise. Studies in a few patients have documented greater than normal exertion-dependent depletion of high-energy phosphate in muscle.

Clinical Manifestations

The inherited form of AMPD1 deficiency has been documented in more than 200 individuals. In most, fatigue, cramps, or myalgias develop following vigorous exercise; myoglobinuria has been reported occasionally. The majority of these patients were first evaluated for these symptoms during childhood or as young adults. Given the high frequency of the exon 2 nonsense mutation in the general population, a large number of homozygous mutant individuals must exist whose symptoms are not sufficient to warrant medical evaluation. It has been postulated that the normal alternative splicing of exon 2, which would suppress the effect of the nonsense mutation, could provide sufficient catalytically active AMPD1 protein to prevent or ameliorate clinical consequences in many homozygous patients. A low level of expression of one of the other AMPD isoforms in skeletal muscle could have the same effect. A secondary deficiency of AMPD1 is found in a number of other muscle diseases, including neurogenic disorders, various myopathies, and collagen-vascular disorders. The clinical symptoms of these individuals are dictated by the primary muscle disease. Because of the clinical heterogeneity associated with AMPD1 deficiency, there may be uncertainty, in any given individual, as to whether the enzyme deficiency state is responsible for symptoms.

Diagnosis

Individuals with AMPD1 deficiency do not produce NH_3 on ischemic exercise of the forearm, and an elevated creatine phosphokinase concentration occurs in 50% of cases. Histochemical stains and determination of enzyme activity demonstrate an absence of AMPD1 in muscle biopsy tissue. The genetic abnormality can be detected by finding an altered restriction enzyme digestion site in genomic DNA.

 ## Treatment

No treatment has been demonstrated to be effective. Oral ribose, administered in an attempt to enhance the synthesis of purine nucleotides, has met with variable subjective improvement.

2,8-DIHYDROXYADENINE RENAL STONES

In the absence of the purine salvage enzyme adenine phosphoribosyltransferase (APRT), the substrate adenine accumulates and is oxidized, although inefficiently, by xanthine oxidase to the very insoluble product 2,8-dihydroxyadenine. Patients with autosomal recessive deficiency of APRT are predisposed to radiolucent renal calculi composed of 2,8-dihydroxyadenine, which may develop within the first months of life or as late as the fifth decade, but stones never develop in many APRT-deficient individuals. The composition of the stones is determined by ultraviolet, infrared, or mass spectrometry, or by x-ray crystallography. Definitive diagnosis requires demonstrating the absence of APRT activity in erythrocyte lysates. No other biochemical or clinical abnormalities have been reported in individuals with APRT deficiency, and heterozygotes have no clinical abnormalities. Relatively few mutations at the 2.8-kb *APRT* locus on chromosome 16q are responsible for causing enzyme deficiency. The disorder is relatively common among individuals of Japanese ancestry, owing mainly to a single base mutation at codon 136 found in 68% of defective alleles, with two other mutations accounting for 28%. APRT mutations in non-Japanese subjects cluster at the intron 4 splice donor site and at codon 87. Therapy for individuals with 2,8-dihydroxyadenine calculi consists of restricting dietary purines, high fluid intake, and treatment with allopurinol to prevent the oxidation of adenine by xanthine oxidase.

XANTHINURIA

Classic, or type I, xanthinuria is an often benign disorder that results from deficiency of the enzyme xanthine oxidase (xanthine dehydrogenase), which catalyzes the conversion of the "oxypurines" xanthine and hypoxanthine to uric acid, the last step in purine catabolism in humans. Clinical consequences are related to the insolubility of xanthine, the predominant compound excreted by these individuals (hypoxanthine is efficiently reutilized by cells via the HPRT salvage reaction). About one third of the approximately 100 individuals in whom xanthinuria has been identified have presented with renal stones composed of xanthine (which in pure form are radiolucent but often also contain calcium). Crystalline deposits of xanthine in muscle have been found in a few xanthinuric individuals with muscle cramps following exercise. Deficiency of xanthine oxidase can be established by direct assay of biopsied liver or small intestinal mucosa, but the diagnosis is strongly suggested by the finding of very low serum and urinary uric acid in conjunction with elevated serum and urinary oxypurines. Xanthine calculi are treated primarily by increasing fluid intake.

A deficiency of xanthine oxidase can also occur in combination with deficiencies of one or both of two other enzymes, aldehyde oxidase and sulfite oxidase, with which it shares a requirement for a molybdenum-containing cofactor for catalytic activity. Xanthine oxidase and aldehyde oxidase have overlapping substrate specificities, and patients deficient in both have so-called type II xanthinuria, which is clinically similar to classic xanthinuria. Patients with type I and type II xanthinuria can be distinguished by a difference in their ability to metabolize allopurinol (type I patients can convert allopurinol to oxypurinol, whereas type II patients cannot) and certain other compounds. Patients with a combined deficiency of xanthine oxidase, aldehyde oxidase, and sulfite oxidase because of defective production of the common molybdenum cofactor have a much more devastating disorder. They present in infancy with severe neurologic dysfunction characterized by seizures, nystagmus, enophthalmos, ocular lens dislocation, and Brushfield spots. These same clinical findings occur in nonxanthinuric patients with isolated deficiency of sulfite oxidase.

ADENYLOSUCCINATE LYASE DEFICIENCY

Variable psychomotor retardation, seizures, autistic features, and, in some cases, growth retardation and muscular wasting have been associated in more than 40 patients with a deficiency of adenylosuccinate lyase (ADSL). Encoded by a gene on chromosome 22q, ADSL catalyzes two late steps in the de novo purine biosynthetic pathway. In each, a nucleotide intermediate formed by the addition of aspartic acid is cleaved to release fumarate and transfer a nitrogen to the growing purine ring. The levels of dephosphorylated ADSL substrates, succinylamidoimidazolecarboxamide (SAICA) riboside and succinyladenosine (S-Ado), may reach 100 to 500 µM in cerebrospinal fluid of affected patients, 20- to 100-fold higher than levels in their plasma. More severe clinical phenotypes are associated with higher SAICA riboside levels and lower ratios of S-Ado/SAICA riboside.

DISORDERS OF PYRIMIDINE METABOLISM

Hereditary orotic aciduria is a rare disorder of de novo pyrimidine biosynthesis associated with macrocytic, hypochromic anemia, leukopenia, retarded growth and development, and the overexcretion of urinary orotic acid. The last feature is often associated with orotic acid crystalluria or renal stones. The disorder results from mutations in the gene for uridine monophosphate (UMP) synthase on chromosome 3q, which encodes a bifunctional enzyme that in two steps catalyzes the conversion of orotic acid to UMP. Depletion of UMP results in diminished ability to synthesize both RNA and DNA. Administering the nucleoside uridine (2 to 4 g/day) is effective treatment, since it can be directly converted to UMP via the salvage enzyme uridine kinase.

Pyrimidine 5′-nucleotidase deficiency is a rare autosomal recessive disorder that results in hemolytic anemia and prominent basophilic stippling of red blood cells. Erythrocytes contain high levels of cytidine and uridine monophosphates, the enzyme substrates, as well as of pyrimidine nucleotide conjugates, including cytidine diphosphate-choline, cytidine diphosphate-ethanolamine, and uridine diphosphate-glucose. Hemolysis is believed to result in part from increased oxidative stress due to inhibition of the pentose phosphate shunt pathway. An acquired pyrimidine 5′-nucleotidase deficiency has been associated with lead toxicity, which is also characterized by anemia and basophilic erythrocyte stippling (due to undegraded

Metabolic Diseases

ribosomal nucleoprotein). Diagnosis of the hereditary disorder is made by measuring erythrocyte pyrimidine 5′-nucleotidase enzymatic activity. A change from normal controls in the ultraviolet absorption spectra of red blood cell lysates, reflecting elevated pyrimidine nucleotides, has been used as a screening test for the disorder.

Dihydropyrimidine dehydrogenase deficiency is a rare autosomal recessive disorder that prevents the degradation of the pyrimidine bases uracil and thymidine. High levels of these metabolites are found in the urine and may be detected during screening for organic aciduria. Although no consistent clinical symptoms have been associated with this defect, administering fluoropyrimidines (5-fluorouracil, 5-fluorodeoxyuridine) to enzyme-deficient patients with malignancy can result in severe and prolonged drug-related neurotoxicity.

SUGGESTED READINGS

Brewerton LJ, Fung E, Snyder FF: Polyethylene glycol-conjugated adenosine phosphorylase: development of alternative enzyme therapy for adenosine deaminase deficiency. Biochim Biophys Acta 2003;1637:171–177. *PEG-AP may be an alternative therapy for adenosine deaminase deficiency.*

Hershfield MS, Mitchell BS: Immunodeficiency diseases caused by adenosine deaminase deficiency and purine nucleoside phosphorylase deficiency. In Scriver CR, Beaudet AL, Sly WS, et al (eds): The Metabolic and Molecular Bases of Inherited Disease, 8th ed. New York, McGraw-Hill, 2001, pp 2585–2625. *Detailed discussion of the clinical, metabolic, and molecular aspects of ADA- and PNP-deficiency states.*

Muul LM, Tuschong LM, Soenen SL, et al: Persistence and expression of the adenosine deaminase gene for 12 years and immune reaction to gene transfer components: long-term results of the first clinical gene therapy trial. Blood 2003;101:2563–2569. *One of two patients had some continuing gene expression.*

Webster DR, Becroft DMO, van Gennip AH, Van Kuilenburg ABP: Hereditary orotic aciduria and other disorders of pyrimidine metabolism. In Scriver CR, Beaudet AL, Sly WS, et al (eds): The Metabolic and Molecular Bases of Inherited Disease, 8th ed. New York, McGraw-Hill, 2001, pp 2663–2702. *An overview of the clinical, biochemical, and genetic aspects of several disorders of pyrimidine metabolism.*

217 LYSOSOMAL STORAGE DISEASES

Margaret M. McGovern
Robert J. Desnick

The lysosomal storage diseases are a family of more than 40 disorders resulting from different defects in lysosomal function. Although most of these disorders are caused by the deficiency of a specific hydrolytic enzyme, others are due to impaired receptors or deficiencies of crucial cofactors or protective proteins. Prevalent among these disorders are Fabry disease, Gaucher disease, and Niemann-Pick disease, that is, lipid storage diseases that result from mutations in specific genes that encode lipid-degrading enzymes. The respective enzymatic defects lead to the storage in lysosomes of specific lipids and their metabolites. All three of these disorders have later-onset forms that can begin in adult life. In addition, Gaucher disease and Niemann-Pick disease have severe, fatal infantile forms that are described briefly.

FABRY DISEASE

Definition

Fabry disease is an X-linked recessive inborn error of glycosphingolipid metabolism characterized by angiokeratomas (telangiectatic skin lesions), hypohidrosis, corneal and lenticular opacities, acroparesthesias, and vascular disease of the kidney, heart, and brain. The disease has an estimated incidence of about 1 in 40,000 males. Atypical hemizygous male subjects with residual α-galactosidase A activity may be asymptomatic or have late onset and mild disease manifestations primarily limited to the heart. Heterozygous female subjects are usually asymptomatic or exhibit mild manifestations.

Pathobiology

The disease results from the deficient activity of lysosomal hydrolase α-galactosidase A (Table 217–1). The course of the disease is more severe in affected male patients with blood group B or AB because the blood group B substances accumulate, since they are normally degraded by α-galactosidase A. The molecular basis of Fabry disease has been identified for a number of patients (Table 217–2). The disease is characterized by marked deposition of globotriaosylceramide and related glycosphingolipids with terminal α-galactosyl moieties primarily in the plasma and in the lysosomes of endothelial, perithelial, and smooth muscle cells of blood vessels. These glycosphingolipid deposits are also prominent in epithelial cells of the cornea, in glomeruli and tubules of the kidney, in muscle fibers of the heart, and in ganglion cells of the dorsal roots and autonomic nervous system. The skin lesions are telangiectasias. Capillaries, venules, and arterioles show pathologic lipid storage, and the capillaries of the dermal papillae just below the epidermis are markedly dilated. The larger lesions are usually located in the upper dermis, where they may produce elevation, flattening, or hypertrophy of the epithelium along with keratosis, hence the term *angiokeratoma*. Ultrastructurally, the glycosphingolipid inclusions in lysosomes have a concentrically arranged lamellar or myelin-like structure.

Clinical Manifestations

Angiokeratomas usually occur in childhood, which may lead to early diagnosis. They increase in size and number with age and range from barely visible to several millimeters in diameter. The lesions are punctate, dark red to blue-black, and flat or slightly raised. They do

Table 217–1 • BIOCHEMICAL AND PHENOTYPIC CHARACTERISTICS OF LYSOSOMAL STORAGE DISEASES

DISEASE	DEFICIENCY	SUBSTANCE ACCUMULATED	SITE	COMPLICATIONS
Fabry	α-Galactosidase A	Primarily globotriaosylceramide	Most cells, particularly vascular endothelial and smooth muscle cells	Ischemia, infarction
Gaucher				
Type 1	Acid β-glucosidase	Primarily glucosylceramide	Macrophage-monocyte system	Infiltration of bone marrow, progressive hepatosplenomegaly, skeletal complications
Type 2	Acid β-glucosidase	Primarily glucosylceramide	Macrophage-monocyte system, CNS	Infiltration of bone marrow, progressive hepatosplenomegaly, skeletal complications, neurodegeneration
Type 3	Acid β-glucosidase	Primarily glucosylceramide	Macrophage-monocyte system, CNS	Progressive neurodegeneration
Niemann-Pick				
Type A	Acid sphingomyelinase	Sphingomyelin	Monocyte-macrophage system, CNS	Hepatosplenomegaly, progressive neurodegeneration
Type B	Acid sphingomyelinase	Sphingomyelin	Monocyte-macrophage system	Progressive hepatosplenomegaly, infiltrative lung disease
Type C	Abnormal cholesterol transport	Primarily cholesterol	Most cells, especially liver, CNS	Hepatosplenomegaly, progressive neurodegeneration

CNS = central nervous system.

Table 217–2 • MOLECULAR GENETICS OF FABRY, GAUCHER, AND NIEMANN-PICK DISEASES

DISEASE	CHROMOSOME ASSIGNMENT	MOLECULAR CHARACTERISTICS	COMMENTS
Fabry	Xq22.1	cDNA, entire genomic sequences, >200 mutant alleles known	More than 200 private mutations detected occurring in single or a few families
Gaucher	1q21	cDNA, functional and pseudogenomic sequences, >200 mutant alleles known	Four mutations (N370S, L444P, 84insG, IVS2$^+$ 1) account for 90 to >95% of mutant alleles in Ashkenazi Jewish patients
Niemann-Pick			
Types A and B	11p15.1 to p15.4	cDNA, entire genomic sequence, >30 mutant alleles known	Four mutations account for >95% of mutant alleles in Ashkenazi Jewish patients with type A disease
Type C	18q11-q12 region	cDNA, entire genomic sequence, >100 mutant alleles known	More than 100 mutations in NPC1 gene

cDNA = complementary DNA; mRNA = messenger RNA.

not blanch with pressure, and the larger ones may show slight hyperkeratosis. Characteristically, the lesions are most dense between the umbilicus and the knees, in the "bathing trunk area," but may occur anywhere, including the oral mucosa. The hips, thighs, buttocks, umbilicus, lower part of the abdomen, scrotum, and glans penis are common sites, and a tendency toward bilateral symmetry is noted. Variants without skin lesions have been described. Sweating is usually decreased or absent. Corneal opacities and characteristic lenticular lesions, observed by slit-lamp examination, are present in affected male patients as well as in about 70 to 80% of asymptomatic heterozygotes. Conjunctival and retinal vascular tortuosity is common and results from systemic vascular involvement.

Pain is the most debilitating symptom in childhood and adolescence. Fabry crises, lasting from minutes to several days, consist of agonizing, burning pain in the hands and feet and proximal parts of the extremities and are usually associated with exercise, fatigue, and fever. These painful acroparesthesias usually become less frequent in the third and fourth decades of life, although in some men they may become more frequent and severe. Attacks of abdominal or flank pain may simulate appendicitis or renal colic.

With increasing age, the major morbid symptoms result from progressive involvement of the vascular system. Early in the course of the disease, casts, red blood cells, and lipid inclusions with characteristic birefringent "Maltese crosses" appear in the urinary sediment. Proteinuria, isothenuria, and gradual deterioration in renal function and the development of azotemia occur in the second to fourth decades. Cardiovascular findings may include hypertension, left ventricular hypertrophy, anginal chest pain, myocardial ischemia or infarction, and congestive heart failure. Mitral insufficiency is the most common valvular lesion. Abnormal electrocardiographic and echocardiographic findings are common. Cerebrovascular manifestations result primarily from multifocal small vessel involvement. Other features may include obstructive airway disease that increases with age, lymphedema of the legs without hypoproteinemia, episodic diarrhea, osteoporosis, retarded growth, and delayed puberty. Death most often results from uremia or vascular disease of the heart or brain. Before the advent of hemodialysis and renal transplantation, the mean age at death for affected men was 41 years. Atypical male variants with residual α-galactosidase A activity who are asymptomatic or mildly affected have been described whose manifestations include late-onset and isolated cardiac disease and proteinuria but normal renal function for age. These patients do not have the early classic manifestations. Those with "cardiac variants" have cardiomegaly, usually involving the left ventricular wall and interventricular septum, and electrocardiographic abnormalities consistent with cardiomyopathy. Others have had hypertrophic cardiomyopathy or myocardial infarction, or both.

Diagnosis

The diagnosis in classically affected male patients is most readily made from a history of painful acroparesthesias, hypohidrosis, characteristic skin lesions, corneal opacities, and lenticular lesions. The disorder is often misdiagnosed as rheumatic fever, erythromyalgia, or neurosis. The skin lesions must be differentiated from benign angiokeratomas of the scrotum (Fordyce's disease) or from angiokeratoma circumscriptum. Angiokeratomas identical to those of Fabry disease

have been reported in cases of fucosidosis, aspartylglycosaminuria, late-onset GM$_1$ gangliosidosis, galactosialidosis, α-N-acetylgalactosaminidase deficiency, and sialidosis. Diagnosis of the mild cardiac variants should be considered in individuals with left ventricular hypertrophy or cardiomyopathy. The diagnosis of classic and variant cases is confirmed biochemically by markedly decreased α-galactosidase A activity in plasma, isolated leukocytes, or cultured fibroblasts or lymphoblasts.

Heterozygous female subjects may have corneal opacities, isolated skin lesions, and low to normal activities of α-galactosidase A in plasma or cell sources. Rare female heterozygotes may have manifestations as severe as those in affected male subjects. However, in asymptomatic, at-risk female members of families affected by Fabry disease, optimal diagnosis should be by direct analysis of the family's specific mutation. Prenatal detection of affected male fetuses can be accomplished by demonstrating deficient α-galactosidase A activity or by detecting the family's specific gene mutation in chorionic villi obtained in the first trimester of pregnancy or in cultured amniocytes obtained by amniocentesis in the second trimester.

 Treatment

Until recently, treatment for Fabry disease has been nonspecific and limited to supportive care. These measures included the use of phenytoin and carbamazepine, which have been shown to decrease the frequency and severity of the chronic acroparesthesias and the periodic crises of excruciating pain. Renal transplantation and long-term hemodialysis also have become life-saving procedures for patients with renal failure. More recently, clinical trials with recombinant α-galactosidase (Fabrazyme, Genzyme Corporation, Cambridge, MA; Replagal, TKT Corporation, Cambridge, MA) have revealed the safety and effectiveness of enzyme replacement therapy for Fabry disease. A phase I/II dose-escalation trial demonstrated that the enzyme was well tolerated and that its use resulted in histologic, biochemical, and ultrastructural reductions in the levels of accumulated tissue globotriaosylceramide. The results of a recent phase III, multicenter, double-blind, randomized, placebo-controlled study of 58 patients with Fabry disease, half of whom received recombinant α-galactosidase and the other half placebo, showed that the treatment group had very significant clearance of globotriaosylceramide from the vascular endothelial cells of the kidney, heart, and skin. The placebo group had no change. After 20 weeks, patients in the placebo group were switched to recombinant α-galactosidase, and all had clearance of the vascular endothelial globotriaosylceramide in these tissues to near-reference-range levels. These studies demonstrated the safety and effectiveness of enzyme replacement therapy for this disease. The enzyme is available in Europe and has been recently approved by the U.S. Food and Drug Administration.

GAUCHER DISEASE

Definition

Gaucher disease is a glycolipid storage disease characterized by the deposition of glucocerebroside in cells of the macrophage-monocyte system. Three clinical subtypes are delineated by the absence or presence and progression of neurologic involvement: type 1, the adult non-neuronopathic form; type 2, the infantile or acute neuronopathic form; and type 3, the juvenile or subacute-neuronopathic form. All three subtypes are inherited as autosomal recessive traits. Type 1 disease is the most common lysosomal storage disease and the most prevalent genetic disorder among Ashkenazi Jewish individuals, with an incidence of about 1 in 1000 and a carrier frequency of about 1 in 16 to 18.

Pathobiology

All three subtypes of Gaucher disease result from deficient activity of the lysosomal hydrolase acid β-glucosidase (see Table 217–1). The molecular basis of Gaucher disease has been identified for more than 95% of Ashkenazi Jewish patients (see Table 217–2). Genotype/phenotype correlations have been noted for the different subtypes, particularly type 1 Gaucher disease. Presumably, the amount of residual enzymatic activity determines disease subtype and severity. For example, type 1 patients homozygous for the milder N370S mutation tend to have a later onset and milder course than do patients with one N370S allele and another mutant allele. However, the wide variability in clinical findings among patients with Gaucher disease cannot be fully explained by the nature of the underlying acid β-glucosidase mutations. The lesions causing the severe type 2 (infantile) disease express little if any enzymatic activity in vitro.

The pathologic hallmark is the presence of the Gaucher cell in the macrophage-monocyte system, particularly in the bone marrow. These cells, which are 20 to 100 μm in diameter, have a characteristic wrinkled-paper appearance resulting from intracytoplasmic substrate deposition. These cells stain strongly positive with periodic acid–Schiff stain, and their presence in bone marrow or other tissues suggests the diagnosis (Fig. 217–1). The accumulated glycolipid glucosylceramide is derived primarily from the phagocytosis and degradation of senescent leukocytes and to a lesser extent from erythrocyte membranes. Glycolipid storage results in organomegaly and pulmonary infiltration. Neuronal cell loss in patients with type 2 and 3 disease is presumably caused by accumulation of the cytotoxic glycolipid glucosylsphingosine in the brain as a result of the severe deficiency of acid β-glucosidase activity. Glucosylceramide accumulation in the bone marrow, liver, spleen, lungs, and kidney leads to pancytopenia, massive hepatosplenomegaly, and occasionally to diffuse infiltrative pulmonary disease and nephropathy or glomerulonephritis. The progressive infiltration of Gaucher cells in the bone marrow causes thinning of the cortex, pathologic fractures, bone pain, bony infarcts, and osteopenia. Central nervous system involvement occurs only in patients with type 2 and 3 disease.

Clinical Manifestations

A broad spectrum of clinical expression is seen in patients with type 1 disease, in part because of a combination of different mutant alleles and unidentified modifier genes. The onset of clinical manifestations occurs from early childhood to late adulthood. At examination, patients may have easy bruisability because of thrombocytopenia, chronic fatigue secondary to anemia, hepatomegaly with or without elevated liver function test results, splenomegaly, and bone pain or pathologic fractures. Occasional patients have pulmonary involvement. Patients whose disease is diagnosed in the first 5 years of life are frequently non-Jewish and typically have a more malignant disease course. Patients with milder disease are discovered later in life during evaluations for hematologic or skeletal problems or are found to have splenomegaly on routine examination. In symptomatic patients, splenomegaly is progressive and can become massive. Clinically apparent bone involvement, which occurs in more than 20% of patients, can be manifested as bone pain or pathologic fractures. Most patients have radiologic evidence of skeletal involvement, including an Erlenmeyer flask deformity of the distal end of the femur and osteopenia, which are early skeletal changes. In patients with symptomatic bone disease, lytic lesions can develop in the long bones, ribs, and pelvis, and osteosclerosis may be evident at an early age. Bone crises with severe pain and swelling can occur. Bleeding secondary to thrombocytopenia may be manifested as epistaxis and bruising and is frequently overlooked until other symptoms become apparent. Children with massive splenomegaly are short of stature because of the energy expenditure required by the enlarged organ.

Type 2 disease, which is rare and panethnic in distribution, is characterized by a rapid neurodegenerative course with extensive visceral involvement and death within the first 2 years of life. The disease presents in infancy and is associated with increased tone, strabismus, and organomegaly. Failure to thrive and stridor from laryngospasm are typical. The progressive psychomotor degeneration leads to death, usually secondary to an intercurrent respiratory infection and respiratory compromise.

Type 3 disease is noted in infancy or childhood. In addition to the organomegaly and bone involvement, patients have neurodegenerative manifestations. Type 3 disease is most frequent in Sweden (1 in 50,000), where it has been traced to a common founder in the 17th century. Type 3 has been further subclassified as types 3a and 3b based on the extent of neurologic involvement and whether progressive myotonia and dementia (type 3a) or isolated supranuclear gaze palsy (type 3b) is present.

Diagnosis

Gaucher disease should be considered in the differential diagnosis of patients with unexplained organomegaly, easy bruisability, or bone pain. Bone marrow examination usually reveals the presence of Gaucher cells; however, all suspected diagnoses should be confirmed by demonstration of deficient acid β-glucosidase activity in isolated leukocytes or cultured cells. For possible genotype/phenotype correlations, the specific acid β-glucosidase mutation may be determined, particularly in Ashkenazi Jewish patients. Carrier identification is best achieved by DNA testing in Jewish families. Testing should be offered to all family members, but it should be kept in mind that heterogeneity even among members of the same kindred can be so great that cases may be diagnosed in asymptomatic affected individuals during such testing. Prenatal diagnosis is possible by determining enzymatic activity or specific mutations in chorionic villi or cultured amniotic fluid cells.

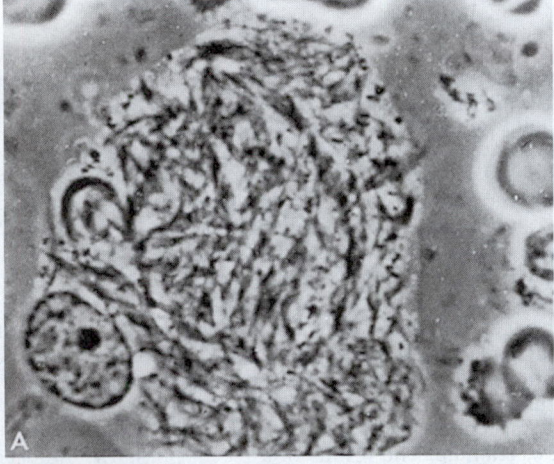

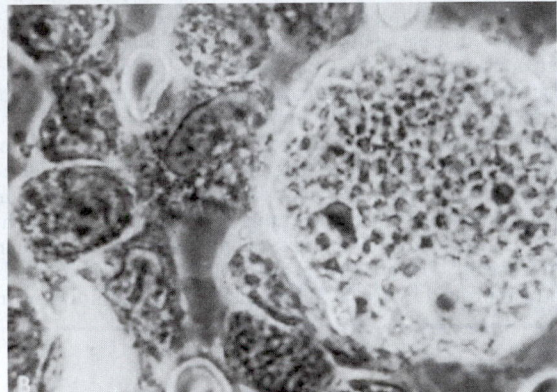

FIGURE 217–1 • Gaucher cell (A) and a foam cell seen in a case of Niemann-Pick disease (B). Both are viewed under phase microscopy with unstained smears of aspirated bone marrow. Magnification can be estimated from adjacent red blood cells.

Rx Treatment

In the past, management of patients with type 1 disease was primarily symptomatic and included blood transfusions for anemia, partial or total splenectomy for severe mechanical cardiopulmonary compromise or hypersplenism, analgesics for bone pain, and orthopedic procedures for joint replacement. A small number of patients have also undergone bone marrow transplantation, which, if successful, is curative. A matched donor is required, however, and significant morbidity and mortality are associated with the procedure. No effective treatment is known for the neurologic involvement in type 2 and 3 disease. More recently, the safety and efficacy of enzyme replacement recombinant acid β-glucosidase have been demonstrated in type 1 disease. Clinical trials have demonstrated that most extraskeletal symptoms are reversed by an initial debulking dose of enzyme (60 IU/kg) administered by intravenous infusion every other week. The effectiveness of enzyme replacement in reversing and preventing bone manifestations is still under study; however, early data indicate that early treatment may be efficacious in normalizing linear growth and bone morphology in affected children. Efforts are also underway to develop gene therapy for type 1 disease.

NIEMANN-PICK DISEASE

Definition

Niemann-Pick disease (NPD) types A and B are lipid storage disorders that result from the deficiency of the lysosomal enzyme acid sphingomyelinase and the subsequent accumulation of its substrate sphingomyelin. The original description of NPD referred to what is now known as type A NPD, which is a fatal disorder of infancy characterized by failure to thrive, hepatosplenomegaly, and a rapidly progressive neurodegenerative course that leads to death by the age of 2 or 3 years. Type B is a non-neuronopathic form observed in children and adults. In addition, several other subtypes of NPD have been described, the major subtype being type C, which results from defective cholesterol transport. Previously, a type D disease was identified in patients from Nova Scotia. Studies have now shown that these type D patients have mutations in the major gene causing type C disease. All the subtypes are inherited as autosomal recessive traits and display variable clinical features.

Pathobiology

Niemann-Pick disease types A and B result from deficient acid sphingomyelinase activity (see Table 217–1). In type C NPD, the genetic defect involves the defective transport of cholesterol from the lysosome to the cytosol. Two different genes causing the altered cholesterol transport in type C disease were recently identified, permitting more precise diagnosis, carrier detection, and prenatal diagnosis in affected families. The pathologic hallmark in NPD types A and B is the histochemically characteristic lipid-laden foam cell, often referred to as the *Niemann-Pick cell*. These cells, which can be readily distinguished from Gaucher cells by their histologic and histochemical characteristics, are not pathognomonic for Niemann-Pick disease because histologically similar cells are found in patients with Wolman's disease, cholesterol ester storage disease, and lipoprotein lipase deficiency, as well as in some patients with GM_1 gangliosidosis type 2. Sphingomyelin is the major lipid that accumulates in the cells and tissues of patients with types A and B Niemann-Pick disease. In most normal tissues, sphingomyelin constitutes 5 to 20% of the total cellular phospholipid content; however, in patients with types A and B disease, sphingomyelin levels may be elevated up to 50-fold and thus constitute about 70% of the total phospholipid fraction. Lysosomal sphingomyelin accumulation in the brain, liver, kidney, and lungs has been documented in organs from patients with NPD types A and B; they contain about the same amount of sphingomyelin, with the notable exception that patients with type B NPD have little or no lipid storage in their central nervous system. In general, patients with type A disease have less than 1% of normal acid sphingomyelinase in cultured fibroblasts and lymphocytes, whereas cells from type B patients typically have some residual activity, which prevents the development of neurologic symptoms.

Clinical Manifestations

The clinical features and course of type A disease are relatively uniform and are characterized by normal appearance at birth, although the newborn period is sometimes complicated by prolonged jaundice. Hepatosplenomegaly, moderate lymphadenopathy, and psychomotor retardation are evident by 6 months of life and are followed by rapid neurodegeneration. The loss of motor function and deterioration in intellectual capabilities are progressive. In later stages, spasticity and rigidity are evident, with affected infants experiencing complete loss of contact with their environment.

In contrast to the predictable natural history of the type A phenotype, the clinical features and course in patients with type B disease are variable. Most cases are diagnosed in infancy or childhood, when enlargement of the liver or spleen or both is detected during routine physical examination. At diagnosis, type B patients also have evidence of mild pulmonary involvement, usually detected as a diffuse reticular or finely nodular infiltration on chest radiography. In most patients, hepatosplenomegaly is particularly prominent in childhood, but with increasing linear growth the abdominal protuberance decreases and becomes less conspicuous. In mildly affected patients, the splenomegaly may not be noted until adulthood, and disease manifestations may be minimal. In most patients with type B disease, decreased pulmonary diffusion secondary to alveolar infiltration becomes evident in childhood and progresses with age. Severely affected individuals may experience significant pulmonary compromise by the age of 15 to 20 years. Such patients have low PO_2 values and dyspnea on exertion. Life-threatening bronchopneumonia may occur, and cor pulmonale has been described. Severely affected patients may also have liver involvement, leading to life-threatening cirrhosis, portal hypertension, and ascites. Clinically significant pancytopenia from secondary hypersplenism may necessitate partial or total splenectomy. However, removal of the spleen can lead to significant worsening of the pulmonary involvement. Typically, patients with type B disease do not have neurologic involvement and are intellectually intact. Patients with NPD type C disease often have prolonged neonatal jaundice, appear normal for 1 to 2 years, and then experience a slowly progressive and variable neurodegenerative course. Their hepatosplenomegaly is less severe than that in patients with type A or B disease, and they may survive into adulthood.

Diagnosis

Type A disease is diagnosed in the patient's first year of life by failure to thrive, organomegaly, and severe psychomotor retardation. In patients with type B disease, splenomegaly is usually noted early in childhood; however, in very mild cases, the enlargement may be subtle and detection may be delayed until adolescence or adulthood. The presence of the characteristic Niemann-Pick cells in the bone marrow supports the diagnosis. However, patients with type C disease also have infiltration of these cells in the bone marrow. Thus, all suspected cases should be evaluated enzymatically to confirm the clinical diagnosis by measuring the acid sphingomyelinase activity in peripheral leukocytes, cultured fibroblasts, and lymphoblasts. Patients with types A and B disease have markedly decreased levels of enzymatic activity (1 to 10% of normal), whereas patients with type C disease may have slightly decreased sphingomyelinase activity (50 to 75% of normal) and patients with Gaucher disease and other storage disorders characterized by hepatosplenomegaly and neurologic involvement have normal or near-normal levels. Type C disease can be biochemically documented by demonstrating the cholesterol transport defect in cultured fibroblasts. The enzymatic identification of types A and B carriers is problematic. However, in families in which the specific molecular lesion has been identified, family members can be accurately tested for heterozygote status by DNA analysis. Heterozygote identification for type C disease also can be accomplished by DNA analysis in families whose mutations have been identified. Prenatal diagnosis of types A and B disease may be reliably made by measuring acid sphingomyelinase activity in cultured amniocytes or chorionic villi. In type C disease, the cholesterol defect can be demonstrated by filipin staining, but DNA diagnosis is most accurate. Thus, in types A, B, and C, prenatal diagnosis can be made by DNA analysis of fetal cells in families in which the specific molecular lesions are known.

Metabolic Diseases

 Treatment

At present, no specific treatment is available for any of the NPD subtypes. Orthotopic liver transplantation in an infant with type A disease and amniotic cell transplantation in several patients with type B disease have been attempted without success. Bone marrow transplantation in a type B patient was successful in reducing the spleen and liver volumes, the sphingomyelin content of the liver, the number of Niemann-Pick cells in the marrow, and radiologically detected infiltration of the lungs. However, no long-term information is available because this patient died 3 months after transplantation. To date, lung transplantation has not been performed in any severely compromised patient with type B disease. Future prospects for treatment of type B disease include enzyme replacement and gene therapy. Treatment of types A and C disease is currently precluded by the severe neurologic involvement.

SUGGESTED READINGS

de Fost M, Aerts JM, Hollak CE: Gaucher disease: from fundamental research to effective therapeutic interventions. Neth J Med 2003;61:3–8. *Intravenous enzyme supplementation therapy is the treatment of choice for moderate or severe disease, but mildly affected patients can consider an oral substrate inhibitor if intravenous treatment is less attractive.*

Desnick RJ, Brady R, Barranger J, et al: Fabry disease, an under-recognized multisystemic disorder: Expert recommendations for diagnosis, management, and enzyme replacement therapy. Ann Intern Med 2003;138:338–346. *Recommendations for clinicians.*

Desnick RJ, Ioannou YA, Eng CM: Fabry disease: α-Galactosidase deficiency and Schindler disease: α-N-acetylgalactosaminidase deficiency. *In* Scriver CR, Beaudet AL, Sly WS, Valle D (eds): The Metabolic and Molecular Bases of Inherited Disease, 8th ed. New York, McGraw-Hill, 2001. *Definitive chapter describing the clinical, pathologic, biochemical, and molecular manifestations of Fabry's disease with more than 400 references.*

Eng CM, Banikazemi M, Gordon RE, et al: A phase 1/2 clinical trial of enzyme replacement in Fabry disease: Pharmacokinetic, substrate clearance, and safety studies. Am J Hum Genet 2001;68:711–722. *Report of the phase I/II trial of enzyme replacement.*

Schuchman EH, Desnick RJ: Types A and B Niemann-Pick disease. *In* Scriver CR, Beaudet AL, Sly WS, Valle D (eds): The Metabolic and Molecular Bases of Inherited Disease, 8th ed. New York, McGraw-Hill, 2001. *The most up-to-date description of the clinical, metabolic, and molecular nature of Niemann-Pick disease types A and B.*

Tayebi N, Stubblefield BK, Park JK, et al: Reciprocal and nonreciprocal recombination at the glucocerebrosidase gene region: Implications for complexity in Gaucher disease. Am J Hum Genet 2003;72:519–534. *Assessment of genotype-phenotype relationships in 240 patients with Gaucher disease.*

218 DISORDERS OF PHENYLALANINE AND TYROSINE METABOLISM

Stephen D. Cederbaum
Charles R. Scriver

Until recently, the inclusion of any disorder of phenylalanine or tyrosine metabolism, save for alkaptonuria, in a textbook of internal medicine would have been considered indulgent wishful thinking. However, the striking success of treatment for phenylketonuria and, more recently, hepatorenal tyrosinemia has thrust them both, either now or in the near future, firmly into the realm of adult metabolic disorders. Phenylketonuria (MIM 261600),* the best known of these disorders, may no longer be considered a disease, although it continues to be a risk factor, because its principal manifestations (mental retardation, pigment dilution, mousy odor, neurotransmitter deficiency) occur only in rare cases escaping early diagnosis and/or effective treatment. This satisfactory turn of events came about because pathogenesis from hyperphenylalaninemia (the risk factor) is offset by treatment (low phenylalanine diet).

Figure 218–1 gives a brief outline of the main catabolic pathway for phenylalanine and tyrosine. The sites of the enzyme deficiency in hyperphenylalaninemia, alkaptonuria, and hepatorenal tyrosinemia are indicated in bold numbers.

*MIM: (Online) Mendelian Inheritance in Man (catalogues of Mendelian traits); the URL is *http://www.ncbi.nlm.nih.gov/OMIM*

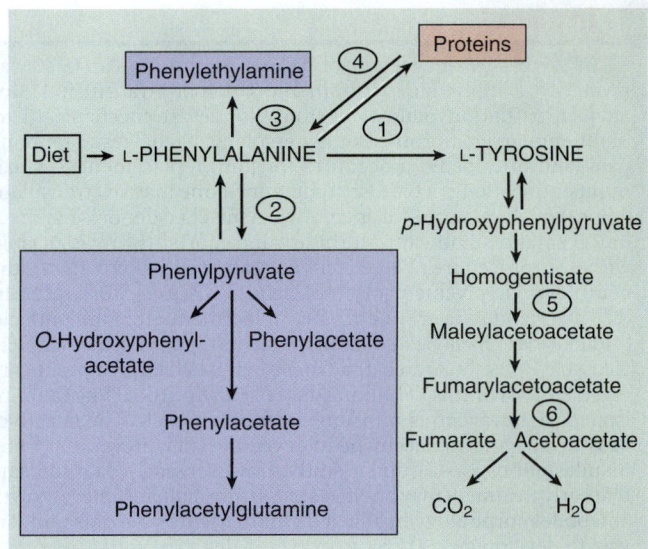

A

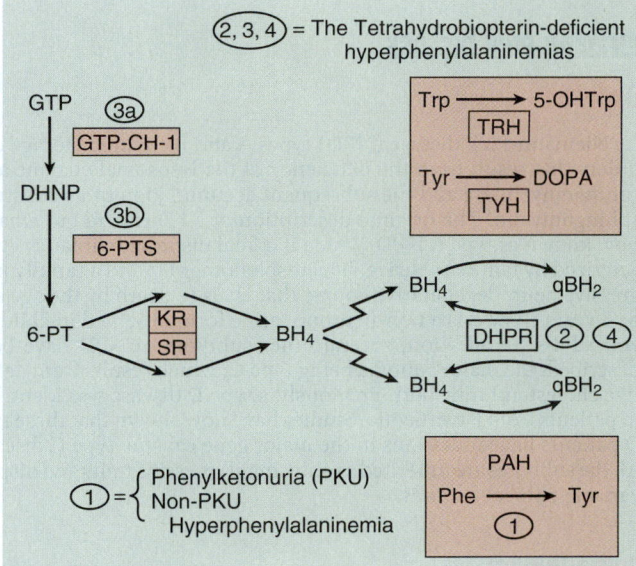

B

FIGURE 218–1 • *A,* Intake of phenylalanine (an essential amino acid supplied only by diet) and its disposal by hydroxylation (1) (representing three fourths of normal runout), transamination (2), decarboxylation (3), and incorporation into proteins (4) (representing a fourth of runout). The subsequent catabolism of tyrosine is depicted on the right side of the panel. The enzymes whose deficiency causes alkaptonuria, homogentisic acid oxidase, and hepatorenal typosinemia, fumarylacetoacetate hydrolase, are indicated by numbers 5 and 6. *B,* Interrelations between phenylalanine hydroxylase (PAH), dihydropteridine reductase (DHPR), and the tetrahydrobiopterin (BH₄) biosynthesis pathway serving aromatic amino acid hydroxylation reactions. Mutations at the relevant chromosomal loci impair the hydroxylation reactions with effects on PAH activity only (1); DHPR activity (2); GTP-cyclohydrolase 1 (GTP-CH-1) activity (3a); 6-pyruvoyltetrahydropterin synthase activity (6-PTS) (3b); and 4α-carbinolamine dehydratase (4). Disorders 2, 3a, 3b, and 4 can impair function of three hydroxylases: PAH, tyrosine hydroxylase (TYH), and tryptophan hydroxylase (TRH). GTP = guanosine triphosphate; DHNP = dihydroneopterin triphosphate; 6-PT = 6-pyruvoyltetrahydropterin; KR = 2′-ketotetrahydropterin reductase; SR = sepiapterin reductase, qBH₂ = quinonoid dihydrobiopterin.

THE HYPERPHENYLALANINEMIAS

Phenylalanine Metabolism

Phenylalanine is an essential amino acid. The normal concentration in plasma is less than 125 μmol/L. Metabolic utilization is largely controlled by a hydroxylation reaction (see Fig. 218–1A), and impaired hydroxylation is the chief explanation for hyperphenylalaninemia.

The reaction requires the apoenzyme phenylalanine hydroxylase (PAH, a monooxygenase), molecular oxygen, and tetrahydrobiopterin cofactor: the last-named is consumed in stoichiometric amounts to form tyrosine, the reaction product. The catalytic property of phenylalanine hydroxylase requires both moment-to-moment regeneration of tetrahydrobiopterin from 4α-carbinolamine and dihydrobiopterin, consecutive byproducts of the hydroxylating reaction, and long-term renewal of the tetrahydrobiopterin pool by synthesis from precursors. The former is achieved by the enzymes 4α-carbinolamine dehydratase (DCOH) and dihydropteridine reductase (QDPR), the latter by a synthesis pathway in which several enzymes act in sequence, guanosine triphosphate cyclohydrolase 1 (GCH1) and 6-pyruvoyl tetrahydrobiopterin synthase (6-PTS). Accordingly, there are several ways to impair phenylalanine hydroxylation. Failure to recognize the biologic heterogeneity of hyperphenylalaninemia may lead to erroneous counseling and the wrong treatment; all of its forms require special management of women during the reproductive years.

Genetic forms of hyperphenylalaninemia are described here; they are all autosomal recessive disorders. About 0.01% of live births are affected. Physicians for adult-age patients must be aware of maternal hyperphenylalaninemia and its consequences for the fetus (see later).

Disorders of Phenylalanine Hydroxylase Integrity

The phenylalanine hydroxylase enzyme is multimeric and homopolymeric. The polypeptide is encoded by a gene on chromosome 12, region q24.1, which is expressed only in liver in humans. *PAH* mutations range from "severe" and cause phenylketonuria (with plasma phenylalanine values >1 mM on a normal diet) to "mild" and cause nonphenylketonuric hyperphenylalaninemia (values <1 mM but >0.125 mM). Phenylketonuria is typically associated with mental retardation in the untreated patient. If there is deficient hydroxylation activity and dietary intake is not curtailed, free phenylalanine accumulates in the body. Overburden of phenylalanine impairs brain development in ways still not fully understood. The risk of mental retardation without treatment is thought to be very low in those individuals whose phenylalanine values are consistently below 625 µM. The incidence and relative frequencies of the two forms (together about 1 per 10,000 births) vary widely among populations.

Phenylketonuria was first described as a clinical entity in 1934. In the following three decades, phenylketonuria was seen as a paradigm for the biochemical basis of mental disease, of disease that could be prevented by deliberately restoring normal metabolism, and of chemical individuality that could be used as the basis for a screening test and early diagnosis. Newborn screening for hyperphenylalaninemia is now one of the most widely applied "genetic" tests. The incidence of the risk factor has not changed, but the frequency of the associated disease is now trivial in screened populations.

Tetrahydrobiopterin-Deficient Forms of Hyperphenylalaninemia

Not every case of persistent hyperphenylalaninemia is explained by a primary hydroxylase deficiency. Tetrahydrobiopterin insufficiency impairs function of three hydroxylases (for phenylalanine, tryptophan, and tyrosine) and synthesis of their products, notably 5-hydroxytryptophan (the precursor of serotonin) and L-dopa (the precursor of catecholamines) (see Fig. 218–1*B*). The products function as neurotransmitters in the brain, and a deficiency of them gives rise to central nervous system disease (including retarded psychomotor development, basal ganglion dysfunction, and unstable body temperature), even when the elevated phenylalanine levels are controlled by diet. Deficient activity of GCH1, 6-PTS, DCOH, or QDPR impairs the synthesis of tetrahydrobiopterin and accounts for about 1% of cases of hyperphenylalaninemia ascertained in the newborn period.

Screening and Diagnosis

Screening newborns for hyperphenylalaninemia is public policy in all developed and in many developing countries. Capillary blood collected on filter paper from heel puncture is analyzed by increasingly modern quantitative methods. Blood phenylalanine values greater than about 350 mM or phenylalanine/tyrosine ratios greater than 1.5 on the first day of life or thereafter are considered abnormal and require

further investigation. The HPA phenotype test is still the most efficient; DNA-based tests detect more than 400 mutations in the *PAH* gene and dozens in the genes controlling tetrahydrobiopterin homeostasis, but none is common to every case of HPA.

Every infant with persistent hyperphenylalaninemia is investigated in specialized centers to rule out disorders of tetrahydrobiopterin homeostasis. Prenatal diagnosis for most of these disorders is possible, particularly if mutations are known.

Mutation databases exist for phenylketonuria (http://www.mcgill.ca/pahdb) and for disorders of tetrahydrobiopterin homeostasis (http://www.unizh.ch/~blau/bh4.html). Routine mutation analysis in the hyperphenylalaninemias is much debated, with the benefits, at the moment, more abstract than real. Progress in the future may tip the balance more heavily toward DNA testing.

 ## Treatment

The mainstay of treatment for primary phenylalanine hydroxylase deficiency is dietary restriction of the amino acid. There are several semisynthetic dietary products ("orphan foods") for this purpose. Phenylketonuric patients can tolerate only 250 to 500 mg of phenylalanine per day (normal intake is greater than 1000 mg) to maintain the blood phenylalanine level below the ideal level of 350 mM. Intake, blood levels of phenylalanine, and growth rate are monitored at frequent intervals to avoid undertreatment or overtreatment. Treatment into adult life is now recommended to maintain normal neuropsychologic function. Well-treated patients have normal or near-normal intellectual development.

The tetrahydrobiopterin-deficient forms require continuous replacement therapy of cofactor alone or in combination with neurotransmitter precursors. Whether postnatal treatment of these disorders is fully effective remains to be seen. Some mutations in the PAH gene may be partially or almost completely responsive to tetrahydrobiopterin as well.

Maternal Hyperphenylalaninemia

Maternal hyperphenylalaninemia is a problem relevant to all practitioners who counsel women about pregnancy. Intrauterine hyperphenylalaninemia places the fetus at risk of microcephaly, mental retardation, and organ malformations (notably cardiac). Accordingly, all females with hyperphenylalaninemia should be identified, followed, counseled about risk when they attain reproductive age, and treated with diet to maintain near-normal blood phenylalanine levels before conception and throughout the pregnancy. When well treated in the mother, pregnancy outcome for the offspring of women with hyperphenylalaninemia is generally good.

Genetics

Mutant alleles (at all relevant loci) are recessive. Their aggregate frequency in the population is about 0.01, meaning that 2% of the population is heterozygous. Observed explanations for the high allelic frequency of this "rare" phenotype include founder effect and genetic drift in some populations and possibly a selective advantage for carriers of the mutant trait.

ALKAPTONURIA

Alkaptonuria (MIM 203500) is an autosomal recessive disorder in which homogentisic acid oxidase activity is deficient (see Fig. 218–1). Homogentisic acid produced during the metabolism of phenylalanine and tyrosine accumulates and is excreted in the urine. It causes pigmentation of cartilage and other connective tissue (ochronosis) and in later years a degenerative arthritis of the spine and the larger peripheral joints. The disease has historical significance, because it was chiefly on the basis of his study of families with alkaptonuria that Sir Archibald Garrod developed the concept of the "inborn error of metabolism." The alkaptonuria gene (symbol *AKU*), encoding homogentisic acid oxidase, has been mapped to human chromosome 3q21-q23, cloned, and characterized, and mutations have been identified—a major advance in the alkaptonuria saga.

Incidence and Prevalence

The trait is rare (<1 per 250,000 births), but cases are still being reported (now >600), including one in a 3500-year-old Egyptian mummy.

Pathogenesis

The activity of homogentisic acid oxidase in the normal adult human liver is sufficient to metabolize more than 1600 g of homogentisic acid per day. Normally, no homogentisic acid can be detected in plasma or urine. In alkaptonuric individuals, there is little or no detectable activity of this enzyme in liver, kidney, or prostate, where it is normally abundant. Plasma levels of homogentisic acid rise to about 175 to 200 μM, and the urinary excretion ranges from 4 to 8 g/day. Mammalian tissue also contains an enzyme called homogentisic acid polyphenyloxidase that catalyzes the oxidation of homogentisic acid to an ochronotic pigment, but pigment can also be produced nonenzymatically in the presence of oxygen and alkali, as, for example, in urine. The homogentisic acid polymer has a high affinity for cartilage and connective tissue macromolecules. The stained tissue is fragile and eventually may break down, leading to degenerative intervertebral disc or joint disease. Homogentisic acid may also have a direct effect on collagen synthesis through inhibition of lysyl hydroxylase.

Pathology

In the adult alkaptonuric patient, costal, laryngeal, and tracheal cartilages are densely pigmented, sometimes appearing coal-black. Pigmentation is also present throughout the body in fibrous tissue, fibrocartilage, tendons, ligaments, epidermis, endocardium, and intima of larger vessels in various organs, including kidney, lung, and prostate.

Clinical Manifestations

Homogentisic acid is present in urine from birth. Urine is colorless when passed but darkens when alkaline or after long exposure to air. Generally, the earliest physical sign is a slight pigmentation of the sclerae or the ears, beginning at age 20 to 30 years. The cartilage of the ears may be slate blue or gray and feel irregular and thickened. Sometimes dusky discolorations of underlying tendons can be seen through the skin over the hands. Pigment in perspiration stains clothing in the axillary and genital regions. The arthritis causes limitation of motion of the hips, knee joints, or shoulders, and there may be periods of acute inflammation. Limitation of motion and ankylosis in the lumbosacral region are late findings. In addition, alkaptonuric patients appear to have a high incidence of cardiovascular disease; at least one degenerated pigmented aortic valve has been replaced with a prosthesis. Other complications include ruptured intervertebral disks, prostatitis, and renal stones. The arthritis must be differentiated from rheumatoid arthritis, osteoarthritis, and gout.

Radiographic Changes

Almost pathognomonic, the changes affect vertebral bodies of the lumbar spine, which show degeneration of the intervertebral discs, narrowing of the space, dense calcification of remaining disc material, and variable fusion of vertebral bodies, but little osteophyte formation and minimal calcification of intervertebral ligaments. The degenerative changes of ochronotic arthritis are most severe in the hip, shoulder, and knee, and there may be calcific deposits in the tendons. The sacroiliac joints and smaller joints of the extremities usually show little or no abnormality. Ear cartilage may be calcified.

Diagnosis and Differential Diagnosis

The diagnosis is suggested by urine discoloration and the presence of nonglucose reducing substance, pigmentation of sclerae or cartilage, arthritic episodes, and typical radiographic changes of the lumbar spine. Homogentisic acid in urine can be identified by chromatographic or enzymatic assays.

 ## Treatment

A low-protein diet for life would be prudent. Dietary restriction of phenylalanine and tyrosine of the degree necessary to reduce homogentisic aciduria is impractical and potentially deleterious. Pharmacologic doses of ascorbic acid, early and continuously, might reduce polymerization and pigmentation because ascorbic acid inhibits the polyphenol oxidase. It does not alter the primary metabolic defect. NTBC (2-(2-nitro-4-trifluoromethylbenzoyl)-1,3-cyclohexanedione), the potent inhibitor of *p*-hydroxyphenylpyruvic acid oxidase, would prevent excess formation of homogentisic acid by blocking the pathway prior to the mutant step, but it requires a reduced protein intake and a synthetic amino acid supplement.

HEPATORENAL TYROSINEMIA (OR TYROSINEMIA TYPE I)

Hepatorenal tyrosinemia (MIM 276700) is an autosomal recessive disorder in which the final enzyme in tyrosine catabolism, fumarylacetate hydrolase (FAH), is deficient. The fumarylacetoacetate that accumulates is converted nonenzymatically to succinylacetone, which is toxic to the liver and kidneys and which inhibits the porphyrin synthetic enzyme ALA dehydratase, causing sudden neurologic crises in some patients.

Incidence

The worldwide incidence is estimated to be less than 1 in 100,000 to 150,000 births. A higher incidence of 1 in 15,000 to 1 in 20,000 occurs in the Canadian Province of Quebec and is as frequent as 1 in 1500 to 1 in 2000 live births in the Sanguenay-Lac St. Jean region. This high frequency is due to the effect of a small, inbred founder population that migrated from France more than 300 years ago.

Clinical Manifestations

The age of onset may vary from infancy to adolescence. Patients present with failure of liver synthetic functions, particularly clotting, but they have proportionately less jaundice and hypoglycemia. Cirrhosis and ascites also occur early in the disease course, but transaminase elevations are more modest. α-Fetoprotein levels are quite astronomical, often exceeding 100,000 ng/mL (normal is less than 10 in children 6 to 9 months of age and thereafter). A more indolent course of gradual onset of cirrhosis occurs as well. Precocious onset of hepatocellular carcinoma is a grave risk, may occur very early, and has led to close scrutiny of surviving patients and, commonly, preemptive liver transplantation.

Neurologic crises resembling those of acute intermittent porphyria occur quite frequently and may be relatively intractable. Renal Fanconi syndrome occurs in all patients and rickets follows in most.

Pathogenesis

The cause of all clinical manifestations is almost certainly the highly toxic succinylacetone that accumulates. Elimination of succinylacetone in humans and in the knockout mouse model substantially eliminates all clinical and biochemical manifestations of the disease.

 ## Treatment

Dietary therapy limiting the intake of phenylalanine and tyrosine improved acute symptoms but had little effect on the long-term outlook of the disorder. The first "cure" for this disorder was liver transplantation, in which one disorder was traded for another. The procedure eliminated succinylacetone from blood (but not from urine), eliminated the renal Fanconi syndrome, and eliminated the neurologic crises. The miracle drug is NTBC (see earlier), which blocks tyrosine catabolism just prior to formation of homogentisic acid and brings succinylacetone levels to below the sensitivity of the analytic procedure. Patients with acute disease may improve within hours and are well enough for discharge from the hospital within days. The longer-term effectiveness of this therapy is unknown. It certainly reduces the incidence of hepatocellular carcinoma but may not eliminate the risk entirely, especially in patients with a longer pretreatment clinical course. All patients must be followed carefully with α-fetoprotein measurement and sensitive liver imaging techniques. Even with NTBC therapy, transplantation specialists particularly are prone to choosing earlier rather than later surgical intervention. Well advanced renal tubular dysfunction may not improve appreciably with treatment.

SUGGESTED READINGS

Elsas LJ II, Acosta PB: Nutritional support of inherited metabolic diseases. *In* Shils ME, Olson JA, Shike M (eds): Modern Nutrition in Health and Disease, 9th ed. Malvern, PA, Lea & Febiger, 1998, pp 1003–1056. *A practical guide to the nutritional aspects of treating this and other metabolic disorders.*

La Du BN: Alkaptonuria; *In* Scriver CR, Beaudet AL, Sly WS, Valle D (eds): The Metabolic and Molecular Bases of Inherited Disease, 8th ed. New York, McGraw-Hill, 2001. *The definitive clinical and molecular discussion of these inborn errors. Also see URL websites for mutation data: http://www.mcgill.ca/pahdb; http://www.unizh.ch/~blau/bh4.html.*

Scriver CR, Eisensmith RC, Woo SL, Kaufman S: The hyperphenylalaninemias of man and mouse. Annu Rev Genet 1994;28:141–165. *A good review.*

Smith I, Lee P: The hyperphenylalaninemias; Kvittingen EA, Holme E: Disorders of tyrosine metabolism. *In* Fernandes J, Saudubray J-M, Van Den Bergh G (eds): Inborn Metabolic Diseases. New York, Springer-Verlag, 2001, pp 171–184; 186–194. *Practical clinical chapters reflecting a transatlantic perspective.*

219 THE HYPERPROLINEMIAS AND HYDROXYPROLINEMIA

James M. Phang

There are three autosomal recessive genetic disorders in the degradative pathways for proline and hydroxyproline. Although these rare disorders are generally benign, the resulting metabolic abnormalities, at least for one of the disorders, are associated with neurologic manifestations in childhood.

The α-nitrogen of the amino acids proline and hydroxyproline is incorporated within a pyrrolidine ring. This feature confers structural and functional properties to proteins. Because of the ring structure, the metabolism of proline, including biosynthesis from glutamate and ornithine and degradation back to glutamate, is catalyzed by a specific set of enzymes. Both synthetic and degradative pathways share Δ^1-pyrroline-5-carboxylate as an intermediate. The cycling of proline may mediate the transfer of reducing-oxidizing potential that may be important under certain conditions. Studies suggest that proline oxidation is increased during apoptosis and can be a source of reactive oxygen species; expression of proline oxidase is reduced or absent in certain cancers. Preformed hydroxyproline is not incorporated into proteins. Instead, hydroxyproline is formed from peptide-linked proline, primarily in collagen.

Hyperprolinemias

The two genetic disorders in proline metabolism are characterized by hyperprolinemia and iminoglycinuria, but they are due to different enzyme deficiencies; type II hyperprolinemia can be diagnosed directly. This disorder is due to a deficiency of Δ^1-pyrroline-5-carboxylate dehydrogenase, which catalyzes the second step in the degradative pathway for proline (Fig. 219–1); the deficiency in enzyme activity can be determined in extracts of circulating leukocytes or cultured fibroblasts. Hyperprolinemia in type II disorder is more marked than in type I, but the distinguishing feature of type II is the accumulation of Δ^1-pyrroline-5-carboxylate in plasma and its excretion in urine. The hyperprolinemia in type I is due to a deficiency of the first enzyme in the pathway, proline oxidase. Although plasma proline is generally lower than in type II, the diagnosis of type I is one of exclusion, that is, hyperprolinemia unaccompanied by Δ^1-pyrroline-5-carboxylate in urine or plasma.

Clinical manifestations have been described with the hyperprolinemias, but the association may be due to chance because, in most cases, hyperprolinemia was identified fortuitously in patients presenting with clinical abnormalities (biased ascertainment). This is especially true for cases of type I hyperprolinemia in which renal

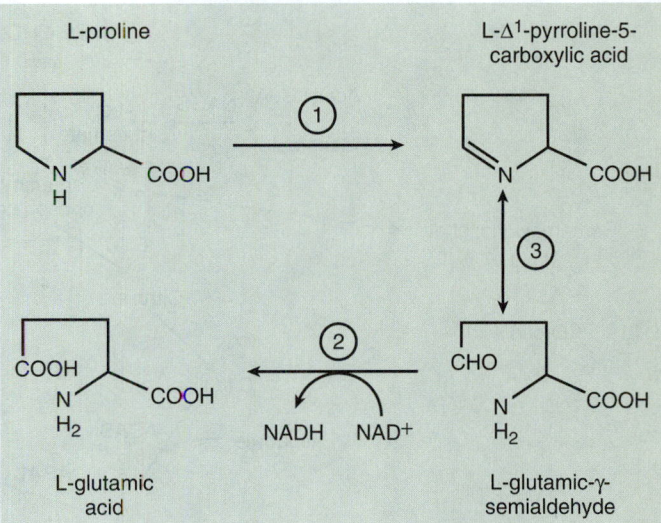

FIGURE 219-1 • Schematic of the degradative pathway for proline. Reaction 1 is catalyzed by proline oxidase (EC number unassigned); reaction 2 is catalyzed by Δ^1-pyrroline-5-carboxylic acid dehydrogenase (EC 1.5.1.12); and reaction 3 is spontaneous. Type I hyperprolinemia is due to blockade at reaction 1 (deficiency of proline oxidase), and type II hyperprolinemia is due to blockade at reaction 2 (deficiency of Δ^1-pyrroline-5-carboxylic acid dehydrogenase).

disease and mental retardation found in some pedigrees were shown to segregate independently of hyperprolinemia. Recent reports suggesting a possible link of proline oxidase to increased susceptibility for schizophrenia have reopened the question. For type II hyperprolinemia, however, clinical associations untainted by biased ascertainment have been identified. Screening a large pedigree in Ireland identified 14 new cases confirmed by elevated plasma Δ^1-pyrroline-5-carboxylate levels and undetectable enzyme activity in leukocytes. Nine of these 14 new subjects had a history of recurrent childhood febrile seizures requiring hospitalization and treatment with anticonvulsants. Thus, the association of type II hyperprolinemia with a predisposition to seizures appears convincing. Adults in this pedigree were fertile and otherwise normal. Although the mechanism for this association remains unclear, the identification of a high-affinity proline transporter in rat brain suggests that proline or its metabolites may have a neuromodulatory function.

Hydroxyprolinemia

Hydroxyprolinemia with hydroxyprolinuria, but without hyperprolinemia or prolinuria, has been described in members of several families. Although the degradation of hydroxyproline parallels that of proline, the pathway enzymes are distinct, except that the second degradation step is catalyzed by a common enzyme that dehydrogenates both Δ^1-pyrroline-5-carboxylate (see earlier) and 3-OH-Δ^1-pyrroline-5-carboxylate. The first step in the degradation, however, is catalyzed by distinct oxidases. The absence of urinary Δ^1-pyrroline-5-carboxylate or its hydroxylated congener leads to the conclusion that this autosomal recessive disorder is due to a deficiency of hydroxyproline oxidase. In this disorder, there are no clinical manifestations related to abnormalities in collagen metabolism or central nervous system function, and therapy is not indicated.

SUGGESTED READINGS

Donald SP, Sun XY, Hu CA, et al: Proline oxidase, encoded by p53-induced gene-6, catalyzes the generation of proline-dependent reactive oxygen species. Cancer Res 2001;61:1810–1815. *Report of proline-dependent generation of reactive oxygen species.*

Liu H, Heath SC, Sobin C, et al: Genetic variation at the 22q11 PRODH2/DGCR6 locus presents an unusual pattern and increases susceptibility to schizophrenia. Proc Natl Acad Sci USA 2002;99:3717–3722. *Genetic evidence linking proline oxidase and schizophrenia.*

Maxwell SA, Rivera A: Proline oxidase induces apoptosis in tumor cells, and its expression is frequently absent or reduced in renal carcinomas. J Biol Chem 2003;278:9784–9789. *Proline oxidase induces apoptosis and is absent in certain cancers.*

Phang JM, Hu CA, Valle D: Disorders of proline and hydroxyproline metabolism. *In* Scriver CR, Beaudet AL, Sly WS, Valle D (eds): The Metabolic and Molecular Basis of Inherited Disease, 8th ed. New York, McGraw-Hill, 2001, pp 1821–1838. *Review of proline metabolism.*

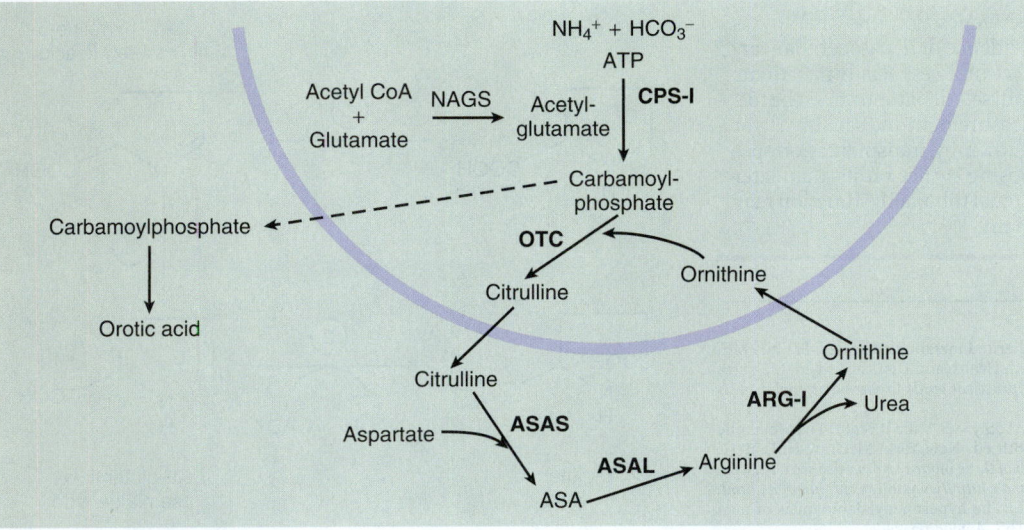

FIGURE 220–1 • Abbreviated pathway for the urea cycle. NAGS = N-acetylglutamate synthetase; CPS-1 = carbamoylphosphate synthetase 1; OTC = ornithine transcarbamoylase; ASAS = argininosuccinate synthetase; ASAL = argininosuccinate lyase; ARG-1 = arginase 1; ASA = argininosuccinate. Enzymes within the colored line function within the mitochondrial matrix.

220 DISEASES OF THE UREA CYCLE

Stephen D. Cederbaum

Ammonia is a highly toxic metabolic product, which, when present at levels no more than two times the upper limits of normal (10 to 25 µM), may cause symptoms. The urea cycle is a five-primary-step metabolic pathway in which two ammonia molecules and one bicarbonate molecule are converted to the relatively easily excreted and nontoxic urea. It is the only major pathway to remove waste nitrogen derived from ingested protein or from normal or augmented protein turnover in the body. The urea cycle occurs predominantly or possibly exclusively in the liver.

In children, the vast majority of cases of hyperammonemia are the result of inborn errors of metabolism, primarily of the urea cycle. In adults, a larger proportion of cases are due to liver failure and less frequently to toxic ingestion and intensive chemotherapy. Nevertheless, with the wider availability of blood ammonia tests, the increased recognition of urea cycle disorders, and more successful treatment modalities, the inherited disorders of ammonia metabolism are being recognized with greater frequency in adolescents and adults with acute or intermittent organic brain syndrome. Hyperammonemia appears to be better tolerated in infants and young children, in part because the cranium is more compliant. Ammonia levels that leave minimal residual damage in infants may be deadly in adults. Ammonia itself and glutamine, an amino acid in equilibrium with ammonia, appear to be the metabolites toxic to the central nervous system. The primary toxic effect appears to be the uptake of fluid into astrocytes, causing cerebral edema. Death is caused acutely by herniation of the brain through the foramen magnum with consequent cerebral ischemia, but survivors may have various degrees of brain damage.

The urea cycle is shown in Figure 220–1. The five primary enzymes generally associated with it are carbamoylphosphate synthetase 1 (CPS-1) and ornithine transcarbamoylase (OTC), both found in the mitochondrion, and argininosuccinate synthetase (ASAS), argininosuccinate lyase (ASAL), and arginase 1 found in the cytoplasm. N-Acetylglutamate synthetase catalyzes the synthesis of N-acetylglutamate, which activates CPS-1 and modulates urea cycle function, the ornithine transporter (ORNT1), which recycles ornithine to the mitochondrion, and a mitochondrial aspartate carrier protein (SLC25A13), which presumably transports aspartate out of the mitochondrion. Deficiency of these latter enzymes has been associated with symptomatic hyperammonemia.

The normal urea cycle can increase its ureagenic capacity greatly in response to ammonia challenge. The genes for all five enzymes have been cloned and are available for defining mutations, prenatal diagnosis, and population studies.

Disorders of the urea cycle are estimated to occur in about 1 in 25,000 births. It is probable that 2 to 4% of the population is heterozygous for a urea cycle defect, although only women who are carriers of ornithine transcarbamoylase deficiency are known to be prone

to symptomatic disease. It is unclear whether patients receiving intensive chemotherapy for leukemia, in whom hyperammonemia occurs rarely, or patients receiving valproate anticonvulsant therapy, in whom it occurs more mildly, are heterozygotes for one or another of these enzyme deficiencies (see later discussion).

Complete deficiency of any of the first four enzymes in the cycle usually leads to severe hyperammonemia in the first 2 to 4 days of life. The patients have irritability, lethargy, and poor feeding that progress rapidly to stupor, seizures, coma, respirator dependence, and death. The plasma ammonia level often exceeds 1000 µM, and urea levels are extremely low. Episodic hyperammonemia occurs in association with periods of endogenous protein catabolism and severely affects patients, such as those with severe OTC deficiency; they almost certainly die or suffer severe neurologic impairment during one of these episodes. Patients with partial deficiency of urea cycle enzymes or those who avoid hyperammonemia in the neonatal period may present at any time later in life, from infancy to adulthood. Older patients have irritability, vomiting, and disorientation, which may progress (as in the infants) to stupor, seizures, coma, and death. These episodes are often precipitated by severe infection, excessive protein intake, parturition, or, rarely, menstruation, or they may have no apparent cause.

Some general genetic characteristics of defects in the urea cycle are presented in Table 220–1.

Enzyme Deficiencies

DEFICIENCY OF CARBAMOYLPHOSPHATE SYNTHETASE (MIM 2373001*). CPS-1, the first enzyme in the urea cycle, constitutes up to 25% of the mitochondrial matrix protein in liver, and ordinarily all of the carbamoylphosphate synthesized from ammonium and bicarbonate by CPS-1 is used to produce urea. Orotic acid and pyrimidines are products of carbamoylphosphate as well, which is synthesized by a second, independently regulated cytoplasmic enzyme. Patients with both the neonatal and the later-onset forms have been described. Diagnosis may be inferred from hyperammonemia, low to absent levels of citrulline in the plasma amino acid profile, and normal or elevated bicarbonate levels. During acute hyperammonemia, there is usually a generalized hyperaminoacidemia with particular prominence of glutamine. Liver transplantation alone offers definitive treatment. Restricting dietary protein, supplementing essential amino acids and citrulline, hospitalizing for "catabolic crises," hemodialysis, or peritoneal dialysis, and administering phenylacetate (or phenylbutyrate) and benzoate to divert ammonia to phenylacetylglutamine and benzoylglycine (hippurate) are used to control symptoms and treat crises (Fig. 220–2). Patients with this and other urea cycle defects are prone to develop severe hyperammonemia with valproate anticonvulsant

---

*MIM = Mendelian Inheritance in Man; the online catalogues of mendelian traits can be found at http://www.ncbi.nlm.gov/OMIM

Table 220–1 • GENETIC CHARACTERISTICS OF DISORDERS OF THE UREA CYCLE

ENZYME DEFECT	INHERITANCE PATTERN	HETEROZYGOTE DETECTION	HETEROZYGOTE SYMPTOMS	PRENATAL DIAGNOSIS*
Carbamoylphosphate synthetase	AR	No[†]	No	Yes
Ornithine transcarbamoylase	X-linked	Yes, in most instances*	Yes	Yes
Argininosuccinate synthetase	AR	No[†]	No	Yes
Argininosuccinate lyase	AR	Yes	No	Yes
Arginase 1	AR	Yes	No	Yes

*With varying degrees of ease.
[†]Heterozygotes for all disorders can be detected, if the specific base change in the gene has been ascertained. This is not practical at this time outside the research laboratory.
AR = Autosomal recessive.

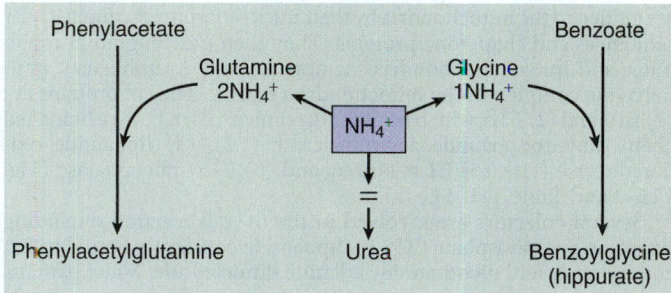

FIGURE 220–2 • Mechanisms of ammonia diversion from the urea cycle with administration of sodium phenylacetate and sodium benzoate.

therapy. A polymorphism at base 4332 in the mRNA (T1405N) reduces enzyme activity and appears to be associated with hepatic veno-occlusive disease and hyperammonemia that occurs with intensive chemotherapy.

DEFICIENCY OF ORNITHINE TRANSCARBAMOYLASE (MIM 311250). This mitochondrial enzyme catalyzes the reaction of carbamoylphosphate with ornithine to form citrulline, which is then transported out of the mitochondrion for further metabolism. The acute form of this X-linked enzyme deficiency usually occurs in male subjects. Uncommonly, a newborn female may be severely affected, which is thought to be due to nonrandom, X-chromosome inactivation. Female carriers of this codominant trait usually escape obvious symptoms, but those who have them usually present later in life or at parturition with hyperammonemic crises, some of which may be severe enough to be fatal. A number of male patients with partial enzyme deficiency may present later as well. Patients with this later-onset form of the disease may suffer from severe and otherwise inexplicable protein intolerance. The amino and organic acid profiles resemble those of CPS-1 deficiency. OTC deficiency is distinguished by extraordinarily high levels of orotic acid in the urine, formed when the excess carbamoylphosphate accumulating in the mitochondrion leaks into the cytoplasm and is channelled into the pyrimidine biosynthetic pathway (see Fig. 220–1). Orotic acid levels may be normal when ammonia has been controlled. Because of this typical clinical biochemical picture, liver biopsy to confirm enzymes is less frequently undertaken than in CPS-1 deficiency. An allopurinol challenge may be necessary to detect carrier females, a test with less than 100% accuracy. The treatment is identical to that described for CPS-1 deficiency.

DEFICIENCY OF ARGININOSUCCINATE SYNTHETASE (CITRULLINEMIA, MIM 215700). This cytoplasmic enzyme condenses the citrulline synthesized by OTC with aspartate to form argininosuccinate in a reaction that introduces the second ammonia nitrogen for excretion as urea. ASAS deficiency leads to hyperammonemia, greatly increased blood citrulline levels, and excretion of excessive amounts of citrulline and orotic acid in the urine. Here, too, neonatal, later-onset, or symptomless deficiency of the enzyme has been reported. Genetic heterogeneity at the ASAS locus has been demonstrated by residual enzyme activity or by study of the gene and its messenger RNA. A second form of citrullinemia has been reported, primarily from Japan and presenting primarily in adulthood. This disorder is due to mutations in an entirely different gene, SLC25A13 (citrin), an apparent mitochondrial carrier protein for aspartate.

Treatment is similar to that for CPS-1 and OTC deficiencies, except that arginine is supplemented instead of citrulline. Citrulline excretion is more complete than that of ammonia, and managing this condition is somewhat easier than managing hyperammonemia.

DEFICIENCY OF ARGININOSUCCINATE LYASE (ARGININOSUCCINIC ACIDURIA, MIM 207900). Argininosuccinate is cleaved into two smaller product molecules, arginine and fumarate, in a reaction catalyzed by ASAL. This enzyme deficiency results in massive accumulation and excretion of argininosuccinate. Variable onset or lack of symptoms characterizes this enzyme deficiency as well. Argininosuccinate is actively secreted by the renal tubules, and its synthesis can be stimulated by stoichiometric amounts of arginine as a source of ornithine to drive the urea cycle. By this means, ammonia levels are rapidly reduced and can be controlled more reliably than in any other urea cycle disorder.

DEFICIENCY OF ARGINASE 1 (HYPERARGININEMIA, MIM 207800). Arginase, the final enzyme in the urea cycle, catalyzes the hydrolysis of arginine to urea and ornithine, the latter returned to the mitochondrion to participate in another cycle of ammonia detoxification (see Fig. 220–1). Clinical symptoms of hyperargininemia, the rarest of the urea cycle defects, are usually of later onset, are more gradual and relentless in progression, and are less frequently or seriously punctuated by apparent episodes of acute hyperammonemia and organic brain syndrome. Rather typically, normal patients begin to develop gait abnormalities and spasticity at 2 to 3 years of age, and cortical and pyramidal tract dysfunction progresses slowly. More than 80% of the reported patients are still alive, some at age 40 or older. The diagnosis is often suspected when arginine levels are found to be elevated in blood or urine. Excess arginine excretion in urine along with secondary cystinuria pattern is more variable and less reliable as a screening method. Hyperammonemia is usually seen only during acute catabolic episodes.

Although most patients have been moderately to severely retarded at detection, treatment by limiting protein and diverting ammonia reverses many of the most severe manifestations of the disease, and presymptomatic treatment has allowed two patients to reach the age of 30 or older without apparent clinical manifestations.

DEFICIENCY OF THE ORNITHINE TRANSPORTER PROTEIN, ORNT1 (HHH SYNDROME, MIM 238970). This inherited predisposition to hyperammonemia is due to deficient activity of the mitochondrial ornithine transporter protein in the recently cloned ORNT1 gene. The first apparent episode of hyperammonemia may occur in childhood or later and, indeed, may not occur at all. Patients may be protein intolerant and many are mildly developmentally delayed, at least. The plasma ornithine level may be no more than two times the upper limit of normal. Treatment of the hyperammonemia is similar to treatment for CPS and OTC deficiencies, but hemodialysis may not be required for the lesser degree of hyperammonemia, and arginine supplementation is not indicated.

Future Treatment

Urea cycle defects, originally considered a pediatric problem, are moving into the realm of internal medicine. Internists must cast aside the lactulose used for hyperammonemia of liver failure and gastrointestinal bleeding in favor of diversion therapy and hemodialysis. Soon, liver replacement, the artificial liver (perhaps stem cells), and gene therapy will be more widely used. As breakthroughs in gene technology allow us to dissect the pathobiology of the acute catabolic process, efforts to control this process, rather than controlling its consequences, will become increasingly important.

SUGGESTED READINGS

Brusilow SW, Horwich AL: Urea cycle enzymes. *In* Scriver CR, Beaudet AL, Sly WS, Valle D (eds): The Metabolic and Molecular Bases of Inherited Disease, 8th ed. New York, McGraw-Hill, 2001, pp 1909–1963. *The definitive clinical and molecular discussion of these inborn errors.*

Kleppe S, Mian A, Lee B: Urea cycle disorders. Curr Treat Options Neurol 2003;5:309–319. *Overview of the genetics, pathophysiology, and treatment, including possible cell and gene therapies.*

Leonard JV: Urea cycle disorders. *In* Fernandes J, Saudubray J-M, Van Den Bergh G (eds): Inborn Metabolic Diseases. New York, Springer-Verlag, 2001, pp 213–222. *A practical clinical chapter on urea cycle disorders reflecting a transatlantic perspective.*

221 BRANCHED CHAIN AMINOACIDURIAS

Louis J. Elsas II

MAPLE SYRUP URINE DISEASE

Maple syrup urine disease (MSUD), also called *branched chain α-ketoaciduria*, derives its name from the burnt sugar smell in the urine and earwax of affected patients. MSUD is caused by impaired branched chain α-ketoacid dehydrogenase (BCKD), which catalyzes decarboxylation of the α-ketoacid derivatives of all three of the branched

chain amino acids: leucine, isoleucine, and valine (Fig. 221–1). They are essential amino acids that share branching, aliphatic chains. If impaired, branched chain α-ketoacids and amino acids accumulate throughout the body. Isovaleric acidemia affects the next metabolic step but only for products of leucine catabolism. Leucine is transaminated to α-ketoisocaproate, which is decarboxylated and transacetylated to isovaleryl coenzyme A (CoA). Isovaleric acidemia is caused by defects in isovaleryl CoA dehydrogenase (Fig. 221–1). Both disorders conform to autosomal recessive patterns of inheritance. The affected homozygote for MSUD exhibits impaired activity in the BCKD multienzyme complex (Fig. 221–2). MSUD is caused by mutations in one of six genes, which code for the six different proteins that make up the BCKD multienzyme complex. A wide range of mutations is defined, along with the severity of impaired enzyme and consequent clinical manifestations (Table 221–1 and Fig. 221–2).

Although they function in mitochondria, the BCKD proteins are encoded in the nuclear genome. Once translated in the cytosol, they are guided to the mitochondria by their intrinsic amino terminal leader sequences and chaperone proteins. They then transmigrate through outer and inner mitochondria membranes and assemble as a multienzyme complex in the mitochondrial matrix. The six proteins are (1) E1α and (2) E1β, which produce the dimeric E1α, β; (3) a branched chain dihydrolipoamide acyltransferase (E2); (4) lipoamide oxidoreductase (E3); (5) E1 α-kinase; and (6) E1 α-phosphatase (Fig. 221–2 and Table 221–1).

Several cofactors are involved in the overall reaction, including thiamine pyrophosphate (TP~P), lipoamide covalently bound to E2, coenzyme A, and nicotinamide adenine dinucleotide. Many patients

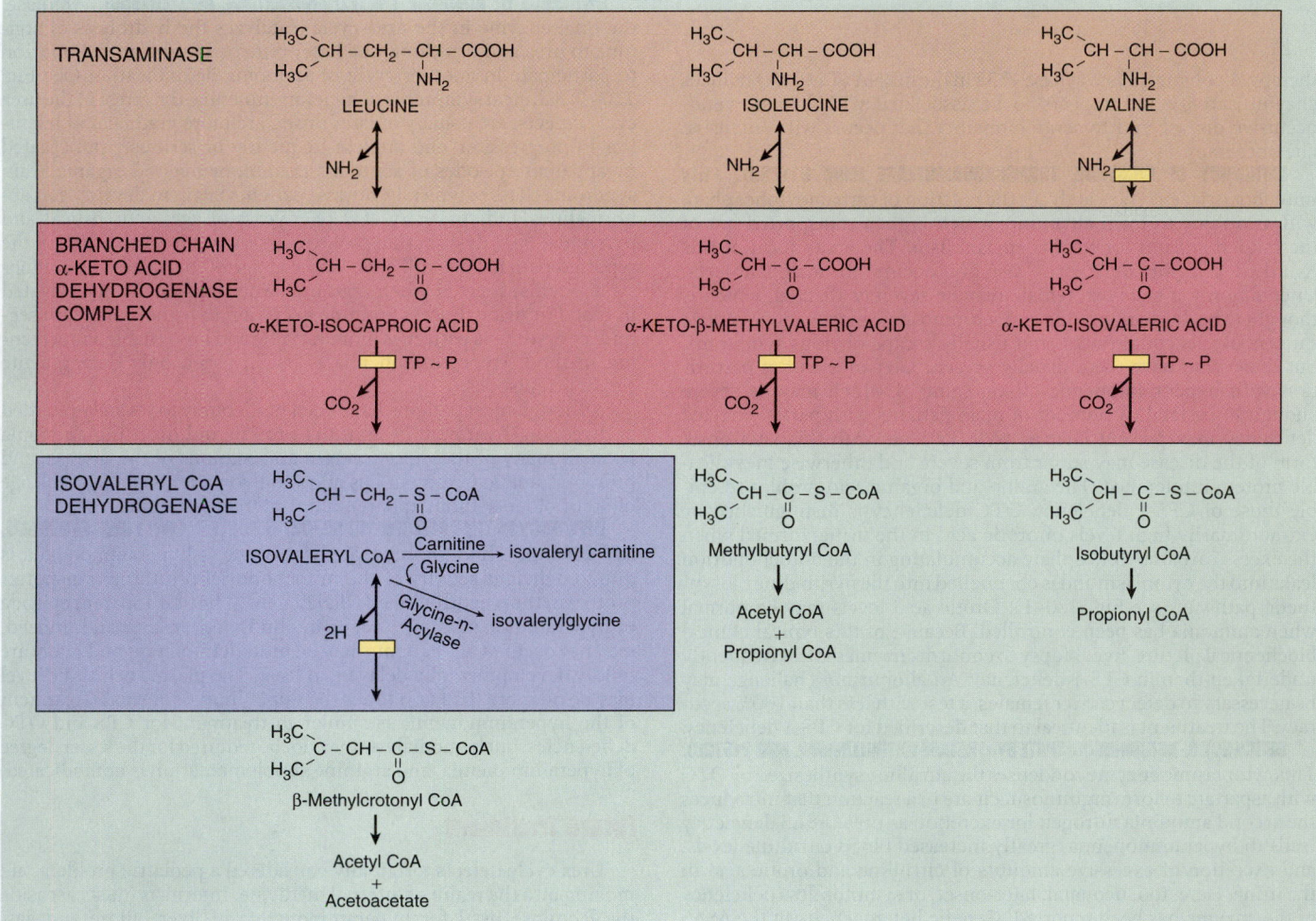

FIGURE 221–1 • Catabolic pathway for the branched chain amino acids. L-leucine, L-isoleucine, and L-valine are transaminated to their branched chain α-keto acids. Valine transaminase may be impaired in hypervalinemia. The branched chain α-keto acids are decarboxylated and transacylated by a mitochondrial multienzyme complex, the branched chain α-keto acid dehydrogenase (BCKD). Impairment of BCKD results in maple syrup urine disease. This enzyme requires thiamine pyrophosphate (TP≈P) as its active cofactor. When isovaleryl CoA dehydrogenase is impaired, isovaleric acidemia occurs. Accumulated isovaleryl CoA can utilize alternate pathways using carnitine transferase and glycine-n-acylase. These alternate pathways are activated as therapeutic interventions in isovaleric acidemia.

Table 221–1 • GENES, PROTEINS, AND MUTATIONS IN THE HUMAN BRANCHED CHAIN α-KETO ACID DEHYDROGENASE COMPLEX

| NAME (FUNCTION) | CHROMOSOME | | MATURE PROTEIN (kD) | MUTATION |
	Locus	Gene Size (kb)		
E1α (decarboxylase)	19q13.3	55	46	Y393N (Mennonite missense mutation)
E1β (stabilizes decarboxylase)	6q1.4	100	38	11-Base pair deletion (frameshift with premature STOP)
E2 (acyltransferase)	1p31	68	46	E163STOP, R183P (common in Ashkenazim)
				F215C (exonic and intronic insertions and deletions)
E3 (dehydrogenase)	7q22	20	50	Affects other substrate-specific dehydrogenases (α-ketoglutarate and pyruvate)
E1α kinase (inactivates)	16p13.12	40	43	Inhibited by tumor necrosis factor-α (may cause cachexia in cancer)
E1α phosphatase (activates)	?	?	?	?

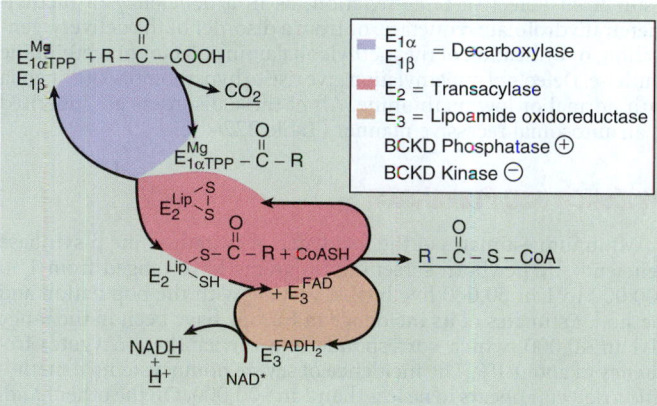

FIGURE 221–2 • The multienzyme complex, branched chain α-keto acid dehydrogenase (BCKD). At least six nuclear encoded proteins are illustrated that assemble in the mitochondrial, inner-membrane matrix. BCKD catalyzes decarboxylation and transacylation of three branched chain α-keto acids and the reoxidation of lipoic acid. The proteins $E_{1\alpha}$ and $E_{1\beta}$ decarboxylase accomplish decarboxylation. $E_{1\alpha}$ is positively regulated by dephosphorylation through the BCKD phosphatase and negatively regulated by BCKD kinase. The E_2 transacylase transfers CoASH to form the branched chain CoA derivative. E_2 contains a lipoic acid that is reduced in this transacylation process and is reoxidized by the E_3 flavoprotein lipoamide oxidoreductase. Impairment of this complex process by mutant genes involved in BCKD assembly, regulation, or function may result in maple syrup urine disease.

respond to pharmacologic excesses of thiamine supplement (8 mg/kg/day). The presumed mechanism is that by saturating binding sites for thiamine pyrophosphate on E1α, the multienzyme complex is stabilized to biologic degradation. Small increases in enzyme function can provide dramatic improvement to the patient, who will continue to require reduced intake of leucine, isoleucine, and valine.

Diagnosis

In typical MSUD, feeding difficulties and apnea develop in a newborn who was normal at birth. Convulsions and decorticate rigidity may develop. Before population-based newborn screening, affected infants died or were severely damaged. With newborn screening, retrieval, diagnosis, and diet intervention before age 2 weeks, these children have reached adulthood with good function.

In surveyed populations, the frequency of MSUD varies from 1:760 (in Mennonites) to an average U.S. figure of 1:185,000 newborns. The disease is more frequent in the Middle East populations, where consanguineous matings are more common than in the United States. Atypical cases with less severe clinical manifestations may be missed in newborn screening and appear with intermittent ataxia in later childhood or early adulthood. The diagnosis should be suspected clinically when a patient has intermittent symptoms related to protein ingestion and sweet smell to the earwax. A positive dinitrophenyl-hydrazine reaction is seen in affected patients' urine, and the

diagnosis is confirmed by the abnormal excesses of branched chain amino acids and keto acids in blood and urine. The enzyme defect is demonstrable in leukocytes and cultured, dermal fibroblasts. Prenatal monitoring is accomplished both biochemically and through DNA analysis of specific mutations. The biochemical phenotype or genotype is required in an affected sibling's cultured cells before attempts at prenatal monitoring.

Rx Treatment

Treatment is aimed at limiting intake of branched chain amino acids to prevent accumulation of neurotoxic branched chain α-keto acids and at maintaining an anabolic state through high caloric intake, limited in leucine, isoleucine, and valine. Branched chain amino acids are essential and must be ingested in quantities sufficient to allow new protein synthesis and normal growth but below levels that result in accumulation of toxic precursors in the blocked reaction. Commercial formulas called *medical foods* are necessary to accomplish this goal. In infancy and early childhood, anabolism is encouraged by providing excess calories and maintaining branched chain amino acid–restricted protein intake at the recommended daily allowance. Treatment is monitored clinically in terms of growth and development and biochemically through analysis of plasma amino acid and urine organic acid concentrations. Because leucine residues are more frequent than isoleucine and valine in natural proteins, care must be taken not to overrestrict isoleucine and valine while attempting to lower blood concentrations of leucine. Thiamine supplements allow increased natural protein intake in thiamine-responsive patients. Chronic acidosis may deplete carnitine, which should also be monitored in blood and supplemented if deficient.

ISOVALERIC ACIDEMIA

Isovaleryl CoA is the product formed from BCKD action on α-ketoisocaproate (leucine's derivative). Isovaleryl CoA is normally converted to β-methylcrotonyl CoA by isovaleryl CoA dehydrogenase (see Fig. 221–1).

When isovaleryl dehydrogenase is impaired, isovaleric acid accumulates in blood and urine and produces a foul odor similar to that of rancid cheese or sweaty feet. In the neonatal form, symptoms are severe in the first week of life and consist of vomiting, acidosis, hypoglycemia, tremors, coma, and death. Leukopenia, anemia, thrombocytopenia, and hyperammonemia may occur during acute attacks. Emergency therapy consists of eliminating dietary leucine and supplementing with intravenous, oral, and colonic infusion of glycine (300 mg/kg/day) to provide an alternate excretory pathway for the nontoxic adduct, isovaleryl glycine. Carnitine (100 mg/kg/day) may provide nontoxic adducts of isovaleryl carnitine (see Fig. 221–1). Both adducts are excreted in the urine. Emergency therapy also requires producing anabolism by using excess calories from carbohydrates, fat, and non–leucine-containing protein. As patients mature, they have less frequent attacks and are developmentally normal. "Attacks" are caused by excess leucine ingestion, starvation, infections, or other causes of catabolism. Chronic intermittent forms of this disorder occur in later life and are less severe but have not been differentiated from acute infantile forms at the biochemical or molecular level of enzyme or gene analysis. These differences in clinical expression may result from epigenetic and environmental phenomena.

Diagnosis

The diagnosis is suspected as a result of the clinical presentation and associated odor and is established by demonstrating excess isovaleric acid and its adducts in the urine by mass spectroscopy. Tandem mass spectroscopy of dried blood is used in some states to screen for isovaleric acidemia in normal newborns. The gene has been cloned and sequenced and some mutations have been defined. The gene is located on chromosome 15q13 and the coding sequence has homology to short- and medium-chain acyldehydrogenase.

 Treatment

> Chronic therapy includes reduced intake of leucine. Unlike in MSUD, valine and isoleucine are catabolized normally and are required as essential nutrients in normal amounts in the diet. Supplements of glycine (90 to 100 mg/kg/day) and carnitine (30 mg/kg/day) are used as part of chronic dietary management. Outcome is excellent in both infantile and later-onset forms of isovaleric acidemia diseases if the acute, irreversible effects of the neonatal disease are prevented.

SUGGESTED READINGS
Ogier de Baulny H, Saudubray JM: Branched-chain organic acidurias. Semin Neonatol 2002;7:65–74. *Overview of pathophysiology and treatment by removing toxic compounds and using special diets and carnitine.*
OMIM—Online Mendelian Inheritance in Man: http://www3.ncbi.nlm.nih.gov/Omim/ *Inclusive reference online to both disorders.*

222 HOMOCYSTINURIA

Bruce A. Barshop

Definitions

Homocysteine is a nonprotein amino acid and an intermediate in methionine metabolism that arises when methionine (through *S*-adenosylmethionine) acts as a donor in methylation reactions (Fig. 222–1). The fate of homocysteine is either remethylation to methionine or transsulfuration (through cystathionine) of serine to cysteine. Homocystinuria results from defective disposal of homocysteine because of a defect in either transsulfuration or remethylation. The classic finding of the disulfide homocystine in urine gives this class of disorders its common name. The free sulfhydryl form, homocysteine, is present in lower amounts in blood; *total homocyst(e)ine* is the term used to described the mix of sulfhydryl and disulfide. The defining finding in blood is hyperhomocyst(e)inemia, which is distributed about 10% as free homocysteine and 90% as protein-bound and soluble disulfides (e.g., homocystine, cysteine-SS-homocysteine).

Etiology

The classic form of homocystinuria is cystathionine β-synthase deficiency, which results in decreased transsulfuration and hypermethioninemic hyperhomocyst(e)inemia. Homocystinuria may also result from defective remethylation, as in a deficiency of methylenetetrahydrofolate reductase, or from a disorder of the delivery, generation, or utilization of the methylcobalamin cofactor of methionine synthase. Defects of remethylation give rise to hyperhomocyst(e)inemia with normal or low methionine. All of these disorders are inherited in an autosomal recessive manner (Table 222–1).

Incidence and Prevalence

Minimum estimates of the incidence of cystathionine β-synthase deficiency by newborn screening programs have ranged from 1 in 300,000 to 1 in 60,000 live births, varying with the population and method. Estimates of its incidence in Europe have been in the range of 1 in 40,000, which corresponds to a carrier (heterozygote) frequency of about 1%. The incidence of severe homocysteine remethylation defects appears to be less than 1 in 500,000. On the other hand, partial remethylation deficiencies seem to have a much greater incidence, which may be clinically relevant in predisposing individuals to thrombotic disorders; evidence of deficiency has been reported in 15 to 30% of some series of patients presenting with vaso-occlusive disease.

Pathogenesis and Mechanisms

Homocysteine has effects on vascular endothelium, platelets, and coagulation factors that predispose to thrombosis. Endothelial dysfunction can be elicited in normal patients when hyperhomocysteinemia is induced transiently, and there is evidence of inflammatory

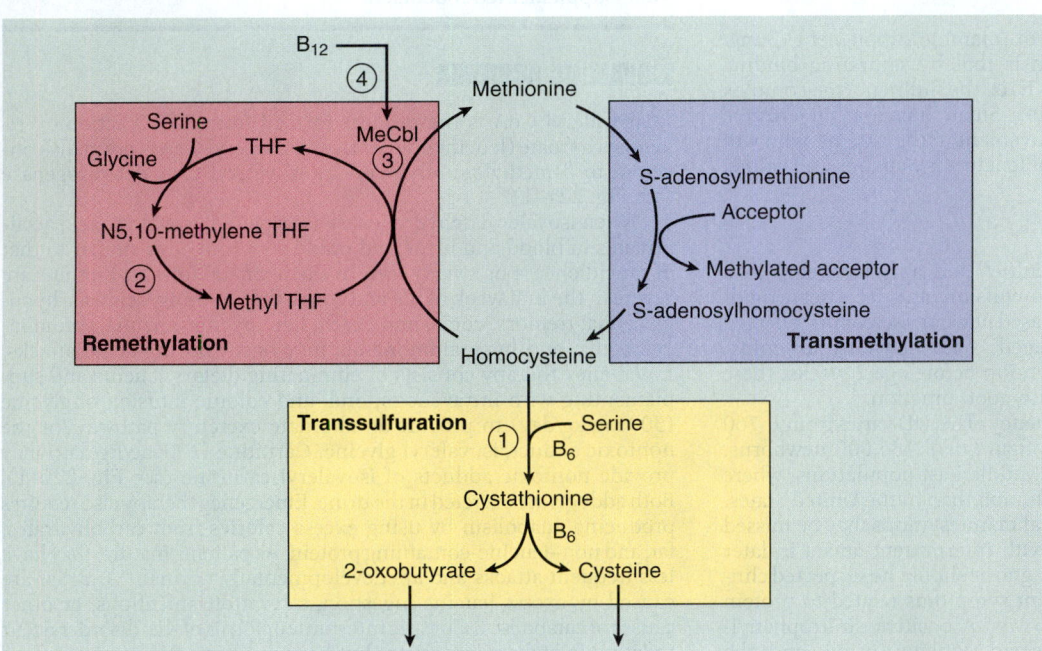

FIGURE 222–1 • Pathways of homocysteine metabolism. The systems of transmethylation, remethylation, and transsulfuration are marked. Steps discussed are numbered: (1) cystathionine β-synthase; (2) methylenetetrahydrofolate reductase; (3) methionine synthase and methyltransferase reductase; (4) systems of cobalamin absorption, distribution, and reduction. THF = tetrahydrofolate; MeCbl = methylcobalamin; B_{12} = cyanocobalamin/hydroxocobalamin; B_6 = pyridoxine.

Table 222–1 • GENETIC DEFECTS ASSOCIATED WITH HOMOCYSTINURIA

FUNCTIONAL DEFECT	COMMON NAME	ENZYME DEFECT	CHROMOSOME LOCUS
Transsulfuration	"Classic" homocystinuria	Cystathionine β-synthase	22q22.3
Remethylation	Folate-dependent homocystinuria	Methylenetetrahydrofolate reductase	1p36.3
	Cbl G	Methionine synthase (methyltransferase)	1q43
	Cbl E	Methyltransferase reductase	5p15.2-p15.3
Cobalamin transport	TC-II	Transcobalamin II	22q11-q13.1
	Cbl F	Lysosomal B$_{12}$ translocase	—
Cobalamin reductase	Cbl C, Cbl D	Unknown	—

mediator activation in experimental systems related to pro-oxidant effects of homocysteine, but there remains some controversy about the relevance of these factors in humans. Modification of connective tissue proteins may cause the skeletal and ocular manifestations associated with homocystinuria. These effects are likely related to fibrillin, which is a component of the matrix of periosteum and perichondrium, the major component of the zonular fibers of the ocular lens, and a protein singularly rich in cysteine. Fibrillin structure may be affected either by cysteine limitation or by homocysteinylation; the result is features of homocystinuria that are also associated with fibrillin mutations (Marfan syndrome). The neurologic effects of homocysteine may be due predominantly to agonism of the N-methyl-D-aspartate receptor by homocysteic acid, although cerebral vascular effects may contribute as well.

Clinical Manifestations

Cystathionine β-synthase deficiency is pleiotropic, with effects in the eye, skeleton, and central nervous and vascular systems (Table 222–2). Eye and skeletal system changes resemble those in Marfan syndrome. Nontraumatic dislocation of the ocular lens can be an initial finding. Some abnormality of the skeletal system develops in almost all untreated patients. Between one third and three fourths of untreated patients have mild or moderate mental retardation, and cerebrovascular thrombosis may play a role in the neurologic picture. Affected patients have a lifelong danger of thromboembolic phenomena, which are the major cause of mortality in cases of untreated disease. Arterial and venous occlusion, in small or large vessels, may occur at any time in life, including infancy. Treatment with pyridoxine, the cofactor of the enzyme, may be effective in nearly half of these patients, particularly those with relatively high residual activity and spared amounts of

immunologically detectable enzyme. Blood total homocyst(e)ine concentrations may be intermediately elevated in heterozygotes, particularly after a methionine load, and heterozygotes are at some increased risk for vaso-occlusive events. Although increased vascular complications have not been formally demonstrated in outcome studies of obligate heterozygotes, a considerable number of studies show a highly disproportionate fraction of patients with various vaso-occlusive complications who manifest either total blood homocyst(e)ine concentrations or fibroblast cystathionine β-synthase activities that fall in the range observed for heterozygotes.

Methylenetetrahydrofolate reductase deficiency has been described in a limited number of patients, with a spectrum of manifestations including neurologic symptoms, thromboses, and lens dislocation, but without conspicuous skeletal changes. Partial deficiencies and thermolabile variants have been observed in otherwise normal subjects who have premature vaso-occlusive disorders. Polymorphisms are also found in the methylenetetrahydrofolate reductase gene in association with spinal closure defects, a class of disease that has been known to be influenced by folate. Cobalamin metabolic disorders generally occur in early childhood and are characterized by neurologic symptoms, megaloblastic anemia, and, in some cases, methylmalonic acidemia.

Diagnosis

Qualitative detection using sodium nitroprusside led to the recognition of homocystinuria early in the history of biochemical genetics, but it is neither specific nor sensitive. Assay of plasma amino acids by routine methods may not reveal homocysteine because of the high degree of protein binding. Because of lower protein

Table 222–2 • CLINICAL FEATURES OF HOMOCYSTINURIA

CLASS	BIOCHEMICAL FEATURES			CLINICAL FEATURES	
	Hcys	met	MMA	System	Signs
Cystathionine β-synthase deficiency	↑	↑	–	Ocular	Ectopia lentis, myopia, glaucoma, optic atrophy, retinal detachment
				Skeletal	Elongated and thinned bones, arachnodactyly, genu valgum, pectus malformation, scoliosis
				Vascular	Thromboembolic events (arterial or venous)
				Neurologic	Mental retardation often in untreated cases
					Cerebrovascular thromboses, seizures
					Psychiatric disorders, personality disorder
Methylenetetrahydrofolate reductase deficiency	↑	↓	–	Ocular	Ectopia lentis
				Vascular	Thromboses
				Neurologic	Variable—psychiatric to severe neurologic
Transcobalamin II deficiency	–/↑	–/↓	+/–	Hematologic	Pancytopenia, macrocytosis
				Pansystemic	MMA, ketoacidosis, stomatitis
Cbl F	–/↑	?	+/–	Pansystemic	MMA, macrocytosis, stomatitis
Cbl C, Cbl D	–/↑	–/↓	+	Hematologic	Pancytopenia
				Neurologic	Mental retardation
Cbl E, Cbl G	↑	–/↓	–	Vascular	Vaso-occlusive phenomena
				Neurologic	Spasticity, dystonia

Hcys = homocyst(e)inemia/homocystinuria; met = plasma methionine; MMA = methylmalonic acidemia; Cbl = cobalamin.

concentrations, routine amino acid analysis of urine is more successful, hence the common name *homocystinuria*. The preferred diagnostic method is total homocyst(e)ine, which is measured in plasma treated with a reducing agent to release bound homocysteine before deproteinization. Plasma amino acids will indicate a transsulfuration or remethylation defect, depending on the presence or absence of hypermethioninemia (see Table 222–2). The clinical diagnosis of remethylation defects is facilitated by detection of urine methylmalonate and blood vitamin B_{12} and folate. The normal range of total homocyst(e)ine in blood extends up to around $15\,\mu mol/L$ and may be more than 50% higher 2 to 4 hours after an oral methionine load. A standard methionine load ($100\,mg/kg$) may identify individuals with partial defects, which could increase the susceptibility to vascular disease.

Rx Treatment

Cystathionine β-synthase deficiency is responsive to the cofactor pyridoxine in about 50% of cases. Doses of 100 to 500 mg/day have been used successfully. Higher doses of pyridoxine should be used cautiously because of the risk of peripheral neuropathy. Responsiveness is documented by the elimination of free homocysteine in blood and urine as pyridoxine is added, but measurement of total homocyst(e)ine demonstrates that the effect is generally far less than complete. Betaine (*N,N,N*-trimethylglycine, Cystadane) is effective in reducing homocysteine through an alternative remethylation step. Betaine is generally given at 6 g/day in divided doses, but considerably higher doses have been used. It is particularly important in pyridoxine-unresponsive cases but may also be used as an adjunct in responsive patients. In the absence of vitamin responsiveness, special diets are adopted to restrict methionine and supplement cysteine. Folic acid may be effective in remethylation defects, and it is also generally used as a supplement (10 to 20 mg/day) in all forms of homocystinuria. Vitamin B_{12} preparations may be lifesaving in disorders of cobalamin metabolism, although their effectiveness in the most common forms of cobalamin C or D defects is generally far from complete. Initial doses are usually $1000\,\mu g/day$, and hydroxocobalamin may be more effective than cyanocobalamin. It is prudent to adopt measures to decrease thrombosis, such as using low-dose aspirin or dipyridamole and avoiding smoking and birth control pills. Nitrous oxide may also be relatively contraindicated inasmuch as it can inhibit methionine synthase. Surgery poses serious risks but can be performed safely as long as attention is paid to hydration and coagulation status.

Prognosis

In cases of cystathionine β-synthase deficiency, pyridoxine responsiveness generally correlates with higher residual activity, and the prognosis is significantly better than that for unresponsive cases, with or without treatment. Skeletal, ocular, vascular, and neurologic risks are all reduced with successful treatment. Without early institution of treatment, the median IQ in a large outcome study was 57 for unresponsive patients and 78 for responsive patients. With early treatment, pyridoxine-unresponsive patients have nearly normal median IQ. With treatment in responsive patients, the prognosis for intellectual development is very good, but significant increases in total homocyst(e)ine generally still persist, and some increased risk of vascular complications probably does remain.

SUGGESTED READINGS

Mudd SH, Levy HL, Kraus J: Disorders of transsulfuration. *In* Scriver CR, Beaudet AL, Sly WS, Valle D (eds): The Metabolic and Molecular Bases of Inherited Disease, vol 2: New York, McGraw-Hill, 2001, pp 2007–2056. *A definitive review with extensive references.*

Jacobsen DW: Hyperhomocysteinemia and oxidative stress: Time for a reality check? Arterioscler Thromb Vasc Biol 2000;20:1182–1184. *Balanced discussion of theories of oxidative stress related to homocysteine.*

Yap S: Classical homocystinuria: Vascular risk and its prevention. J Inherit Metab Dis 2003;26:259–265. *Overview emphasizing that 50% of patients will have a vascular event before age 30 years.*

Yap S, Boers GH, Wilcken B, et al: Vascular outcome in patients with homocystinuria due to cystathionine beta-synthase deficiency treated chronically: A multicenter observational study. Arterioscler Thromb Vasc Biol 2001;21:2080–2085. *A long-term multicenter observational study which demonstrates effectiveness of treatment in reducing vascular risk, despite imperfect biochemical control.*

223 THE PORPHYRIAS

Karl E. Anderson

Porphyrias are due to deficiencies of specific enzymes of the heme biosynthetic pathway and, when clinically expressed, are associated with striking accumulations of heme pathway intermediates. Most porphyrias are inherited, but other factors are important in determining their severity. Porphyrias are more prevalent and more often manifest in adults than most metabolic diseases, and they are likely to be encountered by physicians in many disciplines. The three most common porphyrias differ considerably from each other and are managed very differently.

THE HEME BIOSYNTHETIC PATHWAY AND THE PORPHYRIAS

The genes encoding all eight enzymes of the important heme biosynthetic pathway (Fig. 223–1) have been sequenced and their chromosomal locations identified (Table 223–1). Mutations of the erythroid-specific form of δ-aminolevulinic acid (ALA) synthase, the first enzyme, are found in cases of X-linked sideroblastic anemia. Mutations in genes for the other seven enzymes are found in the porphyrias. (Standard abbreviations for these diseases are given in Table 223–1.) These diseases are all heterogeneous at the molecular level. Therefore, different mutations are to be expected in unrelated families with any given type of porphyria.

Heme is synthesized in largest amounts in bone marrow and liver, where it is used primarily to make hemoglobin and cytochrome P450 enzymes, respectively. Hepatic heme biosynthesis is regulated primarily by ALA synthase, which is rate limiting and under sensitive feedback control by cellular free heme content. Hepatic ALA synthase is induced by many of the same drugs and steroids that induce P450 enzymes. Additional pathway enzymes, and cellular uptake of iron, are important in regulating heme synthesis in erythroid cells.

Intermediates in the pathway (see Fig. 223–1) are normally conserved during heme synthesis and excreted only in small amounts. The porphyrin precursors ALA and porphobilinogen (PBG) are normally excreted in much larger amounts than porphyrins. Porphyrinogens undergo auto-oxidation outside cells and are excreted primarily as porphyrins. ALA, PBG, and porphyrinogens are colorless and nonfluorescent. Porphyrins are reddish and fluoresce when exposed to long-wave ultraviolet light. ALA, PBG, uroporphyrin, heptacarboxyl, hexacarboxyl, and pentacarboxyl porphyrins are excreted mostly in urine, coproporphyrin (a tetracarboxyl porphyrin) in urine and bile, and harderoporphyrin and protoporphyrin in bile and feces.

CLASSIFICATION

Human porphyrias are best classified in terms of their specific enzyme deficiencies. Classification based on clinical manifestations is also useful (see Table 223–1). The acute porphyrias are characterized by *neurologic effects*. In the cutaneous porphyrias, *photosensitivity* results from activation of porphyrins by long-wave ultraviolet light (UVB) with generation of oxygen radicals that damage the skin. Traditionally, porphyrias have also been divided into erythropoietic and hepatic types, based on overproduction of heme pathway intermediates in either bone marrow or liver.

The three most common types of porphyria are likely to be encountered periodically by any physician. They differ markedly from each other with regard to major clinical manifestations, exacerbating factors, tests important for diagnosis, and effective therapies (Table 223–2). Because their features are so distinct, a feature learned about one of these porphyrias will not apply to the others. On the other hand, the first two of these conditions (see Table 223–2) are prototypic: they share some important features with the other less common porphyrias. These important differences are evident in the brief descriptions of each of the porphyrias that follow.

δ-AMINOLEVULINIC ACID-DEHYDRATASE DEFICIENT PORPHYRIA

In this very rare autosomal recessive disorder, ALA-dehydratase is markedly reduced (usually 1 to 2% of normal). Symptoms

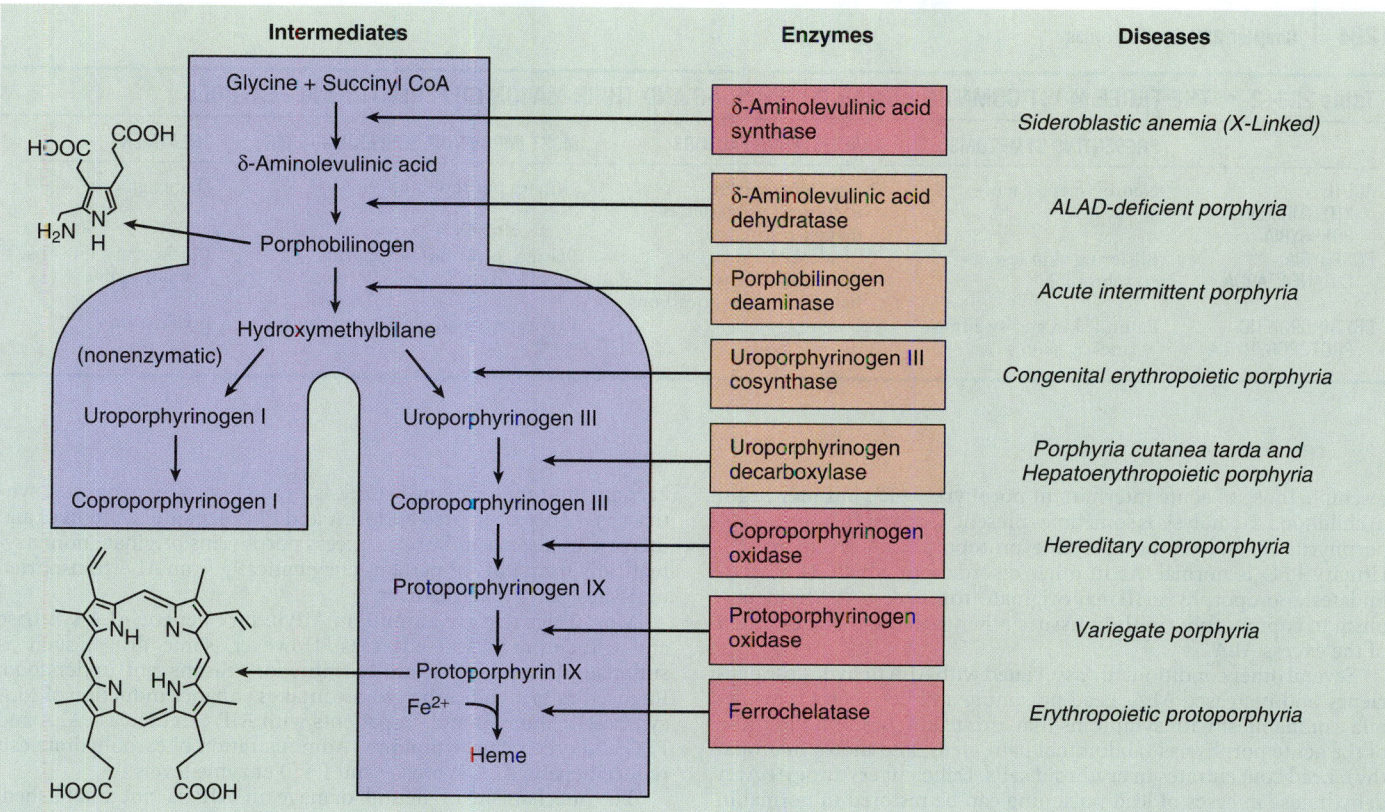

FIGURE 223–1 • Intermediates and enzymes of the heme biosynthetic pathway and the major diseases of porphyrin metabolism that have been associated with deficiencies of specific enzymes. The initial and last three enzymes (in red) are mitochondrial and the other four (in brown) are cytosolic. Heme is synthesized from glycine and succinyl CoA. Intermediates in the pathway include δ-aminolevulinic acid (an amino acid utilized exclusively for heme synthesis), porphobilinogen (a pyrrole), and hydroxymethylbilane (a linear tetrapyrrole). Uroporphyrinogen III cosynthase catalyzes closure of hydroxymethylbilane, with inversion of one of the pyrroles, to form a porphyrin macrocycle, uroporphyrinogen III. (Nonenzymatic closure occurs without inversion of this pyrrole, forming uroporphyrinogen I, which is not metabolized beyond coproporphyrinogen I.) The next two enzymes result in decarboxylation of six of the eight side chains of uroporphyrinogen III, with sequential formation of heptacarboxyl porphyrinogen, hexacarboxyl porphyrinogen, pentacarboxyl porphyrinogen, tetracarboxyl porphyrinogen (coproporphyrinogen III), tricarboxyl porphyrinogen (harderoporphyrinogen), and dicarboxyl porphyrinogen (protoporphyrinogen IX). The final two enzymes catalyze oxidation of protoporphyrinogen IX to protoporphyrin IX, and insertion of ferrous iron into the porphyrin macrocycle to form heme (iron protoporphyrin IX). With the exception of protoporphyrin IX, all porphyrin intermediates are in their reduced forms (hexahydroporphyrins or porphyrinogens). Chemical structures of two intermediates are shown.

Table 223–1 • ENZYMES OF THE HEME BIOSYNTHETIC PATHWAY AND CLASSIFICATION AND INHERITANCE OF DISEASES ASSOCIATED WITH THEIR DEFICIENCIES*

ENZYME	CHROMOSOMAL LOCATION	DISEASE	INHERITANCE	CLASSIFICATIONS OF PORPHYRIAS			
				Hepatic	Erythropoietic	Acute	Cutaneous
ALA synthase							
Erythroid	Xp11.21	Sideroblastic anemia	X-linked recessive				
Nonerythroid	3p21	None known					
ALA dehydratase	9q34	δ-Amino-levulinic acid dehydratase-deficient porphyria (ADP)	Autosomal recessive	?X		X	
Porphobilinogen deaminase†	11q24.1 → q24.2	Acute intermittent porphyria (AIP)	Autosomal dominant	X		X	
Uroporphyrinogen III cosynthase	10q25.2 → q26.3	Congenital erythropoietic porphyria (CEP)	Autosomal recessive		X		X
Uroporphyrinogen decarboxylase	1p34	Porphyria cutanea tarda (PCT)‡	Autosomal dominant	X			X
		Hepatoerythropoietic porphyria (HEP)	Autosomal recessive	X	X		X
Coproporphyrinogen oxidase	3q12	Hereditary coproporphyria (HCP)	Autosomal dominant	X		X	X
Protoporphyrinogen oxidase	1q22 or 23	Variegate porphyria (VP)	Autosomal dominant	X		X	X
Ferrochelatase	18q21.3 or 22	Erythropoietic protoporphyria (EPP)	Autosomal dominant		X		X

*The most precise classification is according to the specific enzyme deficiencies. Other classifications based on the major tissue site of overproduction of heme pathway intermediates (hepatic vs. erythropoietic) or the type of major symptoms (acute neurovisceral vs. cutaneous) are useful but not precise or mutually exclusive.
†This enzyme is also known as hydroxymethylbilane synthase, and formerly as uroporphyrinogen I synthase.
‡Inherited deficiency of uroporphyrinogen decarboxylase is partially responsible for familial (type II) PCT.

Table 223–2 • THE THREE MOST COMMON HUMAN PORPHYRIAS AND THEIR MAJOR DIFFERENTIATING FEATURES

	PRESENTING SYMPTOMS	EXACERBATING FACTORS	MOST IMPORTANT SCREENING TESTS	TREATMENT
ACUTE INTERMITTENT PORPHYRIA	Neurovisceral (acute)	Drugs (mostly P450-inducers), progesterone, dietary restriction	Urinary porphobilinogen	Heme, glucose
PORPHYRIA CUTANEA TARDA	Blistering skin lesions (chronic)	Iron, alcohol, estrogens, hepatitis C virus, halogenated hydrocarbons	Plasma (or urine) porphyrins	Phlebotomy, low-dose chloroquine
ERYTHROPOIETIC PROTOPORPHYRIA	Painful skin and swelling (mostly acute)		Erythrocyte and plasma porphyrins	β-Carotene

resemble those of acute intermittent porphyria (AIP) but may begin in childhood. Hemolysis is sometimes present. Urinary ALA and coproporphyrin III and erythrocyte zinc protoporphyrin are increased. Urinary PBG is normal. As in other disorders in which ALA accumulates, coproporphyrin III may originate from excess ALA by metabolism to coproporphyrin III in tissues other than the tissue of origin of the excess ALA.

Several other conditions are associated with ALA dehydratase deficiency and increased ALA. Lead poisoning and hereditary tyrosinemia can manifest with symptoms that are strikingly similar to those of the acute porphyrias (abdominal pain, ileus, and motor neuropathy). Lead concentrates in erythroid cells. Deficient erythrocyte ALA dehydratase in cases of lead poisoning can be restored to normal in vitro with dithiothreitol. Erythrocyte protoporphyrin and urinary coproporphyrin are increased. In cases of hereditary tyrosinemia, a deficiency of fumarylacetoacetase leads to accumulation of succinylacetone (2,3-dioxoheptanoic acid). This structural analogue of ALA is a potent inhibitor of ALA dehydratase. Other heavy metals or styrene exposure can also inhibit ALA dehydratase.

ACUTE INTERMITTENT PORPHYRIA

Acute intermittent porphyria is an autosomal dominant disorder that results from an approximately 50% deficiency of PBG deaminase. The enzyme is deficient in all individuals who inherit the mutant gene and remains fairly constant over time. The majority of subjects with PBG deaminase deficiency remain asymptomatic.

Prevalence

Cases of AIP occur in all racial groups. The prevalence of AIP in most countries has not been precisely estimated, but it may be most common (perhaps 5 per 100,000) in northern European populations.

Etiology and Pathogenesis

Up to 200 different mutations of the PBG deaminase gene have been identified in unrelated AIP lineages. There are two isoenzymes of PBG deaminase, an erythroid-specific and a nonerythroid or "housekeeping" form. Both are transcribed by alternative mRNA splicing from the same gene, which contains 15 exons. The erythroid-specific isoenzyme is encoded by exons 2 through 15; the erythroid promoter, which functions only in erythroid cells, is found immediately upstream from exon 2. The nonerythroid enzyme is encoded by exons 1 and 3 through 15; the nonerythroid promoter is immediately upstream from exon 1. PBG deaminase is decreased in all tissues of most patients with AIP. But for some mutations—mostly those in or near exon 1—only the nonerythroid isoenzyme is deficient. Therefore, in individuals with this type of mutation, the enzyme activity is deficient in nonerythroid tissues but is normal in erythrocytes. Homozygous AIP is extremely rare.

Most individuals with clinically latent AIP have normal levels of ALA and PBG and apparently normal hepatic cytochrome P450 content. This indicates that the partial deficiency of PBG deaminase does not of itself greatly impair hepatic heme synthesis or induce ALA synthase. However, when the demand for hepatic heme is increased by drugs, hormones, or nutritional factors, the deficient enzyme can become limiting for heme synthesis. Induction of hepatic ALA synthase is then accentuated and ALA and PBG accumulate in liver and increase in plasma and urine. Excess porphyrins originate nonenzymatically from PBG or perhaps enzymatically from ALA transported to tissues other than the liver.

Most drugs that are harmful in AIP induce hepatic ALA synthase and cytochrome P450 enzymes. However, some drugs, such as sulfonamide antibiotics, are harmful for reasons not understood. Reduced caloric and carbohydrate intakes enhance induction of ALA synthase in animals and, in patients with AIP, can increase ALA and PBG and precipitate symptoms. Administration of carbohydrate can reduce hepatic ALA synthase and P450 enzyme levels.

The mechanism of neural damage in AIP is not established. Porphyrias and related disorders associated with increased ALA have similar neurologic manifestations. ALA is structurally analogous to γ-aminobutyric acid (GABA) and can interact with GABA receptors. However, ALA and other products of the heme pathway have not been convincingly shown to be neurotoxic. Alternatively, heme deficiency in nervous tissue may lead to neurologic dysfunction.

Clinical Manifestations

Symptoms rarely occur before puberty and seldom, if ever, recur throughout adult life. Characteristically, attacks last for several days or longer, often require hospitalization, and are followed by complete recovery. Abdominal pain—the most common symptom—is usually steady and poorly localized but may be cramping. Tachycardia, hypertension, restlessness, fine tremors, and excess sweating may be due to sympathetic overactivity. Other manifestations include nausea, vomiting, constipation, pain in the limbs, head, neck, or chest, muscle weakness, and sensory loss. Ileus, with distention and decreased bowel sounds, is common. However, increased bowel sounds and diarrhea may be seen. Because the abdominal symptoms are neurologic rather than inflammatory, tenderness, fever, and leukocytosis are generally absent or mild. Dysuria and bladder dysfunction may occur. Recurrent attacks tend to be similar in a given patient.

Peripheral neuropathy in patients with AIP is primarily motor and results from axonal degeneration. This does not develop in all patients with acute attacks, even when abdominal symptoms are severe. Rarely, neuropathy develops apart from abdominal symptoms. Weakness most commonly begins in proximal muscles (often requiring a careful examination to detect), and more often in the arms than the legs. It can be asymmetric and focal. Tendon reflexes may be little affected or hyperactive in early stages but are usually decreased or absent with advanced neuropathy. Cranial and sensory nerves can be affected. Progression to respiratory and bulbar paralysis and death seldom occurs unless porphyria is not recognized, the use of harmful drugs is not discontinued, and appropriate treatment is not instituted. Sudden death, presumably from cardiac arrhythmia, may also occur.

The central nervous system can be involved. Anxiety, insomnia, depression, disorientation, hallucinations, and paranoia, which can be especially severe during acute attacks, may suggest a primary mental disorder or hysteria. Seizures may occur as an acute neurologic manifestation of AIP, as a result of hyponatremia, or secondary to causes unrelated to porphyria. Hyponatremia may be due to hypothalamic involvement and inappropriate antidiuretic hormone secretion, vomiting, diarrhea and poor intake, or excess renal sodium loss.

After persisting for several days of treatment, an attack may resolve quite rapidly, with abdominal pain disappearing within a few hours and paresis within a few days. Attacks during the luteal phase of the menstrual cycle usually resolve with onset of menses. Even advanced neuropathy seen with a prolonged attack is potentially reversible. Pain, depression, and other symptoms are sometimes chronic.

Chronic hepatic abnormalities are common in patients with AIP. Risk of hepatocellular carcinoma (not associated with hepatitis B or C) is also increased. AIP may predispose a patient to chronic hypertension and be associated with impaired renal function. The mechanisms of these associations are unknown.

Precipitating Factors

Recognition of precipitating factors is important in management. Endogenous steroid hormones, drugs, and nutritional alterations are probably most important. AIP is characterized by rarity of symptoms and excess ALA and PBG before puberty, more frequent clinical expression in women, premenstrual attacks in some women, and exacerbations after administration of sex steroid preparations. Some patients manifest increased proportions of 5β-hydroxysteroid metabolites that are potent inducers of hepatic ALA synthase. Recurrent cyclic attacks are troublesome in some women and occur when progesterone levels are highest. Progesterone and its metabolites are potent inducers of ALA synthase, whereas estrogens are not. Pregnancy is usually well tolerated despite high progesterone levels. Some women are more prone to attacks during pregnancy, possibly partly because of hyperemesis gravidarum and reduced caloric intake.

Drugs remain important as causes of AIP attacks. Barbiturates and sulfonamides are most notorious. Benzodiazepines, which have largely replaced barbiturates in clinical practice, are less hazardous. The major drugs known to be harmful or safe in the acute porphyrias are listed in Table 223–3. Published information is insufficient to allow most drugs to be classified as definitely harmful or safe. Advice can be sought from a center with experience in porphyria with regard to the use of drugs. Some drugs may exacerbate porphyria cutanea tarda (PCT) but not acute porphyrias (see later discussion).

Reduced caloric intake, usually instituted in an effort to lose weight, is a common cause of attacks. Intercurrent infections, major surgery, and other conditions also provoke attacks. Cigarette smoke contains chemicals that can induce hepatic heme synthesis and may predispose to attacks. Attacks are almost always due to two or more factors acting in an additive fashion. Probably for this reason, (1) drugs may produce attacks in adults but are rarely reported to do so in children with PBG deaminase deficiency, (2) anticonvulsants do not produce attacks in some PBG deaminase–deficient subjects, and (3) barbiturate anesthetics more frequently exacerbate porphyria if symptoms are present before anesthetic exposure.

Diagnosis and Differential Diagnosis

Acute intermittent porphyria and other acute porphyrias are uncommon, their symptoms are nonspecific, and their physical findings often minimal. Therefore, a high index of suspicion is necessary for diagnosis. The diagnosis is established by demonstrating a marked increase in urinary PBG by a quantitative assay (see the later discussion of laboratory methods). During an acute attack, PBG excretion is generally in the range of 50 to 200 mg/day (reference range, 0 to 4 mg/day) and ALA excretion is 20 to 100 mg/day (reference range, 0 to 7 mg/day). Such increases virtually ensure a diagnosis of AIP, variegate porphyria (VP), or hereditary coproporphyria (HCP). ALA and PBG excretion generally decrease with clinical improvement. Such decreases are particularly dramatic (but transient) after heme therapy. After an attack, it is unusual for ALA and PBG to decrease to persistently normal levels, except after prolonged periods of latency. In patients with HCP and VP, urinary ALA and PBG may be less increased and may decrease to normal levels more readily than in patients with AIP. Fecal porphyrins are usually normal or minimally increased, which distinguishes AIP from HCP and VP. Urinary uroporphyrin and coproporphyrin are

often considerably increased and erythrocyte protoporphyrin may be slightly increased in patients with AIP, but these findings are not specific.

Decreased PBG deaminase (most conveniently measured in erythrocytes) confirms a diagnosis of AIP. However, as already noted, some mutations of the PBG deaminase gene only reduce the nonerythroid enzyme. Furthermore, erythrocyte PBG deaminase has a wide normal range (up to three-fold) that somewhat overlaps the AIP range and is increased by inapparent concurrent conditions that stimulate erythropoiesis. The enzyme is not reduced in cases of HCP and VP, which is also important to consider when acute porphyria is suspected. For these reasons, measurement of erythrocyte PBG deaminase is not useful in acutely ill patients. On the other hand, its measurement is highly useful for analysis of pedigrees of known AIP patients, if it is established that the propositus has a low value. In screening family members, urinary PBG should also be measured. If the specific mutation of PBG deaminase gene in a family is known, testing for this mutation using DNA methods is useful for detecting relatives who have latent AIP. Diagnosis in utero is possible but is seldom indicated in view of the favorable outlook for most PBG deaminase–deficient subjects.

No single laboratory test fully excludes AIP, HCP, and VP. However, a normal result of a quantitative test for urinary PBG virtually excludes AIP and, when combined with normal ALA and total porphyrins, is strong evidence against HCP and VP as a cause of current symptoms. Attempting to provoke increases in ALA and PBG for diagnostic purposes by glycine loading or administration of phenobarbital may be dangerous and is not definitive.

Table 223–3 • DRUGS CONSIDERED UNSAFE AND SAFE IN PATIENTS WITH ACUTE INTERMITTANT PORPHYRIA, HEREDITARY COPROPORPHYRIA, AND VARIEGATE PORPHYRIA

UNSAFE	SAFE
Angiotensin-converting enzyme inhibitors (especially enalapril)	Acetaminophen
Alcohol	Acetazolamide
Barbiturates*	Allopurinol
Calcium channel blockers (especially nifedipine)	Amiloride
Carbamazepine*	Aspirin
Carisoprodol*	Atropine
Clonazepam	Bromides
Danazol*	Cimetidine
Diclofenac and possibly other nonsteroidal anti-inflammatory drugs	Erythropoietin*[†]
Ergots	?Estrogens*[‡]
Glutethimide*	Gabapentin
Methyprylon	Gentamicin
Ethchlorvynol*	Glucocorticoids
Griseofulvin*	Insulin
Mephenytoin	Narcotic analgesics
Meprobamate (also mebutamate, tybutamate)*	Ofloxacin
Metoclopramide*	Penicillin and derivatives
Phenytoin*	Phenothiazines
Primidone*	Ranitidine*[†]
Progesterone and synthetic progestins*	Streptomycin
Pyrazinamide*	Tetracycline
Pyrazolones (aminopyrine, antipyrine)	
Rifampin*	
Succinimides (ethosuximide, methsuximide)	
Sulfonamide antibiotics*	
Valproic acid*	

*Porphyria is listed as a contraindication, warning, precaution, or adverse effect in U.S. labeling for these drugs. For drugs listed here as unsafe, absence of such cautionary statements in U.S. labeling does not imply lower risk.

[†]Although porphyria is listed as a precaution in U.S. labeling, these drugs are regarded as safe by other sources.

[‡]There is little evidence that estrogens alone are harmful in acute porphyrias. They have been implicated as harmful based mostly on experience with estrogen-progestin combinations and because they can exacerbate porphyria cutanea tarda.

Rx Treatment

Acute attacks usually require hospitalization for treatment of severe pain, nausea, and vomiting and for the administration of intravenous glucose and heme. Hospitalization also facilitates observation for neurologic complications, electrolyte imbalances, and nutritional status and investigation of precipitating factors. Symptomatic therapy includes narcotic analgesics, which are usually required for severe abdominal pain, and small to moderate doses of a phenothiazine for nausea, vomiting, anxiety, and restlessness. Chloral hydrate can be used for insomnia. Benzodiazepines in low doses may be safe if a minor tranquilizer is required. Bladder distention may require catheterization. After recovery, continued treatment with a phenothiazine is seldom indicated.

Heme therapy and carbohydrate loading are specific therapies because they repress hepatic ALA synthase and overproduction of ALA and PBG. Heme therapy is more effective and should be initiated early, but only after the diagnosis of a porphyric attack is confirmed by a marked increase in urinary PBG. Diagnosis is more difficult after heme therapy, which can at least transiently normalize ALA and PBG.

The standard regimen for heme therapy is 3 mg heme per kilogram body weight infused intravenously once daily for 4 days. A longer course of treatment is seldom necessary if treatment is started early. Efficacy is reduced and recovery is less rapid when treatment is delayed and neuronal damage is more advanced. This treatment is not effective for chronic symptoms of AIP. A lyophilized hematin (hydroxy-heme) preparation is available in the United States. The product is unstable when reconstituted with sterile water, and degradation products adhere to endothelial cells, platelets, and coagulation factors, causing a transient anticoagulant effect and frequently phlebitis at the site of infusion. Reconstitution with human albumin enhances the stability of hematin and prevents these side effects. Heme arginate, which is available in Europe and South Africa, is much more stable than hematin and also does not have these side effects.

Carbohydrate loading may suffice for mild attacks and can be given orally as sucrose, glucose polymers, or carbohydrate-rich foods. If oral intake is poorly tolerated or is contraindicated by distention and ileus, intravenous administration of glucose (at least 300 g daily) is usually indicated. A central venous line facilitates more complete parenteral nutrition support and avoids excess fluid volumes.

Treatment of seizures is problematic, because almost all antiseizure drugs can exacerbate AIP. Bromides, gabapentin, and probably vigabatrin can be given safely. β-Adrenergic blocking agents may control tachycardia and hypertension in acute attacks of porphyria, but they may be hazardous in patients with hypovolemia, in whom increased catecholamine secretion may be an important compensatory mechanism. Numerous other therapies have been tried for this disease but have not been consistently useful.

Prognosis

In the past 20 years, attacks of porphyria have rarely been fatal. If acute attacks are treated appropriately, inciting factors are removed, and precautions are taken to prevent further attacks, the outlook for patients with AIP is usually very good. Recurrent attacks of porphyria occur in some patients and can be disabling, but they do not occur throughout adult life. Occasionally, chronic pain and other symptoms develop, but they may improve over the long term. Chronic symptoms and depression increase the risk of suicide and thus require careful management.

Symptoms never develop in the great majority of relatives with PBG deaminase deficiency, especially if they have normal urinary porphyrin precursors. Although such individuals are less sensitive to inducing drugs and other factors than are patients with prior porphyric symptoms, the same precautions should be followed as for patients with AIP. Latent AIP should never be construed as a health risk that limits eligibility for health insurance.

Prevention

Some specific measures are helpful in preventing clinical expression of AIP. (1) Family members should be screened to detect latent cases. (2) Harmful drugs should be avoided. (3) "Crash diets" for weight reduction and even brief periods of starvation (e.g. during postoperative periods or intercurrent illnesses) should be avoided. Diet regimens for obesity should provide for gradual weight loss during periods of clinical remission of porphyria. (4) Attacks can be prevented by administration of gonadotropin releasing hormone analogues (for women with frequent cyclic attacks) or periodic heme infusions. Oophorectomy is not an acceptable option for preventing cyclic attacks. Because suicide is a risk in patients with AIP, a preventive approach is appropriate, especially in patients with chronic symptoms and depression.

CONGENITAL ERYTHROPOIETIC PORPHYRIA

Congenital erythropoietic porphyria (CEP) is an autosomal recessive disorder that is caused by a deficiency of uroporphyrinogen III cosynthase. Fewer than 250 cases have been reported. CEP occurs in several animal species (including all fox squirrels).

Etiology and Pathogenesis

Many different mutations of the uroporphyrinogen III cosynthase gene have been identified in CEP. Most patients have unrelated parents and have inherited a different mutation from each parent. The severity of the disease is variable and relates to the degree of enzyme deficiency caused by the particular mutations. There is considerable accumulation of hydroxymethylbilane (the substrate of the deficient enzyme), which is converted nonenzymatically to uroporphyrinogen I. Uroporphyrin I and other porphyrins accumulate in bone marrow erythroid cells that are actively synthesizing hemoglobin and lead to intramedullary and intravascular hemolysis. Even in the most severe cases, some residual cosynthase activity is present, and heme production is actually increased in response to hemolysis. Excretion of type III porphyrin isomers is also increased. Splenomegaly can contribute to anemia and cause leukopenia and thrombocytopenia. Sunlight, other sources of ultraviolet light, and minor trauma to friable skin are other determinants of clinical expression. Drugs, steroids, and nutrition have little influence.

Clinical Manifestations

Clinical expression is variable. In most cases, reddish urine and severe cutaneous photosensitivity are noted in early infancy. In a few very severe cases, CEP has been manifested as nonimmune hydrops and intrauterine transfusions were administered. If CEP was not recognized, marked photosensitivity resulted when phototherapy was initiated for neonatal jaundice. In some milder cases, symptoms begin in adult life. Cutaneous features resemble those in PCT but are usually more severe. Lesions on sun-exposed skin include bullae and vesicles that are prone to rupture and become infected, hypopigmented or hyperpigmented areas, and hypertrichosis. Loss of digits and facial features and corneal scarring can be severe. Porphyrins are deposited in the teeth (producing a reddish brown color termed *erythrodontia*) and in bone. Bone demineralization can be substantial. Hemolysis and splenomegaly are almost always present, but there are no neurologic manifestations. Life expectancy is often shortened by infections or hematologic complications.

Diagnosis and Differential Diagnosis

In CEP, porphyrin excretion and porphyrin levels in red blood cells and plasma are generally much greater than in other forms of porphyria. Porphyrins in urine are primarily uroporphyrin I and coproporphyrin I, and in feces mostly coproporphyrin I. ALA and PBG are normal. In most cases, uroporphyrin I predominates in erythrocytes. A predominance of protoporphyrin in red blood cells has been described in some cases and is characteristic of bovine CEP. CEP is readily distinguished from erythropoietic protoporphyria (EPP) clinically but may resemble hepatoerythropoietic porphyria and homozygous cases of AIP, VP, and HCP.

Rx Treatment

Protection of the skin from sunlight and minor trauma and prompt treatment of secondary bacterial infections help prevent scarring and mutilation. Improvement may occur after splenectomy. Oral charcoal may be helpful by increasing fecal excretion of porphyrins. Blood transfusions, sometimes combined with hydroxyurea, may suppress erythropoiesis sufficiently to reduce porphyrin overproduction. Bone marrow or stem cell transplantation may be the most effective current therapy. Gene therapy may eventually be possible.

Prevention

In affected families, heterozygotes with intermediate deficiencies of the cosynthase can be detected, and CEP can be diagnosed in utero. Therefore, options are available to prevent genetic transmission.

PORPHYRIA CUTANEA TARDA

Porphyria cutanea tarda is the most common and readily treated form of porphyria. It is caused by a deficiency of uroporphyrinogen decarboxylase in the liver. It is most common in men but has become more frequent in women in association with alcohol and estrogen use.

Etiology and Pathogenesis

Both acquired and inherited factors can play causative roles in PCT. Individual cases can be classified as sporadic (type I) or familial (type II). The majority of cases are type I, in which uroporphyrinogen decarboxylase mutations are not found and the enzyme is deficient in the liver but not in erythrocytes and other tissues. The amount of hepatic uroporphyrinogen decarboxylase protein, as measured immunochemically, is normal, thus suggesting that an acquired process has inhibited (or inactivated) the enzyme. With treatment and remission of the disease, enzyme activity gradually increases to normal. Familial (type II) PCT is distinguished from type I by an inherited, approximately 50% deficiency of the decarboxylase in all tissues, including erythrocytes. This deficiency is an autosomal dominant trait and can result from a number of different mutations of the uroporphyrinogen decarboxylase gene. Apparently, type II PCT is not manifested clinically until the product of the normal allele is inhibited in liver, as in type I PCT. A type III PCT has been described in which the enzyme is deficient in the liver but not in other tissues, and more than one family member is affected. Types I to III are clinically similar and often difficult to distinguish, and they respond to the same therapies.

Examples of *toxic porphyria* have resembled PCT. Most notably, an extensive outbreak of porphyria occurred in eastern Turkey in 1955–1958 after seed wheat containing the fungicide hexachlorobenzene was used for food. Dichlorophenols, trichlorophenols, and 2,3,7,8-tetrachlorodibenzo-*p*-dioxin (TCDD, dioxin) have been implicated in smaller outbreaks and single cases in humans. When administered to animals, these chemicals decrease uroporphyrinogen decarboxylase (only in the liver), and induce a pattern of excess porphyrins resembling PCT. A history of exposure to such chemicals is seldom found in sporadic (type I) PCT.

A notable feature of PCT is massive accumulation of porphyrins in the liver, which may develop over many months. This accumulation precedes the appearance of excess porphyrins in plasma and urine. Hepatic ALA synthase may be little increased because the amount of excess porphyrins produced in PCT is small relative to the rate of hepatic heme formation. By contrast, during attacks of the acute porphyrias, much larger amounts of intermediates are excreted as porphyrin precursors, and ALA synthase is substantially induced. Worsening of PCT by factors (other than alcohol) that induce heme synthesis is seldom reported.

The pattern of porphyrins that accumulate in PCT is complex and characteristic. The enzyme-catalyzed decarboxylation of uroporphyrinogen occurs in four sequential steps. Therefore, when the enzyme is markedly deficient, uroporphyrin and the heptacarboxyl, hexacarboxyl, and pentacarboxyl porphyrins (type I and III isomers derived from the corresponding porphyrinogens) accumulate. In addition, pentacarboxyl porphyrinogen can be metabolized by coproporphyrinogen oxidase to a series of tetracarboxyl porphyrins termed *isocoproporphyrins*. The isocoproporphyrins are excreted primarily in bile and feces and are diagnostic of uroporphyrinogen decarboxylase deficiency.

Multiple factors are believed to contribute to markedly inhibiting hepatic uroporphyrinogen decarboxylase, probably by increasing oxidative stress in the liver. (1) A normal or increased amount of hepatic iron seems essential in this disease. Iron may catalyze the formation of free radicals that lead to formation of an inhibitor of the enzyme protein or oxidize its porphyrinogen substrates to porphyrins. Patients with PCT are homozygous or heterozygous for the *HFE* gene mutations that are associated with genetic hemochromatosis more commonly than expected by chance. (2) Cytochrome P450 enzymes may also be involved in the oxidation of porphyrinogen substrates. (3) Alcohol intake may promote iron absorption, stimulate hepatic heme and porphyrin synthesis, or generate free radicals, leading to inhibition of the decarboxylase. (4) Levels of antioxidants (vitamin C and carotenoids) may be decreased. (5) Estrogens, but apparently not other steroids, can exacerbate PCT, perhaps by an unknown oxidative mechanism. (6) Chronic hepatitis C virus infection may also be associated with oxidative damage to hepatocytes. (7) Drugs may worsen PCT; those so indicated in U.S. labeling are several nonsteroidal anti-inflammatory drugs, sulfonylureas, and busulfan.

Clinical Manifestations

Cutaneous photosensitivity is the major clinical feature. Vesicles and bullae develop most commonly on the dorsum of the hands and on the face, feet, forearms, and legs. Sun-exposed skin becomes friable, and minor trauma may precede the formation of bullae or cause denudation of the skin. Small white plaques ("milia") may precede or follow vesicle formation. Involved skin tends to heal slowly. Hypertrichosis and hyperpigmentation sometimes occur even in the absence of vesicles. Thickening, scarring and calcification of affected skin ("pseudoscleroderma") may be striking. Neurologic effects are not observed.

Porphyria cutanea tarda is associated with clinically identifiable risk factors, including moderate or heavy alcohol intake, smoking, hepatitis C (in as many as 80% of patients in some locations), estrogen use (in women taking oral contraceptives or replacement estrogens or men treated with estrogen for prostate cancer), *HFE* mutations, inherited uroporphyrinogen decarboxylase deficiency, and human immunodeficiency virus infection. At least several of these are found in most patients. An association with systemic lupus erythematosus has also been described. PCT sometimes occurs in patients with advanced renal disease. Skin lesions may be more severe and plasma porphyrin levels much higher in this setting, because urinary excretion of porphyrins is not possible, and they are poorly dialyzed.

Abnormal liver test results—especially of transaminases—are common in PCT and can occur in the absence of hepatitis C. Liver histopathology is nonspecific, other than the finding of fluorescence due to porphyrins, which appear as inclusions in fixed tissue. The liver iron level is often increased. Risk of cirrhosis and hepatocellular carcinoma increases with disease duration. Very rarely, hepatic tumors themselves contain and presumably produce excess porphyrins. Some of these cases have resembled PCT.

Diagnosis and Differential Diagnosis

Skin lesions in cases of PCT, VP, and HCP are indistinguishable clinically and histologically. It is important to differentiate these conditions by laboratory testing before starting therapy. A predominance of uroporphyrin and heptacarboxyl porphyrin in urine and increased isocoproporphyrin in feces is diagnostic of PCT. In PCT, urinary ALA may be slightly increased, whereas PBG is normal. Total fecal porphyrins are less increased in PCT than in VP and HCP. Plasma porphyrins are virtually always increased in patients with skin lesions from any type of porphyria; the fluorescence spectrum of plasma can distinguish VP and EPP from PCT (see later).

Rx Treatment

A course of phlebotomies is the preferred treatment and almost always produces a remission. Patients are also advised to discontinue alcohol, estrogens, iron supplements, or other contributing factors. Because iron stores in PCT are seldom markedly increased, removal of only 5 to 6 units of blood at 1- to 2-week intervals is usually sufficient. Many more phlebotomies may be needed in patients who also have hemochromatosis. Plasma (or serum) ferritin and porphyrin levels should be followed (Fig. 223–2). Deferoxamine, an iron chelator, may be effective but is much less efficient.

A course of low-dose chloroquine 125 mg twice weekly or hydroxychloroquine 100 mg twice weekly for several months is usually effective when repeated phlebotomies are contraindicated. The mechanism of their effects in PCT has not been established. One hypothesis is that chloroquine forms complexes with porphyrins and promotes their removal from the liver. If usual doses of these drugs are given to patients with PCT, marked increases in photosensitivity and porphyrin levels in plasma and urine are seen and may be accompanied by nausea, malaise, fever, and hepatocellular damage. Although these adverse effects are generally transient and are followed by complete remission, it is prudent to avoid them by using a low-dose regimen.

Therapy is more difficult when PCT occurs with advanced renal disease because phlebotomy is usually contraindicated by anemia (usually because of erythropoietin deficiency). Treatment with genetic recombinant erythropoietin can mobilize excess iron, support phlebotomy, and lead to remission of PCT in these patients.

HEPATOERYTHROPOIETIC PORPHYRIA

Hepatoerythropoietic porphyria is a rare autosomal recessive disease that is clinically similar to CEP but is distinguished by excess isocoproporphyrin in feces and urine and decreased uroporphyrinogen decarboxylase activity in erythrocytes (and other tissues). Mild cases may resemble PCT. Mutations in the uroporphyrinogen decarboxylase gene are found in this disease and are associated with some residual enzyme activity. Increased erythrocyte protoporphyrin probably reflects an earlier accumulation of uroporphyrinogen in

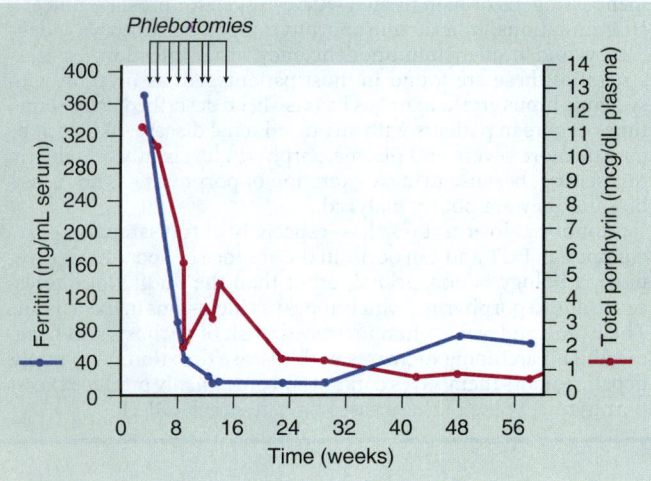

FIGURE 223–2 • Treatment of porphyria cutanea tarda by repeated phlebotomy. The patient was a 37-year-old woman with a history of excess alcohol intake and chronic hepatitis C. Each arrow indicates removal of 450 mL of whole blood. Phlebotomies are stopped when serum ferritin is near the lower limit of normal. Further iron depletion is of no additional benefit and may cause anemia and associated symptoms. Plasma porphyrins become normal and the appearance of new skin lesions ceases within several months. After remission, ferritin can return to normal without recurrence, in most cases. In some cases, relapses occur and respond to another course of phlebotomies. (Modified from Anderson KE: The porphyrias. *In* Zakim D, Boyer T [eds]: Hepatology. Philadelphia, WB Saunders, 2003, pp 291–346.)

erythroblasts, which after completion of hemoglobin synthesis is metabolized to protoporphyrin. A similar explanation can account for increased erythrocyte protoporphyrin in other homozygous forms of porphyria.

HEREDITARY COPROPORPHYRIA AND VARIEGATE PORPHYRIA

The autosomal dominant acute hepatic porphyrias HCP and VP are clinically similar to AIP but are much less common in most countries. Unlike AIP, these disorders can cause cutaneous photosensitivity. VP is quite prevalent in South Africa, where most cases have been traced to a couple who immigrated from Holland in the late 1600s.

Etiology and Pathogenesis

Hereditary coproporphyria and VP are caused by approximately 50% deficiencies of coproporphyrinogen oxidase and protoporphyrinogen oxidase, respectively. Many different mutations in the genes for these enzymes have been described. A specific mutation of the protoporphyrinogen oxidase gene is common in South Africa. ALA and PBG are increased during acute attacks, although the degree and duration of increases are usually less than in AIP. Increases in ALA and PBG occur when hepatic ALA synthase is induced by factors such as endogenous steroids, drugs, and nutritional alterations and because PBG deaminase activity is almost as low as ALA synthase activity even in normal liver. Coproporphyrinogen III may accumulate in patients with VP because of a functional association between coproporphyrinogen oxidase and the deficient protoporphyrinogen oxidase in mitochondria. Furthermore, coproporphyrinogen is more readily lost from the liver than are other porphyrinogens, and its loss increases further when heme synthesis is stimulated. The excess porphyrinogens are autooxidized to the corresponding porphyrins. In one form of HCP, termed *harderoporphyria*, a structurally altered coproporphyrinogen oxidase with reduced substrate affinity results in accumulation of harderoporphyrin as well as coproporphyrin. A few homozygous cases of HCP and VP have been described.

Clinical Manifestations

Drugs, steroids, and nutritional factors that are detrimental in AIP provoke exacerbations of HCP and VP. Neurologic manifestations are identical to those in AIP. Blistering skin lesions are identical to those in PCT and may occur apart from the neurovisceral symptoms. These are much more common in patients with VP than in patients with HCP. Impaired biliary excretion by concurrent liver diseases or drugs such as contraceptive steroids can cause porphyrin retention and worsen photosensitivity.

Diagnosis and Differential Diagnosis

Urinary ALA and PBG are commonly increased during acute attacks. With resolution of symptoms, ALA and PBG normalize more readily than in AIP. Increases in urinary porphyrins are more persistent. A marked, isolated increase in fecal coproporphyrin (especially isomer III) is distinctive for HCP. Fecal coproporphyrin and protoporphyrin are about equally increased in VP. The fluorescence spectrum of plasma porphyrins (at neutral pH) is characteristic and very useful for rapidly distinguishing VP from the other porphyrias. This test is probably the most sensitive porphyrin measurement for detecting VP, including latent cases, at least in adults.

Rx Treatment and Prognosis

Acute attacks of both HCP and VP are treated as in AIP. The striking decreases in attacks and deaths from VP in South Africa have been attributed to identification of latent cases, avoidance of harmful drugs, and better treatment during acute attacks. Measures that protect the skin from sunlight are helpful for photosensitivity. Cholestyramine may decrease the photosensitivity occurring with liver dysfunction. Phlebotomies and chloroquine are not effective.

ERYTHROPOIETIC PROTOPORPHYRIA

Erythropoietic protoporphyria was not clearly described until 1961, perhaps because it seldom causes blistering of the skin, and urine porphyrin levels are not increased. EPP is now recognized as the third most common porphyria. It is caused by a deficiency of ferrochelatase, with increased protoporphyrin in erythrocytes, plasma, bile, and feces.

Etiology and Pathogenesis

Many different mutations in the ferrochelatase gene have been identified in various EPP families. Most of these mutant alleles express little or no ferrochelatase. The pattern of inheritance often appears to be autosomal dominant, but some obligate carriers have little or no increase in red cell protoporphyrin. Coinheritance of a common ferrochelatase allele that expresses low levels of enzyme may explain an incompletely dominant trait, at least in some families.

Ferrochelatase is deficient in all tissues in patients with clinically expressed EPP but becomes rate limiting for protoporphyrin metabolism primarily in bone marrow reticulocytes, which are the primary source of the excess protoporphyrin. Circulating erythrocytes and the liver contribute smaller amounts. The level of protoporphyrin is increased in plasma, and it is excreted in bile and feces. The large amounts of protoporphyrin in erythrocytes of patients with EPP are free (not complexed with zinc), and the protoporphyrin diffuses more readily into plasma as compared with zinc protoporphyrin (found in cases of lead poisoning, iron deficiency, and some homozygous forms of porphyria). Zinc protoporphyrin dissociates less readily from hemoglobin binding sites and persists in the red blood cell as long as it circulates. Disposition of the excess protoporphyrin in EPP depends on hepatic uptake, biliary excretion, and the degree of enterohepatic circulation. These processes are impaired by liver damage.

Clinical Manifestations

Cutaneous manifestations usually begin in childhood and are distinctly different from those of other porphyrias. Burning, itching, erythema, and swelling can occur within minutes of sun exposure. Diffuse edema of sun-exposed areas may resemble angioneurotic edema. Other characteristic skin changes include lichenification, leathery pseudovesicles, labial grooving, and nail changes. Scarring is rarely severe or deforming Vesicles, pigment changes, friability, and hirsutism are unusual. No fluorescence of the teeth, and (except with severe hepatic failure) no neuropathic manifestations are present. Drugs that exacerbate hepatic porphyrias are not known to worsen EPP, although they are generally avoided as a precaution.

Hemolysis is uncommon or very mild in uncomplicated cases. Erythropoiesis and iron metabolism are generally normal. Mild anemia with hypochromia and microcytosis is noted in some cases and is unexplained. Gallstones containing protoporphyrin may develop in patients with EPP.

Liver function is usually normal in patients with EPP. In a minority of patients with EPP, liver disease with protoporphyrin deposition can develop and progress rapidly to death from liver failure. Excess protoporphyrin itself has cholestatic effects and damages hepatocytes. Intercurrent factors such as viral hepatitis, alcohol, iron deficiency, fasting, and oral contraceptive steroids may predispose to protoporphyrin accumulation in liver. Marked photosensitivity and skin blistering and even motor neuropathy have developed in some EPP patients with liver failure. Operating room lights have produced severe skin and peritoneal burns.

Diagnosis and Differential Diagnosis

Protoporphyrin levels are increased in bone marrow, erythrocytes, plasma, bile, and feces of EPP patients. Urinary porphyrins and porphyrin precursors are normal. Hepatic complications of EPP are often preceded by increasing levels of erythrocyte and plasma protoporphyrin, abnormal liver function test results, marked deposition of protoporphyrin in liver cells and bile canaliculi, and increased photosensitivity.

Treatment and Prognosis

β-Carotene (Lumitene, Tishcon) was originally developed primarily for treating EPP and was found to be beneficial in large series of patients. Its mechanism of action may involve quenching of singlet oxygen or free radicals. Carotenemia with mild, dose-related skin discoloration is expected. Cholestyramine may reduce protoporphyrin levels by interrupting its enterohepatic circulation. Iron deficiency, caloric restriction, and drugs or hormone preparations that impair hepatic excretory function should be avoided.

Hepatic complications may resolve spontaneously if a reversible cause of liver dysfunction, such as viral hepatitis or alcohol, is contributing. Transfusions or heme therapy may suppress erythroid and hepatic protoporphyrin production. Plasma exchange, splenectomy, correction of iron deficiency, and cholestyramine or activated charcoal may be beneficial. Liver transplantation is sometimes required.

DUAL PORPHYRIA

Dual porphyria refers to patients with porphyria and deficiencies of more than one enzyme of the heme biosynthetic pathway. Examples include deficiencies of both porphobilinogen deaminase and uroporphyrinogen decarboxylase (with symptoms of AIP, PCT, or both), and deficiencies of both coproporphyrinogen oxidase and uroporphyrinogen III cosynthase.

LABORATORY DIAGNOSIS OF PORPHYRIAS

Porphyrias are readily detected and misdiagnoses avoided by relying primarily on a few first-line tests that are both specific and sensitive. This avoids overuse of tests for porphyria and their misinterpretation. The preferred approach for screening, as outlined in Table 223–4,

---

Table 223–4 • LABORATORY TESTS FOR DIAGNOSIS OF PORPHYRIAS

TESTING	SYMPTOMS SUGGESTING PORPHYRIA	
	Acute Neurovisceral Symptoms	Cutaneous Photosensitivity
First-line (screening for porphyrias)	Urinary ALA, PBG, and total porphyrins (quantitative, random urine)	Total plasma porphyrins*†
Second-line (further evaluation when initial testing is positive)	Urinary ALA, PBG, and total porphyrins† (quantitative, 24-hour urine)	Erythrocyte porphyrins
		Urinary ALA, PBG, and total porphyrins† (quantitative, 24-hour urine)
	Total fecal porphyrins‡	
	Erythrocyte PBG deaminase	
	Total plasma porphyrins*	Total fecal porphyrins‡

*The preferred method is by direct fluorescent spectrophotometry.
†Erythrocyte protoporphyrin should also be measured if erythropoietic protoporphyria is strongly suspected.
‡Urinary and fecal porphyrins are fractionated only if the total is increased.
ALA = δ-aminolevulinic acid; PBG = porphobilinogen.

is to rely on measurement of urinary porphyrin precursors (ALA and PBG) and total porphyrins for patients with neurovisceral symptoms and on a fluorometric measurement of plasma total porphyrins when it is suspected that skin photosensitivity might be due to porphyria. More extensive testing is required if an initial screening test provides a positive result or may also be necessary initially if subclinical porphyria is suspected.

In acutely ill patients, it is important to identify or exclude acute porphyria promptly. Urinary PBG (and ALA) is virtually always markedly increased during acute attacks of AIP. ALA and PBG may be less increased in HCP and VP, but urinary total porphyrins are consistently markedly increased in symptomatic patients. Normal levels of ALA, PBG, and total porphyrins effectively exclude all acute porphyrias as potential causes of current symptoms. Because increases are so striking during an attack, quantitation on a random urine sample is highly informative. Assays for PBG employ Ehrlich's aldehyde (p-dimethylaminobenzaldehyde), which forms reddish purple chromogens with PBG, urobilinogen, and other substances in urine. Qualitative methods (e.g., the Watson-Schwartz and Hoesch tests) are still used to screen for increased PBG but are subject to misinterpretation and false-positive reports, do not quantitate PBG, and are less sensitive and only slightly more rapid than quantitative methods, which separate PBG from interfering substances by ion exchange chromatography. A kit that is reliable for chromatographic screening for increased PBG in urine includes color standards to aid interpretation (ThermoElectron Clinical Chemistry, Noble Park, Australia). Any urine sample that tests positive by a qualitative method for PBG should be retested by a quantitative method.

Total plasma porphyrins are virtually always increased in patients with active, blistering skin lesions due to porphyrias. Normal plasma porphyrin levels exclude porphyria as a cause of cutaneous symptoms, especially if the measurement is carried out by a simple and direct fluorometric method. Plasma porphyrins in VP are mostly covalently bound to plasma porphyrins and may not be detected by other methods. Measurement of erythrocyte protoporphyrin is more sensitive than plasma porphyrins for detecting EPP.

The interpretation of urine, fecal, or erythrocyte porphyrin findings is often problematic. Urine and erythrocyte porphyrins can be increased in many conditions other than porphyria. Fecal porphyrin determinations are semiquantitative and subject to interference by diet and other factors.

Laboratory testing of relatives is usually not appropriate until test results have firmly established a diagnosis of porphyria in the propositus. Results of testing the propositus guide the choice of tests for relatives. Cytosolic heme biosynthetic pathway enzymes (ALA dehydratase, porphobilinogen deaminase, uroporphyrinogen III cosynthase, and uroporphyrinogen decarboxylase) can be measured in erythrocytes. These are not recommended for initial screening of patients with symptoms suggestive of porphyria. The other heme pathway enzymes are mitochondrial and are not reliably measured in erythrocytes. Demonstrating a specific mutation in a family greatly facilitates detection of relatives who carry the same mutation. Consultation with a physician and laboratory with experience in testing for porphyrias is helpful in these situations.

Laboratory data that were the basis for an original diagnosis of porphyria should remain available for future reference. Incorrect diagnoses of porphyria are not uncommon when in fact symptoms are due to other diseases. There is little evidence for the suggestion that porphyria is common in disorders such as multiple chemical sensitivity syndrome.

SUGGESTED READINGS

Andersson C, Innala E, Backstrom T: Acute intermittent porphyria in women: Clinical expression, use and experience of exogenous sex hormones. A population-based study in northern Sweden. J Intern Med 2003;254:176–183. *Emphasizes the risk associated with the common use of oral contraceptives.*

Anderson KE, Sassa S, Bishop DF, Desnick RJ: Disorders of heme biosynthesis: X-linked sideroblastic anemias and the porphyrias. *In* Scriver CR, Beaudet AL, Sly WS, et al (eds): The Metabolic and Molecular Basis of Inherited Disease, vol II, 8th ed. New York, McGraw-Hill, 2001, pp 2991–3062. *A recent, detailed review on the genetic, biochemical, and clinical aspects of the porphyrias.*

Bonkovsky HL, Healey BS, Lourie AN, Gerron GG: Intravenous heme-albumin in acute intermittent porphyria: Evidence for repletion of hepatic hemoproteins and regulatory heme pools. Am J Gastroenterol 1991;86:1050–1056. *This article describes a method for reconstituting and stabilizing lyophilized hematin with human albumin to prevent phlebitis and other side effects.*

Bygum A, Christiansen L, Petersen NE, et al: Familial and sporadic porphyria cutanea tarda: Clinical, biochemical and genetic features with emphasis on iron status. Acta

Derm Venereol 2003;83:115–120. *Daily alcohol intake and use of estrogens are more frequently in the sporadic patients.*

Egger NG, Goeger DE, Payne DA, et al: Porphyria cutanea tarda: Multiplicity of risk factors including HFE mutations, hepatitis C, and inherited uroporphyrinogen decarboxylase deficiency. Dig Dis Sci 2002;47:419–426. *A case series documenting coexisting, multiple risk factors in PCT.*

Mustajoki P, Nordmann Y: Early administration of heme arginate for acute porphyric attacks. Arch Intern Med 1993;153:2004–2008. *A large series of patients treated with intravenous heme, emphasizing the importance of early treatment.*

Schmid R (ed): The porphyrias. Semin Liver Dis 1998;18:1. *A collection of reviews emphasizing recent progress in the cellular and molecular biology of these diseases.*

224 WILSON'S DISEASE

Stephen G. Kaler

Definition

Wilson's disease is an autosomal recessive disorder of copper metabolism. Affected individuals accumulate abnormal levels of copper in the liver and (later) in the brain as a result of mutations in both alleles of the Wilson disease gene (*ATP7B*). The gene was identified in 1993 and encodes a copper-transporting ATPase expressed primarily in the liver where its major function is excretion of hepatic copper into the biliary tract.

The clinical condition was first described in 1912 by S. A. K. Wilson, an American-born neurologist working in England. Thirty-six years later, the pathologist J. N. Cummings proposed an etiologic connection with copper overload and, in 1956, therapy with copper chelation by penicillamine was introduced by J. M. Walshe, a British physician working in Boston.

Epidemiology

The *incidence* of Wilson's disease, defined as the occurrence of new cases, is approximately 1 in 30,000 to 40,000 live births. For special populations in which consanguineous mating is common, the risk of autosomal recessive traits such as Wilson's disease is higher. In the general population, the *prevalence* of heterozygous gene carriers (defined as the ratio of all individuals with one mutant *ATP7B* allele to the population at risk of harboring one, is estimated to be 1 in 90. These individuals may represent a susceptible group for liver disease related to copper overload.

Pathophysiology

Individuals consume 1 to 3 mg of dietary copper daily, of which approximately 50% is absorbed via the gastrointestinal tract. Most diets contain adequate amounts of copper and certain foods (e.g., shellfish, liver, mushrooms, chocolate, nuts) contain particularly high quantities. In normal homeostasis, copper is absorbed from the stomach and duodenum. Absorption is mediated by specific copper uptake genes (e.g., hCTR1). The Menkes' disease gene (*ATP7A*) that encodes a copper-transporting ATPase with high homology to the Wilson gene product transports copper from within intestinal epithelial cells into the blood stream where it is bound by albumin and amino acids and carried to the liver via the portal vein.

Within the liver, copper may be (1) incorporated into ceruloplasmin (a multifunctional α_2-glycoprotein enzyme of molecular weight 132 kD containing 0.3% copper—six copper atoms per molecule), (2) used in the synthesis of other copper-requiring enzymes, (3) bound by metallothionein (a low-molecular-weight cysteine-rich protein that provides a storage and detoxification depot for copper and other trace metal elements), and (4) excreted into the bile. In Wilson's disease, alternative (1) is usually impaired, resulting in low circulating levels of the ceruloplasmin holoenzyme, whereas (4) is invariably impaired, producing massive hepatic copper overload, if the disease is unrecognized. These findings indicate that copper incorporation into ceruloplasmin and biliary excretion of copper are both mediated by the Wilson disease gene product in the normal state.

Circulating levels of functional ceruloplasmin and total serum copper are low in many patients with Wilson's disease. However, these biochemical abnormalities are not necessarily associated with liver disease, as illustrated by the inherited disorders aceruloplasminemia, Menkes' disease, and occipital horn syndrome. A feature that distinguishes Wilson's disease from these conditions is the amount of *non–ceruloplasmin-bound serum copper*, which is about five-fold normal in Wilson's disease patients.

Thus, the major pathophysiologic component of Wilson's disease is hepatic copper overload resulting from defective biliary excretion of the metal. If this diagnosis goes unrecognized, copper overload subsequently involves other tissues, including brain, which is particularly sensitive to perturbations in trace metal homeostasis.

Clinical Manifestations

Presenting clinical features of Wilson's disease include nonspecific liver disease, neurologic abnormalities, psychiatric illness, hemolytic anemia, renal tubular Fanconi' syndrome, and various skeletal abnormalities.

Age influences the specific presentation in Wilson's disease. Nearly all individuals who present with liver disease are younger than 30 years of age, whereas those presenting with neurologic or psychiatric signs may range in age from the first to fifth decade. This reflects the sequence of events in the pathogenesis of this disease (see earlier discussion). However, regardless of clinical presentation, some degree of liver disease is invariably present.

In one series of 400 adult patients with Wilson's disease, approximately 50% presented with neurologic and psychiatric symptoms, 20% with neurologic and hepatic, and 20% with purely hepatic symptoms.

In patients with neurologic presentations, abnormalities include speech difficulty (dysarthria), dystonia, rigidity, tremor or choreiform movements, abnormal gait, and uncoordinated handwriting. Wilson's disease may properly be classified as a movement disorder. The neurologic signs and symptoms reflect the predilection for basal ganglia (e.g., caudate, putamen) involvement in these individuals' brains. Parkinson's disease or other movement disorders may be mistakenly diagnosed.

In psychiatric presentations, changes in personality (irritability, anger, poor self-control), depression, and anxiety are common symptoms. Typically, patients presenting in this fashion are in their late teens or early 20s, a period during which substance abuse is also a diagnostic consideration. Wilson's disease should be formally excluded in all teenagers and young adults with new-onset psychiatric signs.

In hepatic presentations, signs and symptoms include jaundice, hepatomegaly, edema, and ascites. Secondary endocrine effects of liver disease may include delayed puberty or amenorrhea. Viral hepatitis and cirrhosis are often initial diagnostic considerations in individuals with Wilson's disease.

In addition to the brain and liver, the eye is a primary site of copper deposition in Wilson' disease, producing a pathognomonic sign, the Kayser-Fleischer (KF) ring (Fig. 224–1). The KF ring is a golden to greenish-brown annular deposition of copper in the periphery of the cornea. This important diagnostic sign first appears as a superior crescent, then develops inferiorly and ultimately becomes circumferential. Slit-lamp examinations are required to detect rings in their early stage of formation. Copper can also accumulate in the lens and produce "sunflower" cataracts.

Approximately 95% of patients with neurologic signs manifest the KF ring compared with approximately 65% of those with hepatic presentations. Copper chelation therapy causes fading and even disappearance of corneal copper over time.

Hemolytic anemia resulting from the direct toxic effects of copper on red blood cell membranes has been observed in Wilson's disease. This is usually associated with release of massive quantities of hepatic copper into the circulation, a phenomenon that can be sudden and catastrophic.

Renal dysfunction in Wilson's disease is tubular in nature, and leads to abnormal losses of amino acids, electrolytes, calcium, phosphorus, and glucose. Presumably this effect is related to copper toxicity. High copper levels have been noted previously in the kidneys of patients with Wilson's disease. Treatment with copper chelation often improves the renal disturbances.

There can be skeletal effects of Wilson's disease, including osteoporosis and rickets and these may be attributable to renal losses of calcium and phosphorus. Osteoarthritis primarily affecting the knees and wrists also occurs in Wilson's disease patients and may involve excess copper deposition in the bone and cartilage.

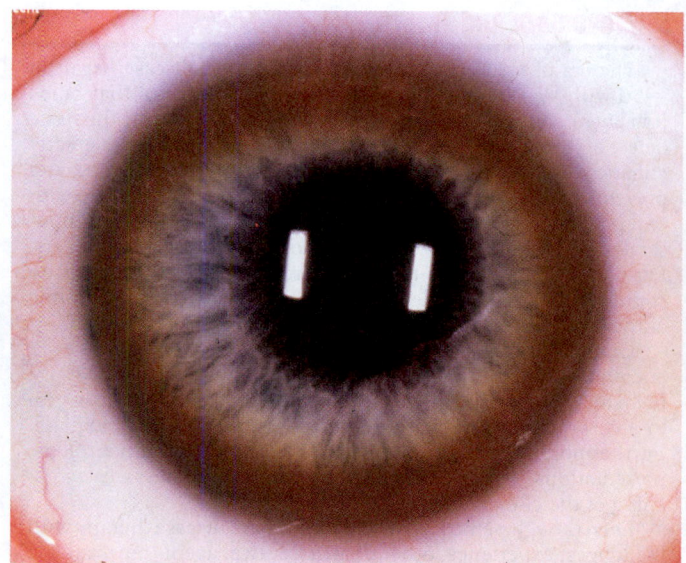

FIGURE 224–1 • Kayser-Fleischer ring in newly diagnosed patient with Wilson's disease.

Diagnosis

The presence of clinical abnormalities described earlier are valuable in the clinical diagnosis of Wilson's disease. Laboratory findings that support the diagnosis include low levels of serum copper and serum ceruloplasmin, elevated hepatic transaminase levels, aminoaciduria, and hemolytic anemia. Incorporation of radiolabeled [64]copper into serum ceruloplasmin, measured as the appearance of copper in the serum after an oral load, is a highly specific diagnostic test; patients with Wilson's disease incorporate very little [64]copper into ceruloplasmin.

Increased urinary excretion of copper (greater than 100 mg per 24 hours) is another easily performed and important diagnostic test for this disorder. Acid-washed (copper free) collection containers should be used. A variation involving serial urine copper measurements is the penicillamine "challenge" in which 500 mg of penicillamine is administered orally after collecting a baseline 24-hr urine specimen. The penicillamine dose is repeated after 12 hours, the midpoint of the second 24-hr urine collection. A several-fold increase in copper excretion in the second collection is suggestive of the diagnosis. Some workers feel that the challenge does not add enormously to diagnostic discrimination compared with the baseline measurement alone.

Percutaneous needle liver biopsy for measurement of hepatic copper remains a "gold standard" albeit an invasive technique for diagnosis. Hepatic copper values greater than 200 mg per gram of dry weight (normal 20 to 50 mg/g dry weight) are characteristic of Wilson's disease. Atomic absorption spectrometry is the preferred method; histochemical stains for copper in a liver biopsy specimen is unreliable.

A Wilson's disease mutation database (*http://www.medgen.med.ualberta.ca/wilson/*) contains more than 200 different mutations reported at the *ATP7B* locus (September 2002). For families in which the mutant alleles have been determined, molecular diagnosis is highly reliable.

In summary, in the absence of formal molecular evidence, the diagnosis of Wilson's disease can be reliably rendered in the presence of two of the following symptoms: (1) positive family history; (2) KF rings; (3) Coombs-negative hemolytic anemia; (4) low serum copper and ceruloplasmin; (5) elevated hepatic copper; (6) increased 24-hr urine copper; and (7) a positive penicillamine challenge.

Rx Prevention and Treatment

The era of successful treatment of Wilson's disease began in 1956 with Walshe's use of penicillamine, a free thiol that binds (chelates) copper. This drug does not formally correct the basic defect of impaired copper excretion in the bile; however, it greatly enhances urinary excretion of copper and thereby corrects and prevents copper overload and its effects. Faithful compliance with oral penicillamine treatment has enabled the good health of thousands of Wilson's disease patients worldwide over the past 45 years. Pyridoxine (vitamin B₆) is usually prescribed concomitantly, to counter the tendency for deficiency of this vitamin to develop during chronic penicillamine administration.

Certain individuals are intolerant of penicillamine however, encountering significant side effects that include nephrotoxicity, hematologic abnormalities, and a distinctive rash, elastosis perforans serpiginosa (which often involves the neck and axillae). Furthermore, in some Wilson's disease patients with neurologic presentations, penicillamine treatment induces paradoxical worsening of the clinical picture.

Even though penicillamine is the Wilson's disease therapy with the longest experience, other pharmaceutical agents are available or in clinical trials that may eventually supplant it as a first-line drug. For example, triethylene tetramine dihydrochloride (Trien) is a suitable alternative chelating agent with a somewhat less significant side effect profile.

Oral zinc acetate has proved highly effective in Wilson' disease, the mechanism of which involves induction of metallothionein synthesis in intestinal epithelial cells; increased metallothionein synthesis results in greater binding of dietary copper and thus decreased absorption. Zinc therapy has particular value in (1) young, presymptomatic patients, (2) patients who are pregnant, given the possible fetal teratogenic effects of other compounds, and (3) as maintenance therapy for patients after their initial "decoppering" is accomplished. Zinc acetate has minimal side effects. The only drawback to its use is the relatively long time (4 to 6 months) needed for restoration of proper copper balance when used as monotherapy in the initial stages of treatment.

Tetrathiomolybdate, a molecule that forms stable tripartite complexes with protein and copper is undergoing clinical trials as therapy for Wilson's disease. This drug both decreases copper absorption and reduces circulating free copper. It is fast acting and can restore normal copper balance within several weeks compared with the several months required with other copper chelators or with zinc.

Regardless of the specific regimen chosen, treatment of Wilson's disease is lifelong. Noncompliance eventually leads to fulminant liver failure.

Liver transplantation is a rare consideration in Wilson's disease because the condition is typically responsive to medical therapy. This is generally only necessary when delayed diagnosis or poor compliance results in irreversible hepatic damage.

Apart from pharmacologic treatment, there are several other important considerations in Wilson's disease treatment. These include dietary restriction of shellfish and liver, both copper-rich foods. The major sources of patients' drinking water should be tested for copper concentration and avoided if levels approach 1.3 mg/L, which is the current maximum contaminant level goal (MCLG) established by the U.S. Environmental Protection Agency. The MCLG for copper in drinking water is set as a concentration at which no known or expected adverse health effects occur and for which there is an adequate margin of safety.

In newly diagnosed patients, there is also frequent need for speech therapy, physical or occupational therapy, and psychiatric counseling.

Wilson's Disease Heterozygotes

There is some debate about the risk for copper overload faced by individuals who are heterozygous for Wilson's disease. Even though Wilson's disease is a classic autosomal recessive trait, that is, requiring two mutant alleles at the *ATP7B* locus for expression of the disease, a recent report from the National Academy of Sciences suggested that heterozygous Wilson's disease carriers could represent a relatively sensitive population in terms of copper overload, particularly when dietary or drinking water copper exposures are higher than usual. Abnormally increased urinary copper excretion has been documented among some siblings of Wilson's disease patients, although genetic confirmation of carrier or noncarrier status for these individuals was not available. Further patient and family studies are needed to formally address these questions.

Prognosis

The prognosis in Wilson's disease is generally favorable; current therapeutic approaches can prevent or reverse most of the significant clinical signs and symptoms, including the KF rings. However, if treatment is stopped, irreversible and potentially fatal liver damage inevitably occurs.

Future Directions

Gene therapy for Wilson disease is a theoretical possibility. Because the Wilson copper transporter is expressed most prominently and functions most critically in the liver, this organ could be specifically targeted using adenoviral, adeno-associated viral, or replication-deficient retroviral vectors. This contrasts with the situation in Menkes' disease, a copper transport disorder in which the normal gene product is highly similar to Wilson's, but for which the target organ would be brain.

Hepatocyte transfer is an alternative to adenoviral, adeno-associated viral, and retroviral-mediated gene transfer, and is gaining credibility for treatment of liver-specific metabolic disorders through a process termed "therapeutic liver repopulation."

SUGGESTED READINGS

Brewer GJ: Recognition, diagnosis, and management of Wilson's disease. Proc Soc Exp Biol Med 2000;223:39–46. *Review emphasizing preference for long-term zinc therapy.*
Committee on Copper in Drinking Water, National Research Council: Copper in Drinking Water. Washington, DC, National Academies Press, 2000. *Review of the data to support EPA guidelines.*
Ferenci P, Caca K, Loudianos G, et al: Diagnosis and phenotypic classification of Wilson disease. Liver 2003;23:139–142. *Consensus report on genetic diagnosis and genotype-phenotype correlations.*
Mercer JFB: The molecular basis of copper-transport diseases. Trends Mol Med 2001;7:64–69. *A review of the relationship between genetics and pathophysiology.*
Sutcliffe RP, Maguire DD, Muiesan P, et al: Liver transplantation for Wilson's disease: long-term results and quality-of-life assessment. Transplantation 2003;75:1003–1006. *Liver transplantation provided excellent results in 21 of 24 patients.*

225 IRON OVERLOAD (HEMOCHROMATOSIS)

Bruce R. Bacon

Hereditary hemochromatosis (HH) is a common inherited disorder of iron metabolism. The genetic abnormality that is responsible for most patients with typical HH is found homozygous in about 1 in 250 persons of Northern European descent. It is characterized by an increase in iron absorption from the upper gastrointestinal tract with subsequent tissue iron deposition in parenchymal cells of the liver, heart, pancreas, joints, and endocrine organs. The autosomal recessive inheritance pattern of HH was clearly shown in the 1970s and the gene responsible for most cases of HH was identified in 1996 by investigators using a positional cloning technique. The gene is called *HFE* and encodes for a novel major histocompatibility complex (MHC) class 1–like molecule that modulates cellular iron transport by binding with transferrin receptor (TfR). Recent prospective population studies have demonstrated that only about 50% of patients who are homozygous for the major mutation found in *HFE* (called C282Y) have evidence of phenotypic expression of iron overload, and only a small percentage (<10%) go on to develop tissue damage from excess iron deposition. These studies have changed modern thinking about HH and must be considered when evaluating patients for the disease in a physician's office, and when developing national health policy regarding screening for this genetic disorder. The discovery of *HFE* has had a tremendous impact in a number of areas. The ability to accurately diagnose disorders of iron overload has been strengthened, family screening is improved, and the evaluation of patients with other forms of liver disease complicated by moderate to severe iron overload is possible. Furthermore, with the discovery of *HFE*, a considerable new body of knowledge regarding the mechanisms of iron absorption has been identified, both in the normal situation and in the pathologic condition seen when *HFE* mutations are present.

Classification of Iron Overload Syndromes

The term *hereditary hemochromatosis* is usually reserved to describe an inherited disorder of iron metabolism that leads to progressive iron deposition in parenchymal cells of the liver, pancreas, and heart. Previously used terms of *primary hemochromatosis* or *idiopathic hemochromatosis* are no longer used because the genetic basis of the disorder has been clarified. When HH is fully developed, organ and tissue damage occur and organ structure and function are impaired. The most common form of HH is caused by homozygosity for the C282Y mutation in the *HFE* gene. However, other inherited forms of iron overload not caused by *HFE* mutations have recently been identified. These disorders appear to be rare and their clinical significance is yet to be determined. Also, many patients who are homozygous for C282Y have no evidence of iron overload. With these issues in mind, four stages of HH have been described:

1. Genetic predisposition with no phenotypic abnormality
2. Iron overload (approximately 2 to 5 g) but without symptoms
3. Iron overload with mild or early symptoms
4. Iron overload with organ damage such as cirrhosis

A classification system that has been used for HH and the other various iron overload syndromes and disorders is provided in Table 225–1.

Genetics and Pathophysiology of Hemochromatosis

Since the classic linkage studies of Simon and colleagues in the mid-1970s, it has been known that the gene for hemochromatosis was located in the human leukocyte antigen (HLA) region on chromosome 6. In 1996, a team of molecular geneticists using a positional cloning technique identified a candidate gene for HH, which is now called *HFE*. *HFE* codes for a novel MHC class 1–like molecule, which, like all MHC proteins, requires interaction with β_2-microglobulin for normal presentation on the cell surface. Two missense mutations were initially identified in *HFE*; one results in a change of cysteine at posi-

tion 282 to tyrosine (Cys282 → Tyr, C282Y); the second results in a change of histidine at position 63 to aspartate (His63 → Asp, H63D). Two other mutations have recently been identified in *HFE* but their frequency is low and their clinical impact appears to be limited. In the original study, 83% of typical phenotypic HH patients were found to be homozygous for the C282Y mutation. Several other studies from around the world in predominantly white populations demonstrated that, of patients with typical hemochromatosis, about 85 to 90% were homozygous for C282Y. Thus, about 10 to 15% of patients with typical HH have some other reason other than C282Y homozygosity for their iron overload. A recent study from Italy has identified a new inherited abnormality of iron overload with no mutations in *HFE*, and studies have shown that mutations in the gene for TfR-2 can result in iron overload that is typical of hemochromatosis.

Immunohistochemical studies have shown that HFE protein is found in the crypt cells of the duodenum associated with β_2-microglobulin and Tfr-1. Current theories are that HFE protein facilitates Tfr-dependent iron uptake into crypt cells in the normal situation. With mutant HFE protein, this ability is lost and there is a relative iron deficiency in duodenal crypt cells. As duodenal crypt cells mature and become villal cells migrating to the villus tip, this relative deficiency of iron results in an increase in the synthesis and expression of a villous iron transport protein called *divalent metal iron transporter 1* (DMT-1, also called DCT-1 or Nramp-2). This transport protein is responsible for dietary iron absorption in the villal cells of the proximal small intestine. Upregulation of DMT-1 expression has been found in an *HFE*-deficient mouse model and in humans with HH, providing supportive evidence for this pathophysiologic mechanism of an inappropriate increase in iron absorption in HH. Once iron transport is increased at the enterocyte luminal surface, then there appears to be a similar compensatory increase in iron transport at the basolateral surface of the enterocyte with an increase in the expression of ferroportin, a newly described membrane-bound iron transport protein. This results in the reductive transfer of iron to the portal circulation where it is avidly bound to diferric transferrin with a high degree of saturation of available iron-binding sites. Excess iron (both transferrin-bound and non–transferrin-bound) is avidly taken up by hepatocytes and stored. Iron stores increase to the point where iron-induced oxidative damage occurs, resulting in cell injury and cell necrosis with phagocytosis by Kupffer cells. Iron-laden Kupffer cells become activated and produce profibrogenic cytokines (e.g., transforming growth factor-β, platelet-derived growth factor), which stimulate stellate cells to synthesize excess collagen and other matrix proteins. Increased fibrosis and then cirrhosis result.

Clinical Manifestations

Several symptoms and clinical findings have been identified in patients with fully established HH and all physicians should be aware of these symptoms and findings. These are summarized in Tables 225–2 and 225–3. Table 225–4 summarizes the typical laboratory findings found in symptomatic and in asymptomatic patients with HH. Recent series have identified that many patients who are C282Y homozygotes are now coming to medical attention without any symptoms or findings because they are being identified by family screening studies, population surveys, or for an evaluation of abnormal iron studies found on routine blood chemistry testing. It is ideal to identify patients who have some phenotypic expression with abnormal iron studies but who do not have evidence of organ damage. A recently reported large population screening study of more than 40,000 ambulatory patients evaluated in San Diego has shown that approximately half of C282Y homozygotes fail to show evidence of phenotypic expression and fewer than 10% of individuals who are C282Y homozygotes actually have signs and symptoms of the disease.

Diagnosis

Because patients with a genetic abnormality can be identified before having evidence of phenotypic expression, the whole discussion of the diagnosis of HH has undergone a change. The role of liver biopsy has lessened considerably with the advent of genetic testing. Nonetheless, some general principles should be acknowledged. If the diagnosis of HH is considered, blood tests including fasting

Table 225–1 • IRON OVERLOAD SYNDROMES

Hereditary hemochromatosis
  HFE-related
    C282Y/C282Y
    C282Y/H63D
    Other mutations
  Non–*HFE*-related
Acquired iron overload
  Anemia caused by ineffective erythropoiesis
    β-thalassemia
    Sideroblastic anemia
    Aplastic anemia
    Pyruvate kinase deficiency
    Pyridoxine-responsive anemia
  Liver disease
    Alcoholic liver disease
    Chronic viral hepatitis B and C
    Porphyria cutanea tarda
    Post-portocaval shunting
  Transfusional and parenteral iron overload
    Red blood cell transfusions
    Iron dextran injections
    Associated with long-term hemodialysis
  Dietary iron overload
Miscellaneous
  Iron overload in sub-Saharan Africa
  Neonatal iron overload
  Aceruloplasminemia
  Congenital atransferrinemia

Table 225–2 • SYMPTOMS IN PATIENTS WITH HEREDITARY HEMOCHROMATOSIS

Asymptomatic
  Abnormal serum iron studies on routine screening chemistry panel
  Evaluation of abnormal liver tests
  Identified by family screening
  Identified by population screening
Nonspecific, systemic symptoms
  Weakness
  Fatigue
  Lethargy
  Apathy
  Weight loss
Specific, organ-related symptoms
  Abdominal pain (hepatomegaly)
  Arthralgias (arthritis)
  Diabetes (pancreas)
  Amenorrhea (cirrhosis)
  Loss of libido, impotence (pituitary, cirrhosis)
  Congestive heart failure (heart)
  Arrhythmias (heart)

Table 225–3 • PHYSICAL FINDINGS IN PATIENTS WITH HEREDITARY HEMOCHROMATOSIS

Asymptomatic
  No physical findings
  Hepatomegaly
Symptomatic
  Liver
    Hepatomegaly
    Cutaneous stigmata of chronic liver disease
    Splenomegaly
    Liver failure: ascites, encephalopathy
  Joints
    Arthritis
    Joint swelling
  Heart
    Dilated cardiomyopathy
    Congestive heart failure
  Skin
    Increased pigmentation
  Endocrine
    Testicular atrophy
    Hypogonadism
    Hypothyroidism

Table 225–4 • LABORATORY FINDINGS IN PATIENTS WITH HEREDITARY HEMOCHROMATOSIS

MEASUREMENTS	NORMAL SUBJECTS	PATIENTS WITH HEREDITARY HEMOCHROMATOSIS	
		Asymptomatic	Symptomatic
BLOOD (FASTING)			
Serum iron level (μg/dL)	60–180	150–280	180–300
Serum transferrin level (mg/dL)	220–410	200–280	200–300
Transferrin saturation(%)	20–45	45–100	80–100
Serum ferritin level (ng/mL)			
Men	20–200	150–1000	500–6000
Women	15–150	120–1000	500–6000
GENETIC (*HFE* MUTATION ANALYSIS)			
C282Y/C282Y	wt/wt	C282Y/C282Y	C282Y/C282Y
C282Y/H63D*	wt/wt	C282Y/H63D	C282Y/H63D
LIVER			
Hepatic iron concentration			
μg/g dry weight	300–1500	2000–10,000	8000–30,000
μmol/g dry weight	5–27	36–179	140–550
Hepatic iron index†	<1.0	1.0 to >1.9	>1.9
Liver histology			
Perls' Prussian blue stain	0, 1+	2+ to 4+	3+, 4+

*Compound heterozygote.
†Hepatic iron index (HII) is calculated by dividing the hepatic iron concentration (in μmol/g dry weight) by the age of the patient (in years). With increased knowledge of genetic testing results in patients with iron overload, the specificity of HII has diminished.

transferrin saturation (TS; serum iron ÷ transferrin or total iron binding capacity × 100%) and ferritin levels should be obtained. In patients with symptoms (see Table 225–2), both of these values are elevated; however, TS is typically the earliest phenotypic marker of HH and may be elevated in young individuals with normal ferritin levels. Serum ferritin can sometimes be elevated in other conditions such as certain cancers and in chronic inflammatory disorders in which there is no evidence of iron overload. Furthermore, in patients with other types of liver disease such as chronic hepatitis C, nonalcoholic steatohepatitis, and alcoholic liver disease, ferritin levels can be elevated in as many as half of the patients studied. Thus, ferritin is relatively sensitive but not specific for iron overload in the presence of these other disorders. The development of a widely available genetic test has contributed to better characterization of patients with underlying liver disease and abnormal serum iron studies.

In the past, if either an elevated TS or ferritin level was identified, a liver biopsy would be performed to establish a diagnosis using histochemical iron stains (Perls' Prussian blue stain) and biochemical determination of hepatic iron concentration (HIC) with calculation of the hepatic iron index (HII). The HII is the ratio of the patient's HIC in μmol/g dry weight divided by the patient's age in years. Previously, when the HII was greater than 1.9, the diagnosis of HH was established. Recent studies with genetic testing have shown that many (>50%) HH patients may have an HII less than 1.9. Thus, the role of the HII is less important in the diagnosis of HH than it was previously.

Currently, when abnormal iron studies are identified, it is reasonable to proceed to genetic testing. If individuals are C282Y homozygotes or compound heterozygotes (C282Y/H63D), liver biopsy is reserved for those patients with elevated liver enzymes or ferritin levels greater than 1000 ng/mL (Fig. 225–1). Several studies have shown that increased fibrosis or cirrhosis is not seen in HH patients when ferritin levels are less than 1000 ng/mL or when liver enzymes are normal. Accordingly, as genetic testing has become more available, liver biopsy is less necessary.

When liver biopsy is performed, iron deposition is found preferentially in a periportal (acinar zone 1) region of the hepatic lobule with a decrease in gradient in acinar zones 2 and 3. With significant iron loading, sinusoidal lining cell (Kupffer cell) iron deposition can be identified and iron can be found in bile duct cells and in fibrous tissue in portal tracts or septa. In patients with secondary iron overload related to alcoholic liver disease or chronic viral hepatitis, iron deposition is typically in Kupffer cells as well as in hepatocytes and is in a panlobular (as opposed to a periportal) distribution. Histologic evaluation of iron-staining patterns provides complementary information to traditional biochemical testing for iron overload along with the available genetic information.

Rx Treatment

Even though there have been advances in the molecular and cell biologic understanding of HH and the impact of *HFE* mutation analysis on diagnosis has been significant, the treatment of HH remains simple, inexpensive, and safe. Patients should have therapeutic phlebotomy of 500 mL of whole blood (approximately 200 to 250 mg of iron, depending on the hemoglobin concentration) done on a weekly basis if tolerated. Therapeutic phlebotomy should be performed until iron-limited erythropoiesis develops, identified by failure of the hemoglobin level and hematocrit to recover before the next phlebotomy. It is reasonable to monitor transferrin saturation and ferritin levels periodically (every 3 months) to predict the return to normal of iron stores and to provide a means of encouragement to patients who are undergoing phlebotomy. Therapeutic phlebotomy should be continued until the transferrin saturation is less than 50% and the ferritin level

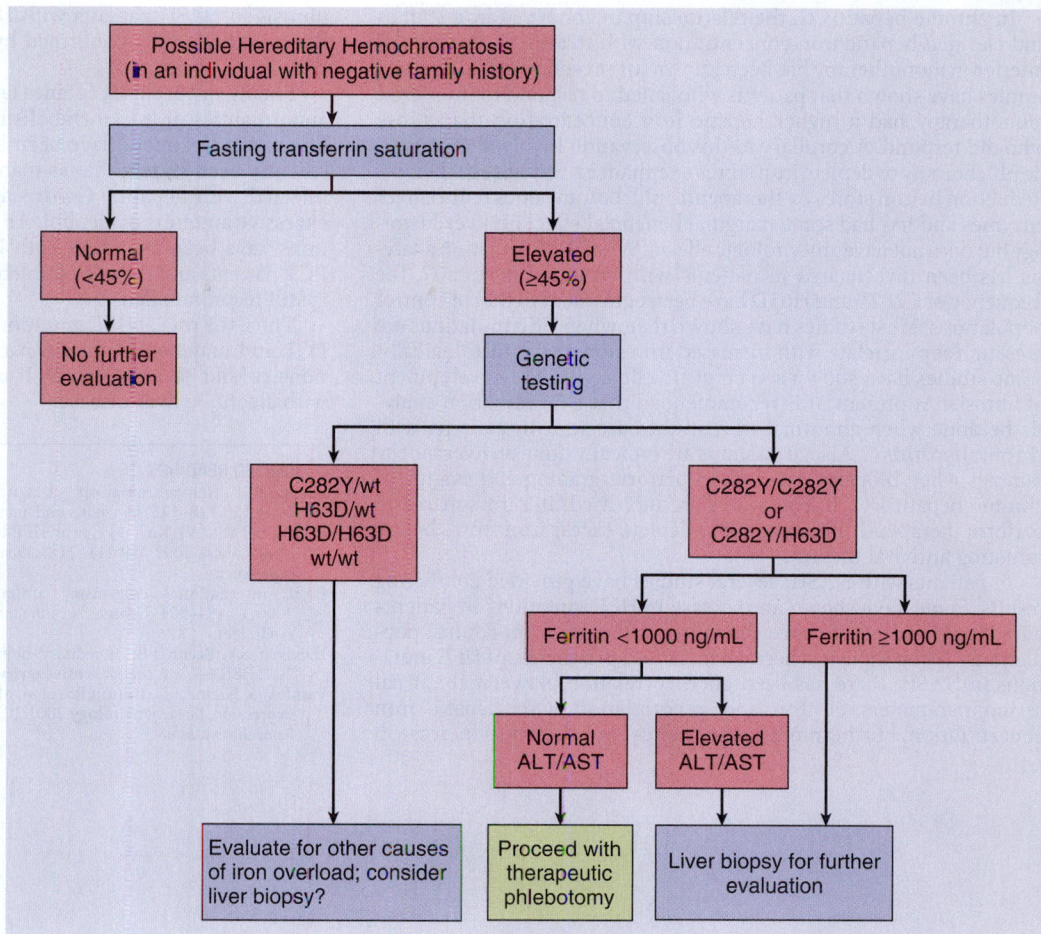

FIGURE 225–1 • Proposed algorithm for evaluation of possible hereditary hemochromatosis in a person with a negative family history.

is less than 50 ng/mL. It is not necessary for patients to become anemic or iron deficient, just depleted of their excess iron stores. Once the initial therapeutic phlebotomy has been completed, most patients require maintenance phlebotomy of 1 unit of blood removed every 2 to 3 months. This requirement is derived empirically with an intent to maintain transferrin saturation at less than 50% and ferritin at less than 50 ng/mL.

With successful iron depletion, patients have an improved sense of well-being, right upper quadrant abdominal pain dissipates, liver test results improve, and diabetes may be easier to manage. Established cirrhosis, arthropathy, and testicular atrophy generally do not improve.

Family Screening

Once an HH proband is recognized, all first-degree relatives should be offered testing. In the past, HLA-haplotyping was performed, but now *HFE* mutation analysis is recommended along with determination of fasting transferrin saturation and ferritin. In probands with children, *HFE* mutation analysis is performed in the spouse to accurately predict the genotype in the child. If the spouse has either mutation, then testing of the child is necessary, although the value and availability of genetic testing in children is debated. If an adult relative of a C282Y homozygote is identified, and is either a C282Y homozygote or a compound heterozygote, and if blood iron studies are abnormal, then a presumptive diagnosis can be made and therapeutic phlebotomy can be initiated using the guidelines already discussed.

Population Screening

Because HH is a common disorder, with a well-described treatment and with a long latent period (i.e., time before disease occurs), it has been suggested that HH would be an ideal disorder to undergo population screening by genetic testing. However, recent studies showing a less than expected phenotypic expression with a decreased number of patients with clinical manifestations of iron-mediated disease being identified have raised questions about this recommendation. This issue may be resolved over the next several years in the context of a large National Institutes of Health–sponsored screening study under way in North America. When screening for iron overload as opposed to screening for *HFE*-linked HH, fasting transferrin saturation should be performed. In this situation, when abnormal iron studies are identified and the patient does not have a mutation in *HFE*, liver biopsy should be considered to clarify the situation relative to iron stores.

HFE Mutation Analysis in Patients with Liver Disease

Many patients with liver disease have abnormalities in serum parameters of iron metabolism. These abnormalities are more commonly seen in patients with hepatocellular liver diseases than in those with cholestatic liver diseases. Several clinical studies have shown that approximately 50% of patients with alcoholic liver disease, chronic viral hepatitis C, and nonalcoholic steatohepatitis (NASH) have abnormalities in serum iron studies. Usually this is an elevation in serum ferritin but occasionally elevated transferrin saturation can be seen as well. When liver biopsy is performed, increased iron deposits can be seen, usually in a panlobular distribution with iron in both hepatocytes and sinusoidal lining cells (Kupffer cells). Hepatic iron concentrations may be slightly increased or normal. When *HFE* mutations have been evaluated in patients with alcoholic liver disease, there has been no increased incidence of either C282Y or H63D (either heterozygote or homozygote) compared with control populations. Furthermore, there was no increase in *HFE* mutations in patients with alcoholic liver disease who had an increased amount of fibrosis. Thus, the abnormal iron studies frequently seen in patients with alcoholic liver disease are most likely due to mechanisms other than mutations in *HFE*.

Metabolic Diseases

In chronic hepatitis C, the relationship of abnormal iron studies and elevated hepatic iron concentration with treatment response to interferon monotherapy has been known for several years. Numerous studies have shown that patients who failed to respond to interferon monotherapy had a higher hepatic iron concentration than those who did respond. A corollary to this observation involved therapeutic phlebotomy to deplete iron stores to enhance a response to therapy. Reduction in iron stores by therapeutic phlebotomy does reduce liver enzymes and has had some marginal beneficial effect on liver histology but does not have any virologic effects. When *HFE* mutation analysis has been investigated in patients with chronic hepatitis C, the frequency of C282Y and H63D have been equivalent to that of control populations. Most studies have shown that, when *HFE* mutations are present, they correlate with increased iron stores seen histologically. Some studies have shown a synergistic effect with the development of fibrosis. At present, it is recommended that *HFE* mutation analysis be done when abnormal iron studies are seen in patients with chronic hepatitis C. Also, iron stains are typically done on liver biopsy samples when biopsies are done to perform grading and staging of chronic hepatitis C. If iron stores are increased, it is reasonable to perform therapeutic phlebotomy to deplete excess iron stores before initiating antiviral therapy.

In patients with NASH, several studies have provided conflicting results. Some have shown an increase in *HFE* mutations in patients with NASH and others have shown no difference from control populations. When there has been an increased prevalence of *HFE* mutations in NASH, there has been good correlation between abnormal serum parameters of iron and a correlation with hepatic iron concentration. Furthermore, some studies have shown an increase in

fibrosis in NASH patients with *HFE* mutations. These observations have not been fully confirmed by others and more investigation in this area is necessary.

Finally, in porphyria cutanea tarda (PCT), the relationship between abnormalities of iron metabolism and the role of therapeutic phlebotomy in treatment have been known for many years. Also, it has recently been shown that as many as 70% of patients with PCT are infected with hepatitis C virus and many patients with PCT drink excessive amounts of alcohol. An increased prevalence of *HFE* mutations have been shown in both European and American studies of PCT patients and the use of phlebotomy to deplete excess iron stores is still recommended.

Thus, the role of *HFE* mutation analysis is of value in patients with PCT and may be of value in patients with chronic hepatitis C and nonalcoholic steatohepatitis. It is probably not of value in patients with alcoholic liver disease.

SUGGESTED READINGS

Bacon BR: Hemochromatosis: Diagnosis and management. Gastroenterology 2001;120:718–725. *Diagnosis and management of patients with hemochromatosis.*

Beutler E, Felitti VJ, Koziol JA, et al: HFE hereditary haemochromatosis mutation in the USA. Lancet 2002;359:211–218. *About 50% of C282Y homozygotes have phenotypic expression.*

EASL international consensus conference on haemochromatosis. J Hepatol 2000;33:485–504. *Consensus conference describing the classification of iron overload syndromes.*

Harrison SA, Bacon BR: Hereditary hemochromatosis: Update for 2003. J Hepatol 2003;38:14–23. *A comprehensive review.*

Parkkila S, Niemela O, Britton RS, et al: Molecular aspects of iron absorption and HFE expression. Gastroenterology 2001;121:1489–1496. *Pathophysiologic mechanisms in hemochromatosis.*

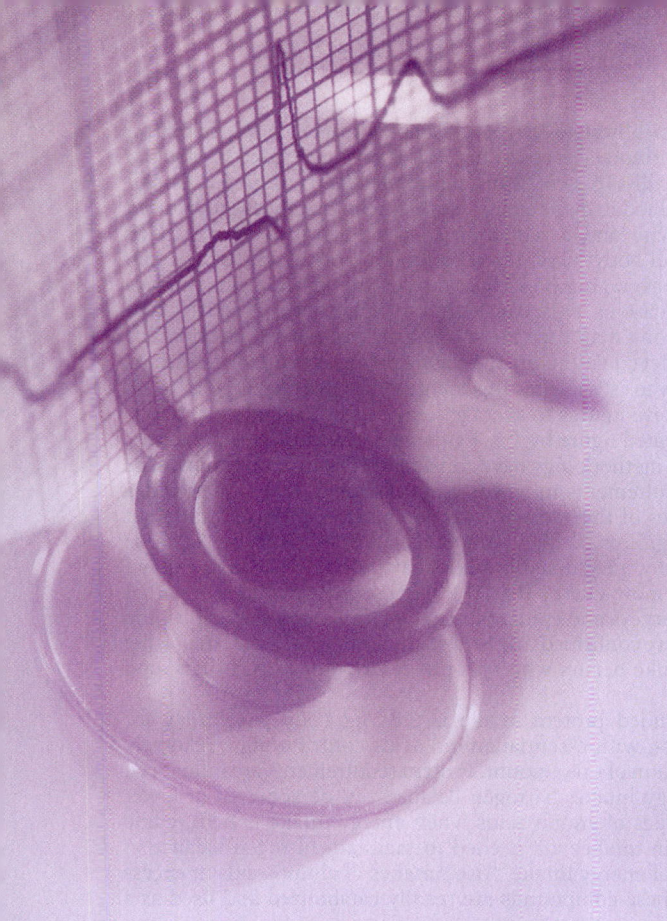

part XVII

Nutritional Diseases

226 NUTRITION IN THE PREVENTION AND TREATMENT OF DISEASE

Cheryl L. Rock

Definition

Nutrition is the process by which the human body utilizes food for the production of energy, for the maintenance of health, for growth, and for the normal functioning of every organ and tissue. Clinical nutrition is focused on the relationship between nutrition and the development and treatment of human disease. Nutrition is an interdisciplinary field of study that is built on a foundation of biomedical and behavioral sciences. Evidence that forms the basis of knowledge in clinical nutrition includes the disease-relevant biochemistry, metabolism, and activities of nutrients and other dietary factors within the tissues and cells; the bioavailability and regulation of nutrients as influenced by disease pathophysiology; the eating patterns and behaviors of the targeted individuals or groups; results from observational and analytic epidemiologic studies; and clinical trials.

Nutrients and other constituents of food constitute a major component of the environmental influences that contribute to risk for disease. However, not all persons exposed to the same nutritional or dietary factors will develop the associated disease. Differential genetic susceptibility is believed to explain the variations in response and outcome among individuals with similar dietary intakes, and the interaction between nutritional and genetic factors is currently an area of intense interest and research.

Principles and General Dietary Recommendations

Constituents of the diet that are essential for sustaining life include water, energy (quantified as kilocalories or kilojoules), certain amino acids, essential fatty acids, vitamins, and minerals (including electrolytes) (Table 226–1). Other dietary constituents, such as carbohydrate and sources of nonspecific nitrogen, must be consumed in amounts sufficient to permit normal metabolic activities and to allow biosynthesis of other compounds that are essential for normal function but can be produced endogenously. Within the past few decades, it has become increasingly clear that several dietary constituents that are not essential nutrients, such as fiber and various phytochemicals (biologically active compounds in plants), may contribute a great deal to disease prevention because of their biologic activities and influence on molecular and physiologic functions.

Major components of energy expenditure include the resting energy expenditure, which is the cost of basic physiologic and involuntary functions (typically 60 to 75% of total expenditure); the thermic effect of food (10% of total expenditure); and energy expended in physical activity (typically 15 to 30% of total expenditure). Aging is associated with a reduction in the energy requirement, mainly due to reduced physical activity and a reduction in the quantity and metabolic activity of lean body mass. Energy requirements of adults are often estimated as averaging 35 kcal/kg/day or calculated using various prediction equations, with consideration of age, level of activity, and other conditions that alter metabolic rate (e.g., fever, injury). The Harris-Benedict equations are the classic predictive equations that are used clinically to estimate resting energy requirements (Table 226–2). To convert these figures to average total energy expenditure, multiply the calculated figure by 1.3. Evidence from studies using doubly labeled water methodology have considerably refined our knowledge of energy requirements in recent years. This methodology provides valid measures of the average total energy expenditure in different age and sex groups of free-living subjects (Table 226–3). In these studies, healthy, weight-stable adults have been observed to expend considerably more energy than the average energy intakes reported in national surveys and epidemiologic or clinical research. Thus, the newer data have confirmed that a substantial amount of underreporting of energy intake occurs when people describe or record their food consumption.

Recommended protein intake is 0.8 g/kg body weight/day for healthy adults, with essential amino acids contributing a relatively small proportion of this amount. Protein requirements are influenced by total energy intake. Nitrogen balance can be achieved at lower levels of intakes of amino acids when energy intake is high, while higher protein intakes are needed to maintain nitrogen balance at lower levels of energy intake. Also, intakes of amino acids in excess of need for these compounds are readily catabolized and used as a

---

Table 226–2 • THE HARRIS-BENEDICT EQUATIONS FOR ESTIMATING RESTING ENERGY EXPENDITURE (REE) IN ADULTS*

For women: REE (kcal/day) = 655 + 9.56 (weight) + 1.85 (height) − 4.68 (age)
For men: REE (kcal/day) = 66.5 + 13.75 (weight) + 5.0 (height) − 6.75 (age)

*Weight is in kilograms, height is in centimeters, and age is in years.

Table 226–1 • ESSENTIAL NUTRIENTS

Water	Riboflavin
Energy (from carbohydrate, protein, and fat)	Thiamin
Essential fatty acids:	Vitamin B_6
Linoleic acid	Vitamin B_{12}
α-Linolenic acid	Biotin
Amino acids:	Pantothenic acid
Histidine	Minerals:
Isoleucine	Calcium
Leucine	Phosphorus
Lysine	Magnesium
Methionine	Iron
Phenylalanine	Zinc
Threonine	Copper
Tryptophan	Manganese
Valine	Iodine
Vitamins:	Selenium
Vitamin A	Molybdenum
Vitamin D	Chromium
Vitamin E	Ultratrace elements
Vitamin K	Electrolytes:
Vitamin C	Sodium
Folate	Potassium
Niacin	Chloride

Table 226–3 • AVERAGE TOTAL ENERGY EXPENDITURE ACROSS AGE AND SEX GROUPS FROM A META-ANALYSIS OF 574 DOUBLY LABELED WATER MEASUREMENTS

AGE GROUP (yr)	N	TOTAL ENERGY EXPENDITURE (kcal/day)
FEMALES		
1–6	21	1316
7–12	24	1914
13–17	26	2727
18–29	89	2488
30–39	76	2392
40–64	47	2345
65–74	24	2057
>75	12	1459
MALES		
1–6	29	1459
7–12	32	2345
13–17	31	3373
18–29	56	3301
30–39	36	3421
40–64	15	2751
65–74	22	2637
>75	34	2201

Adapted from Johnson RK, Coward-McKenzie D: Energy requirement methodology. *In* Coulston AM, Rock CL, Monsen ER (eds): Nutrition in the Prevention and Treatment of Disease. San Diego, Academic Press, 2001, pp 31–42.

source of energy. The amount of protein consumed by most adults in the United States is typically well in excess of requirements (i.e., >50%). Thus inadequate protein intake in noninstitutionalized adults is unlikely to occur unless total food intake is limited, and in those instances, inadequacies of both energy and protein are usually present (Chapter 228).

Essential micronutrients (vitamins, minerals) and other constituents of food can exhibit different biologic activities at physiologic levels of intake (i.e., that can be provided from the diet) compared with pharmacologic dosages. Further, most biologically active constituents of the diet, including essential micronutrients, can promote serious adverse effects at excessive levels of administration or intake (Chapter 231). Nearly half of Americans report use of dietary supplements in national surveys. There are some circumstances in which vitamin and mineral dietary supplements are likely to be beneficial; for example, in a patient with a very limited diet, or in a patient with increased requirements that cannot be met by the diet. In those instances, patients should be monitored for compliance with dosage and regularity of use as prescribed. Currently, many foods in the United States are fortified with vitamins and minerals, as a result of Food and Drug Administration mandates or due to the manufacturer's motivation to produce a product that attracts more buyers. Fortification is the addition during manufacturing of a nutrient that is not normally present in the food. For example, all cereal-grain products in the United States are now fortified with iron, folate, niacin, riboflavin, and thiamin, and refined cereal-grain products have become an important source of iron and folate in the U.S. diet. Many foods in the United States also are calcium-fortified, so meeting the calcium requirement is increasingly feasible even when dairy foods are not consumed.

Adequate intakes of nutrients and other beneficial dietary factors can be obtained from an infinite number of combinations of foods, which is evident in the variety of cuisines that sustain the diverse cultures and populations of the world. Although life stage and the presence of disease are important considerations in defining nutrient needs, a healthy diet is generally one that includes a variety of food types (e.g., vegetables and fruit, grains or other starchy foods, protein-rich foods, sources of essential lipids, and a good source of calcium such as dairy foods). No one food or one food type provides all essential nutrients, and each food type provides a different set of nutrients, but together they can meet nutritional needs. Translated into food choices, a healthy daily diet is one that includes six to 11 servings of bread, cereal, rice, or pasta; three to five servings of vegetables; two to four servings of fruit; two to three servings (or a total of 5 to 9 ounces) of meat, poultry, fish, dried beans, or nuts; and two to three servings of milk, yogurt, or cheese. The range of servings allows for the expected interindividual variability in needs due to different levels of energy and amounts of food that are consumed across age groups and activity levels. With these guidelines, a "serving" for cereal-grain products, vegetables, and fruit is defined most commonly as 1/2 cup, and dairy food servings are defined as 1 cup (milk, yogurt) and 1 ounce (cheese). These general guidelines for good health are based on the typical U.S. dietary pattern, but variations in that pattern also can be nutritionally adequate. For example, a vegetarian diet that excludes meat, poultry, and fish but includes dairy products will still typically provide adequate high-quality protein and all essential micronutrients. A vegan diet (one that excludes all animal foods) needs to include fortified foods, such as fortified soy milk, or dietary supplements to ensure adequate intakes of vitamin B_{12}, calcium, and iron.

Strong evidence for the relationship between diet and risk for major diseases also influences how these general guidelines should be translated into specific food choices. For example, low-fat (rather than regular high-fat) dairy foods are recommended for adults and children older than 2 years of age. Fish, lean meat and poultry, legumes, and nuts are healthier choices than high-saturated-fat sources of protein (high-fat meat and poultry). In general, diets that consist of greater amounts of vegetables, fruit, grains and grain products, legumes, and low-fat dairy foods are associated with lower all-cause mortality rates and lower risk for major diseases, including cardiovascular disease, hypertension, type 2 diabetes mellitus, and many cancers. Also, a high-fiber, reduced-fat diet is low in energy density, which contributes to lower risk for obesity (Chapter 233) and may help to promote weight maintenance rather than weight gain throughout adulthood. Fat is twice as energy-dense as carbohydrate and protein (9, 4, and 4 kcal/g, respectively), and the inclusion of high-fiber foods reduces the energy density of the diet.

Nutrition and Disease

Diet and food choices, and diet modification if indicated, can be a critical component of disease prevention (primary, secondary, and tertiary), an important aspect of the management of a condition or disease, or the primary treatment for some diseases. Dietary intake or nutritional status may be altered as a result of the disease itself or by the treatment modalities that are utilized, such as surgical treatments or medical management, including medications. In the patient who is ill, inadequate intake or altered nutritional needs must be managed with dietary or nutritional interventions to prevent malnutrition or nutrient inadequacies, which can contribute to overall morbidity and mortality associated with the disease or treatments.

CARDIOVASCULAR DISEASE, HYPERTENSION, AND STROKE. Nutritional factors contribute to the prevention and treatment of vascular diseases through several mechanisms. Nutritional factors are important determinants of dyslipidemia, influence blood clotting function and blood pressure, and contribute to other biologic and biochemical mechanisms involved in atherosclerosis and vascular endothelial damage (e.g., oxidative stress, toxic effects of homocysteine). Nutritional guidelines to reduce risk for cardiovascular disease aim to maintain a healthy body weight, a desirable blood cholesterol and lipoprotein profile, and a desirable blood pressure.

The specific dietary pattern recommended to promote a desirable lipoprotein profile is one with limited intake of foods rich in saturated fatty acids (<7% of energy) and cholesterol (<200 mg/day), which are replaced with grains and unsaturated fatty acids from vegetables, fish, legumes, and nuts. Dietary factors that increase low-density lipoprotein (LDL) cholesterol concentration include saturated fatty acids (sources are meat, poultry, dairy fat, coconut, cocoa butter, and palm oil) and *trans*-unsaturated fatty acids (sources are hydrogenated vegetable fat and commercial baked goods). Dietary cholesterol (sources are egg yolk, organ meats, and animal flesh or fat) also can raise LDL cholesterol, but the effect is small compared to that of saturated fatty acids. Dietary factors that lower LDL cholesterol include unsaturated fatty acids, with monounsaturated fatty acids (sources are olive and canola oil, nuts, and avocado) having the most beneficial effects on the lipoprotein profile. Soluble fiber (sources are oats, vegetables, and fruit) and soy protein (at a dosage of 20 to 50 g/day) also lower LDL cholesterol concentration. Obesity and increased carbohydrate intake in the patient with glucose intolerance or uncontrolled type 2 diabetes mellitus are the major nutritional factors that increase plasma triglyceride concentrations. Foods and dietary constituents that are associated with lower risk for cardiovascular disease include vegetables and fruits, which provide antioxidants and folate in addition to fiber, and plant sterols. Dietary recommendations for the treatment of high blood cholesterol are summarized in Table 226–4.

Several nutritional factors contribute to the maintenance of normal blood pressure, and specific guidelines for management of hypertension have been established. In addition to maintaining a healthy body weight and limiting alcohol intake to moderate amounts (two or fewer alcoholic beverages per day), dietary factors shown to be useful in

Table 226–4 • COMPOSITION OF THE DIET RECOMMENDED FOR THE TREATMENT OF HIGH BLOOD CHOLESTEROL IN ADULTS*

Saturated fat	<7% of total energy intake
Polyunsaturated fat	Up to 10% of total energy intake
Monounsaturated fat	Up to 20% of total energy intake
Total fat	25–35% of total energy intake
Carbohydrate intake	50–60% of total energy intake
Protein intake	Approximately 15% of total energy intake
Dietary fiber intake	20–30 g/day
Dietary cholesterol intake	<200 mg/day
Total energy intake	Balanced with expenditure to promote healthy body weight

*Additional therapeutic options include soluble fiber (10–25 g/day) and plant stanols or sterols (2 g/day).

Adapted from Expert Panel on Detection, Evaluation and Treatment of High Blood Cholesterol in Adults: Executive summary of the Third Report of the National Cholesterol Education Program (NCEP) Expert Panel on Detection, Evaluation and Treatment of High Blood Cholesterol in Adults. JAMA 2001;285:2486.

controlling hypertension include limited sodium intake (aiming for 2400 mg/day), and eating fruit and vegetables (five to nine servings per day) and low-fat dairy foods (two to four servings per day). These foods are rich sources of potassium, magnesium, and calcium, nutrients of which higher intakes are associated with lower blood pressure. In epidemiologic studies, vegetable and fruit intake has been observed to be inversely associated with risk for stroke.

Management of the patient with congestive heart failure involves sodium restriction (typically <3000 mg/day). Patients with chronic, severe congestive heart failure are at high risk for cardiac cachexia, a condition in which malnutrition is superimposed on the cardiac condition, which results in further weakness and functional impairment. Dietary counseling aimed toward increased energy and protein intake, usually achieved with small, frequent meals, is a useful adjuvant therapy for these patients.

CANCER. Substantial evidence from epidemiologic, clinical, and laboratory studies suggests that nutritional or dietary factors can influence risk for the development of cancer, prognosis after the diagnosis of cancer, and quality of life during cancer treatment. Current estimates are that one third of cancers in the United States are specifically related to nutritional and dietary factors. Inherited genetic factors alone are believed to explain only 5% of all cancers, with the remainder resulting from interactions between genetic factors and the environment, including diet. Cancers in which the evidence for a link with nutritional factors is strongest include lung, oral and esophageal, stomach, colon and rectal, breast, prostate, ovarian, uterine cervix, and endometrial cancer. Dietary recommendations to reduce risk for cancer are summarized in Table 226–5.

The current direction of research on nutrition and cancer is characterized by increasing interest in protective factors in the diet. Specifically, epidemiologic and laboratory data consistently suggest a protective effect of vegetables and fruit and the various biologically active constituents found in these foods, particularly for cancers of the lung, oral cavity, esophagus, cervix, and breast. Also, randomized controlled trials testing the effects of specific micronutrient supplements (e.g., β-carotene, vitamin E, vitamin C) in high-risk groups have generally not produced results that support this strategy. Exceptions are studies demonstrating that calcium supplementation (1200 mg/day) promotes a modest reduction in risk for recurrence of adenomatous polyps and that selenium supplementation (200 μg/day) may reduce the risk for prostate cancer. However, the latter finding was observed in a clinical trial that was designed to test the effect of selenium supplementation on risk for recurrent skin cancer, rather than prostate cancer, so the association with prostate cancer is now under study in a larger trial better designed for that purpose. Because of the results of the diet supplement trials completed to date,

a food-based approach, which involves changing the overall dietary pattern rather than prescribing diet supplements, is considered more likely to be efficacious in the prevention of cancer.

The presence of cancer and cancer therapy, especially surgery, radiation therapy, and chemotherapy, can have adverse effects on nutritional status. Substantial weight loss and poor nutritional status have been documented in more than 50% of patients at the time of cancer diagnosis in clinical series reports, although the prevalence of weight loss and malnutrition varies widely across cancer types. Cancer and cancer therapy can increase nutritional needs, as well as affect normal digestion, absorption, and metabolism. Many individuals experience treatment-related side effects such as fatigue, loss of appetite, taste alterations, nausea, vomiting, and changes in bowel function that can further impair their ability to consume adequate energy and essential nutrients. Side effects of therapy are usually temporary, although some individuals may have lasting changes that affect their ability to eat and maintain optimal nutritional status. The predominant nutritional problem in patients diagnosed with cancer is a variant of protein-energy malnutrition (Chapter 228).

During times of illness and recovery from cancer treatments, patients can benefit from diet counseling to ensure that nutritional needs are met. Specific counseling strategies that are useful when nausea is a major problem include eating food that is cold or room-temperature, and eating small, more frequent meals. As another example, nutritionally complete enteral supplements or diets with modified food consistency can ensure nutritional adequacy when swallowing is a problem. Individuals who maintain body weight and nutrient stores during cancer treatment may be able to better tolerate treatment-related side effects and recover from therapy more quickly. Improved nutritional status helps to maintain strength and energy, enhance quality of life, and repair and rebuild tissues that have been affected by surgery and other cancer therapies.

Compared with research exploring the relationships between nutritional factors and the risk for primary cancer, there are fewer studies that have examined associations between nutritional factors and recurrence of disease or overall survival in the patient who has successfully completed initial treatments. Overweight or obesity at diagnosis of breast cancer is associated with poorer prognosis in the majority of the studies that have examined this relationship, and there is some evidence that intakes of vegetables or nutrients provided by vegetables and fruit, such as β-carotene and vitamin C, are directly associated with overall survival in this patient population.

DIABETES MELLITUS. Genetic susceptibility sets the stage for type 2 diabetes, but obesity is an important and established risk factor. Diet is a major component of the management of diabetes mellitus, and specific strategies and dietary manipulations to optimize control of diabetes have evolved and been considerably refined over the past few decades. The goal of diet therapy for all persons with diabetes is to attain and maintain optimal metabolic outcomes, including blood glucose levels in the normal or near-normal range, a desirable lipid and lipoprotein profile, and blood pressure levels that are associated with reduced risk for vascular disease. In addition to these indicators of metabolic control, other goals that are considered in diet therapy for patients with diabetes include ensuring normal growth and development, when appropriate, and preventing and treating complications.

Table 226–6 summarizes current dietary recommendations for the management of diabetes. A major focus of interest for both type 1 and type 2 diabetes is carbohydrate intake, owing to the direct effects of this macronutrient on blood glucose. In type 1 diabetes, the best control of blood glucose is achieved when insulin is adjusted to the total carbohydrate content of the meal, rather than vice versa, although day-to-day consistency is helpful when fixed doses of insulin must be used. Cardiovascular disease is a major complication of diabetes, yet the optimal diet to normalize blood lipids in an individual with diabetes can differ from the recommendations for many people without diabetes. Specifically, high-carbohydrate, low-fat diets can be disadvantageous for blood lipids if concurrent weight loss (which is often the goal) does not occur, because this dietary pattern can promote increased triglyceride concentration. However, diets that are high in monounsaturated fat may promote weight gain, if increased total energy intake occurs concurrently. In formulating a diet prescription for patients with either type 1 or type 2 diabetes, the specific distributions of carbohydrate and unsaturated fatty acids in the diet must be

---

Table 226–5 • AMERICAN CANCER SOCIETY GUIDELINES ON DIET, NUTRITION, AND CANCER PREVENTION

1. Eat a variety of healthful foods, with an emphasis on plant sources.
   - Eat five or more servings of a variety of vegetables and fruits each day.
   - Choose whole grains in preference to processed (refined) grains and sugars.
   - Limit consumption of red meats, especially those high in fat and processed.
   - Choose foods that maintain a healthy weight.
2. Adopt a physically active lifestyle.
   - Adults: engage in at least moderate activity for 30 minutes or more on 5 or more days of the week; 45 minutes or more of moderate to vigorous activity on 5 or more days per week may further enhance reductions in the risk of breast and colon cancer.
   - Children and adolescents: engage in at least 60 minutes per day of moderate to vigorous physical activity at least 5 days per week.
3. Maintain a healthful weight throughout life.
   - Balance caloric intake with physical activity.
   - Lose weight if currently overweight or obese.
4. If you drink alcoholic beverages, limit consumption.

Used by permission from Byers T, Nestle M, McTiernan A, et al: American Cancer Society Guidelines on Nutrition and Physical Activity for Cancer Prevention: Reducing the risk of cancer with healthy food choices and physical activity. CA Cancer J Clin 2002;52:92–119.

Table 226–6 • CURRENT DIETARY RECOMMENDATIONS FOR DIABETES MANAGEMENT

DIETARY FACTOR	RECOMMENDATION
Carbohydrate	Carbohydrate and monounsaturated fat should provide 60 to 70% of energy intake, considering the metabolic profile and need for weight loss. Total amount of carbohydrate in meals and snacks is more important than the source or type.
Protein	Usual protein intake (15–20% of energy intake) should not be modified unless renal function is abnormal.
Fat	Saturated fat should provide less than 10% of energy intake (<7% if LDL cholesterol ≥100 mg/dL).
Cholesterol	Limit dietary cholesterol to less than 300 mg/day (<200 mg/day if LDL cholesterol ≥100 mg/dL).
Energy balance	Reduced energy intake and modest weight loss improve insulin resistance and glycemia in type 2 diabetes. Structured programs that emphasize lifestyle changes, including increased physical activity, are recommended as the best treatment approach for promoting weight loss and maintenance of that loss.
Micronutrients	There is no clear evidence that routine vitamin or mineral supplements are beneficial.
Alcohol	Daily intake should be limited (two or fewer alcoholic beverages per day for men, one or fewer alcoholic beverages per day for women). Alcohol should be consumed with food to reduce risk of hypoglycemia.

LDL = low-density lipoprotein.
Adapted from Franz MJ, Bantle JP, Beebe CA, et al: Evidence-based nutrition principles and recommendations for the treatment and prevention of diabetes and related complications. Diabetes Care 2002;25:148.

individualized, based on the metabolic response to these two dietary factors.

Historically, patients with diabetes have been instructed to avoid sugars, especially sucrose and sucrose-containing foods, although studies have now shown that dietary sucrose does not increase glycemia any more than isocaloric amounts of starch. Thus, current guidelines permit the intake of sucrose and sucrose-containing foods within the context of the total carbohydrate in the meal or snack, with these foods simply replacing other carbohydrate sources, if desired. With the goal of optimizing overall nutrient intake, nutrient-dense sources of carbohydrate (e.g., grains, vegetables, fruits, legumes) should remain the major contributors to total carbohydrate, similar to dietary guidelines for the general public.

The glycemic index of foods (the immediate postprandial glucose response to various carbohydrate sources) has been suggested to be applicable for control of diabetes, but current evidence does not suggest consistent or meaningful improvement in blood glucose control when this approach is utilized. Also, current evidence does not support routine supplementation with antioxidant micronutrients, although there is considerable interest in how oxidative stress contributes to the development of complications of diabetes. Moderate intake of alcohol consumed with food has no acute effects on blood glucose or insulin, so the current guidelines advise that alcohol be consumed in moderation as an addition to the regular meal plan, if desired. Evidence does not support routine protein restriction for patients with diabetes. However, a reduction of protein intake to 0.8 to 1.0 g/kg body weight (or adjusted body weight if the patient is more than 115% of desirable weight) per day for those with microalbuminuria, or 0.8 g/kg body weight/day if overt nephropathy is present, is recommended because this strategy may slow the progression of nephropathy.

OTHER DISEASES AND CONDITIONS. Nutritional factors and diet modification play an important role in the prevention and treatment of other chronic diseases. For example, management of chronic renal disease involves restricted intakes of protein, phosphorus, sodium, potassium, and fluids and regular medical monitoring for optimal nutritional management. Malnutrition has been shown to be an important risk for mortality in patients with chronic renal disease, and food choices and total intakes of these patients can be improved with dietary counseling. Protein, sodium, and fluid restrictions are important aspects of the management of chronic liver disease, and supplementation with water-miscible formulations of the fat-soluble vitamins is necessary when fat malabsorption is present. The management of many other diseases of the gastrointestinal tract, such as inflammatory bowel disease, requires special attention to the maintenance of good nutritional status because of the central role of this organ system in absorption, metabolism, and excretion of nutrients. Nutritional factors appear to contribute to risk and progression of chronic neurodegenerative diseases, such as Alzheimer's and Parkinson's disease. Weight loss that occurs in these conditions is primarily due to reduced food intake, often related to dysphasia, which can be prevented with early intervention and diet therapy. Readers are referred to Coulston et al. (see Suggested Readings) for further details on the role of nutrition and the specific strategies utilized in the prevention and treatment of various chronic diseases.

Nutrition in Acute Illness, Surgery, and Injury

Common medical problems that have diverse causes, including infectious diseases, have an adverse impact on nutritional status, and management of these problems is optimized by attention to meeting nutritional needs. Infectious illness promotes increased resting energy expenditure, and tissue catabolism dominates over anabolism, mediated by cytokines and other metabolic factors. When accompanied by reduced food intake, which typically occurs in the acutely ill patient, the resulting energy imbalance results in wasting and an impaired immune response. Malnutrition is associated with increased morbidity due to infectious illness, because malnourished individuals have impaired immunocompetence, which further results in prolonged illness and hospitalization.

Surgery, burn injury, and trauma result in hormonal and other metabolic alterations that affect nutrient metabolism and requirements, and adequate intakes of energy and essential nutrients in these instances are often unlikely without nutritional intervention. Even in the absence of trauma, surgery itself has been shown to result in increased energy expenditure, altered glucose metabolism, and accelerated protein turnover, producing a catabolic condition. Preoperative nutritional deficiencies should be corrected and reserves established if time permits prior to surgery. When malnutrition is present and the delay of surgery is not detrimental, improved nutritional status may reduce complications and improve overall outcome. Nutritional support (enteral or parenteral) should be initiated in patients who are unable to resume normal oral feedings within 10 days post-surgery (Chapters 229 and 230). Provision of adequate energy and amino acids does not appear to alter the hypermetabolic response following surgery, burn injury, and trauma, but the magnitude of weight loss, skeletal muscle loss, and negative nitrogen balance can be attenuated. Further, providing adequate energy, protein, and micronutrients will permit normal healing processes and reduce risk of secondary problems, such as infection.

SUGGESTED READINGS

Byers T, Nestle M, McTiernan A, et al: American Cancer Society Guidelines on Nutrition and Physical Activity for Cancer Prevention: Reducing the risk of cancer with healthy food choices and physical activity. CA Cancer J Clin 2002;52:92–119. *A summary of the nutrition and cancer prevention and specific dietary guidelines for reducing risk for cancer.*

Coulston AM, Rock CL, Monsen ER (eds): Nutrition in the Prevention and Treatment of Disease. San Diego, Academic Press, 2001. *A comprehensive text that includes detailed reviews of principles of clinical nutrition and evidence for the role of nutritional factors in the prevention and treatment of disease, with an emphasis on current scientific evidence, clinical applications, and directions of future research.*

Diabetes Prevention Program Research Group: Reduction in the incidence of type 2 diabetes with lifestyle intervention or metformin. N Engl J Med 2002;346:393–403. *A landmark study that demonstrated that change in diet and physical activity can reduce the incidence of type 2 diabetes in persons at high risk.*

Franz MJ, Bantle JP, Beebe CA, et al: Evidence-based nutrition principles and recommendations for the treatment and prevention of diabetes and related complications. Diabetes Care 2002;25:148–198. *A comprehensive and detailed review of the evidence for the rationale and current dietary guidelines for the management of patients with diabetes mellitus.*

Krauss RM, Eckel RH, Howard B, et al: AHA Dietary Guidelines revision 2000: A statement for healthcare professionals from the Nutrition Committee of the American Heart Association. Circulation 2000;102:2284–2299. *A detailed summary of the rationale and scientific basis of current dietary recommendations for the prevention and treatment of cardiovascular disease, including hypertension.*

227 NUTRITIONAL ASSESSMENT

Bruce R. Bistrian

Nutritional assessment in clinical medicine has three primary goals: to identify the presence and type of malnutrition, to define health-threatening obesity, and to devise suitable diets as prophylaxis against disease later in life. The focus of this chapter is on the diagnosis of protein-energy malnutrition because of its wide prevalence and major impact on disease outcome. Other deficiency diseases are of much less relevance in that most occur in conjunction with protein-energy malnutrition or with specific disease states, such as thiamine deficiency with alcoholic liver disease or fat-soluble vitamin deficiency with malabsorptive states. The classic deficiency diseases, either primary or secondary, are considered elsewhere in this volume. The widespread availability of parenteral and enteral therapeutic measures over the past two decades that can provide adequate feeding regimens for virtually any disease condition makes a rudimentary knowledge of the pathophysiology of protein-energy malnutrition and its nutritional assessment essential for all primary care practitioners (Chapter 228).

Clinical Nutritional Assessment

Clinical assessment of protein nutritional status is based principally on the clinical history, simple anthropometry, and measurement of the levels of several secretory proteins. Although detailed dietary assessment can at times be helpful, in most circumstances physicians can safely limit their diet questions to whether patients have been following a prescribed diet, how much alcohol they drink, and whether they habitually take dietary supplements, including vitamins, minerals, and herbs. In ambulatory patients, the ability to maintain usual and adequate weight generally indicates that serious micronutrient deficiency is probably not due to dietary inadequacy. Isolated vitamin deficiencies in the absence of weight loss or symptoms are rare, except perhaps for folate and vitamin B_{12}. Although nutritional anemias do exist, the role of dietary deficiency in folic acid–related or vitamin B_{12}–related anemias is minimal in the absence of underlying disease or weight loss. Only iron deficiency is a reasonable cause of a dietary anemia. By contrast, full dietary assessment and diet prescriptions are likely to help conditions such as fat malabsorption accompanied by weight loss, cramps, or diarrhea. Such evaluations are most effectively carried out by dietitians. Thus, detailed nutritional assessment of protein-energy malnutrition with secondary assessment of vitamin and mineral deficiencies is usually needed only when protein-energy malnutrition or a specific disorder known to interfere with nutrient metabolism coexists, such as celiac disease, pernicious anemia, or nutrient–drug interactions. Even then, the assessment should emphasize the likely deficiencies. For fat malabsorption, one should check levels of the fat-soluble vitamins A, D, E, and K as well as important divalent and trivalent cations (Ca^{2+}, Zn^{2+}, Mg^{2+}, Fe^{3+}). When ileal resection has occurred, serum B_{12} levels should be measured and the potential for bile salt depletion considered. Weight loss resulting from short-gut syndrome should prompt assessment of the fat-soluble vitamins, folic acid, vitamin B_{12}, calcium, magnesium, zinc, and iron. Measurements of body water status (blood urea nitrogen, serum creatinine, serum sodium) and acid-base balance (serum CO_2 combining power, chloride and potassium, and urine and arterial pH) should be obtained if the diarrhea is profuse.

Clinically obvious marasmus and hypoalbuminemic malnutrition affect 25 to 50% of patients hospitalized for acute care. Many of these patients can benefit from nutritional support and require a thorough clinical nutritional assessment, including a dietary history, physical examination, and laboratory tests that serve to confirm clinical impressions. The history should list information about the timing and amount of weight loss, medical illnesses, medications, gastrointestinal symptoms (abdominal pain, diarrhea, dysphagia), diet habits (eating fewer than two meals per day, alcohol consumption, dietary supplement intake, dental status), social habits (eats alone, needs assistance in self-care), economic status (enough money for food), and mental status, particularly the presence of depressive symptoms. A special focus should be reserved for the elderly, in whom protein-energy malnutrition secondary to these last factors is more common.

Three factors principally determine the timing and appropriateness of nutritional support: (1) the presence and severity of protein-energy malnutrition, defined primarily by weight loss and serum albumin level; (2) the presence and severity of the systemic inflammatory response, also defined by serum albumin level but also by the presence of fever, leukocytosis, and increased band forms; and (3) the actual or expected duration of inadequate nutritional intake. Well-nourished individuals have a 7- to 10-day reserve of energy and protein to withstand a moderate systemic inflammatory response without adverse nutritional consequences. Greater degrees of systemic inflammatory response or preexisting protein-energy malnutrition dramatically shorten the period that semistarvation, defined as consuming less than 50% of the energy and protein needs, can be tolerated.

Weight Loss

A recent unintended weight loss of 10 lb, or more than 5% of usual weight, should prompt efforts to diagnose the underlying disorder or social circumstance. Weight loss alone does not distinguish the composition of tissue loss, which can range from 25 to 30% lean tissue in semistarvation alone to 50% lean tissue loss following semistarvation plus injury. Therefore, unintentional weight loss of more than 10 lb indicates a need for thorough nutritional assessment. Weight loss in excess of 10% of usual weight should be considered to represent protein-energy malnutrition that will impair physiologic function, particularly muscle strength and endurance. Weight loss in excess of 20% should be considered severe protein-energy malnutrition that will substantially impair most organ systems. If major elective surgery is planned, such individuals would benefit from adequate feeding preoperatively or at least early nutritional intervention postoperatively. If palliative or curative radiotherapy or systemic chemotherapy is planned, adequate feeding during therapy with the use of supplemental formulas, tube feeding, or parenteral nutrition (in that order) is indicated. However, if the weight loss represents end-stage systemic illness (e.g., cancer, end-stage liver, renal, or lung disease, acquired immunodeficiency syndrome) for which no primary therapy is planned or is effective, invasive nutritional support is rarely indicated.

Physical Examination

Although the patient's external appearance and a check of the skin, eyes, mouth, hair, and nails often provide a clue to the presence of nutritional abnormalities (Table 227–1), the physical findings of deficiency syndromes of vitamins, essential fatty acids, and trace metals are relatively insensitive and nonspecific. With respect to protein-energy malnutrition, only the marasmic form of semistarvation is evident at examination. Loss of subcutaneous fat and skeletal muscle is manifested by sunken temples, thin extremities, wasting of the muscles of the hand, and, rarely, edema. Although kwashiorkor in children is characterized by severe edema and a potbelly appearance from hepatomegaly and ascites, one rarely encounters these clinical signs in cases of hypoalbuminemic malnutrition.

The most useful element in the physical examination is body weight, which is expressed as a relative value to evaluate the patient in relation to the healthy population. Weight and height are easily obtained, and standards for comparison have been established (Table 227–2). Although newer standards are available, they reflect the increasing prevalence of obesity in the U.S. population. Use of the 1959 standards allows the same tables to be used to diagnose significant protein-energy malnutrition (less than 85% of desirable weight, which approximates the fifth percentile) and significant obesity, defined as obesity predisposing to excessive mortality risk (greater than 130% of desirable weight). Although severe protein-energy malnutrition often occurs at levels greater than 85% of desirable weight because of the greater likelihood of preexisting obesity, this condition is generally detected by percentage weight loss or upper arm anthropometry. Height can be measured in a reclining patient with a tape measure, and in certain situations the patient history may be relied upon. The major confounding variable that limits the value of weight and height as an index of protein-energy malnutrition is the tendency for water retention with disease, and thus weight gain may not reflect an increase in lean body mass or protein content. Fluid retention is particularly a problem in patients with hypoalbuminemic malnutrition because of the effects of aldosterone, antidiuretic hormone, and insulin stimulated by the stress response to cause sodium and fluid retention. Fluid retention, however, is not common in patients first seen at the physician's office or initially at the hospital, except in those with

Table 227–1 • CLINICAL SIGNS AND SYMPTOMS OF NUTRITIONAL INADEQUACY IN ADULT PATIENTS

	CLINICAL SIGN OR SYMPTOM	NUTRIENT
GENERAL	Wasted, skinny	Calorie
	Loss of appetite	Protein-energy, zinc
SKIN	Psoriasiform rash, eczematous scaling	Zinc, vitamin A, essential fatty acids
	Pallor	Folate, iron, vitamin B_{12}, copper
	Follicular hyperkeratosis	Vitamin A, vitamin C
	Perifollicular petechiae	Vitamin C
	Flaking dermatitis	Protein-energy, niacin, riboflavin, zinc
	Bruising	Vitamin C, vitamin K
	Pigmentation changes	Niacin, protein-energy
	Scrotal dermatosis	Riboflavin
	Thickening and dryness of skin	Linoleic acid
HEAD	Temporal muscle wasting	Protein-energy
HAIR	Sparse and thin, dyspigmentation	Protein
	Easy to pull out	Protein
	Corkscrew hairs	Vitamin C
EYES	History of night blindness (also impaired visual recovery after glare)	Vitamin A, zinc
	Photophobia, blurring, conjunctival inflammation	Riboflavin, vitamin A
	Corneal vascularization	Riboflavin
	Xerosis, Bitot spots, keratomalacia	Vitamin A
MOUTH	Glossitis	Riboflavin, niacin, folic acid, vitamin B_{12}, pyridoxine
	Bleeding gums	Vitamin C, riboflavin
	Cheilosis	Riboflavin, pyridoxine, niacin
	Angular stomatitis	Riboflavin, pyridoxine, niacin
	Hypogeusia	Zinc
	Tongue fissuring	Niacin
	Tongue atrophy	Riboflavin, niacin, iron
	Nasolabial seborrhea	Pyridoxine
NECK	Goiter	Iodine
	Parotid enlargement	Protein
THORAX	Thoracic rosary	Vitamin D
ABDOMEN	Diarrhea	Niacin, folate, vitamin B_{12}
	Distention	Protein-energy
	Hepatomegaly	Protein-energy
EXTREMITIES	Edema	Protein, thiamine
	Softening of bone	Vitamin D, calcium, phosphorus
	Bone tenderness	Vitamin D
	Bone ache, joint pain	Vitamin C
	Muscle wasting and weakness	Protein, calorie, vitamin D, selenium, sodium chloride
	Muscle tenderness, muscle pain	Thiamine
NAILS	Spooning	Iron
	Transverse lines	Protein
NEUROLOGIC	Tetany	Calcium, magnesium
	Paresthesias	Thiamine, vitamin B_{12}
	Loss of reflexes, wristdrop, footdrop	Thiamine
	Loss of vibratory and position sense	Vitamin B_{12}
	Ataxia	Vitamin B_{12}
	Dementia, disorientation	Niacin
BLOOD	Anemia	Vitamin B_{12}, folate, iron, pyridoxine
	Hemolysis	Phosphorus, vitamin E

diseases such as cardiac failure, end-stage liver disease, and severe renal disease in whom the disturbance in water metabolism is due to the underlying disease.

The body mass index (BMI), which is the weight in kilograms divided by the height in meters squared, has recently gained favor as a nutritional measure because of two valuable attributes. The measure is relatively independent of height, and the same standards apply to males and females. Normal nutrition is defined as a BMI of 20 to less than 25; significant protein-energy malnutrition, less than 18.5; overweight, from 25 to less than 30; and obesity, 30 or greater. Evidence from less developed countries suggests that the BMI is better correlated with outcome than are weight and height.

Upper Arm Anthropometry

Approximately 50% of body fat is subcutaneous. The use of skinfold calipers to define the triceps skinfold is the most practical technique to estimate body fat. Standards for skinfold measurements are available from the National Health and Nutrition Examination Surveys I and II and were derived from a probability sample of the U.S. population. Generally, less than the fifth percentile is used to define abnormality (Table 227–3). The principal value of the triceps skinfold measurement (TSF) is to determine the arm muscle circumference (AMC) or arm muscle area.

$$\text{AMC (cm)} = \text{arm circumference} - (\pi)(\text{TSF [mm]})/10$$

The arm muscle circumference is a specific measure of protein-energy malnutrition if the fifth or 10th percentile is chosen as the cutoff point, and it is particularly valuable in patients in edematous states or in amputees, in whom weights are inaccurate or insensitive. The triceps skinfold and arm muscle circumference measurements are most useful in initially defining marasmic-type malnutrition

Table 227–2 • DESIRABLE WEIGHT IN POUNDS IN RELATION TO HEIGHT FOR ADULT MEN AND WOMEN 25 YEARS OR OLDER*

MEN, MEDIUM FRAME				WOMEN, MEDIUM FRAME			
Height		Weight (lb)		Height		Weight (lb)	
ft	in.	Range	Midpoint	ft	in.	Range	Midpoint
				4	8	93–104	98.5
				4	9	95–107	101
				4	10	98–110	104
				4	11	101–113	107
				5	0	104–116	110
5	1	113–124	118.5	5	1	107–119	113
5	2	116–128	122	5	2	110–123	116.5
5	3	119–131	125	5	3	113–127	120
5	4	122–134	128	5	4	117–132	124.5
5	5	125–138	131.5	5	5	121–136	128.5
5	6	129–142	135.5	5	6	125–140	132.5
5	7	133–147	140	5	7	129–144	136.5
5	8	137–151	144	5	8	133–148	140.5
5	9	141–155	148	5	9	137–152	144.5
5	10	145–160	153	5	10	141–156	148.5
5	11	149–165	157				
6	0	153–170	161.5				
6	1	157–175	166				
6	2	162–180	171				
6	3	167–185	176				

*Corrected to nude weights and heights by assuming 1-inch heel for men, 2-inch heel for women, and indoor clothing weight of 5 and 3 lbs for men and women, respectively.
Adapted from the Metropolitan Life Insurance Company Statistical Bulletin 1959;4:1.

Table 227–3 • FIFTH, 10TH, AND 50TH PERCENTILE FOR TRICEPS SKINFOLD (TSF) AND MID-UPPER ARM MUSCLE CIRCUMFERENCE (MUAMC) OF AMERICAN MEN AND WOMEN FROM THE NHANES I SURVEY

AGE GROUP	MUAMC (cm)			TSF (mm)		
	Percentile			Percentile		
	5th	10th	50th	5th	10th	50th
MEN						
18–24	23.8	24.8	27.9	4.5	6.0	11.0
18–24	23.5	24.4	27.2	4.0	5.0	9.5
25–34	24.2	25.3	28.0	4.5	5.5	12.0
35–44	25.0	25.6	28.7	5.0	6.0	12.0
45–54	26.0	26.9	28.1	5.0	6.0	11.0
55–64	22.8	26.4	27.9	5.0	6.0	11.0
65–74	22.5	23.7	26.9	4.5	5.5	11.0
WOMEN						
18–24	13.4	19.0	21.8	11.0	13.0	22.0
18–24	17.7	18.5	20.6	9.4	11.0	18.0
25–34	18.3	18.9	21.4	10.5	12.0	21.0
35–44	18.5	19.2	22.0	12.0	14.0	23.0
45–54	18.8	19.5	22.2	13.0	15.0	25.0
55–64	18.6	19.5	22.6	11.0	14.0	25.0
65–74	18.6	19.5	22.5	11.5	14.0	23.0

NHANES = National Health and Nutritional Examination Survey I.
From Bishop CW, Bowen PE, Ritchey SJ: Norms for nutritional assessment of American adults by upper arm anthropometry. Am J Clin Nutr 1981;34:2530–2539.

or the mixed disorder. Nearly all dietitians are skilled in upper arm anthropometry.

Serum Proteins

Despite many concerns, the serum albumin level remains the traditional standard for nutritional assessment by virtue of its extensive history and its continued use to separate the two principal forms of protein-energy malnutrition. Hypoalbuminemia is a strong predictor of risk for morbidity and mortality in both hospitalized and ambulatory patients. In almost all cases, except perhaps for hereditary analbuminemia, excessive loss secondary to nephrosis, and, occasionally, protein-losing enteropathy, hypoalbuminemia identifies the recent or ongoing presence of a systemic inflammatory response with the accompanying effects of anorexia and depression of immune function. Given a half-life for albumin of 18 to 20 days and the fractional replacement rate of about 10% per day, the return of serum albumin to normal takes about 2 weeks of feeding when the stress response remits. Levels of other proteins such as transferrin, prealbumin, and retinol-binding protein with respective half-lives of 7 days, 2 days, and $\frac{1}{2}$ day also fall acutely with injury and respond more quickly when stress remits. Serum transferrin also varies with iron status, however, and prealbumin and retinol-binding protein vary with dietary carbohydrate and renal function. As a result, these proteins do not identify the presence and severity of the stress response any better than albumin does.

Nutritional Therapy and Its Assessment

The same indices that are used in the baseline nutritional assessment can be used to assess response to therapy, provided that certain points are kept in mind. In a stressed, hospitalized patient receiving nutritional support, day-to-day weight changes generally reflect shifts in fluid balance rather than energy balance. In an ambulatory setting, weight increases or decreases are most likely to reflect changes in protein nutritional status and body fat because the underlying illness is usually less severe. Even the most sensitive research methods for assessing changes in lean body mass, however, do not offer major improvements in diagnosis in the more seriously ill patients. Techniques that measure total body water such as isotope dilution and underwater weighing, from which lean tissue is extrapolated, fail to account for the distortion in hydration of lean tissue with illness. Surrogate measures of total body protein to estimate lean tissues such as total body potassium measurement do not adjust for differing potassium/nitrogen ratios with disease. A newer method, multifrequency body impedance, does show promise as a simple, accurate, noninvasive method that may allow distinction between intracellular and extracellular water, with the former used to estimate lean tissue.

In an unstressed patient with marasmus, appropriate protein and calorie intake should cause a positive nitrogen balance of 2 to 6 g/day

(60 to 180 g lean tissue) and slow weight gain, depending on the positive energy balance. For instance, a 300-kcal excess of intake over expenditure would provide approximately 120 g of lean tissue (100 kcal equivalent) plus 200 kcal (22 g) as fat, for a total of around 140 g, or about ⅓ lb of weight per day. Weight gains in excess of this figure usually reflect sodium and water retention from the insulin stimulated by dietary carbohydrate. Such overhydration can be improved by reducing salt and limiting fluid intake. In patients with hypoalbuminemic malnutrition who are no longer stressed, a similar nutritional regimen will lead to a comparable gain of tissue, but weight change is often less as edema becomes mobilized, with normalization of serum albumin in 2 to 4 weeks and of retinol-binding protein, prealbumin, and transferrin more quickly. In stressed patients with hypoalbuminemic malnutrition, appropriate nutritional support often does not restore lean tissue but does improve other important functions, such as wound healing and immunocompetence. However, these are important goals to support specific medical and surgical therapies to improve ultimate clinical outcome. Both the systemic inflammatory response and the limited activity level reduce the efficiency of skeletal muscle repletion, which represents 30% of body weight and 75% of actively metabolizing lean tissue. Functional testing of muscle strength and endurance such as hand dynamometry might be useful as a means of assessing this response but has not found wide clinical acceptance. Similarly, any reduction in other physiologic functions or impairment in the patient's ability to perform the usual activities of daily living will accentuate the consequences of protein-energy malnutrition.

Although caloric expenditure can now be reliably and easily measured with portable indirect calorimeters, estimated energy expenditure is sufficient in most clinical situations. The three components of total energy expenditure are basal energy expenditure (about 55 to 65% of total energy expenditure), thermal effect of feeding (about 10% of total energy expenditure), and activity energy expenditure (the remainder). An energy intake of 30 to 35 kcal/kg of body weight will maintain most sedentary ambulatory patients, with adjustments upward or downward in 200- to 300-kcal increments as prompted by biweekly changes in weight. Although young, severely burned, or traumatized patients may require 35 to 40 kcal/kg in the acute phase to meet total energy expenditure, providing energy intakes principally as carbohydrate that exceed 35 kcal/kg substantially increases the likelihood of hyperglycemia. Recent evidence strongly implicates hyperglycemia in excess of 200 mg/dL as a major risk factor for nosocomial infection, making better glycemic control by the use of insulin or reducing the level of energy intake, or both, important considerations. Most postoperative patients who require invasive nutritional support for mechanical or infectious complications usually require about 25 kcal/kg to meet energy needs and not more than 30 kcal/kg because of their older age and reduced activity and energy expenditure. Overfeeding should be avoided in such patients.

SUGGESTED READINGS

McCowen K, Malhotra A, Bistrian B: Stress-induced hyperglycemia. Crit Care Clin 2001;17:107–124. *In the critically ill, tight control of blood glucose (<110 mg/dL) by intensive insulin therapy has been shown to reduce morbidity and mortality.*

Pablo AM, Izaga MA, Alday LA, et al: Assessment of nutritional status on hospital admission: Nutritional scores. Eur J Clin Nutr 2003;57:824–831. *Malnutrition is common and can be assessed by several different readily available methods.*

van den Berghe G, Wouters P, Weekers F, et al: Intensive insulin therapy in critically ill patients. N Engl J Med 2001;345:1359–1367. *Large randomized clinical trial in critically ill patients demonstrating a 34% reduction in hospital mortality and significant reductions in sepsis, acute renal failure, prolonged ventilatory support, transfusion requirements, and critical illness polyneuropathy with intensive insulin therapy.*

228 PROTEIN-ENERGY MALNUTRITION

Samuel Klein

Normal nutritional status represents a healthy relationship between nutrient intake and nutrient requirements. An imbalance between intake and requirements over time can lead to malnutrition, manifested by alterations in intermediary metabolism, organ function, and body composition. The term protein-energy malnutrition (PEM) has been used to describe macronutrient deficiency syndromes, which include

kwashiorkor, marasmus, and nutritional dwarfism in children, and wasting associated with illness or injury in children and adults.

Primary PEM is caused by lack of access to adequate nutrient intake and usually affects children and elderly persons. The functional and structural abnormalities associated with primary PEM are often reversible with nutritional therapy. However, prolonged primary PEM can cause irreversible changes in organ function and growth.

Secondary PEM is caused by illnesses that alter appetite, digestion, absorption, or nutrient metabolism and can be divided into three general, but often overlapping, categories: (1) diseases that affect gastrointestinal tract function, (2) wasting disorders, and (3) critical illness. Gastrointestinal disease can cause PEM by premucosal (maldigestion), mucosal (malabsorption), or postmucosal (lymphatic obstruction) defects (Table 228–1). The nutritional status of patients with PEM caused by gastrointestinal tract dysfunction can often be restored to normal if adequate nutritional support can be provided by dietary manipulations, enteral tube feeding, or parenteral nutrition. Wasting disorders, such as cancer, acquired immunodeficiency syndrome, and rheumatologic diseases, are characterized by involuntary loss of body weight and muscle mass in the setting of a chronic illness. These patients often experience wasting because of (1) inadequate nutrient intake related to anorexia and possibly gastrointestinal tract dysfunction and (2) metabolic abnormalities caused by alterations in regulatory hormones and cytokines. The alterations in metabolism are responsible for the greater loss of muscle tissue observed in these patients than in those with pure starvation or semistarvation. Restoration of muscle mass is unlikely with nutritional support unless the underlying inflammatory disease is corrected. Weight gain that occurs after nutritional support is initiated is usually caused by increases in fat mass and body water without significant increases in lean tissue. Patients with critical illness exhibit marked metabolic alterations, manifested by increased energy expenditure, endogenous glucose production, lipolytic rates, and protein breakdown. Therefore, protein and energy requirements are increased in critically ill patients. However, providing aggressive nutritional support may ameliorate but does not prevent net lean tissue losses without correction of the underlying illness or injury.

Table 228–1 • CLASSIFICATION OF MALDIGESTIVE AND MALABSORPTIVE DISORDERS

PRIMARY ABNORMALITY	PATHOPHYSIOLOGY	REPRESENTATIVE DISORDERS
Premucosal defect	Pancreatic insufficiency	Chronic pancreatitis
		Cystic fibrosis
		Pancreatic duct obstruction
	Bacterial overgrowth	Motility diseases
		Blind loop syndromes
		Small intestine diverticula
	Rapid gastric emptying and intestinal transit	Postgastric surgery syndrome
Mucosal defect	Inadequate bowel syndrome	Intestinal resection
		Gluten-sensitive enteropathy
		Immunoproliferative small bowel disease
		Radiation enteritis
		Intestinal ischemia
		AIDS enteropathy
Postmucosal defect	Lymphatic obstruction	Congenital intestinal lymphangiectasia
		Milroy's disease
		Secondary intestinal lymphangiectasia
		Retroperitoneal carcinoma
		Lymphoma
		Retroperitoneal fibrosis
		Chronic pancreatitis
		Tuberculosis
		Sarcoidosis
		Crohn's disease
		Whipple's disease
		Constrictive pericarditis
		Chronic congestive heart failure

Protein-Energy Malnutrition in Children

Undernutrition in children differs from that in adults because it affects growth and development. Much of our understanding of undernutrition in children comes from observations and studies in developing nations where poverty, inadequate food supply, and unsanitary conditions lead to a high prevalence of PEM. The Waterlow classification of malnutrition takes into account that children grow and undernutrition affects their growth. Therefore, nutritional status can be assessed by comparing a child's weight for height (wasting) and height for age (stunting) with normal standards (Table 228–2). The characteristics of the three major clinical syndromes of PEM in children are outlined in Table 228–3. Although these three syndromes are classified separately, they may coexist in the same patient.

MARASMUS. Weight loss and marked depletion of subcutaneous fat and muscle mass are the characteristic features in children with marasmus. Loss of fat and muscle makes ribs, joints, and facial bones prominent. The skin is thin, loose, and lies in folds.

KWASHIORKOR. The word *kwashiorkor* comes from the Ga language of West Africa and can be translated as "disease of the displaced child" because it was commonly seen after weaning. The presence of peripheral edema distinguishes children with kwashiorkor from those with marasmus and nutritional dwarfism (Fig. 228–1). Children with kwashiorkor also have typical skin and hair changes (see later sections on hair and skin changes). The abdomen is protuberant because of weakened abdominal muscles, intestinal distention, and hepatomegaly, but there is never ascites. In fact, the presence of ascites should prompt the clinician to search for liver disease or peritonitis. Children with kwashiorkor are typically lethargic and apathetic when left alone but become quite irritable when picked up or held. Kwashiorkor is not caused by a relative deficiency in protein intake as has been previously believed; in fact, protein and energy intakes are similar in children with kwashiorkor and marasmus. Kwashiorkor

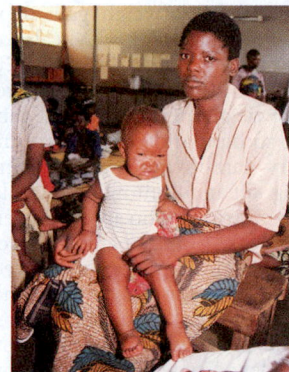

Figure 228–1 • Mother with a child suffering from kwashiorkor in Blantyre, Malawi. The child manifests some of the classic features of kwashiorkor, including leg edema, reddish blond hair discoloration, and irritability. (Photograph courtesy of Mark Manary, MD.)

is related to the physiologic stress of an infection that induces a deleterious metabolic cascade in an already malnourished child. This explains why kwashiorkor is an acute illness compared with the chronicity of undernutrition alone and why there is overlap between marasmus and kwashiorkor. Kwashiorkor is characterized by leaky cell membranes that permit the movement of potassium and other intracellular ions to the extracellular space. The increased osmotic load in the interstitium causes water movement and edema. These changes occur despite increased sodium pump (Na^+,K^+-adenosine triphosphatase [Na^+,K^+-ATPase]) activity, which also contrasts with a slowing down of the sodium pump in pure undernutrition.

NUTRITIONAL DWARFISM. The child with failure to thrive may be of normal weight for height but has short stature and delayed sexual development. Providing appropriate feeding can stimulate catch-up growth and sexual maturation.

Protein-Energy Malnutrition in Adults

The diagnosis of PEM in adults is different from that in children because adults are no longer growing in height. Therefore, undernutrition in adults causes wasting rather than stunting and can be assessed by determining body mass index, defined as the patient's weight (in kg) divided by the patient's height (in m²) (Table 228–4). In addition, although kwashiorkor and marasmus can occur in adults, most studies of adult PEM evaluated hospitalized patients who had secondary PEM and coexisting illness or injury. The current methods that are used clinically to evaluate PEM in hospitalized adult patients shift nutritional assessment from a diagnostic to a prognostic instrument in an attempt to identify patients who can benefit from nutritional therapy. Therefore, common nutritional assessment parameters are affected by non-nutritional factors, making it difficult to separate the influence of the disease itself from the contribution of inadequate nutrient intake. At present, there is no "gold standard" for determining PEM in ill patients. The most commonly used methods include a careful history, physical examination, and selected laboratory tests.

Metabolic Response to Starvation

The adaptive response to starvation involves specific metabolic alterations that enhance the chance for survival by increasing the use

Table 228–2 • WATERLOW CLASSIFICATION OF PROTEIN-ENERGY MALNUTRITION IN CHILDREN

MEASURE	NORMAL	MILD	MODERATE	SEVERE
Weight for height (wasting)				
Percent of median NCHS standard	90–110	80–89	70–79	<70
Standard deviation from the NCHS median	+Z to –Z	–1.1 Z to –2 Z	–2.1 Z to –3 Z	<–3 Z
Height for age (stunting)				
Percent of median NCHS standard	95–105	90–94	85–89	<85
Standard deviation from the NCHS median	+Z to –Z	–1.1 Z to –2 Z	–2.1 Z to –3 Z	<–3 Z

NCHS = National Center for Health Statistics; Z = 1 standard deviation.

Table 228–3 • FEATURES OF PROTEIN-ENERGY MALNUTRITION SYNDROMES IN CHILDREN

CHARACTERISTIC	KWASHIORKOR	MARASMUS	NUTRITIONAL DWARFISM
Weight for age (% expected)	60–80	<60	<60
Weight for height	Normal or decreased	Markedly decreased	Normal
Edema	Present	Absent	Absent
Mood	Irritable when picked up		
	Apathetic when alone	Alert	Alert
Appetite	Poor	Good	Good

Table 228–4 • CLASSIFICATION OF PROTEIN-ENERGY MALNUTRITION IN ADULTS BY BODY MASS INDEX

BODY MASS INDEX (kg/m²)	NUTRITIONAL STATUS
18.5–24.9	Normal
17.0–18.4	Mildly malnourished
15.0–16.9	Moderately malnourished
<15.0	Severely malnourished

of body fat as a fuel, sparing the use of glucose, minimizing body nitrogen losses, and decreasing energy expenditure. A marked shift in fuel use occurs during the first day of starvation. By 24 hours of fasting, the use of glucose as a fuel has decreased; only 15% of liver glycogen stores remain, and the rates of hepatic glucose production and whole body glucose oxidation have decreased. Conversely, endogenous fat stores become the body's major fuel and the rates of adipose tissue lipolysis, hepatic ketone body production, and fat oxidation are increased. After 3 days of fasting, the rate of glucose production is reduced by one half and the rate of lipolysis is more than double the values found at 12 hours of fasting. The increase in fatty acid delivery to the liver, in conjunction with an increase in the ratio of plasma glucagon to insulin concentration, enhances hepatic ketone body production. By 7 days of fasting, plasma ketone body concentrations have increased 75-fold and ketone bodies provide 70% of the brain's energy needs.

In contrast to fatty acids, ketone bodies can cross the blood-brain barrier and provide a water-soluble fuel derived from water-insoluble adipose tissue triglycerides. The use of ketone bodies by the brain greatly diminishes glucose requirements and thus reduces the need for muscle protein degradation to provide glucose precursors. Furthermore, thyroid hormone inactivation and plasma ketones inhibit muscle protein breakdown and prevent rapid protein losses. If postabsorptive protein breakdown rates were to continue throughout starvation, a potentially lethal amount of muscle protein would be catabolized in less than 3 weeks. As fasting continues, the kidney becomes an important site for glucose production; glutamine, released from muscle, is converted to glucose in the kidney and accounts for almost half of total glucose production. Resting metabolic rate decreases by approximately 15% at 7 days.

Adaptation is maximal during more prolonged starvation (>14 days of fasting). At this time, adipose tissue provides more than 90% of daily energy requirements. Total glucose production has decreased to about 75 g/day, providing fuel for glycolytic tissues (40 g/day) and the brain (35 g/day). Muscle protein breakdown has decreased to less than 30 g/day, which causes a marked decrease in urea nitrogen production and excretion. The diminished urea load to the kidneys decreases urine volume to 200 mL/day, thereby minimizing fluid requirements. Resting energy expenditures decreased by approximately 25%.

Undernutrition-Induced Alterations in Tissue Mass and Function

BODY COMPOSITION. All body tissue masses are affected by undernutrition, but fat mass and muscle mass are the most affected. In lean adults, these two tissues account for almost two thirds of body weight. Therefore, the loss of weight that occurs in malnourished patients is principally due to a loss in muscle and fat mass. Body adipose tissue can be almost completely depleted and up to half of muscle mass can be consumed before death from starvation occurs.

BODY WATER. Many patients who are malnourished have intravascular volume depletion because of inadequate water and sodium intake. However, the percentage of body weight that is composed of water may be increased. Decreased plasma proteins, leaky capillaries, leaky cells, and increased interstitial ion content may cause intravascular volume depletion and expansion of the interstitial space. Therefore, malnourished patients may have diminished intravascular volume in the presence of whole body fluid overload.

SKIN. The skin is a large organ that regenerates rapidly: a basal cell of the dermis reaches the cornified layer and dies in 10 to 14 days. Frequently, undernutrition causes the skin to be dry, thin, and wrinkled with atrophy of the basal layers of the epidermis and hyperkeratosis. Severe malnutrition may cause considerable depletion of skin protein and collagen. Patients with kwashiorkor experience sequential skin changes in different locations. Hyperpigmentation occurs first, followed by cracking and stripping of superficial layers, leaving behind hypopigmented, thin, and atrophic epidermis that is friable and easily macerated.

HAIR. Scalp hair becomes thin and sparse and is easily pulled out. In contrast, the eyelashes become long and luxuriant and there may be excessive lanugo hair in children. Children with kwashiorkor experience hypopigmentation with reddish-brown, gray, or blond discoloration. Adults may lose axillary and pubic hair.

GASTROINTESTINAL TRACT. Starvation and malnutrition cause structural and functional deterioration of the intestinal tract, pancreas,

and liver. The total mass and protein content of the intestinal mucosa and pancreas are markedly reduced. Mucosal epithelial cell proliferation rates decrease, and intestinal mucosa become atrophic with flattened villi. The synthesis of mucosal and pancreatic digestive enzymes is reduced. Intestinal transport and absorption of free amino acids are impaired, whereas hydrolysis and absorption of peptides are maintained. Gastric and biliary secretions are diminished. The abdomen may become protuberant because of hypomotility and gas distention. Hepatomegaly is common in severe malnutrition because of excessive fat accumulation caused by decreased very low density lipoprotein synthesis and triglyceride export. There is decreased synthesis of most hepatic proteins.

HEART. Chronic undernutrition affects cardiac mass and function. Cardiac muscle mass decreases, and the decrease is accompanied by fragmentation of myofibrils. Bradycardia (heart rate can decrease to less than 40 beats/min) and decreased stroke volume can cause a marked decrease in cardiac output and low blood pressure. For example, a hypocaloric diet in normal volunteers that caused a 24% decrease in body weight was associated with a 38% decrease in cardiac index.

LUNGS. Respiratory muscle function is altered by malnutrition, as evidenced by a decrease in vital capacity, tidal volume, and minute ventilation.

KIDNEYS. Renal mass and function are relatively well preserved during undernutrition, provided that adequate water is consumed to prevent a severe decrease in renal perfusion and acute renal failure. However, when malnutrition is severe there is a decrease in kidney weight, glomerular filtration rate, the ability to excrete acid, the ability to excrete sodium, and the ability to concentrate urine. Mild proteinuria may also occur.

BONE MARROW. Severe undernutrition suppresses bone marrow red blood cell and white blood cell production and leads to anemia, leukopenia, and lymphocytopenia.

MUSCLE. Muscle function is impaired by malnutrition because of both a loss of muscle mass and impaired metabolism. Decreased sodium pump activity causes an increase in intracellular sodium and a decrease in intracellular potassium, which affects myocyte electrical potential, contributing to fatigue.

BRAIN. The weight and protein content of the brain remain relatively stable during even long-term starvation. Therefore, the integrity of the brain is preserved at the expense of other organs and tissues.

IMMUNE SYSTEM. Severe undernutrition causes atrophy of all lymphoid tissues, including thymus, tonsils, and lymph nodes. Cell-mediated immunity is diminished more than antibody production. Alterations in cell-mediated immunity cause impaired delayed cutaneous hypersensitivity and anergy. The ability to kill bacteria is diminished because of decreased complement and impaired neutrophil function. Gastrointestinal immunoglobulin A secretion is also decreased. Malnourished patients are at increased risk for opportunistic infections and should be considered immunocompromised.

ENDOCRINE SYSTEM. Decreased plasma insulin concentrations and glucose intolerance are common in severe malnutrition. Growth hormone is usually increased and is much greater in the kwashiorkor type than the marasmic type of PEM. Serum thyroxine levels are low, and the conversion of thyroxine to triiodothyronine is decreased, with increased conversion to reverse triiodothyronine. Plasma cortisol concentration is usually greater than normal. The decrease in plasma leptin concentration that occurs early during energy restriction may be an important initiator of the neuroendocrine response to fasting.

ENERGY METABOLISM. Starvation and undernutrition decrease basal energy expenditure because of diminished organ size and function, increased conversion of active thyroid hormone to its inactive form, decreased sodium pump activity, decreased protein turnover, decreased body core temperature, absence of shivering and nonshivering thermogenesis, and suppression of sympathetic nervous system activity. Energy is also conserved by the onset of fatigue, which causes a decrease in physical activity.

Death from Starvation

At the terminal phase of starvation, body fat mass, skeletal muscle mass, and the size of most organs are markedly decreased. During this final phase of starvation, body fat stores are nearly depleted, energy derived from body fat decreases, and muscle protein catabolism is accelerated. The mechanism responsible for death from starvation in humans is not well understood, but many patients ultimately succumb to infection. It has been suggested that there are lethal levels of body weight loss (loss of 40% of body weight), of protein depletion (loss of 30 to 50% of body protein), of fat depletion (loss of 70 to 95% of body fat stores), or of body size (body mass index of 13 kg/m² for men and 11 kg/m² for women) in humans. The duration of survival depends on the amount of available endogenous fuels and the amount of lean tissue. Data from Irish Republican Army hunger strikers demonstrate that death occurs in lean men after approximately 2 months of starvation when more than 35% (~25 kg) of body weight is lost. Obese persons can survive much longer periods of starvation because of their increased fat stores and lean tissue mass. The longest reported fast is that of a severely obese (207 kg) man who safely lost 61% (126 kg) of his initial weight after completing a 382-day fast in which he ingested only acaloric fluids, vitamins, and minerals.

 Treatment

INITIAL EVALUATION. A careful clinical examination is needed to identify life-threatening complications of PEM that require immediate treatment. The presence of fluid, plasma glucose, electrolyte, and acid-base abnormalities should be determined. A search for infections (e.g., obtaining a white blood cell count, urine analysis and culture, blood cultures, and chest radiograph) should be considered even in the absence of physical findings because many patients are not able to mount a normal inflammatory response. The evaluation must also include a careful analysis of the possible route for nutritional support and whether the gastrointestinal tract can be used or parenteral nutrition is needed for refeeding.

INITIAL SUPPORTIVE CARE. Judicious resuscitation with fluids and electrolytes may be necessary before beginning feedings, with frequent evaluations to prevent congestive heart failure from excessive fluid. Vitamin supplementation should be given routinely. Severely malnourished patients are poikilothermic, and warm ambient temperature and warming blankets may be necessary to raise core temperature slowly. However, if warming blankets are being used, patients must be carefully monitored to avoid hyperthermia.

REFEEDING. The goal of feeding the severely malnourished patient can be divided into three phases: (1) to prevent further deterioration and correct life-threatening abnormalities, (2) to restore normal organ function and metabolism, and finally (3) to replete deficient nutrient stores. Oral or enteral tube feedings are preferred to parenteral feeding because of fewer serious complications and enhanced gastrointestinal tract recovery. Feedings should be given in small amounts at frequent intervals to avoid overwhelming the body's limited capacity for nutrient processing and to prevent hypoglycemia, which can occur during brief nonfeeding intervals. Therefore, small amounts of oral feeds should be given frequently (every 1 to 4 hours), enteral tube feeding by continuous drip, or parenteral nutrition by continuous infusion. Sodium intake should be limited during early refeeding, but liberal amounts of phosphorus, potassium, and magnesium should be given to patients who have normal renal function. Daily monitoring of body weight, fluid intake, urine output, and plasma glucose and electrolyte values is critical during the first few days of refeeding so that nutritional therapy can be appropriately adjusted when necessary. Appetite has usually improved during the second phase. Protein and energy intake should be marginally above estimated requirements to provide for adequate maintenance and repair. Additional protein and energy should be provided during phase three for repletion and synthesis of new tissue.

REFEEDING COMPLICATIONS. Refeeding can be harmful and even cause death because of impaired organ function and depleted nutrient stores caused by previous starvation. The adverse consequences caused by initiating feeding too aggressively are known as the refeeding syndrome and usually occur within the first 5 days. Refeeding syndrome complications include fluid overload, electrolyte imbalances, glucose intolerance, cardiac arrhythmias, and diarrhea.

Fluid Overload. Severely malnourished patients are at increased risk for fluid retention and congestive heart failure after nutritional therapy because of compromised cardiac and renal function. Because the ability to excrete sodium is impaired, even normal amounts of dietary sodium intake can be excessive. In addition, carbohydrates increase the concentration of circulating insulin, which stimulates sodium and water reabsorption by the renal tubule. The presence of heart failure requires discontinuation of feeding until cardiac status is stabilized.

Mineral Depletion. Carbohydrate refeeding stimulates insulin release and intracellular uptake of phosphate, which is used for protein synthesis and glucose metabolism. Therefore, plasma phosphorus concentrations can sometimes fall precipitously to below 1 mg/dL after initiating nutritional therapy if adequate phosphate is not given. Severe hypophosphatemia, associated with muscle weakness, paresthesias, seizures, coma, cardiopulmonary decompensation, and death, has occurred in severely malnourished patients after receiving enteral or parenteral nutritional therapy.

Decreased body cell mass and decreased Na⁺,K⁺-ATPase activity or leaky cell membranes in the malnourished patient lead to depletion of the major intracellular cations, potassium and magnesium. Nonetheless, serum potassium and magnesium concentrations may remain normal or near normal during starvation because of their release from tissue and bone stores. During refeeding, increases in protein synthesis, body cell mass, and glycogen stores require generous intakes of potassium and magnesium. In addition, hyperinsulinemia during refeeding increases cellular uptake of potassium and can cause a rapid decline in extracellular concentrations.

Glucose Intolerance. Malnourished patients are predisposed to hypoglycemia because of decreased hepatic glucose production. However, starvation and malnutrition impair insulin's ability to suppress endogenous glucose production and stimulate glucose uptake and oxidation. Therefore, providing enteral or parenteral carbohydrate can cause hyperglycemia, glucosuria, dehydration, and hyperosmolar coma. Furthermore, because of the importance of thiamine in glucose metabolism, carbohydrate refeeding in patients who are thiamine deficient can precipitate Wernicke's encephalopathy.

Cardiac Arrhythmias. Sudden death from ventricular arrhythmias can occur during the first week of refeeding in severely malnourished patients and has been reported in conjunction with severe hypophosphatemia. A prolonged QT interval may be a contributing cause of the rhythm disturbances.

Gastrointestinal Dysfunction. Alterations in gastrointestinal tract function limit the ability of the gastrointestinal tract to digest and absorb food. Mild diarrhea after initiating oral-enteral feeding usually resolves and is not clinically important if fluid and electrolyte homeostasis can be maintained. However, in some severely malnourished patients, oral feeding is associated with severe diarrhea and death. Therefore, aggressive fluid and electrolyte replacement and a search for enteric pathogens should be considered in patients with prolonged or severe diarrhea.

SUGGESTED READINGS

Ashworth A: Treatment of severe malnutrition. J Pediatr Gastroenterol Nutr 2001;32: 516–518. *Reviews the management of severe protein-energy malnutrition, particularly in hospitalized children in underdeveloped countries.*

Golden MHN: Severe malnutrition. *In* Weatherall DJ, Ledington JGG, Warrell DA (eds): Oxford Textbook of Medicine, 3rd ed. New York, Oxford University Press, 1996, pp 1278–1296. *Excellent review of pathophysiology, clinical presentation, and management of malnutrition in children.*

Keusch GT: The history of nutrition: Malnutrition, infection and immunity. J Nutr 2003;133:336S–340S. *This article reviews the relationship between malnutrition and susceptibility to infection.*

Klein S, Jeejeebhoy KN: The malnourished patient: Nutritional assessment and management. *In* Feldman M, Friedman LS, Sleisenger M (eds): Sleisenger and Fordtran's Gastrointestinal and Liver Disease, 7th ed. Philadelphia, WB Saunders, 2002, pp 265–285. *Reviews nutritional assessment and management of severely malnourished adult patients and basic principles of nutritional metabolism.*

Waterlow JC: Protein-Energy Malnutrition. London, Edward Arnold, 1992. *Comprehensive book that carefully discusses all major aspects of protein-energy malnutrition in children in underdeveloped countries.*

229 ENTERAL NUTRITION

John L. Rombeau

Enteral nutrition is the provision of liquid formula diets into the gastrointestinal tract. When compared with total parenteral nutrition, enteral nutrition measurably increases intestinal mucosal growth and function and is less costly. Because of these acknowledged benefits, enteral nutrition is being used with increasing frequency in medical patients. It is therefore incumbent upon physicians to be familiar with the rationale, indications, administration, and complications of enteral nutrition.

Rationale for Provision of Enteral Nutrients

The most important stimulus for gut growth and function is the presence of nutrients within the gastrointestinal tract. Enteral nutrients mediate such effects both directly and indirectly. The presence of nutrients within the intestinal lumen directly increases epithelial proliferation and enhances mucosal cell renewal. In the absence of luminal stimuli or intestinal nutrients, the small and large bowels atrophy not only in the absorptive cells and brush border enzymes but also in the mucus-secreting cells and the gut-associated lymphoid tissue. These entities are important protective components of the intestinal barrier against bacteria, endotoxins, and other antigenic macromolecules and may provide a rationale for using small volumes (e.g., 10 mL/hour) of continuous enteral feeding in critically ill patients even if they cannot tolerate larger volumes and must be fed parenterally as well.

Enteral nutrients mediate many of their indirect enterotropic effects by stimulating gut hormones such as gastrin, neurotensin, bombesin, and enteroglucagon. Gastrin exerts trophic effects on the stomach, duodenum, and possibly the colon. Enteral nutrients given to animal models increase the production of additional enterotropic hormones such as glucagon-like peptide 2. Furthermore, because of reduced manufacturing costs of its nutrient components, enteral feeding is less costly than total parenteral nutrition and may be more cost-effective than hand-feeding disabled or debilitated patients.

Indications

General indications for enteral nutrition include the following: (1) the presence of protein-energy malnutrition (Chapter 228), (2) a gastrointestinal tract that can safely tolerate enteral formulas, and (3) anticipated inadequate oral intake for at least 7 days. Safe use of the gastrointestinal tract is possible in the absence of obstruction, severe intractable diarrhea, or massive bleeding. The anticipated duration of inadequate oral intake is based solely on the clinical judgment of the primary physician. Table 229–1 lists examples of specific medical indications for enteral nutrition. Figure 229–1 gives an algorithm for determining the method of feeding.

Dietary Formulas

Commercial enteral formulas have proliferated rapidly. Table 229–2 outlines the nutrient composition of some of these agents, including polymeric balanced diets, modified formulas, and modular supplements.

POLYMERIC BALANCED FORMULAS. Polymeric formulas are "complete," balanced, isotonic diets containing 100% of the Recommended Dietary Allowance for substrates, vitamins, and minerals when prescribed in

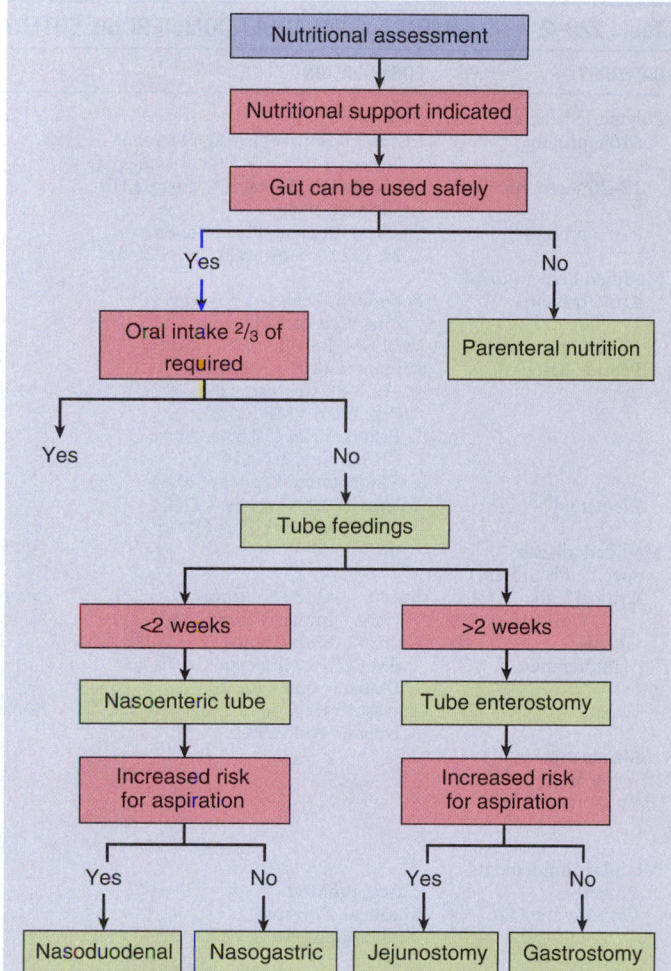

FIGURE 229–1 • Decision approach for the type and route of nutritional support.

the recommended amounts. These formulas are palatable and are the first choice for oral supplementation or tube feeding when digestion and absorption are reasonably normal. The nitrogen source consists of an intact or partially hydrolyzed natural protein (e.g., soy, egg, lactalbumin) that requires the patient's ability to digest protein in addition to carbohydrate and fat. The caloric density of these formulas is usually 1 kcal/mL but can be as high as 1.5 or 2 kcal/mL. Calorie-dense formulas are reasonable choices for patients who have unusually high caloric requirements, can tolerate only limited feeding volumes, or require fluid restriction. Most importantly, polymeric balanced formulas are less expensive than the other formulas. Their major disadvantage is a fixed nutrient composition.

MODIFIED FORMULAS. Conventional modified diets are also "complete" diets. Composed primarily of predigested or elemental nutrients, they require minimal digestion and are almost completely absorbed. Although the protein source can be crystalline amino acids, some pancreatic function is required to digest carbohydrates (oligosaccharides and disaccharides) and fats (up to 30% of which are provided as medium-chain triglycerides). In addition, absorption of glucose, sodium, amino acids, fat, vitamins, and trace elements requires intact mucosal transport systems.

Unlike the polymeric balanced diets, modified diets are hyperosmolar, unpalatable, and relatively expensive, costing between three and 10 times as much per calorie as polymeric balanced formulas. They may produce osmotic diarrhea if administered too rapidly and they require flavoring supplements for oral use. Modified diets may be indicated in patients with conditions of digestive or absorptive insufficiency, in whom polymeric diets are not well tolerated. Examples of such limiting conditions include chronic pancreatitis, short-bowel syndrome, and prolonged ileus.

DISEASE-SPECIFIC FORMULAS. Certain modified formulas are designed for patients with specific nutritional needs. Formulas that contain

Table 229–1 • INDICATIONS FOR THE USE OF ENTERAL NUTRITION IN ADULT MEDICAL PATIENTS

Protein-energy malnutrition with anticipated significantly decreased oral intake for at least 7 days
Anticipated significantly decreased oral intake for 10 days
Severe dysphagia
Massive small bowel resection (used in combination with total parenteral nutrition)
Low-output (<500 mL/day) enterocutaneous fistula

Nutritional Diseases

Table 229–2 • COMMONLY USED ADULT COMMERCIAL ENTERAL FEEDING FORMULAS*

CATEGORY	FORMULATION			
Polymeric balanced	1.0 kcal/mL	1.2 kcal/mL	1.5 kcal/mL	2.0 kcal/mL
≤16% protein	Ensure, Resource, Isocal, Osmolite, Nutren 1.0		Nutren 1.5, Ensure Plus, Resource Plus, Boost Plus, Comply	Nutren 2.0, Deliver, Magnacal
17–20% protein	Osmolite HN, Isocal HN, Ensure HN, Ultracel, Jevity		Ensure Plus HN	TwoCal HN
≥20% protein	Sustacal, Replete, Promote, Protain XL (22%), Isosource VHN (25%)		TraumaCal	
Modified-conventional				
≤16% protein	Peptamen, Reabilan, Vivonex Plus, Criticare HN			
17–20% protein	Vital HN, Reabilan HN, Alitra Q			
Peptide based	Peptamen (16%), Reabilan (12.5%), Criticare HN (14%), Peptamen VMP (25%), Reabilan HN (17.5%), Alitra Q (21%), Vital HN (16%), SandaSource Peptical (20%)		Crucial (25%)	
Elemental	Tolerex (8%), Vivonex T.E.N. (15%), Vivonex Plus (18%)			
Modified–disease specific (% protein)†				
Critical Care	Immun-Aid (32%), Impact (22%), Impact/Fiber (22%)	Perative (20%)		
Glucose intolerance	Glytrol (18%), Choice dM (17%), Glucema (16.7%), Diabeta Source (20%)			
Hepatic	Travasorb Hepatic (11%), Hepatic-Aid (15%)	Hepatic-Aid II (15%)	Nutrihep (11%)	
Malabsorption Renal			Lipisorb (17%), Travasorb Renal (7%)	Renal Cal (6–9%) Amin-Aid (4%)
Pulmonary			NutriVent (18%), Respalor (20%), Pulmocare (16.7%)	
Modular supplements				
Protein	Casec, ProMod			
Carbohydrate fat	Moducal, Polycose Microlipid, MCT oil			

*This table includes only a partial listing of commercial products.
†Manufacturers market these products as disease specific. The author's use of this designation is intended neither to endorse the manufacturer's claims of special efficacy in the diseases specified nor to deny that the polymeric-balanced or modified-conventional formulas might be appropriate or even superior in these conditions.
MCT = medium-chain triglyceride.

only essential amino acids as the protein source are designed for patients with renal failure. Formulas that have a protein source high in branched-chain amino acids and low in aromatic amino acids have been formulated for patients with hepatic encephalopathy, severe trauma, and sepsis. Formulas that are high in fat content (about 55% of calories) and low in carbohydrate content (about 28% of calories) have been recommended for patients with respiratory insufficiency because their oxidation produces less carbon dioxide. The high fat content of these formulas may produce diarrhea in critically ill patients. Recently, diets supplemented with fish oils, arginine, and nucleotides have been developed to allegedly enhance the immune response of critically ill and postoperative patients. These diets are very expensive. Well-controlled and properly designed clinical trials are needed before their use can be recommended. Little objective evidence justifies the use of any of these expensive, disease-specific formulas: Their use should be restricted to patients with specific nutrient needs who cannot tolerate polymeric and conventional modified diets.

MODULAR SUPPLEMENTS. Modular supplements, which consist of single or multiple nutrients, can be added to existing "fixed-ratio" diets without affecting the quality or quantity of other nutrients. They are designed for patients for whom standard fixed-ratio formulas are suboptimal. Commercially available modules include carbohydrate, fat, protein, mineral, electrolyte, and vitamin formulations.

Enteral Nutrition Administration

ACCESS. Selection of the access site for delivery of enteral nutrients is based on the anticipated duration of forced feeding and the potential risk of aspiration. Ideally, enteral nutrition is given by the oral route to conscious patients with intact gag reflexes who require nutritional supplementation only with meals. For patients who cannot tolerate oral nutrition, other access techniques include nasogastric tube, nasoenteric tube, and tube enterostomy.

Nasogastric or nasoenteric tubes are ideal for patients who require short-term (less than 2 weeks) enteral nutrition. To use these access routes safely, patients must have intact gag reflexes and competent lower esophageal sphincters. Ideal candidates are those with poor oral intake such as occurs with cancer of the head and neck and the lung. The stomach is the preferred site of delivery, but the nasoenteric tube should be advanced into the jejunum in patients with gastroparesis and a high risk of aspiration.

Permanent access through tube enterostomies is the preferred route of delivery for long-term enteral nutrition (more than 2 weeks). Tube enterostomies are inserted either endoscopically, laparoscopically, or operatively into the pharynx, stomach, and jejunum.

The percutaneous endoscopic approach is the preferred method for gastrostomy placement. It has the advantage of decreased procedure time, local anesthesia, absence of an incision, and avoidance of ileus. The speed, simplicity, low cost, and low complication rate of percutaneous endoscopic gastrostomy have resulted in its replacement of surgical gastrostomy in most hospitals. Surgical gastrostomy for feeding is indicated for patients unable to tolerate percutaneous endoscopic gastrostomy or for individuals undergoing concomitant gastrointestinal surgery.

Jejunostomy is indicated for patients who need long-term enteral nutrition and have chronic aspiration, gastric outlet obstruction, or stomach or duodenal cancer or for patients who have had a gastrectomy.

DELIVERY. Formulas are delivered intermittently or continuously. Intermittent feeding is preferred for delivery into the stomach because it is more physiologic and "frees" the patient from the feeding equipment. Feedings of polymeric diets in a volume of 240 to 400 mL every 4 hours are well tolerated. The disadvantages of intermittent feedings consist of an initial requirement for nursing supervision, such as monitoring for gastric residuals, and a higher risk of aspiration if delayed gastric emptying is present. Slow administration of small volumes into the stomach (25 to 40 mL/hr) is well tolerated and avoids the abdominal discomfort often caused by the increased rate and volume of intermittent feedings.

Continuous feeding, administered by infusion pump over a period of 18 to 24 hours, requires less nursing supervision and results in smaller residual volumes and a lower risk of aspiration than does intermittent feeding. When feeding into the duodenum or jejunum, continuous feeding is required to avoid distention of the bowel, fluid and electrolyte shifts, and diarrhea, all of which can occur with intermittent feeding. Feedings into the small bowel usually consist of isotonic polymeric solutions, initially at a rate of 30 mL/hour. The rate is increased approximately 25 mL/hour/day until the desired volume is achieved to meet the patient's nutrient requirements. Infusions should be initiated at very low rates (10 mL/hr) in critically ill patients. Disadvantages of continuous feeding include the expense of the volumetric infusion pump and the limitation it places on ambulatory patients.

MONITORING. Patients receiving enteral feedings require the same careful monitoring as do those who receive parenteral nutrition. This need for monitoring is especially true in critically ill patients. Routine monitoring is best accomplished by following a protocol that ensures complete and detailed surveillance to reduce the possibility of error in formula choice and nutrient administration and to assess progress toward nutritional goals (Table 229–3).

Special attention must be paid to gastrointestinal tolerance to the formula. The patient's condition should be evaluated daily for diarrhea, constipation, nausea, cramping, vomiting, and abdominal distention. Clinical evidence of abdominal distention is a contraindication to enteral feeding. One must give close attention to the patient's metabolic status and fluid and electrolyte balance. In many instances, potential complications can be avoided by simple maneuvers such as changing the infusion rate, caloric density, or formulation.

Periodic nutritional assessment is required to evaluate the adequacy of the nutritional support. Nitrogen balance, body weight change, and serum protein status should be monitored and the nutrient prescription amended when indicated. Because of frequent disruptions in feeding attempts, it is not uncommon for hospitalized patients to receive as little as 70% of the enteral calories ordered on a daily basis. These considerations may make it necessary to increase the infusion rate or to supplement infusions with parenteral feeding until satisfactory enteral intake is achieved.

Complications

Clinically significant complications of enteral feeding, although few, should be promptly recognized and treated aggressively. As noted, a standardized monitoring protocol helps prevent and detect possible problems. Complications of enteral feeding are grouped into four major categories: gastrointestinal, metabolic, infectious, and mechanical.

GASTROINTESTINAL. Diarrhea, defined as stool weight (or volume) of more than 200 mL per 24 hours, is the most common complication of enteral nutrition and occurs in 10 to 20% of patients. Its possible causes are listed in Table 229–4. Tube feeding–related factors that have been suggested to predispose to diarrhea but are not documented by controlled studies include formula hyperosmolality, lactose in the presence of relative lactase deficiency, and bacterial contamination of the enteral products and delivery systems. Although contamination is not a frequent cause of diarrhea, formula containers and administration tubing should be changed daily to avoid this complication. High-fat formulas may cause diarrhea when patients suffer from fat malabsorption (as with pancreatic exocrine insufficiency, biliary obstruction, ileectomy, or ileitis). Enterally administered medications, including antibiotics, hyperosmolar drug solutions such as sorbitol-containing elixirs, and magnesium-containing antacids, can cause diarrhea. Many elixir medications contain substantial amounts (up to 65%) of sorbitol, although the agent is listed in alphabetic order in the drug information insert only as an "inactive" ingredient. For this reason, all elixir medications must be considered potential causes of diarrhea in tube-fed patients, and it is often prudent to discontinue them or change them to tablet or intravenous forms to determine their responsibility.

Treatment of diarrhea is directed at the underlying cause; however, several therapeutic options are available when no cause is clearly identifiable. Decreasing the feeding flow rate may alleviate diarrhea by allowing time for intestinal mucosal adaptation to occur when the gastrointestinal tract has not been used for extended periods (in cases of starvation and total parenteral nutrition–induced intestinal atrophy). The flow rate is then slowly increased over several days. Parenteral feeding may be necessary to meet full nutrient requirements during this interval. Nonspecific treatment with antidiarrheal agents can also be tried cautiously. Supplementation of formulas with fiber may help solidify the stool and slow transit time in patients not receiving broad-spectrum antibiotics. The fiber contained in some

---

Table 229–3 • STANDARD ORDER FORM FOR PATIENTS RECEIVING ENTERAL NUTRITION

Obtain an abdominal radiograph to confirm tube location before feeding.

Elevate the head of the bed 30 degrees when feeding into the stomach.

Record the name, volume, and strength of the formula and the duration and rate (mL/hr) of feeding.

Check the gastric residual every 4 hr in patients receiving gastric feedings. Withhold feedings for 4 hr if the residual is greater than 150 mL. Notify the physician if two consecutive measurements detect excessive residual.

Weigh the patient on Monday, Wednesday, and Friday.

Record input and output daily. Every 8 hr, chart the volume of formula administered separately from water or other oral intake.

Change administration tubing daily.

Irrigate the feeding tube with 20 mL of water at the completion of each intermittent feeding, when the tube is disconnected, after delivery of crushed medications, or if feeding is stopped for any reason.

When the patient is ingesting oral nutrients, request calorie counts daily upon request.

Obtain a complete blood cell count with red blood cell indices, SMA-12, serum iron, serum magnesium, albumin, transferrin, and prealbumin every Monday.

Obtain an SMA-6 every Thursday.

Collect urine for 24 hr starting at 8 AM, and analyze for urea nitrogen and creatinine upon request.

Hold feedings for nausea, vomiting, distention. Call a house officer.

SMA-12 = sequential multiple analyzer, 12 tests.

Table 229–4 • CAUSES OF DIARRHEA IN TUBE-FED PATIENTS

Common Causes Unrelated to Tube Feeding
 Elixir medications containing sorbitol
 Magnesium-containing antacids
 Antibiotic-induced sterile gut
 Pseudomembranous colitis
Possible Causes Related to Tube Feeding
 Inadequate fiber to form stool bulk
 High fat content of formula (in the presence of fat malabsorption syndrome)
 Bacterial contamination of enteral products and delivery systems (causal association with diarrhea not documented)
 Rapid advancement in rate (after the gastrointestinal tract is unused for prolonged periods)
Unlikely Causes Related to Tube Feeding
 Formula hyperosmolality (proven not to be a cause of diarrhea)
 Lactose (absent from nearly all enteral feeding formulas)

commercial formulas (usually soy polysaccharide) has not been shown to reduce the incidence of diarrhea.

METABOLIC. Metabolic complications include abnormalities in fluid and electrolyte balance, hyperglycemia, trace element deficiencies, vitamin K deficiency, and abnormalities in protein tolerance.

Overhydration occurs in 20 to 25% of patients receiving enteral nutrition. Cardiac failure and renal insufficiency aggravate the problem and complicate its management. Slowing of the infusion rate or substitution of a 1.5 to 2 kcal/mL formula usually provides adequate treatment, and diuretics are rarely necessary for acute control. Although uncommon, hypertonic dehydration also can occur in patients fed calorie-dense formulas, especially when these patients cannot communicate their thirst.

Hyperglycemia occurs in 10 to 30% of tube-fed patients. High-calorie enteral diets may unmask adult-onset diabetes mellitus. Hyperglycemia is corrected by decreasing the formula flow rate, administering insulin, or implementing both of these measures. Because hyperglycemia can cause osmotic diuresis, the patient's fluid status must be carefully monitored.

Abnormalities of most electrolytes and trace elements have been reported. Routine screening of many of these substances permits early detection before clinical manifestations are apparent. Such screening is especially important in patients with renal, cardiac, or hepatic insufficiency.

INFECTIOUS. The most common infectious complication of enteral nutrition is aspiration pneumonia, which is potentially fatal. Its incidence varies from 1 to 44%, depending on how it is defined. Aspiration can occur subtly, without witnessed episodes of vomiting, and it should be suspected with new onset of tachycardia, tachypnea, fever, hypoxemia, or chest radiographic changes. Patients fed nasogastrically appear to have a higher likelihood of aspiration than do patients fed by gastrostomy or jejunostomy. Those with an endotracheal tube or a tracheostomy have an especially high risk. Feeding beyond the duodenum probably lowers the incidence of aspiration, although no conclusive evidence supports this premise.

Preventive measures include elevating the head of the bed to 30 degrees, periodic measuring of gastric residuals, and inflating the endotracheal tube cuff. Correct techniques to insert the soft feeding tubes and careful observation of the tube's position may prevent potentially lethal bronchopleural complications. A chest radiograph should be obtained before feeding is initiated in every patient with a newly inserted nasogastric or nasoenteric tube if gastric contents cannot be withdrawn through the tube. Methods for detecting "silent" aspiration of enteral formulas in intubated patients include checking tracheal aspirations for the presence of glucose with the use of oxidant reagent strips or placing methylene blue dye in the formula as a potential marker in tracheal aspirates.

MECHANICAL. Mechanical complications associated with enteral nutrition generally relate to the tube itself or to its anatomic position. Nasoenteric tubes can cause nasopharyngeal erosions and discomfort, sinusitis, otitis media, gagging, esophagitis, esophageal reflux, tracheoesophageal fistulas, and rupture of esophageal varices. Feeding tubes can become knotted or clogged. Gastrostomy or jejunostomy tubes can cause mechanical obstruction of the pylorus or small bowel. Additional complications of percutaneous tubes include leakage around the tube, dislodgment to an intraperitoneal position, and occlusion, especially of small-bore needle-catheter jejunostomies.

SUGGESTED READINGS

Jonas CR, Griffith DP, Bergman GF, et al: Nutrient pharmacotherapy. *In:* Rombeau JL, Rolandelli RH (eds): Clinical Nutrition: Parenteral Nutrition, 3rd ed. Philadelphia, WB Saunders, 2001. *A review of the use of nutrients and drugs in improving clinical outcome.*

Klein S: A primer of nutritional support for gastroenterologists. Gastroenterology 2002;122:1677–1687. *A recent review of the scientific basis and clinical utility of nutritional care of hospitalized and home patients.*

230 PARENTERAL NUTRITION

M. Molly McMahon

The notion that patients could receive all of their nutritional requirements intravenously was first appreciated in 1968. This advance was a landmark in the field of nutrition and clinical medicine. Although parenteral nutrition can be essential or even life-saving, its substantial cost and potential for complications necessitate judicious use.

Definition

The term *parenteral nutrition* should be used in place of *intravenous hyperalimentation*, a term coined at a time when provision of an excess of calories was believed to be beneficial. Parenteral nutrition provides amino acids (nitrogen), dextrose (carbohydrate), fat, electrolytes, minerals, trace elements, vitamins, and water by a central vein (central parenteral nutrition) or by a peripheral vein (peripheral parenteral nutrition). The enteral route should always be selected for the provision of nutrition in malnourished patients with a functional gastrointestinal tract because the bowel atrophies when nutrients are provided exclusively by vein. In addition, when compared with parenteral nutrition, tube feeding is less expensive, is associated with fewer metabolic complications, and does not require a central venous catheter for feeding.

Parenteral Nutrition Content

PROTEIN. Nitrogen is required for protein synthesis and is thus an essential component of parenteral nutrition. All currently manufactured parenteral nutrition solutions use crystalline amino acids as the source of nitrogen. Each gram of protein provides 4.0 kcal. Protein solutions are available with or without added electrolytes and minerals. For a well-nourished healthy subject without stress, the recommended dietary allowance of protein is 0.8 g/kg/day, provided that total caloric intake is adequate. Although protein is a metabolic fuel, its structural functions are as important as its fuel functions. At steady state, protein oxidation equals protein intake. Therefore, caloric requirements should be estimated as total calories rather than as nonprotein calories; the latter method includes carbohydrate and fat but excludes protein as a caloric source.

Protein breakdown and synthesis are dynamic processes. During severe illness, protein catabolism exceeds protein synthesis, and a net loss of body protein results. Body protein stores are minimal, and net protein loss results in a loss of tissue function. The increase in proteolysis is primarily caused by the actions of hormones and cytokines, with additional protein losses occurring in specific disease states. Diminished protein synthesis results from bed rest and decreased food intake. The administration of nutrition support to critically ill, immobilized patients can decrease but not prevent the loss of body protein. In general, hospitalized patients with normal renal and hepatic function should receive 1.0 to 1.5 g of protein per kilogram of body weight per day, with stressed patients requiring the higher amount. For the majority of patients, provision of greater amounts of protein does not provide benefit, and the excess protein results in ureagenesis. For obese patients (body mass index greater than or equal to 30), it may be appropriate to provide 1.5 g of protein per kilogram of estimated ideal weight. Data about how to feed obese patients are limited.

Modified amino acid solutions have been formulated for use in specific disease states. For example, the use of branched-chain, low aromatic amino acid solutions (providing up to 36% of amino acids as leucine, isoleucine, and valine) has been suggested for patients with hepatic encephalopathy. These patients have decreased plasma levels of branched chain amino acids and increased levels of aromatic amino acids. Branched-chain amino acids are uniquely oxidized in skeletal muscle and adipose tissue rather than in the liver. Several studies indicate that patients prone to encephalopathy can tolerate more protein being given as branched-chain enriched solutions than as the standard solution. Once the encephalopathy has resolved or if the patient does not receive benefit from this solution, the less costly standard amino acid solution should be used. Patients with liver disease but no encephalopathy can tolerate the less costly standard amino acid solutions. There is insufficient evidence to support the use of branched-chain amino acid solutions for patients with renal failure or severe stress.

Another example of a modified amino acid formulation is a more concentrated (15%) amino acid base solution. Use of this product enables higher caloric and protein supplementation in less volume to patients with excess total body water and salt. The disadvantages of this product are similar to those of branched-chain solutions: its expense and the lack of prospective, randomized trials confirming its efficacy. Parenteral nutrition supplementation with the amino acid glutamine is undergoing investigation. Currently, glutamine is not present in commercially available parenteral nutrition solutions in the United States because it has a shorter shelf life than the more commonly used amino acids and has been considered a nonessential amino acid. During critical illness, however, glutamine appears to be an essential amino acid for the intestinal tract. For patients undergoing bone marrow transplantation, the use of glutamine-supplemented parenteral nutrition (as compared with the standard amino acid solution) has been shown to improve clinical outcome with fewer infections and shortened hospital stay. Additional prospective randomized trials of these modified formulas are needed.

CARBOHYDRATE. Parenteral carbohydrate provided in the form of dextrose is a vital source of fuel and has important nitrogen-sparing effects. Solutions of dextrose in concentrations of 10 to 70% are mixed with the appropriate quantity of amino acids to obtain the desired solution. Each gram of hydrated dextrose monohydrate provides 3.4 kcal. The minimum daily glucose requirement is the amount necessary to meet brain glucose needs (100 to 150 g) because body carbohydrate stores are limited. Providing calories as glucose stimulates insulin secretion, reduces muscle protein breakdown, and decreases hepatic glucose release, thus decreasing the need for skeletal muscle to provide amino acid precursors for gluconeogenesis. Glucose oxidation is also stimulated, thus sparing the oxidation of amino acids.

INTRAVENOUS FAT EMULSION. Fat emulsions provide an intravenous source of fat calories and the essential linoleic and linolenic fatty acids. Currently, intravenous fat emulsions consist of 10% (1.1 kcal/mL) or 20% (2.0 kcal/mL) solutions. The emulsions contain long-chain fatty acids (derived from safflower and/or soybean oil), egg yolk phospholipids as emulsifying agents, and glycerin to make the solution isotonic with plasma. Intravenous fat is calorically dense (9 kcal/g), isotonic, and protein sparing and can prevent essential fatty acid deficiency. In addition, provision of a portion of calories as fat allows lower rates of dextrose infusion, which results in less hyperglycemia and hyperinsulinemia and a lower incidence of abnormalities in liver function tests. The fat can be administered intravenously either by piggyback infusion (10 or 20% only) or as a three-in-one admixture of fat, dextrose, and protein in one container. The fat emulsion is hydrolyzed by lipoprotein lipase to free fatty acids and glycerol. When fatty acids are oxidized for fuel, the respiratory quotient and therefore carbon dioxide production rates are lower than those observed if carbohydrate or protein is oxidized; this feature may be advantageous in certain clinical situations such as severe pulmonary disease.

Adverse effects, including hypoxemia, hepatic dysfunction, and impaired immune function from fat uptake by the reticuloendothelial system, have been reported with high infusion rates of intravenous fat emulsion. At very high infusion rates, enzymatic removal systems for free fatty acids become saturated and hypertriglyceridemia can result. However, all of these effects have been demonstrated at the higher infusion rates achieved during 8- to 12-hour infusions rather than during 24-hour infusions. No data suggest that the continuous infusion of intravenous fat emulsion at recommended rates to normolipidemic patients results in these adverse effects. Thus, continuous fat infusion is preferable to intermittent fat infusion. If the plasma triglyceride concentration exceeds 400 mg/dL, the intravenous fat emulsion infusion rate should be reduced or the infusion discontinued. Although the optimal percentage of calories that should be infused as fat is unclear, provision of 20 to 30% of total calories as fat is generally recommended for stressed patients receiving parenteral nutrition.

The role of fat extends beyond that of energy substrate alone inasmuch as substitution of different fat sources has been reported to beneficially modify the patient's response to illness. Active investigation is underway to determine the optimal type (e.g., medium-chain triglycerides, short-chain triglycerides, structured triglycerides, ω-3 fatty acids) and quantity of fat to be provided in parenteral nutrition solutions.

ELECTROLYTES, MINERALS, TRACE ELEMENTS, AND MULTIVITAMINS. The electrolytes and minerals required for health are sodium, potassium, chloride, calcium, phosphorus, magnesium, and sulfur. The electrolytes are supplied as salts—for example, sodium (chloride, acetate, or phosphate), potassium (chloride, acetate, or phosphate), calcium gluconate, potassium phosphate, and magnesium sulfate—and provide maintenance intake for most adult patients. Most sodium and potassium cations are added to the parenteral nutrition solution as chloride or acetate salts after the phosphate requirement is met. Acetate is further metabolized by the liver to bicarbonate to provide an alkaline buffer.

Trace elements are commercially available as combination products or as single-item injections. The multiple trace element injection contains four, five, six, or seven elements of zinc, copper, manganese, chromium, selenium, iodine, or molybdenum in amounts that are suggested for medically stable adult patients. This amount may be adjusted as needed for individual patients. Because iodine and selenium are not always added to parenteral nutrition solutions, monitoring of levels and supplementation of these trace elements may be required for patients receiving longer-term use of parenteral nutrition. Manganese levels should be checked because the parenteral nutrition provision may need to be decreased or deleted.

The composition of intravenous multivitamin products has been established in accordance with the guidelines of the American Medical Association Nutrition Advisory Group. One adult multivitamin formulation and one pediatric multivitamin formulation are currently available commercially. For years, the adult formulation provided the daily maintenance for three fat-soluble (A, D, and E) and nine water-soluble vitamins. Recently, the Food and Drug Administration amended the adult formulation to increase doses of several water-soluble vitamins and to add vitamin K. Some patients require additional vitamin replacement doses. Serious consequences can result from providing less than the standard replacement amounts of vitamins. During nationwide shortages of intravenous multivitamin preparations, several patients receiving thiamin-deficient parenteral nutrition died with refractory lactic acidosis, clinical courses suggestive of beriberi, and brain lesions diagnostic of acute thiamin deficiency.

Indications for Nutritional Support

Protein catabolism (with eventual depletion of body protein leading to protein-calorie malnutrition) can be a consequence of starvation, severe illness, or a combination of the two. Malnutrition is difficult to define and thus inevitably arbitrary. The need for nutritional support in patients with malnutrition is a reflection of the timing and extent of recent (previous 3- to 6-month interval) unintentional weight loss, the presence or absence of clinical markers of stress, and the anticipated time that the patient will be unable to meet nutritional requirements orally. Studies that have demonstrated a beneficial influence of nutritional support on clinical outcome have provided nutrition for a minimum of 1 week. Currently, no evidence suggests that nutritional support of briefer duration is beneficial. Additional research is needed to develop clinical markers for malnutrition and to identify patients who will benefit from nutritional support.

Delivery of Parenteral Nutrition

INDICATIONS. Once it has been determined that nutrition support should be initiated, the route of nutrient delivery should be selected. Parenteral nutrition should be used whenever nutritional support is indicated in a patient with a nonfunctioning gastrointestinal tract. As examples, parenteral nutrition should be considered in malnourished patients with persistent distal bowel obstruction, serious gastrointestinal motility disorders combined with intolerance of tube feeding, short-bowel syndrome with insufficient intestinal adaptation to maintain nutritional status via the enteral route, and severe pancreatitis, as well as in patients in whom a feeding tube cannot be placed in the desired location. Although it is difficult to establish absolute criteria for the use of parenteral nutrition, the American Society for Parenteral and Enteral Nutrition has published guidelines for the general use of parenteral nutrition, as well as recommendations for its use in selected disease states. Once the decision has been made that parenteral nutrition is required, the clinician is faced with the challenge of selecting peripheral parenteral nutrition or central parenteral nutrition as the preferred form of nutrition.

PERIPHERAL VERSUS CENTRAL PARENTERAL NUTRITION. With the lower caloric and protein requirements that can be provided by this form of nutrition, peripheral parenteral nutrition may be considered in medically stable patients who require short-term (e.g., 7 to 10 days) parenteral nutrition. It is not possible to peripherally administer the high-osmolarity solutions used for central parenteral nutrition because of phlebitis. For this reason, the osmolarity of peripheral parenteral nutrition solutions should not exceed 1000 mOsm/L. The addition of isotonic lipid to dextrose and amino acids may enhance vein tolerance to peripheral parenteral nutrition solutions. Peripheral parenteral nutrition avoids the use of central vein catheterization. However, there are limitations to the use of peripheral parenteral nutrition. The cost of the solution is similar to that of central parenteral nutrition solutions. Furthermore, critically ill patients will not tolerate the high volume rates required to meet nutritional needs. Central parenteral nutrition is necessary to provide adequate nutrition to patients who are moderately or severely stressed or who are anticipated to require longer use of parenteral support.

VASCULAR ACCESS. Selection of the site for catheter insertion should be individualized for each patient. Cannulation of a high-flow central vessel permits infusion of hyperosmolar nutrient solutions that are not tolerated by smaller low-flow peripheral veins. In general, the preferred site of central catheter insertion is the subclavian vein, both for patient comfort and for ease of management. Central vein cannulation for parenteral nutrition should never be considered an emergency procedure. Coagulation studies should be checked before catheterization, and patients should be adequately hydrated. Sterile technique during catheter insertion is mandatory. Whereas placement of double- or triple-lumen catheters is appropriate in patients who require multiple infusions or hemodynamic monitoring in addition to parenteral nutrition, medically stable patients should receive nutrition via a single-lumen catheter. Before initiation of central parenteral nutrition, a chest radiograph should be obtained to confirm catheter tip location in the distal end of the superior vena cava.

A peripherally inserted central catheter for parenteral nutrition may be used effectively in selected adult patients. These radiopaque catheters, inserted in the basilic or cephalic vein via the antecubital fossa and advanced to the distal end of the superior vena cava for infusion of central parenteral nutrition, provide reliable venous access for medically stable patients requiring 1 week to as long as 6 months of central parenteral nutrition. Early reports noted a high incidence of phlebitis with peripherally inserted central catheter use. The use of peripherally inserted central catheters eliminates many of the risks associated with central venous catheter insertion.

ESTIMATION OF DAILY CALORIC REQUIREMENTS. The daily caloric requirement of patients can be estimated by use of a formula such as the Harris-Benedict equation or measured by indirect calorimetry (Table 230–1). For many years, it was believed that patients requiring nutritional support had elevated caloric requirements, especially when stressed by surgery, trauma, or sepsis. Over the last decade, however, numerous studies have shown that the majority of hospitalized patients have surprisingly normal energy expenditure, usually between 100 and 120% of predicted caloric expenditure. Data about how to feed obese patients are limited. Some groups advocate provision of 75% basal caloric requirements based on the obese weight, whereas other groups base the requirement on an adjusted weight.

Overfeeding can result in serious sequelae. Excess calories can increase oxygen consumption, carbon dioxide production, minute

Table 230–1 • GUIDELINES FOR ESTIMATING DAILY CALORIC, PROTEIN, AND FAT REQUIREMENTS OF HOSPITALIZED PATIENTS*

Calories[†]	Basal Harris-Benedict to Harris-Benedict plus 20%
Protein[†]	1.0–1.5 g/kg body weight
Fat	20–30% of total calories during 24-hr infusion

Harris-Benedict equation:
  Females: $655 + (9.6 \times \text{weight in kg}) + (1.8 \times \text{height in cm}) - (4.7 \times \text{age in yr})$
  Males: $66.5 + (13.8 \times \text{weight in kg}) + (5.0 \times \text{height in cm}) - (6.8 \times \text{age in yr})$

*An indirect calorimetric measurement of daily caloric needs may be helpful in the following group of patients: severely stressed patients (e.g., following closed head injury, multiple trauma, severe burn), volume-overloaded patients in whom the "dry weight" estimate is uncertain, nutritionally supported patients in whom weaning from mechanical ventilation is difficult, or patients receiving home parenteral nutrition.
[†]If patient's body mass index (BMI) is ≥30, 75% of the basal Harris-Benedict estimate of caloric needs and 1.5 g of protein per kilogram (based on estimated ideal weight) may be adequate. Ideal body weight can be estimated by the following method: females, 45.4 kg for 1.5 m and 2.3 kg per additional 2.5 cm; males, 48.1 kg for 1.5 m and 2.7 kg per additional 2.5 cm.
[†]Assumes normal or nearly-normal hepatic and renal function.
Modified from McMahon M, Farnell MB, Murray MJ: Nutritional support of critically ill patients. Mayo Clin Proc 1993;68:911–920.

Table 230–2 • ESTIMATING DAILY VOLUME REQUIREMENTS: FIRST STEP IN DESIGNING PARENTERAL NUTRITION FORMULAS

VOLUME STATUS	ESTIMATED DAILY VOLUME REQUIREMENT
Euvolemic patients with normal renal function and no unusual gastrointestinal or renal losses	30 mL of volume per kg body weight is an appropriate initial volume
Patients with increased gastrointestinal (e.g., nasogastric losses, diarrhea, or fistulae output) losses*	Daily volume generally should meet these losses, desired urine output (~1–1.5 L), and insensible losses (500 mL)
Patients with increased total body water and salt stores, critical illness, or syndrome of inappropriate antidiuretic hormone secretion	Maximally concentrated parenteral nutrition formulas should be used

*In general, non-dextrose-containing crystalloid solutions should be used to meet the unusual gastrointestinal losses because the amounts may vary day by day.

ventilation, and the work of breathing, which can fatigue patients with impaired lung function. Overfeeding can also cause hyperglycemia. During hospitalization, hyperglycemia may adversely affect fluid balance, immune function, and outcome. A growing body of clinical evidence links hyperglycemia to nosocomial infection in hospitalized patients. Finally, excessive calories can cause abnormal liver test results.

To design a specific parenteral nutrition program, the clinician should first determine the appropriate volume (Table 230–2) for the individual patient, then estimate the caloric requirement, and finally estimate the protein and fat requirements. The remaining caloric requirements are provided as carbohydrate (Table 230–3).

MONITORING PARENTERAL NUTRITION. Before initiation of parenteral nutrition, patients should have glucose, sodium, potassium, creatinine, urea, aspartate aminotransferase, calcium, phosphorus, and albumin levels measured. Height, weight, and body mass index should be recorded. For patients with pancreatitis or poorly controlled diabetes mellitus or for patients receiving medications formulated in fat emulsion (e.g., propofol), a triglyceride level should be checked before initiation of fat emulsion. For patients with known hypertriglyceridemia, a triglyceride level should be checked before and during intravenous fat emulsion administration. If triglyceride values are greater than 350–400 mg/dL, the fat emulsion dose should be reduced or stopped. Plasma magnesium, zinc, and copper levels should be measured in patients with impaired absorption or increased gastrointestinal (zinc, copper) or renal (magnesium) output. The calcium, magnesium, and zinc values should be interpreted with knowledge of the albumin level because they are albumin bound. In addition, plasma levels may not reflect tissue stores.

After initiation of parenteral nutrition, the patient's vital signs, fluid balance, body weight, and laboratory values must be carefully monitored. The source of fever should always be investigated in a patient with a central venous catheter. Hemodynamic data, fluid balance, and creatinine, urea, and sodium should be reviewed to help determine the appropriate parenteral nutrition volume. Daily weight should be interpreted in light of the fluid balance; weight increases exceeding 0.25 kg over a 24-hour period usually reflect fluid gain. The extent and frequency of biochemical monitoring following initiation of parenteral nutrition should be individualized; at a minimum, plasma glucose, electrolytes, and phosphorus levels should be checked until stable. Glucose control is important in hospitalized patients. [1] During short-term hospitalization, a plasma glucose goal range of 100 to 150 mg/dL is appropriate for medically stable patients in a nonintensive care unit. A goal range of 80 to 120 mg/dL for intensive care unit patients is appropriate. Initiation of a subcutaneous regular insulin algorithm is often necessary. If glycemic control cannot be achieved with parenteral nutrition supplementation of insulin and the regular insulin algorithm, a separate insulin infusion should be initiated.

Table 230–3 • DESIGN OF PARENTERAL NUTRITION PROGRAMS: EXAMPLES

Nonobese patient weighing 60 kg; assume basal Harris-Benedict equation estimate of daily caloric requirements of 1250 kcal/day

Patient characteristics:
1. Euvolemic, normal urine output, and no unusual gastrointestinal losses; therefore, appropriate initial estimate of daily fluid requirement is 30 mL/kg body weight
2. Moderately stressed with normal renal and hepatic function; therefore, appropriate to provide 1.2 g protein per kg body weight
3. Nonobese; therefore, appropriate to provide Harris-Benedict estimate plus 20% for calories, i.e., 1250 kcal plus 20% = 1500 kcal

Program design:
1. Fluid requirement: 30 mL × body weight; 30 × 60 = 1800 mL
2. Caloric requirement: Harris-Benedict estimate plus 20%; 1250 kcal − 250 kcal = 1500 kcal
3. Protein requirement for moderately stressed patient: 1.2 g/kg body weight; 60 × 1.2 = ~70 g protein. 70 g protein × 4 kcal/g protein = 280 kcal
4. Fat requirement: 30% of total calories; 30% × 1500 kcal = 450 kcal
5. Carbohydrate requirement: caloric requirement minus the sum of protein and fat calories: 1500 − (280 + 450 kcal) = 770 kcal. 770 kcal carbohydrate − kcal/g carbohydrate (3.4) = ~225 g carbohydrate
6. Therefore, consider the following parenteral nutrition formula: 1.5 L amino acids, 5%; dextrose, 15%; plus 250 mL of 20% fat emulsion, which provides 1750 mL, 1565 kcal, 75 g protein. 225 g carbohydrate, and 500 fat calories. Note that 5% amino acids equals 50 g protein per liter.
7. If institution uses three-in-one admixture (amino acids plus dextrose plus fat in one container) and stock solutions of 10% amino acids, 70% dextrose, and 20% lipid, a comparable parenteral nutrition program would be 1.5 L amino acids, 5%; dextrose, 15%; fat, 3.5%.

Similar patient characteristics except patients volume-expanded:
1. Consider the following fluid-restricted parenteral nutrition formula: 1 L of amino acids, 7%; dextrose, 20%; plus 250 mL 20% fat emulsion, which provides 1250 mL, 1460 calories, 70 g protein, 200 g carbohydrate, and 500 fat calories.

Table 230–4 • REFEEDING MALNOURISHED PATIENTS, PREVENTING THE REFEEDING SYNDROME

Avoid overfeeding
Avoid excess volume
Measure serum potassium and phosphorus levels and appropriately supplement
Administer thiamine

---

solutions may allow earlier and more adequate nutritional support. A 1-L can of a concentrated commercial solution of 10% amino acids and 70% dextrose, for example, provides 70 g protein and 200 g dextrose (960 total calories) (Table 230–4). Fat should be added when a larger volume can be tolerated. To further restrict volume, the parenteral nutrition admixture may be used as a vehicle for drugs with a stable dose requirement, provided that therapeutic efficacy has been documented for continuous drug infusion. Medications commonly added to the parenteral nutrition admixture include histamine receptor antagonists and regular insulin.

Complications

The complications associated with parenteral nutrition can be categorized into catheter related (mechanical, infectious, and thrombotic), metabolic, and gastrointestinal. Studies have demonstrated that the use of organized interdisciplinary nutrition support teams reduces complications.

Pneumothorax, the most common mechanical complication, is most often related to improper central vein cannulation technique. Anatomic factors (such as cachexia, barrel chest deformity, kyphosis, and morbid obesity) can increase the risk even with satisfactory technique. An important predictor of complications associated with central catheter insertion is the physician's experience in catheter insertion.

Catheter malposition is generally not serious if recognized early. Misdirection most often involves a subclavian catheter traveling up the ipsilateral internal jugular vein. The catheter can usually be repositioned by either the catheter guidewire technique or fluoroscopic manipulation. Other uncommon complications related to catheter placement are air embolism, subclavian or internal carotid artery puncture, hemothorax, hemomediastinum, catheter embolism, thoracic duct injury, and brachial plexus injury.

Bacteremia and fungemia are serious complications, and the catheter should always be evaluated as a potential source of infection. Most catheter-related septicemias begin with focal infections of the catheter wound; organisms from the patient's own cutaneous flora invade the intracutaneous tract when the catheter is inserted and thereafter. Hub contamination may also cause catheter-related septicemia. In addition, hematogenous seeding of the fibrin sheath on the catheter tip can occur during an episode of bacteremia or fungemia. Sterile technique and the use of effective antiseptics during catheter insertion are the most important measures to prevent catheter sepsis.

The two types of infection that occur most often are catheter infection and catheter-related septicemia. Quantitative cultures of the external surface of the catheter differentiate infection from contamination more reliably than the broth culture method does. Infection is diagnosed when culture of the catheter grows more than 15 colony-forming units. Catheter-related septicemia is diagnosed by semiquantitative catheter cultures and blood cultures that are positive for the same species. The most common organisms that cause catheter-related sepsis are coagulase-negative staphylococci, *Staphylococcus aureus,* and yeast. In selected circumstances (unexplained fever or leukocytosis), replacement of the catheter by guidewire exchange technique is appropriate. Catheters should always be removed immediately if patients appear septic. Blood (peripheral and central) and catheter cultures should always be obtained; if applicable, the catheter site should also be cultured. New types of catheters and cuffs are being developed to reduce the risk of device-related infection.

Although subclinical venous thrombosis commonly occurs in patients receiving central parenteral nutrition, clinically significant thrombosis is uncommon during short-term nutrition use. The incidence of thrombosis, however, is greater in patients receiving

---

Parenteral nutrition should not constitute the sole treatment of acute abnormalities in volume or electrolyte disturbances, but it is an effective vehicle to replace chronic losses. Knowledge of the volume of gastrointestinal and renal losses allows an estimation of electrolyte and mineral losses and appropriate parenteral nutrition supplementation. A daily review of the medication profile is essential to anticipate and manage metabolic parameters (e.g., amphotericin: hypokalemia, hypomagnesemia, renal tubular acidosis; corticosteroids: hyperglycemia, hypokalemia; insulin: hypokalemia, hypophosphatemia, hypomagnesemia; diuretics: hypokalemia, hypomagnesemia, metabolic alkalosis; propofol: this anesthetic agent is in a 10% fat emulsion, and its administration may temporarily eliminate or decrease the requirement for additional fat). The acetate and chloride content of the parenteral nutrition admixture should be adjusted for acid-base disturbances. Acetate and chloride balance is best assessed by reviewing the blood gas (arterial or venous) and electrolyte results and by the volume of gastrointestinal or renal losses. For example, the parenteral nutrition acetate content may be increased and the chloride content decreased in cases of metabolic acidosis; the converse is true for metabolic alkalosis. Although the extent of the daily examination must be individualized, the catheter site, heart, and lungs should always be examined and the possible development of peripheral edema assessed. Use of a patient monitoring record that combines information about the composition of the parenteral nutrition solution with biochemical data facilitates prompt recognition of metabolic abnormalities. The daily goal is to determine whether the parenteral nutrition program (volume or composition) needs modification in light of the patient's current condition. Once the gastrointestinal tract regains function, the enteral route should always be used for nutrition.

VOLUME-RESTRICTED PARENTERAL NUTRITION. Patients with excess total body water and salt following major surgery or illness are often those most in need of nutritional support. The ability to concentrate medications, intravenous infusions, and central parenteral nutrition

long-term parenteral nutrition. The diagnosis should always be considered when swelling develops in the arm and neck ipsilateral to the catheter and swollen veins develop in the neck. The use of very low doses of heparin (5000 to 6000 U in parenteral nutrition per day) or warfarin (approximately 1 mg/day) can reduce the incidence of central vein thrombosis without causing adverse hemorrhagic effects and should be considered for patients requiring long-term parenteral nutrition.

Serious metabolic disturbances can result from providing parenteral calories in excess of needs, the exclusive use of dextrose as the caloric source, or an excess or deficiency of nutrients. Serious and life-threatening complications of sudden refeeding, coined the *refeeding syndrome*, have been recognized since the advent of parenteral nutrition therapy (see Table 230–4). The refeeding risk increases when chronically malnourished patients are too rapidly refed. The risks are related to fluid and electrolyte abnormalities, malnutrition-related organ dysfunction, and vitamin deficiencies. The acute increase in plasma insulin concentration caused by feeding can lead to severe hypokalemia, hypomagnesemia, and hypophosphatemia if replacement is inadequate. Hyperinsulinemia promotes the passage of potassium from the extracellular space into the intracellular space and results in hypokalemia. Glucose- and insulin-stimulated glycolysis enhances cellular uptake and the use of phosphorus for the phosphorylation of glycolytic intermediates and for adenosine triphosphate synthesis. Hyperinsulinemia can also increase tissue uptake of magnesium, with subsequent hypomagnesemia. The adverse sequelae resulting from hypokalemia, hypophosphatemia, and hypomagnesemia are discussed in Chapters 112 through 115. In addition, acute hyperinsulinemia promotes renal tubular reabsorption of sodium, which can expand the extracellular fluid and provoke cardiac decompensation in extremely malnourished patients with decreased left ventricular mass. Thiamine supplementation should be provided.

Hepatic abnormalities, the most common gastrointestinal complication associated with parenteral nutrition, may be caused by the therapy itself or by the patient's underlying disease or medications. In adults, parenteral nutrition–related hepatic abnormalities are common and are generally benign and temporary. Some patients requiring long-term parenteral nutrition, however, have persisting abnormalities in liver function tests associated with fibrotic and/or cholestatic damage. Complications may be biochemical (elevation of serum aminotransferase, alkaline phosphatase, or bilirubin) or histologic (steatosis, portal triaditis). Transaminase elevations generally occur early in therapy (1 to 2 weeks after initiation of parenteral nutrition) and often resolve without change in the program. Bilirubin and alkaline phosphatase elevations usually appear slightly later (2 to 3 weeks into therapy).

Although the etiology of parenteral nutrition–related hepatic abnormalities has not been clearly elucidated, many factors have been proposed, including the parenteral nutrition solution (excessive dextrose or total calories or fat-free parenteral nutrition), nutritional deficiencies (carnitine, taurine, essential fatty acid deficiency), and cholestasis. Biliary complications associated with parenteral nutrition include acalculous cholecystitis, gallbladder sludge, and cholelithiasis. Sludge, the most common of these complications, occurs when the gastrointestinal tract is not used. Abnormal liver function test results should not automatically lead to stopping or altering the parenteral nutrition solution inasmuch as abnormal liver function results may not represent true liver dysfunction. Other causes of abnormal hepatic function, such as extrahepatic obstruction, medications, or infection, should be excluded. The nutrition program should be reviewed to be certain that the caloric intake is not excessive and that a mixed-fuel system (i.e., dextrose, protein, and fat) is being infused. Finally, patients receiving long-term parenteral nutrition are at increased risk for developing metabolic bone disease.

1. Van den Berghe G, Wouters P, Weekers F, et al: Intensive insulin therapy in critically ill patients. N Engl J Med 2001;345:1359–1367.

SUGGESTED READINGS

American Gastroenterological Association Clinical Practice and Practice Economics Committee: AGA technical review on parenteral nutrition. Gastroenterology 2001;121:970–1001. *Summarizes the current literature evaluating the clinical use of parenteral nutrition.*

ASPEN Board of Directors: Guidelines for the use of parenteral and enteral nutrition in adult and pediatric patients. J Parenter Enteral Nutr 2002;26:15A–1385A. *Current nutrition guidelines from nutrition society.*

231 CONSEQUENCES OF ALTERED MICRONUTRIENT STATUS

Joel B. Mason

Micronutrients are a highly diverse array of dietary components necessary to sustain health. The physiologic roles of micronutrients are as varied as their composition; some are used in enzymes as either coenzymes or as prosthetic groups, others as biochemical substrates or hormones and, in some instances, the functions are not well defined. Under normal circumstances, the average daily dietary intake for each micronutrient that is required to sustain normal physiologic operations is measured in milligrams or smaller quantities. It is in this manner that micronutrients are distinguished from macronutrients, which encompass carbohydrates, fats, and proteins, as well as the macrominerals, calcium, magnesium, and phosphorus.

For orderly homeostasis to proceed, most dietary nutrients must be ingested in quantities that are neither too small nor too great. Disorders may arise, therefore, when this "physiologic window" is either not met or exceeded. The size of this physiologic window varies for each micronutrient and should be kept in mind, particularly in this era when the administration of large quantities of certain micronutrients is being increasingly explored for possible therapeutic implications. The dietary requirement for a particular micronutrient is determined by many factors, only one of which is the amount needed to sustain those physiologic functions for which it is used (Table 231–1). The U.S. National Academy of Sciences Food and Nutrition Board regularly updates dietary guidelines that define the quantity of each micronutrient that is "adequate to meet the known nutrient needs of practically all healthy persons." These recommended daily allowances (RDAs) underwent revision between 1998 and 2001, and the values for adults appear in Tables 231–2 and 231–3. Also established for the first time were *tolerable upper limits* for each micronutrient, which is the maximal daily level of oral intake that is likely to pose no adverse health risks (see Tables 231–2 and 231–3). *Adequate intake*, which is the amount necessary to prevent a deficiency state, is not necessarily synonymous with *optimal* intake, which is discussed in more detail later.

Vitamins and Trace Elements

VITAMINS. See Table 231–2. Vitamins have long been categorized as either fat-soluble (A, D, E, K) or water-soluble (all the others). This remains a physiologically meaningful manner of categorization. None of the fat-soluble vitamins appear to serve as coenzymes. Absorption of the fat-soluble vitamins is primarily through a micellar route and pathophysiologic conditions associated with fat malabsorption frequently are associated with selective deficiencies of the fat-soluble vitamins. In contrast, most of the functions of the water-soluble vitamins are as coenzymes. Furthermore, the water-soluble

Text continued on p. 1333

Table 231–1 • FACTORS THAT DETERMINE DIETARY REQUIREMENT OF A MICRONUTRIENT

PHYSIOLOGIC FACTORS

Bioavailability: the proportion of a micronutrient that is ingested and is capable of being assimilated and used for physiologic purposes.

Quantity required to fulfill physiologic roles.

Extent to which the body can reuse the micronutrient.

Distribution of nutrient in the body: storage compartments.

Gender.

Stage of life cycle: intrauterine development, childhood, adulthood, elder adulthood, pregnancy, lactation.

PATHOPHYSIOLOGIC AND PHARMACOLOGIC FACTORS

Inborn errors of metabolism: variously affect assimilation, utilization, or excretion of micronutrients.

Acquired disease states that alter the amounts required to sustain homeostasis (e.g., malabsorption, maldigestion, states that increase use).

Lifestyle habits: smoking, ethanol consumption.

Drugs: may alter bioavailability and/or utilization.

Nutritional Diseases

Table 231-2 • VITAMINS AND THEIR FUNCTIONS

	BIOCHEMISTRY AND PHYSIOLOGY	DEFICIENCY [RDA*]	TOXICITY [TUL†]	ASSESSMENT OF STATUS
FAT-SOLUBLE VITAMINS				
Vitamin A	A subset of the retinoid compounds, each member having biologic activity qualitatively similar to retinol, a member of the family. Carotenoids are structurally related to retinoids. Some carotenoids, most notably β-carotene, are metabolized into compounds with vitamin A activity and are therefore considered to be provitamin A compounds. Vitamin A is an integral component of rhodopsin and iodopsins, light-sensitive proteins in rod and cone cells in the retina. Needed for the induction and maintenance of cellular differentiation in certain tissues. Serves as a signal for appropriate morphogenesis in the developing embryo and needed for maintenance of cell-mediated immunity. One microgram of retinol is equivalent to 3.33 international units of vitamin A.	Follicular hyperkeratosis and night blindness are early indicators. Conjunctival xerosis, degeneration of the cornea (keratomalacia), and de-differentiation of rapidly proliferating epithelia are later indications of deficiency. *Bitot spots* (focal areas of the conjunctiva or cornea with foamy appearance) are an indication of xerosis. Blindness, due to corneal destruction and retinal dysfunction, ensues if left uncorrected. Increased susceptibility to infection is also a consequence. [F: 700 μg; M: 900 μg]	In adults, >150,000 μg may cause *acute* toxicity: fatal intracranial hypertension, skin exfoliation, and hepatocellular necrosis. *Chronic* toxicity may occur with habitual daily intake of >10,000 μg: alopecia, ataxia, bone and muscle pain, dermatitis, cheilitis, conjunctivitis, pseudotumor cerebri, hepatocellular necrosis, hyperlipidemia, and hyperostosis are common. Single, large doses of vitamin A (30,000 μg), or habitual intake of >4500 μg/d in early pregnancy can be teratogenic. Excessive intake of carotenoids causes a benign condition characterized by yellowish discoloration of the skin. Habitually large doses of canthaxanthin, a carotenoid, have the additional capability of inducing a retinopathy. [3000 μg]	Retinol concentration in the plasma and vitamin A concentrations in the milk and tears are reasonably accurate measures of adequate status. Toxicity is best assessed by elevated levels of retinyl esters in plasma. A quantitative measure of dark adaptation for night vision or an electroretinogram are useful functional tests.
Vitamin D	A group of sterol compounds whose parent structure is cholecalciferol (vitamin D₃). Cholecalciferol is formed in the skin from 7-dehydrocholesterol (provitamin D₃) by exposure to UV-B radiation. A plant sterol, ergocalciferol (provitamin D₂) can be similarly converted into vitamin D₂ and has similar vitamin D activity. The vitamin undergoes sequential hydroxylations in the liver and kidney at the 25 and 1 positions, respectively, producing the most bioactive form of the vitamin, 1,25-dihydroxy vitamin D. Maintains intracellular and extracellular concentrations of calcium and phosphate by enhancing intestinal absorption of the two ions and, in conjunction with PTH, promoting their mobilization from bone mineral. Vitamin D retards proliferation and promotes differentiation in certain epithelia. One microgram is equivalent to 40 IU.	Deficiency results in disordered bone modeling called *rickets* in childhood and *osteomalacia* in adults. Expansion of the epiphyseal growth plates and replacement of normal bone with unmineralized bone matrix are the cardinal features of rickets; the latter feature also characterizes osteomalacia. Deformity of bone and pathologic fractures occur. Decreased serum concentrations of calcium and phosphate may occur. [5 μg, ages 19–50; 10 μg, ages 51–70; 15 μg, age > 70]	Excess amounts result in abnormally high concentrations of calcium and phosphate in the serum: metastatic calcifications, renal damage, and altered mentation may occur. [50 μg]	The serum concentration of the major circulating metabolite, 25-hydroxy vitamin D, is an excellent indicator of systemic status except in chronic renal failure, in which the impairment of renal 1-hydroxylation results in disassociation of the mono and dihydroxyvitamin concentrations. Measuring the serum concentration of 1,25-dihydroxy vitamin D is then necessary.
Vitamin E	A group of at least 8 naturally occurring compounds, some of which are tocopherols and some of which are tocotrienols. At present, the only dietary form that is thought to be biologically active in humans is alpha-tocopherol. Acts as an antioxidant and free radical scavenger in lipophilic environments, most notably in cell membranes. Acts in conjunction with other antioxidants such as selenium.	Deficiency due to dietary inadequacy rare in developed countries. Usually seen in (1) premature infants, (2) individuals with fat malabsorption, and (3) individuals with abetalipoproteinemia. Red blood cell (RBC) fragility occurs and can produce a hemolytic anemia. Neuronal degeneration produces peripheral neuropathies,	Depressed levels of vitamin K–dependent procoagulants and potentiation of oral anticoagulants has been reported, as has impaired white blood cell (WBC) function. Doses of 800 mg/d have been reported to slightly increase the incidence of hemorrhagic stroke. [1000 mg]	Plasma or serum concentration of alpha-tocopherol is most commonly used. Additional accuracy is obtained by expressing this value per mg of total plasma lipid. RBC peroxide hemolysis test is not entirely specific but is a useful functional measure of the antioxidant potential of cell membranes.

Continued

Table 231–2 • **VITAMINS AND THEIR FUNCTIONS—cont'd**

	BIOCHEMISTRY AND PHYSIOLOGY	DEFICIENCY [RDA*]	TOXICITY [TUL†]	ASSESSMENT OF STATUS
		ophthalmoplegia, and destruction of posterior columns of spinal cord. Neurologic disease is frequently irreversible if deficiency is not corrected early enough. May contribute to hemolytic anemia and retrolental fibroplasia in premature infants. Has been reported to suppress cell-mediated immunity. [15 mg]		
Vitamin K	A family of naphthoquinone compounds with similar biologic activity. Phylloquinone (vitamin K_1) is derived from plants; a variety of menaquinones (vitamin K_2) is derived from bacterial sources. Serves as an essential cofactor in the post-translational gamma-carboxylation of glutamic acid residues in many proteins. These proteins include several circulating procoagulants and anticoagulants as well as proteins in the bone matrix and renal epithelium.	Deficiency syndrome, uncommon except in (1) breast-fed newborns, in whom it may cause "hemorrhagic disease of the newborn," (2) adults with fat malabsorption or who are taking drugs that interfere with vitamin K metabolism (e.g., coumarin, phenytoin, broad-spectrum antibiotics), and (3) individuals taking large doses of vitamin E and anticoagulant drugs. Excessive hemorrhage is the usual manifestation. [F: 90 µg; M: 120 µg]	Rapid intravenous (IV) infusion of K_1 has been associated with dyspnea, flushing, and cardiovascular collapse; this is likely related to the dispersing agents in the solution. Supplementation may interfere with coumarin-based anticoagulation. Pregnant women taking large amounts of the pro-vitamin menadione may deliver infants with hemolytic anemia, hyperbilirubinemia, and kernicterus. [no TUL established]	Prothrombin time is typically used as a measure of functional K status; it is neither sensitive nor specific for vitamin K deficiency. Determination of undercarboxylated prothrombin in the plasma is more accurate but less widely available.
WATER-SOLUBLE VITAMINS Thiamin (vitamin B_1)	A water-soluble compound containing substituted pyrimidine and thiazole rings and a hydroxyethyl side chain. The coenzyme form is thiamin pyrophosphate (TPP). Serves as a coenzyme in many alpha-ketoacid decarboxylation and transketolation reactions. Inadequate thiamin availability leads to impairments of above reactions, resulting in inadequate adenosine triphosphate synthesis and abnormal carbohydrate metabolism, respectively. May have an additional role in neuronal conduction independent of aforementioned actions.	Classical deficiency syndrome ("beriberi") described in Asian populations consuming polished rice diet. Alcoholism and chronic renal dialysis are also common precipitants. High carbohydrate intake increases need for B_1. Mild deficiency commonly produces irritability, fatigue, and headaches. More pronounced deficiency produces various combinations of peripheral neuropathy, cardiovascular dysfunction, and cerebral dysfunction. Cardiovascular involvement ("wet beriberi") includes congestive heart failure and low peripheral vascular resistance. Cerebral disease includes nystagmus, ophthalmoplegia, and ataxia (Wernicke's encephalopathy) as well as hallucinations, impaired short-term memory, and confabulation ("Korsakoff's psychosis") Deficiency syndrome responds within 24 hr to parenteral thiamin but is partially or wholly irreversible after a certain stage. [F: 1.1 mg; M: 1.2 mg]	Excess intake is largely excreted in the urine although parenteral doses of >400 mg/day are reported to cause lethargy, ataxia, and reduced tone of the gastrointestinal tract. [TUL not established]	The most effective measure of B_1 status is the erythrocyte transketolase activity coefficient, which measures enzyme activity before and after addition of exogenous TPP: RBCs from a deficient individual express a substantial increase in enzyme activity with addition of TPP. Thiamin concentrations in blood or urine are also used.
Riboflavin (vitamin B_2)	A compound consisting of a substituted isoalloxazine ring with a ribitol side chain. The vitamin serves as a coenzyme for a diverse array of biochemical reactions. The primary coenzymatic forms	Deficiency is usually seen in conjunction with deficiencies of other B vitamins. Isolated deficiency of riboflavin produces hyperemia and edema of nasopharyngeal	Toxicity not reported in humans. [TUL not established]	The most common method of assessment is determining the activity coefficient of glutathione reductase in RBCs (the test is invalid for individuals with glucose-

Table 231–2 • VITAMINS AND THEIR FUNCTIONS—cont'd

	BIOCHEMISTRY AND PHYSIOLOGY	DEFICIENCY [RDA*]	TOXICITY [TUL†]	ASSESSMENT OF STATUS
	are flavin mononucleotide (FMN) and flavin adenine dinucleotide (FAD). Riboflavin holoenzymes participate in oxidation-reduction reactions in a myriad of metabolic pathways.	mucosa, cheilosis, angular stomatitis, glossitis, seborrheic dermatitis, and a normochromic, normocytic anemia. [F: 1.1; M: 1.3]		6-phosphate dehydrogenase [G6PD] deficiency). Measurements of blood and urine concentrations are less desirable methods.
Niacin (vitamin B₃)	Refers to nicotinic acid and the corresponding amide, nicotinamide. The active coenzymatic forms are composed of nicotinamide affixed to adenine dinucleotide, forming NAD or NADP. More than 200 apoenzymes use these compounds as electron acceptors or hydrogen donors, either as a coenzyme or a cosubstrate. The essential amino acid tryptophan is used as a precursor of niacin; 60 mg of dietary tryptophan yields approximately 1 mg of niacin. Dietary requirements thus depend partly on tryptophan content of diet. Requirement is often determined on basis of caloric intake (i.e., niacin equivalents/1000 kcal). Large doses of nicotinic acid (1.5–3.0 g/day) effectively lower low-density lipoprotein cholesterol and elevate high-density lipoprotein cholesterol.	*Pellagra* is the classic deficiency syndrome and is often seen in populations where corn is the major source of energy. Still endemic in parts of China, Africa, and India. Diarrhea, dementia (or associated symptoms of anxiety or insomnia), and a pigmented dermatitis that develops in sun-exposed areas are typical features. Glossitis, stomatitis, vaginitis, vertigo, and burning dysesthesias are early signs. Reported to occasionally occur in carcinoid syndrome, because tryptophan is diverted to other synthetic pathways. [F:14 mg; M: 16 mg]	Human toxicity known largely through studies examining hypolipidemic effects. Includes vasomotor phenomenon (flushing), hyperglycemia, parenchymal liver damage, and hyperuricemia. [35 mg]	Assessment of status is problematic: blood levels of vitamin not reliable. Measurement of urinary excretion of the niacin metabolites, N-methylnicotinamide and 2-pyridone are thought to be the most effective means of assessment at present.
Vitamin B₆	Refers to several derivatives of pyridine, including pyridoxine (PN), pyridoxal (PL), and pyridoxamine (PM), which are interconvertible in the body. The coenzymatic forms are pyridoxal-5-phosphate (PLP) and pyridoxamine-5-phosphate (PMP). As a coenzyme, B₆ is involved in many transamination reactions (and thereby in gluconeogenesis), in the synthesis of niacin from tryptophan, in the synthesis of several neurotransmitters, and in the synthesis of δ-aminolevulinic acid (and therefore in heme synthesis). It also has functions unrelated to coenzymatic activity: PL and PLP bind to hemoglobin and alter O_2 affinity; PLP also binds to steroid receptors, inhibiting receptor affinity to DNA and thereby modulates steroid activity.	Deficiency usually seen in conjunction with other water-soluble vitamin deficiencies. Stomatitis, angular cheilosis, glossitis, irritability, depression, and confusion occur in moderate to severe depletion; normochromic, normocytic anemia has been reported in severe deficiency. Abnormal electroencephalograms and, in infants, convulsions have also been observed. Some sideroblastic anemias respond to B₆ administration. Isoniazid, cycloserine, penicillamine, ethanol, and theophylline can inhibit B₆ metabolism. [Ages 19–50: 1.3 mg; >50: 1.5 mg for women, 1.7 mg for men]	Long-term use with doses exceeding 200 mg/day (in adults) may cause peripheral neuropathies and photosensitivity. [100 mg]	Many useful laboratory methods of assessment exist. The plasma or erythrocyte PLP levels are most common. Urinary excretion of xanthurenic acid after an oral tryptophan load or activity indices of RBC alanine or aspartic acid transaminases (ALT and AST, respectively) are all functional measures of B₆-dependent enzyme activity.
Folate	A group of related pterin compounds. More than 35 forms of the vitamin are found naturally. The fully oxidized form, folic acid, is not found in nature but is the pharmacologic form of the vitamin. All folate functions relate to its ability to transfer one-carbon groups. It is essential in the de novo synthesis of nucleotides, in the metabolism of several amino acids, and is an integral component for the regeneration of the	Women of childbearing age are most likely to be deficient. The classic deficiency syndrome is megaloblastic anemia. The hematopoietic cells in bone marrow become enlarged and have immature nuclei, reflecting ineffective DNA synthesis. The peripheral blood smear demonstrates macro-ovalocytes and polymorphonuclear leukocytes with an average of more than 3.5 nuclear	Doses >1000 µg/day may partially correct the anemia of B₁₂ deficiency and may therefore mask (and perhaps exacerbate) the associated neuropathy. Large doses also reported to lower seizure threshold in individuals prone to seizures. Parenteral administration is rarely reported to cause allergic phenomena, which is probably due to dispersion agents. [1000 µg]	Serum folate measures short-term folate balance, whereas RBC folate is a better reflection of tissue status. Serum homocysteine rises early in deficiency but is nonspecific because B₁₂ or B₆ deficiency, renal insufficiency, and older age may also cause elevations.

Continued

Nutritional Diseases

Table 231-2 • VITAMINS AND THEIR FUNCTIONS—cont'd

	BIOCHEMISTRY AND PHYSIOLOGY	DEFICIENCY [RDA*]	TOXICITY [TUL†]	ASSESSMENT OF STATUS
	"universal" methyl donor, S-adenosylmethionine. Inhibition of bacterial and cancer cell folate metabolism is the basis for the sulfonamide antibiotics and chemotherapeutic agents such as methotrexate and 5-fluorouracil, respectively.	lobes. Megaloblastic changes also occur in other epithelia that proliferate rapidly (e.g., oral mucosa, gastrointestinal tract, producing glossitis and diarrhea, respectively). Sulfasalazine and diphenytoin inhibit absorption and predispose to deficiency. [400 μg of dietary folate equivalents (DFE); 1 μg folic acid = 1 μg DFE; 1 μg food folate = 0.6 μg DFE]		
Vitamin C (ascorbic and dehydroascorbic acid)	Ascorbic acid readily oxidizes to dehydroascorbic acid in aqueous solution. Because the latter can be reduced in vivo, it possesses vitamin C activity. Total vitamin C is therefore measured as the sum of ascorbic and dehydroascorbic acid concentrations. Because of its reductant properties, it serves primarily as a biologic antioxidant in aqueous environments. Biosyntheses of collagen, carnitine, bile acids, and norepinephrine, as well as proper functioning of the hepatic mixed-function oxygenase system, depend on this property. Vitamin C in foodstuffs increases the intestinal absorption of non-heme iron.	Overt deficiency is uncommon in developed countries. The classic deficiency syndrome is *scurvy*: characterized by fatigue, depression, and widespread abnormalities in connective tissues, such as inflamed gingivae, petechiae, perifollicular hemorrhages, impaired wound healing, coiled hairs, hyperkeratosis, bleeding into body cavities. In infants, defects in ossification and bone growth may occur. Tobacco smoking lowers plasma and leukocyte vitamin C levels. [F: 75 mg; M: 90 mg; increase requirement for cigarette smokers by 35 mg/day]	Quantities 500 mg/day (in adults) sometimes cause nausea and diarrhea. Acidification of the urine with supplementation, and the potential for enhanced oxalate synthesis, have raised concerns about nephrolithiasis but this has yet to be demonstrated. Supplementation may interfere with laboratory tests based on redox potential (e.g., fecal occult blood testing, serum cholesterol, and glucose). Withdrawal from chronic ingestion of high doses of vitamin C supplements should occur gradually over a month because accommodation seems to occur; raising a concern of "rebound scurvy." [2 g]	Plasma ascorbic acid concentration reflects recent dietary intake whereas WBC levels more closely reflect tissue stores. Women's plasma levels are approximately 20% higher than men's for any given dietary intake.
Vitamin B₁₂	A group of closely related cobalamin compounds composed of a corrin ring (with a cobalt atom in its center) connected to a ribonucleotide via an aminopropanol bridge. Microorganisms are the ultimate source of all naturally occurring B₁₂. The two active coenzyme forms are desoxyadenosylcobalamin and methylcobalamin. These coenzymes are needed for the synthesis of succinyl coenzyme A (CoA), which is essential in lipid and carbohydrate metabolism, and for the synthesis of methionine. The latter reaction is essential for amino acid metabolism, for purine and pyrimidine synthesis, for many methylation reactions, and for the intracellular retention of folates.	Dietary inadequacy is a rare cause of deficiency except in strict vegetarians. Most deficiencies arise from loss of intestinal absorption: this may be a result of pernicious anemia, pancreatic insufficiency, atrophic gastritis, small bowel bacterial overgrowth, or ileal disease. Megaloblastic anemia and megaloblastic changes in other epithelia (see "Folate") are the result of sustained depletion. Demyelination of peripheral nerves, posterior and lateral columns of spinal cord, and nerves within the brain may occur. Altered mentation, depression, and psychoses occur. Hematologic and neurologic complications may occur independently. Folate supplementation, in doses of 1000 μg/day, may partly correct the anemia, thereby masking (or perhaps exacerbating) the neuropathic complication. [2.4 μg]	A few allergic reactions have been reported to crystalline B₁₂ preparations and are probably due to impurities, not the vitamin. [TUL not established]	Serum, or plasma, concentrations are generally accurate. Subtle deficiency with neurologic complications, as described in the "Deficiency" column, can best be established by concurrently measuring the concentration of plasma B₁₂ and serum methylmalonic acid, because the latter is a sensitive indicator of cellular deficiency.
Biotin	A bi-cyclic compound consisting of a ureido ring fused to a substituted tetrahydrothiophene ring. Endogenous synthesis by	Isolated deficiency is rare. Deficiency in humans has been produced experimentally (by dietary inadequacy), by prolonged	Toxicity has not been reported in humans with doses as high as 60 mg/day in children. [TUL not established]	Plasma and urine concentrations of biotin are diminished in the deficient state. Elevated urine concentrations of

Table 231–2 • VITAMINS AND THEIR FUNCTIONS—cont'd

	BIOCHEMISTRY AND PHYSIOLOGY	DEFICIENCY [RDA*]	TOXICITY [TUL†]	ASSESSMENT OF STATUS
	intestinal flora may contribute significantly to biotin nutriture. Most dietary biotin is linked to lysine, a compound called biotinyl lysine, or biocytin. The lysine must be hydrolyzed by an intestinal enzyme called biotinidase before intestinal absorption occurs. Acts primarily as a coenzyme for several carboxylases; each holoenzyme catalyzes an ATP-dependent CO_2 transfer. The carboxylases are critical enzymes in carbohydrate and lipid metabolism.	total parenteral nutrition lacking the vitamin, and by ingestion of large quantities of raw egg white, which contains avidin, a protein that binds biotin with such high affinity that it renders it biounavailable. Alterations in mental status, myalgias, hyperesthesias, and anorexia occur. Later, a seborrheic dermatitis and alopecia develop. Biotin deficiency is usually accompanied by lactic acidosis and organic aciduria. [30 µg]		methyl citrate, 3-methylcrotonylglycine, and 3-hydroxyisovalerate are also observed in deficiency.
Pantothenic acid	Consists of pantoic acid linked to β-alanine through an amide bond. Serves as an essential component of CoA and phosphopantetheine, which are essential for synthesis and β-oxidation of fatty acids, as well as synthesis of cholesterol, steroid hormones, vitamins A and D, and other isoprenoid derivatives. CoA is also involved in the synthesis of several amino acids and δ-aminolevulinic acid, a precursor for the corrin ring of vitamin B_{12}, the porphyrin ring of heme, and of cytochromes. CoA is also necessary for the acetylation and fatty acid acylation of a variety of proteins.	Deficiency rare: only reported as a result of feeding semisynthetic diets or an antagonist to the vitamin. Experimental, isolated deficiency in humans produces fatigue, abdominal pain, vomiting, insomnia, and paresthesias of the extremities. [5 mg]	In doses 10 g/day, diarrhea is reported to occur. [TUL not established]	Whole blood and urine concentrations of pantothenate are indicators of status; serum levels are not thought to be accurate.

*Recommended daily allowance (RDA) established for female (F) and male (M) adults by the U.S. Food and Nutrition Board, 1999–2001. In some instances, insufficient data exist to establish an RDA, in which case the adequate intake (AI) established by the board is listed.

†Tolerated upper intake (TUL) established for adults by the U.S. Food and Nutrition Board, 1999–2001.

PTH = parathyroid hormone; UV-B = ultraviolet-B.

Table 231–3 • NUTRITIONAL TRACE ELEMENTS AND THEIR CLINICAL IMPLICATIONS

	BIOCHEMISTRY AND PHYSIOLOGY	DEFICIENCY [RDA*]	TOXICITY [TUL†]	ASSESSMENT OF STATUS
Chromium	Dietary chromium consists of both inorganic and organic forms. Its primary function in humans is to potentiate insulin action. It accomplishes this function as a circulating complex called "glucose tolerance factor," thereby affecting carbohydrate, fat, and protein metabolism.	Deficiency in humans only described in long-term total parenteral nutrition (TPN) patients receiving insufficient chromium. Hyperglycemia or impaired glucose tolerance is uniformly observed. Elevated plasma free fatty acid concentrations, neuropathy, encephalopathy, and abnormalities in nitrogen metabolism are also reported. Whether supplemental chromium may improve glucose tolerance in mildly glucose intolerant but otherwise healthy individuals remains controversial. [F: 25 µg; M: 35 µg]	Toxicity after oral ingestion is uncommon and seems confined to gastric irritation. Airborne exposure may cause contact dermatitis, eczema, skin ulcers, and bronchogenic carcinoma. [no TUL established]	Plasma or serum concentration of chromium is a crude indicator of chromium status; it appears to be meaningful when the value is markedly above or below the normal range.
Copper	Copper is absorbed by a specific intestinal transport mechanism. It is carried to the liver where it is bound to ceruloplasmin, which circulates systemically and delivers copper to target	Dietary deficiency is rare; it has been observed in premature and low-birth-weight infants fed exclusively on a cow's milk diet and in individuals on long-term TPN without copper. Clinical	Acute copper toxicity has been described after excessive oral intake and with absorption of copper salts applied to burned skin. Milder manifestations include nausea, vomiting,	Practical methods for detecting marginal deficiency are not available. Marked deficiency is reliably detected by diminished

Continued

Nutritional Diseases

Table 231–3 • NUTRITIONAL TRACE ELEMENTS AND THEIR CLINICAL IMPLICATIONS—cont'd

	BIOCHEMISTRY AND PHYSIOLOGY	DEFICIENCY [RDA*]	TOXICITY [TUL†]	ASSESSMENT OF STATUS
	tissues in the body. Excretion of copper is largely through bile, and then into the feces. Absorptive and excretory processes vary with the levels of dietary copper, providing a means of copper homeostasis. Copper serves as a component of many enzymes, including amine oxidases, ferroxidases, cytochrome c oxidase, dopamine β-hydroxylase, superoxide dismutase, and tyrosinase.	manifestations include depigmentation of skin and hair, neurologic disturbances, leukopenia, hypochromic microcytic anemia, and skeletal abnormalities. Anemia arises from impaired utilization of iron and is therefore a conditioned form of iron deficiency anemia. The deficiency syndrome, except the anemia and leukopenia, is also observed in Menkes' disease, a rare inherited condition associated with impaired copper utilization. [900 µg]	epigastric pain, and diarrhea; coma and hepatic necrosis may ensue in severe cases. Toxicity may be seen with doses as low as 70 µg/kg/day. Chronic toxicity is also described. Wilson's disease is a rare, inherited disease associated with abnormally low ceruloplasmin levels and accumulation of copper in the liver and brain, eventually leading to damage to these two organs. [10 mg]	serum copper and ceruloplasmin concentrations as well as low red blood cell (RBC) superoxide dismutase activity.
Fluorine	Known more commonly by its ionic form, fluoride. It is incorporated into the crystalline structure of bone, thereby altering its physical characteristics.	Intake of <0.1 mg/day in infants and <0.5 mg/day in children is associated with an increased incidence of dental caries. Optimal intake in adults is between 1.5 and 4 mg/day. [F: 3 mg; M: 4 mg]	Acute ingestion of >30 mg/kg body weight is likely to cause death. Excessive chronic intake (0.1 mg/kg/day) leads to mottling of teeth (dental fluorosis), calcification of tendons and ligaments, and exostoses and may increase the brittleness of bones. [10 mg]	Estimates of intake or clinical assessment are used because no good laboratory test exists.
Iodine	Readily absorbed from the diet, concentrated in the thyroid, and integrated into the thyroid hormones, thyroxine (T_4) and triiodothyronine (T_3). These hormones circulate largely bound to thyroxine-binding globulin. They modulate resting energy expenditure and, in the developing human, growth and development.	In the absence of supplementation, populations relying primarily on food from soils with low iodine content have endemic iodine deficiency. Maternal iodine deficiency leads to fetal deficiency, which produces spontaneous abortions, stillbirths, hypothyroidism, cretinism, and dwarfism. Rapid brain development continues through the second year, and permanent cognitive deficits may be induced by iodine deficiency over that period. In the adult, compensatory hypertrophy of the thyroid goiter occurs along with varying degrees of hypothyroidism. [150 µg]	Large doses (>2 mg/day in adults) may induce hypothyroidism by blocking thyroid hormone synthesis. Supplementation with >100 µg/day to an individual who was formerly deficient occasionally induces hyperthyroidism. [1.1 mg]	Iodine status of a population can be estimated by the prevalence of goiter. Urinary excretion of iodine is an effective laboratory means of assessment. Thyroid-stimulating hormone (TSH) blood level is an indirect, and therefore not entirely specific, means of assessment.
Iron	Conveys the capacity to participate in redox reactions to a number of metalloproteins such as hemoglobin, myoglobin, cytochrome enzymes, and many oxidases and oxygenases. Primary storage form is ferritin and, to a lesser degree, hemosiderin. Intestinal absorption is 15–20% for "heme" iron and 1–8% for iron contained in vegetables. Absorption of the latter form is enhanced by the ascorbic acid in foodstuffs; by poultry, fish, or beef; and by an iron-deficient state. It is decreased by phytate and tannins.	The most common micronutrient deficiency in the world. Women of child-bearing age are the highest risk group because of menstrual blood losses, pregnancy, and lactation. The classic deficiency syndrome is hypochromic, microcytic anemia. Glossitis and koilonychia ("spoon" nails) are also observed. Easy fatigability often is an early symptom, before anemia appears. In children, mild deficiency of insufficient severity to cause anemia is associated with behavioral disturbances and poor school performance. [postmenopausal F and M: 8 mg; premenopausal F: 18 mg]	Iron overload typically occurs when habitual dietary intake is extremely high, intestinal absorption is excessive, repeated parenteral administration occurs, or a combination of these factors exists. Excessive iron stores usually accumulate in the reticuloendothelial tissues and cause little damage ("hemosiderosis"). If overload continues, iron eventually begins to accumulate in tissues such as the hepatic parenchyma, pancreas, heart, and synovium, causing hemochromatosis (Chapter 225). Hereditary hemochromatosis results from homozygosity of a common recessive trait. Excessive intestinal absorption of iron is seen in homozygotes. [45 mg]	Negative iron balance initially leads to depletion of iron stores in the bone marrow: a bone marrow biopsy or the concentration of serum ferritin are accurate and early indicators of such depletion. As the severity of deficiency proceeds, serum iron (SI) decreases and total iron-binding capacity (TIBC) increases: an iron saturation (= SI/TIBC) of <16% suggests iron deficiency. Microcytosis, hypochromia and anemia ensue as latter stages of the deficient state. Elevated levels of serum ferritin or an iron saturation >60% suggest iron overload, although systemic inflammation elevates serum ferritin regardless of iron status.
Manganese	A component of several metalloenzymes. Most manganese is in mitochondria, where it is a component of manganese superoxide dismutase.	Manganese deficiency in the human has not been conclusively demonstrated. It is said to cause hypocholesterolemia, weight loss, hair and nail changes, dermatitis, and impaired synthesis of vitamin K–dependent proteins. [F: 1.8 mg; M: 2.3 mg]	Toxicity by oral ingestion is unknown in humans. Toxic inhalation causes hallucinations, other alterations in mentation, and extrapyramidal movement disorders. [11 mg]	Until the deficiency syndrome is better defined, an appropriate measure of status will be difficult to develop.

Table 231–3 • NUTRITIONAL TRACE ELEMENTS AND THEIR CLINICAL IMPLICATIONS—cont'd

	BIOCHEMISTRY AND PHYSIOLOGY	DEFICIENCY [RDA*]	TOXICITY [TUL†]	ASSESSMENT OF STATUS
Molybdenum	A cofactor in several enzymes, most prominently xanthine oxidase and sulfite oxidase.	A probable case of human deficiency is described as being secondary to parenteral administration of sulfite and resulted in hyperoxypurimenia, hypouricemia, and low sulfate excretion. [45 μg]	Toxicity not well described in the human, although it may interfere with copper metabolism at high doses. [2 mg]	Laboratory means of assessment not meaningful until deficiency syndrome is better described.
Selenium	Most dietary selenium is in the form of an amino acid complex. Nearly complete absorption of such forms occurs. Homeostasis is largely performed by the kidney, which regulates urinary excretion as a function of selenium status. Selenium is a component of several enzymes, most notably glutathione peroxidase and superoxide dismutase. These enzymes appear to prevent oxidative and free radical damage of various cell structures. Evidence suggests that the antioxidant protection conveyed by selenium operates in conjunction with vitamin E because deficiency of one seems to enhance damage induced by a deficiency of the other. Selenium also participates in the enzymatic conversion of thyroxine to its more active metabolite, tri-iodothyronine.	Deficiency is rare in North America but has been observed in individuals on long-term TPN lacking selenium. Such individuals have myalgias and/or cardiomyopathies. Populations in some regions of the world, most notably some parts of China, have marginal intake of selenium. In these regions Keshan's disease, a condition characterized by cardiomyopathy, is endemic; it can be prevented (but not treated) by selenium supplementation. [55 μg]	Toxicity is associated with nausea, diarrhea, alterations in mental status, peripheral neuropathy, loss of hair and nails: such symptoms were observed in adults who inadvertently consumed 27-2400 mg. [400 μg]	Erythrocyte glutathione peroxidase activity and plasma, or whole blood, selenium concentrations are the most commonly used methods of assessment. They are moderately accurate indicators of status.
Zinc	Intestinal absorption occurs by a specific process that is enhanced by pregnancy and corticosteroids and diminished by co-ingestion of phytates, phosphates, iron, copper, lead, or calcium. Diminished intake of zinc leads to an increased efficiency of absorption and decreased fecal excretion, providing a means of zinc homeostasis. Zinc is a component of more than 100 enzymes, among which are DNA polymerase, RNA polymerase, and transfer RNA synthetase.	Zinc deficiency has its most profound effect on rapidly proliferating tissues. Mild deficiency causes growth retardation in children. More severe deficiency is associated with growth arrest, teratogenicity, hypogonadism and infertility, dysgeusia, poor wound healing, diarrhea, dermatitis on the extremities and around orifices, glossitis, alopecia, corneal clouding, loss of dark adaptation, and behavioral changes. Impaired cellular immunity is observed. Excessive loss of gastrointestinal secretions through chronic diarrhea and fistulas may precipitate deficiency. Acrodermatitis enteropathica is a rare, recessively inherited disease in which intestinal absorption of zinc is impaired. [F: 8 mg; M: 11 mg]	Acute zinc toxicity can usually be induced by ingestion of >200 mg of zinc in a single day (in adults). It is manifested by epigastric pain, nausea, vomiting, and diarrhea. Hyperpnea, diaphoresis, and weakness may follow inhalation of zinc fumes. Copper and zinc compete for intestinal absorption: long-term ingestion of >25 mg zinc/day may lead to copper deficiency. Long-term ingestion of >150 mg/day has been reported to cause gastric erosions, low HDL cholesterol levels, and impaired cellular immunity. [40 mg]	No accurate indicators of zinc status exist for routine clinical use. Plasma, RBC, and hair zinc concentrations are often misleading. Acute illness, in particular, is known to diminish plasma zinc levels, in part by inducing a shift of zinc out of the plasma compartment and into the liver. Functional tests that determine dark adaptation, taste acuity, and rate of wound healing lack specificity.

*Recommended daily allowance (RDA) established for female (F) and male (M) adults by the U.S. Food and Nutrition Board, 1999–2001. In some instances, insufficient data exist to establish an RDA, in which case the adequate intake (AI) established by the board is listed.
†Tolerated upper limit (TUL) established for adults by the U.S. Food and Nutrition Board, 1999–2001.

vitamins are not absorbed through the lipophilic phase in the intestine.

TRACE ELEMENTS. See Table 231–3. Fifteen trace elements have been identified as essential for health in animal studies: iron, zinc, copper, chromium, selenium, iodine, fluorine, manganese, molybdenum, cobalt, nickel, tin, silicon, vanadium, and arsenic. Nevertheless, only for the first ten of these has there been compelling evidence that they are essential nutrients in humans. Cobalt seems to be essential solely as a component of vitamin B$_{12}$, but an isolated deficiency state has never been described. Deficiency syndromes for several of the other essential trace elements were not recognized until recently because of their exceedingly small requirements and because of the ubiquitous nature of these elements in foodstuffs. Only under exceptional circumstances, such as long-term reliance on total parenteral nutrition (TPN) lacking the elements, have some of the deficiency syndromes been observed.

The biochemical functions of trace elements have not been as well characterized as those for the vitamins but most of their functions appear to be as components of prosthetic groups or as cofactors for a number of enzymes. Determination of essential trace element status is problematic except in iron, selenium, and iodine. The vanishingly low concentrations of these elements in bodily fluids and tissues, the fact that blood levels frequently do not correlate well with levels in the target tissues, and the fact that functional tests cannot be devised until biochemical functions are better understood preclude an accurate and convenient laboratory method of assessing most of the trace elements.

Conditions that Increase Required Dietary Intake

There are many physiologic, pathophysiologic, and pharmacologic factors that increase the dietary requirements for micronutrients(see

Table 231–1), thereby enhancing the risk of developing a deficiency state.

PHYSIOLOGIC FACTORS. Stages of the life cycle have a significant impact on the requirements of certain nutrients. Phases of rapid growth and development, such as in utero development, infancy, adolescence, and pregnancy are associated with remarkable increases in the utilization of certain micronutrients on a per kilogram basis. Requirements for most micronutrients are increased in pregnancy but, proportionately, the observed increases in the maternal requirements for iron and folate are particularly great, and are related to the rapid proliferation of the placental and fetal tissues. Periods of lactation are similarly associated with remarkable increases in requirements; a lactating woman experiences disproportionately large increases in her requirements for zinc and vitamins A, E, and C, in addition to the aforementioned needs observed in pregnancy to meet the metabolic demands incurred by milk production.

Infancy carries particular vulnerabilities to specific micronutrient inadequacies: Healthy infants in the United States are typically supplemented with vitamin K at birth and with iron and vitamin D during the course of the first year because of their particular susceptibility to deficiencies of these nutrients.

The ability to maintain adequate iron status from menarche through menopause is compromised in women by the additional losses incurred by menstruation, pregnancy, and lactation; therefore, it is not surprising that the subset of populations that displays the highest rate of iron deficiency is women of child-bearing age.

Specific dietary recommendations for the elderly have been formally incorporated into the RDAs because the continuous evolution of physiology that occurs during the life cycle has a concrete impact on the requirements for certain micronutrients. Vitamin B_{12} status, for instance, declines significantly with aging because of the high prevalence of atrophic gastritis and its associated impairment in protein-bound B_{12} absorption. As many as 10 to 30% of the elderly population is thought to be at risk of significant B_{12} deficiency because of this phenomenon; therefore, the elderly should consume some of their B_{12} requirement as the crystalline form rather than solely from the naturally occurring protein-bound forms found in food. The elderly also require greater quantities of vitamins B_6 and D to maintain health compared to younger adults, and this is reflected in the new RDAs (see Table 231–3). For instance, adequate intake for vitamin D in persons aged 51 to 70 years is 10 µg/day (400 international units), double the value for younger adults; this value increases to 15 µg in persons older than 70 years. This appears to be largely due to diminished cutaneous synthesis of vitamin D by senile skin and to decreased sun exposure, the latter of which is particularly important in elderly patients in long-term institutional facilities.

PATHOPHYSIOLOGIC AND PHARMACOLOGIC FACTORS. Intestinal malabsorptive and maldigestive states predispose to multiple micronutrient deficiencies. Both fat-soluble and water-soluble micronutrients (except vitamin B_{12}) are absorbed predominantly in the proximal small intestine. Therefore, diffuse mucosal diseases affecting the proximal portion of the gastrointestinal tract are likely to result in deficiencies. However, even in the absence of mucosal disease of the proximal small intestine, extensive ileal disease, small bowel bacterial overgrowth, and chronic cholestasis can each interfere with the maintenance of adequate intraluminal conjugated bile acid concentrations and thereby impair absorption of fat-soluble vitamins. Maldigestion is usually the result of chronic pancreatitis. Untreated, it frequently causes malabsorption and deficiencies of fat-soluble vitamins. Vitamin B_{12} malabsorption can often be demonstrated in this setting, a result of inadequate R-protein digestion, but clinical B_{12} deficiency is rarely reported.

A myriad of rare inborn errors of metabolism have been described for vitamins and minerals that impair an individual's ability to assimilate, utilize, or retain a particular micronutrient. Such defects are usually partial and can often be overcome, at least in part, by administering doses of the nutrient that are several degrees of magnitude greater than is usually required. Suspicion for such defects should be entertained if (1) a known defect exists in the family, (2) a deficiency syndrome arises at birth or during infancy, or (3) the deficiency syndrome is present despite adequate dietary intake and the absence of any disease that would impair the ability to assimilate the nutrient.

Long-term administration of many drugs may adversely affect micronutrient status and may either induce an overt deficiency syndrome or predispose to one. The manner in which drug-nutrient

Table 231–4 • DRUG-MEDIATED EFFECTS ON MICRONUTRIENT STATUS: EXAMPLES

DRUG	NUTRIENT	MECHANISM OF INTERACTION
Dextroamphetamine, fenfluramine, levodopa	Potentially all micronutrients	Induces anorexia
Cholestyramine	Vitamin D, folate	Adsorbs nutrient, decreases absorption
Omeprazole	Vitamin B_{12}	Modest bacterial overgrowth, decreases gastric acid, impairs absorption
Sulfasalazine	Folate	Impairs absorption and inhibits folate-dependent enzymes
Isoniazid	Pyridoxine	Impairs utilization of B_6
Nonsteroidal anti-inflammatory agents	Iron	Gastrointestinal blood loss
Penicillamine	Zinc	Increases renal excretion

interactions occur varies; some of the more common mechanisms are outlined in Table 231–4. Some drugs exert their therapeutic effects by specifically inhibiting the actions of a micronutrient. Examples include coumarin, which inhibits γ-carboxylation reactions mediated by vitamin K, and methotrexate, which binds tightly to dihydrofolate reductase, thereby inhibiting folate metabolism.

Tobacco smoking alters the metabolism of several vitamins, including folate, C, and E. In large surveys, diminished plasma levels of folate and ascorbic acid have been observed in chronic smokers. Smoking is also associated with diminished levels of folate in cells of the oral mucosa, diminished ascorbic acid levels in leukocytes, and decreased concentrations of vitamin E in the alveolar fluid, providing evidence that many tissues can be affected by smoking and that the effect does not just represent a shift of these micronutrients out of the plasma compartment.

New Frontiers in Marginal Deficiency States of Micronutrients

An interesting and important evolution in the understanding of micronutrient requirements has occurred over the past century: As nutritional science has expanded its appreciation for additional physiologic functions of micronutrients, an ever increasing need to redefine the concept of "deficiency" has ensued. The original means by which the necessary intake of these nutrients was defined was typically based on a disease entity that occurred as a result of a flagrant deficiency of that nutrient, the so-called classic deficiency syndrome. In retrospect, this was quite naive because it is now evident that most micronutrients serve important functions in a wide variety of distinct biochemical systems. As the science of nutrition has come to appreciate such diversity in function, so has the appreciation grown for definitions of new deficiency syndromes based on disordered physiology other than those described by the classic definitions.

Nevertheless, the redefinition of micronutrient deficiencies and the closely related reexamination of recommended daily intakes has proved difficult for several reasons. In some instances, there continues to be less than definitive evidence for the role of a particular micronutrient in a new function that has been proposed. However, even if a novel biochemical or physiologic role is well demonstrated for a nutrient, an appropriate question is whether optimization of such function translates into optimization of health. For example, providing supplemental vitamin E to elderly individuals who are vitamin E replete enhances T-lymphocyte responsiveness to mitogens; nevertheless, it is unclear whether this diminishes infection rates among the elderly. Another difficult problem pertains to the use of micronutrients in supraphysiologic quantities, that is, intakes that greatly exceed all conventional concepts of what is necessary for health. Some micronutrients, when taken in such large quantities, have effects on physiologic functions that impart apparent health benefits; the ingestion of gram quantities of niacin to reduce low-density lipoprotein cholesterol is an example. Such physiologic effects are not observed at more conventional levels of intake and are therefore usually considered to be "pharmacologic" effects of the nutrient. Nevertheless, if the dietary requirement of a nutrient is strictly defined as the minimal dose necessary for the maintenance of optimal health, as has been suggested, then supraphysiologic doses would have to be considered as the dietary requirement in such instances. Thus, the determination of "optimal" nutrient intake is highly dependent on which physiologic effect is sought. Furthermore, if only a segment of the population will benefit from supraphysiologic quantities of a nutrient, should dietary guidelines for the remainder of the population be established according to this effect?

Determining an adequate level of intake implies that there exists a means of measuring nutrient status. In seeking an appropriate measure of nutrient status, the diversity of function often makes it difficult to decide which measurement is the most germane. Tobacco smoking, for example, appears to significantly diminish vitamin E levels in alveolar fluid but not in the serum. Thus, the concepts of "localized" nutrient deficiencies and tissue-specific requirements add an additional level of complexity to the determination of nutrient status.

The remainder of this chapter cites examples of how advances in nutritional science are prompting the redefinition of micronutrient requirements.

FOLATE. A cogent example of the redefinition of vitamin deficiency is the water-soluble vitamin folate. Guidelines regarding the necessary intake of the vitamin were based, until recently, on the prevention of megaloblastic anemia. Measuring serum and erythrocyte folate concentrations has been the most common means of assessing status; maintaining such levels within accepted normative ranges provides good assurance that folate status is adequate to prevent anemia.

It has become increasingly evident, however, that degrees of deficiency that are insufficiently severe to cause anemia may still disturb normal biochemical and physiologic homeostasis. This is, in part, evidenced by an increase in serum homocysteine, an amino acid that is normally metabolized by a folate-dependent pathway. Before the federally mandated fortification of flour in 1998, the median intake of folate among adults was one half of the present RDA and a substantial minority of Americans had significantly elevated serum homocysteine levels. An elevation in homocysteine reflects a less than optimal disposal of homocysteine, an alteration that may increase the development of occlusive vascular disease, as has been suggested by numerous studies. Vitamins B_6 and B_{12} are also important components of the biochemical pathways by which the body disposes of homocysteine, although it is unclear whether dietary intake of B_6 and B_{12} at conventionally recommended levels is adequate to minimize homocysteine levels.

Definitive clinical trials have demonstrated that women taking folate supplements at the time of conception have a markedly lower chance of delivering a baby with a neural tube defect compared with women who are not folate-supplemented but whose folate status generally falls within a conventionally accepted range. It was this observation that compelled the U.S. government to mandate the fortification of flour. Present recommendations are that women of child-bearing age consume 400 µg of folic acid per day in the form of supplements or fortified foods, although the "dose-response curve" of this effect is ill defined. A more controversial observation is the inverse relationship between the ingestion of folate and the incidence of epithelial neoplasia of the uterine cervix, the breast, and the colorectum. This inverse relationship is observed even when folate status (or dietary intake) falls within the range of conventionally accepted normative values.

The aforementioned considerations prompted the U.S. RDA to be raised from 200 to 400 µg of folate per day, and there are some indications that further increases are warranted. Substantial increases in the suggested intake of any micronutrient must be tempered, however, by the consideration of toxicity. With folate, this is primarily related to its ability to mask B_{12} deficiency when taken in doses exceeding 1000 µg/day (see Table 231–2).

ANTIOXIDANT AND FREE-RADICAL SCAVENGING VITAMINS AND PROVITAMINS. Vitamins A, C, and E, as well as many of the carotenoids, are effective antioxidants. In addition, it is clear that vitamins C, E, and some of the carotenoids can scavenge free radicals when taken in adequate quantities. Such properties have long been appreciated, but it is only recently that the roles of oxidation and free radical damage have been

understood to play potentially important roles in common degenerative illnesses such as atherosclerosis, cancer, cataract of the lens, and retinal degeneration. Clinical trials to test the efficacy of antioxidant supplements have largely been disappointing, although growing evidence indicates that populations with marginal antioxidant status have the most to gain and that the adverse effects of the large doses used in many trials may overwhelm the benefits conveyed.

Low-density lipoprotein (LDL) can undergo oxidation in vivo and the LDL thus transformed appears to be particularly atherogenic. Prevention of LDL oxidation, at least in animal models, retards the process of atherogenesis. Supplementation of human subjects with several-fold the RDA of alpha-tocopherol, and perhaps some of the other antioxidant micronutrients, is an effective means of preventing LDL oxidation. However, human intervention trials have largely been unable to demonstrate clinical benefits in the reduction of cardiovascular events.

An enormous body of epidemiologic studies indicates that occurrence of cancers of the oral cavity, lung, esophagus, stomach, and perhaps the colorectum is inversely related to dietary intake of fresh vegetables and fruits. Careful dissection of dietary data suggests that ß-carotene and vitamin E content are the most strongly predictive components of these foodstuffs. High doses of vitamin A and some of its synthetic analogues (e.g., 13-cis-retinoic acid) can effectively reduce the recurrence of head and neck cancers, although hepatic toxicity is sometimes a limiting factor in such cancer preventive therapy. Similarly, these agents, as well as ß-carotene or vitamin E, have been shown to significantly promote the regression of oral leukoplakia, a premalignant lesion, when taken in large doses. Daily supplementation with one to three times the U.S. RDA of ß-carotene, selenium, and vitamin E has been shown to reduce the incidence of adenocarcinoma of the stomach in a region of China where the disease, as well as marginal vitamin status, is particularly prevalent; however, an intervention trial in Finland showed no diminution of lung cancer in smokers with daily supplementation of ß-carotene and vitamin E.

Epidemiologic associations also suggest an inverse relationship between lens cataract, macular degeneration, and the intake of vitamins C, E, and ß-carotene. Considerable experimental evidence indicates that both of these common degenerative conditions of the eye are caused, at least in part, by photo-oxidation and there is some evidence in animal models that these degenerative processes can be retarded by supraphysiologic supplementation with vitamins C or E. Individuals who ingest quantities of vitamin C that exceed the U.S. RDA have a lower incidence of cataract than those ingesting the RDA, suggesting a potential preventive role for larger than conventionally recommended doses of these nutrients. Nevertheless, insufficient interventional data exist to conclusively assume a preventive role for antioxidants in cataract and macular degeneration.

Further investigation is necessary to better define the circumstances under which antioxidant nutrients can be used to prevent or treat chronic, degenerative diseases.

VITAMIN B_{12} AND NEUROPSYCHIATRIC DISEASE: Plasma B_{12} concentrations are considered to be an accurate indication of B_{12} status. The normative range for a healthy population has typically been reported as 150 to 900 pg/mL; values greater than 150 (or 200 in some laboratories) were thought, until recently, to exclude B_{12} deficiency as a cause of neurologic or psychiatric syndromes. Recent observations now indicate that 7 to 10% of individuals who have plasma B_{12} values between 150 and 400 pg/mL may develop neuropsychiatric complications of B_{12} deficiency in the absence of any indications of megaloblastic anemia. Such individuals can be identified by the demonstration of an elevated level of methylmalonic acid in the blood that decreases to normal levels with parenteral B_{12} administration. An elevation in serum methylmalonic acid is both a sensitive and specific indication of cellular B_{12} deficiency. An alternative approach, although one that is less scientifically objective, is to administer several parenteral injections of vitamin B_{12} to an individual who has an otherwise unexplained neuropsychiatric syndrome and whose plasma B_{12} level falls in the 150 to 200 range. Awareness of this phenomenon is particularly important because it is has become clear that atrophic gastritis, an asymptomatic condition that affects approximately 30% of the elderly population, frequently produces a modest decrease in B_{12} status.

Table 231–5 lists several examples of biochemical functions of vitamins that have only recently been identified. As the clinical significance of each of these new roles is defined and as quantities of

Nutritional Diseases

Table 231–5 • NEWLY IDENTIFIED ROLES FOR VITAMINS

VITAMIN OR PROVITAMIN	CLASSICAL ROLE	NEW ROLE
β-Carotene	Pro-vitamin A	Antioxidant, free radical
Niacin	NAD/NADP coenzyme	Reduction of LDL, elevation of HDL and cholesterol
Folate	Hemopoietic factor	Diminishes homocysteinemia
Vitamin A	Transduction of visual input in retina	Induction and maintenance of epithelial differentiation, signal in embryogenesis
Vitamin D	Regulator of calcium	Retards epithelial proliferation; promotes differentiation
Vitamin B_6	Coenzyme for transamination	Modulation of steroid activity

HDL = high-density lipoprotein; LDL = low-density lipoprotein; NAD = nicotinamide adenine dinucleotide; NADP = nicotinamide-adenine dinucleotide phosphate.

each vitamin needed to optimize such functions are determined, redefinition of the desirable range of vitamin status is likely to occur.

SUGGESTED READINGS

Dietary Reference Intakes for vitamin A, vitamin K, arsenic, boron, chromium, copper, iodine, iron, manganese, molybdenum, nickel, silicon, vanadium, and zinc. Washington, DC, Institute of Medicine, National Academy Press, 2001. (www.nap.edu/books/0309072794.html/).

Dietary Reference Intakes for calcium, phosphorus, magnesium, vitamin D, and fluoride. Washington, DC, Institute of Medicine, National Academy Press, 1999. (www.nap.edu/books/0309063507/html/index.html).

Dietary Reference Intakes for thiamin, riboflavin, niacin, vitamin B_6, folate, vitamin B_{12}, pantothenic acid, biotin, and choline. Washington, DC, Institute of Medicine, National Academy Press, 2000. (www.nap.edu/books/0309065542/html/index.html).

Dietary Reference Intakes for vitamin C, vitamin E, selenium, and carotenoids. Washington, DC, Institute of Medicine, National Academy Press, 2000. (www.nap.edu/books/0309069351/html/).

Each of these four books comprehensively and authoritatively reviews the biochemistry, physiology, and nutrition of the indicated nutrients and provides an evidence-based rationale for the new dietary reference intakes (DRIs) and tolerable upper intake levels (TULs).

232 THE EATING DISORDERS

Delia Smith West

Definition

The eating disorders are a group of psychiatric disorders characterized by aberrant eating patterns and disturbed attitudes about the importance of body weight and shape, specifically, the evaluation of self-worth based on weight. The most well known and well characterized of the eating disorders are anorexia nervosa and bulimia nervosa. The hallmark of anorexia nervosa is the pursuit of thinness in the presence of severe emaciation. The defining features of bulimia nervosa are a cycle of binge eating followed by inappropriate compensatory behavior to avoid weight gain (e.g., self-induced vomiting, misuse of laxatives or diuretics, fasting, excessive exercise) and undue concern about body weight.

Etiology

ANOREXIA NERVOSA. Although anorexia nervosa has long been recognized and well described, the origin of the disorder is not well understood. Societal influences promoting an unrealistically thin body size and a cultural environment that associates slimness with happiness and success have been implicated in the development of anorexia nervosa.

Genetic vulnerabilities also appear to play a role in the development of anorexia nervosa. Concordance rates for anorexia nervosa are higher in monozygotic than in dizygotic twins. Furthermore, the prevalence of anorexia nervosa, as well as mood disorders, is higher in first-degree relatives of affected individuals than in the general population, thus suggesting genetic aggregation. Although the indications are strong for genetic influences on the development of anorexia nervosa, the relative contributions of genetics and environmental influences remain unclear.

Neuroendocrine abnormalities have been studied extensively in anorexia nervosa, and questions remain about which aspects of the observed hypothalamic dysfunction are primary and which are secondary to the starvation state. Some patients experience amenorrhea before weight loss and some continue to have abnormal neuroendocrine function after weight restoration.

BULIMIA NERVOSA. As with anorexia nervosa, a sociocultural emphasis on pursuit of an unrealistically thin body weight and unobtainable body shape has been suggested as a causative factor in the origin of bulimia nervosa. Over the previous decades, culturally desirable body shapes have become thinner and more unobtainable for the average woman, in parallel with increases in bulimia nervosa rates. Dieting to lose weight is nearly epidemic in some cultures, and peer pressure to maintain a low body weight is strong. Dieting has been shown to predispose young girls to bulimia nervosa, and a history of obesity, as well as significant fluctuations in weight, has been observed among women in whom the disorder develops. However, being discontented with body size or weight is not uncommon among women in general, and dieting is endemic in our society. Therefore, sociocultural factors alone cannot account for the development of bulimia nervosa in a specific individual.

The aggregation of bulimia nervosa in families suggests a genetic vulnerability. Twin studies indicate that approximately 50% of the variability in the development of bulimia nervosa can be attributed to genetic factors. Depression, anxiety disorders, and substance abuse (particularly alcoholism) have also been shown to be more common in the families of patients with bulimia nervosa than in the general population. Thus, a vulnerability to psychiatric disorders in general and eating disorders in particular may be transmitted genetically. However, the influence of environmental and individual factors remains substantial.

Epidemiology

ANOREXIA NERVOSA. Anorexia nervosa is relatively rare, with lifetime prevalence rates of 0.5% among women and few cases noted in men. The age of onset is bimodal, with peaks around 14 and 18 years of age. The natural course of anorexia nervosa appears to have high mortality rates, with long-term studies reporting 5 to 15% mortality. The disorder appears to be more common among women in higher socioeconomic groups and among whites; furthermore, anorexia nervosa is over-represented in professions that emphasize low body weight, such as fashion models, ballet dancers, and gymnasts.

BULIMIA NERVOSA. Bulimia nervosa is more common than anorexia nervosa and in general has a more optimistic prognosis. Approximately 1 to 2% of women and 0.1% of men will meet the diagnostic criteria for bulimia nervosa sometime in their life. The average age at onset is around 20 years. Although patients with bulimia nervosa from higher socioeconomic groups seek treatment more often than do patients from lower income groups, population-based studies indicate that rates of the disorder are similar. The disorder is more prevalent among whites, but an increasing number of patients from ethnic minority groups have been described in recent years.

Clinical Manifestations

ANOREXIA NERVOSA. Apart from the severe emaciation and amenorrhea central to the disorder, anorexia nervosa has no consistent pathologic or physiologic characteristics. The majority of medical complications seen are sequelae of the starvation state and usually remit with appropriate nutritional remediation. Signs commonly noted on physical examination include hypotension, dry skin or lanugo (downy fine hair), and bradycardia.

Endocrine Abnormalities. Perturbations in endocrine function are invariably present (Chapters 235, 237, and 250). Amenorrhea and hypofunction of the hypothalamic-pituitary axis (reduced luteinizing and follicle-stimulating hormone) develop in females. Secondary amenorrhea is most common, although primary amenorrhea may occur. Amenorrhea may precede weight loss in some patients and may persist after weight restoration. Estrogen metabolism can also be disturbed (low plasma and urinary estrogen levels that rebound with weight gain) and may be associated with irreversible osteopenia and pathologic fractures. Male anorectics have diminished testosterone levels and loss of libido, as well as infertility. Prepubertal patients may have arrested sexual maturation and diminished overall physical growth. Abnormalities in thyroid function test results are common. Low triiodothyronine levels are found consistently, accompanied by normal or low thyroxine levels, and probably reflect adaptations to starvation. Thyroid abnormalities usually reverse with weight restoration, and exogenous thyroid replacement therapy is not indicated.

Cardiovascular Abnormalities. Disturbed cardiovascular function is common and reflects adaptation to starvation. Orthostatic hypotension is frequently observed. Electrocardiograms often reveal bradycardia, ST segment depression, or changes in T wave morphology. Arrhythmias (tachycardia, sinus arrest with ectopic atrial rhythm, nodal escape beats, or junctional rhythms) can develop, even in the absence of electrolyte disturbance. The use of emetics such as syrup of ipecac can cause myopathy, including cardiomyopathy. Sudden death from cardiac failure is a risk but is uncommon.

Fluid and Electrolyte Disturbance/Renal Complications. Dehydration is a common complication, particularly with protracted purging (self-induced vomiting, laxative or diuretic abuse). Hypokalemic, hypochloremic alkalosis is the most frequently occurring electrolyte abnormality. Elevated blood urea nitrogen levels are often found, although the serum creatinine level is usually normal. Chronic hypokalemia can cause proteinuria and renal damage; therefore, renal function should be evaluated in all severely emaciated patients.

Psychiatric Features. In addition to pathologic attitudes about eating and weight that are pathognomonic, patients with anorexia nervosa may display psychiatric features secondary to severe malnutrition, including irritability, mood lability, social withdrawal, anxiety, depression, concentration impairment, food preoccupation, obsessive-compulsive symptoms regarding foods, or bizarre food preferences. These features usually diminish after nutritional replenishment. However, a minority of patients can have comorbid psychiatric disorders (particularly major depression and obsessive-compulsive disorder) that are not secondary to starvation and warrant specific assessment and treatment.

Gastrointestinal Complications. Patients may suffer from gastrointestinal motility problems. Abdominal pain, bloating, and postprandial distress are very common, as is constipation. These complaints can be troublesome for patients who need to eat more to gain weight. Acute gastric dilation and rupture are possible with overaggressive refeeding or large binge episodes.

BULIMIA NERVOSA. The majority of the medical complications associated with bulimia nervosa reflect the binge eating and purgative behavior (self-induced vomiting, laxative and diuretic abuse). No specific signs and symptoms are associated with bulimia nervosa. Patients frequently complain of constipation, bloating and abdominal pain, and lethargy and impaired concentration. Menstrual irregularities are common. Dehydration may be evident, particularly in patients who purge excessively or restrict fluid intake. Erosion of dental enamel and excessive caries are present in some patients. Physical examination seldom reveals the nature of the problem; therefore, a comprehensive history that includes assessment of psychological and behavioral aspects of the disorder is critical.

Serious medical complications can be associated with chronic vomiting or laxative or diuretic abuse. Electrolyte disturbances (metabolic alkalosis, hypochloremia, hypokalemia), elevated serum amylase, gastric and esophageal irritation, and large bowel abnormalities from laxative abuse are the more common physical complications.

Diagnosis

ANOREXIA NERVOSA. The essential features of anorexia nervosa are an intense fear of weight gain or of becoming fat in spite of significantly low body weight (Table 232–1). Two types of anorexia nervosa can be differentiated: restricting, in which weight loss occurs primarily through dieting, fasting, or excessive exercise, and binge-purge, in which the patient engages in binge eating and/or purging. About half of patients with anorexia nervosa are the restricting type, and occasionally some individuals will alternate over time between the restricting and binge-purge types. The diagnostic challenge with

anorexia nervosa is to distinguish it from other causes of malnutrition or starvation. The attitudinal and behavioral features of individuals with anorexia nervosa are therefore vital in making the differential diagnosis. Evaluation of fears of fatness or pursuit of thinness despite significant underweight and undue influence of body weight on self-evaluation is crucial; however, accurate assessment can be challenging because patients often deny the extent of their problems. Thus it is important to probe about weight preoccupations, the potential response to weight regain, and underlying schemas of self-evaluation, in addition to the medical complications associated with low body weight.

BULIMIA NERVOSA. The defining characteristics of bulimia nervosa are the recurrent episodes of binge eating and inappropriate compensatory behavior to avoid weight gain (Table 232–2). An excessive

Table 232–1 • DSM–IV DIAGNOSTIC CRITERIA FOR ANOREXIA NERVOSA

A. Refusal to maintain body weight at or above a minimally normal weight for age and height (e.g., weight loss leading to maintenance of body weight less than 85% of that expected or failure to make expected weight gain during period of growth resulting in body weight less than 85% of that expected).
B. Intense fear of gaining weight or becoming fat even though underweight.
C. Disturbance in the way in which one's body weight or shape is experienced, undue influence of body weight or shape on self-evaluation, or denial of the seriousness of the current low body weight.
D. In post-menarchal females, amenorrhea, i.e., the absence of at least three consecutive menstrual cycles. (A woman is considered to have amenorrhea if her periods occur following only hormone, e.g., estrogen, administration.)

Specify type:
Restricting type: During the current episode of anorexia nervosa, the person has not regularly engaged in binge eating or purging behavior (i.e., self-induced vomiting or the misuse of laxatives, diuretics, or enemas).
Binge eating/purging type: During the current episode of anorexia nervosa, the person has regularly engaged in binge eating or purging behavior (i.e., self-induced vomiting or the misuse of laxatives, diuretics, or enemas).

Reprinted with permission from the Diagnostic and Statistical Manual of Mental Disorders, Fourth Edition. Copyright 1994 American Psychiatric Association.

Table 232–2 • DSM–IV DIAGNOSTIC CRITERIA FOR BULIMIA NERVOSA

A. Recurrent episodes of binge eating. An episode of binge eating is characterized by both of the following:
  1. Eating, in a discrete period (e.g., within any 2-hr period), an amount of food that is definitely larger than most people would eat during a similar period and under similar circumstances.
  2. A sense of lack of control over eating during the episodes (e.g., a feeling that one cannot stop eating or control what or how much one is eating).
B. Recurrent inappropriate compensatory behavior to prevent weight gain such as self-induced vomiting; misuse of laxatives, diuretics, enemas, or other medication; fasting; or excessive exercise.
C. The binge eating and inappropriate compensatory behaviors both occur, on average, at least twice a week for 3 months.
D. Self-evaluation is unduly influenced by body shape and weight.
E. The disturbance does not occur exclusively during episodes of anorexia nervosa.

Specify type:
Purging type: During the current episode of bulimia nervosa, the person has regularly engaged in self-induced vomiting or the misuse of laxatives, diuretics, or enemas.
Non purging type: During the current episode of bulimia nervosa, the person has used other inappropriate compensatory behaviors, such as fasting or excessive exercise, but has not regularly engaged in self-induced vomiting or the misuse of laxatives, diuretics, or enemas.

Reprinted with permission from Diagnostic and Statistical Manual of Mental Disorders, Fourth Edition. Copyright 1994 American Psychiatric Association.

Nutritional Diseases

concern about weight and self-evaluation based on weight are also typical of the disorder. Two types of bulimia nervosa have been identified and are distinguished by the methods used to compensate for excessive calorie intake during binge episodes. Patients with the purging type engage in self-induced vomiting or laxative or diuretic abuse, whereas individuals with the nonpurging type use other methods (e.g., severe caloric restriction, excessive exercise). The purging type is the more common type, and self-induced vomiting is the most common method of purging.

During binge episodes, large amounts of food are consumed, usually in secret. Loss of control over eating (i.e., inability to stop once having started eating) is a defining feature of the binge episode. This loss of control may take the form of frenzied, rapid eating of available food or planned binges for which the patient acquires specific foods in advance for periods when secretive eating can occur. Some patients report dissociative experiences during the binge episode when they "tune out" and are unaware of what or how much they are eating.

Patients with bulimia nervosa are typically of average weight, although both overweight and underweight bulimia nervosa patients exist. Bulimia nervosa is frequently accompanied by depressive symptoms, and patients often meet the diagnostic criteria for major depressive disorder. Depressive symptoms typically remit with successful treatment of the bulimia nervosa and can be viewed as secondary. In a minority of cases, however, concomitant mood disorders precede the bulimia nervosa or fail to improve with adequate treatment and require specific attention. Concurrent substance abuse may occur and often requires assessment and treatment before the bulimia nervosa is addressed.

Rx Treatment

The long-term treatment goal for both disorders is to ameliorate the psychological and behavioral patterns that promote and maintain aberrant eating habits and the attitudinal disturbances. A second goal is to address the medical complications that accompany these behavioral and psychological patterns, particularly for patients with anorexia nervosa, in whom weight restoration is a primary emphasis in the initial treatment.

ANOREXIA NERVOSA. Anorexia nervosa requires a comprehensive, multidisciplinary approach to treatment that integrates medical management, individual psychotherapy, and family therapy. Currently, the best results have been shown with weight restoration accompanied by family therapy for patients with adolescent-onset anorexia nervosa and individual therapy for patients with onset after 18 years of age. Inpatient treatment is often required.

Nutritional Rehabilitation. Weight restoration is a primary initial goal of treatment of a seriously underweight patient. Weight regain programs incorporating behavioral modification strategies appear to be the most effective. Clear goals are outlined (e.g., daily calorie intake, weekly weight gain, abstinence from purging), and patients are rewarded for achieving them by praise and privileges (e.g., time out of bed, time off the unit, visitors, opportunity to exercise). The goal for weight restoration is usually no more than 1 to 2 kg/week, with the ultimate target weight determined individually for each patient. An individually specific healthy weight (i.e., one at which normal reproductive function resumes and bone demineralization ceases) is selected. Weight at discharge in relation to goal weight must also be individually determined, depending on the likelihood of sustained weight regain.

Weight restoration can be accomplished with nutritional hyperalimentation. Daily calorie intake depends on the patient's degree of underweight, and methods of refeeding depend on the condition and approbation of the patient. Oral supplementation can be helpful for patients with moderate malnutrition. Nasogastric tube feeding should not be used routinely; however, this route may be more tolerable for refeeding severely malnourished patients. Those who do not tolerate feeding tubes may require parenteral supplementation. However, this form of feeding should be used only in life-threatening situations and with recognition of the significant dangers associated with parenteral supplementation in this patient population (e.g., severe edema and possible cardiac failure). It is generally recommended that forced nutritional hyperalimentation or supplementation continue only until the patient is out of medical danger. At that time, even if not yet at a healthy body weight, the patient should resume total calorie intake from food. This approach facilitates reestablishment of normal eating patterns and allows hunger and satiety sensations to begin to normalize, both of which are important treatment goals.

Psychotherapy. A first step for psychotherapy is to engage the patient as a motivated and willing partner in the process and to establish a trusting therapeutic relationship. The long-term goals are to address the fear of fatness, which is central to the disorder, as well as to ameliorate self-concept inadequacies, perfectionistic tendencies, disturbed social relationships, and separation or autonomy concerns. Family therapy is particularly effective with younger patients, whereas individual psychotherapy appears most helpful for older patients. Cognitive behavioral treatments have shown promise.

Medication. Although a range of pharmacotherapies for anorexia nervosa have been examined, no pharmacologic agent has demonstrated effectiveness. However, patients with persistent depression may require antidepressant treatment, which should be undertaken with care because malnourished patients with anorexia nervosa may be particularly prone to side effects, especially hypotension and arrhythmia.

BULIMIA NERVOSA. Cognitive behavioral treatment is generally regarded as the treatment of choice for bulimia nervosa. The rationale underlying a cognitive behavioral approach is that dysfunctional beliefs about the importance of weight and shape are primary factors in the development and maintenance of the disorder. Treatment focuses on modifying these cognitions. Behavioral strategies are used to interrupt the cycle of dieting, binge eating, and purging and to gradually resume regular eating habits, as well as expand the range of foods that can be eaten without loss of control. Self-monitoring helps patients identify antecedents that trigger binge eating and purging and the consequences that reinforce the behavior. Cognitive strategies to identify and challenge dysfunctional beliefs are used, specifically strategies to target rigid and perfectionistic attitudes about dieting and self-evaluation. Problem-solving skills and relapse prevention techniques are also provided. Cognitive behavioral treatment is usually offered on an outpatient basis over the course of 16 to 20 sessions. Inpatient treatment is indicated only when a patient's health or safety is of concern (e.g., suicide or medical risk). A longer course of treatment is required for more complicated cases (e.g., patients with concomitant personality disorder). Most patients improve following cognitive behavioral therapy, with reductions of approximately 80% in the frequency of both binge episodes and purging. More than half of treated patients are abstinent from both binging and purging after treatment and remain so at 1 year post-treatment. Preliminary studies indicate that interpersonal psychotherapy can also be effective in treating bulimia nervosa.

Medications. Antidepressant medication has a role in the treatment of bulimia nervosa. When experienced cognitive-behavioral therapists are not available, serotonin reuptake inhibitor, tricyclic, and monoamine oxidase inhibitor antidepressants all have been shown to be effective in reducing binge eating and purging. Antidepressants are effective even among patients who do not have major depression, and doses similar to those used for mood disorders are recommended. However, relapse may occur when the use of these medications is discontinued.

SUGGESTED READINGS

American Psychiatric Association: Practice Guidelines for the Treatment of Patients with Eating Disorders, 2nd ed. Washington DC, American Psychiatric Association, 2000. *Comprehensive details about evidence-based treatment for the eating disorders.*

Fairburn CG, Brownell KD (eds): Eating Disorders and Obesity: A Comprehensive Handbook, 2nd ed. New York, Guilford Press, 2001. *A current, comprehensive compendium that provides chapters on etiology, diagnosis, physiologic manifestations and consequences, and treatment approaches from leading experts in the field.*

Fairburn CG, Harrison PJ: Eating disorders. Lancet 2003;361:407–416. *Reviews prognosis and how little we understand about causes and treatments.*

Keel PK, Dorer DJ, Eddy KT, et al: Predictors of mortality in eating disorders. Arch Gen Psychiatry 2003;60:179–183. *Alcohol use and prior hospitalization for an affective disorder were predictors of mortality.*

233 OBESITY

Michael D. Jensen

Obesity is the most common nutritional disorder in the United States, costing more that $100 billion per year in health-related expenses. Most physicians do not receive specific training in the evaluation and management of obesity despite the fact that more than half the patients they encounter are likely to be overweight or obese. Although progress has been made in understanding the pathophysiology and treatment of obesity, it nonetheless remains a difficult disease to treat. The safest and most effective treatment approaches (lifestyle and behavior modification) are not those commonly employed by physicians.

Definition

The National Institutes of Health/NHLBI report entitled "Clinical Guidelines on the Identification, Evaluation and Treatment of Overweight and Obesity" provides clear, scientifically based definitions of overweight and obesity. Body mass index (BMI) is now the recommended means to categorize weight relative to height for adults. Body mass index is calculated as weight (kg) divided by height squared (m²). To calculate BMI using pounds and inches, the formula is modified as follows: weight (pounds)/height (inches)² × 703. The weight classifications according to BMI are summarized in Table 233–1. Individuals who are overweight (BMI 25.0 to 29.9) may or may not be overfat. Some men may be overweight because of increased muscle mass which is a straightforward clinical judgment. Although in general the risk of developing weight-related health problems increases with a BMI greater than 25, the guidelines point out that intervention or discussion of weight issues with the patient may not be necessary for overweight adults who are entirely healthy and/or are not overfat. On the other hand, some individuals in the BMI 27 to 29.9 range develop serious metabolic complications of obesity that could be expected to improve with weight loss. These individuals are candidates for more aggressive treatment, including pharmacotherapy if needed.

The risk of comorbidities increases considerably once the BMI increases above 30, the level at which obesity is diagnosed. Obesity is divided into three classes, also depending upon BMI. Treatment approaches may differ for those who are overweight and for different classes of obesity. For example, current Food and Drug Administration (FDA) guidelines indicate that pharmacotherapy can be adjunct treatment for any class of obesity, even if medical complications are not present. Although some would argue that treating obese patients without medical complications is a lower priority than treating those with medical complications, familiarity with the guidelines is important; supervisory agencies and third party payers use them to determine who is eligible for treatment benefits. Extreme obesity (BMI >40) is one of the key features that would prompt consideration of a patient for bariatric surgery when medical treatments have failed. Patients with class 2 obesity (BMI 35.0 to 39.9) may be considered for bariatric surgery if medical treatments have failed and if severe, life-threatening complications are present.

The use of BMI to define overweight and obesity is an improvement over previous ideal weight tables, which were based on height/weight percentiles of individuals applying for insurance. In addition to using BMI, the NHLBI Guidelines recommend using the waist circumferences as another office assessment tool that can help with the treatment decision making process. A "large" waist circumference (greater than 102 cm or 40 inches for men and greater than

88 cm or 35 inches for women) is considered an additional indication of risk for overweight and obesity. This measure is primarily relevant to disease risk in overweight and class 1 obesity categories, however. In overweight individuals, a large waist circumference changes the relative risk from "increased" (relative to someone with a normal BMI) to "high." In class 1 obesity, a large waist circumference increases the risk of disease from "high" to "very high." A large waist circumference does not affect disease risk in those persons with class 2 or class 3 obesity.

Prevalence

The number of overweight and obese adults in the United States has increased dramatically over the past 20 years. It is estimated that approximately 60% of adult Americans are either overweight or obese. Approximately 60% of U.S. men and 51% of U.S. women are overweight or obese. It should be noted, however, that a greater percentage of women are obese than men, whereas a larger percentage of men are overweight than women. There are substantial differences in the prevalence of obesity by age, race, and socioeconomic status. The prevalence of obesity in adults tends to rise steadily from ages 20 to 60 years but does not increase and, in fact, begins to decrease in later years. It has been estimated that almost 75% of men aged 60 to 69 years in the United States have a BMI of greater than 25. The increase in mean BMI with age may not be as much of a threat to population health as might first be anticipated. While it is true that young adults with BMIs in the lower part of the normal range have the lowest mortality rates, this changes with age. The BMI associated with the lowest mortality rates is actually at or somewhat above 25 kg/m² for those in their 60s and 70s. Clearly, weight recommendations for a given individual depend on whether adverse health consequences associated with obesity have developed.

The differences in overweight and obesity between African-Americans, Mexican-Americans, and European-Americans are not subtle. African-American women and Mexican-Americans of both sexes have the highest rates of overweight and obesity in the United States. When interpreting these data, however, it is important to keep in mind that there is an inverse relationship between socioeconomic status and obesity, especially among women. Women in lower socioeconomic classes are much more likely to be obese than those in higher socioeconomic classes. This association reduces, but does not eliminate, the racial differences in the prevalence of obesity. Whether the remaining racial differences in the prevalence of obesity are due to genetic, constitutional, or social factors not related to income is not yet clear.

Etiology

In one sense, the etiology of obesity can be considered simplistically; if energy intake exceeds energy expenditure, and if lean body mass remains stable, body fat must increase. Unfortunately, obesity is a much more complex issue. There are significant genetic/constitutional susceptibility aspects to obesity that are heavily influenced by environmental factors. Evidence from family studies and studies of twins strongly supports the concept that within a given environment, a significant portion of the variation in weight is genetic. That said, however, the tremendous increase in the prevalence of obesity in the United States over the last several decades can hardly be ascribed to mass changes in human DNA.

GENETIC ASPECTS. There is strong evidence for a hereditary tendency toward the regulation of body weight. The single gene defects resulting in obesity include a number of classic genetic syndromes such as Prader-Willi and Laurence-Moon-Biedl. The reader is referred to textbooks on genetic disorders for a complete list and description of these conditions. More recently, extremely rare monogenic forms of human obesity due to mutations in the leptin gene and leptin receptor gene have been described. The result is an actual or functional leptin deficiency, much like that seen in *ob/ob* or *db/db* mice, the animal models that stimulated the discovery of leptin. There have also been reports of inherited forms of human obesity due to mutations of genes that regulate appetite neuropeptide synthesis. Doubtless, reports of single gene mutations associated with human obesity will continue to appear; however, the overwhelming majority of cases of human obesity are related to the combination of polygenic susceptibility traits and environmental conditions.

Table 233–1 • CLASSIFICATION OF OVERWEIGHT AND OBESITY BY BODY MASS INDEX (BMI)

	OBESITY CLASS	BMI (kg/m²)
UNDERWEIGHT		<18.5
NORMAL		18.5–24.9
OVERWEIGHT		25.0–29.9
OBESITY	I	30.0–34.9
	II	35.0–39.9
EXTREME OBESITY	III	≥40

CONSTITUTIONAL INFLUENCES. A number of environmental influences can result in long-term, gene-like effects on body weight regulation and the tendency to be susceptible to obesity-related health problems. The effect of the intrauterine environment and the perinatal period on subsequent weight and health is best studied. For example, undernutrition in the last trimester of pregnancy and in the early postnatal period results in a decreased risk of adult obesity. Unfortunately, the low birth weight that is associated with malnutrition in late pregnancy also increases the risk of hypertension, abnormal glucose tolerance, and cardiovascular disease in adulthood. In contrast, undernutrition limited to the first two trimesters of pregnancy is associated with an increased probability of adult obesity. Other early "environmental" effects are that infants of diabetic mothers tend to be fatter than those of nondiabetic mothers, and children of diabetic mothers have a greater prevalence of obesity when they are 5 to 19 years old, independent of their mother's obesity status. Finally, intrauterine exposure to the diabetic environment results in an increased risk of diabetes mellitus and obesity in the offspring. Thus, the issue of the genes versus the environment as regards obesity and metabolic complications of obesity is blurred in the intrauterine and perinatal time intervals. One of the striking and worrisome aspects of these metabolic effects is not only the long-term effects on the individual's weight regulation and health, but the suggestion that these traits can be passed on to future generations.

ENVIRONMENTAL CONTRIBUTORS. Few would argue that there have been dramatic changes in the environment over the last 50 years. These changes promoted a reduction in the amount of physical activity that Americans undertake. In addition, alterations in the food supply have either increased or failed to allow the expected decrease in energy intake that would be needed to match the reduced energy expenditure.

Food. A number of environmental factors can influence food intake (Table 233–2). Consuming energy-dense foods results in greater energy intake, because many adults respond to the volume of food taken in rather than the energy content of food. This factor likely accounts for the association between high-fat diets and excess body weight; many high-fat foods are also energy dense. When humans consume diets that are high in fat but low in energy density, energy intake is not greater than would be expected based on the energy density of the foods. Larger food portion size has also been shown to increase food intake. Given the trend in the United States to serve larger portions of food and beverage, this could be a contributing variable toward obesity. Food variety can also affect energy intake. An increased variety of entrees, sweets, snacks, and carbohydrates in the diet is associated with an increase in body fatness and food intake. In contrast, an increase in variety of vegetables available does not result in an increased food intake and is not associated with increased body fatness. Other factors that may have broad population effects in the United States is the reduced costs of food relative to increased availability and palatability of foods.

Several individual factors may also influence how the properties of food affect energy intake. Individuals vary with respect to their dietary restraint (the tendency to consciously limit food intake to control weight), their feelings of hunger, or their disinhibition (the tendency to overeat opportunistically). It has been proposed that interindividual differences in these factors may modify how food variety, portion size, and so on affect the eating profile. In addition to the environmental influences on food consumption, there are also the effects of the social context under which food is consumed and the emotional state of the individual. These effects are not yet well quantified.

Physical Activity. Physical activity can be broadly divided into exercise (fitness- and sports-related activities) and nonexercise activities. Nonexercise activities include employment-related work and the activities of daily living. Tables are widely available that allow one to calculate energy expenditure based on an individual's weight as well as the type and duration of exercise in which they engage. Unfortunately, only a fraction of Americans engage in exercise at the recommended frequency, intensity, or duration that could be expected to have a protective effect on the development of obesity and other health problems. The portion of Americans who exercise regularly does not appear to be changing; therefore, it seems unlikely that a change in exercise habits over the past several decades is causing the increase in obesity. To the extent that reduced physical activity is contributing to the epidemic of obesity, it is likely the nonexercise component that is changing.

It is difficult to measure the energy expended in nonexercise activity. Although it seems obvious that employment physical activity has decreased with the advent of more automated systems in the workplace, there are surprisingly little data in this regard. One estimate suggests that between 1982 and 1992, energy expenditure at work decreased by approximately 50 kcal/day. The additional changes in the workplace since that time have likely further reduced employment physical activity.

The other component of nonexercise physical activity, the activities of daily living, is equally difficult to measure. A plethora of labor-saving conveniences (e.g., drive-through food and banking, escalators, remote controls, e-mail, on-line shopping) have been introduced into the modern environment. Each of these further reduces the energy humans must expend to get through the day. Again, there are few hard data to assess how much of a change has actually occurred, although a reduction in daily walking trips and an increase in daily automobile trips has been documented.

Perhaps because it is easier to assess, information as to how differences in sedentary activity (television watching, video games, and computer use) relate to obesity is more readily available. There is compelling evidence that more time spent in sedentary pursuits is associated with an increased risk of overweight and obesity. The striking aspect to these studies is that the adverse effect of sedentary activities is independent of participation in traditional exercise activities.

Understanding the contributions of decreased work-related physical activity, decreased activity of daily living, and increases in sedentary behavior can help the physician working with the patient to uncover patterns that may relate to weight gain.

In summary, there are clearly dramatic changes in Western environments that are conspiring to bring out tendencies toward obesity in those with constitutional or genetic susceptibility. Physicians who are aware of these environmental factors are better able to help their obese patients identify which of these environmental factors are contributing to the problem and develop plans for intervention.

Regulation of Body Weight and Energy Balance

Not all of the factors that contribute to the regulation of adult body weight are fully understood; however, this must be a well-balanced process. For example, the typical U.S. adult takes in and expends approximately 2000 to 3000 kcal/day. If there were a consistent error of even 1% in overconsumption of food, this would result in the gain of approximately 25 to 30 pounds of fat every 10 years if there were no change in energy expenditure. Clearly, most adults are able to regulate the average energy balance with much greater precision than 1%. There appears to be regulation both of energy intake and energy expenditure via conscious and unconscious processes.

The excess energy consumed by adults is generally stored as triglyceride in adipocytes. The primary means by which adipose tissue mass expands is to increase the amount of fat stored in each cell (adipocyte hypertrophy). This process can store only a limited amount of fat, however, because there is an upper limit to the size of fat cells. If sufficient fat is deposited, eventually new fat cells are recruited from preadipocytes present in the stromovascular component of adipose tissue. Some adults recruit new adipocytes more readily than others, and thus gain weight more from adipocyte hyperplasia than from hypertrophy. There is evidence that adipose tissue, rather than being static, is slowly but continuously being turned over. Although this may seem surprising, the wide variety of nonfuel activities in which adipocytes are known to participate emphasizes that much of what we once thought we knew about adipose tissue may be incorrect.

Table 233–2 • ENVIRONMENTAL FACTORS PROMOTING OBESITY	
DIETARY	**ACTIVITY**
↑ energy density of foods	↑ sedentary behavior
↑ portion size	↓ activities of daily living
↑ variety*	↓ employment physical activity
↑ palatability	
↑ availability	
↓ cost	
*Variety of sweets/snacks/entrees.	

The discovery of leptin, a protein secreted by adipose tissue that has potent central nervous system effects on food intake as well as diverse peripheral physiologic actions, led to the hope that the problem of body weight regulation had been solved. The leptin-deficient animal model of obesity, the *ob/ob* mouse, is severely obese, hyperphagic, hypometabolic, and sexually immature and has low levels of spontaneous activity. Administering leptin to this animal corrects all of the above-mentioned defects.

What role does leptin play in human obesity? Reports indicate that virtually all individuals with increased body fat have high plasma leptin concentrations; therefore, leptin deficiency is not a common cause of human obesity. Since the discovery of leptin, only two children, the offspring of consanguineous parents, have been found to have congenital leptin deficiency; they were hyperphagic and severely obese. True human leptin deficiency must be extremely rare. Some animal models of genetic obesity (the *db/db* mouse and *fa/fa* rat) have defective leptin receptors, making them unresponsive to leptin. These observations raised the possibility that human obesity, rather than being a condition of leptin deficiency, is a state of leptin resistance. Although an obese human with a defective leptin receptor gene has been reported, it appears that leptin resistance due to leptin receptor defects (or post-signaling genetic abnormalities) is extremely rare.

Much has been learned about the physiology of leptin in humans. Leptin is secreted in a diurnal fashion that appears to be regulated by the effects of insulin and glucose on adipocytes. Leptin secretion can be increased by 30 to 40% with brief periods of overfeeding (prior to changes in body composition), and is reduced by 50% in response to periods of underfeeding that do not result in significant changes in body composition. These rapid and substantial shifts in leptin secretion can potentially account for a large portion of the variability in the normally strong relationship between percentage of body fat and serum leptin concentrations. When blood is collected under carefully controlled circumstances, there is a very strong relationship between plasma leptin concentrations and percentage of body fat (Fig. 233–1). There is no difference in the relationship between leptin and percentage of body fat between women and men. Thus, the assertion that leptin resistance is present in women and in human obesity is not logical; if the normal biologic response to increased body fat is increased leptin secretion, hyperleptinemia merely becomes a different definition of fatness/obesity. Only when deficiency is present does its physiology relate to the development of obesity.

Low or absent leptin results in extreme hunger. Treating patients with congenital leptin deficiency with physiologic doses of recombinant leptin resulted in a remarkable reduction in excessive hunger and significant fat loss. In contrast, treatment of overweight patients with recombinant leptin did not show weight loss, despite achieving peak serum leptin concentrations greater than 30 times basal levels. In animals, leptin plays an important role in modulating the hypothalamic-pituitary response to undernutrition and serves a protective function. Human studies are necessary to confirm this observation. Several of the observed effects of exogenous leptin in *ob/ob* mice were not observed in the single case of human leptin deficiency treated with leptin. In summary, the discovery of leptin has been an important advance in understanding the biology of obesity; however, defects in leptin secretion or inherited defects in leptin action do not appear to be the cause of even a tiny fraction of human obesity.

ENERGY INTAKE

Much has been learned about the biologic regulation of food intake, mostly from the study of animal models. There are a series of peripheral "satiety" signals that act to inhibit further food intake at some point during meal consumption. Some of the signals reach the brain via the vagus nerve and some via the systemic circulation. Examples of the proposed humoral factors modulating appetite are listed in Table 233–3. Many of the compounds are gut- or pancreas-derived hormones (cholecystokinin, glucagon-like peptide 1, insulin, and perhaps other glucagon-related peptides or gut peptides) or peptides (apolipoprotein A-IV, secreted with chylomicrons). The signals are thought to be triggered both by mechanical stimuli (e.g., the fullness of the stomach) and by the presence of nutrients in the jejunum and ileum. It has also been suggested that the drop in leptin concentrations at night may allow the evolution of hunger the following morning.

The central nervous system regulation of food intake is also better understood. A series of neuropeptides and monoamines have been identified that have either anabolic (increased food intake with or without decreased energy expenditure) or catabolic (decreased food intake with or without increased energy expenditure) properties. A list of these compounds is provided in Table 233–4. Understanding

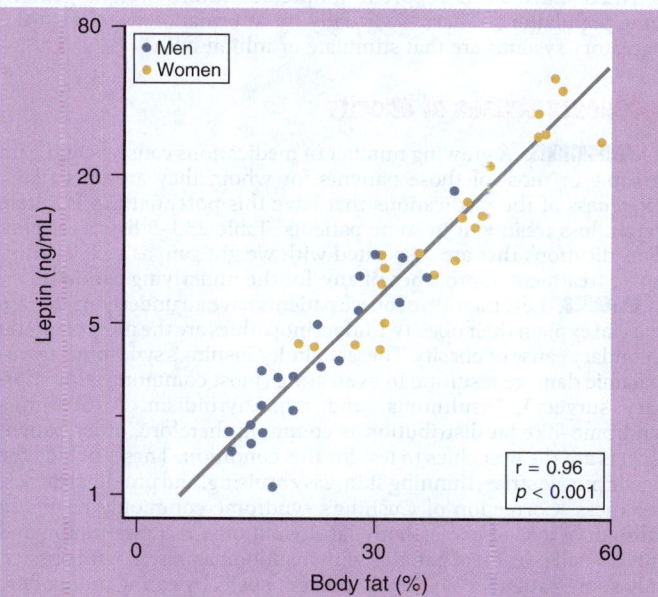

FIGURE 233–1 • The relationship between serum leptin concentrations (log values) and percentage of body fat in 43 lean and obese men and women. [Adapted from Jensen MD, Hensrud D, O'Brien PC, et al: Collection and interpretation of plasma leptin concentration data in humans. Obes Res 1999;7:241–245. © 1999 North American Association for the Study of Obesity. All rights reserved].

Table 233–3 • SUGGESTED BIOLOGIC MODULATORS OF FOOD INTAKE

PERIPHERAL SIGNAL	PROPOSED EFFECT ON FOOD INTAKE
Vagal	(−)
Cholecystokinin	(−)
Apolipoprotein A-IV	(−)
Insulin	(−)
Glucagon-like peptide 1	(−)
Other glucagon related peptides	(−)
Leptin	(+) when leptin ↓↓
Ghrelin	(+)
Tumor necrosis factor-α	(−)
PYY	(−)

(−) inhibits food intake.
(+) stimulates food intake.

Table 233–4 • CENTRAL NERVOUS SYSTEM MODULATORS OF ENERGY BALANCE

CENTRAL ANABOLIC (↑ FOOD INTAKE)	CENTRAL CATABOLIC (↓ INTAKE)
Neuropeptide Y	α-Melanocyte stimulating hormone
Agouti-related protein	Corticotropin releasing hormone
Melanin-concentrating hormone	Thyrotropin releasing hormone
Hypocretins/orexins	Cocaine- and amphetamine-regulated transcript (CART)
Galanin	Interleukin-1β
Norepinephrine	Urocortin
	Oxytocin
	Neurotensin
	Serotonin

the process of appetite regulation may allow the discovery of therapeutic agents that will selectively inhibit or stimulate either anabolic or catabolic central nervous system pathways.

ENERGY EXPENDITURE

Daily energy expenditure in adults varies widely, from less than 1400 kcal/day to more than 5000 kcal/day, with larger, more physically active individuals having the greatest energy needs. Typically, daily energy expenditure is divided into resting (or basal) metabolic rate, the thermic effect of food, and physical activity energy expenditure.

BASAL METABOLIC RATE. The basal metabolic rate (BMR) is the energy expenditure of lying still at rest, awake, in the overnight postabsorptive state. A true BMR is measured after awakening but prior to arising from bed. The resting metabolic rate (RMR) is similarly defined but is not necessarily measured before arising from bed. For most sedentary adult Americans, the RMR represents the major portion of energy expended during the day and may range from less than 1200 to more than 3000 kcal/day. Most (approximately 80%) of the BMR can be related to the amount of lean tissue an individual has.

Not all components of lean tissue consume oxygen at the same relative rates. Visceral, or splanchnic bed, tissues account for approximately 25% of resting metabolic rate but a much smaller proportion of body weight. The brain, which accounts for only a small percent of body weight, accounts for almost 15% of RMR. Likewise, the heart (approximately 7%) and kidneys (approximately 5 to 10%) account for greater portions of resting energy needs than their relative contribution to body mass. In contrast, resting muscle makes up 40 to 50% of lean tissue mass but accounts for only 25% of RMR. This changes dramatically with exercise, however; muscle can account for 80 to 90% of energy expenditure during high-intensity exercise. Adipose tissue is a minor contributor to daily energy expenditure, consuming only approximately 3 kcal/kg/day.

Although the vast majority of RMR can be accounted for by the amount of lean tissue an individual has, there are also other, more subtle, influences on RMR. Age, gender (women have slightly lower BMRs, even corrected for fat-free mass), and fat mass affect RMR. Slight changes in metabolic rate or BMR are observed during the menstrual cycle (luteal phase more than follicular phase). There is also evidence that heritable or family factors do influence BMR, accounting for as much as 10% of interindividual differences.

There are both obligatory and facultative components to RMR. With an energy-restricted diet, significant reductions in BMR relative to the amount of fat-free mass occur. Reductions in the production of triiodothyronine from thyroxine are thought to contribute to this phenomenon. Likewise, during brief periods of overfeeding, it has been found that RMR increases above that which would be expected for the amount of lean tissue present.

It has been proposed that individuals with BMRs lower than predicted are at increased risk of future weight gain. Published data suggest that the relative risk is small, and the clinical effort to identify such patients is not warranted. Measurement of BMR is sometimes helpful in the evaluation of patients who insist they are unable to lose weight while following diets consisting of less than 1000 kcal/day. Almost without fail, their BMR is substantially greater than their reported food intake. This underscores the fact that most adults are notoriously unreliable in assessing their own food intake.

THERMIC EFFECT OF FOOD. Approximately 10% of the energy content of food is expended in the process of digestion, absorption, and metabolism of nutrients. There is significant interindividual variability in this value, ranging from a low of approximately 5% to a high of approximately 15% of meal calories that are "wasted" in the postprandial interval. The thermic effect of a meal is related to the carbohydrate and protein caloric content of the meal (the fat content has little stimulatory effect). Both obligatory and facultative components of the thermic effect of food have been identified. The obligatory components no doubt reflect the energy costs of digestion, absorption, and storage of nutrients. Approximately 60 to 70% of the thermic effect of meals is obligatory, and the remaining 30 to 40% is facultative thermogenesis. The two factors thought to play a role in the facultative component of the thermic effect of food are the postprandial insulin response and activation of the sympathetic nervous system. The thermic effect of food is somewhat lower in insulin-resistant/obese humans, but there have been no reported links between reduced postprandial thermogenesis and future obesity.

PHYSICAL ACTIVITY ENERGY EXPENDITURE. The energy expenditure of physical activity is a product of the amount of work done and the work efficiency of the individual. Because there is not much variability in work efficiency, the published values for estimating the energy costs of work performed are quite accurate. It is common to express the work unit as metabolic equivalents, or METs, which is a multiple of the resting metabolic rate. If an individual's RMR is 1 kcal/min, a workload of 5 METs would be 5 kcal/min. Highly trained athletes can work at extremely high METs (>16) for extended periods, but most sedentary individuals can only work for a limited time at much lower workloads. The peak work capacity refers to the maximum number of calories (or maximum amount of oxygen that can be consumed, $\dot{V}O_{2max}$) that can be expended. There is tremendous variability in peak work capacity that is largely, but not solely, related to how much and what type of physical activity is performed.

Another important concept in understanding the capacity for physical activity (and thus exercise prescriptions) is the lactate threshold. The lactate threshold can be thought of as the level at which exercise begins to become so uncomfortable that it cannot be maintained much longer. The biochemical definition relates to the progressive rise in blood lactate concentrations that are observed. The lactate threshold may range from 50% to 90% of an individual's peak work capacity. Training raises the lactate threshold closer to the maximum workload, and thus allows individuals to work at higher rates for longer periods of time. Obese, sedentary individuals typically have lactate thresholds that are quite low (sometimes on the order of 4 to 5 METs), and the threshold can be even lower in obese patients with type 2 diabetes.

Exercise (fitness- and sports-related activities) is commonly considered the main component of physical activity thermogenesis. Although a large amount of energy can be expended in relatively brief periods in fit individuals, most adults do not exercise at high levels or for a sufficient duration to expend a large amount of energy. Thus, rather than focusing solely on "exercise" as the main component of physical activity energy expenditure, it is important to consider the energy costs of nonexercise activity.

Nonexercise activity thermogenesis (NEAT) is the caloric expense of performing all activities other than exercise. The range of observed NEAT under controlled (metabolic chamber) conditions has been from less than 100 up to approximately 800 kcal/day. There is probably a much wider range in free-living individuals. NEAT is not a static component of daily energy expenditure. It has been shown that NEAT can increase in response to increased food intake in an unconscious manner. In fact, modulation of NEAT can be a significant factor that acts to stabilize weight despite variations in food intake. Low levels of NEAT have been reported to predict future weight gain in some populations. There is virtually no information as to what the regulatory systems are that stimulate or inhibit NEAT.

Secondary Causes of Obesity

MEDICATIONS. A growing number of medications cause weight gain in some or most of those patients for whom they are prescribed. Awareness of the medications that have this potential can facilitate weight loss treatment in some patients. Table 233–5 lists a number of medications that are associated with weight gain as well as alternative treatment approaches, if any, for the underlying condition.

DISEASES. Less than 1% of obese patients have an underlying disease that can explain their obesity. Endocrinopathies are the most common secondary cause of obesity. These include Cushing's syndrome, hypothalamic damage resulting in overeating (most commonly after pituitary surgery), insulinoma, and hypothyroidism. A Cushing's syndrome–like fat distribution is common; therefore, other patient aspects are the best clues to test for this condition. These include the classic purple striae, thinning skin, easy bruising, and proximal muscle weakness. Correction of Cushing's syndrome commonly results in substantial loss of excess body fat. Insulinoma is a rare tumor, and only a small portion of patients with insulinoma present with obesity; only some patients consciously prevent spells by eating more often, and thus become obese. The weight gain associated with hypothyroidism is virtually always due to fluid retention and resolves dramatically with thyroid hormone replacement. Unfortunately, successful treatment is not available for hyperphagia due to hypothalamic damage. Occasionally, adult patients with growth hormone deficiency, most commonly after hypophysectomy, lose excess weight with growth hormone replacement therapy.

Table 233–5 • PHARMACOLOGIC INFLUENCES IN WEIGHT GAIN, AND ALTERNATIVE THERAPIES

DRUGS THAT MAY PROMOTE WEIGHT GAIN	ALTERNATIVE TREATMENTS WITH LESS OR NO WEIGHT GAIN OR THAT PROMOTE WEIGHT LOSS
Psychiatric/Neurologic Medications	Alternative Psychiatric/ Neurologic Medications
Antipsychotics	
Zyprexa, Clozaril	Ziprasodone, risperadone,
Antidepressants	quetapine
Serotonin reuptake inhibitors,	Buproprion, nefazodone
tricyclic antidepressants,	
monamine oxidase inhibitors	
Antiepileptic drugs	
Gabapentin, valproate,	Topiramate, lamotrigine
carbamazepine	
Lithium	
Steroid Hormones	Alternative to Steroid Hormones
Hormonal contraceptives	Barrier methods
Corticosteroids	Nonsteroidal anti-inflammatory drugs
Progestational steroids	Weight loss
Anti-Diabetes Agents	Alternative Anti-Diabetes Agents
Insulin	Metformin
Sulfonylureas	Acarbose, miglitol
Thiazolidinediones	Orlistat, sibutramine
Antihistamines	Decongestants, inhalers
Antihypertensive Agents	Alternative antihypertensive Agents
α- and β-adrenergic receptor blockers	Angiotensin-converting enzyme inhibitors, calcium channel blockers
Highly Active Antiretroviral Therapy	

Adapted from Wadden T, Stankard AJ, eds: Handbook of Obesity Treatment. LJ Aronne, 2002, p 385.

PSYCHOSOCIAL ASPECTS OF OBESITY. Sexual, physical, and emotional abuse, especially in women, can result in long-term adverse consequences that include obesity. The effects of the abuse tend to be most profound if it occurred in childhood and adolescence. These women may be severely obese, suffer from chronic depression, and experience a number of psychosomatic symptoms, particularly chronic gastrointestinal distress. Identifying these issues prior to initiation of weight loss programs is important because successful weight loss may actually aggravate the distress experienced by these women. In addition, appropriate referral for psychiatric help may be needed prior to initiation of treatment for obesity.

Pathophysiology

METABOLIC COMPLICATIONS. The properties of excess adipose tissue that contribute to the metabolic complications of obesity are now better understood. A key observation was that a central or upper body fat distribution, more so than total fat mass, is predictive of the metabolic complications of obesity. It was also noted that obese individuals with enlarged fat cells (adipocyte hypertrophy) were more likely to suffer the metabolic complications than obese persons with normal-sized fat cells (adipocyte hyperplasia). In vitro studies showed that lipolysis, which results in the release of fatty acids and glycerol, is less well regulated in large adipocytes than in normal-sized adipocytes. The finding that upper body obesity is associated with adipocyte hypertrophy and lower body obesity is associated with adipocyte hyperplasia provided a potential link between fat distribution differences and adipose tissue function as regards its fuel export function.

Adipose tissue release of free fatty acids (FFAs) and glycerol into the circulation via lipolysis provides the majority (in a kinetic sense) of circulating lipid fuel. Lipolysis is capable of providing 50 to 100% of daily energy needs. Adipose tissue lipolysis is regulated primarily by insulin (inhibition) and catecholamines (stimulation), although growth hormone and cortisol also can stimulate lipolysis to a lesser extent. Upper body obesity is associated with several abnormalities of adipose tissue lipolysis, most remarkably with higher FFA concentrations due to excess release in the postabsorptive and postprandial periods. Abnormally high FFA concentrations can contribute to or account for a number of the metabolic complications of obesity.

Insulin Resistance. The term *insulin resistance* is typically used when referring to the ability of insulin to promote glucose uptake, oxidation, and storage as well as to inhibit the release of glucose into the circulation. The primary site of insulin-stimulated glucose uptake, oxidation, and storage is skeletal muscle. The principal site of glucose production is the liver. Insulin resistance initially leads to hyperinsulinemia, a possible independent cardiovascular risk factor, and may eventually lead to the development of type 2 diabetes mellitus.

The ability of insulin to stimulate glucose disposal in muscle (and thus maintain normal glucose tolerance) and suppress plasma FFA concentrations is reduced in cases of upper body obesity. High plasma FFA concentrations can induce a state of insulin resistance both in the muscle (glucose uptake) and in the liver (glucose release), independent of obesity. Thus, abnormal regulation of adipose tissue FFA export can potentially explain much of the insulin resistance with respect to glucose metabolism. Although it has been suggested that production of tumor necrosis factor–α (and other peptides) by fat cells may play a role in the development of insulin resistance, there is little experimental evidence from human studies to support this theory.

Islet Cell Failure/Type 2 Diabetes Mellitus. The development of type 2 diabetes requires defects in both insulin secretion and insulin action. Many obese individuals are insulin resistant, yet only a subset develop diabetes mellitus. It follows that those who develop type 2 diabetes develop pancreatic beta cell decompensation with subsequent hyperglycemia. Animal (rodent) studies have suggested that a process referred to as "lipotoxicity" is involved in pancreatic β-cell failure. In this model, increased FFAs are proposed to contribute to the insulin secretory abnormalities seen in obesity and ultimately lead to beta cell failure. Although FFAs have been shown to modulate insulin secretion, it has not been demonstrated that FFA concentration has long-term adverse effect on islet β-cell function in humans. There are a number of important differences between rodent models of diabetes and human diabetes that require consideration of other possibilities. Another explanation for the development of β-cell failure in obesity is the overproduction of islet amyloid polypeptide. This protein is cosecreted with insulin and, because of its tertiary structure (which is different in humans and rodents), can form toxic amyloid deposits in β-cells. Amyloid deposits have been found in the pancreatic islets obtained at autopsy from patients with type 2 diabetes mellitus.

Hypertension. Blood pressure can be increased by a number of mechanisms. Increased circulating blood volume, abnormal vasoconstriction, decreased vascular relaxation, and increased cardiac output may all contribute to hypertension in obesity. The effect of hyperinsulinemia to increase renal sodium absorption has been proposed to contribute to hypertension via increased circulating blood volume. Abnormalities of vascular resistance may also contribute to the pathophysiology of obesity-related hypertension. Under some experimental conditions, elevated FFA levels have been found to cause increased vasoconstriction and reduced NO-mediated vasorelaxation, similar to that seen in the metabolic syndrome. It has also been suggested that there is an increased activity of the sympathetic nervous system in some obesity phenotypes, and that this contributes to obesity-associated hypertension. There are at least two other issues related to the hypertension of obesity that deserve mention. Tumor necrosis factor-α (produced by adipocytes and preadipocytes) has been suggested to contribute to elevated blood pressure, and angiotensinogen (also produced by adipocytes), a precursor of the vasoconstrictor angiotensin II, is positively correlated to blood pressure in some studies.

Dyslipidemia. Upper-body obesity and type 2 diabetes mellitus are associated with increased triglycerides, decreased high-density lipoprotein (HDL) cholesterol, and a high proportion of small, dense low-density lipoprotein (LDL) particles. This dyslipidemia contributes to the increased cardiovascular risk observed in the metabolic syndrome. Fasting hypertriglyceridemia is caused by increased hepatic secretion of very low density lipoprotein (VLDL). The elevated VLDL secretory rate may well be driven by increased delivery of FFAs to the liver (see earlier), which increases triglyceride synthesis and subsequently VLDL apoB-100 secretion. Low HDL cholesterol and the increase in small, dense LDL particles are likely an indirect consequence of elevated triglyceride-rich VLDL mediated via increased cholesterol ester transfer protein (CETP) and hepatic lipase activity. Genetic influences play a significant role in the expression of these lipid abnormalities. Polymorphisms in the genes for apolipoprotein E, lipoprotein lipase, apolipoprotein B-100, and apolipoprotein A-II are reported to affect the expression of increased triglycerides and decreased HDL of upper-body obesity.

Endocrine Manifestations. Obesity can create some abnormalities of the endocrine system. One of the most common abnormalities is polycystic ovarian syndrome (PCOS), which is characterized by mild hirsutism and irregular menses or amenorrhea with anovulatory cycles. It is most commonly linked with obesity and often improves with weight loss and/or other treatments that improve insulin resistance. Thus, it is thought that the insulin resistance associated with obesity may trigger the development of PCOS in susceptible individuals.

Mild to moderate androgen overproduction is a feature of upper body obesity in women; however, in men obesity can be associated with mild hypothalamic hypogonadism. There have been some suggestions that treatment of this central hypogonadism with exogenous testosterone is beneficial, but this is not common practice.

Although estrogens are not elevated in obese premenopausal women, they remain somewhat above postmenopausal levels in obese postmenopausal women. This may contribute to some of the increased prevalence of malignancies (see later).

MECHANICAL COMPLICATIONS OF OBESITY. The excess body weight associated with obesity is thought to be responsible for the increased prevalence of lower extremity degenerative joint disease seen in obese patients. Extreme obesity can result in very premature degenerative joint disease, and this may be especially difficult to treat surgically given the greater stress on joint replacements. Severely obese individuals may also have severe problems with venous stasis, which is occasionally aggravated by right heart failure (see later).

Obstructive Sleep Apnea. Sleep apnea is quite common in severely obese patients, tending to be more common in men generally and in women with an upper body obese phenotype. Sleep apnea is most likely explained by enlargement of upper airways soft tissue, resulting in collapse of the upper airways with inspiration during sleep. The obstruction leads to apneas, with hypoxemia, hypercarbia, and a stress response (high catecholamine and endothelin levels). The frequent arousals to restore breathing result in poor sleep quality. Sleep apnea is associated with an increased risk of hypertension, and, if sleep apnea is severe, it can lead to right heart failure and sudden death. A history of daytime hypersomnolence, loud snoring, restless sleep, or morning headaches is suggestive of obstructive sleep apnea.

Cancer. The risk of breast cancer and endometrial cancer is increased in obese women. It is thought that this may be due to the increased estrogen levels associated with obesity in postmenopausal women. Obese men also have a higher rate of mortality with cancers of the prostate and colon. The reasons for this association are unknown.

Gastrointestinal Disorders. Gastroesophageal reflux disease and gallstones are more prevalent in obese patients. Likewise, fatty liver and nonalcoholic steatohepatitis is more common in obese patients. Nonalcoholic steatohepatitis can eventually progress to cirrhosis and can be a fatal. Weight loss and interventions that improve insulin sensitivity appear to improve fatty liver and nonalcoholic steatohepatitis.

Evaluation

In the office practice, obtaining an accurate height and weight allows calculation of BMI, and under some circumstances measurement of the patient's waist circumference can be useful in assessing risk (see earlier). Accurate measure of blood pressure, which may require a large blood pressure cuff, is important. Identification of the adverse health consequences of obesity should be a routine part of office evaluation of a patient who is overweight or obese. The presence or absence of dyslipidemia (HDL cholesterol <45 mg/dL for women, HDL cholesterol <35 mg/dL for men, or triglycerides >150 mg/dL), hypertension, glucose intolerance/diabetes, and hyperuricemia should be documented. The presence of three or more of these health problems (or two with evidence of insulin resistance) is considered criteria for diagnosis of the dysmetabolic syndrome X. A history suggestive of sleep apnea should prompt a referral for overnight oximetry or a sleep disorder evaluation.

After determining the level of health risk facing the patient with obesity, a review of the patient's lifestyle, including an assessment of physical activity level and eating habits, may help provide information about why the patient is obese. A family history of obesity, or long-standing obesity, provides evidence that there is not a secondary cause of obesity. A careful medication history and social history may help the clinician identify precipitating factors that can be modified to enhance the success of treatment.

Prior to the patient's entering a weight management program, it is important to ensure that he or she has realistic goals and expectations. Often patients expect to lose large amounts of weight in short periods of time with little or no effort. Medical treatment programs, even if they include pharmacotherapy, do not often result in greater than 10% weight loss. A 10% weight loss, however, is sufficient to markedly reduce the medical complications of obesity, although a patient disappointed with this result may quit a medically successful program. Helping the patient to realize and accept that 10% weight loss is reasonable can be one of the more challenging aspects for a physician but can prevent unnecessary disappointment later on.

It is sometimes necessary to delay entry into treatment programs if a patient is not ready to make changes in his or her lifestyle. In this case, a reasonable strategy is to periodically remind the patient of the potential health benefits of improved activity and eating habits. Once a willingness to make changes is apparent, treatment is more likely to succeed.

Rx Treatment

Obesity represents an individual's response to the environment based on genetics and learned behavior. It is seldom a temporary condition and is best viewed as a chronic disease. Therefore, treatment must be considered a long-term issue, much like treatment of diabetes, hypertension, or dyslipidemia. Substantial weight loss can be induced via severe caloric restriction, but without approaches to ensure behavioral changes body fat is invariably regained. Permanent lifestyle changes (eating and activity behavior) can result in permanent weight loss.

Reducing energy intake is the most efficient and effective means to lose weight. For example, creating a 500 kcal/day deficit via reduced food intake can allow the loss of 1 lb of fat per week. Although possible, it is much more difficult to increase energy expenditure by 500 kcal/day through exercise. Higher levels of physical activity can prevent weight gain (or weight regain after weight loss). Some patients are able to change eating and activity habits on their own given the proper information, whereas others require behavior modification interventions (formal or informal) to help make these changes. In some instances, pharmacotherapy or surgery may be needed for treatment of obesity. Figure 233-2 shows how to evaluate and manage overweight and obese patients.

DIET. Changes in eating habits must be permanent if weight loss is to be maintained. An experienced registered dietitian can be helpful in the evaluation of a patient's eating habits and will be able to provide the needed education. The diet history may identify a few eating behaviors that are resulting in excess energy intake. Specific recommendations can then focus on the most blatant poor eating habits. In addition to addressing particular adverse eating behaviors, there are some general principles regarding diet that should be addressed. Reducing the energy density of food (most commonly accomplished by reducing dietary fat) can allow patients to feel satiated while consuming fewer calories. A common mistake, however, is for patients to consume large quantities of easy to eat "non-fat" foods, thereby offsetting the expected benefits of the diet. In addition to reducing the intake of high-fat foods, patients should understand that increasing the consumption of foods high in water and fiber (fruits, vegetables, legumes, and soups) can provide satiety without excess calories. It is also important to avoid the excess intake of beverages containing substantial calories with little or no satiety. Finally, a regular pattern of eating should be encouraged.

New, fad diets are continuously being promoted with the promise of easy weight loss. A common feature of these diets is the claim that special properties of certain foods help people lose weight or are the cause of obesity. If followed, most of these diets result in weight loss because of a reduced energy intake. The reduced intake can be related to the monotony of the diet or, in the case of the low carbohydrate diets, to the appetite suppressant effect of ketosis.

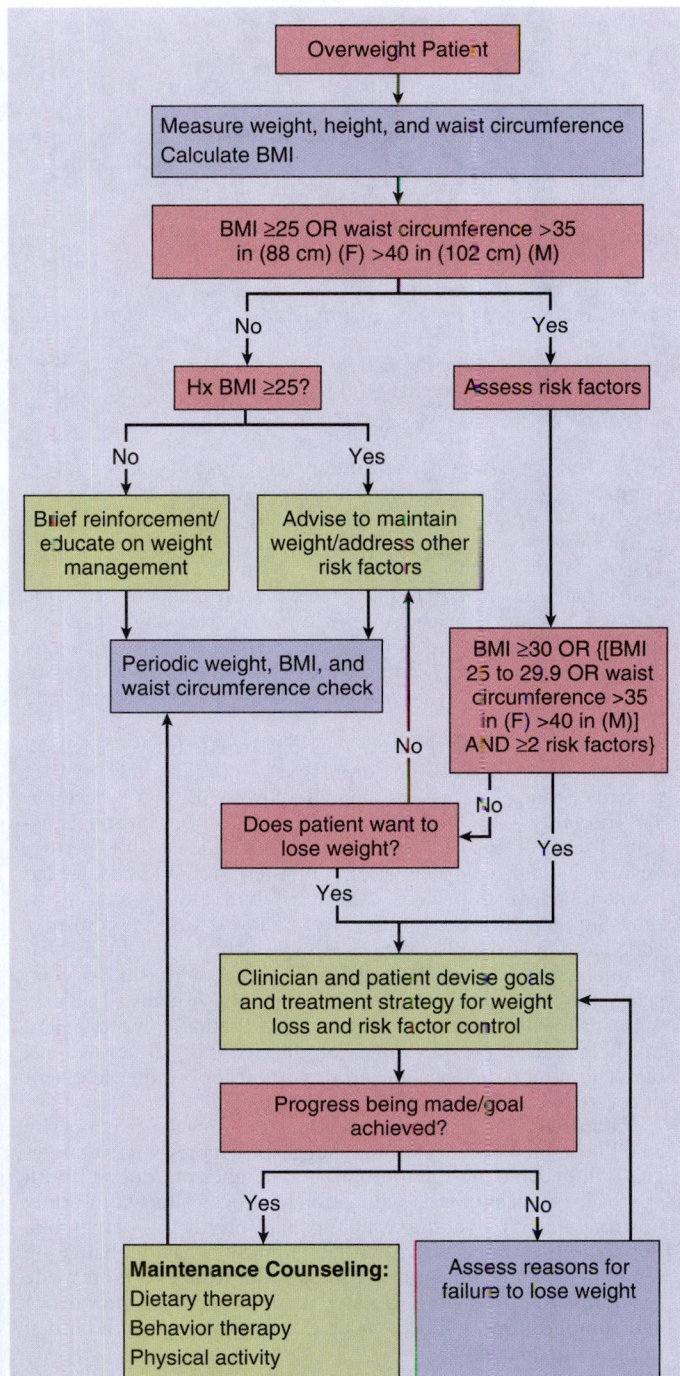

FIGURE 233-2 • Flow diagram for the evaluation and management of overweight and obesity. BMI = body mass index. (Adapted from the NIH/NHLBI: Clinical Guidelines on the Identification, Evaluation and Treatment of Obesity in Adults: The Evidence Report. Obes Res 1998;6:51S–209S).

In small randomized trials, low carbohydrate diets have been at least as effective as conventional diets for weight loss. 🔴

Very low calorie diets (less than 800 calories per day) have been used for years to achieve accelerated weight loss. The rationale for this approach is now in question, given that the long-term results of these diets is no better and sometimes worse than the results from the standard low-calorie diet combined with behavior modification. The expensive laboratory monitoring required for very low calorie diets without an improved long-term outcome raises questions as to the cost-to-benefit ratio of this approach.

PHYSICAL ACTIVITY. Long-term increases in physical activity are necessary to prevent weight regain following successful weight loss. Unfortunately, many overweight and obese patients are quite unfit, being unable to walk even 1 mile continuously. It is not possible for most adults to burn large numbers of calories. For example, only approximately 100 kcal are expended by a 70 kg adult walking 1 mile. Losing weight solely by increasing exercise is impractical for most patients. Increasing physical activity as a means of maintaining weight loss is an attainable goal for most patients, however.

Successful maintenance of weight loss requires that daily energy expenditure be an average of 80 to 90% above RMR. This is a considerable increase for most patients. For example, someone with an RMR of 1500 kcal/day would need to expend approximately 1000 kcal/day in physical activity to meet this target. Activities other than "exercise" are important means to achieve this goal.

There are important health benefits from regular physical activity over and above the effects on weight. These include lower rates of cardiovascular and all-cause mortality, independent of weight. The options for increasing physical activity include exercise (sports or fitness pursuits) or using lifestyle approaches. Both methods can improve fitness and allow weight stability, although persuading obese patients to become more active is not easy. Physicians can begin by asking patients about their current and past activity habits, as well as what barriers they see to increasing physical activity. This accomplishes the goal of stimulating patients to think about the issue in a tactful manner. It can help to ask the patient what personal benefits they envision as a result of increasing their level of activity. If patients agree to begin a exercise/physical activity program, they will need to monitor their activity and set realistic goals for the amount of exercise they are going to achieve.

BEHAVIOR MODIFICATION. Patients who are unable to make changes in eating activity habits on their own or with informal office counseling may benefit from referral to a behavioral therapist. The goals of behavior modification are to help patients modify their eating, activity, and thinking habits that predispose to obesity. The goals of behavioral therapy focus on achieving selected results as regards eating and activity habits and focusing on specific pathways on how to achieve the goals. These pathways may include identifying and removing barriers to developing better eating or activity habits. Small, incremental and consistent changes in behavior are encouraged, as opposed to large, inconsistent changes in behavior. Self-monitoring of food and activity is considered a key feature to success, because most obese patients underestimate food intake and overestimate exercise in the absence of objective measures. Cognitive restructuring has been introduced as a way to help overcome the thought processes that can lead to failure of a weight management program. Patients are taught to identify, challenge, and correct self-defeating thoughts.

PHARMACOTHERAPY. A limited number of drugs are currently available to help patients with weight loss. The disastrous experience with fenfluramine and dexfenfluramine (pulmonary hypertension and cardiac valvular disease) has clearly dampened the enthusiasm of many physicians to prescribe weight loss drugs, even under circumstances that justify their use. Not all overweight or obese patients are candidates for pharmacologic treatment. Table 233–6 provides criteria to help select patients for pharmacologic treatment. Because pharmacologic treatment of obesity exposes patients to some risks and expense, it is reasonable to require an objective benefit. A rational argument can be made that priority should be given to those patients with one or more medical complications or conditions that are likely to improve with weight loss. Medications should not be used alone, but only as a part of a comprehensive program that includes diet, exercise, and behavior modification. When prescribing antiobesity medications, it is important to set clear goals with respect to both weight loss and health benefits. Just as with other classes of medications, continued use of ineffective or suboptimally effective drugs does not serve the patient.

Current Medications. The medications currently available for long-term use act either through appetite reduction (e.g., sibutramine) or via inhibition of intestinal lipase (resulting in fat malabsorption). Phentermine, an appetite suppressant, is currently approved for short-term (3 months) use. Because weight that is lost with

Continued

Nutritional Diseases

Table 233–6 • INDICATIONS FOR PHARMACOLOGIC TREATMENT OF OBESITY

Body mass index >27 kg/m²
One or more complications or conditions that are likely to improve with weight loss
Previous failure of conservative treatment with diet and exercise
Patient agrees to 2- to 4-week trial of making initial changes in diet and exercise before starting pharmacotherapy
Patient agrees to continued treatment with diet, exercise, and behavioral modification while on pharmacologic treatment
Patient agrees to periodic follow-up
Premenopausal women (able to have children) must use some form of contraception
Consider a pregnancy test when initiating treatment if any possibility of pregnancy
No contraindications to the specific drug used for pharmacologic treatment

pharmacotherapy (especially when used without a comprehensive program) is quickly regained once the medication is discontinued, agents that are approved for long-term use (sibutramine and orlistat) are more rational therapeutic choices. **2**

Sibutramine also acts via appetite regulation mechanisms. Patients are typically not less hungry but do experience earlier satiety, resulting is less food intake. The usual starting dose for sibutramine is 10 mg in the morning, with maximum dose of 15 mg if the response is suboptimal. Monthly monitoring for the first 3 months is needed to ensure a good response and to detect adverse effects. A minority of patients develop cardiovascular responses (hypertension and tachycardia) that contraindicate continued use of the medication. Failure to lose weight over the first 1 to 2 months is a strong indicator of drug treatment failure and should prompt the physician to discontinue sibutramine.

Orlistat, a pancreatic lipase inhibitor, facilitates weight loss through a different mechanism. At the typical dose of 120 mg three times daily with meals, approximately 30% of dietary fat is malabsorbed. As expected, adverse gastrointestinal side effects occur. These including oily spotting, abdominal pain, excess flatus, and fecal urgency, together with fatty or oily stools. These side effects decrease with continued use. There is evidence that concomitant use of bulk-forming laxatives (e.g., psyllium, methylcellulose) can reduce the side effects. It is not necessary to use orlistat if a non-fat meal is being consumed.

Both sibutramine and orlistat improve the results of medical treatment programs that include diet, exercise, and behavior modification. **3,4** The addition of either agent results in almost twice as many patients achieving goal weight loss (10% of body weight). There appears to be no additive effect of sibutramine and orlistat.

Success of Medical Therapy. It has been estimated that more than 95% of patients embarking on self-diets or fad diets fail to maintain a significant weight loss for a period of time that would have meaningful health benefits. The published results of commercial programs are not impressively better, mostly because of high dropout rates. In contrast, organized, scientifically based weight management programs that employ behavior modification in addition to dietary instruction, physical activity, and medications (when indicated) can achieve impressive results. Although these programs tend to be more selective (accepting only motivated patients), the dropout rates can be acceptable (<30%) and of those remaining in the program a greater than 10% weight loss can be achieved and maintained for more than 1 or 2 years in 40 to 60% of patients. These results are more impressive than those reported with older, less comprehensive programs, wherein almost all patients regained all weight in less than 6 months.

BARIATRIC SURGERY. Surgical treatment is indicated for severely obese patients with severe medical complications that could be expected to improve with successful weight loss. Patients with a BMI of 35 to 40 with life-threatening complications can be considered, but more typically patients with a BMI greater than 40 and several complications are candidates for surgery, assuming past attempts at medical treatment have failed. Because the risks and costs of surgical treatment are greater than for medical treatment, it is reasonable practice to select patients who stand to obtain more potential benefit from surgery. Contraindications to surgery include active substance abuse, defined noncompliance with previous medical care, and certain psychiatric disorders (schizophrenia, borderline personality disorder, uncontrolled depression).

A multidisciplinary team, including a physician, dietitian, psychologist or psychiatrist with expertise in this area, and a surgeon experienced in bariatric procedures, is important for optimal outcome. Defining realistic expectations is an important part of the evaluation process. Patients undergoing bariatric surgery are not likely to be reduced to their ideal body weight. Successful weight loss is typically defined as losing an average of 50 to 60% of excess body weight; that is, if someone is 150 kg overweight, they might reasonably be expected to lose 75 kg.

A variety of bariatric surgical procedures have been used. The jejunoileal bypass has been abandoned because of delayed severe complications, including liver failure, renal failure, and arthropathy. If these complications are identified, reversal of the procedure can improve or stabilize organ function. Several gastric procedures (gastroplasty, vertical stapling, vertical banded gastroplasty, and gastric banding) are commonly used but are less effective than the roux-en-Y gastric bypass in terms of long-term weight loss and outright surgical failure. A procedure termed the *partial pancreaticobiliary bypass* has become popular in some areas but is associated with sometimes severe, even fatal vitamin and mineral deficiencies.

The results of the roux-en-Y gastric bypass for treatment of morbid obesity have been impressive. Approximately 80% of patients achieve success, as defined above, with this procedure. The mortality (<1%) and morbidity (e.g., infection, wound dehiscence) rates of this procedure are low in centers with expertise, despite the high-risk population. Long-term follow-up is needed to ensure adequate protein, calorie, vitamin, and mineral nutrition. Supplemental vitamin B₁₂, iron, and calcium are routinely added to standard multivitamins. Almost all of the weight loss that occurs happens during the first 1 to 2 years. Long-term (>5 year) success rates are outstanding in good programs. Virtually all patients with successful weight loss experience a dramatic improvement in the medical complications of obesity. For these reasons, bariatric surgery has become an important tool in the treatment of severe, medically complicated obesity.

PREVENTION. The dramatic increase in the prevalence of obesity over the past few decades strongly suggests that preventative strategies will become more important as time goes on. Public health approaches that emphasize education have been almost uniformly unsuccessful at preventing weight gain or producing weight loss. Public health strategies that virtually impose behavior change are more successful in this regard. Unless widespread efforts are made to address the problem of obesity, it is likely that its prevalence and complications will become an ever-increasing health burden in the United States.

1. Foster GD, Wyatt HR, Hill JO, et al: A randomized trial of a low-carbohydrate diet for obesity. N Engl J Med 2003;348:2082–2090.
2. James WP, Astrup A, Finer N, et al: Effect of sibutramine on weight maintenance after weight loss. A randomized trial. Lancet 2000;356:2119–2125.
3. Berkowitz RI, Wadden TA, Tershakovec AM, et al: Behavior therapy and sibutramine for the treatment of adolescent obesity: A randomized controlled trial. JAMA 2003;289:1805–1812.
4. Krempf M, Louvet JP, Allanic H, et al: Weight reduction and long-term maintenance after 18 months' treatment with orlistat for obesity. Int J Obes Relat Metab Disord 2003;27:591–597.

SUGGESTED READINGS

Farooqi IS, Keogh JM, Yeo GS, et al: Clinical spectrum of obesity and mutations in the melanocortin 4 receptor gene. N Engl J Med 2003;348:1160–1163. *These mutations cause a distinct co-dominant obesity syndrome.*
Fontaine KR, Redden DT, Wang C, et al: Years of life lost due to obesity. JAMA 2003;289:187–193. *Obesity markedly reduces life expectancy.*
Friedman JM: A war on obesity, not the obese. Science 2003;299:856–858. *An evolutionary overview.*
Sheehan MT, Jensen MD: Metabolic complications of obesity. Med Clin North Am 2000;84:363–385. *A comprehensive overview.*

part XVIII

Endocrine Diseases

234 PRINCIPLES OF ENDOCRINOLOGY

Gordon N. Gill

Communication is essential for all life processes. Accurate sensing of the environment and appropriate coordinated responses depend on the nervous and endocrine systems, which are tightly interwoven. Nervous system functions are mediated by hormones, and the endocrine system is centrally controlled by the nervous system. Communication between cells is necessary for development from a single fertilized egg to a mature adult, for an orderly reproductive cycle, and for homeostatic adjustments to a constantly changing environment. Hormones, distinct chemical messengers, transmit information from one cell to another to coordinate homeostatic adaptations, growth, development, and reproduction. *Hormones,* a word derived from Greek meaning "excite" or "set in motion," bind with high affinity and specificity to receptors, which are allosteric proteins. Receptor proteins have two essential functional characteristics: (1) a recognition site, which binds hormones with high specificity and affinity, and (2) an activity site, which transduces the information received into a biochemical message. Allosteric receptor proteins adopt various conformational states; binding of the hormone ligand results in the active conformation. The initial event in hormone action is thus a bimolecular reaction dependent on the concentration of hormone, the concentration of receptor, and the affinity of receptor for hormone.

$$[\text{Hormone}] + [\text{Receptor}]_{\text{Inactive}} \underset{k_{-1}}{\overset{k_1}{\rightleftharpoons}} [\text{Hormone} - \text{Receptor}]_{\text{Active}}$$

Factors that control the concentration of both hormone and receptor determine biologic responses of cells, of organs, and of the whole organism.

Classic endocrinology dealt with the glands that produce hormones and the concentration of hormone to which cells expressing receptors are exposed. Biosynthesis, secretion, transport of hormone to target cells, and metabolic inactivation determine the effective hormone concentration. Diseases of endocrine glands that impair hormone production result in deficiency states, whereas diseases that cause excessive production result in hormone excess states. Expression of receptor is equally important in forming the active hormone-receptor complex. Genetic and acquired diseases that impair receptors result in deficiency states, even though hormone concentrations are compensatorily increased. Increased receptor expression results in an excess state, an event that occurs with growth factor receptors in malignant transformation.

Hormones are produced not only by the glands of internal secretion but also by a variety of cells throughout the body. Neurohormones, produced in the hypothalamus, are also produced in cells throughout the nervous system to modulate neuronal function. Gastrointestinal hormones are produced within the nervous system. Hormones that regulate production and maturation of cells of the hematopoietic and immune systems are made in cells of these lineages and in endothelial and mesenchymal cells. Growth-promoting and growth-inhibiting hormones (growth factors and growth inhibitors) are produced by macrophages and mesenchymal cells. Many of these signaling molecules do not travel long distances through the blood to reach target cells as do classic hormones (endocrine) but act on target cells in the vicinity of the producer cell (paracrine) or even on the producer cell itself (autocrine). During development, cell surface hormones may act on the cell surface receptor of a neighbor cell as a cell-cell communication system. Regardless of signaling distance, the same principles of hormone-receptor interactions operate.

HOW HORMONES WORK

Two classes of hormones operate via two types of receptors (Fig. 234–1). Peptide hormones are synthesized as parts of larger protein molecules and are processed as secretory proteins. They act via receptors located in the cell membrane with the recognition/binding site exposed on the cell surface and the activity domain facing the inside of the cell. Activated cell surface receptors use a variety of strategies to transduce signal information, often activating second messengers,

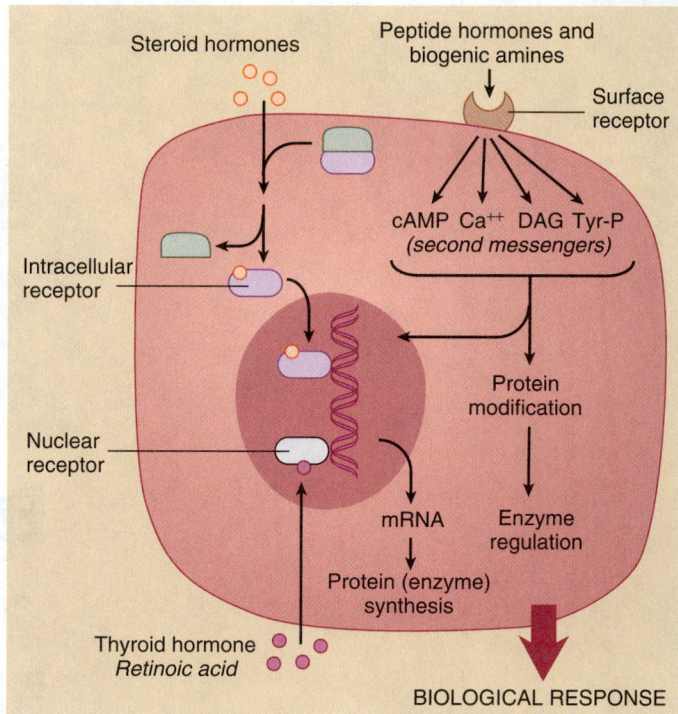

FIGURE 234–1 • Mechanisms by which peptide and steroid hormones signal.

which amplify and distribute the molecular information. Many peptide hormones ultimately signal via regulation of protein phosphorylation. In this most common process through which proteins are covalently modified, a phosphate group is donated to the protein by adenosine triphosphate (ATP). This allows peptide hormones to change rapidly the conformation and thus the function of existing cell enzymes. It also allows somewhat slower changes in gene transcription to regulate the concentration of enzyme proteins. Biogenic amines function like peptide hormones.

Steroid hormones are synthesized from precursor cholesterol. Thyroid hormone, retinoic acid (vitamin A), and vitamin D are synthesized through separate pathways but act through the same family of receptors and mechanisms as do steroid hormones. This group of hormones acts via structurally related receptors that bind to DNA recognition sites to regulate transcription of target genes. They change the concentration of cell proteins, primarily enzymes, and thus the metabolic activity underlying the physiologic response.

Peptide Hormones Act via Cell Surface Receptors

HORMONE BINDING AND SIGNAL TRANSDUCTION

Peptide hormone receptors have one of three general structures (Fig. 234–2): (1) a seven-membrane spanning structure in which the recognition site is formed by exterior sequences between membrane-spanning helices and the activity site is formed by interhelical regions inside the cell; (2) a single membrane-spanning helical structure separating the recognition domain from the cytoplasmic domain, which contains an intrinsic enzyme activity; and (3) a single membrane-spanning helix that separates the recognition domain from an intracellular domain that couples to second messenger systems, as do the seven-membrane spanning receptors. The protein coupled may be an intracellular tyrosine kinase or other enzyme.

Hormone ligands and receptors bind with high affinities (equilibrium dissociation constants [K_D] of nanomolar to picomolar), thus providing the specificity necessary for cells to decode the information provided by the low concentration of hormone present among the many other circulating and extracellular proteins. The conformational change resulting from peptide hormone binding activates receptors to signal from the cell surface. Removal of receptors from the cell surface results in downregulation and attenuation of the response. Binding affinities and dose-response curves for the initial event in cell signaling are the same. Biologic responses consequent

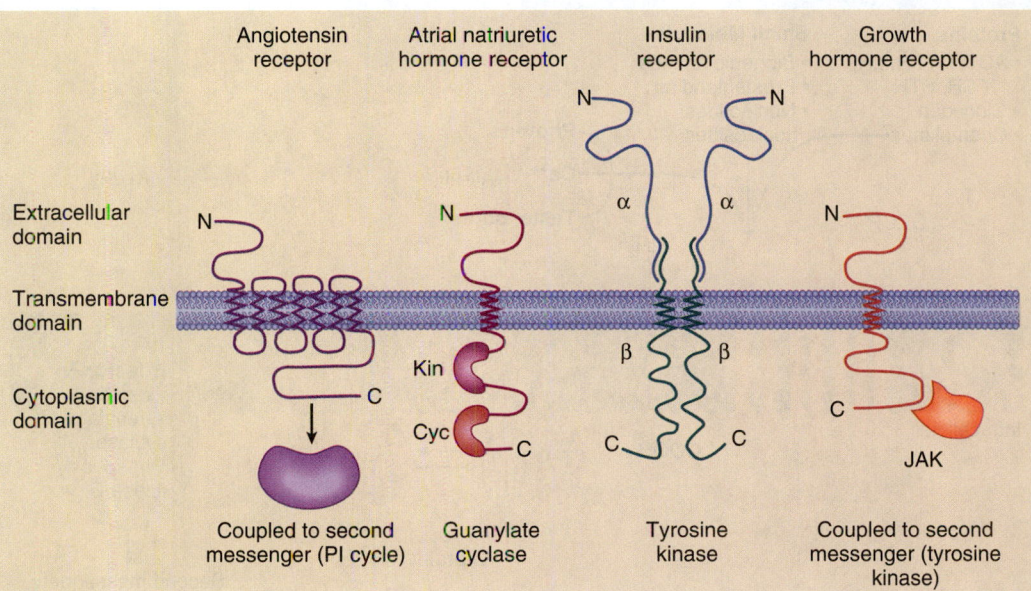

FIGURE 234–2 • Structures of peptide hormone receptors.

to these initial events occur through a series of amplifications, each with its own affinity. The result is a dose-response curve for biologic activities that is more sensitive than that for binding and activation of the initial response. Full biologic responses may thus occur at a low concentration of hormone, resulting in occupancy of only 10% or less of receptors. This provides high sensitivity to small changes in hormone concentration. It also provides significant reserve. Hormone-induced downregulation may remove 90% of receptors from the cell surface. This renders the cell refractory to the initial hormone concentration, but if the need is great enough, hormone concentrations can increase ten-fold and fully activate the residual 10% of receptors to give full biologic responses. Such a response system provides high initial sensitivity, buffering via downregulation against excessive hormone responses, but reserve that can operate when the signal strength is strong enough.

Receptors are mobile in the plane of the membrane. Ligand binding not only transduces signals but also induces downregulation by removing receptors from the cell surface. Ligand binding may induce sequestration of receptors and their retention inside the cell via interactions with cell proteins, as occurs with rhodopsin and adrenergic receptors. Ligand binding may induce endocytosis through clathrin-coated pits with ultimate degradation by lysosomal enzymes, as occurs with insulin and epidermal growth factor receptors. The concentration of cell surface receptors is regulated by interaction with hormone ligand and by other signals that regulate its synthesis and affinity. The concentration of receptors determines the responsiveness of the cells. Antagonists occupy receptors but in general do not induce desensitization. When antagonists are removed, receptor concentrations are high and cells are very responsive to hormone exposure. Effects on receptor concentration are seen clinically as upregulation (e.g., as excessive adrenergic responses when β-blockers are rapidly withdrawn) and as downregulation (e.g., insulin resistance in type II diabetes). Regulation of receptor synthesis is an important mechanism by which one hormone regulates responsiveness to another to coordinate biologic effects.

A class of cell surface receptors serves a nutrient delivery rather than an informational function. These molecules include the low-density lipoprotein (LDL) receptor, the transferrin receptor, and the asialoglycoprotein receptor. LDL and transferrin receptors, which are clustered in coated pits, internalize, deliver LDL (cholesterol) and iron to the cell interior, and then recycle to the cell surface. Such receptors are not downregulated by ligand but undergo repeated rounds of recycling to provide the cell with essential nutrients. The concentration of these receptors is regulated longer term in response to the metabolic state.

INTRACELLULAR SECOND MESSENGERS

CYCLIC ADENOSINE MONOPHOSPHATE AND CYCLIC GUANOSINE MONOPHOSPHATE.

The concept of second messengers was established by Earl Sutherland,

who discovered cyclic adenosine monophosphate (AMP), an intracellular allosteric effector that mediates the action of many peptide hormones. Hormone receptors are coupled to catalytic adenylate cyclase through guanosine nucleotide binding (G) proteins, the β-adrenergic receptor being a paradigm for this signaling pathway (Fig. 234–3). More than 600 human genes encode receptors of this class, mediating responses to a variety of ligands and physical stimuli (hormones, biogenic amines, light, sound, touch, pain, taste, smell). This receptor belongs to the seven-membrane spanning class. On ligand binding, the receptor interacts with a G protein trimer consisting of α, β, and γ subunits. Because G proteins bind guanosine diphosphate (GDP) with higher affinity than guanosine triphosphate (GTP), guanine nucleotide exchange is triggered by proteins that facilitate exchange of GTP for GDP; activity is reversed by hydrolysis of GTP to GDP. Binding of hormones to receptors that operate through the cyclic AMP second messenger system results in a conformational change, causing receptors to bind to G proteins. Ligand-activated receptors facilitate exchange of GTP for GDP so that the activated $G\alpha_s$ (the stimulating GTP-binding subunit) dissociates from the β and γ subunits. The [ligand·hormone receptor]·[$G\alpha_s$·GTP] complex activates adenylate cyclase to catalyze formation of cyclic AMP from ATP. Each hormone ligand induces formation of multiple cyclic AMP molecules through this mechanism. Inhibitory G proteins operate in a similar manner to decrease cyclic AMP formation. In both cases, ligand-activated receptors act to exchange GTP for GDP, analogous to proteins that catalyze this process to regulate protein synthesis.

Adenylate cyclase is a large complex molecule with a 12-membrane spanning structure. The two large cytoplasmic domains have internal sequence similarities and are related to sequences in guanylate cyclase. Eight adenylate cyclases have been identified, and their channel-like structure suggests that they may function as transporters in addition to catalyzing formation of cyclic AMP.

Activation of adenylate cyclase is buffered and terminated by several mechanisms. First, hormone dissociates from receptor. Binding of Gα·GTP to the receptor decreases affinity for hormone about one order of magnitude to facilitate this dissociation. Second, receptors desensitize and are removed from the cell surface by a process involving phosphorylation and interaction with cell proteins termed *arrestins*. If hormone exposure is short, receptors are dephosphorylated and reappear on the cell surface; if exposure is prolonged, receptors are degraded and resensitization requires new receptor synthesis. Third and most importantly, Gα proteins possess intrinsic GTPase activity so that GTP is hydrolyzed to GDP and, on GDP binding, Gα is inactivated and reassociates with the β/γ subunits. A family of proteins, the regulators of G protein signaling (RGS), enhance this GTPase activity to facilitate the "off" switch. There are RGS proteins specific for the various G proteins ($G\alpha_s$, $G\alpha_i$, $G\alpha_q$, $G\alpha_{12}$).

There are many consequences when this mechanism of signal transduction is perturbed. Mutations in seven-membrane spanning receptors may inactivate so that signaling is defective; some

Endocrine Diseases

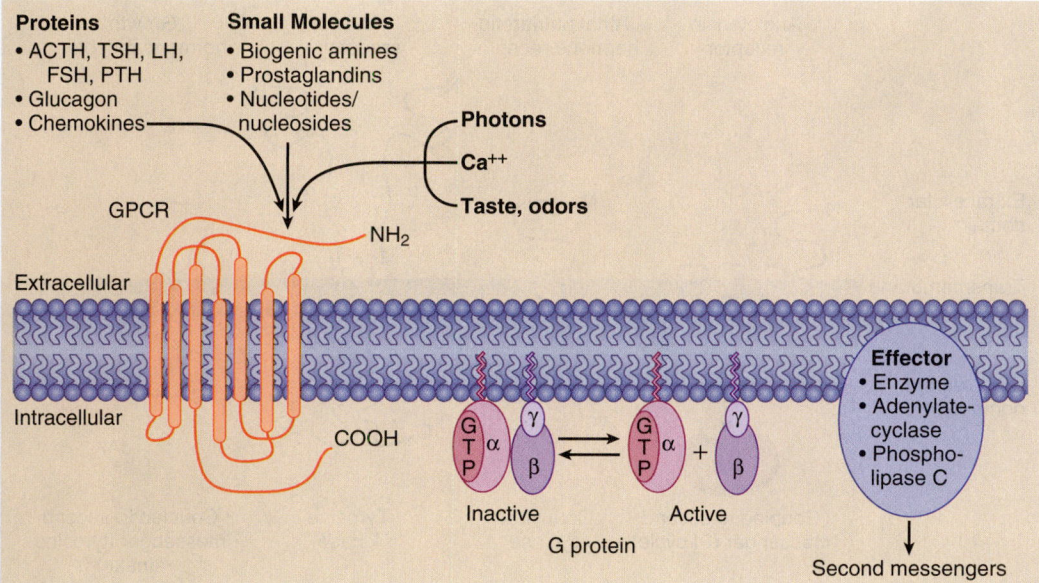

FIGURE 234–3 • G protein-coupled signal transduction. A variety of hormones and other stimuli bind to seven-membrane spanning receptors that activate G protein switches by exchanging guanosine diphosphate for guanosine triphosphate (GTP). GTP-bound G proteins then couple to a variety of signaling machines that transmit information. GTP hydrolysis turns off the switch. (Adapted from Bockaert J, Pin JP: Molecular tinkering of G protein-coupled receptors: An evolutionary process. EMBO J 1999;18:1723–1729, by permission of Oxford University Press.)

mutations, such as those observed in thyroid-stimulating hormone (TSH) receptors in hyperfunctioning thyroid nodules, may activate so that receptors signal in the absence of hormone. Continuous exposure to hormone results in desensitization or tachyphylaxis. Deficiency of G protein, which occurs in certain forms of pseudohypoparathyroidism, results in insensitivity to hormone. Cholera toxin, which activates adenosine diphosphate (ADP) ribosylation of $G\alpha_s$, inhibits GTPase activity and interferes with reversibility so that profound and prolonged elevations in cyclic AMP occur. Mutations in $G\alpha$ proteins that are predicted to impair GTPase activity have been described in endocrine tumors.

Cyclic AMP, an intracellular allosteric effector, binds to the regulatory subunit of cyclic AMP–dependent protein kinase. A-kinase is a tetrameric protein consisting of two regulatory and two catalytic subunits. Binding of cyclic AMP dissociates the inhibitory regulatory subunits as a dimer from the two catalytic subunits. The latter then catalyze the transfer of the γ phosphate of ATP to serine and threonine residues in proteins. This covalent modification by phosphorylation causes an allosteric conformational change in the substrate protein that results in a change in its activity. The hormonal signal is transduced into an alteration in enzyme activity and thus in cell function. Phosphorylation of cytoplasmic proteins results in alterations such as glycolysis; the activated catalytic kinase subunit also migrates to the nucleus to phosphorylate and activate transcription factors such as the cyclic AMP response element binding protein (CREB).

Cyclic AMP actions are reversed by hydrolysis of cyclic AMP by phosphodiesterase to 5′ AMP, and protein phosphorylation is reversed by the action of phosphatases. Phosphodiesterases are regulated and are a frequent target of inhibitor drugs such as methylxanthines, which prolong cyclic AMP action by blocking its degradation. Phosphatases are regulated by phosphatase-inhibitor proteins, which are fine-tuned by phosphorylation of these molecules.

A conceptually similar but structurally distinct system provides signal transduction through the second messenger cyclic guanosine monophosphate (GMP). Two forms of guanylate cyclase catalyze formation of cyclic GMP from GTP. The best characterized mammalian enzyme is the receptor for atrial natriuretic hormone (ANH). The binding site for ANH is located on the extracellular portion of its receptor and separated by a single membrane-spanning domain from the cytoplasmic guanylate cyclase (see Fig. 234–2). In contrast to adenylate cyclase, receptor and catalytic activities reside in the same molecule. Activity is regulated primarily by ligand binding but also depends on phosphorylation of the enzyme, with dephosphorylation causing desensitization. A cytoplasmic form of guanylate cyclase contains a heme moiety and is activated by nitrous oxide and free radicals.

Cyclic GMP acts by binding to the regulatory domain of cyclic GMP-dependent protein kinase. G-kinase, a dimeric enzyme that is evolutionarily related to A-kinase, is allosterically activated on cyclic

GMP binding. Like A-kinase, it catalyzes protein phosphorylation to alter enzyme function and physiologic responses. Reactions are terminated by cyclic GMP phosphodiesterase and protein phosphatases. Cyclic GMP phosphodiesterase is activated by binding of calcium·calmodulin, a mechanism providing biochemical communication between two signaling systems.

CALCIUM AND DIACYLGLYCEROL. Hormone receptors that activate the phosphatidylinositol (PI) cycle transmit information to the interior of the cell by two second messengers: calcium (Ca^{2+}) and diacylglycerol (DAG). The cycle of PI metabolism consists of synthesis of this phospholipid, its breakdown, and its resynthesis. PI is composed of a three-carbon glycerol backbone with long-chain fatty acids esterified at carbons 1 and 2 and an inositol ring esterified via a phosphoester bond at carbon 3. Distinct kinase enzymes catalyze phosphorylation of the inositol ring at positions 3, 4, and 5. Quantitatively, the principal phosphorylations occur sequentially at positions 4 and then 5. The principal function of activated hormone receptors is to stimulate phosphoinositidase (phospholipase C), which releases the phosphorylated inositol to generate inositol trisphosphate (IP_3, inositol 1,4,5 P_3) and DAG (the glycerol backbone with fatty acids attached at carbons 1 and 2). IP_3 increases the concentration of cytoplasmic $[Ca^{2+}]$. It mobilizes stored intracellular Ca^{2+} by binding to specific receptors on intracellular membranes and by facilitating opening of calcium channels. The concentration of basal cytoplasmic Ca^{2+} is at least 1000-fold less than that in storage sites and outside the cell. The release from intracellular stores or entry of Ca^{2+} into the cell rapidly increases cytoplasmic $[Ca^{2+}]$.

Ca^{2+} plays a regulatory role in muscle contraction, in neuromuscular transmission, and in hormone signaling. Ca^{2+} binds to calmodulin and alters its conformation, causing the Ca^{2+}·calmodulin complex to bind to a variety of enzymes to regulate their activities. Ca^{2+}·calmodulin regulates protein kinases, including myosin light chain kinase involved in smooth muscle contraction, phosphorylase kinase involved in breakdown of glycogen, and calmodulin-dependent protein kinase important in synaptic transmission. Ca^{2+}·calmodulin regulates cyclic nucleotide phosphodiesterase and adenylate and guanylate cyclases to influence cyclic AMP and cyclic GMP concentrations, and it is involved in microtubule assembly and disassembly. Ca^{2+}·calmodulin is thus able to bind to a variety of other proteins and to alter their activity in response to information provided by the cytoplasmic Ca^{2+} concentration.

DAG acts as a second messenger by binding to protein kinase C to activate this important regulatory enzyme. Protein kinase C also requires Ca^{2+} for activation, so both second messengers of this pathway cooperate to increase the activity of this enzyme. Tumor promoters, such as active phorbol esters, are DAG analogues and act via protein kinase C.

The components of this second messenger system are diverse and complex. There are several isoenzyme forms of protein kinase C and of phosphoinositidase. Although one isoenzyme form of phospho-inositidase is activated via receptor-coupled G proteins, another is activated by binding to receptor tyrosine kinases and undergoing tyrosine phosphorylation. Additional kinases phosphorylate alternate positions on the inositol ring; PI 3-kinase is activated by certain tyrosine kinases to yield unique PI metabolites with functions distinct from Ca^{2+} mobilization. PtdIns, which is phosphorylated at the 4,5 position, functions in recognizing PH domains to localize and activate kinases and other proteins, and PtdIns 3 (P) binds to FYVE domains in proteins. PX domains also bind to phosphorylated PtdIns. PtdIns kinases thus create membrane docking sites for signal transduction complexes that assemble via proteins that contain PH, FYVE, and PX domains. This process also assembles protein complexes that direct trafficking through the membrane compartments of the cell. Sphingosine, a component of glycosphingolipid metabolism, inhibits protein kinase C, which provides dual regulation of this protein. Specific phosphatases remove the phosphate groups from the inositol ring to terminate its activity; lithium blocks the activity of one of these phosphatases to enhance accumulation of the biologically active inositol phosphates. Like other information pathways, this one is diffused to generate coordinated cellular responses and is buffered and ultimately turned off when the signal strength decreases. Deletion of the PtdIns 3 phosphatase gene *(PTEN),* which occurs frequently in cancer, removes an essential "off" switch, leaving growth and survival signals "on."

PROTEIN TYROSINE KINASES

A group of peptide hormone receptors contains intrinsic protein tyrosine kinase activity. Ligand binding to the extracellular domain results in an allosteric change that is transmitted across the single membrane-spanning segment to activate the cytoplasmic kinase domain (see Fig. 234–2). In a second structural motif, a transmembrane receptor is coupled to a distinct cytoplasmic tyrosine kinase subunit. The growth hormone receptor and JAK2 belong to this second class.

Within the cell, the majority of protein-bound phosphate is attached to serine and threonine residues, with only a small fraction being attached to tyrosine. Numerous kinases, however, covalently modify tyrosine residues in proteins as a central regulatory function in cell proliferation, developmental processes, and differentiated function. The extracellular ligand-binding domains of receptors of this class contain cysteine-rich regions that create the binding sites either as monomers (epidermal growth factor [EGF] receptor) or as dimers (insulin receptor) or contain immunoglobulin-like structures (platelet-derived growth factor [PDGF] and fibroblast growth factor [FGF] receptors). The cytoplasmic protein tyrosine kinase domains are highly homologous, containing ATP and substrate-binding sites, but different receptors recognize distinct substrates to give specific biologic responses. For example, insulin stimulates glucose uptake, whereas EGF stimulates cell proliferation. The tyrosine kinases contain variable domains on both sides of the tyrosine kinase core as well as inserts within the kinase domain, which provide regulatory sites that modulate ligand-activated tyrosine kinase activity.

Information received by a cell surface tyrosine kinase receptor is transmitted through a signal transduction pathway that begins with direct physical coupling of two proteins and proceeds through the GTP-binding protein ras (Fig. 234–4). In response to ligand binding, receptor tyrosine kinases either self-phosphorylate or phosphorylate a linker substrate. Proteins that contain a 100–amino acid domain homologous to a region in *src,* SH2, bind tightly to these sites of tyrosine phosphorylation. The growth factor receptor binding protein 2 (Grb2) is a molecular coupler containing an SH2 domain that plugs into a tyrosine phosphorylation site. Shc is another molecule coupler frequently used. Grb2 also contains two SH3 domains that act as a receptacle for proline-rich domains of the guanine nucleotide exchange protein SOS. These high-affinity protein-to-protein interactions bring SOS to the cell membrane where ras is present in its inactive GDP-bound form. Activated GTP-bound ras then couples to a serine/threonine protein kinase cascade involving first *raf*-1, then MEK and MAP (mitogen-activated protein) kinases. Information is thus relayed, expanded, and diffused to ultimately control gene expression and cell division. Operative mechanisms for this, as for other hormone-signaling pathways, include ligand or protein-protein interactions, activated GTP-bound G proteins, and protein phosphorylation. Receptor tyrosine kinases also couple to additional signaling

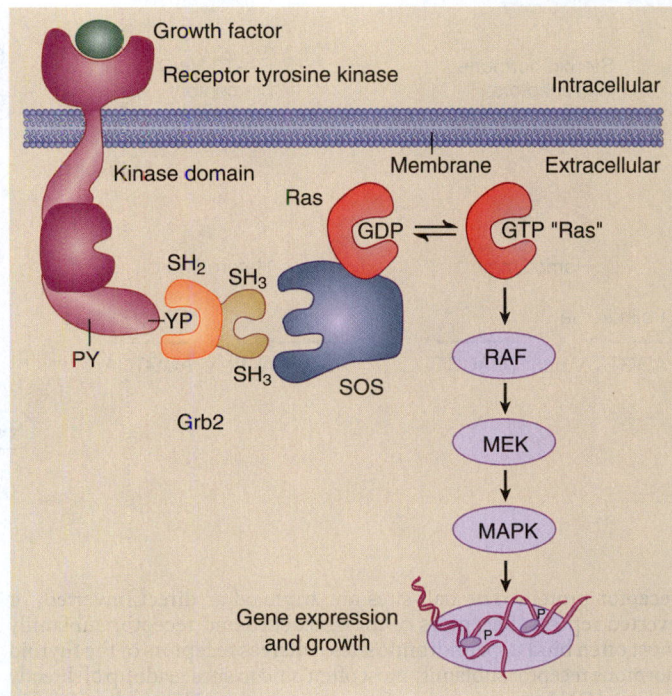

FIGURE 234–4 • Information transfer through a receptor tyrosine kinase pathway. Sites of receptor tyrosine self-phosphorylation, Y-P, are recognized by the SH2 domain of the linker Grb2, which brings the guanine nucleotide exchange factor SOS to the membrane where ras is located. Activated guanosine triphosphate (GTP)-bound ras initiates signaling by contacting raf, a serine threonine kinase, to initiate a cascade of kinase activations.

pathways via SH2 domains in other proteins and via tyrosine phosphorylation of these proteins including phospholipase C-γ, transcription control proteins termed *signal transducers and activators of transcription* (STAT), and PI 3-kinase.

Increased tyrosine kinase activity is reversed by four principal mechanisms: (1) ligand-induced endocytosis and downregulation of surface receptors, (2) tyrosine phosphatases, which specifically remove phosphate from tyrosine residues, (3) reversal of the kinase reaction to transfer the phosphate from tyrosine residues in protein to ADP, and (4) hydrolysis of ras-bound GTP to GDP.

Regulation and reversibility of ligand-activated tyrosine kinases are important. Mutations involving these proteins occur frequently in cells transformed from normal to cancerous patterns of growth. These mutations may bypass regulatory features so that the kinases are constitutively active. The kinases may be overexpressed, most frequently owing to gene amplification but also owing to enhanced transcription, or the ligand may be constitutively expressed to activate receptors continuously. Mutant *ras* proteins may be constitutively active owing to decreased GTPase activity or to a defect in a protein that stimulates the GTPase activity of *ras.* Any of these changes converts a normal regulatory protein into an oncoprotein, one capable of causing neoplastic transformation.

Steroid Hormones Act via Nuclear Receptors

THE SUPERFAMILY OF STEROID HORMONE RECEPTORS. All steroid hormone receptors share structural similarities indicative of a common ancestral molecule. The most conserved structural feature is the DNA-binding domain that contains zinc "fingers." The diagnostic spacing of cysteine residues creates a structure coordinated to a Zn^{2+} atom and a helix that binds to the major groove of DNA. Because the energy of protein-DNA interaction depends on the area of contact, most proteins bind DNA as complexes. Steroid hormone receptors of the glucocorticoid receptor subfamily bind to DNA as homodimers; receptors of the thyroid hormone receptor subfamily may bind as homodimers but more commonly bind as heterodimers with a common partner, the retinoid X receptor (RXR) (Fig. 234–5).

The DNA recognition element consists of two half-sites of six base pairs, each half binding one monomer surface of the dimeric

Endocrine Diseases

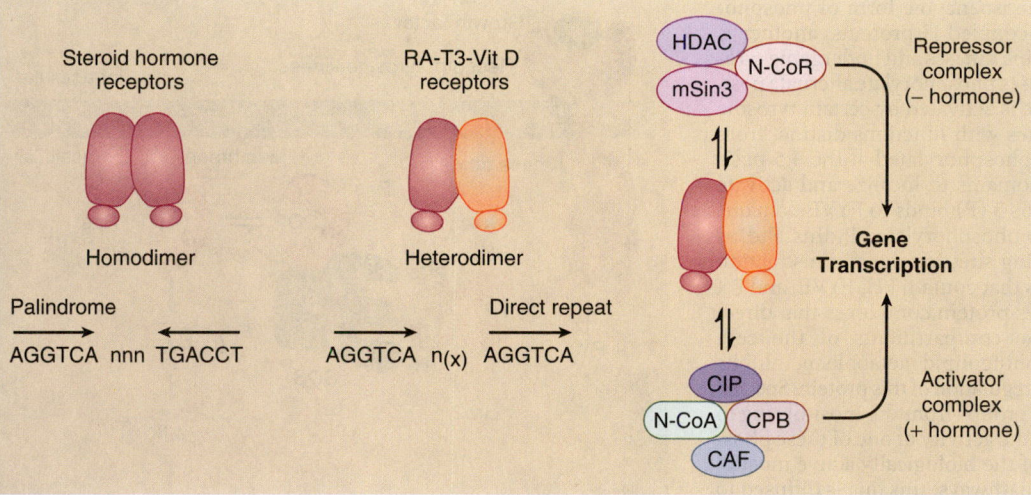

FIGURE 234–5 • How steroid hormone receptors work. *Left,* Glucocorticoid receptor family members bind as homodimers to palindromic DNA sites. Thyroid hormone receptor family members bind primarily as heterodimers with retinoid X receptor to direct repeat DNA sites separated by varying numbers of base pairs. *Right,* As a result of hormone binding, repressor complexes dissociate and activator complexes bind to nuclear receptors. Repressor complexes contain histone deacetylase (HDAC) and activator complexes contain histone acetylase (CAF). The coactivator and corepressor complexes contain multiple proteins; only a few are shown.

receptor protein. The half-sites are arranged as direct, inverted, or everted repeats. Receptors of the glucocorticoid receptor subfamily most often bind to palindromic sites, whereas receptors of the thyroid hormone receptor subfamily most often bind to sites made up of directly repeated DNA sequences. Small variations in the DNA-binding domain and in the DNA recognition element provide specificity for hormone action. One important determinant for receptor binding and activity is the spacing between the two half-sites for dimeric receptor binding. The spacing rules for DNA recognition elements that are arranged as direct repeats (DR) indicate that a spacing of 1 (DR + 1) directs RXR homodimer binding and 9-*cis*-retinoic acid responses, DR + 3 directs vitamin D receptor·RXR binding and vitamin D responses, DR + 4 directs thyroid hormone receptor·RXR binding and thyroid hormone responses, and DR + 5 directs retinoic acid receptor·RXR binding and all-*trans*-retinoic acid responses. RXR binds to the upstream half and the hormone-specific receptor binds to the downstream half of these DNA response elements to mediate hormone-dependent changes in transcription. Spacing between half-sites is crucial for binding homodimeric receptors of the glucocorticoid receptor class, but the sequence of the half-site provides an essential discriminant. Specificity is quantitative, not absolute. For example, progesterone receptors bind to glucocorticoid response elements, and retinoic acid receptors bind to thyroid hormone receptor DNA response elements. Specificity is sufficient for generating hormone-specific responses but may permit overlapping functions as in ligand-activated progesterone receptor induction of glucocorticoid-regulated genes.

Hormone binding activates the biologic function of the receptor. Cortisol receptors exist in inactive complexes with other proteins; cortisol binding induces an allosteric change that facilitates dissociation, allowing the ligand-bound receptor to bind to DNA. Thyroid hormone and retinoic acid receptors exist bound to DNA rather than complexed to protein; hormone binding results in an allosteric change that activates the receptor, so it interacts with other components of the transcription machinery. Binding of triiodothyronine (T_3) to the thyroid hormone receptor results in dissociation of a repressor complex that binds to the empty receptor and binding of an activator complex to the liganded receptor. The thyroid hormone receptor and activator interact with proteins such as the CREB binding protein (CBP) that integrate information from multiple transcription factors, including CREB, STAT, and the thyroid hormone receptor family.

The steroid hormone receptor family is a large one that includes subfamilies of receptors: at least six for retinoic acid, two for thyroid hormone, several for 1,25(OH)$_2$ vitamin D and for fatty acids or metabolites causing perixosome proliferation, and a group of "orphans" whose ligands remain to be identified. As ligands are identified, many orphan receptors are being adopted. Among these are the receptors that heterodimerize with RXR and regulate cholesterol, bile acid, and xenobiotic metabolism. Metabolism of cholesterol to bile acids in the liver, the major route for cholesterol catabolism, is stimulated by oxysteroids acting through LXR receptors (Fig. 234–6). LXRα stimulates transcription of the cytochrome P-450 *CYP7A* gene that catalyzes formation of bile acids. The bile acid receptor FXR, in turn, blocks this activation to provide a feedback loop between cholesterol catabolism

and bile acid formation. This receptor also regulates the transport proteins that facilitate bile acid uptake and egress in gut and liver.

Two receptors that regulate detoxification and elimination of toxic endogenous substances and xenobiotics are the constitutive androstane receptor (CAR), which mediates responses to phenobarbital-like inducers by enhancing transcription of the *CYP2B* gene, and SXR/PXR, which senses xenobiotics and induces *CYP3A* gene expression, metabolizing more than 50% of prescribed drugs and toxic lithocholic bile salts (see Fig. 234–6). SXR/PXR also induces expression of ABC transporters to export toxic compounds from cells. The steroid receptor family of proteins thus regulates many aspects of metabolism beyond those regulated by products of classic endocrine organs.

REGULATION OF GENE TRANSCRIPTION. Hormone-activated receptor proteins bound to their DNA response element targets act as *cis*-active enhancers. They act from various positions relative to the start of transcription and in various combinations with other regulatory proteins to control the rate of initiation of gene transcription. Gene promoters lie upstream of the site where eukaryotic RNA polymerase II initiates transcription of messenger RNA. The best characterized promoter contains a TATA box that binds a protein, transcription factor II-D (TF II-D), which directs accurate transcription by RNA polymerase II about 30 base pairs downstream. Seven proteins (TATA-associated factors [TAFs]) associate with TF II-D in a specific complex that provides a molecular surface for interaction with the transcription-regulatory proteins, which are bound elsewhere to DNA. Other promoter motifs include a basal initiator and GC-rich regions in which multiple transcription start sites exist. Gene expression is induced by increasing the rate of transcription. Mechanisms involved in enhancing rates of initiation of transcription include summing of multiple weak protein·protein interactions and acetylating histones to change their interaction with DNA at the transcription start site.

Hormone-activated receptors can also repress transcription. Negative feedback loops operate through this process. Activated cortisol receptors repress transcription of the gene encoding the adrenocorticotropic hormone (ACTH) precursor; activated thyroid hormone receptors inhibit transcription of both α- and β-TSH subunit genes. The principle of ligand-activated receptors binding to specific DNA target sequences in the regulated gene is the same as that required for inductive responses. The receptor may inhibit transcription by multiple mechanisms, including deacetylating histones, to increase their interaction with DNA.

Many other proteins regulate initiation of transcription, both as inducers and as inhibitors. These bind to DNA through specific sequences, as do steroid receptors, or they may interact with proteins that do. These proteins may be modified in response to hormonal signals initiated at the cell surface. Such alterations account for the changes in gene transcription due to hormones acting through surface receptors. Two general and cooperative mechanisms exist: phosphorylation and translocation of transcription factors from cytoplasm to nucleus. Genes regulated by cyclic AMP contain DNA sequences that specify binding of a specific nuclear transcription regulator (CREB). CREB, which undergoes changes in activity on phosphorylation, is a required final mediator of gene induction by

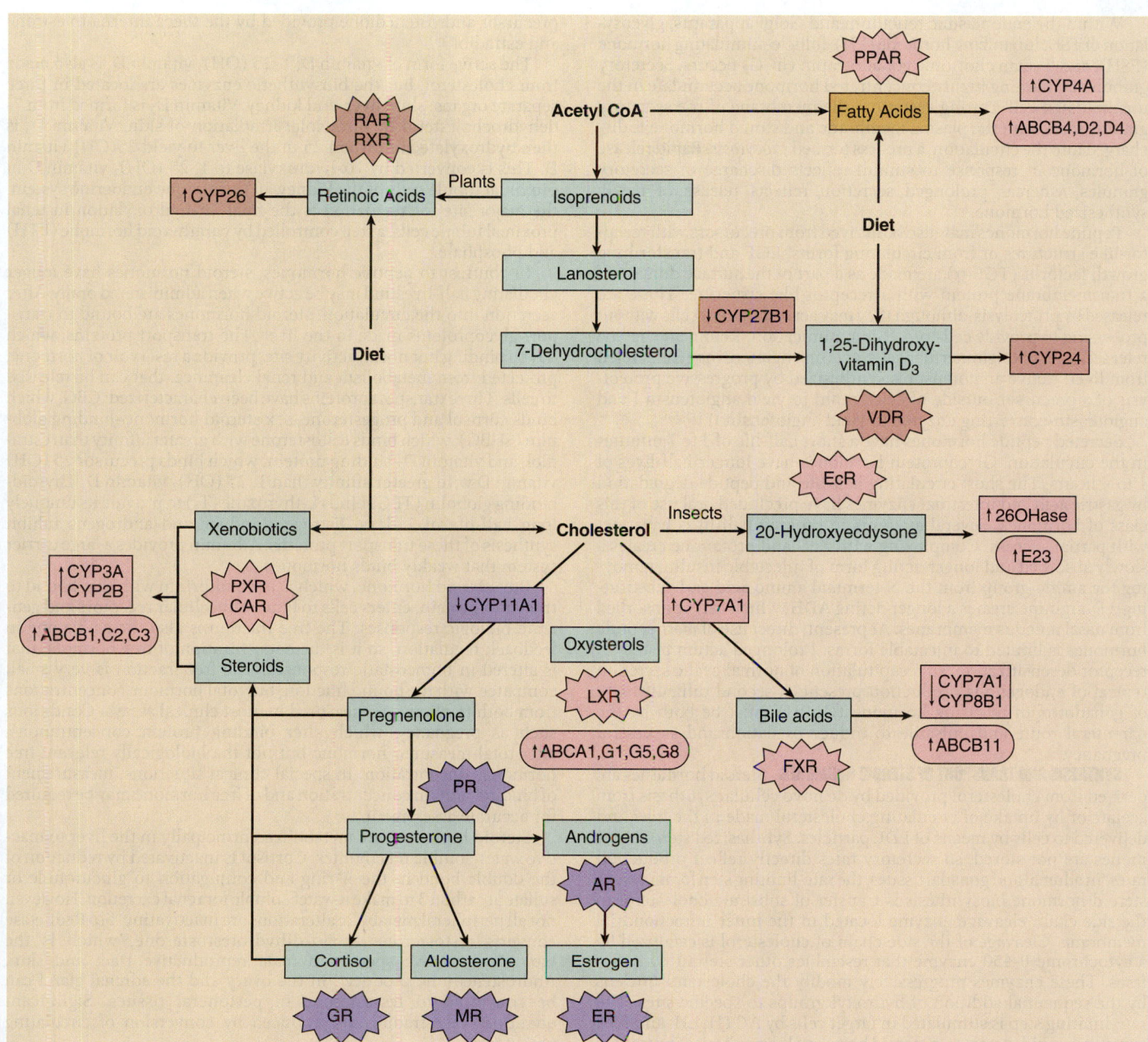

FIGURE 234–6 • Steroid receptor family proteins regulate multiple metabolic processes. *CYP* genes are cytochrome P-450 proteins involved in hepatic metabolism and steroid endocrine gland hormone biosynthesis. PPARs, peroxisome proliferator activated receptors, which are activated by polyunsaturated fatty acids, prostaglandins, eicosanoids, and thiazolidinediones; LXRs, oxysterol (lipid) receptors which are activated by oxidized derivatives of cholesterol; FXR, farnesoid X receptor, which is activated by bile acids; PXR, pregnane X receptor, the rodent orthologue of human SXR, the steroid xenobiotic receptor that binds a variety of xenobiologic ligands; CAR, constitutive androstane receptor, which responds to phenobarbital-like inducers. Classic steroid receptors for androgens (AR), estrogens (ER), glucocorticoids (GR), mineralocorticoids (MR), progesterone (PR), vitamin D (VDR), and retinoic acid (RAR, RXR) are indicated. (Modified from Chawla AJ, Repa J, Evans RM, Mangelsdorf D: Nuclear receptors and lipid physiology: Opening the X-files. Science 2001;294:1866–1870, with permission.)

peptide hormones that act at the cell surface to activate adenylate cyclase and cyclic AMP–dependent protein kinase. STAT and related proteins are phosphorylated on tyrosine residues and, when phosphorylated, enter the nucleus to activate transcription of specific genes. This chain of effects alters transcription of messenger RNAs and cell protein concentrations to dictate changes in cell function and organ physiology.

BIOSYNTHESIS OF HORMONES AND RECEPTORS

SYNTHESIS AND DELIVERY OF PEPTIDE HORMONES. Peptide hormones are small secretory proteins; their biosynthesis and secretion occur via the same processes as other nonhormonal secretory proteins. In general, peptide hormones are synthesized as part of larger precursor proteins that contain additional information. The precursor protein is cleaved, covalently modified, and folded into the form for ultimate secretion.

The precursor structure may have a variety of functions. Precursors for antidiuretic hormone (ADH) and oxytocin contain specific neurophysins that serve as carriers of the peptides from the site of synthesis in the hypothalamus to storage granules in axon terminals in the posterior pituitary. The ACTH precursor, pro-opiomelanocortin, contains information for several peptides that may be coordinately involved in stress responses. Structures in the precursor protein may serve to fold the peptide correctly. The connecting peptide in the insulin precursor between the β and the α subunits facilitates folding for formation of mature insulin with correctly formed disulfide bonds between and within the two chains. The connecting peptide is then excised and removed from mature α-β insulin.

Within the endoplasmic reticulum and Golgi apparatus, glycosylation of TSH, luteinizing hormone (LH), follicle-stimulating hormone (FSH), and human chorionic gonadotropin (hCG) occurs. Secretory granules containing highly concentrated hormone accumulate in the unstimulated cell. During secretion, the membrane of the secretory granule fuses with the plasma membrane and stored hormone is discharged into the circulation, a process termed *exocytosis*. Rapid release of hormone in response to stimuli reflects discharge of secretory granules, whereas prolonged secretion reflects release of newly synthesized hormone.

Peptide hormones may also be derived from precursors with receptor-like structures or from circulating forms. EGF and transforming growth factor-α (TGF-α) are made as a part of the surface domain of a transmembrane protein with a receptor-like structure. These are released by proteolysis, although they may act on adjacent cells without processing to provide cell-to-cell communication. Renin, an enzyme released from juxtaglomerular cells, acts on angiotensinogen secreted from liver. Active angiotensin is synthesized by progressive proteolysis of a precursor outside of cells: renin to yield angiotensin I and angiotensin-converting enzyme to yield angiotensin II.

Secreted peptide hormones have a short half-life of 3 to 7 minutes in the circulation. Glycoprotein hormones have longer half-lives of 1 to 4 hours. The short circulating half-life and peptide degradation by gastric acid and intestinal enzymes have precluded oral use of this class of hormones. Several attempts to prolong half-lives have met with partial success: Complexing with Zn^{2+} and protamine creates a slowly absorbed and longer-acting form of injectable insulin; removing the amino group from the N terminal amino acid and substituting a D-arginine creates a longer-acting ADH, which can be absorbed from nasal mucous membranes. At present, direct use of *most* peptide hormones is limited to injectable forms. Prolonged action results in receptor desensitization, so recapitulation of normal cyclic secretion typical of endogenous production presents a second difficulty. Use of gonadotropin releasing hormone (GnRH) must be both by the parenteral route and pulsatile to induce ovulation and successful pregnancy.

SYNTHESIS AND TRANSPORT OF STEROID HORMONES. Steroid hormones are derived from cholesterol provided by de novo cellular synthesis from acetate or by uptake of circulating cholesterol made in the liver and delivered to cells by means of LDL particles. Synthesized steroid hormones are not stored, so secretory rates directly reflect production rates. In adrenal and gonadal tissues, the rate-limiting step for increased steroid hormone biosynthesis is transfer of substrate cholesterol to the side chain cleavage enzyme located in the inner mitochondrial membrane. Cleavage of the side chain of cholesterol is catalyzed by a cytochrome P-450 enzyme that resembles other steroid hydroxylases. These enzymes progressively modify the cholesterol nucleus by the sequential addition of hydroxyl groups to specific sites. The rate-limiting step is stimulated in target cells by ACTH, LH, and FSH to result in rapid increases in steroid hormone biosynthesis. The trophic stimulatory hormones also maintain the structure of the target glands and induce each of the enzymes involved in hormone biosynthesis. With hypophysectomy or feedback inhibition of pituitary hormone production, the entire steroid biosynthetic pathway decreases and the adrenal, ovary, and testis atrophy. Addition of trophic hormones induces enzymes and regrowth of target glands. Induction of biosynthetic enzymes appears directly mediated through second messenger pathways, primarily cyclic AMP, but growth requires coordinate provision of growth factors because cyclic AMP, in general, inhibits growth.

The pattern of biosynthetic enzymes expressed during cell differentiation determines which steroid hormone is produced and is the basis of the differentiated function of the adrenal and gonads. The fascicularis zone of the adrenal cortex expresses cytochrome P-450 enzymes that catalyze hydroxylations at carbons 21, 17, and 11. They also express 3β-hydroxysteroid dehydrogenase, $\Delta^{4,5}$ isomerase, which forms cortisol. The zona glomerulosa of the adrenal cortex makes aldosterone through a similar series of reactions, but the pathway lacks 17α-hydroxylase and contains an activity that acts at carbon 18. The testis lacks 21- and 11β-hydroxylases, so reactants flow to testosterone. Ovarian synthesis of estradiol requires cooperation between adjacent theca interna and granulosa cells. Granulosa cells express aromatase, the enzyme that catalyzes placement of three double bonds in the A ring of estrogens but cannot provide precursor androstenedione, which is synthesized in the theca interna cell located adjacent to the granulosa cell. Granulosa cells efficiently convert precursor androstenedione provided by the theca interna to estrone and estradiol.

The active form of vitamin D, 1, 25 (OH)$_2$ vitamin D, is also made from cholesterol, but the biosynthetic enzymes are located in three separate organs: skin, liver, and kidney. Vitamin D$_3$ is formed from 7-dehydrocholesterol by ultraviolet irradiation of skin. Vitamin D$_3$ is then hydroxylated at carbon 25 in the liver to yield 25(OH) vitamin D. This is converted by 1α-hydroxylase to 1, 25 (OH)$_2$ vitamin D in proximal tubule cells of the kidney. In this unique endocrine system, the major site for regulation is the final 1α-hydroxylation in renal proximal tubule cells, a step controlled by parathyroid hormone (PTH) and phosphate.

In contrast to peptide hormones, steroid hormones have longer circulating half-lives and may be active when administered orally. After secretion into the circulation, steroid hormones are bound to transport glycoproteins made in the liver. The transport proteins, which have a binding but not an activity site, provide a reservoir of hormone, protected from metabolism and renal clearance, that can be released to cells. Three transport proteins have been characterized: CBG, which binds cortisol and progesterone, sex steroid hormone–binding globulin (SHBG), which binds testosterone with greater affinity than estradiol, and vitamin D–binding protein, which binds precursor 25 (OH) vitamin D with greater affinity than 1, 25 (OH)$_2$ vitamin D. Thyroid-binding globulin (TBG) binds L-thyroxine (T$_4$) to provide its uniquely long half-life of 7 days. Estrogens induce and androgens inhibit synthesis of these transport proteins. Albumin provides a large carrier system that weakly binds hormones.

Free steroid hormone, which is in equilibrium with that bound to transport protein, enters cells to bind intracellular receptors and generate biologic responses. The free fraction is also the active one in feedback regulation, so it is the concentration of free hormone that is altered in homeostatic responses. The free fraction is very small compared with the bound fraction, but total hormone concentrations from both fractions are measured in most clinical assays. Conditions such as pregnancy, which alter binding protein concentrations, alter total measured hormone but not the biologically relevant free hormone concentration. In special clinical situations, measurement of binding protein concentration and of free hormone may be required for accurate assessment.

Steroid hormones are metabolized principally in the liver to inactive water-soluble metabolites. Cortisol is inactivated by reduction of the double bond in the A ring and conjugation to glucuronide or sulfate at carbon 3 to make it water soluble for renal excretion. However, not all peripheral metabolic alterations are inactivating. 5α-Reductase converts testosterone to 5α-dihydrotestosterone, which is the biologically active species in male reproductive tract and skin. Androstenedione produced in the ovary and the adrenal gland can be converted to testosterone in peripheral tissues. Significant quantities of estradiol are produced by conversion of circulating precursors.

Like their hormonal ligands, receptor synthesis is highly regulated to control cellular responses and sensitivity to hormones. Receptor synthesis is increased in response to environmental or developmental need or is repressed in negative feedback loops and during stages of development. Receptor concentration is as important as hormone concentration in determining cell responses. Regulation of receptor synthesis is therefore central to providing coordinated and appropriate endocrine responses.

INTEGRATION OF ENDOCRINE RESPONSES

FEEDBACK LOOPS. Multiple hormones cooperate to coordinate development, reproduction, and homeostasis. When a hormone has elicited an appropriate response, the signal must be terminated. In addition to the buffering that occurs in target cells, feedback control is the principal mechanism through which this occurs (Fig. 234–7). Feedback loops are especially important for communication between organs that are spatially separated. The hormonal products of peripheral endocrine glands such as thyroid, adrenal cortex, ovary, and testis exert negative feedback control over the synthesis and secretion of the stimulatory pituitary hormone. Feedback, which occurs at the level of the pituitary cell and in the hypothalamus, operates by control of several essential steps. The neurohormone thyrotropin-releasing hormone (TRH) stimulates thyrotropes of the anterior pituitary to synthesize and secrete TSH, which, in turn, increases synthesis

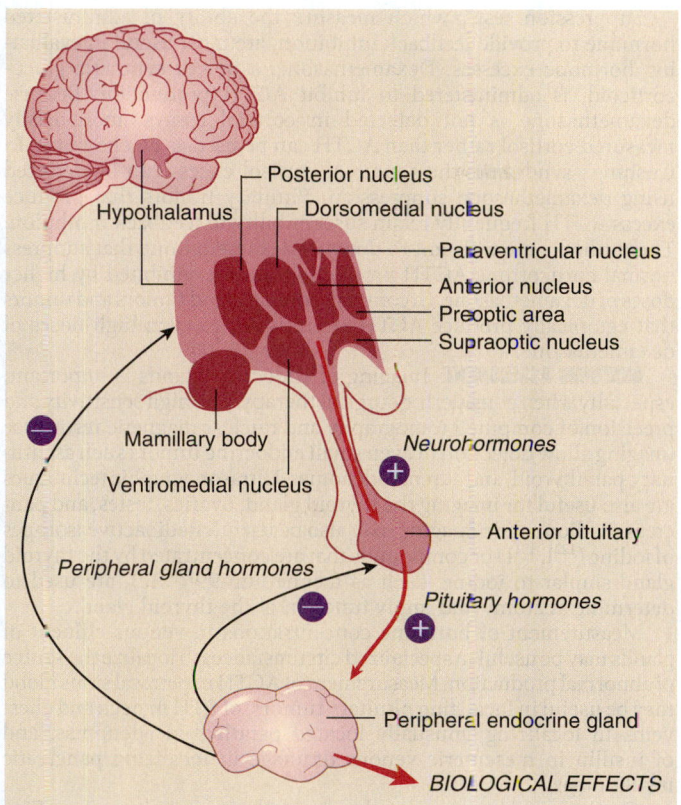

FIGURE 234–7 • Forward regulation and negative feedback.

and secretion of thyroid hormone. Increased production of thyroid hormone induces appropriate metabolic responses in target organs; it also inhibits production of TSH to return the system to baseline. The prohormone T_4 is converted in the pituitary thyrotrope to active T_3, and T_3 binds to nuclear T_3 receptors to inhibit transcription of both α- and β-TSH subunit genes. T_3-bound receptors also decrease synthesis of TRH receptors, rendering cells less responsive to stimulatory TRH. In addition, T_3 inhibits hypothalamic production of TRH. Conversely, when thyroid hormone concentrations are low, feedback inhibition is relieved and TRH stimulates increased production of TSH, which increases production of T_4 and thus reestablishes homeostasis. Feedback principles provide an exquisitely sensitive system for making appropriate changes and then returning to the homeostatic set point.

Feedback operates not only through steroid and thyroid hormones but also through peptides and ions. Pituitary FSH production is feedback regulated by the ovarian steroid hormone estrogen and by the ovarian peptide hormone inhibin. PTH regulates serum Ca^{2+} concentrations; with hypocalcemia, PTH increases and reestablishes normocalcemia. The increase in serum $[Ca^{2+}]$ feedback inhibits PTH synthesis and secretion to reestablish serum PTH concentrations appropriate to normocalcemia. With mutations in the $[Ca^{2+}]$ receptor on parathyroid cell membranes, feedback sensing is impaired and excessive PTH is made.

RECRUITMENT OF COORDINATE RESPONSES. Physiologic responses result from many different cell types and organs acting in concert. The necessary coordination is provided both by a hormone acting at multiple sites and by each hormone eliciting multiple responses, which sum to give the overall effect. Integrated responses require that one hormone regulate the synthesis or action of another; the nervous system is integrated into the overall response. Paradigms of such coordinated responses include stress, fasting, and reproduction.

A major stress, such as trauma with pain and hypovolemia, initiates a central nervous system response that includes synthesis and secretion of corticotropin-releasing hormone (CRH) and ADH. CRH is the major stimulus to increase pituitary secretion of ACTH, which increases adrenal cortisol production. Cortisol maintains not only blood glucose but also vascular responsiveness to epinephrine and norepinephrine. It limits excessive inflammatory responses to prevent further volume loss and tissue damage. CRH acts, in the central nervous

system, to stimulate the peripheral sympathetic nervous system. Increased sympathetic nervous system activity mediates adaptive cardiovascular responses, including increased blood pressure and pulse rate. It also induces appropriate behavioral responses. ADH increases permeability of the collecting duct of the distal nephron to conserve water and intravascular volume. It facilitates CRH-stimulated ACTH secretion. With hypovolemia, the renin-angiotensin-aldosterone system is also activated to enhance vasoconstriction and to conserve sodium and intravascular volume. These responses of the hypothalamus, pituitary, and adrenal cortex together facilitate survival from stresses.

With fasting, blood glucose concentrations are maintained for 12 to 24 hours by glucagon- and epinephrine-mediated release of glucose from glycogen stores. With more prolonged fasting, cortisol-stimulated gluconeogenesis is the major mechanism that sustains blood glucose. Insulin secretion is suppressed. Metabolic demands are decreased by inhibition of 5'-deiodinase to decrease conversion of T_4 to active T_3 in peripheral tissues. Growth-promoting hormones, such as insulin-like growth factor I, are also suppressed under conditions of substrate lack. With starvation, gonadotropin secretion decreases and reproductive capacity is diminished.

Female reproductive cycles result from coordinated signaling by hypothalamic, pituitary, and ovarian hormones. Pulsatile secretion of GnRH stimulates pituitary production of LH and FSH. During the follicular phase of the menstrual cycle these peptide hormones regulate ovarian secretion of estrogen and direct maturation of follicles, one of which increases 1000-fold in diameter and becomes dominant for ovulation. FSH induces LH receptors in ovarian granulosa cells, and both LH and FSH induce aromatase as part of the mechanism that enhances estrogen production. LH and FSH increase during the follicular phase and, with follicle development, estrogen secretion increases. Positive feedback effects of estrogen result in the midcycle surge of LH and FSH, which induces ovulation. The remaining granulosa and theca cells reorganize to form the corpus luteum, which produces progesterone as well as estrogen. Concentrations of these hormones negatively inhibit FSH and LH production and induce additional uterine changes necessary for implantation. Ovarian inhibin also inhibits FSH production. If fertilization and implantation occur, the corpus luteum is regulated by hCG until placental steroidogenesis is established. If fertilization does not occur, negative feedback of estrogen and progesterone inhibits LH and FSH, and the luteal phase of the menstrual cycle ends after about 10 days when the corpus luteum, now deprived of trophic stimulation, decreases estrogen and progesterone production. Menstruation occurs and, in the absence of negative feedback, FSH and LH again increase to initiate a subsequent reproductive cycle.

CYCLES AND RHYTHMS. Nervous system rhythms are evident within feedback loops and coordinate hormonal responses. Several pituitary hormones are secreted with a frequency of 15 to 60 minutes, owing to pulsatile secretion of hypothalamic hormones. Longer rhythms are superimposed on these pulses. Pulsatile secretion of peptide hormones maximizes target cell responses by preventing excessive receptor downregulation. ACTH and, consequently, cortisol exhibit a diurnal rhythm, with early morning secretion exceeding evening secretion at least twofold. Growth hormone is entrained to deep sleep, with maximal daily production occurring coincident with electroencephalographically defined slow-wave sleep. Cycles also occur at different stages of development. At puberty, nocturnal increases in gonadotropins occur, a rhythm much less pronounced in adult life. Measured hormone levels must be interpreted relative to these rhythms and cycles, as well as to stages of the menstrual cycle when assaying reproductive hormones.

ASSESSMENT OF ENDOCRINE FUNCTION

QUANTITATION OF CIRCULATING HORMONES AND METABOLIC PRODUCTS. Endocrine function is assessed by accurately measuring the concentration of hormones present in blood. Even though circulating concentrations are low (nanomolar to micromolar for steroid hormones and thyroxine and picomolar to nanomolar for peptide hormones), precise assays based on competitive protein binding are widely available. Improved sensitivity and accuracy of hormone measurements reduce the need to perform more complex stimulation and suppression tests. Even with sensitive and precise assays of hormone concentration, clinical assessment is essential. Measured values must be interpreted in relation to clinical signs and symptoms. It is also extremely helpful to measure both arms of a feedback loop. Most hormone concentrations exhibit a gaussian distribution of normal values, so an individual measurement at either end of the normal range may be normal or abnormal for that individual. Coincident measurement of TSH and T_4, LH and testosterone, ACTH and cortisol, and PTH and Ca^{2+} gives greater information than either measurement alone. A T_4 value at the lower end of the normal range with an elevated TSH concentration indicates thyroid gland failure, whereas the same T_4 value with a normal TSH value likely indicates a euthyroid state. An elevated cortisol with suppressed ACTH indicates autonomous production of cortisol by an adrenal tumor. Cycles and rhythms of hormone secretion must also be considered. Evening cortisol concentrations are half or less of peak morning values. Coincident measurement of ACTH clarifies whether a low cortisol represents diurnal rhythm or adrenal insufficiency; an elevated ACTH level when the cortisol level is low suggests adrenal insufficiency. Measurement of gonadotropins, estradiol, and progesterone must be related to normal values for follicular and luteal phases of the menstrual cycle.

Steroid and thyroid hormones are bound to carrier proteins. In pregnancy, in which estrogen increases hepatic production of carrier proteins, total cortisol and T_4 values are elevated but ACTH and TSH values are normal. On occasion, it is necessary to measure the free, active hormone concentration. Because the free fraction is very small relative to the total amount, careful separation of bound from free fractions without the use of organic solvents is necessary, and very sensitive detection systems are required. Assays for free T_4 and for ionized Ca^{2+} are available for specialized clinical circumstances. One can assess the amount of binding globulin directly or can indirectly measure unoccupied binding sites (T_3 resin uptake test).

Measurement of urinary excretion of some hormones provides an integrated value for daily production rates. Measurement of urinary free cortisol is particularly useful because cortisol-binding globulin, which binds one cortisol molecule per molecule of protein, is approximately saturated at the peak morning cortisol concentration. Free unbound cortisol that exceeds binding capacity is filtered at the glomerulus, so an elevated 24-hour urine free cortisol determination provides an accurate assessment in cortisol excess syndromes.

Measurement of metabolic effects is an essential component of endocrine evaluation. Insulin function is assessed by measuring plasma and urine glucose concentrations, PTH by measuring serum Ca^{2+}, aldosterone by measuring serum K^+, and ADH by measuring serum and urine osmolalities.

STIMULATION AND SUPPRESSION TESTS. Measurement of both arms of a feedback loop provides sufficient laboratory information in most endocrine deficiency or excess states. Additional diagnostic information can be gained, however, by perturbing the feedback system through administration of hormones. For stimulation tests, a hormone is administered and the ability of the target gland to respond is assessed by measuring its product. This provides an estimate of the ability of the target gland to synthesize hormone, of its trophic maintenance, and of its exposure to feedback inhibition. Baseline measurements are made before hormone administration and at the established normal time of peak target gland response. Ranges of normal responses have been established for comparison. Examples include TRH stimulation tests, in which levels of pituitary-produced TSH are measured. In hypopituitarism, serum TSH fails to increase in response to a standard intravenous injection of TRH. In primary hypothyroidism, in which feedback inhibition by thyroid hormone is small, TSH increases excessively, whereas in hyperthyroidism, excessive feedback inhibition results in minimal or no increases in TSH. For ACTH stimulation tests, $ACTH_{1-24}$ is administered as an intravenous injection to assess the ability of the adrenal cortex to produce cortisol. A low baseline cortisol level that fails to increase indicates adrenal insufficiency. Interpretation requires integration of clinical information because failure to respond to ACTH may also occur when the adrenal cortex has been suppressed, owing to treatment with synthetic glucocorticoids. A variation of stimulation tests involves interruption of the feedback loop by metabolic inhibitors of hormone biosynthesis. Metyrapone, an inhibitor of 11β-hydroxylase, decreases serum cortisol, relieving feedback suppression of ACTH production. The resulting increase in ACTH can be measured directly; or ACTH-stimulated 11-deoxycortisol, the precursor of cortisol, can be measured as an indicator of increased ACTH. The metyrapone test provides an assessment of pituitary corticotrope function and reserve. Stimulation tests are most useful in suspected endocrine deficiency states.

Suppression tests, which measure the ability of administered hormone to provide feedback inhibition, are most useful in evaluating hormone excesses. Dexamethasone, a potent synthetic glucocorticoid, is administered to inhibit ACTH production. Because dexamethasone is not detected in cortisol assays, more easily measured cortisol rather than ACTH can be used as an end point. In Cushing's syndrome, the source of cortisol excess can be deduced using dexamethasone suppression. Pituitary tumors that produce excess ACTH frequently retain susceptibility to feedback inhibition. These tumors are resistant to doses of dexamethasone that suppress normal corticotrope ACTH production but are inhibited by higher doses of dexamethasone. In contrast, adrenal gland tumors and tumors that ectopically produce ACTH are resistant to even high doses of dexamethasone.

ANATOMIC ASSESSMENT. Imaging of endocrine glands is important, especially when considering surgical therapy. The high sensitivity and precision of computed tomography and nuclear magnetic resonance imaging allow detection of even small endocrine tumors such as pituitary, parathyroid, and adrenal adenomas. Ultrasonographic techniques are also useful for imaging the thyroid gland, ovaries, testes, and pancreas. Radionuclide imaging may also be useful. Radioactive isotopes of iodine (^{123}I, ^{131}I) or compounds that are concentrated by the thyroid gland similar to iodine, such as technetium-99 (^{99}Tc), are used to determine anatomy and imply function of the thyroid gland.

Measurement of hormone concentrations in venous effluent of glands may be useful in specialized circumstances to localize the source of abnormal production. Measurement of ACTH in petrosal sinus blood may be useful in localizing pituitary tumors, of PTH in neck and chest veins in localizing unusually located parathyroid adenomas, and of insulin in mesenteric venous drainage in localizing pancreatic insulinomas.

Cytologic and immunocytochemical techniques are important. Fine needle aspiration of thyroid nodules with cytologic examinations analogous to those used in Papanicolaou smears has become the procedure of choice to distinguish benign and malignant thyroid nodules. Staining of surgical tissues with antihormone antibodies provides proof of hormone production and a guide to future therapy.

Receptors are not routinely measured but can be quantitated using immunologic techniques. Recombinant DNA technologies can be used to define inherited defects in receptors. When oncogenes are identified in specific endocrine neoplasms, these can be measured and mutations identified using DNA hybridization techniques. Autoimmune endocrine diseases can be documented by quantitating antibodies directed against specific organs (thyroid-stimulating immunoglobulin, anti-islet cell antibodies, antiadrenal antibodies).

ABERRATIONS IN DISEASE

DEFICIENCY STATES. The most prevalent endocrine disorders result from hormone deficiencies. A variety of disease states impair or destroy endocrine glands: defects in organ development, genetic defects in biosynthetic enzymes, immune-mediated destruction, neoplasia, infections, hemorrhage, nutritional deficits, and vascular insufficiency. Endocrine gland failure may be acute, with rapid development of symptoms, or chronic, with slower development of symptoms but more pronounced physical changes. Defects in a gland such as the thyroid may result in a multisystem disorder resulting from failure to produce a single hormone, whereas defects in the hypothalamus or pituitary may result in a multisystem disorder, including thyroid deficiency, resulting from failure to produce many hormones. Multiple endocrine gland deficiencies may also result from autoimmune-mediated mechanisms in the polyglandular autoimmune deficiency syndromes. Because hormones participate in coordinated responses, secondary changes in other endocrine responses often result from deficiency of a single hormone.

Deficiency states also result from defects in hormone receptors and in signaling mechanisms. Defects may be inherited or acquired. Genetic abnormalities in androgen receptors result in unresponsiveness to androgens and an XY male with a female phenotype; defects in vitamin D receptors result in vitamin D–resistant rickets; defects in thyroid hormone receptors result in the resistance to thyroid hormone of Refetoff's syndrome; defects in growth hormone receptors result in ateliotic dwarfism of Laron's syndrome. Acquired receptor defects most often result from immunologic mechanisms wherein antibodies bind to receptors, blocking ligand access.

Postreceptor defects may occur. A defect in $G\alpha_s$ results in pseudo-hypoparathyroidism, in which unresponsiveness to PTH occurs. Such patients fail to respond normally to other hormones whose receptors couple to adenylate cyclase (TSH, glucagon, LH). Type II diabetes mellitus, which is inherited, is characterized by insulin resistance. The molecular defect has not yet been characterized, but understanding this pathophysiology underlies therapeutic approaches directed at reducing resistance to and augmenting secretion of insulin. Because receptor and postreceptor defects are characterized by hormone resistance, feedback does not occur; and producer glands enlarge and circulating hormone concentrations are high despite clinical evidence for deficiency.

EXCESS STATES. Excessive production of hormone and clinical evidence of such excess implies failure of normal feedback mechanisms. This occurs most commonly with neoplasia and with autoimmunity, in which antireceptor antibodies act as hormone agonists. Tumors of endocrine glands characteristically produce excessive amounts of the hormone made by the cell of origin but are no longer subject to normal feedback controls. Some tumors, such as pituitary adenomas that produce ACTH, retain feedback but require higher concentrations of cortisol to suppress ACTH. Prolactinomas retain dopamine suppression, and both their function and growth can be inhibited by dopamine agonists. Tumors arising in peripheral endocrine glands that are under pituitary trophic hormone regulation are autonomous because they are not normally subject to negative feedback. More undifferentiated tumors may also be insensitive to feedback regulation.

Hormones may be produced in excess by tumors arising from cells that do not normally produce the hormone. Ectopic production of peptide hormones is common in a variety of neoplasms, and symptoms due to the hormone excess may contribute significantly to morbidity. Because steroid hormones are made via a multienzyme pathway, excesses of these hormones occur only with tumors arising in the producer gland or with excessive production of the trophic peptide hormone. Cortisol excess may result from adrenocortical tumors or from excessive stimulation by ACTH produced by pituitary or ectopic neoplasms.

The most prevalent disease resulting from agonistic antibodies is Graves' disease, in which antibodies are produced that activate the TSH receptor. Because many hormones are available as therapeutic agents, some patients take excessive amounts and present with an endocrine excess syndrome.

GENETIC DETERMINANTS OF DISEASE. Many endocrine diseases result from genetic mutations. Genetic defects in biosynthetic enzymes may result in deficiency states: Hypothyroidism may result from thyroid peroxidase or deiodinase enzyme defects; adrenal insufficiency may result from 21-hydroxylase deficiency or a defect in other steroid biosynthetic enzymes; a form of male hypogonadism may result from 5α-reductase deficiency. Receptor defects are thought to be uncommon, but methods to define these have only recently become available. Type II diabetes, the most common endocrine abnormality, is inherited, but its molecular basis is not yet known. Autoimmune endocrine disease also has a genetic basis involving an inherited defect in immune surveillance. Multiple endocrine neoplasia syndromes are due to activating mutations in the *ret* tyrosine kinase receptor so that cell growth and function are constitutively stimulated without ligand.

Methods using nucleic acid probes can be used to make precise diagnoses in disease states and to provide predictive information before overt disease develops. Because genetic defects are present in all DNA, peripheral blood cells or skin fibroblasts provide a ready source of material for assay. Acquired mutations can be assessed by assay of material obtained by biopsy.

SUGGESTED READINGS

Bedecarrats GY, Linher KD, Kaiser UB: Two common naturally occurring mutations in the human gonadotropin-releasing hormone (GnRH) receptor have differential effects on gonadotropin gene expression and on GnRH-mediated signal transduction. J Clin Endocrinol Metab 2003;88:834–843. *Different clinical syndromes can be explained by the responsible mutations.*

Chawla AJ, Repa J, Evans RM, Mangelsdorf D: Nuclear receptors and lipid physiology: Opening the X-files. Science 2001;294:1866–1870. *An overview of the role of many of the steroid receptors in metabolic regulation.*

Hubbard SR, Till JH: Protein tyrosine kinase structure and function. Ann Rev Biochem 2000;69:373–398. *Review of how this class of molecules works. These have become an important new target for design of drug inhibitors, with one anticancer agent now in clinical use.*

Perez DM: Polymorphic G-protein-coupled receptors and associated diseases. Receptors Channels 2002;8:57–64. *A practical review.*

235 NEUROENDOCRINOLOGY AND THE NEUROENDOCRINE SYSTEM

Mark E. Molitch

NEUROENDOCRINE REGULATION

Neuroendocrinology refers to the general area of endocrinology in which the nervous system interacts with the endocrine system to link aspects of cognitive and noncognitive neural activity with metabolic and hormonal homeostatic activity. Neural cells that can secrete hormones, that is, *neurosecretory* cells, serve as the final common pathway linking the brain with the endocrine system. The *neurohypophysial* neurons originate from the paraventricular and supraoptic nuclei, traverse the hypothalamic-pituitary stalk, and release vasopressin and oxytocin from nerve endings in the posterior pituitary. The *hypophysiotropic* neurons, localized in specific hypothalamic nuclei, project their axons to the median eminence to secrete their peptide and bioamine releasing and inhibiting hormones into the proximal end of the hypothalamic-pituitary portal vessels (Fig. 235–1). Neurons from other nuclei within the hypothalamus and other parts of the brain influence pituitary hormone secretion by interacting with these specific neurons. The median eminence receives its blood supply from the superior hypophysial artery, which arborizes into a rich capillary

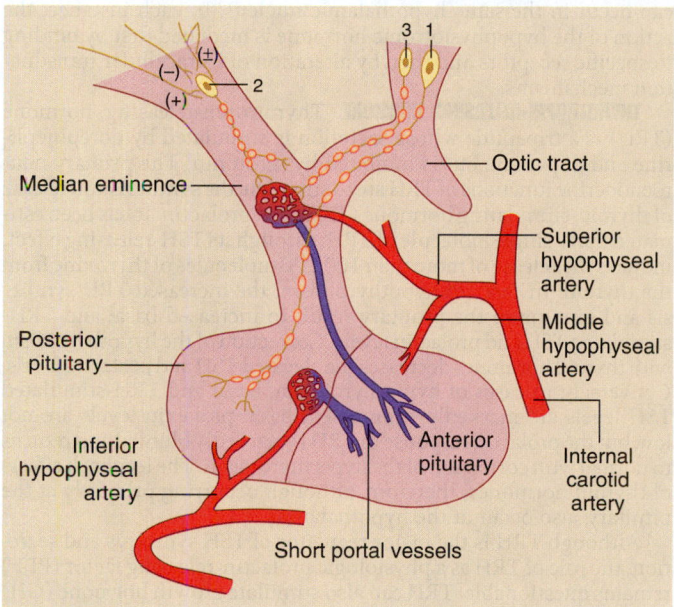

FIGURE 235–1 • Neuroendocrine organization of the hypothalamus and pituitary gland. The posterior pituitary is fed by the inferior hypophyseal artery and the hypothalamus by the superior hypophyseal artery, both branches of the internal carotid artery. A small portion of the anterior pituitary also receives arterial blood from the middle hypophyseal artery. Most of the blood supply to the anterior pituitary is venous by way of the long portal vessels, which connect the portal capillary beds in the median eminence to the venous sinusoids in the anterior pituitary. Hypophysiotropic neuron 3 in the parvocellular division of the paraventricular nucleus and neuron 2 in the arcuate nucleus are shown to terminate in the median eminence on portal capillaries. These neurons of the tuberoinfundibular system secrete hypothalamic releasing and inhibiting hormones into the portal veins for conveyance to the anterior pituitary gland. Neuron 2 is innervated by monoaminergic neurons. Note that the multiple inputs to such neurons, using neuron 2 as an example, can be (a) stimulatory, (b) inhibitory, or (c) neuromodulatory, in which another neuron may affect neurotransmitter release. Neuron 1 represents a peptidergic neuron originating in the magnocellular division of the paraventricular nucleus or supraoptic nucleus and projecting directly to the posterior pituitary by way of the hypothalamic-neurohypophyseal tract. (Reprinted by permission from the American Society for Reproductive Medicine [Fertility and Sterility, 1972, Vol 23, pp 50–63].)

bed. The capillary loops extend into the median eminence and coalesce to form the long portal veins that traverse the pituitary stalk and end in the pituitary. The capillary walls are "fenestrated" and allow entry of the peptides secreted by the axon terminals. At the pituitary end of the stalk, the portal vessels again branch to form an extensive capillary plexus.

The neuroendocrine system operates through a series of feedback loops that control pituitary and target organ hormone levels precisely. Target organ hormones can feed back at both the hypothalamic and the pituitary levels to complete the loop, and efferent controller factors from the hypothalamus may include both stimulatory and inhibitory substances. The feedback loops can be perturbed and result in temporary or prolonged alterations of set points by such factors as length of day (circadian periodicity), stress, nutritional status, and systemic illness. The suprachiasmatic nuclei, located just above the optic chiasm, are important in regulating circadian rhythms of the body.

HYPOPHYSIOTROPIC HORMONES

Regulation of pituitary hormones by the hypophysiotropic hormones is quite complex, in part because of the multiplicity of substances present in the hypothalamus that can affect pituitary hormone secretion and in part because of the redundancy and overlapping nature of the feedback loops alluded to earlier. In addition, some hypophysiotropic hormones exert effects on more than one pituitary hormone (Fig. 235–2). Some of the hypophysiotropic hormones are also found elsewhere in the body, particularly the gastrointestinal tract and placenta, where they may have significant physiologic functions. All of the hypophysiotropic hormones are also present in extrahypothalamic brain tissue and function as neurotransmitters. Several hormones can occur in the same hypothalamic nucleus. In each instance, the action of the hypophysiotropic hormone is mediated first by binding to specific receptors and then by alteration of intracellular transduction mechanisms.

THYROTROPIN-RELEASING HORMONE. Thyrotropin-releasing hormone (TRH) is a tripeptide whose secretion is stimulated by norepinephrine and dopamine but is inhibited by serotonin. The primary neuroendocrine functions of TRH are to stimulate the synthesis and release of thyroid-stimulating hormone (TSH) and prolactin. It has been estimated that a single molecule of TRH, through its TSH-releasing effect, induces the release of more than 100,000 molecules of thyroxine from the thyroid. In cases of hypothyroidism, the increased TRH synthesis and binding to the pituitary result in increased basal and TRH-stimulated TSH and prolactin levels. Correction of the hypothyroidism with thyroid hormones decreases the elevated TSH and prolactin levels. Conversely, in cases of hyperthyroidism, basal and TRH-stimulated TSH levels are markedly suppressed; basal prolactin levels are not low, but the prolactin response to TRH is markedly blunted and returns to normal with correction of the hyperthyroidism. The feedback effects of thyroid hormones, therefore, although occurring primarily at the pituitary, also occur at the hypothalamus.

Although TRH is the major regulator of TSH synthesis and secretion, the role of TRH as a physiologic prolactin-releasing factor (PRF) remains questionable. TRH can also stimulate growth hormone (GH)

secretion in patients with acromegaly, as well as in several states associated with decreased insulin-like growth factor type 1 (IGF-1) feedback on GH secretion, such as cirrhosis, renal insufficiency, anorexia nervosa, poorly controlled type 1 diabetes mellitus, and malnutrition. Such responses are also seen in patients with depression and schizophrenia, which may be associated with disordered central bioaminergic regulation. TRH can also stimulate follicle-stimulating hormone (FSH) secretion in some patients with gonadotroph adenomas, but not in normal individuals. Obviously, somatotroph and gonadotroph cells must have TRH receptors, but "activation" of such receptors, which may involve alteration of intracellular transduction mechanisms, occurs only in special circumstances.

GONADOTROPIN-RELEASING HORMONE. Gonadotropin-releasing hormone (GnRH) is a 10-amino acid peptide. Embryologic studies suggest that GnRH neurons originally develop in the epithelium of the medial part of the olfactory placode. During fetal development, these cells migrate across the cribriform plate, enter the forebrain with the nervus terminalis and vomeronasal nerves, travel medial to the olfactory bulbs, and eventually enter the septal-preoptic region of the hypothalamus. This demonstration of the origin of GnRH-producing neurons from olfactory epithelium is of clinical interest with respect to the entity of Kallmann's syndrome, in which GnRH deficiency is associated with anosmia secondary to agenesis of the olfactory bulbs. At least one form of Kallmann's syndrome has now been found to be caused by a gene defect resulting in loss of function of a protein that facilitates the embryologic migration of these GnRH-producing neurons. GnRH secretion is stimulated by dopamine and norepinephrine and inhibited by serotonin.

The primary function of GnRH is to stimulate the secretion of luteinizing hormone (LH) and FSH. Although early studies suggested the presence of separate LH and FSH releasing factors, only one GnRH has been identified, and the differential secretion of LH and FSH is due to variations in sensitivity of the feedback effects of steroid and peptide hormones and variations in sensitivity to GnRH. GnRH pulsatile secretion also directly upregulates its own receptors; that is, it causes an increase in GnRH receptor number. In contrast, continuous administration of GnRH is associated with a "downregulation" of gonadotropin synthesis and secretion as a result of decreased receptor numbers, as well as postreceptor mechanisms.

In women, positive and negative steroid hormone feedback regulation of the hypothalamic-pituitary-gonadal axis occurs at both the pituitary and the hypothalamic levels, the hypothalamic effects being alteration of GnRH pulse amplitude and frequency and the pituitary effects being modulation of the gonadotropin response to GnRH. In the follicular phase of the menstrual cycle, estrogen feeds back negatively on gonadotropin secretion. At mid-cycle, estrogen feedback becomes positive, and rising estrogen levels from the developing follicle stimulate the ovulatory surge of LH and FSH. Following ovulation, the feedback again becomes negative, and the estrogen and progesterone produced by the corpus luteum result in decreasing levels of LH and FSH. In males, testosterone decreases GnRH pulsatile secretion with a resultant decrease in gonadotropin pulse amplitude and frequency, as well as a decreased gonadotropin response to exogenous GnRH.

The negative-feedback effects of inhibin, a peptide produced by testicular Sertoli cells and ovarian granulosa cells, are predominantly on FSH at the pituitary. Inhibin causes a dose-related decrease in the sensitivity of gonadotrophs to GnRH, but a hypothalamic site of action may also be present. The related ovarian protein activin stimulates basal and GnRH-stimulated FSH synthesis and release from the pituitary, but its primary action is to facilitate the response of ovarian granulosa cells to FSH. Another gonadal peptide, follistatin, also inhibits the oophorectomy- and GnRH-induced rise in FSH selectively, primarily by binding to activin. These ovarian peptides are also found in the pituitary and may therefore have additional local effects on gonadotropin secretion.

The hormone levels and feedback loops mentioned are primarily those of mature adults. In children, gonadotropin and gonadal steroid levels are very low. At puberty, negative feedback of steroid hormones decreases and gonadotropin and steroid levels gradually rise. During this pubertal development, variation in negative and positive estrogen feedback develops in females and eventually precipitates the changes that result in the ovulatory menstrual cycle. At menopause, ovarian estrogen and inhibin production cease, gonadotropin levels rise markedly, and the symptoms associated with estrogen deficiency

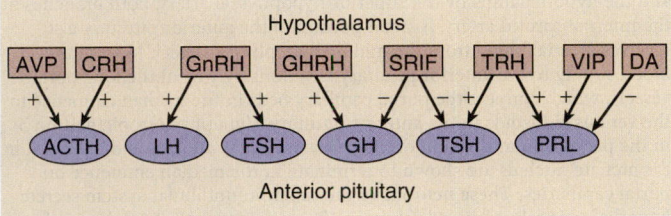

Hypothalamus

| AVP | CRH | GnRH | GHRH | SRIF | TRH | VIP | DA |

Anterior pituitary

ACTH LH FSH GH TSH PRL

FIGURE 235–2 • Interrelationships between hypothalamic and pituitary hormones. Plus signs indicate stimulatory effects and minus signs indicate inhibitory effects. ACTH = adrenocorticotropic hormone; AVP = arginine vasopressin; CRH = corticotropin-releasing hormone; DA = dopamine; FSH = follicle-stimulating hormone; GH = growth hormone; GHRH = growth hormone-releasing hormone; GnRH = gonadotropin-releasing hormone; LH = luteinizing hormone; PRL = prolactin; SRIF = somatotropin release-inhibiting factor (somatostatin); TRH = thyrotropin-releasing hormone; TSH = thyroid-stimulating hormone; VIP = vasoactive intestinal polypeptide.

develop. In men, aging sometimes produces a decrease in testosterone production with a modest rise in gonadotropins, but no clinical syndrome similar to menopause affects men.

GnRH itself has been administered in pulsatile fashion to individuals with hypogonadotropic hypogonadism secondary to GnRH deficiency with great success, that is, restoration of normal sexual function and fertility. Long-acting GnRH agonists have been used to downregulate GnRH receptors and gonadotropin secretion in a variety of conditions, including precocious puberty, prostate cancer, breast cancer, uterine fibroids, and endometriosis. Direct GnRH antagonists that compete for the GnRH receptor are being explored for similar conditions.

SOMATOSTATIN. Somatostatin (also known as *somatotropin release-inhibiting factor*) is a tetradecapeptide: a 28-amino acid precursor that has GH inhibitory properties. Somatostatin blocks the rise in GH that occurs with all stimuli in a dose-dependent fashion. The interaction of somatostatin and growth hormone-releasing hormone (GHRH) on GH secretion is complex. GH secretory episodes are associated with increased GHRH secretion, often accompanied by low somatostatin levels; the basal or trough GH levels are associated with low GHRH levels and more elevated somatostatin levels. Somatostatin also inhibits basal and stimulated TSH secretion. However, dose-response studies using somatostatin infusions in humans have shown that GH is about 10-fold more sensitive to inhibition by somatostatin than is TSH, thus suggesting that the physiologic role of somatostatin in inhibiting TSH secretion is limited.

Somatostatin is also present in the D cells of the pancreatic islets and the gut mucosa, as well as the myenteric neural plexus. Via paracrine and endocrine actions, it suppresses the secretion of insulin, glucagon, cholecystokinin, gastrin, secretin, vasoactive intestinal polypeptide (VIP), and other gastrointestinal hormones, as well as such functions as gastric acid secretion, gastric emptying, gallbladder contraction, and splanchnic blood flow. Analogues of somatostatin have been developed for the treatment of acromegaly, carcinoid tumors, VIP-secreting tumors, TSH-secreting pituitary tumors, islet cell tumors, and diarrhea of a number of causes.

CORTICOTROPIN-RELEASING HORMONE. Corticotropin-releasing hormone (CRH) releases adrenocorticotropic hormone (ACTH), β-endorphin, β-lipotropin, melanocyte-stimulating hormone (MSH), and other peptides generated from pro-opiomelanocortin (POMC) in equimolar amounts. CRH mediates 75% of the ACTH response to stress, and the remaining 25% is due to vasopressin. CRH and vasopressin have synergistic effects on ACTH release. In fact, CRH and vasopressin coexist in about half of the CRH-containing paraventricular neurons and even in the same neurosecretory granules. CRH and vasopressin are not always released coordinately, however, and stress has been shown to selectively activate the vasopressin-containing subset of CRH neurons.

Cortisol feeds back to decrease ACTH secretion at both the hypothalamic and the pituitary levels. ACTH and β-endorphin also feed back negatively to decrease CRH release by the hypothalamus. Morphine suppresses the ACTH response to CRH in humans, presumably acting through opioid μ-receptors. Central bioamines and peptides also influence CRH secretion. Acetylcholine, dopamine, norepinephrine, and epinephrine stimulate and γ-aminobutyric acid inhibits hypothalamic CRH secretion. Norepinephrine and epinephrine also stimulate pituitary ACTH secretion directly and are additive to the stimulatory effect of CRH.

Monokines released by inflammatory tissue, such as interleukin-1, interleukin-6, and tumor necrosis factor–α, stimulate the synthesis and release of CRH and vasopressin from the hypothalamus and the release of ACTH by the pituitary. The consequent increase in cortisol then reduces the intensity of the inflammatory response and release of these monokines, thus completing the feedback loop. Therefore, this neuroendocrine-immune loop serves to modulate the inflammatory response.

Corticotropin-releasing hormone and CRH receptors are widely distributed in the brain, and increases in CRH are associated with activation of the sympathetic and suppression of the parasympathetic nervous system, stimulation of arousal, and increased learning performance. CRH may also be involved in the regulation of body weight; with overfeeding, increased leptin stimulates CRH, which causes decreased food intake and increased energy expenditure.

Biosynthetic human CRH has become available for clinical use. Its major utility is in the differential diagnosis of Cushing's disease versus ectopic ACTH syndrome, with the finding that patients with Cushing's disease respond with a greater than 35% increment, whereas those with ectopic ACTH secretion have a lesser response. If the results are equivocal, CRH testing during bilateral inferior petrosal sinus sampling for ACTH often provides additional discriminatory information.

GROWTH HORMONE-RELEASING HORMONE. GHRH dose-dependently stimulates GH secretion, and in some individuals GHRH is capable of eliciting a small increase in prolactin as well. With repetitive administration every 3 hours, GHRH can cause the release of sufficient GH in children with GHRH deficiency to result in an increase in IGF-I levels and an acceleration of growth. Both IGF-I and GH itself feed back negatively on GH secretion, with the negative feedback mediated by both a decrease in GHRH and an increase in somatostatin. This feedback effect of IGF-I is clinically relevant, as documented by the high circulating GH levels that occur in IGF-I-deficient states, such as renal insufficiency and cirrhosis. In children with mutations of the GH receptor resulting in their not being responsive to GH (GH insensitivity syndrome, also known as Laron-type dwarfism), IGF-I levels are very low and GH levels are correspondingly elevated. α_2-Adrenergic receptors and serotonin activate GHRH and GH secretion, but γ-aminobutyric acid is inhibitory to GHRH secretion.

A recently described, separate GH-stimulating system for GH secretion involves a distinct receptor, termed the *GH secretagogue* (GHS) receptor that interacts with a 28-amino acid peptide called Ghrelin. GHS receptor and Ghrelin mRNA are both present in the pituitary and hypothalamus of humans. How the Ghrelin-GHS receptor system interacts physiologically with GHRH and somatostatin is not yet known. Six-amino acid peptides have been shown to interact with the GHS receptor and cause release of GH; orally active nonpeptide mimetics of these releasing peptides also can release GH. Such substances may have potential diagnostically and therapeutically in the future.

PROLACTIN INHIBITORY FACTOR. The inhibitory component of hypothalamic regulation of prolactin secretion predominates over the stimulatory component. Dopamine is the predominant physiologic prolactin inhibitory factor. It is likely that in most physiologic circumstances that cause a rise in prolactin, such as lactation, a simultaneous fall in dopamine occurs along with a rise in a PRF such as VIP. Blockade of endogenous dopamine receptors by a variety of drugs, such as the neuroleptics, causes a rise in prolactin. Lesions that interrupt the basal hypothalamic neuronal pathways carrying dopamine to the median eminence or that interrupt portal blood flow result in decreased dopamine reaching the pituitary and hyperprolactinemia.

PROLACTIN RELEASING FACTOR. A number of hypothalamic peptides other than TRH have also been shown to have PRF activity. VIP stimulates prolactin synthesis and release at concentrations found in hypothalamic-pituitary portal blood. Within the VIP precursor is another similarly sized peptide known as *peptide histidine methionine*, which also has PRF activity. Complicating the role of VIP as a PRF is the finding that VIP is actually synthesized by anterior pituitary tissue. The precise roles of VIP versus peptide histidine methionine and hypothalamic VIP versus pituitary VIP are still not clear. A 31-amino acid peptide termed PRL-releasing peptide that releases PRL from the pituitary has recently been found to be present in the hypothalamus and pituitary. Its G-protein coupled receptor has also been demonstrated in human pituitaries. At this time, the physiologic importance in humans of PRL-releasing peptide is unclear.

ENDOGENOUS OPIOID PEPTIDES. In the mid-1970s, discovery of the opiate receptors and the fact that some of the endogenous opioid peptide ligands for these receptors were present within POMC, the precursor to ACTH, prompted widespread speculation about the importance of this system in neuroendocrine regulation, as well as the interaction of neuroendocrinology, mental illness, and opiate addiction. Most data now suggest at most a modest role for endogenous opioid peptides in neuroendocrine regulation, however.

The endogenous opioid peptides have a common five-amino acid sequence at their amino termini (Tyr-Gly-Gly-Phe-Met [or Leu]) that is important for their binding to endogenous opioid receptors and bioactivity. Three major opioid peptide receptors and three major groups of opioid peptides (Fig. 235–3) are recognized, but the correspondence is not one for one. The μ-receptor mediates most of the endocrine effects and analgesia; morphine is its prototypic agonist, and naloxone is its prototypic antagonist. The primary peptide ligand for the μ-receptor is β-endorphin, which is derived from POMC, although β-endorphin also binds to the δ-receptor and the enkephalins can also bind to the μ-receptor. The δ-receptor mediates behavioral,

Endocrine Diseases

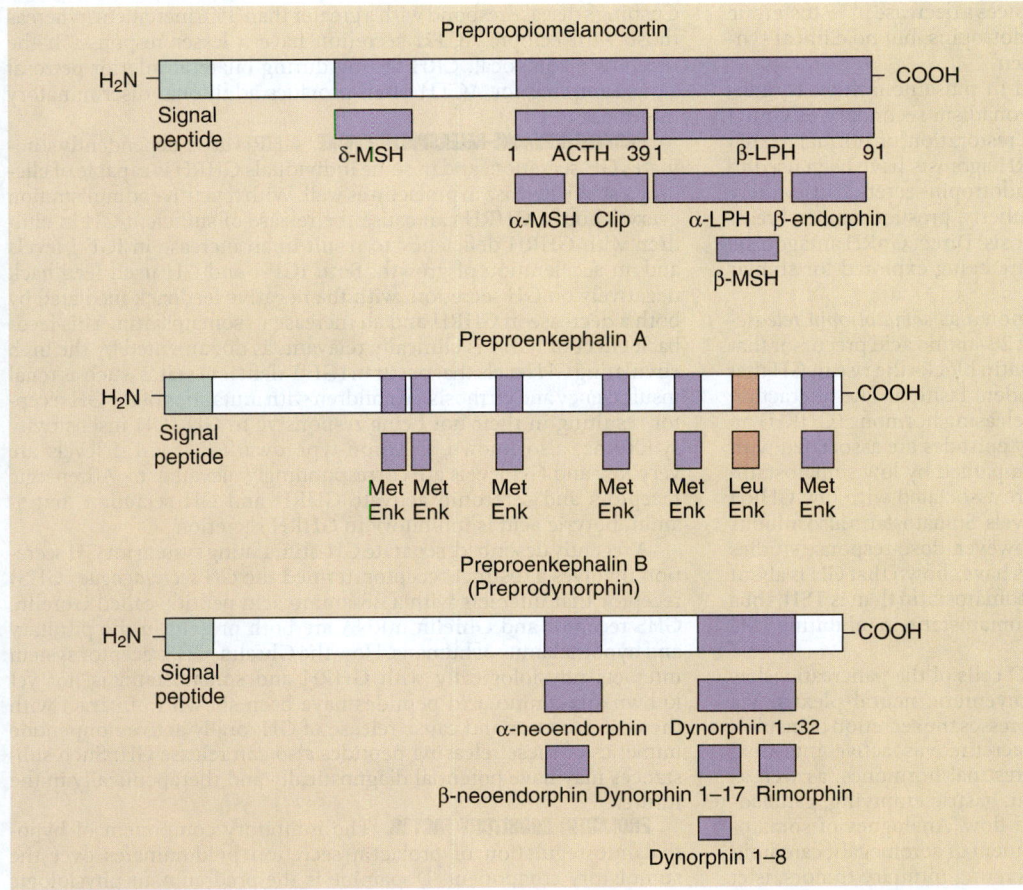

FIGURE 235–3 • Structures of the precursors of the endogenous opioid peptides. Preproopiomelanocortin (POMC) generates several peptides, including β-lipotropin (β-LPH), β-endorphin, adrenocorticotropic hormone (ACTH), α-melanocyte-stimulating hormone (α-MSH), β-MSH, γ-MSH, and corticotropin-like intermediate lobe peptide (CLIP). Preproenkephalin A generates six copies of methionine enkephalin (met-enk) and one copy of leucine-enkephalin (leu-enk). Preproenkephalin B (preprodynorphin) generates α- and β-neoendorphins; dynorphins 108, 1–7, and 1–32; and rimorphin.

analgesic, and some endocrine effects and has as its primary peptide ligands met- and leu-enkephalins, which are derived from proenkephalin A. It is much less well blocked by naloxone than is the μ-receptor. The κ-receptor mediates sedation and ataxia and binds primarily dynorphin and the neo-endorphins, which are derived from proenkephalin B (prodynorphin). A fourth receptor has recently been described that has considerable sequence homology with the δ-receptor and binds to an endogenous 17-amino acid peptide called nociceptin (also known as orphanin FQ).

Pro-opiomelanocortin is a 31-kD precursor peptide that harbors within it ACTH, β-lipotropin, and β-endorphin; the last substance corresponds to the C-terminal 31 amino acids of β-lipotropin. POMC undergoes tissue-specific post-translational processing; that is, in the anterior pituitary the major cleavage products are β-lipotropin and ACTH, with a significant proportion of β-lipotropin being further processed to β-endorphin, but in the pituitary intermediate lobe, the major products are α-MSH, corticotropin-like intermediate peptide, β-endorphin, and γ-lipotropin. Brain POMC, however, is processed primarily to β-endorphin, γ-lipotropin, and ACTH, with most of the ACTH being further processed to corticotropin-like intermediate peptide and α-MSH. All neuronal perikarya containing POMC-derived peptides are located in the arcuate nucleus, from which β-endorphin- and α-MSH-containing fibers project to the median eminence; ventromedial, dorsomedial, paraventricular, and periventricular nuclei of the hypothalamus; amygdala; preoptic area; periaqueductal gray matter; reticular formation; stria terminalis; locus caeruleus; striatum; and hippocampus. The projection to the median eminence results in significant quantities of β-endorphin being found in portal blood. POMC-derived peptides are also found in the placenta, thyroid C cells, pancreas, testes, ovaries, adrenal medulla, gastric antrum, and macrophages. Anterior pituitary β-endorphin is secreted with ACTH after CRH and vasopressin stimulation (see earlier discussion), but the only factors known to decrease hypothalamic β-endorphin are dopamine and estradiol.

The pentapeptide enkephalins are derived from the 28-kD precursor proenkephalin A, which contains six copies of the met-enkephalin sequence and one copy of the leu-enkephalin sequence. Other extended cleavage products with biologic activity may also exist,

and the ratio of met- to leu-enkephalin ranges between 5 : 1 and 10 : 1 in various places in the brain, possibly representing evidence of differences in tissue-specific cleavage and/or degradation. Neuronal perikarya containing the enkephalins are widely distributed throughout the brain, as are fiber networks. Most enkephalinergic neurons are short and have the characteristics of interneurons. Rich enkephalinergic neural fiber networks can be found in the globus pallidus, amygdala, and midbrain, with specific areas of innervation including the origin of the central noradrenergic system, the locus caeruleus, the origin of the central serotoninergic system, the raphe nuclei, and the origin of the striatal dopaminergic system, the substantia nigra. Enkephalinergic neurons in the magnocellular portion of the paraventricular and supraoptic nuclei project to the posterior pituitary. Within the pituitary, enkephalins have been detected primarily in the posterior pituitary. Enkephalins have also been found in the adrenal medulla, gut, heart, lung, sympathetic ganglia, vagus, and retina.

Dynorphin is a 17-amino acid peptide derived from a 28-kD precursor called proenkephalin B or prodynorphin. Shorter peptides termed α- and β-neoendorphin, which have 10 and 9 amino acids, respectively, have also been isolated. These peptides react almost exclusively with the κ-receptor. Dynorphin-containing cells also project from the magnocellular neurons of the paraventricular nucleus to the posterior pituitary. Other tissues containing dynorphin include the gut, lungs, and adrenal medulla.

Nociceptin is a 17–amino acid peptide derived from a κ precursor called pronociceptin. High concentrations of nociceptin and its receptor are present in the hypothalamus as well as in other areas of the brain that serve as the sources of monoamine neurotransmitters, including the locus caeruleus, dorsal raphe, substantia nigra, and ventral tegmental area. In general, nociceptin appears to have an antiopioid or anti-nociceptive effect. When injected into the ventromedial hypothalamus of satiated rats, nociceptin stimulates feeding behavior and it hyperpolarizes GnRH-containing and dopamine-containing neurons in the arcuate nucleus. More detailed experiments involving neuroendocrine regulation have not yet been done, however.

The three main opioid receptors μ, δ, and κ have all been cloned and found to be members of the G protein–coupled, seven-transmembrane class of receptors; they have 61% sequence identity at the amino acid level. The δ-receptors are located predominantly in the thalamus, hippocampus, periaqueductal gray matter, and neocortex, and the receptors are located primarily in the amygdala, nucleus accumbens, and hypothalamus. Dynorphin receptors have been localized to the cerebral cortex, the thalamus, and the caudate nucleus. The anterior pituitary itself is poor in opioid receptors, but the hypothalamus is quite rich, and it has been suggested that the effects of opioid peptides on anterior pituitary hormone secretion are produced via modulation of hypothalamic bioamines and hypophysiotropic factors.

The specific functions of the various opioid peptides and the opioid receptors are still not completely understood, although evidence links them to a number of body functions, including stress, mental illness, narcotic tolerance and dependence, eating, drinking, gastrointestinal function, learning, memory, reward, cardiovascular responses, respiration, thermoregulation, seizures, brain electrical activity, locomotor activity, pregnancy, and neuroimmune activity. More specific functions regarding neuroendocrine regulation have been documented, however. In general, endogenous opioids have an inhibitory influence on gonadotropin secretion through action on GnRH secretion, probably by inhibition of noradrenergic neuronal input. Exogenous β-endorphin and enkephalin analogues increase serum GH and prolactin levels, but blockade of endogenous opioid pathways with naloxone does not alter basal or stimulated GH or prolactin levels. Opioids feed back negatively on ACTH and β-endorphin secretion, and naloxone can increase basal and stimulated ACTH levels. Opioids have virtually no effect on TSH secretion. Overall, the effects of the endogenous opioids on normal physiologic regulation of the various pituitary hormones appear quite minimal. In some states of pathologic gonadotropin dysfunction, it is possible that increased opioid peptidergic tone is present, but this increased tone appears to be somewhat inconsistent.

CENTRAL NERVOUS SYSTEM RHYTHMS AND NEUROENDOCRINE FUNCTION

Pituitary hormones are secreted in a pulsatile fashion with a number of rhythms superimposed. The pulse amplitude of a pituitary hormone reflects the amount of releasing hormone, as well as factors that may alter sensitivity to that releasing hormone. Thus, the amplitude can be altered by the presence of inhibitory factors (e.g., GHRH versus somatostatin), nutritional factors, feedback effects of target organ hormones, and prior stimulation that depletes a readily releasable pool of hormone. The frequency is generally governed by the frequency of release of the hypophysiotropic factor, which is regulated by the hypothalamic pulse generator system.

The pituitary has an intrinsic rhythm of small amplitude with a frequency of every 2 to 10 minutes. Superimposed on this intrinsic rhythm is a rhythm caused by the pulsatile release of hypophysiotropic releasing factors, with or without the withdrawal of a corresponding inhibitory factor. Rhythms that are shorter than a day are referred to as *ultradian* rhythms. The next layer of rhythmicity is the *circadian* rhythm, that is, rhythms with approximately 24-hour periodicity. These rhythms are usually synchronized with the 24-hour period by a periodic environmental cue such as the dark-light cycle. The suprachiasmatic nucleus functions as a circadian pacemaker and receives light-induced electrical impulses from the retina via the retinohypothalamic tract, finally transmitting those impulses to the pineal gland, where they are converted to hormonal signals. Signals for a rhythm with a periodicity longer than 24 hours, an *infradian* rhythm, include the gravitational influence of the moon, which gives rise to the menstrual cycle.

A number of factors may influence circadian and infradian rhythms. One of the most important is the sleep-wake cycle. GH, TSH, prolactin, ACTH, and pubertal LH secretion are all entrained more to the sleep-wake cycle than to the dark-light cycle. Each has an increase and maximal level that occur following sleep onset. The profound diurnal variation in cortisol and ACTH is often used as an index of "normality" of the system. Loss of this diurnal rhythm occurs with disordered regulation by CRH, which may be due to endogenous depression or excessive alcohol intake, as well as autonomous secretion of ACTH in Cushing's disease. Loss of the diurnal rhythm of cortisol has been used as a diagnostic test for Cushing's syndrome.

Interesting changes occur in gonadotropin secretion as a child passes through puberty into adulthood. Early in puberty the amplitude of the pulses increases during sleep at night, especially for LH, but in adulthood this nocturnal rise is lost. In patients with anorexia nervosa, the pattern of gonadotropin secretion often reverts to this pubertal pattern, only to lose this pattern again with weight gain. This phenomenon suggests that body composition may in some way affect regulation of the pulsatile secretion of gonadotropins. In fact, the percentage of body composition that is fat has been proposed as being important in the timing of the onset of puberty. Recent studies implicate leptin as the signal indicating this change in body composition.

Endocrine rhythms appear to reflect a rather primitive organizing influence that helps an animal adapt to the environment. Circadian synchronization with the light-dark cycle and sleep and infradian synchronization with seasonal changes are present very early phylogenetically. However, because humans are able to alter the light-dark cycles, they are less tied to environmental changes. This adaptation has led to new, modern problems with these rhythms, such as jet lag, which involves rapid resynchronization of the rhythms with several-hour time zone displacements. Because not all rhythms resynchronize at the same rates, some of the disorientation and other symptoms associated with jet lag may be due to abnormal phase relationships of various body rhythms to each other and to the dark-light cycle.

NEUROENDOCRINE DISEASE

Diseases of the Hypothalamus

Diseases may affect the hypothalamus by being localized to the hypothalamus, by being part of more generalized central nervous system (CNS) disease such as neurosarcoidosis, or by indirect means such as by causing hydrocephalus (Table 235–1). Furthermore, hormonal changes mediated by functional alterations in hypothalamic regulation may occur in a variety of psychiatric disorders or systemic illnesses.

The axons projecting to the median eminence that contain the various hypophysiotropic factors are concentrated in the basal portion of the hypothalamus. Thus, lesions located within this final common pathway might be expected to cause significant decreases in secretion of some or all of the pituitary hormones except prolactin, which may increase because of the elimination of tonic inhibition by dopamine. Diabetes insipidus may also occur. Other functions of the hypothalamus are more diffusely located, such as the regulation of temperature, food intake, and blood pressure.

Symptoms resulting from hypothalamic dysfunction are related to the size of the lesion and consequently to the area of the hypothalamus involved, as well as to the rapidity of the increase in lesion size. Slowly growing lesions tend to cause problems of hormone dysregulation rather than dramatic symptoms. Large, slowly growing lesions can cause more acute problems, however, when a slight increment in growth eliminates the remaining vestiges of vasopressin or ACTH secretion or completely occludes the aqueduct of Sylvius and precipitates hydrocephalus.

The best way of discerning lesions affecting the hypothalamus is by magnetic resonance imaging (MRI) with gadolinium enhancement, although computed tomographic scanning with intravenous contrast is also quite good. Formal visual field testing may discern impingement of the optic nerves and chiasm by hypothalamic lesions, including the suprasellar extension of pituitary tumors. Detailed testing of hypothalamic-pituitary function may reveal evidence of functional hypothalamic disruption with great sensitivity.

CONGENITAL EMBRYOPATHIC DISORDERS. The most common embryopathic disorders to affect the hypothalamus are the midline cleft syndromes, which cause varying degrees of defects of midline structures, especially the optic and olfactory tracts, the septum pellucidum, the corpus callosum, the anterior commissure, the hypothalamus, and the pituitary. The clinical features of patients with midline cleft defects varies in severity from cyclopia to cleft lip and from isolated hypothalamic hormone defects to panhypopituitarism. The combination of absent septum pellucidum associated with optic nerve hypoplasia is referred to as *septo-optic dysplasia* and is associated with abnormalities of hypothalamic and other diencephalic structures. Some patients with septo-optic dysplasia and hypothalamic hypopituitarism have sexual precocity, presumably caused by a lack of inhibitory influences from other parts of the hypothalamus and intact GnRH-producing structures. Children with very mild midline cleft defects consisting of just

Table 235–1 • ETIOLOGY OF HYPOTHALAMIC DISEASE

NEONATES
Intraventricular hemorrhage
Meningitis: bacterial
Tumors: glioma, hemangioma
Trauma
Hydrocephalus, hydranencephaly, kernicterus

1 MONTH–2 YEARS
Congenital embryopathic disorders: agenesis of the corpus callosum, cleft palate
Congenital disorders: Isolated hormone and receptor mutations, combined pituitary hormone deficiency (Pit-1, Prop-1), Laurence-Moon-Bardet-Biedl, Prader-Labhart-Willi
Tumors: glioma, especially optic glioma, hemangiomas
Infiltrative disease: Langerhans cell histiocytosis, meningitis
Hydrocephalus

2–10 YEARS
Disease associated with midline brain defects: agenesis of corpus callosum
Congenital disorders: Isolated hormone and receptor mutations, combined pituitary hormone deficiency (Pit-1, Prop-1), Laurence-Moon-Bardet-Biedl, Prader-Labhart-Willi, diabetes insipidus, etc.
Tumors: craniopharyngioma, glioma, dysgerminoma, hamartoma, leukemia, ganglioneuroma, ependymoma, medulloblastoma
Infiltrative disease: Langerhans cell histiocytosis, meningitis, tuberculosis, encephalitis
Irradiation: For nasopharyngeal tumors, intracranial tumors, leukemia
Functional: psychosocial deprivation

10–25 YEARS
Congenital disorders: Kallmann's syndrome, gonadotropin-releasing hormone receptor defects
Tumors: craniopharyngioma, pituitary tumors, glioma, hamartoma, dysgerminoma, dermoid, lipoma, neuroblastoma
Trauma: subarachnoid hemorrhage, vascular aneurysm, arteriovenous malformation
Infiltrative diseases: Langerhans cell histiocytosis, sarcoidosis, tuberculosis, meningitis, encephalitis, leukemia
Chronic hydrocephalus or increased intracranial pressure
Functional: hypogonadotropic hypogonadism associated with weight loss, exercise

25–50 YEARS
Tumors: pituitary tumors, meningioma, craniopharyngioma, Rathke's cleft cyst, glioma, lymphoma, angioma, colloid cysts, ependymoma
Infiltrative diseases: sarcoidosis, Langerhans cell histiocytosis, tuberculosis, viral encephalitis
Subarachnoid hemorrhage, vascular aneurysms, arteriovenous malformation
Irradiation: for pituitary adenoma, nasopharyngeal tumors, intracranial tumors
Nutritional: Wernicke's disease
Functional: hypogonadotropic hyogonadism associated with weight loss, exercise

50 YEARS AND OLDER
Tumors: pituitary tumors, meningioma, carniopharyngioma, sarcoma, glioblastoma, lymphoma, colloid cysts, ependymoma
Vascular: infarct, subarachnoid hemorrhage, pituitary apoplexy, aneurysm
Irradiation: for pituitary adenoma, nasopharyngeal tumors, intracranial tumors
Infiltrative diseases: encephalitis, sarcoidosis, meningitis
Nutritional: Wernicke's disease

Modified from Plum F, Van Uitert R: Non-endocrine diseases of the hypothalamus. *In* Reichlin S, Baldessarini RJ, Martin JB (eds): The Hypothalamus. New York, Raven Press, 1978, p 415.

cleft lip, cleft palate, or both have been found to have a markedly increased risk of having GH and other pituitary hormone deficiencies. Recent MRI studies of patients with "idiopathic" GH deficiency show absence of the infundibulum in nearly 50%.

Mutations responsible for these developmental defects are the subject of active investigation. One possible mutation that has been found is in the *Hesx1* gene (also called *Rpx*, for Rathke's pouch homeobox), which is a member of the paired-like class of homeobox genes expressed in the thickened layer of oral ectoderm that gives rise to Rathke's pouch. A C→T substitution in one position in the human *Hesx1* gene was found to cause agenesis of the corpus callosum and panhypopituitarism in one kindred. Many other transcription factors have been described that are expressed sequentially during embryogenesis in Rathke's pouch that are important in the ultimate development of the normal pituitary cell lineages. Mutations have been found in two other homeobox transcription factors genes: *Pit-1*, which causes hypoplasia of somatotrophs, lactotrophs, and thyrotrophs, and *Prop-1*, which causes hypoplasia of these same cell populations and, in addition, gonadotrophs (Chapter 237). Combined pituitary hormone deficiency has an incidence of about 1 in 8000 births and about 10% have an affected relative; it appears that more than half of these cases are due to *Pit-1* or *Prop-1* deficiencies.

Kallmann's syndrome is a condition characterized by anosmia or hyposmia and hypogonadotropic hypogonadism. The diagnosis is made by finding anosmia and low gonadotropin levels, and MRI will show absence or hypoplasia of the olfactory bulbs. The X-linked form of Kallmann's syndrome is due to a gene defect (*KAL*) resulting in loss of function of a protein that facilitates the embryologic migration of GnRH-producing neurons from the olfactory placode to the hypothalamus and the olfactory nerves to the olfactory bulbs. The pituitary is usually intact in this condition, and treatment with pulsatile GnRH therapy or gonadotropins results in spermatogenesis and normal gonadal function. In some patients, other neurologic abnormalities may be present, including cerebellar ataxia, nerve deafness, color blindness, cleft lip and palate, mental retardation, and disordered thirst.

TUMORS. The most common tumors affecting the hypothalamus are *pituitary adenomas* that have significant suprasellar extension. These tumors can cause varying degrees of hypopituitarism, diabetes insipidus, and hyperprolactinemia, either by compressing the normal pituitary or, more commonly, by affecting the pituitary stalk and mediobasal hypothalamus. Evidence that hypopituitarism is caused by pituitary compression includes a low serum prolactin level and a lack of TSH response to TRH; pituitary function in such cases usually does not improve after treatment. In patients with normal or elevated prolactin levels, pituitary function often returns following therapy.

Craniopharyngiomas are the next most common tumors affecting the hypothalamus. Microscopically, craniopharyngiomas consist of cysts alternating with stratified squamous epithelium. The cyst fluid is usually thick and dark and the material is often calcified. They arise from remnants of Rathke's pouch. A closely related lesion is a *Rathke cleft cyst,* which develops from the space between the anterior and rudimentary intermediate lobes. Rathke's cleft cysts are lined with cuboidal as opposed to squamous epithelium, and the cyst fluid is usually a white, mucoid fluid. Craniopharyngiomas may be difficult to remove in their entirety, and postoperative radiation reduces recurrences. Rathke's cleft cysts less commonly recur. Craniopharyngiomas most commonly arise during childhood, but they may also occur in adults and even the elderly. These tumors come to attention because of mass effects, including headache, vomiting, visual disturbance, seizures, hypopituitarism, and polyuria. Some patients have galactorrhea, amenorrhea, and hyperprolactinemia, features suggestive of a prolactinoma. Careful endocrine testing reveals varying degrees of hypopituitarism in 50 to 75% and modest hyperprolactinemia in 25 to 50%. Surgical extirpation of craniopharyngiomas commonly causes a worsening of pituitary function, often resulting in complete panhypopituitarism and diabetes insipidus because of stalk section and may cause damage to hypothalamic centers regulating thirst, body temperature, and food intake. Irradiation may also be helpful, especially in children.

Suprasellar dysgerminomas arise from primitive germ cells that have migrated to the CNS during fetal life and are structurally identical to germ cell tumors of the gonads. They most commonly occur in children, in whom they cause decreased growth because of hypopituitarism, as well as diabetes insipidus and visual problems. Hyperprolactinemia occurs in more than 50% of affected children, and 10% have precocious puberty from the production of human chorionic gonadotropin by the tumor. The finding of an elevated human chorionic gonadotropin level in the spinal fluid may be diagnostic. As opposed to craniopharyngiomas, these tumors are very radiosensitive, and radiation therapy is the preferred treatment.

A hypothalamic *hamartoma* is a nodule of growth of hypothalamic neurons attached by a pedicle to the hypothalamus between the tuber cinereum and the mamillary bodies and extending into the basal cistern. Asymptomatic hamartomas may be present in up to 20% of random autopsies; rarely, these lesions may enlarge and disrupt hypothalamic function because of compression of adjacent tissue. A variant of hamartoma consisting of similar tissue present within the anterior pituitary but without a neural attachment to the hypothalamus is called a choristoma or gangliocytoma. These neuronal tumors are of particular endocrine interest because they can produce hypophysiotropic hormones. A number of cases associated with precocious puberty have been reported in which the hamartomas produced GnRH. Successful treatment has been reported with surgery and with the administration of a long-acting GnRH analogue, which suppresses gonadotropin secretion but does not affect the tumor itself. If the hamartoma does not cause other problems from mass effects, medical therapy with the GnRH analogue may be the best choice, because surgery can be noncurative or even fatal. Some gangliocytomas have been reported that produce GHRH and acromegaly or CRH and Cushing's syndrome.

Other tumors and space-occupying lesions occurring in the suprasellar area include arachnoid cysts, meningiomas, gliomas, astrocytomas, chordomas, infundibulomas, cholesteatomas, neurofibromas, lipomas, and metastatic cancer (particularly from the breast and lung). Any such lesion may be manifested by varying degrees of hypopituitarism, diabetes insipidus, and hyperprolactinemia, and surgical therapy often worsens the hormonal deficit and may cause other hypothalamic damage.

INFLAMMATORY DISORDERS. CNS involvement in cases of *sarcoidosis* occurs in 1 to 5% of patients, as determined on clinical grounds, and in up to 16% of cases at autopsy. Isolated CNS sarcoidosis is quite uncommon, however. When sarcoidosis does involve the CNS, the hypothalamus is involved in 10 to 20% of cases. Sarcoid granulomas can involve the hypothalamus, stalk, or pituitary and may be infiltrative or occur as a mass lesion. Rarely, sarcoid granulomas can be manifested as an expanding intrasellar mass mimicking a pituitary tumor. The most common endocrine findings are varying degrees of hypopituitarism, diabetes insipidus, and hyperprolactinemia. Obesity secondary to hypothalamic involvement by sarcoidosis has also been reported. In patients with isolated CNS sarcoidosis, the diagnosis may be extremely difficult. Examination of cerebrospinal fluid usually shows elevated protein levels, low glucose level, pleocytosis, and variable elevations of angiotensin-converting enzyme. However, biopsy is often necessary. Although corticosteroid therapy has been reported to at least partially reverse the thirst disorders, anterior pituitary hormone deficits usually do not respond.

Langerhans cell histiocytosis or eosinophilic granulomatous infiltration of the hypothalamus may cause diabetes insipidus, varying degrees of hypopituitarism, and hyperprolactinemia. It is the most common cause of diabetes insipidus in children. Usually, this infiltration appears as a thickening of the pituitary stalk, but it may also appear as a mass lesion of the hypothalamus or the pituitary. Osteolytic lesions may be present in the jaw or mastoid, so radiographs of the jaw are a worthwhile part of the diagnostic evaluation of an unknown suprasellar mass or diabetes insipidus for this reason. Therapy consists of local surgery, focal irradiation, or chemotherapy with alkylating agents and high-dose corticosteroids.

VASCULAR DISEASE. An enlarging aneurysm may be manifested as a mass lesion of the hypothalamic-pituitary area and may cause hypopituitarism and visual field defects. Obviously, the distinction must be made before surgery. Tumors and aneurysms may also coexist, and careful radiologic evaluation with MRI is necessary to discern such association. Hypothalamic disease caused by vascular infarction is extremely rare.

TRAUMA. Head trauma can cause defects ranging from isolated ACTH deficiency to panhypopituitarism with diabetes insipidus. Within the first 72 hours of trauma, GH, LH, ACTH, TSH, and prolactin levels may actually be elevated in blood, perhaps because of acute release. These levels subsequently fall, and either patients return to normal or hypopituitarism develops. In patients dying of head injury, anterior pituitary infarction has been found in 16% of cases, posterior pituitary hemorrhage in 34%, and hypothalamic hemorrhage or infarction in 42% of cases. The paraventricular and supraoptic nuclei and median eminence are particularly involved with microhemorrhages, hence the high frequency of panhypopituitarism with diabetes insipidus. With frontal injuries, the brain travels backward but the pituitary cannot move; consequently, the pituitary stalk becomes avulsed, with interruption of the portal vessels. Most patients with head injury are hyperprolactinemic, which clinically confirms that the hypothalamus and/or stalk is the primary site of injury.

IRRADIATION. Whole-brain irradiation for intracranial neoplasms frequently results in hypothalamic dysfunction, as evidenced by endocrine abnormalities and behavioral changes. The most common endocrine abnormality is hyperprolactinemia, but hypopituitarism can also occur. When the radiotherapy is targeted to the hypothalamic area, as in patients with tumors in that area or nasopharyngeal carcinomas, hypopituitarism occurs even more frequently. The frequencies of loss of pituitary function are so high that all patients who have had their pituitary and hypothalamic areas irradiated must be monitored closely for the purpose of detecting these deficits when they occur.

Effects of Hypothalamic Disease on Pituitary Function

Hypothalamic disease can cause both pituitary hyperfunction and hypofunction in varying degrees of severity. Although severe disease can cause absolute deficiencies of the various hormones, milder disease may cause a subtle alteration in feedback loops and timing such that, for example, the integration of signals necessary for menstrual cycling is lost, with subsequent "hypothalamic" amenorrhea. Furthermore, the hypothalamic defects may be interrelated. The rather common finding of hyperprolactinemia occurring with hypothalamic dysfunction causes a hypogonadotropic hypogonadism that is reversible when the elevated prolactin levels are brought down to normal. In many cases, no structural lesion can be found on MRI, and a functional defect caused by altered neurotransmitter regulation is invoked.

GROWTH HORMONE. Loss of normal GH secretion is the most common hormonal defect occurring with structural hypothalamic disease. Congenital idiopathic GH deficiency is a heterogeneous disorder consisting of hypothalamic and pituitary defects. The diagnosis is usually made between 1 and 3 years of age because of impaired growth. Between 5 and 30% of subjects with idiopathic GH deficiency have an affected relative, and thus their defect is thought to have a genetic basis. One autosomal dominant form of complete GH deficiency has been found to be associated with deletion of the gene for GH. About three quarters of cases have a normal GH response to exogenous GHRH, which implies that the defect is probably disordered hypothalamic regulation. Defects in the gene for GHRH have not been found, but a rare form of GH deficiency has been found to be caused by a mutation in the GHRH receptor. As noted earlier, nearly half of children with "idiopathic" GH deficiency have midline cleft defects, and MRI scans should be performed routinely as part of the evaluation.

A reversible form of idiopathic GH deficiency caused by inadequate parental care and affection is referred to as the *emotional deprivation syndrome* or *psychosocial dwarfism*. Restoration of a proper social environment for such a child results in prompt normalization of GH secretion and growth. It has been hypothesized that the disordered GH regulation is due to psychogenic alteration of the neurotransmitter balance necessary for normal GHRH and somatostatin secretion. Other systemic illnesses such as inflammatory bowel disease, often occult, may also cause decreased GH secretion and growth; treatment of the systemic illness will correct the growth abnormality. Treatment of children and adults with GH deficiency is discussed in Chapter 237.

GONADOTROPINS

Hypothalamic Hypogonadism. The primary defect in this group of disorders is thought to involve the secretion of GnRH, with resultant impairment in pituitary gonadotropin secretion and gonadal function. The disorders causing these conditions may be primary, that is, congenital defects, or acquired. Depending on the time of onset, they are manifested as either delayed puberty, interruption of pubertal progression, or loss of adult gonadal function. The lesions causing these disorders may cause loss of other hormones or may be isolated to GnRH. Loss of gonadotropin secretion as the result of hypothalamic structural damage is the second most common defect after GH deficiency. However, a substantial portion of these defects are due to hyperprolactinemia and are reversible with correction of the hyperprolactinemia. In some cases, the defect is idiopathic. Defects in the gene for GnRH have not been found, but mutations in the GnRH receptor occur.

Lesions occurring prepubertally result in the failure of onset of puberty or, if the defect is partial, in incomplete progression of puberty. If the disorder is limited to GnRH and the gonadotropins, prior growth and development are normal, but the growth spurt occurring at puberty is lost. Undescended testes are present in 50% of patients with GnRH deficiency, probably secondary to the absence of gonadotropins during fetal development. The most common congenital lesion causing prepubertal GnRH deficiency is Kallmann's syndrome, which affects 50% of males and 37% of females seen with isolated gonadotropin deficiency. In patients with idiopathic GnRH deficiency, the gene for GnRH appears to be normal but the gene for the GnRH receptor may be abnormal. Indirect measures of functional GnRH secretion show, however, that disorders of pulse amplitude or frequency, or both, may be present. When hyperprolactinemia occurs before puberty, it can prevent the onset of puberty and must always be looked for in this setting.

The ideal therapy for patients with GnRH deficiency is replacement of GnRH via subcutaneous administration every 2 hours with a portable pump. This treatment causes a rapid rise in LH and FSH responses to GnRH, a rise in testosterone to normal, and the development of normal spermatogenesis. Similar approaches in women result in ovulatory cycles in 80%. The success of such therapy confirms the original hypothesis of a primary defect of GnRH secretion. In men, comparable results can be obtained with exogenous gonadotropins given three times per week. GnRH therapy is not successful in those with GnRH receptor mutations. Replacement with testosterone alone causes adequate androgenization but does not result in an increase in testicular size or in spermatogenesis.

Loss of formerly normal GnRH secretion in adults may be due to structural hypothalamic damage such as a tumor, a functional change unassociated with a detectable lesion, or hyperprolactinemia. Structural disease must be excluded in such patients by computed tomography or MRI. Most but not all cases of functional hypogonadotropic hypogonadism occur in women, the most common causes being weight loss, excessive exercise, psychogenic stress, or systemic illness. In some women, the exercise results in a loss of body fat not detected with total body weight measures, and it is unclear whether the hypogonadism is directly due to the loss of body fat or to the exercise per se. Studies of pulsatile gonadotropin secretion in such patients reveal absent pulses. Usually, the gonadotropin response to injected GnRH is normal. Regain of weight and stopping of the exercise result in resumption of normal gonadal function. Hyperprolactinemia occurring postpubertally can also decrease GnRH and the pulsatile secretion of LH and FSH and thereby result in anovulation with oligomenorrhea/amenorrhea in women and impotence and infertility in men.

Therapy should be directed at the underlying process, if possible. Efforts at weight gain and restricting exercise should be made when appropriate. Two goals in the treatment of idiopathic, functional hypogonadotropic amenorrhea are (1) restoration of a normal estrogen status to promote well-being and to prevent osteoporosis and (2) facilitation of ovulation for fertility. The former can generally be achieved with cyclic estrogen and progesterone, whereas the latter may require clomiphene or GnRH or gonadotropin therapy. In men, similar goals may be achieved with testosterone or GnRH or gonadotropins.

Hypothalamic Hypergonadism (Precocious Puberty). Precocious puberty is defined as the onset of puberty before the age of 8 years in girls or 9 years in boys. "Pseudo"-precocious puberty is that resulting from peripheral (gonadal or adrenal) causes. Central, "true," or GnRH-dependent precocious puberty is characterized by hormonal changes similar to those that occur at the time of normal puberty, that is, an increase in the pulsatile release of LH, an increase in the gonadotropin response to GnRH, and an increase in gonadal steroid secretion. GnRH-dependent precocious puberty therefore represents premature activation of this GnRH pulse generator by a variety of lesions, or it may also be idiopathic. Fewer than one quarter of cases of central precocious puberty occur in boys, but they tend to have more serious underlying disease. In boys with central, GnRH-dependent precocious puberty, hypothalamic hamartomas account for 38% of cases, other CNS lesions represent 31%, familial disease accounts for 23%, and idiopathic disease accounts for only 8%. The picture is quite different in girls, however: hypothalamic hamartomas account for only 15% of cases, other CNS lesions represent 14%, the McCune-Albright syndrome (polyostotic fibrous dysplasia) accounts for 6%, and fully 65% are idiopathic. Dysgerminomas in the suprasellar or pineal region can produce chorionic gonadotropin, which acts like LH in its stimulation of gonadal function. Usually such tumors cause increased sex steroid formation but fail to cause ovulation.

Therapy for central GnRH-dependent precocious puberty consists of surgical removal of the tumor or medical therapy with a long-acting GnRH analogue. The latter can suppress gonadotropin and sex steroid hormone levels and cause a stabilization or even regression of secondary sex characteristics and a slowing of growth and bone maturation in most cases. When therapy is discontinued at the normal time of puberty, sex steroid levels increase, secondary sexual characteristics again develop, growth increases, and regular menses develop spontaneously. For patients who do not respond to GnRH analogues, treatment with medroxyprogesterone acetate or testolactone, an aromatase inhibitor, is indicated.

PROLACTIN

Hypothalamic Hyperprolactinemia. Structural or infiltrative lesions of the hypothalamus, such as those discussed earlier, can decrease the amount of dopamine reaching the lactotrophs and thus cause modest hyperprolactinemia. Prolactin elevations resulting from such lesions rarely exceed 150 ng/mL and are usually less than 100 ng/mL. Similar elevations are also seen in patients with the empty-sella syndrome. Because their therapy is quite different, it is very important to differentiate nonsecreting pituitary adenomas with extensive suprasellar extension causing prolactin elevations in this range from prolactin-secreting adenomas, which, when of such a large size, usually cause prolactin elevations 5 to 50 times higher. A number of medications, dopamine in particular, can cause hyperprolactinemia, primarily by interfering with central catecholamines (Table 235–2).

Therapy is generally directed at the underlying cause. The hyperprolactinemia itself may impair gonadal function, so efforts may also be made to lower prolactin levels with dopamine agonists. Prolactin levels usually fall quite readily in such patients. Restoration of gonadal function is not automatic, however, because the primary hypothalamic lesion may also directly impair release of GnRH. In that circumstance, both dopamine agonists and sex steroid replacement may be necessary. When administration of psychotropic medications that cause the hyperprolactinemia cannot be stopped, dopamine agonists may be used but might exacerbate the psychosis. In such cases and in others in which fertility is not an issue, treatment with cyclic estrogen/progestin replacement can be carried out safely.

Idiopathic Hyperprolactinemia. Idiopathic hyperprolactinemia is a diagnosis of exclusion. Prolactin levels in this condition are usually less than 100 ng/mL. In such cases, small pituitary or hypothalamic tumors could exist that are beyond the resolution of current imaging techniques, but when such patients are monitored for many years, it is very uncommon for tumors to later be visualized. Idiopathic hyperprolactinemia can cause amenorrhea, galactorrhea, impotence, infertility, and loss of libido, just as occurs with hyperprolactinemia of other causes, so the idiopathic hyperprolactinemia may need to be treated. Premature osteoporosis related to the estrogen deficiency may also occur. The only possible treatment is dopamine agonists, and these agents are successful in more than 90% of cases. Alternatively, cyclic estrogen/progesterone replacement may be given, but fertility will not be restored.

Table 235–2 • ETIOLOGIES OF HYPERPROLACTINEMIA	
Pituitary Disease	*Other*
Prolactinomas	Pregnancy
Acromegaly	Hypothyroidism
Empty-sella syndrome	Chronic renal failure
Lymphocytic hypophysitis	Cirrhosis
Cushing's disease	Pseudocyesis
Pituitary stalk section	Adrenal insufficiency
Hypothalamic Disease	Idiopathic
Craniopharyngiomas	*Medications*
Meningiomas	Phenothiazines
Dysgerminomas	Haloperidol
Nonsecreting pituitary adenomas	Monoamine oxidase inhibitors
Other tumors	Tricyclic antidepressants
Sarcoidosis	Reserpine
Eosinophilic granuloma	Methyldopa
Neuraxis irradiation	Metoclopramide
Vascular	Amoxapine
Neurogenic	Cocaine
Chest wall lesions	Verapamil
Spinal cord lesions	Fluoxetine
Breast stimulation	Protease inhibitors

Modified from Molitch ME: Disorders of prolactin secretion. Endocrinol Metab Clin North Am 2001;30:585–610.

THYROID-STIMULATING HORMONE. *Hypothalamic hypothyroidism,* also referred to as *tertiary hypothyroidism,* is due to a central lesion that impairs the secretion of TRH, usually along with the loss of other hormones. It occurs considerably less commonly than hypothalamic GH and gonadotropin deficiency. Defects in the gene for TRH have not been detected, but a case has been reported of a TRH receptor mutation causing hypothyroidism. TSH levels in this syndrome are generally normal or even slightly elevated, and the response to TRH is delayed, peaking at 60 to 120 minutes rather than at 20 to 30 minutes. TSH in these patients is biologically less active than normal and binds to the TSH receptor less well because of altered glycosylation as a result of the TRH deficiency. Treatment is with L-thyroxine.

ADRENOCORTICOTROPIC HORMONE. *Hypothalamic ACTH deficiency* caused by hypothalamic lesions is uncommon. It may occur with the loss of other hormones but may also appear as an isolated deficiency. In the absence of CNS lesions or a history of trauma, most cases of isolated ACTH deficiency appear to be a pituitary autoimmune disorder. However, in patients with hypothalamic disease as the cause, basal ACTH levels are low and the ACTH response to injected CRH may be prolonged and exaggerated, much as is the TSH response to TRH. The best test remains a comparison of ACTH responses to hypoglycemia, which is clearly mediated by the hypothalamus, and to CRH. The ACTH response is low in response to hypoglycemia but increased and delayed in response to CRH in most patients with hypothalamic CRH deficiency. Treatment is with glucocorticoids, and mineralocorticoids are not needed.

A transient form of ACTH deficiency may be seen in 10 to 20% of patients with sepsis and possibly other severe illness. Although controlled studies are lacking, treatment with glucocorticoids appears to improve the rate of mortality in those with very low cortisol levels. Upon resolution of the sepsis, the hypothalamic-pituitary-adrenal axis recovers in most patients.

VASOPRESSIN. Diabetes insipidus can develop as a result of destructive lesions in the supraoptic and paraventricular nuclei or in the mediobasal hypothalamus in the path of the neural fibers containing vasopressin (Chapter 238) that are passing on to the posterior pituitary. Irritative lesions can trigger the release of vasopressin in an unregulated fashion and thereby result in the syndrome of inappropriate antidiuretic hormone (vasopressin) secretion.

Effects of Hypothalamic Disease on Other Neurometabolic Functions

A number of functions that affect the internal milieu, in addition to anterior and posterior pituitary function, are regulated, at least in part, by the hypothalamus and include temperature control, behavior, consciousness, memory, sleep, food intake, and carbohydrate metabolism.

ALTERATIONS IN FOOD INTAKE. Body weight is kept relatively constant in nonobese individuals through the integration of a number of factors relating to the intake of nutrients and the output of energy; these functions are also affected by hormonal, environmental, and genetic factors. As with the regulation of hormone secretion, regulation of food intake can be conceptually regarded as an adjustment of food intake and energy expenditure around "set points" that may be different for body weight, total body fat, and lean body mass. The primary regulatory system involves production of the hormone leptin by adipocytes, which binds to hypothalamic leptin receptors and feeds back negatively on food intake and energy expenditure, but a number of other peptides are involved as well (Chapter 233). A number of areas of the hypothalamus are involved in the regulation of energy balance.

Hypothalamic Obesity. Destruction of the mediobasal hypothalamus will sometimes inhibit satiety and may result in hyperphagia and hypothalamic obesity. The hyperphagia is due to destruction of noradrenergic fibers originating in the paraventricular nucleus and passing through the mediobasal hypothalamus. Because of their location, such lesions also usually produce hypopituitarism and diabetes insipidus. In a number of rare syndromes with obesity as a major characteristic, a hypothalamic cause has been postulated. Prader-Willi is the most common of these syndromes and occurs in 1 in 25,000 births. It is characterized by hypotonia, obesity, short stature, mental deficiency, hypogonadism, and small hands and feet. About 70% of patients with Prader-Willi syndrome have a chromosome 15 deletion (15q11-q13) on the paternally derived chromosome.

In the few cases studied at autopsy, no discernible hypothalamic lesions were detected. In the other syndromes (Laurence-Moon-Biedl-Bardet, Alstrom-Hallgren), no specific hypothalamic lesions have been found.

Hypothalamic Anorexia. Lesions of the lateral hypothalamus, which destroy nigrostriatal dopaminergic fibers that pass through this area, produce hypophagia along with an increase in peripheral norepinephrine turnover and metabolic rate. This syndrome is very rare, probably owing to the requirement of bilateral lesions. The hormonal changes that occur in anorexia nervosa appear to all be secondary to the weight loss, and no evidence for a primary hypothalamic disorder in this syndrome has been found.

HYPERGLYCEMIA. Hypothalamic activation as part of the generalized response to stress can cause release of GH, prolactin, and ACTH, which serve as counterregulatory hormones with respect to insulin. These hormones promote lipolysis, gluconeogenesis, and insulin resistance, resulting in glucose elevation. Of more importance in the acute response to stress, this hypothalamic response results in sympathetic activation with release of catecholamines that inhibit insulin secretion and stimulate glycogenolysis. In rare circumstances of acute hypothalamic injury from trauma, stroke, or infection, severe hyperglycemia can occur that is similar to the hyperglycemia seen in animals when the floor of the fourth ventricle is pricked with a needle, a phenomenon referred to as "piqûre" diabetes by Claude Bernard.

TEMPERATURE REGULATION. The anterior hypothalamus and preoptic area contain temperature-sensitive neurons that respond to internal temperature changes by initiating certain thermoregulatory responses necessary to restore a constant temperature. Measures that dissipate heat include cutaneous vasodilation, sweating, panting, and behavioral changes that result in attempts to alter the environment. Measures that increase body heat include increasing metabolic heat production, shivering, cutaneous vasoconstriction, and similar behavioral changes. In humans, much of the increase in metabolic heat production occurs via sympathetic activation. The thermosensitive neurons are affected by endogenous pyrogens and drugs that alter thermoregulation, as well as input from thermoreceptors in the skin and spinal cord.

Rare patients have been reported with anterior hypothalamic lesions that caused sustained hypothermia from failure of heat generation by shivering and vasoconstriction but who had intact heat dissipation or resetting of the temperature set point lower. Paroxysmal hypothermia lasting for minutes to days from the sudden onset of sweating, vasodilation, and a fall in core temperature has been reported in a number of patients in association with demonstrated lesions such as tumors and agenesis of the corpus callosum. Some of these patients had evidence of other hypothalamic dysfunction, including diabetes insipidus, hypogonadism, and precocious puberty.

Fever as a manifestation of hypothalamic disease is uncommon but has been reported in association with trauma or bleeding into the region of the anterior hypothalamus. Such fevers rarely persist more than 2 weeks. Paroxysmal hyperthermia secondary to hypothalamic dysfunction also occurs. Some cases of paroxysmal hypothermia and hyperthermia respond to anticonvulsant medications, which suggests that the neuronal discharge effecting the temperature changes are seizure-like.

Poikilothermy results from an inability to dissipate or generate heat to keep the body temperature constant in the face of varying ambient temperatures. This condition results from bilateral lesions in the posterior hypothalamus and rostral mesencephalon, which are the areas responsible for the final integration of thermoregulatory neural efferents. Patients with this condition do not feel discomfort with temperature changes and are unaware of having a problem. Depending on the ambient temperature, they may experience life-threatening hypothermia or hyperthermia. Poikilothermy is normally present in infants and frequently occurs in elderly individuals.

SUGGESTED READINGS

Beranova M, Oliveira LMB, Bédécarrats GY, et al: Prevalence, phenotypic spectrum, and modes of inheritance of gonadotropin-releasing hormone receptor mutations in idiopathic hypogonadotropic hypogonadism. J Clin Endocrinol Metab 2001;86:1580–1588. *This series of patients shows that new molecular approaches to diagnosis can document the precise mutation in the GnRH receptor causing hypogonadotropic hypogonadism.*

Buller KM: Neuroimmune responses: Reciprocal connections between the hypothalamus and the brainstem. Stress 2003;6:11–17. *Brainstem pathways seem to be important.*

De Kretzer DM, Meinhardt A, Methan T, et al: The roles of inhibin and related peptides in gonadal function. Mol Cell Endocrinol 2000;161:43–46. *A review of inhibin, activin, and follistatin and their interactions in the hypothalamic-pituitary-gonadal axis.*

Habib KE, Gold PW, Chrousos GP: Neuroendocrinology of stress. Endocrinol Metab Clin North Am 2001;30:695–728. *Review of the various interactions between the hypothalamic-pituitary-adrenal axis, stress, and the immune system, including possible therapeutic consequences.*

Kaltsas GA, Powles TB, Evanson J, et al: Hypothalamo-pituitary abnormalities in adult patients with Langerhans cell histiocytosis: Clinical, endocrinological, and radiological features, and response to treatment. J Clin Endocrinol Metab 2000; 85:1370–1376. *This is a report of a series of patients with this infiltrative disorder, with emphasis on its clinical features and treatment.*

Molitch ME: Disorders of prolactin secretion. Endocrinol Metab Clin North Am 2001;30:585–610. *This review covers current knowledge of the regulation of prolactin secretion, various causes of hyperprolactinemia, and the therapeutic options available.*

Mong JA, Krebs C, Pfaff DW: Perspective: Micoarrays and differential display PCR—tools for studying transcript levels of genes in neuroendocrine systems. Endocrinology 2002;143:2002–2006. *Describes the potential power of micoarray technology.*

Warren MP, Fried JL: Hypothalamic amenorrhea: The effects of environmental stresses on the reproductive system—a central effect on the central nervous system. Endocrinol Metab Clin North Am 2001;30:611–629. *This article reviews the various reversible causes of hypothalamic amenorrhea, such as weight loss, intensive physical training, and stress.*

236 CHRONOBIOLOGY (CIRCADIAN RHYTHMS)

Steven M. Reppert

The activities of most physiologic systems, including higher brain function, vary predictably over the 24-hour day and are regulated by a genetically determined circadian clock. Daily rest–activity, sleep–wake, and hunger–satiety cycles are the most overt manifestations of this endogenous clock. The pervasive nature of circadian rhythms means that these variations need to be considered for proper interpretation of diagnostic variables (e.g., daily variations in hormone levels and body temperature). Moreover, knowing the time of day when diseases are most likely to occur helps the clinician anticipate times of increased susceptibility. For example, cardiac output and blood pressure rise rapidly during morning hours, such that acute myocardial infarction, ventricular arrhythmia, and stroke are most frequent at these times. It is also worth emphasizing that physicians and nurses are subject to circadian variations in alertness and performance, and thus hospital staffing practices should take these fluctuations into consideration. Finally, several drugs show circadian rhythms in therapeutic efficacy, such as cancer chemotherapy agents and anesthetics. Understanding these variations has important implications for providing more effective drug treatment schedules.

Anatomical and Molecular Organization

Conceptually, it is useful to divide the circadian timing system into its three components: (1) the clock itself, (2) inputs that synchronize ("entrain") the clock to the environment, and (3) outputs from the clock manifested as time-of-day changes in physiology and behavior (Fig. 236–1). In mammals, the site of the master circadian clock is the suprachiasmatic nuclei (SCN) of the anterior hypothalamus. Light is the dominant environmental stimulus that entrains the circadian clock to the 24-hour day. Photic signals sensed by the retina are communicated to the SCN primarily via the monosynaptic retinohypothalamic tract (RHT). Outputs from the SCN ultimately drive slave oscillators in other brain areas and in peripheral tissues, leading to circadian rhythms in physiology and behavior.

Based on studies in mice, much is known about the molecular organization of the circadian clock. The intracellular 24-hour oscillation is due to the recurrent interactions of clock genes and their protein products (Fig. 236–2). At the beginning of the day, two transcription factors, CLOCK and BMAL1 pair up to drive the expression of the *Period* (*Per1, 2,* and *3*) and *Cryptochrome* (*Cry1* and *2*) genes. In the evening, PER and CRY proteins form PER:CRY complexes necessary for their nuclear translocation. Once in the nucleus, the CRY proteins shut down CLOCK:BMAL1–mediated transcription, while, at the same time, the transcription of *Bmal1* is activated. Increasing BMAL1 then interacts with CLOCK to restart the cycle. Post-translational mechanisms, such as phosphorylation and proteolysis, are important for building appropriate time delays into the molecular oscillations. The molecular machinery of the clock drives SCN neuronal activity, ultimately regulating the output rhythms. Light is thought to entrain the molecular clock by altering the expression of the *Per1* and *Per2* genes.

Circadian Disorders

Because the circadian system regulates the timing of the sleep-wake cycle, and the sleep-wake cycle can, in turn, influence the circadian system, it is often difficult to discern primary circadian disorders from those that disrupt normal sleep patterns or are heightened by sleep state. Examples of such conditions include nighttime epileptic seizures, nocturnal wanderings in Alzheimer's patients, and sleep ailments such as apnea and narcolepsy (Chapter 438). For psychiatric disorders such as depression, seasonal affective disorder, and bipolar illnesses, a role of an altered circadian system in their etiology has been difficult to establish.

INPUT DISORDERS. These conditions can be due to disruption of the input pathway. Blindness caused by retinal destruction is the clearest example of this type of disorder. In these individuals, light is unable to synchronize the circadian pacemaker, but the clock continues to run with its intrinsic period length (slightly longer than 24 hours), unconstrained by the environment. Impairment can result in cyclic insomnia and periodic symptoms similar to jet lag (see later discussion). Some blind individuals whose defects originate in thalamic or cortical brain regions exhibit no symptoms and entrain normally to environmental light-dark cycles, because the RHT is intact.

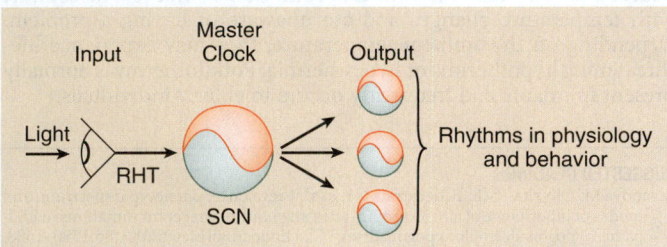

FIGURE 236–1 • Organization of the circadian timing system. Light signals that reset the circadian clock are transduced by retinal photoreceptors and then transmitted to the suprachiasmatic nuclei (SCN) via the retinohypothalamic tract (RHT). Outputs from the SCN ultimately regulate local slave oscillators, giving rise to circadian rhythms in physiology and behavior.

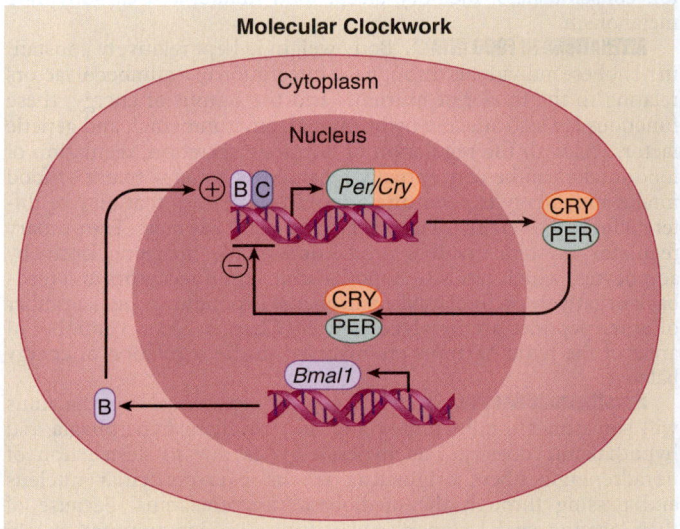

FIGURE 236–2 • The molecular basis of circadian timing. The molecular clock starts with oscillations in *Cryptochrome* (*Cry*) and *Period* (*Per*) gene expression that are driven by the action of CLOCK (C) and BMAL1 (B) heterodimers (+). As CRY and PER proteins accumulate in the cytoplasm, they pair and move to the nucleus, where CRY exerts a negative influence on CLOCK:BMAL1–mediated transcription (–). Increasing BMAL1 levels eventually restart the next clock cycle.

Input disorders can also arise from abnormal perturbations in environmental time. The most well known example is jet lag, which occurs when traveling across three or more time zones. Symptoms include sleep disruption, fatigue, gastrointestinal distress, reduced cognitive skills, and mood alterations. After a few days of adjustment, circadian rhythms resynchronize to the new time zone and symptoms subside. It is not surprising that symptoms associated with night shifts in shift workers (which comprise approximately 25% of the work force) are similar to those of jet lag, the most pronounced being impaired sleep. Standard lighting conditions in the workplace are not sufficient to entrain the circadian pacemaker, leading to chronic symptoms.

CLOCK DISORDERS. Tumors and degenerative lesions that damage the SCN are associated with disrupted circadian rhythms. Sleep preference varies from morning to evening types, and this polygenic variation may be caused by clock gene polymorphisms. At the extremes of morningness and eveningness are people with advanced sleep-phase syndrome (ASPS) and delayed sleep-phase syndrome (DSPS), respectively. These individuals have recalcitrant sleep-wake times, resulting in difficulty adjusting to school and work schedules. The clearest example of a genetic disorder of the SCN clock involves a familial form of ASPS. Genomic linkage analysis has mapped the autosomal dominant condition in one pedigree to a mutation in the *Per2* gene, altering its function in the clockwork.

℞ Treatment

Bright light strategically administered is an effective treatment for the disruption of circadian function occurring in jet lag and shift work, and for adjusting sleep times in some individuals with ASPS and DSPS. Light regimens, however, are not always practical and are not useful for treating circadian disturbances in the blind. Hypnotics such as the benzodiazepines alleviate acute insomnia but their use for treating circadian disorders should be discouraged, as they have substantial side effects. The pineal hormone melatonin has mild hypnotic properties, modestly phase shifts circadian rhythms, and has a minimum of side effects (at least with short-term use). Indeed, melatonin is quite efficacious for treating jet lag and in synchronizing rhythms in some blind people. As our knowledge of the molecular basis of the circadian clock grows, new therapies directed at correcting or rapidly altering circadian timing should emerge.

SUGGESTED READINGS

Cermakian N, Boivin DB: A molecular perspective of human circadian rhythm disorders. Brain Res Brain Res Rev 2003;42:204–220. *Reviews the clock genes and how they influence circadian function.*

Dijk D-J, Lockley SW: Integration of human sleep-wake regulation and circadian rhythmicity. J Appl Physiol 2002;92:852–862. *Review of the relationship between the human sleep-wake cycle and circadian rhythmicity.*

Wijnen H, Boothroyd C, Young MW: Molecular genetics of timing in intrinsic circadian rhythm sleep disorders. Ann Med 2002;34:386–393. *Reviews the key genes and the way they influence sleep/wake behavior.*

237 ANTERIOR PITUITARY

Mark E. Molitch

ANATOMY AND EMBRYOLOGY

The pituitary is a relatively small gland that is located in the sella turcica at the base of the brain. It has a bilobed shape and weighs about 0.6 g (range, 0.4 to 0.9 g), being somewhat larger in women than in men. The pituitary is divided into anterior and posterior lobes, with the anterior lobe accounting for about 80% of the gland. The posterior pituitary, or neurohypophysis, consists of the pituitary stalk as well as the posterior lobe (Chapter 238). Superiorly, the pituitary is covered by the diaphragma sellae, a reflection of the dura mater that forms the roof of the sella and is attached to the clinoid processes. The diaphragma sellae has a central opening that is penetrated by the pituitary stalk and its blood vessels. Importantly, the optic chiasm, formed by the decussation of the optic nerves, is positioned directly above the pituitary gland and below the third ventricle. The exact position of the chiasm is variable, affecting the pattern of visual field changes experienced by patients with pituitary tumors that expand into the suprasellar region. The lateral boundaries of the sella are formed by the cavernous sinuses, which contain the internal carotid artery and cranial nerves III, IV, V_1, V_2, and VI.

The blood supply to the pituitary gland is derived from the superior and inferior hypophyseal arteries, branches of the internal carotid arteries. Specialized vascular structures, referred to as gomitoli, are located in the median eminence of the hypothalamus and consist of short terminal arterioles that drain into portal veins that course down the pituitary stalk to join the sinusoidal capillaries of the anterior lobe. Hypothalamic hormones enter fenestrations in the perigomitolar capillaries to flow from the hypothalamus to the anterior pituitary. Venous drainage from the anterior lobe enters the posterior pituitary capillary bed before draining into the cavernous sinuses. The cavernous sinuses are interconnected by means of channels that encircle the pituitary, and they drain into the petrosal sinuses. The petrosal sinuses can be catheterized for hormone sampling in the diagnosis of adrenocorticotropic hormone (ACTH)–secreting pituitary tumors.

The six major pituitary cell types include somatotrophs (growth hormone [GH] producing), lactotrophs (prolactin [PRL] producing), corticotrophs (ACTH producing), thyrotrophs (thyroid-stimulating hormone [TSH] producing), gonadotrophs (follicle-stimulating hormone [FSH] and luteinizing hormone [LH] producing), and folliculostellate cells that do not produce the classic pituitary hormones but may have paracrine functions. The biochemical characteristics of the major anterior pituitary hormones are summarized in Table 237–1.

The pituitary is formed early in embryonic life from the fusion of Rathke's pouch (which gives rise to the anterior pituitary) and a portion of the ventral diencephalon (which gives rise to the posterior pituitary). Rathke's pouch is an ectodermal evagination in the roof of the primitive oropharynx. There is some evidence, however, that the anterior pituitary may develop from a more rostral neuroectoderm fold rather than this ectodermal tissue. The ontogeny of hormone production during anterior pituitary development has been charac-

Table 237–1 • FEATURES OF THE MAJOR ANTERIOR PITUITARY HORMONES*

HORMONE	AMINO ACIDS	MW (kD)	SERUM HALF-LIFE (min)	CELL TYPE	TARGET GLAND
Growth hormone (GH)	191	22	20	Somatotroph	Multiple
Prolactin (PRL)	198	23	20	Lactotroph	Breast
Adrenocorticotropic hormone (ACTH)	39	4.5	8	Corticotroph	Adrenal
Thyroid-stimulating hormone (TSH)	α-subunit, 92	14	50	Thyrotroph	Thyroid
	β-subunit, 118	17			
Luteinizing hormone (LH)	α-subunit, 92	14	50	Gonadotroph	Gonad
	β-subunit, 121	18			
Follicle-stimulating hormone (FSH)	α-subunit, 92	14	220	Gonadotroph	Gonad
	β-subunit, 111	18			

*The amino acid lengths are based on the cloned complementary DNAs and differ in some cases from the lengths of the sequenced proteins, perhaps because of proteolysis. The indicated molecular weights (MW) include the contributions of the carbohydrates in the case of the glycoprotein hormones (TSH, LH, FSH). The serum half-lives assume single compartment monoexponential decay.

Endocrine Diseases

terized in detail. The pituitary anlage expresses the glycoprotein hormone α gene even as the progenitor cells are arising from Rathke's pouch. Subsequently, proopiomelanocortin (POMC)-producing cells can be seen in the hypothalamus and in the pituitary. An evanescent group of TSH-producing cells appear, but then fade away, to be followed later by a distinct population of TSH cells in a different location in the pituitary. After gonadotrophs develop, GH- and PRL-producing cells appear and later form distinct populations of somatotrophs and lactotrophs. Several homeodomain transcription factors are important in the development of the various types of pituitary cells. Lhx3 is present in somatotrophs, lactotrophs, and thyrotrophs, and mutations in this gene result in complete deficits of GH, PRL, TSH, and the gonadotropins along with a rigid cervical spine. The transcription factor Pit-1, a member of the Pou-Homeodomain family, is produced in somatotrophs, lactotrophs, and thyrotrophs. Mutations in Pit-1 prevent the development of these cells and cause deficiencies of GH, PRL, and TSH. This lineage relationship probably accounts for the observation that some GH-producing tumors also secrete PRL and about one third of TSH-producing tumors co-secrete GH. Prop-1 is another transcription factor critical for the development of somatotrophs, lactotrophs, and thyrotrophs that may in addition be important for gonadotroph differentiation. Mutations in Prop-1 result in deficiencies of GH, PRL, and TSH and in some affected individuals there is delayed puberty. Combined pituitary hormone deficiency (GH, PRL, TSH) has an incidence of about 1 in 8000 births, and about 10% have an affected relative; it appears that more than half of these cases are due to Pit-1 or Prop-1 deficiencies.

Anterior pituitary hormone production is largely established by the ninth week of gestation, and the anatomic and biosynthetic mechanisms that constitute an active hypothalamic-pituitary system appear to be functional by 12 to 17 weeks of gestation. In cases of anencephaly, all anterior pituitary cell types, with the exception of corticotrophs, are capable of hormone synthesis and secretion, indicating that the embryonic pituitary develops relatively normally in the absence of hypothalamic stimulation.

Somatotrophs, which constitute 40 to 50% of anterior pituitary cells, and lactotrophs, which make up 15 to 25%, are located predominantly in the lateral aspects of the anterior pituitary. Corticotrophs constitute 10 to 20% of anterior pituitary cells and are located mainly in the central region of the anterior pituitary. Gonadotrophs, which account for about 10% of pituitary cells, produce both FSH and LH, although a small fraction of gonadotrophs appear to selectively secrete only one of the hormones. Only 5% of pituitary cells are thyrotrophs. The folliculostellate cells have long irregular processes that extend between the hormone-producing cells. They do not contain secretory granules but have been shown to produce growth factors such as basic fibroblast growth factor, vascular endothelial growth factor, and follistatin, among others.

RADIOLOGY OF THE PITUITARY

Radiologic imaging of the pituitary gland primarily involves computed tomography (CT) and magnetic resonance imaging (MRI). CT scans are performed using high-resolution (1.5 mm), contrast-enhanced procedures with direct coronal sections. Although CT provides excellent resolution, problems include artifacts from metallic objects and dental fillings, and some patients have difficulty assuming the position required for coronal sections. Pituitary adenomas are hypodense on both unenhanced and contrast-enhanced CT scans.

Overall, MRI is the technique of choice for evaluating the sellar region. MRI provides multiplanar imaging and excellent resolution of the pituitary and surrounding cerebrospinal fluid and vascular and central nervous system structures. There is less radiation exposure with MRI than with CT, allowing repeated imaging as required for evaluation and follow-up. However, bone structures are not well defined by MRI. The normal anterior pituitary appears isointense with brain white matter, whereas the posterior pituitary exhibits high signal intensity. The optic chiasm can be readily identified superior to the pituitary gland because it is surrounded by hypodense structures. MRI detects pituitary microadenomas in nearly all patients with surgically proven tumors. Pituitary adenomas typically appear hypointense on T1-weighted images and show less enhancement with gadolinium than surrounding normal tissue. Focal hypodense areas are also seen in about one fourth of normal individuals, which may correspond to cysts or small adenomas that have been described in autopsy series,

emphasizing the importance of endocrine evaluation in making the diagnosis of pituitary tumors.

REGULATION OF THE PITUITARY AXIS

The concept of positive and negative feedback control represents a fundamental tenet of endocrinology. The pituitary gland integrates the influences of an array of positive and negative signals to modulate hormone secretion within a narrow range (Table 237–2). The major hypothalamic-pituitary-target gland axes include the thyrotropin-releasing hormone (TRH)–TSH-thyroid hormone axis; corticotropin-releasing hormone (CRH)–ACTH-cortisol axis; gonadotropin-releasing hormone (GnRH)–LH/FSH-gonadal axis; and GH-releasing hormone (GHRH)–GH–insulin-like growth factor (IGF)-1 axis. PRL is the only major pituitary hormone that is not subject to feedback inhibition by hormones produced in target tissues. However, it is controlled by positive and negative input from the hypothalamus.

The principles of feedback regulation are well illustrated by the hypothalamic-pituitary-thyroid axis. Hypothalamic TRH stimulates TSH secretion from the pituitary. TSH increases thyroid hormone secretion, which in turn suppresses hypothalamic TRH as well as pituitary TSH. A typical regulatory loop therefore has both positive (TRH, TSH) and negative (thyroxine [T_4], triiodothyronine [T_3]) components, allowing a high degree of control of hormone levels. In this case, the pituitary gland integrates positive TRH signals and the negative effects of thyroid hormone. The concept of feedback regulation is important not only for understanding pituitary physiology but also because it provides the basis for analyzing pituitary gland function using stimulation and suppression tests.

The feedback regulatory systems just described are superimposed on hormonal rhythms that are used for adaptation to the environment. Seasonal changes, the daily occurrence of the light-dark cycles, and stress are but a few of many environmental events that have major impacts on the secretion of pituitary hormones. Some hormonal pathways, such as ACTH, GH, and PRL secretion, are entrained to the sleep-wake cycle, causing characteristic peaks of ACTH and cortisol production in the early morning with a nadir in the late afternoon and evening. The early pubertal surges of LH occur at night and usually in association with sleep. The menstrual cycle provides an example of a pituitary rhythm that occurs on a much longer time scale (approximately 28 days). The pattern of the menstrual cycle is coupled to cycles of follicular development in the ovary. As follicular development progresses, levels of gonadal steroids and inhibin feed back on the hypothalamus and pituitary to modulate LH and FSH secretion.

Because many hormones are released in a pulsatile manner and in a rhythmic fashion, it is important to be aware of these characteristics of secretion when attempting to relate serum measurements to normal values. Although it is possible to characterize pulsatile patterns of hormone secretion using frequent blood sampling (every 10 minutes) over several hours, this is not practical in a clinical setting. Alternative approaches include stimulation and suppression tests or the use of "integrated" measurements of hormone production such

Table 237–2 • FACTORS THAT REGULATE PITUITARY HORMONE SECRETION

HORMONE	RELEASING FACTORS	INHIBITING FACTORS
Growth hormone	GHRH	Somatostatin, IGF-1
Prolactin	TRH, VIP, E_2	Dopamine
Adrenocorticotropic hormone	CRH, vasopressin	Cortisol
Thyroid-stimulating hormone	TRH	T_4, T_3, somatostatin, dopamine
Luteinizing hormone	GnRH	E_2, testosterone
Follicle-stimulating hormone	GnRH, activin	Inhibin, E_2, testosterone

CRH = corticotropin-releasing hormone; E_2 = estradiol; GHRH = growth hormone-releasing hormone; IGF-1 = insulin-like growth factor-1 (formerly called somatomedin C); T_4 = thyroxine; T_3 = triiodothyronine; TRH = thyrotropin-releasing hormone; VIP = vasoactive intestinal peptide. The gonadal steroids E_2 and testosterone exert much of their inhibitory effects on gonadotropin secretion at the hypothalamic level.

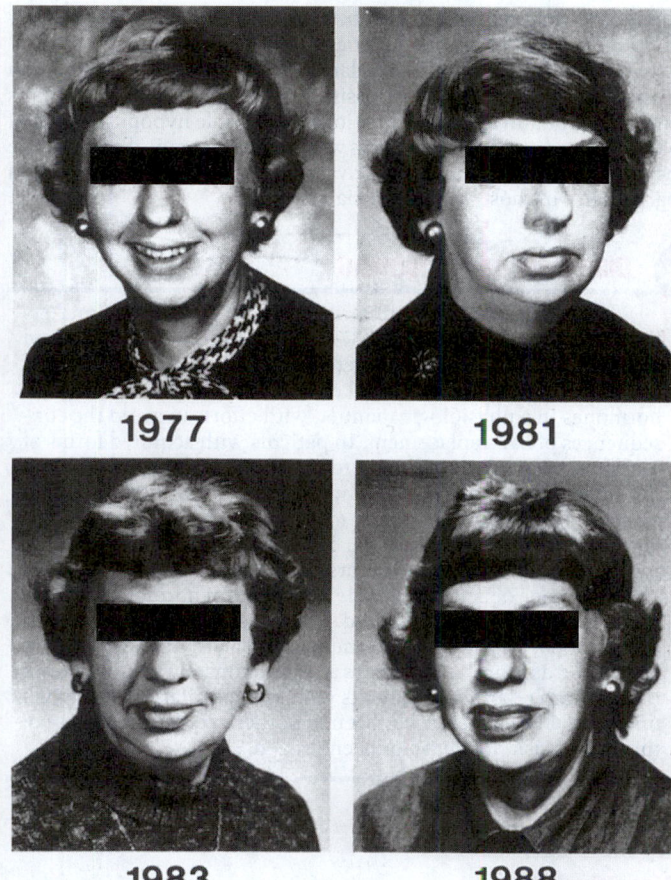

1977 **1981**

1983 **1988**

FIGURE 237–1 • Clinical features of acromegaly. Serial photographs of a 64-year-old woman with acromegaly. Over an 11-year period, there is a progressive coarsening of facial features, including enlargement of the nose and lips and development of prognathism. She also experienced hypertension, arthropathy, and enlargement of the hands (not shown). (From Molitch ME: Clinical manifestations of acromegaly. Endocrinol Metab Clin North Am 1992;21:597–614.)

as 24-hour urine free cortisol as an index of ACTH secretion or IGF-1 as a biologic marker of GH action.

HYPOPITUITARISM

Hypopituitarism implies diminished production of one or more anterior pituitary hormones. Although the recognition of complete or panhypopituitarism is usually straightforward, the detection of partial or selective hormone deficiencies is more challenging. Pituitary hormone deficiencies can be caused by loss of hypothalamic stimulation (tertiary hormone deficiency) or by direct loss of pituitary function (secondary hormone deficiency). The distinction between hypothalamic and pituitary causes of hypopituitarism is important for establishing the correct diagnosis and for applying and interpreting the relevant diagnostic endocrine tests. With improved procedures for testing the hypothalamic-pituitary axis, it is apparent that hypothalamic causes of hypopituitarism are more common than previously appreciated (Chapter 235). When hypopituitarism is accompanied by diabetes insipidus or hyperprolactinemia, one should particularly consider hypothalamic causes of pituitary dysfunction.

Causes of Hypopituitarism

A variety of congenital and acquired causes of hypopituitarism have been described (Table 237–3). Sporadic and familial forms of panhypopituitarism occur, but the underlying genetic or developmental defects have not been elucidated. Congenital combined deficiencies of GH, PRL, and TSH are caused by mutations in the gene encoding Pit-1, a pituitary-specific transcription factor that is involved in the development of somatotroph, lactotroph, and thyrotroph cell

Table 237–3 • CAUSES OF HYPOPITUITARISM

GENETIC DEFECTS
Hypophysiotropic hormone gene defects
Hypophysiotropic hormone receptor gene defects
  GHRH receptor defect
  GnRH receptor defect
  TRH receptor defect
Pituitary hormone gene defects
  Gonadotropins: LH β- and FHS β-subunit gene defects
  Growth hormone: defects in GH gene
  Thyrotropin: defects in TSH β-subunit
  Multiple hormone (GH, PRL, TSH) defects: due to mutation in *Pit-1* gene and *Propl* gene
Pituitary hormone receptor genetic defects
  Growth hormone receptor defects: GH insensitivity syndrome (Laron-type dwarfisin)
  ACTH receptor defects: congenital insensitivity to ACTH
  LH receptor defects
  FSH receptor defects
  TSH receptor defects

CONGENITAL EMBRYOPATHIC DEFECTS
Anencephaly
Midline cleft defects: septo-optic dysplasia, basal encephalocele, cleft lip and palate
Pituitary aplasia
Kallmann's syndrome (GnRH defect with anosmia)

ACQUIRED DEFECTS
Tumors: pituitary adenomas, craniopharyngiomas, dysgerminomas, meningiomas, gliomas, metastatic tumors, hamartomas, Rathke's cleft cysts
Irradiation
Trauma: surgery, external blunt trauma
Empty sella syndrome
Vascular
  Pituitary apoplexy
  Sheehan's syndrome
  Internal carotid aneurysm
  Vasculitis
Inflammatory/infiltrative diseases
  Sarcoidosis
  Langerhans' cell histiocytosis (histiocytosis X, eosinophilic granuloma)
  Tuberculosis, syphilis
  Meningitis
  Lymphocytic hypophysitis, infundibulohypophysitis
Metabolic
  Hemochromatosis
  Amyloidosis
  Critical illness
  Malnutrition
  Anorexia nervosa
  Psychosocial deprivation
Idiopathic

ACTH = adrenocorticotropic hormone; FSH = follicle-stimulating hormone; GH = growth hormone; GHRH = growth hormone releasing hormone; GnRH = gonadotropin-releasing hormone; LH = luteinizing hormone; PRL = prolactin; TRH = thyrotropin-releasing hormone; TSH = thyroid-stimulating hormone.

lineages. Different types of Pit-1 mutations are inherited in an autosomal dominant or recessive pattern. When gonadotrophs are also deficient, mutations may be present in transcription factors that are active earlier in the development of the pituitary lineages, such as Lhx3 and Prop-1. Gene mutations have been found at several steps leading to pituitary hormone secretion, including mutations in the hypophysiotropic releasing factor receptors for GnRH, GHRH, and TRH; mutations in the pituitary hormone structural genes for GH, ACTH, and the β subunits of FSH, TSH, and LH; and mutations in the target organ receptors for GH, ACTH, TSH, and LH. Best studied are mutations of the GH gene, and these have proved to be heterogeneous. Some include large deletions of the GH gene that are inherited in an autosomal recessive manner and involve genetic recombination between related DNA sequences in the duplicated GH gene cluster. Point mutations have also been described in the GH gene, and some of these can be inherited in an autosomal dominant manner, apparently because the mutant hormone impairs GH biosynthesis and normal function of the somatotroph cell. Mutations of the other types described earlier generally cause autosomal recessive forms of selective hormone deficiencies. The congenital embryopathic disorders causing hypopituitarism are discussed in Chapter 235.

Neoplastic lesions, particularly pituitary adenomas, are the most common cause of acquired hypopituitarism. Pituitary adenomas cause hypopituitarism in several different ways. In some cases, there is direct destruction or compression of the normal pituitary. Compression of the pituitary stalk can impair blood supply to the pituitary as well as decrease input from hypothalamic hormones. Hemorrhage into tumors can lead to pituitary infarction. When tested carefully, most patients with macroadenomas have partial deficiencies of one or more pituitary hormones, most often involving GH and gonadotropins. A mild degree of hyperprolactinemia is characteristic of disorders that cause stalk compression, and hyperprolactinemia further impairs gonadotropin secretion. A variety of other neoplasms that occur near the sella, such as craniopharyngiomas, can also cause hypopituitarism (see Table 237–3).

Radiation causes hypopituitarism primarily because of its effects on hypothalamic function, although high-dose radiation (e.g., proton beam) can also cause direct pituitary damage. The sellar region is subjected to radiation in the treatment of pituitary adenomas, craniopharyngiomas, clivus chordomas, optic gliomas, meningiomas, dysgerminomas, and neoplasms of the oropharynx. Importantly, the effects of radiation can be delayed as much as several years, and patients at high risk should be evaluated at about yearly intervals for radiation-induced hypopituitarism. Although GH and gonadotropin deficiencies develop first in most patients, ACTH or TSH deficiencies occasionally occur first, emphasizing the need to evaluate each of the major axes.

Empty sella syndrome can occur as a primary or as an acquired condition. It is caused by defects in the diaphragma sellae that allow herniation of the arachnoid membrane into the hypophyseal fossa. In long-standing cases, sellar enlargement occurs, probably because of persistent transmission of intracranial pressure. With appropriate imaging studies, the pituitary gland can be seen as a flattened rim of tissue along the floor of the sella. Primary empty sella occurs most commonly in women and may be associated with features of benign intracranial hypertension. Pituitary function in patients with primary empty sella syndrome is usually normal, although 15% have mild hyperprolactinemia, probably because of stretching of the pituitary stalk. Acquired forms may occur as a result of surgery, radiation, or pituitary infarction (usually of an adenoma).

Pituitary apoplexy is usually caused by hemorrhage into a tumor with associated infarction. In the absence of a tumor, predispositions to apoplexy include trauma, pregnancy, anticoagulation, sickle cell anemia, and diabetes mellitus. Pituitary infarction in the peripartum period is referred to as Sheehan's syndrome and is usually associated with significant obstetric hemorrhage and hypovolemia. Although Sheehan's syndrome may manifest acutely with vascular collapse, it more commonly has a subacute manifestation consisting of postpartum inability to lactate, amenorrhea, and symptoms of adrenal insufficiency. Sheehan's syndrome is now infrequent, owing to improvements in obstetric care.

Infiltrative diseases such as sarcoidosis, histiocytosis, and tuberculosis usually cause hypopituitarism by infiltrating the hypothalamus and stalk rather than the pituitary and are discussed in Chapter 235. In lymphocytic hypophysitis, there is massive infiltration of the pituitary by lymphocytes and plasma cells with destruction of the parenchyma; it is believed to have an autoimmune basis. The lesion that develops is usually large, and patients present with either symptoms or signs of hypopituitarism or those of a mass lesion (i.e., visual field defects and/or headaches). Some patients may have mild hyperprolactinemia and diabetes insipidus. Almost all cases have been reported in women, and most present during or after pregnancy. Because of the presentation as a mass lesion during pregnancy, such lesions may be confused with prolactinomas, but the mild PRL elevation points to a nonsecretory lesion rather than a prolactinoma. MRI cannot reliably differentiate pituitary adenoma from hypophysitis, although hypophysitis usually manifests with a diffuse enlargement of the pituitary that enhances, rather than as a focal lesion. Diagnosis is usually made by biopsy, but the lesion may be suspected clinically if it manifests during or just after pregnancy. Careful pituitary function testing is mandatory, because many of the patients in the reported cases went undiagnosed and died of adrenocortical insufficiency. Although the prognosis is not clear, a number of cases have resolved spontaneously. An entity with similar histologic findings involving the stalk and posterior pituitary, referred to as *infundibu-* *loneurohypophysitis*, can cause diabetes insipidus. The causes and interrelationships between these entities remain unknown.

The pituitary may undergo damage because of iron deposition in patients with hemochromatosis and amyloid fibrils in patients with systemic amyloidosis. Functional, reversible hypopituitarism of varying degrees occurs in patients with severe systemic illness, severe psychosocial and emotional deprivation, and severe weight loss, and particularly in those with anorexia nervosa.

Rx Diagnosis and Treatment

The diagnosis of hypopituitarism rests on the stimulation tests that are summarized in Table 237–4. Therapy for hypopituitarism depends on the nature and severity of the hormone deficiencies as well as on the desired clinical endpoints. The goal is to replace hormones in a physiologic manner, with efforts to avoid the consequences of overreplacement. In patients with acquired forms of hypopituitarism (e.g., pituitary tumors, radiation treatment), it is not uncommon to encounter a mixture of partial hormone deficiencies. It is generally prudent to provide hormone replacement if partial deficiency is suspected, because patients may experience symptoms over a number of years before an unequivocal diagnosis of hormone deficiency is made. Examples of hormonal replacement paradigms are provided in Table 237–5. Even when conventional hormone replacement (adrenal, thyroid, gonadal) is carried out appropriately, there is an approximately twofold excess risk of death reported in patients with hypopituitarism. Although untreated GH deficiency has been hypothesized to be the cause of this excess risk, this has not been proven.

PITUITARY TUMORS

Classification

Pituitary tumors are classified according to the hormones that they produce and their size: microadenomas, less than 10 mm in diameter; macroadenomas, more than 10 mm in diameter; and macroadenomas with extrasellar extension. In general, the levels of hormones produced by the tumors parallel the size of the tumors, although exceptions occur. The approximate prevalence of the different types of pituitary adenomas, based on surgical data, is summarized in Table 237–6. Immunohistochemical studies, using antibodies specific for each of the major pituitary hormones, have been used to define tumor phenotype. Electron microscopy can provide additional ultrastructural information but is not employed routinely. Pituitary adenomas are very rarely malignant but can be locally invasive.

Theories of Pituitary Tumorigenesis

A long-standing controversy exists concerning the pathogenesis of pituitary tumors. Monoclonal tumors arise from a single progenitor cell, presumably because of a somatic mutation to create an oncogene or to inactivate a tumor suppressor gene. Polyclonal tumors, on the other hand, reflect hyperplasia caused by exogenous stimulation of a group of cells by a growth factor or hypothalamic releasing hormone. By using recombinant DNA techniques to track X-chromosome inactivation as an index of cell lineage, it has been shown that the vast majority of pituitary tumors are monoclonal. This finding does not exclude a role for hormonal stimulation as a predisposing factor for somatic mutations, and the hormonal environment may also affect the rate of tumor growth (e.g., Nelson's syndrome).

Supporting the concept that somatic mutations lead to pituitary tumorigenesis, a subset (35 to 40%) of somatotroph adenomas have mutations in two different amino acids (Arg201 and Glu227) that result in activation of the Gsα-subunit. Either mutation prevents hydrolysis of guanosine triphosphate, causing the Gsα-subunit to stimulate adenylyl cyclase in a constitutive manner. The elevated intracellular cyclic adenosine monophosphate (AMP) levels lead to increased cell growth as well as GH production. Mutations in other oncogenes, such as *ras*, *Rb*, and *p53* are uncommon in pituitary tumors. Thus, the nature of the somatic defects in most pituitary tumors remains unknown.

Two types of inherited predispositions to pituitary tumors are recognized. Patients with McCune-Albright syndrome occasionally develop pituitary adenomas as well as characteristic abnormalities in

Table 237–4 • TESTS OF PITUITARY INSUFFICIENCY

HORMONE	TEST	INTERPRETATION
Growth hormone (GH)	*Insulin tolerance test:* Regular insulin (0.05–0.15 U/kg) is given IV and blood is drawn at −30, 0, 30, 45, 60, and 90 min for measurement of glucose and GH.	If hypoglycemia occurs (glucose <40 mg/dL), GH should increase to >5 µg/L.*
	L-Dopa test: 10 mg/kg PO with GH measurements at 0, 30, 60, and 120 min	Normal response is GH >5 µg/L
	L-Arginine test: 0.5 g/kg (max. 30 g) IV over 30 min with GH measurements at 0, 30, 60, and 120 min.	Normal response is GH >5 µg/L
Adrenocorticotropic hormone (ACTH)	*Insulin tolerance test:* Regular insulin (0.05-0.15 U/kg) is given IV and blood is drawn at −30, 0, 30, 45, 60, and 90 min for measurement of glucose and cortisol.	If hypoglycemia occurs (glucose <40 mg/dL), cortisol should increase by >7 µg/dL or to >20 µg/dL.
	CRH test: 1 µg/kg ovine CRH IV at 8 AM with blood samples drawn at 0, 15, 30, 60, 90, 120 min for measurement of ACTH and cortisol	In most normals, the basal ACTH increases twofold to fourfold and reaches a peak (20-100 pg/mL). ACTH responses may be delayed in cases of hypothalamic dysfunction. Cortisol levels usually reach 20-25 µg/dL.
	Metyrapone test: Metyrapone (30 mg/kg–max. 2 g) at midnight with measurements of plasma 11-deoxycortisol and cortisol at 8 AM. ACTH can also be measured. A 3-day test is also available. Basal cortisol should be >5–6 µg/dL before test.	A normal response is 11-deoxycortisol >7.5 µg/dL or ACTH >75 pg/mL. Plasma cortisol should fall below 4 µg/dL to ensure an adequate response.
	ACTH stimulation test: ACTH 1-24 (Cosyntropin), 0.25 mg IM or IV. Cortisol is measured at 0, 30, and 60 min.	A normal response is cortisol >18 µg/dL. In suspected hypothalamic-pituitary deficiency, a low dose (1 µg) test may be more sensitive.
Thyroid-stimulating hormone (TSH)	*Basal thyroid function tests:* free T₄, free T₃, TSH.	Low free thyroid hormone levels in the setting of TSH levels that are not appropriately increased.
Luteinizing hormone (LH), follicle-stimulating hormone (FSH)	*Basal levels of LH, FSH, testosterone, estrogen*	Basal LH and FSH should be increased in postmenopausal women. Low testosterone levels in conjunction with low or low-normal LH and FSH are consistent with gonadotropin deficiency.
	GnRH test: GnRH (100 µg) IV with measurements of serum LH and FSH at 0, 30, and 60 min.	In most normal persons, LH should increase by 10 IU/L and FSH by 2 IU/L. Normal responses are variable, and repeated stimulation may be required.
	Clomiphene test: Clomiphene citrate (100 mg) is given orally for 5 days. Serum LH and FSH are measured on days 0, 5, 7, 10, and 13.	A 50% increase should occur in LH and FSH, usually by day 5.
Multiple hormones	*Combined anterior pituitary test:* GHRH (1 µg/kg), CRH (1 µg/kg), GnRH (100 µg), are given sequentially IV. Blood samples are drawn at 30, 15, 30, 60, 90, and 120 min for measurements of GH, ACTH, LH and FSH.	Combined or individual releasing hormone responses must be evaluated in the context of basal hormone values and may not be diagnostic (see text).

*Values are with polyclonal assays.

CRH = corticotropin-releasing hormone; GHRH = growth hormone-releasing hormone; GnRH = gonadotropin-releasing hormone; T₃ = triiodothyronine; T₄ = thyroxine; TRH = Thyrotropin-releasing hormone.

Table 237–5 • HORMONAL REPLACEMENT THERAPY IN HYPOPITUITARISM*

PITUITARY AXIS	HORMONAL REPLACEMENTS
Growth hormone (GH)	In children, GH (0.025 mg/kg) SC daily. In adults, GH (0.3–0.8 mg) SC daily. Titrate dose to achieve IGF-1 levels in upper part of normal range.
Prolactin	None
Adrenocorticotropic hormone–cortisol	Prednisone (2.5 mg PO qAM; 2.5 mg PO qPM) or hydrocortisone (10–20 mg PO qAM; 5–10 mg PO qPM). Dose adjusted on clinical basis.
Thyroid-stimulating hormone–thyroid	L-Thyroxine (0.075–0.15 mg) PO qd
Gonadotropins–gonads	Pulsatile GnRH (via pump) can be used for GnRH-deficient subjects, or FSH and LH (or hCG) can be used to induce ovulation in women. hCG alone, or FSH and LH, can be used to induce spermatogenesis in men.
	In men, testosterone enanthate (100–300 mg) IM q1–3 weeks or testosterone cyclopentylpropionate (100–300 mg) IM q1–3 weeks. Testosterone transdermal patches can also be used (5 mg qd). Testosterone gel (1%) 1–2 packets (5–10 g) daily.
	In women, conjugated estrogens (0.625–1.25 mg) or mestranol (35 mg) PO days 1–25 each month cycled with medroxyprogesterone acetate (5–10 mg) PO days 15–25 each month. Low-dose contraceptive pills may also be used. Estrogen-containing transdermal patches are also available.
Posterior pituitary	Desmopressin, 0.05–0.2 mL (5–20 µg) intranasally once or twice daily, or tablets (0.1–0.4 mg every 8–12 hr) or 0.5 mL (2 µg) SC.

*Replacement therapy is dictated by the types of hormone deficiencies and by the clinical circumstances. In each case, the recommended preparations and doses are representative but need to be adjusted for individual patients. Other hormonal preparations are also available.

FSH = follicle-stimulating hormone; hCG = human chorionic gonadotropin; GnRH = gonadotropin-releasing hormone; LH = luteinizing hormone.

other tissues, particularly the ovary, bone, and thyroid. Interestingly, the McCune-Albright syndrome is also caused by mutations in the Gsα-subunit. However, the somatic mutations in McCune-Albright occur early during development, rather than only in the pituitary gland, so that multiple tissues are affected. In multiple endocrine neoplasia type 1 (MEN-1), the predisposition to pituitary tumors is inherited in an autosomal dominant manner and occurs in conjunction with tumors of the parathyroid and pancreas. The *MEN-1* gene has been localized on the long arm of chromosome 11 (11q13) and has been cloned. The *MEN-1* gene codes for a protein called "menin," which is thought to act as a constitutive tumor suppressor. Individuals with *MEN-1* are thought to inherit one mutant allele, with tumorigenesis occurring after a "second hit" mutates or deletes the normal *MEN-1* gene. Deletions of portions of chromosome 11 have also been

Table 237–6 • PREVALENCE OF DIFFERENT TYPES OF PITUITARY ADENOMAS

TYPE OF PITUITARY ADENOMA	DISORDER	HORMONE PRODUCED	PREVALENCE (%)*
Somatotroph	Acromegaly/gigantism	Growth hormone	10–15
Lactotroph (prolactinoma)	Hypogonadism, galactorrhea	Prolactin	25–40
Corticotroph	Cushing's disease	Adrenocorticotropic hormone	10–15
Gonadotroph	Mass effects, hypopituitarism	Follicle-stimulating hormone and luteinizing hormone	15–20
Thyrotroph	Hyperthyroidism	Thyroid-stimulating hormone	<3
Nonfunctioning/null cell	Mass effects, hypopituitarism	None	10–25

*The prevalence rates represent ranges described in several different large series. Mixed tumors (e.g., growth hormone and prolactin) and plurihormonal adenomas are not shown. Rates vary depending on methods used to establish the diagnosis. Prolactinomas were underestimated in most recent pathologic series because they are largely managed medically. Most glycoprotein hormone–producing pituitary tumors were classified as nonfunctioning adenomas until the application of immunohistochemical studies.

described in cases of sporadic pituitary tumors. Deletions of other chromosomal regions (loss of heterozygosity) suggest that several different tumor suppressor genes may play a role in the development of pituitary tumors.

Clinical Manifestations

MASS EFFECTS OF PITUITARY ADENOMAS. Many of the clinical manifestations of pituitary adenomas are related to the hypersecretion of hormones. However, the mass effects of the enlarging tumor can also lead to specific signs and symptoms. Particularly in the case of nonfunctioning tumors or in those that produce gonadotropins, the primary clinical manifestations are related to effects of the tumor on surrounding structures.

Headaches are common in patients with macroadenomas and appear to be caused by expansion of the diaphragma sellae or by invasion of bone. Headaches may be retro-orbital or referred to the top of the skull, but the location is variable. The sudden onset of severe headache associated with nausea, vomiting, and altered consciousness can also be caused by hemorrhagic infarction with sudden enlargement of a pituitary adenoma. In severe cases, pituitary apoplexy can occur, requiring glucocorticoid treatment and possible surgical decompression.

The effects of pituitary tumors on the visual fields are well explained by the relationship of the optic chiasm to the sella turcica. Expansion of macroadenomas into the suprasellar region exerts pressure on the optic chiasm, usually in the central region where nerves emanating from the inferior and medial part of the retina (superior and temporal visual fields) cross. Consequently, bitemporal hemianopsia is the most common visual field abnormality associated with pituitary adenomas. However, the exact pattern of visual field loss is variable and is affected by the location and flexibility of the chiasm as well as by the direction and extent of tumor growth. Large tumors may grow asymmetrically and invade the cavernous sinus or surround an optic nerve, leading to other patterns of visual field changes or loss of visual acuity. The size and direction and degree of extrasellar extension are best evaluated with MRI with gadolinium infusion. If the tumor abuts the chiasm on MRI, then formal visual field testing should be performed by an ophthalmologist. Even long-standing visual field changes may be reversible by surgical or medical decompression.

The normal pituitary is often compressed into a thin rim of tissue by large pituitary adenomas. Hypopituitarism probably results more from compression of the hypothalamic-pituitary stalk than from direct replacement or pressure on the normal pituitary. GH deficiency and hypogonadotropic hypogonadism are particularly common. Slightly elevated PRL levels (generally less than 100 ng/mL) occur in cases of stalk compression because of diminished inhibition by dopamine. It is important not to mistake such tumors for prolactinomas, because they will not decrease in size in response to medical therapy with dopamine agonists. Preoperative hypopituitarism caused by a large pituitary mass is reversible in up to half of patients after surgical decompression. Diabetes insipidus (vasopressin deficiency) is rarely caused by pituitary tumors and should raise the suspicion of a craniopharyngioma or other disorders that are likely to cause hypothalamic dysfunction.

℞ Treatment of Pituitary Adenomas

SURGERY. Except for prolactinomas, surgery is the primary mode of therapy for most pituitary tumors that warrant intervention. Indications for surgery include reduction in hormone levels and decompression to relieve mass effects or to prevent further tumor expansion. Currently, the transsphenoidal route is used almost exclusively for decompression or extirpation of pituitary tumors. Because of substantially greater morbidity, subfrontal craniotomy is reserved for patients with tumors that require extensive exploration of the suprasellar region and surrounding structures, including invasion into the third ventricle. The transsphenoidal approach usually involves a sublabial incision allowing ready access to the sphenoidal sinus that leads to the floor of the sella, but an endoscopic, endonasal approach is becoming used more widely. After the sella is entered, the tumor is identified and resected in fragments under microscopy. Decompression of the sellar contents can allow tumor in the suprasellar region to drop into the surgical field to allow further resection. In experienced hands, transsphenoidal surgery is effective and complications are uncommon (<5% complication rate) but include cerebrospinal fluid leak, hemorrhage, optic nerve injury, hypopituitarism, and sinusitis. Transient diabetes insipidus occurs in about 5% of patients after surgery but rarely persists long-term. Mortality rates are less than 1%. Complication rates increase with increasing size of the tumor and when a craniotomy is performed.

Surgical cure rates are largely a function of the size and location of the pituitary mass. When stringent hormonal criteria are used to assess surgical success rates, less than 30% of macroadenomas are cured by transsphenoidal surgery, although considerable improvements in hormone levels or mass effects can be achieved. On the other hand, hormone hypersecretion by microadenomas can be corrected completely in 80 to 90% of patients, although the cure rates vary considerably at different institutions.

RADIATION THERAPY. Irradiation has been used as a primary mode of treatment of pituitary adenomas and as adjunctive therapy after surgery or in combination with medical therapy. Radiation is typically administered over 5 weeks at a dose of 45 Gy using cobalt-60 or a linear accelerator. Proton-beam therapy has also been used and delivers very high doses of radiation within a localized region, but it is limited to intrasellar lesions and is not widely available. More recently, a radiation therapy technique referred to as "gamma knife" technique or stereotactic radiosurgery has been employed for many patients with pituitary tumors. With this technique, approximately the same dosage of radiation is administered as a single dose through more than 100 ports using a computerized matching of irradiation to tumor geometry. Because response rates are slow (several years, but considerably more rapid with gamma knife) and complete remission is rarely achieved for all of these types of irradiation, primary radiation therapy is generally reserved for patients who cannot or choose not to undergo surgery.

Radiation therapy is more commonly used as adjunctive therapy after incomplete transsphenoidal resection. The decision regarding adjunctive radiotherapy involves a number of issues, including hormone levels, amount and location of residual tumor, rate of tumor growth, and degree of invasiveness. Gamma knife radiotherapy appears to be particularly useful for residual tumor in the cavernous sinus, as the normal structures that course through that area (carotid artery, cranial nerves II, IV, V_1, V_2, VI) are relatively radioresistant. Because the time to recurrence for most nonfunctioning macroadenomas is 5 to 10 years and not all recur, it is often reasonable to follow patients with imaging techniques, reserving irradiation for those with evidence of recurrence. Complications of irradiation are dose related but can also be idiosyncratic. Partial or complete hypopituitarism occurs in 50 to 70% of patients and is primarily due to hypothalamic injury. Second tumors occur in the radiation field in about 2% of patients over a 20-year period. Less common complications include optic nerve damage, brain necrosis, vascular damage, and cognitive dysfunction. Whether gamma knife radiotherapy will have similar rates of complications is at present unknown.

MEDICAL THERAPY. The emergence of medical therapies for pituitary tumors has dramatically affected patient management. Dopamine agonists, which include bromocriptine, pergolide, and cabergoline, have a primary role in the management of prolactinomas. They induce a rapid fall in PRL levels and, importantly, decrease tumor size. Dopamine agonists are also used in the management of acromegaly, although the GH responses and effects on tumor size are generally much less pronounced than in prolactinomas. Somatostatin analogues, such as octreotide and lanreotide, act to suppress the secretion of a number of hormones, including GH and TSH, and have been used to treat acromegaly and TSH-producing tumors. Long-acting GnRH agonists and antagonists have been studied in gonadotropin-producing tumors. Unlike the situation in normal individuals, the long-acting agonists do not cause desensitization and suppression of gonadotropins in most pituitary tumors. GnRH antagonists are more effective, reducing FSH in the majority of patients examined, but these agents have little effect on tumor growth. Medical therapy for Cushing's disease is primarily directed toward inhibition of steroid biosynthesis. These drugs include ketoconazole, metyrapone, aminoglutethimide, mifepristone, etomidate, and mitotane. Because of substantial side effects and because patients with Cushing's disease tend to escape from the cortisol-suppressing effects of these drugs by producing more ACTH, medical therapy is used primarily as an adjunctive treatment or to reduce cortisol levels preoperatively.

GROWTH HORMONE

The pituitary gland contains large amounts of stored GH (5 to 10 mg), a 191-amino acid, single-chain protein that contains two intramolecular disulfide bonds (see Table 237–1). The GH gene is located on chromosome 17 and is part of a five-member gene cluster. In addition to the normal GH gene, the gene cluster includes a GH variant gene that is expressed in the placenta, two placental lactogen (hPL) genes that are also referred to as chorionic somatomammotropin (hCS), and an hPL pseudogene that is not expressed. Highly repetitive sequences within the gene cluster appear to account for the propensity for recombination and deletions of the GH gene, causing one form of GH deficiency.

The predominant circulating form of GH is a 22-kD protein. However, a splicing variant creates a 20-kD form that constitutes 10 to 15% of circulating GH and is biologically active. GH also forms high-molecular-weight oligomers and is complexed in the circulation to two different binding proteins. The high-affinity binding protein has been identified as a circulating form of the extracellular domain of the GH receptor. In addition to greatly reducing the clearance of GH, this binding protein may also modulate GH action.

Production of GH is controlled by a complex interplay of hypothalamic stimulatory and inhibitory peptides, neurotransmitters, growth factors, sex steroids, and nutritional conditions. The most important regulators of GH are the hypothalamic hormones: GHRH, which is stimulatory, and somatostatin, which is inhibitory. A recently identified hypothalamic peptide, Ghrelin, releases GH in humans but is of uncertain physiologic significance. GH increases the production of IGF-1 (also known as somatomedin C), which in turn inhibits GH production. GHRH acts by a G-protein coupled receptor that is structurally related to receptors in the vasoactive intestinal peptide (VIP), glucagon, and secretin family. GHRH stimulates cyclic AMP, activates phospholipase C, and causes an increase in intracellular calcium. GHRH causes somatotroph proliferation as well as increasing GH

biosynthesis and secretion. The Gsα-subunit, which is coupled to the GHRH receptor, is one of the targets for activating mutations that lead to somatotroph adenomas. Somatostatin binds to receptors that inhibit adenylate cyclase and thereby lower cyclic AMP levels. As a result, GHRH and somatostatin act antagonistically at the level of signal transduction. When both hormones are added concomitantly, somatostatin appears to act dominantly and GH secretion is inhibited. Ghrelin has its own receptor.

IGF-1 also inhibits GH secretion, and it acts at both the pituitary and the hypothalamic level. In addition to reflecting GH action (primarily at the liver), serum IGF-1 is also sensitive to nutritional and metabolic changes. In cases of starvation and anorexia nervosa, IGF-1 levels are low, resulting in increased levels of GH. In cases of obesity, GH levels are low and GHRH responses are blunted. Stress, exercise, and a variety of neurogenic stimuli also increase GH secretion. Estrogens stimulate GH secretion, but their effects are less pronounced than for PRL.

Large bursts of GH secretion characteristically occur at night in association with slow-wave sleep. GH levels tend to be greatest during puberty and decline gradually in adulthood. The amplitude of GH pulses is greater in women than in men, likely reflecting the effects of estrogens. Spontaneous GH pulses can reach 50 ng/mL and are cleared rapidly with a half-life of about 20 minutes. Consequently, random GH levels can be very low or high. In addition, GH responses to GHRH are highly variable even within an individual, probably reflecting variations in endogenous somatostatin tone.

Growth hormone acts through a single transmembrane receptor that is structurally related to PRL and cytokine receptors (e.g., erythropoietin and colony-stimulating factors). This group of receptors associates with adaptor tyrosine kinases, one of which is referred to as Janus-associated kinase 2 (JAK2). After GH stimulation, JAK2 is phosphorylated and initiates a signaling cascade. The GH molecule has two distinguishable receptor binding domains that allow it to contact two separate receptor molecules to induce receptor dimerization. Mutations in the GH receptor cause GH resistance and severe growth retardation, a condition referred to as the GH insensitivity syndrome (Laron-type dwarfism). GH levels are elevated and IGF-1 levels are low, reflecting the inability of the mutant receptor to transduce the GH signal.

Many of the growth and metabolic effects of GH are transmitted indirectly through the actions of IGF-1. GH stimulates IGF-1 production in most tissues, where it then exerts autocrine or paracrine effects. Circulating IGF-1 is derived predominantly from the liver and is a useful marker of GH action because it has a longer half-life and integrates the effects of GH pulses. Although IGF-1 levels are used in the diagnosis of acromegaly and to assess the integrity of the GH axis, factors other than GH (e.g., malnutrition) can alter IGF-1 levels. IGF-1 acts through widely distributed receptors that are structurally related to insulin receptors. In addition to its growth-promoting and anabolic effects, IGF-1 also stimulates mitogenesis in many tissues. The bioactivity of IGF-1 is itself modulated by six IGF binding proteins (IGFBPs). These IGFBPs can inhibit or enhance IGF actions and may even function as independent cell regulators. IGFBP-3 is the major IGFBP in plasma; it is regulated by GH, and its levels generally parallel those of IGF-1 itself, both reflecting GH bioactivity.

Growth hormone has its major effects on linear growth but also influences a variety of metabolic pathways. Some of these effects are mediated by GH directly, whereas others are conferred by IGF-1. Although the relative roles of GH and IGF-1 are debated, their actions are cooperative in many cases. The effects of GH on linear growth appear to be mediated largely by IGF-1, which has been used to stimulate growth in patients with GH insensitivity syndrome. Linear growth in the fetus and neonate is not GH dependent, as illustrated by the fact that GH-deficient infants have normal birth lengths, although intrauterine IGF-1 and IGF-2 may be important for fetal growth independent of GH. In contrast, normal postnatal linear growth requires GH, as illustrated by the clinical manifestations of GH deficiency. GH and IGF-1 act together to markedly accelerate linear growth, particularly at the time of puberty when sex steroids enhance GH and IGF-1 levels.

Growth hormone also induces lipolysis and stimulates anabolic activity, including amino acid uptake and protein synthesis. As a result, it reduces body fat, increases lean body mass, and leads to positive nitrogen balance. These properties of GH are most strikingly seen in GH-deficient children who have undergone replacement.

Endocrine Diseases

GH opposes many of the actions of insulin and can be considered diabetogenic. In diabetic individuals, nocturnal GH secretion accounts in large part for the dawn phenomenon, in which there is a decrease in glucose utilization, causing a tendency toward hyperglycemia.

GROWTH HORMONE DEFICIENCY

Causes of GH deficiency include hypothalamic/pituitary disorders, GHRH receptor mutations, GH gene mutations, combined pituitary hormone deficiencies, GH receptor mutations, IGF-1 receptor mutations, radiation, and psychosocial deprivation (Chapter 235). The clinical manifestations of GH deficiency depend on the time of onset and the severity of hormone deficiency. Children with complete GH deficiency have slow linear growth rates (approximately 3 cm/yr), and they rapidly fall below normal on standardized growth charts. GH-deficient children have normal skeletal proportions, and many have a pudgy, youthful appearance because of decreased lipolysis. Particularly in the setting of cortisol deficiency, there is a predisposition to hypoglycemia.

Basal GH does not provide a reliable measure of GH reserve, whereas low IGF-1 and low IGFBP-3 levels are consistent with GH deficiency. GH deficiency is most frequently assessed using insulin-induced hypoglycemia, which activates central nervous system pathways leading to stimulation of both GH and ACTH secretion (see Table 237–4). The insulin tolerance test requires careful monitoring for symptoms of severe hypoglycemia, such as confusion or depressed consciousness. This test should be avoided in patients with seizure disorders or coronary artery disease. Insulin doses (0.1 to 0.15 U/kg) may need to be decreased if glucocorticoid deficiency is suspected or increased in conditions of insulin resistance (e.g., obesity). Alternatives to the insulin tolerance test for evaluation of GH include stimulation by L-dopa or arginine. Stimulation tests with GHRH have not been well standardized and appear to show substantial variation even within an individual, perhaps because of changing somatostatin tone.

Rx Treatment

In children with well-documented GH deficiency, GH replacement is effective and is essential to increase final adult height. In a typical regimen, recombinant GH (0.025 mg/kg) is given daily as subcutaneous injections. The efficacy of GH treatment depends on when it is initiated as well as replacement of other hormone deficiencies, if they coexist. In the setting of multiple hormone deficiencies, replacement of thyroid hormone and cortisol is necessary for effective GH action. On the other hand, sex steroids (estrogen in particular) lead to epiphyseal closure and limit linear growth. Consequently, GH is more effective before puberty; if exogenous sex steroids are given, low doses should be used. GH has also been shown to increase the final height of girls with Turner's syndrome (chromosomal XO state)[1] and children with end-stage renal disease.[2] These uses have been approved by the U.S. Food and Drug Administration (FDA).

Although the potential role of GH replacement in adults is debated, it has been approved by the FDA for the treatment of adults with GH deficiency. Only about one third of children with isolated, idiopathic GH deficiency are found to be GH deficient upon retesting as adults. Thus, all such patients should be retested as young adults before GH therapy is continued or restarted. Short-term studies show that GH treatment can increase lean body mass, decrease fat mass, and improve the sense of well-being in adults with documented GH deficiency, but safety data for long-term GH administration are meager, and data documenting clinically significant increased muscle strength and endurance are lacking. Whether GH treatment in adults will affect the increased mortality rate associated with hypopituitarism remains to be seen. Adverse effects occur at lower doses in adults compared with children, and a starting dose of 0.3 mg/day has been recommended. Although GH therapy has also been approved by the FDA for the treatment of wasting due to the acquired immunodeficiency syndrome, its short-term use to reduce acute catabolism in critically ill patients resulted in increased mortality, so use for such purposes has been curtailed.

GROWTH HORMONE EXCESS: ACROMEGALY AND GIGANTISM

Etiology and Pathogenesis

Growth hormone–producing pituitary tumors involve the neoplastic proliferation of somatotroph cells and account for 10 to 15% of pituitary tumors (see Table 237–6). GH-producing tumors are frequently mixed tumors that secrete more than one hormone. PRL is produced in about 40% of somatotroph adenomas, and some patients may present because of symptoms due to the hyperprolactinemia (i.e., amenorrhea and/or galactorrhea). A subset of these tumors are categorized morphologically as mammosomatotroph adenomas. GH-producing tumors can also co-secrete glycoprotein hormones, most frequently the common α-subunit (10 to 30%) or, rarely, TSH.

Considerable progress has been made concerning the cause of GH-producing pituitary tumors. Ectopic production of GHRH (usually carcinoid or pancreatic islets) is a well-documented but rare (<1%) cause of acromegaly that can result in somatotroph hyperplasia. Gsα-subunit mutations occur in 35 to 40% of somatotroph adenomas. Molecular defects in the remaining 60 to 65% of somatotroph adenomas need to be identified.

Clinical Manifestations

Tumors that secrete GH cause acromegaly in adults and gigantism in children in whom GH excess occurs before epiphyseal closure. The annual incidence of acromegaly has been estimated at about 3 per million. It affects men and women with equal frequency and is most often recognized when patients are in their 30s or 40s, usually after a decade of GH excess. The clinical features of acromegaly are summarized in Table 237–7. The most striking features of acromegaly usually involve the face, hands, and feet. The diagnosis is often suspected because of changes in facial appearance that include enlargement of the lower jaw (prognathism), the nose and lips, and the sinuses (causing frontal bossing) (see Fig. 237–1). Oral cavity changes including malocclusion, increased spacing between the teeth, and enlargement of the tongue may lead to recognition of the disorder by dentists. A hollow, resonant voice is caused by changes in the vocal cords and the soft tissues of the hypopharynx. Sleep apnea may occur in patients with soft tissue obstruction of the pharynx but may also occur because of a central disorder. Few acromegalic patients wear rings because they have long since outgrown them, and they usually have a history of progressive increase in shoe size and width. In addition to bony enlargement, there is a marked increase in the soft tissue of the hands and feet. A moist, doughy, enveloping handshake is characteristic of acromegaly. Heel pad thickness (which can be assessed radiographically) correlates well with IGF-1 levels and other clinical features of the disease. Arthritis (hands, feet, hips, knees) is common (75%) and is caused by cartilage and synovial overgrowth. Some degree of carpal tunnel syndrome is seen in about half of patients. Skin changes include increased skinfolds, particularly over the brow and forehead. The skin is usually oily, owing to increased sebaceous activity and sweating. Skin tags are common, and their presence correlates with the presence of colonic polyps. Galactorrhea may be seen in women, and reproductive dysfunction occurs in both men and women when PRL levels are elevated. Headaches, visual field defects, and other neurologic symptoms depend on the location and extent of tumor growth.

Acromegaly causes as much as a twofold to threefold increase in the rate of mortality. Most of the increased mortality can be attributed to cardiovascular and cerebrovascular diseases and may be related in part to the increased prevalence of hypertension (25 to 35%) and diabetes mellitus (10 to 25%) in patients with acromegaly. There is evidence for cardiac hypertrophy in the majority of acromegalics, and symptomatic heart disease, consisting of coronary ischemia or congestive heart failure or both, occurs in 15 to 20% of patients. Sleep apnea may predispose patients to cardiac dysrhythmias. Some analyses have found an increased risk of premalignant polyps and colon cancer in patients with acromegaly, and screening with colonoscopy is generally recommended in men, particularly those older than 50 years of age and with skin tags. The disfigurement, metabolic complications, and increased mortality associated with acromegaly emphasize the importance of early diagnosis and implementation of appropriate therapy to lower the GH levels into the normal range.

Table 237–7 • CLINICAL FEATURES OF ACROMEGALY

CLINICAL FEATURES	NO. OF SUBJECTS	YEARS OR FREQUENCY
Age at diagnosis	885	42 yr
Delay to diagnosis	680	8.7 yr
Gender (% male)	1331	48%
Acral/facial changes	595	98%
Oligo/amenorrhea (females)	366	72%
Hyperhidrosis	751	64%
Headaches	825	55%
Paresthesias/carpal tunnel	725	40%
Impotence (males)	355	36%
Hypertension	630	28%
Goiter	705	21%
Visual field defects	993	19%

From Molitch ME: Clinical manifestations of acromegaly. Endocrinol Metab Clin North Am 1992; 21:597–614.

Diagnosis

Because GH is secreted in a pulsatile manner, and because the amplitude of normal GH pulses can be large (>50 ng/mL), random GH level measurements are not very useful in making the diagnosis of acromegaly. IGF-1 levels provide an integrated index of GH production and provide a better screening test for acromegaly. IGF-1 levels are normally elevated during puberty and pregnancy and decrease with age, so normal ranges must be age adjusted. IGF-1 levels correlate well with 24-hour GH production rates and with disease activity. The most reliable test for acromegaly is the glucose tolerance test (Table 237–8). In acromegaly, increased glucose levels fail to suppress GH levels to below 1 ng/mL with polyclonal antibody immunoassays and to levels below 0.5 ng/mL using newer monoclonal antibody two-site assays. More than half of patients with acromegaly exhibit a paradoxical stimulation of GH in response to TRH. Co-secretion of PRL should be evaluated, and the common α-subunit of the glycoprotein hormones may provide an additional marker of tumor activity. After the diagnosis of acromegaly is made, radiologic studies, preferably using MRI, should be used to evaluate the extent of tumor

Table 237–8 • SELECTED TESTS OF EXCESS PITUITARY FUNCTION

HORMONE	TEST	INTERPRETATION
Growth hormone (GH)	Basal IGF-1	Elevated IGF-1 levels are consistent with acromegaly when interpreted in the context of age and nutritional status.
	Oral glucose suppression test: After 75-g glucose load, GH is measured at −30, 0, 30, 60, 90, 120 min.	GH should be suppressed to <1 µg/L in normals, with polyclonal radioimmunoassays; <0.5 µg/L with two-site monoclonal assays. GH may paradoxically increase in acromegaly.
Prolactin	Basal prolactin levels	Elevated prolactin (>200 µg/L) is consistent with a prolactinoma. When prolactin levels are between 20 and 200 µg/L, other causes of hyperprolactinemia should be considered.
Adrenocorticotropic hormone (ACTH)	Measurement of 24-hr urine free cortisol	Elevated urine free cortisol level is suggestive of Cushing's syndrome, but it has several other causes as well.
	Overnight dexamethasone suppression test: Dexamethasone (1 mg) PO at midnight followed by 8 AM plasma cortisol.	In normal persons, AM cortisol should be suppressed to <5 µg/dL. Normal dexamethasone suppression excludes Cushing's syndrome. Several other disorders can cause failure to suppress normally.
	Low-dose dexamethasone suppression test: Dexamethasone (0.5 mg) q6h for eight doses with basal and end of treatment measurements that may include 24-hr urine collections for free cortisol or 17-hydroxysteroids and AM plasma cortisol and ACTH.	17-Hydroxysteroids should be suppressed to <4 mg/24 hr; urine free cortisol should be <20 µg/24 hr; serum cortisol should be suppressed to <6 µg/dL. Failure to suppress cortisol production is consistent with the diagnosis of Cushing's syndrome.
	High-dose dexamethasone suppression test: Dexamethasone (2 mg) q6h for eight doses with basal and end of treatment measurements that may include 24-hr urine collections for free cortisol or 17-hydroxysteroids and AM plasma cortisol and ACTH.	The high-dose test is intended to distinguish Cushing's disease (pituitary adenoma), ectopic ACTH production, and adrenal adenoma. The 50% suppression of 17-hydroxy steroids or 90% suppression of urine free cortisol production is suggestive of Cushing's disease. Less than 50% suppression suggests ectopic ACTH or adrenal adenoma. Low ACTH levels are consistent with adrenal adenoma.
	CRH test: Ovine CRH (1 µg/kg) is administered IV and ACTH and cortisol are drawn at −15, 0, 15, 30, 60, 90, and 120 min.	In Cushing's disease, there is usually a 50% increase in ACTH and a 20% increase in cortisol. Adrenal adenoma is associated with suppressed ACTH. Ectopic ACTH is associated with high basal ACTH and cortisol levels that are not affected by CRH.
	Petrosal sinus ACTH sampling: The inferior petrosal sinus is catheterized, ideally bilaterally, and plasma ACTH is compared with simultaneous peripheral samples. The sampling can be done in conjunction with CRH stimulation.	In Cushing's disease, the ratio of ACTH in the petrosal sinus/periphery is at least 2 basally and at least 3 after CRH. In ectopic ACTH, the ratio of petrosal sinus/peripheral level is <1.5.
Thyroid-stimulating hormone (TSH)	Basal thyroid function tests	An inappropriate normal or elevated TSH in the setting of increased free thyroid hormone levels is consistent with a TSH-producing tumor or other causes of inappropriate TSH secretion.
	Free α-subunit level	Elevated free α-subunit levels associated with inappropriately elevated TSH are suggestive of a TSH-producing tumor.
Follicle-stimulating hormone (FSH), luteinizing hormone (LH)	Basal FSH, LH, testosterone	Increased LH and testosterone levels in males are consistent with LH-secreting tumors. Elevated FSH and low-normal testosterone is suggestive of an FSH-producing tumor if primary gonadal failure is not present. In females, assessment of excess hormone secretion is difficult because of changes during the menstrual cycle and at menopause.
	TRH test: TRH (200 µg) is given IV with measurements of serum FSH, LH, FSHβ, and LHβ subunits at 0, 20, 60 min.	Stimulation of LH, FSH, or their free β-subunits is suggestive of a gonadotropin-producing adenoma.

CRH = corticotropin-releasing hormone; IGF = insulin-like growth factor; TRH = thyrotropin-releasing hormone.

growth. Unlike in Cushing's disease and prolactinomas, the majority of patients with acromegaly have macroadenomas. In the absence of an apparent pituitary tumor, the possibility of ectopic GHRH secretion causing somatotroph cell hyperplasia should be considered.

 Treatment

The goals of therapy in acromegaly are to reverse or prevent tumor mass effects and to reduce the long-term morbidity and mortality that result from excess GH production. Correction of the disorder prevents further physical disfigurement and can result in substantial resolution of soft tissue changes and improvements in metabolic derangements. Although reductions in GH levels are associated with improvements in symptoms, the ultimate goal is to achieve normal GH and IGF-1 levels and to prevent tumor recurrence without incurring hypopituitarism.

Transsphenoidal surgery results in GH levels below 5 ng/mL in about 60 to 80% of patients with microadenomas. Not all of these patients are cured of their tumor when assessed by more stringent criteria, such as GH suppression below 2 ng/mL during an oral glucose tolerance test or a normal IGF-1 level. Patients with macroadenomas are less often cured by surgery (<30%) but usually have reductions in GH levels.

Medical therapies for acromegaly include dopamine agonists, such as cabergoline, and somatostatin analogues, such as octreotide and lanreotide. Responsiveness to both classes of these agents depends on the presence and density of receptors on tumor cells. Although cabergoline can reduce GH and IGF-1 levels in many patients, normal levels are achieved in only about one-third. Somatostatin analogues reduce GH and IGF-1 levels in almost all patients, with normal levels of IGF-1 being achieved in more than one half of cases.[3] Tumor size is reduced modestly in about one half of cases. Somatostatin analogues are useful as adjunctive therapy in patients who are not cured by surgery or radiation. Longer-acting preparations of octreotide and other somatostatin analogues that can be given by intramuscular injection every 2 to 4 weeks have now become available. Side effects of somatostatin analogues include diarrhea and increased risk of cholelithiasis, although cholecystitis and need for cholecystectomy are rare. Because of ease of use and lower cost, cabergoline is usually tried before somatostatin analogues but, because of relative efficacies, most patients end up on the latter as adjunctive therapy. In addition, some patients experience additive beneficial effects from combining the two classes of medications while keeping the dose of each drug low enough to avoid adverse effects. Pegvisomant is a new agent that has just become available for the treatment of acromegaly. It is a biosynthetic GH analogue that prevents binding of GH to its receptor. It is capable of normalizing IGF-1 levels in more than 90% of patients with corresponding clinical benefits.[4] Pegvisomant must be given by daily subcutaneous injection and long-term experience with its use is limited, so it generally is held in reserve for those patients not responding optimally to other treatment modalities.

Radiation is not recommended as primary therapy for acromegaly because of the long time (5 to 10 years) required for reductions in GH levels and the high incidence of hypopituitarism and other complications discussed earlier. Adjunctive radiation therapy may be required for patients with macroadenomas when GH levels or mass effects persist after transsphenoidal surgery and medical therapy. Recent data suggest that gamma knife radiotherapy may be the most efficacious form of radiotherapy for acromegaly.

PROLACTIN

Prolactin and GH appear to be derived from a common ancestral gene, which accounts for the similarities in their present-day structures and some overlap in their functional properties. The *PRL* gene is located on chromosome 6 and encodes a 198-amino acid protein (23 kD) that is produced in the lactotroph cells. PRL contains three intramolecular disulfide bonds, and high molecular variants are reported that may represent dimers or protein aggregates. Although the larger molecular weight forms of PRL react in radioimmunoassays, they have diminished biologic potency. Estrogen stimulates lactotroph proliferation, and their number is consequently greater in females than in males and during pregnancy (approximately 70% of pituitary cells).

Secretion of PRL is controlled by tonic inhibition by dopamine, which acts through D_2-type receptors on lactotrophs. PRL biosynthesis and secretion are stimulated by the hypothalamic peptides TRH and VIP. Hypothyroidism causes increased TRH output and increased sensitivity of the lactotrophs to TRH and can result in hyperprolactinemia. VIP, which acts through receptors that increase cyclic AMP, may be responsible, along with a decrease in dopamine, for PRL increases associated with suckling. VIP is also found in the pituitary, where it may act as an autocrine or paracrine regulator of PRL secretion. A new hypothalamic peptide, termed PRL releasing peptide (PRLrp), has been found to release PRL from the pituitary, but its precise physiologic role in humans has not yet been established. On balance, dopamine inhibition is the dominant influence for PRL secretion so that PRL is the one pituitary hormone that increases after pituitary stalk section. A variety of pharmacologic agents can stimulate PRL secretion, in many cases by impairing dopamine secretion or action (see Table 237–2).

Secretion of PRL is pulsatile and increases with sleep, stress, chest wall stimulation, and pregnancy. PRL levels are usually less than 15 to 20 ng/mL in women and 10 to 15 ng/mL in men. The primary function of PRL is to induce and sustain lactation. However, PRL binds to specific receptors that are located in several tissues, including breast, gonads, lymphoid cells, and liver. During pregnancy, PRL levels increase, and, in conjunction with other hormones (estrogens, progesterone, thyroid hormone, cortisol, and insulin), breast epithelium is stimulated to proliferate and milk synthesis is induced. High levels of estrogen and progesterone inhibit lactation during pregnancy. The rapid decline in these steroids in the postpartum period permits lactation to occur. Neural pathways leading to the secretion of oxytocin provide the "let-down" reflex that induces lactation in response to suckling. Early in the postpartum period, PRL secretion is stimulated by suckling, but this response becomes damped with time as the frequency of suckling episodes decreases. PRL also suppresses gonadotropins, probably by a direct action on GnRH-secreting neurons. As a result, breast-feeding can suppress ovulation. The role of PRL in other tissues is not well understood. High levels of PRL are present in amniotic fluid and it is produced in the decidual layer of the placenta.

PROLACTIN DEFICIENCY

Prolactin deficiency is rare and occurs primarily in the setting of combined hormone deficiencies. PRL levels at or below the limits of detection of radioimmunoassays and an absent rise of PRL after TRH stimulation are consistent with the diagnosis. The only recognized consequence of PRL deficiency is the absence of postpartum lactation. No effects on breast development or other tissues have been described in PRL deficiency.

HYPERPROLACTINEMIA

Etiology and Pathogenesis

Hyperprolactinemia can occur as a consequence of pharmacologic alterations in the pathways that control PRL secretion or of physiologic or metabolic effects on PRL production and clearance or as a neoplastic condition (see Table 237–2). Prolactinomas are neoplastic growths of lactotroph cells and are the most common type of pituitary adenoma (25 to 40%). Theories concerning the causes of prolactinomas have centered around hormonal stimuli that influence lactotroph growth and PRL secretion. Estrogen is a potent stimulus for lactotroph proliferation. In rats, chronic estrogen exposure induces lactotroph hyperplasia and prolactinomas, but there is no clear association between estrogens (e.g., oral contraceptive use) and the incidence of prolactinomas in humans. It is possible that estrogen may rarely stimulate the growth of preexisting prolactinomas, and the very high estrogen levels present during pregnancy may cause about 25% of large prolactinomas to increase in size during pregnancy. Diminished dopamine tone results in increased PRL but has not been shown to cause prolactinomas. PRL secretory dynamics are generally restored to normal on resection of prolactinomas, suggesting that an underlying hypothalamic abnormality is not present. Analyses of tumor DNA from a relatively small number of prolactinomas are consistent with a monoclonal origin, but molecular defects in prolactinomas have not been readily identified. Mutations in *ras* and other oncogenes have been found in sporadic case reports but are not found in most prolactinomas.

Microprolactinomas constitute the great majority of tumors in premenopausal women. In contrast, macroadenomas are more commonly seen in men and postmenopausal women. The predominance of smaller tumors in premenopausal women may be accounted for by a bias of ascertainment, because elevated PRL levels in this group lead to clinical manifestations (amenorrhea, galactorrhea, or infertility). It is likely that subclinical prolactinomas exist in men and many older women, because about 10% of individuals have PRL-positive microadenomas in autopsy series.

Clinical Manifestations

Hyperprolactinemia causes galactorrhea and oligo/amenorrhea in premenopausal women. Estrogen facilitates PRL-induced galactorrhea, which explains why it is less common in postmenopausal women and in women with prolonged hypogonadism. Amenorrhea is primarily a consequence of PRL suppression of GnRH, although PRL may also have inhibitory effects at the level of the pituitary and the gonad. Amenorrhea is associated with infertility, and PRL levels should be a routine part of the hormonal evaluation of infertility. Estrogen deficiency can cause decreased libido, vaginal dryness, and dyspareunia. Long-standing estrogen deficiency also leads to osteopenia in some women. A subset of patients have hirsutism and can exhibit elevations of adrenal androgens. Oral contraceptives may mask PRL-induced oligo/amenorrhea that becomes apparent on their discontinuation. In postmenopausal women, prolactinomas are often identified because of mass effects rather than because of their hormonal effects.

In men, hyperprolactinemia causes hypogonadism with suppressed LH and FSH levels and low testosterone levels. Hypogonadism causes diminished libido, impotence, infertility, and, rarely, gynecomastia or galactorrhea. Diminished libido may also reflect suppression of GnRH because testosterone replacement is not as effective as suppression of hyperprolactinemia. Hyperprolactinemia is found in 1 to 2% of men being evaluated for sexual dysfunction.

Diagnosis

There are four primary categories of causes of hyperprolactinemia that must be distinguished if the correct therapy is to be instituted: (1) physiologic/metabolic hyperprolactinemia; (2) pharmacologic hyperprolactinemia; (3) hypothalamic or pituitary stalk compression; and (4) prolactinoma (see Table 237–2). With the exception of pregnancy and renal failure, physiologic causes of increased PRL result in minor elevations in PRL (usually less than 50 ng/mL), which may not be present on repeat testing. Primary hypothyroidism should be excluded as a cause of mild hyperprolactinemia. A careful drug history should be obtained in all patients with hyperprolactinemia because of the large number of agents that can stimulate PRL secretion. Psychotropic medications, in particular, can increase PRL either by reducing dopamine production or by blocking its action. In most cases, the degree of hyperprolactinemia caused by drugs is less than 100 ng/mL. A variety of suprasellar and parasellar mass lesions cause hyperprolactinemia (generally between 20 and 100 ng/mL) because of compression of the hypothalamus or pituitary stalk. Unless there is very good evidence for physiologic or drug-induced hyperprolactinemia, even patients with mild hyperprolactinemia should be evaluated with CT or MRI to distinguish among idiopathic hyperprolactinemia, microprolactinomas, and other large mass lesions that cause stalk compression, resulting in decreased dopamine reaching the lactotrophs. However, a specific caution is needed when two-site assays are used, as patients with very high PRL levels may appear to have PRL levels that are normal or only modestly elevated, due to the "hook effect." To avoid this problem, PRL levels should always be remeasured at 1:100 dilution in patients with macroadenomas and normal to modestly elevated PRL levels, as PRL levels in samples with the "hook effect" will then increase dramatically. When no pituitary lesions are seen by radiographic studies and physiologic and pharmacologic causes of hyperprolactinemia cannot be identified, the diagnosis of idiopathic hyperprolactinemia is made. Idiopathic hyperprolactinemia may represent microprolactinomas too small to be detected accurately by current imaging techniques or altered hypothalamic regulation of PRL secretion. Whether such patients should be treated depends on the clinical effects of hyperprolactinemia. When followed for several years, few of these patients develop large tumors, only 10 to 15% show MRI evidence of microadenomas, and in one third of cases the hyperprolactinemia resolves.

Rx Treatment

The natural history of prolactinomas has been evaluated in several series. Although large prolactinomas clearly must evolve from smaller lesions, it is uncommon (approximately 7%) for microprolactinomas to progress to macroadenomas. When patients with microadenomas are observed over 3 to 5 years but not treated, PRL levels decrease in 20 to 30% and increase in less than 10% of patients. Decreased PRL levels may occur because of spontaneous tumor infarction. Because of the slow rate of growth, it is reasonable to monitor patients with microprolactinomas without treatment unless the hyperprolactinemia is causing symptoms that warrant therapy.

When hyperprolactinemia causes hypogonadism, osteopenia, or infertility, a dopamine agonist such as bromocriptine or cabergoline is the therapy of choice. Dopamine agonists normalize PRL levels and correct amenorrhea-galactorrhea in 80 to 90% of patients. Bromocriptine is usually started as a half tablet (1.25 mg) given at bedtime with a snack to avoid side effects (nausea, dizziness, somnolence, and nasal stuffiness). After the patient has adapted to the drug, the dose can be increased gradually over several weeks. A typical final dose is 2.5 mg, two or three times a day with meals, but up to 20 mg/day may be required. The lowest effective dose should be used after adequate suppression of PRL levels has been achieved. Cabergoline is even more effective and has fewer adverse side effects than bromocriptine and has the additional advantage in only having to be taken once or twice weekly.

Bromocriptine may cause a considerable reduction in tumor size in patients with macroprolactinomas, about 40% having a greater than 50% reduction in tumor size, about 25% having a 25 to 50% reduction in tumor size, and the remainder having little or no response. Cabergoline is even more effective. Visual field defects are a very sensitive index of tumor size, and improvements can be seen in about 90% of patients. Thus, it is reasonable to use cabergoline as first-line therapy even in patients with visual field defects as long as visual acuity is not threatened by rapid progression or recent tumor hemorrhage. Ten to 20% of patients can maintain normal PRL levels after stopping treatment, and 70 to 80% with marked tumor size reduction may not experience tumor re-expansion with cessation of therapy. In patients with very large tumors who have excellent tumor size reduction, stopping therapy must be done very cautiously, if at all. In some cases, prolactinomas appear to be resistant to a dopamine agonist, but it is important to ensure compliance and to be certain that the underlying lesion is a prolactinoma and not some other cause of hyperprolactinemia. In these cases, an alternative dopamine agonist may be successful. Pergolide is another dopamine agonist with proven efficacy in decreasing PRL levels and prolactinoma size, but it has not been approved by the U.S. FDA for treatment of this condition. Alternatively, transsphenoidal surgery may be used. Although initial remission rates (70 to 80%) for transsphenoidal surgery of microprolactinomas are good, there is long-term recurrence in about 20% of patients. For macroprolactinomas, the initial remission rates are closer to 30%, with a similar recurrence rate. Radiation therapy, usually gamma knife, is reserved for those patients with macroadenomas not responding to either medical or surgical treatment.

Continued

Bromocriptine therapy for infertility, or when there is a possibility of pregnancy, deserves special consideration. Bromocriptine can induce ovulation in 80 to 90% of patients with hyperprolactinemia. Although bromocriptine has not been associated with congenital malformations or complications during pregnancy, most physicians and patients prefer to avoid its use during pregnancy if possible. A form of barrier contraception is usually recommended until two to three regular menstrual cycles have occurred. Subsequently, pregnancy can be confirmed if a menstrual period is missed, allowing discontinuation of bromocriptine with exposure of the fetus to the drug for only 3 to 5 weeks. At present, the safety data for pregnancy outcome are much more limited for cabergoline; therefore, bromocriptine is the preferred drug when fertility is desired.

Less than 2% of patients with microadenomas, but 26% of patients with macroadenomas, develop symptoms of tumor enlargement (headaches, visual field defects) during pregnancy. If symptoms develop, MRI and formal visual field testing should be performed. If there is evidence of visual field compromise or tumor growth, bromocriptine therapy should be restarted to shrink the tumor. PRL levels are not very useful because they are normally increased in pregnancy and an enlarging tumor may not cause PRL production to increase substantially. Because problems of tumor growth occur most often in patients with macroadenomas, consideration should be given to the option of transsphenoidal decompression before pregnancy in women with large tumors, as long as fertility can be preserved.

ADRENOCORTICOTROPIC HORMONE

STRUCTURE

Adrenocorticotropic hormone is a 39-amino acid peptide that is derived from a precursor polypeptide POMC (241 amino acids), which encodes several peptides, including an amino-terminal peptide, joining peptide, ACTH, and β-lipotropin (β-LPH) (Chapter 235). The functional roles of the POMC-encoded peptides other than ACTH have not been fully defined. β-LPH, in addition to ACTH, may stimulate melanocytes and contribute to hyperpigmentation in conditions of POMC stimulation. β-LPH can be processed further to yield γ-lipotropin and β-endorphin. The biologically active portion of ACTH resides within the first 18 of its 39 amino acids. However, because a synthetic peptide (cosyntropin) that includes the first 24 amino acids has a longer half-life, it is used clinically to assess adrenocortical function. The half-life of ACTH is relatively short (<10 minutes), and pulses of ACTH secretion are discrete. Levels of precursor peptides, such as β-LPH, do not always parallel those of ACTH because of their slower clearance rates. In cases with neoplastic ectopic production of ACTH, the levels of precursor peptides or their processed products may be elevated. The POMC gene can also be expressed from alternate transcription start sites, giving rise to aberrant POMC transcripts in ectopic tumors.

The primary effect of ACTH is to stimulate the adrenal gland to produce cortisol. It also stimulates secretion of adrenal androgens and mineralocorticoids, although production of mineralocorticoids is controlled primarily through non-ACTH-dependent mechanisms (Chapter 240). Consequently, mineralocorticoid function is preserved in ACTH deficiency, in contrast to primary adrenal insufficiency, which is characterized by loss of glucocorticoid and mineralocorticoid function.

ACTH binds to a high-affinity receptor that is a member of the seven-transmembrane class of receptors that are coupled to G proteins. ACTH acts as a trophic hormone as well as causing the immediate secretion of cortisol and other adrenal steroids. Long-term stimulation by ACTH causes adrenal hyperplasia and enlargement. On the other hand, ACTH deficiency leads to adrenal atrophy, and several days of ACTH stimulation are required before steroid synthesis returns to normal.

The secretion of ACTH is regulated by the hypothalamic-pituitary-adrenal axis. Hypothalamic CRH is the most important stimulator of ACTH secretion. CRH is a 41-amino acid peptide that is produced in the paraventricular nucleus of the hypothalamus and in other sites in the nervous system and peripheral tissues (Chapter 235). The CRH receptor is structurally related to the calcitonin/VIP/GHRH subfamily of seven-membrane-spanning, G protein–coupled receptors. CRH stimulates cyclic AMP production and increases POMC gene transcription as well as ACTH secretion. Chronic stimulation by CRH also causes corticotroph cell hyperplasia, which can be seen in cases of ectopic CRH production.

Arginine vasopressin (AVP) weakly stimulates ACTH when given alone, but it acts synergistically when administered with CRH and functions as a physiologic stimulus to ACTH secretion along with CRH. About half of the CRH-containing paraventricular neurons also contain AVP. CRH and vasopressin are not always released coordinately, however, and stress has been shown to selectively activate the vasopressin-containing subset of CRH neurons. Several other hypothalamic factors (angiotensin II, VIP, gastrin-releasing peptide,

catecholamines) also enhance ACTH secretion, either by stimulating CRH or by acting at the level of the pituitary gland. ACTH secretion is inhibited by glucocorticoids, which act at both the hypothalamic and pituitary levels. Cortisol inhibits POMC gene transcription by binding to glucocorticoid receptors that interact with negative glucocorticoid response elements in the POMC promoter. Cortisol also inhibits ACTH secretion, and it blunts the ACTH response to CRH. Consequently, ACTH responses to CRH stimulation tests are dependent on ambient concentrations of cortisol and are most robust at night when cortisol levels are low. Cortisol inhibits CRH production and may also act at higher central nervous system levels. After prolonged glucocorticoid suppression of the hypothalamic-pituitary-adrenal axis, the amount of endogenous CRH secretion appears to be rate limiting and can require several months to recover.

Plasma ACTH is secreted in discrete pulses (10 to 80 pg/mL) that occur about once an hour. Because of the marked variation in ACTH levels, random measurements are of little value, and most clinical tests are therefore based on levels of cortisol or its metabolites, which tend to integrate the effects of ACTH. ACTH secretion exhibits a marked diurnal rhythm, being greatest at night several hours after the initiation of sleep. ACTH in turn induces a diurnal pattern of cortisol secretion. Cortisol levels are greatest in the early morning and reach a nadir in the late afternoon and evening. Patients with Cushing's disease lose or exhibit a blunted diurnal rhythm of ACTH secretion. ACTH secretion can be stimulated by a variety of different forms of stress, including psychological stimuli such as fright, anticipation of athletic competition, or surgery. Depression is associated with activation of the hypothalamic-pituitary-adrenal axis and impaired dexamethasone suppressibility. Hypoglycemia induces ACTH secretion through a central mechanism. The resulting increase in cortisol secretion represents one of several counter-regulatory mechanisms that increase glucose production. Insulin-induced hypoglycemia provides a mechanism for testing the integrity of the hypothalamic-pituitary-adrenal axis (see Table 237–4). Serious trauma and infection activate an array of cytokines that stimulate CRH and ACTH secretion. Because cortisol levels are often increased up to 10-fold in these circumstances, similar adjustments in cortisol replacement doses may be required in seriously ill patients with adrenal insufficiency.

ADRENOCORTICOTROPIC HORMONE DEFICIENCY: SECONDARY HYPOCORTISOLISM

Secondary hypocortisolism causes symptoms of glucocorticoid deficiency, including nausea, vomiting, weakness, fatigue, fever, and hypotension. In addition to reduced levels of cortisol, abnormal laboratory test findings can include hyponatremia, hypoglycemia, and eosinophilia. Depending on its cause, the severity of cortisol deficiency in cases of secondary adrenal insufficiency is often not as marked as in primary adrenal insufficiency. In addition, mineralocorticoid function is preserved in secondary adrenal deficiency. Consequently, the clinical manifestations of volume depletion are less pronounced, and hyperkalemia is not a feature of ACTH deficiency. Because ACTH levels are low in cases of secondary adrenal insufficiency, hyperpigmentation is not seen, as in primary adrenal insufficiency. In women, reduced adrenal androgens can decrease libido and cause loss of axillary and pubic hair.

The most common cause of ACTH deficiency is treatment with exogenous glucocorticoids, which causes suppression of the hypothalamic-pituitary-adrenal axis. Sudden withdrawal of glucocorticoids or an increased requirement induced by the superimposition of severe illness can elicit symptoms of glucocorticoid deficiency. Congenital forms of ACTH deficiency are rare. When it is present, ACTH deficiency usually occurs in combination with the loss of other pituitary hormones, although acquired, isolated ACTH deficiency does occur, particularly in women with lymphocytic hypophysitis.

ACTH reserve is most often evaluated using CRH or the insulin tolerance test. Caution should be exercised before inducing hypoglycemia in patients with suspected adrenal insufficiency. Insulin-induced hypoglycemia stimulates central responses to neuroglycopenia and mimics some but not all stresses that activate ACTH secretion. CRH testing (ovine CRH 1 mg/kg IV) may be useful for distinguishing hypothalamic and pituitary causes of ACTH deficiency, because it will still induce an ACTH response in most patients with hypothalamic dysfunction and blunted responses to hypoglycemia. The metyrapone test provides an alternative to the insulin tolerance test. By blocking the 11-hydroxylation step, metyrapone inhibits cortisol production, resulting in stimulation of ACTH secretion and an increase in precursor adrenal steroids (e.g., 11-deoxycortisol). Patients should be monitored closely for evidence of adrenal insufficiency, and metyrapone should be used only in patients with at least some evidence of adrenocortical function. ACTH stimulation tests using $ACTH_{1-24}$ (cosyntropin) can accurately evaluate primary adrenocortical insufficiency but do not accurately assess secondary adrenal insufficiency. A variation of the ACTH simulation test using the low dose of 1 μg has been found to be useful for diagnosing secondary adrenal insufficiency in some studies, however.

Deficiency of ACTH is treated by replacement with glucocorticoids. Doses need to be individualized and are based largely on clinical criteria in which symptoms of glucocorticoid deficiency are balanced against features of glucocorticoid excess. Patients should wear MedicAlert tags and be instructed in the warning signs of cortisol deficiency, including nausea, vomiting, abdominal pain, low-grade fever, fatigue, and postural dizziness. Stress doses of steroids should be used during times of illness. Mineralocorticoid replacement is not required in patients with ACTH deficiency.

CUSHING'S DISEASE

Etiology and Pathogenesis

Cushing's disease results from a pituitary adenoma that causes excess production of ACTH (Chapter 240). It should be distinguished from a variety of other causes of Cushing's syndrome (glucocorticoid excess), which include adrenal causes of cortisol excess, ectopic production of ACTH and CRH, and physiologic states that result in overproduction of cortisol. Cushing's disease accounts for 60 to 70% of cases of Cushing's syndrome. Ten to 15% of pituitary tumors secrete ACTH. For unknown reasons, Cushing's disease occurs about eight times more often in women than in men.

The cause of Cushing's disease has been the subject of a long-standing controversy. The observation that CRH stimulates corticotroph hyperplasia and that some patients with Cushing's disease have corticotroph hyperplasia when the pituitary is subjected to pathologic evaluation support the idea of a hypothalamic cause of Cushing's disease. This concept has been used to explain the occasional recurrence of Cushing's disease after apparent cure following transsphenoidal surgery. On the other hand, most ACTH-producing pituitary neoplasms, like other pituitary tumors, are monoclonal. A primary defect in corticotroph cells is also supported by several clinical observations. First, most patients who undergo successful removal of a corticotroph adenoma exhibit suppression of the hypothalamic-pituitary-adrenal axis after surgery, suggesting that CRH is low rather than high. Second, many patients with Cushing's disease respond to exogenous CRH, suggesting that endogenous CRH levels are not high. On balance, the great majority of cases of Cushing's disease likely arise from a primary defect at the level of the pituitary, with rare cases possibly being caused by hypothalamic dysregulation. In addition, there are rare cases of corticotroph hyperplasia causing Cushing's syndrome that are secondary to CRH production by either adjacent CRH-producing intrasellar gangliocytomas or ectopic CRH-producing cancers.

In contrast to other pituitary tumors, the great majority (80 to 90%) of ACTH-secreting tumors are microadenomas at the time of diagnosis. The clinical features of cortisol excess may allow detection of corticotroph adenomas before they have grown to a larger size. High levels of cortisol may also restrain tumor growth. ACTH-secreting macroadenomas tend to be locally invasive.

Clinical Manifestations

The clinical features of Cushing's disease are caused by the effects of excess glucocorticoids and by the hypersecretion of ACTH and other POMC peptide products. The severity of the features of Cushing's disease varies greatly and appears to reflect not only the level of free cortisol but also the duration of the disease and perhaps the sensitivity to glucocorticoid action. In florid cases of Cushing's disease (Fig. 237–2), the constellation of symptoms and physical features is readily recognized. Early in the disease or in mild cases, however, it can be extremely challenging to distinguish the clinical features of Cushing's disease from similar traits that are seen in the normal population. Clinical suspicion is of paramount impor-

Continued

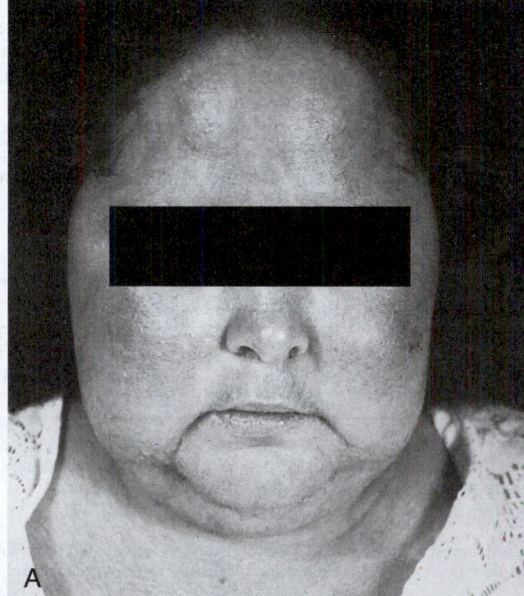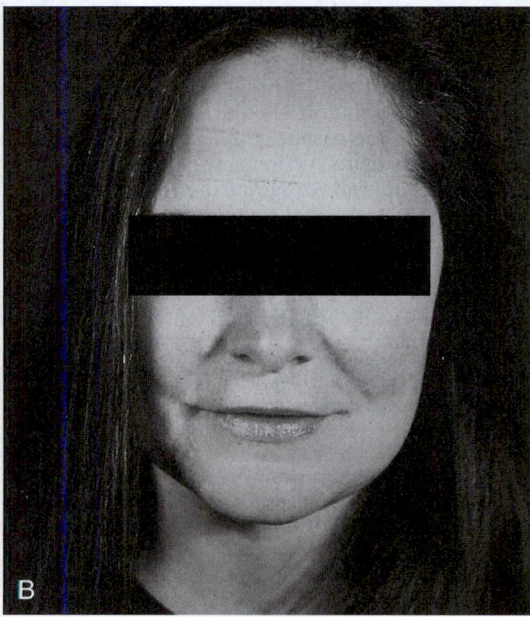

FIGURE 237–2 • Clinical features of Cushing's disease. A 25-year-old woman presented with severe Cushing's disease. *A*, Facial features of Cushing's syndrome including plethora, moon facies, and hirsutism are evident. *B*, Dramatic resolution of the manifestations of cortisol excess after successful transsphenoidal surgery. (Photographs courtesy of Dr. Beverly M. K. Biller.)

tance because it establishes the first screening test before laboratory studies are embarked upon. On the other hand, one must be discriminating and not formally evaluate everyone with obesity, hypertension, and glucose intolerance. Of the many features listed in Table 237–9, some are relatively specific for Cushing's disease. For example, the centripetal distribution of fat with the characteristic "buffalo hump," "moon facies," and deposition in supraclavicular area, with minimal fat in the extremities, is much more specific than generalized obesity. Striae that are wide (>1 cm) and purple reflect steroid-induced thinning of the dermis and can be distinguished from the more common "stretch marks." Numerous spontaneous ecchymoses also occur because of thinning of the skin and capillary fragility. Proximal muscle weakness represents another manifestation of glucocorticoid excess. Osteopenia and hypokalemia, when present, provide objective evidence consistent with ACTH excess. Hypokalemia results from the effects of ACTH on mineralocorticoid production but also from the ability of high levels of cortisol to saturate 11β-dehydrogenase, an enzyme in the kidney that inactivates cortisol. As a result, cortisol can "spill over" and act on mineralocorticoid receptors in the distal tubule. The hyperpigmentation associated with Cushing's disease is not as striking as one encounters with Addison's disease or in ectopic ACTH syndrome; but in association with other findings, it should raise the suspicion of Cushing's disease and help to distinguish it from adrenal causes of hypercortisolemia. Hirsutism and acne are caused by the increased production of adrenal androgens and are more prominent in patients with Cushing's disease than in those with adrenal adenomas, in whom glucocorticoids tend to be the predominant product. Oligo/amenorrhea probably has several causes, including androgen effects on the reproductive axis and glucocorticoid inhibition of GnRH, which may also account for diminished libido. Hypertension and glucose intolerance are caused by glucocorticoid excess. Immunosuppression, opportunistic infections, and impaired wound healing can lead to considerable morbidity. Neuropsychiatric symptoms, including depression, can be prominent effects of Cushing's disease. Suicide occurs with increased frequency in persons who receive no treatment for Cushing's disease.

Diagnosis

The screening tests and differential diagnosis of Cushing's syndrome represent one of the greatest diagnostic challenges in endocrinology (Chapter 240). In most cases, the complete evaluation of Cushing's syndrome can take place in the outpatient setting. The first step is to determine whether a patient truly has cortisol excess. After confirmation of Cushing's syndrome, one must distinguish among (1) adrenal causes of cortisol excess; (2) pituitary causes of ACTH excess (Cushing's disease); (3) ectopic sources of ACTH; and (4) ectopic CRH (Table 237–10).

In screening for hypercortisolism, random cortisol levels are not useful because of diurnal variation of the hormone. The overnight dexamethasone test is the most widely used screening test (see Table 237–8). A normal result of the dexamethasone test essentially excludes Cushing's syndrome. It should be noted, however, that abnormal overnight dexamethasone suppression can be seen in up to 30% of hospitalized patients and in many patients with depression or during alcohol withdrawal. An elevated 24-hour urine free cortisol value

Table 237–9 • CLINICAL FEATURES OF CUSHING'S DISEASE

General
Obesity (centripetal distribution)
"Moon facies" and mild proptosis
Increased supraclavicular fat and "buffalo hump"
Hypertension
Skin
Hyperpigmentation
Facial plethora
Hirsutism
Violaceous striae and thin skin
Capillary fragility and easy bruising
Acne
Edema
Musculoskeletal
Muscle weakness (proximal)
Osteoporosis and back pain
Reproductive
Decreased libido
Oligo/amenorrhea
Neuropsychiatric
Depression
Irritability and emotional lability
Psychosis
Metabolic
Hypokalemia and alkalosis
Hypercalciuria and renal stones
Glucose intolerance or diabetes mellitus
Impaired wound healing
Impaired resistance to infection
Granulocytosis and lymphopenia
Tumor Mass Effects
Headache
Visual field loss
Hypopituitarism

provides an alternative, or additional, screening test for hypercortisolism. Often, two sequential specimens are collected because of day-to-day variations in hormone production. The sensitivity and specificity of urinary free cortisol measurements are greater than those of the overnight dexamethasone suppression test, particularly in hospitalized patients. A third test takes advantage of the observation that there is a loss of diurnal variation of cortisol levels in all forms of Cushing's syndrome. This test consists of finding elevation of a midnight cortisol level in the serum or saliva. Kits are available for patients to obtain a late-night salivary cortisol sample.

After demonstrating that cortisol excess is present, the next step is to determine the source of excess ACTH or cortisol. The classic approach is to perform a low-dose, followed by a high-dose, dexamethasone suppression test (see Tables 237–8 and 237–10). The low-dose dexamethasone test excludes or confirms the presence of Cushing's syndrome. On the second day of the test, normal individuals suppress plasma cortisol to less than 5 μg/dL and reduce the 17-hydroxysteroids to less than 2.5 mg/24 hr or urinary free cortisol to less than 20 μg/24 hr. All forms of Cushing's syndrome fail to suppress according to these criteria.

The high-dose dexamethasone test is one of several means to distinguish ACTH-independent and ACTH-dependent causes of Cushing's syndrome and to discriminate between pituitary and ectopic causes

Table 237–10 • TESTS USED IN THE DIFFERENTIAL DIAGNOSIS OF CUSHING'S SYNDROME*

ETIOLOGY	OVERNIGHT DEXAMETHASONE SUPPRESSION TEST	PLASMA ACTH	LOW-DOSE DEXAMETHASONE	HIGH-DOSE DEXAMETHASONE	CORTICOTROPIN-RELEASING HORMONE STIMULATION OF ACTH	PETROSAL/PERIPHERAL ACTH RATIO
Normal	Suppression	Normal	Suppression		Normal	
Pituitary	No suppression	Normal or high	No suppression	Suppression	Normal or increased	>2
Ectopic	No suppression	High or normal	No suppression	No suppression	No response	<1.5
Adrenal	No suppression	Low	No suppression	No suppression	No response	

*Classic responses are indicated. Certain cases of ectopic adrenocorticotropic hormone (ACTH) production are suppressed by high-dose dexamethasone or are stimulated by corticotropin-releasing hormone. In these cases, petrosal sinus sampling is the most reliable method for distinguishing pituitary and etopic sources of ACTH.

of ACTH-dependent Cushing's syndrome (see Table 237–10). Because adrenal sources of cortisol excess are autonomous and ACTH independent, plasma and urinary cortisol levels are not affected by dexamethasone suppression, even at high doses. In addition, plasma ACTH levels are low in adrenal causes of Cushing's syndrome because the hypothalamic-pituitary axis is suppressed. Pituitary and ectopic causes of Cushing's disease are both ACTH dependent but respond differently to high-dose dexamethasone. Pituitary adenomas have an altered set point for glucocorticoid inhibition but retain a partial ability to respond to high-dose dexamethasone. The exact criteria for dexamethasone suppression in the high-dose test are debated. In most cases of ACTH-producing pituitary adenomas, 17-hydroxysteroids are suppressed to less than 50% of baseline and urinary free cortisol is suppressed below 90% of baseline during the high-dose dexamethasone test.

The ectopic ACTH syndrome should be suspected in patients with known malignancies, particularly small cell carcinoma of the lung; bronchial, thymic, or gastrointestinal carcinoids; islet cell tumors; and medullary carcinoma of the thyroid, among others. Plasma ACTH levels are often very high (>200 pg/mL) and can be associated with hyperpigmentation. Clinical features of Cushing's syndrome may be altered by the rapid onset of extreme hypercortisolemia coincident with elements of tumor cachexia. Pronounced weakness, fluid retention, glucose intolerance, hypokalemia, and poor skin integrity are often seen.

Ectopic ACTH syndrome is readily recognized in its classic form. However, a subset of tumors, particularly carcinoids, exhibit dexamethasone suppression that is similar to that seen with pituitary adenomas. When suspected, carcinoids can sometimes be detected by CT or MRI, but many are too small to be seen even with these techniques. Because of these exceptions to the high-dose dexamethasone test, a variety of procedures have been devised in an attempt to further distinguish ectopic and pituitary dependent sources of ACTH. The metyrapone test takes advantage of the fact that inhibition of 11β-hydroxylase blocks cortisol production. As a result, negative feedback is reduced and pituitary dependent sources of ACTH typically exhibit an increase in ACTH that stimulates the production of precursor adrenal steroids (e.g., 11-deoxycortisol) (see Table 237–4). Although most ectopic causes of ACTH exhibit a blunted response to the decreased cortisol levels, the subset of ectopic tumors that respond atypically to dexamethasone are most likely to give a positive response in the metyrapone test.

In recent years, inferior petrosal sinus sampling has been used to distinguish pituitary and ectopic sources of ACTH when the source of ACTH is not obvious based on the clinical circumstances, biochemical evaluation, and imaging studies. This test requires an experienced radiologist for safe and effective catheterization of the petrosal sinuses (which drain the pituitary venous effluent). Blood samples are taken simultaneously from the left and right petrosal sinuses and from the periphery. In the case of ACTH-producing pituitary adenomas, there is a gradient in ACTH levels between the central and peripheral blood specimens. Administration of CRH stimulates ACTH and tends to enhance the gradient. A gradient of 2:1 (central:peripheral) basally or 3:1 after CRH on either the left or the right is consistent with a pituitary source of ACTH. When clinical and biochemical studies suggest the presence of a pituitary adenoma, pituitary imaging should be performed using CT or MRI. Most ACTH-secreting pituitary adenomas are small and scans are normal in more than half of patients.

Rx Treatment

The efficacy of transsphenoidal surgery for Cushing's disease is greatly aided by making the correct diagnosis preoperatively. In experienced hands, surgical cures of ACTH-producing microadenomas occur in 75 to 90% of patients undergoing a first operation. As in other pituitary tumors, complete remissions with macroadenomas are much less common. In the event of surgical remission or cure, postoperative hypocortisolism is to be expected because of suppression of the hypothalamic-pituitary axis. After coverage for steroid withdrawal in the postoperative period, cortisol replacement should gradually be decreased to allow recovery of the hypothalamic-pituitary-adrenal axis.

If transsphenoidal surgery is unsuccessful, reoperation may be indicated and can result in remission in up to 50% of patients. If transsphenoidal surgery cannot be performed or has failed, alternative forms of therapy should be used to prevent the long-term consequences of hypercortisolism. Pituitary irradiation is usually the second line of treatment for Cushing's disease. It is more efficacious in children and in younger patients, but even in older adults remissions can be achieved in 50 to 60% within 2 years. To prevent the continued ravages of hypercortisolism during this period, however, concomitant medical therapy is usually given. Bilateral adrenalectomy represents another alternative for patients with severe hypercortisolism after transsphenoidal surgery. It rapidly and effectively lowers cortisol levels but is associated with relatively high morbidity and mortality rates (as high as 5%) because of the associated metabolic and immune system alterations caused by hypercortisolism. The morbidity has been reduced in recent years by introduction of the laparoscopic approach. After adrenalectomy, patients must be maintained on glucocorticoids and mineralocorticoids and are at risk for the development of Nelson's syndrome.

Medical therapy for Cushing's disease has its primary role in preparation for surgery or for control of hypercortisolism during the interval when radiation therapy is taking effect. Because most pituitary adenomas are responsive to changes in cortisol levels, they have a tendency to "escape" from adrenal blockade caused by some therapies by producing higher levels of ACTH. The antifungal agent ketoconazole is highly effective in decreasing glucocorticoid biosynthesis and also inhibits ACTH secretion so that it has become the medical therapy of choice. Alternative medications include metyrapone, aminoglutethimide, mifepristone, etomidate, and mitotane.

NELSON'S SYNDROME

Nelson's syndrome was initially described as the appearance of a pituitary adenoma after bilateral adrenalectomy. In addition to an enlarging pituitary mass, the syndrome is characterized by very high ACTH levels and hyperpigmentation. It is caused by a preexisting ACTH-producing tumor that grows in the absence of feedback inhibition by high levels of glucocorticoids. The incidence of clinically significant Nelson's syndrome after adrenalectomy for Cushing's disease varies from 10 to 50% in different series. Patients with Cushing's disease who have undergone adrenalectomy should be followed with imaging studies and plasma ACTH levels because tumors that cause Nelson's syndrome can be very aggressive. When there is evidence of mass effects or rapid growth, transsphenoidal surgery should be performed. Postoperative irradiation may provide additional benefit, although it appears to be less efficacious than in other ACTH-producing adenomas.

GONADOTROPINS (FOLLICLE-STIMULATING HORMONE AND LUTEINIZING HORMONE)

The pituitary glycoprotein hormones include FSH, LH, and TSH. Chorionic gonadotropin, which is structurally very similar to LH, is made in the placenta. Each of the glycoprotein hormones has a specific β-subunit that forms a non-covalent dimer with the common α-subunit. The α- and individual β-subunits are encoded by separate genes. The β-subunit genes are evolutionarily related and share a common gene structure as well as having nucleotide and amino acid sequence homology. Similarities in the structures of the β-subunits account for their ability to form non-covalent dimers with the common α-subunit. The α- and β-subunits each undergo glycosylation, which is important for correct hormone folding, intracellular transport, and secretion. Glycosylation is also required for biologic activity, presumably because of effects on the tertiary structure of the hormones.

The half-life of LH (approximately 50 minutes) is shorter than that of FSH (approximately 220 minutes), accounting for the more rapid secretory dynamics of LH, even though both hormones are secreted together. Differences in FSH and LH sequences between the conserved cysteines provide distinct "determinant loops" that allow the hormones to bind to specific receptors. Receptor contacts are made by both the α- and β-subunits. The receptors for FSH and LH are also structurally related and are members of the G protein–coupled seven transmembrane family. After binding to their receptors, LH and FSH stimulate cyclic AMP production, phosphatidylinositol turnover, and mobilization of calcium.

The gonadotropins are involved in sexual differentiation, sex steroid production, and gametogenesis. The regulation and physiologic roles of gonadotropins are quite different in males and females. In males, receptors for FSH are located on Sertoli cells and seminiferous tubules, whereas LH receptors are located on Leydig cells in the testis. LH stimulates androgen production by the Leydig cells. FSH is involved primarily in sperm maturation in the seminiferous tubules. Thus, FSH and LH act together to induce spermatogenesis (Chapter 247).

In females, ovarian FSH receptors are located on granulosa cells, where they induce enzymes involved in estrogen biosynthesis. LH receptors are located predominantly on thecal cells in the ovary and stimulate the production of ovarian androgens and steroid precursors that are transported to granulosa cells for aromatization to estrogens. The pattern of FSH and LH secretion during the menstrual cycle results in follicular recruitment and maturation (largely FSH-mediated), followed by ovulation (largely LH-mediated) and steroid production by the corpus luteum.

Gonadotropin secretion is regulated primarily by the hypothalamic decapeptide GnRH. The receptor for GnRH is a member of the G protein–coupled seven transmembrane family of receptors. GnRH stimulates an immediate release of intracellular calcium followed by a second phase of extracellular calcium influx. GnRH also activates phosphatidylinositol turnover, resulting in production of diacylglycerol and inositol triphosphate, which act together to stimulate the protein kinase C pathway. The gonadotroph cell is exquisitely sensitive to the pattern of GnRH stimulation. Continuous, rather than pulsatile exposure to GnRH causes gonadotroph desensitization and suppression of LH and FSH. Gonadotroph sensitivity to GnRH is modulated by sex steroids and probably other hypothalamic peptides, such as neuropeptide Y. Increased GnRH secretion in combination with a higher density of GnRH receptors and rising estradiol concentrations accounts in part for the dramatic release of gonadotropins that induces ovulation.

The hypothalamic-pituitary-gonadal axis is activated during fetal development. However, during the first 2 years of life, LH and FSH levels fall and remain suppressed until puberty. The physiologic basis for gonadotropin suppression during early childhood is not well understood but involves tonic inhibition of the GnRH pulse generator by the central nervous system as the pituitary gland is still responsive to exogenous GnRH. Most theories hold that the onset of puberty reflects disinhibition of the pulse generator. Puberty occurs between ages 8 and 13 in girls and between ages 9 and 14 in boys. In the peripubertal period, sleep-associated bursts of LH secretion can first be detected at night. Subsequently, there is a gradual increase in LH pulse frequency and amplitude, such that LH pulses are detected during the day and night.

In women, the pattern of GnRH pulse frequency varies across the menstrual cycle (Part XIX). The combination of GnRH stimulation, in conjunction with ovarian feedback regulation, results in a complex orchestration of positive and negative hormonal signals that converge at the gonadotroph to regulate LH and FSH secretion. The typical 28-day menstrual cycle is divided into follicular and luteal phases that are separated by ovulation on day 14. Unlike chronic exposure to low concentrations of estrogens, which exert negative feedback regulation and inhibit GnRH, the increasing concentration of estrogen before the LH surge exerts positive feedback regulation that results in increased GnRH pulse frequency. Increased GnRH, in combination with increased gonadotroph sensitivity to GnRH, results in the LH/FSH surge. During the luteal phase, the gonadotropin pulse frequency is reduced. In addition to feedback regulation by steroids, ovarian peptides such as inhibin also play a role in control of the reproductive axis. Inhibin causes selective suppression of FSH, without affecting LH secretion. A homodimer of inhibin β-subunits, referred to as *activin*, has opposite actions and selectively stimulates FSH, but its predominant physiologic action is to increase ovarian granulosa cell responsivity to FSH. Circulating inhibin provides one of the negative feedback inputs that leads to FSH suppression as the follicle develops.

The perimenopause is characterized by a gradual cessation of ovarian function. After several years of menstrual cycles that are sometimes anovulatory or irregular, menses cease, thereby defining the menopause. Although there is considerable variation, menopause usually occurs at about age 50. At this point, ovarian follicles have been depleted, and the production of sex steroids changes such that there is minimal production of estrogen and progesterone, but ovarian androgens continue to be made at lesser levels, primarily by stromal cells. The chronic decline in estrogen and progesterone causes loss of feedback inhibition and a marked increase in LH and FSH levels.

In males, the regulation of the hypothalamic-pituitary-gonadal axis is relatively constant. After early puberty, LH and FSH pulses occur about once an hour during the night and day. It is notable that there is considerable variation in LH pulse frequency among normal individuals. Because each pulse of LH stimulates testosterone secretion, one also observes pulses of testosterone after LH, although these pulses are muted somewhat by the presence of serum binding proteins that delay clearance. Nevertheless, testosterone levels can drop below the "normal" range in individuals with slow LH pulse frequencies. Testosterone inhibits the hypothalamic-pituitary axis, although its actions are mediated, in part, by aromatization to estrogens, as has been shown in rare patients who are unable to convert testosterone to estrogen because of a deficiency of aromatase. Much of the inhibition by gonadal steroids occurs at the hypothalamic level, but there is also evidence for weak inhibition of the gonadotroph at the level of the pituitary gland. In contrast to menopause in women, there is no analogous abrupt change in hormone levels in men. There is, however, a gradual decline in testosterone levels associated with an increase in LH and FSH with aging.

HYPOGONADOTROPIC HYPOGONADISM

Clinical features of hypogonadotropic hypogonadism in women are primarily due to estrogen deficiency and include breast atrophy, vaginal dryness, and diminished libido. Hot flashes are uncommon, in contrast to postmenopausal estrogen deficiency. In premenopausal women, normal menstrual cycles provide evidence for an intact hypothalamic-pituitary-gonadal axis. LH and FSH levels should be increased in postmenopausal women. Hypogonadism in men causes decreased libido and sexual function. In men, low testosterone without elevation of LH and FSH is consistent with impaired hypothalamic-pituitary reserve. GnRH stimulation can distinguish hypothalamic and pituitary deficiency but may require multiple injections to prime the pituitary, if GnRH deficiency is of long standing.

In premenopausal women, preparations of estrogen and progestins should be used for hormonal replacement and to allow cyclical growth of the endometrium. Pulsatile GnRH (for GnRH-deficient subjects) or gonadotropins can be given to induce ovulation and fertility when desired. Testosterone can be replaced in men using intramuscular injections that are given at 2- to 4-week intervals. Doses and the intervals between injections should be adjusted on an individual basis using libido and testosterone levels before the next injection as a guide. Oral preparations of androgens should be avoided because of hepatotoxicity. Transdermal patch and gel preparations are also available and give more even testosterone levels but are more expensive than depot injections. However, there is less experience with their long-term acceptance and efficacy. Induction of spermatogenesis requires pulsatile GnRH (for GnRH-deficient subjects) or injections of gonadotropins.

A congenital form of hypogonadotropic hypogonadism is caused by deficiency of GnRH, which in turn causes deficiencies of LH and FSH. When associated with anosmia (absent sense of smell), the condition is referred to as Kallmann's syndrome (Chapter 235). Pulsatile GnRH has been used to induce puberty and fertility in both males and females with Kallmann's syndrome and other forms of GnRH deficiency.

Secondary hypogonadotropic hypogonadism is relatively common. In most cases, it is reversible and is caused by weight loss, anorexia nervosa, stress, heavy exercise, or severe illness. Reversible forms of secondary hypogonadotropic hypogonadism are caused by GnRH deficiency and are more common in women than men. The condition is ideally treated by correcting the underlying cause. Many women have a discrete threshold for weight or exercise level that will cause loss of menstrual periods. When it is not possible to correct the underlying abnormality, hormonal replacement can be used in women for protection against osteopenia and to cycle the endometrium.

A variety of pathologic conditions can cause secondary hypogonadotropic hypogonadism, often in association with deficiencies of other pituitary hormones (see Table 237–3). These include hypothalamic lesions or central nervous system irradiation. Pituitary tumors can suppress gonadotropins because of stalk compression and disruption of pulsatile GnRH input as well as by direct destruction of normal pituitary tissue. Hyperprolactinemia can suppress GnRH and lead to reduced gonadotropin levels. In contrast to the aforementioned causes of hypogonadotropic hypogonadism, which result from GnRH deficiency, primary deficiencies of LH and FSH are uncommon. An acquired form of isolated gonadotroph deficiency is rarely encountered and may have an autoimmune basis. Mutations in the LHβ or FSHβ genes have been described in case reports and cause selective loss of individual gonadotropins. Inactivating mutations in the GnRH receptor and the LH and FSH receptors causing hypogonadotropic hypogonadism have also been reported.

FOLLICLE STIMULATING HORMONE– AND LUTEINIZING HORMONE–PRODUCING TUMORS

Etiology and Pathogenesis

Although most early series suggested that gonadotropin-producing adenomas were relatively uncommon, recent studies using sensitive techniques to characterize tumor phenotype show a prevalence (15 to 20%) that is greater than that of corticotroph or somatotroph adenomas (see Table 237–6). The majority (70 to 80%) of pituitary tumors classified previously as nonfunctioning adenomas can be shown to produce low levels of intact glycoprotein hormones or their uncombined α- or β-subunits. Biosynthetic defects in the tumor cells account for relatively inefficient hormone secretion as well as the propensity to produce uncombined subunits. FSH is produced more commonly than LH. Elevated levels of free α-subunits are noted more often than increased free β-subunits.

Clinical Manifestations

Gonadotropin-producing tumors are somewhat more common in men than women and increase in prevalence with age. FSH- and LH-producing tumors do not usually cause a characteristic hormone excess syndrome. The tumors are typically large macroadenomas and manifest as clinically nonfunctioning tumors with symptoms and signs related to local mass effects. Visual field loss due to suprasellar extension and compression of the optic chiasm is found in more than 70% of patients. Many of these tumors are detected incidentally by CT and MRI performed for unrelated indications. Symptoms of hypopituitarism, including hypogonadism with loss of libido, are also common. Men with predominantly FSH-secreting tumors may present with testicular enlargement from hypertrophy of the seminiferous tubules but also can paradoxically present with hypogonadal features that are related to low levels of testosterone. These patients must be distinguished from those with primary hypogonadism who have testicular dysfunction. Tumors that primarily secrete LH are rare but can cause increased testosterone levels. Premenopausal women with gonadotropin-producing tumors may experience menstrual irregularity or secondary hypogonadism. Postmenopausal women often show reduced gonadotropin levels because the mass effects of the gonadotropin-producing tumors cause stalk compression, impairing GnRH stimulation of gonadotropins from normal pituitary cells.

Diagnosis

Because of the absence of a clinical syndrome in most patients, the preoperative diagnosis of gonadotropin-producing pituitary tumors has relied on imaging studies and laboratory tests. Unfortunately, the laboratory diagnosis of gonadotropin-producing tumors is less than satisfactory. First, the tumors synthesize gonadotropins inefficiently and hormone levels are usually not markedly elevated. Second, because the secretion of gonadotropins is pulsatile, random LH and FSH values are difficult to interpret. Furthermore, gonadotropin levels vary widely and are normally elevated in postmenopausal women. GnRH stimulation tests also do not clearly distinguish subjects with gonadotropin-producing tumors from normal subjects, and suppression tests have not proven useful. However, paradoxical responses to TRH have helped to identify

gonadotropin-secreting tumors. In contrast to its effect on normal persons, TRH stimulates secretion of intact gonadotropins or the uncombined FSHβ- and LHβ-subunits in most patients with gonadotropin tumors. Once identified, the uncombined α- or β-subunits can serve as tumor markers and can be useful for monitoring responses to therapy.

Men with proven gonadotropin-producing tumors typically have high-normal or elevated FSH levels but low levels of testosterone. Moderately elevated PRL levels are common and are caused by tumor mass effects. It is important to distinguish this group from patients with true prolactinomas. As noted earlier, many women, including those in the postmenopausal group, have paradoxically low gonadotropin levels. Thus, the absence of elevated gonadotropins does not exclude the diagnosis of a gonadotropin-producing tumor.

The postoperative diagnosis of gonadotropin-producing tumors can be made based on immunohistochemical analyses or using more sophisticated studies of gonadotropin gene expression. These types of analyses confirm that the great majority of clinically nonfunctioning tumors are composed of gonadotropin-producing cell types.

Rx Treatment

Because the major symptoms of the gonadotropin-producing tumors are due to extrasellar extension and local mass effects, the main aim of treatment is reduction in the size of the tumor. Complete or partial reversal of visual field defects and hypopituitarism can be accomplished by surgery, unless these conditions have been of long standing. Transsphenoidal surgery is rarely curative of this group of macroadenomas, however. Patients with significant residual tumor may benefit from radiation therapy, although there are no large series in which patients have been randomly allocated to treatment groups. Because most tumors are slow growing, one approach when no tumor is visible postoperatively by MRI is to monitor tumor recurrence using visual fields and CT or MRI. If tumor markers such as free α- or β-subunit levels are available, they can be used alone, or in conjunction with TRH testing, to monitor tumor function. When follow-up studies show tumor regrowth, repeat surgery or radiation therapy, or both, is indicated.

There has been great interest in medical therapies that might be useful as adjuncts to surgery or even as primary therapies in patients not requiring immediate decompression. The success of dopamine agonists and somatostatin analogues in treating hormone oversecretion and tumor mass in prolactinomas and acromegaly has not been seen in most patients with gonadotropin-producing tumors, although exceptions have been described in selected patients. The efficacy of long-acting GnRH agonists or antagonists, which suppress LH and FSH in normal individuals, has also been examined. The GnRH agonists stimulate gonadotropin secretion from tumors, without apparent desensitization, and have not been useful. GnRH antagonists have been shown to suppress FSH levels in small series of patients, but these agents have not been found to reduce tumor size.

THYROID-STIMULATING HORMONE

Like the other glycoprotein hormones, TSH is a heterodimer composed of the common α-subunit and the unique TSH β-subunit. Both subunits are glycosylated, and the composition of carbohydrates is thought to alter the biologic activity of the hormone. TSH is produced in thyrotroph cells that account for about 5% of pituitary cell types. TSH is measured by highly sensitive immunoradiometric assays that use antisera directed toward the TSHβ-subunit. Normal levels of TSH range from 0.4 to 4.0μU/mL. The detection limit for current TSH assays is less than 0.01 μU/mL, allowing measurement of suppressed TSH levels in patients with hyperthyroidism.

Thyroid-stimulating hormone controls thyroid hormone (T_4 and T_3) synthesis and secretion from the thyroid gland. TSH receptors are members of the G protein–coupled seven-transmembrane family and are structurally related to LH and FSH receptors. TSH stimulates cyclic AMP production and acts as a trophic hormone as well as stimulating hormone biosynthesis in the thyroid. TSH secretion from the pituitary gland is regulated by the hypothalamic-pituitary-thyroid axis.

Hypothalamic TRH is a tripeptide that stimulates TSH synthesis and secretion. TRH, acting through its G protein–coupled receptor, elicits phosphatidylinositol turnover and induces release of intracellular calcium followed by an influx of extracellular calcium. TSH secretion appears to be modulated by alterations in calcium flux, whereas biosynthesis may be controlled by activation of other pathways, such as protein kinase C. A variety of other hypothalamic hormones including somatostatin and dopamine can inhibit TSH secretion, but their roles in normal physiology have not been clearly elucidated.

Thyroid hormones have an inhibitory effect on the production of TRH and TSH and constitute a powerful negative feedback loop in the hypothalamic-pituitary-thyroid axis. The direct effects of thyroid hormone at the level of the pituitary gland are well illustrated by TSH responses to TRH stimulation tests. In hypothyroidism, TSH responses to exogenous TRH are exaggerated. In hyperthyroidism, TSH responses to TRH are blunted or flat, indicating that the inhibitory effects of thyroid hormone override the stimulatory effects of TRH. Thyroid hormones act via nuclear receptors that function at the transcriptional level to suppress expression of the TRH gene as well as the α- and β-subunit genes of TSH. In hypothyroidism, expression of the TSHα and TSHβ genes is stimulated and hormone production is markedly enhanced.

Secretion of TSH is pulsatile, but the amplitude of the pulses is relatively small and does not create the difficulties in measurement of TSH that are encountered with measurements of other pituitary hormones. TSH levels are elevated in infants in the immediate postpartum period. Thereafter, thyroid function tests remain remarkably constant throughout life. There is a diurnal rhythm of TSH secretion with a small increase at night. Because of the integrated nature of the hypothalamic-pituitary-thyroid axis, thyroid function tests are best interpreted when concentrations of TSH, free T_4, and free T_3 levels are known. Except in conditions of secondary hypothyroidism or TSH-secreting pituitary tumors (see later), TSH levels provide an excellent screening test for thyroid dysfunction. In cases of primary hypothyroidism, TSH levels are elevated as TSH increases logarithmically in response to falling thyroid hormone levels (Chapter 239). In hyperthyroidism, TSH is suppressed to levels below or near the detection limits of most sensitive assays.

CENTRAL HYPOTHYROIDISM

Central forms of hypothyroidism include secondary hypothyroidism, which is caused by TSH deficiency, and tertiary hypothyroidism, which is caused by TRH deficiency. Three different types of congenital TSH deficiency are caused by genetic mutations. One type involves mutations in the TSHβ gene, in which several different types of mutations have been described. A second involves mutations in *Pit-1*, which causes combined deficiencies of GH, PRL, and TSH (see earlier). A third involves a mutation in the gene for TRH. Acquired, central forms of hypothyroidism are often associated with other pituitary hormone deficiencies, and usually there is no goiter because of low TSH levels.

Tests for TSH deficiency are best performed by analyzing free T_4 levels in combination with TSH. Low free T_4 without elevated TSH is consistent with central hypothyroidism. Free T_4 measurements should be used rather than total T_4 to avoid confusion caused by thyroxine-binding globulin (TBG) deficiency (which is suggested by high T_3 resin uptake tests). In some patients with hypothalamic disease, the TSH level is partially elevated in the presence of low levels of free T_4, but the bioactivity of the TSH is reduced. Central forms of hypothyroidism must be distinguished from the sick-euthyroid condition (Chapter 239). Laboratory tests in the sick-euthyroid syndrome progress through several phases but can include prolonged periods when both TSH and free thyroid hormone levels are low. It can be very difficult in these patients to unequivocally exclude central hypothyroidism. In addition to the clinical setting in which thyroid function tests are measured, the presence of normal thyroid function tests before the illness and the absence of known hypothalamic or pituitary disease make true central hypothyroidism unlikely. Increased levels of reverse T_3 are suggestive of sick-euthyroidism, and free T_4 and T_3 may be in the normal or low normal range in sick-euthyroid patients. When TSH deficiency is documented, thyroid hormone is replaced using daily doses of L-thyroxine (0.05 to 0.15 mg/day). Because TSH cannot be used as an end point, one monitors serum levels of free T_4 and T_3.

THYROID-STIMULATING HORMONE–SECRETING TUMORS

Etiology and Pathogenesis

Thyroid stimulating hormone–secreting tumors are rare and account for between 1 and 3% of pituitary tumors. Like gonadotropin-producing tumors, a subset of tumors classified as clinically nonfunctioning tumors can be shown to produce TSH, often at subclinical levels. However, because TSH overproduction can cause hyperthyroidism, TSH-secreting tumors are more readily detected than FSH- and LH-producing tumors. As many as 30% of TSH-producing tumors are plurihormonal. GH and PRL are co-secreted most often, perhaps reflecting a common cellular lineage for thyrotrophs, somatotrophs, and lactotrophs. Long-standing severe hypothyroidism can cause thyrotroph hyperplasia and pituitary enlargement. These hyperplastic masses regress with thyroid hormone replacement therapy, however. Most true TSH-producing tumors are relatively autonomous and respond weakly, if at all, to TRH stimulation or thyroid hormone suppression.

Clinical Manifestations

Thyroid-stimulating hormone–secreting tumors are usually macroadenomas by the time a diagnosis has been made. Consequently, many patients exhibit mass effects of the tumor as well as hyperthyroidism. Now that measurement of TSH is being used as the initial assessment for hyperthyroidism, however, smaller tumors are being seen more commonly than previously. The clinical features of TSH-secreting tumors resemble those of Graves' disease, except that features of autoimmunity such as ophthalmopathy are absent. Circulating levels of T_4 and T_3 range widely but can be elevated as much as twofold to threefold. Diffuse goiter is present in the majority of patients with TSH-producing tumors, and the 24-hour uptake of radioiodine is elevated.

Diagnosis

Because feedback inhibition of TSH is impaired in TSH-producing tumors, TSH levels are inappropriately elevated in the presence of high levels of T_4 and T_3. TSH levels produced by tumors range from the low normal range to as high as 500 μU/mL, but most levels are minimally elevated. Through the use of ultrasensitive TSH assays, it is now possible to detect nonsuppressed TSH levels without the need for TRH testing. Free α-subunit measurements can be very helpful in confirming the diagnosis of a TSH-secreting tumor. Most TSH-producing tumors (>80%) secrete excess free α-subunit. Thus, the diagnosis of a TSH-secreting tumor can usually be made by demonstrating that a hyperthyroid patient has a detectable serum TSH level associated with excess secretion of the free α-subunit. The finding of a mass lesion on CT or MRI confirms the diagnosis. Several other causes of inappropriate TSH secretion should be considered, including resistance to thyroid hormone and familial dysalbuminemic hyperthyroxinemia and other disorders that alter serum thyroid hormone binding proteins.

 Treatment

The goals of therapy are to treat the underlying TSH-secreting tumor and to correct the hyperthyroidism. Transsphenoidal surgery alone is rarely curative because of the large size of most tumors, but it can alleviate mass effects and lower TSH levels. As in other large pituitary tumors, adjunctive irradiation may be required to control tumor growth. Somatostatin analogues have been used as adjunctive medical therapy, and they decrease TSH and α-subunit levels in about 80% of patients with TSH-secreting tumors, but consistent effects on tumor growth have not been demonstrated. Hyperthyroidism caused by TSH-secreting tumors can also be treated using antithyroid drugs or radioiodine.

NULL CELL PITUITARY TUMORS

Null cell adenomas, or clinically nonfunctioning tumors, are variably defined depending on the criteria used to analyze tumor cell phenotype. As noted earlier, the majority of clinically nonfunctioning adenomas can be shown to produce low levels of the free α-subunit, free β-subunits of FSH and LH, and intact FSH and LH when analyzed by immunocytochemistry or for messenger RNA expression. A smaller fraction can be shown to produce low levels of other pituitary hormones, particularly ACTH or GH, that escaped detection based on routine endocrine testing. Even with detailed analyses of hormone production, a subset (10 to 20%) of nonfunctioning adenomas do not appear to produce one of the major pituitary hormones.

The clinical features and management of null cell tumors are similar to those for gonadotropin-producing tumors. The major signs and symptoms result from tumor mass effects that cause visual field defects, headache and other neurologic symptoms, and hypopituitarism. Transsphenoidal surgery is the primary mode of treatment, with a goal of debulking the tumor to relieve mass effects. Because there are no serum tumor markers, patients must be followed by CT or MRI in conjunction with visual field tests.

1. Rosenfeld RG, Frane J, Attie KM, et al: Six-year results of a randomized, prospective trial of human growth hormone and oxandrolone in Turner syndrome. J Pediatr 1992;121:49–55.
2. Fine RN, Kohaut EC, Brown D, et al: Growth after recombinant human growth hormone treatment in children with chronic renal failure: Report of a multicenter randomized double-blind placebo-controlled study. Genentech Cooperative Study Group. J Pediatr 1994;124:374–382.
3. Ezzat S, Snyder PJ, Young WF, et al: Octreotide treatment of acromegaly: A randomized, multicenter study. Ann Intern Med 1992;117:711–718.
4. Trainer PJ, Drake WM, Katznelson L, et al: Treatment of acromegaly with the growth hormone-receptor antagonist pegvisomant. N Engl J Med 2000;342:1171–1177.
5. Webster J, Piscitelli G, Polli A, et al: A comparison of cabergoline and bromocriptine in the treatment of hyperprolactinemic amenorrhea. Cabergoline Comparative Study Group. N Engl J Med 1994;331:904–909.

SUGGESTED READINGS

Arafah BM: Medical management of hypopituitarism in patients with pituitary adenomas. Pituitary 2002;5:109–117. *Review of the treatment of hypopituitarism.*
Beck-Peccoz P, Persani L: Medical management of thyrotropin-secreting pituitary adenomas. Pituitary 2002;5:83–88. *Emphasizes role of somatostatin analogues.*
Boelaert K, Gittoes NJ: Radiotherapy for non-functioning pituitary adenomas. Eur J Endocrinol 2001;144:569–575. *Overview of the risks and benefits.*
Cheung CC, Ezzat S, Smyth HS, et al: The spectrum and significance of primary hypophysitis. J Clin Endocrinol Metab 2001;86:1048–1053. *A review of the clinical presentation and treatment of the various forms of hypophysitis.*
Raff H, Findling JW: A physiologic approach to diagnosis of the Cushing syndrome. Ann Intern Med 2003;138:980–991. *A well-referenced overview that emphasizes the physiology as well as practical diagnosis, with useful flow diagrams.*

238 POSTERIOR PITUITARY

Alan G. Robinson

Anatomy and Hormone Synthesis

The hormones of the posterior pituitary, vasopressin and oxytocin, are synthesized in specialized neurons in the hypothalamus, the magnocellular neurons. There are neurons specific for each hormone and these are noted for their large size. In the hypothalamus, the magnocellular neurons are clustered in the paired paraventricular nuclei and the paired supraoptic nuclei (Fig. 238–1). Vasopressin and oxytocin are also synthesized in parvicellular (small-cell) neurons of the paraventricular nuclei, and vasopressin (but not oxytocin) is synthesized in the suprachiasmatic nucleus. Transcription of vasopressin and oxytocin mRNA and translation of vasopressin and oxytocin prohormone occur entirely in the cell bodies of the hormone-specific neurons. The pre-prohormones are cleaved from the signal peptide in the endoplasmic reticulum, and the prohormones, propressophysin and pro-oxyphysin, are packaged with processing enzymes into neurosecretory granules. In the magnocellular neurons, the neurosecretory granules are transported out of the perikaryon via microtubules down the long axons that form the supraopticohypophyseal tract to terminate in axon terminals in the posterior pituitary. During transport, the processing enzymes cleave propressophysin to vasopressin (eight amino acids), vasopressin-neurophysin (95 amino acids), and vasopressin glycopeptide (39 amino acids). Pro-oxyphysin is similarly cleaved to oxytocin and oxytocin-neurophysin, but there is no glycopeptide for oxytocin. Within the neurosecretory granules,

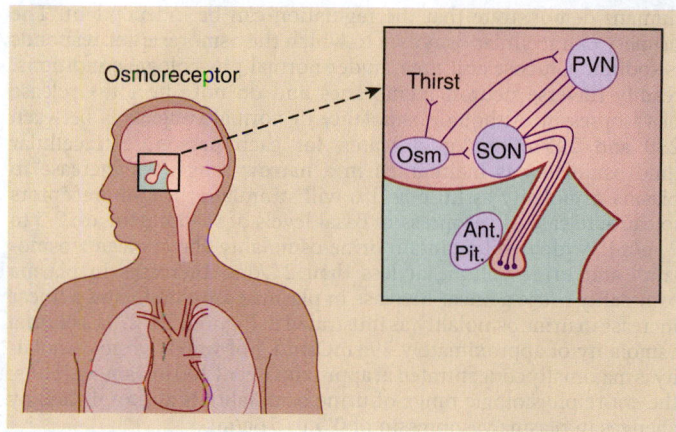

FIGURE 238–1 • Sagittal view of the head demonstrating the position of the neurohypophysis. The magnocellular neurons are clustered in two paraventricular nuclei (PVN) and two supraoptic nuclei (SON). Only one nucleus of each pair is illustrated. The supraoptic nuclei are located lateral to the edge of the optic chiasm, whereas the paraventricular nuclei are central in the wall of the third ventricle. The osmostat (Osm) and thirst center (Thirst) are located in the hypothalamus anterior to the third ventricle. The axons of the four nuclei combine to form the supraopticohypophyseal tract as they course through the pituitary stalk to their storage terminals in the posterior pituitary. Ant. Pit. = anterior pituitary. (From Buonocore CM, Robinson AG: Diagnosis and management of diabetes insipidus during medical emergencies. Endocrinol Metab Clin North Am 1993;22:411–423.)

neurophysins form neurophysin-hormone complexes that stabilize the hormones. Crystallography demonstrates that tetramers of neurophysin form specific binding sites for five molecules of hormone, so hormone in the granules is always bound. Stimulatory (e.g., cholinergic and angiotensin) neurotransmitter terminals and inhibitory (e.g., γ-aminobutyric acid, noradrenergic, atrial natriuretic peptide [ANP]) neurotransmitter terminals control the release of vasopressin by the activity of contacts on the cell body. Physiologic release of vasopressin or oxytocin into the general circulation is at the level of the posterior pituitary, where, in response to an action potential, intracellular calcium is increased to cause the neurosecretory granules to fuse with the axon membrane and to release (via exocytosis into the pericapillary space) the entire contents of the granule. Once released, the hormone has no further association with its respective neurophysin, and each of the peptide products can be independently detected in the general circulation. Factors that stimulate the release of hormone also stimulate synthesis; however, whereas release is instantaneous, synthesis requires a longer time. As synthesis is delayed, the large store of hormone in the posterior pituitary is essential for instantaneous and massive release of hormone as might be necessary with acute hemorrhage (vasopressin) or at delivery (oxytocin). In most species, sufficient vasopressin is stored in the posterior pituitary to support maximum antidiuresis for several days and to maintain baseline levels of antidiuresis for weeks without the synthesis of new hormone.

The axons of the parvicellular neurons of the paraventricular nuclei terminate in the median eminence of the basal hypothalamus, where, similar to other hypothalamic releasing factors, the hormones are secreted into the portal capillary system and where vasopressin serves as one of the regulators of secretion of adrenocorticotropic hormone. Still other axons secrete hormone into the cerebrospinal fluid of the third ventricle; however, the function of this secretion is unknown.

VASOPRESSIN

VASOPRESSIN AND REGULATION OF OSMOLALITY. The primary physiologic action of vasopressin is its function as a water-retaining hormone. The central sensing system (osmostat) for control of release of vasopressin is anatomically discrete, located in a small area of the hypothalamus just anterior to the third ventricle (see Fig. 238–1). The osmostat controls release of vasopressin to cause water retention and also stimulates thirst to cause water repletion. Osmotic regulation of vasopressin release and osmotic regulation of thirst are usually tightly coupled, but experimental lesions and some pathologic situations in humans demonstrate that the regulation can be independent. The primary extracellular osmolyte to which the osmoreceptor responds is sodium. Glucose and urea, under normal physiologic conditions, readily traverse neuron membranes and do not affect the release of vasopressin. Although osmolality in normal subjects is between 280 and 295 mOsm/kg of water, for each person, extracellular fluid osmolality is maintained in a narrow range. An increase in plasma osmolality as little as 1% will stimulate the osmoreceptors to cause release of vasopressin. Basal levels of vasopressin are 0.5 to 2 pg/mL, which will maintain urine osmolality above plasma osmolality and urine volume at less than 2 L/day. Increases in plasma osmolality cause a linear increase in plasma vasopressin and a linear increase in urine osmolality, as illustrated in Figure 238–2. At a plasma osmolality of approximately 294 mOsm/kg of water, urine osmolality is maximally concentrated at approximately 1200 mOsm/kg. Thus, the entire physiologic range of urine osmolality is accomplished by changes in plasma vasopressin of 0.5 to 5 pg/mL.

To maintain fluid balance, water must be not just conserved but consumed as well to replace obligate insensible water loss and obligate urine output. It is thought that thirst is not stimulated until a somewhat higher osmolality than the threshold for release of vasopressin. In a normal day, most humans get sufficient water from catabolism of food and from habitual fluid intake to maintain plasma osmolality below the threshold for thirst. Therefore, water balance (and hence osmolality) is regulated more by secretion of vasopressin than by thirst.

Vasopressin acts on V_2, or antidiuretic, receptors in the kidney to cause water retention. Activation of the V_2 receptors initiates the movement of aquaporin-2 water channels from the cytoplasm to the apical (luminal) membrane of the cells. These channels specifically allow the free movement of water into the cell. Water exits the cell through the basolateral membrane via aquaporin-3 and aquaporin-4 water channels, which are constitutively present. In the absence of vasopressin, the aquaporin-2 channels rapidly move out of the apical membrane. In addition to this "shuttling" of the aquaporin-2 channels, vasopressin also acts via V_2 receptors to regulate synthesis of aquaporin-2; that is, increased vasopressin stimulates aquaporin-2 synthesis and absence of vasopressin suppresses aquaporin-2 synthesis. The hypertonic medullary interstitium determines the maximum concentration of the final urine, which is isotonic with the inner medulla of the kidney (Chapter 111). Whereas the increase in urine osmolality is linear with increases in plasma vasopressin, the changes in urine volume are geometric. The difference is illustrated in Figure 238–2. Urine volume is maintained at less than 4 L/day until plasma vasopressin is nearly absent. When maximum urine osmolality decreases to less than 50 mOsm/kg, urine volume increases rapidly to 18 to 20 L/day.

VASOPRESSIN AND PRESSURE AND VOLUME REGULATION. In contrast to the osmoregulatory system, volume regulation is anatomically diffuse. High-pressure (baro-) receptors are located in the aorta and carotid sinus, and low-pressure volume receptors are located in the left atrium. Stimuli for pressure and volume receptors are carried via the glossopharyngeal (ninth) and vagal (tenth) cranial nerves to the brain stem and through the nucleus tractus solitarii to finally converge on the magnocellular neurons, where there are inhibitory as well as excitatory inputs. Decreases in blood pressure or vascular volume stimulate vasopressin release, whereas maneuvers that increase volume or left atrial pressure (e.g., negative-pressure breathing) decrease secretion of vasopressin. The release of vasopressin in response to changes in volume or pressure is less sensitive than the release in response to osmoreceptors, and a 10 to 15% reduction in blood volume or pressure is needed to stimulate release of vasopressin. However, once arterial pressure falls and vasopressin is stimulated, the increase in response is logarithmic, and levels of vasopressin achieved are markedly above those achieved by osmotic stimulation. Other nonosmotic stimuli such as nausea and intestinal traction probably act through similar nonosmotic neural pathways to release vasopressin. The effector of the pressor component is the V_1 receptor located on vascular smooth muscle. For V_1 receptors, the mechanism of action of vasopressin is to increase intracellular calcium rather than stimulate adenylate cyclase. In intact animals, the pressor activity of vasopressin is weak because of compensatory vasodilatory systems that tend to modulate the action. The action of vasopressin in regulating blood pressure is prominent only when other endocrine systems are deficient (e.g., in autonomic neuropathy). The relatively insensitive regulation of vasopressin secretion by changes in volume and pressure and the modest role of vasopressin to regulate blood pressure are consistent with the notion that regulation of Na^+ (e.g., by renin-angiotensin-aldosterone) is more important to control volume than is regulation of water.

VASOPRESSIN AND ADRENOCORTICOTROPIC HORMONE. Vasopressin in the parvicellular and paraventricular neurons that terminate on the pituitary portal system is released into the pituitary portal capillaries and carried to the anterior pituitary. Anterior pituitary corticotrophs are stimulated via V(1b) receptors to release adrenocorticotropic hormone.

INTERACTION OF OSMOTIC AND VOLUME REGULATION. The vasopressin system has adapted nicely to human behavior. Water is consumed as available without thirst; then, vasopressin regulates water excretion to maintain plasma osmolality; this allows extensive geographic movement without thirst that would produce water-seeking behavior. Yet, thirst is a back-up if dehydration becomes excessive. Similarly, as pressure/volume regulation of vasopressin is less sensitive, modest changes in pressure or volume, which may be exacerbated by upright posture, do not interfere with regulation of osmolality. Usually, the physiologic regulation of osmolality and pressure volume are synergistic. Dehydration causes an increase in osmolality and a decrease in volume, both of which stimulate release of vasopressin. Excess administration of fluid causes both expansion of volume and decrease in osmolality to inhibit vasopressin secretion. Pathologic situations may be characterized by hyponatremia with inadequate volume, as with diuretic use, or a sense of inadequate volume, as with cardiac failure or cirrhosis. In these situations, volume regulation is predominant and vasopressin levels are high. ANP may affect the osmotic release and action of vasopressin. With volume expansion, ANP is

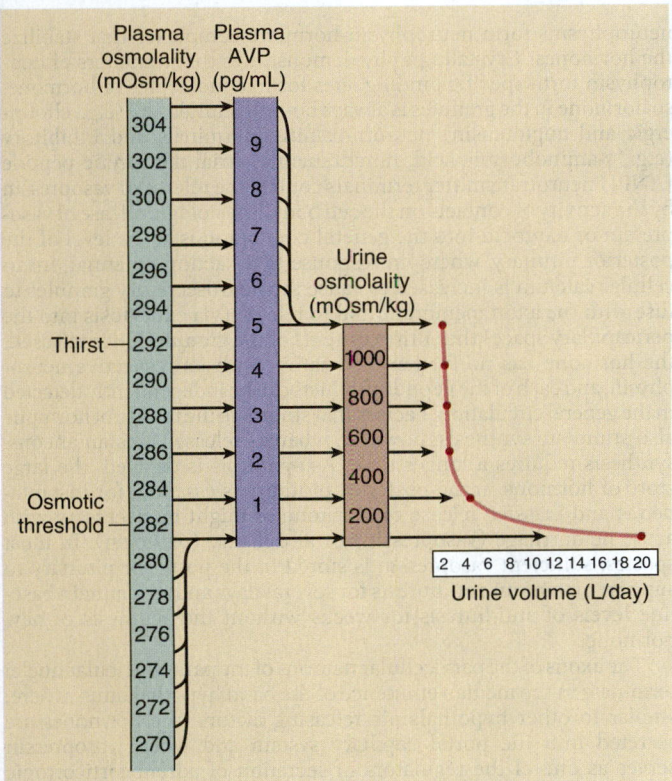

FIGURE 238–2 • Idealized schematic of the normal physiologic relationships among plasma osmolality (mOsm/kg H₂O), plasma vasopressin (pg/mL), urine osmolality (mOsm/kg H₂O), and urine volume (L/day). The entire physiologic range of urine osmolality occurs with 0.5 to 5 pg/mL of vasopressin. Increases in plasma osmolality above approximately 294 mOsm/kg of water result in increases in plasma vasopressin, but no further concentration of the urine, which is limited by the concentration in the renal inner medulla. The relation of volume (calculated based on a constant osmolar load) is logarithmic to the other parameters. Note that urine volume does not change much until there is absent vasopressin, and then volume increases dramatically. The shaded area represents the normal range and interrelationships of the various parameters. (Calculated from formulae presented in Robertson GL, Shelton RL, Athar S: The osmoregulation of vasopressin. Kidney Int 1976;10:25–37. Figure by Robinson AG, UCLA, Los Angeles, CA, with permission.)

released from atrial myocytes and acts at the kidney to induce natriuresis. ANP is also synthesized in the hypothalamus, where it may act to decrease vasopressin secretion. During pregnancy, there is an approximate decrease of osmolality of 10 mOsm/kg, and this is a true reset of the osmostat, where vasopressin increases and decreases appropriately around the lower plasma osmolality. Late in pregnancy, there is a change in the slope of the vasopressin/osmolality curve such that less vasopressin is released. The osmostat for thirst is reset in parallel. Plasma volume is also increased by 7 to 8 L due to profound vasodilatation, and this enlarged volume is similarly sensed as normal. In elderly humans, abnormalities in water and electrolyte balance are common, probably owing to age-related changes in body volume (as much as a 50% decrease in total body water above age 75) and renal function. Diseases that are common in elderly patients and the drugs used as therapy for these diseases affect water balance. Elderly humans have a decreased appreciation for thirst; and, although there is a normal ability to secrete vasopressin, there is a decreased ability to achieve either maximum urine concentration to retain water, or maximum dilution of urine to excrete water. Undetected hyper- or hyponatremia in the elderly can lead to increased morbidity and mortality, so it is important to pay attention to fluid balance problems in these patients.

OXYTOCIN

Oxytocin has similar concentrations in the posterior pituitary of men and women, but a physiologic function for oxytocin has been described only in women. While prolactin is the main hormone for milk production, oxytocin is essential for milk secretion. Suckling stimulates tactile receptors in the nipple, producing an afferent signal to the hypothalamus that causes release of oxytocin from the posterior pituitary. Oxytocin, in turn, induces contraction of specialized myoepithelial cells around the alveoli and ductules to eject milk. The other role of oxytocin is at parturition. This action is more complex and is variable among species. In all species, there is interaction of oxytocin with gonadal steroid hormones, prostaglandins, and relaxin. Additionally, regulation of the uterine receptors for oxytocin dramatically increases the response to oxytocin at the end of pregnancy. The interaction of these various hormones in a cross-stimulation feedforward cascade to support parturition is important to ensure survival of the species, so it is understandable that during parturition, lack of any single hormone (including oxytocin) is not sufficient to inhibit delivery. The greatest release of oxytocin occurs with, not before, delivery of the infant, probably secondary to stretching of the vaginal wall. This "Fergusson reflex" may aid delivery of subsequent fetuses in animals with multiple births; in humans, oxytocin release may be more important to induce uterine contraction to inhibit blood loss after delivery than to initiate parturition. No syndromes of increased or decreased secretion of oxytocin have been defined. Women with diabetes insipidus secondary to traumatic damage of the magnocellular neurons may have normal pregnancy and delivery and breastfeed their infants, but it may be that in these cases oxytocin neurons

survive better than vasopressin neurons. In animal studies, administration of oxytocin to males increases sperm transport, but this function has not been documented in humans. Similar to the receptors for vasopressin, the receptors for oxytocin in the breast and in the myometrium are different and independently regulated. At high plasma levels, oxytocin stimulates vasopressin receptors and vasopressin stimulates oxytocin receptors.

Excessive administration of oxytocin to induce labor can stimulate V_2 receptors of the kidney and cause abnormal water retention and hyponatremia.

DIABETES INSIPIDUS

Definition

Diabetes insipidus is the excretion of a large volume of hypotonic, insipid (tasteless) urine, usually accompanied by polyuria and polydipsia. The large volume, usually greater than 4 L/day, must be distinguished from increased frequency of small volumes and from large volumes of isotonic or hypertonic urine, both of which have other clinical significance. Four pathophysiologic mechanisms are considered in the differential diagnosis of diabetes insipidus: (1) Hypothalamic diabetes insipidus is the inability to secrete (and usually to synthesize) vasopressin in response to increased osmolality. No concentration of the dilute filtrate takes place in the renal collecting duct, and a large volume of urine is excreted. This situation produces an increase in serum osmolality with stimulation of thirst and secondary polydipsia. Levels of vasopressin in plasma are unmeasurable or low. (2) Nephrogenic diabetes insipidus is a disorder in which an otherwise normal kidney is unable to respond to vasopressin. As in hypothalamic diabetes insipidus, the dilute filtrate entering the collecting duct is excreted as a large volume of hypotonic urine. The rise in serum osmolality that occurs stimulates thirst and produces polydipsia. Unlike hypothalamic diabetes insipidus, however, measured levels of vasopressin in plasma are high. (3) Transient diabetes of pregnancy is a rare condition produced by extremely elevated levels of cystine aminopeptidase (oxytocinase or vasopressinase). The rapid destruction of vasopressin produces diabetes insipidus with polyuria and secondary stimulation of thirst to produce polydipsia. Because of the vasopressinase, plasma vasopressin cannot be measured. (4) Primary polydipsia is a primary disorder of thirst stimulation. Ingested water produces a mild decrease in serum osmolality that turns off secretion of vasopressin. In the absence of vasopressin action on the kidney, urine does not become concentrated, and a large volume of dilute urine is excreted. The amount of vasopressin measured in plasma is low. Although the pathophysiologic mechanisms for the four disorders are distinct, patients in each category usually have polyuria, polydipsia, and a normal serum sodium level because the normal thirst mechanism is sufficiently sensitive to maintain fluid balance in the first three disorders and the kidney is normally sufficiently responsive to excrete the water load in the fourth.

Clinical Manifestations

HYPOTHALAMIC DIABETES INSIPIDUS. The sudden appearance of hypotonic polyuria after transcranial surgery in the area of the hypothalamus or after head trauma with basal skull fracture and hypothalamic damage obviously suggests the diagnosis of hypothalamic diabetes insipidus. In these situations, if the patient is unconscious and unable to recognize thirst, hypernatremia is a common accompaniment. However, even in patients with more insidious progression of a specific disease or in patients with idiopathic hypothalamic diabetes insipidus, the onset of polyuria is often relatively abrupt and occurs over a few days. The initial problem is the volume of urine and polydipsia, not the decrease in urine osmolality. Most patients do not report polyuria until urine volume exceeds 4 L/day, and, as illustrated in Figure 238–2, urine volume does not exceed 4 L/day until the ability to concentrate the urine is severely limited and plasma vasopressin is nearly absent. Thus, as few as 10% of the normal number of vasopressinergic neurons may maintain asymptomatic urine volume, but, then, the loss of these few neurons produces a rapid increase in urine volume and symptomatic polyuria. Urine volume seldom exceeds the amount of dilute fluid delivered to the collecting duct (about 18 L in

humans), and in many cases urine volume is less because patients voluntarily restrict fluid intake, which causes some mild volume contraction and increased proximal tubular reabsorption of fluid. Patients often express a preference for cold liquids, which is probably more effective in assuaging thirst. Both thirst and urine output persist through the night. Patients with partial diabetes insipidus have some ability to secrete vasopressin, but this secretion is markedly attenuated at normal levels of plasma osmolality. Therefore, these patients have symptoms and urine volume little different from those of patients with complete diabetes insipidus. Because most patients with hypothalamic diabetes insipidus have sufficient thirst to drink fluid to match urine output, few laboratory abnormalities are present at the time of initial evaluation. Serum sodium level may be in the high normal range, whereas blood urea nitrogen level may be low secondary to large urine volume. Uric acid is relatively high due to the modest volume contraction and the lack of action of vasopressin on V_1 receptors in the kidney, which stimulate clearance of uric acid. Uric acid levels greater than 5 mg/dL are reported to distinguish diabetes insipidus from primary polydipsia.

Continued

A variant of hypothalamic diabetes insipidus is the syndrome of absent osmostat with intact volume receptors. This syndrome is referred to as essential hypernatremia because the patients have increased sodium and absence of thirst. Physiologic maneuvers demonstrate that when the patients are euvolemic, an increase in plasma osmolality produces neither secretion of vasopressin nor sensation of thirst. However, vasopressin is synthesized by the hypothalamus and stored in the posterior pituitary because stimulation of baroreceptors results in prompt secretion of vasopressin; and, the kidney is responsive because vasopressin release by volume receptor stimulation causes urinary concentration. Because patients lack thirst, they are chronically dehydrated, with increased serum sodium levels. It is the dehydration and volume depletion, not the increased osmolality, that stimulate secretion of vasopressin. The amount of urine output depends on the degree of dehydration-induced secretion of vasopressin. If sufficient fluid replacement is given to return extracellular volume to normal, these patients are unable to regulate vasopressin by osmolality and they become markedly polyuric, manifesting the underlying diabetes insipidus.

Hypothalamic diabetes insipidus may be inherited as an autosomal dominant disease that is characterized by an asymptomatic infancy but onset in childhood. (This contrasts with hereditary nephrogenic diabetes insipidus in which polyuria is noted at birth.) Most genetic defects are either in the signal peptide of the pre-prohormone or in the neurophysin portion of the prohormone. Only a single defect has been described in the vasopressin gene itself and none in the glycopeptide. Disruption of cleavage from the signal peptide or abnormal folding of the neurophysin slows trafficking of the mutant prohormone through the endoplasmic reticulum and may produce neuronal cell death. Abnormal packaging of vasopressin and neurophysin may produce increased degradation of both the mutant and the normal wild-type prohormone, and hence inadequate secretion of vasopressin.

Myxedema and adrenal insufficiency both impair the ability to excrete free water by renal mechanisms. The simultaneous occurrence of either of these diseases with diabetes insipidus (as may occur with a tumor of the hypothalamus or pituitary) may decrease the large urine output of diabetes insipidus. Replacement treatment for the anterior pituitary deficiency, especially glucocorticoids, may cause sudden and massive excretion of dilute urine. Similarly, the onset of either hypothyroidism or adrenal insufficiency during the course of diabetes insipidus may decrease the need for vasopressin replacement and even cause hyponatremia. Diabetes insipidus is extremely common in patients who are brain dead, and treatment of the diabetes insipidus along with possible coexistent anterior pituitary deficiency has been advocated to preserve donor organs.

NEPHROGENIC DIABETES INSIPIDUS. The renal response to vasopressin may be impaired by abnormalities of the vasopressin V_2 receptor or the vasopressin-induced water channels, aquaporin-2. The gene for the V_2 receptor has been localized to the Xq28 region of the X chromosome, and familial nephrogenic diabetes insipidus due to V_2 receptor is a rare recessive X-linked disease. Symptoms are noted only in affected males who present with vomiting, constipation, failure to thrive, fever, and polyuria during the first week of life. Hypernatremia is found with a hypo-osmolar urine. The phenotype is identical in patients with mutation of the aquaporin-2 water channel, which should always be suspected when the proband is a girl. Because the

latter is an autosomal recessive disease, consanguinity and a family history of the disease in men and women is common. For mutations of both the receptor and aquaporin-2, it is the disordered synthesis (similar to that described for the vasopressin prohormone in hereditary hypothalamic diabetes insipidus) that produces the disease rather than abnormal function of the protein product per se.

Nephrogenic diabetes insipidus may also be acquired during treatment with certain drugs such as demeclocycline (which is used to treat inappropriate secretion of vasopressin), lithium (used to treat bipolar disorders), and fluoride (previously used in fluorocarbon anesthetics) and from electrolyte abnormalities such as hypokalemia and hypercalcemia. Most of these acquired forms also have decreased synthesis and function of aquaporin-2. Other diseases of the kidney produce polyuria and inability to concentrate the urine secondary to altered renal medullary blood flow or to other disorders that inhibit maintenance of the hypertonic inner medulla. Renal manifestations of sickle cell disease, sarcoidosis, pyelonephritis, multiple melanoma, analgesic nephropathy, and the like are discussed in Chapter 120.

DIABETES INSIPIDUS DURING PREGNANCY. Rarely during pregnancy, women with normal regulation of vasopressin develop diabetes insipidus because of nonphysiologic, extremely elevated levels of cystine aminopeptidase (oxytocinase or vasopressinase), an enzyme produced by the placenta that destroys oxytocin and vasopressin. Concurrent preeclampsia, acute fatty liver, and coagulopathies confirm that the pregnancy is abnormal and, indeed, diabetes insipidus is not found after the pregnancy ends or in subsequent normal pregnancies. In normal pregnancies, there is also an increased metabolism of vasopressin, but this can be overcome by increased synthesis. Polyuria, however, may become manifest in patients who have limited vasopressin reserve because of either a decreased ability to secrete vasopressin (partial hypothalamic diabetes insipidus) or to respond to vasopressin action (compensated nephrogenic diabetes insipidus). Treatment may be required only during the pregnancy, and the patient may return to her previous baseline function without need for therapy when the pregnancy ends. In some patients, hypothalamic diabetes insipidus of another cause first becomes symptomatic during pregnancy and then persists with the usual course of the diabetes insipidus.

PRIMARY POLYDIPSIA. In some patients, primary polydipsia follows acute trauma to the hypothalamus and is severe and unremitting, but in most patients primary polydipsia has a slower onset and more erratic course. Virtually any of the pathologic processes described as causes of hypothalamic diabetes insipidus can cause primary stimulation of thirst. Patients may drink even greater amounts of fluid (e.g., >20 L/day) during the day than patients with hypothalamic diabetes insipidus, yet may sleep through the night with minimal disruption. The disorder may be exacerbated during times of stress yet not be bothersome during normal intervals. Sometimes a lifelong history of habitual excessive water drinking is noted in an entire family. Some patients have obvious psychiatric disorders that contribute to the polydipsia. The physician must always be alert to pharmacologic agents given to treat psychiatric disorders that may result in increased thirst by causing dry mouth, result in nephrogenic diabetes insipidus, or stimulate thirst. Laboratory studies in these patients are normal, although serum sodium may be at the low end of the normal range and the level of uric acid is lower than in patients with hypothalamic diabetes insipidus.

Diagnosis

PHYSIOLOGIC DIAGNOSIS. Although osmotic diuresis secondary to hyperglycemia, an intravenous contrast agent, renal injury, and the like is a more common cause of polyuria, the medical history, isotonic urine osmolality, and routine clinical laboratory tests distinguish these disorders from diabetes insipidus. The diagnosis of diabetes insipidus is considered when urine osmolality is inappropriately low in the presence of elevated serum osmolality from increased serum sodium. These criteria may be met at the initial examination, especially in cases of acute diabetes insipidus occurring after trauma or after surgery in which fluid replacement has not been adequate. In such a patient with hypernatremia and hypotonic urine osmolality with normal renal function, diabetes insipidus is likely and measured plasma vasopressin is low. One need only administer a vasopressin agonist and document a renal response with decreased urine volume

and increased urine osmolality to confirm the diagnosis of hypothalamic diabetes insipidus. Sometimes in the postoperative state a water diuresis occurs from water retention during the surgical procedure. Vasopressin is normally secreted in response to surgical stress, and fluid administered intravenously during the procedure may be retained. During recovery, when vasopressin levels fall, diuresis of the retained fluid occurs. Usually in this case, however, the serum Na^+ level is normal. Yet, if further fluid is administered to match the urine output, persistent polyuria might be mistaken for diabetes insipidus. In this situation, the physician should decrease the rate of fluid administered and observe the urine output and the serum sodium level. If urine output decreases and the serum sodium level remains normal, no treatment is necessary. If serum sodium rises above the normal range and the urine is still hypotonic, the response to a vasopressin agonist will document the diagnosis of diabetes insipidus.

Most outpatients with diabetes insipidus have polyuria, polydipsia, and normal sodium level. In these patients, it is necessary to perform a test to increase serum osmolality and measure the urinary response. The test described is the dehydration test with subsequent response to vasopressin (Fig. 238–3). The test should be carried out under controlled observation in the hospital or an appropriately equipped outpatient area. The timing of the test depends on the symptoms of the patient. If the patient has marked polyuria during the night, it is best to begin the test during the day because the patient may readily become dehydrated. If the patient has only two or three episodes of nocturia per night, it may be best to begin the test in the evening so that the major part of the dehydration takes place when the patient is asleep. In either case, the patient is weighed at the beginning of the test, and the volume and osmolality (usually determined by freezing point depression) of all excreted urine are measured. The patient is weighed after output of each liter of urine. When two consecutive urine samples have osmolality differing by no more than 10% and the patient has lost 2% of body weight, a blood sample is obtained for measurement of serum osmolality, sodium, and plasma vasopressin. The patient is then given 2 mg of desmopressin intravenously or intramuscularly. Patients with normal levels of vasopressin have less than a 5% increase in urine osmolality in response to the administered desmopressin. Patients with complete hypothalamic diabetes insipidus have minimal concentration of the urine with dehydration and a marked increase in urine osmolality in response to administered desmopressin (usually greater than 50%).

Patients with nephrogenic diabetes insipidus usually have no urine concentration in response to administered vasopressin, although in some cases of acquired nephrogenic diabetes insipidus, some urinary concentration may result. Nephrogenic diabetes insipidus is unequivocally distinguished from hypothalamic diabetes insipidus by measurement of vasopressin in plasma. Vasopressin levels are elevated in cases of nephrogenic diabetes insipidus, especially with dehydration.

In patients with partial hypothalamic diabetes insipidus and patients with primary polydipsia, the urine is somewhat concentrated in response to dehydration, but it cannot be expected to be concentrated to the maximum of a normal person because the chronically reduced levels of vasopressin decrease the number of aquaporin-2 water channels, and the large urine volume, regardless of cause, washes out the medullary osmotic gradient that determines the maximum urine concentration. When vasopressin is administered, patients with partial hypothalamic diabetes insipidus have a further increase (usually greater than 10%) in urine osmolality, whereas patients with primary polydipsia have no further increase. The reliability of distinguishing these last two disorders with the controlled dehydration test is debated. Some patients with primary polydipsia may not become sufficiently dehydrated with the test to secrete maximum vasopressin and hence will have an increase in urine osmolality in response to administered

desmopressin. Alternatively, some patients with partial diabetes insipidus may become sufficiently dehydrated that their individual maximal concentration of urine is reached during the test and no further concentration is seen with administered desmopressin. When plasma vasopressin assays become sufficiently sensitive, reliable, and available, plasma vasopressin levels at the end of dehydration may better distinguish these two disorders. In the meantime, it is important to have adequate follow-up of patients with partial diabetes insipidus to ensure that during treatment with vasopressin a good therapeutic response is obtained. In fact, the response to treatment with desmopressin has been considered a continuation of the diagnosis. If, in response to administered desmopressin, there is a decrease in polyuria and thirst with no reduction in sodium, the diagnosis of partial hypothalamic diabetes insipidus is confirmed. If thirst persists and hyponatremia develops, the diagnosis of primary polydipsia is confirmed.

ETIOLOGIC DIAGNOSIS. The dehydration test confirms that inadequate vasopressin level or function is responsible for the polyuria, but the cause must then be determined. Magnetic resonance imaging of the hypothalamic/pituitary area is an important diagnostic tool in these cases. The three areas of interest are the immediate suprasellar region of the hypothalamus, the pituitary stalk, and the posterior lobe within the sella. As noted under Anatomy, vasopressin is synthesized in the paired paraventricular nuclei high on the walls of the third ventricle and the paired supraoptic nuclei lateral to and above the optic chiasm. Vasopressin is synthesized in the magnocellular neurons and carried to the posterior pituitary for storage and release. Section or damage of axons at the level of the posterior pituitary cause reaccumulation of neurosecretory material in the axon proximal to the site of the injury as well as outgrowth of axons in the median eminence, where vasopressin can be secreted into the portal system. Therefore, tumors confined to the sella do not cause diabetes insipidus. To cause hypothalamic diabetes insipidus, tumors in the hypothalamic area immediately above the sella must be either sufficiently large to destroy 80 to 90% of the vasopressin cells or located where the paths of the four nuclear groups converge at the origin of the pituitary stalk just above the diaphragma sellae. Primary tumors, especially craniopharyngioma, suprasellar germinoma, metastatic tumors, and infiltrative diseases may also cause diabetes insipidus by infiltration of the stalk, which is then thickened. Additionally, on T1-weighted images, the stored hormone in neurosecretory granules in the posterior pituitary is visualized as a bright spot in the sella. Most, but not all, normal subjects have this bright spot and in most, but not all, patients with hypothalamic diabetes insipidus the bright spot is lost. Thickening of the stalk and absence of the bright spot is especially suggestive of disease. Infiltrative lesions of the hypothalamic area might have intact anatomy and infiltration that will be demonstrated only if a contrast agent such as gadolinium is used.

Tumors that cause diabetes insipidus are most often benign primary intracranial tumors such as craniopharyngioma, ependymoma (suprasellar germinoma), or pinealoma that arises in the third ventricle. Primary tumors of the anterior pituitary cause diabetes insipidus only when suprasellar extension is present. Metastasis to the hypothalamus from lung, breast, melanoma, and such carcinomas may lodge in the portal capillaries of the median eminence, destroy the supraopticohypophysial tract, and thereby cause diabetes insipidus. Granulomatous diseases, such as Langerhans' cell histiocytosis, sarcoidosis, or tuberculosis may destroy vasopressin cells in the hypothalamus. Leukemic infiltrates and lymphomas of the hypothalamus may cause diabetes insipidus. In patients with diseases with peripheral manifestations, the diagnosis is usually suspected on the basis of general medical findings. Lymphocytic infundibulohypophysitis is similar to lymphocytic hypophysitis of the anterior pituitary and is an autoimmune disease in which lymphocytes infiltrate the neurohypophysis to produce diabetes insipidus, a thickened stalk and absence of the bright spot mimicking a pituitary tumor. The diagnosis was originally demonstrated by pituitary biopsy but now has been made by regression of the thickened stalk and tumor-like appearance with follow-up or by remission when treated with prednisone. When no cause is found, the diagnosis of exclusion is idiopathic diabetes insipidus, but this probably is also an autoimmune disease, and other autoimmune diseases are recognized in affected patients. When central nervous system disease is suspected but not diagnosed by MRI or general physical examination, cerebrospinal fluid obtained by lumbar puncture may be helpful in identifying tumor cells or tumor markers.

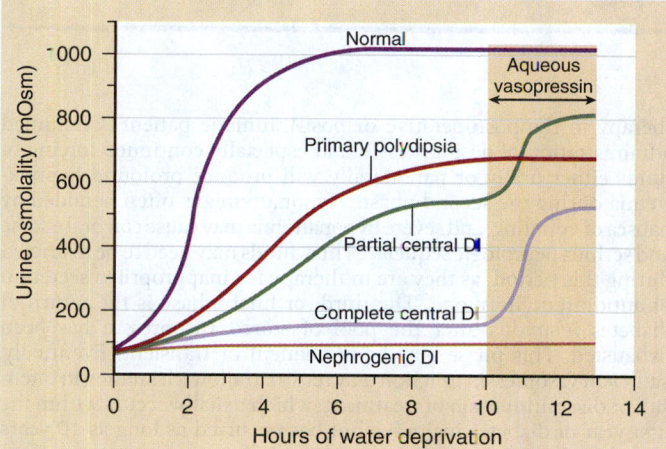

FIGURE 238–3 • Responses to the dehydration test described by Miller and associates (*Annals of Internal Medicine*, 1970) to differentiate various types of diabetes insipidus and primary polydipsia. The response to dehydration shows a plateau, and the subsequent change in urine osmolality in response to administered vasopressin is illustrated. See discussion in the text. DI = diabetes insipidus.

Endocrine Diseases

Rx Treatment

Water diuresis is the primary manifestation of diabetes insipidus, and water replacement in adequate quantities avoids metabolic complications. The aim of therapy is to reduce the amount of polyuria and polydipsia to a tolerable level while avoiding overtreatment, which might produce water retention and hyponatremia. The best therapeutic agent for hypothalamic diabetes insipidus is the vasopressin agonist desmopressin. Desmopressin is different from vasopressin in that the terminal amino group of cystine has been removed to prolong the duration of action and D-arginine is substituted for L-arginine in position 8 to decrease the pressor effect. In therapeutic dosage, this agent acts on V_2, or antidiuretic, receptors with minimal action on V_1, or pressor, receptors. Desmopressin is available in tablets of 0.1 mg or 0.2 mg for oral administration and in either a spray bottle that delivers a fixed dose of 10 μg in 100 μL or in a bottle with a rhinal catheter that can deliver from 50 to 200 μL (5 to 20 μg for intranasal administration). When therapy is initiated, it is best to begin with a low dose—one half of a 0.1-mg tablet, a single spray of 10 μg (100 μL), or 5 μg (50 μL) by the rhinal tube—at night to allow the patient to sleep through the night and then to determine the duration of action by quantifying the polyuria the next day. The duration of action of a single dose varies between patients from 6 to 24 hours, but in most patients a dosage can be determined that gives a good therapeutic response on an every-12-hour schedule for the nasal spray and an 8- or 12-hour schedule for the tablets. If patients are never polyuric on a fixed schedule, it may be advisable to delay administration of a dose once or twice a week to allow diuresis of any accumulated water. Desmopressin is also available for parenteral use in 1-mL vials of 4 μg/mL; 5 to 10% of an intranasal quantity administered intravenously, intramuscularly, or subcutaneously gives an equivalent response. Parenteral administration is especially useful postoperatively or when a patient is unable to take the nasal preparation. In hospitalized patients, some physicians use vasopressin added directly to a crystalloid solution to infuse doses in the range 0.25 to 2.7 mIU/kg/hr to cause modest but persistent urinary concentration as a treatment for diabetes insipidus. References should be checked if this is used and serum sodium levels obtained regularly to prevent hyponatremia.

Some orally administered pharmacologic agents are also useful in treating hypothalamic diabetes insipidus. Chlorpropamide in doses of 100 to 500 mg daily enhances the effect of vasopressin at the renal tubule and is especially useful in patients with partial hypothalamic diabetes insipidus. An antidiuretic effect is noted in 1 to 2 days, but maximum antidiuresis may not be achieved until after several days of administration. This is the only agent used regularly to treat hypothalamic diabetes insipidus. Carbamazepine (Tegretol) in doses of 200 to 600 mg/day causes release of vasopressin. Clofibrate also stimulates the release of endogenous vasopressin in doses of 500 mg every 6 hours. Thiazide diuretics cause sodium depletion and volume contraction and decrease urine volume by increasing proximal tubular reabsorption of glomerular filtrate. Prostaglandin inhibitors (e.g., indomethacin) block the normal action of prostaglandin E to inhibit the action of vasopressin on the kidney. Although use of a prostaglandin inhibitor is not a primary treatment of hypothalamic diabetes insipidus, it may alter the antidiuretic response of other agents. Chlorothiazide, amiloride, or prostaglandin inhibitors may be useful in treating nephrogenic diabetes insipidus. Use of any of these agents is "off label." For each, the prescribing physician should be careful of potential toxicity and side effects. In all cases of drug-induced nephrogenic diabetes insipidus, the most direct therapy is discontinuing the offending agent, if possible. Symptomatic nephrogenic diabetes insipidus is usually treated with a thiazide diuretic, which is enhanced by the coadministration of the potassium-sparing diuretic amiloride. Amiloride may be especially beneficial in cases of nephrogenic diabetes insipidus induced by lithium because the drug decreases the entrance of lithium into cells in the distal tubule. When diuretics are used to treat diabetes insipidus, special attention should be given to the possibility that dehydration will increase the concentration of offending drugs or ions.

Some situations require special attention during therapy. Rarely, if patients with diabetes insipidus are unable to drink or are given a hypertonic solution, severe acute hypernatremia will develop. Osmotic equilibrium with the intracellular water of neurons and glia produces shrinking of the brain. The brain is in a closed vault (skull), and when the brain shrinks, the vasculature of the central nervous system is engorged. Rupture of vessels may produce subarachnoid hemorrhage, gross intracerebral hemorrhage, or intracerebral petechial hemorrhages producing permanent brain damage. If the hypernatremia persists over a longer time, the neurons accommodate by production of "idiogenic osmoles," which decreases the amount of brain neuron shrinkage. If adaptation has occurred, too rapid lowering of osmolality in the extracellular fluid will produce a shift of water into the brain and cause cerebral edema. In this situation, desmopressin can be administered to produce constant antidiuresis, and the amount of water given can be regulated to decrease osmolality by no more than about 1 mEq every 2 hours. Postoperatively or after head trauma, diabetes insipidus may be transient (see Prognosis in the next section), and long-term maintenance therapy cannot be immediately established. During pregnancy, vasopressinase increases the metabolism of vasopressin but not desmopressin, so desmopressin is the drug of choice. The vasopressinase activity subsides by a few weeks after delivery, and patients with the onset of partial diabetes insipidus during pregnancy may become asymptomatic after delivery. The additional advantage of desmopressin is that it has little action on the oxytocin receptors of the uterus. It should be noted that during pregnancy, normal plasma osmolality decreases by 10 mOsm/kg because of changes in serum sodium, and pregnant patients with diabetes insipidus require sufficient desmopressin to maintain serum sodium at this lower level.

Course and Prognosis

The prognosis of properly treated diabetes insipidus is excellent. Historical complications of bladder hypertrophy and hydroureter secondary to voluntarily decreasing urine frequency are largely unseen with modern therapy. If nephrogenic diabetes insipidus is diagnosed and treated early, intracranial calcification and mental retardation are not apparent. When the diabetes insipidus is secondary to a recognized disease process, it is that disease that determines the ultimate prognosis. In some specific clinical situations, the course is different and characteristic. Postoperative or post-traumatic diabetes insipidus is often due to damage of the pituitary stalk and can follow a course referred to as "triphasic" (Fig. 238–4). The first phase is diabetes insipidus secondary to axon shock and lack of release of vasopressin. This phase lasts for 5 to 10 days and is followed by a second phase of antidiuresis, which is thought to be produced by uncontrolled release of vasopressin from the large storage pool in the axon terminals of the posterior pituitary. This store is sufficient to produce constant antidiuresis for an additional 5 to 10 days. The possibility of this course developing is one reason for closely following desmopressin therapy in the postoperative or post-traumatic patient. Continued administration of desmopressin and especially continued forcing of fluids either orally or parenterally will produce profound hyponatremia during the second phase. Hyponatremia is often heralded by nausea or vomiting, and severe hyponatremia may cause cerebral edema and serious neurologic sequelae. Thus, fluids may need to be restricted during this period, as they are in therapy for inappropriate secretion of antidiuretic hormone. The third, or final, phase is the return of diabetes insipidus after the pool of stored vasopressin has been exhausted. This phase may be permanent or transient. Eventually, sufficient vasopressin function may return to allow a lessening in intensity or discontinuation of treatment, which usually occurs within the first year of diabetes insipidus but has occurred as long as 10 years after the initiating event. Potential return of function is another reason for occasionally withholding therapy during long-term treatment. Interestingly, the second phase of excess vasopressin and hyponatremia has been reported without preceding or subsequent diabetes insipidus. This variation is reported as transient postoperative syndrome of inappropriate secretion of antidiuretic hormone. It is probably due to trauma to only some vasopressin axons. Sufficient

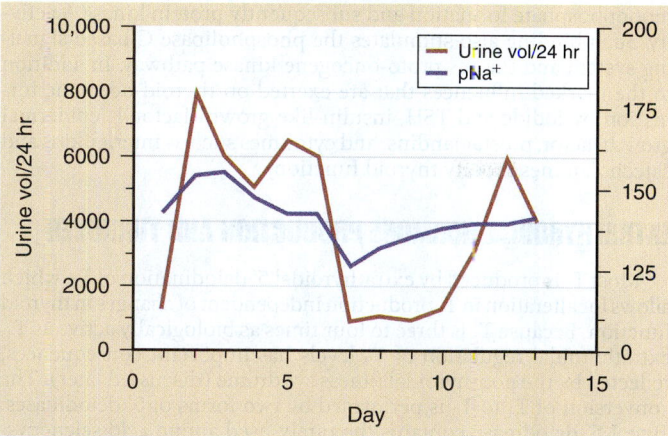

FIGURE 238-4 • Triphasic response of the pituitary stalk to trauma in one patient. Urine output (brown line) and serum Na⁺ (blue line) are illustrated. Note the onset of diabetes insipidus immediately after the head trauma and lasting for 6 days. On days 7 through 10, a marked decrease in diuresis (with elevated urine osmolality) occurred, typical of the second phase with inappropriate release of vasopressin. During this time, the patient actually became hyponatremic and required fluid restriction to treat the hyponatremia. After day 10, a return of diabetes insipidus was noted.

functioning vasopressin neurons are present to prevent the diabetes insipidus of the first and third phases, but sufficient leakage of vasopressin occurs to cause the second phase. It is only the setting and timing that identify this phenomenon as an isolated second phase of the triphasic response.

Diabetes insipidus should not be considered idiopathic until at least 4 years of follow-up. Over this interval, annual computed tomography or MRI scans are indicated to test for the appearance of a tumor or infiltrative process that may not have been detected at the initial examination.

SYNDROME OF INAPPROPRIATE SECRETION OF ANTIDIURETIC HORMONE

Excess secretion of vasopressin can be caused by abnormal secretion from the posterior pituitary or by ectopic synthesis and secretion of vasopressin by a tumor. The excess vasopressin causes water retention, volume expansion, and natriuresis with consequent hyponatremia. This disorder is discussed in Chapters 111 and 112.

SUGGESTED READINGS

Morello JP, Bichet DG: Nephrogenic diabetes insipidus. Annu Rev Physiol 2001;63:607–630. *Review of hereditary nephrogenic diabetes insipidus caused by mutations of the V₂ receptor or aquaporin-2 water channels.*

Pivonello R, De Bellis A, Faggiano A, et al: Central diabetes insipidus and autoimmunity: Relationship between the occurrence of antibodies to arginine vasopressin-secreting cells and clinical, immunological, and radiological features in a large cohort of patients with central diabetes insipidus of known and unknown etiology. J Clin Endocrinol Metab 2003;88:1629–1636. *In one third of cases, an autoimmune cause is likely.*

Robinson AG, Verbalis JV: The posterior pituitary. *In* Larsen PR, Kronenberg HM, Melmed S, Polonsky KS (eds): Williams' Textbook of Endocrinology, 10th ed. Philadelphia, WB Saunders, 2002. *Extensively referenced chapter with a detailed description of the anatomy of the neurohypophysis, synthesis and physiology of vasopressin and oxytocin, and diseases producing diabetes insipidus.*

239 THE THYROID

Wolfgang H. Dillmann

Anatomy and Physiology

The thyroid, the largest endocrine gland in the body, weighs about 20 g with the right lobe usually being larger than the left. Adult size is reached at 15 years of age. The two lateral lobes lie anterior to the thyroid cartilage and are connected by a small isthmus located just below the cricoid cartilage. The lobes have a pointed superior pole and a rounded inferior pole with a thickness of about 2 cm, a length of 4 to 5 cm, and a width of 2 to 3 cm. The lobes are divided by fibrous septa into pseudolobes composed of spherical structures called follicles. A dense capillary network surrounds the follicles, which are richly innervated by sympathetic and parasympathetic nerve endings. The follicles consist of a single layer of epithelial cells surrounding a lumen filled with a proteinaceous colloid material consisting of over 75% thyroglobulin. Thyroglobulin is formed by the epithelial thyroid cells, which both synthesize and store the hormone.

A feedback loop involving the hypothalamus, pituitary, and thyroid gland regulates the glandular secretion of thyroid hormone (Fig. 239-1). The hypothalamus generates thyroid-releasing hormone (TRH) to stimulate pituitary thyroid-stimulating hormone (TSH) production. TSH, in turn, stimulates thyroid hormonal output, which feeds back on both hypothalamus and pituitary to complete the regulatory circle.

Thyroid Hormone Formation

Thyroxine (T_4) is the major secretory product of the thyroid, with a daily production rate of 80 to 100 μg. T_4 is produced only by the thyroid gland. In contrast, only 20% of the daily production rate of triiodothyronine (T_3) is derived from thyroid secretion and 80% from peripheral T_4 conversion (Fig. 239-2). The daily production rate of T_3 is 30 to 40 μg. Normal thyroid hormone formation requires normal levels of TSH and an adequate but not excessive supply of iodine. Optimal iodine intake is 150 to 300 μg/day. In some mountainous areas of the world, daily iodine supplies can be as low as 20 to 30 μg. The United States population, however, has an adequate iodine supply, but this is no longer a country of high iodine intake. For adults, the recommended daily iodine dose is 150 μg/d, which should increase to 200 μg/d for pregnant women. Iodine is reduced to iodide (I⁻) in the gastrointestinal tract and readily absorbed. Iodide is removed from the blood stream by uptake and concentration in the thyroid gland and excretion in the urine. The uptake of iodide into the thyroid cell is mediated by the sodium/iodide symporter (NIS). Under normal conditions, the kidney clears iodide from plasma at about 30 mL/min, whereas thyroid clearance is 8 mL/min, so that only 25% of intake enters the thyroid under normal conditions. Excess iodine intake lowers the percentage of uptake; reduced intake raises it. Thyroid

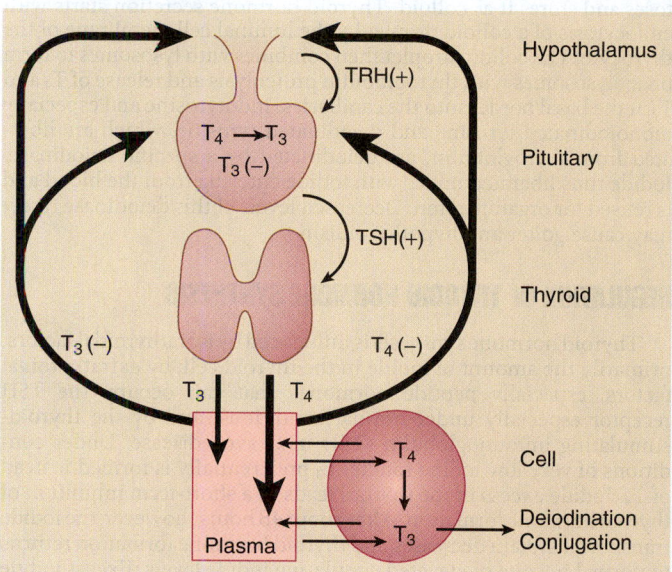

FIGURE 239-1 • Hypothalamic-pituitary-thyroid interrelationship. Thyrotropin releasing hormone (TRH) exerts a positive stimulatory effect on thyroid stimulating hormone (TSH) secretion, which stimulates thyroid hormone formation. Thyroxine (T_4) is the primary thyroid secretory product, which is converted in the cells of specific organs, such as kidney and liver, to triiodothyronine (T_3). T_3 is the most biologically active thyroid hormone and is inactivated by further deiodination or conjugation and biliary excretion.

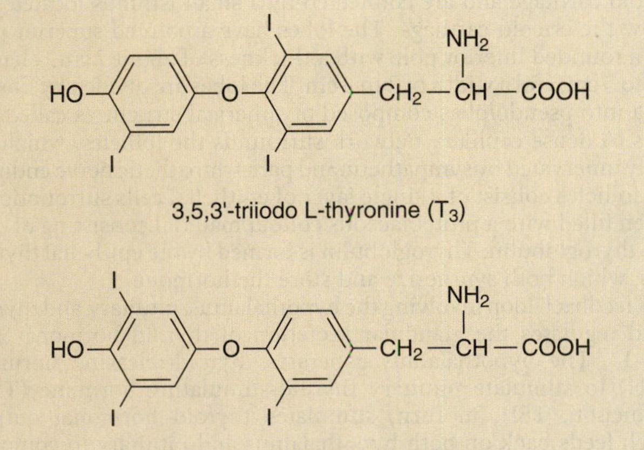

FIGURE 239–2 • Structure of the thyroid hormones.

uptake of iodide varies from 5 to 30%. Other organs such as the salivary glands, mammary glands, gastric mucosa, and choroid plexus also can take up iodine and express NIS but cannot form thyroid hormone. The ability of the thyroid to actively accumulate iodine through an iodide transporter localized in the cell membrane leads to a 20 to 40:1 concentration gradient of cell to plasma. The iodide in the thyroid cells is rapidly oxidized and enzymatically incorporated via thyroid peroxidase into tyrosine molecules of thyroglobulin by a process called *organification*. Thyroid peroxidase requires activation by H_2O_2. A flavoprotein enzyme, presumably an NAPDH cytochrome C reductase, generates H_2O_2, but the precise identity of the H_2O_2-generating system is uncertain. Antithyroid medications such as propylthiouracil (PTU) and methimazole inhibit thyroid peroxidase, thereby decreasing thyroid hormone formation. Thyroid hormone formation occurs on thyroglobulin, a 660-kD glycoprotein, with 25% of its tyrosine residues accessible to iodination. The monoiodinated tyrosine and the deiodinated tyrosine are coupled by the thyroid peroxidase enzyme to form T_4 by linking two DITs or, for T_3 formation, linking one monoiodinated tyrosine and one deiodinated tyrosine molecule. Thyroglobulin contains only 3 or 4 T_4 and 0.2 to 0.3 T_3 residues. The organification and coupling reactions on thyroglobulin occur at the luminal border of the thyrocyte, which then exocytoses and stores it as colloid. Thyroid hormone secretion starts with endocytosis of a colloid droplet by the luminal cell membrane of the thyrocyte. The colloid droplet then combines with lysosomes to form phagolysosomes with thyroglobulin proteolysis and release of T_4 and T_3 at the basal border into the capillaries. Iodotyrosine and especially monoiodinated tyrosine and deiodinated tyrosine, which are liberated from thyroglobulin, are deiodinated by a specific deiodinase. Iodide thus liberated mixes with iodide entering from the blood and is reused for organification. Decreased levels of this deiodinase rarely may cause goiter and hypothyroidism.

REGULATION OF THYROID HORMONE SYNTHESIS

Thyroid hormone synthesis is influenced by intrathyroidal factors, primarily the amount of iodide in the thyroid cell; by extrathyroidal factors, especially peptide hormones that can occupy the TSH receptor especially under normal conditions; and by the thyroid-stimulating immunoglobulin (TSI) in Graves' disease. Under conditions of very low iodine intake, T_3 preferentially is formed instead of T_4. Iodide excess in the thyroid leads to a short-term inhibition of thyroid hormone formation. After about 48 hours, however, the iodide transporter system decreases and thyroid hormone formation returns to normal in spite of elevated circulating iodide levels. Excess iodide also inhibits thyroid hormone release. Increased iodination of thyroglobulin increases its resistance to proteolytic degradation, thereby freeing less T_4 and T_3. Paradoxically, excess iodide can also increase thyroid hormone formation, especially in abnormal thyroid glands. For these reasons, iodine should not be used to treat thyroid diseases except under special conditions. In addition to iodide, TSH influences thyroid function by stimulating all steps of thyroid hormone formation. TSH binding to TSH receptors stimulates cyclic adenosine

monophosphate formation and subsequently protein kinase A activity. Such binding also stimulates the phospholipase C-based signaling system and the *ras* proto-oncogene kinase pathway. In addition to the marked influences that are exerted on thyroid hormone formation by iodide and TSH, insulin-like growth factor-1, epidermal growth factor, prostaglandins, and cytokines such as interleukins and catecholamines modify thyroid function.

EXTRATHYROIDAL HORMONE PRODUCTION AND TURNOVER

Most T_3 is produced by extrathyroidal 5' deiodination of T_4, which allows for alteration in T_3 production independent of changes in thyroid function. Because T_3 is three to four times as biologically active as T_4, extrathyroidal regulation of T_3 levels has important consequences, reflected by the nonthyroidal illness syndrome (discussed later). The conversion of T_4 to T_3 is performed by two forms of 5' deiodinases. Type I 5' deiodinase contains the rarely used amino acid selenocysteine and is most active in liver and kidney. The activity of type I 5' deiodinase declines with hypothyroidism and is inhibited by propylthiouracil and glucocorticoids. Type II 5' deiodinase is active in the central nervous system, pituitary, brown adipose tissue, and placenta. It resists inhibition by PTU and increases with hypothyroidism, resulting in near-normal central nervous system T_3 levels. A third deiodinase, termed 5 deiodinase or type III 5 deiodinase, removes the inner ring iodide to form the biologically inactive reverse T_3 from T_4 and metabolizes T_3 to diiodothyronine. The thyroid hormone derivatives, including reverse T_3 and the di- and monothyronine compounds, have no currently recognized biologic importance.

In addition to deiodination, by which 80% of T_4 is metabolized, thyroid hormones are metabolized by transfer of glucuronyl and sulfate residues to the phenolic hydroxyl group of thyroid hormone and by biliary excretion. Deamination and decarboxylation of the alanine side chain and cleavage of the ether bridge also contribute to thyroid hormone metabolism. Certain specific differences in the metabolism of T_4 and T_3 have clinical importance. The half-life of T_4 is 1 week, and its total body store is $800\,\mu g$, in contrast to the half-life of 1 day for T_3, with total body stores amounting to $50\,\mu g$. These principles make T_4 more suitable than T_3 for chronic thyroid hormone replacement. Hyperthyroidism and vigorous exercise shorten the half-life of thyroid hormones, and hypothyroidism increases it. Drugs listed in Table 239–1 also influence thyroid hormone binding and metabolism.

Hormone Transport

The T_4 and T_3 exist in plasma in free and protein-bound forms. T_4 is strongly protein bound, and only 0.03% is free. T_3, with its higher biologic activity, possesses 10 times less protein binding such that 0.3% is free. Only the free hormone enters cells, exerts its biologic action, and determines thyroid physiologic status. The most important binding proteins are thyroxine-binding globulin (TBG) and transthyretin, formerly known as thyroxine-binding prealbumin albumin; albumin and some lipoproteins play a minor role. In normal

---

Table 239–1 • FACTORS INFLUENCING THYROID HORMONE BINDING TO THYROXINE–BINDING GLOBULIN (TBG)

Increased TBG concentration
  Congenital abnormality
  Hyperestrogenic state
    Pregnancy, estrogen therapy
  Disease related
    Hepatitis, biliary cirrhosis, acute intermittent porphyria
  Drugs
    Tamoxifen, perphenazine, clofibrate
Decreased TBG concentration
  Congenital abnormality
  Drugs
    Glucocorticoids (large doses), androgenic steroids, asparaginase
  Severe systemic illness
    Nephrotic syndrome, chronic liver disease, protein malnutrition
Drugs interfering with binding to normal TBG
  Salicylates, diazepam, phenytoin, furosemide, high levels of free fatty
    acids

plasma, the T_4-binding distribution is 80% of T_4 binding to TBG, 15% to transthyretin, and 5% to albumin and lipoproteins. For T_3, the distribution is 90% bound to TBG and the rest to albumin and lipoproteins, with little binding to transthyretin. Table 239–1 lists conditions leading to alterations in TBG. Changes in total T_4 or T_3 resulting from such alterations may be confused with conditions leading to thyroid hormone excess or deficiency due to hyperthyroidism or hypothyroidism. Elevated or decreased total T_4 or T_3 levels caused by abnormalities in binding proteins are always accompanied by normal free T_4 and free T_3 concentrations and a euthyroid state. Elevated levels of T3G as they occur, for example, in pregnant patients or patients with acute hepatitis lead to increased levels of total T_4 and T_3. Because more T_4 is bound, less T_4 is able to enter the tissue to be metabolized and inhibit TSH secretion. Slightly higher TSH levels result in increased thyroid hormone formation and a new steady state accompanied by normal free thyroid hormone concentrations. Specific drugs also can lower thyroid hormone concentrations without lowering thyroid hormone-binding proteins (see Table 239–1). For example, salicylic acid or phenytoin competes with thyroid hormone for binding to TBG. The effects of phenytoin are more complex in that they both reduce total serum T_4 levels and slightly lower free T_4 concentrations. TSH concentrations remain normal under such circumstances, and the patients are not hypothyroid. In contrast to alterations in binding proteins, increases or decreases in thyroid hormone production lead to abnormalities in both total and free hormone concentrations.

THYROID HORMONE ACTION

Most thyroid hormone effects are mediated by the binding of T_3 to nuclear thyroid hormone receptor proteins. T_3 has a ten-fold higher affinity for this nuclear receptor than T_4, accounting for the higher biologic activity of T_3. T_3 nuclear receptors (TR) belong to the c-erbA proto-oncogene family and are encoded by the genes c-erbAα and c-erbAβ. Each gene has several splice variants, only some of which bind T_3. The T_3 nuclear receptor is a T_3-activated transcription factor that binds to specific nucleotide sequences located upstream or downstream of the transcription start site of T_3-responsive genes. Many T_3-responsive genes show an increase in transcription upon T_3 binding to the nuclear T_3 receptor protein. This leads to increased formation of specific mRNAs and proteins such as those coding for growth hormone, malic enzyme, myosin heavy chain α, and the calcium pump of the sarcoplasmic reticulum. T_3 suppresses transcription of other genes such as the gene coding for the TSH-α and TSH-β subunits. In this scenario, specific mutations of the c-erbAβ receptor lead to the generalized thyroid hormone resistant syndrome: The mutant $T_3\beta$ receptor interferes with the action of normal T_3 receptor proteins. In addition to its effects on transcription, T_3 influences the half-life of mRNA and proteins and affects the translation of mRNA, a step that may lead to rapid changes in ion transport. The genes coding for TR_α, TR_β, and both TR_α and TR_β have been deleted in mice generating null mutants and these mice are viable. TR_α null mutants exhibit bradycardia and hypothermia. TR_β null mutants have elevated T_4 and T_3 levels and deafness and $TR_{\alpha/\beta}$ double null mutants have very markedly elevated T_4 and T_3 levels, deafness, bradycardia, and hypothermia.

EVALUATION OF PATIENTS WITH THYROID DISEASE

The evaluation of patients with thyroid disease includes a physical examination of the thyroid, laboratory tests for thyroid function, and, when indicated, specific other procedures including ultrasonography, radioactive iodine uptake and scan, and fine-needle aspiration.

Physical Examination

Palpation of the thyroid gland is an important part of the general physical examination, and abnormalities in size, consistency, and contour of the gland are common findings. For example, 6% of women have thyroid nodules. An enlargement of the thyroid, however, may be a first clue for Graves' disease; a firm thyroid nodule can represent thyroid cancer. Examination of the thyroid begins by having the patient swallow while the examiner observes the contour of the neck from the side. Thyroid enlargements and irregularities, such as a nodule,

moving up from the substernal area can be identified. One can perform palpation of the thyroid by standing behind the patient and using the fingers of both hands to identify the isthmus lying just below the cricoid cartilage. Moving laterally, the second, third, and fourth fingers can palpate both thyroid lobes. As one exerts gentle pressure during swallowing, the surface of the thyroid moving past the fingers reveals enlargement or the presence of thyroid nodules. A thyroid examination should always include palpation of lateral and submandibular lymph nodes. The size of thyroid nodules can be recorded by measuring their two largest diameters.

Measurement of Thyroid Hormone Values

Techniques employed for measurement of T_4, free T_4, T_3, and TSH by radioimmunoassays or enzyme-coupled immunoassays are rapidly changing. The newer assays are increasingly sensitive. Radioimmunoassays are progressively being replaced by enzyme-linked immunoabsorption assays, and new chemoluminescent compounds are available for supersensitive TSH assays. Serum thyroid hormone concentrations for T_4, free T_4, T_3, and TSH in normal subjects and in patients with thyroid disease are given in Table 239–2. These measurements accurately define thyroid function in most persons, meaning that more specialized tests are rarely needed.

TOTAL AND FREE T_4. Total T_4 values (4.5 to 12.5 µg/dL) are altered by changes in thyroid function or changes in the concentration and affinities of thyroid hormone-binding proteins. Determination of free T_4 levels (nonprotein-bound) corrects for these abnormalities. Current laboratory capacities involve quantitation of nonprotein-bound T_4 by a two-step fluorometric enzyme immunoassay or by equilibrium dialysis. Normal values range from 0.9 to 2 ng/dL. Some of these assays occasionally falsely identify too high free T_4 values in patients with dysalbuminic hyperthyroxemia, but nonprotein-bound T_4 measurement by the two-step immunoassay approach gives a good approximation of free T_4. This free T_4 index is constructed by multiplying the total T_4 by an estimated protein binding (usually the T_3 uptake test). The T_4 index does not adequately reflect the thyroid status in patients with the nonthyroidal illness syndrome (discussed later).

Measurement of total T_3 levels by enzyme-coupled immunoassays has a normal range of 80 to 220 ng/dL and is also influenced by alterations in binding proteins, but to a lesser extent. The total T_3 assay should not be confused with the T_3 uptake or T_3 resin test, which is used to calculate the free thyroxine index.

SERUM REVERSE T_3. Reverse T_3 (rT_3) (normal range, 20 to 40 ng/dL) should be determined only in special situations. Its level is elevated (40 to 120 ng/dL) in patients with various systemic illnesses, leading to the nonthyroidal illness syndrome (NTI). Because of decreased T_4, free T_4, and T_3 levels in some of these patients, its determination can help to distinguish NTI from hypothyroidism. In hypothyroid patients, reverse T_3 levels are decreased.

The levels of the thyroxine hormone-binding proteins, TBG, transthyretin, and albumin can be directly measured by immunoassays. During pregnancy and with estrogen treatment, TBG levels are elevated two- to three-fold owing to a decreased metabolic clearance of TBG molecules, which have an increase in glycosylation. An albumin variant with increased affinity for T_4 exists in the familial dysalbuminic syndrome and leads to elevated T_4 levels with normal T_3 values and uptake. A transthyretin variant with similar effects on T_4 binding has also been described. Table 239–3 lists causes of increased T_4 levels.

SERUM THYROGLOBULIN. Thyroglobulin is produced only by thyroid tissue. Normal persons have low but detectable thyroglobulin levels. Total surgical removal of cancerous thyroid tissue should result in

Table 239–2 • SERUM THYROID HORMONE VALUES IN NORMAL PERSONS AND PATIENTS WITH THYROID DISEASE			
	NORMAL	HYPERTHYROID	HYPOTHYROID
T_4 (µg/dL)	4.5–12.5	>12.5	<4.5
FREE T_4 (ng/dL)	0.9–2	>2	<0.9
T_3 (ng/dL)	80–220	>220	<80
TSH (µU/mL)	0.3–6	<0.3	>6

Table 239–3 • CAUSES OF INCREASED SERUM TOTAL T₄ CONCENTRATION

THYROID STATE CONDITION	T_4	FREE T_4	T_3	TSH	COMMENTS
Hyperthyroid state	H	H	H or N	L	High T_4 combined with hypermetabolic state and hyperthyroidism
Euthyroid state					
Binding abnormalities					
Thyroxine-binding globulin levels increased	H	N	H	N	Autosomal dominant
T_4 binding to albumin increased (familial dysalbuminemic hyperthyroxinemia)	H	N,H*	N	N	*Same "free T_4" methods lead to erroneous results
T_4 binding by transthyretin increased (familial)	H	N	N	N	
T_4 antibodies present	H	N,H	N,L,*H*	N	*Method based, anti–T_3 antibody may also be present
Drug effects					
Inhibitors of 5′-deiodinase					
Oral cholecystographic contrast agents (ipodate, iopanoate)	H	H	L	H	Inhibition of T_3 formation
Amiodarone	H	H	L	L,N	
Propranolol	H	N	L,N	N,H	Only with large doses
Heparin	H	N,H	N	N	Temporary after IV doses
T_4 administration	H	H	N	L	Mild hyperthyroxinemia in patients on T_4 replacement
Various disorders					
Non-thyroidal illness syndrome	H,N	N,L	L	N,L,H	See text for detail
Hyperemesis gravidarum	H	H,N	N	L	During early part of pregnancy; remits
Acute psychiatric illness	H,N	H,N	N	L	During acute phase; remits without treatment
Extrathyroidal deiodinase defect	H	H	N	N	A few case reports but not completely documented
Thyroid hormone resistance syndrome (pituitary and generalized)	H	H	H	H	In generalized resistance syndrome, hypothyroid features can be present, especially related to central nervous system development. If only pituitary resistance, thyrotoxic symptoms

H = high; N = normal; L = low.
*Sequence indicates frequency of occurrence; for example, free T_4 = HN—more frequently free T_4 is high, but normal levels can also be encountered.

undetectable thyroglobulin levels. Determination of thyroglobulin levels by immunoassays has its most useful application after thyroid cancer surgery. The upper normal limit of thyroglobulin is 20 to 25 ng/dL, and levels above that range may indicate a return of thyroid cancer. Thyroglobulin levels also increase when patients become hypothyroid, as occurs, for example, in preparation for radioactive iodine scanning and treatment. Determination of thyroglobulin levels at that time is strongly recommended. Normal thyroglobulin levels do not completely exclude the return of thyroid cancer because in about 10% of patients with thyroid cancer, thyroglobulin is normal in spite of the return of thyroid cancer. Intake of thyroid hormones leads to a decrease of thyroid tissue and thus lowers thyroglobulin levels. Patients with thyrotoxicosis factitia have, therefore, low thyroglobulin levels, in contrast to patients with thyroiditis. In both of these conditions, radioactive iodine uptake is low and thyroglobulin levels can help distinguish between these two conditions. In the presence of antithyroglobulin antibodies, accurate determination of thyroglobulin by immunoassays is not possible.

THYROID-STIMULATING HORMONE. Serum TSH levels correlate inversely with active thyroid hormone concentrations and represent the best single index to the presence of primary hyperthyroidism or primary hypothyroidism. In hypothyroidism with low thyroid hormone concentrations, TSH levels rise above the upper normal limit of 6 μU/mL. In hyperthyroidism with elevated thyroid hormone levels, TSH levels fall below the lower normal limit of 0.3 μU/mL. TSH levels as currently measured fall below the lower limit of normal in patients with hyperthyroidism, whatever the cause. Suppressed TSH levels also can accompany other conditions including first trimester of pregnancy (human chorionic gonadotropin [hCG] secretion); pituitary or hypothalamic disease; nonthyroidal illness; treatment with dopamine, glucocorticoids, and other drugs; and psychiatric illness or recent recovery from hyperthyroidism. In secondary hypothyroidism due to pituitary failure (<5% of all cases of hypothyroidism), the formation and secretion of thyroid hormone is low but TSH levels fail to rise. Similarly, in hypothalamic disease leading to decreased TRH formation, TSH levels are not elevated in spite of decreased T_4 and T_3 concentrations. In patients with hypothalamic or pituitary disease, TSH levels should not be used to assess thyroid status. Elevated TSH levels rarely occur in the absence of hypothyroidism. TSH-producing pituitary tumors

rarely cause hyperthyroidism. In the generalized thyroid hormone resistance syndrome, however, TSH levels are inappropriately elevated in proportion to the markedly elevated T_4 and T_3 levels. In hypothyroidism, markedly elevated TSH levels decline only slowly after thyroxine therapy achieves normal T_4 and T_3 concentrations. Hypothyroidism leads to an increase in the number of TSH-producing thyrotrophs, which decline only slowly after euthyroidism returns. Accordingly, allow 4 to 6 weeks before increasing replacement doses of thyroxine above average on the basis of TSH levels. Severe long-standing hypothyroidism can lead to pituitary enlargement, mimicking pituitary tumors. The availability of sensitive TSH levels allows adequate assessment of pituitary reserves under such circumstances and makes TRH tests less useful.

ANTITHYROID ANTIBODIES. Antibody formation can occur against the thyroid peroxidase enzyme, thyroglobulin, and the TSH receptors T_4, T_3, and NIS. These antibodies can be present in serum. Most frequently, antimicrosomal antibodies occur for which the thyroid peroxidase enzyme is the antigen. In Hashimoto's disease, elevated antibodies occur in more than 80% of patients with no specific therapeutic requirements resulting from high antiperoxidase antibody titers. Antithyroglobulin antibodies are positive in 60% of Hashimoto's disease. Occurrence of antithyroglobulin antibodies precludes using thyroglobulin levels to follow patients after thyroid cancer surgery or radioactive iodine treatment. Different types of TSH receptor antibodies occur, some of which stimulate thyroid hormone formation, whereas others only stimulate DNA synthesis or block TSH action. The TSI is a TSH receptor antibody that stimulates thyroid hormone formation and accompanies more than 90% of cases of Graves' disease. The TSI is related to, but not the same as, the long-acting thyroid-stimulating antibody, a previously used assay. In patients in whom the diagnosis of Graves' disease cannot be made clinically, determination of the TSI may be helpful, but routine TSI determination is not recommended. Persistent high levels of TSI in patients with Graves' disease on long-term antithyroid medication suggests but does not guarantee that stopping the antithyroid medication will not be followed by continuous euthyroidism. Anti-TSH antibodies can cross the placenta and produce neonatal Graves' disease or hypothyroidism. Circulating antibodies to T_4 and T_3 can interfere with the accurate determination of these hormones.

Evaluation of the Thyroid by Radioisotope Tests

RADIOACTIVE IODINE (RAI) UPTAKE. The Na^+/I^- symporter (NIS) in epithelial cells of the thyroid actively transports iodide (I^-) and molecules of similar charge and configuration, such as $^{99m}TcO_4^-$ pertechnetate and ^{201}Th. Only iodide is permanently retained in the thyroid cell by organification. Two separate tests use RAI: total radioactive uptake and thyroid scanning. Both are contraindicated during pregnancy. The RAI uptake only roughly indicates thyroid function. The 24-hour uptake ranges widely from 5 to 20%, and this, along with the markedly decreased uptake in the presence of increased amounts of bodily cold iodine, makes it an unreliable indicator of thyroid function. Patients with subacute thyroiditis have a markedly reduced or absent uptake, whereas patients with active Graves' disease have a normal or increased uptake. Accordingly, the RAI uptake may be useful in diagnosing subacute thyroiditis. Its routine use for the diagnosis of Graves' disease is not recommended.

THYROID SCAN. Thyroid scans give graphic representations of the distribution of RAI in the gland. They are useful in identifying whether thyroid nodules show decreased ("cold") or increased ("hot") accumulation of RAI compared with normal paranodular tissue. Uptake also identifies thyroid tissue outside the gland. The isotopes ^{123}I, ^{131}I, and ^{99m}Tc can be used. ^{123}I is preferred because it provides a much smaller radiation dose to the thyroid than ^{131}I. With a ^{99m}Tc scan, good-quality images can be obtained about 30 minutes after administration. Some thyroid nodules have a normal iodine transporter but lose the ability to organify iodine. Such nodules (about 10%) are not cold on ^{99m}Tc scans, a significant disadvantage of the technique. The ^{131}I isotope is sometimes preferred for identifying thyroid cancer metastases because it has a higher energy gamma ray and better penetrates the tissue. Scans in some patients fail to colocalize palpable nodules adjacent to areas of increased or decreased RAI retention. Such nodules may be autonomously either hot or cold. Because thyroid cancers exist in less than 1% of hot nodules compared with 20% of cold ones, the RAI uptake of thyroid nodules can be useful. In special cases, a suppression scan may be useful. After placing the patient on 150 to 200μg of T_4 per day for 4 to 6 weeks, one repeats the thyroid scan. Thyroid hormone and TSH values should be normal before thyroxine is started. Autonomous nodules continue to show an increased iodine uptake (hot), whereas other nodules lose their RAI retention, becoming cold. Cold nodules need to be further evaluated with fine-needle aspiration. Positron emission tomography has shown some usefulness for the imaging of thyroid cancers in patients with high thyroglobulin levels and negative ^{131}I scans.

THYROID ULTRASONOGRAPHY. Ultrasonography gives a high-resolution image of the thyroid and can identify nodules 1 to 3 mm in diameter. Such small nodules are, however, not clinically relevant. Ultrasonography can distinguish solid from cystic lesions and determine changes in the size of the nodule in response to thyroid hormone suppression therapy. Ultrasound-guided fine-needle aspiration helps in obtaining cytologic material from nodules that are difficult to identify by palpation. Ultrasonography cannot distinguish between benign and malignant thyroid nodules, nor can the technique identify substernal extensions of the thyroid or spread of metastatic disease to this region. For the latter purpose, magnetic resonance imaging (MRI) or computed tomography (CT) can be useful.

Fine-Needle Aspiration of Thyroid Nodules

Aspiration of thyroid nodules with a fine needle (22 to 27 gauge) to obtain material for cytologic examination provides good diagnostic accuracy with minimal side effects. Bleeding into the aspirated nodule is the only unwanted effect and usually has no clinical consequence. Results obtained with this procedure are listed in Table 239–4. Seeding of malignant cells along the needle track does not present a clinical problem with fine-needle aspiration. An experienced cytopathologist is crucial for the successful use of this procedure. Since the advent and wide use of fine-needle aspiration, surgical removal of benign nodules has substantially decreased.

NONTHYROIDAL ILLNESS SYNDROME

Severe systemic illness, physical trauma, and psychiatric disturbances can substantially alter thyroid hormone levels in patients

Table 239–4 • RESULTS OBTAINED BY FINE–NEEDLE ASPIRATION OF THYROID NODULES

RESULT	% OF PATIENTS
Adequate tissue obtained	90
Benign tumor	74
Malignant tumor	4
Suspicious or indeterminate	12
Correct diagnosis	<90
False–negative result	4
False–positive result	1

One fifth of these nodules are malignant after surgery by final pathology.

without intrinsic thyroid disease. Various terms have been used for this condition, including the *nonthyroidal illness syndrome* (NTI), *sick euthyroid syndrome*, and *low T_3 syndrome*. The severity of the illness correlates roughly with the extent of thyroid hormone changes. A decreased serum T_3 concentration is the critical component of the syndrome. The frequent alterations of thyroid hormone levels in severe illness probably make NTI a more common cause of abnormal thyroid hormone values than intrinsic thyroid disease. NTI represents one end of a spectrum of endocrine responses to severe illness which include increases in adrenocorticotropic hormone and cortisol levels. Increases in cytokines, especially tumor necrosis factor, interleukin-1, and interleukin-6, may contribute to the altered thyroid hormone levels. The consequences, if any, of NTI for total body metabolism and the functional status of specific organs are unclear, and therapy is currently not recommended. Diagnosing the simultaneous occurrence of hypothyroidism or hyperthyroidism in patients with NTI is a difficult diagnostic challenge. Different variants of NTI occur.

LOW T_3, NORMAL T_4 VARIANT. A marked decrease in serum total T_3 and free T_3 concentrations accompanied by normal serum T_4 and TSH levels is the most frequently encountered combination of thyroid hormone values in NTI. A rough correlation exists between the severity of the systemic illness and the decrease in T_3 levels. Decreased T_3 levels are most likely caused by an impairment of extrathyroidal T_4 to T_3 conversion. The decline is accompanied by an increase in rT_3 levels. Diminished 5′ deiodinase activity accounts for this reciprocal change, with T_3 no longer being formed from T_4 and reverse T_3 not being metabolized to rT_2. The decrease in T_3 levels may decrease protein turnover and exert a sparing effect on body proteins, but the overall impact on metabolic and organ function is unclear. Because of normal T_4 and TSH levels, this variant of NTI can be clearly distinguished from hypothyroidism.

LOW T_3, LOW T_4 VARIANT. In addition to low T_3 levels, T_4 levels also decline in patients with more severe illness. Several changes contribute (1) decreases in thyroxine-binding proteins (TBG and transthyretin), (2) displacement of T_4 from proteins by fatty acids, and (3) decreased thyroid hormone production because of lowered TSH levels. The degree of lowered T_4 levels correlates with disease severity: Mortality increases in patients with T_4 levels below 4μg/dL and approaches 80% in patients with T_4 levels below 2μg/dL. T_4 administration does not influence outcome, and the low levels reflect the severity of the underlying illness but appear not to contribute directly to mortality. In addition to low T_3 and T_4 levels, T_4 indexes are low but dialysis-measured free T_4 levels remain normal or only minimally lowered. TSH levels are low but may be slightly elevated during recovery from severe illness. TSH levels above 20μU/mL are not compatible with NTI and point to hypothyroidism.

Unusual Variants of Nonthyroidal Illness

Elevated T_4 levels with initially normal T_3 levels that subsequently decline occur with liver disease, especially acute hepatitis. Increased synthesis and release of TBG most likely accounts for the increased T_4 levels. A delayed fall in T_3 levels can affect patients with the acquired immunodeficiency syndrome indicating a poor prognosis; rT_3 levels are not elevated. In psychiatric illness, especially bipolar disorder, elevated T_4 levels occur during the initial disease phase, T_3 levels are normal, and TSH results vary. Elderly patients frequently show low

T_3 levels; possible causes include chronic illness, medication intake, or an adjustment to increasing age. T_3 levels remain normal in selected healthy elderly individuals.

Diagnostic Considerations

The diagnosis of hypothyroidism or hyperthyroidism in severely ill patients with NTI can be difficult. Signs indicating the prior existence of thyroid disease such as a goiter, a thyroidectomy surgical scar, exophthalmos, or pretibial myxedema should be sought. Organ manifestations such as marked bradycardia for hypothyroidism or tachycardia and fine tremor for hyperthyroidism may provide important clues, especially if no other reason for these signs can be identified. As described earlier, NTI-induced alterations in thyroid function tests suppress the standard indices of hypothyroidism or hyperthyroidism, but certain guidelines can help. A TSH level above 20 µU/mL in an NTI patient makes a diagnosis of hypothyroidism highly likely, and thyroxine therapy is indicated. Similarly, TSH levels below 0.03 µU/mL and only moderately elevated T_3 and T_4 levels make hyperthyroidism likely. As systemic illness improves, T_3 and T_4 levels rise further and hyperthyroidism becomes evident. If Graves' disease causes the hyperthyroidism, a TSI determination can be helpful. The preferred treatment for such hyperthyroidism is by medical therapy using PTU or methimazole.

THYROTOXICOSIS

Thyrotoxicosis occurs when tissues are exposed to excess amounts of thyroid hormone, resulting in specific metabolic changes and pathophysiologic alterations in organ function. A distinction can be made between thyrotoxicosis and hyperthyroidism. Hyperthyroidism denotes increased formation and release of thyroid hormone from the thyroid gland, whereas thyrotoxicosis describes the clinical syndrome that results. Excess intake of exogenous thyroid hormone would lead to thyrotoxicosis, but by the definition given above, such a patient would not be hyperthyroid. The terms, however, are frequently used interchangeably. Table 239–5 lists causes for thyrotoxicosis. The major ones are (1) increased occupancy of TSH receptors by TSI, TSH, or hCG; (2) autonomous overproduction of thyroid hormone by thyroid nodules; (3) increased release of thyroid hormone during specific phases of thyroiditis; and (4) excessive thyroid hormone intake or ectopic thyroid hormone formation. The most frequent cause of thyrotoxicosis is Graves' disease, accounting for 60 to 90% of cases and occurring among women with a frequency of 1.9%. Men experience one tenth of the occurrence in women. Other causes in decreasing order of frequency include toxic thyroid nodules, thyroiditis, factitious thyrotoxicosis, iodine-induced thyrotoxicosis, and hCG- and TSH-induced hyperthyroidism.

GRAVES' DISEASE

Graves' disease, also termed *Basedow's* or *Parry's disease*, carries the hallmarks of excess formation and secretion of thyroid hormone and diffuse goiter. Additional characteristics include exophthalmos, dermopathy (especially pretibial myxedema), and rarely thyroid acropachy. These supplementary manifestations seldom appear together and often run a divergent time course.

Etiology and Pathogenesis

Graves' disease is most likely an autoimmune disorder with B lymphocytes producing immunoglobulins, some of which bind to and activate the TSH receptor, stimulating excess thyroid growth and hormone secretion. For these antibodies, the TSH receptor appears to represent the antigenic site, and they act like TSH and are termed *thyroid-stimulating immunoglobulins* (TSI). Other antibodies occur in Graves' and other autoimmune diseases such as Hashimoto's disease. These antibodies bind to the TSH receptor but stimulate only thyroid growth without increasing thyroid hormone secretion. Some antibodies bind to the TSH receptor but block TSH action and lead to thyroid atrophy. A diversity of TSH antibodies occurs in autoimmune thyroid diseases, generating a spectrum of illnesses with Graves' disease and hyperthyroidism at one end and Hashimoto's disease and thyroid atrophy leading to hypothyroidism at the other. The role that specific antibodies play in causing the ophthalmopathy that occurs in a severe form in fewer than 5% of patients with Graves' disease is less clear. Expression of TSH receptor in orbital fibroblast presents an important orbital antigen contributing to the ophthalmopathy. Specific antibodies directed against non-TSH retro-orbital antigens localized on retro-orbital fibroblasts and muscle cells may present a secondary response. Anti-TSH antibodies occur at a low frequency in Hashimoto's disease and in euthyroid relatives of patients with Graves' disease. The simultaneous occurrence of blocking TSH antibodies may prevent hyperthyroidism in such patients.

The precise sequence of events leading to TSH receptor antibody production and factors that initiate antibody formation have not been clearly identified. Genetic risk factors, especially the HLA-DR3 locus, play an important role in susceptibility to develop Graves' disease in whites, but different HLA associations occur with other racial groups. The influence of sex hormones most likely mediate the female preponderance of thyroid autoimmune diseases such as Graves' disease. A potential scenario may be that thyroid cells stimulated by specific cytokines produced in response to a viral infection may express on their cell surface class II molecules of specific HLA-DR types that present fragments of the TSH receptor to T lymphocytes; these then would stimulate B lymphocytes to produce TSH receptor antibodies. The autoimmune response may be promoted by poorly defined factors including the following: (1) iodide excess—for example, the incidence of Graves' disease increases after iodine supplementation in deficient areas; (2) viral or bacterial infection—for example, outbreaks of Graves' disease can follow *Yersinia enterocolitica* infection; (3) glucocorticoid withdrawal or stress—the stress induction has been questioned and may relate to a worsening of symptoms by the combined occurrence of hyperthyroidism and physical or emotional stress, which brings the patients to medical attention; (4) parturition—a state of relative immune tolerance develops during pregnancy and reverses after delivery; (5) lithium therapy; (6) smoking, which is especially a risk factor for ophthalmopathy; (7) cytokine therapy (e.g., interferon γ), which may modify immune responses.

Pathology

The thyroid gland in Graves' disease enlarges diffusely and contains increased vascularity. The parenchyma exhibits hypertrophy and hyperplasia, with follicular cells showing increased height, surrounding a lumen containing a decreased amount of colloid. Infiltration by lymphocytes indicates the autoimmune nature of the disease. These cells probably generate a considerable amount of TSH receptor antibody. Iodide administration increases the colloid accumulation and decreases

---

Table 239–5 • CAUSES OF THYROTOXICOSIS

Dependent on Increased Thyroid Hormone Production
 Dependent on increased occupancy of the TSH receptor by:
  Thyroid-stimulating immunoglobulin (TSI)
   Graves' disease
   Hashitoxicosis
  Human chorionic gonadotropin (hCG)
   Hydatiform mole
   Choriocarcinoma
  Thyroid-stimulating hormone (TSH)
   TSH-producing pituitary tumor
 Autonomous overproduction of thyroid hormone (independent of TSH)
  Toxic adenoma (TSH receptor mutant)
  Toxic multinodular goiter
  Follicular cancer (rare)
 Jod-Basedow effect (excess iodine-induced hyperthyroidism)
Independent of Increased Thyroid Hormone Production
 Increased thyroid hormone release
  Subacute granulomatous thyroiditis (painful)
  Subacute lymphocytic thyroiditis (painless)
 Nonthyroidal source of thyroid hormone
  Thyrotoxicosis factitia
  "Hamburger" thyrotoxicosis
  Ectopic production by:
   Ovarian teratoma (struma ovarii)
   Metastasis of follicular cancer

vascularity, making the gland firmer. A gland that increases in size in patients receiving antithyroid medication indicates either excess medication, inducing hypothyroidism, or too low a dose, providing inadequate receptor blockade and continued thyroid hormone formation and growth. Severe thyrotoxicosis can lead to muscle atrophy with muscle fiber degeneration, cardiac hypertrophy, focal hepatic necrosis with lymphocyte infiltration, a decrease in bone density, and hair loss. In patients with Graves' disease ophthalmopathy, an increase in retro-orbital contents leads to protrusion of the globe. The retro-orbital tissues show marked infiltration by lymphocytes, mast cells, and plasma cells along with increased amounts of mucopolysaccharide, especially hyaluronic acid. Extraocular muscles show edema, round cell infiltration, and mucopolysaccharide deposition eventually resulting in muscle fibrosis. In patients with pretibial myxedema, the skin shows prominent lymphocyte infiltration and mucopolysaccharide deposition.

Clinical Features

Excess thyroid hormone action due to any of the causes listed in Table 239–5 can lead to an increased metabolic rate and changes in the function of several organs. In addition, patients with Graves' disease have specific clinical manifestations resulting from the underlying autoimmune process. The thyrotoxicosis and autoimmune-related manifestations can show independent variations in intensity and time course, causing diagnostic difficulties.

FEATURES OF THYROTOXICOSIS. Table 239–6 lists common signs and symptoms of thyrotoxicosis. The typical patient with Graves' disease is a woman in her mid-20s to 30s experiencing recent onset of nervousness, difficulty in controlling emotions, and a state of agitated tiredness made worse by sleep disturbances. She speaks rapidly and cannot sit still. Problems of recent onset in interaction with others at home or at work are frequently reported. Questioning brings out feelings of heat intolerance with excess sweating, palpitations, muscle weakness, frequent bowel movements, and weight loss in spite of good appetite. Sometimes weight gain ensues because the increased appetite and caloric intake exceed the enhanced caloric consumption. Oligomenorrhea and amenorrhea occur in premenopausal women. On physical examination, the skin is warm and moist and has a fine velvety texture. The hair is fine and, when combed, sheds substantial amounts, leading to thinning of the hair. Onycholysis with separation of the nail from the fingertip is frequent. Gynecomastia can occur in men because of increased estrogen production. Fine tremor is noted on the stretched-out hands, and tendon reflexes become hyperactive. The eye signs of thyrotoxicosis are most likely mediated by an increased sympathetic tone and include a widened distance between the upper and lower lid, lid lag on upward gaze, and frequent blinking. These signs do not indicate Graves' ophthalmopathy and are not accompanied by protrusion of the eyes. Cardiovascular manifestations can be marked, characterized by sinus tachycardia, a widened pulse pressure, and an often elevated systolic blood pressure. True hypertension is not frequent in hyperthyroidism but does occur in hypothyroidism. The heartbeat is vigorous with a hyperactive pericardium. On auscultation, the first sound is increased and a third sound and frequently a systolic murmur are audible. A harsh to-and-fro sound can be audible and is most likely caused by the pleural and pericardial surfaces rubbing each other. Cardiac arrhythmia, especially atrial fibrillation, can contribute to the development of heart failure. Muscle atrophy and weakness develop, and hypokalemic periodic paralysis has a measurable incidence in males of Asian extraction. Bone turnover can be increased, leading to hypercalcemia of as much as 12 mg/dL. Unusual blood-detected abnormalities (<10% of patients) include elevated alkaline phosphatase levels, increased direct bilirubin, mild anemia, and moderate neutropenia. Renal tubular acidosis can occur, and immune complex nephritis has been reported.

In older patients, the manifestations of thyrotoxicosis can be considerably modified. Affected patients frequently appear apathetic rather than nervous. Cardiovascular signs, general muscle weakness, and marked weight loss are more prominent. Cardiac arrhythmias that are refractory to conventional treatment, unexplained heart failure, or the recent onset or marked worsening of preexisting angina pectoris should lead to a determination of thyroid hormone values.

FEATURES SPECIFIC FOR GRAVES' DISEASE. Autoimmune processes mediate the enlargement of the thyroid gland, infiltrative ophthalmopathy, dermopathy, and acropachy, thereby distinguishing Graves' disease from other causes of thyrotoxicosis. Palpation most frequently reveals diffuse and symmetric thyroid enlargement (two to six times normal). Thyroid nodules can occur and should be sampled because, although unusual, thyroid cancer can coincide with Graves' disease. Auscultation of the thyroid frequently reveals a thyroid bruit, reflecting the increased blood supply. In a small number of patients, the thyroid remains of normal size. A hallmark finding of Graves' disease is infiltrative ophthalmopathy. Clinically detectable eye disease occurs in 20 to 40% of patients with Graves' disease, but severe ophthalmopathy requiring aggressive treatment affects only about 5%. Affected persons complain of easy tearing, photophobia, a feeling of sand in the eyes, diplopia, and decreased visual acuity. Ophthalmopathy affects the anterior soft tissue structures of the eye and with progressive severity involves more posterior structures as well. Periorbital edema and chemosis occur early and result from impaired drainage of the orbital veins. The swollen and fibrotic muscles cause lid retraction and restrict ocular movement, leading to diplopia. Upward gaze is most frequently impaired; with limitations of lateral gaze occurring less frequently. Tissue edema and accumulation of hydroscopic hyaluronic acid lead to engorgement of extraocular muscles and swelling of retro-orbital connective tissue, pushing the globe forward and resulting in proptosis and further restriction of eye movement. Proptosis and lid retraction prevent complete closure of the eyes, resulting in exposure keratitis and corneal ulceration. Adequate care to prevent drying and infection of the cornea is important. Compression of the optic nerve at the posterior apex by enlarged muscles may lead to blurring and impaired visual acuity, visual field defects, impairment of color vision, and papilledema. Optic nerve compression can occur in the absence of proptosis. Graves' ophthalmopathy that is clinically apparent in only one eye occurs in 5 to 14% of patients. Sensitive imaging techniques such as computed tomography (CT), however, show that most of these patients have bilateral orbital disease. Most patients with Graves' ophthalmopathy are hyperthyroid, but dissociation can occur with ophthalmopathy appearing in patients of euthyroid or hypothyroid status. More unusual manifestations include coexisting myasthenia gravis with Graves' disease. Other cases may include diffuse lymphadenopathy and splenomegaly. Rarely, other autoimmune disorders occur in patients with Graves' disease.

Diagnosis and Differential Diagnosis

In patients with severe Graves' disease showing typical signs of thyrotoxicosis and autoimmune-mediated manifestations such as ophthalmopathy, the diagnosis is not difficult (see Table 239–6). Gauging the degree of thyroid hormone overproduction guides subsequent therapy. Measurement of free T_4, T_3, and TSH levels constitutes a sufficient laboratory work-up. In all patients with Graves' disease, T_3 levels are markedly elevated, and in most such patients free T_4 levels are elevated as well. In some patients, however, the marked stimulation of TSH receptors leads to higher hormone production rates of T_3 so that serum T_3 levels rise markedly whereas T_4 levels remain normal. This combination of laboratory values is termed T_3 toxicosis and is most frequently found during the initial phases or a relapse of Graves' disease. TSH levels are undetectable and serve to exclude TSH-producing tumors or thyroid hormone resistance as causes for the elevated thyroid hormone levels. In typical Graves' disease, radioactive iodine-based tests and a determination of the TSI are unnecessary. The clinical diagnosis becomes more difficult in patients with milder disease, in older patients manifesting apathetic

Endocrine Diseases

Table 239–6 • TISSUE-SPECIFIC SIGNS AND SYMPTOMS OF THYROTOXICOSIS

TISSUE	SYMPTOMS AND SIGNS
Central nervous system	Nervousness and emotional lability Fine tremor of hands
Cardiovascular	Palpitations, tachycardia, atrial fibrillation, increased difference between systolic and diastolic blood pressure
Gastrointestinal	Hyperdefecation, gastrointestinal hypermotility, diarrhea
Muscle	Proximal muscle weakness, muscle atrophy, hyperreflexia
Skin	Warm moist smooth skin, onycholysis, fine hair, hair loss, excessive perspiration
Metabolic	Heat intolerance, weight loss usually with increased appetite
Thyroid	Enlargement of nodule(s)

thyrotoxicosis, and in patients with coexisting illnesses. Determination of free T_4, T_3, and TSH levels adequately establish the degree of thyrotoxicosis in patients with mild disease and older patients with an apathetic picture. Undetectable TSH levels using an ultrasensitive TSH assay are especially helpful in establishing that the body contains an excess amount of thyroid hormone. Intercurrent illness modifies thyroid hormone values by lowering T_3 levels and, in some patients, T_4 levels. Elevated reverse T_3 levels further implicate an intercurrent illness as a modifier of thyroid hormone values. Obtaining TSI values can be helpful in these patients because their elevation confirms the diagnosis of Graves' disease. The findings on palpation of the thyroid of a nodule, a somewhat painful thyroid, or no palpable thyroid tissue are unusual and require additional diagnostic procedures. A radioactive iodine scan is especially helpful in identifying a cold thyroid nodule surrounded by high uptake in surrounding tissue, a combination compatible with Graves' disease with a cold nodule requiring biopsy. Alternatively, the nodule may be hot, with surrounding areas showing decreased or absent uptake, which makes it more likely that the patient has a toxic adenoma. Very low uptake in patients who experience pain on palpation of the thyroid area indicates thyroiditis. In patients with no palpable thyroid tissue and absent thyroid uptake, ectopic production of thyroid hormone or factitious intake should be suspected. Thyroglobulin levels are very low in such patients.

Discrepancies between the degree of thyrotoxicosis and the extent of autoimmune abnormalities can complicate the diagnosis of Graves' disease. Some patients can exhibit marked bilateral or unilateral ophthalmopathy with minimal or no signs of thyrotoxicosis. In such instances, T_4 and T_3 levels are in the upper normal range and TSH levels are in the low normal or decreased range. The condition has been termed *euthyroid ophthalmopathy* or *euthyroid Graves' disease*. Thyrotoxicosis is mimicked by few clinical syndromes, and thyroid hormone values are normal in most of these. Pheochromocytomas can lead to heat intolerance, profuse sweating, palpitations, tachycardia, elevated glucose levels, and a state of anxiety. Anxiety states by themselves also lead to irritability, tremor, weakness, tachycardia, and weight loss. Thyroid hormone values are normal in these conditions.

℞ Treatment

GRAVES' DISEASE

The ophthalmopathy and dermopathy of Graves' disease require separate therapeutic approaches. The therapy for thyrotoxicosis is aimed at decreasing thyroid hormone formation and secretion. Three different therapeutic approaches are used: (1) antithyroid drugs that inhibit the thyroid peroxidase enzyme involved in thyroid hormone formation, (2) radioactive iodine, and (3) surgery. Both of the latter two treatments decrease the amount of functional thyroid tissue. The most frequently used treatment modalities are antithyroid drugs or radioactive iodine, and the choice between them depends on the phase and severity of the disease, the specific situation of the patient, and the preference and experience of the physician. Spontaneously occurring increases and decreases of the underlying autoimmune abnormality lead to cycles of worsening and improvement of the thyrotoxic symptoms, making the natural history of Graves' disease variable. Consequently, life-long follow-up is recommended. Ten to 20% of patients with Graves' disease experience spontaneous remittance, and about half become hypothyroid after 20 to 30 years in the absence of therapy, most likely due to continued autoimmune destruction of the thyroid. Not treating patients and awaiting a spontaneous remission is not recommended. Therapy directed against the autoimmune process is currently not available.

THYROTOXICOSIS

ANTITHYROID DRUG THERAPY. Amelioration of thyrotoxic symptoms by decreasing thyroid hormone formation and release is the initial task in cases of severe thyrotoxicosis. The thionamide derivatives, PTU and methimazole (MMI), are the preferred initial treatment options in patients with Graves' disease in the absence of contraindications. Radioactive iodine can lead to increased release of thyroid hormone and, infrequently, worsen the thyrotoxic symptoms to the point of inducing thyroid storm. Thyroid surgery is contraindicated in severely hyperthyroid patients. PTU and MMI, as well as carbimazole, which is used in Great Britain and is metabolized to methimazole, interfere with organification and iodotyrosine coupling by inhibiting the peroxidase enzyme. Both compounds may exert a mild immunosuppressive effect; a decrease in the level of TSI occurs after the drugs are started. This could be due to a mild immunosuppressive effect but also could result from decreased thyroid hormone secretion. Both drugs are rapidly absorbed from the gastrointestinal tract and concentrated in the thyroid. PTU inhibits peripheral conversion of T_4 to T_3, contributing 10 to 20% to the decrease in T_3 levels. This effect does not occur with MMI. MMI, however, is at least 10 times more potent than PTU and has a longer intrathyroidal residence time. MMI administered once a day is effective, whereas PTU must be given every 6 to 8 hours to exert its full effect. Both PTU and MMI cross the placenta, but PTU is more water soluble and therefore less well transferred to the fetus. The lowest effective dose of PTU should be given and should not exceed 300 mg/day; given in high doses, PTU and MMI can interfere with fetal thyroid function. The choice between PTU and MMI and particular dosing schemes vary considerably between different centers. PTU is most useful for patients with severe thyrotoxicosis and for the treatment of Graves' disease during pregnancy. Patients with moderate thyrotoxicosis are started on MMI, which comes in 5- and 10-mg tablets. Starting doses of 20 to 30 mg once daily are used. Improvement of thyrotoxic symptoms, in general, takes 2 to 3 weeks and can lag behind the normalization of thyroid hormone values. Euthyroidism can be achieved in 4 to 6 weeks. Thyroid hormone values are checked 4 weeks after the start of therapy and if no decrease in values occurs in spite of compliance, the dose may be increased to 30 to 40 mg/day. Once thyroid hormone levels normalize, the dose is decreased. A decrease in dose that is accompanied by an increase in free T_4 or T_3 levels and symptoms suggesting disease reactivation requires maintenance at higher dose levels for a longer time. Most patients can be maintained on low doses of 2.5 to 5 mg of MMI for 12 to 24 months.

Patients with severe hyperthyroidism are started on PTU (100 to 150 mg every 8 hours). The choice is based on the faster decrease in T_3 levels with PTU than MMI. In some patients, higher doses of 200 to 300 mg every 6 hours are required. PTU comes in 50-mg tablets and, when taken in doses of two or three tablets three times a day, can lead to compliance problems. With improvement, the physician can progressively lower PTU doses and switch to once-a-day MMI. Most patients are then maintained on the lower MMI dose (2.5 to 5 mg/day) for 12 to 24 months. It appears that longer duration of antithyroid therapy bodes well for patients staying euthyroid after the medication is stopped. Most relapses occur within the first 3 to 6 months after discontinuation of antithyroid therapy. In young adults, a second course of antithyroid drug therapy can be tried, but the chance of permanent remission declines.

Undesired occurrences during PTU and MMI therapy include an increase in thyroid size, which may result from overtreatment, shown by low T_4 levels and elevated TSH levels, or undertreatment and reactivation of disease. Unfavorable indicators of disease activity are a requirement for higher PTU and MMI doses and T_3 levels that increase excessively compared with T_4 levels. Favorable prognostic signs are continued normalization of thyroid hormone levels, especially a normal T_4 to T_3 ratio in spite of using lower PTU and MMI doses, and decreasing thyroid size and TSI levels. Routine monitoring of TSI is not recommended. An alternative approach is to maintain patients on high does of PTU or MMI combined with levothyroxine supplementation to prevent hypothyroidism induced by antithyroid drug therapy. Claims of superior remission rates with this approach have not been confirmed in other trials.

Table 239–7 lists side effects of thionamide compounds. These occur most frequently during the initial 3 to 6 months after the therapy is started. The most frequent complications are allergic in nature, and rashes occur in 2 to 3% of patients. The major toxic reaction is agranulocytosis, which develops suddenly and occurs in 0.2 to 0.5% of patients. Routine monitoring of leukocyte counts is not recommended, but a leukocyte count should be obtained before therapy is started. Patients need to be instructed to discontinue their medication and contact their physician when a fever occurs or infections develop, especially in the oropharynx. A white blood cell count below 0.5×10^9/L indicates agranulocytosis and requires both discontinuation of antithyroid drugs and administration of broad-spectrum antibiotics as well as supportive therapy. Other treatment modalities such as radioactive iodine should be chosen for further treatment.

RADIOACTIVE IODINE. RAI therapy (^{131}I) is used most frequently to treat hyperthyroidism in adults in the United States, in contrast to Europe and Japan, where antithyroid medication is the preferred approach. In either event, antithyroid drugs are the preferred initial therapy for thyrotoxicosis. RAI therapy is preferred for older patients with moderate hyperthyroidism and thyroid enlargement, for patients with a prior allergic or toxic reaction to the antithyroid medication, and when frequent medication intake cannot be guaranteed. ^{131}I is also used after a course of antithyroid medication has failed to induce a long-term euthyroid state. RAI treatment is contraindicated during breast feeding and pregnancy; the fetal thyroid becomes able to accumulate iodine at 10 to 12 weeks of gestation. RAI can induce a thyroiditis with glandular swelling leading to potential airway obstruction in patients with large retrosternal goiters. A very low RAI uptake caused by excessive iodine exposure also precludes ^{131}I use.

Before ^{131}I administration, antithyroid drugs should be stopped for 3 or 5 days. Different dosing methods have been proposed for ^{131}I application. One approach is to aim at delivering 80 µCi ^{131}I per gram of thyroid tissue. The 80 µCi is then multiplied by the estimated weight of the gland and corrected for ^{131}I uptake. This delivers 6000 to 8000 rad to the thyroid and most frequently requires doses of 5 to 10 mCi. In patients with low uptake, large glands, and severe thyrotoxicosis leading to rapid intrathyroidal iodine turnover, larger doses often are chosen. Improvement in thyrotoxicosis occurs after 4 to 5 weeks, and 40 to 70% of patients regain normal thyroid functions within 6 to 8 weeks. Almost 80% of patients are cured with one dose. The remaining need a second dose, which should not be given before 6 months have elapsed. After RAI has been given, antithyroid drugs can be added at day 5 so that the patient can reach a euthyroid state more quickly. In addition, β-sympathetic blockade is used to relieve associated symptoms. RAI can induce a painful thyroiditis and lead to acute thyroid hormone release and worsening of thyrotoxicosis. Severe thyroiditis can be treated with antiinflammatory agents such as aspirin; rarely, glucocorticoids are required. RAI treatment-induced worsening of Graves' ophthalmopathy has been reported in some studies but not in others. Administration of glucocorticoids concurrently with RAI treatment may be beneficial, but such treatment is not well enough established to be recommended for routine use. Corticosteroids, however, may be useful for patients with prominent eye disease in whom RAI therapy is the approach of choice. A dose of 40 mg prednisone per day at the time of RAI therapy with subsequent tapering over 2 to 3 months can be used. No increase of thyroid cancer, other malignancies, or malformations in subsequent pregnancies have been documented after RAI therapy. It is recommended, however, that pregnancy not occur for 6 to 12 months after RAI treatment. Hypothyroidism is a consequence of RAI treatment. More than 50% of patients become hypothyroid during the first year after therapy, with an additional 2 to 3% during each subsequent year. Unless otherwise treated, transient hypothyroidism occurs 2 to 3 months after radioactive iodine treatment, with subsequent spontaneous normalization of thyroid hormone values. Patients should be informed of this risk and be followed after the acute phase of treatment every 4 to 6 months and subsequently at least once a year.

SURGERY. Surgical removal of a large part of the thyroid (subtotal thyroidectomy) is indicated in patients with large obstructing glands or glands containing nodules that are identified as malignant or equivocal on fine-needle aspiration. Pregnant women with severe hyperthyroidism, which is difficult to control with antithyroid drugs, can be treated with thyroidectomy during the second trimester. In addition, young patients whose condition is difficult to control on antithyroid drugs, patients with toxic reactions to antithyroid drugs, and patients who are not candidates for antithyroid drugs and refuse radioactive iodine are treated by surgery. Nevertheless, patients must be euthyroid before surgery is undertaken. This is achieved by using PTU or MMI for approximately 6 weeks. In patients on PTU or MMI, a saturated solution of potassium iodide (1 drop three times a day) can be administered daily for 10 days before surgery to reduce the vascularity of the gland. Subtotal thyroidectomy should be performed by an experienced thyroid surgeon. Complications including hypoparathyroidism, recurrent laryngeal nerve paralysis, and hemorrhage should occur in less than 1 to 2% of patients. In addition, transient hypocalcemia, wound infection, and keloid formation leading to unsightly scars may occur. Hypothyroidism occurs to a somewhat lower extent than after RAI, but its frequency may be underestimated. Recurrent hyperthyroidism occurs in about 10% of patients.

ALTERNATIVE AND SUPPORTIVE THERAPIES. In a small number of patients with Graves' disease, the conventional therapies listed above cannot be used. In some, toxic reactions preclude the use of antithyroid drugs and ^{131}I cannot be employed because a very low uptake occurs due to excess iodine exposure or pregnancy. Also, some patients may present a high surgical risk because of underlying medical problems. In such cases, the oral cholecystographic agent iopanoic acid or sodium iopodate (Oragrafin Telepaque), administered at 1 g/day, inhibits T_4 to T_3 conversion and leads to rapid lowering of T_3 levels. In addition, because of release of iodine from the compound, T_4 levels fall. These compounds should be used for only 2 to 3 months because escape from their antithyroid effect occurs. The perchlorate ion (ClO_4^-) of $KClO_4$ is a competitive inhibitor of thyroidal iodide transport. In doses limited to 1 g/day, serious toxic effects such as anaplastic anemia and gastric ulcers can be avoided. The compound is especially effective in iodine-induced hyperthyroidism (Jod-Basedow effect) as occurs, for example, in patients treated with the antiarrhythmic compound amiodarone. Potassium perchlorate should be used for only a short time and with careful supervision. The isolated use of iodine to treat thyrotoxicosis is ill advised because its inhibitory effects on thyroid hormone secretion often fail. Iodine should be used only in patients who are on antithyroid medication and are prepared for thyroid surgery or in the treatment of thyroid storm (see later).

β-Adrenergic blocking agents such as propranolol, 60 to 120 mg/day in three or four divided doses, help to provide relief of symptoms such as tachycardia, tremor, anxiety, and heat intolerance. The rationale for their use is based on an increased sensitivity of the β-sympathetic system in thyrotoxicosis and on a small inhibitory effect of T_4 to T_3 conversion. Patients with a history of asthma or congestive heart failure should not receive propranolol because it constricts bronchial smooth muscle and has a negative inotropic effect. Propranolol should not be used as a sole agent to treat hyperthyroidism because it neither directly inhibits thyroid hormone action nor induces a euthyroid state. Multivitamin supplementation is advisable in patients with severe thyrotoxicosis, especially if nutrition is not well balanced and adequate.

Continued

OPHTHALMOPATHY AND DERMOPATHY

Clinically apparent ophthalmopathy affects 20 to 40% of patients with Graves' disease, but severe symptoms occur in only a minority. For most patients with mild eye signs, only general supportive measures are needed. These include elevation of the head at night and wearing of tinted glasses to protect the eyes from sunlight and foreign bodies. Application of 1% methylcellulose drops to the eyes and taking a diuretic to decrease periorbital swelling provide further relief. Patients with more severe ophthalmopathy should be managed in close consultation between an endocrinologist and an ophthalmologist. Severe inflammatory reactions are treated with 60 to 100 mg of prednisone in divided doses for 2 to 4 weeks, with subsequent tapering of the dose over 8 to 12 weeks. Combinations of prednisone and cyclosporine have also been used. External x-ray therapy to the retro-orbital area is not established as desirable therapy. Signs of optic nerve compression such as papillary edema, decreased color vision, and decreased visual acuity require surgical decompression, for which a transantral approach is frequently favored. After the active inflammatory process subsides, corrective surgical procedures may be beneficial. Retro-orbital muscle surgery may correct for eyeball misalignment and double vision. Eyelid surgery aimed at protecting the cornea, relieving discomfort, and cosmetic improvement should be the last surgical step.

OTHER CAUSES OF THYROTOXICOSIS

TOXIC ADENOMA AND TOXIC MULTINODULAR GOITER. Increased formation and secretion of T_3 and T_4 can occur in a single nodule or in multiple thyroid nodules. The latter condition is also termed *Plummer's disease*. In some toxic adenomas, several point mutations of the TSH receptor gene leading to constitutive activation have been described. A small number of toxic adenomas have mutations in G proteins also resulting in constitutive activation. Single nodules need to be larger than 2 to 3 cm in diameter to engender hyperthyroidism. Histologically, these nodules are follicular adenomas. Frequently, a large nodule is palpable on one side of the thyroid, with atrophy of the other side. In contrast, patients with toxic multinodular goiter may undergo general nodular enlargement. Such persons frequently are older and have had a goiter for a long time before autonomous overproduction of thyroid hormone ensues. The thyrotoxicosis can be precipitated by excess iodine intake (Jod-Basedow effect) and appears to occur particularly frequently in autonomous thyroid tissue, which functions independently of TSH stimulation. On physical examination, multinodular goiters range from small to large with possible substernal extension. Laboratory values show suppressed TSH levels and marked elevation of T_3 levels, with T_4 levels showing a lesser increase. Antibodies against the TSH receptor (TSI) and thyroid peroxidase (anti-TPO) are absent, in contrast to patients with Graves' disease.

On RAI scan, two patterns can be distinguished. Some patients show an irregular and patchy distribution of increased RAI uptake. In others, one or more distinct hot nodules occur with marked, localized increased RAI accumulation and no uptake between the hot nodules. Both patterns are compatible with toxic goiter. Clinically affected patients may be difficult to diagnose because the disease affects elderly patients, who tend to present with apathetic hyperthyroidism. As noted earlier, typical thyrotoxic signs can be minimal in such patients, who often show apathy, lethargy, a depressed mood, weight loss, and cardiac abnormalities.

Radioactive iodine is the treatment of choice for most patients with one toxic adenoma or multinodular toxic goiter. Severely thyrotoxic patients may need a course of antithyroid medication several weeks before they receive RAI to forestall acute worsening and decompensation after ^{131}I administration. The ^{131}I dose is 150 μCi per gram of tissue, twice that used for Graves' disease. Permanent hypothyroidism infrequently develops because remaining thyroid tissue resumes thyroid hormone secretion after ablation of toxic adenomas. Surgery can remove isolated adenomas, especially in younger patients.

RARE CAUSES. Thyrotoxicosis can be caused by TSH-producing pituitary tumors as well as by excess formation of hCG by hydatiform moles or choriocarcinoma. Surgical therapy is appropriate for both pituitary tumors and moles. Choriocarcinoma is treated by appropriate chemotherapy, and persistent thyrotoxicosis may require antithyroid drugs. Ectopic production of thyroid hormone by ovarian teratoma leads to mild thyrotoxicosis. Body scans detect RAI uptake in the location of the ovaries. Surgical removal is corrective. Follicular carcinoma of the thyroid with functioning metastases rarely leads to hyperthyroidism. Therapy is discussed in the section on thyroid cancer. Subacute or chronic thyroiditis can release high amounts of T_4 and T_3 and induce hyperthyroidism lasting for several weeks or months. RAI uptake is very low in such lesions. *Thyrotoxicosis factitia* results from inadvertent or planned ingestion of large amounts of thyroid hormone. It most frequently accompanies efforts at weight loss or occurs in patients with psychiatric problems. Many of these patients have easy access to thyroid hormone because they took it in the past, have relatives or acquaintances who are taking thyroid hormone, or are medical personnel. Ingestion of ground meat products prepared from neck trim containing thyroid tissue has also been reported (hamburger thyrotoxicosis). Patients with thyrotoxic symptoms, suppressed TSH levels, increased T_4 and T_3 levels, low RAI uptake, and suppressed thyroglobulin levels meet the diagnostic criteria for thyrotoxicosis factitia. Patients taking T_3 preparations have elevated T_3 levels but suppressed T_4 levels. Stopping thyroid hormone intake usually suffices as treatment. Additive β-sympathetic blockade or agents such as ipodate to inhibit T_4 to T_3 conversion are rarely needed.

The term *Jod-Basedow effect*, as noted earlier, designates iodine-induced hyperthyroidism. It occurs most frequently in patients with toxic nodular goiter exposed to excess amounts of iodine but has also been reported in Graves' disease. Problems with the autoregulation of thyroid hormone formation usually exist before iodine exposure, but some patients have been reported who exhibited completely normal thyroid function after iodine was withheld. The Jod-Basedow effect typically occurs in iodine-deficient areas after iodine supplementation is provided. Exposure to iodinated radiographic contrast media and iodinated drugs presents a frequent triggering event for the Jod-Basedow effect in the United States. The antiarrhythmic agent amiodarone, which contains 37% iodine, can induce the Jod-Basedow effect. The developing hyperthyroidism can worsen arrhythmias and lead to difficult management problems. In milder cases, antithyroid drugs such as MMI are used. Potassium perchlorate prevents further

Table 239–7 • SIDE EFFECTS OF ANTITHYROID DRUGS

Severe
  Agranulocytosis (0.2–0.5%)
  Only rare cases reported
    Hepatitis (can result in hepatic failure)
    Cholestatic jaundice
    Thrombocytopenia
    Hypoprothrombinemia
    Aplastic anemia
    Lupus–like syndrome with vasculitis
    Hypoglycemia (insulin antibodies)
Less Severe
  Most frequent (1–5%)
    Rash
    Urticaria
    Arthralgia
    Decreased leukocyte level (drop in white blood cell counts by 2–3 × 10³)
    Fever
  Less frequent
    Arthritis
    Diarrhea
    Decreased sense of taste

iodine uptake and inhibits thyroid hormone formation. The usual dose is 200 mg four times a day.

SPECIAL THERAPEUTIC PROBLEMS

THYROID STORM. Thyroid storm or thyrotoxic crisis is a life-threatening form of decompensated hyperthyroidism. Thyroid storm occurs most frequently in patients with severe thyrotoxicosis who develop an intercurrent severe illness such as an infection or sepsis or undergo a major surgical procedure. The distinction between severe thyrotoxicosis with an additional intercurrent illness and thyroid storm cannot be clearly drawn. Patients with severe thyrotoxicosis developing an intercurrent illness should be aggressively treated by the approach outlined in Table 239–8 because the illness can quickly decompensate into thyrotoxic crisis. Thyrotoxic crisis requires no acute increase in thyroid hormone values and it cannot be identified by laboratory tests. An acute increase in tissue availability of free thyroid hormones caused by a decrease in plasma-binding proteins may cause it, but equally likely are coincident increases in cytokines such as tumor necrosis factor-α and interleukin-6. Clinical signs compatible with thyrotoxic crisis are fever in excess of the temperature elevation expected from the intercurrent illness, with temperatures of 41° C (105° F) and even higher. In addition, marked tachycardia, extreme restlessness, agitation, and tremor occur. Patients may experience mental deterioration and become delirious, psychotic, obtunded, and even comatose. Hypotension with congestive heart failure and signs of an acute abdomen can develop. Table 239–8 outlines therapy, which includes high doses of antithyroid medication and iodine after starting antithyroid drugs. Cortisol turnover increases markedly, inducing enhanced formation of 11-keto compounds (cortisone), which are less metabolically active. Administration of 300 mg of hydrocortisone in divided doses is therefore indicated. Propranolol provides effective sympathetic blockade that has a favorable effect on cardiac failure induced by rapid heart rate. The compound has a negative inotropic effect, however, and should be used cautiously in patients with congestive heart failure. A history of asthma attacks precludes the use of β-sympathetic blockers. Treatment of precipitating events and supportive therapy must be started immediately.

THYROTOXICOSIS AND PREGNANCY. The most frequent cause of thyrotoxicosis during pregnancy is Graves' disease, but hyperthyroidism can result from toxic multinodular goiter and, more rarely, an excess of hCG production by hydatiform moles or choriocarcinoma. Hyperthyroidism may be difficult to recognize because pregnancy itself can lead to a hyperdynamic cardiovascular state and heat intolerance. Total T_4 and T_3 levels are increased owing to elevated thyroid hormone-binding protein levels, but T_4 values above 15 μg/dL strongly suggest hyperthyroidism. Hyperemesis gravidarum leads to elevated T_4 levels

(hyperthyroxinemia), with normal T_3 values. In addition to medical problems of the mother resulting from severe thyrotoxicosis, slight increases in neonatal mortality rate and low birth weight in newborns have been reported.

Antithyroid drugs are the initial therapy of choice. RAI is contraindicated, and the patient needs to be euthyroid before surgery can be considered. Because PTU inhibits T_4 to T_3 conversion, is less lipid soluble and crosses the placenta less readily, and is concentrated to a lower extent in the mother's milk than MMI, use of PTU is preferred over MMI in pregnant patients. Isolated cases of aplastica cutis induced by MMI have been reported. At high doses, PTU can induce fetal hypothyroidism and goiter because it crosses the placenta. In contrast, thyroid hormone minimally crosses the placenta. PTU doses are therefore limited to 200 to 300 mg/day; the addition of thyroxine confers no advantage. PTU administered in this way during pregnancy is relatively safe and does not negatively affect either fetal development or the outcome of pregnancy. If adequate control of hyperthyroidism is not possible, subtotal thyroidectomy should be considered, which is best performed during the second trimester. Long-term treatment with propranolol is not recommended because low birth weight can result. In addition, postnatal bradycardia and poor responses to hypoxia have been noted in newborns of mothers treated with propranolol. During the postpartum period, the mother risks developing new Graves' disease, a recurrence of previously quiescent Graves' disease, or postpartum thyroiditis. A state of relative immuno-suppression during pregnancy that disappears with delivery has been implicated. Newborns delivered of mothers with Graves' disease can have a state of transient hyperthyroidism due to placental passage of TSI or less frequently long-term Graves' disease because of a genetic propensity. Mild neonatal thyrotoxicosis requires no therapy because the disease is self-limiting. In severe and more long-term thyrotoxicosis, PTU at doses of 10 to 25 mg every 8 hours is given. Nursing mothers with thyrotoxicosis can safely receive PTU in doses of 200 to 300 mg/day; these doses do not lead to levels in the milk that impair a newborn's thyroid function. MMI is concentrated in the milk at higher levels and should not be used.

CARDIAC DISEASE. Thyrotoxicosis in patients with preexisting cardiac disease can worsen symptoms and induce cardiac decompensation. Rarely, however, does severe hyperthyroidism induce cardiac symptoms in patients without underlying cardiac disease. Nevertheless, angina pectoris or high output failure has been reported after resumption of a euthyroid state in patients with severe thyrotoxicosis without prior evidence of cardiac disease. An increased association exists between Graves' disease and mitral valve prolapse. Most patients with cardiac problems due to hyperthyroidism are elderly, and many have toxic multinodular goiter. It is important to restore a euthyroid state promptly in these patients. This is best achieved by adequate doses of PTU (300 to 600 mg/day). Atrial fibrillation occurs in 10 to 15%; signs of congestive heart failure may be due to the rapid ventricular response and the absence of atrial contraction. Prompt slowing of the ventricular heart rate with digitalis and inducing β-sympathetic blockade with propranolol or atenolol are important. Digitalis must be prescribed with care because thyrotoxic patients are somewhat digitalis resistant, and a narrow margin separates therapeutic and toxic doses. Similarly, β-sympathetic blockers with negative inotropic effects should be used with caution in patients with congestive heart failure. The presence of atrial fibrillation usually requires anticoagulant therapy with aspirin or warfarin sodium. Increased vitamin K metabolism, however, may require lower warfarin doses. Spontaneous reversion from atrial fibrillation to regular sinus rhythm occurs frequently as successfully treated patients achieve a euthyroid state. If sinus rhythm has not returned after a euthyroid period of 4 months, cardioversion should be considered. Angina pectoris can worsen in hyperthyroid patients to the extent that preinfarction angina becomes a concern. In markedly hyperthyroid patients, interventional procedures such as coronary angioplasty or bypass surgery should not be undertaken without prior treatment with antithyroid drugs because of the danger of thyrotoxic crisis. Calcium channel blockers such as diltiazem are useful in patients with contraindications to propranolol. Angiographic procedures using iodinated contrast agents can markedly worsen the thyrotoxicosis because of the induction of the Jod-Basedow effect, which especially endangers patients with toxic multinodular goiter. The antiarrhythmic compound amiodarone also can induce the Jod-Basedow. This condition is termed *amiodarone-induced thyrotoxicosis (AIT) type I*. In other patients, amiodarone activates lysosomal

---

Table 239–8 • MANAGEMENT OF THYROID STORM

GOAL	TREATMENT
Inhibition of thyroid hormone formation and secretion	PTU, 400 mg q8h PO or by nasogastric tube Sodium iodide, 1 g IV in 24 hr, or saturated solution of KI, 5 drops q8h
Sympathetic blockade	Propranolol, 20–40 mg q4–6h, or 1 mg IV slowly (repeat doses until heart rate slows); not indicated in patients with asthma or congestive heart failure that is not rate related
Glucocorticoid therapy	Hydrocortisone, 50–100 mg IV q6h
Supportive therapy	Intravenous fluids (depending on indication: glucose, electrolytes, multivitamins) Temperature control (cooling blankets, acetaminophen; avoid salicylates) O$_2$ if required Digitalis for congestive failure and to slow ventricular response; pentobarbital for sedation Treatment of precipitating event (e.g., infection)

activity, resulting in a destructive thyroiditis. In this AIT type II form, thyroid vascularity by Doppler flow studies is markedly decreased and interleukin-6 levels are increased. The thyroid iodine overload of AIT type I can be treated with potassium perchlorate 200 mg every 6 hours. Agranulocytosis and bone marrow suppression can occur with perchloride, but at doses below 1 g/day the risk is low. In addition, antithyroid medication is used but is frequently of limited effectiveness. In AIT type II, glucocorticoids are used. In some patients, a near total thyroidectomy is required to achieve a euthyroid status and escape the deleterious effects of hyperthyroidism on cardiac arrhythmias.

HYPOTHYROIDISM

Hypothyroidism is the clinical syndrome that results from decreased secretion of thyroid hormone from the thyroid gland. It most frequently reflects a disease of the gland itself (primary hypothyroidism) but can also be caused by pituitary disease (secondary hypothyroidism) or hypothalamic disease (tertiary hypothyroidism). Hypothyroidism leads to a slowing of metabolic processes and, in its most severe form, to the accumulation of mucopolysaccharides in the skin, causing a nonpitting edema termed *myxedema*. The term *myxedema* is reserved by some for a severe form of hypothyroidism, whereas others use the terms interchangeably. The term *cretinism* is reserved for hypothyroidism dating from birth and leading to abnormalities of intellectual and physical development. The generalized thyroid hormone resistance syndrome results from an abnormality in the amino acid sequence of the β form of the nuclear thyroid hormone receptor, leading to decreased T_3 binding. Impairment of thyroid hormone effects in generalized thyroid hormone resistance syndrome is partly overcome by increased thyroid hormone levels, thereby preventing significant hypothyroid symptoms in most patients. The condition is rare.

Incidence, Etiology, and Pathogenesis

The incidence of hypothyroidism varies somewhat with the geographic area. In areas of adequate iodine supply, such as the United States, hypothyroidism occurs in 0.8 to 1.0% of the population. In iodine-deficient areas of the world, the incidence is 10- to 20-fold higher. Neonatal hypothyroidism occurs with a frequency of 0.02% in the white population, whereas among blacks it falls to 0.003%. Additional genetic causes of hypothyroidism have recently been identified, including mutations in the TRH receptor, mutations in pituitary transcription factors regulating TSH expression, mutations in TSH making it biologically inactive, inactivating mutations in the TSH receptor and the α subunit of the Gs protein. These conditions are rare. Table 239–9 lists the causes of hypothyroidism.

Primary hypothyroidism accounts for 90 to 95% of all cases, the remainder being of pituitary or hypothalamic or genetic origin. Most patients with primary hypothyroidism develop thyroid hormone deficiency during adulthood. Only a minority of patients have congenital hypothyroidism resulting from defects in enzymes required for thyroid hormone synthesis, thyroid agenesis, dysgenesis, or ectopic thyroid tissue. Temporary congenital hypothyroidism can be induced by maternal iodine or antithyroid drug administration. Primary hypothyroidism can be of a thyroprivic form, with markedly reduced or absent thyroid tissue, or a goitrous form, with an enlarged thyroid. The most frequent cause of hypothyroidism in adults is autoimmune disease, with goitrous or thyroprivic Hashimoto's disease being the prime example. In autoimmune-based hypothyroidism, antibodies are directed against thyroperoxidase, thyroglobulin, and the TSH receptor and NIS. Antithyroglobulin and antiperoxidase antibodies probably serve as markers of autoimmunity, but anti-TSH antibodies cause disease. TSH receptor antibodies can block TSH action and thus contribute to decreased thyroid hormone formation. In addition to antithyroid antibodies, antibodies can be directed against the proteins of other endocrine organs such as the pancreas, adrenals, parathyroids, and gonads. Affected patients suffer from polyglandular endocrine deficiency states (Chapter 244). A strong family history can be identified in most of these conditions.

Thyroid autoimmune disease also has an increased association with nonendocrine abnormalities such as pernicious anemia, lupus erythematosus, rheumatoid arthritis, Sjögren's syndrome, chronic

Table 239–9 • CAUSES OF HYPOTHYROIDISM
Primary hypothyroidism
Insufficient amount of thyroid tissue
Destruction of tissue by autoimmune process
Hashimoto's thyroiditis (atrophic and goitrous forms)
Graves' disease—end-stage
Destruction of tissue by iatrogenic procedures
^{131}I therapy
Surgical thyroidectomy
External radiation
Destruction of tissue by infiltrative processes
Amyloidosis, lymphoma, scleroderma
Defects of thyroid hormone biosynthesis
Congenital enzyme defects
Congenital mutations in TSH receptor
Iodine deficiency or excess
Drug-induced: thionamides, lithium, sulfonamides, interleukins, tumor necrosis factor, and others
Secondary hypothyroidism
Pituitary
Panhypopituitarism (e.g., neoplasm, radiation, surgery, Sheehan's syndrome)
Isolated TSH deficiency
Hypothalamic
Congenital
Infection
Infiltration (sarcoidosis, granulomas)
Transient hypothyroidism
Silent and subacute thyroiditis
Thyroxine withdrawal
Generalized resistance to thyroid hormone

hepatitis, and myasthenia gravis. Thyroprivic hypothyroidism due to iatrogenic destruction of thyroid tissue by RAI, external beam radiation, or surgery is second only to autoimmune disease in causing hypothyroidism in the United States. Worldwide, hypothyroidism due to iodine deficiencies and goitrogens predominates. Goitrous hypothyroidism develops because TSH hypersecretion results in excessive thyroid growth. Iodine excess also can lead to goitrous hypothyroidism through iodine-induced inhibition of thyroid hormone formation (Wolff-Chaikoff effect). This occurs especially in patients with underlying thyroid disease. The thyroid is unable to reduce iodide uptake in spite of increased iodide stores, and the inability to escape from the Wolff-Chaikoff effect leads to goitrous hypothyroidism. The antiarrhythmic agent amiodarone is very iodine rich, leading to 36- to 40-fold increases in plasma and serum iodine and in this way inducing hypothyroidism.

Secondary hypothyroidism is due to destruction of pituitary thyrotrophs by pituitary or adjacent tumors or by necrosis, as in Sheehan's syndrome. Mutations in the TSH β-subunit can lead to biologically inactive TSH, resulting in secondary hypothyroidism. In addition, mutations in the TSH receptor leading to hypothyroidism are described. Hypothalamic hypothyroidism is due to decreased TRH secretion, resulting in diminished TSH synthesis. TSH produced in the absence of a TRH stimulus does not show normal glycosylation and has decreased biologic activity. In addition to permanent hypothyroidism, transient hypothyroidism affects patients with subacute or painless thyroiditis, including the postpartum variety. Withdrawal of long-time thyroid hormone replacement leads to several weeks of hypothyroidism until the pituitary thyrotroph population is replenished and normal thyroid-pituitary feedback resumes.

Pathologic changes in hypothyroidism depend on the cause. In patients with thyroprivic hypothyroidism, the thyroid atrophies and is replaced by fatty and fibrous tissue. By contrast, in iodine deficiency-induced goitrous hypothyroidism, the gland appears hyperplastic with tall columnar epithelium. Extrathyroidal pathology is more uniform and independent of the cause of hypothyroidism. It is characterized by increased accumulation of glycosaminoglycans in interstitial tissue, giving the skin a waxy appearance. Glycosaminoglycan accumulation occurs because of decreased removal of the substance. With severe long-standing hypothyroidism, increased capillary permeability leads to proteinaceous fluid accumulation, which may involve the pericardium.

Clinical Manifestations

The different causes of hypothyroidism lead to similar symptoms, the most common of which are listed in Table 239–10. The slow and progressive onset in most patients can make clinical diagnosis difficult. This is especially true in elderly patients exhibiting changes such as dry skin, reduced body and scalp hair, and memory difficulties, all of which could be due to the aging process in the absence of hypothyroidism. Typical complaints in hypothyroid patients include increased tiredness and sleep requirement with a depressed mood, feeling cold, gaining weight on the same diet, constipation, increased forgetfulness and increased time needed to fulfill a task, and decreased exercise tolerance associated with muscle cramps on strenuous exercises. Affected patients relate these complaints in a low-pitched, hoarse voice with a slow speech pattern. Frequently the changes are only fully appreciated by the patient after thyroid hormone replacement and return to a euthyroid state. The facial appearance is frequently dull and apathetic, with puffiness around the eyes and loss of lateral eyebrows. The skin takes on a yellow complexion due to carotene accumulation and becomes cold, dry, and rough with nonpitting edema (myxedema). The thyroid may be normal, enlarged, or absent, depending on the cause of hypothyroidism. Cardiovascular changes can include bradycardia and an enlarged cardiac silhouette primarily due to pericardial effusion. Hypertension occurs in 10% of hypothyroid patients and resolves after thyroid hormone replacement. Because of the increased occurrence of hypercholesterolemia and hypertension, hypothyroid patients have more coronary artery disease. Angina pectoris sometimes develops only after starting thyroid hormone replacement. Anemias of different causes accompany hypothyroidism and can contribute to angina symptoms. Iron deficiency anemia results from decreased iron absorption. Absorption of folic acid is decreased. Pernicious anemia results from gastric mucosa atrophy with antibodies directed against the gastric mucosa. The decreased oxygen consumption in the hypothyroid state leads to diminished erythropoietin production, resulting in a mild anemia that can be thought of as an adaptive state. Pulmonary function is characterized by shallow and slow breathing and a decreased respiratory response to hypercapnia and hypoxia. Patients are very sensitive to sedatives that can depress the respiratory drive and lead to CO_2 retention and coma. Gastrointestinal motility decreases markedly and can lead to paralytic ileus and the megacolon of myxedema. The kidneys not only have an impaired ability to excrete a free water load, but a syndrome of inappropriate secretion of antidiuretic hormone can develop and intensify hyponatremia. Slow Achilles tendon reflexes are a hallmark of hypothyroidism. Similarly, severe hypothyroidism can lead to cerebellar ataxia and peripheral neuropathy. Muscle stiffness, cramps, pain, and the carpal tunnel syndrome are of increased frequency. Endocrine and metabolic abnormalities include hyperprolactinemia leading to galactorrhea, heavy menstrual bleeding, menorrhagia, hypoglycemia, and syndrome of inappropriate secretion of antidiuretic hormone. Long-standing and severe hypothyroidism can induce marked thyrotroph hyperplasia, resulting rarely in increased pituitary size and sella enlargement suggesting a pituitary tumor. Hypothyroidism in newborns needs to be treated immediately with thyroxine replacement; otherwise, severe retardation of mental development, short stature, and deaf-mutism can develop.

Diagnosis

Figure 239–3 gives an approach to the diagnosis of hypothyroidism. An elevated TSH level combined with a below-normal free T_4 level is diagnostic of primary hypothyroidism. T_3 levels are not useful in the diagnosis of hypothyroidism because they are frequently normal in mild hypothyroidism and are markedly lowered by the NTI syndrome. In pituitary or hypothalamic hypothyroidism, the TSH level is normal or decreased, and only below-normal T_4 or free T_4 levels are diagnostic. With third-generation sensitive TSH assays, the TRH stimulation test provides little additional information. Using the TRH stimulation test, an absent response of TSH indicates secondary hypothyroidism, whereas a partial or delayed TSH response indicates partial pituitary deficiency or hypothalamic disease. Patients with pituitary hypothyroidism frequently show other signs of pituitary

Table 239–10 • TISSUE-SPECIFIC SIGNS AND SYMPTOMS OF HYPOTHYROIDISM

TISSUE	SIGNS AND SYMPTOMS
Central nervous system	Forgetfulness, stoic appearance, myxedematous dementia, cerebellar ataxia
Cardiovascular	Bradycardia, pericardial effusion, hypertension
Respiratory	Depressed ventilatory drive, pleural effusion, sleep apnea
Gastrointestinal	Constipation, hypomotility
Muscle	Delayed tendon reflexes, muscle stiffness and cramps, increased muscle volume weakness
Skin	Dry, rough, hyperkeratosis; nonpitting puffiness due to mucopolysaccharide deposits
Metabolic	Basal metabolic rate decreased, cold intolerance, decreased T_4 and drug turnover, weight gain

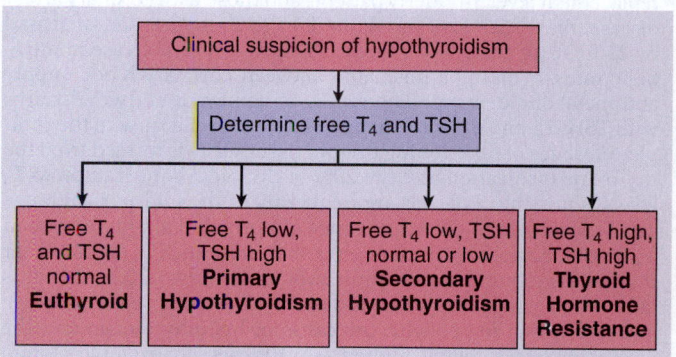

FIGURE 239–3 • Diagnostic approach to hypothyroidism. T_4 = thyroxine; TSH = thyroid-stimulating hormone.

deficiency, including low follicle-stimulating hormone and luteinizing hormone levels in the face of low sex hormone levels. It is especially important to identify deficient adrenocorticotropic hormone secretion and resulting secondary adrenal insufficiency. When present, thyroid hormone replacement cannot be started before initiating cortisol replacement. Low TSH levels can also be found in patients who recently became hypothyroid after a prolonged period of hyperthyroidism that led to a decrease in the pituitary thyrotroph population. Other laboratory manifestations of hypothyroidism include elevated cholesterol, creatine kinase, lactate dehydrogenase, and aspartate transaminase levels.

The presence of antithyroid antibodies is compatible with Hashimoto's disease and presents a risk factor for developing hypothyroidism. During early phases of hypothyroidism, T_4 and free T_4 lie just below the lower normal range. T_3 is normal and TSH is barely elevated. This condition has been termed *subclinical hypothyroidism*, or *the failing gland syndrome*. Patients show minimal or no signs of hypothyroidism because a normal T_3 level maintains their metabolic status. Many such patients later develop clinical hypothyroidism with a further increase in TSH levels and a decrease in T_4 and free T_4 levels. In patients with Hashimoto's disease or after RAI treatment of Graves' disease, this pattern occurs frequently. Transient hypothyroidism frequently occurs in postpartum patients, with subacute thyroiditis, or after RAI treatment for Graves' disease. Changes in TSH levels lag behind alterations in T_4 and T_3 levels; careful follow-up is required to determine whether permanent hypothyroidism ensues.

Differential Diagnosis

Fully developed hypothyroidism presents a distinct clinical picture with few imitations. Patients with renal disease resulting in a nephrotic syndrome and hypoalbuminemia can develop a puffy face, peripheral edema, a pale downy skin, anemia, and hypercholesterolemia. Goiter and thyroid nodules occur with increased frequency in patients with renal disease. Lowering of TBG levels leads to a decrease in total T_4 values. In contrast to hypothyroidism, however, free T_4 is not

Endocrine Diseases

decreased and TSH is not increased. In children, Down syndrome can mimic hypothyroidism. Differential diagnosis is further complicated by an increased incidence of Hashimoto's thyroiditis and resultant

hypothyroidism in patients with Down syndrome, but thyroid hormone values are normal in Down syndrome patients without thyroid disease.

 Treatment

Hypothyroidism is preferentially treated with levothyroxine (T_4), with doses ranging from 0.05 to 0.2 mg/day and an average replacement dose of 1.6 µg/kg/day. T_3 is formed from T_4 by intracellular conversion so that both T_4 and T_3 exist in the body. Synthetic T_4 has a long shelf life and uniform potency. Eighty per cent is absorbed, and once-a-day intake leads to stable T_4, T_3, and TSH levels. Accordingly, thyroxine represents the preferred thyroid hormone preparation for chronic replacement. Patients should be informed that replacement probably is needed for the rest of their lives and that periodic evaluation is required. In young healthy adults without coronary artery disease, a starting dose of 75 to 100 µg/day can be used and then adjusted after 2- to 3-week intervals to reach the final replacement level. In elderly patients and those with coronary artery disease, the initial dose should be 12.5 to 25 µg/day and increased by 25 to 50 µg every 4 to 6 weeks to allow a slow increase in metabolic rates, avoiding a mismatch between coronary blood supply and metabolic demand. The aim is to achieve a euthyroid status with TSH, T_4, and T_3 levels in the normal range. Because in the complete absence of functioning thyroid tissue all T_3 is formed from the thyroxine medication and the 20% of thyroidal contribution to T_3 levels is missing, T_3 levels are frequently in the mid-normal range and T_4 levels are in the upper range of normal. A slight increase in T_4 levels occurs 2 to 6 hours after thyroxine intake, so blood for thyroid hormone determination should be drawn 20 to 24 hours later. The average replacement dose for thyroxine varies with age and to a lesser degree with the cause of hypothyroidism and the level of physical activity. Children (5 to 10 years), for example, require average replacement doses of 3 to 4 µg/kg. Required replacement doses in elderly persons, by contrast, are 20 to 30% lower (1.4 µg/kg/day) than those needed in middle-aged adults. Patients with malabsorption or those taking aluminum preparations (antacids), cholestyramine, lovastatin, ferrous sulfate, and rifampin need higher replacement doses. During pregnancy, especially in the third trimester, thyroxine replacement needs increase by 30 to 50%. After delivery, thyroxine replacement is decreased to standard levels.

The ease of approach, virtual absence of side effects, and observance of a revitalized patient make thyroxine treatment of hypothyroid patients a satisfying therapeutic experience. Thyroxine and T_3 levels normalize within 2 to 3 weeks. TSH levels lag behind for 3 to 4 weeks or more because of the increased number of thyrotrophs in the pituitary after long-standing hypothyroidism. Clinical improvement begins 2 to 3 weeks after therapy, but complete resumption of a euthyroid state can take several months.

Patients receiving chronic T_4 replacement should be evaluated by physical examination and free T_4, T_3, and TSH determination once or twice a year. The TSH level is a good indicator of adequate replacement. In patients with primary hypothyroidism, TSH levels below the normal range indicate over-replacement and levels above the upper normal range indicate under-replacement. Chronic over-replacement with thyroxine can increase bone turnover, which is a special concern in women; however, no evidence currently exists for an increased bone fracture rate. Chronic T_4 over-replacement also can lead to cardiovascular abnormalities, especially arrhythmias and cardiac hypertrophy. The treatment of subclinical hypothyroidism is controversial. Enlargement of the thyroid gland, elevated cholesterol levels (especially with low-density to high-density lipoprotein ratios above 3) or signs of decreased exercise tolerance and mild congestive heart failure warrant treatment.

In addition to T_4, T_3, combinations of T_4 and T_3, desiccated thyroid, and T_4 plus iodine in one tablet are available. The use of a combination of T_4 and T_3 has led in some patients to an improved sense of well-being. The existing combination tablets of T_4 and T_3 contain relatively too much T_3 and are not recommended because their use results frequently in over-replacement. One approach would be to take 50 µg of thyroxine off the total thyroxine dose and replace it by 5 µg T_3 AM and 5 µg T_3 PM (e.g., 150 µg T_4 → 100 µg T_4, 5 µg T_3 AM, 5 µg T_3 PM). Adequate replacement by T_4/T_3 combinations requires the availability of a slow release form of T_3, which is currently not available. In addition, a long-term benefit of T_4/T_3 combination therapy for a significant number of patients is currently not established. Maintenance of TSH levels in the normal range is required to prevent patients from becoming hyperthyroid. The free T_4 levels will be significantly lower than in patients replaced with thyroxine only. The use of T_3 is recommended in special situations. T_3 is useful for short-term treatment of patients with thyroid cancer after thyroid surgery and before RAI administration, because of its short half-life of 1 day versus the half-life of T_4 of 7 days (see section on thyroid cancer). Parenteral T_3 can be used to treat myxedema coma.

SPECIAL CLINICAL CONDITIONS

Angina Pectoris, Cardiac Surgery, and Thyroid Hormone Replacement

Coronary artery disease occurs with increased frequency in hypothyroid patients. The complaint of angina pectoris most often arises with thyroid hormone replacement, which increases cardiac demand and O_2 consumption. Adequate thyroid hormone replacement is strongly recommended in these patients because in addition to the general benefit of a euthyroid state, cholesterol levels may decrease and blood pressure may normalize. Frequently, worsening of the angina precludes adequate thyroid hormone replacement. Treatment with β-sympathetic blockers such as propranolol (20 to 40 mg three times a day) can sometimes ameliorate the problem but may lead to significant bradycardia. Also, β-blockade fails to solve the basic dilemma between inadequate thyroid hormone replacement and angina production. In such patients with persistent mild to moderate hypothyroidism, percutaneous coronary transluminal angioplasty or coronary bypass surgery can be undertaken. Several studies have shown no deleterious consequences of a mild to moderate hypothyroid state on clinical outcome.

 Treatment of Myxedema Coma

Patients with severe myxedema, either spontaneously or because of cold exposure, intake of analgesics or sedatives, or infection, may become progressively obtunded and lapse into coma. Myxedema coma is rare but presents a life-threatening emergency with a 20 to 50% mortality rate. It is best treated in an intensive-care unit. Treatment should be instituted immediately; if T_4 and TSH levels cannot be readily obtained, therapy may be started on clinical suspicion. Increasing obtundation and elevated PCO_2 levels especially indicate the need for thyroid hormone administration. Assessment of adrenal function should also be undertaken, because giving hydrocortisone can disturb pituitary-adrenal feedback and make subsequent diagnosis difficult. Vigorous thyroid hormone replacement is required. Thyroxine can be given as a single 300 µg T_4 bolus followed by daily 50- to 100-µg intravenous T_4 maintenance doses. A T_3 replacement schedule using 10 µg T_3 intravenously every 4 hours until the patient greatly improves and oral therapy can be resumed has been advocated. T_3 administration offers the potential advantage that no conversion of T_4 to T_3 is required, a step that may be impaired in severely ill patients. Excess T_3 can, however, also induce cardiac arrhythmia. A combination of thyroxine (200 µg) and T_3 (25 µg) has also been advocated. The treatment of myxedema coma is outlined in Table 239–11.

Table 239–11 • TREATMENT OF MYXEDEMA COMA

Thyroid Hormone Administration
  300 µg T₄ over 5–10 minutes initially, followed by 100 µg T₄ IV q24h
    until oral T₄ therapy can be started *Alternatively,* 10 µg T₃ IV q4h
    until oral T₄ therapy can be started
Glucocorticoid Administration
  Hydrocortisone, 100 mg IV bolus followed by 25 mg q6h by IV drip
  Cover to conserve heat
  Intravenous fluids, electrolytes, and glucose to correct electrolyte
    abnormalities and hypoglycemia
  Tracheal intubation and mechanical ventilation as required
  Treat precipitating conditions (infection)
  Avoid sedatives, narcotics, and overhydration

Pregnancy and Hypothyroidism

Normal fetal brain development during the first and part of the second trimester, a time period before the fetal thyroid develops, depends on placental thyroxine transfer from the mother. It is, therefore, important to ensure that women with a risk for hypothyroidism are euthyroid before conception and during early pregnancy. Hypothyroidism in the mother during the second trimester can lead to decreased IQ scores in the offspring. Prompt diagnosis of hypothyroidism and thyroxine replacement is therefore required. The dose of thyroxine may need to be increased by 30 to 50% in hypothyroid women during pregnancy, especially in the second and third trimester. After delivery, thyroxine doses are decreased to prior levels.

THYROIDITIS

Thyroiditis includes infectious and autoimmune inflammatory diseases of the thyroid. Thyroiditis is divided into acute (suppurative), subacute painful (granulomatous), subacute painless (lymphocytic), chronic lymphocytic (Hashimoto's), and chronic fibrous (Riedel's) thyroiditis. Postpartum thyroiditis is classified as a variant of subacute painless lymphocytic thyroiditis.

ACUTE (SUPPURATIVE) THYROIDITIS

Acute suppurative thyroiditis consists of a rare infection of the gland by bacteria, fungi, *Pneumocystis carinii,* or other organisms. Symptoms include tender swelling, sometimes with fluctuation and an erythematous skin overlying the area. Fever with leukocytosis frequently occurs. Identification of the microbial agent may require fine-needle aspiration of the lesion. Appropriate antibiotics and sometimes drainage of the abscess are required. Long-term sequelae are rare, but when a large part of the thyroid gland is involved, hypothyroidism may occur.

SUBACUTE PAINFUL (GRANULOMATOUS) THYROIDITIS

Incidence, Etiology, and Pathology

Subacute painful thyroiditis, also referred to as *de Quervain's thyroiditis, giant cell thyroiditis, subacute nonsuppurative thyroiditis,* or *granulomatous thyroiditis,* is the most frequent cause of severe thyroid pain and tenderness. Subacute painful thyroiditis is not rare, resulting in 5% of all medical consultations for thyroid disease. It is most common in women 40 to 50 years old and shows an association with HLA-B35. The disease frequently follows a viral infection, and elevated titers to mumps, adeno-, entro-, echo-, influenza, coxsackie-, measles, and other viruses have been found. Increased thyroid antibody titers (antimicrosomal, antithyroglobulin, anti-TSH receptor) occur in 10 to 20% of patients during the subacute phase and disappear as the disease fades. Such antibodies are polyclonal and most likely arise secondary to thyroid damage caused by viral infection. The thyroid is enlarged and edematous with destruction of follicular architecture and the presence of histocytes that coalesce into giant cells.

Clinical Manifestations

The disease frequently follows by 1 to 3 weeks the occurrence of viral pharyngitis, mumps, measles, or other viral syndromes. Severe pain develops over the thyroid area, radiates to the ear, and is enhanced by swallowing. A feeling of general malaise with muscle aches, pain, anorexia, and fever is present. On palpation, the thyroid is very tender and may be generally enlarged but can contain unilateral painful areas. Cervical lymphadenopathy rarely occurs. Characteristic laboratory findings are an elevated sedimentation rate, often above 100 mm/hr Westergren, and a markedly decreased RAI uptake (<2% at 24 hours). The levels of free T₄ and TSH depend on the phase of the disease, with high T₄ levels occurring during the early stage owing to follicle disruption and hormone release. At later stages, transient hypothyroidism may follow, with elevated TSH levels. Rarely, permanent hypothyroidism ensues. Thyroglobulin levels are elevated during the acute phase.

Subacute thyroiditis is an inflammatory, self-limiting disorder that at most requires symptomatic therapy. In mild cases, no therapy or analgesics such as aspirin (2 to 3 g/day) is sufficient treatment. Prednisone, 40 to 60 mg/day, can suppress more severe symptoms and bring relief. Within 8 to 10 days, symptoms markedly decrease, and the dose can be tapered and completely stopped after 4 weeks. Sometimes symptoms flare up again and the prednisone taper needs to be reversed. In some patients, more than one attack may occur, leading to an increased risk of permanent hypothyroidism. During the initial phase, the patient may be thyrotoxic and need treatment with β-sympathetic blocking agents such as propranolol. Rarely, hepatitis develops, requiring careful follow-up.

SUBACUTE PAINLESS (LYMPHOCYTIC) THYROIDITIS WITH TRANSIENT HYPERTHYROIDISM

Incidence, Etiology, and Pathology

Subacute painless thyroiditis with transient hyperthyroidism is also called subacute lymphocytic thyroiditis with spontaneously revolving hyperthyroidism and silent thyroiditis. The hallmark of the disorder is a self-limiting episode of thyrotoxicosis and a histologic picture of lymphocytic infiltration that differs from the changes found in Hashimoto's disease. Both postpartum thyroiditis and the sporadic disease occurring in the general population are forms of subacute lymphocytic thyroiditis. The incidence of sporadic subacute painless thyroiditis shows some geographic variability, with the sporadic form occurring more frequently in previously iodine-deficient areas that are now iodine replete, such as the Great Lakes area of the United States, where the disease may account for 5 to 15% of all cases of thyroiditis. Postpartum thyroiditis occurs in 2 to 6% of all pregnant women in the United States. The incidence is even higher in Sweden and Japan, reaching 7 to 12%. Eighty per cent of cases of the sporadic form affect women between the ages of 30 and 40 years. The disease is most likely autoimmune and independent of a preceding viral illness. Subacute lymphatic thyroiditis is distinguished from chronic lymphocytic thyroiditis (Hashimoto's disease) by a self-limiting course and a lower extent of lymphocyte infiltration with the absence of germinal centers.

Clinical Manifestations and Diagnosis

Typical symptoms include an abrupt onset with signs of thyrotoxicosis such as nervousness, heat intolerance, tachycardia, and weight loss. A small, firm, but painless goiter is noted in about half the patients. Some may present in a hypothyroid state after the initial hyperthyroid phase was unnoticed. Postpartum thyroiditis usually occurs 3 to 6 months after delivery and is probably due to a rebound of immune activity after it was suppressed during pregnancy. One finds an initial transient hyperthyroid phase followed by hypothyroidism. The latter condition lasts 1 to 3 months, and most patients make a spontaneous recovery. During the initial hyperthyroid phase, which can last 2 to 4 months, T₄ and T₃ levels are elevated, with relatively higher T₄ levels due to thyroid hormone release from damaged follicles. Thyroid anti-

Continued

Endocrine Diseases

bodies, especially antiperoxidase, are frequently positive. The sedimentation rate is normal or only slightly elevated, in contrast to the marked elevation occurring in subacute painful thyroiditis. The RAI uptake is suppressed. Signs of Graves' disease, such as ophthalmopathy and pretibial myxedema, are absent, and the level of TSI, which is the hallmark of Graves' disease, is normal. Thyroid biopsy shows a typical histologic picture with abundant lymphocyte infiltration, but the procedure is not required for routine diagnosis. Treatment aims at sympathetic blockade using, for example, propranolol to alleviate symptoms during the thyrotoxic phase. Glucocorticoids are not needed. Prolonged hypothyroid episodes may be treated with thyroxine replacement, but with subsequent tapering of the dose and final withdrawal because most patients regain euthyroid status. Increased incidences of goiter and persistent hypothyroidism have been noted in patients who continue to show antiperoxidase antibodies. Similarly, the recurrence of postpartum thyroiditis has been noted in some patients with continued presence of antiperoxidase antibodies after the initial phase of the disease.

DRUG-INDUCED THYROIDITIS

With the increased therapeutic use of cytokines such as interlukin-2 for various malignancies and interferons such as interferon-α for chronic hepatitis B or C, thyroid dysfunction has been noted in 5 to 10% of patients. A thyroiditis-like picture with hyper- and hypothyroidism has been observed with interleukin-2. Interferon-γ can lead to expression of class II HLA molecules resulting in Graves' disease. The cardiac antiarrhythmic drug amiodarone can induce a destructive thyroiditis, resulting in hyperthyroidism and elevated interleukin-6 levels.

CHRONIC LYMPHOCYTIC THYROIDITIS (HASHIMOTO'S THYROIDITIS)

Chronic lymphocytic thyroiditis is the most prevalent form of thyroid autoimmune disease, affecting 3 to 4% of the population in the United States. It is three times more common in women and most frequently diagnosed between the third and fifth decade of life. A genetic propensity for the disease is demonstrated by an increased familial incidence and an association with major histocompatibility antigens such as HLA-B8. The goitrous variant of Hashimoto's thyroiditis occurs more frequently in patients positive for HLA-DR5, whereas the atrophic variant is associated with HLA-DR3. The presence of antiperoxidase and antithyroglobulin antibodies indicates the autoimmune nature of the disease. Very high levels of thyroid antibodies distinguish Hashimoto's thyroiditis from other forms. In addition, anti-TSH receptor antibodies can occur that are frequently of the blocking variety, impairing TSH action. Rarely, TSIs are present, leading to hyperthyroidism and the combined occurrence of Graves' disease and Hashimoto's disease called *hashitoxicosis*. Thyroid pathology is dominated by heavy lymphocyte infiltration destroying the normal follicular architecture. Lymph follicles and germinal centers can be identified. The presence of copious lymphocytes is a hallmark of the disease that distinguishes it from other forms of autoimmune thyroiditis. Differential diagnosis between the abundant lymphocyte infiltrates of Hashimoto's disease and the occurrence of a primary thyroid lymphoma is sometimes difficult. Thyroid lymphomas occur with an increased frequency in Hashimoto's disease but overall are rare. Also, the pathology of the thyroid gland in Hashimoto's disease is characterized by extensive fibrosis throughout the gland. Different manifestations of Hashimoto's disease can be distinguished. The occurrence of a goitrous versus an atrophic variant may be explained by the prevailing autoimmune antibodies. For example, in patients with atrophic thyroiditis, high titers of TSH receptor-blocking antibodies are found. In other patients with Hashimoto's disease, a goiter and features of Graves' disease occur that result from the TSI presence.

Clinical Manifestations and Diagnosis

In Hashimoto's thyroiditis, thyroid enlargement is the most frequent manifestation, with 75% of patients having a euthyroid goiter; the remainder have the atrophic variety and may not have a palpable gland. Hypothyroidism occurs as an initial manifestation in 20% of patients. Hyperthyroidism occurs in less than 5% of patients and can be either self-limiting or long standing, representing hashitoxicosis. The principal abnormalities in the immune system discussed for Graves' disease also apply to Hashimoto's disease. The prevalence of specific forms of TSH receptor antibodies with a predominance of the TSI in Graves' disease versus the occurrence of TSH receptor-blocking antibodies in Hashimoto's disease distinguishes the two autoimmune diseases. In addition, lymphocyte infiltration is much more destructive to the architecture of the normal gland than in Graves' disease. Other autoimmune diseases occur with increased frequency in Hashimoto's patients, including autoimmune diseases of the endocrine system with adrenal, parathyroid, pituitary, and gonad destruction and damage to β cells of the pancreas. Furthermore, an association occurs with pernicious anemia, Sjögren's syndrome, lupus erythematosus, and idiopathic thrombocytopenic purpura. Graves' disease can occur in conjunction with the same illnesses.

On physical examination, a painless symmetrically enlarged thyroid gland is noted that feels firm and rubbery with an irregular surface. The gland can reach a size and firmness that leads to pressure symptoms, impairing swallowing and resulting in inlet obstruction with tracheal compression. Sometimes only one firm lobe or a single firm thyroid nodule may be palpable, representing the only remnant, with other parts of the gland destroyed by the autoimmune process. On laboratory examination, 90% of patients have positive antiperoxidase antibodies and 50% have antithyroglobulin antibodies. T_4 and TSH levels can be normal. In patients with the hypothyroid form, TSH levels are elevated and T_4 and free T_4 levels are decreased. RAI scans are not required for routine work-up and are not diagnostic. They can show normal, increased, or decreased overall uptake with local patchy areas of increased and decreased iodine accumulation. Fine-needle aspiration is not routinely used but can be helpful in differentiating a firm nodule as a thyroid remnant in Hashimoto's disease versus a benign thyroid adenoma or thyroid cancer. The incidence of thyroid cancer is not increased in Hashimoto's disease except for the increased occurrence of lymphomas, a rare event.

Rx Treatment

The autoimmune abnormality underlying Hashimoto's disease is currently not amenable to therapy. Therapy is directed at achieving a euthyroid state and dealing with mechanical problems resulting from the goiter. Thyroxine replacement is initiated when T_4 levels are low and TSH levels are high. In some patients, only the TSH is slightly elevated and the T_4 is low-normal, with signs of hypothyroidism being absent. These patients can be treated with thyroxine replacement to forestall further thyroid gland enlargement and future clinical hypothyroidism. In some patients, thyroxine therapy cannot decrease the goiter size, and obstructive symptoms may require surgery for relief. During the early phases of Hashimoto's disease, transient hyperthyroidism can occur and requires only symptomatic treatment with sympathetic β-blockers. Hyperthyroidism developing in well-established Hashimoto's disease is treated like Graves' disease, with antithyroid medication as the treatment of choice.

FIBROUS THYROIDITIS (RIEDEL'S THYROIDITIS)

In fibrous thyroiditis, thyroid tissue is replaced by dense, chronically inflamed fibrous tissue. The thyroid is rock hard on palpation, a finding that can be compatible with thyroid cancer. Thyroid aspiration can clarify the diagnosis. Tracheal obstruction can occur and may require surgery. Sclerosing mediastinitis, retroperitoneal fibrosis, sclerosis of the biliary tract, and pseudotumors of the orbit have been described in such patients. When hypothyroidism exists, thyroxine replacement is required.

NONTOXIC DIFFUSE AND NODULAR GOITER

The term *nontoxic* or *simple goiter* indicates an increase in the mass of the thyroid gland resulting from excessive replication of benign thyroid epithelial cells. In patients with nontoxic goiter, thyroid hormone values usually are normal. The increase in thyroid size is a slow process evolving over many years, starting with a diffuse initial enlargement, which frequently becomes multinodular with time. Nontoxic goiter is the most common thyroid disease in America, affecting about 5% of the population. Its incidence increases with age and affects women three to five times more frequently than men. Goiters have been classified according to the epidemiologic pattern in which they occur as endemic or sporadic goiters. Thyroid enlargement occurring in more than 10% of a population is termed *endemic goiter* and is presumed to result from environmental factors, such as iodine deficiency or the presence of goitrogens in the food chain that inhibit thyroid hormone formation. *Sporadic goiter* indicates thyroid enlargement in a small fraction of the population. The cause of sporadic goiter varies, with thyroid growth most frequently stimulated by extrathyroidal growth factors. TSH is the most frequent stimulator. The observation that goiters also occur in patients with adequate thyroid hormone levels and normal or low TSH levels indicates either that the sensitivity of thyroid cells to TSH can increase markedly or that other factors drive thyroid cell growth. Stimulatory effects of IGF-I and EGF on thyroid cell growth have been reported. In addition, TSH receptor-directed antibodies that have only a growth-stimulating effect have been described. Different thyroid cells also have a varying propensity to grow and enter the mitotic cycle independent of stimulation by growth factors. Specific thyroid cells and their descendants that possess an increased noncancerous propensity to divide and grow can form new thyroid follicles. These different factors that contribute to goiter formation explain why not all goiters shrink or stop growing on thyroxine supplementation and resultant TSH suppression.

The pathology of the goitrous thyroid varies, depending on the stage and cause of the goiter. Initially, hypertrophic follicles with hypervascularity are prevalent throughout the gland. With increasing duration, follicle size varies. Some follicles become involuted, whereas others enlarge with colloid accumulation. Fibrotic areas sometimes separate hypertrophic from atrophic and involuted areas. This mixed pattern of follicle activity is reflected in RAI scans with patchy areas of increased and decreased uptake.

Clinical Manifestations

Patients with nontoxic simple goiter can be asymptomatic or present with symptoms due to mechanical pressure exerted by the enlarged thyroid gland. Structures exposed to pressure are the trachea, esophagus, recurrent laryngeal nerve, and large cervical veins. Substernal goiters are most frequently responsible for tracheal pressure symptoms leading to deviation, narrowing, and chondromalacia. The trachea must be narrowed to 20 to 30% of its normal diameter to produce respiratory symptoms, especially inspiratory stridor. Pull and pressure on the laryngeal nerve leading to hoarseness can occur with benign goiters but should raise the suspicion of malignancy. The presence of a substernal goiter is made evident when patients raise both arms above the head, which pulls the goiter upward into the thoracic inlet. The resultant impediment of jugular venous return leads to a livid suffusion of the face and discomfort for the patient (Pemberton's sign). An acute painful enlargement of an area of the thyroid frequently reflects sudden bleeding into a thyroid nodule; symptoms improve as resorption of the hemorrhage occurs. In a slow and progressively developing dominant nodule, thyroid cancer must be excluded by cytologic examination of a fine-needle aspirate.

Congenital goiter in endemic areas results most frequently from insufficient thyroid hormone formation due to iodine deficiency or the presence of goitrogens and resultant TSH stimulation of the gland. Sporadic congenital goiter is often due to biosynthetic abnormalities in thyroid hormone formation resulting from defects in (1) iodide transport into the thyroid, (2) deficient peroxidase activity, (3) deficient iodotyrosine coupling, (4) formation of abnormal thyroglobulin, (5) impaired thyroglobulin proteolysis, or (6) deiodinases being deficient or absent and not allowing for intrathyroidal iodide conservation. These defects are rare and account for

10% of all congenital hypothyroidism. If these patients are left untreated, goiter and cretinism can result. In other patients, nontoxic goiter with mild hypothyroidism develops. The combination of congenital hypothyroidism and eighth nerve deafness has been termed *Pendred's syndrome*. The gene for Pendred's syndrome has been identified and the protein that it encodes, termed *pendrin*, has been cloned.

Diagnostic Procedures

The most sensitive index to evaluate thyroid status in patients with goiter is the TSH level. TSH can be elevated in the face of normal or low-normal T_4 levels and mid-normal T_3 values. Most such patients benefit from thyroxine replacement, with TSH decreasing into the normal range and removing the thyroid growth stimulus. The thyroid status of patients with nontoxic goiter needs to be evaluated once or twice a year because some thyroid nodules develop autonomy over time, and toxic adenomas can develop with resulting thyrotoxicosis. In addition, ingestion of excess iodine can induce thyrotoxicosis because of the Jod-Basedow effect. With progressive involution of the goiter, TSH values increase progressively and hypothyroidism develops. The presence of pressure symptoms requires evaluation for substernal extension of the thyroid gland, which is best performed by computed tomography or magnetic resonance imaging. In the absence of such imaging, radiography reveals tracheal deviation, and pulmonary function tests can document inspiratory impairment. In patients with endemic goiter, especially due to iodine deficiency, laboratory values show low T_4, normal T_3, and elevated TSH levels stimulating the thyroid gland for further compensatory growth. The amount of iodine intake can be documented by determining iodide excretion in the urine, which is correspondingly low in iodine-deficiency regions.

 ## Treatment

The aim of therapy is to decrease the size of the thyroid, relieve pressure-induced symptoms, and achieve a euthyroid state. The approach to the patient with a goiter is outlined in Figure 239–4. In patients with sporadic goiter and elevated TSH levels, a clear rationale for thyroxine therapy is given. Thyroxine is started at 100 μg/day with subsequent dose adjustments to bring TSH into the low-normal but not the undetectable range. In patients with large, nontoxic diffuse goiters and normal T_4 and TSH levels, the same approach is chosen. The efficiency of this approach is indicated by a 20% decrease in thyroid volume after 1 year of treatment. In patients showing a response to therapy, treatment may be indefinite.

Treatment of multinodular goiter, especially in older patients, provides a more difficult problem. The TSH level must be determined, and if it is suppressed or in the low-normal range, thyroxine therapy should not be started. Thyroxine therapy also can be guided by results of an RAI scan and the suppression test, as described earlier. Identification of autonomous areas excludes thyroxine therapy. In patients with multinodular goiter without autonomous areas and high-normal or elevated TSH levels, a trial of thyroxine therapy can be undertaken. In older patients, the initial dose of thyroxine should not be higher than 50 μg, and dose increases should be staggered at 25-μg steps at 4- to 6-week intervals. The results of thyroxine suppression therapy in patients with long-standing multinodular goiter are frequently disappointing, with little or no decrease in goiter size. Because thyroid tissue between nodules can decrease considerably, however, the nodules may appear more prominent. If no discernible decrease in size of multinodular goiter occurs after 6 to 12 months, thyroxine therapy should be stopped. In such patients, symptoms of temporary hypothyroidism can occur 1 month after stopping the medication and last for an additional month.

Endemic goiter is best treated by iodine supplementation, providing approximately 200 μg of iodine per day, or by the removal of identifiable goitrogens. Iodine supplementation can induce thyrotoxicosis due to the Jod-Basedow effect. Surgical therapy of a goiter should be undertaken only if significant obstructive symptoms occur and goiter size cannot be reduced by thyroxine therapy.

Continued

Endocrine Diseases

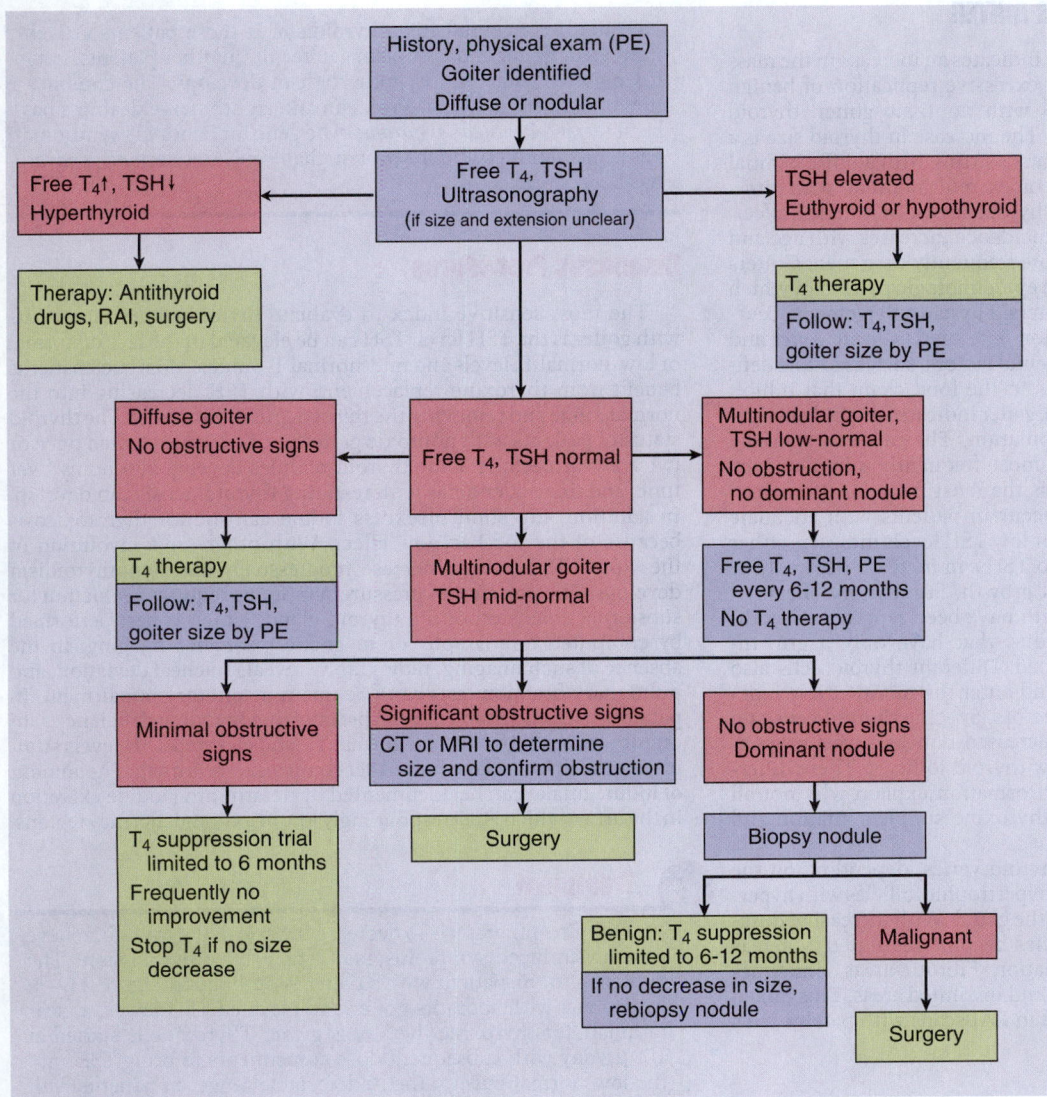

FIGURE 239–4 • Evaluation and management of patients with non-toxic diffuse and nodular goiter and undetermined thyroid status. CT = computed tomography; MRI = magnetic resonance imaging; RAI = radioactive iodine; T_4 = thyroxine; TSH = thyroid-stimulating hormone.

After partial thyroidectomy, thyroxine at $1.6\,\mu g/kg/day$ should be supplied to prevent regenerative hyperplasia. RAI therapy for large goiters has been tried with some success. More than one ^{131}I treatment may be needed. [131]I can induce a thyroiditis and thyroid swelling, leading to an acute increase in obstructive symptoms, and should therefore be performed only in carefully observed patients.

BENIGN AND MALIGNANT THYROID NODULES

A thyroid nodule is a single palpable abnormality in the thyroid gland that can be a benign adenoma or thyroid cancer. Thyroid nodules are frequent and occur in about 5% of the population. In contrast, thyroid cancer is much less frequent, and among 100 patients with thyroid nodules only 4 have thyroid cancer. Distinguishing between benign and malignant lesions is an important task that is best accomplished by sampling cells from the lesions by fine-needle aspiration. This distinction is required to perform selective surgery.

SOLITARY THYROID NODULES

Incidence, Etiology, and Pathology

Thyroid nodules must be at least 1 cm in diameter to be palpable. Such clinically detectable nodules occur in 6% of women and about 1.5% of men. The prevalence rises to 40 to 50% if smaller nodules are included that are discovered by autopsy or high-resolution

ultrasonography: Ultrasonographic studies also reveal that abnormalities that appear as single nodules on palpation often represent conglomerates of multiple nodules. A solitary thyroid nodule identified on palpation is, therefore, a rather nonspecific finding. The most common benign lesion forming a single thyroid nodule is a thyroid adenoma. Most likely such adenomas result from clones of follicular cells that progress more quickly through the cell cycle but show benign growth characteristics. An adenoma is defined as a solitary encapsulated nodule composed of follicular cells arranged in an architecture that differs from that of the adjacent gland. The definition distinguishes adenomas from adenomatous nodules, which represent the early stage of a multinodular goiter. Adenomatous nodules lack a well-defined capsule or an architecture similar to the surrounding gland; clinically, adenomatous nodules and thyroid adenomas have a similar appearance. Adenomas vary in size, cell architecture, and appearance of follicular cells. Cell architecture nearly always follows a follicular pattern, with papillary adenomas being very rare. Follicular adenomas are classified into microfollicular or macrofollicular lesions and an embryonal variant containing almost no collagen. Hürthle cell adenomas are made up of follicular cells containing a large amount of mitochondria and have an eosinophilic staining pattern. No clear correlation between functional behavior or a propensity for malignant degeneration has been established for these different types of adenomas, and they are not precursors of thyroid cancer. Because adenomas are often hypercellular and contain mitotic figures, differentiation of a benign follicular adenoma from a follicular carcinoma on cytologic material obtained by aspiration is frequently not possible. Capsular invasion and vessel infiltration are hallmarks of a malignant lesion, and these can be assessed only by histologic examination of the entire nodule. Frequently, nodules outgrow their blood supply and undergo cystic degeneration. Ultimate pathologic evaluation of follicular neoplasms identifies benign adenomas in 85% and carcinomas in 15%.

Clinical Manifestations

Most thyroid nodules are discovered on routine physical examination. A systematic approach to thyroid nodules is outlined in Figure 239–5. Only rarely do solitary nodules become large enough or extend below the sternum to cause pressure symptoms. Bleeding into a nodule can lead to acute pain and enlargement. Most patients with thyroid nodules are euthyroid because 85 to 90% of the adenomas concentrate iodine very poorly and do not actively form thyroid hormone. The evaluation of a thyroid nodule includes a history, especially inquiries about the occurrence of specific risk factors such as radiation to the head and neck area. Examination reveals the presence of the nodule and should evaluate lymph nodes in the head and neck area as well as the clinical thyroid status of the patient. Blood determinations of free T_4 and TSH should be obtained to confirm the thyroid status. Fine-needle aspiration of the thyroid nodule to provide material for evaluation by a cytopathologist provides the most accurate assessment. Results to be expected from fine-needle aspiration are listed in Table 239–4.

Rx Treatment

Identification of a nodule as a papillary carcinoma requires thyroid surgery. If a suspicious result is obtained and cannot distinguish between a follicular adenoma and a carcinoma, an RAI scan can be performed: 85 to 90% of thyroid nodules are nonfunctional or "cold" and 20% of such nodules contain a malignancy. Identification of a nodule with a suspicious cytologic result as nonfunctional on RAI scan should result in surgical removal. Ten to 15% of thyroid nodules are functional or "hot"; the incidence of thyroid cancer is less than 1% in such lesions. In a majority of solitary hyperfunctioning nodules, acquired somatic activating mutations of the TSH receptor occur continuously, stimulating thyroid hormone formation even when the TSH receptor is not occupied by TSH. A smaller number of adenomas have activating mutations of the $Gs\alpha$ signaling protein. The TSH receptor or $Gs\alpha$ mutations occur in more than 90% of solitary hyperfunctioning nodules. Patients who are euthyroid can be followed with careful evaluation of thyroid size and functional status. Sooner or later, 25% of these patients become hyperthyroid. Nodules in such patients are surgically removed after the patient is made

euthyroid by treatment with PTU or MMI. In older patients or in patients with a high surgical risk, such nodules can be ablated with RAI. Ultrasonographically directed ethanol injection to ablate hyperfunctioning nodules has also been used.

In about 75% of patients, a thyroid nodule aspirate indicates a benign thyroid nodule. Most such patients have few or no pressure symptoms. In patients with a normal TSH level, thyroxine should be given, starting at 100 µg/day but choosing lower doses in elderly patients and those having cardiovascular symptoms, as discussed earlier. Approximately a one-fifth reduction in the size of these nodules occurs in a majority of patients within 6 to 12 months. If no response to thyroxine occurs, the medication can be stopped. The size of the nodule should then be followed carefully, and a growing nodule should be reaspirated at 1- to 2-year intervals. Rapid growth of a nodule, especially in a patient on thyroxine, requires reaspiration. Increase in nodule size can be due to the accumulation of fluid in a cystic lesion. Although the cyst can be aspirated, fluid frequently reaccumulates and the nodule progressively enlarges. Benign enlarging nodules can be removed surgically.

THYROID CANCER

Incidence and Etiology

Thyroid cancer almost always manifests as a palpable thyroid abnormality. Although most thyroid nodules are benign, about 1 in 25 contains a thyroid cancer. In every 100,000 adults, about six women and two men each year develop thyroid cancer. Such cancers can progress aggressively, especially by local invasion, and lead to much suffering; about 9% are fatal. The incidence of clinically apparent thyroid cancer contrasts to reports that small (<10 mm in diameter), asymptomatic thyroid cancers are found in 5 to 10% of the population at autopsy. These small lesions are considered occult neoplasms of unclear clinical significance. Rarely, such small lesions metastasize to lymph nodes. The cause of thyroid cancer remains unknown, but they are monoclonal in origin, and in papillary thyroid cancer activation of kinase, genes *ret* and *trk* have been reported. The activation of the *ret* gene occurs through rearrangement, bringing the gene under the control of other, stronger promoters. Rearrangement of *ret* occurs in 20 to 40% of papillary thyroid cancer and were found in patients with papillary thyroid cancer arising after the Chernobyl radiation exposure. In follicular cancer, mutations of the *ras* gene occur. A recent report describes a rearrangement derived fusion gene of Pax 8 and PPAR$_\gamma$1 in follicular cancer but not in follicular adenomas. Anaplastic cancer shows inactivating mutations of the *p53* repressor gene. Despite these beginnings, however, a conclusive relationship between

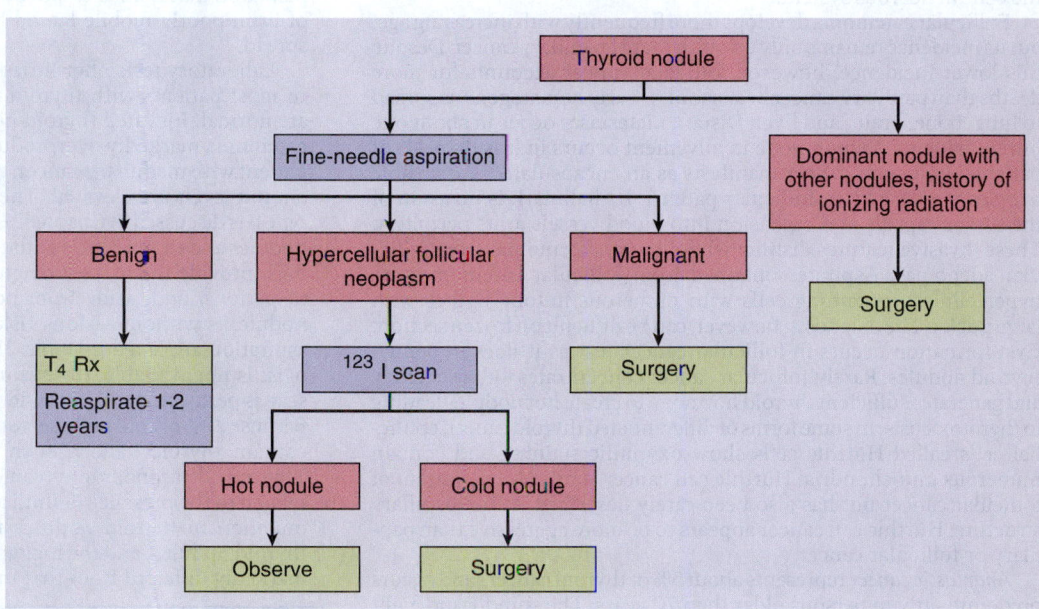

FIGURE 239–5 • Work-up of thyroid nodules. Rx = therapy; T_4 = thyroxine.

specific gene alterations and particular forms of thyroid cancer has not been established.

Certain risk factors for thyroid cancer can be identified. Radiation to the head and neck area, especially during early childhood, leads to a 30-fold increase in thyroid cancer with radiation doses up to 1500 rad. Higher radiation doses of 5000 rad or more, as are delivered to the thyroid by ^{131}I therapy for Graves' disease, do not lead to an increased incidence of thyroid cancer. Other risk factors are primarily genetic and include familial forms of papillary cancer, Gardner's and Cowden's syndrome for papillary cancer, and the multiple endocrine neoplasia (MEN) type II syndrome for medullary cancer. Thyroid cancer is twice as frequent in women as in men, but men have a worse prognosis. The prognosis of thyroid cancer is worse in young (less than 20 years) and old (more than 60 years) patients. Most thyroid cancers are of follicular epithelial cell origin; chronic TSH stimulation appears to play a permissive but not causative role in differentiated papillary and follicular thyroid cancers. Papillary cancer is the least aggressive malignancy and represents about 70 to 90% of all thyroid cancer, with follicular cancers having varying incidents. In iodine-deficient areas, follicular cancer is more frequent. The rest are made up of medullary cancer, anaplastic cancer, lymphomas, and other rare tumors. Metastases to the thyroid occur primarily from malignant melanomas and cancers of breast, lung, and kidney.

Pathology

Papillary cancer is the most common thyroid cancer in the United States, being two to three times more common in women and relatively more common in young patients. The absolute incidence is higher in the fourth to seventh decades. Papillary cancers occur most frequently in parts of the world where iodine supply is adequate. Papillary cancers generally are not encapsulated, and they grow slowly by infiltrative local spread, initially affecting other parts of the thyroid and extending to regional lymph nodes in the neck. Microscopically, papillary cancer is characterized by epithelial cells with large, irregular, frequently clear nuclei covering fibrovascular stalks. In the nucleus, folds or grooves are frequently visible, which are hallmarks of papillary thyroid cancer. The papillae, which give the tumor its name, may not be present in parts of the tumor, and some parts may have a follicular structure. About half of papillary carcinomas contain laminated, calcified spherules called *psammoma bodies*. Variants of papillary cancer with good prognosis include the micropapillary encapsulated, solid, and follicular variants. A poor prognosis is associated with tall cells and diffuse sclerosing variants. Although one study has reported a higher mortality rate with lymph node metastases, local lymph node invasion is not necessarily a bad prognostic sign in papillary cancer because it occurs even with occult tumors less than 1 cm in diameter, which have a favorable prognosis. In patients older than 50 years of age, papillary cancers undergo a more aggressive local spread, leading to death from local invasions in over half of the patients. Distant metastases are uncommon (2 to 3% of patients), with the lung more frequently involved than bone or the central nervous system.

Follicular carcinoma develops more frequently with increasing age, but its incidence remains only one fifth that of papillary cancer. Despite this lower incidence, however, follicular cancer accounts for more deaths than papillary cancer because of its early hematogenous spread to lung, bone, brain, and liver. Distant metastases occur in about one fifth of patients. Lymph node involvement occurs in less than 1% of patients. Follicular cancer manifests as an encapsulated, expansible neoplasm with a microfollicular pattern. Its hallmark is invasion of the tumor capsule and extension into blood vessels at its periphery. These invasive features distinguish follicular carcinomas from follicular adenomas. Aspirates obtained from follicular carcinomas are hypercellular, containing cells with numerous mitotic figures with large nuclei. The diagnosis, however, can be difficult on frozen section. Cyst formation occurs in follicular cancer just as it does in benign thyroid nodules. Rarely, follicular cancer concentrates iodine actively and generates sufficient thyroid hormone to create hot nodules leading to thyrotoxicosis. In some forms of differentiated thyroid cancer, epithelial cells called Hürthle cells show oxyphilic staining and contain numerous mitochondria. Hürthle cell cancer is primarily a variant of follicular cancer but has also been rarely described with a papillary structure. Hürthle cell cancer appears to be more aggressive than papillary or follicular cancer.

Anaplastic cancer represents about 5% of thyroid cancers and occurs predominantly in persons older than 70 years. The spindle and giant cell variants are most frequent, and the rare small cell variant can be confused with lymphomas or medullary cancer. Almost one third of anaplastic cancers arise in preexisting differentiated cancers. The prognosis is dismal, with a mean survival of 7 to 12 months. Death most commonly results from aggressive local invasion causing progressive tracheal obstruction or massive hemorrhage. Distant metastases occur, but the local spread is so rapid that metastatic foci have little clinical importance.

Medullary carcinoma is a malignant tumor of calcitonin-secreting C cells that accounts for 2 to 3% of all thyroid cancer. Point mutations occur in the *ret* gene in medullary cancer instead of the rearrangements found in papillary cancer. The tumor produces calcitonin, calcitonin-related peptide, chromogranin A, adrenocorticotropic hormone, prostaglandins, and carcinoembryonic antigen. Densely packed cells form solid masses separated by hyalinized tumor stroma. Amyloid deposits occur frequently. Several variants of the tumor have been described, with the sporadically occurring form accounting for 80% and genetic or familial variants making up the remainder. The familial variants can be subdivided into those occurring with MEN IIa, MEN IIb, and a familial non-MEN variant. In MEN IIa, the medullary cancer occurs together with pheochromocytomas and parathyroid adenomas; in MEN IIb, pheochromocytomas and ganglioneuromas occur. In the familial form, the tumor is multicentric in origin and C-cell hyperplasia precedes cancer development. The tumor metastasizes via the lymphatic route and the blood stream. The peak incidence of the sporadic form is in the sixth and seventh decades. At the time of diagnosis, lymphatic spread has frequently developed. Medullary carcinoma is quite aggressive, and fewer than half of its carriers survive for 10 years.

Thyroid lymphoma most frequently consists of the diffuse B-cell variant and occurs most frequently in patients with Hashimoto's disease. Such lymphomas manifest as rapidly growing masses replacing thyroid tissue and extending through the capsule into adjacent soft tissue. Secondary involvement of the thyroid by malignant lymphoma arising elsewhere occurs in about one fifth of patients with advanced generalized lymphoma.

Clinical Manifestations and Diagnosis

Thyroid nodules are frequent, but only about 1 in 20 contains a thyroid cancer. Figure 239–5 outlines the approach to such lesions. The task is to identify the cancerous lesion in order to perform selective surgery. Specific features in the patient's history and symptoms and signs can point to the occurrence of cancer but are not conclusive. Thyroid cancer is more likely in a nodule developing in a child or a patient older than 60 years of age, especially men. A single hard nodule showing rapid, painless growth is more likely to be a cancerous lesion. A history of radiation to the head and neck area during childhood, a family history of thyroid cancer, Gardner's syndrome, Cowden's syndrome, and MEN II syndrome all represent strong risk factors. A single hard nodule noted on palpation that is fixed to surrounding tissue and the identification of firm, poorly mobile lateral lymph nodes may indicate cancer spread.

Laboratory tests offer little in the diagnosis of thyroid cancer. In most patients with thyroid nodules, thyroid hormone values are normal. Elevated thyroid hormone levels indicate a follicular carcinoma markedly overproducing thyroid hormone. In the rare patient with medullary cancer, calcitonin-related peptides and calcitonin levels are elevated. The evaluation of patients with MEN type II is discussed in Chapter 244. Fine-needle aspiration of thyroid nodules and examination of the obtained material by a cytopathologist provide the highest diagnostic yield. The procedure is easy to perform and, aside from occasional bleeding in the thyroid nodule, is without serious risk. Results obtained by fine-needle aspiration are listed in Table 239–4. When a trained cytopathologist is not available, the evaluation needs to be modified. A ^{123}I scan is performed to determine whether the thyroid nodule is cold. Because 20% of cold nodules coming to attention in a referral center contain thyroid cancer, such nodules are surgically removed. Thyroid ultrasonography can provide further detail, especially related to the presence of fluid and cystic lesions. Most fluid accumulation in thyroid nodules represents cystic degeneration of thyroid nodules, and the incidence of cancer in such lesions is not markedly different from that in solid nodules.

Rx Treatment

Thyroid surgery should be performed by an experienced thyroid surgeon. Some diversity of opinion exists related to the extent of the operation. For example, some thyroid surgeons treat a 1.5- to 2.0-cm papillary cancer only with a lobectomy, whereas others prefer a near-total thyroidectomy. I prefer the removal of such lesions by near-total thyroidectomy. In the hands of an experienced surgeon, complications from permanent hypoparathyroidism (2%) or vocal cord paralysis (2%) are no greater for a near-total thyroidectomy than for a lobectomy. A near-total thyroidectomy has the advantage that only small remnants of thyroid tissue remain, which can be ablated with RAI. Because normal thyroid tissue accumulates RAI much more avidly than any thyroid cancer, it is not possible to treat thyroid cancer successfully by ^{131}I therapy in the presence of a large amount of normal thyroid tissue. In addition, after near-total thyroidectomy, the patient can be followed with thyroglobulin levels. Increases in the level of thyroglobulin indicate a return of thyroid cancer.

^{131}I ablation is used in patients who undergo near-total thyroidectomy, especially if the primary lesion is a papillary cancer greater than 2 cm in diameter or a follicular cancer. The regimen goes as follows: One day after surgery, patients are started on triiodothyronine (liothyronine sodium [Cytomel] 25 µg every day or twice a day) and maintained on this dose of T_3 for 4 to 6 weeks. T_3 has a half-life of 1 day and the patient becomes hypothyroid much more quickly than with thyroxine treatment. When medication is stopped at the end of the 4- to 6-week healing period, the patient becomes markedly hypothyroid, documented by an elevated TSH level. After the TSH has attained levels of at least 40 µU/mL, a scanning dose of 3 mCi of ^{123}I is administered. If a small remnant of thyroid tissue is left in the bed of the thyroid, an ablative dose of 29 mCi of ^{131}I is administered. Identification of a larger amount of thyroid tissue or lymph node metastases leads to the administration of a higher dose of ^{131}I, ranging from 75 to 125 mCi according to the amount of remaining tissue. Seven to 10 days after treatment, a second RAI scan can be performed. This post-treatment scan identifies areas of ^{131}I uptake that were not detected by the initial lower-dose diagnostic scan.

When patients become hypothyroid for RAI scanning, it is important to obtain a thyroglobulin measurement: elevated levels indicate that a sizable mass of thyroid tissue was left after surgery. Patients who had considerable thyroid tissue left or tumor spread to lymph nodes should be rescanned 6 months after the initial scan to ensure that the initial RAI treatment ablated all thyroid tissue. Patients who had only a small amount of tissue left can be rescanned within 1 year. Patients whose thyroglobulin levels remain normal should be rescanned 3 years after surgery. If no evidence of RAI accumulation occurs, no subsequent rescanning is necessary and patients can be followed with thyroglobulin values. With recombinant TSH (rTSH), the follow-up approach for patients with thyroid cancer has been modified. The administration of 0.9 mg rTSH on two consecutive days with the patient continuing to take his thyroxine replacement stimulates ^{131}I uptake and increase thyroglobulin levels to the same extent as making the patient hypothyroid. This approach avoids inducing a hypothyroid state with its undesirable symptoms and with prolonged TSH stimulation of thyroid cancer remnants. The use of rTSH is especially indicated in patients with low, detectable thyroglobulin levels (Tg <3 ng/ml), in high-risk cancer patients, in patients with medical contraindications of a hypothyroid state (e.g., chronic obstructive pulmonary disease), and in the absence of a pituitary TSH response. Currently, rTSH is not approved for thyroid cancer treatment. The ^{131}I dose would need to be 40 to 50% higher than with the conventional approach. In euthyroid patients, less ^{131}I goes to the thyroid than in a hypothyroid state because of a relatively higher renal ^{131}I clearance. In about 10% of patients, thyroid cancer can dedifferentiate, resulting in a discrepancy between a positive RAI scan and undetectable thyroglobulin levels. Similarly, patients with elevated thyroglobulin level and minimal or absent RAI uptake on scans have been identified. Such individuals need to be followed carefully and may require additional RAI treatment because the elevated thyroglobulin level can indicate the presence of thyroid cancer. The best initial treatment of patients with near-total thyroidectomy for papillary cancer consists of giving sufficient thyroxine to suppress TSH into the low-normal range combined with RAI therapy. This regimen markedly decreases the late recurrence of papillary cancer. Follicular carcinoma is more aggressive and should be treated more vigorously than papillary cancer. External beam radiation therapy is used to treat bone metastases especially if they lead to pain or pressure-induced neurologic injury. Medullary cancer does not respond to RAI therapy and must be treated with surgery plus external radiation and chemotherapy, especially if bone metastases occur. Anaplastic cancer has a poor prognosis; attempts to increase survival time by treatment with chemotherapy and external radiation therapy have been unsuccessful, although palliative external radiation can especially alleviate obstruction.

SUGGESTED READINGS

Acharya S, Sarafoglou K, LaQuaglia M, et al: Thyroid neoplasms after therapeutic radiation for malignancies during childhood or adolescence. Cancer 2003;97:2397–2403. *Most of these malignancies may not become evident for decades after radiation therapy, so all individuals at risk require life-long follow-up.*

Alexander EK, Hurwitz S, Heering JP, et al: Natural history of benign solid and cystic thyroid nodules. Ann Intern Med 2003;138:315–318. *Most solid, benign thyroid nodules grow, so an increase in size is not a reliable predictor of malignancy.*

Caki M, Samanci N, Balci N, et al: Musculoskeletal manifestations in patients with thyroid disease. Clin Endocrinol (Oxf) 2003;59:162–167. *Review of the musculoskeletal disorders that often accompany thyroid dysfunction.*

Corvilain B, Van Sande J, Dumont JE, et al: Somatic and germline mutations of the TSH receptor and thyroid diseases. Clin Endocrinol (Oxf) 2001;55:143–158. *Overview of genetic abnormalities leading to thyroid dysfunction.*

Danese MD, Ladenson PW, Meinert CL, et al: Clinical review 115: Effect of thyroxine therapy on serum lipoproteins in patients with mild thyroid failure: A quantitative review of the literature. J Clin Endocrinol Metab 2000;85:2993–3001. *Treatment lowers LDL but does not affect HDL or triglycerides.*

Derwahl M, Studer H: Nodular goiter and goiter nodules: Where iodine deficiency falls short of explaining the facts. Exp Clin Endocrinol Diabetes 2001;109:250–260. *Goiter nodules and nodular goiters are benign neoplasms arising by mechanisms common to all benign endocrine and nonendocrine neoplasms, but superimposed iodine shortage greatly enhances their incidence.*

Fewins J, Simpson CB, Miller FR: Complications of thyroid and parathyroid surgery. Otolaryngol Clin North Am 2003;36:189–206. *Most complications are related to metabolic derangements or to injury to the recurrent laryngeal nerve.*

Kinder BK: Well differentiated thyroid cancer. Curr Opin Oncol 2003;15:71–77. *Review of established and experimental therapies.*

Krohn K, Paschke R: Clinical review 133: Progress in understanding the etiology of thyroid autonomy. J Clin Endocrinol Metab 2001;86:3336–3345. *A physiologic overview.*

Marqusee E, Benson CB, Frates MC, et al: Usefulness of ultrasonography in the management of nodular thyroid disease. Ann Intern Med 2000;133:696–700. *Ultrasonography altered the clinical management for 63% of patients with abnormal physical examinations.*

Pasieka JL: Anaplastic thyroid cancer. Curr Opin Oncol 2003;15:78–83. *Surgical resection is usually inadequate, so evaluation for multimodal therapy in the setting of a clinical trial is recommended.*

Peeters RP, Wouters PJ, Kaptein E, et al: Reduced activation and increased inactivation of thyroid hormone in tissues of critically ill patients. J Clin Endocrinol Metab 2003;88:3202–3211. *Reviews the physiologic and clinical implications of the thyroid function test abnormalities seen in critically ill patients.*

Ross DS: Serum thyroid-stimulating hormone measurement for assessment of thyroid function and disease. Endocrinol Metab Clin North Am 2001;30:245–264. *Third generation thyroid stimulating hormone assays are the best screening test of thyroid function.*

Shoup M, Stojadinovic A, Nissan A, et al: Prognostic indicators of outcomes in patients with distant metastases from differentiated thyroid carcinoma. J Am Coll Surg 2003;197:191–197. *Age over 45 years, a site other than lung only or bone only, and symptoms were associated with poorer outcomes.*

Silva JE: The thermogenic effect of thyroid hormone and its clinical implications. Ann Intern Med 2003;139:205–213. *Explains the interrelationship between physiology and clinical symptoms.*

Stockigt JR: Free thyroid hormone measurement. A critical appraisal. Endocrinol Metab Clin North Am 2001;30:265–289. *Reviews the use of this assay.*

Thomusch O, Machens A, Sekulla C, et al: The impact of surgical technique on postoperative hypoparathyroidism in bilateral thyroid surgery: A multivariate analysis of 5846 consecutive patients. Surgery 2003;133:180–185. *Emphasizes the benefit of experienced, high volume thyroid surgeons.*

Titton RL, Gervais DA, Boland GW, et al: Sonography and sonographically guided fine-needle aspiration biopsy of the thyroid gland: Indications and techniques, pearls and pitfalls. AJR Am J Roentgenol 2003;181:267–271. *Overview of the currently recommended approach to diagnosis.*

Yen PM: Physiological and molecular basis of thyroid hormone action. Physiol Rev 2001;81:1097–1142. *A scholarly overview of the molecular mechanisms of thyroid hormone's action and the occasional resistance to it.*

240 THE ADRENAL CORTEX

D. Lynn Loriaux

The two adrenal glands lie either on top of or next to the kidneys (Fig. 240–1). Each gland, between 6 and 8 g in weight, is composed of a cortex and a medulla. The cortex makes steroid hormones and the medulla, in essence a sympathetic ganglion, makes catecholamines. The cortex is composed of three histologic zones in the adult: zona glomerulosa, zona fasciculata, and zona reticularis (Fig. 240–2). Each zone can be thought of as an independent organ. The outermost zona glomerulosa produces aldosterone, the primary mineralocorticoid in humans. The zona fasciculata produces mainly cortisol, the major glucocorticoid in humans, and the zona reticularis produces the "adrenal androgens." The adrenal androgens are in fact androgen and estrogen precursors, the parent compound being dehydroepiandrosterone and its sulfate conjugate. The biologic actions of these steroid hormones are effected via intracellular receptors, cytoplasmic or nuclear in location, that regulate gene transcription on binding with the appropriate ligand. Dehydroepiandrosterone has no known receptor. The distribution of these receptors defines the responsive tissues for each hormone. Aldosterone regulates sodium balance, primarily acting on the distal tubule of the nephron. Cortisol maintains physiologic integrity in ways that remain poorly understood, and its receptors are found in virtually every cell in the body. Dehydroepiandrosterone has no identifiable biologic action. The synthesis and secretion of each of these hormones are regulated, in the main, by a separate "feedback" system. The major trophic hormone for aldosterone secretion is renin; for cortisol, it is adrenocorticotropic hormone (ACTH); and for dehydroepiandrosterone, it is cortical androgen-stimulating hormone, which is not yet fully characterized. Thus, in the case of the zona glomerulosa and the zona fasciculata, the functional status of each can be assessed by measuring two hormones: aldosterone and plasma renin for the former and cortisol and ACTH for the latter.

The adrenal medulla, in essence a sympathetic ganglion, produces catecholamines in response to neural input. Disorders of the adrenal medulla are discussed in Chapter 241.

DISORDERS OF ADRENOCORTICAL FUNCTION

Disorders of adrenocortical function can be thought of as disorders of overproduction or underproduction of the four classes of steroid hormones produced by the adrenal gland: cortisol, aldosterone, androgen, and estrogen. In addition, "mixed" disorders, the congenital adrenal hyperplasias, are characterized by a clinical picture of combined hormone excess and deficiency. These disorders are considered separately.

The diagnosis of disorders of adrenocortical function, like that of other endocrine syndromes, requires a compatible clinical picture with biochemical confirmation of the associated underlying abnormality. In years past, the tests used in the diagnosis of adrenal disease were both confusing and many. Fortunately, the last several years have brought order and simplification to the process.

Tests of Adrenocortical Function

THE PORTER-SILBER CHROMOGENS. The three-carbon side chain of cortisol reacts with *m*-dinitrobenzene to form a colored adduct with an absorption maximum at 410 μm. Other adrenal steroids having this configuration in the side chain include cortisone, 11-deoxycortisol, tetrahydrocortisone, tetrahydro-11-deoxycortisol, and tetrahydrocortisol (Fig. 240–3). This reaction, called the Porter-Silber chromogen reaction, was the basis of the first test to provide some measure of cortisol production. It is still in widespread use. Because urinary metabolites are, for the most part, conjugated to glucuronic acid and sulfuric acid, measurement of Porter-Silber chromogens

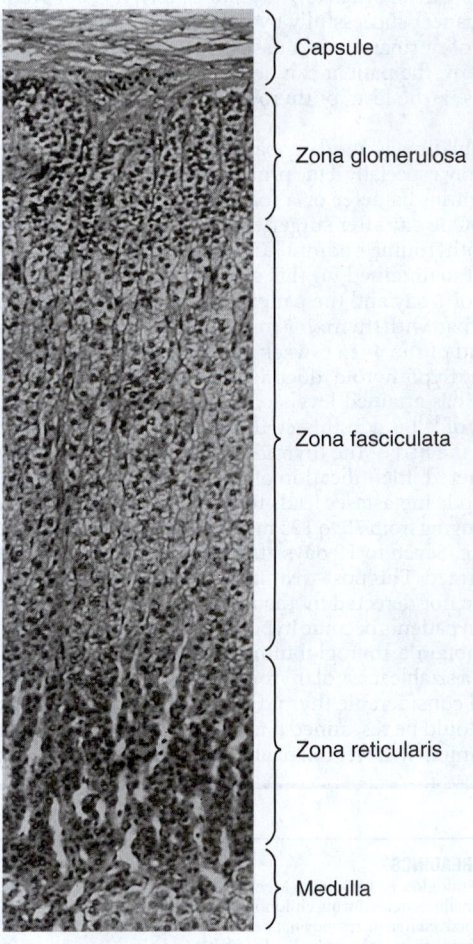

Capsule

Zona glomerulosa

Zona fasciculata

Zona reticularis

Medulla

FIGURE 240–2 • Histologic section through a normal adult adrenal gland showing the progression, outside in, of the zona glomerulosa, zona fasciculata, and zona reticularis.

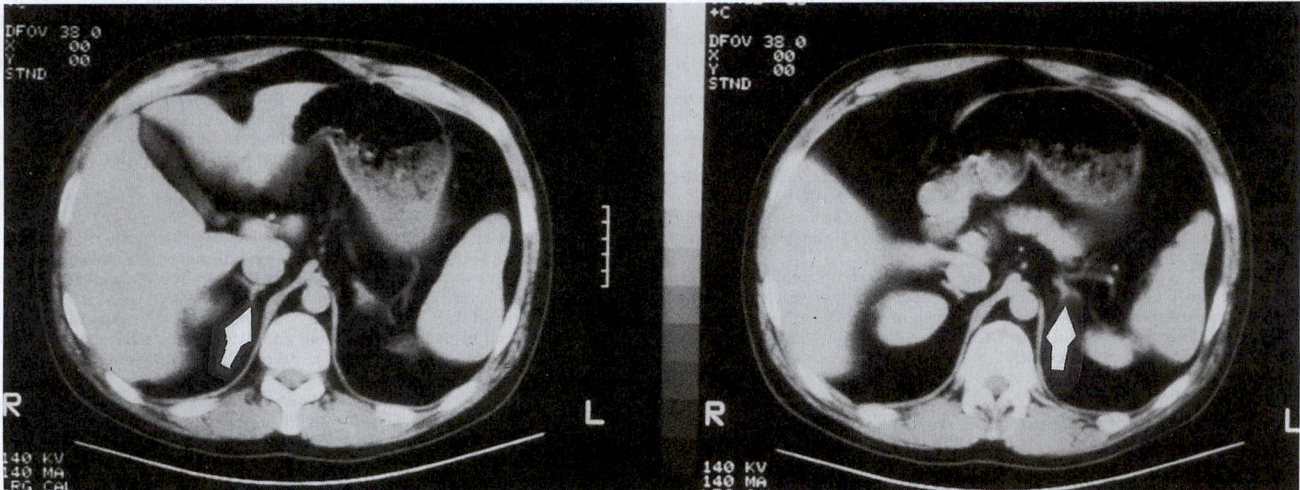

FIGURE 240–1 • Magnetic resonance images of the abdomen showing the position and relative size of the normal adrenal glands.

initially involves an acid hydrolysis to cleave these conjugates. This step is followed by lipid extraction with a solvent such as dichloromethane. The Porter-Silber reaction is performed on the steroids in the lipid extract. The absorption maximum is quantitated spectrophotometrically. The normal range for Porter-Silber chromogen excretion is 2 to 12 mg/day. Excretion of these steroids is markedly affected by body size, and the normal range is considerably narrowed by normalizing the measurement against urinary creatinine excretion. With this correction, the normal range is the same for all ages, 4.5 ± 1 (SD) mg/g creatinine per day. The normal range includes the extinction point for the assay, which means that values below the normal range cannot be measured reliably with this assay.

URINE FREE CORTISOL. Urine free cortisol is that fraction of urinary cortisol that is neither conjugated to glucuronic or sulfuric acid nor bound to a circulating protein. Accordingly, it is filtered by the renal glomerulus and can be extracted directly from urine with a lipid solvent. The detection limit of this assay also lies in the normal range of cortisol excretion and hence the assay is not a reliable test for adrenal insufficiency.

PLASMA CORTISOL. Intuitively, measurement of circulating plasma cortisol should provide the most direct assessment of adrenal cortisol secretion. The secretion of cortisol is pulsatile, with a steady frequency of about one pulse per hour in adults. The amplitude of these pulses, however, varies markedly, with 8 to 10 high-amplitude pulses clustering in the early morning hours. This pattern creates a diurnal secretory rhythm in plasma cortisol concentration. Cortisol circulates predominantly bound to a glycosylated 59-kD α_2-globulin, cortisol-binding globulin (transcortin). This binding protein protects circulating cortisol from hepatic clearance and gives cortisol a relatively long plasma half-life of 60 to 80 minutes. Normal plasma cortisol concentrations range between 5 and 20 µg/dL. At some time each day, normal subjects have plasma cortisol concentrations that cannot be differentiated from zero. These biologic complexities make interpretation of isolated plasma cortisol determinations hazardous. If cortisol is measured at frequent intervals (30 minutes) over a 24-hour period and the values are averaged, the mean plasma cortisol concentration amounts to 7.5 ± 1 µg/dL. To work within this narrow confidence interval, however, requires the measurement of a large number of plasma cortisol concentrations, which is prohibitive except in extraordinary circumstances.

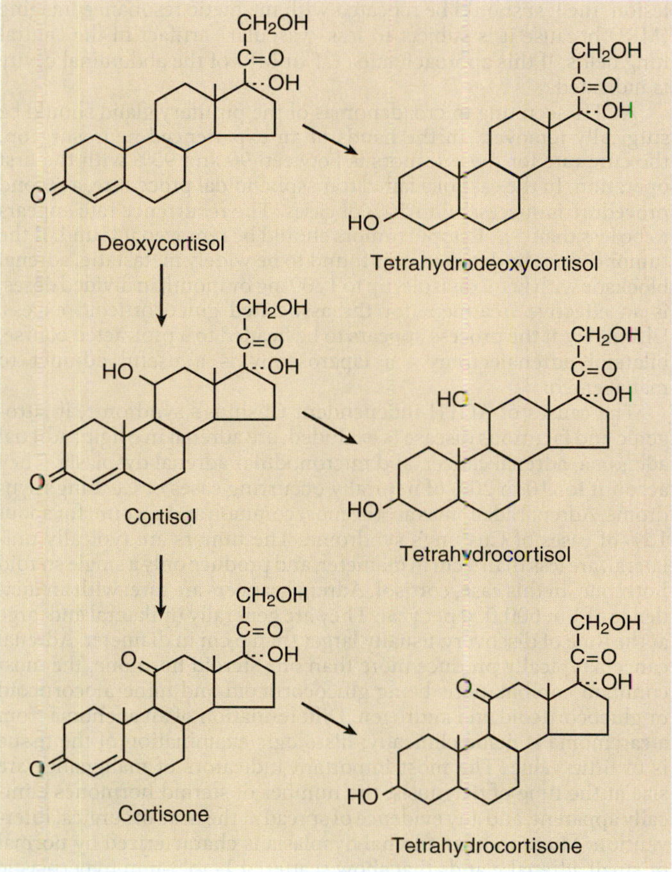

PLASMA ACTH CONCENTRATION. Development of the two-site immunoradiometric assay for ACTH considerably simplified the differential diagnosis of adrenal disease. The normal range of plasma ACTH extends up to 100 pg/mL.

PROVOCATIVE TESTS OF ADRENAL FUNCTION. Three provocative tests of adrenal function are in common use. The ACTH stimulation test is the most reliable screening test for adrenal hypofunction. It is also the standard method by which suspected enzymatic deficiencies in adrenal steroidogenesis are examined. The test is performed by administering 250 µg of synthetic ACTH (cosyntropin; Cortrosyn) intravenously and measuring the serum steroids of interest 45 and 60 minutes later. The normal adrenal gland produces plasma cortisol concentrations greater than 20 µg/dL in response to this challenge. *Corticotropin-releasing hormone,* the 41–amino acid hypothalamic secretagogue for ACTH, is a useful test for separating ACTH-dependent from ACTH-independent hypercortisolism and is an essential component of the inferior petrosal sinus sampling procedure for localizing the site of ACTH secretion (Chapter 237). The test is performed by infusing corticotropin-releasing hormone, 1 µg/kg, intravenously over a period of 1 minute and measuring the ACTH response between 3 and 30 minutes thereafter.

The *dexamethasone suppression test* is widely used to screen for adrenal hyperfunction. The test has so many false-positive and false-negative results (sensitivity and specificity of about 0.8), however, that it is superseded by the other tests mentioned. The test retains some value in the differential diagnosis of mineralocorticoid excess. Many iterations of this test are available, the simplest being 0.5 mg dexamethasone administered by mouth every 6 hours for 2 days.

Plasma and urine aldosterone and plasma renin activity are important tests for evaluating states of apparent mineralocorticoid excess and deficiency.

The differential diagnosis of congenital adrenal hyperplasia requires the measurement of specific steroid biosynthetic intermediates that accumulate proximal to the responsible enzymatic deficiencies in the steroid biosynthetic cascade. The most commonly measured are 17-hydroxyprogesterone (21-hydroxylase deficiency) and 11-deoxycortisol (11-hydroxylase deficiency). These steroids are most reliably measured in the context of an ACTH stimulation test, as described earlier.

ADRENAL HYPERFUNCTION

Four syndromes of adrenal hyperfunction are differentiated: Cushing's syndrome, hypokalemic metabolic alkalosis, masculinization, and feminization. These syndromes result from the excessive secretion of cortisol, mineralocorticoid, androgen, and estrogen, respectively. These disorders can occur in isolation or, more commonly, in combination with one or more of the others.

Glucocorticoid Excess: Cushing's Syndrome

DIAGNOSIS. Cushing's syndrome is caused by glucocorticoid excess. The "classic" syndrome is defined clinically: weight gain, plethora,

FIGURE 240–3 • Family of steroids known as the Porter-Silber chromogens, commonly referred to as the 17-hydroxysteroids.

Table 240–1 • CLINICAL FEATURES OF GLUCOCORTICOID EXCESS	
FEATURE	**FREQUENCY (%)**
Weight gain	90
"Moon facies"	75
Hypertension	75
Violaceous striae	65
Hirsutism	65
Glucose intolerance	65
Proximal muscle weakness	60
Plethora	60
Menstrual dysfunction	60
Acne	40
Easy bruising	40
Osteopenia	40
Dependent edema	40
Hyperpigmentation	20
Hypokalemic metabolic alkalosis	15

striae, hypertension, and proximal muscle weakness (Table 240–1). The weight gain is predominantly truncal, with increased fat deposited in a yokelike pattern around the neck leading to the well-known dorsocervical fat pad ("buffalo hump") and filling in of the supra-clavicular fossae. Plethora is evident as a ruddy complexion. The striae of Cushing's syndrome are characteristically violaceous and occur in thin skin. Proximal muscle weakness is best assessed by testing the ability of the patient to rise unassisted from a squatting position. The biochemical diagnosis depends on the demonstration of an elevated plasma concentration of "bioactive" cortisol, which is best reflected in the excretion of urine free cortisol. If the clinical picture is "strong," urine free cortisol concentrations above the normal range are adequate for the diagnosis. If the clinical picture is "weak," urine free cortisol excretion must be above the levels found in "physiologic" causes of adrenal activation such as stress and depression. This level is generally taken to be 250 μg/day. This approach to the diagnosis of Cushing's syndrome occasionally identifies patients with an "atypical" picture. At one extreme are patients with minimal clinical manifestations of Cushing's syndrome but very high levels of free cortisol excretion. This constellation of findings is characteristic of Cushing's syndrome associated with systemic malignancy, typically a small cell carcinoma of the lung. The clinical picture is dominated by the "cachexia" of malignancy, and the typical "anabolic" features of Cushing's syndrome such as weight gain and dorsocervical fat distribution fail to develop. At the other extreme are patients with well-established clinical signs of Cushing's syndrome but without sufficient urine free cortisol excretion to confirm the diagnosis. This situation is usually the result of iatrogenic or surreptitious exogenous glucocorticoid administration. A careful history and review of systems usually reveal the source of the glucocorticoid. In the rare case of surreptitious glucocorticoid abuse, measurement of the commonly prescribed synthetic glucocorticoids in randomly obtained serum samples is necessary for the diagnosis. Rarely, naturally occurring Cushing's syndrome can be cyclic or even intermittent. In this case, repeated measurement of urine free cortisol at frequent intervals of 3 to 5 days is necessary to establish the diagnosis.

DIFFERENTIAL DIAGNOSIS AND TREATMENT. The causes of Cushing's syndrome are shown in Table 240–2. They can be conveniently divided into ACTH-dependent and ACTH-independent causes. This differentiation is made on the basis of the plasma ACTH concentration following the administration of corticotropin-releasing hormone. Values greater than 10 pg/dL indicate ACTH-dependent disease; values less than 10 pg/dL indicate ACTH-independent disease.

The causes of ACTH-dependent Cushing's syndrome include Cushing's disease caused by an ACTH-secreting pituitary tumor and the ectopic secretion of ACTH from a neoplasm not of pituitary origin. Cushing's disease, the most common cause of Cushing's syndrome, accounts for 70 to 80% of all noniatrogenic cases (Chapter 237). Ectopic secretion of ACTH by a nonpituitary neoplasm accounts for about 10% of cases. The common causes of ectopic ACTH secretion are listed in Table 240–3. More than 90% of these tumors are found in the chest. The most common cause is the bronchial carcinoid. Other neoplasms include small cell cancer of the lung, medullary cancer of the thyroid, islet cell tumors of the pancreas, and pheochromocytoma.

Two forms of the ectopic ACTH syndrome can be differentiated. In the first, Cushing's syndrome occurs as classically described by Harvey Cushing. It can be thought of as the anabolic form of ectopic ACTH secretion because it is associated with weight gain and the characteristic central obesity of the disorder. It is usually caused by slow-growing benign tumors such as bronchial carcinoid tumors. The second form, the catabolic form, has none of the anabolic features associated with "classic" Cushing's syndrome. Weight loss, hypertension, edema, and hypokalemia dominate the clinical picture. This form of the disease is commonly associated with advanced and widely metastatic tumors that impair caloric intake and prevent weight gain and the development of central obesity.

Differentiating the two ACTH-dependent forms of Cushing's syndrome from each other depends on localizing the source of the ACTH secretion. The most effective method of doing so is by sampling inferior petrosal sinus blood for the measurement of ACTH levels. Pituitary venous blood drains into the cavernous sinuses on either side of the sella turcica and thence into the internal jugular veins by way of the inferior petrosal sinuses. These sinuses can be readily cannulated via catheters inserted into the femoral vein. Blood sampled simultaneously from both sinuses and a peripheral vein allows the ratio of ACTH between the sites to be determined. The test is most precise when the blood is sampled after the administration of corticotropin-releasing hormone. The lowest central-to-peripheral ratio of ACTH compatible with Cushing's disease is 3. The highest ratio seen with ectopic ACTH-secreting tumors is 1.8.

When ACTH secretion is localized to the pituitary gland, therapeutic intervention is recommended without further delay (Chapter 237). If the ACTH originates from an ectopic site, an attempt to define the specific lesion is undertaken. The most direct course is to examine the entire chest by computed tomography (CT) at 0.5-cm intervals. If this approach fails to identify a suspicious lesion, the test should be repeated with magnetic resonance imaging (MRI) because it is subject to less "vascular" artifact in the central lung fields. If this approach fails, CT or MRI of the abdominal cavity is indicated.

ACTH-secreting microadenomas of the pituitary gland should be surgically removed. In the hands of an experienced neurosurgeon, the cure rate for these tumors is between 90 and 95% with the first operation. In the case of a failed transsphenoidal procedure, a second procedure is successful in 50% of cases. The recurrence rate appears to be less than 5%. Ectopic tumors should be removed if found. If the tumor cannot be detected or is found to be widely metastatic, adrenal blockade with ketoconazole, up to 1200 mg by mouth in divided doses, is an effective treatment for the associated glucocorticoid excess. Ultimately, if the process appears to be headed to a protracted course, bilateral adrenalectomy via laparoscopy is a useful adjunct to management.

The causes of ACTH-independent Cushing's syndrome, if iatrogenic and factitious disease is excluded, are adrenal in origin: adrenal adenoma, adrenal cancer, and micronodular adrenal dysplasia. They account for 10 to 20% of naturally occurring cases of Cushing's syndrome. Adrenal adenomas are the most common and account for about 15% of cases of Cushing's syndrome. The tumors are typically unilateral, are less than 4 cm in diameter, and produce only a single steroid hormone, in this case, cortisol. Adrenal cancers are rare, with an incidence of 1 in 600,000 per year. They are generally unilateral and large at the time of discovery, usually larger than 6 cm in diameter. Adrenal cancers typically produce more than one steroid hormone, the most common combinations being glucocorticoid and mineralocorticoid or glucocorticoid and androgen. Differentiation of an adenoma from a carcinoma is made clinically; histologic examination of the tissue is of little value. The most important indicators of malignancy are size at the time of diagnosis, the number of steroid hormones clinically apparent, and any evidence of spread at the time of surgical intervention. Micronodular adrenal dysplasia is characterized by normal or small adrenal glands that show scattered 1- to 3-mm hyperplastic nodules separated by atrophic adrenal cortex. This disease can be sporadic or part of a larger syndrome, Carney's complex, in which

Table 240–2 • CAUSES OF CUSHING'S SYNDROME

ACTH-Dependent Causes
  ACTH-secreting pituitary tumor (Cushing's disease)
  Nonpituitary ACTH-secreting neoplasm (ectopic ACTH syndrome)
ACTH-Independent Causes
  Adrenal adenoma
  Adrenal carcinoma
  Micronodular adrenal disease
  Factitious or surreptitious glucocorticoid administration

ACTH = adrenocorticotropic hormone.

Table 240–3 • COMMON CAUSES OF ECTOPIC ADRENOCORTICOTROPIC HORMONE SECRETION

CAUSE	FREQUENCY (%)
Small cell carcinoma of the lung	30
Endocrine tumors of foregut origin	53
Thymic carcinoid	
Islet cell tumor	
Medullary carcinoma, thyroid	
Bronchial carcinoid	
Pheochromocytoma	5
Ovarian tumors	2

the adrenal disease is associated with pigmented lentigines, atrial myxoma, and germ cell tumors (see references).

The differential diagnosis of ACTH-independent Cushing's syndrome depends almost exclusively on the findings produced by CT or MRI. Small unilateral lesions with no evidence of metastasis should be removed by a unilateral flank excision or by a laparoscopic procedure. Large lesions should be removed via a transabdominal approach so that the abdominal organs can be carefully examined and the liver biopsied at the time of surgery. Treatment of micronodular adrenal dysplasia is bilateral adrenalectomy.

Metastases should be surgically excised until no longer feasible. The only known chemotherapy effective against this cancer is *o,p'*-dichlorodiphenyldichloroethane. It is given orally to tolerance, usually a dose between 6 and 10 g/day. Side effects are neuropsychiatric and gastrointestinal, with somnolence, ataxia, reduced attention span, nausea, and diarrhea predominating. One fourth of patients have an objective remission, and the remissions average 7 months. No one has been cured of metastatic adrenocortical carcinoma.

Mineralocorticoid Excess

DIAGNOSIS. No reliable symptoms are known for mineralocorticoid excess. Signs include arterial hypertension and dependent edema. Laboratory findings are more specific. The mineralocorticoid effect on the distal nephron is sodium retention at the expense of potassium and hydrogen excretion. Excess mineralocorticoid produces an expanded vascular volume in association with hypokalemia and metabolic alkalosis. Mineralocorticoid excess can be renin-angiotensin independent or dependent. The aldosterone-secreting tumor is an example of renin-angiotensin–independent disease. In renin-angiotensin–dependent disease, the mineralocorticoid is produced in response to the renin-angiotensin trophic signal. This trophic signal is commonly encountered in states of contracted arterial volume such as congestive heart failure or cirrhosis with ascites. The two forms of mineralocorticoid excess can be differentiated on the basis of plasma renin activity. If resting plasma renin activity is high, the mineralocorticoid excess is renin-angiotensin dependent. If plasma renin activity is low and cannot be stimulated by 4 hours of upright posture, the mineralocorticoid excess is renin-angiotensin independent.

Renin-Angiotensin–Independent Mineralocorticoid Excess

DIFFERENTIAL DIAGNOSIS AND TREATMENT. Table 240–4 lists the causes of renin-angiotensin–independent mineralocorticoid excess. Aldosterone is the offending mineralocorticoid in most but not all of these disorders. The initial task is to differentiate cases caused by aldosterone excess from those caused by another mineralocorticoid. Urine and plasma aldosterone measurements provide the answers for this differentiation. If the aldosterone concentration is normal or above normal, aldosterone is the causative agent. If the aldosterone concentration is below the normal range or undetectable, the disorder is caused by a mineralocorticoid other than aldosterone.

Two common causes of aldosterone-mediated renin-angiotensin–independent mineralocorticoid excess are aldosterone-producing adenoma and bilateral hyperplasia of aldosterone-secreting cells. Dexamethasone-suppressible hyperaldosteronism is a rare cause of aldosterone-mediated renin-angiotensin–independent mineralocorticoid excess. It can be excluded by finding normal or high levels of circulating aldosterone after 2 days of dexamethasone, 2 mg/day by mouth in divided doses. The remaining causes of renin-angiotensin–independent aldosterone excess must be separated from one another to guide the appropriate therapeutic intervention. Aldosterone-

secreting adenomas respond well to surgical removal, whereas bilateral hyperplasia does not. The most direct approach to this differentiation is to measure cortisol-aldosterone ratios in adrenal venous blood sampled simultaneously from both glands following the administration of ACTH. The diagnostic accuracy of this test approaches 100%. Aldosterone-secreting adenomas are characterized by high levels of aldosterone from one side and low levels from the other, the secretion from the nonaffected side being suppressed by the volume-expanded state. Bilateral hyperplasia is characterized by comparable aldosterone levels from each gland, and therefore cortisol-to-aldosterone ratios in effluent adrenal blood are roughly equal on the two sides.

Unilateral adrenal adenomas should be surgically excised. In the hands of an experienced surgeon, the cure rate is very high. Bilateral hyperplasia does not respond well to surgery and is best treated with spironolactone to address the metabolic sequelae of mineralocorticoid excess and with antihypertensive medications if spironolactone inadequately controls blood pressure.

The causes of nonaldosterone-mediated renin-angiotensin–independent mineralocorticoid excess are rare (see Table 240–4). The initial task is to exclude adrenocortical carcinoma, which is best done by imaging the adrenal glands with CT or MRI. Failure to find adrenal asymmetry and the presence of a dominant mass, usually larger than 4 cm in diameter, essentially excludes the diagnosis. Symmetrically enlarged adrenal glands of moderate degree suggest congenital adrenal hyperplasia. The two congenital adrenal hyperplasias that lead to hypertension are 11-hydroxylase deficiency and 17-hydroxylase deficiency. The former can be diagnosed by measuring the circulating concentration of 11-deoxycortisol. Normally, this steroid does not circulate in plasma. 17-Hydroxylase deficiency is best diagnosed by a unique clinical picture (hypertension, pubertal delay, and genital ambiguity) coupled with an inappropriately elevated plasma progesterone concentration.

The enzyme 11β-hydroxysteroid dehydrogenase (11β-HSD) catalyzes the conversion of cortisol to cortisone. Cortisol interacts with the mineralocorticoid receptor as an agonist; cortisone does not. Because the circulating concentrations of cortisol are 1000 times those of aldosterone, cortisol can have considerable mineralocorticoid activity in humans. Excess activity is prevented by the action of 11β-HSD, which converts cortisol to its inactive metabolite, cortisone. If the activity of this enzyme is impaired, cortisol assumes the role of aldosterone. Because cortisol secretion is not regulated by the renin-angiotensin system, a state of mineralocorticoid excess at normal plasma cortisol concentrations results. The appropriate treatment is to suppress cortisol secretion with an exogenous glucocorticoid having little or no mineralocorticoid activity, such as dexamethasone or prednisone.

The active ingredient in licorice, glycyrrhizic acid, is a competitive inhibitor of 11β-HSD. Thus, licorice intoxication can cause hypertension by the same mechanism as spontaneously occurring 11β-HSD deficiency. Licorice intoxication can usually be excluded by history. The most common source of licorice in the United States is chewing tobacco.

All causes of nonaldosterone-mediated renin-angiotensin–independent mineralocorticoid excess except for malignancy should "respond" to adrenal suppression with dexamethasone, 2 mg/day. If this measure fails, especially in the presence of an adrenal mass, adrenal malignancy is suggested. When adrenal suppression is successful, hydrocortisone, 12 to 15 mg/m²/day, should be used for long-term treatment.

Renin-angiotensin–dependent mineralocorticoid excess is seen with common disorders (Table 240–5).

Table 240–4 • COMMON CAUSES OF RENIN-ANGIOTENSIN–INDEPENDENT MINERALOCORTICOID EXCESS

Aldosterone-secreting adenoma
Adrenal cancer
Congenital adrenal hyperplasia
   11-Hydroxylase deficiency
   17-Hydroxylase deficiency
   11β-Hydroxysteroid dehydrogenase deficiency
Licorice intoxication
Glucocorticoid-suppressible hyperaldosteronism

Table 240–5 • COMMON CAUSES OF RENIN-ANGIOTENSIN–DEPENDENT MINERALOCORTICOID EXCESS

Vomiting
Diuretics
Edematous disorders
   Congestive heart failure
   Hepatic cirrhosis
   Nephrotic syndrome
Renal ischemia
Bartter's syndrome
Renin-secreting tumors

ADRENAL HYPOFUNCTION

Glucocorticoid Deficiency

DIAGNOSIS. A broad spectrum of signs and symptoms can herald the presence of glucocorticoid deficiency. At one extreme is the chronic syndrome, characterized by symptoms of malaise, anorexia, and orthostatic hypotension. Occasionally, vague abdominal pain can occur. Signs include weight loss, hypotension with an orthostatic component, and, in certain cases, a melanin-based hyperpigmentation of the skin. The routine laboratory picture reveals a normochromic normocytic anemia, relative lymphocytosis, often with an unexplained eosinophilia, mild prerenal azotemia, and hyponatremia. If aldosterone secretion is impaired by the process, hyperkalemia can also be observed. At the other extreme is the acute syndrome, characterized by rapidly evolving agitation, confusion, fever, and abdominal pain, all associated with arterial hypotension. As the hypotension evolves into shock, it is relatively unresponsive to volume replacement and pressor agents and imitates the hemodynamic characteristics of pump failure in association with decreased vascular resistance. The laboratory findings are the same as those found in the chronic syndrome. Untreated, the acute syndrome quickly leads to coma and death. When initially seen, the symptoms and signs of most patients with adrenal insufficiency lie somewhere on the continuum between these two extremes.

The diagnosis of glucocorticoid deficiency is confirmed by the inability of the adrenal glands to respond normally to an ACTH challenge. Synthetic ACTH, 250 μg, is administered intravenously, and plasma cortisol is determined 45 and 60 minutes later. The normal adrenal gland produces plasma cortisol concentrations of 20 μg/dL or more. Any value lower than 20 μg/dL implies a degree of adrenal compromise. Because the differential diagnosis of adrenal insufficiency relies on the plasma concentration of ACTH, it is prudent to draw a blood sample for ACTH before the administration of ACTH and "hold" the sample in the laboratory pending results of the plasma cortisol determination.

DIFFERENTIAL DIAGNOSIS AND TREATMENT. The initial task in the differential diagnosis of glucocorticoid deficiency is to define whether or not the process is ACTH dependent (Table 240–6). ACTH-dependent glucocorticoid deficiency implies disordered function of the hypothalamus and/or pituitary gland leading to ACTH deficiency. ACTH-independent glucocorticoid deficiency is caused by disordered adrenal function, such as destruction of the gland by an infectious process such as tuberculosis. This distinction is best made on the basis of plasma ACTH concentrations measured at the time of glucocorticoid deficiency (i.e., before treatment with glucocorticoid has been initiated). ACTH concentrations in or below the normal range imply an ACTH-dependent process. ACTH concentrations above the normal range imply an ACTH-independent process.

GLUCOCORTICOID DEFICIENCY RELATED TO ADRENAL SUPPRESSION

The most common cause of ACTH-dependent glucocorticoid deficiency is hypothalamic-pituitary-adrenal "suppression" by exogenously administered glucocorticoids, either iatrogenic or factitious. Whether adrenal suppression develops as a result of exogenous glucocorticoid administration depends on three variables: the dose of the glucocorticoid administered, the duration of administration, and the schedule of administration. It is unusual for clinically manifest adrenal suppression to develop with doses of glucocorticoid equal to or less than the daily replacement dose of the preparation used—20 mg/day of hydrocortisone, 5 mg/day of prednisone or prednisolone, and 0.5 mg/day of dexamethasone. Given doses that exceed these limits, it is unusual for clinically manifest glucocorticoid deficiency to develop if the duration of administration is less than 3 weeks. Finally, the dosage schedule can affect the rapidity with which the final state of adrenal suppression is reached. Glucocorticoids given as a single dose upon awakening in the morning are the least suppressive; glucocorticoids given in divided doses throughout the day are the most suppressive. Thus, at one extreme are patients given decreasing doses of prednisone for 14 days to treat an acute inflammatory process such as poison ivy. Signs and symptoms of glucocorticoid deficiency following cessation of the medication are extremely unlikely. At the other extreme are patients treated with large doses of glucocorticoid given in divided doses for long periods for the treatment of disorders such as chronic obstructive pulmonary disease. Many of the stigmata of Cushing's syndrome develop in these patients. These patients will develop the signs and symptoms of glucocorticoid deficiency within 48 hours if the glucocorticoid treatment is stopped for any reason. The clinical manifestations of this deficiency can range from the chronic syndrome at one extreme to the acute syndrome at the other.

GLUCOCORTICOID DEFICIENCY CAUSED BY HYPOTHALAMIC-PITUITARY DISEASE

Destructive lesions of the hypothalamus and pituitary gland are a rare cause of ACTH-dependent glucocorticoid deficiency. Although this condition is uncommon, diagnosis is imperative because early therapeutic intervention can prevent many of the serious sequelae of these tumors, including blindness. Examples include pituitary tumor, metastatic tumors to the region, sarcoid, amyloid, craniopharyngioma, and Rathke's pouch cyst. Pituitary infections such as actinomycosis and nocardiosis and vascular accidents such as Sheehan's syndrome also can lead to adrenal insufficiency. The most direct approach to the diagnosis of these lesions is imaging with CT scan using contrast enhancement or with MRI following gadolinium administration. A rare cause of ACTH-dependent glucocorticoid deficiency is autoimmune lymphocytic hypophysitis.

Treatment of chronic ACTH-dependent glucocorticoid insufficiency consists of replacing the missing hormones. Glucocorticoid should be replaced in the form of hydrocortisone, the naturally occurring glucocorticoid in humans, at a rate of 12 to 15 mg/m^2/day. Cortisol is secreted in bursts, between 7 and 10 per day, clustering in the morning hours. To reproduce this pattern with replacement steroid is impossible with the currently available methods. Empirically, however, it has been found that patients do as well with a single morning dose of cortisol as with divided doses, and compliance is simplified with this regimen. Clinical measures best monitor the adequacy of replacement: anorexia, weight loss, and hyponatremia suggest underreplacement; weight gain, plethora, and supraclavicular fat deposition suggest over-replacement. The current standard of practice is to increase the cortisol dose in the context of "stress," actual or anticipated. The dose of cortisol is doubled for the duration of the stress and returned to replacement levels immediately upon cessation of the stress. Typical stresses include febrile illness; nausea and vomiting; trauma such as lacerations, contusions, and fractures; and surgical procedures, including dental extraction. Acute glucocorticoid deficiency is treated with large doses of cortisol given intravenously, 100 mg every 6 hours, coupled with emergency support of blood pressure with volume expansion and pressors when indicated.

Table 240–6 • CAUSES OF GLUCOCORTICOID DEFICIENCY

ACTH-Independent Causes
  Tuberculosis
  Autoimmune (idiopathic)
  Other rare causes
    Fungal infection
    Adrenal hemorrhage
    Metastases
    Sarcoidosis
    Amyloidosis
    Adrenoleukodystrophy
    Adrenomyeloneuropathy
    HIV infection
    Congenital adrenal hyperplasia
    Medications (ketoconazole, o,p'-DDD)
ACTH-Dependent Causes
  Hypothalamic-pituitary-adrenal suppression
    Exogenous
      Glucocorticoid
      ACTH
    Endogenous—cure of Cushing's syndrome
  Hypothalamic-pituitary lesions
    Neoplasm
      Primary pituitary tumor
      Metastatic tumor
    Craniopharyngioma
    Infection
      Tuberculosis
      Actinomycosis
      Nocardiosis
  Sarcoid
  Head trauma
  Isolated ACTH deficiency

ACTH = adrenocorticotropic hormone; HIV = human immunodeficiency virus; o,p'-DDD = o,p'-dichlorodiphenyl dichloroethane.

Primary Adrenal Insufficiency

The most common cause of primary adrenal insufficiency worldwide is tuberculosis. Tuberculosis causes adrenal insufficiency by destroying the adrenal cortex and replacing it with caseating granulomas. The most common cause of adrenal insufficiency in the industrialized West is an autoimmune process, usually as part of the polyglandular deficiency syndrome. In this disorder, an autoimmune "adrenalitis" leads to destruction of the adrenal cortex. This disease has two forms, types I and II. The relative features of the two forms are detailed in Table 240–7. Type I is a disease of childhood with a mean age of onset of 12 years. Type II begins at an average age of 24 years. The dominant features of type I disease are adrenal insufficiency, hypoparathyroidism, and mucocutaneous candidiasis. The dominant features of type II disease are adrenal insufficiency, autoimmune thyroid disease, and insulin-dependent diabetes mellitus. Other important differences include the patterns of inheritance. Type I is transmitted as an autosomal recessive trait occurring across sibships, whereas type II has a "dominant" pattern of inheritance appearing in multiple generations of an affected family. Also, type I disease has no HLA association, whereas type II is associated with the DR3/DR4 haplotypes. Both disorders appear to be mediated by an autoimmune process. For example, circulating antibodies to one or more endocrine organs are found in most patients, and defects in T-lymphocyte function such as a decrease in "suppressor" activity are described.

All of the clinically important fungi except *Monilia* can cause adrenal destruction. The most common cause is histoplasmosis, which is due to an organism particularly prominent in the Ohio and Tennessee valleys and along the Piedmont Plateau of the Mid-Atlantic states. South American blastomycosis is the next most common fungal cause of adrenal insufficiency, followed by North American blastomycosis, coccidioidomycosis, and cryptococcosis. The pathophysiology of fungal adrenalitis is much like that of tuberculosis—destruction leading to adrenal enlargement with caseating granuloma formation. If healing occurs, the adrenal glands can shrink in size, sometimes resuming a relatively normal volume. The healing process is often accompanied by calcification.

The advent of CT has revealed adrenal hemorrhage as a more frequent cause of adrenal insufficiency than had been recognized previously. The usual setting is a stressed individual receiving long-term anticoagulation for the prevention of pulmonary or cardiac emboli or other thrombotic phenomena. Typically, affected patients complain of back pain, followed in a few days by onset of the initial signs and symptoms of adrenal insufficiency.

Metastases to the adrenal gland are common, with a frequency as high as 70% in patients with disseminated breast or lung cancer. Adrenal insufficiency as a result of metastases, however, is uncommon, although moderate abnormalities in adrenal function can often be detected in patients with bilateral adrenal metastases. Tumors commonly associated with adrenal insufficiency are cancers of the breast, lung, stomach, colon, melanoma, and some lymphomas.

Acquired immunodeficiency syndrome can be associated with adrenal insufficiency in its late stages. Cytomegalovirus infection of the adrenal glands commonly accompanies this condition, as does infection with *Mycobacterium avium-intracellulare* and the various fungi that can colonize and destroy the adrenal glands. The plasma cortisol response to ACTH administration is abnormal in 10 to 15% of patients with AIDS and its advanced complications.

Adrenoleukodystrophy is an inborn abnormality of long-chain fatty acid metabolism that causes adrenal insufficiency in association with several neurologically impaired phenotypes. Newborn adrenoleukodystrophy is transmitted as an autosomal recessive trait. Adrenoleukodystrophy, also known as brown Schilder's disease (brown being an adjective describing the hyperpigmentation of the skin) or sudanophilic leukodystrophy, is an X-linked disease of children characterized by rapidly progressive central demyelination leading to seizures, dementia, cortical blindness, coma, and death. Death usually occurs before puberty is complete. X-linked adrenomyeloneuropathy is a disease of young adults characterized by a slowly progressive mixed upper and lower motor and sensory neuropathy leading to an ascending spastic paraparesis. Signs and symptoms of spinocerebellar degeneration appear in some cases. Both forms of the disease are associated with progressive failure of all steroid-secreting cells leading to adrenal and gonadal failure. The metabolic marker for these diseases is an elevated circulating level of long-chain fatty acids, C_{26} and greater in length. The cause of this abnormality seems to be an abnormal peroxisomal transporter protein that prevents appropriate metabolism of the very long chain fatty acids. Several treatments have been tried, but only autologous bone marrow transplantation appears to have any chance of success.

Other rare causes of primary adrenal insufficiency include amyloidosis, congenital unresponsiveness to ACTH, congenital adrenal hypoplasia, and familial glucocorticoid insufficiency.

Treatment of ACTH-independent glucocorticoid deficiency is the same as that outlined for ACTH-dependent glucocorticoid deficiency, except that the addition of a mineralocorticoid is usually required because adrenal cortical destruction impairs both cortisol and aldosterone secretion. The available orally active mineralocorticoid is fludrocortisone acetate (Florinef). It is equipotent with aldosterone. The secretion rate of aldosterone in salt-replete humans is about 100 μg/day. Thus, fludrocortisone, 100 μg/day, is the appropriate replacement dose. The drug has a wide therapeutic window, and no specific monitoring for treatment effect is necessary other than an occasional plasma potassium concentration.

Mineralocorticoid Deficiency

DIAGNOSIS. The major clinical manifestations of mineralocorticoid deficiency are hyponatremia, hyperkalemia, and mild metabolic acidosis. These disorders can lead to profound muscle weakness and cardiac arrhythmias. Combined glucocorticoid and mineralocorticoid deficiency is a common cause of this picture and should initially be excluded with an ACTH stimulation test. If that test result is normal, the diagnosis of isolated hypoaldosteronism depends on the demonstration of an inappropriately low circulating aldosterone level. The causes of isolated hypoaldosteronism are listed in Table 240–8.

DIFFERENTIAL DIAGNOSIS AND TREATMENT. Selective hypoaldosteronism was, until recently, believed to be rare. Recent studies, however, show that it accounts for as many as 10% of cases of unexplained hyperkalemia. The causes of hypoaldosteronism can be divided into renin-angiotensin–dependent (hyporeninemic) and renin-angiotensin–independent (hyper–reninemic) causes. Differentiation is based on plasma renin activity. The usual test is a measurement of plasma renin activity following 4 hours of upright posture. Levels in the normal or low range identify cases that are renin-angiotensin dependent, whereas high levels identify cases that are renin-angiotensin independent.

Renin deficiency, overall, is the most common cause of selective aldosterone deficiency. It is usually found in elderly subjects with mild, nonoliguric renal disease. Many such patients have insulin-dependent diabetes, and diabetic nephropathy is thought to be an important contributing abnormality. Other causes of

Table 240–7 • POLYENDOCRINE DEFICIENCY SYNDROMES		
FEATURE	**TYPE I**	**TYPE II**
Age of onset	12 yr	24 yr
Adrenal insufficiency	+	+
Diabetes mellitus	–	+
Autoimmune thyroid disease	–	+
Hypoparathyroidism	+	–
Mucocutaneous candidiasis	+	–
Hypogonadism	+	+/–
Chronic active hepatitis	+	–
Pernicious anemia	+	–
Vitiligo	+	+

Table 240–8 • CAUSES OF ISOLATED HYPOALDOSTERONISM
Renin-Angiotensin–Dependent
Hyporeninemic hypoaldosteronism
Autonomic neuropathy
Prostaglandin synthesis inhibitors
Renin-Angiotensin–Independent
Inhibition of aldosterone synthesis
Heparin
Cyclosporine
Calcium channel blockers
Following resection of an aldosterone-secreting adenoma
18-Hydroxylase deficiency
Aldosterone resistance (pseudohypoaldosteronism)

renin-angiotensin–dependent hypoaldosteronism include autonomic dysfunction associated with prolonged bedrest and, rarely, treatment with prostaglandin synthesis inhibitors such as indomethacin.

The causes of renin-angiotensin–independent hypoaldosteronism include all causes of ACTH-independent adrenal insufficiency listed in Table 240–6. In this setting, selective hypoaldosteronism can result if treatment is confined to glucocorticoid replacement. The other causes of this disorder center on alterations in the synthesis and secretion of aldosterone and include long-term heparin administration and the "salt-wasting" forms of congenital adrenal hyperplasia (21-hydroxylase deficiency, 3β-hydroxysteroid dehydrogenase deficiency, and 17-hydroxylase deficiency). Again, treating these disorders with glucocorticoid alone is a common cause of selective hypoaldosteronism. Finally, any defect in the conversion of corticosterone to aldosterone, such as 18-hydroxylase deficiency, leads to selective hypoaldosteronism.

Treating selective hypoaldosteronism of any cause is straightforward. Aldosterone deficiency does not produce clinical symptoms unless the subject is "salt deprived." This condition is unlikely to occur at levels of salt intake greater than 10 mEq/kg/day. For adults, this amount equals about 4 g of sodium chloride per day, which is characteristic of the average American diet. Thus, a simple way to treat selective hypoaldosteronism is to ensure adequate dietary salt intake, which in the United States is not a problem in young and otherwise healthy subjects. This approach fails, however, in patients with "fetish" diets or those who cannot maintain an adequate oral intake of salt for any reason. Important in this regard are the dietary restrictions that frequently accompany old age and those often imposed on infants and toddlers. In these cases, it is advisable to supply exogenous mineralocorticoid. Fludrocortisone is the only available preparation of orally active mineralocorticoid. It is equipotent with aldosterone and is given in doses that approximate the daily production rate of aldosterone in a salt-replete individual, 100 μg/day. The preparation can be given as a single daily dose with the morning meal. The drug's therapeutic window is wide, so overtreatment is unlikely. Thus, an occasional serum potassium concentration measurement is adequate to monitor the efficacy of treatment.

DISORDERS OF COMBINED INSUFFICIENCY AND EXCESS

The Congenital Adrenal Hyperplasias

Defects in the synthesis of cortisol lead to compensatory stimulation of adrenal steroidogenesis to maintain normal plasma cortisol concentrations. Such stimulation inevitably leads to an accumulation of the steroid biosynthetic intermediate immediately before the enzymic defect in the biosynthetic cascade. Clinically, the result is expressed as glucocorticoid deficiency (which can be so mild as to be inapparent or so severe as to be life threatening) in association with mineralocorticoid excess or deficiency and androgen excess or deficiency. These disorders are usually classified as "salt wasting," "hypertensive," "virilizing," or "feminizing," depending on the combination of hormone excess and deficiency. They are presented in detail in Chapter 246. Only the attenuated or "nonclassic" form of 21-hydroxylase deficiency is presented here.

21-Hydroxylase deficiency is one of the most prevalent autosomal recessive disorders, with a heterozygote frequency that may be as high as one in five. Although congenital in nature, the disorder usually makes its initial appearance with the onset of puberty. Hirsutism, oligomenorrhea, and cystic acne are the most common clinical manifestations. The disorder is identical in clinical presentation to idiopathic hirsutism–polycystic ovarian disease and cannot be differentiated from this disorder without specifically examining adrenal steroidogenesis to look for the 2l-hydroxylase block. Such examination is best done in the context of an ACTH stimulation test performed in the usual way, with measurements of 17-hydroxyprogesterone made 45 and 60 minutes after administration of the ACTH. Normal subjects do not exceed 17-hydroxyprogesterone levels of 350 ng/dL, but patients with the disorder achieve plasma levels greater than 1500 ng/dL. The incidence of this disorder in young hirsute patients varies between 1 and 30%, depending on ethnic background, and averages about 5% for the population as a whole.

As with the other congenital adrenal hyperplasias, treatment consists of exogenous glucocorticoid replacement to circumvent the deficiency in cortisol biosynthesis. The usual approach is to administer cortisol (Cortef), 12 to 15 mg/m²/day as a single morning dose. Care should be taken that the adrenal gland is not completely suppressed by the replacement regimen chosen, which can be assessed by an ACTH stimulation test 3 to 6 months following the initiation of treatment.

DISORDERS OF TISSUE RESPONSIVENESS

The Steroid Resistance Syndromes

Two disorders of end-organ resistance are relevant to a discussion of disorders of adrenal function: glucocorticoid resistance and mineralocorticoid resistance.

Glucocorticoid resistance is rare; only 17 separate probands have been described to date. The disease is characterized by markedly elevated indices of cortisol production (increased urine free cortisol excretion) in the absence of any of the clinical stigmata of Cushing's syndrome. Occasionally, signs and symptoms of mineralocorticoid and androgen excess are responsible for bringing the patient to medical attention. Like the situation in congenital adrenal hyperplasia, androgen and mineralocorticoid concentrations are elevated in this syndrome as a byproduct of the increased adrenal steroidogenesis necessary to produce enough cortisol to maintain life. The cause of the disease, which has not been proved in all cases, is a defect in the ligand-binding domain of the glucocorticoid receptor. The disease is transmitted as an autosomal recessive trait, with heterozygote subjects sometimes manifesting attenuated forms of the disorder.

The diagnosis is suggested by finding elevated rates of urine free cortisol excretion in a subject with none of the stigmata of Cushing's syndrome. The diagnosis is confirmed by demonstrating abnormal binding characteristics of the glucocorticoid receptor, usually in mononuclear leukocytes. Treatment should be reserved for persons manifesting signs and symptoms of androgen or mineralocorticoid excess and consists of the exogenous administration of a synthetic glucocorticoid, usually dexamethasone, in doses sufficient to bring the urine free cortisol excretion into the normal range. Such treatment is usually accompanied by remission of the associated steroid excess syndromes.

Mineralocorticoid resistance is characterized by elevated levels of aldosterone and increased plasma renin activity in association with signs and symptoms of mineralocorticoid deficiency. The disorder is generally referred to as *pseudohypoaldosteronism*. It is commonly divided into two subtypes, but only type I appears to fulfill the usual criteria for receptor-mediated end-organ resistance.

Type I pseudohypoaldosteronism is a rare inherited disorder characterized by salt loss and failure to thrive in infancy, most commonly between 5 and 7 days of age. The cause appears to be an abnormal mineralocorticoid receptor, with decreased binding affinity and decreased receptor number both described. Hyponatremia, hyperkalemia, and metabolic acidosis in association with elevated plasma and urine aldosterone and elevated plasma renin activity make the diagnosis. Treatment is to replace salt at a rate of 10 to 40 mEq/kg/day.

SUGGESTED READINGS
Arlt W, Allolio B: Adrenal insufficiency. Lancet 2003;361:1881–1893. *An overview including presentation, diagnosis, and therapy.*
Berger J, Moser HW, Forss PS: Leukodystrophies: Recent developments in genetics, molecular biology, pathogenesis, and treatment. Curr Opin Neurol 2001;14:305–312. *The latest on this devastating disease.*
Dorin RI, Qualls CR, Crapo LM: Diagnosis of adrenal insufficiency. Ann Intern Med 2003;139:194–204. *A practical overview with emphasis on the cosyntropin test.*
Hallfeldt KK, Mussack T, Trupka A, et al: Laparoscopic lateral adrenalectomy versus open posterior adrenalectomy for the treatment of benign adrenal tumors. Surg Endosc 2003;17:264–267. *Laparoscopic adrenalectomy is technically demanding but safe in high-volume centers.*
Lamberts SW: Hereditary glucocorticoid resistance. Ann Endocrinol (Paris) 2001;62:164–167. *A thorough review of this unrecognized condition.*
Malchoff CD: Carney complex: Clarity and complexity. J Clin Endocrinol Metab 2000;85:4010–4012. *Good update on the syndrome.*
Raff H, Findling JW: A physiologic approach to diagnosis of the Cushing syndrome. Ann Intern Med 2003;138:980–991. *A well-referenced overview that emphasizes the physiology as well as practical diagnosis, with useful flow diagrams.*

241 THE ADRENAL MEDULLA, CATECHOLAMINES, AND PHEOCHROMOCYTOMA

Daniel T. O'Connor

The catecholamines (norepinephrine, epinephrine, and dopamine) serve as neurotransmitters and circulating hormones. Catecholamines acquire their name by the catechol (3,4-dihydroxyphenyl) modification of their aromatic (phenyl) rings. *Norepinephrine* is the amine neurotransmitter released from terminals of postganglionic axons of the sympathetic nervous system, as well as from central nervous system noradrenergic axons. Adrenal medullary chromaffin cells store both epinephrine and norepinephrine in catecholamine secretory vesicles.

Chromaffin cells derive embryologically from neuroectoderm. Precursor cells differentiate in the center of the adrenal gland in response to cortisol, after which the precursors again differentiate into sympathetic neurons in response to nerve growth factor. A few such cells also migrate to form paraganglia, collections of chromaffin cells on both sides of the aorta. The largest such periaortic cluster, often found near the level of the inferior mesenteric artery, is referred to as the organ of Zuckerkandl. Both chromaffin cells and postganglionic sympathetic axons are part of the effector limb of the sympathetic branch of the autonomic nervous system and are innervated by thoracolumbar preganglionic axons emerging from the spinal cord.

Catecholamines are released from the adrenal medulla into the circulation through the adrenal vein. Norepinephrine from sympathetic neurons is released presynaptically and acts as a cell-to-cell neurotransmitter. Circulating plasma norepinephrine influences blood pressure and heart rate under only the most extreme circumstances of sympathetic activation. Relatively selective adrenal catecholamine release occurs during syncope and insulin-evoked hypoglycemia, whereas active, dynamic exercise selectively stimulates sympathetic neuronal norepinephrine release.

CATECHOLAMINE BIOSYNTHESIS AND METABOLISM

Catecholamine biosynthesis starts with the essential dietary amino acid phenylalanine, which is converted to tyrosine by phenylalanine hydroxylase. Tyrosine is hydroxylated to dihydroxyphenylalanine (DOPA) by the action of tyrosine hydroxylase, the rate-limiting enzymatic step in catecholamine biosynthesis. DOPA decarboxylase then converts DOPA to dopamine, which is carried by the vesicular monoamine transporter from the cytosol into the catecholamine storage vesicle, where dopamine β-hydroxylase converts it to norepinephrine. In sympathetic axons and in 15 to 20% of chromaffin cells, norepinephrine is the final catecholamine product. In 80 to 85% of chromaffin cells, a further enzymatic step occurs: phenylethanolamine-N-methyltransferase, a cytosolic enzyme, catalyzes the N-methylation of norepinephrine to epinephrine.

Catecholamines in noradrenergic axons and chromaffin cells are sequestered from the cytosol in membrane-limited organelles called *catecholamine storage vesicles* (or chromaffin granules in chromaffin cells). Chromaffin granule cores contain not only catecholamines but also soluble proteins such as dopamine β-hydroxylase and chromogranin A.

The process of catecholamine discharge from chromaffin cells and sympathetic axons is *exocytosis,* wherein all soluble components of the granule are co-released and ultimately make their way to the circulation.

Neuronal uptake ("reuptake") is the major route of norepinephrine removal from synaptic clefts (Fig. 241–1). Characteristics of this process are its location at the presynaptic axonal membrane, high affinity, stereoselectivity, saturability, dependence on extracellular sodium, and specific pharmacologic inhibition by agents such as tricyclic antidepressants (e.g., desipramine) and cocaine. Non-neuronal uptake may be mediated by the organic cation transporter (OCT) family, especially OCT3. After neuronal uptake, cytosolic catecholamines can be either retransported into storage vesicles or deaminated by the enzyme monoamine oxidase (MAO) to yield the unstable intermediate dihydroxyphenylglycolaldehyde, which is then metabolized to dihydroxyphenylglycol (DHPG). The enzyme catechol O-methyltransferase (COMT), which acts on both catecholamines and DHPG, is present mainly in the cytosol of liver and kidney cells and also in chromaffin cells. COMT adds a methyl group to one of the hydroxyl oxygens on the catecholamines' dihydroxyphenyl rings to yield either metanephrine (i.e., methoxyepinephrine from epinephrine), normetanephrine (i.e., methoxynorepinephrine from norepinephrine), or methoxytyramine (from dopamine). The metanephrines can then be deaminated by MAO to yield vanillylmandelic acid (VMA), whereas deamination of methoxytyramine by MAO yields homovanillic acid. DHPG is also a substrate for COMT in the formation of methoxyhydroxyphenylglycol (MHPG). In the liver, alcohol dehydrogenase oxidizes MHPG to VMA. Thus, complete enzymatic degradation of catecholamines to VMA (from epinephrine or norepinephrine) or homovanillic acid (from dopamine) involves the sequential action of two enzymes (MAO and COMT), either of which may initiate the process, followed by an alcohol dehydrogenase step in the liver. In the blood stream, catecholamines have a very short half-life, 1 to 2 minutes. They are cleared from the circulation largely by neuronal uptake, but in addition are subject to direct renal excretion or sulfoconjugation of a ring hydroxyl group by SULT1A3 in the gastrointestinal tract.

CATECHOLAMINE ACTION

Catecholamine receptors are specific for ligands and are classified as subtypes of the α ($\alpha_{1a,b,c}$, $\alpha_{2a,b,c}$) and β ($\beta_{1,2,3}$) classes. The hemodynamic effects of circulating norepinephrine require extreme concentrations. Whereas plasma norepinephrine may vary normally over a range of 200 to 1000 pg/mL during physiologic stimulation of sympathetic neuronal activity, far higher concentrations of infused norepinephrine (in excess of 1000 to 2000 pg/mL) are required to substantially affect the blood pressure or heart rate. At β-receptors,

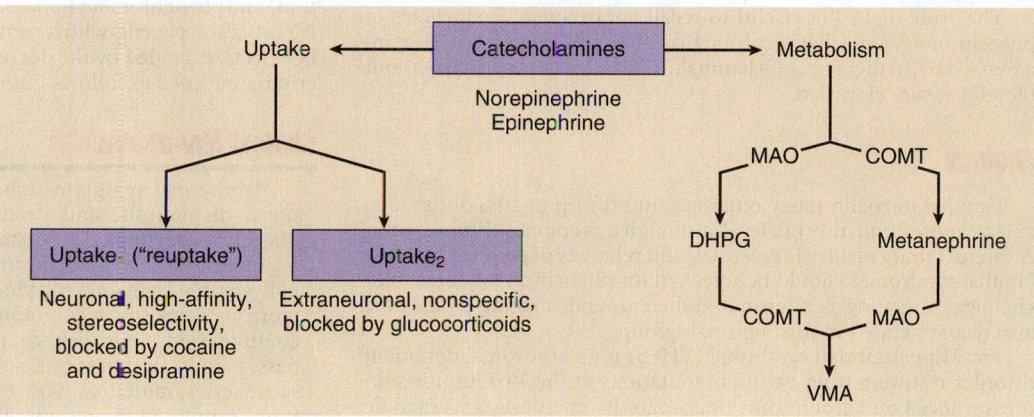

FIGURE 241–1 • Catecholamine disposition and metabolism. COMT = catechol-O-methyltransferase; DHPG = dihydroxyphenylglycol; MAO = monoamine oxidase; VMA = vanillylmandelic acid.

norepinephrine is a strong agonist at β_1 (cardiac inotropic and chronotropic) sites, although a relatively weak agonist at β_2 (vascular, vasodilatory) sites. At α-receptors, norepinephrine is an effective agonist at both α_1 (vascular, vasoconstrictive) and α_2 (neuronal and vascular) sites. Infused norepinephrine acutely raises both systolic and diastolic blood pressure by actions on both β_1- and α-adrenergic receptors, with vasoconstriction accompanied by reflex bradycardia. The hemodynamic effects of circulating epinephrine (50 to 500 pg/mL) differ from those of norepinephrine. At β-receptors, epinephrine is an agonist at both the β_1 and β_2 sites. It is also a more potent agonist than norepinephrine at both the α_1 and α_2 sites. During acute infusion, it increases systolic blood pressure, heart rate, and cardiac output, with a fall in diastolic blood pressure and systemic resistance, the latter effects resulting from actions at β_2-adrenergic receptors.

With chronic excess of circulating catecholamines, the hemodynamic profile may change substantially, in part as a consequence of desensitization of catecholamine target organs resulting from adaptive changes in both receptor and postreceptor responses.

PHEOCHROMOCYTOMA

Pheochromocytoma is a chromaffin cell neoplasm that typically causes symptoms and signs of episodic catecholamine release, including paroxysmal hypertension. The tumor is an unusual cause of hypertension and accounts for at most 0.1 to 0.2% of cases of high blood pressure. In population-based cancer studies, its frequency was about two cases per million population. The diagnosis of pheochromocytoma is typically made in young to middle-aged adults, most commonly in the fourth or fifth decade of life; about 10% of diagnoses are made in children (usually male). Autopsy series indicate that the incidence of pheochromocytoma increases progressively with age. In adults, no gender difference is seen in the incidence of pheochromocytoma.

About 90% of pheochromocytomas exist as solitary, unilateral, encapsulated adrenal medullary tumors. About 10% are bilateral, more commonly seen in several members of a family, 40 to 70% of whose members may have bilateral tumors. The tumors are vascular, and large ones often contain internal hemorrhagic or cystic areas. Reported sizes have ranged from less than 1 g to several kilograms; the average is about 40 g. About 10% of tumors are extra-adrenal (paragangliomas), and 90% of these are intra-abdominal, most commonly arising from chromaffin cells near the aortic bifurcation in the organ of Zuckerkandl or near the kidney. Other sites include the paravertebral sympathetic ganglia, the urinary bladder, other autonomic ganglia (celiac, superior, or inferior mesenteric), the thorax (including the posterior mediastinum, the heart, and paracardiac regions), and the neck (in sympathetic ganglia, the carotid body, cranial nerves, or the glomus jugulare). Bilateral and extra-adrenal tumors are more common in children. Histologically, oval groups of cells, in clusters or "nests," stain for chromogranin A; a less frequently used stain identifies neuron-specific enolase. Fewer than 10% of the tumors are malignant; malignancy occurs more frequently in extra-adrenal tumors and is diagnosed by local invasion or distant metastases but cannot be judged reliably from the histologic appearance. Local invasion commonly involves adjacent vascular structures such as the inferior vena cava. Distant metastatic sites include bone, lung, lymph nodes, and liver. Bilateral adrenal medullary hyperplasia has been reported in gene carriers from kindreds with multiple endocrine neoplasia (MEN) type 2. This hyperplasia may be a precursor of pheochromocytoma.

The "rule of 10s" is useful to recall approximate frequencies of pheochromocytoma that vary from the usual: 10% bilateral, 10% extra-adrenal, 10% malignant, 10% familial, 10% pediatric, and 10% without blood pressure elevation.

Etiology

Familial pheochromocytomas account for up to 10% of the total and are more frequently bilateral, although less commonly malignant. A careful family history is essential, and relatives of patients with the familial syndromes should be screened for pheochromocytoma; biochemical screening is often not sufficient, and imaging studies are also recommended in this high-risk group.

Von Hippel-Lindau syndrome (VHLS) is an autosomal dominant disorder resulting from germline mutations at the *VHL* tumor suppressor locus on chromosome 3p25-p26. Its manifestations include pheochromocytoma (in about 14% of gene carriers), retinal angioma,

cerebellar hemangioblastoma, renal cysts and carcinoma, pancreatic cysts, and epididymal cystadenoma. Accordingly, all patients with pheochromocytoma deserve careful funduscopic examination. Pheochromocytoma occurs in cases of type 2 VHLS, in which missense mutations (especially Arg238Trp or Arg238Gln) lie in a region of the *VHL* gene product that binds transcriptional elongation factors. Pheochromocytomas do not occur in type 1 VHLS, which is caused by deletion or premature termination (nonsense) *VHL* mutations.

The MEN type 2A and type 2B (Sipple's syndrome) are autosomal dominant disorders arising from germline mutations on chromosome 10q11.2 in the *RET* proto-oncogene, which encodes a neurotrophin coreceptor tyrosine kinase. The features of MEN type 2A include pheochromocytoma (in about 40% of gene carriers), medullary thyroid carcinoma, and primary hyperparathyroidism (adenoma or hyperplasia). Because of this syndrome, it is wise to screen all pheochromocytoma patients for medullary thyroid carcinoma with serum calcitonin. MEN type 2B features include pheochromocytoma, medullary thyroid carcinoma, multiple mucosal neuromas (of the lips, tongue, buccal mucosa, eyelids, conjunctivae, corneas, and gastrointestinal tract), and a marfanoid body habitus (but without lens or aortic abnormalities). *RET* mutations in MEN type 2A affect one of five Cys residues in the juxtamembrane extracellular domain, perhaps resulting in intermolecular disulfide formation and consequent constitutive activation of the kinase. The most common *RET* mutation in MEN type 2B, Met981Thr, seems to alter the substrate specificity of the kinase.

The clinical presentation of pheochromocytoma may differ in MEN type 2 versus VHLS: MEN type 2 patients may be more symptomatic, have a higher incidence of hypertension, and have higher plasma metanephrines, but have lower plasma catecholamines than VHLS patients. Pheochromocytomas in VHLS patients exhibit a more noradrenergic phenotype characterized by selective increases in urinary and plasma normetanephrine and sometimes norepinephrine, whereas tumors in MEN type 2 patients exhibit an adrenergic phenotype, characterized by additional and consistent increases in plasma and urinary metanephrine, sometimes associated with increases in epinephrine.

Hereditary neurofibromatosis (von Recklinghausen's disease), an autosomal dominant disorder resulting from mutations at the *NF1* (neurofibromin) locus on chromosome 17q11.2, is manifested as neurofibromas and cafe au lait spots; about 1% of patients with neurofibromatosis have pheochromocytoma. Inactivating germline mutations at the SDHB (succinate dehydrogenase small subunit D) locus on chromosome 11q23 may also cause susceptibility to familial pheochromocytoma, as well as familial paraganglioma. Familial pheochromocytoma may also occur in isolation; whether such families represent disease processes etiologically distinct from VHLS or MEN is not clear.

In the 90 to 95% of pheochromocytomas that are sporadic, the cause of the neoplastic process remains obscure, although loss of heterozygosity on chromosomes 1p, 3p, 17p, and 22q suggests somatic cell deletion mutation of one autosomal allele at as-yet uncharacterized tumor suppressor loci.

Diagnosis

Because pheochromocytoma is a potentially curable form of hypertension, the diagnosis is worth considering in each new case of hypertension. However, because hypertension is so commonly encountered in clinical practice (approximately 20 to 25% of the adult population) and pheochromocytoma is so distinctly unusual (approximately 0.1 to 0.2% of patients with hypertension), laboratory evaluation should be selective, guided by the degree of clinical suspicion, and based on criteria outlined as follows (Table 241–1).

Clinical Manifestations

Paroxysmal symptoms (such as the triad of episodic palpitations, diaphoresis, and headache) are the classic features of pheochromocytoma. These paroxysmal "attacks" characteristically begin abruptly, may last for minutes to hours, and subside gradually, with a frequency varying from many times daily to one or more per week (most commonly) or even every few months. Less common symptoms include apprehension or anxiety, tremulousness, pain in the chest or abdomen, weakness, or weight loss. In some series, more than 90% of patients have experienced paroxysmal symptoms of one or more of the classic triad. Autopsy series

Table 241–1 • DIAGNOSTIC APPROACH TO PHEOCHROMOCYTOMA

Clinical clues or "tipoffs"
  History
    Paroxysmal symptoms (classic triad is headache, diaphoresis, palpitations)
    History of extraordinarily labile or refractory hypertension
    Family history of pheochromocytoma, von Hippel-Lindau syndrome, or multiple endocrine neoplasia
    Incidental adrenal abnormality on abdominal imaging test (rarely)
  Physical examination
    Labile, refractory hypertension
    Orthostatic hypotension
    von Hippel-Lindau syndrome– or multiple endocrine neoplasia–associated findings (retinal angiomas, thyroid enlargement, mucosal neuromas)
Biochemical confirmation (only after clue or tipoff; begin with urinary tests)
  Urinary catecholamines and metabolites (24-hr sample or 2-hr sample after a paroxysm; metanephrines, the initial screening test)
  Plasma catecholamines (if urinary values are equivocal; take care to obtain a basal, resting sample)
  Clonidine suppression test (if plasma catecholamines are in the equivocal 1000 to 2000 pg/mL range)
  Plasma chromogranin A (storage vesicle protein released with catecholamines; also elevated by renal failure)
Anatomic localization (only after biochemical confirmation)
  By morphology (most sensitive, less specific)
    Computed tomography (the imaging test most frequently obtained)
    Magnetic resonance imaging (may have advantages for extra-adrenal tumors)
  By function (most specific, less sensitive)
    Radiolabeled metaiodobenzylguanidine scanning (accumulates in functioning chromaffin tissue)

indicate that as many as 50 to 75% of pheochromocytomas may be undiagnosed during life, thus suggesting that many pheochromocytomas do not give rise to these classic symptomatic features. Patients older than 60 years with pheochromocytoma are especially likely to report minor or no symptoms.

Other features in the history may suggest pheochromocytoma. Affected patients may report an increase in blood pressure after receiving certain antihypertensive drugs, especially β-adrenergic antagonists and guanethidine, or they may experience a remarkable fall in blood pressure after receiving α_1-adrenergic antagonists such as prazosin. Hypertension in such patients is relatively refractory to medical management. A history of extreme blood pressure lability during intubation, surgery, or induction of general anesthesia also suggests possible pheochromocytoma. A family history of pheochromocytoma, VHLS, or MEN type 2 should prompt an evaluation for pheochromocytoma. Paroxysmal symptoms on micturition or bladder distention, or painless gross hematuria may suggest pheochromocytoma of the bladder; the diagnosis is confirmed by cystoscopy.

Hypertension, usually severe and refractory to antihypertensive medications, is the cardinal sign of pheochromocytoma, although it is nonspecific and may be insensitive. In about half of patients, hypertension is sustained, with intermittent blood pressure surges in half or more of these; in about 40%, hypertension is paroxysmal, with relatively normal blood pressure between surges. Hypertensive surges may be precipitated by abdominal manipulation, but generally no antecedent is noted. The heart rate is usually elevated during blood pressure surges but may decline as a result of physiologic reflex bradycardia. Orthostatic hypotension is variably observed. As many as 15 to 20% of patients may have cholesterol gallstones.

Diagnosis

LABORATORY DIAGNOSIS

Because hypertension is so common and pheochromocytoma so rare, further biochemical evaluation for pheochromocytoma in hypertensive patients should be selective and focused on subjects who display

some relevant clue to pheochromocytoma on history, physical examination, or screening laboratory evaluation. If interpretation of urinary measurements is not clear-cut, evaluation should proceed to plasma measurements, which require more careful sampling technique. The number and diversity of biochemical tests obtained should parallel the clinical index of suspicion. If suspicion is low, a single screening test may suffice, usually 24-hour urinary metanephrine excretion. If suspicion is high, multiple tests, both urine and plasma, are in order. Because anatomic or imaging studies may detect nonspecific adrenal abnormalities in up to 2% of the population, such studies should not be undertaken unless biochemical tests are positive.

ROUTINE TESTS. Results of routine screening tests obtained for other purposes (such as general health maintenance) may provide tipoffs. Hyperglycemia is common, and about half of patients with pheochromocytoma manifest carbohydrate intolerance; frank diabetes requiring insulin is unusual. Lactic acidosis occurs rarely, even without shock. Serum lactate dehydrogenase activity may be elevated from adrenal isoenzyme 3. Rarely, pheochromocytoma may be an incidental finding on computed tomography (CT) or magnetic resonance imaging (MRI) scans of the abdomen undertaken for other indications.

URINE TESTS. Widely available tests measure urinary free (unconjugated) catecholamines and catecholamine metabolites: the metanephrines and VMA. A 24-hour urine sample is collected, and creatinine is measured in the same sample as an index of adequacy and completeness of collection. Of the available urinary tests, increased fractionated metanephrines (separately measured normetanephrine and metanephrine) have the highest diagnostic sensitivity for pheochromocytoma. Normal test results for urinary fractionated metanephrines are therefore useful for excluding pheochromocytoma. Inadequate specificity makes it difficult to reliably confirm pheochromocytoma from an increased test result. Urinary VMA is less sensitive than metanephrines. Urinary excretion of metanephrines and VMA remains normal until the very end stage of renal disease, so elevated levels validly diagnose pheochromocytoma.

Artifactual false-positive assay results have been greatly minimized in recent years with the introduction of more specific assay methods based on separation of catecholamines and metabolites in urine by high-pressure liquid chromatography. False-positive increases in free catecholamines may result from exogenous sources, such as catecholamines (which may be administered surreptitiously), α-methyldopa (but VMA excretion is characteristically normal), L-DOPA, labetalol, sympathomimetic amines (which release endogenous catecholamines from their stores), and fluorescent drugs such as tetracycline. Misleading elevations of endogenous catecholamines may occur as a consequence of the sympathoadrenal responses to shock, hypoglycemia, physical exertion, increased intracranial pressure, or withdrawal of central α_2-agonists such as clonidine. False-positive metanephrine elevations may result from excessive catecholamines (exogenous or endogenous) or the use of tricyclic antidepressants, MAO inhibitors, or propranolol (which interferes with the spectrophotometric assay). False-positive elevations in VMA levels may occur after the patient ingests carbidopa (a peripheral DOPA decarboxylase inhibitor) or MAO inhibitors.

BLOOD TESTS. Biochemical tests on blood samples offer the advantage of patient convenience but the disadvantage that even minor physical or mental stress can result in false-positive elevations. Plasma catecholamines are best sampled from a supine, resting patient in whom an indwelling antecubital venous cannula has been in place for at least 15 minutes. Plasma assay methods generally provide reliable results with the usual normal resting norepinephrine value being 200 to 400 pg/mL and the normal resting epinephrine value being 20 to 60 pg/mL. Most patients with pheochromocytoma have markedly elevated (>2000 pg/mL) resting plasma catecholamine (norepinephrine plus epinephrine) values; plasma concentrations elevated beyond this point strongly suggest pheochromocytoma. The upper limit of normal (norepinephrine plus epinephrine) is less than 1000 pg/mL. Values between 1000 and 2000 pg/mL are equivocal and may represent either pheochromocytoma or sympathoadrenal activation by physical or mental stress. In these subjects, the clonidine suppression test is of particular value.

False-positive plasma catecholamine elevations may result from the same factors that produce false-positive urinary elevations but are a more severe problem because measurements are made at only one point. These factors include physical stress, such as trauma, surgery, upright posture, acute venipuncture, hypoglycemia, hypovolemia, hypotension, cold, and sodium depletion, or mental stress, such as anxiety or pain. Drugs that increase plasma catecholamines include sympathomimetic amines, which release catecholamines from their stores; cocaine, which blocks catecholamine reuptake; and abrupt clonidine withdrawal. Illnesses known to elevate plasma catecholamines include both acute (e.g., myocardial infarction, diabetic ketoacidosis, or sepsis) and chronic conditions (e.g., congestive heart failure, anemia, respiratory failure, or hypothyroidism). Factors that diminish plasma catecholamines include drugs (clonidine, reserpine, and α-methylparatyrosine), autonomic neuropathy, and congenital deficiency of dopamine β-hydroxylase activity.

As with urine biochemical tests, plasma catecholamine sampling during a paroxysmal attack of hypertension is of value. A finding of normal plasma catecholamines when blood pressure is elevated is quite a useful negative result. Because only extreme elevations of plasma norepinephrine perturb blood pressure, the finding of normal plasma catecholamines while blood pressure is elevated argues strongly against pheochromocytoma as the cause.

Plasma metanephrine measurements are also highly sensitive and specific for diagnosis of pheochromocytoma, although the measurements are not as widely available as plasma catecholamines. Other components of the catecholamine storage vesicle core are released into the blood stream by pheochromocytomas. The plasma concentration of chromogranin A is elevated in patients with pheochromocytoma, with a diagnostic sensitivity of 83% and specificity of 96%. It is not substantially elevated by acute venipuncture, nor is it affected by drugs used in the treatment or diagnosis of pheochromocytoma. Because chromogranin A is released by a variety of neuroendocrine secretory vesicles, its plasma concentration is also elevated in other cases of neuroendocrine neoplasia. Chromogranin A values are also elevated in cases of renal insufficiency because of retained immunoreactive fragments of the protein.

PHARMACOLOGIC DIAGNOSTIC TESTS: SUPPRESSIVE AND PROVOCATIVE

Pharmacologic tests for pheochromocytoma are generally not necessary because the diagnosis can usually be confirmed by urine and plasma biochemical measurements at rest or during spontaneous blood pressure surges.

The *clonidine suppression test* is of value if plasma catecholamine elevations in a patient with suspected pheochromocytoma are equivocal (that is, from 1000 to 2000 pg/mL). The rationale for the test is that pheochromocytoma chromaffin cells, unlike normal adrenal medullary chromaffin cells, are not innervated; hence, catecholamine release from pheochromocytoma chromaffin cells is autonomous and not susceptible to manipulation by drugs that decrease efferent sympathetic outflow, such as the central α_2-agonist clonidine. Blood is obtained for plasma catecholamines before and 3 hours after a single oral dose of 0.3 mg clonidine. In a subject without pheochromocytoma, plasma norepinephrine should fall to less than 500 pg/mL after clonidine. A positive test (failure of catecholamines to decline after clonidine) is sensitive but may not be entirely specific for pheochromocytoma. Although catecholamine levels do not fall after clonidine administration in cases of pheochromocytoma, the blood pressure fall is comparable to that seen in patients with essential hypertension. To prevent inordinate falls in blood pressure during the test, prior volume depletion should be avoided; the test is most safely done in subjects whose diastolic blood pressure before clonidine is 100 mm Hg or higher. Because β-blockers such as propranolol diminish circulating norepinephrine clearance (and hence plasma norepinephrine responses to clonidine), their use should be discontinued 48 hours before and during the test. The test remains valid during α-blockade.

Catecholamine provocative tests (such as the glucagon or tyramine tests) are used in only a few centers because of the potential hazard posed by inordinate catecholamine release.

Anatomic Localization

Tumor location must be known to plan the proper surgical route. Ninety-five per cent of pheochromocytomas are in the abdomen, and the great majority of these can be visualized by one of three modalities: CT, MRI, or [^{131}I]-metaiodobenzylguanidine (MIBG) scintigraphy. CT and MRI are highly sensitive, although they are nonspecific because they visualize any mass lesion, not just pheochromocytoma.

Iodine-131-MIBG, a radiolabeled analogue of guanethidine, is transported into chromaffin cells by the reuptake cell membrane catecholamine carrier. Because it accumulates in chromaffin cells, an MIBG abnormality is extraordinarily specific (about 98%) for pheochromocytoma, although somewhat less sensitive (85 to 90%) than CT or MRI. [^{123}I]-MIBG is used extensively outside the United States. MIBG imaging is especially useful for metastatic, recurrent, or extra-adrenal tumors.

Abdominal ultrasonography is a safe imaging tool but is less sensitive than CT or MRI. Plain abdominal radiography, intravenous urography (pyelography), air insufflation retroperitoneal pneumography, arteriography, and venography are no longer used to localize pheochromocytoma. Indeed, arteriography or venography of the tumor may trigger hypertensive crises.

Differential Diagnosis

Because many conditions can mimic the diagnostic features of pheochromocytoma, as many as 90% of patients who have some feature of the tumor turn out not to have one after diagnostic testing. Examples include certain drugs, such as surreptitiously self-administered epinephrine or isoproterenol. Abrupt withdrawal from clonidine can provoke a sympathoadrenal discharge with "rebound" blood pressure elevation. Subjects treated with MAO inhibitors for depression may have hypertensive crises if they inadvertently ingest foods rich in tyramine.

Disease states causing or simulating catecholamine excess and hypertension include thyrotoxicosis; acute intracranial disturbances such as subarachnoid hemorrhage or posterior fossa masses; hypertensive crisis of paraplegia, which can be initiated by visceral manipulation or bladder distention; and hypoglycemia, especially in the presence of β-blockade. Damage to carotid sinus baroreceptors by surgery or tumor may result in baroreflex failure, with episodic blood pressure and plasma catecholamine surges; clonidine is the drug of choice. Episodic surges in plasma dopamine have been described in some patients with episodic blood pressure elevation but without pheochromocytoma; the mechanism has not been established. Some patients with symptomatic blood pressure surges have underlying unrecognized emotional trauma, which may respond to psychotherapy.

Pathophysiology and Complications

Although circulating catecholamine excess is the ultimate cause of hypertension in patients with pheochromocytoma, the correlation of blood pressure with plasma catecholamines is modest. Desensitization to catecholamine effects may contribute to underdiagnosis of the tumor in elderly patients. In addition to catecholamines, pheochromocytomas also release a number of potentially vasoactive substances that may modify blood pressure. Hemodynamic studies suggest that elevations in systemic vascular resistance rather than cardiac output account for the blood pressure rise.

Acute norepinephrine infusion leads to plasma volume contraction, and a past mainstay of pheochromocytoma management has been an effort to re-expand plasma volume, either spontaneously after therapeutic α-blockade or with preoperative saline infusion. However, recent careful measurements of plasma volume indicate that on average it is not as contracted as once believed. Orthostatic hypotension is variably observed in pheochromocytoma. It cannot be clearly attributed to plasma volume contraction and probably reflects catecholamine desensitization, the effects of vasodilator peptides and catecholamines, and dysautonomia.

The major catecholamine secreted by most pheochromocytomas is norepinephrine. Small intra-adrenal tumors (especially early in the course of MEN type 2) may secrete predominantly epinephrine. Pure epinephrine secretion by pheochromocytomas is rare.

Cardiomyopathy (myocarditis) occurs in a minority of patients with pheochromocytoma, presumably as a consequence of catecholamine excess. This process is generally reversible after tumor removal, and congestive heart failure responds to preoperative α-adrenergic blockade. In most patients, however, the degree of myocardial left ventricular hypertrophy on cardiac ultrasonography is no different from that seen in essential hypertension.

Rx **Treatment**

PREOPERATIVE PREPARATION AND DRUG TREATMENT. Once pheochromocytoma has been diagnosed, the patient is prepared for surgery with adrenergic blockade for a period of 1 to 4 weeks. During α-blockade, any catecholamine-induced plasma volume contraction is allowed to correct itself. α-Blockade is usually accomplished with oral phenoxybenzamine, an irreversible, noncompetitive antagonist that acts predominantly (though not exclusively) at α_1-receptors. The drug is begun at 5 mg twice daily, and the dose is adjusted gradually upward by increments of 10 mg every 1 to 4 days to a maximum of 50 to 100 mg twice daily. The usual dose range required is 30 to 80 mg/day. Treatment goals are to normalize blood pressure (<160/<90 mm Hg), prevent paroxysmal hypertension, and abolish tachyarrhythmias (ventricular extrasystoles, fewer than five per minute) without inducing intolerable orthostatic hypotension (i.e., orthostatic falls of >85/>45 mm Hg). Side effects of an adequate phenoxybenzamine dosage include orthostatic hypotension, tachycardia, nasal congestion, dry mouth, diplopia, and ejaculatory dysfunction. In patients intolerant of phenoxybenzamine, one can use the α_1-selective antagonist doxazosin (at 2 to 8 mg orally once daily) or prazosin (at 0.5 to 16 mg/day, orally two to four times daily). Some authorities advocate the initial use of the newer, more selective α_1-selective antagonists (e.g., doxazosin) in preference to phenoxybenzamine, since phenoxybenzamine's alkylation of α-receptors may cause prolonged α-blockade contributing to postoperative hypotension, and its minor action on presynaptic α_2-receptors may contribute to increased sympathetic neuronal norepinephrine release, causing undesirable chronotropic and inotropic effects in the heart.

If blood pressure or tachyarrhythmias, including sinus tachycardia, are not fully controlled by α-blockade, β-blockade is instituted with oral propranolol, 10 to 40 mg four times daily. β-blockade must not be undertaken before α-blockade has been instituted; after blockade of vasodilatory vascular β_2-adrenergic receptors, catecholamines' continued access to vasoconstrictive α_1-receptors may induce unopposed vasoconstriction and exacerbation of hypertension. β-Blockade may be especially useful for predominantly epinephrine-secreting tumors. The more β_1-selective antagonists atenolol (50 to 100 mg/day) or metoprolol (50 to 200 mg/day), or the combined α/β-antagonist labetalol (100 to 400 mg/day), are alternatives to propranolol and are preferable in the view of some authorities. In subjects with contraindications to β-blockade, lidocaine or amiodarone can be used for tachyarrhythmias.

If combined management with α- plus β-adrenergic antagonists is not fully effective (especially in patients with widespread, unresectable malignant pheochromocytoma), the tyrosine hydroxylase inhibitor α-methylparatyrosine is added at an oral dose of 0.25 to 1.0 g four times daily. Its use may be complicated by sedation, fatigue, anxiety, diarrhea, or extrapyramidal reactions.

For acute management of severe hypertensive crises, intravenous nitroprusside is effective. Intravenous nonselective α_1/α_2-blockade with phentolamine (1 to 2 mg bolus, then by further incremental doses or continuous infusion) is also useful. If a pressor response is accompanied by tachycardia, the combined α/β-adrenergic antagonist labetalol (intravenous 5-mg incremental doses) may also be useful. Calcium channel blockade with sublingual nifedipine (10 mg broken under the tongue) has also been used.

Opiates (narcotic analgesics), narcotic antagonists (such as naloxone), histamine, adrenocorticotropic hormone, saralasin, glucagon, or indirect sympathomimetic amines (such as phenylpropanolamine or tyramine) should be avoided. All of these agents may provoke hypertensive surges by releasing catecholamines from the tumor. Drugs that block catecholamine reuptake, such as tricyclic antidepressants (e.g., desipramine), cocaine, or guanethidine, may worsen hypertension. β-Adrenergic antagonists, by blocking vasodilatory vascular β_2-receptors, may cause unopposed α-mediated vasoconstriction by circulating catecholamines and thereby result in severe hypertension, unless α-blockade is instituted beforehand. Dopaminergic antagonists (such as metoclopramide or sulpiride) may result in hypertension and should be avoided.

OPERATIVE AND PERIOPERATIVE MANAGEMENT. Autopsy series of pheochromocytoma indicate that even clinically unsuspected cases can be lethal. At least 90% of pheochromocytomas are benign, and surgical resection provides a cure, although up to 25% of patients may retain some lesser degree of hypertension. Residual tumor may be diagnosed by urinary catecholamine measurement 1 to 2 weeks postoperatively. The operative mortality rate of pheochromocytoma resection should not exceed 2 to 3%. Patients should be followed for at least 10 years postoperatively, because of the small (approximately 5%) risk of late tumor recurrence. Perioperative complications were more frequent in patients with higher blood pressures, higher catecholamine and metabolite excretion, recurrent or multiple surgical excisions, or prolonged anesthesia. In cases of malignant pheochromocytoma, the individual course is highly variable, but the long-term 50% survival is less than 5 years.

Several surgical approaches are feasible, depending on the particular characteristics of the pheochromocytoma; the experience of the surgeon is crucial. Laparoscopic adrenalectomy is increasingly used in recent years and may result in faster postoperative recovery. The entire adrenal gland harboring a pheochromocytoma is usually excised, but during excision of bilateral pheochromocytomas, a section of cortex from one adrenal gland may be left in place, to prevent steroid dependency. Anesthetic management is guided by selection of agents that do not cause catecholamine release or potentiate catecholamine's dysrhythmic effects. Intravenous glucose replacement (5% dextrose in water or saline) should be given to prevent hypoglycemia, a frequent occurrence after tumor removal. Times at which hypertensive surges are likely to occur include anesthetic induction, intubation, tumor palpation, and ligation of tumor veins. If intraoperative hypotension occurs, the initial treatment should be saline infusion to expand intravascular volume. Norepinephrine infusion is appropriate only after plasma volume expansion to euvolemia.

For intraoperative blood pressure surges, intravenous nitroprusside is often used. Alternatively, α-blockade can be accomplished with intravenous phentolamine (an α_1- and α_2-antagonist), starting with a 1- to 2-mg dose and proceeding to infusion. The calcium channel antagonist nicardipine has also been used.

In the postoperative period, several problems occur with some frequency:

1. Hypotension. Most commonly, hypotension results from hypovolemia and responds to saline infusion; several liters may be required, often with the guidance of central pressure measurements. After volume repletion, norepinephrine can be infused if needed.
2. Hypertension. Plasma catecholamine levels remain elevated for several days even after complete pheochromocytoma resection. Even 2 weeks postoperatively, up to one fourth of patients still have hypertension. At this time, the differential diagnosis includes residual unresected tumor, essential hypertension, or hypertension secondary to renal damage caused by prior hypertension. A urine collection for catecholamines, obtained at least 1 to 2 weeks after tumor resection, will clarify matters.
3. Hypoglycemia. After correction of catecholamine excess, insulin release may be increased and end-organ responsiveness to insulin augmented, resulting in hypoglycemia. Hypoglycemia may masquerade as refractory hypotension. Infusion of glucose (5% dextrose in water or saline) during the intraoperative and immediate postoperative period is useful.

MALIGNANT PHEOCHROMOCYTOMA. Although most pheochromocytomas are well-encapsulated, localized growths, approximately 5 to 10% are malignant. Malignancy is diagnosed by the biologic behavior of the tumor in the form of adjacent tissue invasion or distant metastatic spread. Extra-adrenal tumors are more likely to metastasize than are primary adrenal ones. Catecholamine biosynthesis tends to be especially deranged in malignant tumors, with secretion of substantial amounts of DOPA and dopamine (metabolized to homovanillic acid, which can be detected in the urine). Increased plasma DOPA in patients with pheochromocytoma suggests malignancy. Extreme elevations in plasma norepinephrine or chromogranin A may suggest malignant pheochromocytoma; serial

Continued

chromogranin A measurements can then be used to gauge tumor response to treatment.

In patients with malignant pheochromocytoma, α- and β-adrenergic blockade with phenoxybenzamine and propranolol remains the mainstay of management of the symptoms and signs of catecholamine excess. If catecholamine effects are not controlled, the tyrosine hydroxylase inhibitor α-methylparatyrosine can be effective at 0.25 to 1.0 g four times daily.

Metastases tend to be slow-growing, and the natural history of malignant pheochromocytoma is variable; the 5-year survival rate is less than 50%. Common sites of metastasis are the retroperitoneum, skeleton (bone), lymph nodes, and liver. Periodic surgical debulking may help control symptoms. The response to chemotherapy has generally been disappointing, but the combination of vincristine, cyclophosphamide, and dacarbazine shows promise in many patients. Skeletal metastases show some response to irradiation, although the neoplasm is not particularly susceptible to radiation therapy. High-dose (approximately 500 mCi cumulative dose) repeated radiation therapy with intravenous [^{131}I]-MIBG remains experimental but is of value in some patients.

CATECHOLAMINE DEFICIENCY DISEASE STATES

Loss of even both adrenal glands seldom produces a catecholamine deficiency state. In diabetic patients receiving insulin, the usual counter-regulatory response to hypoglycemia involves the actions of epinephrine and glucagon to trigger hepatic glycogenolysis. In diabetic patients who also have autonomic neuropathy, deficient epinephrine release during hypoglycemia coupled with deficient glucagon responses may result in impairment of the usual counter-regulatory response to hypoglycemia and prolong its duration.

Several individuals have been described with hereditary deficiency of dopamine β-hydroxylase; such individuals have greatly diminished or undetectable norepinephrine and epinephrine levels in blood, urine, and cerebrospinal fluid. The initial features of this lifelong syndrome include severe orthostatic hypotension, ptosis, nasal stuffiness, hyperextensible joints, and retrograde ejaculation. The diagnosis is made in patients with severe orthostatic hypotension, a plasma norepinephrine/dopamine ratio of less than 1, and undetectable plasma dopamine β-hydroxylase enzymatic activity and immunoreactivity. During sympathoadrenal activation in these subjects, increments in efferent sympathetic nerve traffic occur, but sympathetic axons release the precursor dopamine instead of norepinephrine, perhaps compounding the hypotension.

THE INCIDENTAL ADRENAL MASS (OR "INCIDENTALOMA")

About 2% of all abdominal CT scans, as well as 9% of autopsies, incidentally discover minimal adrenal gland abnormalities. Rarely do these lesions require further attention.

Occasionally, the appearance of an adrenal mass on CT or MRI scan is sufficiently characteristic for a firm diagnosis; an example is adrenal myelolipoma, a benign accumulation of bone marrow elements in an otherwise normally functioning adrenal gland with a characteristic fat-density image on CT or MRI scan. Myelolipoma requires no treatment.

If an adrenal mass is larger than 4 cm in span, its chance of malignancy (especially adrenocortical carcinoma) increases, and such masses should be resected unless they have a clearly benign appearance (such as myelolipoma) on CT or MRI scan. In smaller lesions, adrenal carcinoma is unlikely unless other signs or symptoms of adrenocortical hormone excess are apparent. Incidental masses smaller than 4 to 6 cm in span are monitored by periodic CT scanning. In subjects with known metastatic carcinoma, adrenal abnormalities are likely to be adrenal metastases. In subjects with recent major abdominal trauma, adrenal abnormalities probably represent hemorrhage and should resolve with time.

Because not all pheochromocytomas manifest hypertension at all times, all patients with incidental adrenal masses should be screened for pheochromocytoma with a 24-hour urine collection for catecholamine metabolites.

Virtually all patients with aldosterone-producing adrenal adenoma have hypertension, although hypokalemia may not be constant. Screening for primary aldosteronism can be readily accomplished with an ambulatory morning plasma aldosterone concentration to plasma renin activity ratio (PAC [ng/dL]/PRA [ng/mL/hour] ratio). A PAC/PRA ratio of greater than 20 and PAC greater than 15 ng/dL constitutes a positive screening test result.

Whereas frank Cushing's disease is heralded by classic signs or symptoms, preclinical Cushing's disease may lack the typical signs and symptoms of hypercortisolism. In either case, the diagnosis is made by giving 1 mg of oral dexamethasone at 11 PM and sampling serum cortisol the next morning at 8 AM; a cortisol value of less than 5 μg/dL is normal.

SUGGESTED READINGS

Eisenhofer G, Huynh T-T, Hiroi M, Pacak K: Understanding catecholamine metabolism as a guide to the biochemical diagnosis of pheochromocytoma. Rev Endocrine Metab Disord 2001;2:297–311. *A comprehensive approach to enzymes, pathways, sites, and products of catecholamine metabolism.*

Grumbach MM, Biller BM, Braunstein GD, et al: Management of the clinically inapparent adrenal mass ("incidentaloma"). Ann Intern Med 2003;138:424–429. *Recommendations of a consensus panel.*

Noshiro T, Shimizu K, Watanabe T, et al: Changes in clinical features and long-term prognosis in patients with pheochromocytoma. Am J Hypertens 2000;13:35–43. *Patients should be followed postoperatively for at least 10 years, because of the small (approximately 5%) risk of late tumor recurrence.*

Prys-Roberts C: Phaeochromocytoma: Recent progress in its management. Br J Anaesth 2000;85:44–57. *An experienced anesthesiologist details how pheochromocytoma management has evolved over the past 30 years.*

242 DIABETES MELLITUS

Robert S. Sherwin

Overview

Diabetes mellitus is a chronic disorder characterized by the impaired metabolism of glucose and other energy-yielding fuels as well as by the late development of vascular and neuropathic complications. Diabetes comprises of a group of disorders involving distinct pathogenic mechanisms, for which hyperglycemia is the common denominator. Regardless of its cause, the disease is associated with a common hormonal defect, namely, insulin deficiency, which may be total, partial, or relative when viewed in the context of coexisting insulin resistance. Lack of insulin *effect* plays a primary role in the metabolic derangements linked to diabetes, and hyperglycemia in turn plays an important role in disease-related complications.

In 1998, the United States Centers for Disease Control and Prevention estimated that 16 million Americans (or nearly 6% of the U.S. population) fulfilled the diagnostic criteria for diabetes mellitus; more than one third of these cases were thought to be undiagnosed. The number of affected patients continues to rise as the 21st century begins, with current estimates exceeding 800,000 new cases per year. Diabetes is the fourth most common reason for patient contact with an American physician, accounting for approximately 12% of U.S. health care dollars and total annual costs exceeding 100 billion dollars. Worldwide, diabetes affects more than 135 million people; this figure is projected to reach 300 million cases by 2025. Unfortunately, the rate of growth of diabetes is largest in developing nations, where barriers exist to proper diagnosis and treatment.

Diabetes is a leading cause of both mortality and early disability; in the United States, it is the leading cause of blindness among working-age adults, of end-stage renal disease, and of nontraumatic limb amputations. Diabetes increases the risk of cardiac, cerebral, and peripheral vascular disease two- to seven-fold and in the obstetric setting is a major contributor to neonatal morbidity and mortality. On the bright side, a growing body of evidence suggests that most (if not all) of the debilitating complications of diabetes (Fig. 242–1) can be prevented or delayed by the prospective treatment of hyperglycemia and other cardiovascular risk factors. When treating diabetes, the timing of

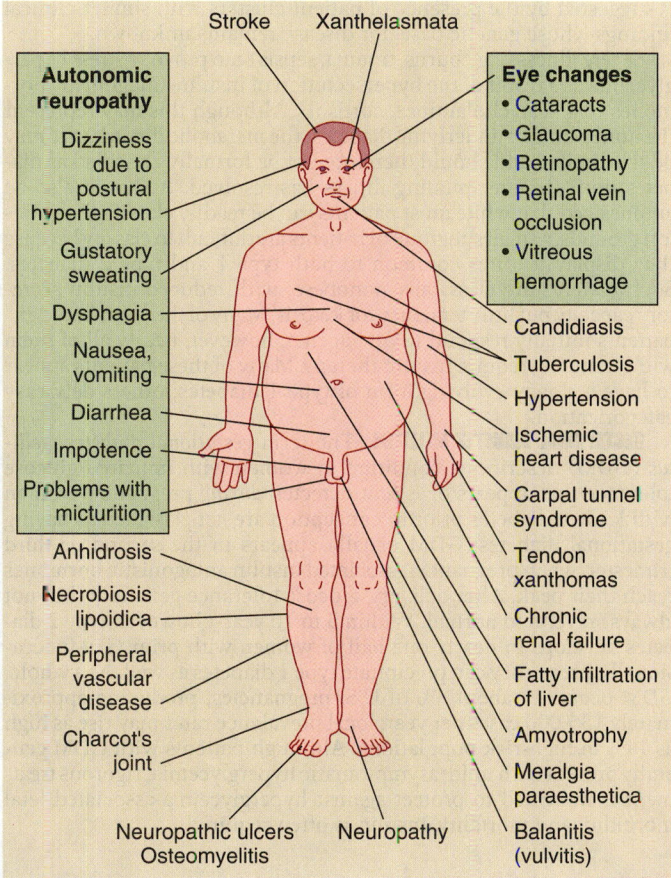

FIGURE 242–1 • Long-term complications of diabetes mellitus. (From Forbes CD, Jackson WF: Color Atlas and Text of Clinical Medicine, 3rd ed. London, Mosby, 2003, with permission.)

Table 242–1 • **CLASSIFICATION OF DIABETES MELLITUS**

ESTABLISHED DIABETES MELLITUS

I. Type 1 diabetes, formerly known as insulin-dependent diabetes mellitus (IDDM) or "juvenile-onset diabetes" (primarily due to β-cell destruction, usually leading to absolute insulin deficiency)
   A. Immune mediated
   B. Idiopathic
II. Type 2 diabetes, formerly known as non-insulin-dependent diabetes (NIDDM) or "adult-onset diabetes" (may range from predominantly insulin resistance with relative insulin deficiency to predominantly secretory defect with insulin resistance)
III. Other specific types
   A. Genetic defects of β-cell function (e.g., maturity-onset diabetes of the young [MODY] types 1–6 and point mutations in mitochondrial DNA)
   B. Genetic defects in insulin action (e.g., type A insulin resistance, leprechaunism, Rabson-Mendenhall syndrome, lipoatrophic diabetes)
   C. Disease of the exocrine pancreas (e.g., pancreatitis, trauma, pancreatectomy, neoplasia, cystic fibrosis, hemochromatosis, fibrocalculous pancreatopathy)
   D. Endocrinopathies (e.g., acromegaly, Cushing's syndrome, hyperthyroidism, pheochromocytoma, glucagonoma, somatostinoma, aldosteronoma)
   E. Drug- or chemical-induced (e.g., vacor, pentamidine, nicotinic acid, glucocorticoids, thyroid hormone, diazoxide, β-adrenergic agonists, thiazides, phenytoin, α-interferon)
   F. Infections (e.g., congenital rubella, cytomegalovirus)
   G. Uncommon forms of immune-mediated diabetes (e.g., "stiff-man" syndrome, anti-insulin receptor antibodies)
   H. Other genetic syndromes (e.g., Down sydrome, Klinefelter's syndrome, Turner's syndrome, Wolfram's sydrome, Friedrich's ataxia, Huntington's disease, Laurence-Moon-Biedl syndrome, myotonic dystrophy, porphyria, Prader-Willi syndrome)
IV. Gestational diabetes mellitus

RISK CATEGORIES FOR DIABETES MELLITUS

I. Impaired fasting glucose (IFG)
II. Impaired glucose tolerance (IGT)

therapy is crucial; clinical outcomes depend critically on early recognition and treatment of the disease.

Classification

The newly revised American Diabetes Association (ADA) classification scheme for diabetes mellitus is summarized in Table 242–1. Clinical diabetes is divided into four general subclasses, including (1) type 1, primarily caused by autoimmune pancreatic β-cell destruction and characterized by absolute insulin deficiency; (2) type 2, characterized by insulin resistance and relative insulin deficiency; (3) "other" specific types of diabetes, associated with identifiable clinical conditions or syndromes; and (4) gestational diabetes mellitus. In addition to these clinical categories, two "risk conditions"—*impaired glucose tolerance (IGT)* and *impaired fasting glucose (IFG)*—have been defined to describe metabolic states in between normal glucose homeostasis and overt diabetes. Both IGT and IFG significantly increase the future risk of developing diabetes mellitus, and in many cases are part of the disease's natural history. It should also be noted here that patients with any form of diabetes may require insulin therapy; for this reason, the previously used terms "insulin-dependent" (for type 1) and "non-insulin-dependent" (for type 2) diabetes have been eliminated.

TYPE 1 DIABETES MELLITUS. Patients with type 1 diabetes mellitus have little or no insulin secretory capacity and depend on exogenous insulin to prevent metabolic decompensation and death. Classically, symptoms appear abruptly (i.e., over days or weeks) in previously healthy, nonobese children or young adults; in older patients, however, the disease may manifest more gradually. At the time of initial evaluation most type 1 diabetic patients are ill and symptomatic, most commonly presenting with polyuria, polydipsia, polyphagia, and weight loss; such patients may also present with ketoacidosis. Type 1 diabetes is believed to have a prolonged asymptomatic preclinical phase (often lasting years), during which pancreatic β cells are gradually destroyed by an autoimmune attack influenced by HLA and other

genetic factors, as well as by the environment (Fig. 242–2). In some patients, an acute illness may speed the transition from the preclinical phase to clinical disease. Initially, most type 1 patients require high-dose insulin therapy to restore a disordered metabolism. A so-called "honeymoon period" (lasting weeks or months) may follow, however, during which small doses of insulin are needed due to partial recovery of β-cell function and reversal of the insulin resistance caused by acute illness. Thereafter, insulin secretory capacity is gradually lost; this process may take several years. That type 1 diabetes is an autoimmune disease is supported by its association with specific immune response (HLA) genes and by the presence of autoantibodies to islet cells and their constituents (e.g., insulin, glutamic acid decarboxylase). Type 1 diabetes accounts for less than 10% of cases of diabetes in the United States.

TYPE 2 DIABETES MELLITUS. Type 2 accounts for over 90% of cases of clinical diabetes. Patients with type 2 disease retain some endogenous insulin secretory capacity; however, their insulin levels are low relative to their ambient glucose levels and magnitude of insulin resistance. Type 2 patients are not dependent on insulin for immediate survival, and ketosis rarely develops, except under conditions of great physical stress. Nevertheless, many of these patients do require insulin therapy for proper glycemic control. Although found with increasing frequency in adolescents, type 2 diabetes is usually associated with advancing age; most cases are diagnosed after age 45. Type 2 diabetes has a high rate of genetic penetrance unrelated to HLA genes and is associated with a high-fat diet, obesity, and/or a lack of physical activity. The clinical features of type 2 diabetes can be quite insidious; classic symptoms may be mild (fatigue, weakness, dizziness, blurred vision, and other nonspecific complaints may dominate the clinical picture) or may be tolerated for many years before a patient seeks medical attention. Moreover, if the degree of hyperglycemia is insufficient to produce symptoms, the diagnosis may be made only after the development of vascular or neuropathic complications.

OTHER SPECIFIC TYPES OF DIABETES. This category encompasses a wide variety of diabetic syndromes attributed to a specific disease, drug,

Endocrine Diseases

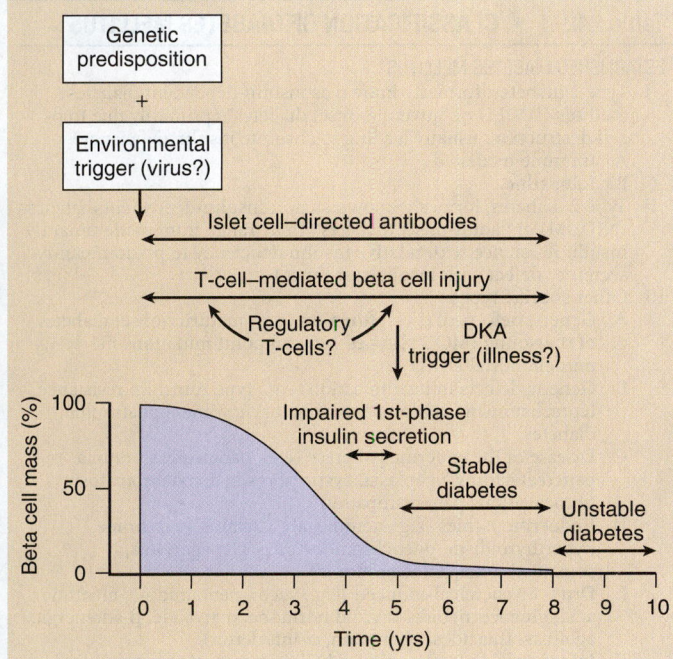

FIGURE 242–2 • A summary of the sequence of events that lead to pancreatic β-cell loss, and ultimately to the clinical appearance of type 1 diabetes. DKA = diabetic ketoacidosis.

or condition (see Table 242–1). Categories include genetic defects of β-cell function or insulin action, diseases of the exocrine pancreas, endocrinopathies, drug- or chemical-induced diabetes, infections, and other immune-mediated and genetic syndromes associated with diabetes mellitus.

Maturity-onset diabetes of the young (MODY), formerly classified as a subtype of type 2 diabetes, has now been more accurately described as a consequence of genetic research. Clinically, patients with MODY generally present in adolescence or young adulthood; unlike patients with classic type 2 diabetes, they are usually nonobese, normotensive, and normolipidemic at the time of diagnosis. MODY is a heterogeneous disorder encompassing several monogenic defects of β-cell function, with autosomal dominant inheritance and penetrance exceeding 80%. Mutations at several genetic loci have been identified. The most common form—MODY type 3—is associated with a mutation of hepatocyte nuclear factor 1a (HNF-1a), a gene transcription factor encoded on chromosome 12. MODY type 2 patients share a mutation in the gene encoding glucokinase, the key enzyme responsible for the phosphorylation of glucose within the β cell and the liver. A variety of glucokinase mutations have been identified in different families, each capable of interfering with the transduction of the glucose signal to the β cell. Other described forms of MODY are shown in Table 242–2; the existence of additional forms of MODY

is suggested by the presence of patient clusters with similar clinical findings whose genetic basis for disease remains unknown.

Severe illness (e.g., burns, trauma, sepsis) can provoke stress hyperglycemia as a result of the hypersecretion of insulin antagonistic hormones (e.g., catecholamines, cortisol). Although this may represent the unmasking of underlying diabetes, the metabolic disturbance may be self-limited and should therefore not be formally classified as diabetes until the precipitating illness has resolved. It should also be emphasized that while most patients can be readily classified on clinical grounds, a small subgroup of patients are difficult to classify because they display features common to both type 1 and type 2 diabetes. Such patients are classically nonobese, with reduced insulin secretory capacity but little tendency for ketosis. Many of these "in-between" patients initially respond to oral agents; however, nearly all of them will eventually require insulin therapy. Many of these patients appear to have a slowly evolving form of type 1 diabetes; others defy easy categorization.

GESTATIONAL DIABETES MELLITUS. The term *gestational diabetes mellitus* (GDM) describes a condition in women with impaired glucose tolerance that appears or is first detected *during* pregnancy. Women with known diabetes prior to conception are *not* classified as having gestational diabetes. GDM usually appears in the second or third trimester, when pregnancy-associated insulin antagonistic hormones reach their peak. After delivery, glucose tolerance generally (but not always) reverts to normal. Within 5 to 10 years, however, type 2 diabetes develops in nearly one half of women with prior GDM; occasionally, pregnancy can precipitate type 1 diabetes as well. As a whole, GDM occurs in about 4% of U.S. pregnancies, producing approximately 135,000 cases per year; local prevalence rates may rise as high as 14% in high-risk populations. Although patients with GDM generally present with mild, asymptomatic hyperglycemia, rigorous treatment is indicated to protect against hyperglycemia-associated fetal morbidity and mortality. Insulin is often required.

Diagnosis and Screening

The diagnosis of diabetes mellitus is straightforward when classic symptoms of polyuria, polydipsia, and unexplained weight loss are present. In these cases, a random plasma glucose measurement of 200 mg/dL or greater is sufficient to clinch the diagnosis; confirmatory testing is unwarranted and may delay treatment. Although glycosuria is strongly suggestive of diabetes, urine test results should never be used exclusively to diagnose diabetes, since an altered renal threshold for glucose can produce similar findings. If suspected diabetes is not confirmed through random glucose determination, additional diagnostic testing should be performed.

An 8-hour (overnight) fasting plasma glucose measurement is most convenient; diabetes is established if fasting glucose levels are 126 mg/dL or greater on two separate occasions. Alternatively, a 75 g oral glucose tolerance test (oGTT) may be employed. The oGTT should be performed after an overnight fast, using a glucose load containing 75 g of anhydrous glucose dissolved in water; 2-hour postload glucose levels of 200 mg/dL or greater confirm the presence of diabetes. An important note about the oGTT: while able to detect diabetes in its earliest stage, this test should be performed under controlled conditions to ensure its accuracy. Common factors that nonspecifically

Table 242–2 • CLASSIFICATION OF CURRENTLY RECOGNIZED GENETIC DEFECTS OF β-CELL FUNCTION: MATURITY-ONSET DIABETES OF THE YOUNG (MODY)

MODY	CHROMOSOME	DEFECTIVE GENE PRODUCT	MOLECULAR DEFECT	MOST COMMON TREATMENT
1	20q	HNF-4α	β-Cell mass, insulin secretion	OHA, insulin
2	7p	Glucokinase	Glucose phosphorylation	Diet and exercise
3	12q	HNF-1α	β-Cell mass, insulin secretion	OHA, insulin
4	13q	IPF-1 (PDX-1)	β-Cell development and function	OHA, insulin
5	17cen-q	HNF-1β	β-Cell mass, insulin secretion	Insulin
6	2q	Neuro D1 (BETA2)	β-Cell development and function	Insulin

HNF = hepatocyte nuclear factor; IPF = insulin promoter factor; Neuro D1 = neurogenic differentiation factor 1; OHA = oral hypoglycemic agent.
Adapted from Fajans SS, Bell GI, Polonsky KS: Molecular mechanisms and clinical pathophysiology of maturity-onset diabetes of the young. N Engl J Med 2001;345:971–980.

deteriorate the oGTT include (1) carbohydrate restriction (<150 g for 3 days), (2) bed rest or severe inactivity, (3) medical or surgical stress, (4) drugs (e.g., thiazides, β-blockers, glucocorticoids, or phenytoin), (5) smoking, and (6) anxiety from repeated needlesticks. As a result, the oGTT should not be performed in acutely ill patients, and patients taking the oGTT should ideally stop smoking and consume a liberal carbohydrate diet for at least 3 days prior to testing. The current American Diabetes Association criteria for the diagnosis of diabetes mellitus are shown below; in the absence of unequivocal hyperglycemia with acute metabolic decompensation, each criterion used should be confirmed by repeat testing on a separate occasion.

1. Classic symptoms of diabetes (polyuria, polydipsia, and unexplained weight loss) *PLUS* random glucose concentration of 200 mg/dL or greater (≥11.1 mmol/L) *OR*
2. Fasting (≥8-hour) plasma glucose concentration of 126 mg/dL or greater (≥ 7.0 mmol/L) *OR*
3. 2-hour postload glucose concentration of 200 mg/dL or greater (≥11.1 mmol/L) during a 75 g oGTT

In recent years, increasing emphasis has been placed on two "risk categories" for diabetes, IFG and IGT. Since both conditions are associated with an increased risk of developing diabetes and subsequent vascular disease, all patients with IFG or IGT should be treated with diet and exercise and should be screened annually for progression to diabetes. The recent report of the NIH-funded Diabetes Prevention Program as well as studies from Finland and China have demonstrated that modest changes in life style sharply reduced the development of type 2 diabetes in patients with IGT. As detailed earlier, diabetes mellitus is established if fasting glucose levels are 126 mg/dL or greater; however, a fasting glucose concentration of 109 mg/dL, not 125 mg/dL, has been designated as the upper limit of normal. While somewhat arbitrary, this level was chosen because it approximates the level above which acute-phase insulin secretion is suppressed in response to intravenous glucose. More importantly, fasting glucose levels above 109 mg/dL are associated with an increased risk of developing diabetes. Patients with fasting glucose levels between 110 and 125 mg/dL are classified as having IFG (Table 242–3). Because individuals with IFG may exhibit severe postprandial hyperglycemia, a 75 g oGTT should be performed in all such patients to rule out diabetes. During the 75 g oGTT, 2-hour postload glucose concentrations of 200 mg/dL or greater are diagnostic of diabetes, whereas patients with levels between 140 and 199 mg/dL are defined as having IGT. Table 242–3 summarizes the diagnosis of IFG, IGT, and overt diabetes mellitus.

Because patients with diabetes may harbor the disease for many years before symptoms are appreciated, the ADA has endorsed the screening of "high-risk" individuals at 3-year intervals (Table 242–4). By current ADA criteria, "high-risk" patients include those with a personal history of IFG, IGT, GDM, obesity, hypertension, or dyslipidemia. Patients in high-risk ethnic groups and patients with first-degree relatives with diabetes also qualify for screening. In most cases, a fasting plasma glucose level is the screening test of choice; however, the oGTT has the distinct advantage of detecting patients with IGT.

Table 242–3 • DIAGNOSTIC CATEGORIES: IMPAIRED FASTING GLUCOSE, IMPAIRED GLUCOSE TOLERANCE, AND DIABETES MELLITUS*

	2-HOUR (75-G) OGTT RESULT		
	<140 mg/dL	140–199 mg/dL	>22 mg/dL
FASTING PLASMA GLUCOSE			
<110 mg/dL	Normal	IGT	DM
110–125 mg/dL	IFG	IGT *and* IFG	DM
≥125 mg/dL	DM	DM	DM

*These diagnostic categories are based on the combined results of a fasting plasma glucose level and a 2-hour, 75-g oral glucose tolerance test. Note that a confirmed random plasma glucose level of ≥200 mg/dL in the appropriate clinical setting is diagnostic of diabetes and precludes the need for further testing.

DM = diabetes mellitus; IFG = impaired fasting glucose; IGT = impaired glucose tolerance; oGTT = oral glucose tolerance test.

Table 242–4 • CRITERIA FOR DIABETES SCREENING IN ASYMPTOMATIC INDIVIDUALS*

1. Testing for diabetes should be considered in all individuals at age 45 years and older and, if results are normal, it should be repeated at 3-year intervals.
2. Testing should be considered at a younger age or be carried out more frequently in individuals who
   • Are obese (>120% desirable body weight or a body mass index >27)
   • Have a first-degree relative with diabetes
   • Are members of a high-risk ethnic population (e.g., African-American, Hispanic American, Native American, Asian American, Pacific Islander)
   • Have delivered a baby weighing >9 pounds or have been diagnosed with gestational diabetes mellitus
   • Have systemic hypertension (blood pressure >140/90)
   • Have a high-density lipoprotein cholesterol level <35 mg/dL and/or a triglyceride level >250 mg/dL
   • On previous testing, had impaired glucose tolerance or impaired fasting glucose

*A fasting plasma glucose (FPG) or an oral glucose tolerance test (OGTT) can be used for diagnosis. In most clinical settings, the FPG is preferred because of ease of administration, convenience, acceptability to patients, and lower cost.

Adapted from Report of the expert committee on the diagnosis and classification of diabetes mellitus. Diabetes Care 2000;23(Suppl 1):S4–S19.

GESTATIONAL DIABETES MELLITUS. Since even mild glucose elevations can have serious adverse effects on a developing fetus, an aggressive screening approach is recommended during pregnancy. Women with a high clinical risk of gestational diabetes (personal history of GDM, obesity, glycosuria, or a strong family history of diabetes) should undergo screening as soon as possible after conception; in these patients, screening *prior* to pregnancy is preferred if possible. At 24 to 28 weeks of gestation, screening is recommended for *all* pregnant women, except those in the lowest risk category who meet *all* of the following clinical characteristics:

• Age less than 25 years
• Weight normal before pregnancy
• Member of an ethnic group with a low risk of GDM (e.g., European)
• No known diabetes in first-degree relatives
• No history of abnormal glucose tolerance
• No history of poor obstetric outcome

In pregnant women, a casual plasma glucose level of 200 mg/dL or greater or a confirmed fasting plasma glucose level of 126 mg/dL or greater establishes the diagnosis of GDM and precludes the need for a glucose challenge. In the absence of obvious hyperglycemia, a screening 1-hour 50 g oGTT should be performed between 24 and 28 weeks of gestation. If the fasting glucose level is 105 mg/dL or greater or the 1-hour postload value is 140 mg/dL or greater, a diagnostic 100 g oGTT is indicated. Gestational diabetes is then diagnosed if two or more values equal or exceed the upper limits of normal: fasting, 95 mg/dL; 1-hour, 180 mg/dL; 2-hour, 155 mg/dL; and 3-hour, 140 mg/dL. To save time and effort, proceeding directly to the 100 g diagnostic oGTT is an acceptable alternative.

Prevalence/Epidemiology

TYPE 1 DIABETES. Prevalence rates for type 1 diabetes are relatively accurate, since these patients invariably become symptomatic; current estimates for the United States hover between 0.3 and 0.4%. Type 1 diabetes is more prevalent in Finland, Scandinavia, and Scotland, less prevalent in Southern Europe and the Middle East, and uncommon in Asian nations. The annual incidence appears to have risen in the last half-century, which could imply the introduction of an unidentified environmental factor. Prevalence rates are strikingly different among ethnic groups living in the same geographic region, likely due to genetic differences in susceptibility to the disease.

Recent recognition that type 1 diabetes has a protracted preclinical phase has shed new light on some epidemiologic characteristics of the disease. Type 1 diabetes has an increased incidence in the winter months and may be associated with specific viral epidemics. These

Endocrine Diseases

observations may in part be explained by the superimposition of illness-provoked insulin resistance in patients with marginal β-cell function. Similarly, the common appearance of type 1 diabetes during puberty may also be attributed to insulin resistance; even under normal circumstances, puberty is accompanied by impaired insulin-stimulated glucose metabolism. New methods for tracking islet-directed autoimmunity have led to a reappraisal of the age at which type 1 diabetes first appears. Although the age-specific incidence rises progressively from infancy to puberty and then declines, incidence rates persist at lower levels for many decades; in fact, about 30% of patients are diagnosed after the age of 20 years. In the later-onset patients, the clinical syndrome tends to evolve more slowly; in addition, islet-directed antibody titers may be lower, and HLA types may be different from those of younger patients. As a result, type 2 diabetes mellitus is initially misdiagnosed in many of these patients.

TYPE 2 DIABETES. Systematic screening for asymptomatic diabetes mellitus is generally limited to high-risk populations, rendering broader prevalence estimates imprecise. Total U.S. prevalence has been estimated at 6% but likely exceeds 10 or 15% in persons older than 50 years of age; one third of these cases are thought to be undiagnosed. Type 2 diabetes is more common in Native Americans, Hispanic Americans, and African Americans than in people of European heritage; these patients also typically present at an earlier age. Prevalence rates also vary worldwide, where type 2 diabetes has a propensity for Asiatic Indians, Polynesians/Micronesians, and Latin Americans. Interestingly, African blacks, Australian Aborigines, Asians, and Pacific Islanders all have an increased risk of diabetes after emigration to the United States; this may be attributable to a genetically determined inability to metabolically adapt to "Western" behavior patterns, such as reduced physical activity and a high-fat, high-calorie diet.

Although relatively little is known about the specific genetic abnormalities associated with type 2 diabetes, the personal factors promoting disease expression are well established. Increased age, reduced physical activity, and especially obesity promote the expression of disease in genetically susceptible persons. The severity and duration of obesity contribute significantly to diabetes risk; patients with high waist-hip ratios (i.e., central or upper body obesity) are also more prone to the disease. Family history is also very important, since type 2 diabetes occurs more frequently in persons with diabetic parents or siblings. Identical twin concordance rates approach 100%; in these cases, affected twins will even develop diabetes at a similar age.

IMPAIRED FASTING GLUCOSE AND IMPAIRED GLUCOSE TOLERANCE. Precise statistical data regarding the prevalence of these diagnostic categories are lacking. In the United States, it is estimated that about 10–12 million people have impaired fasting glucose levels, while about 20 million have impaired glucose tolerance. The diagnoses often overlap as well: approximately 37% of patients with IFG also have IGT, and approximately 24% of patients with IGT also have IFG. Owing to the insidious nature of both conditions, precise rates of progression to overt diabetes are difficult to establish; current estimates approach 5 to 8% per year for each condition, with even higher rates if both conditions are present. In general, IGT and IFG have similar capacity to predict the future development of diabetes. IGT is also an independent risk factor for cardiovascular complications.

Pathophysiology

INSULIN SECRETION AND ACTION. The gene coding for human insulin is located on the short arm of chromosome 11. Insulin is initially synthesized in pancreatic β cells as *proinsulin*, a single-chain, 86 amino acid polypeptide. Subsequent cleavage of proinsulin removes a connecting strand (*C-peptide*) to form the smaller, double-chain insulin molecule, which contains 51 amino acid residues. Both insulin and the C-peptide remnant are packaged in membrane-bound storage granules; stimulation of insulin secretion results in the discharge of equimolar amounts of insulin and C-peptide (and a small amount of proinsulin) into the portal circulation. Although insulin is heavily metabolized during its first pass through the liver, the C-peptide fragment largely escapes hepatic metabolism; as a result, peripheral C-peptide levels provide a more precise marker of endogenous insulin secretion.

Glucose concentration is the key regulator of insulin secretion. To activate secretion, a glucose molecule must first be transported by a protein (GLUT 2) into the β cell, phosphorylated by the enzyme glucokinase, and metabolized. The precise triggering process is poorly understood but probably involves activation of signal transduction

pathways and mitochondrial signals, closure of adenosine triphosphate–sensitive potassium channels, and calcium entry into the cytoplasm of the β cell. Normally, when blood glucose rises even slightly above fasting levels, β cells secrete insulin, initially from preformed (stored) insulin and later from de novo insulin synthesis. The magnitude of the insulin response is determined by the amount of glucose available as well as by the mode of glucose entry; compared with intravenous administration, higher insulin levels are produced when glucose is given orally because of the simultaneous release of gut peptides (e.g., glucagon-like peptide I, gastric inhibitory polypeptide), which amplify the insulin response. Other insulin secretagogues include amino acids (e.g., leucine), vagal stimulation, sulfonylureas, repaglinide, and nateglinide (see later). Once secreted into the portal vein, 50% or more of insulin is removed by first pass through the liver. The consequence of this hepatic metabolism is that portal vein insulin levels are at least two- to four-fold higher than levels in the peripheral circulation. This point has clinical relevance with regard to insulin therapy; whereas insulin secreted by pancreatic β cells directly enters the portal circulation, peripherally administered insulin does not raise portal insulin levels and therefore may be less efficient in inducing hepatic effects.

Insulin acts on its target tissues (liver, muscle, and fat, primarily) through a specific insulin receptor, which is a heterodimer containing two α- and two β-chains linked by disulfide bridges. The α-subunits of the receptor reside on the extracellular surface and are the sites of insulin binding. The β-subunits span the membrane and can be phosphorylated on serine, threonine, and tyrosine residues on the cytoplasmic face. The intrinsic protein tyrosine kinase activity of the β-subunit is essential for the function of the insulin receptor. Rapid receptor autophosphorylation and tyrosine phosphorylation of cellular substrates are important early steps in insulin action. Thereafter, a series of phosphorylation and dephosphorylation reactions are triggered that produce insulin's ultimate effects. A variety of postreceptor signal transduction pathways are activated by insulin, including PI3 (phosphatidylinositol 3′) kinase, an enzyme whose product appears to be critical for the eventual translocation of glucose transport proteins (GLUT 4) to the cell surface to facilitate glucose uptake.

A number of so-called "counter-regulatory" hormones oppose the metabolic actions of insulin, including glucagon, growth hormone, cortisol, and catecholamines. Among these, glucagon (and to a lesser extent, growth hormone) plays the most important role in the development of diabetes. Glucagon is normally secreted by pancreatic α cells in response to hypoglycemia, amino acids, and activation of the autonomic nervous system. Its chief effects are on the liver, where it stimulates glycogenolysis, gluconeogenesis, and ketogenesis via cyclic adenosine monophosphate–dependent mechanisms. Glucagon release is normally inhibited by hyperglycemia and hyperinsulinemia; however, in both types of diabetes, glucagon levels are absolutely or relatively *elevated* despite the presence of hyperglycemia. Growth hormone secretion by the anterior pituitary gland is also inappropriately increased in type 1 diabetes, a result (at least in part) of the body's attempt to overcome a defect in insulin-like growth factor type 1 generation caused by insulin deficiency. The major metabolic actions of growth hormone are on peripheral tissues, where it acts to promote lipolysis and inhibit glucose consumption. In type 1 diabetic patients with reduced portal insulin levels, growth hormone is also capable of stimulating hepatic glucose production.

METABOLIC EFFECTS OF INSULIN. Insulin deficiency—be it relative or absolute—plays a pivotal role in the pathophysiology of diabetes mellitus. The effects of insulin lack are best appreciated by first examining the normal role of insulin in fuel homeostasis.

Fasted State. After an overnight fast, low basal insulin levels result in diminished glucose uptake in peripheral insulin-sensitive tissues (e.g., muscle and fat). In the fasted state, most glucose uptake occurs in non-insulin-sensitive tissues, primarily the brain, which, because of its inability to use free fatty acids, is critically dependent on a constant supply of glucose for oxidative metabolism. Maintenance of stable blood glucose levels is achieved through the release of glucose by the liver (and to a small extent, by the kidney); production rates of 7 to 10 g per hour (~2 mg/kg/min) match those of the consuming tissues. The hepatic processes involved are glycogenolysis and gluconeogenesis; both play a significant role, and both depend critically on the balance between insulin and glucagon in the portal circulation. Reduced portal insulin levels decrease glycogen synthesis, which allows glucagon's stimulatory effect on glycogenolysis to prevail. Glucagon predominance also stimulates gluconeogenesis, while concurrent low insulin levels promote the peripheral mobilization of glucose precursors (amino acids, lactate, pyruvate, glycerol) and fuels (free fatty acids) for gluconeogenesis.

Fed State. Ingestion of a large glucose load triggers multiple homeostatic mechanisms to minimize glucose excursions, including (1) suppression of endogenous glucose production, (2) stimulation of hepatic glucose uptake, and (3) acceleration of glucose uptake by peripheral tissues, predominantly muscle. Each of these mechanisms depends principally on insulin. In the liver, meal-stimulated insulin levels rapidly suppress glucose production. At least 30% of ingested glucose is deposited directly in the liver, via glycogen synthesis and storage; concurrently, hepatic triglyceride synthesis increases. Peripherally, insulin-stimulated glucose transport across the plasmalemma of both adipose and muscle tissue is attributable to the recruitment of glucose transport proteins (i.e. GLUT 4) from the cytosolic compartment to the plasma membrane. In muscle, glucose may then be metabolized, or it may be converted to glycogen for storage. In adipose tissue, glucose is used primarily for the formation of α-glycerophosphate, which is necessary for the esterification of free fatty acids to form triglycerides for storage in adipose tissue.

The scenario described—the ingestion of large quantities of pure glucose—is not representative of conditions during ordinary meals. If the quantity of carbohydrate consumed and resulting insulin response are small, glucose homeostasis is maintained largely by reduced hepatic glucose production rather than by increased glucose uptake, because glucose production is much more sensitive than glucose uptake to the effects of small changes in insulin secretion. The rise in insulin that accompanies the consumption of mixed meals also facilitates protein and fat storage. Because muscle is in negative nitrogen balance in the fasting state, repletion of muscle nitrogen depends on the net uptake of amino acids in response to protein feeding. In muscle, insulin acts to promote positive nitrogen balance by facilitating amino acid uptake, by inhibiting the breakdown of protein, and (to a lesser extent) by stimulating new protein synthesis. In adipose tissue, the action of insulin accelerates triglyceride incorporation by stimulating lipoprotein lipase, while simultaneously inhibiting the hormone-sensitive lipase that catalyzes the hydrolysis of stored triglycerides. In adipose tissue, the net effect of insulin is to promote the synthesis and storage of triglycerides.

METABOLIC DEFECTS IN DIABETES. In both type 1 and type 2 diabetes, fasting hyperglycemia is accompanied by an inappropriate increase in hepatic glucose production; this effect is magnified in type 1 diabetes due to absolute portal insulin deficiency. In addition, total body glucose uptake is generally increased in diabetes, largely due to mass action induced by hyperglycemia. Increased hepatic glucose production in both types of diabetes is due mostly to accelerated gluconeogenesis; the loss of insulin's restraining effect on the α cell also leads to a relative increase in portal glucagon levels, resulting in increased uptake and conversion of glycogenic substrates to glucose within the liver. Insulin deficiency also leads to the hypersecretion of growth hormone, which further accentuates glucose overproduction. In the extreme situation of total insulin lack, excessive counter-regulatory hormone release further stimulates gluconeogenesis, while blocking compensatory increases in glucose disposal. The clinical correlate is profound hyperglycemia and glycosuria (Fig. 242–3).

Diabetes is also characterized by marked postprandial hyperglycemia. In type 2 diabetes, delayed insulin secretion and hepatic insulin resistance join forces to impair both suppression of hepatic glucose production and the liver's ability to store glucose as glycogen. Hyperglycemia ensues, even though insulin levels may eventually rise to levels above those seen in nondiabetic individuals (insulin secretion remains deficient relative to the prevailing glucose level), because insulin resistance reduces the capacity of myocytes to extract and store the excess glucose released from the liver. Under normal circumstances, muscles show increased levels of glucose-6-phosphate after sensing insulin; this rise is markedly attenuated in diabetes, which implies that the block in glycogen synthesis precedes glucose-6-phosphate formation, and thus is mediated at the level of either glucose transport (by GLUT 4) or the conversion of glucose to glucose-6-phosphate (by hexokinase). These defects are more pronounced in patients with severe hyperglycemia, in whom insulin secretion is further reduced. Type 1 patients show the most marked and prolonged elevations in blood glucose after ingestion of carbohydrate. These individuals have low portal vein insulin levels, which cannot be reversed by subcutaneous insulin therapy. Consequently, during hyperglycemia, the liver fails to arrest glucose production and fails to

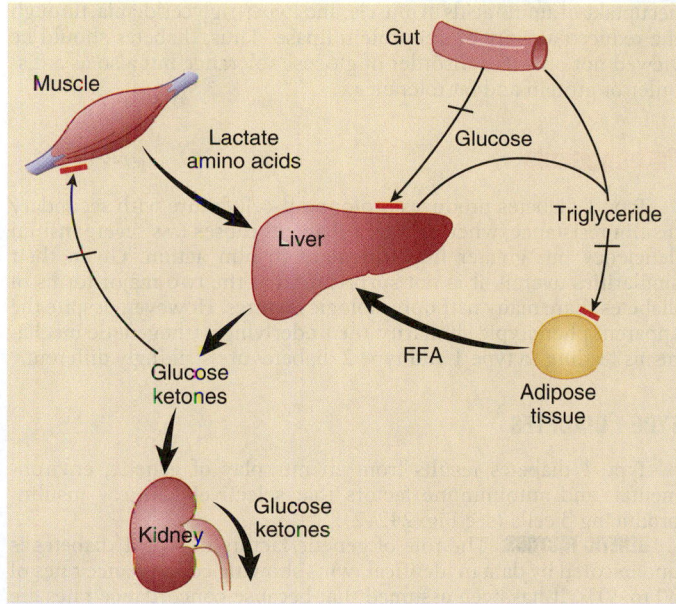

FIGURE 242–3 • The effects of severe insulin deficiency on body fuel metabolism. Lack of insulin leads to mobilization of substrates for gluconeogenesis and ketogenesis from muscle and adipose tissue, accelerated production of glucose and ketones by the liver, and impaired removal of endogenous and exogenous fuels by insulin-responsive tissues. The net results are severe hyperglycemia and hyperketonemia that overwhelm renal removal mechanisms. FFA = free fatty acids.

appropriately take up glucose for storage as glycogen. In addition, glucose uptake by peripheral tissues is impaired by the lack of insulin and by the development of insulin resistance secondary to chronic insulin deprivation and the toxic effects of chronic hyperglycemia. The net result is a gross defect in glucose disposal that can be only partially compensated by renal glycosuria.

In addition to hyperglycemia, fasting free fatty acid levels are also elevated in diabetes, because of accelerated mobilization of fat stores. In type 2 diabetes, elevated free fatty acid levels occur in the presence of normal or even increased insulin levels, suggesting that adipocytes become resistant to insulin's inhibitory effect on lipolysis. This adipocyte resistance ultimately leads to the mobilization and inappropriate deposition of triglyceride into liver and muscle, which in turn is associated with insulin resistance in these organs.

Although free fatty acids are not directly converted to glucose, they do promote hyperglycemia by providing the liver with energy to support gluconeogenesis, as well as by interfering with muscle glucose uptake (predominantly by inhibiting glucose transport). Endogenous insulin secretion in type 2 diabetes provides sufficient portal levels of insulin to suppress the conversion of free fatty acids to ketones in the liver. In type 1 diabetes, however, mobilized free fatty acids are more readily converted to ketone bodies. The combined effects of insulin deficiency and the presence of glucagon suppress fat synthesis in the liver. This suppression of fat synthesis reduces intrahepatic malonyl coenzyme A, which together with carnitine stimulates the activity of acyl acylcarnitine transferase I and thereby facilitates the transfer of long-chain fatty acids into mitochondria, where they are broken down via β-oxidation and converted to ketone bodies. In addition, hypoinsulinemia, by decreasing ketone turnover, enhances the magnitude of the ketosis for any given level of ketone production. During diabetic ketoacidosis, ketone levels are further increased because of the concurrent release of counter-regulatory hormones. The rise in glucagon accelerates hepatic ketogenesis, whereas elevations of catecholamines, growth hormone, and cortisol act in concert to increase lipolysis and subsequent delivery of free fatty acids to the liver (see Fig. 242–3). The increase in substrate delivery may become so pronounced that it saturates the oxidative pathway, thus leading to hepatic steatosis and severe hypertriglyceridemia.

In addition to disordered glucose disposal, type 1 diabetic patients may exhibit defects in the disposal of ingested proteins and fats as well. In the absence of the normal rise in insulin, meal ingestion may produce hyperaminoacidemia, because of a failure to stimulate the net uptake of amino acids in muscle, and hypertriglyceridemia, through the reduced activity of lipoprotein lipase. Thus, diabetes should be viewed not only as a disorder of glucose tolerance but also as a disorder of protein and fat tolerance.

Pathogenesis

Type 1 diabetes produces profound β-cell failure with secondary insulin resistance, whereas type 2 diabetes causes less severe insulin deficiency but greater impairment of insulin action. Given their similarities overall, it is not surprising that the two major forms of diabetes share many pathophysiologic features. However, despite the apparent phenotypic similarity, the underlying pathogenetic mechanisms leading to type 1 and type 2 diabetes are strikingly different.

TYPE 1 DIABETES

Type 1 diabetes results from an interplay of genetic, environmental, and autoimmune factors that selectively destroy insulin-producing β cells (see Fig. 242–2).

GENETIC FACTORS. The role of genetic factors in type 1 diabetes is underscored by data in identical twins showing concordance rates of 30 to 40%. It has been assumed that because concordance rates are not 100%, environmental factors must be important for disease expression. Although the presence of an environmental trigger is likely, it should be recognized that even identical twins do not express identical T-cell receptor and immunoglobulin genes; therefore, total concordance would not be expected for autoimmune diseases such as type 1 diabetes.

Many of the genes linked to type 1 diabetes have not been identified, but some are known. HLA genes, located on the short arm of chromosome 6, clearly play a dominant role; in nonaffected siblings, the risk of developing diabetes is 15 to 20% if they are HLA-identical, approximately 5% if they share one HLA gene, and less than 1% if no HLA genes are shared. Specific HLA haplotypes have been linked to type 1 diabetes: 90 to 95% of type 1 patients express DR3 and/or DR4 class II HLA molecules (as compared with 50 to 60% of the general population), whereas 60% express both alleles, a rate more than 10-fold that of the general population. Another class II allele, DQB1*0602, has a negative association with the disease. Specific class II DQ haplotypes (e.g., DQ8 and DQ2) even more strongly correlate with disease susceptibility in caucasian individuals; this susceptibility is associated with polymorphisms of the allele encoding the β-chain of the DQ class II HLA molecule. The presence of aspartic acid at position 57 protects against disease, while substitution of a neutral amino acid at this position is associated with higher disease frequency. Other polymorphisms, such as the substitution of arginine at position 52 of the DQ α-chain, may confer additional risk. Overall, it seems clear that significant genetic heterogeneity exists, and that no single class II HLA gene accounts for all HLA-associated susceptibility to disease. Association of the disease with specific class II HLA genes implies the involvement of CD4+ T cells in the autoimmune process, because these molecules are critical for both the presentation of antigenic peptides to CD4+ T cells and the selection of the CD4+ T-cell repertoire in the thymus.

Other genes likely to contribute genetic susceptibility to type 1 diabetes include *IDDM 2* (chromosome 11p), a noncoding promoter region of the insulin gene that may influence insulin gene expression in the thymus (and may therefore affect thymic selection of insulin-reactive T cells), and *CTLA-4* (chromosome 2q), which plays a role in T-cell action and regulation. Many other genes have also been implicated, underscoring the polygenic nature of this disease.

ENVIRONMENTAL FACTORS. Although environmental factors such as diet and toxins have been proposed as triggers of diabetes, most of the scientific attention has focused on putative viruses. Epidemics of mumps, congenital rubella, and coxsackievirus have been associated with an increased frequency of type 1 diabetes. In one instance, coxsackievirus B4 was isolated from the pancreas of a child who died of diabetic ketoacidosis, and inoculation of the virus into mice caused diabetes, fulfilling Koch's postulates. However, it is likely that acute, lytic viral infections are responsible for only an occasional case of diabetes. Instead, if viruses are involved, it is far more likely that they trigger an autoimmune response. If a virus contains an epitope resembling a β-cell protein, viral infection could theoretically abrogate self-tolerance and trigger autoimmunity.

AUTOIMMUNE FACTORS. About 80% of patients with new-onset type 1 diabetes have islet cell antibodies. Antibodies to a variety of β-cell constituents have been identified, including insulin, isoforms of glutamic acid decarboxylase (GAD 65 and GAD 67), and the secretory granule protein ICA 512 or IA-2, which contains a tyrosine phosphatase-like domain. The idea that type 1 diabetes is a chronic autoimmune disease with acute manifestations is supported by the fact that islet antigen-directed antibodies are present in approximately 3% of asymptomatic first-degree relatives of patients; such antibody-positive individuals are at high risk for the development of type 1 diabetes, although clinical onset may be delayed by many years. The likelihood of type 1 diabetes is greater than 50% if autoantibodies are present to more than one β-cell antigen (i.e., insulin, GAD 65, ICA 512), whereas diabetes rarely develops in antibody-negative relatives. If antibodies appear at a young age, the risk for clinical diabetes is particularly high.

The listed antibodies appear to be markers for, rather than the cause of, β-cell injury. β-Cell destruction (by apoptotic and cytotoxic mechanisms) is mediated by a variety of cytokines, or by direct T lymphocyte activity. Supporting this notion, type 1 diabetes has been transferred through bone marrow cells from a diabetic patient to a nondiabetic recipient. Additionally, autopsies performed on patients dying soon after disease onset have shown islet-restricted monocytic cellular infiltrates (termed insulitis) that are composed of CD8+ and CD4+ T cells, macrophages, and B cells. Usually, as the disease progresses, the islets become completely devoid of β cells and inflammatory infiltrates; α, δ, and pancreatic polypeptide cells are left intact, thus illustrating the exquisite specificity of the autoimmune attack. At the time of clinical diagnosis, about 5 to 10% of the original β-cell mass typically remains (see Fig. 242–2).

A critical role for T cells is supported by studies involving pancreatic transplantation in identical twins. Monozygotic twins with diabetes who received kidney and pancreas grafts from their nondiabetic, genetically identical sibling required little or no immunosuppression for graft acceptance. Nevertheless, the islets were soon selectively invaded with mononuclear cells, predominantly CD8+ T cells, with the subsequent recurrence of diabetes. Thus, decades after the original onset of disease, the immune system retained the ability to selectively destroy β cells. Evidence implicating T cells also derives from clinical trials using immunosuppressive drugs. Drugs such as cyclosporine slow or prevent the progression of recent-onset diabetes, but immunosuppression must be continuous to maintain the effect. Further supporting data for a primary role for T cells derives from NOD mice, in which insulitis and islet autoantibodies develop at about 4 weeks of age, and diabetes ultimately develops after 12 to 24 weeks; in these mice, a variety of treatments designed to deplete T cells can prevent diabetes. Most importantly, adoptive transfer of T cells isolated from diabetic mice donors into immune-incompetent NOD mice rapidly produces diabetes. Both CD4+ and CD8+ T cells are generally required for transfer of disease, which suggests that both are necessary for disease expression. These diabetogenic T cells target specific β-cell antigens, including insulin and GAD. A likely role for GAD and/or insulin is also suggested by data showing that if NOD mice are made tolerant to GAD or to insulin (or to peptides derived from these molecules) early in life, insulitis and diabetes fail to develop. Finally, the chronic, smoldering nature of type 1 diabetes suggests the presence of regulatory or protective influences. In keeping with this observation, T cells that protect the islet cell from immune attack have been isolated from the islets of NOD mice. Such findings suggest that the rate of appearance and clinical expression of disease may be modulated by the balance between diabetogenic and protective populations of T cells. "Tipping the scales" in favor of protective T-cell proliferation is the goal of protective immunization.

TYPE 2 DIABETES

Hyperglycemia in type 2 diabetes likely results from complex genetic interactions, the expression of which is modified by environmental factors such as body weight and exercise. With type 2 diabetes, identical twin concordance rates approach 100%, although disease onset and course can vary greatly based on environmental factors. Hyperglycemia itself is known to impair insulin secretion and action; elevated free fatty acid levels also play a pathogenic role. By the time that hyperglycemia is detected, nearly all type 2 patients exhibit both defective insulin secretion and insulin resistance; this makes it

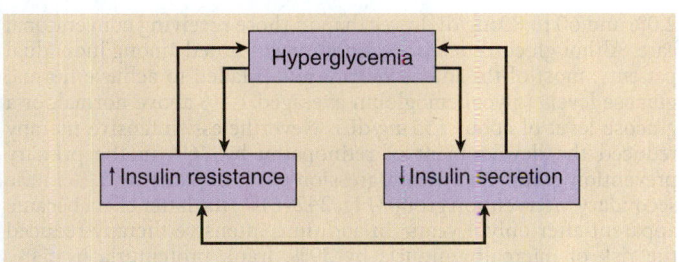

FIGURE 242–4 • Elevations of circulating glucose initiate a vicious cycle in which hyperglycemia begets more severe hyperglycemia.

difficult to determine which of the two factors is primarily responsible for the vicious cycle leading to disease (Fig. 242–4).

GENETIC FACTORS. Although monogenic forms of diabetes have been identified (e.g., MODY types 1 through 6), the vast majority of cases are polygenic in nature. Type 2 diabetes shows clear familial aggregation but does not segregate in classic mendelian fashion; this implies that the disease results either from a combination of genetic defects or from the simultaneous presence of multiple susceptibility genes in the presence of predisposing environmental factors. Candidate gene mutations for polygenic forms of type 2 diabetes include mutations of the coding region of the insulin gene, peroxisome proliferator-activated receptor gamma (PPAR-γ), intestinal fatty acid binding protein 2 (FABP 2), calpain 10, and the β-3-adrenergic receptor. These and other mutations have been associated with isolated patient clusters of type 2 diabetes.

INSULIN SECRETION. Fasting insulin levels in type 2 diabetes are generally normal or elevated, yet they are *relatively* low given the degree of coexisting hyperglycemia. As the disease progresses and hyperglycemia becomes more severe, basal insulin levels eventually fail to keep up and may even decline. The insulin secretory defect usually correlates with the severity of fasting hyperglycemia and is more evident following carbohydrate ingestion. In its mildest form, the β-cell defect is subtle, involving the loss of the first-phase insulin response and the normal oscillatory pattern of insulin secretion. Although the overall insulin response may be fairly intact, this "normal" response is actually inadequate to maintain glucose tolerance when viewed in the context of simultaneous insulin resistance. During this early stage, the β-cell defect is usually specific for glucose; other secretagogues (e.g., amino acids) maintain their potency, and insulin deficiency is thus less pronounced during the ingestion of mixed meals. Patients with more severe fasting hyperglycemia lose this capacity to respond to the other insulin secretagogues; thus, their secretory defect worsens as their disease progresses. Unfortunately, the underlying cause of the secretory defect remains uncertain and is likely multifactorial.

Studies in rodents suggest that the loss of glucose-stimulated insulin secretion is followed by a decreased expression of GLUT 2, the primary glucose transport protein of the pancreatic β-cell. Such a loss of GLUT 2 during the clinical transition to diabetes would likely accelerate the decline of glucose-stimulated insulin secretion. Pathologic studies of islets from patients with long-standing type 2 diabetes have demonstrated amyloid-like deposits composed of islet amyloid polypeptide, or *amylin*, a peptide synthesized in the β-cell and cosecreted with insulin. Chronic hypersecretion of amylin may lead to precipitation of the peptide, which over time might also contribute to impaired β-cell function. Recent experiments in gene knockout mice suggest a potential role for impaired insulin receptor signaling in the development of impaired β-cell function. A link between insulin resistance and secretion is also suggested by data showing that accumulation of fat within the β-cell (as a result of hyperglycemia, insulin resistance, and increased fatty acid turnover) may further reduce insulin secretion.

INSULIN RESISTANCE. With few exceptions (e.g., a subgroup of African American patients), type 2 diabetes is characterized by impaired insulin action. The insulin dose-response curve for augmenting glucose uptake in peripheral tissues is shifted to the right (representing decreased insulin sensitivity), and maximal response is reduced, particularly in the setting of severe hyperglycemia. Other insulin-dependent processes, such as inhibition of hepatic glucose production and lipolysis, also show reduced sensitivity to insulin. The mechanisms responsible for insulin resistance remain poorly understood.

Early studies of insulin resistance focused on defects of the insulin receptor. Mutation of the insulin receptor gene can produce leprechaunism, characterized by severe growth retardation, extreme insulin resistance, and early infant death. Other syndromes related to mutated insulin receptors include the Rabson-Mendenhall syndrome, also associated with tooth and nail abnormalities and pineal gland hyperplasia, and "type A insulin resistance," most often affecting young females with acanthosis nigricans, polycystic ovaries, and hirsutism. Another example of extreme insulin resistance involves the presence of anti-insulin receptor antibodies, which is associated clinically with acanthosis nigricans and other autoimmune phenomena.

Although insulin receptors are rarely abnormal in type 2 patients, defects in more distal "post-receptor" pathways play a far greater role in insulin resistance. One important aspect of resistance is a reduced capacity for translocation of GLUT 4 to the cell surface in muscle cells. A separate defect in glycogen synthesis is also likely to be present. Whether the defects uncovered are primary or secondary to the disturbance in glucose metabolism is uncertain; possibly, a variety of genetic abnormalities in cellular transduction of the insulin signal may individually or in concert produce an identical clinical phenotype. It is uncertain whether mechanisms of insulin resistance in nonobese patients are identical to those of their obese counterparts; however, the coexistence of obesity clearly accentuates the severity of the resistant state. In particular, upper body or abdominal (as compared with lower body or peripheral) obesity is associated with insulin resistance and diabetes. Intra-abdominal visceral fat deposits, detected by computed tomography or magnetic resonance imaging, have a higher lipolysis rate and are more resistant to insulin than peripheral fat. The resulting increase in circulating free fatty acid levels promotes fat deposits in the liver and muscle, worsening insulin resistance. Intracellular free fatty acid metabolites appear to promote insulin resistance through complex mechanisms, involving serine (rather than tyrosine) phosphorylation of insulin signaling molecules. Cortisol hypersecretion and/or hereditary factors may also influence the distribution of body fat, the latter contributing an additional genetic influence on the expression of disease.

ADIPOCYTE-DERIVED HORMONES AND CYTOKINES. Adipocytes, once thought of as inert fat storage cells, are now known to produce a number of metabolically active hormones that may affect insulin sensitivity. *Leptin*, for example, acts on the hypothalamus to promote satiety and energy expenditure and may accelerate glucose metabolism. *Adiponectin* (Acrp30), another fat-derived hormone, circulates at levels that correlate inversely with both adiposity and degree of insulin resistance. The administration of adiponectin to obese mice causes a transient, dose-dependent, insulin-independent decrease in circulating glucose levels; adiponectin also improves insulin sensitivity by decreasing triglycerides in the liver and muscle, likely by increasing the expression of molecules involved in fatty acid combustion and energy dissipation. Finally, adipose tissue is an abundant source of the cytokine tumor necrosis factor-α, which is known to inhibit muscle glucose metabolism by inducing serine phosphorylation of insulin signalling molecules. The precise impact that these and other adipocyte-derived factors exert on insulin resistance has yet to be established; these proteins may well play an important role in the pathogenesis of diabetes.

GLUCOTOXICITY AND LIPOTOXICITY. Hyperglycemia per se impairs the β-cell response to glucose and promotes insulin resistance. Reversal of glucotoxicity can disrupt the vicious cycle that perpetuates hyperglycemia (see Fig. 242–4). Circulating lipids can also adversely affect glucose metabolism; increased free fatty acid levels accelerate hepatic gluconeogenesis, inhibit muscle glucose metabolism, and may impair pancreatic β-cell function. As is the case with glucotoxicity, the reversal of lipotoxicity can rapidly improve metabolic control and facilitate favorable therapeutic outcomes.

WHAT IS THE PRIMARY DEFECT? It remains uncertain whether insulin resistance or defective insulin secretion is the primary defect in type 2 diabetes. This issue is difficult to resolve once diabetes has developed; therefore, research attention has focused primarily on high-risk, nondiabetic subjects. Studies in high-risk populations (e.g., Pima Indians, Mexican Americans) have suggested that insulin resistance is the initial defect; similar findings have been reported in first-degree relatives of type 2 diabetic patients and in healthy prediabetic offspring of two diabetic parents. Interestingly, hyperinsulinemia has been detected in prediabetic subjects as early as one to two decades before clinical onset, suggesting that the development of diabetes can be exceedingly slow. Although these studies support the view that

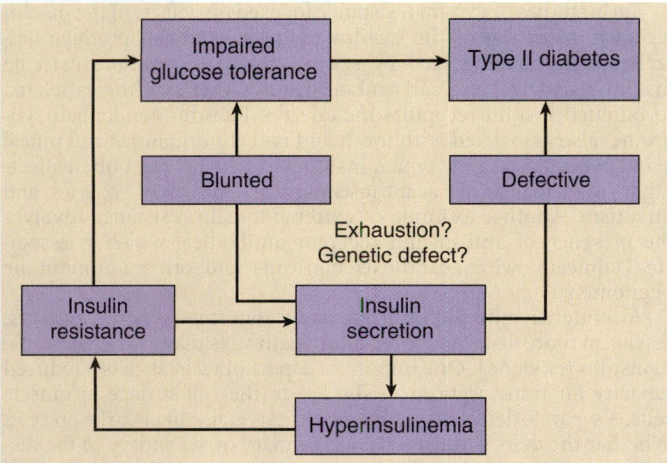

FIGURE 242-5 • A proposed sequence of events leading to the development of type 2 diabetes: insulin resistance resulting from genetic influences, central obesity, inactivity, or a combination of these factors leads over time to a progressive loss of the β-cell's capacity to compensate for this defect.

insulin resistance generally antedates insulin deficiency, the presence of insulin resistance alone is generally insufficient to generate disease; this implies that for diabetes to occur, impaired insulin secretion is also required (Fig. 242-5). It is possible that the appearance of a secretory defect is a secondary phenomenon, possibly resulting from "β-cell exhaustion," excess fatty acid delivery, and/or amylin accumulation. Alternatively, diminished insulin secretion may result from an independent defect that becomes evident only upon chronic β-cell stimulation, such as a subtle genetic defect in insulin signaling.

The sequence of events described—underlying insulin resistance followed by a secretory defect—is common but clearly does not describe all type 2 diabetic patients. For example, a subgroup of African American patients exhibits little or no insulin resistance. Additionally, diminished glucose-stimulated insulin secretion is seen in women with gestational diabetes in whom type 2 diabetes later develops. Finally, the demonstration of functional β-cell–associated gene mutations in patients with MODY indicates that primary β-cell defects are capable of producing a similar phenotype. Taken together, these lines of evidence strongly suggest that type 2 diabetes cannot be explained by insulin resistance alone or by any single pathogenic mechanism.

Relationship Between Diabetes Control and Its Complications

Whether the vascular and neuropathic complications of diabetes mellitus can be prevented or delayed by improved glycemic control was debated for more than a half century. To answer the question, the National Institutes of Health initiated the Diabetes Control and Complications Trial (DCCT), a 9-year multicenter study involving 1441 type 1 patients aged 13 to 39 years who were randomly assigned to either intensive insulin therapy or conventional care. Intensive therapy consisted of three or more insulin injections per day (or an insulin pump), self-monitoring of blood glucose at least four times per day, and frequent contact with a diabetes health care team. Conventional care consisted of one or more (commonly two) injections of insulin per day, less frequent glucose monitoring, standard education, and less frequent health care visits. The target goals of therapy were different as well. The intensive therapy group sought pre-meal blood sugar levels of 70–120 mg/dL, postprandial blood levels of less than 180 mg/dL, and glycohemoglobin values as close to normal as possible. In the conventional care group, the primary goal was simply to maintain clinical well-being. Patients were divided into two groups: (1) a primary prevention group, with diabetes for 1 to 5 years and no detectable complications, and (2) a secondary intervention group, with diabetes for 1 to 15 years and mild nonproliferative retinopathy. Remarkably, nearly 99% of enrolled patients completed the trial.

The DCCT achieved a clear separation of glucose levels between the groups over the entire study period. Glycohemoglobin (Hb A_{1c}) and mean glucose levels in the intensive therapy group were 1.5 to 2.0% and 60 to 80 mg/dL lower than in those receiving conventional care. Although considerable variability was noted among individual patients, most of the intensive care group failed to achieve normal glucose levels (glycohemoglobin averaged 1.1% above normal, or a glucose level of about 155 mg/dL). Nevertheless, intensive therapy reduced the development of retinopathy by 76% in the primary prevention group, and the progression of retinopathy by 54% in the secondary intervention group (Fig. 242-6) **1**; the latter effect became apparent after only 4 years. In addition, intensive therapy reduced the risk of microalbuminuria by 39%, frank proteinuria by 54%, and clinical neuropathy by 60%. The incidence of major cardiovascular events also tended to be lower, but the number of events was insufficient for statistical proof; at the very least, intensive therapy did not pose a *risk* for macrovascular complications. An exponential relationship over time between the average blood glucose level (as reflected by Hb A_{1c}) and the progression of retinopathy in the intensive care group suggests that there may be no threshold level at which complications occur. These findings imply that *any degree of improvement in glycemic control has benefit*, and that normalization of glucose levels is not required to slow the progression of diabetic complications.

The benefits achieved by intensive control in the DCCT were not without risk. Weight gain was more common, and most importantly, the frequency of severe hypoglycemia (including multiple episodes in some patients) was three-fold higher in the intensive care group. In many cases, such episodes occurred without classic warning symptoms, often while the patient was asleep. Thus, in some patients, the risks of intensive therapy may outweigh the benefits; possibly included are patients with recurrent severe hypoglycemia, patients with advanced complications, young children, and patients who are unable or unwilling to participate in their management (e.g., self-monitoring of blood glucose). Such individuals are likely to benefit from less aggressive therapy designed to moderately lower glucose levels without the risk of hypoglycemia. It is noteworthy that despite

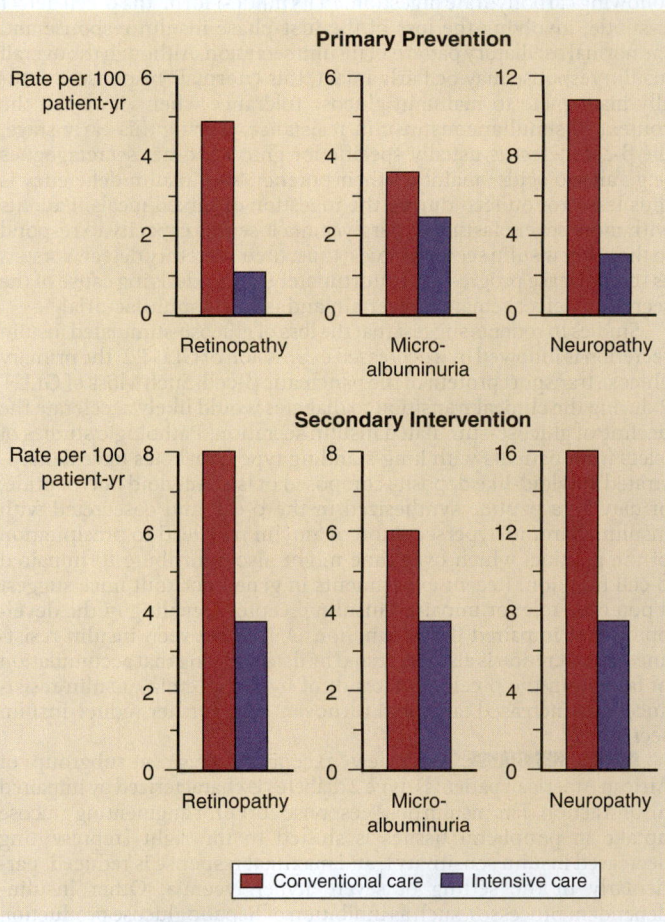

FIGURE 242-6 • A summary of the results of the Diabetes Control and Complications Trial.

the higher rate of hypoglycemia, intensive therapy in the DCCT had no detectable long-term effects on cognitive function.

Although the DCCT did not involve type 2 diabetic patients, a small study using a similar experimental design in lean Japanese patients with type 2 diabetes showed similar results. More conclusive evidence that improved control of blood glucose is beneficial for type 2 diabetic patients derives from the United Kingdom Prospective Diabetes Study (UKPDS). The UKPDS recruited 5102 patients with newly diagnosed type 2 diabetes between 1977 and 1991. After 3 months of diet therapy, the 3867 patients with fasting glucose levels between 6.1 and 15.0 mmol/L (110 and 270 mg/dL) were randomized to a more intensive regimen consisting of sulfonylurea, metformin (for obese patients only) or insulin, or a conventional treatment regimen focused primarily on symptom reduction. Subjects were monitored for an average of 10 years. Although glycemic control gradually deteriorated in both groups, the intensified treatment group had lower mean Hb A_{1c} than their conventionally treated counterparts (7.0% versus 7.9%). This modest improvement significantly reduced microvascular complications by 25% and reduced all diabetes-related events by 12%. **[2]** The intensified treatment group also had a 16% reduction in a combined end point—nonfatal or fatal myocardial infarction or sudden death—that did not quite reach statistical significance ($P=.052$). A continuous relationship was again noted between glycemic control and diabetic complications; also similar to the DCCT, no glycemic threshold for microvascular complications was observed. Importantly, serious adverse events were rare for all of the treatment arms in the UKPDS, and only a single death from hypoglycemia occurred in more than 27,000 patient years of intensive therapy.

What conclusions can be drawn from the DCCT and the UKPDS? The primary message is that "glucose matters." In both type 1 and type 2 diabetic patients who are willing and able to actively participate in their management, the goal should be to achieve the best possible level of glycemic control as rapidly as possible without undue risk. The DCCT and UKPDS also demonstrate that most patients benefit from lower glucose levels, even if normalization is not achieved; for most type 2 patients, effective glucose reductions can be achieved by diet, oral agents, or less complicated insulin regimens than are required in type 1 patients. The greatest challenge for the clinician is how to effectively apply the DCCT and UKPDS results in practice, a formidable task. Both study groups were highly motivated and compliant. Furthermore, management was supervised by an experienced health care team that was able to devote more time to patients than is usually feasible. An important lesson from these studies was that successful treatment of diabetes was largely accomplished through the efforts of the patients themselves, as well as by nurse educators, dietitians, and diabetes counselors. It makes sense, then, to encourage the use of physician-directed health care *teams* to translate the findings of the DCCT and UKPDS into clinical practice.

Rx Treatment

Treatment of diabetes mellitus involves changes in lifestyle and may require pharmacologic intervention with insulin or with oral glucose-lowering drugs. In type 1 diabetes, the primary focus is to replace lost insulin secretion; lifestyle changes are required to facilitate insulin therapy and to optimize health. For patients with type 2 diabetes, changes in lifestyle are the cornerstone of treatment (especially in the early stages of disease), and pharmacologic intervention is a secondary treatment strategy. Although therapeutic strategies differ for the two common forms of diabetes, the treatment goals are essentially identical. In the short term, the goals of diabetes treatment are to optimize metabolic control and improve the patient's sense of clinical well-being. Long-term therapeutic goals focus on the prevention of complications, including cardiovascular disease, nephropathy, retinopathy, and neurologic disease.

TYPE 1 DIABETES

INSULIN PREPARATIONS AND PHARMACOKINETICS. A variety of highly purified insulin preparations are commercially available that differ mainly in their pharmacokinetics (Table 242–5). Premixed insulin preparations are also available and may offer added convenience for selected patients. Nearly all insulin preparations contain 100 U/mL (U-100), although a more concentrated 500 U/mL preparation of regular insulin

Table 242–5 • INSULIN PREPARATIONS: EFFECT ONSET, PEAK, AND DURATION AFTER SUBCUTANEOUS ADMINISTRATION

CLASS	PREPARATION EFFECT	ONSET OF EFFECT	PEAK (HRS)	DURATION OF ACTION (HRS)
Rapid-acting	Lispro or Aspart	10–15 min	1–2	3–4
Short-acting	Regular (R)	30 min	2–4	5–8
Intermediate-acting	NPH (N) or Lente	2–4 hours	5–10	16–20
Long-acting	Ultralente (U)	4–6 hours	6–16	~24
	Glargine	2–4 hours	no peak	>30

(U-500) for severely resistant patients can be obtained. Human insulin is now the only form of insulin sold in North America and other industrialized countries, largely because of immunologic concerns. Because human insulin generates lower titers of insulin antibodies than porcine or bovine insulin, it acts more rapidly after injection and has a shorter duration of action, allowing better synchrony between insulin peaks (after premeal injection of rapid-acting insulin) and the absorption of meals. It is noteworthy that the same insulin preparation can produce variable responses in a single patient, since the peak and duration of most insulin preparations are influenced by the site of administration, skin temperature, the depth of injection, and the magnitude of the insulin dose.

Rapid- and Short-Acting Insulin Preparations. After subcutaneous injection, regular (R) insulin begins to act in about 30 minutes and should therefore be administered 25 to 30 minutes before a meal. Because it acts quickly and has a relatively short duration of action (5–8 hours), it is effective for blunting postprandial glucose excursions and for facilitating rapid dose adjustments based on measured blood glucose values. The properties of regular insulin are especially helpful in managing glucose elevations that occur during illness, or after the consumption of large meals. Given intravenously, regular insulin is also effective in the perioperative period and in the management of severely ill patients and acute hyperglycemic complications.

In regular insulin preparations, insulin molecules exist predominantly in hexameric form. Before being absorbed, insulin hexamers must first be diluted in subcutaneous interstitial fluid, then dissociate into single molecules; this property accounts for the slightly delayed absorption of regular insulin from subcutaneous injection sites. Recently, advances in recombinant DNA technology have led to the development of insulin analogues intended to bypass this property, allowing for more rapid absorption. In 1996, lispro insulin was introduced. This insulin analogue, in which the amino acids in positions B28 (lysine) and B29 (proline) have been reversed, has a reduced capacity for hexameric self-association and is therefore more rapidly absorbed. Its effects begin within 10 to 15 minutes of administration, and generally wane within 3 to 4 hours. Because of its rapid onset, lispro can be given just before eating (as opposed to 30 minutes prior), a feature that greatly simplifies the planning and consumption of meals; also, because its effects wane more rapidly, there is a reduced risk of "late" hypoglycemia if the next meal is delayed. Using lispro insulin, postprandial glucose and hemoglobin A_{1c} reductions are equal to or better than those achieved with regular insulin, and there is a reduced incidence of delayed hypoglycemia. For these reasons, and because of greater convenience and flexibility, lispro is being used with increasing frequency in intensive treatment regimens.

Insulin aspart, the second rapid-acting insulin analogue approved by the Food and Drug Administration (FDA), was released in 2001. In insulin aspart, a neutral proline residue at position B28 is replaced by negatively charged aspartic acid, resulting in a reduced capacity for self-association and faster absorption. The pharmacokinetic properties of insulin aspart are similar to those of insulin lispro; insulin aspart may have a slightly longer duration of effect.

Intermediate- and Long-Acting Insulin Preparations. The longer-acting insulin preparations have been modified to delay their absorption from injection sites, resulting in a longer duration of insulin activity. The addition of protamine and zinc yields intermediate-acting Neutral Protamine Hagedorn (NPH) insulin, whereas enlarging the size of the zinc-insulin crystal yields Lente (intermediate-acting) and Ultralente (long-acting) insulins. NPH and Lente, the intermediate-acting insulins, have a similar time course of action; when given twice per day, they offer a compromise between some degree of meal coverage (coinciding with peak activity) and the provision of basal insulin levels. Ultralente insulin, because of its longer duration and somewhat less evident peaks, offers possible advantages for basal insulin replacement and can be given once daily in some patients. However, the pharmacokinetics of Ultralente are less predictable in clinical practice (even within a single patient), and its effects commonly require twice-daily dosing, limiting its utility.

Insulin glargine, approved by the FDA in 2001, differs from human insulin both at position A21, where asparagine is replaced by glycine, and at the C-terminus of the B-chain, where two arginine residues have been added. Insulin glargine is soluble at acidic pH and less so in physiologic conditions; injected at a pH of 4, it is neutralized in subcutaneous tissue and forms microprecipitates, delaying its absorption and prolonging its duration of activity. The primary advantages of glargine insulin are greater than 24-hour activity (allowing once-daily dosing) and the lack of peak concentrations; both characteristics are desirable for the provision of consistent basal insulin levels. Disadvantages include higher cost, a higher incidence of mild injection site discomfort, and the inability to mix glargine with other insulins. Clinical trials in type 1 diabetic patients suggest that insulin glargine produces similar or slightly larger reductions in hemoglobin A_{1c} as compared with NPH; comparative trials have also shown a reduced incidence in nocturnal hypoglycemia when insulin glargine is used. In type 2 diabetic patients, the clinical differences between glargine and NPH are less significant; in comparative trials, hemoglobin A_{1c} reductions are generally equivalent, and there are smaller differences in the incidence of hypoglycemia. Other long-acting insulins, intended for use in basal insulin therapy, are currently in development.

INSULIN REGIMENS. While a simple concept, the clinical use of insulin to treat diabetes mellitus can be extraordinarily complex. There are many important inter-patient (and intra-patient) variables, so a predictable algorithm cannot be uniformly applied to all patients, nor to a single patient at all times. In general, subcutaneous insulin regimens for type 1 diabetes may be classified as "conservative" or "intensive." Modes of continuous subcutaneous insulin infusion (i.e., insulin pumps) have also gained popularity in recent years.

Conservative Insulin Therapy. Through the early stages of type 1 diabetes, some degree of β-cell function is usually preserved, allowing many patients to achieve glycemic control with less intensive effort. Because intermediate-acting insulins are not generally sustained over a 24-hour period, and because insulin requirements tend to increase early in the morning, these patients should start with two daily injections, consisting of a mixture of intermediate-acting and rapid-acting human insulins administered before breakfast and before dinner. Although Lente insulin has a theoretic advantage over NPH in that it does not contain a foreign protein (protamine), this difference seems to have negligible clinical significance. In fact, NPH may be preferable to Lente when insulins are mixed, because the excess zinc in Lente preparations can cause regular insulin to precipitate out of solution, delaying its absorption.

There are many acceptable approaches to the initiation of conventional insulin therapy (see the section on the treatment of type 2 diabetes). Regardless of the initiation method used, insulin dose adjustments will inevitably be required. Initially, doses of the intermediate-acting insulin should be adjusted to optimize pre-dinner and fasting (morning) glucose levels. Once these goals are accomplished, rapid-acting insulin doses should then be adjusted to optimize postprandial, pre-lunch, and bedtime glucose values. Patients should generally inject in the same anatomic region at the same time each day (i.e., in the abdomen in the morning, in the thigh at night) to ensure consistent insulin delivery; an effort should also be made to avoid exact duplication of injection sites within a 1-week period. Some patients may experience a brief "honeymoon" period, during which β-cell function partially recovers and insulin needs are temporarily reduced. Such an improvement should not be used as a signal to reduce efforts aimed at glycemic control, since continuation of optimal insulin therapy will help to preserve residual β-cell function.

Multiple Subcutaneous Injections. Several years after the onset of type 1 diabetes, residual insulin secretion typically ceases. When this occurs, twice-daily insulin injections are no longer acceptable, even if they continue to successfully control diabetic symptoms. For optimal glycemic control, insulin delivery should more closely simulate the "normal" pattern of insulin secretion; namely, continuous or "basal" insulin levels are required throughout the day, while brief increases

in insulin levels ("boluses") should coincide with the ingestion of meals. The primary problem with twice-daily insulin regimens is that the glucose-lowering effect of the pre-dinner intermediate-acting insulin is greatest at the time when insulin requirements are at their lowest (i.e., around 3:00 AM). Additionally, when requirements are increasing in the pre-dawn hours, insulin levels are declining. The net results of this poorly matched insulin supply and demand are the production of nocturnal hypoglycemia and/or fasting (morning) hyperglycemia.

Successful management of diabetes begins with fasting glucose control. Failure to control morning sugars often results in the stubborn perpetuation of hyperglycemia throughout the day. Once hepatic gluconeogenesis has been activated in the morning, it is not readily suppressed by insulin injections. The key factors responsible for fasting hyperglycemia are inadequate overnight delivery of insulin and sleep-associated growth hormone release. The "dawn phenomenon" is most pronounced in patients with type 1 diabetes because of their inability to compensate by raising endogenous insulin secretion. The magnitude of the dawn phenomenon can be attenuated by designing insulin regimens to ensure that the effects of exogenous insulin do not peak in the middle of the night and dissipate by morning. Several approaches to insulin therapy can deal with this problem; some of the more common regimens are displayed in Figure 242–7. One common approach is to use three injections: a mixture of intermediate- and rapid- or short-acting insulin before breakfast, rapid- or short-acting insulin before dinner, and intermediate-acting insulin at bedtime. The primary disadvantage of this approach is that meal sizes and schedules must be fixed rather rigidly. Alternative multidose regimens incorporate short- or rapid-acting insulin injections before each meal, with one or two daily doses of intermediate- or long-acting insulin (e.g., glargine). Pen-style insulin injectors are also available; these may help to make multidose regimens more convenient and tolerable for patients.

Continuous Subcutaneous Insulin Infusion (CSII). In CSII, rapid-acting insulin is administered around the clock by a battery-powered, externally worn, computer-controlled infusion pump (see Fig. 242–7). The

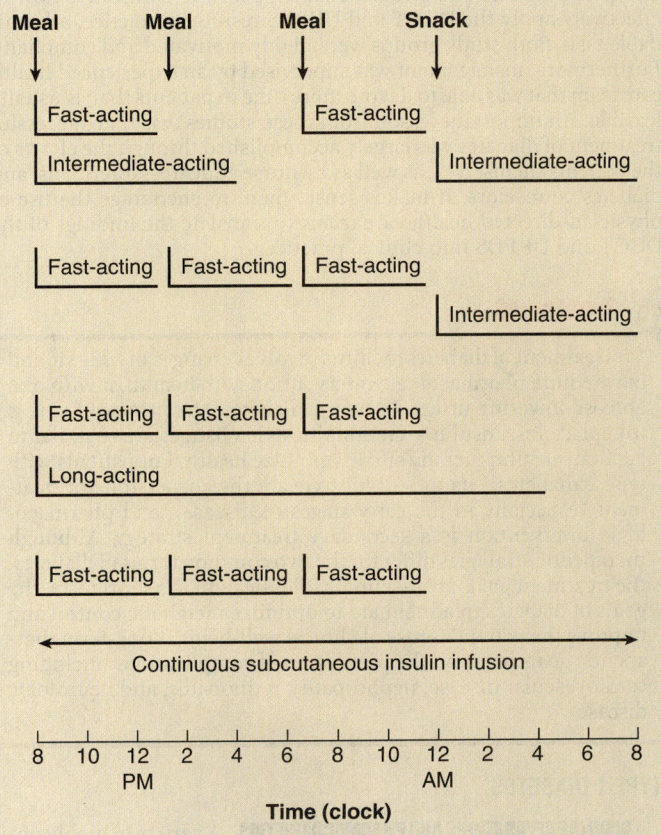

FIGURE 242–7 • Several intensive insulin regimens commonly used in the treatment of diabetes. Each is designed to provide a continuous supply of insulin around the clock and to make extra insulin available at the time of meals, thereby simulating more closely the normal physiologic pattern of insulin secretion.

pump delivers a continuous basal rate and can be programmed to vary the flow rate automatically for set time periods, such as reducing the flow rate after bedtime and increasing flow to compensate for increased insulin requirements in the pre-dawn hours. Boluses, determined by self-monitoring of blood glucose and expected meals, are given by manual pump activation. Most insulin pumps contain an insulin reservoir attached to a subcutaneous catheter (the catheter is inserted using an introducing needle, which is then removed). Catheters are generally best placed in the abdomen, to standardize absorption and maximize visibility. Overall, the CSII method provides diabetic patients with the highest degrees of lifestyle flexibility and glucose control.

The CSII approach has several limitations. One obvious disadvantage of pump therapy is the wearing of the pump itself; the device may be undesirable for patients during intense exercise, contact sports, submersion in water, or personal intimacy. Furthermore, because CSII uses rapid- or short-acting insulin, any interruption in flow (most commonly because of insulin precipitation within the catheter) can lead to rapid deterioration of metabolic control. Local infections at the catheter site occasionally occur, necessitating a site change every 2 to 3 days. Furthermore, maintenance of the pump and appropriate insulin infusion rates requires significant patient effort and sophistication.

The intensive treatment regimens described above are not for everyone. In appropriate patients, however, intensive insulin therapy should be strongly encouraged to reduce the risk of late diabetic complications. It should also be noted that pregnancy is an absolute indication for intensive therapy, and that reduction of the excess neonatal morbidity and mortality associated with diabetic pregnancies requires tight glycemic control. Ideally, intensive insulin therapy should be instituted in type 1 patients before conception, to minimize the risk of fetal anomalies. After conception, blood glucose targets are more stringently applied than at other times, with the specific aim of maintaining glucose levels in the normal range.

LIFESTYLE CHANGES. Diet and exercise contribute importantly to the care of patients with type 1 diabetes. Patients should be educated about balancing caloric intake (diet) with energy expenditure (exercise) and should understand the basic concepts of insulin therapy as it relates to stress and physical activity. If properly managed and sufficiently motivated, diabetic patients should be able to consume the foods they enjoy and should be able to fully participate in exercise and sports.

Diet. The introduction of intensive insulin regimens has increased meal flexibility by allowing more latitude in varying the size, content, and timing of meals. New approaches offer the opportunity for a more normal lifestyle, thus minimizing compliance problems and optimizing patient acceptance and satisfaction. Meals should be nutritionally sound and should provide sufficient calories to meet the energy needs of growing children, active young adults, and pregnant women; the 1800-kcal diet classically prescribed for type 2 patients is grossly insufficient in these and other individuals. Furthermore, diabetic diets should be specifically aimed at minimizing long-term cardiovascular risk by minimizing the ingestion of sodium, cholesterol, and saturated fats (Table 242–6).

Because type 1 patients depend on exogenous insulin, proper management is facilitated by a meal plan designed to match the time course of the selected insulin regimen. Patients should learn to compensate for meal-plan departures by adjusting their insulin doses and for periods of altered activity by adjusting their consumption of food. Effort should be made to avoid long delays between meals, and small snacks may be needed at times of peak insulin action to avoid hypoglycemia. Most patients, regardless of their regimen, should incorporate a bedtime snack to reduce the risk of nocturnal hypoglycemia. Finally, the potential for insulin-induced weight gain requires special emphasis on portion control; to control hypoglycemia, patients should master the use of appropriate carbohydrate intake and avoid overcompensation.

Exercise. Regular exercise is important to promote overall health and to reduce cardiovascular complications. Surprisingly, there is little evidence to suggest that exercise itself substantially improves glycemic control in type 1 diabetes, although it is known to reduce overall insulin requirements by enhancing insulin sensitivity. Through accelerated insulin absorption (due to increased local blood flow at the injection site) and increased muscle glucose consumption, exercise can rapidly reduce blood glucose levels, particularly when it coincides with the peak action of an insulin injection. In nondiabetic individuals, blood glucose levels remain stable during exercise, as decreased

Table 242–6 • LIFESTYLE MODIFICATIONS FOR PATIENTS WITH DIABETES

I. Dietary prescription
  1. Weight reduction, gain, or maintenance, to achieve and maintain ideal body weight
  2. Restriction of saturated fat to <10% of total calories, to be replaced in the diet by carbohydrates and monounsaturated fats. If LDL reduction is also desired, saturated fats should be further restricted to <7% of daily caloric intake
  3. Decreased cholesterol intake to <300 mg per day. If LDL reduction is also desired, cholesterol intake should be further restricted to <200 mg per day
  4. Sodium restriction (<2.4 g per day) in patients with hypertension; in those with overt nephropathy, sodium intake should be further restricted to <2.0 g per day
  5. Protein restriction to <20% of total calories; with nephropathy, protein intake should be further restricted to <0.8 mg/kg/day, or to ~10% of daily caloric intake

II. Exercise prescription*
  1. A combination of aerobic exercise and resistance training is preferred. Avoid heavy lifting, straining, and Valsalva maneuvers, which can raise blood pressure and may aggravate proliferative diabetic retinopathy.
  2. Intensity: Increase heart rate "moderately" to at least 55% of "maximal" heart rate (220 minus age in years), with adjustments based on the patient's cardiovascular fitness. Patients with improved cardiovascular fitness can proceed to "harder" activities, achieving heart rates exceeding 70% of maximum.
  3. Duration: 30 minutes, preceded and followed by stretching and flexibility exercises for a minimum of 5–10 minutes.
  4. Frequency: at least 3 days per week. Results are best if exercise occurs nearly every day.
  5. Avoid strenuous exercise if fasting glucose levels are ≥250 mg/dL. Avoid all forms of exercise if glucose levels are ≥300 mg/dL and/or ketosis is present.
  6. Monitor blood glucose before, during, and after exercise, to learn responses to different exercise conditions and to identify when changes in insulin and/or food intake are necessary.
  7. Consume added foods as needed to avoid hypoglycemia. A rapidly-absorbed carbohydrate source should be readily available during exercise and for up to 8 hours after exercise is completed.

*Exercise limitations are imposed by preexisting coronary or peripheral vascular disease, proliferative retinopathy, peripheral or autonomic neuropathy, and/or poor glycemic control.
LDL = low-density lipoprotein.

endogenous insulin secretion promotes increased hepatic glucose production to match the increased rate of glucose consumption. In diabetic patients receiving exogenous insulin, however, this "finely tuned" homeostatic mechanism is greatly disturbed. The continued presence of exogenous insulin during exercise further accelerates glucose uptake and (more importantly) blocks the compensatory increase in glucose production; as a result, circulating glucose levels can fall precipitously during exercise. Because the magnitude of this fall is not easily titrated, hypoglycemia may occur if the patient is unable to appropriately adjust diet and insulin before, during, and after physical activity (Table 242–6).

TYPE 2 DIABETES

Nonpharmacologic Measures

In many type 2 diabetic patients, diet and exercise are the only therapeutic interventions required to restore metabolic control. As a result, the temptation to use pharmacologic agents should be restrained at the outset, unless the patient is symptomatic or hyperglycemia is severe. On the other hand, the clinician must also resist the temptation to be satisfied by the elimination of symptoms, which is simply the first of many steps in the comprehensive treatment of diabetes. The combination of lifestyle changes and medications can reduce both cardiovascular and microvascular events by about 50%. [3]

DIET. Irrespective of initial weight, modest weight reduction (on the order of 5 kg) in obese diabetic patients leads to improved glycemic control. The dramatic impact of weight loss is mediated by changes in insulin-responsive tissues, as well as by enhanced β-cell activity; insulin resistance diminishes, glucose production declines, and

Endocrine Diseases

lower glucose levels improve glucose-stimulated insulin secretion. The beneficial effects of weight loss are not restricted to glucose; dietary therapy also yields improved lipid profiles and reductions in systemic blood pressure. In general, it matters little how weight loss is achieved, provided that good health is preserved and adequate nutrition is maintained. Successful weight loss is best achieved by the combination of a supportive environment that emphasizes long-term goals, regular exercise to increase energy expenditure, and long-term behavior modification.

In sedentary diabetic patients, maintenance caloric requirements can be as low as 20 to 25 kcal per kilogram of body weight per day. In these individuals, the classically prescribed 1800-kcal diet will be ineffective in producing weight loss. It is sensible to begin with a nutritionally sound, individually tailored diet that is aimed at producing a caloric deficit of about 500 kcal per day. Because a caloric deficit of approximately 3500 kcal is required to lose 1 lb of body fat, weight loss using this method can be expected at 1 lb per week. For obese patients with a history of multiple failed weight loss attempts, very low calorie diets (<1000 kcal/day) can be useful when carried out under medical supervision. Orlistat, a gastrointestinal lipase inhibitor that reduces dietary fat absorption, can be an effective adjunct for achieving weight loss in some patients; it may also improve glycemic control and lipoprotein profiles. Regardless of the method used, experience tells us that most patients are unable to maintain low-calorie diets for an extended period of time; if successful, the majority of patients regain lost weight. In patients with type 2 diabetes, metabolic factors may also contribute to difficulty maintaining weight loss. Dieting reduces glycosuria and therefore lessens urinary caloric loss. Also, the expected decrease in basal metabolic rate during weight loss is accentuated in diabetic patients, because weight loss reverses both accelerated gluconeogenesis and the futile cycling of substrates; these conditions, commonly seen in poorly controlled diabetes, waste a good deal of energy in the hyperglycemic state.

Even when diabetic patients cannot lose weight, a careful meal plan is a valuable tool for reducing their risk of cardiovascular disease. This benefit is best achieved by restricting saturated fats and cholesterol and by raising the dietary content of carbohydrates and monounsaturated fats. It was originally thought that carbohydrate intake should be restricted in diabetes; however, it is now appreciated that a diet high in carbohydrate (>50%) may improve insulin action and glycemic control, particularly in patients with mild hyperglycemia. In patients with more severe fasting hyperglycemia or with triglyceride elevations aggravated by high-carbohydrate diets, reduced carbohydrate intake (<45% of total calories) and greater reliance on monounsaturated fats may be preferable. It has also been assumed that carbohydrate intake should be focused on complex carbohydrates (starches), and that sucrose should be avoided; however, evidence supporting these assumptions is scarce. Simple sugars appear to raise glucose levels to a similar extent as complex carbohydrates; thus, total carbohydrate intake, rather than type of carbohydrate, should be the primary consideration. Fiber-containing carbohydrates such as oats, gums, legumes, and fruit pectin may also be beneficial, since fiber blunts meal-induced glucose excursions by delaying gastric emptying and carbohydrate absorption. Fiber helps to prevent constipation and may also contribute to lowering of triglyceride and low-density lipoprotein (LDL) cholesterol levels.

Another key component of the diabetic meal plan is to alter patterns of dietary fat. The typical Western diet, high in saturated animal fat, likely contributes to the development of atherosclerosis. Diabetic patients with normal lipid profiles are encouraged to follow the recommendations of the National Cholesterol Education Program (NCEP) by limiting total fat intake to less than 30% of total calories, with less than 10% of calories as saturated fat and less than 300 mg/day of dietary cholesterol (see Table 242–6). If low-density lipoprotein levels are elevated, stricter recommendations apply (NCEP Step II diet), with less than 7% of calories as saturated fat and less than 200 mg/day of dietary cholesterol. As mentioned earlier, if elevated triglycerides are of concern, one should consider a moderate *increase* in monounsaturated fats, to replace dietary carbohydrates; of course, increasing fat intake should always be recommended with caution in patients with obesity. Despite a lack of supporting scientific evidence, moderation of dietary protein is also currently recommended for patients with diabetes; this issue assumes greater importance in patients with proteinuria and overt diabetic nephropathy.

EXERCISE. Regular exercise is a powerful adjunct in the treatment of type 2 diabetes. Long-term studies demonstrate consistent beneficial effects of regular exercise on carbohydrate metabolism and insulin sensitivity, which can be maintained for several years. Exercise also facilitates weight loss and its maintenance, which further improves glycemic control and also has beneficial effects on cardiovascular risk: regular exercise lowers triglyceride-rich very low density lipoprotein levels, raises high-density lipoprotein levels, and improves fibrinolytic activity. In general, "moderate" levels of exercise should be prescribed most days of the week (see Table 242–6). Limitations may be imposed by preexisting coronary or peripheral vascular disease, proliferative retinopathy, peripheral or autonomic neuropathy, and poor glycemic control.

Pharmacologic Intervention

ORAL GLUCOSE-LOWERING AGENTS. The hypoglycemic effect of sulfonylureas was first noted in the 1940s, during the development of sulfa antibiotics. Chlorpropamide, the first oral agent approved for use in the United States, was released in 1954. With the exception of phenformin (which was briefly available before being pulled from the market in the 1970s), sulfonylureas were the only oral agents available in the United States for more than 40 years. In contrast, since the 1995 approval of metformin by the FDA, several new classes of oral agents have become available for the treatment of type 2 diabetes (Table 242–7 and Fig. 242–8). Oral agents are indicated in patients in whom diet and exercise fail to achieve treatment goals and may be favored over insulin in older patients with relatively mild degrees of hyperglycemia. Patients with more severe hyperglycemia generally require insulin during the initial phases of treatment; once glucose levels have stabilized and the "toxic" effects of severe hyperglycemia on β-cell function and insulin action have been minimized, many of these patients can then be converted to oral agents.

Sulfonylureas. Sulfonylureas are insulin "secretagogues," which act through specific sulfonylurea receptors on the β-cell surface. Drug-receptor binding acts to close adenosine triphosphate–dependent potassium channels, resulting in cellular depolarization, calcium influx, and the translocation of insulin secretory granules to the β-cell surface. The resulting release of insulin into the portal vein rapidly suppresses hepatic glucose production, and later facilitates peripheral glucose utilization; insulin resistance commonly diminishes as a result of the reversal of glucotoxicity. Because sulfonylureas rely on a preserved β-cell response, they are ineffective in the treatment of type 1 diabetes.

Although the sulfonylureas differ in relative potency, effective dosage, metabolism, and duration of action, from a clinical standpoint these differences have marginal significance (see Table 242–7). Each drug has similar hypoglycemic effects: at maximally effective doses, an average drop in hemoglobin A_{1c} of 1 to 2% is expected, correlating to average fasting plasma glucose reductions of 40 to 80 mg/dL. Drugs with hepatic metabolism and a shorter duration of action have

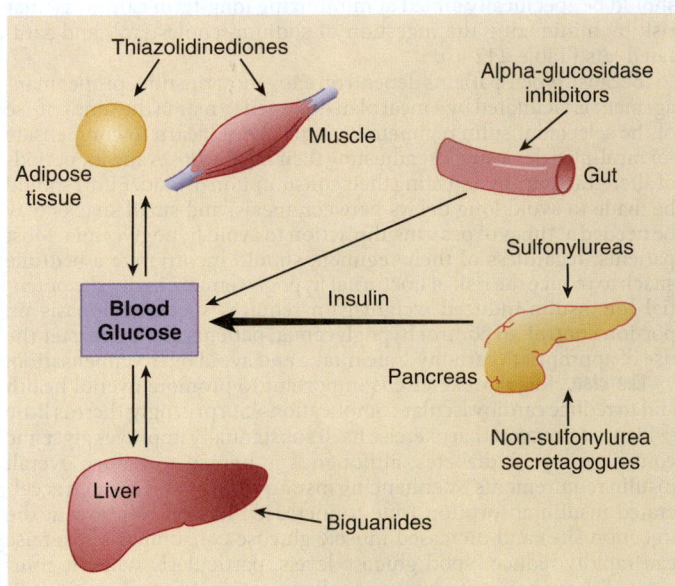

FIGURE 242–8 • Mechanism of action of oral glucose-lowering agents.

Table 242–7 • CHARACTERISTICS OF ORAL GLUCOSE–LOWERING AGENTS

CLASS/AGENT	ACTION	ADMINISTRATION	TOTAL DAILY DOSE (MG/D)	DOSES/DAY	METABOLISM AND EXCRETION	DURATION OF ACTION (HRS)	PRINCIPLE SIDE EFFECTS
Sulfonylureas	Insulin secretagogues	30 minutes prior to meals					Hypoglycemia, weight gain, hyperinsulinemia
First generation							
Chlorpropamide			100–500	1	K > L	~60	
Tolazamide			100–1000	1–2	L > K	12–24	
Tolbutamide			500–3000	2–3	L > K	6–12	
Second generation							
Glimepiride			1–8	1	L > K	24	
Glyburide			1.25–20	1–2	L > K	Up to 24	
Glyburide micronized			1.5–12	1–2	L > K	Up to 24	
Glipizide			5–40	1–2	L > K	Up to 24	
Glipizide GITS			5–20	1	L > K	24	
Biguanide	Inhibits hepatic gluconeogenesis	With meals					Gastrointestinal disturbances (abdominal pain, nausea, diarrhea), lactic acidosis
Metformin			500–2550	2–3	K	Up to 24	
Metformin XR			500–2000	1	K	24	
Metformin/ Glyburide			1.25–20/ 250–2000	2	K/L > K	Up to 24	
Thiazolidinediones	Insulin sensitizers (PPAR-γ agonists)	With meals					Fluid retention, weight gain, congestive heart failure, edema, anemia. Due to the troglitazone experience, periodic monitoring of LFTs is recommended
Pioglitazone			15–45	1	L	24	
Rosiglitazone			4–8	1–2	L	Up to 24	
Alpha-glucosidase inhibitors	Delay carbohydrate absorption	Just prior to meals					Gastrointestinal disturbances (abdominal pain, nausea, diarrhea),? LFT elevation
Acarbose			75–300	3	Gut/K*	Local effect	
Miglitol			75–300	3	K	Local effect	
Non-sulfonylurea secretagogues	Insulin secretagogues	15 minutes prior to meals					Hypoglycemia, weight gain, hyperinsulinemia
Repaglinide			1.5–16	3	L > K	<4	
Nateglinide			180–360	3	K > L	<4	

*The small fraction (<2%) of acarbose that is absorbed is eliminated by the kidneys.
K = kidney; L = liver; LFT = liver function test.

advantages in elderly patients with impaired renal function (who are more vulnerable to hypoglycemia) but may be less effective in practice because of noncompliance with multiple dosing schedules. Conversely, longer-acting agents can be dosed once daily, enhancing compliance but increasing the risk of prolonged hypoglycemia. After the appropriate drug is chosen, treatment is initiated at low doses, with dose increases every 1 to 2 weeks until either treatment goals are met or "maximally effective" doses are reached. Note that for all sulfonylureas, efficacy plateaus at about 50% of the listed maximum dose; above these "maximally effective" doses, there is little clinical benefit derived from dose escalation, and alternative therapies should be considered.

The majority of type 2 patients initially respond to sulfonylureas with improved glycemic control. However, 10 to 20% of patients show little or no response; these cases are known as "primary" drug failures. Additionally, many other patients will experience the loss of drug effect after years of successful therapy; these "secondary" drug failures occur at rates of 5 to 10% per year, because of progressive β-cell failure, drug tolerance, lack of enthusiasm for diet and exercise, and/or the superimposition of comorbid illness. Glucotoxicity itself can also contribute to worsening glucose control. In clinical practice, early signs of secondary drug failure should provoke renewed attempts to reinforce diet and exercise, as well as a reassessment of drug dosage. The re-appearance of hyperglycemia despite maximally effective drug doses signals the need to add another class of oral agent, or to insti-

tute insulin therapy. Overall, only approximately 25% of patients reach glucose targets with a sulfonylurea alone; stated another way, three in four patients will require additional modes of therapy.

Advantages of sulfonylureas include low cost (especially with generics), convenience (once-daily dosing), and the proven reduction of microvascular endpoints (retinopathy, nephropathy, and probably neuropathy) in the UKPDS. Disadvantages include hypoglycemia, weight gain, and the theoretical acceleration of so-called "β-cell exhaustion."

Non-sulfonylurea Secretagogues. Repaglinide, a non-sulfonylurea that interacts with a different portion of the sulfonylurea receptor to stimulate insulin secretion, was approved by the FDA in 1998. A similar agent, nateglinide, was released 2 years later. The major advantage of the nonsulfonylurea secretagogues over sulfonylureas is their rapid and relatively short duration of action, which may attenuate postprandial glucose excursions and reduce the risk of fasting hypoglycemia. Both drugs require frequent daily dosing and should be taken 0 to 15 minutes before meals. Repaglinide and nateglinide exhibit similar or diminished glucose-lowering power compared with the sulfonylureas. Both agents have a favorable side effect profile and typically produce less clinical hypoglycemia than traditional sulfonylureas. The primary disadvantages of the nonsulfonylurea secretagogues are their higher cost and multiple dosing schedules.

Biguanides. Metformin is the only biguanide available for use in the United States. Unlike sulfonylureas, this agent is an "insulin sensitizer," which acts mainly to reduce hepatic glucose production by suppressing gluconeogenesis. Metformin may also augment peripheral glucose utilization, although this effect may be secondary to reversal of glucotoxicity. Metformin exhibits a similar glucose-lowering effect to the sulfonylureas, with expected hemoglobin A_{1C} reductions of 1 to 2%. Metformin has a relatively short half-life (it is eliminated exclusively by the kidney) and is therefore given in two or three divided doses with meals. An extended-release metformin product, released in 2001, allows for more convenient daily dosing.

Because the effects of metformin are extrapancreatic, insulin levels generally fall, a potential advantage if the theory implicating hyperinsulinemia in the development of atherosclerosis proves correct. Other advantages of metformin include mild weight loss, mild (<10%) low-density lipoprotein and triglyceride reductions, and little induced hypoglycemia. Side effects are primarily gastrointestinal, including abdominal pain, bloating, nausea, diarrhea, and anorexia; these may be partially responsible for the weight loss effect. Metformin can also rarely produce lactic acidosis (approximately 0.03 cases per 1000 patient years) and should therefore not be given to patients with renal insufficiency (serum creatinine ≥1.5 in males or ≥1.4 in females), liver disease, congestive heart failure, metabolic acidosis, or a history of alcohol abuse. The drug should also be held in dehydrated patients, and for 48 to 72 hours prior to either surgery or the administration of intravenous radiocontrast agents.

With regard to evidence-based medicine, metformin has the most proven track record among the oral agents. Like sulfonylureas, metformin reduced microvascular end points in the UKPDS; unlike sulfonylureas, it may also have produced reductions in myocardial infarction, diabetes-related death, and overall mortality. Furthermore, in the recently released results of Diabetes Prevention Program (see below), metformin showed an ability to delay the progression to diabetes in patients with impaired glucose tolerance.

Thiazolidinediones. Thiazolidinediones (TZDs) reduce insulin resistance, most likely through activation of PPAR-γ (peroxisome proliferator-activated receptor gamma), a nuclear receptor that regulates the transcription of several insulin-responsive genes that regulate carbohydrate and lipid metabolism. The biologic effect of TZDs is principally mediated by stimulation of peripheral glucose metabolism. PPAR-γ activation also reduces lipolysis and enhances peripheral adipocyte differentiation, thereby redistributing fat stores from the liver, muscle and visceral depots to subcutaneous depots, an effect that likely contributes to the "insulin-sensitizing" effects of the TZDs. In 1997, troglitazone was the first TZD approved for use in the United States; although effective, the drug was withdrawn from the market in 1999 because of concerns over idiosyncratic hepatotoxicity. Two new TZDs, rosiglitazone and pioglitazone, were FDA-approved in 1999; these agents have negligible hepatotoxicity and are currently in widespread use.

Used as monotherapy, TZDs have slightly milder (and more slowly developing) glucose-lowering effects as compared with sulfonylureas and metformin, with expected hemoglobin A_{1C} reductions of 1.0 to 1.5%. Clinical advantages of TZDs include convenience (once-daily dosing), little hypoglycemia, and reduced levels of circulating insulin. TZDs have many other beneficial effects, including (1) lower triglyceride levels (particularly with pioglitazone), (2) higher high-density lipoprotein levels, (3) reductions in small, dense low-density lipoprotein cholesterol, (4) small reductions in blood pressure, (5) improved endothelial function, and (6) enhanced fibrinolytic activity. Studies suggest that TZDs may also slow the growth of atherosclerotic plaque in carotid arteries; ongoing clinical trials are investigating their use in cardiovascular risk reduction. Finally, there is some evidence that TZDs may also slow the decline of β-cell function, thus delaying the clinical progression from impaired glucose tolerance to overt diabetes mellitus.

Compared to other oral hypoglycemic agents, TZDs are more costly. Side effects of the TZDs are largely related to fluid retention and fat redistribution and include weight gain, edema, mild anemia, and worsening of congestive heart failure. These drugs are therefore not recommended for use in patients with moderate-to-severe congestive heart failure or those with severe anemia. As mentioned earlier, the two newer agents appear to be relatively free of hepatic toxicity; however, because of the troglitazone experience, they should not be used in patients with active liver disease or with elevated serum transaminases (ALT ≥2.5 times the upper limit of normal). The manufacturers of both rosiglitazone and pioglitazone currently recommend monitoring liver function tests every 2 months during the first year of therapy, with "peri-odic" testing thereafter. TZDs should be discontinued if transaminases are three or more times the upper limit of normal.

α-GLUCOSIDASE INHIBITORS. Acarbose and miglitol are competitive inhibitors of α-glucosidases, brush-border enzymes in the proximal small intestine that serve to break down complex carbohydrates into monosaccharides. These agents delay the absorption of carbohydrates such as starch, sucrose, and maltose but do not affect the absorption of glucose and other monosaccharides. To be effective, acarbose and miglitol must be taken at the beginning of each carbohydrate-containing meal, usually three to four times per day. Acarbose is minimally absorbed systemically, while miglitol is absorbed and rapidly excreted (unchanged) in the urine. Perhaps as a result of improved glycemic control, both of these agents are associated with modest (<10%) reductions in circulating triglyceride levels and have no appreciable effects on low-density or high-density lipoprotein cholesterol.

In controlled trials performed in patients with type 2 diabetes, α-glucosidase inhibitors reduced postprandial glucose excursions and produced small (0.5 to 1.0%) but meaningful reductions in hemoglobin A_{1C}. The most common side effects associated with both acarbose and miglitol are abdominal pain, bloating, flatulence, and diarrhea; these adverse events can be minimized by initiating therapy at low doses and by using a slowly escalating dose titration schedule. Still, the manufacturers of both drugs discourage their use in patients with inflammatory bowel disease, colonic ulceration, or any other significant chronic gastrointestinal disorder.

INSULIN THERAPY. Insulin is commonly used as first-line therapy for nonobese, younger, or severely hyperglycemic patients with type 2 diabetes and is often temporarily required during times of severe stress (e.g., injury, infection, surgery) or during pregnancy. Insulin should not be used as a first-line therapy for patients who are poorly compliant, unwilling to self-monitor glucose levels, or at high risk for hypoglycemia (e.g., the very elderly). In obese patients, profound insulin resistance often necessitates the use of large doses of insulin, which can interfere with efforts to restrict caloric intake and achieve weight loss. In leaner patients, and in patients with relatively mild fasting hyperglycemia (who continue to maintain endogenous insulin secretory capacity), relatively small doses of basal insulin (e.g., 0.3 to 0.4 U/kg of body weight per day) given once or twice per day may be sufficient to achieve glucose targets. Many of these patients retain some degree of meal-stimulated endogenous insulin secretion and may therefore require less rapid-acting insulin as well.

Although it is common practice to administer a single dose of intermediate-acting insulin in the morning, the glucose-lowering effect of this regimen does not usually extend over a full 24-hour period. Because a key element of successful insulin treatment is to counteract accelerated rates of endogenous glucose production in the morning, it is generally more effective to split the dose and administer sufficient amounts of intermediate-acting insulin in the evening (preferably at bedtime) to optimize control. Alternatively, a single dose of intermediate-acting insulin given at bedtime or of insulin glargine may be effective throughout the following day in patients who have retained the capacity to secrete insulin with meals. This approach has the advantage of greater simplicity and compliance and can be combined with oral glucose-lowering agents during the day to facilitate endogenous insulin release and action.

With regard to the *initiation* of insulin therapy, there are many acceptable approaches. As a first step, the total daily dose of insulin should be estimated from body weight; total insulin requirements typically range between 0.5 and 1.0 U/kg/day. One classic method for starting insulin is to divide the total daily dose unevenly, with two thirds given before breakfast and the remaining one third before dinner. Each of the two doses is then further subdivided: at breakfast, two thirds of the dose is given as intermediate-acting insulin and the other one third as a rapid-acting preparation, while at dinner, the dose is divided into two equal parts. As an example, for a 90 kg man with estimated requirements of 0.67 U/kg/day, 60 U of insulin may be required. Using the above method, this patient might receive 27 units of NPH with 13 units of regular insulin before breakfast, then 10 units of NPH with 10 units of regular insulin before dinner. Please note that this is only one of many "rule-of-thumb" methods for the initiation of insulin; with the advent of intensive therapy, such methods have become largely obsolete. Furthermore, in the absence of hyperglycemic symptoms, clinicians should generally begin with more conservative doses of insulin, to minimize hypoglycemia and to smooth the patient's transition to subcutaneous insulin therapy.

In clinical practice, most insulin-treated patients are obese, have more severe hyperglycemia, and have already failed oral therapy. Such patients have higher degrees of both insulin deficiency and insulin resistance; as a result, they may require multiple-dose insulin regimens similar to those of type 1 patients. In these patients, it is best to distribute the insulin as evenly as possible throughout the day and to provide sufficient coverage overnight to control fasting hyperglycemia. The complexity of the regimen should be individualized according to the clinical context, the patient's ability to perform self-care, and most importantly, the patient's level of education and motivation.

In many cases, the combination of intensive insulin therapy with oral hypoglycemic agents (TZDs or metformin) may reduce insulin dose requirements and improve glycemic control. While growing in acceptance, the potential benefit of reducing circulating insulin levels (using combination therapy) on the development of atherogenesis remains to be established. Experience with the use of intensified insulin treatment, including continuous subcutaneous insulin infusion pumps and multiple subcutaneous injection regimens, is growing in patients with type 2 diabetes. Preliminary results suggest that intensified treatment may be successfully applied to many of these patients.

Treatment Strategies for Type 2 Diabetes

In contrast to type 1 diabetes, in which insulin therapy is required, several pharmacologic options exist for the management of type 2 diabetes. The pros and cons of the various oral hypoglycemic agents have already been discussed; often, it is difficult to justify the use of one oral agent over another. In the literature, many studies have compared the glucose-lowering power of one oral agent to another; however, few studies have compared the drugs in terms of relevant clinical outcomes such as mortality, cardiovascular disease, or microvascular complications. To date, the largest study to address such outcomes in type 2 diabetes was the UKPDS.

In the UKPDS, improved outcomes produced by intensified therapy were similar for patients given insulin, sulfonylureas, or metformin therapy. The ability of the study to detect differences among the various treatments was limited because of drug crossovers and because of the frequent need for drug combinations as the study progressed. The use of metformin in the UKPDS deserves specific mention here because of conflicting results. In the study, patients initially assigned to metformin therapy showed decreased rates of microvascular complications, combined diabetes-related end points, diabetes-related deaths, all-cause deaths, and myocardial infarction as compared with conventionally treated patients; in contrast, patients treated with insulin or sulfonylureas demonstrated reductions in only two of the five categories: microvascular complications and combined diabetes-related end points. Thus, metformin therapy appeared advantageous. Late in the study, however, 537 patients failing sulfonylurea therapy were randomly assigned to either continue the sulfonylurea alone or to add metformin. Compared to the sulfonylurea subgroup, this combined-therapy subgroup had an unexpected 60% *increase* in all-cause mortality. The results of this "substudy" have been called into question, since it was unblinded and lacked a placebo control. In addition, 25% of the patients assigned to continue monotherapy eventually required metformin to achieve glucose targets. In summary, based on the UKPDS, it is difficult to offer an unequivocal recommendation for metformin as compared to sulfonylureas or insulin therapy.

The choice of initial pharmacologic therapy for type 2 diabetes should be influenced mainly by the severity of fasting hyperglycemia, the degree of obesity, and the presence and magnitude of hyperglycemic symptoms. Other factors such as age, education, motivation, and comorbid conditions should also be considered. To determine the effectiveness of the therapy selected, drug regimens should be adjusted over a 3-month period based on glucose self-monitoring; failure to meet glucose targets within 3 months suggests the need for combination therapy (Fig. 242–9). Published clinical trials comparing drug combinations to monotherapy have generally shown additive reductions in hemoglobin A_{1c}; with few exceptions, the magnitude of A_{1c} reduction is similar to that achieved when the added agent is used as monotherapy. As is the case with monotherapy, there is no convincing evidence favoring one combination regimen over another, and most combinations have been approved by the FDA. "Triple-therapy," or combining three agents to achieve glucose targets, is also used frequently in clinical practice (although not yet with FDA

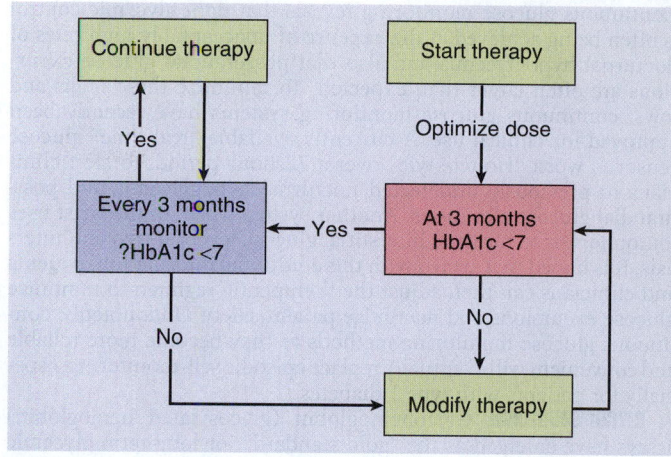

FIGURE 242–9 • Strategy for the treatment of type 2 diabetes.

approval) and appears to be effective. Ultimately, if glucose targets cannot be met by combining oral agents, insulin remains an effective treatment option.

MONITORING

SELF-MONITORING OF BLOOD GLUCOSE. Self-monitoring of blood glucose has revolutionized the management of diabetes. It actively involves patients in the treatment process, allows more rapid treatment adjustments, and reinforces dietary changes. Self-monitoring provides the patient with the tools necessary to assist in managing their disease and is especially useful during periods of stress and for patients who are susceptible to hypoglycemia. Urine glucose testing is unreliable and should not be used.

Newer glucose meters are small, portable, and reliable, give a digital readout, and have computerized memory to facilitate record keeping. Blood sampling is facilitated (and made less painful) by automated, spring-operated lancet devices; recent "off-the-finger" products also allow for more comfortable testing. Self-monitoring of blood glucose is of maximal value if the patient performs tests on a regular basis, can accurately measure glucose levels, and can make use of the results. The patient must become familiar with what a normal glucose value is, what the glucose targets are, and how levels can vary with changes in diet, activity, and insulin absorption. For most insulin-dependent patients, day-to-day adjustments in short-acting insulin based on pre-meal values and a "sliding scale" can be readily accomplished. These patients also need to examine the effects of their longer-acting insulin injections, and to make adjustments if glucose levels (e.g., pre-breakfast, pre-dinner, and bedtime values) are not within the target range. At a minimum, patients should be able to adjust to repetitive patterns of hypoglycemia or hyperglycemia, as well as to periods of stress and illness ("sick days"). For patients in the latter circumstance, urine testing for ketones should also be routinely performed.

The success of insulin therapy depends on the frequency with which the patient performs self-monitoring. Patients with type 1 diabetes should be encouraged to monitor before each meal and at bedtime and whenever symptoms occur. Periodic checks 90 to 120 minutes after meals help to control postprandial hyperglycemia, and patients should occasionally monitor pre-dawn (e.g, 3 AM) glucose levels to avoid nocturnal dips. Currently, no clear guidelines have been established regarding the frequency of blood glucose monitoring for type 2 diabetes. Type 2 patients who are treated with insulin should self-test daily, usually before breakfast, before dinner, and at bedtime. The frequency of blood glucose self-monitoring will depend largely on the stability of metabolic control; testing should be more frequent during the initiation of treatment, after changes in therapy, and during all times that altered metabolic control is suspected. Type 2 patients maintained on dietary therapy should, at the very least, learn self-monitoring of blood glucose to prevent metabolic decompensation. These patients also benefit from periodically monitoring glucose levels so that they may better appreciate how changes in their diet can adversely affect glycemic control.

CONTINUOUS GLUCOSE MONITORING. Traditional self-monitoring of blood glucose is often inadequate to optimize metabolic control.

Continuous glucose monitoring reveals that tight glycemic control is often being achieved at the expense of unacceptably high rates of nocturnal hypoglycemia and also that postprandial glucose excursions are often larger than expected. To minimize these highs and lows, continuous glucose monitoring systems have recently been approved for clinical use. A currently available "real-time" glucose sensor is worn "Holter-style" over a 72-hour period, to alert clinicians to previously undetected nocturnal hypoglycemia and postprandial glucose elevations. Another system worn on the wrist uses iontophoresis to measure interstitial glucose levels at frequent intervals. It is hoped that armed with this additional information, patients and clinicians can then adjust the therapeutic regimen to minimize glucose excursions and maximize patient safety. Undoubtedly, continuous glucose monitoring methods as they become more reliable and convenient will eventually replace episodic self-monitoring, especially for patients with type 1 diabetes.

GLYCOHEMOGLOBIN. Glycohemoglobin (glycosylated hemoglobin) assays have emerged as the "gold standard" for long-term glycemic control. The test does not rely on a patient's ability to self-monitor blood glucose levels and is not influenced by acute glycemic changes or by recent meals. Glycohemoglobin is formed when glucose reacts nonenzymatically with the hemoglobin A molecule; it is composed of several fractions, the largest being hemoglobin A_{1C}. Hemoglobin A_{1C} (expressed as the percentage of total hemoglobin) varies in proportion to the average level of glucose over the lifespan of the red blood cell, thereby providing an index of glycemic control during the preceding 6 to 12 weeks. Several assay methods have been developed that yield different ranges for nondiabetic control subjects; clinicians should therefore become familiar with the specific assays used for testing their patients.

Although ambient glucose levels are the dominant influence on glycohemoglobin levels, other factors can confound the interpretation of the test. For example, any condition that increases red blood cell turnover (e.g., pregnancy, hemolytic anemia) spuriously lowers glycohemoglobin levels, regardless of the assay used. Some assays yield spuriously low values in patients with hemoglobinopathies (e.g., sickle cell disease or trait, hemoglobin C or D), or high values when either hemoglobin F is increased (e.g., thalassemia, myeloproliferative disorders) or when large doses of aspirin are consumed. Thus, for unexpectedly high or low values encountered in clinical practice, factors that alter the specific assay should be excluded. In most cases, discrepancies between self-monitoring of blood glucose and glycohemoglobin results reflect problems with the former rather than the latter. Although glycohemoglobin provides the most accurate estimate of overall glycemic control, it has limited value in guiding specific changes in therapy; in clinical practice, frequent blood glucose measurements are essential to properly adjust the therapeutic regimen.

MANAGEMENT PLAN/TREATMENT GOALS. A management plan should take into consideration the life patterns, age, work and school schedules, psychosocial needs, educational level, and motivation of each individual patient. The plan should include lifestyle changes, a meal plan, medications, monitoring instructions (including "sick day" management), and education regarding the prevention and treatment of hypoglycemia. Importantly, all components of the plan must be both understood and accepted by the patient. Active patient participation in problem solving, as well as ongoing support from a health care team, is critical for the successful management of diabetes. At each visit, the management plan should be reviewed, and an assessment should be made of the patient's progress in achieving glucose targets; if goals are not being met, causes need to be identified, and the plan should then be modified accordingly. At each visit, the history and physical examination should focus on early signs and symptoms of retinal, cardiovascular, neurologic, and podiatric complications, and on reinforcement of the diet and exercise prescription. A complete ophthalmologic examination, assessment of cardiovascular risk factors, and measurement of urinary albumin excretion (through either a timed collection or two "spot" urine albumin-to-creatinine ratios) should all be performed annually. Specialized podiatric care is also recommended for all patients with evidence of pedal neuropathy.

Formulation of individual glycemic goals must take into account the results of the DCCT (type 1 diabetes) and the UKPDS (type 2 diabetes) in the context of the patient's capacity to implement the treatment plan, risk for hypoglycemia, and other factors that would alter the risk-benefit ratio. Table 242–8 presents target glycemic guidelines

Table 242–8 • THERAPEUTIC TARGETS FOR NONPREGNANT DIABETIC PATIENTS

PARAMETERS	NORMAL	TARGET*	INTERVENTION SUGGESTED†
Preprandial plasma glucose (mg/dL)	<110	80–120	<80 or >140
2-hour postprandial glucose (mg/dL)	<140	<160	>180
Bedtime plasma glucose (mg/dL)	<120	100–140	<100 or >160
Hemoglobin A_{1c} (%)	<6	<7†	>7
Low-density lipoprotein cholesterol (mg/dL)	<130	<100	>100
High-density lipoprotein cholesterol (mg/dL)	>40	>45 (men), >55 (women)	<40
Fasting triglycerides (mg/dL)	<150	<150	>150
Blood pressure (mg Hg)	<140/90	<130/85	>130/85

*Clinical targets vary for individual patients, depending on assessment of overall health and risk-to-benefit ratio.
†Interventions may include dietary therapy, exercise prescription, and/or pharmacologic intervention.
‡Hemoglobin A_{1c} control to <6.5% is advocated by some authorities, especially in type 2 diabetics.

for nonpregnant diabetic patients as well as targets for other clinical factors (e.g., blood pressure, lipids) that increase the potential for diabetic complications.

PANCREAS TRANSPLANTATION

Intensive insulin therapy rarely (if ever) restores glucose homeostasis to levels achieved in nondiabetic individuals. As a result, the search for more effective methods of treatment remains a crucial long-term goal of diabetes research. Pancreas transplantation is promising in this regard; with growing experience in recent years, there have been substantial improvements in the outcome of pancreas transplant surgery. In major centers, 80 to 90% of patients emerge from the perioperative period with a functioning graft; once insulin independence is established, the majority of patients remain stable for several years. Successful pancreas transplantation improves the quality of life of patients with diabetes, primarily by eliminating the need for dietary restrictions, insulin injections, and frequent glucose self-monitoring. Although pancreas transplantation is only partially able to reverse long-term diabetic complications, it effectively eliminates acute complications such as hypoglycemia and diabetic ketoacidosis.

Unfortunately, because of the need for long-term immunosuppression, pancreas transplantation is at present an option for only a select group of patients, mainly for type 1 diabetics who will already require immunosuppression for a renal allograft. In such individuals, successful pancreas transplantation is also effective in preventing nephropathy in the grafted kidney. In the absence of indications for a kidney transplant, pancreas transplantation should generally be considered only in diabetic patients with a history of frequent, severe metabolic complications (e.g., hypoglycemia, ketoacidosis), in whom insulin therapy consistently fails to achieve metabolic control.

Pancreatic islet cell transplantation holds many potential advantages over the whole-gland transplant, since it is simpler to perform and less costly. Until recently, islet transplantation has had disappointing results with regard to long-term insulin independence; however, a recent series published out of Edmonton, Alberta, Canada, suggests that outcomes may be improving and that islet transplantation may become a therapeutic option. In this 12-patient series (median follow-up, 10 months), 4 patients had normal glucose tolerance, 5 had IGT, and 3 had a stable diabetes characterized by endogenous insulin production and a low risk of hypoglycemia. Interestingly, compared with diabetic patients, islet-cell transplantation has been easier in patients with chronic pancreatitis, many of whom have successfully undergone total pancreatectomy followed by intraportal injection of pancreatic islets. The implication here is that with diabetes, the use of immunosuppressive drugs, chronic low-grade rejection of the foreign islet grafts, and/or the activation of an autoimmune response may account for transplant failure. If these inferences are correct, the future of islet transplantation therapy for diabetes depends mainly on manipulating the islet and/or the immune response and the availability of donor islets, rather than on technical surgical advances.

Prevention of Diabetes

As the pathogenesis of both types of diabetes becomes better understood, the potential for prevention of these diseases is more realistic. Two large, multicenter disease prevention trials have already been completed in the United States, and several more are planned.

In the Diabetes Prevention Program, more than 3000 overweight subjects with IGT were randomized into four treatment arms: (1) intensive lifestyle changes aimed at reducing body weight by 7% through a low-fat diet and 150 minutes of weekly exercise; (2) treatment with metformin, 850 mg twice per day; (3) treatment with placebo pills, twice per day; and (4) treatment with troglitazone, 400 mg once per day (this arm was discontinued because of concerns over liver toxicity). The latter three groups also received standard information regarding diet and exercise. On the advice of the Diabetes Prevention Program's external data monitoring board, the trial was stopped a year early because of definitive results: 29% of patients in the placebo group developed diabetes during the average follow-up period of 3 years, compared with 22% of patients taking metformin and only 14% of patients undergoing intensive diet and exercise. [4] Put another way, patients taking metformin reduced their risk of diabetes by 31% versus standard care, whereas patients undergoing intensive lifestyle interventions reduced their risk by an impressive 58%. This suggests that patients with IGT (more than 20 million patients in the United States alone, according to recent estimates) can sharply lower their immediate risk of diabetes with intensive lifestyle changes (or in some cases with metformin), and puts the onus on clinicians to screen, identify, and appropriately treat patients with IGT. Postmenopausal estrogen and progestin can reduce the incidence of type 2 diabetes by 35%, [5] but the adverse effects of such therapy may outweigh its benefits (Chapter 256).

Results of the Diabetes Prevention Trial Type 1 have also been recently published. In this study, "high-risk" relatives of type 1 diabetic subjects (based on antibody screening and HLA typing) were randomly assigned to no treatment or to low-dose insulin injections, a therapy used successfully in rodent models of spontaneous autoimmune diabetes to prevent disease expression. After 5 years of observation, nearly 60% of these "high-risk" patients developed diabetes, as predicted by clinical models; unfortunately, there was *no* difference in incidence between the insulin and no treatment arms. [6] Another substudy of the Diabetes Prevention Trial Type 1, testing the prevention of diabetes using *oral* insulin in patients at more moderate risk for disease, is still underway. Other putative preventive strategies are also under investigation.

ACUTE METABOLIC COMPLICATIONS

HYPERGLYCEMIC STATES

Metabolic decompensation in diabetes is generally classified into one of two broad clinical syndromes: diabetic ketoacidosis (DKA) or the hyperosmolar hyperglycemic state (HHS). Although DKA is generally seen in type 1 patients and the HHS affects type 2 patients, lines of classification are commonly blurred; for example, the HHS can present with variable degrees of ketosis and acidosis, while DKA is being seen with increasing frequency in obese type 2 patients. Despite aggressive treatment, mortality rates remain high for both conditions, approaching 5% for DKA and 15% for the HHS. Mortality is associated with advanced age and comorbidity and is usually due to an associated catastrophic illness (e.g., myocardial infarction, cerebrovascular accident, sepsis) or to acute complications, including aspiration, cardiac arrhythmias, or cerebral edema. Treatment of hyperglycemic states therefore involves far more than the administration of insulin to reverse hyperglycemia; it also depends critically on the detection and treatment of precipitating illness, as well as prompt attention to fluid and electrolyte disturbances.

DIABETIC KETOACIDOSIS. DKA may herald the onset of type 1 diabetes but most often occurs in established diabetic patients as a result of an intercurrent illness (e.g., infection), an inappropriate reduction in insulin dosage, or missed insulin injections (especially in adolescents). A common scenario is a patient who fails to adjust insulin therapy and consume extra fluids during an illness. Other common precipi-

tants of DKA (and the HHS) include myocardial infarction, cerebrovascular accident, and alcohol intoxication or abuse; a more extensive list of common precipitants appears in Table 242–9. Prevention of DKA requires extensive education in "sick day" insulin and fluid management as well as home-based assessment of urine ketones whenever severe hyperglycemia or physical illness is noted.

The three cardinal biochemical features of DKA—hyperglycemia, ketosis, and acidosis—result from the combined effects of deficient circulating insulin activity and the excessive secretion of counter-regulatory hormones. These hormonal imbalances mobilize the delivery of substrates from muscle (amino acids, lactate, pyruvate) and adipose tissue (free fatty acids, glycerol) to the liver, where they are actively converted to glucose or to ketone bodies (β-hydroxybutyrate, acetoacetate, acetone); both are ultimately released into the circulation at rates that greatly exceed the capacity of tissues to use them. The end results are hyperglycemia (>250 mg/dL), ketoacidosis (pH <7.30), and an osmotic diuresis that promotes dehydration and electrolyte loss. Typically, the clinical history of DKA involves deterioration over days, with advancing polyuria, polydipsia, and other symptoms of worsening hyperglycemia; other common clinical features include weakness, lethargy, nausea, and anorexia. Abdominal pain in the setting of DKA is classically periumbilical and can mimic the acute abdomen. Reduced motility of the gastrointestinal tract or (in severe cases) paralytic ileus may further contribute to diagnostic confusion. Vomiting is an ominous symptom because it precludes oral replacement of fluid losses; severe volume depletion follows quickly. Physical findings in DKA are mainly secondary to dehydration and acidosis and include dry skin and mucous membranes, reduced jugular venous pressure, tachycardia, orthostatic hypotension, depressed mental function, and Kussmaul (deep, rapid) respirations. Ketosis is often recognizable by a sweet, sickly smell on the patient's breath.

The diagnosis of DKA is usually straightforward and should be made promptly. The clinical picture and the presence of hyperglycemia should alert the clinician to test for ketones and to measure arterial pH. Initial laboratory information to be gathered should include a complete blood cell count with differential, urinalysis, serum chemistries (a "Chem-10," including divalent cations), and cardiac enzymes; liver and pancreatic function tests should also be considered. An electrocardiogram and a chest radiograph should be performed, and cultures should be taken from blood, urine, and other potential sources as clinically indicated. In DKA, glucose levels vary from 250 to greater than 1000 mg/dL, serum bicarbonate drops below 18 mEq/L, and there is an excess anion gap that is generally proportional to the decrease in serum bicarbonate. Hyperchloremia may be superimposed if the patient maintains an adequate glomerular filtration rate (GFR) and is able to exchange ketoacid anions for chloride in the kidney. The degree of

---

Table 242–9 • PRECIPITANTS OF DIABETIC KETOACIDOSIS AND/OR THE HYPEROSMOLAR HYPERGLYCEMIC STATE

THE THREE MOST COMMON PRECIPITANTS
Infections (30–50%): pneumonia, urinary tract infections, sepsis, gastroenteritis, etc.
Inadequate insulin treatment (20–40%): includes noncompliance, insulin pump failure
Myocardial ischemia/infarction (3–6%): often clinically "silent" in diabetic patients

OTHER PRECIPITANTS
Cerebrovascular accident
Intracranial bleeding (e.g., subdural hematoma)
Acute pulmonary embolism
Intestinal/mesenteric thrombosis
Intestinal obstruction
Acute pancreatitis
Alcohol intoxication/abuse
Renal failure (± peritoneal dialysis)
Severe burns, hyperthermia, or hypothermia
Endocrine disorders: Cushing's syndrome, thyrotoxicosis, acromegaly
Total parenteral nutrition
Drugs:
  Cardiovascular: beta-blockers, calcium channel blockers, diuretics, diazoxide, encainide
  Immunosuppressant drugs, including corticosteroids
  Miscellaneous: antipsychotics, phenytoin, cimetidine, pentamidine, L-asparaginase

depression of arterial pH depends largely on respiratory compensation. In mild cases, the pH may range from 7.25 to 7.30, while in severe cases it can fall below 7.00. In general, clinical severity of DKA depends more on the magnitude of acidosis than on hyperglycemia; as a result, arterial pH is widely used as a reference indicator of DKA severity. Occasionally, a degree of superimposed metabolic alkalosis (e.g., caused by vomiting or diuretic use) may obscure the true severity of ketoacidosis. An increased anion gap out of proportion to the fall of bicarbonate should suggest this possibility. Other laboratory abnormalities commonly seen in DKA include a reduced measured serum sodium level (due to hyperosmolarity and the resulting osmotic shift of water into the intravascular space), prerenal azotemia, and hyperamylasemia, which is usually of nonpancreatic origin and can lead to an erroneous diagnosis of pancreatitis. Normal, elevated, or reduced concentrations of potassium, phosphate, and magnesium may exist when DKA is diagnosed; however, large deficits of these electrolytes invariably accompany the osmotic diuresis and become readily apparent during the course of treatment.

Special care should be taken when interpreting serum or urine ketone results. Because quantitative measurements of β-hydroxybutyrate and acetoacetate are not readily available, rapid diagnosis usually requires *qualitative* assessment of serum ketones using serum dilutions and reagent strips (Ketostix) or tablets (Acetest), which depend on a nitroprusside reaction with acetoacetate. Acetone, however, reacts weakly with nitroprusside and β-hydroxybutyrate reacts not at all; as a result, qualitative testing for ketones can be misleadingly low. Furthermore, because of the presence of intracellular acidosis, β-hydroxybutyrate levels are often much higher than levels of acetoacetate, which may further conceal the true degree of ketoacidosis. Conversely, after insulin therapy begins, the nitroprusside reaction gives the "false" impression of sustained ketoacidosis for hours or even days, for two reasons: (1) β-hydroxybutyrate is converted to acetoacetate, creating an illusion of rising ketone levels, and (2) nonacidic acetone is cleared slowly from the peripheral circulation.

HYPEROSMOLAR HYPERGLYCEMIC STATE. The metabolic state formerly known as the hyperglycemic hyperosmolar nonketotic state/coma has been renamed the hyperosmolar hyperglycemic state (HHS), to highlight two important points: (1) ketosis (and acidosis) may be present to varying degrees in HHS, and (2) alterations in sensorium most commonly occur in the absence of coma. In fact, only 10% of HHS patients present with frank coma, and an equal percentage show no signs whatsoever of mental obtundation. The hallmarks of the HHS are severe hyperosmolarity (>320 mOsm/L) and hyperglycemia (>600 mg/dL). Severe hyperglycemia occurs because patients cannot drink enough liquid to keep pace with a vigorous osmotic diuresis; the resulting impairment in renal function further reduces glucose excretion through the kidney, leading to remarkable blood glucose elevations. In contrast to DKA, severe acidosis and ketosis are generally absent in the HHS; however, some type 2 patients with depressed endogenous insulin secretion may be unable to fully suppress ketone production in the face of elevated counter-regulatory hormones produced by physical illness. Because HHS patients have higher portal vein insulin concentrations than patients with DKA, ketoacid production by the liver is relatively mild, yielding only mild acidosis. In the HHS, in the absence of concurrent acid-base disturbances, arterial pH rarely drops below 7.30, and serum bicarbonate levels rarely fall below 18 mEq/L.

In the hyperosmolar hyperglycemic state, clinical severity and levels of consciousness generally correlate with the severity and duration of hyperosmolarity. Clinical signs indicate profound dehydration; gastrointestinal symptoms are less frequently seen than in diabetic ketoacidosis. A variety of often reversible neurologic abnormalities may exist, including grand mal or focal seizures, extensor plantar reflexes, aphasia, hemisensory or motor deficits, and/or worsening of a preexisting organic mental syndrome. The laboratory picture is dominated by the effects of uncontrolled diabetes and dehydration; renal function is impaired, hemoglobin is elevated, and liver function test results may be abnormal because of baseline hepatic steatosis. Although severe hyperglycemia would be expected to lower measured serum sodium, it is not uncommon to see "normal" or even "elevated" sodium levels because of the severity of dehydration. The serum osmolarity itself can be measured directly or can be estimated using the following formula, which excludes urea, since it is freely diffusible throughout the body and therefore has little influence on the osmotic pressure gradient:

$$\text{Effective osmolarity (mOsm/L)} = 2[\text{measured serum Na}^+ + \text{K}^+ \text{(mEq/L)}] + [\text{glucose (mg/dL)}/18]$$

Rx Treatment

The initial goals of therapy for both hyperglycemic states are to replace fluid and electrolyte deficits and to slowly correct hyperglycemia. Unless severe, ketoacidosis will generally correct with these measures and requires no specific therapy. ADA management guidelines are presented in Figure 242–10 and summarized here. In the treatment of hyperglycemic states, special attention must be paid both to treatment of precipitating illness and to potential complications that may arise during (or as a result of) appropriate medical therapy.

In the early hours of treatment, the primary consideration is to restore intravascular volume, to correct tissue hypoperfusion and restore insulin sensitivity. With DKA, there can exist massive total-body deficits of water (5 to 10 L), sodium (5 to 10 mEq/kg), and other electrolytes (see later); losses are even more profound in the HHS. Although water loss usually exceeds the loss of sodium, it is almost always preferable to begin fluid replacement with isotonic normal saline (0.9% NaCl solution) for efficient volume restoration. Fluid replacement regimens vary, but it is common to administer 1 L of normal saline within the first hour, followed by continuous infusion with either 0.45% NaCl or 0.9% NaCl depending on the corrected serum sodium and the patient's hemodynamic status. Likewise, the rate of infusion (commonly 250 to 500 mL/hour) should be adjusted according to both biochemical responses and the clinical status of the patient (e.g., oliguria or underlying cardiovascular disease). In pediatric patients with DKA, isotonic solutions are generally preferred, since they are less likely than hypotonic solutions to accelerate water shifts into the intracellular space and contribute to cerebral edema. During the course of treatment, once blood glucose falls to below 250 or 300 mg/dL, glucose should be added to intravenous fluids to avoid eventual hypoglycemia and to minimize the risk of cerebral edema.

Although insulin resistance is present in both DKA and the HHS, supraphysiologic doses of insulin are unnecessary and are more likely to provoke hypokalemia, hypophosphatemia, and delayed hypoglycemia. A typical insulin replacement regimen uses an intravenous bolus of 0.15 U/kg of rapid-acting (e.g., regular) insulin, followed by 0.1 U/kg/hour thereafter. Smaller doses may be used in HHS. Intravenous administration is the most predictable way of delivering insulin to target tissues, particularly in severely hypovolemic patients with reduced peripheral blood flow. If intravenous administration is not possible, the intramuscular or subcutaneous routes of administration can be used. It is ideal if blood glucose levels fall at a steady and predictable rate (50 to 80 mg/dL/hour), so it is important to monitor blood glucose hourly during insulin therapy to ensure an appropriate rate of decline. Blood glucose should not fall too rapidly, especially in young children, in whom accelerated glucose correction has been associated with cerebral edema.

When reviewing the progress of treatment, it is important to consider a failure in insulin delivery if blood glucose fails to drop appropriately. In some patients, persistent hyperglycemia may be due to severe insulin resistance and necessitates an increase in the insulin dose. However, because the primary mechanism for lowering plasma glucose in the early stages of treatment is urinary glucose disposal (rather than insulin-stimulated glucose consumption), the problem may simply reflect inadequate replacement of intravascular volume, in which case insulin rates may not need to be increased. After a stable blood glucose level below 250 mg/dL has been achieved, subcutaneous administration of insulin can be started, and the intravenous insulin infusion may be discontinued. With DKA, it is best to overlap the intravenous and subcutaneous routes by 1 to 2 hours, to avoid the return of ketoacidosis. Following the return of normoglycemia, long-term medical management should be initi-

Continued

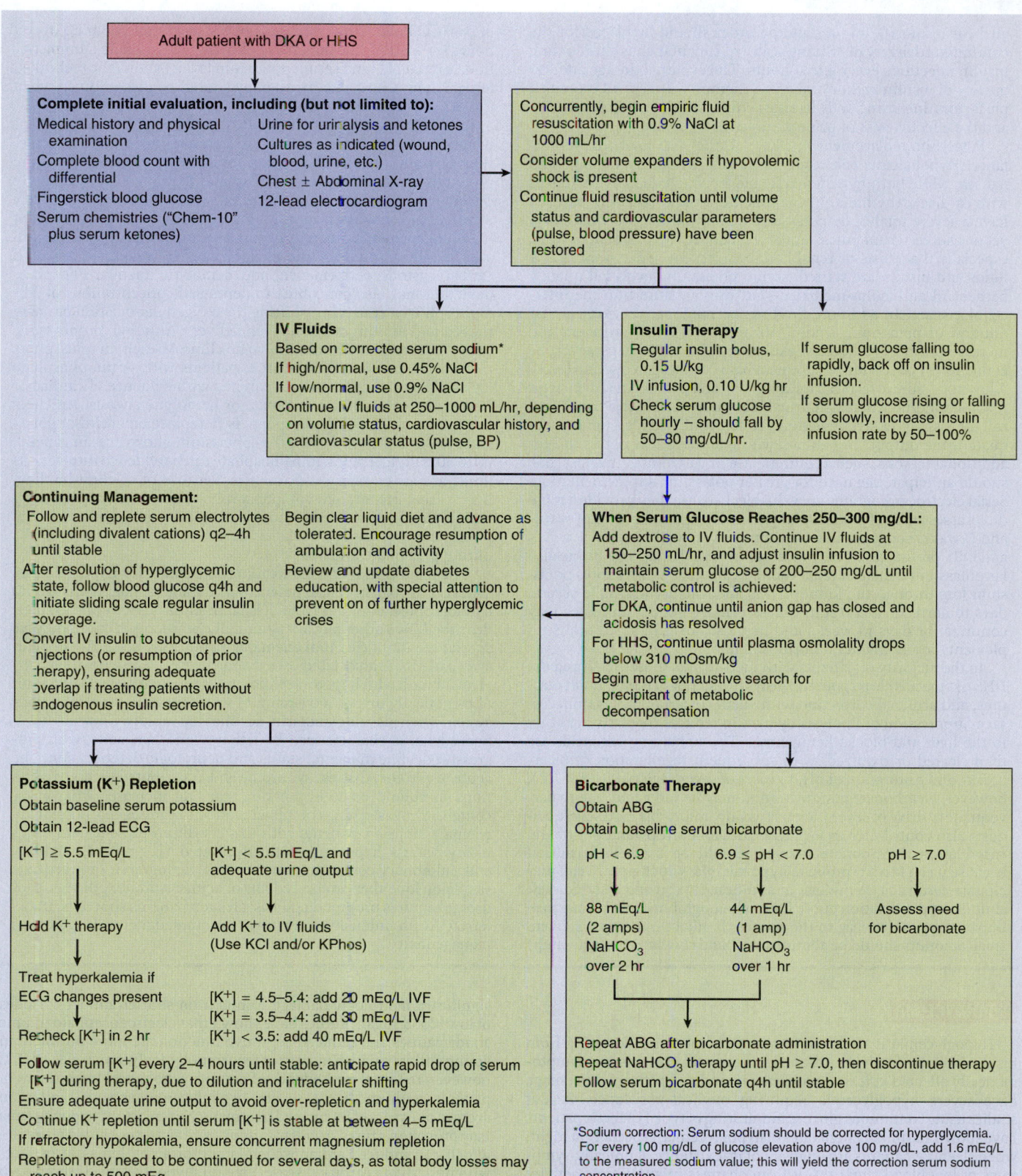

FIGURE 242–10 • Management of diabetic ketoacidosis (DKA) and hyperosmolar hyperglycemic state (HHS).

ated (or resumed), and a standing order should be placed for the continuous delivery of "sliding scale" of subcutaneous short-acting insulin injections every 4 to 6 hours. The eventual dosage and frequency of insulin and/or oral agent therapy will depend on multiple factors, including body habitus, comorbidity, insulin sensitivity, and the effectiveness of prior therapeutic regimens.

Potassium replacement in DKA and the HHS is of vital importance. Hypokalemia can result in muscle weakness, cramps, and nausea, while both hyperkalemia and hypokalemia are associated with cardiac arrhythmia. At the time of initial evaluation, patients have a severe total-body potassium deficit (about 3 to 7 mEq/kg), yet measured serum potassium levels may be low, normal, or high, especially if acidosis or renal failure is present. Once intravenous fluids and insulin are started, serum potassium levels fall quickly because of an insulin-mediated shift of potassium into the intracellular space. In addition, fluid replacement causes extracellular dilution of potassium, leading to improved renal perfusion and increased urinary potassium excretion. This rapid decline can be countered by potassium replacement based on measured serum levels. A low potassium level (<3.5 mEq/kg) requires prompt treatment with up to 40 mEq/hr, whereas "normal" serum levels (3.5 to 5.5 mEq/kg) call for less aggressive repletion (10 to 30 mEq/hr), assuming adequate urine output. In patients who may have lost potassium for additional reasons, such as diuretic use or gastrointestinal loss, one should anticipate the need for greater potassium supplementation. Serial electrocardiograms are valuable, because they provide a more direct assessment of *intracellular* potassium; flat-to-inverted T waves and U waves suggest a low potassium level, while peaked T waves and QRS prolongation may indicate hyperkalemia. The intracellular potassium deficit in renal tubular cells further promotes potassium loss through the kidneys; this abnormality may take several days to correct. As a result, excess urinary potassium losses may continue for days to weeks and may call for prolonged oral supplementation to maintain normokalemia.

In the majority of patients with mild-to-moderate DKA (and the HHS), ketoacids clear spontaneously with standard therapeutic measures, and artificial correction with alkali (bicarbonate) is unnecessary. Suppression of lipolysis by insulin reduces free fatty acid flux to the liver and blocks ketogenesis. The remaining ketoacids are then cleared or oxidized, with subsequent regeneration of bicarbonate and restoration of pH. In cases of severe acidosis (pH < 7.0), however, bicarbonate administration may be indicated; the hyperventilatory drive of severe acidosis is uncomfortable, and severe acidosis also contributes to negative cardiac inotropy and peripheral vasodilation. Bicarbonate therapy should be used with caution because it can further provoke hypokalemia, which in turn can precipitate cardiac arrhythmias. In addition, by causing a sudden left shift of the dissociation curve for oxyhemoglobin, bicarbonate may impair oxygen delivery to the tissues. If alkaline therapy is given, small amounts should be administered, and slowly: 44 mEq (1 amp)

of $NaHCO_3$ over 1 hour for a pH of 6.9 to 7.0, and 88 mEq over 2 hours for a pH of less than 6.9. Following bicarbonate administration, arterial pH (and serum potassium levels) should be rechecked every 2 hours, and alkaline therapy should be discontinued when the pH rises above 7.0.

In the setting of DKA, phosphate losses average 3 to 7 mmol/kg, whereas magnesium losses reach 1 to 2 mEq/kg; magnitudes of depletion for both ions may be greater for the HHS because of a more prolonged osmotic diuresis. Phosphate is shifted extracellularly during hyperosmolar states, so initial serum levels may be falsely elevated and may drop rapidly during therapy. Complications of hypophosphatemia generally occur at serum levels below 1.0 mg/dL and include respiratory and skeletal muscle weakness, impaired cardiac systolic performance, and hemolytic anemia. Phosphate depletion may also contribute to depressed concentrations of 2,3-diphosphoglycerate, thus shifting the oxygen dissociation curve to the left and limiting tissue oxygen delivery. Although prophylactic phosphate replacement has shown no clinical benefit in trials, phosphate repletion should be given to patients with serum phosphate levels below 1.0 mg/dL and to patients with evidence of cardiac or respiratory compromise, hypoxia, or hemolytic anemia. An effective means of replacing phosphate is to replace one third of potassium losses (discussed earlier) as potassium phosphate; in general, 20 to 30 mEq/L of potassium phosphate can be added to intravenous fluids and given over several hours. Because of calcium binding, hypocalcemic tetany may complicate phosphate therapy unless magnesium supplements are also provided; for this reason, serum calcium, phosphate, and magnesium levels should be monitored periodically during phosphate infusion.

The most common complications of therapy for hyperglycemic states are hypoglycemia, hypokalemia, hypophosphatemia, and fluid overload; precautions to avoid these complications have already been described. Two other rare but potentially fatal complications deserve special mention. Cerebral edema, which occurs primarily in pediatric patients, is associated with overaggressive correction of hyperglycemia and with hypotonic fluid replacement; it is likely the result of osmotically driven movement of water into the central nervous system when plasma osmolarity declines too rapidly. Clinically, cerebral edema is characterized by lethargy and headache, with progressive decline in mental status and neurologic deterioration. The acute respiratory distress syndrome is also attributed to rapid reductions in colloid osmotic pressure, causing increased lung water content, decreased lung compliance, and noncardiogenic pulmonary edema. Clinically, patients with this condition present with respiratory distress, hypoxemia with an elevated A-a gradient, and bilateral pulmonary congestion on the chest radiograph. In practice, a suspicion for either cerebral edema or acute respiratory distress syndrome requires prompt diagnosis; all such patients should be transferred to an intensive care unit for immediate and aggressive management.

HYPOGLYCEMIA

Hypoglycemia is the most frequent complication resulting from insulin therapy for type 1 diabetes; nearly all patients are symptomatically affected at least once per year, and a significant percentage have severe hypoglycemia requiring medical assistance. Recent studies using continuous glucose monitoring of type 1 diabetic patients have shown alarmingly high rates of hypoglycemia, especially at night, when sleeping patients are unaware of its existence. Clinically, symptoms of low blood sugar result from changes in autonomic activity and brain function. Autonomic symptoms, including sweating, tremor, and palpitations, are often the earliest subjective warning signs of hypoglycemia. Central nervous system symptoms and signs of glucose deficiency, termed neuroglycopenia, may be nonspecific (e.g., fatigue or weakness) or more clearly neurologic (e.g., double vision, oral paresthesias, slurring of speech, apraxia, or behavioral disturbances). Hypoglycemia affects type 2 patients as well; most cases occur during treatment with insulin or insulin secretagogues, especially the longer-acting sulfonylureas. Because of the long-acting nature of the oral agents, low blood sugar levels can recur up to 48 hours after drug withdrawal, and a more extended course of therapy is often required.

It is well known that prolonged, severe hypoglycemia can cause irreversible brain damage. What is less clear, however, is whether

significant neurologic damage results from shorter, milder episodes of low blood sugar. Studies have shown that electroencephalographic abnormalities and reduced cognitive function are more prevalent in young children with a history of recurrent hypoglycemia. The DCCT, however, reported no evidence of neuropsychological impairment in patients with recurrent severe hypoglycemic episodes, after an average of 7 years of intensified treatment. Nevertheless, hypoglycemia may provoke seizures, accidental injury, and a catecholamine response, which can induce cardiac ischemia and/or arrhythmias in patients with underlying cardiac disease. Overall, hypoglycemia is thought to account for 3 to 4% of deaths in insulin-treated diabetic patients. Hypoglycemia also has far-reaching social implications: on a personal level, it can induce great fear, preclude comfortable engagement in routine activities (e.g., driving), and lead both patient and clinician to aim deliberately for less than optimal glycemic control. From a practical standpoint, the growing body of evidence that tight glucose control prevents long-term complications of diabetes has led to more aggressive treatment regimens, inevitably resulting in a greater incidence of clinical hypoglycemia. This, in turn, has necessitated further study of the physiology, consequences, and prevention of hypoglycemia in diabetic patients.

In *non*diabetic persons, hypoglycemia provokes a rapid, multitiered metabolic response intended to restore normal blood glucose levels. The brain cannot store more than a few minutes' supply of energy; in the short term, its function is exclusively dependent on a constant supply of glucose for fuel. To preserve central nervous system function, spontaneous recovery from hypoglycemia involves both the activation of endogenous glucose production and reduced peripheral glucose utilization. Three fundamental mechanisms are responsible for this process: (1) the dissipation of endogenous insulin, (2) counterregulatory hormone activity, and (3) the subjective awareness of hypoglycemia, resulting in hunger and subsequent carbohydrate ingestion. Early hormonal changes are triggered when plasma glucose approaches the hypoglycemic range (65 to 70 mg/dL). A rise in glucose production, attributable mainly to stimulation of hepatic glycogenolysis, is initiated by the release of glucagon from pancreatic α-cells in conjunction with falling levels of endogenous insulin. Catecholamines are also released, which produce "alarm" symptoms for hypoglycemia (e.g., hunger, tremor, palpitations) and further promote the synthesis of glucose, via stimulation of hepatic glycogenolysis, mobilization of substrates for gluconeogenesis, and further suppression of insulin production. When hypoglycemia is sustained, additional counterregulatory hormones such as growth hormone and corticosteroids are released; through a variety of complimentary mechanisms, these hormones also help to promote continued glucose availability. Reduced peripheral glucose uptake results from an interplay of factors, including low circulating insulin levels, epinephrine's inhibitory effect on insulin-stimulated glucose uptake, elevated free fatty acid levels, and hypoglycemia per se. For a more in-depth discussion of metabolic responses to hypoglycemia, Chapter 243.

Type 1 diabetic patients are more prone to hypoglycemia for several reasons. First of all, injected insulin enters the circulation from a nonphysiologic source (e.g., a subcutaneous depot) and is therefore unaffected by counter-regulatory responses to falling glucose levels. In addition, type 1 patients lose their glucagon response to hypoglycemia, for unclear reasons; this appears to be a stimulus-specific phenomenon, since their glucagon response to other stimuli may be unaffected. Defective glucagon responses develop in most type 1 patients 2 to 5 years after diagnosis (usually at about the same time that they become severely insulin-deficient), after which time counterregulation relies heavily on epinephrine release. Unfortunately, one-half of type 1 patients also undergo a stimulus-specific diminution in their epinephrine response to hypoglycemia, further predisposing them to severe hypoglycemia. Finally, the ability of type 1 diabetics to recognize hypoglycemia and take corrective action may also be impaired. In some cases, the irritability and confusion that occur during hypoglycemia may prevent the patient's awareness of its cause. In others, patients may lose the autonomic warning symptoms of hypoglycemia and may recognize (or fail to recognize) the condition only when somatic neurologic function becomes impaired. This so-called "hypoglycemic unawareness" syndrome has been associated with a number of factors, including a history of severe hypoglycemia, long duration of diabetes, and autonomic neuropathy.

Hypoglycemia unawareness commonly occurs when patients are switched to intensive insulin regimens. The introduction of intensified treatment regimens can lower the glucose threshold that triggers epinephrine release and adrenergic symptoms, which at least partly explains the increased frequency of severe hypoglycemia reported in the DCCT. The mechanism underlying the changes is an increased incidence of iatrogenic hypoglycemia during intensified insulin therapy. It has been shown that even brief periods of antecedent hypoglycemia can suppress counter-regulatory responses during subsequent hypoglycemic episodes; this effect persists for several days or weeks. On the bright side, defective glucose counter-regulation induced by intensive insulin regimens appears to be reversible, via scrupulous avoidance of hypoglycemia and readjustment of treatment goals; this underscores the need to prevent iatrogenic hypoglycemia by improving patients' self-management skills. Continuous glucose monitoring, by allowing more precise adjustments in the insulin regimen, can be expected to improve hypoglycemia unawareness and the diminished counter-regulatory response.

PATHOGENESIS OF CHRONIC DIABETIC COMPLICATIONS

The pathogenesis of the microvascular and neuropathic complications of diabetes is complex and poorly understood. Two well-researched mechanisms proposed for glucose-induced cell injury are advanced glycosylation end-products (AGEs) and an accelerated polyol pathway with consequent protein kinase C activation. These and other potential contributors are briefly discussed.

Proteins are readily glycosylated in vivo in direct proportion to prevailing levels of glucose. This nonenzymatic glycosylation is nonspecific, involving a wide range of proteins, including hemoglobin, collagen, laminin, low-density lipoproteins, and peripheral nerve proteins (tubulin). The consequent AGEs accumulate in a variety of tissues (including the kidneys and blood vessels) and are thought to contribute to cell injury through a variety of mechanisms, including stimulation of cytokines, complement activation, and upregulation of growth factor synthesis. AGEs also stimulate oxidative reactions, and their cross-linking capabilities render them resistant to natural degradation. In experimental diabetic animals, inhibition of AGE formation reduces tissue deposition of these end products and inhibits both the expansion of glomerular volume and urinary protein excretion.

In the polyol pathway, increased activity of intracellular aldose reductase leads to an accumulation of sorbitol and fructose, resulting in osmotic cell injury, decreased glutathione antioxidant activity (via decreased NAD+), and the enhanced formation of diacylglycerol. Diacylglycerol formation can in turn activate specific isoforms of protein kinase C, which stimulate transforming growth factor-β release and play an important role in cell proliferation and vascular permeability. Beneficial effects of both aldose reductase inhibitors and specific protein kinase C inhibitors have been consistently demonstrated in animal models of diabetes. To date, their value in human subjects is uncertain.

Other potential mechanisms through which glucose could impair cell function include (but are not limited to) (1) formation of reactive oxygen species (hydrogen peroxide, superoxide), (2) activation of cytokines (angiotensin II, endothelin), (3) growth factor stimulation (transforming growth factor-β, vascular endothelial growth factor), and (4) depletion of basement membrane glycosaminoglycans. Interventions directed at each of these mechanisms are currently under investigation.

Hemodynamic changes in the microcirculation may also contribute to microangiopathy. In the diabetic kidney, GFR is increased out of proportion to renal plasma flow, owing to an elevation in the transglomerular pressure gradient. It is assumed that raised glomerular pressures promote the passage of proteins and AGEs; with time, their accumulation in the mesangium could trigger the proliferation of mesangial cells and matrix production, eventually leading to glomerulosclerosis. Compensatory hyperfiltration would develop in less affected glomeruli, but even these would ultimately succumb because of progressive glomerular damage. Clinical studies support this view. Unilateral renal artery stenosis diminishes diabetic pathologic lesions in the affected kidney, and angiotensin converting enzyme (ACE) inhibitors (which reduce transglomerular pressure) are known to slow the progression of diabetic nephropathy. The diabetes-associated increase in microcirculatory hydrostatic pressure may also contribute to generalized capillary leakage of macromolecules in diabetic patients.

These theories would predict the benefits of optimal glycemic control reported by the DCCT in patients with mild or no complications. Whether similar benefits can be expected once severe damage has occurred is less clear. Extensive glycosylation of proteins with slow turnover rates would not be readily affected by correction of hyperglycemia. Moreover, the hemodynamic theory for nephropathy predicts that once glomerular injury causes compensatory hyperfiltration, progressive injury may continue in the remaining glomeruli, regardless of the prevailing metabolic state.

DIABETIC RETINOPATHY

Diabetic retinopathy refers to progressive pathologic alterations in the retinal microvasculature, leading to areas of retinal nonperfusion, increased vascular permeability, and the pathologic proliferation of retinal vessels. In the United States, diabetes is the leading cause of blindness in persons aged 20 to 74 years. Retinopathy in patients with poorly controlled type 1 diabetes occurs in about 25% of patients 5 years after diagnosis, in 60% at 10 years, and in more than 95% at 15 years. Blindness occurs 25 times more frequently in diabetic patients than in control subjects and is seen most often after the disease has been present for at least 15 years, in the setting of advanced retinopathy. Approximately 10 to 15% of type 1 diabetic patients will become legally blind (visual acuity of 20/200 or worse in the better eye). In type 2 diabetes, though the incidence of blindness is lower, higher disease prevalence results in an even larger number of patients affected with severe visual loss.

The earliest pathologic changes associated with retinopathy are termed *mild nonproliferative diabetic retinopathy* (*mild NPDR*). In type 1 patients, these changes generally begin 3 to 5 years after diagnosis. The first signs of mild NPDR are microaneurysms, which arise most often in areas of capillary occlusion. Subsequently, increasing vascular permeability leads to retinal blot hemorrhages (round, with blurred edges) and "hard" exudates (sharply defined and yellow). Infarctions of the nerve fiber layer, known as "soft" exudates or "cotton-wool spots," appear as white or gray, rounded swellings. At this early stage of retinopathy, visual acuity is generally unaffected, and the risk of progression to high-risk proliferative diabetic retinopathy (PDR) (see later) is about 15% at 5 years. *Moderate NPDR* is characterized by intraretinal microvascular abnormalities, including venous caliber changes, beading, and increased capillary dilatation and permeability. Later changes, termed *severe* or *very severe NPDR*, include progressive retinal capillary loss and ischemia, with further development of extensive hemorrhages, exudates, and microaneurysms. At 5 years, moderate and severe NPDR are associated with a 30% and 60% risk of progression to high-risk PDR, respectively.

Proliferative diabetic retinopathy involves neovascularization, the growth of fine tufts of new blood vessels and fibrous tissue from the inner retinal surface or the optic head. Early proliferative changes are confined to the retina, but later invasion of the vitreous body constitutes *high-risk PDR*; during this end stage, fibrosis and contracture of the neovasculature results in retinal detachment and hemorrhage, the most important determinants of blindness. Occasionally, new vessels can invade the iris and anterior chamber, leading to sight-threatening closed-angle glaucoma.

Clinically significant macular edema (CSME) results from vascular leakage at the macula and can occur either with or without the stages of retinopathy described earlier. CSME is suggested by hard macular exudates on fundoscopic examination and can be confirmed with slit lamp biomicroscopy. In general, maculopathy is more common in type 2 patients, in whom it is an important contributor to the loss of visual acuity. As will be discussed, the treatment of CSME runs parallel to the treatment of other forms of diabetic retinopathy.

 Treatment

At present, medical management of diabetic retinopathy is aimed at controlling risk factors for progression. The value of tight glycemic control was proven by the DCCT, whose primary prevention arm demonstrated an impressive 76% risk reduction for the onset of retinopathy with intensive therapy. In the secondary prevention arm, patients with early NPDR undergoing intensive therapy demonstrated a 47% risk reduction in the development of severe NPDR or PDR, a 51% risk reduction in the need for laser treatment, and a 26% risk reduction in the development of CSME. Other targets for medical management, all associated with accelerated retinal damage, include (1) hypertension, (2) hyperlipidemia, (3) treatment of nephropathy, and (4) careful follow-up during pregnancy, where accelerated retinal pathology has been linked to preexisting diabetes (but not gestational disease).

Surgical management of retinopathy is aimed at slowing disease progression, as baseline visual acuity is difficult to recover. In the 1980s, large-scale prospective clinical trials such as the Diabetic Retinopathy Study and the Early Treatment Diabetic Retinopathy Study established photocoagulation as the treatment of choice when retinopathy threatens vision. Most patients with PDR, and selected patients with severe NPDR, are now treated primarily with scatter (panretinal) photocoagulation; cryotherapy or vitrectomy may be required if laser treatment is unfeasible for technical reasons or because of extensive disease. CSME is near-universally treated with focal photocoagulation, with the possible exception of patients exhibiting no or minimal NPDR. In such patients, close follow-up at 2- to 4-month intervals is an acceptable option. A treatment chart, adapted from a thorough technical review by Aiello et al, is shown in Table 242–10. Note that the decision to treat depends not only on stage of retinopathy and extent of CSME but also on general medical status, compliance with follow-up, and status of the contralateral eye.

These considerations make it imperative for physicians to prospectively identify diabetic patients at risk for retinopathy and visual loss. Nonspecialists, including house officers, internists, and diabetologists, are known to have difficulty diagnosing the stages of retinopathy; studies show that such physicians arrive at the correct diagnosis in fewer than half of cases. Accordingly, patients should be referred to an experienced ophthalmologist for a complete examination, to include a dilated fundoscopic examination, tonometry, and slit lamp biomicroscopy. The most recent ADA position statement recommends initial eye examination within 3 to 5 years of diagnosis of type 1 diabetes, and at the time of diagnosis in type 2 patients. Two special circumstances deserve a footnote here: (1) since children rarely develop retinopathy before puberty, early-onset type 1 patients generally do not require screening before 10 years of age, and (2) the acceleration of retinopathy during pregnancy demands that all patients with preexisting diabetes be examined during the first trimester. Follow-up of all patients should occur at least on a yearly basis, with the possible exception of retinopathy-free type 2 diabetics. Even in the latter cases, the ADA does recommend yearly examinations to avoid lost follow-up and to identify patients with more aggressive ocular disease.

DIABETIC NEPHROPATHY

End-stage renal disease (ESRD) from diabetic nephropathy (Chapter 118) is a major cause of morbidity and mortality, particularly in patients with type 1 diabetes, affecting 30 to 35% of patients in the United States. Although nephropathy is about one half as frequent in type 2 diabetics (partially due to a shortened life expectancy), type 2 diabetes still makes up the vast majority of diabetic patients seeking therapy for ESRD. Overall, diabetes is the leading cause of ESRD in the United States, accounting for more than one third of cases.

Details are less clear in patients with type 2 diabetes, but the natural history of diabetic nephropathy in type 1 diabetes is well described (Fig. 242–11). The period immediately following diagnosis is best characterized by glomerular hyperfiltration. During this time, there is renal hypertrophy, increased renal blood flow, increased glomeru-

---

Table 242–10 • GUIDELINES FOR TREATMENT AND FOLLOW-UP OF DIABETIC RETINOPATHY

STAGE OF RETINOPATHY	PANRETINAL PC	IF CSME, FOCAL PC*	FOLLOW-UP
No to minimal NPDR	*Not* recommended	Possible	12 months[†]
Mild to moderate NPDR	*Not* recommended	Probable	6–12 months[†]
Severe to very severe NPDR	Possible	Recommended	2–4 months
Early PDR	Probable	Recommended	2–4 months
High-risk PDR	Recommended	Recommended	2–4 months

*If retinopathy and CSME coexist, focal PC for CSME should always precede panretinal PC.
[†]In these patients, follow-up is recommended in just 2–4 months if CSME is also present.
CSME = clinically significant macular edema; NPDR = nonproliferative diabetic retinopathy; PC = photocoagulation; PDR = proliferative diabetic retinopathy.
Adapted from Aiello LP, et al: Diabetic retinopathy (Technical Review). Diabetes Care 1998;21:143–156.

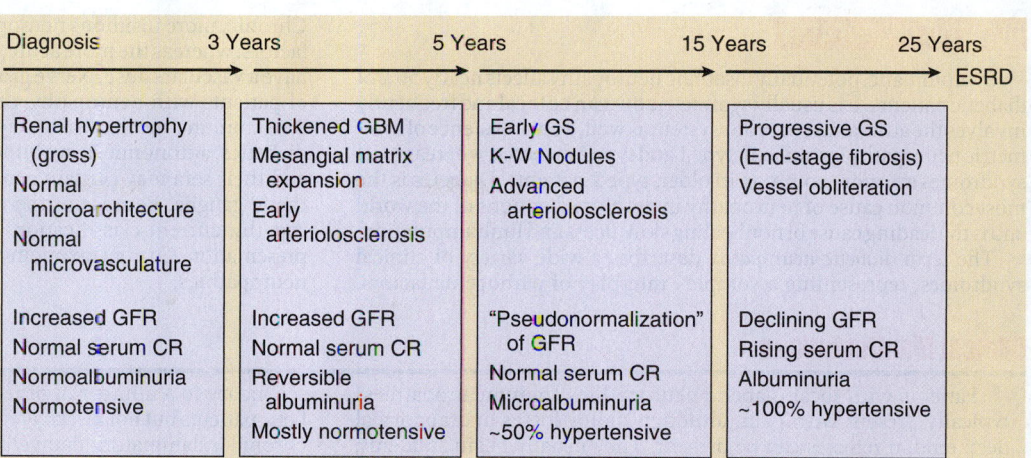

FIGURE 242-11 • The natural history of diabetic nephropathy in type 1 diabetic patients. Left untreated, end-stage renal disease (ESRD) develops in most patients within 10 years after a rise in serum creatinine (reflecting an approximately 50% decline in GFR). Fortunately, early intervention with glycemic control, angiotensin converting enzyme inhibitors, and antihypertensive therapy can slow the progression of disease. CR = creatinine; GBM = glomerular basement membrane; GFR = glomerular filtration rate; GS = glomerulosclerosis.

lar volume, and an increased transglomerular pressure gradient, all contributing to a rise in GFR. Importantly, these changes depend at least in part on hyperglycemia, as they are diminished by intensive diabetes treatment. Three to 5 years after diagnosis, early glomerular lesions appear, characterized by thickening of glomerular basement membranes, mesangial matrix expansion, and arteriosclerosis. Albumin excretion remains low during early glomerular changes; however, as pathologic changes mount, the glomeruli lose their functional integrity, resulting in glomerular filtration defects and increased glomerular permeability. Although results of routine tests of renal function (creatinine and urinalysis) still remain normal, microalbuminuria (30 to 300 mg/day) appears. Systemic hypertension is also present at this time in more than 50% of cases.

After several years, most diabetic patients exhibit diffuse glomerulosclerosis, although a minority have pathognomonic Kimmelstiel-Wilson nodular lesions. Although pathologic changes continue to mount throughout the disease, glomerulosclerosis extensive enough to cause ESRD develops in a minority of patients; in these cases, overt albuminuria (>300 mg/day) begins approximately 15 years after diagnosis. Soon after, following a variable period on the order of 3 to 5 years, the GFR begins a relentless decline (≥10 mL/min/year), which is eventually reflected by an increase in serum creatinine. The appearance of massive proteinuria and the nephrotic syndrome is common in this context and often heralds progression to ESRD. Once the serum creatinine rises (reflecting an approximately 50% decline in GFR), ESRD develops in most patients within 10 years. This course is highly variable, however, particularly in type 2 diabetics, who may exhibit moderate proteinuria for several years without a substantial deterioration of renal function. A simple but useful method of monitoring progression to renal failure is to plot the reciprocal of the serum creatinine as a function of time. This technique allows better assessment of both therapeutic interventions and the time when renal replacement therapy will become necessary.

There are several known risk factors for the development of diabetic nephropathy, including duration of disease, elevated glycohemoglobin levels, and the presence of concurrent hypertension, hyperlipidemia, and tobacco use. Race is known to play a major role as well, as demonstrated by a higher prevalence of nephropathy in African American, Hispanic, and Native American patients. There is also a high concordance rate in families, with studies in both type 1 and type 2 diabetic families revealing a three- to four-fold increase in the prevalence of nephropathy with affected siblings.

 Treatment

Treatment of nephropathy has become an important focus of recent research and depends heavily on stage of disease. Early in the course of diabetes (before the onset of microalbuminuria), strict glycemic control is of the utmost importance. The DCCT demonstrated that intensive therapy reduced microalbuminuria by 39% and overt albuminuria by 54% in type 1 diabetic patients. A similar result was demonstrated in the UKPDS of type 2 diabetic patients, in which a less dramatic improvement in glycemic control reduced microalbuminuria and overt albuminuria by 24% and 33%, respectively. In normotensive type 2 diabetic patients, treatment with ACE inhibitors retards microalbumin production, and blood pressure lowering appears to be responsible for only part of this effect. Randomized trials using ACE inhibitors and angiotensin II receptor blockers have consistently shown a delay in the progression of both proteinuria and declining GFR,[7-9] and these classes of drugs have become the first choice for lowering blood pressure to 120 mm Hg or lower in diabetic patients (Chapter 63).

Once clinical nephropathy becomes evident, aggressive efforts at strict glycemic control have marginal value in slowing the progression of nephropathy. As described earlier, efforts aimed at reducing hypertension and glomerular pressure become the mainstay of therapy. Dietary protein restriction (i.e., 0.8 g/kg of body weight) may add limited benefit, and aggressive lipid management is useful in preventing both renal and extrarenal vascular complications. As ESRD approaches, long-term treatment plans should proceed much as they would in nondiabetic uremic patients, but therapy should be initiated sooner. It is well known that diabetic patients have a poorer tolerance for uremia than their nondiabetic counterparts; protein wasting is accelerated, hypertension becomes more difficult to control, and there is acceleration of generalized atherosclerosis with extensive cardiovascular morbidity. Current options for ESRD patients include hemodialysis, peritoneal dialysis, kidney transplantation, and a combined kidney-pancreas transplantation. Decisions among these options are complex (and beyond the scope of this chapter) and must be made on an individual basis. Finally, it should be noted that mortality associated with both dialysis and organ transplantation is higher in diabetic than nondiabetic patients, usually because of cardiovascular comorbidity and the more rapid development of complications such as vascular insufficiency.

It should be briefly noted here that glomerular nephropathy is not the only entity that commonly affects the genitourinary system in diabetic patients. Asymptomatic bacteriuria and pyelonephritis are twice as common in diabetic women, owing to several factors, including autonomic bladder dysfunction, impaired organ perfusion, and glycosuria. Papillary necrosis is associated with diabetes in more than one half of cases, and renal artery stenosis is more common as well. Hyperkalemia is another frequent complication of diabetes, due to a variety of factors including insulin deficiency, metabolic acidosis, reduced GFR, use of ACE inhibitors, and the syndrome of hyporeninemic hypoaldosteronism commonly seen in elderly patients with impaired renal function. Finally, diabetic patients are at notable risk for azotemic complications following the injection of contrast dye for radiologic studies. For this reason, aggressive pre- and post-radiology hydration with intravenous fluids is critical in these cases.

DIABETIC NEUROPATHY

Symptomatic, potentially disabling neuropathy affects nearly 50% of diabetic patients. It is usually symmetric but can be focal and frequently involves the autonomic nervous system as well. The prevalence of symmetric neuropathy is similar in type 1 and type 2 diabetes, whereas focal syndromes are more common in older, type 2 patients. Diabetes is the most common cause of neuropathy in developed nations of the world and is the leading cause of nonhealing skin ulcers and limb amputation.

The term *diabetic neuropathy* describes a wide variety of clinical syndromes, representing a complex interplay of pathogenic factors.

Chronic, more insidious neuropathies may be mediated by metabolic factors, whereas the more acute, self-limiting neuropathies most likely have a vascular cause. Nerve growth factor is diminished in the nerves of patients with neuropathy, perhaps limiting regenerative capacity. Autoimmune mechanisms may also be involved: in affected type 1 diabetics, autonomic nerve bundles may show monocytic infiltration, and their sera may contain complement-fixing antibodies to sympathetic ganglia. Because of the multifactorial nature of diabetic neuropathy, current classification schemes are based largely on clinical presentation. Current taxonomy includes focal, diffuse, and autonomic neuropathies.

Clinical Manifestations

Patients with focal diabetic neuropathies (mononeuropathies) typically present with pain, although motor losses and abnormal deep tendon reflexes can be present. They usually begin suddenly, suggesting a vascular cause. Although any cranial or peripheral nerve can be involved, the most common sites include the oculomotor, median, radial, and lateral popliteal nerves. Painful radiculopathy may also occur in the distribution of one or more spinal roots and can easily be confused clinically with internal organ disease or postherpetic neuralgia. Because of the self-limited nature of focal neuropathy, treatment is generally aimed at pain control, with physical therapy as needed to maintain function of affected muscle groups. Focal neuropathies are generally self-limited, with an average duration of 6 to 8 weeks; chronicity can occur but is less common. Entrapment syndromes are more common in diabetic patients and may be distinguished by their more gradual onset, slow progression, and persistence with time. Entrapment sites include the median (carpal tunnel syndrome), ulnar, and radial nerves; lower extremity nerves such as the lateral popliteal, peroneal, and plantar nerves can also be involved. Conservative treatment of entrapment syndromes involves splinting and the use of anti-inflammatory medication. Surgical correction can be curative.

Distal symmetric (sensorimotor) polyneuropathy is the most common neurologic syndrome seen in diabetes. This process involves all somatic nerves but has a strong predilection for distal sensorimotor nerves of the feet and hands. Sensory fibers are generally preferentially affected; disease affects both small, unmyelinated C fibers (transmitting pain and temperature) and larger, myelinated Aδ/Aβ fibers, which carry touch, vibration, and proprioception. Early on, most patients with distal neuropathy are asymptomatic, with subtle abnormalities on examination, including the loss of vibration sense, light touch, two-point discrimination, and thermal sensitivity. Once symptomatic, patients typically report numbness and tingling of the distal extremities, often in the classic "stocking-glove" distribution. Pain is also common and can be C-fiber pain (burning, dysesthesia, and allodynia) or the large-fiber variety, usually described as "gnawing" or like a toothache. Severe, spontaneous, short-lived lancinating pains may also occur. Left unchecked, all types of pain may gradually gain in intensity, with a tendency to worsen at night, and there may be progressive loss of sensorimotor function as well. Later stages of disease can involve severe sensory loss, small muscle wasting of the hands and feet, sensory ataxia, and neuropathic arthropathy (Charcot joints). Foot ulceration can occur anywhere in the course of disease but is more common in advanced stages. Treatment, as will be discussed, is generally aimed at pain control and the slowing of symptom progression. Acute sensory neuropathy, a rapid-onset variant of symmetric polyneuropathy, usually occurs in the setting of altered metabolic control (e.g., DKA) or during initiation of insulin therapy ("insulin neuritis"). In this condition, C-fiber symptoms predominate. Acute sensory neuropathy carries a better prognosis than its chronic counterpart, with many patients achieving complete resolution.

Proximal motor neuropathy (diabetic amyotrophy), although classified as a polyneuropathy, is a unique condition that deserves special mention. This syndrome primarily affects elderly type 2 patients and is more common in men. It classically begins with pain in the thighs, hips, and buttocks, followed by weakness and atrophy of the proximal pelvic muscle groups. Iliopsoas, obturator, and adductor muscles of the pelvis are preferentially affected, with relative preservation of the hamstrings and gluteal muscles. In advanced cases, patients exhibit the inability to rise from a seated position (Gower's maneuver). Proximal motor neuropathy can be secondary to a number of other diseases, all more common in diabetic patients but not directly related to hyperglycemia. These include chronic inflammatory demyelinating polyneuropathy, monoclonal gammopathy, and vasculitis, all of which should be ruled out before the diagnosis of diabetic amyotrophy is made. This form of neuropathy has a good prognosis, with most cases resolving spontaneously in 12 to 24 months. Therapy is primarily supportive.

Symptomatic autonomic diabetic neuropathy carries a poor prognosis. Autonomic neuropathy typically accompanies other chronic complications of diabetes and may play a pathogenetic role through disturbed regulation of local blood flow. The manifestations of autonomic neuropathy are protean. Common syndromes are discussed here, grouped by organ system.

CARDIAC. Common cardiovascular abnormalities seen with autonomic neuropathy include resting tachycardia, diminished heart rate variability, and prolonged QTc. Diabetic patients often have defective heart rate and blood pressure responses to exercise, and their lack of autonomic regulation places them at high risk for silent myocardial ischemia, congestive heart failure, and sudden cardiac death. Unfortunately, no specific treatments are available for these conditions. Recent efforts to identify patients at risk for cardiac complications allow only for closer follow-up and appropriate treatment of coexisting cardiovascular risk factors.

VASCULAR. Postural hypotension is likely caused by an impaired sympathetic vasoconstrictor response and impaired cardiac reflexes. Non-neurogenic causes of orthostasis, such as volume depletion, impaired cardiac function, and infectious causes should be ruled out before the diagnosis is made. Tilt table testing can be useful to confirm the diagnosis. Nonpharmacologic measures, such as a raised-head position at night, reduction of rapid positional changes, and supportive elastic garments can be useful in mild cases. Disabling disease may require pharmacologic intervention; first-line agents include mineralocorticoids (9-α-fluorohydrocortisone), α-agonists (midodrine), and β-blockers with intrinsic sympathomimetic activity (pindolol). Clonidine, ergotamine-caffeine combinations, yohimbine, octreotide, and desmopressin can also be useful in selected cases. Often, the side effects of these agents limit their use; one must exercise caution before prescribing any of these agents to patients with diabetes.

GASTROINTESTINAL. Altered gastrointestinal function is commonly seen in patients with diabetes. Constipation is the most common clinical syndrome. Diarrhea is another frequent complaint and can be caused by a variety of conditions, including hypermotility (impaired sympathetic inhibition), hypomotility with bacterial overgrowth, pancreatic insufficiency, and bile salt irritation. Treatment is generally aimed at the underlying condition and may include antidiarrheals, broad-spectrum antibiotics, pancreatic enzymes, and bile acid sequestrants (cholestyramine). Gastroparesis is a particularly disabling condition, often manifesting with bloating, early satiety, nausea, and vomiting. Treatment of gastroparesis begins with small, frequent meals and the use of metoclopramide, a central dopaminergic agonist with gastric cholinergic activity. Early treatment is useful, but the drug's effect may diminish over time. Erythromycin, which acts on the motilin receptor to promote gastric motility, can also be considered.

GENITOURINARY. Impaired parasympathetic innervation leads to bladder hypotonia, incomplete bladder emptying, dribbling, and overflow incontinence. Bethanechol, a parasympathomimetic agent, can be helpful in reversing these symptoms, but its use is often limited by side effects including salivation, lacrimation, diarrhea, and bronchoconstriction. α-Blockers help by relaxing the urinary sphincter, but these agents can potentiate postural hypotension, already prevalent in diabetic patients. Advanced cases of bladder dysfunction often require intermittent catheterization or the placement of an indwelling catheter. Erectile dysfunction is commonly seen in male diabetic patients. Injections of locally acting vasomotor agents, such as alprostadil and papaverine, have been used with moderate success but carry the risk of priapism, infection, and local fibrosis with repeated use. Sildenafil, a selective inhibitor of phosphodiesterase type 5, inhibits local breakdown of cyclic guanosine monophosphate, which in the presence of nitric oxide leads to selective engorgement of the corpus callosum. Sildenafil has demonstrated efficacy in the context of diabetes, but caution should be used in patients with suspected coronary disease, and the drug is contraindicated in combination with nitrate therapy. In refractory cases, referral to a urologist for a penile prosthetic implant should be considered.

SUDOMOTOR DYSFUNCTION. Abnormal sweat production in diabetic patients can result in xerosis and cracking of the skin, further predisposing these patients to cutaneous infections. Distal anhydrosis with compensatory truncal-facial sweating may occur, whereas generalized anhydrosis can produce heat intolerance and increase the risk of hyperthermia and heat stroke. An impaired sweat response can also further impair the diabetic patient's ability to recognize hypoglycemia. Current therapy for sudomotor dysfunction is limited to behavioral modification (i.e., heat avoidance), topical moisturizers, and intensive skin care. Local sympathectomy for hyperhydrosis should be considered only in severe, refractory cases.

Diagnosis

Diagnosing diabetic neuropathy can be a difficult task. It begins with a careful history and detailed neurologic examination, including detailed sensory testing (Semmes-Weinstein monofilament, two-point discrimination, 128 cps tuning fork, thermal discrimination), motor/gait examination, and documentation of deep tendon reflexes. Electrophysiologic studies, such as nerve conduction velocity studies and electromyography, are of use in firming up the diagnosis, although it should be noted that unmyelinated C-fiber neuropathy is undetectable with these methods. Nerve biopsy can occasionally be helpful to rule out other causes of neuropathy but is generally not recommended for diagnosis. If diffuse neuropathic symptoms are predominantly sensory in nature, work-up for additional causes of neuropathy should include testing for human immunodeficiency virus, vitamin B_{12} levels, SPEP/SIEP (serum protein electrophoresis/serum immunoelectrophoresis), and additional testing where indicated in suspected cases of porphyria, heavy metal intoxication, and paraneoplastic syndromes.

Treatment

Early treatment of diabetic neuropathy should include tight glycemic control. In the DCCT, intensive therapy slowed the onset of neuropathy by 70% and slowed the progression of early neuropathy by 57%, while in the UKPDS, glucose control was associated with improved vibratory sensation. The potential use of recombinant nerve growth factor treatment has been quelled for the moment, after large multicenter trials failed to demonstrate clinical efficacy. Other potential treatments still in the investigational stage include aldose reductase inhibitors, ACE inhibitors, the antioxidant α-lipoic acid, and γ-lineoleic acid, an important constituent of neuronal membrane phospholipics.

There are several therapies for neuropathic pain whose use has been supported by randomized controlled trials. Tricyclic antidepressants, including amitriptyline, desipramine, and nortriptyline, are moderately effective and well tolerated at low doses, but dose escalation can result in drowsiness, anticholinergic effects, potentiation of cardiac arrhythmias, and worsening of glaucoma. Anticonvulsants, such as carbamazepine and gabapentin, may also be effective, although the former can cause hematologic abnormalities, whereas patients taking the latter may report dizziness, fatigue, headaches, or diarrhea. Topical therapies, such as capsaicin (which depletes stores of axonal substance P), clonidine, and lidocaine can be moderately effective. Additional oral agents to be considered include mexiletine, an oral lidocaine analogue, and tramadol, a centrally acting reuptake inhibitor with opiate activity. In refractory cases, long-term opiate use and consultation with a specifically trained pain specialist may be required.

DIABETIC FOOT

The diabetic foot is characterized by slowly healing plantar ulcers that result from apparently insignificant trauma. Left untreated, superficial ulcers may penetrate to underlying tissues, leading to complications including cellulitis, abscess formation, joint sepsis, and osteomyelitis. Gangrene may occur, and in severe cases amputation may be required. Overall, about 15% of diabetic patients experience clinically significant foot ulceration. Risk factors for ulcer development include long-standing diabetes, poor glycemic control, and concurrent diabetic complications; visual loss may also contribute to difficulties with self-care. Affected diabetic patients may eventually require amputation, with diabetes accounting for more than one half of nontraumatic lower extremity amputations in the United States. In the United States, the total costs of caring for diabetic foot ulcers are estimated at more than 6 billion dollars annually.

To varying degrees, the diabetic foot is characterized by chronic sensorimotor neuropathy, vascular disease, autonomic neuropathy, and impaired immune function. Sensory neuropathy prevents the detection of minor traumatic events, so that ill-fitting shoes (or sharp objects in the shoe) may erode the skin surface without signaling pain. Pedal neuropathy also produces abnormalities in both proprioception and intrinsic muscle motor function, pathologically altering weight distribution on the metatarsal heads and leading to "clawing" of the metatarsophalangeal joints. In advanced cases, abnormal loading of the foot can result in repeated painless fractures and the displacement of normal joint surfaces, producing so-called Charcot joints. Aortic and peripheral vascular disease often coexist. Diminished cardiac output and/or disturbed autoregulatory mechanisms of the microcirculation may further contribute to impaired blood flow and delay ulcer healing. Finally, abnormal immune function (secondary to severe hyperglycemia) can predispose to infection, further slowing wound closure and increasing the likelihood of ulcer complications.

Prevention of the diabetic foot parallels general diabetic care, with emphasis on proper nutrition, tight glycemic control, and medical risk factor modification, including smoking cessation. A general foot care prescription (Table 242–11) is valuable, and office visits should routinely include careful examination of the feet. In affected patients, a specialist examination is recommended at least once per year. In cases of deformed feet, pressure relief (off-loading) is essential and may include the use of orthotics, specialty shoes, assistive devices, and a total contact cast to direct pressure away from a high-risk area. Once an ulcer has formed, it should be treated aggressively with antibiotics, appropriate local wound care, and débridement of necrotic tissue. In selected cases, newer FDA-approved treatments should also be considered. Local application of recombinant human platelet-derived growth factor can moderately accelerate wound healing. Bioengineered tissue therapies, containing human dermal-epidermal components,

---

Table 242–11 • FOOT CARE PRESCRIPTION FOR DIABETIC PATIENTS WITH LOWER EXTREMITY SENSORY NEUROPATHY

Never walk barefooted
Do not apply hot water or heating pads to the feet
Inspect the feet daily, using a mirror for plantar surfaces
Wash the feet daily, drying thoroughly between the toes
Lubricate dry skin to avoid cracking
Wear properly fitting, well-cushioned shoes (insoles)
Break in new shoes slowly
Consider a second pair of shoes at night (larger size for dependent edema)
Cut toenails straight across, to conservative lengths
Schedule regular visits to a diabetic footcare specialist

have also shown some efficacy in early clinical trials; these products act as biologic dressings and contain live human fibroblasts, which deliver growth factors and extracellular matrix components directly to damaged skin. For extensive cases of gangrene or deep tissue infections, surgical amputation may be required. A compromised peripheral circulation makes such an outcome more likely. If poor circulation is present, a vascular surgeon should be consulted for consideration of angioplasty or vascular bypass.

HYPERTENSION, DYSLIPIDEMIA, AND CARDIOVASCULAR DISEASE

Atherosclerosis involving the coronary, cerebral, and peripheral (lower extremity) arteries is the predominant cause of diabetes-related mortality. The atherosclerotic process in diabetes is indistinguishable from that of the nondiabetic population but begins earlier and is often more severe. A predilection to cardiovascular disease is observed over the entire spectrum of diabetes, from poorly controlled insulin-dependent patients to those with mild, diet-controlled hyperglycemia or IGT. For unclear reasons, the disparity between diabetic and nondiabetic subjects is more pronounced in women. When accompanied by other major cardiovascular risk factors such as hypertension, dyslipidemia, and smoking, diabetes markedly increases the incidence of macrovascular complications. For example, the observed two- to three-fold greater risk of myocardial infarction with diabetes rises to eight-fold in the presence of hypertension, and to nearly 20-fold if both hypertension and dyslipidemia are present; smoking raises these risks even further. As a result, the diagnosis of diabetes mellitus should quickly prompt both an exhaustive search for coexisting cardiovascular risk factors and the initiation of aggressive preventive measures. This view is supported by recent data demonstrating that intensive intervention that targets multiple risk factors decreases the risk of cardiovascular events in patients with type 2 diabetes.

Diabetes is an independent risk factor for accelerated atherosclerosis. Its association with vascular disease is not solely attributable to an increased prevalence of other recognized vascular risk factors such as hypertension, smoking, and dyslipidemia. Many abnormalities induced by the diabetic state may contribute to atherosclerosis, including lipid abnormalities (e.g., increased total very low density lipoprotein, increased small dense [atherogenic] low-density lipoprotein, decreased high-density lipoprotein, increased lipoprotein oxidation, increased lipoprotein glycosylation, decreased lipoprotein lipase activity), accentuated platelet aggregation and adhesion, endothelial cell dysfunction, and an induced procoagulant state (e.g., increased clotting factors and fibrinogen, decreased levels of antithrombin III, protein C, and protein S, and decreased fibrinolytic activity). These changes are thought to be in large part due to the presence of insulin resistance. It has been suggested that hyperinsulinemia per se might also contribute to macrovascular disease; proposed pathogenetic mechanisms include insulin-induced stimulation of vascular endothelial and smooth muscle cells, enhanced insulin-like growth factor 1 expression, and the augmented synthesis of atherogenic factors such as endothelin and plasminogen activator inhibitor.

In patients with diabetes, systemic hypertension is an important cofactor in the development of cardiovascular disease, nephropathy, and retinopathy (Chapter 63). In type 2 patients, the prevalence of hypertension is more than twice that of the nondiabetic population, largely due to the clustering of both disorders in patients with obesity and insulin resistance. Type 1 patients, in contrast, are usually normotensive in the absence of renal disease; if nephropathy develops, the majority of affected patients will then develop secondary hypertension. The importance of aggressive blood pressure management in diabetes has been established by the UKPDS (see earlier): in the study, blood pressure reduction (with ACE inhibitors or β-blockers) in type 2 diabetic patients with hypertension produced striking decreases in both cardiovascular and microvascular outcomes. Subsequent prospective trials, including the Systolic Hypertension in the Elderly Program (SHEP), the Systolic Hypertension in Europe (Sys-Eur) Trial, and the Hypertension Optimal Treatment (HOT) trial, have confirmed the value of aggressive blood pressure goals in reducing major cardiovascular events in diabetic patients. Based on these and other studies, the Joint National Committee VI (JNC VI) has established blood pressure targets of less than 130/85 for patients with diabetes mellitus; even stricter reductions (<125/75) are recommended in the presence of established nephropathy.

Rx Treatment

The choice of antihypertensive agent for diabetic patients has for years been the subject of considerable research and debate. Among the various therapeutic options, ACE inhibitors and angiotensin II receptor blockers may offer special advantages, as they have consistently demonstrated the ability to lower intraglomerular pressures and to slow the progression of albuminuria and diabetic nephropathy. JNC VI has endorsed α-adrenergic antagonists, calcium channel antagonists, and low-dose diuretics as the preferred alternative agents for use in diabetic patients, due to neutral or favorable effects on insulin sensitivity and glucose control. β-Blockers should also be strongly considered, particularly in the setting of concurrent cardiovascular disease, including prior myocardial infarction, mild-to-moderate congestive heart failure, and cardiac arrhythmias. Prospective trials comparing antihypertensive agents in diabetic patients have yielded mixed results. In the UKPDS, β-blockers were as effective as ACE inhibitors in reducing adverse cardiac and microvascular outcomes; other studies using calcium channel blockers have shown comparable results as well. On the flip side, several well-known studies, including the Appropriate Blood Pressure Control in Diabetes (ABCD) trial, the Captopril Prevention Project (CPP), and the Fosinopril versus Amlodipine Cardiovascular Events Trial (FACET) suggest improved cardiovascular outcomes with the specific use of ACE inhibitors as first-line therapy (Chapter 63). Based on currently available evidence, ACE inhibitors are recommended as first-line antihypertensive therapy in patients with diabetes, especially in the presence of microalbuminuria or overt nephropathy. Angiotensin II receptor antagonists are an excellent alternative, especially in patients who are unable to tolerate ACE inhibitors.

Dyslipidemia is another crucial therapeutic target in the management of diabetes. The most common lipid disorder associated with diabetes is an increased level of triglyceride-rich lipoproteins (e.g., very low density lipoprotein); depressed levels of high-density lipoprotein are also common, as are the presence of "small dense" atherogenic low-density lipoprotein molecules. The third report of the National Cholesterol Education Program (NCEP) Expert Panel continues to identify low-density lipoprotein cholesterol as the primary target for therapy, based on overwhelming evidence from clinical trials. This panel has recently established diabetes as a coronary heart disease "equivalent," meaning that all diabetic patients should strive for low-density lipoprotein levels below 100 mg/dL; high-density lipoprotein levels should exceed 40 mg/dL in men and 50 mg/dL in women, while triglyceride levels should fall below 200 mg/dL (ideally, below 150 mg/dL). Initial steps in treating diabetic dyslipidemia should include optimization of glycemic control, dietary reinforcement, and a prescription of aerobic exercise. Strict dietary parameters for diabetic patients with dyslipidemia call for less than 35% of daily calories as fat, with less than 7% of total calories as saturated fat and less than 200 mg/day of dietary cholesterol (the NCEP Step II diet). Regular aerobic exercise helps by raising high-density lipoprotein levels, and weight loss achieved through exercise can further attenuate lipid abnormalities.

Hydroxymethylglutaryl coenzyme A reductase inhibitors (i.e., "statins") are generally used first-line for lowering low-density lipoprotein cholesterol in patients with diabetes; of note, many of the statins have a modest triglyceride-lowering effect as well. Controlled trials specifically document the beneficial effect of statins on patients with diabetes, even in the absence of coronary disease.[10] If statins are contraindicated, or poorly tolerated, the cholesterol absorption inhibitor ezetimibe or bile acid sequestrants are an alternative means of lowering low-density lipoprotein. Bile acid sequestrants, however, can actually raise triglyceride levels and should therefore be used with caution. Nicotinic acid, while also effective at lowering low-density lipoprotein (and triglycerides), is less useful in diabetic patients, since it can worsen insulin resistance and adversely affect glycemic control. Low-density lipoprotein, of course, is not the only appropriate target for lipid-lowering therapy. Recent prospective trials using fibric acid derivatives (e.g., gemfibrozil, fenofibrate) to lower triglyceride levels and raise high-density lipoprotein have also produced substantially improved cardiovascular outcomes.

The measures described are largely aimed at preventing coronary artery disease in diabetic patients; once coronary artery disease has been established, it should also be aggressively treated. Compared to the general population, a higher proportion of diabetic patients die within a year of an acute myocardial infarction. Furthermore, while there has recently been a considerable decline in overall coronary artery disease–related mortality, a similar decline in patients with diabetes has not been observed. Low-dose aspirin therapy (81 to 325 mg/day) should be routinely recommended for the majority of adult patients with diabetes (especially with concurrent CAD), because of proven reductions in cardiovascular morbidity and mortality. After myocardial infarction, particularly in the setting of left ventricular systolic dysfunction, β-blockers and ACE inhibitors (or angiotensin II receptor blockers) may offer additional benefits. Finally, although angioplasty is an option in diabetic patients with coronary disease, there is evidence to suggest that diabetic patients may derive greater-than-expected comparative benefit from coronary bypass procedures. With the recent development of advanced stenting procedures and adjunctive antiplatelet therapy, however, this distinction may become less important in the future.

Unfortunately, the known association between diabetes mellitus and premature atherosclerosis may only be the "tip of the iceberg" with regard to linking glucose metabolism and vascular risk. Insulin resistance (i.e., impaired insulin-stimulated glucose metabolism) is quite common in "healthy" people living in Western nations; in such individuals, insulin resistance is often counterbalanced by increased insulin secretion, preventing the emergence of overt diabetes mellitus. Although this state of chronic hyperinsulinemia

may successfully defend against diabetes, a heavy price may be paid; compensatory hyperinsulinemia has been postulated to have adverse effects on other insulin-related systems, such as sympathetic nervous system activity, renal sodium reabsorption, hepatic triglyceride synthesis, and arterial smooth muscle proliferation. This much is known: nonobese, nondiabetic individuals with insulin resistance and hyperinsulinemia have higher blood pressure, glucose levels, and triglyceride levels (and lower high-density lipoprotein cholesterol concentrations) than matched subjects with normal insulin levels. The term *metabolic syndrome* (formerly known as "syndrome X") was coined to describe this phenomenon, namely, the clustering within one person of hyperinsulinemia, centrally distributed adiposity, mild glucose intolerance, dyslipidemia, and hypertension, each of which is likely an independent risk factor for atherosclerosis (Fig. 242–12). Prospective population studies have confirmed that chronic hyperinsulinemia predicts the development of cardiovascular disease. Although such statistical associations do not prove causality, they suggest that insulin resistance itself may play a role in promoting atherosclerosis. If true, this hypothesis further underscores the importance of lifestyle changes in the treatment of patients with more subtle metabolic abnormalities (i.e., metabolic syndrome, impaired glucose tolerance, and/or impaired fasting glucose).

An important final note: concerns about hyperinsulinemia should *not* be interpreted as a signal to reduce therapeutic insulin doses, because the long-term adverse effects of poor glycemic control are undoubtedly much greater than those possibly caused by hyperinsulinemia. This point is clearly supported by the UKPDS, in which intensive treatment with insulin or sulfonylureas tended to reduce cardiovascular events despite inducing hyperinsulinemia. Treatment of impaired glucose tolerance with the α-glucosidase inhibitor acarbose is a promising new approach for reducing hypertension and cardiovascular events in patients with impaired glucose tolerance. ■

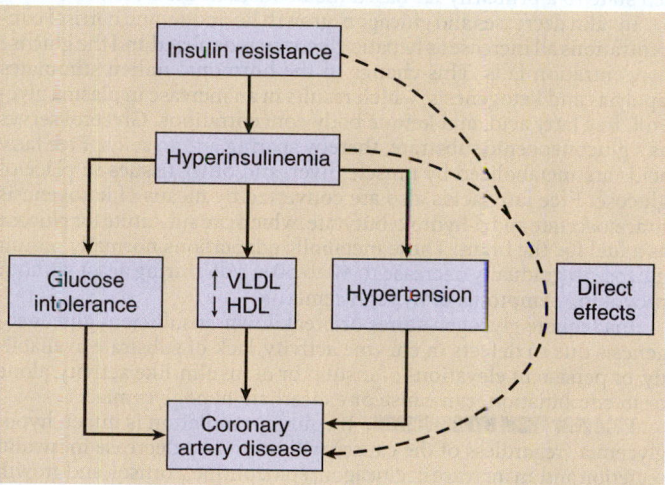

FIGURE 242–12 • The metabolic syndrome. Insulin resistance may account for a clustering of cardiovascular risk factors, including hypertension, dyslipidemia, and syndromes of glucose intolerance. HDL = high-density lipoprotein; VLDL = very low density lipoprotein.

Table 242–12 • **KEY ELEMENTS OF A COMPREHENSIVE MANAGEMENT PLAN FOR PATIENTS WITH DIABETES MELLITUS**

Lifestyle changes
  Proper diet
  Aerobic exercise
  Weight control
  Smoking cessation
Control of modifiable metabolic factors
  Glucose control
  Lipid control
  Blood pressure control
  Aspirin ("thrombotic control")
Preventive care
  Regular medical/neurologic screening exams
  Regular screening for albuminuria
  Regular ophthalmologic examinations
  Regular podiatric examinations (and self-examinations)
  Regular dental check-ups

Summary

In caring for patients with diabetes mellitus, the primary long-term goals are to minimize complications and to preserve the patients' sense of clinical well-being. These goals are attained most easily through early detection and treatment, perhaps even before the patient meets formal diagnostic criteria. In view of the wide array of problems encountered in diabetes, patient care must be thorough and comprehensive and involves far more than simple glycemic control. Lifestyle modification should be the primary focus of patient care, and special attention should be devoted to concurrent risk factors that compound the adverse effects of diabetes on atherogenesis and cardiovascular disease. Lastly, because most complications of diabetes develop slowly and are not easily reversible, it is crucial for clinicians to take a prospec-

tive, preventive approach to diabetes care. Key elements of a comprehensive management plan for the care of diabetic patients are summarized in Table 242–12.

1. Diabetes Control and Complications Trial Research Group: The effect of intensive treatment of diabetes on the development and progression of long-term complications of insulin-dependent diabetes mellitus. N Engl J Med 1993;329:977–986.
2. Turner RC, Holman RR, Cull CA, et al: Intensive blood-glucose control with sulphonylureas or insulin compared with conventional treatment and risk of complications in patients with type 2 diabetes (UKPDS 33). Lancet 1998;352:837–853.
3. Gaede P, Vedel P, Larsen N, et al: Multifactorial intervention and cardiovascular disease in patients with type 2 diabetes. N Engl J Med 2003;348:383–393.
4. Knowler WC, Barrett-Connor E, Fowler SE, et al: Reduction in the incidence of type 2 diabetes with lifestyle intervention or metformin. N Engl J Med 2002; 346:393–403.
5. Kanaya AM, Herrington D, Vittinghoff E, et al: Glycemic effects of postmenopausal hormone therapy: The Heart and Estrogen/progestin Replacement Study. A randomized, double-blind, placebo-controlled trial. Ann Intern Med 2003;138:1–9.

6. Diabetes Prevention Trial—Type 1 Diabetes Study Group: Effects of insulin in relatives of patients with type 1 diabetes mellitus. N Engl J Med 2002;346:1685–1691.
7. Gerstein HC: Reduction of cardiovascular events and microvascular complications in diabetes with ACE inhibitor treatment: HOPE and MICRO-HOPE. Diabetes Metab Res Rev 2002;18(Suppl 3):S82–S85.
8. Lewis EJ, Hunsicker LG, Bain RP, et al: The effect of angiotensin-converting-enzyme inhibition on diabetic nephropathy. N Engl J Med 1999;329:1456–1462.
9. Brenner BM, Cooper ME, de Zeeuw D, et al: RENAAL Study Investigators: Effects of losartan on renal and cardiovascular outcomes in patients with type 2 diabetes and nephropathy. N Engl J Med 2001;345:861–869.
10. Collins R, Armitage J, Parish S, et al, for the Heart Protection Study Collaborative Group: MRC/BHF Heart Protection Study of cholesterol-lowering with simvastatin in 5963 people with diabetes: A randomised placebo-controlled trial. Lancet 2003;361:2005–2016.
11. Chiasson JL, Josse RG, Gomis R, et al: Acarbose treatment and the risk of cardiovascular disease and hypertension in patients with impaired glucose tolerance: The STOP-NIDDM trial. JAMA 2003;290:486–494.

SUGGESTED READINGS
American Diabetes Association: Clinical practice recommendations 2000. Diabetes Care 2000;23(Suppl):1–8. *An up-to-date summary of the current classification of diabetes and standards of care for the management of diabetic patients, including goals of treatment.*
Estacio RO, Schrier RW: Diabetic nephropathy: Pathogenesis, diagnosis, and prevention of progression. Adv Intern Med 2001;46:359–408. *A concise, comprehensive review of the issues surrounding the pathogenesis, diagnosis, and treatment of diabetic nephropathy.*
Expert Committee on the Diagnosis and Classification of Diabetes Mellitus: Report of the expert committee on the diagnosis and classification of diabetes mellitus. Diabetes Care 2003;26 Suppl 1:S5–S20. *Updated diagnostic criteria.*
Jeffcoate WJ, Harding KG: Diabetic foot ulcers. Lancet 2003;361:1545–1551. *A practical review.*
Kazlauskaite R, Fogelfeld L: Insulin therapy in type 2 diabetes. Dis Mon 2003;49:377–420. *A comprehensive review.*
Kitabachi AE, et al: Management of hyperglycemic crises in patients with diabetes (Technical Review). Diabetes Care 2001;24:131–153. *A thorough technical review of the pathophysiology, diagnosis, and treatment of acute hyperglycemic crises in patients with diabetes.*

243 HYPOGLYCEMIA/PANCREATIC ISLET CELL DISORDERS

Robert A. Rizza
F. John Service

HYPOGLYCEMIA

Hypoglycemia is a clinical syndrome of diverse causes in which low levels of plasma glucose eventually lead to neuroglycopenia.

Regulation of Carbohydrate Metabolism

INTERACTIONS BETWEEN INSULIN AND COUNTER-INSULIN HORMONES. Under normal circumstances, plasma glucose concentration averages 70 to 100 mg/dL before meals and rarely exceeds 140 to 150 mg/dL after meals. The brain is almost totally dependent on glucose for energy, although over the long term it can adapt to substrates other than glucose (e.g., ketone bodies). Because severe hypoglycemia can impair mental function and, if prolonged, can cause permanent brain damage, a series of well-developed, and at times redundant, homeostatic processes defend against hypoglycemia. Insulin suppresses glucose production by inhibiting both glycogenolysis and gluconeogenesis. Insulin also stimulates glucose uptake in muscle, liver, and fat. Glucagon, epinephrine, cortisol, and growth hormone, collectively referred to as the counter-regulatory or counter-insulin hormones, oppose the effects of insulin.

In healthy nondiabetic subjects, insulin concentration increases as glucose concentration increases and falls as glucose concentration falls. In contrast, counter-regulatory hormone concentrations change (in general) in the opposite direction of insulin, falling as glucose rises and rising as glucose falls. By doing so, insulin and the counter-insulin hormones act in concert to ensure that the amount of glucose entering and leaving the blood stream is closely matched in both the fed and the fasted state. Excess amounts of insulin or insulin-like material (e.g., insulin-like growth factor [IGF]-1 or IGF-2), inadequate secretion of counter-insulin hormones, insufficient substrate, or defects in the gluconeogenic or glycogenolytic pathways alone or in combination can disrupt this balance and cause hypoglycemia.

REGULATION OF GLUCOSE CONCENTRATION IN THE FED STATE. After an overnight fast (e.g., 8 to 10 hours), rates of glucose production and utilization average about 2 mg/kg/min. At this time, the majority of the glucose is released from the liver, with a small amount being produced by the kidney. Carbohydrate ingestion increases glucose concentration, which stimulates secretion of insulin from the pancreatic β cells and suppresses secretion of glucagon from the pancreatic α cells. The resultant rise in the insulin-to-glucagon ratio increases hepatic glycogen synthesis and inhibits both glycogenolysis and gluconeogenesis, thereby resulting in a increase in hepatic glycogen content. Glucose concentrations continue to rise until the rate of glucose uptake by peripheral tissues exceeds the net amount of glucose (meal-derived and endogenously produced) being released from the splanchnic bed. Glucose concentration then begins to fall toward prandial levels. This results in a progressive fall in insulin and a progressive rise in glucagon concentrations, which in turn permits a gradual increase in endogenous glucose production and a gradual fall in glucose utilization to basal rates. Depending on the amount and type of food ingested, both glucose concentration and turnover are generally back to basal levels sometime between 4 and 6 hours after the start of a meal.

Thus, the rate of carbohydrate absorption, the timing as well as the amount of insulin and glucagon secreted, the ability of the liver to store and subsequently release glucose, and the response of the liver, muscle, and fat to insulin and counter-insulin hormones all interact to minimize the rise in glucose concentration after a meal as well as to ensure a smooth return of glucose concentrations to preprandial levels during the transition from the fed to the postabsorptive state.

REGULATION OF GLUCOSE CONCENTRATIONS IN THE FASTED STATE. The contribution of gluconeogenesis becomes progressively more important as the duration of fast is extended and hepatic glycogen stores are depleted. The rate of glycogen depletion depends on a variety of factors, including antecedent diet and exercise, but is nearly complete after 24 to 48 hours of fasting. Anything that lowers the demand for glucose lessens the need to break down protein stores. This is accomplished by changing from a primarily carbohydrate-based metabolism in the fed state to a primarily fat-based metabolism in the fasted state.

Insulin decreases and glucagon, growth hormone, and cortisol concentrations all increase as hepatic glycogen is depleted and the glucose concentration falls. This change in the hormonal milieu stimulates lipolysis and ketogenesis, which results in an increase in plasma glycerol, free fatty acid, and ketone body concentrations. Glycerol serves as a gluconeogenic substrate, thereby sparing amino acids. Free fatty acids are metabolized by muscle, liver, and other tissues in place of glucose. Free fatty acids also are converted by means of ketogenesis to acetoacetate and β-hydroxybutyrate, which can substitute for glucose as a fuel for the brain. These metabolic adaptations normally permit glucose to gradually decrease to 40 to 50 mg/dL during a fast without provoking symptoms of hypoglycemia.

Inadequate glycogen stores or breakdown, insufficient gluconeogenesis due to defects in enzyme activity, lack of substrate availability, or persistent elevations of insulin or of insulin-like activity, alone or in combination, can cause or exacerbate hypoglycemia.

RECOVERY FROM HYPOGLYCEMIA. If counter-regulation is intact, hypoglycemia (regardless of the cause) will result in a decrease in insulin secretion and an increase in glucagon, epinephrine, cortisol, and growth hormone secretion. Glucagon provides the major defense against acute hypoglycemia. Epinephrine appears to become progressively more important when hypoglycemia is prolonged or severe. Permissive amounts of cortisol and growth hormone are required for a normal hepatic response to glucagon and epinephrine. Drugs or diseases that inhibit counter-regulatory secretion or action predispose to hypoglycemia.

Clinical Manifestations

Symptoms of hypoglycemia have been classified into two major groups: those arising from activation of the autonomic nervous system (autonomic) and those related to insufficient glucose supply to the brain (neuroglycopenic).

During acute insulin-induced hypoglycemia in healthy persons, autonomic symptoms are recognized at a threshold of approximately 60 mg/dL (3 mM) and impairment of brain function manifested by neuroglycopenic symptoms occurs at a threshold of approximately 50 mg/dL (2.8 mM) in arterialized venous blood (Fig. 243–1). Comparable venous levels would be about 3 mg/dL

(0 16mM) less. The rate of glucose descent has little if any influence on the occurrence of symptoms and signs of hypoglycemia in nondiabetic persons.

Variations among reports regarding allocation of symptoms to the autonomic and neuroglycopenic types may be ascribed to the types of patients examined, diabetic versus nondiabetic, type 1 versus type 2 diabetes, clinical versus experimental conditions, and, probably most importantly, differences among persons regarding their perceptions of symptoms. During experimentally induced hypoglycemia in 20 persons with and 25 persons without diabetes, a principal component analysis allocated sweating, trembling, warmness, anxiety, and nausea to the autonomic group and dizziness, confusion, tiredness, difficulty with speaking, headache, and inability to concentrate to the neuroglycopenic group. Hunger, blurred vision, drowsiness, and weakness could not be allocated to either group with any confidence. In another study of 10 nondiabetic persons, partitioning of symptoms during insulin-induced hypoglycemia allocated shaky/tremulous, heart pounding, nervous/anxious, sweaty, hungry, and tingling to the autonomic group and warm, weak, difficulty thinking/confused, and tired/drowsy to the neuroglycopenic group.

In a retrospective analysis of 60 patients with insulinoma, 85% had various combinations of diplopia, blurred vision, sweating, palpitations, and weakness; 80% had confusion or abnormal behavior; 50% were amnesic for the episode or had coma; and 12% had generalized seizures. None of the symptoms noted earlier, regardless of type, is specific for hypoglycemia.

It is highly unlikely that autonomic symptoms alone, in the absence of at least one event of neuroglycopenia, is indicative of a hypoglycemic disorder.

Classification of Hypoglycemia

A useful approach for the clinician is a classification based on clinical characteristics (Table 243–1). Persons who appear healthy are likely to have hypoglycemic disorders that are different from those of persons who are ill. Hospitalized patients are at additional risk for hypoglycemia, often from iatrogenic factors.

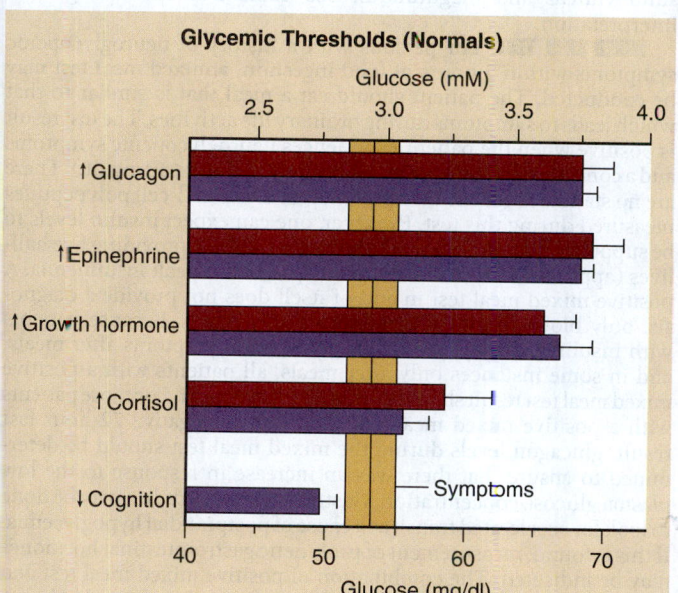

Glycemic Thresholds (Normals)

FIGURE 243–1 • Arterialized venous glycemic (mean ± standard error) thresholds for increments in plasma glucagon, epinephrine, growth hormone, and cortisol for symptoms of hypoglycemia and for impairment of cognitive function during decrements in plasma glucose in normal humans from two independent studies. (From Cryer PE: Glucose counterregulation: The physiological mechanisms that prevent or correct hypoglycemia. In Frier B, Fisher BM [eds]: Hypoglycaemia and Diabetes: Clinical and Physiological Aspects. London, Boston, Edward Arnold, 1993, pp 34–55; with permission.)

Table 243–1 • CLINICAL CLASSIFICATION OF HYPOGLYCEMIC DISORDERS

I. Patient Appears Healthy*
   A. No coexistent disease
      1. Drugs
         a. Ethanol
         b. Salicylates
         c. Quinine
         d. Haloperidol
      2. Insulinoma
      3. Islet hypertrophy/nesidioblastosis
      4. Factitial hypoglycemia from insulin or sulfonylurea use
      5. Exercise
      6. Autoimmune insulin syndrome
   B. Compensated coexistent disease
      1. Drugs
         a. Dispensing error
         b. Disopyramide
         c. β–Adrenergic blocking agents
II. Patient Appears Ill
   A. Drugs
      1. Pentamidine and *Pneumocystis pneumonia*
      2. Sulfamethoxazole/trimethoprim and renal failure
      3. Propoxyphene and renal failure
      4. Quinine and cerebral malaria
      5. Quinine and malaria
      6. Topical salicylates and renal failure
      7. Unripe ackee fruit and undernutrition
   B. Predisposing illness
      1. Small-for-gestational-age infant
      2. Beckwith-Wiedemann syndrome
      3. Erythroblastosis fetalis
      4. Infant of diabetic mother
      5. Glycogen storage disease
      6. Defects in amino acid and fatty acid metabolism
      7. Reye's syndrome
      8. Cyanotic congenital heart disease
      9. Hypopituitarism
      10. Isolated growth hormone deficiency
      11. Isolated adrenocorticotropic hormone deficiency
      12. Addison's disease
      13. Galactosemia
      14. Hereditary fructose intolerance
      15. Carnitine deficiency
      16. Defective type 1 glucose transporter in the brain
      17. Acquired severe liver disease
      18. Non–islet cell tumor hypoglycemia
      19. Sepsis
      20. Renal failure
      21. Congestive heart failure
      22. Lactic acidosis
      23. Starvation
      24. Anorexia nervosa
      25. Postoperative removal of pheochromocytoma
      26. Insulin receptor antibody hypoglycemia
      27. Spinal muscular atrophy
   C. Hospitalized patient
      1. Diseases predisposing to hypoglycemia
      2. Total parenteral nutrition and insulin therapy
      3. Questran interference with glucocorticoid absorption
      4. Shock

*Mutations in the β-cell sulfonylurea receptor gene, glutamate dehydrogenase gene, and glucokinase gene are rare causes of hyperinsulinemic hypoglycemia, usually manifested in infancy or childhood.

Evaluation of Hypoglycemia

The direction and extent of evaluation is dependent on the clinical presentation. The healthy-appearing patient with no coexistent disease who has a history of episodic symptoms suggestive of hypoglycemia requires an approach quite different from the hospitalized patient with acute hypoglycemia.

HEALTHY-APPEARING PATIENT

PLASMA GLUCOSE. Because symptoms from hypoglycemia are not specific, it is essential to document a low plasma glucose concentration at the time of the occurrence of spontaneous symptoms and relief of symptoms through correction of the low plasma glucose concentration (Whipple's triad) before concluding that a patient has a hypoglycemic disorder. Furthermore, reliance solely on a low blood glucose value to diagnose a hypoglycemic disorder fails to take into consideration the possibility of laboratory error, artifactual hypoglycemia, and, indeed, that normal persons may have plasma glucose levels well below 50 mg/dL (2.8 mM) during prolonged fasting. It is important to recognize that a normal plasma glucose concentration (when measured reliably) obtained during the occurrence of spontaneous symptoms absolutely eliminates the possibility of a hypoglycemic disorder; no further evaluation is required. Although hypoglycemic disorders are uncommon, symptoms suggestive of hypoglycemia are quite common.

Often, measurement of plasma glucose is not feasible during the occurrence of spontaneous symptoms during ordinary life activities. Under such circumstances, a judgment about whether to proceed with further evaluation depends on a detailed history. Elicitation of a history of neuroglycopenic symptoms or evidence for a confirmed low plasma glucose concentration warrants further testing.

SEVENTY-TWO-HOUR FAST. The prolonged supervised (72-hour) fast is the classic diagnostic test. It should be conducted in a standardized fashion. A suggested protocol is shown in Table 243–2. For patients who experience signs or symptoms of hypoglycemia and have simultaneously measured plasma glucose in the hypoglycemic range, the fast should be terminated at that point. Studies in patients who have neither should not be extended beyond 72 hours nor truncated prior to 72 hours.

The decision to end the fast may not be easy. Some patients have slightly depressed glycemic levels without symptoms or signs of hypoglycemia. Other patients may experience the symptoms they have had in ordinary life but have plasma glucose levels above the hypoglycemic range. Young, lean, healthy women and, to a lesser degree, men, may have plasma glucose levels in the range of 40 mg/dL during prolonged fasting. Careful examination and testing for subtle signs of symptoms of neuroglycopenia should be conducted repeatedly when the patient's plasma glucose level is near or in the hypoglycemic range. The 72-hour fast may be ended when plasma glucose is 55 mg/dL or less if Whipple's triad had previously been demonstrated. β-Cell polypeptides are suppressed in healthy persons when plasma glucose is 55 mg/dL or less. Although most patients with insulinoma become hypoglycemic prior to 72 hours (33% in 12 hours, 65% in 24 hours, 84% in 36 hours, 93% in 48 hours, and 99% in 72 hours in a group of 170 insulinoma patients), continuation of the fast to 72 hours is necessary to rule out the likelihood of organic hypoglycemia. Although the 72-hour fast has usually been considered to be an inpatient procedure, we have been initiating the fast in an endocrine testing center after an overnight fast. Forty per cent of patients have had positive results of the fast in the outpatient setting. Those patients whose fast result is not positive by the end of the business day are admitted to the hospital to complete the 72-hour fast.

The interpretation of concentrations of β-cell polypeptides (insulin, C peptide, and proinsulin) during the prolonged supervised fast is predicated on the concomitant plasma glucose concentration. The normal overnight fasting ranges for these polypeptides do not apply when the plasma glucose level is low (e.g., ≤55 mg/dL).

Table 243–2 • PROTOCOL FOR 72-HOUR FAST

1. Date onset of fast as of last ingestion of calories; discontinue all nonessential medications.
2. May drink calorie-free and caffeine-free beverages.
3. Must be active during waking hours.
4. Measure plasma glucose, insulin, and C-peptide (on the same venipuncture specimen) every 6 hours until plasma glucose reaches ≤60 mg/dL (3.3 mM), when frequency should be every 1 to 2 hours.
5. End the fast when the plasma glucose is ≤45 mg/dL (2.5 mM) and the patient has symptoms and/or signs of hypoglycemia, or plasma glucose is ≤55 mg/dL if Whipple's triad had been demonstrated previously.
6. At the end of the fast, measure plasma glucose, insulin, C-peptide, β-hydroxybutyrate, and sulfonylurea (on the same venipuncture specimen); then inject glucagon 1 mg intravenously and measure plasma glucose q10 min × 3. After this, feed the patient.

Insulin-mediated hypoglycemic disorders are characterized by plasma insulin concentrations greater than or equal to 3 μU/mL (immunochemiluminometric assay) (Fig. 243–2).

Persons with insulinomas have insulin concentrations that rarely exceed 100 μU/mL. Values of 1000 μU/mL or greater suggest recent insulin administration or the presence of insulin antibodies. Ratios of glucose to insulin, and vice versa, including the "amended ratio," have been used in an effort to identify relative hyperinsulinemia when the insulin concentration is in the normal overnight fasting range. Unfortunately, these ratios have very poor diagnostic utility (see Fig. 243–2).

Criteria for hyperinsulinemia using C-peptide and proinsulin (each measured by immunochemiluminometric assays) are 200 pmol/L or more and 5 pmol/L or more, respectively (see Fig. 243–2). The molar ratio of insulin to C-peptide is the same for patients with insulinomas and healthy individuals (approximately 0.2). Although the molar ratio of proinsulin to insulin is increased in patients with insulinoma, it has no diagnostic utility.

Because of the antiketogenic effect of insulin, plasma β-hydroxybutyrate measurement at the end of the fast (72 hours in normal individuals and at Whipple's triad in patients with a hypoglycemic disorder) is useful. This parameter is considered to be an insulin surrogate. Patients with insulin-mediated hypoglycemia have concentrations of less than 2.7 mmol/L, whereas others (normal individuals or those with non-insulin-mediated hypoglycemia) have higher levels (see Fig. 243–2). Another insulin surrogate is the response of plasma glucose to 1 mg of glucagon injected intravenously at the end of the fast. The rationale for this procedure is that insulin is glycogenic and antiglycogenolytic. Patients with insulin-mediated hypoglycemia have a maximum increment of 25 mg/dL or more above the terminal fasting plasma glucose, whereas others (normal individuals or those with non-insulin-mediated hypoglycemia) have lower increments (see Fig. 243–2). When the plasma glucose concentration exceeds 60 mg/dL at the end of the fast, measurement of the β-cell polypeptides and insulin surrogates is uninformative and unnecessary.

Measurement of sulfonylureas in the plasma at the end of the fast is an essential component of the prolonged supervised fast. The pattern of plasma glucose and β-cell polypeptides in sulfonylurea-induced hypoglycemia is identical to that observed in persons with insulinoma. A liquid chromatographic tandem mass spectrography method provides a sensitive measurement of first and second-generation sulfonylureas and meglitinides. See Table 243–3 for diagnostic interpretation.

MIXED MEAL TEST. For persons with a history of neuroglycopenic symptoms within 5 hours of food ingestion, a mixed meal test may be conducted. The patient should eat a meal that is similar to that which leads to symptoms during ordinary life activities. The test result is positive when the patient experiences neuroglycopenic symptoms and a concomitant plasma glucose level is low (e.g., ≤50 mg/dL). There are no standards for the interpretation of levels of β-cell polypeptides measured during this test. However, one can expect insulin levels to be suppressed during postprandial hypoglycemia, providing five half-lives (approximately 30 min) have elapsed from peak insulinemia. A positive mixed meal test in and of itself does not provide a diagnosis, only biochemical confirmation of the history. Because patients with insulinoma may have neuroglycopenic symptoms after meals, and in some instances only after meals, all patients with a positive mixed meal test result should undergo a 72-hour fast. For those patients with a positive mixed meal test result and a negative 72-hour fast result, glucagon levels during the mixed meal test should be determined to ensure that there was an increase in response to the low plasma glucose concentration. Gastric emptying studies may be done to look for accelerated transit as a cause of postprandial hypoglycemia. If this is found, measurement of prokinetic gastrointestinal hormones may be indicated. The combination of positive mixed meal test and negative 72-hour fast in a patient with a history of postprandial hypoglycemia suggests the presence of noninsulinoma pancreatogenous hypoglycemia syndrome (NIPHS). The 5-hour oral glucose tolerance test should never be used as a diagnostic test for hypoglycemia because a substantial percentage of healthy persons may have a plasma glucose nadir less than or equal to 50 mg/dL.

C-PEPTIDE SUPPRESSION TEST. The C-peptide suppression test can be used to provide additional diagnostic information, especially if data from the 72-hour fast are not conclusive. This test can also be used as a screening test: when the likelihood of a hypoglycemic disorder

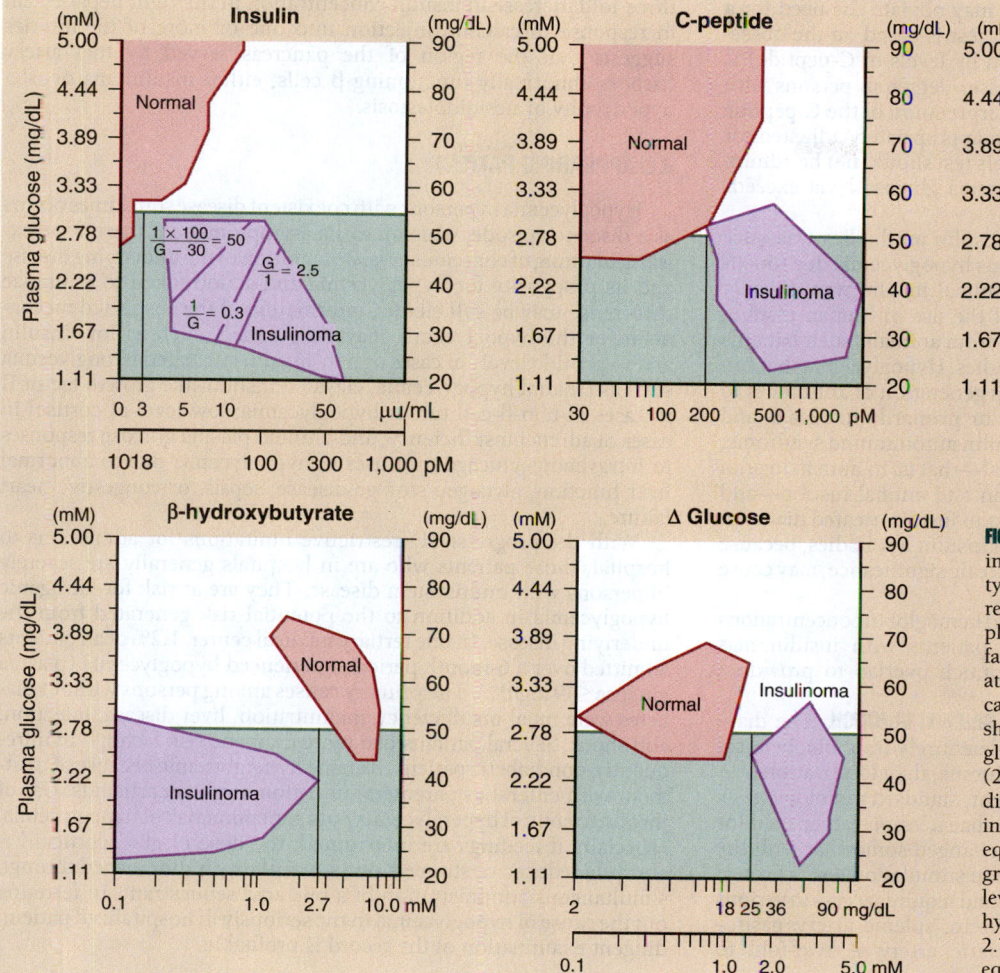

FIGURE 243–2 • Distributions of plasma insulin, C-peptide proinsulin, β-hydroxybutyrate, and plasma glucose (Δ glucose) response to intravenous glucagon versus plasma glucose at the end of the prolonged fast (72 hours in normal persons [N = 25] or at Whipple's triad for patients with histologically confirmed insulinoma [N = 40]) are shown. The shaded area represents plasma glucose level less than or equal to 50 mg/dL (2.8 mM). The vertical line represents the diagnostic level for insulinoma. Criteria for insulinoma are insulin level greater than or equal to 3 μU/mL (18 pM), C-peptide level greater than or equal to 200 pM, proinsulin level greater than or equal to 5 pM, β-hydroxybutyrate level less than or equal to 2.7 mM, and Δ glucose level greater than or equal to 25 mg/dL (1.4 mM).

Table 243–3 • DIAGNOSTIC INTERPRETATION OF THE RESULTS OF A 72-HOUR FAST*

	SIGNS AND SYMPTOMS	GLUCOSE[†] (mg/dL)	INSULIN[§] (μU/mL)	C-PEPTIDE[§¶] (pmol/L)	PROINSULIN[§∥] (pmol/L)	B-HYDROXYBUTYRATE (mmol/L)	CHANGE IN GLUCOSE** (mg/dL)	SULFONYLUREA IN PLASMA
Normal	No	≥40	<3	<200	<5	>2.7	<25	No
Insulinoma	Yes	≤45	≥3[††]	≥200	≥5	≤2.7	≤25	No
Factitious hypoglycemia from insulin	Yes	≤45	≥3[§§]	<200	<5	≤2.7	≥25	No
Sulfonylurea-induced hypoglycemia	Yes	≤45	≥3	≥200	≥5	≤2.7	≥25	Yes[‡‡]
Hypoglycemia mediated by insulin-like growth factor	Yes	≤45	<3	<200	<5	≤2.7	≥25	No
Non-insulin–mediated hypoglycemia	Yes	≤45	<3	<200	<5	>2.7	<25	No
Inadvertent feeding during the fast	No	≤45	<3	<200	<5	≤2.7	≥25	No
Nonhypoglycemic disorder	Yes	≥40	<3	<200	<5	>2.7	<25	No

*Measurements are made at the point the decision is made to end the fast.
†Sequential plasma glucose measurements in the hypoglycemic range fluctuate. Plasma glucose levels ≤45 mg/dL at the time a decision is made to end the fast may rise to as much as 56 mg/dL when the fast is actually ended approximately 1 hour later. Plasma glucose levels may be as low as 40 mg/dL during prolonged fasting in normal women.
‡Measured by ICMA, lower limit of detection is 0.1 μU/mL.
§In normal subjects, plasma insulin, C-peptide, and proinsulin levels may be higher if the plasma glucose level is >60 mg/dL.
¶Measured by the immunochemiluminometric technique (lower limit of detection, 33 pmol/L).
∥Measured by the immunochemiluminometric technique (lower limit of detection, 0.2 pmol/L).
**In response to intravenous glucagon (peak value minus value at end of fast).
††Ratios of insulin to glucose are of no diagnostic value in patients with insulinomas.
‡‡Unlike the first generation of sulfonylurea drugs, which were easily measured, second-generation drugs are difficult to measure.
§§Plasma insulin levels may be very high (>100 μU/mL or even ≥1000 μU/mL) in factitious hypoglycemia produced by insulin.
Reprinted with permission from Service FJ: Hypoglycemia Disorder. N Engl J Med 1995;332:1144–1152. © 1995, Massachusetts Medical Society. All rights reserved.

is not high, a normal result on this test may obviate the need for a 72-hour fast. The C-peptide suppression test is based on the observation that β-cell secretion (as measured by levels of C-peptide) is suppressed during hypoglycemia to a lesser degree in persons with insulinomas than in normal persons. Interpretation of the C-peptide suppression test requires normative data appropriately adjusted for the patient's body mass index and age. This test should not be administered unless the immediate pretest plasma glucose level exceeds 60 mg/dL.

INSULIN ANTIBODIES. The detection of insulin antibodies was once considered to be firm evidence of factitious hypoglycemia due to self-administered insulin, especially when animal insulin was the only commercially available type. Because of the use of human insulin, which is less antigenic than that derived from animals, such patients usually have no detectable insulin antibodies. Hypoglycemia that can be directly attributed to the spontaneous generation of antibodies to native insulin has been reported to occur primarily in Asians and rarely in whites. In patients with the insulin autoimmune syndrome, the insulin antibodies may be monoclonal—that is, to human insulin alone—or polyclonal—that is, to human and animal insulin—and are present in very high titers, in contrast to insulin-treated diabetes. It is important to test for the presence of insulin antibodies, because even low titers, which may have no diagnostic significance, may cause spurious results of the assay for insulin.

GLYCATED HEMOGLOBIN. Although glycated hemoglobin concentrations are statistically significantly lower in patients with insulinomas than in control subjects, there is too much overlap to provide a diagnostic criterion.

INSULIN RESPONSE TO SELECTIVE ARTERIAL CALCIUM INJECTION. The diagnosis of a hypoglycemic disorder is made entirely from biochemical evidence. Should the data point to insulinoma, then localization procedures are undertaken. Up to the present, standard radiologic tests have been done solely in an effort to localize a lesion rather than for diagnostic purposes. This position has changed somewhat with the availability of the selective arterial calcium stimulation test. This test is conducted in a vascular radiology suite and requires access to various intra-abdominal vessels: right hepatic vein, splenic artery, gastroduodenal artery, and superior mesenteric artery. A two-fold to three-fold increase in insulin concentration in the right hepatic vein in response to calcium injection into one or more of the arteries suggests that the region of the pancreas served by that artery harbors abnormally functioning β cells, either insulinoma or islet hypertrophy or nesidioblastosis.

ILL-APPEARING PATIENT

Hypoglycemia in persons with coexistent disease sometimes occurs as a discrete episode, which may be asymptomatic if there is preexisting blunting of consciousness. Recognition of the underlying disease and its propensity for hypoglycemia and action taken to minimize recurrence may be sufficient. Confirmation of the suspected mechanism for the hypoglycemia may be pursued, such as low insulin and C-peptide levels in cases of non-insulin-mediated hypoglycemia such as ethanol hypoglycemia; elevated insulin-like growth factor II in cases of non-β-cell tumor hypoglycemia; low level of cortisol in cases of adrenal insufficiency; and blunted plasma glucose responses to intravenous glucagon in cases of hypoglycemia due to abnormal liver function, glycogen storage disease, sepsis, or congestive heart failure.

With the progressively restrictive limitations for admissions to hospital, those patients who are in hospitals generally are severely ill persons with multisystem disease. They are at risk for iatrogenic hypoglycemia in addition to the potential risk generated from the underlying disease. In one tertiary medical center, 1.2% of all patients admitted over a 6-month period experienced hypoglycemia (plasma glucose ≤49 mg/dL). The primary causes among persons without diabetes were renal insufficiency, malnutrition, liver disease, infection, and shock. Several patients had more than one risk factor. Not infrequently, nondiabetic patients become hyperglycemic because of treatment with enteral or parenteral nutrition or glucocorticoids. Use of insulin to control hyperglycemia puts patients at risk of hypoglycemia, especially if feedings are interrupted, the dose of glucocorticoid is abruptly reduced or stopped, or its availability is diminished through simultaneous administration of a bile acid sequestrant. In ferreting out the cause of hypoglycemia in the seriously ill hospitalized patient, diligent examination of the record is profitable.

Rx Treatment

The treatment of hypoglycemic disorders encompasses two distinct components: (1) relief of neuroglycopenic systems by restoration of the low plasma glucose level to the normal range and (2) correction of the underlying cause of the hypoglycemia. Unlike diabetes, in which restoration of euglycemia or hypoglycemia is the ideal goal, overtreatment of hypoglycemia in a nondiabetic person has no sequelae. For the as-yet undiagnosed patient, blood by venipuncture should be obtained for measurement of glucose, β-cell polypeptides, and β-hydroxybutyrate before treatment. Both diagnosis and treatment can be achieved by intravenous injection of glucagon and the plasma glucose response monitored. Depending on the response, the patient may require intravenous glucose administration as a bolus of 50% or a continuous infusion of 5 or 10% or recover sufficiently to take oral nutrition.

Treatment of the underlying cause of the hypoglycemia depends on the specific cause. Once a biochemical diagnosis of insulinoma has been made, preoperative localization should be attempted. Because of the rarity of insulinoma, only a few referral centers have generated sufficient experience to assess the effectiveness of various localization procedures: computed tomography, magnetic resonance imaging, endoscopic and transabdominal ultrasonography, octreotide scan, celiac axis angiography, and selective arterial calcium stimulation and transhepatic portal venous sampling. Experts differ in their preferred approaches because of differences in experience and skill level. Ultrasonography has the advantage of precise localization, especially in relation to the pancreatic duct. Magnetic resonance imaging and octreotide scanning are not useful. Transhepatic portal venous sampling has been abandoned in those centers that had once used this technique. There is general agreement that intraoperative ultrasonography combined with careful palpation of the pancreas by an experienced surgeon provides the highest success rate in localization.

SPECIFIC CAUSES. Insulinoma is a rare tumor, the incidence of which is estimated to be 4 cases per 1 million person years, an incidence similar to that of pheochromocytoma. Insulinoma occurs at any age, is slightly more common in women (59%), and is associated with low rates of malignancy (6%), multiplicity (9%), multiple endocrine neoplasia syndrome (8%), and recurrence (8%). After successful removal of an insulinoma, the patient can look forward to normal life expectancy. Medical therapy for the patient whose insulinoma is missed at pancreatic exploration, for the patient unsuitable for surgery, or for the patient with metastatic insulinoma may include diazoxide, verapamil, phenytoin, propranolol, or octreotide. Insulinoma is occasionally suspected in patients with labile diabetes, especially when insulin therapy has apparently been suspended. There is one case of documented insulinoma in a person with type 1 diabetes and a few cases in persons with type 2 diabetes. Optimal treatment is surgical resection.

Very rarely, adults with episodes of hyperinsulinemic hypoglycemia resulting in neuroglycopenia harbor islet hypertrophy/nesidioblastosis but no insulinoma (NIPHS). Their clinical features are uniquely different from those of insulinoma: predominance of males, postprandial neuroglycopenia, negative 72-hour fast result, negative radiologic localization studies, positive selective arterial calcium stimulation test, and relief of symptoms with gradient guided partial pancreatectomy.

Insulin factitial hypoglycemia usually is manifested by neuroglycopenic symptoms that occur erratically. This disorder is observed more often in women, usually those in a health-related occupation. Once confronted with the diagnosis, about half of the patients admit to self-abuse and most cease this activity. Insulin autoimmune hypoglycemia may be very difficult to distinguish from insulin factitial hypoglycemia because of similar biochemical features. However, some patients with the former have

Table 243-4 • CHARACTERISTICS OF FUNCTIONING ISLET CELL CARCINOMAS

SYNDROME	CLINICAL PRESENTATION	BIOCHEMICAL DIAGNOSIS	RATE OF MALIGNANCY (%)	METASTASES AT DIAGNOSIS (%)	LOCALIZATION (RADIOGRAPHIC)	ECTOPIC SITES (NON-PANCREATIC)
Insulinoma	Neuroglycopenia Andrenergic response	Blood glucose ≤45 mg/dL Insulin >6 μU/mL Absence of insulin antibodies Nl/elevated C-peptide	<10	<10	Ultrasonography, spiral CT, selective calcium stimulation test	Rare
Zollinger-Ellison syndrome	Dyspepsia/ulcer Diarrhea	Elevated basal gastrin Elevated basal acid output Positive secretin test	50–60	50–80	Ultrasonography, CT, angiography, PVS	Duodenum Rarely other
WDHA (VIPoma)	Profuse, secretory diarrhea Hypokalemia Hypo/achlorhydria, hypercalcemia, hyperglycemia	Elevated VIP	50	50	CT, occasionally, angiography PVS	Retroperitoneum Lung
Glucagonoma	Dermatitis Diabetes Weight loss Anemia	Elevated glucagon	75	60–70	CT	Rare
Somatostatinoma	Diabetes Cholelithiasis Diarrhea Steatorrhea	Elevated somatostatin	90–100	50–75	CT	Duodenum

WDHA = watery diarrhea, hypokalemia, achlorhydria; VIP = vasoactive intestinal pepide; PVS = portal venous sampling; CT = computed tomography.
Modified from Grant CS: Surgical management of malignant islet cell tumors. World J Surg 1993;17:498–503.

evidence of other autoimmune disease, and the insulin antibody titers are very high.

Mutations in the β-cell sulfonylurea receptor gene, glutamate dehydrogenase gene, and glucokinase gene have been reported to cause hyperinsulinemic hypoglycemia (i.e., inappropriately elevated insulin and C-peptide concentrations), primarily at an early age and often in a familial pattern. Physical exercise–induced hypoglycemia also has been described in some families.

ISLET CELL TUMORS

Tumors of the endocrine pancreas generally are malignant. Insulin-producing tumors are the exception because they are usually benign. Islet cell tumors are commonly referred to as either functioning or nonfunctioning. Functioning tumors release one or more hormones in amounts sufficient to raise plasma concentrations. Nonfunctioning tumors may contain one or more hormones but, by definition, do not release substantial amounts into the systemic circulation. Functioning tumors generally manifest with symptoms relating to the hormones being secreted, whereas nonfunctioning tumors generally manifest as a pancreatic mass or as a metastasis. Nonfunctioning tumors tend to be larger and more advanced at the time of diagnosis because their presence is not heralded by symptoms generated by hormone excess.

Functioning islet cell tumors are commonly associated with one of five widely recognized syndromes (Table 243–4). The insulinoma, Zollinger-Ellison, glucagonoma, VIPoma, and somatostatinoma syndromes are believed to be due (at least in part) to excess secretion of insulin, gastrin, glucagon, vasoactive intestinal polypeptide (VIP), and somatostatin, respectively. However, a number of additional symptoms also can occur because these tumors frequently secrete more than one hormone (e.g., pancreatic polypeptide, adrenocorticotropin, calcitonin, neurotensin, human chorionic gonadotropin, growth hormone-releasing factor, prostaglandins, and parathyroid hormone) and the amount and type of the hormone being secreted can change over time. Islet cell tumors are either sporadic or can occur in association with other known genetic syndromes, such as multiple endocrine neoplasia type 1. Sporadic tumors occur at any age but most commonly are detected between 40 and 60 years of age. The diagnosis can be confirmed by obtaining tissue during surgical resection or by means of a needle biopsy.

With the exception perhaps of insulinomas, the optimal treatment of islet cell tumors is currently not known because their rarity has made the conduct of randomized therapeutic trials extremely difficult. Furthermore, in the absence of metastases, there are no reliable histologic criteria that can distinguish benign from malignant lesions. Islet cell tumors most commonly metastasize to the liver and adjacent lymph nodes. Metastases to lung, bone, adrenal gland, kidney, and ovary may also occur. Fortunately, the rate of growth of malignant islet cell tumors is generally slow. Therefore, many clinicians recommend surgery if the pancreatic tumor is resectable and if the extent of metastatic disease (if present) is limited. "Debulking" of metastases, whether by surgery or by hepatic embolization, may improve symptoms by lowering circulating hormone concentrations. Treatment with chemotherapeutic agents such as streptozotocin (alone or in combination with 5-fluorouracil), doxorubicin, dacarbazine, or interferon-β also may improve symptoms and, in some instances, perhaps improve survival. Somatostatin is a potent inhibitor of hormone secretion. Treatment with long-acting analogues of somatostatin can result in a dramatic, albeit at times temporary, decrease in symptoms, particularly those associated with glucagonomas and VIPomas.

SUGGESTED READINGS

Carroll MF, Burge MR, Schade DS: Severe hypoglycemia in adults. Rev Endocr Metab Disord 2003;4:149–157. *Review of the common causes.*

Otonkoski T, Kaminen N, Ustinov J, et al: Physical exercise-induced hyperinsulinemic hypoglycemia is an autosomal-dominant trait characterized by abnormal pyruvate-induced insulin release. Diabetes 2003;52:199–204. *A newly-described syndrome.*

Vella A, Service FJ, O'Brien PC: Glucose counterregulatory hormones in the 72-hour fast. Endocr Pract 2003;9:115–118. *Approach to the diagnosis of glucagon deficiency.*

244 POLYGLANDULAR DISORDERS

Henry M. Kronenberg

Internists need to recognize diseases that involve independent abnormalities of more than one endocrine gland for a number of reasons:

First, the known patterns of multiglandular disease can alert the clinician to look for a second disorder when one is diagnosed. Second, the treatment of many of the individual diseases in polyglandular disorders may differ from the treatment appropriate for the same diseases when they manifest in isolation. Third, because many of these diseases appear in characteristic familial patterns, the recognition of the syndromes can lead to useful family screening. Fourth, an understanding of the pathogenesis of these unusual disorders is likely to clarify the pathogenesis of more common single-gland disorders as well. This chapter discusses the best-characterized polyglandular disorders with these four considerations as the primary focus. Other chapters should be consulted for more detailed discussion of the diseases of individual glands.

NEOPLASTIC SYNDROMES

Three mechanistically distinct neoplastic syndromes involve more than one endocrine gland. Although given a variety of different names in the past, they are now most frequently called *multiple endocrine neoplasia type 1*, *multiple endocrine neoplasia types 2a and 2b*, and *McCune-Albright syndrome*.

Multiple Endocrine Neoplasia Type 1

Multiple endocrine neoplasia type 1 (MEN 1) is an autosomal dominant disorder characteristically involving the parathyroid glands, the pancreatic islets, and the anterior pituitary. Less commonly, adrenal cortical neoplasia, foregut carcinoids (primarily of thymus and lung), lipomas, and facial angiofibromas and collagenomas occur.

PARATHYROID DISEASE. Hyperparathyroidism is the most common abnormality in MEN 1, found in more than 90% of patients. Elevation of blood calcium levels generally first appears between the ages of 20 and 40 years, considerably earlier than in sporadic primary hyperparathyroidism; this is not usually a disease of children, however. At first, the disease is asymptomatic but then can lead to all the expected consequences of primary hyperparathyroidism. Unlike sporadic hyperparathyroidism, the disease is relentlessly progressive and, with prolonged follow-up, always involves all four parathyroid glands. The involvement is characteristically asymmetrical and asynchronous. This pattern can lead to inappropriately limited parathyroid surgery. If fewer than three parathyroid glands are removed, hypercalcemia always recurs, although not necessarily immediately. Surgical results in cases of MEN 1 are generally less satisfactory than in sporadic four-gland parathyroid disease. At some centers, all four glands are removed, and a portion of one gland is reimplanted in the easily accessible forearm in an attempt to avoid the hazards of too much or too little surgery. The difficulty in attaining long-term normocalcemia has led many clinicians to postpone surgery when the disease is asymptomatic. This strategy may need to be modified if the patient develops Zollinger-Ellison syndrome (see later), because hypercalcemia can dramatically increase the gastrin levels in such patients.

PANCREATIC ISLET DISEASE. As many as 80% of patients have pancreatic abnormalities at autopsy; a large number correspondingly have increased blood levels of gastrin, insulin, pancreatic polypeptide, somatostatin, vasoactive intestinal polypeptide, or glucagon during stimulation or suppression tests. The pancreas is often diffusely involved with microadenomas and macroadenomas and apparently hyperplastic lesions. Characteristically, more than one islet hormone is secreted from these multiple tumors. Despite this underlying pattern of multiple cellular involvement, patients characteristically present with symptoms of only one hormonal disorder. The most common disease is Zollinger-Ellison syndrome, a peptic ulcer disease associated with gastrin-producing tumors. Identification of disease-causing tumors has proven difficult. The gastrinomas in MEN 1 are often multiple, very small, and found in the duodenal wall. Macroadenomas observed in the pancreas by computed tomography or intraoperative ultrasonography may well synthesize hormones other than gastrin.

Although some centers continue to experiment with aggressive attempts at surgical cure, the high recurrence rate after surgery has limited the role for surgery in this disease. Medical therapy with H_2 receptor antagonists and H^+, K^+-ATPase inhibitors can usually adequately control the secretion of stomach acid. The tumors are slow-growing but frequently metastasize locally and to the liver. Chemotherapy is only partially effective and never cures the disease.

Insulinomas are the second most common clinically important islet tumor in cases of MEN 1. These tumors are often small and multiple and are much less frequently malignant than the gastrinomas. Despite the frequently diffuse nature of the disease, dominant insulin-producing tumors can often be identified by selective portal venous sampling. Removal of the dominant tissue or, if necessary, subtotal (80%) pancreatectomy is the primary therapeutic strategy.

PITUITARY DISEASE. As in sporadic disease, pituitary disease can manifest with a hypersecretion syndrome or with symptoms due to a sellar mass or hypopituitarism. Pituitary tumors occur in one half of MEN 1 patients. Prolactinomas are the most common tumors. Adrenocortical hyperfunction can result from a pituitary adenoma or from production of adrenocorticotropic hormone or corticotropin-releasing hormone by a foregut carcinoid. Although nonfunctioning adrenal neoplasms are common in cases of MEN 1, primary adrenal neoplasms causing glucocorticoid excess are rare. Acromegaly can result from a pituitary neoplasm or as a consequence of production of growth hormone–releasing hormone by pancreatic islet tumors. After consideration of ectopic hormone and releasing hormone production by nonpituitary tumors, the course and treatment of pituitary disease in MEN 1 resemble those of sporadic pituitary disease.

PATHOGENESIS. The gene for MEN 1 is located at chromosome 11, band 11q13, and it encodes a 610–amino acid protein called menin. Menin is a nuclear transcription factor expressed in most tissues. Although the normal function of menin is unknown, the pattern of menin gene abnormalities in MEN 1 suggests that the menin gene is a tumor suppressor gene. The inherited mutations in the menin gene, which vary widely and are found throughout the gene, often generate truncated, presumably nonfunctional menin peptides. In addition to this genetic abnormality, inherited by all cells in the body, MEN 1 tumors usually harbor deletions of the normal allele of the menin gene. Presumably, loss of both copies of the tumor suppressor gene—one by inherited mutation and one by mutation of one particular cell—confers a selective advantage to the cell that proliferates to become a clonal tumor. Such clonal deletions have been found in 100% of parathyroid tumors removed at surgery from MEN 1 patients. Other acquired genetic abnormalities accumulate in these tumors; thus, the tumors in MEN 1 follow the pattern of multistep tumorigenesis found in malignant tumors.

The two-hit tumor suppressor model can explain many of the features of MEN 1. Clinical presentation of an inherited disorder in adulthood can be explained by the requirement for second mutations before clonal expansion. The asymmetrical but relentless nature of the parathyroid disease may be explained by asynchronous but inevitable somatic mutations in each of the parathyroid glands. Multiple islet tumors might result from the same process.

The menin gene is mutated in about 20% of sporadic parathyroid adenomas, a fraction of sporadic malignant endocrine tumors of the pancreas, and some sporadic carcinoid tumors of the lung as well. Because these mutations occur only in the tumor and not in the patients' normal cells, no familial clustering occurs.

Genetic screening for menin gene mutations is now available commercially. Because inactivating mutations can occur anywhere within the gene, standard surveys of the borders of exons and introns detect only 85% of the genetic abnormalities in MEN 1 families. Thus, the specific mutation in an index case should be ascertained before family members are screened. Because no safe and effective therapies are available for asymptomatic MEN 1 tumors, the precise role for genetic screening has not been established. To detect active disease, the most useful single test to complement a thorough history and physical examination is measurement of blood calcium, particularly ionized calcium, at intervals after the age of 15 years. Prolactin, gastrin, and fasting blood sugar measurements can also be useful.

Multiple Endocrine Neoplasia Types 2a and 2b

Multiple endocrine neoplasia type 2a is an autosomal dominant disease that manifests with medullary carcinoma of the thyroid (MCT), pheochromocytoma, and, less commonly, hyperparathyroidism. MEN 2b is closely related to MEN 2a because it also manifests with MCT and pheochromocytoma and because both diseases involve mutations in the *RET* proto-oncogene (see later). Patients with MEN 2b present with a number of abnormalities not found in patients with MEN 2a, however. These include mucosal neuromas of the tongue, lips, eyelids, and gastrointestinal tract and a marfanoid habitus. Hyperparathyroicism rarely occurs in cases of MEN 2b. MEN 2b is less common than MEN 2a; both diseases are rarer than MEN 1.

In MEN 2a and 2b, the MCTs and the pheochromocytomas often appear bilaterally. Careful prospective analysis of MEN 2a families has demonstrated that diffuse C cell hyperplasia precedes a clinically obvious appearance of MCT. C cell hyperplasia can be detected during the first decade of life by measurement of calcitonin after administration of gastrin, although this test has been supplanted clinically by genetic screening (see later). Virtually all MEN 2a patients eventually develop C cell disease. Complete thyroidectomy of patients with C cell hyperplasia has dramatically decreased the incidence of MCT, which has been the major cause of death in patients with MEN 2a.

Half of patients with MEN 2a develop pheochromocytomas. Family screening allows the detection of pheochromocytoma before the development of hypertension. Plasma metanephrine levels are elevated consistently in patients with MEN 2a pheochromocytomas, as they are in patients with sporadic pheochromocytomas. The tumors are usually found in the adrenal glands and can be documented preoperatively by computed tomography, magnetic resonance imaging, and [^{131}I]-metaiodobenzylguanidine scanning.

Almost all patients with MEN 2a have been found to harbor point mutations in the *RET* proto-oncogene, found in the pericentromeric region of chromosome 10. *RET* encodes a member of the tyrosine protein kinase family of cell surface receptors. The gene is expressed in spinal cord, in certain cultured blood cell lines, and in all tested medullary thyroid cancer and pheochromocytoma cell lines (both from MEN 2 patients and from sporadic tumors). *RET* interacts with other transmembrane receptors which, in turn, bind ligands of the glial cell line–derived neurotrophic factor (GCNF) family. This complicated system of ligands and receptors controls the migration, proliferation, and survival of neural crest cells that populate the thyroid gland, the adrenal gland, and the intrinsic nervous system of the gut. Mutations in *RET* have been found in five different cysteines located in the portion of the receptor that forms the extracellular, ligand-binding domain. The mutant *RET* gene signals in a ligand-independent manner, thereby acting as an oncogene. The mutant *RET* genes can transform cultured cells and cause medullary cancer of the thyroid in transgenic mice.

The transition from diffuse hyperplasia of C cells or adrenal medullary cells to clonal neoplasms of the thyroid or adrenal gland probably requires subsequent somatic mutations. Such mutations include the loss of genetic markers on chromosomes 1p, 3p, 3q, and 22q that frequently occur in these tumors.

Patients with MEN 2b harbor point mutations in the substrate binding pocket of the *RET* kinase, most commonly a change of methionine-918 to threonine. These mutations activate the kinase and change its substrate specificity.

Familial medullary cancer of the thyroid, without tumors of the adrenal or parathyroid gland, is also caused by mutations of the *RET* gene. These mutations include the same mutations that cause MEN 2a, as well as unique mutations in the *RET* gene's kinase domain. Systematic analysis of the *RET* gene has demonstrated that inheritable *RET* gene abnormalities occur in patients with apparently sporadic medullary cancer of the thyroid as well. Inherited *RET* gene abnormalities are not found in patients with isolated pheochromocytomas or parathyroid adenomas, however. Remarkably, some patients with familial Hirschsprung's disease, associated with absence of neurons in the enteric sympathetic nervous system, have inactive *RET* genes.

Direct genetic testing has now replaced calcitonin testing as a screening tool in MEN 2 families. These genetic studies have shown that calcitonin testing and even histologic analysis of thyroid tissue can lead to false-positive and false-negative assignment of disease within families. The limited number of sites in the *RET* gene that cause inherited disease make genetic testing now routinely feasible. Surgery to prevent medullary thyroid cancer is now performed before the age of 5 years in MEN 2a patients and before 6 months of age in patients with the more severe MEN 2b disease.

McCune-Albright Syndrome

The McCune-Albright syndrome is a noninherited disorder consisting of the triad of polyostotic fibrous dysplasia, light brown pigmented skin lesions (café-au-lait spots), and endocrinopathy, usually precocious puberty. Multiple endocrine abnormalities can occur. The precocious puberty, more often seen in girls than boys, is gonadotropin-independent. Hyperthyroidism is caused by autonomous thyroid nodules. Acromegaly is caused by pituitary adenomas that produce growth hormone and, usually, prolactin. Adrenocortical hyperfunction is caused by ACTH-independent adrenal adenomas. Hypophosphatemic rickets, with normal blood calcium level, phosphate wasting, and low or inappropriately normal levels of $1,25(OH)_2D_3$, may result from release of a humoral factor from the dysplastic fibrous tissue.

This somewhat bewildering array of endocrine abnormalities has been rationalized by the observation that cells in the involved tissues harbor mutations in the α subunit of the G$_S$ protein. The G$_S$ protein links cell surface receptors to the activation of adenylate cyclase. The mutations in McCune-Albright syndrome are point mutations at arginine-201 in the G$_S$ subunit; these mutations lead to prolonged activity of G$_S$ and inappropriate activation of adenylate cyclase. Increased levels of cyclic adenosine monophosphate lead to cellular proliferation and hormone secretion. McCune-Albright patients are genetic mosaics. Presumably, at an early stage in embryonic development, a point mutation occurs in the G$_S$ gene of a cell that then proliferates, differentiates, and variably populates normal bone, skin, and endocrine tissues. In cell types in which elevations in cyclic adenosine monophosphate lead to proliferation, abnormal cells become predominant and lead to disease. Because the disease is never inherited, the mutation is presumably lethal when present in all cells of the embryo. In contrast, the very same mutations at arginine-201 have been found in cases of isolated acromegaly and autonomous thyroid nodules. One can, therefore, speculate that McCune-Albright syndrome is the most dramatic example of a spectrum of disorders that vary in severity and presentation, depending on the stage of development of the original mutant cell.

AUTOIMMUNE SYNDROMES

Organ-specific autoimmune disease, characterized by lymphocytic infiltration and organ-specific autoantibodies, commonly results in endocrine hypofunction or hyperfunction. Clinical manifestations of disease are usually limited to one gland. Not uncommonly, however, disorders of more than one endocrine gland appear in families or in individual patients. Characteristic patterns of disease presentation and genetic inheritance allow the definition of two syndromes with overlapping manifestations (Table 244–1).

Autoimmune Polyglandular Syndrome Type 1

Autoimmune polyglandular syndrome type 1 is a rare disease that is also known as autoimmune polyendocrinopathy, candidiasis,

Table 244–1 • CLINICAL FEATURES OF AUTOIMMUNE POLYGLANDULAR SYNDROMES

FEATURE	TYPE 1	TYPE 2
Mucocutaneous candidiasis	Very common	Not seen
Hypoparathyroidism	Common	Rare
Addison's disease	Common	Common
Primary hypogonadism	Common	Occurs
Autoimmune thyroid disease	Rare	Common
Autoimmune diabetes	Occurs	Common
Hypophysitis	Occurs	Occurs
Autoimmune hepatitis	Occurs	Not seen
Pernicious anemia	Occurs	Occurs
Vitiligo	Occurs	Occurs
Malabsorption syndrome	Occurs	Occurs in celiac disease
Alopecia	Common	Occurs
Myasthenia gravis	Not seen	Occurs
Keratopathy	Common	Not seen
Tympanic membrane calcification	Common	Not seen
Inheritance	Autosomal recessive	HLA association
Age at onset	Usually childhood	Usually adulthood

and ectodermal dystrophy syndrome. It typically manifests in early childhood. Mucocutaneous candidiasis occurs in virtually all patients and is usually the first manifestation of disease. Hypoparathyroidism and Addison's disease are the most common endocrine manifestations; each of these diseases occurs in 70 to 80% of patients. Hypoparathyroidism usually precedes Addison's disease; both diseases typically manifest before the age of 15 years. Premature ovarian failure (in 60% of affected women) usually appears as secondary amenorrhea; testicular failure occurs less frequently. Insulin-dependent diabetes mellitus occurs in 12% of patients, usually in adulthood; hypothyroidism is uncommon.

Nonendocrine components of this syndrome, in addition to the mucocutaneous candidiasis, include alopecia, vitiligo, corneal opacities, autoimmune hepatitis, enamel hypoplasia of teeth, tympanic membrane calcification, nail dystrophy that correlates only loosely with obvious candidiasis, parietal cell atrophy and vitamin B_{12} malabsorption, and more general intestinal malabsorption with steatorrhea. Asplenism, with Howell-Jolly bodies on peripheral blood smears, has been noted in several patients.

Each of the disease components should be sought when any patient presents with hypoparathyroidism, primary adrenal insufficiency, or mucocutaneous candidiasis. The hypoparathyroidism is treated like the sporadic disease with oral calcium and 1,25-dihydroxyvitamin D, although variable intestinal malabsorption can present a particular therapeutic challenge. The candidiasis can be satisfactorily controlled with ketoconazole.

Autoimmune polyglandular syndrome type 1 is an autosomal recessive disorder, caused by a variety of inactivating mutations in the gene encoding a transcription factor, autoimmune regulator-1 (AIRE-1). AIRE-1 is expressed in lymphoid tissue, including epithelial cells of the thymus. The appearance of organ-specific autoantibodies precedes disease presentation and predicts the development of specific end-organ damage. The role of these antibodies and the precise pathogenesis of the syndrome are unknown, however.

Autoimmune Polyglandular Syndrome Type 2

Autoimmune polyglandular syndrome type 2 is considerably more common than the type 1 syndrome and typically manifests in adulthood. Insulin-dependent diabetes mellitus and thyroid dysfunction—either autoimmune hypothyroidism or Graves' disease—are the most frequent manifestations. Addison's disease is the third major endocrine component of this disorder. Although most patients who present with autoimmune diabetes or thyroid disease have clinical involvement of only one gland, a large fraction of patients with autoimmune Addison's disease develop clinically evident disease in other endocrine glands. Less common components of the type 2 polyglandular syndrome include primary hypogonadism and hypophysitis. Pernicious anemia, vitiligo, celiac disease, alopecia, and myasthenia gravis are also associated with this syndrome.

The treatment of each component of this syndrome is identical to the treatment of each disorder in isolation, although possible clustering of diseases must be kept in mind during the evaluation and follow-up of all patients with each individual component disorder. Thyroid hormone therapy can precipitate symptoms of adrenal insufficiency in patients with both disorders, for example. Consequently, careful history, including family history, physical examination, and a low threshold for specific laboratory testing for adrenal insufficiency should be part of the evaluation of every patient with autoimmune hypothyroidism. Further, combinations of hypothyroidism, adrenal insufficiency, and hypogonadism can mimic hypopituitarism, although specific hormonal testing can easily distinguish these disorders. Because multiple components of the syndrome can appear asynchronously, periodic evaluation for early appearance of further disease components is indicated.

Autoimmune polyglandular syndrome type 2 is usually inherited in families with characteristic HLA associations. The HLA associations do not predict disease absolutely, even in identical twins, so environmental factors must contribute to disease presentation. Typically, several different autoimmune diseases occur in each family. Autoimmune vulnerability rather than specific organ disease is inherited. Diabetes, as part of the polyglandular syndrome, usually manifests at an older age and develops more slowly than isolated autoimmune diabetes. The characteristic pattern of association with

specific DQ loci does not differ between polyglandular and isolated diabetes, however.

Organ-specific antibodies appear before clinical disease and predict subsequent disease. The role of these antibodies in organ hypofunction has not been established, however.

SUGGESTED READINGS

Agarwal SK, Kester MB, Debelenko LV, et al.: Germline mutations of the MEN1 gene in familial multiple endocrine neoplasia type 1 and related states. Hum Molec Genet 1997;6:1169–1175. *The first large series of menin gene abnormalities.*

Brandi ML, Gagel RF, Angeli A, et al: CONSENSUS guidelines for diagnosis and therapy of MEN type 1 and type 2. J Clin Endocrinol Metab 2001;86:5658–5671. *A thorough and succinct summary of an international conference.*

Eisenhofer G, Walther, MM, Huynh T-T, et al: Pheochromocytomas in von Hippel–Lindau syndrome and multiple endocrine neoplasia type 2 display distinct biochemical clinical phenotypes. J Clin Endocrinol Metab 2001;86:1999–2008. *A large series contrasting the biology and diagnosis of two familial pheochromocytoma syndromes.*

Gibril F, Chen Y-J, Schrump DS, et al: Prospective study of thymic carcinoids in patients with multiple endocrine neoplasia type 1. J Clin Endocr Metab 2003;88:1066–1081. *This prospective series documents the natural history of an uncommon but sometimes lethal MEN 1 tumor and provides suggestions for prevention, diagnosis, and treatment.*

Hansford JR, Mulligan LM: Multiple endocrine neoplasia type 2 and RET: From neoplasia to neurogenesis. J Med Genet 2000;37:817–827. *A thorough review of the molecular pathogenesis of RET-associated diseases.*

Lips CJ, Landsvater RM, Hoppener JW, et al: Clinical screening as compared with DNA analysis in families with multiple endocrine neoplasia type 2A. N Engl J Med 1994;331:828–835. *The first "field" demonstration of the advantage of using DNA testing instead of calcitonin testing in MEN 2a families.*

Lumbroso S, Paris F, Sultan C: McCune-Albright syndrome: Molecular genetics. J Pediatr Endocrinol Metab 2002;15(Suppl 3):875–882. *An updated overview.*

245 MULTIPLE-ORGAN SYNDROMES: CARCINOID SYNDROME

John A. Oates
Kenneth R. Hande

Carcinoid syndrome is the constellation of systemic signs and symptoms associated with malignant neoplasms of enterochromaffin cells. Cutaneous flushing, diarrhea, and cardiac valvular lesions are the most common endocrine consequences of these tumors.

The Neoplasms

Tumors that cause the carcinoid syndrome are neuroendocrine cells of the enterochromaffin type. The neurosecretory granules of these cells typically contain 5-hydroxytryptamine (serotonin) and tachykinins such as substance P. The metastatic tumors associated with carcinoid syndrome usually arise from primary tumors in the ileum. The syndrome also can be produced by neoplasms arising from the remainder of the small intestine, from organs derived from the embryonic foregut (e.g., bronchus, stomach, pancreas, and thyroid), and from ovarian or testicular teratomas. The usual carcinoid tumor arising from the ileum has the histologic pattern of dense nests of cells with uniform size and nuclear appearance. Histochemically, they typically exhibit an argentaffin reaction in which the cells convert a silver salt to metallic silver. A positive argentaffin reaction is not required for the diagnosis, however, as carcinoid tumors arising from organs of the embryonic foregut may contain few if any argentaffin cells. Ultrastructural examination of carcinoid tumors reveals the electron-dense secretion granules.

Carcinoid tumors have a proclivity to metastasize to the liver and may involve this organ extensively and predominantly. Extrahepatic metastases occur in bone, where they are often osteoblastic, and in the lung, pancreas, spleen, ovaries, adrenals, and other organs.

Primary carcinoid tumors of the appendix are common, but they rarely metastasize. Those from the large intestine may metastasize but almost never exhibit endocrine effects.

Clinical Manifestations

Carcinoid tumors typically have a slow rate of growth, and many patients with carcinoid syndrome survive for a decade after the disease is recognized. For much of the duration of the illness, morbidity results largely from the endocrine functions of the tumor. Death usually is caused by cardiac or hepatic failure and by complications associated with tumor growth.

VASODILATOR PAROXYSMS. Cutaneous flushing is the most common clinical feature. The typical flush is erythematous and involves the head and neck (blush area). Some patients exhibit vivid color changes from red to violaceous to pallor. Prolonged flushing attacks may be associated with lacrimation and periorbital edema. The flush may be accompanied by tachycardia, and the blood pressure usually falls or does not change. A rise in blood pressure during flushing is rare, and carcinoid syndrome is not a cause of sustained hypertension. Flushing may be provoked by excitement, exertion, eating, and ethanol ingestion.

TELANGIECTASIA. In addition to paroxysms of cutaneous vasodilatation, some patients also develop telangiectasia, primarily on the face and neck, which is most marked in the malar area.

GASTROINTESTINAL SYMPTOMS. Intestinal hypermotility with borborygmi, cramping, and explosive diarrhea may accompany the episodic flushes. Chronic diarrhea is more common and may have a secretory component. When this is severe, malabsorption may occur.

CARDIAC MANIFESTATIONS. Plaquelike thickening of the endocardium of the valvular cusps and cardiac chambers occurs primarily on the right side of the heart but may involve the left side to a minimal degree. The endocardial thickening is composed of smooth muscle cells embedded in a stroma rich in mucopolysaccharides. The thickening and deformation of the valve cusps, chordae tendineae, and papillary muscles interfere with valvular function and may lead to regurgitation, stenosis, or combined functional lesions. The fibrosing process has a tendency to produce incompetence of the tricuspid valve and stenosis of the smaller pulmonary orifice, a deleterious hemodynamic combination. Cardiac function may be further compromised by impaired atrial and ventricular compliance and by the occasional occurrence of a high cardiac output that probably results from continuing release of a vasodilator.

PULMONARY SYMPTOMS. Bronchoconstriction, usually most pronounced during flushing attacks, is a less common feature of the syndrome, but it may be severe.

GENERAL. Intestinal obstruction may result from the primary tumor or from the desmoplastic reaction in the surrounding mesentery; infrequently, the primary tumors cause gastrointestinal bleeding. Necrosis of hepatic tumor masses may produce an acute syndrome of abdominal pain, tenderness, fever, and leukocytosis. Hepatomegaly from the metastatic disease is usually present, but extensive metastatic involvement of the liver by the slowly growing tumors may occur before liver function tests become abnormal. Generalized fatigue and debilitation are underappreciated features of carcinoid syndrome. Attacks of severe and sustained flushing with life-threatening hemodynamic compromise and bronchoconstriction may occur and are referred to as *carcinoid crisis*. Precipitating factors include anesthesia/surgery, tumor necrosis, and catecholamine infusion.

Endocrine Function of Carcinoid Tumors

SEROTONIN. The most constant biochemical feature of carcinoid tumors is the presence of tryptophan hydroxylase, which catalyzes the formation of 5-hydroxytryptophan (5-HTP) from tryptophan (Fig. 245–1). The typical ileal carcinoid tumor also contains aromatic L-amino-acid decarboxylase, which catalyzes the conversion of 5-HTP to 5-hydroxytryptamine (serotonin). Gastric carcinoids, however, are frequently deficient in this decarboxylase and release 5-HTP from the tumor.

Following its release from the tumor, serotonin is inactivated primarily by monoamine oxidase; uptake in the platelets also contributes to removal of free serotonin from blood. Monoamine oxidase oxidizes serotonin to 5-hydroxyindoleacetaldehyde, which is rapidly converted to 5-hydroxyindoleacetic acid (5-HIAA) by aldehyde

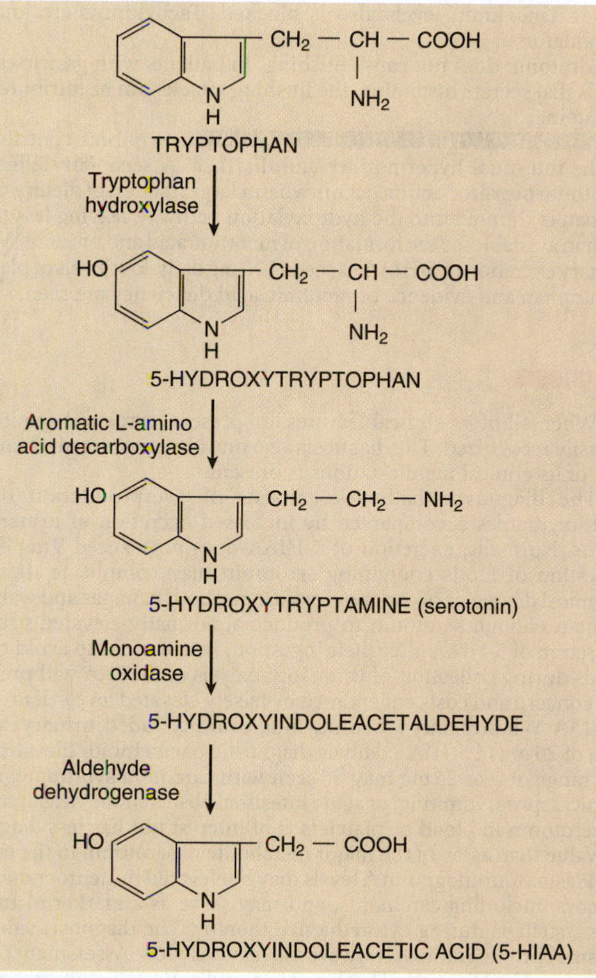

FIGURE 245–1 • Synthesis and degradation of serotonin.

dehydrogenase (see Fig. 245–1). This acid is rapidly excreted into the urine, and almost all circulating serotonin can be accounted for as urinary 5-HIAA.

TACHYKININS. Peptides of the tachykinin family are stored in carcinoid tumors and are released during flushing. Several tachykinins are derived from a common precursor β-preprotachykinin; of these, neuropeptide K, neurokinin A, and substance P have been identified in tumors and blood from patients with the carcinoid syndrome.

OTHER BIOLOGICALLY ACTIVE SUBSTANCES. Some carcinoid tumors, particularly those of gastric origin, release excessive amounts of histamine. This can be detected by an increased urinary excretion of histamine or its metabolite, N-methylhistamine.

Carcinoid tumors have been associated with a number of ectopic endocrine syndromes, including hyperadrenocorticism that results from ectopic production of adrenocorticotropic hormone and acromegaly due to secretion of growth hormone-releasing hormone by the tumor.

MECHANISM OF THE FLUSH. Flushing can be triggered by catecholamines, and this probably accounts for the association of flushing with exercise and emotional stimuli. For experimental induction of flushing, injection of isoproterenol in amounts of as little as 0.5 µg may be effective. Pentagastrin, in doses as small as 0.25 µg, also can trigger flushing, an action that may explain the provocation of flushes by eating in some patients. Because the hemodynamic changes associated with such pharmacologically induced attacks can be severe, epinephrine and other β-adrenergic amines as well as pentagastrin should be administered with great caution. Flushing episodes can be blocked by somatostatin.

Most of the evidence points to the tachykinins as mediators of the carcinoid flush. Tachykinins, particularly neuropeptide K, can be identified in plasma during flushing. Tachykinin levels have been shown to be increased during pentagastrin-induced flushing, and when pentagastrin-induced flushing is inhibited by somatostatin, the rise in tachykinin levels also is blocked. Tachykinins are known vasodilators.

Serotonin does not cause flushing. In patients with gastric carcinoids that secrete histamine, the flushing attacks can be attributed to histamine.

PATHOPHYSIOLOGY OF SEROTONIN OVERPRODUCTION. Serotonin contributes to the intestinal hypermotility and diarrhea. A secondary effect of serotonin overproduction occurs when a large fraction of dietary tryptophan is shunted into the hydroxylation pathway, leaving less tryptophan available for the formation of nicotinic acid and protein. When urinary excretion of 5-HIAA exceeds 100 mg daily, low levels of plasma tryptophan and evidence of nicotinic acid deficiency are seen.

Diagnosis

When all of its clinical features are present, carcinoid syndrome is easily recognized. The diagnosis also must be considered when any one of its clinical manifestations is present.

The diagnostic hallmark consists of overproduction of 5-hydroxyindoles accompanied by increased excretion of urinary 5-HIAA. Normally, excretion of 5-HIAA does not exceed 9 mg daily. Ingestion of foods containing serotonin may complicate the biochemical diagnosis of carcinoid syndrome; both bananas and walnuts contain enough serotonin to produce abnormally elevated urinary excretion of 5-HIAA after their ingestion. Instructions to avoid these foods during collection of urine for analysis of 5-HIAA will prevent the concern and costs engendered by falsely elevated levels of urinary 5-HIAA. When dietary 5-hydroxyindoles are excluded, urinary excretion of 25 mg of 5-HIAA daily is diagnostic of carcinoid. Elevation in the range of 9 to 25 mg may be seen with carcinoid syndrome, nontropical sprue, vomiting, or acute intestinal obstruction. Measurement of serotonin in blood or platelets is of interest but has less diagnostic value than assay of the major metabolite of serotonin in the urine.

Plasma chromogranin A levels may be elevated by neuroendocrine tumors, including carcinoids, and may serve as a marker of tumor mass, such as during cytoreductive therapy. The diagnosis value of plasma chromogranin A, however, is relatively low. Assessment of the extent and localization of both primary and metastatic tumor is aided by computed tomographic scans of the abdomen and chest and by imaging with radionuclide-labeled somatostatin receptor ligands.

DIFFERENTIAL DIAGNOSIS. Attacks of flushing in a patient with normal urinary excretion of 5-HIAA raises other diagnostic possibilities. Systemic mastocyte activation disorders, including systemic mastocytosis and idiopathic anaphylaxis, produce flushing and diarrhea and should be considered when 5-HIAA excretion is not elevated. Flushing also occurs in genetically predisposed individuals following ethanol ingestion, in the postmenopausal state, and in conjunction with other neuroendocrine tumors such as VIPomas and medullary carcinoma of the thyroid.

VARIANTS OF THE CARCINOID SYNDROME. The origin of the tumor influences the biologically active substances produced and their storage and release. The typical carcinoid syndrome usually results from tumors of midgut origin, which almost invariably secrete serotonin. Tumor serotonin content is likely to be high, and the tumor usually contains dense nests of argentaffin-positive cells. In contrast, tumors arising from the embryonic foregut contain fewer argentaffin cells, have lower serotonin content, and may secrete 5-HTP. Ectopic hormone production (e.g., Cushing's syndrome and acromegaly) and multiple endocrine adenomas are more likely to be associated with tumors of embryonic foregut.

Patients with gastric carcinoids frequently exhibit unique flushing, which begins as a bright, patchy erythema with sharply delineated serpentine borders; these patches tend to coalesce as the blush heightens. Food ingestion is especially likely to produce flushes. The tumors are usually deficient in decarboxylase enzyme and secrete 5-HTP; histamine secretion is also common, as is a high incidence of peptic ulceration. In these patients, histamine is the principal factor causing flushing.

With carcinoid tumors arising from the bronchus, attacks of flushing tend to be prolonged and severe and may be associated with periorbital edema, excessive lacrimation and salivation, hypotension, tachycardia and tachyarrhythmias, anxiety, and tremulousness. Nausea, vomiting, explosive diarrhea, and bronchoconstriction may progress to a severe degree. This group is therapeutically unique in that severe flushes often can be prevented by corticosteroids.

 Treatment

Treatment of the carcinoid syndrome is directed toward (1) pharmacologic therapy for humorally mediated symptoms and (2) the reduction of tumor mass.

The discovery that somatostatin can prevent the flushing and other endocrine manifestations of the carcinoid syndrome has provided the basis for a major advance in the treatment of these patients. The development of analogues of somatostatin, with longer biologic half-lives than the native hormone, has made subcutaneous administration a feasible route of therapy. One of the somatostatin analogues, octreotide, has been found to markedly improve the flushing and other endocrine manifestations of most patients with carcinoid syndrome. This is frequently associated with a reduction in urinary 5-HIAA excretion and in tachykinin levels in blood. With the improvement of these endocrine symptoms, including fatigue, a considerable improvement in quality of life may be achieved. Octreotide can be administered subcutaneously at intervals of approximately 8 hours, usually beginning with 75 to 150 µg and titrating upward until maximum inhibition of flushing and other symptoms is achieved, which usually occurs at single doses of 750 µg or less. A long-acting octreotide formulation (octreotide LAR), consisting of microspheres containing octreotide, permits once-monthly dosing. Two to 3 months may be required to achieve steady-state levels of octreotide from administration of octreotide LAR, during which time supplementation with subcutaneous octreotide may be needed. An uncommon but severe adverse effect of octreotide is hypoglycemia, probably as a result of the inhibition of glucagon and growth hormone secretion. The suppression of pancreatic exocrine function by octreotide can cause steatorrhea, and inhibition of the release of cholecystokinin can cause cholelithiasis. In patients receiving octreotide, about 5% achieve tumor regression, and in the group as a whole, less tumor progression and a longer median survival are seen in comparison with historical control subjects. The progression of carcinoid heart disease is slowed by octreotide treatment. Octreotide can prevent or treat carcinoid crises that accompany the massive release of mediators that sometimes occurs during operative procedures and tumor necrosis. In patients with histamine-secreting gastric carcinoids, blockade of both H_1- and H_2-histamine receptors markedly ameliorates flushing.

Early diagnosis of the carcinoid syndrome has led to complete surgical cure of a few patients with tumors arising in ovarian or testicular teratomas or in the bronchus. By releasing their humoral mediators directly into the systemic circulation, these tumors can produce the syndrome before metastatic disease occurs. In contrast, tumors that release humoral substances into the portal circulation to be largely metabolized by the liver usually produce the syndrome only after liver metastases occur. Given the slow progression of this neoplasm, however, effective reduction in tumor mass can ameliorate morbidity and improve the quality of life even after metastases have occurred. In selected patients, this can be achieved by surgical debulking of tumor, including hemihepatectomy for unilobar metastases, excision of large superficial hepatic metastases, and removal of the primary tumor together with regional lymph nodes containing metastases. Elective cholecystectomy during the surgical intervention will prevent the complications of cholelithiasis that may result from octreotide treatment. As the blood supply of hepatic metastases is largely arterial, percutaneous embolization of the hepatic arterial supply to the most involved hepatic lobe sometimes can reduce inoperable hepatic metastases; the procedure carries a high risk of complications. Chemotherapy with single or combination cytotoxic agents given acutely has produced little benefit except perhaps intra-arterially in conjunction with hepatic arterial embolization. For patients who exhibit tumor progression or whose clinical syndrome has failed to improve following cytoreduction and octreotide, interferon-α may be considered as adjunctive therapy.

A concerted strategy consisting of removal of the primary tumor, reduction in tumor bulk, and the administration of octreotide (with or without interferon-α) can lead to considerable amelioration of symptoms and improvement in the quality of life, reduction of the release of the humoral substances that engender the cardiac lesions, and prolongation of survival.

SUGGESTED READINGS

Crocetti E, Paci E: Malignant carcinoids in the USA, SEER 1992–1999. An epidemiological study with 6830 cases. Eur J Cancer Prev 2003;12:191–194. *Thirteen percent of patients had metastases at diagnosis, 24% had multiple tumors, and 5-year survival was 82%.*

Eriksson B, Oberg K: Summing up 15 years of somatostatin analog therapy in neuroendocrine tumors: Future outlook. Ann Oncol 1999;10(Suppl 2):S31–S38. *Describes a large experience with the use of somatostatin analogues in neuroendocrine tumors, including carcinoid syndrome.*

Modlin IM, Lye KD, Kidd M: A 5-decade analysis of 13,715 carcinoid tumors. Cancer 2003;97:934–959. *The incidence rate of diagnosed carcinoid is increasing.*

Moller JE, Connolly HM, Rubin J, et al: Factors associated with progression of carcinoid heart disease. N Engl J Med 2003;348:1005–1015. *Higher serotonin levels and need for chemotherapy carry a worse diagnosis.*

Tomassetti P, Migliori M, Simoni P, et al: Diagnostic value of plasma chromogranin A in neuroendocrine tumors. Eur J Gastroenterol Hepatol 2001;12:55–58. *Measurement of plasma chromogranin A is of limited value in the diagnosis of carcinoid syndrome.*

246 DISORDERS OF SEXUAL DIFFERENTIATION

Maria I. New
Nathalie Josso

Gonads, genital ducts, and external genitalia become sexually dimorphic during fetal life, depending on the presence or absence of genetic and endocrine factors, nearly all of which actively impose maleness. This asymmetrical mechanism of sex differentiation has an important bearing on the pathogenesis of intersex disorders: Male pseudohermaphroditism, defined as incomplete virilization of a 46,XY male, results from defects in the synthesis, metabolism, or action of one or several masculinizing factors. In contrast, female pseudohermaphroditism results from inappropriate exposure of female anlagen to masculinizing agents.

ANATOMY OF NORMAL SEX DIFFERENTIATION

Male Sex Differentiation

TESTICULAR DIFFERENTIATION. The gonadal primordium is represented by the gonadal ridge, which is progressively colonized by extraembryonic primordial germ cells. The first recognizable event of testicular differentiation, at 7 weeks' gestation, is the development of primordial Sertoli cells, which aggregate to form seminiferous tubules and produce antimüllerian hormone (AMH), also called *müllerian-inhibiting substance.* Leydig cells differentiate at 8 weeks' gestation and increase until 12 to 14 weeks, when they begin to degenerate. At birth, few remain in the interstitial tissue; the Leydig cell population reappears at puberty.

SOMATIC SEX DIFFERENTIATION. After gonadal differentiation, the internal reproductive tract consists of two pairs of ducts: the wolffian ducts and the müllerian ducts. In males, müllerian duct regression begins at 8 weeks and is more or less complete at 10 to 12 weeks. The wolffian ducts develop into the vasa deferentia, epididymides, and seminal vesicles. Prostatic buds develop around the opening of the ducts at 10 to 11 weeks' gestation, and fusion of outgrowths of the urogenital sinus forms the prostatic utricle, the male equivalent of the vagina (Fig 246–1). At 10 weeks' gestation, elongation of the genital tubercle and fusion of the urethral folds over the urethral groove lead to formation of the penile urethra, whereas the genital swellings move posteriorly and fuse to form the scrotum. Male anatomic development is completed by 90 days' gestation, but penile growth occurs mainly between 20 weeks and term, at a time when, paradoxically, serum testosterone levels are declining. Several other growth factors are also involved.

Female Differentiation

OVARIAN DIFFERENTIATION. Slower than the testis to differentiate initially, the fetal ovary eventually reaches a more advanced stage of maturation. At 12 to 13 weeks' gestation, some oogonia located in the deepest layer of the cortex have entered the meiotic prophase. By

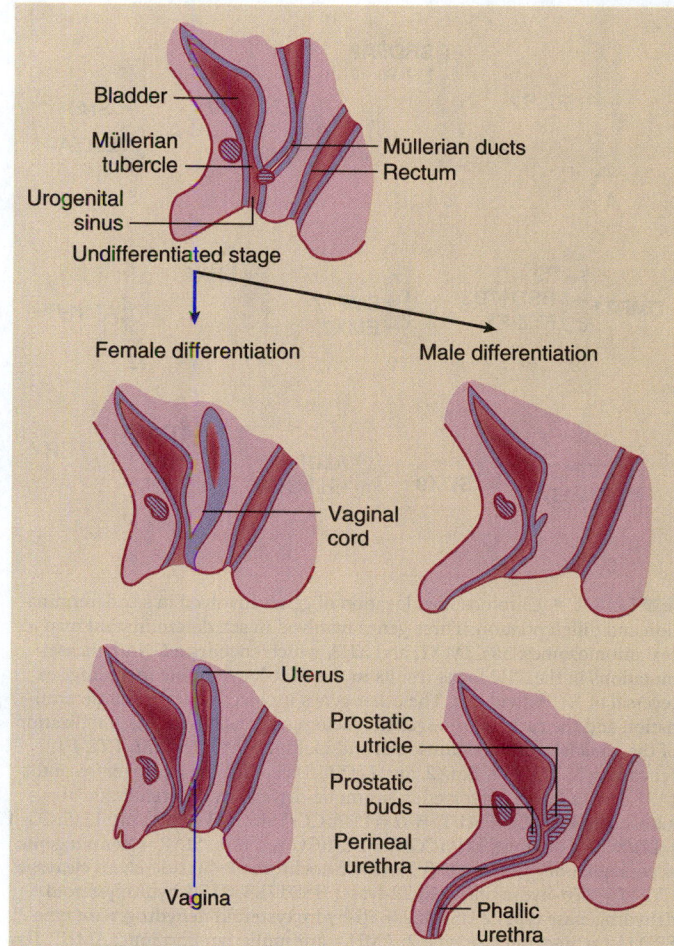

FIGURE 246–1 • Differentiation of the urogenital sinus. (From Josso N: Physiology of sex differentiation: A guide to the understanding and management of the intersex child. In Josso N [ed]: The Intersex Child. Basel, Karger, 1981, p 1.)

7 months' gestation, all germ cells have entered or completed the meiotic prophase. Fetal granulosa cells produce estrogen at the same developmental stage at which fetal testes produce testosterone, but ovarian production of AMH can be demonstrated only after birth.

SOMATIC SEX DIFFERENTIATION. Female fetal sex differentiation is characterized by degeneration of the wolffian ducts at 10 weeks, whereas the müllerian ducts develop into fallopian tubes, uterus, and the upper part of the vagina. The vagina differentiates at the level of the müllerian tubercle, between the openings of the wolffian ducts where the prostatic utricle forms in males. Whereas in males the prostatic utricle opens just beneath the neck of the bladder, in females, the lower end of the vagina slides down the posterior wall of the urethra to acquire a separate opening on the body surface (see Fig. 246–1). Feminization of the external genitalia begins with formation of the dorsal commissure between the genital swellings, which in the female do not migrate posteriorly or fuse and give rise to the labia majora. Because the genital folds do not fuse, they become the labia minora, and the genital tubercle becomes the clitoris. In the female, these steps occur in the absence of hormonal stimulation but the signaling molecule WNT4 is required for the initial formation of the müllerian ducts.

MECHANISMS OF SEX DIFFERENTIATION

GENETICS OF SEX DETERMINATION: SRY AND ITS PARTNERS. Testicular differentiation is usually called *sex determination* because it determines whether testicular hormones, responsible for subsequent somatic sex differentiation, will be produced. Sex determination in mammals is governed primarily by SRY, a transcription factor expressed by Sertoli cells and encoded by a gene located on the Y chromosome proximal to the pseudoautosomal boundary (Fig. 246–2). The pseudoauto-

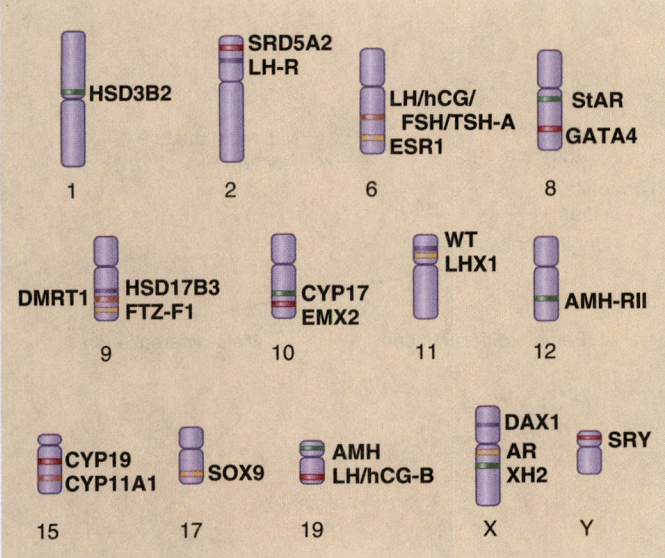

FIGURE 246-2 • Chromosomal location of genes involved in sex determination and differentiation. Three genes involved in sex determination map to sex chromosomes: *SRY, DAX1,* and *XH2,* which encodes a DNA helicase; mutations in the *XH2* locus results in the ATR-X syndrome including sex reversal of XY individuals. The other genes involved in testicular determination and the early morphogenetic factors responsible for the stabilization of the gonadal ridge are autosomal and include *SOX9, DMRT1, FTZ-F1* (encoding SF1), *WT1, EMX2,* and *LHX1.* Except for the androgen receptor *(AR)* gene, all genes involved in hormone-driven sex differentiation are autosomal. LH/hCG/FSH/TSH-α = LH/hCG/FSH/TSH α-subunit; LH/hCG-β = LH/hCG β-subunit; LH/hCG-R = LH/hCG receptor, StAR = steroidogenic acute regulatory protein; CYP11A1 = cytochrome P450 side-chain cleavage; CYP17 = 17α-hydroxylase/20,22-lyase; HSD17B3 = 17β-hydroxysteroid dehydrogenase type 3; HSD3B2 = 3β-hydroxysteroid dehydrogenase type 2; SRD5A2 = 5α-reductase type 2; AMH = antimüllerian hormone; AMHR-II = AMH receptor type II. Although not involved in normal sex differentiation, mutated CYP19 (cytochrome P450 aromatase) and ESR1 (estrogen receptor-α) can result in abnormal sex phenotypes. Abbreviations are those used by the National Center for Biotechnology Information-Online Mendelian Inheritance in Man (NCBI-OMIM); http//www.ncbi.nlm.nih.gov/Omim.

mal regions of the sex chromosomes enter into homologous recombination at meiosis, and it is essential that the testis-determining gene be situated in the non-recombining Y-specific region. Mutations of *SRY* are encountered in approximately 15% of XY sex-reversed females, and conversely, translocation of *SRY* on an X chromosome leads to maleness in XX individuals.

However, normal *SRY* transcripts, although necessary, do not guarantee normal testicular differentiation. SRY target genes, not yet identified, are probably important and, in addition to SRY, many other transcription factors are required for testicular development (see Fig. 246-2). and often for other functions as well. For example, mutations of Wilms' tumor type 1 *(WT-1)* gene lead to Wilms' tumor and renal insufficiency, SOX-9 mutations are associated with campomelic dysplasia. The orphan nuclear receptors steroidogenic factor type 1 (SF-1), also known as FTZ-F1, and DAX-1, also known as Ahch, are required for normal adrenal and pituitary development. As shown in the mouse, Dax-1 acts in a dose-dependent manner to repress *Sry* and is also necessary to the integrity of testicular germinal epithelium. Chromosomal location of genes involved in sex determination is shown in Figure 246-2.

BIOSYNTHESIS AND ACTION OF TESTICULAR HORMONES. Virilization of the reproductive tract is mediated by AMH and testosterone; in their absence or inactivity, female differentiation proceeds unimpeded (Fig. 246-3). AMH, a glycoprotein synthesized by immature Sertoli and postnatal granulosa cells, is responsible for müllerian regression. The gene, located on chromosome 19, is a member of the transforming growth factor-β (TGF-β) family and acts via a type II AMH receptor whose gene is located on chromosome 12q13. For signaling, AMH uses three type I receptors of the bone morphogenetic protein family, ALK2, 3, and 6, all activating cytoplasmic effectors SMADs 1 and 5.

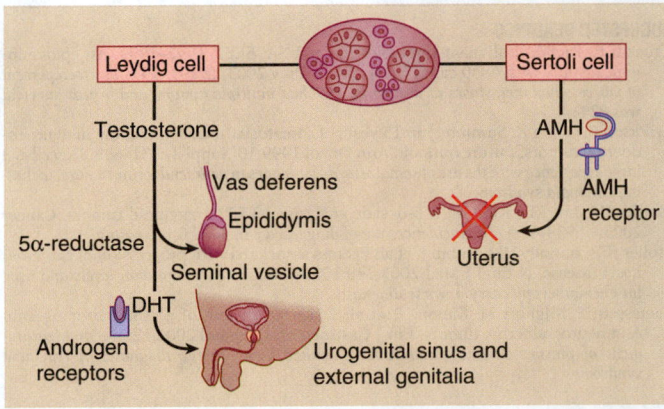

FIGURE 246-3 • Hormones involved in male differentiation of the reproductive tract. Testosterone, synthesized by Leydig cells, maintains the wolffian ducts and virilizes the urogenital sinus and external genitalia after reduction to dihydrotestosterone by 5α-reductase. Antimüllerian hormone (AMH), produced by fetal Sertoli cells, inhibits development of the müllerian ducts, which would otherwise develop into the uterus and fallopian tubes. DHT = dihydrotestosterone. (Modified from Josso N: Physiology of sex differentiation: A guide to the understanding and management of the intersex child. *In* Josso N [ed]: The Intersex Child. Basel, Karger, 1981, p 1.)

Androgens are responsible for maintenance of the wolffian ducts and virilization of the urogenital sinus and external genitalia. Testosterone is produced from cholesterol by gonadotropin stimulation of fetal Leydig cells through the coordinated action of steroidogenic enzymes, most of which are also expressed in the adrenal gland. P-450 side-chain cleavage enzyme, which is responsible for the initial step in the steroidogenic pathway, is located at the inner mitochondrial membrane. Translocation of cholesterol into the mitochondrion is dependent on steroidogenic acute regulatory protein, a phosphoprotein coded by a gene located on chromosome 8p11.2. Steroidogenic acute regulatory protein (StAR), steroidogenic P-450 enzymes, and AMH are positively regulated by SF-1, whose action is opposed by DAX-1.

Testosterone production by the fetal testis is detectable at 9 weeks in the human fetus, increases to a peak at 15 to 18 weeks, and then falls sharply, so the serum concentrations of testosterone overlap in males and females in late pregnancy. When human chorionic gonadotropin (hCG) declines in the third trimester, the hypothalamic-pituitary axis gains control over testicular functional activity.

Testosterone is the major steroid released by fetal testes in the blood stream and enters cells by passive diffusion or pinocytosis. Testosterone is converted intracellularly to dihydrotestosterone (DHT) by the enzyme 5α-reductase (see Fig. 246-3). Two distinct isoforms of 5α-reductase have been cloned: Type 1 is present in very low levels in the prostate and the sebaceous glands; type 2 is present in high levels in the prostate and in the area of the external genitalia. DHT binds to the androgen receptor with greater affinity and stability than does testosterone. Therefore, in tissues equipped with 5α-reductase at the time of sex differentiation, such as the prostate, urogenital sinus, and external genitalia, DHT is the active androgen. However, at high concentrations, testosterone interacts with the androgen receptor similarly to DHT.

STAGES OF SEX DIFFERENTIATION

Normal sex differentiation occurs at various levels (Fig. 246-4). Genetic sex is established at fertilization by the nature of the sex chromosome donated by the spermatozoon. The presence or absence of sex-determining genes dictates gonadal sex, whereas the presence or absence of fetal testicular hormones determines somatic sex. Gender identity is established early in life but can be disrupted at puberty by hormonal factors.

DISORDERS OF GONADAL SEX

Gonadal sex disorders may or may not be associated with sex chromosome abnormalities.

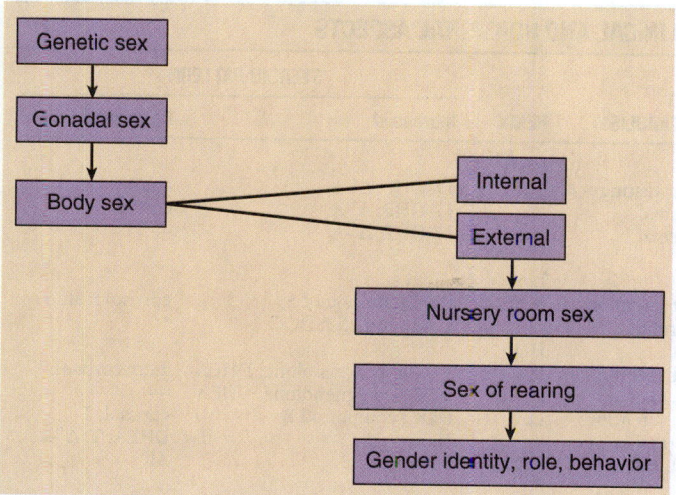

FIGURE 246–4 • Stages of sex differentiation. Genetic sex specified at fertilization determines gonadal sex, which in turn determines somatic and legal sex. Gender identity is usually determined by the sex of rearing. (From New MI, Levine LS: Congenital adrenal hyperplasia. In Harris H, Hirschhorn K [eds]: Advances in Human Genetics. New York, Plenum Press 1973, p 251.)

TURNER'S SYNDROME. Patients with Turner's syndrome have normal female genitalia, short stature, and typical dysmorphic features. The dysmorphism includes an increased carrying angle of the arms, sphinx-like neck, low hairline, shield chest, widely spaced nipples, and typical facies characterized by low-set ears and micrognathia. The chromosomal complement is 45,X, and the incidence is about 1 in 2500 births. Treatment with human growth hormone has improved the final height of patients with Turner's syndrome. The patients are infertile because the ovaries are dysgenetic and have become bilateral streaks without follicles. Thus, these patients have primary amenorrhea and are infertile. Because the internal genitalia include a normal uterus and fallopian tubes, patients may benefit from in vitro fertilization.

KLINEFELTER'S SYNDROME. In this condition, males have normal development of the penis and scrotum, but the testes are small and firm. At adolescence, gynecomastia is frequent and infertility is common as a result of azoospermia. The usual karyotype is 47,XXY. Hormonal findings include elevated gonadotropin levels and a decreased serum testosterone concentration. Klinefelter's syndrome is a common disorder that occurs in 1 in 500 men.

XX MALE SYNDROME. Males with a 46,XX karyotype have normal external and internal male genitalia; however, they resemble patients with Klinefelter's syndrome in that they have small testes, azoospermia, and infertility. Translocation of the *SRY* gene on the X chromosome is detected in 90% of sporadic cases but not when XX maleness and true hermaphroditism are transmitted as an autosomal recessive condition in the same family.

TRUE HERMAPHRODITISM. True hermaphroditism, a rare and usually sporadic disorder, is defined as the coexistence of seminiferous tubules and ovarian follicles in the same subject. Most patients have an ovotestis with either an ovary or a testis on the opposite side; a testis is usually in the scrotum, an ovotestis more seldom.

The genitalia are usually ambiguous; rare cases of completely masculine or feminine genitalia have been reported. The anatomy of the internal reproductive tract depends on the nature of the gonads. A uterus is present in approximately 90% of cases. Testosterone response to hCG is variable, and AMH levels are usually low. Most patients experience breast development, ovulation, and even menstruation at puberty; pregnancy and successful childbirth are possible if selective removal of testicular tissue is feasible. Unless gender has already been assigned, male orientation should be restricted to patients with no uterus and descended testicular tissue because testicular tissue is usually dysgenetic and prone to malignant degeneration. Most true hermaphrodites have a 46,XX karyotype. To resolve the discrepancy between the presence of testicular tissue and the lack of a Y chromosome, the DNA of 46,XX true hermaphrodites has been probed for *SRY*. True hermaphrodites usually lack *SRY*, which suggests that the condition, at least in familial cases, is due to constitutive activation of a gene normally triggered by *SRY*.

TESTICULAR DYSGENESIS. Testicular dysgenesis is characterized by seminiferous tubule degeneration and invasion by connective tissue arranged in whorls as in a streak gonad. Germ cells are rare or absent; the gonad is often maldescended and prone to malignant degeneration. The clinical picture, as in true hermaphroditism, combines defects of AMH- and testosterone-dependent steps of sex differentiation, depending on the extent and timing of testicular degeneration. The incidence of gonadal tumors may reach 30%, thus making castration and subsequent hormonal replacement the safest therapeutic option.

Mixed Gonadal Dysgenesis. Mixed gonadal dysgenesis, a frequent cause of sexual ambiguity, is characterized by the presence of a testis on one side and a fibrous streak on the other. The karyotype is either 46,XY or mosaic 45,X/46,XY; however, many such mosaics, discovered fortuitously by prenatal diagnosis, have normally developed testes and are clinically normal. Otherwise, Turner-like malformations may be present, the genitalia are ambiguous, and a gonad may or may not be palpable on one side. A fallopian tube is present on the side of the streak gonad. Leydig cell function, evaluated by testosterone response to hCG, and Sertoli cell function, evaluated by serum AMH levels, range from minimal to normal.

Dysgenetic Male Pseudohermaphroditism. Patients with dysgenetic male pseudohermaphroditism have bilaterally differentiated dysgenetic testes. Their external genitalia are always ambiguous, and müllerian derivatives are always present. The clinical, endocrine, and cytogenetic picture is similar to that of mixed gonadal dysgenesis.

PURE GONADAL DYSGENESIS, TESTICULAR REGRESSION SYNDROME. Patients with pure gonadal dysgenesis have a normal female phenotype, including uterus and fallopian tubes, but have fibrous streaks instead of gonads; they are free of Turner-like malformations and attain normal height. Familial cases have been described with either a 46,XX or, more frequently, a 46,XY karyotype; in the latter, mutations of the *SRY* gene have been identified in 15% of cases. Other 46,XY patients with absent gonads have various degrees of sexual ambiguity and no müllerian derivatives. The implication that some testicular tissue was functional at least up to 10 weeks and subsequently regressed has led to the name "fetal testicular regression syndrome." Testicular regression may occur in late pregnancy or even postnatally; these fully virilized males have only bilateral cryptorchidism. This condition is also known as *anorchia*.

DISORDERS OF PHENOTYPIC SEX

FEMALE PSEUDOHERMAPHRODITISM

Female pseudohermaphroditism, defined as the sexual ambiguity of a 46,XX fetus with two normal ovaries, is the most frequent type of intersex. Rarely, the female fetus is masculinized because of transplacental transfer of androgens from an ovarian or adrenocortical tumor in the mother or from exogenous steroids. Most female pseudohermaphrodites have been exposed to endogenous androgens prenatally as a result of congenital adrenal hyperplasia (CAH).

Virilization caused by androgen excess is limited to the androgen-responsive external genitalia (the lower part of the vagina, genital folds and swellings, and phallus). Masculinization ranges from minimal clitoromegaly and a mild degree of posterior labial fusion to the formation of a urogenital sinus with the orifice located distally along the urethral groove and ending, in extreme cases, at the tip of the phallus. Because no testicular tissue is present, AMH is not produced; therefore, the fallopian tubes, uterus, and upper portion of the vagina are normal. Thus, with proper medical treatment and vaginal reconstruction, normal childbearing is possible.

CAH should be suspected in sexually ambiguous newborns with a uterus but no palpable gonadal tissue. Such patients should be karyotyped and have endocrine evaluation done immediately because of the life-threatening salt loss found in many cases of CAH.

CONGENITAL ADRENAL HYPERPLASIA

CAH is a family of monogenic autosomal recessive disorders of steroidogenesis in which defective enzymatic steps result in impaired synthesis of cortisol by the adrenal cortex (Table 246–1). Subsequent adrenocorticotropic hormone (ACTH) oversecretion via the negative feedback system stimulates the adrenal to become hyperplastic. As a result, both precursor steroids proximal to the enzyme block and hormonal products of unimpeded pathways are overproduced. In some

Endocrine Diseases

Table 246–1 • FORMS OF CONGENITAL ADRENAL HYPERPLASIA: CLINICAL AND HORMONAL ASPECTS

DEFICIENCY	GENITAL AMBIGUITY	POSTNATAL VIRILIZATION	SALT METABOLISM	RENIN	STEROID PATTERN Increased	Decreased
21-Hydroxylase				High		
A. Classic salt wasting	F	Yes	Salt wasting		17-OHP; Δ⁴-A	aldo; cortisol
Simple virilizing	F	Yes	Normal		17-OHP; Δ⁴-A	cortisol
B. Nonclassic (symptomatic and asymptomatic)	No	Yes	Normal		17-OHP; Δ⁴-A	—
11β-Hydroxylase				Low		
A. Classic	F	Yes	Salt retention		DOC; compound S	cortisol ± aldo
B. Nonclassic	No	Yes	Normal		Compound S ± DOC	
3β-Hydroxysteroid dehydrogenase				High		
A. Classic	M/F	Yes	Salt wasting		17-OH-pregnenolone; DHEA	aldo: cortisol; T
B. Nonclassic	No	Yes	Normal		17-OH-pregnenolone; DHEA	—
17α-Hydroxylase	M	No	Salt retention	Low	DOC; compound B	cortisol; T
17,20-Lyase	M	No	Normal		None	DHEA; T; Δ⁴-A
Cholesterol desmolase	M	No	Salt wasting	High	None	All

17-OHP = 17-hydroxyprogesterone: Δ⁴-A = Δ⁴-androstenedione; aldo = aldosterone; B = corticosterone; compound S = 11-deoxycortisol; DOC = deoxycorticosterone; DHEA = dehydroepiandrosterone; T = testosterone.

forms, diversion of precursor steroids into androgen pathways results in excessive levels of potent androgens and virilization of the female fetus. In other forms, underproduction of sex steroids in both the adrenal and the testes leads to ambiguous genitalia in genetic males. Abnormal secretion of mineralocorticoids in some cases results in disturbances in the regulation of electrolytes, plasma volume, and blood pressure, with the risk of decompensation and shock.

STEROID 21-HYDROXYLASE DEFICIENCY

CLASSIC 21-HYDROXYLASE DEFICIENCY. Steroid 21-hydroxylase deficiency is the most common enzymatic defect causing CAH. Classic 21-hydroxylase deficiency occurs in about 1 in 15,000 live births, but the incidence may vary by population and geographic area (Fig. 246–5). The classic disorder has two forms: salt wasting and simple virilizing (non–salt wasting); both result in sexual ambiguity in the newborn genetic female. In the salt-wasting form, which occurs in about three fourths of cases, adrenal production of aldosterone and cortisol is inadequate. Salt-wasting crises are associated with hyponatremia, hyperkalemia, and hypovolemia, with metabolic acidosis, loss of vascular tone, and in some cases, shock and death. Crises usually arise between 7 days and 2 weeks of life, after discharge from the hospital. Thus, an affected first-born male who has normal genitalia is particularly at risk for a salt-wasting crisis at home. Ambiguous genitalia in a female usually prompt diagnostic procedures, thus placing females at lower risk. Salt wasting should be carefully ruled out even in newborns with mild genital ambiguity. Unlike salt wasters, simple virilizers can synthesize sufficient amounts of aldosterone for salt retention.

NONCLASSIC 21-HYDROXYLASE DEFICIENCY. Nonclassic 21-hydroxylase deficiency, a genetic variant of the classic form, is associated with a milder enzyme defect and does not cause prenatal virilization in a genetic female. However, signs of androgen excess may appear postnatally in both sexes. Nonclassic 21-hydroxylase deficiency occurs in 1 in 100 people in the general population, with a higher frequency in specific ethnic groups (e.g., 1 in 27 Ashkenazi Jews, 1 in 40 Hispanics, 1 in 50 Slavs, 1 in 300 Italians), which makes this deficiency the most frequent autosomal recessive disease in humans.

Clinical Manifestations

In 21-hydroxylase deficiency, 17α-hydroxyprogesterone (17-OHP) and progesterone are overproduced and are converted to the androgens dehydroepiandrosterone, Δ⁴-androstenedione, and testosterone, which cause virilization. Postnatally, in children with untreated classic and nonclassic 21-hydroxylase deficiency, growth accelerates in the early years but the epiphyses close prematurely, which results in a tall child but a short adult. Even when treated, most patients do not reach the height potential indicated by family height. Pubertal development under hypothalamic-

pituitary control may be suppressed by excess adrenal androgens, and fertility potential may not be achieved until proper treatment is instituted to suppress ACTH and adrenal androgen secretion. Without treatment, males may have evidence of pseudopuberty marked by phallic growth, small testes, and precocious growth of pubic, axillary, and body hair. Male internal and external genital development is normal. Untreated females may suffer from excessive androgenic symptoms such as cystic acne, menstrual/ovulatory irregularities, or polycystic ovarian syndrome (Fig. 246–6).

Molecular Genetics

The gene encoding 21-hydroxylase is located on the short arm of chromosome 6 within the human major histocompatibility complex. The gene locus for the 21-hydroxylase enzyme, termed *CYP21,* has a closely neighboring homologue, the pseudogene *CYP21P,* that is not expressed. Two forms of mutations observed are gene deletions, which result from chromosomal misalignment as well as unequal crossing over during meiosis, and gene conversions, which apparently involve the transfer of short sequences resident on the pseudogene to the active gene. Although in most patients the severity of the *CYP21* mutation correlates with the severity of disease and the disease type, among apparently mutation-identical groups, genotype does not always correlate with phenotype.

Diagnosis

Screening of newborns for elevated serum 17-OHP identifies males and females with classic 21-hydroxylase deficiency irrespective of genital phenotype. In the United States, newborns are currently screened in 22 states. In suspected cases, the chromosomal or genetic sex should be determined by buccal smear for Barr bodies, karyotyping, fluorescent Y, or *SRY* analysis. Elevated 17-OHP, which may be several hundred times normal, confirms the enzyme defect. Routine screening at random does not detect the nonclassic form of 21-hydroxylase deficiency. In the nonclassic form, 17-OHP levels may be elevated in early morning readings but normal in midmorning and afternoon. Thus, the deficiency is best diagnosed with an ACTH stimulation test (an intravenous bolus injection of 0.25 mg of synthetic ACTH and assay for serum 17-OHP at 0 and 60 minutes). The coordinates of the baseline and the ACTH-stimulated 17-OHP concentrations aggregate on a regression line into three diagnostic groups. Classic cases fall into the highest group on the regression line, nonclassic cases aggregate lower than classic cases, and an overlap of heterozygote carriers and unaffected cases appears in the lowest group (Fig. 246–7).

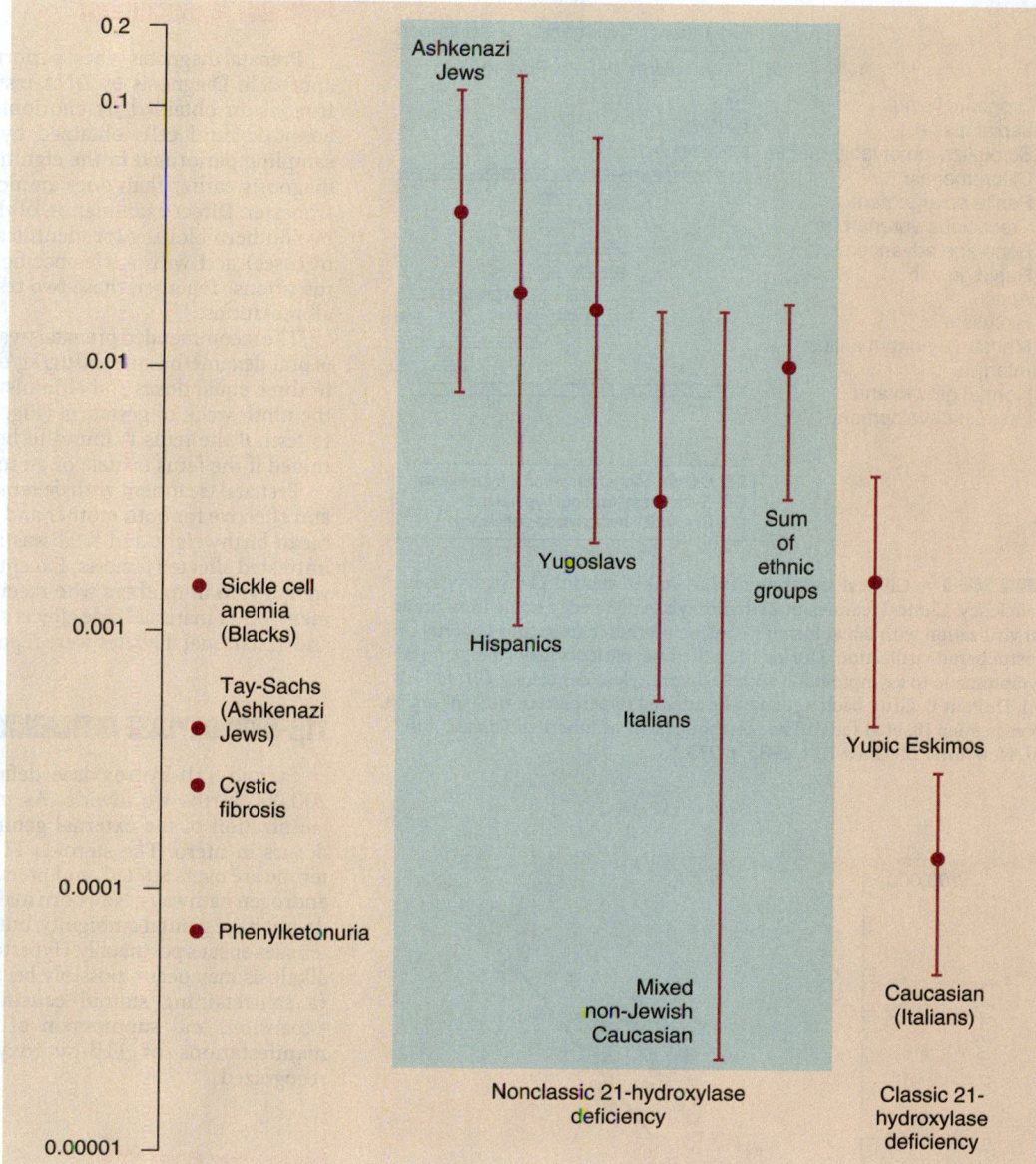

FIGURE 246-5 • Disease frequencies of classic 21-hydroxylase deficiency (in two populations), nonclassic 21-hydroxylase deficiency (in five ethnic groups), and four other relatively common autosomal recessive disorders are compared. (From Speiser PW, DuPont B, Rubinstein P, et al: High frequency of nonclassical steroid 21-hydroxylase deficiency. Am J Hum Genet 1985;37:650.)

Rx Treatment

Females with classic 21-hydroxylase deficiency should almost always be assigned to the female gender because they have the potential for normal sexual and reproductive function. In classically affected females who were not prenatally treated, surgical correction of genital ambiguity is required. Recent experience indicates that early one-stage vaginal and perineal reconstruction, which avoids a second-stage surgical procedure and decreases delayed vaginal stenosis, is effective in correcting the ambiguity in certain cases.

Postnatal management involves lifelong hormonal replacement. It is necessary to monitor the 17-OHP serum concentration (or daily urinary excretion of pregnanetriol) as well as plasma renin activity in the classic salt-wasting form. Hydrocortisone is generally given in infancy and childhood in a dose range of 10 to 25 mg/m²/day to maintain the serum 17-OHP concentration between 500 and 1000 ng/dL. Attempts to bring the 17-OHP concentration to normal result in cushingoid features and retarded growth. In adolescence and adulthood, hydrocortisone may be replaced with dexamethasone or prednisone. Mineralocorticoid (9α-fluorohydrocortisone) administration and added salt to the diet are necessary in patients with salt-wasting disease and may improve hormonal control in simple virilizers. Unfortunately, in a sizable number of children with CAH, it has proved difficult to maintain satisfactory adrenal suppression without producing an unacceptable degree of hypercortisolism. Unfavorable outcomes include short stature, reduced fertility, polycystic ovaries, irregular menses, acne, hirsutism, frontal balding, and progressive obesity. Although erratic compliance with prescribed substitution therapy is undeniably a major cause of escape from pituitary suppression, much of the problem is inherent in our limited ability to control ACTH secretion. For this reason, it has been suggested that the more severely affected children (severely virilized and salt wasting with double-null mutations in the 21-hydroxylase gene) will have a better quality of life if they are adrenalectomized at an early age and reared as patients with Addison's disease would be, who require modest doses of daily steroids (with provision for increased dosages in the face of stress). To date, this approach shows promise in the limited number of cases documented.

Recently, growth hormone therapy alone or in combination with gonadotropin-releasing hormone has been shown to decrease height deficit in CAH patients with a poor height prognosis.

Treatment of symptomatic nonclassic 21-hydroxylase deficiency with dexamethasone in low doses (0.25 mg at bedtime) is usually effective in reversing the symptoms of androgen excess, including reduced fertility.

In recent years, gene therapy technology has greatly advanced such that gene therapy using *CYP21* complementary DNA may become a viable treatment alternative.

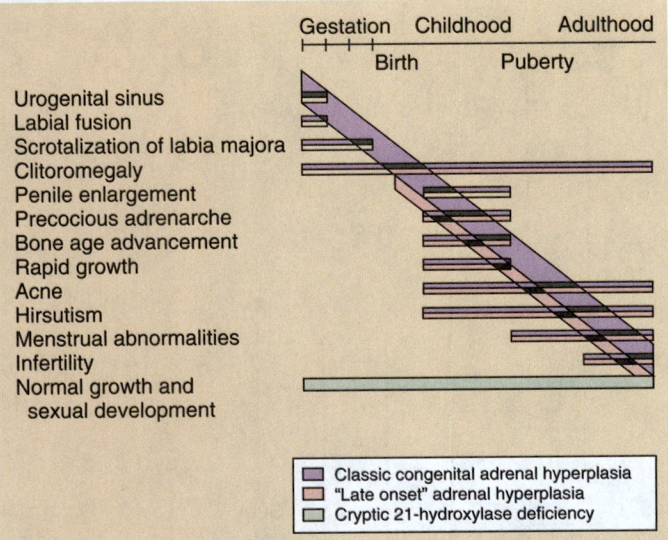

FIGURE 246–6 • Clinical spectrum of HLA-linked steroid 21-hydroxylase deficiency. Clinical features in 21-hydroxylase deficiency range from prenatal virilization with labial fusion to precocious adrenarche and pubertal or postpubertal virilization. During their lifetime, patients may change from symptomatic to asymptomatic with 21-hydroxylase deficiency. (From New MI, DuPont B, Grumbach K, et al: The adrenal hyperplasias. *In* Stanbury JB, Wyngaarden JB, et al [eds]: The Metabolic Basis of Inherited Disease, 5th ed. New York, McGraw-Hill, 1983, p 973.)

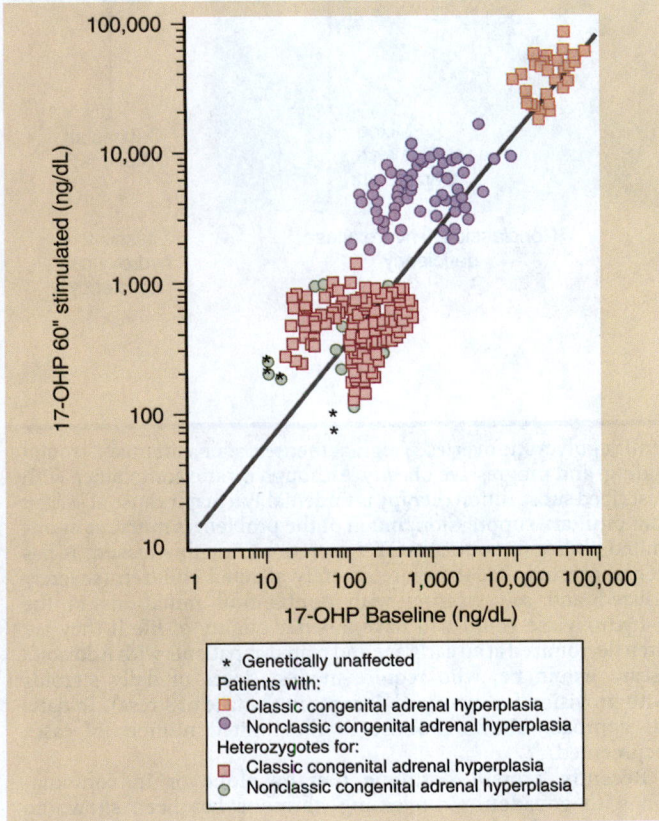

FIGURE 246–7 • Nomogram relating baseline to adrenocorticotropic hormone–stimulated serum concentrations of 17-hydroxyprogesterone (17-OHP). The scales are logarithmic. A regression line for all data points is shown. The data for this nomogram were collected between 1982 and 1991 at the Department of Pediatrics, The New York Presbyterian Hospital–Weill Cornell Medical Center, New York.

Prenatal Management

Prenatal diagnosis is best performed with a direct molecular genetic approach. Diagnosis by DNA testing requires sampling of chorion frondosum obtained by chorionic villus sampling or sampling of amniotic fluid cells obtained by amniocentesis. Chorionic villus sampling performed in the eighth to tenth week of gestation allows diagnosis earlier than does amniocentesis performed in the second trimester. Direct examination of the *CYP21* gene locus is carried out by Southern blotting for identification of gene deletions (10 to 35% of cases) and with allele-specific oligonucleotide probes for point mutations. Together, these two tests routinely identify about 90% of all mutations.

The recommended prenatal treatment of 21-hydroxylase deficiency is oral dexamethasone, 20 μg/kg/day (prepregnancy weight) divided in three equal doses and administered to the mother starting before the ninth week of gestation (Fig. 246–8). Therapy should continue to term if the fetus is found to be an affected female but is discontinued if the fetus is male or an unaffected female.

Prenatal treatment with dexamethasone has been shown to be safe and effective for both mother and child in the largest human studies. Mean birthweight and fetal wastage were the same for treated and untreated affected females. Except for a statistically significant higher weight gain in mothers who received prenatal dexamethasone treatment, other maternal side effects such as striae, edema, hypertension, and gestational diabetes were reported to be the same in both groups.

11β-HYDROXYLASE DEFICIENCY

Steroid 11β-hydroxylase deficiency occurs in 1 in 100,000 to 200,000 births worldwide. As in 21-hydroxylase deficiency, masculinization of the external genitalia in classically affected females occurs in utero. The steroids 11-deoxycortisol and deoxycorticosterone are oversecreted, and precursors are shunted into uninhibited androgen pathways. Newborn males with 11β-hydroxylase deficiency do not have genital ambiguity, but virilization in untreated males and females ensues postnatally. Hypertension with or without hypokalemic alkalosis may occur, possibly because of excess deoxycorticosterone (a salt-retaining steroid causing hypokalemia), plasma volume expansion, and suppression of plasma renin activity. Nonclassic manifestations of 11β-hydroxylase deficiency have also been recognized.

Molecular Genetics

Two genes located on the long arm of chromosome 8 encode the 11β-hydroxylase enzyme proteins CYP11B1 (expressed in the zona fasciculata) and CYP11B2 (expressed in the zona glomerulosa). Mutations in the *CYP11B1* gene, which has regulatory sequences responsive to ACTH, impair cortisol synthesis and cause CAH. Mutations in the *CYP11B2* gene, which normally expresses the enzyme aldosterone synthase, impair aldosterone synthesis but not cortisol synthesis. This rare condition, termed *aldosterone synthase type II deficiency* (Persian salt-wasting disease), causes salt-wasting symptoms in early life that often resolve by adulthood. Because the *CYP11B* genes are homologues, splicing mutations create a chimeric gene having regulatory sequence features of *CYP11B1* and structural coding features of *CYP11B2*; the result is a rare form of low-renin hypertension called *dexamethasone-suppressible hyperaldosteronism.*

Diagnosis

In 11β-hydroxylase deficiency, serum 11-deoxycortisol (compound S) and deoxycorticosterone are elevated. Plasma renin activity is suppressed and/or plasma aldosterone levels are low. In genetic females with ambiguous genitalia, 11β-hydroxylase deficiency can be distinguished from 21-hydroxylase deficiency by elevated levels of compound S and deoxycorticosterone, as well as by suppressed plasma renin activity.

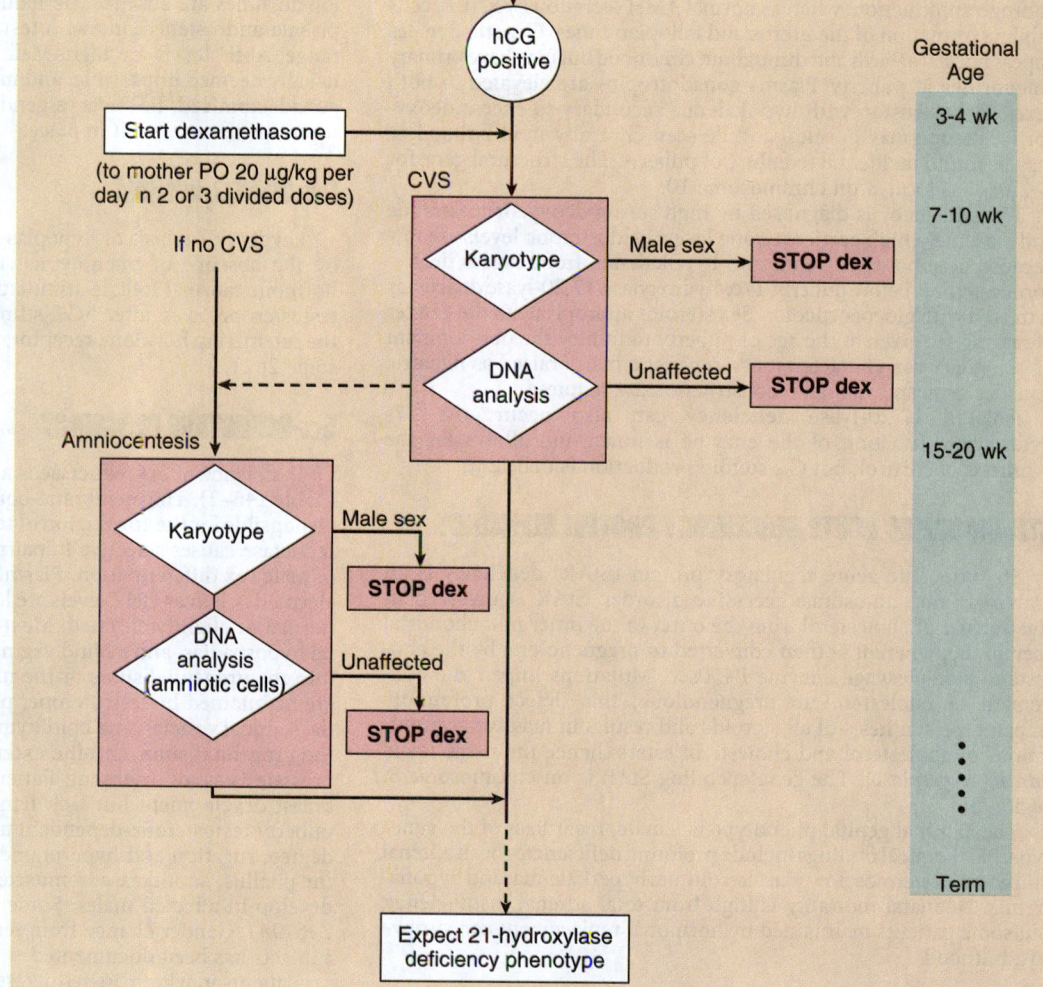

FIGURE 246–8 • Algorithm depicting prenatal management of pregnancy in families at risk for a fetus affected with 21-hydroxylase deficiency. CVS = chorionic villus sampling; dex = dexamethasone; hCG = human chorionic gonadotropin; 17-OHP = 17α-hydroxyprogesterone. (From Speiser PW, Laforgia N, Kato K, et al: First trimester prenatal treatment and molecular genetic diagnosis of congenital adrenal hyperplasia [21-hydroxylase deficiency]. J Clin Endocrinol Metab 1990;70:838–848. © The Endocrine Society.)

 **Treatment**

Treatment of 11β-hydroxylase deficiency with glucocorticoids leads to reduced levels of deoxycorticosterone with natriuresis, a rise in plasma renin activity, and normotension. Because the renin-angiotensin system is no longer suppressed, aldosterone levels rise to normal. Surgical correction may be necessary in untreated genetic female genitalia. In recent years, prenatal diagnosis and treatment of 11β-hydroxylase deficiency have been carried out with the same protocol as in steroid 21-hydroxylase deficiency and have achieved the same success.

MALE PSEUDOHERMAPHRODITISM

Male pseudohermaphroditism occurring in the absence of testicular dysgenesis is due to biochemical defects impairing the biosynthesis or action of either testosterone or AMH and is usually genetically transmitted in an autosomal recessive fashion, with the notable exception of androgen insensitivity, which is X linked. The chromosomal location of genes involved in sex differentiation is shown in Figure 246–2; only the most important ones are mentioned in the text.

3β-HYDROXYSTEROID DEHYDROGENASE DEFICIENCY

A defect in 3β-hydroxysteroid dehydrogenase, an enzyme that acts early in the pathway of cortisol synthesis, impairs sex steroid synthesis in both the adrenal and the gonads. Because the synthesis of testosterone is impaired in 3β-hydroxysteroid dehydrogenase deficiency, males are incompletely masculinized and are born with ambiguous genitalia. In a genetic female fetus, Δ⁴-androgens formed peripherally from the excess secretion of dehydroepiandrosterone may produce mild clitoral enlargement. In the case of a severe enzyme deficiency in either sex, salt wasting secondary to aldosterone deficiency may develop.

A gene for the peripheral form of 3β-hydroxysteroid dehydrogenase (type I) and a gene for the adrenal-gonadal form of 3β-hydroxysteroid dehydrogenase (type II) have been identified and mapped to chromosome 1. Mutations in the type II gene have been described only in the classic form of the disorder.

Steroid 3β-hydroxysteroid dehydrogenase deficiency is diagnosed by a high ratio of Δ^5- to Δ^4-steroids. Elevated levels of pregnenolone, 17-hydroxypregnenolone, and dehydroepiandrosterone are evident in serum; the urinary Δ^5-metabolites pregnanetriol and 16-pregnanetriol are elevated. Steroid values in the newborn period may not be informative inasmuch as Δ^5-steroid levels are normally high during this time in unaffected persons. Glucocorticoid administration, with the addition of a mineralocorticoid to correct salt wasting, is effective.

Some women exhibiting clinically significant signs of androgen excess show a pattern of elevated Δ^5- to Δ^4-steroids; this condition may represent an underlying mild (nonclassic) 3β-hydroxysteroid dehydrogenase defect. No mutation has been identified to date in the nonclassic form. The nonclassic defect is diagnosed by 60-minute ACTH testing. Treatment consists of oral dexamethasone administration in small doses (0.25 mg at bedtime).

17α-HYDROXYLASE/17,20-LYASE DEFICIENCY

Combined 17α-hydroxylase/17,20-lyase deficiency, a rare form of CAH, impairs the synthesis of cortisol and sex steroids. Males at birth may have ambiguous genitalia and be mistakenly assigned to the female gender. Wolffian duct formation is incomplete because of deficient androgen production, whereas normal AMH secretion by Sertoli cells inhibits formation of the uterus and fallopian tubes. Genetic females appear normal at birth and throughout childhood but may have primary amenorrhea at puberty. Plasma gonadotropins are elevated in both sexes. Hypertension with hypokalemia secondary to excess deoxycorticosterone may develop and be seen clinically in childhood or may be found incidental to failure of puberty. The structural gene for P-450c17 is located on chromosome 10.

The deficiency is diagnosed by high serum deoxycorticosterone and extremely high corticosterone levels. Aldosterone levels are low because of suppressed renin and hypokalemia from excess deoxycorticosterone. Before puberty, 17α-hydroxylase/17,20-lyase deficiency is treated with glucocorticoids. Sex steroids appropriate to the gender of rearing are given at the age of puberty to induce the development of secondary sex characteristics. In genetic males raised as females, gonadectomy and vaginal reconstruction are required.

Isolated 17,20-lyase deficiency can also occur; the 17-hydroxylase function of the enzyme is intact and allows for the synthesis of cortisol, but C_{19}-steroid production is deficient.

STEROIDOGENIC ACUTE REGULATORY PROTEIN DEFICIENCY

Steroidogenic acute regulatory protein (StAR) deficiency is an extremely rare autosomal recessive disorder. StAR is involved in the transfer of cholesterol from the outer to the inner mitochondrial membrane, where it is then converted to pregnenolone by the cholesterol side-cleavage enzyme P450scc. Mutations impair the conversion of cholesterol to pregnenolone; this defect profoundly impairs the synthesis of all steroids and results in massive accumulations of cholesterol and cholesterol esters, hence the name *lipoid adrenal hyperplasia*. The gene encoding StAR is on chromosome 8, region p11.2.

The external genital phenotype is female, regardless of the genotype. Biochemical findings include profound deficiencies of all adrenal and gonadal steroids, low plasma volume, hyperkalemia, and hyponatremia. Neonatal mortality is high from total adrenal insufficiency, but some patients maintained by hormonal replacement can survive to adulthood.

17β-HYDROXYSTEROID DEHYDROGENASE TYPE 3

17β-Hydroxysteroid dehydrogenase type 3 promotes the conversion of androstenedione to testosterone, the last step in the testosterone biosynthetic pathway. It is predominantly expressed in the testes and its gene is located on chromosome 9q22. Mutations in XY patients lead to isolated male pseudohermaphroditism without CAH. The external genitalia are usually unambiguously female. At puberty, marked virilization occurs because of the activity of the ubiquitously expressed type 1 isoform of 17β-hydroxysteroid dehydrogenase. Breast

development occurs in half of the cases. At surgery, testes and epididymides are found in the inguinal canal, and the uterus and fallopian tubes are absent. The hallmark of the condition is elevated plasma androstenedione with testosterone levels in the lower male range; AMH levels are high. Male reconstruction of the genitalia is usually deemed impossible, and most patients are raised as girls and gonadectomized; however, a gender role change has been reported when the testes are left in place.

LEYDIG CELL APLASIA

Leydig cell aplasia or hypoplasia is a rare syndrome characterized by the absence of phenotypic virilization, high basal luteinizing hormone, normal follicle-stimulating hormone, high AMH, and low testosterone, even after hCG stimulation. It is due to mutations of the luteinizing hormone receptor, whose gene is located on chromosome 2p21.

5α-REDUCTASE DEFICIENCY

Deficiency of 5α-reductase is a rare autosomal recessive disorder (Table 246–2). The membrane-bound enzyme 5α-reductase type 2 is responsible for the conversion of testosterone to DHT. A defect in 5α-reductase causes selective impairment of the DHT-dependent steps of male sex differentiation. Plasma testosterone levels are normal to elevated, whereas DHT levels are low. Luteinizing hormone levels are normal or slightly elevated. Most patients have severe perineoscrotal hypospadias, and a blind vaginal pouch may be present and open into the urogenital sinus or the urethra. Because the wolffian ducts are maintained by testosterone, patients have normal vasa deferentia, seminal vesicles, and epididymides. DHT-mediated virilization of the urogenital sinus and the external genitalia is impaired, and the prostate is small or absent. Patients have a female habitus without breast development but lack female internal genital structures. At puberty, testosterone-dependent masculinization occurs to a variable degree; rugation and hyperpigmentation of the scrotum, growth of the phallus, an increase in muscle mass, and deepening of the voice develop in affected males. Some may have testicular descent (Fig. 246–9A). Gender change from female to male in untreated affected subjects has been documented.

Patients in whom 5α-reductase deficiency is diagnosed in infancy and early childhood are best reared as males once the hypospadias and cryptorchidism are surgically corrected. Because DHT is not available for general use, adults are usually treated with high doses of testosterone esters. In the absence of 5α-reductase, 19-nortestosterone is active and can be given by injection in an esterified form.

5α-Reductase isoform 2 is the major isoenzyme expressed in genital tissues, and a deletion in the type 2 gene has been found in affected subjects. Eighteen different mutations have been identified in 25 families, and approximately 40% of affected individuals are compound heterozygotes.

Table 246–2 • DISORDERS OF SEXUAL DIFFERENTIATION IN MALES

DISORDER	DEFECTIVE PROTEIN	GENE LOCALIZATION	PHENOTYPE				ENDOCRINOLOGY	
			Müllerian Ducts	Wolffian Ducts	External Genitalia	Other	Testosterone	AMH
Defects in enzymes involved in testosterone synthesis or metabolism	Side-chain cleavage	15q23–24	Absent	Present	Ambiguous		Low	Normal
	17α-Hydroxylase	10	Absent	Present	Female	Hypertension	Low	Normal
	3β-HSD type 2	1p13	Absent	Present	Ambiguous	Salt loss	Low	High*
	17β-HSD type 3	9q22	Absent	Present	Female		Low	Normal
	5α-Reductase type 2	2p23	Absent	Present	Ambiguous		High	Normal
Androgen metabolism insensitivity								
A. CAIS	Androgen receptor	Xq11–12	Absent	Absent	Female		Normal	High*
B. PAIS	Androgen receptor	Xq11–12	Absent	Present	Ambiguous		Normal	High*
Persistent müllerian duct syndrome	AMH	19p13	Present	Present	Male		Normal	Low
	AMH receptor	12q13	Present	Present	Male		Normal	Normal

*In the neonatal and pubertal periods; normal at other times.
AMH = antimüllerian hormone; CAIS = complete androgen insensitivity; HSD = hydroxysteroid dehydrogenase; PAIS = partial androgen insensitivity.

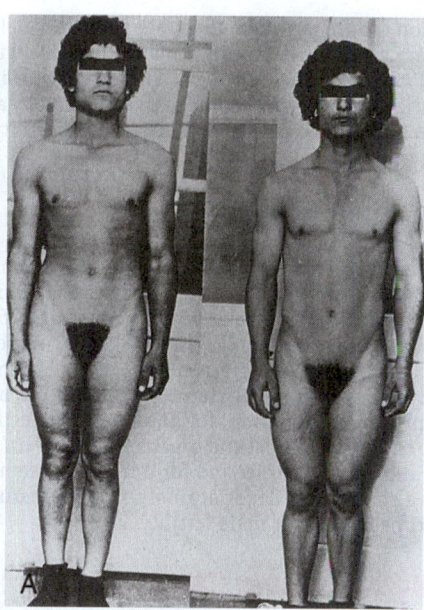
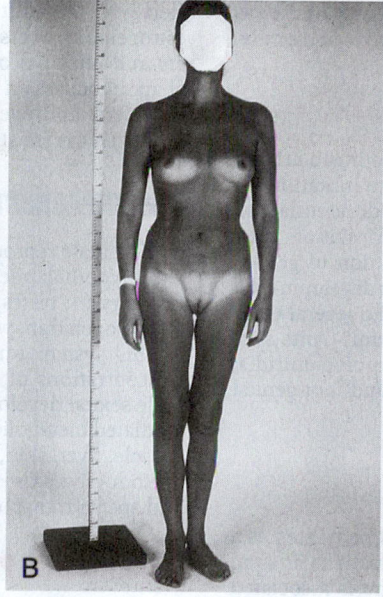
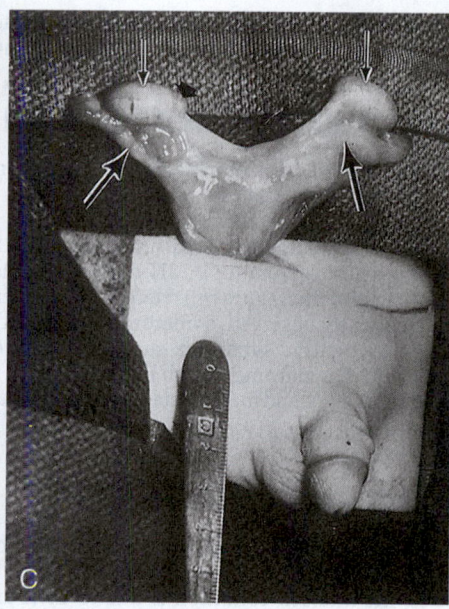

FIGURE 246—9 • *A*, Pubertal virilization in brothers with 5α-reductase deficiency. *B*, Patient with complete androgen insensitivity. *C*, A case of persistent müllerian duct syndrome—operative field. Above the normal, infantile male genitalia are the contents of the right hernia sac, which consists of the testes (small arrows) and fallopian tubes (large arrows) separated by the uterus. A portion of an epididymis (arrowhead) caps the right testis. The vas deferens was palpable posteriorly on both sides. (*A*, From Savage MO, Preece MA, Jeffcoate SL, et al: Familial male pseudohermaphroditism due to deficiency of 5α-reductase. Clin Endocrinol 1980;12:397; *B* and *C*, from Harbison MD, Magid MLS, Josso N, et al: Antimüllerian hormone in three intersex conditions. Ann Genet 1991;34:226.)

ANDROGEN INSENSITIVITY

Masculinization of the reproductive tract depends on androgen binding to the androgen receptor protein. Mutations of the X-linked gene coding for the androgen receptor in subjects hemizygous for the mutated gene therefore lead to androgen insensitivity (see Table 246–2), formerly known as *testicular feminization syndrome*. Androgen insensitivity is one of the most frequent forms of male pseudohermaphroditism; estimates of incidence vary from 1 in 20,000 to 64,000 male births. It causes a spectrum of phenotypic abnormalities.

Clinical Manifestations

Subjects affected by the complete form of androgen insensitivity have a normal female phenotype. They are rarely discovered before puberty unless masses are palpated in the groin or labia and discovered to be testes at surgical exploration. The vagina is usually shallow and ends blindly. Internal genital structures are generally absent, although some cases with residual müllerian derivatives have been described. The testes may be located in the abdomen or in the labia majora and do not undergo spermatogenesis. Pubic and axillary hair is scant or absent (Fig. 246–9B). AMH levels are elevated during the first year and after puberty. Testosterone and luteinizing hormone levels are elevated as a result of defective feedback regulation caused by androgen resistance at the level of the hypothalamus. Estrogen production is usually increased; when coupled with androgen insensitivity, the increased estrogen production results in an unopposed estrogen effect and is the most likely explanation for breast development at puberty.

Partial androgen insensitivity, also termed *Reifenstein's syndrome*, is characterized by a variable degree of genital ambiguity, and both virilization and breast development occur at puberty (see Table 246–2). Partial androgen insensitivity is also consistent with a male phenotype with gynecomastia and infertility as the sole manifestations. Mutations of the androgen receptor have also been reported in prostate cancer.

Molecular Genetics and Prenatal Diagnosis

The androgen receptor gene is located on the long arm of the X chromosome between Xq12 and Xp11, consistent with the sex-linked recessive mode of inheritance observed in affected families. De novo cases are not uncommon. Most mutations in androgen-insensitive individuals are located within exons 2 to 8, which encode the DNA and androgen-binding domain; mutations in exon 1 are rare, mostly deletions or insertions that lead to premature termination of translation and hence to complete androgen insensitivity. Prenatal diagnosis of androgen receptor defects is possible with chorionic villus tissue biopsy and DNA analysis.

Rx Treatment

Management depends on the severity of the androgen receptor defect. Patients with complete androgen insensitivity should be raised as girls, and the testes should be removed to avoid malignant degeneration, which occurs in 1 to 2% of cases. The optimal time for castration is controversial. Some physicians prefer to delay it until after adolescence to allow spontaneous feminization to occur. Estrogen treatment is then required to preserve breast development. Management of patients with partial androgen insensitivity is less straightforward because the diagnosis cannot always be confirmed by molecular studies in the neonatal period. When the phallus is very small and other causes of male pseudohermaphroditism have been excluded, female gender assignment may be the best option. Patients with partial androgen insensitivity who are raised as girls should have their testes removed early to avoid unwanted virilization.

PERSISTENT MÜLLERIAN DUCT SYNDROME

Male pseudohermaphroditism caused by an isolated defect of AMH synthesis or action is a rare autosomal recessive disorder characterized by the presence of a uterus and tubes tightly linked to the testes in otherwise normally virilized males. When these structures are held in the pelvis by the round ligament, they prevent the testes from descending and lead to bilateral cryptorchidism (Fig. 246–9C). In most cases, however, müllerian derivatives are mobile and are dragged into the inguinal canal and scrotum by the descending testis; the result is an apparent inguinoscrotal hernia with contralateral cryptorchidism. The condition is usually discovered only at surgery.

A dozen different mutations of the gene coding for AMH have been described in patients with low or undetectable serum concentrations of the hormone. Mutations of the AMH receptor gene are involved in subjects with normal serum levels of AMH. Treatment should aim at preserving fertility through early correction of cryptorchidism while paying great attention to the integrity of the vas deferens, which is often incorporated in the wall of the uterus and cervix.

UNEXPLAINED MALE PSEUDOHERMAPHRODITISM

More than 50% of cases of male pseudohermaphroditism are not explained by molecular analysis. They could be due to mutations of yet unknown genes specifically involved in sex differentiation. Alternatively, sex ambiguity could represent a malformation masquerading as a testosterone or AMH defect. Association of genital ambiguity with intrauterine growth retardation or other developmental defects is frequently observed, sometimes as one of the several components of a recognized syndrome such as Smith-Lemli-Opitz syndrome; the WAGR syndrome, which include Wilms' tumor, aniridia, gonadal abnormalities, and mental retardation; or the hand-foot-genital syndrome.

CONCLUSIONS AND GENERAL MANAGEMENT

Sexual ambiguity, at least in the newborn, should be treated as a pediatric emergency. It may threaten the life of the patient if, as in most cases, the intersex condition is due to CAH and is associated with salt loss. Even if such is not the case, it is important to reach a diagnosis as early as possible.

Three diagnostic clues are helpful: gonadal location, presence of a uterus, and karyotype. If no gonads are palpable in a 46,XX chromatin–positive baby, CAH should be suspected before the possibility of true hermaphroditism or idiopathic female pseudohermaphroditism is entertained. In patients with at least one palpable gonad, if a uterus can be visualized by ultrasonography, the most likely diagnosis is testicular dysgenesis in 46,XY subjects and true hermaphroditism or XX maleness in 46,XX subjects. If no müllerian derivatives are present, testosterone insensitivity should be ruled out, if possible, before steroidogenic defects or malformative male pseudohermaphroditism, are considered. If the sex of rearing is debatable, it is prudent to wait until the results of a quick work-up, including an hCG test and AMH assay, are obtained and the various issues have been thoroughly discussed with the parents. However, once gender has been assigned, there should be no ambiguity in the sex of rearing to avoid confusion of gender.

SUGGESTED READINGS

Hughes IA: Minireview: Sex differentiation. Endocrinology 2001;142:3281–3287. *A comprehensive review of the factors involved in sex determination and differentiation.*
Josso N, Rey R, Gonzales J: Sexual differentiation. *In* DeGroot L (ed): Pediatric Endocrinology. http://www.endotext.org/pediatrics/pediatrics7/pediatricsframe7.htm. 2003. *This chapter carefully describes human sexual differentiation, the underlying molecular genetic basis, and associated abnormalities.*
Migeon CJ, Wisniewski AB, Brown TR, et al: 46,XY intersex individuals: Phenotypic and etiologic classification, knowledge of condition, and satisfaction with knowledge in adulthood. Pediatrics 2002;110:616–621. *The purpose of this study was to identify and study adults who have a 46,XY karyotype and presented as infants or children with variable degrees of undermasculinization of their genitalia.*
New MI, Carlson A, Obeid J, et al: Update on prenatal diagnosis for congenital adrenal hyperplasia in 532 pregnancies. J Clin Endocrinol Metab 2001;86:5651–5657. *Prenatal dexamethasone was effective in this large case series.*
New MI, Crawford C, Wilson RC: Genetic disorders of the adrenal gland. *In* Rimoin DL, Connor JM, Pyeritz RE (eds): Emery and Rimoin's Principles and Practice of Medical Genetics, 3rd ed. New York, Churchill Livingstone, 1996, pp 1441–1476. *An overview of the molecular genetics of adrenal disorders.*
Yu RN, Ito M, Saunders TL, et al: Role of *Ahch* in gonadal development and gametogenesis. Nat Genet 1998;20:353–357. *Transgenic mouse technology sheds a new light on the role of Dax-1 in sex determination and spermatogenesis.*

247 THE TESTIS AND MALE SEXUAL FUNCTION

Ronald S. Swerdloff
Christina Wang

The testis is a bifunctional organ serving as the site of sex steroid (i.e., testosterone synthesis) and sperm production in the male. Thus, the testis controls both sexuality and the perpetuity of the species

(fertility). In addition, androgens and their metabolites (including estrogens) serve essential metabolic roles and may be important inducers and effectors of brain function in men. The discussion in this chapter focuses on the issues of male reproductive physiology and its disorders: androgen deficiency, sexual dysfunction, infertility, and androgen excess states.

MALE REPRODUCTIVE PHYSIOLOGY

The male reproductive axis consists of six main components: (1) extrahypothalamic central nervous system, (2) hypothalamus, (3) pituitary, (4) testes, (5) sex steroid–sensitive end organs, and (6) sites of androgen transport and metabolism (Fig. 247–1). The components of this system function in an integrative fashion to control the concentrations of circulating gonadal steroids required for normal male sexual development and function; for androgen- and estrogen-mediated metabolic effects on critical end organs such as brain, bone, muscle, liver, skin, and bone marrow; and for immune systems. The reproductive axis is also responsible for normal germ cell maturation and sperm transport necessary for male fertility.

Hypothalamic Pituitary Function (Chapter 235)

The hypothalamus is the principal integrative unit responsible for the normal pulsatile secretion of gonadotropin-releasing hormone (GnRH), which is delivered through the hypothalamic-hypophyseal portal blood system to the pituitary gland. Although GnRH has been identified in many areas of the central nervous system (CNS), it is most concentrated in the medial basal, arcuate, and suprachiasmatic nuclei in the hypothalamus and travels by axonomic flow to the axon terminals of the median eminence. The pulsatile release of GnRH provides the signals for the timing of the release of luteinizing hormone (LH) and follicle-stimulating hormone (FSH), which in normal circumstances occurs approximately every 60 to 90 minutes. The secretion of GnRH is regulated in a complex fashion by neuronal input from higher cognitive and sensory centers and by circulating levels of sex steroids and peptide hormones such as prolactin and leptin. The local effectors of GnRH synthesis and release include a number of neuropeptides, catecholamines, indolamines, nitric oxide and excitatory amino acids, γ-aminobutyric acid, dopamine, neuropeptide Y, vasoactive intestinal peptide, and corticotropin-releasing hormone. Testosterone either directly or through its metabolic products (i.e., estradiol and dihydrotestosterone) has inhibitory effects on the secretion and release of GnRH as well as direct inhibitory effects on

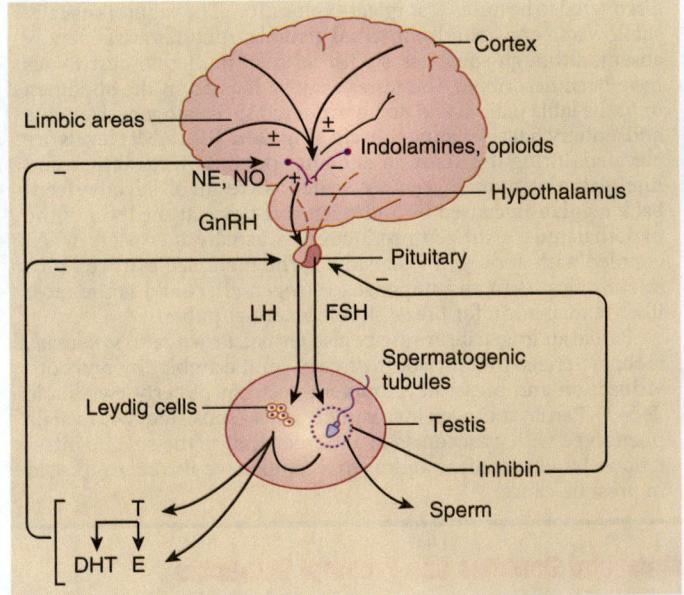

FIGURE 247–1 • The hypothalamic-pituitary-gonadal axis in the male. DHT = dihydrotestosterone; E = estrogen; FSH = follicle-stimulating hormone; GnRH = gonadotropin-releasing hormone; LH = luteinizing hormone; NE = norepinephrine; NO = nitric oxide; T = testosterone.

secretion and release of LH and FSH. Prolactin is a potent inhibitor of GnRH secretion, thus explaining its role in inhibiting LH and testosterone secretion in conditions of hyperprolactinemia.

Luteinizing hormone and FSH are glycopeptides consisting of two subunits (α and β). They share the same α-subunit, with specificity endowed by the β-subunit. The heterodimer is required for biologic activity; the subunits can be detected in serum and may be increased in certain pathologic conditions (e.g., α-subunit elevations in gonadotropin-secreting pituitary adenomas). LH and FSH are synthesized in the same pituitary cell (gonadotrophs) and secreted in a pulsatile pattern. The clearance of these two gonadotrophic hormones differs, with LH having a shorter half-life than FSH. While blood levels of testosterone demonstrate a robust diurnal rhythm in young, healthy adult men, the circadian pattern of LH is highly individualized and blunted relative to testosterone. Puberty is heralded by nighttime pulsatile serum patterns before obvious increases are noted in the daytime. Feedback regulation of LH and FSH secretion also occurs at the pituitary, with testosterone, dihydrotestosterone (DHT), and estrogens inhibiting the synthesis and/or release of both gonadotropins. Circulating testicular peptide products of the Sertoli cell (i.e., inhibin) also produce selective inhibition of FSH. LH and FSH circulate unbound to carrier proteins and act predominantly through specific cell surface receptors on the Leydig and Sertoli cells of the testes, respectively.

Testis Function

The testis is a complex organ consisting of (1) seminiferous tubules containing Sertoli cells and germ cells in various stages of maturation and (2) the interstitium where the steroid-secreting cells (Leydig), macrophages, and blood vessels reside (Fig. 247–2). The Leydig cells synthesize steroid hormones under the regulation of LH. The LH receptors on the cell surface of the Leydig cells lead to G protein/cyclic adenosine monophosphate–mediated events. This process involves a steroid acute regulatory (StAR) protein essential for steroidogenesis in the gonads and adrenal glands (Fig. 247–3).

TESTOSTERONE SYNTHESIS. Testosterone is the principal male hormone secreted by the testes, with about 7 mg produced per day in adult males. Testosterone synthesis occurs in the human testes through either the delta 4 or the delta 5 pathway (see Fig. 247–3), with the latter pathway predominant. The enzymatic rate-limiting step in the process is the LH-inducible StAR protein and the conversion of cholesterol to pregnenolone by the cholesterol side-chain cleavage enzyme.

TESTOSTERONE TRANSPORT IN BLOOD. Testosterone circulates mainly bound to two plasma proteins: sex hormone–binding globulin (SHBG; also known as testosterone-binding globulin) and albumin. In young adult men, about 54% of testosterone is bound to albumin, 44% is bound to SHBG, and 2 to 3% is unbound, or free. The SHBG-testosterone fraction is tightly bound and serves a storage role.

Bioavailable testosterone refers to the sum of albumin-bound and free testosterone and is measured by separating SHBG-bound testosterone from the total testosterone in the serum. Serum SHBG levels are increased in endogenous and exogenous hyperestrogenemic states, hyperthyroidism, aging, phenytoin treatment, anorexia nervosa, and prolonged stress. SHBG levels are lowered with androgen treatment, obesity, acromegaly, and hypothyroidism. In most instances, measurement of serum total testosterone will detect individuals with androgen deficiency. In conditions with abnormal SHBG levels, the total testosterone measurement (usual laboratory test requested) may be misleading. Testosterone secretion has a diurnal variation and is highest in the morning in young adult men; this rhythm is lost with aging.

TESTOSTERONE ACTION. Testosterone exerts its effects at different end organs either through direct action or after conversion to an active metabolite such as DHT by 5α-reductase or estradiol by the aromatase enzyme (Fig. 247–4). Thus, testosterone can act as an androgenic

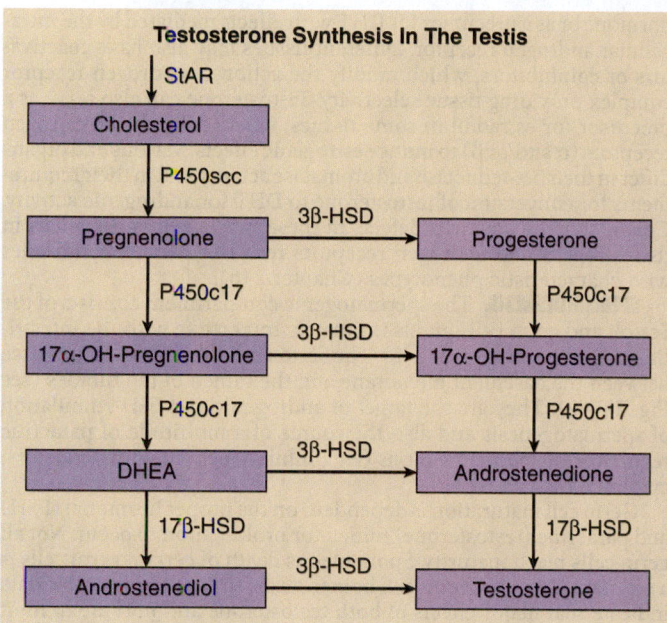

Testosterone Synthesis In The Testis

FIGURE 247–3 • The steroid acute regulatory (StAR) protein mobilizes cholesterol from cellular stores to the mitochondria. Intratesticular steroidogenic pathways for synthesis of testosterone. Although both the delta 5 (left) and delta 4 (right) pathways exist, the delta 5 pathway predominates in the testis. HSD = hydroxysteroid dehydrogenase.

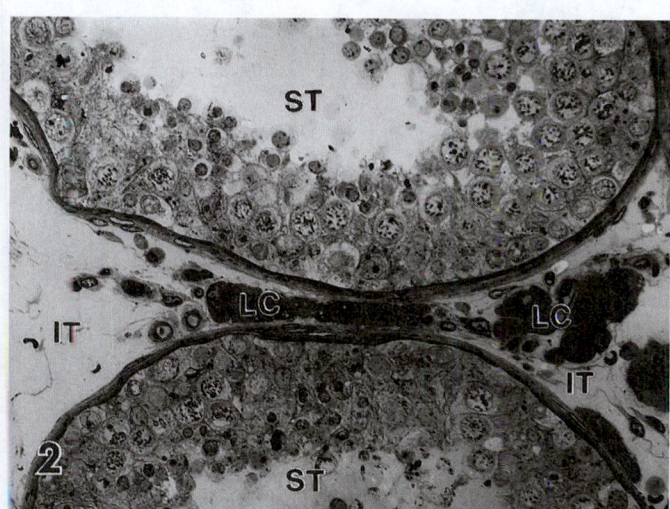

FIGURE 247–2 • Testis. Light micrograph of the glutaraldehyde-fixed, epoxy-embedded testicular section from a normal man showing seminiferous tubules (ST) and interstitium (IT). The seminiferous tubules contain Sertoli cells and germ cells at various phases of maturation. The interstitium consists of Leydig cells (LC), blood vessels, and lymphatic space.

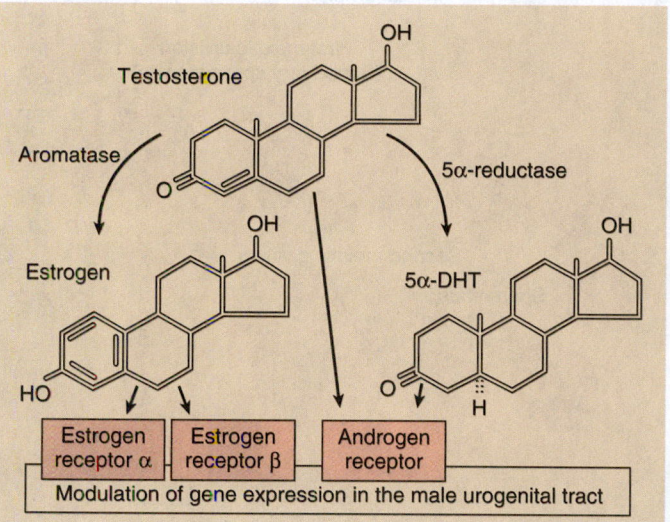

FIGURE 247–4 • Testosterone action is mediated either directly (androgen receptor), after conversion to estradiol (estrogen receptor α or β), or after conversion to dihydrotestosterone (DHT) (androgen receptor). (From Kuiper GCJM, Carlquist M, Gustafsson JA: Estrogen is a male and female hormone. Sci Med 1998;5:36–45; with permission.)

hormone or as a precursor for DHT with effects mediated by the intracellular androgen receptor. Different tissues may also have coactivators or coinhibitors, which modify the action of androgen-receptor complex providing tissue selectivity. Testosterone can also serve as a precursor for estradiol in some tissues, where it binds the estrogen receptors (α and/or β) to induce estrogenic effects. Various end organs differ in their 5α-reductase and aromatase activity and in their requirements for conversion of testosterone to DHT for androgenic activity. Congenital and acquired defects in these two enzymes as well as in the estrogens and androgen receptors result in distinct syndromes with characteristic phenotypes (Chapter 246).

SPERMATOGENESIS. The spermatogenic compartment consists of the Sertoli and germ cells and is intimately interactive with the interstitial compartment (Fig. 247–5). The Sertoli cells bridge the entire space between the basement membrane and the lumen of the tubules (see Fig. 247–2). They are the target of androgenic and FSH stimulation of spermatogenesis and also the source of a multitude of paracrine regulators of spermatogenesis (e.g., inhibin, activin, growth factors, cytokines).

Germ cell maturation is dependent on the proper hormonal (FSH) and paracrine (testosterone) milieu for proliferation to occur. Not all germ cells reach maturity. Spontaneous death of certain germ cells is a constant feature of germ cell homeostasis. In fact, considerable data indicate that major effects of both testosterone and FSH are to limit the amount of germ cell death (apoptosis).

SPERM TRANSPORT. After spermatogenesis is completed, mature spermatozoa are released into the excretory system and travel through the rete testes and epididymis, where they functionally mature before traversing the vas deferens. The semen gains constituents from the seminal vesicles, prostate, and bulbourethral glands before ejaculation.

Normal Sexual Function and Erectile Physiology

Normal sexual function in men requires normal sexual desire (libido) and erectile, ejaculatory, and orgasmic capacity. The process is complex, involving cognitive, sensory, hormonal, autonomic neuronal, and penile vascular integrative actions for normal function.

Defects occur at multiple levels. Although considerable progress has occurred in the past few years in therapeutic options, an understanding of the normal physiology is essential for proper assessment and treatment of men with sexual dysfunction.

The brain is the integrative center of the sexual response system. It processes sensory input, stored fantasy information, purposeful thoughts, spontaneous nocturnal reflex activity, and hormonal signals (e.g., testosterone) to create the hypothalamic neuronal message that traverses the spinal cord to the thoracic 9–12 sympathetic and sacral parasympathetic outflow tracts. The nonadrenergic, noncholinergic autonomic plexus nerves initiate vasodilatation of the cavernosal arterial and corporal cavernosa sinusoids of the penis through release of local vasodilators such as nitric oxide (NO) and vasoactive intestinal peptide from the vascular endothelium and the smooth muscle cells of the sinusoids (Fig. 247–6). A family of enzymes (nitric oxide synthetases) regulates NO synthesis, which produces smooth muscle dilatation through activation of cyclic guanosine monophosphate (GMP) and modification of calcium flux. Cyclic GMP levels are rapidly reversible through inactivation by phosphodiesterase. The neurogenic mechanisms leading to vasodilatation of the cavernosal arterioles and sinusoids lead to a rapid increase in penile blood flow and expansion of the vascular channels; this, in turn, inhibits venous return through compression of the venous channels against the tunica albuginea and limits drainage of the obliquely penetrating veins. After orgasm, detumescence occurs, owing to less vasodilation (NO) and greater vasoconstrictive signals (α_2-adrenergic, endothelins).

Testosterone seems to have its primary effect on erectile function by enhancing libido with secondary effects on penile NO synthase activity. Sexual desire and fantasy are highly sensitive to testosterone, thus explaining the preservation of erectile capacity in many men with partial androgen deficiency. In contrast, erectile dysfunction is common in older men despite normal serum testosterone levels; the latter effect appears to be the result of impaired penile vasodilatory capacity. This is often reversible through local (intracavernosal or transurethral) administration of potent vasodilators (prostaglandins, papaverine, and phentolamine) or by oral administration of penile-specific phosphodiesterase-5 inhibitors (sildenafil). Combined androgen deficiency with decreased libido and decreased penile responsiveness due to impaired NO synthesis activity may be common in elderly men. With the availability of effective penile vasodilatory medications to ensure erectile capacity, complaints of diminished libido may be effectively treated with androgen supplementation.

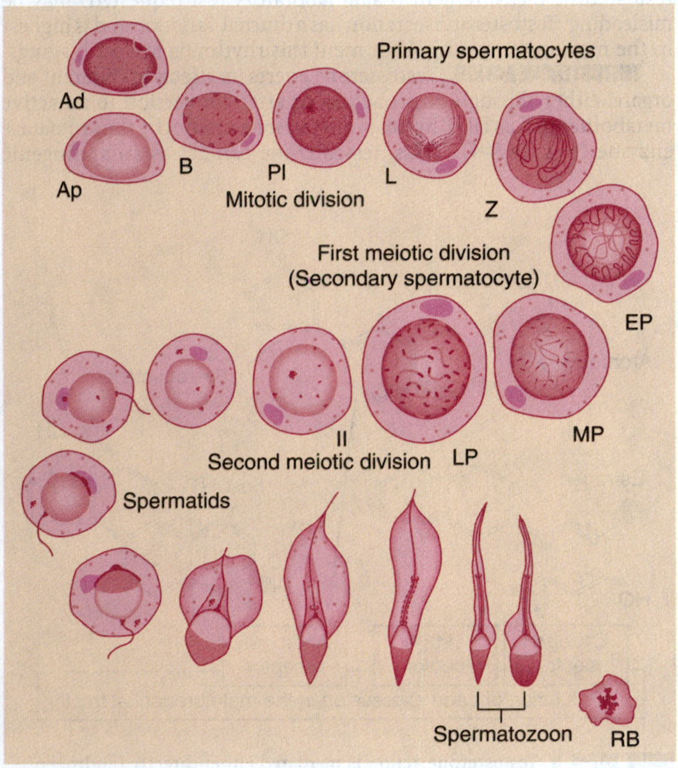

FIGURE 247–5 • Stages of human spermatogenesis. (From Hermo L, Clemont Y: How are germ cells produced and what factors control their production? In Robaine B, Pryor J, Trasler J [eds]: Handbook of Andrology. New York, American Society of Andrology, 1995, pp 13–15.)

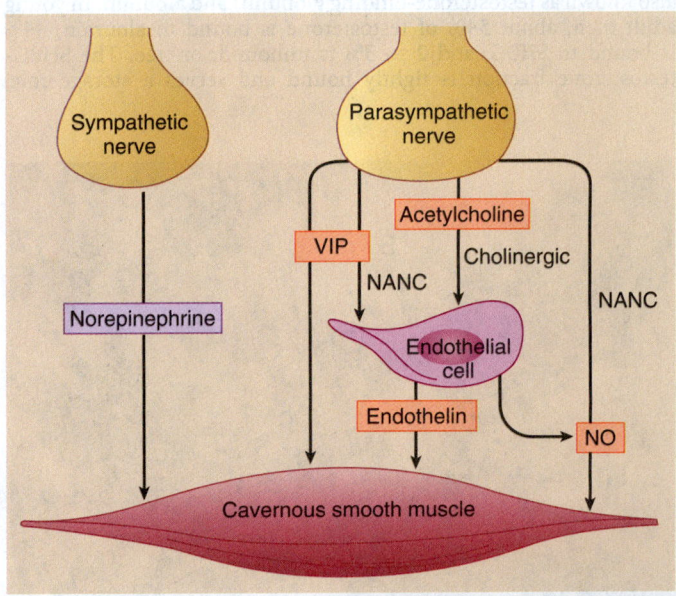

FIGURE 247–6 • The interaction among cholinergic, adrenergic, and nonadrenergic, noncholinergic (NANC) neuronal pathways and their contribution to penile smooth muscle contraction (patterned arrows) and dilation (open arrows). NO = nitric oxide; VIP = vasoactive intestinal polypeptide. (From Lue TF: Physiology of penile erection and pathophysiology of erectile dysfunction and priapism. In Walsh P, Retick A, Vaughn E, Wein A [eds]: Campbell's Urology, 7th ed. Philadelphia, WB Saunders, 1998, p 1164.)

REPRODUCTIVE AXIS DURING FETAL DEVELOPMENT, CHILDHOOD, AND PUBERTY

SEXUAL DIFFERENTIATION IN THE FETUS. Normal male sexual differentiation is complex and includes the establishment of genetic and phenotypic sex (Chapter 246).

ADRENARCHE AND PUBERTY. Adrenarche occurs at about 7 or 8 years of age when the zona reticularis of the adrenal gland undergoes maturation, leading to increased secretion of androgen precursors, such as androstenedione, dehydroepiandrosterone (DHEA), and DHEA sulfate (DHEA-S). Although the physiologic events initiating adrenarche are incompletely understood, the process is probably under the control of adrenocorticotropic hormone and independent of the control of LH and FSH. Adrenarche usually heralds subsequent activity in the hypothalamic-pituitary-gonadal axis. Androstenedione and DHEA are technically androgenic prehormones and do not bind to the androgen receptor. In part, the prepubertal growth spurt and the early development of pubic and axillary hair are mediated by conversion of these precursors to testosterone and DHT at the peripheral tissue sites.

Puberty occurs when a hypothalamic clock gets activated, resulting in increased GnRH and gonadotropin secretion. In the interval before the onset of puberty, LH and FSH are secreted in low amounts and are subject to feedback control by the small amounts of circulating testosterone from the testes. Initiation of puberty is determined by increase in the pulsatile pattern of hypothalamic GnRH secretion. This is marked by nocturnal bursts of LH secretion when puberty begins. As puberty progresses, feedback sensitivity of the hypothalamus and pituitary to circulating steroids lessens, and increasing concentrations of both gonadotropins and gonadal steroids ensue. The increasing concentrations of intratesticular testosterone and circulating FSH stimulate the Sertoli cell to produce factors leading to the maturation of spermatogenesis and inhibition of germ cell apoptosis. The phenotypic equivalents of the hormonal changes in puberty have been well documented. Pediatricians and endocrinologists routinely perform staging of the genital and pubic hair development (Table 247–1). The majority of the extratesticular end organ events of puberty are secondary to the increased circulating levels of testosterone and its metabolic products (DHT and estradiol). The penis and scrotum grow and become pigmented. As spermatogenesis advances, the testes increase in size from 1 to 2 mL at the outset of puberty to 15 to 35 mL in adulthood. There is a progressive increase in facial, axillary, chest, abdominal, thigh, and pubic hair; frontal scalp hair regresses, and the voice deepens (Fig. 247–7). Genital and sexual hair development requires conversion of testosterone to DHT for its full effects.

ABERRATIONS OF TIMING OF PUBERTY. Delayed puberty in boys is usually defined as a temporary (physiologic) form of hypothalamic hypogonadotropic hypogonadism in which sexual development has not begun by age 13.5 years. Usually these children have a height age (the age

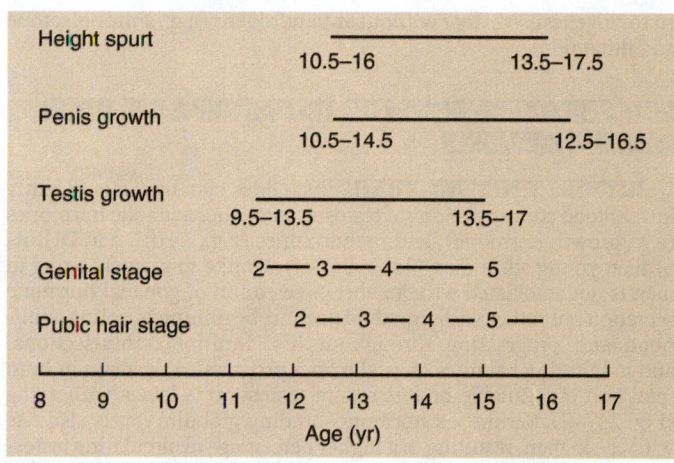

FIGURE 247–7 • Diagram of the timing of the various components of puberty. The range of ages in which each parameter begins and is completed is shown for each bar. These data are from European children obtained 30 years ago. There may be a slight trend for earlier onset of puberty over the past 30 years. (From Marshall WA, Tanner JM: Variations in the pattern of pubertal changes in boys. Arch Dis Child 1970;45:13–23.)

that is representative for 50% of normal children at the patient's height) that is delayed with respect to their chronologic age and is concordant with their bone age. Once initiated, puberty should be completed within 4.5 years. Although delayed sexual maturation is an inevitable component of prepubertal onset of hypogonadism or androgen resistance, the majority of boys with delayed development have a constitutional delayed physiologic clock and eventually attain full sexual adulthood. There is often a family history of a parent or sibling being a "late bloomer." Careful documentation of changing physical findings and measurement of serum LH, FSH, and testosterone may prove valuable clues of the beginning of puberty. Inquiring and testing for hyposmia or anosmia and other midline defects may indicate a common variant of congenital hypogonadotropic hypogonadism (Kallmann's syndrome). A family history of delay in puberty may encourage patience and observation. The decision of how early to treat depends on the perceived degree of psychological stress associated with the maturational delay. The major concern about treatment is early fusion of the epiphyses, which compromises optimal height. With proper dosing and monitoring of bone age, this is unusual, because bone age is usually retarded in delayed puberty. In adolescent boys with delayed puberty and low levels of gonadotropins, periodic withdrawal of treatment is used to determine whether spontaneous puberty has occurred. Many adult men diagnosed and treated for hypogonadotropic hypogonadism at ages 15 to 19 have proved to have normal reproductive function when taken off testosterone therapy many years later.

Precocious puberty in boys is defined as the onset of pubertal (genital and secondary sexual) development beginning before 9 years of age (2.5 SD above the mean age of progression to stage 2). Sexual precocity can be subcategorized to true (complete and incomplete) isosexual precocious puberty and pseudoprecocious puberty. The distinction is that true precocious puberty is associated with increases in GnRH-stimulated LH and FSH secretion (hypothalamic-pituitary origin), whereas pseudoprecocious puberty is independent of GnRH stimulation of LH and FSH secretion. True precocious puberty is often associated with CNS disease (two thirds of boys and <10% of girls), including hypothalamic tumors, cysts, inflammatory conditions, and seizure disorders. The diagnosis is based on the finding of sexual precocity, inappropriately elevated serum LH levels, and associated elevations of serum testosterone. CNS visualizations by magnetic resonance imaging can localize most lesions. Pseudoprecocious puberty is characterized by increased testosterone with suppressed β-LH levels. Diagnoses include human chorionic gonadotropin secretory tumors (i.e., testicular, hepatic, hypothalamic, and pineal tumors), congenital virilizing adrenal hyperplasia, testicular testosterone-secreting neoplasms, and constitutively active LH receptor mutations, resulting in uncontrolled testosterone (testitoxicosis) secretion. Treatment of true precocious puberty is removal of the CNS lesion if possible and treatment with GnRH analogues. Treatment of pseudoprecocious puberty depends on the cause but includes glucocorticoids for congenital virilizing adrenal hyperplasia and ketoconazole (suppresses

Table 247–1 • PUBERTAL STAGES IN BOYS

	PUBIC HAIR	GENITAL
STAGE 1	Absence of pubic hair.	Childlike penis, testes, and scrotum (testes 2 mL).
STAGE 2	Sparse, lightly pigmented hair mainly at the base of the penis.	Scrotum enlarged with early rugation and pigmentation. Testes begin to enlarge (3–5 mL).
STAGE 3	Hair becomes coarse, darker, and more curled and more extensive.	Penis has grown in length and diameter. Testes now 8–10 mL. Scrotum more rugated.
STAGE 4	Hair adult in quality but distribution does not include medial aspect of thighs.	Penis further enlarged with development of the glans. Scrotum and testes (10–13 mL) further enlarged.
STAGE 5	Hair is adult and extends to thighs.	Penis and scrotum fully adult. Testes 15 mL and greater.

Modified from Marshall WA, Tanner JM: Variation in pattern of pubertal changes in boys. Arch Dis Child 1970;45:13–23.

steroidogenesis) with or without antiandrogens (e.g., spironolactone and flutamide).

MALE SENESCENCE: DECREASED TESTOSTERONE AND OTHER ANABOLIC HORMONES

TESTOSTERONE DEFICIENCY IN THE ELDERLY. Older men have significantly lower blood concentrations of testosterone, other anabolic hormones (e.g., growth hormone), and prehormones (e.g., DHEA and DHEA-S) than young adult men (Table 247–2). Unlike in women, aging in men is not associated with an abrupt cessation of gonadal hormone secretion but rather with a gradual decline, beginning in young adulthood and progressing throughout life. Multiple cross-sectional and longitudinal studies have shown a progressive decrease in both total and bioavailable or free serum testosterone levels with aging (Fig. 247–8). Serum sex hormone–binding globulin levels also rise with age in men, resulting in a higher percentage of circulating testosterone tightly bound and less bioavailable. Recent data indicate that between 40% and 80% of men older than 70 years of age have blood levels of bioavailable or free testosterone below the normal range for young adults (Fig. 247–9).

The effects of low testosterone levels in aging men are similar to those observed in younger hypogonadal men. These include decreases in muscle mass, muscle strength, bone mass, libido, and erectile function and impaired mood and sense of well-being. Older men have increased body fat, particularly visceral fat. The effect of reduced androgen levels on cognition and memory are unknown, but it is possible that androgens may have similar positive effects on brain functions as estrogen does in older women. In recent years, a number of studies have demonstrated the beneficial effects of testosterone replacement in elderly men with relatively low serum testosterone levels. Testosterone replacement therapy (up to 3 years), in most studies, decreases fat mass, increases lean body mass, improves strength, and increases bone mineral density. Data on fracture rates with androgen replacement therapy of older men with low serum biologically active testosterone levels are not yet available. Because erectile dysfunction in the older man is multifactorial, with impaired vasodilatory function in the penis predominating in many cases (see section on sexual dysfunction), testosterone replacement therapy in older men may enhance libido but often does not improve erectile dysfunction. Improved sense of well-being and increased energy levels are also generally observed after treatment with testosterone.

Digital rectal examination should be performed and a prostate-specific antigen level obtained to ensure that there are no findings suggestive of severe benign prostatic hypertrophy or prostate cancer (nodules, irregularities).

ADRENAL DEFICIENCY OF ANDROGEN PRECURSORS IN OLDER MEN. In recent years, a marked decline in the circulating levels of adrenal androgens, especially DHEA and its sulfate DHEA-S, has been recognized in elderly men and women (see Fig. 247–9) (Chapter 246). Serum levels of DHEA and DHEA-S peak at about the third decade of life and then decline at about 2% per year, resulting in levels 10 to 20% of baseline by age 80. This decline in DHEA and DHEA-S is not accompanied by a decrease in adrenocorticotropic hormone. DHEA is a precursor to true androgens such as testosterone and DHT but does not bind to the androgen receptor itself. It is unclear whether DHEA binds to a unique nuclear receptor to initiate its action. Studies have been reported that DHEA administered to aging experimental animals

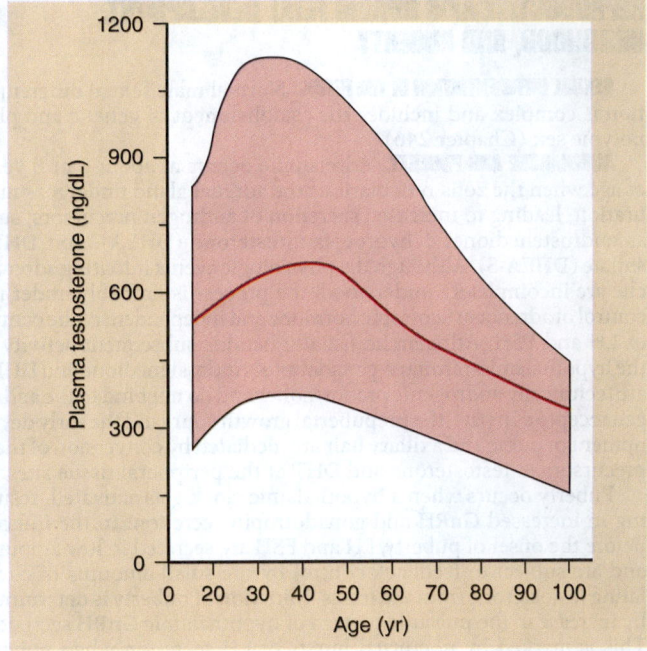

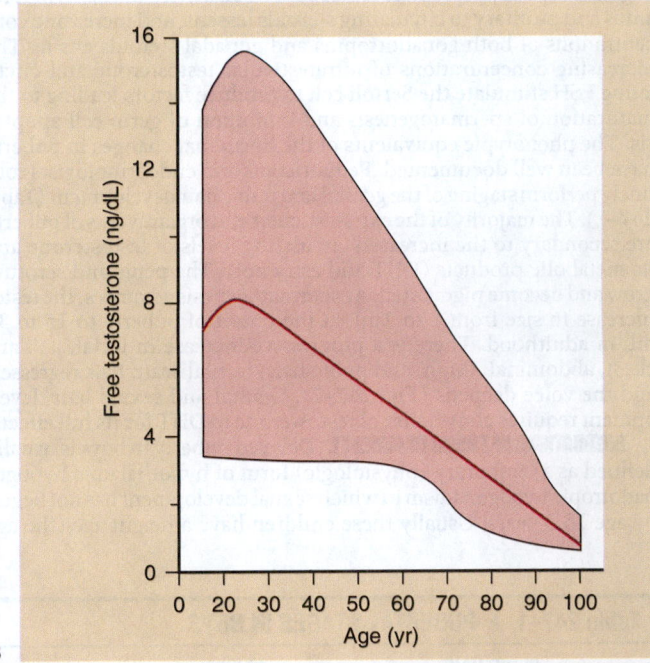

FIGURE 247–8 • Relationship between plasma testosterone (upper) and free testosterone (lower) levels and age in normal males. (From Baker HWG, Berger HG, DeKretser DM, et al: Changes in the pituitary-testicular system with age. Clin Endocrinol 1996;5:349–372.)

and humans may improve the sense of well-being, reduce anxiety and depression, enhance memory, prevent development of cancer, decrease body fat, decrease risk of cardiovascular disease, and provide other beneficial effects on immune function. Most studies in humans used oral doses of 1 to 5 mg/kg/day. An oral dose of 50 mg/day will increase testosterone and DHT to or above the normal physiologic range for women but not men. Much higher doses of DHEA can increase testosterone to male ranges but at the expense of very high serum DHEA concentrations. Recent studies showed that oral administration of 50 mg of DHEA to older men raised serum DHEA and DHEA-S concentrations to the levels found in young men but had no beneficial effects on quality of life, sexual function, mood, body composition, or exercise capacity. In the United States, DHEA is available without prescription as a health supplement and is widely used, creating a situation in which large-scale multicenter, prospective, placebo-controlled trials are difficult to perform. There is no substantial reason to administer DHEA to older men who may have low serum DHEA levels.

Table 247–2 • HORMONAL CHANGES ASSOCIATED WITH AGING

GnRH-LH/FSH/T	CRH-ACTH-DHEA(S)	GHRH-GH-IGH AXIS
↑ LH,* ↑ FSH	No change in ACTH	↓ GHRH message and receptor
↓ T (↓ Leydig cells)	↓ DHEA and DHEA-S	↓ GH secretory pulses
↓ Free T	↓ DHEA and DHEA-S	↓ Circulating GH
↑ SHBG	Response to ACTH	↓ Serum IGF-I

*↓ LH pulse amplitude and ↓ responsiveness to GnRH.
ACTH = adrenocorticotropic hormone; CRH = corticotropin-releasing hormone; DHEA = dehydroepiandrosterone; DHEA-S = DHEA sulfate; FSH = follicle-stimulating hormone; GH = growth hormone; GHRH = growth hormone–releasing hormone; GnRH = gonadotropin-releasing hormone; IGF-1 = insulin-like growth factor-1; LH = luteinizing hormone; SHBG = sex hormone–binding globulin; T = testosterone.

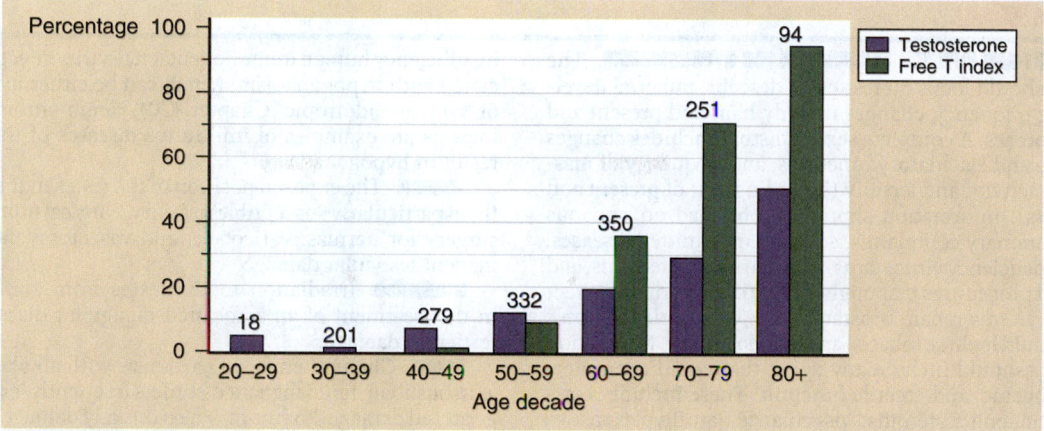

FIGURE 247–9 • Hypogonadism in aging men. Bar height indicates the percentage of men in each 10-year interval, from the third to the ninth decades, with at least one testosterone value in the hypogonadal range. The criteria used for these determinations are as follows: total testosterone less than 11.3 nmol/L (325 ng/dL) (shaded bars) or testosterone and sex hormone–binding globulin (free T index) less than 0.153 nmol/nmol (striped bars). The numbers above each pair of bars indicate the number of men studied in the corresponding decade. The fraction of men who are hypogonadal increases progressively after age 50 by either criterion. More men are hypogonadal by free T index than by total testosterone after the age of 50, and there seems to be a progressively greater difference, with increasing age, between the two criteria.

GROWTH HORMONE/INSULIN-LIKE GROWTH FACTOR-1 DEFICIENCY IN OLDER MEN.

Hypothalamic growth hormone–releasing hormone messenger RNA, pituitary growth hormone–releasing hormone receptor concentrations, pituitary secretion of growth hormone (GH), and serum insulin-like growth factor-1 levels decrease with aging (see Table 247–2). Part of the decline may be related to falling testosterone levels, because testosterone is known to enhance GH secretion. GH is an anabolic and lipolytic hormone, and many of its actions on peripheral tissues are mediated by insulin-like growth factor-1. GH deficiency in adults results in changes in body composition and mood (decreased muscle mass, increased body fat, decreased strength, and a decline in sense of well-being), which are very similar to the changes observed with aging. Studies show that although GH induced changes in body composition compared with placebo, the individual's muscle strength, exercise endurance, mood, and cognitive function remained unchanged. The side effects of GH treatment are dose related but include edema of lower extremities, diffuse arthralgias, hand stiffness, and tiredness.

MALE HYPOGONADISM

Definition

Hypogonadism refers to low circulating levels of testosterone. Most androgen-deficient men are infertile. Primary hypogonadism indicates that the abnormality originates in the testis; secondary hypogonadism indicates a defect at the hypothalamus or pituitary, resulting in decreased gonadotropins (LH and/or FSH) and secondary impairment of testicular function. Combined primary and secondary hypogonadism occurs in aging and in a number of systemic diseases, such as alcoholism, liver disease, and sickle cell disease. Decreased androgen action mimicking androgen deficiency may occur in patients with androgen receptor defects (androgen resistance), postreceptor signaling abnormalities, and inability to convert testosterone to the active metabolite DHT (5α-reductase abnormalities).

Etiology

Many of the causes of primary and secondary hypogonadism are listed in Tables 247–3 and 247–4 (see also Chapter 246).

Table 247–3 • **CAUSES OF PRIMARY TESTICULAR FAILURE AND END ORGAN RESISTANCE**

Congenital disorders
  Chromosomal disorders
  Klinefelter's and related syndromes (e.g., XXY, XXY/XY, XYY, XX males)
  Testosterone biosynthetic enzyme defects
  Myotonia dystrophy
Developmental disorders
  Prenatal diethylstilbestrol syndrome
  Cryptorchidism
Acquired defects
  Orchitis
  Mumps and other viruses
  Granulomatous (e.g., tuberculosis, leprosy)
  Human immunodeficiency virus
Infiltrative diseases (i.e., hemochromatosis, amyloidosis)
Surgical, traumatic injuries, and torsion of testis
Irradiation
Toxins (i.e., alcohol, fungicides, insecticides, heavy metals, cottonseed oil, DDT and other environmental estrogens)
Drugs
  Cytotoxic agents
  Inhibitors of testosterone synthesis and antiandrogens (e.g., ketoconazole, cimetidine, flutamide, cyproterone, spironolactone)
  Ethanol, opioids and other recreational drugs
Autoimmune testicular failure
  Isolated
  Associated with other organ-specific disorders (i.e., Addison's disease, Hashimoto's thyroiditis, insulin-dependent diabetes)
Systemic diseases (e.g., cirrhosis, chronic renal failure, sickle cell disease, acquired immunodeficiency syndrome, amyloidosis)
Androgen resistance syndromes
5α-Reductase deficiency

Table 247–4 • **CAUSES OF HYPOGONADOTROPIC HYPOGONADISM**

IDIOPATHIC OR CONGENITAL
Isolated deficiency of GnRH
  With anosmia (Kallmann's syndrome)
  With other abnormalities (Prader-Willi syndrome, Laurence-Moon-Biedl syndrome, basal encephalocele)
Partial deficiency of GnRH (fertile eunuch syndrome)
Multiple hypothalamic/pituitary hormone deficiency
Pituitary hypoplasia or aplasia

ACQUIRED
Trauma, postsurgery, postirradiation
Neoplastic
Pituitary adenomas (prolactinomas, other functional and nonfunctional tumors)
Craniopharyngiomas, germinomas, gliomas, leukemia, lymphomas
Pituitary infarction, carotid aneurysm
Infiltrative and infectious diseases of hypothalamus and pituitary (sarcoidosis, tuberculosis, coccidioidomycosis, histoplasmosis, syphilis, abscess, histiocytosis X, hemochromatosis)
Autoimmune hypophysitis
Malnutrition and systemic disease
Anorexia nervosa, starvation, renal failure, liver failure
Exogenous hormones and drugs
Antiandrogens, estrogens and antiestrogens, progestrogens, glucocorticoids, cimetidine, spironolactone, digoxin, drug-induced hyperprolactinemia (metoclopramide, tranquilizers, antihypertensives)

Endocrine Diseases

Clinical Manifestations

CLINICAL HISTORY AND PHYSICAL EXAMINATION FOR HYPOGONADISM. The medical history should focus on testicular descent, pubertal development, shaving frequency, changes in body hair, and present and past systemic illnesses. A complete sexual history includes changes in libido, erectile and ejaculatory functions, and frequency of masturbation, coital activity, and fertility (including that of present and previous partners). Information should be obtained on previous orchitis, sinopulmonary complaints, sexually transmitted diseases, human immunodeficiency virus status, genitourinary infections, and previous surgical procedures that might affect the reproductive tract (e.g., vasectomy, hernia repair, prostatectomy, varicocele ligation). Social history should include tobacco and alcohol intake. Medication and drug history should include any agent that could affect hormonal, spermatogenic, and erectile function. These include recreational drugs; anabolic steroids; psychiatric, antihypertensive, antiandrogenic, cytotoxic, and alternative medicine therapies; environmental toxins; and exposure to heat (including saunas and Jacuzzis) and radiation.

The general physical examination is supplemented by height and span measurements; assessment of muscle mass and adiposity; characterization of facial, pubic, and body hair distribution; presence of acne and facial wrinkling; breast examination for gynecomastia; examination of the scrotal contents; measurement of penile length and urethral integrity; digital rectal prostate examination; and visual field assessment. The scrotal examination should include assessment of midline fusion (e.g., bifid scrotum, hypospadias); measurement of testicular size (ruler will suffice but Prader or Takihara orchidometers are preferred) and consistency; presence of intratesticular masses; abnormalities of the epididymis; bilateral presence of vas deferens; and presence of varicoceles, hydroceles, or hernias. Normal testicular size ranges from 3.6 to 5.5 cm in length, 2.1 to 3.2 cm in width, and 15 to 35 mL in volume in white and black men. Asian men have slightly smaller mean testicular size. A decrease in testicular volume usually implies decreased spermatogenic cells because the seminiferous tubules account for more than 80% of testicular volume.

LABORATORY TESTS. Because a strong diurnal rhythm in testosterone secretion results in the highest serum levels in the morning hours and lowest levels in the evening, the measurement of testosterone, LH, and FSH is routinely determined from morning blood samples. Elevated LH and FSH levels distinguish primary from secondary hypogonadism (both have low serum testosterone levels). Serum prolactin levels should be measured in all cases of hypogonadotropic hypogonadism, pituitary mass lesions, and galactorrhea. DHT is measured in cases of abnormal differentiation of the genitalia and when DHT administration is suspected. Serum estradiol should be measured in cases of gynecomastia. Assessment of other testosterone precursors and products may be required in special circumstances, including suspected congenital enzyme defects. The semen analysis is the "cornerstone" of the laboratory examination for infertility.

HYPOGONADISM AND ANDROGEN RESISTANCE

Primary Testicular Hypogonadism

Primary hypogonadism refers to a condition of androgen deficiency with or without infertility in which the pathologic process lies at the testis level. A list of common causes is given in Table 247–3.

CONGENITAL DISORDERS (CHAPTER 246), ACQUIRED DEFECTS
Mumps, Orchitis, Leprosy, Human Immunodeficiency Virus Infection, and Hematochromatosis. After puberty, mumps is associated with clinical orchitis in 25% of cases, and 60% of those affected become infertile. During acute orchitis, the testes are inflamed, painful, and swollen. After the acute inflammatory phase, the testes gradually decrease in size, although swelling can persist for months. The testes may return to normal size and function or undergo atrophy. Spermatogenic changes occur more often and earlier than Leydig cell dysfunction. Thus, patients with postorchitic infertility may have normal testosterone and LH levels with increased serum FSH levels. With time, elevations in LH and lowered serum testosterone levels may appear. Leprosy may also cause orchitis, and gonadal

insufficiency human immunodeficiency virus infection is often associated with hypogonadism, which can be either hypogonadotropic or hypergonadotropic (Chapter 420). Hemo-chromatosis and amyloidosis are examples of infiltrative diseases of the testis that can result in hypogonadism.

Trauma. The exposed position of the testes in the scrotum makes them particularly susceptible to injury. Surgical injury during scrotal surgery for hernias, varicocele, and vasectomy can result in permanent testicular damage.

Irradiation. Irradiation to the testes from accidental exposure in the treatment of an associated malignant disease will produce testicular damage.

Drugs. Chemotherapy, in particular with alkylating agents such as in busulfan, for malignant disorders frequently leads to irreversible germ cell damage. Toxins may also directly damage the testes. Many agents such as fungicides and insecticides (e.g., DBCP, metabolites of DDT), heavy metals (lead, cadmium), and cottonseed oil (gossypol) produce damage to the germ cells. Leydig cells are relatively less susceptible to most chemotherapeutic drugs than Sertoli and germ cells. Serum testosterone levels are usually normal despite infertility in the exposed men.

Some medications may interfere with testosterone biosynthesis (e.g., ketoconazole, spironolactone) or action (cyproterone, flutamide). Ethanol, independent of its effect in causing liver disease, will inhibit testosterone biosynthesis. Marijuana, heroin, methadone, medroxyprogesterone acetate, other progestins, and estrogens all lower testosterone, but mainly by decreasing the pituitary secretion of LH. Medical treatment or illicit use (e.g., in athletes, body builders) with androgens such as testosterone, dihydrotestosterone, and synthetic anabolic steroids will lower serum LH and FSH and lower sperm counts in the absence of clinical signs and symptoms of androgen deficiency. Serum testosterone levels will be normal to elevated after testosterone treatment but will be low after use of DHT and synthetic anabolic agents.

Autoimmune Testicular Failure. Antibodies against microsomal fraction of the Leydig cells may occur either as an isolated disorder or as part of a multiglandular disorder involving, to variable degrees, the thyroid, pituitary, adrenals, pancreas, and other organs.

Testicular Defects Associated with Systemic Diseases. Abnormalities of the hypothalamic-pituitary-testicular axis occur in a number of systemic diseases. These include liver failure, renal failure, severe malnutrition, sickle cell anemia, advanced malignancies, cystic fibrosis, and amyloidosis. About one half of men undergoing chronic hemodialysis for renal failure experience decreased libido, infertility, and impotence. The effects of cirrhosis of the liver on testicular function are complex and may be either independent or associated with direct toxic effects of continued use of alcohol. Gynecomastia, testicular atrophy, and impotence are concomitant signs of cirrhosis. Decreased spermatogenesis with peritubular fibrosis occurs in at least 50% of patients. In contrast to the decrease in serum testosterone levels, estradiol levels are usually elevated. This results in an increased ratio of serum estradiol to testosterone with an increased proclivity for gynecomastia. Patients with sickle cell anemia often have impaired testicular function. Boys with sickle cell anemia may have impaired sexual maturation, and men are often infertile. The defect in sickle cell anemia seems to be ischemic in origin, probably with accelerated apoptosis; it may occur either at the testicular or at the hypothalamic-pituitary level.

Secondary Gonadal Insufficiency (Hypogonadotropic Hypogonadism)

Hypogonadotropic hypogonadism represents a deficiency in the secretion of gonadotropins (LH and FSH) due to an intrinsic or functional abnormality in the hypothalamus or pituitary glands (see earlier and Chapter 246). Such disorders result in the secondary Leydig cell dysfunction (see Table 247–4). The clinical manifestations depend on the age of the patient at the onset of the disorder.

ACQUIRED HYPOGONADOTROPIC DISORDERS, FUNCTIONAL DISORDERS. Anorexia nervosa and weight loss are examples of functional defects resulting in low serum testosterone levels. Anorexia nervosa, predominantly a disorder of adolescent girls, is characterized by excessive weight loss as a result of dietary restriction and/or bulimia.

Occasionally, anorexia nervosa is seen in men, but in such an instance it usually implies a variant of a more severe psychiatric disorder. Men and women present with manifestations of hypo-gonadotropic hypogonadism. Starvation from other than a psychological basis may also reduce gonadotropic secretion, although women seem more susceptible to this disorder. Although strenuous exercise commonly produces reproductive dysfunction in female athletes (e.g., long-distance runners and dancers), it has minimal effects on testicular function in men. Severe stress and systemic illness also lower gonadotropin and testosterone levels. Organic hypothalamic-pituitary disorders include neoplastic, granulomatous, infiltrative, and post-traumatic lesions in the region of the hypothalamus and pituitary.

Prolactinomas present differently in men and women (Chapter 237). Unlike in women, in whom small tumors can be detected early because of symptoms of amenorrhea and galactorrhea, in men the tumors are usually large (>1 cm in diameter [macroadenomas]) by the time they are detected. It is unclear whether the large size of the adenoma at the time of presentation in men is due to the late diagnosis, caused by failure of patients and physicians to appreciate early signs, or to more rapid growth of these tumors in men. Male patients with prolactin-secreting macroadenomas usually present with hypogonadism, erectile dysfunction, and visual manifestations from suprasellar extension. Hypogonadism in microprolactinomas is usually the result of prolactin suppression of GnRH secretion. In macroadenomas, the suppression of gonadotropins and hypogonadotropic hypogonadism may be due to the GnRH suppressive effects described earlier or due to mass effect damaging the non-neoplastic gonadotrophs.

Large non–prolactin-secreting pituitary tumors (GH, adrenocorticotropic hormone, glycopeptide, and null cell) may also produce gonadotropin insufficiency from damage of the adjacent normal pituitary gland (Chapter 237), resulting in decreased serum LH and testosterone levels.

ANDROGEN RESISTANCE (ANDROGEN-SENSITIVE END ORGAN DEFICIENCY). Certain conditions have clinical phenotypes mimicking testosterone deficiency in the absence of lowered testosterone levels. These are either drug induced (antiandrogens) or congenital defects in the androgen receptor, postreceptor defects, or 5α-reductase deficiency (Chapter 246).

Rx Treatment of Androgen Deficiency

INDICATIONS. The main medical indication for androgen replacement therapy is male hypogonadism (Table 247–5). The diagnosis is based on clinical symptoms and signs and a reduced serum testosterone level. The most available and commonly used blood measurement of testosterone is serum total testosterone. The normal range of a young adult male population varies for different laboratories but should be in the general range of 300 to 1000 ng/dL (10 to 38 nmol/L). Total testosterone measurements may be misleading indicators of Leydig cell status in conditions in which SHBG levels are abnormal (see earlier section). Under these circumstances, a measurement of free testosterone (by dialysis method), bioavailable testosterone (free + albumin bound), or calculated free testosterone (utilizing total testosterone and SHBG measurements) is useful to characterize circulating bioactive testosterone levels.

The following rules apply to most young and middle-aged men suspected of hypogonadism. If a morning serum total testosterone level is repeatedly less than 250 ng/dL (8.5 nmol/L), the patient is most probably hypogonadal, and testosterone replacement is indicated. If the serum testosterone level is between 250 and 300 ng/dL with normal serum LH levels, the patient may not be hypogonadal, and androgen replacement may not improve the symptoms (e.g., sexual dysfunction). Thus, when serum total testosterone is borderline and LH is not increased, measurement of one of the bioactive testosterone level levels is indicated. The guidelines for men over the age of 60 years are less certain; since SHBG levels are increased in this age group, total testosterone levels may overestimate the biologically active forms of circulating testosterone. In men older than 60 years with signs and/or symptoms of androgen deficiency, a serum total testosterone level greater than 400 ng/dL argues strongly against hypogonadism; a serum level less than 200 ng/dL is almost always a clinically significant level, and total testosterone concentrations between 200 and 400 ng/dL deserve further testing with one of the tests of bioactive testosterone.

CONTRAINDICATIONS TO TESTOSTERONE THERAPY. Absolute contraindications for androgen replacement therapy include carcinoma of the prostate and the male breast. These cancers are androgen dependent for growth and proliferation. Androgens should be used with caution in older men with enlarged prostates and urinary symptoms, elevated hematocrit, and sleep-related breathing disorders.

ANDROGEN PREPARATIONS. Testosterone esters such as testosterone enanthate (or cypionate) are the most widely used preparations in the United States and throughout the world (Table 247–6). The recommended dose is 150 to 200 mg administered intramuscularly once every 2 to 3 weeks.

Modified 17α-alkylated androgens, which are available in oral preparations, are not recommended as androgen replacement. These agents may lead to abnormalities in liver function tests and marked decreases in high-density lipoprotein cholesterol and increases in total cholesterol levels compared with the testosterone esters. Orally active testosterone undecanoate is not available in the United States but is used in Canada, Europe, and other places in the world. This ester is absorbed into the lymphatics and has variable bioavailability.

Implants are pellets of crystalline testosterone. The serum testosterone levels are maintained in the physiologic range for 4 to 6 months. Implants are not popular in the United States but are widely used in Australia and the United Kingdom.

Transdermal skin patches are a relatively recent development in androgen treatment. Skin patches and hydroalcoholic gels are available and are widely used. The nonscrotal patches deliver 5 mg of testosterone per day, which is the physiologic production rate. Some patches use alcohol-based absorption enhancement systems that decrease the patch size. These patches deliver levels of testosterone within the normal range but have a high incidence of skin irritability (redness, swelling, and blisters). Other patches are large and less prone to skin irritation but have a tendency to fall off with activity. Hydroalcoholic testosterone gels have been developed for transdermal application. They give reasonably constant serum concentrations and cause little skin irritation.

BENEFITS VERSUS RISKS OF ANDROGEN THERAPY. Table 247–7 shows the benefits and potential side effects of androgen treatment. In hypogonadal men, androgen replacement leads to the development and maintenance of secondary sexual characteristics. Testosterone has important anabolic effects on muscle and bone and improves libido and sexual dysfunction. It has less effect on erectile dysfunction (see later section on sexual dysfunction).

MALE INFERTILITY

Definition

Infertility is defined as the failure of a couple to achieve a pregnancy after at least 1 year of frequent unprotected intercourse. If a pregnancy has not occurred after 3 years, infertility most likely will persist without medical treatment.

Prevalence and Incidence

Studies in the United States and Europe showed a 1-year prevalence of infertility in 15% of couples. The prevalence in developing countries is likely to be higher because of the higher prevalence of genital tract infection. As shown in multicenter studies, 30 to 35% of subfertility can be attributed to predominantly female factors, 25 to 30% to male factors, and 25 to 30% to

Endocrine Diseases

Table 247-5 • INDICATIONS FOR ANDROGEN THERAPY

Androgen deficiency (hypogonadism)
Microphallus (neonatal)
Delayed puberty in boys
Elderly men with low total or bioavailable or free testosterone levels
Angioneurotic edema
Other possible uses or under investigation:
   Hormonal male contraception
   Wasting disease associated with cancer/human immunodeficiency
     virus/chronic infection
   Postmenopausal female

Table 247-6 • ANDROGEN PREPARATIONS

ROUTE	PREPARATION	DOSE AND FREQUENCY OF ADMINISTRATION
Oral*	Testosterone undecanoate (not available in United States; available in Canada, Mexico, Europe, Asia)	40 to 80 mg orally two to three times per day
Injectable	Testosterone enanthate and cypionate	100 mg intramuscularly per week or 150–200 mg intramuscularly per 2–3 weeks
Implants	Testosterone implants	200-mg pellets, three inserted once every 4 to 6 months
Transdermal	Scrotal patch	One patch delivering 4 or 6 mg testosterone per day
	Nonscrotal patch, Androderm	Two patches delivering 2.5 mg testosterone each per day or one patch delivering 5 mg testosterone per day
	Testoderm TTS	One patch delivering 5 mg testosterone per day

*Oral modified 17α-alkylated androgens such as methyltestosterone, fluoxymesterone, oxymetholone, stanozolol, and oxandrolone are not recommended for use in treatment of androgen deficiency states because of potential hepatotoxicity and adverse effects on serum lipids.

Table 247-7 • ANDROGEN THERAPY: RISKS VERSUS BENEFITS

BENEFITS	RISKS
Development or maintenance of secondary sex characteristics	Fluid retention
Improves libido and sexual function	Gynecomastia
Increases muscle mass and strength	Acne/oily skin
Increases bone mineral density	Increases hematocrit
Decreases body and visceral fat	Decreases high-density lipoprotein cholesterol (cardiovascular risk?)
Improves mood	Sleep apnea
Effect on cognition (?)	Prostate diseases
Effect on quality of life (?)	Benign prostate hyperplasia
	Carcinoma of prostate
	Aggressive behavior (?)

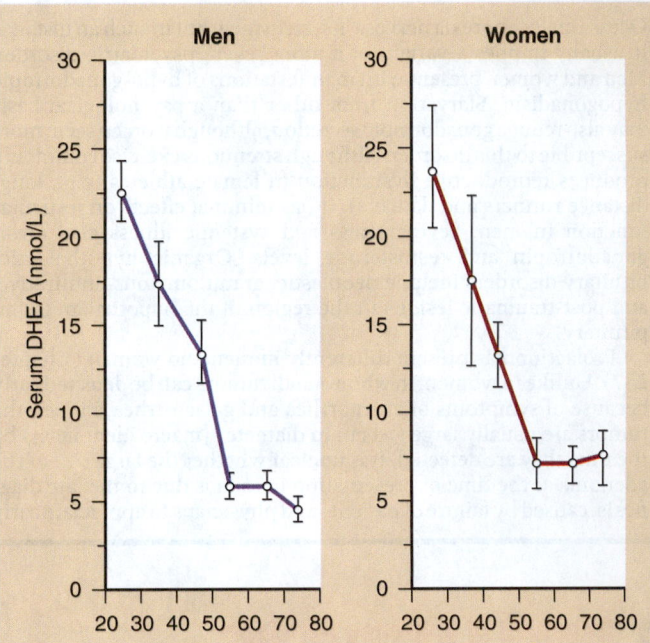

FIGURE 247-10 • Declining serum dehydroepiandrosterone (DHEA) with aging. Serum DHEA sulfate levels (not shown) parallel the decrease in DHEA. (Adapted from Labrie F, et al: Marked decline in serum concentrations of adrenal C19 sex steroid precursors and conjugated androgen metabolites during aging. J Clin Endocrinol Metab 1997;82:2396–2402. © The Endocrine Society.)

Table 247-8 • MALE INFERTILITY: BASIC LABORATORY TESTS

SEMEN ANALYSES	HORMONE ANALYSES (IN PATIENTS WITH ABNORMAL SEMEN ANALYSES)
Volume, pH	Serum/luteinizing hormone/follicle-stimulating hormone
Microscopy: agglutination, debris	Serum testosterone
Sperm: concentration, motility, morphology, vitality	If luteinizing hormone and testosterone low, serum prolactin
Leukocytes	
Immature germ cells	
Sperm autoantibodies (sperm/semen biochemistry, sperm function tests)	

Diagnosis

The approach to the diagnosis of an infertile couple includes management of the male and the female partner (Figs. 247–10 and 247–11). Examination of the ejaculate is the cornerstone for the investigation of an infertile man (Table 247–8). Semen samples are collected when possible at the physician's office or at home, preferably after 2 to 7 days' abstinence from sexual intercourse.

The generally accepted reference values for a semen analysis are given in Table 247–9. A normal sperm concentration is greater than 20 million/mL; however, men with lower sperm counts can be fertile. More than 50% of the spermatozoa should be motile and more than 25% should demonstrate a rapidly progressive motility pattern.

Numerous studies have demonstrated that considerable overlap is observed in the semen quality of fertile and subfertile men, and no definite threshold is defined below which a man would be infertile except when azoospermia is present.

In patients with abnormal semen analyses, measurements of serum FSH, LH, and testosterone are indicated (see Fig. 247–10). Elevated FSH levels usually indicate severe germinal epithelium damage and may be associated with guarded prognosis. A decreased serum inhibin β level also reflects poor Sertoli cell dysfunction and may be a marker

problems in both partners; in the remaining cases, no cause can be identified.

Etiology

Hypothalamic-pituitary disorders are infrequent causes of male infertility and are discussed in the section on hypogonadism and androgen deficiency. Primarily, testicular disorders are the most frequent identifiable cause of infertility (see Table 247–3).

Endocrine Diseases

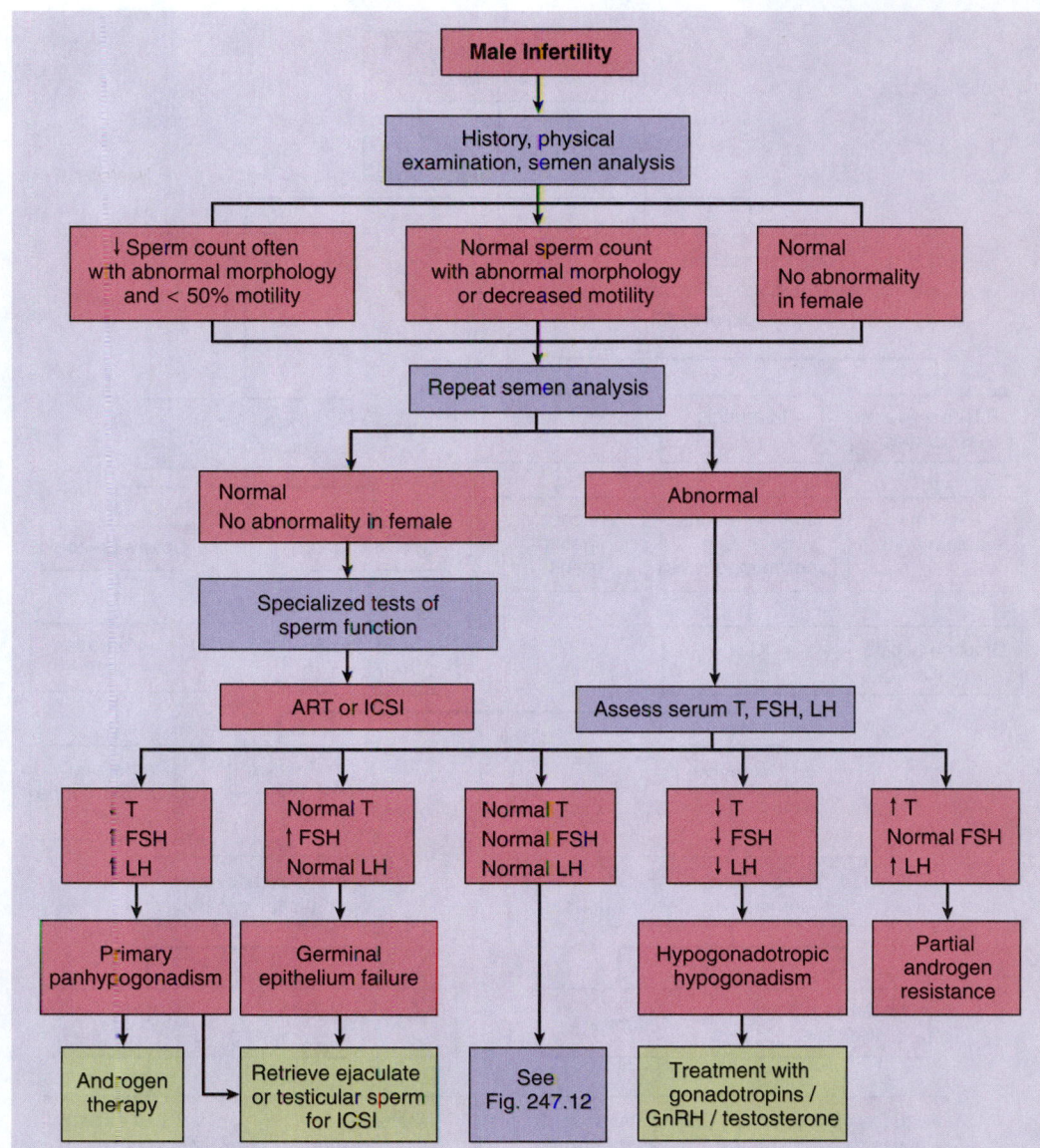

FIGURE 247–11 • Algorithmic approach to the diagnosis and treatment of male infertility. ART = assisted reproductive technology; FSH = follicle-stimulating hormone; GnRH = gonadotropin-releasing hormone; ICSI = intracytoplasmic sperm injection; LH = serum luteinizing hormone; T = serum testosterone.

Table 247–9 • SEMEN ANALYSIS: REFERENCE RANGE

PARAMETER	REFERENCE RANGE
Semen volume	>2 mL
Sperm	
Concentration	>20 million/mL
Total count	>40 million/ejaculate
Motility	>50% motile
	>25% rapid progressively motile
Morphology	>15% normal*
Vitality (live)	>75%
Leukocytes	<1 million/mL

*This value is based on using the strict criteria for assessment of sperm morphology in studies using in vitro fertilization as an endpoint.

From World Health Organization Laboratory Manual for Examination of Human Semen and Sperm Cervical Mucus Interaction, 4th ed. Cambridge, Cambridge University Press, 1999.

of spermatogenic dysfunction. Elevated serum LH and FSH together with a low serum testosterone level indicate pantesticular failure. Low serum FSH, LH, and testosterone suggest hypothalamic pituitary dysfunction; a serum prolactin level should be measured and additional appropriate investigations (as discussed in the section on secondary hypogonadism) may be required. The presence of low sperm concentration and suppressed LH level with increased, normal, or low serum testosterone level (without clinical manifestations of androgen deficiency) may suggest exogenous androgen therapy. The

hormonal pattern in androgen insensitivity (an uncommon cause of male infertility) is elevated LH, normal FSH, and high normal to increased serum testosterone levels.

Rx Treatment

An algorithmic approach to the treatment of male infertility is illustrated in Figures 247–11 and 247–12. The principles of management of male factor infertility can be summarized as follows: (1) Men with mild to moderate oligozoospermia with or without decreased sperm motility and some impairment of motility are subfertile rather than infertile. Spontaneous pregnancies occur in this group. (2) Reliable medical treatment is limited to the 1 to 2% of infertile men with gonadotropin insufficiency. (3) Assisted reproductive technologies including in vitro fertilization and intracytoplasmic sperm injection have dramatically improved the pregnancy rates in partners of men with severe oligozoospermia, very poor morphology, and poor to absent motility. (4) Azoospermia (absence of sperm with the ejaculate) may occur in men with obstruction of the ejaculatory system. In these patients, in vitro fertilization and intracytoplasmic sperm injection after either percutaneous epididymal sperm extraction or microsurgical epididymal sperm extraction give comparable and highly successful results. (5) Azoospermia due to impaired spermatogenesis may not be a futile state, as sperm may be present within the testes. These sperm can be extracted by testicular sperm extraction and intracytoplasmic sperm injection performed with good success.

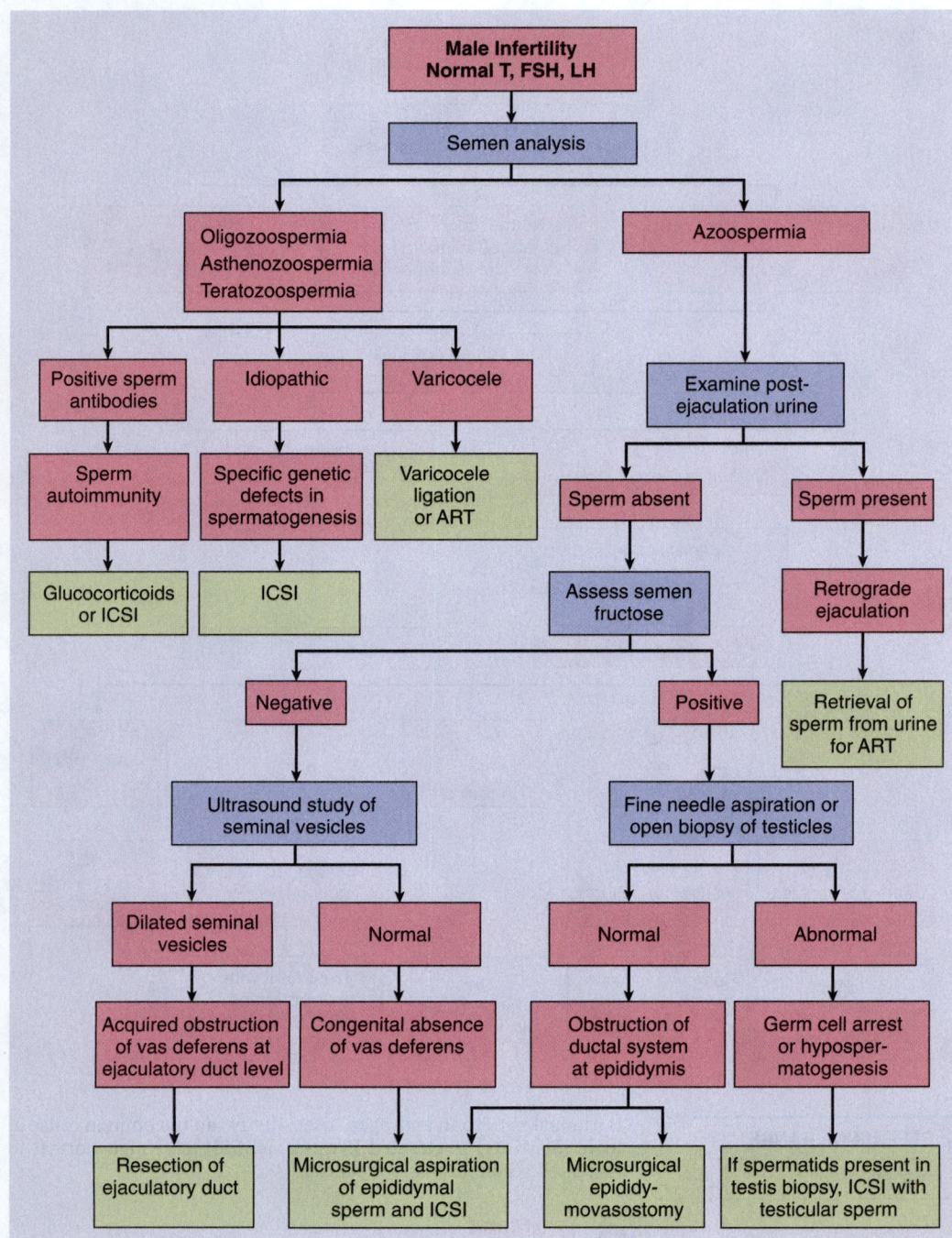

FIGURE 247–12 • Algorithmic approach to the diagnosis and treatment of male infertility in patients with normal serum hormone concentrations. ART = assisted reproductive technology; FSH = follicle-stimulating hormone; ICSI = intracytoplasmic sperm injection; LH = serum luteinizing hormone; T = serum testosterone.

SEXUAL DYSFUNCTION

Sexual dysfunction can be divided into four main categories: (1) loss of desire (libido), (2) erectile dysfunction, (3) ejaculatory insufficiency, and (4) anorgasmic states.

DECREASED LIBIDO

Loss of libido refers to reduction in sexual interest, initiative, and frequency and intensity of responses to internal or external erotic stimuli. Causal factors include psychogenic factors, CNS disease, androgen deficiency and resistance, and side effects from medications (e.g., antihypertensives, psychotropics, alcohol, narcotics, dopamine blockers, antiandrogens). Treatment is directed toward the causal mechanism.

EJACULATORY FAILURE AND IMPAIRED ORGASM

Ejaculatory insufficiency refers to absent or reduced seminal emission and/or impaired ejaculatory contraction. It is usually associated with neurologic conditions and medication therapy. Anorgasmic state is a distressing but relatively uncommon condition in men when the normal process of erection and ejaculation occurs in the absence of the subjective sensation of pleasure initiated at the time of emission and ejaculation. Premature ejaculation is the most common form of male sexual dysfunction. Estimates of prevalence vary, but 25 to 30% seems a reasonable estimate. The Diagnostic and Statistical Manual of Mental Disorders VI defines the diagnostic criteria for premature ejaculation as follows: persistent or recurrent ejaculation with minimal sexual stimulation that (1) occurs before, upon, or shortly after penetration and before the person wishes; (2) is associated with marked distress or interpersonal difficulty; and (3) is not a direct effect of substance abuse such as opiate withdrawal.

ERECTILE DYSFUNCTION

Definition

Erectile dysfunction can be defined as the inability of a man to obtain rigidity sufficient to permit coitus of adequate duration to satisfy himself and his partner.

Prevalence

Current estimates suggest that 10 to 15% of all American men suffer from erectile dysfunction, with the incidence progressively increased as men get older. Data from the Massachusetts Aging Study report that 52% of men 40 to 70 years of age experience some degree of erectile dysfunction.

Etiology

The causes of erectile dysfunction are many but can be generally categorized in the following areas: psychological, endocrine, systemic illness, neurologic, iatrogenic, drug related, and aging.

 ## Treatment

ORAL MEDICATIONS. Oral sildenafil is a widely used and very effective drug for this disorder. Sildenafil is a competitive and selective inhibitor of cyclic GMP phosphodiesterase-5 (the primary phosphodiesterase in cavernosal tissue). Inhibition of phosphodiesterase-5 causes persistence of normally (sexually) stimulated GMP in the corpora cavernosa, resulting in protracted cavernosal tumescence and rigidity. Early reports indicate that sildenafil is effective in 60 to 80% of treated men. Patients with diabetes mellitus, spinal cord injuries, prostatic surgery, and pelvic irradiation also benefit but with a somewhat lower response rate. The usual starting dose of sildenafil is 50 mg, increasing in 25-mg increments up to 100 mg when required. The most serious side effect is cardiovascular collapse, particularly in patients taking long-acting nitrate or nitroglycerin preparations. Because of its mechanism of action, sildenafil is used on demand, with administration 20 to 60 minutes before intercourse. Two additional phosphodiesterase-5 inhibitors (vardenafil and tadalafil) have been approved for treatment of erectile dysfunction. Vardenafil has a relatively faster onset of action (4 to 6 hours) while tadalafil has a much longer action (17.5 hours). Apomorphine is a selective dopamine receptor agonist that stimulates the CNS, generating an arousal response that includes a penile erection. Apomorphine has not been approved by the Food and Drug Administration. Yohimbine is an indolalquinolonic alkaloid with central-acting effects, including α_2-adrenergic blockade and cholinergic and dopaminergic stimulation. Despite its widespread use, placebo-controlled studies have shown variable degrees of success and yohimbine seems most useful in conditions in which there is a mechanism of organic disease. Trazodone possesses both serotonin and α_2-adrenergic antagonistic properties. It appears to be moderately effective in approximately one third of patients, with the main side effect being sedation.

The intraurethral prostaglandin E_1 suppository alprostadil is believed to work locally on the corpora cavernosa as a vasodilatory agent. The suppository is apparently successful in improving erectile function in one third to two thirds of cases.

INTRACAVERNOSAL INJECTIONS OF VASODILATING DRUGS. Until the recent availability of oral sildenafil, intracavernosa injection with prostaglandin E_1 and other vasodilators (papaverine, phentolamine) was the mainstay of pharmacologic therapy for erectile dysfunction. The medications are injected using a 27- to 30-gauge needle.

SUGGESTED READINGS

Bacon CG, Mittleman MA, Kawachi I, et al: Sexual function in men older than 50 years of age: Results from the health professionals follow-up study. Ann Intern Med 2003;139:161–168. *The prevalence of erectile dysfunction was 33% (age standardized) in the prior three months; physical activity and leanness were protective.*

Harman SM, Metter EJ, Tobin JD, et al: Longitudinal effects of aging on serum total and free testosterone levels in healthy men. J Clin Endocrinol Metab 2001;86:724–731. *Largest longitudinal evaluation of the effects of normal aging on circulating gonadal hormone levels.*

Kandeel FR, Koussa VKT, Swerdloff RS: Male sexual function and its disorders: Physiology, pathophysiology, clinical investigation and treatment. Endocrine Rev 2001;22:342–388. *Comprehensive review of pathogenesis, evaluation, and management of sexual dysfunction.*

Khorram O, Patrizio P, Wang C, Swerdloff R: Reproductive technologies for male infertility. J Clin Endocrinol Metab 2001;86:2373–2379. *Updated review of the important role of advanced reproductive technologies such as in vitro fertilization, intracytoplasmic sperm injection, and epididymal and testicular sperm extraction on the management of couples with male factor infertility.*

Salonia A, Rigatti P, Montorsi F: Sildenafil in erectile dysfunction: A critical review. Curr Med Res Opin 2003;19:241–262. *A practical review of the data.*

Wang C, Swerdloff RS: Androgen replacement therapy. Ann Med 1997;29:365–370. *Discussion of risks and benefits of androgen treatment with information on available androgen preparations.*

Wu FCW, von Eckardstein A: Androgens and coronary artery disease. Endocrine Rev 2003;24:187–217. *There seems to be no major effect of androgens on coronary disease.*

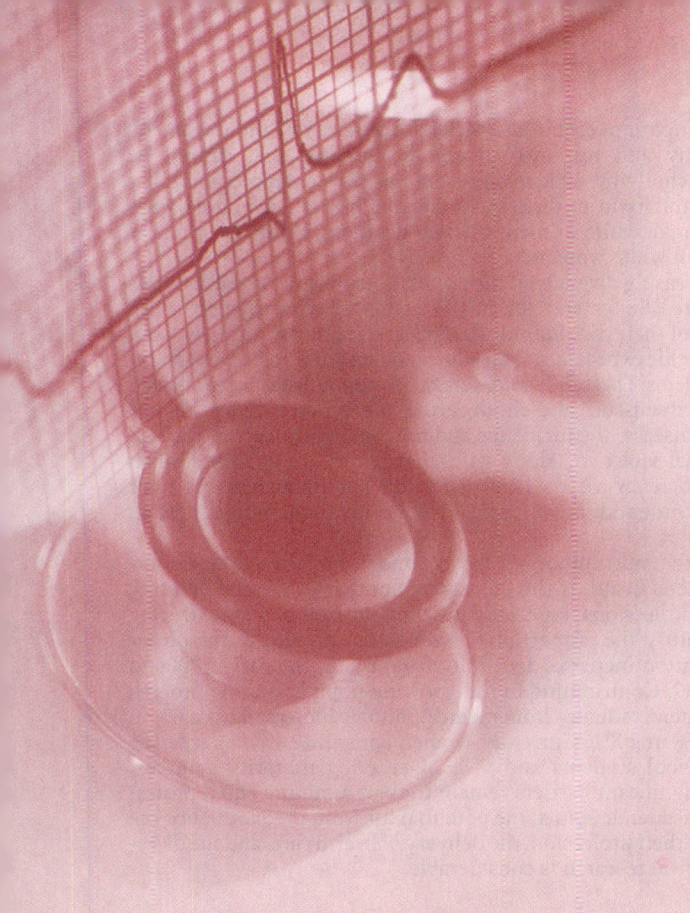

part XIX

Women's Health

248 APPROACH TO WOMEN'S HEALTH

Janet B. Henrich

Over the past decade, women's health has emerged as a rapidly expanding field of scientific inquiry and knowledge with important implications for clinical practice and for the education and training of physicians. Women's health can be viewed broadly as the study of the effect of sex and gender on health and disease that occurs across the spectrum of the biologic, behavioral, and social sciences. Increasing scientific information about the influence of sex and gender differences on health and disease has expanded our concept of women's health beyond the traditional focus on reproductive organs and their function. This broader interdisciplinary perspective of women's health has created a new area of knowledge and scholarship that is distinct from or more detailed than the knowledge base of existing disciplines. It has provided a new model to study the interactions between biologic mechanisms and psychosocial and environmental factors and their influence on human growth and development and response to health challenges. The clinical application of this information to women across all age groups highlights the interdisciplinary nature of this field.

Basic Principles Underlying Women's Health

The importance of the effect of sex and gender differences on health and disease is outlined in a recent Institute of Medicine Report, "Exploring the Biological Contributions to Human Health: Does Sex Matter?" Complex interactions exist among sex hormones, normal and abnormal physiology, and the physical and emotional well-being of women. As early as the embryonic period, there are structural differences between female and male brains. Many of these differences are programmed during fetal life by hormones. During the reproductive years, the influence of sex hormones on sexual development and reproductive function differentiates a category of health issues that are unique to women. As women age and sex hormones decrease during the menopause, women's risk factors for disease change dramatically and become more similar to men's. Although women develop the diseases that affect men, biologic mechanisms and psychosocial factors influence the course of disease differently in women.

Until recently, most of the information used to make clinical decisions in women was based on studies conducted primarily in men. Women were excluded from research on diseases that are important to both sexes because of misconceptions about women's health, legal and ethical issues, and cultural biases. Because women, on average, live longer than men and are affected by major diseases at a later age, it was often perceived incorrectly that women were healthier than men. In fact, throughout life women experience poorer health than men, especially in the advanced years. The lack of information concerning women had important implications. Information based primarily on studies done in men was often applied inappropriately to women or resulted in different standards of care. To rectify this gap in knowledge, the National Institutes of Health (NIH) implemented a policy in 1994 that requires the inclusion of women and minorities in all human research studies funded by the NIH. Substantial progress has been made in this area. Recent efforts have focused on ensuring that adequate numbers of women are included, and that findings related to sex and gender differences are reported.

Efforts to increase our knowledge about women's health issues require an integrated approach that acknowledges the diversity among women and considers the social factors that influence their lives. One of the important social trends over the past 50 years is the increasing participation of women in the work force. Since World War II, the number of women who work has more than doubled. Currently, it is estimated that 65% of women ages 16 to 64 years work during any week, and close to 45% work full time throughout the year. The full effects of multiple roles, work stress, and new environmental exposures on women's health and reproductive status are largely unknown but are certain to have important health and social ramifications. Paralleling the growing numbers of women in the work force is the increasing number of single-parent families headed by women, especially minority women. Many of these families live in poverty. Increasing evidence indicates that socioeconomic factors are major indicators of health and that, for some health outcomes, poverty and lack of education are more important determinants of health than ethnicity.

However, important ethnic and racial differences remain in women's susceptibility and response to certain diseases that cannot be explained wholly by socioeconomic status. For example, mortality rates for coronary heart disease, stroke, and breast cancer are higher in black than in white women, whereas death rates from lung cancer are higher in white women.

The increasing diversity of the population will affect health trends in the United States and the health status of women specifically. Regardless of their racial/ethnic designation, minority group women have a lower life expectancy than white women and experience greater health problems. These differences are most pronounced in areas related to reproductive issues and childbearing, the occurrence and course of chronic disease, the incidence and outcome of cancer, and acts of interpersonal violence. Along with changes in our society, human immunodeficiency virus (HIV) infection and homelessness have recently become additional special health concerns of minority group women.

One of the most important factors underlying the current interest in women's health is the increasing number of women entering the health professions, especially the discipline of medicine. During the last century, the proportion of women represented in the physician population increased four-fold, from 6% in the early 1900s to 24% in 2000. Contributing to this growing population, the proportion of women graduates from medical schools increased from 6% in 1960 to 43% in 2001. Currently, women constitute 46% of entering medical school students and 50% of entering minority students. Although significant barriers remain to their attaining equal professional and academic status, the potential for women to influence the structure of their profession, the delivery of health care, and the direction of medical research is considerable.

Morbidity and Mortality in Women

At the turn of the 20th century, the average lifespan of women in the United States was 48 years, compared with 46 years in men. Since then, the life expectancy in women has increased more than 30 years and is now close to 80 years, compared with 74 years in men. Because of the gender gap in life expectancy, women currently comprise close to two thirds of the population over the age of 65 and three fourths of the population over the age of 85. The reasons for the dramatic increase in overall life expectancy are thought to be related to the control of infectious diseases and progress in the treatment of chronic diseases such as diabetes and cardiovascular disease. The reasons for the disparity in life expectancy in women and men are less well established but are thought to be primarily biologic.

Table 248–1 shows the leading causes of death in women of all ages and races. Despite a dramatic decline in mortality rates for heart disease that has occurred in both sexes over the past two decades, heart disease remains the leading cause of death for women and accounts for 30% of all deaths in women. Heart disease occurs 10 to 15 years later in women than in men. This delayed onset is thought to be due primarily to the protective effect of estrogens in premenopausal women and accounts for the fact that 90% of heart disease

Table 248–1 • LEADING CAUSES OF DEATH IN WOMEN: UNITED STATES, 2000

CAUSE OF DEATH	DEATHS	PERCENTAGE OF TOTAL DEATHS
All causes	1,225,773	100.0
Cardiovascular diseases	365,953	29.9
Malignant neoplasms	267,009	21.8
Cerebrovascular diseases	102,892	8.4
Chronic lung diseases	62,005	5.1
Diabetes mellitus	37,699	3.1
Pneumonia/influenza	36,655	3.0
Alzheimer's disease	35,120	2.9
Accidents (unintentional injuries)	34,083	2.8
Nephritis/nephrotic syndrome/nephrosis	19,440	1.6

From Anderson RN: Deaths: Leading Causes for 2000. National Vital Statistics Reports; vol 50, no 16. Hyattsville, MD: National Center for Health Statistics, 2002.

mortality in women occurs after the menopause. There are significant racial and ethnic differences in mortality among women. Black women are more likely to die from heart disease than white women up to the age of 75 years; thereafter, death rates are higher in white women. In contrast, Hispanic, Native American, and Asian/Pacific Islander women have significantly lower rates of death from heart disease. Evidence suggests that heart disease, once it develops, is more serious in women than in men, resulting in higher mortality rates. In addition to biologic factors, the poorer survival of women may be due to the older age and increased prevalence of comorbid conditions in women at the time of diagnosis, as well as to less well defined social factors that influence the diagnosis and treatment of heart disease in women.

Cancer is the second leading cause of death in women and is the most common cause of premature death. The mortality rate for all cancers combined in women changed little during the last half of the 20th century. Major advances in the diagnosis and treatment of cervical and uterine cancers in women were offset by an increase in mortality rates for lung and breast cancer. Although breast cancer is still the most common cancer diagnosed in women, lung cancer is now the leading cause of cancer deaths. It is estimated that 90% of lung cancer deaths can be attributed to cigarette smoking and are therefore potentially preventable. Whereas deaths from lung cancer in men have begun to decline due to a decrease in male cigarette use, death rates for women continue to rise.

Breast cancer is the second leading cause of cancer deaths in women. Whereas the incidence of breast cancer continued to rise over the past decade, mortality rates declined for the first time since cancer registries began tracking this disease in the 1940s. This disparity is thought to be related partly to the widespread use of screening mammography and the detection of cancers in earlier stages that have a more favorable prognosis. There are significant racial differences in breast cancer incidence. White women continue to have the highest rates of breast cancer, followed closely by black women. Hispanic and Asian/Pacific Islander women are at intermediate risk, and Native American women are at lowest risk. There are also significant racial differences in breast cancer mortality. Although breast cancer incidence rates are 19% lower in black women than in white women, mortality rates are 32% higher in black women. Mortality rates in other racial/ethnic groups correspond to the lower incidence rates in these groups. Reasons for these racial differences in breast cancer incidence and mortality are unclear but may be related to socioeconomic and biologic factors as well as certain health behaviors, such as participation in screening mammography. Although it has been shown that breast cancer screening with mammography and clinical breast examination decreases mortality from breast cancer in women older than 50 years of age, and that 69% of American women 50 years of age and older report having had a recent mammogram, screening rates are lower in women who are poor or are less well educated.

Although stroke-related deaths have declined by almost 60% in the United States over the past 25 years, deaths from stroke still account for 8% of all deaths in women and rank third as a cause of mortality. Striking racial differences exist in stroke mortality: death rates in black women are almost twice those for white women. Most of the stroke deaths in women result from thromboembolic disease and occur in older women. However, aneurysmal subarachnoid hemorrhage, a less frequent form of stroke that is more common in women than in men, contributes to stroke mortality, particularly in younger or pregnant women.

Death rates from chronic pulmonary diseases have increased steadily for both women and men during the past 25 years; however, the increase has been greater in women. Because this increase has been linked to patterns in cigarette smoking, the increase in death rates in women for pulmonary disease, as well as for lung cancer, are expected to continue to rise. Death rates from pneumonia and influenza closely parallel pulmonary-related deaths and vary over time based on the epidemiology of these acute illnesses.

Diabetes has consistently ranked as a leading cause of death in women. Moreover, the reported death rate from diabetes most likely underestimates the impact of this disease on mortality because of its strong association with other life-threatening medical conditions, such as cardiovascular disease, stroke, and kidney failure. It is estimated that 8% of all women 20 years or older have diabetes; however, prevalence rates are higher in black, Hispanic, and Native American women. Separate from disease-related death rates, diabetes is a significant cause of morbidity and, in women of childbearing age, has important adverse effects on pregnancy and pregnancy outcome, resulting in an increased risk of toxemia, macrosomia, hydramnios, congenital malformations, cesarean section, and fetal and perinatal mortality.

Although mortality rates from HIV infection and acquired immunodeficiency syndrome (AIDS) began to decline in the mid-1990s as a result of highly effective combination treatment for HIV infection and better prevention of opportunistic infections, HIV remains a leading cause of death in women in the age group of 25 to 44 years. Women overall account for an increasing proportion of AIDS cases, and ethnic minority women are disproportionately affected. As the features of this epidemic change, with heterosexual transmission accounting for the majority of new HIV cases in women, these rates are expected to continue to rise.

Mortality rates alone do not provide a complete picture of women's health status. Although women live longer than men, overall measures of health status are worse in women. Based on estimates from the 1997 National Health Interview Survey (NHIS), more women than men report symptoms or seek care for acute medical conditions, such as urinary tract infections and respiratory and digestive disorders, and are more disabled by these self-limited illnesses as measured by number of bed days or days lost from work. In addition, several chronic conditions occur more frequently in women and cause significant disability, such as arthritis, thyroid disease, migraine, bladder disorders, chronic respiratory disorders (including chronic bronchitis, sinusitis, and asthma), and chronic intestinal problems (including gastritis, colitis, and constipation). Data from other sources show that affective disorders, especially major depressive episodes, and the anxiety disorders are significantly more prevalent in women. Most importantly, women's perception of their health status is lower than men's. According to estimates from the NHIS, only 35% of women describe their health as excellent, compared with 40% of men.

Life Span Groups

Many of the important health issues in women have their onset or greatest impact at certain ages and are intricately linked with women's psychosocial and sexual development. To develop a more integrated concept of women's health, it is instructive to look at the important health issues in women within the major life span groups. Several governmental and institutional sources were used to compile this information. Of these, the themes developed by the "Report of the National Institutes of Health: Opportunities for Research on Women's Health," known as the Hunt Valley Report, form the basis of this section.

BIRTH TO YOUNG ADULTHOOD. As young women reach puberty, the health issues that emerge are related primarily to developmental changes involving physical and sexual growth and changing relationships within and outside the family. Central to the psychosocial development of young women is the process of gender identification and orientation and the development of self-esteem. Intentional and unintentional injuries, including an increasing frequency of acts of physical and sexual violence, are the primary cause of death and disability in young women and account for half of all deaths in women in this age group. A small proportion of girls develop a chronic disease or disability. Most of these conditions are related to autoimmune disorders, such as lupus erythematosus, juvenile rheumatoid arthritis, and thyroid disease. Because of hormonal influences, many of these conditions first occur or are exacerbated during puberty.

AGES 15 TO 44 YEARS. During young adulthood, mortality rates in women are relatively low and deaths due to injury predominate. As women progress through this age group, cancer of the breast and reproductive tract emerge as the leading cause of death, followed by unintentional injury and heart disease. Among the unintentional and intentional injuries in this age group, motor vehicle accidents, homicide, and suicide account for three fourths of all injury deaths. The death rate from motor vehicle accidents is highest in women 15 to 24 years of age; more than half of these deaths are alcohol related. A major tragedy in the United States is the rapidly increasing death rate from homicide and suicide in young women. Black women, similar to black men, are most likely to be homicide victims, and firearms are used in more than half of these deaths. Because 30% of murders in women are perpetrated by a family member or acquaintance, the contribution of ongoing family violence to these fatal events is thought to be substantial.

The most dramatic trend in this age group, beginning in the 1980s and peaking in the mid-1990s, was the emergence and rapid rise of

HIV infection as a major cause of death. Although overall AIDS incidence and mortality rates have decreased yearly since 1996, the rate of decline has been smaller in women. The biologic and social aspects of HIV infection are difficult to separate; however, current evidence suggests that gender differences in the presentation and clinical course of HIV infection are related more to women's limited access to care and lower acceptance of, or adherence to, treatment than to true biologic differences. The consequences of this disease for gynecologic care and reproductive counseling in women are unique. Because of the interrelationships between the degree of immunosuppression related to HIV infection, the presence of coinfection with human papillomavirus, and an increased risk of cervical neoplasia, the Centers for Disease Control and Prevention and the Agency for Health Care Policy and Research recommend that newly diagnosed HIV-infected women have an initial pelvic examination and Pap smear that are repeated in 6 months. If the findings of these examinations and prior Pap smears are normal, and the woman has no AIDS-defining condition or evidence of human papillomavirus infection, subsequent annual screening is adequate. Women who are at higher risk because they do not meet these criteria require more frequent surveillance or additional studies, depending on the Pap smear findings.

Primary physicians play a unique role in counseling HIV-infected women of childbearing age. Since HIV can be transmitted during pregnancy, and more than 40% of pregnancies are unintended, routine medical care should include discussions about effective contraceptive methods, the effects of pregnancy on HIV infection and treatment, and the potential for perinatal transmission of HIV. Treatment strategies in women who may become or are pregnant should take into consideration regimens that maximally suppress maternal viral load and reduce transmission to the fetus while minimizing toxicity. In 1994, the Pediatric AIDS Clinical Trials Group demonstrated that a three-part regimen of zidovudine reduces the risk of perinatal transmission by 70% and is effective even in women with advanced disease. Current U.S. Public Health Service recommendations for antiretroviral chemoprophylaxis to reduce perinatal HIV transmission are evolving rapidly and take into consideration the now standard use of more aggressive combination drug therapies to treat HIV, as well as the clinical status and antiviral drug history of the woman. Zidovudine should be part of the antepartum drug regimen in all pregnant HIV-infected women if feasible. Despite these advances, the social consequences of this disease are enormous and result in loss of productive life, disruption of family structure, and premature death. The challenge to primary physicians to help control the transmission of HIV is an essential part of national prevention efforts.

An important role of physicians in the care of young women is to recognize and reduce risk-taking and other unhealthy behaviors. Health habits become established during early adulthood. Unhealthy behaviors not only place women at risk for life-threatening events but also have important implications for the development of illness later in life. For example, early or unprotected sexual activity increases women's risk for sexually transmitted diseases. Not only are these diseases transmitted more easily from men to women, but women are disproportionately affected because of infectious complications that can lead to disorders of reproductive function, such as pelvic inflammatory disease, ectopic pregnancy, and infertility. Unfortunately, efforts at risk reduction, particularly in the use of harmful substances, are hampered by industry and market forces and other social factors that influence women's lives. For example, the adverse effects of cigarette smoking on lung cancer and other respiratory diseases, heart disease, osteoporosis, and reproductive function are well documented, yet women become established smokers at an earlier age and have longer lifetime smoking histories than men. It is unclear what effect recent restrictions in advertising will have on women's tobacco use.

Social and cultural factors have also contributed to the increasing prevalence of dieting and eating disorders. Based on strict diagnostic criteria of the Diagnostic and Statistical Manual of Mental Disorders (DSM-IV), it is estimated that 2% of young women suffer from anorexia nervosa or bulimia, and an additional 5% have less specific eating disorders characterized by aberrant eating patterns and weight management habits. These disorders are often refractory to treatment and can be life-threatening. The statistics most likely underestimate the prevalence of eating disorders in young women. According to findings from the 1999 Youth Risk Behavior Surveillance System developed by the Centers for Disease Control and Prevention, 60% of adolescent women reported that they had attempted dieting in the previous month, 19% had gone more than 24 hours without eating,

11% had taken diet aids without professional advice, and close to 8% had induced vomiting or taken laxatives for weight control.

This life span group delineates women's reproductive years. In addition to traditional childbearing and family responsibilities, women are increasingly assuming new roles. The effect of multiple and often conflicting roles on women's mental and physical health remains to be determined but is closely linked to reproductive freedom and health. Thus, physicians need to understand the safety, effectiveness, and acceptability of current methods of contraception in culturally diverse women. Because of an increased understanding of many other common disorders of reproductive function, it is also clear that general physicians can no longer view these disorders as exclusively gynecologic problems. The association of polycystic ovary disease with insulin resistance and the hyperandrogenic state and the contribution of nonreproductive causes to chronic pelvic pain highlight the general medical nature of these disorders.

One of the themes that links together many of the medical disorders that have the highest prevalence in women in this age group is the role of autoimmunity. Most of the autoimmune diseases are more common in women than in men and cause greater morbidity. Many are influenced by changes in estrogen levels, particularly during pregnancy. Among the collagen vascular diseases, rheumatoid arthritis, systemic lupus erythematosus, and scleroderma have prevalence rates that are three to nine times higher in women. Many autoimmune-related endocrinopathies, such as Hashimoto's thyroiditis and Grave's disease, have a female-to-male ratio as high as $10:1$. Other autoimmune diseases that are more prevalent in women include type 1 diabetes mellitus, idiopathic adrenal failure, multiple sclerosis, and myasthenia gravis. Less well recognized is the role of autoimmunity in recurrent pregnancy loss and infertility in women.

Among the mental disorders, depressive illnesses are twice as common in women as men. An estimated 6% of women experience a major depressive episode sometime during their lifetime, and twice that many have chronic low-grade symptoms of depression. The excess risk of depression in women increases from childhood to adolescence and extends throughout life; however, the genetic, biologic, and environmental contributions to this gender effect are not fully understood. Women are also three times as likely as men to be diagnosed with an anxiety disorder, including agoraphobia, simple phobia, and panic disorder as well as with somatization disorders. In addition, many women experience mood, cognitive, or behavioral changes associated with cyclic changes in hormone levels during the menstrual cycle, or with marked changes in levels during the postpartum period or at the menopause.

A major cause of psychosocial morbidity in women is physical and sexual abuse. Based on the National Violence Against Women Survey conducted by the National Institute of Justice and the Centers for Disease Control and Prevention in 1998, 52% of women have been physically assaulted at some time during their life, and 18% have experienced a rape. Young women are at particular risk for rape; of those women who have been raped, more than half were younger than 18 years of age when rape first occurred. Physical and sexual assault in women is primarily a problem of partner violence. Three fourths of women who experience physical or sexual abuse after the age of 18 years are assaulted by a current or former spouse or male intimate. Based on this finding, states are developing legal and other preventive strategies to protect women. Unfortunately, owing to lack of knowledge and training and misconceptions about physical and sexual violence, physicians often fail to recognize or address symptoms of abuse. Adequate screening tools are especially crucial in the emergency department, where up to one third of women who have been assaulted seek care. To ensure widespread detection of abuse, screening should become a regular part of the medical history in any setting.

AGES 45 TO 64 YEARS. Death rates for women in this age group have declined by 30% in the past 25 years. Previously, the leading cause of death was heart disease; however, cancer is now ranked number one, with lung cancer emerging as the leading cause of cancer deaths. These shifts in mortality rates reflect primarily a decline in death rates for heart disease that has been observed in both sexes and is attributed to changes in lifestyle, such as better control of hypertension and lower blood cholesterol levels.

Many of the important chronic conditions in women first appear in this age group, and the prevalence of some increase markedly during this time period. There are significant racial and ethnic differences in the prevalence of many of these conditions. The prevalence of obesity especially is disproportionately high in minority women; close to 70% of black and Mexican American women are overweight, compared with 47% of white women. Because obesity is a major risk factor for diabetes, heart disease, stroke, gallbladder disease, and some cancers and may be a factor in osteoarthritis, weight control in women is an important public health issue.

The emergence of many of these conditions, such as heart disease, osteoporosis, and cancer, is inextricably linked to the menopause and the marked decline in estrogen levels that occurs during this age period. The role of hormone-replacement therapy (HRT) in altering the risk of developing these disorders is an area of intense research activity. HRT is the most effective therapy for vasomotor and genitourinary symptoms associated with the menopause and decreases bone loss and the risk of osteoporotic fracture. Because earlier observational data suggested that HRT might also have a protective effect on the heart, it was used increasingly over the past decade to prevent these conditions. However, recently released findings from the NIH-sponsored Women's Health Initiative, the first large randomized clinical trial designed to look at these outcomes, call this practice into question. The combined estrogen-progesterone arm of this multicenter study was halted early because of an increased incidence of breast cancer in women receiving active therapy, a potentially adverse outcome of HRT that was confirmed in the study. **1** Rates of heart disease, stroke, and dementia were also increased in women on HRT compared with women taking placebo, whereas rates of hip fracture and colon cancer were reduced. Because the risks of HRT use outweigh its benefits, combined estrogen and progesterone should no longer be used as preventive therapy in postmenopausal women. The data for estrogen use alone await the completion of the rest of the trial.

While the menopause encompasses many of the physiologic changes that define this period, women also experience major transitions in social roles and life circumstances that profoundly affect their physical and mental health. Children leave home, many women become widowed or divorced, parenting roles change as women are called upon to care for aging parents, and disabilities increase, making it difficult for some women to function within and outside the home. Not surprisingly, many women experience a major depressive episode during this period. An understanding of these life events is essential to the comprehensive care of mature women.

AGES 65 YEARS AND OLDER. Heart disease is the leading cause of death in older women, followed by cancer and stroke. Mortality rates for all three disorders rise steeply after the age of 65 years and begin to approach the rates for men. Chronic pulmonary disease and pneumonia continue to cause high death rates because of the increase and severity of infections associated with an age-related decline in immune function. Injury is the sixth leading cause of death in older women; most of these deaths are related to falls.

After the age of 65, many other chronic illnesses, such as hypertension, the arthritides, most digestive disorders, and thyroid disease, are more common in women than men of the same age and cause significant morbidity. As women's longevity increases, they bear the burden of illnesses that are seen primarily in the very old. Of these, the neurologic degenerative diseases, such as dementia, sleep disorders, and neurosensory and movement disorders, are particularly common in women. Unfortunately, the added years of life in women are often spent in a frail or dependent state and often result in institutionalization. Currently, women residing in nursing homes outnumber men by three to one. In particular, urinary incontinence and osteoporosis put women at high risk for institutionalization. Prevalence rates of urinary incontinence are twice as high in women as in men and affect up to one half of community-dwelling women. Osteoporosis is associated with deformity and pain secondary to vertebral fractures; however, hip fracture, usually the result of a fall, is the most serious consequence of osteoporosis in older women. According to the National Osteoporosis Foundation, one half of women with a hip fracture never walk independently again, one third never live independently again, and one fifth die within a year of the fracture.

The social and psychological changes that women experience as they age add to the burden of illness. Social isolation increases due to death of loved ones, loss of financial stability, and increasing physical disabilities. In addition to an increasing incidence of dementia with age, mental health problems become more prevalent or serious. The role of the primary physician is to recognize and help reduce the impact of these accumulated conditions on women's ability to function and on their quality of life.

Women's Health Education and Training

Among academic medical institutions, there is increasing awareness of the importance of women's health. However, there is often uncertainty about what actually constitutes women's health and the best way to train physicians to provide more comprehensive care to women.

Data from the 1998 National Ambulatory Medical Care Survey provide insight into the complex nature of the way women receive care and the content and provision of that care. In an analysis of differences in the delivery of medical care to women among the medical disciplines, primary care physicians in family practice, internal medicine, and obstetrics and gynecology provide the majority of office-based care to women ages 15 years and older (57%). Physicians in the surgical and nonsurgical subspecialties provide the remaining services. As women age, however, the proportion of care provided by primary physicians decreases to 45% or less in women 65 years of age and older. These findings have important implications for the health care of women. The lack of uniform standards of care, especially regarding preventive services, and the splintering of routine care among disciplines, may result in poorly coordinated and incomplete care. The multiprovider approach that this system fosters does not necessarily mean improved services to women and is antithetical to the concept of primary care.

To address these concerns, the Council on Graduate Medical Education recommends that all physicians, regardless of their educational level and specialty interest, be educated in the fundamentals of women's health and demonstrate competence in providing care to women. To provide models that may assist academic institutions in implementing these recommendations, the U.S. Department of Health and Human Services has funded the establishment of eighteen National Centers of Excellence in Women's Health within academic health centers. These centers are designed to facilitate the development of innovative clinical models, integrated curricula, and interdisciplinary research in women's health and to foster the development of women faculty. The impact of the Centers on curriculum reform, clinical care, and research initiatives is currently being evaluated.

Recommendations for a Core Women's Health Curriculum

As a foundation for addressing women's health conditions, it is essential that physicians understand basic female physiology and reproductive biology. In addition, they need to appreciate the complex interaction between the environment and the biology and psychosocial development of women. Among the conditions that are not specific to women, physicians need to be aware of those aspects of disease that are different in women or have important gender implications. The ability to apply this information requires that physicians adopt attitudes and behavior that are culture and gender sensitive. Women's relationship to the medical system is also changing and requires physicians to understand women's patterns of health seeking and forms of communication and interaction, as well as to appreciate gender differences in clinical decision making.

To assist academic medical institutions in implementing curricular changes, the Public Health Service Office on Women's Health, in collaboration with the National Institutes of Health Office of Research on Women's Health and the Health Resources and Services Administration, published a report in 1996 that provides the rationale for the development of a women's health curriculum and outlines the educational philosophy, scope, and content of a core curriculum. The report's recommendations are designed to augment and enhance rather than duplicate or replace existing curricula in the traditional disciplines. Although the report is directed to undergraduate medical education, its concepts and content can be applied broadly across the educational spectrum and may be helpful in modifying and updating residency training in the traditional medical disciplines.

1. Writing Group for the Women's Health Initiative Investigators: Risks and benefits of estrogen plus progestin in healthy postmenopausal women: Principal results from the Women's Health Initiative randomized controlled trial. JAMA 2002;288:321–333. *This large multicenter trial provides the first randomized controlled data on which to base treatment decisions in postmenopausal women with an intact uterus.*

SUGGESTED READINGS

Chlebowski RT, Hendrix SL, Langer RD, et al: WHI Investigators. Influence of estrogen plus progestin on breast cancer and mammography in healthy postmenopausal women: The Women's Health Initiative Randomized Trial. JAMA 2003;289:3243–3253. *Hormonal therapy increased incident breast cancers, which were diagnosed at a more advanced state compared with placebo.*

Committee on Understanding the Biology of Sex and Gender Differences: Exploring the biological contributions to human health: Does sex matter? *In* Weizmann T, Pardue ML (eds): Board on Health Sciences Policy, Institute of Medicine. Washington DC, National Academy Press, 2001. *This report presents compelling evidence to support the study of sex and gender differences and offers recommendations to promote research in this area.*

Manson JE, Hsia J, Johnson KC, et al: Women's Health Initiative Investigators. Estrogen plus progestin and the risk of coronary heart disease. N Engl J Med 2003;349:523–534. *Hormonal therapy was detrimental in the first year and of no benefit overall.*

Pandey SK, Hart JJ, Tiwary S: Women's health and the internet: Understanding emerging trends and implications. Soc Sci Med 2003;56:179–191. *Women, especially in higher income households, are more likely to use the internet for health information than are men.*

Shumaker SA, Legault C, Thal L, et al: WHIMS Investigators. Estrogen plus progestin and the incidence of dementia and mild cognitive impairment in postmenopausal women: The Women's Health Initiative Memory Study: A randomized controlled trial. JAMA 2003;289:2651–2662. *Hormone therapy increased the risk of probable dementia.*

249 OVARIES AND DEVELOPMENT

Robert W. Rebar
Gregory F. Erickson

The ovaries episodically release female gametes (oocytes or eggs) and secrete sex steroid hormones, principally androstenedione, estradiol, and progesterone. Oocytes are released only during the adult reproductive years, when sex steroid secretion is also greatest, but the ovaries are physiologically active throughout life.

Sex steroids affect the growth, differentiation, and function of a variety of tissues and organs throughout the body; therefore, abnormalities of the ovaries and of sex steroid secretion should be recognized by all physicians. A rational approach to the diagnosis and treatment of reproductive disorders in women requires an understanding of the functions of the ovaries and of their most important unit, the follicle, throughout life.

EMBRYOLOGY AND ANATOMY OF THE OVARIES

EMBRYOGENESIS AND DIFFERENTIATION. Organogenesis of the ovaries occurs during fetal life. Ovarian cells are derived from two very different sources: (1) primordial germ cells (PGCs) originate at a site outside the prospective gonads and (2) somatic cells differentiate from the coelomic epithelium and gonadal mesenchyme. In females, PGCs become oocytes, whereas somatic cells differentiate into a variety of cell types, including granulosa, theca, and vascular cells.

PGCs in the human embryo can be distinguished at the gastrula stage (Fig. 249–1). Shortly after formation, PGCs migrate through the dorsal mesentery to the genital ridges. Chemotaxis plays a role in directing PGCs to the gonads. During migration, PGCs proliferate in response to growth factors, most notably kit ligand. The importance of kit is demonstrated by the finding that loss-of-function mutations result in a paucity of PGCs, which in turn results in premature ovarian failure.

The genital ridges are characterized by a thickening of the coelomic epithelium and underlying primary mesenchyme. Initially, the gonads are sexually indifferent. Male gonadal differentiation is triggered by the Y chromosome–encoded testis-determining factor, SRY. SRY expression results in the differentiation of Sertoli cells and the secretion of müllerian inhibiting substance (MIS), which induces regression of the müllerian ducts. Testicular interstitial cells differentiate into Leydig cells, which secrete testosterone, which in turn stimulates wolffian duct development. In the female, absence of MIS and testosterone leads to the degeneration of the wolffian ducts and to the development of the müllerian ducts. Thus, the development of the ovaries and female reproductive system is considered a "default" pathway.

When PGCs enter the genital ridges, they begin gametogenesis (see Fig. 249–1). In females, this process is termed *oogenesis* and involves the differentiation of PGCs into oogonia and oocytes. When sex-specific differentiation of the ovary commences, the inactive X chromosome in the PGCs becomes active. This denotes the formation of mitotically active oogonia. The importance of two functional X chromosomes during oogenesis is emphasized by the fact that 45,X females lack oocytes and undergo premature menopause.

After repeated mitosis, oogonia initiate meiosis and become oocytes (see Fig. 249–1). At approximately the same time, granulosa cells differentiate within the gonadal mesenchyme and establish intimate associations with oocytes. Oocytes that become surrounded by granulosa cells stop meiosis after diplotene, and the bivalents enter an interphase state known as dictyotene. If an oocyte is not surrounded by granulosa cells, meiosis continues to diakinesis and the oocyte dies by apoptosis. Granulosa cells, therefore, are critical for oocyte survival. The vast majority of oocytes die during fetal ovary development (Fig. 249–2), apparently from a lack of contact with granulosa cells.

With further development, the oocyte/granulosa cell complex becomes a primordial follicle. This occurs between the sixth and ninth months of gestation (Fig. 249–3). A primordial follicle consists of a single layer of squamous granulosa cells, a small (about 15 μm in diameter) dictyotene oocyte, and a thin basal lamina (see Fig. 249–3). In the human female, all potential future eggs have entered diplotene of meiosis at the time of birth, and no reserve oogonia remain.

THE ADULT OVARY: ANATOMY. The ovaries of normal cycling women are oval bodies that each measure 2.5 to 5.0 cm in length, 1.5 to 3 cm in width, and 0.6 to 1.5 cm in thickness. The medial edge is attached by the mesovarium to the broad ligament, which in turn extends from the uterus laterally to the wall of the pelvic cavity. The ovary is covered by cuboidal epithelium. Beneath the epithelium is a layer of dense connective tissue, the tunica albuginea, which contains the primordial follicles.

The ovaries are organized into two principal parts: a central zone, the medulla, which is surrounded by a particularly prominent peripheral zone, the cortex (Fig. 249–4). Growing follicles at different stages of development are present in the cortex. Typically, one follicle per cycle reaches maturity and ovulates its ovum. After ovulation, the follicle transforms into a corpus luteum. The corpus luteum of the cycle lasts for about 7 days, after which it dies and becomes a nodule of dense connective tissue, the corpus albicans (see Fig. 249–4).

The medulla is composed of loose connective tissue with numerous blood vessels and associated nerves. The arterial supply to the ovary originates from two principal sources: the ovarian artery and the uterine artery. These two vessels, which enter the medulla from opposite directions, form an anastomotic trunk and become a common vessel called the ramus ovaricus artery. This artery gives rise to a series of primary branches (spiral arteries) that enter the hilum. In the hilum, numerous secondary and tertiary branches are given off to supply the medulla and the follicles and luteal tissue in the cortex (see Fig. 249–4). The hilum also contains the hilus cells (see Fig. 249–4), which, like

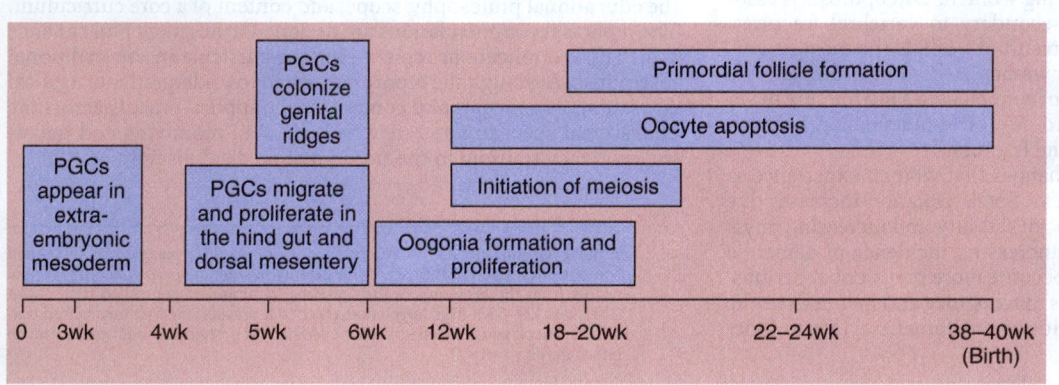

FIGURE 249–1 • Diagram illustrating the developmental timetable of the major events that ultimately lead to the formation of primordial follicles during the process of human ovary organogenesis.

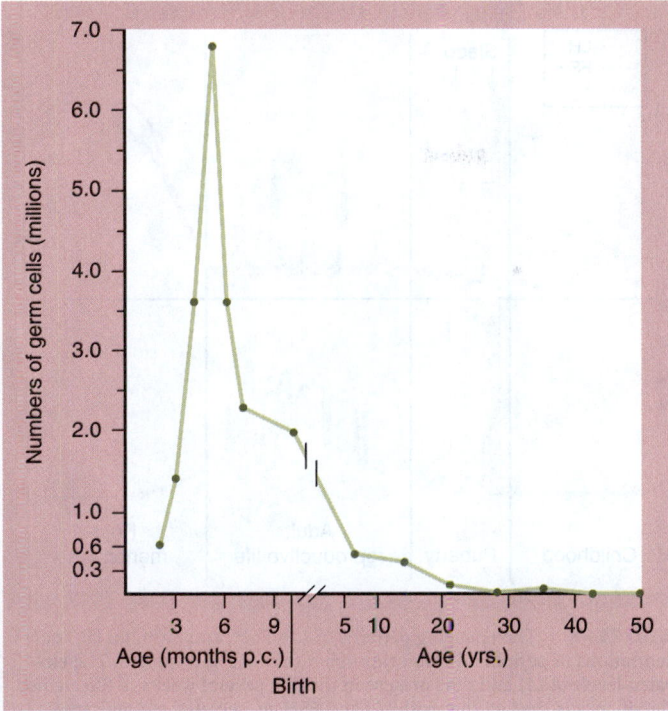

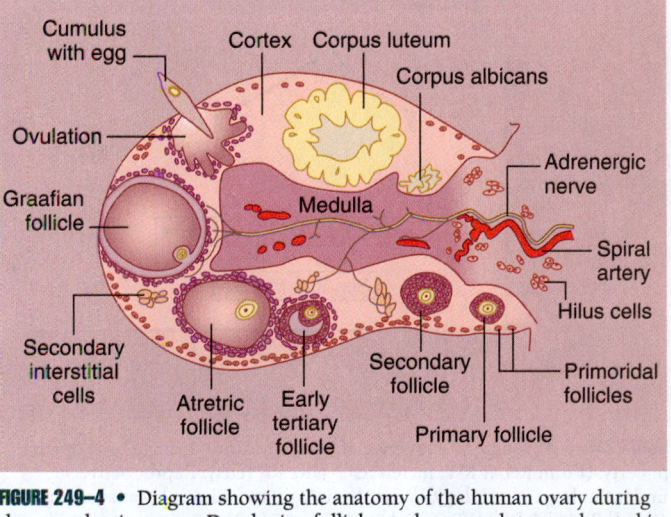

FIGURE 249–4 • Diagram showing the anatomy of the human ovary during the reproductive years. Developing follicles and corpora lutea are located in the cortex, while the hilus cells, autonomic nerves, and spiral arteries are present in the medulla. (From Erickson GF: The ovary: Basic principles and concepts. *In* Felig P, Baxter JD, Broadus AE, et al [eds]: Endocrinology and Metabolism, 3rd ed. New York, McGraw-Hill, 1995, with permission.)

FIGURE 249–2 • Changes in the total number of germ cells in the human ovaries during aging. At early to midgestation, the number of germ cells increases to almost 7 million; shortly thereafter, the number declines rapidly to about 2 million at birth. The number continues to decline until no oocytes are detected at 50 years of age. (From Baker TG: Radiosensitivity of mammalian oocytes with particular reference to the human female. Am J Obstetr Gynecol 1971;110:745–761, with permission.)

the testicular Leydig cells, contain Reinke crystals and secrete testosterone. The physiological role of the hilus cells is still unknown.

SUGGESTED READINGS

Erickson GF: The role of growth factors in ovary organogenesis. J Soc Gynecol Investig 2001;8:S13–S16. *Overview that emphasizes the role of the primordial follicles, which vary in number among women, and how this number influences fertility and menopause.*

OVARIAN FUNCTION IN CHILDHOOD AND PUBERTY

PHYSICAL CHANGES AT PUBERTY. Puberty extends from the earliest signs of sexual maturation until the attainment of physical, mental, and emotional maturity. Pubertal changes in girls result directly or indirectly from maturation of the hypothalamic-pituitary-ovarian unit. Hormonally, human puberty is characterized by a resetting of the negative gonadal steroid feedback loop, the establishment of new circadian and ultradian (frequent) gonadotropin rhythms, and the acquisition in the female of a positive estrogen feedback loop controlling the menstrual cycle as interdependent expressions of the gonadotropins and ovarian steroids. In girls, pubertal development generally occurs between 8 and 14 years of age. The age at onset and the rate of progress through puberty are variable and depend on genetic, socioeconomic, nutritional, physical, and psychological factors.

Physical changes occur in an orderly sequence over a definite time frame during puberty (Fig. 249–5). Breast budding in girls is usually the first pubertal change, followed shortly by the appearance of pubic hair, with menarche occurring late in pubertal development. The time from breast budding (median age at onset, 9.8 years) to menarche

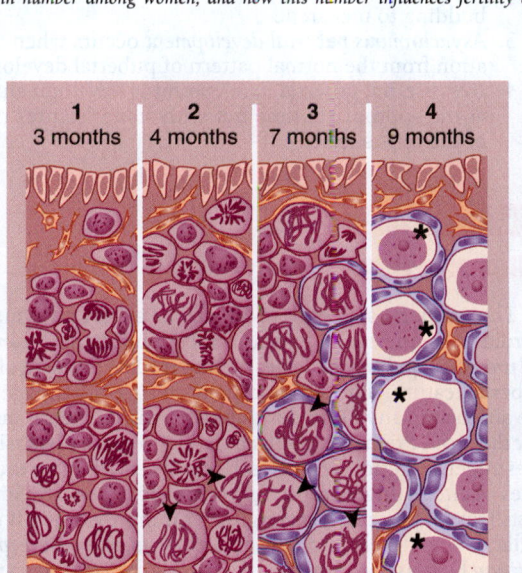

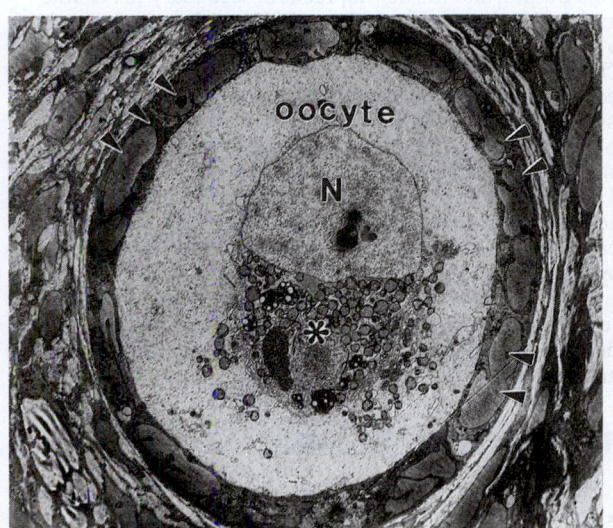

FIGURE 249–3 • *A,* Drawing showing gametogenesis in the human fetal ovary leading to the formation of primordial follicles. At 3 months (1), oogonia divide mitotically. At 4 months (2), some oogonia deep within the cortical cords enter meiosis (arrowheads). At 7 months (3), the cords are no longer distinct and all germ cells are in meiotic prophase I. At 9 months (4), some oocytes become associated with granulosa cells and appear as primordial follicles (asterisks). *B,* Electron micrograph of human primordial follicle. Granulosa cells (arrowheads), oocyte nucleus (N), and Balbiani body (asterisk) are shown. (From Erickson GF: The ovary: Basic principles and concepts. *In* Felig P, Baxter JD, Broadus AE, et al [eds]: Endocrinology and Metabolism, 3rd ed. New York, McGraw-Hill, 1995, with permission.)

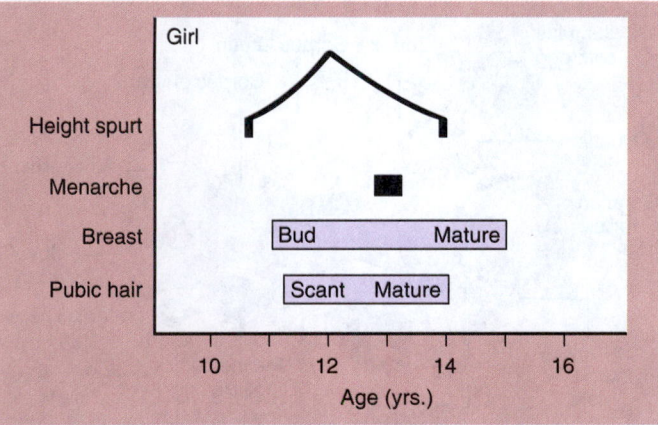

FIGURE 249–5 • Temporal sequence of events for the "average" girl during puberty. (From Rebar RW: *In* Yen SSC, Jaffe RB [eds]: Reproductive Endocrinology: Physiology, Pathophysiology, and Clinical Management, 4th ed. Philadelphia: WB Saunders, 1999, p 710.)

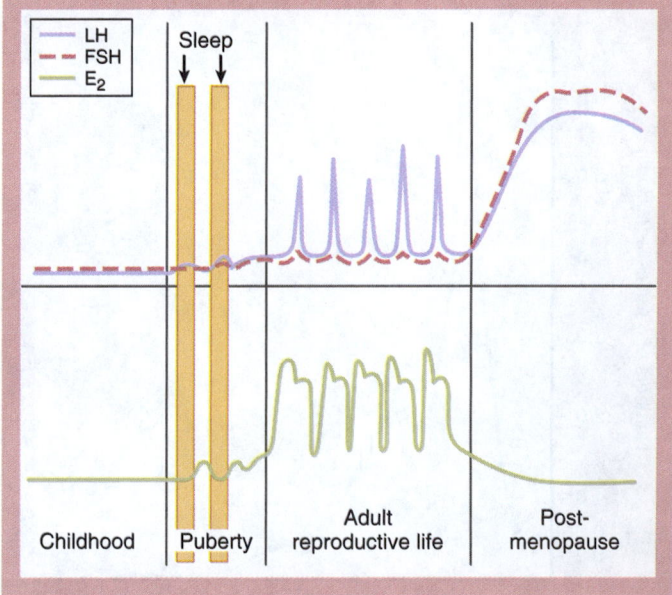

FIGURE 249–6 • The changing patterns of LH, FSH, and estradiol (E_2) concentrations in peripheral blood throughout the life of a woman. The elevated levels of LH and FSH present in the first several weeks of life are not shown, nor is the fact that both LH and FSH are secreted in a pulsatile fashion. The pubertal period has been expanded to illustrate the sleep-associated increases in LH and FSH followed by morning increases in E_2 that are observed during puberty. (Reprinted with permission from Endocrine and Metabolism Continuing Education Quality Control Program, 1982. Copyright American Association for Clinical Chemistry, Inc.)

approximates 2 years. Breast development results from increasing ovarian estrogen production and pubic and axillary hair from increasing ovarian androgen production. Estrogens are required for growth of pubic hair as well.

The ovarian sex steroids join with growth hormone and adrenal androgens to produce the adolescent growth spurt. Peak growth velocity is achieved relatively early with little growth observed after menarche. Lean body mass, skeletal mass, and body fat are equal in prepubertal boys and girls, but by maturity, women have twice as much body fat as men and less lean body mass and skeletal mass, as a result of differences in sex steroid secretion beginning at puberty. Estrogens are necessary for normal formation, mineralization, and maturation of bones. Well-established standards exist for determining radiographically, typically by examining radiographs of the bones of the wrist, whether bone age is appropriate for chronologic age. Estrogen deficiencies retard and excesses advance bone age in relation to chronologic age.

HORMONAL CHANGES. The ovaries function even in early childhood. The low levels of luteinizing hormone (LH) and follicle-stimulating hormone (FSH), which are normally present, increase if the ovaries are removed before puberty, just as they do later in life, indicating exquisite sensitivity of the hypothalamic-pituitary unit to extremely low circulating sex steroid levels. As puberty nears, there is a progressive decrease in sensitivity of the hypothalamic-pituitary unit to sex steroids, leading to increased secretion of pituitary gonadotropins, stimulation of sex steroid output, and the development of secondary sex characteristics. Increased secretion of both LH and FSH initially occurs at night with sleep and is associated with increased estradiol secretion the next morning (Fig. 249–6). As is true for most hormones, both LH and FSH are secreted in an episodic or pulsatile rather than a continuous fashion. It is possible that the sleep-entrained pulsatile secretion of gonadotropins commences in response to increased pulsatile secretion of gonadotropin-releasing hormone (GnRH). Later in puberty, secretion of LH and FSH is increased, relative to childhood, throughout the 24-hour period, except during the early follicular phase, when nighttime increases still occur. Basal levels of estradiol, the major estrogen secreted by the ovaries, increase throughout puberty. A "critical body mass" may be required for positive estrogen feedback and ovulation. During the first 2 years after menarche, up to 90% of menstrual cycles may be anovulatory because of a delay in the synchronization of the hypothalamic-pituitary-ovarian axis.

ABERRATIONS IN PUBERTAL DEVELOPMENT

Abnormalities of pubertal development can be divided into four major categories (Table 249–1), as follows.

1. *Precocious puberty* represents any pubertal changes before the age of 9 years in white girls and before the age of 8 years in African American girls. This is quite controversial. Some clinicians believe evaluation is warranted only if pubertal development begins before age 7. The nearer that pubertal development begins to the mean age of onset of puberty, the less

likely is it to have a pathologic basis. The precocious development is *isosexual* when the development is common to the phenotypic sex of the individual and *heterosexual* when the development is characteristic of the opposite sex. *True* or *central precocious puberty* is due to premature maturation of the hypothalamic-pituitary axis. In the absence of increased hypothalamic-pituitary activity, *precocious pseudopuberty* (also known as precocious puberty of peripheral origin) exists.

2. *Delayed* (or *interrupted*) *puberty* is defined as the absence of any secondary sex characteristics by the age of 13 years or of menarche by age 16 years or by passage of 5 or more years from breast budding to menarche.

3. *Asynchronous pubertal development* occurs when there is deviation from the normal pattern of pubertal development.

4. *Heterosexual pubertal development* is development that occurs at the appropriate time but with some features characteristic of the opposite sex.

PRECOCIOUS PUBERTY

Differential Diagnosis

The temporal sequence in which the signs and symptoms of sex steroid hormone excess appear is most important. *Incomplete isosexual precocious puberty* indicates premature development of only a single pubertal feature. If breast budding occurs before the age of 8 years in the absence of any other development, the diagnosis may be *premature thelarche*. Premature thelarche is believed due to transient increases in estrogen secretion or increased breast sensitivity to the small quantities of circulating estrogens present before puberty. Simple ovarian cysts may be present in some girls with this disorder. If pubic and/or axillary hair develops alone and persists, *premature pubarche* and *adrenarche* must be considered. These abnormalities are associated with slight increases in adrenal androgen secretion but not with clitorimegaly or other signs of virilization. These syndromes require no treatment, and affected girls typically begin true puberty at the usual age. Careful follow-up is required to distinguish these disorders from true precocious puberty.

When precocious development is isosexual, the purpose of evaluation is to determine if the cause is central (true precocious puberty)

Table 249–1 • ABERRATIONS OF PUBERTAL DEVELOPMENT

I. Precocious development
  A. Isosexual precocity
    1. Incomplete sexual precocity
      a. Premature thelarche
      b. Premature pubarche
      c. Premature adrenarche
    2. True (central) precocious puberty
      a. Idiopathic (constitutional)
      b. Due to central nervous system lesions
      c. Primary hypothyroidism
      d. Silver-Russell syndrome
    3. Precocious pseudopuberty (of peripheral origin)
      a. Ovarian neoplasms
      b. Adrenal neoplasms
      c. Iatrogenic (estrogen-containing preparations)
      d. hCG-secreting neoplasms distinct from central nervous system and ovarian tumors
      e. McCune-Albright syndrome
  B. Heterosexual precocity
    1. Ovarian neoplasms
    2. Adrenal neoplasms
    3. Congenital adrenal hyperplasia
    4. Other rare disorders of sexual differentiation
II. Delayed pubertal development (no development by age 13 yr; absence of menarche by age 16 yr; passage of 5 yr or more from breast budding without menarche)
  A. Anatomic abnormalities
    1. Müllerian agenesis or dysgenesis (Rokitansky-Küster-Hauser syndrome)
    2. Distal genital tract obstruction
      a. Transverse vaginal septum
      b. Imperforate hymen
      c. Vaginal agenesis
  B. Hypergonadotropic hypogonadism (follicle-stimulating hormone >30–40 mIU/mL)
    1. Gonadal dysgenesis
      a. With stigmata of Turner's syndrome
      b. Pure (46,XX or 46,XY)
      c. Mixed
    2. Ovarian failure with normal ovarian development
      a. Autoimmune disorders
      b. Gonadotropin receptor and/or postreceptor defects (? resistant ovary or Savage syndrome)
      c. Enzymatic defects (17α-hydroxylase deficiency, galactosemia)
      d. Physical causes
        i. Irradiation
        ii. Chemotherapeutic agents
        iii. Viral agents
      e. Idiopathic
  C. Hypogonadotropic or normogonadotropic hypogonadism (luteinizing hormone and follicle-stimulating hormone <10 mIU/mL or luteinizing hormone and follicle-stimulating hormone 6–25 mIU/mL with at least one being >10 mIU/mL)
    1. Isolated gonadotropin deficiency
      a. In association with midline defects (Kallmann's syndrome)
      b. Independent of associated disorders
    2. Neoplasms of the hypothalamic-pituitary axis
      a. Craniopharyngiomas
      b. Pituitary tumors
      c. Others
    3. Infiltrative processes (Langerhans-type histiocytosis)
    4. Idiopathic hypopituitarism
    5. "Hypothalamic" forms of amenorrhea
      a. Psychogenic
      b. Exercise associated
      c. Associated with malnutrition
      d. Anorexia nervosa
    6. Miscellaneous disorders
      a. Prader-Labhardt-Willi syndrome
      b. Lawrence-Moon-Bardet-Biedl syndrome
      c. Primary hypothyroidism
    7. Constitutional delayed puberty
III. Asynchronous pubertal development
  A. Incomplete forms of androgen insensitivity
  B. Complete forms of androgen insensitivity
IV. Heterosexual pubertal development
  A. Polycystic ovary syndrome
  B. Congenital adrenal hyperplasia (female pseudohermaphroditism)
    1. 21-Hydroxylase deficiency
    2. 11β-Hydroxylase deficiency
    3. 3β-ol-Hydroxysteroid dehydrogenase deficiency
  C. Male pseudohermaphroditism due to 5α-reductase deficiency
  D. Male pseudohermaphroditism due to partial androgen insensitivity
  E. Mixed gonadal dysgenesis
  F. Androgen-producing neoplasms
    1. Ovarian
    2. Adrenal
  G. Cushing's syndrome

or not. Careful questioning of the patient and her parents may indicate inadvertent ingestion or absorption of sex steroids (iatrogenic or factitious). About 10% of individuals with true precocious puberty have one of several organic brain diseases, including neoplasms, tuberous sclerosis, neurofibromatosis, encephalitis, meningitis, and hydrocephalus. The seriousness of intracranial lesions mandates that girls with precocious puberty have radiographic evaluation of the central nervous system, most effectively by magnetic resonance imaging (MRI). In almost 90% of girls with true precocious puberty, however, no cause is identified (idiopathic or constitutional).

The physical examination may also provide critical information about the cause of the precocious development. Cutaneous café-au-lait spots, facial asymmetry, polyostotic fibrous dysplasia and other skeletal abnormalities, cranial nerve deficits, and multiple ovarian follicular cysts suggest *McCune-Albright syndrome* in a girl with precocious puberty. It is now known that various clones of cells in the endocrine glands of girls with this disorder function autonomously with respect to cyclic adenosine monophosphate (cAMP) production as a consequence of a mutation within exon 8 of the G protein α subunit. This same mutation probably accounts for the bone lesions and café-au-lait hyperpigmentation. Precocious development associated with short stature, congenital bodily asymmetry, triangular facies, and clinodactyly suggests the *Silver-Russell syndrome*. Characteristic signs and symptoms may suggest the coexistence of primary hypothyroidism and precocious puberty, especially if galactorrhea is also present. In these patients, thyroid hormone replacement therapy halts progression of pubertal development until the expected age of puberty. (Enigmatically, primary hypothyroidism may also lead to delayed pubertal development. Thyroid hormone replacement permits the onset of puberty.)

Abdominal and rectal examination may reveal a mass, suggesting an adrenal or ovarian tumor. Because palpable ovarian cysts may develop rarely before ovulation in true precocious puberty, the presence of a mass need not confirm the diagnosis of precocious pseudopuberty.

When vaginal bleeding is the only sign of development, the diagnosis of sexual precocity should be suspect. Common causes of bleeding in this age group include irritation from a vaginal infection or foreign body, sexual assault, prolapse of the urethral meatus, and ingestion of estrogen-containing medications (most commonly, oral contraceptive preparations). A vaginal or cervical neoplasm is also a rare possibility. Thus, vaginal bleeding dictates the need for vaginal examination, often best performed under anesthesia, before further evaluation is undertaken.

Heterosexual precocity in an apparent prepubertal female is almost always due to congenital adrenal hyperplasia or to an androgen-secreting adrenal or ovarian neoplasm. Only very rarely must another disorder of sexual differentiation be considered (Chapter 246). It is important to examine the external genitalia carefully because congenital adrenal hyperplasia is usually associated with some degree of sexual ambiguity.

Excessive androgens produced endogenously by abnormal fetal adrenal glands in utero or diffusing across the placenta to the fetus from the mother can virilize the external genitalia and result in female pseudohermaphroditism. The extent of virilization varies from an enlarged clitoris only to sexual ambiguity sufficient to make gender assignment difficult.

Excessive maternal androgen secretion, typically from an ovarian or adrenal neoplasm, can lead to virilization of a female fetus. This occurs very rarely, because of the great capacity of the placenta to aromatize naturally occurring androgens to estrogens. Virilization of a female fetus is much more likely to occur if a pregnant woman has ingested a synthetic steroid preparation with androgenic properties because available synthetic compounds generally cannot be aromatized.

Excessive androgen secretion beginning in utero is usually associated with defective cortisol synthesis. As a consequence, pituitary corticotropin secretion is increased, resulting in congenital adrenal hyperplasia and excessive androgen secretion. The three different enzyme defects in the steroidogenic pathway that can lead to virilization of the female fetus are described in Chapter 246. 21-Hydroxylase deficiency is the most common form of congenital adrenal hyperplasia, accounting for the disorder in more than 90% of affected individuals. The defect may vary from partial to complete deficiency of the enzyme.

Diagnostic Tests

MEASUREMENT OF PEPTIDE AND STEROID HORMONES. Increased levels of immunoreactive human chorionic gonadotropin (hCG) may suggest an hCG-secreting neoplasm, most commonly an ovarian teratoma or dysgerminoma. In such cases, the hCG, which is antigenically and biologically similar to LH, stimulates ovarian steroid secretion and pseudopubertal development. Because even specific LH immunoassays show some cross-reactivity with hCG, values for serum LH may be elevated in individuals with hCG-secreting tumors. Immunoreactive hCG is always elevated in the presence of such tumors. Levels and ratios of FSH and LH typical of pubertal as opposed to prepubertal girls help in diagnosing true precocious puberty. Timed urine collections rather than blood samples can be used to measure gonadotropin secretion if necessary. The use of exogenous GnRH to stimulate endogenous LH and FSH secretion can be useful in differentiating gonadotropin-dependent from gonadotropin-independent precocious puberty. Excessively high circulating levels of estrogen suggest an estrogen-producing neoplasm. High levels of serum testosterone suggest an ovarian source of excess androgen in girls with heterosexual development, whereas increased levels of dehydroepiandrosterone (DHEA) or its sulfate (DHEA-S) (the principal precursors of 17-ketosteroids) suggest an adrenal source. High levels of serum 17-hydroxyprogesterone imply congenital adrenal hyperplasia (CAH) secondary to 21-hydroxylase deficiency, whereas high levels of serum 11-deoxycortisol imply an 11β-hydroxylase deficiency. In CAH these hormone levels should decrease promptly after oral administration of suppressive doses of dexamethasone. Suppression in response to exogenous corticoids occurs much less consistently in individuals with adrenal cortical adenomas and carcinomas and rarely in those with ovarian androgen-secreting neoplasms (Chapters 240 and 246).

ADDITIONAL STUDIES. Ultrasonic scanning of the adrenals and ovaries and computed tomography (CT) of the adrenals may be indicated to confirm clinical suspicions. In girls with ovarian or adrenal neoplasms, the tumor can almost always be localized radiographically. Catheterization of the ovarian and adrenal veins and measurements of the effluent steroids from each gland should be pursued only when CT, ultrasonography, or MRI fails to identify what is suspected to be a neoplasm. Although plain skull films are of use in screening for pituitary and parapituitary tumors, CT or MRI of the skull is indicated in the presence of definite neurologic deficits or if true precocious puberty is suspected. Radiographic estimation of bone age is indicated in all cases and serves as a useful tool to follow the results of treatment.

Treatment

Treatment for precocious puberty should be initiated promptly so that (1) the patient's ultimate height is not compromised as a result of sex steroid-induced premature epiphyseal closure and (2) emotional disturbances in the patient and her parents are prevented or attenuated.

GnRH analogues are now the preferred therapy for suppressing gonadotropin secretion and also may prevent early bone maturation. The analogues are not effective in children with McCune-Albright syndrome, and ketoconazole or testolactone has been only marginally successful. Aqueous depot medroxyprogesterone acetate (100 to 200 mg IM every 2 to 4 weeks) also may be used to suppress gonadotropin secretion. Medroxyprogesterone acetate, however, does not always prevent premature epiphyseal closure and the resultant short stature.

Individuals with CNS or steroid-secreting neoplasms must undergo therapy appropriate for the particular lesion. Girls with congenital adrenal hyperplasia are appropriately managed with glucocorticoids (plus mineralocorticoids when indicated) as outlined in Chapter 246.

DELAYED PUBERTY

Typically girls with delayed puberty present at age 16 years or later because of primary amenorrhea, but younger girls may present because of failure to initiate pubertal development. Because of the anxiety generated by delayed puberty, some evaluation is always indicated regardless of the age of the patient.

When pubertal development progresses normally but menstruation does not begin, an abnormality in the genital tract should be considered. Congenital malformations of the müllerian ducts are uncommon, occurring in 0.02% of all women. Most do not cause amenorrhea, and many do not impair reproduction. The anomalies associated with amenorrhea vary in severity from an imperforate hymen to complete aplasia of all müllerian duct derivatives with vaginal atresia. Although aplasia generally involves all of the müllerian duct derivatives, defects may involve only a single part of the distal genital tract.

A müllerian duct anomaly is suggested by (1) normal levels of serum gonadotropins and steroids, (2) an abnormal outflow tract, (3) a history of cyclic abdominal pain with or without a palpable mass, and (4) normal development of secondary sex characteristics. Normal ovarian function still induces endometrial growth and shedding after menarche if the uterus is normal. In the absence of a normal outflow tract, however, the menstrual effluent is retained and may or may not be able to escape into the abdominal cavity. Free in the abdominal cavity, the effluent may cause endometriosis. Constrained in the uterine cavity, the effluent causes hematometra and a large abdominal mass. In the absence of a mass or cyclic pain, a karyotype is indicated in girls with evidence of an abnormal genital tract to rule out any of several disorders of sexual differentiation (Chapter 246). Such disorders, however, almost never occur together with completely normal pubertal development. In girls with a normal karyotype and a genital tract anomaly, examination under anesthesia and diagnostic laparoscopy should be undertaken to delineate the extent of the defect. When the abnormality consists of an imperforate hymen or transverse vaginal septum only, surgical restoration can be accomplished relatively simply. Attempts to provide an outflow tract for the uterus should not be undertaken if there is no cervix, because of the high risk of recurrent pelvic infection. Even with a functional cervix, the creation of an outflow tract that permits successful pregnancy is unlikely. A functional vagina can be created surgically or by the daily use of ever-larger dilators. To prevent shrinkage and scarring, surgery should be deferred until the patient is willing to use dilators postoperatively on a daily basis or she is about to become sexually active.

Other causes of delayed puberty and primary amenorrhea are the same as those that may cause amenorrhea in older women (see later). When no apparent cause for delayed development is found, constitutional delayed puberty must be entertained as a diagnosis of exclusion. A strong family history of delayed maturation adds support to this presumption. Small doses of estrogen may be administered to induce some pubertal development but may obscure a pathologic cause for the delay and may compromise linear growth and ultimate height.

ASYNCHRONOUS PUBERTAL DEVELOPMENT

Asynchronous pubertal development is characteristic of male pseudohermaphroditism due to androgen insensitivity, especially complete testicular feminization. This syndrome of androgen insensitivity is inherited either as an X-linked recessive or as a sex-limited autosomal dominant trait. Despite the presence of intra-abdominal or inguinal testes, there is complete failure of virilization. Affected individuals develop breasts (but only to Tanner stage 3) and a typical female habitus with unambiguous female external genitalia but with absence of internal female structures, generally having only a foreshortened blind-ending vagina. Little or no pubic and axillary hair develops. The karyotype is obviously 46,XY in these individuals.

Circulating testosterone levels are equivalent to or higher than those found in normal men, and LH levels are elevated while FSH levels are normal compared to those in menstruating women. This syndrome is discussed further in Chapter 246.

HETEROSEXUAL PUBERTAL DEVELOPMENT

Polycystic ovary (PCO) syndrome, by far the most common cause of heterosexual pubertal development, is associated with the development of some secondary sex features characteristic of males at the normal age of puberty. Feminization occurs in affected girls, and they develop normal breasts and a typical female habitus, but masculinization also occurs. (In contrast, girls with congenital adrenal hyperplasia generally show little if any female development at puberty.) A heterogeneous syndrome, PCO syndrome most typically begins at or near puberty with hirsutism and irregular menses from the time of menarche. Menarche may be delayed as well, so that young women may present with primary amenorrhea. Basal LH levels tend to be somewhat elevated in perhaps 80% of cases, and circulating levels of all androgens are elevated moderately. Some degree of insulin resistance is almost invariably present as well, and hypercholesterolemia may predispose to cardiovascular disease later in life.

Congenital adrenal hyperplasia is generally diagnosed before puberty, and heterosexual precocious pseudopuberty is typical. However, if the defect is mild and changes to the external genitalia are minimal, masculinization may occur at the expected age of puberty. This attenuated or nonclassic form of 21-hydroxylase deficiency seems to occur in families with a strong family history of hirsutism. Affected girls generally have some defeminization with flattening of the breasts, severe hirsutism, relatively short stature, and obesity.

Mixed gonadal dysgenesis designates asymmetrical gonadal development, with a germ cell tumor or a testis on one side and an undifferentiated streak, rudimentary gonad, or no gonad on the other. The extent of genital virilization before puberty is variable in this rare disorder. The vast majority are reared as girls, in whom virilization occurs at puberty; some may note breast development as well. Affected individuals generally have a mosaic karyotype, with 45,X/46,XY being most common. Short stature and other stigmata associated with a 45,X karyotype in Turner's syndrome are less common in patients with tumors than in patients with testes. Gonadectomy is indicated in all individuals with a Y chromosome to eliminate the increased neoplastic potential of such dysgenetic gonads and in all patients in whom virilization occurs at puberty to remove the source of androgen. Estrogen replacement therapy is warranted following gonadectomy. Other causes of male pseudohermaphroditism associated with heterosexual pubertal development are described in Chapter 246.

An androgen-producing neoplasm or Cushing's syndrome may occur rarely during the pubertal years and lead to heterosexual development.

SUGGESTED READINGS

Chumlea WC, Schubert CM, Roche AF, et al: Age at menarche and racial comparisons in U.S. girls. Pediatrics 2003;111:110–113. *Analysis of the most recent developmental data in U.S. girls.*

Elmlinger MW, Kuhnel W, Ranke MB: Reference ranges for serum concentrations of lutropin (LH), follitropin (FSH), estradiol (E₂), prolactin, progesterone, sex hormone–binding globulin (SHBG), dehydroepiandrosterone sulfate (DHEAS), cortisol and ferritin in neonates, children and young adults. Clin Chem Lab Med 2002;40:1151–1160. *A useful guide to normal values of reproductive hormones in children and adolescents.*

Hamilton AS, Mack TM: Puberty and genetic susceptibility to breast cancer in a case-control study in twins. N Engl J Med 2003;348:2313–2322. *Age of puberty did not influence breast cancer risk.*

Selevan SG, Rice DC, Hogan KA, et al: Blood lead concentration and delayed puberty in girls. N Engl J Med 2003;348:1527–1536. *Environmental lead exposure may delay puberty.*

Simpson JL, Rebar RW: Normal and abnormal sexual differentiation and development In Becker KL, et al (eds): Principles and Practice of Endocrinology and Metabolism, 3rd ed. Philadelphia, Lippincott Williams and Wilkins, 2001, pp 852–885. *A detailed discussion of the disorders of sexual differentiation organized similarly to the discussion in this chapter.*

Wang Y: Is obesity associated with early sexual maturation? A comparison of the association in American boys versus girls. Pediatrics 2002;110:903–910. *The importance of obesity in the timing of pubertal development is documented in this analysis of data from a national U.S. survey.*

250 MENSTRUAL CYCLE AND FERTILITY

Robert W. Rebar
Gregory F. Erickson

THE NORMAL MENSTRUAL CYCLE

Characteristics of the Menstrual Cycle

Between menarche at approximately age 12 years and the menopause at about age 51 years, the reproductive organs of normal women undergo a series of closely coordinated changes at approximately monthly intervals that together constitute the normal menstrual cycle. The menstrual cycle is the expression of the coordinated interactions of the hypothalamic-pituitary-ovarian axis, with associated changes in the target tissues (endometrium, cervix, vagina) of the reproductive tract.

A menstrual cycle begins with the first day of genital bleeding (day 1; menses) and ends just prior to the next menstrual period. The median menstrual cycle length is 28 days, but normal ovulatory menstrual cycles may range from about 21 to 40 days in length. Menstrual cycles vary most greatly in length in the years immediately following menarche and in the years immediately preceding menopause, largely because of an increased incidence of anovulatory cycles. Irregularities in menstrual cycle length may also be caused by abrupt changes in diet, exercise, or environment; by serious emotional disturbances; and following parturition or abortion. The menstrual cycle can be divided into three distinct phases: *follicular, ovulatory,* and *luteal.*

FOLLICULAR (PREOVULATORY) PHASE. Variable in length, the follicular phase begins with the first day of menstrual bleeding and extends to the day prior to the preovulatory luteinizing hormone (LH) surge. A rise in serum follicle-stimulating hormone (FSH) begins in the late luteal phase of the previous menstrual cycle, continues into the early follicular phase, and initiates growth and development of a group of follicles (Fig. 250–1). The preovulatory follicle destined for ovulation is selected from this cohort in a manner that is not yet understood. Circulating LH levels rise slowly throughout the follicular phase, but FSH levels fall after the early follicular phase increase. Approximately 7 to 8 days before the preovulatory LH surge, estradiol and estrone begin to increase, generally reaching a maximum on the day before or the day of the LH surge. The divergence in LH and FSH levels may be related to the follicular secretion of *inhibin,* a hormone that specifically inhibits the release of FSH. Several days before the LH surge, plasma androgens (androstenedione and testosterone) and some progestins (17α-hydroxyprogesterone and 20α-dihydroprogesterone) begin to increase. They peak on the day of the LH surge. Progesterone itself does not increase until just prior to the onset of the LH surge.

OVULATORY PHASE. During this phase the ovum is released from the mature graafian follicle about 32 to 34 hours after the onset of the preovulatory surge of LH by the pituitary gland. The ovulatory phase extends from 1 day prior to the LH surge to 1 day following the LH surge (see Fig. 250–1). Some women experience brief (a few minutes to a few hours in length), dull, unilateral pelvic pain near the time of ovulation, termed *mittelschmerz.* The association of this pain with ovulation is unknown, but it may be due to leakage of follicular fluid into the abdominal cavity at ovulation. Mittelschmerz may occur before or after actual ovulation or not at all in ovulatory women. During the ovulatory phase a rapid rise in plasma LH in response to positive estrogen feedback leads to final maturation of the follicle and to ovulation. As peak LH levels are reached, estradiol levels drop but progesterone levels continue to increase.

LUTEAL (POSTOVULATORY) PHASE. The more constant half of the menstrual cycle, the luteal phase, is approximately 14 days in length and ends with the onset of menses (see Fig. 250–1). This phase represents the functional lifespan of the corpus luteum ("yellow body") of the ovary, which supports the released ovum by secreting progesterone. In the luteal phase, progesterone secretion increases to a peak 6 to 8 days after the LH surge. Parallel but smaller increases in 17α-hydroxyprogesterone, estradiol, and estrone levels also occur. Progesterone levels decrease toward menses unless the ovum is fertilized and pregnancy results. The finding of serum progesterone levels greater than 10 ng/mL 1 week prior to menses is probably diagnostic of normal ovulation. Progestins increase basal morning body

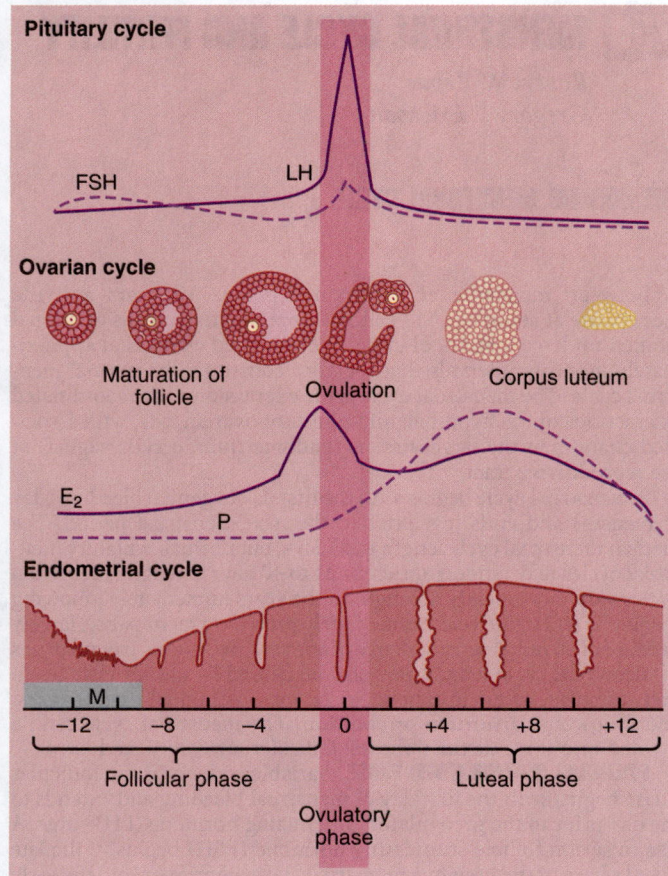

Pituitary cycle

FSH   LH

Ovarian cycle

Maturation of follicle   Ovulation   Corpus luteum

E₂

P

Endometrial cycle

M

−12   −8   −4   0   +4   +8   +12

Follicular phase   Luteal phase

Ovulatory phase

FIGURE 250–1 • The idealized cyclic changes observed in gonadotropins, estradiol (E₂), progesterone (P), and uterine endometrium during the normal menstrual cycle. The data are centered on the day of the luteinizing hormone (LH) surge (day 0). Days of menstrual bleeding are indicated by M. FSH = follicle-stimulating hormone. (Reprinted with permission from Endocrine and Metabolism Continuing Education Quality Control Program, 1982. Copyright American Association for Clinical Chemistry, Inc.)

temperature so that a "thermogenic shift" of more than 0.3° C occurring after a nadir is a presumptive sign of ovulation and progesterone secretion. Unfortunately, taking basal temperatures on a daily basis is tedious, subject to error, and not very reliable.

Cyclic Changes in Target Organs

ENDOMETRIUM

During the menstrual cycle the endometrium undergoes remarkable histologic and cytologic changes, which culminate with menstrual bleeding when the corpus luteum ceases to secrete progesterone (see Fig. 250–1). The *basal layer of the endometrium,* which is not lost during menses, then regenerates the *superficial layer* of compact epithelial cells lining the uterine cavity and an *intermediate layer of spongiosa,* both of which are shed at each menstruation. Endometrial glands in these layers proliferate under the influence of estrogen in the follicular phase so that the mucosa thickens. In the luteal phase, under the influence of progesterone, the glands become coiled and secretory, with increased vascularity and edema of the stroma. As both estradiol and progesterone decline in the late luteal phase, the stroma becomes increasingly edematous, endometrial and blood vessel necrosis occurs, and endometrial bleeding ensues. Local release of prostaglandins may initiate vasospasm and ischemic necrosis in the endometrium as well as the uterine contractions accompanying menstrual flow. Thus, prostaglandin synthetase inhibitors can relieve dysmenorrhea (menstrual cramping). Fibrinolytic activity in the endometrium also peaks at the time of menstruation, accounting for the noncoagulability of menstrual blood. Because the histologic changes during the menstrual cycle are so characteristic, endometrial biopsies are used to date the stage of the cycle and to assess the tissue response to gonadal steroids.

CERVIX AND CERVICAL MUCUS

During the follicular phase, cervical vascularity, congestion, and edema increase progressively under the influence of estrogen. The external cervical os opens to a diameter of 3 mm at ovulation and then decreases to 1 mm. Cervical mucus increases in quantity (10- to 30-fold) and in elasticity. "Palm leaf" arborization (ferning) becomes prominent just prior to ovulation (if cervical mucus is allowed to dry on a glass slide and is examined microscopically). Under the influence of progesterone during the luteal phase, cervical mucus thickens, becomes less watery, and loses its elasticity and ability to fern. The characteristics of cervical mucus are useful clinically to evaluate the stage of the cycle and the amount of estrogen present.

VAGINA

When ovarian estrogen secretion is low, as in the early follicular phase, vaginal epithelium is pale and thin. In the follicular phase under the influence of estrogens the epithelium thickens, and the number of mature cornified epithelial cells increases. During the luteal phase, progesterone causes a decrease in the percentage of cornified cells and an increase in the number of precornified intermediate cells and polymorphonuclear leukocytes. There is also increased cellular debris and clumping of shed desquamated cells. Histologic changes in the vaginal epithelium and in the cervical mucus are the most sensitive indicators of estrogen status in the body. However, the reliability of vaginal smears depends on the absence of infection or exogenously administered steroid hormones that have antiestrogenic effects. Steroid hormones also facilitate progression of spermatozoa toward the ovaries and of ova toward the uterine cavity through effects on the fallopian tubes.

OVARY

During the reproductive years, the human ovaries regularly produce a single dominant graafian follicle that grows and develops to the preovulatory stage during the follicular phase of the menstrual cycle. This process is brought about by combined action of FSH and LH on the follicle wall to cause the biosynthesis of increasing quantities of estradiol. At about midpoint in the menstrual cycle, the surge of LH acts on the preovulatory follicle to cause the secretion of a mature fertilizable oocyte by a process termed ovulation. After ovulation, the follicle wall transforms into the corpus luteum, which produces considerable quantities of progesterone and estradiol during the luteal phase of the cycle. If implantation does not occur, the corpus luteum undergoes luteolysis and stops hormone production. In the late luteal phase, another dominant follicle develops and a new menstrual cycle begins. The potential to produce a dominant follicle stops at the menopause when few or no reserve oocytes remain.

CHRONOLOGY OF FOLLICULOGENESIS. The preovulatory follicle arises by folliculogenesis. It begins its development when a primordial follicle is recruited into the pool of growing follicles. As a consequence of successive primordial follicle recruitments, the ovaries contain a pool of small graafian follicles with the potential to develop into the preovulatory follicle. In the human female, folliculogenesis is a long process. In each menstrual cycle, the preovulatory follicle arises from a primordial follicle that was recruited to grow about 1 year earlier (Fig. 250–2). The mechanism responsible for recruitment is poorly understood, but studies in laboratory animals indicate that specific molecules from the granulosa cells, namely kit ligand and müllerian inhibiting substance, play stimulatory and inhibitory roles, respectively.

There are two major phases of folliculogenesis: the preantral (gonadotropin-independent) and the antral or graafian (gonadotropin-dependent) period. The first phase is characterized by growth of the oocyte within the follicle and the onset of granulosa proliferation. The early stages of preantral folliculogenesis (class 1, primary and secondary follicle states; class 2, tertiary or cavitation state) proceed slowly. It requires 300 days or more for a recruited primordial follicle to complete the preantral or gonadotropin-independent period of folliculogenesis (see Fig. 250–2). During the second phase of folliculogenesis, the granulosa and theca cells proliferate extensively and the antrum enlarges greatly. The size of the graafian follicle increases relatively rapidly as it grows and develops through the small (class 3, 4, 5), medium (class 6, 7), and large (class 8) stages. The mature graafian follicle that will ovulate requires 40 to 50 days to complete the antral phase of follicular growth. The follicles that do not participate in ovulation undergo atresia and die by apoptosis. Atresia can

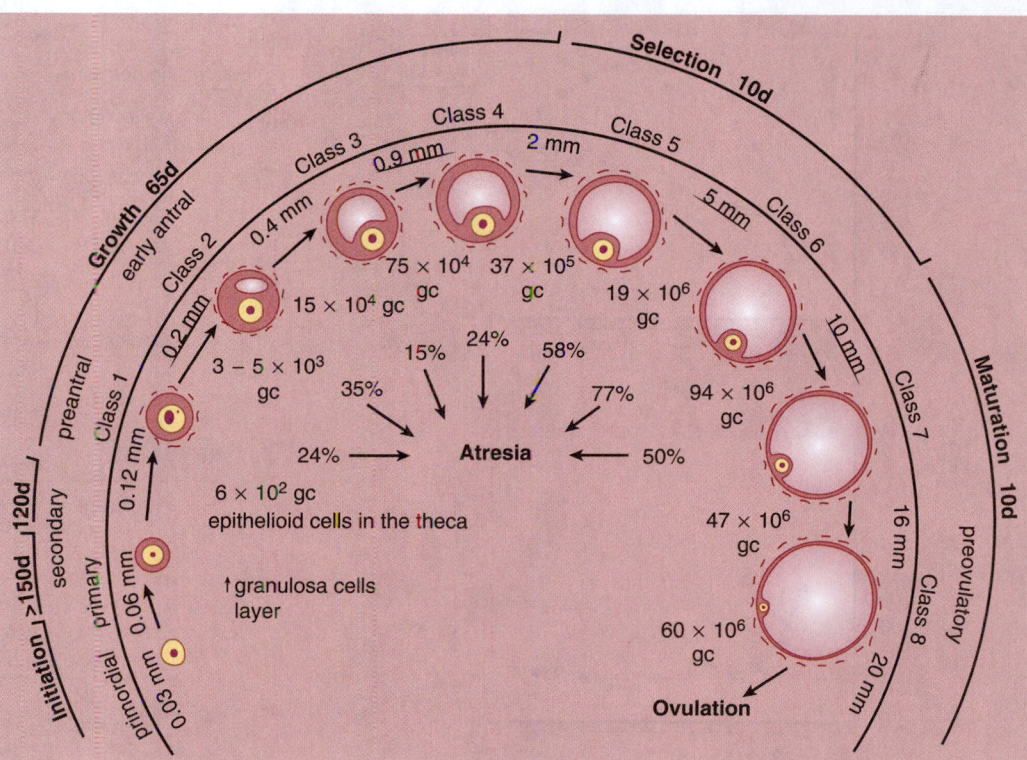

FIGURE 250–2 • The chronology of folliculogenesis in the human ovary. Folliculogenesis is divided into two major periods, preantral (gonadotropin independent) and antral (gonadotropin dependent). In the preantral period, a recruited primordial follicle develops to the primary-secondary (class 1) and early tertiary (class 2) stage, at which time cavitation or antrum formation begins. The antral period includes the small graafian (0.9 to 5 mm, class 4 and 5), medium graafian (6 to 10 mm, class 6), large graafian (10 to 15 mm, class 7), and preovulatory (16 to 20 mm, class 8) follicles. Time required for completion of preantral and antral periods is approximately 300 and approximately 40 days, respectively. Gc = number of granulosa cells; mm = follicle diameter; % atresia indicated. (Modified from Gougeon A: Dynamics of follicular growth in the human: A model from preliminary results. Hum Reprod 1986;1:81–87.)

occur at any stage of antral follicle development but appears most prominent in the small graafian follicles at the class 5 stage.

SELECTION. In women, the dominant follicle is selected from a cohort of class 5 follicles (4.7 ± 0.7 mm in diameter) at the end of the luteal phase of the menstrual cycle. A typical class 5 follicle consists of a fully grown oocyte surrounded by a zona pellucida, about 1 million granulosa cells, a theca interna containing several layers of differentiated theca interstitial cells, and a band of smooth muscle cells termed the theca externa (Fig. 250–3). Once selected, it requires about 20 days for a dominant follicle to develop to the ovulatory stage.

The mechanism responsible for selection involves a high sustained rate of granulosa and theca cell proliferation. Shortly after the mid-luteal phase of the cycle, the granulosa cells in all of the cohort class 5 follicles show a sharp increase (~twofold) in the rate of granulosa mitosis. The first indication of a selection is that the granulosa cells within the chosen follicle continue dividing at a high rate while proliferation slows in the other cohort follicles. Because this event occurs in the late luteal phase, it is believed that the selection occurs at this point in the menstrual cycle. As a consequence of the high sustained mitotic rate and the progressive accumulation of follicular fluid, the dominant follicle undergoes remarkable growth, reaching 6.9 ± 0.5 mm in diameter at days 1 to 5, 13.7 ± 1.2 mm at days 6 to 10, and 18.8 ± 0.5 mm at days 11 to 14 of the menstrual cycle. In nondomi-

nant follicles, growth and expansion proceed more slowly, and with time atresia becomes increasingly more evident. Rarely does an atretic human follicle reach 9 mm or greater in diameter.

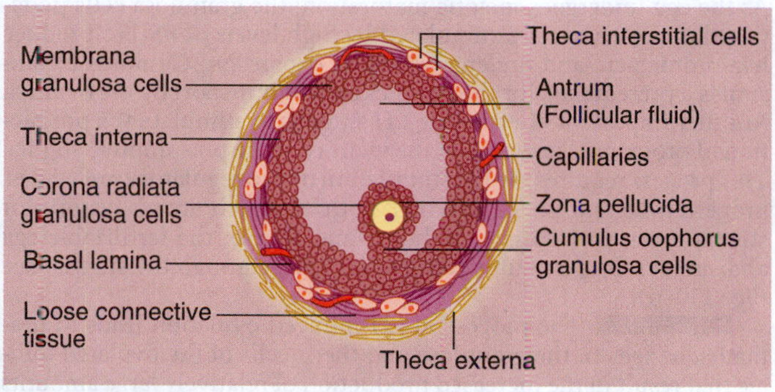

FSH is obligatory for selection and there is no other ligand known that can serve in this regulatory capacity. In women, it is the increase in plasma FSH levels that begins at the end of luteal phase and continues through the early follicular phase that evokes follicle selection (Fig. 250–4). This rise in plasma FSH is accomplished by an increase in the concentration of FSH in the follicular fluid of the healthy (dominant) follicle as it moves through the cycle. By contrast, the levels of FSH remain low or undetectable in the follicular fluid of the nondominant atretic follicles. Such evidence has led to the concept that selection is controlled by a selective increase in the concentration of FSH in the follicular fluid of one cohort follicle. The manner in which this selective increase in FSH is controlled remains one of the quintessential problems of ovary physiology.

Mechanism of FSH Action. FSH exerts its influence on follicle growth and development by stimulating granulosa cell mitosis and cytodifferentiation. FSH regulates biologic responses through activation of specific high-affinity FSH receptors on the surface of the granulosa cell. The binding event is transduced into an intracellular signal through the cyclic adenosine monophosphate (AMP)–dependent protein kinase A signal transduction pathway (Fig. 250–5). This process leads to the activation of a large body of genes that result in increases in cell number and regulatory molecules leading to cytodifferentiation.

In women, the granulosa cells in the chosen follicle continue to divide at a relatively rapid rate throughout the follicular phase of the cycle, increasing from about 1×10^6 cells at selection to over 50×10^6 cells at ovulation. The role of FSH in this mitogen response has been established. The high mitotic rate in the granulosa cells during dominant follicle growth can be accounted for by the relatively high concentrations of FSH in follicular fluid.

The concept that FSH is also the major inducer of granulosa cytodifferentiation in the dominant follicle is clear. The $P450_{Aromatase}$ ($P450_{Arom}$) gene is one of the physiologically important genes whose expression is induced by FSH (see Fig. 250–5). The temporal pattern of expression of $P450_{Arom}$ is a critical determinant of when and how much estradiol is produced by the developing dominant follicle during the follicular phase of the menstrual cycle. Another major FSH-dependent transcriptional event is the expression of LH receptors. Typically, this expression is delayed until the dominant follicle is fully differentiated at around day 12 of the cycle. The presence of a large number of LH receptors in the granulosa cells is essential for the

Membrana granulosa cells

Theca interna

Corona radiata granulosa cells

Basal lamina

Loose connective tissue

Theca interstitial cells

Antrum (Follicular fluid)

Capillaries

Zona pellucida

Cumulus oophorus granulosa cells

Theca externa

FIGURE 250–3 • Schematic cross section of a healthy graafian follicle. (From Erickson GF: Primary cultures of ovarian cells in serum-free medium as models of hormone-dependent differentiation. Mol Cell Endocrinol 1983;29:21–49.)

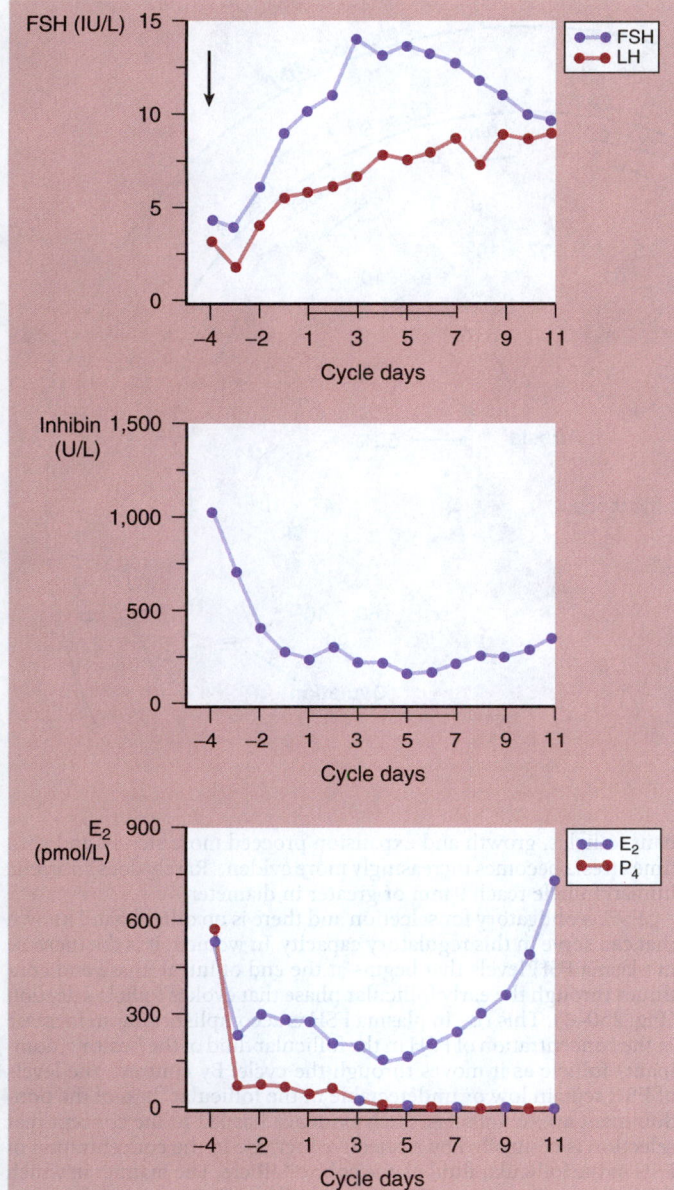

FIGURE 250–4 • The endocrinology of the luteal-follicular transition in women. Data are means ± SE of daily serum concentrations of follicle-stimulating hormone (FSH), luteinizing hormone (LH), estradiol (E$_2$), progesterone (P$_4$) and immunoreactive inhibin in women with normal cycles. Note the secondary rise in plasma FSH in the late luteal phase (−2 days before menses). (Modified from Roseff SJ, Bangah ML, Kettel LM, et al: Dynamic changes in circulating inhibin levels during the luteal-follicular transition of the human menstrual cycle. J Clin Endocrinol Metab 1989;69:1033–1039.)

LH–human chorionic gonadotropin (hCG) surge to trigger ovulation. The terminal differentiation of the granulosa cells is also characterized by the increasing synthesis and accumulation of a wide variety of FSH-regulated gene products in addition to P450$_{Arom}$ and LH receptors. Examples include inhibin B, activin, and follistatin.

Mechanism of LH Action. The primary function of LH in follicle development is to stimulate androgen production by the theca interstitial cells (see Fig. 250–5). There is great clinical interest in this LH response because of (1) its crucial role in estrogen biosynthesis and (2) its involvement in infertility and hyperandrogenism in women with polycystic ovary (PCO) syndrome. The mechanism of LH action involves binding to LH-hCG receptors located on theca cells. Upon activation, the LH receptors interact with G proteins, which then activate adenylate cyclase leading to the synthesis of cyclic AMP, which in turn is capable of stimulating gene expression through protein kinase A. At the gene level, LH signaling elicits increases in a variety of genes including the steroidogenic acute regulatory (StAR), P450C22, 3β-

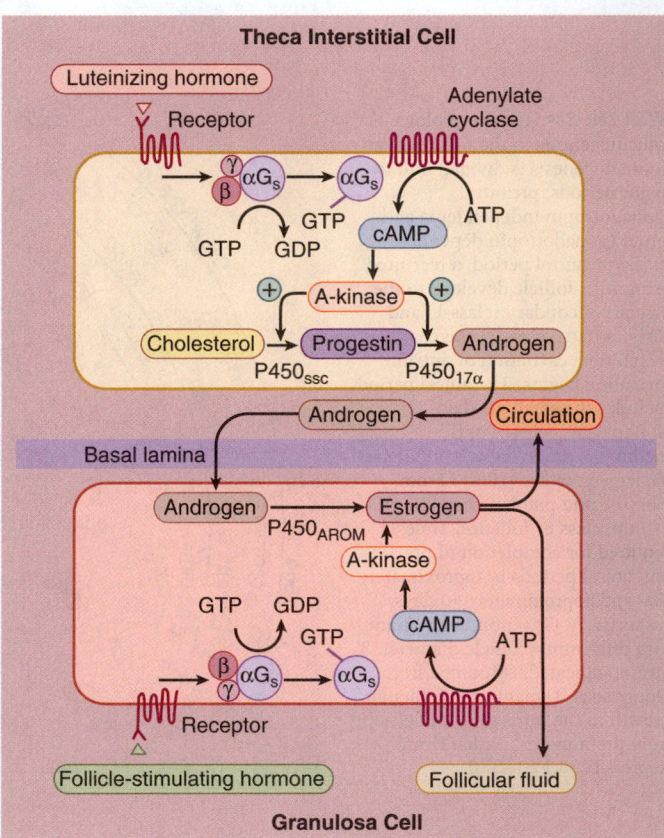

FIGURE 250–5 • The two gonadotropin–two cell concept of follicle estrogen production. ATP = adenosine triphosphate; cAMP = cyclic adenosine monophosphate; GDP = guanosine diphosphate; GTP = guanosine triphosphate. (Modified from Erickson GF: Normal ovarian function. Clin Obstet Gynecol 1978;21:31–52.)

hydroxysteroid dehydrogenase (3β-HSD), and P450C17 genes. The biologic outcome of this LH response is increased conversion of cholesterol to androstenedione. Theca cells express insulin receptors with protein tyrosine kinase activity. Activation of the insulin receptor signaling pathway leads to increased theca androgen production. The cross talk between the insulin and LH receptor signaling is clinically relevant because of the relationship between hyperinsulinemia and hyperandrogenism in women.

One of the most important physiologic consequences of FSH and LH action on the dominant follicle is the production of estradiol. This physiologically important process is called the *two gonadotropin–two cell concept* of follicular estrogen production (see Fig. 250–5). This is a basic principle in ovary physiology.

OVULATION. At about midpoint in the menstrual cycle, the preovulatory surges of LH and FSH act on the preovulatory follicle to initiate the events leading to ovulation (Fig. 250–6). During this process, the LH surge induces meiotic maturation, a process that converts the oocyte into a fertilizable egg arrested at the second meiotic metaphase. As the egg undergoes meiotic maturation, the granulosa cells juxtaposed to the oocyte are stimulated by high levels of FSH to produce hyaluronic acid and undergo cumulus expansion. Cumulus expansion is a prerequisite for the egg pickup and transport by the oviduct. Another important effect of the LH surge is to stimulate the production of proteolytic enzymes in the vicinity of the presumptive stigma. This process requires the LH stimulation of two regulatory molecules, progesterone and prostaglandins, both of which are obligatory for stigma formation. After a 36-hour time course, the fertilizable egg and surrounding cumulus cells are secreted through the stigma (see Fig. 250–6).

LUTEOGENESIS. The process of LH-induced ovulation leads to dramatic changes in the granulosa and theca cells of the ovulated follicle that result in the increased production of relatively large amounts of progesterone and estradiol during the first week of the luteal phase. This event, termed *luteinization*, is of great importance for the formation and development of a secretory endometrium. Three major

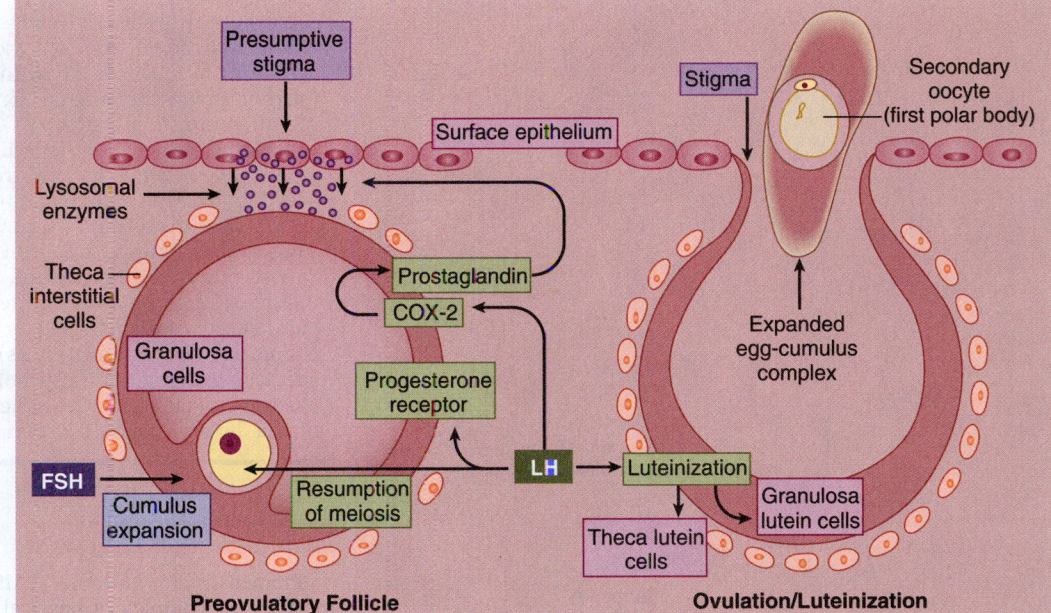

FIGURE 250–6 • The mechanism of ovulation. COX-2 = cyclooxygenase 2; FSH = follicle-stimulating hormone; LH = luteinizing hormone. (Modified from Erickson GF: The ovary: Basic principles and concepts. *In* Felig P, Baxter JD, Broadus AE, Frohman LA [eds]:Endocrinology and Metabolism, 3rd ed. New York, McGraw-Hill, 1995, pp 973–1015.)

physiologic mechanisms are responsible for luteinization: (1) removal of the luteinization inhibitors emanating from the oocyte, (2) secretion of LH by the pituitary, and (3) delivery of high levels of cholesterol present in low-density lipoprotein. The underlying basis for progesterone production by the corpus luteum involves the induction of StAR, P450C22, and 3β-HSD in the granulosa lutein cells. The two cell–two gonadotropin mechanism is responsible for estradiol production by the human corpus luteum.

If implantation does not occur, the corpus luteum initiates luteolysis. This event is reflected in decreases in progesterone and estradiol biosynthesis and the expression of apoptosis. The physiologic mechanism underlying luteolysis in unknown, but it is clear that hCG released by the implanting embryo is able to prevent luteolysis. When luteolysis occurs, another dominant follicle is selected and a new menstrual cycle begins.

THE AUTOCRINE-PARACRINE CONCEPT. An important concept to emerge in the past decade is that the follicle and luteal cells produce regulatory molecules that can modulate, either amplify or attenuate, FSH and LH action. This is the autocrine-paracrine concept (Fig. 250–7). Much of what we know about this concept has come from studies conducted in animal models. One finding of great interest is that folliculogenesis and female fertility are critically dependent on two oocyte-derived factors: growth differentiation factor-9 and bone morphogenetic protein-15. Although these autocrine-paracrine molecules have been identified in human oocytes, there is at present little evidence available for deciding their importance in the human ovary. The current challenges are to understand how the autocrine-paracrine molecules are regulated and how the activities are integrated into the overall pathways that govern ovarian physiology and pathophysiology.

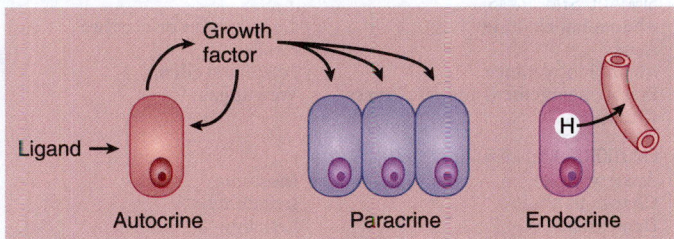

FIGURE 250–7 • Comparison of autocrine-paracrine and endocrine concepts. H = hormone. (Modified from Erickson GF: Nongonadotropic regulation of ovarian function: Growth hormone and IGFs. *In* Filicori M, Flanigni C [eds]: Ovulation Induction: Basic Science and Clinical Advances [Excerpta Medica International Congress Series]. Amsterdam, Elsevier Science Publishers, 1994, pp 73–84.)

Neuroendocrine Regulation of the Ovaries

Neurons containing various peptide hormones that can release or inhibit secretion of the gonadotropins are found in the hypothalamus (Chapter 235). Specifically, cells containing gonadotropin-releasing hormone (GnRH) occur in the area including the arcuate nucleus and median eminence and the preoptic area. Axons from these neurons run in the tuberoinfundibular tract and terminate on capillaries within the median eminence, which allows delivery of their products through the portal vascular system to the anterior pituitary gland. It appears that classical neurotransmitters, including norepinephrine, dopamine, and serotonin, as well as neuromodulators, such as endogenous opiates and prostaglandins, influence secretion of GnRH by the hypothalamus. In addition, estrogens and androgens bind to cells in the hypothalamus and the anterior pituitary, and progestins bind to cells in the hypothalamus to influence hypothalamic-pituitary regulation of ovarian function.

GnRH is secreted in a pulsatile fashion (perhaps because of an inherent oscillator within the arcuate nucleus) and is responsible for pulsatile release of gonadotropins. Pulsatile gonadotropin release in turn appears to account for the pulsatile secretion of sex steroids from the ovaries. The ovarian sex steroids then feed back on the hypothalamic-pituitary unit to modulate both the frequency and amplitude of the gonadotropin pulse (Fig. 250–8). Thus, gonadotropin pulses vary throughout the menstrual cycle. Pulses occur at approximately 60- to 90-minute intervals in the follicular phase and at intervals of more than 180 minutes in the luteal phase.

Gonadal steroids can exert both negative and positive feedback effects on gonadotropin secretion. Among ovarian steroids, 17β-estradiol is the most potent inhibitor of gonadotropin secretion, acting on both the hypothalamus and the pituitary. For women to ovulate, estradiol must also elicit a positive feedback effect on gonadotropin release. The feedback effects are both time and dose dependent. In the normal menstrual cycle the positive feedback action of estradiol leading to the LH surge is preceded by a period when lower estradiol levels are present with their negative feedback effects.

It appears that the ovary is the "clock" for the timing of ovulation, with the hypothalamus stimulating pulsatile release of the gonadotropins. The follicle complex and corpus luteum develop in response to gonadotropin stimulation. For appropriate ovarian regulation of reproductive function in women, three biologic characteristics are necessary: (1) an appropriate balance and sequence of negative and positive feedback actions, (2) differential feedback effects on the release of LH and FSH, and (3) local intraovarian controls on follicular growth and maturation, separate from but interrelated with the effects of gonadotropins on the ovaries.

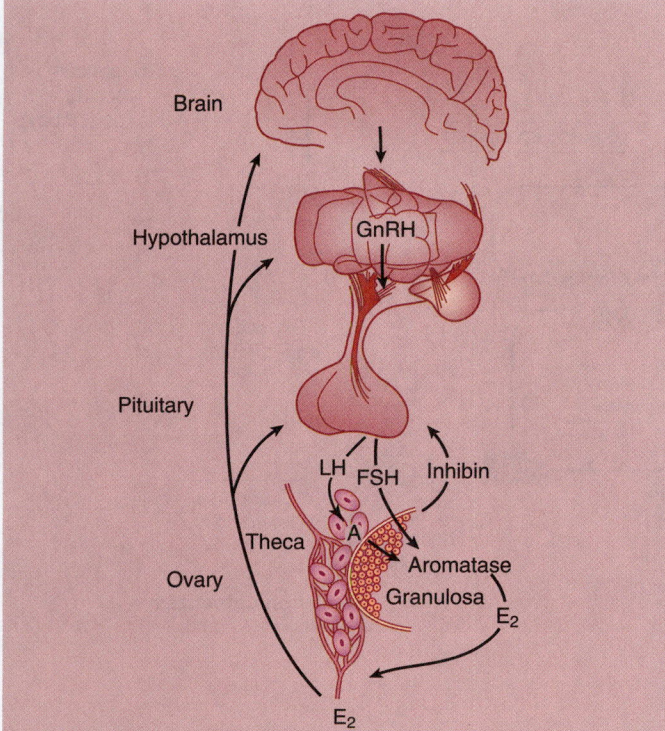

FIGURE 250–8 • The hypothalamic-pituitary-ovarian axis in the regulation of follicular maturation and steroidogenesis. A = androgens; E_s = estradiol; FSH = follicle-stimulating hormone; GnRH = gonadotropin-releasing hormone; LH = luteinizing hormone. (Modified from Endocrine and Metabolism Continuing Education Quality Control Program, 1982. Copyright American Association for Clinical Chemistry, Inc.)

ABNORMALITIES OF THE REPRODUCTIVE YEARS

DYSMENORRHEA AND ENDOMETRIOSIS

Dysmenorrhea, perhaps the most common of all gynecologic disorders, affects about 50% of postpubertal women. Dysmenorrhea can be classified as primary or secondary.

Primary dysmenorrhea occurs only in ovulatory cycles. Prostaglandins that are released from the endometrium just prior to and during menstruation cause contraction of uterine smooth muscle and produce dysmenorrhea by initiating painful, exaggerated uterine contractions and myometrial ischemia. Associated systemic symptoms include nausea, diarrhea, headache, and emotional changes. Primary dysmenorrhea is much more common than secondary dysmenorrhea.

In *secondary dysmenorrhea* there is a pathologic cause for the dysmenorrhea. Endometriosis, the ectopic occurrence of endometrial tissue generally within the abdominal cavity, is the most common cause in severe cases. Other possible causes include pelvic inflammatory disease, congenital abnormalities such as atresia of a portion of the distal genital tract and cystic duplication of the paramesonephric ducts, and cervical stenosis.

 Treatment

Prostaglandin synthetase inhibitors such as naproxen, ibuprofen, mefenamic acid, and indomethacin are the mainstays of treatment. If the dysmenorrhea is still severe, addition of an oral contraceptive preparation to inhibit ovulation and limit prostaglandin release is generally effective. In cases in which the pelvic pain still remains intractable, additional evaluation is warranted. If thorough evaluation of the gastrointestinal and urinary tracts fails to reveal a definitive cause, examination under anesthesia and diagnostic laparoscopy may be indicated.

If endometriosis is diagnosed at laparoscopy, treatment varies, depending on the severity of the disease and the goals of the patient regarding fertility. It may be possible to fulgurate implants or lyse adhesions through the laparoscope. In general, endometriosis should be treated medically, with additional surgery deferred until infertility (if present) becomes manifest. Medical therapy can consist of continuous suppression with GnRH analogues, progestins, oral contraceptive agents, or danazol for 3 to 6 months. GnRH analogues have become the most frequent form of medical suppressive therapy. After a course of therapy, use of oral contraceptive agents should probably be continued until fertility is desired. Conservative surgical resection of endometriotic tissue should almost always be deferred until it is established as the cause of infertility. Surgery may be required, however, for continuing severe pain, severe endometriosis, or large ovarian cysts containing endometriosis (endometriomas). If symptoms continue despite adequate treatment or if psychological overlay is suspected, psychiatric evaluation may be indicated. Medical causes of dysmenorrhea, however, should be eliminated first.

PREMENSTRUAL SYNDROME

Premenstrual syndrome (PMS), also known as premenstrual tension, is a complex of physical and/or emotional symptoms that occur repetitively in a cyclic fashion before menstruation and that diminish or disappear with menstruation. Typically these cyclic symptoms are sufficiently severe to interfere with some aspects of life. Women with established psychiatric disturbances probably should not be included among those with PMS. More than 150 different symptoms are now thought to vary with the menstrual cycle (Table 250–1). Estimates of the prevalence of PMS range from 25 to 100%. The American Psychiatric Association has defined a disorder that should be regarded as similar to but more severe than PMS and termed it premenstrual dysphoric disorder (PMDD). Certain specific symptoms must be present to diagnose PMDD. For most women, PMS is merely annoying; severe PMS (or PMDD) causes serious difficulties for no more than 5 to 10% of women of reproductive age. The diagnosis of PMDD is best established by requiring patients to keep prospective daily records of symptoms over a 2- to 3-month period. Fewer than 50% of women complaining of PMS are found to have the syndrome when such records are examined.

Most women seek help for PMS in their 30s after 10 or more years of symptoms. Many report that their symptoms began at menarche; approximately half state that symptoms followed childbirth. Severity and duration of symptoms are often reported to increase after each successive pregnancy and to become more severe with advancing age. Women with severe long-standing PMS almost always describe associated psychological reactions, including social difficulties, such as marital discord, difficulty relating to their children, difficulty maintaining friendships, and withdrawal from social activities.

Table 250–1 • COMMON SYMPTOMS OF CYCLIC PREMENSTRUAL SYNDROME

SOMATIC SYMPTOMS

Abdominal bloating	Constipation or diarrhea
Acne	Headache
Alcohol intolerance	Peripheral edema
Breast engorgement and tenderness	Weight gain
Clumsiness	

EMOTIONAL AND MENTAL SYMPTOMS

Anxiety	Insomnia
Change in libido	Irritability
Depression	Lethargy
Fatigue	Mood swings
Food cravings (especially salt and sugar)	Panic attacks
Hostility	Paranoia
Inability to concentrate	Violence toward self and others
Increased appetite	Withdrawal from others

Rx Treatment

The cause of PMS is unknown, and patients should be informed that no one therapy has been effective in all women. Women with mild premenstrual symptoms often benefit from simple changes in lifestyle, including daily mild aerobic exercise; reduction in intake of xanthine-containing beverages, salt, and refined sugar in the day, particularly in the luteal phase; stress reduction; and adequate rest. Women with more severe PMS may benefit from treating predominant complaints symptomatically. Thus, bromocriptine* (generally 2.5 mg twice a day) or danazol (100 to 400 mg/day in two divided doses) may be given continuously for relief of mastalgia, with the understanding that both may have unpleasant side effects. Prostaglandin synthetase inhibitors may help reduce dysmenorrhea and may alleviate headaches. Mild sedatives and tranquilizers may help reduce insomnia and anxiety. Low doses of fluoxetine (20 mg) and other selective serotonin reuptake inhibitors, administered either daily or for the last 2 weeks of each menstrual cycle, often reduce the emotional symptoms associated with PMS. Mild diuretics (especially spironolactone at doses up to 100 mg each morning) may benefit cyclic edema if that can be confirmed.

Because PMS requires the occurrence of cyclic ovulation, oophorectomy is occasionally considered for patients with particularly intractable symptoms. However, oophorectomy may create new problems related to estrogen deficiency for women with PMS treated in this permanent fashion. Several trials employing a GnRH agonist together with exogenous steroids (so-called add-back therapy) have been described as reducing PMS. Whether such therapy can be utilized in the long term remains to be determined.

Natural progesterone, particularly in the form of vaginal suppositories given at doses of up to 800 mg/day, has been used, but results of double-blind placebo-controlled trials have provided no evidence of efficacy. Likewise, the use of large quantities of multiple vitamins or of oil of evening primrose, containing the essential fatty acid γ-linolenic acid, a precursor of prostaglandins, is unsubstantiated.

ABNORMAL UTERINE BLEEDING

Differential Diagnosis

The causes of abnormal uterine bleeding in the reproductive years include complications from the use of oral contraceptives, complications of pregnancy (especially threatened, incomplete, or missed abortion and ectopic pregnancy), coagulation disorders (most commonly idiopathic thrombocytopenic purpura and von Willebrand's disease), and pelvic disease such as intrauterine polyps, leiomyomas, and tumors of the vagina and cervix. Clear cell adenocarcinoma of the vagina or cervix may occur in women exposed to diethylstilbestrol (DES) during fetal life as a result of maternal ingestion. Affected women may also have congenital abnormalities of the upper vagina, cervix, and uterus. Because a history of DES exposure is not always obtained and because this malignant tumor may be fatal, clinical suspicion should remain high. Women with a history of DES exposure should be reassured, however, that the incidence of malignancy is extremely low. Trauma (coital or otherwise), foreign bodies, systemic illnesses including various endocrinopathies (such as diabetes mellitus, hypothyroidism and hyperthyroidism, Cushing's syndrome, and Addison's disease), leukemia, and renal disease may also be associated with abnormal bleeding as the presenting manifestation.

Dysfunctional uterine bleeding, abnormal uterine bleeding with no demonstrable organic genital or extragenital cause (75% of cases), is most frequently associated with anovulation. Postmenarchal bleeding in adolescents secondary to immaturity of the hypothalamic-pituitary-ovarian axis accounts for about 20% of all cases, and perimenopausal bleeding consequent to incipient ovarian failure constitutes more than half of the cases. Most anovulatory bleeding is due to either estrogen withdrawal or estrogen breakthrough bleeding. In anovulatory women, estrogen stimulates the endometrium unopposed by progesterone. As a consequence, the endometrium proliferates, becomes thicker, and may shed irregularly, especially if estrogen levels

---

*This use is not listed in the manufacturer's directive.

drop. Anovulatory bleeding tends to occur at less frequent intervals, and organic lesions tend to cause bleeding more frequently than cyclic menses.

Evaluation

All cases of abnormal bleeding should be evaluated, including obtaining a thorough history with special emphasis on the amount and duration of blood loss. Prospective charting of the days on which bleeding occurs may be required to evaluate the bleeding pattern. Complications of pregnancy or a bleeding diathesis must always be ruled out.

The physical examination (including the Papanicolaou smear) is normal in dysfunctional bleeding except for signs of anemia in the more severe cases. Laboratory tests should include a complete blood count, platelet count, coagulation studies, thyroid function tests, and fasting blood glucose. Dysfunctional uterine bleeding must be a diagnosis of exclusion. Management of dysfunctional uterine bleeding depends on the age of the patient and the extent of the bleeding. A sample of the endometrium should be obtained by biopsy or by dilatation and curettage from all women older than 35 years and from those at increased risk for endometrial carcinoma because of prolonged anovulatory bleeding.

Rx Treatment

Even profuse bleeding in anovulatory women can almost always be successfully treated by administering one combination oral contraceptive pill every 6 hours for 5 to 7 days. Bleeding should cease within 24 hours, but patients should be warned to expect heavy bleeding 2 to 4 days after stopping therapy. If anemia and signs of acute blood loss are profound, blood transfusion may be necessary. If the bleeding continues despite therapy, curettage can be carried out. Recurrence can be prevented by giving the patient combination oral contraceptive agents cyclically for 3 or more months. If spontaneous cyclic menses do not resume and pregnancy is not desired, the patient can be treated with cyclic progestin (medroxyprogesterone acetate, 5 to 10 mg for 10 to 14 days each month) or oral contraceptive agents. If pregnancy is desired, ovulation can be induced, as discussed subsequently.

Acute episodes of anovulatory bleeding can also be treated with conjugated estrogens administered intravenously (25 mg every 4 hours for up to three doses) until bleeding ceases. Progestin therapy (medroxyprogesterone acetate, 5 to 10 mg orally for 10 days) should be started simultaneously. Withdrawal bleeding occurs after cessation of therapy, and the patient can then be treated with oral contraceptive agents for at least three cycles.

For individuals with anovulatory bleeding without an episode of profuse bleeding, treatment with cyclic oral contraceptive agents or progestin can be provided unless pregnancy is desired, in which case ovulation must be induced.

Endometrial ablation by any of several methods is being used increasingly to treat persistent bleeding, especially because it is not a major operation. However, ablation is not 100% effective, and medical management remains the first line of therapy for most women. Hysterectomy may be an appropriate choice for a small number of women.

AMENORRHEA

Definition and Etiology

Amenorrhea is the absence of menstruation for 3 or more months in women with past menses (*secondary amenorrhea*) or the absence of menarche by the age of 16 years regardless of the absence or presence of secondary sex characteristics (*primary amenorrhea*). If an intact genital outflow tract exists and there is no primary disease of the uterus, amenorrhea is a sign of failure of the hypothalamic-pituitary-ovarian axis to produce cyclically the hormones necessary for menses. Amenorrhea is a sign of any of several disorders involving different organ systems. Amenorrhea is physiologic in the prepubertal girl, during pregnancy and early in lactation, and after the menopause. At any other time it is pathologic and demands evaluation. Use of the term *postpill amenorrhea* to refer to failure to resume menses within

3 months of discontinuing oral contraceptives is inappropriate. Women so affected should be evaluated in the same manner as any woman with amenorrhea. Similarly, individuals with menses occurring at infrequent intervals of greater than 40 days or having fewer than nine menses per year, termed *oligomenorrhea*, should be evaluated identically to women with amenorrhea.

Clinical Evaluation

In patients with amenorrhea, even subtle hormonal abnormalities may be manifested by obvious signs and symptoms. Breast development indicates exposure to estrogens, and the presence of pubic and axillary hair indicates androgenic stimulation.

Patients should be questioned especially closely for evidence of psychological disturbances, dietary and exercise habits, lifestyle, environmental stresses, a family history of genetic anomalies, and abnormal growth and development. Patients should also be asked about and examined for any signs of hyperandrogenism, including hirsutism, temporal balding, deepening of the voice, increased muscle mass, clitorimegaly, and increased libido, as well as for signs of defeminization, including decreasing breast size and vaginal atrophy. Any history of galactorrhea, the nonpuerperal secretion of milk from the breasts, should be determined (Chapter 237). A history of symptoms related to thyroid and adrenal dysfunction should also be sought.

The physical examination should focus on evaluating (1) body dimensions and habitus, (2) the extent and distribution of body hair, (3) breast development and secretions, and (4) the genitalia.

In normal adult women the arm span is similar to the height, whereas in hypogonadal women the span is generally more than 5 cm greater than the height. The general appearance of the patient should be evaluated to determine whether the habitus is that of an adult female. The distribution and quantity of body hair should be considered in view of the family history. The extent of any hirsutism should be recorded, preferably by photographs. Other signs of virilization should be sought carefully. Breast development should be graded according to the method of Tanner (Table 250–2). Breast secretion should be sought by applying pressure to the breasts while the patient is seated. Any secretion should be examined microscopically for the presence of perfectly round fat globules of varying size, which are always present in milk and indicate galactorrhea. Finally, the female genitalia should be examined carefully because they are such sensitive indicators of hormonal milieu. The Tanner stage of pubic hair development should be noted (Table 250–2).

Because the sensitivity of the genitalia to androgens decreases onward from early in fetal development, the extent of any virilization is important. Fusion of the labia and enlargement of the clitoris with or without formation of a penile urethra are observed in women exposed to androgens during the first 3 months of fetal development (Chapter 246). Significant clitorimegaly in the absence of other signs of sexual ambiguity and in the presence of other signs of virilization requires marked androgenic stimulation and strongly implicates an androgen-secreting neoplasm in the absence of a history of ingestion of exogenous steroids. The development of the labia minora in postpubertal women indicates the influence of estrogens. Overt anomalies of the distal genital tract and especially any evidence of obstruction to the escape of menstrual blood should be sought in the remainder of the pelvic examination. The vaginal mucosa and the cervical mucus are exquisitely sensitive to estrogen. Under the influence of estrogen, the vaginal mucosa changes during sexual maturation from a tissue with a shiny, bright red appearance with sparse, thin secretions to a dull, gray-pink rugated surface with copious, thick secretions.

The history and physical examination quickly differentiate among several causes of amenorrhea, regardless of the age of the patient (Table 250–3). The various disorders of sexual differentiation and the other anatomic causes are often apparent on inspection. Distal genital tract obstruction should be identified at the time of pelvic examination even if the specific abnormality is not obvious. The physical stigmata of Turner's syndrome, discussed subsequently, generally make the diagnosis simple. Any sexual ambiguity indicates the need for chromosomal analysis and the measurement of 17α-hydroxyprogesterone to rule out congenital adrenal hyperplasia. Pregnancy and gestational trophoblastic disease may be suspected and confirmed by measuring circulating concentrations of hCG. The possibility of intrauterine synechiae or adhesions (Asherman's syndrome) must be considered in individuals in whom amenorrhea develops after curettage or

endometritis. Tuberculous endometritis, especially in younger women, may also lead to this disorder. Without hormonal measurements it may be impossible to distinguish among individuals with chronic anovulation, in whom hypothalamic-pituitary-ovarian function is insufficiently coordinated to produce cyclic ovulation, and those with ovarian failure, in whom in most cases the ovaries are devoid of oocytes.

Table 250–2 • CRITERIA FOR DISTINGUISHING TANNER STAGES 1 TO 5 DURING PUBERTAL MATURATION

TANNER STAGE	BREAST	PUBIC HAIR
1 (Prepubertal)	No palpable glandular tissue or pigmentation of areola; elevation of areola only	No pubic hair; short, fine vellus hair only
2	Glandular tissue palpable with elevation of breast and areola together as a small mound; areolar diameter increased	Sparse, long, pigmented terminal hair chiefly along the labia majora
3	Further enlargement without separation of breast and areola; although more darkly pigmented, areola still pale and immature; nipple generally at or above midplane of breast tissue when individual is seated upright	Dark, coarse, curly hair, extending sparsely over mons
4	Secondary mound of areola and papilla above breast	Adult-type hair, abundant but limited to mons and labia
5 (Adult)	Recession of areola to contour of breast; development of Montgomery's glands and ducts on areola; further pigmentation of areola; nipple generally below midplane of breast tissue when individual is seated upright; maturation independent of breast size	Adult-type hair in quantity and distribution; spread to inner aspects of the thighs in most racial groups

Data from Ross GT: Disorders of the ovary and female reproductive tract. *In* Wilson JD, Foster DW (eds): Textbook of Endocrinology, 7th ed. Philadelphia, WB Saunders, 1985, p 206; Speroff L, Glass RH, Kase N: Clinical Gynecologic Endocrinology and Infertility, 3rd ed. Baltimore, Williams & Wilkins, 1983, p 377; and Kustin J, Rebar RW: Menstrual disorders in the adolescent age group. Primary Care 1987;14:139–166.

Table 250–3 • CAUSES OF AMENORRHEA

ANATOMIC CAUSES
Pregnancy
Various disorders of sexual differentiation
   Distal genital tract obstruction (müllerian agenesis or dysgenesis)
   Gonadal dysgenesis*
   Ambiguity of external genitalia (male and female pseudohermaphroditism)
Intrauterine adhesions (Asherman's syndrome)
Gestational trophoblastic disease

CHRONIC ANOVULATION
Due to CNS-hypothalamic-pituitary dysfunction
With inappropriate steroid feedback (e.g., polycystic ovary syndrome)
Due to thyroid or adrenal disorders

OVARIAN "FAILURE"
Menopause
Genetic abnormalities
Physical and environmental causes (e.g., chemotherapeutic agents, irradiation)
Idiopathic

*Gonadal dysgenesis may be viewed as both a disorder of sexual differentiation and a form of gonadal "failure."
CNS = central nervous system.

Still, it is generally possible to form some strong clinical impressions about the cause of the amenorrhea. It can be noted whether the patient has absence of, incomplete, or complete development of secondary sex characteristics. The presence of excess body hair or galactorrhea may provide clinical evidence of the pathogenesis of the amenorrhea. Signs and symptoms of adrenal or thyroid dysfunction may be important as well.

Administration of a progestin (typically medroxyprogesterone acetate, 5 to 10 mg given orally for 5 to 10 days, or progesterone in oil, 100 mg given intramuscularly) has been advocated to assess the level of endogenous estrogen. This test is of limited value, however, because almost half the young women with premature ovarian failure experience withdrawal bleeding in response to progestin.

To ascertain whether the outflow tract is intact, an orally active estrogen, such as 2.5 mg of conjugated estrogen daily for 21 days, with 5 to 10 mg of oral medroxyprogesterone acetate for the last 5 to 10 days, may be administered. Withdrawal bleeding should occur if the endometrium is normal. Still, hysterosalpingography and hysteroscopy may be required to diagnose Asherman's syndrome because some patients continue to have some withdrawal bleeding.

Laboratory Evaluation

Basal levels of FSH, prolactin, and TSH should be measured in all amenorrheic and oligomenorrheic women to confirm the clinical impression (Fig. 250–9).

Increased thyroid-stimulating hormone (TSH) levels with or without increased levels of prolactin imply primary hypothyroidism, and further evaluation for this disorder is indicated (Chapter 237). Although hypothyroidism commonly results in anovulation, amenorrhea occurs in only some hypothyroid women. Menorrhagia and oligomenorrhea may occur as well. The sensitive immunoassays for TSH permit identification of women with hyperthyroidism as well because TSH levels are suppressed in those individuals.

If the prolactin concentration is increased (typically >20 to 30 ng/mL) and the TSH level is normal (generally <5 μU/mL),

measurement of the prolactin concentration in the basal state should be repeated before more extensive evaluation is undertaken. This is the case because prolactin levels are increased by nonspecific stressful stimuli, sleep, and food ingestion. Prolactin levels may be elevated in as many as one third of women with amenorrhea.

Increased FSH levels (generally >30 to 40 mIU/mL) imply ovarian failure and require further evaluation. Chromosomal evaluation is indicated in all individuals with elevated FSH levels who are younger than 30 years at the time the amenorrhea begins.

If prolactin and TSH concentrations are within normal ranges and FSH levels are low or normal, the measurement of total testosterone levels may be helpful whether or not there is any evidence of hirsutism or virilization. Hyperandrogenic women need not be hirsute because some have relative insensitivity of the hair follicles to androgens. Mildly increased levels of testosterone (and perhaps dehydroepiandrosterone sulfate [DHEAS] as well) suggest polycystic ovary (PCO) syndrome. However, total circulating androgen levels are rarely not elevated because of the alterations in metabolic clearance rate and sex hormone–binding globulin that are present in PCO syndrome. Consequently, some clinicians prefer to measure circulating free testosterone levels.

Circulating levels of LH and FSH may aid in differentiating PCO syndrome from hypothalamic-pituitary dysfunction. LH levels are frequently elevated in PCO syndrome so that the ratio of LH to FSH is increased; however, LH levels may be identical to those observed in normal women in the follicular phase. In contrast, levels of LH and FSH are normal or slightly reduced in hypothalamic-pituitary dysfunction. There is some overlap between women with "PCO-like" disorders and those with hypothalamic-pituitary dysfunction. Radiographic assessment of the sella turcica is indicated in all amenorrheic women in whom both LH and FSH levels are very low (both <10 mIU/mL) to exclude a pituitary or parapituitary neoplasm. Other pituitary functions should be evaluated in any individual with significantly impaired LH and FSH secretion, as detailed subsequently. Both total testosterone and DHEAS levels should be measured in hirsute or virilized women. Testosterone levels greater than 200 ng/dL should lead to investigation for an androgen-producing neoplasm, most likely

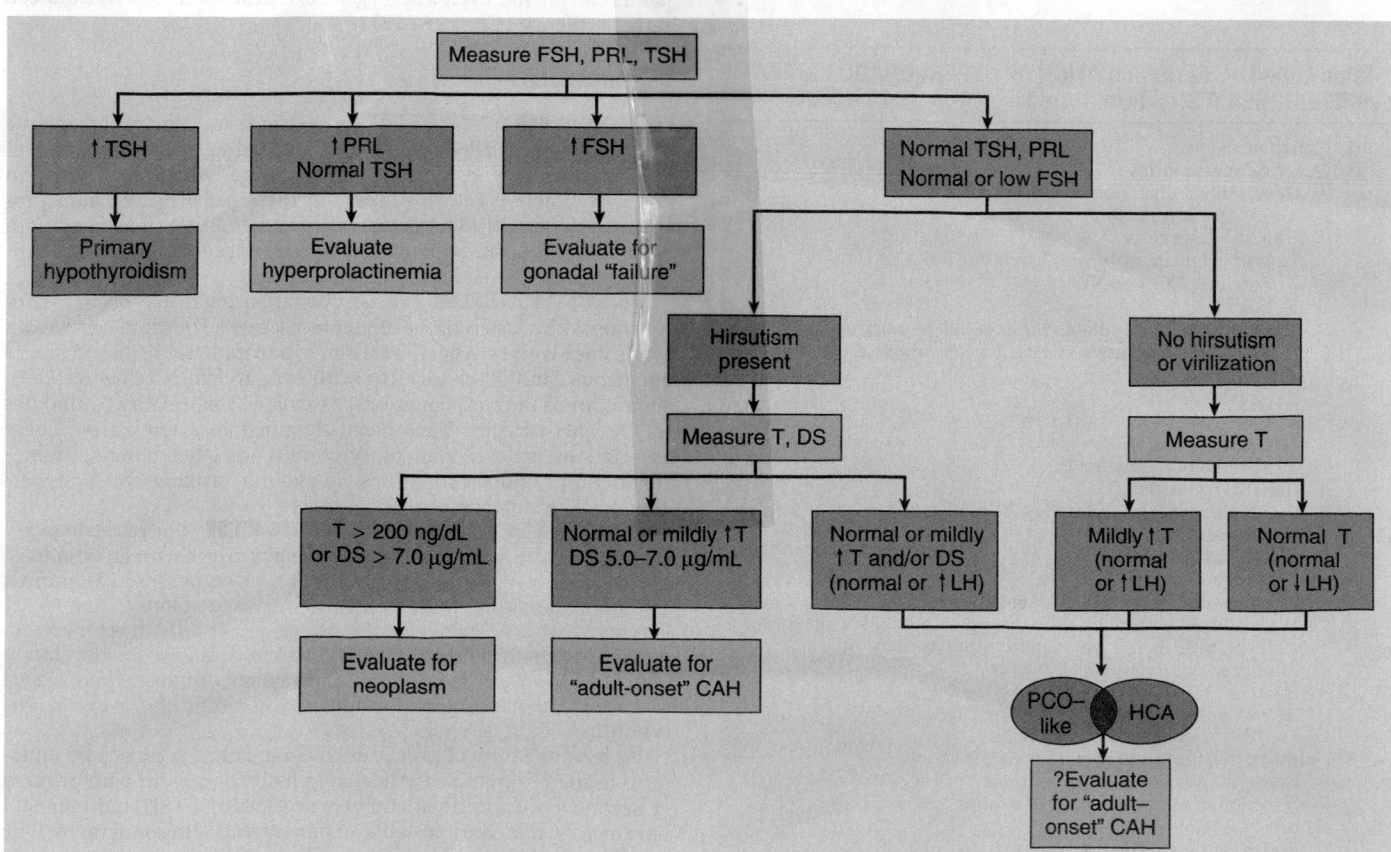

FIGURE 250–9 • Biochemical evaluation of amenorrhea. This schema must be considered as an adjunct to the clinical evaluation of the patient. See text for details. CAH = congenital adrenal hyperplasia; DS = dehydroepiandrosterone sulfate; FSH = follicle-stimulating hormone; HCA = hypothalamic chronic anovulation; LH = luteinizing hormone; PCO-like = polycystic ovarian–like; PRL = prolactin; T = testosterone; TSH = thyroid-stimulating hormone.

of ovarian origin. DHEAS levels greater than 7.0 μg/mL should lead to evaluation for an adrenal neoplasm, and DHEAS levels between 5.0 and 7.0 μg/mL should lead to evaluation for adult-onset congenital adrenal hyperplasia (Chapter 246).

HYPERGONADOTROPIC AMENORRHEA (PRESUMPTIVE OVARIAN FAILURE, PRIMARY HYPOGONADISM)

Differential Diagnosis

Gonadal failure may begin at any time during embryonic or postnatal development and may result from many causes (Table 250–4). Normally, the ovaries fail at menopause when virtually no functioning follicles remain. However, premature loss of oocytes prior to age 40 may occur and lead to premature ovarian failure, possibly from abnormalities in the recruitment and selection of oocytes. Because FSH is the principal regulator of folliculogenesis, most causes of premature ovarian failure may somehow involve FSH secretion or action. Circulating gonadotropin levels increase whenever ovarian failure occurs because of decreased negative estrogen feedback to the hypothalamic-pituitary unit.

GENETIC ABNORMALITIES

Several pathologic conditions with dysgenetic gonads involve elevated gonadotropin levels and amenorrhea. The term *gonadal dysgenesis* refers to individuals with undifferentiated streak gonads without any association with either extragonadal stigmata or sex chromosomal aberrations. Because individuals with gonadal dysgenesis have the normal complement of oocytes at 20 weeks of fetal age but virtually none by birth, this disorder is a form of premature ovarian failure.

Turner's syndrome describes patients with streak gonads composed of fibrous stroma and four cardinal features: (1) a female phenotype, (2) sexual infantilism, (3) short stature, and (4) several physical abnormalities, sometimes including a webbed neck, low-set ears, multiple pigmented nevi, double eyelashes, micrognathia, epicanthal folds,

shield-like chest with microthelia, short fourth metacarpals, an increased carrying angle of the arms, and certain renal and cardiovascular defects (most commonly coarctation of the aorta and aortic stenosis). The diagnosis can sometimes be made at birth because of unexplained lymphedema of the hands and feet. The syndrome is associated with an abnormality of sex chromosome number, morphology, or both. Most commonly the second sex chromosome is absent (45,X). This is the single most common chromosomal disorder in humans, but more than 95% of such fetuses are aborted, so that the incidence in newborns is approximately 1 in 3000 to 5000. Chromosomal breakage and mosaicism occur frequently as well. In mosaic individuals with a normal 46,XX cell line, sufficient follicles may persist postnatally to initiate pubertal changes and to cause ovulation so that pregnancy is possible.

Pure gonadal dysgenesis is the term given to phenotypically female individuals with streak gonads who are of normal stature and have none of the physical stigmata associated with Turner's syndrome. Such individuals have either a 46,XX or 46,XY karyotype. The 46,XX defect may be inherited as an autosomal recessive, with 10% having associated nerve deafness. The 46,XY defect may be inherited as an X-linked recessive, with clitorimegaly occurring in 10 to 15% and gonadal tumors developing in 25% if the gonads are not removed.

Trisomy X (46,XXX karyotype) is also associated with premature menopause, although many such individuals actually have normal reproductive lives. Premature menopause can also occur in mosaic individuals with cell lines with excess X chromosomes. When gonadal abnormalities occur in women with excess X chromosomes, they seem to occur after ovarian differentiation so that some ovarian function is possible. Only later in life do such women develop secondary amenorrhea and premature ovarian failure.

In girls with the rare syndrome of 17α-hydroxylase deficiency who survive until the expected age of puberty, sexual infantilism and primary amenorrhea occur together with elevated levels of gonadotropins. Increased synthesis of desoxycorticosterone leads to hypertension with hypokalemic alkalosis; serum progesterone levels are elevated as well. As with other causes of congenital adrenal hyperplasia, the hypertension is controlled by replacement therapy with glucocorticoids (Chapter 246). Women with galactosemia also experience ovarian failure early in life, even when a galactose-restricted diet is introduced early in infancy (Chapter 212).

OTHER CAUSES

PHYSICAL AND ENVIRONMENTAL. Irradiation and chemotherapeutic agents, especially alkylating agents, utilized to treat various malignant diseases may also cause premature ovarian failure. Ovulation and cyclic menses return in some of these patients even after prolonged intervals of hypergonadotropic amenorrhea associated with signs and symptoms of profound hypoestrogenism. Rarely, mumps affects the ovaries and causes ovarian failure.

AUTOIMMUNE DISORDERS. Premature ovarian failure may occur in conjunction with a variety of autoimmune disorders. The most well-known syndrome involves hypoadrenalism, hypoparathyroidism, and mucocutaneous candidiasis together with ovarian failure (Chapter 244). Thyroiditis is the most commonly associated abnormality. Antibodies to the FSH receptor have been identified in a few cases. These associations make it mandatory to rule out other potentially life-threatening endocrinopathies in young women with hypergonadotropic amenorrhea.

DEFECTIVE GONADOTROPIN SECRETION AND/OR ACTION. The resistant ovary (Savage) syndrome occurs in young amenorrheic women who have (1) elevated peripheral gonadotropin concentrations, (2) normal (although immature) follicles present on ovarian biopsy, (3) a 46,XX karyotype with no evidence of mosaicism, (4) fully developed secondary sex characteristics, and (5) ovarian resistance to stimulation with human menopausal or pituitary gonadotropins. There seems to be some block to gonadotropin action within the ovary in this syndrome.

At least one form of premature ovarian failure is caused by mutations in the FSH receptor. Affected individuals present with primary or secondary amenorrhea and elevated levels of FSH and may still have ovarian follicles detectable on transvaginal ultrasonography. One specific mutation on chromosome 2p (C566T:alanine to valine) in exon 7 of the FSH receptor has been identified in several Finnish families, but the mutation has not been detected in any other populations.

Table 250–4 • CLASSIFICATION OF HYPERGONADOTROPIC AMENORRHEA (FSH > 30 mIU/mL)

I. **Menopause**
II. **Genetic abnormalities**
   A. Genetically reduced germ cell endowment
   B. Accelerated atresia
   C. Gonadal dysgenesis
      1. With stigmata of Turner's syndrome (45,X)
      2. Pure (46,XX or 46,XY)
      3. Mixed
   D. Trisomy X with or without chromosomal mosaicism
   E. In association with myotonia dystrophica or other abnormalities
   F. Enzymatic defects
      1. 17α-Hydroxylase deficiency
      2. Galactosemia
III. **Physical and environmental causes**
   A. Gonadal irradiation
   B. Chemotherapeutic (especially alkylating) agents
   C. Viral agents
   D. Surgical extirpation
IV. **Autoimmune disorders**
   A. Polyglandular, involving ovarian failure and any combination of thyroiditis, hypoadrenalism, hypoparathyroidism, diabetes mellitus, myasthenia gravis, vitiligo, mucocutaneous candidiasis, and pernicious anemia
   B. Isolated ovarian failure
   C. In association with congenital thymic dysplasia
   D. Circulating gonadotropin antibodies
V. **Defective gonadotropin secretion and/or action**
   A. Resistant ovary or Savage syndrome
   B. Secretion of biologically inactive forms
   C. α or β subunit defects
   D. FSH receptor (FSHR) mutations
VI. **Idiopathic premature ovarian failure**

FSH = follicle-stimulating hormone.

Rx Treatment

Women with hypergonadotropic amenorrhea and ovarian failure should be treated identically whether or not they have signs of hypoestrogenism or desire pregnancy. Ovarian biopsy is not indicated to document the existence of follicles because only a small portion of each ovary can be sampled and because pregnancies have resulted in patients who had biopsies devoid of follicles. Estrogen replacement is warranted to prevent the accelerated bone loss known to occur in affected women (Chapter 258). The estrogen should be given sequentially with a progestin to prevent endometrial hyperplasia. Young women with ovarian failure may require twice as much estrogen as postmenopausal women for relief of signs and symptoms of hypoestrogenism.

Women with hypergonadotropic amenorrhea are rarely able to become pregnant. It is not clear why pregnancy may rarely occur in such women, but the pregnancy rate is less than 10%. The most successful treatment of young women with hypergonadotropic amenorrhea involves hormone replacement to mimic the normal menstrual cycle and embryo transfer utilizing donor oocytes. Pregnancy rates are higher than in other women undergoing in vitro fertilization and typically exceed 30% per cycle.

CHRONIC ANOVULATION

Chronic anovulation, the most frequent form of amenorrhea encountered in women of reproductive age, implies that functional ovarian follicles remain and that cyclic ovulation can be induced or reinitiated with appropriate therapy (Table 250–5). Appropriate management requires that the cause of the anovulation be determined.

Table 250–5 • CAUSES OF CHRONIC ANOVULATION

I. Chronic anovulation of hypothalamic-pituitary origin
  A. Hypothalamic chronic anovulation
    1. Psychogenic
    2. Exercise associated
    3. Associated with diet, weight loss, and/or malnutrition
    4. Anorexia nervosa and bulimia
    5. Pseudocyesis
  B. Forms of isolated gonadotropin deficiency (including Kallmann's syndrome)
  C. Due to hypothalamic-pituitary damage
    1. Pituitary and parapituitary tumors
    2. Empty sella syndrome
    3. Following surgery
    4. Following irradiation
    5. Following trauma
    6. Following infection
    7. Following infarction
  D. Idiopathic hypopituitarism
  E. Hypothalamic-pituitary dysfunction or failure with hyperprolactinemia (multiple causes)
  F. Due to systemic diseases
II. Chronic anovulation due to inappropriate feedback (i.e., polycystic ovary syndrome)
  A. Excessive extraglandular estrogen production (i.e., obesity)
  B. Abnormal buffering involving sex hormone–binding globulin (including liver disease)
  C. Functional androgen excess (adrenal or ovarian)
  D. Neoplasms producing androgens or estrogens
  E. Neoplasms producing chorionic gonadotropin
III. Chronic anovulation due to other endocrine and metabolic disorders
  A. Adrenal hyperfunction
    1. Cushing's syndrome
    2. Congenital adrenal hyperplasia (female pseudohermaphroditism)
  B. Thyroid dysfunction
    1. Hyperthyroidism
    2. Hypothyroidism
  C. Prolactin and/or growth hormone excess
    1. Hypothalamic dysfunction
    2. Pituitary dysfunction (microadenomas and macroadenomas)
    3. Drug induced
  D. Malnutrition

The pathophysiologic bases for several forms of anovulation are unknown, but the anovulation can be interrupted transiently by non-specific induction of ovulation in the majority of affected women. It is important to recognize that anovulation can result in either amenorrhea or irregular (generally less frequent) menses.

Hypothalamic Chronic Anovulation

Hypothalamic chronic anovulation (HCA) represents a heterogeneous group of disorders with similar manifestations. Emotional and physical stress, exercise, diet, weight loss, body composition, malnutrition, environment, and other unrecognized factors may contribute in varying proportions to the anovulation. Abrupt cessation of menses in women younger than 30 years who have no anatomic abnormalities of the hypothalamic-pituitary-ovarian axis and no other endocrine disturbances suggests a diagnosis of HCA. Affected individuals tend to be bright, educated, and engaged in intellectual occupations and may well give a history of psychosexual problems and socioenvironmental trauma. HCA is characterized by low to normal levels of gonadotropins and relative hypoestrogenism. Rarely, however, do affected women present with signs and symptoms of estrogen deficiency. Psychological counseling and/or a change in lifestyle, especially for women engaged in strenuous exercise programs, may be effective in inducing cyclic ovulation and menses. For women desiring pregnancy, ovulation can also be induced with clomiphene citrate (50 to 100 mg/day for 5 days beginning on the third to fifth day of withdrawal bleeding). Treatment with exogenous purified or synthetic gonadotropins to induce follicular maturation followed by hCG to induce follicular rupture or GnRH administered in a pulsatile fashion may be effective in women who do not ovulate in response to clomiphene.

Most physicians advocate the use of exogenous steroids to prevent osteoporosis. A regimen can be used consisting of daily oral conjugated or esterified estrogens (0.625 to 1.25 mg), ethinyl estradiol (20 μg), or micronized estradiol-17β (1 to 2 mg) or transdermal estradiol-17β (0.05 to 0.10 mg) daily, with oral medroxyprogesterone acetate (5 to 10 mg) added for the first 12 to 14 days of each month. Sexually active women can be given oral contraceptive agents as an alternative. If steroid therapy is administered, patients must be informed that the amenorrhea will probably be present when therapy is discontinued. Other physicians believe that only periodic observation is indicated, with barrier methods of contraception recommended for fertility control. Adequate ingestion of calcium should be ensured regardless of therapy. Contraception is needed for sexually active women with HCA because the functional defect is mild in these disorders and may resolve spontaneously at any time, with ovulation occurring prior to any episode of menstruation.

Individuals with amenorrhea and significant weight loss should be examined for the possibility of *anorexia nervosa* (Chapter 232). This disorder may be the most severe form of functional HCA, or it may be a distinct entity.

Kallmann's syndrome (isolated gonadotropin deficiency or familial hypogonadotropic hypogonadism) is a familial disorder consisting of gonadotropin deficiency, anosmia or hyposmia, and color blindness in men or, more rarely, in women. Other midline defects such as cleft lip and palate can occur in the affected individual or in family members. The trait is transmitted as an X-linked recessive or a male-limited autosomal dominant trait, but genetic heterogeneity may occur. Partial or complete agenesis of the olfactory bulb is present on autopsy, accounting for use of the term *olfactogenital dysplasia*. The disorder affects only gonadotropin secretion, and all other pituitary hormones are secreted normally. Isolated gonadotropin deficiency in the absence of anosmia occurs as well. Sexual infantilism with a eunuchoid habitus is the clinical hallmark of this disorder, but moderate breast development may occur. Circulating LH and FSH levels are quite low but almost always detectable. Ovulation induction requires use of exogenous gonadotropins and hCG or pulsatile GnRH. Estrogen replacement therapy is indicated in these women until pregnancy is desired. It may not be possible to distinguish between partial isolated gonadotropin deficiency and functional HCA in all cases.

Hypopituitarism may be obvious on cursory inspection or sufficiently subtle to require endocrine testing (Chapter 237). The clinical presentation depends on the age of onset, the cause, and the nutritional status of the individual. Failure of development of secondary sex characteristics or of development to progress once puberty is initiated must always raise the question of hypopituitarism. Ovulation can be induced successfully with exogenous gonadotropins when pregnancy is desired and after the hypopituitarism is treated appropriately. Replacement therapy with estrogen is indicated to prevent signs and symptoms of estrogen deficiency.

Galactorrhea associated with hyperprolactinemia, whatever the cause, almost always occurs together with amenorrhea caused by hypothalamic-pituitary dysfunction or failure. Many conditions can cause excess prolactin secretion (Chapter 237). Hirsutism may be observed occasionally in association with amenorrhea-galactorrhea and hyperprolactinemia. Elevated levels of the adrenal androgens DHEA and DHEAS may be observed and may account for the PCO-type ovaries present in some hyperprolactinemic women.

The hypothalamic-pituitary unit may also fail to function normally in a number of stressful, debilitating, systemic illnesses that interfere with somatic growth and development. Chronic renal failure, liver disease, and diabetes mellitus are the most prominent examples.

Chronic Anovulation Related to Inappropriate Feedback

PCO syndrome, which causes anovulation because of inappropriate feedback signals to the hypothalamic-pituitary unit, is a heterogeneous disorder in which there is considerable clinical and biochemical variability among affected individuals. Although patients usually present with amenorrhea, hirsutism, and obesity, affected women may instead complain of irregular and profuse uterine bleeding, may not have hirsutism, and may be of normal weight. Excess androgen from any source or increased extraglandular conversion of androgens to estrogens can lead to the typical findings of PCO syndrome. Included are such diverse disorders as Cushing's syndrome, mild congenital adrenal hyperplasia, virilizing tumors of adrenal or ovarian origin, hyperthyroidism and hypothyroidism, obesity, and primary PCO syndrome with no other recognizable cause.

In the primary syndrome the irregular menses, mild obesity, and hirsutism begin during puberty and typically become more severe with time. Obesity alone can lead to a PCO-like syndrome, with the degree of obesity required to cause anovulation varying widely from individual to individual. All such patients are well estrogenized regardless of whether they present with primary or secondary amenorrhea or dysfunctional bleeding. As noted, LH concentrations tend to be elevated, with relatively low and constant FSH levels, but both may be in the normal range compared with levels in women in the follicular phase of the menstrual cycle. Levels of most circulating androgens, especially testosterone, tend to be mildly elevated. The cause of PCO syndrome is unknown, but current evidence suggests that the hypothalamic-pituitary unit is intact and that a functional derangement, perhaps involving insulin-like growth factors such as IGF-I within the ovary, results in abnormal gonadotropin secretion. PCO is characterized by insulin resistance and compensatory hyperinsulinemia. The insulin resistance has been found in affected women of many racial and ethnic groups, implying that it is a universal characteristic and that a common defect may be present. There is increasing evidence of specific genetic abnormalities in some women with PCO.

The aim of the diagnostic evaluation is to rule out any causes (such as neoplasms) that require definitive therapy. Hirsutism should be evaluated as detailed in Chapter 255. PCO syndrome itself is a benign disorder. Patients generally require therapy for hirsutism, for induction of ovulation if pregnancy is desired, and for prevention of estrogen-induced endometrial hyperplasia and cancer. No ideal therapy exists; the therapeutic approach must be individualized to the needs of each patient. In addition, the risks of cardiovascular disease and of diabetes mellitus are increased in women with PCO, presumably at least in part because of the increased androgens and insulin resistance invariably present. Moreover, many affected women have elevated cholesterol levels, related at least in part to the other metabolic alterations present.

In the anovulatory woman not desiring pregnancy who is not hirsute, therapy with intermittent progestin administration (such as medroxyprogesterone acetate, 5 to 10 mg orally for 10 to 14 days each month) or oral contraceptives can be provided to reduce the increased risk of endometrial carcinoma that is present in such a woman with unopposed estrogen. All women utilizing intermittent progestin administration should be cautioned about the need for effective contraception

if they are sexually active because these agents do not inhibit ovulation when administered intermittently.

It is now apparent that improvements in insulin sensitivity in women with PCO, either through lifestyle changes (i.e., exercise and diet) or through pharmacologic intervention, consistently result in improvements in the reproductive and metabolic abnormalities associated with PCO. Resumption of ovulation may occur in up to 60 to 70% of affected women.

The longest and largest published experiences with any agent that improves insulin sensitivity in PCO is with metformin, a biguanide that works primarily by suppressing hepatic gluconeogenesis and also improves insulin sensitivity in the periphery (primarily skeletal muscle). Its use in women with PCO leads to reductions in circulatory insulin and androgen levels and resumption of menses in some women. Divided doses of 1500 to 2000 mg/day have proved effective.

Some clinicians advocate giving metformin (or another insulin sensitizing agent) to all women with PCO, whereas others would administer such an agent only to those with documented insulin resistance. Some clinicians also advocate giving metformin first to women who desire pregnancy and then adding an agent to induce ovulation if the metformin proves ineffective. This is an evolving field; it is important to remember that these agents are not approved for use in pregnant women or for the induction of ovulation.

The approach to the hirsute anovulatory woman not desiring pregnancy is detailed in Chapter 255. Oral contraceptive agents are the first line of therapy for such women with mild hirsutism and offer protection from endometrial hyperplasia.

In women with PCO syndrome desiring pregnancy, clomiphene citrate can be used to induce ovulation. Approximately 75 to 80% conceive with such therapy. In addition to insulin sensitizing agents, other possible methods of inducing ovulation include use of exogenous gonadotropins and hCG, pulsatile GnRH, wedge resection of the ovaries at laparotomy, and laser or cautery destruction of follicles at laparoscopy. Surgical treatment is warranted rarely and only in women in whom all other methods fail, in whom there is a question of an ovarian tumor because of ovarian size or circulating androgen levels, and in whom fertility is not an issue (because of the risk of pelvic adhesions from the surgery leading to infertility).

A particularly severely affected subset of women present with marked obesity, anovulation, mild glucose intolerance and high levels of circulating insulin with insulin resistance, acanthosis nigricans, hyperuricemia, and severe hirsutism with markedly elevated circulating androgen levels. These women have *hyperthecosis of the ovaries* in which the androgen-producing cells in the stromal, hilar, and thecal components of the ovaries are increased greatly in number. Although considered a separate entity by some clinicians, hyperthecosis should probably be viewed as a part of the spectrum of disorders constituting PCO syndrome.

CHRONIC ANOVULATION RELATED TO OTHER ENDOCRINE AND METABOLIC DISORDERS

Adrenal hyperfunction appears to cause chronic anovulation by inducing a PCO-like syndrome secondary to increased adrenal androgen secretion, but other possible mechanisms also exist.

Both hyperthyroidism and hypothyroidism are associated with a variety of menstrual disturbances, including dysfunctional uterine bleeding and amenorrhea as a result of alterations in the metabolism of androgens and estrogens. These metabolic changes in turn result in inappropriate steroid feedback and chronic anovulation.

DISORDERS OF FOLLICULOGENESIS

Recognized disorders of folliculogenesis cannot be identified before ovulation begins. They are believed to reflect abnormalities in follicular development.

Luteinized Unruptured Follicle Syndrome

The luteinized unruptured follicle syndrome refers to the development of a dominant follicle without its subsequent disruption and release of the ovum. The abnormality can be diagnosed by ultrasonography or by the absence of evidence of ovulation when the ovary is viewed at laparoscopy. The disorder is believed to occur infrequently and sporadically and is probably not a significant cause of infertility. Menstrual cycles in which no ovum is released are characterized by presumptive evidence of ovulation, including biphasic basal body temperatures, secretory endometrium, a normal LH surge, and normal progesterone production in the luteal phase. In fact, although the syndrome is believed to occur, data to substantiate its existence are only circumstantial (although strongly suggestive) at present.

Luteal Phase Dysfunction

Progesterone secretion in the luteal phase may be reduced in duration (termed luteal phase insufficiency) or in amount (termed luteal phase inadequacy). More rarely the endometrium may be unable to respond to secreted progesterone because of the absence of progesterone receptors. These disorders are believed to represent causes of infertility (because of inability of fertilized ova to implant) in approximately 5% of infertile couples. Abnormalities of the follicular phase, especially in the frequency of gonadotropin pulses, may account for most luteal phase defects. Luteal phase defects may also occur sporadically in normally ovulating women approximately once each year.

Luteal phase dysfunction may be associated with several clinical entities, including mild or intermittent hyperprolactinemia (of any cause), strenuous physical exercise, inadequately treated 21-hydroxylase deficiency, and habitual abortion. Luteal dysfunction occurs more commonly at the extremes of reproductive life and in the first menstrual cycles following full-term delivery, abortion, or discontinuation of oral contraceptives. It may also occur during ovulatory cycles induced with clomiphene citrate or exogenous gonadotropins and hCG.

The diagnosis of luteal phase dysfunction can be made either by endometrial biopsy or by serial progesterone determinations. Endometrial biopsies obtained from the uterine fundus in the late luteal phases of two different cycles must be at least 2 days out of phase from the expected date of bleeding, as judged from the subsequent menstrual cycle, for the diagnosis to be made. The absolute concentration that progesterone must achieve and the length of time progesterone must be increased in the luteal phase to exclude luteal dysfunction are unclear. Luteal dysfunction is extremely rare in women with menstrual cycles greater than 25 days in length in whom a single random progesterone determination is greater than 15 ng/mL.

Rx Treatment

Treatment of luteal dysfunction is controversial. Any underlying defect should be treated. If subsequent luteal function depends on prior follicular development, modification of follicular development with either clomiphene citrate (25 to 100 mg daily by mouth for 5 days beginning on cycle day 3 to 5) or FSH (75 to 300 IU intramuscularly for 3 to 5 days beginning on cycle day 3 to 5) is reasonable. hCG (2500 to 5000 IU intramuscularly at 2- to 3-day intervals beginning with the shift in basal body temperature) or progesterone (12.5 mg intramuscularly in oil daily or 25 mg twice a day as rectal or vaginal suppositories) can be utilized as well. Bromocriptine may correct the abnormality in individuals with hyperprolactinemia. Synthetic progestational agents should not be used to treat luteal phase defects because of their possible (although unproven) association with congenital anomalies. Furthermore, the synthetic progestins produce an abnormal endometrium. None of these agents has been shown to increase the pregnancy rate.

INFERTILITY

Infertility may be defined as involuntary inability to conceive. *Sterility* is total inability to reproduce. In either case the situation may or may not be correctable, especially for each particular couple. Failure to reproduce thwarts a basic human instinct and causes anger, guilt, and depression. More than 10% of couples in the United States seek medical assistance for infertility.

The requirements for pregnancy to occur are several:

1. The male must produce adequate numbers of normal, motile spermatozoa.

2. The male must be capable of ejaculating the sperm through a patent ductal system.
3. The sperm must be able to traverse an unobstructed female reproductive tract.
4. The female must ovulate and release an ovum.
5. The sperm must be able to fertilize the ovum.
6. The fertilized ovum must be capable of developing and implanting in appropriately prepared endometrium.

Infertility is too frequently viewed primarily as a problem of the female. In fact, in approximately 40% of cases, infertility is caused by the male (Table 250–6). In perhaps one third of couples, more than one cause contributes to the infertility.

Peak age for fertility in the female is 25 years. For nulliparous women of this age, the average time during which unprotected intercourse occurs until conception is 5.3 months. For parous women, the average duration of intercourse until conception is 2.7 months. The reproductive performance of couples is influenced by the ages of the female and male partners, the frequency of intercourse, and the length of time the couple has been attempting to conceive. There is a decline in both female and male reproductive performance after age 25 years.

Couples who complain of infertility merit evaluation regardless of the length of infertility. If the couple believes there is a problem, it is the physician's responsibility to reassure them by appropriate

Table 250–6 • CAUSES OF INFERTILITY AND THEIR APPROXIMATE INCIDENCE (%)

I. Male factors (40%)
  A. Decreased production of spermatozoa
    1. Varicocele
    2. Testicular failure
    3. Endocrine disorders
    4. Cryptorchidism
    5. Stress, smoking, caffeine, nicotine, recreational drugs
  B. Ductal obstruction
    1. Epididymal (postinfection)
    2. Congenital absence of vas deferens
    3. Ejaculatory duct (postinfection)
    4. Postvasectomy
  C. Inability to deliver sperm into vagina
    1. Ejaculatory disturbances
    2. Hypospadias
    3. Sexual problems (i.e., impotence), medical or psychological
  D. Abnormal semen
    1. Infection
    2. Abnormal volume
    3. Abnormal viscosity
  E. Immunologic factors
    1. Sperm-immobilizing antibodies
    2. Sperm-agglutinating antibodies
II. Female factors
  A. Fallopian tube pathology (20-30%)
    1. Pelvic inflammatory disease or puerperal infection
    2. Congenital anomalies
    3. Endometriosis
    4. Secondary to past peritonitis of nongenital origin
  B. Amenorrhea and anovulation (15%)
  C. Minor ovulatory disturbances (<5%?)
  D. Cervical and uterine factors (10%)
    1. Leiomyomas and polyps
    2. Uterine anomalies
    3. Intrauterine synechiae (Asherman's syndrome)
    4. Destroyed endocervical glands (postsurgery or postinfection)
  E. Vaginal factors (<5%)
    1. Congenital absence of vagina
    2. Imperforate hymen
    3. Vaginismus
    4. Vaginitis
  F. Immunologic factors (<5%)
    1. Sperm-immobilizing antibodies
    2. Sperm-agglutinating antibodies
  G. Nutritional and metabolic factors (5%)
    1. Thyroid disorders
    2. Diabetes mellitus
    3. Severe nutritional disturbances
III. Idiopathic or unexplained (<10%)

evaluation and subsequent explanation of all findings and the prognosis.

The evaluation begins with a detailed history obtained from both partners and physical examinations of both individuals. The couple should be seen together for the first visit. Each couple should be questioned together and separately because separate interviews may uncover information that would not be imparted in the presence of the partner.

Initial evaluation for infertility generally includes (1) assessment of semen; (2) documentation of ovulation by basal body temperature, serum progesterone determination approximately 6 to 8 days before menses, or endometrial biopsy less than 3 days before onset of menses; and (3) evaluation of the female genital tract by hysterosalpingography or sonohysterography, also known as saline infusion sonography. Basal serum levels of thyroid hormones should be measured. Diagnostic laparoscopy with tubal dye instillation should be performed if results of all previous tests are normal because 30 to 50% of women are found to have endometriosis or tubal disease on surgical evaluation. Treatment must be predicated on the findings of the infertility evaluation.

Induction of Ovulation

Induction of ovulation should never be attempted until serious disorders precluding pregnancy are ruled out or treated. Furthermore, ovulation induction should be utilized only in women with chronic anovulation because women with ovarian failure are unresponsive to any form of ovulation induction. In general, the use of pharmaceutical agents does not improve the quality of an ovum, and thus the chance of pregnancy is not improved in women who ovulate regularly.

Clomiphene citrate is the agent that usually induces ovulation most easily. Clomiphene should be utilized in individuals without hyperprolactinemia who have the ability to release LH and FSH. A typical course of clomiphene therapy is begun on the fifth day following either spontaneous or induced uterine bleeding. The initial dosage is 50 mg daily for 5 days. Clomiphene appears to act as an antiestrogen and stimulates gonadotropin secretion by the pituitary gland to initiate follicular development. If ovulation is not achieved in the first cycle of treatment, the daily dosage is increased to 100 mg. If ovulation is still not achieved, dosage is increased in a stepwise fashion in 50-mg increments to a maximum of 200 to 250 mg daily for 5 days. The highest dose should be continued for 3 to 6 months before the patient is regarded as unresponsive to clomiphene. The quantity of drug and the length of time that it can be used, as suggested here, are greater than those recommended by the manufacturers but conform with published series.

The ovulatory surge of LH may occur 5 to 12 days (average, 7 days) after the completion of the last day of clomiphene treatment in each course. Couples are advised to have intercourse every other day during this interval. Ovulation can be documented by monitoring changes in basal body temperature or preferably by measuring serum progesterone approximately 14 days after the last clomiphene tablet is taken. In addition, menses should occur about 3 weeks after the last day of therapy. Withdrawal bleeding with progestin can be induced if the patient fails to bleed within 4 weeks of therapy and if a serum hCG level documents that the patient is not pregnant. Testing the urine for an LH surge with any of several commercially available tests may also be useful in timing ovulation.

Some clinicians give 5000 to 10,000 IU of hCG intramuscularly 7 days after the last day of clomiphene therapy to trigger ovulation, but this approach has not been established to increase effectiveness. The administration of hCG, however, does serve to time ovulation and may be helpful in selected couples. Ovulation can be expected to occur approximately 36 hours after hCG administration.

Of appropriately selected patients, 75 to 80% ovulate and 40 to 50% can be expected to become pregnant. About 15% of pregnancies can be expected with each ovulatory cycle. The multiple pregnancy rate is about 8%, with almost all being twins. The incidence of congenital anomalies is not increased.

Side effects of clomiphene are uncommon and rarely serious. The most serious ones include vasomotor flushes (10%), abdominal discomfort (5%), breast tenderness (2%), nausea and vomiting (2%), visual symptoms (1.5%), and headache (1%). Ovarian enlargement may occur but is rare (5%). Concern has been raised about the potential for clomiphene to increase the risk of epithelial ovarian cancer. The bulk of the evidence now indicates that clomiphene does not increase this risk, but research in this area continues.

The addition of dexamethasone, 0.5 mg orally at bedtime to blunt the nighttime secretion of adrenocorticotropic hormone, may be useful in hyperandrogenic women with an adrenal component who fail to ovulate in response to clomiphene. Other individuals who do not respond to clomiphene typically require exogenous gonadotropins and hCG or perhaps pulsatile GnRH to induce ovulation.

Both bromocriptine and cabergoline, two dopamine agonists, are effective in inducing ovulation in hyperprolactinemic women. The drug should be stopped when pregnancy is confirmed. Ovulatory menses and pregnancy are achieved in about 80% of patients with galactorrhea and hyperprolactinemia. The majority of women with prolactin-secreting pituitary tumors remain asymptomatic during pregnancy. It is rare for a patient with either a microadenoma or a macroadenoma to develop a problem related to the tumor that affects either the mother or the fetus during pregnancy. Monitoring during pregnancy need consist only of questioning the patient about the development of visual symptoms and headaches. Formal assessment of visual fields and computed tomography or magnetic resonance imaging should be carried out in any patient experiencing suspicious symptoms. Symptoms generally abate with institution of therapy with a dopamine agonist. No adverse effects of dopamine agonists on fetuses or pregnancies have been reported.

Several preparations of purified and synthetic biochemically engineered gonadotropins for use for induction of ovulation now exist. Synthetic preparations consist entirely of FSH, whereas most purified preparations contain some LH as well. Each vial typically contains 75 IU of the appropriate gonadotropin. Individuals with gonadotropin deficiency require a preparation containing some LH. Exogenous gonadotropins are typically administered at doses of two to four vials (intramuscularly or subcutaneously depending on the preparation) for 5 to 12 days to achieve follicular development as monitored by ultrasonography and serum or urinary estradiol concentrations; hCG, 5000 to 10,000 IU, is administered as a single intramuscular dose when follicular maturation is apparent. The hCG should be withheld if more than three follicles mature together. GnRH analogues are now being utilized to suppress endogenous follicular activity before initiating therapy with exogenous gonadotropins and continued until hCG is given in older women and those with poor responses to exogenous gonadotropins. Use of the analogues necessitates administration of larger quantities of exogenous gonadotropins. Success rates, however, seem to be somewhat improved with this combined therapy. GnRH analogues are also being used experimentally to induce an endogenous LH surge.

Because of the expense and the complication rate, thorough evaluation should be carried out to exclude other causes of infertility before exogenous gonadotropins and hCG are used. Ovulation can be induced in almost 100% of patients, but pregnancy occurs in only 50 to 70%. There is no increased risk of congenital anomalies with exogenous gonadotropins and hCG. Concerns have been raised that exogenous gonadotropins may increase the risk of ovarian epithelial cancer, but more data do not support this possibility.

The rate of multiple pregnancies with exogenous gonadotropins and hCG may approach 30%, with 5% being triplets or more. Ovarian hyperstimulation is the major side effect and may be life threatening. The ovaries enlarge remarkably in this treatment-induced syndrome, and multiple follicle cysts, stromal edema, and multiple corpora lutea are present. There is a shift of fluid from the intravascular space into the abdominal cavity with resultant hypovolemia and hemoconcentration. The cause of the ascites is unknown. Treatment is conservative, with monitoring of fluid and electrolyte status. Pelvic examinations should not be performed for fear of rupturing the ovaries. The hyperstimulation generally resolves slowly over about 7 days.

GnRH, administered intravenously or less effectively subcutaneously at doses of 5 to 20 μg every 60 to 120 minutes, can also be used to induce ovulation in women with an intact pituitary gland. It is most effective in individuals with HCA. hCG can be administered to support the corpus luteum after ovulation at a dose of 1500 IU intramuscularly every 3 days for three to four doses. The advantage of GnRH rests in the fact that hyperstimulation is extremely unlikely. However, reported pregnancy rates have been no greater than those achieved with exogenous gonadotropins and hCG. Furthermore, some patients do not tolerate wearing the infusion pump that must be utilized. GnRH is no longer marketed for this use in the United States.

Use of clomiphene citrate or exogenous gonadotropins together with intrauterine insemination of spermatozoa is increasing in women with unexplained infertility. The intent is to stimulate several oocytes to be ovulated, but multiple (sometimes high order) gestations are a significant risk. At this time there is no evidence that this approach helps more couples to conceive than would spontaneously, but the time to pregnancy seems reduced.

SEXUAL FUNCTION AND DYSFUNCTION

Although sexual responses begin following puberty, they can continue for the duration of a woman's life. Sexual responses historically have been divided into four phases: excitement, plateau, orgasm, and resolution.

With sexual arousal and excitement, vasocongestion and muscular tension increase progressively, primarily in the genitals, manifested by vaginal lubrication in the female. The lubrication is due to formation of a transudate in the vagina. Sexual excitement is initiated by any of a variety of psychogenic or somatogenic sexual stimuli and must be reinforced to result in orgasm. With continued stimulation, the excitement phase increases in intensity into a plateau phase during which a high state of sexual interest is maintained. The plateau phase may be short or long, and it is from this phase that an individual can shift to orgasm. The orgasmic phase tends to be brief and is characterized by rapid release from the developed vasocongestion and muscular tension. The orgasmic release is also known as the climax because peak psychological and physical intensity is achieved and there is an attendant feeling of satisfaction. Copious secretions and transudate may flow during orgasm in women. Although women may resolve toward sleep following orgasm, many remain responsive to sexual stimulation and may return to plateau and subsequent orgasm.

Characteristic genital and extragenital responses occur during these phases. Estrogens magnify the sexual responses, but responses may occur in estrogen-deficient women. For women these changes occur in the breasts and in the pudendal region and are variable from one response cycle to another. For some women, excitement proceeds quickly through plateau to orgasm, and orgasm is explosive and accompanied by vocalization and involuntary contractions of the pelvic skeletal muscles. For other women, the responses are slow in building, controlled in amplitude, and long lasting. For a few women orgasm never occurs; for many it is intermittently absent.

The somatic sensate focus enabling orgasmic release is variable and may include stimulation of the breasts, vagina, or clitoris. The psychological aspect of coitus may involve concentration on the current partner or act or fantasies about other times and persons. Although orgasms may vary in physiologic intensity, what is important is psychological satisfaction. Satisfaction for both men and women may be had without orgasm.

Many clinicians have noted several limitations of this traditional human sex response cycle. In general, the genital focus and the linear sequence do not accurately reflect women's sexual experiences. Moreover, this model fails to reflect the various relationships between the mind and the body when men and women are sexual. Sexual motivation is complex, influenced by many cognitive, societal, and emotional factors. More and more clinicians and researchers see the cycle as circular with stimuli of different types leading to arousal.

Women may seek consultation because of disturbances in normal sexual arousal or orgasm. Such sexual dysfunction may be due to either organic or functional disturbances.

A variety of diseases affecting neurologic function, including diabetes mellitus and multiple sclerosis, may prevent sexual arousal. So, too, may local pelvic disorders, such as endometriosis and vaginitis, which cause dyspareunia and lead to sexual avoidance. Estrogen deficiency causing vaginal atrophy and dyspareunia is a relatively common cause of sexual dysfunction. Debilitating systemic diseases such as malignant disease may also affect sexual function indirectly.

In most cases the cause of sexual dysfunction is psychological. For instance, vaginismus involves involuntary contractions of the muscles surrounding the introitus and leads to dyspareunia. It is a conditioned response engendered by a previous imagined or real traumatic sexual experience. Feelings of guilt, caused by incest or rape as examples; of inadequacy, caused by hysterectomy or mastectomy; or of depression or anxiety may lead to failure to be aroused. Failure to achieve orgasm may be viewed as a dysfunction if the woman is frustrated or dissatisfied.

Treatment of sexual dysfunction is best accomplished by eliminating functional causes and providing the patient, often together with her partner, with appropriate psychological counseling. Behavioral modification is effective in treating many women with psychological sexual dysfunction.

SUGGESTED READINGS

Aboulghar MA, Mansour RT, Serour GI, et al: Diagnosis and management of unexplained infertility: An update. Arch Gynecol Obstet 2003;267:177–188. *A practical overview.*

Bain C, Cooper KG, Parkin DE: Microwave endometrial ablation versus endometrial resection: A randomized controlled trial. Obstet Gynecol 2002,99.983–987. *The two were equally effective.*

Barbieri RL: Endometriosis. *In* Becker KL (ed): Principles and Practice of Endocrinology and Metabolism, 3rd ed. Philadelphia, Lippincott Williams & Wilkins, 2001, pp 972–976. *A succinct summary of this enigmatic disorder.*

Barbieri RL: Metformin for the treatment of polycystic ovary syndrome. Obstet Gynecol 2003;101:785–793. *A balanced discussion of the role of insulin-sensitizing agents in the treatment of polycystic ovary syndrome.*

Basson R: The female sexual response: A different model. J Sex Marital Ther 2000;26:51–65. *A detailed outline of a cycle model of female sexual response.*

Basson R, Berman J, Burnett A, et al: Report of the international consensus developmental conference on female sexual dysfunction: Definitions and classifications. J Urol 2000;163:888–893. *A summary of the classification of disorders of female sexual function.*

Erickson GF: Ovarian androgen biosynthesis: Endocrine regulation. *In* Azziz R, Nestler JE, Dewailly D (eds): Androgen Excess Disorders in Women. Philadelphia, Lippincott-Raven, 1997, pp 3–11. *A detailed overview.*

Erickson GF, Shimasaki S: A summary of the cellular basis of ovary androgen production. Fertil Steril 2001;76:943–949. *A physiologic overview.*

Grady-Weliky TA: Clinical practice. Premenstrual dysphoric disorder. N Engl J Med 2003;348:433–438. *A practical overview of the pathophysiology, diagnosis, and therapy of this common disorder.*

Harborne L, Fleming R, Lyall H, et al: Descriptive review of the evidence for the use of metformin in polycystic ovary syndrome. Lancet 2003;361:1894–1901. *The widespread clinical use of this drug seems to be premature based on the paucity of the evidence to support it.*

Hunter MS, Ussher JM, Browne SJ, et al: A randomized comparison of psychological (cognitive behavior therapy), medical (fluoxetine) and combined treatment for women with premenstrual dysphoric disorder. J Psychosom Obstet Gynaecol 2002;23:193–199. *Cognitive behavior therapy and fluoxetine are equally effective, but there was no additional benefit of combining them.*

Nugent D, Watson AJ, Killick SR, et al: A randomized controlled trial of tubal flushing with lipiodol for unexplained infertility. Fertil Steril 2002;77:173–175. *A single flush was associated with a significantly higher pregnancy rate in couples with unexplained infertility.*

Parsanezhad ME, Alborzi S, Motazedian S, et al: Use of dexamethasone and clomiphene citrate in the treatment of clomiphene citrate-resistant patients with polycystic ovary syndrome and normal dehydroepiandrosterone sulfate levels: A prospective, double-blind, placebo-controlled trial. Fertil Steril 2002;78:1001–1004. *Dexamethasone was safe and effective, so the authors recommend it before gonadotropin therapy or surgical intervention.*

Rapkin A: A review of treatment of premenstrual syndrome and premenstrual dysphoric disorder. Psychoneuroendocrinology 2003;28(Suppl 3):39–53. *A comprehensive review.*

Suh CS, Sonntag B, Erickson GF: A novel analysis of the life of the ovary from embryogenesis through menopause. Rev Endocr Metab Disord 2002;3:5–12. *Explains the life-long evolution of ovarian function.*

Surrey ES, Schoolcraft WB: Management of endometriosis-associated infertility. Obstet Gynecol Clin North Am 2003;30:193–208. *Emphasizes an individualized approach.*

Timmreck LS, Reindollar RH: Contemporary issues in primary amenorrhea. Obstet Gynecol Clin North Am 2003;30:287–302. *The most common causes remain ovarian failure, congenital absence of the uterus and vagina, GnRH deficiency, and constitutional delay of puberty.*

Weigert M, Krischker U, Pohl M, et al: Comparison of stimulation with clomiphene citrate in combination with recombinant follicle-stimulating hormone and recombinant luteinizing hormone to stimulation with a gonadotropin-releasing hormone agonist protocol: A prospective, randomized study. Fertil Steril 2002;78:34–39. *Clomiphene plus recombinant FSH + recombinant LH led to comparable pregnancy rates despite lower gonadotropin doses with less need for monitoring and less ovarian hyperstimulation.*

Williams C, Giannopoulos T, Sherriff EA: ACP best practice no 170. Investigation of infertility with the emphasis on laboratory testing and with reference to radiological imaging. J Clin Pathol 2003;56:261–267. *Suggested approach to laboratory testing and monitoring in fertility diagnosis and treatment.*

Zapantis G, Santoro N: The menopausal transition: Characteristics and management. Best Pract Res Clin Endocrinol Metab 2003;17:33–52. *A summary of characteristic features and bleeding disorders occurring during the later reproductive years just prior to menopause.*

251 CONTRACEPTION

Daniel R. Mishell, Jr.

Contraceptive Use and Effectiveness

Reversible contraception, the temporary prevention of fertility, includes all contraceptive methods except sterilization. Sterilization should be considered to be permanent, despite the possibility of surgical reversal. There are advantages and disadvantages for each contraceptive method. During contraceptive counseling, these advantages and disadvantages should be thoroughly explained so that the individual will choose the most acceptable method and not discontinue use prematurely and have an unwanted pregnancy.

In the United States in 1995, there were about 60 million women in the reproductive age group (15 to 44), and 39 million (65%) were using a method of contraception. Of the remainder, about 5% were sterile (prior hysterectomy), 9% were pregnant or trying to conceive, 11% were never sexually active, and 6% had no recent sexual activity. Only 5% who were sexually active were not using a method of contraception.

In the United States in 1995, the most common methods of fertility prevention were female sterilization and oral contraceptives (OCs), each used by about 10 million women. Next in frequency of use was the male condom, followed by male sterilization (Table 251–1). The injectable progestin was used by about 1 million women, but the intrauterine device (IUD) and progestin implants, the two most effective methods of reversible contraception, were used by less than 1 million women. Since 1982, there has been a marked decrease in diaphragm and IUD use and a continuous increase in condom use. Nearly 80% of reproductive-age women have used OCs at some time.

Despite an increased use of contraceptive methods by U.S. women since 1982, more than half the pregnancies that occur are unwanted. Of the 6.3 million pregnancies that occurred in the United States in 1994, 3.1 million were unwanted and 1.4 million of them were terminated by elective abortion. Of the women with an unwanted pregnancy, 50% stated they were using a method of contraception in the month they conceived.

The terms *method effectiveness* and *use effectiveness* (or *method failure* and *patient failure*) were previously used to describe the frequency of conceptions that occurred while the method was being used correctly or incorrectly. These terms have been replaced by the terms *typical* and *perfect use*. Methods used at the time of coitus have failure rates in the first year of use of about 5% or more, whereas OCs, implants, injections, the IUD, and sterilization have first-year typical use failure rates of 3% or less (Table 251–2). Cumulative failure rates for use of long-acting methods are low. The pregnancy rate for 5 years of use of the progestin implants is 1.1%, and for 10 years' use of the Copper T380 IUD it is 2.2%. The cumulative failure rate of all types of tubal sterilization is 1.31% during the first 5 years after the procedure and 1.85% after 10 years, being highest for tubal fulguration and lowest for segmental resection. When women conceive while using these long-acting methods, the ectopic pregnancy rates are high: about 30% with tubal sterilization failure, 25% with implant failure, and 5% with copper IUD failure.

Table 251–1 • PERCENTAGE DISTRIBUTION AND NUMBER (IN MILLIONS) OF CONTRACEPTIVE USERS AGED 15-44, BY CURRENT METHOD, 1982-1995

METHOD	1982 %	1982 No.	1988 %	1988 No.	1995 %	1995 No.
Sterilization	34.1	10,295	39.2	13,686	38.6	14,942
Female	23.2	6,998	27.5	9,614	27.7	10,727
Male	10.9	3,298	11.7	4,069	10.9	4,215
Pill	28.0	8,431	30.7	10,734	26.9	10,410
Implant	NA	NA	NA	NA	1.3	515
Injectable	NA	NA	NA	NA	3.0	1,146
IUD	7.1	2,153	2.0	703	0.8	310
Diaphragm	8.1	2,436	5.7	2,000	1.9	720
Male condom	12.0	3,608	14.6	5,093	20.4	7,889
Foam	2.4	711	1.1	371	0.4	161
Periodic abstinence	3.9	1,166	2.3	806	2.3	883
Withdrawal	2.0	588	2.2	778	3.0	1,178
Other*	2.5	754	2.1	733	1.3	508
Total	100.0	30,142	100.0	34,912	100.0	38,663
Sample n	NA	4,242	NA	5,176	NA	7,145

*Other consists of douche, sponge, jelly or cream alone, and other methods.
From Piccinini LJ, Mosher WD: Trends in contraception use in the United States 1982-1995. Fam Plann Perspect 30:4-10 and 46, 1998. With permission of the Alan Guttmacher Institute.

Table 251–2 • PERCENTAGE OF WOMEN EXPERIENCING A CONTRACEPTIVE FAILURE DURING THE FIRST YEAR OF TYPICAL USE AND THE FIRST YEAR OF PERFECT USE

METHOD	% OF WOMEN EXPERIENCING AN ACCIDENTAL PREGNANCY WITHIN THE FIRST YEAR OF USE Typical Use	Perfect Use
Chance	85	85
Spermicides	26	6
Periodic abstinence	25	
Calendar		9
Ovulation method		3
Symptothermal		2
Postovulation		1
Withdrawal	19	4
Cap		
Parous women	40	26
Nulliparous women	20	9
Diaphragm	20	6
Condom		
Female	21	5
Male	14	3
Pill	5	
Progestin only		0.5
Combined		0.1
IUD		
Progesterone T	2.0	1.5
Copper T380A	0.8	0.6
Depo-Provera	0.3	0.3
Norplant and Norplant 2	0.05	0.05
Female sterilization	0.5	0.5
Male sterilization	0.15	0.10

From Hatcher RA: Contraceptive Technology, 17th ed. New York, Ardent Media, 1998.

Spermicides and Barriers

All spermicidal agents contain a surfactant, usually nonoxynol 9, that immobilizes or kills sperm on contact. They also provide a mechanical barrier and need to be placed into the vagina before each coital act. There is no increased risk of birth defects in the offspring of women who conceive while using spermicides.

A diaphragm must be carefully fitted by the health care provider. The largest size that does not cause discomfort or undue pressure on the vagina should be used. The diaphragm should not be left in place for more than 24 hours, because it may cause ulceration of the vaginal epithelium. Diaphragm users have an increased risk of urinary tract infection.

The cervical cap, a cup-shaped plastic or rubber device that fits around the cervix, can be left in place longer than the diaphragm and is more comfortable. The various types of caps are manufactured in different sizes and should be fitted to the cervix by a clinician. The cap should be left on the cervix for no more than 48 hours, and a spermicide should always be placed inside the cap before use.

Use of the male condom by individuals with multiple sex partners should be encouraged because it is the most effective way to prevent sexually transmitted diseases.

The female condom consists of a soft, loose-fitting prelubricated sheath and two flexible polyurethane rings. The female condom can be inserted before beginning sexual activity and be left in place for a longer time period after ejaculation occurs than the male condom. Because the female condom covers the external genitalia, it may prevent transmission of genital herpes. Because polyurethane is stronger than the latex used in male condoms, the female condom is less likely to rupture. Polyurethane does not allow virus transmission and should reduce the risk of acquiring human immunodeficiency virus infection.

Oral Steroid Contraceptives

There are three major types of OC formulations: fixed-dose combination, combination phasic, and daily progestin. The combination formulations are the most widely used and most effective. They consist of tablets containing both an estrogen and a progestin given continuously for 3 weeks. No steroids are given for the next 7 days (except for one formulation in which estrogen alone is given for an additional 5 days), after which time the active combination is given for an additional 3 weeks. The endometrium usually begins to slough 1 to 3 days after steroid ingestion is stopped, causing withdrawal bleeding, which usually lasts 3 to 4 days. The uterine blood loss with OC use averages about 25 mL per cycle, less than the 35 mL average for ovulatory cycles.

All formulations are made from synthetic steroids. There are two major types of synthetic progestins: derivatives of 19-nortestosterone (which are used in OCs) and derivatives of 17α-acetoxyprogesterone (pregnanes). Pregnanes are structurally related to progesterone and are used in injectable contraceptives but are not used in OCs.

The 19-nortestosterone progestins used in OCs are of two major types, estranes and gonanes, and both have androgenic activity. The estranes currently used in several OCs are norethindrone and its acetates, norethindrone acetate and ethynodiol diacetate. Gonanes have greater progestational activity per unit weight than estranes, and thus a smaller amount of these progestins are used in OC formulations. The parent compound of the gonanes is DL-norgestrel, but only the levo isomer is biologically active. Gonanes used in OCs include both norgestrel and levonorgestrel and three less androgenic derivatives of levonorgestrel: desogestrel, norgestimate, and gestodene. One other progestin that is structurally related to spironolactone has been formulated in an OC. This progestin is called drospirenone and has some diuretic activity as well as progestational activity without androgenic activity.

With the exception of two daily progestin-only formulations, the progestins are combined with varying dosages of two estrogens, ethinyl estradiol and its 3-methyl ether, called mestranol. All the older higher-dosage OC formulations contained mestranol, and this steroid is still present in some 50 μg formulations. All formulations with less than 50 μg of estrogen (20 to 35 μg) contain ethinyl estradiol.

The estrogen-progestin combination is the most effective type of OC formulation because these preparations consistently inhibit the midcycle gonadotropin surge and thus prevent ovulation. The progestin-only formulations have a lower dose of progestin than the combined agents and do not consistently inhibit ovulation, even though they are ingested every day. Both types of formulations also act on the cervical mucus and tubal motility to interfere with sperm transport. Progestins also alter the endometrium to interfere with implantation if fertilization occurs. To maintain contraceptive effectiveness with the combination formulations, it is very important that the pill-free interval be limited to no more than 7 days. This is best accomplished by ingestion of either a placebo or an iron tablet daily during the steroid-free interval.

METABOLIC EFFECTS. The synthetic steroids in OC formulations have many metabolic effects in addition to their contraceptive actions. These effects can cause the more common, less serious side effects as well as the rare, serious complications. The magnitude of these effects is directly related to the dosage and potency of the steroids in the formulations. The most frequent symptoms produced by the estrogen component include nausea, breast tenderness, and fluid retention. The progestins can produce certain androgenic effects, such as weight gain, acne, and nervousness. Because estrogens decrease sebum production, women who have acne should be given a formulation with a low progestin-estrogen ratio. Unscheduled (breakthrough) bleeding is usually produced by insufficient estrogen, too much progestin, or a combination of both. This problem is more common with formulations containing 20 μg of estrogen than those containing 30 to 35 μg and is increased in women who also smoke cigarettes.

The synthetic estrogens used in OCs cause an increase in the hepatic production of several proteins. The progestins do not affect protein synthesis except to reduce levels of sex hormone-binding globulin. Some of the proteins that are increased by ethinyl estradiol, such as factors V, VIII, and X and fibrinogen, may enhance thrombosis, whereas an increase in angiotensinogen levels may elevate blood pressure in some users. Blood pressure should be monitored in all users of OCs and the agent discontinued if there is a clinically significant increase. The incidence of both venous and arterial thrombosis in OC users is directly related to the dose of estrogen. Changes in the coagulation parameters with most low-dose OCs are very small or nonexistent.

The effect of OCs on glucose metabolism is directly related to the dose, potency, and type of progestin. Although high-progestin dose formulations caused peripheral insulin resistance, the low-progestin formulations in current use do not significantly alter levels of glucose, insulin, or glucagon after a glucose load. The risk of developing diabetes mellitus is not increased in women with a history of gestational diabetes who take OCs compared with control subjects. The risk of development of type 2 diabetes is not increased among current or former OC users compared with age-matched control subjects.

The estrogen component of OCs causes an increase in high-density lipoprotein cholesterol levels, a decrease in low-density lipoprotein cholesterol levels, and an increase in total cholesterol and triglyceride levels. The progestin component causes a decrease in high-density lipoprotein levels, an increase in low-density lipoprotein levels, and a decrease in total cholesterol and triglyceride levels. High-progestin formulations have an adverse effect on the lipid profile; because of the direct beneficial effect of estrogen on the arterial wall, however, users of these agents do not have an increased risk of cardiovascular disease. The newer combination formulations with less androgenic progestins have a more favorable effect on the lipid profile.

COMPLICATIONS AND RISK FACTORS. The cause of the increased incidence of both venous and arterial cardiovascular disease in users of OCs is thrombosis, not atherosclerosis. The background rate of venous thrombosis and embolism in women of reproductive age is about 0.8 per 10,000 woman years. Among users of OCs with 30 or 35 μg ethinyl estradiol, it is 3 per 10,000 woman years, about four times the background rate but one half the rate of 6 per 10,000 woman years that occurs in association with pregnancy. Although the risk of venous thrombosis and embolism is higher among women ingesting OCs with 50 μg of ethinyl estradiol than those with 30 to 35 μg, studies to date indicate that the risk of venous thrombosis and embolism with OCs containing 20 μg ethinyl estradiol is similar to that of OCs with 30 to 35 μg ethinyl estradiol. In the presence of an inherited coagulopathy disorder, the risk of venous thrombosis is increased severalfold. Because only 1 in 300 women with activated protein C resistance will develop venous thrombosis with OC use, it is not recommended that screening for coagulation deficiencies be undertaken before patients are started on OC use unless the individual patient has a personal or strong family history of thrombotic events.

The use of high-dose OCs by women who smoke cigarettes significantly increases the risk of myocardial infarction. Therefore, combination OCs should not be prescribed to women older than 35 years who smoke cigarettes or use alternative forms of nicotine. Recent epidemiologic studies indicate that use of low-dose OCs by nonsmoking women without hypertension is not associated with a significantly increased incidence of either myocardial infarction or hemorrhagic or thrombotic stroke.

For about 2 years after the discontinuation of contraceptives, the rate of return of fertility is slightly lower for users of OCs than for users of barrier methods. OCs do not cause permanent infertility or adversely affect pregnancies that occur after their discontinuation. OCs are not teratogenic if accidentally ingested during pregnancy.

The risk of breast cancer diagnosis is increased by about 25% in young women who are currently using OCs, but this increased risk is no longer present 10 or more years after they stop using OCs. Because there is no relationship between risk of breast cancer and dose or duration of use of estrogen, it is unlikely that OCs initiate breast cancer. Furthermore, there is no significant increase in risk of breast cancer with initiation of OC use at a very young age, use before a first birth, or use by women with a family history of breast cancer (Chapter 204). A recent study among women ages 35 to 64 showed no significant increased risk of breast cancer among current and former OC users.

The epidemiologic data regarding the risk of invasive cervical cancer as well as cervical intraepithelial neoplasia and OC use is conflicting. Nonetheless, the majority of well-controlled studies indicate that there is no change in risk of cervical intraepithelial neoplasia and OC use. However, it is likely that a causal relationship exists between OC use and a reported increased risk of cervical adenocarcinoma. OC users need annual cervical cytologic screening (Chapter 205).

Several studies have shown that the use of OCs has a protective effect against endometrial cancer. This decrease in risk persists for many years after OCs are stopped. Women who use OCs for at least 1 year have a 50% reduced risk of endometrial cancer development between the ages of 40 and 65 years as compared with nonusers. This protective effect is related to duration of use, increasing from a 20% reduction with 1 year of use to a 60% reduction with 4 years of use.

In addition, OCs reduce the risk of developing epithelial ovarian cancer as well as cancers with low malignant potential. The magnitude of the decrease in risk is directly related to the duration of OC use, increasing from about a 40% reduction with 4 years of use to a 60% reduction with 12 years of use. The protective effect continues for at least 20 years after the use of OCs ends. As with endometrial cancer, the protective effect occurs only in women of low parity (fewer than four), who are at greatest risk for this type of cancer. Recent studies have reported that OCs significantly reduce the risk of developing colorectal cancer by about 20%.

The development of a benign hepatocellular adenoma was a rare occurrence in long-term users of high-dose OCs containing mestranol but is not increased by use of ethinyl estradiol OCs. There is no increased risk of liver cancer associated with OC use. OC use also does not increase the risk of development of malignant melanoma or prolactin-secreting pituitary adenomas.

The OCs can be prescribed for the majority of women of reproductive age. Absolute contraindications include a history of vascular disease, including systemic diseases that affect the vascular system, such as lupus erythematosus or diabetes with retinopathy or nephropathy. Cigarette smoking by OC users older than 35 years of age and uncontrolled hypertension are also contraindications, as are a personal history of cancer of the breast or endometrium and cholestatic jaundice of pregnancy. Pregnancy and any undiagnosed cause of uterine bleeding are also contraindications. Women with functional heart diseases should not use OCs because the fluid retention could result in congestive heart failure. There is no evidence, however, that individuals with asymptomatic mitral valve prolapse should not use OCs. Women with active liver disease should not take OCs. However, women who have recovered from liver disease, such as viral hepatitis, and whose liver function test results have returned to normal, can safely take OCs. Relative contraindications to OC use include classic but not common migraine headaches, undiagnosed causes of amenorrhea, and depression. Use of OCs does not cause enlargement of prolactin-secreting pituitary microadenomas or worsen functional hyperprolactinemia (Chapter 237), as was previously believed.

INITIATION OF THERAPY AND SURVEILLANCE. If a healthy woman has no contraindications to OC use, it is unnecessary to perform any laboratory tests, including cervical cytology, before use unless these are necessary for routine health maintenance. Routine use of laboratory tests is not indicated unless the woman has a family history of diabetes or arterial vascular disease at a young age, in which case a fasting glucose or lipid panel should be obtained. After the first three cycles of OC use, a nondirected history should be obtained and blood pressure measured. After this visit, the woman should be seen annually; at each visit, a nondirected history should again be taken, blood pressure and body weight measured, and a physical examination (including breast, abdominal, and pelvic examination with cervical cytology) performed. It is not necessary to measure lipids, other than the routine cholesterol screening every 5 years, in women with no cardiovascular risk factors, even if they are older than 35 years. If the woman has a history of liver disease, a liver panel should be obtained to make certain that liver function is normal before OCs are started. There is no reason to discontinue OC use unless pregnancy is desired. Intermittent discontinuation is unnecessary and may result in an unwanted pregnancy.

Although synthetic sex steroids can retard the biotransformation of certain drugs (e.g., phenazone and meperidine) as a result of substrate competition, such interference is usually not important clinically. However, some drugs can interfere clinically with the action of OCs by inducing liver enzymes that convert the steroids to more polar and less biologically active metabolites. These drugs include barbiturates, sulfonamides, cyclophosphamide, griseofulvin, and rifampin. There is a high incidence of OC failure in women ingesting rifampin, and these two agents as well as systemic griseofulvin should not be given concurrently. There is no reliable evidence that other antibiotics (including ampicillin and tetracycline), analgesics, or barbiturates inhibit OC effectiveness. Products containing St. John's wort reduce contraceptive effectiveness and cause breakthrough bleeding. Women taking medication for epilepsy should be treated with 50 μg estrogen formulations, because many antiepileptic medications lower ethinyl estradiol levels and cause breakthrough bleeding, which may cause premature discontinuation of use. Because of their many health benefits, including reduction in risk of endometrial and ovarian cancer and induction of regular cyclic uterine bleeding, the continued use of OCs until menopause should be encouraged in women without contraindications.

Transdermal and Intravaginal Steroid Contraceptives

Two novel methods of delivering contraceptive steroids other than the oral route have received regulatory approval for marketing in the United States. One of these is a transdermal patch with an area of 20 cm², which delivers 150 μg of the progestin norelgestromin, the active metabolite of norgestimate, and 20 μg of ethinyl estradiol daily into the systemic circulation for 7 days. After this time span, the patch is removed and another is attached to a different area of the skin. The steroids are absorbed into the circulation at a constant rate, yielding fairly constant circulatory levels of each steroid while the patch is attached. This differs from the peaks and valleys of steroid levels that occur after ingestion of an OC. After three patches are applied, no patch is used for the fourth week to allow withdrawal bleeding. Contraceptive efficacy, bleeding patterns, and side effects are similar to those associated with OCs, but in one comparative study compliance was better with the patch than with the OC.

Another method of administering contraceptive steroids at a constant rate is by use of a flexible vaginal ring, which is 58 mm in outside diameter and 4 mm thick. The ring is composed of ethinyl vinyl acetate and contains the progestin etonogestrel and ethinyl estradiol. The rings are all the same size and do not have to be fitted. The ring is inserted and removed by the woman herself and is left in place for 3 weeks, after which time it is removed for 1 week to allow withdrawal bleeding. Each day, 120 μg of etonogestrel and 15 μg of ethinyl estradiol is released from the ring, and bleeding with the ring in place is uncommon. Contraceptive efficacy and side effects are similar to those of OCs.

INJECTABLE STEROID CONTRACEPTIVES. Several types of injectable steroid formulations are in use for contraception throughout the world. The one most widely used in the United States is depomedroxyprogesterone acetate (DMPA). This contraceptive is administered as an intramuscular injection of 1 mL of an aqueous suspension containing 150 mg of crystalline medroxyprogesterone acetate once every 3 months. Other injectable contraceptives include norethindrone enanthate, given in a dose of 200 mg every 2 months, and several once-a-month injections of combinations of different progestins and estrogens. DMPA has a low failure rate, 0.1% at 1 year and 0.4% at 2 years. Its major contraceptive action consists of inhibition of ovulation. It also impedes sperm transport by keeping the cervical mucus thick and inhibits endometrial growth and glycogen production. Serum medroxyprogesterone levels rise steadily to contraceptively effective blood levels (>0.5 ng/mL) within 24 hours after the injection. Levels plateau for about 3 months, after which there is a gradual decline until levels become undetectable 7 to 9 months after the injection. Endogenous estradiol levels remain above the postmenopausal range, and symptoms of estrogen deficiency do not occur. Although many women using DMPA have a decreased amount of bone mineral density during use, bone density increases after DMPA is stopped, and there are no reports of an increased risk of fracture with DMPA use.

Because of the lag time it takes to clear DMPA from the circulation, resumption of ovulation is delayed for a variable period of time after the last injection. It may take as long as 1 year for ovulatory cycles to return. After this initial delay, fecundity resumes at a rate similar to that found after discontinuing a barrier contraceptive.

The major side effect of DMPA is complete disruption of the menstrual cycle. Since this formulation contains only a progestin, without an estrogen, endometrial integrity is not maintained and uterine bleeding occurs at irregular and unpredictable intervals. The bleeding is usually light in amount and does not cause anemia. As duration of therapy increases, the incidence of frequent bleeding steadily declines and the incidence of amenorrhea steadily increases, so that at the end of 2 years, about 70% of users are amenorrheic. Women who use this method of contraception should be counseled that with time the irregular bleeding episodes will cease and amenorrhea will most likely occur. Most DMPA users gain between 1.5 to 4 kg in their first year of use and continue to gain weight thereafter. If weight gain occurs, caloric intake should be decreased. Because there is no estrogen in DMPA, its use does not cause hypertension or thromboembolism.

In cycling women, the initial injection should be given no later than day 5 of the cycle to be certain to inhibit ovulation in the initial treatment cycle. The first injection should be given within 5 days after delivery in nonlactating women but not until after 6 weeks in lactating women.

Because the major reason for discontinuance of all progestin-injectable contraceptives is menstrual irregularity, several combined progestin-estrogen injectables that are given once monthly and produce regular withdrawal bleeding have been developed. A combination of medroxyprogesterone acetate, 25 mg, and an estradiol ester, estradiol cypionate 5 mg, was marketed for use in the United States after extensive clinical trials but is currently unavailable. A 0.5 mL aqueous suspension of this formulation is injected intramuscularly, into the deltoid, thigh, or gluteal muscle once every 28 days ±5 days. Pregnancy rates are reported to be about 0.1% after 1 year of use. The estradiol is cleared about 2 weeks after the injection, and withdrawal bleeding usually occurs between 2 and 3 weeks after each injection. Because the amount of medroxyprogesterone is markedly less than that used in DMPA, the progestin is cleared more rapidly and ovulation and resumption of fertility occur within a few months of discontinuation.

SUBDERMAL IMPLANTS. Several types of subdermal implants containing only progestins are effective long-acting methods of contraception. The initial formulation that was marketed consisted of six 3.4 cm polydimethylsiloxane (Silastic) capsules, each containing 36 mg of levonorgestrel, and was very effective. Subcutaneous insertion in the upper arm is performed in an outpatient setting utilizing a small skin incision with local anesthesia. The capsules are removed when desired by the user or at the end of 5 years, which is the duration of maximal contraceptive effectiveness. Return to ovulation is prompt after implant removal. These capsules are no longer marketed in the United States.

Annual pregnancy rates for the first 5 years of use are about 0.2 per 100 women, whereas the cumulative 5-year pregnancy rate is 1.1%.

The major side effect is the totally irregular pattern of uterine bleeding. Bleeding episodes are more prolonged and irregular during the first year of use, after which they become more regular as ovulatory cycles occur. A formulation containing levonorgestrel in two 4 cm Silastic rods has a similar pharmacologic pattern as the six capsules with similar effectiveness and side effects. The two rods are easier to insert and remove than the six capsules. These rods are not marketed in the United States. A single 4 cm by 2 mm ethylene vinyl acetate rod containing 68 µg of etonogestrel, the active metabolite of desogestrel, provides effective contraception for 3 years. This rod is packaged in a disposable metal trochar inserter and does not require a skin incision for insertion, only for removal. Ovulation is inhibited by the circulating etonogestrel levels, and no pregnancies were reported in three large clinical trials. As with other progestin-only implants, irregular bleeding is the most common clinical complaint.

Emergency Contraception

For a woman not using contraception, if emergency contraception is given within 72 hours after a single coitus in midcycle, about 75% of pregnancies will be prevented. If more than one episode of coitus has occurred, or if treatment was initiated later than 72 hours after coitus, the method is less effective. Until recently, the most common currently used regimen is ingestion of four tablets of the OC containing 50 µg of ethinyl estradiol and 0.5 mg DL-norgestrel, in doses of two tablets 12 hours apart. The pregnancy rate with this regimen is 2%, about one fourth that of the 8% expected rate. Another formulation consisting of a 750 µg single tablet of levonorgestrel given once every 12 hours is slightly more effective than the two tablets of the combination steroid formulation without the estrogenic side effects. This formulation is marketed in the United States and elsewhere and prevents about 85% of the expected pregnancies for a pregnancy rate of 1%.

Intrauterine Devices

The main benefits of IUDs are (1) a high level of effectiveness, (2) a lack of systemic metabolic effects for copper IUDs, and (3) the need for only a single act of motivation for long-term use. Despite these advantages, less than 1% of married women of reproductive age use the IUD for contraception in the United States, compared with 15% to 30% in most European countries and Canada. The Copper T380A IUD is the only copper-bearing IUD currently marketed in the United States, but the Multiload CU 375 is widely used in Europe. The Copper T380A is approved for use in the United States for 10 years and maintains its high levels of effectiveness for at least 12 years. A levonorgestrel-releasing IUD is also marketed in the United States. A dose of 20 µg of levonorgestrel diffuses from the device into the endometrial cavity each day. Because of the progestational effect on the endometrium,

the amount of uterine bleeding is markedly reduced with use of this device, and it has been used therapeutically to treat menorrhagia. The previously marketed progesterone-releasing IUD needed to be replaced annually, but the levonorgestrel-releasing IUD has a high level of effectiveness for 5 years, which is the approved duration of use.

The main mechanism of contraceptive action of copper-bearing IUDs is spermicidal. This effect is caused by a local sterile leukocytic response produced by the copper as well as the plastic IUD itself. Because of the spermicidal action of IUDs, very few, if any, spermatozoa reach the oviducts, and the ovum usually does not become fertilized. The levonorgestrel-releasing IUD acts mainly by preventing transport of spermatozoa through the cervical mucus and thus preventing fertilization of the ovum. After removal of each type of IUD, the inflammatory reaction rapidly disappears and resumption of fertility is prompt. In the first year of use, IUDs have less than a 1% pregnancy rate, a 10% expulsion rate, and a 15% rate of removal for medical reasons, mainly bleeding and pain. The incidence of each of these events, especially expulsion, diminishes steadily in subsequent years. Mefenamic acid ingested in a dosage of 500 mg three times a day during the days of menstruation has been shown to significantly reduce the amount of uterine bleeding in IUD users.

Development of acute salpingitis more than a month after insertion of the IUD is due to infection with a sexually transmitted pathogen and is unrelated to the presence of the device. All IUD-related upper genital tract infections occur only during the insertion process. If there is clinical suspicion that cervicitis is present, the endocervix should be cultured and the insertion delayed until the results reveal that no pathogenic organisms are present. It is not cost-effective to routinely administer antibiotics with IUD insertion.

The IUD is not associated with an increased incidence of either endometrial or cervical carcinoma. The IUD is a particularly useful method of contraception for women who have completed their families and do not desire permanent sterilization and have contraindications to, or do not wish to use, other effective methods of reversible contraception. It was calculated that after 5 years of use, the IUD is the most cost effective of all methods of contraception, including sterilization.

SUGGESTED READINGS

Haggai DN: Emergency contraception: The journey so far. BJOG 2003;110:339–345. *Overview of the history and current status of this important, controversial type.*
Marchbanks PA, McDonald JA, Wilson HG, et al: Oral contraceptives and the risk of breast cancer. N Engl J Med 2002;346:2025–2032. *Women ages 35–64 who were current or former users of oral contraceptives did not have higher breast cancer rates.*

252 PREGNANCY: NEOPLASTIC DISEASES

Edward C. Grendys, Jr.

Although uncommon in a relative sense, cancer remains a leading cause of death in women of reproductive age (Table 252–1). Overall cancer-related deaths account for 13% of mortality in women between the ages of 15 and 34 years and 38% in women aged 35 to 54 years. In this reproductive age group, cancer is expected to complicate approximately 3500 pregnancies in the United States, with an incidence of 1 in 1000. However, it has been suggested that as women continue to delay childbearing, this incidence may begin to rise in concordance with the direct relationship of age on cancer incidence (Fig. 252–1).

Table 252–1 • REPORTED DEATHS IN U.S. WOMEN AGED 15-54

CAUSE	NO. CASES/YEAR
Cancer	34,361
Cardiac disease	13,900
Trauma	12,154

Data from American Cancer Society, Cancer Statistics, 1998.

Women's Health

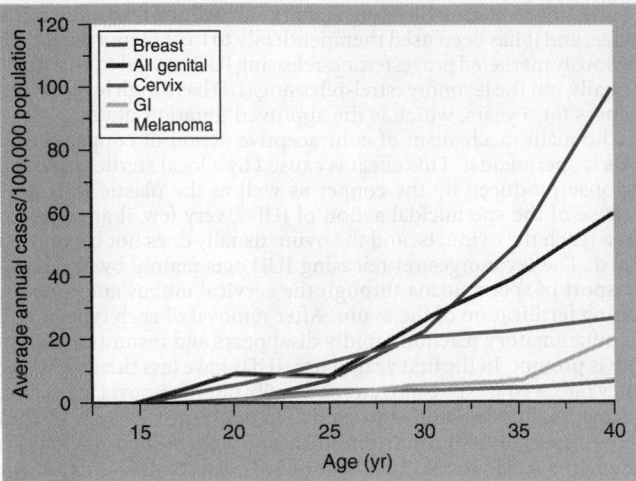

FIGURE 252–1 • Incidence of common malignancies seen in pregnancy. (Data from American Cancer Society, Cancer Statistics, 1998.)

SITE/TYPE	ESTIMATED INCIDENCE PER 1000 PREGNANCIES
Table 252–2 • INCIDENCE OF CANCER IN PREGNANCY	
Cervix uteri	
Noninvasive	1.3
Invasive	1.0
Breast	0.33
Melanoma	0.14
Ovary	0.10
Colorectal	0.02
Leukemia	0.01
Lymphoma	0.01

From Allen HH, Nisker JA (eds): Cancer in Pregnancy: Therapeutic Guidelines: Mt. Kisco, NY, Futura, 1986.

Given these statistics, it is imperative that primary care physicians (i.e., family practitioners, internists, and obstetricians/gynecologists) be knowledgeable in current screening recommendations, especially regarding the cervix, colon, and breast malignancies. Subtle signs of malignancy can occasionally be mistaken for side effects of pregnancy, thus possibly leading to diagnostic and treatment delay.

When a cancer occurs in a gravid woman, it obviously carries with it enormous pressures on both the patient and her family, as well as on the treating team of physicians. The diagnosis alone is certainly anxiety provoking enough without the burden of the treatment decision that is about to affect two lives.

The approach to a pregnant patient diagnosed with a concomitant malignant process requires a concerted multidisciplinary approach. This team should include, at a minimum, obstetricians with experience in high-risk pregnancies and oncologists with a keen understanding of fetal development and maturation. Also, significant input from psychosocial, religious, and even legal personnel can be invaluable to maximize the outcome of mother, fetus, and family. An integrated care plan should be formulated, and communication between all team members must be encouraged. The medical and psychological sequelae of this process are complex and not to be taken lightly. Decisions ranging from pregnancy preservation, type and timing of diagnostic and therapeutic interventions, use of antepartum lung-maturing corticosteroids, and timing and mode of delivery must all be carefully planned and executed.

The most common malignancies encountered during pregnancy are uterine/cervical cancer, breast cancer, melanoma, ovarian cancer, thyroid cancer, leukemia, lymphoma, and colorectal cancer (Table 252–2). Specific reviews of these common malignancies encountered in this population are presented here, along with various strategies employed in their management.

Two fundamental issues must be contemplated when one approaches the care of a gravid patient diagnosed with a malignant process. The impact of the disease state on the patient is of obvious paramount importance, and an understanding of the natural history of the disease is therefore critical. Treatment options, success rates, and risk of treatment modifications or delays must be considered. Equally important is the maternal and paternal desires of pregnancy

preservation and the risk of the chosen treatment regimens on fetal health, including sequelae resulting from elective early delivery or potential for in utero fetal harm from toxic side effects of therapy. Patients need to be presented with unbiased information regarding risks to both mother and fetus and with all potential options of intervention, including pregnancy termination if it is required and desired. Most likely, these management issues are best left to a tertiary care center with a high-risk neonatal nursery (level III) that can adequately manage a preterm yet viable infant if necessary.

Fetal Development

Physicians involved with the treatment of cancer in the pregnant patient must possess an in-depth understanding of embryonic development as well as of the disease process and the available therapeutic options. The terminology adopted by embryologists and clinical obstetricians must also be understood.

Fetal age is the most critical in terms of prediction of fetal survival and subsequent morbidity. In clinical obstetrics, estimated gestational age (EGA) is defined as the time from the last day of the last menstrual period (Fig. 252–2). Embryonic age from a developmental biologist's viewpoint begins at fertilization and is thus 2 weeks shorter in duration. This 2-week differential is critical and potentially legally important when considering fetal viability and age at which termination (abortion) can be legally performed. It must be remembered that ovulation and subsequent fertilization does not occur until approximately 2 weeks after the last menstrual period. Thus, the normal gestation is 40 weeks and clinical viability generally has been defined as greater than 25 weeks' EGA. For accurate clinical communication, fetal age should be documented in terms of EGA (in weeks). Gestation is further subdivided into 14-week trimesters, as shown in Figure 252–2. In most states, abortion can legally be performed in the first trimester, whereas some states allow termination until 24 weeks (late abortion).

The most vulnerable portion of development is believed to be during the embryonic period (see Fig. 252–2). During this time, major organ systems are forming (organogenesis) and it appears that the conceptus is susceptible to outside teratogenic influences. For this reason, most clinicians believe that therapeutic intervention is best delayed until after this period to lessen fetal risk in a patient desirous of preserving her pregnancy.

After the embryonic period, fetal development is focused on organ growth and maturation. Certain basic physical and metabolic

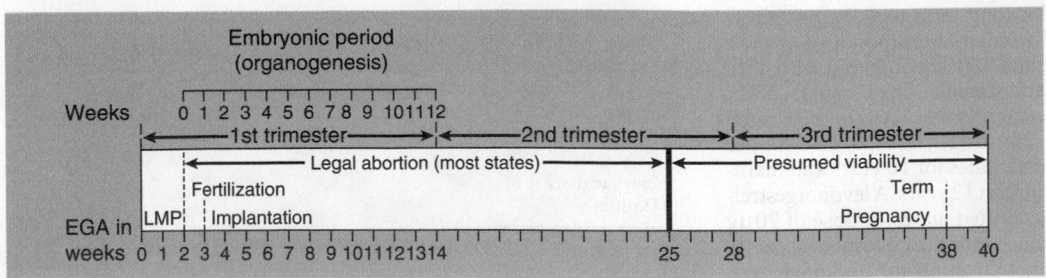

FIGURE 252–2 • Fetal development.

Table 252–3 • INCIDENCE OF FETAL MORTALITY, HYALINE MEMBRANE DISEASE (HMD), BRONCHOPULMONARY DYSPLASIA (BPD), AND INTRAVENTRICULAR HEMORRHAGE (IVH) AS ASSOCIATED WITH FETAL AGE

EGA (WEEKS)	MORTALITY (%)	HMD (%)	BPD (%)	IVH (%)
24–25	66	93	59	36
26–27	32	86	59	32
28–29	20	71	34	34
30–31	9	46	13	7
32–33	1.2	33	2.4	1.8

EGA = estimated gestational age.

Table 252–4 • SURVIVAL STATISTICS IN RELATION TO ESTIMATED GESTATIONAL AGE (EGA)

EGA (WEEKS)	% SURVIVAL
25	24.0
26	57.1
27	66.7
28	84.9
29	82.9
30	80.7
31	94.2
32	92.1
33	92.2
34	94.8
35	98.1
36	98.1
37	93.3
38	97.7

capabilities appear to be required to maintain extrauterine life. Most commonly, viability is defined as 25 weeks of EGA although reports of fetal survival before this age have been noted. Subsequent fetal morbidity and mortality are linearly correlated with gestational age (Table 252–3). Obviously, preterm infants require care in a specific neonatal unit prepared for such complicated management (level III nurseries). A review of 600 preterm infants without associated congenital anomalies demonstrated a mortality rate of approximately 32% for a fetus delivered at 26 weeks' EGA compared with 2.7% when the fetus was allowed to develop to 34 weeks of age (Table 252–4). Significant literature supports the concept of maximizing in utero fetal life to decrease fetal morbidity, mortality, and long-term developmental delay.

Although the short-term major risk to the fetus appears to be secondary to poor lung development, subsequent development of hyaline membrane disease, and bronchopulmonary dysplasia (see Table 252–3), recent reports are confirming increased risk of intraventricular hemorrhage and significant long-term motor and neurologic sequelae associated with surviving a preterm delivery. Infants weighing less than 1500 g at birth appear to suffer from significant long-term deficiencies in intelligence quotient, visual motor integration, and reading performance. Similar data reveal significant neurologic impairment in infants documented with intraventricular hemorrhage. In one study, only 26% of low-birth-weight children with subsequent intraventricular hemorrhage had normal developmental abilities at the time of preschool testing. It appears that predelivery use of corticosteroids decreases the risk of pulmonary complications as well as intraventricular hemorrhage. It is important for parents to understand the potential ramifications of early delivery on their child and realize that survival can be associated with significant long-term morbidity.

Diagnostic and Therapeutic Procedures in the Pregnant Patient with Cancer

Commonly accepted practices of diagnostic imaging, surgery, therapeutic radiation therapy, and chemotherapy have profoundly different implications in the pregnant versus nonpregnant patient. The risk-benefit profiles of each modality must be carefully considered before implementation.

RADIATION AND PREGNANCY

Radiation can cause both direct and indirect intracellular damage. Direct radiation damage is believed to be a relatively minor component of these detrimental effects. Indirect damage is initiated by free water radiation-induced ionization. This leads to free radical formation with subsequent chemical intracellular reaction and damage. Because the major component of cells is water, this is believed to be the major mechanism of action. In vitro studies indicate that dividing cells, specifically near the mitotic phase, appear to be most vulnerable.

At therapeutic doses, radiation does not significantly directly damage cellular microstructures, membranes, or metabolic processes. The primary toxic effects appear to result primarily from free radical–induced damage at the DNA level. The damage is most likely secondary to double-stranded breaks in DNA leading to replication errors, which are presumably lethal and potentially teratogenic.

At doses of radiation less than 100 cGy, cellular death results from direct inhibition of cell division and is most prevalent in cells undergoing active division. The induction of radiation-induced mutations increases as a linear function of single doses of 400 to 600 cGy. Because of the acute toxicity to cells, radiation is considered a weak teratogen. Clinical retrospective studies suggest some association of spontaneous abortion with early fetal irradiation.

The fetal effects of radiation appear to be related to the gestational age at the time of exposure, as well as total dose received. An analysis of children exposed in utero to atomic bomb–produced radiation revealed that most long-term neurologic sequelae occurred in children exposed between 8 and 15 weeks' EGA, with no cases reported in children exposed before 8 weeks' EGA. Exposure at an earlier gestational age most likely resulted in miscarriage.

Fetal exposure to radiation between 11 and 16 weeks' gestation appears to result in an increased risk of microcephaly and mental retardation. Exposure in the third trimester may be associated with longer term developmental abnormalities (Tables 252–5 and 252–6). In general, third-trimester fetal doses should not exceed 100 cGy.

The maternal effects of radiation are well documented. Direct ovarian exposures of 1000 cGy are associated with permanent sterilization in more than 90% of women. Lower doses also result in

Table 252–5 • CRITICAL PERIODS FOR FETAL IRRADIATION

DISORDER/PROBLEM	RADIATION DOSE	
	100 to 500 cGy	500 to 1000 cGy
Embryonic death		0–1 week
Malformation	1–8 weeks	1–8 weeks
Microcephaly	1–15 weeks	1–15 weeks
Mental retardation	8–15 weeks	8–25 weeks
Growth retardation	1–15 weeks	1–25 weeks
Late-onset cancer		1–39 weeks
Genetic aberrations		

Table 252–6 • ESTIMATED TOTAL RADIATION EXPOSURE RESULTING IN MAJOR ABNORMALITIES

GESTATION (MONTHS)	RADIATION DOSE (cGy)
1	40
2	90
3	140
4	200
5	250
6	350
8	500
9	600

sterility but appear to be dependent on patient age and menstrual and reproductive history. Ovarian suppression with oral contraceptives or gonadotropin hormone antagonists may help preserve ovarian function and subsequent reproductive potential, especially in the adolescent female. This effect appears to be less pronounced as age increases.

Estimated fetal radiation exposures for standard radiographic procedures are listed in Table 252–7. A risk-benefit assessment must be performed before any radiographic evaluation is undertaken in a pregnant patient.

Because of the relatively high fetal exposure associated with pelvic abdominal computed tomography (CT), it is not recommended in early pregnancy. If limited CT pelvic imaging to evaluate pelvic outlets for term vaginal delivery has been used, fetal risk should be minimal at this gestational age.

Mammography, as noted in Table 252–7, presents essentially no risk to the developing fetus. Therefore, its use as a diagnostic modality in the patient with a clinically suspicious breast lesion is recommended if clinically warranted.

Perhaps the most commonly employed imaging procedure in the pregnant patient is real-time ultrasonography. Its use in fetal anatomic observation and age determination has been well studied and is considered safe throughout the gestational period.

It can also be an important instrument for maternal evaluation of suspected renal, abdominal, pelvic hepatic, cardiac, vascular, and breast tissues. Hepatic ultrasonographic evaluation can detect occult liver metastasis with a sensitivity of 76% without fetal risk. Breast ultrasonography is a useful adjunct in characterizing breast lesion architecture noted on physical examination or mammography (see section on breast carcinoma in pregnancy).

Magnetic resonance imaging, because of its lack of ionizing radiation, is believed to be acceptable in pregnancy, and to date no adverse fetal or maternal sequelae have been described.

Therapeutic megavoltage radiation therapy has a pivotal role in the management of many malignancies, such as breast and cervical cancer and lymphoma. Its use in pregnancy must be regarded as a completely separate entity from diagnostic radiographic procedures. Depending on the specific anatomic area to be treated, the fetal exposure can range from minimal to substantial (Table 252–8).

SURGERY IN PREGNANCY

Of the common solid tumor cancers affecting the pregnant patient, most are treatable and many curable by a surgical approach. Fetal risk appears to be most dependent on the anatomic location of the neoplasm and the risk of subsequent stimulation of preterm labor, which is most affected by timing of the procedure. Pelvic and abdominal radical procedures can be safely undertaken if appropriate planning is used.

Surgical approaches to breast, ovarian, gastrointestinal, thyroid, melanoma, neurologic, and vulvar cancer have been well described, along with a multitude of benign surgical conditions. The current anesthetic agents in common use are believed to be without risk of fetal teratogenicity, and certainly minor procedures with local or

Table 252–8 • ESTIMATED FETAL DOSES FROM EXTRAPELVIC AND EXTRA-ABDOMINAL MATERNAL IRRADIATION

RADIATION SITE/ PRESCRIBED DOSE	ESTIMATED GESTATIONAL AGE	FETAL DOSE (cGy)
Tibia sarcoma/50 Gy	25 weeks	1.5
Brain glioblastoma/60 Gy	13 weeks	3.9
Hodgkin's disease (mantle fields)/38 Gy	34 weeks	42
Hodgkin's disease with mediastinum/neck/40 Gy	18–31 weeks	20
Breast cancer/50 Gy	Ovarian dose	9

Data from Greer BE, Goof BA, Kuh W, et al: Cancer in the pregnant patient. *In* Hoskins WJ, Perez CA, Young RC (eds): Principles and Practice of Gynecologic Oncology, 2nd ed. Philadelphia, Lippincott-Raven, 1997, pp 463–485.

regional analgesia (epidural, spinal, nerve block) are essentially without risk. Exclusive of cesarean section, it has been estimated that approximately 35,000 pregnant women undergo some surgical procedure per year.

An issue that should be considered is the critical nature of the uteroplacental unit, which is susceptible to blood pressure changes and intravascular volume depletion. Major changes in blood flow to the placenta can lead to subsequent fetal hypoxia and potentially precipitate neurologic sequelae. Therefore, the supine position is best avoided in the gravid patient (especially after 20 weeks' EGA) owing to decreased cardiac return associated with uterine compression on the inferior vena cava. Patients are best maintained in the left lateral decubitus position (30 degrees) to decrease this compressive effect. Diagnostic procedures including fine-needle aspiration, core biopsy, and/or surgical removal of suspicious lesions should rarely, if ever, be deferred due to pregnancy. As described earlier, a surgeon and anesthesiologist with appropriate understanding of uteroplacental dynamics should be sought to provide optimal care.

Equally critical is the increased thrombogenic state associated with pregnancy as brought about by decreases in plasma fibrinolytic activity, increases in coagulation factors, and increased pelvic and lower extremity stasis. These factors combine for a five- to six-fold increased risk of thromboembolic phenomena in the pregnant patient, and thus appropriate thromboprophylaxis should be undertaken. Current acceptable techniques include subcutaneous heparin 5000 units three times a day, low-molecular-weight heparin (enoxaparin, 40 mg/day), or inflatable compression stockings. Non-custom fit elastic stockings (TedHose) have no role in thromboprophylaxis.

CHEMOTHERAPY IN PREGNANCY

Chemotherapy, by definition, is the use of chemical agents to treat or control disease. Therefore, any medication from acetaminophen to zinc has the potential to cause fetal effects, both beneficial and harmful. The United States Food and Drug Administration has established labeling of prescription drugs to provide information regarding potential fetal risks. These five categories (A, B, C, D, and X) indicate risk of fetal teratogenicity (Table 252–9). A similar classification system has been adopted by the Australian Drug Evaluation Committee (ADEC) as well as by the German health care administration. From a practical standpoint, drugs in Food and Drug Administration categories A, B, and C are prescribed with impunity.

Chemotherapy specifically as an antineoplastic agent has an integral role in the management of many of the cancers encountered during pregnancy. Some agents are used as adjuvant therapy after primary surgery (e.g., breast cancer), whereas others are the primary treatment modality (e.g., Hodgkin's disease). The potential toxicity to the developing fetus must be considered when discussing potential treatment regimens in the pregnant patient.

All chemotherapeutic agents, by virtue of their mechanism of action, have the ability to be both mutagenic and teratogenic to the actively dividing cells of the embryo and fetus. The vast majority are considered category D or X agents. Unfortunately, controlled data on their effects on the developing fetus are limited. Most information has come

Table 252–7 • ESTIMATED FETAL DOSE FROM COMMON DIAGNOSTIC RADIOGRAPHIC PROCEDURES

EXAMINATION	FETAL DOSE IN cGy (RAD)
Chest (posteroanterior/lateral)	0.00006
Abdomen	0.15–0.26
Lumbar spine	0.65
Pelvis	0.2–0.35
Hip	0.13–0.2
Intravenous pyelography	0.47–0.82
Upper gastrointestinal tract	0.17–0.48
Barium enema	0.82–1.14
Mammography	Undetectable
CT of head	0.007
CT of abdomen (early pregnancy)	0.04
CT of pelvis	2.5
^{99m}Tc-MDP bone scan	0.15

CT = computed tomography.

Table 252–9 • UNITED STATES FOOD AND DRUG ADMINISTRATION PREGNANCY CATEGORY DEFINITIONS

CATEGORY	DEFINITION
A	Controlled studies in women fail to demonstrate a risk to the fetus in the first trimester, and the possibility of fetal harm appears remote.
B	Animal studies do not indicate a risk to the fetus and there are no controlled human studies. Animal studies do show an adverse effect on the fetus but well-controlled studies in pregnant women have failed to demonstrate a risk to the fetus.
C	Studies have shown that the drug exerts animal teratogenic or embryocidal effects, but there are no controlled studies in women, or no studies are available in either animals or women.
D	Positive evidence of human fetal risk exists, but benefits in certain situations may make use of the drug acceptable.
X	Studies in animals or humans have demonstrated fetal abnormalities or there is evidence of fetal risk based on human experience and the risk of drug administration clearly outweighs any possible benefit.

Table 252–11 • SPECIFIC CHEMOTHERAPEUTIC AGENTS AND THEIR ACTIONS

AGENT	CELL-CYCLE ACTION	POTENTIAL FETAL TOXICITY
Alkylating agent: cyclophosphamide, ifosfamide, chlorambucil, nitrogen mustard, cisplatin	Nonspecific	14% fetal malformations in first trimester; chlorambucil syndrome of renal aplasia, cleft palate, skeletal anomalies
Antitumor antibiotics: dactinomycin, mitomycin C, bleomycin, doxorubicin	Variable	None reported
Animetabolites: 5-fluorouracil, methotrexate, cytarabine	Cell cycle specific	Multiple defects: cranial dysostocia, hypertelorism, micrognathia, cleft palate; contraindicated in pregnancy
Taxanes: paclitaxel	Cell cycle specific	No data in pregnancy
Biologic response modifiers: interleukins, interferons	Nonspecific	Contraindicated in pregnancy
Hormones: tamoxifen, megestrol	Nonspecific	Contraindicated in pregnancy

from retrospective reviews, clinical observation, and laboratory experiments on gravid animals.

It appears that the first trimester is the most susceptible to deleterious chemotherapy influences. Overall, it appears that approximately 20% of fetuses exposed to cytotoxic agents in the first trimester will manifest major anomalies, as compared with 3% in an unexposed population.

Chemotherapeutic agents primarily act by interrupting various portions of vital cell processes. This reproductive cell cycle is divided into five phases, each with specific actions leading to cell duplication (Table 252–10). Cancer cells are thought to replicate at a higher rate and therefore should be more susceptible to the cytotoxic or cytostatic effects of chemotherapy. Specific chemotherapeutic agents are often categorized by their interaction within the cell cycle and are traditionally classified into alkylating agents, antitumor antibiotics, antimetabolites, vinca alkaloids, biologic response modifiers, hormones, and taxanes. Specific agents and their actions are listed in Table 252–11.

The timing of chemotherapy administration in relationship to anticipated delivery must be carefully planned to avoid delivery around the time of the maternal hematopoietic nadir. Hematopoietic suppression (anemia, leukopenia, and thrombocytopenia) may occur in the fetus as a result of transplacental passage of cytotoxic agents from the mother to the fetus, and the neonatology team should be advised accordingly.

Taxanes (paclitaxel and docetaxel) have significant activity in many solid tumor malignancies. Case reports describing safe administration of paclitaxel (Taxol) have been published, but great caution must still be exercised. Appropriate consent must be obtained prior to administration and careful risk-versus-benefit analysis be undertaken. Given its activity of microtubular assembly, concern for its effect on fetal development is significant.

Breast-feeding is contraindicated during chemotherapeutic administration because these systemically administered antineoplastic agents may reach significant levels in breast milk.

SPECIFIC MALIGNANCIES IN PREGNANCY

CERVICAL CANCER

Cervical cancer remains the most common malignancy encountered during pregnancy. It occurs with an incidence of approximately 1.2 cases per 10,000 pregnancies. With the expanded knowledge of the natural history of this disease, the majority of patients with early cervical carcinoma can be managed with fetal preservation (if desired) without undue maternal morbidity or mortality.

Initial prenatal evaluation should routinely include a Papanicolaou (Pap) smear. This simple, inexpensive, and extremely effective screening procedure has significantly decreased the incidence of invasive squamous cell carcinoma of the cervix in the United States. In countries where this procedure is not widely practiced, cervical cancer remains one of the leading causes of death. After intense investigation and numerous clinical observations, the natural progression from a preinvasive dysplastic lesion to overt invasive cervical carcinoma is well understood. The purported rationale of the Pap smear is as a screening, and not a diagnostic, procedure. The success of Pap smear screening has been in its ability to diagnose dysplastic lesions, thus allowing for simple ablative and curative measures.

All clinicians who practice Pap smear screening should have an understanding of the Bethesda system of Pap smear interpretation as well as diagnostic and treatment algorithms. The Bethesda classification system is listed in Table 252–12. In general, a diagnosis of atyp-

Table 252–10 • CELL CYCLE

CELL PHASE	APPROXIMATE TIME (HOURS)	ACTIVITY
G1 (gap 1)	Variable	RNA manufacture, preparation for DNA synthesis
S (synthesis)	8	DNA duplication
G2 (gap 2)	3	Spindle apparatus formation
M (mitosis)	1	Mitosis
G0 (gap 0)		Resting (quiescent)

Table 252–12 • COMPARISON OF PAPANICOLAOU SMEAR CYTOLOGIC NOMENCLATURE

BETHESDA SYSTEM	CIN SYSTEM	HISTOLOGY
Normal	Normal	Normal
Benign cellular changes: requires specific annotation	Inflammatory atypia	Atypical cells
Squamous cell abnormalities		
Atypical squamous cells of undetermined significance (ASCUS)	CIN I	Mild dysplasia
Low-grade squamous intraepithelial lesion	CIN I	Mild dysplasia
High-grade squamous intraepithelial lesion	CIN II or III	Moderate or severe dysplasia

ical squamous cells of undetermined significance on an initial Pap smear can usually be managed with a simple repeat smear in 3 months. A Pap smear diagnosis of atypical glandular cells is, however, significantly different. (Persistent smears showing atypical squamous cells of undetermined significance, squamous intraepithelial lesions, or evidence of carcinoma mandates colposcopic evaluation of the cervix and vagina.) Atypical glandular cells on Pap smears are associated with a high incidence (11%) of invasive cancer and must be evaluated aggressively.

Cytologic evidence of squamous intraepithelial lesions is most commonly evaluated with cervical colposcopy. Colposcopy during pregnancy is safe and effective and in the vast majority (>90%) provides adequate diagnostic information. As in the nonpregnant patient, any area of gross abnormality, even in the presence of a normal Pap smear, requires biopsy.

Rx Treatment

Given the knowledge of the natural history of cervical dysplasia, observational strategies have been developed to allow the pregnancy to continue without need for intervention. Even in the patient with biopsy-proven carcinoma in situ, excision or cervical ablation can most commonly be deferred until after delivery. Importantly, a diagnosis of cervical dysplasia is not an indication for cesarean delivery, because there has been no demonstrable increased risk to mother or fetus with vaginal delivery.

Locally advanced cervical carcinoma, not amenable to surgical resection, requires treatment with radical radiation therapy. The standard external high-energy teletherapy radiation often exceeds 4500 cGy and is not compatible with fetal life. Again, decisions regarding fetal age, risk of early delivery versus waiting, and parental desires must be weighed, given the curability of this disease. With most lesions confined to the cervix, careful observation and expedited delivery after fetal maturation followed by radical treatment appears reasonable.

OVARIAN NEOPLASMS

The incidence of adnexal masses associated with pregnancy has been reported to range from 1 in 81 to 1 in 2500. With the use of ultrasonography for routine fetal surveillance, the detection of previously unrecognized adnexal masses in both early and late gestation is likely to increase.

Of the adnexal masses noticed in pregnancy, approximately 50% are smaller than 5 cm in diameter, whereas 25% are between 5 and 10 cm and 25% are greater than 10 cm at the time of discovery. Ninety-five per cent of these also are unilateral.

Unilateral, mobile, noncomplex masses smaller than 5 cm, noticed in the first trimester, will resolve in more than 90% of cases. It therefore is reasonable to observe nonsuspicious neoplasms conservatively with repeat ultrasonography into the second trimester (when elective surgical intervention is safest) to document spontaneous resolution.

A subgroup of patients undergoing assisted reproductive therapy with various ovulation-inducing medications present a unique situation. Because of the induced ovarian hyperstimulation and increased ultrasonographic surveillance, these patients commonly have ovarian cysts noted in the first trimester. Spontaneous resolution of benign-appearing ovarian cysts can be expected in more than 90% of patients who have undergone ovulation induction. Recent reports of possible associations between ovulation induction and an increased incidence of ovarian neoplasms should, however, be kept in mind, although this is considered to most likely be a long-term effect.

Adnexal masses can originate from multiple sources, and the differential diagnosis is complex, including multiple gynecologic and nongynecologic entities. Fortunately, modern pelvic imaging, especially ultrasonography, aids greatly in differentiating the primary origins of these masses. The common types of neoplastic and non-neoplastic ovarian masses noticed during pregnancy are described in Tables 252-13 and 252-14. Most ovarian tumors occurring during early pregnancy are benign, with the most common neoplastic ovarian mass being a benign cystic teratoma.

The lifetime risk of ovarian carcinoma for an American woman is approximately 1 in 70, with an age-adjusted annual incidence of approximately 13.7 cases per 100,000 women. This results in

Table 252-13 • DIFFERENTIAL DIAGNOSIS OF THE PELVIC MASS

Gynecologic
Ovary
 Benign (functional)
 Neoplastic (benign, malignant)
Fallopian tube
 Hydrosalpinx
 Tubo-ovarian abscess
 Ectopic pregnancy
Uterine
 Benign (leiomyomata)
 Malignant (sarcoma)
Nongynecologic
Gastrointestinal
 Colon (including stool, diverticular disease)
 Small bowel
 Appendix
Mesothelial tumors
Lymphoma
Retroperitoneal neoplasm
Pelvic kidney
Urachal cyst
Mesenteric cyst
Metastatic disease
Sacral meningocele
Distended bladder

Table 252-14 • HISTOLOGIC TYPE OF NON-NEOPLASTIC OVARIAN TUMORS IN PREGNANCY

HISTOLOGIC TYPE	FREQUENCY (%)
Endometriotic	14.0
Paraovarian	11.0
Simple cyst	12.0
Corpus luteal	50.0
Unknown	6.0
Miscellaneous	
Luteoma	1.0
Ovarian edema	1.0
Thecal lutein	5.0

Data from Stedman C, Kline R: Intraoperative complications and unexpected pathology at the time of cesarean section. Obstet Gynecol Clin North Am 1988;15:745–769.

approximately 24,000 new cases of ovarian cancer and 14,500 deaths per annum.

These malignancies can occur at any age, including infancy and childhood; however, the overall age-specific incidence increases dramatically with age. In women 40 years of age, there are approximately 10 cases per 100,000, increasing to a peak incidence of approximately 45 cases per 100,000 women between the ages of 60 and 65 years. Given this age distribution, the discovery of ovarian carcinoma in pregnancy is still distinctly uncommon.

Evaluation

PELVIC IMAGING. The key to evaluation of the pelvic/adnexal mass in pregnancy is to attempt to differentiate benign from malignant processes, to avoid unnecessary intervention. Given the widespread use of ultrasonography for fetal evaluation, many patients are noted to have adnexal masses as incidental findings. Fortunately, the vast majority of these are functional in nature and tend to resolve spontaneously. Other than the acute presentation of abdominal pain associated with ovarian torsion, most common between the sixth and 14th weeks of gestation, these masses often are clinically inapparent and may be accompanied only with the vague nonspecific abdominal discomfort common to pregnancy. Discovery of a mass in the first trimester in most situations should prompt repeat ultrasonography in the early second trimester to confirm resolution or stability.

Two to 5% of adnexal masses persisting after the first trimester are pathologically confirmed as being malignant, resulting in an overall malignancy rate of 1 in 5000 to 1 in 18,000 live births.

TUMOR MARKERS (Chapter 189). The use of CA-125 to differentiate malignant from benign adnexal masses has been well described. Unfortunately, in the premenopausal woman, the high rate of false-positive serum elevations in CA-125 makes this a relatively poor screening test. It is also commonly elevated due to the pregnancy itself, and therefore its use in the pregnant patient to aid in the differentiation of benign from malignant ovarian neoplasm is not recommended.

 Treatment

The discovery of an asymptomatic adnexal mass in the first trimester should be viewed with cautious optimism. As described earlier, many of these are functional in nature (corpus luteum) and most resolve spontaneously. Observation of nonsuspicious (simple, noncomplex, without excrescences, without ascites) lesions into the second trimester with repeat ultrasonographic assessment is appropriate.

PELVIC SURGERY. The timing of the surgical intervention cannot always be controlled, and emergency situations occasionally arise.

If laparotomy is required during the first trimester, spontaneous abortion is more likely, possibly because of disruption of the delicate corpus luteum. After 7 to 10 weeks of gestation, the trophoblast is capable of supplying sufficient quantities of specific steroid hormones for the maintenance of the gestation.

Should surgical extirpation of the corpus luteum be required in the first trimester, progestin support is recommended. A daily intramuscular injection of 100 mg of progesterone in oil or a 100 mg transvaginal suppository every 12 hours provides adequate progestin replacement. A mass that is first noted in the third trimester is best managed by awaiting fetal maturity if the clinical suspicion of malignancy is low.

The optimal timing of elective surgical intervention is during the second trimester. Apparent risk of preterm labor with subsequent fetal morbidity seems to be lessened. Uterine size at this gestational age does not preclude appropriate aortic and upper abdominal surgical exposure. Severe third-trimester complications are associated with failure to remove significant ovarian masses during mid-pregnancy.

OVARIAN CARCINOMA. Although uncommon, there are unfortunate instances in which both epithelial and germ cell carcinomas are diagnosed during pregnancy. The mainstay of management is still surgery, with removal of the neoplasm as well as appropriate surgical staging and debulking as indicated. It is strongly recommended that this procedure be undertaken as a team approach, including both an experienced gynecologic oncologist and a maternal-fetal medicine specialist. The nuances of the surgical approach are beyond the scope of this text.

After completion of the initial surgical effort, consideration of chemotherapy is warranted, depending on stage of disease, estimated fetal age, and desires of the mother. Chemotherapeutic intervention, most commonly with a platinum-based regimen (cisplatin) has been well described and appears to be safe to both mother and fetus. Taxanes (paclitaxel and docetaxel) have significant activity in many solid tumor malignancies, including epithelial ovarian cancer. Case reports describing safe administration of paclitaxel (Taxol) have been published, but great caution must still be exercised. Appropriate consent must be obtained prior to administration and careful risk-versus-benefit analysis must be undertaken.

BREAST CANCER IN PREGNANCY (Chapter 204)

Cancer of the breast occurring during pregnancy or within the first year after delivery is considered pregnancy-associated breast carcinoma. Breast carcinoma remains the second most common malignancy occurring in the pregnant patient and affects approximately 1 in 3000 pregnancies in the United States.

Traditionally, pregnancy-associated breast carcinoma has been thought to carry a poorer prognosis, although recent matched controlled data do not support this claim. Women with pregnancy-associated breast carcinoma are, however, more commonly diagnosed with locally advanced node-positive disease at the time of diagnosis (61% vs. 38%). The obvious adverse effect of advanced disease is

reflected by a decrease in the 5-year survival rate from 82% in the node-negative group to 47% in the node-positive group. Pregnant patients are also 2.5 times more likely to present with distant metastatic disease at the time of diagnosis, as compared with their nonpregnant counterparts.

Both the patient and the clinician must be continually vigilant to subtle breast changes. Most pregnancy-associated breast carcinomas initially manifest as a painless mass, and more than 90% are detected during patient self-breast examination. Similar diagnostic algorithms should be applied in both the pregnant and the nonpregnant patient with a suspicious breast lesion. Fine-needle aspiration, diagnostic mammography, ultrasonography, and open-breast biopsy pose no documented fetal risk. The historical reluctance to aggressively pursue histologic diagnosis of breast masses in pregnancy is unwarranted and perhaps detrimental.

A recent series of 134 breast biopsies performed during pregnancy revealed a 21% incidence of malignancy, thereby confirming the need for aggressive measures. As in nonpregnant women, infiltrating ductal carcinoma continues to be the most common histologic subtype encountered.

Breast ultrasonography is an important adjunct in the evaluation of the palpable or mammographically demonstrated breast lesion. Its ability to differentiate cystic from solid lesions can provide useful information and can guide subsequent diagnostic decisions. On characterization of a breast mass, the most common initial diagnostic modality of choice is the fine-needle aspiration.

 Treatment

The initial approach to breast carcinoma is most commonly surgical. Depending on the clinical stage, either breast-conserving lumpectomy or mastectomy, both with axillary lymph node dissection, is classically undertaken.

After surgical resection and lymph node evaluation, a decision about adjuvant therapy must be made. In surgically documented, early-stage disease, a complete metastatic work-up is not warranted given the low yield. Therefore, decisions regarding the need for adjuvant therapy are usually based on the initial choice of surgical procedure. Again, given the potential harm of radiation therapy to the developing fetus, a radical mastectomy with lymph node dissection is usually the procedure of choice, thereby eliminating the need for postoperative radiation therapy.

Chemotherapeutic intervention has been advocated in cases of locally advanced and advanced carcinoma of the breast. As described previously, it is prudent to avoid chemotherapeutic intervention during the critical period of organogenesis in a desired pregnancy (see section on chemotherapy in pregnancy).

MELANOMA (Chapter 209)

The overall incidence of cutaneous melanoma appears to be increasing, and it has been estimated that 1 in 90 persons were diagnosed with this neoplasm in 2000. Some literature suggests that the incidence of melanoma complicating pregnancy will exceed that of cervical carcinoma.

Risk factors documented to increase the risk of melanoma development are outlined in Table 252–15. Increased awareness among physicians and patients as well as improved screening appears to have led to a tendency toward earlier diagnosis. These lesions tend to occur in sun-exposed areas; however, it must be recalled that 17% of

Table 252–15 • RISK FACTORS ASSOCIATED WITH DEVELOPMENT OF CUTANEOUS MELANOMA

Fair complexion
Tendency toward easy sunburning
Early age of first sunburn
Inability to tan
Familial history of malignant melanoma
Personal history of melanoma
Environmental exposure to ultraviolet B irradiation

melanomas diagnosed in the female population are found on the vulva and perineum. This high incidence provides the basis for aggressive biopsy of suspicious pigmented vulvar lesions.

Initial treatment of a melanotic lesion is the same in a pregnant or a nonpregnant patient. Wide local excision with adequate surgical margins remains the procedure of choice. Adjuvant therapy remains controversial in this setting.

The fetal risk of maternal melanoma is not well defined. It remains the most common malignancy to metastasize to the placenta and fetus. Although overall the incidence appears to be extremely low (approximately 60 cases reported), careful pathologic examination of the placenta is warranted. In documented cases of placental spread, the fetal risk appears to be as high as 40 or 50%. An altered clinical course in the pregnant patient with melanoma has also been suggested. Observational data imply a potential hormonal influence on the melanotic process. Given the well-documented cutaneous manifestations of pregnancy, including increased pigmentation of the vulva, areola, and linea nigra, some investigators have postulated that the increased levels of estrogen, progesterone, adrenocorticotropic hormone, and melanin-stimulating hormone may somehow influence melanoma growth.

THYROID CANCER (Chapter 239)

Thyroid cancer is the most commonly diagnosed endocrinologic malignancy, with approximately 16,100 cases noted in 1997, of which about 11,000 were in women. Of these cases, almost half were documented in reproductive-aged women (15 to 44 years); thus, thyroid carcinoma complicating pregnancy is not uncommon. Thyroid nodules are common and are often encountered during initial prenatal evaluation (they represent benign entities in approximately 90% of cases).

Diagnostic evaluation of a thyroid nodule in a pregnant patient is usually limited to physical examination, laboratory studies, and thyroid ultrasonography followed by fine needle or excisional biopsy. Specifically, nuclear medicine scintigraphy scans are omitted because of concerns about the effects of radioactive ^{123}I or ^{131}I on the fetal thyroid. Transplacental passage of iodine is well documented.

After an appropriate diagnosis, surgical resection remains the primary mode of treatment. The timing of this intervention remains an important decision. A recent retrospective review suggests equivalent outcomes in patients who undergo thyroidectomy during pregnancy and those who wait until the postpartum state. Radionuclide thyroid ablation is contraindicated during pregnancy.

COLORECTAL CANCER IN PREGNANCY (Chapter 200)

The lifetime risk of colorectal carcinoma in women is 1 in 17 (6%), with the vast majority of these being diagnosed after the age of 50 years. Only 8% of cases are noted in the reproductive age group (<40 years). A similar increase in incidence may be noted as childbearing is delayed.

More than 80% of colorectal carcinomas associated with pregnancy occur in the rectum (commonly below the peritoneal reflection and thus palpable on digital rectal examination). Diagnostic delays are usually attributed to the increased frequency of rectal bleeding episodes common to pregnancy (usually hemorrhoid related) and thus decreased clinical suspicion. Symptoms associated with advanced disease such as abdominal pain, distention, and constipation are rarely encountered.

The diagnosis of colorectal carcinoma depends on a detailed history of risk factors such as history of polyps or family history of carcinoma (including gastrointestinal, breast), a complete lymph node survey, a digital rectal examination with Hemoccult testing, and sigmoidoscopy or colonoscopy. Determination of a serum marker such as carcinoembryonic antigen is of no value in pregnancy because it is elevated in the normal gestation.

Management of colorectal carcinoma is most commonly surgical, and similar surgical practices as outlined previously should be followed.

The prognosis for a woman diagnosed with colorectal carcinoma in pregnancy is similar to that of matched nonpregnant control subjects. Postoperative local adjuvant pelvic radiation therapy is obviously contraindicated in a desired pregnancy.

HEMATOLOGIC MALIGNANCY IN PREGNANCY (Chapters 194 and 195)

Hematologic malignancies complicating pregnancy are rare. Hodgkin's disease, considered a primary lymph node malignancy, commonly affects young adults and is the most common hematologic malignancy associated with pregnancy. An incidence of 1 in 5000 live births has been reported.

More than 70% of patients diagnosed with Hodgkin's disease initially present with painless lymphadenopathy, commonly noted in the cervical, submaxillary, or axillary chains. Systemic signs often associated with advanced disease include night sweats, fever, weight loss, and fatigue. Diagnosis depends on appropriate lymph node biopsy and documentation of the pathognomonic Reed-Sternberg cell.

Staging modalities include physical examination, CT of chest, abdomen, and pelvis, lymphangiography, and occasional staging laparotomy with splenectomy. The use of abdominopelvic CT is not recommended in pregnant patients, although magnetic resonance imaging can be performed safely. Both the surgeon and the oncologist must carefully consider the risk versus benefit for both fetus and mother when making decisions about using staging laparotomy.

Chemotherapy can be toxic to ovarian function, and its risk seems to be related to patient age. Commonly used protocols consisting of mechlorethamine, vincristine, procarbazine, and prednisone (MOPP) result in amenorrhea in one third of patients, with permanent ovarian failure occurring in 75% of patients older than 30 years of age at the time of treatment. It appears that the doxorubicin, bleomycin, vinblastine, dacarbazine (ABVD) regimen is potentially less toxic, with an approximate risk of amenorrhea of 5%. The role of ovarian suppression and subsequent functional preservation has already been described.

PHEOCHROMOCYTOMA (Chapter 241)

Although only rarely encountered in pregnancy, a pheochromocytoma represents a unique neoplastic event with significant morbidity and mortality to both mother and fetus. It most commonly represents a nonmalignant entity, although malignant differentiation can occur. Pheochromocytomas are most commonly found within the adrenal medulla, although they can also arise from the chromaffin cell within sympathetic ganglia.

In pregnancy, the syndrome is usually manifested by severe episodes of hypertension usually not associated with significant proteinuria. It can be easily confused with an atypical presentation of preeclampsia. Associated signs and symptoms include tachycardia, palpitations, headache, diaphoresis, and anxiety. Given its rarity, the diagnosis is often unsuspected. If the pheochromocytoma is undiagnosed and therefore not treated, maternal and fetal mortality rates exceed 16 and 26%, respectively.

CONCLUSION

The diagnosis of cancer in pregnancy presents a unique management dilemma that ultimately affects two patients. The decision process is complicated by the significant risks to the fetus in terms of developmental abnormalities and preterm delivery and to the mother in terms of the malignant process itself. Multiple social, ethical, moral, and religious issues also play an important part in the decision tree.

The treatment of these patients should remain unbiased, well researched, and, above all, multidisciplinary. Basic aspects of cancer screening must be maintained even during pregnancy, and signs and symptoms of serious neoplastic processes must not be overlooked.

SUGGESTED READINGS
Lishner M: Cancer in pregnancy. Ann Oncol 2003;14(Suppl 3):iii31–36. *A practical overview of management strategies.*
Oduncu FS, Kimmig R, Hepp H, et al: Cancer in pregnancy: Maternal-fetal conflict. J Cancer Res Clin Oncol 2003;129:133–146. *Reviews the effects of cancer on the mother and fetus, with emphasis on an interdisciplinary approach.*
Rugo HS: Management of breast cancer diagnosed during pregnancy. Curr Treat Options Oncol 2003;4:165–173. *Despite the frequency of this problem, the limited prospective data cannot accurately assess the risks of various options.*

253 PREGNANCY: HYPERTENSION AND OTHER COMMON MEDICAL PROBLEMS

Diane L. Elliot

Caring for women of reproductive age requires knowing how to diagnose pregnancy and the appropriate initial care during a pregnancy. Managing medical problems during gestation necessitates understanding pregnancy's influence on illnesses, a condition's effects on pregnancy, and the appropriate management to optimize the well-being of both mother and fetus.

DIAGNOSIS AND MANAGEMENT OF PREGNANCY

Laboratory testing for pregnancy is suggested for women with suspected pregnancy, amenorrhea, pelvic pain, and scheduled radiographic studies. Historical information (e.g., last menses, sexual activity, contraceptive practices) will not reliably exclude pregnancy. For example, when seen in an acute care setting, approximately 10% of pregnant adolescents reported no sexual activity.

Serum and urine pregnancy tests use monoclonal antibodies for the intact human chorionic gonadotropin (hCG) molecule or its beta-subunit. At implantation, the syncytiotrophoblast begins producing hCG. Two weeks after conception, the hCG level is approximately 80 mIU/mL, with comparable serum and urine values. During a normal early intrauterine pregnancy, the level doubles every 2 days. Monoclonal assays can detect hCG at a level of approximately 30 mIU/mL, resulting in a sensitivity for pregnancy of more than 90% at the time of the first missed menses. Home pregnancy tests also use monoclonal antibodies. Although these claim 99% accuracy, for inexperienced users, pregnancy was diagnosed with a sensitivity of 80% and a specificity of 70%. Clinical assessment and home pregnancy test results should be confirmed with measurement of hCG.

Transvaginal ultrasonography can detect a gestational sac 5 weeks after conception or when the hCG level is greater than 2000 mIU/mL. Before that time, sequential hCG levels may be needed to distinguish an ectopic from an intrauterine pregnancy. A fetal heartbeat is detectable by ultrasonography by 7 to 8 weeks and is audible with Doppler ultrasonography at 10 to 12 weeks. Quickening and fetal heart tones by fetoscope both occur between 16 and 20 weeks of gestation.

When pregnancy is diagnosed, important issues to address include the woman's feelings about the pregnancy and the importance of early and continuous prenatal care. The clinician should assess the patient's nutrition, review her medications for contraindicated drugs, and emphasize discontinuing smoking and alcohol. Supplemental folic acid prior to conception and early in gestation reduces the risk of neural tube defects, such as spina bifida and anencephaly, by one half. All women of childbearing age should receive additional folate, either as a daily multivitamin or as fortified breakfast cereal. Laboratory tests, such as a complete blood cell count; Rh determination; screening for rubella, hepatitis, cytomegalovirus, and toxoplasmosis antibodies; and Papanicolaou smear and vaginal cultures, usually are deferred and obtained by the health care provider who will care for the woman during pregnancy and delivery.

HYPERTENSION

Definition and Epidemiology

Hypertension (Chapter 63) is the most common medical problem during pregnancy, with a prevalence of 6 to 8%. It is the second leading cause of maternal mortality in the United States, accounting for 15% of those deaths. It is diagnosed when the blood pressure is greater than 140/90 mm Hg measured with the patient in the sitting position on two occasions. Previously, an increase of more than 30/15 mm Hg during pregnancy also was considered a criterion for hypertension, and although patients with such an increase need close follow-up, that finding alone has poor predictive value.

Diagnostic Classification

Hypertension during pregnancy can be classified as (1) preeclampsia, (2) chronic hypertension, (3) chronic hypertension plus preeclampsia, and (4) gestational hypertension or nonproteinuric hypertension of pregnancy. During a normal pregnancy, blood pressure declines during the first and second trimesters, rising to prepregnancy levels near term. Because of the initial blood pressure decrement, when readings before pregnancy are not known, an elevation during the third trimester could represent either preexisting chronic or transient gestational hypertension.

PREECLAMPSIA AND GESTATIONAL HYPERTENSION

Definition and Epidemiology

Preeclampsia usually develops during the third trimester, often after 32 weeks. Its incidence varies in different groups of women, with a prevalence of 6 to 10% in Western countries. Risks include prior preeclampsia, chronic hypertension, multifetal gestation, and diabetes. Typically, diastolic pressure increases more than systolic, and systolic levels often are less than 160 mm Hg. Blood pressures that, although elevated, would not be alarming for nonpregnant individuals should not be considered reassuring. Severe organ system dysfunction can occur with what would be only moderate hypertension among nonpregnant women. In addition to a blood pressure greater than 140/90 mm Hg, another criterion for preeclampsia is proteinuria (greater than 0.3 g/24 hours or 1+ on a random specimen). The manifestations vary, however. Among women with eclampsia (preeclampsia plus seizures), 20% did not have proteinuria. Edema was removed as a criterion for preeclampsia because of its high prevalence during pregnancy and lack of specificity for preeclampsia.

Hypertension without other manifestations of preeclampsia is termed *gestational hypertension* or *nonproteinuric hypertension* of pregnancy. By definition, gestational hypertension resolves by 3 months post partum. Women with nonproteinuric hypertension are at increased risk for preeclampsia and require close monitoring for its other manifestations, as approximately one fourth develop that disorder during the pregnancy.

Pathogenesis

During a normal pregnancy, the implanted placenta replaces the endothelium and internal elastic lamina of the maternal uterine spiral arteries with fetal trophoblastic tissue. These altered arteries dilate to five times their prepregnant state and are no longer responsive to circulating vasoconstrictors. This trophoblastic invasion does not occur with preeclampsia, and the arteries do not dilate. Accordingly, the placenta is chronically underperfused. This is thought to result in secondary widespread endothelial dysfunction, with activation of platelets and the coagulation cascade. In addition, women with preeclampsia fail to develop the normal increased blood volume and reduced systemic vascular resistance of pregnancy. Women develop an imbalance of vasoactive prostaglandins, with an increase in the ratio of thromboxane A_2 (vasoconstriction) to prostacyclin (vasodilatation), leading to vasospasm. The organ damage that occurs is more due to organ ischemia caused by the underlying systemic changes than it is to the elevated blood pressure. The rationale for preventing preeclampsia with low-dose acetylsalicylic acid was its inhibition of cyclooxygenase and selective reduction in thromboxane synthesis.

Clinical Manifestations

Clinical criteria subdivide preeclampsia into severe and nonsevere, based on the degree of blood pressure elevation and the presence of seizures (eclampsia) or other end-organ damage (renal dysfunction, pulmonary edema, thrombocytopenia, hepatic abnormalities, or central nervous system effects). Intravascular coagulation and hepatic ischemia can cause a constellation of findings, called the HELLP (hemolysis, elevated liver functions, and low platelets) syndrome. Although delivery is the treatment of preeclampsia, a small percentage of manifestations are seen immediately post partum.

Laboratory tests do not reliably predict development of preeclampsia, nor do they differentiate among the different hypertensive disorders. Serum uric acid levels were considered useful in identifying preeclampsia. However, when evaluated in a nested-case control study, an individual's uric acid level could not be used to classify her hypertension.

Treatment

Transient gestational hypertension is treated with bed rest, close monitoring of mother and fetus, and medications, when necessary. When to initiate antihypertensive drug treatment is controversial. Many authorities recommend drug therapy when the blood pressure persistently exceeds 140/90 mm Hg. Drug therapy reduces perinatal deaths and severe maternal hypertension. However, for women with preexisting hypertension, it has not been shown to affect development of preeclampsia. The experience with antihypertensive medication in pregnancy appears in Table 253–1. The definitive treatment of preeclampsia and transient gestational hypertension is delivery. Before 34 weeks of gestation, that benefit is weighed against the fetal advantages of prolonging intrauterine development.

Prevention

Although use of supplemental calcium and low-dose acetylsalicylic acid to prevent preeclampsia appeared promising, in studies, at least in the United States, these agents have not been effective.

CHRONIC HYPERTENSION

Etiology and Epidemiology

Chronic hypertension is present in 1 to 5% of pregnant women. This includes women known to be hypertensive before pregnancy, hypertension developing during the first 20 weeks of pregnancy, and

pregnancy-induced hypertension persisting more than 3 months after delivery. Most cases are due to essential hypertension. For the unusual individual with secondary hypertension, causes include intrinsic renal disease, renal artery stenosis, aortic coarctation, connective tissue diseases, and Cushing's disease.

Although there are fewer than 250 reported cases, pheochromocytoma during pregnancy produces significant morbidity and mortality. Its features (headache, excessive perspiration, and palpitations) overlap with those of pregnancy, and evaluation with measurement of urinary catecholamines is indicated for all women with newly diagnosed hypertension before 34 weeks of pregnancy.

Treatment

Women with chronic hypertension who are considering pregnancy should not receive angiotensin-converting enzyme inhibitors. Among women with preexisting hypertension, the usual blood pressure decrease during the first trimester often allows the stopping of antihypertensive medications. Pharmacologic treatment has not been shown to prevent preeclampsia or improve pregnancy outcome. Accordingly, blood pressure can be monitored, and medications reinstituted if needed, at a threshold of 150 to 160/100 to 110 mm Hg. Chronic hypertension newly diagnosed during pregnancy can be differentiated from transient gestational hypertension, because the former persists post partum.

Prognosis and Prevention

Although the majority of hypertensive women have uncomplicated pregnancies, risk is increased for abruptio placentae,

Table 253–1 • ANTIHYPERTENSIVE DRUG USE DURING PREGNANCY*

MEDICATION	SAFETY OF USE DURING PREGNANCY	COMMENTS
CENTRAL SYMPATHOLYTIC		
Methyldopa	++++	Extensive use, most study, and best safety record of any antihypertensive used during pregnancy. It reduces vascular resistance while preserving maternal cardiac output and uteroplacental perfusion. Considered safe to use when breast-feeding.
Clonidine	+++	Not assessed for chronic hypertension during pregnancy. No adverse effects when used for hypertension during the third trimester. Potential for rebound when discontinued abruptly.
α- AND β-BLOCKERS		
Labetalol	++++	Used in several trials without adverse effects. α-Blocking results in vasodilation (including uteroplacental blood vessels), and β-blockade prevents reflex tachycardia. Cardiac output is unchanged. Low concentration in breast milk.
β-BLOCKERS		
Atenolol, metoprolol, pindolol, propranolol	+++	Probably safe for third trimester use, but neonatal bradycardia, respiratory distress, and hypoglycemia have been reported. Use earlier in gestation may result in intrauterine growth retardation. Atenolol and metoprolol concentrated in breast milk; propranolol has low concentrations in breast milk.
DIRECT ARTERIAL VASODILATOR		
Hydralazine	++++	Extensively used during pregnancy. It causes vascular dilatation and a reflex tachycardia. Primarily used parenterally for acute management of hypertension or with methyldopa or a β-blocking agent.
CALCIUM CHANNEL BLOCKERS		
Nifedipine (most commonly used, due to its primarily peripheral effects), diltiazem, verapamil	+++	Probably safely used in the third trimester. Their use maintains uteroplacental perfusion; may also have tocolytic effects. Sublingual nifedipine has been associated with hypotension and fetal distress. Avoid use with magnesium sulfate, because combination risks profound hypotension.
DIURETICS		
Hydrochlorothiazide, chlorthalidone, furosemide	++	Use during pregnancy is controversial and often discontinued as blood pressure decreases, early in pregnancy. If used before pregnancy, it can be continued, but its use should not be initiated during pregnancy. Concentrations in breast milk are low and may reduce milk production.
ANGIOTENSIN-CONVERTING ENZYME INHIBITORS AND ANGIOTENSIN II RECEPTOR BLOCKERS		
Captopril, lisinopril, benazepril, enalopril, losartan, valsartan, candesartan	0	Use is contraindicated during pregnancy, because it affects renal development in second and third trimesters. Miscarriage, fetal death, malformations, and neonatal renal failure can result. No reports of adverse effects from brief use, limited to the first trimester. No data on the effects of angiotensin II receptor antagonists, but presumed similar and also contraindicated.

*Drugs listed have established effects during pregnancy. Antihypertensive agents not listed may be safe during pregnancy; however, until that is known, those drugs should be switched to one of the safely used listed agents.

intrauterine growth restriction, preterm delivery, perinatal death, and superimposed preeclampsia. The preeclampsia rate varies with the severity of hypertension, with some series reporting an incidence of more than 50%. For women with mild hypertension, however, the incidence is approximately 15%. Women with chronic hypertension, especially those with long-standing disease and coincident additional medical problems, are followed at least twice weekly during gestation, often with additional home blood pressure monitoring. Superimposed preeclampsia is suggested by a sudden increase in blood pressure, elevations of more than 160/110 mm Hg, new or worsening proteinuria, or new laboratory abnormalities, including platelet count less than 100,000/mm, abnormal liver functions, and creatinine level increasing to more than 1.2 mg/dL.

CARDIAC DISEASE

Etiology and Epidemiology

The prevalence of heart disease during pregnancy is approximately 1%. In Western countries, congenital problems have surpassed rheumatic heart disease as its most common cause. (The chapters of Part VIII discuss cardiovascular disease in detail.)

Pathogenesis

Understanding the hemodynamic changes during normal pregnancy permits interpretation of history and physical examination findings and anticipation of pregnancy's effect on preexisting cardiac abnormalities. During gestation, cardiac output increases 30 to 50%, peaking near week 27. This is due to increases in heart rate and stroke volume, plus a decrease in systemic vascular resistance. Blood volume also expands, with a greater increase in plasma volume than red blood cell mass, resulting in the physiologic anemia of pregnancy.

A woman's previous cardiac functional status is a guide to the effects of pregnancy. Women with New York Heart Association Functional Class I or II disease (no symptoms with normal daily activities) usually can withstand pregnancy. Because of the decreased systemic vascular resistance, regurgitant lesions are tolerated better than stenotic abnormalities. At greatest risk are women with pulmonary hypertension (either primary or Eisenmenger's syndrome), with limitations in right-sided output. The mortality rate during pregnancy among this last group approaches 50%.

Clinical Manifestations and Management

Normal pregnancy results in effects that can mimic heart disease. More than half of normal pregnant women report dyspnea. Physical findings of congestive heart failure also are common during pregnancy. The increased stroke volume results in a systolic flow murmur in the majority of pregnant women, and an S_3 also is audible in a significant percentage. The electrocardiogram can show anterior T-wave changes, owing to the heart's leftward rotation late in gestation. However, clinical findings should not be dismissed, as up to half of cardiac problems first become apparent with the additional cardiac demands of pregnancy. Echocardiography, including transesophageal studies, is well tolerated, retains its utility, and may be needed to characterize abnormal findings during pregnancy.

Pregnancy is proarrhythmic, and both atrial and ventricular ectopy increase. Among women with structurally normal hearts, premature contractions are benign and managed expectantly. Drug therapy is needed only for intolerable symptoms or threats to maternal or fetal well-being. The therapy for most arrhythmias is not altered during pregnancy. Most antiarrhythmic drugs are not contraindicated during pregnancy, and cardioversion does not present increased risk for the mother or fetus. Adenosine can be used safely for terminating atrioventricular node-dependent tachyarrhythmias. Most class I agents also are safe. Digoxin dosage usually requires an increase, owing to the reduced protein binding and increased renal excretion during pregnancy. Amiodarone should be avoided during gestation. As with most antiarrhythmic drugs, it crosses the placenta and can cause fetal goiter, growth retardation, and neonatal hypothyroidism. Beta-blocker and calcium channel blocker use is discussed in the preceding section on hypertension.

Certain cardiac abnormalities pose unique considerations. For women with Marfan syndrome, pregnancy's connective tissue changes and hyperdynamic state can increase their risk for aortic dissection. However, the risk is acceptably low when the prepregnancy aortic diameter is less than 40 mm. Women with repaired aortic coarctation usually have successful pregnancies and a preeclampsia incidence similar to that of the general population, when the arm-to-leg blood pressure difference is less than 20 mm Hg. Ischemic cardiac disease is rare during gestation, with a prevalence of 1 in 10,000 pregnancies. When present, it usually is associated with cocaine use or accelerated atherosclerotic vascular disease (e.g., long-standing type I diabetes or untreated hyperlipidemia).

Peripartum cardiomyopathy is defined as onset of a global dilated cardiomyopathy during the third trimester to 6 months post partum. Its prevalence is 1 in 4000 pregnancies. Risk factors for peripartum cardiomyopathy include obesity, African American heritage, and multiple prior pregnancies. Its cause is not understood, and prognosis is variable. Overall, approximately one third of patients stabilize, one third progress, and one third improve. Both recurrence and normal outcomes have been described with subsequent pregnancies.

Prognosis

A retrospective review of 276 pregnancies among 221 women with heart disease (excluding isolated mitral valve prolapse) showed that 96% of individuals had functional class I or II disease. Overall, approximately 25% of pregnancies resulted in a maternal and/or neonatal cardiac adverse event. Based on clinical and echocardiographic assessment, independent predictors of cardiac problems during pregnancy were prior cardiac events, previous arrhythmias, functional class greater than II, left-sided heart obstruction, and myocardial dysfunction. With no, one, or more than one of those five factors, the rate of maternal events was 3, 30, and 66%, respectively. These predictors have not been prospectively validated, and few women with certain cardiac problems were included in the cohort. However, the results are consistent with pregnancy's hemodynamic changes and can be combined with lesion-specific considerations when one advises women with heart disease about the risk of pregnancy.

An additional prognostic consideration for women with congenital heart disease is the risk of similar problems in their children. For this group, congenital heart disease is six times more likely among their offspring or a risk of approximately 10%. However, because this rate varies with different abnormalities, referral for genetic counseling is appropriate.

THROMBOEMBOLIC DISEASE

Epidemiology

Thromboembolism (deep venous thrombosis and pulmonary emboli) is uncommon during pregnancy, with a prevalence of 1 per 1500 pregnancies. When they do occur, however, maternal morbidity is high. Thromboemboli are the leading nonobstetric cause of maternal mortality.

Pathogenesis

Pregnancy results in physical and biochemical changes that increase clot formation. During gestation, the venous system dilates, and stasis is increased further by venous obstruction from the gravid uterus. The plasma concentrations of coagulation factors, fibrinolysis inhibitors, and procoagulants shift to promote coagulation. Those women with a hereditary thrombophilic disorder (such as activated protein C resistance, protein C and S deficiency, factor V mutations, and antithrombin III deficiency) have high rates of thrombosis during pregnancy.

Antiphospholipid antibodies result in platelet activation and, despite these patients' prolonged partial thromboplastin time, lead to thrombosis. During pregnancy, these patients are prone to placental thrombosis and infarction, causing recurrent pregnancy loss, intrauterine growth retardation, fetal death, severe preeclampsia, and maternal arterial and venous thromboemboli.

Clinical Manifestations

The symptoms and signs of deep venous thrombosis (DVT) and pulmonary emboli retain their low sensitivity and specificity during pregnancy, and findings are limited further by the fact that lower extremity edema is a feature of many normal pregnancies. In addition, for unexplained reasons, the pulmonary alveolar-arterial oxygen gradient may be normal in more than 50% of pregnant women with documented pulmonary emboli. That percentage is much greater than that rate of 2 to 20% observed among nonpregnant patients. Patient position should be noted when arterial blood gases are measured, because during the third trimester, arterial PO_2 when the subject is sitting is approximately 15 mm Hg higher than it is when the subject is supine.

Diagnosis

Pregnancy does not alter the range of diagnostic options for DVT and pulmonary embolism, which include noninvasive lower extremity studies (e.g., compression ultrasonography, Doppler studies, and impedance plethysmography), lung ventilation-perfusion scanning, computed tomography and magnetic resonance imaging and pulmonary angiography. The operating characteristics of noninvasive studies of the lower extremities appear similar to results in nonpregnant women, provided the women are evaluated in the lateral decubitus position to minimize the effects of the gravid uterus. Magnetic resonance imaging has been used successfully to detect iliac and ovarian vein thrombosis during pregnancy.

Fetal radiation exposure is a consideration when selecting diagnostic tests. However, most procedures can be performed with minimal risk. Ventilation and perfusion scanning is a sensitive but not specific test for pulmonary emboli. A normal scan effectively excludes the diagnosis. However, low and indeterminate scans are frequent and necessitate additional testing. Ventilation and perfusion lung scans result in fetal radiation of approximately 40 mrads. Fetal radiation exposure during chest computed tomographic scanning depends on the height of the uterus and how low on the lung the images are obtained. The radiation exposure to the fetus can be up to 200 mrads but often is less than 20 mrads. Pulmonary angiography is the "gold standard" means to diagnose pulmonary emboli. Its use (by the brachial route with appropriate shielding) exposes the fetus to approximately 100 mrads. These are low amounts of radiation; for comparison, the fetal exposure during plain abdominal radiography is 240 mrads. Although the threshold for harmful effects is not established firmly, fetal risk is thought to increase after approximately 5 rad of radiation exposure.

Rx Treatment

Traditional therapy for thromboemboli has been initial anticoagulation with intravenous unfractionated heparin, followed by oral anticoagulation with warfarin. Warfarin (Coumadin) causes an embryopathy, especially if used between the sixth and 12th weeks, and as a result, its use is avoided during pregnancy. Unfractionated heparin contains large charged molecules that do not cross the placenta or cause fetal problems, and as a result, fixed or adjusted subcutaneous unfractionated heparin has been used for anticoagulation during pregnancy.

Despite its higher cost, a more uniform dose response, reduced needs for monitoring therapy, and lower complication rates have resulted in low-molecular-weight (LMW) heparin replacing unfractionated heparin use. LMW heparin also does not cross the placenta. Although studies during pregnancy are few, as with nonpregnant patients, subcutaneous LMW heparin is as effective as traditional unfractionated heparin therapy. Because dosing is not well established during pregnancy, antifactor Xa levels should be obtained 6 hours after injection to monitor therapy, and the dose should be reassessed every 2 weeks until delivery.

During labor and delivery, subcutaneous dosing can be held or changed to low-dose intravenous heparin (500 U/hr). Intravenous unfractionated heparin can be discontinued immediately and predictably reversed with protamine, if necessary. Eight hours after delivery, subcutaneous LMW heparin therapy can be resumed and continued for an additional 6 to 12 weeks. Alternatively, warfarin

can be started the evening of delivery, overlapped with heparin therapy, and monitored as usual. Women may breast-feed safely while taking warfarin, because only an inactive metabolite is excreted into breast milk.

Risks of heparin therapy include thrombocytopenia and, during pregnancy, osteopenia. Heparin-induced thrombocytopenia develops in 2% of those treated with unfractionated heparin. Despite thrombocytopenia, arterial and venous thromboses characterize the disorder. It should be suspected when platelets decrease and confirmed by assaying for the causative heparin-induced antibody. The disorder's risk is less with LMW heparin, but once thrombocytopenia is present, LMW heparin cannot be substituted for unfractionated heparin. Heparin-associated osteoporosis can occur when individuals receive more than 20,000 U/day for more than 3 months. This risk for significant bone loss also may be less with LMW heparin.

Prevention

Women with a DVT during pregnancy should be evaluated for a hypercoagulable state. When a woman has experienced a previous DVT during pregnancy, has a hereditary thrombophilic disorder, or has antiphospholipid antibodies, her DVT risk during pregnancy is increased significantly. The indications for and preferred method of prophylaxis are not established. Subcutaneous unfractionated heparin, at a dose of 5000 to 7500 U twice a day, has been used. For prophylaxis, the heparin level should be 0.08 to 0.20 U/mL, measured 3 hours after an injection. Often, the dose must be increased by 2500 U each trimester to achieve that level. More recently, LMW heparin has been replacing that therapy, using a fixed dose slightly less than used that for DVT treatment and comparable to the prophylactic dose used in surgical patients. The management of pregnant women with antiphospholipid antibodies is dependent on the presence of prior problems and associated conditions. At a minimum, low-dose acetylsalicylic acid is administered. Aspirin and prophylactic heparin are given if the woman has experienced thromboembolic problems during a prior pregnancy. When heparin is contraindicated (e.g., with preexisting thrombocytopenia), low-dose acetylsalicylic acid plus prednisone and intravenous immunoglobulin G may be used.

ASTHMA

Epidemiology

Asthma (Chapter 84) is the most common chronic respiratory illness during pregnancy, with a prevalence of 1 to 7%.

Pathogenesis and Clinical Manifestations

Pregnancy is accompanied by physiologic alterations that both alleviate and exacerbate reactive airway disease. In general, however, pulmonary function does not change during gestation, including FEV_1 and peak expiratory flow rate. The course of asthma during pregnancy is variable and cannot be predicted well from patient characteristics. Overall, one third of women with asthma remain stable, one third improve, and one third worsen. Those with more severe disease and a history of prior exacerbation during pregnancy are at greater risk for deterioration during gestation. The unpredictability necessitates that all women with asthma be monitored more closely when pregnant.

Rx Treatment

Management is similar to that of asthma in general. Table 253–2 lists therapies commonly prescribed for asthma, with comments about their use during pregnancy. Up to 50% of women with asthma do not require drug treatment during pregnancy. When indicated, medication use is similar to use by nonpregnant individuals. Inhaled and oral β_2-agonists can be used during pregnancy. These agents are tocolytic in higher doses and rarely have been reported to inhibit labor. Inhaled cromolyn sodium can be continued. Theophylline crosses the placenta, but other than rare reports of newborn jitteriness, it is safely used during pregnancy. Its clearance is reduced as pregnancy progresses, and serum levels should be monitored. Values of 5 to 12 µg/mL are optimal during pregnancy. Branded products are preferred to reduce variability in absorption.

Maternal hypoxia, hypocapnia, and alkalemia are detrimental to the fetus. Asthma exacerbations should be treated early and aggressively, with a lower threshold for hospitalization. Oxygen is needed if maternal pulse oximetry is less than 95% or PaO_2 is less than 75 mm Hg. Fetal well-being should be assessed continuously with an external electronic monitor. The typical triggers for asthma worsening are respiratory infections and gastroesophageal reflux. Hormonal changes during pregnancy relax the lower esophageal sphincter, and more than one third of pregnant women experience reflux symptoms. Histamine type-2 receptor antagonists, other than nizatidine, are safely used during pregnancy, and ranitidine is the preferred drug. Experience with proton pump inhibitor use during gestation is minimal. While they appear safe, their use is reserved for failures with H_2 blockers. The rate of sinusitis is six times greater during pregnancy, and because it may not be manifest with its usual findings, a higher index of suspicion is needed. During pregnancy, bronchopulmonary infections can be treated with erythromycin (avoiding the estolate esters), penicillins, and first- and second-generation cephalosporins. Azithromycin is an alternative for patients who cannot use penicillins and cephalosporins. Tetracycline, trimethoprim/sulfamethoxazole, and fluoroquinolones are contraindicated.

Corticosteroids, both inhaled and systemically administered, can be used during pregnancy. The use of inhaled corticosteroids decreases the number of asthma exacerbations during pregnancy. Among inhaled corticosteroids, beclomethasone has been used most extensively and is the preferred agent. The risk of an asthma exacerbation compromising pregnancy far outweighs any potential corticosteroid risk. Prednisone is metabolized by the placenta, which limits fetal exposure to the active drug, and the maternal-fetal gradient for prednisone is 10:1. Women using oral corticosteroids near term require "stress doses" at the time of delivery. Asthma treatment is not altered for lactating mothers. For medications used to treat reactive airway disease, the amount reaching an infant through breast milk is less than exposure before birth through the placenta.

Prognosis

With current therapy and avoidance of hypoxia, the maternal and fetal morbidity associated with asthma usually is low. Risk of antepartum and postpartum hemorrhage is increased slightly, and women requiring corticosteroids are more likely to develop gestational hypertension. Offspring of asthmatic women are more subject to hyperbilirubinemia.

THYROID DISORDERS (Chapter 239)

The placenta is impermeable to thyroid hormones and thyroid-stimulating hormone (TSH), and the fetus independently produces and regulates thyroid hormone levels. The critical period for thyroid hormone's effects on fetal brain maturation is 1 month before birth through the first year of life. Pregnancy alters certain indices of maternal thyroid function. Thyroid binding globulin increases during gestation, leading to an elevation of total thyroxine and a decreased T_3 resin uptake. However, free thyroxine and the calculated thyroid index accurately reflect thyroid function during pregnancy. TSH levels are altered only slightly and remain a useful means of screening for hypothyroidism and for assessing the adequacy of thyroid hormone replacement therapy.

HYPOTHYROIDISM

Epidemiology

Hypothyroidism frequently is associated with anovulation, resulting in reduced fertility. Hence, the coexistence of untreated hypothyroidism and pregnancy is rare.

Table 253–2 • DRUG TREATMENT OF ASTHMA DURING PREGNANCY

THERAPY	COMMENTS
Desensitization or immunotherapy ("allergy shots")	Ongoing therapy can be continued. However, skin testing, initiating treatment, and increasing therapy should be avoided. Reducing exposure to environmental irritants and allergens remains important.
Antihistamines (chlorpheniramine and tripelennamine preferred, and nonsedating agents used when sedation must be minimized)	More information is available for older antihistamines. Recommendations for newer agents, with less sedation, are based on limited animal and human data.
Disodium cromoglycolate (no data on nedocromil)	Less than 10% of drug is absorbed. No reported adverse effects from use during pregnancy.
Theophylline	Distribution and clearance altered during pregnancy, and levels should be checked monthly. It crosses the placenta; rarely, neonatal toxicity has been reported, despite therapeutic maternal levels.
β-Agonists (albuterol, metaproterenol, terbutaline; no data on salmeterol)	Use is safe during pregnancy. Rare report of tocolytic effects.
Inhaled ipratropium	Little data on use during pregnancy, although it probably is safe.
Antileukotriene (zafirlukast, montelukast, zileuton)	No human information; zileuton had adverse effects in animal studies and not recommended for use during pregancy.
Inhaled corticosteroids (beclomethasone [best studied agent], budesonide)	Regular use reduces asthma exacerbations during pregnancy.
Oral corticosteroids	May be used safely, when indicated. Ninety per cent of prednisone is inactivated by the placenta, reducing fetal exposure. Betamethasone does not undergo placental 11–oxidation and is the preferred corticosteroid when promoting fetal lung maturation.

 Management

Women on thyroid replacement should have their TSH levels monitored each trimester. Approximately 20% will require a dose increase during pregnancy. The absorption of levothyroxine is inhibited by iron, and women should be reminded to let at least 2 hours pass between taking thyroid replacement medicine and prenatal vitamins, which contain additional iron.

HYPERTHYROIDISM

Epidemiology

Hyperthyroidism develops during 0.02 to 0.3% of pregnancies, and it follows diabetes as the most common endocrine disorder during pregnancy.

Etiology

Women who are hyperthyroid during pregnancy are presumed to have Graves' disease. hCG and TSH share the same β subunit, and hCG weakly cross-reacts with TSH. That resemblance is of clinical importance with a molar pregnancy, during which extremely high hCG levels can be a rare cause of hyperthyroidism.

Women's Health

Clinical Manifestations

Certain findings of hyperthyroidism (e.g., tachycardia, sensation of warmth, fatigue) are features of a normal pregnancy. Rather than the traditional symptoms of weight loss, hyperthyroidism during pregnancy can cause an inappropriately low weight gain. Treating gestational hyperthyroidism significantly improves maternal and fetal outcomes. Thus, a low threshold for obtaining thyroid function tests is appropriate.

Treatment

Thyroid scanning is contraindicated during pregnancy. The hyperthyroid pregnant woman is treated medically with propylthiouracil (PTU) or methimazole. Radioactive iodine is absolutely contraindicated during pregnancy, because it also will affect the fetus. Surgical treatment of hyperthyroidism is reserved for the unusual individual who has complications from medical therapy.

In the United States, medical therapy usually is initiated with a PTU dose of 100 mg three times a day, with tapering based on measured thyroid hormone levels. PTU is preferred because of the rare report of aplasia cutis with methimazole and PTU's lower placental permeability. β-Blockers may be necessary transiently to control initial symptoms. PTU treatment usually reduces the thyroid hormone level within 3 to 4 weeks, at which time the dose is tapered to 50 mg three times a day. Thyroid function is monitored monthly, and the therapeutic goal is the lowest PTU dose needed to maintain maternal thyroid hormone levels in the high normal range.

Propylthiouracil crosses the placenta, whereas thyroid hormones and TSH do not. Infants are at risk for a neonatal goiter when prenatal PTU dosage is more than 100 mg/day. Because of the "immunosuppression" of pregnancy, tapering the PTU dose usually is possible later in pregnancy, and approximately one third of women can discontinue PTU therapy in the last trimester. PTU (at a dose less than 450 mg/day) and methimazole (up to 20 mg/day) appear safe with breast-feeding. To minimize potential effects, the mother should take antithyroid drugs just after breast-feeding.

Prognosis

Graves' disease may become worse post partum. Because fetal exposure is no longer a consideration, many clinicians empirically increase the PTU dose after delivery. Neonatal Graves' disease is uncommon and occurs in approximately 2% of offspring. Because of residual effects of maternal PTU, the disorder may not be apparent at birth and may manifest 2 weeks after birth.

POSTPARTUM THYROID DYSFUNCTION

Epidemiology

Postpartum thyroid dysfunction follows 5 to 10% of pregnancies. Risk is increased with a family or personal history of postpartum thyroid dysfunction, a goiter (which are not normally present during pregnancy), and the presence of antimicrosomal antibodies. The recurrence rate in subsequent pregnancies is approximately 50%.

Pathogenesis, Treatment, and Prognosis

Postpartum thyroid dysfunction is associated with a "flare" of the woman's preexisting autoimmune thyroid disease. Affected individuals typically develop transient hyperthyroidism, associated with a low iodine uptake, 6 to 12 weeks following delivery. Because the hyperthyroidism is self-limited, the usual treatment is symptomatic with β-blockers. Hyperthyroidism usually is followed by hypothyroidism, and that condition also often is temporary. Despite hypothyroidism not being permanent, thyroid hormone replacement should not be withheld. However, 6 months after initiating replacement, it is appropriate to attempt stopping therapy. For some individuals, the hypothyroidism will be permanent.

DIABETES MELLITUS

Definition, Diagnosis, and Epidemiology

Diabetes (Chapter 242) is present among 3% of pregnant women, more than 90% of whom have gestational diabetes mellitus (GDM). GDM is defined as glucose intolerance detected during pregnancy, and it affects 14% of pregnant women. Risk factors for GDM include obesity, age older than 35 years, family history of type II diabetes, and prior delivery of a large (more than 9 lbs) infant. Of those with diabetes prior to pregnancy, the majority have type 2 diabetes.

Gestational diabetes is asymptomatic when diagnosed. The decision to screen for GDM remains controversial. Recently, the Fourth International Workshop Conference on Gestational Diabetes Mellitus removed the recommendation for screening among women with low (less than 2%) risk for GDM. This includes women who are younger than 25 years, not obese, have no personal history of diabetes or poor obstetric outcome, and have no first-degree relatives with diabetes. The Centers for Disease Control and Prevention recommend screening all pregnant women at 24 to 28 weeks' gestation with a glucose measurement obtained 1 hour after ingestion of 50 g of oral glucose. A serum glucose level greater than 140 mg/dL or whole blood glucose level greater than 170 mg/dL is considered positive. This cutoff value is 90% sensitive and 80% specific. A 100 g 3-hour glucose tolerance test result confirms the presence of GDM.

White's classification stratifies diabetes during pregnancy based on duration of diabetes, therapy, and the presence of retinopathy, nephropathy, or heart disease. Class A refers to women with GDM. Classes B and C include women requiring insulin but without other complications from diabetes. The greatest potential for complications is among women with diabetes and benign retinopathy (class D), nephropathy (class F), proliferative retinopathy (class R), and heart disease (class H).

Pathogenesis

Organogenesis occurs early in the first trimester. Because "tight" blood glucose control during this interval decreases congenital malformations and miscarriages, optimal blood glucose is especially appropriate when diabetic women are considering pregnancy and early in gestation. Hemoglobin A_{1c} should be normal for at least 2 months before conception. Women taking oral hypoglycemic agents should be switched to insulin prior to pregnancy, because these agents cross the placenta, may be teratogenic, and can cause prolonged fetal hyperinsulinemia.

Treatment

The therapeutic goal is "tight" glucose control, with fasting and preprandial capillary blood glucose values of approximately 65 mg/dL (equivalent to a plasma concentration of 75 mg/dL) and 1-hour postprandial value less than 120 mg/dL (plasma less than 140 mg/dL). Women must be able to monitor their blood glucose and obtain several values per day (fasting, following breakfast, late afternoon, evening, and middle of the night testing, when morning values are elevated). Monthly glycosylated hemoglobin values should parallel changes seen among normal women and decrease by approximately 20% during pregnancy. Ketonemia adversely affects the fetus, and care must be taken to prevent starvation ketosis and weight loss. Hospitalization for intense patient education and glucose control may be appropriate early in gestation. Additional indications for hospitalization include nausea and vomiting, poor glucose control that is unresponsive to insulin adjustments, and persistent ketonuria.

The recommended diet during gestation is 30 to 35 kcal/kg/day based on ideal body weight, with a composition of 40 to 50% carbohydrate, 20% protein, and 30 to 40% fat. Calories are divided as three meals and three snacks a day: 10% breakfast, 30% lunch, 30% dinner, and 10% each snack. Low-intensity aerobic exercise is being studied for its benefits for GDM, and obese women with GDM should avoid excessive weight gain and may be advised to use a mild caloric restriction (e.g., 25 kcal/kg/day).

Approximately 15% of women with GDM will require insulin therapy during pregnancy. Insulin treatment usually is initiated when the fasting blood glucose level is greater than 105 mg/dL or

Continued

Table 253–3 • CAUSES OF NEW-ONSET JAUNDICE DURING PREGNANCY*

DIAGNOSIS	PREVALENCE	SYMPTOMS AND SIGNS	LABORATORY FINDINGS	MANAGEMENT	MATERNAL & FETAL OUTCOME
Viral hepatitis (A, B, C, and D)	Leading cause of jaundice during pregnancy, accounting for half of pregnant women with jaundice. Acute hepatitis B in 2 per 1000 pregnancies, and acute A or C in 1 per 1000.	Natural history of viral hepatitis is unchanged by pregnancy. The typical symptoms and signs occur. Chronic HBV carriers usually have normal pregnancies, unless they also have chronic hepatitis. Unless cirrhosis is present, chronic hepatitis C does not affect pregnancy, nor does pregnancy influence the natural history of hepatitis C.	Serologic diagnosis is not changed with pregnancy. Liver function abnormalities are comparable to those in nonpregnant individuals.	Supportive and similar to guidelines for viral hepatitis in nonpregnant patients. Any potential for transmission of HBV at delivery is an indication for passive (hepatitis B immunoglobulin) and active (hepatitis B vaccine) immunization of the newborn. No analogous treatment is available for hepatitis C.	Maternal outcomes with hepatitis A, B, C, and D comparable to outcomes in a nonpregnant individual. Newborn concern is potential vertical transmission at the time of delivery.
Intrahepatic cholestasis of pregnancy (IHCP)	Second leading cause of jaundice during gestation. Occurrence rate varies with ethnicity (e.g., 0.1% of pregnancies in the U.S, 20% among pregnant Chilean women, and rare among black women).	Usually, in the third trimester, women develop pruritus of their entire body, usually beginning with palms and soles. Thirty per cent become jaundiced approximately 2 weeks after onset of pruritus.	Bilirubin not elevated greater than 5 mg/dL, transaminase levels increased two- to 10-fold, alkaline phosphatase increased four-fold.	Parenteral vitamin K plus ursodeoxycholic acid (UDCA), which reduces pruritus and liver function abnormalities but is not proved to alter outcome. Small trials demonstrate no benefits for S-adenosylmethionine (SAMe), dexamethasone, and Guar gum.	No increase in maternal morbidity, but associated with increased prematurity, fetal distress, and perinatal infant death. Resolves 2 days to 2 weeks after delivery. Disorder recurs in most subsequent pregnancies.
Preeclampsia with the HELLP (*h*emolysis, *e*levated *l*iver functions, and *l*ow *p*latelets) syndrome plus the rare occurrence of associated hepatic rupture	Preeclampsia occurs during the late second or third trimesters, (usually earlier in gestation than AFLP). HELLP seen in 4 to 12% of women with preeclampsia. Hepatic rupture seen with 5 per 10,000 pregnancies.	Nausea, vomiting, right upper quadrant pain, along with other findings of preeclampsia (hypertension, hyperreflexia) occur. Acute abdominal pain and shock signal hepatic rupture. Imaging rupture has been reported using ultrasonography; computed tomography, and magnetic resonance imaging.	Transaminase increased two- to 10-fold, and alkaline phosphatase increased one to 10 times normal. Platelets are less than 100,000 mm³, with microangiopathic hemolytic anemia, and disseminated intravascular coagulation. Hemolysis results in elevated bilirubin and lactate dehydrogenase levels.	Delivery and other therapeutic measures for preeclampsia. Condition may transiently worsen following delivery, then improve over several days.	Maternal mortality is 2%, and prematurity and perinatal mortality 5 to 30%. Recurrence rate is approximately 5%. Maternal mortality with hepatic rupture is more than 50%, and therapy is supportive, with surgery when needed.
Acute fatty liver of pregnancy (AFLP)	Occurs in 1 per 13,000 pregnancies, with onset late in the third trimester. Case reports suggest that some women's AFLP is caused by an inborn error of mitochondrial fatty acid metabolism.	Malaise, nausea, vomiting, epigastric pain; may be findings of hepatic encephalopathy. Right upper quadrant is tender.	Transaminase level increased one- to five-fold, and alkaline phosphatase increased two to eight times normal. White blood cell count greater than 15,000; platelets often less than 100,000. Hypoglycemia and disseminated intravascular coagulation may be present. Ultrasonography and computed tomography can suggest AFLP, but sensitivity is less than 50% for that diagnosis.	Delivery and supportive care.	Maternal mortality and fetal mortality approximately 20%. If mother survives, normal liver function is restored soon after delivery. Based on limited information, usually does not recur during next pregnancy. Because some offspring of mothers with AFLP were noted to be homozygous for long-chain 3-hydroxyacyl-CoA dehydrogenases (a devastating error of mitochondrial fatty acid metabolism), being heterozygous for the disorder may predispose to AFLP.
Choledocholithiasis	Accounts for approximately 7% of jaundice during pregnancy.	Manifestations are not altered by pregnancy.	Laboratory findings similar to when not pregnant. Ultrasonography can reveal abnormality, with same limitations in visualizing the problem as when not pregnant.	Uterine enlargement makes surgery more difficult in the third trimester, and endoscopic retrograde cholangiopancreatography and sphincterotomy, performed while minimizing fluoroscopy and with appropriate shielding, has been used successfully in that setting.	If obstruction relieved, maternal and fetal outcomes are not adversely affected by the disorder.

*Additional considerations are drug-induced hepatitis, Budd-Chiari syndrome, and pre-existing chronic liver disease.

2-hour postprandial glucose exceeds 120 mg/dL on two occasions within 2 weeks. The initial human insulin dose is 0.3 to 0.7 U/kg (based on prepregnancy weight), administered as a combination of short- and intermediate-acting insulin, given in two to four injections per day. These are general guidelines, and individual requirements vary. Insulin requirements usually decrease slightly during the first trimester, then increase until term. During the ninth month, insulin needs are approximately 50% greater than at preconception, and the increase is greater among patients with type 2 diabetes. Obese women with type 2 diabetes may need much higher insulin doses because of the additional insulin resistance of pregnancy, with requirements up to 2 U/kg/day.

Insulin requirements decrease after delivery, and no insulin may be required for 1 to 3 days. A week after delivery, insulin needs are reduced by approximately 50%. To avoid hypoglycemia, intravenous glucose should be constantly infused, with hourly glucose monitoring. A few days post partum, insulin requirements are reduced to 0.6 U/kg/day, and caloric requirements are approximately 27 and 25 kcal/kg/day for nursing and nonlactating women, respectively.

Prognosis

Most women with uncomplicated type I diabetes (White's classes B and C) do well during pregnancy. However, maternal risks (including accelerated retinopathy, preeclampsia, and pyelonephritis), sudden fetal death, and perinatal mortality are increased slightly. Despite careful management, congenital malformations complicate 6 to 10% of diabetic women's pregnancies. Risk factors for maternal morbidity and relative contraindications to pregnancy include established renal disease (creatinine greater than 2.0 mg/dL or proteinuria of more than 2 g/day), uncontrolled hypertension, severe gastroparesis, and atherosclerotic vascular disease. If the creatinine clearance is less than 80 mL/min or urine protein is greater than 2 g/day, up to 50% of women will experience permanent further renal impairment during pregnancy. Because diabetic retinopathy progresses in 10 to 50% of pregnant women, patients should be examined by an ophthalmologist each trimester.

Women with GDM usually normalize their blood glucose immediately post partum. Follow-up fasting glucose values should be obtained approximately 2 months post partum. Two thirds of these women will have GDM in subsequent pregnancies, and up to 50% will develop diabetes over the next 15 years.

HEPATIC DISEASE

Most liver function test results are unchanged by pregnancy. The mean levels of alanine aminotransferase, aspartate aminotransferase, γ-glutamyl transpeptidase, and bilirubin are slightly lower during pregnancy. Alkaline phosphatase, coming primarily from the placenta, increases slowly during the first and second trimester and rises to four times the prepregnant values at term. Because of the expanded plasma volume, the serum albumin value decreases 10 to 50%.

NEW-ONSET JAUNDICE DURING PREGNANCY

Etiology and Epidemiology

Jaundice is seen in approximately 1 in 2000 pregnancies. Its occurrence alters the evaluation due to consideration of conditions unique to pregnancy, including gestation-associated life-threatening hepatic disorders. The features of the usual causes for newly occurring jaundice during pregnancy are listed in Table 253–3.

℞ Diagnosis and Treatment

Viral hepatitis is the most common cause of jaundice during pregnancy, accounting for 50% of such cases, and episodes are distributed evenly among trimesters. The natural history of most viral hepatitides (types A, B, C, and D) is not altered by pregnancy, nor are their serologic diagnoses changed. Hepatitis B can be transmitted to the newborn at the time of delivery. Treating newborns

with hepatitis B immunoglobulin and hepatitis B vaccine can prevent vertical transmission of hepatitis B. The rates of hepatitis C vertical transmission vary, with some figures as high as 36%. Quantitative virus RNA may allow stratification of that risk. Women with undetectable levels are unlikely to transmit the infection, whereas those whose titers are more than 1 million copies/mL have the greatest risk. Preventive therapy, as used for hepatitis B, is not available for hepatitis C. Hepatitis E is a water-borne infection that can occur in developing areas after flooding. For reasons that are not understood, the fatality rate among pregnant women with hepatitis E is markedly higher than other hepatitis types, reaching 20%.

Other causes of pregnancy-associated jaundice are intrahepatic cholestasis of pregnancy, the HELLP syndrome, hepatic rupture, and acute fatty liver of pregnancy. Each typically occurs in the third trimester. During the first trimester, hyperemesis gravidarum may cause jaundice. However, its clinical manifestations usually suggest this diagnosis, and abnormalities resolve within days of improved nutrition.

Ultrasonography is an important noninvasive assessment tool during pregnancy. It can detect biliary tract disease, duct dilation, and hepatic subcapsular hematomas. In addition, the liver's appearance can suggest fatty infiltration, mass lesions, and cirrhosis. However, although findings of acute fatty liver are helpful, ultrasonography and computed tomography each have low sensitivity in detecting acute fatty liver of pregnancy, and liver biopsy may be needed to confirm that diagnosis.

Cholelithiasis occurs during approximately 5% of pregnancies, and choledocholithiasis accounts for approximately 7% of jaundice during pregnancy. Symptoms of cholelithiasis are not changed by gestation. During the first and second trimesters, laparoscopic cholecystectomy can be performed safely. Uterine enlargement makes surgery more difficult in the third trimester, and endoscopic retrograde cholangiopancreatography and sphincterotomy, performed while minimizing fluoroscopy and with appropriate shielding, has been used successfully in that setting.

SUGGESTED READINGS

Lee RV, Rosene-Montella K, Barbour LA, et al: Medical Care of the Pregnant Patient. Philadelphia: American College of Physicians, 2000. *Well written and comprehensive general reference for medical problems during pregnancy.*

Maynard SE, Min JY, Merchan J, et al: Excess placental soluble fms-like tyrosine kinase 1 (sFlt1) may contribute to endothelial dysfunction, hypertension, and proteinuria in preeclampsia. J Clin Invest 2003;111:649–658. *Data suggesting that excess circulating sFlt1 contributes to the pathogenesis of preeclampsia.*

Reimold SC, Rutherford JD: Clinical practice. Valvular heart disease in pregnancy. N Engl J Med 2003;349:52–59. *A practical review.*

Roberts JM, Pearson GD, Cutler JA, et al: Summary of the NHLBI Working Group on Research on Hypertension During Pregnancy. Hypertens Pregnancy 2003;22:109–127. *A consensus overview.*

254 HIV IN PREGNANCY

Stephen A. Spector

The World Health Organization and UNAIDS estimated that by the end of 2001, more than 40 million people were living with human immunodeficiency virus (HIV) infection, including 1 in every 100 adults in the sexually active ages of 15 to 49 years. Overall, approximately 15,000 new HIV infections occur daily, of which 47% affect women and more than 95% are in developing countries. In the United States, approximately 15% of the more than 600,000 cases of the acquired immunodeficiency syndrome (AIDS) reported to the Centers for Disease Control and Prevention (CDC) were in girls and women, and AIDS is the fifth most common cause of death in women between 24 and 44 years of age (Chapter 412).

Pregnant women are at risk of transmitting HIV to their newborns, with approximately 25% of exposed infants becoming infected unless intervention occurs. The exact timing of HIV transmission from mother to infant is unknown. The best estimate is that in developed countries, approximately one third of infections occur in utero whereas two thirds occur intrapartum. Risk factors for increased mother-to-infant transmission include women with low CD4+ lymphocyte counts, high HIV RNA loads, the presence of active sexually transmitted diseases, rupture of amniotic membranes beyond 4 hours, and prematurity of birth. Of all risk factors, plasma HIV RNA load is most important in determining the risk for mother-to-infant transmission.

Women can also transmit HIV through their breast milk, and such transmission accounts for one third of all infant infections in developing countries, where a majority of HIV-infected women breast-feed their infants. In developing countries, the benefits of exclusive breast-feeding are believed by some experts to outweigh the risk of transmission of HIV through milk (estimated to be 5% within the first 6 months to 24 months). The claim by some investigators that exclusive breast-feeding decreases the risk of transmission from an infected mother to her infant is yet to be supported through a prospective clinical trial. Therefore, most experts believe that substitute feeding should be used whenever possible to prevent mother-to-infant transmission of HIV. HIV-infected women in developed countries should be strongly discouraged from breast-feeding their newborns.

USE OF ANTIRETROVIRAL AGENTS DURING PREGNANCY

Treatment recommendations for HIV-infected pregnant women are based on the premise that therapies known to be of benefit should not be withheld during pregnancy unless they are known to be harmful to the mother or fetus (Chapter 421). Thus, unless there are specific reasons for withholding antiretroviral therapy, pregnant women should be given optimal combination therapy, usually including two reverse transcriptase inhibitors and a protease inhibitor. When possible, one of the reverse transcriptase inhibitors should include zidovudine because it has clearly been demonstrated to decrease vertical transmission and to be safe for mother and infant. In a controlled trial conducted by the Pediatric AIDS Clinical Trials Group (PACTG 076), HIV infection occurred in 25% of infants when the mother and infant received placebo compared with 8% of infants when mother and infant received zidovudine.[1] The treatment regimen used for the PACTG 076 study and the currently used preferable zidovudine regimens are summarized in Figure 254–1. The intervention involves three parts: (1) treatment of the mother with oral zidovudine during pregnancy, (2) administration of intravenous zidovudine during labor, and (3) 6 weeks of oral zidovudine administered to the infant after birth.[2] Each of these three parts is thought to contribute to decreasing transmission and all three parts of the intervention should be administered whenever possible.

In another study (PACTG 185), blocking mother-to-infant transmission with zidovudine intervention was shown to be even more effective, decreasing transmission to approximately 5%. The use of HIV-specific immunoglobulin provides no additional benefit over the use of zidovudine alone. A study in Thailand found that mother-to-infant transmission can be reduced when women receive zidovudine only in their last month of pregnancy. These data indicate that HIV-infected women identified at *any* stage of pregnancy should receive zidovudine to decrease the risk of perinatal transmission.[3] However,

this approach is suboptimal, and women and infants should receive the full PACTG 076 regimen whenever possible.

The treatment regimen of zidovudine, 100 mg, administered five times daily in the PACTG 076 study was based on the standard dose of zidovudine for adults in 1989. The current recommended dosing for zidovudine of 200 mg three times daily or 300 mg twice daily has been associated with a comparable clinical response and is the recommended dosing schedule for use by pregnant women.

A short-course regimen of zidovudine in non-breast-feeding women in Thailand consisting of zidovudine 300 mg twice daily from 36 weeks' gestation and 300 mg administered every 3 hours during labor decreased transmission to 9%. Another study using a four-arm factorial design compared administration of zidovudine antenatally starting at 28 or 36 weeks' gestation, orally intrapartum, and to the neonate for 3 days or 6 weeks. The long-long arm (beginning at 28 weeks antenatally and 6 weeks' treatment to the infant) was found to be significantly superior to the other arms, with a resulting transmission rate of 4%. A third study (performed in Africa) in HIV-infected women of whom 73% breast-fed their infants demonstrated that the combination of zidovudine and lamivudine (3-TC) beginning at 36 weeks' gestation, orally intrapartum, and for 1 week postpartum to the mother and infant reduced transmission to 6% for infants at 6 weeks of age. However, with the high rate of breast-feeding, by 18 months of age, 15% of infants were identified as infected, and 19% were infected or had died.

Additional trials have demonstrated that intrapartum/postpartum regimens with either zidovudine and lamivudine or nevirapine are also useful in decreasing transmission when administered to an HIV-infected pregnant woman late in pregnancy or while in labor. In an African cohort of women and infants, the intrapartum administration of zidovudine to the mother and postpartum to the breast-feeding mother and infant for 1 week decreased transmission at 6 weeks of age from 17% in the placebo group to 6% in the treated group. It should be noted that in this trial, the administration of zidovudine and lamivudine to the mother alone failed to decrease transmission to the infant. In another study performed in Uganda, the administration of a single 200 mg dose of nevirapine to the mother at onset of labor combined with a single 2 mg/kg dose of nevirapine to her infant at 24 to 72 hours of age reduced transmission at 6 weeks to 12%.[4]

In the United States and other developed countries, combination therapy, usually comprising two nucleoside reverse transcriptase inhibitors and a protease inhibitor, when administered to a woman beginning in the second trimester of pregnancy combined with intrapartum zidovudine and 6 weeks of zidovudine administered to the infant has decreased mother-to-infant transmission to less than 2%. The addition of nevirapine was of no further benefit in circumstances in which women receive perinatal care and antenatal antiretroviral therapy and in which cesarean section can be safely performed (PACTG 316).

Optimal medical management of the HIV-infected pregnant woman should include treatment with antiretrovirals, usually including two nucleoside reverse transcriptase inhibitors and a protease inhibitor, to achieve an HIV plasma RNA load of less than 400 copies per milliliter. Studies done prior to the availability of combination antiretroviral therapy generally demonstrated a reduction in HIV mother-to-infant transmission when the infant was delivered by cesarean section prior to rupture of amniotic membranes. More recent data indicate that for women with plasma HIV RNA less than 1000 copies/mL, there is no additional benefit to cesarean section. Additionally, nonelective cesarean section performed after the onset of labor or rupture of amniotic membranes has not been associated with a significant reduction in infant infection when compared with vaginal delivery.

Although the use of antiretroviral agents has been shown to be highly effective in decreasing mother-to-infant transmission and in the short term to be safe for both mother and infant, the long-term impact on infants, the vast majority of whom are uninfected with HIV, is unknown. Thus, a decision to use any antiretroviral therapy during pregnancy should be made by the woman after a thorough discussion of risks and benefits with her health care provider. Infants born to HIV-infected women should be followed by or in consultation with health care providers experienced in the care of HIV-infected children. Infants identified as infected should be treated as outlined in the Centers for Disease Control and Prevention's "Guidelines for the Use of Antiretroviral Agents in Pediatric HIV Infection."

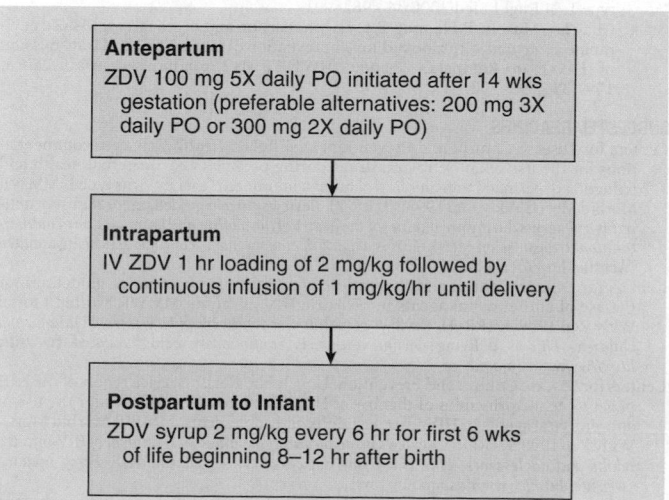

Antepartum
ZDV 100 mg 5X daily PO initiated after 14 wks gestation (preferable alternatives: 200 mg 3X daily PO or 300 mg 2X daily PO)

Intrapartum
IV ZDV 1 hr loading of 2 mg/kg followed by continuous infusion of 1 mg/kg/hr until delivery

Postpartum to Infant
ZDV syrup 2 mg/kg every 6 hr for first 6 wks of life beginning 8–12 hr after birth

FIGURE 254–1 • PACTG 076 zidovudine (ZDV) regimen for prevention of mother-to-infant transmission of HIV.

SCENARIOS THAT MAY REQUIRE ADJUSTMENTS TO THE STANDARD CARE OF WOMEN INFECTED WITH HUMAN IMMUNODEFICIENCY VIRUS

HIV-INFECTED PREGNANT WOMEN WITHOUT PRIOR ANTIRETROVIRAL THERAPY. The recommendation for antiretroviral therapy should be made after standard clinical, immunologic, and virologic evaluation. The three-part zidovudine chemoprophylaxis regimen should be recommended for all pregnant women. If the woman's HIV plasma RNA load is greater than 1000 copies/mL, combination therapy with an additional nucleoside reverse transcriptase inhibitor and a protease inhibitor is recommended. Decisions regarding combination antiretroviral treatment should be made after a full review of risks and benefits of treatment. At present, most HIV experts recommend combination antiretroviral therapy, including zidovudine, although recent studies indicate that other nucleoside reverse transcriptase inhibitors, including didanosine and stavudine, may also provide benefit. Some HIV experts recommend beginning antiretroviral therapy after the first trimester (the period of organogenesis) in an attempt to minimize risk to the fetus. If a woman's HIV disease status has not progressed to meet the current guidelines for initiation of antiretroviral therapy (i.e., her CD4+ lymphocyte count is greater than 350 cells/μL and plasma HIV RNA is less than 55,000 copies/mL), some experts recommend the discontinuation of therapy after delivery. If HIV treatment is to be discontinued, all antiretroviral agents should be stopped at the same time so as to minimize the risk for development of antiretroviral resistance.

HIV-INFECTED WOMEN PRESENTING IN LATE PREGNANCY (AFTER APPROXIMATELY 36 WEEKS OF GESTATION) KNOWN TO BE HIV-INFECTED BUT NOT RECEIVING ANTIRETROVIRAL THERAPY. A woman who presents late in pregnancy should have her plasma HIV RNA level and CD4+ lymphocyte count evaluated. The woman should be started on antiretroviral therapy including at least zidovudine; however, most experts recommend instituting three antiretrovirals, including two nucleoside reverse transcriptase inhibitors and a protease inhibitor. If the RNA load around the expected delivery date is not less than 1000 copies/mL, an elective cesarean section should be considered. During delivery and postpartum to the infant, the PACTG 076 regimen is recommended.

HIV-INFECTED WOMEN WHO HAVE VIRAL LOADS GREATER THAN 1000 COPIES/mL DESPITE RECEIVING ANTIRETROVIRAL THERAPY AT 36 WEEKS' GESTATION. If the plasma HIV RNA load is declining at the time of assay, the current antiretroviral therapy should be continued. However, if the viral load is considerably greater than 1000 copies/mL, it is unlikely that it will decline to less than 1000 copies/mL at the time of delivery. The woman should be counseled that elective cesarean section may be of benefit in decreasing the risk of intrapartum transmission. During delivery and postpartum to the infant, the PACTG 076 regimen is recommended.

HIV-INFECTED WOMEN RECEIVING ANTIRETROVIRAL THERAPY DURING THE CURRENT PREGNANCY. Women receiving antiretroviral therapy and identified as being pregnant should continue their current antiretroviral therapy, provided that plasma HIV RNA levels are less than 400 copies/mL. Women who are identified as pregnant during the first trimester should be counseled regarding the potential risks of taking an antiretroviral agent during this period. If therapy is discontinued, all drugs should be stopped and reintroduced at the same time to avoid the development of resistance. If the current antiretroviral regimen does not include zidovudine, substituting zidovudine or adding it to the regimen should be considered after 14 weeks' gestation. If the previous antiretroviral therapy had not resulted in plasma HIV RNA levels less than 400 copies/mL, a regimen usually consisting of three drugs of at least two different classes including at least two new drugs should be instituted during pregnancy. If resistance testing is available, pregnant women should be begun on antiretrovirals to which their virus is known to be susceptible.

HIV-INFECTED PREGNANT WOMEN IN LABOR WHO HAVE HAD NO PRIOR THERAPY. Several treatment options are available for women who present in labor; however, it should be noted that transplacental infection of the fetus may have already occurred. Treatment regimens include administration of intrapartum intravenous zidovudine, followed by the 6-week zidovudine regimen for the newborn. Some experts also add nevirapine in a single dose prior to delivery to the pregnant woman and following delivery to the infant. Cesarean section prior to rupture of amniotic membranes is recommended by some experts for this situation to prevent transmission. The benefit to the infant must be weighed against the potential risk to the mother of a cesarean section. After delivery, the woman should have a full evaluation of her HIV status and, when appropriate, have antiretroviral therapy recommended for her own health.

INFANTS BORN TO MOTHERS WHO HAVE RECEIVED NO ANTIRETROVIRAL THERAPY DURING PREGNANCY OR INTRAPARTUM. The 6-week neonatal course of zidovudine is recommended as soon after birth as possible for infants born to HIV-infected women. Many HIV experts recommend three-drug combination regimens, including two reverse transcriptase inhibitors and an antiprotease compound for 6 weeks. Following delivery, the woman should have a full evaluation of her HIV status and, when appropriate, have antiretroviral therapy recommended for her own health.

All pregnant women, regardless of plasma HIV RNA load, should be advised that the use of antiretroviral prophylaxis has been found to provide benefit in preventing perinatal transmission.

TESTING AND SUPPORTIVE CARE

After delivery, HIV-infected women should receive comprehensive care and support services required for management of their HIV infection and for care of their family. This care should begin before pregnancy, with continuity of care ensured throughout pregnancy and postpartum.

Testing for HIV and counseling are essential to any successful plan for identification of treatment of pregnant women. All pregnant women, regardless of their sexual or social history, should be offered HIV antibody testing (Chapter 410). Patients whose test results are negative should be informed that false-positive or false-negative results may occur due to the latent phase between HIV exposure and development of antibody. The false-negative rate depends on the prevalence of risk-related behavior in the tested population. Patients whose test result is negative should be encouraged to practice low-risk behavior to minimize their risk of infection. A pregnant woman whose test result is positive should have a confirmatory test performed. After confirmation, the patient should have counseling regarding whether to continue the pregnancy, potential risks to the fetus, and benefits of antiretroviral intervention and treatment for herself and her newborn. After identification of HIV infection, care for the infected woman should be the same as for any other person newly identified as HIV positive. Prophylaxis for opportunistic pathogens and treatment of infections should be as recommended for others infected with HIV.

1. Shapiro DE, Sperling RS, Mandelbrot L, et al: Risk factors for perinatal human immunodeficiency virus transmission in patients receiving zidovudine prophylaxis. Pediatric AIDS Clinical Trials Group protocol 076 Study Group. Obstet Gynecol 1999;94:897–908.
2. Connor EM, Sperling RS, Gelber R, et al: Reduction of maternal-infant transmission of human immunodeficiency virus type 1 with zidovudine treatment. N Engl J Med 1994;331:1173–1180.
3. Lallemant M, Jourdain G, Le Coeur S, et al: A trial of shortened zidovudine regimens to prevent mother-to-child transmission of human immunodeficiency virus type 1. N Engl J Med 2000;343:982–991.
4. Guay LA, Musoke P, Fleming T, et al: Intrapartum and neonatal single-dose nevirapine compared with zidovudine for prevention of mother-to-child transmission of HIV-1 in Kampala, Uganda. HIVNET 012 randomised trial. Lancet 1999;354:795–802.

SUGGESTED READINGS

Centers for Disease Control and Prevention: U.S. Public Health Service recommendations for the use of antiretroviral drugs during pregnancy for maternal health and reduction of perinatal transmission of human immunodeficiency virus type 1. MMWR Morbid Mortal Wkly Rep 1998;47(RR-2). *Reviews current guidelines for the use of antiretroviral agents during pregnancy for the health of the mother and for reduction of mother-to-infant transmission of HIV. This is a living document that is continuously being updated* (website: http://www.aidsinfo.nih.gov).

Centers for Disease Control and Prevention: U.S. Public Health Service guidelines for the use of antiretroviral agents in pediatric HIV infection. MMWR Morbid Mortal Wkly Rep 1998;47(RR-4). *Reviews guidelines for treatment of HIV-infected infants and children. This is a living document that is continuously being updated* (website: http://www.aidsinfo.nih.gov).

Centers for Disease Control and Prevention: U.S. Public Health Service report of the NIH panel to define principles of therapy of HIV infection and guidelines for the use of antiretroviral agents in HIV-infected adults and adolescents. MMWR Morbid Mortal Wkly Rep 1998:47(RR-5). *Reviews principles and guidelines for treatment of HIV-infected adults and adolescents. This is a living document that is continuously being updated* (website: http://www.aidsinfo.nih.gov).

Richardson BA, John-Stewart GC, Hughes JP, et al: Breast-milk infectivity in human immunodeficiency virus type 1-infected mothers. J Infect Dis 2003;187:736–740. *This study demonstrated that the risk of transmission of HIV depends on the viral load within breast milk and not on infant age.*

Sperling RS, Shapiro DE, Coombs RW, et al: Maternal viral load, zidovudine treatment, and the risk of transmission of human immunodeficiency virus type 1 from mother to infant. N Engl J Med 1996;335:1621–1629. *This study demonstrated that a high maternal plasma concentration of HIV RNA is a risk factor for mother-to-infant transmission. However, women transmit the virus at every level of plasma HIV RNA. To prevent HIV transmission, initiating maternal treatment with zidovudine is recommended regardless of the plasma HIV RNA level or CD4+ lymphocyte count.*
UNAIDS/WHO AIDS Epidemic Update 2001. *Reviews worldwide AIDS epidemic to December 2002 (website: http://www.unaids.org).*

255 HIRSUTISM

Roger S. Rittmaster

Definition

NORMAL HAIR GROWTH. Most body hair can be classified as vellus or terminal. Vellus hairs are fine and unpigmented, such as those that cover the face of children. Terminal hairs, pigmented and coarser, may be sex hormone–dependent (such as those over the chin and abdomen of men) or sex hormone–independent (such as eyebrows and eyelashes) (Fig. 255–1). Androgens convert vellus hair to terminal hair in sex hormone–dependent areas.

HIRSUTISM. Hirsutism is the presence of excess hair in women. This is usually an androgen-dependent process. Twenty-five to 35% of young women have terminal hair over the lower abdomen, around the nipples, or over the upper lip. Most women gradually develop more androgen-dependent body hair with age. Nevertheless, "normal" patterns of female hair growth are unacceptable to many women. At the other extreme, severe hirsutism may, rarely, be the earliest sign of masculinizing diseases. More often, however, severe hirsutism reflects only increased androgen production in women with no serious underlying disorder.

Etiology

Causes of hirsutism can be divided into androgen-dependent and androgen-independent. Androgen-dependent hirsutism is restricted to areas where men typically become hirsute and often begins with adolescence. In women, androgens arise from the ovaries, the adrenal glands, or exogenous sources such as anabolic steroids (Table 255–1). Often, no definite abnormality exists; the hirsutism simply results from modestly increased androgen production and/or increased skin sensitivity to androgens.

Androgen-independent hirsutism (also termed "hypertrichosis") is caused by drugs (cyclosporine, glucocorticoids, minoxidil, diazoxide, and possibly phenytoin) or starvation (anorexia nervosa); it may be associated with the skin lesions of porphyria; or it may be an inher-

ited condition. Androgen-independent hirsutism is characterized by long, fine hairs occurring over much of the body, including such areas as the forehead and flanks. Androgens may exacerbate androgen-independent hirsutism, giving rise to a clinically confusing presentation. The pathophysiology of androgen-independent hirsutism is unknown.

Table 255–1 • CAUSES OF ANDROGEN-DEPENDENT HIRSUTISM

Ovarian causes
  Severe insulin resistance
  Virilizing ovarian tumors
Adrenal causes
  Congenital adrenal hyperplasia
  21-Hydroxylase deficiency
  3β-Hydroxysteroid dehydrogenase deficiency
  11-Hydroxylase deficiency
  Cushing's disease
  Ectopic adrenocorticotropic hormone–producing tumors
  Virilizing adrenal tumors
Combined ovarian and adrenal causes
  Polycystic ovary syndrome
  "Idiopathic" hirsutism
Exogenous androgens
  Anabolic steroids
  Danazol
  Postmenopausal hormone replacement formulations containing androgens

Pathophysiology of Androgen-Dependent Hirsutism

To be active in skin, testosterone, the major circulating androgen, must first be converted to dihydrotestosterone by the enzyme 5α-reductase. Hirsute women have elevated skin 5α-reductase compared with nonhirsute women. They may also have polymorphisms of the androgen receptor leading to increased androgen effect.

Hirsute women as a group also have increased androgen production from the adrenal glands, the ovaries, or both. Either testosterone itself is secreted, or androgen precursors such as androstenedione are secreted, which are then converted in the liver or skin to active androgens. Many hirsute women simply fall at one end of the normal spectrum of androgen production and skin sensitivity to androgens.

The ovarian and adrenal causes of hirsutism listed in Table 255–1 lead to increased androgen production. Virilizing tumors secrete androgens directly. The pituitary adenomas in Cushing's disease release adrenocorticotropic hormone, which stimulates the adrenals to secrete both cortisol and androgens (Chapter 240). The virilizing forms of congenital adrenal hyperplasia involve enzyme defects that impair cortisol synthesis, leading to increased adrenocorticotropic hormone secretion (Chapter 240). The enzyme block causes shunting of cortisol precursors to androgens. The most common form, 21-hydroxylase deficiency, leads to an overproduction of 17-hydroxyprogesterone. Whereas severe forms of 21-hydroxylase deficiency cause ambiguous genitalia in female infants, milder forms may lead only to hirsutism and/or irregular menses. This "nonclassic" form of 21-hydroxylase deficiency is present in about 1% of hirsute women.

In the polycystic ovarian syndrome, both the ovaries and the adrenal glands secrete excess androgens, although the majority of the androgens are usually of ovarian origin (Chapter 250).

Clinical Manifestations

Androgen-induced hirsutism of benign origin usually begins in adolescence and becomes gradually worse with time. Family history is often positive. The hirsutism may vary from mild to severe. Usually hair growth begins over the lower abdomen, on the breasts, and over the upper lip. Widespread hirsutism over the upper back, upper abdomen, and upper chest implies severe hyperandrogenism. Some women have only facial hair or other unusual patterns of hirsutism, probably due to local variation in skin 5α-reductase activity.

Severe, rapidly progressive hirsutism, beginning in childhood or beyond adolescence, suggests an androgen-secreting tumor. Such

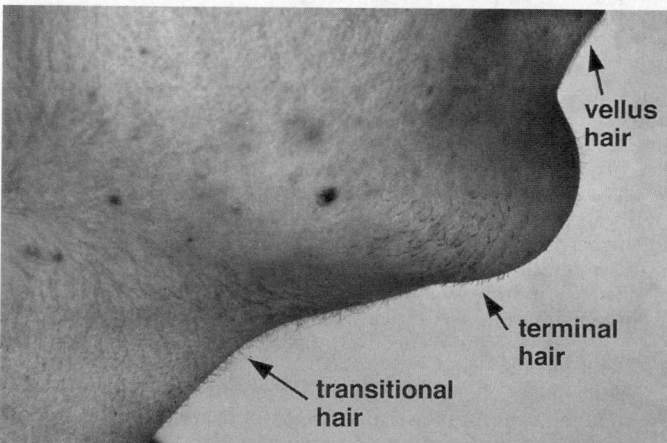

FIGURE 255–1 • Facial hair growth in a hirsute woman. Vellus hair is fine, unpigmented hair. Terminal hair is coarse and pigmented. Transitional hair is intermediate between vellus and terminal. This woman also has mild acne, another androgen-dependent process. (From Rittmaster RS: Hirsutism. Med Clin North Am 1987;14:2686, with permission.)

Continued

tumors can cause signs of virilization: deepening of the voice, excess muscle development, and marked clitoral enlargement. Signs of virilization, however, simply imply severe hyperandrogenism and can occasionally be seen with all causes of hirsutism. Androgen-secreting tumors are rare, and most severely hirsute women have either polycystic ovarian syndrome or hirsutism alone.

Nonclassic congenital adrenal hyperplasia is clinically indistinguishable from simple hirsutism or polycystic ovarian syndrome, and the diagnosis must be made biochemically. Cushing's disease may be suspected when the patient presents with central obesity, hypertension, diabetes, and/or thinning of the skin (Chapter 237).

Diagnosis

The diagnostic evaluation of hirsutism is directed at ruling out a significant underlying cause. Important historical points include a drug history, age of onset, and rate of progression of hirsutism, presence of thinning of scalp hair or deepening of the voice, menstrual history, history of obesity, and family history of hirsutism. The physical examination should include an assessment of the quality and distribution of hair growth, signs of virilization or Cushing's syndrome, and presence of abdominal or pelvic masses in women suspected of having an androgen-secreting tumor.

LABORATORY EVALUATION. In women with androgen-dependent hirsutism, regular ovulatory menses, and no physical signs of Cushing's syndrome, hormonal evaluation is usually unnecessary. Virilizing tumors have not been reported in such patients, and hirsutism associated with nonclassic congenital adrenal hyperplasia need not be treated differently from other benign forms of hirsutism (see treatment section).

In hirsute women with irregular menses, a reasonable laboratory evaluation includes measurement of serum testosterone, 17-hydroxyprogesterone, prolactin, luteinizing hormone, and follicle-stimulating hormone. A testosterone level less than 170 ng/dL (6 nmol/L) makes an androgen-secreting tumor highly unlikely, although re-evaluation may be necessary if the hirsutism continues to progress or signs of virilization appear. Testosterone levels greater than 170 ng/dL may also be seen with polycystic ovarian syndrome. To rule out nonclassic 21-hydroxylase deficiency, serum 17-hydroxyprogesterone should be measured between 7 and 9 AM during the first week of the menstrual cycle (values may be elevated during the luteal phase). Values less than 200 ng/dL (6 nmol/L) rule out this diagnosis. Mildly elevated values (<1000 ng/dL) (30 nmol/L) may be seen in both heterozygous and homozygous 21-hydroxylase deficiency (the heterozygous disorder is not associated with hirsutism) and in polycystic ovarian syndrome. To distinguish between these conditions, 17-hydroxyprogesterone should be measured 30 to 60 minutes after the intravenous administration of 250 μg synthetic adrenocorticotropic hormone. Levels are usually greater than 1500 ng/dL (45 nmol/L) in homozygous 21-hydroxylase deficiency. Other forms of nonclassic congenital adrenal hyperplasia are too rare to justify routine hormonal screening. Serum prolactin, luteinizing hormone, and follicle-stimulating hormone levels are used to evaluate the possibility that a prolactinoma, ovarian failure, or polycystic ovarian syndrome is contributing to the irregular menses. These tests are not directly relevant to the evaluation of hirsutism itself. Measurement of dehydroepiandrosterone sulfate as an index of adrenal androgen production is generally unhelpful.

Rx Treatment

Hirsutism is a cosmetic problem that may have severe psychosocial consequences. Because it is not a disease in itself, the benefits and risks of any therapy should be carefully weighed and the treatment individualized.

MECHANICAL HAIR REMOVAL. For mild hirsutism, bleaching and mechanical hair removal are adequate and safe. Shaving is the easiest method of temporarily removing visible hair. Although shaving does not increase hair growth rates, it may leave a stubble and is unacceptable to many women. Plucking and waxing may control mild hirsutism, but they may lead to scarring. Electrolysis can provide a safe, effective alternative for localized mild to moderate hirsutism and is a useful adjunct to medical therapy in more severe cases. Electrolysis is expensive, however, and long-term treatment may be necessary. Laser hair removal is a new option for treatment of hirsutism. It is expensive but less time-consuming than electrolysis. Beneficial treatment results have been demonstrated up to a year after therapy, but long-term outcomes have yet to be reported.

DRUG TREATMENT. Successful medical therapy results in a gradual return of terminal hair to finer, less pigmented vellus hair. Younger women with mild hirsutism of brief duration respond best to medical therapy. More severe hair growth can be prevented, and resolution of the hirsutism is possible. Nevertheless, drug treatment is not a cure, and lifelong therapy may be necessary to prevent recurrence. Generally, 6 months is needed to judge the efficacy of a given therapy, although improvement may continue indefinitely. No oral drug is approved by the Food and Drug Administration specifically for treatment of hirsutism.

Antiandrogens. Antiandrogens (spironolactone, cyproterone acetate, flutamide) block the androgen receptor and are the drug treatment of choice for hirsutism. They are effective in reducing hair growth in at least 70% of women, and hirsutism stabilizes in the remaining percentage. Spironolactone is usually given in a starting dose of 50 mg twice daily. The most common side effect is increased frequency of menses, which can be controlled by combining spironolactone with an oral contraceptive. Spironolactone should not be given to women with renal insufficiency, because it can cause severe hyperkalemia in such individuals. Cyproterone acetate, a potent antiandrogen and progestin, is often given as 25 to 50 mg daily for the first 10 days of a birth control pill cycle. Although widely used in Europe and Canada, it is not available in the United States. Flutamide is given as 125 to 250 mg twice daily. Flutamide can cause a drug-induced hepatitis, and all antiandrogens should be avoided in pregnant women. Flutamide is more expensive than other antiandrogens. Efficacy for these antiandrogens is similar.[1]

5α-Reductase Inhibitors. Finasteride blocks the formation of dihydrotestosterone and is approved for treatment of benign prostatic hyperplasia and male pattern baldness. It also effectively treats idiopathic hirsutism and hirsutism in the polycystic ovary syndrome.[2] All studies to date have used 2.5 or 5 mg daily, although 1 mg daily should be as effective. It would be expected to cause ambiguous genitalia in the male offspring of women taking the drug during pregnancy.

Ovarian Suppression. Although oral contraceptives are often used to control menstrual cycles in women given antiandrogens, they are usually ineffective for treating hirsutism when used alone (although they may prevent the hirsutism from becoming worse). Birth control pills differ in the androgenicity of the progestational component, but this difference is less important than the ability of the progestin to suppress ovarian androgen secretion. For treatment of women with polycystic ovary syndrome, a progestin-dominant pill should be used. Gonadotropin-releasing hormone analogues suppress the ovary by suppressing luteinizing hormone and follicle-stimulating hormone secretion. They are effective in treating hirsutism associated with polycystic ovarian syndrome but are expensive and lead to menopausal symptoms unless estrogens are given concurrently.

Glucocorticoids. Glucocorticoids suppress adrenal cortisol and androgen secretion. They are frequently ineffective in low doses, and higher doses can cause Cushing's syndrome. They also can cause a drug-induced hirsutism in some women and cannot be recommended as a routine treatment. Although glucocorticoids have traditionally been used to treat congenital adrenal hyperplasia, antiandrogens are more effective in treating the hirsutism associated with this disorder.

Other. Topical eflornithine cream has recently been approved by the Food and Drug Administration (FDA) for treatment of hirsutism. Eflornithine inhibits ornithine decarboxylase, an enzyme essential for hair growth. It is modestly effective, although the improvement rapidly reverses once the drug is stopped. There have been no trials comparing eflornithine, or use of it in combination, with other treatments for hirsutism.

Women's Health

Prognosis

Untreated, hirsutism usually becomes gradually worse with time, and most therapies need to be continued indefinitely. However, worsening hirsutism is easily prevented with antiandrogen therapy, and most women experience a satisfactory improvement with the judicious use of mechanical and medical therapies.

1. Moghetti P, Tosi F, Tosti A, et al: Comparison of spironolactone, flutamide and finasteride efficacy in the treatment of hirsutism: A randomized, double blind, placebo-controlled trial. J Clin Endocrinol Metab 2000;85:89–94.
2. Lakryc EM, Motta EL, Soares JM Jr, et al: The benefits of finasteride for hirsute women with polycystic ovary syndrome or idiopathic hirsutism. Gynecol Endocrinol 2003;17:57–63.

SUGGESTED READINGS
Azziz R: The evaluation and management of hirsutism. Obstet Gynecol 2003;101:995–1007. *A detailed review of the pathophysiology of idiopathic hirsutism and a good overview of the treatment.*
Carmina E: A risk-benefit assessment of pharmacological therapies for hirsutism. Drug Safety 2001;24:267–276. *A concise overview of therapeutic options for hirsutism.*

256 MENOPAUSE

Rogerio A. Lobo

Menopause is defined as the last menstrual period; the median age is 51.4 years, and the age distribution ranges from 40 to 58 years. Age at menopause has not changed over the past few centuries, whereas there has been a gradual increase in life expectancy. Thus, although in previous centuries women were not expected to live beyond menopause, women now spend one third to one half of their lives after menopause. Because menstrual cycles rarely cease abruptly, there is a period of time, termed the *perimenopause* or *menopausal transition,* during which there is a wide fluctuation in the hormonal profiles. In general, the perimenopause begins a few years before the last menstrual period (menopause) when cycles become irregular and there are often, but not always, symptoms suggesting a declining estrogen status. Although estrogen levels can be higher than normal early in the perimenopause, an abrupt decline in estrogen occurs 6 months before menopause. The perimenopause also extends for a few years beyond the menopause, a time during which transient and episodic bursts of ovarian activity may occur that may result in some vaginal bleeding.

The total group of postmenopausal women in the United States is increasing. In 2000, it is estimated that there were 31.2 million women older than age 55, compared with 28.7 million in 1990. It is estimated the size of this group will grow to 45.9 million by 2020.

REPRODUCTIVE DECLINE AND MENOPAUSE

The time from the decline in reproductive capacity onward is often referred to as the *climacteric.* Reproductive aging occurs rapidly after the third decade, and fecundity is extremely low before menopause. Thus, reproductive aging precedes menopause by 5 to 10 years, at a "young" chronologic age. This is signified by an increase in serum follicle-stimulating hormone (FSH) level in the early follicular phase of regular cycles. These values may be elevated only intermittently before they continue to rise at the time of menopause. Decreasing ovarian estrogen, but particularly inhibin B, is responsible for the rise in FSH (Chapter 237).

HORMONAL CHANGES WITH ESTABLISHED MENOPAUSE

Figure 256–1 depicts the typical hormonal changes of postmenopausal women compared with those of ovulatory women in the early follicular phase. The most significant findings are the marked reductions in estradiol (E_2) and estrone (E_1). Serum E_2 is reduced to a greater extent than E_1. Serum E_1, on the other hand, is produced primarily by peripheral aromatization from androgens, which decline principally as a function of age. Levels of E_2 average 15 pg/mL and range from 10 to 25 pg/mL. In oophorectomized women, values are usually 10 pg/mL or less. Serum E_1 values average 30 pg/mL but may be higher in obese women because aromatization increases as a function of the mass of adipose tissue. Estrone sulfate (E_1S) is an estrogen conjugate that serves as a stable-circulating reservoir of estrogen, and its levels are the highest of any estrogen. In premenopausal women, values are usually above 1000 pg/mL; in postmenopausal women, levels average 350 pg/mL. Apart from elevations in FSH and luteinizing hormone (LH), pituitary hormones are not affected. Specifically, growth hormone, thyroid-stimulating hormone, and adrenocorticotropic hormone (ACTH) levels are normal. Serum prolactin levels may be very slightly decreased because prolactin is somewhat influenced by estrogen status. Both the postmenopausal ovary and the adrenal gland continue to produce androgen. The ovary continues to produce androstenedione and testosterone but not E_2, and this production has been shown to be at least partially dependent on LH. Androstenedione and testosterone levels are lower in women who have experienced bilateral oophorectomy, with values averaging 0.8 ng/mL and 10 ng/dL, respectively. The adrenal gland also continues to produce androstenedione, dehydroepiandrosterone, and dehydroepiandrosterone sulfate, and, primarily as a function of aging, these

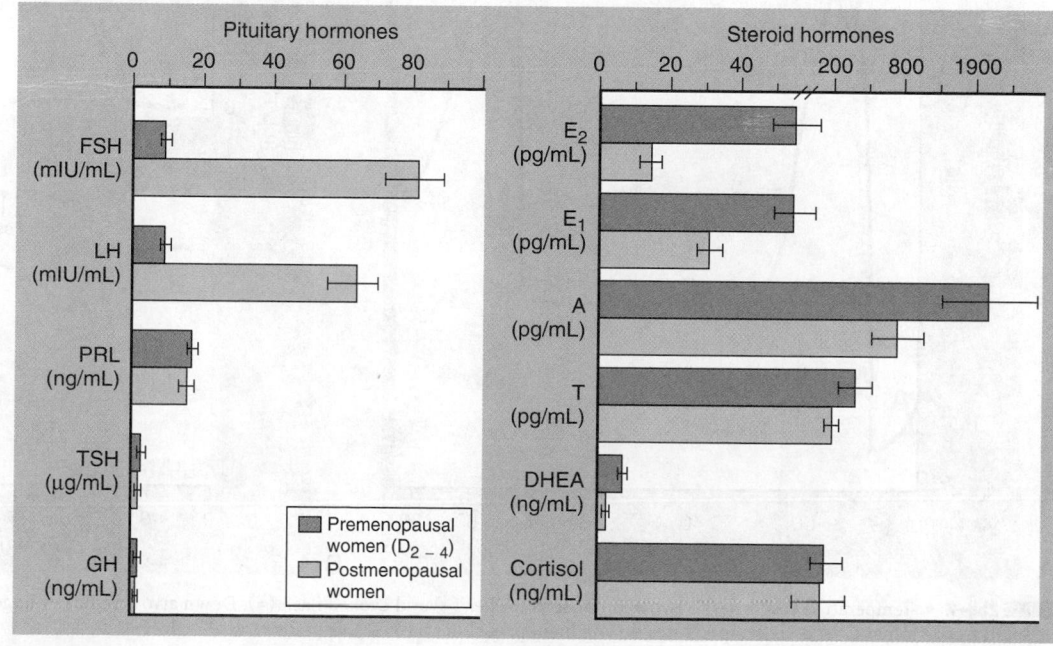

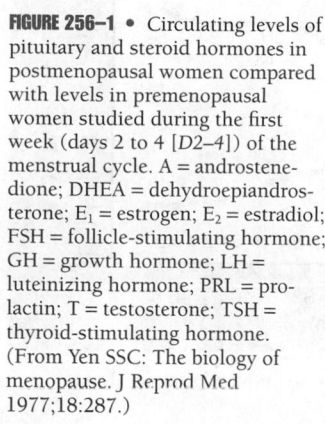

FIGURE 256–1 • Circulating levels of pituitary and steroid hormones in postmenopausal women compared with levels in premenopausal women studied during the first week (days 2 to 4 [*D2–4*]) of the menstrual cycle. A = androstenedione; DHEA = dehydroepiandrosterone; E_1 = estrogen; E_2 = estradiol; FSH = follicle-stimulating hormone; GH = growth hormone; LH = luteinizing hormone; PRL = prolactin; T = testosterone; TSH = thyroid-stimulating hormone. (From Yen SSC: The biology of menopause. J Reprod Med 1977;18:287.)

values decrease somewhat (adrenopause), although cortisol secretion remains unaffected.

Whether an androgen "deficiency" occurs after menopause is still debated. Data obtained across the perimenopause have suggested very little early change in secreted androstenedione and testosterone. Indeed, as sex hormone binding globulin (SHBG) decreases after menopause, levels of unbound or free testosterone are higher in the first few years after menopause. Androstenedione declines more rapidly, and both decline as a function of age. This age decline can be demonstrated between young premenopausal and postmenopausal women on the basis of 24-hour mean values. Nevertheless, on an individual basis, some younger perimenopausal and postmenopausal women exhibit very low androgen levels, prompting the consideration for androgen replacement. Women receiving oral estrogen tend to have low levels of unbound testosterone because of the increase in SHBG.

EFFECTS OF DECLINING ESTROGEN

Estrogen receptors are abundant throughout the body; therefore, the absence of estrogen potentially influences virtually all systems in some way.

BRAIN AND CENTRAL NERVOUS SYSTEM. In the brain, because estrogen receptors are abundant (predominantly ERβ) in the cortex and hippocampus and estrogen is known to influence many brain processes, the absence of estrogen can result in symptomatic as well as physiologic changes. Estrogen is important for blood flow, synaptic activity, neuronal growth, the survival of cholinergic neurons, and many other functions, including cognition. Hot flushes are an early and acute symptom of estrogen deficiency. This can occur in the perimenopause when levels characteristically fluctuate widely. It is the rapid fall in estrogen levels that precipitates the symptoms. Although the proximate cause of the flush remains elusive, the episodes result from a hypothalamic response (probably mediated by catecholamines) as a result of a change in estrogen status. The flush has been well

characterized physiologically. It results in heat dissipation by an increase in peripheral temperature (finger, toe); a decrease in skin resistance, associated with diaphoresis; and a reduction in core body temperature (Fig. 256–2). There are hormonal correlates of flush activity such as an increase in serum LH and plasma pro-opiomelanocortin peptides (ACTH, β-endorphin) at the time of the flush, but these occurrences are thought to be epiphenomena that result as a consequence of the flush and are not related to its etiology.

In general, estrogen has a positive effect on mood and contributes to a sense of well-being. In an estrogen-deficient state such as occurs after the menopause, a higher incidence of depression (clinical or subclinical) is manifest. Dementia increases as a function of age and has a higher prevalence in women compared with men. Some of this trend may be related to estrogen deficiency. Thus, the risk of Alzheimer's disease may be reduced with estrogen in postmenopausal women. However, once dementia is established, estrogen does not appear to reverse cognitive decline. Estrogen is also thought to have an overall positive effect on verbal memory.

COLLAGEN. Estrogen has a positive effect on collagen that is important for bone, the skin, and other sites such as the pelvis and urinary system. Both estrogen and androgen receptors have been identified in skin fibroblasts. Thirty percent of skin collagen is lost within the first 5 years after menopause. There is a decrease in collagen of approximately 2% per year for the first 10 years after menopause. This statistic, which is similar to that of bone loss after menopause, strongly suggests a link between skin thickness, bone loss, and the risk of osteoporosis. It is claimed that estrogen restores collagen content after menopause, and after 2 years of treatment improves skin thickness. The supportive effect of estrogen on collagen has important implications for bone homeostasis as well as for the pelvis after menopause. Here, reductions in collagen support and atrophy of the vaginal and urethral mucosa have been implicated in a variety of symptoms of prolapse and urinary incontinence. Uterine prolapse and other gynecologic symptoms related to poor collagen support as well as urinary complaints may improve with estrogen. Restoration of bladder control

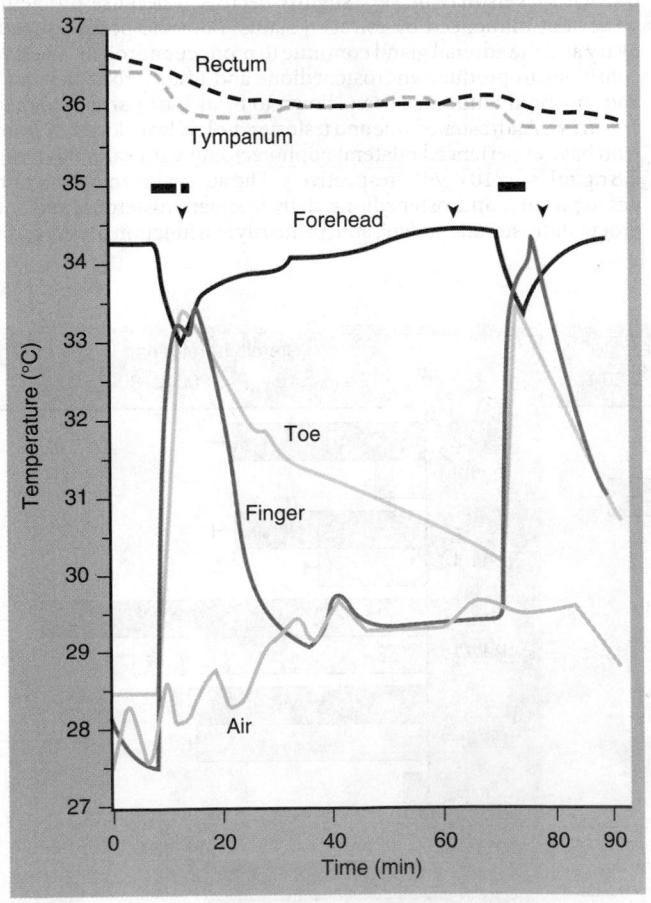

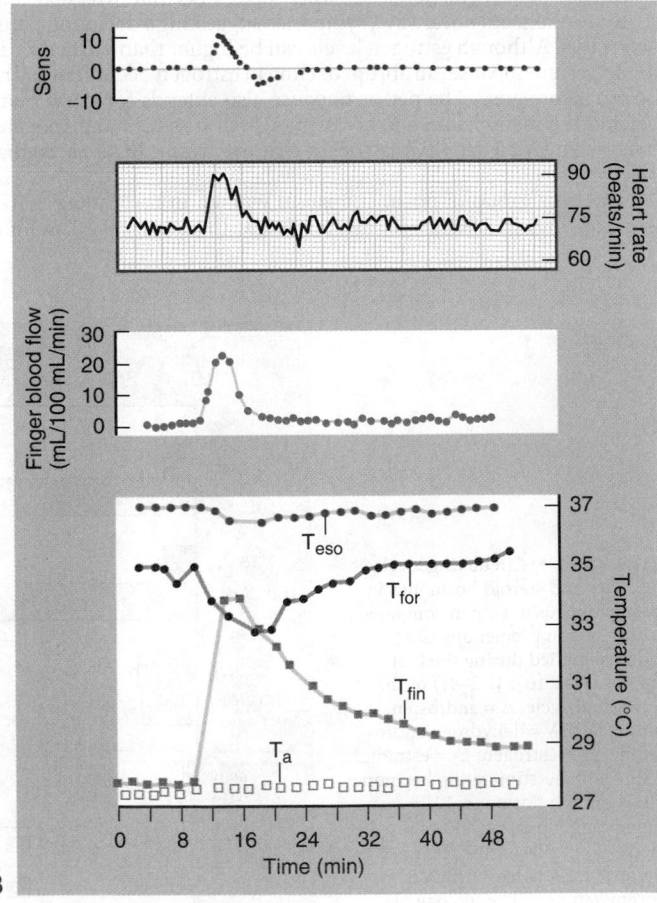

FIGURE 256–2 • Temperature responses to two spontaneous flashes (−) and evoked flash (=). Down arrow indicates finger stab for blood sample. (Data adapted from Molnar GW: Body temperatures during menopausal hot flashes. J Appl Physiol 1975;38:499–503.)

with estrogen in older women has been shown to decrease the need for admission to nursing homes in Sweden.

GENITAL ATROPHY. Vulvovaginal complaints are often associated with estrogen deficiency. It is generally stated, however, that these symptoms occur only several years after estrogen levels decline. With this change, an increase in sexual complaints also occurs. Estrogen deficiency results in a thin and paler vaginal mucosa. The moisture content is low, the pH increases (usually >5), and the mucosa may exhibit inflammation and small petechiae. With estrogen treatment, it has been documented that vaginal cytology changes from a profile of predominantly parabasal cells to one with an increased number of superficial cells. Along with this, the vaginal pH decreases, vaginal blood flow increases, and the electropotential difference across the vaginal mucosa increases to premenopausal levels.

BONE LOSS. It is well established that estrogen deficiency leads to bone loss (Chapter 258). This can be noted for the first time with irregularity of menstrual cycles before menopause. It has been shown that from 1.5 years before the menopause to 1.5 years after menopause, spine bone mineral density decreases by 2.56% per year, compared with a premenopausal loss rate of 0.13% per year. Loss of trabecular bone (spine) is greater with estrogen deficiency than is loss of cortical bone.

At the time of menopause there is an accelerated loss of bone that results in a 3% reduction in bone mass per year for the first 5 years. Therefore, the rate of loss of bone is in the range of 1 to 2% per year. Dramatic changes in bone architecture accompany this loss in bone, greatly increasing the risk of fracture. For every standard deviation of reduction in bone mass there is a two-fold or greater risk of fracture. The rate at which a woman reaches the fracture threshold is dependent on many factors, such as genetics, nutrition, activity level, and lifestyle; also extremely important is the total amount of bone a woman has at the time of menopause. Peak bone mass is achieved by the second decade and begins to decrease thereafter.

Estrogen deficiency at the time of menopause results in an accelerated decline in bone mass, and this is mediated by a variety of mechanisms. The primary deficit is one of increased resorption (osteoclastic activity) that outsteps and is therefore uncoupled from bone formation (osteoblastic activity). In old age, bone formation also lags further. Estrogen action on bone is both direct and indirect. Direct effects are mediated through receptor (predominantly ERα) mechanisms as well as cellular membrane effects, and these include specific effects on bone collagen. There are also effects mediated through the androgen receptor that are important for bone formation. Indirect effects that increase bone resorption are mediated through the effects of parathyroid hormone (PTH) and cytokines, although intermittent PTH is now known to stimulate bone formation. Positive influences also involve the effects of other growth factors, calcitonin, vitamin D metabolism, and calcium absorption. In an estrogen-deficient state, these positive effects are diminished.

Osteoporosis is a devastating and debilitating disease. The only way to accurately access bone mass is with direct measurements. Historical information about risk factors and biochemical urinary analyses are only partially helpful. Dual x-ray absorptiometry remains the best approach at present and has high precision, reproducibility, and low radiation exposure (Chapter 241).

CARDIOVASCULAR EFFECTS. It appears clear that after menopause, there is an increase in the risk of cardiovascular disease in women. Data from the Framingham study have been used to compare the incidence of cardiovascular disease in men and women as they age. Although the incidence is three times lower in women than in men before the menopause (3.1:1000 per year in women aged 45 to 49), it is approximately equal in men and women aged 75 to 79, being 53:1000 and 50.4:1000 per year, respectively. This trend also pertains to gender differences in mortality due to cardiovascular disease. Coronary artery disease is the leading cause of death in women, and the lifetime risk of death is 31% in postmenopausal women versus a 3% risk of dying of breast cancer.

Although cardiovascular disease becomes more prevalent only in later years following a natural menopause, premature cessation of ovarian function (before menopause) constitutes a significant risk. Premature menopause, occurring before age 35, has been shown to increase the risk of myocardial infarction two- to three-fold, and premature oophorectomy (before age 35) increases the risk sevenfold.

When the possible reasons for the increase in cardiovascular disease are examined, the most prevalent finding is that of the rise in total cholesterol at an accelerated rate in postmenopausal women. Although

changes with age, weight, blood pressure, and blood glucose levels are not thought to be substantially different in men and women, the rate of rise in total cholesterol after menopause is significantly different. This increase in total cholesterol is explained by increases in levels of low-density lipoprotein cholesterol (LDL-C). The oxidation of LDL-C is also enhanced, as are levels of very low density lipoproteins and lipoprotein(a). HDL-C levels trend downward with time, but these changes are small and inconsistent relative to the increases in LDL-C.

Coagulation balance is not altered significantly as a counterbalance of changes occurs; some procoagulation factors increase (factor VII, fibrinogen) but so do factors such as antithrombin III, plasminogen, and proteins C and S. Blood flow in all vascular beds decreases after menopause; prostacyclin production decreases, endothelin levels increase, and vasomotor responses to acetylcholine challenges are constrictive, reflecting reduced nitric oxide synthetase activity. With estrogen, all these parameters improve and coronary arteries respond to acetylcholine by dilating, with a commensurate increase in blood flow. Circulating plasma nitric oxide has also been shown to increase and levels of angiotensin-converting enzymes to decrease. Estrogen and progesterone receptors have been found in vascular tissues, including coronary arteries (predominantly ERβ). In addition, there are membrane effects mediated by estrogen that may or may not relate to ERα or ERβ. Overall, the direct vascular effects of estrogen are viewed to be as important as, or more important than, the changes in lipid and as lipoproteins after menopause.

In normal, nonobese postmenopausal women, carbohydrate tolerance also decreases as a result of an increase in insulin resistance. This, too, is partially reversed by estrogen. Biophysical and neurohormonal responses to stress (stress reactivity) are exaggerated in postmenopausal women compared with premenopausal women, and this heightened reactivity is blunted by estrogen replacement as well. Whether these changes influence cardiovascular risk with estrogen deficiency is not known, but clearly estrogen replacement returns many parameters into the range of premenopausal women.

There are probably subtle effects of estrogen on the musculoskeletal system, the eyes, the ears, and the sensory organs, but these systems have been incompletely studied. It is known, however, that the rate of macular degeneration increases after menopause, and this rate may be attenuated in users of estrogen. Similarly, there is an important effect of estrogen on immune function, but this, too, warrants further investigation.

THE DECISION TO USE ESTROGEN

Whether or not hormonal "replacement" should be considered is a very individual decision. This takes into account symptoms, risk factors, and individual preferences and needs. Alternatives should also be considered. If hormonal therapy is chosen, there should be flexibility in prescribing because there is no ideal regimen for all women.

RISK-BENEFIT ASSESSMENT. Estrogen "replacement" therapy, previously referred to as ERT, now should be called estrogen therapy (ET). ET is indicated for the relief of hot flushes and urogenital atrophy and for the prevention of osteoporosis. For these indications, a titration of dose is important, with the most common dose being 0.625 mg of conjugated equine estrogen (CEE) or its equivalent. Most recently there has been a trend to use lower doses than this, to reduce potential risks and side effects with demonstration of effectiveness for several indications. ET may be divided into short-term relief of symptoms such as hot flushes, for which a larger dose may sometimes be required, and long-term prophylaxis against the morbidity and mortality from osteoporosis and other degenerative diseases including cognitive decline.

To address the potential long-term benefits of ET and hormonal therapy (HT), which includes the use of a progestin, the NIH launched two large randomized trials as well as other studies known collectively as the Women's Health Initiative (WHI). CEE 0.625 mg or placebo was used in hysterectomized women in one trial, which is still ongoing; and CEE 0.625 mg together with medroxyprogesterone acetate (MPA) 2–5 mg or placebo was used continuously in women with a uterus. This latter trial was terminated prematurely in 2002 at 5.2 years.

The primary end points of the trial were to assess whether there are cardioprotective effects of HT and whether these treatments increase the risk of breast cancer. Data for other end points such as osteoporotic fracture were also assessed. At 5.2 years, the Data and Safety Monitoring Board terminated the HT trial because the rates of breast cancer had crossed over the preset monitoring boundary, and there was no beneficial effect on coronary disease and, indeed, some increased risk was observed in the first year of use. [1,2] The breast cancer rates had not crossed the preset boundary for risk in the ET trial in 2002, and it is planned to continue until 2005.

Although virtually all observational trials had shown previously that ET and HT decrease coronary risk by 30 to 50%, recent secondary prevention trials and data from WHI suggest that there is no benefit, and potentially some increased risk, in the first two years of use, particularly in those women not using statins. This finding is consistent with earlier results from the Health and Estrogen/Progestin Replacement Study. [3] Thus, ET/HT should not be used for the indication of cardio-protection. However, no trial to date has assessed whether ET/HT begun at the onset of menopause in younger, healthier women (as was the case in the observational trials) may be of benefit. The secondary prevention trials treated women in their 60s and 70s who had significant risk factors. In the completed WHI trial, the mean age of women was 63 years, with only 16% of the women being within 5 years of menopause. Recent data suggest that the timing of initiation of ET/HT is extremely important for certain proposed benefits, specifically coronary disease and cognitive decline.

Virtually all other findings of WHI are consistent with observational trials in terms of risks and benefits (summarized in Table 256–1). Most notably, hormonal therapy increased the risk of breast cancer, [4] and it did not improve cognitive function. [5] The overall risks of breast cancer were confined only to previous users of estrogen, and the magnitude of risk is consistent with previous reports, suggesting some increased risk in certain women related to the dose and duration of therapy. For these reasons the approach to ET/HT should be to use the lowest possible dose. Lower dose therapy has been shown to be effective for relief of symptoms as well as preservation of bone mass.

CHANGES IN MORTALITY WITH ESTROGEN USE. In several cohort studies, an overall 40% reduction in all-cause mortality has been observed with long-term estrogen use. Two studies have shown that the benefit in mortality is related to the duration of use, but one has suggested that the effect is decreased beyond 10 years of use because of an increase in breast cancer mortality (reported only in this cohort and not in the others). Most studies have shown either no change in breast cancer mortality with estrogen use or a decrease in mortality. In these observational cohorts looking at all-cause mortality, the overall reduction was found to be attributable to a reduction in cardiovascular mortality, although there was a small effect in cancer mortality as well. For example, several studies have shown a protective effect of ET on colon cancer mortality. This protection of approximately 50% (relative risk, 0.5) is also greater with a longer duration of use.

In WHI, there was no overall change in mortality. [1] If ET/HT decreases all-cause mortality, it will be in the setting of long-term use when initiated in young, healthy women at the onset of menopause (as in the observational trials). This will never be proven because the

current recommendation after the WHI study is to use the lowest dose of ET/HT for the shortest duration of time to control symptoms of menopause.

RISKS ASSOCIATED WITH ET/HT. Among the risks that have been associated with ET/HT are endometrial disease, breast cancer, venous thrombosis, and stroke with higher doses of estrogen, side effects such as vaginal bleeding, somatic complaints, and idiosyncratic reactions, including hypertension. All of these risks are in part dose related, lending to the credence of using lower doses. Endometrial disease occurs with unopposed estrogen therapy in women who have a uterus. Although a woman's risk of developing endometrial cancer with unopposed estrogen use is two- to eight-fold higher than that for the general population, in most patients, precursor lesions, primarily endometrial hyperplasia, signal the presence of an abnormality (Chapter 205). Thus, the risk is far less for endometrial cancer than it is for varying degrees of hyperplasia. One study showed that the risk of endometrial hyperplasia was 20% after 1 year of use of 0.625 mg of oral CEE. In another study, the 3-year postmenopausal Estrogen/Progestin Interventions Trial, this risk was approximately 40% at the end of 3 years. No cancers were reported in either of these two studies, and the addition of a progestin essentially eliminated the hyperplasia. Using a dose of 0.3 mg of CEE results in a risk in the range 5 to 10% after 2 to 3 years. With the same dose of esterified estrogens that is less potent, no hyperplasia was found after 2 years.

The risk of developing endometrial cancer is the same for a woman taking estrogen and progestin (HT) as for the general population. The addition of a progestin merely eliminates the excess risk induced by estrogen. Other endometrial cancers occurring in postmenopausal women are not thought to be hormonally related. Although the risk of developing endometrial cancer is increased significantly in estrogen users, the risk of death from this type of endometrial cancer does not increase proportionately. Endometrial cancers associated with estrogen use are thought not to be as aggressive as spontaneously occurring cancers or that tumors in women taking estrogen are likely to be discovered and treated at an earlier stage, thus improving survival rates.

More controversial is the risk of breast cancer with estrogen as discussed above. Several case-control studies found no increase with ET alone but in the same study showed a statistical increase with progestin use (HT) in the range of 1.3 or 1.4 (relative risk). [4] Although the ET trial from WHI is ongoing, when the HT trial was terminated at 5.2 years in part because of breast cancer risk, no such data were evident with ET. Although the cancer risk is unproven, there is biologic plausibility that progesterone increases the risk of breast mitotic activity and HT increases mammographic tissue density more than with ET.

If estrogen is to be implicated in cancer risk, then both the estrogen dose and its duration of use need to be factored into risk estimates. For moderate doses of estrogen, the risk of breast cancer is probably in the range of 20 to 30% in those women who are susceptible. Unfortunately, such women cannot be identified before therapy is initiated.

Table 256–1 • **SUMMARY OF MAIN OUTCOMES FROM WHI**

OUTCOME	RELATIVE RISK VS PLACEBO (95% CL)*	INCREASED ABSOLUTE RISK PER 10,000 WOMEN/YR‡	INCREASED ABSOLUTE BENEFIT PER 10,000 WOMEN/YR
CHD	1.29 (1.02–1.63)	+7	
Invasive breast cancer	1.26 (1.00–1.59)	+8	
Stroke	1.41 (1.07–1.85)	+8	
PE	2.13 (1.39–3.25)	+8	
Colorectal cancer	0.63 (0.43–0.92)		−6
Hip fracture	0.66 (0.45–0.98)		−5
Global index†	1.15 (1.03–1.28)		

*Relative hazards are depicted with the nominal 95% confidence limits (CL).
†The global index was an attempt to take into account the specific risks and benefits chosen above.
‡Note the risks and benefits are depicted as the absolute rates (increase or decrease) per 10,000 women annually.
CHD = coronary heart disease
PE = pulmonary embolism

One of the greatest concerns of women receiving estrogen is the return of menstrual bleeding. Somatic complaints such as breast tenderness and bloating may also occur with ET but can be alleviated by alterations in dose and type of preparation. Such concerns should be discussed with the patient, and the choice of regimen should remain flexible.

Idiosyncratic reactions including hypertension and allergic manifestations have been observed in users of estrogen, particularly oral estrogen. Hypertension with estrogen use, the cause of which is not entirely clear, occurs in about 5% of oral contraceptive users. Estrogen usually causes no change in blood pressure; it may actually reduce blood pressure, a finding that has relevance for normotensive as well as hypertensive individuals. However, an increase in both diastolic and systolic blood pressures has been noted in susceptible individuals and is rapidly reversible with discontinuation of ET. A different form of estrogen may eliminate the problem. Alterations in the route of estrogen administration and dose have resulted in improved blood pressure in such individuals.

In susceptible individuals, ET/HT increases the risk of venous thrombosis in a fashion similar to that of oral contraceptive use. This risk is approximately two-fold with oral standard doses of estrogen. It is unclear if this risk is related to an unknown thrombophilia. However, this increased risk does not increase mortality, and the rate for pulmonary embolism is low (background prevalence of 11:100,000 women). Nevertheless, it is important to inform all patients of these findings. In women with the history of thrombosis, however, there is an increased risk with estrogen administered orally, a risk that is not easily identifiable except by reviewing the patient's history and by measuring coagulation factors. Women who have a family history of thrombosis or have had thrombotic events with oral contraceptives or any prior estrogen use should be counseled very carefully and monitored closely. Nonoral estrogen is a consideration for these patients and may be used if there are no alternatives.

There is an unexplained increase in the risk of unstable angina, and potentially myocardial infarction within 1 to 2 years of initiating estrogen in women with established coronary disease. There is some evidence that concurrent statin use eliminates this early risk. Nevertheless, standard ET/HT should not be initiated within 2 years of a coronary event even if used to treat symptoms. **2,3** There is no indication that ET/HT prevents heart disease.

HORMONAL REGIMENS

Estrogen Therapy

The aim of ET is to provide "replacement" in a fashion that is as physiologic as possible. Follicular phase levels of E_2 during the normal menstrual cycle range between 40 and 100 pg/mL. Threshold levels of E_2 for achieving benefit for osteoporosis and cardiovascular disease are in the range of 50 to 60 pg/mL for most women. Nevertheless, any increment of estrogen levels from baseline is expected to exert some significant effect, thus leading to the concept of a minimal effective dose.

Oral ET results in higher levels of E_1 than E_2. This is true for oral estradiol as well as estrone products. CEE is a mixture of at least 10 conjugated estrogens derived from equine pregnant urine. Estrone sulfate is the major component, but the biologic activities of equilin, 17a-dihydroequilin, and several other B-ring estrogens, including Δ–dihydroestrone, have been documented. Table 256–2 compares the standard doses of the most frequently prescribed oral estrogens and the levels of E_1 and E_2 achieved.

Synthetic estrogens, given orally, are vastly more potent. Ethinyl estradiol is used in oral contraceptives. A dose of 5 µg is equivalent to the standard ET doses used (0.625 mg CEE or 1 mg micronized estradiol). Standard ET doses are five or six times less than the amount of estrogen used in oral contraceptives.

Oral estrogens have a potent hepatic ("first-pass") effect that results in the loss of approximately 30% of its activity with a single passage after oral administration. However, this results in stimulation of hepatic proteins and enzymes. Some of these changes are not particularly beneficial (an increase in procoagulation factors), whereas other changes are beneficial (an increase in high-density lipoprotein cholesterol [HDL-C] and a decrease in fibrinogen and plasminogen activator inhibitor-1).

Table 256–2 • MEAN SERUM ESTRADIOL (E_2) AND ESTRONE (E_1)

ESTROGEN DOSE (mg)	LEVEL (pg/mL)	
	E_2	E_1
CEE (0.3)*	18	76
CEE (0.625)	39	153
CEE (1.25)	60	220
Micronized E_2 (1)	35	190
Micronized E_2 (2)	63	300
E_1 sulfate (0.625)	34	125
E_1 sulfate (1.25)	42	220

*Conjugated equine estrogen (CEE) contains biologically active estrogens other than E_2 and E_1.

Nonoral estrogen delivers estrogen in the form in which it is formulated. E_2 is administered in patches, in gels, and subcutaneously. This synthetic administration is not subject to major hepatic effects as with oral therapy. Standard doses in the United States of alcohol-based or matrix patches are 0.05 or 0.1 mg. Lower-dose patches of 0.025 mg are also available for administration once a week or twice a week. Matrix patches are preferable because there is less skin reaction and estrogen delivery is more reliable. Although levels of E_2 vary widely among women, levels with transdermal therapy are more constant in individual women than with oral ET. With the 0.05-mg patch, E_2 levels are in the 40 to 50 pg/mL range, and with the 0.1-mg patch, levels are typically 70 to 100 pg/mL. It is not unusual, however, for some women to have levels in excess of 200 pg/mL.

In women with vulvovaginal or urinary complaints, vaginal therapy is most appropriate. Creams of estradiol or CEE are available as well as tablets and an estrogen ring. With creams, systemic absorption occurs but with levels that are one fourth of that achieved after similar milligram doses administered orally. Absorption is less the more estrogenized the mucosa is. For CEE, only 0.5 g (0.3 mg) is necessary; for micronized E_2, doses as low as 0.25 mg are sufficient. Other products (tablets and rings) are available that have been designed to limit systemic absorption. A Silastic ring of E_2 is available that delivers E_2 to the vagina for 3 months with only minimal systemic absorption.

With oral and transdermal methods, estrogen is administered every day, although it is still acceptable to consider cyclic regimens of every 25 to 26 days of therapy.

Use of a Progestin

In women with a uterus, a progestin is necessary to "oppose" the proliferative effects of estrogen on the endometrium. A regimen that includes progestins is usually referred to as HT rather than ET. Progestins are usually administered orally but may be used vaginally or as an intrauterine device. The dose of progestins should be kept low to prevent attenuating the beneficial effects of ET on the cardiovascular system and brain.

There are many ways to administer progestins. The most commonly used oral progestins are medroxyprogesterone acetate (MPA) in doses of 5 to 10 mg, norethindrone in doses of 0.3 to 1 mg, and micronized progesterone in doses of 100 to 300 mg. Equivalent doses to prevent hyperplasia when administered for at least 10 days in a woman receiving ET (equivalent to 0.625 mg CEE) are as follows: MPA 5 mg, norethindrone 0.7 mg, and micronized progesterone 200 mg. Larger doses of estrogen may require larger doses and more prolonged regimens of progestins. In sequential administration of progestins, the number of days (length of exposure) is more important than the dose. Thus, if a woman is receiving oral ET continuously, a regimen of at least 10 to 12 days of exposure is preferable to a 7-day regimen.

When progestins are administered sequentially (10 to 14 days each month), withdrawal bleeding occurs in about 80% of women. Continuous administration of both estrogen and progestin (continuous combined therapy) was developed to achieve amenorrhea. In the first 3 to 6 months, breakthrough bleeding and spotting is common. In some women on this regimen, amenorrhea is never completely achieved. The most common combination, in the United States, is a single tablet containing 0.625 mg CEE and 2.5 mg MPA. A similar tablet with 5 mg MPA is also available. Currently, the only marketed sequential regimen is one that contains 0.625 mg CEE and 5 mg MPA, which is added for 14 days each cycle. Other regimens are under review by the Food and Drug Administration (FDA). With the trend of using lower doses of estrogen, various low-dose fixed combinations of CEE with MPA have recently been approved by the FDA. Equal efficacy to standard doses has been demonstrated for these combinations in terms of reduction of hot flushes, maintenance of bone mass, metabolic profiles, and a reduction in the incidence of bleeding in the first year of treatment has been observed.

Progesterone administered vaginally (in low doses) avoids systemic effects and results in high concentrations of progesterone in the uterus. Intrauterine delivery of progestins is ideal for targeting the uterus but is not approved in the United States.

Progestins, particularly when taken orally, may lead to problems of continuance or compliance because of side effects, including mood alterations and bleeding. These have to be dealt with effectively and usually require more flexibility in prescribing habits. Most short-term clinical trials have demonstrated an attenuating effect of progestins on cardiovascular end points that are improved with estrogen. These include lipoprotein changes (an attenuation of the rise in HDL-C) as well as arterial and metabolic effects. A reduction in blood flow and some brain effects may also be found. Nevertheless, observational cohort studies have not demonstrated any difference in benefit between ET and HT. It would be prudent, however, to use the lowest dose of progestin necessary to prevent hyperplasia until more data are available. Except in rare circumstances (e.g., previous endometrial cancer, recent diagnosis of endometriosis) progestins should not be prescribed in women who have undergone hysterectomy.

Androgen Therapy

In a very subtle way, some women are relatively androgen deficient. Clinicians have proposed adding androgen to ET or HT for complaints or problems relating to libido and energy that are not relieved by adequate estrogen. Although well-controlled trials using parenteral testosterone have shown benefit in younger oophorectomized women, there have been few data showing benefit using more physiologic therapy, until recently. Recent data using a testosterone patch or pellet (with near physiologic levels) have shown improvement in several scales of well-being and sexual function. An oral preparation (esterified estrogens 0.625 mg with 1.25 mg of methyl testosterone) was shown to improve sexual motivation and enjoyment in women with hypoactive sexual desire who were unresponsive to estrogen alone. The latter findings correlated with an increase in circulating androgen levels. As newer forms and doses of androgen become available, perhaps more women may benefit from this approach. At present, androgen therapy should be individualized and considered for those women who have symptoms that are not adequately relieved with traditional ET or HT. At lower doses, androgenizing side effects are very infrequent but should be discussed before prescribing testosterone. At present, small doses of methyltestosterone (1.25 and 2.5 mg) added to esterified estrogens are available in tablets, as are testosterone patches that are available for men (and therefore require dose reductions) and testosterone subcutaneous pellets.

Administration of dehydroepiandrosterone at 25 to 50 mg/day may also be an option.

Selective Estrogen Receptor Modulators and Other Alternatives (Chapter 258)

If women chose not to receive estrogen or should not because of an estrogen-responsive disease such as breast cancer, there are several alternatives. For osteoporosis, estrogen therapy is an effective preventive strategy,[6] but bisphosphonates are also an effective therapy. Alendronate, in daily doses of 5 mg (for prevention) and 10 mg (for treatment; 70 mg once a week is now available) or risedronate 5 mg may be highly beneficial as a primary agent but may also be used as an adjunctive to estrogen for women with low bone mass. [7] Obviously, calcium, vitamin D, and exercise are important adjuncts as well but when used alone are not as effective as other measures discussed here. Nevertheless, all postmenopausal women should receive adequate vitamin D and ingest at least 1000 mg of calcium and up to 1500 mg if not receiving other measures. Statins, used for lipid disorders, may be beneficial for decreasing bone resorption. Androgen therapy may enhance bone formation as well. In the future, PTH therapy offers great promise for increasing bone mass.

Selective estrogen receptor modulators (SERMs) such as tamoxifen and raloxifene have mixed agonist and antagonistic properties. Both of these first- and second-generation SERMs antagonize estrogen action in the breast and induce hot flushes. Raloxifene, but not tamoxifen, is also antagonistic to the uterus (endometrium). Both have agonist properties on bone and liver. This leads to a protective effect against osteoporosis and beneficial lipid and lipoprotein effects but a two- to three-fold increase in venous thrombosis. Table 256–3 provides an appreciation of the current agonistic and antagonistic effects that are important for postmenopausal health.

Raloxifene has been shown to be beneficial for the prevention of bone loss,[8] although the bone density effects are less than those of ET. Prospective trials have demonstrated a significant decrease in vertebral fractures. Both tamoxifen and raloxifene, although having beneficial effects on bone resorption, also reduce cholesterol and LDL-C but do not increase HDL-C. Raloxifene, as a more potent estrogen antagonist, may not have beneficial vascular effects. Raloxifene, by virtue of being antagonistic at the level of the breast, has been shown in prospective studies to reduce the incidence of estrogen-responsive (ER-positive) breast cancers (but not ER-negative tumors). Raloxifene may be viewed to be an alternative that is keenly suited for the woman with a uterus who is asymptomatic but needs protection against osteoporosis. More long-term data on these alternatives will be available shortly.

Another SERM-like compound (not depicted in the table) that is used worldwide but is not approved (as yet) in the United States is tibolone. This progestin-like compound exhibits estrogenic, antiestrogenic, and androgenic effects by virtue of its structure and metabolites. At 2.5 mg, tibolone suppresses hot flushes, prevents osteoporosis, and has a positive effect on mood and sexual function. There also is very limited (or no) uterine stimulation. However, there is a suppression of HDL-cholesterol but at the same time a decrease in triglycerides. In the monkey, there is no deleterious effect of tibolone on coronary arteries.

Table 256–3 • EFFECTS OF ESTRADIOL AND SERMS ON VARIOUS ORGAN SYSTEMS AS PERTINENT TO POSTMENOPAUSAL USE

	BRAIN	UTERUS	VAGINA	BREAST	BONE	CARDIOVASCULAR SYSTEM
E_2	++	++	++	++	++	++
Pure antiestrogen	–	–	–	–	–	–
"Ideal"	++	–	++	–	++	++
Tamoxifen	–	+	–	–	+	+
Raloxifene	+–	–	–	–	+	+
Isoflavones	+–	–	+–	–	+–	+

SERM = selective estrogen receptor modulator.

Other SERMs are also in development that have a purely antagonist effect on breast and endometrium and a favorable effect on the brain, bone, and cardiovascular systems. A potential concern of using a very antagonistic SERM on the uterus is increasing the risk of uterine prolapse in older women.

In recent years, more natural products such as phytoestrogens have gained popularity for use in postmenopausal women. Isoflavonoids in dietary products (e.g., soy) or as supplements have been shown to alleviate hot flushes to some limited degree but require fairly large doses (60 to 80 mg/day). Nevertheless, lower doses (25 to 50 mg) are beneficial for lowering cholesterol. However, in opposition to animal data, there are very weak or negligible effects on bone mass in women with standard doses. Effects on the brain (cognition, mood) in the human have not been proved, as is the case for an antiestrogenic protective effect on the breast and uterus.

Hot flashes, the most common menopausal symptom, can be disabling psychologically. Paroxetine, an antidepressant unrelated to the tricyclics or selective serotonin uptake inhibitors, can reduce these symptoms significantly when used at 12.5 or 25 mg per day. [9]

1. Writing Group for the Women's Health Initiative Investigators: Risks and Benefits of estrogen plus progestin in healthy postmenopausal women: Principal results from the Women's Health Initiative randomized controlled trial. JAMA 2002;288:321–333.
2. Manson JE, Hsia J, Johnson KC, et al: Women's Health Initiative Investigators. Estrogen plus progestin and the risk of coronary heart disease. N Engl J Med 2003;349:523–534.
3. Hulley S, Grady D, Bush T, et al: Randomized trial of estrogen plus progestin for secondary prevention of coronary heart disease in postmenopausal women. Heart and Estrogen/Progestin Replacement Study (HERS) Research Group. JAMA 1998;280:605–613.
4. Chlebowski RT, Hendrix SL, Langer RD, et al: WHI Investigators: Influence of estrogen plus progestin on breast cancer and mammography in healthy postmenopausal women: The Women's Health Initiative Randomized Trial. JAMA 2003;289:3243–3253.
5. Shumaker SA, Legault C, Thal L, et al: WHIMS Investigators: Estrogen plus progestin and the incidence of dementia and mild cognitive impairment in postmenopausal women. The Women's Health Initiative Memory Study: A randomized controlled trial. JAMA 2003;289:2651–2662.
6. Lindsay R, Gallagher JC, Kleerekoper M, Pickar JH: Effect of lower doses of conjugated equine estrogens with and without medroxyprogesterone acetate on bone in early postmenopausal women. JAMA 2002;287:2668–2676.
7. Liberman UA, Weiss SR, Broll J, et al: Effect of oral alendronate on bone mineral density and the incidence of fractures in postmenopausal osteoporosis. N Engl J Med 1995;333:1437–1443.
8. Ettinger B, Black DM, Mitlak BH, et al: Reduction of vertebral fracture risk in postmenopausal women with osteoporosis treated with raloxifene. Results from a 3-year randomized clinical trial. JAMA 1999;282:637–645.
9. Stearns V, Beebe KL, Iyengar M, et al: Paroxetine controlled release in the treatment of menopausal hot flashes: A randomized controlled trial. JAMA 2003;289:2827–2834.

SUGGESTED READINGS

Grimes D, Lobo RA: Perspectives on the Women's Health Initiative trial of hormone replacement therapy. Obstet Gynecol 2002;100:1344–1353. *A comprehensive overview of the evidence.*

Nelson HD, Humphrey LL, Nygren P, et al: Postmenopausal hormone replacement therapy: Scientific review. JAMA 2002;288:872–881. *A comprehensive overview of the evidence.*

Wu L-JW, Tice JA, Bellino FL: Phytoestrogens and healthy aging: gaps in knowledge. A workshop report. Menopause 2001;8:157–170. *Overview of these food and dietary supplements.*

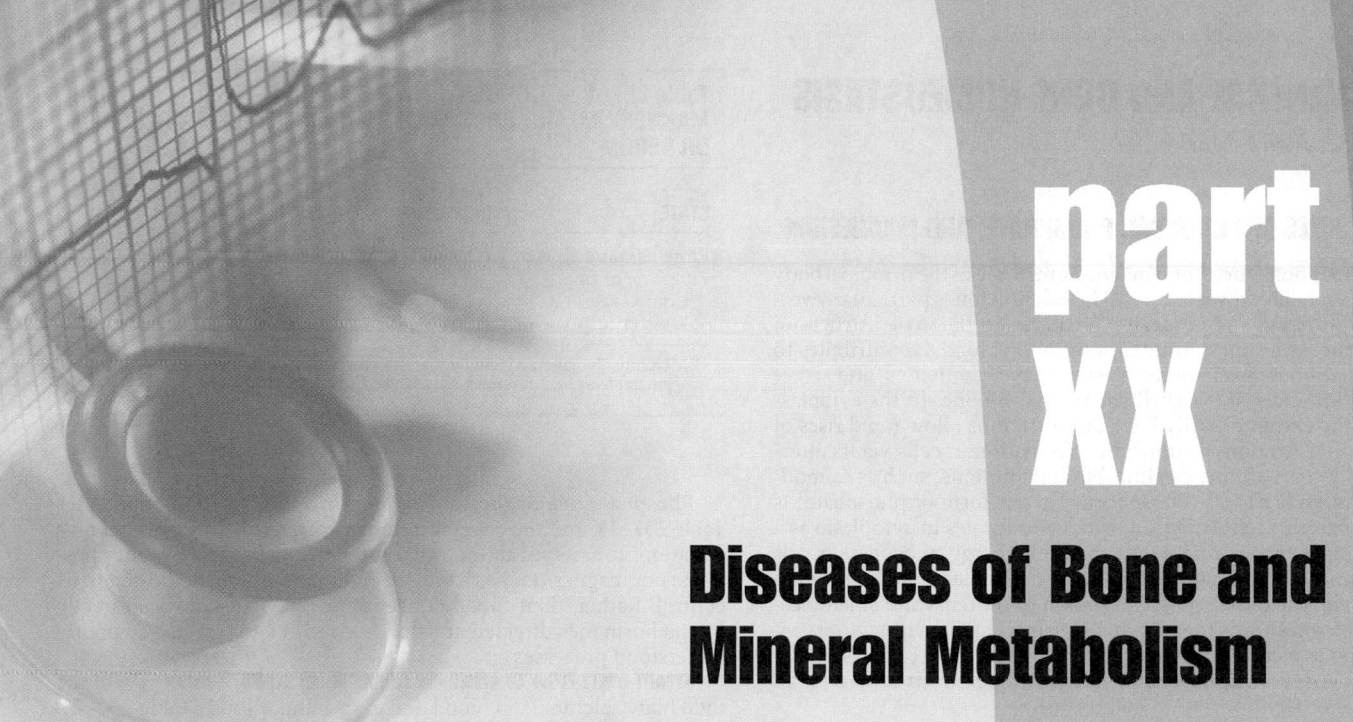

part XX

Diseases of Bone and Mineral Metabolism

257 MINERAL AND BONE HOMEOSTASIS

Stephen J. Marx

DIVERSE ROLES FOR CALCIUM, PHOSPHATE, AND MAGNESIUM

Calcium, phosphorus, and magnesium, three of the principal body elements, each have diverse roles. The calcium ion is particularly versatile. In the crystalline phase, it contributes to the varied structural roles of bone. In a supersaturated solution in blood, it contributes to cellular membrane excitability, plasma enzyme activities, and accretion of all minerals in extracellular matrix of bone. In the cytoplasmic fluid, its extraordinarily low concentrations allow rapid rises of its local concentrations to transmit information in cells via its interactions with high-affinity calcium-binding proteins, such as calmodulin or protein kinase C. Phosphorus (in the form of phosphate) is the principal intracellular anion, with central roles in cytoplasm as a buffer, energy carrier (mainly via the high-energy phosphate bonds of adenosine triphosphate [ATP]), and molecular switch (through phosphorylation and dephosphorylation of proteins and small messengers). Magnesium is the principal divalent cation in the cytoplasm, functioning as a cofactor in many chemical reactions (e.g., as a magnesium–adenosine triphosphate [ATP] complex or as a cofactor in many steps of DNA or RNA metabolism).

MINERALS IN BLOOD

THE STATES OF CALCIUM, PHOSPHATE, AND MAGNESIUM IN BLOOD. Total calcium concentration in blood is tightly regulated so that typical diurnal fluctuations are not more than 5% from the mean value. Calcium in blood is divided similarly among protein-bound, complexed, and ionized fractions (Table 257–1). Calcium in blood is principally bound to albumin, and this binding is decreased by more acidic pH. The ionized calcium fraction is the focus for metabolic control by the parathyroid gland, and measurements of ionized calcium in blood give the most valid index of pathologic disruptions of blood calcium homeostasis.

Table 257–1 • CONCENTRATIONS AND STATES OF CALCIUM, MAGNESIUM, AND PHOSPHATE IN NORMAL HUMAN PLASMA OR SERUM*

STATE	CALCIUM (mM)	MAGNESIUM (mM)	PHOSPHATE (mM)
Protein bound	1.15 (47)	0.26 (31)	0.15 (13)
Filterable or free[†]			
Complexed	0.25 (10)	0.06 (7)	0.40 (35)
Ionized	1.06 (43)	0.52 (62)	0.60 (52)

*Number in parentheses indicates percentage of total for that mineral.
†Filterable or free = complexed + ionized.

Phosphate and magnesium in blood are principally unbound (see Table 257–1), and the concentration of each spans a broader relative variation from its mean than that for calcium. Neither serum phosphate nor magnesium has a known endocrine system dedicated to its control. Rather, their blood concentrations are sustained indirectly by the hormones directed at calcium control and directly by poorly understood processes.

STEADY-STATE FLOW OF MINERALS TO AND FROM BLOOD. Only 0.1% of the total body calcium is in blood and extracellular fluid (Table 257–2). This calcium pool is in a rapidly exchanging equilibrium with large calcium pools controlled by three organs: bone, intestine, and kidney. The rate of these daily fluxes (Fig. 257–1) is sufficiently large that disturbance of calcium flux to or from any of these three organs can result in abnormally high or low concentrations of calcium in blood.

ORGANS EXCHANGING MUCH MINERAL WITH BLOOD

Bone

FUNCTION AND ARCHITECTURE. Major functions of bone include support, encasement of hematopoietic or central nervous system tissue, and serving as a reservoir for calcium, phosphate, and magnesium. The

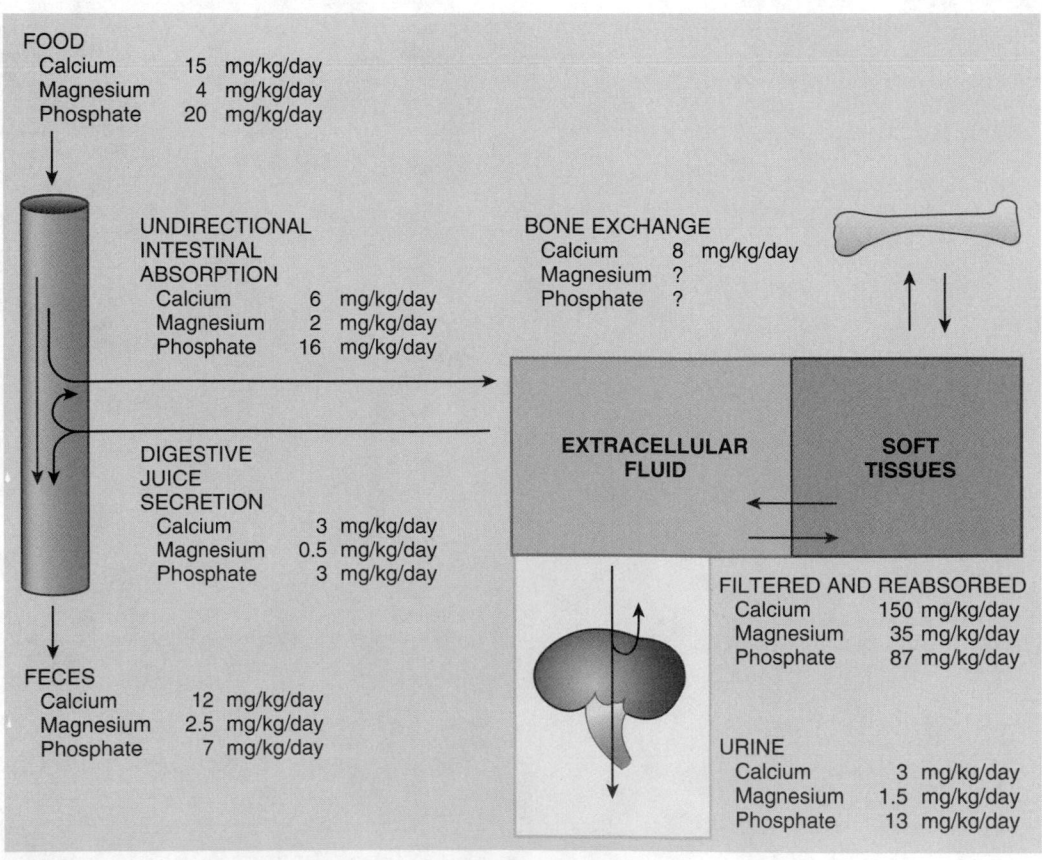

FIGURE 257–1 • Typical mineral fluxes in adults. (Modified from Aurbach GD, Marx SJ, Spiegel AM: Parathyroid hormone, calcitonin, and the calciferols. *In* Wilson JD, Foster DW [eds]: Williams Textbook of Endocrinology, 7th ed. Philadelphia, WB Saunders, 1985, p 1144.)

Table 257–2 • DISTRIBUTION OF CALCIUM, MAGNESIUM, AND PHOSPHATE IN THE BODY OF A 70-KG ADULT*

COMPARTMENT	CALCIUM (g)	MAGNESIUM (g)	PHOSPHATE (g)
Bone and teeth	1300 (99)	14.0 (54)	600.0 (86)
Extracellular fluid	1 (0.1)	0.3 (1)	0.2 (0.03)
Cells	7 (1.0)	12.0 (46)	100.0 (14)

*Most of calcium is in bone; almost half of magnesium is in cells. Phosphate, as the principal counterion to calcium and magnesium in their dominant pools, has an intermediate proportional distribution. Number in parentheses is the percentage of total for that mineral.

it is able to accumulate minerals. The mineral phase of bone extracellular matrix is a mixture of multiple amorphous and crystalline states, the latter principally as hydroxyapatite crystals: $Ca_5(OH)(PO_4)_3$. From 90 to 95% of osteoid protein is composed of bundles of type I collagen, a long triple helix of two α_1 (type I) chains and one α_2 (type I) chain. The principal collagen of cartilage matrix is type II as a homotrimer of three α_1 (type II) chains. Fibrils of collagen play a major role in the strength of bone (type I collagen), cartilage (type II collagen), and elastic tissues (type III collagen). Their disruption results in characteristic disturbances: osteogenesis imperfecta (type I collagen), chondrodysplasia (type II collagen), Ehlers-Danlos syndrome or arterial aneurysms (type III collagen), and even certain variants of familial osteoarthritis (type II collagen). The second most prominent protein in bone matrix is osteocalcin (or bone Gla-protein); it has a molar content of three residues of γ-carboxyglutamic acid, an unusual amino acid that confers high affinity for calcium on bone crystals. The role of osteocalcin is unknown, but its concentration in blood is a potential index of osteoblast activity. Many other proteins (phosphoproteins, and glycoproteins in bone matrix) with uncertain functions have been identified in the search for molecules regulating bone mineral accumulation and bone growth. Some are covered later.

CELLS. Several cells are highly characteristic of bone. A flat bone-lining cell (perhaps derived from marrow stroma) with few organelles covers many bone surfaces thought not to be undergoing modification. This cell may be a precursor of the osteoblast. The osteoblast is a cuboidal bone matrix-synthesizing cell, derived from bone stromal cells. It lines any periosteal, endosteal, or trabecular surface at which bone formation takes place. Its plasma membrane is highly enriched with a bone-specific isoform of the alkaline phosphatase enzyme. This enzyme promotes bone mineralization by catalyzing, in supersaturated extracellular fluid of bone, the hydrolysis of pyrophosphate and related inhibitors of calcium-phosphate crystallization.

The osteocyte is the principal stable cell inside mature bone. It is probably derived from an osteoblast that has differentiated otherwise to encase itself in bone. Osteocytes are interconnected with one another via long processes that traverse bone canaliculi. Encased in crystals, the osteocyte has unknown roles but is appropriately located to modulate local mineral fluxes.

The chondrocyte, also derived from bone stroma, is the dominant cell of cartilage; it releases to the extracellular matrix type II collagen and vesicles that are rich in alkaline phosphatase and that may be a central organelle for accumulating calcium in preparation for mineralization of cartilage. By its locations such as in embryonic bone and in the cartilaginous growth plate, one likely role is control of bone morphogenesis.

The osteoclast is the main bone-resorbing cell. It is derived from precursors of the premonocyte lineage. It is a highly motile, multinucleated giant cell with several features, specialized for bone. These include organelles that mediate cell attachment to bone surface (podosomes), a strikingly redundant ruffled border for ion transport at its bone face, many enzymes that function in bone resorption, and a high concentration of carbonic anhydrase II, which helps acidify the extracellular pocket between the osteoclast ruffled border and the skeletal resorption surface. Excess osteoclastic activity is central in several important and diverse disorders (Paget's disease, osteoporosis, boney metastases). These are sometimes managed with inhibition of osteoclastic activity, particularly by bisphosphonate drugs.

LOCAL REGULATORS OF BONE CELLS. Bone cells are under systemic and local regulation. Known systemic regulators include parathyroid hormone (PTH), calcitonin, and calcitriol, which are considered later in this chapter. There is also a highly complex network of local controls. The term *osteoclast-activating factors* was applied in the 1980s to incompletely characterized components in fluids that could activate bone resorption in vitro. Some of their active components have been identified. For example, interleukin-1 and lymphotoxin/tumor necrosis factor-β (TNFβ) are potential stimulators of bone resorption that are released locally by some tumors in bone. They cannot act directly on mature osteoclasts but can act through nearby cells, such as osteoblasts or marrow stromal cells, that communicate with osteoclasts. At least three molecules in the TNF and TNF-ligand family form the main pathway that can mediate osteoblastic activation of the osteoclast; these are RANK-ligand on the osteoblast, RANK, the osteoclastic surface receptor for RANK-ligand, and osteoprotegerin, a mimic of membranous RANK in bone extracellular fluid. Specific drugs directed at this pathway are under development. Parathyroid

architecture of bone responds to changes in mechanical load. Mature bone adopts one of two macroscopic organizations (Fig. 257–2). The cortices of all bones and the interior of certain bones have a continuous layered structure termed *cortical* or *lamellar* bone. Lamellar bone, which is predominant in the long bones, is characterized by little metabolic activity and few cells. It has a highly organized extracellular matrix of mineral and parallel protein bundles, mainly of type I collagen. During embryonic development, or in states with pathologic increase of bone turnover, bone assumes a less organized "woven" architecture. Within the vertebral bodies and in portions of the interior of other bones, bone tissue is organized as a series of thin, interdigitating plates; this is termed *trabecular, cancellous,* or *spongy bone*. Its higher cellularity and higher ratio of surface to volume are better suited to rapid turnover.

EXTRACELLULAR MATRIX. Newly deposited osteoid, the nonmineralized or organic component of the skeletal extracellular matrix, undergoes a poorly understood maturation process for 1 to 3 weeks until

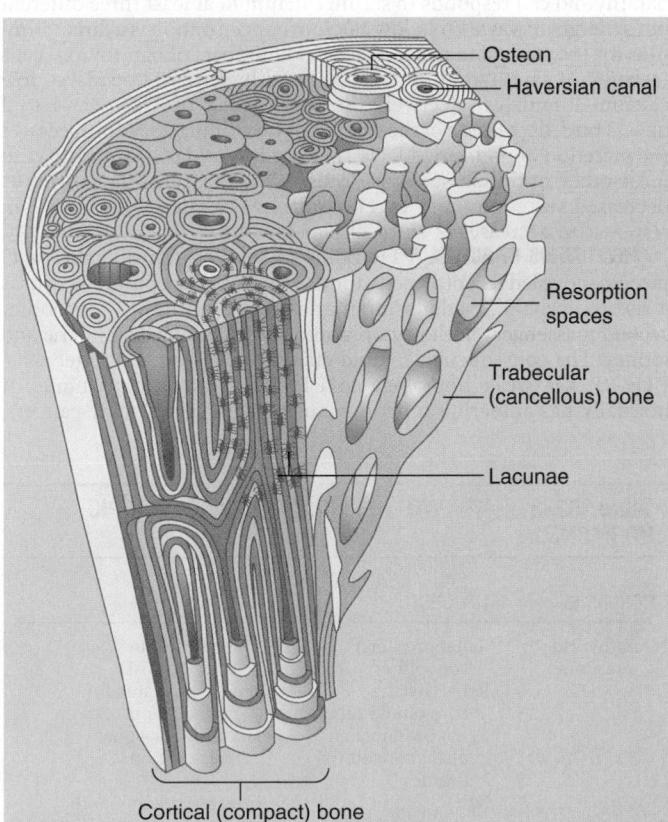

FIGURE 257–2 • Bone organization. Microstructure of mature bone; areas of cortical (lamellar) and trabecular (cancellous) bone are shown. The central area in the transverse section shows differences in mineral density as degrees of shading. Note the organization of osteons, the distribution of osteocyte lacunae, and the organization of bone lamellae. (Adapted from Warwick R, Williams PL [eds]: Gray's Anatomy, 35th ed. Edinburgh, Churchill Livingstone, 1973, p 217.)

hormone-related protein (PTH-RP) is a local mediator of diverse functions in many tissues. For example, it regulates chondrocyte differentiation. When oversecreted by a tumor into blood, PTH-RP can be the principal cause of humoral hypercalcemia of malignancy. Like the activators of bone resorption, the activators of bone formation are poorly understood, particularly because this process involves an interplay of osteoblast proliferation and differentiation. Some local contributors to this process include insulin-like growth factor I and transforming growth factor-β; the latter is present selectively and at high concentrations in osteoblasts and osteocytes. In addition, bone morphogenetic proteins are a family of major embryo pattern determinants (homologues of transforming growth factor-β) that can induce bone formation in soft-tissue sites. Prostaglandins can stimulate bone formation or bone resorption, and they may be important mediators in inflammatory processes of the skeletal system.

REMODELING. Bone growth or modeling occurs initially within a membrane or along the edge of cartilage (e.g., periosteum or epiphyseal growth plate). Although it contains few cells, cortical bone is constantly undergoing slow and orderly cycles of localized resorption and then rebuilding. This process is described as the local remodeling unit (alternately termed *osteon* [see Fig. 257–2] or *basic multicellular unit*). Remodeling begins with osteoclasts excavating a cavity in mature bone; as this resorption tunnel advances, osteoclasts are replaced by other cells and eventually osteoblasts. Over an interval of several months, new bone is deposited in cylindric lamellae around the rim of the cavity until it is refilled to complete this cycle. This cycle is an important example of the coordinated relation between the bone resorption and bone formation processes. Most perturbations that modify one component of these two processes also modify the other in the same direction. The determinants of this coupling between bone resorption and formation are not well known, but they probably include a host of growth factors present at high local concentrations in bone extracellular matrix and exposed or released by the skeletal resorption process.

Intestines

MINERAL ABSORPTION. The intestinal absorption of magnesium and phosphate is not subject to fine regulation and has not been studied intensively. By contrast, intestinal absorption of calcium is tightly regulated and has been analyzed in detail. Most calcium absorption is accomplished in the small bowel. Over a wide range of calcium intakes, approximately 10% of dietary calcium is absorbed passively; the remainder of net intestinal absorption of calcium is regulated by active vitamin D metabolites, especially 1a,25(OH)$_2$D, in blood. With a normal diet, approximately 30% of calcium is absorbed. With low dietary calcium, the secondarily high blood 1a,25(OH)$_2$D level can drive fractional calcium absorption to approach 90%.

Kidney

ION FILTRATION AND REABSORPTION. The non–protein-bound fractions of calcium, magnesium, and phosphate from plasma cross the glomerulus. The distal portions of the nephron have efficient and selective systems that can complete the reabsorption from tubular fluid of more than 99% of any one of these minerals. Tubular calcium reabsorption is stimulated principally by PTH; thiazides or lithium can also increase tubular calcium reabsorption. Saline loading, with or without loop diuretics, can inhibit this. Tubular phosphate reabsorption is mainly under negative influence by PTH. FGF23 (23rd member of the fibroblast growth factor gene family) is a phosphaturic peptide oversecreted by some tumors. It also contributes to some nontumoral hypophosphatemias.

Integrated Fluxes: Mineral Balance and Nutrition

Skeletal growth is maximal throughout childhood and nears completion during adolescence. Until this time, the rate of skeletal calcium accretion is typically 200 to 400 mg (5 to 10 mmol)/day. Fetal mineralization during the last trimester or milk secretion during lactation imposes similar total daily increments on calcium efflux from maternal blood. The skeleton remains in a state of approximately zero mineral balance between ages 20 and 35 years, after which it slowly loses mass. This loss is greatest in the trabecular bone of the vertebrae, attaining peak loss rates about the menopause. This is most

striking (e.g., 3 to 10% per year) during the first 1 to 4 years after surgically induced menopause.

Normal adults can sustain zero calcium balance with daily calcium intakes between 400 and 1500 mg (10 to 37.5 mmol), mainly as dairy products. Typical daily calcium intakes in the United States are 500 to 800 mg (12.5 to 20 mmol), and there is uncertainty over the minimal calcium intake level to sustain optimal skeletal health. With a typical daily calcium intake of 700 mg (17.5 mmol), about one fourth, or 175 mg (4.37 mmol), is absorbed; during skeletal balance, this amount must equal the amount lost in urinary excretion (disregarding the small amount of calcium lost from skin).

Because of the large mineral fluxes between blood and the three principal exchanging pools (bone, renal tubular lumen, and intestinal lumen), it is often difficult to attribute mild disruptions to one pool. For example, there is uncertainty whether the slow bone losses with age-associated osteoporosis reflect primary disturbances of calcium flux in bone, in the intestine, or in combinations of these.

HORMONAL REGULATORS OF MINERAL HOMEOSTASIS

Parathyroid Hormone

SYNTHESIS, SECRETION, AND METABOLISM. PTH is a rapidly regulated hormone that sustains calcium and 1α,25(OH)$_2$D in blood and depresses phosphate in blood (Table 257–3). PTH is stored in the parathyroid cell mainly as a native peptide of 84 amino acids. The parathyroid cell secretes PTH as the native molecule or as fragments, only some of which are biologically active. Fragments are also generated after secretion of PTH into blood. The amino terminus of PTH (residues 1 to 34) is required for PTH receptor binding and biologic activity.

BLOOD CALCIUM EFFECT ON PARATHYROID GLAND. The parathyroid gland regulates blood levels of PTH and consequently of 1α,25(OH)$_2$D and is exquisitely sensitive (through its membrane-bound receptor for extracellular calcium) to changes of ionized calcium in blood. The parathyroid cell responds to serum calcium in at least three different but synergistic ways. First, low calcium concentration is a direct stimulus for the gradual increase in size and numbers of parathyroid cells (secondary parathyroid hypertrophy and hyperplasia). Second, low calcium stimulates selectively the biosynthesis of PTH over 1 to 2 days. Third, depression of the calcium level stimulates within seconds the secretion of preformed PTH. The parathyroid cell contrasts with most other hormone secretory cells, which exhibit unchanged or decreased secretion (e.g., C-cell control of calcitonin secretion) in response to decreases of extracellular calcium.

MECHANISMS OF ACTION. PTH binds to a seven-transmembrane G protein–coupled receptor; activation of that PTH receptor then causes a rise of cyclic 3′,5′-adenosine monophosphate (cAMP) and other second messengers in the cytoplasm of PTH target cells in bone and kidney. The consequence is rapid effects of PTH on the target cells. PTH-RP has weak homology to PTH at the amino terminus; it normally has autocrine functions but is secreted by many cancers,

Table 257–3 • EFFECTS OF PRINCIPAL CALCIOTROPIC HORMONES

HORMONE	PRINCIPAL TARGET TISSUES	ACTION
Parathyroid hormone	Renal proximal convoluted tubule	Increase serum 1α,25(OH)$_2$D
	Renal distal convoluted tubule	Increase calcium reabsorption
	Renal proximal and distal convoluted tubules	Decrease phosphate reabsorption
	Bone	Increase calcium and phosphate resorption
Calcitonin	Bone	Decrease calcium and phosphate resorption
1α,25(OH)$_2$D	Small bowel	Increase calcium absorption
	Bone	Increase calcium and phosphate resorption
	Parathyroid gland	Decrease synthesis of PTH

causing hypercalcemia through its interactions with the same PTH receptors.

ACTION IN BONE. PTH in bone stimulates osteoblasts and osteoclasts. The effects on osteoclasts are indirect because these cells lack receptors for PTH. Stimulation of RANK-ligand on the osteoblast is an indirect mediator of osteoclast activation by PTH. Very high PTH levels result in a clear excess of bone resorption over bone formation. With exogenous administration, PTH analogs can increase bone density.

ACTION IN KIDNEY. PTH acts in the kidney to stimulate the synthesis of $1\alpha,25(OH)_2D$ by increasing the activity of $25OHD_31\alpha$-hydroxylase in the proximal tubules. PTH acts in the distal portions of the nephron to increase tubular reabsorption of calcium. In addition, PTH inhibits phosphate reabsorption in the distal and proximal tubules. PTH also inhibits bicarbonate reabsorption.

ACTION ON INTESTINE. PTH has no important direct action on the intestine. However, the direct renal effect of PTH to increase serum $1\alpha,25(OH)_2D$ causes highly important secondary effects through calcitriol action on intestinal calcium absorption.

Calcitonin

SYNTHESIS AND SECRETION. Calcitonin is a peptide of 32 amino acids that is normally synthesized and secreted by the parafollicular or C cells, which are neuroectodermal cells around the follicles in the thyroid gland. Calcitonin secretion is stimulated by calcium and by certain intestinal peptides (gastrin and glucagon) (Chapter 261).

ACTIONS. Calcitonin, at high concentrations, can directly inhibit osteoclast function. Calcitonin can also act in the kidney to cause mild natriuresis. These calcitonin actions are not important in normal human physiology. The principal interests in calcitonin are as a tumor marker, particularly for familial parafollicular or C-cell neoplasia, or as a pharmacologic agent to treat osteolytic bone disorders, such as Paget's disease.

Vitamin D and Its Metabolites

SYNTHESIS OF VITAMIN D. Vitamin D_3 is a secosteroid (i.e., a steroid with one ring opened) synthesized from 7-dehydro-cholesterol in the epidermis (Fig. 257–3), in a reaction catalyzed by ultraviolet (UV) light derived from the sun. UV exposure depends on time outdoors, latitude, season, and atmospheric particles. Vitamin D_2, produced synthetically from the plant sterol ergosterol, is a vitamin D_3 analogue used as a dietary supplement or drug. The metabolism and actions of vitamin D_3 and vitamin D_2 are similar in humans. The more widespread use of vitamin D_2 in place of D_3 in the United States is a coincidence, the result of the earlier discovery of D_2 around 1930. Vitamin D fortification of foods and the resulting prevention of vitamin D deficiency, rickets, and osteomalacia was a major public health milestone.

HYDROXYLATIONS OF VITAMIN D METABOLITES. Vitamin D ("D" herein refers to combinations of the D_3 and D_2 isoforms) is converted to 25OHD in hepatocytes. This reaction is not under metabolic control and is determined principally by the serum levels of its precursor, vitamin D. 25OHD is normally converted to $1\alpha,25(OH)_2D$ (calcitriol) only in the renal proximal tubule by a cytochrome P450 enzyme system (CYP27B1) stimulated by PTH. Thus, deficient production of calcitriol is a component of PTH deficiency and many renal disorders. A similar PTH-independent 1α-hydroxylation occurs in the normal placenta and abnormally in granuloma tissues, as in sarcoidosis. 25OHD and $1\alpha,25(OH)_2D$ can also be hydroxylated at other residues (C-23, C-24, C-26), but these and other conversions serve mainly to inactivate vitamin D metabolites. The 1α-hydroxylase, in addition to being stimulated by PTH, is inhibited by $1\alpha,25(OH)_2D$. Also, $1\alpha,25(OH)_2D$ activates the hydroxylases that inactivate vitamin D metabolites, completing a feedback loop.

ABSORPTION AND TRANSPORT OF VITAMIN D METABOLITES. Vitamin D metabolites enter the bloodstream like other sterols, and a small fraction of all vitamin D metabolites undergoes an enterohepatic recirculation. When cutaneous synthesis of vitamin D is marginal, any cause of intestinal malabsorption can result in vitamin D deficiency. Vitamin D metabolites are lipid soluble; they circulate in plasma bound to a specific 25OHD binding protein and, to a lesser degree, to other carriers.

MECHANISM OF ACTION OF VITAMIN D METABOLITES. Vitamin D is an inactive precursor; its derived 25OHD and $1\alpha,25(OH)_2D$ forms are both active. Although the concentration of total 25OHD is about 1000-fold higher than that of total $1\alpha,25(OH)_2D$ in blood, the latter has higher comparative affinity for the vitamin D receptor and normally determines the degree of vitamin D receptor activation. Calcitriol binds to intracellular receptors in target cells. The vitamin D receptor is highly homologous to the receptors for true steroids and to those for thyroid hormone and retinoic acid. All are DNA-binding regulators of transcription from selected genes.

INTESTINAL ACTIONS OF CALCITRIOL. Calcitriol increases the flux of calcium from the intestinal lumen to blood. This is its one principal direct action on normal physiology. Calcitriol, to a much lesser extent, increases the flux of phosphate and magnesium from intestinal lumen to blood.

SKELETAL EFFECTS OF CALCITRIOL. The principal effects of calcitriol on bone (antirachitic effects) are indirect results of its action to promote calcium influx from intestinal lumen to blood. The deficient bone mineralization in vitamin D deficiency states is the consequence of the combination of low calcium in blood and low phosphate in blood, the latter resulting from the renal phosphate-wasting effects from secondary hyperparathyroidism. Any direct anabolic effect of calcitriol on bone cells is controversial.

Although physiologic calcitriol levels help move calcium to bone, the supraphysiologic concentrations of vitamin D metabolites sometimes reached during pharmacotherapy can raise blood calcium in part by increasing osteoclast numbers and activity and thereby paradoxically increasing bone resorption and calcium flux from bone to blood.

OTHER EFFECTS OF CALCITRIOL. Calcitriol, independent of blood calcium, can inhibit PTH biosynthesis and secretion; these direct negative effects of calcitriol might contribute a form of short-loop negative feedback to parathyroid function. Calcitriol controls concentrations of renal enzymes that hydroxylate 25OHD; calcitriol decreases the $25OHD_3$ 1α-hydroxylase and increases the other hydroxylases that catabolize 25OHD in the renal tubule and in other tissues. Possibly important effects of calcitriol in skin and hair are suggested by its protective effect on psoriatic skin at pharmacologic doses and by the striking association of total alopecia with the rare hereditary syndrome of severely defective vitamin D receptors. Vitamin D receptors are present in many additional organs and osteoclast precursors, but no role for them has been identified in normal physiology except in the small intestine.

Other Hormones

SEX STEROIDS. Sex steroids, particularly estrogens, have slow but extremely important anabolic effects on bone. Estrogen deficiency results in accelerated bone remodeling with disproportionate bone resorption, particularly in trabecular bone.

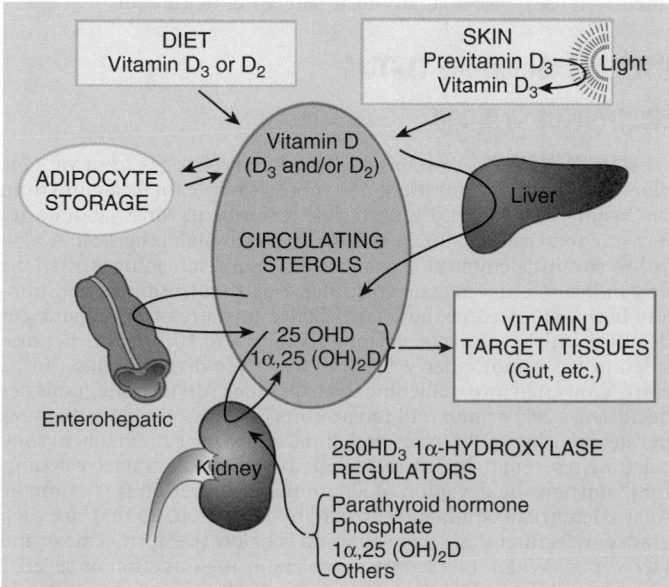

FIGURE 257–3 • The vitamin D activation pathway. This involves steps in many different organs. Dysfunction at any step can have clinically important consequences.

GLUCOCORTICOIDS. Glucocorticoids affect many of the tissues that contribute to mineral metabolism. The most striking effect is bone thinning that results from pathologic or pharmacologic high glucocorticoid concentrations. This thinning is probably a consequence mainly of inhibited osteoblasts. In addition, glucocorticoids antagonize the actions of vitamin D metabolites by unknown mechanisms.

THYROID HORMONE. Thyroid hormones also have direct effects on bone cells. Excess of thyroid hormones causes increased release of calcium from bone. The skeletal consequences of deficient thyroid hormone are most evident in the disordered growth of cartilaginous epiphyses associated with congenital hypothyroidism.

GROWTH HORMONE. Growth hormone stimulates the growth of bone and cartilage, in part by stimulating local production of IGF-1 by osteoblasts and chondrocytes. The result is termed *gigantism* in adolescents and *acromegaly* in adults.

ADAPTATIONS TO DISRUPTIONS OF MINERAL METABOLISM

The two principal calciotropic hormones, PTH and calcitriol, interact with each other and in multiple target tissues to control the metabolism of calcium, phosphate, and, to a lesser degree, magnesium (Fig. 257–4; see Table 257–3). These hormones allow for adaptations over intervals that are short (minutes) or long (months).

Blood levels of ionized calcium are sustained at nearly invariant levels, with minimal diurnal changes reflecting mainly the sudden rises of calcium influx with meals. Serum levels of PTH and calcitriol also show only modest diurnal changes under normal conditions. Serum phosphate typically has broad diurnal fluctuations, with a nadir around 9:00 AM and peaks at around 6:00 PM and 4:00 AM.

Hypercalcemias

States with long-term increase of serum calcium are associated with primary and secondary deviations at multiple steps of the integrated mineral homeostasis system. The most common cause of hypercalcemia is primary overfunction of the parathyroid gland. This has the potential to distort most of the normal calcium regulatory processes. Primary hyperparathyroidism results in high blood levels of PTH and often of $1\alpha,25(OH)_2D$ as well. The results are combinations of increased calcium influx to blood dependent on the evoked dysfunctions in intestinal, skeletal, and renal lumenal pools of calcium. A different integrated metabolic pattern results when hypercalcemia is caused

by dysfunction outside the parathyroid; for example, with osteolytic metastases, skeletal immobilization, or dietary calcium overload (milk-alkali syndrome). In the latter disturbances, the parathyroid gland reacts appropriately and becomes suppressed by the increase of ionized calcium in blood; blood concentrations of PTH and $1\alpha,25(OH)_2D$ become low. The abnormally high renal filtered load of calcium without the anticalciuric effects of PTH results in severe hypercalciuria; with such hypercalciuria, irreversible renal damage can occur over a period of only a few weeks.

Hypocalcemias

Hypocalcemia, if not caused by hypoparathyroidism, results in the parathyroid gland's recognizing the signal of a low ionized calcium level in blood. Increased PTH secretion (within seconds), increased PTH biosynthesis (within days), and parathyroid cell hyperplasia (within weeks) activate its homeostatic pathways. The consequences of this secondary hyperparathyroidism are increased renal tubular secretion of $1\alpha,25(OH)_2D$ (if there is not underlying deficiency of 25OHD or of the 25OHD 1α-hydroxylase) and increased net calcium flux into blood from the intestinal lumen, from bone, and from the renal tubular lumen. The relative contribution of each calcium pool to this integrated response depends in part on the chronic state of that pool and on the relative levels of PTH and calcitriol. Serum calcium typically begins to fall below normal only when the osteolytic response to PTH or to $1\alpha,25(OH)_2D$ becomes weakened (from depletion of readily exchangeable calcium pools or other types of tachyphylaxis). Secondary hyperparathyroidism has important effects on phosphate homeostasis by directly affecting bone and kidney, increasing phosphate influx from bone, and causing a similar increase in phosphate efflux into urine. With hypoparathyroidism, some residual components of mineral homeostasis can be sustained despite a deficiency or complete absence of PTH and secondarily of $1\alpha,25(OH)_2D$.

Metabolic Bone Diseases

Certain forms of metabolic bone disease are associated with dramatic imbalances in mineral flux to or from blood; these include increased calcium influx to blood with aggressive osteolytic processes and decreased calcium influx with many forms of osteomalacia. Osteomalacia is bone softening from a deficiency of mineral in bone matrix; it has diverse causes, many of which are understood. Other forms of metabolic bone disease, because they do not dramatically compromise the readily exchangeable pools of bone mineral, may have little or no long-term impact on the blood homeostatic system. For example, idiopathic osteoporosis has been categorized into two major forms (perimenopausal and aging-associated), but in either form no clear changes in blood PTH or $1\alpha,25(OH)_2D$ have been identified as causes of or adaptations to altered bone calcium.

USES OF LABORATORY TESTING

Electrolytes in Blood

CALCIUM IN BLOOD. To stabilize the calcium changes from variable blood albumin concentration, one should sample total calcium from the fasting patient, who is seated or recumbent. Most laboratories measure total calcium inexpensively and with high precision. A high or low serum calcium value from multichannel screening is often the first indication of a treatable disorder. Serum calcium has traditionally been expressed in the United States in units of milligrams per deciliter, with a typical normal range being 8.8 to 10.2 mg/dL. Because calcium has a molecular weight of 40 and is divalent, this can be easily converted into milliequivalents per liter (divide milligrams per deciliter by 2.0) or into millimolar units (SI units; divide milligrams per deciliter by 4.0). Simple equations allow measurements of total calcium in serum to be "corrected" (to better reflect ionized calcium) for distortions by deviation of albumin concentration (for example, total calcium can be adjusted upward by 1 mg/dL [0.25 mM] for each gram per deciliter that serum albumin is below the normal mean and vice versa). When uncertainty exists about the direction or severity of an abnormality of blood calcium, the ionized calcium fraction should be evaluated directly as it is a more valid and direct reflection of pathophysiology. This is a more demanding laboratory procedure than is total calcium, and the reproducibility is generally worse. An

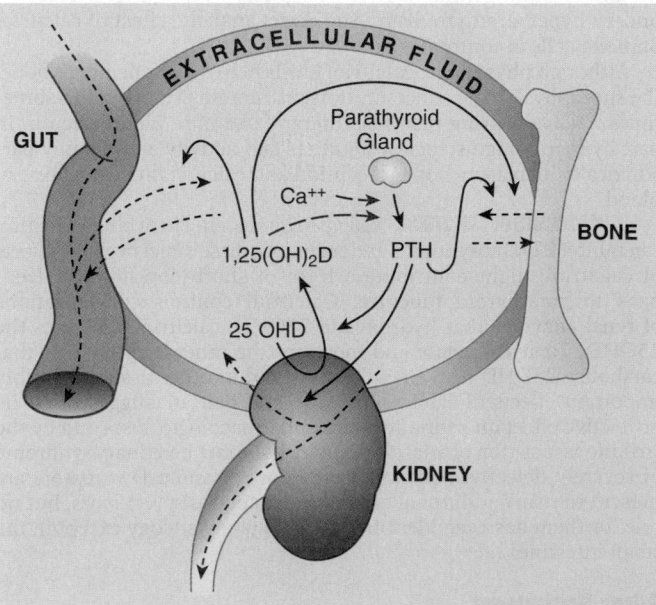

FIGURE 257–4 • Integrated control of secretion and actions of parathyroid hormone (PTH) and calcitriol [$1\alpha,25(OH)_2$ vitamin D = $1\alpha,25(OH)_2D$] with emphasis on calcium fluxes. Solid lines show secretion and targets of PTH and calcitriol. Interrupted black lines are calcium fluxes. Interrupted red lines show inhibitory effects.

abnormality of blood calcium can arise from an abnormal flux to or from the major sites of calcium turnover—bone, gut, and renal luminal fluid.

PHOSPHATE IN BLOOD. Phosphate measurements in serum represent only the 30% that is in inorganic compounds. By convention, phosphate is reported in units of elemental phosphorus. These conventions avoid some of the confusion that would result from efforts to consider molar anion content (phosphate in serum is in a variable equilibrium between its monobasic and dibasic states). Its principal determinants are PTH, age, gender, food ingestion, and diurnal rhythm. Serum phosphate is only a weak index of intracellular phosphate stores. Its fractional swings about its average are far wider than those for calcium. Thus the morning fasting state is preferred.

MAGNESIUM IN BLOOD. Serum magnesium, like phosphate, is determined by its threshold for renal excretion and by total body pools. Primary disturbance of magnesium in blood is unusual, but important abnormalities can occur during major illnesses; for example, in association with chemotherapy or with extensive burns; tissue necrosis may increase blood magnesium, while large fluid losses could depress it.

Hormones in Blood

PARATHYROID HORMONE. PTH is often the first parameter that should be examined when evaluating a possible disturbance of mineral homeostasis. A two-site immunoassay can give a result that is a practical index of intact, biologically active PTH although the assay also cross-reacts with a minority component of inactive PTH forms, missing the far amino terminus. Clinical correlations are excellent with this assay, and only small adjustment is generally needed for renal compromise.

CALCITONIN. Calcitonin is also measured by immunoassay. Clinical uses are limited. When calcitonin assays are used in management of C-cell neoplasia, it is particularly important to use normal ranges, adjusted for the selected C-cell challenge protocol and the patient's age. *RET* gene sequencing is the preferred test for diagnosis of multiple endocrine neoplasia, type 2.

25-HYDROXYVITAMIN D. Vitamin D, the inactive precorsor, is rarely measured in clinical settings. However, two different vitamin D metabolites can be measured. It is essential to understand that these two metabolites, 25OHD and $1\alpha,25(OH)_2D$, are usually indicators of two entirely different types of process. Serum 25OHD is a useful index of vitamin D nutritional status and of the efficacy of selected vitamin D analogs as drugs. It is also a good index of sterol absorption. Low levels can result from deficiency of sunlight, from deficiency of vitamin D nutritional supplementation, from fat malabsorption, and from accelerated hepatic catabolism of vitamin D metabolites. Because the body easily compensates for 25OHD concentrations well above normal, dangerously high levels occur only with intake of pharmacologic doses of vitamin D or of 25OHD.

$1\alpha,25$-DIHYDROXYVITAMIN D. $1\alpha,25(OH)_2D$ (calcitriol) measurement in serum gives an index of this secosteroid hormone, whose renal production is usually finely regulated by blood PTH. Even with vitamin D intoxication and high blood 25OHD, the serum levels of $1\alpha,25(OH)_2D$ may be appropriately low because of its regulatory system. Serum $1\alpha,25(OH)_2D$ has only limited diagnostic use. However, certain states can be associated with otherwise unexplainable mineral disturbances that reflect high levels of $1\alpha,25(OH)_2D$ (sarcoidosis and other granulomatous diseases) or low levels (certain renal tubular disorders, such as X-linked hypophosphatemia). Because of rapid half-time in blood (3 to 6 hours), calcitriol levels are rarely used as a monitor of its pharmacologic efficacy.

BLOOD INDICES OF BONE DISTURBANCE. Alkaline phosphatase in serum is an index of its sources in bone, liver, and placenta and of its excretion by the biliary tree. With increased osteoblastic activity, the amount of skeletal alkaline phosphatase in serum can rise dramatically. Skeletal alkaline phosphatase can be measured selectively through its physicochemical properties (it is the heat-labile component of total alkaline phosphatase) or otherwise (e.g., by immunoassay, a topic for research in several centers). High skeletal alkaline phosphatase levels can point to high bone turnover (hyperparathyroidism, Paget's disease). Specific portions of procollagen type I and other bone-specific proteins are also under investigation as possible specific indicators of skeletal processes. Osteocalcin (sometimes called bone Gla-protein) is another osteoblast-specific protein that has been useful in some long-term studies of bone turnover, but its insensitivity to diffuse bone pathology has compromised its broad clinical use.

Direct Measurements on the Skeleton

BONE RADIOGRAMS AND BONE SCANS. Standard radiography is often the starting point in evaluating bone disorders. Images can be specific for numerous conditions or can direct further diagnostic procedures (i.e., bone biopsy) to sites of focal disturbance. A bone scan with technetium-99m diphosphonate may identify a local disturbance that is not accompanied by radiographic change; the label adsorbs to bone mineral, and increased local blood flow without fracture is sufficient to give a positive signal.

BONE MASS INDICES. Bone mass can be measured noninvasively with a variety of techniques. These include dual-channel radiographs, single- and dual-channel photon absorptiometry, radiographs with computed tomography, and other methods under development. The choice of one over another should depend largely on local expertise and cost. For sequential studies in a patient, these methods are compromised, to varying degrees, by high cost, lack of precision, and poor correlation between institutions.

BONE BIOPSY. Bone biopsy is not used widely. It can be the final diagnostic tool in identifying local or generalized bone disturbances, such as myeloid neoplasia. It can be particularly useful in distinguishing osteomalacia from osteoporosis. Maximal information about the bone formation process can be obtained after prior administration of two pulses of tetracyclines 14 days apart (tetracyclines selectively adsorb to the mineralization front of osteoid and provide a fluorescent signal in the biopsy sample). When considering this test, the clinician should consult persons knowledgeable about its indications and the details of its processing.

Analyses of the Intestines in Mineral Metabolism

Specific tests of intestinal function are rarely used in current clinical practice. Metabolic balance studies are time consuming and expensive. Calcium absorption studies with radioactive or stable isotopes are not applied outside research settings. Several indices of intestinal function are considered in other chapters.

Analyses of the Kidney and Urine

Renal biopsy should be done only for the standard indications related to intrinsic or systemic diseases in the kidney. Urinary excretion of hydroxyproline and other collagen metabolites is a useful index of bone resorption rates because 60% of urinary hydroxyproline is normally derived from collagen in bone. Pyridinium cross-links, another collagen byproduct in urine, may prove to be a more useful index of bone resorption.

Urinary excretion of calcium, magnesium, or phosphate is useful in screening for total body excess or deficiency of any of these minerals. Urinary excretion of calcium is central in the evaluation of urolithiasis. More detailed discussion of the work-up of urolithiasis is presented elsewhere.

SUGGESTED READINGS

Bilezikian JP, Raisz LG, Rodan GA (eds): Principles of Bone Biology, 2nd ed. New York, Academic Press, 2003. *A multiauthored book, particularly strong in basic principles of bone pathophysiology.*

DeGroot LJ (ed): Endocrinology, 4th ed. Philadelphia, WB Saunders, 2001. *Section IV on the parathyroids has 20 very detailed chapters covering the parathyroids and metabolic bone disease.*

Favus MJ (ed): Primer on the Metabolic Bone Diseases and Disorders of Mineral Metabolism, 4th ed. New York, Lippincott-Raven, 1999. *Concise chapters that quickly advance the reader to current research on a topic.*

258 OSTEOPOROSIS

Joel S. Finkelstein

Definition

Osteoporosis, the most common type of metabolic bone disease, is characterized by a parallel reduction in bone mineral and bone matrix so that bone is decreased in amount but is of normal

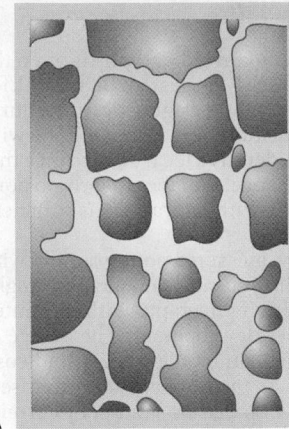 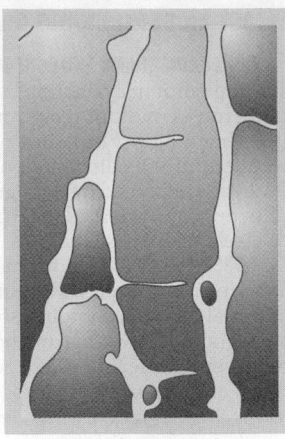

A   B

FIGURE 258–1 • The microarchitecture of normal bone (*A*) and osteoporotic bone (*B*). There is thinning and a loss of trabeculae. (Redrawn from Kumar P, Clark M: Clinical Medicine, 5th ed. London, WB Saunders, 2002.)

composition (Fig. 258–1). As a result, the strength of bone is reduced and the risk of fracture is increased. The World Health Organization's nomenclature uses the term *osteopenia* to refer to a condition in which bone mineral density is between 1 and 2.5 standard deviations below peak bone mass and the term *osteoporosis* to refer to a condition in which bone mineral density is more than 2.5 standard deviations below peak bone mass.

Epidemiology

Osteoporosis affects over 20 million Americans and leads to approximately 1.5 million fractures in the United States each year. During the course of their lifetime, women lose about 50% of their trabecular bone and 30% of their cortical bone, and 40% of all postmenopausal white women eventually sustain osteoporotic fractures. By extreme old age, one third of all women and one sixth of all men will have a hip fracture. The annual cost of health care for osteoporosis is nearly $14 billion in the United States.

Pathobiology

At any point in time, bone density in adults depends on both the peak bone density achieved during development and the subsequent bone loss (Fig. 258–2). Thus, osteopenia can result from deficient pubertal bone accretion, accelerated adult bone loss, or both.

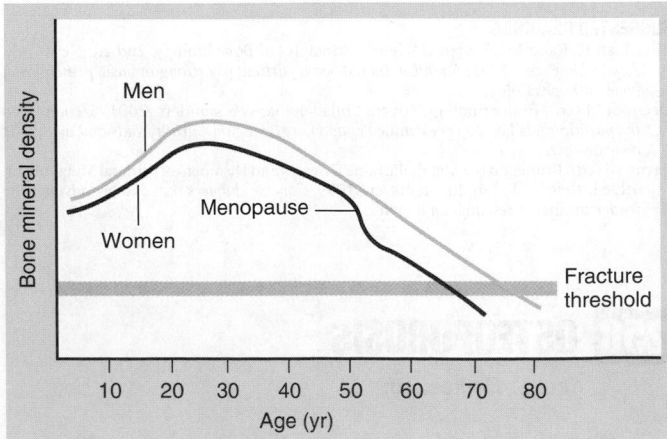

FIGURE 258–2 • Cortical bone mineral density versus age in men and women. Women have lower peak cortical bone density than men and experience a period of rapid bone loss at the time of the menopause, thus reaching the fracture threshold (the level of bone density at which the risk of developing osteoporotic fractures begins to increase) earlier than men.

Table 258–1 • FACTORS THAT MAY AFFECT PEAK BONE MASS
Gender
Race
Genetic factors
Gonadal steroids
Growth hormone
Timing of puberty
Calcium intake
Exercise

DETERMINANTS OF PEAK BONE DENSITY

Bone density is the amount of bone tissue per unit volume. In operational terms, bone density is usually defined as the amount of bone mineral per unit area, so that areal rather than volumetric density is actually measured. Bone density increases dramatically during puberty in response to gonadal steroids and eventually reaches values in young adults that are nearly double those of children. Other factors that influence peak bone density are listed in Table 258–1. Of these, genetic factors account for up to 80% of the variance in peak bone mass. The impact of genetic factors on bone density has been demonstrated in several ways. For example, bone density is lower in the daughters of women with osteoporosis than in the daughters of women without osteoporosis. Moreover, the concordance of bone density is much higher among monozygotic than dizygotic twins. Several genes, including the vitamin D receptor gene, the estrogen receptor gene, the type I procollagen genes, and the low-density lipoprotein receptor-related protein 5 (LRP 5) gene have been implicated as determinants of bone density.

Men have higher bone density than women, and African Americans have higher bone density than Americans of European heritage. These differences are, at least in part, due to differences in bone size and body size and may account for a lower incidence of osteoporotic fractures in men and in African Americans. Peak bone mineral density is reduced in men with histories of constitutionally delayed puberty, a finding that may be important in the pathogenesis of osteoporosis in some men. Similar findings have been reported in women with delayed menarche. Studies in identical twins suggest that moderate calcium supplementation can enhance prepubertal bone accretion. Associations between peak bone density and physical activity during development have also been reported.

PHYSIOLOGIC CAUSES OF ADULT BONE LOSS

After peak bone density is reached, bone density remains stable for years and then declines. Bone loss begins before menses cease in women, although the precise time of onset is unknown. Once menses cease, the rate of bone loss is accelerated several-fold in women. During the first 5 to 10 years of the menopause, trabecular bone is lost faster than cortical bone, with rates of approximately 2 to 4% and 1 to 2% per year, respectively. A woman can lose 10 to 15% of her cortical bone and 25 to 30% of her trabecular bone during this time, a loss that can prevented by estrogen therapy. Furthermore, rates of bone loss vary considerably between women. It is not clear why some postmenopausal women are "fast losers" of bone. A subset of women in whom osteoporosis is more severe than expected for their age are said to have type I, or "postmenopausal," osteoporosis. In these women, accelerated bone resorption is thought to suppress parathyroid hormone, which in turn reduces 1,25-dihydroxyvitamin D formation, which then limits intestinal calcium absorption. Clinically, type I osteoporosis often presents with vertebral "crush" fractures or Colles' fractures. Although the mechanisms whereby estrogen deficiency leads to bone loss are still not established, recent evidence suggests that the skeletal effects of estrogen may be mediated through a system of molecules called receptor activator of nuclear factor-κB ligand (RANKL), its cell surface receptor, receptor activator of nuclear factor-κB (RANK), and its soluble (decoy) receptor osteoprotegerin (OPG) (Fig. 258–3). RANKL is expressed on the surface of osteoblast precursors and RANK is expressed on the surface of osteoclast precursors. Binding of RANKL to RANK, in the presence of permissive levels of macrophage colony-stimulating factor, stimulates the differentia-

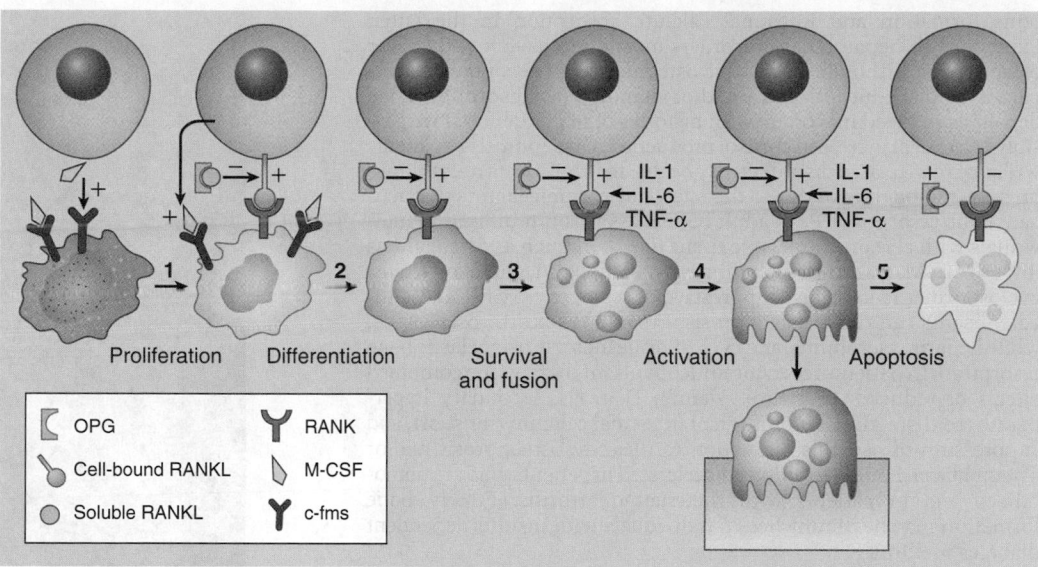

FIGURE 258–3 • Regulation of osteoclast development by receptor activator of nuclear factor-κB ligand (RANKL), receptor activator of nuclear factor-κB (RANK), and osteoprotogerin (OPG). M-CSF = macrophage colony-stimulating factor; c-fms = receptor for M-CSF; IL-1 = interleukin-1; IL-6 = interleukin-6; TNF-α = tumor necrosis factor alpha. (From Hofbauer LC, Heufelder AE: The role of receptor activator of nuclear factor-κB ligand and osteoprotogerin in the pathogenesis and treatment of metabolic bone diseases. J Clin Endocrinol Metab 2000;85:2355–2363.)

tion of osteoclast precursors to mature osteoclasts (see Fig. 258–3). OPG, a circulating protein produced by many cell types, including osteoblasts, binds to RANKL, thereby inhibiting osteoclast development. Estrogen deficiency reduces OPG production and increases RANKL expression on osteoblast precursor cells, actions that should increase osteoclast development and increase bone resorption. In contrast, estrogen administration increases OPG production, and OPG administration abolishes ovariectomy-induced bone loss in rodents. Estrogen deficiency also increases skeletal production of bone-resorbing cytokines such as interleukin-1, interleukin-6, and tumor necrosis factor and reduces skeletal production of growth factors that stimulate bone formation, such as insulin-like growth factor-1 and transforming growth factor-β. The effects of estrogen on the RANK/OPG system may, at least in part, be mediated by its effects on local or systemic production of such cytokines or growth factors. Estrogen deficiency also increases the skeleton's sensitivity to the resorptive effects of parathyroid hormone. Finally, the discovery of estrogen receptors on osteoblasts suggests that estrogen deficiency may also alter bone formation directly.

Once the period of rapid postmenopausal bone loss ends, bone loss continues at a more gradual rate throughout life. The osteoporosis that results from normal aging, which occurs in both women and men, has been termed type II, or "senile," osteoporosis. Because type II osteoporosis is associated with a more balanced decrease in cortical and trabecular bone mass, fractures of the hip, pelvis, wrist, proximal humerus, proximal tibia, and vertebral bodies all occur commonly. Factors that may be important in the pathogenesis of type II osteoporosis include (1) a primary defect in the ability of the kidney to make 1,25-dihydroxyvitamin D and/or decreased intestinal sensitivity to 1,25-dihydroxyvitamin D, leading to diminished calcium absorption and mild secondary hyperparathyroidism; and (2) a decrease in osteoblastic bone formation with aging. The distinctions between type I and type II osteoporosis are often quite arbitrary and there may be considerable overlap between these syndromes. For example, bone loss can be arrested by estrogen administration even in the elderly.

SECONDARY CAUSES OF ADULT BONE LOSS

A large number of disorders can lead to osteoporosis independent from the normal effects of the menopause in women and aging in both women and men (Table 258–2). For example, young women who develop estrogen deficiency due to hyperprolactinemia, anorexia nervosa, or hypothalamic amenorrhea frequently lose bone in a manner similar to that which occurs at the onset of the natural menopause. Hypogonadism is also an important secondary cause of osteoporosis in men. Other endocrine disorders such as hyperthyroidism, hyperparathyroidism, hypercortisolism, and growth hormone deficiency are important secondary causes of osteoporosis primarily due to increased bone resorption in the former two disorders and decreased

Table 258–2 • SECONDARY CAUSES OF OSTEOPOROSIS

Endocrine diseases
  Female hypogonadism
    Hyperprolactinemia
    Hypothalamic amenorrhea
    Anorexia nervosa
    Premature and primary ovarian failure
  Male hypogonadism
    Primary gonadal failure (e.g., Klinefelter's syndrome)
    Secondary gonadal failure (e.g., idiopathic hypogonadotropic hypogonadism)
    Delayed puberty
  Hyperthyroidism
  Hyperparathyroidism
  Hypercortisolism
  Growth hormone deficiency
  Vitamin D deficiency
  Idiopathic hypercalciuria
  Diabetes mellitus
Gastrointestinal diseases
  Subtotal gastrectomy
  Malabsorption syndromes
  Chronic obstructive jaundice
  Primary biliary cirrhosis and other cirrhoses
  Alactasia
Bone marrow disorders
  Multiple myeloma
  Lymphoma
  Leukemia
  Hemolytic anemias
  Systemic mastocytosis
  Disseminated carcinoma
Connective tissue diseases
  Osteogenesis imperfecta
  Ehlers-Danlos syndrome
  Marfan's syndrome
  Homocystinuria
Drugs
  Alcohol
  Heparin
  Glucocorticoids
  Thyroxine
  Anticonvulsants
  Gonadotropin-releasing hormone agonists
  Cyclosporine
  Tacrolimus
  Chemotherapy
Miscellaneous causes
  Immobilization
  Rheumatoid arthritis
  Renal tubular acidosis

Diseases of Bone and Mineral Metabolism

bone formation and intestinal calcium absorption in the latter. Patients with hepatobiliary disorders most often have low-turnover osteoporosis, although some have osteomalacia or secondary hyperparathyroidism due to calcium and/or vitamin D malabsorption. Bone density is reduced in women with histories of major depression, possibly because of increased cortisol production. Osteoporosis in patients with marrow-related disorders may be due to local effects of cytokines on bone remodeling or due to the release of systemic factors that activate bone resorption. Peak adult bone mass is compromised in individuals with certain connective tissue disorders such as osteogenesis imperfecta. Many drugs, including ethanol, heparin, glucocorticoids, cyclosporine, tacrolimus, suppressive doses of thyroxine, and anticonvulsants can cause osteoporosis. Ethanol is toxic to osteoblasts, while heparin, tacrolimus, and cyclosporine increase osteoclastic bone resorption. In patients receiving anticonvulsant therapy, the combined effects of reduced 25-hydroxyvitamin D levels, secondary hyperparathyroidism, direct inhibition of intestinal calcium transport, and suppression of osteoblast function can lead to osteoporosis and/or osteomalacia. Bone resorption is accelerated in patients who are immobilized and in patients with rheumatoid arthritis. Finally, bone formation may be diminished in individuals with insulin-dependent diabetes mellitus.

Clinical Manifestations

Osteoporosis is asymptomatic unless it results in a fracture—usually a vertebral compression fracture or a fracture of the wrist, hip, ribs, pelvis, or humerus. Vertebral compression fractures often occur with minimal stress, such as with sneezing, bending, or lifting a light object. The middle and lower thoracic and upper lumbar regions are most frequently involved. Back pain usually begins acutely and often radiates laterally to the flanks and anteriorly. The pain subsides gradually over a period of weeks to months and recurs with the occurrence of new fractures. Patients with fractures that result in spinal deformity may have a chronic backache that is made worse by standing. Such patients lose height and may develop the characteristic dorsal kyphosis and cervical lordosis known as the "dowager's hump." In some patients, vertebral collapse can occur slowly and without symptoms. Fractures of the femoral neck and intertrochanteric region are the most devastating complication of osteoporosis. Hip fractures are associated with falls, occurring either as a result of modest trauma or, in some instances, prior to the fall. The likelihood of suffering a hip fracture during a fall is also related to the direction of the fall, so that fractures are more likely to occur when the person falls to the side, probably because there is less soft tissue available to dissipate the impact. Secondary complications of hip fractures, such as pulmonary thromboembolism or nosocomial infections, carry a mortality rate of 15 to 20% in elderly patients, and an additional 30% of hip fracture victims require long-term nursing home care.

A characteristic radiograph of osteoporosis of the spine is shown in Figure 258–4. With the loss of trabecular bone in the vertebral bodies, the vertebral end plates appear to be accentuated. The normal contrast between the radiodensity of the spinal column and the adjacent soft tissues also may be lost. Vertebral deformity may take the form of collapse (reduction in both anterior and posterior height), anterior wedging (reduction in anterior height), or the so-called "codfish" deformity (due to weakening of the subchondral plates and expansion of the intervertebral discs). Protrusion of the intervertebral discs in the vertebral bodies produces Schmorl's nodules. In the absence of fractures, radiographs are insensitive indicators of bone loss because a substantial reduction in bone mass is required before it is visible on radiographs.

Diagnosis

The diagnosis of osteoporosis can be made by either documenting a typical fragility fracture or measuring bone mineral density. The World Health Organization nomenclature uses the term *osteopenia* for bone mineral density between 1 and 2.5 standard deviations below peak bone mass and the term *osteoporosis* for bone mineral density more than 2.5 standard deviations below peak bone mass. Bone densitometry cannot distinguish between osteoporosis and osteomalacia.

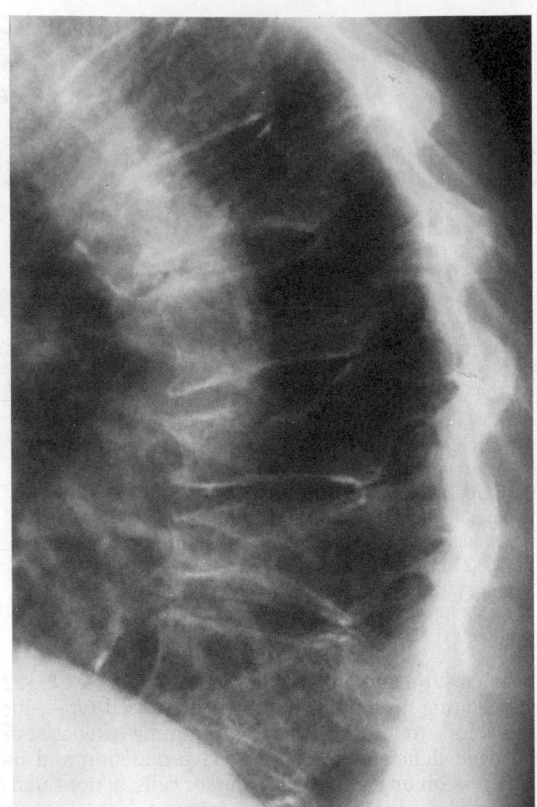

FIGURE 258–4 • Radiograph showing radiolucency, compression fractures, and kyphosis in the spine of a patient with osteoporosis.

BONE DENSITOMETRY

Several techniques are available for measuring bone mineral density in the axial and appendicular skeleton. Large prospective studies have demonstrated that bone density measurements of the distal and proximal radius, os calcis, proximal femur, or spine can predict the development of the major types of osteoporotic fractures, including hip fractures. In general, for every 1 standard deviation that bone mineral density decreases, the risk of all future osteoporotic fractures increases by about 50%, regardless of the technique or the skeletal site used to assess bone density. A bone density measurement at a specific skeletal site predicts fractures at that site better than bone density measurements made at a different skeletal site, however.

Bone density results are traditionally expressed as either the T or the Z score. The T score is the number of standard deviations by which the patient's bone density differs from the peak bone density of individuals of the same gender and ethnicity. The Z score is the number of standard deviations by which the patient's bone density differs from bone density of age-matched individuals of the same gender and ethnicity.

Techniques for assessing bone density differ greatly in their reproducibility, radiation exposure, examination time, cost, and sensitivity for detecting osteoporosis. Because it measures trabecular bone in the vertebral bodies, quantitative computed tomography of the spine is the most sensitive method for diagnosing osteoporosis. However, because the expense and radiation dose of quantitative computed tomography are high and its reproducibility is relatively poor, it is not an ideal technique when repeat measurements aimed at detecting small changes in bone density are needed. Single photon absorptiometry of the proximal forearm has good precision and low radiation exposure but is relatively insensitive for detecting osteoporosis because it measures cortical bone, which is lost more slowly than trabecular bone in the early menopause. For most patients, dual energy x-ray absorptiometry (DEXA) of either the lumbar spine or the proximal femur is the method of choice for measuring bone mineral density. Because DEXA scans of the spine in the posterior-anterior projection include both the trabecular-rich vertebral bodies and the cortical-rich posterior spinal elements, DEXA measurements of the spine are not as sensitive as quantitative computed tomography for detecting early trabecular bone loss. However, its far greater precision, low radiation dose, rapid examination time, and lower cost make DEXA preferable to quantitative computed tomography in most situations. Most DEXA scanners can measure spinal bone mineral density in both the posterior-anterior and lateral projections. Lateral spine DEXA is more sensitive than posterior-anterior spine DEXA for detecting osteoporosis, although its reproducibility is somewhat lower. In men older than 50 years of age, degenerative changes in the posterior spinous elements are so common that posterior-anterior spine DEXA is often unreliable. DEXA measurements of the proximal femur predict hip fractures better than measurements made at other sites and may be preferred in elderly patients in whom focal osteosclerosis associated with degenerative changes of the posterior spine can mask decreases in bone mineral density of the vertebral bodies. DEXA of the spine is clearly superior to DEXA of the proximal femur for assessing changes in bone density over time.

BIOCHEMICAL MARKERS OF BONE TURNOVER

In recent years, there has been considerable interest in tests for biochemical markers of osteoblast (serum osteocalcin, bone-specific alkaline phosphatase, type-1 procollagen amino-terminal propeptide, and type-1 procollagen carboxy-terminal propeptide) and osteoclast (urine hydroxyproline, urine pyridinium cross links, urine cross-linked C-telopeptides of type 1 collagen, urine cross-linked N-telopeptides of type 1 collagen, and carboxyterminal telopeptide of type 1 collagen) activity. In theory, a simple blood or urine test that could predict rates of bone loss or the response to therapy would be of great value. The clinical utility of routine measurements of these biochemical markers of bone turnover has not been established, however. Some data suggest that measurements of bone formation or resorption markers, either alone or in combination, can predict rates of bone loss in postmenopausal women receiving calcium or other antiresorptive agents whereas other data do not. Bone turnover markers may also be independent predictors for osteoporotic fracture after adjusting for bone mineral density. At present, routine use of bone turnover measurements is not recommended because they do not predict clinical end points sufficiently well in individual patients.

SECONDARY CAUSES OF OSTEOPOROSIS

Secondary causes of osteoporosis should be sought in patients with an established diagnosis of osteoporosis, particularly when the bone density is significantly lower than that of age- and sex-matched individuals. A history and physical examination that focuses on the factors that may affect peak bone mass (see Table 258–1) and secondary causes of osteoporosis (see Table 258–2), and selected laboratory tests, are sufficient in most patients. Levels of serum calcium, inorganic phosphate, and alkaline phosphatase are usually normal in patients with osteoporosis, although alkaline phosphatase may be elevated transiently after a fracture. A sustained elevation of the alkaline phosphatase level, in the absence of liver disease, may suggest osteomalacia, Paget's disease, or skeletal metastases. Other routine chemistry tests can help exclude renal or hepatic diseases, and a complete blood cell count may help uncover a hematologic or myeloproliferative disorder. Because multiple myeloma can mimic involutional osteoporosis, it should be considered when evaluating patients with osteoporosis, particularly those with unexpectedly severe disease. Measuring serum parathyroid hormone and 25-hydroxyvitamin D levels is recommended to exclude hyperparathyroidism and vitamin D deficiency. A serum thyroid-stimulating hormone level should be checked when thyroid disease is suspected. Because a patient with Cushing's syndrome can present with osteoporosis, a 24-hour urinary free cortisol or an overnight dexamethasone suppression test may be useful. In men with unexplained osteoporosis, a serum testosterone level and a 24-hour urine sample for calcium and creatinine should be measured. Measurements of bone turnover markers may be useful when evaluating patients with osteoporosis of unknown cause or of unexplained severity. Finally, in selected patients, iliac crest bone biopsy after double tetracycline labeling may be useful, particularly for distinguishing osteoporosis from osteomalacia.

Prevention and Treatment

At present, it is not possible to reverse established osteoporosis. Early intervention, however, can prevent osteoporosis in most people,

and later intervention can halt the progression of osteoporosis once it has developed. The choice of treatment for osteoporosis depends on its cause and the stage of the illness. If a secondary cause of osteoporosis is present, specific treatment should be aimed at correcting the underlying disorder. During the acute phase of vertebral compression, attention is directed toward relieving pain with analgesics, muscle relaxants, heat, massage, and/or rest. Many patients with discomfort related to osteoporotic fractures or deformity benefit from a well-designed program of physical therapy. Some patients appear to benefit from a corset or an orthopedic back brace. Both weight-bearing and non-weight-bearing exercises appear to have beneficial effects on bone mass. For most patients, exercises to strengthen the abdominal and back muscles are appropriate, and referral to a physical therapist with expertise in treating osteoporotic patients is often helpful. Precautions to prevent falls, including a review of medications that can affect stability, a survey of the home environment to ensure proper lighting, railings, and stable walking surfaces, and exercises to improve muscle strength and tone, should be taken. Pharmacologic therapy is aimed at preventing further bone loss and decreasing the likelihood of future fracture.

CALCIUM

Both dietary calcium intake and fractional intestinal calcium absorption decrease with age. Most postmenopausal women consume less than 500 mg of calcium in their diet each day. The effects of calcium supplementation on bone mass in early postmenopausal women have been examined in several prospective, randomized trials. In general, it appears that calcium can retard, but not arrest, cortical bone loss from the forearm in women who are within the first several years of the menopause. Most studies have failed to demonstrate a protective effect of calcium on spinal bone loss in early postmenopausal women. Calcium therapy appears to be more effective in arresting bone loss in late than in early postmenopausal women, although most studies indicate that administering calcium does not halt their bone loss completely. Calcium supplementation, however, is clearly less effective than estrogen or other antiresorptive agents. Overall, it appears that calcium therapy is somewhat beneficial in both early and late postmenopausal women. Additional therapy is needed, however, if the goal of therapy is to prevent bone loss completely. Calcium supplementation, together with vitamin D, reduces the risk of nonvertebral fractures in men and women older than 65 years of age. [1,2] In the United States, the recommended daily calcium intake for adolescents and young adults between the ages of 11 and 24 years is 1200 to 1500 mg. The recommended daily calcium intake for men between 25 and 65 years and women between 25 and 50 years is 1000 mg. Postmenopausal women up to the age of 65 years should consume 1000 mg of calcium per day if they are also on hormone replacement therapy and 1500 mg of calcium per day in the absence of estrogen replacement. All adults over the age of 65 should consume 1500 mg of calcium daily.

ESTROGEN

Estrogen therapy inhibits osteoclastic bone resorption. It prevents both cortical and trabecular bone loss in estrogen-deficient women and is effective if administered orally or topically. Estrogen therapy prevents bone loss in both early and late postmenopausal women. On average, spinal bone mineral density increases 3 to 5% during the first 3 years of estrogen therapy and significant bone loss is rare among women who are compliant with their treatment regimen. Because bone loss is most rapid in the first years of the menopause, the benefits of estrogen therapy probably are greater if started during this time before a substantial amount of bone loss has occurred. Case-control studies suggest that estrogen therapy significantly reduces the risk of forearm, vertebral, pelvic, and hip fractures in postmenopausal women. Data from the Women's Health Initiative demonstrate that hormone therapy reduces the risk of both vertebral and hip fractures in postmenopausal women. [3] Conjugated estrogens, with or without medroxyprogesterone acetate, prevent bone loss when administered in doses of 0.3 mg per day or higher. How long a woman should remain on estrogen replacement therapy has not been established. In the United States, estrogen is approved by the Food and Drug Administration for prevention of postmenopausal bone loss.

Although the beneficial effects of estrogen therapy on bone mass are well established, less than 15% of postmenopausal women in the

United States take estrogen replacement. The decision to treat with estrogen is influenced by other factors and should be individualized. In some women, estrogen is prescribed to alleviate menopausal symptoms. In others, the prospect of adhering to a treatment program that may produce menstruation is unacceptable. When given without concomitant progestin, estrogen replacement therapy increases the risk of endometrial carcinoma. Thus, in a woman whose uterus is intact, estrogen therapy should be combined with a progestin, administered either cyclically (e.g., 5 to 10 mg medroxyprogesterone acetate for 10 to 14 days each month) or continuously (e.g., 2.5 mg medroxyprogesterone acetate per day). The latter regimen often eliminates menstrual bleeding after an initial period of 3 to 6 months, during which irregular bleeding may occur. Progestins may also enhance the osteoprotective effect of estrogens. In a woman who has had a hysterectomy, unopposed estrogen should be given daily.

The relationships between estrogen therapy and breast cancer or cardiovascular disease have been the subject of many case-control and cohort studies and, more recently, randomized, controlled trials. Although many studies, including at least one meta-analysis, concluded that long-term (greater than 15 years) estrogen therapy is associated with approximately a 30% increase in the risk of breast cancer in postmenopausal women. In the Women's Health Initiative, conjugated estrogen plus medroxyprogesterone acetate therapy increased the risk of invasive breast cancer by 26% over a 5.2-year period of follow-up.[3] The increased risk of breast cancer became evident after 4 years of follow-up. Thus, estrogen therapy is generally contraindicated in women with a history of breast cancer, and all postmenopausal women receiving estrogen therapy should have regular breast examinations and annual mammograms. Numerous case-control and cohort studies reported that estrogen therapy decreases the risk of major coronary disease by approximately 50%. The potential for bias due to patient selection or uneven diagnostic surveillance in these nonrandomized studies cannot be excluded, however. Two major randomized controlled trials have now demonstrated that data from observational studies examining the effects of estrogen on cardiovascular disease in women were clearly biased in ways that have not yet been clarified. In the Heart and Estrogen/Progestin Replacement Study (HERS), a randomized controlled trial that examined the effects of hormone replacement therapy on cardiovascular disease in postmenopausal women with preexisting coronary artery disease, conjugated equine estrogens plus medoxyprogesterone acetate did not reduce the overall rate of myocardial infarction or death from cardiovascular disease over a 4-year period. In fact, hormone therapy tripled the overall risk of thromboembolic disease and increased the risk for coronary events in the first year. In the Women's Health Initiative, combined estrogen plus progestin therapy increased the risk nonfatal myocardial infarction or death from coronary heart disease by 29% in women largely free of cardiovascular disease on entry to the study.[3] At present, estrogen therapy is indicated primarily to treat menopausal symptoms. In postmenopausal women who are being treated with estrogen to alleviate menopausal symptoms, additional skeletal benefits are likely to occur. If the primary reason for therapy is prevention or treatment of osteoporosis, agents other than estrogen should generally be used.

SELECTIVE ESTROGEN RECEPTOR MODULATORS

Tamoxifen, a selective estrogen receptor modulator, prevents bone loss from the spine and proximal femur in postmenopausal women with breast cancer and lowers serum low-density lipoprotein cholesterol levels. Tamoxifen blocks the actions of estrogen on the breast but acts like an estrogen agonist on the endometrium. Recent data suggest that tamoxifen reduces the risk of breast cancer in women at high risk for developing breast cancer, although it increases the risk of endometrial cancer and venous thromboembolic disease.

Another selective estrogen receptor modulator, raloxifene, prevents bone loss from the spine, proximal femur, and total body in early postmenopausal women and reduces serum total and low-density lipoprotein cholesterol levels. Raloxifene reduces the risk of vertebral fractures in late postmenopausal women with established osteoporosis but has no effect on the incidence of nonvertebral fractures.[4] Like tamoxifen, raloxifene blocks the effect of estrogen on the breast. In postmenopausal women with osteoporosis, raloxifene reduced the risk of breast cancer by more than 70% over a 4-year period. In contrast to tamoxifen and estrogen, however, raloxifene does not

cause endometrial hyperplasia. There are several possible explanations for the tissue selectivity of raloxifene. Raloxifene and estrogen both bind to the same region of the estrogen receptor. The binding of raloxifene and estrogen induces different conformational changes in the estrogen receptor, however, which allows the ligand-receptor complexes to recruit distinct arrays of coactivating and corepressing proteins. It appears that these differences in recruited transcription factors ultimately allow raloxifene and estrogen to induce transcription of different genes in some cell types. The tissue selectivity of raloxifene may also be related to differences in transcription factors between tissues and the differential expression of the two distinct estrogen receptors. Raloxifene is approved by the FDA both for prevention of bone loss in early postmenopausal women and for treatment of women with established osteoporosis. The recommended dosage is 60 mg once daily. It is well tolerated by most women. Raloxifene slightly increases the risk of vasomotor flushes and muscle cramps and, like estrogen and tamoxifen, increases the risk of venous thromboembolic disease.

BISPHOSPHONATES

Bisphosphonates are carbon-substituted analogues of pyrophosphate that bind tightly to hydroxyapatite crystals and inhibit osteoclastic bone resorption. Several bisphosphonates have been reported to increase bone mineral density in postmenopausal women, although only alendronate and risedronate are approved by the FDA for prevention of bone loss or for treatment of established osteoporosis in postmenopausal women.

Alendronate and risedronate are second-generation aminobisphosphonates and are much more potent inhibitors of bone resorptions than etidronate, a first-generation bisphosphonate. Aminobisphosphonates inhibit the conversion of farnesyl pyrophosphate to geranylgeranyl pyrophosphate, a step in the mevalonate pathway that is required for prenylation of GTP-binding proteins. As a result, osteoclast apoptosis is increased. Oral alendronate and risedronate, in a dose of 5 mg per day, increase bone mineral density of the lumbar spine and proximal femur in early postmenopausal women. In late postmenopausal women with established osteoporosis, alendronate, in a dose of 10 mg per day, increases bone mineral density of the lumbar spine and proximal femur by 9% and 4%, respectively, over 3 years and reduces the incidence of osteoporotic fractures, including hip fractures and symptomatic vertebral fractures, by approximately 40 to 50%.[5] Similar effects have been reported with risedronate in a dose of 5 mg per day, although the increases in bone density may be slightly smaller than with alendronate.[6] Both agents appear to prevent hip fractures most effectively in women with severe osteoporosis, such as in women with preexisting vertebral fractures. Although bone loss probably resumes after alendronate therapy is discontinued, there is no evidence that the rate of bone loss is accelerated and the rate of loss is slower than after discontinuation of hormone therapy.

Both alendronate and risedronate have long biologic half-lives. When given once weekly, in doses that are seven times their usual daily dose, changes in bone mineral density are similar to those observed with daily dosing. The frequency of side effects appears to be similar with daily or weekly dosing of each drug. Alendronate is approved by the FDA in both a dosage of 10 mg once daily and a dosage of 70 mg once weekly. Risedronate is approved at a dosage of 5 mg daily and a dosage of 35 mg once weekly. Because alendronate and risedronate are poorly absorbed in the presence of food, both drugs must be given by themselves after an overnight fast and patients should remain fasting for at least 30 minutes. Occasional patients may develop esophagitis or other gastrointestinal problems during oral bisphosphonate therapy. To decrease the incidence of these side effects, alendronate and risedronate should be taken with at least 8 oz of water and patients should remain upright for at least 30 minutes after taking the medication.

Like alendronate and risedronate, cyclic etidronate administration prevents bone loss in early postmenopausal women and increases spinal bone mineral density and decreases the incidence of vertebral fractures in late postmenopausal women. Etidronate is much less potent, however, than alendronate or risedronate and inhibits normal bone mineralization when given continuously for many months. Although initial reports suggested that cyclic etidronate administration reduces the incidence of spine fractures by 50%, further follow-up of these patients indicates that the reduction in vertebral fracture risk is considerably less than reported originally, and that the benefits of etidronate therapy may be restricted to a subgroup of women at particularly high risk for fracture. Etidronate is well tolerated. The best documented effects of etidronate are with a dose of 400 mg per day for the first 2 weeks of every 3-month period. To ensure adequate absorption, patients should not eat for 2 hours before or after etidronate administration. Etidronate has not been approved by the FDA to treat osteoporosis at the time of this writing.

Patients with osteoporosis who cannot tolerate or absorb oral bisphosphonates are frequently given intravenous pamidronate in doses ranging from 30 mg every 3 months to 90 mg every 6 months. In noncontrolled studies, intravenous pamidronate has been reported to increase spine bone mineral density by about 9% over 2 years, a change that is similar to that reported with oral alendronate. The effect of intravenous pamidronate on the risk of fractures in unknown, and the drug has not approved for treatment of osteoporosis by the FDA.

Other intravenously administered bisphosphonates, including zoledronate and ibandronate, are currently under development. A single 4 mg infusion of zoledronate, administered over 15 minutes once yearly, increases spine and hip bone mineral density by approximately 5% and 3%, respectively, after 1 year, changes that are similar to those seen with oral bisphosphonates. If zoledronate reduces fractures as effectively as alendronate and risedronate, it may become an important treatment alternative for women with postmenopausal osteoporosis.

CALCITONIN

Calcitonin is a 32-amino-acid peptide that is normally produced by the thyroid C cells. Osteoclasts have calcitonin receptors, and calcitonin rapidly inhibits osteoclastic bone resorption. Calcitonin from salmon is more potent than human calcitonin and is therefore preferred in most circumstances. The effects of salmon calcitonin therapy on bone loss in women who are within the first 5 years of the menopause have been inconsistent. Some groups have demonstrated that intranasal salmon calcitonin therapy prevents spinal bone loss for up to 3 years, whereas others have been unable to demonstrate such an effect. Salmon calcitonin appears to prevent spinal bone loss in late postmenopausal women, although appendicular (i.e., cortical) bone loss continues. One study reported that a daily dose of 200 IU of intranasal calcitonin reduced the risk of new vertebral fractures in women with postmenopausal osteoporosis, although a higher dose was ineffective. Calcitonin is approved by the FDA for treatment of late postmenopausal women with low bone mineral density and is available for both parenteral and intranasal use. The recommended dose is 100 IU subcutaneously or 200 IU intranasally each day, given with adequate calcium and vitamin D. It is not approved for prevention of postmenopausal bone loss. Side effects of injected calcitonin administration, including nausea, flushing, and local inflammatory reactions, occur in 10 to 15% of patients and can often be minimized by administering the medication at bedtime, starting at low doses (i.e., 25 IU), and increasing the dosage gradually over a period of several weeks. Side effects are uncommon with intranasal calcitonin. In occasional patients, calcitonin may have significant analgesic effects. Overall, calcitonin is less potent and less effective than other antiresorptive medications, and its use should be reserved for patients with osteoporosis who cannot be treated with other agents.

VITAMIN D AND ITS METABOLITES

Vitamin D is important for absorption of calcium from the gastrointestinal tract. Vitamin D deficiency is common yet infrequently diagnosed in the United States. More than half of general medical inpatients and half of patients who experience a hip fracture have hypovitaminosis D. A serum 25-hydroxyvitamin D level below 15 ng/mL is considered deficient, and many experts believe that serum 25-hydroxyvitamin D levels should be 20 or even 30 ng/mL for optimal skeletal health. Most Americans consume diets with a vitamin D content well below the recommended daily intake. Elderly people are at particular risk for vitamin D deficiency because calcium absorption decreases with age and the ability of the skin to synthesize vitamin D is reduced. Furthermore, the ability to convert 25-hydroxyvitamin D to 1,25-dihydroxyvitamin D is impaired in many elderly people.

Decreased vitamin D formation and calcium absorption may lead to secondary hyperparathyroidism and accelerated bone loss.

Small doses of vitamin D (800 IU per day) plus calcium dramatically reduce the incidence of hip fractures and other nonspine fractures in elderly women. [1] Similar results have been found in a group of men and women older than 65 years of age in the United States. Because toxicity from such doses of vitamin D has not been reported, this therapy can be recommended to virtually all postmenopausal women. Smaller doses of vitamin D (400 IU per day) may not produce the same benefit. The current recommended daily intake of vitamin D is 200 IU for adults 19 to 50 years old, 400 IU for adults 51 to 70 years old, and 600 IU for adults older than 70. Many experts, however, recommend that all adults consume 800 IU of vitamin D each day.

The role of 1,25-dihydroxyvitamin D therapy in postmenopausal osteoporosis is more controversial. At high doses (0.8 μg per day), 1,25-dihydroxyvitamin D plus calcium increases bone mass but most patients develop hypercalciuria and/or hypercalcemia. At doses of 0.5 to 0.6 μg per day, 1,25-dihydroxyvitamin D plus calcium preserves spinal bone mass and decreases the rate of both vertebral and nonvertebral fractures with little toxicity. It is unclear, however, whether 1,25-dihydroxyvitamin D therapy is superior to treatment with small doses of vitamin D. Because the therapeutic index of 1,25-dihydroxyvitamin D therapy is small, its use should probably be reserved for patients who are not candidates for other forms of pharmacologic therapy. Other analogues of vitamin D are being investigated as potential therapies for postmenopausal osteoporosis.

PARATHYROID HORMONE

All currently available therapies for osteoporosis inhibit osteoclastic bone resorption. In contrast, parathyroid hormone, when given intermittently in low doses, stimulates osteoblastic bone formation. The bone formed in response to parathyroid hormone administration is histologically normal and its strength is increased. Many animal studies have demonstrated that parathyroid hormone can prevent or reverse estrogen-deficiency osteoporosis. Parathyroid hormone increases bone mineral density of the spine and prevents bone loss from the proximal femur and total body in young women with estrogen deficiency induced by gonadotropin releasing hormone (GnRH) analogue therapy. A recent large, multicenter, randomized, controlled trial demonstrated that once-daily parathyroid hormone therapy increases bone density of the spine by 10 to 14% and increases femoral neck bone density by 3 to 5% in women with postmenopausal osteoporosis treated for a median of 21 months. [7] In these same women, parathyroid hormone reduced the risk of vertebral fractures by nearly 70% and reduced the risk of nonvertebral fractures by 54%. In osteoporotic women who are also receiving estrogen therapy, parathyroid hormone therapy may have even more dramatic effects with increases in spine bone density of nearly 30% over 2 years in one study. Some women treated with parathyroid hormone experience nausea, headaches, dizziness, and leg cramps, and transient mild hypercalcemia is sometimes seen several hours after its administration. Parathyroid hormone is the only true anabolic therapy for osteoporosis that has been approved by the FDA.

HIP PROTECTORS

In addition to bone mineral density, falls are a major risk factor for hip fractures. One randomized, controlled trial demonstrated that anatomically designed external hip protectors dramatically reduce the risk of hip fractures in frail, elderly adults, although another trial did not, probably due to poor compliance in the latter study. Hip protectors should be strongly considered for all osteoporotic people who are at risk of falling.

FUTURE THERAPIES

Several therapeutic agents are currently in clinical trials. It is well known that sodium fluoride increases spinal bone density. Bone formed in response to fluoride, however, is qualitatively abnormal, and cortical bone density sometimes decreases. A randomized controlled trial demonstrated that a standard formulation of sodium fluoride therapy failed to reduce the risk of vertebral fractures and actually increased the incidence of fractures of the appendicular skeleton despite large increases in spinal bone mineral density. One study suggested that sodium fluoride reduces the risk of vertebral fractures without accelerating cortical bone loss when administered in a lower dose as a slow-release preparation. The risk of vertebral fractures was not reduced, however, in a second study that used a similar dose of sodium fluoride.

Some recent epidemiologic studies suggest that HMG-CoA reductase inhibitor (statin) use is associated with a lower risk of osteoporotic fractures, although other studies have failed to demonstrate a similar association. Both statins and aminobisphosphonates inhibit steps in the mevalonate pathway. Thus, it is possible that statins, like bisphosphonates, might inhibit bone resorption. Prospective, controlled studies are needed to determine whether statins increase bone mineral density and reduce fracture risk. Other potential future therapies to prevent or reverse osteoporosis include OPG, growth factors (insulin-like growth factors, transforming growth factor-β, fibroblast growth factor, platelet-derived growth factor, and bone morphogenetic proteins), agents that suppress or antagonize the effects of bone-resorbing cytokines, vitamin D analogues, prostaglandin E_2, strontium salts, agents that interfere with osteoclast attachment to bone such as integrin antagonists, and phytoestrogens, particularly the isoflavones such as ipriflavone.

Osteoporosis in Men

Although osteoporosis is less common in men, men lose about 30% of their trabecular bone and 20% of their cortical bone during the course of their lifetimes. Thirty percent of all hip and vertebral fractures occur in men. By extreme old age, one in every six men will have a hip fracture.

Secondary causes of osteoporosis in men are similar to those in women. Epidemiologic studies suggest that hypogonadism, prior glucocorticoid use, gastric resection, idiopathic hypercalciuria, and ethanol abuse are among the most common identifiable causes of osteoporosis in men. Between 15 and 25% of men with hip or vertebral fractures are androgen deficient. Androgens have important effects on skeletal development. Peak bone mass is reduced in men who were androgen deficient during adolescence due to idiopathic hypogonadotropic hypogonadism or Klinefelter syndrome and in men with histories of constitutionally delayed puberty. In adult men, castration or induction of androgen deficiency with long-acting GnRH analogues increases bone resorption and leads to rapid bone loss. Osteoporosis is frequently observed in men with primary gonadal failure, hemochromatosis, hyperprolactinemic hypogonadism, or other disorders of the pituitary-hypothalamic axis.

Androgens may stimulate bone formation directly, since osteoblastic cells possess androgen receptors. Androgens stimulate osteoblastic cell proliferation and differentiation, an effect that may be mediated by transforming growth factor-β or fibroblast growth factor. Androgens also inhibit bone resorption, probably through mechanisms that involve alterations in the local production of bone-resorbing cytokines such as interleukin-1 and interleukin-6. In the majority of eugonadal osteoporotic men, bone formation and osteoblastic cell proliferation are reduced.

Aromatization of testosterone into estrogens may be essential for many of the effects of testosterone on bone. Estrogen therapy can maintain bone mass in castrated male-to-female transsexuals. More importantly, severe osteopenia has been reported both in a man with estrogen resistance due to a genetic defect in his estrogen receptor and in men with estrogen deficiency due to a mutation in aromatase P-450, despite normal or high serum testosterone levels in both circumstances. No clear effects of androgens on calcium regulatory hormones have been demonstrated. Further studies are needed to clarify the physiologic roles of androgens and estrogens on bone metabolism in men.

In men with androgen-deficiency osteoporosis, androgen replacement is usually indicated. Beneficial effects of androgen therapy on bone mass have been demonstrated in men with hyperprolactinemic hypogonadism, idiopathic hypogonadotropic hypogonadism, and acquired hypogonadism. In elderly men whose serum testosterone levels are in the lower portion of the normal range, testosterone replacement does not improve bone density, although it is probably effective in a subset of men whose serum testosterone levels are frankly reduced. In men with prostate cancer with severe hypogonadism due to therapy with a long-acting GnRH analogue, intravenous pamidronate completely prevents bone loss. The degree of androgen deficiency that leads to bone loss is currently unknown.

Alendronate therapy, in a dose of 10 mg per day, increases lumbar spine and proximal femur bone mineral density and reduces the risk of vertebral fractures in men with idiopathic osteoporosis. ■ The magnitude of these effects appears similar to that seen in women with postmenopausal osteoporosis. Alendronate is approved by the FDA to treat men with idiopathic osteoporosis. Parathyroid hormone, in a dose of 20 µg subcutaneously each day, also increases lumbar spine and proximal femur bone mineral density in men with idiopathic osteoporosis. It is also approved by the FDA for use in men with osteoporosis.

Glucocorticoid-Induced Osteoporosis

Bone loss is a common complication of glucocorticoid excess, whether due to endogenous Cushing's syndrome or the administration of exogenous glucocorticoids. The most important adverse effects of glucocorticoids on bone metabolism appear to be suppressed osteoblast activity and a vitamin D–independent inhibition of intestinal calcium absorption. Glucocorticoids also suppress gonadotropin secretion, leading to secondary hypogonadism. The ability of glucocorticoids to suppress bone formation appears to be mediated, at least in part, by suppression of local secretion of insulin-like growth factor-1 in bone, an effect that may help explain why glucocorticoids promote osteoblast apoptosis. Glucocorticoids also increase RANKL and reduce OPG production, effects that should promote osteoclastogenesis and may be related to the increase in bone resorption that has sometimes been reported in the first few months of glucocorticoid therapy.

The predominant effect of administering glucocorticoids on the skeleton is a loss of trabecular bone, although cortical bone mass also decreases. Thus, lateral spine DEXA is more sensitive than posterior-anterior spine DEXA for detecting bone loss in glucocorticoid-treated patients. Data from epidemiologic studies suggest that doses of prednisone as low as 2.5 mg per day increase the risk of fractures. Bone loss is most rapid in the first 6 to 12 months of therapy, but accelerated bone loss appears to continue as long as therapy is continued.

Because the bone loss associated with glucocorticoids is largely irreversible, the decision to administer them should be made carefully. When they are used, the dosage should be maintained as low as possible. If it is anticipated that glucocorticoid therapy will be maintained for several months or longer, treatment to prevent bone loss should be considered, particularly in estrogen-deficient women and when a high dosage of glucocorticoids is needed.

Several studies have demonstrated that either calcitonin or bisphosphonates can prevent bone loss from the spine and proximal femur in patients receiving glucocorticoid therapy for 1 to 2 years. Cyclic etidronate, alendronate, and risedronate therapy all reduce the incidence of vertebral fractures in patients receiving glucocorticoid therapy. Risedronate and alendronate are both approved by the FDA to treat patients with glucocorticoid-induced osteoporosis. The recommended dose of risedronate is 5 mg per day. For men and estrogen-sufficient women, the recommended dose of alendronate is also 5 mg per day, whereas estrogen-deficient women should receive 10 mg of alendronate daily.

The effects of gonadal steroids on glucocorticoid-induced bone loss have not been well studied, although gonadal steroid replacement is reasonable in hypogonadal subjects. Studies of the effects of vitamin D and its metabolites on glucocorticoid-induced bone loss have produced inconsistent results. One controlled study demonstrated that 0.5 to 1.0 µg of calcitriol plus 1000 mg of calcium per day prevents spinal bone loss for at least 1 year in patients who are starting treatment with glucocorticoids. Because of the potential for hypercalciuria and/or hypercalcemia, patients receiving calcitriol therapy require careful monitoring. Calcitriol therapy seems most logical in patients with low urinary calcium excretion, suggesting poor intestinal absorption of calcium, and should be avoided in patients with hypercalciuria. Physiologic vitamin D replacement (400 to 800 IU per day), can be safely recommended in all patients receiving glucocorticoids, and calcium supplementation (1000 mg per day) should be added unless the urinary calcium excretion is excessive. Finally, one small study reported that daily parathyroid hormone administration increases spine bone mineral density in postmenopausal women also receiving hormone replacement therapy. Because glucocorticoids reduce local skeletal production of insulin-like growth factor-1, and parathyroid hormone increases local skeletal production of insulin-like growth factor-1, parathyroid hormone appears to be an attractive potential therapy for glucocorticoid-induced osteoporosis.

1. Chapuy MC, Arlot ME, Duboeuf F, et al. Vitamin D₃ and calcium to prevent hip fractures in elderly women. N Engl J Med 1992; 327:1637–1642.
2. Prince RL, Smith M, Dick IM, et al: Prevention of postmenopausal osteoporosis. A comparative study of exercise, calcium supplementation, and hormone-replacement therapy. N Engl J Med 1991;325:1190–1195.
3. Rossouw JE, Anderson GL, Prentice RL, et al: Risks and benefits of estrogen plus progestin in healthy postmenopausal women: Principal results From the Women's Health Initiative randomized controlled trial. JAMA 2002;288:321–333.
4. Ettinger B, Black DM, Mitlak BH, et al: Reduction of vertebral fracture risk in postmenopausal women with osteoporosis treated with raloxifene: Results from a 3-year randomized clinical trial. JAMA 1999;282:637–645.
5. Liberman UA, Weiss SR, Broll J, et al: Effect of oral alendronate on bone mineral density and the incidence of fractures in postmenopausal osteoporosis. N Engl J Med 1995;333:1437–1443.
6. McClung MR, Geusens P, Miller PD, et al. Effect of risedronate on the risk of hip fracture in elderly women. N Engl J Med 2001; 344:333–340.
7. Neer RM, Arnaud CD, Zanchetta JR, et al: Effect of parathyroid hormone (1–34) on fractures and bone mineral density in postmenopausal women with osteoporosis. N Engl J Med 2001;344:1434–1441.
8. Orwoll E, Ettinger M, Weiss S, et al. Alendronate for the treatment of osteoporosis in men. N Engl J Med 2000; 343:604–610.

SUGGESTED READINGS

American College of Rheumatology Ad Hoc Committee on Glucocorticoid-Induced Osteoporosis: Recommendations for the prevention and treatment of glucocorticoid-induced osteoporosis: 2001 update. Arthritis Rheum 2001;44:1496–1503. *A thorough review of current therapies for glucocorticoid-induced osteoporosis that contains the latest official recommendations from the American College of Rheumatology.*

Cauley JA, Black DM, Barrett-Connor E, et al: Effects of hormone replacement therapy on clinical fractures and height loss: The Heart and Estrogen/Progestin Replacement Study (HERS). Am J Med 2001;110:442–450. *There was no evidence of a reduction in the incidence of fractures or rate of height loss in older women without osteoporosis.*

Greenspan SL, Emkey RD, Bone HG, et al: Significant differential effects of alendronate, estrogen, or combination therapy on the rate of bone loss after discontinuation of treatment of postmenopausal osteoporosis. A randomized, double-blind, placebo-controlled trial. Ann Intern Med 2002;137:875–883. *Accelerated bone loss is seen after withdrawal of estrogen therapy but not after withdrawal of alendronate or combination therapy.*

Hofbauer LC, Heufelder AE: The role of receptor activator of nuclear factor-κB ligand and osteoprotegerin in the pathogenesis and treatment of metabolic bone diseases. J Clin Endocrinol Metab 2000;85:2355–2363. *A comprehensive and well-organized review of the literature related to this important and rapidly developing area of bone biology.*

Horwitz MJ, Tedesco MB, Gundberg C, et al: Short-term, high-dose parathyroid hormone-related protein as a skeletal anabolic agent for the treatment of postmenopausal osteoporosis. J Clin Endocrinol Metab 2003;88:569–575. *PTH-related protein administered subcutaneously in high doses for only 3 months appears to be a potent anabolic agent, producing a 4.7% increase in lumbar spine bone density.*

Lafage-Proust MH, Boudignon B, Thomas T: Glucocorticoid-induced osteoporosis: Pathophysiological data and recent treatments. Joint Bone Spine 2003;70:109–118. *Review emphasizing that bisphosphonates are effective in preventing and treating glucocorticoid-induced osteoporosis.*

Lindsay R, Gallagher JC, Kleerekoper M, et al: Effect of lower doses of conjugated equine estrogens with and without medroxyprogesterone acetate on bone in early postmenopausal women. JAMA 2002;287:2668–2676. *Doses lower than 0.625 mg/d effectively increase bone mineral density and content in early postmenopausal women.*

Roy DK, O'Neill TW, Finn JD, et al, for the European Prospective Osteoporosis Study (EPOS). Determinants of incident vertebral fracture in men and women: Results from the European Prospective Osteoporosis Study (EPOS). Osteoporos Int 2003;14:19–26. *None of the lifestyle factors studied including smoking, alcohol intake, physical activity or milk consumption showed any consistent associations with incident vertebral fracture.*

Stein E, Shane E: Secondary osteoporosis. Endocrinol Metab Clin North Am 2003;32:115–134. *Describes the causes and diagnostic investigation of suspected secondary osteoporosis.*

259 OSTEOMALACIA AND RICKETS

Marc K. Drezner

Definition

Rickets and osteomalacia are diseases characterized by defective bone and cartilage mineralization in children and bone mineralization in adults. The abnormal calcification of cartilage occurs at epiphyseal growth plates that also exhibit delayed maturation of the cartilage cellular sequence and disorganization of cell arrangement. The resultant profusion of disorganized, nonmineralized, degenerating cartilage causes widening of the epiphyseal plates with flaring or cupping and irregularity of the epiphyseal-metaphyseal junctions. The abnormal calcification of bone is restricted to the organic matrix at the bone-osteoid interfaces of remodeling tissue. The insufficient mineralization of newly formed matrix paradoxically results in enhanced bone volume and increased susceptibility to fractures or bone deformities. The various disorders associated with rickets and osteomala-

cia that have been identified and characterized to date are numerous (Table 259–1). Although the phenotypic expression of the defective bone and cartilage mineralization is similar in each of these disorders, the associated biochemical abnormalities and the therapeutic approaches differ according to the pathogenetic defect. Therefore, when diagnosing rickets and/or osteomalacia, further systematic analysis is needed to determine cause and appropriate therapy for the disorder.

Etiology and Pathogenesis

Mineralization of cartilage and bone is a complex process in which the calcium-phosphorus inorganic mineral phase is deposited in an organic matrix in a highly ordered fashion. Such mineralization depends on (1) the availability of sufficient calcium and phosphorus from the extracellular fluid; (2) adequate metabolic and transport function of chondrocytes and osteoblasts to regulate the concentration of calcium, phosphorus, and other ions at the mineralization sites; (3) the presence of collagen with unique type, number, and distribution of cross-links, remarkable patterns of hydroxylation and glycosylation, and abundant phosphate content, which collectively permits and facilitates deposition of mineral at gaps, hole zones, and between the distal ends of two collagen molecules; (4) maintenance of an optimal pH (approximately 7.6) for deposition of calcium-phosphorus complexes; and (5) low concentration of calcification inhibitors (e.g., pyrophosphates, proteoglycans) in bone matrix.

Many of the disorders of mineralization occur secondary to known defects in these control steps. In this regard, most diseases resulting in rickets and/or osteomalacia result from abnormalities in the vitamin D endocrine system. Traditionally, a direct role has been assumed for vitamin D or, more properly, its active metabolite, 1,25-dihydroxyvitamin D, on production of normal collagen matrix and regulation of bone mineralization. However, it is more likely that the abnormal mineralization in these disorders results from an associated calcium and phosphorus deficiency that diminishes the driving force for calcification. Primary disorders of phosphate homeostasis also underlie a large number of the rachitic/osteomalacic disorders. Diminished gastrointestinal absorption or renal wasting of phosphorus limits this essential mineral in such disorders. The isolated deficiency of phosphorus alone or in conjunction with a frequently occurring aberration in vitamin D metabolism underlies defective mineralization. In accord with the complex regulation of bone mineralization, however, decreases in calcium or phosphorus do not account for rickets and osteomalacia in all forms of the disease. Indeed, certain forms of rickets and osteomalacia occur in spite of a normal or even elevated calcium-phosphate product. In such diseases, altered pH, abnormal collagen matrix, or excessive concentration of calcification inhibitors underlies the abnormal mineralization. In other forms of the disease, the precise mechanism causing the defective mineralization remains unknown.

Inadequate mineralization in rickets occurs in the matrix of cartilage in the growing epiphyseal plate. These characteristic changes are confined to the maturation zone of the cartilage, whereas the resting and proliferative zones of the epiphyses exhibit normal histologic features. In the maturation zone, the height of the cell columns is increased and the cells are closely packed and irregularly aligned. Moreover, calcification in the interstitial regions of this hypertrophic zone is defective.

In bone, the abnormal mineralization results in accumulation of excess osteoid, a sine qua non for the diagnosis of osteomalacia in most instances (Fig. 259–1). A supranormal amount of osteoid, however, may also occur in disease states associated with accelerated bone turnover, such as hyperparathyroidism. In addition, reduced mineralization activity may be observed without hyperosteoidosis in osteoporosis. Establishing the diagnosis of osteomalacia histopathologically, therefore, requires documenting abnormal mineralization with excess osteoid. These defects are manifest in bone by an increase in the forming surface covered by incompletely mineralized osteoid, an increase in osteoid volume and thickness, and a decrease in the mineralization front (the percentage of osteoid-covered bone-forming surface undergoing calcification) or the mineral apposition rate. The amount of osteoid in bone and the mineralization dynamics are determined in 3- to 5-μm thick sections of undecalcified bone by special stains and the fluorescence of previously ingested tetracycline that is deposited at calcification fronts.

Table 259–1 • THE RICKETS AND OSTEOMALACIA SYNDROMES

I. Disorders of the vitamin D endocrine system
  A. Decreased bioavailability of vitamin D
    1. Deficient endogenous production
      a. Inadequate sunlight exposure
      b. Aging
    2. Nutritional deficiency
    3. Loss of vitamin D metabolites
      a. Nephrotic syndrome
      b. Peritoneal dialysis
  B. Vitamin D malabsorption
    1. Gastrointestinal disorders
      a. Partial/total gastrectomy
      b. Small bowel disease (e.g., celiac disease)
      c. Intestinal bypass
    2. Pancreatic insufficiency
    3. Hepatobiliary disease
      a. Biliary atresia
      b. Biliary obstruction
      c. Biliary fistula
      d. Cirrhosis
  C. Abnormal vitamin D metabolism
    1. Impaired hepatic 25-hydroxylation of vitamin D
      a. Liver disease
      b. Anticonvulsant therapy
    2. Impaired renal 1α-hydroxylation of 25-hydroxyvitamin D
      a. Hereditary vitamin D–dependent rickets type 1 (pseudo-vitamin D deficiency)
      b. Chronic renal failure
      c. Pseudohypoparathyroidism
  D. Target organ resistance to vitamin D and metabolites
    1. Hereditary vitamin D–dependent rickets type 2
      a. Hormone binding negative
      b. Defect in hormone-binding capacity
      c. Defect in hormone-binding affinity
      d. Deficient hormone-receptor nuclear localization
      e. Decreased affinity of the hormone-receptor complex
II. Disorders of phosphate homeostasis
  A. Dietary
    1. Low phosphate intake
    2. Ingestion of phosphate-binding antacids
  B. Impaired renal tubular phosphate reabsorption
    1. Hereditary
      a. X-linked hypophosphatemic rickets/osteomalacia
      b. Hereditary hypophosphatemic rickets/osteomalacia with hypercalciuria
      c. Autosomal dominant hypophosphatemic rickets
      d. Hypophosphatemic bone disease (nonrachitic hypophosphatemic osteomalacia)
      e. Adult-onset hypophosphatemic rickets
      f. Autosomal recessive hypophosphatemic rickets (X-linked hypercalciuric nephrolithiasis)
      g. X-linked recessive hypophosphatemic rickets (X-linked hypercalciuric nephrolithiasis)
    2. Acquired
      a. Tumor-induced osteomalacia (oncogenous osteomalacia)
        i. Mesenchymal, epidermal, and endodermal tumors
        ii. Fibrous dysplasia of bone
        iii. Neurofibromatosis
        iv. Linear nevus sebaceous syndrome
        v. Light-chain nephropathy
      b. Sporadic hypophosphatemic osteomalacia
  C. General renal tubular disorders
    1. Fanconi's syndrome type 1
      a. Hereditary
        i. Familial idiopathic
        ii. Cystinosis (Lignac-Fanconi syndrome)
        iii. Hereditary fructose intolerance
        iv. Tyrosinemia
        v. Galactosemia
        vi. Glycogen storage disease
        vii. Wilson's disease
        viii. Oculocerebral renal syndrome (Lowe's syndrome)
      b. Acquired
        i. Renal transplantation
        ii. Multiple myeloma
      c. Intoxication
        i. Cadmium
        ii. Lead
        iii. Tetracycline (outdated)
    2. Fanconi's syndrome type 2
III. Metabolic acidosis
  A. Distal renal tubular acidosis
    1. Primary
      a. Sporadic
      b. Familial
    2. Secondary
      a. Galactosemia (after galactose ingestion)
      b. Hereditary fructose intolerance with nephrocalcinosis (after chronic fructose ingestion)
      c. Hypergammaglobulinemic states
      d. Medullary sponge kidney
    3. Acquired
      a. Ureterosigmoidostomy
      b. Drug-induced
        i. Acetazolamide
        ii. Ammonium chloride
IV. Disorders of calcium homeostasis
  A. Dietary calcium deficiency
V. Abnormal bone matrix
  A. Fibrogenesis imperfecta ossium
  B. Axial osteomalacia
VI. Primary mineralization defects
  A. Hereditary
    1. Hypophosphatasia
      a. Perinatal disease
      b. Infantile disease
      c. Childhood disease
      d. Adult-onset disease
      e. Pseudohypophosphatasia
VII. Mineralization inhibitors
  A. Etidronate
  B. Fluoride
  C. Aluminum

Clinical Manifestations

The clinical features of rickets, although variable to some degree according to the underlying disorder, are primarily related to skeletal pain and deformity, bone fractures, slipped epiphyses, and abnormalities of growth. In addition, hypocalcemia, when present, may be severe enough to produce tetany, laryngeal spasm, and seizures.

In infants and young children, symptoms include listlessness, irritability, and, in some forms of metabolic rickets, profound hypotonia and proximal muscle weakness. Indeed, as the disease progresses and muscle weakness is present, children often are unable to walk without support. Throughout early life, classic skeletal deformities appear. By 6 months of age, frontal bossing with flattening at the back is evident. Later, a lateral collapse of both chest walls (Harrison's sulcus) and rachitic rosary may appear. If untreated, progressive bony deformities result in bowing (see Fig. 259–1)—particularly in the tibia, femur, radius, and ulna—and fractures. In addition, dental eruption may be delayed and, in those forms of the disease with hypocalcemia or hereditary hypophosphatemia, enamel defects and inadequate dentin calcification occur, respectively.

In contrast, clinical signs of osteomalacia are nondescript. Indeed, the disease-specific abnormalities may be overlooked and features of an underlying disorder (e.g., malabsorption) may predominate. Symptoms, when present, may include diffuse skeletal pain and muscular weakness. The pain, often described as dull and aching, is generally worsened by activity and prominent around the hips, resulting in an antalgic gait. The muscle weakness is primarily proximal and frequently associated with wasting, hypotonia, and a waddling gait. This myopathy is seen in almost all forms of rickets and osteomalacia, X-linked hypophosphatemic rickets and osteomalacia notably excepted. Clinical improvement in the myopathy usually results from specific therapy, such as vitamin D repletion in cases of nutritional osteomalacia, phosphate supplementation in disorders marked

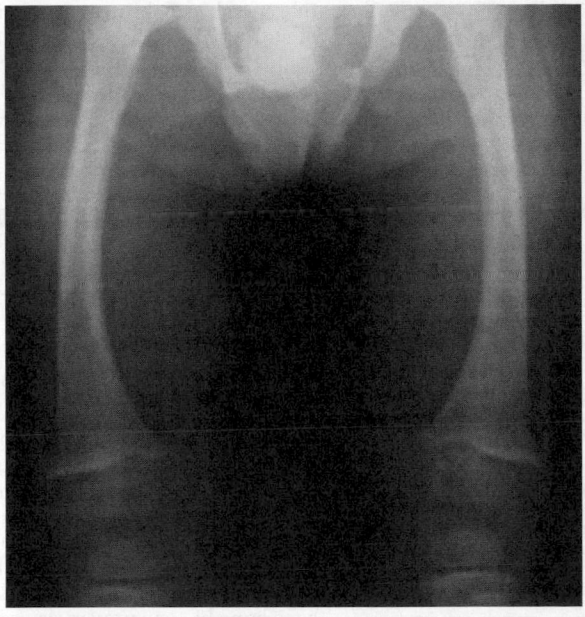
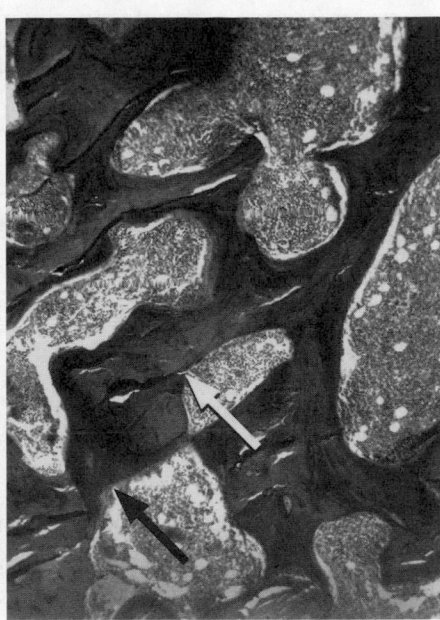

A   B

FIGURE 259–1 • *A*, Radiographic appearance of the lower extremities in a youth with rickets. The bowed femurs are evident bilaterally. In addition, at the distal ends of the femurs, the growth plates are wide and flared and display an irregular hazy appearance at the diaphyseal line secondary to uneven invasion of the recently calcified cartilage by adjacent bone tissue. *B*, Microscopic appearance of bone biopsy sections from a patient with osteomalacia. Stained sections exhibit mineralized bone (white arrow) covered by unmineralized osteoid seams (black arrow). Such observations are representative of the abnormal mineralization that characterizes the osteomalacic bone disorder.

by renal phosphate wasting, or correction of acidosis. Fractures of the ribs, vertebral bodies, and long bones may occur and lead to progressive deformities as well as point tenderness on palpation.

The radiographic abnormalities in both rickets and osteomalacia reflect the histopathologic changes. In rickets, alterations are most evident at the growth plate, which is wide and flared and displays an irregular hazy appearance at the diaphyseal line secondary to uneven invasion of the recently calcified cartilage by adjacent bone tissue (see Fig. 259–1). The trabecular pattern of the metaphyses is also abnormal, the cortices of the diaphyses are thinned, and the shafts frequently are bowed (see Fig. 259–1).

In osteomalacia, a moderate decrease in bone density is usually associated with coarsening of trabeculae and blurring of their margins. When secondary hyperparathyroidism is present, subperiosteal resorption in the phalanges and metacarpals, erosion of the distal ends of the clavicles, and bone cysts may be observed. A more specific radiographic abnormality is the presence of Looser's zones, also called *pseudofractures* or *Milkman's fractures*, in the shafts of long bones. These are ribbon-like zones of rarefaction, ranging from a few millimeters to several centimeters in length and usually oriented perpendicular to the bone surface. Often, they occur symmetrically and most commonly are present at the medial aspect of the femurs near the femoral heads, in the metatarsals, or in the pelvis. Long-standing osteomalacia may also result in additional characteristic radiographic abnormalities, including biconcave collapsed vertebrae and a trefoil (or triangular) pelvis.

In patients with renal tubular disorders (Chapter 122), increased rather than decreased bone density may be present. Despite the increased bone mass, histopathologic evaluation of biopsies reveals an abundance of unmineralized osteoid, and bones remain subject to fracture. Thus, the increased density likely reflects replacement of marrow air space with osteoid.

Biochemical abnormalities in patients with rickets and osteomalacia vary with the cause of the disorder. However, the rachitic and osteomalacic syndromes may be divided into calcipenic and phosphopenic forms, as well as those in which mineral availability is apparently normal. In general, patients with the calcipenic dis-

eases exhibit a low or marginally normal serum calcium level, a decreased serum phosphorus concentration, and (secondary) hyperparathyroidism. If vitamin D deficiency prevails, the serum 25-hydroxyvitamin D levels are characteristically low, generally less than 10 ng/mL but occasionally 10 to 20 ng/mL. In contrast, the serum 1,25-dihydroxyvitamin D concentration may not be overtly decreased secondary to the prevailing hyperparathyroidism. Alternatively, a defect in vitamin D metabolism often results in an isolated deficiency of 1,25-dihydroxyvitamin D, whereas end-organ resistance to this active vitamin D metabolite increases the circulating level of calcitriol.

A primary abnormality of transepithelial phosphate transport in the nephron, resulting in renal phosphate wasting, underlies the majority of the phosphopenic disorders. As a rule, patients with these disorders maintain a normal serum calcium concentration, whereas the serum phosphorus level is characteristically low. In contrast to the calcipenic forms of disease, the serum 25-hydroxyvitamin D and parathyroid hormone levels are normal in patients with hypophosphatemic disease. Moreover, affected subjects commonly maintain a normal (or mildly decreased) serum 1,25-dihydroxyvitamin D level despite the prevailing hypophosphatemia, which should increase production of this active vitamin D metabolite. However, an elevated serum 1,25-dihydroxyvitamin D concentration was recently reported in several rare genetic phosphopenic disorders, hereditary hypophosphatemic rickets with hypercalciuria, Fanconi's syndrome type 2, and X-linked recessive hypophosphatemic rickets. Whereas the elevated calcitriol level underlies increased gastrointestinal absorption of calcium and hypercalciuria in these diseases, the impact of abnormal vitamin D metabolism on the phenotypic expression of the phosphopenic disorders is less certain. In those diseases with normal serum calcium and phosphorus concentrations, laboratory abnormalities are unique to each form of the disease. Nevertheless, alkaline phosphatase activity in plasma is generally elevated in all forms of rickets and osteomalacia. Even severe forms of disease, however, particularly those due to renal tubular disorders, may be associated with normal or only marginally elevated enzyme activity.

DISORDERS OF THE VITAMIN D ENDOCRINE SYSTEM

Rickets and osteomalacia due to disorders of the vitamin D endocrine system comprise a wide variety of calcipenic diseases. The variable biochemical abnormalities associated with these disparate disorders are summarized in Table 259–2. Although many of these diseases are no longer common causes of rickets and osteomalacia,

others are often hidden causes of bone disease in a varying population of patients.

Decreased Bioavailability of Vitamin D

INADEQUATE SUNLIGHT AND NUTRITIONAL VITAMIN D DEFICIENCY. Adequate exposure to sunlight and fortification of dairy products with vitamin

Diseases of Bone and Mineral Metabolism

Table 259–2 • BIOCHEMICAL ABNORMALITIES OF THE CALCIOPENIC RACHITIC/OSTEOMALACIC DISORDERS

	VDDR	CRF	HVDDR 1	HVDDR 2	HP	PSH
BIOCHEMICAL FINDINGS						
Calcium	⇓	⇓	⇓	⇓	⇓	⇓
Phosphorus	N/⇓	⇑	N/⇓	N/⇓	⇑	⇑
Alkaline phosphatase	⇑	⇑	⇑	⇑	N/⇑	N/⇑
Parathyroid hormone	⇑	⇑	⇑	⇑	⇓	⇑
25(OH)D	⇓	N/⇓	N	N	N	N
$1,25(OH)_2D$	⇑	⇓	⇓	⇑	⇓	⇓
RENAL FUNCTION						
Urinary phosphorus	⇑	⇓	⇑	⇑	⇓	⇓
Urinary calcium	⇓	⇓	⇓	⇓	⇓	⇓
GASTROINTESTINAL FUNCTION						
Calcium absorption	⇓	⇓	⇓	⇓	⇓	⇓
Phosphorus absorption	⇓	⇓	⇓	⇓	⇓	⇓

VDDR = vitamin D–deficiency rickets (including sunlight or nutritional deficiency, vitamin D malabsorption, inhibition of 25-hydroxylation); CRF = chronic renal familure; HP = hypoparathyroidism; HVDDR 1 = hereditary vitamin D–dependent rickets type 1; HVDDR 2 = hereditary vitamin D–dependent rickets type 2; N = normal; PSH = pseudohypoparathyroidm; ⇓ = decreased; ⇑ = increased; N/⇓ = normal or decreased; N/⇑ = normal or increased.

D have eliminated vitamin D deficiency secondary to inadequate endogenous production or nutrition in the majority of countries. However, in several populations, such as Asian immigrants in Britain, rickets and osteomalacia secondary to vitamin D deficiency occurs in neonates and infants, adolescents during pubertal growth, and, less frequently, among adults. Insufficient vitamin D intake secondary to using unfortified foods, naturally dark pigmentation (which interferes with ultraviolet transmission through the skin), genetic factors, and social customs (such as avoiding sun exposure) contribute to the development of disease in these subjects. Moreover, occurrence of disease in neonates is virtually always the result of vitamin D deficiency in mothers with ethnocultural risk factors for such deficiency. In the United States and other developed countries, a surprisingly frequent occurrence of vitamin D deficiency osteomalacia has also been recognized recently in alcoholics, institutionalized patients, and the elderly. Poor diet, in some cases including avoiding milk and milk products due to lactose intolerance, lack of sunlight exposure, and an age-related decline in the dermal synthesis of 7-dehydrocholesterol are among the factors predisposing to the vitamin D deficiency and consequent bone disease.

The clinical sequelae of decreased vitamin D bioavailability are generally preceded by a fall in circulating 25-hydroxyvitamin D levels. While such a deficiency is due in most patients to inadequate circulating vitamin D, Asian Indians in the United States also manifest increased 25-hydroxyvitamin D–24-hydroxylase activity, which may limit circulating 25-hydroxyvitamin D levels. In any case, measurement of 25-hydroxyvitamin D serves to identify populations at risk for, and facilitates early detection of, vitamin D deficiency rickets and osteomalacia.

Studies in vitamin D receptor–null mice suggest that abnormal renal CaBP-D9k protein-mediated tubular calcium reabsorption may be the chief factor underlying the hypocalcemia when vitamin D bioavailability is compromised. Regardless, introducing vitamin D supplements (400 to 800 U/day) may, under these circumstances, prevent development of clinically significant disease.

Treating clinically evident vitamin D–deficient rickets and osteomalacia invariably results in healing of the bone disease. The disorder is best treated with vitamin D and restoration of normal dietary calcium and phosphorus intake. Ergocalciferol (vitamin D_2) is preferred because it provides the missing substrate that submits to physiologic regulation of vitamin D metabolite production.

Vitamin D Malabsorption

Gastrointestinal malabsorption associated with diseases of the small intestine, hepatobiliary tree, and pancreas may result in decreased absorption of vitamin D and/or depletion of endogenous 25-hydroxyvitamin D stores due to abnormal enterohepatic circulation.

In general, malabsorption of vitamin D occurs as a consequence of steatorrhea, which disturbs fat emulsification and chylomicron-facilitated absorption (Chapter 141). Such abnormalities often are associated with rickets and/or osteomalacia. However, most affected patients are asymptomatic, and many exhibit only reduced bone volume rather than evidence of defective bone mineralization. Intestinal bypass surgery and adult celiac disease are common examples of disorders in which vitamin D malabsorption occurs and in which the suspicion for osteomalacia should remain high. In contrast, patients with cholestatic liver disease, extrahepatic biliary obstruction, and diseases of the distal portions of the small intestine, such as regional enteritis, may develop bone disease secondary not only to poor vitamin D absorption but also to disruption of enterohepatic circulation.

Osteomalacia may also develop in patients who have had partial or total gastrectomy for peptic ulcer disease or other indications. Loss of gastrointestinal acidity or malfunction of the proximal small bowel underlies the vitamin D malabsorption in such circumstances. Absence of sufficient absorbing surface or failure of intestinal mucosal cells to respond to vitamin D or its metabolites may also cause vitamin D malabsorption and consequent bone disease.

The prevalence of osteomalacia in patients with gastrointestinal malabsorption varies widely from country to country. However, as many as 25 to 50% of British and European patients with partial gastrectomy, inflammatory bowel disease, and cholestatic liver disease have bone biopsy–proven osteomalacia.

Treatment of established disease generally requires pharmacologic amounts of vitamin D or its metabolites to overcome the defective absorption and/or the aberrant enterohepatic circulation or to offset end-organ resistance at the intestinal mucosa. Most patients respond well to calcium supplements, 1 to 1.5 g/day, and ergocalciferol, 1250 to 5000 μg/day. If the severity of malabsorption makes oral vitamin D ineffective, parenteral ergocalciferol, 12,500 to 25,000 μg, given intramuscularly once a month, is a practical alternative. Because magnesium deficiency often coexists in patients with malabsorptive diseases and may slow healing of the osteomalacia, adjunctive therapy with magnesium oxide may facilitate bone mineralization.

Abnormal Vitamin D Metabolism

LIVER DISEASE. Because vitamin D is hydroxylated in the liver to form 25-hydroxyvitamin D, patients with severe parenchymal or obstructive hepatic disease (Chapter 154) may have reduced production of this metabolite. These patients, however, rarely manifest biochemical or histologic evidence of osteomalacia. Indeed, an overt decrease of 25-hydroxyvitamin D generally requires concomitant nutritional deficiency or interruption of the enterohepatic circulation. Consequently, therapy for biopsy-proven osteomalacia, when present, is similar to therapy for osteomalacia that is secondary to malabsorption of vitamin D.

DRUG-INDUCED DISEASE. Decreased circulating levels of 25-hydroxyvitamin D may also occur in patients treated with drugs such as phenytoin or phenobarbital. This defect in vitamin D metabolism is due to induction of hepatic microsomal enzymes that metabolize 25-hydroxyvitamin D to inactive metabolites. Secondary to this abnormality and/or to the direct inhibitory effects of these drugs on intestinal calcium absorption and parathyroid hormone (PTH)–mediated calcium mobilization from bone, treated subjects often exhibit a decreased level of ionized calcium. These multiple influences commonly result in a bone disorder that may be mild osteomalacia or hyperparathyroid bone disease. Treatment of the bone disease and hypocalcemia generally requires modest vitamin D supplementation (150 to 400 μg/week).

VITAMIN D–DEPENDENT RICKETS TYPE 1 (PSEUDOVITAMIN D DEFICIENCY). Limited production of 1,25-dihydroxyvitamin D due to hereditary or acquired diseases represents another abnormality of vitamin D metabolism that invariably results in rickets or osteomalacia. Vitamin D–dependent rickets type 1 is such a genetic disorder, transmitted as an autosomal recessive trait and characterized by hypocalcemia, hypophosphatemia, and elevated alkaline phosphatase activity. As a result of the hypocalcemia, PTH levels are elevated and, consequently, urinary excretion of amino acids and phosphate is enhanced. In addition to these biochemical abnormalities, within the first year of life patients exhibit muscle weakness and hypotonia, motor retardation, and stunted growth. With progression, patients develop the classic radiographic signs of vitamin D–deficiency rickets and bone biopsy evidence of osteomalacia. Further, affected subjects have a decreased serum 1,25-dihydroxyvitamin D concentration, due to inactivating missense and null mutations in the 1α-hydroxylase gene, localized to chromosome 12q13.3, which abolish enzyme activity and limit production of this active vitamin D metabolite. This abnormality has been substantiated by (1) experiments in humans that demonstrate that serum calcitriol levels do not increase in response to classic stimuli of enzyme activity, (2) the absence of enzyme activity in renal cortical homogenates from the porcine homologue of this disease, and (3) the development of classic disease in mice following targeted ablation of 25-hydroxyvitamin D–1α-hydroxylase activity. Consistent with these observations, a physiologic dose of calcitriol (1 μg/day) generally promotes complete healing of the bone disease and resolution of the biochemical abnormalities, whereas a pharmacologic dose of vitamin D (20,000 to 100,000 U/day) or 25-hydroxyvitamin D (0.1 to 1.0 mg/day) is required to achieve similar effects. Regardless of the therapy used, in the majority of affected patients, therapy with vitamin D or its metabolites must be continued for life to prevent relapse. In a minority of subjects with a syndrome clinically identical to vitamin D–dependent rickets type 1, however, stopping treatment does not result in the reappearance of biochemical or radiographic signs of the disease.

CHRONIC RENAL FAILURE. Osteomalacia is common in patients with chronic renal failure and often tends to be the predominant type of renal osteodystrophy in younger patients (Chapter 262). The abnormal mineralization may be part of mixed uremic osteodystrophy or exist in isolation as a low-turnover osteomalacia. In the latter, the defect in mineralization almost certainly results in part from a decreased conversion of 25-hydroxyvitamin D to 1,25-dihydroxyvitamin D. Such abnormal vitamin D metabolism occurs secondary to either insufficient viable renal cortical tissue or the inhibitory effects of hyperphosphatemia on renal 25-hydroxyvitamin D–1α-hydroxylase activity. In addition, in some patients aluminum accumulated in bone underlies the abnormal mineralization. Indeed, the presence of aluminum may render the bone abnormality vitamin D–resistant. Under such circumstances, treatment with deferoxamine may be necessary to mobilize the aluminum from bone and other tissues and improve mineralization.

HYPOPARATHYROIDISM. Osteomalacia only rarely occurs in patients with hypoparathyroidism (Chapter 260). Hypocalcemia and low or low-normal serum 1,25-dihydroxyvitamin D are usually present and appear important in the pathogenesis of the bone disease. However, the underlying reason for the variable occurrence of bone pathology remains uncertain. The low serum 1,25-dihydroxyvitamin D concentration results from the PTH deficiency. Bone pain suggests the diagnosis, and generally the diagnosis depends on histomorphometric analysis of a bone biopsy. The majority of patients respond well to treatment with vitamin D and calcium supplements, but for reasons that are not clear, some require therapy with 1,25-dihydroxyvitamin D.

PSEUDOHYPOPARATHYROIDISM. In pseudohypoparathyroidism, apparent bone and kidney resistance to PTH results in hypocalcemia, retention of phosphate, and low serum 1,25-dihydroxyvitamin D levels (Chapter 260). Surprisingly, however, affected patients often manifest bone disease marked by increased resorptive activity and osteomalacia. Indeed, severe demineralization, including frank osteitis fibrosa cystica and occasionally rickets or osteomalacia, has been observed in 24 patients with pseudohypoparathyroidism. More commonly, the bone disease is silent and diagnosis often depends on histomorphometric analysis of a bone biopsy sample. Undoubtedly, hypocalcemia, secondary hyperparathyroidism, and low serum 1,25-dihydroxyvitamin D levels are important cofactors in the pathogenesis of the disease. Patients respond well to pharmacologic amounts of vitamin D or replacement doses of 1,25-dihydroxyvitamin D.

Target Organ Resistance to Calcitriol

VITAMIN D–DEPENDENT RICKETS, TYPE 2. Patients with clinical and biochemical abnormalities similar to those of subjects with vitamin D–dependent rickets type 1, but elevated 1,25-dihydroxyvitamin D levels, have recently been described. They have not only calcipenic rickets and osteomalacia but also variably associated abnormalities, including alopecia (in 60% of patients) and, in a minority of subjects, additional ectodermal anomalies, such as multiple milia, epidermal cysts, and oligodontia. The disease is a rare autosomal recessive disorder caused by mutations in the DNA and ligand-binding domains of the vitamin D receptor, which results in a decreased target organ responsiveness to 1,25-dihydroxyvitamin D through heterogeneous mechanisms. The genetic defects identified to date consist largely of point mutations in the conserved zinc finger region that reduce or abolish the affinity of the receptor for the DNA response element and, less often, point mutations that introduce a premature stop codon in the hormone-binding domain of the receptor, which limits binding of 1,25-dihydroxyvitamin D to the receptor. As a consequence, affected patients manifest (1) failure of 1,25-dihydroxyvitamin D binding to available receptors; (2) a reduction in 1,25-dihydroxyvitamin D receptor-binding sites; (3) abnormal binding affinity of 1,25-dihydroxyvitamin D to receptor; (4) inadequate translocation of 1,25-dihydroxyvitamin D–receptor complex to the nucleus; and (5) diminished affinity of the 1,25-dihydroxyvitamin D–receptor complex for the DNA-binding domain secondary to changes in the structure of receptor zinc-binding fingers. The role of the vitamin D receptor in the pathogenesis of this disorder has been confirmed in mice by targeted ablation of the DNA-binding domain of the receptor, which results in hypocalcemia, hyperparathyroidism, and alopecia within the first month of life. Effective treatment of this disease likely depends on the nature of the underlying abnormality. Thus, patients with deficient affinity of 1,25-dihydroxyvitamin D to receptor and inadequate nuclear translocation respond to high-dose vitamin D or 1,25-dihydroxyvitamin D with complete clinical and biochemical remission. In contrast, patients with other forms of the disease generally remain refractory to treatment with vitamin D or its analogues. However, every patient should receive a 6-month trial of therapy with supplemental calcium (1 to 3 g/day) and vitamin D (400,000 to 1,200,000 U/day), 25-hydroxyvitamin D (0.05 to 1.5 mg/day), or, in more severe cases, 1,25-dihydroxyvitamin D (5 to 60 μg/day). If the abnormalities of the syndrome do not normalize in response to this treatment, clinical remission might be achieved by administering high-dose oral calcium or long-term intracaval infusion of calcium. In addition, recent studies indicate that phosphate restriction in vitamin D–resistant null mice, the murine homologue of the human disease, effects normal bone mineralization.

DISORDERS OF PHOSPHATE HOMEOSTASIS (Chapter 220)

Rickets and osteomalacia occur in association with a variety of disorders in which phosphate depletion predominates. Most typically, these diseases have in common abnormal proximal renal tubular function, which results in an increased renal clearance of inorganic phosphorus and hypophosphatemia. However, the biochemical abnormalities characteristic of these disorders are quite variable (Table 259–3).

Table 259–3 • BIOCHEMICAL ABNORMALITIES OF THE PHOSPHOPENIC RACHITIC/OSTEOMALACIC DISORDERS

	XLH	HHRH	ADHR	XRHR	FS 1	FS 2	TIO
BIOCHEMICAL FINDINGS							
Calcium	N	N	N	N	N	N	N
Phosphorus	⇓	⇓	⇓	⇓	⇓	⇓	⇓
Alkaline phosphatase	N/⇑	N/⇑	N/⇑	N/⇑	N/⇑	N/⇑	N/⇑
Parathyroid hormone	N	⇓	N	⇓	N	⇓	N
25(OH)D	N	N	N	N	N	N	N
1,25(OH)₂D	(⇓)	⇑	(⇓)	⇑	(⇓)	⇑	⇓
RENAL FUNCTION							
Urinary phosphorus	⇑	⇑	⇑	⇑	⇑	⇑	⇑
Urinary calcium	⇓	⇑	⇓	⇑	⇓	⇑	⇓
GASTROINTESTINAL FUNCTION							
Calcium absorption	⇓	⇑	⇓	⇑	⇓	⇑	⇓
Phosphorus absorption	⇓	⇑	⇓	⇑	⇓	⇑	⇓

AOHR = autosomal dominant hypophosphatemic rickets; FS 1 = Fanconi's syndrome type 1; FS 2 = Fanconi's syndrome type 2; HHRH = hereditary hypophosphatemic rickets with hypercalciuria; N = normal; TIO = tumor-induced osteomalacia; XLH = X-linked hypophosphatemic rickets; XRHR = X-linked recessive hypophosphatemic rickets; ⇓ = decreased; ⇑ = increased; (⇓) = decreased relative to the serum phosphorus concentration; N/⇑ = normal or increased.

Modified from Econs MJ, Drezner MK: Bone disease resulting from inherited disorders of renal tubule transport and vitamin D metabolism. *In* Coe FL, Favus MJ: Disorders of Bone and Mineral Metabolism. New York, Raven Press, 1992, p 937.

Impaired Renal Tubular Phosphate Reabsorption

X-LINKED HYPOPHOSPHATEMIC RICKETS/OSTEOMALACIA. X-linked hypophosphatemic (XLH) rickets/osteomalacia represents the prototypic phosphate-wasting disorder, characterized in general by progressively severe skeletal abnormalities, growth retardation, and X-linked dominant inheritance. However, the clinical expression of the disease varies widely. The mildest abnormality is hypophosphatemia without clinically evident bone disease, and the most common clinically evident manifestation is short stature. Nevertheless, the majority of children with the disease exhibit enlargement of the wrists and/or knees secondary to rickets, as well as bowing of the lower extremities. Additional early signs of the disease may include late dentition, tooth abscesses secondary to poor mineralization of the interglobular dentine, and premature cranial synostosis. Despite marked variability in the clinical presentation, bone biopsies in affected children and adults invariably reveal osteomalacia, the severity of which has no relationship to gender, the extent of the biochemical abnormalities, or the severity of the clinical disability. In untreated youths and adults, the serum 25-hydroxyvitamin D level is normal and the concentration of 1,25-dihydroxyvitamin D is in the low-normal range. The paradoxical occurrence of hypophosphatemia and normal serum calcitriol levels is due to aberrant regulation of renal 25-hydroxyvitamin D–1α-hydroxylase activity, most likely caused by abnormal phosphate transport. Indeed, studies in *Hyp* mice, the murine homologue of the human disease, have established that defective regulation is confined to enzyme localized in the proximal convoluted tubule, the site of the abnormal phosphate transport. Alternatively, a circulating factor central to the genesis of the disease (see later) may impair vitamin D metabolism in the kidney.

A primary inborn error that results in an expressed abnormality in the renal proximal tubule (and perhaps the intestine), which impairs phosphate reabsorption (and absorption), underlies the pathogenesis of XLH. Although controversy exists regarding the character of the inborn error, studies in *Hyp* mice suggest that elaboration of a humoral factor underlies the observed inhibition of phosphate transport in affected patients. In this regard, recent investigations resulted in the cloning and identification of the disease gene as PHEX, a *phos*-phate-regulating gene with homologies to endopeptidases located on the X chromosome. Deactivating mutations of this membrane-localized gene clearly underlie the phenotypic expression of XLH by a mechanism that is as yet poorly understood. However, recognition of a humoral factor as essential to the pathogenesis of the disease suggests that the PHEX gene product may function normally to inactivate phosphatonin, a presumed phosphaturic hormone. An excess of this hormone would occur secondary to PHEX protein dysfunction and result in renal phosphate wasting and perhaps abnormal bone mineralization. Despite these apparent advances, further progress has been limited by the inability to identify physiologically relevant PHEX substrates, which may function as phosphatonins. The search for candidate substrates has been guided, in part, by the knowledge that related endopeptidases have substrates that are coexpressed in an organ/cell type-specific fashion. In this context, physiologically relevant PHEX substrate is likely produced in osteoblasts, the site of predominant *PHEX* expression. Indeed, genes regulating extracellular matrix production, bone mineralization, and renal P transport (i.e., stanniocalcin I) are colocalized to the osteoblast. However, efforts to date have not identified a PHEX/Phex substrate in osteoblasts, which influences renal P transport or bone mineralization.

Regardless, choice of therapy for this disease has been remarkably influenced by an increased understanding of the pathophysiologic factors that affect its phenotypic expression. Thus, current treatment strategies for children directly address the combined calcitriol and phosphorus deficiency characteristic of the disease. Generally, the regimen includes a period of titration to achieve a maximum dose of calcitriol, 40 to 60 ng/kg/day in two divided doses and phosphorus, 1 to 2 g/day in four or five divided doses. Although youths occasionally prove refractory to such therapeutic intervention, combined therapy often improves growth velocity, normalizes lower extremity deformities, and induces healing of the attendant bone disease. Of course, treatment involves a significant risk of toxicity that is generally expressed as abnormalities of calcium homeostasis and/or detrimental effects on renal function. Therapy in adults is reserved for episodes of intractable bone pain and refractory nonunion of bone fractures. Recent observations that long-term growth hormone administration in affected youths may benefit growth, phosphate retention, and bone density suggest that a subgroup of patients may benefit from adjunctive treatment with this hormone.

HEREDITARY HYPOPHOSPHATEMIC RICKETS WITH HYPERCALCIURIA (HHRH). This rare genetic disease is marked by hypophosphatemic rickets with hypercalciuria. In contrast to other diseases in which renal phosphate transport is limited, patients with HHRH exhibit increased 1,25-dihydroxyvitamin D production. The resultant elevated serum calcitriol levels enhance the gastrointestinal calcium absorption, which in turn increases the filtered renal calcium load and inhibits PTH secretion. The clinical expression of the disease is heterogeneous, although initial symptoms generally consist of bone pain and/or deformities of the lower extremities. Additional features of the disease include short stature, muscle weakness, and radiographic signs of rickets/osteomalacia and/or osteopenia. The various symptoms and signs may exist separately or in combination and may be present in a mild or severe form. In general, the severity of the bone mineralization defect correlates inversely with the prevailing serum phosphorus concentration. Relatives of patients with evident HHRH may exhibit an additional mode of disease expression. These subjects manifest hypercalciuria and hypophosphatemia, but the abnormalities are less marked and occur in the absence of discernible bone disease. The preponderance of evidence indicates that HHRH is inherited by autosomal recessive transmission.

To date, the genetic defect underlying this disease remains unknown. Although targeted inactivation in mice of Npt2 (a renal-specific, brush border membrane Na^+-phosphate cotransporter expressed in the proximal convoluted tubule) leads to severe renal phosphate wasting, hypercalciuria, and skeletal abnormalities, extensive study has revealed no putative disease-causing mutations in the *NPT2* gene, and linkage analysis has failed to link HHRH to the *NPT2* gene region.

Patients with HHRH have been treated successfully with high-dose phosphorus (1 to 2.5 g/day in five divided doses) alone. In response to therapy, bone pain disappears and muscular strength improves substantially. Moreover, the majority of treated subjects exhibit accelerated linear growth, and radiologic signs of rickets are completely absent within 4 to 9 months. Despite this favorable response, limited studies indicate that such treatment does not completely heal the associated osteomalacia. Therefore, further studies are necessary to determine whether phosphorus alone is truly sufficient for this disorder.

AUTOSOMAL DOMINANT HYPOPHOSPHATEMIC RICKETS (ADHR). Although many investigators assume that all familial renal phosphate wasting disorders are X-linked, several studies have documented an autosomal dominant inheritance of a hypophosphatemic disorder similar to XLH. The phenotypic manifestations of this disorder include the expected hypophosphatemia due to renal phosphate wasting, lower extremity deformities, and rickets/osteomalacia. Affected patients also demonstrate normal serum levels of parathyroid hormone and 25-hydroxyvitamin D, while maintaining an inappropriate normal concentration of 1,25-dihydroxyvitamin D, in the presence of hypophosphatemia. Long-term studies indicate that a few of the affected female patients demonstrate delayed penetrance of clinically apparent disease and an increased tendency for bone fracture, which are uncommon occurrences in XLH. In addition, among patients who manifest disease in childhood, rare individuals lose the renal phosphate-wasting defect after puberty. Limited information is available regarding other aspects of the disease. However, recent studies have identified the gene locus for this disease on chromosome 12p13 in an 18-cM interval between the flanking markers D12S100 and D12S397. Moreover, mutations in FGF-23 have been discovered in patients with ADHR. These mutations protect the protein from proteolysis, thereby potentially elevating circulating levels of the FGF-23, which likely leads to P wasting. This discovery suggests that FGF-23 may not only function as a phosphaturic factor in ADHR but also serve as a PHEX substrate and phosphatonin in XLH.

An apparent forme fruste of ADHR (autosomal dominant) hypophosphatemic bone disease has many of the characteristics of XLH and ADHR, but recent reports indicate that affected children display no evidence of rachitic disease. Because this syndrome is described in only a few small kindreds, and radiographically evident rickets is not universal in children with familial hypophosphatemia, these families may have ADHR. Further observations are necessary to discriminate this possibility.

X-LINKED RECESSIVE HYPOPHOSPHATEMIC RICKETS (X-LINKED HYPERCALCIURIC NEPHROLITHIASIS). The initial description of X-linked recessive hypophosphatemic rickets involved a family in which males presented with rickets or osteomalacia, hypophosphatemia, and a reduced renal threshold for phosphate reabsorption. In contrast to patients with XLH, affected subjects exhibited hypercalciuria, elevated serum 1,25-dihydroxyvitamin D levels, and proteinuria of up to 3 g/day. Patients also developed nephrolithiasis and nephrocalcinosis with progressive renal failure in early adulthood. Female carriers in the family were not hypophosphatemic and lacked any biochemical abnormalities other than hypercalciuria. Three related syndromes have been reported independently: X-linked recessive nephrolithiasis with renal failure, Dent's disease, and low-molecular-weight proteinuria with hypercalciuria and nephrocalcinosis. These syndromes differ in degree from each other, but common themes include proximal tubular reabsorptive failure, nephrolithiasis, nephrocalcinosis, progressive renal insufficiency, and, in some cases, rickets or osteomalacia. Identification of mutations in the voltage-gated chloride-channel gene *CLCN5* in all four syndromes has established that they are phenotypic variants of a single disease and are not separate entities. However, the varied manifestations that may be associated with mutations in this gene, particularly the presence of hypophosphatemia and rickets/osteomalacia, underscore that environmental differences, diet, and/or modifying genetic backgrounds may influence phenotypic expression of the disease.

TUMOR-INDUCED OSTEOMALACIA (ONCOGENOUS OSTEOMALACIA). Since initial recognition of this disease, reports have been published of approximately 110 patients in whom rickets and/or osteomalacia have been associated with a coexisting tumor. The coexistent tumors have been of mesenchymal origin in the majority of patients. The cardinal feature of this disease is remission of the unexplained bone disease after tumor resection. In general, affected patients present with bone and muscle pain, muscle weakness, and, occasionally, recurrent fractures of long bones. Biochemical abnormalities include renal phosphate wasting marked by an abnormally low renal tubular maximum for the reabsorption of phosphate per liter of glomerular filtrate, decreased gastrointestinal absorption of phosphate, and consequent hypophosphatemia. In general, serum 25-hydroxyvitamin D levels are normal and serum calcitriol is profoundly decreased or inappropriately normal relative to the hypophosphatemia. Generalized osteopenia, pseudofractures, and coarsened trabeculae, as well as widened epiphyseal plates in children, comprise the common radiographic abnormalities of the syndrome.

Most investigators agree that tumor production of a humoral factor or factors that may affect multiple functions of the proximal renal tubule, particularly phosphate reabsorption (resulting in hypophosphatemia), underlies the pathogenesis of this syndrome. This possibility is supported by (1) the presence of phosphaturic activity in tumor extracts in patients with tumor-induced osteomalacia; (2) the occurrence of hypophosphatemia and increased urinary phosphate excretion in heterotransplanted tumor-bearing athymic nude mice; and (3) the demonstration that extracts of the heterotransplanted tumor inhibit renal 25-hydroxyvitamin D–1α-hydroxylase activity in cultured kidney cells. Indeed, extensive analysis of tumors from patients with tumor-induced osteomalacia have revealed excessive production of FGF23, proteins with known functions related to bone matrix formation (osteopontin, dentin matrix protein, and fibronectin) and mineralization (MEPE/osteoregulin) or mineral ion transport (Glvr-1, Ank-A), as well as those with potential bone-related activity (e.g., Frizzled Related Protein 4). Continued study of these proteins will undoubtedly reveal that one or more of them is central to the pathogenesis of this disease. Indeed, based on these observations, it is likely that the tumor-induced osteomalacia syndrome is heterogeneous and that "phosphatonin" may be a family of hormones. Regardless, recent studies indicate that in a substantial proportion of affected patients the secretion of the phosphatonins may be modulated by somatostatin receptors. Hence, tumor identification is possible upon octreotide scanning and octreotide therapy (50 to 100 μg SC three times a day) may ameliorate the biochemical and perhaps bone abnormalities of the syndrome if tumor resection is not possible.

Adding to the complexity of the syndrome, patients with tumor-associated osteomalacia secondary to hematogenous malignancy exhibit abnormalities of the syndrome secondary to a distinctly different mechanism. In these subjects, the nephropathy associated with light-chain proteinuria results in decreased renal phosphate reabsorption and consequent hypophosphatemia. At least 15 patients with this form of the disorder have been reported.

The primary treatment of this disorder is complete resection of the associated tumor. However, recurrence or metastases of tumors often preclude such definitive therapy. In such cases, calcitriol (1.5 to 3.0 μg/day) alone or combined with phosphorus supplementation (2 to 4 g/day) completely heals the attendant bone disease or significantly improves the biochemical and histologic abnormalities. Careful serial assessment of parathyroid function, serum and urinary calcium, and renal function are essential to ensure safe therapy in affected subjects.

Fanconi's Syndrome (Chapter 122)

Rickets and osteomalacia are frequently associated with Fanconi's syndrome, a disorder characterized by phosphaturia and consequent hypophosphatemia, aminoaciduria, renal glycosuria, albuminuria, and proximal renal tubular acidosis. Although a wide diversity of congenital and acquired diseases are associated with this syndrome (see Table 259–1), damage to the proximal renal tubule represents the common underlying mechanism of disease. Resultant dysfunction results in renal wasting of those substances primarily reabsorbed at the proximal tubule. The associated bone disease in this disorder is likely secondary to hypophosphatemia and/or acidosis, abnormalities that occur in association with aberrantly regulated (Fanconi's syndrome, type 1) or normally regulated (Fanconi's syndrome, type 2) vitamin D metabolism. In any case, regardless of the underlying cause, patients with osteomalacia associated with adult-acquired Fanconi's syndrome appear to respond well to treatment with phosphate and vitamin D replacement. In fact, these patients do not appear to require 1,25-dihydroxyvitamin D.

METABOLIC ACIDOSIS

Osteomalacia occurs secondary to renal tubular acidosis and the acidosis that follows ureterosigmoidoscopy. The bone disease results from the multifactorial influence of acidosis, which decreases the conversion of amorphous calcium phosphate to hydroxyapatite at the mineralization front, induces renal phosphate wasting, and possibly interferes with calcitriol production. Systemic acidosis also enhances dissolution of bone and results in hypercalciuria. Affected patients have a normal serum calcium level, a low-normal or decreased serum phosphorus level, and an elevated alkaline phosphatase level. Secondary to hypercalciuria, nephrocalcinosis and renal lithiasis often occur. Bicarbonate therapy alone effectively treats the osteomalacia associated with metabolic acidosis, although administering vitamin D and calcium when starting therapy facilitates healing of the bone disease.

PRIMARY DISORDERS OF BONE MATRIX

Intrinsic disorders of bone in which apparently abnormal matrix is produced but is not normally mineralized are extremely rare and are poorly understood. These diseases may result from presumed abnormalities of collagen or other proteins in the matrix or aberrant enzyme activity essential for normal mineralization.

Abnormal Bone Matrix

FIBROGENESIS IMPERFECTA OSSIUM. Fibrogenesis imperfecta ossium is a rare, sporadically occurring disorder characterized by the gradual onset of intractable skeletal pain in middle-aged men and women. Pathologic fractures are a prominent clinical feature, and patients typically become bedridden. Although the serum calcium and phosphorus levels are normal, the alkaline phosphatase level is invariably elevated. The bones have a dense, amorphous, mottled appearance radiologically and a disorganized arrangement of collagen with decreased birefringence histologically. Most likely, the disorganized collagen matrix limits normal bone mineralization.

AXIAL OSTEOMALACIA. Axial osteomalacia is another unusual sporadically occurring disorder that generally affects only middle-aged men. The majority of patients present with only vague, dull, chronic axial discomfort that typically affects the cervical region most severely. Abnormal radiographic findings are limited to the pelvis and spine, where the coarsened trabecular pattern is characteristic of osteomalacia. Although the alkaline phosphatase level may be increased, histopathologic studies reveal a normal lamellar pattern of collagen.

However, the osteoblasts appear flat and inactive, suggesting that an osteoblastic defect, and perhaps an attendant abnormal matrix, inhibits normal mineralization.

Abnormal Enzyme Activity

HYPOPHOSPHATASIA. Hypophosphatasia is a heritable disorder characterized by a deficiency of the tissue-nonspecific (liver, bone, kidney) isoenzyme of alkaline phosphatase, increased urinary excretion of phosphorylethanolamine, and skeletal disease that includes osteomalacia and rickets. The severity of clinical expression is remarkably variable and spans intrauterine death from profound skeletal hypomineralization at one extreme to lifelong absence of symptoms at the other. As a consequence, six clinical disease types are distinguished (see Table 259–1). The age at which skeletal disease is initially noted delineates, in large part, the perinatal (lethal), infantile, childhood, and adult variants of the disorder. However, affected children and adults may manifest only the unique dental abnormalities of the syndrome and, accordingly, are classified as having odontohypophosphatasia. Finally, patients with the rare variant, pseudohypophosphatasia, have the clinical-radiologic-biochemical features of the classic disease without a decrease in the circulating levels of alkaline phosphatase. These individuals have defects in cellular localization and substrate specificity of the enzyme.

Affected infants exhibit hypercalcemia, hypercalciuria, enlarged sutures of the skull, craniosynostosis, delayed dentition, enlarged epiphyses, and prominent costochondral junctions. Genu valgum or varum may develop subsequently. In older children, disease may be limited to rickets. Surprisingly, the disorder in adults is mild despite the presence of osteopenia. Indeed, the disease may be limited to slowly healing metatarsal fractures or loss or fracture of teeth. Nevertheless, 50% of patients have an history of early exfoliation of deciduous teeth and/or rickets, and disease may reflect re-expression of the childhood disorder.

The perinatal and infantile forms of disease are inherited as autosomal recessive traits. The modes of inheritance for odontophosphatasia, adult hypophosphatasia, and childhood hypophosphatasia remain unclear, although an autosomal dominant disease transmission has been described in some kindreds with mild or severe disease. In many of these families, recent studies indicate that the existent mutations exhibit a negative dominant effect, inhibiting the enzymatic activity of the heterodimer. The variability in disease apparently depends on the degree of heterodimeric inhibition with highly negative dominant effects associated with severe hypophosphatasia. The physiologic basis for the bone disease likely relates to the role of alkaline phosphatase in cleaving pyrophosphate, an inhibitor of bone mineralization. Failure to hydrolyze this physiologic substrate results in inorganic pyrophosphate elevated to levels sufficiently high to inhibit the mineralization process. The consequence of this pathophysiologic process is a block of the vectorial spread of mineral from initial nuclei within matrix vesicles outward into the matrix of growth cartilage and bone.

Therapy of this disease has been generally unrewarding. Thus, supportive treatment is important and may include craniotomy in children (to manage craniosynostosis) and, in adults, insertion of load-sharing intramedullary rods to treat fractures. Expert dental care is also crucial to minimize tooth loss and prevent consequent malnutrition in youths.

MINERALIZATION INHIBITORS

ETIDRONATE. Disturbances in mineralization may be seen in patients who consume etidronate daily at doses greater than 5 mg/kg of body weight. The etidronate is deposited at the bone surface and inhibits osteoblast function; it also directly inhibits calcium-phosphate crystallization.

FLUORIDE. Although multiple studies document that fluoride stimulates new bone formation, administering the drug in high doses without adequate calcium supplementation results in poorly mineralized bone, consistent with osteomalacia. The mechanisms by which fluoride alters osteoblast function and/or directly inhibits mineralization remains unknown.

ALUMINUM. Excess aluminum accumulation in bone inhibits mineralization and is a potential mechanism for the osteomalacia

observed in patients with chronic renal failure, as discussed earlier. In addition, accumulation of aluminum in bone likely underlies the osteomalacia observed in patients treated with total parenteral nutrition. In such cases, aluminum contamination of casein hydrolysate, as well as albumin, phosphate, and calcium solutions, provides the major source of the mineral. Changing total parenteral nutrition solutions from those with casein hydrolysate to those with purified amino acids has markedly reduced the incidence of clinically evident bone disease.

SUGGESTED READINGS

Bai XY, Miao D, Goltzman D, et al: The autosomal dominant hypophosphatemic rickets R176Q mutation in fibroblast growth factor 23 resists proteolytic cleavage and enhances in vivo biological potency. J Biol Chem 2003;278:9843–9849. *Direct in vivo evidence that missense mutations from ADHR kindreds are gain-of-function mutations that retain and increase the protein's biological potency. For the first time a potential role for FGF23 in dissociating parathyroid hormone actions on mineral fluxes and vitamin D metabolism in the kidney is defined.*

Baroncelli GI, Bertelloni S, Ceccarelli C, Saggese G: Effect of growth hormone treatment on final height, phosphate metabolism, and bone mineral density in children with X-linked hypophosphatemic rickets. J Pediatr 2001;138:236–243. *Review of the underlying concepts and the specific details of treatment for hypophosphatemic rickets, including use of growth hormone.*

Gartner LM, Greer FR, for the Section on Breastfeeding and Committee on Nutrition. American Academy of Pediatrics. Prevention of rickets and vitamin D deficiency: New guidelines for vitamin D intake. Pediatrics 2003;111:908–910. *Recommends 200 IU of vitamin D per day be continued throughout childhood and adolescence.*

Jonsson KB, Zahradnik R, Larsson T, et al: Fibroblast growth factor 23 in oncogenic osteomalacia and X-linked hypophosphatemia. N Engl J Med 2003;348:1656–1663. *FGF-23, a growth factor, can be markedly elevated in oncogenic osteomalacia or X-linked hypophosphatemia and may have a role in phosphate homeostasis.*

Thakker RV: Pathogenesis of Dent's disease and related syndromes of X-linked nephrolithiasis. Kidney Int 2000;57:787–793. *Review of the interrelationships and common themes (including rickets/osteomalacia) between the various X-linked recessive syndromes that are caused by mutations in the chloride channel gene.*

260 THE PARATHYROID GLANDS, HYPERCALCEMIA, AND HYPOCALCEMIA

Allen M. Spiegel

THE PARATHYROID GLANDS

EMBRYOLOGY AND ANATOMY. Normally, there are four parathyroids, averaging 120 mg in total weight, but as many as 5% of normal individuals may have more than four glands. The superior parathyroids are derived from the fourth (more caudal) branchial pouches and remain almost stationary during embryologic development. Their typical final location is near the upper poles of the thyroid. Aberrant locations include the tracheoesophageal groove and the retroesophageal space. The inferior parathyroids develop (in association with the thymus) from the third branchial pouches. During normal development, they migrate caudally, assuming a final position near the lower poles of the thyroid. The inferior parathyroids may fail to descend, remaining near the angle of the jaw or, at the other extreme, may descend into the anterior mediastinum in association with the thymus.

SYNTHESIS AND SECRETION OF PARATHYROID HORMONE. Parathyroid hormone (PTH), together with vitamin D (Chapter 260), is the principal regulator of ionized calcium in extracellular fluid. PTH is synthesized in the parathyroid glands as "preproparathyroid hormone," a precursor composed of 115 amino acids. A hydrophobic "leader" peptide of 25 amino acids is first cleaved from the amino-terminus to yield the prohormone, followed by cleavage of a basic amino-terminal hexapeptide to yield the mature 84-amino-acid hormone. The latter is the principal secreted form of the hormone. There is no evidence for secretion of either the preprohormone or the prohormone. The prohormone possesses less than 0.2% of the biologic activity of the native 84-amino-acid hormone. The full biologic activity of the intact hormone resides within the amino-terminal 1-34 fragment, whereas fragments from the midregion and carboxy-terminal regions lack biologic activity (Fig. 260–1).

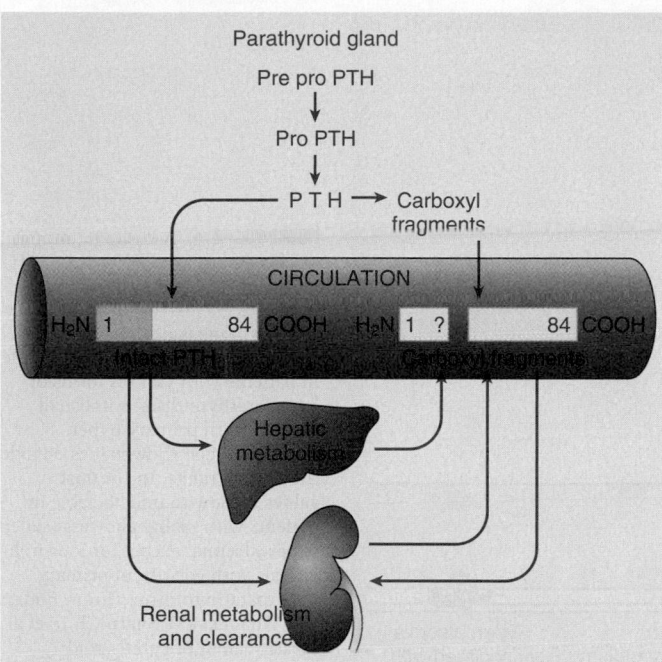

Parathyroid gland

Pre pro PTH

Pro PTH

P T H → Carboxyl fragments

CIRCULATION

H₂N 1   84 COOH   H₂N 1 ?   84 COOH

Intact PTH   Carboxyl fragments

Hepatic metabolism

Renal metabolism and clearance

FIGURE 260–1 • Secretion, metabolism, and clearance of parathyroid hormone (PTH). *Top:* PTH is synthesized as a preprohormone and undergoes successive cleavages within the parathyroid to the mature (1–84), major secreted form of the hormone. Under certain conditions (e.g., hypercalcemia), some of the hormone is cleaved intracellularly into biologically inactive, carboxy-terminal fragments, which are also secreted. *Middle:* The major circulating forms of the hormone are the intact 1–84 species (the shaded region corresponds to the amino-terminal 1–34 portion possessing full biologic activity) and biologically inactive carboxy-terminal fragments. The presence of amino-terminal fragments in the circulation is unclear (indicated by "?"). *Bottom:* Peripheral metabolism of the hormone occurs in liver and kidney. The kidney also clears intact hormone and carboxy-terminal fragments from the circulation. (From Endres DE, Villanueva R, Sharp CF Jr, et al: Measurement of parathyroid hormone. Endocrinol Metab Clin North Am 1989;18:611–629.)

Secretion of PTH is regulated primarily by the concentration of ionized calcium in the extracellular fluid. Normally, PTH secretion is regulated at a "set point" that maintains serum ionized calcium within a relatively narrow range. Deviations below the set point stimulate hormone secretion, and deviations above the set point inhibit hormone secretion. Effects of calcium on hormone secretion occur acutely (within minutes); low calcium levels have a slower stimulatory action on hormone synthesis. At high calcium concentrations, there is evidence for intracellular degradation of synthesized hormone and possible release of biologically inactive fragments. High magnesium ion concentrations in extracellular fluid, like high calcium concentrations, inhibit PTH secretion, but hypomagnesemia, unlike hypocalcemia, may inhibit hormone secretion and action. The active metabolite of vitamin D, $1,25(OH)_2D$ (dihydroxycholecalciferol), suppresses both secretion and synthesis of PTH. Reduction in $1,25(OH)_2D$ is a major factor contributing to increased PTH secretion in renal failure.

FORMS OF PARATHYROID HORMONE IN PLASMA. PTH circulates in plasma as the intact hormone secreted from the gland and as fragments derived either from glandular secretion (particularly in hypercalcemic states) or from peripheral metabolism of the intact hormone. Most of these fragments lack biologic activity but may, depending on antibody specificity, contribute to immunoreactivity in plasma (see Fig. 260–1).

PARATHYROID HORMONE ACTION. PTH acts directly on kidney and bone, and indirectly on the gut, to maintain the normal concentration of serum ionized calcium (see Chapter 257 for a complete discussion of mineral homeostasis). In the kidney, PTH (1) enhances reabsorption of calcium and of magnesium from the glomerular filtrate; (2) increases excretion of phosphate and of bicarbonate; (3)

activates the enzyme (1α-hydroxylase) that forms the active metabolite $1,25(OH)_2D$ of vitamin D. In bone, PTH causes the release of calcium and phosphate into the extracellular fluid. The hormone acts directly on osteoblasts, which secondarily affect osteoclast activity. The hypercalcemic action on bone and the anticalciuric action on kidney combine to raise the serum calcium level. The phosphatemic action on bone tends to blunt the hypercalcemic effect of the hormone owing to formation of calcium phosphate complexes, but the phosphaturic action counteracts the tendency to hyperphosphatemia. Stimulation of $1,25(OH)_2D$ formation promotes enhanced intestinal absorption of calcium, which also serves to maintain a normal serum calcium level. The clinical consequences of PTH excess (or in the opposite direction, hormone deficiency) follow directly from the actions of the hormone: (1) hypercalcemia, (2) a tendency to hypophosphatemia, (3) a tendency to reduced serum bicarbonate levels and hyperchloremia, (4) increased serum levels of $1,25(OH)_2D$, and (5) relative reduction in urinary calcium excretion and increase in urinary phosphate excretion for a given filtered load.

MECHANISM OF PARATHYROID HORMONE ACTION. The first step in PTH action is binding to specific plasma membrane–bound receptors on target cells in bone and kidney. Such receptors are coupled to guanosine triphosphate–binding proteins—in particular, the Gs protein that links receptors to stimulation of adenylyl cyclase (for a more general description of the mechanism of polypeptide hormone action, see Chapter 234). Adenylyl cyclase catalyzes the formation of the "second messenger," cyclic adenosine monophosphate (cAMP), which mediates hormone action by stimulating the phosphorylation of critical intracellular proteins. A diagnostically useful peculiarity of PTH action on proximal renal tubular cells is that, not only are cAMP levels increased intracellularly but, because of overflow into the extracellular fluid, urinary cAMP excretion is also increased. "Second messengers" other than cAMP may also mediate certain actions of PTH.

ASSAY OF PARATHYROID HORMONE IN PLASMA. Normally, the concentration of biologically active PTH circulating in plasma is low (<50 pg/mL). Bioassays sensitive enough to detect such low levels include a renal cytochemical assay and several assays based on stimulating cAMP formation in bone or kidney cells. Unfortunately, such assays are too cumbersome for routine clinical use. Total urinary cAMP excretion (normalized to creatinine clearance by simultaneously measuring serum and urinary creatinine) is an easily measured and sensitive index of circulating PTH bioactivity. It is elevated in primary hyperparathyroidism, is low in hypoparathyroidism, and falls within 1 hour of successful parathyroidectomy in patients with hyperparathyroidism. Increased urinary cAMP excretion, however, is not absolutely specific for PTH hypersecretion; parathyroid hormone–related peptide, secreted by many malignancies, similarly increases urinary cAMP excretion, which must be taken into account when interpreting urinary cAMP measurements in subjects with hypercalcemia (see Hypercalcemia Associated with Malignancy).

Radioimmunoassays are sufficiently sensitive and practical for routinely measuring circulating PTH. Interpretation of assay results requires an understanding of what a particular antiserum is measuring. Immunoreactivity need not correlate with biologic activity. Indeed, the bulk of circulating PTH consists of biologically inactive midregion and carboxy-terminal fragments. Because such fragments are cleared by the kidney, renal impairment causes them to accumulate at even higher concentrations (see Fig. 260–1). Antisera with predominant specificity for midregion and carboxy-terminal regions, therefore, measure predominantly biologically inactive hormone fragments. Such assays are reasonably useful for discriminating normal from hyperparathyroid subjects, but their utility is much more limited in subjects with renal failure. Even with normal renal function, such assays may show considerable overlap between patients with parathyroid-mediated hypercalcemia and those with non–parathyroid-mediated hypercalcemia. In part, this may reflect the release of inactive hormone fragments by the parathyroid gland in non–PTH-mediated hypercalcemic states.

Most of these problems have been circumvented by the development of highly sensitive "two-site" immunoradiometric assays. Such assays employ two distinct antibodies, one against the amino-terminal region and one against the carboxy-terminal region. Effectively, only intact, biologically active hormone is measured. Such assays allow measurement of circulating hormone in most normal

Diseases of Bone and Mineral Metabolism

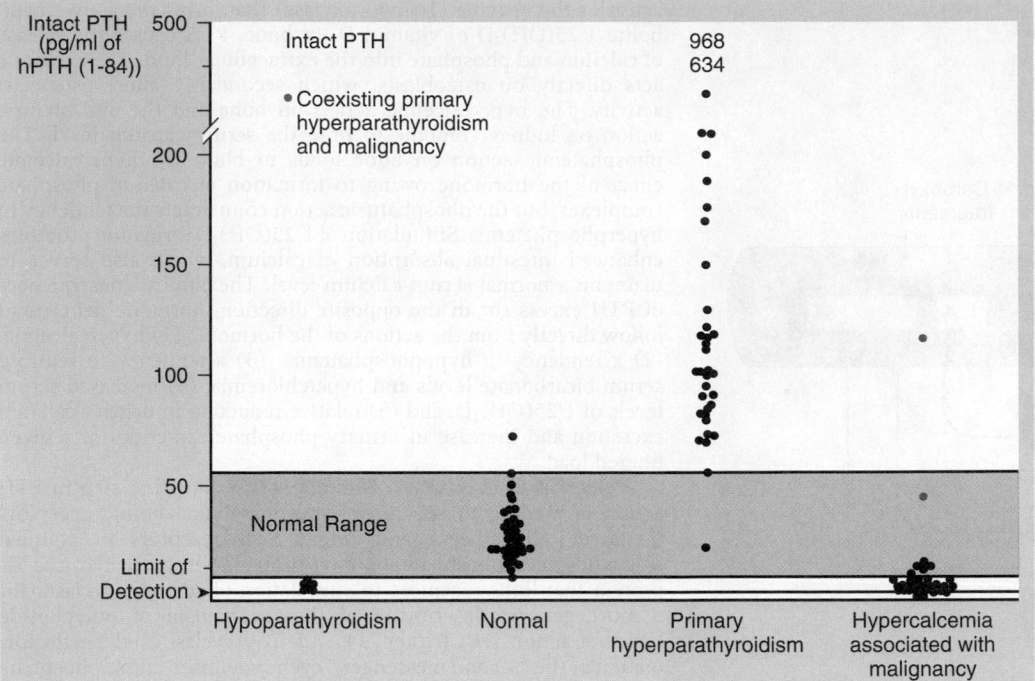

FIGURE 260–2 • Two-site immunoassay for parathyroid hormone (PTH) in serum. The two-site method measures exclusively intact PTH. The hormone is detectable in most normal subjects and is undetectable in patients with various forms of hypoparathyroidism. Almost all patients with primary hyperparathyroidism show values outside the normal range. In contrast, values are low to undetectable in patients with malignancy-associated hypercalcemia, except for four individuals with coexistent primary hyperparathyroidism. (From Endres DB, Villanueva R, Sharp CF Jr, et al: Measurement of parathyroid hormone. Endocrinol Metab Clin North Am 1989;18:611–629.)

individuals, are scarcely affected by renal impairment, and allow excellent discrimination between PTH-mediated and non–PTH-mediated causes of hypercalcemia (Fig. 260–2).

HYPERCALCEMIA

Definition

Hypercalcemia is an abnormal elevation in serum ionized calcium concentration. Because total, rather than ionized, calcium is generally measured, one must be aware of factors that influence the fraction of total serum calcium that is ionized. Of these, serum albumin concentration is of greatest clinical relevance because albumin is the chief circulating calcium-binding protein. "Normal" total serum calcium concentration associated with a significant reduction in serum albumin (e.g., in patients with malignancy) may actually represent abnormally elevated levels of serum ionized calcium. Acid-base status also influences the proportion of total serum calcium that is protein bound (alkalosis decreases the ionized calcium concentration, and acidosis increases it).

Etiology

Many different diseases are potential causes of hypercalcemia. Of these, the most common are primary hyperparathyroidism (particularly in asymptomatic individuals whose hypercalcemia is detected by routine serum chemistry measurement) and malignancy (particularly in hospitalized individuals). These disorders, as well as some of the rarer causes of hypercalcemia, are considered in the following discussion.

Pathogenesis

Hypercalcemia results from excessive calcium influx into the extracellular fluid from bone and decreased efflux from the kidneys into the urine. Calcium mobilization from bone is mediated by activators of bone resorption. These activators include systemic factors (e.g., PTH, $1,25(OH)_2D$) and locally acting factors, such as various lymphokines. Reduced renal calcium excretion may lead to hypercalcemia, particularly in states of increased bone turnover. Renal impairment, volume depletion, and anticalciuretic agents, such as thiazide diuretics and PTH, are clinically relevant factors that can reduce renal calcium excretion and provoke hypercalcemia.

Clinical Manifestations

Many manifestations are not specific to the underlying cause (specific disease manifestations are discussed under individual disease headings). Extreme hypercalcemia leads to coma and death. Neurologic manifestations in less severe cases may include confusion, lethargy, weakness, and hyporeflexia. Hypercalcemia may be detected by shortening of the QT interval on the electrocardiogram. Arrhythmias are rare, but bradycardia and first-degree heart block have been reported. Acute hypercalcemia may be associated with significant hypertension. Gastrointestinal manifestations include constipation and anorexia; in severe cases, there may be nausea and vomiting. Acute pancreatitis has been reported in association with hypercalcemia of various causes. Hypercalcemia interferes with antidiuretic hormone action, thereby leading to polyuria and polydipsia. Reversible reduction in renal function associated with significant hypercalcemia is followed by more permanent damage if hypercalcemia persists. Particularly if serum phosphorus is also increased, hypercalcemia can lead to nephrocalcinosis and interstitial nephritis. Hypercalciuria and nephrolithiasis may also occur. Deposition of calcium in other soft tissues, including skin and cornea, is most likely to occur in patients with associated hyperphosphatemia.

Differential Diagnosis

Potential causes of hypercalcemia are listed in Table 260–1. These may be divided into PTH-mediated (primary hyperparathyroidism) and non–PTH-mediated diseases (all others). Although ectopic secretion of PTH by tumors was long considered a potential cause of PTH-mediated hypercalcemia, there is general agreement that ectopic secretion of authentic PTH (as opposed to PTH-related peptides; see later text) by tumors is extremely rare. The first step in the differential diagnosis of hypercalcemia is to establish whether PTH hypersecretion is present because subsequent diagnostic maneuvers and definitive therapy critically depend on this distinction.

Readily measured blood and urine chemistries may offer some clues to diagnosis. In theory, PTH hypersecretion should be reflected by hypophosphatemia, hyperchloremia, hypobicarbonatemia, increased urinary phosphate excretion, and urinary calcium excretion that is relatively low for the filtered load. PTH secretion suppressed by hypercalcemia of nonparathyroid etiology should, in theory, reverse these parameters. In practice, there is considerable overlap

Table 260-1 • CAUSES OF HYPERCALCEMIA

Parathyroid hormone-mediated causes
Primary hyperparathyroidism
   Sporadic, familial (multiple endocrine neoplasia types I and II; hyperparathyroidism–jaw tumor syndrome; familial isolated hyperparathyroidism?)
Familial hypocalciuric hypercalcemia*
Ectopic secretion of parathyroid hormone by tumors (very rare)
Non–parathyroid hormone-mediated causes
Malignancy associated
   Local osteolytic hypercalcemia
   Humoral hypercalcemia of malignancy
Vitamin D–mediated
   Vitamin D intoxication
   Excessive production of $1,25(OH)_2D$ in granulomatous disorders
Other endocrinopathies
   Thyrotoxicosis
   Hypoadrenalism
Immobilization with increased bone turnover (e.g., Paget's disease)
Acute renal failure with rhabdomyolysis
Calcium carbonate ingestion (milk-alkali syndrome)
Jansen-type metaphyseal chondrodysplasia (activating mutation of parathyroid hormone receptor)

*Parathyroid hormone secretion is necessary for hypercalcemia but is not the primary defect.

Table 260-2 • DIAGNOSTIC APPROACH TO HYPERCALCEMIA

1. Distinguish parathyroid hormone (PTH)-mediated forms of hypercalcemia from non–PTH-mediated forms: *PTH immunoassay (preferably two-site type) is the definitive test.*
2. If the PTH level is elevated, primary hyperparathyroidism is the most likely diagnosis: *Family history for hypercalcemia should be checked to distinguish sporadic from familial (multiple endocrine neoplasia syndromes, hyperparathyroidism–jaw tumor syndrome, and hypocalciuric hypercalcemia) disease. Marginal elevation in PTH levels, particularly in young, asymptomatic individuals, should prompt urine calcium measurement to exclude familial hypocalciuric hypercalcemia. In patients with coexisting malignancy, selective venous sampling can be done to exclude ectopic PTH secretion, but the latter is extremely rare.*
3. If PTH is low or undetectable, further laboratory tests (in addition to complete history, physical, and radiologic studies) are needed to distinguish among the various forms of non–PTH-mediated forms of hypercalcemia: *Increased urinary cAMP excretion suggests tumor secretion of PTH-related peptide (direct radioimmunoassays for this peptide are now available). Increased $1,25(OH)_2D$ suggests granulomatous disease (including some types of lymphoma).*

cAMP = cyclic adenosine monophosphate.

in each of these parameters between patients with parathyroid-mediated forms of hypercalcemia and those with non–parathyroid-mediated forms. This situation may reflect confounding variables, such as vomiting, diuretic treatment, and renal failure, as well as the ability of certain hypercalcemic agents to mimic many actions of PTH. Most important in this respect is PTH-related peptide, first isolated from tumors associated with the syndrome of humoral hypercalcemia. This peptide mimics all of the known actions of PTH on kidney and bone, including increasing urinary cAMP excretion and stimulating renal formation of $1,25(OH)_2D$. Decreased urinary cAMP excretion (with normal renal function) strongly suggests non–PTH-mediated hypercalcemia, but increased urinary cAMP excretion is compatible with both primary hyperparathyroidism and tumor secretion of PTH-related peptide. Serum $1,25(OH)_2D$ concentration also does not allow definitive diagnosis. It may be elevated in primary hyperparathyroidism and vitamin D–related causes of hypercalcemia and may be reduced in other non–parathyroid-mediated causes of hypercalcemia. For reasons that are not entirely clear, the serum $1,25(OH)_2D$ level is often low in patients with malignancies secreting PTH-related peptide, despite the ability of the peptide to stimulate $1,25(OH)_2D$ formation.

Definitive distinction between parathyroid- and non–parathyroid-mediated causes of hypercalcemia relies primarily on PTH immunoassay. As discussed earlier, this distinction is best made with the two-site type of assays that measure intact PTH and are unaffected by renal function (see Fig. 260-2). An elevated PTH level secures the diagnosis of primary hyperparathyroidism. In selected cases with coexistent malignancy, the unlikely possibility of ectopic PTH secretion may be excluded by selective venous sampling and assay of PTH, but generally this testing is unnecessary. Hormone levels in the normal range suggest the possibility of familial hypocalciuric hypercalcemia. This entity is discussed further in the section on hyperparathyroidism. Low to undetectable values for PTH place the patient in the non–parathyroid-mediated category. Additional testing is necessary to establish a specific diagnosis within this group. Immunoassays for PTH-related peptide have been developed, and these may allow the diagnosis of hypercalcemia caused by a tumor secreting this agent. Complete clinical evaluation, including history (e.g., vitamin ingestion, chronicity of symptoms), physical examination (masses, lymphadenopathy), radiologic studies, and other blood tests (e.g., thyroid and adrenal function), may point to a diagnosis. An unusual cause of non–parathyroid-mediated hypercalcemia is Jansen-type metaphyseal chondrodysplasia, in which an activating mutation of the PTH receptor mimics the effects of excess PTH. The diagnostic approach to hypercalcemia is summarized in Table 260-2.

 Treatment

The definitive treatment of hypercalcemia depends on the specific diagnosis and treatment of the underlying disease (e.g., parathyroidectomy for primary hyperparathyroidism, chemotherapy for a malignancy). The initial treatment of hypercalcemia can be instituted (and in acute hypercalcemic crisis often *must* be instituted) without a specific diagnosis, but cumulative toxicity and loss of efficacy preclude long-term nonspecific treatment. Measures aimed at reducing the serum calcium level act by increasing urinary calcium excretion and by decreasing bone resorption. General measures applicable to every patient include mobilization as soon as feasible (because immobility increases bone resorption) and hydration (because significant hypercalcemia causes dehydration). Volume depletion, by limiting renal calcium excretion, perpetuates a vicious circle that can lead to acute hypercalcemic crisis. Volume expansion with isotonic saline often significantly reduces the serum calcium level by enhancing renal calcium excretion. Only after volume repletion should diuretics be used to enhance sodium and thereby calcium excretion. With a vigorous saline diuresis, calcium excretion in the range of 1 to 2 g/day can be achieved as a temporary measure to reduce the serum calcium level. In patients with renal failure, dialysis can be used almost as effectively to remove calcium from extracellular fluid. Careful monitoring of cardiac function and serum electrolytes is necessary with both saline diuresis and dialysis treatment.

Measures aimed at reducing bone resorption by inhibiting osteoclast function are most effective in treating hypercalcemia, regardless of the specific factor causing increased bone resorption. Available agents include calcitonin, bisphosphonates (diphosphonates), plicamycin (mithramycin), and gallium nitrate. Calcitonin has low toxicity and acts most rapidly, but even in doses up to 32 MRC U/kg/day by intravenous infusion, lowering of serum calcium is generally limited and transient. Bisphosphonates must be given parenterally, and their effect is both significant and often prolonged (days). Pamidronate (dose 30 to 90 mg intravenously over 24 hours) is potent and effective. A newer generation bisphosphonate, zoledronic acid, has been approved by the Food and Drug Administration. In randomized, double-blind controlled trials, zoledronic acid (4 mg) proved slightly more effective than pamidronate (90 mg). Zoledronic acid should be infused over no less than 15 minutes with careful monitoring of serum creatinine because of potential renal toxicity. Plicamycin (25 μg/kg intravenously) effectively lowers serum calcium, but it has cumulative toxicity in liver, kidney, and platelets and can no longer be justified as initial therapy. Intravenous phosphate poses a serious danger of metastatic calcification in the hypercalcemic patient and should probably no longer be used, given availability of other safer and effective agents. Oral phosphate is safer and useful in patients with

Continued

significant hypercalcemia who are awaiting definitive treatment and in whom hypercalcemic crisis should be prevented. Dosages in the range of 2 g/day of elemental phosphorus (10 g of phosphate salts) in divided doses can be given. Serum phosphate and renal function should be carefully monitored.

Glucocorticoids are highly effective in treating hypercalcemia caused by vitamin D–related mechanisms (vitamin D intoxication, overproduction of 1,25(OH)$_2$D in granulomatous disorders) and certain malignancies (cytokine release associated with myeloma), but are ineffective in most other forms of hypercalcemia, including hyperparathyroidism and most malignancies. Forty to 100 mg/day of prednisone or the equivalent is the usual dose range.

PRIMARY HYPERPARATHYROIDISM

Definition

Primary hyperparathyroidism is a disorder in which hypercalcemia is due to hypersecretion of PTH.

Etiology

In most cases (about 85%), hyperparathyroidism is caused by sporadic, solitary adenomas. Hyperplasia of all four glands occurs in about 10% of cases, and these are most often familial, in the context of four distinct autosomal dominant inherited diseases: multiple endocrine neoplasia (MEN) types I and II, hyperparathyroidism–jaw tumor syndrome, and familial hypocalciuric hypercalcemia. There may also exist a form of familial isolated hyperparathyroidism whose genetic basis is unclear. Parathyroid carcinoma occurs rarely (<5% of cases), but has clearly been associated with the hyperparathyroidism-jaw tumor syndrome. The latter syndrome includes fibro-osseous jaw tumors, renal cysts, and solid renal tumors. The gene for MEN type I has been identified on chromosome 11q13. Enlarged glands in this disease contain monoclonal tumors with germline loss-of-function mutations in one allele of the MEN I gene and somatic loss of the second, normal allele. This suggests that the MEN I gene is a "tumor suppressor" whose loss leads to tumorigenesis. About 30% of sporadic parathyroid tumors also show allele loss at 11q13, and in a subset, somatic loss-of-function mutations of the MEN I gene have been identified, suggesting a similar pathogenesis. The gene for MEN type II has been identified as the *RET* proto-oncogene on chromosome 10q11. Identification of the MEN type I and type II genes facilitates genetic diagnosis and studies of pathogenesis. The gene responsible for hyperparathyroidism–jaw tumor syndrome has been localized to chromosome 1q25-q31 and identified and named *parafibromin*. Very rarely, a rearrangement involving the PTH gene on the short arm of chromosome 11 and a cell cycle control gene termed *cyclin D* or *PRAD 1* on the long arm of chromosome 11 appears to cause parathyroid adenoma formation. Epidemiologic evidence suggests that a history of neck irradiation predisposes to parathyroid tumor formation. Specific molecular defects have not been identified. Finally, long-standing secondary hyperparathyroidism (e.g., in response to renal failure) may evolve into autonomous hypersecretion, so-called tertiary hyperparathyroidism.

Incidence

The incidence of hyperparathyroidism has increased substantially, largely as a result of routine blood calcium measurement. Age-adjusted incidence rates are between 25 and 50 per 100,000, based on recent surveys. A prevalence between 0.1 and 0.5% has been estimated, with females affected about twice as commonly as males. The incidence rises sharply after age 40 years.

Pathology

Microscopic distinction between adenoma and hyperplasia is difficult, if not impossible. The distinction between single-gland and multigland disease relies on gross surgical identification of more than one enlarged gland. In MEN types I and II, there is always multigland involvement, although asymmetric gland enlargement is often present.

The chief cell generally predominates in parathyroid tumors; oxyphil cell tumors are much rarer.

Pathophysiology

The primary disturbance is inappropriate secretion of PTH for the level of serum calcium. Studies (in vitro) with isolated parathyroid cells show that most adenomas either fail to suppress secretion at high calcium levels or show an altered set point, that is, a higher calcium level is required to suppress secretion than for normal cells. Cells from hyperplastic glands may show a normal calcium set point for secretion. Hypersecretion of PTH in such cases may be due to a primary defect causing cellular proliferation and to an inability to suppress hormone secretion completely because of increased cell mass.

Slight increases in PTH secretion act on bone to increase turnover and may reduce cortical rather than trabecular bone density. At very high levels, PTH causes radiographically detectable subperiosteal bone resorption and, eventually, marrow fibrosis and cystic, reparative bone lesions termed "brown tumors." This is the classic form of the disease called *osteitis fibrosa cystica*. PTH increases renal calcium reabsorption, but nonetheless, at high filtered loads of calcium, hypercalciuria develops. Enhanced 1,25(OH)$_2$D formation by the kidneys is prominent in some patients and is associated with increased intestinal calcium absorption. Such patients may be at particular risk for renal stones.

Clinical Manifestations

Most patients either are asymptomatic at presentation (discovered through incidental blood calcium measurement) or have vague, nonspecific symptoms, such as fatigue, weakness, and mental disturbance. Patients with significant hypercalcemia show many of the signs and symptoms of hypercalcemia previously discussed. Nephrolithiasis, with or without renal colic, is not specifically associated with hyperparathyroidism but is most commonly seen in this setting. Subperiosteal bone resorption is rarely seen, and osteitis fibrosa cystica even less commonly. Neuromuscular abnormalities, particularly proximal muscle weakness affecting the lower limbs, may be prominent. Joint manifestations include chondrocalcinosis that may lead to pseudogout. It has been claimed that hypertension and peptic ulcer disease are manifestations of hyperparathyroidism, but these are common, and there is no firm evidence for a causal relationship. No specific physical findings are present in hyperparathyroidism. A neck mass, if present, most commonly represents a coincidental thyroid nodule, less commonly a benign or malignant parathyroid tumor. "Band keratopathy," calcification at 3- and 9-o'clock positions of the cornea, is best seen by slit-lamp examination and occurs most often when hypercalcemia is accompanied by hyperphosphatemia—thus, less commonly in hyperparathyroidism than in other hypercalcemic disorders. Radiologic findings include subperiosteal resorption, which, when present, is best seen at the radial sides of the phalanges, distal phalangeal tufts, and distal clavicles. Lucent bone lesions, representing brown tumors, are seen in rare, severely affected patients. Soft tissue calcification may be evident in the joints, kidneys, and lungs. The calcification is best appreciated on bone scans.

Diagnosis

The differential diagnosis of hypercalcemia is discussed earlier. PTH immunoassay, preferably one of the newer two-site assays, is the key to diagnosis. In distinguishing between hyperparathyroid and normal states (e.g., in patients presenting with nephrolithiasis), repeated careful serum calcium and PTH (including the midregion type of assay) measurements are most useful. Hypercalcemic subjects taking lithium or thiazides should be retested for hyperparathyroidism after discontinuing the drug (this may not be feasible in some patients on lithium), because both drugs may alter serum calcium and PTH secretion. In relatively young, asymptomatic individuals, or if the serum PTH level is marginally elevated, hypercalcemia may be due to familial hypocalciuric hypercalcemia rather than hyperparathyroidism (see Familial Hypocalciuric Hypercalcemia).

Rx Prognosis and Treatment

Surgical parathyroidectomy is the only definitive treatment for hyperparathyroidism. Oral phosphate treatment can lower the serum calcium level, but the long-term safety and efficacy of this approach are unclear. In mildly affected older women, estrogen treatment has been advocated, particularly to blunt bone resorption, but, again, long-term efficacy is unknown. Thus, the only alternative to surgery at present is conservative medical follow-up. Most experts recommend surgery for all patients with symptomatic disease and even for asymptomatic patients meeting other, somewhat arbitrary, criteria, such as age younger than 40 years or a serum calcium level greater than 11.5 mg/day. The appropriate management of patients not fitting any of these criteria is controversial; some advocate surgery for all, and others conservative follow-up. The long-term course of untreated hyperparathyroidism is unknown. Controlled studies comparing surgery versus medical follow-up have not been performed. Small series of patients followed conservatively for several years suggest that mild biochemical disease rarely progresses to severe symptomatic disease. Bone densitometry is an important component of the evaluation of patients with hyperparathyroidism, because it is much more sensitive than plain radiographs. Reduction in cortical bone density (measured in the forearm) greater than 2 standard deviations below the mean of age-matched control subjects is an indication for surgery. Evidence exists for a substantial increase in bone density following parathyroidectomy in a subset of patients with low vertebral bone density at presentation, so surgery may be indicated in such patients as well. Because definitive treatment recommendations are not possible, therapy must be individualized. The author personally follows a policy of recommending surgery for all but older patients with only mild biochemical disease.

If the decision is to perform surgery, a highly experienced parathyroid surgeon must be found. A success rate as high as 95% can be expected for initial neck exploration by a skilled surgeon. The success rate is substantially lower with inexperienced surgeons. Preoperative localization is not needed by the skilled surgeon performing initial exploration. Neither localization studies nor neck exploration itself should serve as *diagnostic* maneuvers. Only after the diagnosis has been established biochemically (by PTH assay) should one recommend surgery. In patients undergoing repeat neck exploration for recurrent or persistent disease, localization studies are extremely helpful. Noninvasive studies include ultrasonography, technetium-99m sestamibi scanning, computed tomography (CT), and magnetic resonance imaging. Invasive techniques include fine-needle aspiration of imaged lesions for PTH assay, selective arteriography, and selective venous catheterization for hormone assay. The latter techniques are best performed by radiologists with specialized experience.

After successful surgery, hypocalcemia is generally mild and transient, and rarely requires treatment. In the rare case of subjects with extensive bone disease, severe, prolonged hypocalcemia secondary to "bone hunger" occurs. Persistent relative hypophosphatemia suggests that bone hunger, rather than hypoparathyroidism, is the cause of hypocalcemia in this setting. Acute treatment with calcium infusions and long-term treatment with vitamin D and oral calcium may be needed. Eventually, treatment can be discontinued if normal parathyroid tissue remains. In patients without residual normal parathyroid tissue, lifelong vitamin D therapy is necessary. Autotransplantation of parathyroid tissue in the forearm is an experimental alternative in such cases. Successful surgery generally halts formation of renal stones in patients with nephrolithiasis and allows skeletal remineralization in patients with bone disease. There is no definitive evidence that surgery corrects hypertension or other nonspecific manifestations of hyperparathyroidism.

FAMILIAL HYPOCALCIURIC HYPERCALCEMIA

Definition

Familial hypocalciuric hypercalcemia is an autosomal dominant genetic disease with essentially complete penetrance that causes hypercalcemia and relatively low urinary calcium excretion for the filtered load.

Etiology

The disease is caused by mutations in a gene on the long arm of chromosome 3 encoding a calcium-sensing receptor. In some families, the disease may be caused by a gene localized to a different chromosome.

Incidence

The disorder is relatively rare, but it is over-represented among patients presenting with unsuccessful neck exploration because of the difficulty in achieving normocalcemia by surgery.

Pathophysiology

The primary disturbance appears to be in divalent cation transport and/or "sensing" in at least the kidneys and parathyroids. The kidneys show an exaggerated reabsorption of filtered calcium (and magnesium) that leads to hypercalcemia. The parathyroids, however, fail to suppress fully hormone secretion despite hypercalcemia. The process is PTH-dependent because totally parathyroidectomized subjects become hypocalcemic, but even small amounts of parathyroid tissue are sufficient to maintain hypercalcemia. Parathyroid gland mass is generally only mildly increased.

Clinical Manifestations

The disease leads to few, if any, clinical manifestations—hence its other name, *familial benign hypercalcemia*. Nephrolithiasis and bone disease are, in general, not seen. Pancreatitis has been reported, but the specificity of this association is unclear. Hypercalcemia is present at birth. In some neonates, a clinically severe form of the disease is present. This severe form may be due to inheritance of a double dose of the abnormal gene. Otherwise, the main morbidity is that resulting from unsuccessful neck exploration that has failed to distinguish this disorder from conventional hyperparathyroidism. There is no evidence of associated endocrinopathies, as in the MEN syndromes.

Diagnosis

A high index of suspicion is needed to recognize this disease. Hypercalcemia associated with relatively young age, with only slight elevation in the serum PTH level, or with a family history of unsuccessful neck exploration should trigger further evaluation. Hypermagnesemia is suggestive; urinary calcium-creatinine ratios less than 0.01:1 strongly support the diagnosis. Screening first-degree relatives for hypercalcemia may also be helpful. For those families in which the disease gene is localized to chromosome 3q, specific genetic diagnosis is possible by screening for mutations in the calcium-sensing receptor gene. Distinct mutations in this gene have already been identified in several kindreds.

Prognosis and Treatment

Because the disease is compatible with normal life expectancy and is associated with little, if any, morbidity, neck exploration appears to be contraindicated. Successful surgical treatment, moreover, is difficult, with permanent hypoparathyroidism or, more commonly, recurrent hypercalcemia being the usual result.

HYPERCALCEMIA ASSOCIATED WITH MALIGNANCY

Etiology and Pathogenesis

Malignancies can cause hypercalcemia through two nonmutually exclusive mechanisms. First, local osteolytic hypercalcemia is caused by tumor metastatic to bone. Tumor cells may release bone-resorbing factors or so-called osteoclast-activating factors, which indirectly lead to bone resorption. Cytokines such as lymphotoxin and interleukin-1 are potent osteoclast-activating factors. Second, humoral hypercalcemia of malignancy is caused by tumor-secreting factors into the circulation that act systemically to increase bone resorption. Such factors may show other PTH-like actions, including increasing urinary cAMP and phosphate excretion and decreasing renal calcium excretion. This condition leads to a syndrome with biochemical features closely resembling those of primary hyperparathyroidism. One such factor commonly associated with many tumors has recently been identified as a polypeptide roughly twice as large as PTH and homologous in amino acid sequence to the biologically active amino-terminus of PTH. This so-called PTH-related peptide may also be secreted by tumors metastatic to bone, so that humoral and local osteolytic mechanisms may combine to cause hypercalcemia. Some tumors cause hypercalcemia through excessive synthesis of $1,25(OH)_2D$, in a manner analogous to that seen in sarcoidosis (see later text). A role for additional, as yet unidentified, bone-resorbing agents secreted by tumors has not been excluded.

Incidence

Malignancy-associated hypercalcemia occurs most commonly in patients with bone metastases. Breast carcinoma is one of the most frequent causes. Most subjects with bone metastases are not hypercalcemic because of adequate renal compensatory mechanisms. Slight renal impairment may then provoke hypercalcemia. Treatment of women with breast cancer metastatic to bone with tamoxifen has been associated with acute sharp increases in the serum calcium level. Certain hematogenous neoplasms, such as myeloma and human lymphotropic virus type I–associated leukemia/lymphoma, are frequently associated with hypercalcemia. Humoral hypercalcemia of malignancy is much rarer. It is seen most frequently with squamous carcinomas, but biochemical evidence indicates that almost any tumor type, including breast carcinoma, can produce PTH-related peptide.

Clinical Manifestations

Malignancy-associated hypercalcemia often develops acutely, may be severe (hypercalcemic crisis), and is frequently a grave prognostic sign. In most cases, particularly of the local osteolytic hypercalcemia variety, the underlying neoplasm is clinically evident. An otherwise occult neoplasm may occasionally manifest with humoral hypercalcemia of malignancy. Accurate and rapid diagnosis is critical in such cases because successful tumor removal may be feasible.

Diagnosis

As discussed earlier, PTH radioimmunoassay is the crucial test for excluding coexistent primary hyperparathyroidism. PTH-related peptide fails to cross react in such assays. Specific immunoassays for this peptide have been developed, and these facilitate diagnosis of tumor secretion of the peptide. Increased urinary cAMP excretion (coupled with low or undetectable PTH measurement) also favors tumor secretion of PTH-related peptide. If both PTH and urinary cAMP levels are low, one is dealing with a vitamin D–mediated or local osteolytic hypercalcemia.

 ## Treatment and Prognosis

Acute, nonspecific treatment of hypercalcemia is instituted if the diagnosis is unclear (see above). Definitive treatment must be directed at the underlying neoplasm, if feasible. When tumor treatment is not possible, vigorous treatment of hypercalcemia may be irrelevant. In those cases mediated by vitamin D or lymphokine release, glucocorticoids are often uniquely effective in lowering the serum calcium level.

HYPERCALCEMIA DUE TO GRANULOMATOUS DISEASES AND TO VITAMIN D INTOXICATION

Etiology and Pathogenesis

Hypercalcemia is caused by unregulated formation of $1,25(OH)_2D$ in granuloma-associated macrophages. Normally, 1-hydroxylation takes place in the kidney and is sensitive to feedback suppression by high serum calcium levels. Unregulated synthesis of $1,25(OH)_2D$ in patients with granulomatous diseases renders them hypersensitive to vitamin D (from the diet or through sun exposure). Ingestion of excessive amounts of vitamin D or its metabolites can lead to hypercalcemia by overcoming normal feedback mechanisms.

Incidence and Prevalence

Hypercalcemia has been observed in almost any disease capable of causing granulomas. These diseases include sarcoidosis, tuberculosis, fungal infections, berylliosis, and some lymphomas, such as Hodgkin's disease. Overt hypercalcemia may be seen in only about 10% of patients with sarcoidosis, but hypercalciuria and intestinal hyperabsorption of calcium may occur in almost half of such individuals. Hypercalcemia due to vitamin D intoxication is relatively rare outside of the context of treatment for hypocalcemia.

Clinical Manifestations

Manifestations are those of the underlying disease, as well as the superimposed effects of hypercalcemia. Because this form of hypercalcemia often coexists with relatively higher serum phosphorus levels than those seen in hyperparathyroidism, soft tissue calcification, nephrocalcinosis, and renal impairment are more common. Patients may present with hypercalcemia and relatively few other findings (e.g., subtle hilar adenopathy in sarcoidosis).

Diagnosis

PTH and urinary cAMP are suppressed. The serum level of $1,25(OH)_2D$ is elevated. In cases of vitamin D intoxication, the serum $1,25(OH)_2D$ level may be normal and only serum $25(OH)D$ is increased.

 ## Treatment and Prognosis

The prognosis depends on that of the underlying disease. Glucocorticoids are extremely effective in lowering the serum calcium level in such cases. Chloroquine has been used effectively in subjects who cannot tolerate glucocorticoid treatment. When the cause of hypercalcemia is vitamin D intoxication, ingestion of all forms of vitamin D should be stopped.

HYPOCALCEMIA

Definition

Hypocalcemia is an abnormal reduction in serum ionized calcium concentration. (See Chapter 261 and Part XXVIII for calcium and phosphorus reference range values.) Reduction in total serum calcium, as may occur in patients with hypoalbuminemia, does not necessarily reflect a reduction in ionized calcium. Ionized, not total, serum calcium affects neuromuscular function and is therefore the clinically relevant parameter.

Etiology And Pathogenesis

Normal serum ionized calcium concentration is maintained by the direct actions of PTH on kidney and bone and by the indirect actions, through $1,25(OH)_2D$, on the intestine (Chapter 261). Hypocalcemic disorders can be divided according to pathogenesis into two broad categories: (1) primary hypoparathyroidism, in which hypocalcemia is due to deficient secretion and/or action of PTH (specific subtypes are discussed under individual headings); and (2) hypocalcemia due to target organ malfunction (e.g., renal failure, intestinal malabsorption, vitamin D deficiency). Hypocalcemia occurs in this category despite normal or even increased PTH secretion (secondary hyperparathyroidism). In hypoparathyroidism, there is reduced mobilization of calcium from bone, reduced renal reabsorption of calcium, lowered phosphaturia, and reduced $1,25(OH)_2D$ formation with a resultant decrease in intestinal calcium absorption. The end results are hypocalcemia and hyperphosphatemia. Renal failure (Chapter 103) and acute phosphate loads (as may occur with

Table 260–3 • CAUSES OF HYPOCALCEMIA

HYPOPARATHYROIDISM
Deficient parathyroid hormone secretion
　Idiopathic (autoimmune)
　Parathyroid hormone gene mutation
GCMB transcription factor gene mutation
　Activating calcium-sensing receptor mutation (autosomal dominant
　　hypoparathyroidism)
Surgical
Infiltrative (iron overload, Wilson's disease)
Functional
Hypomagnesemia
Transient postoperative
Deficient parathyroid hormone action (hormone resistance)
Pseudohypoparathyroidism types Ia and Ib

NORMAL OR INCREASED PARATHYROID HORMONE FUNCTION
Renal failure
Intestinal malabsorption
Acute pancreatitis
Osteoblastic metastases
Vitamin D deficiency or resistance

chemotherapy of certain tumors, such as Burkitt's lymphoma) are other causes of hypocalcemia with hyperphosphatemia. With vitamin D deficiency or malabsorption, hypocalcemia occurs with normal or low serum phosphorus levels (the latter reflecting secondary hyperparathyroidism). Hypocalcemia with low or normal serum phosphorus levels is also seen in acute pancreatitis (attributed to calcium soap formation, but this is unproved) and in some patients with osteoblastic tumor metastases. Table 260–3 summarizes the causes of hypocalcemia.

Clinical Manifestations

Hypocalcemia of any cause is associated with certain typical signs and symptoms. Most prominent among these is increased neuromuscular excitability. Paresthesias of the fingers, toes, and circumoral region are mild manifestations; in more extreme cases, there may be muscle cramping, carpopedal spasm, laryngeal stridor, and convulsions. Symptoms reflect not only the degree of hypocalcemia but also the acuteness of the decrease in serum calcium concentration. Patients with long-standing severe hypocalcemia may show surprisingly few symptoms. Factors that acutely alter the balance between ionized and protein-bound calcium may precipitate symptoms. For example, alkalosis lowers ionized calcium; thus, hyperventilation may provoke symptoms of tetany. Signs of latent tetany include Chvostek's sign (twitching of the upper lip after tapping on the facial nerve below the zygomatic arch) and Trousseau's sign (carpal spasm after inflating a cuff on the upper arm above systolic blood pressure for 2 to 3 minutes).

Various mental disturbances, such as irritability, depression, and even psychosis, have been attributed to hypocalcemia. Papilledema and other signs of increased intracranial pressure have been reported. Intracranial calcifications, particularly of the basal ganglia, may be seen on plain radiographs and even more frequently on CT scan. Increased sensitivity to the dystonic effects of phenothiazines has been attributed to basal ganglia calcification. Long-standing hypocalcemia may lead to cataract formation. Cardiac effects of hypocalcemia include a prolonged QT interval and, rarely, congestive heart failure. Dental anomalies depend on age of onset; in children, hypocalcemia can cause enamel hypoplasia and failure of the adult teeth to erupt.

Differential Diagnosis

Measuring serum calcium, phosphorus, and creatinine levels allows one to categorize the form of hypocalcemia. Hypocalcemia and hyperphosphatemia with normal renal function are pathognomonic of hypoparathyroidism. Low or undetectable PTH by immunoassay despite hypocalcemia confirms the diagnosis. (Rare forms of PTH-resistant hypoparathyroidism show elevated levels of PTH and are discussed further later.) Hypocalcemia and hyperphosphatemia caused by renal failure pose no diagnostic problem. Hypocalcemia with normal or low serum phosphorus levels should prompt measurement of vitamin D metabolites and assessment of gastrointestinal function to check for vitamin D deficiency and malabsorption, respectively. Measurements of PTH should show increased values in such patients, because the normal parathyroids attempt to compensate for hypocalcemia.

Rx Treatment

Acute, symptomatic hypocalcemia requires emergency treatment in the form of intravenous calcium infusion. Ten to 20 mL of 10% calcium gluconate solution (contains 10 mg of elemental calcium per milliliter) may be given over 10 to 20 minutes (this may be hazardous in patients taking cardiac glycosides). In less urgent settings, a slow intravenous infusion (over 4 to 8 hours) of 20 mg of elemental calcium per kilogram of body weight may be given. As with hypercalcemic disorders, definitive resolution of hypocalcemia requires treating the underlying disease. In patients with hypoparathyroidism, life-long therapy with vitamin D (with or without oral calcium) is required. This is discussed further under treatment of hypoparathyroidism.

HYPOPARATHYROIDISM

Definition

Hypoparathyroidism is defined as deficient PTH secretion and/or action. This condition may lead to overt hypocalcemia and hyperphosphatemia, as discussed earlier, or it may only predispose to hypocalcemia (decreased parathyroid reserve) in times of increased calcium demand, such as pregnancy.

Etiology and Pathogenesis

PERMANENT DEFICIENCY IN PARATHYROID HORMONE SECRETION. This deficiency may result from surgical removal of the parathyroids, from glandular destruction by iron overload (e.g., transfusions in thalassemia) or copper overload (Wilson's disease), and from glandular destruction through a presumed autoimmune mechanism. The latter often has a genetic basis. The parathyroids may fail to develop as part of DiGeorge's syndrome. Some cases termed *idiopathic hypoparathyroidism* may be due to inherited mutations in the PTH gene that prevent synthesis and secretion of PTH. Other cases may be due to homozygous mutation of GCMB, a transcription factor predominantly expressed in parathyroid cells. Activating mutations of the calcium-sensing receptor lead to inhibition of PTH secretion at inappropriately low serum ionized calcium levels and are a cause of autosomal dominant hypoparathyroidism.

TRANSIENT DEFICIENCY IN PARATHYROID HORMONE SECRETION. Reversible hypoparathyroidism can be caused by hypomagnesemia. The latter may compromise both PTH secretion and action. Magnesium replacement corrects the defect. Transient hypoparathyroidism may also result from suppression of normal parathyroids by parathyroid adenomas or other causes of hypercalcemia. This condition rarely lasts more than 1 week. Surgical injury to the parathyroids is another postulated cause of transiently reduced hormone secretion.

DEFICIENCY IN PARATHYROID HORMONE ACTION. Target-organ resistance to PTH appears to be the major cause of this form of hypoparathyroidism, which was termed *pseudohypoparathyroidism* by Albright, who described it as the first example of a hormone-resistance disorder. Subsequent studies indicated that the defect in this disease occurs before formation of cAMP (a second messenger of PTH action) because affected subjects lack the normal brisk increase in urinary cAMP excretion observed after infusing PTH in normal individuals. There are at least two forms of pseudohypoparathyroidism. In type Ia disease, a 50% deficiency has been found in the Gs protein that couples PTH (and many other) receptors to the enzyme that forms cAMP, adenylyl cyclase. This deficiency may limit normal cAMP production in response to PTH as well as to other hormones, such as thyroid-stimulating hormone. As a result, patients with this form of the disease show endocrine abnormalities (e.g., hypothyroidism, hypogonadism) in addition to hypoparathyroidism. In affected subjects from several families with type Ia disease, distinct mutations that prevent synthesis of normal Gs protein have been found in the gene encoding the Gs protein. Inheritance of the mutation is autosomal dominant, but there is evidence for imprinting of the gene. When the mutant gene is inherited from the mother, pseudohypoparathyroidism type Ia results in both hormone resistance and Albright's hereditary osteodystrophy. If the mutant gene is inherited from the father, only features of Albright's hereditary osteodystrophy are present, a condition termed *pseudopseudohypoparathyroidism*. In subjects with type Ib disease, hormone resistance is limited to PTH. Again, PTH resistance only occurs when the disease is inherited maternally. Several studies have shown that patients with type Ib disease have a defect in imprinting of the *Gs* gene.

Incidence

All forms of hypoparathyroidism are relatively rare. The incidence of surgical hypoparathyroidism varies widely as a function of the skill of the surgeon.

Clinical Manifestations

The manifestations generally associated with hypocalcemia have been discussed above. The clinical features unique to each form of hypoparathyroidism reflect the underlying disease. In autoimmune forms, there may be associated endocrine deficiency, most frequently Addison's disease, as well as a T-cell defect predisposing to mucocutaneous candidiasis. Alopecia and vitiligo may also be seen. In pseudohypoparathyroidism type Ib, the appearance is normal, but in type Ia disease, affected individuals show Albright's hereditary osteodystrophy, a constellation of abnormal physical findings (Fig. 260–3) including obesity, short stature, round face and short neck, metacarpal and metatarsal shortening (most often fourth and fifth), shortening and broadening of the distal phalanges, and subcutaneous calcifications. Such individuals often show slight mental retardation and associated endocrine abnormalities, most commonly hypothyroidism (without goiter) and hypogonadism. First-degree relatives of patients with pseudohypoparathyroidism type Ia may show the physical features of Albright's osteodystrophy without evidence of hormone resistance. This condition has been termed *pseudopseudohypoparathyroidism*. Rarely, individuals with pseudohypoparathyroidism (more often of the Ib type) have radiographic evidence of osteitis fibrosa cystica and elevated serum levels of bone-derived alkaline phosphatase. This finding suggests selective renal, as opposed to skeletal, resistance to PTH action.

Differential Diagnosis

Low or undetectable serum PTH in the face of hypocalcemia, hyperphosphatemia, and normal renal function establishes the diagnosis of hormone-deficient hypoparathyroidism. Diagnosis of the underlying disease depends on history (e.g., neck surgery), physical findings (e.g., candidiasis, alopecia), and additional laboratory tests (e.g., evidence for hypoadrenalism). Inappropriately elevated urine calcium in subjects with hypoparathyroidism (with or without a family history) suggest the diagnosis of autosomal dominant hypoparathyroidism caused by activating mutation of the calcium-sensing receptor. Such mutations cause not only inappropriate suppression of PTH secretion but also inappropriate increase in renal calcium excretion. DNA diagnosis is possible but is not routinely available for clinical use. Antibodies to parathyroid antigens have been detected in the autoimmune form of the disease, but this test is not available for routine clinical use. An elevated level of serum PTH measured by immunoassay in a subject with hypocalcemia, hyperphosphatemia, and normal renal function suggests hormone-resistant hypoparathyroidism. PTH infusion (at present with commercially available synthetic 1-34 peptide) and measurement of urinary cAMP excretion can be performed to confirm PTH resistance. Physical appearance can help distinguish type Ia from type Ib pseudohypoparathyroidism, as can testing for other endocrinopathies, such as hypothyroidism. Measurement of Gs protein and detection of mutations in the corresponding gene are not routinely available tests.

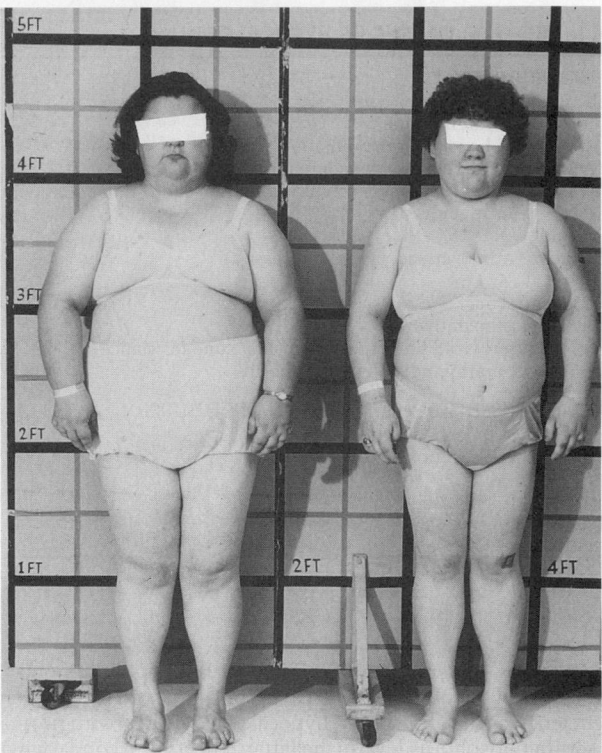

FIGURE 260–3 • Phenotypic features of Albright's hereditary osteodystrophy. A mother (*left*) and daughter display many of the features of Albright's osteodystrophy, including obesity, short stature, round face, and short neck. Metacarpal and metatarsal shortening manifest as shortened fourth and fifth fingers (right hands of both subjects) and shortened fourth toes (left feet of both subjects), respectively. Both subjects show resistance to parathyroid hormone (PTH) and thyroid-stimulating hormone, as well as deficient Gs protein activity, characteristic of pseudohypoparathyroidism type Ia. (From Spiegel AM, Weinstein LS: Pseudohypoparathyroidism. *In* Scriver CR, Beaudet AL, Sly WS, Valle D [eds]. The Metabolic & Molecular Basis of Inherited Disease, 8th ed. New York, McGraw-Hill, 2001, p 4205.)

 Treatment

Transient forms of hypoparathyroidism may not require treatment. Reversible forms should be treated appropriately, that is, magnesium replacement for hypomagnesemia. In permanent hormone-deficient hypoparathyroidism, hormone replacement therapy is not practical. Parathyroid autografting is effective in some patients with surgical hypoparathyroidism. When this is not feasible, and also in subjects with pseudohypoparathyroidism, life-long treatment with oral vitamin D is required. Vitamin D_2 ergocalciferol (generally 50,000 U/day), is inexpensive in comparison to the active metabolite $1,25(OH)_2D$ (generally 0.25 µg/day). The latter has the theoretical advantage of more rapid onset (and in case of toxicity, offset) of action, but with appropriate monitoring, vitamin D_2 can be used very effectively. Oral calcium salts (1 to 2 g of elemental calcium per day in divided doses) may be added for individuals whose dietary calcium intake is highly variable or inadequate. The goal of treatment is the lowest serum calcium concentration compatible with avoidance of symptoms, because without PTH, urinary calcium excretion (and the possibility of nephrolithiasis) is increased at any filtered load of calcium. Both serum and urine calcium levels, as well as renal function, must be monitored. In patients with autosomal dominant hypoparathyroidism due to calcium-sensing receptor mutation, particular care must be taken to avoid overcorrecting hypocalcemia, because such patients are particularly susceptible to renal calcification and nephrolithiasis given the tendency to hypercalciuria in this disease. In forms of hypoparathyroidism that have associated endocrinopathies, appropriate hormone replacement therapy should be instituted.

SUGGESTED READINGS

Brown EM, MacLeod RJ: Extracellular calcium sensing and extracellular calcium signaling. Physiol Rev 2001;81:239–297. *Detailed review of calcium-sensing receptor, its role in extracellular calcium homeostasis, and derangements in the receptor in familial hypocalciuric hypercalcemia and other disorders.*

Ding C, Buckingham B, Levine MA: Familial isolated hypoparathyroidism caused by a mutation in the gene for the transcription factor GCMB. J Clin Invest 2001;108:1215–1220. *Genetic basis for one form of hypoparathyroidism and discussion of other inherited forms.*

Jofre R, Gomez JM, Menarguez J, et al: Parathyroidectomy: Whom and when? Kidney Int Suppl 2003;85:97–100. *Overview of surgical options in patients on maintenance dialysis.*

Misof BM, Roschger P, Cosman F, et al: Effects of intermittent parathyroid hormone administration on bone mineralization density in iliac crest biopsies from patients with osteoporosis. A paired study before and after treatment. J Clin Endocrinol Metab 2003;88:1150–1156. *Intermittent PTH stimulates bone matrix formation.*

Sidhu S, Neill AK, Russell CF: Long-term outcome of unilateral parathyroid exploration for primary hyperparathyroidism due to presumed solitary adenoma. World J Surg 2003;27:339–342. *Scan-directed unilateral surgery was successful in 98% of cases.*

Simonds WF, James-Newton LA, Agarwal SK, et al: Familial isolated hyperparathyroidism: clinical and genetic characteristics of 36 kindreds. Medicine 2002;81:1–26. *Extensive study clarifying genetic basis for inherited forms of hyperparathyroidism.*

Vestergaard P, Mosekilde L: Fractures in patients with primary hyperparathyroidism: Nationwide follow-up study of 1201 patients. World J Surg 2003;27:343–349. *There was no difference in the risk of fractures in those with versus without parathyroidectomy.*

Weinstein LS: The stimulatory G protein alpha-subunit gene: Mutations and imprinting lead to complex phenotypes. J Clin Endocrinol Metab 2001;86:4622–4626. *Genetic basis for pseudohypoparathyroidism types 1a and 1b.*

Wellington K, Goa KL: Zoledronic acid: A review of its use in the management of bone metastases and hypercalcaemia of malignancy. Drugs 2003;63:417–437. *This drug may be the treatment of choice.*

261 MEDULLARY THYROID CARCINOMA AND CALCITONIN

Leonard J. Deftos
Robert F. Gagel

Medullary thyroid carcinoma (MTC) is a tumor of the calcitonin-producing cells of the thyroid gland. Calcitonin is a 32-amino acid peptide secreted primarily by the thyroidal C-cells in mammals and by the embryologically related ultimobranchial gland in submammals. The main biologic effect of calcitonin is to decrease bone resorption by inhibiting the osteoclast. This effect, along with a lesser calciuric action, decreases the concentration of blood calcium, with a nadir directly related to bone turnover; thus, the hypocalcemia may be slight in normal adults but considerable when bone resorption is increased pathologically in disease states or physiologically during bone growth. This property of calcitonin makes it an effective drug for hyperresorptive diseases, such as Paget's disease, osteoporosis, and hypercalcemia. The physiologic significance of other reported effects of calcitonin is not well established. The calciuric effect of calcitonin is seen primarily with pharmacologic doses of the hormone. An analgesic effect of calcitonin continues to receive considerable attention and may be related to neuroendocrine actions of the hormone. In addition to its role in skeletal physiology and treatment, calcitonin is a serum and tumor marker for MTC, the signal tumor of multiple endocrine neoplasia (MEN) type 2 and its variants (Table 261–1).

Table 261–1 • COMPONENTS OF MULTIPLE ENDOCRINE NEOPLASIA TYPE 2 AND THEIR FREQUENCY BASED ON AVERAGE FIGURES FROM THE LITERATURE

COMPONENT	MEN TYPE 2A (%)	MEN TYPE 2B (%)
Medullary thyroid carcinoma	95	90
Pheochromocytoma	50	45
Hyperparathyroidism	25	Rare
Mucosal neuroma syndrome	—	90
Mixed type		
Overlap of MEN 1 and 2		
Other endocrine tumors		
associated		
Neurofibromatosis		
von Hippel-Lindau		

CALCITONIN

BIOCHEMISTRY. The 32-amino acid structure of calcitonin, determined for several species, reveals a common 1,7 amino-terminal disulfide bridge and carboxy-terminal proline. Seven of the nine amino-terminal residues are identical in all calcitonin molecules. The interspecies structural differences in the rest of the molecule cause the submammalian (ultimobranchial) calcitonin molecules to be more potent in mammals than the mammalian calcitonin molecules. Thus, the potent salmon form of the hormone is the one used for treatment of osteoporosis, hypercalcemia, and Paget's disease of bone. The greater chemical basicity of these submammalian calcitonin species probably accounts for their increased potency. In contrast to the other major bone active peptides, parathyroid hormone and parathyroid hormone–related protein, a biologically active fragment of calcitonin has not been identified, and the entire molecule seems to be necessary for biologic activity.

SECRETION AND PRODUCTION. The most important secretory regulation of calcitonin is mediated by ambient calcium. An acute increase in blood calcium concentration increases the secretion of calcitonin, and an acute decrease in blood calcium level decreases the secretion of calcitonin. This action is mediated through the calcium-sensing receptor expressed by the thyroidal C-cells. The effects of chronic changes in blood calcium concentration on secretion have not been as well defined. Chronic hypercalcemia may stimulate calcitonin production, but this compensatory response may be limited. Chronic hypocalcemia seems to increase calcitonin storage in C-cells. Although a variety of other factors have been reported to stimulate calcitonin secretion, only pentagastrin and its related peptides are consistent additional secretagogues. The high concentration of pentagastrin necessary to stimulate secretion does not support the presence of a normal entero–C-cell secretory pathway. Nevertheless, pentagastrin and calcium are clinically important agents for evaluating calcitonin secretion by both normal and malignant C-cells, and both are used for provocative testing of calcitonin secretion, although the former is not widely available.

The effect of gonadal steroids and age on calcitonin production remains controversial. It is well established that blood concentrations of calcitonin are higher in males than females and in children than adults. Some studies report a decline in calcitonin secretion during adulthood and a stimulation of calcitonin secretion by estrogens and testosterone. These observations have led to the hypothesis that age- and menopause-related declines in calcitonin production contribute to the corresponding declines in bone mass seen in the elderly, especially in postmenopausal women. These observations support the use of calcitonin in treating osteoporosis, but more complex hormonal abnormalities underlie this skeletal disorder.

MEDULLARY THYROID CARCINOMA

Medullary thyroid carcinoma is a rare tumor of the calcitonin-producing C-cells of the thyroid gland, accounting for about 5 to 10% of thyroid cancers. These cells migrate from the neural crest to the thyroid gland and to other sites of the diffuse neuroendocrine system during embryogenesis in mammals. In submammals, these cells form their own distinct organ, the ultimobranchial gland. The neural crest origin of C-cells accounts for their production of a variety of biologically active substances. This embryologic origin may also explain the common association of MTC with other neuroendocrine tumors. Thus, MTC can occur as part of MEN type 2 or sporadically. Whereas early reports emphasized sporadic tumors, the growing appreciation of the inherited nature of the tumor has resulted in an increased diagnosis of familial cases. Even in apparently sporadic cases with no family history of the tumor, approximately 6% are found to have a genetic basis.

Pathology

A palpable tumor is the most common physical finding in the patient with MTC. The tumor is usually firm and located in the middle or upper lobes of the gland. Bilateral tumors are common in cases of MEN. Calcification can be present in the tumor, and this may result in a radiographic pattern that is characteristic enough to help in its clinical diagnosis. Similarly, amyloid present in the tumor can assist in histologic diagnosis. However, cytologic diagnosis is made difficult by the fact that the cells of MTC can be arranged in a variety of patterns. Therefore, the diagnosis of MTC is conclusively made by demonstrating calcitonin in the tumor by immunohistology with a calcitonin antibody. The presence of abnormal calcitonin-producing cells may be revealed by diagnostic fine-needle aspiration of the thyroid. Hyperplasia of the C-cells antedates the frank malignancy of MTC, especially in the familial forms of the tumor. C-cell hyperplasia is often too subtle to be appreciated by light microscopy, and immuno-histology for calcitonin is necessary to make this diagnosis. The advent of genetic testing for MEN provides additional strategies for distin-guishing MTC from other thyroid tumors.

Tumor Behavior

The natural history of the tumor is variable. The clinical behav-ior of MTC is usually intermediate between that of aggressive anaplas-tic thyroid cancer and that of indolent papillary and follicular thyroid cancer. Local lymph node spread is common, and metastases to lung and bone can occur. MTC in which all or most of the cells produce calcitonin may have a better prognosis than a more heterogeneous tumor in which calcitonin production is not uniform. Even in the most aggressive tumors, calcitonin production is usually sufficient to serve as a specific marker for this thyroid cancer. However, there may be rare instances in which calcitonin production has ceased. The 5-year survival rate of patients with metastatic MTC approximates 50%. Survival can vary from several months to three decades after diag-nosis. Patients younger than 2 years of age with metastatic disease and older than 50 years of age with only localized disease have been reported. C-cell hyperplasia can occur in patients as young as 2 years and as old as 45 years. Therefore, the tumor can be rapidly aggres-sive, leading to death within months after diagnosis, or it can be indo-lent and compatible with survival for decades. In the latter case, serum calcitonin levels remain elevated but stable or slowly increasing.

Clinical Manifestations

PHEOCHROMOCYTOMA. Pheochromocytoma is a component of MEN type 2A and 2B, in which the tumor can be bilateral or unilateral. Bilateral and multifocal pheochromocytomas are very common in this clinical setting, with an incidence of more than 70%. This figure contrasts with a bilateral incidence of usually less than 10% for spo-radic pheochromocytomas and only 20 to 50% for familial pheochro-mocytomas. Other hereditary forms of bilateral pheochromocytoma include von Hippel-Lindau disease and isolated hereditary pheochromocytoma. Pheochromocytomas are seen occasionally in patients with MEN 1. Adrenal medullary hyperplasia is a prede-cessor of the pheochromocytomas seen with MTC. The increase in adrenal medullary mass results from diffuse or multifocal prolifer-ation of adrenal medullary cells, primarily those found within the head and body of the glands. The biochemical as well as clinical manifestations of this tumor may be elusive, so diagnostic tests for pheochromocytoma should be pursued vigorously in MEN type 2 with appropriate testing and retroperitoneal imaging. Three decades of routine screening for pheochromocytomas in MEN 2 has led to a change in the clinical presentation. Large pheochromocytomas that put patients at high risk for sudden death are seen only in the rare patient with previously undiscovered MEN 2 or in a patient with known MEN 2 who declines screening. More commonly, patients are identified by subtle clinical features or modest abnormalities of catecholamine or metanephrine production. Early diagnosis and appropriate treatment combined with the routine use of adrenergic blockade has made death or serious morbidity from pheochromo-cytoma in this disorder uncommon.

HYPERPARATHYROIDISM. Hyperparathyroidism occurs in 10 to 20% of MEN 2 patients, being more common in MEN type 2A and rarely occurring in MEN type 2B (and it also occurs in MEN type 1). The presence of hyperparathyroidism thus should always make one con-sider the possibility of MEN. The differential diagnosis of heredi-tary hypercalcemia includes familial hypercalcemic hypocalciuria, familial parathyroid adenoma—jaw tumor syndromes, familial parathyroid hyperplasia, MEN 1, and MEN 2A. Parathyroid hyper-

---

Table 261–2 • MULTIPLE ENDOCRINE NEOPLASIA TYPE 2 (MEN 2)

Multiple endocrine neoplasia type 2A (MEN 2A)*
   Medullary thyroid carcinoma
   Pheochromocytoma
   Parathyroid neoplasia
Variants of MEN 2A
   MEN 2A with cutaneous lichen amyloidosis (MEN 2A/CLA)
   MEN 2A with Hirschsprung's disease
Familial medullary thyroid carcinoma (FMTC)
Multiple endocrine neoplasia type 2B (MEN 2B)
   Medullary thyroid carcinoma
   Pheochromocytoma
   Parathyroid disease (rare)
   Marfanoid habitus
   Intestinal ganglioneuromatosis and mucosal neuromas

*Sipple syndrome.

MULTIPLE ENDOCRINE NEOPLASIA (Chapter 244)

In addition to sporadic tumors, MTC can occur in association with other endocrine tumors as part of a multiple endocrine neopla-sia, designated MEN type 2, to distinguish it from MEN type 1, which consists of parathyroid, pancreatic, and pituitary tumors. MEN type 2 (Sipple's syndrome) is an autosomal dominant syndrome that can be clinically classified into two subtypes, type 2A and 2B (Table 261–2).

plasia is more common than adenoma, an important consideration for surgical exploration of all parathyroid glands. The *RET* proto-oncogene is expressed in parathyroid tissue and is likely to account for the neoplastic changes.

MULTIPLE MUCOSAL NEUROMAS. The presence of neuromas with a cen-trofacial distribution is the most consistent component of MEN type 2B. The most common location of neuromas is the oral cavity. The oral lesions are almost invariably present by the first decade and in some cases even at birth. Mucosal neuromas can also be present in the eyelid, conjunctiva, cornea, and other mucosal surfaces. The most prominent microscopic feature of neuromas is an increase in the size and number of nerves. These hypertrophied nerve fibers are readily seen with a slit lamp and occasionally by direct oph-thalmologic examination. Hypertrophied corneal nerves have also been identified in MEN 2A, although there has been no report of mucosal neuromas in this syndrome.

Gastrointestinal tract abnormalities are part of the multiple mucosal neuroma syndrome. The most common of these is gas-trointestinal ganglioneuromatosis, which usually occurs in the small and large intestines but has also been noted in the esophagus and stomach. The associated neurologic dysfunction is frequently asso-ciated with swallowing abnormalities, megacolon, diarrhea, and con-stipation, and may be the most common presenting manifestation in childhood. The diarrhea may also be due to excess production of bioactive substances by the MTC. In any case, diarrhea is the most common symptom of MTC. The association of MTC with Hirschsprung's disease has become recently appreciated.

MARFANOID HABITUS. Some MEN 2B patients have a tall, slender body with long arms and legs, an abnormal ratio of upper to lower body segments, and poor muscle development. Other features asso-ciated with the marfanoid habitus may include dorsal kyphosis, pectus excavatum or pectus carinatum, pes cavus, and high-arched palate. In contrast to patients with true Marfan's syndrome, these patients do not have aortic arch abnormalities, ectopia lentis, homo-cystinuria, or mucopolysaccharide abnormalities.

Pathogenesis

HEREDITARY MTC (FAMILIAL MTC AND MEN 2). Genetic linkage studies mapped the gene for MEN 2 to a centromeric chromosome 10 locus, and *RET* proto-oncogene mutations were subsequently identified for the associated clinical syndromes (Tables 261–1 and 261–2). The gene encodes a receptor tyrosine kinase. Two broad classes of mutations have been identified (Fig. 261–1). Six specific codons (609, 611, 618, 620, 630, and 634) in the extracellular domain of the tyrosine kinase receptor encoded by *RET* change a conserved cysteine to another amino acid. Codon 634 mutations, and by inference other extracellular domain mutations, cause receptor dimerization and activation and initiate the transformation of C-cells. A second class of rarer mutations involve the intracellular domain, with the most common located at codon 918 (see Fig. 261–1). This coding change results in receptor activation in the absence of dimerization. Other intracellular domain mutations occur at codons 768, 790, 791, 804, 883, and 891. Identification of the mutation in a family member can be a guide to the appropriate genetic diagnosis. The clinical syndromes associated with each of these mutations is described in Figure 261–1. Mutations of other components of the *RET* signaling system (glial cell-derived neurotrophic factor and the glial cell-derived neurotrophic factor-α1 receptor) have not been identified in MTC (see Fig. 261–1).

In familial MTC, the earliest identified histologic abnormality associated with the *RET* proto-oncogene mutations is C-cell hyperplasia. It appears that a second genetic event at the *RET* locus may hasten or facilitate transformation. These events include loss of the normal *RET* allele or amplification of the mutant *RET* allele. The specific somatic mechanisms for amplification include trisomy 10 (two mutant chromosome 10 copies) or tandem duplication of the mutant *RET* gene. Evidence for loss of normal copies of genes on chromosomes 1p, 3q, 13q, and 22q suggest that other as yet unidentified genes are likely to be involved in the progression observed in hereditary MTC.

Since the majority of familial cases will have identifiable *RET* mutation, as can even apparently sporadic cases, screening should be vigorously pursued with routine testing of *RET* exons 10, 11, 13, 14, 15, and 16, with sequencing of the remaining 15 exons if indicated. The clinician should be aware that there can be technical errors in testing and should be prepared to use more than one laboratory for confirmation studies.

GERMLINE MUTATIONS IN APPARENTLY SPORADIC MTC. The discovery of *RET* proto-oncogene mutations in MTC has uncovered unidentified kindreds with hereditary MTC in which the proband masqueraded as sporadic MTC. Approximately 6% of patients with apparently sporadic MTC have germline *RET* mutations indicative of familial MTC. Although most are members of previously unidentified kindreds, some are examples of de novo mutations, most commonly of codon 634. This has led to the identification of additional family members at risk for development of MTC. These studies recommend *RET* proto-oncogene testing of all patients with apparently sporadic MTC.

SOMATIC MUTATIONS IN SPORADIC MTC. Somatic mutations (nongermline mutations acquired during cell growth and differentiation) of *RET* codon 918 are found in approximately 25% of sporadic tumors (see Fig. 261–1), and evidence suggests that sporadic MTCs with this mutation are more aggressive and are associated with shorter survival. In the aggressive tumors with a codon 918 mutation, it is not clear whether the mutation is the initiating abnormality or one that is acquired in the progression from a less to a more malignant phenotype.

Diagnosis

GENETIC TESTING. Genetic testing is used to identify individuals, especially children, at risk for development of familial MTC and MEN 2. These tests are available from a variety of commercial sources (http://www.genetests.org). The test can be performed on a single peripheral blood sample. The presence of a specific mutation and the propensity to develop the clinical syndrome of MEN 2 or familial MTC essentially indicates full concordance. Genetic testing can be complicated by a variety of laboratory or sampling errors. Since genetic testing has become the "gold standard" for diagnosis of hereditary MTC and decisions regarding thyroidectomy are based on these results, it is prudent to repeat the genetic test on a separate peripheral blood sample, preferably in more than one laboratory. It is reasonable to exclude an individual with two or more negative genetic test results from further screening efforts. Although genetic testing will have a great impact on the diagnosis and treatment of MTC, it will have little impact on management of adrenal medullary and parathyroid disease, where manifestations generally develop later.

CALCITONIN. Overexpression of the calcitonin gene is the molecular hallmark of MTC. This overexpression results in the increased production of calcitonin by the tumor and increased secretion of the hormone into blood. As a result, most patients with MTC have an increased circulating concentration of calcitonin that can be detected by radioimmunoassay and increased tumor concentrations that can be demonstrated directly by immunohistology or through increased messenger RNA (mRNA) expression by in situ hybridization. Usually, the basal blood concentration of calcitonin is sufficiently elevated to be diagnostic of the presence of the tumor. In the early stages of the disease, however, the basal concentrations of calcitonin cannot be readily distinguished from normal. In these circumstances, provocative testing of calcitonin secretion can reveal the presence of the abnormal C-cells. Such testing is also clinically indicated for the relative of a patient with familial MTC when early diagnosis is sought; although, as discussed, genetic testing has largely replaced calcitonin testing in MEN 2 kindreds with an identifiable *RET* mutation. Family screening is also recommended for apparently sporadic tumors because family history can be unreliable. However, the predicted probability of a patient with sporadic MTC with a negative *RET* test having hereditary MTC is very low—probably in the 0.1% range. Thus, calcitonin testing in this situation may be unneeded.

The two most commonly used provocative agents for calcitonin secretion are calcium and the synthetic gastrin analogue pentagastrin (not available for clinical use in United States at present), alone or in combination. Most tumors respond to either agent with a diagnostic increase in calcitonin secretion. Calcitonin blood measurements can also be used to evaluate therapy and monitor tumor recurrence. Interpretation must be made according to the specific parameters of the procedure used.

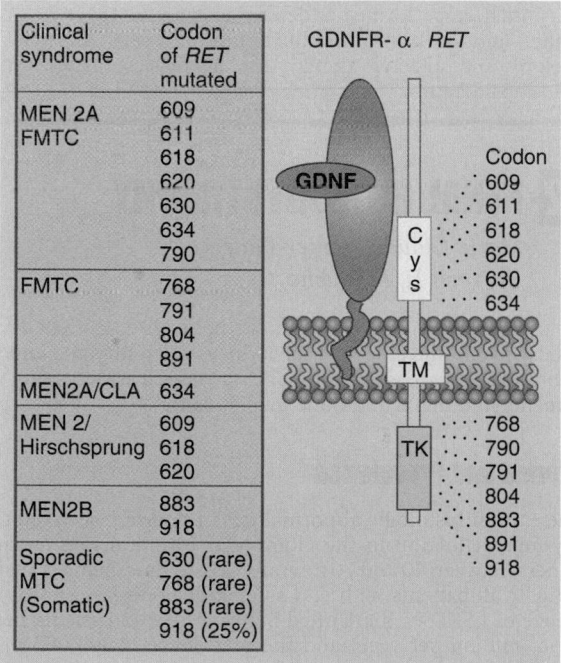

Clinical syndrome	Codon of *RET* mutated
MEN 2A FMTC	609 611 618 620 630 634 790
FMTC	768 791 804 891
MEN2A/CLA	634
MEN 2/ Hirschsprung	609 618 620
MEN2B	883 918
Sporadic MTC (Somatic)	630 (rare) 768 (rare) 883 (rare) 918 (25%)

FIGURE 261–1 • The *RET* proto-oncogene/glial cell-derived neurotrophic factor receptor (GDNFR)-α1 complex. Mutations of the *RET* proto-oncogene receptor are causative for multiple endocrine neoplasia type 2A (MEN 2A), familial medullary thyroid carcinoma (FMTC), MEN 2A/cutaneous lichen amyloidosis (MEN 2A/CLA), MEN 2 associated with Hirschsprung's disease, or MEN 2B. Mutations of the extracellular cysteine-rich region of the receptor (Cys) and intracellular tyrosine kinase domain (TK) have been identified as germline mutations in the indicated syndromes. Somatic mutations of the *RET* proto-oncogene have also been identified in sporadic MTC. GDNF = glial cell-derived neurotrophic factor, which is a small peptide ligand for the RET/GDNF receptor complex.

℞ Treatment

SURGERY. Surgery is the treatment of choice for the three types of neoplasia in MEN 2. Because all are potentially lethal, especially MTC and pheochromocytoma, but can be cured in their early stages, aggressive therapy is warranted. Early surgery is effective treatment and can be curative. Management of the individual components of MEN 2 generally follows the accepted procedures for each neoplasm. The sequence of treatment, however, is guided by several important principles. In adults with the fully formed MEN 2A syndrome, pheochromocytomas, commonly bilateral, should be treated first because they can be life threatening. Management of thyroid and parathyroid disorders follows. Accepted surgical procedures include unilateral or bilateral adrenalectomy for diseased glands by anterior, posterior, or laparoscopic approaches or unilateral cortical sparing adrenalectomy in an attempt to preserve adrenal cortical function. Bilateral adrenalectomy at an early age is mandatory in the rare kindred with malignant pheochromocytoma. In adults with palpable MTC (>1 cm), metastasis to local lymph nodes is common, and a total thyroidectomy and compartment-oriented lymph node dissection should be performed to enhance the likelihood of complete removal of all tumor. Hyperparathyroidism may be managed by either subtotal parathyroidectomy or total parathyroidectomy with transplantation of parathyroid tissue to the nondominant forearm.

GENETIC TESTING AND MANAGEMENT. Hereditary MTC is currently unique among genetic malignancies in that identification of a genetic abnormality leads to a specific therapeutic intervention. In other genetic malignancies such as colon or breast carcinoma, the identification of a germline mutation leads to increased surveillance, but this information is only rarely used to direct a specific therapy.

The identification of a mutation of the *RET* proto-oncogene indicates that the affected individual has a greater than 90% probability of development of MTC at some point during life. A 25-year history of prospective screening for MEN 2 has provided reasonable evidence that more than 85% of children who have had total thyroidectomy in the teenage years currently have no evidence of disease. This experience has been sufficiently positive that there is consensus in the endocrine community that a total thyroidectomy should be performed in most children with MEN 2A and a germline *RET* mutation (codons 611, 618, 620, or 634) by the age of 6 years. Other rarer mutations (609, 768, 790, 791, 804, and 891) that cause

MEN 2A or familial MTC appear to be associated with less aggressive MTC, and there are a number of kindreds with these mutations in which death or serious morbidity from MTC is rare. Deferral of thyroidectomy until the teenage years or until there are calcitonin abnormalities in these unique kindreds may be appropriate.

It is important to keep in mind that death from MTC in MEN 2A or hereditary MTC before prospective screening with calcitonin testing occurred in the fourth or fifth decade, with rare deaths caused by MTC in the third or fourth decade. Thus, the results of prospective studies that were initiated 25 years ago are only now providing meaningful evidence that early intervention is beneficial. Despite the fact that a still longer period of observation will be required before definitive conclusions can be drawn, there is growing confidence that early thyroidectomy combined with appropriate care of pheochromocytomas can approximate a normal life span for most patients with hereditary MTC and render death from metastatic MTC a rare event.

MANAGEMENT OF PERSISTENT POSTOPERATIVE CALCITONIN MEASUREMENTS IN PATIENTS WITH MTC. A vexing problem for clinicians is the persistence of calcitonin elevations following primary surgical management. The major question is whether reoperation to remove all identifiable lymph nodes in the neck (compartment-oriented dissection) has value. A recent body of experience supports reoperative strategy in patients with persistent disease. In the selection of these patients, it is important to perform a careful search for distant metastatic disease and to exclude hepatic, bone, and pulmonary metastasis by appropriate imaging studies. Some physicians perform laparoscopy with direct hepatic visualization or selective catheterization of the arterial and venous supply of the liver with measurement of pentagastrin-stimulated calcitonin in hepatic venous effluent to exclude hepatic metastasis. In patients with no evidence of distant metastatic disease, reoperative compartment-oriented lymphadenectomy may be appropriate. Approximately one of five carefully selected patients will have the serum calcitonin level normalized following microsurgical dissection (calcitonin values nondetectable following pentagastrin). No long-term follow-up studies in this group of patients has been performed to determine whether this type of surgical intervention affects morbidity or mortality related to MTC, yet the lack of other effective therapy for this disease makes it a reasonable consideration.

SUGGESTED READINGS

Brandi ML, Gagel RF, Angeli A, et al: Guidelines for diagnosis and therapy of MEN type 1 and type 2. J Clin Endocrinol Metab 2001;86:5658-5671. *A review of the recommendations of a consensus meeting.*

Cohen MS, Moley JF: Surgical treatment of medullary thyroid carcinoma. J Intern Med 2003;253:616–626. *Emphasizes that most patients with a palpable primary tumor have nodal disease, often bilateral, so resection of the primary and cervical lymph nodes is important. Nevertheless, more than half of the patients will have recurrent disease, for which there is no good therapy.*

Clayman GL, el-Baradie TS: Medullary thyroid cancer. Otolaryngol Clin North Am 2003;36:91–105. *Review of molecular genetics, with an emphasis on prognosis and therapeutic options, including interdisciplinary management.*

Deftos LJ, Sherman SI, Gagel RF: Multiglandular endocrine disorders. In Felig P, Frohman LA (eds): Endocrinology and Metabolism, 4th ed. New York, McGraw Hill, 2001, pp 1355-1382. *A detailed and contemporary discussion of polyglandular endocrine disease, including MTC and MEN 2.*

Diez JJ, Iglesias P: Somatostatin analogs in the treatment of medullary thyroid carcinoma. J Endocrinol Invest 2002;25:773–778. *These drugs were not effective in recurrent medullary thyroid carcinoma.*

Huang SC, Koch CA, Vortmeyer AO, et al: Duplication of the mutant RET allele in trisomy 10 or loss of the wild-type allele in multiple endocrine neoplasia type 2-associated pheochromocytomas. Cancer Res 2000;60:6223-6226. *Introduction of the concept of the wild-type or normal RET receptor functioning to suppress the transforming potential of the mutant receptor.*

Mulligan LM, Kwok JBJ, Healey CS, et al: Germ-line mutations of the RET proto-oncogene in multiple endocrine neoplasia type 2A. Nature 1993;363:458–460. *Identification of the genetic abnormality in MEN IIA.*

Pellegriti G, Leboulleux S, Baudin E, et al: Long-term outcome of medullary thyroid carcinoma in patients with normal postoperative medical imaging. Br J Cancer 2003;88:1537–1542. *A clinical study of prognostic factors in medullary thyroid carcinoma patients with normal postoperative imaging and either elevated or undetectable serum calcitonin levels, showing that elevated postoperative calcitonin levels and evidence of tumor extension were critical prognostic factors for a high risk of imaging-detected relapse.*

Sanso GE, Domene HM, Garcia R, et al: Very early detection of RET proto-oncogene mutation is crucial for preventive thyroidectomy in multiple endocrine neoplasia type 2 children. Cancer 2002;94:323–330. *Potential use of this diagnostic approach to select patients for prophylactic thyroidectomy.*

262 RENAL OSTEODYSTROPHY

Marie-Claude Monier-Faugere
Hartmut H. Malluche

Renal osteodystrophy is a metabolic bone disease that develops secondary to chronic failure of the kidneys' excretory and endocrine functions. Renal osteodystrophy encompasses a wide variety of derangements in mineral and bone metabolism.

Incidence and Prevalence

The earliest histologic abnormalities of bone are seen after a relatively mild reduction in the glomerular filtration rate (creatinine clearances between 40 and 70 mL/min). Histologic changes are found in virtually all patients with end-stage kidney disease (ESKD). The incidence of ESKD in the United States is 79,102 patients per year (287 per million per year) and the prevalence is 304,083 patients (1105 per million).

Pathogenesis and Histopathology

PATHOGENETIC FACTORS

The kidneys have a well-established pivotal role in maintaining mineral homeostasis and hormonal balance. With progressive loss of excretory kidney function, abnormalities in divalent ions and secondary hyperparathyroidism typically develop early.

FACTORS IMPLICATED IN THE DEVELOPMENT OF SECONDARY HYPERPARATHYROIDISM. In advanced kidney failure, a variety of factors have been identified as direct stimulators of parathyroid hormone (PTH) secretion, including hypocalcemia, low levels of circulating calcitriol (the active vitamin D metabolite), and more recently, hyperphosphatemia. However, most patients with mild chronic kidney failure exhibit increased serum PTH levels without alterations in serum levels of calcium, phosphorus, and calcitriol.

Early Kidney Failure. The early sequence of events is still not fully elucidated. However, the early stages of kidney failure are marked by some signs of end-organ resistance to vitamin D, such as a mild decrease in intestinal calcium absorption and an altered calciuric response to oral supplementation of calcitriol. Calcitriol exerts its action by binding to vitamin D receptors, which interact with specific sequences of nuclear DNA, the vitamin D response elements that control genomic synthesis of many proteins including PTH. In early renal failure, binding of the hormone–vitamin D receptor complex to the vitamin D response element has been found to be reduced, which could lead to less suppressive effects of physiologic blood levels of calcitriol on PTH synthesis and therefore PTH overproduction. The exact mechanisms implicated in impaired binding of the hormone–vitamin D receptor complex to the vitamin D response element are not fully elucidated. In experimental studies on rats, alterations in the vitamin D receptor heterodimer partner (retinoid X receptor) have been observed; however, this mechanism has not been proved in humans. Other alterations in accessory nuclear factors, abnormal phosphorylation, and changes in conformation of the vitamin D receptor or chemical alteration of the DNA binding domain may be involved in the impaired vitamin D receptor response to calcitriol.

Advanced Kidney Failure. With more advanced nephron loss, the phosphate load of the remaining functioning nephrons progressively increases. This increased load results in inhibition of C1-α-hydroxylase, the enzyme responsible for the conversion of 25-hydroxyvitamin D to its active metabolite 1,25-dihydroxyvitamin D (calcitriol). Calcitriol deficiency in turn further decreases intestinal calcium absorption and thus results in hypocalcemia. Calcitriol deficiency in cases of advanced kidney failure is associated with a decreased number of vitamin D receptors, in particular, receptors in parathyroid glands. Because calcitriol has been shown to suppress the expression of pre-pro-PTH mRNA, lower circulating calcitriol levels together with a low number of vitamin D receptors in patients with ESKD result in stimulation of both synthesis and secretion of PTH. Low blood levels of ionized calcium rapidly stimulate PTH secretion, whereas high calcium concentrations suppress it. The relationship between ionized calcium and PTH follows a sigmoidal pattern. The action of calcium on parathyroid gland cells is associated with modulation of intracellular cyclic adenosine monophosphate (cAMP). The short-term stimulation induced by low calcium is due to release of stored preformed hormone and an increase in the number of cells that secrete PTH. More prolonged hypocalcemia induces changes in intracellular PTH degradation with reutilization of degraded hormone and mobilization of the secondary storage pool. Within days or weeks of the onset of hypocalcemia, pre-pro-PTH mRNA expression is stimulated. This effect is exerted through a recently described negative calcium response element located in the upstream flanking region of the gene for PTH. Calcium exerts its effects on parathyroid gland cells through a recently isolated G protein–coupled calcium-sensing receptor located on the cell membrane. Expression of the calcium receptor has been shown to be suppressed by calcitriol deficiency and stimulated by calcitriol administration, thus suggesting an additional regulatory mechanism of the active vitamin D metabolite on PTH production. The decreased number of calcium-sensing receptors with low circulating calcitriol may, at least in part, explain the relative insensitivity of parathyroid gland cells to calcium in patients undergoing dialysis (higher set point).

When the glomerular filtration rate reaches levels of less than 25% of normal, the serum phosphorus content rises. At this level of reduced renal function, the ability of the remaining nephrons to increase phosphate excretion is exhausted. Increased serum phosphorus levels further decrease serum calcium through physicochemical binding and suppress C1-α-hydroxylase activity, which results in further lowering of the circulating levels of calcitriol. Moreover, a direct stimulatory effect of phosphorus on parathyroid gland cells, independent of calcium and calcitriol, has recently been observed in patients with ESKD. The mechanism of the direct action of phosphorus on PTH secretion has not been fully elucidated.

All of these mechanisms result in increased production of PTH and increased parathyroid gland mass. The size of the parathyroid glands progressively increases with time in dialyzed patients and parallels serum PTH levels. This increase in size is mainly due to diffuse cellular hyperplasia. Monoclonal cell growth may also develop and result in the formation of tumor-like nodules that have less or no vitamin D and calcium-sensing receptors and that promote parathyroid gland resistance to calcitriol and calcium.

FACTORS AFFECTING PARATHYROID HORMONE PRODUCTION AND ITS EFFECTS ON BONE. Other systemic factors such as α-adrenergic agonists, dopamine, prostaglandin E, secretin, and phosphodiesterase inhibitors that alter the cAMP content of parathyroid cells may increase PTH secretion. Recently, the inflammatory cytokine interleukin-8 was found to stimulate PTH secretion. The effect of magnesium in regulating PTH secretion is similar to that of calcium, but not as potent. Moreover, peripheral degradation of PTH is reduced in uremia and numerous PTH fragments circulate, thus prolonging the effects of PTH on target organs.

Accumulation of aluminum in bone and other organs such as the parathyroid glands may occur in patients undergoing dialysis or before the initiation of dialysis. Aluminum accumulation in the parathyroid glands results in decreased secretion of PTH and suppression of bone turnover. In addition, aluminum inhibits renal and intestinal C1-α-hydroxylase activity and may thus further contribute to reduced levels of calcitriol. Possible sources of aluminum include high concentrations in the water used for dialysis, prescription of aluminum-containing phosphate binders, and aluminum in drinking water, infant formula, and other liquids or solid food.

Bone is an important buffer for excess acid production in patients with ESKD. Metabolic acidosis has been shown to stimulate bone resorption and suppress bone formation, thereby resulting in negative bone balance.

Patients with ESKD are in a hypogonadal state, and some are treated with glucocorticoids, which have an impact on bone metabolism. Patients maintained on chronic dialysis have retention of β_2-microglobulin and alterations in cytokines, growth factors, PTH, and vitamin D receptors that may be involved in the regulation of bone remodeling, thus affecting the histologic pattern of renal osteodystrophy.

HISTOLOGIC PATTERN

Renal osteodystrophy is not a uniform bone disease. Depending on the relative contribution of the different pathogenic factors, patients with ESKD have different histologic patterns.

PREDOMINANT HYPERPARATHYROID BONE DISEASE. Excess parathyroid hormone results in a marked increase in bone turnover. Osteoclasts, osteoblasts, and osteocytes are found in abundance (Fig. 262–1). Disturbed osteoblastic activity results in a disorderly production of collagen, which is deposited not only toward the trabecular surface

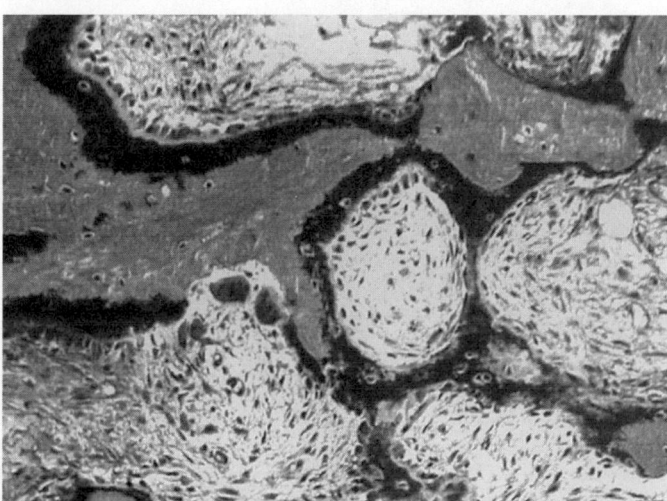

FIGURE 262–1 • Predominant hyperparathyroid bone disease with a high fraction of the trabecular surface covered by osteoid seams, many osteoblasts and osteoclasts, and marrow fibrosis; undecalcified 3 μm thick section of iliac bone (brightfield light microscopy, modified Masson-Goldner stain, original magnification × 125).

but also in the marrow cavity, thereby causing peritrabecular and marrow fibrosis. The nonmineralized component of bone, osteoid, is increased, and the normal three-dimensional architecture of osteoid is frequently lost. Osteoid seams no longer exhibit their usual birefringence under polarized light; instead, a disorderly arrangement of woven osteoid and woven bone with a typical crisscross pattern under polarized light is seen. The mineral apposition rate and number of actively mineralizing sites are increased, as documented under fluorescent light after the administration of time-spaced tetracycline markers.

LOW-TURNOVER BONE DISEASE. Low-turnover uremic osteodystrophy is the other end of the spectrum of renal osteodystrophy. The histologic hallmark of this group is a profound decrease in bone turnover, that is, low number of active remodeling sites resulting in bone resorption and suppressed bone formation. The majority of trabecular bone is covered by lining cells, with few osteoclasts and osteoblasts. Bone structure is predominantly lamellar. The extent of mineralizing surfaces is markedly reduced. Usually only a few thin single labels of tetracycline are observed. Two histologic subgroups can be identified in this type of renal osteodystrophy, depending on the sequence of events leading to a decline in the number and/or activity of the osteoblasts: low-turnover osteomalacia and adynamic bone disease.

Low-turnover osteomalacia is characterized by an accumulation of unmineralized matrix in which a diminution in mineralization precedes or is more pronounced than the inhibition of collagen deposition. Unmineralized bone represents a sizable fraction of trabecular bone volume. The increased lamellar osteoid volume is due to the presence of wide osteoid seams that cover a large portion of the trabecular surface (Fig. 262–2). The occasional presence of woven bone buried within the trabeculae indicates past high bone turnover. When osteoclasts are present, they are usually seen within trabecular bone or at the small fraction of trabecular surface left without osteoid coating.

With adynamic uremic bone disease, the reduction in mineralization is coupled with a concomitant and parallel decrease in bone formation. Adynamic uremic bone disease is characterized by few osteoid seams and few bone cells (Fig. 262–3).

MIXED UREMIC OSTEODYSTROPHY. Mixed uremic osteodystrophy is caused primarily by hyperparathyroidism and defective mineralization with or without increased bone formation. These features may coexist in varying degrees in different patients. Increased numbers of heterogeneous remodeling sites can be seen (Fig. 262–4). The number of osteoclasts is usually increased. Because active foci with numerous cells, woven osteoid seams, and peritrabecular fibrosis coexist next to lamellar sites with a more reduced activity, greater production of lamellar or woven osteoid causes an accumulation of osteoid with normal or increased thickness of osteoid seams. Whereas

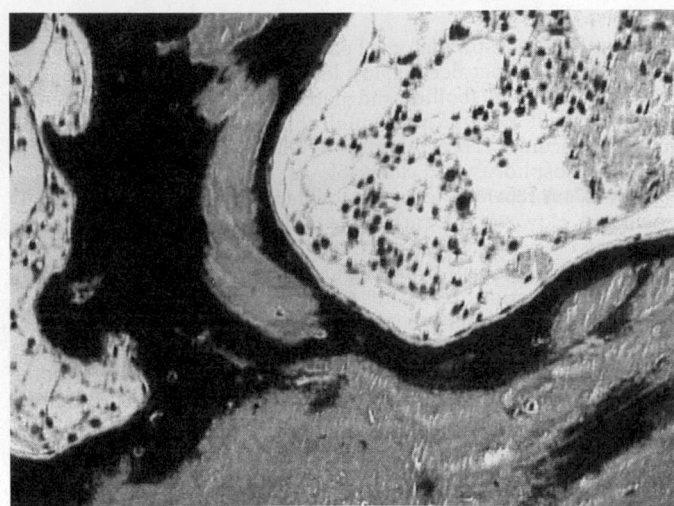

FIGURE 262–3 • Adynamic bone disease with no accumulation of osteoid, and absence of osteoblasts and osteoclasts; undecalcified 3 μm thick section of iliac bone (brightfield light microscopy, modified Masson-Goldner stain, original magnification × 125).

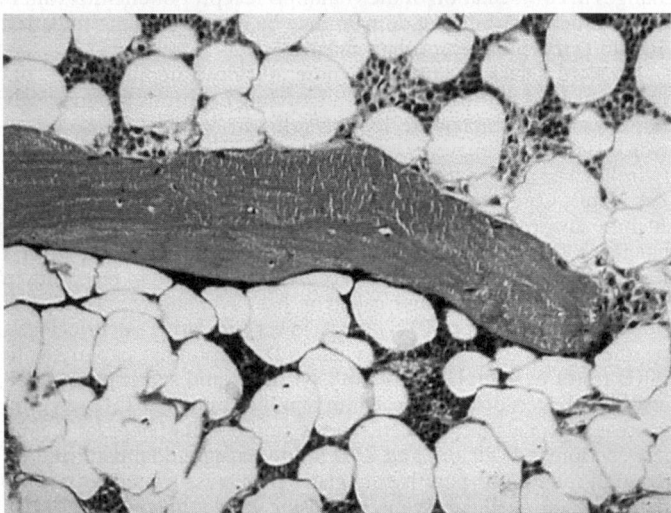

FIGURE 262–4 • Mixed uremic osteodystrophy. Few osteoblasts, several osteoclasts, and mild peritrabecular fibrosis; undecalcified, 3-μm thick section of human iliac bone (brightfield light microscopy, modified Masson-Goldner stain, original magnification × 125).

active mineralizing surfaces increase in woven bone with a higher mineralization rate and diffuse labeling, mineralization surfaces may be reduced in lamellar bone with a decreased mineral apposition rate.

ASSOCIATED FEATURES
Bone Aluminum Accumulation. Aluminum accumulates in bone at the mineralization front, at the cement lines, or diffusely. The extent of stainable aluminum at the mineralization front correlates best with histologic abnormalities in mineralization. Aluminum deposition is most severe in cases of low-turnover osteomalacia. However, it can be observed in all histologic forms of renal osteodystrophy. In patients in whom an increased aluminum burden develops, bone mineralization and bone turnover progressively decrease. These abnormalities are reversed with removal of the aluminum.

Osteoporosis and Osteosclerosis. With progressive loss of renal function, cancellous bone volume is increased along with a loss of cortical bone. Patients undergoing chronic dialysis might have a loss or gain in bone volume depending on bone balance. In the case of negative bone balance, bone loss occurs in cortical and cancellous bone and is more rapid when bone turnover is high. When the bone balance is positive, osteosclerosis may be observed when osteoblasts are active in depositing new bone, thus superseding bone resorption. When bone turnover is low, however, positive bone balance results in hypercalcemia and possibly extraosseous calcification.

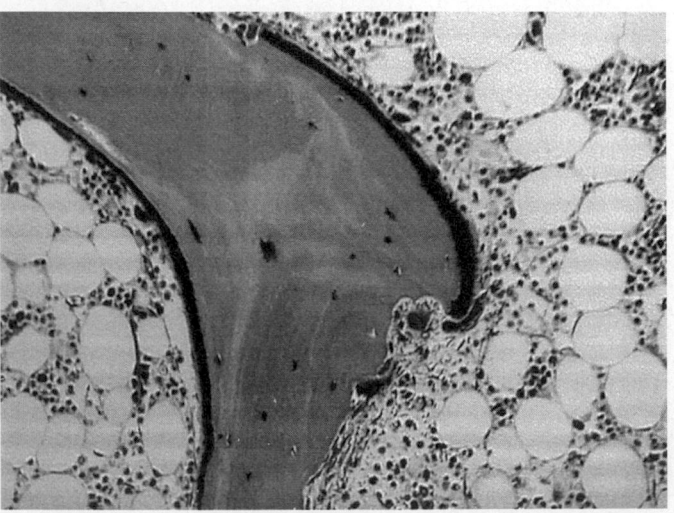

FIGURE 262–2 • Low-turnover osteomalacia demonstrating an accumulation of osteoid, a high ratio of osteoid surface to bone surface, thick osteoid seams, and absence of active osteoblasts or osteoclasts; undecalcified 3 μm thick section of iliac bone (brightfield light microscopy, modified Masson-Goldner stain, original magnification × 160).

Clinical Manifestations

Patients with mild to moderate kidney insufficiency are rarely symptomatic. Symptoms appear in patients with advanced kidney failure. Clinical manifestations are preceded, however, by an abnormal biochemical profile that should alert the physician and prompt steps to prevent more severe complications. When symptoms occur, they are usually insidious, subtle, nonspecific, and slowly progressive. Patients with ESKD are prone to a variety of symptoms related to alterations in bone and mineral metabolism.

BONE PAIN, FRACTURES, AND SKELETAL DEFORMITIES. Bone pain is usually vague, ill defined, and deep seated. It may be diffuse or localized in the lower part of the back, hips, knees, or legs. Weight bearing and changes in position commonly aggravate it. Bone pain may progress slowly to the degree that patients are completely incapacitated. Bone pain in patients with ESKD usually does not cause physical signs; however, local tenderness may be apparent with pressure. Occasionally, pain can occur suddenly at one joint of the lower extremities and mimic acute arthritis or periarthritis not relieved by heat or massage. A sharp chest pain may indicate rib fracture. Spontaneous fractures or fractures after minimal trauma may also occur in vertebrae (crush fractures) and in tubular bones.

Bone pain and bone fractures can be observed in all patients with ESKD independent of the underlying histologic bone disease, especially when osteoporosis is present. However, low-turnover osteomalacia and aluminum-related bone disease are associated with the most severe bone pain and the highest incidence of fractures and incapacity.

Skeletal deformities can be observed in children and adults. Most children with ESKD have growth retardation, and bone deformities may develop from vitamin D deficiency (rickets) or secondary hyperparathyroidism. In rickets, bowing of the long bones is seen, especially the tibiae and femora, with typical genu valgum that becomes more severe with adolescence. Long-standing secondary hyperparathyroidism in children may be responsible for slipped epiphyses secondary to impaired transformation of growth cartilage into regular metaphyseal spongiosa. This complication most commonly affects the hips, becomes obvious in preadolescence, and causes limping but is usually painless. When the radius and ulna are involved, ulnar deviation of the hands and local swelling may occur. In adults, skeletal deformities can be observed in cases of severe osteomalacia or osteoporosis and include lumbar scoliosis, thoracic kyphosis, and recurrent rib fractures.

MYOPATHY. Proximal muscle weakness is fairly common in dialysis patients, particularly those with aluminum toxicity, severe hyperparathyroidism, or osteomalacia. Its onset is usually gradual and mainly affects the lower extremities. Proximal myopathy is manifested by difficulty in rising out of a chair or climbing stairs. Patients may have a characteristic waddling gait.

PRURITUS. Itching affects 40 to 90% of patients with ESKD. Pruritus can occur before the institution of dialysis and can disappear after regular dialytic therapy. However, symptoms more often begin about 6 months after the start of dialysis and persist thereafter. Pruritus may be localized and mild or generalized and severe and prevent sleep and interfere with the patient's normal activities.

The mechanisms underlying pruritus in patients with ESKD are poorly understood. Several possible factors have been implicated (alone or in combination), such as secondary hyperparathyroidism, hypercalcemia, and increased calcium phosphate production, in addition to dry skin (xeroderma), intradermic microprecipitation of divalent ions, peripheral neuropathy, allergic reactions, hypersensitivity, histamine, proliferation of skin mast cells, hypervitaminosis A, iron deficiency, and abnormal fatty acid metabolism.

SOFT TISSUE CALCIFICATIONS, TUMORAL CALCINOSIS, AND CALCIPHYLAXIS. Asymptomatic vascular calcification is common in patients with ESKD. Soft tissue calcification may occur in the eyes and manifest as band keratopathy in the sclerae or induce an inflammatory response known as the red eye syndrome in the conjunctiva. These types of calcifications are usually associated with hyperparathyroidism or increased calcium phosphate product. Calcium deposits are also found in the lungs and lead to restrictive lung disease. Deposits in the myocardium might cause arrhythmias, annular calcifications, or myocardial dysfunction. Most soft tissue calcifications are attributed to secondary hyperparathyroidism or to the increased calcium phosphate product associated with it. However, they have also been described in patients with adynamic bone disease. This diversity could be explained by increased calcium and/or phosphate release from bone in patients with severe hyperparathyroidism and an inability to maintain normal mineral accretion in patients with adynamic bone disease.

Tumoral calcinosis is a form of soft tissue calcification that usually involves the periarticular tissues. Calcium deposits may grow to enormous size and interfere with the function of adjacent joints and organs. Although this type of calcification is usually associated with high calcium phosphate product, its exact pathogenesis is poorly understood. It may also be associated with certain ill-defined intrinsic factors. Similar to soft tissue calcification, it is observed with severe hyperparathyroidism and low-turnover bone disease.

The syndrome of calciphylaxis is characterized by vascular calcification in the tunica media. These calcifications induce painful violaceous skin lesions that progress to ischemic necrosis. This syndrome is associated with serious complications and often death. Calciphylaxis has been associated with high serum calcium phosphate product and severe secondary hyperparathyroidism. However, it can also be seen in patients with normal or mildly elevated serum phosphate or PTH levels. The pathogenesis of calciphylaxis is probably multifactorial because hyperparathyroidism, high calcium phosphate production, steroid therapy, vitamin D therapy, iron overload, aluminum toxicity, and protein C deficiency have all been implicated.

DIALYSIS DEMENTIA. Clinically, dialysis dementia is a form of progressive neurologic abnormality and includes dysarthria, dysphagia, amnesia, apraxia, mutism, myoclonic jerks, facial grimacing, seizures, and ultimately, severe dementia and death. This condition is usually associated with severe aluminum accumulation.

Diagnosis

The only unequivocal tool for the exact diagnosis of renal osteodystrophy is bone biopsy for histologic examination of mineralized bone after tetracycline double labeling and aluminum staining. Biopsy determines the precise level of bone formation, mineralization, bone resorption, and bone turnover and the extent of bone aluminum deposition, if present. The results serve as a basis for appropriate use of tailored therapeutic regimens.

In the absence of bone biopsy, the physician needs to estimate the level of bone turnover, the presence of osteomalacia, and the possibility of bone aluminum toxicity. Abnormalities in serum calcium, phosphorus, and alkaline phosphatase levels indicate severe renal osteodystrophy but are useless when used alone to indicate bone turnover or osteomalacia. Hypercalcemia may be observed in cases of severe hyperparathyroidism or adynamic bone disease, especially with vitamin D therapy. Hyperphosphatemia is an indication of noncompliance with phosphate binders and/or severe hyperparathyroidism secondary to increased release of phosphorus from bone. High serum levels of alkaline phosphatase are usually seen in both osteomalacia and predominant hyperparathyroidism.

Skeletal radiographic abnormalities are seen when the disease is advanced and include erosive cortical defects in the skull (pepper pot skull), acro-osteolysis of the clavicula, and erosion of the terminal finger phalanges. A rugger-jersey appearance of the spine and a ground-glass appearance of the skull, ribs, pelvis, and metaphysis of tubular bones reflect advanced cancellous changes. In severe hyperparathyroid bone disease, pseudocysts or brown tumors may be observed. It is common to underestimate the extent of disease on x-ray. Signs of increased bone resorption may be seen on radiographs reflecting past resorption activity, which may have been succeeded by the accumulation of osteoid. Because osteoid is radiolucent, the superimposed osteomalacia will be missed by radiographic examination. Looser zones, straight bands of radiolucency abutting the cortex and running perpendicular to the long axis of bone, are of relatively low sensitivity and low specificity for the diagnosis of osteomalacia.

Serum PTH levels are better indicators of bone turnover, especially when measured with the immunoradiometric "intact" assay that detects only the intact hormone. However, careful assessment of the predictive value of serum PTH levels for bone turnover shows that all patients with serum PTH levels within or below the normal range (<65 pg/mL) have low bone turnover and that values of serum PTH levels above 500 pg/mL are 100% and 95.5% specific for high bone turnover in patients maintained on hemodialysis and peritoneal dialysis, respectively. For the majority of dialyzed patients, that is, those with serum PTH levels between 65 and 500 pg/mL, bone turnover unfortunately cannot be predicted accurately. In addition to serum PTH values, certain risk factors for low bone turnover have been isolated and include peritoneal dialysis, diabetes, advanced age, high calcium content in the dialysate, high doses of phosphate binders, aggressive vitamin D therapy, or previous parathyroidectomy. However, in individual patients, discrepancies between risk factors, PTH levels, and bone turnover are frequent; this situation calls for bone biopsy. Recently, with the development of a new PTH assay that measures exclusively PTH-(1–84), it has been shown that the "intact" PTH assay detects not only PTH-(1–84) but also large C-PTH fragments. These large fragments have the potential of antagonizing the effects of PTH-(1–84) on serum calcium and bone turnover. The PTH-(1–84)/C-PTH fragments ratio has been shown to be the best indicator of bone turnover in a selected cohort of ESKD patients without presenting conditions or medication treatment (vitamin D or other) known to affect bone. It awaits further studies to determine whether the PTH-(1–84)/C-PTH fragments ratio can predict bone turnover in all ESKD patients.

Aluminum accumulation may be seen at any level of bone turnover or any serum PTH level. Although correlations exist between random serum aluminum levels and the extent of stainable aluminum in bone, no threshold value allows a clear-cut distinction between patients with and patients without aluminum-related bone disease. The deferoxamine infusion test is advocated to improve the sensitivity of random serum aluminum levels. An increase in serum aluminum levels of greater than 200 µg/L 48 hours after a standardized infusion constitutes a positive result. This test does improve the sensitivity of predicting aluminum-related bone disease, but the specificity is greatly reduced. Having both a positive deferoxamine test and a PTH level less than 200 pg/mL will make the diagnosis of aluminum-related bone disease with almost absolute certainty. However, the sensitivity is greatly reduced and many patients will have false-negative results.

Rx Prevention and Treatment

Therapeutic intervention should begin before far-advanced bone disease develops, that is, not later than at the time of institution of dialysis. Secondary hyperparathyroidism can be prevented by avoiding deviations of serum phosphorus and calcium levels from normal.

CONTROL OF SERUM PHOSPHORUS AND CALCIUM. None of the available dialytic methods is efficient in removing phosphorus because of compartmentalization and slow efflux of phosphorus from the intracellular space. Dialysis removes approximately 3 g of phosphorus per week. Therefore, in patients with ESKD, dietary phosphate restriction has to be implemented. However, because phosphate is present in most protein-containing food products, phosphate restriction is limited by the need for appropriate dietary protein intake. With the current recommendations, the protein intake of dialyzed patients should be at least 1.2 g/kg/day (hemodialysis) and 1.3 g/kg/day (peritoneal dialysis), which provides a minimum of 1 g of phosphorus per day. Therefore, the addition of phosphate binders is needed in most patients. Currently used phosphate binders are calcium carbonate and calcium acetate. They are most effective when given with meals and in proportion to the size of the meal. Calcium citrate should be avoided because it promotes intestinal aluminum absorption. Aluminum-containing phosphate binders, although more potent than calcium salts, should not be used because of the risk of aluminum-related bone disease. However, in severe cases of hyperphosphatemia, when calcium-containing phosphate binders have proved to be insufficient, low doses of aluminum-containing phosphate binders can be used in addition to calcium salts for a limited period. Recently, non–calcium-containing sevelamer hydrochloride (Renagel) became available as an alternative phosphate binder. This drug has been shown to be associated with less progression of coronary and aortic calcifications than are calcium-containing binders.

Hypocalcemia in chronic renal failure may be corrected by control of serum phosphorus and vitamin D treatment. If these measures are insufficient or patients are symptomatic, administration of calcium salts between meals is indicated.

USE OF VITAMIN D AND ITS METABOLITES. Replacement of the missing hormone calcitriol in patients with chronic renal failure is an established practice. Calcitriol therapy is effective in suppressing secondary hyperparathyroidism. In moderate hyperparathyroidism with or without mineralization defects, daily oral administration of calcitriol (0.25 to 0.5 µg/day of Rocaltrol) usually decreases serum PTH levels, suppresses bone turnover, and improves mineralization. It is advisable to start with low doses and increase the daily dose in steps of 0.25 µg if serum calcium levels do not increase (at least 0.5 mg/dL) after 2 weeks of therapy. Even so, episodes of hypercalcemia may occur but can be circumvented by decreasing oral calcium salts and/or by lowering the dialysate calcium content. Despite these measures, however, hypercalcemia may persist. Alternative approaches have been developed and include pulse oral (Rocaltrol) or intravenous (Calcijex) calcitriol administration two or three times per week at doses as high as 5 µg. Both measures are effective even though the positive response is clearly reduced if deposits of stainable aluminum are present in bone or when the parathyroid glands undergo monoclonal growth transformation and become refractory to the action of calcitriol. Newly developed vitamin D analogues with similar potency to calcitriol have been introduced: 19-Nor-1-α-25-dihydroxyvitamin D_2 (Zemplar) and doxercalciferol (Hectorol) for control of secondary hyperparathyroidism. Their effects on bone in dialysis patients are not known at this time, however.

To prevent severe osteomalacia, deficiency in the parent vitamin D, 25-hydroxyvitamin D, should be ruled out and corrected if found abnormally low.

PARATHYROIDECTOMY. Despite treatment, overt secondary hyperparathyroidism develops in some patients and may necessitate parathyroidectomy. Indications for parathyroidectomy include (1) persistent hypercalcemia despite no vitamin D treatment and modulation of the dialysate calcium concentration, (2) persistent hyperphosphatemia and high calcium phosphate production despite aggressive dietary counseling and compliance with prescriptions, (3) progressive and symptomatic soft tissue calcification with high bone turnover (including calciphylaxis), (4) severe progressive and symptomatic hyperparathyroidism when rapid reduction in PTH is required and vitamin D pulse therapy has failed, and (5) refractory pruritus. Before parathyroidectomy, histologic evidence of severe hyperparathyroidism and absence of aluminum accumulation need to be documented.

The most frequently used surgical approaches to parathyroidectomy are subtotal parathyroidectomy and total parathyroidectomy with parathyroid autotransplantation. Subtotal parathyroidectomy risks the possibility of inadequate reduction in parathyroid gland mass or the recurrence of hyperparathyroidism in the remaining tissue. These complications might require re-exploration of the neck, which can be difficult because of the formation of scar tissue. Re-exploration may be facilitated by marking the remaining gland with a metallic clip or a suture. Total parathyroidectomy with parathyroid autotransplantation in the forearm allows easy access to the residual parathyroid tissue if necessary. However, migration of the transplanted cells into the venous circulation and the muscles of the forearm has been reported. The success of both techniques relies on the expertise and experience of the surgeon.

Patients undergoing parathyroidectomy require careful follow-up and meticulous management. Postoperative hypocalcemia should be anticipated and treated with oral and intravenous calcium. The use of calcitriol may minimize the need for large doses of calcium salts; however, it may interfere with successful uptake of the transplanted gland. A reasonable approach would be the use of intravenous calcitriol administered at the end of each dialysis treatment for two to three treatments before parathyroidectomy, followed by the lowest dose of oral calcitriol needed.

REMOVAL OF ALUMINUM. Any therapeutic maneuver that lowers plasma aluminum levels and creates a concentration gradient across the bone-extracellular fluid membrane will be able to move aluminum from bone to blood. Aluminum is 80% protein bound; therefore, only 20% of total aluminum is ultrafilterable. Elimination of aluminum from bone through normal turnover and by completely withdrawing aluminum sources is very slow and may take years. However, aluminum removal is greatly enhanced by use of the chelator agent deferoxamine (Desferal*). Deferoxamine increases the complex bound fraction of aluminum and facilitates its removal through dialysis. An appropriate dose appears to be 5 mg/kg one to three times per week infused slowly over a 2-hour period. Deferoxamine is relatively safe, but rare ocular complications such as cataracts, altered color vision, night blindness, or scotoma have been reported. Episodes of hypotension caused by a vasodilatory effect of the drug can occur during deferoxamine therapy. Hypotension can be precipitated by rapid infusion and the use of low-calcium dialysate. This condition is usually easily reversible; however, in some cases angina has been reported. Nausea, vomiting, and neuromuscular excitability are usually transient. The association between deferoxamine therapy and infection has been a subject of controversy. Although numerous case reports of bacteremia and mucormycosis occurring with deferoxamine therapy have been published, a large survey did not confirm that deferoxamine increases the risk of bacteremia in dialysis patients. The possible relationship between deferoxamine therapy and mucormycosis—although rare—represents a very serious complication. Therefore, unequivocal documentation of aluminum overload is required before long-term deteroxamine therapy is begun.

TREATMENT OF ADYNAMIC BONE DISEASE. When adynamic bone disease is not the result of bone aluminum toxicity, measures to avoid oversuppression of PTH and bone turnover are indicated. These measures include discontinuation of vitamin D therapy and reduction in calcium-containing phosphate binders and/or the dialysate calcium content. However, no specific treatment is available for adynamic bone disease at present. Thus, preventive measures should be carefully considered because of the morbidity and risk of hypercalcemia associated with this condition.

*Deferoxamine is approved by the Food and Drug Administration for the chelation and thus removal of iron, but not for aluminum removal.

SUGGESTED READINGS

Elder G: Pathophysiology and recent advances in the management of renal osteodystrophy. J Bone Miner Res 2002;17:2094–2105. *A practical overview emphasizing the increasing number of effective therapies that can reduce the morbidity associated with this common problem.*

Ho LT, Sprague SM: Percutaneous bone biopsy in the diagnosis of renal osteodystrophy. Semin Nephrol 2002;22:268–275. *Although multiple biochemical markers are available, definitive diagnosis requires percutaneous bone biopsy, especially if parathyroidectomy is being considered.*

Horl WH: Renal osteodystrophy: Role of calcimimetics. Am J Kidney Dis 2003;41(3 Suppl 1):S104–S107. *Active vitamin D may be necessary for intestinal absorption of calcium and normocalcemia in patients with chronic renal failure who are taking calcimimetics to suppress parathyroid hormone secretion.*

Monier-Faugere M-C, Geng Z, Mawad H, et al: Improved assessment of bone turnover by the PTH-(1–84)/large C-PTH fragment ratio in ESRD. Kidney Int 2001;60:1460–1468. *Presents novel information on the value of the PTH-(1–84)/ C-PTH fragments ratio in predicting bone turnover in dialyzed patients.*

263 PAGET'S DISEASE OF BONE (OSTEITIS DEFORMANS)

John A. Kanis

Definition

Paget's disease of bone is a focal disorder of skeletal metabolism in which all the elements of skeletal remodeling (resorption, formation, and mineralization) are increased. Increased bone formation results in the disorganized assembly of collagen, which gives rise to bony enlargement and deformity.

Etiology

The cause is unknown. A viral infection of osteoclasts is postulated on the basis of finding viral nucleocapsids of the Paramyxoviridae in affected osteoclasts. Such findings are, however, not specific and are seen in some other rare disorders of bone turnover (pyknodysostosis and some cases of osteopetrosis [Chapter 258]). A positive family history in approximately 10% of patients suggests a dominant pattern of susceptibility, with weak associations with the HLA Dqwl antigens in the United States and with A9 and B15 in the United Kingdom. A homozygous deletion of the *TNFRSF11B* gene appears to cause a juvenile form of the disease.

Prevalence and Epidemiology

Paget's disease is the second most common disorder of bone, outstripped only by osteoporosis. It is most commonly found in the United Kingdom, where the prevalence is 5% of the population older than 55 years and is roughly equal between genders. The frequency of symptomatic disease increases with age. The paucity of evidence for the occurrence of new lesions in symptomatic disease, however, suggests a high modal incidence in early middle age that declines rapidly thereafter, but with a variable latency between onset of the disorder and its radiographic or clinical expression.

Although most common in the United Kingdom, it is also common in places such as Australia, New Zealand, South Africa, and the United States, where significant British immigration occurred in the past, but the disease occurs with a lower frequency in native-born individuals than in immigrants. The disorder is extremely rare in the Nordic countries, the Arab Middle East, China, and Japan and among Australian aboriginals. Intermediate rates are found in France, Germany, Italy, and Spain. Some evidence suggests that the incidence of Paget's disease is decreasing.

Pathophysiology and Histopathology

The disease is characterized by increased metabolic activity of bone surfaces. Bone remodeling normally occupies 10 to 15% of bone surfaces, and at affected sites this activity may be increased five- to ten-fold. Osteoclast numbers are increased, as is their size, and they may contain up to 100 nuclei. Osteoclast competence is decreased, but their plethora results in an increase in bone resorption with crenated erosion cavities subsequently filled in by the activity of osteoblasts. The irregular cement lines give rise to a mosaic patchwork appearance at bone histologic examination. New bone that is formed is often woven rather than lamellar and is thus structurally less competent and occupies more space. Mineralization rates are normal, but because abnormally large volumes of bone are undergoing mineralization, the surface covered with unmineralized osteoid is increased. Marrow fibrosis and hypervascularity are also features.

Remodeling throughout the cortex increases its porosity and blurs the distinction between cortical and cancellous bone. An imbalance between formation and resorption variably results in osteopenia or osteosclerosis.

Clinical Manifestations

The extent of disease involvement is markedly heterogeneous. Paget's disease may involve only one bone. More frequently, multiple sites are involved, typically in an asymmetric distribution. The most common sites are the pelvis, lumbar spine, and femur; one or more of these sites are affected in more than 75% of cases.

More than 95% of patients with Paget's disease are asymptomatic. The most common problems encountered are bone pain, skeletal deformity, and fracture (Table 263–1). Apart from fracture, the onset is insidious and 30% of patients have had symptoms for more than 10 years before diagnosis. It may be difficult to distinguish bone pain arising from Paget's disease from that caused by arthritis, particularly of the hip and the spine. Deformity is an initial complaint in one fifth of patients. Obvious bone enlargement is seen, particularly in the limbs and in the skull and facial bones. Bone enlargement contributes significantly to the neurologic complications and more uncertainly to joint disease. The most frequent deformity of long bones is bowing, which is

Continued

Table 263–1 • CLINICAL FEATURES AND COMPLICATIONS OF PAGET'S DISEASE

COMMON
Bone pain—pagetic, articular
Fracture—long bones, vertebral bodies
Neurologic—deafness
Deformity and enlargement of bones

UNCOMMON
Pain—fissure fracture
Spinal neurologic syndromes
Hypercalciuria of immobilization or fracture
Vascular bleeding from bone during surgery
Extraskeletal (aortic) calcification
Osteosarcoma and other bone tumors

RARE
Cardiovascular disease
Cranial nerve lesions (except VIII)
Brain stem and cerebellar lesions
Hypercalcemia of immobilization
Extramedullary hematopoiesis
Epidural hematoma

SIGNIFICANCE UNCERTAIN
Gout
Pseudogout
Angioid streaks
Hyperparathyroidism
Urolithiasis

From Kanis JA: Pathophysiology and Treatment of Paget's Disease of Bone, 2nd ed. London, Martin Dunitz, 1998.

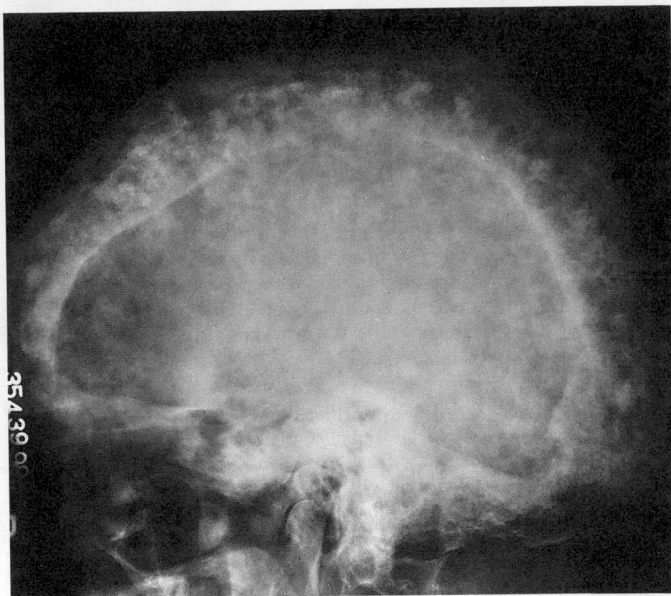

FIGURE 263–1 • Advanced involvement of the skull with marked thickening of the entire vault, areas of osteolysis, and patchy new bone formation resulting in a "cotton-wool" appearance.

characteristically lateral in the case of the femur and anterior in the case of the tibia.

The incidence of fissure fractures is significantly greater in patients with bowing. Fissure fractures may be symptomatic and may herald complete fractures, but many patients have indolent pain, particularly on weight bearing associated with local tenderness. Complete fractures of the long bones occur most commonly in the femur, followed by the tibia and the forearm, which together account for up to 90% of pathologic fractures of long bones. They commonly follow trivial injury, and unlike the case in osteoporosis, femoral fractures are less frequently cervical and more usually subtrochanteric or involve the shaft.

Neurologic complications are common and are among the more serious clinical problems. A variety of neurologic problems arise from platybasia. Cranial disease also results in deafness, vertigo, and tinnitus. Spinal syndromes most frequently occur when Paget's disease affects the thoracic spine. They are usually associated with enlarged vertebrae and decreased diameter of the spinal canal with cord or root compression. Also, the highly vascular pagetic bone may divert the blood supply from neural tissue.

Cardiac output may be increased and give rise to high-output failure in patients with extensive disease when 30% or more of the skeleton is involved. Sarcoma arising in pagetic bone, a rare but serious complication of the disorder, accounts for most cases of sarcoma in the population 50 years or older. The pelvis and femora are common sites, followed by the humerus, face, and skull. Benign and malignant giant cell tumors may also occur. New pain developing in a patient with long-standing Paget's disease not attributable to microfractures should arouse a high degree of suspicion. Other manifestations include the development of a large mass or pathologic fracture.

Laboratory Findings

RADIOGRAPHIC FEATURES. The early phase of osteolytic activity is sometimes seen clearly in the skull as osteoporosis circumscripta or as a V-shaped advancing front in a long bone. A second mixed phase shows evidence of patchy osteolysis and sclerosis, which is the most common radiographic finding. The third phase is that of predominant bone sclerosis (Fig. 263–1). Thickening of the cortices is characteristic,

along with enlargement of the long bones (Fig. 263–2). Intracortical resorption results in a loss of the corticomedullary junction and accentuation of trabecular markings. The combination of all these features is virtually diagnostic, so bone biopsy is rarely required. The average patient has six lesions affecting 14% of the skeleton. In approximately 10 to 20% of symptomatic patients, the disorder is mono-ostotic. As a general rule, scintigraphy is more sensitive than radiography, but 2 to 3% of radiographically overt lesions may not be associated with increased scintigraphic uptake (so-called burnt-out Paget's disease).

The pelvis is the most common site affected; evidence is found in approximately two thirds of patients. Narrowing of the joint space of the hip is common. Most patients show medial or concentric narrowing of the joint space; degenerative osteoarthrosis more frequently causes narrowing of the superior aspect. Computed tomography is also useful to assess the cause of pain at the spine and in the investigation for osteosarcoma.

BIOCHEMICAL MANIFESTATIONS. Extracellular calcium homeostasis is almost invariably normal despite the massive increase in bone turnover. Hypercalciuria and more rarely hypercalcemia may occur with prolonged immobilization or fracture. Serum activity of alkaline phosphatase, in part derived from osteoblasts, is most often used to measure the extent of skeletal involvement. Increased bone resorption can be assessed by the urinary excretion of hydroxyproline, which in Paget's disease is derived largely from the collagen destruction of bone. Urinary excretion of pyridinoline cross links is a more specific and sensitive marker. In untreated patients, serum activity of alkaline phosphatase and urinary excretion of hydroxyproline are closely correlated, and both correlate with the extent of disease. Up to 10% of patients with symptomatic Paget's disease have values of alkaline phosphatase within the laboratory reference range, and this figure is even higher in the case of hydroxyproline.

℞ Treatment

Data are insufficient to recommend medical treatment to asymptomatic patients, except in the presence of rapidly advancing osteolytic disease in the long bones of the lower limb, where the risk of pathologic fracture is high. Medical treatment has centered on specific inhibitors of osteoclast-mediated bone resorption, including the bisphosphonates, calcitonins, mithramycin, and gallium nitrate.

CALCITONINS. A variety of calcitonins have been used. The most common is synthetic salmon calcitonin (salcatonin), which may be given by subcutaneous injection, 50 to 100 U daily or on alternate days. In several European countries, salcatonin is available

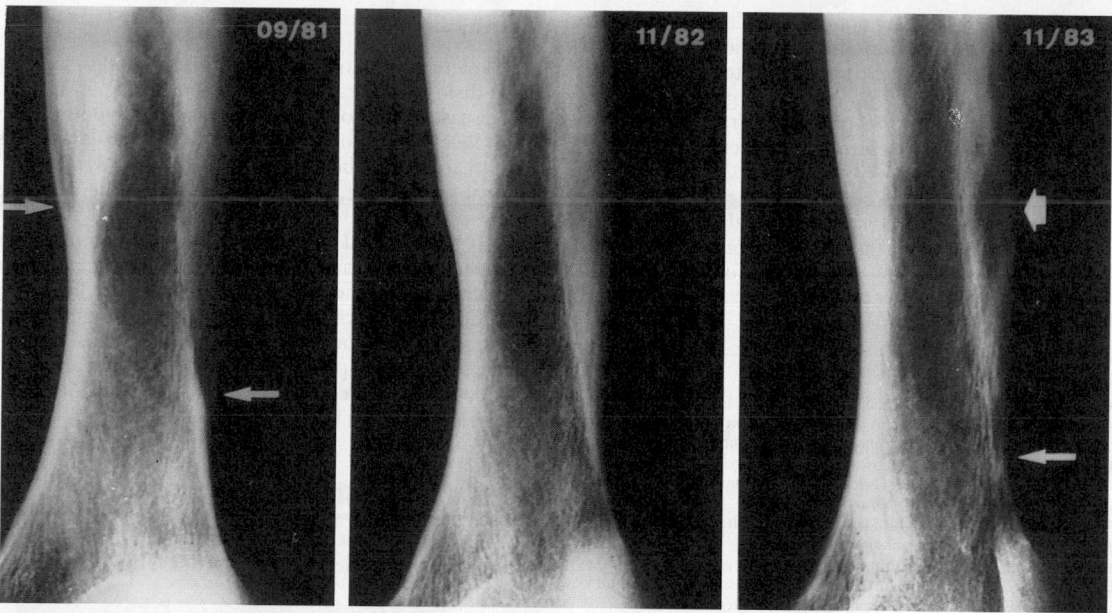

FIGURE 263–2 • Sequential radiographs of the distal end of the femur at the dates shown. *Left,* Distinction between Paget's and normal bone *(arrows),* the osteolytic front, and expansion of bone diameter at the affected site. Treatment with a bisphosphonate *(center)* induced in-filling of the resorption font. Relapse after treatment *(right)* was associated with a new area of osteolysis *(thick arrow)* and progression of the resorption front. (From Kanis JA: Pathophysiology and Treatment of Paget's Disease of Bone, 2nd ed. London, Martin Dunitz, 1998.)

as a nasal spray. Treatment results in an early decrease in bone resorption, which can be monitored by the decrease in urinary excretion of hydroxyproline and, after several weeks, a decrease in the serum activity of alkaline phosphatase. On average, these indices decrease to 40 to 50% of pretreatment values. Treatment is associated with relief of bone pain, healing of osteolytic lesions, decreased cardiac output, and improvement of neurologic disease. Deafness is rarely reversed, but progression may be prevented.

Disease activity recurs once treatment is stopped, so if long-term control is required, calcitonin must be given indefinitely. In the case of bone pain, relief may occur for many months or years after treatment is stopped, and therefore intermittent treatment is worthwhile. The escape phenomenon describes failure to maintain a biochemical response despite continued treatment or even increasing the dose. In some cases, this acquired resistance appears to be associated with the development of salcatonin antibodies, in which case a biochemical response is elicited with an alternative calcitonin. No serious side effects of calcitonin are reported, but transient nausea or flushing develops in up to one third of patients, and in 5 to 10% of patients, long-term treatment cannot be tolerated.

BISPHOSPHONATES. These pyrophosphate analogues are adsorbed onto hydroxyapatite, particularly at sites of resorption. As with calcitonin, an early effect of treatment is to decrease bone resorption, followed by a later decrease in bone formation, as marked by alkaline phosphatase. Unlike the calcitonins, their effects persist for many months or years when treatment is stopped, so the bisphosphonates (Table 263–2) have largely replaced the use of calcitonin. Etidronate has activity comparable to that of calcitonin, and higher doses may impair the mineralization of bone. Other bisphosphonates induce more complete effects on disease activity, symptoms, and radiographic abnormalities (see Fig. 263–2) than in the case of the calcitonins or etidronate. Oral bisphosphonates are not absorbed in the presence of food or calcium-containing liquids. Other nonapproved treatments include mithramycin, gallium nitrate, and the combination of calcium with thiazide diuretics.

SURGICAL MANAGEMENT. Elective surgery is often undertaken despite effective medical treatment to decrease bone vascularity and provide a more normal environment for prosthetic implants. Apart from fractures, the most common indication for surgery is joint disease at the hip. In the case of hip pain and some of the spinal neurologic syndromes, surgery can be avoided by effective medical treatment. Osteotomy has a role in managing deformities or the pain associated with fissure fractures in the presence of deformity.

Table 263–2 • BISPHOSPHONATES USED IN THE TREATMENT OF PAGET'S DISEASE

AGENT	ROUTE	DOSE (mg/day)	DURATION
Alendronate	Oral	40	6 mo
Clodronate*	Oral	1600	3-6 mo
	IV	300	5 d
Etidronate	Oral	400	6 mo
Pamidronate	IV	30-60[†]	3 d
Risedronate	Oral	30	2 m
Tiludronate*	Oral	400	3 m

*Has not been approved by the Food and Drug Administration at the time of publication.

[†]Lower dose approved; higher dose used by investigators.

Prognosis

Pagetic bone pain almost invariably responds to medical treatment. In practice, it may be difficult to distinguish the pain in Paget's disease from pain caused by coexisting osteoarthropathy or joint pain arising from deformity. In patients in whom pain at the hip is not controlled by analgesics or specific treatment, replacement arthroplasty is the treatment of choice.

Long-term treatment results in the resumption of lamellar bone formation, and in the case of the calcitonins and newer bisphosphonates, more normal radiographic appearances. Overall, there appears to be good correlation between the degree of biochemical control and attaining clinical improvement, so biochemical monitoring of disease activity is of value. Decreased bone enlargement and deformity have been reported following long-term treatment with the bisphosphonates. Effective medical management improves spinal neurologic syndromes when they are slowly progressive. The long-term results are as good as those from surgery without the mortality of the latter. The rate of neurologic improvement seen with drug treatment is often more rapid than can be accounted for by remodeling of bone but is due to a decrease in soft tissue swelling and redistribution of blood flow.

No good evidence indicates that medical treatment significantly alters the natural history of fissure fractures. These fractures may be indolent, occasionally giving rise to pain and complete fracture. Limited experience suggests that in these patients pain decreases following osteotomy. Pathologic fractures of long bones generally heal well, but the incidence of delayed union and nonunion is higher than normal. The occurrence of fracture provides an opportunity to correct deformity when managed either conservatively or with surgery. Long-term treatment may decrease the frequency of pathologic fracture, but this potential advantage has not been assessed by long-term prospective studies.

The prognosis of patients with osteosarcoma is extremely poor, and no evidence indicates that medical treatment alters its natural history. Indeed, the role of radiation therapy, chemotherapy, or surgical intervention has not been established except for symptomatic treatment.

SUGGESTED READINGS

Doyle T, Gunn J, Anderson G, et al: Paget's disease in New Zealand: Evidence for declining prevalence. Bone 2002;31:616–619. *The declining prevalence over the past two decades suggests that there are important environmental determinants in its development.*

Selby PL, Davie MW, Ralston SH, et al, for the Tooth Society of Great Britain; National Association for the Relief of Paget's Disease: Guidelines on the management of Paget's disease of bone. Bone 2002;31:366–373. *A practical overview.*

Whitehouse RW: Paget's disease of bone. Semin Musculoskelet Radiol 2002;6:313–322. *An overview of the approach to radiologic diagnosis.*

Whyte MP, Obrecht SE, Finnegan PM, et al: osteoprotegerin deficiency and juvenile Paget's disease. N Engl J Med 2002;347:175–184. *Juvenile Paget's disease caused by homozygous deletion of TNFRSF11B, resulting in osteoprotegerin deficiency.*

264 OSTEONECROSIS, OSTEOSCLEROSIS/HYPEROSTOSIS, AND OTHER DISORDERS OF BONE

Michael P. Whyte

OSTEONECROSIS

Osteonecrosis (aseptic, avascular, or ischemic necrosis of bone) refers to skeletal infarction. Bone infarcts may be asymptomatic, cause self-limited discomfort, or engender painful collapse of subarticular bone leading to joint destruction.

Etiology

Many conditions are associated with osteonecrosis (Table 264–1). In adults, the most common causes are ethanol abuse and long-term glucocorticoid therapy, both of which demonstrate dose-dependent effects.

Table 264–1 • CAUSES OF ISCHEMIC NECROSIS OF CARTILAGE AND BONE

ENDOCRINE/METABOLIC
Ethanol abuse
Glucocorticoid therapy
Cushing's disease
Diabetes mellitus
Hyperuricemia
Osteomalacia
Hyperlipidemia

STORAGE DISEASES (E.G., GAUCHER'S DISEASE)
Hemoglobinopathies (e.g., sickle cell disease)
Trauma (e.g., dislocation, fracture)
HIV infection
Dysbaric conditions (e.g., caisson disease)
Collagen-vascular disorders
Irradiation
Pancreatitis
Organ transplantation
Hemodialysis
Burns
Intravascular coagulation
Idopathic, familial

Pathogenesis

Skeletal infarction may result from blood vessel destruction (e.g., joint dislocation, fracture), obstruction (e.g., thromboemboli, sickle cell disease, fat emboli, caisson disease), or, hypothetically, compression from local expansion of fatty tissue (e.g., ethanol abuse, glucocorticoid treatment, diabetes mellitus). However, symptoms may not occur unless, weeks later, resorption of dead bone during skeletal repair leads to pathologic fracture. Certain skeletal sites (often subarticular) are predisposed to osteonecrosis but differ for traumatic and nontraumatic processes and for children and adults. *Osteochondrosis* refers to necrosis of ossification centers; more than 50 eponymic types are recorded. The susceptibility of children to osteochondrosis and its pathogenesis are poorly understood. At all ages, however, the femoral head is especially prone to infarction. Nontraumatic osteonecrosis also commonly affects the femoral condyles, distal end of the tibia, humeral head, and talus.

Clinical Manifestations

Pain occurs acutely on skeletal collapse. Chronic arthralgia results from desquamated necrotic tissue and articular destruction.

Diagnosis

Magnetic resonance imaging (MRI) demonstrating marrow edema is especially sensitive for detecting early osteonecrosis. Bone scintigraphy discloses skeletal reconstitution with or without fracture. Relatively late in the pathologic process, radiographs first show patchy areas of osteopenia and osteosclerosis that reflect skeletal repair. A linear subchondral radiolucency (crescent sign) indicates bony collapse.

 ## Treatment

Non–weight-bearing is advisable for an affected limb. Decompression by trephine insertion is used for some sites. Arthrotomy to remove debris, transpositional osteotomy, arthroplasty, or joint replacement may be necessary.

OSTEOSCLEROSIS/HYPEROSTOSIS

Many conditions are associated with radiographic evidence of increased bone density. Skeletal dysplasias, metabolic disturbances, and a variety of other disorders can cause generalized or focal increases in bone mass (Table 264–2). Aberrations in skeletal growth, modeling (shaping), and/or remodeling (turnover) may be at fault. *Osteosclerosis* refers to thickening of trabecular (spongy, cancellous) bone. *Hyperostosis* describes widening of cortical (compact) bone. Increases in trabecular or cortical bone or both may augment skeletal density.

OSTEOSCLEROSIS

Neoplastic, hematologic, and metabolic disorders may preferentially cause sclerosis in trabecular bone because it houses marrow and remodels more rapidly than cortical bone.

FIBROGENESIS IMPERFECTA OSSIUM

This rare, sporadic condition features generalized osteopenia, but coarsening of remaining trabeculae places it among disorders of increased bone mass.

Etiology and Pathogenesis

The cause is unknown. Subperiosteal bone formation and collagen synthesis in nonosseous tissues seem to be normal.

Table 264–2 • DISORDERS THAT CAUSE DENSE BONES
DYSPLASIAS
Central osteosclerosis with ectodermal dysplasia
Craniodiaphyseal dysplasia
Craniometaphyseal dysplasia
Dysosteosclerosis
Endosteal hyperostosis
van Buchem's disease
Sclerosteosis
Frontometaphyseal dysplasia
Infantile cortical hyperostosis (Caffey's disease)
Lenz-Majewski syndrome
Melorheostosis
Metaphyseal dysplasia (Pyle's disease)
Mixed sclerosing-bone dystrophy
Oculodento—osseous dysplasia
Osteodysplasia of Melnick and Needles
Osteoectasia with hyperphosphatasia (hyperostosis corticalis)
Osteopathia striata
Osteopetrosis
Osteopoikilosis
Progressive diaphyseal dysplasia (Engelmann's disease)
Pycnodysostosis
METABOLIC
Carbonic anhydrase II deficiency
Fluorosis
Heavy metal poisoning
Hepatitis C–associated osteosclerosis
Hypervitaminosis A, D
Hyperparathyroidism, hypoparathyroidism, and pseudohypoparathyroidism
Hypophosphatemic rickets or osteomalacia
Milk-alkali syndrome
Renal osteodystrophy
OTHER
Axial osteomalacia
Fibrogenesis imperfecta ossium
High bone mass with torus palatinus
Ionizing radiation
Lymphoma
Mastocytosis
Multiple myeloma
Myelofibrosis
Osteomyelitis
Osteonecrosis
Paget's disease
Sarcoidosis
Skeletal metastases
Tuberous sclerosis

From Whyte MP: Skeletal disorders characterized by osteosclerosis or hyperostosis. *In* Avioli LV, Krane SM (eds): Metabolic Bone Disease, 3rd ed. San Diego, Academic Press, 1998.

Clinical Manifestations

Typically, intractable skeletal pain begins gradually during middle age or later and then rapidly increases with a debilitating course and immobility. Spontaneous fractures are a prominent complication. Physical examination reveals marked bony tenderness.

Diagnosis

On radiographic study, only the skull is spared. Initially, osteopenia and a slightly abnormal appearance of trabecular bone are noted. Subsequently, the changes suggest osteomalacia. Corticomedullary junctions become indistinct as compact bone is replaced by an abnormal cancellous pattern. Generalized osteopenia causes the remaining spongy bone to appear coarse and dense in a fishnet pattern of mixed lytic and sclerotic areas.

Alkaline phosphatase activity in serum is increased.

Histopathologic Findings

The skeletal lesion is a localized form of osteomalacia that varies considerably in severity from area to area. In diseased regions, polarized light microscopy shows collagen fibrils that lack birefringence, and electron microscopy reveals that they are thin and randomly organized.

HYPEROSTOSIS

PROGRESSIVE DIAPHYSEAL DYSPLASIA (CAMURATI-ENGELMANN DISEASE)

This skeletal dysplasia affects all races and is inherited as an autosomal dominant trait with variable penetrance. New bone formation gradually envelops both the periosteal and endosteal surfaces of long bone diaphyses. With severe disease, osteosclerosis also occurs in the axial skeleton.

Etiology and Pathogenesis

Mutations compromise the gene that encodes transforming growth factor-β. Osteoblast differentiation may also be deranged.

Clinical Manifestations

During childhood, limping or a broad-based and waddling gait is noted. Muscular dystrophy can be diagnosed erroneously. Severely affected individuals may have a characteristic body habitus featuring an enlarged head with prominent forehead, proptosis, and thin limbs with little subcutaneous fat or muscle mass and tender thickened bones. Cranial nerve palsies and raised intracranial pressure can occur. Some patients have hepatosplenomegaly, Raynaud's phenomenon, and additional findings suggestive of vasculitis. Symptoms may remit after puberty.

Diagnosis

Irregular hyperostosis of the diaphyses of the major long bones slowly develops as a result of periosteal and endosteal new bone formation. Femora and tibiae are most commonly affected. Metaphyses may eventually become involved. The age of onset, rate of progression, and severity are variable. Clinical, radiographic, and bone scan findings are generally concordant. Routine biochemical parameters of bone and mineral metabolism are typically normal, although serum alkaline phosphatase activity, urinary hydroxyproline levels, and the erythrocyte sedimentation rate can be elevated. Histopathologic study reveals newly formed woven bone that matures and becomes incorporated into cortical bone. Electron microscopy of muscle may show myopathic changes and vascular abnormalities.

Treatment

Glucocorticoid therapy (typically a low dose of prednisone on alternate days) can relieve bone pain and may normalize skeletal histology. Bisphosphonates have sometimes been useful.

ENDOSTEAL HYPEROSTOSIS

Sclerosteosis and van Buchem's disease, autosomal recessive disorders, are the principal types of endosteal hyperostosis.

Etiology and Pathogenesis

Sclerosteosis and van Buchem's disease both map to chromosome 17q12-q21. Sclerosteosis is caused by mutations in a gene called *SOST*. Van Buchem's disease involves a downstream deletion. Enhanced osteoblast activity with failure of osteoclasts to compensate for the increased bone formation seems to explain the skeletal changes.

Clinical Manifestations

Sclerosteosis (cortical hyperostosis with syndactyly) occurs primarily in Afrikaners of South Africa. Elsewhere, Dutch ancestry is also common. Gender distribution appears equal. Patients are tall and heavy beginning in childhood, have a prominent mandible of square configuration, and have deafness and facial nerve palsy from cranial nerve entrapment. Raised intracranial pressure and headache may reflect a small cranial cavity that can shorten life expectancy. Van Buchem's disease causes progressive asymmetric enlargement of the jaw during puberty, but prognathism is not a feature. Patients may be symptom free or, beginning as early as infancy, have recurrent facial nerve palsy, deafness, and optic atrophy from narrowing of cranial foramina. Long bones may hurt with applied pressure but are not fragile.

Diagnosis

In sclerosteosis, the skeleton is radiographically normal in early childhood except when bony syndactyly is present. Syndactyly, most often involving the index and third fingers, is common. Progressive bony thickening widens the skull and causes prognathism. Long bones have thickened cortices. The pelvis, vertebral pedicles, ribs, and other tubular bones may become dense. Computed tomography has shown fusion of ossicles and narrowing of the internal auditory canals and cochlear aqueducts. In van Buchem's disease, endosteal thickening homogeneously widens diaphyseal cortices and narrows medullary canals. Bones are properly modeled. Osteosclerosis involves the skull base, facial bones, vertebrae, pelvis, and ribs.

Serum alkaline phosphatase activity can be increased from enhanced skeletal formation.

 Treatment

Surgical decompression of narrowed foramina may alleviate cranial nerve palsies.

PACHYDERMOPERIOSTOSIS

Pachydermoperiostosis (hypertrophic osteoarthropathy, primary or idiopathic) is an autosomal dominant disorder that features clubbing of the digits, hyperhidrosis with thickening of the skin (especially of the face), and periosteal new bone formation prominently in the distal ends of the limbs. Autosomal recessive inheritance also seems to occur. Not all patients manifest all three principal features.

Etiology and Pathogenesis

The genetic defect is unknown. A controversial hypothesis suggests that initially some circulating factor acts on the vasculature to cause hyperemia and thereby alters soft tissues, but later blood flow is reduced.

Clinical ManifestationS

Men seem to be more severely affected than women and blacks more commonly than whites. Symptoms typically begin during adolescence, intensify during the next decade, but then become quiescent. Arthralgia and fatigue are common. Stiffness and limited mobility occur in both the appendicular and the axial skeleton. Clubbing with slowly progressive enlargement of the hands and feet results in a paw-like appearance. Cutaneous changes include thickening, furrowing, pitting, and oiliness, especially of the scalp and face.

Radiologic Features

Periostitis thickens the distal portions of the tibia, fibula, radius, and ulna. Clubbing is obvious, and acro-osteolysis can occur. Periosteal proliferation is exuberant, with irregular texture, and often involves the epiphyses, whereas secondary hypertrophic osteoarthropathy (pulmonary or otherwise) typically causes a smooth and undulating periosteal reaction. Ankylosis of joints, especially in the hands and feet, may trouble

older patients. Bone scanning in either condition reveals symmetric, diffuse, regular uptake along the cortical margins of long bones, especially in the legs, called a "double stripe" sign.

 Treatment

Painful synovial effusions may respond to nonsteroidal antiinflammatory drugs. Contractures or neurovascular compression by osteosclerotic lesions may require surgical intervention.

OSTEOSCLEROSIS WITH HYPEROSTOSIS

OSTEOPETROSIS

Osteopetrosis (marble bone disease) occurs in two major clinical forms—the autosomal recessive or "malignant" type, which kills during infancy or early childhood if untreated, and the autosomal dominant or "benign" type, which causes fewer problems. Other autosomal recessive types feature intermediate severity, neuronal storage disease, stillbirth, or renal tubular acidosis with cerebral calcification secondary to carbonic anhydrase II isoenzyme deficiency. Recently, bisphosphonate-induced osteopetrosis has been reported.

Etiology and Pathogenesis

The defective gene causing autosomal dominant osteopetrosis encodes a chloride channel important for osteoclast activity. Abnormalities in this gene or one that encodes a subunit of a vacuolar proton pump can also result in malignant disease. Carbonic anhydrase II deficiency is due to deactivating mutations in the gene that encodes this isoenzyme.

Histopathologic studies show that all true forms of osteopetrosis feature profound deficiency of osteoclast action. Primary spongiosa (calcified cartilage deposited during endochondral bone formation) persists away from growth plates and constitutes the pathognomonic finding. Defective endosteal bone resorption impairs the formation of marrow space. Quiescent skeletal remodeling leads to bone fragility from diminished interconnection of osteons and from delayed conversion of immature (woven) bone to mature (compact) bone. Studies of animal models of osteopetrosis suggest that rarely some patients may have abnormalities as distal as the marrow microenvironment that compromise osteoclast precursor cell growth and differentiation, or abnormalities as proximal as bone tissue itself, with resistance to degradation. Neuronal storage disease (ceroid lipofuscin) could reflect a lysosomal defect. Deficient superoxide production (necessary for bone resorption) may also be a pathogenetic factor. Viral-like inclusions in osteoclasts are of uncertain significance.

Clinical Manifestations

Malignant osteopetrosis can first manifest during infancy as nasal "stuffiness" from underdeveloped mastoid and paranasal sinuses. Small cranial foramina may cause optic, oculomotor, or facial nerve palsy. Failure to thrive, delayed dentition, and fracture are common. Hypersplenism and recurrent infection, bruising, and bleeding reflect myelophthisis. Short stature, large head, frontal bossing, nystagmus, hepatosplenomegaly, and genu valgum are characteristic physical features. Untreated children usually die during the first decade of life from hemorrhage, pneumonia, severe anemia, or sepsis. Benign osteopetrosis occasionally causes fracture, facial palsy, deafness, mandibular osteomyelitis, bone marrow failure, impaired vision, psychomotor delay, carpal tunnel syndrome, or osteoarthritis. Carbonic anhydrase II deficiency can result in failure to thrive, fracture, developmental delay, mental subnormality, and short stature. Cerebral calcification develops during childhood, but defective skeletal modeling and osteosclerosis may correct spontaneously. Both proximal and distal renal tubular acidosis has been described.

Diagnosis

A generalized increase in bone density is the radiographic hallmark. In severe disease, modeling defects in long bones produce

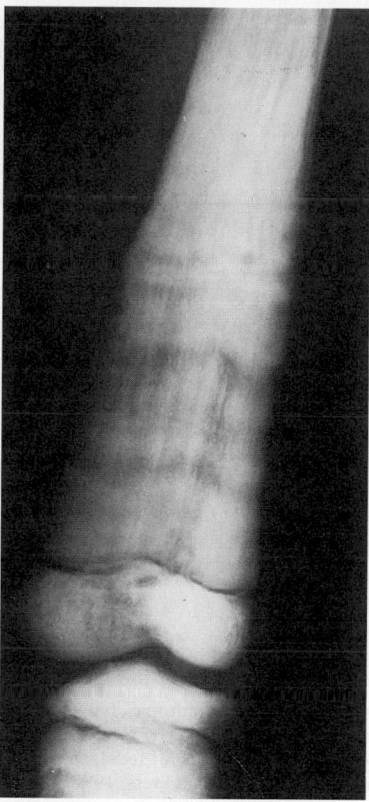

FIGURE 264–1 • Osteopetrosis. An anteroposterior radiograph of the distal end of the femur shows a widened metadiaphyseal region with characteristic alternating dense and lucent bands. (From Whyte MP, Murphy WA: Osteopetrosis and other sclerosing bone disorders. *In* Avioli LV, Krane SM [eds]: Metabolic Bone Disease, 2nd ed. Philadelphia, WB Saunders, 1990.)

an "Erlenmeyer flask" deformity (Fig. 264–1). Alternating dense and lucent bands commonly occur in the metaphyses and pelvis. The cranium is usually thickened and dense, especially at the base, and the paranasal and mastoid sinuses are underpneumatized. Vertebrae may show, on lateral view, a "bone-in-bone" (endobone) configuration or end-plate sclerosis causing a "rugger-jersey" appearance. Skeletal scintigraphy can disclose fractures and osteomyelitis. MRI helps monitor the response to bone marrow transplantation because successful engraftment normalizes marrow signals.

Serum levels of acid phosphatase and creatine kinase (brain isoenzyme), apparently from osteoclasts, are abnormal. In malignant osteopetrosis, hypocalcemia with secondary hyperparathyroidism and elevated serum concentrations of calcitriol can accompany radiologic changes that resemble rickets. In benign osteopetrosis, biochemical indices of mineral homeostasis are typically unremarkable, although serum parathyroid hormone levels may be increased.

 Treatment

Because the etiology, pathogenesis, and prognosis of the osteopetroses differ, correct classification is crucial. It may be necessary to evaluate disease progression and study the family. For the malignant form, HLA-identical bone marrow transplantation to supply functional osteoclasts has remarkably benefited some children. Calcium-deficient diets have been used but may be limited by hypocalcemia and rickets. Massive oral doses of calcitriol (1,25-dihydroxyvitamin D_3) together with dietary calcium restriction (to prevent hypercalciuria/hypercalcemia) or human interferon-γ, which enhances superoxide production, have successfully stimulated osteoclast activity. Prednisone alone, or with a low-calcium, high-phosphate diet, may also be effective. Glucocorticoid therapy stabilizes pancytopenia and hepatosplenomegaly. Hyperbaric oxygenation helps treat osteomyelitis. Surgical decompression of optic and facial nerves can be beneficial. Early prenatal diagnosis, radiographically or by ultrasound, has not been successful. Mutation analysis is now useful in some affected families.

PYCNODYSOSTOSIS

Pycnodysostosis is believed to have troubled the French impressionist painter Henri de Toulouse-Lautrec (1864–1901). Most descriptions have come from Europe and the United States, but the disorder seems to be especially common in Japan.

Etiology and Pathogenesis

This autosomal recessive condition is caused by defects in the gene that encodes cathepsin K. Diminished rates of collagen degradation and skeletal turnover are reported. In chondrocytes and osteoblasts, abnormal inclusions have been described.

Clinical Manifestations

Characteristic features seen during infancy or early childhood are a disproportionate short stature, relatively large cranium, fronto-occipital prominence, proptosis, bluish sclerae, a beaked and pointed nose, small facies and chin, obtuse mandibular angle, a high-arched palate, and dental malocclusion with retention of primary teeth. Cranial sutures remain open. Fingers are short and clubbed from acro-osteolysis or aplasia of the terminal phalanges, and the hands are small and square. Repeated fractures cause knock-knee deformity. Mental retardation is noted in approximately 10% of patients. Adult height ranges from 4 ft 3 in to 4 ft 11 in. Life expectancy can be shortened by recurrent respiratory infections and right-sided heart failure from chronic upper airway obstruction secondary to micrognathia.

Laboratory Findings

Osteosclerosis is uniform, first becoming apparent in childhood and increasing with age. Skeletal modeling defects do not occur, although long bones appear to have thick cortices because of narrow medullary canals. Clavicles are gracile and hypoplastic at their lateral segments. The calvarium and base of the skull are sclerotic, orbital ridges are dense, and wormian bones are present. Serum calcium and inorganic phosphate levels and alkaline phosphatase activity are typically normal. Anemia is not a problem.

Rx Treatment

No effective medical therapy is documented. Fractures of the long bones usually mend satisfactorily. Internal fixation of long bones is formidable because of their hardness. Tooth extraction is difficult. Osteomyelitis of the mandible may require antibiotic, surgical, and/or hyperbaric therapy.

HEPATITIS C–ASSOCIATED OSTEOSCLEROSIS

Rarely, achy and tender limbs develop in individuals who are infected with hepatitis C virus. Radiographic studies reveal a marked generalized increase in bone mass from osteosclerosis and hyperostosis. Disturbances in the insulin-like growth factor system may explain the enhanced bone formation. Calcitonin or bisphosphonate therapy has benefited some patients.

FOCAL OSTEOSCLEROSIS/HYPEROSTOSIS

OSTEOPOIKILOSIS

Osteopoikilosis ("spotted bones") is a radiologic curiosity inherited as a highly penetrant autosomal dominant trait. The bony lesions are asymptomatic. However, incorrect diagnosis may lead to confusion with serious conditions, including metastatic disease. Some patients have connective tissue nevi called *dermatofibrosis lenticularis disseminata* (i.e., Buschke-Ollendorff syndrome).

Radiologic Features

Numerous small round or oval foci of bony sclerosis appear in cancellous bone in the tarsal, carpal, pelvic, and metaepiphyseal regions of tubular bones.

OSTEOPATHIA STRIATA

This autosomal dominant curiosity features linear striations in the metaphyseal regions of long bones and in the ilium. Clinically important syndromes include osteopathia striata with cranial sclerosis or with focal dermal hypoplasia (Goltz's syndrome). Goltz's syndrome is an X-linked recessive condition featuring widespread linear areas of dermal hypoplasia and various bony defects in the limbs of affected males.

MELORHEOSTOSIS

Melorheostosis causes bony changes likened to melted wax dripping down a candle. No Mendelian basis for this disorder has been established. The anatomic distribution suggests a segmentary embryogenic defect.

Clinical Manifestations

Usually, monomelic involvement is noted; bilateral disease is generally asymmetric. Cutaneous changes over affected bones are common (e.g., linear scleroderma-like areas and hypertrichosis). Soft tissue abnormalities often appear before the hyperostosis. Symptoms typically begin during childhood, with pain and stiffness being the major complaints. Joints may become contracted and deformed. Leg length inequality results from soft tissue contractures and premature fusion of epiphyses. Skeletal changes seem to progress most rapidly throughout childhood. During adult life, melorheostosis may or may not gradually spread, although pain is especially common.

Radiologic Features

Irregular, very dense, eccentric periosteal and endosteal hyperostosis affects a single bone or several adjacent bones. The lower limbs are most commonly involved. Endosteal thickening predominates during infancy and childhood and periosteal new bone formation during adulthood. Ectopic bone formation may occur, particularly near joints.

 Treatment

Surgical correction of contractures is difficult; recurrent deformity is common.

MIXED SCLEROSING-BONE DYSTROPHY

This typically sporadic disorder features combinations of osteopoikilosis, osteopathia striata, melorheostosis, cranial sclerosis, or other skeletal defects in one individual. Patients may experience problems associated with the individual patterns of osteosclerosis or hyperostosis, such as nerve palsy with cranial sclerosis and bone pain with melorheostosis.

OTHER DISORDERS OF BONE

FIBROUS DYSPLASIA

This sporadic, developmental disorder features an expansile fibrous lesion(s) within bone. Polyostotic disease is typically seen before the age of 10 years; monostotic disease begins in adolescence or early adult life. McCune-Albright syndrome refers to polyostotic fibrous dysplasia, café au lait spots (Fig. 264–2), and endocrine hyperfunction.

Etiology and Pathogenesis

Somatic mosaicism for an activating mutation in the gene that encodes the α subunit of the receptor/adenylate cyclase-coupling G protein causes fibrous dysplasia and the McCune-Albright syndrome. Imperfect bone forms because mesenchymal cells do not fully differentiate to osteoblasts. Endocrinopathy generally results from end-organ hyperactivity.

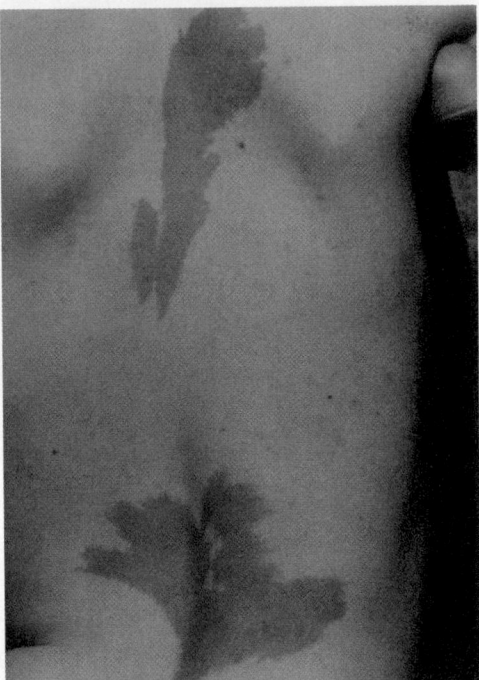

FIGURE 264–2 • McCune-Albright syndrome. Typical rough-border ("coast-of-Maine") pigmented café au lait spots. (From Whyte MP: Metabolic and dysplastic disorders. *In* Coe FL, Favus MJ [eds]: Disorders of Bone and Mineral Metabolism. New York, Raven Press, 1992.)

Clinical Manifestations

Monostotic fibrous dysplasia is more common than polyostotic disease. The skull and long bones are affected most often. The skeletal lesions can deform bone, cause fractures, and occasionally entrap nerves. Sarcomatous degeneration is rare (incidence, <1%) but typically occurs within the facial bones or femur and is more frequent when polyostotic disease is present. Pregnancy may "reactivate" previously quiescent lesions. McCune-Albright syndrome usually causes pseudoprecocious puberty in girls. Less commonly there is pseudoprecocious puberty in boys or thyrotoxicosis, Cushing's disease, acromegaly, hyperprolactinemia, or hyperparathyroidism. In some patients, acquired renal phosphate wasting causes hypophosphatemic rickets or osteomalacia.

Radiologic Features

In the long bones, lesions are found in either the metaphysis or the diaphysis. They are typically well defined with thin cortices and have a ground-glass appearance (Fig. 264–3). Occasionally, the defects are lobulated with trabeculated areas of radiolucency.

 Treatment

With mild disease, bone lesions may not expand. In severe cases, individual defects can progress and new ones appear. Spontaneous healing does not occur, but pathologic fractures generally mend well. Stress fractures, however, can be difficult to detect and treat. When the skull is involved, nerve compression may require surgical intervention. In the McCune-Albright syndrome, the aromatase inhibitor testolactone helps control pseudoprecocious puberty in girls. Intravenous infusions of the bisphosphonate pamidronate have helped some patients.

HEREDITARY MULTIPLE EXOSTOSES

This relatively common, highly penetrant, autosomal dominant disorder features irregular bony excrescences that protrude from expanded metaphyses. The gene defect is known in some families.

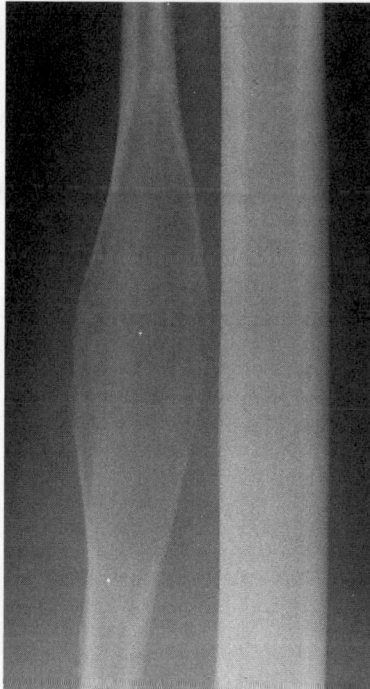

FIGURE 264-3 • Fibrous dysplasia. A characteristic expansile lesion with a ground-glass appearance has caused thinning of the cortex in the mid-diaphysis of the fibula. (From Whyte MP: Fibrous dysplasia. *In* Favus MJ [ed]: Primer on the Metabolic Bone Diseases and Disorders of Mineral Metabolism, 3rd ed. Philadelphia, Lippincott-Raven, 1996.)

Osteocartilaginous exostoses arise from growth plates and increase in size until linear growth ceases. Lesions may or may not become detached from the parent bone. Their structure is relatively unremarkable, with an outer cortex and an inner spongiosa. Disability results primarily from limb length discrepancies when linear bone growth suffers at the expense of transverse expansion. Compression of nerves, the spinal cord, or the vascular system occurs occasionally. Sarcomatous degeneration (0.5 to 2% of patients) should be suspected when an exostosis enlarges rapidly, especially during adult life.

ENCHONDROMATOSIS (DYSCHONDROPLASIA, OLLIER'S DISEASE)

This sporadic disorder features cartilaginous masses within the trabecular bone that arise from growth plates. The condition begins in childhood with localized swelling and interferes with linear bone growth. At puberty, expansion of cartilage masses ceases, and they can be replaced by mature bone. Enchondromas appear radiographically as lucent defects in flat bones or in metaphyses of tubular bones, often with central calcific stippling. When enchondromatosis occurs with multiple hemangiomas (Maffucci syndrome), the enchondromas or hemangiomas undergo malignant transformation in about 15% of cases.

ACHONDROPLASIA

Chondrodystrophies are disorders of cartilage growth that result in disproportionate short stature. Achondroplasia is the most common. There is a defect in the gene that encodes fibroblast growth factor receptor type 3. About 80% of cases are new mutations for this autosomal dominant defect, which increases in frequency with increasing paternal age. Short, tubular bones form because of abnormal endochondral ossification in the limbs. In the chondrocranium, membranous ossification is undisturbed—thus the skull vault is normal. However, the cranial base and foramen magnum are small. Lumbar lordosis is greatly exaggerated, and the spinal canal narrows from the upper to lower segments of the vertebral column. This disturbance is revealed radiographically by decreasing interpediculate distance. The head is large with frontal bossing and midface hypoplasia. The trunk is of relatively normal length, but the limbs show rhizomelic shortening and the hands have a trident configuration. The long bones appear massive owing to their disproportionately normal width. Surprisingly, growth plates are not grossly disorganized in achondroplasia, and chondrocytes appear normal. Complications can include hydrocephalus or compression of the brain stem, spinal cord, or nerve roots. Minimal impingement by a disk or osteophyte on the small spinal canal can cause neurologic disturbances. Despite its problems, achondroplasia is compatible with good health and a normal life span.

SUGGESTED READINGS

Hernigou P, Bachir D, Galacteros F: The natural history of symptomatic osteonecrosis in adults with sickle-cell disease. J Bone Joint Surg Am 2003;85-A:500–504. *When osteonecrosis develops, the deterioration is rapid and, in most patients, operative intervention is necessary because of intractable pain.*

Lieberman JR, Berry DJ, Mont MA, et al: Osteonecrosis of the hip: Management in the 21st century. Instr Course Lect 2003;52:337–355. *Recommended procedures include core decompression, vascularized and nonvascularized bone grafting procedures, and arthroplasty.*

Mader R: Clinical manifestations of diffuse idiopathic skeletal hyperostosis of the cervical spine. Semin Arthritis Rheum 2002;32:130–135. *Often presents with abnormalities of the pharynx, larynx, and the esophagus.*

part XXI

Diseases of Allergy and Clinical Immunology

265 APPROACH TO THE PATIENT WITH ALLERGIC OR IMMUNOLOGIC DISEASE

Stephen I. Wasserman

Allergic diseases and disorders of the immune system affect multiple organ systems and may arise in a variety of manners. The reader is directed to Chapters 41 to 45 for detailed discussion of the immune system and for specific autoimmune and acquired immune disorders. This chapter addresses allergic disorders, the most common manifestation of immune system dysfunction, and primary immune deficiencies, which are uncommon manifestations of immune system problems. For clarity, these two issues are treated separately.

ALLERGIC

Allergic disorders are common and their prevalence is increasing, particularly in urbanized, Western societies. It is said that allergic diseases are the most common disorders presenting to a primary care physician and therefore an appreciation of how to approach the diagnosis and treatment of allergic patients is of major importance to the practice of internal medicine. The increase in allergic diseases noted in the past two decades is thought to be due to advancing hygienic conditions, decreases in infant and childhood infections, and an increasingly sedentary and indoor lifestyle. These changes appear to inhibit activation of the innate immune system and thereby prevent effective maturation of the acquired immune system. The immune bias in utero and infancy is toward a type 2 T helper (Th2)—directed immune response, which is the immune pathway required for the expression of allergic disease. It is therefore postulated that without sufficient early childhood infection to induce a switch to a protective, Th1 immune bias, allergic disease is more likely to emerge during childhood. Substantial epidemiologic evidence has been gathered to support this concept, now termed the *hygiene hypothesis*. Thus, allergy is more prevalent in individuals of higher socioeconomic status, in those living in urban areas, in less polluted communities (i.e., Western Germany), in first-born compared with later siblings, and in those multiply immunized and those free of mycobacterial disease. Conversely, those living on farms, in rural communities, in more highly polluted areas (i.e., Eastern Germany); those with mycobacterial infection; and children who have experienced multiple early childhood infections are less likely to develop allergic disorders.

The persistence or aberrant activation of Th2 lymphocytes leads to the generation of cytokines (i.e., interleukins 4, 5, 13) that stimulate B-lymphocyte synthesis of immunoglobulin E (IgE) antibody and the production of eosinophilic polymorphonuclear leukocytes. The expression of allergic disorders is due to the interaction of specific allergen with allergen-reactive IgE bound to high-affinity receptors on mast cells and basophils. This interaction leads to activation of these target cells and their release of preformed, granule-associated mediators (exemplified by histamine), synthesis of lipid mediators from membrane lipids (sulfidopeptide leukotrienes), and the transcription and secretion of cytokines including tumor necrosis factor-α and interleukins 4, 5, and 13. These mediators directly induce smooth muscle contraction, vascular dilatation, and endothelial leakage; cause vascular adhesion molecule expression; and attract and activate inflammatory leukocytes, particularly CD4+ T lymphocytes, basophils, and eosinophils. Other IgE-dependent mediators are thought to be responsible for stimulating smooth muscle proliferation and tissue remodeling.

It is important to recognize that allergy is a systemic immune disorder and thus its expression can be multisystemic. It is essential to remember this fact during the approach to the patient with suspected allergic problems because a focus only upon the major presenting symptom may be insufficient to identify all of the pertinent medical issues present in a given patient.

History

Allergic disorders are those caused by the interaction of a sensitized host (one who has made IgE antibody recognizing a specific antigen) with a specific allergen. Not all patients possessing specific IgE antibody react adversely upon interaction with the allergen, and such individuals are termed sensitized but not allergic. The primary allergic conditions are seasonal allergic rhinoconjunctivitis (hay fever), perennial allergic rhinitis or sinusitis, asthma, anaphylaxis (especially secondary to foods, medications, and hymenopteran stings), urticaria or angioedema and atopic dermatitis (eczema), and food allergy or intolerance. It is currently estimated that more than 40% of the population are atopic (i.e., able to mount an IgE immune response and to exhibit a positive prick puncture immediate hypersensitivity response to common aeroallergens), 10 to 20% have allergic rhinoconjunctivitis, 5 to 7% have active asthma, and 20% have experienced urticaria at some time during their life. There is a high degree of heritability of allergic disease with a great degree of concordance in identical twins, and the risk of expressing allergic disease is highest if both parents are atopic. The inheritance of specific manifestations of allergy and the specific allergen to which a patient is sensitized is less simple.

Quite often the diagnosis of allergic disorders is straightforward after asking about the nature of the patient's complaints, when and where reactions occur, and what exposures the patient believes are relevant to symptom induction and/or exacerbation (Table 265–1). Patients with seasonal and perennial rhinitis commonly present with complaints of itchy nose and palate, sneezing, watery rhinorrhea, itching, watery and burning eyes, and nasal obstruction, which, when severe, may cause anosmia. In the evaluation of possible causes of seasonal rhinoconjunctivitis or sinusitis, the time of the year when symptoms occur is pertinent to the association of symptoms with pollination of trees (early spring), grasses (late spring and summer), and weeds (fall). In some patients with perennial symptoms, the multiple overlapping pollen seasons are responsible for most of their symptoms. Indoor exposures to furred animals, house dust mites or insects, and mold at home, school, workplace, or recreational site should be assessed particularly in the search for additional causes of perennial symptoms. Molds and mites are to be expected in humid environments, and mites are nearly ubiquitous in bedding and in homes with pets, carpeting, and overstuffed furnishings. Additional occupational or recreational exposures may be pertinent in selected situations (i.e., bakers, health care workers, food handlers, horse fanciers, laboratory animal handlers, and others) where specific, inciting allergens may be identified. As many patients with rhinitis have concomitant asthma, it is important to obtain historical information regarding its presence in all patients presenting with rhinitis.

Patients with asthma (Chapter 84) may present with cough and/or wheeze with dyspnea, which is reversible spontaneously or with treatment. In addition to the historical associations noted for rhinitis, the influence of exercise, exposure to tobacco smoke, the effect of respiratory infection, occupational exposures (i.e., up to 30% of atopic animal handlers develop asthma), and medication use (i.e., β-adrenergic blocking drugs) are of particular pertinence. As the vast majority of patients with asthma have concurrent rhinitis, it is essential that the physician evaluate this issue in all asthmatic patients.

Patients with urticaria (Chapter 269) describe pruritic, erythematous cutaneous lesions with regular or irregular borders occurring anywhere on the body, which may be very small (1×1 mm) or extremely large. Lesions are often preceded by intense intertriginal pruritus. Individual urticarial lesions generally persist for a few hours and almost never for more than 24 hours. Angioedema (Chapter 269)

Table 265–1 • SYMPTOMS AND SIGNS SUGGESTING ALLERGIC DISEASE

SYMPTOMS
Cutaneous: itch, rash
Ocular: gritty sensation, itch
Upper respiratory: palatal pruritus, clear rhinorrhea, sneeze, nasal obstruction
Lower respiratory: wheeze, cough, dyspnea
Gastrointestinal: nausea, vomiting, cramping pain

SIGNS
Cutaneous: flushing, urticaria, angioedema, eczema
Ocular: conjunctival erythema, chemosis
Upper respiratory: pallor, edema, clear rhinorrhea, polyps
Lower respiratory: wheeze

is most frequently appreciated in the face, hands, and other soft tissues and is generally accompanied by symptoms of stretching and tightness of the skin rather than pruritus. Lesions, especially in the face, typically last 24 to 36 hours. Although the large majority of urticaria or angioedema is non–IgE mediated, it is nonetheless important to identify foods and medications used by patients with acute urticaria-angioedema, particularly those ingested within 2 to 4 hours of the development of lesions, and to inquire about insect stings. Chronic urticaria is less often IgE mediated; questions about medications, especially nonsteroidal anti-inflammatory drugs, recent infection (especially Epstein-Barr virus), and the presence of autoantibodies to the IgE receptor must be addressed. In angioedema the use of angiotensin-converting enzyme inhibitors must be sought. Atopic dermatitis is another allergic cutaneous disorder in which patients complain of intense pruritus, especially in flexural surfaces. In adults, foods (IgE mediated) and cutaneous infection with *Staphylococcus aureus* (superantigen mediated) are the most commonly identified precipitating events.

Anaphylaxis (Chapter 270) is the most important allergic emergency and is potentially fatal. It is an acute allergic response associated with cutaneous (urticaria, angioedema, flushing), respiratory (laryngeal edema, asthma), cardiovascular (arrhythmia, hypotension, extravascular fluid loss), gastrointestinal (nausea, vomiting, abdominal pain, diarrhea), and nonspecific symptoms (metallic taste, sense of impending doom) that may occur singly or together. Historical information of note includes all medications, foods, and other encounters occurring within 2 hours of the reaction. Epidemiologic data suggest that foods (especially peanuts, tree nuts, shellfish, milk, and egg), hymenoptera stings, and medications (antibiotics, muscle relaxants, radiocontrast media) are the most frequently identified causes of this important problem.

Patients presenting with food allergy often complain of the specific gastrointestinal manifestations of nausea, vomiting, diarrhea, and abdominal pain. Eczema, urticaria, and anaphylaxis, as noted previously, may also be consequences of food allergy. In general, allergic symptoms consequent to foods occur within minutes to 2 hours of ingestion of the causative food; delayed symptoms are unlikely to be mediated by IgE-allergen interaction. Other symptoms attributable to foods are less easily explained by allergic mechanisms and are termed food intolerance.

Physical Examination

The physical examination of the patient with suspected allergic disease should emphasize the organ systems pertinent to the complaints of the patient.

The skin should be examined for the presence of urticarial or angioedematous lesions and for signs of atopic dermatitis including flexural papules, excoriations, and lichenification. Keratosis pilaris, particularly on the outer aspect of the upper arm, commonly accompanies atopic dermatitis. Urticaria typically consists of small, pink, irregular lesions that blanch on pressure and clear, leaving normal skin. In a patient with urticaria a simple test for dermatographism should be undertaken. Angioedematous lesions are larger and more diffuse, pale, and most often found affecting the face and acral areas.

The eyes, ears, nose, and throat should be examined in all patients suspected of having allergic disease, particularly those whose symptoms suggest seasonal or perennial allergic rhinoconjunctivitis-sinusitis or asthma. In allergic disease the conjunctivae are often injected and may be edematous. There may be "cobblestoning" of the epithelium. The periorbital tissues may be swollen and darkened. Examination of the nares may show pale and edematous nasal mucous membranes and swollen turbinates, and polyps may be seen. Secretions, generally clear, may be seen in the nasal passages or in the posterior pharynx. Such secretions generally contain copious numbers of eosinophils (see later), and their absence is a point against allergic causation. Fever and discolored secretions, particularly thick and yellow or green, in the presence of neutrophilic polymorphonuclear leukocytes suggest infection. Percussion over the maxillary or frontal sinuses may elicit tenderness in acute sinusitis, and in such a case transillumination of the sinus, albeit a test of low sensitivity, may be impaired. In chronic sinusitis the physical examination may be unrevealing. In acute otitis media there may be erythema and bulging or perforation of the tympanic membrane with fluid in the canal, and in chronic cases there may be scarring and retraction of the drum. Alteration in air-bone conduction may be noted as well.

In acute asthma patients may display tachypnea, auditory wheezes, and be unable to speak in full sentences because of shortness of breath. Use of accessory muscles of respiration and evidence of cyanosis should be sought. Examination of the chest includes inspection for evidence of chronic hyperinflation and auscultation for wheezing (which, if unilateral, might suggest a foreign body or tumor). In mild asthma the examination might be normal or the only physical finding may be wheezing on forced expiration and a slight prolongation of the expiratory phase.

Patients experiencing acute anaphylaxis usually demonstrate flushing, and concomitant urticaria-angioedema is often present. Assessment of vital signs may disclose hypotension and tachycardia. In some situations, hoarseness or stridor related to laryngeal edema or wheezing secondary to asthma can be identified. Hyperactive bowel sounds may be noted. Progressive hypoxia and cyanosis may ensue. In severe anaphylaxis, cardiovascular collapse secondary to hypoxia and hypotension may result in death.

Laboratory Evaluation

In the evaluation of patients with allergic disorders, the laboratory may be of assistance in both the identification and quantification of the degree of specific organ dysfunction and in the assessment of the presence and specificity of IgE antibody.

ASSESSMENT OF TOTAL AND ALLERGEN-SPECIFIC IMMUNOGLOBULIN E. Essentially all (>95%) IgE antibody is bound to specific high-affinity receptors on tissue mast cells and circulating peripheral blood basophils. The small amount of serum IgE antibody circulates in nanogram quantities and can be identified only with techniques of sufficient sensitivity. Generally, such tests employ a solid phase to which an antibody to human IgE is coupled. The patient's serum is then added, the contained IgE is bound, and nonbound materials are removed by washing. The amount of IgE bound is then determined by addition of a second antibody to IgE to which a quantifying reagent, such as a radioactive isotope or an enzyme capable of creating a colorimetric end point, is bound. A large proportion of IgE in a given individual may be directed toward a single antigen. Because total serum IgE levels may still be normal in the presence of allergic manifestations, the measurement of total serum IgE is rarely of help in diagnosis. In a few situations, such as adult atopic dermatitis or allergic bronchopulmonary aspergillosis, measurement of total serum IgE levels may give insight into disease severity or to the risk of disease exacerbation.

Of more importance is the identification of allergen-specific IgE in a patient in whom allergic disease is suspected. Such specific IgE may be identified in vitro or in vivo. Such a search for allergen-specific IgE is particularly useful in the evaluation of patients with suspected allergic rhinitis, asthma, eczema, food reactions, and anaphylaxis. In vitro assessment is performed much as for the quantification of total IgE except that the initial capture reagent bound to a solid phase is a specific pollen, mold, or mite constituent or a venom, food, or other allergen in question. Development of the assay is identical to that used to quantify total IgE, and results are generally reported in a semiquantitative manner. The magnitude of the reaction is weakly correlated to the degree of sensitization and expression of allergy, although for certain foods more precise correlative data exist on the risk of allergy and the amount of the allergen-specific IgE detected. The in vivo assessment of allergen-specific IgE is undertaken by introducing into the skin a minute quantity of the allergen in question by a prick puncture technique and assessing the cutaneous response 15 to 30 minutes thereafter. A positive response is one in which a wheal and flare at least 2 mm larger than that caused by a saline control occurs at the injection site. In vivo tests are rapid and inexpensive; they require the absence of dermatographism, that patients not be using antihistaminic medications, and that patients display a positive response to a control employing histamine. In some situations, (i.e., penicillin or hymenopteran), a more diluted allergen is directly injected intradermally and wheal-and-flare responses are assessed similarly. The presence of allergen-specific IgE antibody and a clear temporal correlation of exposure to allergen and genesis of symptoms are required to conclude that a patient is allergic to a specific allergen. In the absence of symptoms, the patient with allergen-specific IgE is termed sensitized but not allergic.

Specific in vivo challenge tests may also be used to identify allergen responsiveness. Such tests in the presence of specific IgE antibody may be useful in research settings or may be used clinically to clarify the exact relationship between exposure and symptoms. Such tests may be dangerous as they introduce the allergen to which the patient is presumed allergic. In food allergy such challenges, best done in a double-blind and placebo-controlled manner, may be useful in separating allergy from sensitization. However, food challenge tests are unnecessary in the situation of anaphylaxis and a positive test for IgE antibody to the putative allergen. As many patients falsely believe foods are responsible for their symptoms, such double-blind challenges may be useful in directing patients' concerns into more productive directions. Inhalation tests employing specific allergens or chemicals have been helpful in elucidation of some cases of occupational allergy or asthma.

OTHER LABORATORY AIDS IN ALLERGIC DISEASE. In a patient with acute asthma, chest radiographs generally demonstrate hyperinflation. In some instances the evidence of bronchiectasis may be present, a finding that raises the specter of allergic bronchopulmonary aspergillosis. The presence of a tumor or radiopaque foreign body may be noted and should be sought in a patient with unilateral localized wheezing. In the examination of the patient with asthma, assessment of both airflow and volumes can provide a clear picture of the severity of asthma and its response to treatment. Flow volume loops can also identify the presence of vocal cord dysfunction. When patients with airway obstruction are evaluated, their response to inhaled β_2-adrenergic agonist medication can be helpful in elucidating the reversible nature of their disorder. Essentially all asthmatic patients exhibiting bronchoconstriction display a bronchodilatory response to inhalation of such agents. In suspected cases of asthma, when pulmonary function is normal, challenge with histamine or methacholine can be performed. These agents take advantage of the nonspecific bronchial hyperresponsiveness characteristic of asthmatic patients. Failure of a patient to develop bronchoconstriction upon inhalation of either of these agents strongly argues against the diagnosis of asthma.

Other laboratory tools may be of benefit to the clinician in the identification and classification of allergic disorders. Audiometry may clarify the degree hearing loss caused by otitis media in a patient with allergic rhinitis. When sinusitis is suspected, computed tomography (CT) of the sinuses gives the most complete imaging and has the highest degree of sensitivity for the identification of mucosal thickening, opacification of air spaces, and the presence of polyps and of bone erosions. Sinus CT is particularly useful in the examination of the ethmoid and sphenoid sinuses, which are often affected in chronic allergic disease and difficult to assess on physical examination or with plain radiographs.

The hematology and biochemistry laboratory may also be helpful in the evaluation of a patient with allergic disease. The quantification of blood, sputum, nasal mucus, or tissue eosinophilia and the response to corticosteroid therapy is a useful correlate in the identification and management of allergic disease. The quantification of tryptase, a mast cell–specific protease with a serum half-life of 2 hours, if performed on serum or plasma obtained within hours of a systemic response with associated hypotension, can assist in diagnosis when anaphylaxis is suspected.

IMMUNOLOGIC DISEASE

Diseases related to disordered immune function (immunodeficiency) are far less common than allergic disorders. The most frequent is IgA deficiency, which occurs in approximately 1 in 1000 individuals and is often asymptomatic. Next most frequently encountered are disorders of B and/or T lymphocytes such as common variable hypogammaglobulinemia (CVH), and other disorders including DiGeorge syndrome and severe combined immunodeficiency (Chapters 298). Much less common are defects in neutrophil function or complement. In essence, the expression of immune deficiency disorders is infection related to impaired host defense. Thus, the evaluation of suspected immune deficiency is the evaluation of recurrent, persistent, severe, and otherwise unexplained infections. Although many immune disorders arise in early childhood, not all do so, and with improved management many patients live into adulthood. It is important for the general internist and internal medicine subspecialist to be cognizant of their presentation.

History

The most important historical information includes the age of onset of the problem in question; family history of frequent infection or

---

Table 265–2 • KEY POINTS REGARDING IMMUNOLOGIC DISORDERS

ANTIBODY DEFICIENCY DISORDERS
Onset after 6 months of age
Recurrent respiratory infection
Infection with bacteria, especially encapsulated organisms
Absence of isohemagglutinins
Evaluation of B-cell function, not numbers

CELLULAR IMMUNE DEFECTS
Onset prior to 6 months of age
Recurrent viral, fungal, or parasitic (opportunistic) infection
Defective delayed hypersensitivity skin responses
Malabsorption or diarrhea

COMPLEMENT DEFICIENCIES
Recurrent bacterial infection
Recurrent neisserial infection (deficiency of late components)
Associated rheumatic disorder (especially systemic lupus erythematosus)

FACTORS SUGGESTING NEUTROPHIL DYSFUNCTION
Late separation of umbilical cord
Persistent neutrophilic leukocytosis
Recurrent/persistent gingivitis or peridontitis
Recurrent bacterial infection with granuloma formation

---

death at an early age from infection; the number, sites, and type of infection; and the presence of other physical abnormalities (Table 265–2). The earlier the onset of infections, the more severe the immune defect is likely to be. T-lymphocytic defects, with or without B-cell deficiencies, usually arise in the first 3 to 5 months of life, whereas B-cell function is supported by maternal antibody until after the first 6 months of life. Many of the immune disorders are X linked, and a careful family history is critical in such situations. Death related to infection of a male sibling of the patient's mother should lead to the question of such an X-linked disorder.

In a patient with a T-cell disorder, viral, fungal, mycobacterial, and other opportunistic infections (*Pneumocystis carinii*, *Toxoplasma gondii*) are most commonly noted and live virus vaccination may be associated with disseminated and progressive viral disease. Persistent thrush, diarrhea, malabsorption, and failure to thrive occurring in early childhood may suggest the presence of T-cell abnormalities.

In B-cell or antibody deficiency, pyogenic bacterial infections predominate, particularly involving encapsulated microorganisms. Usually such infections affect the upper and lower respiratory tract and skin and are severe and persistent. Infections with unusual organisms, with unexpected complications, or involving multiple sites (lung, sinus, joint, bone, meninges, abscess formation, or sepsis) should raise the index of suspicion. In adults the most common disorder in this class is CVH.

As in any patient with infection, information should be sought about exposure to ill individuals or to irritants such as tobacco smoke, the hygiene of the environment to which the patient is exposed, and the presence of an anatomic abnormality or allergy that might predispose to infection.

Physical Examination

Physical examination beyond that necessary to assess the extent and severity of a particular infection should be focused on immune organs. Assessment of tonsillar tissue, presence and size of lymph nodes, spleen, and liver is important. Patients with CVH often present with hepatosplenomegaly and lymph node hyperplasia, whereas in X-linked hypogammaglobulinemia lymph tissue is absent. Telangiectasia (ataxia telangiectasia), cardiac defects (DiGeorge syndrome), chronic eczema (Wiskott-Aldrich syndrome), and chronic periodontitis (neutrophil defects) all suggest immune deficiency syndromes.

Laboratory Evaluation

The proper use of the laboratory is essential in the elucidation of a suspected immune deficiency disorder. Screening tests appropriate to the generalist's initial approach include complete blood count, total neutrophil and lymphocyte enumeration, quantitative immunoglobulin levels, and assessment of isohemagglutinins (especially when CVH is suspected). In some situations, quantification of IgG subclasses may be warranted to identify specific subclass deficiency. In consideration of T-lymphocyte defects, it is important to enumerate total T cells and specific T-cell subsets. Delayed hypersensitivity skin testing to recall antigens is also helpful in assessing cellular immunity. When neutrophil defects are suspected, a nitroblue tetrazolium test or measurement of phagocytic potency can be performed. Complement defects are best addressed by obtaining a CH50 level CH50 is the amount of patient serum required to cause lysis of 50% of test erythrocytes. It is compared with the amount of pooled normal serum required to cause the same degree of lysis.

Additional tests of antibody production to defined stimuli, including vaccinations, may be helpful when selective antibody deficiency is suspected or when borderline immunoglobulin levels are encountered in the presence of frequent infection. In some situations the assessment of T-cell proliferation to mitogens or antigen may be of benefit. Further testing could include assessment of natural killer cell function and the production of cytokines by activated lymphocytes. In general, such additional laboratory tests should be performed in conjunction with consultation with an expert in immune disorders.

SUGGESTED READINGS

Moneret-Vautrin DA, Kanny G, Fremont S: Laboratory tests for diagnosis of food allergy: Advantages, disadvantages and future perspectives. Allerg Immunol (Paris) 2003;35:113–119. *Overview of their use and limitations.*

Paul MD, Shearer WT: Approach to the evaluation of the immunodeficient patient. *In* Rich RR, Fleisher TA, Shearer WT, et al (eds): Clinical Immunology: Principles and Practice, 2nd ed. London, Mosby, 2001, pp 33.1–33.11. *A comprehensive book chapter.*

Shearer WT, Li JT: Preface to the Fifth Primer on allergic and immunologic diseases. J Allergy Clin Immunol 2003;111:441–778. *An overview of and approach to allergy/immunologic disease.*

266 DISEASES OF THE THYMUS

Barton T. Haynes
Max D. Cooper

Normal Development and Function

The role of the thymus is to generate clonally diverse T lymphocytes that can recognize a vast array of foreign proteins presented as peptides on host cells. Essential parallel thymic functions are elimination of self-reactive T-cell clones that could damage normal tissue and production of regulatory T cells that migrate to the periphery and suppress autoreactive B cells that escape elimination in the thymus.

The embryonic thymus is formed initially from epithelial cells lining the third and fourth pharyngeal pouches. These specialized epithelial cells migrate through the neck region to form bilateral thymic lobes in the upper anterior mediastinum. The epithelial thymus begins to attract hematopoietic stem cells from the circulation around the 8th week of fetal life. Within the epithelial thymus, these precursor cells are influenced to proliferate and differentiate along T-lymphocyte lines. This lifelong process begins in the outer cortex of the thymus and the immature thymocytes migrate toward the medullary region as they proliferate and mature. Cortical regions of the lobules that collectively form the bilateral thymic lobes thus become filled with immature T lymphocytes, the extraordinary clonal diversity of which is manifested by differences in their T-cell receptor (TCR) specificities. Each developing T cell is selected for survival or death depending on the affinity of its receptor for self-peptides, which are presented initially on the surface of cortical epithelial cells. As maturing thymocytes approach the corticomedullary junction, they encounter macrophages or dendritic cell immigrants that can also present peptide fragments of antigenic proteins. Thymocytes that fail to receive any TCR-mediated signal are programmed to die. Immature thymocytes also receive a death signal if their TCR has relatively high affinity for a self-peptide, whereas moderate affinity for a self-peptide selects for survival. Only 1% or so of the thymic T cells survive this

selection process to seed the peripheral lymphoid tissues. After binding to dendritic cells and macrophages via TCR/major histocompatibility complex (MHC) interactions, thymocytes that are negatively selected become sensitive to death signals delivered by *fas* molecules (CD95) and undergo *apoptosis* (a term for programmed cell death). Mouse strains defective in fas expression (MRL/lpr) or fas ligand (gld/gld) have large thymuses and lymph nodes and defective negative selection of thymocytes and are prone to autoimmune syndromes. A molecule important for positive thymocyte selection is the oncogene product *bcl-2*. High levels of expression of bcl-2 in thymocytes promote cell survival by conferring resistance to programmed cell death.

Thymocytes also possess an array of non-TCR cell surface glycoproteins that they use to interact with their environment. Progression of thymocyte maturation can be conveniently monitored by the expression of CD4 and CD8 molecules. The most immature thymocytes lack detectable CD4 and CD8. Intermediate-stage thymocytes express both CD4 and CD8; these double-positives predominate in the thymic cortex. Clonal selection occurs during this stage of differentiation, and the CD4 and CD8 molecules play key roles in the selection process. The peptide fragments of antigenic proteins are presented within the α-helical grooves of MHC class II and class I molecules. CD4 has an affinity for MHC class II molecules on specialized antigen-presenting cells, whereas the CD8 molecules can bind class I molecules present on all nucleated cells. The CD4 or CD8 molecules thus serve as coreceptors in the positive clonal selection, which leads to the development of either mature CD4+ cells with helper (CD11/CD25−) or suppressor (CD4+/CD25+), also called T regulatory cells, function or CD8+ T cells with cytotoxic potential. Most of the positively selected T cells exit the thymus via the small blood vessels in the corticomedullary region and via thymic lymphatics. Thymic function can be monitored throughout life by a surrogate marker for recent thymic emigrants in the circulation, namely the levels of DNA excision circles that are created in the thymus during TCR V(D)J gene rearrangements.

THE THYMUS FUNCTIONS THROUGHOUT LIFE. The lymphoid thymus reaches its maximal size of approximately 30 g by around age 1 year, and it gradually decreases in size thereafter to 3 g or less in most older individuals. Because the thymus-derived T-cell clones may have lifespans of several decades, normally there is little need for constant thymic replenishment. Nevertheless, thymocyte differentiation and T-cell migration to the periphery persist throughout life, albeit at levels that vary according to the thymic central compartment mass and an individual's hormonal balance (Fig. 266–1).

CENTRAL AND PERIPHERAL THYMIC COMPARTMENTS. The thymus can be thought of as a chimeric organ composed of a central lymphoid compartment that lies within the true epithelial thymus and a peripheral lymphoid compartment located in the extrathymic perivascular space (Fig. 266–2). At birth, the thymic epithelial component is filled with developing thymocytes, whereas the thymic perivascular space contains only vessels and scattered peripheral lymphoid and myeloid cells (see Fig. 266–2A). From early childhood onward the thymic perivascular space begins to accumulate peripheral lymphoid and myeloid cells, as well as gradually increasing numbers of mature adipose cells (see Fig. 266–2B). The aging process within the thymus leads to progressive atrophy of the true epithelial thymus, loss of peripheral cells within the thymic perivascular space, and eventual filling of the perivascular space with adipocytes (see Fig. 266–2C). An appreciation of the central and peripheral compartmentalization of the thymus and the age-related changes in these compartments is essential for the interpretation of disease-related alterations in thymic histology and function.

Developmental Defects of the Thymus

DiGeorge syndrome, also called the third and fourth pharyngeal pouch syndrome, features hypoplastic thymus and parathyroid development in addition to facial and cardiac abnormalities, which may include a ventricular septal defect and aortic abnormalities. DiGeorge syndrome occurs in both males and females, a majority of whom may have submicroscopic deletions of chromosome 22q11. The initial clinical manifestations are neonatal seizures secondary to hypocalcemia or cyanosis and other signs of cardiac insufficiency. Immunodeficiency is a later manifestation, the severity of which depends on the degree of thymic hypoplasia. Most affected individuals have a small ectopic but functionally normal thymus that can

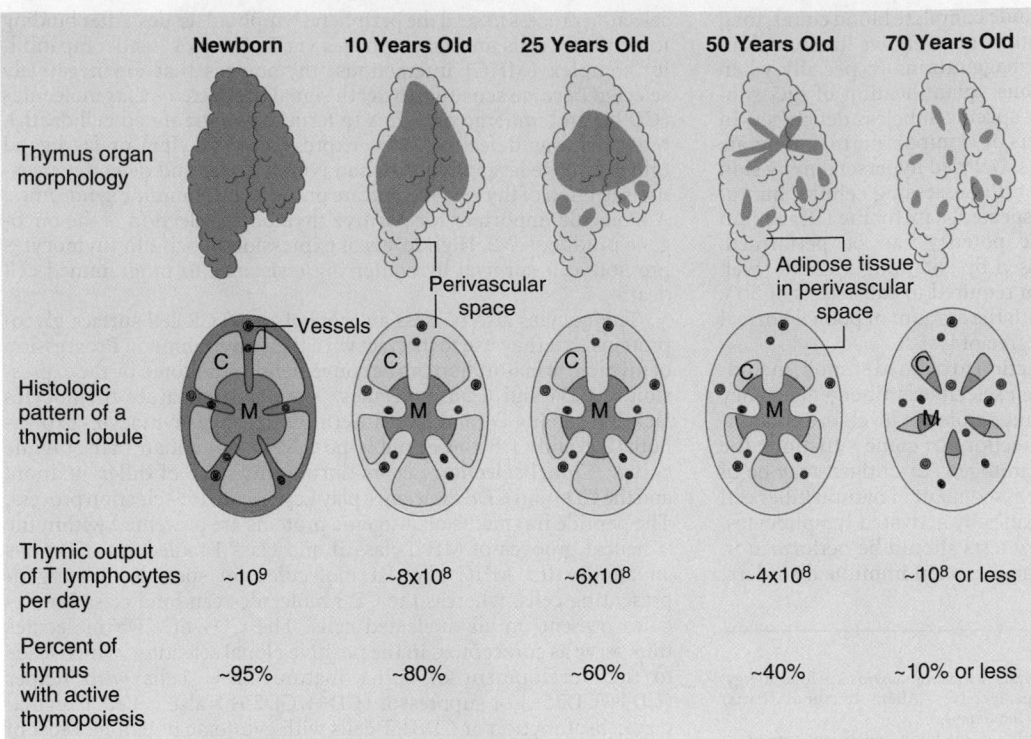

FIGURE 266–1 • Morphology, histology, and T lymphocyte output of the human thymus during aging. Shaded areas are thymic epithelial space (site of thymopoiesis). C = cortex; M = medulla. (From Haynes BF, Sempowski GD, Wells AF, Hale LP: The human thymus and aging. Immunol Res 2000;22:253–261.)

seed T cells to the periphery in numbers that may or may not be sufficient for immune defense. In rare instances, affected infants have no detectable thymus or peripheral T cells, and thymic transplantation must be considered in these cases. Thymic grafts and all blood products given to these patients need to be rigorously depleted of donor T cells by high-dose irradiation or other means because of the threat of lethal graft-versus-host disease.

Ataxia-telangiectasia is a hereditary disorder in which thymic hypoplasia and variable T-cell deficiency are seen in association with oculocutaneous telangiectasia and truncal ataxia (Chapter 272).

Acquired Abnormalities of Thymic Function

THYMIC HYPERPLASIA. Striking variability in thymic size can occur in apparently normal adults. The physiologic basis for thymic enlargement may include hormonal influences on thymopoietic activity. Pituitary hormones that can enhance thymic growth include growth hormone, luteinizing hormone, and follicle-stimulating hormone, whereas thyrotropin may inhibit thymic growth. Interleukin-7 (IL-7), a product of thymic stromal cells, is an important thymocyte growth factor. Other locally produced factors, including epithelial growth factor and transforming growth factor α, may regulate thymic epithelial cell production of cytokines that can affect T-cell proliferation, such as IL-1 and IL-6. Thymic enlargement can occur in adults without demonstrable pathology and patients with thyrotoxicosis, Addison's disease, or following orchidectomy.

THYMIC ATROPHY. Thymic atrophy is a well-known consequence of stressful illnesses, including severe infections, burns, and other conditions that result in elevated levels of adrenal corticosteroids. The atrophy is due to the relative susceptibility of immature thymocytes to lysis by corticosteroids of endogenous or exogenous origin. Thymic function is rapidly restored to normal following cessation of steroid therapy. Temporary thymic atrophy also occurs as a consequence of irradiation or treatment with cytotoxic drugs. Thymic atrophy is a physiologic consequence of pregnancy and elevated levels of estrogen.

MYASTHENIA GRAVIS. Myasthenia gravis is characterized by muscle weakness attributable to an autoimmune response against acetylcholine receptors (Chapter 464). Improvement in this disease is frequently observed after thymectomy, thus implying a causal link between the thymus and the autoreactive T- and B-cell clones. Germinal center

formation is seen in the thymic perivascular space of most patients with myasthenia gravis, and the morphology of the thymus in myasthenia is similar to that seen in early human immunodeficiency virus (HIV) infection (see Fig. 266–2E and F). Thymic B cells make antiacetylcholine receptor antibodies. However, the precise reason why thymectomy works in the treatment of myasthenia gravis is not known because after thymectomy, serum antiacetylcholine receptor antibody levels frequently do not decrease. Thymic epithelial tumors (thymomas) are diagnosed in approximately 10% of individuals with myasthenia gravis.

INFECTION. HIV infection can affect thymic function by several mechanisms. First, thymocyte maturation can be diminished because of infection of activated CD4+, chemokine receptor 5-bearing (CCR5+) developing thymocytes. Second, thymic myeloid cells, such as macrophages and dendritic cells, also express CD4 and CCR5 and are infectible by HIV. Third, macrophages, B cells, and CD8+ cytotoxic effector T cells migrate into the thymic perivascular space, with the formation of perivascular space germinal centers (see Fig. 266–2F) and corresponding reduction in thymopoiesis. Peripheral perivascular space CD4+ cells (mature T cells as well as macrophages) and developing thymocytes within the true epithelial thymus become infected with HIV. Active thymocyte development decreases over time in HIV-induced acquired immune deficiency syndrome (AIDS), which can result in empty thymic epithelium encased in CD8+ cytotoxic T-cell infiltrates (see Fig. 266–2F).

Thus, the capacity for thymic production of CD4+ T cells can be severely compromised in both pediatric and adult HIV-infected patients and may eventually be lost entirely. Consequently, severe immunodeficiency may occur relatively early in congenital HIV infection. In contrast, in adults, the peripheral pool of memory T cells becomes well established by adolescence. The extraordinary regenerative capacity of peripheral T cells in adults is temporarily able to compensate for the accelerated rate of T-cell death induced by HIV. After an average of 8 to 10 years, however, untreated HIV infection results in increased CD4 and CD8 T-cell proliferation and apoptotic death, leading to CD4+ T-cell lymphopenia with severe immunodeficiency and fullblown AIDS results (Chapter 411). After combination antiretroviral therapy, both the thymus and peripheral lymph nodes can regenerate, resulting in reconstitution of near normal peripheral T-cell number and function in many AIDS patients.

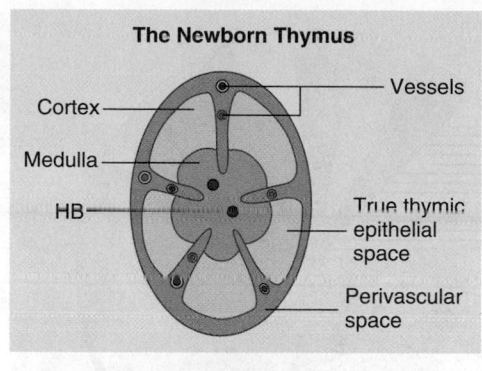

The Newborn Thymus

Cortex
Medulla
HB
Vessels
True thymic epithelial space
Perivascular space

A

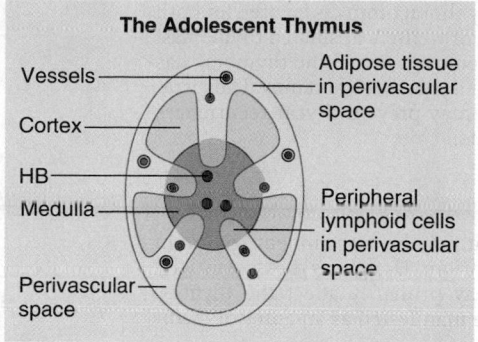

The Adolescent Thymus

Vessels
Cortex
HB
Medulla
Perivascular space
Adipose tissue in perivascular space
Peripheral lymphoid cells in perivascular space

B

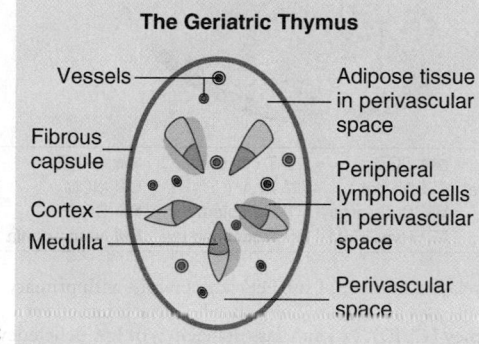

The Geriatric Thymus

Vessels
Fibrous capsule
Cortex
Medulla
Adipose tissue in perivascular space
Peripheral lymphoid cells in perivascular space
Perivascular space

C

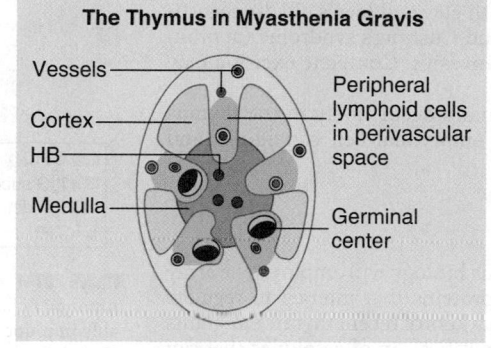

The Thymus in Myasthenia Gravis

Vessels
Cortex
HB
Medulla
Peripheral lymphoid cells in perivascular space
Germinal center

D

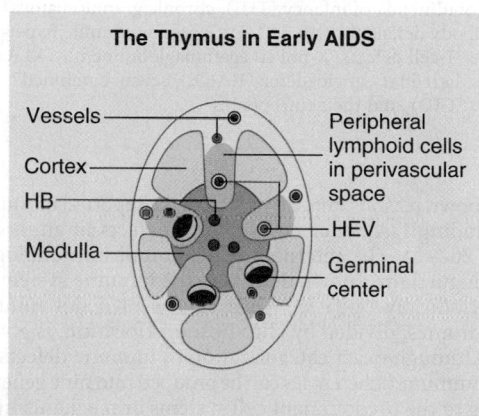

The Thymus in Early AIDS

Vessels
Cortex
HB
Medulla
Peripheral lymphoid cells in perivascular space
HEV
Germinal center

E

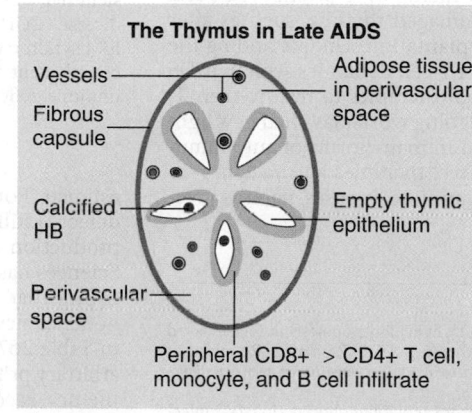

The Thymus in Late AIDS

Vessels
Fibrous capsule
Calcified HB
Perivascular space
Adipose tissue in perivascular space
Empty thymic epithelium
Peripheral CD8+ > CD4+ T cell, monocyte, and B cell infiltrate

F

FIGURE 266–2 • Morphology of the human thymus during normal aging and in myasthenia gravis and human immunodeficiency virus (HIV) infection. Panels show schematic representations of a thymic lobule at birth (*A*), during adolescence and young adulthood (*B*), and in old age (*C*). At birth, the epithelial thymus contains most of the thymus tissue, and the perivascular space has only vessels and scattered peripheral lymphoid and myeloid cells (*A*). From age 5 years to approximately age 25 years, the thymic perivascular space normally contains infiltrations of peripheral T and B cells and macrophages, as well as foci of adipocytes (*B*). As thymic atrophy progresses, the perivascular space fills up with adipocytes, peripheral immune cells decrease, and the true epithelial thymus lobes shrink in volume (*C*). Panels show schematic representations of the human thymus in myasthenia gravis (*D*), early HIV infection (*E*), and late HIV infection (*F*). The changes seen in myasthenia gravis are similar to those seen in early HIV infection and include germinal center formation in the thymic perivascular space, as well as perivascular space expansion of peripheral lymphoid and myeloid infiltrations (*D* and *E*). In late HIV infection, the true epithelial thymus can be depleted of developing thymocytes and is surrounded by large cellular infiltrates containing peripheral B cells, macrophages, and CD8+ cytotoxic effector T cells (*F*). (From Haynes BF, Hale LP: The human thymus: A chimeric organ comprised of central and peripheral lymphoid components. Immunol Res 1998;18:175–192.)

THYMECTOMY. Removal of the thymus after the peripheral lymphoid compartments have been seeded with T-cell clones may have no discernible effects for many years, presumably because of the regenerative capacity of T lymphocytes. Thymectomy is rarely complete, moreover, in part because approximately 30% of individuals have extramediastinal thymic arrests. Nevertheless, the potential need for thymic function later in life dictates careful consideration before undertaking thymectomy.

THYMOMA. The term *thymoma* is usually reserved for thymic epithelial cell tumors, which, although rare, are the most commonly diagnosed tumors of the anterior superior mediastinum. Thymomas are frequently associated with myasthenia gravis. They also occur in rare individuals with acquired hypogammaglobulinemia who stop producing B-lineage cells; bone marrow insufficiency in these individuals may also extend to the erythroid and myeloid lineages.

The diagnosis of thymoma is suggested when these associated conditions occur or when an anterior mediastinal mass is detected, which may be an incidental finding because approximately one third of affected individuals are asymptomatic. Others with thymoma may have chest pain, dysphagia, signs of tracheal impingement, or superior vena cava obstruction. The extent of the tumor mass can be estimated by imaging procedures, but accurate diagnosis depends on obtaining tissue for histologic assessment. Even when an adequate sample is available, the diagnosis may be difficult, however. No reliable markers for neoplastic epithelial clones are known, and thymomas are rarely composed of obviously neoplastic epithelial cells. Instead, they are usually formed by a mixture of apparently normal lymphoid thymocytes and epithelial cells that are either spindle shaped or ovoid. Consequently, the most reliable prognostic indication is evidence for or against invasiveness by the epithelial tumor. For this reason, direct tumor visualization by thoracotomy is favored for both diagnosis and treatment. In the case of well-encapsulated thymomas, tumors rarely occur after surgical removal. When the thymoma has invaded the capsule or surrounding tissue, surgical removal and irradiation or intensive chemotherapy may prevent 5-year recurrences in more than half of affected patients.

Other Tumors of the Thymus

LYMPHOMAS. Thymic involvement may be a prominent feature in lymphoblastic neoplasms of T-cell origin. Hodgkin's disease, usually of the nodular sclerosing type, may primarily affect the thymus. Histiocytic lymphomas may also be manifested as an anterior mediastinal mass in adults.

CARCINOID TUMORS. See Chapter 245. Carcinoid tumors rarely arise in the thymus: Those associated with elevated levels of adrenocorticotropic hormone-like hormones and Cushing's syndrome (approximately one third) are particularly invasive. Complete excision may be curative.

GERM CELL TUMORS. Germ cell tumors occur rarely in the thymus but include seminoma, teratoma, embryonal cell carcinoma, and choriocarcinoma.

Future Directions

Future research in human thymus biology will employ gene array technology to identify genes and proteins that interact to regulate thymopoiesis or that may serve as markers of recent thymic emigrants in the periphery. The successful identification of cytokines that can drive thymopoiesis could lead to new therapies to promote safe and rapid regeneration of the aging or damaged thymus, such as after chemotherapy or bone marrow transplantation. Understanding the role of thymic function in the complex T-cell dynamics seen in AIDS patients may allow the development of therapies to restore their T-cell numbers and function. Finally, ongoing work may shed new light on the disordered T-cell function seen in many forms of autoimmunity. This could potentially lead to novel therapies and vaccines for the treatment and prevention of autoimmune diseases, such as juvenile onset diabetes.

SUGGESTED READINGS

Markert ML, Alverez-McLeod AP, Sempowski GD, et al: Thymopoiesis in HIV-infected adults after highly active antiretroviral therapy. AIDS Res Hum Retroviruses 2001;17:1635–1643. *Thymopoiesis contributes to immune reconstitution even in patients who have had prolonged CD4(+) lymphosemia.*

Mohri H, Perelson AS, Tung K, et al: Increased turnover of T lymphocytes in HIV-1 infection and its reduction by anti-retroviral therapy. J Exp Med 2001;194:1277–1287. *CD4(+) lymphocyte depletion is due to increased cellular destruction not decreased cellular production.*

Sempowski GD, Haynes BF: Immune reconstitution in patients with HIV infection. Annu Rev Med 2002;53:269–284. *Immune reconstitution with return of thymic function can occur.*

267 PRIMARY IMMUNODEFICIENCY DISEASES

Charlotte Cunningham-Rundles

The first genetic defect involving the immune system was reported in 1952, but about 100 primary immunodeficiency syndromes have now been described, and others are likely to be identified in the future. The immune-based diseases involve abnormalities of structure or function of the specialized lymphocytes, monocytes, phagocytic cells, or the complement proteins or may result from systemic defects that impinge on the immune system. Deficiencies of neutrophils and of the complement system, and the acquired immunodeficiency syndrome (AIDS), are described separately; this chapter concentrates on defects of lymphocytes.

One of the first principles is that primary immune defects can be diagnosed in infants, children, or adults. Although the spectrum of molecular defects may vary, many of the clinical findings are similar, regardless of the age of the patient. The overall incidence of primary immunodeficiency diseases has been estimated at about 1 : 10,000, excluding selective IgA deficiency, but this is likely to be an under

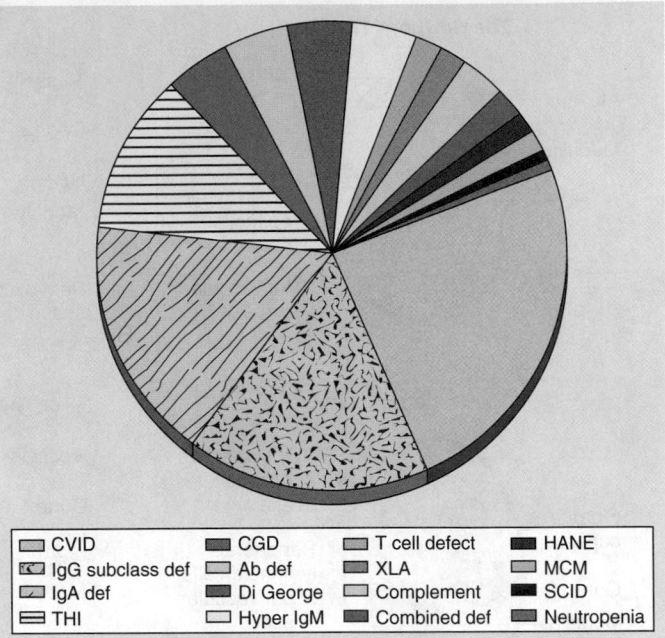

CVID	CGD	T cell defect	HANE
IgG subclass def	Ab def	XLA	MCM
IgA def	Di George	Complement	SCID
THI	Hyper IgM	Combined def	Neutropenia

FIGURE 267–1 • The relative number of subjects who present with primary immune deficiency diseases are shown. Subjects who have common variable immune deficiency (CVID), IgG subclass deficiency, or IgA deficiency (IgA def) represent about half of the total group. Other defects include transient hypogammaglobulinemia of infancy (THI), chronic granulomatous disease (CGD), antibody deficiency (Ab def), DiGeorge syndrome, hyper-IgM syndrome, other T-cell defects, X-linked agammaglobulinemia (XLA), complement defects, hereditary angioedema (HANE), severe combined immune deficiency (SCID), and the neutropenias.

estimate. For unknown reasons, more than half of the reported immune defects (still excluding IgA deficiency) involve defects in antibody production (Fig. 267–1). The International Union of Immunologic Sciences has catalogued the known defects of the immune system, a listing that is periodically updated. An overview of major immunodeficiency syndromes, divided by chromosomal location, is given in Table 267–1. Although exact categorization of immune defects is arbitrary, primary immune deficiencies can be grouped into nine general themes, according to the predominant cell systems or mechanism(s) that are defective.

1. *Antibody deficiency (B-cell) disorders* comprise 50 to 65% of primary immune deficiencies, excluding selective IgA deficiency. Rarely, antibody deficiency with normal serum immunoglobulin concentrations occurs. These defects may be broad (both protein and polysaccharide antigens) or more restricted (e.g., to carbohydrate bacterial capsular antigens).
2. *Cellular deficiency (T-cell) disorders* are uncommon and account for at most 5 to 10% of primary immune deficiencies. Although it is useful to classify these as isolated T-cell disorders, when T-cell function is significantly impaired antibody formation is also deficient.
3. *Combined cellular and antibody (T- and B-cell) deficiencies* comprise 20 to 25% of all primary immune deficiencies. This is a heterogeneous group, characterized by the defects of both T- and B-cell function, often associated with decreased numbers of T lymphocytes and reduced immunoglobulin levels. Examples are severe combined immune deficiency diseases (SCIDs) or combined T and B defects that are more restricted in phenotype.
4. *Interferon γ (IFNγ)–associated immune deficiencies.* These defects involve components of the IFNγ receptor, production of interleukin (IL)-12, or defects of the IL-12 receptor, all of which result in deficiencies of IFNγ and result in susceptibility to mycobacterial disease.
5. *Defects of lymphocyte apoptosis.* These are defects that involve a failure of lymphocyte homeostasis due to impaired cell death and produce a heterogeneous syndrome of lymphadenopathy, splenomegaly, and autoimmunity.

Table 267–1 • CHROMOSOME LOCATIONS AND PRIMARY IMMUNODEFICIENCY DISEASES

CHROMOSOME	GENE PRODUCT	NAME	FEATURES
1p31.2	IL-12 RB2	IL-12 receptor defect	Mycobacterial infections
1q 23–q 24	Fas ligand	Autoimmune lymphoproliferative disorder	Hepatosplenomegaly, ITP, hemolytic anemia
1q 21.1–q21.3	RFX-5	MHC class II antigen deficiency	Low Ig level, lack of T-cell responses to antigens, CD4 deficiency
1q25	p67^{phox}	Autosomal recessive CGD	Lack of bacterial and fungal killing by phagocytic cells
1q42–43	Vesicle membrane component, LYST	Chediak-Higashi syndrome	Lack of intracellular killing, T-cell or NK-cell cytotoxicity; giant lysosomes
2q12	ZAP 70	CD8 lymphocytopenia	Failure of CD4$^+$ T cells to respond to T cell receptor stimulation
5p13	IL-7R	T-B$^+$ NK$^+$ SCID	Absence of T- and B-cell functions
6p21.3 TAP2	MHC class I antigen deficiency	A form of bare lymphocyte syndrome	Marked deficiency of CD8$^+$ T cells; combined B- and T-cell defects
7q11.23	p47^{phox}	Autosomal recessive CGD	Lack of bacterial and fungal killing by phagocytic cells
8q21	Nibrin	Nijmegen breakage syndrome	Combined B- and T-cell defects; resembles A-T
9p21–p13	RNA processing enzyme	Cartilage-hair hypoplasia	Combined T- and B-cell defects of varying severity
10p13	Unknown	DiGeorge's/velocardiofacial syndrome	Low numbers of T cells and impaired T-cell function
10p14–15	IL-2Rα	Lymphoproliferative syndrome	Poor T-cell responses; impaired apoptosis; increased bcl-2; autoimmunity
10q 24.1	Fas (CD95) ligand	Autoimmune lymphoproliferative disorder	ITP, hemolytic anemia, lymphadenopathy, splenomegaly
11p13	*RAG*-1 or *RAG*-2	T$^-$ B$^-$ NK$^+$ SCID	Absence of T- and B-cell functions
11q22.3	DNA-dependent kinase (ATM)	A-T	Ig deficiency; T-cell deficiency
13q.14	RFXAP	MHC class II antigen deficiency	Low Ig level; lack of T-cell responses to antigens; CD4 deficiency
14q13.1	Purine nucleosidase	PNP deficiency	Severe T-cell deficiency; may have Igs; neurologic defect in some
14q32.3	Immunoglobulin heavy chains	B cell–negative agammaglobulinemia (μ) or selective deficiencies of other isotypes	Absence of antibody production and lack of B cells in μ chain mutations; subclasses missing but B cells present in others
15q21	myosin-Va	Griscelli's disease	Partial combined T- and B-cell immunodeficiencies, partial albinism
16p13	CIITA	MHC class II antigen deficiency	Low Ig level; lack of T-cell responses to antigens; CD4 deficiency
16q24	p22^{phox}	Autosomal recessive CGD	Lack of bacterial and fungal killing by phagocytic cells
19p13.1	JAKIII	T$^-$ B$^+$ NK$^-$ SCID	Absence of T-, B-, and NK-cell functions
20q13.11	ADA	T$^-$ B$^-$ NK$^-$ SCID	Absence of T- and B-cell functions, bone abnormalities
21q 22.3	AIRE	Mucocutaneous candidiasis with endocrinopathy	Oral and/or cutaneous candidiasis, hypoparathyroid, hypothyroid/hypoadrenalism, diabetes, hepatitis, vitiligo, alopecia
21q22.1–q22.2	IFN-γR1	Disseminated mycobacterial infections	Failure of macrophages and other cells to produce TNF-α in response to IFN-γ
21q22.3	CD18	LAD 1	Absence of cytotoxic T- and NK-lymphocyte function; lack of phagocytic cell adhesion
Xp21.1	Gp91^{phox}, cytochrome b-245 polypeptide	X-linked CGD	Lack of bacterial and fungal killing by phagocytic cells
Xp11.23–q13.3	Immune-specific DNA binding protein, MP3, FOX P3	IPEX	Early diabetes, autoimmunity, diarrhea, eczema, infections, nephrosis
Xp11.23	Cytoskeletal protein, WASP	Wiskott-Aldrich syndrome	Thrombocytopenia; poor anti-polysaccharide antibody production; T-cell deficiency
Xq13.1	Common γ chain (γc) of cytokine receptors	T$^-$ B$^+$ NK$^-$ SCID	Absence of T- and NK-cell functions
Xq22	BTK	X-linked (Bruton's) agammaglobulinemia	Absence of antibody production; lack of B cells
Xq28	NEMO IKK gamma protein	Incontinentia pigmenti	Alopecia, abnormal tooth eruption, skin lesions, pigmentation, infections
Xq24–26	CD40 ligand, CD154	Hyper-IgM syndrome	IgG and IgA low, IgM high or normal, no class switch, poor memory, germinal centers poorly formed, *Pneumocystis carinii* cryptosporidia, neutropenia
Xq25.	SAP; SLAM enhances T-cell functions	X-linked lymphoproliferative syndrome	Lack of anti-EBNA and long-lived T-cell immunity to EBV; low Ig levels in some, B-cell lymphoma
Xq26	CD154 (CD40 ligand)	X-linked hyper-IgM syndrome	Failure to produce IgG, IgA, and IgE antibodies

ADA = adenosine deaminase deficiency; AIRE = autoimmune regulator; A-T = ataxia-telangiectasia; BTK = Bruton tyrosine kinase; CGD = chronic granulomatous disease; CIITA = class II transactivator; EBNA = Epstein-Barr nuclear antigen; EBV = Epstein-Barr virus; FOX P3 = forkhead box p3; IFN-γ = interferon-γ; Ig = immunoglobulin; IKK = I-kappa-B kinase; IL = interleukin; IPEX = X-linked immune dysfunction enteropathy polyendocrinopathy; ITP = immune thrombocytopenia purpura; JAKIII = Janus kinase III; LAD 1 = leukocyte adhesion deficiency type 1; LYST = lysosomal tracking regulator; MHC = major histocompatibility complex; NEMO = NF kappa B essential modulator; NK = natural killer; PNP = purine nucleoside phosphorylase; *RAG* = recombinase-activating gene; RFXAP = regulatory factor X-associated protein; RFX-5 = regulatory factor X, 5; SCID = severe combined immunodeficiency; SAP = SLAM-associated protein; SLAM = signaling lymphocyte activation molecule; TAP = transporter-associated protein; T-B = no T cells and no B cells; TNF-α = tumor necrosis factor α; WASP = Wiskott-Aldrich syndrome protein; ZAP 70 = zeta-associated protein 70.

6. *Diseases of cytolytic pathways.* These diseases involve abnormalities of cell killing, due to defects in the structural components involved in cytotoxicity.

7. *Phagocytic disorders* (granulocytes, monocytes) constitute approximately 10 to 15% of all primary immune deficiencies. Defects of neutrophil and monocyte maturation and differentiation, chemotaxis, phagocytosis, and intracellular killing have all been described.

8. *Other well-defined defects.* There are other well-described immune defects, some known for years and others only recently described. The central immunologic mechanisms that are defective have not yet been elucidated. Examples include autoimmune polyendocrinopathy syndrome with candidiasis (APCED), mucocutaneous candidiasis, the hyper-IgE syndrome, and X-linked immune polyendocrinopathy (IPEX.)

9. *Complement deficiencies* result in inadequate coating of bacteria or viruses with antibody (opsonization), reduced or absent phagocytosis, or impaired lysis of microorganisms predisposing to infections. The most common complement defect involves the C1 inhibitor, which results in recurrent attacks of angioedema but not infections. Complement disorders account for a small percentage of primary immune deficiencies (<2%) and may coexist with autoimmune diseases, such as systemic lupus erythematosus (SLE).

APPROACH TO THE PATIENT WITH SUSPECTED IMMUNE DEFICIENCY

Clinical History in Immune deficiency Disorders

The most frequent clinical indicator of an immune defect is the occurrence of "too many infections." When frequent and prolonged infections are coupled with weight loss and/or failure to thrive or if unusual infections appear, an evaluation of the immune system is indicated. A confirmed report of an immunodeficiency disease occurring in a sibling or first-degree relative should also prompt careful clinical assessment and laboratory investigation, even without a history of severe or unusual infections. Common and less common clinical features are outlined on Table 267–2.

Physical Examination

The physical examination can reveal pertinent clues to the nature of an immune defect. Young children with significant immunodeficiencies often appear chronically ill and exhibit pallor and sometimes loss of subcutaneous fat. For adults, however, it is not unusual for there to be few or no physical signs that an immune defect is present. The physical examination should include height and weight, with special attention paid to examination of the conjunctiva, lymphoid tissue and tonsils, ears, sinuses, lungs, joints, gingiva, gums, skin, and nails. Table 267–3 includes some of the physical findings of patients with primary immune defects.

SELECTED IMMUNE DEFECTS

DEFECTS OF ANTIBODY PRODUCTION

Defects of antibody production are quite heterogeneous and, overall, are the most common of the primary immune deficiency diseases (see Fig. 267–1).

X-LINKED AGAMMAGLOBULINEMIA

Males with X-linked agammaglobulinemia (XLA) usually present with infections such as bacterial pneumonia, acute otitis, septic arthritis, bacterial meningitis, and/or septicemia after 6 months of age when maternal immune globulin has been depleted. The most common organisms found include pneumococci, streptococci, *Pseudomonas*, and *Haemophilus* species. Opportunistic infections such as *Pneumocystis carinii* pneumonia or fungal or parasitic diseases are rarely encountered. Patients with XLA generally exhibit normal anti-viral immunity, although infections with enteroviruses (ECHO and polio viruses) can lead to chronic or fatal infections of the central nervous system. Since killed polio vaccines have been reintroduced, very few cases of polio have appeared.

The diagnosis of XLA is confirmed by finding very low concentrations of serum IgG, IgA, and IgM for a patient's age. Tests for antibodies to vaccine antigens show little, if any, antibody protection; isohemagglutinins are absent. Levels of B cells in peripheral blood are very low or absent (<3%, and often undetectable), and numbers of T cells are increased. Due to the lack of lymph node germinal centers, tonsils and adenoids are almost absent, lymph nodes are small, and plasma cells are rare or absent. The gene on the X chromosome, which is abnormal in XLA, codes for a tyrosine kinase, named Bruton tyrosine kinase (or BTK), a kinase involved in signal transduction pathways essential for B-cell maturation. Many different mutations in BTK have been identified in subjects with XLA.

 Treatment

The overall prognosis in XLA appears good if intravenous immunoglobulin (IVIg) treatment is started early and at adequate doses, such as 400 mg/kg body weight IVIg every 3 to 4 weeks. An occasional patient may develop severe sinopulmonary disease while receiving this therapy, for unclear reasons. Chronic (rotating) antibiotic therapy is then also necessary.

COMMON VARIABLE IMMUNODEFICIENCY

Patients with common variable immunodeficiency (CVID) (previously called acquired or adult-onset hypogammaglobulinemia) also have levels of IgG, IgA, and/or IgM that are significantly lower than the mean for age. B-cell numbers are generally normal or slightly reduced; antibody production, as measured before and after vaccine challenge, is reduced or absent. T-cell numbers are generally normal, although some subjects are lymphopenic with moderate reductions of T-cell subsets, especially CD4⁺ and B cells. Unlike patients with XLA, patients with CVID have normal sized or enlarged lymph nodes; an enlarged spleen is found in about a third of patients.

Although this disorder may occur in children, most patients are adults at the time of diagnosis. The mean age at diagnosis is 29 years for males and 33 years for females. Most subjects present with a history of recurrent pneumonia, often leading to empyema or bronchiectasis. This condition is also been associated with autoimmune conditions in about 23% of cases; idiopathic thrombocytopenic purpura (ITP), hemolytic anemia, rheumatoid disease, or pernicious anemia are the most common. Gastrointestinal diseases also occur, including giardiasis, a sprue-like syndrome, with or without nodular lymphoid hyperplasia, gastric atrophy, achlorhydria, and inflammatory bowel disease. Other complications include gastric carcinoma and

Table 267–2 • COMMON CLINICAL FEATURES OF IMMUNODEFICIENCY

Usually present	Recurrent upper respiratory infections
	Severe bacterial infections
	Persistent infections with incomplete or no response to therapy
Often present	Persistent sinusitis or mastoiditis (*Streptococcus pneumoniae, Haemophilus, Moraxella catarrhalis, Staphylococcus aureus, Pseudomonas* spp.)
	Recurrent bronchitis or pneumonia
	Failure to thrive or growth retardation for infants or children; weight loss for adults
	Intermittent fever
	Infection with unusual organisms
	Skin lesions: rash, seborrhea, pyoderma, necrotic abscesses, alopecia, eczema, telangiectasia
	Recalcitrant thrush
	Diarrhea and malabsorption
	Hearing loss due to chronic otitis
	Chronic conjunctivitis
	Arthralgia or arthritis
	Bronchiectasis
	Evidence of autoimmunity, especially autoimmune thrombocytopenia or hemolytic anemia
	Hematologic abnormalities: aplastic anemia, hemolytic anemia, neutropenia, thrombocytopenia
	History of prior surgery, biopsy
Occasionally present	Paucity of lymph nodes and tonsils
	Lymphadenopathy
	Hepatosplenomegaly
	Severe viral disease (e.g., varicella, herpes simplex)
	Chronic encephalitis
	Recurrent meningitis
	Deep infections: cellulitis, osteomyelitis, organ abscesses
	Chronic gastrointestinal disease, infections, lymphoid hyperplasia, sprue-like syndrome, atypical inflammatory bowel disease
	Autoimmune disease such as autoimmune thrombocytopenia, hemolytic anemia, rheumatologic disease, alopecia, thyroiditis, pernicious anemia
	Pyoderma gangrenosum
	Adverse reaction to vaccines
	Delayed umbilical cord detachment
	Chronic stomatitis or peritonitis

Table 267–3 • **SPECIAL PHYSICAL FEATURES ASSOCIATED WITH IMMUNODEFICIENCY DISORDERS**

CLINICAL FEATURES	DISORDERS
DERMATOLOGIC	
Eczema	T-cell defects, T- or B-cell immune deficiency, Wiskott-Aldrich syndrome, IPEX
Sparse and/or hypopigmented hair	Cartilage hair hypoplasia, Chediak-Higashi syndrome, Griscelli's syndrome
Ocular telangiectasia	Ataxia-telangiectasia
Oculocutaneous albinism	Chediak-Higashi syndrome
Severe dermatitis	SCID with acute GVHD
Recurrent abscesses, of lung especially	Hyper-IgE syndrome
Recurrent organ abscesses, liver and rectum especially	Chronic granulomatous disease
Recurrent skin infections, abscesses	Leukocyte adhesion defect, hyper-IgE syndrome
Oral ulcers	Hyper-IgM syndrome, AID (cytokine deaminase)
Peridontitis, gingivitis, stomatitis	Neutrophil defects, hyper-IgM syndrome
Oral or nail candidiasis	T-cell immune defects; combined defects; mucocutaneous candidiasis, hyper-IgE syndrome
Vitiligo	B-cell defects, mucocutaneous candidiasis
Alopecia	B-cell defects, mucocutaneous candidiasis
Chronic conjunctivitis	B-cell defects
EXTREMITIES	
Clubbing of the nails	Chronic lung disease due to antibody defects
Arthritis	Antibody defects; Wiskott-Aldrich syndrome, hyper-IgM
ENDOCRINOLOGIC	
Hypoparathyroidism	DiGeorge's syndrome, mucocutaneous candidiasis
Endocrinopathies (autoimmune)	Mucocutaneous candidiasis
Growth hormone deficiency	X-linked agammaglobulinemia
Gonadal dysgenesis	Mucocutaneous candidiasis
HEMATOLOGIC	
Hemolytic anemia	B- and T-cell immune defects, ALPS
Thrombocytopenia, small platelets	Wiskott-Aldrich syndrome
Neutropenia	Hyper-IgM syndrome, Wiskott-Aldrich variant
Immune thrombocytopenia	B-cell immune defects, ALPS
SKELETAL	
Short-limb dwarfism	Short-limb dwarfism with T- and/or B-cell immune defects
Bony dysplasia	ADA deficiency, SCID

ADA = adenosine deaminase deficiency; AID = activation-induced cytidine deaminase; ALPS = autoimmune lymphoproliferative syndrome; GVHD = graft-versus-host disease; Ig = immunoglobulin; IPEX = X-linked immune dysfunction enteropathy polyendocrinopathy; SCID = severe combined immunodeficiency.

non-Hodgkin's lymphoma. If noncaseating granulomas of the lungs, spleen, skin, and liver are found in an initial evaluation, the diagnosis of sarcoidosis is sometimes applied, which may delay the diagnosis of immune deficiency.

In CVID there are circulating B lymphocytes, but these cells differentiate poorly into immunoglobulin-producing plasma cells. CVID and selective IgA deficiency may be related conditions; both defects may be present in the same family, and an occasional IgA-deficient person may later become hypogammaglobulinemic. This theory is supported by the increased incidence of the same major histocompatibility (MHC) haplotypes in many people with CVID and selective IgA deficiency, suggesting that there may be a susceptibility gene in the class II or class III region of the MHC on chromosome 6. However, such a gene has not been identified.

Complicating the etiology of CVID, certain drugs such as phenytoin and gold can cause severely lowered serum immunoglobulin levels; paradoxically, a few human immunodeficiency virus (HIV)–infected CVID subjects have demonstrated resolution of the antibody deficiency. Thus, external factors may initiate CVID or selective IgA deficiency, or potentially reverse the defect.

Rx **Treatment**

The treatment of CVID is the same as that for subjects with XLA: IVIg in doses of at least 300 to 400 mg/kg every 3 or 4 weeks, with the addition of antibiotics as needed.

SELECTIVE IGA DEFICIENCY

Selective IgA deficiency (operationally serum IgA levels <7 mg/dL) is the most common of the congenital immune defects. The incidence

of IgA deficiency is about 1:500, but there is great variability in the prevalence in different ethnic groups. Although most people who are IgA deficient do not have any illnesses, a lack of IgA is also associated with a variety of illnesses. Autosomal dominant and autosomal recessive inheritance are found, but most cases are sporadic. The cause(s) of this defect are unknown but are present at the stem cell level, because transfer of bone marrow from an IgA-deficient donor to a normal recipient results in IgA deficiency in the recipient and transfer of bone marrow from a normal individual to an IgA-deficient patient corrects the defect.

Although there are substantial amounts of IgA in serum, most of the IgA-producing B cells are in the mucosa of the sinopulmonary, genital, or gastrointestinal tracts, where they produce secretory IgA. Recurrent sinopulmonary infections are the most frequent illnesses associated with selective IgA deficiency and are often the reason why quantitative serum immunoglobulin levels are first obtained. Allergic disorders, allergic conjunctivitis, rhinitis, urticaria, atopic eczema, and bronchial asthma are common. Gastrointestinal diseases, especially infection with *Giardia lamblia*, also occur. Nodular lymphoid hyperplasia and malabsorption can also develop, but malabsorption can be present without nodular lymphoid hyperplasia. Patients with celiac disease have a high incidence of IgA deficiency. In a review of 604 subjects with celiac sprue, 14 had IgA deficiency (2.3%); response to a gluten-free diet was similar to that of celiac sprue patients without this deficiency. Finally, autoimmunity is commonly found in selective IgA deficiency; the most frequent of these conditions include rheumatoid arthritis, SLE, vitiligo, hemolytic anemia, ITP, and various neurologic diseases.

Concomitant IgG$_2$ subclass deficiency may be found in about 12% of patients with IgA deficiency, resulting in deficient antibody production. Some IgA-deficient individuals have anti-IgA antibodies in their serum—generally only those who have no detectable IgA in their serum. Although IgA/anti-IgA reactions resulting from blood or plasma infusions are potentially severe, such reactions are actually extremely rare.

 Treatment

There is no specific therapy for patients with IgA deficiency, except antibiotics as needed or treatment of the gastrointestinal or autoimmune disease by standard means. Concentrates of IgA, if available, would not permit transport of IgA into the external secretions, because secreted IgA is produced locally.

IMMUNODEFICIENCY WITH ELEVATED IGM LEVELS

Males with immune deficiency with elevated IgM levels (hyper-IgM syndrome) have very low serum levels of IgG and IgA but normal or elevated levels of IgM. (The name is somewhat of a misnomer.) Due to the lack of immune globulin and antibody, males usually become ill in the first year of life with otitis, sinusitis, pneumonia, or severe diarrhea. Although in XLA there are few palpable lymph nodes, patients with hyper-IgM syndrome may have lymphoid hyperplasia. Neutropenia (transient, cyclic, or chronic) is common, as well as hemolytic anemia or thrombocytopenia. B-cell numbers are normal. The abnormal (X-linked) gene codes for a gene product (CD154), a surface receptor found on activated T cells that is the ligand for CD40, an antigen present on the surface of B cells. Cross-linking of CD40 by CD154, in the presence of cytokines such as IL-2, IL-4, or IL-10, is required for B-cell proliferation, differentiation, and isotype switch from IgM to IgG and IgA production. CD154 is a transmembrane protein with significant homology to TNF.

Mutations of CD154 are not the only cause of the hyper-IgM syndrome. An occasional male or female hyper-IgM patient has normal T-cell CD154; mutations of an enzyme, activation-induced cytidine deaminase (AID), may also produce this disease. As in other patients with hyper-IgM syndrome, a lack of immunoglobulin somatic hypermutation and lymph node hyperplasia are seen. Another related, recently described defect involves an impaired cytoplasmic signaling molecule, nuclear factor κB (NF-κB), due to mutations in the *NF-κB essential modulator* (NEMO) gene. In this X-linked defect, there is an association of a skin disease and a congenital disorder of tooth formation, hair, and eccrine sweat glands, with a variable immune deficiency.

 Treatment

Patients with hyper-IgM syndrome (and related defects) are unable to make IgG antibodies; therefore, treatment with IVIg is required in the same doses as for agammaglobulinemia or CVID, at least 400 mg/kg/month. Because of the incidence of *Pneumocystis carinii* infections, patients with hyper-IgM syndromes are maintained on chronic antibiotic prophylaxis. Because liver disease due to cryptosporidia is common, especially in older patients, use of sterile water may be an added protective measure.

DEFECTS OF THE T-CELL SYSTEM

THYMIC HYPOPLASIA (DIGEORGE SYNDROME)

This is the most common of the chromosomal deletion syndromes, affecting males or females perhaps as many as 1:2000 to 1:4000 births. Thymic hypoplasia results from abnormal development of the third and fourth pharyngeal pouches. Hypoplasia of parathyroid or thyroid glands may also occur. Infants may present with hypocalcemic seizures in the first month of life. Associated anomalies include congenital heart disease (right-sided aortic arch or atrial or ventricular septal defects), cleft palate, small mouth, short philtrum, low-set ears, and hypertelorism. This syndrome is associated with an increased frequency of learning disabilities.

Complete DiGeorge syndrome is quite rare; these infants resemble patients with SCID, presenting with bacterial, viral, and parasitic infections or graft-versus-host disease (GVHD) if nonirradiated blood transfusions have been given. The most common form of DiGeorge syndrome (partial DiGeorge syndrome) arises when there is a milder

degree of hypoplasia of the thymus and parathyroid glands; residual thymic tissue may lie in the neck or high mediastinum. In these cases, T-cell numbers may be mildly depressed but increase with age. Cell-mediated immunity (T-cell responses to mitogens and antigens) may be absent, reduced, or normal. Serum immunoglobulin levels in partial DiGeorge syndrome are usually normal for age.

Approximately 90% of patients have a large deletion of about 30 genes in the region of chromosomal 22q11.2. This deletion may present with a variety of phenotypes including Shprintzen or velo-cardiofacial syndromes or isolated outflow tract defects of the heart (tetralogy of Fallot, truncus arteriosus, or interrupted aortic arch). Diagnosis of DiGeorge syndrome is usually made by in situ hybridization using probes to identify the responsible chromosomal region. Other deletions have also been associated with DiGeorge and velo-cardiofacial syndromes on chromosome 10p13; these genes are also unknown.

 Treatment

Infants with partial DiGeorge syndrome do not appear to require any specific treatment except as indicated for endocrinologic or cardiac defects. For the rare patient with complete DiGeorge syndrome, immune reconstitution been achieved by HLA-identical bone marrow transplantation or by thymic tissue transplantation in a few.

COMBINED DEFECTS

SEVERE COMBINED IMMUNE DEFICIENCY DISORDERS

Severe combined immune deficiency syndromes (SCIDs) are caused by a number of genetic mutations, any of which are essential in T and B immune and/or natural killer (NK) functions. The clinical phenotypes are similar in all cases. Male or female infants with SCID demonstrate a failure to thrive, and bacterial, viral, or parasitic infections affect the respiratory and gastrointestinal tracts or skin. Infections with opportunistic organisms, *Candida albicans, P. carinii,* atypical mycobacteria, varicella, and/or cytomegalovirus are common. Administration of bacille Calmette-Guérin (BCG) vaccine can lead to death. The thymus is absent, and lymph nodes and tonsils are tiny or absent. The lymphopenia is due to a profound lack of T cells (although maternal T cells may be present), but there are variable numbers of B and NK cells depending on the type of mutation that is present. Due to the lack of T-cell immunity, maternal T cells that have crossed the placenta, or T cells from nonirradiated blood or blood products, can lead to GVHD. Infants with SCID are almost always lymphopenic, have no proliferative responses to mitogens or antigens, and have low levels of serum immune globulins with absent antibody production.

 Treatment

The treatment of the SCID syndromes is transplantation of bone marrow or stem cells from HLA-identical donors. Other techniques include the use of haploidentical (usually parental) bone marrow or stem cells. Pretransplantation chemoablation and GVHD prophylaxis may not be required in all cases for successful engraftment. SCID is a fatal immune defect, and an early diagnosis and transplantation are essential.

Patients with SCID syndrome are perhaps the best possible candidates for gene therapy. Correction of the gene defect in a few lymphocyte precursors would be capable of generating high numbers of lymphocytes with a long life expectancy. Ex vivo gene transfer into autologous marrow hematopoietic cells has led to a full correction of X-linked SCID but leahemia in two patients.

Descriptions of Various Combined Defects

Some of the forms of SCID are described here and in Table 267–1.
X-LINKED RECESSIVE SEVERE COMBINED IMMUNODEFICIENCY DISEASE (XSCID).
About half of all cases of SCID are X-linked recessive in inheritance due to mutations of the common gamma chain (γ_c) of cytokine receptors, including IL-2, IL-4, IL-7, IL-9, IL-15, and IL-21; γ_c is encoded

on the X chromosome. These patients appear similar to those with other forms of SCID, with profound lymphopenia due to very low numbers of T and NK cells in the peripheral blood, and an elevated percentage of B cells. The shared γ_c chain increases the affinity of the receptor for these cytokines and enables the receptor to stimulate effective intracellular signaling; in its absence, multiple cytokine deficiencies coincide and lead to the profound immune deficiency state.

JANUS KINASE 3 (JAK3) DEFICIENCY. About 7% of SCID patients have a mutation in an intracytoplasmic kinase called Janus Kinase 3 (JAK3). These infants have an immunologic phenotype similar to that of patients with X-linked SCID, with elevated numbers of B cells and few if any T and NK cells. JAK3 is an essential signaling molecule associated with the common γ chain (γ_c); thus, a defect in this cytoplasmic kinase mimics the defect in the γ_c chain.

ADENOSINE DEAMINASE (ADA) DEFICIENCY. About 15% of infants with SCID have a mutation of the enzyme ADA. ADA deficiency results in the accumulation of toxic levels of adenosine, 2′-deoxyadenosine, and 2′-O-methyladenosine in lymphocytes, leading to T-cell death. Infants with ADA deficiency clinically have the same phenotype as other forms of SCID, but there also are often bone abnormalities resulting in rib cage abnormalities and chondro-osseous dysplasia. ADA-deficient patients have a profound lymphopenia (<500/mm³) with very low numbers of both T and B cells. Milder forms of this condition have been reported in a few adults, leading to T-cell defects, very low CD4 T-cell numbers, and hypogammaglobulinemia.

In addition to bone marrow or stem cell transplant, enzyme replacement therapy (with polyethylene glycol conjugated bovine adenosine deaminase) is available but less effective: it has not been used if bone marrow transplantation is possible. Gene therapy has been attempted but has thus far been marginally useful in the few cases in which it was tried.

RAG-1 OR RAG-2 DEFICIENCIES. Infants with mutations of recombinase activating genes RAG-1 or RAG-2, essential in the recombination of variable regions genes for both T- and B-cell receptors, lack both B and T lymphocytes but have NK cells in the peripheral blood. Mutations in RAG-1 or RAG-2 genes effectively prevent the formation of T- and B-cell antigen receptors. In some cases, mutations in the same genes have also been found in a partial form of SCID, Omenn's syndrome, in which some T- and B-cell development occurs but full immunity is not achieved.

SCID WITH RADIOSENSITIVITY. Another form of SCID, associated with increased cellular radiosensitivity, results from mutation of a gene encoding a protein involved in V(D)J recombination and DNA repair, Artemis.

ZAP-70 DEFECT. Stimulation of the T-cell antigen receptor results in tyrosine phosphorylation of a number of cellular substrates, one of which is the T-cell receptor-ζ chain. Mutations of the ζ chain–associated protein (Zap-70) result in a form of SCID in which there is a selective defect of T-cell signaling and very low numbers of CD8 T cells.

IL-7 RECEPTOR DEFICIENCY. The secretion of IL-7 from thymic stromal cells is critical for thymic development. Mutations of the IL-7 receptor α chain result in an SCID phenotype in which there are very few T cells and normal or elevated numbers of both B and NK cells.

CD45 SCID. The transmembrane protein tyrosine phosphatase CD45 is involved in the transduction of the T- and B-cell antigen receptor signal; mutations of CD45 also lead to SCID.

RETICULAR DYSGENESIS. One of the most rare and severe forms of SCID is reticular dysgenesis, the cause of which remains unknown. In this phenotype, there is a total lack of both lymphocytes and granulocytes in peripheral blood and bone marrow and lack of thymic development.

OTHER COMBINED IMMUNE DEFICIENCY DISORDERS (CIDs). In addition to the SCID syndromes, in which there is a severe lack of both T- and B-cell development, there are other less severe immune deficiencies sometimes called combined immune defects. Like in the SCID syndromes, these infants have recurrent or chronic sinopulmonary infections, failure to thrive, diarrhea, oral or cutaneous candidiasis, recurrent skin infections, bacterial sepsis, severe varicella or other viral infections, and an increased incidence of lymphomas and other cancers.

CID WITH PURINE NUCLEOSIDE PHOSPHORYLASE DEFICIENCY. The enzyme purine nucleoside phosphorylase (PNP) catalyzes the phosphorolytic cleavage of inosine to hypoxanthine. Similar to ADA deficiency, patients with PNP deficiency have an immune defect involving primarily T cells, also with severe hypouricemia and hypouricosuria. PNP-deficient patients are as lymphopenic as those with ADA deficiency, with

a marked deficiency of T cells but increased numbers of NK cells. T-cell function is low but not absent. Serum immunoglobulins levels are normal or elevated. PNP deficiency is often accompanied by a neurologic disorder with pyramidal signs, extensor plantar responses, and exaggerated reflexes or spastic diplegia. Deaths have resulted from generalized vaccinia and varicella infections. GVHD may develop if non-irradiated allogeneic blood is transfused. This condition is fatal, and bone marrow or stem cell transplantation has been used, although not with great success.

DEFECTIVE EXPRESSION OF MHC ANTIGENS. This defect is sometimes called bare lymphocyte syndrome due to the lack of MHC antigens on lymphocytes. There are three main forms: (1) class I MHC deficiency, (2) class II MHC deficiency, and (3) combined MHC class I and II deficiencies.

MHC Class I Antigen Deficiency. This condition is quite rare and not accompanied by pathologic manifestations during the first years of life; chronic lung disease (bronchiectasis, emphysema, and bronchial obstruction) develops in late childhood. Patients do not appear to be susceptible to systemic infections, but there often is involvement of the nasal sinuses leading to granulomatous changes and nasal polyps. There is a deficiency of CD8+ but not of CD4+ T cells. This defect is due to mutations of one of two genes (TAP1 and TAP2) within the MHC locus on chromosome 6 that encodes the protein TAP. TAP proteins are associated with the transport of peptides of digested antigens from the cytoplasm across the Golgi apparatus to the MHC class 1 antigens on the cell surface.

MHC Class II Antigen Deficiency. Infants with MHC class II deficiency present with diarrhea often due to cryptosporidiosis, as well as sepsis, candidiasis, bacterial pneumonia, and enteroviral or pneumocystis infections. Hallmarks of this disease are moderate lymphopenia, very low number of CD4+ T cells, and normal or elevated numbers of CD8+ T cells. The MHC class II antigens (HLA-DP, -DQ, and -DR) are absent on B cells and monocytes. Patients are hypogammaglobulinemic and antibody deficient. Lymphocyte proliferation to mitogens is preserved, but lymphocytes are anergic to antigen stimulation. The MHC genes are normal in this defect, and the lack of MHC class II is due to mutations of genes that coordinate the expression of MHC Class II molecules on the surface of antigen presenting cells. These molecules include a protein named RFX5, which binds to the MHC class II gene promoter region, a second protein, RFXAP, and a third, a novel MHC class II transactivator (CIITA).

IMMUNE DEFICIENCY WITH THROMBOCYTOPENIA AND ECZEMA (WISKOTT-ALDRICH SYNDROME) AND VARIANTS. Wiskott-Aldrich syndrome (WAS) is an X-linked recessive disease with the hallmarks of eczema, thrombocytopenic purpura, and susceptibility to bacterial and other infections. Bloody diarrhea is common during infancy. Platelets are small and function poorly. Atopic dermatitis and otitis media, pneumonia, or meningitis caused by encapsulated bacteria often develop during the first year of life. Autoimmune disorders occur in about 40% of patients. In a retrospective survey of 154 individuals, the average age at diagnosis was 21 months and the average age at death was 8 years. With adequate therapy, the prognosis for this disorder has improved. The major causes of death have been infections, uncontrolled bleeding, and Epstein-Barr virus (EBV)–induced lymphomas.

Serum immunoglobulins are variable in WAS; a low IgM, elevated IgA and IgE, and a normal or slightly reduced level of serum IgG are characteristic. Patients exhibit poor or no responses after immunization with polysaccharide (pneumoccocal) vaccines and absent or markedly diminished isohemagglutinin titers. Lymphopenia is common, and lymphocyte proliferation to mitogens is depressed.

The mutated gene on the X chromosome that codes for the Wiskott-Aldrich syndrome protein (WASP) is a cytoplasmic protein involved in actin polymerization. The actin cytoskeleton plays critical roles in cell morphologic changes following activation and during cell motility.

In addition to the classic forms of WAS, several mutational variants have been described with a different phenotype and not requiring the same treatment. The first variant is isolated X-linked thrombocytopenia, in which the essential finding is thrombocytopenia but with no immune deficiency. The second variant, X-linked neutropenia, is due to a mutation in the region of WASP encoding the conserved GTPase binding domain, resulting in constitutive activation of the WAS protein.

Corrections of platelet and immunologic abnormalities in patients with WAS can be achieved by HLA-identical sibling bone marrow transplantation, with less success for T-cell–depleted haploidentical stem cell transplantation. Splenectomy can improve platelet counts. Prophylactic antibiotics and IVIg are standard therapies in WAS.

ATAXIA-TELANGIECTASIA (AT). The hallmarks of this syndrome are progressive cerebellar ataxia, occular and cutaneous telangiectasias, and chronic sinopulmonary disease. Ataxia usually becomes evident before the age of 3 and telangiectasias usually appear by age 6. Chronic sinopulmonary infections are very common. Patients with AT have a strong predisposition to develop a malignancy. In general, lymphomas in AT patients tend to be of B-cell origin (B-CLL), whereas the leukemias tend to be of the T-CLL type. The function of the mutated gene (*ATM*) is not entirely understood; however, it is a DNA-dependent protein kinase involved in signal transduction, telomere maintenance, and initiation of p53-dependent apoptosis.

Serum IgG2 or IgA levels are diminished or absent in 80% and 60% of patients, respectively. IgA and/or IgE levels can be diminished, and IgM levels are diminished or normal. Specific antibody levels may be decreased or normal. Peripheral lymphopenia, as well as decreased cellular immunity, is common. The severity of sinopulmonary infections is not always correlated with the degree of immunodeficiency. The thymus is hypoplastic. An elevated serum alpha-fetoprotein level is found in most patients. No satisfactory treatment has been found, although immune globulin is usually given to those with antibody defects. Cells from patients and heterozygous carriers demonstrate increased sensitivity to ionizing radiation, defective DNA repair, and frequent chromosomal abnormalities. Radiation is to be avoided.

CARTILAGE HAIR HYPOPLASIA (CHH). This autosomal recessive condition consists of short-limbed dwarfism, thin and fine-caliber hair, and frequent and severe infections. Patients may have incomplete extension at the elbows, an anterolateral chest deformity (Harrison grooves), genu varum, and excessively long fibula distally relative to the tibia. Severe or fatal varicella infections, generalized vaccinia, and vaccine-associated poliomyelitis have occurred. Predisposition to several cancers has been reported. Variable immune deficiency may be present, including defective antibody-mediated immunity, defective cellular immunity, or SCID. The defect is due to mutations of an endoribonuclease with at least two functions: cleavage of RNA in mitochondrial DNA synthesis and nucleolar cleaving of pre-rRNA. Bone marrow transplantation results in immunologic reconstitution in some CHH patients with the SCID phenotype. Some patients with the milder types of immune deficiency have lived to adulthood with no significant infections.

DISEASES OF CYTOLYTIC PATHWAYS

X-LINKED LYMPHOPROLIFERATIVE DISEASE. X-linked lymphoproliferative disease (XLP, or Duncan disease) is characterized by extreme sensitivity to EBV infections, resulting in severe or fatal infectious mononucleosis, hypogammaglobulinemia, and/or malignant lymphoma. In one large study, 50% of patients had developed fatal infectious mononucleosis at an average age of 2.5 years, 33% developed hypogammaglobulinemia, and another 25% developed malignant lymphoma. The malignant lymphomas were most often of Burkitt type and involved the ileocecal region. In patients surviving the primary infection, multiple cellular immune defects involving T, B, and NK cells develop. There has been 100% mortality by the age of 40.

The defective gene in XLP encodes a protein called SAP (SLAM-associated protein) that normally acts as a negative regulator of SLAM (signaling lymphocyte activation molecule), a protein that is present on the surfaces of activated T and B cells. SLAM mediates expansion of activated T cells during immune responses, and mutations in SAP result in uncontrolled lymphocyte activation. Males with this defect have a marked impairment in production of antibodies to the EBV nuclear antigen (EBNA), although antibody titers to the viral capsid antigen have ranged from zero to markedly elevated. A few patients with XLP transplanted with HLA-identical related or an unrelated bone marrow have had restored immunity, including normal immune response to EBV.

HEMOPHAGOCYTIC LYMPHOHISTIOCYTOSIS. This is a rare autosomal disorder with a striking clinical picture of hepatomegaly, splenomegaly, jaundice, variable neurologic signs, lymphadenopathy, anemia, leukopenia, and thrombocytopenia. Overproduction of IFN-γ and TNF-α by T lymphocytes and macrophages, with reduced T-cell and NK-cell cytotoxicity, all occur. Hemophagocytosis appears in bone marrow, lymph nodes, spleen, liver, and central nervous system, as well as a nonmalignant lymphohistiocytic infiltration of the reticuloendothelial system. In 20 to 40% of patients, there is a mutation in perforin, one of the major proteins of cytolytic granules. Acute treatment may include etoposide and cortical steroids alone or in combination with cyclosporin. Allogeneic bone marrow transplantation has been successful.

CHEDIAK-HIGASHI SYNDROME (CHS). Decreased pigmentation of hair and eyes resulting in partial albinism, photophobia, and nystagmus characterizes this syndrome. The phenotype includes neutropenia, abnormal susceptibility to infection, and malignant lymphoma. From 85 to 90% of CHS patients develop a lymphoproliferative syndrome, the "accelerated phase" of the disorder, characterized by generalized lymphohistiocytic infiltrates, fever, jaundice, hepatosplenomegaly, lymphadenopathy, pancytopenia, and bleeding. Chediak-Higashi syndrome is caused by mutations in the lysosomal trafficking regulator gene *LYST*. Bone marrow transplantation is curative.

GRISCELLI SYNDROME. This is a rare autosomal recessive disorder that results in pigmentary dilution of the skin and hair, the presence of silvery hair with large clumps of pigment in hair shafts, and an accumulation of melanosomes in melanocytes. Patients develop uncontrolled T lymphocyte and macrophage activation syndrome, which can lead to death in the absence of bone marrow transplantation. This disease is caused by mutations in the gene encoding myosin Va, a member of an unconventional myosin family.

INTERFERON-γ–ASSOCIATED IMMUNE DEFICIENCIES

Disseminated BCG and low-grade mycobacterial infections occur in patients with severe T-cell defects (SCID) but also are seen in certain cytokine receptor defects that eliminate the use of IFN-γ. Disseminated infections due to salmonella, another group of reduced-virulence intracellular bacteria, also occur in approximately half of these cases, but other viral microorganisms do not appear to cause clinical disease. These mutations include the gene that encodes the IFN-γ receptor (IFN-γR1) and the β1 chain of the IL-12 receptor (IL-12Rβ1). IL-12 is a potent inducer of IFN-γ production by T and NK cells. The susceptibility of these patients to mycobacterial infections illustrates the essential role of IFN-γ in the control of mycobacteria.

DISEASES RESULTING FROM ABNORMAL APOPTOSIS

AUTOIMMUNE LYMPHOPROLIFERATIVE SYNDROME (ALPS). This disorder encompasses autoimmune features with marked and chronic lymphadenopathy and splenomegaly due to defective lymphoid apoptosis, resulting from mutations in either the *FAS* gene (CD95) or mutations in the FAS ligand (*FASL*) gene (CD95L). A third form, called type II ALPS, is caused by mutation in the caspase-10 gene, a member of the apoptosis cascade. The average age of ALPS onset is 5 years, with prominent cervical lymphadenopathy and enlarged spleen being almost universal. Autoimmune hemolytic anemia and autoimmune thrombocytopenia are very common; splenectomy has often been performed. Autoimmune manifestations of the disease, such as hemolytic anemia and thrombocytopenia, may persist into adolescence. B- and T-cell lymphomas may appear in some with this syndrome. However, FAS mutations are compatible with long-term survival, and the intermittent lymphadenopathy may diminish over time.

INTERLEUKIN-2 RECEPTOR α CHAIN (IL-2Rα, CD25). This defect resulted from a mutation in the IL-2 receptor α chain (CD25), a subunit of the high-affinity receptor for IL-2, resulting in opportunistic infections. Hepatosplenomegaly and lymphocytic infiltration of lung, liver, gut, and bone also occurred, presumably due to lack of lymphocyte apoptosis. Allogeneic bone marrow transplant resulted in recovery of immune functions.

PHAGOCYTIC DEFECTS

Defects of neutrophils are described in detail in Chapter 163. Of the most clinical significance are the neutropenias, followed by chronic granulomatous disease.

OTHER IMMUNE DEFICIENCIES

HYPERIMMUNOGLOBULINEMIA E SYNDROME (HIE). This syndrome is a well described but poorly understood defect that leads to recurrent staphylococcal abscesses and markedly elevated serum IgE concentrations. Patients develop severe staphylococcal abscesses predominantly involving the skin and lungs. Pulmonary involvement is very common and often results in pneumatocoeles. The syndrome can sometimes be confused with severe atopic dermatitis, but HIE has a much earlier onset and almost always includes lung involvement. Patients with HIE may develop cutaneous (and nail) candidal infections, which is usually not a feature of atopy. Other clinical features of HIE include hyperextensible joints, scoliosis, easy breakage of bones, osteoporosis, midline anomalies, craniosynostosis, delayed shedding of primary teeth due to a lack of root resorption, unusual facies with a broad nasal bridge, rough facial skin, and a tubular and prominent nose. Most cases are sporadic, but an autosomal-dominant form of inheritance with variable expressivity has been described. Laboratory features include high levels of serum IgE (<2000, but perhaps reducing with age), normal levels of IgG, IgA, and IgM, eosinophilia, and reduced anamnestic antibody responses to some vaccine antigens. The nature of this disorder remains unknown. The only therapy is prophylactic therapeutic doses of a penicillinase-resistant antibiotic and treatment of other infections as appropriate.

MUCOCUTANEOUS CANDIDIASIS, AND AUTOIMMUNE POLYENDOCRINOPATHY SYNDROME WITH CANDIDIASIS (APCED).
This is an autosomal recessive or sporadic disorder in which nail and mucosal candidiasis appear. In almost all cases, the candidal infections do not become systemic and there are no other significant infections. A closely related disease is autoimmune polyglandular syndrome, also an autosomal-recessive disorder caused by mutation in the "autoimmune regulator" (AIRE) gene, characterized by Addison's disease and/or hypoparathyroidism or other autoimmune disorders. Candidiasis usually appears in childhood, and the primary endocrine diseases develop in the first 20 years of life; other accompanying diseases may not appear until at least the fifth decade.

The primary biochemical defect in APCED is unknown, but the gene codes for a novel nuclear protein possibly involved in transcriptional regulation. The treatment of mucocutaneous candidiasis is chronic oral antifungal agents. Treatments of the autoimmune components are those normally appropriate.

X-LINKED IMMUNE ENDOCRINOPATHY (IPEX).
This is an X-linked syndrome including intractable diarrhea, eczema, diabetes mellitus, or thyroid autoimmunity. Death in infancy or early childhood has been noted, but some males have survived for long periods. The disease is named X-linked polyendocrinopathy, immune dysfunction, and diarrhea (IPEX.) The mutation affects a gene (MP3 or FOXP3) of still unclear function. Supportive therapy includes total parenteral nutrition, insulin if needed, and blood transfusions as required. Prolonged immunosuppressive therapy with steroids and cyclosporin has been used with some benefit. Allogeneic bone marrow transplantation from an HLA-identical family member has been successful.

COMPLEMENT DEFICIENCIES

In addition to congenital or hereditary disorders of lymphoid cells, genetically determined deficiencies have been described for all of the components of complement. Undue susceptibility to infection is a characteristic of deficiencies of C2, C3, C5, C6, and C7. These are described in detail in Chapter 45. The most prevalent of the complement defects involves the C1 inhibitor, leading to hereditary angioedema.

TESTS USED TO INVESTIGATE IMMUNE FUNCTIONS

The number of patients suspected of having primary immune deficiency exceeds the actual incidences of these diseases. Thus, it is important that the tests selected for immunologic assessment be pertinent to the patient, informative, and cost-effective and performed in appropriate stages. The clinical history and the age of the patient should guide the laboratory evaluation. For sick infants with many signs of severe compromise (opportunistic infections, severe failure to thrive), an evaluation of the cellular immune system needs to be performed as soon as possible. The most informative initial test is the complete blood cell count because most infants with SCID and those with severe DiGeorge syndrome will have lymphopenia. A severe T-cell defect would be very unlikely if the absolute lymphocyte count is normal. A normal platelet count excludes the diagnosis of Wiskott-Aldrich syndrome, and a normal absolute neutrophil count excludes the neutropenias. The evaluation of the immune system is best approached in stages, performing the basic screening tests first, and turning to more complex testing as indicated. An overview of this approach is given in Table 267–4.

CLINICAL HISTORY AND INITIAL PROCEDURES.
Aside from the initial history and physical examination (including height and weight), the first immune test is the complete blood cell count with differential. The first visit should also include obtaining all previous medical records, pathology reports or slides, and results of previous cultures and X-rays. Immune deficiency, especially if it has persisted for some time, will often affect the lung so pulmonary function should be tested, even if the chest radiograph is normal.

SERUM IMMUNOGLOBULINS AND ANTIBODY PRODUCTION.
Because antibody deficiency diseases are more common than other immune defects, an emphasis should be placed on the investigation of immunoglobulins and antibody production, especially for older children and adults. The relevant test is quantification of serum IgG, IgA, and IgM levels as related to age-matched controls. Serum protein electrophoresis or immunoelectrophoresis is not useful for this purpose. Serum IgG subclasses may add information, but tests of specific antibody production is essential; assessment of antibody responses to both protein and polysaccharide antigens is performed. This is particularly important if there is a consideration of treatment with immunoglobulin; if immunoglobulin is given before this is done, it will be difficult to verify the need for treatment, aside from stopping and reassessing antibody production after 5 or more months have elapsed. Determination of antibody titers to diphtheria/tetanus/pertussis (DPT), DT, or dT immunization before and after immunization (3 to 4 weeks) are used to determine IgG antibody responses to protein antigens. Because most patients have already received primary DPT immunizations, this is a measure of anamnestic antibody responses. Immunization with live viral vaccines is contraindicated in patients with suspected immune disorders; this includes measles, mumps, rubella, all attenuated polio, BCG, and chickenpox vaccines. To measure antibody responses to polysaccharide antigens using a non–protein-conjugated pneumococcal vaccine, antibody titers are

Table 267–4 • LABORATORY TESTS FOR IMMUNODEFICIENCY

	FIRST LEVEL	SECOND LEVEL
Antibody/ immunoglobulin (Ig) deficiency	Quantitative immunoglobulins: IgG, IgA, and IgM Preexisting antibodies to prior immunizations: tetanus, diphtheria, rubella, *Haemophilus influenzae*, and polio Isohemagglutinins (IgG subclass levels)	IgE level, B-cell enumeration Antibody response to pneumococcal polysaccharide vaccination
T-cell or cellular immunodeficiency	Total lymphocyte count Delayed-type hypersensitivity skin tests	T-cell and subpopulation enumeration Proliferative responses to mitogens, antigens, allogeneic cells Acquisition of activation molecules; *in situ* hybridization for chromosome 22 defect
Phagocytic	White blood cell count and morphology IgE level	Nitroblue tetrazolium reduction; or oxidative burst by flow cytometer
Complement	CH_{50} C3 and C4 levels	Individual complement levels

determined before and 3 to 4 weeks postimmunization. Antibody responses to carbohydrate antigens are typically poor in children younger than 2 years old and may be depressed up to 5 years of age. Isohemagglutinins (anti-A or anti-B blood group substance) can be used as another test of antibody production. These antibodies develop in subjects over the age of 2 and are usually found in a titer of 1:16 or greater.

DELAYED-TYPE HYPERSENSITIVITY. Commonly used to assess T-cell function, delayed-type hypersensitivity skin tests have been widely used in general screening. Although these tests are not always easy to interpret, they may yield some information. In adults, about 85% will have one or more positive reactions, but such tests are not useful for infants under the age of 2. A positive test to recall antigens can eliminate the presence of a more severe T-cell defect.

QUANTIFICATION OF T, B, AND NK CELLS. Analysis of lymphocyte phenotypes using monoclonal antibodies and flow cytometry identifies T and B cells, subpopulations of T cells, NK cells, and monocytes/macrophages, in comparison to the laboratory-established normal controls of similar age.

T-CELL FUNCTIONAL ASSESSMENT. The functional capability of T cells is determined by testing in vitro proliferative responses to mitogens, antigens, or allogeneic cells; the cells are transformed into large, blast-like cells with synthesis of DNA and eventual cell division that is measured by various means. Mitogens are plant extracts that stimulate both CD4 and CD8 positive T cells to divide; specific antigens, tetanus, diphtheria, and *Candida* are commonly used to study specific T-cell responses. Sufficient exposure to the antigen is required for a positive response; proliferation to antigenic stimuli is uncommon in infant during the first year of life.

COMPLEMENT DEFICIENCY ASSESSMENT. Although deficiencies of complement proteins are uncommonly found, they may lead to recurrent bacterial infections. Screening tests include total hemolytic complement (called CH50) and serum levels of C3 and C4. It is important that the serum or plasma reach the laboratory in optimum condition for testing.

POLYMORPHONUCLEAR LEUKOCYTE ANALYSES. Aside from neutropenia, a major polymorphonuclear leukocyte disorder is chronic granulomatous disease (CGD). In the presence of a suggestive history, this diagnosis should be considered on the first clinic visit. The nitroblue tetrazolium test (NBT) is the classic laboratory method for screening for CGD, but it has been replaced in many laboratories by a flow cytometer equivalent that is better suited to the study of clinical samples.

FUTURE DIRECTIONS

In the past 10 years, the genetic and molecular bases of many of the primary immune deficiency disorders have been elucidated, and a growing number of new syndromes have been identified. These remarkable advances have meant that diagnoses can be made much more accurately, and novel and targeted treatments designed. The recent and ongoing analyses of these "experiments of nature" have also opened up new fields of investigation for the basic immunologist, and have provided significant insights into a number of organ-based immune-mediated diseases. In the coming decade, it is likely that additional immune defects with a genetic origin will be described, and that some of the complex immune deficiency diseases that have so far resisted clarification will be elucidated.

SUGGESTED READINGS

Buckley RH: Advances in immunology: Primary immunodeficiency diseases due to defects in lymphocytes. N Engl J Med 2000;343:1313–1324. *A comprehensive review.*
Cunningham-Rundles C, Bodian C: Common variable immunodeficiency: Clinical and immunological features of 248 patients. Clin Immunol 1999;92:34–48. *Mortality in 248 patients was related to lower IgG levels, fewer peripheral B cells, and poorer T-cell responses.*
Fischer A: Primary immunodeficiency diseases: An experimental model for molecular medicine. Lancet 2001;357:1863–1869. *Of about 100 primary immunodeficiency diseases, about 75% can be reliably diagnosed with molecular probes.*
Hammarstrom L, Vorechovsky I, Webster D: Selective IgA deficiency (SIgAD) and common variable immunodeficiency (CVID). Clin Exp Immunol 2000;120:225–231. *A detailed review.*

268 ALLERGIC RHINOSINUSITIS

Richard D. deShazo

Definition

Allergic rhinitis is a symptom complex characterized by paroxysms of sneezing; itching of the eyes, nose, and palate; rhinorrhea; and nasal obstruction. It is often associated with postnasal drip, cough, irritability, and fatigue. Symptoms develop when persons inhale airborne antigens (allergens) to which they have previously been exposed and have made immunoglobulin E (IgE) antibodies. These IgE antibodies bind to IgE receptors on mast cells in the respiratory mucosa and to basophils in the peripheral blood. When IgE molecules on their surface are bridged by allergen, mast cells release preformed and granule-associated chemical mediators. They also generate other mediators and cytokines that lead to nasal inflammation and, with continued allergen exposure, chronic symptoms.

Epidemiology

Allergic rhinitis is common and accounts for at least 2.5% of all physician visits, 2 million lost school days per year, 6 million lost work days, and 28 million restricted work days per year. Allergic rhinitis results in the expenditure of $2.4 billion on prescription and over-the-counter medications for allergy and $1.1 billion in physician billings, with a total indirect and direct cost of $7 billion per year. Between 10 and 20% of the U.S. population is affected, and the prevalence in urban areas is increasing. The prevalence is lowest in children younger than 5 years, rises to a peak in early adulthood (as high as 24% in the United States), and declines thereafter. The 4-year remission rate is reported to be 10% in males and 5% in females.

Clinical Manifestations

The swollen nasal mucosa of patients with acute allergic rhinitis is pale and blue but becomes erythematous and indurated with chronic allergen exposure. Clear rhinorrhea may be visible anteriorly or, with nasal obstruction, dripping down a cobblestone-appearing posterior pharynx. Giemsa or Hansel stains of these nasal secretions show cell populations to be predominantly eosinophils. A transverse nasal crease, a high arched palate, mouth breathing, and dental malocclusion are common, especially in children. Venous dilation of the subcutaneous skin beneath the eyes may produce "allergic shiners." Purulent rhinitis, purulent postnasal drip, and pain in a maxillary tooth are independent predictors of complicating sinusitis.

Complications and Associations

Allergic nasal inflammation associated with allergic rhinitis can cause obstruction of the sinus osteomeatal complex and lead to sinusitis (Fig. 268–1). As much as 30% of acute maxillary and 78% of chronic sinusitis results from this mechanism. Allergic rhinitis is also strongly associated with secretory otitis media, sleep disorders, and anosmia. Allergic rhinitis often occurs concomitantly with other common allergic conditions, including allergic conjunctivitis, allergic asthma, and atopic dermatitis (eczema). Twenty-eight to 50% of patients with asthma and up to 30% with eczema have allergic rhinitis. These conditions have been termed *atopic diseases*, and patients who have them are often called *atopic*.

Differential Diagnosis

Syndromes of rhinitis may be divided into allergic, infectious, perennial nonallergic, and miscellaneous categories (Table 268–1). Allergic rhinitis should be differentiated from other forms of rhinitis because the approach to management is different. Episodic exposure to inhaled allergens such as cat salivary proteins, horse dander, murine urinary proteins, pollen, or house dust mite feces may provoke acute allergic symptoms that are easily diagnosed as *acute allergic rhinitis*. If allergen exposure is seasonal, for instance, tree and grass pollen in

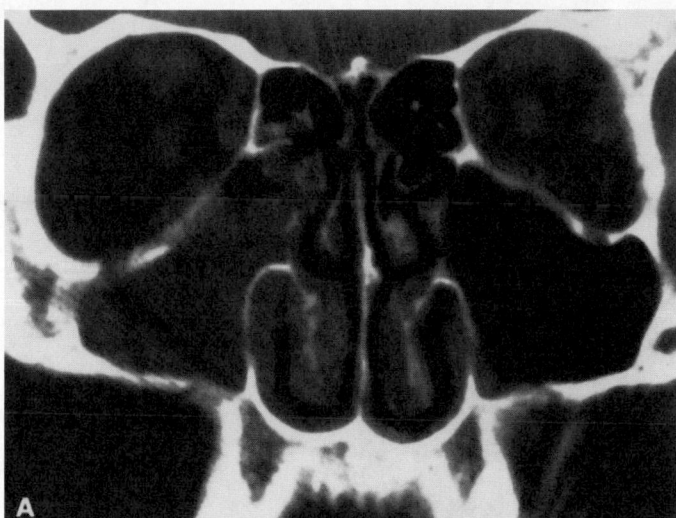

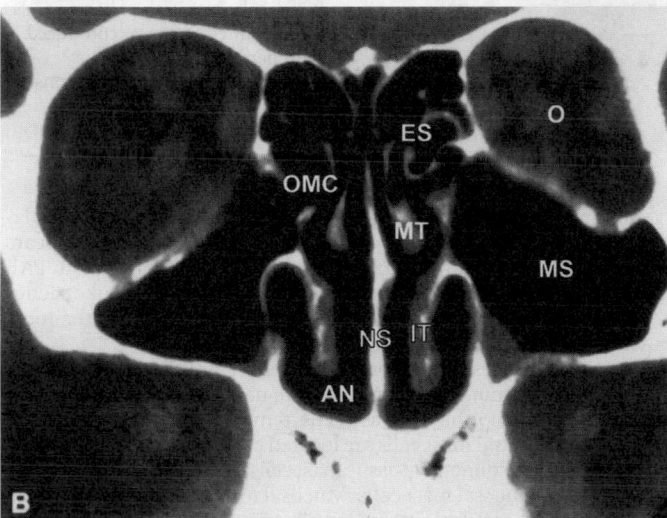

FIGURE 268–1 • Coronal computed tomography of a patient with allergic rhinosinusitis. *A,* There is opacification of the right maxillary sinus (MS) and obstruction of the right osteomeatal complex (OMC) from generalized mucosal hypertrophy associated with allergic inflammation. *B,* After 6 weeks of topical nasal corticosteroids and oral antihistamines, there is nearly complete resolution of the OMC obstruction. AN = anterior nares; ES = ethmoid sinus; IT = inferior turbinate; MT = middle turbinate; NS = nasal septum; O = orbit. (Modified from Orlandi RR, Kennedy DK: Am J Med Sci 1998;316:29–38.)

Table 268–1 • CLASSIFICATION OF RHINITIS

ALLERGIC
Acute
Seasonal
Perennial
Occupational

INFECTIOUS
Acute: Viral, bacterial
Chronic:
    Specific: Bacterial, fungal
    Nonspecific: Associated with immune deficiency (antibody deficiency, cystic fibrosis, ciliary abnormalities)

PERENNIAL NONALLERGIC
Idiopathic (vasomotor rhinitis)
Nonallergic rhinitis with eosinophilia syndrome (NARES)

MISCELLANEOUS FORMS
Hormonal: Pregnancy, hypothyroidism, etc.
Drug induced: Associated with aspirin sensitivity, rhinitis medicamentosa (vasoconstrictor nose sprays), antihypertensives, etc.
Food associated: Gustatory, immunoglobulin E mediated, preservative induced
Atrophic rhinitis (*Klebsiella ozaenae*)
Mechanical: Hypertrophied turbinates, deviated nasal septum, foreign body, nasal polyps
Granulomatous: Wegener's granulomatosis, sarcoidosis, midline granuloma

the spring (rose fever) or ragweed pollen exposure in the fall (hay fever), symptoms are predictable and reproducible and thus *seasonal allergic rhinitis* may be diagnosed by the history (Fig. 268–2). When allergen exposure is chronic, *perennial allergic rhinitis* may result. This form is common in subtropical regions with long pollinating seasons and ever-present mold and dust mite allergens and with occupational allergen exposure. Perennial allergic rhinitis may be difficult to distinguish from nonallergic forms and may require certain testing (discussed later) for accurate diagnosis. Of all patients with rhinitis, 11% have seasonal symptoms, with 78% of these patients having an apparent allergic cause. Thirty-three per cent of patients with rhinitis have perennial symptoms with a seasonal exacerbation, and 68% of these patients have a probable allergic cause. Fifty-six per cent of patients with rhinitis have perennial symptoms alone, but only about 50% of them have symptoms that can be attributed to allergens. Most patients with allergic rhinitis have allergic symptom triggers, eosinophil-rich nasal secretions, allergen-specific IgE to inhalant allergens, and a family history of allergic disease.

Nasal eosinophilia is not diagnostic for allergic rhinitis because nasal eosinophilia occurs in the *nonallergic rhinitis with nasal eosinophilia syndrome* (NARES). NARES occurs in as many as 15% of patients with rhinitis and is characterized by perennial symptoms, an

older average age than that of patients with allergic rhinitis (39 versus 25 years), and milder symptoms of nasal itching and sneezing. The clear nasal secretions contain more than 25% eosinophils, but the role of eosinophils in the disorder is unclear. Fifty per cent of patients with NARES have sinusitis, 33% have nasal polyps, and 14% have asthma. IgE to inhalant allergens is usually absent. Another frequent form of perennial nonallergic rhinitis is commonly called vasomotor rhinitis. Patients with this disorder complain predominantly of chronic nasal congestion intensified by rapid changes in temperature and relative humidity, odors, or alcohol. Several lines of evidence suggest that they have nasal autonomic nervous system dysfunction. For instance, they have abnormal nasal responses to temperature stimuli applied to the skin and excess nasal sensitivity to topically applied acetylcholine congeners. They have little nasal itching or sneezing, but headaches, anosmia, and sinusitis are common. A family history of allergy or allergic symptom triggers is uncommon. Positive immediate hypersensitivity skin tests to inhalant allergens and nasal eosinophilia are unusual. *Atrophic rhinitis* is a syndrome of progressive atrophy of the nasal mucosa in elderly patients, who report chronic nasal congestion and constantly perceive a bad odor. It also occurs after chronic nasal inflammation such as that seen with sarcoidosis or after multiple sinus surgeries. *Rhinitis medicamentosa* is a complication of chronic use of vasoconstrictor nasal sprays or intranasal cocaine abuse. Chronic nasal obstruction and nasal inflammation develop and are manifest as beefy red nasal membranes on physical examination. Rhinitis of pregnancy and rhinitis associated with birth control pills or hypothyroidism reflect nasal obstruction that occurs on a *hormonal basis*. Nasal obstruction may also be a side effect of antihypertensive drugs. Unilateral rhinitis or nasal polyps are uncommon in uncomplicated allergic rhinitis. *Unilateral rhinitis* suggests the possibility of nasal obstruction by a foreign body, tumor, or polyp. The presence of nasal polyps suggests chronic bacterial sinusitis, allergic fungal sinusitis, aspirin hypersensitivity, cystic fibrosis, or immobile cilia syndrome.

Mechanisms of Allergic Reactions

The expression of allergic diseases reflects an autosomal dominant pattern of inheritance with incomplete penetrance. This inheritance pattern is manifest as a propensity to respond to inhalant allergen exposure by producing high levels of allergen-specific IgE. The IgE response appears to be controlled by immune response genes located within the major histocompatibility complex (MHC) on chromosome 6. The immunologic mechanisms for atopy have been studied in murine models and in humans and appear to center on the expression of a

Diseases of Allergy and Clinical Immunology

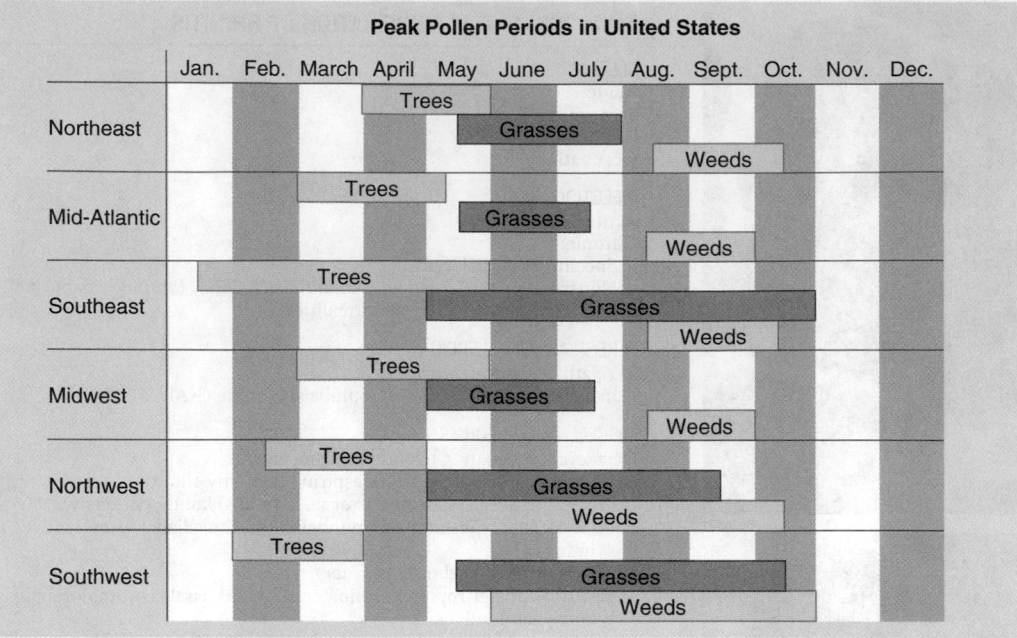

FIGURE 268–2 • Peak pollen periods in the United States. (Reproduced with permission from Fisons Pharmaceuticals. © 1989, Fisons Corporation.)

repertoire of responses associated with the Th2 type of T helper lymphocyte, which is summarized in the following.

PRODUCTION OF IMMUNOGLOBULIN E. Sensitization to allergen is necessary to elicit an IgE response (Fig. 268–3). After inhalation, the allergen must first be internalized by antigen-presenting cells, which include macrophages, dendritic cells, activated T lymphocytes, and B lymphocytes. After allergen processing, peptide fragments of the allergen are presented with class II (MHC) molecules of host antigen-presenting cells to CD4+ T lymphocytes. These lymphocytes have receptors specific for the particular MHC-peptide complex. This interaction results in the release of cytokines by the CD4+ cell.

T helper lymphocytes (CD4+) appear to be of two classes: Th1 and Th2. If the CD4+ cells that recognize the allergen are of the Th2 class, a specific repertoire of mediators is released, including interleukin-4 (IL-4), IL-5, and IL-9. Other cytokines, including IL-2, IL-3, IL-10, IL-13, and granulocyte-macrophage colony-stimulating factor (GM-CSF), are also released in the process of antigen recognition but are not specific to activation of the Th2 class. IL-4, IL-5, and IL-6 are cytokines involved in B-cell proliferation and differentiation. Activated B lymphocytes, having bound allergen by their allergen-specific IgM variable-region binding sites, are stimulated by these cytokines to proliferate and secrete IgM. IL-4, IL-6, IL-10, and IL-13 from Th2 cells promote B-cell isotype switching to IgE antibody synthesis. Thus, atopy appears to be the result of a predisposition toward Th2-type responses, which result in the formation of large quantities of allergen-specific IgE.

BINDING TO MAST CELLS AND EOSINOPHILS. After IgE antibodies specific for a certain allergen are synthesized and secreted, they bind to mast cells and basophils. When allergen is inhaled into the nose, the allergen or a hapten-allergen complex cross-links these allergen-specific cell-bound IgE antibodies on the mast cell surface, whereupon rapid degranulation and mediator release occur.

Mast cell mediators are either preformed, associated with granules, formed during degranulation, or generated after transcription (Fig. 268–4). The most important preformed mediator is histamine, which reproduces all of the symptoms of acute allergic rhinitis when sprayed nasally into normal volunteers. Histamine causes mucus secretion, vasodilation leading to nasal congestion, increased vascular permeability leading to tissue edema, and sneezing through stimulation of sensory nerve fibers. The cross-linking of IgE antibody on mast cells activates phospholipase A_2 and releases arachidonic acid from the A_2 position of cell membrane phospholipids. Mast cells then metabolize arachidonic acid, either by the cyclooxygenase pathway to form prostaglandin and thromboxane mediators or by the lipoxygenase pathway to form leukotrienes. Prostaglandin D_2 (PGD_2); the sulfidopeptide leukotrienes LTC_4, LTD_4, and LTE_4 (slow reacting substance of anaphylaxis); platelet-activating factor (PAF); and bradykinin

(generated by the action of tryptase) are formed during degranulation. PGD_2 is synthesized by mast cells but not basophils and appears to be more potent than histamine in causing nasal congestion. PAF is a potent chemotactic factor, and the sulfidopeptide leukotrienes and bradykinins are vasoactive. One leukotriene, LTB_4, is the most potent chemotactic factor in humans.

Mast cells are present in concentrations of $7000/mm^3$ in the normal nasal submucosa but only $50/mm^3$ in the nasal epithelium. The total number of nasal epithelial mast cells remains constant during the allergy season. Nasal mast cells are located predominantly in the nasal lamina propria as connective tissue mast cells, although 15% are epithelial and called mucosal mast cells. Mucosal mast cells express tryptase without chymase and proliferate in allergic rhinitis under the influence of Th2 cytokines. The superficial nasal epithelium in patients with allergic rhinitis has 50-fold more basophilic cells (mast cells and basophils) per specimen than epithelium from nonallergic subjects. Increased concentrations of mast cells are found near postcapillary venules, where they increase vascular permeability; near sensory nerves, where they initiate the sneeze reflex; and near glands, where they facilitate secretion.

When allergic reactions begin, mast cells amplify them by releasing not only vasoactive agents but also cytokines, including GM-CSF, tumor necrosis factor α (TNF-α), transforming growth factor β, IL-1 to IL-6, and IL-13. These cytokines further promote IgE production, mast cell growth, and eosinophil growth, chemotaxis, and survival. For instance, IL-5, TNF-α, and IL-1 promote eosinophil movement by increasing their expression of adhesion receptors on endothelium. In turn, eosinophils secrete IL-1, which favors Th2 cell proliferation, and the mast cell growth factor IL-3. Eosinophils release oxygen radicals and proteins that are toxic to the nasal epithelium, including eosinophil major basic protein.

Mechanisms of Nasal Allergic Reactions

ANATOMY AND PHYSIOLOGY OF THE NOSE. Under normal conditions, the nose accounts for nearly 50% of the resistance to airflow in the airway. It is lined by pseudostratified epithelium resting on a basement membrane that separates it from deeper submucosal layers. The submucosa contains mucous, seromucous, and serous glands. The small arteries, arterioles, and arteriovenous anastomoses determine regional blood flow. Capacitance vessels consisting of veins and cavernous sinusoids determine nasal patency. The cavernous sinusoids lie beneath the capillaries and venules, are most dense in the inferior and middle turbinates, and contain smooth muscle cells controlled by the sympathetic nervous system. Withdrawal of sympathetic tone or, to a lesser degree, cholinergic stimulation causes this sinusoidal erectile tissue to become engorged. Cholinergic stimulation causes arterial

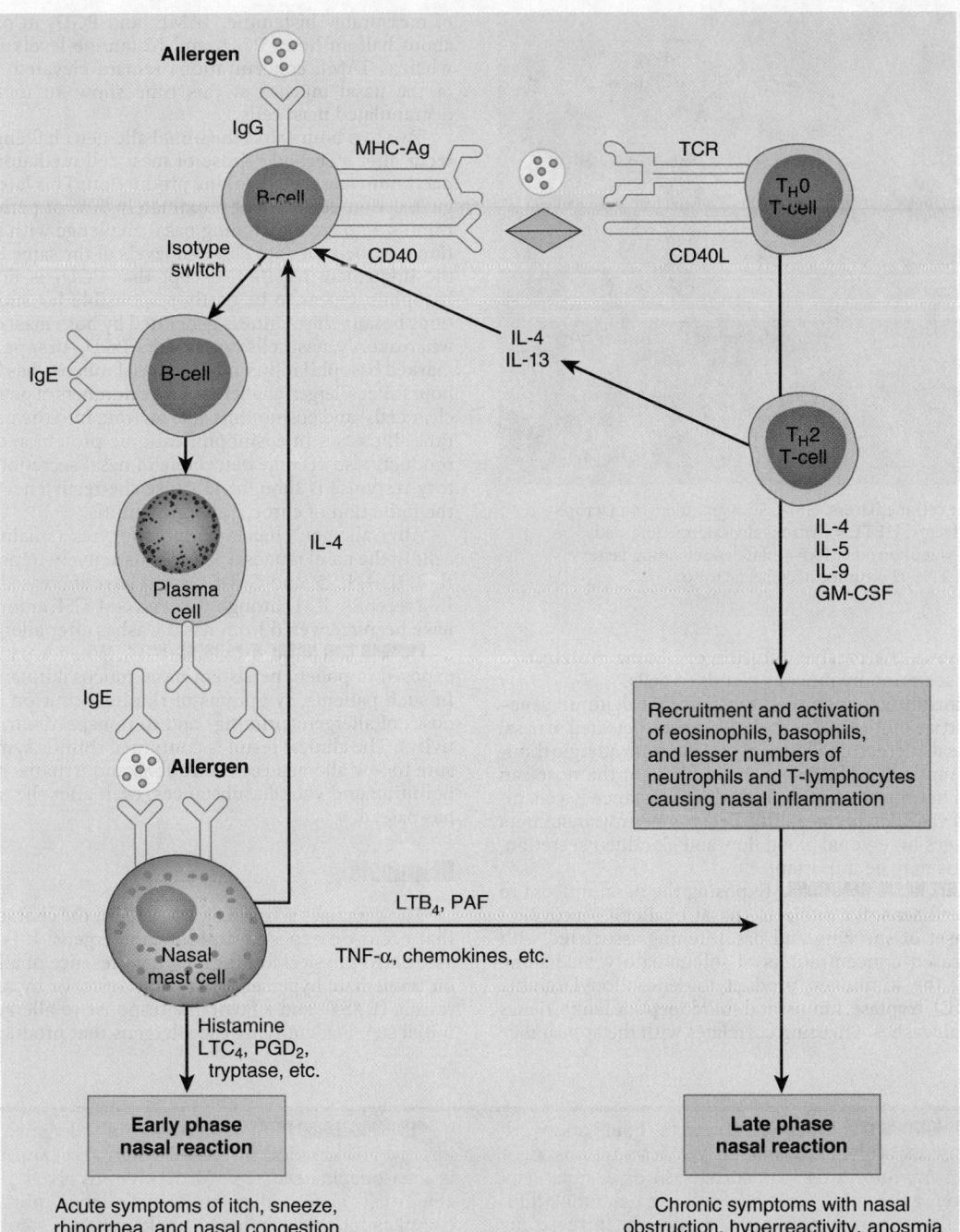

FIGURE 268–3 • Pathophysiology of allergic rhinitis. Allergen is presented to Th2 helper T lymphocytes by antigen-presenting cells (such as macrophages or B lymphocytes) in the context of major histocompatibility complex (MHC) proteins. In atopic individuals, this process leads to the production of cytokines, including interleukin-4 (IL-4), IL-5, IL-6, IL-9, IL-10, and IL-13. The IL-4 from these Th2 lymphocytes works in concert with other cytokines to induce B-cell isotype switching to immunoglobulin E (IgE). This isotype switch requires contact-dependent help from T cells through interaction of the CD40 molecule on B cells and the CD40 ligand (CD40L) on T cells. B cells that produce allergen-specific IgE mature into plasma cells that produce IgE, which binds to mast cells in the nasal mucosa. When inhaled allergens bridge IgE molecules on mast cells, mast cell degranulation occurs and preformed mediators are released. These mediators induce the *early-phase nasal reaction*, characterized by rhinorrhea, sneezing, itching, and nasal obstruction. A second release of mast cell mediators may occur 2 to 6 hours later and lead to recurrence of symptoms. This late-phase reaction is associated with an inflammatory response in the nose and the ongoing symptoms. Inflammation is promoted by the release of mast cell chemotactic factors such as leukotriene B$_4$ (LTB$_4$) and cytokines from mast cells and Th2 lymphocytes. These cytokines promote inflammatory cell migration into the nasal mucosa by upregulation of cellular adhesion receptors such as intercellular adhesion molecule 1 on epithelial cells and vascular cell adhesion molecule on vascular endothelium. They also facilitate eosinophil differentiation, activation, and survival. GM-CSF = granulocyte-macrophage colony-stimulating factor; PAF = platelet-activating factor; TCR = T-cell receptor; TNF = tumor necrosis factor.

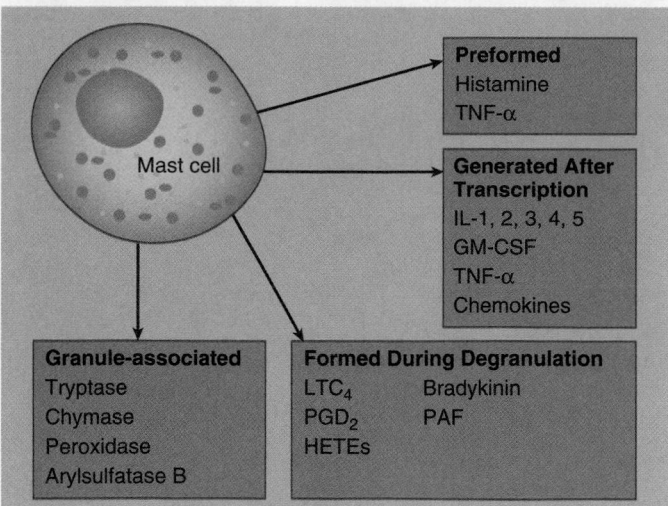

FIGURE 268–4 • Mast cell mediators. GM-CSF = granulocyte-macrophage colony-stimulating factor; HETE = hydroxyeicosatetraenoic acid; IL = interleukin; LT = leukotriene; PAF = platelet-activating factor; PG = prostaglandin; TNF-α = tumor necrosis factor α.

dilation and promotes the passive diffusion of plasma protein into glands and active secretion by mucous glands in cells.

Novel neurotransmitters, including substance P, calcitonin gene–related peptide, and vasointestinal peptide, have been detected in nasal secretions after nasal allergen challenge of patients with allergic rhinitis. Antidromic stimulation of sensory nerve fibers in the nose can release a variety of neurotransmitters, including substance P, a chemical that increases vascular permeability. Because neurotransmitters also produce changes in regional blood flow and glandular secretion, their role in rhinitis may be important.

IMMEDIATE AND LATE NASAL REACTIONS. Exposing the nasal mucosa to ragweed in ragweed-sensitive subjects (nasal challenge) provokes the immediate onset of sneezing and nasal itching associated with significantly increased concentrations of inflammatory mediators. Histamine, PGD$_2$, the kininogen product toluenesulfonylarginine methyl ester (TAME), tryptase, kinins, and sulfidopeptide leukotrienes are present in nasal washes. Sneezing correlates with the appearance

of measurable histamine, TAME, and PGD$_2$ in nasal washes. After about half an hour, PGD$_2$ and histamine levels return to baseline, whereas TAME concentrations remain elevated. Biopsy specimens of the nasal mucosa at this time show an increased number of degranulated mast cells.

Two to 6 hours after the initial allergen challenge, symptoms may recur after a second release of mast cell mediators coincident with maximum mast cell cytokine production. This late-phase nasal allergic reaction occurs in approximately 50% of patients with seasonal rhinitis who are undergoing nasal challenge with allergen. The reaction is associated with elevated levels of the same mediators noted in the immediate reaction, except that PGD$_2$ is not detected. Thus, basophils appear to be partly responsible for such late-phase reactions because histamine is generated by both mast cells and basophils whereas only mast cells can produce PGD$_2$. In support of this concept, marked basophil influx into the nasal mucosa has been noted 3 to 11 hours after allergen challenge. Large numbers of neutrophils, mononuclear cells, and eosinophils also migrate into the nasal mucosa at this time. Increases in eosinophil cationic protein and other eosinophil products also become detectable in nasal secretions. This inflammatory response is thought to cause the recurrence of symptoms and the induction of chronic allergic rhinitis.

After allergen challenge, lymphocytes remain the predominant cells in the nasal mucosa. These cells actively transcribe messages for IL-3, IL-4, IL-5, and GM-CSF and have increased expression of the IL-2 receptor. IL-1 through IL-5 and GM-CSF, among other cytokines, have been recovered from nasal washes after allergen challenge.

PRIMING AND NASAL HYPERREACTIVITY. When a patient is continually exposed to pollen, persistent nasal mucosal inflammation develops. In such patients, symptoms of rhinitis occur on exposure to lower doses of allergen (priming) and to nonspecific irritants (hyperreactivity). The clinical result is continued rhinitis symptoms with exposure to low allergen concentrations and irritants such as particulate pollution and volatile substances, even after the peak pollen season has passed.

Diagnosis

The diagnosis is based on a history of the characteristic symptoms that occur on exposure to known allergens. It is supported by the associated physical findings, by the presence of allergen-specific IgE on immediate hypersensitivity skin tests, or by radioallergosorbent testing (RAST) and a favorable response to allergen avoidance. The initial step is identifying the allergens that produce symptoms.

 Treatment

ALLERGEN IDENTIFICATION AND AVOIDANCE. A careful home and work environmental history is often informative. When symptoms occur acutely, such as symptoms after exposure to cat or occupational allergens, identifying the culprit may be simple. In perennial rhinitis, identifying allergens by history may be difficult. In these circumstances, carefully performed immediate hypersensitivity skin testing (prick skin tests) is a quick, inexpensive, and safe way to identify the presence of allergen-specific IgE. In sensitive patients, testing with selected extracts of tree, grass, or weed pollen, mold, house dust mite, and/or animal allergens results in a wheal-and-flare reaction at the skin test site within 20 minutes. Although less sensitive and more expensive, RAST is a surrogate test that gives similar information from a serum sample. Neither total serum IgE levels, elevated in only 30 to 40% of patients, nor peripheral blood eosinophil counts are sensitive enough for routine diagnosis of allergic rhinitis. Stained nasal smears detect eosinophilia, which is helpful in narrowing the diagnosis to allergic rhinitis or NARES, and neutrophilia (>50%) associated with sinusitis.

Simple measures to avoid allergens include maintaining the relative humidity at 50% or less to limit house dust mite and mold growth and avoiding exposure to irritants such as cigarette smoke. Air conditioners decrease concentrations of pollen, mold, and dust mite allergens in indoor air. Avoiding exposure to the feces of the house dust mite, the most common cause of perennial allergic rhinitis, is facilitated by covering mattresses, box springs, and pillows with plastic and washing bedding in water hotter than 70° F once weekly. Synthetic pillows should also be used. Furry pets should be removed from the home unless testing shows they are not the source of symptoms.

PHARMACOLOGIC TREATMENT. If avoiding allergens does not result in improvement, topical nasal corticosteroids or antihistamine therapy is a reasonable next step. Corticosteroids given orally or parenterally usually abolish all symptoms of allergic rhinitis. The potential complications of such therapy make systemic steroids unacceptable for treating allergic rhinitis except in unusual circumstances. Topical intranasal steroid therapy is at present the most effective single maintenance therapy and causes few side effects when used at recommended doses (Table 268–2). Although first-generation intranasal corticosteroids such as beclomethasone and budesonide are as efficacious as second-generation products such as fluticasone propionate and mometasone furoate, the latter have less systemic bioavailability, which decreases potential systemic effects. In experimental nasal allergen challenge, they decrease the amount of histamine released in the early nasal response to allergen by 75% and increase the threshold dose for a positive response to allergen. With regular use, they inhibit both immediate and late-phase nasal reactions. Their maximal therapeutic effects are seen as quickly as 3 to 5 days. Corticosteroids have both vasoconstrictor and anti-inflammatory effects, including inhibition of mediator release and inflammatory cell chemotaxis. Topical nasal steroids are more effective than cromolyn and second-generation antihistamines and improve the symptoms of seasonal asthma in patients with both seasonal allergic rhinitis and seasonal allergic asthma. These preparations are available in both aqueous and fluorocarbon (Freon)-propelled preparations. The aqueous preparations may be particularly useful in patients in whom Freon preparations cause mucosal drying, crusting, or epistaxis. Rarely, nasal steroids are associated with nasal septal perforation,

Table 268–2 • INTRANASAL STEROIDS AVAILABLE IN THE UNITED STATES

NAME/TRADE NAME	DOSE	APPROVED FOR CHILDREN (yr)
Dexamethasone sodium phosphate (Decadron, Turbinaire*)	2 sprays (168 µg) in each nostril bid–tid, max, 1008 µg/day	>6
Flunisolide (Nasalide)	2 sprays (50 µg) in each nostril bid–tid, max, 400 µg/day	>6
Beclomethasone dipropionate (Beconase, Vancenase, Beconase AQ, Vancenase AQ)	1 spray (42 µg) in each nostril bid–qid; max, 336 µg/day	>6
Triamcinolone acetonide (Nasacort)	2 sprays (110 µg) in each nostril once a day; max, 440 µg/day	>6
Budesonide (Rhinocort)	2 sprays (64 µg) in each nostril once a day; max, 256 µg/day	>6
Fluticasone (Flonase)	2 sprays (100 µg) in each nostril once a day; max, 200 µg/day	>4
Mometasone furoate monohydrate (Nasonex)	2 sprays (50 µg) in each nostril once a day; max, unclear	>12

*For short term use only.

Table 268–3 • REPRESENTATIVE ANTIHISTAMINES*

DRUG	SEDATIVE EFFECTS	ANTIHISTAMINE EFFECTS	DOSING INTERVALS (h)
Ethanolamines			
Clemastine (Tavist)	2+	1–2+	12
Diphenhydramine (Benadryl)	3+	1–2+	6–8
Ethylenediamines			
Pyrilamine (Histadyl)	1+	1–2+	6–8
Alkylamines			
Chlorpheniramine (Chlor-Trimeton)	1+	2+	4–6
Phenothiazines			
Promethazine (Phenergan)	3+	3+	6–24
Piperidines			
Loratadine (Claritin)†	±	2–3+	24
Desloratadine (Clarinex)	±	2–3+	24
Fexofenadine (Allegra)†	±	2–3+	12–24
Azatadine (Optimine)	2+	2+	12
Cyproheptadine (Periactin)	3+	2+	8
Piperazines			
Hydroxyzine (Atarax)	3+	3+	12
Cetirizine (Zyrtec)†	1+	2–3+	24
Miscellaneous			
Azelastine‡	±	2–3+	12
Levocabastine‡	±	2–3±	12

*Antihistamines in this listing have specific contraindications that require review before prescribing.
†Second-generation antihistamines.
‡Nasal spray.
©2000 by Facts and Comparisons. Used with permission and modified from Drug Facts and Comparisons, 2000 ed. St Louis, Facts and Comparisons, a division of the JB lippincott Company, Effects were graded 1 to 4.

probably secondary to nasal septal wall damage from inappropriate use of the pressurized aerosol. Mucosal atrophy has not been noted even after years of usage. Treatment failures occur if mucus or other debris is not cleaned from the nose before application. This cleaning can be facilitated by saline nasal sprays or washes.

Antihistamines help control sneezing, rhinorrhea, and itching but may provide inadequate relief from nasal obstruction (Table 268–3). Oral antihistamines that contain the decongestant pseudoephedrine have been shown to be of added benefit.[2] Because the latter agents may cause palpitations, insomnia or irritability, exacerbation of glaucoma, and urinary retention and are contraindicated in patients receiving monoamine oxidase therapy, they should be used cautiously. Nasal decongestant sprays are not recommended as tachyphylaxis develops after 5 to 7 days and rebound nasal congestion results. Continued use leads to rhinitis medicamentosa.

The first-generation H₁-receptor antagonists produce sedation and other central nervous system symptoms in 20% of patients and may cause drying of the mouth and urinary hesitancy. Adverse effects on intellectual and motor function, including driving, occur. Newer second-generation antihistamines are less lipophilic, less likely to cross the blood-brain barrier, and therefore less sedating. Some of the second-generation H₁ antihistamines inhibit mast cell mediator release and inflammatory cell movement and function, perhaps explaining their salutary effects in asthma when present. Likewise, leukotriene receptor antagonists used in asthma treatment may have additive effects with antihistamines on allergic rhinitis. There is no evidence for the development of pharmacologic tolerance to antihistamines. Thus, rotating from one antihistamine to another is not beneficial. Furthermore, clinical studies do not support the use of combinations of H₁- and H₂-antagonists to treat allergic rhinitis.

Cromolyn inhibits mast cell degranulation and mediator release from mast cells and has other anti-inflammatory actions. This over-the-counter medication is useful prior to expected allergen exposure and inhibits both immediate and late-phase nasal reactions. It is as effective as antihistamines in treating allergic rhinitis but must

be used frequently and takes 2 to 6 weeks to reach full efficacy. It has no side effects.

Ipratropium bromide, a congener of atropine, has been found to reduce rhinorrhea when used intranasally. It does not block sneezing or nasal obstruction and is thus of greater use in nonallergic rhinitis with predominantly rhinorrhea.

ALLERGEN IMMUNOTHERAPY. Allergen immunotherapy involves the subcutaneous administration of increasing concentrations of allergen to which the patient has demonstrated sensitization and symptoms by skin test (or RAST) and history, respectively. Immunotherapy should be considered when pharmacotherapy and avoidance of allergens fail to resolve the symptoms or when pharmacotherapy produces unacceptable side effects or is not cost-effective. High-dose immunotherapy for allergic rhinitis has been shown to relieve symptoms of allergic rhinitis effectively in controlled studies.[3] Allergen immunotherapy should be strongly considered for patients with perennial symptoms, perennial rhinitis with seasonal exacerbations, or constitutional symptoms (such as severe fatigue) or patients with associated sinusitis, allergic conjunctivitis, or asthma. It is time consuming and associated with a risk of anaphylaxis, especially when administered by health care professionals not properly trained in its use.

Allergen immunotherapy blocks both the immediate and the late-phase nasal reaction. The specific mechanism by which it relieves symptoms is unclear, although it increases allergen-specific IgG, reduces allergen-specific IgE, decreases allergen-induced mediator release, decreases eosinophil chemotaxis, and appears to favor a shift to cytokine profiles associated with Th1 responses to allergen.

NOVEL THERAPIES. Because cytokines mediate allergic inflammation, downregulation of the proinflammatory cytokines IL-1, IL-4, IL-5, IL-13, and TNF-α or upregulation of anti-inflammatory cytokines IL-10 and IL-12 or interferon-γ is logical. Clinical trials using anti–IL-4 and IL-1 receptor antagonist, among others, are in progress in patients with allergic disease. Therapy with monoclonal anti-IgE is also under investigation.

Grade 4

1. Corren J, Harris AG, Aaronson D, et al: Efficacy and safety of loratadine plus pseudoephedrine in patients with seasonal allergic rhinitis and asthma. J Allergy Clin Immunol 1997;100:781–788.
2. Weiner JM, Abramson MJ, Puy RM: Intranasal corticosteroids versus oral H1 receptor antagonists in allergic rhinitis: A systematic review of randomized controlled trials. BMJ 1998;317:1624–1629.
3. Durham SR, Walker SM, Varga E-V, et al: Long term efficacy of grass pollen immunotherapy. N Engl J Med 1999;341:468–475.

SUGGESTED READINGS

Casiano RR: Treatment of acute and chronic rhinosinusitis. Semin Respir Infect 2000;15:216–226. *An excellent review of syndromes of rhinosinusitis and treatment from the perspective of the otolaryngologist.*

Christodoulopoulos P, Cameron L, Durham S, Hamid Q: Molecular pathology of allergic disease: Upper airway disease. J Allergy Clin Immunol 2000;105:211–223. *An excellent review article with an extensive discussion of the pathophysiology of allergic disease.*

Corren J: Allergic rhinitis: Treating the adult. J Allergy Clin Immunol 2000;105:S610–S615. *A practical and well-written overview of treatment of rhinitis.*

Dykewicz MS: Rhinitis and sinusitis. J Allergy Clin Immunol 2003;111:S520–S529. *An excellent brief review article with up-to-date references.*

Weber RW: Immunotherapy with allergens. JAMA 1997;278:1881–1887. *A well-written review of the rationale for and mechanism of action of allergen immunotherapy in allergic respiratory disease.*

269 URTICARIA AND ANGIOEDEMA

Michael M. Frank

Urticaria is defined as the transient appearance of elevated, erythematous pruritic wheals (hives) or serpiginous exanthem, often surrounded by an area of erythema. It commonly involves the trunk and extremities, sparing palms and soles, but it may involve any epidermal or mucosal surface. The wheals are thought to result from local subcutaneous and intradermal leakage of plasma filtrate from postcapillary venules. In most cases, there is associated increased blood flow to the localized area of swelling, resulting in a surrounding erythema or flare. The lesions blanch on pressure, reflecting this pathogenetic process. The appearance of urticaria is believed to reflect in most cases an ongoing immediate hypersensitivity reaction.

Angioedema is formed by a similar extravasation of fluid, but in this case the leakage of fluid involves deeper dermal and subdermal sites. Because of its location in deeper cutaneous structures, it appears as brawny, nonpitting edema, usually without well-defined margins. Although urticaria is almost always pruritic, indicating stimulation of nociceptive nerves in the region, angioedema may be unassociated with itching. Unlike other forms of edema, angioedema is not commonly distributed in dependent areas of the body. It often involves the lips, tongue, eyelids, genitalia, or hands or feet but also may involve any epidermal or mucosal surface. The transient nature of involvement is important in defining both urticaria and angioedema; these manifestations appear and peak in minutes to hours and disappear over hours to days.

Incidence and Prevalence

Acute episodes of urticaria/angioedema are arbitrarily defined as those lasting less than 6 weeks. More prolonged episodes are defined as chronic. Acute urticaria and angioedema are common clinical problems, occurring in as much as 10 to 20% of the population at one time or another. The acute episodes may occur at any age and are the most common form seen in childhood. They occur in persons of either gender and of all races and occupations and at all seasons of the year. Chronic urticaria/angioedema also can occur in individuals of any age, but the peak incidence is noted in young adults.

In general, symptoms of urticaria are more striking and more easily recognized than those of angioedema, and these symptoms are often the presenting complaint. At presentation, about 50% of patients have both urticaria and angioedema, approximately 40% have urticaria alone, and about 10% have only angioedema. Although in most patients the lesions clear spontaneously or respond rapidly to treatment with H_1 antihistamines, a minority of patients continue to have lesions over a period that may last years. Of patients with chronic urticaria and angioedema, 75% have symptoms for longer than 1 year, 50% have symptoms for longer than 5 years, and 20% have symptoms for decades. At times, these symptoms can be debilitating. This clinical syndrome represents a final common pathway of multiple initiating stimuli, and the natural course of disease reflects multiple initiating factors.

Pathogenesis and Pathology

Urticaria/angioedema results from dilatation of small vessels with associated leakage of plasma from local postcapillary venules. Experimentally, such leakage can be induced by multiple stimuli. Degranulation of cutaneous mast cells is thought to be the most frequent cause of disease. Mast cells are found in high frequency within the subcutaneous tissues and dermis. Their distribution is particularly rich around blood vessels. These cells stain poorly with the commonly used histopathologic stains and often must be visualized by specific staining techniques. Upon being activated by any of a number of stimuli, these cells degranulate, releasing over a period of seconds preformed mediators present in the granules, like histamine, that induce capillary permeability. They also synthesize various mediators in response to the activation signal that increase capillary permeability, including prostaglandins, hydroxyeicosatetraenoic acids (HETEs), leukotrienes B_4, C_4, and D_2, and platelet-activating factor (PAF). With appropriate stimuli, cellular regulatory factors such as the cytokines (interleukin [IL]-4, IL-5, IL-6, and THF α are synthesized and may be released without degranulation and release of preformed mediators; these cytokines may control the function of other cells within the lesion. The various activation factors lead to upregulation of various cellular adhesion molecules that promote the immigration of immune and inflammatory cells, resulting in the formation of longer lasting lesions.

Many stimuli induce mast cells to degranulate. Probably most important is the interaction of mast cell membrane–bound IgE antibody with specific antigen. Mast cells have on their surface a number of receptors, including the high-affinity receptor for IgE (FcϵRI), and in tissues mast cells are often found coated with IgE antibody derived from plasma. Interaction of IgE antibody with its specific multivalent antigen cross-links IgE receptors, a required step in initiating the degranulation process. In fact, anything that cross-links IgE receptors can cause the cells to degranulate, including IgG autoantibody to the IgE receptor (discussed later). In addition, a series of peptides derived from various plasma mediator molecules can interact with specific receptors for them on mast cells, triggering degranulation. For example, peptides derived from activated complement proteins including C3a, C4a, and C5a and small fragments of C2 can induce mast cell degranulation. Similarly, peptides such as bradykinin, derived from activation and cleavage of proteins of the kinin-generating system, neuropeptides such as substance P, and PAF can induce mast cell degranulation. Leukotrienes were originally identified by their ability to induce delayed smooth muscle contraction in test systems and were encompassed by the phrase "slow releasing substance of anaphylaxis." Incompletely defined cellular products derived from circulating mononuclear cells and neutrophils can cause mast cell degranulation as well. Moreover, toxic products from neutrophils and monocytes, whose release is induced by many factors including mast cell products, can upon injection induce a typical hive.

Inducing an immediate hypersensitivity response in an allergic individual by intradermally injecting a sensitizing antigen leads to rapid mast cell degranulation and the immediate appearance of a wheal and flare response that gradually fades. In many individuals, 4 to 6 hours later a "late-phase" response is noted with an increase in local inflammation and swelling. Biopsy of such a late-phase reaction reveals that neutrophils, some lymphocytes, and eosinophils are accumulated in the inflamed area and later are gradually replaced by mononuclear cells. The factors that induce the late-phase reaction are not completely defined, but the recent demonstration that chemotactic cytokines are produced some hours after mast cell triggering suggests that these factors contribute to late-phase inflammation.

An understanding of these experimental findings helps explain biopsy findings in patients with acute and chronic urticaria/angioedema. Although the disease may be chronic, individual lesions usually are evanescent, lasting hours to days. In most cases on biopsy, subcutaneous edema is prominent, with flattened rete pegs, widened dermal papillae, and swollen collagen fibers also being seen. There is increased histamine content of skin, and some studies demonstrate an increased number of cutaneous mast cells when compared with normal individuals. Even uninvolved skin from a patient with urticaria may show higher histamine content than does the skin of normal persons. Mast cell degranulation is seen on biopsy of lesions. A small subset of patients have a neutrophil predominance and the lesion appears inflammatory in nature. In chronic urticaria, a modest mononuclear cell infiltrate around vessels containing lymphocytes (predominantly CD4+ helper T cells), basophils, and a few monocytes/macrophages is noted. An increase in eosinophils may also be seen. Patients with physical urticaria tend to have more neutrophils and eosinophils on biopsy than are observed in chronic urticaria/angioedema. In a minority of cases with typical urticarial lesions, leukocytoclastic vasculitis is observed. In these patients the urticarial lesions may be less evanescent than in typical urticaria and rarely may be associated with purpura. Many of these patients have an elevated erythrocyte sedimentation rate. This syndrome is reported to be associated with the formation of IgG anti-C1q autoantibody, indicating that the underlying diagnosis is vasculitis and placing the patient in a different diagnostic and therapeutic group.

Causes of urticaria/angioedema are listed in Table 269–1. However, in most reported series, the cause is never found. In several large series, approximately 70% of all cases remained in the idiopathic group after all other urticarial syndrome complexes were eliminated. It is believed that most acute urticaria/angioedema cases represent hypersensitivity reactions to drugs, foods, or, less commonly, inhalants, because when a cause is defined it commonly involves one of these sensitizing agents. Penicillin is the drug still most commonly associated with acute urticaria; aspirin and other nonsteroidal anti-inflammatory drugs (NSAIDs) may rarely exacerbate urticaria, possibly by inhibiting prostaglandin synthesis, and diuretics, radiocontrast dyes, food additives, sulfonamides, and muscle relaxants all are associated with acute urticaria. Opioids can trigger direct mast cell release of histamine and cause urticarial lesions. Among foods, nuts, milk, eggs, chocolate, citrus fruits, tomatoes, fish, shellfish, and food dyes have all been associated with onset of acute urticaria in some individuals. Nevertheless, because many different antigens, including food additives, drugs, foods, and food contaminants, have been defined as causative in individual cases and because little antigen may be required to precipitate attacks, it may be difficult or impossible to define the causative agent. In many cases in which the disease becomes chronic, the patient is asked to keep a diary to determine whether a particular food or commercial product is involved in an attack. If it is impossible to define the precipitating agent by this means, a severely restricted elimination diet, limiting foods to boiled rice and lamb, may be tried for several weeks to determine whether eliminating an offending ingested agent terminates the attacks. Often these attempts are unsuccessful.

There are defined clinical situations in which urticaria and/or angioedema is a common presenting problem. Patients undergoing immune complex–mediated reactions, as occur in active systemic lupus erythematosus and serum sickness, may experience waves of urticarial lesions, in this case believed to be due to activation of mediator pathways by circulating immune complexes with generation of kinins and complement-derived anaphylatoxins.

Autoantibodies of various sorts interacting with antigen may induce urticarial reactions. Reports suggest that as many as 40% of patients with chronic urticaria have IgG autoantibodies to the IgE Fc receptor Ia chain. This receptor is a four-chain molecule present on mast cells and eosinophils to which IgE binds with high affinity, setting the stage for an allergic attack. Multivalent antigen interacting with cell-bound IgE triggers the release of mediators. IgG autoantibodies to the high-affinity IgE receptor, perhaps augmented by the action of complement, is thought to trigger receptor aggregation, releasing mediators in the absence of specific IgE antibody. IgG anti-IgE is also present in a small number of patients; in this case, autoantibody cross-links receptors that have IgE bound to them, causing release of mediators from IgE-coated mast cells. Thyroid autoantibodies have been associated with urticaria in many studies, probably reflecting the propensity of some patients to form multiple autoantibodies. As many as 30% of patients with chronic urticaria in some studies possess antithyroglobulin or antimicrosomal antibodies, the patients being either hyperthyroid or hypothyroid. Similarly, blood transfusions and infusions of fresh frozen plasma (FFP) are often associated with hives caused by antibodies in the plasma encountering host antigen or circulating host antibodies binding antigens in the blood products. Some cancers—for example, lymphomas—may be associated with urticarial lesions, thought to be due to an antibody response to tumor antigens. A similar mechanism is clearly responsible for the hives associated with some infectious agents, particularly viral agents. Here, antigens on or released from infectious agents are bound to antibodies induced in the patient and hives result. Hives are a frequent response to the antibodies formed in the early response to hepatitis A and B and Epstein-Barr virus infection. There are a number of anecdotal reports of *Helicobacter* infection leading to the release of antigens that cause chronic hives. These reports still require confirmation in a controlled study. Rarely, fungal antigens such as those derived from *Candida albicans* may precipitate hives or angioedema. Given the rarity of this latter observation, nystatin treatment is inappropriate in patients with chronic urticaria/angioedema unless a clear association with a hypersensitivity response to candidal antigens can be demonstrated. Although rare in the United States, many parasitic diseases can, at times, be associated with urticaria/angioedema with or without hypereosinophilia. Presumably, the presence of the urticaria/angioedema reflects an ongoing immediate hypersensitivity reaction to parasite antigens.

The complex of urticaria, bone pain, and lymphadenopathy is termed *Schnitzler's syndrome*. Affected patients often have greatly increased IgM levels, suggesting an ongoing immunologic reaction, but the cause of the syndrome is unknown.

Physical Urticarias and Angioedemas

It is important to consider the physical urticaria/angioedema complex when evaluating patients with chronic recurrent urticaria or angioedema because in one large series these represented 16% of all chronic urticaria/angioedema patients seen. In some cases a highly specific diagnosis can be made, a clear precipitating factor can be defined, and the patient can learn to avoid attacks. Moreover, specific therapy may be available. These causes of urticaria/angioedema appear to be so easily defined that it seems unlikely that they could be missed. However, in practice, this is not the case; a detailed history is required to identify these factors. Indeed, it is common for these patients to go years before a correct diagnosis is made. The physical urticarias have in common urticaria/angioedema precipitated by a known physical cause. The response may follow exposure to cold, heat, elevated body temperature, pressure, vibration, specific-wavelength ultraviolet rays, or, rarely, even water on the skin. In some cases, these reactions are believed to be IgE-mediated, because they can be passively transferred with serum of an affected donor to the skin of an unaffected recipient. In other cases, the cause is unknown.

Table 269–1 • CLASSIFICATION OF URTICARIA/ANGIOEDEMA

I. Manifestation of hypersensitivity to a defined agent
  A. Drug reactions
  B. Foods and food additives
  C. Inhaled and contact allergens
II. Presumed immune complex–induced
  A. Collagen disease
  B. Endocrine disease (thyroid disorders)
  C. Serum sickness
  D. Transfusion-induced
  E. Malignancy (tumor antigen-induced)
  F. Infectious agents
  G. Urticarial vasculitis
III. Physical urticarias
  A. Dermatographism
  B. Familial and acquired cold urticaria
  C. Localized heat urticaria
  D. Cholinergic urticaria
  E. Exercise-induced anaphylaxis/urticaria
  F. Delayed pressure urticaria/angioedema
  G. Familial and acquired vibratory angioedema
  H. Solar urticaria
  I. Aquagenic urticaria
IV. Urticaria pigmentosa and systemic mastocytosis
V. Chronic urticaria and angioedema
VI. Defined complement-related disorders
  A. Hereditary angioedema
  B. Acquired C1 inhibitor deficiency
  C. Hereditary angioedema type III
  D. Complement factor I deficiency
VII. Angioedema induced by angiotensin-converting enzyme inhibitors and interleukin-2

SYMPTOMATIC DERMATOGRAPHISM. As much as 2 to 5% of the general population may be dermatographic, with the appearance of blanching followed by a linear streak of edema and erythema within 2 to 5 minutes of stroking the skin. A small proportion of such individuals have sufficiently severe dermatographism that they become symptomatic. In some cases, the symptoms can be transferred to a normal recipient by passive transfer of plasma, suggesting that in some way IgE antibody plays a role. In general, these individuals can be treated successfully with H_1 and H_2 antihistamines.

COLD URTICARIA. Patients with cold urticaria experience urticaria/angioedema on exposure to cold and may become hypotensive on diving into a cold swimming pool. Careful studies have shown that mast cell degranulation with histamine release occurs in these patients on cold exposure. Degranulation may be even more extensive when the patient's tissues are warmed after cold exposure. Placing an ice cube on the skin for 5 minutes and then removing it reveals an area of blanching in the shape of the cube followed by edema formation in the same area surrounded by an erythematous flare caused by local hyperemia. During attacks, blood histamine and tumor necrosis factor-α levels are elevated. In some of these patients, passive transfer of the sensitivity to the skin of normal persons has been demonstrated. It has been suggested that on cold exposure, certain dermal antigens undergo a conformational change that allows specific IgE autoantibody to bind and initiate mast cell degranulation. These patients are typically treated with cyproheptadine, sometimes with the addition of hydroxyzine. Cold urticaria has been described in a number of diseases associated with pathologic globulins, such as cryoglobulins or cryofibrinogens. The symptom complex, however, is not associated with the presence of cold agglutinins. When cold urticaria is associated with underlying disease, treatment of those diseases is an essential part of therapy.

In some patients, disease manifestations are atypical in that the patient gives a history of urticarial symptoms but the ice cube test is negative. In occasional patients, dermatographism is brought out by cold exposure; in others, exercise-induced urticaria is noted only in the cold. There is a rare familial type of cold urticaria inherited as an autosomal dominant trait in which patients develop urticarial lesions 9 to 18 hours after cold exposure. This response cannot be passively transferred with plasma, and the cause is unknown.

CHOLINERGIC OR GENERALIZED HEAT URTICARIA. Typically, these patients, representing about 4% of all patients with chronic urticaria, develop small (several millimeters), intensely pruritic wheals on an erythematous base on their upper trunk and arms after exercise with sweating or after hot showers. An increase in core body temperature is essential for the development of lesions. It is generally believed that the parasympathetic nervous system supply to cutaneous vessels releases acetylcholine as well as a neuropeptide such as vasoactive intestinal peptide, causing mediator release. There is no evidence of an IgE-mediated reaction. In support of this hypothesis is the fact that 30 to 50% of these patients develop typical lesions as well as a series of local satellite lesions when intracutaneously injected with methacholine. Atropine may inhibit the skin test but does not successfully treat the disease. These patients are typically highly responsive to hydroxyzine therapy. There is a subset of patients who respond to heat exposure by developing large urticarial lesions rather than the typical lesions of cholinergic urticaria. These patients tend not to develop their hives with exercise and are less responsive to hydroxyzine therapy.

Localized heat urticaria has been described with a wheal-and-flare response noted 2 to 5 minutes after applying localized heat to the skin.

EXERCISE-INDUCED URTICARIA ANAPHYLAXIS. These patients note urticarial lesions appearing 5 to 30 minutes after the onset of exercise that last for 1 to 3 hours. In severe cases, anaphylactic reactions may be noted. This is an illness generally of young adults. At times, symptoms are difficult to distinguish from those of cholinergic urticaria; however, these patients do not develop urticaria upon increasing core body temperature, and they tend to respond poorly to antihistamines. A β-agonist or mast cell–stabilizing agent, such as cromolyn, taken before exercise may prevent attacks.

PRESSURE-INDUCED URTICARIA. For unknown reasons, urticarial lesions are common at pressure points on the body, such as where clothing is tight. Some patients note that marked urticarial lesions develop 4 to 6 hours after pressure is applied to the body. For example, these individuals may note urticarial lesions on buttocks after sitting for a long time on a hard chair or angioedema or urticaria on their feet after prolonged standing in one place. The lesions may be provoked by placing a 1-inch strap weighted at the ends with 15-pound weights over the shoulders for 20 minutes. A systemic response with malaise and even fever may be noted. The response to antihistamines is often poor. The urticaria but not the systemic toxicity may respond to antihistamine therapy. The most severely affected of these patients may require every-other-day glucocorticoid administration for partial relief. In general, these patients are unresponsive to NSAIDs.

Similarly, some patients respond to local vibration by developing urticarial lesions. Typically, symptoms are induced by placing a vibrator or vortex mixer on the arm for 5 minutes; urticaria appears in 1 to 5 minutes.

SOLAR URTICARIA. In these patients, urticarial responses develop shortly after exposure to sunlight; the patients are divided into subgroups by the wavelength of light that provokes attacks. Patients whose attacks are provoked by light at 280 to 320 nm (type 1) and 400 to 500 nm (type 4) typically have disease that can be passively transferred with serum to nonaffected recipients, suggesting the presence of an IgE-dependent mechanism. Type 6, provoked by light at 400 nm, is present in some patients with erythropoietic protoporphyria. Glass absorbs light with a wavelength less than 320 nm, and patients with urticaria in response to light wavelengths less than 320 nm are protected by a pane of glass. Preparations containing zinc oxide or titanium dioxide block all light transmission but are white and present cosmetic difficulties. The erythema-causing band of the solar spectrum, UVB, is at wavelength 290 to 320 nm, and these patients can sometimes be helped considerably by sunscreens containing paraaminobenzoic acid (PABA), which absorb light in this range. However, many of these persons are not protected by the PABA sunscreens. Sunscreen preparations containing butyl methoxydibenzoyl methane or terephthalylidene dicamphor sulfonic acid absorb light in the ultraviolet A range and may be more useful for this patient group.

There are many types of light sensitivity, and sorting these out may be confusing. Light sensitivity reactions may include metabolic abnormalities (erythrogenic porphyria), in which products of metabolism absorb light energy and undergo chemical alteration that renders them toxic; photoallergic reactions, in which drugs that can sensitize skin induce allergic reactions when altered by sunlight; and phototoxic reactions, in which drugs localized in cutaneous tissues directly cause tissue-damaging reactions when exposed to light of the proper wavelength. In many of these cases, the light energy is absorbed by a complex ring structure in the drug, which subsequently releases photons and electrons that lead to local generation of toxic products such as singlet oxygen, hydrogen peroxide, and chloramines. In each case, the clinician attempts to identify the cause of the urticaria and eliminate the offending agent.

AQUAGENIC URTICARIA. These patients respond within 2 to 30 minutes with urticaria when water is applied to the skin. Typically, this is noted in the course of baths or showers, even with water at tepid temperature. In most cases, these individuals are probably exquisitely sensitive to additives in the water (e.g., chlorine), but it is reported that rare individuals develop urticaria in response to distilled water.

Chronic Urticaria/Angioedema

Chronic urticaria/angioedema has many causes, and identifying the causative agent may be difficult or impossible. If attempts at identifying the cause of the urticaria have failed, a patient may require treatment. H_1 antihistamines are usually the agents of first choice. Other therapeutic agents are listed earlier in the chapter; in patients with chronic disease, high-dose hydroxyzine and cyproheptadine are often effective.[1] These agents make patients drowsy and may not be well tolerated initially, but drowsiness may pass if the drug is continued. Optimally, the dose is increased until drowsiness persists and then the dosage is reduced slightly. It is common to find patients who, because the drugs have not been used properly, claim to have been unresponsive to these agents. Many more conveniently used and less sedating antihistamines have become available and have been shown in controlled studies to be effective. These include fexofenadine, loratadine, and cetirizine.[2] H_2 inhibitory drugs are often added to H_1 inhibitors if the clinical response is not adequate. Leukotriene antagonists were superior to placebo in limited trials. Other agents reported to be beneficial in individual cases include doxepin, a tricyclic antidepressant with anti-H_1 and anti-H_2 properties; nifedipine, a calcium-channel blocker; and ketotifen, a drug shown to be efficacious in physical urticaria. Recently, a number of case reports indicated response to cyclosporin. ❸ If these agents fail, a course of glucocorticoids may be required. In general, therapy begins with 20 mg of prednisone per day in divided doses for 1 week. The dosage is then consolidated to a single dose a day, and then the drug is rapidly tapered on an every-other-day schedule until the patient is receiving glucocorticoids only once every other day. The dose of glucocorticoids should be tapered to the lowest dose that maintains the patient's condition with minimal symptoms. After a course of glucocorticoid therapy, patients often remain in remission for a prolonged time. The illness may recur at a later time or when glucocorticoids are tapered.

Differential Diagnosis

This set of diseases is multifactorial. Usually the diagnosis of urticaria/angioedema does not present a problem in the patient with clear episodes of pruritic wheals or localized brawny edema. Because many agents can cause these lesions, considerable detective work is required to define these diseases and to develop a suitable specific therapy. During the initial evaluation, a number of points must be explored. A history of a fixed rather than evanescent eruption or the presence of burning, bruising, or vesiculating lesions should prompt early biopsy. Similarly, fever or systemic signs and symptoms, including arthralgias, pulmonary symptoms, and abdominal pain, suggest that further exploration is needed. Patients with idiopathic chronic urticaria typically have a normal sedimentation rate, white blood cell count, and differential count; these should be determined. In appropriate cases, antinuclear antibodies (ANA), heterophile antibodies, serologic tests for syphilis (STS), rheumatoid factor level, cryoglobulins and cryofibrinogen, cold hemolysin, C4, and C1 inhibitor levels should be studied for further clues to the underlying diagnosis. In the patient who responds poorly to therapy or who has atypical disease, a biopsy is clearly indicated. Patients with urticarial vasculitis are treated for the underlying vasculitis.

 Treatment

The use of antihistamines and glucocorticoids is discussed under the various entities and in the section on chronic urticaria/angioedema. Epinephrine is clinically useful in acute management of urticaria/angioedema. In this case, the drug is administered as a series of injections: 0.2 to 0.3 mL of a 1:1000 dilution subcutaneously, repeated at half-hour intervals two or three times until symptoms are controlled. The use of epinephrine is contraindicated in certain patient groups, such as patients with severe cardiovascular disease. Longer acting epinephrine preparations such as epinephrine in oil (Sus-Phrine) may be useful.

Urticaria Pigmentosa and Systemic Mastocytosis

Urticaria pigmentosa is characterized by the local accumulation of intradermal masses of infiltrating mast cells (Chapter 280). The lesions may resemble freckles superficially but are raised, as might be expected of infiltrative lesions, and may be somewhat erythematous. They may urticate when stroked (Darier's sign). Systemic mastocytosis is associated with massive accumulation of mast cells in other organs, particularly the bone marrow and gastrointestinal tract. Although some affected patients may present with acute or chronic urticaria, that presentation is rare; systemic signs of histamine toxicity, gastrointestinal disorders, or disorders consequent to destruction of bone marrow or bone are more common.

Hereditary Angioedema

Hereditary angioedema (HAE) presents clinically as episodic attacks of brawny nonpitting edema that usually involve the extremities but may affect any external body surface including the genitalia. Mucosal surfaces are affected as well, and patients frequently have attacks of severe abdominal pain due to swelling of the submucosa of the gastrointestinal tract. On rare occasions, attacks may affect the airway and cause respiratory obstruction and asphyxiation. Although attacks are sporadic, about half the patients note that trauma, particularly associated with local pressure, precipitates an attack, and half the patients note a marked increase in attack frequency at times

of emotional stress. About one third of patients note an erythema marginatum–like rash at the onset of attacks that they often describe as nonraised, nonpruritic circles on the skin. In general, attacks become progressively more severe over about 1.5 days and then regress over a similar time period, but the duration of an attack may be longer, with swelling moving from region to region of the body.

Although relatively rare (incidence about 1:10,000), this disease has received a great deal of attention because of the high incidence of lethal complications. Its pathophysiologic basis is best understood of all of the angioedemas, and adequate therapy is available for most patients. Presence of this disease is associated with either low levels or abnormal function of a plasma regulatory protein, the C1 inhibitor. This protein controls activation of the complement, kinin-generating, fibrinolytic, and intrinsic clotting pathways. Although the precise cause of the capillary leakage is unknown, it is believed that a peptide formed during activation of the kinin-generating mediator pathway is the responsible factor. HAE has an autosomal dominant inheritance pattern, affecting 50% of the offspring of a patient and occurring with equal frequency in males and females. This autosomal dominant inheritance reflects the presence of one normal and one abnormal gene for C1 inhibitor on chromosome 11. This abnormal gene may yield no gene product (85% of patients; type 1) or may code for a nonfunctional protein (15% of patients; type 2).

HAE tends to be mild in childhood, becoming more severe at puberty. The factors that initiate attacks are unknown. There is no direct relationship between the level or activity of C1 inhibitor and the severity of disease. Patients are described who presumably possessed the defect from birth but whose attacks began at age 70 years. Diagnosis is established by finding low levels of C1 inhibitor antigen (type I) or function (all patients) and low levels of the complement protein C4 and/or C2. C1 inhibitor inhibits the function of activated C1 of the classic complement pathway. C1 inhibitor acts by binding to the substrate to be inhibited, and the product of one normal gene is insufficient to control mediator activation. When activated, C1 cleaves the next two proteins in the cascade, C4 and C2. Because the function of activated C1 is unregulated in the presence of a relative C1 inhibitor deficiency, C1 continues to cleave C4 and C2. Patients always have low levels of circulating C4 and C2 during attacks and usually have low levels between attacks. Interestingly, because of the presence of other control proteins, the levels of C3, the most commonly measured complement protein, are always normal. Presumably because of the constant complement activation present in these patients, they may develop an immune dysregulation shown by the higher-than-normal incidence of autoimmune diseases. These include endocrinopathies, granulomatous bowel disorders, arthritides, and systemic lupus erythematosus.

Attacks of hereditary angioedema respond poorly to epinephrine, antihistamines, and glucocorticoids—the mainstays of treatment of urticaria and angioedema caused by immediate hypersensitivity reactions. Nevertheless, acute attacks are treated with epinephrine, both nebulized racemic epinephrine in the airway (1:1000 given by nebulization) and subcutaneous injections (0.2 to 0.3 mL 1:1000 repeated q20 to 30 min × 3). Epinephrine administered very early in an attack often produces some improvement, and the use of antihistamines for sedation may be helpful. Patients often relate that attacks are terminated by intravenously administered FFP to supply the missing inhibitor protein. Nevertheless, a rare patient becomes more edematous after FFP, presumably reflecting increased availability of mediator substrates, and FFP, therefore, is not recommended for treating life-threatening laryngeal edema. In this circumstance, nasotracheal intubation in the operating room under conditions in which tracheostomy can be performed is indicated. FFP can be given in nonemergency situations, such as for preoperative patients to prevent attacks. The usual dose of FFP is 2 units, an arbitrary amount that has been used extensively and has proved to be effective.

The preponderance of evidence suggests that infusions of purified C1 inhibitor terminate attacks, but this material is not available in the United States. ❹ Although short-term therapy with purified C1 inhibitor and treatment of acute attacks of HAE have not been generally satisfactory, long-term therapy has been quite successful. Patients respond to all of the acetylated artificial androgens with increased C1 inhibitor levels that in some cases approach normal values, a correction of serum C4 and C2, and a marked amelioration of symptoms. In the rare patient in whom the drug is ineffective or in whom drug toxicity is a problem, plasmin inhibitors such as aminocaproic acid are also effective. These agents are more difficult to use clinically and have greater toxicity than androgens. Their mechanism of action is unknown and there is no change in the extent of complement activation reflected in the persistent reduction in the serum level of C4 and C2. With all of these agents, there is a high degree of patient-to-patient variation in drug dosage, and the lowest dose that controls symptoms is chosen. Women are often treated with danazol (200 to 600 mg/day) or stanozolol (2 to 6 mg/day); danazol and stanozolol are synthetic androgens that have few masculinizing side effects.[5] Men are often treated with the less expensive but more androgenic agent methyltestosterone (10 to 30 mg/day orally). A number of agents, given to patients for other conditions, greatly increase the severity and number of HAE attacks. These include estrogens (often given in birth control agents) and angiotensin-converting enzyme inhibitors given for control of hypertension.

Other Hereditary Angioedema-Like Syndromes

A number of syndromes are associated with a typical HAE symptom complex. In some cases, these syndromes appear to be inherited and in others they are a reflection of acquired disease. Some patients with malignancies, including lymphosarcoma, leukemia, lymphoma, and paraproteinemia, develop circulating or cellular factors that activate C1 and deplete the C1 inhibitor activity in serum. Also, rare patients with circulating immune complexes develop massive activation of the complement cascade, with C1 inhibitor utilization and an HAE-like clinical picture. Perhaps the most common of these rare individuals are patients who form monoclonal or polyclonal autoantibodies to the C1 inhibitor, which destroy its activity. Clinically these patients cannot be distinguished from patients with HAE. However, their laboratory test results usually make separation possible. These patient groups in general have profound depressions in functional levels of C1, C4, and C2. Patients with HAE commonly have normal C1 levels. Although their plasma C1 inhibitor antigen level may be normal, these patient groups have marked depression of C1 inhibitor function. Their treatment focuses on the underlying disease when possible. Some of these patients respond to danazol or other anabolic steroids. Several of the patients with anti-C1 inhibitor autoantibody have responded to glucocorticoid therapy, and several have responded to cytotoxic therapy. One report suggests that plasmin inhibitors are more effective than the androgens in patients with anti-C1 inhibitor antibody.

Recently a patient group has been defined with typical HAE symptoms, but with normal C1 inhibitor and complement function, termed HAE type 3. Like HAE, this symptom complex is inherited as an autosomal dominant trait but appears to be estrogen dependent and affects only women. Like for HAE, estrogen therapy exacerbates disease and some of these patients have had severe disease during pregnancy. Some patients have responded to danazol therapy. The pathophysiology of the disease is unknown.

Factor I Deficiency

Factor I is one of the control proteins of the complement activation pathway. The rare individuals with an inherited deficiency of this protein continuously activate and cleave C3, generating the anaphylatoxins C3a and perhaps C5a. In vitro, these cleavage peptides induce mast cell degranulation and cause chronic urticaria that disappears when the patient is infused with factor I. In general, this form of urticaria is relatively mild and is treated symptomatically with antihistamines.

Angioedema Induced by Angiotensin-Converting Enzyme Inhibitors and Interleukin-2

Within hours to 1 week of therapy with angiotensin-converting enzyme inhibitors, or more rarely later, patients may note angioedema that becomes life-threatening. In general, these patients have normal C1 inhibitor function. Angiotensin-converting enzyme plays an important role in the degradation of bradykinin and the neuropeptide substance P, and these mediators may be important in angioedema formation. Patients are treated with antihistamines and/or epinephrine as appropriate, and the angiotensin-converting enzyme inhibitor is discontinued. Recently, a patient has been described with congenital angiotensin-converting enzyme deficiency. This patient presented as an adult with recurrent angioedema of the upper airway,

emphasizing the importance of this enzyme in the proper metabolism of mediators of edema. It is important to determine whether other such patients exist. It has also been noted that systemic capillary leak or angioedema may follow the systemic infusion of interleukin-2 used to treat malignancy. This cytokine activates both the complement- and kinin-generating pathways. It also activates T cells, and it has been suggested that these activated cells directly damage the endothelium.

---

1. Breneman DL: Cetirizine versus hydroxyzine and placebo in chronic idiopathic urticaria. Ann Pharmacother 1996;30:1075–1079.
2. Finn AF Jr, Kaplan AP, Fretwell R, et al: A double-blind, placebo-controlled trial of fexofenadine HCl in the treatment of chronic idiopathic urticaria. J Allergy Clin Immunol 1999;103:1071–1078.
3. Grattan CE, O'Donnell BF, Francis DM, et al: Randomized double-blind study of cyclosporin in chronic idiopathic urticaria. Br J Dermatol 2000;143:365–372.
4. Waytes AT, Rosen FS, Frank MM: Treatment of hereditary angioedema with a vapor-heated C1 inhibitor concentrate. N Engl J Med 1996;334:1630–1634.
5. Gelfand JA, Sherins RJ, Alling DW, Frank MM: Treatment of hereditary angioedema with danazol. Reversal of clinical and biochemical abnormalities. N Engl J Med 1976;117:208–215.

SUGGESTED READINGS

Bork K, Barnstedt S-E, Koch P, Traupe M: Hereditary angioedema with normal C1 inhibitor activity in women. Lancet 2000;356:213–217. *First description of hereditary angioedema type 3.*

Gonzalez E, Gonzalez S: Drug photosensitivity, idiopathic photodermatoses and sunscreens. J Am Acad Dermatol 1996;35:871–885. *Discussion of all aspects of light sensitivity.*

Kaplan AP: Chronic urticaria and angioedema (clinical practice). *N Engl J Med* 2002;346:175–179. *Clear practice guidelines with appropriate references.*

Kontou-Fili K, Borici-Mazi R, Kapp A, et al: Physical urticaria: Classification and diagnostic guidelines. Allergy 1997;52:504–513. *Excellent practice guide to the physical urticarias.*

Kozel MM, Bossuyt PM, Mekkes JR, et al: Laboratory tests and identified diagnoses in patients with physical and chronic urticaria and angioedema: A systematic review. J Am Acad Dermatol 2003;48:409–416. *Overview of the current literature showing that the evidence is limited.*

Lee CW, Sheffer AL: Primary acquired cold urticaria. Allergy Asthma Proc 2003;24:9–12. *Review of clinical presentation, pathogenesis, diagnosis, and management.*

Ortonne JP: Chronic idiopathic urticaria for the generalist. Eur J Intern Med 2003;14:148–157. *Reviews treatments, including desloratadine, a once-daily, nonsedating treatment.*

Tedeschi A, Airaghi L, Lorini M, et al: Chronic urticaria: A role for newer immunomodulatory drugs? Am J Clin Dermatol 2003;4:297–305. *Overview of therapeutic options, including newer drugs.*

270 SYSTEMIC ANAPHYLAXIS

Lawrence B. Schwartz

Definition

Systemic anaphylaxis arises when mast cells are provoked to secrete mediators that evoke a systemic response. Although mast cells in any organ system may be involved, depending on the distribution of the instigating stimulus, the principal targets include the cardiovascular, cutaneous, respiratory, and gastrointestinal systems, all sites where mast cells are most abundant. The terms *anaphylactic* and *anaphylactoid*, respectively, attempt to distinguish between mast cell activation initiated by allergen and IgE, classic immediate hypersensitivity, versus mast cell activation by alternative pathways. Although the mediators elicited from mast cells overlap extensively in anaphylaxis and anaphylactoid reactions, thereby invoking similar acute therapies, understanding differences in causation will likely affect therapeutic interventions aimed at preventing future attacks.

Cells other than mast cells also undoubtedly participate in systemic anaphylaxis, particularly those armed with antigen-specific IgE. Basophils, like mast cells, constitutively express substantial amounts of the high-affinity receptor for IgE and FcεRI, and when activated through this pathway, also release mediators within minutes. Eosinophils, monocytes, antigen-presenting cells, and epithelial cells may be induced to express this receptor, thereby affecting the intensity, duration, or character of anaphylactic reactions. Whether some cases of systemic anaphylaxis occur through one or more of these cell types without involving mast cells is theoretically possible, but remains controversial.

Precipitating Factors

Most IgE-dependent mast cell activation events occur at local sites and result in local disease. For example, allergic conjunctivitis, allergic rhinitis, or allergic asthma typically occurs when an allergen interacts with the corresponding mucosal surface of a sensitive individual. Systemic anaphylaxis presumably requires the allergen (or nonallergen agonist) to distribute systemically before mast cells at remote sites are activated. This is most likely to occur with parenteral allergen administration and is less likely with administration by the oral route, by inhalation, or by direct cutaneous or ocular contact. Activation of mast cells in perivascular locations should have the greatest effect on systemic vascular responses, even though large amounts of mediators released locally in theory could spill into the circulation and affect remote sites. Accordingly, intravenous penicillin is more likely than oral penicillin to elicit a severe anaphylactic reaction. However, the precise distributions of mast cells that are activated during anaphylactic reactions are undetermined.

ALLERGENS. The most common allergens causing systemic anaphylactic reactions include drugs (e.g., penicillin), insect venoms, foods, radiocontrast media, allergen immunotherapy injections, latex, and autoantigens. Most allergens are typically proteins or glycoproteins that serve as complete antigens. In contrast, most drugs act as haptens, becoming covalently linked to self proteins in the circulation, in tissues, or on cells, with the complexes acting as multivalent allergens. Multivalency is important, because cross-linking of IgE on the surface of cells brings together at least two FcεRI molecules that then transmit an activating signal into the cell. A monovalent antigen rather than activating cross-linking would block cross-linking, thereby inhibiting activation.

An allergen exposure must lead to sensitization before an immediate hypersensitivity reaction can occur. Allergen exposure leads to antigen processing and presentation to Th cells, with subsequent class switching of allergen-specific B cells to IgE, a process that takes between 1 and 2 weeks. Consequently, anaphylaxis does not occur upon first exposure to an allergen, but may occur after subsequent exposures.

NON–IgE-DEPENDENT AGONISTS. Most non–IgE-dependent foreign agents do not require antigen processing and can elicit a mast cell activation response upon first exposure. These include radiocontrast dyes, narcotics such as codeine and morphine, and vancomycin. The dose and rate of administration and individual variations in sensitivity are determinants of severity. For radiocontrast dyes, low ionic strength media are less likely than high ionic strength media to elicit a systemic reaction. Vancomycin produces a mast cell activation event known as red man's syndrome, typically involving urticaria without cardiovascular compromise, and usually can be avoided by reducing the rate of administration of the antibiotic.

Endogenous mast cell activators include neuropeptides such as substance P, neurokinin A, and calcitonin gene-related peptide, and the complement anaphylatoxins C3a and C5a. Whether a magnitude of mast cell activation sufficient to cause systemic anaphylaxis can result from endogenous secretion or generation of these peptides by themselves is unproven. For example, an anaphylactic shocklike syndrome occurred in hemodialysis patients exposed to a contaminated hemodialysis membrane and was associated with complement activation, but mast cell activation was not detected.

Aspirin hypersensitivity can manifest as either a respiratory or a cardiovascular reaction. Respiratory reactions include bronchospasm, nasal congestion, and rhinorrhea, and may extend beyond the respiratory tract to include abdominal cramping, watery diarrhea, and urticaria. Cardiovascular reactions clinically identical to allergen-induced systemic anaphylaxis also can occur. In most cases, such reactions appear to be pharmacologically (not IgE) mediated, and in sensitive subjects can occur to any of the cyclooxygenase (COX)-1 inhibitors. Although COX inhibitors (i.e., nonsteroidal anti-inflammatory drugs) may shunt arachidonic acid metabolism down a lipoxygenase pathway, a mechanism to explain mast cell activation has not yet emerged. COX-2-selective inhibitors appear to be relatively safe in aspirin-sensitive asthmatics, but they have not been adequately tested in aspirin-sensitive anaphylaxis subjects. Less commonly, sensitivity occurs to only one of the drugs within this class and is due to IgE against a unique chemical moiety.

AUTOIMMUNITY. Some patients present with spontaneous episodes of anaphylaxis. In some cases, this may be an extension of a physical urticaria, occurring in response to stimuli such as exercise or cold.

Progesterone-induced anaphylaxis, which tends to occur just before menses, although uncommon, has been well documented. In other cases, occurrences are not associated with an obvious stimulus. Some cases of chronic urticaria are known to be associated with IgG and IgM antibodies against FcεRI or IgE. In such cases, complement activation and generation of complement anaphylatoxins at the surface of mast cells has been postulated to synergize with FcεRI-mediated activation. This mechanism explains why these urticarial reactions occur preferentially in the skin—because complement anaphylatoxins act on skin-derived but not on lung-derived mast cells. An analogous autoimmune process might activate mast cells localized in blood vessel walls, the result being anaphylaxis, but such a mechanism for systemic anaphylaxis remains unproven.

Epidemiology

Assessing the annual incidence of systemic anaphylaxis and the prevalence of those at risk for systemic anaphylaxis are compromised by imprecise diagnostic measures. Approximately 1500 to 2000 deaths occur per year from systemic anaphylaxis in the United States. Nonfatal cases are much more common, estimated to occur in about 0.2% of the population per year. Further analyses suggest that between 3 and 43 million (1 and 15% of the population) may be at risk for such reactions. Drug reactions account for most cases. β-Lactam antibiotics and radiocontrast media provoke most such events, but the list of offending agents is lengthy and ever increasing. During general anesthesia, systemic anaphylactic reactions occur with a frequency of about 1 in 3500, and muscle relaxants, latex, and induction drugs are the three classes of agents most commonly implicated. Food and insect sting reactions each account for about 100 deaths per year. Among foods, peanuts and tree nuts are the most common inducers of anaphylaxis, whereas shellfish, milk, eggs, soy, and wheat are somewhat less common causes; but as with drugs, the list of implicated foods is long. Honey bees, bumble bees, hornets, yellow jackets, paper wasps, and fire ants are the insects primarily responsible for anaphylactic reactions. Finally, latex provokes anaphylaxis in a small but significant group of individuals, particularly patients who had undergone multiple surgical procedures early in life, such as those with spina bifida or congenital urinary tract disorders. Over a 5-year period, the Food and Drug Administration collected approximately 1100 reports of latex-induced anaphylaxis, including 15 deaths.

Pathophysiology

Mast cells participate in both acquired and innate forms of immunity. They develop in peripheral tissues from bone marrow progenitors primarily under the influence of stem cell factor, the ligand for the tyrosine kinase receptor called Kit. Armed with allergen-specific IgE, they are activated by multivalent allergens that cross-link IgE and associated FcεRI molecules on the mast cell surface. This may be important in host defense against certain parasites that elicit a strong IgE response. Experiments performed in rodents suggest that mast cells also can be activated directly by certain bacterial products, leading to the secretion of mediators that recruit neutrophils. This response may restrain bacterial dissemination until a more potent acquired immune response develops. Activation of mast cells by endogenous peptides such as substance P or calcitonin gene-related peptide may influence basic biologic processes such as wound healing and angiogenesis. Whether mast cells have a critical, nonredundant role in these biologic and immunologic processes remains controversial. However, their central role in immediate hypersensitivity is clear.

Mediators released by mast cells include preformed molecules stored in secretory granules, newly generated products of arachidonic acid, and an array of cytokines and chemokines. Histamine, formed from histidine by histidine decarboxylase, is the sole biogenic amine stored in all granules of human mast cells and human basophils. From 1 to 5 pg of histamine is found per cell. Levels of histamine in normal plasma range from 1 to 10 nM. In skin, lung, and intestine, where mast cell concentrations normally range from 1 to 20 million per mL, local concentrations of histamine after mast cell degranulation theoretically may approach 100 μM. Concentrations of histamine inside secretory granules as high as 100 mM can be calculated.

Histamine released by mast cells or basophils diffuses freely and interacts with H_1, H_2, H_3, and H_4 receptors. H_1 receptors are found on endothelial and smooth muscle cells, and in the central nervous system (CNS). Bronchial and gastrointestinal smooth muscle contraction, vascular smooth muscle relaxation, and increased permeability of post-capillary venules account for many of the signs and symptoms of systemic anaphylaxis, and are in part mediated by histamine acting on H_1 receptors. In the CNS, blocking H_1 receptors appears to cause drowsiness. Some investigators have speculated that excessive levels of histamine in the CNS account for the sense of doom that many victims of anaphylaxis notice at onset. H_2 receptors reside on gastric parietal cells, and at lower levels on inflammatory cells, bronchial epithelium, endothelium, and in the CNS. Increased acid production in the stomach, albeit transient, may occur during systemic anaphylaxis, but is more likely to become clinically significant when histamine levels are chronically elevated, as observed in patients with systemic mastocytosis. The anti-inflammatory and potential CNS effects of H_2 receptor stimulation appear to be somewhat modest. Stimulation of H_3 and H_4 receptors, the least well studied of the histamine receptors, may increase motor activity, enhance acid production in the stomach, and modulate inflammation. Histamine, after its secretion from mast cells and basophils, is rapidly metabolized to methyl histamine and indoleacetic acid.

Prostaglandin D_2 (PGD_2) is the principal COX-catalyzed product of arachidonic acid secreted by activated mast cells, but it is not made by basophils. PGD_2 binds to the G protein–coupled receptors CRTH2 and DP. Both COX-1 and COX-2 are involved in PGD_2 production by mast cells. Consequently, a COX inhibitor that is bipotent might be better than one that is selective at blocking PGD_2-mediated responses during anaphylaxis, which may include hypotension, bronchospasm, and inhibition of platelet aggregation.

Leukotriene C_4 (LTC_4) is released by both mast cells and basophils after its formation from arachidonic acid and glutathione is sequentially catalyzed first by 5-lipoxygenase and 5-lipoxygenase activating protein and then by LTC synthase. Conversion of LTC_4 to LTD_4 and LTE_4, which also are bioactive, occurs in the extracellular space. These sulfidopeptide leukotrienes bind to $CysLT_1$ (smooth muscle, epithelial and endothelial cells, lung macrophages, eosinophils) and to $CysLT_2$ (endothelial and epithelial cells), both G protein–coupled receptors. Sulfidopeptide leukotrienes cause bronchoconstriction, mucus secretion, eosinophil recruitment, increased vasopermeability, diminished cardiac contractility, vasoconstriction of coronary and peripheral arteries, and vasodilation of venules.

Mast cells also are the sole or principal source of heparin proteoglycan and the proteases, α-tryptase, β-tryptase, chymase, and mast cell carboxypeptidase. Like neutrophils and monocytes, they also contain cathepsin G. Basophils are relatively deficient in these enzymes. Mature β-tryptase is stored in the secretory granules of all mast cells, where it accounts for about 20% of the entire protein content of the cell; it is released during degranulation of activated cells. In contrast, precursor forms of both α- and β-tryptases are spontaneously secreted by mast cells at rest. The other proteases appear together in a subset of mast cells. Those mast cells possessing tryptase alone are called MC_T cells and are the predominant type of mast cell in the lung and small intestinal mucosa. Those mast cells possessing all proteases are called MC_{TC} cells and account for most of the mast cells in skin, intestinal submucosa, conjunctiva, and blood vessel walls. The roles of these molecules in the pathophysiology of anaphylaxis are undefined.

Cytokines (tumor necrosis factor-α, interleukin-4, -5, -6, -13, and -16, granulocyte-macrophage colony-stimulating factor) and chemokines (interleukin-8, monocyte chemotactic protein-1, monocyte inflammatory protein-1α) represent another dimension of the mediators released by mast cells and basophils. Although not selectively produced by these cell types, the vasoactive and inflammatory potential of such mediators could affect the severity and duration of anaphylaxis. As selective antagonists of the relevant cytokines and chemokines become available and are tested for therapeutic benefits, their roles in the pathogenesis of anaphylaxis will be better understood.

Diagnosis and Differential Diagnosis

Systemic anaphylaxis includes various combinations of hypotension, tachycardia, urticaria, bronchoconstriction, laryngeal edema, colic, diarrhea, and a sense of doom, and its onset is within minutes of the provoking stimulus. Systemic anaphylaxis can be confirmed by demonstrating antigen-specific IgE (sensitization) and an elevated serum level of β-tryptase (mast cell activation). Skin testing or in vitro measurements of antigen-specific IgE should be delayed for at least 2 weeks after the precipitating event to prevent false-negative results. An increased level of mature β-tryptase in serum obtained within several hours after a hypotensive event, normal levels being undetectable, strongly suggests that mast cell activation has occurred. During a study of experimental insect sting–induced anaphylaxis, the increased serum level of β-tryptase correlated closely with the decrease in the mean arterial pressure, indicating that the magnitude of mast cell activation is a primary determinant of clinical severity. Objective criteria, such as a β-tryptase level, provide greater precision for the diagnosis of anaphylaxis than clinical signs and symptoms alone and may be useful for distinguishing anaphylaxis from other conditions. However, some cases of putative anaphylaxis, particularly after food ingestion, are not associated with an elevated level of β-tryptase. This observation raises the question of whether there are anaphylactic pathways not involving mast cell activation, invoking instead possible basophil activation. Measuring plasma levels of histamine, because it is rapidly metabolized, is not a practical test for anaphylaxis. Urinary histamine levels reflect the small portion of histamine not metabolized in the circulation before renal clearance and are affected by ingested histamine-containing foods and histamine-producing mucosal bacteria, compromising the utility of this test.

Anaphylaxis should be distinguished from a variety of disorders with overlapping presentations. Vasovagal syncope presents with diaphoresis, nausea, hypotension, and bradycardia, but without urticaria. Flushing disorders may be benign and unrelated to anaphylaxis, or they could be a manifestation of pathologic conditions such as the carcinoid syndrome, in which urticaria and profound hypotension are not typically associated, and pheochromocytoma, which causes episodic hypertension. Precise detection of these latter conditions involves determining the serum levels of serotonin and urinary levels of 5-hydroxyindole acetic acid, catecholamines, and vanillylmandelic acid. Panic attacks and vocal cord dysfunction can be a challenge to distinguish from anaphylaxis, especially by history alone, but they must be considered. Acute attacks of hereditary and acquired angioedema due to C1 esterase inhibitor deficiency are not associated with pruritic urticaria, and they persist longer than attacks of anaphylaxis. Shock due to complement activation by contaminated hemodialysis tubing, without involving mast cell activation, also has been reported. Scombroidosis occurs 5 to 90 minutes after ingestion of histamine in poorly stored fish and presents with flushing, palpitations, headache, and gastrointestinal symptoms. The condition lasts several hours, with both duration and severity depending on the amount of histamine ingested. Scombroidosis usually responds to H_1 receptor and H_2 receptor antihistamines but occasionally requires epinephrine and intravenous fluids. Acute serum sickness, genetic cell activation syndromes, endotoxin-mediated septic shock, and superantigen-mediated toxic shock syndromes all present with fever, which is not characteristic of anaphylaxis. Also, hypoglycemia, seizure, and primary pulmonary or cardiac events should be considered in the differential diagnosis of anaphylaxis.

In some cases, systemic anaphylaxis may occur together with another disorder. For example, a 65-year-old man after being stung by a wasp complained of dizziness and shortness of breath, was hypotensive with urticaria, responded to treatment with subcutaneous epinephrine, then complained of chest pressure, and had an electrocardiogram indicating an inferior wall infarction. Serum levels of both a β-tryptase and cardiac enzymes were elevated, indicating both anaphylaxis and myocardial infarction had occurred.

Systemic mastocytosis is an important condition to consider in the differential diagnosis of anaphylaxis. In adults, somatic activating mutations in the gene for Kit in mast cell progenitors result in an excessive body burden of mast cells. In children with this disorder the disease may regress spontaneously, possibly due to the lack of this activating mutation. Patients with too many mast cells are at increased risk for anaphylaxis, and anaphylaxis may be a presenting manifestation of systemic mastocytosis. For example, anaphylaxis to an insect sting in the absence of venom-specific IgE should suggest the possibility of systemic mastocytosis. Diagnostic tests for systemic mastocytosis might include a biopsy of a skin lesion suspected to be urticaria pigmentosa, a bone marrow biopsy stained for mast cells (antitryptase immunohistochemistry being most sensitive), detection of bone marrow mast cells expressing surface CD2 and CD25, and an elevated serum level of total tryptase (mature plus immature forms of α- and β- tryptases) during a nonacute interval.

Diseases of Allergy and Clinical Immunology

Rx Prevention and Therapy

Acutely, treatment of systemic anaphylaxis first requires that airway patency, blood pressure, and cardiac status be addressed. Intubation, tracheostomy, volume expanders, and vasopressors may be needed. Epinephrine administered subcutaneously or intramuscularly (0.2 to 0.5 mg for adults, 0.01 mg/kg up to 0.5 mg for children, repeated every 10 to 15 min as needed) is the most critical drug to administer, the earlier during the course of an anaphylactic event the better. Epinephrine improves the loss of vasomotor tone and the increased vasopermeability, thereby counteracting hypotension and tissue edema. However, the benefits of epinephrine need to be weighed against its disadvantages in elderly subjects and in those with cerebrovascular and coronary artery disease, hypertension, diabetes, hyperthyroidism, cardiomyopathy, and narrow angle glaucoma, wherein it can precipitate myocardial infarction, stroke, and pulmonary edema. Also, patients taking a β-blocker may be resistant to epinephrine; in such a case, glucagon (1 mg intravenously (IV), 1 to 5 mg/hour IV) may be used. Oxygen may be administered by nasal cannula. Parenteral administration of H$_1$ receptor (diphenhydramine, 1 to 2 mg/kg up to 50 mg) and H$_2$ receptor (ranitidine, 300 mg IV over 5 min) antihistamines may reverse or prevent progression of some of the signs and symptoms of acute anaphylaxis. Prednisone (20 mg orally) or Solu-Medrol (40 mg IV) may reduce the risk of protracted or recurrent anaphylaxis but is unlikely to be of benefit acutely.

Patients who have experienced an anaphylactic reaction are at greatest risk to suffer another episode. Such individuals should wear a Medic-Alert bracelet and be instructed in the use of epinephrine (e.g., EpiPen), which they should carry. Avoidance of β-blockers and ACE inhibitors is recommended, because both may worsen the severity of an anaphylactic episode and β-blockers clearly interfere with β-agonist treatment. In subjects with recurrent anaphylaxis, prophylactic use of H$_1$ and H$_2$ receptor antihistamines is beneficial. A leukotriene antagonist and COX inhibitor theoretically would provide additional benefit, but they have not been systematically studied. Finally, cyclosporin A (3 to 5 mg/kg) might be considered in difficult cases of recurrent anaphylaxis because of its ability to inhibit mast cell activation in vitro. Glucocorticosteroids, which do not inhibit experimental mast cell activation, are unlikely to provide a major benefit in most patients with recurrent anaphylaxis.

Specific anaphylactic syndromes have unique therapeutic considerations. The sensitivity to peanuts in allergic patients may be reduced from the equivalent of half a peanut to almost nine peanuts after treatment using a specific humanized monoclonal antibody. Insect venom sensitivity can be selectively treated by immunotherapy. Radiocontrast media reactions can be prevented or attenuated by prior administration of prednisone and H$_1$ and H$_2$ receptor antihistamines. Patients hypersensitive to penicillin, in general, should avoid β-lactam antibiotics but can be desensitized when an antibiotic in this class is critically needed (e.g., penicillin for neurosyphilis). However, desensitization is temporary; once the drug has cleared, sensitivity is likely to return. Progesterone-induced anaphylaxis may respond to the luteinizing hormone-releasing hormone analogue, Lupron, or to oophorectomy. Systemic mastocytosis patients, in addition to prophylactic pharmacologic measures, should avoid using direct mast cell agonists such as codeine, morphine, and vancomycin. Food, aspirin, and latex sensitive subjects must practice avoidance of the provocative agent. One looks to the future to bear more effective and long-lasting desensitization therapies than are currently available for most patients at risk for IgE- and non–IgE-mediated anaphylaxis.

1. Leung DY, Sampson HA, Yunginger JW, et al: Effect of anti-IgE therapy in patients with peanut allergy. N Engl J Med 2003;348:986–993.

SUGGESTED READINGS
Kikuchi Y, Kaplan AP: A role for C5a in augmenting IgG-dependent histamine release from basophils in chronic urticaria. J Allergy Clin Immunol 2002;109:114–118. *Insightful study showing complement involvement in autoimmune-mediated activation of basophils.*
Neugut AI, Ghatak AT, Miller RL: Anaphylaxis in the United States: An investigation into its epidemiology. Arch Intern Med 2001;161:15–21. *A recent comprehensive survey of the burden of people at risk for anaphylaxis in the USA.*
Schwartz LB: Clinical utility of tryptase levels in systemic mastocytosis and associated hematologic disorders. Leuk Res 2001;25:553–562. *Molecular and practical insight into the clinical utility of serum tryptase measurements in disorders of mast cell activation and mast cell hyperplasia.*
Valent P, Horny HP, Escribano L, et al: Diagnostic criteria and classification of mastocytosis: A consensus proposal. Leukemia Res 2001;25:603–625. *Practical guide to diagnosing systemic mastocytosis, a risk factor for anaphylaxis.*

271 INSECT STING ALLERGY

Lawrence M. Lichtenstein

Stings of insects of the order Hymenoptera have long been recognized as a potential cause of severe, often life-threatening reactions in susceptible individuals. These reactions are unrelated to toxic chemicals in the venom, instead being due to allergic sensitization. Insect sting allergy has recently become the most intensely studied model of anaphylaxis in humans, and study of this model has resulted in important advances that have had rapid clinical applications.

Epidemiology

The incidence of immediate hypersensitivity to insect stings based on history is 3%; more than 20% of the population, however, has positive skin test reactions to insect venom. Other allergies do not seem to predispose to insect sting sensitivity. The frequency varies with exposure and is therefore greater in children and males, as well as in those inclined to outdoor activities. Systemic reactions to insect stings cause few fatalities, but the morbidity, fear, and change in lifestyle caused by these reactions are significant. A large number of people suffer prolonged and unusually severe local inflammatory reactions to insect stings that are allergic in nature. As with other allergies, there appears to be an inherited predisposition inasmuch as multiple family members are often affected.

Etiology

The only insects possessing true stingers are those of the order Hymenoptera. The two families of importance are the bees (honeybees, bumblebees) and the vespids (yellow jackets, hornets, wasps). Bees have barbed stingers that remain in the skin after a sting. Yellow jackets are the most common culprits, but honeybees are more commonly implicated in the western United States. Wasps are more common in the south central United States (especially Texas). Sensitivity develops to antigens in the insect venom, most of which have enzymatic activity. A major allergen in both insect families is phospholipase A, but these allergens do not cross-react with one another.

Pathogenesis

Injection of foreign proteins commonly causes the production of specific antibodies of the IgE and IgG classes. Venom-specific IgE antibodies may develop after any sting, with this response sometimes persisting for less than 3 months and in other instances persisting for more than 25 years. Tissue mast cells and circulating basophils bind IgE antibody, thereby becoming sensitized so that a repeat encounter with the offending allergen triggers release of the mediators of anaphylaxis (Chapter 270). Initiation and persistence of this sensitization are related to inheritable and other unknown determinants. Sensitization may occur at any time in life, even after many uneventful stings. The sensitizing sting itself causes no unusual reaction and is often so remote as to evade recollection.

Generalized mediator release from sensitized basophils and mast cells (Chapter 270) causes the many manifestations of anaphylaxis. Localization of symptoms to specific target tissues is not well understood. The pathology observed in fatal cases includes upper airway edema and obstruction, the visceral consequences of hypotension, or, occasionally, no discernible abnormality (see Chapter 270 for a discussion of anaphylaxis).

Large local reactions are IgE dependent; their prolonged time course is characteristic of the so-called late-phase response to antigen. These reactions involve a cascade of events beginning with mediator release from mast cells and culminating in local inflammation involving many cell types and numerous mechanisms. The potential roles of eosinophils, basophils, lymphocytes, and cytokines and chemokines are being elucidated.

The venom-specific IgG antibody response to a sting is usually short lived, lasting only a few months. Repeated stings (as occurs in beekeepers) are associated with high titers of IgG antibodies, which protect against allergic reactions. Beekeepers who do not have anaphylactic reactions have high IgG titers, as do affected individuals immunized with venom. Passive transfer of these IgG antibodies protects sensitive patients from a sting. These protective antibodies are thought to block the allergic reaction by competing with IgE for the allergenic venom proteins and have therefore been termed "blocking" antibodies.

Clinical Manifestations

Allergic reactions to insect stings are either generalized (systemic) or large local reactions. Systemic sting reactions present the classic manifestations of anaphylaxis described in Chapter 270. The observed frequency of the most common symptoms in adult patients is presented in Table 271–1. The risk of a fatal outcome increases, as expected, with age and the use of certain drugs, especially antagonists of β-adrenergic receptors. Fatal anaphylaxis may occur without a history of sting allergy.

The onset of systemic symptoms is rapid, within 2 to 3 minutes, and rarely occurs more than 30 minutes after a sting. Symptoms occurring hours later (except large local reactions) are not usually associated with immediate hypersensitivity or IgE antibodies. Unusual reactions such as vasculitis, nephropathies, encephalitis, and other neurologic manifestations have been reported, but no causal relationship has been established. Allergic respiratory symptoms may occur in beekeepers and their families through sensitization to the dust in the hives, which contains bee body protein. This sensitivity is unrelated to sting reactions.

Large local reactions are slow in onset and occur with or without concomitant early systemic reaction. The area of induration increases in size progressively for the first 24 to 48 hours and then resolves gradually over several days. These reactions may be so large as to immobilize an entire limb and are a significant cause of morbidity in sensitive individuals. Red streaks resembling lymphangitis may be observed and are often treated with antibiotics despite a lack of evidence for true cellulitis.

Natural History

The natural history of insect sting allergy has been incompletely documented. The prevalence of venom sensitization in the general population is noted earlier. It is estimated that about 20% of those at risk by virtue of positive skin tests (but with no history of a systemic reaction) will react on sting. There is considerable variability in the reaction to a sting among those who are clearly allergic as demonstrated by positive skin tests and a history of a previous reaction. Recent studies indicate that 25 to 60% of adults had a systemic reaction when stung by the appropriate insect. In children, on the other hand, a repeat sting causes a reaction in only 8%. The incidence in adolescents and young adults must lie between these extremes.

Table 271–1 • SYMPTOMS REPORTED BY 245 PATIENTS

SYMPTOM	PERCENTAGE
Cutaneous only	14
Urticaria/angioedema	78
Dizziness/hypotension	61
Dyspnea-wheezing	53
Throat tightness/hoarseness	40
Loss of consciousness	33

This variability confounds the prediction of risk associated with sensitization.

Although many patients and physicians believe that allergic sting reactions become progressively more severe with every sting, such is not true. Most of those affected maintain a similar pattern of symptoms with every sting. Factors favoring a systemic reaction include multiple stings, as well as stings in close temporal proximity (only weeks apart).

Sensitization generally decreases or disappears in time, much more so in children than in adults. However, resensitization has been observed upon re-sting.

Diagnosis

Acute anaphylaxis is easily diagnosed by the presence of classic symptoms and signs. The insect sting may be inapparent. The differential diagnosis is more difficult in localized reactions such as acute chest pain and dyspnea or syncope without urticaria.

Skin tests are performed intradermally with venom diluted to concentrations in the range of 1 to 1000 ng/mL. Five types of venom are used: honeybee, yellow jacket, yellow hornet, white-faced hornet, and *Polistes* wasp. A positive intradermal skin test, a wheal larger than 5 mm in diameter with at least 20 mm of erythema, develops within 20 minutes. The degree of skin test sensitivity does not correlate with clinical sensitivity. Within a few months after a systemic sting reaction, skin tests are almost uniformly positive. Stings more remote in time are more commonly associated with an apparent loss of sensitivity (similar to the situation in penicillin-related anaphylaxis).

Honeybee venom sensitivity occurs independent of other venom allergies, but about 10% of patients are sensitive to both bee and vespid venom. Vespid venom is highly cross-reactive, so almost all vespid-sensitive patients have positive yellow jacket, yellow hornet, and white-faced hornet skin tests, even though most have been stung only by yellow jackets. Half of these patients are also sensitive to *Polistes* venom. Very few individuals are allergic to only one or two of the vespid venoms. In vitro radioallergosorbent test (RAST) inhibition techniques are useful to distinguish cross-reactivity from specific sensitivity. This issue is clinically relevant in patients with a positive skin test to *Polistes*, which is often due to cross-reactivity, and the patient may be spared considerable expense and unnecessary immunization by RAST inhibition analysis.

Rx Treatment

The treatment of choice for anaphylactic reactions is subcutaneous epinephrine, 1:1000, 0.5 mL initially and repeated twice at 10-minute intervals, if necessary, to reverse the progression of symptoms. Antihistamines and glucocorticoids do not contribute to the management of life-threatening symptoms but may reduce the duration and severity of cutaneous manifestations. Their use should not be considered until the acute episode has ended. Intravenous volume expansion or airway maintenance may be necessary. In a few individuals, the process is resistant to epinephrine; in such instances, an α-adrenergic agent (i.e., norepinephrine) may be tried. Affected persons not yet protected by immunotherapy are advised to carry and are instructed in the use of a kit containing a syringe device preloaded with one or two recommended doses of epinephrine.

Venom immunotherapy is successful in virtually all patients. Fewer than 2% of those immunized have any systemic symptoms after a challenge sting, and these are uniformly less severe than their previous reactions. The indications for venom immunotherapy are based on an improved understanding of the natural history of the disease. Those with a history of life-threatening reactions should be treated. The risk of progression from strictly cutaneous to life-threatening respiratory or vascular reactions is rare (<1%) in adults and children. Cutaneous reactors who are more likely to be stung in their daily activities or who for a variety of reasons (location, age, cardiovascular disease) can ill afford a reaction should be treated. The cost and inconvenience of treatment may deter other cutaneous reactors from undergoing immunotherapy. Children, much more commonly than adults, have cutaneous symptoms only. These children may be left untreated.

Until the recent realization that the venom skin tests are not specific, venom immunotherapy was contraindicated in the absence of a positive venom skin test or RAST. This must now be reconsidered. If the skin test is negative, a RAST may well be helpful. However, there are rare individuals whose skin and RAST tests are negative but who are still at risk. A clinical decision must be made as to whether these patients should be treated. Sting challenge is becoming increasingly important because of the skin test problems. The nonspecialist may consider referring the patient to a specialist who is able to carry out these sting tests. Although other mechanisms may contribute, induction of increased serum levels of venom-specific IgG antibodies is the most apparent mechanism of protection for venom immunotherapy; less than 3 mg/mL is associated with an increased risk of sting anaphylaxis. In many European centers, the patient is restung in the hospital before therapy is begun.

Rapid immunization in 6 to 8 weekly visits is recommended to take advantage of a significantly greater and more rapid immune response with fewer adverse reactions than a slower (>20 weeks) regimen. The maintenance dose of 100 μg of each venom is repeated monthly for at least 6 months and then continued at 6- to 8-week intervals for 5 years. If treatment is interrupted for more than 3 months, it is likely that protection will diminish to inadequate levels. Loss of venom sensitivity during maintenance immunotherapy occurs in some patients during the initial 3 to 5 years of treatment. Skin tests should therefore be repeated every 2 years. After 5 years, it appears that patients can stop therapy and suffer a sting without serious sequelae. Possible exceptions include patients with extremely severe reactions or those with complicating medical conditions. After stopping venom immunotherapy, venom sensitivity continues to decline and is not increased even after stings.

Adverse reactions to venom immunotherapy may be early or late. Immediate reactions include all the manifestations of anaphylaxis. During the initial course of treatment, 10 to 15% of patients report systemic complaints, only half of which require epinephrine. At maintenance doses, systemic reactions occur rarely. After a systemic reaction, the dose should be reduced by up to 50% on the subsequent visit and then increased gradually toward 100 μg again.

Large local reactions occur frequently—50% of treated patients experience at least one such reaction. These reactions occur after 10 of every 100 injections in the induction phase, most commonly in the midrange of doses (10 to 50 μg) and much less often at maintenance doses. Large local reactions do not presage systemic reactions and require a reduction in dose only for the most severe reactions. Long-term side effects have not been observed with venom immunotherapy or in beekeepers stung frequently for over 30 years.

SUGGESTED READINGS

Frew AJ. Immunotherapy of allergic disease. J Allergy Clin Immunol 2003;111:S712–S719. *Specific immunotherapy can provide long-lasting relief.*
Hamilton RG, Adkinson NF Jr: Clinical laboratory assessment of IgE-dependent hypersensitivity. J Allergy Clin Immunol 2003;111:S687–S701. *How to improve the diagnosis and management of IgE-dependent allergic diseases.*

272 MASTOCYTOSIS

Dean D. Metcalfe

Definition and Epidemiology

Mastocytosis is a rare disease characterized by an abnormal increase in mast cells in the bone marrow, liver, spleen, lymph nodes, gastrointestinal tract, and skin. Mastocytosis may occur in any age group and demonstrates a slight male preponderance (1.5:1.0). The prevalence of the disease is unknown, and familial occurrence is unusual.

The disease is subdivided into categories on the basis of clinical features, pathologic findings, and prognosis (Table 272–1). Patients with cutaneous mastocytosis and patients with indolent systemic mastocytosis (ISM) have the best prognosis. Patients with other forms of mastocytosis do poorly. ISM usually manifests with skin involvement, and systemic disease is then documented. In most cases, patients with ISM gradually accrue more mast cells with progression of symptoms but can be managed successfully for decades with medications that provide symptomatic relief. The next most common form of systemic mastocytosis is associated with clonal hematologic non-mast cell lineage disease (SM-AHNMD), in which examination of the bone marrow and peripheral blood reveals the hematologic abnormality. The prognosis in these patients is determined by the associated hematologic disorder. Aggressive systemic mastocytosis (ASM), mast cell leukemia, mast cell sarcoma, and extracutaneous mastocytoma are rare forms, generally associated with fulminant behavior. Mast cell leukemia is distinguished by its unique pathologic and clinical picture. The peripheral blood smear shows immature mast cells. In ASM, individuals experience a rapid increase in mast cell numbers and have poor prognostic features but do not have a distinctive hematologic disorder or mast cell leukemia. Mast cell sarcoma is exceedingly rare, with an initial localized growth and metastatic potential. An extracutaneous mastocytoma is unifocal, nondestructive, and usually found in the lung.

Etiology and Pathogenesis

Mast cells originate from pluripotent bone marrow stem cells and migrate through the blood stream and lymphatics to specific sites, where they mature into fully granulated cells. Targeting of mast cells to defined locations is determined by the sequential expression of cell-surface adhesion molecules. Mast cells are often found along the endothelial and epithelial basement membrane, along nerves, and around glandular structures. Tissues at interfaces between the external and internal environment, such as the skin and gastrointestinal tract, are particularly rich in mast cells.

Mast cell number and differentiation are regulated by factors produced both in the hematopoietic marrow and by cells in the tissues in which mast cells finally reside. Mast cell growth and differentiation depend on Kit ligand, or stem cell factor, and are inhibited by interferon-γ. Mutations in Kit that lead to ligand-independent phosphorylation of this receptor with resultant growth enhancement and chemotaxis have been described in patients with mastocytosis. The most common of these mutations is a point mutation (Asp816Val) in the catalytic domain. Other genetic polymorphisms such as the Q576R polymorphism in the interleukin-4 receptor α chain may mitigate disease expression.

Regardless of the cause of the increased burden of mast cells, the pathogenesis of the disease is largely the result of the increased production of mast cell mediators, which have effects both at the site of their production and at remote sites. Mast cell mediators are of three categories, all of which produce biologic effects typical of those observed in patients with mastocytosis (Table 272–2).

Table 272–1 • WORLD HEALTH ORGANIZATION CLASSIFICATION OF MASTOCYTOSIS

Cutaneous mastocytosis (CM)
  Urticaria pigmentosa (UP)/maculopapular cutaneous mastocytosis (MPCM)
    Typical UP
    Plaque form
    Nodular form
    Telangiectasia macularis eruption perstans (TMEP)
  Diffuse cutaneous mastocytosis (DCM)
  Solitary mastocytoma of skin
Indolent systemic mastocytosis (ISM)
Systemic mastocytosis with an associated clonal hematologic non-mast cell lineage disease (SM-AHNMD)
Aggressive systemic mastocytosis (ASM)
Mast cell leukemia (MCL)
Mast cell sarcoma (MCS)
Extracutaneous mastocytoma

Table 272–2 • REPRESENTATIVE MAST CELL PRODUCTS AND THEIR BIOLOGIC EFFECTS

PRODUCT	EFFECT
GRANULE ASSOCIATED	
Histamine	Pruritus, increased vasopermeability, gastric hypersecretion, bronchoconstriction
Heparin	Local anticoagulation
Tryptase, chymotryptic proteases	Degradation of local connective tissues
LIPID DERIVED	
Sulfidopeptide leukotrienes	Increased vasopermeability, bronchoconstriction, vasoconstriction (LTC_4); increased vasopermeability, bronchoconstriction, vasodilation (LTD_4 and LTE_4)
Prostaglandin D_2	Vasodilation, bronchoconstriction
Platelet-activating factor	Increased vasopermeability, vasodilation, bronchoconstriction
CYTOKINES	
Proinflammatory factors	Fibrosis (TGF-β); activation of vascular endothelial cells, cachexia (TNF-α; IL-6); IgE synthesis (IL-4)
Growth enhancing	Colony-stimulating factor (IL-3), eosinophilia (IL-5)

IL = interleukin; LTC = leukotriene; TGF = transforming growth factor; TNF = tumor necrosis factor.

Clinical Manifestations

The variants of mastocytosis in general share similar clinical features, although some patterns of disease may predominate in a specific category. The skin, gastrointestinal tract, liver, spleen, lymph nodes, bone marrow, and skeletal system yield the most significant management problems. The respiratory tract and endocrine system are generally spared. Patients with mastocytosis do not suffer from recurrent infections.

The most common skin manifestation of mastocytosis is urticaria pigmentosa (UP) (Fig. 272–1). It is seen in more than 90% of patients with ISM and in fewer than 50% of patients with SM-AHNMD or ASM. The lesions of UP appear as scattered small reddish brown macules or slightly raised papules. Scratching or rubbing the lesions usually causes urtication and erythema around the macules, a phenomenon known as Darier's sign. UP is associated with pruritus, which may be exacerbated by changes in climatic temperature, skin friction, and ingestion of hot beverages, spicy foods, ethanol, and certain drugs. The diagnosis is confirmed by characteristic skin histopathologic findings. Diffuse cutaneous mastocytosis consists of a diffuse mast cell infiltration of the skin. Solitary lesions called *mastocytomas* do occur but are quite rare. Young children with UP or diffuse cutaneous mastocytosis may have bullous eruptions.

Gastrointestinal disease often develops in patients with mastocytosis. The most common problem is gastric hypersecretion caused by elevated plasma histamine with resultant gastritis and peptic ulcer disease. Diarrhea and abdominal pain are common and are followed by the onset of malabsorption in approximately one in three patients. Radiographic abnormalities fall into three major categories: peptic ulcers; abnormal mucosal patterns such as mucosal edema, multiple nodular lesions, coarsened mucosal folds, or multiple polyps; and motility disturbances. Histopathologic examination of jejunal biopsy specimens has shown moderate blunting of the villi; however, significant mast cell hyperplasia is uncommon.

Hepatic and splenic involvement in indolent systemic mastocytosis is relatively common, although liver function tests are often normal. The most common chemical abnormality is an elevated alkaline phosphatase concentration, which must be distinguished from bone-derived alkaline phosphatase, levels of which may also be elevated. The most serious manifestation of hepatic and splenic involvement is portal hypertension and ascites associated with fibro-

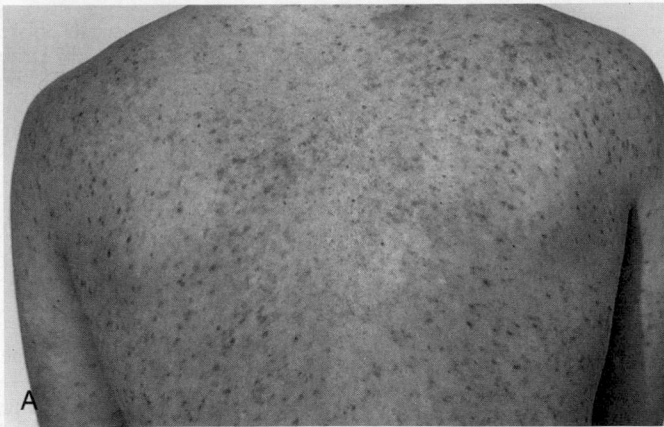

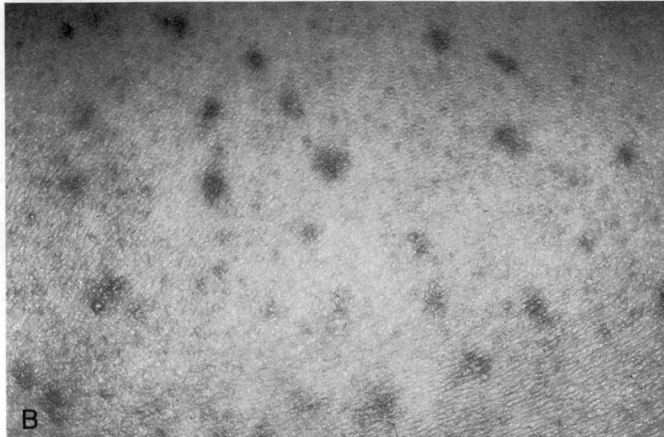

FIGURE 272–1 • *A,* Urticaria pigmentosa in a patient with indolent systemic mastocytosis. *B,* Close-up view of urticaria pigmentosa.

sis of the liver and spleen. These conditions appear most commonly in patients who have mastocytosis with an associated hematologic disorder or in those with ASM.

Bone marrow lesions most commonly consist of focal aggregates of spindle-shaped mast cells, often mixed with eosinophils, lymphocytes, and occasional plasma cells, histiocytes, and fibroblasts (Fig. 272–2). Mast cells in bone marrow aspirates from patients with mastocytosis often express CD2 and CD25. Anemia, leukopenia, thrombocytopenia, and eosinophilia may occur in association with systemic disease. Bone marrow infiltration with mast cells may induce bone changes that cause radiographically detectable lesions in up to 70% of patients. The proximal long bones are most often affected, followed by the pelvis, ribs, and skull. Musculoskeletal pain is the most common symptom and is present in 19 to 28% of patients. Skeletal scintigraphy (bone scan) is more sensitive than radiographic surveys in detecting and locating active lesions. In severe or advanced disease, pathologic fractures do occur.

Patients with every category of mastocytosis sometimes experience flushing or systemic hypotension. In occasional patients, hypotension may be provoked by alcohol, aspirin, exercise, stinging insects, radiocontrast media, or infections.

Neuropsychiatric abnormalities have been reported. Problems include a decreased attention span, memory impairment, and irritability. Depression as a consequence of chronic disease or perhaps mediated by mast cell products is a possibility.

Diagnosis

The diagnosis of mastocytosis rests on histology, supported by clinical, biochemical, and radiographic data. Mast cells may be overlooked on histologic sections, depending on the fixative and/or stain used. The most useful stain for mast cells is tryptase, which highlights the granules in the cytoplasm of the mast cell.

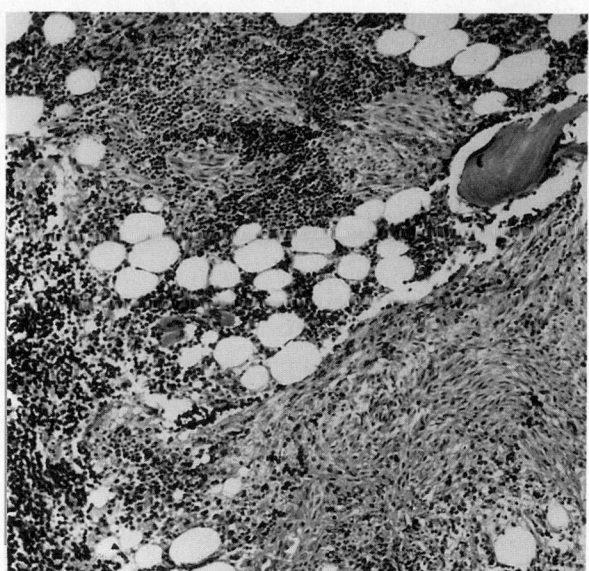

FIGURE 272–2 • Bone marrow biopsy shows a characteristic lesion of systemic mastocytosis with a nodular, paratrabecular infiltrate of mast cells.

The majority of patients with mastocytosis have UP. This diagnosis should be confirmed by skin biopsy. Blind skin biopsies are not recommended because other skin conditions, including eczema, are associated with an increase in numbers of dermal mast cells.

In the absence of skin lesions, mastocytosis may be suspected in patients with one or several of the following: unexplained ulcer disease or malabsorption, radiographic or ^{99m}Tc bone scan abnormalities, hepatomegaly, splenomegaly, lymphadenopathy, peripheral blood abnormalities, and unexplained flushing or hypotension. Elevated levels of plasma or urinary histamine or histamine metabolites, prostaglandin D$_2$ metabolites in the urine, or plasma mast cell tryptase are not diagnostic but do raise the index of suspicion for mastocytosis. Elevated serum levels of soluble Kit and/or CD25 are directly associated with severity of disease and bone marrow pathology.

Patients suspected of having mastocytosis in the absence of skin lesions should have bone marrow biopsy and aspirate samples taken for diagnosis. Patients with UP or diffuse cutaneous mastocytosis should also have this procedure if they have peripheral blood abnormalities, hepatomegaly, splenomegaly, or lymphadenopathy to determine whether they have an associated hematologic disorder. Other tissue specimens such as from lymph nodes, liver, and gastrointestinal mucosa define the extent of mast cell involvement but are obtained only as necessary.

Patients suspected of having mastocytosis should have 24-hour urine 5-hydroxyindoleacetic acid measured to help eliminate the possibility of a carcinoid tumor. Patients with mastocytosis do not excrete increased amounts of 5-hydroxyindoleacetic acid. Idiopathic anaphylaxis and flushing must also be considered. Patients with these disorders do not have histologic evidence of significant mast cell proliferation, and have normal levels of plasma mast cell tryptase between attacks.

 Treatment

In all categories of mastocytosis, a primary objective of treatment is to control mast cell mediator–induced signs and symptoms such as hypotension, gastrointestinal cramping, and pruritus. H$_1$ receptor antagonists such as hydroxyzine and fexofenadine are helpful in reducing pruritus, flushing, and tachycardia. If insufficient relief occurs, adding an H$_2$ antagonist such as ranitidine or cimetidine may be beneficial. However, many patients continue to complain of bone pain, headaches, and flushing, which result in part from the inability to block other mast cell mediators. Disodium cromoglycate (cromolyn sodium) inhibits the degranulation of mast cells and may have some efficacy in the treatment of mastocytosis. Epinephrine is used to treat episodes of hypoten-

sion. Patients should be prepared to self-administer this drug. If subcutaneous epinephrine is insufficient, intensive therapy as recommended for anaphylaxis should be instituted. Patients with recurrent episodes of systemic hypotension may have H$_1$ and H$_2$ antihistamines prescribed to lessen the severity of attacks. Episodes of profound hypotension may be spontaneous but have also been observed following stings from insects or the administration of radiocontrast media. The latter observation has led to the suggestion that patients with mastocytosis be premedicated with antihistamines and a glucocorticoid before receiving radiocontrast media.

Treatment of gastrointestinal disease is directed at controlling peptic symptoms, diarrhea, and malabsorption. Gastric acid hypersecretion leading to peptic symptoms and ulcerations is controlled with H$_2$ antagonists and proton pump inhibitors. Diarrhea is difficult to manage, and H$_2$ antagonists are generally not effective. Anticholinergics may give partial relief. In patients with severe malabsorption, systemic glucocorticoids have been shown to be effective. Ascites is also difficult to manage. One patient with portal hypertension was successfully managed with a portacaval shunt. Another patient with exudative ascites was treated successfully with systemic glucocorticoid therapy.

Patients with SM-AHNMD are treated as dictated by the specific hematologic abnormality. In mast cell leukemia, chemotherapy has not yet been shown to produce remissions. Chemotherapy has no place in the treatment of cutaneous mastocytosis or ISM. One study suggests that splenectomy may improve survival in patients with poor prognostic forms of mastocytosis.

Prognosis

Prognosis must be addressed separately for each variety of mastocytosis. One study found seven variables that were strongly associated with poor survival, including constitutional symptoms, anemia, thrombocytopenia, abnormal liver function test results, lobated mast cell nucleus, a low percentage of fat cells in the bone marrow biopsy sample, and an associated hematologic disorder. Other poor prognostic variables include the absence of UP, male gender, absence of skin and bone symptoms, hepatomegaly, splenomegaly, and normal bone radiographic findings.

As a group, patients with cutaneous mastocytosis or ISM alone have the best prognosis. Among children with isolated UP, at least 50% improve by adulthood. Adults with UP usually progress gradually to systemic disease and may rarely convert to SM-AHNMD. Diffuse cutaneous mastocytosis is usually associated with indolent systemic disease. Patients with SM-AHNMD have a variable course, depending on the prognosis of their hematologic disorder. With mast cell leukemia, mean survival is less than 6 months. Survival with ASM is 2 to 3 years without therapy. The prognosis appears to improve with aggressive symptomatic management.

Future Directions

There is much interest in identifying compounds of small molecular weight that preferentially inhibit mutated Kit over wild-type Kit. Nonmyeloablative matched sibling donor bone marrow transplantation is being examined in clinical trials as an option for patients in advanced categories of systemic mastocytosis and impending marrow failure.

SUGGESTED READINGS

Akin C, Schwartz LB, Kitoh T, et al: Soluble stem cell factor receptor (CD117) and IL-2 receptor (CD25) levels in the plasma of patients with mastocytosis: relationships to disease severity and bone marrow pathology. Blood 2000;96:1267–1273. *sKit and sCD25 are markers of the severity of disease in patients with mastocytosis.*

Ma Y, Zeng S, Metcalfe DD, et al: The c-KIT mutation causing human mastocytosis is resistant to STI571 and other KIT kinase inhibitors: kinases with enigmatic site mutations show different sensitivity profiles than wild type kinases and those with regulatory type mutations. Blood 2002;99:1741–1744. *Demonstration that kinase inhibitors may not effectively inhibit Kit with an activating mutation in the kinase domain.*

Metcalfe DD, Akin C: Mastocytosis: Molecular mechanisms and clinical disease heterogeneity. Leuk Res 2001;25:577–582. *A detailed review of mutations in Kit and their relevance in disease pathogenesis and diagnosis.*

Valent P, Akin C, Sperr WR, et al: Aggressive systemic mastocytosis and related mast cell disorders: current treatment options and proposed response criteria. Leuk Res 2003;27:635–641. *A summary of current treatment options in the treatment of the multiple variants of mastocytosis and recommended response criteria to use in evaluating the degree to which a given treatment plan results in a clinical response.*

Valent P, Horny H-P, Li C, et al: Mastocytosis. *In* Jaffee ES, Harris NL, Stein H, Varderman JW (eds): World Health Organization Classification of Tumours: Pathology and Genetics in Tumours of Haematopoietic and Lymphoid Tissues. Lyon, IARC Press, 2001, pp 291–302. *Presentation of the World Health Organization Classification of mastocytosis along with detailed classification criteria.*

Worobec AS, Akin C, Scott LM, et al: Mastocytosis complicating pregnancy. Obstet Gynecol 2000;95:391–395. *A useful source of information for those with mastocytosis considering extending their family.*

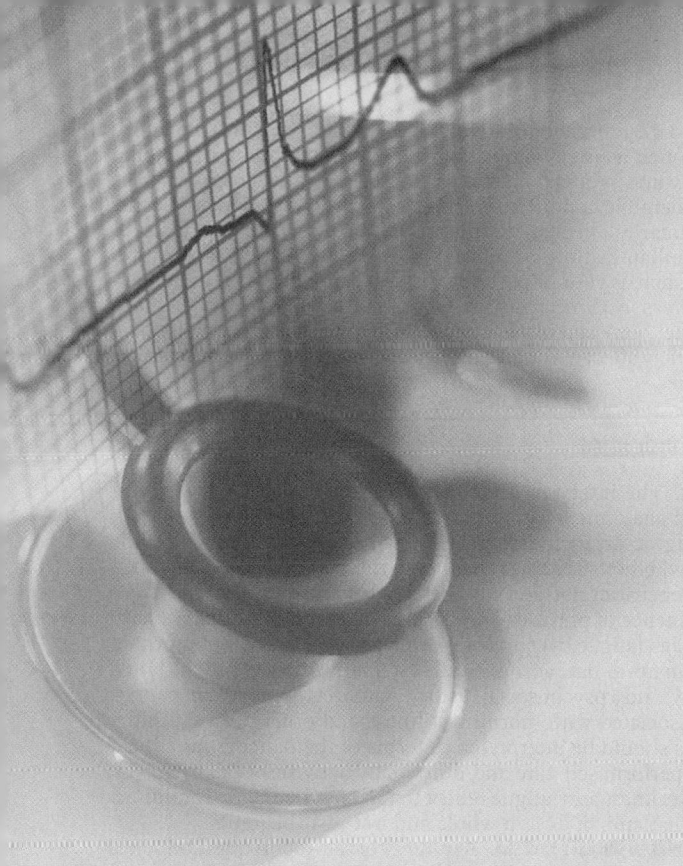

part XXII

Rheumatic Diseases

273 APPROACH TO THE PATIENT WITH RHEUMATIC DISEASE

Duncan A. Gordon
William P. Arend

Rheumatic diseases of the musculoskeletal system are common, disabling, and costly to the economy. This chapter provides a guide for approaching the patient with rheumatic symptoms by outlining the components necessary for identifying the patient's problems, formulating the diagnosis, and initiating treatment.

The pain, stiffness, and joint swelling of musculoskeletal disorders may manifest as acute, subacute, or chronic problems due to inflammatory, metabolic, or degenerative conditions alone or in combination. For the patient, however, it is the functional interference with daily activities that determines the impact of the condition. The value of a general medical approach to the patient with rheumatic complaints is paramount, keeping specialized assessment in perspective. At times, a limited work-up may suffice, whereas in other instances, assessment by a number of laboratory, imaging, and other disciplines may be necessary. Before clinical approaches are considered, it is helpful to review the anatomy and pathophysiology of the structures affected.

Anatomy

Knowledge of the anatomic structures will answer the question, Where is the lesion? In the case of musculoskeletal diseases, the joints are primarily affected. The structures that may be involved are shown in Figure 273–1A, the articular structures of the musculoskeletal system. Foremost is the joint cavity and lining membrane known as the *synovium*. Hyaline cartilage overlying the bony end plates provides the lubricating surface for the joint. An intact bony end plate is required to support the cartilage. The joint capsule and ligaments provide further support and blend with the periosteum.

The nonarticular anatomy of the musculoskeletal system is equally important (see Fig. 273–1A). This includes local structures such as tendons, bursae, or muscles associated with various joint regions or, more generally, the collagen, elastin, and ground substance known as the *connective tissue system*. These tissues are so widespread that any organ system of the body may be involved.

Pathophysiology

After determining which anatomic structures of the musculoskeletal system are involved, whether articular, nonarticular, or both, one must answer the question, What is the lesion? The usual pathology is either inflammatory, metabolic, degenerative, or some combination thereof (Fig. 273–1B). Joint neoplasms are exceptional. With inflammatory disorders such as rheumatoid arthritis (RA) or septic arthritis, the joint cavity and synovial membrane are primarily affected, whereas with degenerative conditions such as osteoarthritis (OA), the cartilage is primarily affected. Cartilage loss also may be secondary to synovial inflammation or trauma. Metabolic crystal deposition disorders such as gout or pseudogout also cause articular inflammation, whereas osteonecrosis of bone is associated with cartilage damage after bony end plate collapse. Moreover, the same pathologic processes may affect extra-articular systems such as skin, muscle, and vasculature.

Patient Evaluation

HISTORY. The interview should provide a detailed chronology of the illness: anatomic location of the pain, whether local or referred; aggravating factors including the effects of activity, rest, or sleep; type of onset, whether sudden or insidious; the pattern of joint involvement, symmetric or not, and whether axial or affecting upper or lower limbs; influence of previous and current treatments; systemic symptoms such as fatigue, weight loss, or fever and duration of morning stiffness; an up-to-date account and systematic review of all the joints of the body; and a psychosocial history. A nonrestorative sleep pattern may be associated with morning stiffness and other diffuse aching. Symptoms should be interpreted in terms of the patient's functional ability to perform self-care and other daily activities (Table 273–1). General weakness and fatigue reflect that many rheumatic conditions affect the patient's body as a whole and not just the joints.

FUNCTIONAL DISABILITY INDICES. A number of self-report questionnaires such as the Stanford Health Assessment Questionnaire, Functional Disability Index, Arthritis Impact Measurement Scales, or modifications of these have been developed for ongoing evaluation of patients with arthritis (see Table 273–1). These instruments document the patient's functional status with results comparable with traditional measures of joint disease activity, such as tender joint count, radiographic joint erosion score, and erythrocyte sedimentation rate.

DEMOGRAPHY. An appreciation of the age, gender, and personal history, including marital status, occupation, and other psychosocial factors, of the patient is helpful. The age of the patient is relevant to developmental and heritable disorders of connective tissue. For example, arthritis is a major manifestation of hemophilia with onset during childhood. Juvenile RA refers to polyarthritis coming on before the age of 16 years. In young adults, seropositive, seronegative, and septic arthritic conditions may arise, whereas OA is exceptional. The onset for RA is the middle years, whereas the elderly are more prone to OA. RA and the collagen diseases are more common in women, whereas ankylosing spondylitis and the other B27 spondyloarthropathies are more common in men. Gouty arthritis is more common in men and rarely attacks women before menopause. Arthritis in the elderly is often assumed to be degenerative, when in fact the

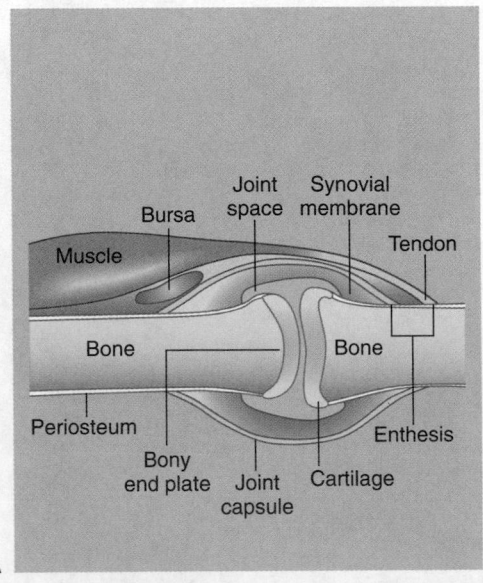

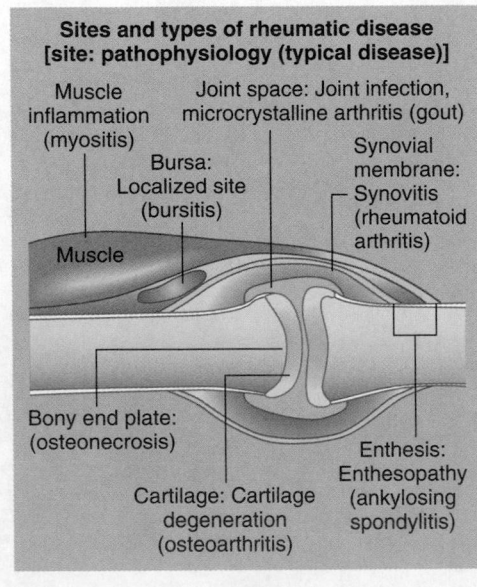

FIGURE 273–1 • *A,* Anatomic structures of the musculoskeletal system. *B,* Location of rheumatic disease processes.

Table 273–1 • SELF-REPORT QUESTIONNAIRE FOR ARTHRITIS

Please check (✓) the ONE best answer for your abilities.

At this moment, are you able to:	Without Any Difficulty	With Some Difficulty	With Much Difficulty	Unable to Do
a. Dress yourself, including tying shoelaces and doing buttons?				
b. Get in and out of bed?				
c. Lift a full cup or glass to your mouth?				
d. Walk outdoors on flat ground?				
e. Wash and dry your entire body?				
f. Bend down to pick up clothing from the floor?				
g. Turn regular faucets (taps) on and off?				
h. Get in and out of a car?				

From Pincus T, Callahan LF, Brooks RH, et al: Self report questionnaire scores in rheumatoid arthritis compared with traditional physical, radiographic, and laboratory measures. Ann Intern Med 1989; 100:259.

patient may suffer from an inflammatory process such as polymyalgia rheumatica, RA, or systemic lupus erythematosus. Occupation is also important because of associated physical and psychological stresses. The clinician should find out exactly what the patient's job entails to determine how demanding it is. Occupational factors are also important with repetitive joint trauma in individuals susceptible to OA. Symptoms may be associated with jogging or trauma from sports activities.

PHYSICAL EXAMINATION. The physical examination includes a record of the patient's gait and posture as well as examination of the spine and skeletal muscles.

The joints shown in Figure 273–2 should be examined systematically, region by region, to determine whether any are inflamed or damaged. The pattern of joint involvement, whether symmetrical, axial, or peripheral, should be recorded using the diagram.

Because many rheumatic disorders are systemic, physical examination may document the presence of extra-articular features. In RA, these include subcutaneous nodules, digital vasculitis, and other systemic features described in Chapter 278. Any one of these may be mistaken for a nonrheumatic condition, and their presence may indicate more ominous disease. Any number of systemic features may be the result of an adverse drug reaction.

JOINT INFLAMMATION. Key signs of joint inflammation are tenderness and swelling. These may be associated with local heat, but erythema is not a feature of rheumatoid inflammation, whereas tenderness, heat, and erythema may be seen with septic or gouty arthritis. A joint is considered active if it is tender on pressure or passive movement with stress. Joint swelling may be periarticular or intra-articular. Intra-articular swelling is associated with a joint effusion detected by showing fluctuation (Fig. 273–3). It is important to note the difference between tender *joints* and deep referred tender *points* characteristic of a nonarticular syndrome known as *fibromyalgia* (Chapter 289).

JOINT DAMAGE AND DESTRUCTION. This may be assessed clinically or radiologically. Common observations include loss of range of movement, collateral instability, malalignment, subluxation, or cartilage loss causing bone-on-bone crepitus. One should record a separate count of damaged joints, as with actively inflamed joints.

Diagnosis

Clinical evaluation enables us to establish which anatomic structures are inflamed, which are damaged, and how function is impaired.

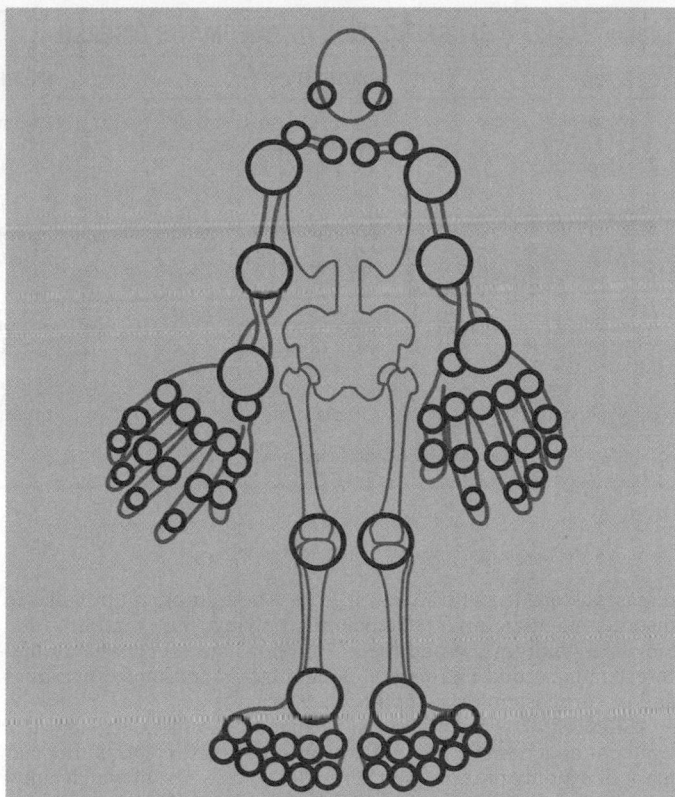

FIGURE 273–2 • A pictorial method for indicating joint disease activity or destruction. The sketch can be used on a printed form or rubber stamp to chart which joints are active or deformed at the time of each assessment. (Courtesy of Dr. Hugh A. Smythe, Toronto.)

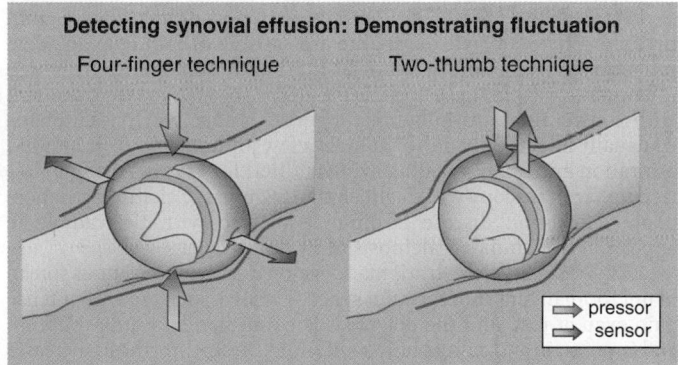

Detecting synovial effusion: Demonstrating fluctuation

Four-finger technique   Two-thumb technique

⟹ pressor
⟹ sensor

FIGURE 273–3 • A demonstration of fluctuation for detecting a synovial effusion. An increase in fluid tension induced by finger pressure in one area is transmitted so that the sensor fingers can detect it elsewhere. In the two-thumb or four-finger technique, the pressure should be in a slightly different direction to the sensor finger to avoid false-positive results. (From Klippel JH, Dieppe PA: Rheumatology, 2nd ed. London, Mosby, 1998, section 5, p 3.7.)

Nine specific types of rheumatic involvement can be identified as a framework for various diagnostic possibilities or hypotheses to be considered (see Fig. 273–1B). The nine categories presented in the following paragraphs are listed in Table 273–2 along with typical diseases, examples of laboratory tests, and treatments. Table 273–2 and the descriptions below provide the basis for more detailed information contained in the following chapters of this section.

SYNOVITIS. Inflammation of the synovial membrane lining of the joint is typical of inflammatory polyarthritis such as RA. If synovitis is persistent, irreversible joint damage results. The polyarthritis of RA is more severe than that found in the diffuse connective tissue

Rheumatic Diseases

Table 273–2 • CLASSIFICATION OF RHEUMATIC DISEASE

CATEGORY	PROTOTYPES	USEFUL TESTS	TREATMENTS
Synovitis	Rheumatoid arthritis	Rheumatoid factor, erythrocyte sedimentation rate	Methotrexate
	Autoimmune collagen diseases	Antinuclear antibody test	Prednisone
Enthesopathy	Ankylosing spondylitis, B27 spondylarthropathies	Sacroiliac radiographs	NSAIDs
Crystal-induced synovitis	Gout	Joint fluid crystal examination	NSAIDs
	Pseudogout	Radiographic chondrocalcinosis	NSAIDs
Joint space disease	Septic arthritis	Joint fluid culture	Antibiotics
Cartilage degeneration	Osteoarthritis	Radiographs of affected area	Physical therapy
			Analgesics
Osteoarticular disease	Osteonecrosis	Radiographs, magnetic resonance imaging	Prosthetic joint replacement
Polymyositis	Dermatomyositis	Muscle enzymes, electromyography, muscle biopsy	Corticosteroids
	Inclusion body myositis		
Local conditions	Tendinitis	None, radiographs of affected area	Local
General conditions	Fibromyalgia	Erythrocyte sedimentation rate	Fitness exercises

NSAIDs = nonsteroidal anti-inflammatory drugs.

diseases associated with autoantibodies. These autoimmune collagen disorders include lupus, scleroderma, polymyositis, vasculitis, and Sjögren's syndrome. When these conditions are progressive or life-threatening, second-line disease-modifying immunosuppressive drugs and/or corticosteroids are appropriate.

ENTHESOPATHY. The enthesis is the anatomic transition zone where ligament attaches to bone. Inflammation in this region is the hallmark of a family of seronegative rheumatic diseases, of which ankylosing spondylitis is the prototype. Other members of this group include postinfectious enteric or venereal reactive arthritis, psoriatic arthritis, and the arthropathy associated with inflammatory bowel disease. All these conditions have in common the presence of the human leukocyte antigen HLA-B27. In ankylosing spondylitis, the sacroiliac joints and apophyseal joints of the spine show characteristic inflammation with a tendency to bony ankylosis. An exercise program along with nonsteroidal anti-inflammatory drugs is usually effective, whereas prednisone is rarely needed.

CRYSTAL-INDUCED SYNOVITIS. Crystals of monosodium urate, calcium pyrophosphate, or hydroxyapatite are capable of inducing an acute inflammatory reaction in synovial fluid and joint lining. Although inflammation from these crystals may clear spontaneously, treatment with nonsteroidal anti-inflammatory drugs is effective. Crystal arthritis usually affects only one or at most a few joints at a time. Joint fluid aspiration and analysis of the synovial fluid for crystals using polarized light microscopy will establish the diagnosis. Calcium pyrophosphate deposition disease is often associated with the radiologic appearance of chondrocalcinosis of hyaline cartilage.

JOINT SPACE. Septic arthritis may develop from hematogenous spread of microorganisms into the joint space. This is associated with intense pain even at rest, and the diagnosis is confirmed by joint aspiration and Gram stain and culture of synovial fluid. A joint prosthesis increases susceptibility to infection in that joint. Although systemic antibiotics are usually sufficient, arthroscopic débridement and surgical drainage may be required.

Blood in the joint space, known as *hemarthrosis*, may result from microfractures, coagulopathy, or tumor.

CARTILAGE DEGENERATION. OA is defined as loss of articular cartilage with bony repair leading to formation of osteophytes. It should be considered a final pathway for persistent inflammatory conditions such as RA, ankylosing spondylitis, septic arthritis, and metabolic disorders with chondrocalcinosis. Joint hypermobility and previous trauma are other mechanical factors that may predispose to OA. Although hereditary OA may affect the distal interphalangeal joints of the fingers, it usually only involves one or two larger joints such as a hip or knee. For this reason, OA disability can be more readily controlled by physical or orthopedic measures than can RA. Although nonsteroidal anti-inflammatory drugs and analgesics may provide pain relief, they are largely palliative.

OSTEOARTICULAR CONDITIONS. Osteonecrosis results after collapse of the bony end plate from vascular insufficiency. The consequence is crush and fragmentation of cartilage. Osteonecrosis may be idiopathic, or associated with systemic conditions such as sickle cell disease or fatty liver after treatment with high-dose corticosteroids. Osteopenia/

osteoporosis may complicate many rheumatic conditions and is dealt with in Chapter 287.

Inflammation of the periosteum, known as *periostitis*, may be associated with hypertrophic pulmonary osteoarthropathy and clubbing. This syndrome may be a clue to underlying lung cancer.

POLYMYOSITIS. Inflammation and weakness of the proximal skeletal muscles are characteristic of polymyositis; with rash, it is called *dermatomyositis*. Elevated creatine kinase levels, electromyographic abnormalities, and histologic abnormalities on muscle biopsy are characteristic. Corticosteroids and immunosuppressive agents may control polymyositis, but older patients with dermatomyositis may have hidden malignancy and steroid resistance.

LOCAL CONDITIONS. Nonarticular disorders such as tendinitis, bursitis, and neck and low-back strains are common problems. Local signs of inflammation are characteristic of these conditions, which usually respond to analgesics or nonsteroidal anti-inflammatory drugs, physical therapy, protective splints, or injection of corticosteroids.

GENERAL CONDITIONS. These nonarticular or extra-articular disorders are not usually associated with arthritis. This group includes polymyalgia rheumatica, complex regional pain syndrome/reflex sympathetic dystrophy, and fibromyalgia. Polymyalgia rheumatica affects the elderly with persistent neck, shoulder, and hip pain; chronic fatigue; and high erythrocyte sedimentation rate. Sometimes it is associated with underlying giant cell or temporal arteritis. In the case of temporal arteritis, corticosteroids are mandatory because of the risk of blindness from ophthalmic arteritis.

Fibromyalgia refers to a common syndrome of widespread polyarthralgias associated with chronic fatigue and a nonrestorative sleep pattern. It is characterized by the presence of deep referred tender points, as described in Chapter 289.

Rx Treatment

Treatment should be based on a correct diagnosis, which may not be initially obvious (see Table 273–2). Also important is whether the patient's problem is urgent, or whether treatment can be postponed until the diagnosis is established. For example, acute monarthritis due to sepsis or gout requires immediate attention, whereas widespread smouldering polyarthritis does not. However, a patient with polyarthritis who is systemically ill requires prompt investigation to exclude a diffuse connective tissue disease, underlying infection, or hidden malignancy.

Regardless of the diagnosis, educating the patient and family is crucial to successful management of any chronic musculoskeletal illness. The informed patient is more likely to comply with treatment and hold realistic expectations of outcome. For the patient with musculoskeletal disease, the goal of management is to control pain and maintain independence. For this reason, treatment should be individualized and based on early identification of problems, a firm diagnosis, and continued monitoring of response to treatment.

SUGGESTED READINGS

Holte HH, Tambs K, Bjerkedal T: Time trends in disability pensioning for rheumatoid arthritis, osteoarthritis and soft tissue rheumatism in Norway 1968–97. Scand J Public Health 2003;31:17–23. *Disability pensioning for osteoarthritis and soft tissue rheumatism is rising faster, whereas disability for rheumatoid arthritis is declining, compared with other causes.*

Klippel JH (ed): Primer on the Rheumatic Diseases, 12th ed. Atlanta, Arthritis Foundation, 2001. *Classic, authoritative, current descriptions of all rheumatic diseases and of all rheumatology, available as a public service at nominal cost.*

Sharma L, Dunlop DD, Cahue S, et al: Quadriceps strength and osteoarthritis progression in malaligned and lax knees. Ann Intern Med 2003;138:613–619. *In malaligned knees and lax knees, greater quadriceps strength at baseline increases progression of tibiofemoral osteoarthritis.*

274 DIAGNOSTIC TESTS IN RHEUMATIC DISEASES

Joseph E. Craft

The approach to diagnosis of rheumatic diseases requires a careful history and physical examination as these illnesses can involve multiple organ systems, and the diagnostic tests available are an adjunct to these most basic skills. Laboratory and imaging tests should not be performed without a properly formed pretest suspicion. Indeed, the majority of diagnostic tests performed in the work-up of possible rheumatic diseases are not specific for any one illness. Nevertheless, some tests, such as antinuclear antibodies (ANAs), can be quite sensitive. The results of the tests should always be interpreted within the clinical context.

Arthrocentesis and Joint Fluid Analysis

Arthrocentesis is an essential technique in the diagnosis and treatment of inflammatory and septic arthritis. The analysis of synovial fluid is needed to differentiate inflammatory arthritis from noninflammatory arthritis, thereby focusing treatment options. For example, the importance of arthrocentesis as a technique to establish the diagnosis of septic arthritis cannot be overemphasized, because serious complications, including joint destruction and sepsis, can occur if diagnosis is delayed. Arthrocentesis also may be administered for therapeutic reasons in any disease causing joint effusions, because relief of pressure in the synovial capsule may provide significant decrease in pain. Indeed, repeated aspirations are part of the therapy for septic arthritis in combination with antibiotics, shortening the time to joint sterilization and ultimate recovery. In addition, intra-articular steroid injections for the treatment of acute or chronic inflammatory arthritis, such as gout and rheumatoid arthritis (RA), can be administered at the end of arthrocentesis.

Arthrocentesis is a relatively safe and minimally invasive procedure. Arthrocentesis-associated septic arthritis is the complication of greatest concern, occurring at a rate of 1:10,000 aspirations. A small amount of bleeding may occur at the aspiration site. Contraindications to arthrocentesis include a bleeding diathesis, which can be corrected with appropriate coagulation factors or platelets, and overlying skin infection. Although arthrocentesis of the hip joint may require fluoroscopic guidance, other diarthroidal joints can be aspirated without special equipment. A person who performs arthrocentesis should be familiar with the local anatomy of the joint to be aspirated to avoid potential damage to underlying neurovascular structures. Arthrocentesis should be done under sterile conditions following careful skin cleansing with iodine. A local anesthetic such as 1% lidocaine should be generously infiltrated into the soft tissues toward the joint capsule. This will minimize discomfort accompanying the procedure, because a properly performed arthrocentesis should be relatively pain free. For aspiration of large joints (knee, elbow, shoulder, or hip), typically a 1.5-inch 18- to 19-guage needle is used attached to a syringe capable of holding the estimated volume of synovial fluid. Using this large-gauge needle facilitates draining the synovial fluid, which can be thick due to excessive cellularity or crystals, making arthrocentesis difficult. Smaller joints, such as metacarpophalangeal, can be drained with a small 23- to 25-gauge needle. On removal, the fluid should be placed aseptically into a sterile container and sent for Gram-stain and cultures. The remaining fluid is placed into an ethylenediaminetetraacetic acid (EDTA)–treated tube and sent for cell count and crystal analysis. Even a few microliters can be used to look for crystals under polarized microscopy.

Cell counts are crucial in differentiating an inflammatory from a noninflammatory cause of joint pain and effusion (Fig. 274–1), but the cell number should not be used to make a specific diagnosis such as infection. There is some debate over the number of white blood cells required for a diagnosis of inflammation; however, a synovial fluid with a cell count greater than 2000 white blood cells/mm^3 is generally regarded as an inflammatory fluid. Red pigment from hemoglobin can come from the inflammatory process or blood from trauma to local vessels during arthrocentesis. Truly bloody aspirates have a finite differential, including trauma, tumors such as pigmented villonodular synovitis, and bleeding disorders.

Traditionally, a number of tests, including gross appearance, protein, glucose, mucin clot, and viscosity, were performed with synovial fluids. However, these tests are no longer routinely performed because, in most cases, they do not add any more information to the results of cell counts, culture, and Gram-staining. For example, the clarity of the fluid may indicate the level of inflammation; however, fibrinous material may also increase the opaque appearance of synovial fluid. Barely visible turbidity indicates less than 1000 cells/mm^3 in the fluid. The viscosity of the synovial fluid is derived from the normal proteoglycan components making the fluid thick, normally the consistency of corn syrup. During inflammation, this matrix can be broken down and the synovial fluid can appear less viscous. A mucin clot derived from acidic precipitation of the proteoglycan content of the synovial fluid can be used as an estimate of inflammation; however, interobserver variability limits the usefulness of this measurement. Glucose and lactic acid levels can reflect an infectious etiology, but their use in ruling out infection is limited as RA and crystal-induced arthropathies can reduce glucose levels and raise lactic acid levels.

Similar to the joint, enlarged bursae should be aspirated when inflammation or infection is suspected. The drainage technique is

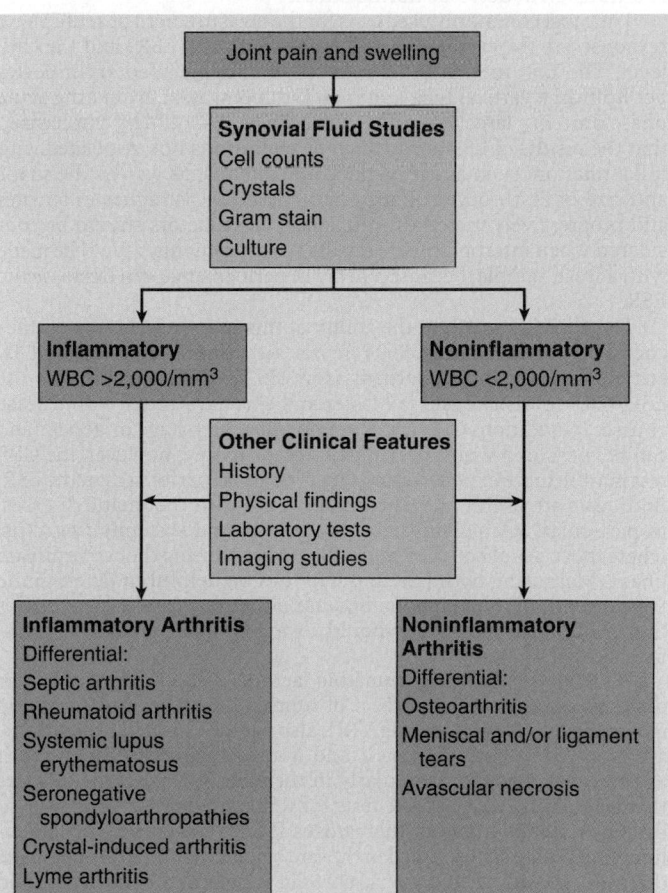

FIGURE 274–1 • Diagnostic approach for swollen joints.

(Figure contents:)

Joint pain and swelling

Synovial Fluid Studies
Cell counts
Crystals
Gram stain
Culture

Inflammatory
WBC >2,000/mm^3

Noninflammatory
WBC <2,000/mm^3

Other Clinical Features
History
Physical findings
Laboratory tests
Imaging studies

Inflammatory Arthritis
Differential:
Septic arthritis
Rheumatoid arthritis
Systemic lupus erythematosus
Seronegative spondyloarthropathies
Crystal-induced arthritis
Lyme arthritis

Noninflammatory Arthritis
Differential:
Osteoarthritis
Meniscal and/or ligament tears
Avascular necrosis

analogous to that described for arthrocentesis, but the bursa location is usually more superficial than a joint capsule. Cell counts, crystal analysis, and Gram-staining and culture should also be done on the bursal fluid.

Arthroscopy

Arthroscopy is used for both diagnostic and therapeutic purposes. The knee is the joint mostly commonly evaluated with arthroscopy, but other joints can also be examined. Diagnostically, the procedure is used to detect mechanical abnormalities, including meniscal or ligamentous tears and loose bodies, and to obtain tissues to rule out an indolent infection, such as from mycobacteria or fungi. Therapeutically, arthroscopy has largely replaced arthrotomy. It is frequently used for synovectomy, as well as for repairs of torn menisci and/or ligaments. In rheumatology, arthroscopic synovectomy can be used in a patient with chronic monoarticular synovitis refractory to medical treatment such as local steroid injections. There are two commonly used techniques: traditional arthroscopy using glass lenses and "needle" arthroscopy using fiberoptic technology. The traditional method allows for more instrumentation such as meniscal repairs, débridement, and excisions, whereas the smaller arthroscope is limited to smaller manipulations. In general, arthroscopy is performed in the ambulatory setting and patients are fully functional in a few days. Possible complications include hemarthrosis, infections, and venous thrombosis.

Laboratory Tests

ACUTE PHASE REACTANTS. Acute phase reactants are proteins produced by the liver in response to stress and include fibrinogen, C-reactive protein (CRP), amyloid A, albumin, transferrin, complement C3 and C4, ferritin, and haptoglobin. Hepatic synthesis of these proteins is altered during infection, inflammation, or tissue necrosis. Macrophages and monocytes primarily synthesize proinflammatory cytokines, such as interleukin (IL)-6, IL-1β, and tumor necrosis factor (TNF)-α, that are responsible for changes in the levels of acute phase proteins via hepatic effects. In contrast to most acute phase proteins, serum albumin and transferrin decrease during stress.

The most commonly used tests for the measurement of acute phase response are the erythrocyte sedimentation rate (ESR) and the CRP level. The ESR measures the rate of fall of aggregated erythrocytes per hour in a vertical tube and is an indirect way of evaluating acute phase proteins, largely fibrinogen. However, it should be emphasized that the results of ESR are affected by conditions not associated with inflammation, such as age, gender, and anemia, as well as the shape and size of erythrocytes. For example, the ESR is higher in females and progressively increases with aging; these factors should be considered when interpreting the results. Measurements should be made with a fresh sample, because a delay in performance can decrease the ESR.

The CRP is named for the ability of this protein to bind pneumococcal C-polysaccharide. CRP levels are commonly measured by enzyme-linked immunosorbent assay (ELISA). Compared with the ESR, CRP levels rise and fall faster and correlate better with disease course. In addition, CRP levels are not affected by age or gender and can be measured with a previously stored sample; however, the CRP test may be more expensive and takes longer to perform than the ESR. Both tests are useful in evaluating patients with rheumatic diseases, in particular, RA, polymyalgia rheumatica, and systemic vasculitis, where the levels of both ESR and CRP increase during the active disease phase. Measuring both ESR and CRP can be helpful in determining the presence of inflammation because either test can be falsely positive or negative; the results should always be interpreted in the clinical context.

RHEUMATOID FACTORS. Rheumatoid factors (RFs) are autoantibodies directed against the Fc portion of human IgG. The most common isotype is IgM, but IgG and IgA RFs also occur. Elevated levels of RFs are reported in both rheumatic and nonrheumatic diseases, as well as in healthy people, particularly in the elderly. Rheumatic diseases that frequently have positive tests for RFs include RA, Sjögren's syndrome, systemic lupus erythematosus (SLE), and mixed cryoglobulinemia. RFs are also detected in the sera of patients with nonrheumatic diseases, including infections, chronic inflammatory diseases, and malignancy. About 75 to 85% of patients with RA have RFs. These patients tend to have a more aggressive form of the disease with joint erosions and a higher frequency of extra-articular manifestations such as subcutaneous nodules and vasculitis. Methods used for the measurement of RFs are agglutination, precipitation, radioimmunoassay, and ELISA, with the latter two methods being more precise in quantifying levels. Overall, it should be kept in mind that the test for RF is neither sensitive nor specific for any rheumatic disease, including RA.

ANTINUCLEAR ANTIBODIES. ANAs often signal the presence of an underlying connective tissue disease (Table 274–1). The term *ANA* is a bit of a misnomer, because these autoantibodies are directed against self-antigens found in the nucleus of mammalian cells (ANA) as well as antigens found in the cytoplasm. Although the latter would more appropriately be termed *anti-cytoplasmic antibodies*, they should not be confused with *anti–neutrophil cytoplasmic antibodies* (ANCAs), described later, and they are generally subsumed under the more common acronym ANA. ANAs are quite a sensitive measure for the presence of connective tissue diseases. They are found in virtually all patients with SLE, and the vast majority of individuals with systemic sclerosis, either diffuse or limited disease (so-called CREST syndrome: calcinosis, Raynaud's syndrome, esophageal dysfunction, sclerodactyly and telangiectasias), Sjögren's syndrome, mixed connective tissue disease (MCTD, a disease with features of scleroderma, SLE, myositis and/or rheumatoid arthritis), and adult polymyositis and dermatomyositis. ANAs occur as well in patients with RA, in a subset with juvenile RA (young girls with pauciarticular involvement and eye inflammation), in juvenile dermatomyositis, in patients with the chronic liver diseases primary biliary cirrhosis and autoimmune hepatitis, and in individuals with drug-induced lupus, regardless of the precipitating drug. ANAs may also be present in a variety of other conditions, including acute viral infections such as infectious mononucleosis, chronic infections such as endocarditis or parasitic diseases, chronic inflammatory states such as Crohn's disease, and in a variety of neoplasms, including melanoma and hepatocellular carcinoma. A small percentage of otherwise healthy young women, approximately 5 to 7%, and of the healthy elderly also have ANAs in their serum.

Given the broad range of conditions in which ANAs occur and the frequency of a positive test in the connective tissue diseases, the test may be considered to lack specificity. However, it is now well established that ANAs represent not merely one specificity of autoantibody; rather, multiple different ANAs develop that bind different intracellular (intranuclear or intracytoplasmic) antigens. For example, ANAs in patients with SLE typically bind to chromatin, composed of DNA and DNA-binding proteins such as histones, or to ribonucleoproteins, such as the so-called Sm antigen, the RNP antigen, or the Ro antigen. By contrast, ANAs in systemic sclerosis target kinetochores (proteins that bind centromeric regions of DNA) or other nonhistone proteins associated with DNA structure or transcription, and ANAs in polymyositis or dermatomyositis patients are directed against antigens in the cytoplasm of cells. Identification of specific ANAs, such as anti-DNA, is used to enhance the specificity of the test.

ANAs are generally detected using indirect immunofluorescence. Serum from a patient is diluted in buffer and applied in serial dilutions to slides on which human epithelial cells (Hep-2 cells) have been fixed; the fixation allows potential ANAs to enter the cell and to bind to target antigens in the nucleus or cytoplasm. Bound antibody from the patient's serum is detected by a second anti-human antibody to which a fluorescent tag has been placed, allowing for detection with a fluorescent microscope. Because the various antigenic targets of ANAs have different intracellular locations, different ANAs reveal different staining patterns, such as rim, speckled, nucleolar, and cytoplasmic (see Table 274–1). The ANA patterns may provide a clue to the antigen that is being detected and, as outlined earlier, the potential associated disease. Total ANAs can now be detected by ELISA, a sensitive procedure, but ELISA cannot reveal different staining patterns. However, using ELISA to detect specific ANAs, as discussed earlier, is quite helpful diagnostically.

ANTI-PHOSPHOLIPID ANTIBODIES. Anti-phospholipid antibodies occur in patients with connective tissue diseases such as SLE, and in patients without apparent connective tissue diseases, the primary antiphospholipid syndrome (APLS). Anti-phospholipid antibodies are associated with a syndrome of thrombosis, recurrent fetal loss, and thrombocytopenia. Four types of anti-phospholipid antibodies are reported: antibodies responsible for a false-positive Venereal Disease Research Laboratories (VDRL) result, lupus anticoagulants,

Table 274–1 • SELECTED AUTOANTIBODIES AND RHEUMATIC DISEASES

IMMUNOFLUORESCENCE PATTERN	ANTIBODY	ANTIGEN	DISEASE ASSOCIATION	COMMENTS
Human epithelial cells (Hep-2) homogeneous ANA	Anti-histone	Histones H1, H2A, H2B, H3, H4	Drug-induced lupus (>95%), infectious mononucleosis (5–10%), "normals" (1–2%)	Low titer (<1:320) in "normals"
Hep-2 rim ANA	Anti–double-stranded DNA	Double-stranded DNA	SLE (50%)	Double-stranded DNA antibodies highly specific for SLE (rarely seen on Hep-2 cells)
Hep-2 speckled ANA	Anti-Smith	Proteins associated with small nuclear ribonucleoprotein particle	SLE (30%)	Highly specific for SLE
	Anti–U1-RNP	U1 small ribonuclear ribonucleoprotein	SLE (30%); MCTD (>95%)	High titer in MCTD
	Anti-Ro (SS-A)	Two proteins complexed to small RNAs Y1-Y5	SLE (30%); Sjögren's (70–80%)	Missed on Hep-2 ANA; common in "ANA-negative" SLE
	Anti-La (SS-B)	Single protein plus RNA polymerase III transcript	SLE (15%); Sjögren's (50–70%)	
	Anti-Ku	DNA binding protein	SLE (10%)	
	Anti–SCL-70	DNA topoisomerase I	PSS (40–70%); CREST (10–20%)	
Hep-2 nucleolar ANA	Anti–PM-Scl	Nucleolar protein complex	PSS (3%); PM (8%)	May identify overlap syndrome
	Anti–Mi-2	Nuclear protein complex	DM (15–20%)	Rare in PM
	Anti–RNA polymerase I	Subunits of RNA polymerase I	PSS (4%)	
Hep-2 dividing cell-specific patterns	Anticentromere	Centromere/kinetocore protein	CREST (80%); PSS (30%)	In patients with isolated Raynaud's, may predict progression to CREST
	Anti–proliferating cell nuclear antigen	Auxillary protein of DNA polymerase δ	SLE (3%)	
Hep-2 cytoplasmic staining	Antisynthetase Anti–Jo-1	Histidyl tRNA synthetase	PM/DM (18–25%) PM/DM (3%)	Often with ILD
	Anti–PL-7	Threonyl tRNA synthetase	PM/DM (3%)	Often with ILD
	Anti–PL-12	Alanyl tRNA synthetase		Often with ILD
	Anti-SRP	Signal recognition particle	PM (4%)	No Raynaud's rare ILD, poor prognosis
	Anti–ribosomal P	Large ribosomal subunit	SLE (10%)	May be associated with central nervous system manifestations
	Anti-mitochondrial	E2 component of pyruvate dehydrogenase complex at inner mitochondrial membrane	Primary biliary cirrhosis (PBC: 90–95%); "normals" (<1%)	PBC may show CREST, Sjögren's features
Alcohol-fixed human neutrophils Cytosolic	C-ANCA	Serine protease	Wegner's granulomatosis (90%)	
Perinuclear	P-ANCA	Myeloperoxidase	Microscopic PAN; Churg-Strauss	

ANA = antinuclear antibodies; ANCA = antineutrophil cytoplasmic antibodies; CREST = calcinosis, Raynaud's phenomenon, esophageal dysmotility, sclerodactyly, and telangectasia; DM = dermatomyositis; ILD = interstitial lung disease; MCTD = mixed connective tissue disease; PM = polymyositis; PSS = progressive systemic sclerosis (diffuse scleroderma); SLE = systemic lupus erythematosus; SS = single-stranded DNA.

anti-cardiolipin antibodies, and anti–β2 glycoprotein (GP) I antibodies (the latter two antibodies are detected by ELISA). Patients with primary or secondary APLS, the latter, for example, in SLE, can have one or all of these antibodies.

Lupus anticoagulants are antibodies that bind plasma proteins like prothrombin bound to anionic phospholipids. The presence of a lupus anticoagulant is suggestive of APLS and, in the appropriate clinical situation, should be investigated with in vitro clotting assays such as the dilute Russell viper venom time (dRVVT), the kaolin clotting time, and the activated partial thromboplastin time (aPTT). These tests are protracted by the blocking of prothrombin and are used for the diagnosis of primary and secondary APLS. The prolonged clotting time is not corrected by mixing with normal plasma but rather by adding phospholipids. Although patients with lupus anticoagulants have prolonged coagulation times, they have an increased incidence of thrombosis, not bleeding. Anti–β2 glycoprotein and anti-cardiolipin antibodies are measured by ELISA. The target antigens of anti-cardiolipin antibodies are phospholipids such as cardiolipin; three isotypes, IgG, IgM, and IgA, are reported, with IgG having the strongest relation with thrombosis. The target of anti–β2–GP I antibodies is β2-GP I, a coagulant, and appears to be more specific than anti-cardiolipin antibodies for the diagnosis of primary or secondary APLS.

Antibodies leading to a biologically false-positive VDRL are not directly associated with clinical disease and should not be used for the diagnosis of APLS.

ANTI-NEUTROPHIL CYTOPLASMIC ANTIBODIES. Anti-neutrophil cytoplasmic antibodies (ANCAs) are autoantibodies that bind antigens present in the cytoplasm of neutrophils (see Table 274–1). They are measured by ELISA and by immunofluorescent staining with ethanol-fixed human neutrophils. Two forms of ANCA are of clinical importance: cytoplasmic (c)-ANCA and perinuclear (p)-ANCA. The measurement of ANCA is useful in diagnosing systemic vasculitis. The presence of c-ANCA is highly sensitive for the diagnosis of Wegener's granulomatosis, with around 90% of such patients having c-ANCA during the active phase of the disease. The target antigen of c-ANCA is proteinase-3, and antibodies to this neutrophil protein can be detected by ELISA. By contrast to c-ANCA, the presence of p-ANCA is rather nonspecific, with these antibodies arising in pauci-immune glomerulonephritis, microscopic polyangiitis, Churg-Strauss syndrome, sclerosing cholangitis, and ulcerative colitis. Myeloperoxidase is the target antigen of p-ANCA in patients with pauci-immune glomerulonephritis, microscopic polyangiitis, and Churg-Strauss syndrome, whereas the target antigens of p-ANCA in patients with nonvasculitic conditions include lactoferrin, cathepsin G, and lysozyme.

Diagnostic Imaging

ROENTGENOGRAPHY. Roentgenography, synonomous with plain radiography, plays an important role in diagnosing arthritis, serves as an initial diagnostic procedure of low cost, and provides information on alignment, bony structures, and soft tissues. These abnormalities may present themselves as joint space narrowing, erosions, periarticular soft tissue swelling, new bone formation (osteophytes), and calcifications. Often, these findings are sufficient to establish a rheumatologic diagnosis; however, conventional radiography does not detect the early bone changes of avascular necrosis or osteomyelitis; in both cases, radiographic changes in bone occur only later in the disease course. The major drawback to conventional radiography is exposure to ionizing radiation; however, in most circumstances this is minimal for x-rays of the extremities. Generally two views perpendicular to each other are required for accurate assessments, as some bony abnormalities may be missed by x-rays done in one plane. Weight-bearing joints should have at least one view under stress. For example, at least one view of the knees should be done standing, because this view can identify joint space narrowing, which cannot be detected on the supine view.

Arthrography is performed with the injection of radiopaque contrast material or air, or both, into a joint. This procedure is useful in diagnosing soft tissue injuries such as a rotator cuff tear. However, it has largely been replaced by MRI, which is less invasive and more reliably details soft tissue abnormalities. Conventional tomography takes multiple x-ray images on a film rotated around an axis to capture multiple angles of an image. In particular, this technique can be useful in identification of fractures, assessment at the odontoid process, and the visualization of the sternoclavicular, temporomandibular, and costovertebral joints. Now, however, computed tomography (CT) is often preferred.

COMPUTED TOMOGRAPHY. CT scanning is a technique in which x-rays are used to generate multiple images of an area of the body and are then reconstructed by computer with excellent contrast resolution. This technique is useful for analysis of soft tissues, deeper structures obscured by other organs, osteonecrosis of the femoral head, and joints hard to image radiographically. The advantage of CT is that the soft tissue images and bony structures are easily analyzed together. In rheumatologic lung disease, a high resolution CT can guide therapy when a classic "ground glass" appearance implies an active inflammatory process in the lungs. The disadvantages are expense and ionized radiation exposure.

SCINTIGRAPHY. Scintigraphy uses radioactive tracer uptake as a marker of disease activity. The radioactive isotope decay is then captured by a gamma camera. Bone scanning uses radioactive technetium 99m methylene diphosphate and shows areas of increased bone formation, high vascular flow, or calcium deposition. Although it is quite sensitive to inflammation and infection, it is not specific for any one disease; however, it is useful in the diagnosis of osteomyelitis and RA. Three-phase bone scans take serial images at different time points (early vascular phase, intermediate blood pooling phase, and, finally, late phase) to further delineate the disease process. Increased uptake at a particular phase can increase the diagnostic specificity for osteonecrosis, inflammation, and infection. Other forms of scintigraphy include the indium 111–labeled white cell scan, the gallium 67 citrate scan, and the technetium 99m sulfur colloid scan.

ULTRASONOGRAPHY. Ultrasonography has drawn attention from inflammatory arthritis rheumatologists. Ultrasonography uses sound waves to delineate the anatomy. It is a quick and noninvasive procedure and does not expose the patient to ionizing radiation. It is excellent for detecting fluid in cysts, joints, or bursae and is commonly used to direct arthrocentesis. Ultrasonography is an operator-dependent technique and has a potential for interobserver variability in interpretation of results; nevertheless, it has been used to detect rotator cuff tears and joint erosions.

MAGNETIC RESONANCE IMAGING. MRI uses the physical characteristics of protons in tissues to develop a high contrast resolution image of the body. MRI provides excellent soft tissue images because the amount of water in soft tissues and neighboring structures varies. MRI is quite useful for analyzing joints, bursae, tendons, and ligaments and is often performed for the diagnosis of rotator cuff pathologies and meniscal tears. The synovium can be visualized using gadolinium as a contrast agent. MRI can detect avascular necrosis earlier than CT and bone scans. In spinal diseases, this technique is useful in delineating soft tissues such as discs and nerve roots as well as the spinal cord. The major drawback of MRI is that metal implants can affect the quality of the image and can be a contraindication to its use. The procedure can be claustrophobic and is more expensive than CT scanning; however, MRI lacks exposure to ionizing radiation.

BONE DENSITOMETRY. Bone density is commonly measured to survey for osteoporosis and is done in two ways: dual energy X-ray absorptiometry (DEXA) and quantitative computed tomography (QCT). DEXA measures the absorption of low-level X-rays through bone to calculate bone density. DEXA is relatively inexpensive and can be used to measure bone density at any location. The results are then compared to standard curves from age- and sex-matched controls. QCT uses known standards while scanning the desired bone to determine bone density. It has the benefit of measuring cancellous bone, not just the overlying cortical bone; however, it has some ionizing radiation exposure although less than regular CT scanning.

SUGGESTED READINGS

Kane D, Balint PV, Sturrock RD: Ultrasonography is superior to clinical examination in the detection and localization of knee joint effusion in rheumatoid arthritis. J Rheumatol 2003;30:966–971. *Imaging was better than an experienced rheumatologist.*

Levine JS, Branch DW, Rauch J: Antiphospholipid antibody syndrome. N Engl J Med 2002;346:752–763. *A comprehensive review of the biology, diagnosis, therapy, and prognosis of the full spectrum of the syndrome.*

Maiden NL, Hurst NP, Lochhead A, et al: Medically unexplained symptoms in patients referred to a specialist rheumatology service: Prevalence and associations. Rheumatology (Oxford) 2003;42:108–112. *About 30% of referred patients had no obvious rheumatologic disease.*

Myckatyn SO, Russell AS: Outcome of positive antinuclear antibodies in individuals without connective tissue disease. J Rheumatol 2003;30:736–739. *Over a median of five years, less than 10% of patients developed connective tissue disease.*

Smolen JS, Breedveld FC, Schiff MH, et al: A simplified disease activity index for rheumatoid arthritis for use in clinical practice. Rheumatology (Oxford) 2003;42:244–257. *A valid and sensitive method.*

van Tubergen A, Heuft-Dorenbosch L, Schulpen G, et al: Radiographic assessment of sacroiliitis by radiologists and rheumatologists: Does training improve quality? Ann Rheum Dis 2003;62:519–525. *Sensitivity and specificity were modest, with large intra-observer variations and no improvment after individual or group training.*

275 CONNECTIVE TISSUE STRUCTURE AND FUNCTION

Richard F. Loeser

Connective tissue forms the architectural framework of the musculoskeletal system and serves as a scaffold that supports various organs and tissues. Many important structures within the body are composed primarily of connective tissue (Table 275–1). For example, articular cartilage is made up exclusively of a specialized dense connective tissue without blood vessels, nerves, or lymphatics. Tendons, ligaments, intervertebral discs, and fascia are structures also consisting of dense connective tissue, although of a different composition than cartilage. Bone contains both dense and loose connective tissue; the latter provides support for bone marrow cells and helps to fill the space within the bone cavity. Adipose tissue is also often considered to be a specialized connective tissue that has both metabolic and structural functions.

What connective tissues have in common is that they contain cells, usually of mesodermal origin, that have an abundant extracellular matrix. The cells within a particular connective tissue control the composition of the extracellular matrix, which in turn determines the physical properties of the tissue. There are many types of connective tissue cells, ranging from fibroblasts, which are present in the connective tissue found in skin, synovium, tendons, ligaments, and fascia, to more specialized cells such as chondrocytes and osteoblasts, which are found in cartilage and bone, respectively (see Table 275–1). Basement membranes are a more special form of connective tissue in that they are produced by epithelial and endothelial cells rather than mesenchymal cells. The connective tissue matrix consists of an intricate mixture of proteins and other macromolecules, which are responsible for the unique function of each particular type of connective tissue. Connective tissues that must withstand high tensile loads, such as tendons, have a high content of collagen fibers, whereas tissues that must resist compression, such as cartilage, have a high proteoglycan content.

Because of the wide distribution of connective tissues within the human body, diseases that affect connective tissue cells or

Table 275–1 • THE DIVERSITY OF CONNECTIVE TISSUE-CONTAINING STRUCTURES

STRUCTURE	FUNCTION	CELLS	KEY MATRIX COMPONENTS
Adipose tissue	Energy storage, organ protection	Adipocytes, fibroblasts	Fine reticular fibers
Basement membrane	Support and filtration barrier	Epithelial and endothelial cells	Type IV collagen, laminin
Bone	Skeletal support, blood cell production	Osteoblasts, osteoclasts, osteocytes	Type I collagen, osteocalcin, bone sialoprotein, hydroxyapatite
Cartilage	Allows joint motion, transmits loads	Chondrocytes	Type II collagen, aggrecan
Dermis	Support and resiliency	Fibroblasts	Type I collagen, elastin
Ligament	Connects bone to bone	Fibroblasts	Type I collagen, small PGs
Tendon	Connects muscle to bone	Fibroblasts	Type I collagen, small PGs
Stroma	Support of organs	Fibroblasts, organ specific cells	Type I, VI collagen, fibronectin
Synovium	Joint lining, produces synovial fluid	Fibroblasts, macrophages	Type I, III collagen
Vessel wall	Structural support of blood vessels	Vascular smooth muscle cells	Type III collagen, elastin

PG = proteoglycan.

extracellular matrix proteins often have systemic effects. These connective tissue disorders can be divided into three general types: those that arise from a mutation within a gene encoding a connective tissue protein (e.g., Marfan's syndrome), those that are the result of an inflammatory, sometimes autoimmune process, centered in connective tissues (e.g., rheumatoid arthritis), and those that are the result of a degenerative type of process, often associated with aging (e.g., osteoarthritis). A basic understanding of the composition of the various connective tissues and how this composition relates to structure and function is important for understanding the clinical presentation, as well as management, of the spectrum of musculoskeletal and connective tissue disorders.

Connective Tissue Proteins and Macromolecules

Each different type of connective tissue has a unique composition based on the amount and specific forms of extracellular matrix proteins and macromolecules. The extracellular matrix components can be grouped into families that include the collagens, proteoglycans, elastins, and other noncollagenous glycoproteins. These extracellular matrix components not only provide the scaffolding that forms the tissue, but, importantly, they also create an information-rich environment that provides external cues to the connective tissue cells. Intracellular signaling, initiated through the interaction of extracellular matrix components with cell surface receptors, regulates a number of important processes, including cell growth, differentiation, and survival and remodeling of the matrix. The integrins, named for their ability to integrate the extracellular matrix with intracellular cytoskeletal components, are a large and important family of cell-surface receptors that recognize and bind a number of different extracellular matrix proteins initiating intracellular signaling. The signals generated by extracellular matrix proteins are integrated with signals generated by soluble mediators, also present in the matrix, including growth factors and cytokines. In normal functioning connective tissues, the cells, extracellular matrix proteins, and soluble mediators all work beautifully in concert to maintain the tissue and to adapt the tissue to meet changes in physical or biomechanical demands.

COLLAGENS. Collagen is a major component of the extracellular matrix and is the most abundant protein in the body, accounting for about 25 to 30% of the total protein mass. Collagens are triple helical proteins formed when three polypeptide chains, called alpha chains, wind around each other to form a collagen molecule. The alpha chains are rich in the amino acids proline and glycine, which are important in forming the helical conformation of the polypeptide chain. Because of its ring structure, proline stabilizes the helix. Glycine, the smallest of the amino acids, is spaced at every third position in the chain such that it occupies the tightly spaced inside portions of the triple helix. Mutations that result in the substitution of a much larger amino acid for glycine can severely disrupt the triple helical structure. Post-translational modifications, including hydroxylation of specific proline and lysine residues, occur during the processing of the collagen molecules and are important in stabilizing the collagen structure and in forming interchain and intrachain cross-links.

There are more than 30 collagen genes coding for the collagen alpha chains. Alpha chains specific for each collagen type combine to form at least 19 different collagens. The types of collagen can be grouped by structure and function (Table 275–2). In the fibrillar collagens (collagen types I, II, III, V, and XI), individual collagen molecules are packed in a staggered and ordered fashion to form a collagen fibril, which has a characteristic banding pattern when observed by high-power microscopy. Fibril formation occurs outside the cell after the N-terminal and C-terminal propeptides present on procollagen molecules are proteolytically removed to form mature collagen. The fibrils in turn are packed together to form fibers. Further cross-linking of collagen fibrils strengthens the structure. These rather stiff, rope-like structures provide the tensile strength for connective tissues. The fibril-associated collagens (collagen types IX, XII, XIV) help to form and stabilize the collagen fibrils. Unlike the fibrillar collagens, this group of collagens contains regions where the triple helical structure is interrupted, which can result in a bend in the collagen molecule, thus the name *fibril-associated collagens with interrupted triple helixes*. Type IV collagen is the classic basement-membrane collagen that forms in aggregates to provide structural support to the basement membrane.

The type and amount of collagen found in a particular connective tissue has an important contribution to tissue function. Tissues such as bone, tendon, and cartilage, which must withstand high biomechanical loads, are packed with large amounts of long fibrillar collagens, primarily type I collagen in bone and tendons and type II collagen in cartilage. The loose connective tissues, such as basement membranes and organ stroma, experience much less mechanical force but require a matrix that allows more rapid diffusion of molecules and so contain a higher content of aggregating or anchoring types of collagen and less fibrillar collagen. Recent work correlating mutations in particular collagen genes with disease phenotypes in humans as well as studies of phenotype after gene disruption in transgenic mice have added to our knowledge of collagen function (see Table 275–2). Some examples include "brittle-bone disease" or osteogenesis imperfecta resulting from type I collagen mutations, severe premature osteoarthritis from type II collagen mutations, and fragile blood vessel and visceral walls in Ehlers-Danlos syndrome type IV from mutations in type III collagen. Excess collagen production can also disrupt tissue function usually by causing tissue fibrosis as seen in scleroderma. Finally, fragile connective tissues can result from inadequate collagen production and cross-linking as occurs in scurvy from vitamin C deficiency. Vitamin C (ascorbic acid) serves as a cofactor for the hydroxylation reaction necessary to modify specific prolyl and lysyl residues in procollagen and a deficiency reduces collagen secretion, stability, and cross-linking.

PROTEOGLYCANS. These matrix macromolecules consist of a protein core to which short oligosaccharides and longer chains of glycosaminoglycans are covalently attached. There is a large variety of proteoglycans based on the types and lengths of glycosaminoglycans as well as the sequence and length of the protein core. Chondroitin sulfate, keratan sulfate, heparin sulfate, and dermatan sulfate are four different forms of glycosaminoglycans that consist of repeating disaccharide units. The sulfates present on the glycosaminoglycans create a highly negatively charged environment that is hydrophilic. Thus, connective tissues that contain large amounts of proteoglycans will also contain relatively large amounts of water bound to the proteoglycans. In addition to water, proteoglycans bind cationic proteins,

Table 275–2 • CONNECTIVE TISSUE COLLAGENS

COLLAGEN TYPE	CHAINS	MOLECULES	TISSUE DISTRIBUTION	SELECTED DISEASES FROM MUTATIONS
FIBRILLAR COLLAGENS				
I	α1(I)	[α1(I)]$_2$α2(I)	Skin, bone, tendon, organ	Osteogenesis imperfecta, Ehlers-Danlos
	α2(I)	[α1(I)]$_3$	capsules, arteries	type VIIA
II	α1(II)	[α1(II)]$_3$	Cartilage, vitreous humor	Stickler syndrome, osteoarthritis
III	α1(III)	[α1(III)]$_3$	Skin, vessels, uterus	Ehlers-Danlos type IV, aortic aneurysms
V	α1(V)	[α1(V)]$_3$	Skin, vessels, placenta, chorion, uterus	
	α2(V)	[α1(V)]$_2$α2(V)		
	α3(V)	α1(V)α2(V)α3(V)		
XI	α1(XI), α2(XI)	α1(XI)α2(XI)α1(II)	Cartilage	
BASEMENT-MEMBRANE COLLAGENS				
IV	α1-α5(IV)	[α1(IV)]$_2$α2(IV)	Basement membranes	Alport syndrome
FIBRIL-ASSOCIATED COLLAGENS WITH INTERRUPTED TRIPLE HELIXES (FACIT)				
IX	α1-α3(IX)	α1(IX)α2(IX)α3(IX)	Cartilage, intervertbral discs	Degenerative disc disease, osteoarthritis
XII	α1(XII)	[α1(XII)]$_3$	Tendons, ligaments, other soft tissues	
XIV	α1(XIV)		Ubiquitous	
NETWORK-FORMING COLLAGENS				
VIII	α1(VIII),α2(VIII)		Cornea, vessels	
X	α1(X)	[α1(X)]$_3$	Growth plate cartilage	Spondylometaphyseal dysplasia
LONG-CHAIN, ANCHORING-FIBRIL COLLAGEN WITH INTERRUPTED TRIPLE HELIX				
VII	α1(VII)	[α1(VII)]$_3$	Anchoring fibrils	Epidermolysis bullosa
OTHERS				
VI	α1-α3(VI)	α1(VI)α2(VI)α3(VI)	Cartilage, stroma	
XIII	α1(XIII)		Skin, gut	

which in some cases include growth factors, resulting in a mechanism by which tissues can store growth factors in the matrix.

Aggrecan is a very large (molecular weight of more than 200,000 kD) proteoglycan found in cartilage that contains a protein core of over 2000 amino acids to which are attached about 100 long chondrotin sulfate chains, about 30 shorter keratan sulfate chains, and approximately 50 short oligosaccharides. Decorin, biglycan, fibromodulin, and lumican are examples of small proteoglycans that have much shorter protein cores (30 to 60 kD) and fewer glycosaminoglycan side chains. These small proteoglycans interact with collagen and function to regulate the formation of collagen fibrils and help stabilize the collagen network. Although their functions are not completely understood, they likely have other roles as well due to their ability to bind matrix molecules, in addition to collagen, and due to their affinity for growth factors.

Hyaluronic acid is a nonsulfated glycosaminoglycan that is synthesized in very long linear polymer strands. Hyaluronic acid is produced by chondrocytes and by synovial cells and is a major component contributing to the viscosity of the synovial fluid. Unlike the other glycosaminoglycans, hyaluronic acid is not attached to a protein core and so it is not directly used to form proteoglycans. In cartilage, however, strands of hyaluronic acid bind aggrecan molecules through a non-covalent interaction with a globular portion of the N-terminus of the aggrecan core protein and a second small protein called link protein. The resulting macromolecular complex containing 100 or more aggrecan molecules linked to each long strand of hyaluronic acid forms a gel-like substance in cartilage due to its high sugar and water content.

The proteoglycan aggregates provide articular cartilage with resiliency. When cartilage is compressed during joint loading, water is pushed out from the proteoglycans and the negative charges on the glycosaminoglycans become closer, which helps to resist further compression through charge repulsion. When the load is released, water is drawn back to the proteoglycans, resulting in a fluid flow that is responsible for part of the biomechanical stimulation of the cells. The fluid flow also helps to move nutrients through the tissue, which is particularly important for articular cartilage, a connective tissue that depends on diffusion from the synovial fluid for most of its nutrition. The network of collagen fibers that surrounds aggrecan prevents the proteoglycans from swelling beyond a certain size, thus creating a swelling pressure in cartilage, which also helps resist compression.

NONCOLLAGENOUS FIBRILLAR PROTEINS. Elastic fibers are composed of elastin and proteins, often referred to as microfibrils, such as fibrillin, because their fibrils are much smaller than the classic collagen fibrils. Elastic fibers must withstand repeated stretching and deformation and be capable of returning to a relaxed state. Tropoelastin is the precursor to elastin and is synthesized by several cell types, including vascular smooth muscle cells and dermal fibroblasts, where it contributes to the elasticity of the blood vessel wall and skin, respectively. Elastin also plays a similar role in the lung. Elastin, like collagen, forms interchain and intrachain cross-links that help to stabilize and strengthen the elastic fibers, although the stiffness of the elastin fibers is less than that of the collagen fibers. Many of the cross-links in elastin are formed through the hydroxylation of two unique amino acids found in tropoelastin, desmosine and isodesmosine. Fibrillin is found in several elastic tissues and is particularly abundant in the aorta, suspensory ligament of the lens, and periosteum. Fibrillin was a little-known protein until it was discovered that fibrillin mutations are the cause of most cases of Marfan's syndrome.

NONCOLLAGENOUS GLYCOPROTEINS. Along with the proteoglycans, the many other noncollagenous matrix glycoproteins found in connective tissues form much of what is sometimes described as the "ground substance" in histologic terms. This rather inert-sounding description should in no way be taken to suggest that these matrix components simply fill in or hold the tissue together. Rather these proteins participate actively in creating the information-rich environment described earlier. Proteins in this group include fibronectin, vitronectin, osteopontin, laminin, and thrombospondin. Fibronectin is found in most connective tissues throughout the body. Laminin is particularly prominent in basement membranes, and osteopontin is found in greater amounts in cartilage and bone. All of these proteins bind to cells through specific cell-surface receptors to promote attachment of cells to the matrix. The proteins also interact with other matrix proteins, such as collagen and proteoglycans, to further integrate the cells with the extracellular matrix. Through the interactions with cell receptors and other matrix proteins, the noncollagenous glycoproteins function in regulating tissue morphogenesis as well as tissue repair and remodeling. They also appear to play a role in other diverse processes, including tumor growth and metastasis.

OTHER MATRIX PROTEINS. Many other matrix proteins are present in connective tissues, such as tenascin, osteonectin, matrix Gla protein, and osteocalcin, that are less completely understood but probably no less important. Matrix Gla protein and osteocalcin are both found in bone, whereas matrix Gla protein is also present in cartilage and other soft tissues, including blood vessel walls. Both proteins require reduced vitamin K as a cofactor for a post-translational carboxylation reaction important to the cation binding properties of the proteins.

Inhibition of vitamin K reduction by the drug warfarin interferes with this reaction, as it does for the coagulation factors. Warfarin is contraindicated in pregnancy because it has been shown to cause an embryopathy, which includes abnormalities in skeletal formation, likely secondary to effects on matrix Gla protein and/or osteocalcin.

EXTRACELLULAR MATRIX PROTEIN RECEPTORS. Connective tissue cells use several different types of cell-surface receptors to bind extracellular matrix proteins. The major types of receptors include integrins, CD44, and proteoglycan-family receptors such as the syndecans (Table 275-3). CD44 is expressed by several different connective tissue cell types as well as by nonconnective tissue cells such as lymphocytes. On connective tissue cells, CD44 is the principal receptor for hyaluronan. CD44 binding of hyaluronan is particularly important in forming a gel-like pericellular coat found around certain connective tissue cells such as chondrocytes. Syndecans contain a transmembrane protein core to which heparin sulfate proteoglycans are attached to the extracellular domain. The proteoglycans bind growth factors such as fibroblast growth factor. Syndecans also appear to interact with integrins and may modulate integrin function.

The integrins represent the largest family of extracellular matrix receptors and have been found to be the primary receptors for many matrix proteins, including collagens, fibronectin, laminin, vitronectin, osteopontin, and thrombospondin (see Table 275-3). Integrins are heterodimeric transmembrane proteins consisting of one alpha and one beta subunit. There are more than 20 known integrins formed by 14 types of alpha subunits and at least nine types of beta subunits. There are two major subfamilies of integrins that function in mediating cell extracellular matrix interactions. These are the $\beta1$ subfamily and the αV subfamily. The specificity of extracellular matrix protein binding is determined by both the alpha and the beta subunit, although more than one integrin type can bind to the same matrix protein, often at different sites within the protein. For example the $\alpha1\beta1$, $\alpha2\beta1$, $\alpha3\beta1$, and $\alpha10\beta1$ integrins are all capable of binding collagen, whereas $\alpha3\beta1$, $\alpha4\beta1$, $\alpha5\beta1$, and $\alpha V\beta3$ can all bind fibronectin. Also, each type of integrin can bind more than one different type of extracellular matrix protein; for example $\alpha V\beta3$ can bind vitronectin, osteopontin, or fibronectin.

Each connective tissue cell expresses a combination of integrins that is regulated, at least in part, by the mix of proteins present in the extracellular matrix. Also, integrin expression and affinity for matrix ligands can change in response to cues from the matrix, including stimulation by growth factors and cytokines. The exact function of each particular integrin is currently a topic of investigation by a number of research laboratories. Research in bone has found that the $\alpha V\beta3$ integrin present on osteoclasts plays an important role in the ability of these cells to resorb bone. For this reason, chemical inhibitors of $\alpha V\beta3$ are being tested in early clinical trials for the treatment of osteoporosis.

Binding of extracellular matrix proteins to integrins activates a number of signal transduction pathways that regulate cell responses to the matrix, including changes in gene expression. Signaling complexes are formed at sites, often referred to as focal adhesions, where close contact is made between the integrins and the extracellular matrix. The signaling complexes include activation of several different tyrosine and serine-threonine kinases, phosphoinositide and arachidonic acid pathways, as well as ion fluxes. Accompanying, and intimately tied to, activation of cell signaling are changes in the organization of the cytoskeleton. In this way, integrins can mediate processes that require changes in cytoarchitecture such as cell migration and wound repair. Integrins also provide signals necessary to promote cell survival in cells that require attachment to a matrix to survive. Given their diverse roles in mediating events important to connective tissue development, repair, and remodeling, studies of integrin function should provide important new information needed to understand connective tissue in health and disease.

Specialized Connective Tissue Structures

CARTILAGE. There are several different types of cartilage, including hyaline, elastic, and fibrocartilage. Hyaline cartilage includes articular cartilage, which is present at the ends of bones and is responsible for the normal smooth gliding motion of the joints. Elastic cartilage, which is more flexible than hyaline, is found in the external ear and epiglottis. Fibrocartilage is found in the menisci and in ligaments at the site of insertion to bone or where tendons wrap around a bony pulley. Cartilage contains only one cell type, the chondrocyte, which is responsible for the synthesis and breakdown of the cartilage matrix. Very little to no cell division occurs in normal adult cartilage and so the resident chondrocytes must maintain the tissue for the lifetime of the individual.

The extracellular matrix is very abundant in cartilage where the cells make up only about 2 to 5% of the volume of the tissue. The matrix contains large amounts of type II collagen and the large aggregating proteoglycan aggrecan. The high aggrecan content is accompanied by a high water content, making cartilage about 70 to 80% water. Articular cartilage must resist compressive forces that occur during joint loading and so the proteoglycan content is appropriately high. In the superficial region of cartilage, the collagen fibers are arranged parallel to the surface of the tissue to withstand the shear forces occurring at the joint surface during movement. The surface of cartilage is very smooth with a very low coefficient of friction (less than that of ice on ice), which is critical for providing smooth and rapid joint movements. A protein called superficial zone protein, produced by chondrocytes and synovial cells, appears to be important for this function. When cartilage is damaged, it interferes with normal movement but it is not a direct source of pain because of the lack of a nerve supply. Pain, which occurs during the development of arthritis, results from pathologic lesions in other tissues such as bone, synovium, and the joint capsule.

TENDONS AND LIGAMENTS. Tendons connect muscle to bone and ligaments connect bone to bone. Both are composed of connective tissue, which must withstand the high tensile loads that occur during movement. Tendons transmit the force from muscle contraction to bone, resulting in movement. Ligaments serve to stabilize joints, allowing for a certain degree and direction of movement but resisting excessive displacement between bones. Tendon and ligament fibroblasts are responsible for the synthesis and maintenance of the matrix. Tendons and ligaments contain a very high content of type I collagen, which is found in long and densely packed parallel fibers. The noncollagenous proteins include proteoglycans such as decorin and biglycan, which are much smaller than the aggrecan found in cartilage, giving them a comparatively reduced water content.

SYNOVIUM. The synovium lines diarthrodial joints and is composed of loose connective tissue. In most places within normal joints, it is only a few cell layers thick. Unlike cartilage, synovium contains blood vessels, lymphatics, and nerves. It is the major source of nutrients for the cartilage and produces many of the major constituents found in the synovial fluid, including hyaluronic acid. There are two types of cells in the synovial matrix: fibroblasts (sometimes called type B synovial cells) and macrophages (type A cells). The synovial fibroblasts are responsible for matrix protein production. The macrophages are responsible for removing cell debris and any microorganisms that might gain entrance. The synovium is a major site of inflammation in arthritic diseases, where it becomes thickened by proliferation of resident cells and by an influx of inflammatory cells from the

Table 275–3 • CELL-SURFACE RECEPTORS FOR EXTRACELLULAR MATRIX COMPONENTS

RECEPTOR	LIGANDS
CD 44	Hyaluronan
Syndecan (1–4)	Tenascin, fibronectin, fibroblast growth factor (FGF)
Integrins	
$\alpha1\beta1$	Collagen, laminin, cartilage matrix protein
$\alpha2\beta1$	Collagen, laminin, chondroadherin
$\alpha3\beta1$	Laminin, fibronectin, collagen, epiligrin
$\alpha4\beta1$	Fibronectin, VCAM-1
$\alpha5\beta1$	Fibronectin
$\alpha6\beta1$	Laminin
$\alpha7\beta1$	Laminin
$\alpha8\beta1$	Tenascin, nephronectin, fibronectin, vitronectin
$\alpha9\beta1$	Laminin, collagen, tenascin
$\alpha10\beta1$	Collagen
$\alpha V\beta1$	Fibronectin, vitronectin
$\alpha V\beta3$	Vitronectin, fibrinogen, osteopontin, fibronectin, thrombospondin
$\alpha V\beta5$	Vitronectin, fibronectin
$\alpha V\beta6$	Fibronectin, tenascin
$\alpha V\beta8$	Vitronectin, laminin, collagen, fibronectin

circulation. In inflammatory arthritis, activated synovial fibroblasts produce enzymes, including the matrix metalloproteinases (MMPs), which degrade joint structures, whereas inflammatory cells produce cytokines, such as tumor necrosis factor-α and interleukin-1 among others, which stimulate MMP production and drive the inflammatory process.

INTERVERTEBRAL DISKS. The intervertebral disks, which assist in movement and provide flexibility to the spine, have distinct regions consisting of the inner nucleus pulposus and an outer fibrosis rim, the annulus, along with an intermediate area between the two. Blood vessels are present in the outer region of the annulus but not in the nucleus pulposus, which must obtain its nutrients by diffusion. The annulus contains denser connective tissue to provide structural support whereas the nucleus pulposus has a higher water content and is more gel-like. Discs contain both types I and II collagen along with proteoglycans, including aggrecan, found predominately in the nucleus pulposus. The cells in this region are more chondrocyte-like, whereas those in the outer fibrosis regions are more fibroblast-like. By adulthood, very few cells are present in the nucleus pulposus, which, along with the changes associated with aging discussed in the next section, make discs very susceptible to degeneration and unable to repair damaged matrix.

Changes in Connective Tissues Associated with Aging

Aging has an important impact on both the structure and the function of connective tissues. General aging changes in connective tissue cells include a reduced mitogenic response and a reduced synthetic capacity, likely the result of a reduction in the cellular response to growth factor stimulation. In the extracellular matrix, there is an accumulation of modified and, in some cases, degraded matrix components. The matrix changes appear to reduce the capacity of aging connective tissues to resist tensile forces and to reduce resiliency. Age-related changes in elastin contribute to a loss in tissue elasticity. These changes make connective tissues more susceptible to injury and less capable of repairing damage and in this way contribute to age-associated conditions.

Evidence is mounting that age-related nonenzymatic glycation occurs in the collagen found in several different connective tissue structures, including cartilage, tendons, ligaments, and intervertebral disks. Because collagen has such a long half-life (estimated to be more than 100 years for type II collagen in cartilage), there is a progressive accumulation of collagen that contains advanced glycation end-products, which can in turn form intrachain and interchain cross-links stiffening the collagen fibers. Increased collagen stiffness may contribute to the reduced flexibility noted in ligaments and tendons with age. Although the collagen is stiffer with age, it appears to be less able to resist tensile forces and so could be characterized as being more brittle.

Changes in proteoglycan size and sulfation also occur with age. These changes result in a reduced capacity for binding water, which contributes to an age-related decrease in hydration of connective tissues. Decreases in water content with age have been measured in articular cartilage and in intervertebral discs. Reduced hydration makes the tissues less able to respond to compression. The decreased water content of the discs, along with increased collagen cross-linking from nonenzymatic glycation, may offer an explanation for why disc herniations are less common in older adults but disc degeneration is more common. Less is known about age-related changes in matrix proteins other than fibrillar collagen and the large proteoglycans. There is an increase in fibronectin in some connective tissues with age, but the consequences of this increase are not known.

Connective Tissue Degradation

There is a need for repair and remodeling of connective tissues in response to injury, growth, and changes in the biomechanical demands at specific tissue sites. Repair and remodeling of connective tissues require that some components of the tissue be removed and replaced with new components. Healing of wounds in the skin also requires migration of cells into the damaged area, and cell migration is facilitated by matrix degradation. To accomplish these tasks, a set of enzymes capable of degrading extracellular matrix proteins is required (Table 275–4). These enzymes are produced by connective tissue cells and released, where they act locally to degrade specific

Table 275–4 • MATRIX DEGRADING ENZYMES

PROTEINASE	SUBSTRATES
MATRIX METALLOPROTEINASES (MMPS)	
MMP-1, MMP-8, MMP-13 (collagenase 1, 2, 3)	Fibrillar collagens, fibronectin, aggrecan
MMP-3, MMP-10, MMP-11 (stromelysin 1, 2, 3)	Proteoglycan, procollagenase, fibronectin
MMP-2, MMP-9 (gelatinase A, B)	Denatured collagen, aggrecan, fibronectin
MMP-7 (matrilysin)	Proenzymes, fibronectin, other matrix proteins
MMP-12 (macrophage elastase)	Elastin, fibronectin, laminin
MMP-14, MMP-15, MMP-16, MMP-17 (MT1-MT4-MMP)	Procollagenase
ADAM-17 (TACE)	Tumor necrosis factor-α
ADAMTS-4, ADAMTS-5 (aggrecanase 1, 2)	Aggrecan
SERINE PROTEASES	
Plasmin	Fibrin, pro-MMPs
Plasminogen activators	Plasminogen
Neutrophil elastase	Elastin
CYSTEINE PROTEASES	
Cathepsin K	Type I collagen
Cathepsin B	Broad specificity
ASPARTATE PROTEASES	
Cathepsin D	Aggrecan, denatured collagen
Pepsin	Broad specificity

MT-MMP = membrane type-MMP; ADAM = a disintegrin and a metalloproteinase; TACE = tumor necrosis factor-α converting enzyme; ADAMTS = a disintegrin and a metalloproteinase with a thrombospondin motif.

Modified from Mort JS, Poole AR: Mediators of inflammation, tissue destruction, and repair. D. Proteases and their inhibitors. In Klippel JH (ed): Primer on the Rheumatic Diseases, 12th ed. Atlanta, Arthritis Foundation, 2001, pp 72–81.

matrix components. In certain disease states—for example, osteoarthritis and rheumatoid arthritis—excess production of matrix-degrading enzymes occurs, overwhelming the capacity of the cells to replace the lost matrix components, which results in net tissue destruction and loss.

The largest family of matrix-degrading enzymes, the MMP family, consists of enzymes that share functional domains, require zinc for activity, and are active at neutral pH. The MMPs are either released into the extracellular matrix or, in some cases, such as the membrane-type MMPs, directly anchored to the cell. MMP-1, MMP-8, and MMP-13 are collagenases, which are the primary enzymes capable of degrading native collagen, whereas MMP-2 and MMP-9 are gelatinases, which degrade denatured collagen. MMP-3, MMP-10, and MMP-11 are stromelysins responsible for degrading noncollagen proteins such as proteoglycans and fibronectin, whereas MMP-12 functions as an elastase. The membrane-type MMPs can serve to activate other MMPs at the cell surface. More recently discovered members of the MMP family include the ADAMs (a disintegrin and a metalloproteinase) and the ADAMTSs (a disintegrin and a metalloproteinase with a thrombospondin motif). The ADAMS are localized to the cell surface, at least in part through the disintegrin domain. ADAM-17 is also known as TACE (tumor necrosis factor-α converting enzyme) because of its ability to cleave tumor necrosis factor-α to an active form. Finally, the ADAMTSs utilize the thrombospondin motif to interact with proteoglycans, which can serve as substrates for these enzymes. ADAMTS-4 and ADAMTS-5 are aggrecanases that have been shown to cleave the large proteoglycan aggrecan.

The MMPs are normally kept in an inactive state by a propeptide region that interacts with the zinc moiety at the active site. Cleavage of the propeptide by other MMPs or members of other protease families results in the release of active enzyme. Further control of MMP activity is provided by specific inhibitors of MMPs present in the extracellular matrix, including the tissue inhibitors of metalloproteinases (TIMPs). The expression of MMPs and TIMPs is regulated at the transcriptional level by cytokines, growth factors, and matrix components, including, in some cases, fragments of proteins degraded by MMPs, providing for a feedback loop during matrix remodeling.

Other matrix-degrading enzymes are the serine proteases, which include plasmin and elastase, the aspartic proteases, which include pepsin and cathepsin D, and the cysteine proteases, including papain and cathepsins B, C, K, L, and S. Plasmin, the cleavage product of plasminogen, can cleave MMP propeptides, resulting in MMP activation. Elastase, often a product of neutrophils, can degrade elastin and some fibrillar collagens. Cathepsin K has been recognized as a key mediator of bone resorption, where it functions to cleave collagen under the acidic conditions found at the osteoclast ruffled border. Like the MMPs, production and secretion of these proteases is controlled by signals from growth factors, cytokines, and matrix components. Thus, a fine and intricate balance exists in connective tissues that controls the integrity of the tissue and the response to injury. This balance is disturbed in disease states that cause connective tissue destruction.

Research advances that have improved our knowledge of the biology of connective tissue are being applied in the design of new therapies. We are witnessing the emergence of anticytokine therapies, such as anti-tumor necrosis factor-α and antagonists to interleukin-1 aimed not only at reducing inflammation in connective tissues but also halting tissue destruction. Growth factors capable of stimulating repair are being studied for treatment of chronic wounds, non-healing bone defects, and cartilage lesions. Small molecule inhibitors of MMPs and other matrix-degrading enzymes are in development and early testing. Finally, advances in tissue engineering should make it possible to reconstruct or replace many damaged connective tissue structures. Undifferentiated mesenchymal precursor cells found in the bone marrow and some connective tissues, including adipose, can be induced in vitro to differentiate into cells capable of producing bone, cartilage, muscle, or adipose tissue, depending on culture conditions. These exciting advances will certainly lead to better treatments for the many common conditions affecting connective tissues.

SUGGESTED READINGS

Bornstein P, Sage EH: Matricellular proteins: Extracellular modulators of cell function. Curr Opin Cell Biol 2002;14:608–616. *A review of the extracellular matrix proteins that mediate interactions between the cell and the matrix.*

Kresse H, Schonherr E: Proteoglycans of the extracellular matrix and growth control. J Cell Physiol 2001;189:266–274. *Describes the mechanisms by which proteoglycans regulate cellular functions, including interactions with growth factors.*

Miranti CK, Brugge JS: Sensing the environment: A historical perspective on integrin signal transduction. Nat Cell Biol 2002;4:E83–E90. *An overview of how integrins regulate cell function. This issue contains additional reviews in the field of cell-extracellular matrix biology.*

Myllyharju J, Kivirikko KI: Collagens and collagen-related diseases. Ann Med 2001;33:7–21. *Detailed review of the various collagen types found in connective tissues and the disorders caused by collagen gene mutations.*

Vu TH, Werb Z: Matrix metalloproteinases: Effectors of development and normal physiology. Genes Dev 2000;14:2123–2133. *Review of the matrix metalloproteinase family of matrix-degrading enzymes and their involvement in processes that involve remodeling of connective tissue extracellular matrix.*

276 INHERITED DISEASES OF CONNECTIVE TISSUE

Reed E. Pyeritz

MUCOPOLYSACCHARIDOSES

Definition

Proteoglycans are ubiquitous components of the extracellular matrix (ECM) and the surfaces of cells and are among the largest and most complex of human molecules. Proteoglycans consist of a protein core to which are covalently bound glycosaminoglycans (GAG; mucopolysaccharides) of several types: dermatan sulfate, heparan sulfate, keratan sulfate, and chondroitin sulfate. These four polymeric molecules are cleaved from their protein core in lysosomes; then they, plus hyaluronan (a GAG lacking a protein core), are catabolized further in lysosomes in a stepwise fashion by 10 enzymes. Genetic defects in any one of these enzymes lead to accumulation of GAG metabolites in lysosomes, with profound disruption of cellular physiology. The phenotypes resulting from deficiencies of these catabolic enzymes are termed *mucopolysaccharidoses* (MPSs) and are classified into seven types (Table 276–1). Several additional disorders, termed *mucolipidoses* (MLs), are due to a genetic defect in post-translational modification of lysosomal enzymes and share features with MPS.

Etiology and Pathogenesis

With the exception of MPS II (Hunter syndrome), which is X-linked, each of these disorders is autosomal recessive. All MPSs are due to deficiency of a single lysosomal enzyme responsible for a specific step in GAG metabolism. Catabolism of GAG proceeds normally until the step requiring the defective enzyme, where further normal metabolism halts. Although a minor degree of nonspecific breakdown occurs, which results in urinary excretion of cleaved GAG that can be useful diagnostically, accumulation of GAG within lysosomes of cells of mesenchymal origin, endothelium, and, in most cases, neurons causes widespread, progressive cellular dysfunction and clinical effects. Lysosomal enzymes are targeted to lysosomes by post-translational addition of mannose 6-phosphate. Deficiency of the phosphotransferase that catalyzes the first step in this reaction results in an inability to catabolize all GAG. The catabolic enzymes, which normally would be transported into lysosomes, instead are secreted from the cell and are found in unusually high concentration in plasma, providing one diagnostic test for ML.

Prevalence

All MPS disorders are rare, on the order of 1 per 100,000 or less, without ethnic predilection.

Pathology

All pathologic manifestations of MPS and ML disorders worsen with age, and some are present from early developmental stages. Gross anatomic hallmarks are hepatosplenomegaly, marked skeletal alterations termed *dysostosis multiplex* that result in short stature and thoracic cage deformity, thickening and narrowing of airways and arteries, and coarsening of facial features. Although mental retardation is a prominent feature of some of these conditions, the brain may show only ventriculomegaly secondary to communicating hydrocephalus. Mesenchymal cells show a cytoplasm full of apparently empty vacuoles; these are lysosomes from which GAG has been removed by fixation. Cells cultured from patients show greatly enlarged lysosomes filled with granular material. In the severe form of ML, dense inclusions are present, which gave rise to the common name, *I-cell disease.*

Clinical Manifestations

Each of the disorders in Table 276–1 shows a wide spectrum of clinical severity. This wide spectrum has led to a classification that gives the impression of separate disorders within some of the MPS and ML types, but these represent the apparent ends of the continuum. Some of the disorders result in death by adolescence (Hurler syndrome, severe Hunter syndrome, ML II), whereas others are commonly compatible with survival to adulthood. The latter group is emphasized here.

The milder end of the MPS I spectrum, Scheie syndrome, may not be diagnosed until adulthood, with stiffened joints, corneal clouding and glaucoma, carpal tunnel syndrome, and aortic valvular disease. Stature and intelligence are not affected. The main health risks are valvular involvement, thickening of meninges that can produce a myelopathy, and thickening of the upper airways that can produce obstructive symptoms and sleep apnea.

The milder form of MPS II, Hunter syndrome, is distinctive because it is X-linked (affecting virtually only males), and the cornea shows little overt clouding. Cervical myelopathy, obstructive airway disease, and cor pulmonale are important concerns. A combined conductive-neurosensory hearing loss is common.

Neither MPS IV (Morquio syndrome) nor MPS VI (Maroteaux-Lamy syndrome) affects intelligence. Both syndromes often are associated with severe skeletal changes, which are distinct radiographically, but produce similar problems of kyphoscoliosis, pectus

Continued

Table 276–1 • MUCOPOLYSACCHARIDOSES AND MUCOLIPIDOSES

TYPE	EPONYM OR COMMON NAME	CLINICAL FEATURES	INHERITANCE	OMIM*	ENZYMATIC DEFECT
MPS IH	Hurler syndrome	DM and short stature; MR; corneal clouding; HS; heart disease; death in childhood	AR	252800	α-L-iduronidase
MPS IS	Scheie syndrome	Coarse facies; stiff joints, corneal clouding; aortic valve disease; normal intelligence and lifespan	AR	252800	α-L-iduronidase
MPS II	Hunter syndrome	Severe form: coarse facies, DM and short stature, HS; MR; no corneal clouding; death by late adolescence Mild form: coarse facies, short stature; normal intelligence; survival to adulthood	XL	309900	Iduronate sulfatase
MPS IIIA	Sanfilippo A	Severe MR and hyperactivity; mild somatic changes	AR	252900	Heparan N-sulfatase
MPS IIIB	Sanfilippo B	Same as MPS IIIA	AR	252920	α-N-acetylglucosaminidase
MPS IIIC	Sanfilippo C	Same as MPS IIIA	AR	252930	Acetyl-CoA:α-glucosaminide acetyltransferase
MPS IIID	Sanfilippo D	Same as MPS IIIA	AR	252940	N-acetylglucosamine 6-sulfatase
MPS IVA	Morquio A	Short stature and distinct skeletal dysplasia with odontoid hypoplasia and myelopathy; corneal clouding; normal intelligence; valvular heart disease	AR	253000	Galactose 6-sulfatase
MPS IVB	Morquio B	Same as MPS IVA	AR	253010	β-Galactosidase
MPS VI	Maroteaux-Lamy	DM and short stature; corneal clouding; normal intelligence; aortic stenosis; leukocyte inclusions; hydrocephalus in severe form	AR	253200	N-acetylgalactosamine
MPS VII	Sly syndrome	DM; HS; widely variable, including MR;	AR	253220	β-Glucuronidase
MPS IX	—	short stature; periarticular soft tissue masses	AR	601492	Hyaluronidase
ML II	I-cell disease	Similar to but more severe than MPS IH but cellular inclusions; no mucopolysacchariduria	AR	252500	UDP-N-acetylglucosamine: lysosomal enzyme N-acetylglucosaminyl-1-phosphotransferase
ML III	Pseudo-Hurler polydystrophy	Short stature and mild DM; stiff joints, arthropathy, coarse facies; variable but mild MR; survival to adulthood	AR	252500	Same as ML II

*Entries in Online Mendelian Inheritance in Man, OMIM. McKusick-Nathans Institute for Genetic Medicine, Johns Hopkins University (Baltimore, MD) and National Center for Biotechnology Information, National Library of Medicine (Bethesda, MD), 2000. World Wide Web URL: http://www.ncbi.nlm.nih.gov/omim/.
AR = autosomal recessive; DM = dysostosis multiplex; HS = hepatosplenomegaly; MR = mental retardation; XL = X-linked.

carinatum, restrictive lung disease, and severe short stature and joint degeneration. Cervical myelopathy from thickened dura is common to both and is accentuated by odontoid hypoplasia in MPS IV. Thickening of the aortic and mitral valves may produce severe dysfunction requiring replacement. General anesthesia is especially hazardous because of the narrow upper and middle airways.

Patients with ML III (pseudo-Hurler polydystrophy) resemble patients with MPS VI but often have mild-to-moderate mental retardation. Aortic regurgitation is common.

Differential Diagnosis

Diagnosis of these conditions is difficult in the young child before most of the clinical features have progressed but should be considered in any person with hepatosplenomegaly and coarsening of the facial features. Evaluation requires a pedigree analysis, skeletal radiographic survey, echocardiogram, and analysis of the urine for excretion of GAG. Often the specific MPS is evident from radiographs, the presence or absence of corneal clouding, and the pattern of mucopolysacchariduria. Enzymatic analysis of leukocytes confirms the diagnosis. MLs do not show mucopolysacchariduria but have marked elevation of all the GAG catabolic lysosomal enzymes in plasma.

℞ Treatment and Care

Ventriculoperitoneal shunting is necessary when intracranial pressure is elevated. Close attention to hearing and visual problems is essential throughout life. Many adults with MPS and ML require surgery for carpal tunnel. Cardiovascular surgery for valvular or coronary disease may be necessary. All anesthesia is high risk because of the narrow airways and, in the case of MPS IV, atlantoaxial instability. For patients who remain ambulatory, selective joint replacement can be beneficial. Because of the morbidity associated with thoracic cage deformity, consideration should be given to stabilizing spinal deformity before it becomes severe.

Replacement of the deficient enzyme via intravenous infusion is being studied for most of the MPS disorders. Recently, laronidase (Aldurazyme) was approved in the United States for treatment of MPS I. An infusion every 2 weeks for 1 year in adolescent and adult patients resulted in substantial reduction in hepatosplenomegaly and modest improvement in pulmonary function, sleep apnea, and joint mobility. Whether early institution of therapy in young children will modulate mental retardation in the Hurler variant of MPS I is uncertain.

MARFAN SYNDROME

Definition

Marfan syndrome is an autosomal dominant, pleiotropic disorder caused by defects in the principal component of the extracellular microfibril, the large glycoprotein fibrillin-1. The features occur in multiple systems, especially the eye, skeleton, heart, aorta, lung, and integument. Notable features include dislocation of the ocular lens, tall stature with particularly long limbs and digits, deformity of the thoracic cage from pectus carinatum or excavatum and abnormal curvature of the spine, mitral and tricuspid valve prolapse, dilation of the sinuses of Valsalva and predisposition to aortic dissection, spontaneous pneumothorax, abnormal skin stretch marks, hernias, and dural ectasia. When untreated, patients often die before age 30 or 40 from aortic dissection or congestive heart failure.

Etiology and Pathogenesis

Mutations in *FBN1,* which maps to human chromosome 15q21.1 and encodes fibrillin-1, cause Marfan syndrome and related connective tissue disorders. Several hundred distinct mutations have been found, and few occur in more than one family. Patients are heterozygous for mutations in *FBN1,* hence the autosomal dominant inheritance. Because extracellular microfibrils are polymers of many fibrillin-1 molecules, the molecular pathogenesis operates by a dominant-negative mechanism, whereby virtually all microfibrils contain mutant monomers. Microfibrils are ubiquitous in the ECM of most tissues and perform different functions. In elastic tissues, microfibrils are intimately associated with elastin to form elastic fibers. Microfibrils, in the absence of elastin or collagen, form the ocular zonules that hold the lens to the ciliary body. At the dermal-epidermal junction, microfibrils are oriented perpendicularly and likely perform some role in adhesion of the layers.

The features of Marfan syndrome are highly variable, even among relatives who share the same mutation in *FBN1.* This variability persists after accounting for the effects of age. Men tend to be affected more severely, for unclear reasons.

Prevalence

Marfan syndrome is a common mendelian disorder, with an estimated incidence of about 1 per 5000. Marfan syndrome is found throughout the world, without ethnic or geographic predilection.

Pathology

The features of Marfan syndrome are age dependent. Some severely affected infants have flagrant features and often die of mitral regurgitation and heart failure despite aggressive management. At the other end of the clinical spectrum, Marfan syndrome merges with several related disorders, and patients may not come to medical attention, let alone receive a definitive diagnosis, until adulthood.

None of the gross or microscopic pathologic changes is specific for Marfan syndrome. The medial degeneration of the aortic wall, characterized by disarray and fragmentation of the elastic fibers and increased proteoglycan (often inappropriately termed *cystic medial necrosis*) also can be seen in other disorders and in older people with hypertension. Aortic dissection usually begins just superior to the aortic valve (type A) and often progresses to the bifurcation. Death usually results from retrograde dissection and hemopericardium. About 10% of dissections begin in the descending thoracic aorta (type B).

Clinical Manifestations

The lens tends to be displaced superiorly, and usually the zonules remain intact. The retina is at increased risk of detachment, especially in patients who are highly myopic. Tubular bones overgrow, accounting for the disproportionate tall stature (dolichostenomelia), long digits (arachnodactyly), and sternal deformity. Ligaments may be lax, causing scoliosis and joint hypermobility. Alternatively, congenital contractures are common, especially of the elbows and digits. The palate typically is highly arched, and the dentition can be crowded and maloccluded. Mitral valve prolapse occurs in about 80%, and the valve leaflets become progressively thickened (myxomatous on histopathology). The mitral annulus may dilate and calcify. Aortic root dilation begins in the sinuses of Valsalva and progresses with age, albeit at highly variable rates. Most males with Marfan syndrome have an aortic root dimension above the upper limit of normal for their body surface area by adolescence. Some females show a slower progression and may have a root diameter around the upper limit of normal well into adulthood. The dilation usually does not involve the distal ascending aorta. Spontaneous pneumothorax, resulting from rupture of apical blebs, occurs in about 5% of patients. Stretch marks (striae atrophicae) occur over areas of flexural stress, such as the shoulders, breasts, and lower back. The neural canal in the lumbosacral region is enlarged in most people with Marfan syndrome; this may be visible on plain radiographs, especially if the neuroforamina are widened. Imaging by computed tomography or magnetic resonance imaging is diagnostic and should be used in patients with back pain and radicular symptoms. Large anterior meningoceles in the pelvis are a severe manifestation of dural ectasia.

Differential Diagnosis

The conditions that overlap clinically and genetically with Marfan syndrome include familial aortic aneurysm, familial ectopia lentis, MASS phenotype (which includes many families with mitral valve prolapse syndrome), and Shprintzen-Goldberg syndrome. All of these conditions are diagnosed clinically, so differentiating them one from another is arbitrary. A careful family history is essential to this process. Molecular genetic testing has a limited role. If the mutation in *FBN1* is known in a family, however, analysis of DNA can be used effectively for presymptomatic or prenatal diagnosis.

A question of Marfan syndrome arises most commonly in the tall, lanky adolescent who has several minor skeletal features, nearsightedness, and athletic desires. A detailed ophthalmologic examination with full pupillary dilation and a transthoracic echocardiogram are essential components in the evaluation. If these tests are negative, and no one in the family has a history of Marfan syndrome or aortic dissection, the patient likely can be reassured.

Rx Treatment and Care

Life expectancy in Marfan syndrome has improved markedly to the point that many patients can expect survival to advanced years. All patients should be seen at least annually by a physician who manages the overall care. Most patients require annual ophthalmologic and cardiologic consultation and orthopedic consultation as required by specific problems. Some evidence supports the prophylactic use of β-adrenergic blockade from an early age to slow the rate of aortic root dilation and protect from aortic dissection. Prophylactic surgical repair of the aortic root has had the greatest beneficial impact. The composite graft, involving a prosthetic valve in a Dacron tube and implantation of the coronary ostia into the graft, was the first approach to show markedly improved survival. More recently, replacement of the aneurysm and preservation of the native aortic valve has shown promise. For the adult, aortic root surgery should be recommended when the maximal aortic diameter reaches 50 to 55 mm; a strong family history of aortic dissection should prompt earlier repair.

EHLERS-DANLOS SYNDROMES

Definition

The Ehlers-Danlos syndromes (EDSs) are clinically variable and genetically heterogeneous. Diagnoses still are based largely on the bedside examination, and the classification scheme and diagnostic criteria have been revised more recently. The unifying themes among these disorders are fragility of tissues, joint hypermobility, and skin hyperextensibility.

Etiology and Pathogenesis

Defects in collagen and other proteins in the ECM of various tissues underlie all forms of EDS that have been elucidated so far. The specific genetic mutations occur in a variety of genes, with the effect of altering the structure, synthesis, post-translational modifications, or stability of the collagens involved. The known molecular defects are listed in Table 276–2.

Prevalence

No accurate data exist, but an incidence of about 1 in 5000 births is a reasonable estimate of how many individuals qualify for one of the EDS diagnoses. Each of the types represents something of a clinical spectrum, with the mild end merging with what might be considered normal variation. Just as the diagnostic criteria are arbitrary, so would any determination inherited prevalence based on phenotypic criteria. The extent to which normal variation in joint hypermobility, skin elasticity, and tissue fragility represents genetic variation at loci that encode collagen or other ECM genes requires considerable research.

Table 276-2 • EHLERS-DANLOS SYNDROMES

TYPE	FORMER NAME	CLINICAL FEATURES*	INHERITANCE	OMIM†	MOLECULAR DEFECT
Classic	EDS I and II	Joint hypermobility; skin hyperextensibility; atrophic scars; smooth, velvety skin; subcutaneous spheroids	AD	130000 130010	Structure of type V collagen ?COL5A1, COL5A2
Hypermobility	EDS III	Joint hypermobility; some skin hyperextensibility, with or without smooth, velvety texture	AD AR	130020 225320	? Tenascin-X (TNX)
Vascular	EDS IV	Thin skin; easy bruising; pinched nose; acrogeria; rupture of large-caliber and medium-caliber arteries, uterus, and large bowel	AD	130050 (225350) (225360)	Deficient type III collagen (COL3A1)
Kyphoscoliotic	EDS VI	Joint hypermobility; congenital, progressive scoliosis; scleral fragility with globe rupture; tissue fragility, aortic dilation, MVP	AR	225400	Deficiency of lysyl hydroxylase
Arthrochalasia	EDS VII A and B	Joint hypermobility, severe, with subluxations, congenital hip dislocation; skin hyperextensibility; tissue fragility	AD	130060	No cleavage of N-terminus of type I procollagen due to mutations in COL1A1 or COL1A2
Dermatosparaxis	EDS VII C	Severe skin fragility; decreased skin elasticity easy bruising; hernias; premature rupture of fetal membranes	AR	225410	No cleavage of N-terminus of type I procollagen due to deficiency of peptidase
Unclassified types	EDS V	Classic features	XL	305200	?
	EDS VIII	Classic features and periodontal disease	AD	130080	?
	EDS X	Mild classic features, MVP	?	225310	?
	EDS XI	Joint instability	AD	147900	?
	EDS IX	Classic features; occipital horns	XL	309400	Allelic to Menkes' syndrome
	EDS, progerioid form	Classic features and premature aging	AR	130700	Deficiency of galactosyltransferase I

*Listed in order of diagnostic importance.
†Entries in Online Mendelian Inheritance in Man, OMIM. McKusick-Nathans Institute for Genetic Medicine, Johns Hopkins University (Baltimore, MD) and National Center for Biotechnology Information, National Library of Medicine (Bethesda, MD), 2000. World Wide Web URL: http://www.ncbi.nlm.nih.gov/omim/.
AD = autosomal dominant; AR = autosomal recessive; EDS = Ehlers-Danlos syndrome; MVP = mitral valve prolapse; XL = X-linked.

Pathology

Little of routine pathologic evaluation distinguishes among the various types of EDS or even distinguishes individual types from normal. Thickness of the dermis is decreased in some forms, especially the vascular type, and the walls of arteries are reduced in thickness in this type. By electron microscopy, the classic, hypermobile, and kyphoscoliotic types have abnormal collagen fibers, especially when viewed in cross section (variable and often increased fiber diameter with an irregular outline). In the vascular type, some patients have dilated endoplasmic reticulum consistent with aberrant secretion of type III collagen molecules.

Clinical Manifestations

The major and minor features of each EDS are detailed in Table 276-2. Infants with classic EDS often are born prematurely by 4 to 8 weeks because of rupture of fetal membranes. Diagnosing the vascular and kyphoscoliotic types is important because of their cardiovascular features. The vascular type, previously termed *EDS IV*, is characterized by a troublesome tendency of spontaneous rupture of large arteries and hollow organs, especially the colon and uterus. Because these events carry considerable morbidity, life expectancy is reduced, on average, by more than half. During pregnancy, women with this form of EDS are especially vulnerable to rupture of major arteries and the uterus. In the kyphoscoliotic type, aortic root dilation and aortic regurgitation can develop. Patients with most forms of EDS are prone to develop mitral valve prolapse, and progression to mitral regurgitation occurs more often than in the common form of mitral valve prolapse.

Differential Diagnosis

By carefully adhering to the clinical features shown in Table 276-2 and judicious use of laboratory tests, the various defined types of EDS can be differentiated. Many specific non-EDS syndromes need to be excluded. Infants with the kyphoscoliotic type of EDS share some features with severe Marfan syndrome. Patients with Larsen's syndrome may resemble patients with the arthrochalasis type of EDS. The skin redundancy and loss of elasticity of the dermatosparaxis type of EDS is reminiscent of autosomal dominant cutis laxa, which is not associated with easy bruising or tissue fragility.

The most difficult decision is whether a person warrants any diagnosis of EDS. Patients who have only joint hypermobility without skin changes should not be labeled with EDS; a diagnosis of familial joint hypermobility might be more appropriate. Familial joint instability involves a predisposition to dislocations of major joints that is rare in most types of EDS except for arthrochalasis.

Rx Treatment and Care

Management of most skin and joint problems should be conservative and preventive. Sutures need to be placed with careful attention to approximating the margins and avoiding tension; removable sutures should be left in place for twice the usual time. Most joint hypermobility and pain in EDS does not require surgical treatment. Benefit often is derived from physical therapy designed to strengthen the muscles that need to provide support for the loose ligaments. All patients should receive genetic counseling about the mode of inheritance and their risk of having children affected with EDS. The possibility of prenatal diagnosis exists for all of the types with defined molecular or biochemical defects.

The vascular type of EDS requires particular surgical care; the ruptured arteries are difficult to repair because of the pronounced vascular fragility. Rupture of the bowel is a surgical emergency. Because the risk of uterine and vascular rupture is especially high during pregnancy in women with the vascular form, these women should be advised of a substantial risk of dying related to pregnancy. Patients should be advised to avoid contact sports and to treat blood pressure elevations aggressively. Biochemical and genetic screening holds the potential for relieving relatives at risk by discovering that they do not have a defect in type III collagen.

The kyphoscoliotic type of EDS may improve with large doses of ascorbic acid (1 to 4 g/day) because vitamin C is a cofactor for the enzyme that is deficient. No other metabolic or genetic therapy is effective in other forms of EDS.

OSTEOGENESIS IMPERFECTA SYNDROMES

Definition

The heterogeneous group of disorders called *osteogenesis imperfecta* (OI) includes, at one end of the severity spectrum, a type lethal prenatally or in the neonatal period and, at the other, such mild features that distinguishing affected individuals from the general population is difficult. The unifying feature is hereditary osteopenia (insufficient bone), with primary defects in the protein matrix in bone and other tissues. The clinical syndromes all involve osteoporosis with liability to fracture.

Etiology and Pathogenesis

Patients in whom mutations have been found all have defects of one sort or another in the two genes that encode the procollagen chains of type I collagen, *COL1A1* and *COL1A2*. Type I collagen is composed of two α1(I) and one α2(I) procollagen chains; the mature fiber requires considerable post-translational modification that occurs appropriately only if the three procollagen chains have intertwined to form a triple helix that is perfect and completed at the right speed. A mutation that affects formation of the triple helix, such as substitution of one of the mandatory glycine residues that occurs at every third position, also has adverse effects on modifications that render the molecule capable of forming effective mature fibers. As a result, a single nucleotide change resulting in a missense mutation may have profound effects on the ECM and produce a severe condition. Alternatively and at first glance paradoxically, a mutation that eliminates an entire allele, or at least production of any product capable of intertwining with normal procollagen chains, has a much milder effect on the ECM and the severity of OI. Examples of the most common classes of mutations are shown in Table 276–3. Hundreds of mutations have been described.

Prevalence

No careful epidemiologic study has been performed, and the milder forms of type I OI merge with the phenotypes found in the general population. A crude estimate of its overall prevalence is 1 to 2 per 20,000. The neonatal lethal form (type II), which is nearly always due to a new mutation in a parental gamete, has an incidence of about 1 in 50,000.

Pathology

Other than the gross pathology associated with the clinical manifestations, the most characteristic pathology is a primary reduction in bone matrix with secondary undermineralization.

Clinical Manifestations

The major phenotypic features of OI are shown in Table 276–3. The most severe type is II, followed in decreasing order by III, IV, and I. In type II, infants either are stillborn or die soon after birth of pulmonary failure secondary to the small thorax, which usually is compromised further by myriad rib fractures. A few infants have survived for at least a few years but require enormous attention to their medical needs.

Type III OI may be confused with type II at birth, but survival alone helps make the distinction. Bony deformity is pronounced and not necessarily due to fractures. Mobility is impaired, and most patients require a wheelchair at an early age. Stature may be severely compromised. Because of progressive vertebral column deformity and rib fractures, restrictive lung disease is a common problem as patients age; many die of pulmonary complications. Basilar impression causing compression of the brainstem and the craniocervical junction can produce central sleep apnea, headache, and upper motor neuron signs.

Patients with type IV OI generally have reduced stature, some bony deformity, and abnormal teeth that are opalescent and wear easily (dentinogenesis imperfecta). As in type I OI, the tendency to fracture is highest in childhood and lessens with adolescence. A distinguishing characteristic of type IV OI is a normal scleral hue.

Type I OI is probably the most common form and is associated with a bluish or blue-gray scleral hue. People with type I OI who also have dentinogenesis imperfecta tend to have more severe skeletal problems. The risk of fracture diminishes during adulthood but re-emerges as a major concern for women after menopause. Hearing impairment in all forms of OI is common and age-related, being rare before adolescence. The deficits are of either a mixed or a predominantly conductive form.

Differential Diagnosis

The range of diagnostic possibilities in a person with multiple fractures largely depends on age. In infancy, the genetic conditions hypophosphatasia, severe osteochondrodysplasias (e.g., achondrogenesis and forms of spondyloepiphyseal dysplasia), and Menkes' syndrome need to be excluded when a diagnosis of type II or III OI is considered. The radiographic features eventually become entirely diagnostic, but often the neonatologist has to arrive at a definitive answer in short order. Analysis of serum alkaline phosphatase and copper can be helpful. In childhood, the most common situation leading to a consideration of a mild form of OI is child abuse. In this situation, the pattern of fracture is usually distinct, and bone mineralization should be normal if the child is the object of nonaccidental or repeated

Table 276–3 • OSTEOGENESIS IMPERFECTA

TYPE	CLINICAL FEATURES	INHERITANCE	OMIM*	BASIC DEFECTS
I	Fractures variable in number; little deformity; stature normal or nearly so; blue sclerae; hearing loss common but not always present; DI uncommon	AD	166200	Typically, one nonfunctional *COL1A1* allele
II	Lethal in utero or shortly after birth; many fractures at birth typically involving ribs (may appear "beaded") and other long bones; little calvaria; pulmonary hypertension	AD	166210	*COL1A1* or *COL1A2*: substitution of glycyl residues; occasionally deletions of a portion of the triple-helical domain
		AR	259400	Deletion in *COL1A2* plus a nonfunctional allele
III	Fractures common, but long bones progressively deform starting in utero; stature markedly reduced; sclerae often blue, but become lighter with age; DI and hearing loss common	AD, AR (rare)	259420 259440	One single–amino acid substitution Two mutations in *COL1A1* and/or *COL1A2* (rarely)
IV	Fractures common; stature usually reduced; bone deformity common, but rarely severe; scleral hue normal to grayish; hearing loss variable; DI common	AD	166220 166240	Point mutations in *COL1A1* or *COL1A2* Exon skipping mutations in *COL1A2*

*Entries in Online Mendelian Inheritance in Man, OMIM. McKusick-Nathans Institute for Genetic Medicine, Johns Hopkins University (Baltimore, MD) and National Center for Biotechnology Information, National Library of Medicine (Bethesda, MD), 2000. World Wide Web URL: http://www.ncbi.nlm.nih.gov/omim/.

AD = autosomal dominant; AR = autosomal recessive; DI = dentinogenesis imperfecta.

Rheumatic Diseases

accidental trauma. Abnormal scleral hue, dentinogenesis imperfecta, and wormian bones (microfractures along the cranial sutures) all support the diagnosis of OI. The legal and child-protective systems often request exclusion of OI, however, by analysis of collagen production from cultured skin fibroblasts. In older children, the disorder idiopathic juvenile osteoporosis should be considered in any patient seen initially with repeated fractures. Occasionally, studies of skin fibroblasts are needed to document whether a defect in type I collagen (which would be characteristic of OI) is present. Many osteochondrodysplasias are associated with short stature, skeletal deformity, and a tendency to fracture. Pyknodysostosis and osteopetrosis are associated with sclerotic bones, however, rather than osteoporotic ones. In adulthood, early-onset osteoporosis may be confused with OI. Mutations in type I collagen also cause familial osteoporosis, and the skeletal phenotypes merge; patients with true OI may have scleral, hearing, or dental abnormalities and a positive family history.

Treatment and Care

Management of the skeletal complications largely depends on orthopedic, physical, and occupational therapy approaches. Although no medical treatment has yet been proved to improve the quality of the bone, studies of growth hormone, mesenchymal stem cell transplantation, and bisphosphonates are under way. The long-term goals are for the patient to maintain function and independence as an individual. These goals can be advanced in some patients by judicious use of intramedullary rods in the long bones of the legs; if mobility and especially ambulation can be maintained, the demineralization associated with inactivity can be avoided.

Unaffected parents of a child with OI and all affected individuals should have genetic counseling. For the parents of a child with type II OI, the possibility of germinal mosaicism (which has been well documented in this condition) should not be overlooked. If one parent has a "new" mutation in one of the type I procollagen genes and multiple gonadal cells carry this mutation, the risk of recurrence in future children is not negligible. If the mutation in the affected child can be defined, the risk of recurrence can be quantified (through molecular analysis of sperm) if the mutation arose in the father.

PSEUDOXANTHOMA ELASTICUM

Definition

Pseudoxanthoma elasticum (PXE) is a heritable disorder of connective tissue with pleiotropic manifestations wherever elastic fibers are found but primarily in the skin, eye, and vasculature. Life expectancy is reduced on average because of a predisposition to myocardial infarction and gastrointestinal hemorrhage.

Etiology and Pathogenesis

At least two forms of PXE exist, autosomal recessive (the more common form) and autosomal dominant. A gene for both forms maps to human chromosome 16 and has been identified as encoding one of the adenosine triphosphate (ATP)–binding cassette transporters. Because of the prominent histopathologic feature of calcification of elastic tissue, this gene may be important in calcium homeostasis. It is unclear, however, whether calcification is a primary or secondary phenomenon.

Prevalence

The exact frequency of PXE is unknown, but it is probably underdiagnosed. Rough approximations suggest a prevalence of 1 in 25,000 to 100,000. Males and females are equally affected, although women are more likely to seek medical attention out of concern for the skin changes.

Pathology

The hallmark of PXE, and an important diagnostic clue, is the histopathologic finding of hyperproliferated elastic fibers in the mid-dermis; these fibers become fragmented, clumped, and calcified. An arteriolar sclerosis develops in the media of muscular arteries and arterioles; the lumen may become progressively and concentrically narrowed. Alternatively, microaneurysms can form. Thickening of the endocardium, especially atrial endocardium, develops in some patients. In the eye, Bruch's membrane becomes calcified and fragmented.

Clinical Manifestations

Because of the pleiotropic nature of PXE, the diagnosis initially is suspected by any of a variety of clinicians, especially dermatologists, ophthalmologists, cardiologists, and gastroenterologists. The condition gains its name from the dermatologic feature of yellowish papules that appear at areas of flexural stress, especially the neck, groin, popliteal and cubital fossae, and periumbilical regions and on the buccal mucosa. The appearance of affected skin has been likened to that of a "plucked chicken." Over time, affected areas coalesce and become thickened.

Changes in the eye begin as a generalized, subtle mottled pattern in the retina (peau d'orange) and progress to the characteristic angioid streaks. The latter changes are not specific for PXE and can be seen in diabetes mellitus, sickle cell disease, and a variety of other conditions. Streaks represent breaks in Bruch's membrane, an elastic lamina that lies between the retinal vasculature and the choroid. Spontaneous hemorrhages, especially those involving the macula, lead to progressive visual loss.

Involvement of arteries of various caliber produces problems because of occlusion and hemorrhage. The lifetime risk of serious gastrointestinal hemorrhage from any site, but especially the stomach, is about 10%. Hypertension is relatively common, in part because of involvement of the renal vasculature. Progressive occlusion of peripheral arteries leads to absence of pulses; acral ischemia is rare because of the development of collaterals. The risk for stroke, myocardial infarction, abdominal angina, and intermittent claudication is increased independent of other risk factors.

Differential Diagnosis

An acquired form of PXE has been reported and is also of unclear etiology. This form is difficult to differentiate from a sporadic case potentially caused by a new mutation or heterozygous parents, but it tends to affect only the skin. As suggested by the name, the cutaneous features of PXE need to be differentiated from true xanthoma resulting from a disorder of lipid metabolism. The dermatologic manifestations need to be differentiated from Miescher's elastoma, elastic tissue nevi (Buschke-Ollendorff syndrome), and solar elastosis.

Treatment and Care

No cure for or means of preventing PXE is known. Based on one report of an association between calcium intake in early life and later severity of PXE, restriction of dietary calcium, primarily dairy products, may have a role. No clinical trials have been performed, however. In many instances, careful attention to the ocular features by a retinal specialist experienced in PXE can delay but not prevent loss of vision. The risk of gastrointestinal hemorrhage suggests that patients should avoid gastric irritants, such as aspirin, nonsteroidal anti-inflammatory drugs, and excessive alcohol. Stool should be checked regularly for occult blood, and angiography may be necessary to detect the source of bleeding. All standard risk factors for atherosclerosis should be managed aggressively. Complaints of chest pain should prompt a rigorous investigation for coronary artery disease. Angioplasty has not been reported to be effective, and the coronary lesions tend to be diffuse. Coronary artery bypass graft surgery has been performed, but long-term results have not been reported. It may be theoretically advantageous to use vein grafts rather than the internal mammary artery for bypass. The excessive wrinkling and pseudoxanthoma in exposed areas can be ameliorated by plastic surgery.

FUTURE DIRECTIONS

Each of these disorders poses special considerations in clinical diagnosis, utility of molecular testing, genetic counseling, and

Rheumatic Diseases

management. For the storage disorders, the clinical utility of enzyme replacement therapy is actively being pursued by several pharmaceutical companies. For several of the other conditions, somatic stem cell therapy offers some promise, but is years away from routine clinical use. Considerable progress will be made over the next few years in delineating the milder ranges of the phenotypes in Marfan syndrome, OI, and EDS. Molecular testing may have a role in specific circumstances, as will close medical management for individuals detected as being at heightened risk for cardiovascular, skeletal, and ocular complications.

---

1. Shores J, Berger KR, Murphy EA, Pyeritz RE: Chronic β-adrenergic blockade protects the aorta in the Marfan syndrome: A prospective, randomized trial of propranolol. N Engl J Med 1994;330:1335–1341.

SUGGESTED READINGS
Gott VL, Greene PS, Alejo DE, et al: Surgery for ascending aortic disease in Marfan patients: A multi-center study. N Engl J Med 1999;340:1307–1313. *Follow-up of nearly 700 patients documents the good long-term outcome of prophylactic repair of the dilated aortic root.*
Le Saux O, Beck K, Sachsinger C, et al: A spectrum of *ABCC6* mutations is responsible for pseudoxanthoma elasticum. Am J Hum Genet 2001;69:749–764. *An extensive array of changes in the gene encoding a protein in a family of ATP-binding cassette transporters.*
Mao J-R, Bristow J: The Ehlers-Danlos syndrome: On beyond collagen. J Clin Invest 2001;107:1063–1069. *How mutations in specific genes affect the extracellular matrix and produce complex phenotypes such as EDS.*
Miller DC: Valve-sparing aortic root replacement in patients with the Marfan syndrome. J Thorac Cardiovasc Surg 2003;125:773–778. *A critical review of the various approaches to preserving the native aortic valve while replacing the dilated proximal ascending aorta.*
Pyeritz RE: Marfan syndrome and other disorders of fibrillin. *In* Rimoin DL, Connor JM, Pyeritz RE, Korf BR (eds): Principles and Practice of Medical Genetics, 4th ed. Edinburgh, Churchill Livingstone, 2002, p 3977. *A review of the clinical, pathologic, and molecular aspects of Marfan syndrome and related disorders.*
Rauch F, Plotkin H, Zeitlin L, Glorieux FH: Bone mass, size, and density in children and adolescents with osteogenesis imperfecta: Effect of intravenous pamidronate therapy. J Bone Miner Res 2003;18:610–614. *Compared to historical controls, children and adolescents who received an average of 4 years of treatment had significantly higher bone mass, size, and density; those most severely affected at baseline had the greatest improvement.*
Steinmann B, Royce PS, Superti-Furga A: The Ehlers-Danlos syndrome. *In* Royce PM, Steinmann B (eds): Connective Tissue and Its Heritable Disorders: Molecular, Genetic, and Medical Aspects, 2nd ed. New York, Wiley-Liss, 2002, p 431. *An excellent review chapter of all aspects of EDS.*
Uitto J, Pulkkinen L: Heritable diseases affecting the elastic tissues: Cutis laxa, pseudoxanthoma elasticum and related disorders. *In* Rimoin DL, Connor JM, Pyeritz RE, Korf BR (eds): Principles and Practice of Medical Genetics, 4th ed. New York, Churchill Livingstone, 2002, p 4044. *A comprehensive review of all aspects of pseudoxanthoma elasticum and related disorders.*
Wenstrup RJ, Meyer RA, Lyle JS, et al: Prevalence of aortic root dilation in the Ehlers-Danlos syndrome. Genet Med 2002;4:112–117. *Echocardiographic screening detected asymptomatic and generally mild dilation of the aortic root in 28% of patients.*

---

277 BURSITIS, TENDINITIS, AND OTHER PERIARTICULAR DISORDERS

Dennis W. Boulware

Tendinitis, bursitis, and other periarticular structures can cause regional pain near joints that is often confused with arthritis. Through an understanding of the musculoskeletal anatomy and a careful clinical examination, the true cause of pain can often be determined at the bedside. The tendons, bursae, and other articular structures are readily accessible to the clinician during the physical examination and offer the examiner an opportunity to delineate the origin of the pain. The presence and location of soft tissue swelling, the effect of passive and active range of motion on pain, and the location of the point of maximal tenderness assist in making the correct diagnosis. When the cause of pain is not apparent, non-musculoskeletal causes should be considered, especially in proximal locations, because referred neurogenic pain could mimic shoulder or hip girdle problems.

The presence and localization of soft-tissue swelling can be very helpful in identifying the cause of regional pain. Arthritis, or synovitis, causes effusions in the synovial space or diffuse swelling of the synovium, producing global joint swelling. Bursitis elicits an effusion or swelling similar to that of synovitis but limited to the bursa only. As a rule, tendinitis causes little swelling and if present is limited to the tenosynovial structure.

Examination for tenderness should be done by direct palpation, passive and active range of motion, and isometric loading against resistance. Synovitis, tendinitis, and bursitis all elicit tenderness on direct palpation but differ in where the tenderness is localized. In synovitis, direct palpation of the synovium elicits diffuse tenderness that is present over the entire synovial surface area. In bursitis, palpation localizes the tenderness to the bursal structure and spares the synovium. The tenderness in tendinitis is elicited best by active range of motion and active isometric loading against resistance but can be detected by direct palpation. Tendinitis is painful with active or passive range of motion as the inflamed tendon experiences loading. Passive range of motion elicits tenderness only if the inflamed tendon is stretched and passively loaded, and active range of motion or isometric testing elicits tenderness by actively loading the tendon.

With a fundamental knowledge of the musculoskeletal anatomy and awareness of which musculoskeletal structures are loaded during the examination, a proper diagnosis can be made. Once the correct diagnosis is made, appropriate therapy can be prescribed, ensuring a greater likelihood of successful improvement. Table 277–1 lists each anatomic region and the more common periarticular conditions for each region.

Shoulder

The most common causes of shoulder pain are disorders of the periarticular structures: the biceps and rotator cuff tendons, the subacromial and subdeltoid bursa, and the articular capsule (Fig. 277–1). Patients with rotator cuff tendon problems, including the supraspinatus tendinitis, describe pain on active abduction of the shoulder but often report pain at night. This pain is usually focused over the lateral aspect of the shoulder but can be difficult for the patient to localize. Rotator cuff tendon disorders are the most common cause of shoulder pain and are usually due to unaccustomed overuse of the arm in overhead activities, which impinges the cuff between the acromion and the humeral head, resulting in injury. Falling on the arm or shoulder can injure the rotator cuff and can cause an acute impingement, occasionally with a partial or complete tear. On examination, the patient has full passive range of motion, with more tenderness on active, resisted abduction or external rotation than on passive abduction or external rotation. Passive forward flexion to 90 degrees impinges the inflamed rotator cuff and confirms the diagnosis (Fig. 277–2). Chronic impingement can occur from bony encroachment of an acromioclavicular joint inferior osteophyte, resulting in attenuation of the cuff or eventually a tear.

Bicipital tendinitis involves the long head of the biceps tendon as it traverses the humeral bicipital groove. Clinically, the patient experiences anterior shoulder pain, especially on active use of the biceps—flexion of the elbow, supination of the hand, or flexion of the shoulder. Tenderness is elicited by direct palpation of the tendon in the bicipital groove or by sudden active loading of the biceps. With the elbow placed passively in full flexion, the patient is asked to resist the examiner, who will suddenly attempt to extend the elbow and pronate the hand. Chronic bicipital tendinitis can cause attrition and complete rupture of the tendon of the bicipital long head.

The subacromial or subdeltoid bursa is the largest and most frequently inflamed shoulder bursa. Subacromial or subdeltoid bursitis causes pain in the lateral aspect of the shoulder as the bursa extends

---

Table 277–1 • TENDINITIS OR BURSITIS BY REGION

Shoulder	**Knee**
Subacromial bursitis	Pes anserine
Rotator cuff (including supraspinatus tendinitis)	Prepatellar bursitis
	Patellar tendinitis
Biceps tendinitis	Iliotibial band bursitis
Elbow	**Ankle**
Olecranon bursitis	Retrocalcaneal bursitis
Epicondylitis	Achilles tendinitis
Wrist and hand	**Foot**
de Quervain's disease	Plantar fasciitis
Trigger finger	
Hip	
Trochanteric bursitis	
Iliopsoas bursitis	

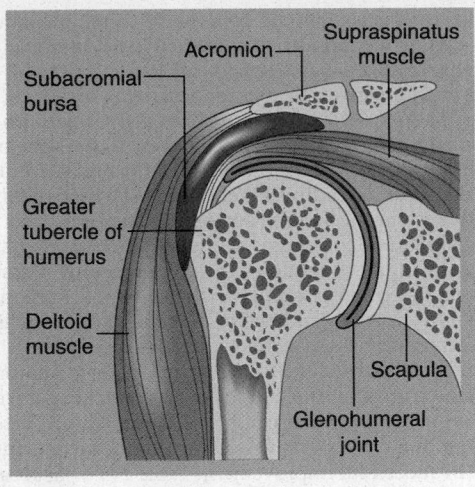
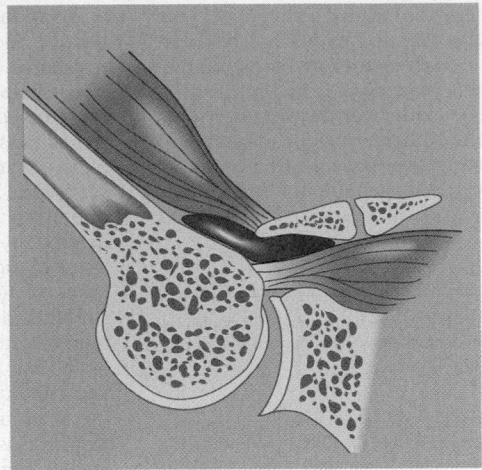

FIGURE 277–1 • Relationship of subacromial bursa (shown in blue) to supraspinatus muscle and acromion process. *A*, In the position of adduction of the humerus. To show this bursa more clearly, the synovial membrane of the glenohumeral joint is not shown in blue. *B*, In the position of abduction of the humerus, the acromion impinges on the subacromial bursa and the insertion of the supraspinatus tendon. (From Polley HF, Hunder GG [eds]: Rheumatologic Interviewing and Physical Examination of the Joints, 2nd ed. Philadelphia, WB Saunders, 1978, p 65.)

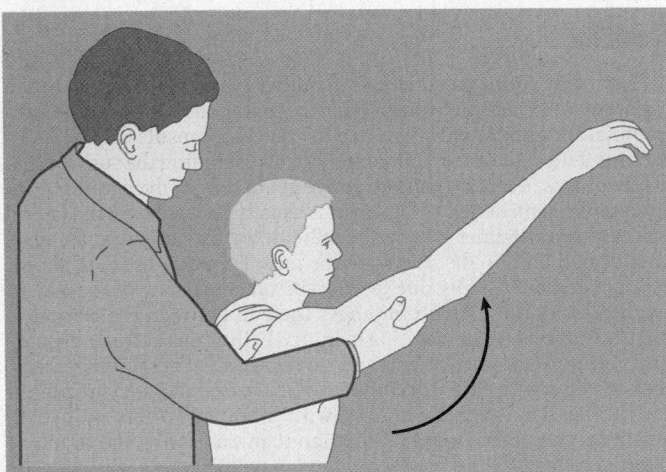

FIGURE 277–2 • The impingement sign is elicited by forced forward elevation of the arm. Pain results as the greater tuberosity impinges on the acromion. The examiner's hand prevents scapular rotation. This maneuver may be positive in other periarticular disorders. (From Neer CS II: Impingement lesions. Clin Orthop 1983;173:70–77.)

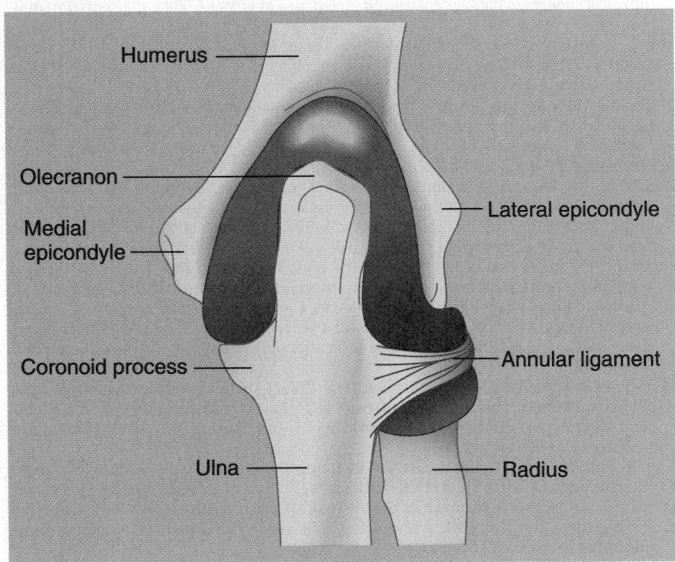

FIGURE 277–3 • Posterior aspect of the elbow showing the relationship of the humerus, radius, ulna, olecranon process, and synovium (in blue). (From Polley HF, Hunder GG [eds]: Rheumatologic Interviewing and Physical Examination of the Joints, 2nd ed. Philadelphia, WB Saunders, 1978, p 82.)

beneath the deltoid muscle. It differs from a rotator cuff tendinitis by the presence of tenderness on direct palpation beneath the acromion process. Similar to tendinitis, a shoulder with isolated bursitis should have full passive range of motion with more tenderness on active resisted abduction than on passive abduction.

Another periarticular cause of shoulder pain is adhesive capsulitis, or frozen shoulder. This condition is initially painful but progresses through an adhesive phase with loss of passive and active range of motion in all directions, especially external rotation and abduction. After several years, the pain subsides and the range of motion may return slowly. Adhesive capsulitis is associated with diabetes mellitus, tuberculosis, cervical spine disease, upper extremity injuries, coronary artery disease, and chronic pulmonary disease. It is similar to the reflex sympathetic dystrophy syndrome when there is diffuse involvement of the entire limb and vasomotor instability.

Glenohumeral arthritis causes synovitis with tenderness on passive range of motion, especially rotation. Since the glenohumeral joint lies deep beneath the deltoid muscle, soft-tissue swelling is not easily apparent on physical examination.

Elbow

Elbow pain is more commonly caused by epicondylitis and olecranon bursitis than by true elbow arthritis. The lateral and medial epicondylar areas serve as the origins for all of the forearm's muscles, and overuse of these muscle groups can result in medial or lateral epicondylitis, commonly known as tennis or golfer's elbow (Fig.

277–3). A specific examination to elicit tenderness is essential in making a diagnosis. Since the elbow joint has two articulations, each one can develop arthritis and be a source for pain. In arthritis, passive extension and flexion of the ulnohumeral articulation and passive supination and pronation of the radiohumeral articulation cause tenderness. These passive manipulations cause little if any tenderness in epicondylitis. Tenderness from epicondylitis is elicited by direct palpation over the inflamed area or by stretching of the involved muscle group combined with active isometric contraction against resistance. Swelling is not a common feature in epicondylitis.

The olecranon bursa exists on the dorsal surface of the olecranon process (Fig. 277–4). In olecranon bursitis, tenderness and swelling are localized by palpation to the olecranon bursa. This bursitis can be differentiated from elbow arthritis, which causes swelling and tenderness in the paraolecranon grooves.

Wrist and Hand

The first dorsal extensor compartment is a common site for tendinitis at the wrist, known as de Quervain's disease. This extensor compartment houses the extensor pollicis brevis and the abductor pollicis longus tendons. Typically affecting middle-aged women, de Quervain's disease manifests as pain along the radial aspect of the wrist, usually worsened by active use of the involved hand. The con-

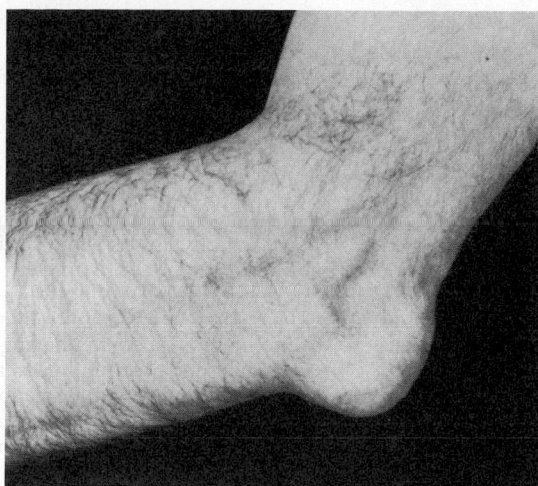

FIGURE 277–4 • Olecranon bursitis in a patient with tophaceous gout. (From Polley HF, Hunder GG [eds]: Rheumatologic Interviewing and Physical Examination of the Joints, 2nd ed. Philadelphia, WB Saunders, 1978, p 83.)

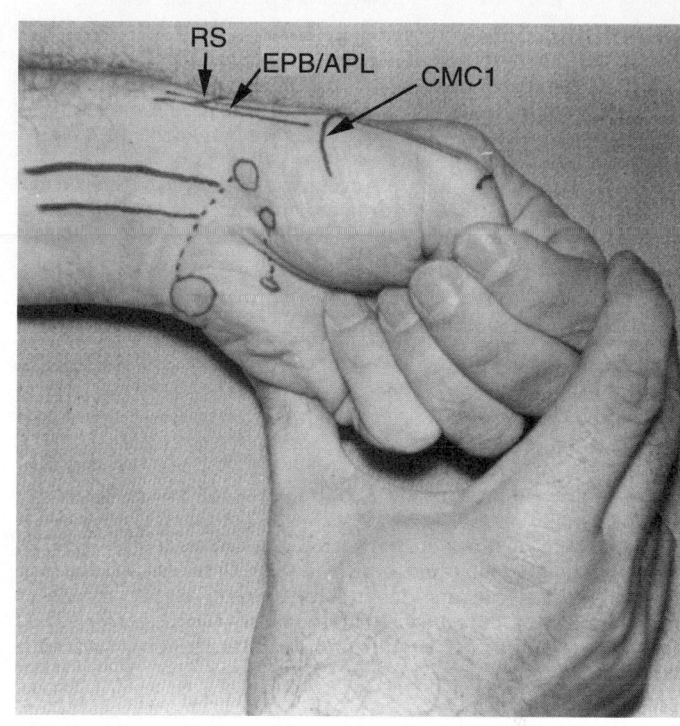

FIGURE 277–5 • Finkelstein's test for de Quervain's tenosynovitis. Radial deviation of the wrist stretches the inflamed common sheath of the extensor pollicis brevis/abductor pollicis longus (EPB/APL), causing acute pain. RS = radial styloid; CMC1 = first carpometacarpal joint. (From Canoso JJ [ed]: Rheumatology in Primary Care. Philadelphia, WB Saunders, 1997, p 219.)

dition can be confirmed by Finkelstein's test, in which the thumb is held within the fist and the hand is deviated passively in an ulnar direction (Fig. 277–5). In patients with de Quervain's disease, the test elicits exquisite tenderness. Swelling and tenderness are common and localized to the involved tendons overlying the distal radius.

Trigger fingers cause painful clicking in the fingers during active use and can cause locking sensations when one attempts to extend a flexed finger. This condition is caused by thickening of the A1 retinacular pulley in the palm, causing an entrapment of the tendon within the tendon sheath.

Hip

The trochanteric area has three main bursae, of which the most clinically relevant one is the gluteus maximus bursa between the gluteus maximus muscle and the greater trochanter (Fig. 277–6). The patient reports hip pain, but the differentiation between a hip joint pathologic lesion and trochanteric pain can be made quickly by examination. Passive rotation of the hip joint may be limited and elicits tenderness in a case of hip joint pathology but not trochanteric bursitis. Direct palpation laterally and posterolaterally over the greater trochanter elicits tenderness in cases of trochanteric bursitis but not hip joint pathology.

The iliopsoas bursa lies anterior to the true hip joint and can be a source of anterior hip pain. Tenderness in the anterior groin, or

anterior hip joint, accompanied by enlargement in the area, could be caused by iliopsoas bursitis and must be differentiated from an inguinal hernia.

Knee

The knee has many bursal structures that can become inflamed from overuse, trauma, or infection. The bursa overlying the patella can become injured from trauma or infection, causing prepatellar bursitis. In prepatellar bursitis, the swelling and tenderness are limited to the prepatellar area overlying the patella. Palpation along the medial and lateral knee yields unremarkable findings. In cases of arthritis, the entire synovium is swollen from synovitis or an effusion.

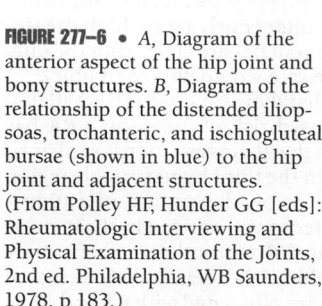

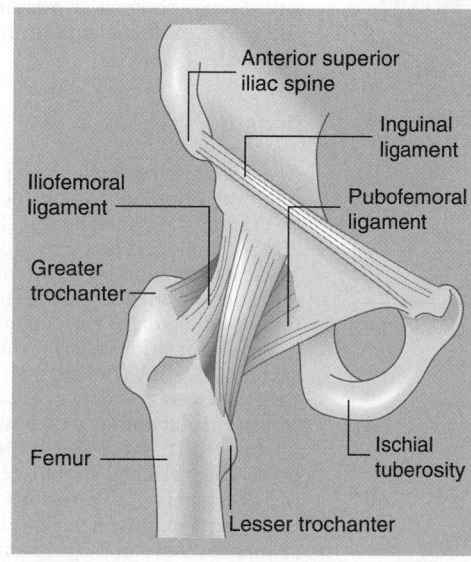

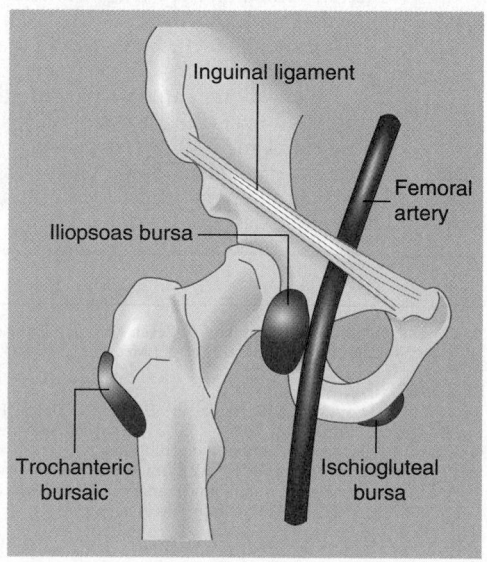

FIGURE 277–6 • A, Diagram of the anterior aspect of the hip joint and bony structures. B, Diagram of the relationship of the distended iliopsoas, trochanteric, and ischiogluteal bursae (shown in blue) to the hip joint and adjacent structures. (From Polley HF, Hunder GG [eds]: Rheumatologic Interviewing and Physical Examination of the Joints, 2nd ed. Philadelphia, WB Saunders, 1978, p 183.)

Pes anserine bursitis causes pain along the medial aspect of the knee below the medial tibial plateau, as the bursa lies medial to the anterior tibial tuberosity and several centimeters inferior to the medial joint line. Swelling is not often observed, but tenderness is localized by palpation to the bursa only, and tenderness is unaffected by passive range of motion of the knee.

Patellar tendinitis commonly occurs from overuse of the patellar tendon and manifests as anterior knee pain exacerbated by active use of the quadriceps, such as jumping. Examination reveals tenderness to palpation localized to the patellar tendon.

Iliotibial band bursitis caused by a tight iliotibial band elicits pain over the lateral aspect of the knee and clicking as the band passes over the lateral femoral condyle. Examination of the knee finds the tenderness confined to the lateral area of the knee with an absence of any knee effusion.

Ankle

Retrocalcaneal bursitis and Achilles tendinitis both cause posterior ankle pain reproduced by active loading of the Achilles tendon. The retrocalcaneal bursa lies between the calcaneus and the Achilles tendon, and differentiating these two conditions can be done on examination by localizing the tenderness to the Achilles tendon or the retrocalcaneal bursal area. The prognoses for these two conditions are very different, as rupture of the Achilles tendon is a risk with Achilles tendinitis only.

Foot

Plantar fasciitis is a common condition associated with many biomechanical abnormalities of the foot, including pes cavus deformities, pes planus deformities, and Achilles tendon tightness. Pain along the plantar surface of the medial heel is the most common complaint, and the diagnosis can be confirmed by reproducing the pain with deep palpation of the plantar surface of the heel.

Imaging

Imaging is of little utility in acute cases of tendinitis or bursitis but may be helpful in chronic or treatment-resistant cases. Radiography, ultrasonography, and magnetic resonance imaging may be helpful in certain cases but should not be ordered routinely.

 Treatment

In general, treatment for bursitis, tendinitis, and other periarticular conditions is very similar and usually conservative, starting with rest. Physical therapy is helpful in most cases and more successful when therapy includes a combination of passive modalities, such as ice and heat, and active modalities, such as strengthening exercises to improve any biomechanical imbalances. Nonsteroidal anti-inflammatory drugs are helpful as analgesics but are of limited usefulness in alleviating chronic conditions. Judicious intralesional injections of steroids are helpful but have obvious adverse consequences. Furthermore, caution should be exercised when considering intralesional steroids for bicipital and Achilles tendinitis because tendon rupture is a risk. Ultrasound is sometimes helpful and is of proven benefit in symptomatic calcific tendinitis of the shoulder.❶ Surgery may be required but should be reserved for recalcitrant, refractory, and functionally limiting conditions.

 1. Ebenbichler GR, Erdogmus CB, Resch KL, et al: Ultrasound therapy for calcific tendonitis of the shoulder. N Engl J Med 1999;340:1533–1538.

SUGGESTED READINGS

Koopman WJ, Boulware DW, Heudebert GR (eds): Clinical Primer of Rheumatology. Lippincott, Williams & Wilkins, 2003. *A textbook written specifically for busy clinicians with emphasis on treatment and diagnosis.*

Speed CA, Richards C, Nichols D, et al: Extracorporeal shock-wave therapy for tendonitis of the rotator cuff. A double-blind, randomised, controlled trial. J Bone Joint Surg Br 2002;84:509–512. *This therapy was of no benefit.*

278 RHEUMATOID ARTHRITIS

James R. O'Dell

Definition

Rheumatoid arthritis (RA) is a chronic systemic inflammatory disease of unknown etiology that primarily targets synovial tissues. It is relatively common with a prevalence of approximately 1% in adults all over the world. RA shortens survival and significantly impacts on quality of life in most affected patients. As this definition implies, RA is a systemic disease with essentially all patients having some systemic features such as fatigue, low-grade fevers, anemia, and elevations of acute phase reactants (erythrocyte sedimentation rate [ESR] or C-reactive protein [CRP]). Despite these systemic features, the primary target of this disease is the synovium that is responsible for most of the protean clinical features. Synovial tissues proliferate in an uncontrolled fashion, resulting in excess fluid production and erosion of surrounding bone, as well as tendon and ligament damage.

Fortunately, the last decade has seen the landscape of treatment of RA change dramatically. Current therapies will result in substantial clinical benefit for most patients, particularly if they are diagnosed early and started on appropriate therapy.

Epidemiology

RA is seen all over the world with a remarkably consistent prevalence of 0.5 to 1% of adults. For reasons that are still unclear, the prevalence in women is two or three times greater than in men. RA can occur at any age, but onset before the age of 45 in men is uncommon. The relatively few, well-done inception cohorts that are available suggest that the yearly incidence of RA is approximately 40/100,000 for women and about half of that for men. These figures vary significantly based on the age of the cohort. The best available data suggest that the incidence of RA in women increases with age until approximately 45, then it plateaus. The incidence rate is much lower in young men, approximately one third that of women but increases steadily with age and approaches that of women in the over-65 age group. Since the incidence of RA increases or is stable with age and RA is a lifelong disease, the prevalence of RA increases with each decade. Recent data strongly suggest that the incidence of RA, particularly rheumatoid factor-negative RA, is decreasing. The reason or reasons for this are unclear, but if elucidated, could provide valuable insight into the etiology/pathogenesis of RA and would allow us to think, for the first time, about preventive strategies.

RA has a significant genetic component; therefore, it is not surprising that certain populations have been reported where RA is very unusual and others where it is very common. Most notably, cohorts have been described in rural Nigeria where no individuals are affected with RA; in contrast, a prevalence of RA of 5% in some studies of Chippewa, Yakima, and Inuit Native American tribes has been reported.

Genetics

Genetics clearly play a significant role in determining both the risk of developing RA and the severity of the disease. Twin studies reveal a concordance rate for RA that averages approximately 15 to 20% for monozygotic twins and approximately 5% for dizygotic twins. These data in monozygotic twins simultaneously reveal both the significance of genetics and the fact that genetics are clearly not the only important factor, or the concordance rate would approach unity.

The association of certain human leukocyte antigen (HLA) alleles, specifically HLA-DR4, and an increased risk of developing RA has long been recognized. It is now known that this association is explained by a particular amino acid sequence in the third hypervariable region on the DRβ1 chain. DR molecules sit on the surface of antigen-presenting cells and allow T cells to recognize antigen in the context of DR. Hypervariable regions on the DR molecule are particularly important for antigen recognition. Table 278–1 details the amino acid sequence of several DRβ1 chains that are associated with RA and some that are not. This amino acid sequence associated with RA has been

Table 278–1 • HLA ASSOCIATIONS WITH RHEUMATOID ARTHRITIS (RA)

	HLA TYPES (ALLELES) AND METHODS OF DETECTION			THIRD HYPERVARIABLE REGION AMINO ACID SEQUENCES					MOST COMMON ETHNIC GROUPS
	Alloantisera (DR)	MLC (Dw)	DNA (DRB1)	70	71	72	73	74	
Associated with RA	DR4	Dw4	*0401	Q	K	R	A	A	Whites (west Europe)
	DR4	Dw14	*0404	·	R	·	·	·	Whites (west Europe)
	DR4	Dw15	*0405	·	R	·	·	·	Japanese, Chinese
	DR1	Dw1	*0101	·	R	·	·	·	Asian Indians, Israelis
	DR6 (14)	Dw16	*1402	·	R	·	·	·	Yakima Native Americans
	DR10	—	*1001	R	R	·	·	·	Spanish, Greeks, Israelis
Not associated with RA	DR4	Dw10	*0402	D	E	·	·	·	Whites (East Europe)
	DR4	Dw13	*0403	·	R	·	·	E	Polynesians
	DR2	Dw2	*1501	D	A	·	·	·	Whites
	DR3	Dw3	*0301	·	·	·	G	R	Whites

Q = glutamine, K = lysine, R = arginine, A = alanine, D = aspartic acid, E = glutamic acid; · = the same amino acid in that position as DRB1*0401.

called the "shared epitope" or the "at-risk allele." It has been shown by a number of investigators that individuals with the "shared epitope" have more severe RA and more extra-articular manifestations than those patients that are shared epitope negative. Furthermore, individuals with two copies of the shared epitope, particularly those associated with HLA-DR4, have a further increased risk for the development of severe and destructive RA. This association with a particular antigen recognition site may ultimately help us understand the antigen or antigens that are important for triggering RA. Conversely, others have suggested that perhaps patients develop RA because the shared epitope prevents them from recognition of certain arthrogenic antigens. The importance of certain DRβ1 types in RA supports the concept that T cells are integrally involved in the pathogenesis.

Population-based studies have suggested that only about one third of the genetic risk for RA is explained by genes located in the HLA region. Large studies of siblings concordant for RA have suggested that ultimately at least five or six genes will be identified that are important for the development of RA. Currently, genes controlling tumor necrosis factor-α (TNF-α) are receiving significant attention.

The shared epitope is present in approximately 20% of the white population, and individuals that carry this allele have only about a 1 in 20 chance of developing RA. Therefore, this test has little if any clinical utility. In addition to genetics, a number of other factors have been associated with the incidence, and in some cases the severity, of RA including estrogen use, smoking, and coffee consumption.

The use of oral contraceptives has been associated with a decrease in the incidence of RA; since this effect seems to be strongest with oral contraceptives that have a high estrogen content, it is postulated that estrogen is responsible for this protective effect. Studies that have tried to address the question of postmenopausal estrogen use and its effect on RA have yielded conflicting results.

Smoking has been associated with a significant increase in the risk of developing RA. This association has been particularly strong in men and in those with rheumatoid factor-positive disease. Recently, investigators in Europe have reported that coffee consumption is a risk factor for developing RA; investigators in North America have suggested that this risk may be limited to decaffeinated coffee.

Etiology/Pathogenesis and Pathology

RA appears to require the complex interaction of genetic and environmental factors with the immune system and ultimately the synovial tissues throughout the body (Fig. 278–1). RA clearly has a significant genetic component, but only approximately 1 in 20 whites with the so-called shared epitope develop RA. Furthermore, even if one monozygotic twin has RA, there is only approximately a 1 in 4 chance that the other twin will develop the same disease. Clearly, other factors, in addition to genetics, are active in precipitating or triggering RA. Triggers for RA have long been the target of active research. Purported triggers have included bacteria (*Mycobacteria*, *Streptococcus*, *Mycoplasma*, *Escherichia coli*, *Helicobacter pylori*), viruses (rubella, Epstein-Barr virus, parvovirus), superantigens, and many others.

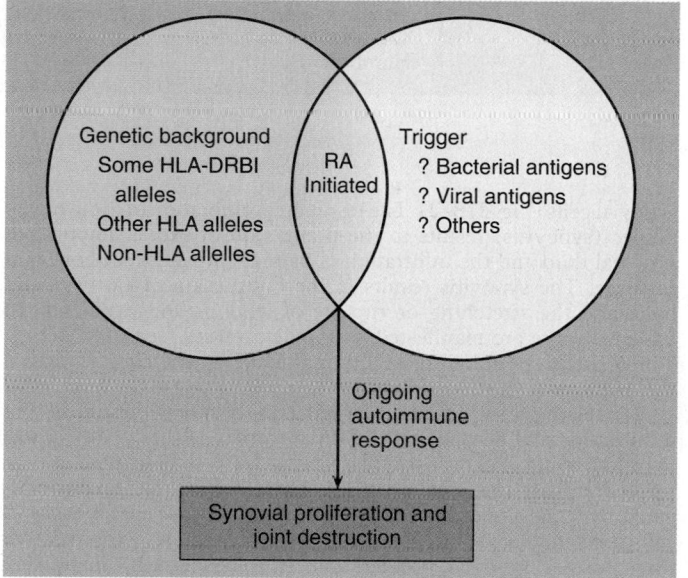

FIGURE 278–1 • Rheumatoid arthritis (RA): Initiation.

Rheumatic fever, reactive arthritis (Reiter's syndrome), and, more recently, Lyme arthritis are examples of arthritic syndromes where infectious triggers have clearly been demonstrated, but these triggering agents are often difficult or impossible to isolate at the time when the arthritic syndromes occur. Many other examples exist in animal models of arthritis, including mycobacterial and streptococcal-induced syndromes. Reactive arthritis is perhaps the most relevant example for RA. Reactive arthritis has clearly been shown to occur when any one of a host of different but specific infectious triggers are presented to a specific location in the body, the gastrointestinal or genitourinary tract, of individuals with a certain genetic background (HLA-B27 in most cases). Additionally, in this syndrome, the age and gender of the individual and hence the maturity of the immune system may be critical for the development of this syndrome, which occurs primarily between the ages of 15 and 40 years in males. Once unraveled, the pathophysiology of RA may be similar.

Despite the absence of clear evidence linking any infectious agent to RA, it is widely believed that ultimately an important triggering role will be elucidated for infectious or other environmental agents. Once a trigger or triggers for RA are identified, we will be able to think about strategies for prevention, but this information may not help individuals with established disease.

The synovial tissues are the primary target of the autoimmune inflammatory process that is RA; why this is true remains elusive. Once RA is initiated, the synovial tissues throughout the body become the site of a complex interaction of T cells, B cells, macrophages, and

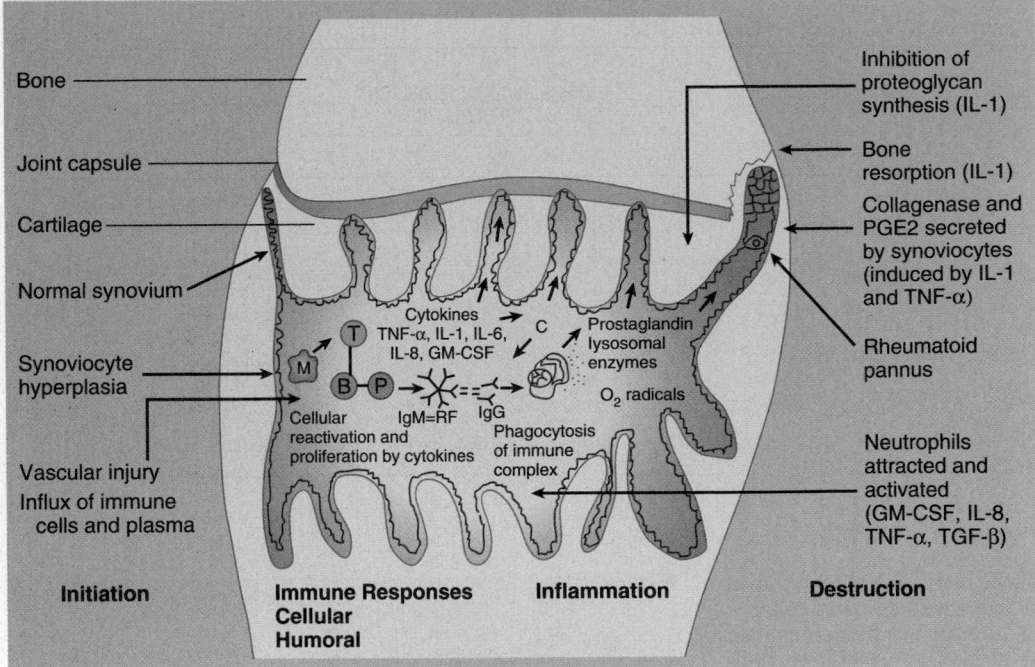

FIGURE 278–2 • Events involved in the pathogenesis of rheumatoid synovitis progress from left to right. M = macrophage; T = T lymphocyte; B = B lymphocyte; P = plasma cell; IL = interleukin; TNF-α = tumor necrosis factor-α; TGF-β = transforming growth factor-β; GM-CSF = granulocyte-macrophage colony-stimulating factor; RF = rheumatoid factor; PGE₂ = prostaglandin E₂; C = complement.

synovial cells (Fig. 278–2). The resultant proliferation of the synovial tissues (synovitis) results in the production of excess amounts of synovial fluid and the infiltration of pannus into adjacent bone and cartilage. The synovitis results in the destruction of cartilage and bone and the stretching or rupture of tendons and ligaments. In patients, these are manifested by the deformities (see Figs. 278–4, 278–5, and 278–9) and disability that make up the clinical picture that is RA.

The relative roles of the cellular versus the humoral immune system in initiation and perpetuation of RA are much debated; both appear to be important. T cells, particularly of the activated Th1 type, appear to predominate in synovial tissues. These T cells presumably activated by some yet unknown antigen presented by macrophages, B cells, or synoviocytes in the context of DR, secrete cytokines that drive further synovial proliferation. It is believed by many that although RA may initially be triggered by exogenous antigen, once initiated, the process may be perpetuated by autoantigens. Macrophage-derived cytokines, particularly interleukin-1 (IL-1) and TNF-α, play central roles in this ongoing inflammatory process. As definitive proof, biological products directed against either of these cytokines have shown significant efficacy in animal models of RA, as well as in patients.

The humoral immune system is also playing a role. Rheumatoid factor has long been a serologic marker of RA and is well known to correlate with more severe disease, including erosions of bone and extra-articular features. Why rheumatoid factor is produced in excess and the exact role that it plays remains elusive. Rheumatoid factor production may increase complement activation and result in the release of lysosomal enzymes, kinins and oxygen-free radicals. A host of other autoantibodies that are relatively specific for RA have recently been reported and include antibodies to type II collagen, human cartilage gp39, and citrullinated proteins. Although in many cases the levels of these antibodies are associated with more severe disease, their overall significance remains to be elucidated.

Diagnosis

All current treatment paradigms for RA stress the early aggressive use of disease-modifying antirheumatic drugs (DMARDs). Therefore, the importance of accurate early diagnosis of RA can not be overemphasized. Unfortunately, there is no one single finding on physical examination or laboratory testing that is pathognomonic of RA. Instead, the diagnosis of RA is a clinical one, requiring a collection of historical and physical features, as well as an alert and informed clinician.

Table 278–2 • CLASSIFICATION CRITERIA FOR RHEUMATOID ARTHRITIS*

1. Morning stiffness (≥1 hr)
2. Swelling (soft tissue) of three or more joints
3. Swelling (soft tissue) of hand joints (PIP, MCP, or wrist)
4. Symmetrical swelling (soft tissue)
5. Subcutaneous nodules
6. Serum rheumatoid factor
7. Erosions and/or periarticular osteopenia in hand or wrist joints seen on radiograph

*Criteria 1 to 4 must have been continuous for 6 weeks or longer and criteria 2 to 5 must be observed by a physician. A classification as rheumatoid arthritis requires that four of the seven criteria be fulfilled.
MCP = metacarpophalangeal; PIP = proximal interphalangeal

Table 278–2 lists the classification criteria for RA, and although not designed specifically for the purpose of diagnosis, they are ubiquitously used as a diagnostic aid. The first five criteria are all clinical; in other words, they are met by physical examination or talking to the patient. Only the last two criteria require laboratory tests or radiographs. It is critical to note that the first four criteria need to be present for at least 6 weeks before a diagnosis of RA can be made. This is true because a host of conditions, including many viral-related syndromes, often cause self-limited polyarthritis syndromes that look identical to RA, including at times the presence of rheumatoid factor. These syndromes, which usually last 2 to 3 weeks, have caused many physicians to be overly cautious and delay the diagnosis of RA for months and sometimes years, resulting in delays in therapy. The goal for most RA patients should be to establish a diagnosis and to start DMARD therapy by 3 months of disease.

Although variable, most patients with RA present with an insidious onset of pain, stiffness, and/or swelling in multiple joints over the course of weeks to months. The joint manifestations of RA may be accompanied by systemic features such as fatigue, low-grade fevers, and weight loss. Less commonly, the onset can be fulminant and occur almost overnight, or patients may have persistent monoarthritis or oligoarthritis for prolonged periods before manifesting the more typical pattern of joint involvement. Rarely, patients may present with extra-articular features of RA before the joint problems occur.

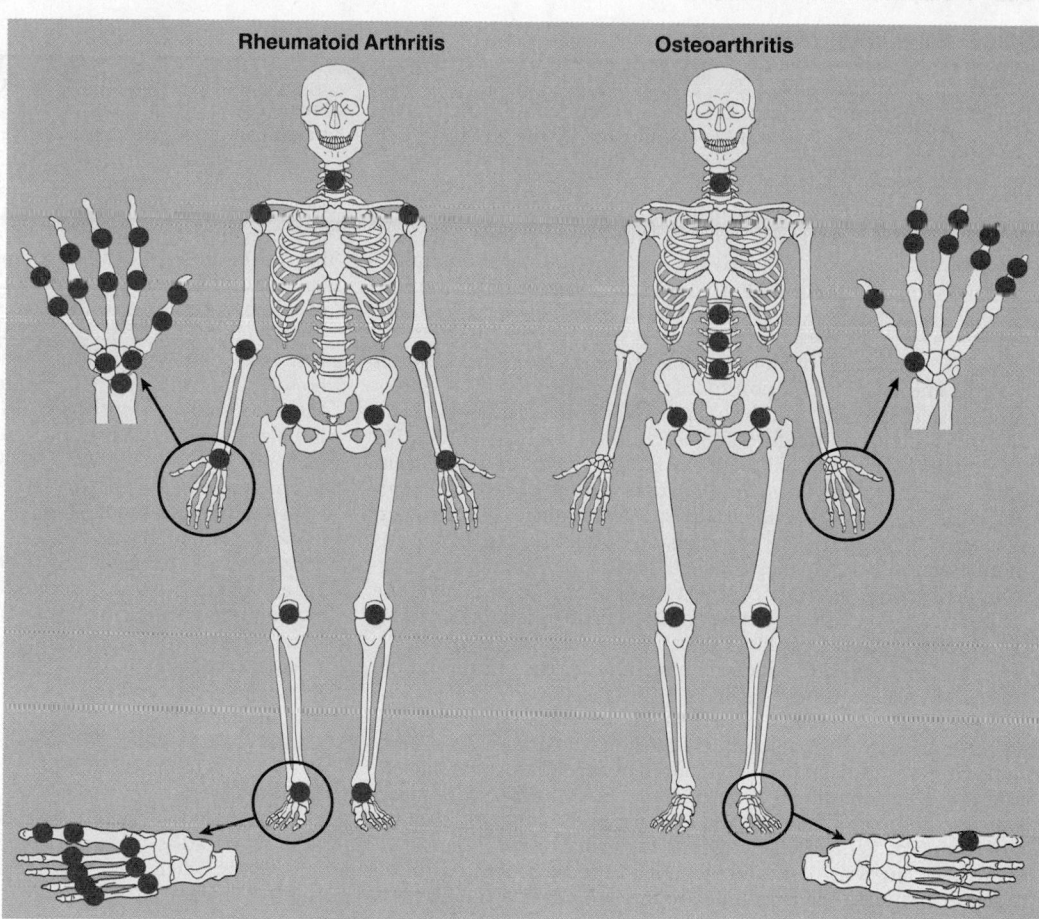

Rheumatoid Arthritis   Osteoarthritis

FIGURE 278–3 • The joint distribution of the two most common forms of arthritis—rheumatoid arthritis and osteoarthritis—are compared and contrasted. Joints involved in these arthritides are noted by the black circles over the involved joint areas.

The distribution of involved joints is a critical clue to the underlying diagnosis (Fig. 278–3). The joints that are involved in patients with RA at presentation are also variable; typically the symptoms start in the small joints of the hands (proximal interphalangeal [PIPs] and metacarpophalangeal [MCPs]) and the toes (metatarsalphalangeal [MTPs]). Importantly, RA spares the distal interphalangeal (DIPs) and small joints of the toes (see Fig. 278–3). If DIP involvement is a prominent finding, consider a different diagnosis (e.g., osteoarthritis [OA] or psoriatic arthritis). Later, RA moves, or some would say "metastasizes," to larger joints: wrists, knees, elbows, ankles, hips, and shoulders (roughly in that order). Although the patient's history of joint symptoms (arthralgia) is important, the diagnosis of RA requires the presence of inflammation (swelling and/or warmth) on examination of the joints.

Morning stiffness is a hallmark of inflammatory arthritis and is a prominent feature of RA. Patients with RA are characteristically at their worst first thing in the morning or after prolonged periods of rest. This stiffness, in and around joints, often lasts for hours, and quantifying it is one way to measure improvement. Stiffness is relieved by warmth and activity, and reducing or eliminating it is a clear goal of therapy.

Differential Diagnosis

The accurate diagnosis of RA early in its course, although challenging, is critical if patients are to benefit maximally from therapeutic intervention. Once disease has been present and active for a number of years and the characteristic deformities on physical examination and radiographic changes have occurred, the diagnosis in most cases is all too obvious. Unfortunately, once patients have progressed to that point, many, if not all, of the deformities no longer are amenable to medical therapy.

Many diseases can mimic RA (Table 278–3). Early in the course of disease, self-limited viral syndromes need to be considered, especially hepatitis B and C, parvovirus, rubella (infection or

Table 278–3 • DIFFERENTIAL DIAGNOSIS OF RHEUMATOID ARTHRITIS

DISORDER	SUBCUTANEOUS NODULES	RHEUMATOID FACTOR
Viral arthritis (hepatitis B and C, parvovirus, rubella, others)	–	+/–
Bacterial endocarditis	+/–	+
Rheumatic fever	+	–
Sarcoidosis	+	+
Reactive arthritis	–	–
Psoriatic arthritis	–	–
Systemic lupus erythematosus	+/–	+
Primary Sjögren's syndrome	–	+
Chronic tophus gout	+	–
Calcium pyrophosphate disease	–	–
Polymyalgia rheumatica	–	–
Osteoarthritis (erosive)	–	–

– = not present; + = frequently present; +/– = occasionally present.

vaccination), and Epstein-Barr virus. At any time systemic lupus erythematosus, psoriatic arthritis, and reactive arthritis may present diagnostic challenges. In the case of these three mimics, a targeted history and examination to elucidate their associated clinical features, such as rashes, oral ulcers, nail changes, dactylitis, urethritis, and renal, pulmonary, gastrointestinal or ophthalmologic problems is critical. Especially in the elderly, with fulminant-onset RA, remitting seronegative symmetrical synovitis with pitting edema, or paraneoplastic syndromes should be considered. Chronic tophaceous gout may also mimic severe nodular RA. Hypothyroidism not only causes many rheumatic manifestations but also occurs commonly in conjunction with RA and, therefore, should be kept in mind.

Clinical Manifestations

ARTICULAR MANIFESTATIONS. RA can affect any of the synovial (diarthrodial) joints (see Fig. 278–3). Most commonly, the disease starts in the MCPs, PIPS, and MTPs followed by the wrists, knees, elbows, ankles, hips, and shoulders in roughly that order. Early treatment helps limit the number of joints involved. Less commonly, and usually later, RA may involve the temporomandibular, cricoarytenoid, and sternoclavicular joints. RA may involve the upper part of the cervical spine, particularly the C1-C2 articulation, but unlike the spondyloarthropathies, does not involve the rest of the spine. RA patients are, however, at an increased risk of osteoporosis, and this risk should be considered and dealt with early.

Hands. The hands are a major site of involvement in almost all patients and a significant portion of the disabilities that RA causes is because of damage and dysfunction of the hands. Typical early disease is pictured in Figure 278–4, with the swelling of the PIPs and MCPs easily seen. The DIPs are rarely involved; significant involvement of the DIPs should make one think about a different diagnosis. Figure 278–5 illustrates the classic ulnar deviation and swan-neck deformities (hyperextension of the PIPs) that are commonly seen in late, more established disease. Boutonniere (or buttonhole) deformities also occur as a result of hyperextension of the MCPs. If the clinical disease remains active, hand function will slowly deteriorate. Sudden loss of function of individual fingers may occur from tendon ruptures, which require the expertise of a carefully selected hand surgeon to repair.

Feet. Feet, particularly the MTPs, are involved early in almost all patients with RA. Radiographic erosions occur at least as early in the feet as in the hands. Subluxation of the toes is common and leads to the dual problem of the breakdown of the skin with ulcers on the top of the toes and painful ambulation because of loss of the cushioning pads that usually protect the heads of the MTPs.

Wrists. The wrist joints are involved in most patients with RA; radial deviation is the rule, and patients with severe involvement may progress to volar subluxation. Even early in the course of the disease, synovial proliferation in and around the wrists may compress the median nerve, causing carpal tunnel syndrome (Fig. 278–6). Later, this synovial proliferation may invade tendons and lead to rupture.

Large Joints. Involvement of knees, ankles, elbows, hips, and shoulders is common. Characteristically, the whole joint surface is involved in a symmetrical fashion. Therefore, RA is not only symmetrical from one side of the body to the other but symmetrical within the individual joint with the whole joint surface area involved. In the case of the knee (Fig. 278–7A) the medial and lateral compartments are both severely narrowed (RA) contrasted with a knee involved with OA (Fig. 278–7B), where only one compartment is involved.

Synovial cysts may occur around any of the joints (large or small) and occasionally present as soft, fluctuant masses that are diagnostic challenges. Synovial cysts from the knee are perhaps the best examples of this phenomenon. When the knee produces excess synovial fluid, it may accumulate in the popliteal space (popliteal or Baker's cyst) (Fig. 278–8). These cysts may cause problems by pressing on the popliteal nerve, artery, or veins; they may dissect into the tissues of the calf (usually posteriorly); or they may rupture. Dissections may produce only minor symptoms such as a feeling of fullness; ruptures of the cyst with extravasation of the inflammatory content produces significant pain and swelling and may be confused with thrombophlebitis, the so-called pseudothrombophlebitis syndrome. Ultrasonography of the popliteal fossa and calf are useful to confirm the diagnosis and to rule out thrombophlebitis, which may be precipitated by popliteal cysts. Treatment of popliteal (Baker's) cysts should be directed at interrupting the inflammatory process in the knee through an intra-articular injection of corticosteroid.

Neck. Although most of the axial skeleton is spared in RA, the cervical spine and especially the C1-C2 articulation is not. As with RA elsewhere, bony erosions and ligament damage can occur in this area and may lead to subluxation (Fig. 278–9). Most often, subluxation is minor, and patients and caregivers need only be cautious and avoid forcing the neck into positions of flexion: occasionally it may be severe and lead to compromise of the cervical cord and in some cases death.

Other Joints. Wherever synovial tissue exists, RA may cause problems. The temporomandibular, cricoarytenoid, and sternoclavicular joints are examples. The cricoarytenoid joint is responsible for abduction and adduction of the vocal cords. Involvement of this joint may lead to a feeling of fullness in the throat, to hoarseness and, rarely, when the cords are essentially fused in a closed position, to a syndrome of acute respiratory distress with or without stridor. In this latter situation, emergent tracheotomy may be life-saving.

EXTRA-ARTICULAR MANIFESTATIONS. Systemic features of RA such as fatigue, weight loss, and low-grade fevers occur frequently, and like all the other extra-articular features, tend to be more common in those patients with rheumatoid factor (seropositive).

Skin. Subcutaneous nodules are seen in approximately one quarter of patients with RA: almost exclusively in patients that are seropositive. Patients with nodules without rheumatoid factor should be carefully scrutinized for a different diagnosis such as chronic tophaceous gout. Nodules may occur almost anywhere (e.g., lungs, heart, eye), but most commonly occur subcutaneously on extensor surfaces (particularly forearms) (Fig. 278–10), over joints, or over

Continued

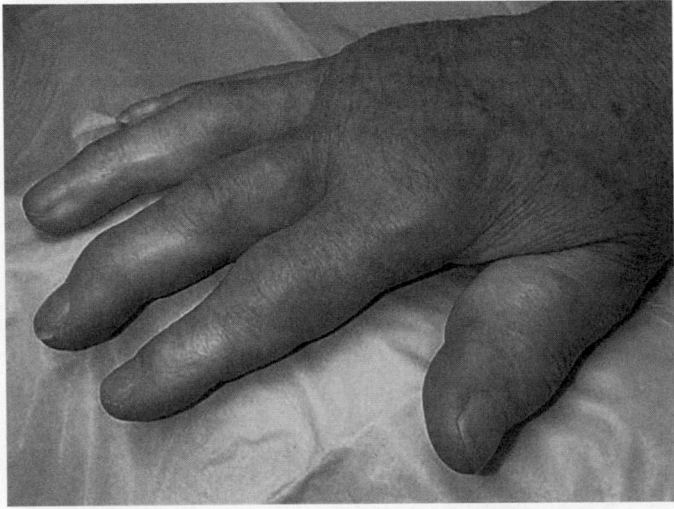

FIGURE 278–4 • Early rheumatoid arthritis manifested as soft tissue swelling of the proximal interphalangeal and metacarpophalangeal joints of the hand. Radiographs at this time would show soft tissue swelling and juxta-articular osteoporosis and occasionally even may show early marginal erosions.

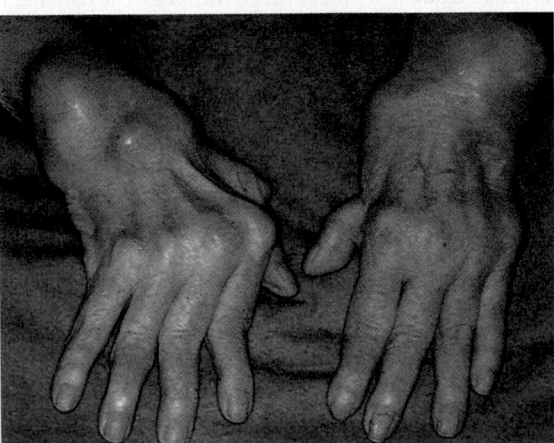

FIGURE 278–5 • Severe advanced rheumatoid arthritis of the hands. There is massive tendon swelling over the dorsal surfaces of both wrists, severe muscle wasting, ulnar deviation of the metacarpophalangeal joints, and swan-neck deformity of the fingers. (From Forbes CD, Jackson WF: Color Atlas and Text of Clinical Medicine, 3rd ed. London, Mosby, 2003.)

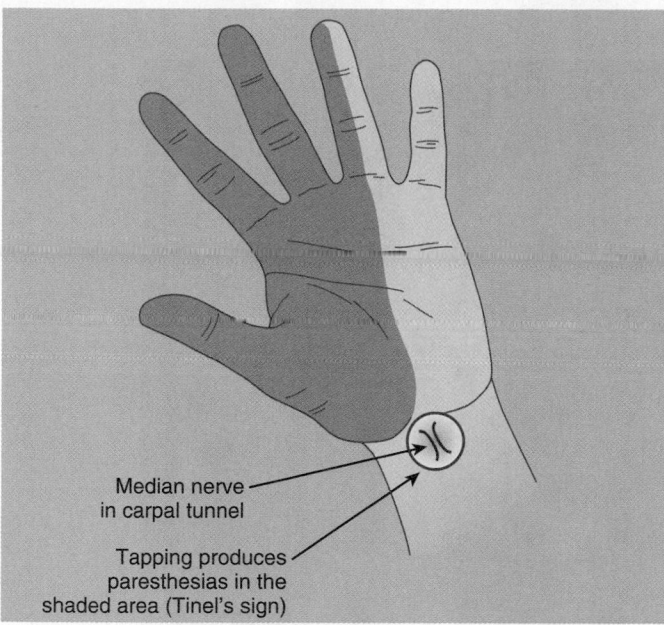

Median nerve
in carpal tunnel

Tapping produces
paresthesias in the
shaded area (Tinel's sign)

FIGURE 278–6 • Distribution of pain and/or paresthesias (shaded area) when the median nerve is compressed by swelling in the wrist (carpal tunnel).

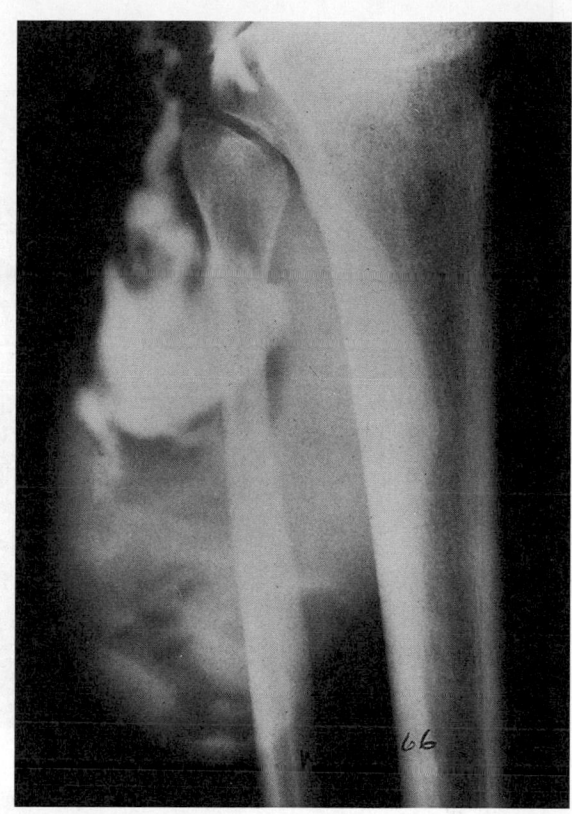

FIGURE 278–8 • Arthrogram with a radiocontrast agent injected into the knee. The dye flows into the popliteal space and through a narrow channel into a large synovial cyst (Baker's cyst) that has dissected into the soft tissue of the calf.

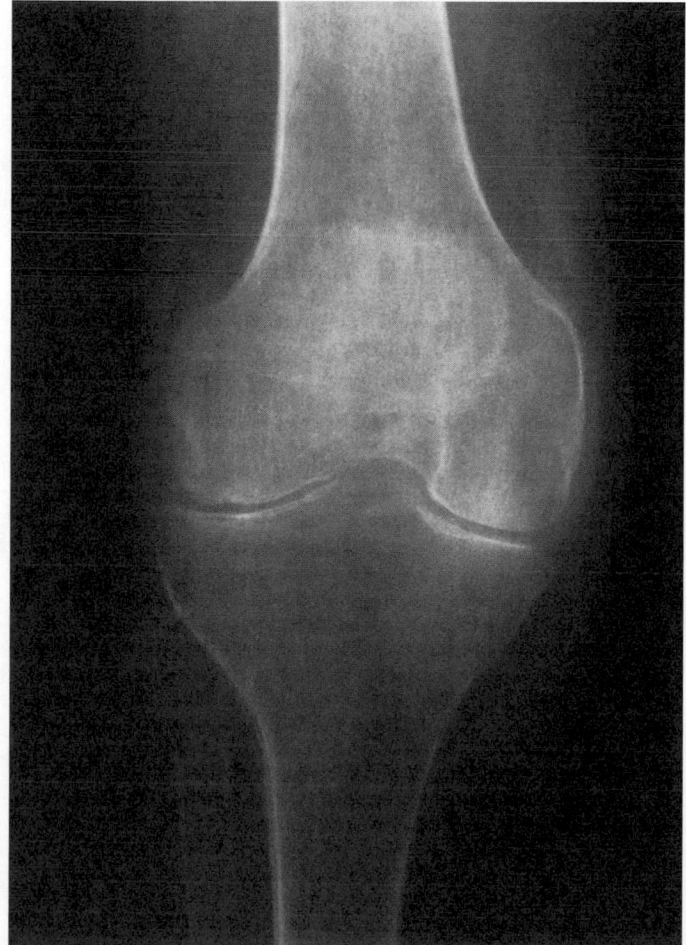

A

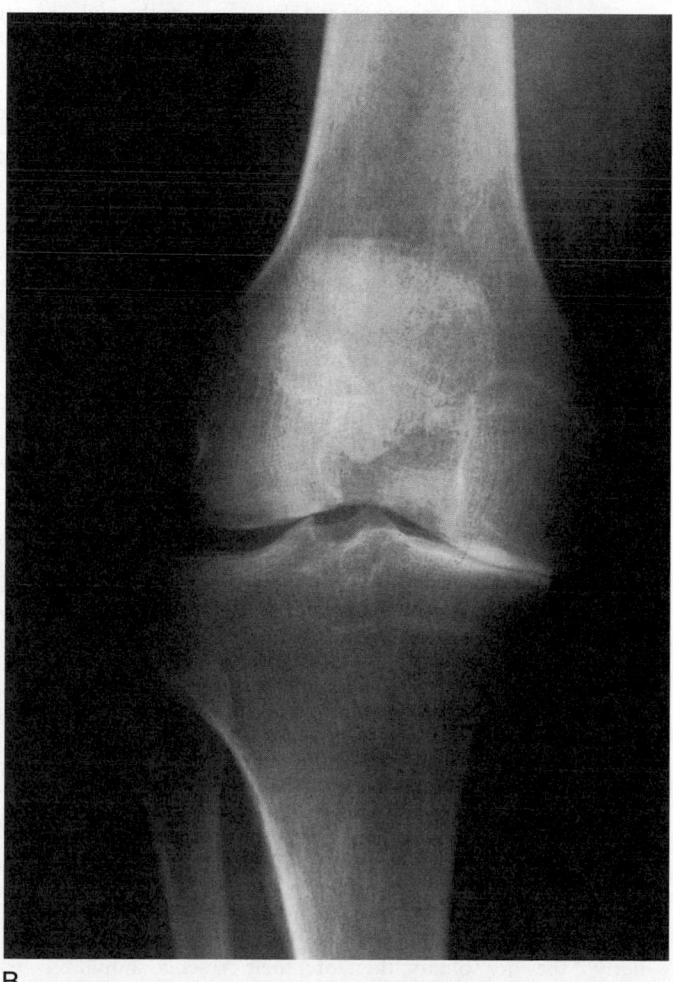

B

FIGURE 278–7 • Radiographs of the knees in the two most common forms of arthritis—rheumatoid arthritis and osteoarthritis—are compared and contrasted. *A,* Severe involvement in rheumatoid arthritis, with almost complete symmetrical loss of joint space in both the medial and lateral compartment, with little subchondral sclerosis or osteophyte formation. *B,* Typical osteoarthritis, with severe, near-total loss of joint space of one compartment and a normal or actually increased joint space of the other compartment. Note also the significant subchondral sclerosis in the involved area typical of osteoarthritis.

1649

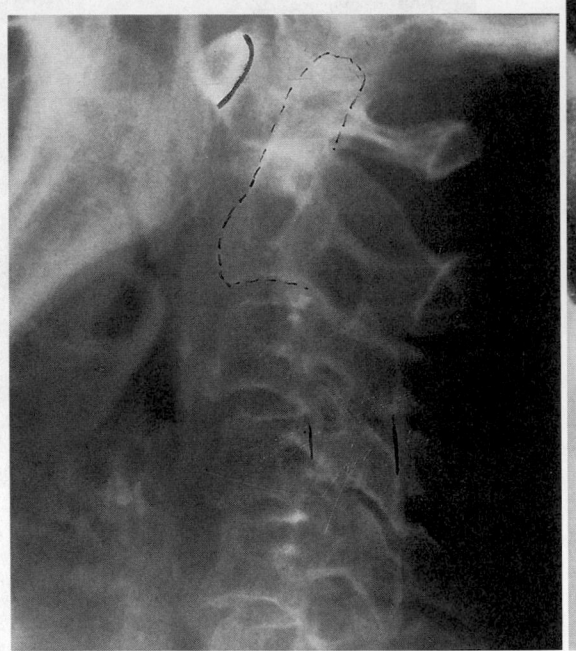

A   B

FIGURE 278–9 • Lateral radiograph and lateral pathologic specimen of the cervical spine in patients with rheumatoid arthritis are shown. *A,* The body of C2 and its odontoid process are outlined by the broken lines, and the posterior aspect of the anterior segment of C1 is indicated by a solid line. Normally a space of only 2 to 3 cm separates C1 from C2. The space between C1 and the odontoid of C2 is markedly increased, indicative of subluxation of C1 and C2. *B,* A pathologic specimen from a patient who died from C1-C2 subluxation. The horizontal arrow shows the odontoid process that subluxed posteriorly, severely compressing and almost severing the cord. The vertical arrow shows a bone graft that had been put in place posteriorly to try and keep this patient from subluxing. Below the arrow you can see a nonhealing area through the bone graft, and inferior to that a wire fixation suture is still in place.

pressure points. They are firm on examination, are usually nontender (unless traumatized), have a characteristic histologic picture, and are thought to be triggered by small vessel vasculitis. A syndrome of increased nodulosis, despite good control of the disease, has been described with methotrexate therapy (Fig. 278–11).

Small vessel vasculitis, manifested as digital infarcts, or leukocytoclastic vasculitis may be seen (Fig. 278–12) and should prompt more aggressive DMARD treatment. A vasculitis of small and medium arteries, which is indistinguishable from polyarteritis nodosa can be seen and requires aggressive systemic therapy. Finally, pyoderma gangrenosum is seen with increased frequency in association with RA.

Cardiac. Although clinically important, cardiac involvement directly related to RA is uncommon: patients with RA have significantly increased morbidity and mortality from coronary artery disease. The reasons for this are not clear, but chronic inflammation, some of the medications used, and sedentary lifestyle all may be significant risk factors. Pericardial effusions are common (50% of patients by echocardiography) but are usually asymptomatic. Rarely, long-standing pericardial disease may result in a fibrinous pericarditis, and patients may present clinically with constrictive pericarditis. Uncommonly, rheumatoid nodules may occur in the conduction system and cause heart block.

Pulmonary. Pulmonary manifestations of RA include pleural effusions, rheumatoid nodules, and parenchymal lung disease. Pleural effusions occur more commonly in men and are usually small and asymptomatic. Of interest, pleural fluid in RA is characterized by low levels of glucose and pH and, therefore, may at times be confused with empyema. Rheumatoid nodules may occur in the lung, especially in men (Fig. 278–13); they are usually solid but may calcify, cavitate, or become infected. Rarely, nodules may rupture and produce a pneumothorax. If RA patients are exposed to coal dust, diffuse nodular densities may occur (Caplan's syndrome). Differentiating rheumatoid nodules from lung cancer may be problematic, particularly if they are solitary; therefore, their presence should precipitate an aggressive diagnostic work-up.

Diffuse interstitial fibrosis occurs in RA and may progress to a honeycomb appearance on radiograph with increasing dyspnea.

Rarely, bronchiolitis obliterans can be seen with or without organizing pneumonia. Bronchiolitis obliterans carries a poor prognosis and may occur more often in association with D-penicillamine or gold therapy.

Ophthalmologic Manifestations. The most common manifestation of RA in the eye is keratoconjunctivitis sicca (dry eyes) from secondary Sjögren's syndrome. Patients may have associated xerostomia (dry mouth), parotid gland swelling, or occasionally lymphadenopathy. Scleritis can also occur and may be painful with progression to thinning of the sclera (seen on physical examination with deep pigment showing through). Scleritis may progress to perforation of the orbit (scleromalacia perforans). Rarely, tendinitis of the superior oblique muscles may result in double-vision (Brown's syndrome).

Neurologic Manifestations. Peripheral nerve entrapment syndromes, including carpal tunnel syndrome (median nerve at the wrist) and tarsal tunnel syndrome (entrapment of the anterior tibial nerve at the ankle), are common in RA, particularly carpal tunnel syndrome. Vasculitis can lead to mononeuritis multiplex and a host of neurologic problems. Subluxations at C1-C2 may produce myelopathy (see Fig. 278–9). Rheumatoid nodules in the CNS have been described but are rare and usually asymptomatic.

Felty's Syndrome. Felty's syndrome is the triad of RA, splenomegaly, and neutropenia. This complication is seen in patients with severe, seropositive disease and may be accompanied by hepatomegaly, thrombocytopenia, lymphadenopathy, and fevers. Most patients with Felty's syndrome do not require special therapy, but instead treatment should be directed towards their severe RA. If severe neutropenia exists (<500 cells/µL) accompanied by recurrent bacteria infections or chronic, nonhealing leg ulcers, splenectomy may be indicated.

Some RA patients, who were previously thought to have Felty's syndrome have peripheral white blood cell counts dominated by large granular lymphocytes with almost complete absence of neutrophils. This condition is known as the *large granular lymphocyte syndrome* and is thought to be a variant of T-cell leukemia. When seen in the setting of RA, these patients have a good prognosis with the neutropenia often responding dramatically to methotrexate therapy.

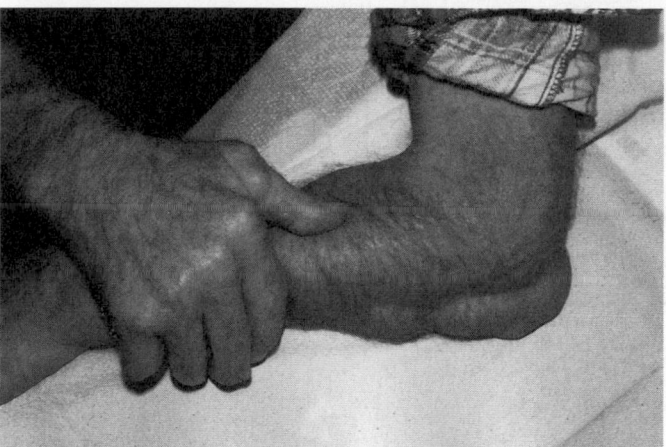

FIGURE 278–10 • Rheumatoid nodules. In this patient large rheumatoid nodules are seen in a classic location along the extensor surface of the forearm and in the olecranon bursa.

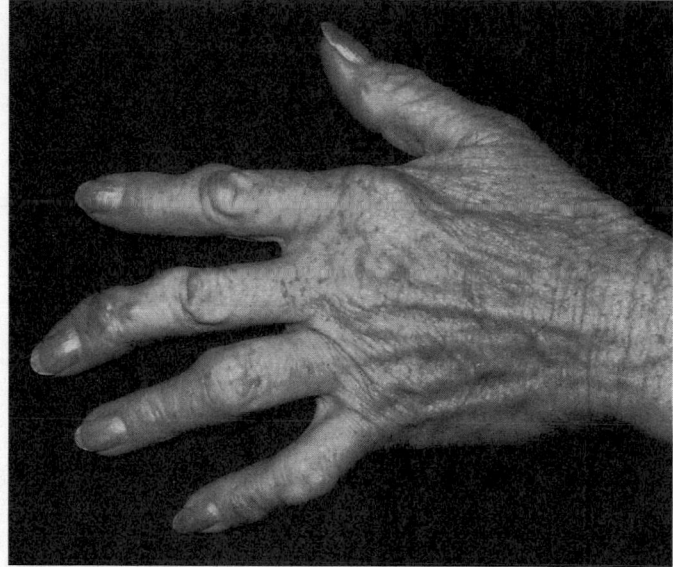

FIGURE 278–11 • Rheumatoid nodulosis. In this patient multiple rheumatoid nodules are present over joints. In some cases, the nodules may dominate the clinical picture. Rarely, this may be seen as a side effect of methotrexate therapy.

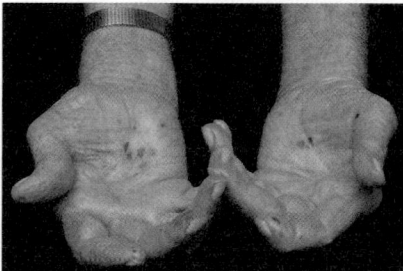 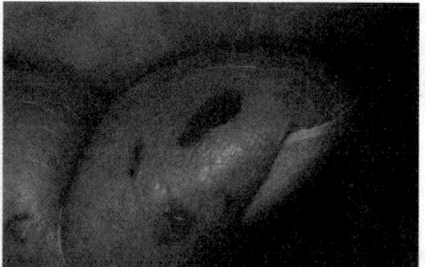

FIGURE 278–12 • *Left* and *Right*, Rheumatoid vasculitis with small brown infarcts of palms and fingers in chronic rheumatoid arthritis. (*Left* and *Right*, Courtesy of Dr. Martin Lidsky, Houston, TX.)

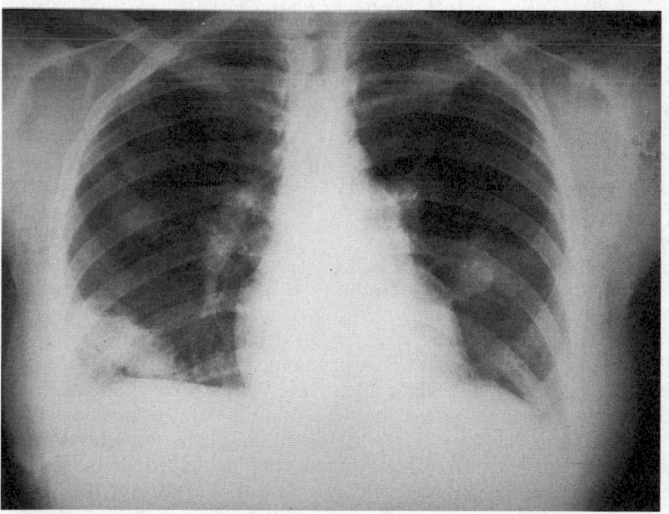

FIGURE 278–13 • Chest radiograph demonstrates discrete rheumatoid nodules in both the right and left lower lobes of the lungs. (Courtesy of Dr. Martin Lidsky, Houston, TX.)

Laboratory Features

The most characteristic laboratory abnormality in RA is the presence of rheumatoid factor, which is found in approximately 80% of patients. Rheumatoid factor, first described in the 1930s, is an antibody that recognizes IgG as its antigen. The presence of rheumatoid factor is strongly associated with more severe articular disease as well as essentially all of the extra-articular features previously discussed. The exact role that rheumatoid factor plays in the etiology/

pathogenesis of RA remains to be elucidated. Rheumatoid factor is seen in association with many diseases other than RA, particularly in disease processes that provide chronic stimulation of the immune system (see Table 278–3). RA is associated with multiple other autoantibodies, including antinuclear antibodies ($\approx$30% of patients) and antineutrophil cytoplasmic antibodies, particularly of the perinuclear type ($\approx$30% of patients).

Most patients with RA have an anemia of chronic disease. The degree of anemia is proportional to the activity of the disease, and therapy that controls the disease or erythropoietin administration may normalize the hemoglobin. Thrombocytosis is common, with platelet counts returning to normal as the inflammation is controlled. Acute-phase reactants, ESR, and CRP levels also parallel the activity of the disease, and their persistent elevation portends a poor prognosis, both in terms of joint destruction and mortality. White blood cell counts may be elevated or normal, or in the case of Felty's syndrome, profoundly depressed.

Synovial fluid in RA is characterized by white blood cell counts in the 5000- to 100,000/mm^3 range with approximately two thirds of the cells being polymorphonuclear leukocytes. Unfortunately, there are no synovial fluid findings that are pathognomonic of RA.

Disease Course and Prognosis

Until recently, RA was thought to be a relatively benign disease. Unfortunately, it is now clear that once established, RA is a lifelong progressive disease that produces significant morbidity in most patients and premature mortality in many. Long-term studies have found that 50% of RA patients have had to stop working after 10 years (approximately ten times the average rate). Patients who are rheumatoid factor positive and those who are shared epitope positive have a worse prognosis with more erosions and more extra-articular disease (Table 278–4). Once deformities are found on examination or erosions on radiography, the damage is largely irreversible. It has been clearly

Table 278–4 • EXTRA-ARTICULAR MANIFESTATIONS OF RHEUMATOID ARTHRITIS

SITE	MANIFESTATIONS
Skin	Nodules, fragility, vasculitis, pyoderma gangrenosum
Heart	Pericarditis, premature atherosclerosis, vasculitis, valvular, and valve ring nodules
Lung	Pleural effusions, interstitial lung disease, bronchiolitis obliterans, rheumatoid nodules, vasculitis
Eye	Keratoconjunctivitis sicca, episcleritis, scleritis, scleromalacia perforans, peripheral ulcerative keratopathy
Neurologic	Entrapment neuropathy, cervical myelopathy, mononeuritis multiplex (vasculitis), peripheral neuropathy
Hematopoietic	Anemia, thrombocytosis, lymphadenopathy, Felty's syndrome
Kidney	Amyloidosis, vasculitis
Bone	Osteopenia

Table 278–5 • KEYS TO OPTIMIZE OUTCOME OF RA TREATMENT

Early, accurate diagnosis
Early DMARD therapy
Strive for remission in all patients
Monitor carefully for treatment toxicities
Consider and treat comorbid conditions*

---

*Important comorbid conditions include cardiovascular disease, increased susceptibility to infections, and osteoporosis.
DMARD = disease-modifying antirheumatic drug; RA = rheumatoid arthritis.

Table 278–6 • GLUCOCORTICOID GUIDELINES

Avoid use of glucocorticoids without DMARDs
Prednisone >10 mg/day rarely indicated for articular disease
Taper to the lowest effective dose
Use as "bridge therapy" until DMARD therapy effective
Remember prophylaxis against osteoporosis

DMARD = disease-modifying antirheumatic drug.

shown that erosions occur in most patients in the first 1 to 2 years and that the rate of radiographic damage can be affected by early therapy. Therefore, early DMARD therapy is critical. Although, long-term data are not yet available, short-term data strongly suggest that current patients have the opportunity to benefit greatly if the newer principles of therapy are practiced.

Treatment

GENERAL. RA is a lifelong disease process that has no known cure; the diagnosis is made based on clinical criteria and many different options exist for treatment. All of these factors magnify the importance of the patient-physician interaction and place a premium on the art rather than the science of medicine. The optimal care for patients with RA requires an effective interaction between primary care physicians and rheumatologists, and in some cases physical therapists (PT), occupational therapists (OT), and orthopedic surgeons. Because of the serious nature of the disease, the rapid introduction of new treatments, and the need for expertise in monitoring these therapies, all patients with RA should be followed by a rheumatologist.

The goal of therapy for RA is to put the disease in remission and to maintain this remission by continuing therapy (Table 278–5). Using currently available therapies, if RA is treated early, this is possible in 20 to 35% of patients. Unfortunately, remissions require the ongoing use of medications and even then are not always durable. Some combination of nonsteroidal anti-inflammatory drugs (NSAIDs), steroids, and DMARDs is necessary in almost all patients. In many, perhaps most, combinations of different DMARDs or DMARDs plus biologicals are necessary for optimal control. It is of critical importance that therapy be escalated rapidly to ensure maximal suppression of disease with minimal toxicity and expense. Additionally, all patients with RA should be educated about their disease and the therapies that will be used. In most cases, patients should have an opportunity to spend time with PT and OT to learn about range-of-motion exercises, joint protection, and assistive devices. When treating RA, four types of medical therapies are used: NSAIDs, glucocorticoids, DMARDs, and biological DMARDs.

NSAIDs. NSAIDs are important for the symptomatic relief provided to RA patients; however, they play only a minor role, if any, in altering the underlying disease process. Therefore, NSAIDs should rarely, if ever, be used to treat RA without the concomitant use of DMARDs. Many clinicians waste valuable time switching from one NSAID to another before starting DMARD therapy.

Much has been written about the gastrointestinal toxicity of NSAIDs, and many of these concerns are particularly relevant to RA patients who have a significant number of risk factors that are associated with toxicities. Therefore, cyclooxygenase-2 (COX-2) selective agents have been particularly popular in this group of patients. Several caveats should be kept in mind: RA patients have a significantly increased risk for cardiovascular problems, and since COX-2 drugs provide little antiplatelet activity, many of these patients will need to take low-dose aspirin therapy in addition to their COX-2 selective drug, and the effect this has on gastrointestinal toxicity is unclear. Additionally, the COX-2 drugs appear to differ little from the nonselective COX agents in terms of their effects on the kidney and on blood pressure. Both of these issues are of particular concern for RA patients because of their significantly increased risk of cardiovascular disease.

GLUCOCORTICOIDS. Glucocorticoids have had a significant role in the treatment of RA for over half a century. Indeed, RA was chosen as the first disease to test this new therapy in 1948, partly because it was thought that RA was a disease of glucocorticoid deficiency (an issue that remains unresolved). As was the case with the first patient treated in 1948, glucocorticoid therapy can be dramatically and rapidly effective in patients with RA. Glucocorticoids are not only useful for symptomatic improvement but significantly decrease the radiographic progression of RA.■ Unfortunately, the toxicities of long-term steroid therapy are legend. Therefore, the optimal use of these drugs requires an understanding of the principles of steroid use in RA (Table 278–6).

Glucocorticoids remain among the most potent, anti-inflammatory treatments available: because of this and their rapid onset of action, they are ideally suited to help control the inflammation in RA while the much slower-acting DMARDs are starting to work. Prednisone, the most commonly used glucocorticoid, should rarely be used in doses higher than 10 mg/day to treat the articular manifestations of RA. This dose should be slowly tapered to the lowest effective dose, and the concomitant DMARD therapy should be adjusted to make this possible. Glucocorticoids should rarely, if ever, be used to treat RA without concomitant DMARD therapy. The paradigm is to shut off inflammation rapidly with glucocorticoids and then to taper them as the DMARD is kicking in ("bridge therapy"). In all patients on glucocorticoids, strong consideration should be given to the prevention of osteoporosis, and bisphosphonates have been shown to be particularly effective in this regard. Higher doses of glucocorticoids may be necessary for extra-articular manifestations, especially for vasculitis and scleritis.

DMARDs. DMARDs are a group of medications that have the ability to modify or change the disabling potential of RA. In most cases, drugs included in this class have met the "gold standard," which is the ability to halt or slow the radiographic progression of RA. Included in this group of medications are methotrexate, sulfasalazine (Azulfidine), gold, antimalarials, leflunomide (Arava), azathioprine, penicillamine, and minocycline. It is critically important that clinicians and patients alike understand that these medications take 2 to 6 months to exert their maximal effect. Therefore, other measures such as glucocorticoid therapy may be needed to control the disease while these medications are starting to work.

All of these DMARDs have been shown to be effective in treating both early and more advanced RA. The choice of which to start first depends on patient and physician concerns about toxicity and monitoring issues, as well as the activity of disease and comorbid conditions. Until additional research elucidates factors that allow us to select the best initial therapy for each patient, there are many reasonable choices for initial therapy. The critical factor is not which DMARD to start first but the fact that DMARD therapy is started early in the disease process.

Methotrexate is the preferred DMARD of most rheumatologists, in part because patients have a more durable response and when monitored correctly, serious toxicities are rare. Methotrexate is dramatically effective in slowing the radiographic progression of RA and is usually given orally in doses ranging from 5 to 25 mg/week, given as a single dose. This once-a-week administration is worthy of emphasis; prior experience with daily therapy in psoriasis has taught us the importance of allowing the liver time to recover between doses. Oral absorption of methotrexate is variable; therefore, subcutaneous injections of methotrexate may be effective when oral treatment is not. Side effects of methotrexate include oral ulcers, nausea, hepatotoxicity, bone marrow suppression, and pneumonitis. With the exception of pneumonitis, these toxicities respond to dose adjustments. Monitoring of blood counts and liver blood tests (albumin and aspartate aminotransaminase or alanine aminotransferase) should be done every 4 to 8 weeks with dosage adjustments as needed. Renal function is critical for clearance of methotrexate; previously stable patients may experience severe toxicities when renal function deteriorates. Pneumonitis, although rare, is less predictable and may be fatal, particularly if the methotrexate is not stopped or is restarted. Folic acid in the dose of 1 to 4 mg/day can significantly decrease most methotrexate toxicities without apparent loss of efficacy against RA. Methotrexate in combination with sulfasalazine and hydroxychloroquine has been shown to be more effective than methotrexate alone.**2**

Leflunomide, a pyrimidine antagonist, is the newest DMARD approved for use in RA. It has very long half-life and therefore a loading dose of 100 mg/day for three days may be given before daily therapy of 10 to 20 mg/day is started. The most common toxicity is diarrhea, which may respond to dose reduction. Also, because of its long half-life and its teratogenic potential, women wishing to become pregnant who have previously received leflunomide, even if therapy was stopped years ago, should have blood levels drawn. If toxicity occurs or if pregnancy is being considered, leflunomide can be rapidly eliminated from the body with cholestyramine.

Antimalarials, hydroxychloroquine (Plaquenil) or chloroquine, are frequently used for the treatment of RA. They have the least toxicity of any of the DMARDs and do not require monitoring of blood tests. Yearly or twice-yearly monitoring by an ophthalmologist is recommended to detect any signs of retinal toxicity (rare). Hydroxychloroquine is the most commonly used preparation and is given orally 200 to 400 mg/day. These drugs are frequently used in combination with other DMARDs, particularly methotrexate.

Sulfasalazine is the most commonly used DMARD in Europe. It is an effective treatment when given in doses of 1 to 3 g/day. Monitoring of blood counts, particularly white blood cell counts, in the first 6 months is recommended. Minocycline, 100 mg twice daily, has been shown to be an effective treatment for RA, par-

ticularly when used in early, seropositive disease. Chronic therapy (>2 years) with minocycline may lead to cutaneous hyperpigmentation.

Gold, the oldest DMARD, when given intramuscularly, remains an extremely effective therapy for a small percentage of patients. It is less commonly used because of its slow onset of action, need for intramuscular administration, frequent monitoring required (complete blood count and urinalysis) and frequent toxicities. Toxicities include skin rashes, bone marrow suppression, and proteinuria.

BIOLOGICAL DMARDs. Recent research has continued to elucidate the central role that cytokines, most notably TNF-α and IL-1, play in the pathophysiology of RA. This has led directly to the development and clinical use of biological agents directed against TNF-α (etanercept [Enbrel] and infliximab [Remicade]) and IL-1 (anakinra [Kineret]). Etanercept is a recombinant TNF receptor fusion protein and is administered by subcutaneous injection 25 mg twice weekly. Infliximab is a mouse/human chimeric monoclonal antibody against TNF-α that is given intravenously (3 to 10 mg/kg) every 4 to 8 weeks. Both have been shown to be highly effective against both clinical symptoms and radiographic progression of RA.**3,4** A rapid onset of action (days to weeks) is apparent with both of these agents and is a significant advantage that these treatments have over conventional DMARDs. Current disadvantages include cost and concern about long-term toxicities, in particular, infections (especially tuberculosis) and demyelinating syndromes. Adalimumab, a newer anti-TNF agent, improves disease in patients who already are taking methotrexate.**5**

Anakinra, a recombinant human IL-1 receptor antagonist, is given subcutaneously 100 mg/day. It has been shown to be effective against signs and symptoms of RA as well as radiographic progression. Its onset of action is somewhat slower and less dramatic than the TNF inhibitors. Toxicities include injection site reactions and pneumonia (especially in patients with asthma).

COMORBIDITY. Optimal care of patients with RA requires a recognition of the associated comorbid conditions, including an increased risk of cardiovascular death, osteoporosis, infections (especially pneumonia), and an increased risk of certain cancers. Increasingly, cardiovascular disease is being recognized as the cause of much of the excess mortality in RA. A number of factors probably contribute to this mortality, including sedentary lifestyle, glucocorticoid therapy, and treatments that increase homocysteine levels such as methotrexate and sulfasalazine. However, with the recent identification of the strong association between chronic inflammation and cardiovascular disease, it is likely that this may be the most significant factor. Therapies that control RA earlier and better can be expected to decrease cardiovascular morbidity and mortality. Clinicians should consider RA a risk factor for cardiovascular disease and should aggressively address other cardiovascular risk factors in their rheumatoid patients.

Osteoporosis is ubiquitous in patients with RA, and early therapy results in long-term dividends. Patients with RA are at an increased risk for infections, and this risk is further increased by some of our therapies. Patients should be cautioned to seek medical attention early for even minor symptoms suggestive of infection, especially if receiving anti-TNF therapy. All patients with RA should receive a pneumococcal and yearly influenza vaccinations. Finally, patients with RA have an increased risk of lymphomas. Occasionally, B-cell lymphomas may be associated with immunosuppression and regress after immunosuppression is discontinued. RA patients have significantly decreased risk (odds ratio, 0.2) of developing colon cancer. This is thought to be secondary to chronic inhibition of COX by NSAIDs in this group of patients.

Future Directions

Significant advances in our ability to effectively treat RA have come from our understanding of the cytokine imbalance that accompanies this disease. Much research is focused on the further development of biological products to modulate this balance. There is a critical need for a cytokine thermostat that would allow us to titrate the desired cytokine balance to control disease without altering critical immune functions. Even with existing therapies, there are many different effective options for patients with RA. The challenge to the clinician is to pick the right option for each patient. Unfortunately, there are little data

to aid in this choice and, therefore, parameters, genetic or otherwise, that would allow us to select the best initial option for each patient would be a major breakthrough. Finally, elucidation of the trigger or triggers for RA may allow us to begin to think about prevention.

1. Kirwan J: The effect of glucocorticoids on joint destruction in rheumatoid arthritis. The Arthritis and Rheumatism Council Low-Dose Glucocorticoid Study Group. N Engl J Med 1995;333:142–146.
2. O'Dell JR, Haire CE, Erickson N, et al: Treatment of rheumatoid arthritis with methotrexate alone, sulfasalazine and hydroxychloroquine, or a combination of all three medications. N Engl J Med 1996;334:1287–1291.

3. Bathon JM, Martin RW, Fleischmann RM, et al: A comparison of etanercept and methotrexate in patients with early rheumatoid arthritis. N Engl J Med 2000;343:1586–1593.
4. Lipsky PE, Van der Heijde D, St. Clair EW, et al: Infliximab and methotrexate in the treatment of rheumatoid arthritis. N Engl J Med 2000;243:1594–1602.
5. Weinblatt ME, Keystone EC, Furst DE, et al: Adalimumab, a fully human anti-tumor necrosis factor alpha monoclonal antibody, for the treatment of rheumatoid arthritis in patients taking concomitant methotrexate: The ARMADA trial. Arthritis Rheum 2003;38:35–45.

SUGGESTED READINGS

American College of Rheumatology Subcommittee on Rheumatoid Arthritis Guidelines: Guidelines for the Management of Rheumatoid Arthritis, 2002 Update. Arthritis Rheum 2002;46:328–346. *Consensus guidelines, including traditional and newer therapies, with a flow diagram to guide the non-rheumatologist.*

Arend WP: Physiology of cytokine pathways in rheumatoid arthritis. Arthritis Rheum 2001;45:101–106. *Summary of cytokine pathways and how they can guide the development of new therapies, especially monoclonal antibodies.*

Mikuls TR, Saag KG: Comorbidity in rheumatoid arthritis. Rheum Dis Clin North Am 2001;27:283–303. *Emphasizes how comorbid conditions contribute to a patient's disability.*

279 THE SPONDYLOARTHROPATHIES

Robert D. Inman

The spondyloarthropathies (SpAs) encompass a group of clinical syndromes that are linked in terms of disease manifestations and in terms of genetic susceptibility. The clinical subsets most commonly recognized are ankylosing spondylitis, reactive arthritis, psoriatic arthritis, and enteropathic arthritis (Fig. 279–1). In addition, there is a sizable population of patients that does not fit into one of these distinct diagnostic categories but shares some of the common clinical features described in this chapter. The syndrome associated with this subset is termed undifferentiated SpA, which over time may evolve into a classical pattern such as ankylosing spondylitis but which may remain in an undifferentiated pattern in long follow-up studies.

Family studies in which there are multiple individuals with an SpA have emphasized some of the commonality between the four distinct subsets just mentioned. The impression from such studies is that there is a shared common path of immunogenetic susceptibility upon which various genetic and environmental influences lead to characteristic clinical subsets. Thus, if enteropathic arthritis occurs in such a family, in another family it may be psoriatic arthritis. In this sense, the SpAs seem to "breed true." It should be recognized, however, that some distinct feature can be clinically very close in their manifestations (e.g., guttate psoriasis and keratodermia blennorrhagica), making simple discrimination sometimes difficult.

There are several common features in the family of SpAs, which at once link them and serve to distinguish them from the other major contributor to chronic polyarthritis, RA. The arthropathies have a strong predilection for the spine, in particular the sacroiliac joints.

There is a shared predilection for new bone formation at sites of chronic inflammation, with joint ankylosis as a consequence. When peripheral arthritis occurs, it is commonly lower extremity and asymmetrical. There is a predilection for sites of tendon insertion into bone (entheses), so that enthesitis becomes one of the most specific clinical manifestations of the SpA. The basis for this target organ involvement has invoked biomechanical factors, innervation, local vascularity, and bone marrow–derived inflammatory mediators, but the precise mechanism for this relationship remains incompletely defined. Whatever the reason, inflammation in the enthesis and contiguous subchondral bone is a characteristic feature of this arthritis, and the appearance of this inflammation on magnetic resonance imaging (MRI) is distinct enough to lead some investigators to use such imaging for diagnostic purposes.

Predilection for ocular inflammation, particularly acute anterior uveitis, is a common feature of all subsets and indeed is considered by some to be a member of SpA in its own right because it may occur in the same susceptible populations of patients even in the absence of joint involvement. Finally, all subsets have an association with the class I human leukocyte antigen (HLA) allele B27, with the strength of the association varying somewhat between them.

Increasingly, diagnostic criteria (Table 279–1) are being used that emphasize the clinical common features, namely inflammatory spinal pain or asymmetrical, lower extremity synovitis. There are several distinctive features that differentiate the SpA from rheumatoid arthritis (RA), the other main contributor to the differential diagnosis of chronic polyarthritis (Table 279–2). These include sex predilection, HLA association, pattern of joint involvement, and the presence of rheumatoid factor, which becomes the serologic borderline between seropositive disease (RA) and seronegative disease (SpA).

At the level of joint histopathology, sites of chronic inflammation in the former are associated with erosions but in the latter are associated with new bone formation. This suggests a fundamental difference in the cytokine profile in the microenvironment of the joint, and although there is some evidence that SpAs reflect more of a type 2 T helper cell (Th2) cytokine profile as opposed to the Th1 profile of RA, this has not been resolved, and the mediators of neo-ossification await identification.

HLA-B27

The major histocompatibility complex (MHC), on the short arm of chromosome 6 in humans, is one of the most polymorphic regions of the human genome. This is particularly so for the B locus, which constitutes part of the class I MHC genes in this complex. There are probably more than 200 different alleles at this locus, of which B27 is one. As with all HLA alleles, there is codominant expression of B locus genes, so that most individuals who are "B27 positive" are heterozygous for the B locus and there appears to be little clinical or prognostic significance associated with the less common homozygous B27 state. The conventional role of class I HLA antigens is to present a processed peptide to the T-cell receptor of a specific CD8+ cytotoxic T cell, thereby initiating an immune response against the pathogen from which that peptide was derived by intracellular proteolysis and processing. This function places the HLA antigens in a critical role in host defense against pathogens, and it is the hetero-

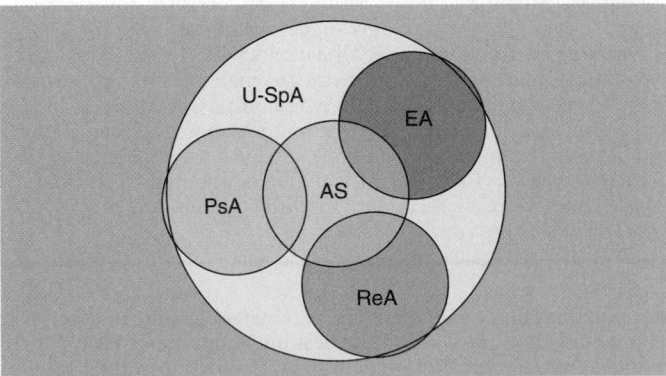

FIGURE 279–1 • Schematic relationships among the different SpA subsets. Ankylosing spondylitis (AS) is considered the classical SpA, encompassing the essential features of this family of diseases. AS may overlap with psoriatic arthritis (PsA), enteropathic arthritis (EA), or reactive arthritis (ReA). There are many patients with clinical features of SpA who do not meet diagnostic criteria for the four defined subsets. Such cases are termed undifferentiated SpA (U-SpA).

Table 279–1 • EUROPEAN SPONDYLOARTHROPATHY STUDY GROUP CRITERIA FOR SPONDYLOARTHROPATHY

Inflammatory spinal pain
  OR
Synovitis (asymmetrical or predominantly in the lower limb)
  PLUS
Any one of the following:

Any one of the following:	Positive family history
	Psoriasis
	Inflammatory bowel disease
	Urethritis, cervicitis, or acute diarrhea within 1 month before arthritis
	Alternating buttock pain
	Enthesopathy
	Sacroiliitis

Table 279-2 • CONTRAST OF RHEUMATOID ARTHRITIS AND SPONDYLOARTHROPATHY

FEATURE	RHEUMATOID ARTHRITIS	ANKYLOSING SPONDYLITIS	ENTEROPATHIC ARTHRITIS	PSORIATIC ARTHRITIS	REACTIVE ARTHRITIS
Male/female ratio	1:3	3:1	1:1	1:1	10:1
HLA association	DR4	B27	B27(axial)	B27(axial)	B27
Joint pattern	Symmetric, Peripheral	Axial	Axial and peripheral	Axial and asymmetric peripheral	Axial and asymmetric peripheral
Sacroiliac	0	Symmetric	Symmetric	Asymmetric	Asymmetric
Syndesmophyte	0	Smooth, marginal	Smooth, marginal	Coarse, nonmarginal	Coarse, nonmarginal
Eye	Scleritis	Iritis	+/−	0	Iritis and conjunctivitis
Skin	Vasculitis	0	0	Psoriasis	Keratoderma
Rheumatoid factor	>80%	0	0	0	0

HLA = human leukocyte antigen.

geneity of cellular immune responses that is alleged to be an advantage for a species (such as humans) with an extensive polymorphism region of the genome. This idea has led to the concept that infectious diseases have driven allelic polymorphism in the MHC. Such a hypothesis postulates selective advantage in the extensive peptide-binding capabilities conferred by different alleles of the B locus, but what of the disadvantages?

It is clear that HLA is strongly associated with the SpAs. Yet prevalence of HLA-B27 varies widely in different racial and ethnic clusters around the world. It is virtually absent in aboriginal populations in Australia, occurs in 1% of the population in Japan, 7% of northern European countries, and 50% of some of the native tribes in western Canada. The environmental-genetic interaction that may account for the expansion or restriction of this gene in human populations is unknown. There is practical impact of this variability for the clinician. Because the relative risk conferred by a gene reflects the prevalence of the gene in the affected individuals versus the prevalence of the gene in the normal population, the relative risk for SpA is higher in a population where the gene is uncommon (e.g., Japan) than in a population where B27 is more common (e.g., Scandinavia). In North American whites, the prevalence of the gene is approximately 7%. Thus, there is a 7% "false-positive" rate if one is attempting to use the gene as a diagnostic marker to decipher the cause of chronic back pain in an unselected population of patients. On the other hand, 90% of patients with ankylosing spondylitis (AS) are B27 positive, so there is a 10% "false-negative" rate in the use of the test diagnostically. The key factor is pretest probability. In a patient with chronic back pain that is clearly inflammatory in character, the addition of a positive B27 combines to strengthen the likelihood of AS accounting for the back problem.

It had been held that the prevalence of AS in various parts of the globe closely parallels the prevalence of B27 in that population, and in general this pattern is valid. But what has introduced complexity into this has been the recognition that there is not just one B27, but in fact there are more than 20 subtypes of B27 (ranging from B*2701 to B*2724 at present). In terms of the evolution of molecular variability, B*2705 is regarded as the primordial subtype with variability developing over time on the basis of alterations in the genomic DNA. The amino acid substitutions occurring as a result are generally reflected in the peptide-binding cleft of the B27 molecule, arguing that there has been a functional change concurrent with the structural change. This notion has been lent support by the observation that some subtypes, notably B*2706 and B*2709, do not seem to confer increased susceptibility to development of AS. As an extension of genetic epidemiology, this observation has led to a search for "arthritogenic peptides" that can be presented by the disease-associated subtypes such as B*2705 and B*2704 but not by the non–disease-associated subtypes. To date, no simple peptide-susceptibility relationship has been demonstrated, but this is an important clue to the pathogenic role of B27 and studies are ongoing to mine this relationship.

There have been other approaches to defining the mechanism whereby B27 confers disease susceptibility in addition to that of uniquely presenting an arthritogenic peptide to T cells. According to the theory of molecular mimicry, an autoimmune response can ensue after an infection if the immune response against the pathogen cross-reacts with host antigens. There is a degree of sequence homology between B27 and several candidate gram-negative enteric bacteria and there is evidence for cross-reacting monoclonal antibodies, but the significance of such homology for disease pathogenesis remains unresolved. There has also been investigation into alteration of primary host-pathogen interactions, such as modulation of invasion, intracellular replication, and pathogen clearance, but no definitive allele-specific relationships have been demonstrated in these studies, although this remains an area of active study. In B27-transgenic rats, the spontaneous development of pathology strikingly similar to human SpA has supported the notion that B27 itself is the critical genetic factor in disease pathogenesis. These animals develop a Crohn's-like pathology in the gastrointestinal tract, spondylitis, peripheral arthritis, uveitis, and psoriasiform skin and nail changes. Of interest, if such animals are raised in a germ-free environment, there is a marked reduction of joint and gut disease, implying a dynamic interrelationship between microbial triggers and background host genes that seems to recapitulate the situation seen clinically.

Genome-wide screening studies of multiplex families with SpA, particularly AS, are ongoing in several countries in order to identify other important genes that are involved in predisposing to these diseases. Several candidate loci have been identified, although considerable variability between different studies is apparent. The common observation, however, is that the strongest association is with the HLA complex, so that at least in familial AS, B27 may at least be necessary, if not sufficient, to confer disease susceptibility. MRI studies in asymptomatic B27-positive individuals indicate that there is a much higher prevalence of sacroiliitis than previously recognized, and studies are continuing to define that prevalence and indeed the prevalence of SpA in the general population. Some investigators have concluded that SpAs are as common as RA in the population.

Ankylosing Spondylitis

AS is the most common inflammatory disorder of the axial skeleton. Although prevalence is under study in several centers, the following is a useful rule of thumb: AS occurs in 0.2% of the general population, in 2% of the B27-positive population, and in 20% of B27-positive individuals with an affected family member. A male predominance in the disease is evident with a male/female ratio ranging from 2.5:1 to 5:1. The basis for this gender bias is not resolved. It is held, however, that AS is under-recognized in women, perhaps because of milder axial disease and a more delayed disease onset, but alternative diagnoses of pelvic and low back pain in women may hinder clinician awareness of the disease in female patients.

AS typically begins in young adulthood, but symptoms may arise in adolescence or earlier. Up to 15% of children with juvenile chronic polyarthritis are classified as having juvenile ankylosing spondylitis, or JAS. Such children may present with a pauciarticular pattern, with a predilection for the tarsal joints. During the adolescent years there is an increasing prevalence of radiographic sacroiliitis, with almost all patients manifesting this feature by the end of the teenage years. At the other end of the age spectrum, there is a small number of patients with late-onset AS who may present with sacroiliitis and oligoarthritis. The axial involvement and asymmetrical lower extremity involvement may serve to differentiate such patients from those with late-onset RA, although clinically there may be overlapping features.

The classical presentation of AS is the insidious onset of low back pain, which persists more than 3 months, is accompanied by early morning stiffness, and is typically improved by exercise (Table 279–3). Some investigators would also include a response to nonsteroidal anti-inflammatory drug (NSAID) therapy as a feature further differentiating AS from mechanical low back pain. Back pain that awakens the patient from sleep is often a clue to inflammatory back pain that may have been previously misdiagnosed as the pain of degenerative disc disease, the latter being the much more common cause of low back pain in the population at large. The pain is typically in the region of the sacroiliac joints, with or without slight radiation to the buttock area. Mid-thoracic pain and cervical pain, particularly at night, are less common but strongly suggest inflammatory back pain when they occur. Fatigue is also a suggestive symptom and is often highlighted by these patients because the typical young male patient sets a high functional norm in terms of sports and recreation. If inflammation is inadequately controlled, there is increasing stiffness, which may persist most of the day, as well as progressive loss of mobility and flexibility.

A peripheral oligoarthritis is seen in up to 30% of patients with AS. Typically, this is asymmetrical oligoarthritis with a predilection for the lower extremities. It is important to ask about concurrent or previous tendinitis (e.g., Achilles tendinitis) or heel pain (e.g., plantar fasciitis) because either may reflect a enthesitis that is part of the clinical picture. Involvement of the hip can occur at any point in the course of AS and can follow a course to joint destruction. A hip flexion contracture on this basis may contribute to increasing stoop on standing and walking, which otherwise may be attributed to spinal involvement in the disease.

Extra-articular features involve primarily the eye. Ocular involvement may occur in up to 40% of AS patients, most typically acute anterior uveitis (iritis). The uveitis is often manifest by slight impairment in visual acuity, and photophobia and eye pain may accompany this. Typically, it is unilateral and recurrent. Uncommon manifestations include aortic insufficiency, cardiac conduction defects, and pulmonary fibrosis.

Physical examination of the spine characteristically reflects restricted movement, which early on may reflect in part paraspinal muscle spasm but late in the course reflects ankylosis of the zygapophyseal joints and syndesmophyte bridging of the vertebral bodies. Forward flexion is restricted and can be monitored by measuring the finger-to-floor distance on bending forward. Schober's test is used to measure mobility in the lower back. With the patient standing upright, a 10-cm span is marked from the fifth lumbar vertebra upward. Upon maximal forward flexion, the distance between the marks is remeasured. With normal spinal mobility the flexed distance should register as 15 cm, or an increment of 5 cm. Thoracic involvement is measured in chest expansion, with the chest circumference at maximum inspiration being more than 5 cm greater than the circumference at maximal expiration. Changes in cervical mobility can be measured as occiput-to-wall distance, with the patient's heels against the wall and the patient attempting to touch the back of the head to the wall. Inflammation in the sacroiliac joint may be reflected in joint line tenderness to direct pressure or by the fabere or Gaenslen maneuver. In the former, the patient lies supine while the examiner flexes and externally rotates the hip. In the latter, the examiner extends the hip by letting the leg dangle off the side of the examining table. In both cases, stress is placed on the sacroiliac joint and may reproduce the back pain if it derives from this site.

Laboratory tests in the evaluation of inflammatory back pain are relatively nonspecific. The erythrocyte sedimentation rate and C-reactive protein are typically elevated, but normal levels do not exclude inflammatory back pain and typically the degree of elevation is less than would be seen in acute RA. The anemia of chronic disease may be observed if the condition is long-standing. Serum immunoglobulin A levels may be elevated, but autoantibodies are notable for their absence. HLA-B27 is rarely the definitive factor for diagnosis, and the false-positive and false-negative rates have already been discussed. In the setting of characteristic back symptoms, the test has reasonably high sensitivity and specificity.

The radiographic assessment is important for disease confirmation, but early in the course of the disease there may be no radiographic changes in the sacroiliac joints. If there is a high index of suspicion in such cases, the use of a bone scan, computed tomography (CT) scan, or MRI may improve on the sensitivity of the plain radiograph. Views of the sacroiliac joints should be requested because the obliquity of the joint renders it difficult to assess on a routine anteroposterior pelvis radiograph. The classical changes are bilateral changes in the sacroiliac joints (Fig. 279–2). Changes include erosions in the joint line, pseudowidening, subchondral sclerosis, and finally ankylosis.

Radiographs of the spine may reveal squaring of the vertebral bodies (loss of the normal anterior concavity of the lumbar vertebra) and "shiny corners" (subchondral sclerosis at the upper edge of the vertebral body), both being manifestations of an enthesitis. Syndesmophytes, representing marginal bridging of the vertebrae (Figs. 279–3 and 279–4), eventually develop and make the diagnosis clear. Because ankylosis of the apophyseal joints may occur without syndesmophyte formation, it is important to assess the posterior joints on the lateral lumbosacral spine views as well as the anterior margin of the vertebrae. Eventually, the changes may result in a "bamboo spine," so called because the bridging syndesmophytes can indeed mimic the appearance of bamboo. It is now appreciated that osteoporosis is a significant feature of AS, probably reflecting both the local chronic inflammation and the abnormal biomechanical loading of the vertebrae as the disease progresses.

The differential diagnosis includes the other SpAs, osteitis condensans ilii, diffuse idiopathic skeletal hyperostosis, synovitis-acne-pustulosis-hyperostosis-osteomyelitis (SAPHO) syndrome, and some induced hyperostotic states (vitamin A intoxication, fluorosis). New bone formation occurs in degenerative disc disease, but the bulky, horizontal appearance of osteophytes is easily distinguished

---

Table 279–3 • MODIFIED NEW YORK CRITERIA FOR ANKYLOSING SPONDYLITIS (1984)

1. Clinical criteria
   a. Low back pain and stiffness for more than 3 months, which improves with exercise but is not relieved by rest.
   b. Limitation of motion of the lumbar spine in both the sagittal and frontal planes.
   c. Limitation of chest expansion.
2. Radiologic criteria.
   Sacroiliitis: Grade ≥2 bilateral *or* Grade 3 or 4 unilateral.

Grading
1. Definite AS if the radiologic criterion is associated with at least one clinical variable.
2. Probable AS if:
   a. The three clinical criteria are present.
   b. The radiologic criterion is present without the clinical criteria.

AS = ankylosing spondylitis.

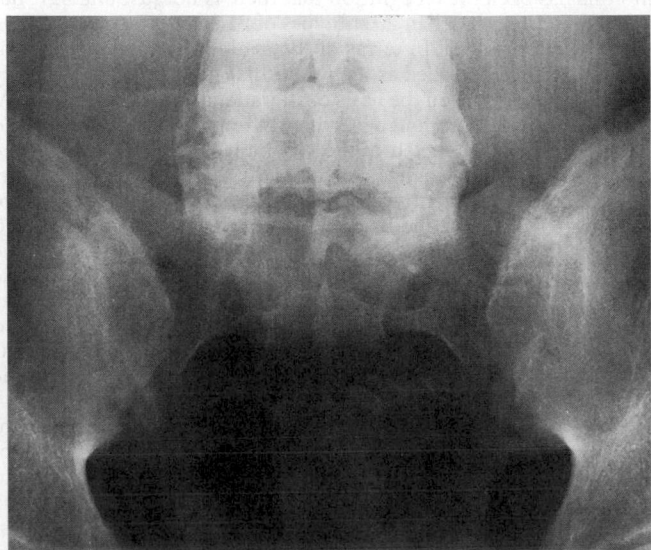

FIGURE 279–2 • Bilaterally symmetrical sacroiliitis in ankylosing spondylitis.

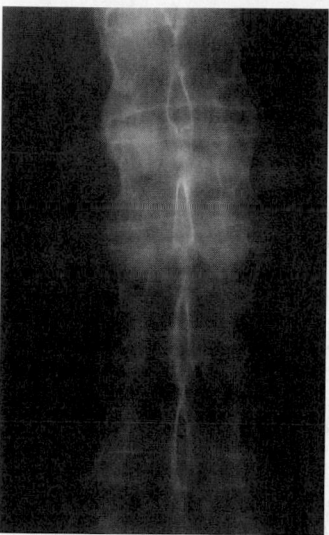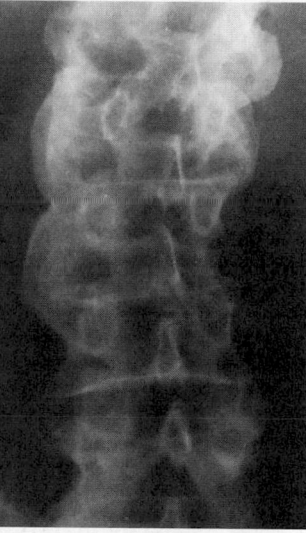

FIGURE 279–3 • *Left*, Lumbar spondylitis in ankylosing spondylitis with symmetrical, marginal bridging syndesmophytes and calcification of the spinal ligament. *Right*, The bulky, nonmarginal, asymmetrical syndesmophytes of reactive arthritis with lumbar spondylitis.

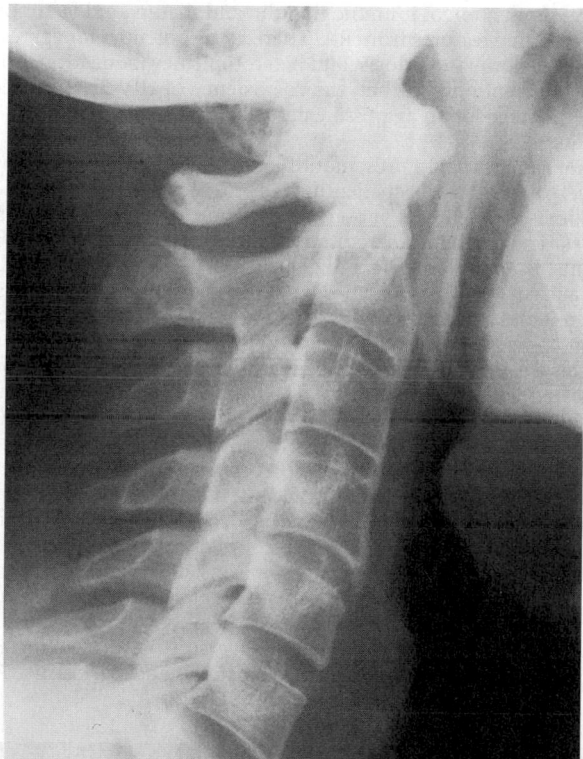

FIGURE 279–4 • A 34-year-old male who had ankylosing spondylitis for 9 years and neck pain. Radiographs demonstrate narrowing of the C2-C3 apophyseal joints posteriorly and anterior bridging marginal syndesmophytes extending from C2 to C5.

from that of syndesmophytes, and the narrowing of the disc space is not a feature of AS.

The clinical course and disease severity of AS are highly variable. Inflammatory back pain and stiffness dominate the picture in the early stages, whereas chronic pain and deformity may develop over time. It may be only a minority of patients who go on to develop the full-blown picture of a bamboo spine, but at present there are few variables that can reliably aid in prognosticating the course. In AS patients in whom new, refractory spinal pain develops, intervertebral fracture should be considered and may occur after minimal trauma.

Additional late complications may include cauda equina syndrome, osteoporotic compression fractures, spondylodiscitis, and restrictive lung disease.

Reactive Arthritis

Reactive arthritis (ReA) is an aseptic arthritis that occurs subsequent to an extra-articular infection, most typically of the gastrointestinal (GI) or genitourinary (GU) tract. In the former, the key pathogens are *Salmonella typhimurium, Yersinia enterocolitica, Shigella flexneri*, and *Campylobacter jejuni*. For the latter, *Chlamydia trachomatis* is the commonest offender. The true incidence and prevalence of ReA are not well defined. In epidemics involving *Salmonella* or *Yersinia*, it is estimated that ReA develops in 2 to 7% of infected individuals but as many as 20% of B27+ infected individuals. In such epidemic studies, B27 confers risk not only for the onset of arthritis but also for axial involvement and chronicity. The variability in determining the rate of ReA is determined by the heterogeneity of the cohorts reported. Even in the setting of an epidemic point source outbreak, the inoculum varies widely among the exposed individuals, and the genetic makeup of the population at risk (e.g., the prevalence of B27) may differ greatly between different studies. Case ascertainment, and relative risk, is even more difficult for post-*Chlamydia* ReA. Among young adults in the United States there is a high prevalence of asymptomatic *Chlamydia* carriage in the GU tract, and establishing a causal link between *Chlamydia* and synovitis can be difficult. Nevertheless, it is with *Chlamydia* that ReA has most intensively been studied. Whereas immunofluorescence studies have identified bacterial antigens in joints of patients with ReA after both GI and GU infections, it is primarily in post-*Chlamydia* ReA that polymerase chain reaction results on synovial tissues have most consistently been positive, suggesting that viable *Chlamydia* may persist in the joints of such patients, albeit in a metabolically altered state.

Typically, the arthritis has its onset 1 to 3 weeks after the GI or GU infection, but the temporal details are often difficult to define precisely.

Although the definition of aseptic arthritis following an extra-articular infection may include a broader range of pathogens (e.g., *Chlamydia pneumoniae*), sites of infection (e.g., streptococcal pharyngitis), and types of infections (e.g., *Giardia* infections of the GI tract), these clinical scenarios have generally not been included in the ReA roster. They lack the other associated clinical features of the SpA group of diseases, and they lack an association with B27.

The pattern of joint involvement in ReA is one of asymmetrical oligoarthritis with a predilection for the lower extremity, a pattern shared by most SpA syndromes. Enthesitis may arise as Achilles tendonitis or plantar fasciitis. Dactylitis, arising as a sausage digit, may also be seen. Dactylitis is the net result of inflammatory changes affecting the joint capsule, entheses, periarticular structures, and periosteal bone. Sacroiliitis may be seen in the acute phase, but radiographic changes are seen largely in the patients with a more chronic course.

When ReA is accompanied by certain extra-articular features such as urethritis, conjunctivitis, or mucocutaneous lesions, the term Reiter's syndrome may be applied, but increasingly investigators are using ReA to refer to this symptom complex. The urethritis may be manifest as dysuria or discharge and the rash as circinate balanitis. This appears as vesicles or shallow ulcerations on the glans penis. Painless lingual or oral ulcerations may also be seen. The fact that the cervicitis may be less symptomatic may account in part for the underdiagnosis of this entity in women. The classical skin manifestation is keratoderma blennorrhagicum, a painless papulosquamous eruption on the palms or soles (Fig. 279–5). Occasional nail dystrophy with pitting and onycholysis or subungual keratosis can be seen. The conjunctivitis can be bilateral and painful in contrast to the acute anterior uveitis that can also be seen in this setting, which tends to be painless and unilateral.

Radiographic findings in ReA can be seen in the involved peripheral joints, with soft tissue swelling and juxta-articular osteopenia the early findings. Areas of periostitis and new bone formation may develop in peripheral joints. When sacroiliac changes are seen they are typically asymmetrical, in contrast to the symmetrical pattern seen in AS (Fig. 279–6). In the chronic phase, syndesmophytes may develop, but they are described as bulky, nonmarginal, often asymmetrical formations that differ from the classical syndesmophytes of AS.

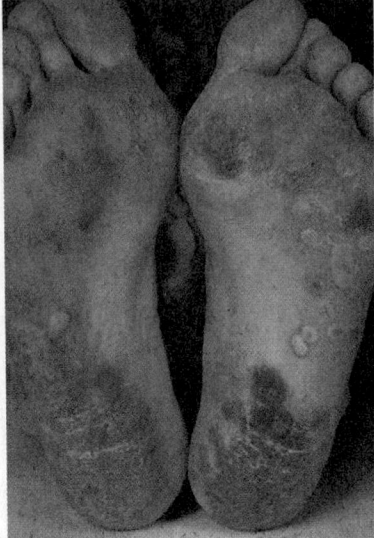

FIGURE 279–5 • Keratoderma blennorrhagicum of the feet in Reiter's syndrome.

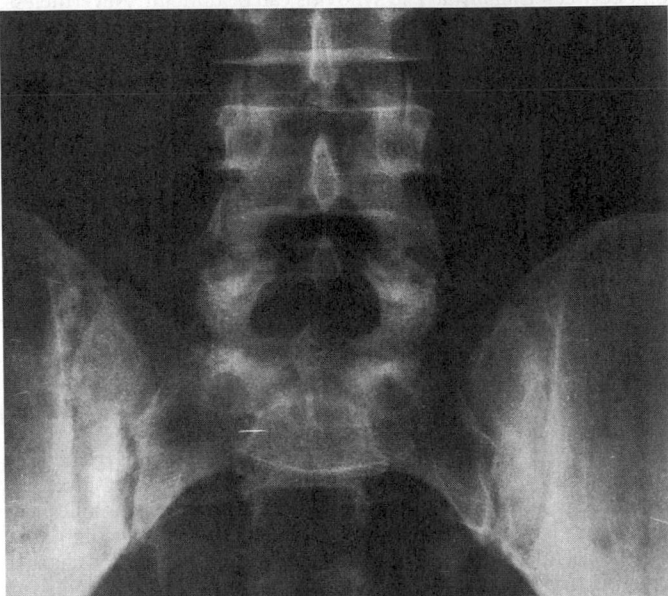

FIGURE 279–6 • Bilaterally asymmetrical sacroiliitis in Reiter's syndrome. Erosions, pseudowidening, and ileal sclerosis are present.

The most important differential diagnosis for such reactive arthropathies is septic arthritis. Both *Yersinia* and *Salmonella* can induce a septic arthritis, so an appropriate culture of synovial fluid should precede the diagnosis of ReA whenever possible. The course of ReA is variable, and few prognostic markers are available for the clinician to predict the course in any individual case. The majority of patients have an initial episode lasting 2 to 3 months, but synovitis may persist for a year or longer. In one 5-year follow-up of a point source cohort of post-*Salmonella* ReA, 20% of patients had ongoing inflammatory joint disease at this time, and some degree of functional disability was observed in 30% of patients 5 years after the onset of disease.

HUMAN IMMUNODEFICIENCY VIRUS AND REACTIVE ARTHRITIS

An aggressive form of SpA may be seen in patients who have concomitant infection with human immunodeficiency virus (HIV). It appears that there is no increased frequency of ReA or Reiter's syndrome in patients infected with HIV, but HIV may alter the course of these arthropathies, with a tendency for a more aggressive and more refractory course of joint disease. Aggressive skin and joint disease

may be seen in patients who develop psoriatic arthritis (PsA) in the setting of HIV. Most North American patients with the HIV-ReA constellation are B27 positive, but studies of comparable patients in Africa have found a sizable B27-negative component in such groups of patients. The arthritis in such patients falls into two clinical patterns: (1) an additive, asymmetrical polyarthritis or (2) an intermittent oligoarthritis that most commonly affects the lower extremities. Enthesitis, fasciitis, conjunctivitis, and urethritis can all be seen in such patients. Sacroiliitis can occur, although extensive spinal syndesmophyte formation is not common.

Psoriatic Arthritis

PsA develops in 5 to 7% of patients with psoriasis. Although most cases arise in patients with established cutaneous disease, some patients (particularly children) have arthritis that antedates the appearance of the skin lesions. Although the extent of psoriatic skin disease correlates poorly with the development of arthritis, the risk of PsA increases with a family history of SpA. The age of onset can range from 30 to 55 years, with a equal predilection for women and men. Psoriatic spondylitis has a slight male predominance.

The genetic associations with PsA are complex. Psoriasis itself is associated with HLA-B13, HLA-B16, HLA-B17, and HLA-Cw6. By contrast, HLA-B39 and HLA-B27 have been associated with sacroiliitis and axial involvement. No etiologic agent has been proved, although some investigators have proposed that the process represents a ReA in response to cutaneous bacteria. The histopathology of the synovitis of PsA is comparable to that of the other SpAs, with the absence of local production of immunoglobulin and rheumatoid factor being differentiating features from RA. There is the potential for aggressive osteolysis, fibrous ankylosis, and heterotopic new bone formation to occur. As mentioned earlier, the coexistence of HIV and PsA seems to set the stage for an aggressive course of joint destruction in some patients.

PsA has a variable presentation and disease course, but several clinical patterns have been identified in prospectively followed cohorts of patients. The clinical subsets are not mutually exclusive, nor are they static over time. The commonest form, affecting 30 to 50% of patients, is an asymmetrical oligoarthritis, which may involve both large and small joints. Dactylitis, arising as sausage digits, can be seen in fingers and toes and actually represents an enthesitis. In the second subset, there is selective targeting of the distal interphalangeal joints, and this is seen in 10 to 15% of patients. These changes are strongly associated with nail dystrophy, of which the features are onycholysis, subungual keratosis, pitting, and oil drop–like staining (Fig. 279–7). In the third subset (15 to 30% of patients) there is a symmetrical polyarthritis, mimicking RA in many ways except for the absence of rheumatoid nodules and rheumatoid factor. The fourth clinical variant is psoriatic spondylitis, occurring in 20% of patients; 50% of such patients are B27 positive. Finally, arthritis mutilans (5% of patients) is a destructive, erosive arthritis affecting large and small joints. It can be associated with marked deformities and significant disability.

Radiographic changes in PsA involve soft tissue swelling (particularly in the case of dactylitis), erosions, and periostitis. Axial

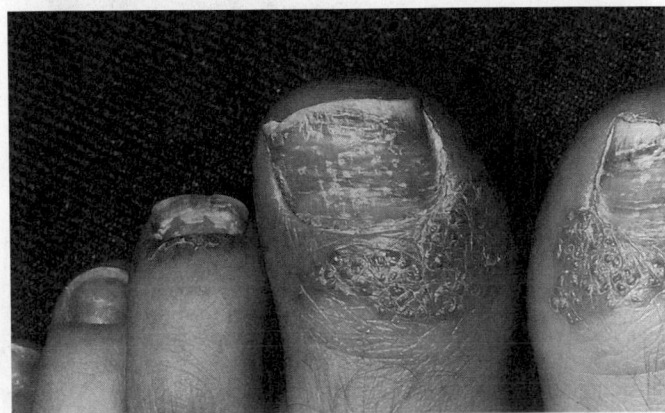

FIGURE 279–7 • Nail pitting, onycholysis, and transverse ridging in psoriatic arthritis. Dactylitis of the second toe is present.

Table 279–4 • ENTEROPATHIC ARTHRITIS

FEATURE	PERIPHERAL ARTHRITIS	SACROILIITIS, SPONDYLITIS
CROHN'S DISEASE AND ARTHRITIS		
Frequency in CD	10–20%	2–7%
HLA-B27 associated	No	Yes
Pattern	Transient, symmetrical	Chronic
Course	Related to activity of CD	Unrelated to activity of CD
Effect of surgery	Remission of arthritis uncommon	No effect
Effect of anti-TNF therapy	Effective	Effective
ULCERATIVE COLITIS AND ARTHRITIS		
Frequency in UC	5–10%	2–7%
HLA-B27 associated	No	Yes
Pattern	Transient	Chronic
Course	(More common in pancolitis than proctitis)	
	Related to activity of UC	Unrelated
Effect of surgery	Remission of arthritis	No effect

CD = Crohn's disease; HLA = human leukocyte antigen; TNF = tumor necrosis factor; UC = ulcerative colitis.

involvement may present the image of asymmetrical sacroiliitis and syndesmophytes that are bulky, asymmetrical, and nonmarginal. The classical "pencil-in-cup" deformity may be seen in patients with distal interphalangeal joint disease or arthritis mutilans. Acro-osteolysis is seen in a minority of patients and reflects an aggressive erosive process.

The diagnosis of PsA depends on finding the typical skin or nail changes in association with one of the articular variants described previously. The differential for the skin lesions can include seborrheic dermatitis, dyshidrotic eczema, fungal infection, keratodermia blennorrhagica, and palmoplantar pustulosis.

Enteropathic Arthritis

Enteropathic arthritis (EA) refers to the arthritis associated with Crohn's disease (CD) or ulcerative colitis (UC) (Table 279–4). All extraenteric manifestations, including arthritis, occur more commonly in CD than in UC. Peripheral arthritis occurs in 10 to 20% of CD patients and 2 to 7% of UC patients. This pattern of arthritis occurs more commonly in patients with other extraenteric features (e.g., erythema nodosum, iritis). This is typically an inflammatory, nonerosive polyarthritis, predominantly of large joints. In general, the peripheral arthritis activity parallels the activity of the gut inflammation, and measures that control the GI disease usually control the joint disease concomitantly. The arthritis is not associated with B27.

In contrast, the sacroiliitis or spondylitis follows a pattern in which the joint inflammation waxes and wanes independently of the bowel inflammation. The axial disease occurs in 2 to 7% of CD patients and 2 to 7% of UC patients. HLA-B27 is found in 50% of patients with the axial arthritis. The course tends to be chronic as opposed to the transient course of the peripheral arthritis.

The association of bowel inflammation and arthritis is supported by ileocolonoscopic studies, which have demonstrated subclinical inflammation of the bowel in patients covering the entire spectrum of the SpAs. Histology demonstrates that changes of acute ileitis are seen in postdysenteric ReA, whereas chronic inflammatory changes are more likely to be seen in patients with AS. As mentioned earlier, the abnormalities in the bowel of B27-transgenic rats have strong similarity to lesions of CD, and the germ-free environment minimizes inflammatory changes in both the gut and the joints. This finding has argued that altered bowel permeability, with enhanced bacteremia or antigenemia, may provide the link in both cases. It is important to recognize that the joint finding of EA may precede any GI symptoms or signs. Conversely, the diarrhea preceding the onset of peripheral or axial arthritis in a young patient could as likely represent a foodborne pathogen (such as *Salmonella* or *Yersinia*) with secondary ReA, as inflammatory bowel disease and an accompanying EA. In the initial assessment of such a patient, it is important to carry out careful and complete stool cultures. If the GI symptoms persist, it often falls to a diagnostic colonoscopy to resolve the issue.

Undifferentiated Spondyloarthropathy

Despite careful clinical and radiographic assessment, there are still a substantial number of patients who do not fall easily into one of the classical diagnostic subsets outlined previously. These patients are often defined as having undifferentiated spondyloarthropathy (USpA), presenting with peripheral enthesitis; or asymmetrical arthritis or sacroiliitis; or iritis, in the absence of identifiable antecedent infection or concurrent inflammatory bowel disease or psoriasis. The natural history of USpA has not been well defined, and case heterogeneity and diagnostic dilemmas plague a systematic or multicenter approach to the problem. When the clinical course has been examined, a number of such patients finally meet diagnostic criteria for AS, but many remain with a distinct USpA pattern for prolonged periods of time.

 Treatment

GENERAL APPROACH. The SpA group of diseases necessitate a global approach to management in which education of patients is the cornerstone. With the typical onset during young adulthood and with a male predominance, these patients may express significant frustration or depression if their acute arthritis evolves into a chronic course that may significantly impair their functional capabilities and their quality of life. The clinician managing patients with SpA should be aware that these psychosocial aspects of the disease are an important part of the burden of illness.

Exercise forms an important part of the treatment plan for patients with AS. Generally, high-impact sports should be avoided, and swimming is an ideal exercise. Stretching to maintain mobility and maintenance of posture should be emphasized, and an experienced physiotherapist can greatly assist in instructing the patient in daily exercises. Long car trips and air travel should include periodic stretching. Sleep position should emphasize a straight back position rather than one curled on the side. Deep breathing exercises and avoidance of cigarettes should be stressed.

One key area of concern for patients is prognosis because the SpAs, and particularly ReA, often occur in young, active individuals for whom athletic activity is a priority. There is general recognition that ReA has a greater propensity for chronicity than was previously appreciated, and this should temper a too optimistic projection on the natural history of the disease. At a 5-year follow-up of a cohort of patients with point source *Salmonella*-induced ReA, two thirds continued to have subjective complaints and one third demonstrated objective changes in the joints. Variability in prognosis in the large group of patients falling into the diagnostic category of USpA is perplexing for the patients in this category. At present, there is a lack of reliable predictors of progression in patients with this heterogeneous cluster of articular and extra-articular features.

NONSTEROIDAL ANTI-INFLAMMATORY DRUGS. In general, there is significant improvement in joint inflammation after the introduction of NSAIDs, the exception being salicylates, which seem less effective in control of pain and stiffness. Indomethacin and diclofenac, up to 200 mg daily in divided doses, are generally well tolerated in this population of patients. These agents have to be used with caution in EA because of concern about exacerbating the underlying inflammatory bowel disease. In the case of AS, the goal with anti-inflammatory treatment is to achieve sufficient control of pain and stiffness to allow an active, sustained program of exercise and physical activity that maintains posture in addition to improvements in quality of life.

CORTICOSTEROIDS. The response to the commonly used intra-articular steroid injection of peripheral joints in SpA patients is often

Continued

neither as dramatic nor as sustained as in patients with RA. Corticosteroid injection into the sacroiliac joints is usually performed under imaging guidance (fluoroscopy or CT). One study observed that in 24 such injections there was a good response in 79% of patients and that improvement could persist for many months. Systemic corticosteroids (either orally or by an intravenous bolus protocol) have been used for severe symptomatic flares, but controlled trials to validate effectiveness are lacking. The goal should be prompt tapering of the dose when symptomatic control is achieved. The recognition that osteoporosis is a significant problem in AS provides further impetus to use corticosteroids sparingly. Topical steroids are usually effective for treatment of the mucous membrane and skin manifestations of RS. For uveitis, topical corticosteroid eye drops are an integral component of management, and treatment should be monitored jointly with an ophthalmologist.

SULFASALAZINE. Randomized, placebo-controlled trials have provided evidence to support the role of sulfasalazine (SSZ), particularly in PsA.**1** Three 36-week, randomized, double-blind multicenter studies of patients with AS, PsA, or RS, respectively, were undertaken, comparing SSZ (2 g/day) with placebo in each case. The different response rates in the placebo arms of these trials highlight the variability in clinical course of the SpAs. An analysis of these studies with SSZ stratified the patients into those having axial or peripheral disease. Among patients with only axial disease, response criteria were met equally in the SSZ group and the placebo group. Among the patients with peripheral arthritis, responses were seen in 59% of the SSZ group and 43% of the placebo group ($P < .0005$). These findings are useful in guiding selection of patients for SSZ treatment options.

METHOTREXATE. Concurrent with the widespread use of methotrexate (MTX) in patients with RA, there has been increasing use of MTX in patients with SpA. Generally, responses have been good, particularly for peripheral joint disease, but there have been few controlled trials to substantiate these clinical impressions. There is little evidence that MTX changes the course of axial diseases in AS. Experience with long-term MTX therapy for 38 patients with PsA has been reported, and although there was an improvement in joint count, there was no evidence of slowing of radiographic progression. It may require long-term follow-up to resolve whether MTX has a joint-sparing effect in PsA.

OTHER DISEASE-MODIFYING AGENTS. There have been several therapeutic approaches to control of PsA including chloroquine, intramuscular gold, and cyclosporine, all of which show some clinical efficacy, but long-term studies are needed to evaluate them more comprehensively. The response of SpA patients to SSZ may be attributable to the antibiotic moiety of this compound (sulfapyridine) or to the anti-inflammatory moiety (5-aminosalicylic acid [5-ASA]). A study reported that of SpA patients who had been taking SSZ and

then were switched to 5-ASA, most maintained their response profile, supporting the notion that 5-ASA may be the active moiety in SSZ. A open study of intravenous pamidronate for refractory AS showed a significant improvement in disease activity scores.

ANTIBIOTIC THERAPY. The current concept of the pathogenesis of ReA postulates that a bacterial infection, usually GI or GU, is the triggering event in an immunogenetically susceptible host. For the other SpAs there is less compelling evidence to implicate infection in a causal role. It is sound clinical practice to treat any culture-proven *Chlamydia* urethritis in conjunction with treatment of the sexual partner. For this indication, azithromycin 1 g as a single dose is as effective as doxycycline 100 mg twice a day for 7 days. The role of antibiotics in the management of SpA has been controversial. An earlier retrospective review concluded that 37% of episodes of urethritis not treated with anti-*Chlamydia* agents were associated with subsequent RS, whereas only 10% of such episodes when treated with tetracycline progressed to RS. In a 3-month, double-blind, placebo-controlled study of chronic ReA, lymecycline significantly decreased the duration of illness in patients with *Chlamydia*-induced ReA but not in patients with ReA triggered by enteric pathogens. Two controlled trials of ciprofloxacin demonstrated no significant difference from placebo in ReA and undifferentiated oligoarthritis.**2** Ciprofloxacin was not effective in *Yersinia*- or *Salmonella*-induced ReA, but there was a trend toward response in *Chlamydia*-induced ReA. Definitive conclusions on the role of antibiotic treatment in *Chlamydia*-induced ReA await a controlled trial.

ANTI–TUMOR NECROSIS FACTOR THERAPY. The role of immunomodulatory cytokines in the pathogenesis of SpA has been controversial. Some studies have implicated as an AS susceptibility marker genetic polymorphism associated with a relative impairment of tumor necrosis factor α (TNF-α) production, but not all studies have supported this notion. Despite the uncertainties about the role of proinflammatory cytokines in AS, some of the newer biologic agents such as the chimeric monoclonal antibody to TNF-α (infliximab) or the soluble TNF receptor (etanercept) have been used in the treatment of SpA. In a randomized trial, use of etanercept for four months resulted in an 80% response rate compared with 30% in the placebo group, a highly significant result.**3** This and other studies have reported a prompt response in clinical outcome measures as well as laboratory indicators of inflammation, and MRI evaluations have showed improvement in local inflammation in the sacroiliac joints and spine. The treatments have been well tolerated with no serious adverse events, but patients appear to relapse when treatment is discontinued. Whether these encouraging short-term results are borne out in the long-term management of AS and whether anti-TNF treatment can alter the progressive ankylosis of this disease over time await further study.

---

1. Clegg DO, Reda DJ, Abdellatif M: Comparison of sulfasalazine and placebo for the treatment of axial and peripheral articular manifestations of the seronegative spondyloarthropathies. Arthritis Rheum 1999;42:2325–2329.
2. Sieper J, Fendler C, Laitko S, et al: No benefit of long-term ciprofloxacin treatment in patients with reactive arthritis and undifferentiated oligoarthritis. Arthritis Rheum 1999;42:1386–1396.
3. Gorman JD, Sack KE, Davis JC Jr: Treatment of ankylosing spondylitis by inhibition of tumor necrosis factor alpha. N Engl J Med 2002;346:1349–1356.

SUGGESTED READINGS

Anandarajah AP, Ritchlin CT: Etanercept in psoriatic arthritis. Expert Opin Biol Ther 2003;3:169–177. *This therapy also is effective in psoriatic arthritis.*
Brandt J, Khariouzov A, Listing J, et al: Six-month results of a double-blind, placebo-controlled trial of etanercept treatment in patients with active ankylosing spondylitis. Arthritis Rheum 2003;48:1667–1675. *Confirms benefit of etanercept but shows patients relapse when it is discontinued.*
Braun J, Sieper J, Breban M, et al: Anti TNF-α therapy for ankylosing spondylitis: International experience. Ann Rheum Dis 2002;61:51–60. *Describes anti-TNF agents, which have dramatically changed the therapeutic landscape in the spondyloarthropathies.*
Flores D, Marquez J, Garza M, et al: Reactive arthritis: Newer developments. Rheum Dis Clin North Am 2003;29:37–59. *An overview of causes and treatments.*
Stone MA, Salonen D, Lax M, et al: Clinical and imaging correlates of response to treatment with infliximab in ankylosing spondylitis. J Rheumatol 2001;28:1605–1614. *Confirmation of the effectiveness of this new therapy.*

280 SYSTEMIC LUPUS ERYTHEMATOSUS

Peter H. Schur

Systemic lupus erythematosus (SLE) is a disease of unknown cause that may produce variable combinations of fever, rash, hair loss, arthritis, pleuritis, pericarditis, nephritis, anemia, leukopenia, thrombocytopenia, and central nervous system (CNS) disease. The clinical course is characterized by periods of remissions and acute or chronic relapses. Characteristic immune abnormalities, especially antibodies to a number of nuclear and other cellular antigens, develop in patients with SLE. The diagnosis is facilitated by determining whether the patient has 4 of the 11 clinical and/or laboratory criteria developed for the classification of SLE (Table 280–1).

Epidemiology

Systemic lupus erythematosus can occur at any age but has its onset primarily between the ages of 16 and 55 years. It occurs more frequently in women. In children, the female-to-male ratio is 3 : 1; in adults, it ranges from 10 : 1 to 15 : 1; and in older individuals, the ratio

Table 280–1 • CRITERIA FOR CLASSIFICATION OF SYSTEMIC LUPUS ERYTHEMATOSUS*

CRITERION	DEFINITION
1. Malar rash	Fixed erythema, flat or raised, over the malar eminences, tending to spare the nasolabial folds
2. Discoid rash	Erythematous raised patches with adherent keratotic scaling and follicular plugging; atrophic scarring may occur in older lesions
3. Photosensitivity	Skin rash as a result of unusual reaction to sunlight, by patient history or physician observation
4. Oral ulcers	Oral or nasopharyngeal ulceration, usually painless, observed by a physician
5. Arthritis	Nonerosive arthritis involving two or more peripheral joints and characterized by tenderness, swelling, or effusion
6. Serositis	a. Pleuritis—convincing history of pleuritic pain or rub heard by a physician or evidence of pleural effusion OR b. Pericarditis—documented by electrocardiogram or rub or by evidence of pericardial effusion
7. Renal disorder	a. Persistent proteinuria >0.5 g/day or >3+ if quantitation not performed OR b. Cellular casts—may be red blood cell, hemoglobin, granular, tubular, or mixed
8. Neurologic disorder	a. Seizures—in the absence of offending drugs or known metabolic derangements, e.g., uremia, ketoacidosis, or electrolyte imbalance OR b. Psychosis in the absence of offending drugs or known metabolic derangements, e.g., uremia, ketoacidosis, or electrolyte imbalance
9. Hematologic disorder	a. Hemolytic anemia with reticulocytosis OR b. Leukopenia <4000/mm^3 total on two or more occasions c. Lymphopenia <1500/mm^3 on two or more occasions OR d. Thrombocytopenia <100,000/mm^3 in the absence of offending drugs
10. Immunologic disorder	a. Anti-DNA: antibody to native DNA in abnormal titer OR b. Anti-Sm: presence of antibody to Sm nuclear antigen OR c. Positive findings of antiphospholipid antibodies based on (1) an abnormal serum level of IgG or IgM anticardiolipin antibodies, (2) a positive test result for lupus anticoagulant with the use of a standard method, or (3) a false-positive result on serologic test for syphilis known to be positive for at least 6 mo and confirmed by *Treponema pallidum* immobilization or fluorescent treponemal antibody absorption test
11. Antinuclear antibody	An abnormal titer of antinuclear antibody by immunofluorescence or an equivalent assay at any point and in the absence of drugs known to be associated with "drug-induced lupus" syndrome

*The classification is based on 11 criteria. For the purpose of identifying patients in clinical studies, a person shall be said to have systemic lupus erythematosus if any 4 or more of the 11 criteria are present, serially or simultaneously, during any interval of observation.

is 8:1. The prevalence of SLE is estimated to be between 40 to 50 cases per 100,000 population. In the United States, the highest incidence is among Asians in Hawaii, blacks, and certain Native Americans (Sioux, Crow, Arapahoe). The risk of SLE developing in a black American female has been estimated to be 1 in 250. The prevalence is about the same worldwide; the disease appears to be common in China, in Southeast Asia, and among blacks in the Caribbean but is seen infrequently in blacks in Africa. Limited observations suggest that the incidence of discoid lupus erythematosus is the same as the incidence of SLE.

Etiology

The cause of SLE remains unknown, although many observations suggest a role for genetic, hormonal, immunologic, and environmental factors. The evidence for a genetic role is summarized in Table 280–2. Some of these genetic marker associations are found more frequently in SLE patients of different races and ethnicities. It has been calculated that at least four genes, possibly as many as 20, are involved in predisposing individuals to SLE. Each gene presumably affects some aspect of immune regulation, protein degradation, peptide transport across cell membranes, immune response, complement, the reticuloendothelial system (including phagocytosis), immunoglobulins, apoptosis, and sex hormones. Thus, combinations of dissimilar gene defects may result in distinct abnormal responses and produce separate pathologic processes and different clinical expression.

The evidence for hormonal abnormalities is based primarily on the observation that SLE is much more common among women in their childbearing years. In addition, SLE has been observed in some males with Klinefelter's syndrome, and some abnormalities of estrogen metabolism have been noted in both men and women with SLE. However, the clinical expression of SLE is similar in men and women. Furthermore, a lupus-like disease of New Zealand mice is more common and more severe and has an earlier onset in females, and it is ameliorated by oophorectomy or treatment with male hormones. In other strains of mice with a lupus-like disease, however, this gender difference is not noted.

Numerous immune system abnormalities occur in patients with SLE, the etiology of which remains unclear; nor do we know which are primary and which are secondary to the disease process. Some of these immune defects are episodic, and some correlate with disease activity. SLE is primarily a disease with abnormalities of immune system regulation. These abnormalities are thought to be secondary to a loss of "self" tolerance; that is, SLE patients (either before or during disease evolution) are no longer totally tolerant of all their "self" antigens, and consequently an immune response develops to these antigens. The number of suppressor T cells also decreases; these would normally be down-regulating (maintaining homeostasis) immune responses. Furthermore, mice with lupus and possibly humans with SLE have a (genetic) defect in apoptosis that results in abnormal programmed cell death (apoptosis). Cells break down abnormally, and certain (especially nuclear) antigens are processed by antigen-presenting cells (i.e., macrophages, B lymphocytes, dendritic cells) into peptides. The peptide-major histocompatibility complex stimulates the expansion of helper (i.e., CD4) autoreactive T cells that, through release of cytokines (i.e., interleukin-6, interleukin-4, and interleukin-10), cause autoreactive B cells to become activated, proliferate, and differentiate into antibody-producing cells and make an excess of antibodies to many nuclear antigens (Fig. 280–1).

Table 280–2 • GENETIC RISK FACTORS FOR SYSTEMIC LUPUS ERYTHEMATOSUS

High concordance rate (14–57%) in monozygotic twins
Increased frequency (5–12%) of LE, autoantibodies, suppressor cell defects in 1st-degree relatives
Increased frequency: HLA-B8, DR2, DR3, DQA1, DQB1
    C2, C4 (especially C4A), CR1 deficiency
    Certain genetic markers on IgG (Immunoglobulin G)
    Fc receptor genes
    Chromosome markers in the Iq41-q42 region
Anti-DNA associated with DR2, DR3, DR7, DQB1
Anti-Sm associated with DR4, DR7, DQw6
Anti-RNP associated with DQw5, DQw8
Anti-Ro (SS-A) associated with DR2, DR3, DQA1/DQB1, C2D
Anti-La (SS-B) associated with DR3, DQw2.3
Antiphospholipid associated with DR4, DR7, DR53, DQw7

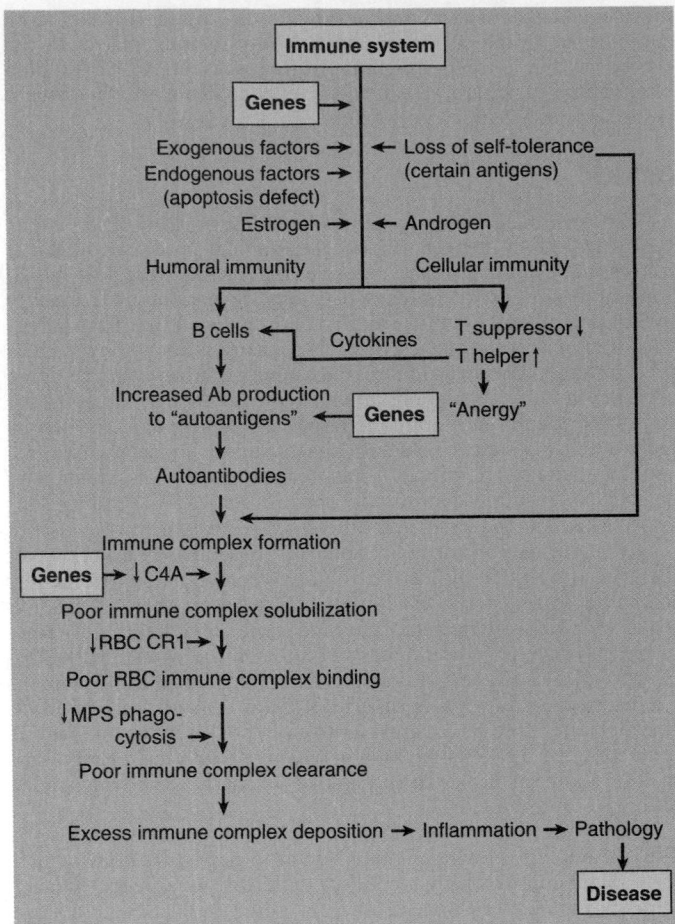

FIGURE 280–1 • Pathogenetic events in systemic lupus erythematosus.

With continued pressure over time from "self" antigens, the immune response switches from low-affinity, highly cross-reactive IgM antibodies—via somatic (hyper)mutation—to high-affinity IgG antibodies and to more limited epitopes on "self" antigens. Unique idiotypes of antibodies may stimulate autoreactive T cells to expand, thereby helping unique clones of B cells to expand and thus making more specific ANAs with unique idiotypes.

Female hormones promote B-cell hyperactivity, whereas androgens may have the opposite effect. Environmental factors such as microorganisms (i.e., viruses) may stimulate specific cells in this immune network. Furthermore, ultraviolet (UV) light—known to exacerbate lupus skin lesions—may stimulate keratinocytes to secrete more interleukin-1, which in turn stimulates B cells to make more antibody. Not all autoantibodies cause disease. In fact, all normal individuals make autoantibodies, albeit in low levels. The variability in clinical disease (different organs in specific patients) may thus reflect variability in the quality and quantity of the immune response. Although these observations suggest possible triggering factors for disease, it remains unclear what causes exacerbations—although clinically they often follow infections and other stressful events—and what causes perpetuation of the immune abnormalities with waxing and waning of the disease.

Pathogenesis

Many manifestations are mediated by antibodies. The classic example is that of diffuse proliferative glomerulonephritis. Immune complexes, which consist of nuclear antigens (especially DNA) and ANAs (especially antibodies to DNA), form in the circulation and are deposited in the glomerular basement membrane (GBM) or form in situ; histone may facilitate immune complex deposition. The complement system is then activated and chemotactic factors are generated. These factors induce the attraction and infiltration of leukocytes, which then phagocytose immune complexes and cause the release of mediators (such as activators of the clotting system), which further perpetuate the glomerular inflammation. With continuing immune complex deposition, chronic inflammation may ensue, ultimately leading to fibrinoid necrosis and scarring (crescents) and loss of renal function. In lupus membranous glomerulonephritis, similar mechanisms occur, although immune complex–containing, poorly complement-fixing IgG form primarily in situ on the GBM; there is no cellular infiltrate. The mechanism for the GBM protein leakage, which results in the nephrotic syndrome, may be secondary to injury to glomerular epithelial cells. In lupus mesangial glomerulonephritis, mesangial cells (macrophage-like cells) have phagocytosed immune complexes, thus preventing them from being deposited on the GBM.

Immune complexes have been detected (by immunofluorescence and/or electron microscopy) at the dermal-epidermal junction in both skin lesions and normal skin, in the choroid plexus, in the pericardium, and in the pleural cavity. The pathogenic potential of immune complexes depends on the antibody (its specificity, affinity, charge, and ability to activate complement or other mediators of inflammation), the nature of the antigen (size, charge), the ability of the immune complex to be solubilized by complement or bound to and cleared by red blood cells (RBCs) (both systems may be defective in SLE), the clearance ability of the mononuclear phagocytosis system, and other factors.

Patients with SLE also make antibodies to cell-surface antigens. RBCs, white blood cells (WBCs), and platelets coated with such antibodies are cleared from the circulation either through Fc receptors on macrophages of the reticuloendothelial system, by complement-mediated cytotoxicity, or by antibody-dependent cellular cytotoxicity, resulting in hemolytic anemia, leukopenia, and thrombocytopenia. Antibodies to endothelial cells have been implicated in vasculitis, and antibodies to neuronal cells have been associated with neuropsychiatric lupus. Of recent particular interest are antibodies to the phospholipid-β_2-glycoprotein I complex. These antibodies appear to interfere with the normal anticoagulant effect of β_2-glycoprotein I and are thus implicated in the arterial and venous thromboses (causing strokes and thrombophlebitis) and placental infarcts (causing miscarriages) complicating SLE.

Skin lesions are thought to be multifactorial in origin. UV light has multiple effects, including (1) damage to DNA (the patient makes antibodies to DNA, immune complexes form, complement is

Alternatively, T cells respond (abnormally) to nuclear material (over)expressed on apoptotic blebs of cells; or microorganisms may be broken down within antigen-presenting cells into "mimicry peptides" that have similar antigenic structures to self peptides. Thus, a characteristic immune profile develops in patients with SLE: the development of elevated levels of antinuclear antibodies (ANAs) especially to DNA, Sm, RNP, Ro, La, and others (Chapter 274) (Table 280–3). ANAs are made to molecules involved in essential cellular functions (e.g., RNA splicing); antigens are active sites on these molecules.

Table 280–3 • AUTOANTIBODIES IN PATIENTS WITH SYSTEMIC LUPUS ERYTHEMATOSUS

TEST	SENSITIVITY (%)	SPECIFICITY (%)	PREDICTIVE VALUE (%)
ANA	99	80	15–35
dsDNA	70	95	95
ssDNA	80	50	50
Histone	30–80	Moderate	Moderate
Nucleoprotein	58	Moderate	Moderate
SM	25	99	97
RNP (U1-RNP)	50	87–94	46–85
Ro (SS-A)	25–35		
La (SS-B)	15		
PCNA	5	95	95

Cytoplasm: mitochondria, lysosomes, microsomes, ribosomes. RNA: dsRNA, ssRNA, rRNA. Cell membranes: red blood cells, white blood (T and B) cells, platelets, brain. Other: clotting factors (antiphospholipid antibodies), thyroid, rheumatoid factors, biologic false-positive serologic test for syphilis. In SLE, anti-DNA and anti-Sm are associated with renal disease, anti-RNP with Raynaud's, and anti-Ro with photosensitivity. Anti-RNP is seen in SLE, rheumatoid arthritis, scleroderma, Sjögren's syndrome, and mixed connective tissue disease. Anti-Ro (SS-A) is seen in SLE, Sjögren's syndrome, primary photosensitivity, and primary biliary cirrhosis. Anti-La (SS-B) is seen in SLE and Sjögren's syndrome.

activated, and a local inflammatory response ensues); (2) increases in binding of anti-Ro, anti-La, and anti-RNP to UV-activated keratinocytes; (3) alterations in cellular membrane phospholipid metabolism; (4) increases in interleukin-1 release from cutaneous keratinocytes and Langerhans' cells; and (5) effects on suppressor T cells.

Pathology

Few unique pathologic features are associated with SLE. In patients with arthritis, the synovial histopathology tends to be nonspecific, with superficial fibrin-like material and local or diffuse cell lining proliferation. Vascular changes include perivascular mononuclear cells, lumen obliteration, enlarged endothelial cells, and thrombi, but fibrinoid necrosis is uncommon. Biopsies of the malar erythema may reveal some minor basal layer abnormalities as well as immune complex deposits at the dermal-epidermal junction. Discoid skin lesions are characterized by hyperkeratosis, follicular plugging, and more basal cell layer changes, including immune complexes at the dermal-epidermal junction. Pleura and pericardium are infiltrated by mononuclear cells. Lupus pneumonitis is characterized by alveolar wall injury, hemorrhage, and edema, hyaline membrane formation, and immune complex deposits. Coronary arteries often demonstrate premature-onset atherosclerosis. Libman-Sacks endocarditis is characterized by the accumulation of immune complexes, mononuclear cells, hematoxylin bodies, and fibrin and platelet thrombi. Pathologic examination of the spleen often reveals an "onion skin" appearance of the splenic arteries, which is thought to represent healed arteritis.

RENAL DISEASE. Minimal disease (type IIA mesangial disease) of glomeruli has immune complex deposits only in mesangial cells. Type IIb mesangial nephritis also has mesangial hypercellularity. Focal proliferative nephritis (type III) has segmental proliferation in glomerular tufts and in the mesangium, immune complex deposits in the mesangium, and scattered granular deposits in subendothelial, subepithelial, and intra-GBM distributions. Active diffuse proliferative glomerulonephritis (type IV) affects more than 50% of glomeruli with cellular proliferation, necrosis, "wire loops," subendothelial deposits, and hematoxylin bodies. When chronic, the process involves sclerosis, adhesions, crescents, and tubular atrophy. Extensive "lumpy and bumpy" deposits of immune complexes are present. In membranous nephritis (type V), diffuse, uniform thickening of the GBM is seen, with a fine granular deposition of immune complexes in the subendothelial region beneath fused foot processes. Tubular degenerative changes with interstitial mononuclear cells are not uncommon. Extensive crescent formation, representing scarring, indicates a poor prognosis.

The brain is notable for the paucity of pathologic changes. Some minor blood vessel abnormalities, an occasional microinfarct, and some perivascular infiltration have been noted.

Clinical Manifestations

Systemic lupus erythematosus is highly variable in onset as well as in course. The initial symptoms may be nonspecific (Table 280–4) and include myalgia, nausea, vomiting, headaches, depression, easy bruising, or more specific symptoms or any combination thereof. These symptoms may be mild or severe, fleeting or persistent.

GENERAL SYMPTOMS. Fatigue occurs in virtually all patients with SLE. Fatigue may parallel the onset of SLE or its relapse but should be distinguished from the fatigue associated with other factors, such as increased workload, sleep disturbance, depression, unhealthy habits, stress, deconditioning, anemia, the use of certain medications (including prednisone), and any intercurrent disease. Fever is seen in 80% of patients; it is usually episodic. Infections, which occur commonly in SLE patients, must always be considered.

MUSCULOSKELETAL MANIFESTATIONS. Arthralgias and arthritis have been noted in 95% of patients with SLE. Symptoms tend to be asymmetrical and migratory, with complaints in a particular joint often gone in 1 to 3 days. Fingers, hands, wrists, knees, and, less frequently, ankles, elbows, shoulders, and hips are affected. Morning stiffness is generally measured in minutes, in contrast to the hours associated

Table 280–4 • CLINICAL FEATURES IN SYSTEMIC LUPUS ERYTHEMATOSUS

MANIFESTATION	APPROXIMATE FREQUENCY (%)	
	At Onset	At Any Time
Nonspecific		
Fatigue	—	90
Fever	36	80
Weight loss	—	60
Arthralgia/myalgia	69	95
Specific		
Arthritis	—	90
Skin		
Butterfly rash	40	50
Discoid LE cells	6	20
Photosensitivity	29	58
Mucous ulcers	11	30
Alopecia	—	71
Raynaud's phenomenon	18	30
Purpura	—	15
Urticaria	—	9
Renal	16	50
Nephrosis	—	18
Gastrointestinal	—	38
Pulmonary	3	50
Pleurisy	—	45
Effusions	—	24
Pneumonia	—	29
Cardiac	—	46
Pericarditis	—	48
Murmurs	—	23
Electrocardiographic changes	—	34
Lymphadenopathy	7	50
Splenomegaly	—	20
Hepatomegaly	—	25
Central nervous system	12	75
Functional	—	Most
Psychosis	—	20
Seizures	—	20
Hematologic	—	90

with rheumatoid arthritis. Although joint deformities are considered to be more a feature of rheumatoid arthritis, damage to periarticular tissue can cause flexion deformities, ulnar deviation, soft tissue laxity, and swan neck deformities, particularly in patients with long-standing disease. Joint erosions are rare. Tenosynovitis is noted in 10 to 13% of patients. Synovial effusions are infrequent and usually small.

Avascular necrosis may occur, especially in the femoral head and less frequently in the humeral head, tibial plateau, and scaphoid navicular. Involvement is often bilateral. High prednisone dosage and prolonged use are risk factors for avascular necrosis. The first symptom of hip involvement may be groin pain. Radiographic findings may be negative or equivocal, but magnetic resonance imaging is usually diagnostic. Osteoporosis is common, especially in trabecular bones, and is worsened by corticosteroids. Muscle weakness may represent myositis (uncommon) or may be due to medications (corticosteroids, antimalarials). Myalgia is very common.

MUCOCUTANEOUS LESIONS. Photosensitivity, implying a rash after exposure to UVB light (e.g., sunlight, fluorescent light), occurs in more than 50% of patients. Some patients are also sensitive to UVA light—the clue is rash after exposure to sun filtered through glass. Fair-skinned individuals tend to be more susceptible. Photosensitivity may develop at any time or may vary in intensity during the course of SLE. The classic butterfly rash, that is, erythema over the cheeks and nose (Fig. 280–2A), develops after UV exposure in more than 50% of patients. The skin may feel warm and slightly edematous. Application of alcohol, found in many sunscreens, may cause vasodilation and thereby more erythema. The rash may last for hours or days and often recurs. A maculopapular eruption with fine scaling may ensue and last longer, although it generally heals without residue.

Discoid lesions develop in 25% of patients with SLE but may also occur in the absence of any other feature of SLE. Discoid lesions are characterized by discrete round, annular, erythematous, slightly

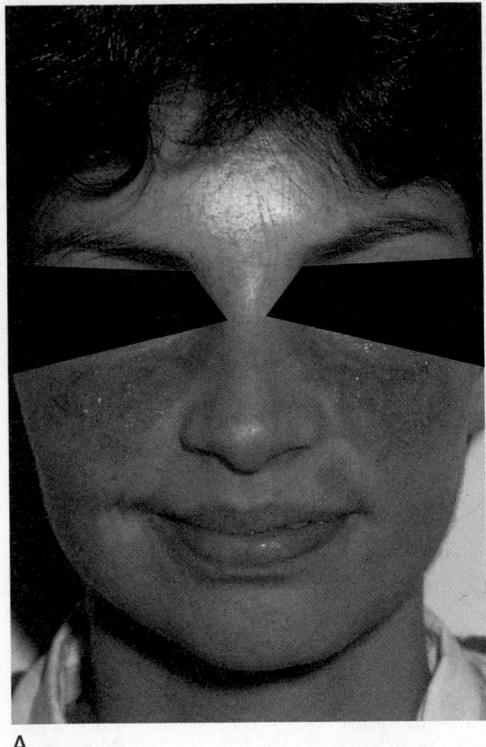

A

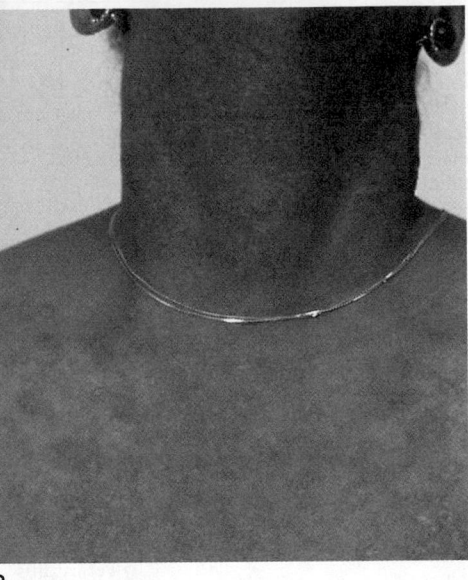

B

FIGURE 280–2 • Cutaneous manifestations of SLE. *A,* Erythematous malar rash. Note that the rash does not cross the nasolabial fold. *B,* Discoid lupus involving neck and upper chest. The lesions have characteristic central scarring. (From Gladman DD, Urowitz MB: Systemic lupus erythematosus: Clinical features. *In* Klippel JH, Dieppe PA: Rheumatology, 2nd ed. London, Mosby, 1998, with permission.)

infiltrated plaques covered by a well-formed adherent scale that extends into dilated hair follicles. Follicular plugging is prominent. Lesions slowly expand with active inflammation at the periphery, and in their wake are left depressed scars, telangiectasia, and depigmentation; central scarring with atrophy is characteristic. Lesions tend to occur on the face, scalp, neck, and ears and around the shoulders (see Fig. 280–2B). Some lesions may be hyperkeratotic and thus be confused with psoriasis. Patients with isolated discoid lupus have about a 10% chance of eventually developing SLE.

Subacute cutaneous lupus erythematosus occurs in about 10% of patients with SLE. The lesions are small, erythematous, slightly scaly papules that evolve into psoriasiform or annular forms. Lesions typically appear on the forearms and upper part of the torso; atrophy or scarring rarely develops, although telangiectasia does. A strong association is seen with HLA-DR3 and anti-Ro antibodies.

Lupus profundus/panniculitis is a rare manifestation of SLE. Typically, painful nodules develop under a skin lesion on the scalp, face, arms, chest, back, thighs, and buttocks and resolve as a depression. Ulcerations are uncommon. The presence of immune complex deposits at the dermal-epidermal junction helps distinguish these lesions from those of the Weber-Christian syndrome. Bullous lesions are rare and can be distinguished from other bullous diseases by the difference in serum antibodies and dermal immune deposits.

Hair loss, on the scalp or elsewhere, occurs in 71% of SLE patients. The most common is premature hair loss (telogen effluvium) characterized by a diffuse thinning of the scalp. Such hair loss may follow a flare of SLE, stress, pregnancy, or the use of steroids; the hair generally grows back. Some patients have "lupus hair," hair that easily fractures and is thin and unruly. Discoid lesions of the scalp usually result in permanent hair loss.

Mucous membranes are frequently affected. Discoid lesions may appear on the lip. The soft or hard palate may be involved by discoid plaques, by areas of erythema, and especially by painless ulcers. These lesions should be distinguished by biopsy from lichen planus, candidiasis, aphthous stomatitis, bites, leukoplakia, and malignancy. Nasal ulcers have been noted in 20% of patients.

VASCULAR LESIONS. Livedo reticularis, secondary to spasm of the dermal ascending arterioles, is often seen on the forearms, legs, and even the torso. Occlusion may result in ulcers. A strong association is seen with Raynaud's phenomenon and with antiphospholipid antibodies. Telangiectasias are found commonly on the face and trunk. They represent dilated blood vessels and *not* an active inflammatory lesion. Telangiectasias appear more prominent when the patient blushes, is in a hot environment (shower), or takes a vasodilator (e.g., alcohol, calcium channel blocker). Telangiectasias may also be associated with solar damage, aging, hypertension, diabetes, and other rheumatic diseases.

Raynaud's phenomenon occurs in 17 to 30% of patients. It is characterized by blanching of the nail beds, fingers, toes, and occasionally the ears, nose, and tongue. The vasospasm of small to medium-sized arteries may be induced by cold, cigarette smoke, caffeine, decongestants, stress, and other factors. After ischemia, there may be bluing and graying followed by vasodilation with warming and reddening. Gangrene is rare.

Vasculitis of post-capillary venules with neutrophil or lymphocyte accumulation develops in 20% of patients and is manifested as urticaria or purpura. When small arteries are affected, microinfarcts of the fingertips, toes, nail cuticles, forearms, or ankles may develop; the lesions about the ankle may ulcerate. The blood vessels typically have fibrinoid necrosis, thrombosis, and a variable cellular infiltrate. Patients with vasculitis have low serum levels of complement and high serum immune complex levels and may have antiphospholipid antibodies.

Other less common vascular lesions seen in SLE include Janeway's spots on the palms, Osler's nodes on the fingertips, atrophie blanche lesions, and chilblain lupus (pernio) on the fingers and toes.

PULMONARY MANIFESTATIONS. Pulmonary involvement occurs in most patients with SLE and is manifested as pleurisy, cough, dyspnea, abnormal pulmonary function tests, or chest radiographic abnormalities. Pleurisy occurs in more than 50% of patients; the most common cause is chest wall pain on local pressure and/or movement. Pleuritis (inflammation of the pleura) also causes pleurisy. It is diagnosed by the presence of a pleural friction rub and/or the radiographic presence of a pleural effusion. Effusions typically have low complement and protein levels, few WBCs (the pleura has mononuclear cells), glucose levels approximating plasma levels (by contrast, they are low in rheumatoid arthritis), and lupus erythematosus (LE) cells. Cough usually represents an infection, but pulmonary edema secondary to cardiac or renal failure or fluid overload in a patient receiving corticosteroids should be considered.

Acute lupus pneumonitis occurs in 5 to 12% of SLE patients and is characterized by fever, cough (even hemoptysis), pleurisy, and dyspnea. Radiography shows diffuse acinar infiltrates, especially in the lower lobes. Subsequently, interstitial infiltrates and fibrosis may develop, with pulmonary function abnormalities. The prognosis is poor.

Pulmonary hypertension may complicate SLE but is more frequent with scleroderma or mixed connective tissue disease. Raynaud's phenomenon is common. Late findings include dyspnea, hypoxemia, restrictive lung disease, and reduced CO_2 diffusing capacity.

The shrinking or vanishing lung syndrome has been described in some patients. It is believed to result from weakening and elevation of the diaphragm (lung fields are radiographically clear).

CARDIOVASCULAR MANIFESTATIONS. Pericardial effusion is observed by echocardiography in most patients with SLE, and clinical pericarditis, manifested as substernal chest pain, a pericardial rub, and electrocardiographic changes, has been noted in up to 18% of patients. Tamponade and restrictive pericarditis are rare. The pericardial fluid has characteristics similar to those of SLE pleural fluids.

Myocarditis, characterized by resting tachycardia, arrhythmias, electrocardiographic nonspecific ST-T wave abnormalities, and unexplained cardiomegaly with congestive heart failure, has been noted in 8 to 78% of large series.

Coronary artery disease is being recognized increasingly in SLE, particularly in patients with long-standing disease, especially those receiving chronic corticosteroids. As a result, a greater number of younger patients with angina, myocardial infarctions, and congestive heart failure are being seen. The cause of the premature atherosclerosis remains unclear, but steroid-induced lipid abnormalities, immune complex deposition along blood vessels, and hypertension may all play a role. Hypertension is common, especially with flares of nephritis, chronic renal disease, and steroid use.

Valvular disease has been noted in up to 25% of patients; most common is mitral valve prolapse. Murmurs are even more common and may represent valvular disease or may be due to anemia, fever, and/or cardiomegaly. Echocardiography is very useful to detect Libman-Sacks verrucous endocarditis. Verrucae are typically near the edge of the valve. Bacterial endocarditis may develop on damaged valves.

Thrombophlebitis occurs in more than 10% of patients with SLE. It most commonly affects the lower part of the leg and is often associated with antiphospholipid antibodies and the use of oral contraceptives. The renal veins and inferior vena cava are rarely involved, but when involved may cause nephrotic syndrome; pulmonary embolisms are uncommon.

HEMATOLOGIC CONSIDERATIONS. Abnormalities of the formed elements of blood and the clotting and fibrinolytic systems are common in SLE. Anemia occurs in at least 50% of patients. The most common cause is chronic disease; RBCs are normochromic and normocytic, the reticulocyte count is low, and iron stores are adequate. Anemia may reflect chronic gastrointestinal blood loss secondary to the use of nonsteroidal anti-inflammatory drugs (NSAIDs) and/or steroids or secondary to excessive menstrual bleeding. Hemolytic anemia frequently occurs, and the reticulocyte count and lactate dehydrogenase level are elevated, haptoglobin levels are low, and the Coombs' test is positive. A positive Coombs' test with both immunoglobulin and complement on RBCs is associated with hemolysis, whereas a positive complement Coombs' test with no other findings rarely accompanies hemolysis. Antibodies are usually anti-Rh and are "warm." Medications, especially immunosuppressive drugs, may induce anemia; in such a case, reticulocyte counts are low and haptoglobin levels normal.

Leukopenia with a WBC count less than 4500 has been noted in more than 50% of patients with SLE, whereas counts less than 4000 occur in only 17%. Granulocytes are affected more than lymphocytes. Leukopenia usually results from immune mechanisms (i.e., antineutrophil antibodies, immune complexes) or medications. Lymphocytopenia (which may be due to complement-fixing IgM or cold-reactive antibodies) may occur during active disease. Leukocytosis, or an excess of neutrophils, generally reflects infection or steroid use. An increase in activated T cells and a decrease in natural killer cells are noted, especially during active disease.

Thrombocytopenia with platelet counts less than 150,000 per cubic millimeter has been noted in more than 50% of patients, whereas counts less than 50,000 have been noted in only 10%. Thrombocytopenia may reflect myeloproliferative diseases, ineffective thrombopoiesis (e.g., megaloblastic anemia), abnormal platelet distribution (e.g., splenomegaly), and abnormal immune mechanisms (antiplatelet antibodies, disseminated intravascular coagulation, and idiopathic thrombocytopenic purpura [ITP]). ITP may be the first manifestation of SLE. Most patients with both hemolytic anemia and ITP (Evans' syndrome) have SLE. In SLE-associated ITP, platelets are sensitized by IgG antibodies, which then bind to (splenic) macrophage Fc receptors with resulting phagocytosis. Thrombocytopenia ensues when production fails to keep up with accelerated destruction. Platelet counts less than 50,000 may rarely cause symptomatic bleeding, whereas counts less than 20,000 per cubic millimeter may cause petechiae, purpura, nosebleeds, and gum bleeding.

Lymphadenopathy occurs in 50% of patients with SLE, especially during active disease. Nodes are typically small, soft, nontender, and discrete in the neck, axillary, and inguinal areas. Biopsies may reveal follicular hyperplasia. Infection and malignancy should always be considered. When in doubt, a biopsy should be done.

Splenomegaly occurs in 10 to 20% of patients, especially during active disease and in association with lymphadenopathy. Splenomegaly does not necessarily cause hemolytic anemia but is usually associated with leukopenia. A slight increase in lymphoproliferative malignancies is observed in patients with SLE.

Antibodies to many clotting factors have been described in patients with SLE, including factors VIII, IX, XI, XII, and XIII. These antibodies may induce bleeding. Antiphospholipid antibodies are found in about 25% of patients with SLE (Chapter 187). They should be suspected when the patient has a prolonged partial thromboplastin time, arterial and venous thromboses, thrombocytopenia, false-positive results to tests for syphilis, or recurrent midtrimester miscarriages. Weaker associations have been noted with livedo reticularis, renal disease, pulmonary hypertension, and cardiac valvular disease. Antiphospholipid antibodies can be present in individuals who do not have SLE. Antiphospholipid antibodies can be detected as a lupus anticoagulant, as anticardiolipin antibodies, and as antibodies to β_2-glycoprotein I, prothrombin, and other phospholipid cofactors. Clinical risks increase with higher titers.

False-positive results of tests for syphilis have been noted in 25% of SLE patients and in fact may precede SLE by years. The "false" nature is confirmed when a *Treponema pallidum* immobilization test or fluorescent treponemal antibody absorption test finding is negative. There is no rationale for performing tests for syphilis in patients with SLE unless syphilis is suspected.

The erythrocyte sedimentation rate is elevated in most patients with SLE and is thought by some observers to correlate with clinical disease activity (Chapter 282).

RENAL MANIFESTATIONS. Clinical lupus nephritis is observed in about 50% of SLE patients and is characterized by either urinary or functional (e.g., clearance) abnormalities. Also, many more patients have electron microscopic and/or immunofluorescence evidence of immune complex deposits in the glomeruli (Fig. 280–3), even in the absence of light microscopic abnormalities. The presence of clinical lupus nephritis is of concern because of its potential for increased morbidity and mortality.

Minimal or mesangial nephritis (type II) develops in about 10 to 20% of patients. Patients may have some urinary abnormalities, the glomerular filtration rate is usually normal, complement levels may

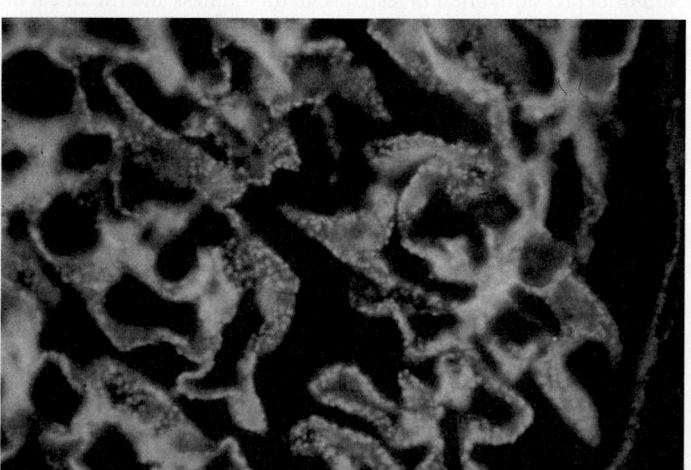

FIGURE 280–3 • Immunofluorescence shows immune complex deposits in a capillary distribution. (From Gladman DD, Urowitz MB: Systemic lupus erythematosus: Clinical features. *In* Klippel JH, Dieppe PA: Rheumatology, 2nd ed. London, Mosby, 1998, with permission.)

be somewhat depressed, and anti-DNA antibodies may be somewhat elevated. The prognosis is very good. Focal proliferative nephritis (type III) develops in 10 to 20% of patients; the clinical picture is similar to that of mesangial (type IIB) disease but is somewhat more severe. The prognosis is good.

Diffuse proliferative glomerulonephritis (type IV) occurs in more than 50% of patients. Active urinary sediment is noted, proteinuria may be marked, glomerular clearance is diminished, complement levels are significantly diminished, anti-DNA antibody and immune complex levels are elevated (especially during active nephritis), and patients are usually hypertensive. Initial creatinine levels greater than 1.2 mg/dL indicates a poor prognosis with regard to long-term renal function.

Membranous glomerulonephritis (type V) occurs in about 10 to 20% of patients. Proteinuria is marked, with little urinary sediment; complement, anti-DNA antibody, and immune complex levels are normal; glomerular filtration is normal; lipid levels are elevated; and hypertension is a late event. Mild proteinuria has a good prognosis, but nephrotic syndrome with persistent edema and high lipid levels has a poor prognosis.

Biopsies are useful in patients with clinical nephritis to determine the pathologic type of nephritis, to detect whether active inflammation (which has the potential for reversal) is present versus fibrosis and sclerosis, and to distinguish lupus nephritis from other forms of renal disease.

Urinary tract infections are common. Azotemia (slight) may result from use of NSAIDs.

GASTROINTESTINAL MANIFESTATIONS. The gastrointestinal tract may be involved in 25 to 40% of patients with SLE. Up to 25% of patients have esophageal complaints, including difficulty swallowing. The lack of radiographic abnormalities suggests stress as a cause, whereas if radiographic abnormalities are present in the esophagus, scleroderma-overlap syndrome should be considered. In addition, dysphagia may result from hiatal hernia and gastric reflux. Dyspepsia is common, especially with stress and with NSAID and steroid use. Abdominal pain, nausea, and vomiting are also common. In the absence of peptic ulcers and adverse medication effects, a cause is rarely determined. On the other hand, one should always consider mesenteric vasculitis, which is characterized by intermittent lower abdominal pain eventually progressing to an acute abdomen. The diagnosis is usually confirmed by angiography. Pancreatitis (up to 8% of patients) should also be considered in the presence of upper abdominal pain, nausea, and vomiting. Pancreatitis may reflect vasculitis. Hepatomegaly is uncommon, but liver chemistry abnormalities (lactate dehydrogenase, serum glutamate pyruvate transferase) are common, especially in patients with active disease or those taking NSAIDs. Persistent liver chemistry abnormalities may suggest cirrhosis; chronic, active, or persistent hepatitis; granulomatous hepatitis; cholestasis; infection (e.g., hepatitis); or drug toxicity and may warrant a liver biopsy.

NEUROPSYCHIATRIC MANIFESTATIONS. These symptoms occur in virtually all patients with SLE (Table 280–5). Many patients manifest anxiety and/or depression, often in response to their illness and the threat of loss of health, family, and job, disfigurement, disability, dependency, and death. Symptoms may include psychosomatic complaints such as insomnia, anorexia, constipation, myalgia, arthralgia, fatigue, palpitations, diarrhea, dizzy spells, hyperventilation, memory loss, emotional lability, confusion, decreased concentration, headaches, and cognitive defects. These psychological responses to illness should be differentiated from organic brain disease, which may cause the same symptoms. Most useful in discriminating functional from organic disease are tests of cognitive function and psychological status (e.g., the Minnesota Multiphasic Personality Inventory); other tests such as magnetic resonance imaging, electroencephalography with evoked potentials, and antiribosomal P-protein antibody determinations may also be useful. Cerebrospinal fluid analysis is most useful to exclude infection, although some physicians note a correlation of elevated levels of interleukin-6, total proteins, and antineuronal antibodies with CNS disease activity.

Psychosis is said to occur in about 24% of patients with SLE. Psychosis can also be caused by renal failure (uremic encephalopathy), hypertension (with multiple cerebral infarcts), metabolic abnormalities, infection, or drugs (tranquilizers, antidepressants, narcotics, β-blockers, NSAIDs, cimetidine, antimalarials, alcohol, caffeine, benzodiazepine, and others). Steroids may cause or help clear a psychosis; clearing of a psychosis after steroid therapy suggests that the

Table 280–5 • NEUROPSYCHIATRIC MANIFESTATIONS—DIAGNOSTIC MANEUVERS

FUNCTIONAL ETIOLOGY	FUNCTIONAL OR ORGANIC	ORGANIC ETIOLOGY
CENTRAL NERVOUS SYSTEM		
Depression	Psychosis	Aseptic meningitis
Hypomania/mania	Cognitive defects	Cerebrovascular disease
Anxiety	Dysesthesia	Demyelinating syndromes
Conversion reaction	Headache	Headache, including migraine and benign intracranial hypertension
Affective disorder		Movement disorder (chorea)
Mood swings		Myelopathy
Adjustment disorder		Seizure disorders
Psychiatric testing	Electroencephalography-evoked potentials	Acute confusion state
	Computed tomography	Anxiety disorder
	Brain scan	Cognitive dysfunction
		Mood disorder
		Psychosis
PERIPHERAL NERVOUS SYSTEM		
		Acute inflammatory demyelinating polyradiculopathy (Guillain-Barre syndrome)
		Autonomic disorder
		Mononeuropathy, single/multiplex
		Myasthenia gravis
		Neuropathy, cranial
		Plexopathy
		Polyneuropathy

psychosis had an organic cause. Medications may cause other problems: aseptic meningitis from azathioprine, ibuprofen, and other NSAIDs and, rarely, headaches, hallucinations, mental confusion, psychosis, seizures, and neuromyopathy from antimalarial drugs.

Headaches are a frequent complaint and are usually due to stress and tension; migraine has been noted in 10 to 37% of patients. Other causes of headache include ingesting cold food, nitrites, or monosodium glutamate; hangover; hunger; sinusitis; dental or eye disease; and malignancies.

Seizures are said to occur in 15 to 20% of patients with SLE and include grand mal, petit mal, temporal lobe, focal, and jacksonian seizures. Seizures may reflect an old scar or an acute inflammatory episode or may be due to metabolic imbalances, uremia, hypertension, infections, tumors, head trauma, or vasculopathy. When associated with other aspects of a lupus exacerbation, a CNS cause should be suspected. CNS vasculitis is rare.

Cranial or peripheral neuropathies develop in 10 to 15% of patients. They usually occur coincident with lupus exacerbation. Cranial neuropathies include those affecting eye muscles, trigeminal neuralgia, facial weakness, and vertigo. Peripheral neuropathy is usually asymmetrical and mild and affects more than one nerve (mononeuritis multiplex).

Stroke has been noted in up to 15% of patients secondary to hemorrhage or thrombosis, antiphospholipid antibodies, hypertension, and thrombocytopenia. Less common are movement disorders (e.g., ataxia, choreoathetosis, hemiballismus) and transverse myelitis. Meningitis is not uncommon and may be due to either infection or medication.

The eye is frequently involved by rash involving the eyelid, conjunctivitis, or keratoconjunctivitis. A characteristic finding on fundoscopic examination is retinal "cotton wool" exudates (cytoid bodies), usually near the disk. They reflect a microangiopathy of retinal capillaries and localized microinfarction of the superficial nerve fiber layers of the retina. Whereas old textbooks cited a frequency of 10 to 25%, cotton wool exudates are now seen only rarely.

MENSES AND PREGNANCY. Some patients think that their SLE flares with menses. Some patients have heavy menses, which may reflect the presence of antiphospholipid antibodies, the use of NSAIDs or steroids, or hormonal abnormalities. Lupus may become less active after menopause.

Approximately 25 to 30% of pregnancies in patients with SLE result in miscarriage; overall fetal loss approaches 35%, and patients are more likely to have a premature delivery. Increased fetal mortality is more likely (three times) to occur in the presence of major organ involvement, especially renal disease. Antiphospholipid antibodies predispose to recurrent midtrimester fetal loss. Preeclampsia is a frequent complication and is difficult to distinguish from a lupus flare.

Neonatal lupus is a rare condition characterized by typical skin lesions shortly after exposure to UV light in a nursery. The rash generally clears within months; SLE rarely develops later in life. Sera from the infants (and their mothers) have antibodies to Ro and La. The risk of neonatal lupus developing is about 1 to 5% in infants of mothers with anti-Ro antibodies. If the mothers have other specific antibodies, hemolytic anemia or thrombocytopenia may ensue. Congenital heart block is very rare but is associated with anti-Ro and anti-La antibodies, and with HLA-DR3 in the mother.

DRUG-INDUCED LUPUS. Some medications such as sulfonamides, penicillin, and oral contraceptives may exacerbate lupus. Hydralazine and procainamide can induce a lupus-like disease, especially in patients who are slow acetylators and/or are HLA-DR4 positive. Minocycline also appears to cause a lupus-like syndrome, especially in young women treated for acne. Other medications may possibly induce lupus or just ANAs, but the evidence is less convincing (Table 280–6). The symptoms and serology of drug-induced lupus are quite similar to those of SLE, with notable differences (Table 280–7). Furthermore, drug-induced lupus tends to be mild, is not life threatening, and is reversible. ANAs develop in 50 to 100% of patients taking procainamide, whereas lupus develops in only 25% of those with ANAs. Therefore, a positive finding on an ANA test does not preclude continued use of these medications. The mechanism for drug-induced lupus is unknown.

Differential Diagnosis

Systemic lupus erythematosus usually begins with the nonspecific or specific symptoms and signs listed in Table 280–4 but can also first manifest with easy bruising, splenomegaly, peripheral neuritis, myoendocarditis and endocarditis, interstitial pneumonitis,

Table 280–6 • LUPUS-INDUCING DRUGS

DEFINITE	POSSIBLE	UNLIKELY
Hydralazine	Phenytoin	Griseofulvin
Procainamide	Penicillamine	Phenylbutazone
Minocycline	Isoniazid	Oral contraceptives
	Chlorpromazine	Gold salts
	α-Methyldopa	Penicillins
	Quinidine	Hydrazine
	Sulfonamides	L-Canavanine
	Propylthiouracil	Aminosalicylic acid
	Practolol	Streptomycin
	Acebutolol	Other tetracyclines
	Lithium carbonate	Methylthiouracil
	p-Aminosalicylate	Oxyphenisatin
	Nitrofurantoin	Tolazamide
	Tartrazine	Methysergide
	Atenolol	Reserpine
	Metoprolol	Isoquinazepan
	Oxprenolol	
	Mephenytoin	
	Primidone	
	Trimethadione	
	Ethosuximide	
	Methimazole	
	Captopril	
	Chlorthalidone	
	Carbamazepine	
	Phenylethylacetylurea	

Table 280–7 • CLINICAL AND LABORATORY FEATURES OF DRUG-INDUCED LUPUS

CLINICAL FEATURES	SPONTANEOUS SLE (%)	DRUG-INDUCED LUPUS (%)
Age	20–40	50
Sex (F:M)	9	1
Race	All	"No blacks"
Acetylation type	Slow-fast	Slow
Onset of symptoms	Gradual	Abrupt
Constitutional-symptoms (fever, malaise, myalgia)	90	50
Arthritis/arthralgia	95	95
Pleuropericarditis	50	50
Skin rash	74	10–20
Renal disease	50	5
Central nervous system disease	75	0
Hematologic disease	Common	Unusual
Immune abnormalities		
ANA	95	95
LE cells	90	90
Anti-dsDNA	80	Rare
Anti-ssDNA	80	Common
Anti-histone	25	90
Anti-Sm	20–30	Rare
Anti-RNP	40–50	Rare
Complement	Reduced	Normal
Immune complexes	Elevated	Normal

ANA = antinuclear antibody; SLE = systemic lupus erythematosus.

Table 280–8 • DISORDERS RESEMBLING SYSTEMIC LUPUS ERYTHEMATOSUS

COMMON	LESS COMMON
Drug-induced lupus	Polymyositis/dermatomyositis
Scleroderma	Rheumatic fever
Wegener's granulomatosis	Sarcoidosis
Cutaneous (discoid) lupus	Relapsing polychondritis
Rheumatoid arthritis	Weber-Christian disease
Chronic active hepatitis (lupoid hepatitis)	Mixed cryoglobulinemia
Vasculitis	Whipple's disease
Felty's syndrome	Familial Mediterranean fever
Juvenile (rheumatoid) arthritis	
Sjögren's syndrome	
Mixed connective tissue disease	
Fibromyalgia chronic fatigue syndrome	

aseptic meningitis, or a positive Coombs' test result. The presence of anemia (71%), leukopenia (56%), thrombocytopenia (11%), proteinuria, hematuria, pyuria, azotemia, hypergammaglobulinemia, immune complexes, cryoglobulins, antiphospholipid antibodies, and the Biologic False-Positive Serologic Test for Syphilis should also make one suspect SLE. On first examination, patients are often thought to have other connective tissue, rheumatic, or immune disorders (Table 280–8). Children tend to have more renal disease; patients who are older at disease onset have less rash, arthritis, and renal disease but more keratoconjunctivitis sicca (Sjögren's syndrome); and males tend to have more serositis and less arthritis.

Most physicians use the American Rheumatism Association criteria for the classification of SLE (see Table 280–1) to help make a diagnosis—it should be noted that these criteria were developed for the *classification* of SLE, not for individual diagnosis. The sensitivity and specificity of these criteria are approximately 96% when compared with other rheumatic syndromes when patients have four of these criteria; however, their predictive value is less. Patients with three criteria can be said to have "probable" SLE, and in those with two criteria, "possible" SLE.

Table 280–9 • CONDITIONS ASSOCIATED WITH ANTINUCLEAR ANTIBODIES

Lupus erythematosus
Sjögren's syndrome
Rheumatoid arthritis
Juvenile arthritis
Leprosy
Infectious mononucleosis
Scleroderma
Liver disease
Primary pulmonary fibrosis
Vasculitis
Dermatomyositis/polymyositis
Mixed connective tissue disease
Mixed cryoglobulinemia
Aging
Medications

The ANA test is a useful screening test for SLE. If the test result is negative, the patient has a 0.14% probability of having SLE. A positive test result has a 15 to 35% predictive value for SLE (see Table 280–3). Table 280–9 gives a list of other diseases associated with a positive ANA test result. Low titers (i.e., 1/40 to 1/80) have less predictive value. If the ANA test result is positive, it is useful to test for antibodies to double-stranded DNA and the Sm, RNP, Ro (SS-A), and La (SS-B) nuclear RNA proteins. Their sensitivity, specificity, and predictive value for SLE (as well as for some other specific ANAs) are detailed in Table 280–3.

Determining serum complement levels is also often helpful, both diagnostically and to assess lupus disease activity. Serum complement levels are rarely depressed in other rheumatic diseases. Decreases in levels of CH50 (total hemolytic complement), C4, and C3 tend to parallel or even precede activity, especially renal disease.

Rx Treatment

Treatment must be individualized for each patient. Not all patients require steroids, as this medication has the potential of doing more harm than good. The goals for each therapy and the potential of each for benefit and risk should be considered carefully. The goal is to improve and/or maintain organ function and prevent permanent organ injury. The threat of a chronic disease can be very stressful for the patient, as can visiting a physician frequently and having many laboratory tests—and waiting for the results. Thus, emotional support is essential, as well as counseling and the provision of written (and other) material. Patients should be assured that SLE is mild in most patients, that it is rarely life threatening, and that serious organ involvement can usually be prevented or treated. Support by family, friends, and organizations such as the Lupus Foundation and the Arthritis Foundation is often helpful.

It is important to determine whether the symptoms and signs are due to SLE or to another disease (Table 280–10). For instance, fever is more likely to be due to an infection and fatigue due to a lack of sleep. Low serum complement levels and/or high anti-DNA antibody levels suggest the presence of active SLE.

Preventive measures are useful. Patients with SLE should avoid using sulfonamides, penicillin, and high-estrogen birth control pills, which may exacerbate the lupus. Exercise has been demonstrated to ameliorate the fatigue associated with SLE. Patients should be questioned regarding their degree of photosensitivity; not all patients have photosensitivity, and the degree may vary, including variation over time. Photosensitive patients should use sunscreens daily with an SPF of at least 30. For those who are very photosensitive, sunscreen should be used twice daily. Photosensitizing medications (e.g., tetracyclines, psoralens) should be avoided. Immunization with flu and pneumococcal vaccines is advisable.

In treating SLE, one should consider which organ is involved and to what degree ("severity"). Table 280–11 provides an outline of therapy based on organ involvement; treatment starts conservatively and if the response is inadequate, becomes more aggressive.

Treatment of lupus nephritis (Table 280–12) should be based on whether the disease is considered active, the type of nephritis (see earlier), and the severity. The goal of treatment should be to improve, maintain, and prevent deterioration in renal function. For mesangial or focal glomerulonephritis, bed rest or a short course of prednisone (30 mg/day) usually suffices to clear the urinary and serologic abnormalities. For diffuse proliferative glomerulonephritis, more vigorous treatment is usually necessary. Patients are generally treated with 1 mg/kg of prednisone. If azotemia is present (especially if the creatinine level is greater than 1.2 mg/dL), an immunosuppressive drug should be added, either azathioprine in doses of 50 to 200 mg/day (a dose to achieve slight leukopenia) or cyclophosphamide. Pulse cyclophosphamide with or without pulse prednisone is more effective than pulse prednisone alone for proliferative glomerulonephritis. Pulse steroids (1 g of IV methylprednisolone per day for one to three doses) may be useful acutely until the immunosuppressive drug starts working (which may be 7 to 10 days). Cyclophosphamide given intravenously (in the morning) once

monthly (for 6 months) and then every 3 months (for eight doses) appears to be as effective and less toxic than the same drug given by mouth. The risks of this therapy (malignancy, infections, hair loss, infertility) should be discussed with patients. The initial dose is 0.85 g/1.7 m² body surface area. The WBC count is determined 7 to 10 days later, and the next dose is adjusted (to a maximum of 2 g/1.7 m²) to achieve a WBC count of about 4000. Another option is to treat with azathioprine or mycophenolate maleate (2000 mg/day) after 6 months of intravenous cyclophosphamide. Acute membranous glomerulonephritis usually responds to high doses of oral prednisone (1 mg/kg of prednisone per day) or to pulse steroids. If there is no response to steroids, a trial of an immunosuppressive drug should be instituted. Hypertension should be treated vigorously; angiotensin-converting enzyme inhibitors appear to help proteinuria. Diuretics are useful to control edema and hypertension. There is no evidence that plasmapheresis benefits the management of lupus nephritis. For active renal disease, patients should be monitored frequently with urinalysis, serum creatinine determination, and immune function tests (complement, anti-DNA). When the disease becomes inactive, monitoring can be less frequent, depending on the degree of residual damage; patients with nephrotic-range proteinuria or those with azotemia need to be monitored more closely.

Acute lupus psychosis should be treated aggressively and quickly in the hope of reversing the process, which usually means high doses of prednisone (1 to 2 mg/kg), as well as antipsychotics. Once the psychosis has cleared, the dosage of steroids should be tapered rapidly because patients are at high risk for infection; adding an immunosuppressive drug, particularly cyclophosphamide, may be beneficial. Steroids themselves may induce psychosis; therefore, it is important to serially monitor the patient with objective measures, including electroencephalography and magnetic resonance imaging, as well as cerebrospinal fluid protein. However, often one must rely on clinical judgment. Cognitive defects may respond to a short course of steroids. Seizure disorders are treated with anticonvulsants (e.g., phenytoin, phenobarbital, carbamazepine, clonazepam, valproic acid, and gabapentin); no evidence exists that these medications exacerbate SLE. Multiple small strokes may be due to a vasculopathy caused by antiphospholipid antibodies.

Treatment of the antiphospholipid antibody syndrome continues to be an evolving field. Low levels of these antibodies rarely cause symptoms. Patients with high levels and no symptoms should be treated with low-dose aspirin (81 mg/day); with symptoms, chronic warfarin (Coumadin) therapy is used at a dosage to maintain an International Normalized Ratio (INR) between 3 and 4. Pregnant patients with a previous history of a midtrimester miscarriage are treated with aspirin 81 mg/day and subcutaneous heparin, 10,000 U every 12 hours.

Patients started on prednisone therapy should receive high doses only until the inflammation has subsided; therefore, the patient should be assessed frequently regarding specific organ function, as well as immune status (complement, anti-DNA antibodies). For acute, severe lupus, multiple daily doses are recommended, followed by a switch to a daily morning dose. For long-term management, the benefit-risk issue needs to be discussed. The prednisone dosage should then be tapered, the rate depending on the severity of organ inflammation and damage, the maximum dose, and side effects from prednisone (i.e., psychological changes, insomnia, weight gain, hypertension, diabetes, peptic ulcer, infections such as acne, cushingoid features, adrenal suppression, osteonecrosis, myopathy, impaired wound and fracture healing, skin atrophy, cataracts, atherosclerosis, growth retardation, and osteoporosis). Patients receiving long-term steroids should be monitored for osteoporosis and treated aggressively with calcium, vitamin D, bisphosphonates, or combinations thereof. Patients taking antimalarial drugs should have an ophthalmologic examination regularly; those taking NSAIDs should be watched for gastrointestinal and renal toxicity.

Prognosis

The prognosis for SLE patients in the United States has improved dramatically since the 1950s, when the survival rate was approximately 50% at 5 years. Currently the survival rate is approximately 90% at 10 years. The prognosis is worse for patients with CNS involvement, hypertension, azotemia, and early age of onset. The major cause of death is infection. Although there is an impression of greater awareness of the disease, its clinical expression has not changed in 20 years; nor is there evidence that it is being diagnosed earlier.

Future Directions

A greater understanding of the pathophysiology of SLE is anticipated to emerge over the next 10 years. Of particular interest are on-going studies on the genetic influences that appear to predispose to acquiring the disease, and to the development of certain patterns of organ involvement. SLE is a polygenic disease, with subsets of patients exhibiting differing clinical symptoms and severity. It is highly likely that this clinical heterogeneity is influenced, at least in part, by different groups of genes. Studies in spontaneous animal models of

---

Table 280–10 • SYMPTOMS AND SIGNS SUGGESTING ACTIVE SYSTEMIC LUPUS ERYTHEMATOSUS

SYMPTOMS	SIGNS
Malaise	Anemia
Poor appetite	Leukopenia
Weight loss	Thrombocytopenia
Fatigue	Hematuria
Pallor	Pyuria
Abnormal menses	Proteinuria
Fever	Azotemia
Arthritis	ESR elevation
Seizures	Decreased complement (C3, C4, CH50)
Chest pain	Immune complexes
Edema	Anti-dsDNA
Hair loss	
Oliguria	
Rashes	
Mouth sores	

ESR = erythrocyte sedimentation rate.

Table 280–11 • TREATMENT OF SPECIFIC PROBLEMS IN LUPUS

Fever: NSAIDs → antimalarials → steroids
Arthralgia/myalgia: NSAIDs → acetaminophen → amitriptyline
Arthritis: NSAIDs → antimalarials → steroids (alternate day) or methotrexate
Rashes: Sunscreens → topical steroids → antimalarials → injection
Oral ulcers: Antimalarials
Raynaud's: No smoking, caffeine, decongestants → warm clothing → biofeedback → (long-acting) nifedipine → prazosin
Serositis: Indomethacin → steroids
Pulmonary: Steroids
Hypertension: Diuretics → ACE inhibitors → calcium channel blockers → β-blockers → vasodilators
Thrombocytopenia/hemolytic anemia: Steroids → IV γ-globulin → immunosuppressives → splenectomy
Renal disease: Steroids → pulse steroids → immunosuppressives
CNS disease
  Organic: Steroids → antiseizures drugs → immunosuppressives
  Functional: Antianxiety/antidepression drugs

ACE = angiotensin-converting enzyme: CNS = central nervous system; NSAIDs = nonsteroidal anti-inflammatory drugs.

Table 280–12 • TREATMENT OF RENAL LUPUS

PATHOLOGY	SYMPTOMS	URINE	GFR	COMPLEMENT	TREATMENT	GOAL
Mesangial	0	RBC, WBC, protein	nl	± ↓	Monitor	Watch for progression
Membranous	Edema	Protein	nl	nl	Trial of prednisone immunosuppression, diuretic	Decrease proteinuria and edema
Focal — Active	0	RBC, WBC, protein	↓	↓	Prednisone	Improve renal function
Focal — Chronic	BP ↑	Protein	↓	nl	Antihypertensive, ACE inhibitor	
Proliferative						
Diffuse — Active	Edema BP	RBC, WBC, protein	↓ ↓	↓ ↓	Prednisone (pulse) Azathioprine, 50–200 mg Cyclophosphamide, 0.85–2 g/1.7 m²	Improve renal function
Diffuse — Chronic	Uremia	Protein	↓ ↓	nl	Antihypertensive, ACE inhibitor	Prevent deterioration of renal function
Failure	Uremia	None	0	nl	Dialysis transplant	Decrease uremia

ACE = angiotensin-converting enzyme; BP = blood pressure; GFR = glomerular filtration rate; nl = normal; RBC = red blood cell; WBC = white blood cell.

Rheumatic Diseases

SLE are beginning to clarify predisposing genes and the mechanisms of their effects. The results of initial human studies indicate the presence of similar types of immune system abnormalities involving T and B cell dysfunction as well as defects in clearance of immune complexes. New therapeutic directions in SLE include the development of molecules that tolerize the anti-DNA antibody response, immune ablative therapy with or without stem cell transfer, and anti-IL-10 antibodies. The treatment of non-life-threatening manifestations, and the prevention of some organ complications of SLE and its treatment, should also evolve over the next decade.

1. Illei GG, Austin HA, Crane M, et al: Combination therapy with pulse cyclophosphamide plus pulse methylprednisolone improves long-term renal outcome without adding toxicity in patients with lupus nephritis. Ann Intern Med 2001;135:248–257.

SUGGESTED READINGS

The American College of Rheumatology: Nomenclature and case definitions for neuropsychiatric lupus syndromes. Arthritis Rheum 1999;42:599–608. *Consensus definitions to guide reliable diagnosis.*

The American College of Rheumatology: Guidelines for referral and management of systemic lupus erythematosus in adults. Arthritis Rheum 1999;42:1785–1796. *Consensus guidelines.*

Bijl M, Horst G, Bootsma H, et al: Mycophenolate mofetil prevents a clinical relapse in patients with systemic lupus erythematosus at risk. Ann Rheum Dis 2003;62:534–539. *This drug prevented clinical relapses in a non-randomized study.*

Cervera R, Khamashta MA, Font J, et al: Morbidity and mortality in systemic lupus erythematosus during a five year period. A multicenter prospective study of 1000 patients. Medicine 1999;78:167–175. *A large case series.*

Esdaile JM, Abrahamowicz M, Grodzicky T, et al: Traditional Framingham risk factors fail to fully account for accelerated atherosclerosis in systemic lupus erythematosus. Arthritis Rheum 2001;44:2331–2337. *The risk of clinical coronary and cerebrovascular disease is about 10-fold higher than predicted.*

Fiehn C, Hajjar Y, Mueller K, et al: Improved clinical outcome of lupus nephritis during the past decade: Importance of early diagnosis and treatment. Ann Rheum Dis 2003;62:435–439. *Outcome is improving likely owing to earlier diagnosis and treatment.*

Gladman DD, Goldsmith CH, Urowitz MB, et al: The Systemic Lupus International Collaborating Clinics/American College of Rheumatology (SLICC/ACR) Damage Index for Systemic Lupus Erythematosus International Comparison. J Rheumatol 2000; 27:373–376. *A valid index for assessing severity.*

Hebert LA: Management of lupus nephropathy. Nephron Clin Pract 2003;93:C7–C12. *An evidence-based review.*

Keane MP, Lynch JP: Pleuropulmonary manifestations of systemic lupus erythematosus. Thorax 2000;55:159–166. *A comprehensive overview.*

Kuiper-Geertsma DG, Derksen RH: Newer drugs for the treatment of lupus nephritis. Drugs 2003;63:167–180. *Comprehensive review of newer therapies, including immunosuppressants used in organ transplantation and monoclonal antibodies directed at immune cells, cytokines, and components of the complement system.*

Sanchez-Guerrero J, Villegas A, Mendoza-Fuentes A, et al: Disease activity during the premenopausal and postmenopausal periods in women with systemic lupus erythematosus. Am J Med 2001;111:464–468. *Disease is less active during the menopausal and postmenopausal periods.*

281 SCLERODERMA (SYSTEMIC SCLEROSIS)

Fredrick M. Wigley

Definitions

Scleroderma (systemic sclerosis) is a chronic, systemic disease that targets the skin, lungs, heart, gastrointestinal tract, kidneys, and musculoskeletal system. The disorder is characterized by three features: (1) tissue fibrosis, (2) a small blood vessel vasculopathy, and (3) a specific autoimmune response associated with autoantibodies. Because thickening of the skin is the most prominent clinical feature, *scleroderma* ("hard skin") has become the most popular name for this disease. Scleroderma is classified into two major subsets that are distinguished by the extent of skin thickening: (1) limited and (2) diffuse cutaneous scleroderma (Table 281–1). Patients with diffuse disease have widespread skin involvement, including areas proximal to the elbows or knees and/or the trunk. In limited scleroderma, the skin changes are restricted to the face, neck, and areas distal to the elbows and/or knees, sparing the trunk. The CREST syndrome (an acronym for subcutaneous *c*alcinosis, *R*aynaud's phenomenon, *e*sophageal dysfunction, *s*clerodactyly [scleroderma limited to the fingers], and *t*elangiectasia) is a form of limited scleroderma associated with anticentromere antibodies. Patients with limited scleroderma generally follow a more benign disease course than do patients with diffuse

Table 281–1 • CRITERIA AND CLASSIFICATION FOR SCLERODERMA (SYSTEMIC SCLEROSIS)

Definite scleroderma: Scleroderma skin changes proximal to the metacarpophalangeal joints or metatarsophalangeal joints *OR* (2 of 3): (1) sclerodactyly (scleroderma limited to the fingers); (2) digital pitting scars or loss of finger pad; (3) bibasilar pulmonary fibrosis

Diffuse cutaneous scleroderma: Scleroderma skin changes above the elbows or knees and/or on the trunk (abdomen or chest)

Limited cutaneous scleroderma: Scleroderma skin changes distal to the elbow, knees, and above the clavicles

CREST syndrome: Subcutaneous *c*alcinosis, *R*aynaud's phenomenon, *e*sophageal dysfunction, *s*clerodactyly, and *t*elangiectasia (3 of 5 must be present)

Overlap syndromes: Diffuse or limited scleroderma plus typical features of one or more of another connective tissue or autoimmune disease

Mixed connective tissue disease: Features of scleroderma, systemic lupus erythematosus, polymyositis, rheumatoid arthritis, and the presence of anti-U1snRNP

Systemic sclerosis sine scleroderma: Systemic features without skin involvement

Undifferentiated connective tissue disease: Features of scleroderma but no definite clinical or laboratory findings to make a definite diagnosis

Localized scleroderma: Asymmetric plaques of fibrotic skin without systemic disease

Morphea: Limited (single plaque); generalized (multiple plaques)

Linear scleroderma: Longitudinal fibrotic bands

Nodular scleroderma: Keloid-like nodules

cutaneous disease. A diagnosis of scleroderma can be suspected when a patient presents with Raynaud's phenomenon associated with findings of typical nailfold capillary abnormalities seen in scleroderma, and/or scleroderma specific autoantibodies even in the absence of the usual skin changes.

Overlap syndromes, defined as features of two or more rheumatic diseases occurring in the same patient, frequently include findings suggestive of scleroderma. The most common overlap syndromes involve scleroderma with inflammatory polymyositis, Sjögren's syndrome, symmetrical polyarthritis, and lupus-like reactions. Mixed connective tissue disease (MCTD) is an overlap syndrome with features of scleroderma, polymyositis, lupus-like rashes, and rheumatoid-like polyarthritis. Patients with MCTD have a specific antibody response to ribonuclear protein (anti-U1snRNP). Either severe interstitial lung disease or isolated pulmonary hypertension (PHTN) may develop in these patients, which is similar to what occurs in patients with diffuse and limited scleroderma, respectively.

Localized scleroderma is a nonsystemic skin disease that is primarily seen in children. The most common form of localized scleroderma is an isolated circular patch of thickened skin called *morphea*. Multiple morphea lesions can occur, and they occasionally coalesce, mimicking the skin changes of systemic sclerosis. Active morphea lesions present as enlarging geographic lesions with raised violaceous borders and ivory-white sclerotic centers. Infiltration of the dermis with lymphocytes and collagen deposition is seen in the morphea lesion. Localized scleroderma can also present as a linear streak (*linear scleroderma*) that crosses dermatomes and is associated with tracking of fibrosis from the skin into deeper tissues, including muscle and fascia. In severe cases, linear scleroderma leads to dramatic growth deformities of affected regions. Hemifacial atrophy caused by linear scleroderma has been called a *coup de sabre* ("sword stroke") lesion. Although localized scleroderma may be disfiguring and disabling, it is generally a self-limited process not associated with a systemic illness. Patients with localized scleroderma have antinuclear antibodies most often directed against histone of chromatin, suggesting the presence of an underlying autoimmune process.

Etiology

Autoimmune, genetic, hormonal, and environmental factors may all play a role in the development of scleroderma. The presence of disease-specific autoantibodies (e.g., anti-topoisomerase in the diffuse form; anticentromere in the limited form) and evidence of activated immune cells in tissues places scleroderma in the family of autoimmune disorders. Furthermore, autoimmune diseases are frequently evident in the family members of scleroderma patients (e.g., systemic lupus erythematosus, rheumatoid arthritis, and Hashimoto's thyroiditis). Scleroderma-like skin changes are seen in patients with chronic graft-versus-host disease, suggesting a role for a cellular immune process in scleroderma. Scleroderma is most likely a complex multigenetic disease influenced by environmental and epigenetic factors. Familial aggregation is rare (2%) and monozygotic twins are usually discordant for disease. Although no clear human leukocyte antigen association with scleroderma is defined, genealogy data suggest Oklahoma Choctaw Native Americans with scleroderma inherited a common haplotype, making them susceptible to the disease. Hormonal influence on the disease is suggested by the fact that women are more likely than men to develop scleroderma, as they are for other autoimmune diseases. Finally, environmental factors may trigger the disease in the susceptible host. For example, silica exposure among miners has been associated with typical scleroderma. Certain chemical exposures (e.g., vinyl chloride, organic solvents) can cause scleroderma-like reactions.

Incidence and Prevalence

Scleroderma is a rare disease, with an incidence of approximately 20 per million population per year and a prevalence of 100 to 300 per million population. The average age at onset is between 35 and 50 years, and it is more common among women (3 to 7 : 1 female-to-male ratio). Although well described in the elderly, it is uncommon for the disease to become manifest before age 25 years, particularly the CREST variant. Scleroderma is found in all races and in various geographic areas. Urban to rural differences in occurrence are not apparent. The prevalence of scleroderma is higher in Native Americans and it appears to be more severe in expression among both African Americans and Native Americans. Females have a higher mortality rate than males; this finding has not changed over decades of follow-up.

Natural History

The natural history of this disease is variable, but scleroderma is typically a chronic disease that evolves over many months or years. Scleroderma tends to be a monophasic disease that rarely relapses (~5%) after remitting. The initial phase is manifest by active inflammation that is associated with progressive fibrosis of the skin and other organs; the disease activity lasts from several months to several years. As the disease activity remits, patients encounter a variety of complications resulting from skin and internal organ fibrosis. The degree of skin involvement predicts the subsequent course of events (Table 281–2). Patients with diffuse scleroderma (arms, legs, and trunk)

Table 281–2 • CHARACTERISTICS OF SUBSETS OF SCLERODERMA

DIFFUSE SCLERODERMA
Widespread skin thickening involving distal and proximal body
Rapid onset (within 1 yr) of skin and other features following appearance of Raynaud's phenomenon
Significant visceral involvement including the heart, lungs, gastrointestinal tract, or kidneys
High scores on disability and organ damage indices secondary to extensive fibrosis of tissues
Poor prognostic signs include later age at onset, female gender, African American or Native American race, presence of large pericardial effusion, or tendon friction rubs
Associated with antinuclear antibodies and the absence of anticentromere antibody
Highly variable disease course but overall poorer prognosis with 10-yr survival of 40–60%

LIMITED SCLERODERMA
Limited to no skin thickening
Several year interval or slow progression of disease from the onset of Raynaud's phenomenon
Late visceral disease with unique features of isolated pulmonary hypertension and digital amputations secondary to severe ischemic vascular disease
CREST is a variant of limited scleroderma
Associated with primary biliary cirrhosis
Associated with anticentromere antibody
Relatively good prognosis with 10-yr survival of >70%

---

have a worse prognosis than those with limited scleroderma (distal arms and legs only). Patients with limited disease have normal life expectancies, with the exception of those who develop severe isolated PHTN (approximately 10%). In contrast to limited scleroderma, patients with diffuse scleroderma have a rapid progression of skin disease over several months to involve the fingers, hands, arms, trunk, and legs with thickened, immobile skin. In concert with skin disease, patients with diffuse scleroderma frequently develop signs of pulmonary, musculoskeletal, gastrointestinal, cardiac, and renal dysfunction, some of which may lead to organ failure and/or death.

Pathogenesis

Raynaud's phenomenon (episodic color changes of the skin triggered by cold exposure or emotional stress) is a nearly universal symptom of scleroderma. Raynaud's phenomenon occurs early in the disease process, sometimes years before the diagnosis is suspected. The universality of Raynaud's phenomenon in scleroderma suggests that vascular perturbation is an early event in the pathogenesis of scleroderma (Fig. 281–1). Although the cause of this abnormality remains unknown, blood vessels in scleroderma patients are overly sensitive to cold temperatures and other sympathetic stimuli. In vitro studies of cutaneous vessels from patients with scleroderma show a 300-fold increase in α_2-adrenergic smooth muscle activity compared to that in normal vessels. Blood vessels in scleroderma also show evidence of endothelial cell dysfunction, including defects in the control of intravascular coagulation and platelet activation, enhanced trafficking of inflammatory cells into tissues, and increased production of inflammatory mediators (e.g., oxygen radicals and cytokines). Dysfunctional endothelium also causes an imbalance in the secretion of important vasoconstrictors (e.g., increased endothelin-1) or vasodilators (e.g., decreased nitric oxide and prostacyclin). Events of ischemia-reperfusion, evidenced by the clinical occurrence of Raynaud's phenomenon, are associated with cutaneous ulcers or, on occasion, digital amputation. Digital ischemia is the most overt manifestation of widespread microvascular dysfunction affecting not only the skin but all of the organs targeted in scleroderma. For example, disease of the pulmonary vessels may cause severe PHTN and progressive right-sided heart failure. Episodic vasospasm and disease of the endomyocardial vessels of the heart causes contraction-band necrosis, or focal areas of fibrosis that can result in arrhythmia or cardiomyopathy. Vasospasm of the small arteries of the kidneys may be associated with severe hypertension, renal infarction, and, occasionally, renal failure. Gastrointestinal dysfunction is also thought to be secondary to small artery disease in the vessels to the esophagus and lower gastrointestinal tract coupled with neuromuscular abnormalities. Histologic examination of the arteries of these organs demonstrates endothelial disruption, intimal proliferation, excessive collagen deposition, and overabundant extracellular matrix, all of which narrow the vessel lumen. This vasculopathy of small and medium arteries is fundamental in most pathologic findings in scleroderma (Fig. 281–2).

Almost every patient with scleroderma develops a fibrotic reaction in tissue ranging from the skin to the heart. This fibrosis results from excessive production of collagen and other extracellular molecules by activated tissue fibroblasts. Excess tissue collagen causes decreased flexibility and malfunction of the affected organ. Most evidence suggests that the fibroblast is an innocent bystander, activated by profibrotic cytokines made during other biologic events. For

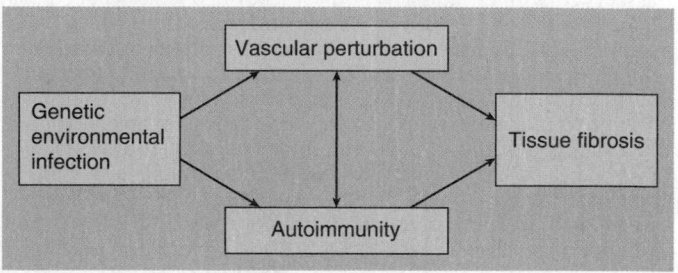

FIGURE 281–1 • Schematic diagram of the major pathophysiologic processes thought to occur in scleroderma: vascular disease with abnormal regional blood flow, autoimmunity, and tissue fibrosis.

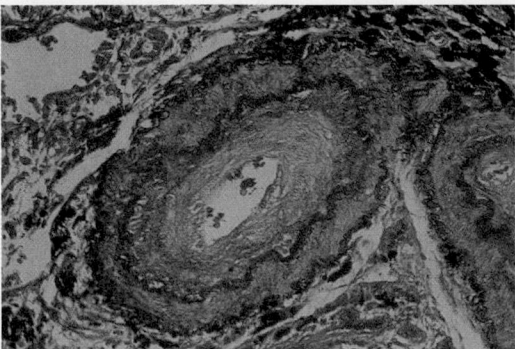

FIGURE 281–2 • Slide of small artery in the lung of a patient with scleroderma. Marked proliferation of the intimal layer of the vessel narrows the lumen and alters local blood flow. Endothelial cell dysfunction is also known to occur.

Table 281–3 • AUTOANTIGENS IN SCLERODERMA

Topoisomerase I (SCL–70/TOPO1): 25–40% of patients with diffuse scleroderma; associated with severe lung disease; seen more frequently in blacks than in whites

Centromere (ACA): 55–96% of patients with the CREST syndrome; targets CENP-B (100%) and CENP-C (50%); associated with Raynaud's phenomenon and seen in 10% of patients with biliary cirrhosis; presence of ACA and anti-TOPO1 is mutually exclusive

RNA polymerase I, II, and III: 4–20% of patients; associated with diffuse skin disease, renal involvement, and less lung or muscle disease

Fibrillarin (U3snRNP): 8–10% of patients; high frequency in blacks and Native Americans and associated with muscle and cardiopulmonary disease

Th RNP (endoribonuclease): 10% of patients with limited scleroderma

Nor-90 (nucleolus organizer protein): Rare

PM–Scl (A nucleolar complex): Associated with inflammatory muscle disease in scleroderma

Nucleolin: Rare

U1snRNP (U1 RNA and polypeptides): Associated with the overlap syndrome mixed connective tissue disease

B-23 (nucleophosmin, a nucleolar phosphoprotein): Associated with pulmonary hypertension and overlap syndrome

example, cytokines made by activated T cells or other immune or inflammatory cells (e.g., macrophages, mast cells, or platelets) activate fibroblasts (see Fig. 281–2). Platelet-derived growth factor (released by activated platelets), transforming growth factor-β, (TGF-β) and interleukin-1 are examples of profibrotic cytokines implicated in scleroderma. Endothelin-1, produced by the activated endothelium of injured blood vessels, also activates fibroblasts. A genetic defect may be acquired that alters fibroblast function by activation of an autocrine factor, development of abnormal matrix signaling, or clonal selection of highly activated tissue fibroblast populations. Finally, fibroblasts may be activated by tissue hypoxia or oxygen radicals produced during the ischemic-reperfusion events associated with the vascular disease of scleroderma.

Scleroderma patients also have evidence of ongoing autoimmunity: namely, disease-specific autoantibodies (Table 281–3). In diffuse scleroderma, autoantibodies are directed against topoisomerase (formerly called Scl-70) as well as fibrillarin and RNA polymerases I, II, and III. In the CREST syndrome, the antibodies are directed against centromere structures (CENP A-C). The immune response in scleroderma is driven by self-antigens and is T cell–dependent. T cells (both CD4 and CD8) are found in abnormal numbers in the tissue

(e.g., skin, heart, lungs) of patients with scleroderma. However, it is conceivable that the autoimmune process in scleroderma is a biologic process that amplifies rather than initiates the principal disease process.

Accumulating data indicate that naive autoreactive T cells are available to react with newly exposed self-antigens. Cryptic epitopes of autoantigens can be exposed to autoreactive T cells during apoptotic cell death, thus triggering an autoimmune process. In vitro studies demonstrate that granzyme B derived from T cells can cleave scleroderma-specific autoantigens into fragments that reveal cryptic epitopes. Fragmentation of scleroderma autoantigens by reactive oxygen species (ROS) has also been shown.

Thus, tissue injury due to ischemia reperfusion or cellular apoptosis can propagate a chronic inflammatory process by driving the autoimmune process. The activated immune cells in turn can propagate tissue fibrosis or vascular disease by secretion of proinflammatory cytokines.

Clinical Manifestations

RAYNAUD'S PHENOMENON

The diagnosis of Raynaud's phenomenon is based on clinical criteria. The patient must give a history of excessive cold sensitivity and recurrent events of sharply demarcated pallor and/or cyanosis of the skin of the digits. Although a number of methods exist to quantitate attacks of Raynaud's phenomenon objectively, no test is considered practical or reproducible enough to replace the clinical criteria in diagnosis. Raynaud's phenomenon occurs in 3 to 15% of the general population. It is more common among females (3 to 4:1) and is likely to begin before age 20 years. During cold exposure (particularly during shifting temperatures and winter months) Raynaud's attacks increase in frequency and intensity. Primary Raynaud's phenomenon occurs when no disease process is associated with the events. Distinguishing primary Raynaud's from that associated with an underlying disorder is frequently challenging. Young age at onset (<30 years), symmetrical manifestation of symptoms, mild to moderate severity and no association with tissue gangrene, normal nailfold capillary examination, and a negative antinuclear antibody (ANA) titer are all indicative of primary Raynaud's phenomenon. Secondary Raynaud's phenomenon occurs in a variety of settings, including connective tissues diseases (e.g., systemic lupus erythematosus, MCTD, vasculitis), occupational trauma (e.g., hypothenar hammer syndrome), the use of certain drugs, disorders that alter normal flow properties of blood, and other conditions that damage vessels (Table 281–4). The presence of intense Raynaud's attacks, especially when accompanied by skin gangrene or ulceration, warrants a thorough diagnostic evaluation for secondary causes.

In scleroderma, Raynaud's phenomenon and digital ischemia are the clinical manifestations of both fixed structural vascular disease and abnormal regulation of local blood flow. The intima of small and medium vessels is thickened with an increase in collagen content, causing a loss of vessel flexibility and obliteration of its lumen (Color Plate 7C). Despite significant vascular disease, there remains sufficient vascular reserve to provide adequate blood flow and nutrition during periods of rest and in a warm ambient temperature. Digital pitting with loss of fingertip tissue and small, painful, superficial ulcerations are very common and are usually secondary to disease in the small arteries and arterioles of the skin. Large, deep ulceration of the distal finger is a consequence of larger vessel (e.g., digital artery) occlusion associated with severe vasospasm. The latter event usually presents as a sharp demarcation of the distal digit with intense, localized pain secondary to ischemia. Failure to reverse these events may lead to loss of the whole digit or limb with deep tissue infarction.

The most important therapeutic intervention for Raynaud's phenomenon is the maintenance of warmth. A warm ambient temperature reduces the frequency and severity of Raynaud's phenomenon. All patients with Raynaud's phenomenon should understand that clothing should be layered and loose-fitting, with the goal of maintaining a warm core body temperature, not just warmth of the affected extremities. Avoidance of aggravating factors, including smoking, sympathomimetic drugs (e.g., preparations for the common cold), nonselective β-blockers (e.g., propranolol), and narcotics, is also crucial. Biofeedback alone is not helpful for Raynaud's phenomenon. Drug therapy for Raynaud's phenomenon includes oral or systemic vasodilators, antiplatelet agents, and antioxidants. The calcium-channel blockers are first-line therapy for

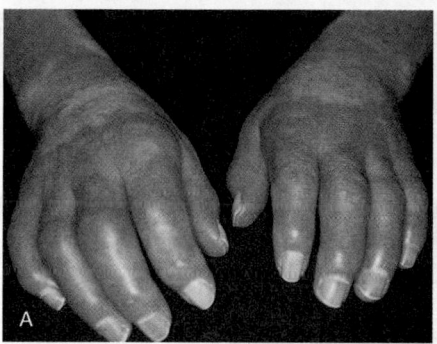
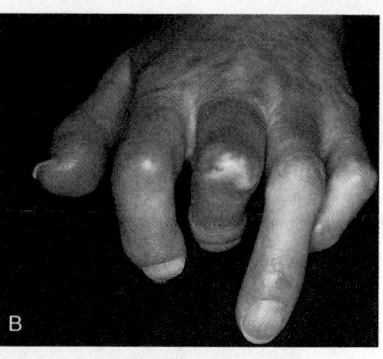

FIGURE 281–3 • Scleroderma involving the hands. *A,* Edematous phase with diffuse swelling of fingers. *B,* Atrophic phase with contracture and thickening sclerodactyly (thick skin over the fingers).

Table 281–4 • CHARACTERISTICS OF SUBSETS OF SCLERODERMA: CONDITIONS ASSOCIATED WITH RAYNAUD'S PHENOMENON

RHEUMATIC DISEASES
Scleroderma (95%)
Systemic lupus erythematosus (30–40%)
Dermatomyositis and polymyositis (30%)
Sjögren's syndrome (30%)
Rheumatoid arthritis (controversial)

DRUGS/CHEMICALS
Chemotherapeutic agents
Polyvinyl chloride
Ergotamines
Clonidine
Interferons
Nonselective β-blockers
Estrogen

AGENTS EXPECTED TO AGGRAVATE RAYNAUD'S PHENOMENON
Nicotine
Narcotics
Sympathomimetic agents
Cyclosporin
Cocaine

TRAUMA OR INJURY TO DIGITAL HAND VESSELS
Frostbite
Repetitive occupational stress
Thenar hammer syndrome
Thoracic outlet syndrome

CONDITIONS CAUSING ARTERIAL DISEASE
Vasculitis
Arteriosclerosis
Thromboangiitis obliterans
Emboli disease

OTHER
Hypothyroidism
Malignancy
Migraine headaches
POEMS syndrome
Prinzmetal's angina
Cryoproteinemias
Cold agglutinins
Reflex sympathetic dystrophy
Carpal tunnel syndrome

severe Raynaud's phenomenon. Short-acting nifedipine administered three times per day reduces the severity of Raynaud's attacks and the number of ischemic digital ulcers. Sustained-release calcium-channel blockers have become popular (e.g., nifedipine, amlodipine, diltiazem) because of ease of administration and general safety. Although the calcium-channel blockers are the agents most likely to be effective, a host of other vasodilators have been used, including nitrates (topical and oral) and sympatholytic agents (e.g., prazosin, phenoxybenzamine, and others). Combinations of agents are tried in refractory cases, but this strategy is generally disappointing.

Intravenous vasodilating prostaglandins (prostaglandin E_1, epoprostenol, iloprost) reduce the severity and frequency of Raynaud's attacks and are most helpful during periods of sustained critical ischemia. Oral prostaglandins, drugs that enhance nitric oxide, inhibitors of endothelin and selective α-adrenergic receptor antagonists are other experimental approaches to the problem. Patients with critical digital ischemia should be hospitalized to reduce activity, maintain warmth, and permit the rapid initiation of vasodilator therapy. Antiplatelet therapy with low-dose aspirin may be useful, but its benefit is unproven. Heparinization may be considered during acute ischemic crises of the digits, but chronic anticoagulation in scleroderma is not recommended. For refractory cases, temporary cervical or lumbar sympathectomy can reverse vasospasm. Chemical sympathectomy of the affected digit, performed by local infiltration with either lidocaine or bupivacaine, may provide immediate relief. If temporary chemical sympathectomies prove efficacious, a surgical approach to sympathectomy can be considered. Local, at the level of the digit, rather than proximal surgical sympathectomy is considered safe and effective. Studies on long-term responses to sympathectomies suggest that Raynaud's attacks eventually recur. Ischemic digital lesions should be treated with topical antibiotics and daily cleansing with soap and water. Digits that progress to dry gangrene should be permitted to undergo autoamputation. Surgical amputation is best done only for intractable pain or deep tissue infection.

SKIN INVOLVEMENT

The most overt clinical manifestation of scleroderma, particularly in patients with diffuse disease, is cutaneous fibrosis. Cutaneous involvement with scleroderma begins with an edematous phase that is associated with an active inflammatory process. This phase persists for several weeks to months and is characterized by nonpitting edema of the affected limbs, erythema of the skin, and intense pruritus (Fig. 281–3A). The edematous phase eventually gives way to a fibrotic stage, which may last months or years. Excessive collagen in the dermis thickens the skin, making it inflexible and causing dysfunction of skin appendages. Sweating is decreased, and hair growth on the involved area ceases. In the late stages of disease, atrophy and permanent contractures develop (see Fig. 281–3B). Patients with diffuse cutaneous scleroderma develop masked facies, small oral apertures, and vertical furrowing of the perioral skin (Fig. 281–4). As the gums atrophy and facial skin tightens, the teeth appear more prominent. Flexion contractures of fingers, wrists, and elbows often appear secondary to dermal sclerosis and atrophy of underlying tissues. Ulceration of the skin is a late complication. Hypopigmentation and hyperpigmentation of the skin ("salt-and-pepper" appearance) may accompany the fibrotic reaction of the skin, particularly on the face, arms, and trunk. A general tanning of the skin is also common.

Despite evidence of active inflammation in the edematous phase, systemic corticosteroids do not appear to be effective. In the early

Continued

Rheumatic Diseases

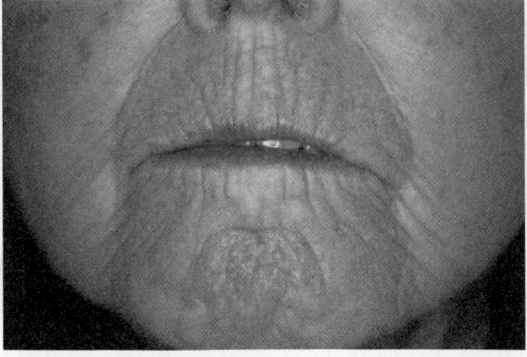

FIGURE 281–4 • Facial features in scleroderma. Note the vertical lines or furrowing around the mouth in this patient with diffuse scleroderma.

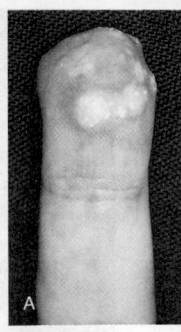
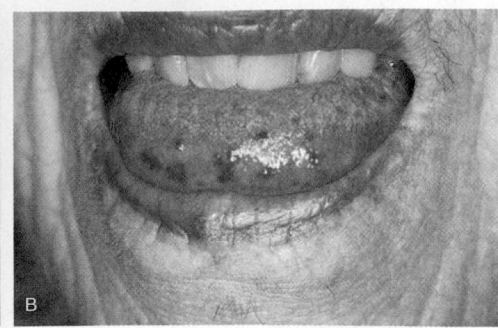

FIGURE 281–5 • Features of CREST syndrome. A, Subcutaneous calcinosis on tip of finger. B, Telangiectasia on mucous membrane and tongue.

active stage of diffuse scleroderma, pruritus can be one of the most distressing symptoms. Antihistamines, analgesics, or cyclic antidepressants are often used but usually are only partially effective. Over some weeks to months, the skin becomes progressively thickened, secondary to excess collagen deposition. Drying of the skin surface results from loss of natural oils, causing pruritus and repetitive skin trauma from scratching. Ulceration and secondary tissue infection may result. Treatment is best done with frequent topical application of an emollient, periodic cleansing with soap and water, and topical antibiotics to any traumatic skin ulcerations. Ischemic ankle ulceration occurs in a subset of patients.

Telangiectasias of the skin appear as erythematous spots that blanch on pressure and are a manifestation of abnormal dilated capillaries. Telangiectasias on the face, fingers, palms, and mucous membranes are prominent in the CREST syndrome (Fig. 281–5) and may resemble Osler-Weber-Rendu disease (hereditary hemorrhagic telangiectasia). Nailfold capillary abnormalities can be viewed using microscopy done after applying immersion oil to the skin surface. In early scleroderma, the nailfold capillaries appear enlarged. In later stages of scleroderma, the nailfold capillaries are attenuated and irregular.

GASTROINTESTINAL INVOLVEMENT

Almost every scleroderma patient has symptoms or signs of gastrointestinal disease. Patients may complain that chewing is difficult because of decreased facial flexibility, a decreased oral aperture, or dry mucous membranes. Poor dental health may result from difficulty with routine dental care. Upper pharyngeal function is usually normal, but dysphagia resulting from esophageal disease sometimes mimics neuromuscular disease. Approximately 90% of patients have symptoms of esophageal disease. Heartburn, regurgitation, or dysphagia for pills and solids (more than liquids) is caused by the loss of normal smooth muscle function and dysmotility of the lower two thirds of the esophagus. If untreated, gastrointestinal reflux may lead to esophagitis, bleeding, esophageal strictures, and/or Barrett's esophagus. The severity of symptoms may not accurately reflect the seriousness of the esophageal disease.

A barium swallow and cine-esophagogram are both sensitive tests for esophageal strictures. However, direct measurement of esophageal motility via esophageal manometry may be needed if the cause of symptoms is not clear. Direct endoscopy may be appropriate to rule out Barrett's esophagus. Most patients benefit from an aggressive antireflux program. Education about standard nondrug antireflux measures is critical. Patients often do well by eating frequent, smaller meals. Treatment of esophagitis by suppression of gastric acid with H_2-blockers has been disappointing in scleroderma. However, protein-pump inhibitors (e.g., omeprazole or lansoprazole) can be effective and usually need to be used long term. A prokinetic drug should be added when symptoms of dysphagia or endoscopic findings of esophagitis are present, despite the use of effective acid suppression. The prokinetic drug metoclopramide is more effective in early disease, but is less likely to help in later, advanced esophageal dysfunction.

Delayed gastric emptying often causes early satiety, anorexia, or the sensation of bloating. Occasionally, dilatation of the gastric microvasculature gives the mucosa a "watermelon stomach" appearance on endoscopy. Laser therapy may be necessary to control bleeding from these abnormal vessels.

Bloating, abdominal distention, diarrhea, and/or constipation are common complaints caused by dysmotility of the small and large bowel. Sluggish or atonic bowel function allows bacterial overgrowth to result in serious diarrhea with malabsorption, weakness, and progressive loss of weight. Management includes the use of cyclic antibiotics and prokinetic drugs. Recurrent bouts of pseudo-obstruction are one of the most serious bowel problems in scleroderma. These episodes are sometimes mistaken for surgical emergencies. Pseudo-obstruction is the manifestation of profound loss of bowel smooth muscle function causing regions of dysmotility. Pneumatosis cystoides intestinalis sometimes complicates scleroderma of the bowel when gas leaks into the diseased intestinal wall and tracks into the mesentery of the gut or the peritoneal cavity, mimicking a bowel perforation. Asymptomatic large-mouthed diverticula, pathognomonic of scleroderma, also result from fibrosis and atrophy of the bowel wall. Volvulus, stricture, or perforation are uncommon complications of severe bowel involvement. Incontinence of stool can result from fibrosis of both upper and lower rectal sphincters. Total parenteral nutrition may be necessary for patients who have severe scleroderma-related bowel disease without response to other medical therapy.

PULMONARY INVOLVEMENT

Pulmonary disease has become one of the most difficult-to-treat end-organ manifestations of scleroderma. It is associated with significant morbidity and has become the leading cause of mortality in this disease. Lung injury in scleroderma results from one of two processes: (1) fibrosing alveolitis (leading to restrictive lung disease) or (2) obliterative vasculopathy of medium and small pulmonary vessels (associated in some cases with PHTN). Both interstitial fibrosis and pulmonary vascular disease are present to some degree in most patients. However, interstitial lung disease is more characteristic of diffuse scleroderma, and isolated PHTN is more closely associated with limited disease. Obstructive airway disease and pleural reactions are uncommon in scleroderma. Spontaneous pneumothorax, adult respiratory distress syndrome, and pulmonary hemorrhage have been reported rarely.

The most common symptom of scleroderma lung disease is dyspnea in the absence of chest pain. Nonproductive cough is a late manifestation. Active fibrosing alveolitis may be asymptomatic and undetectable by chest radiograph. Pulmonary function testing is the most sensitive method for detecting early lung dysfunction but may be normal during the early phase of active disease. Eventually, lung function testing is abnormal in more than 60% of patients. Isolated low diffusing capacity and reduced lung volume are the most common findings in early disease. A major challenge is to accurately gauge the activity of alveolitis. Activity can be defined by serial pulmonary function testing, by high-resolution computed tomography, or by analysis of cell counts from bronchoalveolar lavage (BAL) fluid. Patients with an excess percentage of neutrophils or eosinophils (>3%) on BAL tend to have worsening lung function over several months, whereas those with normal BAL findings generally do not show progressive worsening. If alveolitis is present, treatment with immunosuppressive drugs (e.g., cyclophosphamide) is indicated. Uncontrolled studies suggest that daily oral cyclophosphamide (2 mg/kg) reduces the alveolitis and prevents progressive lung disease in scleroderma. The outcome of untreated alveolitis is pulmonary fibrosis, severe restrictive ventilatory defects, and ineffective gas exchange. Progressive restrictive disease occurs in 20 to 30% of patients and is more likely to occur in patients with diffuse scleroderma, those of African-American ethnicity, and those with antibodies to topoisomerase I (Scl-70 antibodies).

Severe isolated PHTN (i.e., PHTN in the absence of interstitial lung disease) occurs in 10% of patients with the CREST syndrome but is uncommon in diffuse scleroderma. The natural history of mild to moderate PHTN is not well defined in scleroderma, but rapid progression to life-threatening disease occurs in a subset of patients, usually with limited skin disease. Detection of PHTN by bedside examination is most difficult until it has progressed to an advanced stage. Echocardiography is a sensitive and useful noninvasive method of detecting mild to moderate PHTN early. A survey of echocardiography in 691 scleroderma patients found 15.3% had mild PHTN, 6.9% had moderate PHTN (mean pulmonary artery pressure 46 to 55 mm Hg), and 11.1% had severe PHTN (>55 mm Hg). Mild PHTN is usually not treated in the absence of signs of right heart failure; however, new oral pulmonary vasodilators may allow early intervention in selected patients. Moderate to severe PHTN with clinical status of New York Heart Association class II–IV should be managed more aggressively. Right-sided heart catheterization provides confirmation of the diagnosis and permits the measurement of pulmonary hemodynamics with and without a vasodilator challenge (e.g., adenosine, nitric oxide, or epoprostenol). Patients who respond to the challenge with a decrease in pulmonary vascular resistance or pulmonary artery pressure are candidates for treatment with oral calcium-channel blockers. The dose of calcium-channel blockers in such patients should be increased to the maximum dose tolerated. Patients who do not respond to a vasodilator challenge are candidates for continuous infusion of prostacyclin (epoprostenol, iloprost) via a centrally placed intravenous line, subcutaneous delivery of prostaglandin E_1, or the oral administration of an endothelin receptor inhibitor (bosentan) [1,2] Aerosolized prostaglandins (e.g., iloprost) are also under study. Prognosis for patients with severe PHTN with or without fibrosis remains poor. Patients with PHTN in the setting of severe lung fibrosis are less likely to respond to any vasodilator therapy. Lung transplantation may be necessary for patients with progressive, severe PHTN.

CARDIAC INVOLVEMENT

Symptoms of cardiovascular disease in scleroderma are nonspecific and usually present as dyspnea on exertion or as congestive heart failure. Although symptoms of the cardiac involvement are often appreciated in later stages of the disease, objective noninvasive testing can demonstrate heart involvement early in the disease course. Asymptomatic pericardial effusions or clinically silent arrhythmias may be demonstrated, particularly in diffuse scleroderma. Pericardial disease is symptomatic in approximately 10% of patients, whereas pericardial disease can be demonstrated by echocardiography or at postmortem in 40 to 60% of cases. Acute pericarditis usually presents with chest pain, fever, and dyspnea. Tamponade is rare. Although pericardial disease may be present without symptoms, the presence of a large pericardial effusion is associated with poor overall prognosis.

Myocardial fibrosis can lead to a cardiomyopathy and heart failure. The fibrosis is distributed in patches of contraction band necrosis on both sides of the heart. Coronary circulation vasospasm has been demonstrated during attacks of cold-induced Raynaud's phenomenon. This suggests that myocardial fibrosis is associated with reversible vasospasm of the coronary circulation and repeated bouts of ischemia-reperfusion injury. Echocardiography demonstrates myocardial disease in approximately 50 to 70% of cases, but in most patients, cardiac dysfunction is clinically silent until late in the disease. Myocarditis associated with diffuse inflammatory polymyositis may affect the heart function in scleroderma patients.

Defects in conduction and cardiac rhythm occur as a consequence of myocardial fibrosis. Estimates of the prevalence of electrocardiographic abnormalities suggest that 50% of scleroderma patients will have some conduction defect or arrhythmia, most of which are asymptomatic. Scleroderma-related syncope is an ominous symptom of either late-stage PHTN or an important arrhythmia. Valvular heart disease and coronary artery disease is not part of scleroderma; therefore, typical angina should make one consider atherosclerosis of the coronary vessels or another process. Atypical chest pain is usually caused by musculoskeletal problems, esophageal reflux disease, or PHTN mimicking cardiac disease.

RENAL INVOLVEMENT

Before the discovery of angiotensin-converting enzyme (ACE) inhibitors, hypertensive renal crisis was the leading cause of death in scleroderma. In contrast, death or end-stage renal disease resulting from scleroderma renal crisis is now rare. Mild proteinuria or microscopic hematuria without loss of renal function or evidence of glomerular disease is the most common sign of renal disease. Approximately 10% of patients with diffuse scleroderma have a renal crisis that mimics malignant hypertension, with rapidly progressive renal failure secondary to microvascular disease, vasospasm, and tissue ischemia. Microangiopathic hemolytic anemia, thrombocytopenia, and rapidly progressive loss of renal function can accompany scleroderma renal crisis. Studies demonstrate high levels of serum renin associated with vasospasm and intrinsic renal vessel disease. Neither microscopic urinary findings nor baseline serum renin levels are predictors of a renal crisis. However, new anemia or thrombocytopenia, with or without hypertension, should alert the physician to scleroderma kidney disease. A renal crisis is associated with use of corticosteroids or can be precipitated in situations that compromise renal blood flow (e.g., dehydration). Any hypertension ($\geq$140/90) in a scleroderma patient should be carefully evaluated because a renal crisis is potentially reversible with appropriate management. Indeed, the patients presenting with serum creatinine level of 3.0 mg/dL or greater have a poor prognosis. The key to successful therapy is early detection and rapid intervention. Some patients continue to have progressive renal failure despite control of blood pressure. Patients who progress to renal failure and dialysis can recover renal function after months of therapy. Successful renal transplantation has been done in patients with scleroderma.

MUSCULOSKELETAL INVOLVEMENT

Musculoskeletal symptoms are almost always present in scleroderma and are often the initial symptom of the disease. The most common symptoms are pain, stiffness, and diffuse muscular discomfort that mimics a flulike syndrome. The pain is more intense around joints, including the fingers, wrists, elbows, shoulders, knees, and ankles, yet inflammatory signs of synovitis are infrequent. A sense of weakness in the muscles of the hands, arms, and legs can be subtle or profound. On physical examination, a coarse rub can be palpated or auscultated over the wrists, knees, or ankles. These "tendon friction rubs" are secondary to fibrin deposition and fibrosis in the tissues. They occur almost exclusively in diffuse scleroderma and their presence is predictive of a poor overall prognosis. Musculoskeletal symptoms in scleroderma often fail to respond to traditional anti-inflammatory medications.

The muscle disease of scleroderma may be multifactorial. Weakness is often caused by muscle atrophy secondary to the inflexibility of fibrotic skin and lack of normal exercise. It can also occur because of malnutrition resulting from scleroderma bowel disease. Finally, muscle weakness in scleroderma may be secondary to direct muscle disease. In diffuse scleroderma, fibrosis can extend into the striated muscle, causing muscle atrophy and clinical weakness. Approximately 5 to 10% of scleroderma patients have an inflammatory muscle disease that can follow the same course as polymyositis and other forms of idiopathic inflammatory myopathy.

OTHER MANIFESTATIONS

Dry eyes (keratoconjunctivitis sicca) and/or mucous membranes (xerostomia) occur in 25% of patients. Minor lip biopsy can demon-

Continued

strate fibrosis or the lymphocytic infiltration typical of Sjögren's syndrome. The central nervous system is generally spared in scleroderma, but unilateral or bilateral trigeminal neuralgia is known to occur. Carpal tunnel syndrome can complicate diffuse scleroderma while other forms of peripheral neuropathy are uncommon. Autoimmune hepatitis and biliary cirrhosis are reported in patients with the CREST syndrome. Abnormal thyroid function in scleroderma is frequent (~20%), particularly in limited scleroderma, and is associated with thyroid tissue fibrosis. Avascular necrosis of carpal bones of the wrist can occur secondary to the peripheral vascular disease. An inflammatory polyarthritis that mimics rheumatoid arthritis is seen in a subset of scleroderma patients. Most data suggest normal fertility in scleroderma, but there is an increased risk during pregnancy of hypertension, scleroderma renal crisis, or premature fetal loss.

Psychosocial aspects are most important and are often overlooked. Scleroderma is a disfiguring disease that alters virtually every aspect of the patient's life. The chronic nature of the disease and the threat of death have significant psychological impact on the patient. Evidence suggests that depression in scleroderma patients is related more to the patient's personality, the degree of pain, and social support than to disease severity. Sexual perfor-mance is often affected significantly, particularly in patients with diffuse disease. Impotence among male scleroderma patients is common, resulting from neurovascular disease.

Diagnosis (with Differential Diagnosis)

The early symptoms of scleroderma, unexplained fatigue, arthralgia, myalgia, and the new onset of Raynaud's phenomenon are nonspecific and mimic other rheumatic diseases such as systemic lupus erythematosus, polymyositis, rheumatoid arthritis, and Sjögren's syndrome. Some patients ultimately diagnosed with scleroderma defy classification at the time of presentation. These patients' conditions are best classified as "undifferentiated connective tissue disease" with features of scleroderma. The presence of severe Raynaud's phenomenon with digital ulcers, nailfold capillary changes, gastrointestinal symptoms (e.g., esophageal reflux), and cutaneous changes begin to distinguish scleroderma from other rheumatic diseases.

A number of disorders mimic scleroderma. Scleredema is characterized by thick, indurated skin that begins on the trunk, especially over the upper back and shoulders, and can spread to arms, legs, and face. Scleredema can be a transient condition following infection or a more persistent disorder associated with insulin-dependent diabetes. Eosinophilic fasciitis (EF), also called Shulman's syndrome, can also mimic scleroderma. Eosinophilic fasciitis is more common in males and presents as a progressive stiffening of the arms, legs, and trunk. Inflammation and fibrosis within fascia create puckering of the skin (Fig. 281–6) and deep venous tracks (the "groove sign"). Because the inflammatory process is deep to cutaneous tissues, skin may be pinched readily in EF, in contrast to the thickened skin involved in scleroderma. Scleromyxedema (papular mucinosis) closely mimics the cutaneous manifestations of scleroderma (Fig. 281–7). Patients are usually between 30 and 70 years old and have an associated paraproteinemia that consists of IgG type with λ light chains. Scleroderma-like skin changes have been reported in a number of other disorders, including the carcinoid syndrome, chronic graft-versus-host disease, porphyria cutanea tarda, POEMS syndrome (polyneuropathy, organomegaly, endocrinopathy, monoclonal gammopathy, and scleroderma-like skin changes), bleomycin exposure, Werner's syndrome, and phenylketonuria. Eosinophilia-myalgia syndrome and toxic oil syndrome are toxin-induced disorders that have scleroderma-like features.

 ## Treatment

No drug or treatment has proved safe and effective in altering the underlying disease process in scleroderma. Treatment should be done during the early, inflammatory stage of the disease, before irreversible sclerosis has been established. The natural course of the disease is highly variable, and most effective therapy targets disease in specific organs. Strategy for treatment has included antifibrotic agents, anti-inflammatory drugs, immunosuppressive therapy, vascular drugs, and a variety of agents without clear mechanisms of action.

The most popular drug has been D-penicillamine, which is thought to work as an antifibrotic and immunosuppressive agent. A recent controlled trial of D-penicillamine found no difference

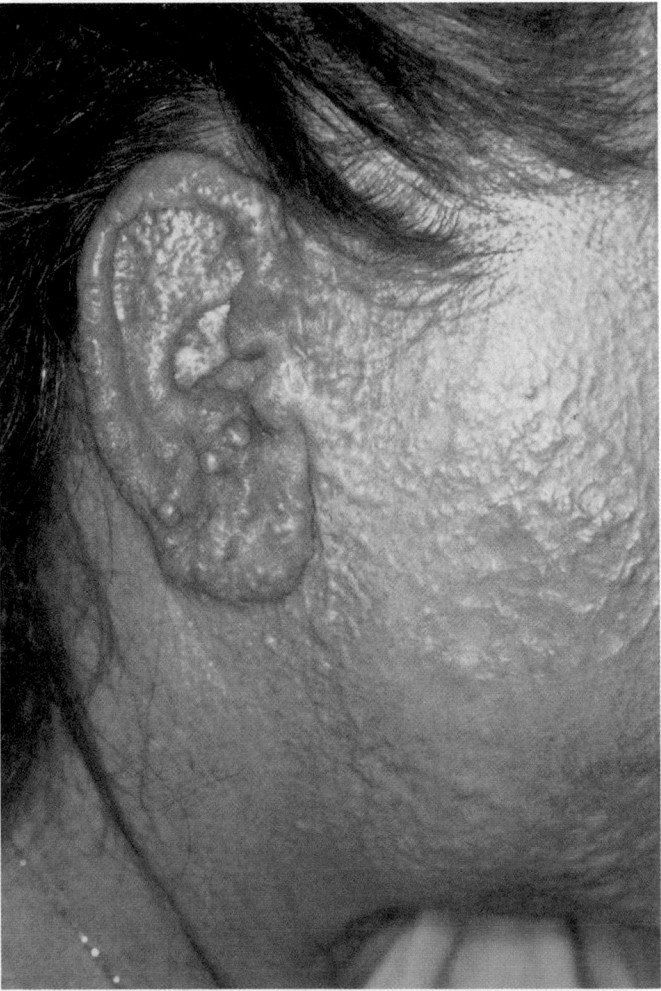

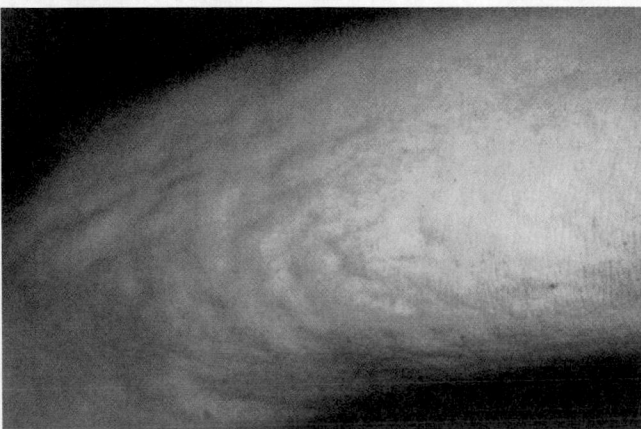

FIGURE 281–6 • Photograph of arm of a patient with eosmorphic fasciitis demonstrating puckering of skin of the upper arm due to inflammation, increased collagen and extra-matrix in the fasciae.

FIGURE 281–7 • Photograph of the face of a patient with scleromyxedema (papular mucinosis) demonstrating thickened skin with cobblestone-like appearance.

between high and low doses, suggesting that D-penicillamine is not effective treatment.[3] Low-dose weekly methotrexate has become popular for many inflammatory diseases including scleroderma. Although methotrexate may control myositis or inflammatory arthritis, evidence that it prevents or reverses skin or other organ fibrosis is lacking.[4] Colchicine, potassium para-aminobenzoate, interferon, antithymocyte globulin, cyclosporin, tacrolimus (FK-506), dimethyl sulfoxide, relaxin, photopheresis, and corticosteroids have all been reported to be beneficial for scleroderma, but evidence of clear benefit is either lacking or a clinical trial with control subjects has negated initial enthusiasm. New agents under study include immunosuppressive therapy (e.g., mycophenolate mofetil, cyclophosphamide), oral tolerance therapy, thalidomide, autologous bone marrow transplantation, TGF-β antagonist, halofuginone, endothelin-1 receptor blockade, and long-term prostaglandin therapy. The long list of agents under study points out that no single strategy has proved satisfactory. Disease modification therapy is best done in the setting of specialized centers and research protocols.

Prognosis

The prognosis for patients with diffuse scleroderma may be improving. Estimates have suggested that the 5-year survival has improved from 60 to 70% to greater than 80%, and the 10-year survival from 40 to 50 to 60%. Patients with limited scleroderma generally have a normal survival, unless severe PHTN is present. Patients with later age at onset, diffuse skin disease, presence of tendon friction rubs, and anti-topoisomerase antibody have a worse prognosis.

Future Directions

Major studies are underway to better define clinical and biologic markers of disease activity in scleroderma. Early detection of active disease will allow prevention of disease progression by the use of new therapeutic agents including immunosuppressive agents, vasoactive drugs (e.g., prostaglandins), and new biologic agents (e.g., monoclonal autoantibodies against TGF-β). Continued investigations into the biologic processes causing scleroderma should further clarify the roles of the fibroblast, immune system, and blood vessel in the disease.

1. Channick RN, Simonneau G, Sitbon O, et al: Effects of a dual endothelin-receptor antagonist bosentan in patients with pulmonary hypertension: A randomized placebo-controlled study. Lancet 2001;358:1119–1123.
2. Badesch DB, Tapson VF, McGoon MD, et al: Continuous intravenous epoprostenol for pulmonary hypertension due to the scleroderma spectrum of disease: A randomized controlled trial. Ann Intern Med 2000;132:425–434.
3. Clements PJ, Furst DE, Wong WK, et al: High-dose versus low-dose D-penicillamine in early diffuse systemic sclerosis: Analysis of a two-year, double-blind, randomized, controlled clinical trial. Arthritis Rheum 1999;42:1194–1203.
4. Pope JE, Bellamy N, Seibold JR, et al: A randomized controlled trial of methotrexate versus placebo in early diffuse scleroderma. Arthritis Rheum 2001;44:1351–1358.

SUGGESTED READINGS

Benrud-Larson LM, Haythornthwaite JA, Heinberg LJ, et al: The impact of pain and symptoms of depression in scleroderma. Pain 2002;3:267–275. *Pain and depression are common and worsen function and social adjustment.*

Geirsson AJ, Wollheim FA, Akesson A: Disease severity of 100 patients with systemic sclerosis over a period of 14 years: Using a modified Medsger scale. Ann Rheum Dis 2001;12:1117–1122. *Organ disease, which usually appears within five years of diagnosis and then stabilizes, predicts poor outcomes from skin involvement.*

Steen VD, Medsger TA Jr: Improvement in skin thickening in systemic sclerosis associated with improved survival. Arthritis Rheum 2001;12:2828–2835. *In two thirds of patients, skin thickening diminishes; these patients have a better prognosis.*

Sule SD, Wigley FM: Treatment of scleroderma: An update. Expert Opin Investig Drugs 2003;12:471–482. *A comprehensive update, including experimental therapies.*

Wigley FM: Clinical practice: Raynaud's phenomenon. N Engl J Med 2002;347:1001–1008. *A practical review, based on a case discussion.*

282 SJÖGREN'S SYNDROME

Stanley Naguwa
M. Eric Gershwin

Definition

Sjögren's syndrome (SS) is an autoimmune disease characterized by immune-mediated destruction of exocrine glands, particularly salivary and lacrimal glands, with subsequent development of keratoconjunctivitis and xerostomia. These clinical features all are secondary to exocrine gland dysfunction. A primary and a secondary form of SS have been defined. Primary SS occurs in the absence of a connective tissue disease; secondary SS occurs most commonly in association with a systemic connective tissue disorder, particularly rheumatoid arthritis, but also including systemic sclerosis, systemic lupus erythematosus, and polymyositis.

Epidemiology

SS initially was characterized and described in 1933. For many years, SS was considered relatively uncommon and primarily a disease of older women, often associated with rheumatoid arthritis. More recent data, obtained using standardized criteria, suggest, however, that SS may affect 0.5 to 2% of women. Nonetheless, the incidence of SS increases with age, and SS is virtually absent in children. Nearly 2% of women older than age 60 have features of primary SS, particularly dry eyes and dry mouth. Other exocrine glands also can be affected with subsequent development of pancreatic dysfunction, vaginal dryness, and dry cough. SS occurs in 10 to 25% of patients with SLE and 30 to 50% of patients with rheumatoid arthritis.

Diagnostic Criteria

The diagnostic criteria of SS continue to evolve, but currently a revised European study of classification is employed (Table 282–1). These criteria cannot be employed if the patient has compounding medical problems, including preexisting lymphoma, acquired immunodeficiency syndrome, sarcoidosis, amyloidosis, graft-versus-host disease, and sialadenosis, diseases commonly included in the differential diagnosis. A Sjögren's-like disease is associated with graft-versus-host disease and diffuse infiltrative lymphocytosis syndrome. The diagnosis of graft-versus-host disease is clinically obvious, based on the history. Diffuse infiltrative lymphocytosis syndrome occurs more commonly in males in the absence of the unique autoantibody profile of SS. The classification criteria are helpful in distinguishing between SS and sicca syndrome secondary to medications. The presence of a positive lip biopsy and/or the presence of autoantibodies suggests a systemic autoimmune disease. SS is found more commonly associated with several other autoimmune diseases, including Hashimoto's thyroiditis, primary biliary cirrhosis, chronic active hepatitis, celiac sprue, myasthenia gravis, and pernicious anemia.

Clinical Manifestations

SS most commonly presents as xerophthalmia (dry eyes) and xerostomia (dry mouth) in women in their 30s to 50s. The dry mouth leads to difficulty in swallowing, recurrent dental infections, pain on eating salty or spicy foods, and difficulty in talking. In many patients, the impairment of fluid secretion within the nasal and throat passage predisposes to oral thrush. Dry eyes result in complaints of ocular itching, a grittiness, and an exaggerated sensitivity to ocular insults such as smoke. Other upper and lower respiratory symptoms also are secondary to dryness and include a nonproductive cough and occasionally tracheobronchitis.

Classically, SS is manifested by a painless enlargement of salivary glands, often beginning unilaterally. The enlargement may be dramatic, may be cyclic in nature, and is generally absent in patients with coincidental rheumatoid arthritis. The symptoms develop insidiously, and often the diagnosis is not considered for several years because the complaints of sicca are attributed to medications (e.g., antihistamines, antidepressants), a dry environment,

Continued

or aging. The neurologic components of SS include peripheral and cranial neuropathies and a multiple sclerosis—like central nervous system disease. Skin manifestations include palpable/nonpalpable purpura, papules, urticarial lesions, or annular lesions. Xerosis is a frequently noted finding on examination. A nonerosive arthritis, polyarthralgias, and Raynaud's phenomena all are typically seen in SS. In addition to tracheobronchitis, lung involvement in SS may include bronchiectasis, interstitial pneumonitis, and fibrosis. Smoking is an additional major risk factor for pulmonary disease in patients with SS. Renal involvement may include interstitial nephritis, renal tubular acidosis, and hyposthenuria. Autoimmune liver disease and pancreatitis are seen occasionally.

The classic exocrine symptoms of SS are listed in Table 282–2, but SS theoretically can affect all major organ systems (Table 282–3). Patients initially may present only with extraglandular symptoms, especially a nonerosive rheumatoid factor—positive arthritis. In addition, and as a component of the inflammatory process and proinflammatory cytokine release, patients may manifest chronic fatigue and low-grade fevers. Finally, B-cell lymphoma has been described as a secondary event in SS. The incidence of lymphoma in SS varies among studies and may depend on local referral patterns (selection bias); lymphoma develops in approximately 5% of patients.

Table 282–1 • CLASSIFICATION CRITERIA FOR SJÖGREN'S SYNDROME

I. **Ocular symptoms:** a positive response to at least one of the three selected questions:
  1. Have you had daily, persistent, troublesome dry eyes for >3 months?
  2. Do you have a recurrent sensation of sand or gravel in the eyes?
  3. Do you use tear substitutes more than three times a day?
II. **Oral symptoms:** a positive response to at least one of the three selected questions:
  1. Have you had a daily feeling of dry mouth for >3 months?
  2. Have you had recurrent or persistently swollen salivary glands as an adult?
  3. Do you frequently drink liquids to aid in swallowing dry food?
III. **Ocular signs:** objective evidence of ocular involvement defined as a positive result in at least one of the following two tests:
  1. Schirmer's test (≤5 mm in 5 minutes)*
  2. Rose bengal score (≥4 according to van Bijsterveld's scoring system)
IV. **Histopathology:** a focus score ≥1 in a minor salivary gland biopsy. (A focus is defined as an agglomerate of at least 50 mononuclear cells; the focus score is defined by the number of foci in 4 mm^2 of glandular tissue.)
V. **Salivary gland involvement:** objective evidence of salivary gland involvement defined by a positive result in at least one of the following three diagnostic tests:
  1. Salivary scintigraphy
  2. Parotid sialography
  3. Unstimulated salivary flow (≤1.5 mL in 15 minutes)*
VI. **Autoantibodies:** presence in the serum of the following autoantibodies:
  1. Antibodies to Ro(SS-A) or La(SS-B) antigens, or both

Rules for classification: In patients without any potentially associated disease, the presence of any four of the six items indicates primary Sjögren's syndrome. In patients with a potentially associated disease (e.g., another connective tissue disease), item I or item II plus any two from among items III, IV, V indicates secondary Sjögren's syndrome.

Exclusion criteria: Preexisting lymphoma, AIDS sarcoidosis, graft-versus-host disease, sialadenosis. Use of antidepressant and antihypertensive drugs, neuroleptics, parasympatholytic drugs.

*Because it has been shown that this test may be reduced in normal subjects >60 years old, it should be excluded from the criteria or not considered indicative for a diagnosis of Sjögren's syndrome in elderly subjects.

From Vitali C, Bombardier: S, Moutsopoulos HM, et al (The European Study Group on Diagnostic Criteria for Sjögren's Syndrome): Assessment of the European Classification Criteria for Sjögren's syndrome in a series of clinically defined cases: Results of a prospective multicentre study. Ann Rheum Dis 1996; 55:116.

Table 282–2 • SYMPTOMS OF SJÖGREN'S SYNDROME SECONDARY TO EXOCRINE GLAND DYSFUNCTION

EYE (XEROPHTHALMIA)
Burning
Blurring
Foreign body sensation
Photosensitivity

ORAL (XEROSTOMIA)
Burning (especially with atypical thrush)
Difficulty chewing
Dysphonia
Inability to "spit"
Increased dental carries
Nocturnal awakening to drink water
Pain with "spicy" and salty food (e.g., mustard)
Sialadenitis

NOSE, THROAT
Difficulty swallowing (especially dry foods)
Epistaxis/dry nares
Hoarseness

CARDIOPULMONARY
Tracheobronchitis, including a dry cough

GENITOURINARY
Dyspareunia
Dysuria
Vaginal dryness

SKIN
Xerosis

Laboratory Findings

The most commonly used test for the diagnosis of SS is Schirmer's test, performed without anesthetic eye drops, measuring the wetting of standardized tear test strips that are applied between the eyeball and the lateral inferior lid. Salivary flow and labial salivary biopsy also commonly are used for diagnosis. Patients with SS have antinuclear antibodies of either homogeneous or speckled patterns (80 to 90% frequency), antibodies to Ro (SSA) (60 to 75% frequency) and La (SSB) (40% frequency), antibodies to rheumatoid factor (70 to 90% frequency), a mixed cryoglobulin with rheumatoid factor activity (type II) (<5%), and antibodies to centromere (<5%). The presence of mixed cryoglobulinemia suggests hepatitis C infection; these complexes contain rheumatoid factor, hepatitis C antigen, and complement. Antibodies to mitochondria likewise have been described but are found reliably only in patients with coexistent primary biliary cirrhosis.

Patients with SS exhibit a dramatic polyclonal B-cell activation. Several other autoantibodies have been described with variable frequencies, including antibodies to carbonic anhydrase, α-fodrin, proteosomal subunits, and the muscarinic M3 receptor; the last-mentioned is found on salivary glands and may explain glandular dysfunction. There also is evidence for altered B-cell differentiation. An SS-like disorder develops in mice transgenic for BAFF (a member of the tumor necrosis factor [TNF]-α superfamily that regulates B-cell proliferation). Anemia, including autoimmune hemolytic anemia; leukopenia; and thrombocytopenia all occur in SS, most commonly found in patients with chronic disease.

The serious immune system abnormalities in SS include lymphadenopathy, pseudolymphoma, and lymphoma. The transition from a rheumatoid factor—positive, polyclonal gammopathy to a rheumatoid factor—negative, oligoclonal/monoclonal gammopathy augers a change from a benign to a malignant process. This process can be enhanced if the V κ III b–related and the G-6 (VH1-related) idiotypes are present. Histologically the intense lymphoid infiltration includes the presence of germinal centers in the exocrine glands; the intense lymphocytic infiltrate is predominantly CD4+ T-cell TCRαβ CD45 RO cells. Finally, the degree of inflammation seems to be associated with a Th1 response with striking production of interferon-γ, interleukin-2, and interleukin-10. The development of severe histologic changes may be a prodrome of lymphoma. The migration of mononuclear cells to exocrine glands is mediated by chemokines and their cognate receptors, particularly MIP-1 and RANTES.

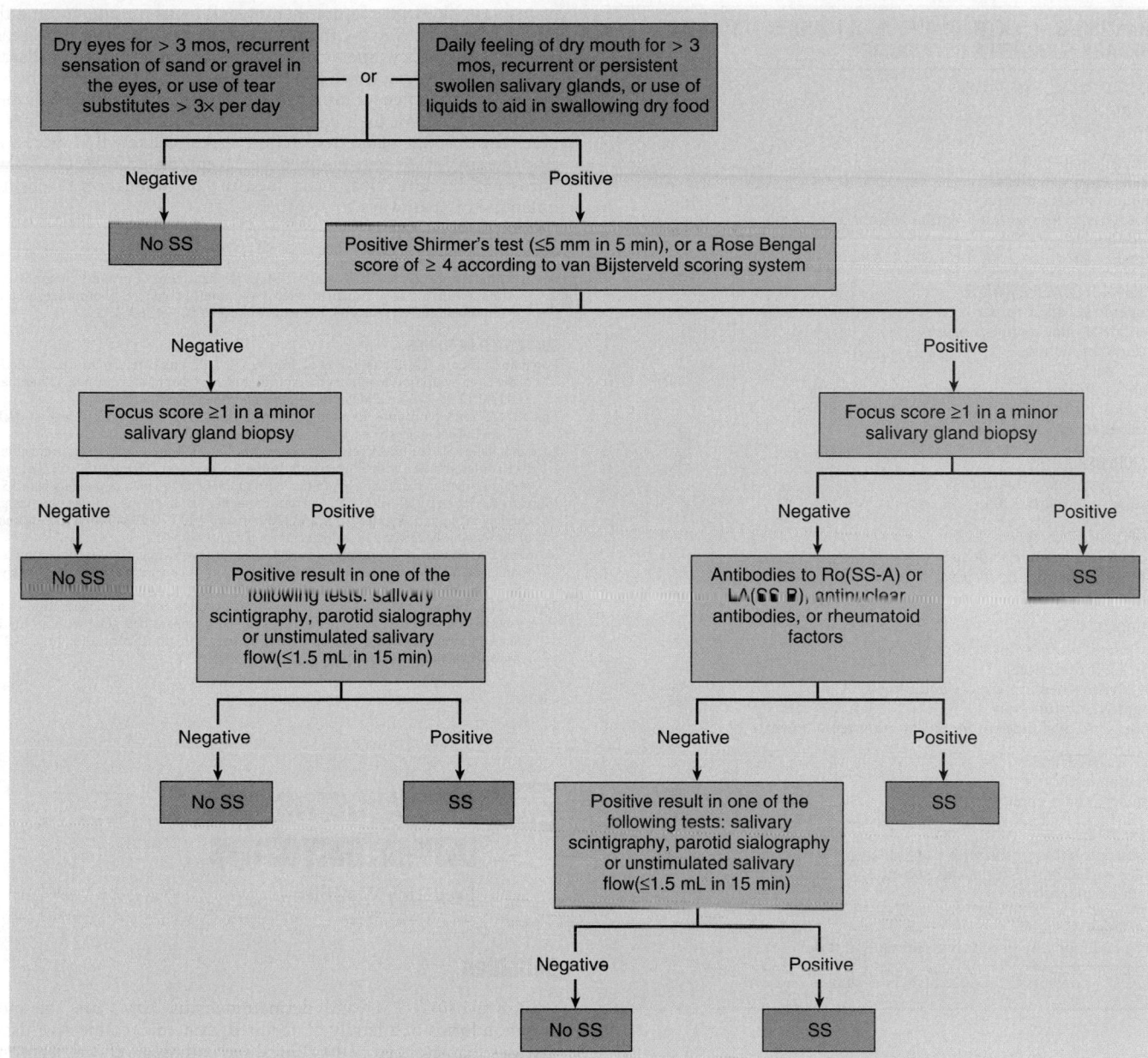

FIGURE 282–1 • Algorithm for the diagnosis of Sjögren's syndrome. (From Tzoufas AG, Moutsopoulos HM: Sjögren's syndrome. *In* Klippel JH, Dieppe PA [eds]: Rheumatology, 2nd ed. London, Mosby, 1998, with permission.)

Etiology

Some observations suggest that a retroviral infection may be a primary factor in either the cause or the modulation of SS. No cause-and-effect relationship has been established yet, however, between a retroviral infection and SS. Multiple other viruses have been incriminated in SS, including Epstein-Barr virus. SS does have a strong immunogenetic basis, however, and was one of the first autoimmune diseases associated with specific major histocompatibility complex genes. Several genetic alleles have been described to occur more commonly in patients with SS, particularly HLA class II antigens. As with other autoimmune diseases, the specific HLA gene association varies, however, according to the ethnic background of the individual. Patients with primary biliary cirrhosis have a higher frequency of HLA DRB1*15-DRB1*0301 (white) (17.8% compared with 3.5%); this is in linkage disequilibrium with DQB1 (0201), DPB1*0201 and TAP1 (0101), TAP2 (0101), and TNF-α2. The responsible mechanisms are unknown, and more extensive studies are required to map class II genes precisely, particularly in the DQB1 first hypervariable region.

The significance of anti-Ro and La antibodies in SS is speculative. These antibodies are found deposited in the salivary glands of affected patients. The Ro proteins colocalize to the blebs of apoptotic cells

and may become an immune target or function as a primary immunogen. Nonetheless, the levels of antibodies to Ro and La in serum do not correlate with disease activity. A pathologic role of anti-Ro antibodies has been described because their passive transfer in pregnancy leads to neonatal congenital heart block. In fetuses of mothers with anti-Ro antibodies and heart block, therapy with dexamethasone, which readily passes the placenta, is preferred over prednisone.

Rx Treatment

The primary treatment of SS is to minimize discomfort by using substitutes for the dysfunctional exocrine secretions (e.g., artificial tears, artificial saliva, increased oral fluids, ocular lubricants, vaginal lubricants). Ocular steroids are not recommended because they predispose to serious secondary infections. Goggles and punctal occlusion also are used to slow the loss of tears. Oral pilocarpine and cevimeline may stimulate functional exocrine glands and improve symptoms, but the response varies greatly among patients. The appearance of thrush warrants prompt treatment because it severely aggravates oral symptoms; nystatin is gener-

Continued

Rheumatic Diseases

Table 282–3 • EXTRAGLANDULAR MANIFESTATIONS OF PRIMARY SJÖGREN'S SYNDROME

CONSTITUTIONAL SYMPTOMS
Fatigue
Low-grade fever

SKIN AND VASCULAR
Small vessel vasculitis
Raynaud's phenomenon
Photosensitivity reactions similar to subacute cutaneous systemic lupus erythematosus
Xerosis

UPPER AND LOWER AIRWAYS
Pyogenic sialadenitis/parotitis
Interstitial pneumonitis/fibrosis
Chronic bronchitis
Bronchiectasis
Bronchiolitis obliterans organizing pneumonia
Pseudolymphoma with intrapulmonary nodules
Chronic obstructive pulmonary disease

MUSCULOSKELETAL
Polyarthralgias, polyarthritis
Myopathy/polymyositis

RENAL
Type I renal tubular acidosis
Tubular interstitial nephritis
Hyposthenuria

NEUROLOGIC
Peripheral motor sensory neuropathy
MS-like focal lesions
Transient ischemic attacks, including CVA
Cognitive dysfunction
Spinal cord dysfunction, including transverse myelitis

GASTROINTESTINAL
Hepatomegaly
Primary biliary cirrhosis

ENDOCRINE
Hashimoto's thyroiditis with possible hypothyroidism
Other endocrine dysfunctions secondary to autoimmune endocrinopathy

NEOPLASIA
Lymphadenopathy/pseudolymphoma/lymphoma

CVA = cerebrovascular accident; MS = multiple sclerosis.

ally effective. Finally, regular dental examinations and oral hygiene are crucial for reducing subsequent oral health issues (i.e., caries and periodontal disease associated with xerostomia). TNF-α inhibitors have been effective in small randomized trials for up to 24 weeks in improving xerostomia,█ but larger studies are needed to assess this therapy fully.

Extraglandular manifestations of SS also are managed in a symptomatic fashion. Treatment of arthritis includes nonsteroidal anti-inflammatory drugs, prednisone, hydroxychloroquine, methotrexate, and TNF-α inhibitors. Constitutional symptoms are treated with hydroxychloroquine and/or prednisone. Inflammatory organ system disease (involving the lung, liver, neurologic system, hematologic system, and kidney) is treated individually with prednisone, methotrexate, azathioprine, or TNF-α inhibitors. Careful surveillance for infectious complications and neoplasia is crucial because the risk of both is increased in SS. Intravenous immunoglobulin has been suggested as a treatment for SS, but there is no evidence to support its use. The mortality of patients with SS has been estimated as being 2.7-fold greater than a control population.

Future Directions

It is ironic that although much has been learned about the effector mechanisms of SS, little is known about the inductive mecha-

nisms. It is likely that future therapy will focus on interrupting the inflammatory pathways without ever understanding how the disease begins. If the latency time for development of an autoimmune disease is measured in years, it will be extremely difficult to identify the etiologic agents involved. Future work will focus on specific cytokines, chemokines, and/or their cognate receptor interactions in efforts to block the exocrine gland destruction. It is also likely that more specific therapy for the anti-Ro–mediated complete heart block of newborns will be developed, again focusing on abrogation of effector inflammatory pathways.

1. Cummins MJ, Papas A, Kammer GM, et al: Treatment of primary Sjögren's syndrome with low-dose human interferon alfa administered by the oromucosal route: Combined phase III results. Arthritis Rheum 2003;49:585–593.

SUGGESTED READINGS
Bowman SJ, Booth DA, Platts RG, et al, for the UK Sjögren's Interest Group: Validation of the Sicca Symptoms Inventory for clinical studies of Sjögren's syndrome. J Rheumatol 2003;30:1259–1266. *Validates a symptom questionnaire.*
Fox RI: Sjögren's syndrome: Evolving therapies. Expert Opin Investig Drugs 2003;12:247–254. *Comprehensive review, including experimental therapies.*
Groom J, Kalled SL, Cutler AH, et al: Association of BAFF/BLys overexpression and altered B cell differentiation with Sjögren's syndrome. J Clin Invest 2002;109:59–68. *An important contribution that may explain the hypergammaglobulinemia in patients with SS.*
Johnson R, Haga H-J, Gordon TP: Current concepts on diagnosis, autoantibodies and therapy in Sjögren's syndrome. Scand J Rheumatol 2000;29:341–348. *A concise source of the autoantibodies and their frequency in patients with SS.*
Skopouli FN, Kassan SS, Moutsopoulos HM: Sjögren's syndrome: Causes, detection, and management. J Musculoskeletal Med 2000;17:33. *A concise review of the therapy of SS.*
Tapinos NI, Polihronis M, Thyphronitis G, Moutsopoulos HM: Characterization of the cysteine-rich secretory protein 3 gene as an early-transcribed gene with a putative role in the pathophysiology of Sjögren's syndrome. Arthritis Rheum 2002;46:215–222. *A well-written article on the pathophysiology of SS.*

283 POLYMYOSITIS AND DERMATOMYOSITIS

Frederick W. Miller

Definition

Polymyositis (PM) and dermatomyositis (DM) are the most common forms of a family of acquired, systemic, connective tissue diseases characterized by the clinical and pathologic effects of chronic muscle inflammation of unknown cause, known as the idiopathic inflammatory myopathies (IIM). Other forms of IIM include inclusion body myositis (IBM) and myositis seen in association with cancer or with other connective tissue diseases (such as scleroderma, systemic lupus erythematosus, or rheumatoid arthritis) as a myositis overlap syndrome. The IIM, also known as the myositis syndromes, are diagnosed based on a combination of clinical, laboratory, and pathologic findings (Table 283–1).

Epidemiology

PM and DM are rare disorders described more than a century ago in Europe; they are now known to be worldwide in distribution and likely increasing in frequency. The estimated annual incidence ranges from 5 to 10 per million and estimated prevalence is 50 to 90 per million. PM and DM peak in prevalence in childhood (7 to 15 years) and in midlife (30 to 50 years), whereas the malignancy-associated forms and IBM are more common after age 50 years. Current studies suggest, however, that the prevalence, frequency of clinical forms, and risk factors for developing IIM likely differ in different parts of the world. There is an approximately 3 : 1 female predominance in all forms except in IBM in which the female:male ratio is inverted (approximately 1 : 3). Certain ethnic groups, including persons of African or Hispanic descent, may be at increased risk for IIM with poorer outcomes compared with whites. Anecdotal clusterings of PM and DM onset in time and space suggest strong environmental influences, but the specific agents involved remain elusive.

Table 283–1 • CRITERIA FOR THE DIAGNOSIS OF POLYMYOSITIS AND DERMATOMYOSITIS*

1. Symmetric, often progressive, proximal muscle weakness
2. Characteristic electromyographic triad
   Short duration, small, low-amplitude polyphasic potentials
   Fibrillation potentials, seen even at rest
   Bizarre high-frequency repetitive discharges
3. Elevations of serum levels of muscle-associated enzymes
   Creatine kinase
   Aldolase
   Lactate dehydrogenase
   Transaminases
4. Evidence of chronic inflammation in muscle biopsy
   Necrosis of type I and type II muscle fibers
   Degeneration and regeneration of myofibers with variation in myofiber size
   Focal collections of interstitial or perivascular mononuclear cells
5. Characteristic rashes of dermatomyositis
   Scaly erythematous palpable eruptions over the metacarpophalangeal or interphalangeal joints, knees, elbows, or medial malleoli (Gottron's papules)
   Scaly erythematous macules over the metacarpophalangeal or interphalangeal joints, knees, elbows, or medial malleoli (Gottron's sign)
   Periorbital purplish discoloration (heliotrope rash)

Definite disease – For PM, all of the first four criteria
                    For DM, any three of the first four criteria plus the rash
Probable disease = For PM, any three of the first four criteria
                    For DM, any two of the first four criteria plus the rash
Possible disease = For PM, any two of the first four criteria
                    For DM, any one of the first four criteria plus the rash
*Criteria originally proposed by Bohan and Peter in 1975.

Pathogenesis

An immune-mediated component to the myositis syndromes is suggested by (1) the inflammatory pathology, (2) the frequent finding of autoantibodies and other immune abnormalities, (3) the overlap with autoimmune diseases such as systemic lupus erythematosus in some patients, (4) the immunogenetic risk factors, and (5) the clinical response to anti-inflammatory agents. Nonetheless, by definition, the pathogeneses remain unknown. Many lines of evidence suggest that chronic immune activation in genetically susceptible individuals, following exposure to environmental triggers, plays a pivotal role in the development of IIM.

The pathology in the muscle, skin, and other affected tissues is characterized by focal collections of mononuclear cells. Lymphocytes are the most common cells in the infiltrates, but macrophages, plasma cells, basophils, and neutrophils are sometimes present. In certain variants, eosinophils (eosinophilic myositis) or granulomas (granulomatous myositis) predominate. The muscle cells (myocytes) show evidence of necrosis with degeneration and regeneration (Fig. 283–1) and there is often increased connective tissue or fibrosis in the interstitial areas around the myocytes.

Immunohistochemical and other studies implicate different pathogeneses in the various forms of myositis. In PM and IBM, the pathology suggests a cytotoxic T lymphocyte–mediated process with CD8+ T cells surrounding and invading otherwise normal-appearing myocytes in endomysial areas. In DM, however, the infiltrate is predominantly composed of B-lymphocytes and CD4+ helper T cells in perimysial areas around the fascicles and small blood vessels. Blood vessel pathology with endothelial cell damage from complement deposition and atrophy of the myofibers at the periphery of the fascicle (called *perifascicular atrophy* and caused by the more tenuous blood

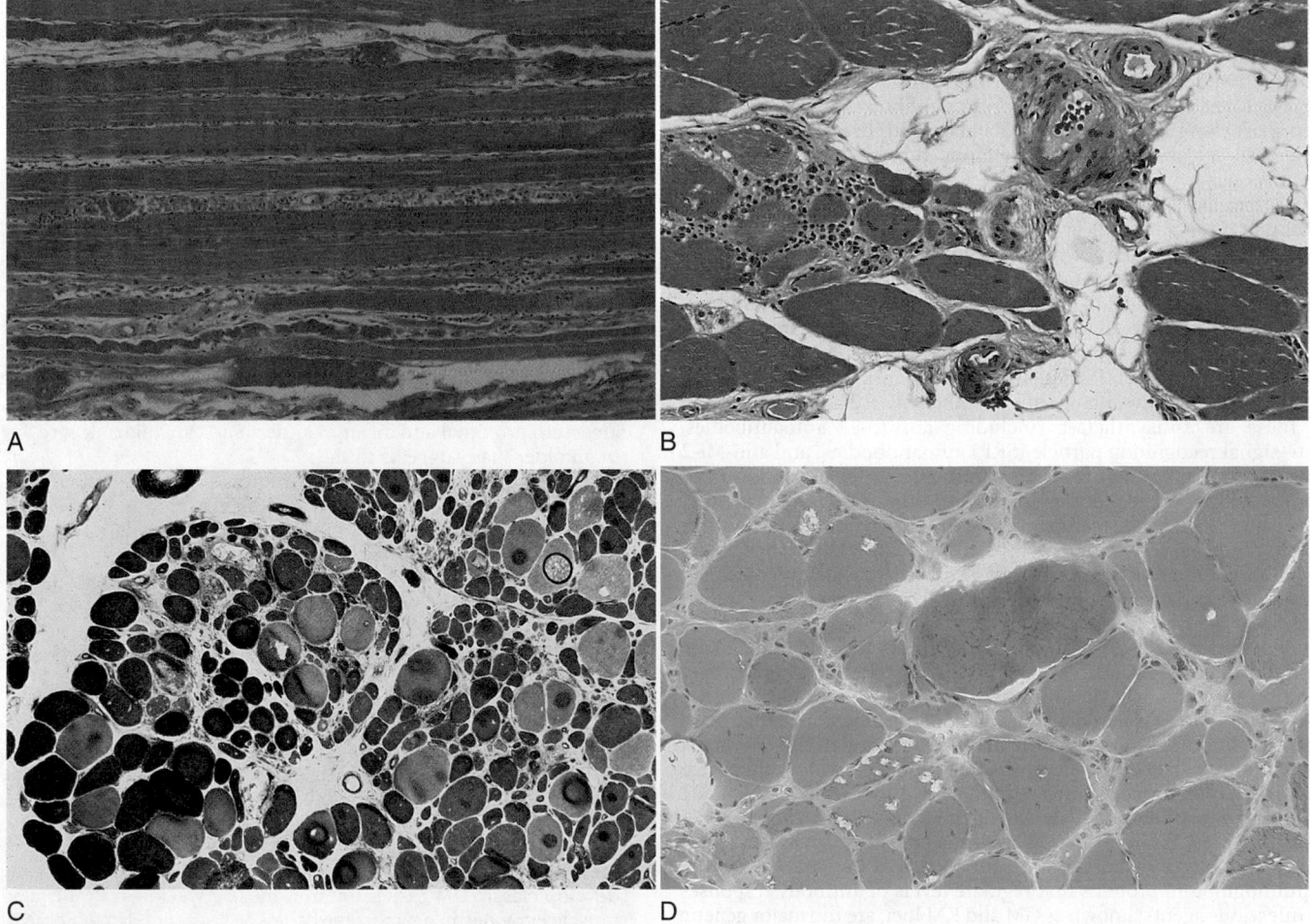

A

B

C

D

FIGURE 283–1 • Pathologic changes in myositis by light microscopy. *A* and *B*, Longitudinal and cross-sectional views of inflammatory myopathy show variation in cell size, necrosis, regeneration, and inflammation (hematoxylin and eosin stain). *C*, Perifascicular atrophy in dermatomyositis (ATPase stain). *D*, Red-rimmed inclusions, marked cell size variation, and relatively sparse inflammation in inclusion body myositis (trichrome stain). (Photos courtesy of Dr. J. Nelson and Dr. L. Love; from Klippel JH, Dieppe PA: Rheumatology, 2nd ed. London, Mosby, 1998, with permission.)

Table 283–2 • CLASSIFICATIONS OF THE IDIOPATHIC INFLAMMATORY MYOPATHIES

CLASSIFICATION GROUP	ASSOCIATED CLINICAL FEATURES	SEVERITY OF MYOSITIS	RESPONSE OF MYOSITIS TO THERAPY	PROGNOSIS (5-YR SURVIVAL)
CLINICAL GROUPS				
Polymyositis	None of the features below	Variable	Variable	Moderate (~80%)
Dermatomyositis	Gottron's papules or heliotrope	Mild-moderate	Good	Moderate (~85%)
Connective tissue myositis	Overlap with other connective tissue diseases	Mild	Excellent	Good (~90%)
Cancer-associated myositis	Cancer diagnosed within 2 yr of idiopathic inflammatory myopathy	Variable	Moderate to poor	Poor, secondary to cancer (~60%)
Juvenile myositis	Diagnosis before age 18 years Dermatomyositis (DM) >> polymyositis (PM) Subcutaneous calcifications Gastrointestinal vasculitis	Variable	Moderate to good	Good (>95%)
Inclusion body myositis	Insidious onset in older white males Distal involvement, atrophy, and asymmetrical weakness Poor response to therapy	Mild but progressive	Poor	Few deaths, but significant morbidity (>85%)
SEROLOGIC GROUPS				
Anti-synthetases	Acute onset in PM or DM Interstitial lung disease, fever, dyspnea on exertion, arthritis, mechanic's hands, Raynaud's phenomena	Moderate to severe	Moderate, but flares with taper	Poor (~75%)
Anti-SRP (signal recognition particle)	Acute onset in black female Palpitations, cardiac disease, severe weakness No rash (clinically PM)	Severe	Poor	Very poor (~30%)
Anti-Mi-2	Classic DM "V" and "shawl" rashes, cuticular changes	Mild	Good	Good (>95%)

supply in this area) are also characteristic findings in DM. IBM differs from PM and DM by the presence of characteristic reddish inclusions and vacuoles, rimmed by purple granules, inside the myocytes as demonstrated in trichrome-stained frozen muscle sections. Additional IBM features include frequent endomysial fibrosis, amyloid deposition, marked variation in myofiber diameter, and characteristic intranuclear and intracytoplasmic filamentous tubules seen on electron microscopy.

Autoantibodies are found in more than 90% of PM and DM patients, although it remains unclear what role, if any, they play in pathogenesis. The most frequent of these are antinuclear antibodies (ANA), but many others are commonly seen, including rheumatoid factor, anti-U1RNP, anti-La, anti-Ro, anti-PM/Scl, and anti-Ku autoantibodies. None of these are diagnostic for PM or DM, but, if present, they do assist in distinguishing the IIM from the other forms of myopathy. About one third of IIM patients have autoantibodies that are diagnostic, known as *myositis-specific autoantibodies*. The most common of these are antisynthetase (including anti-Jo-1) autoantibodies, anti–signal recognition particle (SRP) autoantibodies, and anti-Mi-2 autoantibodies. Each of these autoantibodies is strongly associated with a distinct clinical presentation, response to therapy, and prognosis, suggesting that each may represent a truly different myositis syndrome (Table 283–2). The myositis-specific autoantibodies are available commercially but need not be obtained in all patients. They may be particularly useful in diagnosing perplexing cases or in predicting prognosis.

As is the case for other autoimmune conditions, PM and DM are complex disorders whose etiologies likely involve the interaction of multiple genetic and environmental risk factors. The strongest genetic risk factors identified to date are the polymorphic genes that regulate the immune responses in the major histocompatibility complex known as human leukocyte antigen (HLA) genes. In whites, the ancestral HLA haplotype containing A1, B8, DRB1*0301, and DQA1*0501 alleles is most strongly associated with all forms of myositis. In other ethnic groups, though, such as Koreans and Mesoamericans, HLA genes are not risk factors, but certain alleles of the genes encoding immunoglobulin proteins that regulate levels of antibody responses to infectious agents, known as GM and KM loci, are the major genetic risk factors for PM and DM. Alleles of other polymorphic genes, including those that regulate cytokine responses to environmental exposures, such as tumor necrosis factor (TNF)-α and interleukin-1 receptor antagonist (IL-1Ra) alleles, have recently been associated with the childhood myositis syndromes. The environmental triggers for PM and DM are not known, but selected viral and bacterial infections, as well as certain drugs, dietary supplements, vaccines, medical implants, and occupational exposures have been implicated in case reports.

Clinical Manifestations

Myositis may present acutely, subacutely, or insidiously, and patients can have single or multiple episodic attacks or persistent disease activity. The IIM may be divided into groups based on clinical-pathologic or serologic features and each of these groups has characteristic clinical and prognostic associations (see Table 283–2). Therefore, the way in which the disease presents can suggest the form of IIM present. For example, an acute, severe onset of PM with cardiac involvement may herald a particularly difficult course with persistent disease as is often seen in patients with anti-SRP autoantibodies. Alternatively, a slowly progressive onset associated with proximal and distal weakness and thigh muscle atrophy in an older man suggests IBM.

Symmetric, proximal muscle weakness is present in most cases and results in difficulty arising from chairs, getting out of cars, reaching overhead, or combing hair. Many patients also report generalized fatigue or muscle pain. DM patients can present with a variety of photosensitive rashes over the face, chest, and hands. *Gottron's papules* are raised, often scaly, palpable lesions overlying an erythematous base on extensor surfaces such as the metacarpophalangeal and proximal interphalangeal joints, elbows, and knees; these are virtually pathognomonic for DM. Other characteristic rashes of DM are *Gottron's sign* (macules in a distribution similar to Gottron's papules) and a characteristic purplish rash over and sometimes surrounding the upper eyelids known as the *heliotrope rash*. Patients may also develop a rash in the V of the neck (V-sign) or in the distribution of a shawl (shawl-sign). A roughening, scaling, and erythematous fissuring of the palmar and lateral aspects of the fingers, known as *mechanic's hands*, may be seen in either PM or DM patients. Occasionally, patients may develop classic DM rashes without muscle weakness or elevated muscle enzymes in a syndrome called DM sine myositis. Some of these individuals, however, have subclinical myositis, as demonstrated by magnetic resonance imaging (MRI) studies of muscle or muscle biopsy, whereas in others clinical myositis develops over time. Children with DM are particularly at risk for the development of subcutaneous calcifications and intestinal vasculitis.

Although the patient and physician often focus on skeletal muscle involvement in these conditions, the IIM are systemic diseases with frequent extramuscular manifestations (Table 283–3). Patients may suffer from arthralgias and arthritis, a variety of skin disorders, and general symptoms such as fatigue, weight loss, Raynaud's phenomenon, or fever. The gastrointestinal, pulmonary, or cardiac system may also be involved, which can both complicate therapy and adversely affect prognosis. The development of these extramuscular manifestations may precede or follow the development of the myositis and their severity may be independent of the degree of myositis.

Diagnosis

Muscle pain and weakness are frequent patient complaints arising from many causes. These can be the result of intrinsic muscle diseases (myopathies), pathology of the nerves innervating the muscle (neuropathies), or the effects of drugs, toxins, or infectious agents. All these entities must be carefully considered and excluded to allow the diagnosis of PM or DM (Table 283–4). A careful medical and family history, complete physical examination, and directed laboratory testing with electromyography and muscle biopsy should reveal

---

Table 283–3 • EXTRAMUSCULAR MANIFESTATIONS OF POLYMYOSITIS AND DERMATOMYOSITIS

General
  Fatigue
  Malaise
  Weight loss
  Raynaud's syndrome
Musculoskeletal
  Arthralgias, usually symmetric and involving the hand joints
  Nonerosive polyarthritis, usually symmetric and involving the hand joints
  Deforming arthropathy of hand joints
  Carpal tunnel syndrome
  Osteopenia
Cutaneous
  Characteristic dermatomyositis rashes: Gottron's papules, Gottron's sign, heliotrope rash
  Other rashes: V-sign and shawl-sign rashes; linear extensor erythema; roughening, scaling, and erythematous fissuring of the palmar and lateral aspects of the fingers (mechanic's hands)
  Photosensitivity
  Periungual abnormalities including telangiectasias and cuticular overgrowth
  Irregular indurated plaques over the fingers with mucin accumulation in the dermis
  Subcutaneous and intradermal calcification, which may ulcerate with secondary infection
  Vasculitis with infarcts and digital ulcers
Gastrointestinal
  Abnormal pharyngeal and cricopharyngeal function, often leading to dysphonia
  Esophageal dysphagia with occasional nasal regurgitation or aspiration
  Delayed gastric emptying and reflux
  Dysmotility of the small and large intestines
  Malabsorption
  Vasculitis with infarcts and necrosis of the bowel
Pulmonary
  Ventilatory insufficiency due to respiratory muscle weakness
  Atelectasis
  Aspiration pneumonia
  Interstitial lung disease
  Pulmonary hypertension
  Drug-related pneumonitis
  Opportunistic infections in immunocompromised patients
Cardiac
  Myocarditis with arrhythmias and congestive failure
  Cardiomyopathy
  Cor pulmonale
  Rare pericarditis and pericardial effusions

Table 283–4 • DIFFERENTIAL DIAGNOSIS OF IDIOPATHIC INFLAMMATORY MYOPATHY

Drug- and toxin-induced myopathies
  Corticosteroids
  Ethanol
  Lipid-lowering agents (HMG-CoA reductase inhibitors and fibrates)
  D-Penicillamine
  Colchicine
  Cocaine
  Cyclosporin
  Ipecac
  Chloroquine/hydroxychloroquine
  Zidovudine (AZT)
  L-Tryptophan (eosinophilia-myalgia syndrome)
Endocrine diseases
  Hypothyroidism
  Hyperthyroidism
  Acromegaly
  Diabetes mellitus
Neurologic disorders
  Amyotrophic lateral sclerosis
  Myasthenia gravis
  Eaton-Lambert syndrome
  Multiple sclerosis
  Guillain-Barré syndrome
  Motor neuron disease
Other immunologic or connective tissue diseases
  Hypereosinophilic syndrome
  Polyarteritis nodosa and other forms of vasculitis
  Polymyalgia rheumatica
  Still's disease
  Rheumatoid arthritis
  Systemic lupus erythematosus
  Systemic sclerosis
  Tendonitis and overuse syndromes
Acquired metabolic abnormalities
  Hypokalemia
  Hypercalcemia
  Hypocalcemia
Inherited metabolic myopathies
  Acid maltase deficiency
  Phosphorylase deficiency (McArdle's disease)
  Lipid metabolic defects (primary and secondary carnitine deficiency)
  Palmityltransferase deficiency
  Phosphofructokinase deficiency
Mitochondrial myopathies
  Mitochondrial encephalomyopathy; lactic acidosis; stroke (MELAS)
  Neuropathy ataxia, retinitis pigmentosa (NARP)
  Myoclonic epilepsy, ragged red fibers (MERRF)
  Kearns-Sayre syndrome
Inherited muscle structural protein defects (dystrophies)
  Duchenne and Becker dystrophy
  Fascioscapulohumeral dystrophy
  Limb-girdle dystrophy
  Myotonic dystrophy
  Other dystrophies
Infectious myopathies
  Bacterial (pyomyositis, gangrene, Lyme disease)
  Parasitic (trichinosis, toxoplasmosis, sarcosporidiosis, trypanosomiasis)
  Fungal (candida, cryptococcus, sporotrichosis, actinomycosis, histoplasmosis)
  Viral (influenza, adenovirus, coxsackievirus, echovirus, Epstein-Barr virus, retroviruses including HIV and HTLV-I and -II, hepatitis B and C)

---

the cause of muscle weakness in most cases. Given that the muscle pathology of IIM is often focal and not evenly distributed, MRI of the muscle can be useful to identify where inflammation is present and to increase the yield of muscle biopsy.

Population-based studies have confirmed a two- to three-fold increased relative risk of a variety of cancers in roughly equal distribution to those in the population, within 2 years of the development of DM, and to a lesser extent PM. PM and DM patients at onset should therefore be carefully assessed for malignancies, especially cancers for which they have other risk factors. The cancer workup should be directed and include a thorough history for any changes in habits that might suggest a neoplasm, careful physical examinations and screening rectal examinations, fecal occult blood tests, urinalysis, blood chemistry studies, chest radiograph, and prostate-specific antigen testing in men. Women should undergo serial gynecologic examinations, Papanicolaou's stain, and CA-125 testing. Physicians should have a low threshold for performing pelvic ultrasonography or computed tomography to exclude ovarian cancer given its frequency in women with DM. Any abnormalities in these initial studies should be followed by appropriate investigations to conclusively exclude malignancy.

 Treatment

The therapy of PM and DM is directed at decreasing inflammation in target tissues, relieving symptoms, and rebuilding endurance and muscle strength. Corticosteroids are the initial and primary therapy for these diseases. Several factors are important in determining corticosteroid responses. These are, in addition to the clinical and serologic group of the patient, an adequate initial dose (at least 1 mg/kg/day of prednisone or equivalent), continuation of prednisone until or after the serum creatine kinase normalizes, and a slow rate of prednisone tapering (approximately 10 mg/month or about 15% of the existing dose per month). High-dose intravenous corticosteroids (1 g/day for 3 days) and additional immunosuppressive therapy may be useful as initial treatments in severe cases.

There is no consensus on the best treatment for corticosteroid-resistant patients. Oral methotrexate and azathioprine are the major therapeutic options used in practice, but intravenous gamma-globulin,[1] cyclosporin A, cyclophosphamide, anti-TNF agents, or combinations of these may also be beneficial in difficult cases. With the exception of the use of hydroxychloroquine and sunscreens for the treatment of the DM rash, no specific treatment other than therapy for the underlying myositis is known to improve the systemic manifestations of the IIM. Rehabilitation and physical therapy are important in maintaining range of motion and preventing contractures during active disease. Exercise probably improves strength and endurance when initiated in a graded way during disease remission.

The treatment of IBM is controversial. Retrospective reviews of corticosteroid and cytotoxic therapy, as well as several prospective trials, suggest that the rate of deterioration may be decreased or stabilized and strength improved by treating IBM patients with evidence of active myositis.[2] Physical therapy, however, plays the most important role in longer term IBM care.

Prognosis

The prognosis of PM and DM is poorly studied, but current information suggests that each clinical and serologic group may differ in response to therapy and outcome (see Table 283–2). Myositis patients who also have another connective tissue disease (the overlap group) tend to have the mildest myositis, best clinical responses, and fewest exacerbations of disease over time. DM patients have more severe disease, followed by PM patients. Patients with IBM do not respond to therapy as well as patients in the other clinical groups. The serologic groups are also different in their disease courses and prognosis. Patients with anti-Mi-2 autoantibodies tend to have mild myositis with good responses to therapy and few disease exacerbations with tapering of therapy. Anti-synthetase autoantibody patients have more severe disease, moderate therapeutic responses, but frequent exacerbations with tapering of therapy. Anti-SRP patients have the most acute onset, and the most severe myositis, with the least response to therapy, and the most persistent disease.

Any patient with an unexpectedly unresponsive or perplexing clinical course, however, should be reevaluated for possible misdiagnosis or the development of another cause of muscle weakness.

Future Directions

Given the current incurable nature of the myositis syndromes and the poor outcomes in many patients, future directions will likely be focused on improved classification criteria to separate the IIM from dystrophies and metabolic myopathies through the use of molecular genetic and immunologic information. A more complete understanding of the pathogenesis of these disorders may result in more focused therapies. Because these complex diseases likely arise from interactions of genetic and environmental risk factors, defining these elements may provide insight into the mechanisms of development of myositis. This knowledge could possibly allow for prevention of some myositis cases by avoidance of certain environmental exposures in genetically susceptible individuals or via gene therapy.

1. Dalakas MC, Illa I, Dambrosia JM, et al: A controlled trial of high-dose intravenous immune globulin infusions as treatment for dermatomyositis. N Engl J Med 1993;329:1993–2000.
2. Leff RL, Miller FW, Hicks J, et al: The treatment of inclusion body myositis: A retrospective review and a randomized, prospective trial of immunosuppressive therapy. Medicine (Baltimore) 1993;72:225–235.

SUGGESTED READINGS
Briemberg HR, Amato AA: Dermatomyositis and polymyositis. Curr Treat Options Neurol 2003;5:349–356. *A current review of established and experimental approaches.*
Marie I, Hachulla E, Hatron PY, et al: Polymyositis and dermatomyositis: Short term and long term outcome, and predictive factors of prognosis. J Rheumatol 2001;28:2230–2237. *Lung and esophageal involvement are predictors of poor prognosis.*
Stockton D, Doherty VR, Brewster DH: Risk of cancer in patients with dermatomyositis or polymyositis, and follow-up implications: A Scottish population-based cohort study. Br J Cancer 2001;85:41–45. *Risk is increased 7-fold, mostly during the first two years.*
Wakata N, Kurihara T, Saito E, et al: Polymyositis and dermatomyositis associated with malignancy: A 30-year retrospective study. Int J Dermatol 2002;41:729–734. *Most cancers appeared in one to at most four years but often were very advanced when diagnosed.*

284 THE SYSTEMIC VASCULITIDES

John H. Stone

Definition

The vasculitides are a heterogeneous group of disorders linked by the common finding of destructive inflammation within blood vessel walls. Based on current classification schemes, approximately 20 different forms of primary vasculitis are recognized (Table 284–1).

Table 284–1 • CLASSIFICATION SCHEME OF VASCULITIDES ACCORDING TO SIZE OF PREDOMINANT BLOOD VESSELS INVOLVED

Predominantly Large-Vessel Vasculitides
Takayasu's arteritis
Giant cell arteritis
Cogan's syndrome
Behçet's disease[†]

Predominantly Medium-Vessel Vasculitides
Classic polyarteritis nodosa
Cutaneous polyarteritis nodosa
Rheumatoid vasculitis*
Buerger's disease
Kawasaki's disease
Primary angiitis of the central nervous system

Predominantly Small-Vessel Vasculitides
Immune-complex mediated
  Cutaneous leukocytoclastic angiitis ("hypersensitivity" vasculitis)
  Henoch-Schönlein purpura
  Urticarial vasculitis
  Cryoglobulinemia*
  Erythema elevatum diutinum
"ANCA-associated" disorders
  Wegener's granulomatosis*
  Microscopic polyangiitis*
  Churg-Strauss syndrome*
Miscellaneous small-vessel vasculitides
  Connective tissue disorders*
  Paraneoplastic diseases
  Infection
  Inflammatory bowel disease

*Frequent overlap of small- and medium-sized blood vessel involvement.
†May involve small-, medium-, and large-sized blood vessels.
ANCA = antineutrophil cytoplasmic antibody.

CLASSIFICATION BY VESSEL SIZE. The etiologies of most forms of vasculitis remain unknown. Because of the major gaps in understanding, the most valid basis for classifying the vasculitides is the size of the predominant blood vessels involved. The vasculitides are categorized initially by whether the vessels affected are *large, medium,* or *small* (see Table 284–1). Within individual cases, there is frequently overlap in the size of the blood vessels affected.

ADDITIONAL CONSIDERATIONS IN CLASSIFICATION. Several other considerations are relevant to the classification of vasculitis (Table 284–2). These are (1) the age, gender, and ethnic background of the patient; (2) the disease's tropism for particular organs; (3) the presence or absence of granulomatous inflammation; (4) the participation of immune complexes in disease pathophysiology; and (5) the detection of characteristic autoantibodies in the patients' serum, such as antineutrophil cytoplasmic antibodies (ANCAs).

The organ tropisms of these disorders are illustrated by the following examples: Whereas Henoch-Schönlein purpura (HSP) typically affects the skin, joints, kidneys, and gastrointestinal tract, Wegener's granulomatosis (WG) classically involves the upper airways, lungs, and kidneys. In contrast to both of these, Cogan's syndrome (CS) involves the eyes, the audiovestibular apparatus of the inner ear, and the large arteries (in 10 to 15% of cases). The granulomatous features of some forms of vasculitis resemble fungal and mycobacterial infections, or the inflammation induced by the presence of a foreign body, suggesting a role for chronic antigenic stimulation.

Immune complexes are essential to the pathophysiology of some small- and medium-vessel vasculitides. Complexes of IgA1 are found in HSP. Immune complexes consisting of IgG, IgM, complement components, and the hepatitis C virion characterize most cases of mixed cryoglobulinemia. In contrast, "pauci-immune" types of small- and medium-vessel vasculitis such as WG and microscopic polyangiitis (MPA) have little immunoglobulin or complement deposition within diseased tissues. Many but not all patients with pauci-immune forms of vasculitis are ANCA positive.

Epidemiology

The epidemiologic features of individual forms of systemic vasculitis vary tremendously by geography (Table 284–3). This may reflect genetic influences, variation in environmental exposures, and other unknown disease risk factors. For example, whereas Behçet's disease (BD) is rare in North Americans, affecting only 1 person in approximately 300,000, this condition is several hundred times more common among inhabitants of countries bordering the ancient Silk Route. Similarly, although Takayasu's arteritis (TA) is rare in the United States—on the order of 3 new cases per million people per year—this disease is reportedly the most common cause of renal artery stenosis in India, where the incidence may be as high as 200 to 300 per million per year.

Age is an important consideration in the epidemiology of vasculitis. Eighty percent of patients with Kawasaki's disease (KD) are younger than 5 years of age. In contrast, giant cell arteritis virtually never occurs in patients younger than 50 years of age, and the mean age of patients with this disease is 72 years. Age may also impact disease severity and outcome. In HSP, the overwhelming majority of cases in children (who comprise 90% of all cases) have self-limited courses, resolving within several weeks. In adults, however, HSP has a higher likelihood of chronicity and a greater likelihood of a poor renal outcome.

The distribution of gender varies across many forms of vasculitis. Buerger's disease is the only form of vasculitis with a striking male predominance. The greater prevalence of smoking among males in most societies probably explains this predilection. In contrast, TA has an overwhelming tendency to occur in females (a 9:1 female-male ratio). The pauci-immune forms of vasculitis such as WG, MPA, and Churg-Strauss syndrome (CSS) occur in males and females with approximately equal frequencies.

The strongest link between any single gene and vasculitis is the association of HLA-B51 with BD. In BD, 80% of Asian patients have the HLA-B51 gene. The prevalence of HLA-B51 is significantly higher among patients with BD in Japan than among non-disease controls (55% vs. < 15%). Among the sporadic cases of BD involving whites in the United States, however, HLA-B51 occurs in fewer than 15% of cases.

With the exception of Buerger's disease and smoking, no true associations between disease and environmental or occupation exposures have been confirmed. Associations have also been reported but not confirmed between exposures to silica and some types of pauci-immune vasculitis. However, precise definitions of relationships between exposures and vasculitis are complicated by difficulties in obtaining reliable measurements of the levels of such exposures, the likelihood of recall bias among patients who are diagnosed with vasculitis, and the choice of appropriate control groups.

Pathology

Table 284–4 illustrates the pathologic characteristics of selected forms of vasculitis. Specific pathologic features are discussed in the subsections on each disease. The type of inflammatory cell infiltrate in vasculitis is independent of the size of blood vessels involved. Mixed cell infiltrates in vasculitis are the rule rather than the exception, and histopathologic patterns of vasculitis may include leukocytoclasis,* granulomatous findings (with or without giant cells), lymphoplasmacytic infiltrates, varying degrees of eosinophilic infiltration, necrosis, and combinations of all of these findings.

Individual forms of vasculitis may demonstrate more than one set of histopathologic findings. For example, giant cell arteritis may be associated with a lymphocytic infiltrate in the media and adventitia in some cases but also with a panarteritis characterized by granulomatous inflammation, giant cell formation, and intimal proliferation in others. Conversely, the same inflammatory pattern may occur in several types of disease. Leukocytoclastic vasculitis may be observed by light microscopy in such disparate disorders as medication-induced cutaneous leukocytoclastic angiitis (CLA), HSP, and WG. Distinction among these disorders may be facilitated by histologic findings on biopsy but often requires rigorous clinicopathologic correlation.

Pathophysiology

Regardless of the size of the predominant blood vessels involved, some pathophysiologic mechanisms are common to many different forms of vasculitis. Immune complex deposition, for example, is present in several types of both medium- and small-vessel vasculitis. In this section, the general concepts related to the pathogenesis of large vessel vasculitides are discussed separately from those of medium- and small-vessel vasculitides.

PATHOPHYSIOLOGY OF LARGE-VESSEL VASCULITIDES. The pathologic process in large-vessel vasculitis appears to begin in the adventitia. Here, in both TA and giant cell arteritis, abundant numbers of activated T lymphocytes are found within inflamed arterial walls, centering on the adventitia. In TA, most of these T cells appear to be of the CD8+ subtype. Current evidence suggests that the cytotoxic functions of these cells, mediated by perforin and granzyme B, contribute to smooth muscle cell damage in this disease. CD4+ T-cell responses in TA have not been well defined.

In giant cell arteritis, much evidence now suggests an antigen-driven disease with the site of immunologic recognition events being

Table 284–2 • CONSIDERATIONS IN THE CLASSIFICATION OF SYSTEMIC VASCULITIS

Size of predominant blood vessels affected
Epidemiologic features
  Age
  Gender
  Ethnic background
Pattern of organ involvement
Pathologic features
  Granulomatous inflammation
  Immune complex deposition vs. "pauci-immune" histopathology
Presence of ANCA in serum

    ANCA = antineutrophil cytoplasmic antibody.

*Leukocytoclasis is the degranulation of polymorphonuclear leukocytes within blood vessel walls, leaving small nuclear fragments and karyorrhexis (i.e., "nuclear dust") in and around the vessels.

Table 284–3 • EPIDEMIOLOGY OF SELECTED VASCULITIDES

DISEASE	UNITED STATES	ELSEWHERE	AGE/GENDER/ETHNIC PREDISPOSITIONS
Giant cell arteritis	Incidence: 240/million (Olmsted County, MN)	220–270/million (Scandinavian countries)	Age > 50 yr, mean age 72; females 3 : 1; northern European ancestry
Takayasu's arteritis	Incidence: 3/million	200–300/million (India)	Age < 40 yr; females 9 : 1; Asian
Behçet's disease	Prevalence: 3/million	3000/million (Turkey)	Silk Route countries
Polyarteritis nodosa	Incidence: 7/million	7/million (Spain)	Slight male predominance
Kawasaki's disease	Incidence: 100/million*	900/million (Japan)	Children of Asian ancestry
Wegener's granulomatosis	Incidence: 4/million	8.5/million (United Kingdom)	Whites >> blacks

*Among children < 5 years of age.
From Gonzalez-Gay MA, Garica-Porrua C: Epidemiology of the vasculitides. Rheum Clin North Am 2001;27:729–749.

Table 284–4 • PATHOLOGIC CHARACTERISTICS OF SELECTED FORMS OF VASCULITIS

	TAKAYASU'S ARTERITIS	POLYARTERITIS NODOSA	WEGENER'S GRANULOMATOSIS	CHURG-STRAUSS SYNDROME	HENOCH-SCHÖNLEIN PURPURA	CUTANEOUS LEUKOCYTOCLASTIC ANGIITIS
Vessels involved	Elastic (large) or muscular (medium-sized) arteries	Medium- and small-sized muscular arteries	Small-sized arteries and veins; sometimes medium-sized vessels	Small-sized arteries and veins; sometimes medium-sized vessels	Capillaries, venules, and arterioles	Capillaries, venules, and arterioles
Organ involvement	Aorta, aortic arch and major branches, and pulmonary arteries	Skin, peripheral nerve, GI tract, and other viscera	Upper respiratory tract, lungs, kidneys, skin, eyes	Upper respiratory tract, lungs, heart, peripheral nerves	Skin, joints, GI tract, kidneys	Skin, joints
Type of vasculitis and inflammatory cells	Granulomatous with some giant cells; fibrosis in chronic stages	Necrotizing, with mixed cellular infiltrate	Necrotizing or granulomatous (or both); mixed cellular infiltrate, plus occasional eosinophils	Necrotizing or granulomatous (or both); prominent eosinophils, and other mixed infiltrate	Leukocytoclastic, with some lymphocytes and variable eosinophils IgA deposits in affected tissues	Leukocytoclastic, with occasional eosinophils

GI = gastrointestinal.

the adventitia. CD4+ T cells that secrete interferon-γ appear to be recruited to the adventitia by a specific antigen(s), the identity of which remains unknown. Both the T cells that orchestrate the transmural inflammation and the inciting antigen(s) are theorized to reach the adventitia through the vasa vasorum. Subsequently, T-cell signals from the adventitia stimulate macrophages and multinucleated giant cells to elaborate an array of downstream mediators, such as metalloproteinases and platelet-derived growth factor. The results of this inflammatory cascade are granulomatous inflammation, fibrinoid necrosis, destruction of the internal elastic lamina, arterial wall hyperplasia, smooth muscle cell proliferation, intimal thickening, vascular occlusion and, in some cases, weakening of the vessel wall leading to dilation and aneurysm formation.

MEDIUM- AND SMALL-VESSEL VASCULITIDES. Several different pathophysiologic mechanisms are operative among the medium- and small-vessel vasculitides. In many cases, the mechanisms outlined in the following sections (and other mechanisms) overlap.

Immune Complex–Mediated Vascular Injury. Immune complex–mediated tissue injury does not produce a single clinical syndrome but rather applies to many forms of vasculitis and overlaps with injuries caused by other immune mechanisms. Numerous variables influence the nature of immune complex–mediated injury, including the physical properties of the complexes (e.g., size), the ability of the immune complexes to activate complement, the antigen/antibody ratio, and the hemodynamic features of specific vascular beds. Immune complexes participate in the pathophysiology of some forms of both medium- and small-vessel forms of vasculitis, including polyarteritis nodosa (PAN), cryoglobulinemia, HSP, CLA, and rheumatoid vasculitis.

Hepatitis B virus (HBV) surface antigen/antibody complexes are present in the circulation of patients with HBV-associated PAN. Moreover, deposits of HBV surface antigen, immunoglobulin, and complement are found in the vasculitic lesions of muscular arteries, dermal

capillaries, glomeruli, and vasa nervorum. In what was formerly known as "essential" mixed cryoglobulinemia, anti-hepatitis C virus (HCV) antibodies and HCV RNA have been detected in cryoprecipitates of patients with cryoglobulinemic vasculitis, as well as in dermal lesions.

Role of ANCA. ANCA are directed against antigens that reside within the primary granules of neutrophils and monocytes. Two types of ANCA are relevant to vasculitis: (1) ANCA directed against proteinase-3 (PR-3), and (2) ANCA directed against myeloperoxidase (MPO). ANCAs interact with cytokines, neutrophils, monocytes, and other elements of the immune system to amplify ongoing inflammation in certain forms of vasculitis. However, evidence for a primary etiologic role of these antibodies in pauci-immune vasculitis is lacking.

The three types of vasculitis often associated with ANCA are WG, MPA, and CSS. WG is typically associated with antibodies to PR-3, which cause a cytoplasmic ANCA (C-ANCA) pattern of staining on immunofluorescence testing of serum. Between 55 and 90% of patients with WG are ANCA positive. Seventy percent of patients with MPO have ANCA, typically with an antigen specificity for MPO. These antibodies usually cause perinuclear ANCA (P-ANCA) staining on immunofluorescence testing. Only about 50% of patients with CSS are ANCA positive, with a slight tendency toward anti-MPO antibodies.

In WG, abnormal cytokine regulation interacts with the production of ANCA to fuel the inflammatory response. Tumor necrosis factor (TNF) and other Th1 cytokines appear to play central roles. In animal models, granuloma formation is markedly impaired by antibodies to TNF. Under the direction of interleukin-12, CD4+ T cells from patients with WG produce elevated levels of TNF, and peripheral blood mononuclear cells secrete increased amounts of interferon-γ. Serum levels of soluble receptors for TNF are elevated in patients with active WG and normalize with the induction of remission. Finally, in vitro priming of activated neutrophils with TNF markedly enhances the ability of ANCA to stimulate neutrophil degranulation.

Superantigen Model. The degree of immune activation in KD, and the acute but generally self-limited nature of this illness, imply a potential role for superantigens. Superantigens are proteins produced by microbial pathogens (e.g., *Staphylococcus aureus* or *Streptococcus* species) that are capable of stimulating large populations of T cells in an unrestricted, class II major histocompatibility complex (MHC)-dependent manner. Superantigens bind directly to conserved amino acid residues outside the antigen-binding groove on class II MHC molecules, thereby selectively stimulating T cells that express particular β-chain variable gene segments. Through the binding of this MHC-superantigen complex to its cognate T-cell receptors, as many as 20% of circulating lymphocytes may become activated, leading to a potentially enormous outpouring of cytokines. Substantial attention has focused on toxic shock syndrome toxin-1, an exotoxin produced by *S. aureus*. Superantigens have also been postulated to play roles in the susceptibility to disease flares in WG. Nasal carriage of *S. aureus* and superantigens associated with these organisms have been linked to a greater likelihood of disease flares.

ANTIENDOTHELIAL CELL ANTIBODIES. Antiendothelial cell antibodies can induce endothelial cell injury and lysis through either complement-mediated cytotoxicity or antibody-dependent cellular cytotoxicity. Both of these mechanisms have been demonstrated to cause endothelial injury in in vitro assays employing sera from patients with systemic vasculitis. The ability of these antibodies to damage endothelial cells is an appealing argument for their potential role in forms of vasculitis in which the endothelium is the focus of the inflammation (as opposed to the more external vessel wall layers). However, the true relevance of antiendothelial cell antibodies to human disease and their importance within the larger context of other disease mechanisms remain unclear.

Systemic Vasculitis and Infection. Since the 1970s, persistent HBV infection has been linked to some cases of PAN. During the 1990s, firm links were established between HCV infections and 90% of the cases of essential mixed cryoglobulinemia. Recently described animal models of spontaneous vasculitides induced by viral infections heighten the likelihood that similar mechanisms are operative in human disease.

Clinical Manifestations

LARGE-VESSEL VASCULITIDES

Takayasu's Arteritis

TA has a predilection for the aorta and its major branches. In contrast to atherosclerosis, which is characterized by focal, irregular lesions, the lesions of TA are long, smooth, tapered stenoses (Fig. 284–1A). The most commonly involved arteries in TA are the subclavian and innominate arteries. Because of its ability to obliterate peripheral pulses (particularly in the upper extremities), TA has been termed the "pulseless disease." Exuberant collateral circulation tends to develop in response to the narrowing of major arteries. The pulmonary circulation is involved in approximately 50% of cases of TA.

TA patients with severe narrowing of the aortic arch vessels supplying the head may develop Takayasu's retinopathy, a hypotension retinopathy leading to neurovascularization. In contrast, patients with prolonged hypertension associated with renal artery stenosis demonstrate the classic ocular features of hypertension: copper-wiring and multiple retinal infarctions. TA involvement of the ascending aorta may lead to aortic dilation, aneurysm formation, and aortic rupture (Fig. 284–1B). TA may also cause intrinsic cardiac disease, including cardiomyopathy and valvular dysfunction secondary to valvulitis.

The cornerstone of treatment of TA is corticosteroids. For patients with marked symptoms and signs of an inflammatory phase, prednisone 1 mg/kg/day is usually effective in controlling the disease. This dose should be tapered within 8 to 12 weeks to less than 20 mg/day, and ultimately to less than 10 mg/day as a maintenance dose. In patients with TA that is refractory to moderate doses of corticosteroids, methotrexate (up to 25 mg/week) and mycophenolate mofetil (1500 mg twice daily) may be useful.

Cogan's Syndrome

The combination of inflammatory eye disease and vestibuloauditory dysfunction is the sine qua non of CS. In addition to inflammatory disease of the eyes and ears, up to 15% of CS patients have a large- to medium-vessel vasculitis. Although the ocular manifestations vary, the classic presentation is that of interstitial keratitis and sensorineural hearing loss. CS may appear first in either the eyes or the ears. Although intervals as long as 1 to 2 years have been described between the start of disease in one organ and the appearance of disease in the other, the time between disease manifestations in these organs is usually only a matter of months. The vascular disease in CS resembles TA. Medium- and large-vessel arteritis may lead to a host of complications in patients with CS, including aortitis, aortic regurgitation, coronary artery inflammation, mesenteric vasculitis, limb claudication, and other manifestations. Interstitial keratitis generally responds well to topical corticosteroid therapy. Rapidly progressive sensorineural hearing loss requires early, aggressive therapy with high doses of systemic corticosteroids. Cytotoxic agents may be added for patients with suboptimal responses to corticosteroids who still have salvageable hearing.

Behçet's Disease

BD may affect small-, medium-, and large-sized vessels, in either the venous or the arterial circulation. The most typical lesions in BD are mucocutaneous, reflecting the involvement of small-sized blood vessels. The triad of recurrent mouth ulcers, genital ulcers, and eye inflammation is the classic presentation. The criteria of the International Study Group for the Diagnosis of BD consist of one required manifestation—recurrent oral ulceration—plus at least two of the following: recurrent genital ulceration, characteristic eye or skin lesions, or a positive pathergy test. However, the spectrum of BD includes other disease manifestations not included in the diagnostic criteria. Large-vessel complications of BD may include aneurysms in the pulmonary and/or systemic arterial systems. Venous complications include deep venous, vena caval, portohepatic vein, and cerebral sinus thromboses. Pathergy—the development of pustules at the sites of sterile needle pricks—is a distinctive feature in many patients with BD, particularly those of Turkish origin. The arthritis of BD is a nondeforming, oligoarticular, asymmetrical arthritis of large joints. Gastrointestinal lesions in BD typically consist of ulcerations of the distal ileum or cecum. Crohn's disease, which can cause genital ulcers as well as gastrointestinal tract pathology, may be particularly difficult to distinguish from BD.

Colchicine (up to 1.5 to 2 mg/day) is sometimes effective for mild oral and genital ulcers in BD. Thalidomide (100 mg/day) is also useful for mucocutaneous disease manifestations. Severe disease in any organ system almost always requires high doses of prednisone (e.g., 1 mg/kg/day). Chlorambucil (0.2 mg/kg/day, increased as tolerated) or cyclophosphamide (2 mg/kg/day) is indicated for the most severe forms of uveitis or meningoencephalitis. Azathioprine (2 mg/kg/day), cyclosporine (3 to 5 mg/kg/day in two divided doses), methotrexate (up to 25 mg/week), interferon-α (3 million to 5 million units three times a week), and pentoxifylline (300 mg three times/day) have also been employed in BD.

MEDIUM-VESSEL VASCULITIDES

Polyarteritis Nodosa

First described in 1866 by Kussmaul and Maier, PAN was the only widely recognized form of vasculitis for decades. The 1994 International Consensus Conference on the Nomenclature of Systemic Vasculitides defined classic PAN as necrotizing inflammation of medium- or small-sized arteries that spares the smallest blood vessels (arterioles, venules, and capillaries). PAN has a striking predilection for certain organs, particularly the skin, peripheral nerves, gastrointestinal tract, and kidneys.

PAN usually begins with nonspecific symptoms that may include malaise, fatigue, fever, myalgias, and arthralgias. Overt signs of

Continued

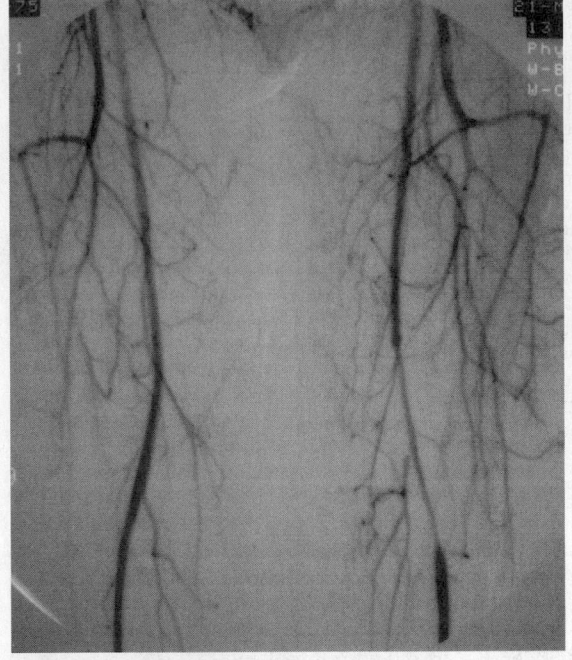

A(i)

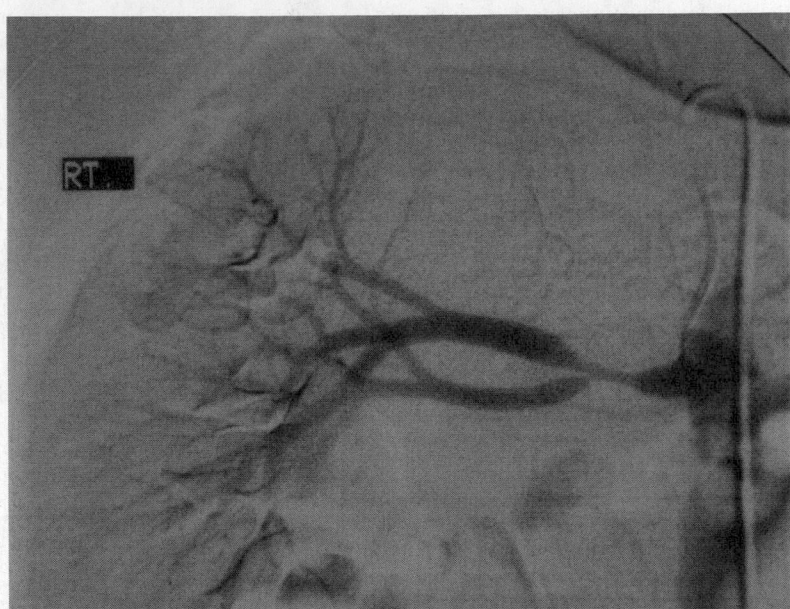

A(ii)

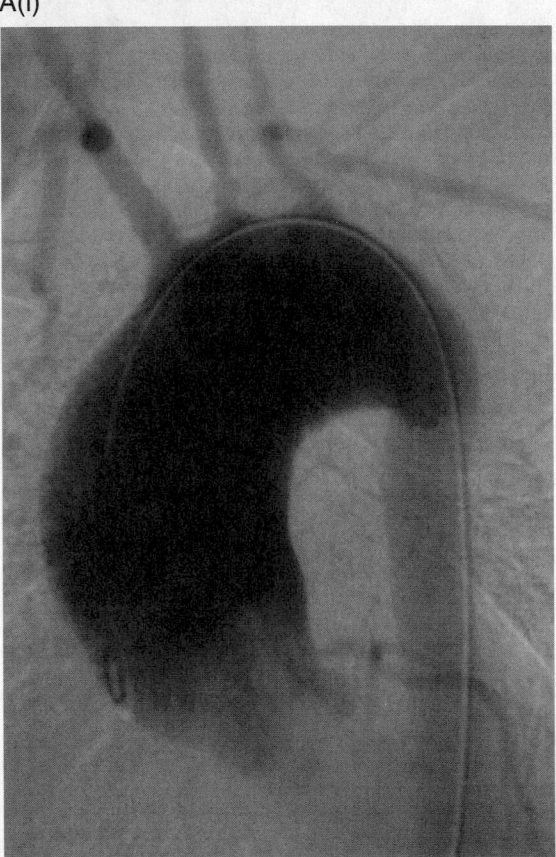

B

FIGURE 284–1 • Large-vessel disease in Takayasu's arteritis. *A*, Long, smooth taperings in the left common femoral artery (*i*) and the right renal artery (*ii*). *B*, Dilation of the ascending aorta. Aortic regurgitation necessitated an aortic valve replacement and replacement of the ascending aorta with a Gore-Tex graft.

vasculitis may not occur until weeks or months after onset of the first symptoms. Skin lesions of PAN include livedo reticularis, subcutaneous nodules, ulcers, and digital gangrene. A majority of patients with PAN (>80% in some series) have vasculitic neuropathy, typically in the pattern of a mononeuritis multiplex.

The classic gastrointestinal manifestation of PAN is "intestinal angina," the occurrence of postprandial abdominal pain. PAN can also affect individual gastrointestinal tract organs such as the gallbladder or appendix, presenting as cholecystitis or appendicitis. The typical renal manifestation of PAN is vasculitic involvement of the medium-sized intrarenal arteries, leading to renin-mediated hypertension and renal infarctions. Cardiac lesions, which usually remain subclinical, may lead to myocardial infarction or con-gestive heart failure. For reasons that are not understood, PAN usually spares the lungs.

The diagnosis of PAN requires either a tissue biopsy or an angiogram that demonstrates microaneurysms (Fig. 284–2). Simultaneous nerve/muscle biopsies (e.g., sural nerve and gastrocnemius muscle) are of high yield if there is a clinical suspicion of vasculitic neuropathy. The pathologic changes in PAN are limited to the arterial circulation. The lesions of PAN are segmental and favor the branch points of arteries. In gross pathologic specimens, aneurysmal bulges of the arterial wall may be visible. Histologic sections reveal infiltration and destruction of the blood vessel wall by inflammatory cells, accompanied by fibrinoid necrosis. Granulomatous inflammation is absent.

Approximately one half of patients with PAN achieve remissions or cures with high doses of corticosteroids alone. Cyclophosphamide (2 mg/kg/day, adjusted for renal dysfunction) is indicated for patients whose disease is refractory to cortico-steroids or who have serious involvement of major organs. In recent years, therapeutic regimens involving lamivudine have improved the treatment of HBV-associated PAN substantially. Because of increasing use of the HBV vaccine, fewer cases of PAN are associated with HBV infections than in previous eras (<10% now).

Rheumatoid Vasculitis

Rheumatoid vasculitis is a severe complication of rheumatoid arthritis that sometimes occurs in patients with long-standing, erosive rheumatoid arthritis. The typical patient has a history of seropositive disease, rheumatoid nodules, and arthritis that is no longer active. Risk factors for rheumatoid vasculitis include male gender; a high titer of rheumatoid factor; history of erosive, joint-destructive arthritis; the presence of rheumatoid nodules; history of extra-articular disease features; the occurrence of Felty's syndrome; and possibly possession of the HLA-DRB1*04 allele. Rheumatoid vasculitis closely mimics PAN in its behavior. Rheumatoid vasculitis usually requires treatment with cyclophosphamide and prednisone. In addition to the PAN-like form of rheumatoid vasculitis, a milder form of vasculitis exists in rheumatoid arthritis. The benign form typically leads to minor nailbed infarctions but does not herald the onset of systemic vasculitis and does not require additional treatment beyond that required to treat the underlying arthritis.

Buerger's Disease

Buerger's disease, also known as *thromboangiitis obliterans*, has a remarkably strong yet poorly understood association with cigarette smoking. Buerger's disease does not occur in the absence of exposure to tobacco. The vessels affected by Buerger's disease are the distal, medium-sized arteries and veins, particularly vessels at the levels of the ankles and wrists. The disease is characterized by thrombotic obliterations that begin distally and proceed proximally. Buerger's disease tends to be segmental in nature, involving 5- to 10-cm lengths of blood vessels. Arterial obliteration leads to the development of collateral vessels with a "corkscrew" appearance on angiography. Vascular occlusion in Buerger's disease often leads to the loss of digits and, if smoking persists, larger amounts of tissue (e.g., hands or feet). Despite the intense involvement of the extremities in Buerger's disease, internal organ disease almost never occurs.

Complete abstinence from tobacco is essential to the treatment of Buerger's disease. Failure to stop smoking is associated with a dramatic increase in the risk of limb loss by amputation. No other therapeutic interventions, including corticosteroids or anticoagulation, have dramatic effects on Buerger's disease.

Kawasaki's Disease

KD occurs exclusively in young children. Because of its striking mucocutaneous findings and lymphadenopathy, KD is also known as *mucocutaneous lymph node syndrome*. Features of KD include high fevers, cervical adenopathy, conjunctival congestion, buccal erythema, protuberance of the tongue papillae ("strawberry tongue"), a polymorphous truncal rash, erythema of the palms and soles, and desquamation of skin from the fingertips occurring days to weeks into the illness. In its acuity and severity, KD resembles toxic shock syndrome and scarlet fever, both of which are mediated by superantigens (see Pathophysiology).

In a small number of patients, severe panvasculitis in the coronary vessels leads to acute cardiac complications. Coronary arteritis leads to narrowing of the vessel lumen by the migration of myointimal cells from the media through the fragmented internal elastic lamina. Direct complications include aneurysmal dilation and thrombosis of the coronary arteries, leading to myocardial infarction and possibly to death (in 1 to 2% during the acute illness). Late mortality from myocardial infarction may occur from the thrombosis of coronary artery aneurysms formed during the initial inflammatory stage.

The recommended therapeutic regimen in KD is the combination of intravenous immunoglobulin (IVIG) (400 mg/kg/day on 4 consecutive days) and acetylsalicylic acid (ASA) (100 mg/kg/day, lowered to 3 to 5 mg/kg/day after resolution of the fever). IVIG prevents the formation of coronary aneurysms in most cases. Corticosteroids are reserved for salvage therapy in patients who fail IVIG and ASA.

Vasculitis of the Central Nervous System

Central nervous system (CNS) vasculitis includes two major categories of disease: (1) true CNS vasculitis (also known as *primary angiitis of the CNS* [PACNS]); and (2) "benign" angiopathy of the CNS (BACNS). BACNS should be regarded as a vasculopathy, not a true vasculitis. Both PACNS and BACNS are syndromes that have many potential causes.

PRIMARY ANGIITIS OF THE CNS. Patients with PACNS may manifest the triad of headache, encephalopathy, and multifocal strokes that the disorder develops in a subacute fashion. The first symptom is usually headache, often severe and sometimes associated with nausea and vomiting. If untreated, almost all patients eventually develop lethargy, confusion, and memory loss. Some develop multifocal strokes, seizures, evidence of increased intracranial pressure, or myelopathy. Routine laboratory tests (e.g., the erythrocyte sedimentation rate) are often normal in PACNS. Lumbar puncture demonstrates abnormalities of the cerebrospinal fluid in approximately 80% of cases, usually a modest monocytosis and elevated protein.

The classic abnormality on angiography is the "string of beads" pattern produced by segmental arterial narrowing alternating with dilations. Vascular occlusions, collateral formation, and prolonged circulation time may also be seen. However, no angiographic pattern is pathognomonic. Other disorders, particularly those that cause vasospasm, can produce identical angiographic abnormalities. Angiograms are falsely negative in about 35% of patients with PACNS. Magnetic resonance imaging (MRI) is more sensitive than computed tomography in the evaluation of possible CNS vasculitis. Typical findings are multiple bilateral infarctions. Hemorrhagic lesions and mass lesions also occur.

Biopsies should be directed toward radiologically evident lesions. The yield of biopsy procedures may be increased by sampling the leptomeninges as well at the underlying cortex. Histopathologic specimens of the leptomeninges and cortex in PACNS show vasculitis of the small- and medium-sized arteries. Prednisone and cyclophosphamide are recommended for patients who have positive brain biopsies. Treatment courses of 6 to 12 months are recommended.

BENIGN ANGIOPATHY OF THE CNS. An increasing number of cases of CNS "vasculitis" are reported in which the diagnosis is based on angiography alone, without the performance of a brain biopsy. These patients differ from biopsy-confirmed cases in that 80% are women, the onset of their symptoms is comparatively abrupt, their neurologic signs are less severe (encephalopathy is less common), and their lumbar punctures are normal. The term "benign" may be misleading, however, because strokes and significant neurologic dysfunction sometimes occur in BACNS. However, patients with BACNS are less likely than those with PACNS to require cyclophosphamide or prolonged treatment with corticosteroids.

Three fourths of the patients have abnormal brain MRI studies. Angiographic findings in BACNS, consisting of vascular narrowing or beading, are generally indistinguishable from those of PACNS and conditions that mimic PACNS. The most distinctive angiographic feature of BACNS is that the abnormalities are completely reversible, usually within 4 to 8 weeks. Thus, these abnormalities are believed to reflect vasospasm rather than true vasculitis. In the evaluation of patients with potential BACNS, the essential test is often a repeat CNS angiogram at 4 to 8 weeks. Angiographic abnormalities due to BACNS should resolve in this interval.

Continued

Prednisone alone (beginning at 1 mg/kg per day) is adequate therapy for some patients with BACNS. The corticosteroids can be tapered off over 3 to 6 months. Calcium-channel blockers have been added in attempts to reduce vasospasm. Cytotoxic therapy is not indicated for this group of patients.

SMALL-VESSEL VASCULITIDES

Wegener's Granulomatosis

Classic WG involves the upper respiratory tract, the lungs, and the kidneys. Distinctive features may also occur in the eyes, ears, and other organs. The three pathologic hallmarks of WG are (1) granulomatous inflammation in the upper and/or lower respiratory tract; (2) necrotizing vasculitis affecting arteries or veins; and (3) segmental glomerulonephritis, associated with necrosis and thrombosis of capillary loops, with or without granulomatous lesions.

Approximately 90% of patients with WG have nasal involvement, including crusting, bleeding, and obstruction. Cartilaginous inflammation may lead to nasal septal perforation and collapse of the nasal bridge ("saddle-nose" deformity). Erosive sinus disease and subglottic stenosis (narrowing of the trachea just below the vocal cords) are highly characteristic of WG.

Two principal forms of ear disease—conductive and sensorineural hearing loss—are typical of WG. Conductive hearing loss, caused by middle ear disease, is more common. Orbital masses ("pseudotumors") and scleritis are the signature ocular lesions of WG. Scleritis may lead to scleromalacia perforans and visual loss. The clinical manifestations of WG in the lung range from asymptomatic nodules to fulminant alveolar hemorrhage. The most common radiographic findings are pulmonary infiltrates and nodules. The infiltrates, which may wax and wane, are often misdiagnosed initially as pneumonia. Nodules are usually multiple and bilateral and often result in cavitation.

Renal involvement is the most ominous clinical manifestation of WG. The clinical presentation of renal disease in WG is that of rapidly progressive glomerulonephritis: hematuria, red blood cell (RBC) casts, and proteinuria (usually non-nephrotic). Without appropriate therapy, end-stage renal disease may ensue within days to weeks.

Sixty percent of patients with WG have musculoskeletal symptoms during their disease courses. Arthralgias/arthritis are frequently the presenting complaint. Splinter hemorrhages, digital ischemia, and digital gangrene all may occur in WG. Skin lesions in WG include the full panoply of lesions associated with cutaneous vasculitis, including purpura (Fig. 284-3). Meningeal inflammation, presenting with headaches, cranial neuropathies, and a clinical picture compatible with chronic meningitis, is perhaps the most common CNS manifestation of WG. Mononeuritis multiplex may affect the peripheral nervous system.

WG is the prototype of conditions associated with C-ANCA. Positive immunofluorescence tests for ANCA should be confirmed by enzyme immunoassays for antibodies to either PR-3 or MPO. However, a negative ANCA assay does not preclude the diagnosis of WG. Up to 40% of patients with WG lack these antibodies. Furthermore, ANCA titers do not correlate reliably with disease activity. Titers of ANCA tend to decline following the institution of immunosuppressive therapy but do not always become

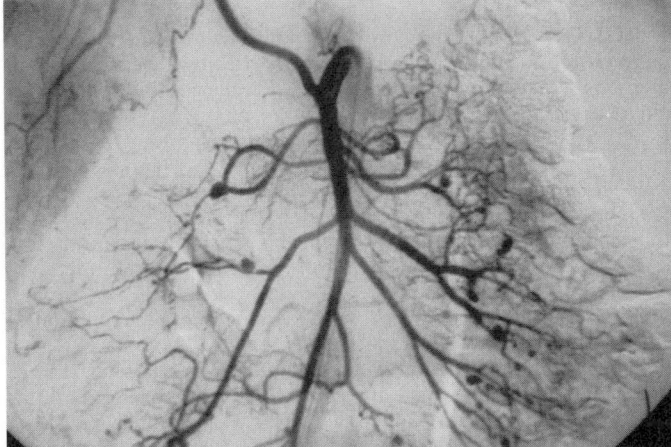

A

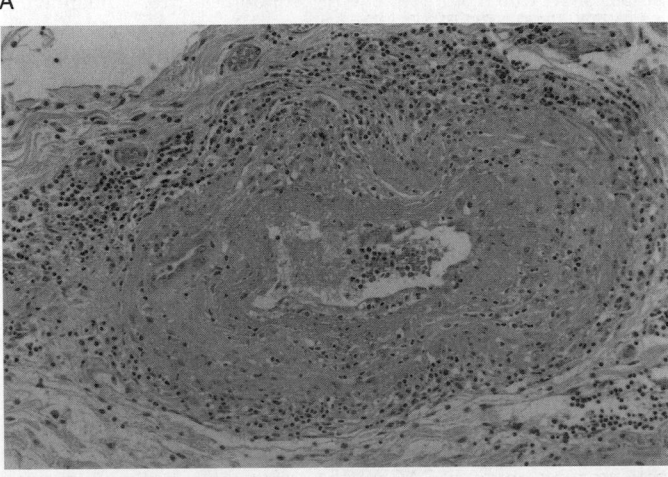

B

FIGURE 284-2 • Vasculitis of medium-sized arteries in polyarteritis nodosa. *A,* Mesenteric angiogram, showing numerous aneurysms in medium-sized arteries. *B,* Fibrinoid necrosis in a jejunal artery from a patient who required surgical resection of necrotic bowel.

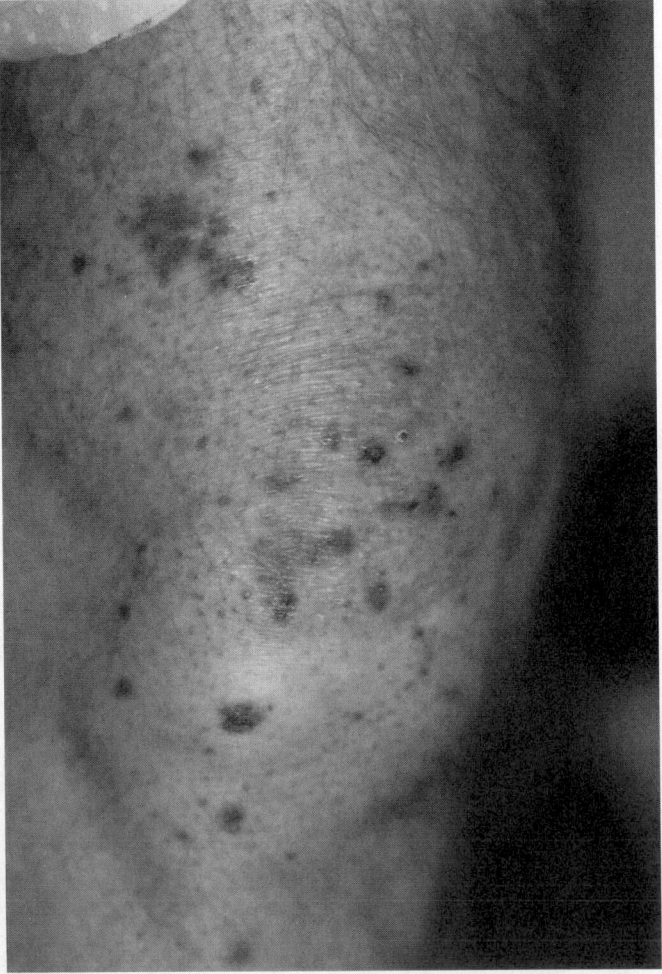

FIGURE 284-3 • Palpable purpura in a patient with small-vessel vasculitis of the skin.

negative. Despite advances in ANCA testing techniques, the cornerstone of diagnosis in WG remains the combination of typical clinical features and histopathology.

WG manifestations that constitute immediate threats to either the function of a vital organ or to the patient's life require urgent treatment with both a cytotoxic agent (usually cyclophosphamide, 2 mg/kg orally daily) and high doses of corticosteroids (1 mg/kg orally daily, tapered over 6 to 12 months). Limited forms of WG may respond to the combination of methotrexate (up to 25 mg/week) and corticosteroids. Methotrexate is not an appropriate first-line treatment for patients with severe involvement of the kidney, lung, or other vital organs.

Microscopic Polyangiitis

MPA is characterized by (1) nongranulomatous, necrotizing vasculitis with few or no immune deposits; (2) small-sized (and possibly medium-sized) blood vessel involvement in the arterial and/or venous circulations; and (3) a tropism for the kidneys and lungs. Cases of small-vessel vasculitis once regarded as PAN are now classified more properly as MPA. In contrast to PAN, an ANCA-negative disorder, 70% of MPA patients are ANCA positive. The ANCA in MPA, usually directed against MPO, cause a perinuclear pattern of staining on immunofluorescence testing (P-ANCA).

MPA is commonly implicated in pulmonary-renal syndromes. A dominant feature of MPA is necrotizing glomerulonephritis, which occurs in nearly 80% of patients. Glomerulonephritis leads to crescent formation, RBC cast formation within the renal tubules, and RBC casts in the urinary sediment. Without prompt treatment, rapidly progressive glomerulonephritis leads to irreversible renal damage. Pulmonary capillaritis may lead rapidly to life-threatening alveolar hemorrhage. Glomerulonephritis (79%), weight loss (73%), mononeuritis multiplex (58%), and fever (55%) are the most common disease manifestations of MPA. Upper respiratory tract symptoms in MPA are much milder than those associated with WG.

The approach to the treatment of MPA is similar to the treatment for WG. Some evidence indicates, however, that MPA may be treated as effectively and more safely with monthly intravenous cyclophosphamide (750 mg/m² of body surface area) rather than the daily cyclophosphamide regimen preferred for WG. Cyclophosphamide may be continued for 6 to 12 months or replaced by methotrexate or azathioprine at an earlier time once the disease has clearly entered remission.

Churg-Strauss Syndrome

CSS is an eosinophil-rich form of granulomatous inflammation that involves the respiratory tract and other organs. The disease is associated with necrotizing vasculitis of small- to medium-sized vessels. Two hallmarks of CSS are asthma and eosinophilia. Several phases of CSS are described as follows:

- A prodromal phase, characterized by the presence of allergic disease (typically asthma or allergic rhinitis), which may last from months to many years
- An eosinophilia/tissue infiltration phase, in which remarkably high peripheral eosinophilia may occur and tissue infiltration by eosinophils is observed in the lung, gastrointestinal tract, and other tissues
- A vasculitic phase, in which systemic necrotizing vasculitis afflicts a wide range of organs, ranging from the heart and lungs to peripheral nerves and skin

CSS must be distinguished from a group of hypereosinophilic disorders: Löffler's syndrome, the hypereosinophil syndrome, eosinophilic gastroenteritis, chronic eosinophilic pneumonia, and eosinophilic leukemia. Associations between the use of leukotriene antagonists and CSS are probably related to the reduction in the dose of corticosteroids afforded by these medications rather than any truly causal relationship. Patients with mild disease may be treated with prednisone. Those with evidence of neurologic, cardiac, renal, or gastrointestinal involvement should be treated with cyclophosphamide in addition to corticosteroids. Although clinical remissions may be obtained in more than 90% of patients with CSS, disease

recurrences occur in 25%. In most cases, relapses are heralded by the return of eosinophilia.

Henoch-Schönlein Purpura

HSP is characterized by non-thrombocytopenic purpura, arthritis, abdominal pain, and glomerulonephritis. The histopathologic findings are those of a leukocytoclastic vasculitis with IgA deposition. HSP can develop at any age, but 80 to 90% of the cases occur in children. Although the cause is unknown, the disease's seasonal variation and the fact that two thirds of patients with HSP experience antecedent acute upper respiratory illnesses suggest an infectious trigger. The diagnosis of HSP can be confirmed only by demonstration of IgA deposition within and around blood vessel walls.

The classic HSP patient presents with the acute onset of fever, palpable purpura on the lower extremities and buttocks, abdominal pain, arthritis, and hematuria. The clinician must be alert to the possibility of HSP even when only parts of the syndrome are present. In some patients, the cutaneous involvement takes the form of maculopapular lesions, blisters, and ulcers. HSP causes arthralgias or arthritis in large joints, especially the knees and ankles, and to a lesser degree, the wrists and elbows. Migratory patterns are typical. The abdominal pain is often colicky and may worsen after eating. Some patients experience nausea, vomiting, and upper or lower gastrointestinal bleeding. Unlike gastrointestinal disease and arthritis, which occasionally precede the onset of purpura, glomerulonephritis almost always follows the appearance of skin disease. Approximately 60% of patients have elevated levels of serum IgA. Although there are two subclasses of IgA, HSP is associated with increases only in IgA1.

Most patients, especially children, have self-limited disease courses that last an average of 4 weeks. Corticosteroids ameliorate the joint and gastrointestinal symptoms in most cases and improve the cutaneous manifestations in some. The efficacy of corticosteroids in the glomerulonephritis of HSP is controversial. Uncontrolled studies suggest that high-dose methylprednisolone followed by oral prednisone combined with azathioprine or cyclophosphamide may be useful in severe glomerulonephritis associated with HSP.

Cutaneous Leukocytoclastic Angiitis

CLA has also been termed *hypersensitivity vasculitis*. CLA is the preferred name, because no hypersensitivity or allergy is evident in many cases. Histories of exposure to new medications or to infections may be elicited, however, and immune complex deposition is central to disease pathophysiology. Although occasionally associated with synovitis, other signs of systemic involvement are absent.

The skin lesions in CLA occur in "crops" because of identical timing in exposure to the inciting antigen. The lesions typically occur first in dependent regions, such as the lower extremities or buttocks. The rash may be asymptomatic but is usually accompanied by burning or tingling sensations. A wide array of skin lesions may occur, including palpable purpura, papules, urticaria/angioedema, erythema multiforme, vesicles, pustules, necrosis, and (rarely) ulcers. Most cases with clearly identified precipitants resolve over 1 to 4 weeks, often with some residual hyperpigmentation. A subset of patients, however, has recurrent disease that remains confined to the skin and requires prolonged therapy.

Keys to the management of CLA include (1) exclusion of any underlying form of vasculitis that may cause subclinical involvement of other organs; and (2) removal of any agent (e.g., a medication) that may have triggered the vasculitis. For patients in whom a precipitant can be identified, removal of the offending agent usually leads to resolution of the vasculitis within days to weeks. The type, intensity, and duration of drug therapy are based on the degree of disease severity. Mild cases may be treated simply with leg elevation and the administration of nonsteroidal anti-inflammatory agents (and/or H₁ antihistamines). For persistent disease not associated with cutaneous gangrene, colchicine, hydroxychloroquine, or dapsone may be tried. For severe cases immunosuppressive agents may be indicated, generally begin-ning with corticosteroids. Azathioprine is commonly used as a steroid-sparing agent.

Continued

Urticarial Vasculitis

At least three subtypes of urticarial vasculitis (UV) are known: (1) a normocomplementemic form, which is generally idiopathic and benign (which may be viewed as a manifestation of CLA); (2) a hypocomplementemic form, which is often associated with a systemic inflammatory disease; and (3) hypocomplementemic urticarial vasculitis syndrome (HUVS), a potentially severe condition usually associated with autoantibodies to the collagen-like region of C1q. Most patients with the hypocomplementemic subtype have an underlying systemic disorder such as systemic lupus erythematosus or Sjögren's syndrome. Many HUVS patients have C1q "precipitins," that is, IgG autoantibodies to the collagen-like region of C1q. The role of anti-C1q antibodies in disease pathogenesis remains unclear.

The lesions of UV must be distinguished from those of the far more common chronic idiopathic urticaria. Unlike idiopathic urticaria, the lesions of UV last more than 48 hours, often have a purpuric component (i.e., they do not blanch), and resolve with postinflammatory hyperpigmentation. In UV, lesions associated with vasculitis are often accompanied by stinging or burning. UV affects the capillaries and postcapillary venules, showing leukocytoclastic vasculitis on light microscopy. Immunofluorescence reveals both immunoglobulin and complement deposition in or around blood vessels of the upper dermis and/or the dermoepidermal junction.

Patients whose serum complement levels remain normal during attacks often have self-limited disease and require little therapy. Other cases, especially HUVS, may cause life-threatening involvement of the lungs or other organs and require periods of intensive immunosuppression. Treatment decisions in HUVS must be individualized according to the patient's clinical status.

Cryoglobulinemia

Cryoglobulins (CGs) are antibodies that precipitate from serum under conditions of cold and resolubilize on rewarming. CG are classified into types I, II, or III based on whether or not monoclonality and/or rheumatoid factor activity (the ability to bind to the Fc portion of IgG) are present. Type I CGs, which are monoclonal but lack rheumatoid factor activity, are associated with certain hematopoietic malignancies and often lead to hyperviscosity rather than to vasculitis. In contrast, types II and III CG may be associated with systemic vasculitis involving small-sized (and often medium-sized) blood vessels. Vasculitis results from the deposition of CG-containing immune complexes in blood vessel walls and the activation of complement.

CG types II and III are termed "mixed" CG because they consist of both IgG and IgM antibodies. The IgM components in types II and III cryoglobulinemia both possess rheumatoid factor activity (i.e., assays for rheumatoid factor are positive). Whereas the IgM component in type II CG is monoclonal, the IgM in type III is polyclonal. Ninety percent of patients with vasculitis secondary to mixed CG are hypocomplementemic, with C4 levels characteristically more depressed than C3. Infection with HCV accounts for at least 80% of the vasculitis cases associated with mixed CG.

The optimal therapy for most cases of cryoglobulinemic vasculitis is the successful treatment of the underlying HCV. For CG patients with relatively mild disease (e.g., frequent purpuric lesions, shallow cutaneous ulcers), interferon-α (beginning at 3 million units three times a week) alone or combined with ribavirin (1000 to 1200mg/day) may be effective. For patients with mononeuritis multiplex or other manifestations of severe disease, corticosteroids and cyclophosphamide are required. Plasmapheresis may be a useful adjunctive therapy.

Differential Diagnosis

The major categories of diseases that can mimic vasculitis are displayed in Table 284–5. Certain features of a patient's case should raise the diagnostic suspicion for vasculitis. First, most cases of vasculitis do not begin suddenly but rather unfold subacutely, over weeks or months. Second, pain is usually a prominent feature of vasculitis, resulting from arthritis/arthralgias, myalgias, headaches, vasculitic neuropathy, testicular infarction, digital ischemia, sinusitis, otalgia, back pain (caused by aortic inflammation), postprandial abdominal pain (caused by mesenteric vasculitis), or other disease manifestations. Third, signs of inflammation, such as fever, skin rash, weight loss, and elevated acute-phase reactants are highly characteristic. These signs of inflammation are frequently so apparent that many patients undergo empirical treatment with antibiotics for infections before the correct diagnosis is made. Finally, multiorgan system involvement is the rule in vasculitis. Cases of systemic vasculitis in which problems are isolated to individual organs are exceptional.

Ideally, the diagnosis of vasculitis is established through biopsy of an involved organ. Diagnoses based on angiography alone have many potential pitfalls. Angiographic findings that are "consistent with vasculitis" must be interpreted in the proper context. A diverse array of other diseases, ranging from atherosclerosis to vasospasm to pheochromocytoma, may mimic vasculitis angiographically. Systemic vasculitis is frequently mimicked by two or more common medical problems occurring simultaneously in the same patients. Finally, high on the differential diagnosis of any individual form of vasculitis are other forms of vasculitis. For example, digital ischemia and splinter hemorrhages may be secondary to idiopathic PAN. They may also be caused by PAN associated with HBV, WG, cryoglobulinemia, MPA, CSS, Buerger's disease, or some other form of vasculitis. Because the appropriate interventions for these conditions vary widely, careful distinction among these potential etiologies is essential.

Table 284–5 • MAJOR DISEASE CATEGORIES IN THE DIFFERENTIAL DIAGNOSIS OF VASCULITIDES

Other forms of vasculitis
Simultaneous occurrence of common medical problems in the same patient
Infections
  Bacterial, viral, mycobacterial, fungal
Occlusive processes
  Hypercoagulable states
  Atheroembolic disease
Malignancies
  Lymphoma (including lymphomatoid granulomatosis)
  Castleman's disease
  Amyloidosis
  Paraproteinemias
Connective tissue disorders
  Systemic lupus erythematosus/mixed connective tissue disease
  Systemic sclerosis
  Rheumatoid arthritis
Miscellaneous
  Atrial myxoma
  Calciphylaxis
  Fibromuscular dysplasia
  Neutrophilic dermatoses
  Pyoderma gangrenosum
  Sarcoidosis

℞ Treatment

This section briefly reviews the major principles of vasculitis treatment. Disease-specific treatments were provided earlier under the discussions of the clinical manifestations of each disease. The intensity of treatment in patients with vasculitis must be guided by the degree of disease activity. Specifically, the treatment of vasculitis should not be predicated only on abnormal laboratory tests but rather on clear evidence of active disease. In addition, the intensity of treatment must be adapted to the type of vasculitis. Whereas giant cell arteritis responds to high doses of corticosteroids in essentially all cases, for example, WG nearly always requires an additional agent (usually either cyclophosphamide or methotrexate) to obtain disease control. In contrast, most cases of HSP and CLA require no immunosuppressive treatment at all.

Conventional therapies such as corticosteroids, immunomodulating agents, and cytotoxic drugs induce remissions and control vasculitis in most cases. Moreover, in some cases—a variable percentage, depending on the type of vasculitis—the disease is curable. Unfortunately, the treatments for vasculitis have enormous potential for toxicity. Regular monitoring of patients' bone marrow, renal, and hepatic function is essential to avoid treatment-induced toxicity. Prophylaxis against opportunistic infections, particularly *Pneumocystis carinii* pneumonia, is an important part of many vasculitis treatment regimens. During the tapering of immunosuppressive medications, disease flares are common in many forms of vasculitis.

A common error is treating patients with high doses of immunosuppressive agents for too long. The most appropriate use of medications such as cyclophosphamide and corticosteroids is to induce remission as quickly as possible with early, aggressive treatment regimens and then to convert patients to safer treatments for the maintenance of remission.

Prognosis

Assuming that the diagnosis is made before the patient has become catastrophically ill, the prognosis in systemic vasculitis is determined largely by the answers to four questions:

1. Was the diagnosis established before the occurrence of major, irreversible organ damage?
2. Was aggressive (but appropriately dosed) treatment begun in a timely fashion?
3. Was there careful monitoring during treatment, and were specific steps taken to avoid drug-induced toxicity (e.g., opportunistic infection)?
4. Were the potentially toxic medications that induced remission stopped at an appropriate juncture and substituted for less dangerous medications (or simply stopped altogether)?

For most forms of vasculitis, the factors that determine long-term, drug-free remissions remain poorly understood. The likelihood of achieving sustained remissions off all medications (or cures) varies according to the specific type of vasculitis.

Future Directions

Compelling laboratory and spontaneously occurring animal models of disease, combined with the known associations among HBV, HCV, and vasculitis in humans, suggest that additional links between infection and systemic vasculitis may be established in the future. Ongoing studies in WG and cryoglobulinemia will also elucidate genetic risk factors for these and other forms of vasculitis. Enormous strides have been made in the description of cytokine and chemokine pathways relevant to inflammation. Specific studies in vasculitis will elucidate important disease mechanisms and identify new potential targets for therapy. Proteomic studies will hasten progress in this area. Finally, multicenter collaborations among vasculitis investigators, established in only the past few years, will enhance the ability to test new treatments for vasculitis in rigorous clinical trials.

1. Hamuryudan V, Mat C, Saip S, et al: Thalidomide in the treatment of the mucocutaneous lesions of the Behçet syndrome: A randomized, double-blind, placebo-controlled trial. Ann Intern Med 1998;128:443–450.

SUGGESTED READINGS

Hoffman GS, Kerr GS, Leavitt RY, et al: Wegener's granulomatosis: An analysis of 158 patients. Ann Intern Med 1992;116:488–498. *Definitive report on the longitudinal experience with WG at the National Institutes of Health.*

Jennette JC, Falk RJ, Andrassy K, et al: Nomenclature of systemic vasculitides: Proposal of an international consensus conference. Arthritis Rheum 1994;37:187–192. *Results of a consensus conference that offers the most current views on nomenclature for the vasculitides, particularly considering the role of ANCA.*

Noth I, Strek ME, Leff AR: Churg-Strauss syndrome. Lancet 2003;361:587–594. *Review of pathology, diagnosis, and treatment.*

Regan MJ, Hellmann DB, Stone JH: Treatment of Wegener's granulomatosis. Rheum Dis Clin North Am 2001;27:863–886. *Thorough description of the current standard of care for WG, with many lessons applicable to other forms of vasculitis. Guidelines with regard to the use of immunosuppressive medications in vasculitis.*

Stone JH, Calabrese LH, Hoffman GS, et al: Vasculitis: A collection of pearls and myths. Rheum Dis Clin North Am 2001;27:677–728. *Practical advice distilled from the experience of several vasculitis experts related to the evaluation and management of patients with vasculitis.*

Stone JH, Nousari HC: "Essential" cutaneous vasculitis: What every rheumatologist should know about vasculitis of the skin. Curr Opin Rheumatol 2001;13:23–34. *A well-illustrated, concisely organized approach to the complex subject of cutaneous vasculitis.*

285 POLYMYALGIA RHEUMATICA AND TEMPORAL ARTERITIS

Stephen A. Paget

Definition

Polymyalgia rheumatica (PMR) and temporal arteritis (TA; also called giant cell arteritis) are companion systemic inflammatory disorders of unknown etiology that represent a spectrum from severe proximal aches and pains and constitutional symptoms to an occlusive granulomatous vasculitis of medium and large vessels that can lead to permanent blindness or other organ and tissue damage. These disorders occur solely in patients older than 50 years of age, in women more than men, are propagated by antigen-driven, cell-mediated (Th1) immune mechanisms associated with specific genetic markers, and are highly responsive to corticosteroids.

Epidemiology

In the United States, the average annual incidence of PMR is 52.5 per 100,000 patients age 50 years and older and increases with age. The prevalence is about 0.5 to 0.7%. Internationally, the frequency varies according to country, with the highest rates occurring in the Scandinavian countries. The incidence and prevalence of TA is approximately one third that of PMR.

Pathobiology

The etiology of PMR and TA is unknown, but both demonstrate familial aggregation and have a genetic association with HLA-DR4 and a demonstrated sequence polymorphism encoded within the hypervariable region of the HLA-DRβ1*04 gene. Disease in genetically predisposed patients may be triggered by environmental factors such as viruses or internal antigens such as elastin, and their inflammatory manifestations are directed by specific patterns of cell-mediated, Th1-associated cytokines. The cytokine production by the mononuclear cells in the involved tissues appears to influence the clinical phenotype. Cytokine profiles characterized in temporal artery biopsy specimens obtained from patients with PMR and TA differ. In TA tissue, one finds the T lymphocyte products interferon (IFN)-γ and interleukin (IL)-2 and the macrophage products IL-1β, IL-6, and transforming growth factor (TGF)-β. In PMR vascular tissue, transcripts for TGF-β, IL-1, and IL-2, but not for IFN-γ are found. Patients with TA who present with fever of unknown origin and who do *not* have ischemic symptoms such as visual loss have low IFN-γ levels. Arteries that express high IFN-γ levels typically have multinucleated giant cells present, and these cells remove debris and secrete cytokines that stimulate intimal hyperplasia and lead to angiogenesis.

The adventitia is considered the immunologic center in the pathogenesis of TA. Macrophages and T lymphocytes enter the vessel wall via the vasa vasorum with the aid of adhesion molecules and come into contact with an inciting antigen. Here, it is likely that clonal proliferation of CD4+ T cells is triggered by the presentation of unknown antigens by antigen-presenting cells. The activated CD4 cells produce IFN-γ that attracts macrophages to the arterial wall. Some of these macrophages fuse at the intima-media to form multinucleated giant cells. These cells produce vascular endothelial growth factor, which triggers neovascularization both in the intima-media junction and at the level of the vasa vasorum, sprouting from the adventitia to the media. The subsequent immunologic events lead to a characteristic topography of mononuclear cells throughout the vessel wall. Products of the giant cells and macrophages at the intima-media junction include enzymes such as collagenase and nitric oxide, both of which likely contribute to tissue damage. The pathologic impact of cytokines leads not only to the characteristic medial damage but also to the significant intimal hyperplasia that eventually, if not treated, may cause luminal narrowing and tissue ischemia.

In TA, a transmural (involving all layers of the vessel), inflammatory infiltrate, predominantly of mononuclear cells and commonly with giant cells, is found in the superficial temporal arteries as well as other large and medium-sized arteries. In elderly patients, fragmentation of the internal elastica is characteristic and helps to differentiate this vascular lesion from that of atherosclerosis. Often, macrophages containing fragments of elastic tissue are found at the intima-media junction, the histologic center of the inflammatory process. As mentioned earlier, immunochemical techniques demonstrate differing patterns of cells and their proinflammatory and profibrotic products in the adventitia, media, and intima. Intimal proliferation may be prominent and lead to luminal narrowing. Fibrinoid necrosis, a common histologic feature in polyarteritis nodosa, is not seen in TA.

In PMR, mononuclear cell inflammation can be found not only in the proximal joints such as the shoulders but also in the surrounding tendons, bursae, and soft tissues consistent with enthesitis. Although muscle pains may be present, no muscle inflammation is found.

Clinical Manifestations

PMR and TA are systemic inflammatory disorders that occur primarily in patients older than 50 years of age, in women more than men (2:1), and in whites. PMR and TA are particularly uncommon in African-Americans.

Shared characteristics of the two disorders include significant cytokine-driven constitutional symptoms such as fever, fatigue, and weight loss, as well as a markedly elevated erythrocyte sedimentation rate (ESR), anemia, and thrombocytosis. The musculoskeletal hallmark of PMR is proximal, severe, and symmetrical morning and even day-long stiffness, soreness, and pain in the shoulder, neck, and pelvic girdles. Fifty percent of patients with TA share this characteristic proximal pain syndrome. Carpal tunnel syndrome and hand and knee synovitis may be seen in patients with PMR, but the overall presentation remains predominantly proximal, as opposed to rheumatoid arthritis, in which peripheral synovitis dominates. Whereas PMR patients may appear to have proximal muscle weakness, this is invariably due to pain, not muscle inflammation.

Specific signs and symptoms of TA are best appreciated in their anatomic and physiologic contexts. TA preferentially affects certain blood vessels, including the branches of the external carotid artery, the ophthalmic artery and particularly its posterior ciliary branches, and large arteries that arise from the aortic arch and abdominal aorta. Headache and scalp pain are probably the most frequent symptoms, occurring in 50 to 75% of patients. Headache is often the first manifestation of TA and is described as boring, severe, and constant, unresponsive to simple pain medications and persisting through the night. Classically, patients complain of persistent and prominent temporal headaches, but occipital pains can also occur. Ear, pinna, or parotid gland pain may occur secondary to involvement of the posterior auricular artery. Jaw claudication and pain due to masseter muscle ischemia on chewing occurs in 50% of patients. Lingual and maxillary artery involvement can lead to jaw or tongue pain on chewing or talking. The superficial temporal artery may become tortuous, prominent, nodular, or tender, but these findings are not invariable and a positive temporal artery biopsy may be found in vessels that appear normal.

Fixed or intermittent symptoms related to vasculitic involvement of the ophthalmic arteries and its branches are the most dreaded in this illness and demand immediate therapeutic intervention. These symptoms are related to vascular narrowing due to both active inflammation and endothelial injury–derived vasospasm. Decreased vision secondary to arteritis is the most common serious consequence of TA, occurring in 20 to 50% of patients who present to ophthalmologists. It is the presenting symptom in 60% of patients with TA who develop visual loss. A careful history of most patients who present with "sudden" visual loss reveals that preceding headache, constitutional symptoms, and PMR occurred in approximately 40% of patients. Even the evolution of the visual loss was often staggered with amaurosis fugax in 10% and a partial field defect progressing to complete blindness over days. If TA remains untreated, the second eye may become involved within 1 to 2 weeks. The posterior ciliary arteries are the most frequently involved; thus, anterior ischemic optic neuropathy is the most common lesion, which can be easily defined by an ophthalmologist. Occlusion of the central retinal artery and its branches are uncommon; thus, exudates, hemorrhages, and frank vasculitis are infrequent. Five percent of patients may present with diplopia or ptosis, which may precede visual loss. The final visual abnormality can be a composite of many ischemic events occurring together in the optic nerve, extraocular muscles, chiasm, and the brain itself. Because TA primarily involves arteries that contain elastica and the elastic lamina is lost as vessels pierce the dura, intracerebral lesions such as strokes are uncommon but not unheard of.

Large artery involvement most commonly presents as arm or leg claudication with rarer manifestations being stroke, subclavian steal syndrome, intestinal infarction, and symptomatic aortic aneurysm. Thus, a subclinical arteritis can exist and demands long-term monitoring.

Steroid-treated PMR and TA are self-limited illnesses lasting 1 to 2 years in most patients. However, a subgroup of patients with both disorders can have active inflammatory disease as manifested by persistent symptoms and blood test signs of active inflammation for 7 to 10 years. Of note is the fact that thoracic aneurysms with giant cells in the tissue can develop as long as 15 years after the diagnosis, successful treatment, and discontinuation of steroids. In most studies, survival in both disorders is similar to that of unaffected persons of the same age. However, one recent study did show that survival was decreased in a group of patients with TA that had permanent visual loss and required more than 10 mg of prednisone/day at 6 months. This probably supports the experience that the morbidity and mortality is caused by steroid-related treatment complications in this high-risk, elderly group of patients with many comorbidities.

Diagnosis

The diagnoses of PMR and TA are based on clinical facts, with supporting but not diagnostic aid obtained from laboratory tests and temporal artery biopsy. No physician should await a positive temporal artery biopsy or demand the presence of an elevated ESR before making the definitive diagnosis of TA in the setting of a characteristic clinical picture. This said, the laboratory hallmark of PMR and TA is an elevation in IL-6 stimulated acute phase reactants such as the ESR and the C-reactive protein (CRP). The ESR is usually in excess of 50 mm/hour and may exceed 100 mm/hour. An ESR in the low 20s or 30s, however, does not exclude a diagnosis of PMR or GCA if other characteristic clinical features are present and especially if the patient is already taking steroids.

Normocytic, normochromic anemia and thrombocytosis occur in approximately 50% of patients with both disorders and are excellent guides to the state of inflammation. In both PMR and TA, the frequency of rheumatoid factor, antinuclear antibody, complement levels, monoclonal proteins, and cryoglobulins are not higher than in age-matched controls. An elevated alkaline phosphatase level may be elevated in one third of patients, primarily in TA. Although these tests are not indicated in these illnesses, muscle enzymes and electromyography are normal and muscle biopsy shows type II fiber atrophy but no inflammation.

SUPERFICIAL TEMPORAL ARTERY ASSESSMENT. Color duplex ultrasonography has been employed in the diagnosis of TA. A hypoechoic halo around the superficial temporal artery has been reported in 73% of patients with biopsy-proven TA. The halo, representing edema in the arterial wall, was observed bilaterally in a significant subset of patients and disappeared in a mean of 16 days after the initiation of steroids. The presence of the halo had a sensitivity of 73% and was 100% specific for TA. Most rheumatologists still use the temporal artery biopsy as the diagnostic "gold standard" in TA.

Temporal artery biopsy continues to be an important diagnostic test for the presence of TA. However, a few caveats must be stated. First, in a patient in whom the clinical diagnosis is strong, treatment with steroids should be instituted immediately without waiting for the biopsy results. Second, because of the skipped nature of the pathologic inflammatory lesions in the vessel wall, as many as 20 to 30% of biopsies may be negative, despite an overwhelming diagnostic likelihood of TA. However, because the biopsy is helpful in confirming the diagnosis of TA in which high doses of steroids are employed, the following guidelines are given. Patients with pure PMR and no TA signs or symptoms do *not* need a biopsy. However, because 10% of them may develop such clinical manifestations of TA within the next year, they should be told to report them immediately. When TA is likely, an outpatient biopsy should be performed on the symptomatic side of the head, preferably including inflamed areas with tenderness or nodularity and incorporating 2 to 3 cm of vessel. Multiple sections should be requested because of the segmental nature of the disease process. Some rheumatologists routinely perform bilateral biopsies, while others obtain a contralateral biopsy if the first is negative. Diagnostic biopsy findings continue to be present for as long as 2 to 4 weeks after the diagnosis is made and steroid treatment instituted.

Differential Diagnosis

The systemic nature of these disorders and the fact that they occur in the elderly demand careful diagnostic scrutiny to avoid missing a malignancy or major infection and treating patients inappropriately with high-dose steroids. This is true in PMR because there is no diagnostic test and in TA because the TA biopsy may be negative in the face of active, vision-threatening vasculitis. Infections that must be considered and ruled out if clinically appropriate include tuberculosis, endocarditis, and hepatitis B and C. Malignancies such as lymphoma and multiple myeloma are look-alikes, and an age-appropriate cancer evaluation is always indicated in this age group. Autoimmune disorders such as elderly onset rheumatoid arthritis (RA) and systemic lupus erythematosus as well as dermatomyositis and other types of vasculitis must be considered in the differential diagnosis and sorted out by employing clinical information and serologic testing. There is support for the concept that elderly onset RA is the same disorder as PMR with negative rheumatoid factor, a more proximal focus of joint inflammation, and a good response to low-dose prednisone. PMR and TA should always be thought of in the setting of a fever of unknown origin because their symptoms and signs can be occult or the history incomplete.

 **Treatment**

Both PMR and TA are highly responsive to corticosteroids, and this medication is the preferred treatment choice. This response is so characteristic that an immediate and dramatic improvement in PMR and TA symptoms within 1 to 3 days after steroid institution supports the diagnosis. Thus, a lack of rapid and significant improvement in signs, symptoms, and function within 5 to 7 days should be considered a major point against the diagnosis. The physician should then consider an alternative diagnosis (e.g. tumor or infection) or the presence of TA in PMR patients that might demand a higher steroid dose. Because the inflammatory set point of the two disorders is different, different doses of steroids are employed at the onset of treatment. Whereas PMR usually responds to 15 mg of prednisone (two or three times a day), TA usually requires 60 to 80 mg prednisone per day in divided doses or higher doses if organ or tissue damage is present or threatened. In TA, if visual symptoms are present as a fixed loss or amaurosis fugax, the patient should be treated with high-dose intravenous Solu-Medrol with doses ranging from 40 mg every 8 hours to 1 g/day for 3 days, followed by high-dose oral steroids in divided doses.

Within 2 to 3 days after the institution of steroids, most symptoms of PMR or TA clear rapidly and patients describe a miraculous improvement. The steroid dose is then maintained for 2 to 3 weeks, during which the ESR, CRP, hemoglobin, and platelet counts normalize. Steroid taper is then instituted and guided by the clinical response. In PMR, taper is commonly by 1 mg every 7 to 10 days; in TA, taper is by 5 to 10 mg every 7 to 10 days. It is important that the taper be guided primarily by clinical findings (e.g., PMR stiffness, headache, fatigue) and that the ESR be placed into that clinical context. One should never "chase the ESR" because the elderly patient would be subjected inappropriately to a dangerously high cumulative dose of steroids with their attendant side effects. An increased dose of prednisone should be based on a change in symptoms, not solely on an increase in the ESR. The effective dose demanded for a flare often can be as low as 5 to 10 mg prednisone, and uncommonly does one have to go to 60 mg/day to control symptoms (e.g., visual abnormalities). A persistently elevated ESR (>50 mm/hour) without PMR or TA symptoms should alert the physician to look for alternative causes such as infection. Treatment is a careful balancing act between disease control and avoidance of steroid-related toxicity. The overall goal of the patient and the physician is to attain the best disease control with the lowest dose of steroids. In most patients, prednisone can be tapered off safely in 1 to 2 years. However, other patients may need to take low doses of steroids for 2 or more years. The higher the initial dose and cumulative dose, the greater the likelihood that the patient will develop a major steroid side effect such as sepsis, osteoporosis, osteonecrosis, diabetes, emotional lability, or myopathy. Appropriate immunizations, osteoporosis regimens (calcium, vitamin D, and bisphosphonates), and metabolic monitoring are mandatory in all patients started on chronic steroid therapy.

Alternative immunosuppressive agents have been tested in both PMR and TA patients in an attempt to "spare steroids" and control the inflammatory state. Results of randomized, controlled studies are mixed on whether methotrexate is an effective drug in attaining both goals when started along with prednisone, but the largest, most recent study showed no incremental benefit from combined therapy. However, in patients with refractory disease that demands too high a chronic dose of prednisone (≥10 to 20 mg) to control disease activity, weekly RA-type doses of methotrexate (7.5 to 20 mg/week) or azathioprine (2 mg/kg) are often employed. Multicenter studies are underway to define the role of tumor necrosis factor (TNF) blockade in the treatment of TA.

Future Directions

Better understanding of the disease-causing roles of immunologically active cells and their cytokine products, along with genetics and correlations with clinical subsets, will lead to more focused treatment modalities, such as anti-TNF agents, and the avoidance of the need for long-term treatment with steroids.

1. Hoffman GS, Cid MC, Hellmann DB, et al: International Network for the Study of Systemic Vasculitides. A multicenter, randomized, double-blind, placebo-controlled trial of adjuvant methotrexate treatment for giant-cell arteritis. Arthritis Rheum 2002;46:1309–1318.

SUGGESTED READINGS
Bjornsson J: Clues to the pathogenesis of giant cell arteritis from the study of the vessel wall. Arthritis Care Res 2000;13:286–290. *A review of the pathogenetic mechanisms involved in the evolution of the dreaded vascular occlusion in giant cell arteritis from one of the pioneers in the field.*
Cantini F, Salvarani C, Olivieri I, et al: Arthritis Rheum 2000;44:1155–1159. *An ultrasound and magnetic resonance imaging study demonstrating that the prominent proximal musculoskeletal symptoms so characteristic of PMR reflect glenohumeral joint synovitis, subacromial and subdeltoid bursitis, and biceps tenosynovitis.*
Hachulla E, Boivin U, Pasturel-Michon A-L, et al: Prognostic factors and long-term evolution in a cohort of 133 patients with giant cell arteritis. Clin and Exp Rheumatol 2001;19:171–176. *An excellent clinical study of a large cohort of giant cell arteritis patients with a focus on their clinical courses, relapses, and factors that alter survival.*
Myklebust G, Wilsgaard T, Jacobsen BK, et al: Causes of death in polymyalgia rheumatica. A prospective longitudinal study of 315 cases and matched population controls. Scand J Rheumatol 2003;32:38–41. *The disease was not associated with increased mortality but rather with increased survival, perhaps due to the type of patients in whom the diagnosis is estalished.*
Salvarani C, Fabrizio C, Boiardi L: Polymyalgia rheumatica and giant-cell arteritis. N Engl J Med 2002;32:261–271. *A comprehensive review.*
Salvarani C, Hunder GG: Giant cell arteritis with low erythrocyte sedimentation rate: Frequency of occurrence in a population-based study. Arthritis Care Res 2001;45:140–145. *Giant cell arteritis is a clinical diagnosis and should be considered in classic patients even if the sedimentation rate is normal; an important reminder from the Mayo Clinic.*

Rheumatic Diseases

286 INFECTIOUS ARTHRITIS

Luis R. Espinoza

Infectious or septic arthritis is an inflammatory reaction resulting from a direct invasion of the joint space by pathogenic microorganisms, resulting in pain, swelling, redness, limitation of joint motion, and eventually joint destruction and permanent disability if untreated. It remains a relevant issue in clinical medicine, and despite significant advances in diagnostic approaches and the development of newer and more powerful antibiotics, its impact in terms of human morbidity and mortality remains unchanged.

NONGONOCOCCAL BACTERIAL ARTHRITIS

Epidemiology, Pathogenesis, and Risk Factors

Septic arthritis occurs in all age groups but is more common in children than adults. Males are usually affected more commonly than females, although in patients with underlying rheumatoid arthritis (RA), females are affected more often. An annual incidence of culture-proven septic arthritis of 1 in 62,500 has recently been shown in a well-conducted prospective study in the United Kingdom. In another community, in a prospective study conducted in the Netherlands, an incidence of bacterial arthritis was found to be 5.7 per 100,000 inhabitants per year.

Any microorganisms including bacteria, fungi, viruses, and protozoa may invade joints; however, the overwhelming majority (90%) of cases of septic arthritis are caused by pyogenic bacteria (i.e., staphylococci, streptococci; Table 286–1). Bacteria may reach the joint by various routes, the most common being hematogenous spread. Other less common routes include direct inoculation during diagnostic or therapeutic arthrocentesis or arthroscopies, trauma, and contiguous osteomyelitis, cellulitis, abscesses, tenosynovitis, and/or septic bursitis. Once the microbial agent penetrates the joint space, it initiates a series of inflammatory reactions that may lead to joint destruction and permanent joint damage. Viable microorganisms and/or their products activate the release of proinflammatory cytokines, such as tumor necrosis factor (TNF)-α and interleukin-1, and proteolytic enzymes, such as metalloproteinases and other collagen-degrading enzymes. These substances may induce synovial membrane proliferation, granulation tissue, neovascularization, and infiltration by polymorphonuclear (PMN) cells and may result, if untreated, in cartilage and bone destruction. The articular damage may progress even after eradication of microorganisms by antibiotic therapy because persistence of bacterial antigens and metalloproteinases within the joint will continue to promote an inflammatory response. Important risk factors for the development of septic arthritis include age older than 60 years, diabetes mellitus, immunodeficiency states, preexistent joint damage (particularly RA), skin infection, intravenous drug use, debilitating conditions, hemoglobinopathy, and joint prostheses (Table 286–2).

Clinical Manifestations

The onset of septic arthritis is usually acute, and more than 75% of the patients have monoarticular arthritis. Any joint can be affected in septic arthritis, although the knee joint followed by the hip and ankle are most commonly affected. Involvement of the sacroiliac, costochondral, or sternoclavicular joints is more commonly seen in intravenous drug users. Constitutional complaints are relatively common and include chills, fever, malaise, and anorexia. On physical examination, the affected joints can be extremely painful, warm, swollen, and filled with fluid. These inflammatory signs, however, may be masked in debilitated, severely ill patients or in those receiving corticosteroids or immunosuppressive agents. Polyarthritis may occur in patients with underlying connective tissue disease, particularly RA, or an immunosuppressive state and carries a worse prognosis, with a mortality rate of approximately 30%.

Diagnosis

Septic arthritis should be suspected in the presence of an appropriate clinical picture, imaging findings, and examination of the synovial fluid. A definite diagnosis is made in the presence of a positive synovial fluid culture.

Early recognition of infection is the most important step in the management of septic arthritis. Arthrocentesis is mandatory in the presence of a joint effusion, particularly when an infectious process is considered. All fluid aspirated should be sent for a Gram stain, aerobic and anaerobic bacterial cultures, and cell count with a leukocyte differential. The synovial fluid leukocyte count is usually between 40,000 and 50,000 cells per cubic millimeter, with a predominance (>80%) of PMN cells. Glucose, protein, and lactate levels are not very helpful and for the most part are nonspecific. The yield of organisms from joint fluid culture is approximately 50 to 60%. The erythrocyte sedimentation rate, C-reactive protein levels, and peripheral blood white cell count are elevated in most patients, and the latter two may be helpful in the follow-up of patients. A persistently elevated C-reactive protein and/or white blood cell count may imply persistence of joint infection. Plain radiographs are seldom useful early in the disease, although they may reveal joint abnormalities, such as loss of articular cartilage and bone erosion in untreated patients or in patients with aggressive disease. In patients suspected of deep-seated joint infections such as sacroiliac or facet joint involvement, scintigraphy, computed tomography, or magnetic resonance imaging studies may be helpful.

Table 286–1 • **MICROORGANISMS RESPONSIBLE FOR ACUTE NONGONOCOCCAL BACTERIAL ARTHRITIS (ALL AGES)**

MICROORGANISM	FREQUENCY (%)
GRAM POSITIVE	60–90
Staphylococcus aureus	50–70
Group A, B, C streptococci	15–30
Staphylococcus epidermidis	6–20
Streptococcus pneumoniae	1–3
Enterococcus spp.	<1
Corynebacterium spp.	<1
GRAM NEGATIVE	5–25
Salmonella spp.	
Pseudomonas aeruginosa	
Escherichia coli	
Klebsiella pneumoniae	
Enterobacter spp.	
Brucella spp.	
Haemophilus influenzae	
Kingella kingae	
ANAEROBES	1–2
Fusobacterium spp.	
Bacteroides fragilis	

Table 286–2 • **PREDISPOSING RISK FACTORS FOR JOINT INFECTION**

Preexisting joint damage
    Osteoarthritis
    Rheumatoid arthritis
Intravenous drug use
Diabetes mellitus
Elderly, debilitated state
Neoplasia
Immunosuppressive therapy
Immunodeficiency
    Human immunodeficiency virus infection
    Hypogammaglobulinemia
    Complement deficiency
Menses and pregnancy—gonococcemia
Prosthetic joint
Cirrhosis
Leg ulcers

 **Treatment**

Prompt institution of appropriate antibiotic therapy and joint drainage of the purulent fluid is essential in the management of septic arthritis. Even so, the treatment of septic arthritis remains unsatisfactory. Antibiotics should be given to all patients suspected of having septic arthritis, even before results of bacteriologic studies become available. Initial selection of antibiotics should be based on Gram stain results of joint fluid or other body fluids or secretions. If no microorganisms are identified, empirical treatment should be given with the age, risk factors, and clinical picture of the patient taken into consideration. Normal individuals should be treated initially for infections with Gram-positive organisms, whereas broad-spectrum antibiotics are indicated in debilitated, severely ill, and immunocompromised individuals. Once culture results become available, antibiotics can be changed if indicated. A 3-week treatment period (1 week of parenteral followed by 2 weeks of oral antibiotics) is currently the norm for most patients with septic arthritis. Parenteral, not intra-articular, therapy with either a β-lactamase–resistant penicillin or a first-generation cephalosporin should initially be given. Vancomycin should be used to treat methicillin-resistant *Staphylococcus aureus* infection. Gram-negative organisms should be treated with a third-generation cephalosporin such as cefotaxime or ceftriaxone, or an aminoglycoside. Long-term administration of oral antibiotics is recommended in patients with chronic bone and joint infections (e.g., prosthetic joints).

Closed needle aspiration on a daily basis or as often as necessary is an important part of medical management. Most patients can be treated in this manner, although surgical draining is indicated in deep-seated joints (including hip and shoulders), joints with preexistent damage, joints not responding to appropriate medical management, or joints with loculated effusion or contiguous osteomyelitis. Arthroscopic rather than open surgery is recommended. Joint immobilization is not indicated except in patients with incapacitating pain or after surgical drainage. Joint immobilization and functional splinting of the affected joints are recommended to prevent muscle atrophy and contractures and to preserve joint function. Polymerase chain reaction (PCR) analysis of synovial fluid may be used to monitor the presence of bacterial DNA, the absence of which may assist in the decision to discontinue antibiotic treatment.

GONOCOCCAL ARTHRITIS

Neisseria gonorrhoeae is the most common cause of septic arthritis in the United States, particularly in young sexually active individuals. Women are affected two to three times as often as men. Its incidence has decreased in the past several years, coinciding with the changes in sexual behavior that have occurred since the advent of the human immunodeficiency virus (HIV) epidemic. Disseminated gonococcal infection occurs in from 0.5 to 3% of cases of mucosal infection and is the most common reason for hospital admission as a result of septic arthritis in the United States, with an estimated incidence of 2.8 cases per 100,000 population per year.

Disseminated gonococcal infection is always preceded by mucosal infection with *N. gonorrhoeae*. The infection commonly involves the endocervix or urethra but may involve the pharynx and rectum and may or may not be symptomatic. The risk for gonococcal dissemination following a mucosal infection depends on the patient's immunologic status and on the virulence of the microorganism.

Clinical Manifestations

Gonococcal arthritis may present as part of a disseminated infection or as a monoarticular infection. Disseminated gonococcal infection usually presents with migratory arthralgias, fever, chills, dermatitis, and tenosynovitis. Asymptomatic genital, anal, or pharyngeal gonococcal infection is usually the norm. A variety of skin lesions may be present, including small erythematous papules that progress to vesicular, pustular, and/or necrotizing lesions. Skin rash may be observed in any region, including palms. The tenosynovitis may be transitory and is characterized by pain, swelling, and periarticular erythema. Septic arthritis affecting one or a few joints, or frank polyarthritis, may be seen in the absence of skin involvement and is clinically indistinguishable from other forms of septic arthritis.

Diagnosis

N. gonorrhoeae is seldom found in synovial fluid or skin lesions. In most patients, the diagnosis is made indirectly by finding a positive culture from the genitourinary tract or, much less frequently, from the rectum or pharynx. In the presence of a negative Gram stain and/or synovial fluid culture, a presumptive diagnosis can be made by the characteristic clinical picture associated with a rapid response to antibiotics. PCR allows identification of the microorganism in the synovial fluid. Other laboratory findings are nonspecific.

 **Treatment**

Hospitalization is recommended, particularly if serious complications such as endocarditis and meningitis are present. A third-generation β-lactamase–resistant cephalosporin such as ceftriaxone, 1 g intramuscularly or intravenously every 24 hours, is initially recommended. Alternative regimens include cefotaxime or ceftizoxime, 1 g intravenously every 8 hours. Spectinomycin, 2 g intramuscularly every 12 hours, is the treatment of choice for individuals allergic to β-lactam drugs. If organisms are sensitive to penicillin, treatment may be switched to ampicillin, 1 g intravenously every 6 hours, or penicillin G, 10 million U intravenously daily in divided doses. Ceftriaxone and spectinomycin are safe and effective for treatment of gonorrhea in pregnancy. Parenteral therapy should be given until evidence of clinical improvement is seen, usually 2 to 4 days, and then oral antibiotics can be substituted; a penicillin derivative and cephalosporin should be given for another 7 to 10 days. Because of the high prevalence of coexistent chlamydia infection, concomitant therapy with oral doxycycline or another tetracycline should be given. Tests for syphilis, chlamydia, and HIV infection should be considered after completion of therapy.

VIRAL ARTHRITIS

This group of arthritides constitutes the second most common cause of infectious arthritis after bacterial arthritis. Multiple viral infections are accompanied by inflammatory articular involvement including hepatitis viruses, parvovirus, rubella virus, and HIV. Acute and, much less commonly, chronic arthritis and vasculitis have all been described with viral infections. Acute arthritis usually lasts 3 to 4 weeks, may affect small and large joints, may be extremely painful and nonerosive in nature, and may disappear without sequelae. It is seldom accompanied by serologic and radiologic changes, and it can be monoarticular, oligoarticular, and, less frequently, polyarticular and symmetric, mimicking RA.

Patients with hepatitis C virus and parvovirus may exhibit a more chronic, symmetric arthritis of the small and large joints, with a positive rheumatoid factor indistinguishable from RA. Hepatitis B and C and, to a lesser degree, hepatitis A virus may cause other immune-complex–mediated rheumatic syndromes including mixed cryoglobulinemic-related vasculitis.

Rubella-associated arthritis occurs within days of the appearance of skin rash in natural infection or 2 to 4 weeks after vaccination. The pattern of joint inflammation is frequently that of a migratory polyarthralgia and less often that of polyarthritis. It may mimic RA, and small joints of the hands as well as knees are affected more commonly. The acute episode usually lasts 3 to 21 days, but it may persist for months. Rubella virus has been isolated from peripheral blood and synovial fluid from affected individuals, but its role as an etiologic agent in RA and other chronic arthritides is highly questionable.

Rheumatic manifestations are relatively frequent during the course of HIV infection. They may occur at any time during the course of the disease, although they tend to be more common in late stages. In Central Africa, rheumatic manifestations are usually the initial clinical manifestation of HIV infection. A wide spectrum of inflammatory articular disorders can be seen, ranging from arthralgias to distinct rheumatologic disorders such as reactive arthritis and psoriatic arthritis. Osteoarticular infections are rarely seen, but when present in HIV-infected patients, they tend to occur in the presence of low CD4+ cell counts. Septic arthritis and polymyositis can be seen. In general, the clinical picture and response to therapy is similar to that for patients without HIV infection. Causal microorganisms are also similar to those found in non-HIV populations, with *S. aureus* being the most common etiologic agent.

Most patients with viral-associated arthritis do respond well to anti-inflammatory and analgesic therapy. Second-line anti-inflammatory agents or immunosuppressive agents including steroids, methotrexate, azathioprine, or cyclosporin may need to be used in those cases refractory to conventional therapy.

Other viruses less commonly causing arthralgias and arthritis include herpes zoster, cytomegalovirus, Epstein-Barr virus, echovirus, adenovirus, and coxsackievirus. Chi-Kunguya, O'nyong-nyong, and Ross River viruses are all alpha viruses responsible for major epidemics of febrile polyarthritis in Africa, Australia, Europe, and Latin America.

MISCELLANEOUS FORMS OF INFECTIOUS ARTHRITIS

MYCOPLASMA ARTHRITIS. Mycoplasma-induced monoarthritis or oligoarthritis is relatively common in children and in immunocompromised patients, particularly those with agammaglobulinemia. The exact prevalence of mycoplasma-related arthritis is unknown.

LYME DISEASE. Arthritis is the most common clinical manifestation of late (persistent) or stage 3 infection. The knee joint is involved in almost all cases. Symmetric or rheumatoid arthritis–like joint involvement in association with HLA-DR4 usually does not respond to antibiotic therapy. Laboratory diagnosis is based on serologic techniques. Treatment with appropriate antibiotics is effective in most patients with the correct diagnosis. Identified risk factors leading to failure of antibiotic treatment include older age at the time of diagnosis and prior administration of intra-articular steroids. Some cases are refractory to conventional therapy, and in these patients newer modalities such as vaccination may be required.

TUBERCULOUS ARTHRITIS. Both pulmonary and extrapulmonary tuberculosis have had a resurgence in the past several years. The major reason for this resurgence is the HIV pandemic, considering that HIV specifically affects cellular immunity, which is the first line of defense against tuberculosis. Active pulmonary involvement is often not detected, but the PPD skin test is usually positive. Direct histologic evidence and culture of synovial fluid are required for diagnosis—particularly in patients presenting with chronic monoarthritis or oligoarthritis of the large joints unresponsive to conventional anti-inflammatory therapy. Tuberculous arthritis is a potential complication in RA patients being treated with the newer biologic agents such as inhibitors of TNF-α. Joint involvement with atypical *Mycobacterium* infection should be considered in immunocompromised patients, after repeated intra-articular steroid injections, and in certain occupations (e.g., fisherman). Long-term therapy with isoniazid, ethambutol, and/or rifampin is indicated.

SYPHILIS. Joint involvement may occur at any stage of congenital, secondary, and tertiary syphilis. It may also present itself in association with HIV infection. A wide clinical spectrum is seen including osteochondritis, osteitis, periostitis, and bilateral hydrarthrosis, usually involving the knees and painless joints (Clutton's joints) in children with congenital syphilis. Polyarthralgia, polyarthritis, tenosynovitis (not as common or as painful as in disseminated gonococcal infection), unilateral sacroiliitis, and spondylitis may occur in patients with secondary syphilis. Charcot's joints, gummatous arthritis, osteitis, and chronic arthritis may all be seen in patients with tertiary syphilis. Diagnosis can be difficult, especially in the setting of HIV infection, in which repeated serologic analysis is often necessary. Penicillin is the agent of choice in syphilitic arthritis and usually provides good results.

FUNGAL ARTHRITIS. Musculoskeletal involvement secondary to fungal infection is a rare occurrence, although an increased incidence of pathogenic and opportunistic fungal infections and the emergence of new species, particularly in immunosuppressed patients, have been described. Chronic course and delayed diagnosis are common. The use of biologic agents such as TNF-α inhibitors may also be accompanied by systemic fungal infection, including articular. Therefore, the possibility of fungal arthritis should be kept in mind in patients treated in this manner.

The most common fungi affecting the musculoskeletal system are *Coccidioides immitis, Histoplasma capsulatum, Blastomyces dermatitides,* *Sporothrix schenckii,* and in immunocompromised patients, *Candida, Aspergillus, Cryptococcus,* and *Histoplasma.* Diagnosis requires identification of the organism in synovial tissue or isolation from synovial fluid or tissue. Long-term therapy with amphotericin-B and the newer antimycotic agents, with or without surgical débridement, is often effective.

FUTURE DIRECTIONS

The infecting microorganism is detectable by routine culture techniques or Gram staining in only 50% of cases of septic arthritis. Therefore, there is a need for the development of rapid and sensitive methods of identification and antimicrobial susceptibility of the responsible microorganism, including PCR and DNA analysis. The treatment of septic arthritis needs to be fully defined, particularly the duration and routes of administration of antibiotics and the type of drainage. Further development of imaging techniques capable of discriminating between infection and sterile inflammation is needed for an improved diagnosis.

SUGGESTED READINGS
Bentas W, Karch H, Huppertz H-I: Lyme arthritis in children and adolescents: Outcome 12 months after initiation of antibiotic therapy. J Rheumatol 2000;27:2025–2030. *The outcome is more benign in younger children.*
Dubost JJ, Soubrier M, De Champs C, et al: No changes in the distribution of organisms responsible for septic arthritis over a 20 year period. Ann Rheum Dis 2002;61:267–269. *Staphylococci and streptococci remain the leading causes.*
Gupta MN, Sturrock RD, Field M: A prospective 2-year study of 75 patients with adult-onset septic arthritis. Rheumatol 2001;40:24–30. *Prospective investigation aimed to assess clinical features, treatment strategies, and outcome of septic arthritis.*
Keane J, Gershon S, Wise RR, et al: Tuberculosis associated with infliximab, a tumor necrosis factor α–neutralizing agent. N Engl J Med 2001;345:1098–1104. *Excellent report alerting the clinician about the possible development of disseminated tuberculosis following treatment with TNF-α inhibitors.*
Nolla JM, Gomez-Vaquero C, Corbella X, et al: Group B streptococcus (*Streptococcus agalactiae*) Pyogenic arthritis in nonpregnant adults. Medicine 2003;82:119–128. *Identifies group B streptococcus (GBS), or Streptococcus agalactiae, as a significant etiologic agent (10%) of pyogenic arthritis in nonpregnant adults. Monoarthritis is the most common clinical presentation, and penicillin is the drug of choice.*
Stengel D, Bauwens K, Sehouli J, et al: Systematic review and meta-analysis of antibiotic therapy for bone and joint infections. Lancet Infect Dis 2001;1:175–188. *Emphasizes the lack of high-quality evidence to support specific approaches.*

287 OSTEOARTHRITIS

Thomas J. Schnitzer
Nancy E. Lane

Osteoarthritis (OA) is a disorder of diarthrodial joints characterized clinically by pain and functional limitations, radiographically by osteophytes and joint space narrowing, and histopathologically by alterations in cartilage and subchondral bone integrity. The most common of all joint diseases, its importance derives from its economic impact, in terms of both productivity (single greatest cause of days lost from work) and cost of treatment (chronic use of analgesics and anti-inflammatory drugs). Although the etiology of the disorder is still not clearly understood, OA has been shown to be a family of disorders with cartilage as a target organ in which biomechanical factors play a central role and with risk factors such as age, weight, and occupation also of major importance. Since there is currently no treatment to prevent or ameliorate the basic disease process, medical treatment is aimed primarily at relieving pain and improving joint function, with orthopedic intervention largely reserved for those situations that cannot be controlled with more conservative therapy.

Epidemiology

OA is by far the most common joint disorder, one of the most common chronic diseases in the elderly, and a leading cause of disability. Because OA can be defined both radiographically and clinically and because there is little correlation between the two, the prevalence of this condition has been variously estimated in epidemiologic studies. Using radiographic criteria, prevalence of the joint findings steadily increases from less than 2% in women younger than 45 years of age to 30% in those aged 45 to 64 years and to 68% in those older than 65 years of age. Prevalence in men is slightly higher in the younger age groups (<45 years of age), whereas women are affected more commonly at ages older than 55 years, except for disease of the hip.

The pattern of joint involvement in OA is strikingly affected by age, gender, previous joint injury, and occupational history. Prior to age 55, there is little difference in joint pattern between men and women. In older men, hip OA is more common, whereas older women tend to have more involvement of the proximal interphalangeal (PIP) joints and the base of the thumb (first carpometacarpal [CMC] joint). Joints subjected to repeated trauma or overuse demonstrate a higher prevalence of OA. Cotton and mill workers have increased OA of the hand and involved fingers; miners and warehouse workers who bend, squat, and lift heavy loads frequently demonstrate increased knee and spine involvement; and pneumatic drill workers experience increased elbow and wrist disease.

Racial and genetic factors are also important in OA prevalence and pattern. Chinese, Jamaican blacks, South African blacks, and Asian Indians have a lower incidence of OA of the hip than whites, whereas Japanese have an increased incidence, apparently related to the more frequent occurrence of congenital hip dysplasia. Black women have a higher prevalence of knee OA than white women but a lower prevalence of involvement of the distal interphalangeal (DIP) joints of the hand (Heberden's nodes). Involvement of the DIP joints of the hands is particularly common in women and is often found to have a familial pattern of inheritance, with the female relatives of the proband having similar joint findings with a twofold to fivefold increased prevalence.

Modifiable risk factors for OA also have been identified in recent studies. Increased weight is the most significant independent predictor of both incidence and progression of OA in weight-bearing joints, and weight reduction has been shown to reduce the development and progression of knee OA. Certain types of high-impact repetitive activities are associated with an increased risk for the development of OA in the stressed joint (see earlier), whereas other activities are not. In particular, there appears to be an increased risk of knee OA in elite, highly competitive runners. In contrast, there appears to be no increased prevalence of knee OA in low-impact activities like marathon running. However, this may be due to a self-selection process, with those experiencing knee pain unable to continue the activity. Smoking and osteoporosis have both been shown to be negatively associated with OA, but the explanations for these associations are unknown.

Pathology

The hallmarks of OA on gross or arthroscopic examination are focal ulcerated areas of cartilage exposing underlying eburnated (ivory appearing) bone that occur at the load-bearing areas of the joint surface, as well as juxta-articular osteophytes that grow at the joint margins. These states represent the end stage of a continuum, and OA is a pathologic *process*. At its earliest stage, it presents as softening of the cartilage surface, progressing to fibrillation of the surface layers, loss of cartilage thickness, the development of clefts into the depth of cartilage, and eventual loss of cartilage integrity with release of shards of cartilage. Bone participates in this process as well, with reactive changes (bony subchondral sclerosis) underlying the areas of cartilage loss, the development of subchondral bone cysts that may communicate with the joint space and expand into geodes, and marginal osteophytes (new cartilage and bone growth) at non–weight-bearing areas.

The earliest histologic changes reveal loss of extracellular cartilage matrix, loss of chondrocytes in the surface layers of articular cartilage, and reactive changes in the deeper chondrocytes manifested by cellular division and "cloning" in an apparent attempt at repair. Later, there is progressive loss of chondrocytes at all levels, with marked thinning of the cartilage matrix and, in some instances, the development of fibrocartilage in place of lost hyaline articular cartilage. The surrounding synovium is largely unaffected, although in later disease cartilage fragments may incite focal inflammatory lesions without the progressive and destructive pannus seen in typical inflammatory arthropathies.

Pathogenesis

Articular cartilage serves two major functions: (1) to permit nearly frictionless joint motion, and (2) to act as a "shock absorber" and transmit loads across joint surfaces to the surrounding tissues. The requisite properties of elasticity and high tensile strength are imparted by proteoglycans and collagen of the extracellular matrix that comprise more than 90% of the cartilage macromolecules. The proteoglycan elements of the matrix are actively being metabolized and turned over with a half-life of weeks. The highly negatively charged sulfated glycosaminoglycan components of the proteoglycans impart the elastic properties to cartilage. The collagen component of cartilage matrix is characterized by a unique structure (type II collagen) that provides the tensile strength and tightly constrains the proteoglycan molecules in a three-dimensional framework. The collagen fibers are covalently linked by other matrix molecules believed to provide the "glue" to hold the matrix intact. Collagen itself is metabolized very slowly (half-life of many years) in the normal state.

In OA, there is an initial phase when chondrocyte metabolic activity is upregulated (enhanced proteoglycan synthesis) followed by eventual chondrocyte loss (apoptosis). The reason for failure of repair is unclear but may relate to the inability to re-form, once disrupted, the three-dimensional architecture of cartilage in mature individuals.

Degradation of collagen and proteoglycans in OA is carried out by proteolytic enzymes (metalloproteinases [MMPs]) synthesized by and released from the chondrocytes themselves. A number of cytokines and other mediators of inflammation, including interleukin-1β (IL-1β), tumor necrosis factor-α, IL-6, IL-8, nitric oxide (NO), and prostaglandins, can be produced by the chondrocyte and act within the cartilage to promote a catabolic state by activating MMPs. The subsequent activation of these potent enzymes overwhelms the natural matrix defenses and ultimately results in collagen breakdown and proteoglycan cleavage. Fragments from these molecules are then released into the synovial fluid and enter the circulation, where they provide "markers" of degradation and can be used as a means to detect and measure the disease activity.

The factors responsible for activating chondrocytes to release MMPs are currently being elucidated. However, those conditions causing biomechanical alteration of cartilage are known to lead to OA: joint injury, abnormal joint loading due to neuropathic changes (Charcot joint) or ligamentous damage (anterior cruciate ligament [ACL] or meniscus injuries), altered joint surface congruity as in dysplasias, and muscle atrophy in the elderly. A number of metabolic conditions are known to predispose to the early onset of OA: ochronosis with the deposition of homogentisic acid and hemochromatosis with the deposition of iron. Gene defects affecting matrix structures would be expected to possibly lead to OA, but thus far genetic factors have been shown to play a role only in the development of dysplasias with secondary OA. The pathogenetic mechanisms and feedback loops associated with altered cartilage structure and biomechanics are demonstrated in Figure 287–1.

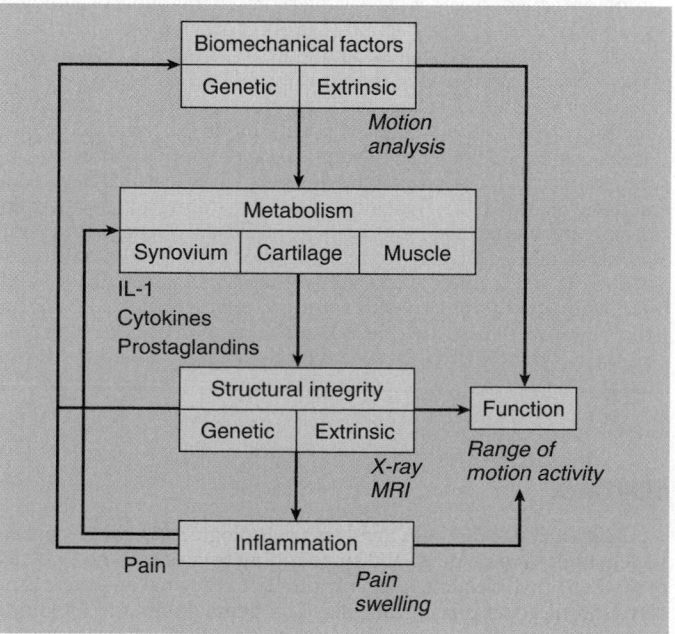

FIGURE 287–1 • Pathogenetic pathways in osteoarthritis. IL-1 = interleukin-1; MRI = magnetic resonance imaging.

Clinical Manifestations

The initial stages of the OA disease process are clinically silent, which explains the high prevalence of radiographic and pathologic signs of OA in clinically asymptomatic patients. Even in later stages of OA, there is a poor correlation between clinical symptoms and alterations in cartilage and bone integrity, defined arthroscopically or by indirect imaging techniques (radiography, magnetic resonance imaging [MRI]). The factors or events that make the OA disease process clinically apparent are unknown but are likely to be heterogeneous in nature and invoke changes within the synovium, bone, and surrounding supporting structures (muscle, ligaments) that produce pain. Pain does not derive from cartilage itself, a completely aneural tissue.

Pain is the predominant symptom that prompts the diagnosis of OA, initially often involving only one joint, with others becoming painful subsequently. The pain of OA is most often described as a deep ache, accompanied frequently by joint stiffness that follows periods of inactivity (on arising in the morning or after sitting). Pain is aggravated by using the involved joints, may radiate, or may be referred to surrounding structures. In the early stages of the disease, pain is commonly relieved by rest. With more severe disease, pain may be persistent, interfering with normal function and preventing sleep, even with medical management. Even in severe disease, systemic manifestations such as fever, weight loss, anemia, and elevated erythrocyte sedimentation rate (ESR) are not present.

The joints most commonly involved in OA are the metatarsophalangeal (MTP) joint of the great toe (hallux valgus or "bunion"); the PIP and DIP joints of the fingers, the CMC joint of the thumb, hips, knees, and both lumbar and cervical spine (Fig. 287–2). Other joints, even major weight-bearing joints such as the ankle, are regularly spared unless involved in secondary forms of OA (Table 287–1). On physical examination, the joints may demonstrate tenderness, crepitus, and a limited range of motion. Joint swelling may be due to an accompanying synovial effusion or to bony enlargement and the presence of osteophytes. Joint instability is seen only in severe disease or after internal derangement of the knee with disruption of one or more of the major supporting structures (e.g., ACL or medial collateral ligament). Patients with far-advanced disease exhibit gross deformity, with subluxation of the involved joints. Although OA is thought to be a uniformly progressive disease that invariably leads to joint replacement, this is not the case. The disease appears to stabilize in many patients with no worsening of signs or symptoms, and there may be actual improvement in some patients.

SPECIFIC JOINT INVOLVEMENT

HAND. Firm, slowly progressive bony enlargements of the DIP joints are called *Heberden's nodes* and represent marginal osteophytic spurs (Fig. 287–3). Occasionally, the onset of symptoms in the hand is acute, with sudden redness and tenderness in the involved joint. These changes can lead to deformity, with lateral and flexor deviation at these joints. A related disorder, erosive OA, is associated with repetitive episodes of acute symptoms and is differentiated by the additional finding of erosive changes on radiographs of the involved joints and a tendency to bony ankylosis. A genetic basis for Heberden's nodes appears to exist, the condition demonstrating a distinct female-dominant familial tendency (women are affected 10 times more commonly than men). Changes similar to those in the DIP joints occur in the PIP joints and are termed *Bouchard's nodes* (see Fig. 287–2). The only other joint to be commonly involved is the CMC joint of the thumb, often eliciting complaints of pain on use (wringing out clothes [washerwoman's hands] and grasping objects such as screwdrivers and doorknobs) and leading to a squared appearance of the base of the hand.

KNEE. Idiopathic knee OA is a leading cause of painful ambulation and is more common in women than in men. The medial compartment of the femorotibial joint space is most commonly affected, resulting in varus deformity (bow legs). Lateral compartment disease may lead to valgus deformity (knock-knee). Patellofemoral disease is also quite common and may represent a substantial portion of knee pathology in patients presenting with knee pain. It is important to exclude other causes of knee pain such as internal derangements of the knee (e.g., meniscal tears or ligament tears) that may lead to secondary knee OA), soft tissue sprains, bursal inflammation, and Baker's cysts (which may coexist with knee OA). In young women, the possibility of chondromalacia patellae should always be considered. Its cause is not known; it is almost always self-limited and is not thought to lead to OA. In idiopathic knee OA, physical examination of the involved joint often elicits crepitation of the tibiofemoral joint, pain, and decreased range of motion. Effusions are not infrequently present but are often small and may be difficult to appreciate.

HIP. Although congenital (Legg-Calvé-Perthes disease) and developmental (slipped femoral capital epiphysis) abnormalities have long been implicated in secondary hip OA, the majority of primary hip OA is now believed to be the consequence of mild dysplasia of the femoral head and/or acetabulum resulting in incongruity of the articulating surfaces. With use of the joint, there is progressive cartilage degeneration and secondary bony productive changes typical of OA. Pain is typically referred to the groin, with anterior thigh and knee symptoms occasionally predominant. Many patients presenting with pain in their "hip" may have referred pain from degenerative disc disease or OA of the lumbar spine. The earliest physical finding in hip OA is loss of internal rotation; with progressive disease, range of motion is limited further in all directions, the affected leg shortens and significant functional limitation occurs, often necessitating surgery.

FOOT. The first MTP joint is the primary joint involved with associated bony swelling and deformity (bunion). Significantly more common in women than men, these changes have been attributed to abnormal stresses imposed on the joint by footwear. In extreme cases, the joint space may be destroyed, leading to a condition known as *hallux rigidus*, which may interfere with normal ambulation and necessitate surgical correction.

SPINE. Technically, OA of the spine relates strictly to changes in synovial-lined joints (apophyseal and uncovertebral joints) that can lead to localized pain as well as irritation of adjacent nerve roots with referred pain in the form of radiculopathy. Nerve root compression resulting from apophyseal joint subluxation, prolapse of an intervertebral disc, or osteophytic spurring may occur and the patient may present with muscle weakness, hyporeflexia, and paresthesia or hypesthesia. In the cervical region, spinal involvement can lead to cord impingement with long tract signs or may affect the vertebral artery, producing insufficiency of the posterior circulation with associated symptoms. OA of the spine should be differentiated from diffuse skeletal hyperostosis in which there is marked calcification of the paraspinous ligaments and sparing of the arthrodial spinal joints.

PRIMARY GENERALIZED OA. The pattern of involvement of three or more joints or joint groups with OA has been given this name and is seen most commonly in older women. Typically, the DIP and PIP joints of the hand, the knees, and the spine are involved. Whether this represents a distinct subset of OA is not known but has been suggested.

Diagnosis

LABORATORY FINDINGS. OA involves a pathologic process that appears largely limited to cartilage and surrounding tissues with no evidence of systemic involvement. Typically the ESR is normal and there is no elevation of acute-phase reactants. The hemoglobin and leukocyte counts remain within normal limits. The synovial fluid itself demonstrates no evidence of an inflammatory reaction, with few leukocytes (typically < 3000/mm^3) and good viscosity. Occasionally, fragments of cartilage and crystals of calcium hydroxyapatite or calcium pyrophosphate dihydrate are seen in the synovial fluid. Rheumatoid factor is absent in the majority of OA patients, but a significant number of older individuals exhibit low titer elevations that are not diagnostic of rheumatoid arthritis but are a common accompaniment of aging.

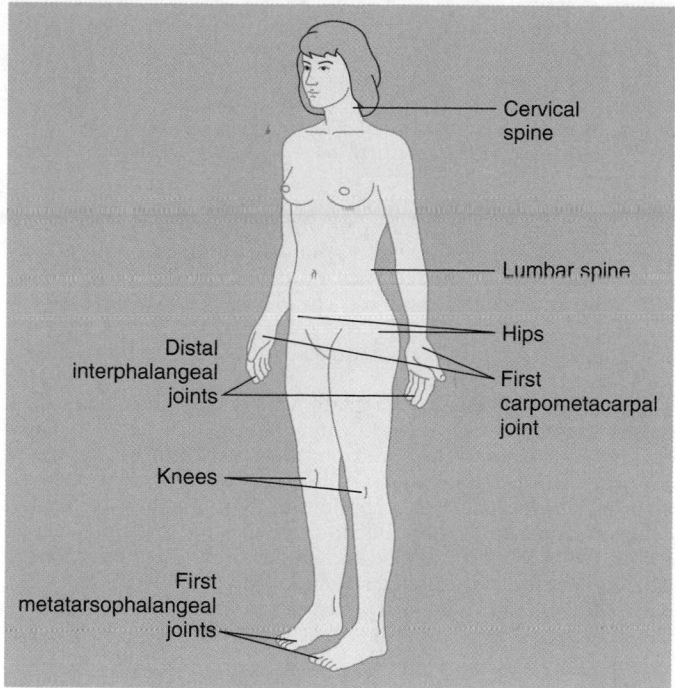

FIGURE 287–2 ◆ Joints commonly affected by osteoarthritis.

Labels: Cervical spine, Lumbar spine, Hips, First carpometacarpal joint, Distal interphalangeal joints, Knees, First metatarsophalangeal joints

Table 287–1 ● ETIOLOGIC CLASSIFICATION OF OSTEOARTHRITIS

Idiopathic (primary)
Localized
  Hands: Heberden's nodes, erosive interphalangeal arthropathy
  Feet: hallux valgus, hammer toes; talonavicular osteoarthritis
  Knees: medial, lateral, patellofemoral compartments
  Hips: sites of cartilage loss—eccentric (superior), concentric (axial, medial), diffuse
  Spine: zygoapophyseal joints, osteophytes, intervertebral discs (spondylosis); ligaments, e.g., disseminated idiopathic skeletal hyperostosis
Other single sites: shoulder, temporomandibular, carpometacarpal joints
Generalized—includes three or more areas listed above
Mineral deposition diseases
  Calcium pyrophosphate deposition disease
  Hydroxyapatite arthropathy
Destructive disease (e.g., Milwaukee shoulder)

Secondary
Post-traumatic
Congenital or developmental
  Legg-Calvé-Perthes hip dislocation
  Epiphyseal dysplasias
  Articular cartilage disorders associated with a gene deficiency (e.g., association with type II procollagen gene mutation)
Disturbed local tissue structure by primary disease, e.g., ischemic necrosis, tophaceous gout, hyperparathyroid cysts, Paget's disease, rheumatoid arthritis, osteopetrosis, osteochondritis
Miscellaneous additional diseases
  Endocrine: diabetes mellitus, acromegaly, hypothyroidism
  Metabolic: hemochromatosis, ochronosis, Gaucher's disease
  Neuropathic arthropathies
  Miscellaneous: frostbite, Kashin-Beck disease, caisson disease
  Mechanical: obesity, unequal lower extremity length; valgus/varus deformities, ligamentous laxity (including associations with type I procollagen gene mutations of Ehlers-Danlos syndrome).

Compiled in part by Osteoarthritis Diagnostic Criteria Committee, American Rheumatism Association, 1983.

Cartilage matrix components unique to the joints have been identified, and sensitive assays have been developed to detect these "markers" in synovial fluid, serum, and urine. Further clinical correlations need to be performed to determine the relationship of these markers to the disease process, activity, and state and their possible use for earlier diagnosis and management of OA.

RADIOLOGY AND IMAGING FINDINGS. Pathognomonic findings on plain radiography of involved joints include the presence of osteophytes at the margins of involved joints, associated joint space narrowing representing areas of cartilage thinning or loss, and evidence of bony reaction marked by subchondral sclerosis and bone cysts in more progressive disease. Some patients may lack one or more of these findings.

Radiography has been shown to be insensitive to the pathologic processes occurring in the cartilage. Many patients having normal radiographs with destructive cartilage changes documented by arthroscopy. However, performing a weight-bearing knee radiograph with the knee flexed to 20 degrees allows a more reliable assessment of joint space narrowing, and repeating this radiograph can be used to assess changes in joint space narrowing over time. Other techniques have therefore been developed with greater potential sensitivity to detect cartilage change. In particular, MRI has the advantage of demonstrating cartilage as a positive image and has been used widely to document major cartilage injuries such as meniscal tears. Further refinement of this technology will enhance the resolution as well as increase sensitivity to detect changes in hydration, which mark the earliest cartilage abnormalities in OA. It is anticipated that such technology will be important in the future in assessing disease progression and the efficacy of therapeutic interventions.

Other technologies being developed to evaluate the OA joint include scintigraphy and ultrasonography.

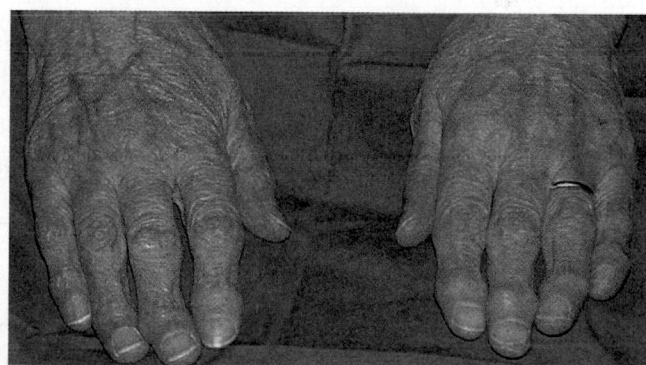

FIGURE 287–3 ● Typical hand deformities in osteoarthritis. Heberden's nodes are seen on the distal interphalangeal joints, and Bouchard's nodes are at the proximal interphalangeal joints. (From Forbes CD, Jackson WF: Color Atlas and Text of Clinical Medicine, 3rd ed. London, Mosby, 2003.)

 Treatment

People with OA seek pain relief and improved physical function. Because at this time there is no known therapy in humans that affects the basic disease process (to inhibit cartilage degradation or enhance synthesis), medical therapy has focused on providing symptomatic relief. Largely because of ease of administration and acceptance by patients, an unwarranted reliance has been placed on pharmacologic intervention, particularly non-steroidal anti-inflammatory drugs (NSAIDs), as initial therapy at the expense of physi-cal measures that have less morbidity and may provide longer-term benefit. The American College of Rheumatology has recently formulated evidence-based guidelines for progressive, step-wise treatment of patients with knee and hip OA that incorporates this approach.

PHYSICAL MEASURES. Although often overlooked, physical therapy and exercise programs provide important benefit and should be prescribed as baseline therapy for all patients with OA. Muscle atrophy

Continued

commonly accompanies OA. Because muscles serve to reduce load on cartilage, maintaining muscle function is crucial for cartilage integrity and pain reduction. Both muscle strength and range of motion can be improved with appropriate physical therapy. Isometric exercises are preferred to isotonic because they place less stress on the involved joint.

Heat and cold are both used with varying effectiveness to provide symptomatic relief to OA patients and as an important adjunct to physical therapy regimens. Using transcutaneous nerve stimulation, particularly to relieve back pain, and acupuncture is effective in some patients and provides an attractive alternative to pharmacologic intervention.

Periods of rest throughout the day may be an important adjunct in the routine of patients with OA. Reduction in joint loading, either by resting or appropriately using a cane, often permits increased periods of activity with reduced pain. Using cushioned shoes (commercial running or walking shoes) also may help lower extremity joint symptoms. Back pain may be reduced by muscle-strengthening exercises as well as by a well-fitted brace. However, the fitted brace should be used only intermittently to prevent abdominal and paraspinal muscle atrophy.

PHARMACOLOGIC THERAPY (Table 287–2). Symptomatic relief of joint pain in patients with OA may be achieved with simple analgesic agents such as acetaminophen. Particularly in the elderly with decreased renal reserve and an increased incidence of upper gastrointestinal bleeding, acetaminophen and other simple analgesics should be the drugs of initial choice. If inflammation is present (erosive OA) or symptoms are not well controlled with simple analgesics, lower doses of NSAIDs may prove to be effective.

A newer class of NSAIDs (cyclooxygenase-2 [COX-2] inhibitors) that inhibits inflammatory-mediated production of prostaglandins (COX-2 mediated) but permits constitutive prostaglandin production (COX-1 mediated) is available. They appear to have less gastrointestinal toxicity than traditional nonselective NSAIDs. Therefore, their use may be preferred to nonselective NSAIDs, particularly in patients at high risk of gastrointestinal side effects. **1,2**

Controlled studies of intra-articular steroid injections have demonstrated safety and benefit when given every three months for up to two years. **3** Intra-articular injections of steroids should not be repeated more than three or four times per year in any given joint because of the possibility of the steroids potentiating cartilage breakdown. Systemic use of steroids has no place in the treatment of OA. In knee OA, intra-articular hyaluronan has been shown to produce modest improvement in pain that may persist for a few months.

Topical treatment with capsaicin, a substance-P inhibitor, has been shown to relieve localized pain in some patients with OA. The development of agents that can stimulate cartilage synthesis or prevent degradation is actively being pursued and may provide the next generation of agents used to treat OA. For example, intra-articular hyaluronate can improve joint symptoms. **4** Oral glucosamine and chondroitin is controversial but appears to be effective based on a meta-analysis. **5**

ORTHOPEDIC SURGERY. Joint replacement surgery has been the single biggest advance in the treatment of OA in the past half century. Patients in whom optimal medical management has failed and who continue to have pain that interferes with sleep or activity or who have significant limitations of joint function are candidates for an operation. Those individuals with altered limb alignment and early OA of a hip or knee may benefit from osteotomy. Most patients have more advanced disease and require total joint replacement. Ideal candidates for total joint arthroplasty exhibit well-maintained muscle strength and should be older than 60 years of age. Younger patients are discouraged from undergoing joint replacement because of the small but real incidence of long-term failure of joint implants, mainly due to loosening. Revision arthroplasty is possible but has a higher failure rate and can be avoided by delaying initial arthroplasty as long as possible and putting less load on the replaced joint.

Arthroscopic surgery is useful for removing loose bodies and repairing intrinsic defects of the knee as well as shoulder (rotator cuff) and ankle pathology. Arthroscopic lavage (flushing of saline to remove cartilage debris) in patients with knee OA may provide pain relief. Abrasion arthroplasty (chondroplasty) has been widely used in patients with knee OA, but no data exist to demonstrate its efficacy, and it cannot be recommended currently.

Future Directions

In the next few years, the focus of OA treatment will most likely change from use of only analgesic agents to agents that may alter the course of the disease. These future drugs may include MMP inhibitors, cartilage growth factors, NO inhibitors, or agents that may prevent chondrocyte apoptosis. In addition, research is currently being carried out in biosynthetic cartilage replacement and in improved materials for total joint replacement. Therefore, the future holds promise not only to slow the joint degeneration in OA but possibly also to reverse it.

Grade **A**

1. Geba GP, Weaver AL, Polis AB, et al: Efficacy of rofecoxib, celecoxib, and acetaminophen in osteoarthritis of the knee: A randomized trial. Vioxx, Acetaminophen, Celecoxib Trial (VACT) Group. JAMA 2001;287:64–71.
2. Day R, Morrison B, Luza A, et al: A randomized trial of the efficacy and tolerability of the COX-2 inhibitor rofecoxib versus ibuprofen in patients with osteoarthritis. Rofecoxib/Ibuprofen Comparator Study Group. Arch Intern Med 2000;160:1781–1787.
3. Raynauld JP, Buckland-Wright C, Ward R, et al: Safety and efficacy of long-term intraarticular steroid injections in osteoarthritis of the knee: A randomized, double-blind, placebo-controlled trial. Arthritis Rheum 2003;48:370–377.
4. Altman R, Moskowitz R: Intra-articular sodium hyaluronate (Hyalgan) in the treatment of patients with osteoarthritis of the knee: A randomized clinical trial. Hyalgan Study Group. J Rheumatol 1998;25:2203–2212.
5. Richy F, Bruyere O, Ethgen O, et al: Structural and symptomatic efficacy of glucosamine and chondroitin in knee osteoarthritis: A comprehensive meta-analysis. Arch Intern Med 2003;163:1514–1522.

SUGGESTED READINGS

American College of Rheumatology Subcommittee on Osteoarthritis Guidelines: Recommendations for the medical management of OA of the hip and knee. Arthritis Rheum 2000;43:1905–1915. *Consensus guidelines.*

Brosseau L, MacLeay L, Robinson V, et al: Intensity of exercise for the treatment of osteoarthritis. Cochrane Database Syst Rev 2003;(2):CD004259. *High intensity and low intensity aerobic exercise are equally effective in improving functional status and osteoarthritis of the knee.*

Pelletier PJ, Pelletier JM, Abramson SB: Osteoarthritis, an inflammatory disease. Arthritis Rheum 2001;44:1237–1247. *Emphasizes the inflammatory component of OA and its importance for selecting treatment.*

Table 287–2 • RECOMMENDATIONS FOR THE PHARMACOLOGIC MANAGEMENT OF OSTEOARTHRITIS OF THE HIP AND KNEE

Pharmacologic Therapy*
Oral
  Acetaminophen
  COX-2 specific inhibitor
  Nonselective NSAID plus misoprostol or a proton pump inhibitor[†]
  Nonacetylated salicylate
  Other pure analgesics
    Tramadol
    Opioids
Intra-articular
  Glucocorticoids
  Hyaluronan
Topical
  Capsaicin
  Methylsalicylate

*The choice should be individualized for each patient.
[†]Misoprostol and proton pump inhibitors can be used in patients who are at increased risk of upper gastrointestinal adverse events.
COX-2 = cyclooxygenase-2; NSAID = nonsteroidal anti-inflammatory drug.
From the American College of Rheumatology Subcommittee on Osteoarthritis Guidelines. Arthritis Rheum 2003;43:1905–1915.

288 CRYSTAL DEPOSITION DISEASES

Robert Terkeltaub

Supersaturation of body fluids with a variety of solutes may result in the deposition of different forms of crystals and calculi. Pathologic crystallization can be a clinical problem within not only extracellular fluids (e.g., biliary tract and urinary tract calculi) but also within the matrix of certain connective tissues (e.g., arterial wall calcification in atherosclerosis). In gout, systemic elevation of uric acid promotes deposition of the monosodium salt of uric acid at stereotypic locations including synovium and cartilage of peripheral joints, the olecranon bursa, and the helix of the ear. The loose avascular connective tissue of articular cartilage is particularly susceptible to calcification with aging in idiopathic chondrocalcinosis, with osteoarthritis, and with an intra-articular excess of inorganic pyrophosphate (PPi) in these conditions and certain metabolic disorders. This chapter discusses crystal deposition diseases that predominantly manifest as joint disease (with the principal focus on gout, calcium pyrophosphate dihydrate [CPPD] crystal deposition disease, hydroxyapatite [HA] crystal deposition, and the articular manifestations of oxalate crystal deposition).

GOUT AND HYPERURICEMIA

Definition

The term *gout* refers to heterogeneous disorders resulting from tissue deposition of monosodium urate crystals or crystallization of uric acid in the urinary tract. Fundamental to the development of gout is a substantial increase in total body uric acid stores, reflected in the metabolic disorder hyperuricemia. The definition of hyperuricemia is a serum uric acid level at least two standard deviations above the norm established by individual laboratories according to gender. Serum urate levels rise with puberty, and then, in females, remain relatively stable overall until menopause, at which time concentrations begin to rise associated with a loss of the ability of estrogen to promote renal excretion of uric acid. Typically, hyperuricemia is defined as a serum uric acid greater than 7.0 mg/dL in adult men and 6.0 mg/dL in premenopausal women.

Epidemiology

Gout is predominantly an idiopathic or multifactorial disease of adult men, with a peak incidence in the fifth decade. Gout rarely occurs in men before adolescence or in women before menopause. The disease is common. In 1986, the prevalence of self-reported gout in America was 13.6 per 1000 men and 6.4 per 1000 women. The prevalence has increased over the past few decades in countries that have an improving standard of living. In association with increased longevity and common use of hyperuricemia-promoting thiazide diuretics, the prevalence of gout also is rising among aging women, particularly in association with chronic renal insufficiency. Prevalence among persons of Pacific Islander ethnic extraction appears substantially higher than among whites.

Hyperuricemia can be documented in at least 5% of the asymptomatic U.S. population on at least one occasion during adulthood. The duration and magnitude of hyperuricemia directly correlate with the risk of development of gout. However, a minority of individuals with sustained hyperuricemia go on to develop clinical gout, partly because increases in serum urate levels are relatively mild (i.e., serum urate < 9.0 mg/dL) in most individuals or occur transiently in response to dietary and pharmacologic changes. Therefore, asymptomatic hyperuricemia without gout is not a disease.

Pathobiology

Uric acid is normally produced as an end product of the degradation of purine compounds (Fig. 288–1). However, the solubility of the principal physiologic salt of uric acid, monosodium urate, in connective tissues is normally close to 7 mg/dL at 37° C, and urate solubility declines progressively at cooler temperatures such as those in distal peripheral joints. Thus, in humans, "normal" serum urate concentrations provide only a narrow safety margin for urate crystal deposition. Humans, like other high mammals, lack uric acid oxidase (uricase), which oxidizes uric acid to the more soluble compound allantoin. Significantly, genetically engineered uricase knockout mice demonstrate not only a marked increase in serum urate (from ~1.0 to ~11.0 mg/dL) but also develop severe uric acid nephrolithiasis with renal function compromise in early life.

Miscible total body urate stores are approximately 1.2 g (range, 800 to 1600 mg) in healthy men and about half this value in healthy women. Yet urate synthesis averages approximately 750 mg/day in men, and dietary purine intake stimulates additional uric acid production. Gastrointestinal (GI) elimination of uric acid via gut bacterial urate oxidation can remove a few hundred milligrams of uric acid daily, but this elimination pathway has a limited potential for adaptive increases in capacity. Renal urate excretion in normal adult men receiving a purine-free diet averages approximately 400 mg/day, and the normal range is between 250 and 750 mg/day on a typical Western diet. Renal urate excretion can increase substantially in adaptation to increased uric acid generation. However, physiologic limits to renal elimination of uric acid constrain the capacity of this urate removal pathway, and excessive uric filtration is nephrotoxic, as discussed further later. Therefore, the majority of total body urate stores is normally turned over daily, providing a narrow physiologic window for urate balance with the potential for substantial expansion of total body urate stores.

Multiple social, environmental, and genetic factors influence uric acid formation and removal. The familial occurrence of gout is reported in approximately 20% of affected patients. Family and twin studies suggest that both hyperuricemia and renal handling of uric acid are polygenic traits. In a given individual, single and combined disorders of uric acid formation and excretion can be responsible for hyperuricemia and gout (Table 288–1). A minority of patients with gout have urate overproduction alone as the primary abnormality. The most common defect identifiable in patients with gout is renal

---

Table 288–1 • HYPERURICEMIA: CAUSES AND CLASSIFICATION*

Uric Acid Overproduction
Primary hyperuricemia
  Idiopathic
  HGPRT deficiency (partial and complete)
  PRPP synthetase superactivity
Secondary hyperuricemia
  Excessive dietary purine intake
  Increased nucleotide turnover (e.g., myeloproliferative and
    lymphoproliferative disorders, hemolytic diseases, psoriasis,
    Paget's disease of bone)
  Accelerated ATP degradation
    Ethanol abuse
    Glycogen storage diseases (types I, III, V, VII)
    Fructose ingestion, hereditary fructose intolerance
    Hypoxemia and tissue underperfusion
    Severe muscle exertion
    ? Hypertriglyceridemia (via metabolism of excess acetate)

Uric Acid Underexcretion
Primary hyperuricemia
  Idiopathic (influenced by gender and ethnicity)
  Familial juvenile hyperuricemic nephropathy
Secondary hyperuricemia
  Diminished glomerular filtration rate
  Enhanced tubualr urate reabsorption
    Dehydration
    Diuretics
    Insulin resistance (syndrome X)
  Inhibition of tubular urate secretion
    Competitive anions (e.g., ketoacidosis and lactic acidosis)
  Mechanism incompletely defined
    Hypertension
    Hyperparathyroidism
    Hypothyroidism
    Certain drugs (e.g., cyclosporine, pyrazinamide, ethambutol, low-
      dose salicylates)
    Lead toxicity with nephropathy

*Increased uric acid production and diminished uric acid excretion by the kidney, alone or in combination, promote hyperuricemia in patients with gout. Classification of patients with gout by the mechanism(s) causing hyperuricemia helps in directing diagnosis of unsuspected, underlying disorders and is useful to guide therapy. This table provides such a classification scheme, in which *primary hyperuricemia* refers to inherently disordered uric acid metabolism not associated with a distinct acquired disorder such as ethanol abuse or diuretic therapy.

ATP = adenosine triphosphate; HGPRT = hypoxine-guanine phosphoribosyl-transferase; PRPP = 5-phosphoribosyl-1-pyrophosphate.

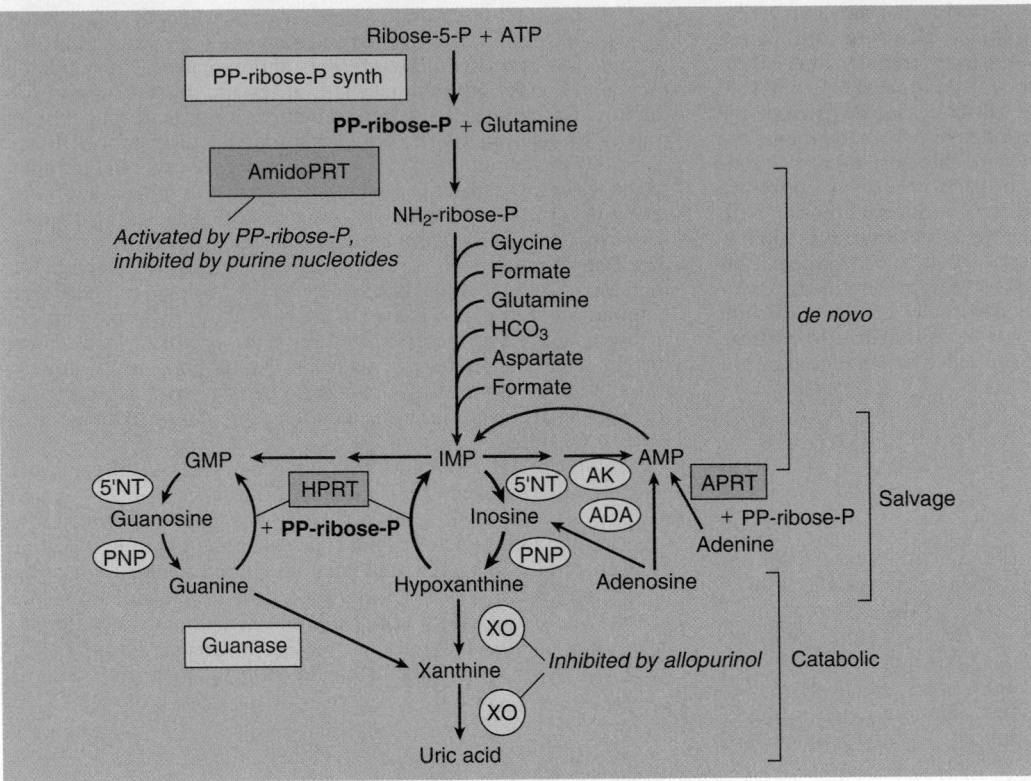

FIGURE 288–1 • Intracellular purine metabolism and how uric acid is generated. The synthesis of purine nucleotides involves closely regulated biochemical pathways, termed "de novo" and "salvage." In the "de novo path," a purine ring is synthesized from small molecule precursors, sequentially added to a ribose-phosphate backbone donated by 5-phosphoribosyl-1-pyrophosphate (PP-ribose-P). The first reaction of the de novo path is catalyzed by amidophosphoribosyltransferase (AmidoPRT). This reaction is the main site of pathway regulation via antagonistic interaction involving inhibition by relatively abundant purine nucleotide products and activation by PP-ribose-P, which is normally relatively sparse. At inosine monophosphate (IMP), the pathway branches and gives rise to adenosine monophosphate (AMP) and guanosine monophosphate (GMP) and their derivatives. Control of purine nucleotide production also occurs at distal points in the pathways governing formation of adenylate and guanylate derivatives. In the "salvage" pathway, the preformed purine bases hypoxanthine, guanine, and adenine, derived from turnover of IMP, GMP, and AMP, are directly condensed with PP-ribose-P by hypoxine-guanine phosphoribosyltransferase (HGPRT) and adenine phosphoribosyltransferase (APRT). Factors that govern the relationship between rates of purine-base salvage and purine synthesis include the availability of PP-ribose-P and concentrations of the nucleotide products common to both pathways. The catabolic steps that generate uric acid from nucleic acids and free purine nucleotides involve degradation to hypoxanthine and xanthine through purine nucleoside intermediates. Some of the hypoxanthine formed by nucleotide turnover is diverted to the liver and catabolized in sequential reactions catalyzed by xanthine oxidase (XO) to uric acid; the remainder is salvaged by HGRPT. Operation of the salvage pathway reduces de novo path activity. This is because HGRPT and APRT have greater affinity for PPRP than does AmidoPRT, because base salvage lowers the concentration of PP-ribose-P, and because the nucleotide end products of the HRPT and APRT reactions directly inhibit AmidoPRT. Clinically, inherited mutations or regulatory defects for PP-ribose-P synthetase associated with superactivity of this enzyme are associated with hyperuricemia. Deficiency of HGPRT promotes hyperuricemia via enhanced conversion of hypoxanthine and guanine to uric acid and a compensatory increase in de novo path activity because of reduced formation of inhibitory nucleotides and increased availability of PP-ribose-P for the AmidoPRT reaction. Clinically, increased net ATP breakdown can cause hyperuricemia by increasing the production of XO substrates and by releasing inhibition of AmidoPRT. Hyperuricemia associated with net ATP catabolism in muscle and liver may occur acutely in certain conditions (including severe hypoxia and tissue ischemia, and hereditary fructose intolerance) (Table 288–1) and chronically in association with excessive alcohol consumption, which places increased demands on hepatocellular ATP stores for metabolism of alcohol. Therapeutically, allopurinol, by blocking XO-catalyzed uric acid generation, enhances salvage of hypoxanthine, further inhibiting de novo activity. This action reduces purine excretion more than expected from inhibition of uric acid formation alone. ADA = adenosine deaminase; AK = adenosine kinase; 5'NT = 5'-nucleotidase; PNP = purine nucleoside phosphorylase.

underexcretion of urate, via an undefined mechanism. The recent cloning of renal urate transporters, including URATI, may help in elucidating the molecular basis for this common observation.

ABNORMAL RENAL HANDLING OF URATE. Almost all plasma urate is filtered at the glomerulus, with more than 95% of the filtered load undergoing proximal tubular (presecretory) reabsorption. Subsequent proximal tubular secretion of about 50% of the filtered urate load contributes to most of the uric acid excreted. Postsecretory tubular reabsorption of about 40% of the filtered urate load is another primary mechanism of renal uric acid handling. Decreased glomerular filtration rate and heredity and the effects of hydration, a variety of organic acids including ketoacids and lactate, drugs, exogenous toxins such as lead, and tubular handling of uric acid all can impair renal excretion of uric acid (see Table 288–1). Among the offending pharmacologic agents are diuretics, cyclosporine, and low-dose acetylsalicylic acid (see Table 288–1). Patients with gout tend to have a relatively high incidence of other diseases that predispose to renal insufficiency, including hypertension, which can increase tubular urate reabsorption. A substantial fraction of patients with both hyperuricemia and

primary gout has "syndrome X" (or metabolic syndrome) in which insulin resistance (IR) is a central factor. In syndrome X, IR promotes abdominal (visceral) obesity, glucose intolerance, and dyslipidemia. Syndrome X also is strongly associated with essential hypertension and atherosclerosis. Insulin normally stimulates the renal tubular sodium-hydrogen exchanger, thereby facilitating secretion of hydrogen and reabsorption of sodium, bicarbonate, chloride, and certain organic anions including uric acid. Thus, IR in syndrome X is associated with increased renal urate reabsorption. Type IV hyperlipidemia in syndrome X also could promote increased uric acid generation via augmented provision of acetate from triglycerides.

INCREASED URATE PRODUCTION. The pathways by which uric acid is generated in the metabolism of purine nucleotides are illustrated in Figure 288–1. In addition, the legend to Figure 288–1 summarizes the clinical implications of disordered activity of uric acid synthetic pathways and the therapeutic mechanisms of action of allopurinol. Between 10 and 20% of patients with gout produce excessive uric acid. In approximately 10% of patients with gout, an excess of uric acid production can be readily documented by excretion of more than

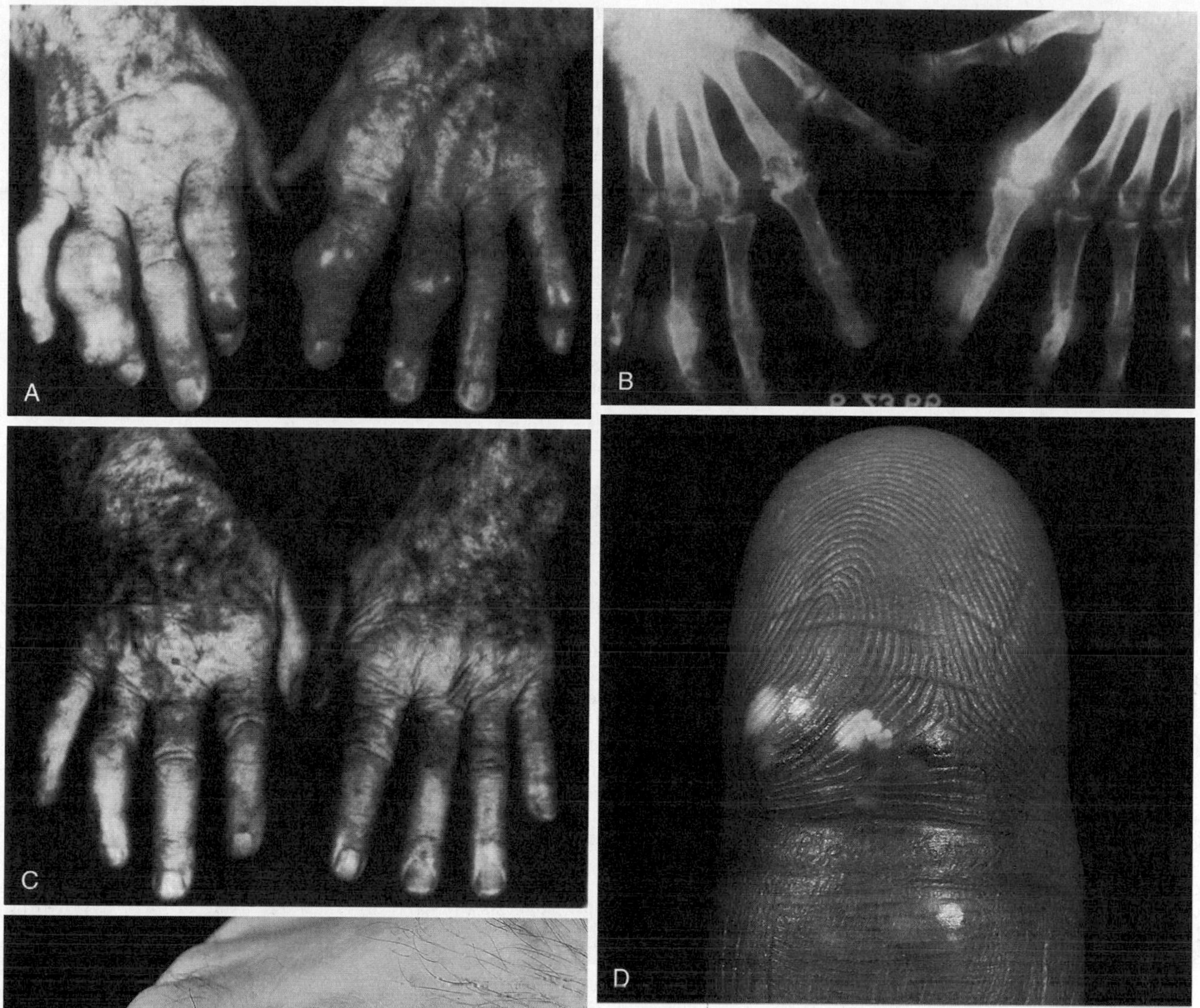

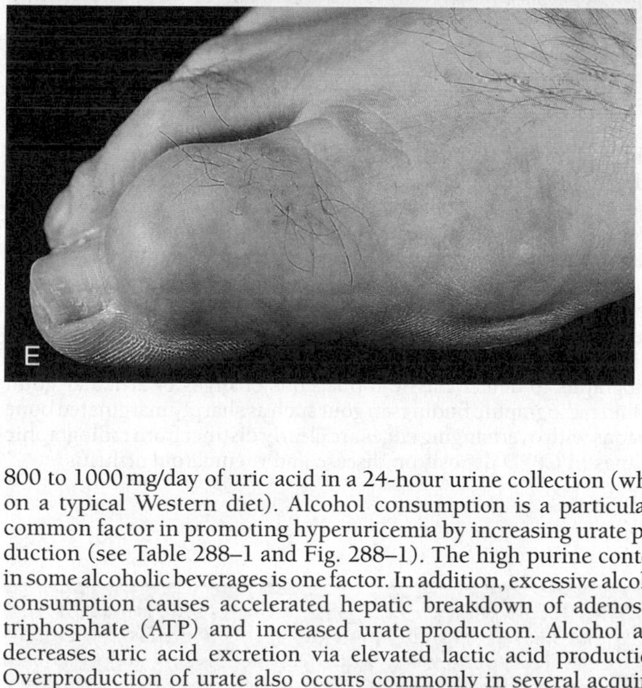

FIGURE 288–2 • Tophaceous gout. *A to C*, Chronic gouty arthritis with tophaceous destruction of bone and joints (*A* and *B*) and improvement after 3 years of treatment with allopurinol, prophylactic colchicine, and a moderately low purine diet (*C*). *D*, Tophaceous deposits in the digital pad of a 28-year-old man with systemic lupus erythematosus under treatment with diuretics. A single attack of gout had occurred 2 years earlier. *E*, Tophaceous enlargement of the great toe in a 44-year-old man with a 4-year history of recurrent gouty arthritis.

800 to 1000 mg/day of uric acid in a 24-hour urine collection (while on a typical Western diet). Alcohol consumption is a particularly common factor in promoting hyperuricemia by increasing urate production (see Table 288–1 and Fig. 288–1). The high purine content in some alcoholic beverages is one factor. In addition, excessive alcohol consumption causes accelerated hepatic breakdown of adenosine triphosphate (ATP) and increased urate production. Alcohol also decreases uric acid excretion via elevated lactic acid production. Overproduction of urate also occurs commonly in several acquired and genetic disorders that are characterized by excessive rates of cell and, therefore, nucleic acid turnover (see Table 288–1). Inherited derangements in mechanisms regulating purine nucleotide synthesis (see Table 288–1 and Fig. 288–1) account for a small fraction of patients with urate overproduction.

PATHOGENESIS OF TISSUE DEPOSITION OF URATE CRYSTALS AND INFLAMMATORY DISEASE IN GOUT. Tophaceous deposits of urate crystals and the morphology of individual urate crystals are seen in Figures 288–2 and 288–3, respectively. Tophi commonly develop in osteoarthritic interphalangeal joints, suggesting roles of connective tissue matrix

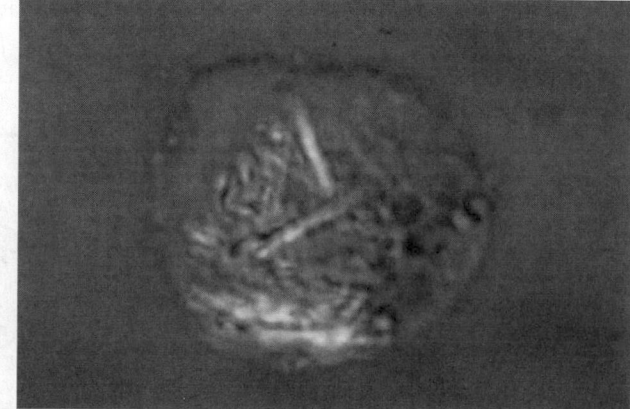

FIGURE 288–3 • Sodium urate monohydrate crystals phagocytosed by a leukocyte in synovial fluid from acute gouty arthritis, examined by polarized light.

structure and turnover in urate crystal deposition. The predilection for marked urate crystal deposition in the first metatarsophalangeal (MTP) joint may also relate to repetitive minor trauma at that site. Microscopic tophaceous deposits of urate crystals are often present in the synovial membrane at the time of the first gouty attack and may also be detected within cartilage. Abrupt rises and declines in serum urate levels, as stimulated by diuretics, alcohol use, and with initiation of therapy with antihyperuricemic drugs, may promote release of urate crystals from tophi via changes in packing of crystals in tophaceous deposits. Free urate crystals have considerable pro-inflammatory potential, via the ability to activate synovial lining cells and leukocytes and to trigger multiple inflammatory cascades. Yet in some individuals with gout, urate crystals can be found in asymptomatic MTP and knee joints that have never been involved in an acute attack or in noninflamed joints between acute attacks of gout at those sites. These findings reinforce that urate deposition in tissues can be asymptomatic.

Urate crystals activate cells partly via nonspecific activation of signal transduction pathways (e.g., mitogen-activated protein kinase activation) and induce cellular release of cyclooxygenase- and lipoxygenase-derived metabolites of arachidonic acid and cytokines including tumor necrosis factor-α, interleukin-1 (IL-1), and IL-8. The ingress of neutrophils into the joint is central in triggering acute gouty arthritis, and effects on neutrophil-endothelial cell interactions likely represent a major locus for the prophylactic and therapeutic effects of colchicine. IL-8 and closely related chemokines that bind the IL-8 receptor CXCR2 (including GRO-α) appear to be critical in initiating and perpetuating neutrophil ingress in acute gouty inflammation. The acute gouty attack often is spontaneously self-limited by 7 to 10 days, likely mediated by an altered balance between proinflammatory and anti-inflammatory mediators in the joint. Low-grade synovitis may persist in affected joints. Inflammatory mechanisms in gout, especially in untreated disease, can lead to chronic synovial proliferation, cartilage loss, and bone erosion.

Clinical Manifestations

Gout classically presents as recurrent attacks of acute arthritis characterized by often excruciatingly painful articular and periarticular inflammation, including erythema and edema of the skin that can mimic bacterial cellulitis. Acute gouty arthritis is typically monoarticular or oligoarticular. Stereotypic involvement of the first MTP joint is termed *podagra*. Acute polyarticular gout also may occur, particularly in the elderly and in transplant patients on cyclosporine. This presentation can be associated with substantial systemic leukocytosis and temperature elevation that mimics sepsis. Chronic gouty inflammation and proliferative, erosive arthritis in gout also can mimic rheumatoid arthritis.

Gouty tophi (see Fig. 288–2) can involve not only synovium and cartilage of joints but also subchondral bone and soft tissues including the olecranon bursa, the first MTP joint bursa, and the helix of the ear. Olecranon bursitis may occur in gout, but often the olecranon bursa tophi remain clinically quiescent. Uric acid urolithiasis is a common manifestation of gout, particularly in acid urine of urate overproducers. Excessive excretion in the urinary tract of uric acid also may promote calcium oxalate lithiasis. Interstitial nephropathy, characterized by deposition of monosodium urate in the renal medulla at physiologic pH, is currently a rare manifestation of gout, largely because of advances in recognition and treatment of hyperuricemia and hypertension.

Onset of gout (with or without tophaceous crystal deposits) in early adulthood and a high incidence of uric acid urinary tract stones constitute the common clinical phenotype in both partial deficiency of hypoxine-guanine phosphoribosyltransferase (HGPRT) and milder forms of superactivity of 5-phosphoribosyl-1-pyrophosphate (PP-ribose-P) synthetase. Severe HGPRT deficiency is associated with spasticity, choreoathetosis, mental retardation, and self-mutilation (Lesch-Nyhan syndrome). In some subjects, regulatory defects in PP-ribose-P synthetase are accompanied by sensorineural deafness and neurodevelopmental defects. Both HGPRT and PP-ribose-P synthetase are X-linked genes. Thus, homozygous males are affected, and postmenopausal gout and urinary tract stones can occur as the phenotype of carrier females. Hyperuricemia in prepubertal boys always suggests the need to determine if one of these enzymatic defects is the etiology.

Diagnosis

The combination of the classic picture of acute gouty arthritis described earlier, or urolithiasis, with evidence of past or current hyperuricemia, is highly suggestive of gout. The serum uric acid level may fluctuate and is often normal at the time of an acute gout attack. The synovial fluid in acute gout typically demonstrates leukocytosis and other nonspecific features of joint inflammation. The ability of gout to mimic septic arthritis and vice versa is noteworthy, and free and intracellular urate (or CPPD crystals) are sometimes found as a secondary effect of joint inflammation in septic joints. Thus, the diagnostic importance of arthrocentesis with adequate synovial fluid crystal analysis, and in many instances, concomitant exclusion of joint infection is emphasized (Fig. 288–4). As illustrated in Figure 288–3, urate crystals (needle-shaped, brightly negatively birefringent crystals, many of them within neutrophils) can be identified by compensated polarized light microscopy of wet preparations of synovial fluid in the vast majority of cases of gouty arthritis. Though weakly birefringent relative to urate crystals and often rhomboid in shape, CPPD crystals can be rod shaped and intracellular and thereby resemble urate crystals. Thus, the use of compensated polarized light microscopy is also needed to exclude positively birefringent CPPD crystals. Other investigations of diagnostic value that also can assist in management decisions include measurement of 24-hour urine uric acid and use of radiographs to detect classic tophaceous changes of articular gout. Certain radiographic findings in gout such as sharply marginated bone erosions with overhanging edges are clearly distinct from radiographic findings in CPPD deposition disease and rheumatoid arthritis.

Rx Prevention and Treatment

The principal goal of therapy in acute gout is rapid and safe resolution of the painful, inflammatory attack. Related but distinct goals in the longer-term management of gout are to limit recurrences of acute gouty arthritis, to prevent disabling tissue consequences of monosodium urate crystal deposition and urolithiasis, and to recognize and appropriately treat medical conditions commonly associated with gout (e.g., hypertension, obesity, hyperlipidemia, alcohol abuse, chronic renal insufficiency, and possibly hypothyroidism). Uricosuric drugs and allopurinol used to reduce serum urate levels do not possess anti-inflammatory properties. Moreover, initiation of uric acid–lowering treatment with these drugs during the inflammatory phase of acute gout should not be done because it often worsens the arthritis.

ACUTE GOUTY ARTHRITIS. Acute gouty arthritis generally responds well to nonsteroidal anti-inflammatory agents (NSAIDs) or certain other treatments, particularly when treatment is initiated within 1 or 2 days of onset (see Fig. 288–4). One cost-effective NSAID regimen for acute gout is indomethacin (50 mg three or four times daily for 2 or 3 days, with subsequent rapid tapering and discontinuation by 1 week). However, headache and GI side effects may limit indomethacin use. Naproxen (375 or 500 mg orally twice a day) or sulindac (150 or 200 mg orally twice a day) are reasonable NSAID alternatives. Evidence-based data for use in gout of the cyclooxygenase-2 (COX-2)-selective NSAIDs, particularly in patients on anticoagulants or with substantial GI risk factors, are awaited at the time of this writing. Use of both COX-2-nonselective and COX-2-

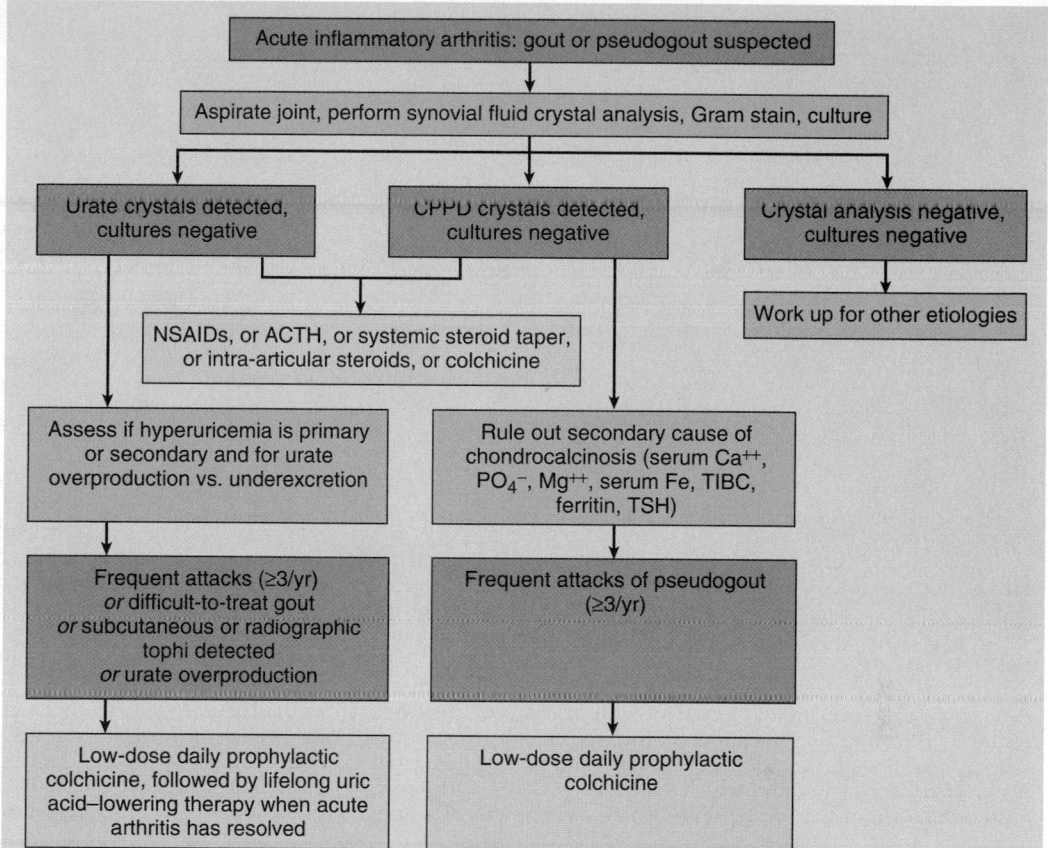

FIGURE 288–4 • Algorithm for clinical approach to acute gouty arthritis and pseudogout. In this scheme, which is further discussed in the text, central emphasis is placed on the diagnostic importance of arthrocentesis and synovial fluid analysis. ACTH = adrenocorticotropic hormone; CPPD = calcium pyrophosphate dihydrate; Gm = Gram; NSAIDs = nonsteroidal anti-inflammatory drugs; Sub-Q = subcutaneous; TIBC = total iron-binding capacity; TSH = thyroid-stimulating hormone.

selective NSAIDs is potentially problematic with significant renal insufficiency. Alternative approaches to the acute therapy of monoarticular gouty arthritis include the local intra-articular injection of a glucocorticosteroid ester. Regardless of the prior duration of the acute attack, such treatment is effective and pragmatic for involvement of a single large joint. Synthetic adrenocorticotrophic hormone (ACTH) is an excellent alternative in patients without preexisting adrenal suppression, particularly for acute polyarticular gout or when the administration of other agents is contraindicated. A typical dose for podagra is 25 USP units of ACTH injected subcutaneously. With larger joint involvement or for polyarticular gout, ACTH 40 USP units intramuscular or by slow intravenous effusion is generally effective as a single dose. Occasionally, a second dose may be required. Peripheral anti-inflammatory effects of ACTH as well as induction of adrenal glucocorticoid release both appear to contribute to the rapid and reliable efficacy of ACTH for acute gout. An alternative strategy for acute gout employs systemic anti-inflammatory doses of corticosteroids (oral prednisone, at least 30 mg/day to start, with a typical regimen being 60 mg/day with a steady taper over 14 days). Alternatively, a short course of intravenous methylprednisolone at up to double these prednisone doses is effective in severe cases.

Colchicine at low doses (e.g., 0.6 mg twice daily with normal renal and hepatic function) is a useful adjunct to NSAIDs, ACTH, and corticosteroids for the therapy of severe or refractory acute attacks of gout and may help prevent clinical rebound on discontinuation of the primary anti-inflammatory treatment. To abort early recurrences of acute gout, patients can also be instructed to initiate therapy with either low-dose oral colchicine (e.g., 0.6 mg once every hour for up to 3 hours) or an NSAID at the first premonition or symptom of an impending episode. Use of larger doses of oral colchicine as a primary modality for acute gouty arthritis has fallen out of favor because the therapeutic benefit/toxicity ratio is most often inferior for colchicine relative to NSAIDS, glucocorticoids, and ACTH. In general, the use of intravenous colchicine is not advisable. Potentially fatal marrow suppression may occur even with low doses (<2 mg) of intravenous colchicine in patients with renal insufficiency and hepatobiliary disease, particularly in older subjects.

TREATMENT BETWEEN GOUTY ATTACKS (INTERVAL THERAPY) AND FOR CHRONIC GOUT AND HYPERURICEMIA. Colchicine (0.6 mg once or twice daily) is effective for prophylaxis of recurrent attacks of acute gout, though low-dose NSAID treatment also may be beneficial. As illustrated in Figure 288-4, certain findings support the institution of uric acid–lowering therapy for gout. Antihyperuricemic therapy in gout is potentially toxic and requires lifelong continuation. Thus, the therapeutic aims and the potential benefit/risk ratio of treatment should be weighed on a case-to-case basis. In some individuals, the serum urate concentration can be successfully normalized without antihyperuricemic drugs by cessation of alcohol, substitution of another class of antihypertensive agent for a thiazide in antihypertensive treatment, or better control of obesity. A low-carbohydrate diet specifically tailored to treat syndrome X (metabolic syndrome) can substantially diminish hyperuricemia in this condition. But purine-restricted diets are generally unpalatable and typically fail to lower serum uric acid by more than 1 mg/dL. Avoidance of particularly purine-rich foods such as organ meats is advised when they are identified to be provocative agents in acute attacks.

Accepted indications for pharmacologic antihyperuricemic therapy in patients with well-documented gout are (1) frequent attacks (≥ three per year) of acute gout; (2) the occurrence of acute gout that is difficult to safely manage, such as polyarticular gout and gout associated with transplantation, or evidence of chronic renal insufficiency; (3) subcutaneous or intra-articular tophaceous deposits; and (4) documented urate overproduction. A common side effect of initiating uric acid–lowering therapy is triggering of gout attacks, particularly in the first few months of treatment. Thus, prophylactic low-dose colchicine (0.6 mg orally once or twice a day) is typically continued for 6 months after starting uric acid–lowering treatment. Patients with diminished renal function taking customary prophylactic doses of colchicine over prolonged periods may develop a reversible proximal myopathy, often accompanied by elevated levels of serum creatine kinase; severe bone marrow depression also can occur. Thus, guidelines for safe prophylactic colchicine dosing in renal failure include reducing colchicine to

Continued

0.6 mg orally every 2 days with a serum creatinine of 2.0, and to 0.6 mg orally every 3 days with a serum creatinine of 3.0.

Reduction of the total body urate stores, the size of tophi, and the risk for ongoing precipitation of supersaturated urate is best achieved by long-term reduction of serum urate concentration to 6 mg/dL or less. However, serum urate lowering to this extent is generally not readily achievable in patients with significant renal dysfunction (creatinine clearance < 60) without reaching toxic doses of uric acid–lowering agents. Uricosuric drugs such as probenecid and sulfinpyrazone (and benzbromarone, which is not currently available in the United States) increase renal clearance of uric acid by inhibiting tubular reabsorption. The widely employed xanthine oxidase inhibitor allopurinol inhibits urate synthesis (see Fig. 288–1).

Uricosuric agents are effective as first-line agents for patients with gout associated with normal urinary uric acid excretion. Allopurinol is the first-line drug in patients with excessive uric acid excretion, with previous histories of uric acid stones, or with renal insufficiency. Allopurinol can be given on a once-a-day basis, and it may promote more rapid dissolution of tophi than uricosuric drugs. Thus, allopurinol is the preferred choice of many physicians, regardless of whether the patient is a urate overproducer or underexcreter. Minor hypersensitivity reactions to allopurinol including pruritus and dermatitis are common. Approximately half of the patients with such minor reactions can successfully be desensitized to allopurinol or treated with oxypurinol, the major active metabolite of allopurinol. But adverse effects with allopurinol are potentially more dangerous and occur more often than with uricosuric drugs. For example, there can be substantial morbidity and sometimes mortality in cases of allopurinol hepatotoxicity, and in the allopurinol hypersensitivity syndrome, which typically presents with fever, eosinophilia, dermatitis, elevation of hepatic enzymes, renal failure, and sometimes vasculitis. The risk of allopurinol hypersensitivity is greatly augmented in patients with diminished renal function. Therefore, such subjects should be treated with an allopurinol dose adjusted downward, from the usual dose of 300 mg a day, in a manner proportional to the impairment in creatinine clearance.

Marked hyperuricemia, rapid tophus development, and difficulties in management of gout are prevalent problems associated with the use of cyclosporine in transplantation medicine. Uricosuric effects (in addition to antihypertensive effects) of the angiotensin-1 receptor blocker losartan may be therapeutically useful as an adjunct to allopurinol for uric acid lowering in cyclosporine-treated patients with renal insufficiency.◼ The clinical urate-lowering effect of losartan appears to be maximal at a dose of 50 mg orally daily; this effect is selective as it is not shared with irbesartan. The uricosuric effect of losartan appears to diminish as a new steady-state of lower serum uric acid is reached.

Acute, massive uric acid precipitation within renal tubules can be catastrophic in patients undergoing cytotoxic chemotherapy for certain malignancies and thus requires prophylactic use of allopurinol. However, in the population at large, hyperuricemia alone is not related to the development of clinically significant renal disease. The cause of asymptomatic hyperuricemia should be diagnostically considered; however, treatment of asymptomatic hyperuricemia is not indicated unless there is evidence of chronic uric acid overproduction.

PROGNOSIS. Recognition of gout is important because the disease frequently leads to painful and destructive arthropathy and urolithiasis and because gout is associated with a variety of potentially serious medical conditions. However, the inflammatory manifestations of gout are most often satisfactorily managed, and treatment of hyperuricemia is most often effective in preventing and reversing many of the long-term consequences of the disease.

Future Directions

Further clinical development of uric acid–lowering drug alternatives to allopurinol and the current generation of uricosuric drugs should assist in treatment of refractory patients with gout. Patients with gout in association with renal failure and hypersensitivity to allopurinol can be difficult to manage successfully. Investigation for the possible therapeutic efficacy of recombinant uric acid oxidase infusions in such patients will be of interest.

CARTILAGE CALCIFICATION: CPPD CRYSTAL DEPOSITION DISEASE AND ARTICULAR HA CRYSTAL DEPOSITION

Definition

Calcium-containing crystals deposited in the pericellular matrix of cartilage are often in the form of CPPD, a disorder termed *chondrocalcinosis*, *pyrophosphate arthropathy*, and, when associated with acute arthritis, *pseudogout*. Crystals of the basic calcium phosphate (BCP) HA, the mineral phase deposited in growth cartilage and in bone, also may be deposited in articular cartilage. Deposition of HA and closely related BCP crystals in periarticular structures, and in loci other than cartilage, such as the rotator cuff and subacromial bursa of the shoulder (calcific tendonitis and bursitis), also can present as painful inflammatory conditions.

Epidemiology

Radiographic and autopsy studies have indicated that knee chondrocalcinosis is present in approximately 15% of people who are 65 years old and 50% or more of those aged 85 years or older. Most elderly individuals with CPPD deposition disease in the United States have a primary (idiopathic) disorder. Studies of synovial fluids and cartilage specimens from osteoarthritis have suggested that HA crystalline material is frequently present, often in conjunction with CPPD crystals. The presence of HA crystalline material within the joint space appears to correlate directly with the severity of osteoarthritis.

Pathobiology

Articular cartilage, unlike growth plate cartilage, is specialized to not undergo matrix calcification. However, certain features of growth cartilage chondrocyte differentiation shared by chondrocytes in degenerative and aging cartilages (including foci of proliferation, hypertrophy, and apoptosis) appear to stimulate articular chondrocalcinosis. The ability of chondrocytes to mineralize their pericellular matrix also depends on the concentrations of calcium, inorganic phosphate (Pi), PPi, and the solubility products of these solutes, as well as certain alterations in the extracellular matrix and other promineralizing factors, including activation of tissue (type 2) transglutaminase and the tissue form of factor XIIIa transglutaminase. In aging and osteoarthritic cartilages, activity of PPi-generating nucleoside triphosphate pyrophosphohydrolase (NTPPPH) isozymes including PC-1, as well as PPi generation, are markedly increased (Fig. 288–5). Depending on cartilage ATP concentration, and the level of activity of Pi-generating adenosine triphosphatases and pyrophosphatases (which also degrade PPi), HA crystal formation may be promoted (see Fig. 288–5). It does not appear that all HA crystalline deposits in cartilage are directly made by chondrocytes in osteoarthritis. Some of the HA crystalline material in osteoarthritic cartilage is derived from bone shards embedded in cartilage.

Several metabolic disorders associated with CPPD crystal deposition disease (Table 288–2) may help induce chondrocalcinosis in part by promoting intra-articular PPi excess. These include genetic deficiency of the PPi-degrading enzyme tissue-nonspecific alkaline phosphatase in hypophosphatasia, acquired tissue excess of the pyrophosphatase inhibitor iron in hemochromatosis, and deficiency of the pyrophosphatase cofactor magnesium in hypomagnesemia. Chondrocalcinosis secondary to hyperparathyroidism appears to be mediated not only by hypercalcemia but also by the ability of excess parathyroid hormone (PTH) to activate and alter the differentiation of articular chondrocytes, which normally express PTH/PTH-related protein receptors.

CPPD and HA crystals can stimulate chondrocytes and intra-articular leukocytes, can traffic to the synovium, can promote

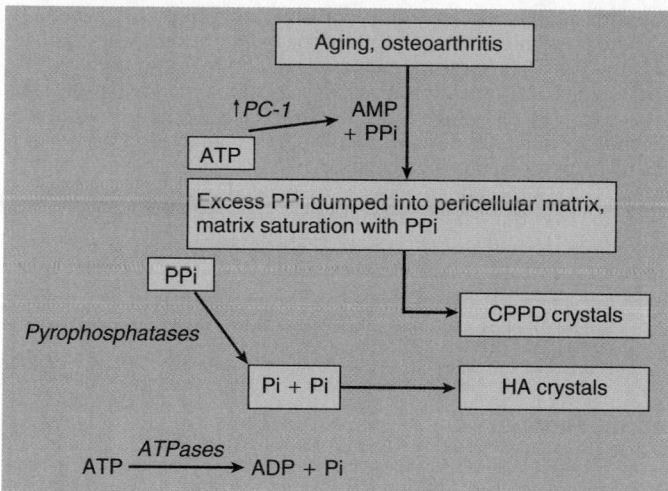

FIGURE 288–5 • Proposed inorganic pyrophosphate (PPi)-dependent mechanisms stimulating calcium pyrophosphate dihydrate (CPPD) and hydroxyapatite (HA) crystal deposition in aging and osteoarthritis. Roles of adenosine triphosphate (ATP) and PPi metabolism and inorganic phosphate (Pi) generation in cartilage calcification are shown. In this model, excess PPi generation in aging cartilages in idiopathic CPPD deposition disease of aging and in osteoarthritic cartilages is mediated in part by marked increases in nucleoside triphosphate pyrophosphohydrolase (NTPPPH) activity, mediated in part by the NTPPPH isozyme PC-1. In idiopathic chondrocalcinosis of aging, mean cartilage PPi and NTPPPH levels are double normal. As discussed in one of the reading citations (Terkeltaub R, 2002), PC-1 is markedly upregulated at sites of meniscal cartilage calcification in vivo, and PC-1 not only directly induces elevated PPi but also matrix calcification by chondrocytes in vitro. Depending on the extracellular availability of substrate PPi and the activity of pyrophosphatases, the availability of substrate (ATP) and the activity of adenosine triphosphatases (ATPases), and other factors such as substantial local Mg^{2+} concentrations, HA crystal deposition, as opposed to CPPD deposition, may be stimulated in this model. AMP = adenosine monophosphate.

Table 288–2 • CPPD CRYSTAL DEPOSITION DISEASE: COMMON ETIOLOGIES AND CLINICAL PRESENTATIONS

Etiologies of CPPD Crystal Deposition Disease
High Prevalence
  Idiopathic in association with aging (most frequent)
  Complication of established osteoarthritis
  Long-term consequence of mechanical joint trauma or knee
    meniscectomy
Less prevalent
  Familial
  Associated with systemic metabolic disease (hyperparathyroidism,
    hemochromatosis, hypomagnesemia, myxedematous
    hypothyroidism, ochronosis)

Common Clinical Presentations of CPPD Crystal Deposition Disease
Asymptomatic or incidental finding (e.g., asymptomatic knee
  fibrocartilage chondrocalcinosis)
Recurrent acute inflammatory monoarticular arthritis ("pseudogout")
  (e.g., knee, wrist)
Chronic degenerative arthritis ("pseudo-osteoarthritis" or
  "pseudoneuropathic arthritis")
Chronic symmetrical inflammatory polyarthritis ("pseudo–rheumatoid
  arthritis")
Recurrent acute hemarthrosis
Carpal tunnel syndrome
Ligamentum flavum involvement (has the potential to cause spinal
  canal stenosis and myelopathy)

CPPD = calcium pyrophosphate dihydrate.

the expression of connective tissue–degrading enzymes, and can trigger inflammation, thereby contributing to cartilage degradation and worsening of osteoarthritis. Many of the same mechanisms described earlier in gout mediate inflammatory manifestations associated with CPPD and HA crystal deposition.

Clinical Manifestations

Clinical presentations and primary and secondary etiologic factors associated with CPPD deposition disease are summarized in Table 288–2. As in gout, acute attacks of severely painful inflammatory synovitis (pseudogout) in patients with CPPD deposition disease can be provoked by minor trauma or intercurrent medical or surgical illness. Leukocyte counts in the synovial fluid are substantially elevated and intraleukocytic CPPD crystals are most often detectable by compensated polarized light microscopy in pseudogout. CPPD disease patients can present with episodes of hemarthrosis, often post-traumatic and in the knee. Some patients with CPPD disease demonstrate "pseudorheumatoid" joints that reflect local synovial and periarticular tenosynovial proliferation. Ingestion of not only CPPD but also HA crystals by synovial lining cells, and lysosomal catabolism of such ingested crystals, stimulates synovial proliferation, in part via solubilization of the crystalline calcium.

CPPD deposition disease can present as a chronic degenerative arthropathy that commonly affects certain joints that are not usually spared in primary osteoarthritis (e.g., metacarpophalangeal joints, wrists, elbows, glenohumeral joints). Concentrated CPPD crystal deposition can also occur in tendons, ligaments, bursae, and occasionally in bone. CPPD deposits in tendons (e.g., Achilles, triceps, obturator tendons) are usually fine and linear on radiographs. CPPD deposits within the ligamentum flavum can be sizable and can progress to cause canal stenosis and myelopathy. Similarly, carpal tunnel syndrome can be provoked by deposits of CPPD in tendons.

Familial CPPD deposition disease has been described in certain countries and ethnic groups, including kindreds from Spain, Czechoslovakia, Holland, France, England, Germany, Sweden, Israel, the United States, Canada, Chile, and Japan. In an English kindred with CPPD disease, recurrent childhood seizures were strongly associated with later development of CPPD deposition disease. Familial chondrocalcinosis could be more prevalent in Spain. It has been proposed that a mutation originating in Spain may have been spread across Europe and into South America along military and trade routes highly traveled in the 17th century. The pattern of inheritance and clinical presentation of familial CPPD deposition disease is variable. Some families manifest early-onset polyarthritis, which can include ankylosing intervertebral and sacroiliac joint disease. In others, a late-onset chondrocalcinosis occurs, and the disease can be indistinguishable from common, idiopathic CPPD deposition disease. Predisposition to CPPD disease in several geographically dispersed kindreds has been linked to an area within chromosome 5p bearing the *ANK* gene. ANK appears to function as a membrane channel for PPi.

Unlike the case for urate and CPPD crystal deposition, acute synovitis due to HA crystal deposition is unusual. But acute inflammatory syndromes, including pseudopodagra, may occur in association with periarticular HA crystal deposition in tendons, ligaments, and soft tissues, which may occur in certain post-traumatic conditions and the systemic autoimmune diseases scleroderma and dermatomyositis. Shoulder rotator cuff tendonitis and subacromial bursitis associated with HA are common. A distinctive non-inflammatory syndrome of rotator cuff tear and marked cartilage degeneration associated with abundant intra-articular HA and related BCP crystalline material also has been described. In this entity (termed *cuff tear arthropathy* or *Milwaukee shoulder syndrome*), the crystal deposition may function as a significant etiopathogenic factor.

Diagnosis

Because CPPD deposition disease can imitate several other conditions (see Table 288–2), a precise diagnosis is essential. Idiopathic CPPD deposition disease of aging is the most common form of the disease. Diagnosis of CPPD deposition disease prior to age 50 years, particularly if CPPD deposition is widespread, should prompt diagnostic consideration of a metabolic or familial disorder (see Table 288–2). The demonstrable presence of CPPD crystals in synovial fluid or in tissues using compensated polarized light microscopy (as discussed earlier for gout vs. pseudogout) is definite evidence for the disease. The appearance and number of CPPD crystals can change with storage. The clinician must be careful to examine relatively fresh specimens collected in vials free of calcium-chelating anticoagulants.

A thorough laboratory evaluation of the newly diagnosed CPPD disease patient routinely includes serum levels of calcium, phosphorus, magnesium, alkaline phosphatase, ferritin, iron and total iron-binding capacity, and thyroid-stimulating hormone. Patients with arthritis who are suspected of having CPPD deposition disease can be adequately screened radiologically by obtaining an anteroposterior (AP) view of each knee, an AP view of the pelvis (to detect symphysis pubis involvement), and posteroanterior views of both hands that include visualization of both wrists. Chondrocalcinosis, typically as linear calcific deposits, may or may not be detectable by radiographic screening of these areas in CPPD deposition disease. Radiographic evidence other than chondrocalcinosis may point to the correct diagnosis, including subchondral cyst formation, scaphoid-lunate widening in the wrist secondary to ligamentous degeneration, and patellofemoral joint space narrowing (often isolated, with the patella "wrapped around" the femur).

HA crystal deposition may be detected via radiographic evidence of calcifications. Unlike urate and CPPD crystals, HA crystals are non-birefringent. HA crystals stain with alizarin red and may be visualized as globules within cells in synovial fluid. However, specialized techniques including transmission electron microscopy may be needed to confirm HA crystal deposition.

Prevention and Treatment

There is no specific treatment for idiopathic CPPD deposition disease, unlike the case for CPPD deposition secondary to certain metabolic disorders (e.g., hyperparathyroidism, hypomagnesemic conditions). The potential benefits for prevention of cartilage degeneration in the appropriate treatment of secondary causes of established CPPD deposition disease are unclear, because the ability to detect chondrocalcinosis radiologically is usually indicative of advanced deposition of CPPD crystals and significant replacement of cartilage matrix.

Episodes of pseudogout generally respond to NSAIDs and/or intra-articular injections of steroids, though sometimes more slowly than in gout. ACTH and systemic glucocorticosteroids, also given as described earlier for acute gout, are effective in most cases of acute pseudogout. The response to colchicine is less consistent than that usually seen in acute gout, but pseudogout episodes can be diminished in frequency by low-dose daily colchicine prophylaxis, as for gouty arthritis.

NSAIDs and local steroid injection are effective treatment options for HA crystal–associated calcific tendonitis and subacromial bursitis. Ultrasound as a therapeutic modality promotes short-term clinical improvement and helps stimulate dissolution of calcific deposits of HA in the rotator cuff.

Prognosis

Only a small fraction of patients with CPPD deposition disease have prolonged, recurring polyarticular inflammation. Progressive degenerative arthropathy is more common. Though CPPD deposition disease appears to be a common and significant public health problem in the elderly, the "disease impact," and the long-term course of CPPD-associated degenerative arthropathy in an unselected population have not been extensively evaluated.

Future Directions

The potential to develop therapies based on new molecular targets has been raised by the recent identification of specific molecular mediators of cartilage calcification, including PC-1, ANK, the tissue form of factor XIIIa and tissue (type 2) transglutaminase.

OXALATE CRYSTAL DEPOSITION AND JOINT DISEASE

Joint tissues are one of the sites of deposition of oxalate crystals in patients with primary hyperoxaluria and secondary hyperoxalemia in patients with dialysis-dependent renal failure. Articular and periarticular clinical manifestations of oxalate crystal deposition include

chondrocalcinosis, acute and chronic arthritis (typically symmetrical, and involving the small joints of the hands, but sometimes affecting large joints), flexor tenosynovitis, ligamentum flavum involvement, and inflammatory manifestations due to skin and vascular deposits of oxalate crystals. A high index of clinical suspicion is important in diagnosis, which can be confirmed by crystal analysis of tissue specimens and synovial fluids. The classic shape of oxalate crystals is bipyramidal (like a postal envelope), associated with strong positive birefringence. But oxalate crystals are commonly polymorphic and can mimic HA and CPPD crystals in appearance.

1. Kamper AL, Nielsen AH: Uricosuric effect of losartan in patients with renal transplants. Transplantation 2001;72:671–674.
2. Ebenbichler GR, Erdogmus CB, Resch KL, et al: Ultrasound therapy for calcific tendinitis of the shoulder. N Engl J Med 1999;340:1533–1538.

SUGGESTED READINGS

Dessein PH, Shipton EA, Stanwix AE, et al: Beneficial effects of weight loss associated with moderate calorie/carbohydrate restriction and increased proportional intake of protein and unsaturated fat on serum urate and lipoprotein levels in gout: A pilot study. Ann Rheum Dis 2000;59:539–543. *Weight reduction from this diet was associated with lower uric acid levels and fewer gouty attacks.*

Fam AG: Difficult gout and new approaches for control of hyperuricemia in the allopurinol-allergic patient. Curr Rheumatol Rep 2001;3:29–35. *A thorough review of management of allopurinol hypersensitivity and other difficult management issues in uric acid lowering for gout.*

Maldonado I, Prasad V, Reginato AJ: Oxalate crystal deposition and arthropathy. Curr Rheumatol Rep 2002;4:257–264. *A valuable review of the etiology and clinical manifestations of oxalate crystal deposition.*

Ritter J, Kerr LD, Valeriano-Marcet J, Spiera H: ACTH revisited: Effective treatment for acute crystal-induced synovitis in patients with multiple medical problems. J Rheumatol 1994;21:696–699. *Useful in gout or pseudogout when patients cannot tolerate other therapies.*

Rott KT, Agudelo CA: Gout. JAMA 2003;289:2857–2860. *A practical review.*

Terkeltaub R: What does cartilage calcification tell us about osteoarthritis? J Rheumatol 2002;29:411–415. *Reviews recent advances in the pathogenesis of chondrocalcinosis.*

289 FIBROMYALGIA

Robert M. Bennett

Definition

Fibromyalgia is a multisymptomatic syndrome defined by the core feature of chronic widespread pain. Many of these patients also have severe fatigue and associated symptoms related to visceral hyperalgesia, such as irritable bowel and bladder.

Epidemiology

Chronic musculoskeletal pain (CMP) commonly is encountered in the general population with an estimated prevalence of about 35%. CMP is subdivided into chronic regional pain (CRP), with a prevalence of about 25%, and chronic widespread pain (CWP), with a prevalence of about 10%.

Fibromyalgia is conceived as a subset of CWP and has a prevalence of about 2% in women and 0.5% in men. There is a steady increase of fibromyalgia with age, reaching about 12% of women in their 60s. CMP is associated with a reduction in overall health status, with fibromyalgia patients having more impairment than CMP and CRP. The prevalence of fibromyalgia in the medical setting is much greater, accounting for about 20% of rheumatology visits in the United States. Israeli patients on internal medicine wards had a 21% prevalence of CWP and 15% prevalence of fibromyalgia.

Pathobiology

Contemporary research has provided a pathobiologic paradigm for understanding fibromyalgia in terms of abnormalities of sensory processing within the central nervous system which interact with peripheral pain generators and neuroendocrine pathways to generate the wide spectrum of patient symptoms. The term that is used for magnification of sensory impulses within the central nervous system (CNS) is *central sensitization*.

AMPLIFIED SENSORY PROCESSING. The magnification of sensory stimuli that would not normally elicit pain is a distinctive feature of fibromyalgia patients. This is most clearly demonstrated by an increase in somatosensory potentials in fibromyalgia subjects. Temporal summation may be a critical event in the development of central sensitization. This occurs when unmyelinated C fibers are stimulated at a rate of one impulse every 2 to 3 seconds. This has been demonstrated in fibromyalgia after repetitive thermal stimulation of the skin and after intramuscular electrical stimulation. Several studies have shown reduced thalamic blood flow in fibromyalgia subjects. This finding is in accord with other chronic pain states, and is postulated to be associated with a loss of a tonic disinhibition of thalamic activity that occurs in chronic pain. Two neurotransmitters involved in pain transmission are elevated in the cerebrospinal fluid (CSF) of fibromyalgia subjects. There is a two- to three-fold increase of substance P and a four-fold elevation of nerve growth factor in the CSF.

NEUROENDOCRINE DYSFUNCTION. Fibromyalgia is not a hormonal deficiency state, but there is evidence that the hypothalamic-pituitary and the sympathoadrenal stress axes are impaired in fibromyalgia patients. About 30% of patients have neurally mediated hypotension.

Clinical Manifestations

PAIN. The core *symptom* of fibromyalgia is chronic widespread pain and stiffness. Characteristically, the pain is described as a constant dull ache that is worsened by muscle overactivity. Fibromyalgia related pain is usually perceived as arising from muscle; however, many patients also report joint pain, but have no objective evidence of arthritis.

FATIGUE. Easy fatigability from physical exertion, mental exertion, and psychologic stressors are typical of fibromyalgia. Patients with the chronic fatigue syndrome (CFS) have many similarities with fibromyalgia patients; about 75% of patients meeting the diagnostic criteria of CFS also meet the criteria for diagnosis of fibromyalgia.

DISORDERED SLEEP. Fibromyalgia patients have nonrestorative sleep. Even if they sleep continuously for 8 to 10 hours, they awake feeling tired. Many exhibit an alpha-delta electroencephalographic pattern that would explain their never achieving the restorative stages 3 and 4 of non–rapid eye movement sleep. A poor night's sleep is often followed by a worsening of fibromyalgia symptoms the next day.

COGNITIVE DYSFUNCTION. Cognitive dysfunction is a prominent complaint of many fibromyalgia patients. They commonly describe difficulties with short-term memory, concentration, logical analysis, and motivation. Recent studies have documented defects in working memory and verbal fluency. These changes have been estimated to be equivalent to 20 years of aging.

ASSOCIATED DISORDERS. It is not unusual for fibromyalgia patients to have an array of somatic complaints other than musculoskeletal pain. It is thought that these symptoms are in part a result of the abnormal sensory processing and the neuroendocrine effects of chronic stress.

PSYCHOLOGIC DISTRESS. Having a chronic painful disorder, for which there is currently no generally accepted cure, often produces an existential crisis. Approximately 30% of fibromyalgia patients have significant depression at any given time, and about 60% have a lifetime prevalence of depressive illness. Psychologic distress in fibromyalgia may in part determine who becomes a patient. Although psychiatric disorders are common in fibromyalgia patients, they do not seem to be intrinsically related to the pathophysiology of fibromyalgia, but rather appear to be a result of symptom severity.

INITIATION AND MAINTENANCE OF FIBROMYALGIA. Fibromyalgia seldom emerges "out of the blue." Many patients relate an acute injury, repetitive workload, stress, infections, and toxins to its onset. It is not uncommon for a regional pain state to evolve into fibromyalgia. Fibromyalgia is commonly found as an accompaniment of rheumatoid arthritis, low back pain, systemic lupus erythematosus, Sjögren's syndrome, inflammatory bowel disease, and osteoarthritis. There is a 22% prevalence of fibromyalgia 1 year after whiplash injuries. There is a variable familial prevalence of fibromyalgia, suggesting that subjects destined to develop fibromyalgia are either genetically predisposed (nature), or have past life events or experiences that favor its later development (nurture).

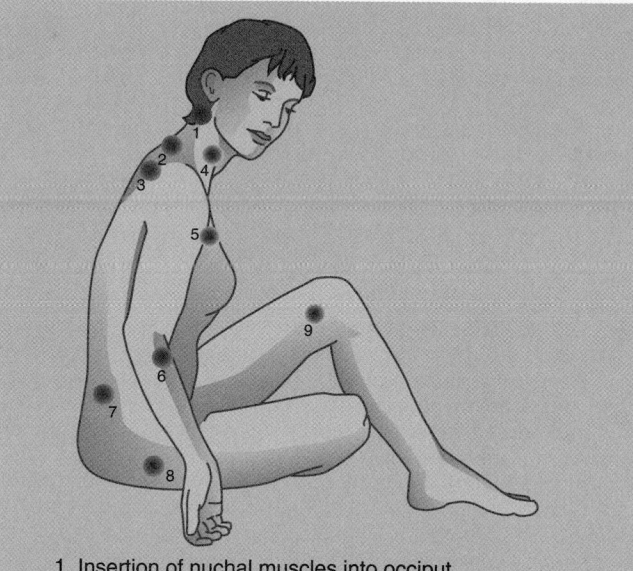

1. Insertion of nuchal muscles into occiput
2. Upper border of trapezius-mid-portion
3. Muscle attachments to upper medial border of scapula
4. Anterior aspects of the C5, C7 intertransverse spaces
5. 2nd rib space - about 3 cm lateral to the sternal border
6. Muscle attachments to lateral epicondyle
7. Upper outer quadrant of gluteal muscles
8. Muscle attachments just posterior to greater trochanter
9. Medial fat pad of knee proximal to joint line

A total of eleven or more tender points in conjunction with a history of widespread pain is characteristic of the fibromyalgia syndrome.

FIGURE 289–1 • Recommended tender point locations, American College of Rheumatology, 1990 criteria. A total of 11 or more tender points in conjunction with a history of widespread pain is characteristic of the fibromyalgia syndrome. (From Bennett RM: Fibromyalgia. *In* Wall PD, Melzack R [eds]: Textbook of Pain, 4th ed. Edinburgh, Churchill Livingstone, 1999.)

Diagnosis

The diagnosis of fibromyalgia is usually based on the 1990 recommendations of the American College of Rheumatology (ACR) classification criteria. These criteria comprise one historical feature and one physical finding. The historical feature is widespread pain of 3 months' duration or more. The physical finding is the finding of numerous tender points. The ACR diagnosis requires the patient to experience pain in at least 11 of 18 specified tender point sites on digital palpation at a force of 4 kg (the amount of pressure required to blanch a thumbnail). The locations of the 18 tender points are shown in Figure 289–1. Fibromyalgia is not a diagnosis of exclusion; thus, laboratory tests and imaging studies play no role in establishing the diagnosis according to the 1990 ACR criteria.

Rx Prevention and Treatment

The successful management of fibromyalgia requires a thorough analysis in terms of the biopsychosocial model of disease. The major management issues that require attention are listed in Table 289–1.

EDUCATION. There is evidence that higher educational attainments are associated with a better prognosis in many chronic disorders, such as fibromyalgia. Education has a positive effect through cognitive behavioral strategies, such as goal setting and reassessment of priorities. Educated patients are more likely to take an active role in self-management.

PAIN. In considering the management of pain in fibromyalgia, it is logical to focus on the major sites of pain processing; namely

Continued

peripheral pain generation, dorsal horn sensitization, psychologic influences, and the descending pain pathway. There is no specific tissue pathology, at least in peripheral tissues, that can be said to be characteristic of fibromyalgia. However the CNS is sensitized, peripheral pain generators are not only perceived as being more painful but also prolong and amplify the machinery of central sensitization. Although some peripheral pain generators, notably arthritic disorders, may be helped by nonsteroidal anti-inflammatory drugs, central pain is not very responsive to these agents. Specific treatments for other pain generators include, for example, gabapentin in neuropathic pain and $5-HT_{1D}$ antagonists in vascular headaches. Some pain generators, such as osteoarthritis of the knees or bursitis, may be helped by local corticosteroid injections. In other instances, surgery may be appropriate (e.g., in severe osteoarthritis of the hips). The most common pain generators, in most fibromyalgia patients, are myofascial trigger points. These need to be identified and treated by stretching, improved physical conditioning, acupressure, and physician intervention with procaine injections.

The modulation of central sensitization is mainly pharmacologic. Currently the only drugs approved by the Food and Drug Administration that modulate central reactivity are those that activate or amplify the descending pain system; these include opioids, tricyclic antidepressants, and α_2-adrenergic agonists.

Antidepressants such as amitriptyline have long been a mainstay in the treatment of chronic pain states, including fibromyalgia. Despite their widespread use, the long-term efficacy of antidepressants in managing fibromyalgia pain has not been well established.

Opioids are often used in the treatment of fibromyalgia, but there have been no controlled clinical trials. They should not be the first choice of analgesia, but they should not be withheld if less powerful analgesics have failed. Tramadol (Ultram) is proving to be a useful drug to treat fibromyalgia; it is a weak opioid agonist and also inhibits the reuptake of serotonin and noradrenaline at the level of the dorsal horn.■ α_2-Adrenergic agonists such as tizanidine (Zanaflex) have been used successfully in some chronic pain disorders. There have been no controlled trials in fibromyalgia. 5-HT3 antagonists have been the subject of several encouraging short-term trials in fibromyalgia patients. Long-term studies in fibromyalgia patients are needed before the efficacy of this class of drugs can be fully evaluated. Drugs that modulate the ascending pain system are less commonly used. However, there is evidence, in the experimental setting, that blocking NMDA receptors with ketamine and/or dextromethorphan ameliorates pain in fibromyalgia subjects.

FATIGUE. The common treatable cause of chronic fatigue in fibromyalgia patients are (1) inappropriate dosing of medications, (2) depression, (3) aerobic deconditioning, (3) primary sleep disorder (e.g., sleep apnea), (4) nonrestorative sleep, (5) neurally mediated hypotension, and (6) growth hormone deficiency. There are anecdotal reports that modafinil (Provigil), a nonamphetamine drug used in narcolepsy and sleep deprivation situations, is of some benefit in improving nonspecific fatigue.

SLEEP. Low-dose tricyclic antidepressants (TCAs), such as amitriptyline, trazodone, doxepin, and imipramine, have been the mainstay of sleep pharmacotherapy in fibromyalgia patients. Many patients cannot tolerate TCAs due to unacceptable levels of daytime drowsiness or weight gain. In these patients, short-acting benzodiazepine-like medications such as zolpidem may be beneficial. About 25% of male and 15% of female fibromyalgia patients have sleep apnea that usually requires treatment with continuous positive airway pressure or surgery. By far the most common sleep disorder in fibromyalgia patients is restless leg syndrome/periodic limb movement disorder. Treatment is usually with L-DOPA/carbidopa (Sinemet 10/100 mg at supper time) or clonazepam (Klonopin 0.5 or 1.0 mg at bedtime).

PSYCHOLOGICAL DISTRESS. Fibromyalgia patients often develop stressors related to psychosocial/economic and health issues. Psychologic intervention in terms of improving the internal locus of control and more effective problem solving are important in such patients. Cognitive-behavioral therapy is particularly well suited to effect these changes. Although antidepressant medications are commonly used in the treatment of pain and sleep in fibromyalgia patients, the doses used are usually suboptimal for treating depressive illness. Patients with bipolar disorder, suicidal ideation, psychosis, and severe post-traumatic stress disorder should be managed in conjunction with a psychiatrist.

DECONDITIONING. The benefits of exercise are based on reasonable scientific evidence, but exercise may also be deleterious. Overtraining results in a syndrome of chronic fatigue, reduced performance, depression, impaired hormonal stress responses, increased susceptibility to muscle damage, and infections. A carefully planned individual exercise program is always needed to optimize the benefits and minimize increased pain and fatigue.

ENDOCRINE DYSFUNCTION. There is no good evidence that fibromyalgia is primarily due to an endocrine disorder. However, common problems such as hypothyroidism and menopausal symptoms often aggravate pain and fatigue, and appropriate replacement therapy is usually indicated. Fibromyalgia patients have a reduced hypothalamic pituitary axis (HPA) responsiveness to stressors. However, replacement therapy with prednisone (15 mg/day) was not of any therapeutic benefit. About one third of fibromyalgia patients are growth hormone deficient and replacement therapy has been reported to benefit such patients.

ASSOCIATED DISORDERS. Recognition and treatment of problems that are commonly associated with fibromyalgia are important in the overall management scheme. These disorders are discussed in other chapters.

Prognosis

Fibromyalgia symptoms usually persist over many years. However, patients seen in the community rather than in tertiary care centers have been reported to have a 24% remission rate after 2 years. The consequences of pain and fatigability influence motor performance; every-day activities take longer in fibromyalgia patients, who need more time to get started in the morning and often require extra rest periods during the day. The adaptations that fibromyalgia patients have to make to minimize their pain often has a negative impact on both vocational and avocational activities. A survey of fibromyalgia patients seen in academic centers reported that 70% perceived themselves as being disabled and 16% were receiving Social Security benefits.

Future Directions

Fibromyalgia is often referred to as a "poorly defined disorder." However, the recent demonstration of central sensitization and neuroendocrine dysfunction has provided some insight into its pathobiology. There is persuasive clinical evidence that individuals destined to acquire fibromyalgia have a vulnerability to its development. This vulnerability will probably emerge as having a complex genetic component interacting with environmental insults. The current challenge is to understand fibromyalgia symptoms in terms of environmental influences on gene transcription and interacting proteonomic networks. A particular focus of recent research has been the mechanism whereby proinflammatory cytokines (especially interleukin-8) can lead to chronic pain states. Future directions will probably integrate the central neuroendocrine abnormalities of fibromyalgia with dysfunctional responses to both physical and psychologic stresses.

Table 289–1 • MAJOR ISSUES IN THE MANAGEMENT OF FIBROMYALGIA PATIENTS

Education	Psychological distress
Pain	Deconditioning
Fatigue	Endocrine dysfunction
Sleep	Associated disorders

 1. Bennett RM, Kamin M, Karim R, et al: Tramadol and acetaminophen combination tablets in the treatment of fibromyalgia pain: A double-blind, randomized, placebo-controlled study. Am J Med 2003;114:537–545.

SUGGESTED READINGS
Bradley LA, McKendree-Smith NL, Alarcon GS, et al: Is fibromyalgia a neurologic disease? Curr Pain Headache Rep 2002;6:106–114. *A review of the literature on the cause and development of abnormal pain sensitivity in fibromyalgia.*
White KP, Harth M: Classification, epidemiology, and natural history of fibromyalgia. Curr Pain Headache Rep 2001;5:320–329. *An overview of fibromyalgia.*

290 THE AMYLOIDOSES

Joel N. Buxbaum

Definition

The amyloidoses are a subset of diseases produced by the aggregation of misfolded proteins. The aggregates are generally deposited extracellularly, usually at a distance from the site of synthesis, ultimately compromising the function of the target organ producing clinical disease. Kidney involvement, seen in several forms of amyloidosis (Table 290–1), is manifested by proteinuria, progressing to the nephrotic syndrome, renal failure, or both. Cardiac deposits result in congestive heart failure, arrhythmias, or anginal syndromes. Peripheral nerve infiltration produces symptomatic neuropathy, whereas central nervous system deposition may produce dementia or cerebral hemorrhage when the deposits are primarily vascular.

Amyloid deposits are identified in pathologic specimens by their homogeneous appearance when stained with hematoxylin and eosin and a discrete fibrillar ultrastructure on electron microscopy. The deposits bind the dye Congo red, yielding a characteristic positive birefringence when viewed with polarized light. They also bind metachromatic dyes like thioflavine T and S. These properties belong to the major fibrillar component, because fibrils isolated from tissue by low ionic strength extraction show the same characteristics. The deposits also contain a set of accessory molecules that can be detected by staining with specific antibodies. These include the serum amyloid p component (SAP), apolipoprotein E (apoE), and the heparan sulfate proteoglycan perlecan. The aggregates in other disorders of protein conformation, notably Huntington's and Parkinson's diseases, are predominantly intracellular with characteristic nuclear or nuclear and cytoplasmic inclusions. They are generally non-Congophilic. Intracellular or extracellular nonamyloid aggregation diseases have not been shown to contain the same accessory molecules.

Pathogenesis

More than 20 proteins form clinically relevant amyloid deposits (see Table 290–1). The precursors appear to have no common amino acid sequences. The dominant structural feature of the deposited fibril, regardless of the precursor, is the beta pleated sheet. In vitro studies with many of the precursors have begun to elucidate the steps involved in the aggregation process. In each case, a critical early event appears to be the formation of a misfolded monomer that may be facilitated by structural change secondary to a mutation. When there is no mutation, deposition may result from increased synthesis, a decrease in a normal process of degradative proteolytic cleavage, or an abnormal cleavage of a normal protein, any or all of which increase the absolute amount of misfolded conformer. In the case of the prion diseases, there may be other mechanisms that have not yet been identified.

Diagnosis

Specific organ involvement can be determined by a variety of diagnostic techniques, including computed tomography (CT) scans, echocardiograms, peripheral nerve conduction studies, renal sonograms, and biochemical assays of liver function. The attribution of the dysfunction to amyloid deposition and the nature of the precursor can only be made by appropriate examination of involved tissue (Fig. 290–1). Staining with Congo red with examination under polarized and fluorescent light to reveal the characteristic birefringence

Table 290–1 • CHEMICAL CLASSIFICATION OF HUMAN AMYLOID

AMYLOID PROTEIN	PRECURSOR*	CLINICAL SYNDROMES	INVOLVED TISSUES
AA	(Apo)serum AA	Chronic/inflammation; familial Mediterranean fever; familial amyloid nephropathy with urticaria and deafness; tumors (Muckle-Wells syndrome)	Kidney, liver, spleen
AL	Ig light chain, κ or λ	Primary/myeloma-associated	Kidney, heart, peripheral nerve, tongue, bone marrow
AH	Ig heavy chain	Primary/myeloma-associated	Kidney, heart, peripheral nerve, tongue, bone marrow
ATTR	Transthyretin	Familial amyloidotic polyneuropathy; familial amyloidotic cardiomyopathy; senile systemic (cardiac) amyloid	Peripheral and autonomic nerves, heart, kidney
AApoA1	Apolipoprotein A1	Familial amyloidotic polyneuropathy	Heart, skin, larynx, vessels, liver, kidney, nerve
AApoA2	Apolipoprotein A2	Familial nephropathy	Kidney
AGel	Gelsolin	Finnish corneal lattice dystrophy with cranial neuropathy	Cornea, cranial and peripheral nerves, kidney
ACys	Cystatin C	Hereditary cerebral hemorrhage with amyloid	Cranial vessels
Aβ	Aβ protein precursor (AβPP)	Alzheimer's disease, aging	CNS
Aβ₂M	β₂-Microglobulin	Dialysis related amyloid	Synovium, carpal tunnel, tongue
APrP	Prion protein	Creutzfeld-Jakob, Gerstmann-Sträussler-Scheinker disease, fatal familial insomnia	CNS
ABri†	BRI gene product	Familial neurodegeneration	Central nervous system, blood vessels
ACal	Procalcitonin	Medullary thyroid carcinoma	Thyroid
AANF	Atrial natriuretic factor	Atrial amyloid of aging	Atria
AIAPP	Islet amyloid polypeptide	Senile amyloid of the pancreas	Pancreas
ALys	Lysozyme	Ostertag renal amyloid	Kidney, liver, salivary glands
AFib	Fibrinogen α-chain	Hereditary renal amyloid	Kidney
APin	To be named	Odontogenic tumor	Pindborg tumors
Ack	Cytokeratins	Cutaneous	Skin
Apro	Prolactin	Aging pituitary	Pituitary
AIns	Insulin	Iatrogenic	Pancreas
ALac	*Lactoferrin*	Corneal deposition	Cornea
Amed	Lactadherin	Atherosclerosis	Aorta
AKer	Kerato-epithelin	Familial corneal deposition	Cornea

*Proteins in italic are preliminary.
†ADan is from the same gene as ABri and has identical N-terminal sequence. ADan is, therefore, not included in the nomenclature as a separate protein.

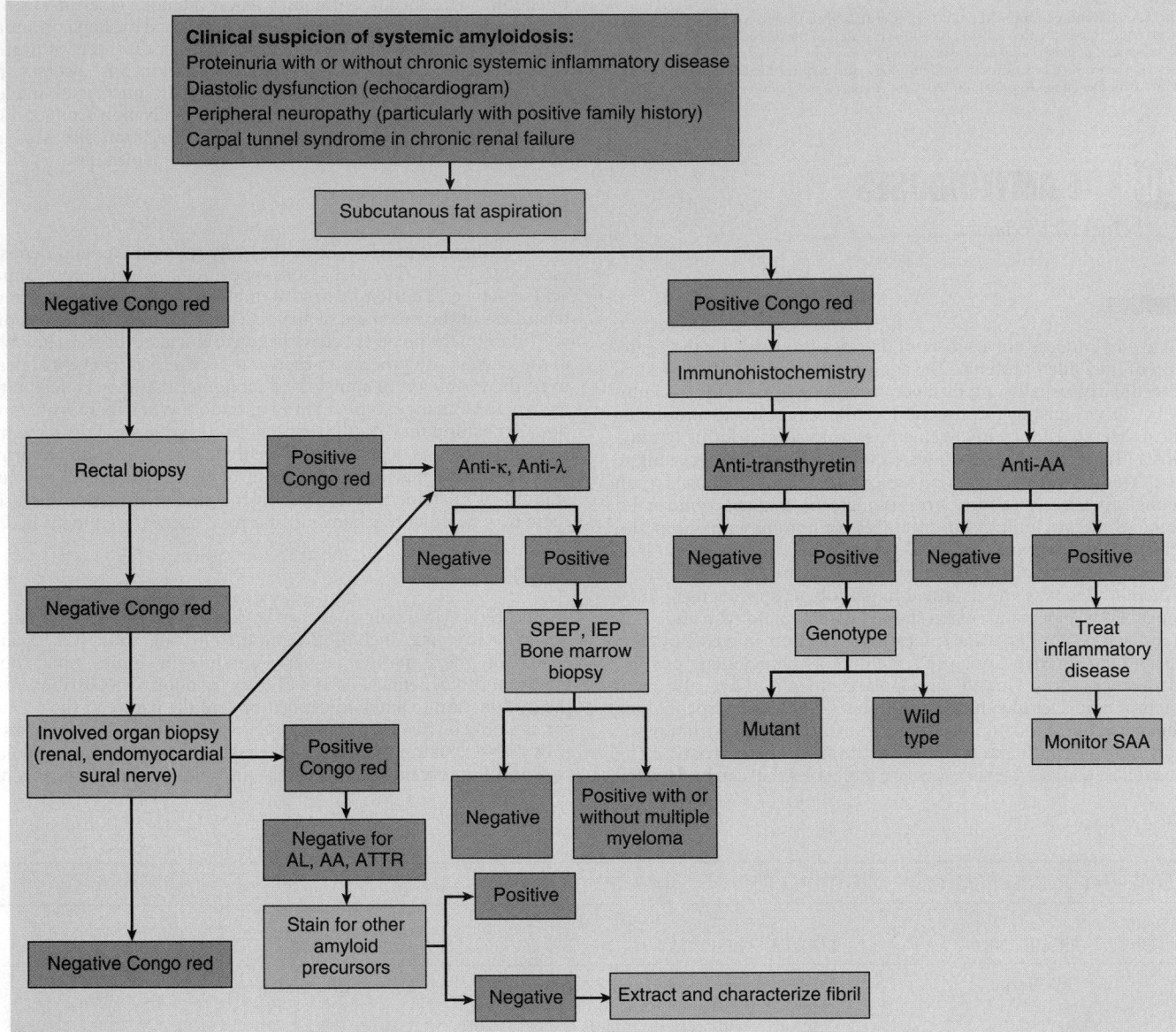

FIGURE 290–1 • Approach to the patient with possible systemic amyloidosis.

and fluorescence, followed by more detailed immunohistochemical analysis using antibodies to specific precursors, allows a definitive diagnosis in almost all cases. Examination of an involved organ using these techniques has great sensitivity, as well as specificity, yielding a diagnosis in more than 90% of cases. Errors in tissue handling or staining, particularly related to antibody specificity, are the most common causes of diagnostic failure. Tissue sampling in early disease, when involvement may be patchy, may also lead to false-negative results. In some circumstances, notably early familial amyloidotic polyneuropathy (FAP) or monoclonal immunoglobulin deposition disease, nonamyloid tissue aggregates stain with specific antiprecursor antibodies and do not bind Congo red. This finding implies the presence of a nonamyloidotic, but nonetheless pathogenic, precursor state.

The diagnosis of the amyloidoses has been facilitated by the development of relatively benign methods of tissue sampling. Rectal biopsy and subcutaneous fat aspiration are safe and efficient means of obtaining tissue for pathologic examination. Labial gland and gastric biopsies also are useful but have not yet been widely used in the United States. Samples obtained by any of these techniques can be stained with Congo red and specific antiprecursor antibodies. A combination of rectal biopsy and subcutaneous fat aspiration has a diagnostic yield greater than 80%. In the absence of technical mishaps, biopsy of a clinically involved organ (notably liver or kidney) gives a diagnosis in more than 90% of cases. A summary of results from current sampling procedures is listed in Table 290–2.

Table 290–2 • DIAGNOSTIC YIELD OF TISSUE SAMPLING PROCEDURES IN THE MAJOR AMYLOIDOSES

TISSUE	AL	AA	ATTR
Subcutaneous fat aspiration*	541/689 (79%)	56/91[†] (62%)	58/71 (82%)
Rectal biopsy*	146/194 (75%)	54/65 (85%)	—
Bone marrow biopsy	221/394 (56%)	12/26 (46%)	—
Stomach and small bowel biopsy	19/23 (83%)	15/16 (94%)	—
Labial salivary gland biopsy	13/16 (81%)	13/14 (93%)	—

*Neither subcutaneous fat aspiration nor rectal biopsy is useful in $A\beta_2$-microglobulin.
[†]The results of subcutaneous fat aspiration in AA amyloid do not include patients with familial Mediterranean fever who are generally not positive from this site.

Epidemiology

Current data indicate that the most common form of systemic amyloidosis worldwide is amyloid A (AA), secondary to either infectious or noninfectious inflammation. In the United States, light chain amyloid (AL) is the most commonly seen clinically, but recent autopsy studies suggest that late-onset deposition of transthyretin amyloid in the heart is more common, particularly in African Americans. Transthyretin amyloid has been reported to occur in 2% of autopsies in individuals older than age 60 years, a frequency far higher than that of AL in autopsy or death certificate studies. In some geographic areas, notably the northern coastal region of Portugal, several districts in northern Sweden, and the Arao and Nagano prefectures in Japan, FAP secondary to a mutation in the transthyretin gene is the most common amyloid seen in clinical practice.

Amyloid, derived from β_2-microglobulin, is deposited in the periarticular soft tissues, the carpal tunnel, the skeleton, and, rarely, the tongue of patients undergoing long-term hemodialysis. The mechanism is unclear. It may represent a combination of membrane pore size small enough to retain the β_2-m dimer and a reactive process involving macrophage activation. After 15 years of dialysis, virtually all patients show some evidence of $A\beta_2$-m deposition with symptoms related to nerve compression and joint immobilization secondary to synovial deposition.

The amyloid proteins derived from normal sequence islet amyloid polypeptide (IAPP) and $A\beta$ are seen with increasing frequency in the elderly, although the true incidence of either amyloid protein is unknown. The impact of $A\beta$ deposition as the cause of Alzheimer's disease is well known. The role of IAPP deposition in the pathogenesis of type II diabetes is less certain, although evidence suggests that it is a factor contributing to increasing insulin deficiency in the elderly.

Clinical Manifestations

The clinical features and course of the systemic amyloidoses are a function of the site and rate of deposition. Each protein seems to have a characteristic hierarchy of tissue deposition. The kidney is the most frequent site of deposition in both AL and AA, is common in some ATTR mutants, and is the only site in some of the hereditary amyloidoses. The most common presentation is proteinuria, with the full nephrotic syndrome found in many cases. Renal tubular acidosis may also occur early. Without effective treatment, the course is one of progressive renal failure. In some cases, the initial presentation is renal failure. The complications of renal failure are a frequent cause of death, regardless of the nature of the precursor producing the renal disease.

Cardiac deposition is common in AL, with approximately 20% of patients having arrhythmias or congestive heart failure as an initial manifestation. Many of the mutant transthyretin amyloidoses also have cardiac infiltration as the dominant clinical feature (familial amyloidotic cardiomyopathy, or FAC). Myocardial deposition of wild type TTR in the elderly (senile systemic amyloidosis) is probably the most common form of amyloid heart disease. Whatever the precursor, ventricular myocardial deposition leads to diastolic dysfunction, congestive heart failure, and a variety of arrhythmias including atrial standstill, atrial fibrillation, complete heart block, and sudden death, presumably related to ventricular irritability or abnormalities of autonomic control. Cardiac transthyretin amyloidosis appears to progress at a far slower rate than that related to AL deposition, presumably as a function of the concentration of the amyloidogenic precursor.

The diagnosis of cardiac amyloid can be suspected on the basis of low voltage on the electrocardiogram and characteristic echocardiographic features including ventricular septal thickening and an increase in the E/A (early atrial to ventricular flow/flow related to atrial contraction) consistent with ventricular noncompliance. There is also distortion of the normal relationship between left ventricular mass (as determined by echocardiogram) and left ventricular voltage on the electrocardiogram. Frequently, cardiac binding of technetium-99 is noted during the course of a soft tissue CT scan in a patient with amyloid. Even though the finding is not sensitive, its occurrence should raise one's level of suspicion and suggest further investigation. The definitive diagnostic test is endomyocardial biopsy with specific analysis for Congophilia and the presence of known amyloid precursors by immunohistochemical or immunoelectron microscopic techniques.

Approximately 10% of patients with AA disease have cardiac involvement. In most of these individuals, the coronary and intramyocardial vessels are affected, with angina pectoris or myocardial infarction being the presenting manifestation of the disease.

Peripheral neuropathy is seen in FAP, with mutant transthyretins, and in AL disease. The symptoms are usually sensorimotor and can result in painless ulcerations or Charcot joints. Dysesthesias are a troubling symptom in some patients. FAP patients also have striking autonomic involvement. This is frequently the most disabling feature of the entire FAP symptom complex.

Although not a true polyneuropathy, carpal tunnel syndrome may be seen in AL, FAP, and dialysis-related amyloid. Only a small proportion of all patients with isolated carpal tunnel syndrome have amyloid deposition. In most cases, the protein is TTR, frequently with no evidence of disease elsewhere.

Hepatic and splenic deposition is common in AL and AA, but clinical consequences are uncommon. Visceral infiltration presents a risk in closed liver biopsy, in which hepatic rupture or excessive bleeding has been reported. Coagulopathies occur in AL. Severe factor X deficiency has been related to sequestration of the protein by fibrils, but recent reports have suggested that this might not be the entire explanation. Nonetheless, because of the vascular fragility related to deposition within vessel walls, bleeding may be severe in these patients and coagulation parameters should be monitored regularly.

Rx Treatment

The critical step in the treatment of any of the amyloidoses is the accurate recognition of the precursor. Even though the nature of the precursor allows the identification of the primary pathologic process, effective specific treatments are not yet available for most of the individual amyloidoses, so it is possible to mistreat an individual patient. The Hippocratic caveat "above all do no harm" is particularly applicable in this set of disorders. For example, cardiac involvement by AL or late onset TTR deposition may have identical clinical features at the time of clinical presentation, including the presence of a coincidental monoclonal Ig in individuals with TTR disease. Whereas the supportive treatment of both conditions is identical (i.e., loop diuretics and avoidance of digoxin and calcium channel blocking agents), the use of potentially toxic antineoplastic therapy is only appropriate in AL. Thus, the immunohistologic identification of the deposited protein as Ig light chain or TTR-derived is critical for adequate care.

Once the nature of the protein is definitively established, the institution of protein-specific therapies, to the extent that they exist, can be initiated. AL, as either the primary disease or in association with multiple myeloma, is treated as a clonal disorder of plasma cells (Chapter 196). In randomized controlled trials, a combination of melphalan and prednisone prolonged survival after diagnosis. Colchicine alone or added to the melphalan/prednisone regimen had no effect. ☐ High-intensity chemotherapy with stem cell replacement is currently being extensively used in the treatment of myeloma. Data thus far suggest that this treatment may be effective in AL patients without significant cardiac involvement. However, studies examining outcomes to date indicate that the patients who appear to benefit are in the group that would do well anyway, even with less aggressive treatment.

Because AA occurs in the course of a variety of inflammatory diseases, the primary goal of any treatment is to suppress the inflammatory process. There is an increasing amount of circumstantial data indicating that more aggressive treatment of both adult and juvenile rheumatoid arthritis is associated with a lower frequency of amyloid renal disease. In addition, there is a well-established body of data showing that suppression of the inflammatory episodes of familial Mediterranean fever with colchicine prevents the development of renal AA, formerly the main cause of death in these patients. It appears that reduction and maintenance of the SAA level less than 10 mg/mL is sufficient to allow absorption of the deposits. If renal failure does not resolve, renal transplantation, after adequate suppression of inflammation, can be effective treatment.

Treatment of the amyloidoses related to mutations in the TTR gene is accomplished by a crude form of gene therapy in which the patients receive a liver transplant containing two normal TTR alleles.

Continued

Progression of the disease is arrested in most instances. Post-transplant functional status is related to the degree of nutritional and visceral compromise present at the time of transplantation. For reasons that are unclear, cardiac involvement in patients with mutations other than TTR val30met responds poorly to liver transplant, and combined heart and liver transplantation may be a more effective procedure.

There has been some progress toward prevention of the β_2-m amyloidosis associated with dialysis. Even though data regarding the frequency of deposition with different dialysis membranes are not yet available, there is a suggestion that high-flux dialysis decreases amyloid morbidity.

A variety of agents have been employed to specifically scan for amyloid deposits as a way to measure therapeutic response. The longest experience has been with iodinated SAP. Liver, spleen, renal, and adrenal deposits of amyloid are well visualized by this technique, although it has not been consistently useful in cardiac scanning. Labeled aprotinin seems to have better affinity for cardiac deposits. The usefulness of this technique in primary diagnosis has not yet been established, but in patients with a positive initial scan reduction in binding of the agent has been associated with clinical response. Neither of these technologies is currently available in the United States.

Supportive measures include antibiotics when indicated, careful fluid management and diuresis for congestive heart failure and the edema of the nephrotic syndrome, dialysis, and renal transplantation for end-stage renal disease. Nutritional status should be maintained with supplements if necessary.

Future Directions

Despite its increasing use, high-intensity chemotherapy with stem cell autotransplantation for AL is still experimental and is best carried out in a center experienced in both the supportive therapy of amyloidosis and transplantation as part of a research protocol. It is likely that the indications and benefits of this treatment modality will not become clear in the absence of a randomized prospective study. In FAP, a variety of compounds have been shown to inhibit TTR fibril formation in vitro and represent potential effective therapeutic agents. Some of these should reach clinical trial status over the next few years, perhaps obviating or reducing the need for liver transplantation. In β_2-m amyloidosis, current studies of high-flux dialysis and the role of different dialysis membranes should provide conclusive data regarding prevention of deposition.

1. Kyle RA, Gertz MA, Greipp PR, et al: A trial of three regimens for primary amyloidosis: Colchicine alone, melphalan and prednisone, and melphalan, prednisone and colchicine. N Engl J Med 1997;336:1202–1207.

SUGGESTED READINGS
Abraham RS, Katzmann JA, Clark RJ, et al: Quantitative analysis of serum free light chains. A new marker for the diagnostic evaluation of primary systemic amyloidosis. Am J Clin Pathol 2003;119:274–278. *This assay may be used to follow the response to therapy.*
Buxbaum JN, Tagoe CE: The genetics of the amyloidoses. Annu Rev Med 2000;51:543–569. *A comprehensive review of the genetics of the amyloidoses with particular emphasis on the systemic, genetically influenced or determined disorders, and Alzheimer's disease.*
Gershoni-Baruch R, Brik R, Zacks N, et al: The contribution of genotypes at the MEFV and SAA1 loci to amyloidosis and disease severity in patients with familial Mediterranean fever. Arthritis Rheum 2003;48:1149–1155. *A genotype-phenotype correlation.*
Gillmore JD, Lovat LB, Persey MR, et al: Amyloid load and clinical outcome in AA amyloidosis in relation to circulating concentration of serum amyloid A protein. Lancet 2001;358:24–29. *An excellent study of how the Centre for Amyloidosis and Acute Phase Proteins (UK) monitors their patients with AA.*
Goeminne A, Missault L, Bauwens F, et al: Clinical experience with cardiac amyloidosis. Acta Cardiol 2003;58:143–147. *Cardiac amyloidosis carries an ominous prognosis.*
Hazenberg BPC, van Rijswijk MH: Where has secondary amyloid gone? Ann Rheum Dis 2000;59:577–579. *A review discussing the apparent decrease in AA secondary to systemic inflammatory diseases.*
Mumford AD, O'Donnell J, Gillmore JD, et al: Bleeding symptoms and coagulation abnormalities in 337 patients with AL-amyloidosis. Br J Haematol 2000;110:454–460. *Coagulation abnormalities in AL, a comprehensive analysis.*
Poullos PD, Stollman N: Gastrointestinal amyloidosis: Approach to treatment. Curr Treat Options Gastroenterol 2003;6:17–25. *Emphasizes symptom-directed therapy.*
Sanchorawala V, Wright DG, Seldin DC, et al: An overview of the use of high-dose melphalan with autologous stem cell transplantation for the treatment of AL amyloidosis. Bone Marrow Transplant 2001;28:637–642. *A review of high-intensity chemotherapy plus autologous stem cell transplantation from the center with the most experience.*

291 SYSTEMIC DISEASES IN WHICH ARTHRITIS IS A FEATURE

Sterling G. West

Arthritis, arthralgias, and/or myalgias can be significant features of several systemic diseases and may be the presenting symptoms for some of these disorders (Table 291–1). Appropriate evaluation of these musculoskeletal symptoms, including selected laboratory tests and radiographs, provide clues for the earlier diagnosis of these diseases. Brief descriptions of the arthritic manifestations for some of these systemic disorders follows; more detailed discussion of each entity is found in other chapters devoted to these diseases. Because of the rarity of many of these diseases, evidence-based treatments with Food and Drug Administration–approved medications are lacking.

HEMOCHROMATOSIS

Joint involvement occurs in 40 to 75% of patients with hereditary hemochromatosis (HH). The metacarpophalangeal (MCP) joints (espe-

Table 291–1 • SYSTEMIC DISEASES ASSOCIATED WITH ARTHRITIS

DISEASE	TEST*
GASTROINTESTINAL DISEASES	
Hemochromatosis	Iron studies, radiographs, *HFE gene*
Autoimmune hepatitis	Liver-associated enzymes, *anti-F1 actin Ab*
Primary biliary cirrhosis	Alkaline phosphatase, *anti-mitochondrial Ab*
Pancreatitis-arthritis syndrome	Lipase, amylase, *abdominal CT scan*
Whipple's disease	—*PCR for* T. whippleii *DNA*
Gluten-sensitive enteropathy	—*Anti-transglutaminase Ab*
Inflammatory bowel disease	Stool guaiac, *colonoscopy*
Hepatitis B/hepatitis C	Liver-associated enzymes, *hepatitis serology*
Intestinal bypass arthritis	—*Cryoglobulins*
HEMATOLOGIC DISORDERS	
Hemophilia	PTT, *factor VIII and IX levels*
Hemoglobinopathies	CBC, *Hgb electrophoresis*
Hypogammaglobulinemia	Low total protein, *SPEP*
Plasma cell dyscrasias	High total protein, *SPEP*
ENDOCRINE DISORDERS	
Diabetes mellitus	Glucose, *Hgb A1C*
Thyroid disorders	TSH, *T4*
Parathyroid disorders	Calcium, phosphorus, *PTH*
Acromegaly	Radiographs, *growth hormone*
Hyperlipoproteinemia	Lipid panel
Paget's disease	Alkaline phosphatase, radiographs
MALIGNANT DISORDERS	
Hypertrophic osteoarthropathy	Radiographs (hands, wrists, chest)
Leukemia and lymphoma	CBC, LDH
Carcinomatous polyarthritis	—*Cancer screen*
Palmar fasciitis and arthritis	—*CA-125, pelvic CT scan*
OTHER DISEASES	
Multicentric reticulohistiocytosis	Radiographs
Sarcoidosis	Chest radiograph, *ACE level*
Relapsing polychondritis	—*Cartilage biopsy*
Cystic fibrosis	Chest radiograph, *sweat chloride*
Familial Mediterranean fever	—*MEFV gene*
Pigmented villonodular synovitis	Synovial fluid analysis, *MRI*
Systemic infections	Cultures, serologies, (RPR, HIV, parvovirus)

*Tests listed are common laboratory tests and radiographs that are frequently ordered that should provide a clue that a systemic disease is a possible cause of the patient's musculoskeletal symptoms. These tests, coupled with the history and physical examination, should be followed by more specific serologies and biopsies (listed in italics) to confirm the diagnosis.

ACE = angiotensin-converting enzyme; CBC = complete blood cell count; CT = computed tomography; HIV = human immunodeficiency virus; LDH = lactate dehydrogenase; MRI = magnetic resonance imaging; PCR = polymerase chain reaction; PTH = parathyroid hormone; PTT = partial thromboplastin time; RPR = rapid plasmin reagin; SPEP = serum protein electrophoresis; TSH = thyroid stimulating hormone.

cially second and third MCPs), wrists, knees, hips, and ankles are most often involved in a symmetric pattern. The arthropathy resembles osteoarthritis with joint swelling resulting from bony enlargement but is separated clinically by involvement of atypical joints, such as MCP joints, wrists, and ankles. Radiographs show joint space narrowing, subchondral cysts, sclerosis, and osteophytes that are hook-like at the MCP joints. Chondrocalcinosis is present in up to 50% of patients. It is typically asymptomatic but in some patients leads to attacks of acute inflammatory synovitis (pseudogout), which may result in the misdiagnosis of rheumatoid arthritis (RA). The prevalence of overt arthritis increases with age and may be only minimally symptomatic when the disease presents in other organs. However, it is not uncommon for articular pain to be the initial presenting complaint. Consequently, all patients (especially male) presenting with premature osteoarthritis occurring in atypical joints, especially MCP joints and wrists, should be screened for HH with iron studies. Treatment is symptomatic with nonsteroidal anti-inflammatory drugs (NSAIDs) and, when severe, total joint arthroplasties. Phlebotomy for iron removal does not alter the course of the arthritis. Additional rheumatic manifestations in patients with hemochromatosis include osteoporosis due to hypogonadism and osteomalacia due to vitamin D deficiency when liver disease is severe.

AUTOIMMUNE HEPATITIS

Patients with type I autoimmune hepatitis may present with a syndrome resembling systemic lupus erythematosus (SLE). Patients are frequently young and female, who complain of polyarthralgia and occasionally fever. Laboratory examination may show leukopenia, a positive antinuclear antibody (70 to 90%), elevated erythrocyte sedimentation rate, polyclonal gammopathy, and elevated liver-associated enzymes. Antibodies against double-stranded DNA are not seen, whereas antibodies against the smooth muscle antigen (F1 actin) support the diagnosis. Joint radiographs show soft tissue swelling without erosions or deformity. Joint pain resolves with corticosteroid therapy for the liver disease.

PRIMARY BILIARY CIRRHOSIS

Up to 50% of patients with primary biliary cirrhosis (PBC) have other autoimmune disorders including RA, Sjögren's syndrome, limited scleroderma, and autoimmune thyroiditis. In addition to antimitochondrial antibodies, rheumatoid factor and antinuclear antibodies are often present. More than 10% of PBC patients have a symmetric or asymmetric small joint inflammatory arthritis. Unlike RA, it can involve distal interphalangeal joints and is rarely erosive or deforming. Other musculoskeletal manifestations include osteomalacia due to vitamin D deficiency, osteoporosis due to renal tubular acidosis, and hypertrophic osteoarthropathy associated with liver disease.

WHIPPLE'S DISEASE

An inflammatory arthritis occurs in 60 to 90% of patients with Whipple's disease and may precede the clinical manifestations by years. The joint involvement typically is an intermittent, migratory oligoarthritis affecting large more than small joints, lasting from several hours to days. The synovial fluid is inflammatory with a predominance of mononuclear cells. Subcutaneous nodules are occasionally seen, contributing to an erroneous diagnosis of rheumatic fever or RA. However, patients consistently test negative for rheumatoid factors and antinuclear antibodies. Synovial biopsies show rod-shaped bacilli on electron microscopy, which have been identified as *Trophermyma whippleii*. Diagnosis can now be made by polymerase chain reaction to detect DNA of the organism in peripheral blood, cerebrospinal fluid, or tissue biopsy specimens. Typically, the arthritis does not cause radiographic changes or deformities. Prolonged antibiotic therapy results in resolution of musculoskeletal as well as other symptoms of this disease.

GLUTEN-SENSITIVE ENTEROPATHY (CELIAC DISEASE)

A symmetric polyarthritis may precede the enteropathic symptoms of celiac disease. Large joints such as knees and ankles, more than hips and shoulders, are most commonly involved. The arthritis

does not cause deformities or radiographic changes and resolves with a gluten-free diet in 40% of cases. Another musculoskeletal manifestation is osteomalacia due to vitamin D malabsorption, which may mimic diffuse fibromyalgia.

PANCREATIC-ARTHRITIS SYNDROME

Pancreatic panniculitis is a systemic syndrome occurring in some patients with pancreatic acinar cell carcinoma and less commonly in patients with pancreatitis. This syndrome is characterized by tender, red nodules usually on the extremities, which are frequently misdiagnosed as erythema nodosum but in reality are areas of lobular panniculitis with fat necrosis. Arthritis occurs in 60% of patients and usually involves the ankles and knees. Synovial fluid is typically noninflammatory and creamy in color. It contains multiple lipid droplets due to necrosis of fat in the synovial membrane. Other manifestations include osteolytic lesions from bone marrow fat necrosis, pleuropericarditis, fever, and eosinophilia. The prominent fat necrosis is due to release of lipase, amylase, and trypsin from the diseased pancreas. Another musculoskeletal manifestation resulting from pancreatic disease is osteomalacia from vitamin D deficiency due to malabsorption from insufficiency of the pancreas.

HEMOPHILIA

Hemophilia A (factor VIII deficiency) and hemophilia B (factor IX deficiency) are associated with hemarthrosis. Almost all patients with factor levels less than 5% of normal experience recurrent hemarthroses spontaneously or after minor trauma. Intramuscular hemorrhage can also occur. Recurrent hemarthrosis can lead to proliferative synovitis and cartilage degradation, resulting in both erosive and degenerative changes on radiographs. Physical examination shows bony enlargement, crepitus, atrophic muscles, and joint contractures. Treatment of acute monoarthritis is with factor replacement to achieve a level of 30% or greater, given at the first sign of joint swelling. Patients with fever or who fail to respond to factor replacement need joint aspiration to rule out septic arthritis, whose incidence is increased with hemophilia. Chronic arthritis is treated with NSAIDs that do not inhibit platelet function, arthroscopic synovectomy for chronic synovitis, and total joint arthroplasty for end-stage joint disease.

HEMOGLOBINOPATHIES

Patients with sickle cell anemia (S-S) or the heterozygous state of sickle-beta-thalassemia, sickle-C (S-C), and sickle-D (S-D) disease frequently experience polyarthralgia. Local sickling of cells leads to obstruction of the microcirculation and to bony infarctions. Patients most commonly experience painful crises causing chest, back, and joint pain. A painful large joint arthritis often with noninflammatory synovial effusions lasting days to weeks can also occur. Bony infarcts in the metaphyses of bones are commonly found on joint radiographs. Femoral and humeral head osteonecrosis can occur in up to 33% of S-S and S-C cases. Because of splenic dysfunction, septic arthritis and osteomyelitis (50% caused by *Salmonella*) have been associated with sickle cell disease. In adults, gout has been reported, whereas in children younger than 2 years old, an acute, painful, nonpitting swelling of the hands and feet (hand-foot syndrome) associated with fever and leukocytosis may be the first manifestation of sickle cell anemia. Treatment includes intravenous hydration, oxygen, and analgesics. In patients with beta-thalassemia major (Cooley's anemia), significant expansion of bone marrow develops as a result of increased erythroid precursors, leading to osteoporosis and microfractures that affect primarily the lower extremities.

HYPOGAMMAGLOBULINEMIA

Patients with congenital X-linked hypogammaglobulinemia (Bruton's disease) or acquired common variable immunodeficiency can develop a nonerosive, noninfectious large joint oligoarthritis that responds to intravenous gamma globulin therapy. However, septic arthritis caused by common pathogens or *Mycoplasma* can also occur and must be rigorously excluded. Selective IgA deficiency is associated with various rheumatic manifestations, including positive autoantibodies, in the absence of clinical disease. Systemic autoimmune disorders, including SLE and juvenile rheumatoid arthritis, and organ-specific autoimmune disorders, such as type I diabetes mellitus and myasthenia gravis, also occur in IgA-deficient individuals.

DIABETES MELLITUS

Diabetic stiff hand syndrome of limited joint mobility (diabetic cheirarthropathy) occurs in 30 to 75% of patients with long-standing, poorly controlled type I or type II diabetes mellitus. Patients present with the insidious development of flexion contractures and thickened skin of the fingers, which may be confused with scleroderma. These changes may be due to excess glycosylation of tendinous structures and accumulation of sugar alcohols producing excess water content in the skin, leading to increased stiffness. As a result of the inability to fully extend the fingers, the "prayer sign" is observed on physical examination. Charcot, or neuropathic, joints occur in less than 1% of all patients with long-standing diabetes. All patients have a diabetic peripheral neuropathy and most commonly present with painless swelling of the feet caused by destruction most commonly of the tarsometatarsal joints. Deformities can occur with mid-tarsal collapse ("rocker bottom" feet), predisposing to ulceration and infection of the skin over desensate bony prominences. Radiographs are diagnostic, and treatment should include supportive footwear and protected weight bearing. Unlike the Charcot joint, diabetic osteolysis and diabetic amyotrophy are unique to diabetes. The osteolysis is characterized by resorption of the distal metatarsal bone and proximal phalanges of the feet, giving radiographs a characteristic "licked candy" appearance. Pain is variable and treatment conservative, because the process may terminate on its own. Diabetic amyotrophy presents with severe pain and dysesthesias of the proximal muscles of one or both thighs. Carpal tunnel syndrome, adhesive capsulitis of the shoulder (frozen shoulder), flexor tenosynovitis of the hands, diffuse idiopathic skeletal hyperostosis, and septic joints are all musculoskeletal conditions that occur with increased frequency in diabetic patients.

THYROID DISORDERS

Musculoskeletal symptoms occur in 33% of patients with clinical hypothyroidism (thyroid-stimulating hormone >20 μU/mL). Patients can present with carpal tunnel syndrome, Raynaud's phenomenon, and/or muscle aching similar to fibromyalgia. Patients with severe hypothyroidism can experience a noninflammatory myopathy with proximal muscle weakness and elevated creatine kinase, which may be confused clinically with polymyositis. Similarly, myxedematous patients can develop a symmetric arthropathy of the large joints, especially the knees, associated with noninflammatory synovial fluid with increased viscosity. The association of hypothyroidism with chondrocalcinosis is controversial, but clearly patients initiating treatment with thyroid replacement can experience an acute attack of pseudogout. Patients with hyperthyroidism can develop proximal myopathy (70%), adhesive capsulitis of the shoulder (10%), osteoporosis, and/or thyroid acropachy. Thyroid acropachy occurs in less than 1% of patients with Graves' disease and consists of soft tissue swelling of the hands, digital clubbing, and periostitis, particularly involving the metacarpal and phalangeal bone shafts. Pain is usually mild, radiographs are characteristic, and there is no effective therapy.

PARATHYROID DISORDERS

Primary hyperparathyroidism can present with osteoporosis and fractures, or with chondrocalcinosis and episodes of acute pseudogout. In severe hyperparathyroidism, which is rare, vague myalgias resembling fibromyalgia, a reversible, painless, proximal myopathy, and osteitis fibrosa cystica can be seen. Osteitis fibrosa cystica has a characteristic appearance radiographically with subperiosteal resorption on the radial side of the phalanges, small erosions in the hands and distal clavicles, and discrete lytic bone lesions (Brown tumors). Ectopic calcifications, joint laxity, and tendon ruptures have also been reported in patients with severe hyperparathyroidism. Hypoparathyroidism has also been associated with a myopathy and ectopic calcifications. Patients with pseudo- and pseudo-pseudohypoparathyroidism have a shortened fourth metacarpal bone bilaterally.

ACROMEGALY

Up to 75% of patients with acromegaly develop an atypical form of osteoarthritis. The knees, shoulders, hips, and lumbosacral and cervical spine are the most frequently symptomatic areas, although the hands reveal the most characteristic radiographic changes. Carpal tunnel syndrome (50%), Raynaud's phenomenon (33%), and proximal muscle weakness with normal creatine kinase can also occur.

HYPERLIPOPROTEINEMIA

Type II familial hypercholesterolemia is associated with tendinous and tuberous xanthomas and episodic Achilles tendinitis. An acute, migratory inflammatory arthritis persisting up to a month and resembling rheumatic fever occurs in up to 50% of patients. Large more than small joints are predominantly affected. Additionally, a self-limited, acute monoarticular or oligoarticular arthritis involving the knee or ankle can also occur. In all hyperlipidemias, gout must be excluded before ascribing the symptoms to hyperlipoproteinemia. Therapy with NSAIDs and treatment of the underlying lipid disorder should be pursued.

PAGET'S DISEASE

Paget's disease can cause bony pain and deformity. Joint pain caused by secondary osteoarthritis in areas of pagetic involvement of bone most commonly occurs in the hip, knee, or vertebrae. Spinal stenosis from Paget's disease of the spine has been reported.

HYPERTROPHIC OSTEOARTHROPATHY

Hypertrophic osteoarthropathy (HOA) is a syndrome that includes clubbing of the fingers and toes, periostitis of long bones (distal tibia, femur, and radius), and arthritis. HOA is classified into primary (hereditary) and secondary forms. Between 80 and 90% of secondary HOA is associated with non–small cell lung cancer. Other causes include other neoplasms (mesothelioma), chronic pulmonary infections, congenital heart disease, cirrhosis, and inflammatory bowel disease. Patients with HOA present with bone pain and noninflammatory arthritis caused by the periarticular periostitis. Radiographs show diagnostic changes of periosteal elevation and/or new bone formation along the distal ends of long bones. Therapy is symptomatic, and HOA resolves with successful treatment of the underlying primary disease.

LEUKEMIA AND LYMPHOMA

Leukemia can present as a symmetric or migratory polyarthritis, monoarthritis (rare), back pain (10%), or nocturnal bone pain. Articular manifestations occur in 15 to 60% of children and 4 to 6% of adults with acute leukemia. Joint pain is attributed to leukemic synovial infiltration and usually involves the ankle or knee. The joint pain is disproportionally more severe than the clinical findings. Synovial effusions are uncommon, and evidence of leukemic cells in the synovial fluid is rare. The peripheral white blood cell count may be normal, but lactate dehydrogenase is always elevated, frequently to very high levels. Radiographs are normal in 50%. The musculoskeletal symptoms resolve with successful therapy of the leukemia. Nocturnal bone pain is the most common presenting musculoskeletal complaint of patients with lymphoma. Patients with T-cell lymphoma may occasionally develop a chronic, nonerosive polyarthritis with erythroderma.

CARCINOMATOUS POLYARTHRITIS

Polyarthritis can rarely be the presenting manifestation of an occult malignancy. It may precede the discovery of the malignancy by several months. Breast cancer and other non-intrathoracic malignancies are the most common associated cancers. Clinical features suggesting carcinomatous polyarthritis include explosive onset of a seronegative, asymmetric polyarthritis predominantly involving the lower extremities in a patient older than age 60 years. Polymyalgia rheumatica and RA must be excluded. Treatment of the underlying malignancy results in improvement of the arthritis.

PALMAR FASCIITIS AND ARTHRITIS SYNDROME

Ovarian carcinoma is the most common malignancy found in patients with palmar fasciitis and arthritis. Patients present with a severe painful and symmetric inflammatory polyarthritis and fasciitis involving primarily the hands and less commonly the feet. Patients may have vasomotor instability causing diagnostic confusion with reflex sympathetic dystrophy syndrome or RA. This syndrome portends a poor prognosis, because it typically manifests after tumor metastasis. Response to treatment is variable, although clinical improvement can be seen with successful eradication of the underlying tumor.

MULTICENTRIC RETICULOHISTIOCYTOSIS

Multicentric reticulohistiocytosis (MRH) is a chronic, symmetric, inflammatory polyarthritis, most commonly affecting the hands and cervical spine. It may resemble RA but has prominent distal interphalangeal joint synovitis and can cause a severely deforming arthritis mutilans in 50% of cases. Firm, reddish-brown or yellow papulonodular lesions ("coral beads") that wax and wane occur around the nailbeds and on the face, hands, ears, and other areas predominantly above the waist. The skin lesions have a diagnostic histology. However, in 66% of patients, these diagnostic nodules follow the onset of arthritis by months to years. Additional associations include xanthelasma (33%) and malignancies of various types (25%), which may precede or follow the onset of MRH. Treatment may include cytotoxic therapy if the arthritis is aggressive.

SARCOIDOSIS

Joint manifestations including arthritis, periarthritis, and arthralgias occur in 2 to 38% of patients with sarcoidosis. Rheumatic involvement is divided into acute and chronic types. The first consists of the triad of arthritis, erythema nodosum, and hilar adenopathy on chest radiograph (Lofgren's syndrome), which may be accompanied by fever. Arthritis arises most often in the knees and ankles, and periarticular pain can be severe. Treatment is with NSAIDs and/or colchicine, and symptoms usually remit spontaneously over several weeks. The less common type of joint involvement consists of synovitis that accompanies the slower onset, more chronic, and systemic form of sarcoidosis. The arthritis is usually polyarthritis, oligoarthritis, or monoarthritis involving the small or large joints and is typically nondestructive, but in some cases can be aggressive. Dactylitis resulting from sarcoid bone and soft tissue involvement can occur. In contrast to the acute type, chronic sarcoid arthropathy is characterized by inflammatory synovial fluid and histologic granulomas on synovial biopsy. Treatment consists of NSAIDs, low-dose corticosteroids, hydroxychloroquine, and methotrexate or azathioprine. Other musculoskeletal manifestations include lytic or sclerotic bone lesions and a myopathy.

RELAPSING POLYCHONDRITIS

Relapsing polychondritis (RP) is an uncommon multisystem disorder characterized by recurrent episodes of inflammation of cartilaginous tissues. Patients typically first present with the sudden onset of pain and erythema involving the cartilage of the external ear, larynx/trachea, or nose. A nonerosive, seronegative polyarthritis or oligoarthritis affecting small, large, or costochondral joints (23 to 47%), ocular inflammation including episcleritis/scleritis, and audiovestibular disturbances may also be presenting symptoms. RP is presumably due to a cell-mediated immune response against cartilage components; biopsies showing acute and chronic inflammation destroying cartilage support the diagnosis. Late sequelae of RP include deformity of the pinnae or nose, reduced vision or hearing, tracheal narrowing or collapse, and aortic insufficiency resulting from

aortic ring dilatation as well as other cardiovascular abnormalities. Patients with RP frequently have associated coexisting diseases, such as systemic vasculitis, various connective tissue diseases (e.g., RA), myelodysplastic syndromes and other cancers, and thyroid disease. Treatment depends on the severity of the presentation and whether major organs are involved. Mild episodes of inflammation are treated with NSAIDs, colchicine, dapsone, and low-dose corticosteroids. Life-threatening or organ-threatening complications are treated with high-dose corticosteroids and immunosuppressive agents, such as methotrexate or cyclophosphamide.

CYSTIC FIBROSIS

In up to 40% of patients with cystic fibrosis, an episodic, nondestructive, inflammatory oligoarthritis develops, most commonly involving the fingers and lower extremity joints. This arthritis is thought to be due to immune complex deposition caused by chronic lung infections. Attacks last for a few days and may be associated with fever and erythema nodosum. Other musculoskeletal manifestations include osteoporosis and osteomalacia due to malabsorption and, more rarely, hypertrophic osteoarthropathy and a small vessel vasculitis.

FAMILIAL MEDITERRANEAN FEVER

Familial Mediterranean fever (FMF) is an autosomal recessive disorder associated with the MEFV gene on chromosome 16 and characterized by irregular attacks, lasting 1 to 3 days, of fever and one or more inflammatory manifestations. Between 50 and 75% of patients have arthritis with the attacks. Intermittent monoarticular arthritis involving the knee or other large joints is the most typical, although a polyarthritis can occur in 20% of patients. Localized joint pain and exquisite tenderness out of proportion to the swelling, erythema, or warmth is common. Treatment of the arthritis is with analgesics because glucocorticoids are ineffective. Recovery of joint function between attacks usually occurs, and joint destruction is rare. However, up to 10% of patients have prolonged arthritic episodes lasting weeks to months, which may lead to joint (especially hip) damage requiring surgery. Colchicine is used prophylactically to prevent attacks of FMF and the long-term complication of amyloidosis.

PIGMENTED VILLONODULAR SYNOVITIS

Pigmented villonodular synovitis (PVNS) is characterized by the onset in middle age of pain and swelling of the knees or hips, or even of tendons and bursae. The synovial fluid characteristically is hemorrhagic, and radiographs may show soft tissue swelling, osteolysis, subchondral cysts, and bony erosions. PVNS is a nonmalignant condition that may be simulated by hemangiomas, lipomas, and xanthomas, and the cells usually are of a mixed nature. The treatment for PVNS is synovectomy.

FUTURE DIRECTIONS

With the advances being made in immunology and genetics, there will be an increased understanding of the pathogenesis of many of these diseases. Treatments such as immunomodulating biologic agents or cartilage-preserving therapy with metalloproteinase inhibitors will be developed based on new discoveries elucidating the etiology of these unusual disorders.

SUGGESTED READINGS

Barnard J, Newman LS: Sarcoidosis: Immunology, rheumatic involvement, and therapeutics. Opin Rheumatol 2001;13:84–91. *An updated review on the spectrum and treatment of joint, bone, and muscle involvement in sarcoidosis.*

Slot O, Locht H. Arthritis as presenting symptom in silent adult coeliac disease. Two cases and review of the literature. Scand J Rheumatol 2000;29:260–263. *An updated review of rheumatic symptoms as the presenting symptom of gluten-sensitive enteropathy.*

Smith LL, Burnet SP, McNeil JD: Musculoskeletal manifestations of diabetes mellitus. Br J Sports Med 2003;37:30–35. *An overview emphasizing that good glucose control appears to improve or prevent the development of rheumatic conditions.*

von Kempis J: Arthropathy in hereditary hemochromatosis. Curr Opin Rheumatol 2001;13:80–83. *A concise review of the genetics and pathogenesis of hemochromatotic arthropathy.*

Rheumatic Diseases

292 IDIOPATHIC MULTIFOCAL FIBROSCLEROSIS

Wilmer L. Sibbitt, Jr.

Definition

Idiopathic multifocal fibrosclerosis (IMF) is an inflammatory disease characterized by the development of inflammatory pseudo-tumors, resulting in some combination of retroperitoneal fibrosis, mediastinal fibrosis, orbital pseudotumor, Dupuytren's contracture, lymphoid hyperplasia, Peyronie's disease, vasculitis, thyroiditis, primary biliary cirrhosis, testicular fibrosis, and pachymeningitis. Retroperitoneal fibrosis (Ormond's disease) is a subset of IMF and is characterized by fibrosis of the retroperitoneum that entraps and distorts retroperitoneal structures including the great vessels, ureters, nerves, kidneys, and biliary tree.

Epidemiology

IMF is a rare condition with a prevalence estimated at less than 20/100,000, and an incidence of less than 3/100,000 per year. However, in relevant populations with predisposing conditions, these figures are considerably higher. For example, methysergide is associated with an incidence of IMF at the rate of 1 case in 5000 users per year. Mean age at presentation is 56 years, and the male : female ratio is 3 : 1. The cumulative actuarial survival rate is 86% at 1 year and 78% at 2 years.

Pathobiology

The histopathology of IMF is characterized by multifocal fibrosis, granulation tissue, B cells, T helper cells, large numbers of spindle-shaped cells expressing macrophage markers, and activated fibroblasts. T-cell receptor gene rearrangements have been reported as has a 40% association with HLA-B27, but these associations have not been proven. Degenerative and inflammatory diseases of the aorta (atherosclerosis, aortitis, inherited diseases of collagen, trauma, infection, aortic aneurysm) shed inflammatory lipids and oxidized lipoproteins through the aortic adventitia into the retroperitoneum, resulting in an intense inflammatory process. Thus, the presence of IMF should trigger an evaluation for aortic disease. Confounding syndromes including lymphoma, crystal-storing histiocytosis, immunocytoma, neuroblastoma, diffuse retroperitoneal carcinoma (pancreatic, scirrhous gastric, prostate, ovarian, renal, uterine cervix, carcinoid), Wegener's granulomatosis, xanthogranulomatous pyelonephritis, chronic pyelonephritis, tuberculosis, guinea worm infestation, sarcoidosis, and aortic graft infection should be excluded by appropriate imaging, biopsy, aspiration, and/or serology tests. Secondary retroperitoneal fibrosis can be caused by drugs and toxins (methysergide, methyldopa, levodopa, ergot, bromocriptine, pergolide, asbestos, fluoropyrimidine), aortic aneurysm, malignant tumors (metastatic carcinomas, carcinoid, lymphoma), retroperitoneal injury (hemorrhage, infection, radiation, surgery, stenting, angioplasty), autoimmune disease, Erdheim-Chester disease, tuberculosis, sarcoidosis, biliary tract disease, gonorrhea, and ascending lymphangitis.

Clinical Manifestations

IMF commonly presents as (1) isolated retroperitoneal fibrosis; (2) retroperitoneal, mesenteric, pulmonary, and periarticular fibrosis accompanied by subcutaneous panniculitis; (3) a triad of sclerosing cholangitis, retroperitoneal fibrosis, and Riedel's thyroiditis; and (4) other less common combinations. The retroperitoneal form of IMF typically presents as (1) ill-defined pain in the lower abdomen, lumbosacral region, or flank; (2) visceral obstruction resulting in vomiting, diarrhea, or dehydration; (3) hydronephrosis, renal insufficiency; (4) severe peripheral edema and venous varicosities; or (5) claudication, pain, dysesthesias, weakness, or spasticity resulting from nerve entrapment and epidural cord compression. Pulmonary emboli, deep venous thrombosis, and obstruction of the bowel, bladder, or bronchi can occur.

Mediastinal fibrosis may result in a lymphoma-like mass and superior vena caval syndrome with edema and venous dilatation of the arms, neck, and head. Extrahepatic portal vein obstruction, portal hypertension, esophageal varices, and uveitis may occur. A definitive diagnosis should be undertaken rapidly and therapy seriously considered.

Diagnosis

Computed tomography (CT), magnetic resonance imaging, and urogram with appropriate contrast demonstrate a retroperitoneal inflammatory reaction, obstruction of ureters, great vessels, biliary tree, or pancreatic ducts, or the presence of diffuse or discrete unifocal or multifocal retroperitoneal masses. Fibrosis may extend into the root of the mesentery, the bladder, and peribronchial areas, resulting in traction, distortion, and obstruction of the gut, urethra, and bronchi. Indium-111 labeled leukocyte or gallium radionuclide scans are useful to exclude abscess, demonstrate inflammatory processes, and follow disease activity. The presence of autoimmune diseases, drug use, and toxin exposure should be excluded by appropriate history and serologic testing. After suspicious masses are identified, biopsy is usually essential to confirm the diagnosis and to exclude confounding conditions, especially neoplasia and infection. Biopsy may be guided by CT, ultrasound, mediastinoscopy, laparoscopy, or retroperitoneal exploration and can often be accomplished by percutaneous needle biopsy.

Rx Prevention and Treatment

All recommendations for prevention and treatment of IMF are based on relatively small series and case reports. The most important therapy or prevention of IMF is removal of the cause, most commonly an offending drug. Otherwise, treatment of IMF is largely empirical but may be necessary because the disease is often progressive and fatal. Nonsurgical therapies include high-dose oral corticosteroids, pulse methylprednisolone, penicillamine, azathioprine, cyclophosphamide, and cyclosporine, all of which have had some success. Tamoxifen has been used as primary therapy on a limited basis with some success and very little toxicity. Lifelong anticoagulation is required for those patients with large vein involvement and associated deep venous thrombosis. Surgical interventions include lysis of fibrotic masses and stenting of ureteral, biliary, venous, and arterial obstructions. Surgical repair or stenting of an abdominal aortic aneurysm may be either an exacerbating or ameliorating factor for IMF; thus, therapy for aneurysm must be individualized.

Future Directions

The inflammatory and cytokine networks that are triggered by drugs, crystals, or anatomic changes associated with IMF are poorly understood but likely parallel those of other fibrotic diseases. Animal models of IMF need to be developed and validated. National registries and interinstitutional cooperative studies are also necessary to support basic and clinical research in this rare disease. New treatments to prevent cellular inflammation and biologic-derived therapies directed at individual cytokines may be applicable in the therapy of IMF. Antilipid agents, especially the statins, may have some effect in halting the local dissemination of cholesterol crystals from atherosclerotic aortas, thus preventing IMF. New interventional modalities including transcutaneous biopsy, retroperitoneoscopy, intravascular and intraureteral stenting, and angioplasty and areteroplasty done together may also by helpful in treating IMF.

SUGGESTED READINGS

Al-Nafussi A, Wong NA: Intra-abdominal spindle cell lesions: A review and practical aids to diagnosis. Histopathology 2001;38:387–402. *An excellent review of this disorder with an emphasis on histopathology.*

Katz R, Golijanin D, Pode D, et al: Primary and postoperative retroperitoneal fibrosis—experience with 18 cases. Urology 2002;60:780–783. *Overview of treatment with nephrostomy drainage, ureteral stenting, ureterolysis, and re-implantation.*

Oguz KK, Kiratli H, Oguz O, et al: Multifocal fibrosclerosis: A new case report and review of the literature. Eur Radiol 2002;12:1134–1138. *Emphasizes the relationships among retroperitoneal fibrosis, mediastinal fibrosis, sclerosing cholangitis, and Riedel's thyroiditis.*

293 SURGICAL TREATMENT OF JOINT DISEASES

Joseph A. Buckwalter

Musculoskeletal conditions, particularly arthritis of weight-bearing joints, are a common cause of chronic pain, deformity, and functional impairment. As the mean life expectancy of the population continues to increase, clinically significant arthritis is becoming increasingly more prevalent. Debilitating joint pain that is not relieved by nonoperative treatment is the most common indication for surgical intervention. Approximately 250,000 total knee replacements are performed annually in the United States, and the rate of total hip arthroplasty is approximately 60 per 100,000 population.

While total joint arthroplasty of the hip and knee are among the most successful of all surgical procedures in terms of pain relief and functional improvement, joint procedures are not without risk. A thorough understanding of potential perioperative and postoperative complications is imperative in assessing an individual's surgical risk versus expected benefits. Reasonable short-term and long-term expectations as well as the importance of continued follow-up must be communicated with the patient. Nonetheless, surgical treatment offers dramatic relief to many patients with pain and deformity from arthritis and who fail to improve with nonoperative treatments.

Indications for Surgery

The principle indication for surgery in the treatment of arthritis is pain that is unrelieved by nonoperative modalities. Another indication is loss of function, such as with a hip that has become fused from chronic disease. Less commonly, surgery may be performed to prevent disease progression. Examples include core decompression to reduce the risk of collapse of a hip with avascular necrosis, or osteotomy after a malunited fracture to slow the progression of degenerative change in an adjacent joint.

Except for some arthritic conditions that lead to spinal instability and neurologic compromise, operative treatment of arthritis is elective. Patients should therefore understand and exhaust all viable nonoperative options before considering surgery. Moreover, the patient's symptoms and/or deformity should be severe enough to warrant surgery. In addition, the patient should be capable of rehabilitating the treated joint enough to enjoy the benefits of the operation. For example, a nonambulatory patient with incapacitating hip pain from arthritis may be better treated by simple resection of the hip joint as opposed to total hip replacement.

Preoperative Evaluation

Many patients with arthritis suffer from involvement of multiple joints or organ systems. Therefore, determination of the exact cause of a patient's symptoms is not always straightforward. Patients with avascular necrosis or arthritis of the hip with collapse of the femoral head often present with severe knee pain, and yet may have minor if any hip symptoms. Similarly, concomitant hip and lumbar arthritis or shoulder and cervical arthritis may present a diagnostic dilemma. Furthermore, many forms of arthritis cause such severe deformity and altered range of motion that neurologic involvement or even sepsis may be difficult to discern. In such cases, joint aspiration, differential joint injections, electrodiagnostic studies, and additional radiographic imaging may be required in addition to routine plain radiographs.

As with all surgical patients, the orthopedic patient should have a careful history and general physical examination with routine hematology and chemistry profiles obtained preoperatively. The need for a chest radiograph and electrocardiogram are dictated by anesthesia guidelines according to the individual's age and past medical history. Many candidates for surgical treatment of arthritis are elderly or have disease processes with the potential for multisystem involvement. Cardiac, pulmonary, renal, and peripheral vascular function should be evaluated and treated preoperatively.

Urinalysis is generally performed before arthroplasty to detect bacteriuria, which may increase the risk of postoperative infection.

Asymptomatic bacteriuria may simply require additional antibiotic prophylaxis, whereas any systemic signs of infection, such as fever or leukocytosis, may require more prolonged treatment and delay of the elective procedure. Carious teeth or other periodontal infection, pharyngitis, and other potential sources of hematogenous postoperative infection should be evaluated and treated preoperatively.

Patients with a history of rheumatoid arthritis (RA), Down syndrome, or other conditions known to be associated with cervical instability should have screening flexion and extension lateral radiographs of the cervical spine performed. Any evidence of instability should be further evaluated by a spine surgeon. Clinically significant cervical subluxation could then be addressed surgically before any other elective surgery, or it may dictate the use of regional instead of general endotracheal anesthesia.

Certain medications may need to be withheld in the perioperative period. Some popular herbal supplements and megadose vitamins are thought to increase the risk of anesthesia and may interfere with thromboembolic prophylaxis postoperatively. Patients taking antithrombotic medications may need to hold or alter their medications preoperatively. Depending on the patient's risk of thromboembolism and the condition being treated, the prescribing physician may simply withhold coumadin until the prothrombin normalizes, or may substitute intravenous heparin or subcutaneous fractionated heparin for 4 to 5 days before surgery. The relatively short and predictable half-life of heparin allows it to be stopped a few hours before the operation. For more serious conditions, such as a history of pulmonary emboli, consideration may be given to placing an inferior vena cava filter.

Obesity

An estimated 3 to 4 lb of pressure are translated to lower extremity joints for each pound of body weight during normal walking. It is therefore not surprising that obesity has been associated with early onset knee osteoarthritis and with an increased incidence of meniscal tears. Some obese patients appreciate varying degrees of relief from symptoms of arthritis with weight loss. Weight reduction may also increase the probability of a successful operation with a decreased incidence of infection, wound complications, and blood loss. Whether obesity is correlated with early loosening of a total hip or knee replacement is controversial, possibly because obese patients may be less active. Weight control may be more difficult for the patient whose one or more arthritic joints preclude aerobic exercise. For these individuals, the surgeon may recommend proceeding with operative treatment despite the increased risks associated with obesity.

DISEASE-RELATED FACTORS

Surgical options and indications vary according to the rheumatic condition (Table 293–1). Patients with certain forms of arthritis have

Table 293–1 • OPERATIVE TREATMENT OPTIONS FOR ARTHRITIS

TYPE OF ARTHRITIS	AFFECTED JOINT	FAVORED SURGICAL OPTIONS
Osteoarthritis	Knee, hip, shoulder	Arthroscopic débridement Osteotomy (hip, knee) Arthrodesis Arthroplasty
	Interphalangeal, wrist	Synovectomy Arthrodesis
	Ankle	Arthroscopy Arthrodesis Arthroplasty (infrequently)
	Elbow	Arthroscopy for loose bodies Arthroplasty
Rheumatoid and other inflammatory arthritides	Knee, hip, shoulder	Arthroscopic synovectomy Arthroplasty
	Wrist	Arthroscopic synovectomy Arthrodesis Arthroplasty (infrequently)
	Ankle	Arthrodesis Arthroplasty (more often)
	Elbow	Arthroscopic synovectomy

an increased incidence of surgical complications or are predisposed to conditions that require special attention perioperatively.

Osteoarthritis

Osteoarthritis is responsible for more surgical procedures than any other form of arthritis. The goal of these procedures is to alleviate pain while preserving or restoring a functional articulation. In patients with a remaining joint space, débridement of loose bodies and tears of the meniscal or chondral surface can alleviate pain and restore a mechanically smooth articular surface. Defects in the surface may further be repaired with osteochondral allografts or by stimulating ingrowth of fibrocartilage by perforating the subchondral bone. Transplantation of chondrocytes or whole tissue grafts with chondrogenic potential, including periosteum and perichondrium, may be particularly useful in young patients with isolated articular defects. All of these procedures, although potentially helpful with less severe disease, are not indicated for patients with advanced osteoarthritis. Many of the procedures discussed later in this chapter, including osteotomy, arthrodesis, and arthroplasty, are the mainstays of surgical intervention for advanced osteoarthritis.

Rheumatoid Arthritis

Patients with RA often have involvement of multiple joints and organ systems. They require careful perioperative evaluation to prevent complications and establish the sequencing of surgical sites. The medications used to treat RA may also require specific perioperative consideration.

Approximately 1% of the population of the United States has RA; of these, approximately 10% require surgery for atlantoaxial subluxation. Significant atlantoaxial subluxation, atlantoaxial impaction, and/or subaxial subluxation is present in 61% of patients with RA who present for total joint arthroplasty. Half of patients with these findings may have no clinical signs or symptoms of instability of the cervical spine or of neurologic compromise. Therefore, it is important that all patients with RA have screening flexion and extension lateral radiographs of the cervical spine obtained before any operative procedure. Instability, as determined by a difference on the flexion and extension radiographs of 7 to 10 mm at the atlantoaxial joint or greater than 4 mm at subaxial levels, generally requires surgical stabilization before any other elective procedure. Patients with lesser degrees of cervical involvement should be carefully evaluated by the anesthesiologist and considered for an intubation while awake or for a regional anesthetic.

Patients with debilitating involvement of multiple joints require careful planning to optimize their potential for rehabilitation. The patient being considered for lower extremity surgery requires use of the upper extremities for transferring, rising from a chair, climbing stairs, and ambulating with a walker or other assistive device. It may therefore be prudent to stabilize a severely arthritic wrist or treat a debilitating shoulder before replacing a hip, for example. In addition, patients with multiple lower extremity joint involvement may benefit from sequential or simultaneous joint operations. The patient with ipsilateral hip and knee involvement often finds some relief of knee pain and easier rehabilitation of the knee if the hip is addressed first. However, the patient with severe arthritis and contractures of both knees should be considered for simultaneous total knee arthroplasty. Otherwise, a flexion contracture in an untreated knee prevents the patient from standing straight and potentially compromises the rehabilitation of the operated knee.

Long-term use of corticosteroids, nonsteroidal anti-inflammatory drugs (NSAIDs), and methotrexate may complicate the surgical treatment of patients with RA. Patients who have been taking corticosteroids often require "stress dose" steroids perioperatively because of adrenal inhibition. In addition, steroid use combined with long-term effects of the disease itself often make blood vessels, skin, and connective tissues more friable. Therefore, caution must be exercised in handling the skin and soft tissues both intraoperatively and postoperatively because even mild pressure or adhesive tape may cause bleeding or even ulceration.

Many patients with RA are treated with methotrexate. A comparison study of rheumatoid patients undergoing total joint arthroplasty showed a similar incidence of wound complications among patients who were treated with methotrexate and those who were not. Moreover,

it has been shown that there is no benefit in terms of infection or wound complications associated with interrupting methotrexate therapy perioperatively.

Many patients who present for orthopaedic surgery have been taking NSAIDs for arthritis pain. Patients receiving NSAIDs at the time of hospital admission for total hip arthroplasty have a higher incidence of gastrointestinal bleeding. Consideration should be given both to interrupting NSAID treatment perioperatively and to treating prophylactically for a gastrointestinal ulcer with an H_2 blocker.

Osteonecrosis

Osteonecrosis, or aseptic necrosis, most commonly involves the femoral head, but is also not uncommon in the medial femoral condyle and humeral head. Treatment remains controversial, due, at least in part, to a lack of understanding of the natural history of the disorder. Anti-inflammatory agents, intra-articular steroid injections, and periods of protected weight bearing may provide temporary symptomatic relief, but they are not thought to alter the long-term outcome. Similarly, arthroscopic débridement of resultant fragments in the knee can improve mechanical pain but does not prevent progression.

Most surgical treatments for osteonecrosis have been developed for the hip. Core decompression involves removing a core of bone from the lateral femoral cortex into the center of the osteonecrotic lesion. This is typically performed under fluoroscopic guidance with a cannulated drill and is reserved for patients who have not yet experienced collapse of the femoral head or associated acetabular changes. The durability of the results may be slightly increased with the addition of a vascularized fibular graft, but at the expense of considerable operative time and donor site morbidity.

For patients whose femoral head is already collapsed, redirectional osteotomy may allow placement of an intact portion of the femoral head into a weight-bearing position, thereby alleviating pain and preserving joint function. This technically demanding procedure is not an option for patients with larger lesions or whole head involvement, in which case arthrodesis or arthroplasty should be used.

Ankylosing Spondylitis

Joint replacements decrease pain and improve function for patients with advanced hip disease due to ankylosing spondylitis (AS). Osteotomies that correct spinal deformities can also benefit some patients. Spinal involvement can lead to extensive ligamentous calcification and heterotopic ossification that make regional anesthesia difficult, if not impossible. Patients with prolonged disease also develop severe kyphotic deformities of the cervical, thoracic, and lumbar spine that impede endotracheal intubation. Restricted chest excursion may further complicate intraoperative and postoperative care. Patients with AS tend to bleed more during and after surgery than similar, otherwise healthy individuals. The explanation for this bleeding tendency appears to be that, compared with normal tissues, the ossified soft tissues are less capable of contracting to assist in hemostasis. There does not appear to be an associated defect in blood coagulation or platelet function.

Patients with AS, diffuse idiopathic skeletal hyperostosis, or posttraumatic osteoarthrosis are at increased risk for postoperative heterotopic ossification. Although patients with AS have excellent pain relief after total hip arthroplasty, gains in total range of motion are often limited by periarticular heterotopic ossification, as well as long-standing soft tissue contractures and muscle atrophy. Various regimens have been tried to prevent postoperative soft tissue ossification, but radiation therapy delivered locally appears to be the most effective means of preventing heterotopic bone formation after surgery. Fractionated and single low-dose radiation therapy to the hip and abductor musculature has been effective when begun early in the postoperative period.

Psoriatic Arthritis

Patients with psoriatic arthritis present a unique perioperative risk known as *isomorphic* or *Koebner's phenomenon*, whereby a psoriatic flare may occur at the surgical site as a result of the physiologic and/or psychological stress of surgery. This process may predispose the patient to a generalized flare of psoriasis as well. Whether patients with psoriasis are at increased risk of postoperative infections remains controversial.

Hemophilic Arthropathy

Joint disease may begin early in life for the hemophilic patient. Relatively minor injury can lead to hemarthroses with resultant chronic synovitis and contractures. Despite the risk of perioperative bleeding, patients with hemophilia can experience significant benefits from operative intervention. Synovectomy is commonly performed in the knee and elbow, and typically provides excellent pain relief, increased range of motion, and a decrease in recurrent hemarthroses. Patients with hemophilic arthropathy appear to be at increased risk of late infection after a total joint arthroplasty, probably related to the development of hemarthrosis. It is important to promptly distinguish between septic arthritis and hemarthrosis and to treat the patient appropriately.

SURGICAL OPTIONS

Even though there are many variations in surgical approaches according to the joint involved, some definitions and principles may be widely applied. Arthroscopy, arthrodesis, osteotomy, and arthroplasty are the most widely used procedures for arthritis.

Arthroscopy

Arthroscopic surgery has seen many advances in the past 3 decades. In general, two small incisions are made into the joint; an arthroscope is placed through one, and one of many different arthroscopic tools is placed through the other. Many times, the incisions are small enough that they do not require sutures. Certain arthroscopic procedures can even be performed without the use of general anesthesia.

At its inception, arthroscopy was used as a diagnostic tool to avoid unnecessary arthrotomy of the knee. Advances in arthroscopic techniques have subsequently allowed for a variety of minimally invasive procedures to be performed in many joints throughout the body, often with better results than with open procedures. For example, the recovery period was often weeks or months and early degenerative changes of the knee were common after arthrotomy and meniscectomy. However, most patients are nearly recovered in 2 to 3 weeks and are functioning well at 12-year follow-up of knee arthroscopy performed for partial meniscectomy.

Whereas the accuracy of magnetic resonance imaging approaches 90% for meniscal tears, the sensitivity and accuracy for chondral surface lesions, such as occur with osteoarthritis, is low. One must therefore depend on clinical evaluation in determining whether to perform arthroscopy for joint pain. Arthroscopy is particularly useful in the arthritic knee, shoulder, or wrist that has symptoms directly attributable to a mechanical source, such as a meniscal tear (Fig. 293–1), chondral lesion, labral tear, or loose body. Arthroscopy also allows removal of anterior talotibial osteophytes that cause post-traumatic anterior ankle impingement. With advanced osteoarthritis, arthroscopic débridement and chondroplasty may provide short-term relief of symptoms but does not affect the natural history of the disease.

Arthroscopy also provides a minimally invasive method for synovectomy. This operation has proven particularly useful for reducing pain and increasing function in patients with synovitis due to inflammatory disease, hemophilic arthropathy, and pigmented villonodular synovitis. Arthroscopic synovectomy also appears to reduce the incidence of hemarthrosis in patients with hemophilia.

Arthroscopy of the hip is far less common than arthroscopy of the knee and shoulder. This is due, in part, to limited experience among surgeons and controversy regarding the indications. The three-dimensional architecture of the hip and surrounding soft tissues make it difficult to enter with an arthroscope. Complications, including transient nerve palsy, are not uncommon. However, in experienced hands, hip arthroscopy can be useful in removing loose bodies, débriding labral tears, and defining pathology in hips with pain of unknown etiology.

Osteotomy

An osteotomy is performed by cutting and realigning a bone. Common indications include correcting deformity from a malunited

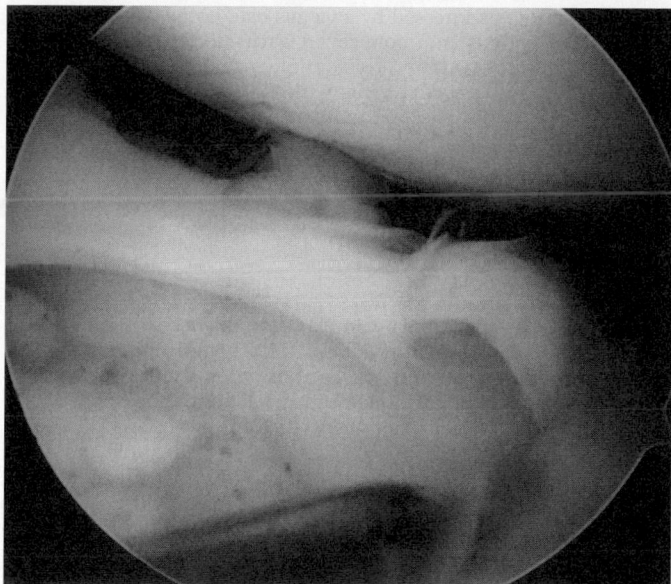

A

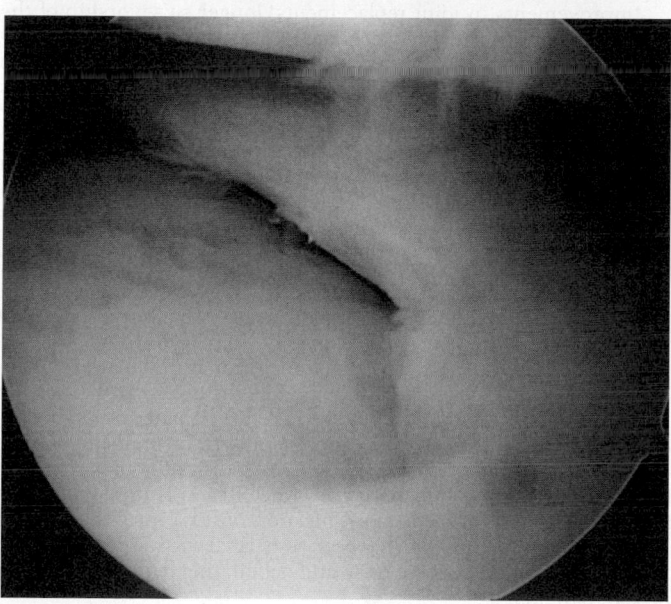

B

FIGURE 293–1 • Arthroscopic views of a degenerative medial meniscal tear before (*A*) and after (*B*) arthroscopic resection.

fracture, shortening to correct a limb length discrepancy, and redirecting weight-bearing forces from a diseased area of a joint to a healthy one.

HIP. Osteotomies are currently performed around the hip to relieve pain from dysplasia or osteonecrosis. In the dysplastic hip, the femoral head is covered by an abnormally small amount of acetabular surface area. This increases the overall pressure on the articular cartilage. A patient with a symptomatic dysplastic hip in whom the cartilage space is still preserved on plain radiographs may benefit from rotation of the acetabulum, femoral head, or both to distribute weight-bearing forces through a larger joint surface area. Similarly, in selected cases of symptomatic osteonecrosis of the femoral head, rotational osteotomy of the proximal femur allows displacement of the necrotic portion of the femoral head out of the weight-bearing area. Hip osteotomies are technically demanding and should only be performed in young patients with debilitating pain, despite residual cartilage thickness.

KNEE. Osteotomy in an arthritic knee is intended to redirect the weight-bearing axis away from a degenerative portion of the tibiofemoral articulation and through a portion where normal cartilage remains. This may also stimulate development of fibrocartilage in the newly unloaded degenerative areas. Arthritis with moderate varus deformity is addressed by a valgus osteotomy of the proximal tibia, whereas valgus and more severe varus deformities are treated by distal femoral osteotomy. This option is generally considered for young, heavy, and active patients with isolated unicompartmental, noninflammatory disease. Approximately 60 to 65% of patients continue to function well 10 years after the operation. Improvements in total knee arthroplasty function and longevity have led to a substantial decline in the number of osteotomies performed in the United States.

Arthrodesis

Arthrodesis, or fusion of a joint, is accomplished by removing the adjoining surfaces of two articulating bones and immobilizing the joint either externally or internally until union occurs. Arthrodesis is the surgical treatment of choice for intractable arthritic pain of subtalar and interphalangeal joints where replacement options are lacking. Despite recent developments in arthroplasty of the ankle and wrist, arthrodesis is still the principle operation for end-stage arthritis of these joints as well. Each has a high rate of fusion with predictable long-term durability. Recent data indicate that even with follow-up as long as 44 years, ankle arthrodesis is a durable solution for ankle arthritis and is not associated with ipsilateral knee pain or degeneration.

Improvements in joint replacements, longer survivorship of the prosthesis, improved revision techniques, and increasing patient expectations have led to a decline in the percentage of patients who choose arthrodesis over arthroplasty of the hip, knee, or shoulder. Arthrodesis may still be considered for a young person with severe monarticular arthritis who performs manual labor and is likely to outlive one or more prostheses in these joints. This procedure is effective both in relieving joint pain and in providing a stable and durable junction between two bones, even in the absence of neuromotor or ligamentous function. For these reasons, arthrodesis remains a useful operation for the treatment of shoulder dysfunction associated with brachial plexus injury, loss of deltoid function, or intractable instability. Knee fusion similarly provides relief of pain and a stable lower extremity in the absence of quadriceps or hamstring function.

Fused joints have obvious functional limitations that are unacceptable to many patients. Although elbow fusion can be reliably obtained, shoulder and wrist motion are inadequate to completely compensate for loss of elbow motion. Similarly, knee fusion is associated with many functional limitations, including difficulty in driving a car or using public transportation. Knee fusion is now typically a salvage operation for intractable infection or for a knee that cannot be reconstructed. Hip fusion has been associated with difficulty sitting, altered gait, ipsilateral knee pain, and debilitating back pain in up to 60% of patients.

Resection Arthroplasty

Resection arthroplasty is performed by removing one or both articular surfaces of a joint and allowing the bone ends to articulate. Initially described as the treatment for tuberculous arthritis of the hip, resection arthroplasty is now reserved for salvage of a persistently infected joint, a joint that cannot be reconstructed, or for treatment of hip arthritis in a motor compromised patient. An example of the latter is the patient with painful hip arthritis secondary to polio whose motor deficit does not provide the necessary soft tissue stability to permit total hip arthroplasty. The most common indication, however, remains recalcitrant infection after total hip arthroplasty. Despite the obvious associated limb shortening, most otherwise neurologically intact patients have complete eradication of any infection and remain ambulatory with the assistance of a shoe lift and walking aides.

Arthroplasty

HIP. Early arthroplasty involved placement of interposition materials between the acetabulum and the resected proximal femur of an arthritic or septic hip. Various materials were used, including wood, Pyrex, metal, and local soft tissues. From that point, a "cup," or mold arthroplasty was developed. It approximated the size and shape of the native femoral head that was removed with special gouges. While long-term successes have been reported, the majority of patients experienced prosthetic loosening, acetabular osteolysis, and early failure.

Hip arthroplasty was revolutionized when Sir John Charnley described low friction arthroplasty of the hip in the 1960s. His model of an acetabulum resurfaced with high-molecular-weight polyethylene matched with a small metal femoral head fixed to an intramedullary stem has been the basis of modern day total hip replacement.

It is estimated that more than 200,000 total hip arthroplasties are performed in the United States each year. Three decades of clinical experience and laboratory research have led to improved functional results and long-term durability. With dramatic reduction in the incidence of infection and other postoperative complications, aseptic loosening remains the predominant cause of failure over the life of the prosthesis. Extensive research with cell cultures, animal studies, and retrieved arthroplasty components have led to a better understanding of the sources of wear, characteristics of the particles, and the body's response to them. Particulate debris, the majority of which appears to come from wear of the polyethylene surface, stimulates osteoclastic bone resorption at the interface between the polymethylmethacrylate and bone in cemented devices, and between the porous-coated prosthesis and bone in cementless implants. Periprosthetic osteolysis can then lead to bone resorption, loosening, and even fracture of the bone or prosthesis. The development of radiographic evidence of osteolysis is usually slow and seldom presents before 5 years. It is therefore imperative that patients have regular clinical and radiographic follow-up for the remainder of their lives to detect impending failure early.

Improved cement techniques have led to a decreased incidence of loosening of the femoral component, such that successful femoral fixation may exceed 20 years. However, despite improved cement techniques, cemented acetabular components continue to have a high rate of failure. Cementless designs, which allow bone ingrowth into a porous surface on the component, have given rise to improved acetabular results, with loosening of less than 6% at 10 to 15 years after implantation. Therefore, cementless fixation is currently used almost universally for acetabular components. Femoral results have not had such a clear distinction. Although loosening rates as low as 3.4% at 15 years have been obtained with cementless femoral components, concerns about thigh pain and fixation in osteoporotic bone have led many surgeons to reserve them for younger patients.

KNEE. Although the majority of pioneering research in the field of total joint arthroplasty focused on the hip, the knee has become the most common site of joint replacement (Figs. 293–2 and 293–3). Total knee arthroplasty entails replacing the articular surfaces of the femur, tibia, and patella. Most total knee arthroplasties are performed with a tourniquet; thus, intraoperative blood loss is minimal. Component survivorship has been commonly reported as 95 to 97% at 10 years after implantation and up to 94.1% at 15 years. Similar to total hip arthroplasty, total knee arthroplasty may be performed with cement or bone ingrowth as the means of fixation. Regardless of the means of tibial and femoral fixation, clinical results and durability are excellent. Uncemented patellar components, however, require a metal-back for ingrowth, and therefore have a relatively thin polyethylene surface, as opposed to cemented patellar components, which are all polyethylene. The resultant mechanical problems with uncemented patellar designs have led to many early failures and a decrease in their use.

SHOULDER. Arthroplasty is performed much less commonly in the shoulder than in the hip or knee, possibly because it is a non–weight bearing joint. Thus far, results are promising with an estimated 92% survivorship of the component 5 years after implantation. Nearly all patients report substantial decrease in pain and increase in function. Glenoid component loosening is the most common mode of failure. To this end, hemiarthroplasty is commonly performed; that is, the humeral head is replaced but a congruent glenoid is left unresurfaced. Early data indicate similar pain relief and functional improvement whether or not the glenoid is replaced in patients with osteoarthritis and inflammatory disease.

ELBOW. Although there is less experience than with total hip and knee replacements, total elbow arthroplasty has seen significant advances in recent years. Loosening rates are high in young active patients with post-traumatic osteoarthritis, but 86% good or excellent results have been reported at 10- to 15-year follow-up in rheumatoid patients. In addition, the results approach those for total hip and knee arthroplasty, with approximately 90% survivorship of the elbow prosthesis more than 10 years after implantation.

ANKLE. The results with total ankle arthroplasty have been less encouraging than those in other major joints. Failures approach 50%

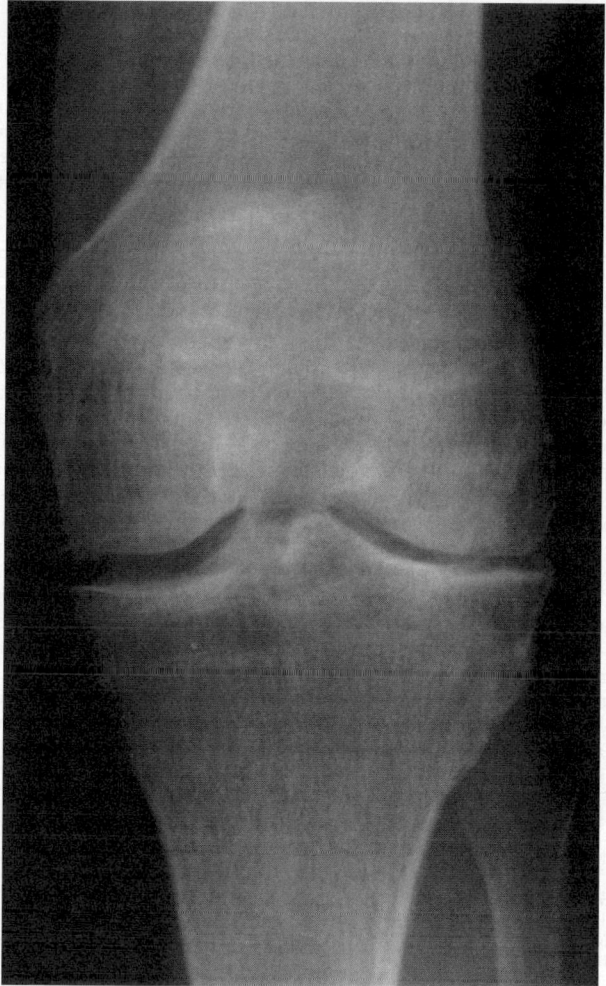

FIGURE 293–2 • Severe osteoarthritis of the knee. Classic radiographic findings include loss of joint space, osteophytes, and subchondral sclerosis. There is also varus deformity.

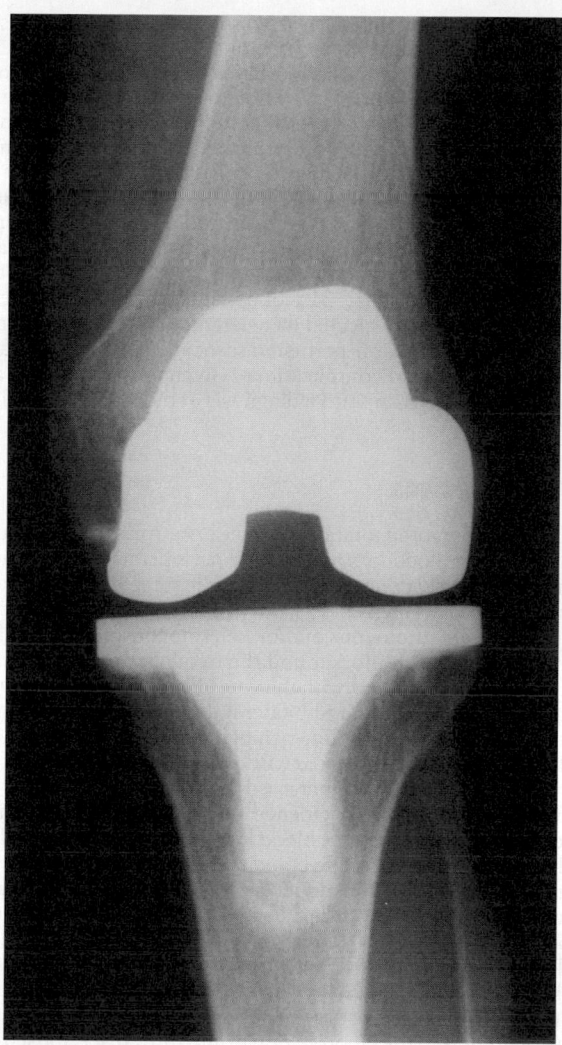

FIGURE 293–3 • Patient from Figure 293–2 after total knee arthroplasty. The distal femur and proximal tibia have been replaced with cemented metallic surfaces. The polyethylene spacer between the components is radiolucent.

at intermediate term follow-up, and some authors have recommended against various ankle prostheses. Newer techniques, including adjuvant fusion of the distal tibiofibular syndesmosis, may lead to improved longevity of the prosthesis, but long-term results are lacking. Most surgeons restrict ankle arthroplasty to elderly patients with inflammatory involvement of multiple joints.

PERIOPERATIVE COMPLICATIONS

Infection

The first major obstacle to joint arthroplasty was infection, which led to failure of total hip replacement in nearly 30% of early cases. Advances in the understanding and use of prophylactic antibiotics, body exhaust suits, laminar flow operating suites, and surgical efficiencies to reduce the time that the wound is open have all contributed to a reduction in postoperative infections. The accepted incidence of deep prosthetic infection now ranges from 0.5 to 2%. The most important risk factors include absence of prophylactic antibiotics, history of previous infection, multiple operations, and a draining wound postoperatively. The risk associated with persistent wound drainage is one reason that postoperative hematomas should be treated aggressively.

An infected total joint prosthesis requires surgical management. Deep infection of an otherwise stable prosthesis can be successfully treated with surgical irrigation and intravenous antibiotics if detected early. Chronic infections and those associated with one or more loose components typically require extirpation of all hardware and cement. An antibiotic-laden cement spacer provides a vehicle for high-dose local antibiotics and maintains soft tissue tension in the resected joint until eradication of infection is established.

The risk of deep infection of a total joint arthroplasty due to transient bacteremia from surgical and diagnostic procedures is controversial. Several reports have suggested that joint prostheses can be seeded by the bacteremia associated with dental procedures. For this reason, it is often recommended that 2 g of penicillin be given 1 hour before a dental procedure, followed by 1 g at 6 hours later. Erythromycin may be substituted for penicillin-sensitive patients. Oral antibiotics targeted at the local flora should be considered for other procedures likely to evoke a bacteremia.

Thromboembolic Disease

Thromboembolism is among the most serious potential complications of spine and major lower extremity procedures. The incidence of deep venous thrombosis (DVT) after hip or knee replacement is between 50 and 80%. The first peak incidence of DVT appears 48 to 72 hours postoperatively, followed by a second peak at 5 to 7 days, and even a third smaller peak at 6 weeks. More importantly, fatal pulmonary embolus may occur in up to 1% of knee replacement patients and 3% of hip replacement patients without appropriate prophylaxis.

Prophylactic measures include pharmaceutical agents and mechanical devices. Sequential compression devices are mechanical stockings that create a pressure gradient to enhance venous return. A meta-analysis of more than 10,000 patients has shown a significant reduction in postoperative thromboembolic events, including pulmonary embolism, with warfarin, pneumatic compression, and low-molecular-weight heparins. ◼ Warfarin, long considered the gold standard, was reported to be the safest and most effective agent. Low-molecular-weight heparins are convenient because they do not require

Rheumatic Diseases

laboratory monitoring, but they are associated with clinically significant postoperative bleeding in 3.5% of cases.

Whereas the morbidity and mortality associated with postoperative pulmonary embolism are well documented, it is equally important to understand the potential complications of heparin use. Approximately 45% of total joint arthroplasty patients have clinically significant bleeding if heparin is administered within the first week after surgery. Patients managed with heparin in the acute postoperative period have also been shown to be more likely to develop gastrointestinal bleeding, hematologic complications, hematoma formation, and early prosthetic loosening and revision. In a recent series from the Mayo Clinic, 31% of patients given heparin after pulmonary embolus was suspected were later found to have a normal or low probability ventilation-perfusion scan, and 52% of these patients had heparin-associated complications. Given these risks, it is advisable to withhold heparin until a diagnosis of pulmonary embolism is confirmed.

Blood Transfusions

Patients undergoing total hip or knee arthroplasty may incur clinically significant blood loss and require perioperative transfusion. In a recent multicenter survey of 330 orthopedic surgeons, 57% of patients who had a hip replacement and 39% of patients who had a knee replacement received an autologous and/or heterologous blood transfusion postoperatively. The authors found the frequency of allogenic blood transfusion to be associated with the type of operative procedure (revision total hip arthroplasty and bilateral total knee replacement were the most common) and baseline hemoglobin of 130 g/L or less. Blood transfusions were also associated with an increased incidence of infection, volume overload, and increased hospital stay.

Efforts to reduce the incidence of allogenic transfusion have included techniques to reduce blood loss intraoperatively, autologous blood donation, postoperative blood salvage, and the use of erythropoietin perioperatively. Tourniquet use is nearly universal in total knee replacement surgery; therefore, intraoperative blood loss is minimal. The peripheral vasodilatory effects of regional anesthetic and reduced blood loss with hypotensive anesthesia further help with intraoperative blood conservation. However, articular bone and soft tissue surfaces continue to bleed postoperatively. Combined with the effects of reentry of fluids into the blood stream from a third space, most patients continue to experience a decline in their hemoglobin for 2 to 3 days postoperatively.

Predonation of autologous blood has helped reduce the use of allogenic blood substantially, but is associated with significant cost as well as discomfort and inconvenience for the patient. In addition, there is the problem of overdonation, with approximately 50% of predonated autologous units being discarded after total hip or knee arthroplasty. Another alternative that has been recently revisited is the use of drains that collect blood postoperatively and allow its reinfusion. Postoperative blood salvage significantly reduces the risk of blood transfusion after total joint arthroplasty and is relatively inexpensive. In addition, recombinant DNA technology has recently made erythropoietin more readily available. Through optimization of the preoperative hematocrit, erythropoietin can further reduce the risk of postoperative transfusion, even in the patient undergoing revision surgery.

Heterotopic Ossification

Heterotopic ossification is not uncommon around the hip and elbow postoperatively. Fortunately, a small fraction of the patients with radiographic changes actually have clinical symptoms, which include decreased range of motion and sometimes pain from the associated inflammatory response. Prophylactic radiation should be considered for patients at high risk, including those with central nervous system injury, a history of traumatic dislocation, or diffuse idiopathic skeletal hyperostosis.

FUTURE DIRECTIONS

Arthroscopic débridement of articular lesions is a relatively minor surgical procedure with limited risks. Thermal instruments are currently being investigated in an effort to produce a more mechanically smooth surface without damaging underlying or surrounding cartilage. Further investigation is also underway to produce implants, living and artificial, to fill articular voids and restore the cartilaginous surface.

Even though arthroplasties have enjoyed terrific initial success in most patients, considerable attention continues to be directed at increasing the longevity of the implants. Increased cross-linking of the polyethylene through improved manufacturing and sterilization techniques may prove to be a critical step in reducing wear debris. Alternative bearing surfaces, including improved ceramic and metal-on-metal articulations, are also being explored. In addition to minimizing the production of wear particles, means of reducing the response to that debris are also being explored. One day, inhibition of various cell mediators may prove useful in the treatment or prevention of wear debris-induced osteolysis.

1. Freedman KB, Brookenthal KR, Fitzgerald RH, et al: A meta-analysis of thromboembolic prophylaxis following elective total hip arthroplasty. J Bone Joint Surg 2000;82–A:929–938.

SUGGESTED READINGS

Callaghan JJ, Albright JC, Goetz DD, et al: Charnley total hip arthroplasty with cement. Minimum twenty-five year follow-up. J Bone Joint Surg 2000;82:487–497. *Demonstrates the durability of this approach.*

Engh CA, Claus AM, Hopper RH, Engh CA. Long-term results using the anatomic medullary locking hip prosthesis. Clin Orthop 2001;393:137–146. *Cementless hips had less than a 10% loosening rate at a mean follow-up of 12.2 years.*

Fardet L, Messow M, Maillefert JF, et al: Primary glenohumeral degenerative joint disease: Factors predisposing to arthroplasty. Clin Exp Rheumatol 2003;21:13–18. *Osteonecrosis and non-eccentric glenohumeral head osteoarthritis increased the likelihood of arthroplasty.*

Gill GS, Mills D, Joshi AB: Mortality following primary total knee arthroplasty. J Bone Joint Surg Am 2003;85:432–435. *This study determined the mortality rate for patients undergoing primary total knee arthroplasty in a private practice setting involving one surgeon in a nonteaching institution. Increasing patient age and the presence of associated cardiovascular comorbid conditions were indentified as risk factors for mortality.*

Harris WH: Wear and periprosthetic osteolysis. The problem. Clin Orthop 2001;393:66–70. *Overview of how wear on the polyethylene leads to osteolysis, including radiologic diagnosis.*

Waters TS, Bentley G: Patellar resurfacing in total knee arthroplasty. A prospective, randomized study. J Bone Joint Surg Am 2003;85:212–217. *This study compared the outcome of resurfacing and nonresurfacing of the patella in patients undergoing total knee arthroplasty. Patients without a resurfaced patella had a significantly higher rate of anterior knee pain and the authors recommended patellar resurfacing at the time of total knee replacement.*

part XXIII

Infectious Diseases

294 INTRODUCTION TO MICROBIAL DISEASE

W. Michael Scheld
Gerald L. Mandell

Infectious diseases have profoundly influenced the course of human history. The "black death" (caused by *Yersinia pestis*) changed the social structure of medieval Europe, eliminating approximately one third of the population in the process. The outcomes of military campaigns have been altered by outbreaks of diseases such as dysentery and typhus. Examples include Napoleon's retreat from Russia after typhus did more damage to his army than the opposition forces, the decision by the French to sell the Louisiana territory following deaths of French soldiers from yellow fever in Cuba and the Gulf coast, and the introduction of smallpox to the nonimmune population of the New World by Europeans, thus facilitating the "conquest" and the dawn of the colonial age. Malaria influenced the geographic and racial pattern and distribution of hemoglobins and erythrocyte antigens in Africa. The development of *Plasmodium falciparum* is inhibited by the presence of hemoglobin S, and Duffy blood group–negative erythrocytes are resistant to infection with *Plasmodium vivax*. Thus, populations with these erythrocyte factors are found in areas where malaria is common.

Infections are the major cause of morbidity and mortality in the world. Of the approximately 53 million deaths worldwide in 2002, at least one third were due to infectious diseases. In the United States, pneumonia is the fifth leading cause of death overall, and the most common cause of death related to infection. In addition, invasive disease caused by *Streptococcus pneumoniae* and community-acquired pneumonia overall have increased in incidence over the past decade. The acquired immunodeficiency syndrome (AIDS) threatens to disrupt the social fabric in many countries of Africa, and is severely distressing the health care system in the United States and in other parts of the world.

Infection may be defined as multiplication of microbes (e.g., viruses to multicellular parasites) in the tissues of the host. The host may or may not be symptomatic. For example, infection with the human immunodeficiency virus (HIV) may cause no overt signs or symptoms of illness for years. The definition of infection should also include instances of multiplication of microbes on the surface or in the lumen of the host, causing signs and symptoms of illness or disease. For example, toxin-producing strains of *Escherichia coli* may multiply in the gut and cause a diarrheal illness without invading tissues. Microbes can cause diseases without actually coming in contact with the host by virtue of toxin production. *Clostridium botulinum* may grow in certain improperly processed foods and produce a toxin that can be lethal on ingestion. A relatively trivial infection such as that caused by *Clostridium tetani* in a small puncture wound can cause devastating illness because of a toxin released from the organism growing in the tissues. It has now become apparent that multiple virulence factors of microorganisms may be carried in tandem on so-called pathogenicity islands of the genome.

We live in a virtual sea of microorganisms, and all our body surfaces have an indigenous bacterial flora. This normal flora actually protects us from infection. Reduction of gut colonization increases susceptibility to infection by pathogens such as *Salmonella enteritidis* serovar *typhimurium*. Bacteria that constitute the normal flora are thought to exert their protective effect by several mechanisms: (1) utilizing nutrients and occupying an ecologic niche, thus competing with pathogens; (2) producing antibacterial substances that inhibit the growth of pathogens; and (3) inducing host immunity that is cross-reactive and effective against pathogens. In addition to the normal flora, transient colonization may be seen with known or potential pathogens. This may be a special problem in hospitalized patients, leading to nosocomial infection (Chapter 299).

Only a small proportion of microbial species may be considered to be primary or professional pathogens, and even among these species a relatively small number of clones have been shown to cause disease (Chapter 301). For example, epidemic meningococcal meningitis and meningococcemia are due to a small number of clones of *Neisseria meningitidis*, and the worldwide explosion of penicillin-resistant *Streptococcus pneumoniae* can be traced to a few clones originating in South Africa and Spain. This observation supports the concept that pathogenic organisms are highly adapted to the pathogenic state and have developed characteristics that enable them to be transmitted, to attach to surfaces, to invade tissue, to avoid host defenses, and, thus, to cause disease. In contrast, opportunistic pathogens cause disease principally in impaired hosts, and these organisms, which may be harmless members of normal flora in healthy persons, may act as virulent invaders in patients with severe defects in host defense mechanisms.

Pathogenic organisms may be acquired by several routes. Direct contact has been implicated in the acquisition of staphylococcal disease. Airborne spread, usually by droplet nuclei, occurs in respiratory diseases such as influenza and in severe acute respiratory syndrome (SARS). Contaminated water is the usual vehicle in *Giardia* infection and typhoid fever. Foodborne toxic illnesses may be caused by extracellular toxins, produced by *Clostridium perfringens* and *Staphylococcus aureus*. Blood and blood products may be vectors for transmitting hepatitis B and C viruses as well as HIV. Sexual transmission is also important for these agents and for a variety of pathogens including *Treponema pallidum* (syphilis), *Neisseria gonorrhoeae* (gonorrhea), and *Chlamydia trachomatis* (nonspecific urethritis). The fetus may be infected in utero, and the infection may be devastating if the agent is rubella virus or cytomegalovirus. Arthropod vectors may be important, as illustrated by mosquitoes for malaria, ticks for Lyme disease and ehrlichiosis, and lice for typhus.

Pathogens are able to cause disease because of a finely tuned array of adaptations. These include the ability to attach to appropriate cells, often mediated by specialized structures such as the pili on gram-negative rods. Microbes such as *Shigella* species have the ability to invade cells and cause damage. Toxins may act at a distance or may intoxicate only infected cells. Pathogens have the ability to thwart host defenses by a variety of ingenious maneuvers. The antiphagocytic coat of the pneumococcus is an example. Organisms may change their surface antigen display at an astonishingly rapid rate to outmaneuver the host immune system. Examples include influenza virus and trypanosomes. Certain pathogens have the ability to inhibit the respiratory burst of phagocytes (*Toxoplasma gondii*), and others can destroy phagocytic cells that have engulfed them (e.g., *Streptococcus pyogenes*). The environment plays an important role in infection, both in transmission and in the ability of the host to combat the invader. The humidity and temperature of air may affect the infectivity of airborne pathogens. The sanitary state of food and water, woefully lacking in many areas of the developing world, is an important factor in the acquisition of enteric pathogens, one of the major causes of mortality and morbidity, such as physical and mental developmental delay leading to poor performance in school and other consequences. The malaria associated with the "bad air" of swamps is, in fact, due to the mosquitoes, but the environmental association was appropriate. The nutritional status of the host is clearly a significant factor in certain infectious diseases. It is likely that micronutrient deficiency contributes to the invasion and multiplication of certain bacterial pathogens. The establishment of infection is a complicated interplay of factors involving the microbe, the host, and the environment.

Host reaction to infection may result in illness. For example, prior infection with *Campylobacter jejuni* is responsible for about 40% of cases of Guillain-Barré syndrome. The mechanism is thought to be production of antibodies against *C. jejuni* lipopolysaccharides that cross-react with gangliosides in peripheral nerves. Similarly, much of the damage resulting from meningitis is due to the host response to invading bacterial pathogens.

With unusual exceptions, infectious diseases are often treatable and curable. Thus, it is important to make an accurate etiologic diagnosis and institute appropriate therapy promptly. In acute infections such as pneumonia, meningitis, or sepsis, rapid institution of therapy may be life-saving and thus a presumptive etiologic diagnosis should be established before a definitive diagnosis. This presumptive diagnosis is based on the history, physical examination, epidemiology of illness in the community, and rapid techniques such as microscopic examination of appropriate Gram-stained specimens. Antimicrobial therapy can then be instituted for the presumptive etiologic agents, but must be reevaluated as more definitive diagnostic information becomes available.

Finally, at risk of alienating colleagues in other disciplines, it must be stated that infectious disease is by far the most dynamic of subspecialties of internal medicine. A number of factors or themes of current interest contribute to this conclusion, including the following:

1. *Emerging infections.* The most obvious is AIDS, but scores of pathogens, new diseases, and new syndromes have been described in the past 2 decades. West Nile virus is now firmly entrenched in the Western Hemisphere. Since 2002, several new pathogens have been described, including a human metapneumovirus responsible for upper and lower respiratory tract infections and perhaps occasional asthma in both children and adults. A novel coronavirus is associated with SARS, a new worldwide epidemic of atypical pneumonia first described in March 2003. A roundworm associated with raccoons that can cause fatal encephalitis is now evident. The second report from the Institute of Medicine on emerging infections (February 2003) will undoubtedly shape the framework for a response by the Centers for Disease Control and Prevention and other agencies.

2. *Genomics.* The exact sequence of the genome of more than 150 pathogens relevant to humans has been determined in less than a decade. This new information, in concert with genomic information from multicellular organisms such as the *Anopheles* mosquito, offers significant promise for the development of new therapies and vaccines.

3. *Genetic factors altering susceptibility to infection and the response to infectious diseases.* This field, although in its infancy, promises new and significant information relevant to the wide variety of responses to infectious diseases among humans. For example, an overvigorous response with generation of tumor necrosis factor-α may accentuate the development of cerebral complications in falciparum malaria.

4. *Antimicrobial resistance.* It is perhaps surprising (if not frightening) that the development of new antimicrobial agents has slowed despite the burgeoning problem of antimicrobial resistance. This disconnect has been the focus of meetings among the pharmaceutical industry, the Infectious Disease Society of America, and the Food and Drug Administration. Multiresistant pneumococci, vancomycin resistance in *Staphylococcus aureus*, and vancomycin-resistant enterococci are just a few examples among many that have emerged.

5. *The role of infectious agents in chronic diseases.* Many so-called idiopathic diseases may in fact have an infectious basis. A list of conditions for which there is some evidence (but not conclusive evidence) includes diabetes, atherosclerosis, acute leukemia, collagen vascular diseases, and inflammatory bowel disease. In addition, we know that hepatitis C virus and human papillomavirus cause human cancers.

6. *New therapies.* The number of antivirals has more than quadrupled since the 19th edition of this textbook. Furthermore, immunotherapy or adjunctive agents hold promise for the treatment of various diseases. Examples include activated protein C (drotrecogin alfa) for sepsis and septic shock and, perhaps, interleukin-2 in the therapy of advanced AIDS.

7. *Bioterrorism.* The anthrax attacks of late 2001 in the eastern United States have brought this issue to the attention of politicians, public health authorities, physicians in general, and the public. This situation has been expressed well by George F. Will in contrasting one of the greatest scientific achievements of the 20th century with our current predicament as, "No human achievement has done more to lessen suffering for a larger number of people than has the conquest of infectious diseases, such as smallpox. And nothing more succinctly sums up the odiousness of our enemies than their contemplated reintroduction of some of the indiscriminate promiscuous killers into the human story" (*Newsweek*, November 11, 2002). Experts within and outside the discipline of infectious diseases are currently struggling with smallpox vaccination policies. A vaccine with considerable adverse effects is to be utilized in military personnel and health care workers in a setting where the natural disease does not exist. This is a unique experiment. The consequences are not insignificant because the actual risk of a deliberate smallpox event is unknown at present. The benefit of smallpox vaccination in this setting is not measurable in the absence of the disease, whereas the adverse effects are readily measurable and may lead to the reluctance of the public to accept vaccination against other pathogens. This would be an unfortunate outcome because vaccination to prevent infection is probably the greatest achievement of medical science.

295 THE FEBRILE PATIENT

David C. Dale

Fever, or *pyrexia*, is an elevation of body temperature to a level greater than normal—that is, greater than 37.5° C (99.5° F)—caused by resetting of the thermoregulatory center in the medulla. To detect fever, oral, rectal, tympanic membrane, and pulmonary artery measurements are more reliable than axillary temperatures. Fever is a useful marker of inflammation; usually the height of the fever reflects the severity of the inflammatory process. Anorexia, malaise, myalgias, headache, and other constitutional symptoms often occur at the same time. When the body temperature changes rapidly, chills and sweats are also observed. Fever with night sweats is a feature of many chronic inflammatory conditions. *Hyperthermia* is a term for fever caused by a disturbance in thermal regulatory control: excessive heat production (e.g., with vigorous exercise or as a reaction to some anesthetics), decreased dissipation (e.g., with dehydration), or loss of regulation (e.g., from injury to the hypothalamic regulatory center).

Most febrile patients have pain, tenderness, redness, and swelling at the site of inflammation, and the cause of the fever is readily identified. In a general medical practice, the most common causes of fever are upper respiratory illnesses, urinary tract infections, cellulitis, superficial abscesses, and pneumonia. In otherwise healthy individuals, fever alone is not a cause for hospitalization unless the temperature is high (>39° C or 102° F) or accompanied by shaking, chills, hypotension, a change in sensorium, or other symptoms suggesting bacteremia. However, in immunosuppressed individuals, the elderly, and patients with recent surgery, in intensive care units, or living in long-term care facilities, greater caution is indicated.

FEVER OF UNEXPLAINED ORIGIN

An unexplained fever is usually defined in adults as an illness lasting more than 3 weeks with temperatures greater than 101° F (38.3° C) in which a diagnosis has not been made despite a good hospital or office evaluation. Ordinarily, by this time the work-up has included a history, physical examination, routine blood and urine tests and cultures, radiographs, and some specialized serologic tests. With careful further evaluation, a diagnosis can be made in 70 to 90% of these cases.

Diagnoses for unexplained fevers fall into six general categories: infections, noninfectious inflammatory conditions, neoplastic diseases, drug fevers, factitious illnesses, and a group of less common causes (Table 295–1). The pattern of fever is only occasionally helpful in pointing to a specific diagnosis, such as the alternate-day fever in established *Plasmodium vivax* infections, the sustained fever in untreated *Salmonella typhi* infections and other continuous bacteremias, and the relapsing (Pel-Ebstein) fever in Hodgkin's disease and other lymphomas.

Evaluation of Patients

In patients with persistent fever, it is important initially to review carefully the medical history and repeat the physical examination. New clues may be found in the social, occupational, travel, and medication history. On physical examination, special attention should be given to the skin, lymph nodes (including epitrochlear, postauricular and axillary), mucous membranes (including the conjunctivae), and abdominal region (masses, tenderness, and size of the liver and spleen). Usually the basic laboratory tests—complete blood count, differential, sedimentation rate, urinalysis, liver function tests, skin tests for delayed hypersensitivity (e.g., purified protein derivative, mumps), and stool for occult blood—should be repeated. Most patients with active inflammation are anemic, and the leukocyte differential can provide valuable clues. Neutrophilia suggests an occult bacterial infection. Monocytosis suggests tuberculosis, brucellosis, inflammatory bowel disease, or other chronic inflammatory conditions. Severe lymphopenia suggests immunodeficiency or a malignancy. A very elevated sedimentation rate suggests giant cell/temporal arteritis, polymyalgia rheumatica, Still's disease, bacterial endocarditis, or other occult infections, and a normal test rarely occurs with any of these illnesses. If the alkaline phosphatase level is elevated, obstructive or infiltrative disease of the liver is the most likely cause, although

Table 295–1 • CAUSES OF FEVER OF UNKNOWN ORIGIN

INFECTIONS

Abscesses—hepatic, subhepatic, gallbladder, subphrenic, splenic, periappendiceal, perinephric, pelvic, and other sites
Granulomatous—extrapulmonary and miliary tuberculosis, atypical mycobacterial infection, fungal infection
Intravascular—catheter-related endocarditis, meningococcemia, gonococcemia, *Listeria*, *Brucella*, rat-bite fever, relapsing fever
Viral, rickettsial, and chlamydial—infectious mononucleosis, cytomegalovirus, human immunodeficiency virus, hepatitis, Q fever, psittacosis
Parasitic—extraintestinal amebiasis, malaria, toxoplasmosis

NONINFECTIOUS INFLAMMATORY DISORDERS

Collagen vascular diseases—rheumatic fever, systemic lupus erythematosus, rheumatoid arthritis (particularly Still's disease), vasculitis (all types)
Granulomatous—sarcoidosis, granulomatous hepatitis, Crohn's disease
Tissue injury—pulmonary emboli, sickle cell disease, hemolytic anemia

NEOPLASTIC DISEASES

Lymphoma/leukemia—Hodgkin's and non–Hodgkin's lymphoma, acute leukemia, myelodysplastic syndrome
Carcinoma—kidney, pancreas, liver, gastrointestinal tract, lung, especially when metastatic
Atrial myxomas
Central nervous system tumors

DRUG FEVERS

Sulfonamides, penicillins, thiouracils, barbiturates, quinidine, laxatives (especially with phenolphthalein)

FACTITIOUS ILLNESSES

Injections of toxic material, manipulation or exchange of thermometers

OTHER CAUSES

Familial Mediterranean fever, Fabry's disease, cyclic neutropenia

---

nonspecific elevation is not uncommon. Other tests (e.g., antinuclear antibodies, febrile agglutinins, complement assays) may be positive but are rarely helpful in evaluation of unexplained fever.

A definitive diagnosis is usually made through a combination of imaging studies, microbiologic tests, and/or biopsies. Previous radiographs should be carefully reviewed for evidence of sinusitis, apical inflammation or small nodules in the lungs, hilar adenopathy, or an intra-abdominal mass. Abdominal ultrasonography, gallium and radioisotopically labeled leukocyte scans, computed tomography, and magnetic resonance imaging are helpful in examining the liver, gallbladder, spleen, and pelvic areas for tumors and abscesses. These tests have reduced the need for exploratory laparotomies.

Cultures of blood (including for *Mycobacterium avium* in human immunodeficiency virus–infected patients), urine (including mycobacterial cultures if tuberculosis is suspected), and other body fluids (e.g., cerebrospinal, peritoneal, pleural) should be obtained if suggested by clinical examination. It is useful to perform anaerobic cultures of material from suspected abscess cavities and to examine blood cultures for fastidious bacteria, yeast, and fungi in difficult cases. A tissue diagnosis can often be made from a biopsy of abnormal skin, lymph nodes, or the bone marrow. Biopsy or needle aspiration of liver, lung, bone, or other deep tissue sites is also valuable when abscesses or tumors are suspected.

Rx Therapy

Antipyretics are regularly prescribed for febrile patients, but the evidence for benefit from reducing fever is limited. Therapeutic trials with antibiotics, corticosteroids, or antipyretics in patients with unexplained fever before the diagnosis is clear can confuse the evaluation. In some instances, a trial may be justified but should be time limited (about 2 weeks). In patients with deep tissue abscesses, fever usually persists despite antibiotics. In patients with noninfectious inflammatory diseases (e.g., sarcoidosis, Still's disease, or vasculitis), a good clinical diagnosis can usually be made before such therapy is begun. In patients with malignancies, rational therapy depends on a tissue diagnosis. Patients with factitious illness often have serious underlying psychiatric

disorders. Careful management is essential to prevent desperate acts, including suicide.

Extensive work-ups of unexplained fevers can be very expensive. In every patient, the need for hospital care and testing should be continually reassessed. When the patient is not severely ill, it is frequently worthwhile to use observation alone as a diagnostic tool. Sometimes even a short period of observation allows an obscure diagnosis to become obvious. In other cases, the fever disappears without the necessity for further diagnostic tests.

SUGGESTED READINGS

Arnow PM, Flaherty JP: Fever of unknown origin. Lancet 1997;350:575–580. *A succinct summary of the causes of unexplained fever category by category.*
Bentley DW, Bradley S, High K, et al: Practice guideline for evaluation of fever and infection in long-term care facilities. Clin Infect Dis 2000;31:640–653. *An excellent review for care of patients in long-term care and skilled nursing facilities, including evidence-based recommendations.*
Bodey GP, Rolston KV: Management of fever in neutropenic patients. J Infect Chemother 2001;1:1–9. *A careful review focusing on management of fever and neutropenia after chemotherapy for cancer.*
de Kleijn EM, van Lier HJ, van der Meer JW: Fever of unknown origin (FUO). II. Diagnostic procedures in a prospective multicenter study of 167 patients. The Netherlands FUO Study Group. Medicine (Baltimore) 1997;76:401–414. *A report on the value of diagnostic tests and procedures in a series of 167 patients recently evaluated for unexplained fever.*
Knockaert DC, Vanderschueren S, Blockmans D: Fever of unknown origin in adults: 40 years on. J Intern Med 2003;253:263–275. *A useful summary of adults with fever of unknown origin including comments on newer imaging modalities for the diagnosis of FUO.*
Mackowiak PA: Diagnostic implications and clinical consequences of antipyretic therapy. Clin Infect Dis 2000;31:S230–S233. *A scholarly report on antipyretic drugs. Part of a special issue of this journal on antipyretic pharmacotherapy.*
Marik PE: Fever in the ICU. Chest 2000;117:855–869. *An excellent review of temperature measurements and their clinical implications for patients in intensive care units.*
Mourad O, Palda V, Detsky AS: A comprehensive evidence-based approach to fever of unknown origin. Arch Intern Med 2003;163:545–551. *An excellent analytical review pointing to the best approach to the diagnosis of fever of unknown origin.*
Sullivan M, Fineberg J, Bartlett JG: Fever in patients with HIV infection. Infect Dis Clinic North Am 1996;10:149–165. *A good summary of the causes of fever in patients with HIV infection. This issue also contains a series of other excellent articles on evaluating patients with fever.*
Tal S, Guller V, Gurevich A, et al: Fever of unknown origin in the elderly. J Intern Med 2002;252:295–304. *A comprehensive review of FUO in the elderly.*
Vanderschueren S, Knockaert D, Adriaenssens T, et al: From prolonged febrile illness to fever of unknown origin: The challenge continues. Arch Intern Med 2003;163:1003–1004. *A careful review of 290 immunocompetent patients referred for evaluation of fever of unknown origin.*

296 THE PATHOGENESIS OF FEVER

Bruce Beutler
Steven M. Beutler

Definition

Fever (pyrexia) is defined as an elevation of core body temperature above the level normally maintained by the individual. Under normal circumstances, core body temperature (the temperature of blood in the right atrium) is tightly regulated, with circadian variations over a range that usually does not exceed 1° F (0.6° C) and a mean value of 98.6° F (37° C) (the normal "set-point"). An array of thermoregulatory mechanisms, described in detail here, ensure that this temperature is maintained. During episodes of fever, the thermoregulatory set-point is shifted such that the same thermoregulatory mechanisms are used to maintain an abnormally elevated temperature.

It is important to realize that fever is not equivalent to an elevated core temperature but to an elevated set-point. Under many circumstances, ranging from intense physical exertion to immersion in hot liquids, core temperature may be elevated yet fever does not exist because the body is attempting to cope with the departure from homeostasis. Failure of thermoregulation may also be associated with elevated core temperature; this problem too (which occurs in malignant hyperthermia) is distinct from fever.

Thermoregulatory Mechanisms

Core body temperature is determined by two opposing processes, each of which is regulated by the central nervous system. On the one

Table 296–1 • FEVER PATTERNS AS DIAGNOSTIC CLUES

FEVER PATTERN	CAUSE
Alternate-day fever	*Plasmodium vivax, P. ovale*
Fever every third day	*P. malariae*
Relapsing fever: daily for 3 to 6 days; fever-free interval for about 1 week supervenes	*Borrelia* spp., rat-bite fever (*Streptobacillus moniliformis; Spirillum minus*)
Continuous "undulating fever"	Brucellosis; typhoid
Periodic pyrexia (Pel-Ebstein phenomenon) with variable cycles	Hodgkin's disease

hand, energy in the form of heat is generated by living tissues ("thermogenesis"). Energy may be passively absorbed from the environment as well. On the other hand, energy is inevitably lost to the environment, chiefly through the emission of infrared radiation and through transfer of energy to the surrounding medium. The temperature at which tissues are maintained is related to heat capacity (e.g., to the amount of energy required to elevate temperature by a defined increment) and to the quantity of energy lost or gained by the system.

Metabolic reactions proceed more rapidly at an elevated temperature. Therefore, the passive warming effect of a febrile state leads to accelerated energy production in the form of heat: for each temperature increment of $1°$ F ($0.6°$ C), the basal metabolic rate increases by approximately 10%. This increase may at times be quite significant from a nutritional point of view.

Muscle is a particularly flexible transducer of chemical energy. "Shivering thermogenesis" refers to the unconscious process whereby muscles are recruited to produce energy through the exercise of activity. Such induction of energy leads to enhanced metabolic demand, which is one mechanism responsible for the rise in body temperature in fever. Hence a sharp "chill" often heralds the onset of fever.

Conservation of energy is effected through piloerection in mammals other than humans. In humans, "gooseflesh" is the equivalent response. "Flushing" represents a redistribution of circulation to dermal vessels and facilitates heat loss; a blanched appearance of the skin indicates an attempt to conserve heat.

Initiation of Fever

The neural pathways responsible for thermoregulation originate in the hypothalamus. A local sensing mechanism exists wherein the temperature of blood is coupled to the development of autonomic discharge. Elevation of body temperature depends primarily on sympathetic outflow and leads to shivering thermogenesis and dermal vasoconstriction, whereas cooling mechanisms (sweating and dermal vasodilation) involve a mixture of sympathetic and parasympathetic pathways.

Certain neurotropic drugs can disrupt the hypothalamic thermosensory mechanism—or blunt the hypothalamic response—and thus may interfere with the development of fever. Among these drugs, phenothiazines are the best known for their "poikilothermic" effect. These agents are not specifically active in febrile states; rather, they act to disable thermoregulatory mechanisms.

Clinical Manifestations

Although fever patterns tend to be nonspecific, they may sometimes provide diagnostic clues (Table 296–1). Intermittent fevers are seen in many conditions and are, therefore, of little help in discriminating between various disorders. Intermittent fever may also occur when a continuous fever is interrupted with antipyretics or cooling measures: such interventions must be taken into account in analysis of a temperature curve.

In addition to considering patterns of pyrexia, it is worthwhile to note the relationship between core temperature and other vital signs. For example, dissociation between the temperature and pulse is sometimes seen in cases of typhoid fever, Legionnaires' disease, psittacosis, and brucellosis. Factitious fever is also accompanied by an inappropriately low pulse. In addition, the respiratory rate may remain normal, and superimposed diurnal variations in temperature may be absent.

Drug fever may occur in association with nearly any medication. No fever pattern is characteristic. Fevers caused by drug allergy tend to be well tolerated and may be accompanied by other allergic phenomena such as rash, nephritis, or neutropenia in 20 to 60% of patients. Neoplasia is often associated with fever, which frequently responds dramatically to one or two doses of nonsteroidal anti-inflammatory agents. Other noninfectious causes of fever include adrenal insufficiency, especially in cases of adrenal crisis; thyroid storm; and a variety of rheumatologic conditions.

Extreme pyrexia (characterized by a core temperature higher than $106°$ F) often indicates failure of a distal mechanism of thermoregulation occurring alone or in combination with infection. Examples of noninfectious causes of such extreme pyrexia include heat stroke (Chapters 97), neuroleptic malignant syndrome (Chapters 105 and 460), and malignant hyperthermia associated with succinylcholine.

Initial Events During Infection

ACTIVATION OF THE INNATE IMMUNE RESPONSE

The innate immune system of the host is ultimately responsible for the development of infectious fevers. The initial events that occur to permit this are now understood in considerable detail. The most impressive advance in this area has been the identification of cell surface receptors that actually "sense" microbial infection by interacting with molecules of microbial origin. These receptors are the *causa causans* of fevers (and for that matter, all forms of inflammation) that attend infection.

Macrophages and dendritic cells are among the first components of the innate immune system to encounter infectious agents or their products. These cells sense infection chiefly through a family of single-spanning plasma membrane proteins known as Toll-like receptors (TLRs). The human genome contains 10 TLR genes, and each TLR recognizes a limited repertoire of microbial molecules that are represented across a broad range of microbial taxa and indispensable for microbial survival. For example, TLR4 recognizes lipopolysaccharides, the major component of the outer membrane of virtually all gram-negative bacteria. TLR2 recognizes peptidoglycan, an essential structural component of all gram-negative and gram-positive bacterial cell walls. TLR5 recognizes flagellin, and TLR9 recognizes DNA lacking methyl groups on the cytosine of CpG dinucleotides—a form of DNA represented in all microorganisms. Upon contact with these diverse microbial inducers, TLRs generate signals that lead to the elaboration of inflammatory cytokines such as tumor necrosis factor (TNF) and interleukin-1, -6, and -12. These, in turn, abet both the innate immune response and the adaptive immune response, and mediate fever. Because microbial inducers and secreted cytokines can both gain access to the plasma, a localized infection can cause effects at a distance. Fever induction is among these effects.

CYTOKINES AND FEVER

Hypothalamic dysregulation and fever result when cytokines of innate immune origin interact with cells of the central nervous system (Fig. 296–1). This communication between the immune system and the nervous system is perhaps the most thoroughly studied "neuroimmunoendocrine" link. During the past two decades, several of the cytokines active in the pathogenesis of fever have been isolated, and their structures have been determined by molecular cloning. As of this writing, 11 proteins with pyrogenic activity have been identified (Table 296–2). Although mononuclear phagocytes are the principal source of pyrogenic cytokines, the same proteins may sometimes originate from nonimmune cells of neoplastic tissue through autonomous production and secretion.

The pyrogenic cytokines are structurally diverse proteins with well-established effects in hematopoiesis, inflammation, and regulation of cell metabolism. Individual agents are often markedly pleiotropic in their actions. In addition to their involvement in mediating fever, cytokines mediate the "acute-phase response" (Chapter 297), which is characterized by increased production of "acute-phase reactants" in the liver (fibrinogen, C-reactive protein, complement proteins B, C3, C4, α_2-acid glycoprotein, serum amyloid A, and a variety of proteinase inhibitors among them), decreased production of albumin

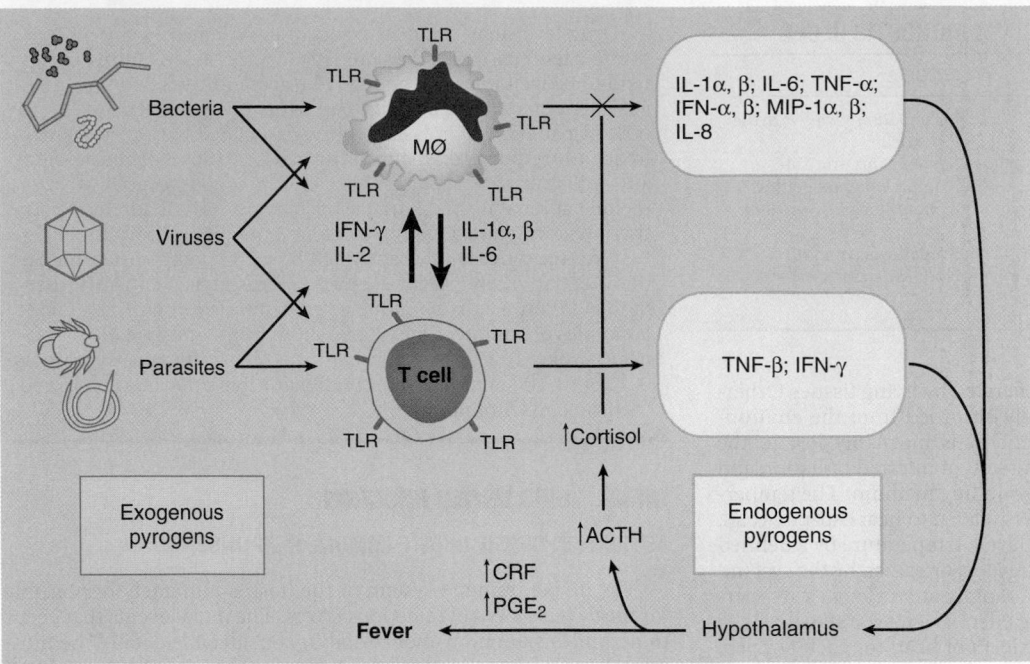

FIGURE 296–1 • Production of endogenous pyrogens by macrophages and T lymphocytes. A variety of microbial pathogens produce molecules that function as exogenous pyrogens and trigger the release of endogenous pyrogens from mononuclear cells. IL = interleukin; TNF = tumor necrosis factor; IFN = interferon; MIP = macrophage inflammatory protein; ACTH = adrenocorticotropic hormone; CRF = corticotropin releasing factor; PGE₂ = prostaglandin E₂.

Table 296–2 • PROTEINS WITH PYROGENIC ACTIVITY

ENDOGENOUS PYROGEN	PRINCIPAL SOURCE	INDUCED BY	PRINCIPAL EFFECTS IN ADDITION TO PYROGENESIS	PHYSICAL CHARACTERISTICS
Tumor necrosis factor α	Macrophages	LPS, other microbial products	Fever, shock, anorexia, tumor necrosis, bone resorption, ↓ adipocyte lipoprotein lipase, neutrophils activation, ↑ endothelial cell adhesiveness/procoagulant effect	Homotrimer; 17 kD subunit size (nonglycosylated) ↓26% identity
Lymphotoxin/tumor necrosis factor	Lymphocytes (T & B)	Antigenic/mitogenic stimulation		Homotrimer; 20–25 kD subunit size (glycosylated)
Interleukin-1α	Macrophages and many other cell types	LPS, other microbial products, TNF	Fever, interleukin-2 production, bone resorption, pannus formation, neutrophil activation, ↑ endothelial cell adhesiveness/procoagulant effect	Monomer; 17 kD (glycosylated) ↓26% identity
Interleukin-1β				Monomer; 17 kD (glycosylated)
Interferon-α	Leukocytes (esp. monocyte-macrophages)		Induction of antiviral state	22 kd (glycosylated) ↓23% identify
Interferon-β	Fibroblasts	LPS, viral infection, double-stranded RNA		22 kD (glycosylated)
Interferon-γ	T lymphocytes		Macrophage activation Up-regulation of class I and class II MHC molecules	20–25 kD (glycosylated)
Interleukin-6	Many cell type	LPS, TNF	↑ Synthesis of acute-phase reactants Weak antiviral effect Terminal differentiation of B cells; T-cell activation	21–26 kD (glycosylated)
Macrophage inflammatory protein 1α		LPS		7.9 kD (nonglycosylated) ↓57% identify
Macrophage inflammatory protein 1β	Macrophages		Neutrophil chemotaxis	7.8 kD (nonglycosylated)
Interleukin-8		LPS, TNF; interleukin-1		8.0 kD (nonglycosylated)

LPS = liposaccharide; TNF = tumor necrosis factor.

and transferrin, hypoferremia, hypertriglyceridemia, and other metabolic changes.

Pyrogenic cytokines are presumed to bind to receptors present on vascular endothelial cells that lie within the hypothalamus. They act to reset the hypothalamic thermoregulatory center by prompting an elevation in core body temperature. The resetting is believed to depend largely on endothelial cells producing prostaglandins (PGE₂ and perhaps PGE₂α). Thromboxanes and lipoxygenase products may also affect the set-point. Cytokines can also interact directly with neural tissues; some evidence suggests that the release of corticotropin-releasing factor may trigger thermogenesis in response to at least one cytokine (interleukin-1β).

Although no single cytokine is capable of provoking fever of a magnitude equivalent to that elicited by endotoxin, it is probable that the combined production of several cytokines is sufficient to explain most fevers.

One cytokine, known as TNF-α, seems capable of producing many of the physiologic derangements observed in septic shock and thus appears to mediate most of the deleterious effects of bacterial endotoxin, including fever. A lymphokine known as lymphotoxin (also referred to as TNF-β) is homologous to TNF-α, binds to the same receptors as TNF-α, and elicits many of the same effects. Two other cytokines (interleukin-1α and interleukin-1β), although incapable of causing shock by themselves, produce many effects similar to those of TNF-α, and in some instances, synergistic responses have been noted. Similarly, interferons of the α/β type can synergize with TNF-α in some of its effects.

Many of the cytokines are mutually inducing, and the concept of a "cytokine cascade" has been offered to describe the production of several factors occurring in response to the elaboration of one member of the group. The temporal sequence of induction may be reflected in the course of fever in vivo. For example, injecting a bolus of TNF-α into a rabbit will immediately raise body temperature and cause a delayed rise, apparently related to secondary production of interleukin-1.

Mechanisms of Antipyresis

Nonsteroidal antipyretic agents inhibit fever by blocking the synthesis of prostaglandins within the endothelium of the hypothalamic vasculature, which is accomplished through inhibition of cyclooxygenase. However, they do not diminish the elaboration of endogenous pyrogens and may actually increase the production of some of these proteins (notably TNF-α). Nonsteroidal antipyretics do not produce poikilothermic effects; they can reduce fever but cannot lower body temperature beneath its normal set-point. It may reasonably be inferred from this observation that prostaglandins do not normally act to maintain core body temperature.

Glucocorticoid hormones directly impede the production of endogenous pyrogens by mononuclear phagocytic cells. Cytokine synthesis is inhibited at more than one level and has been studied most thoroughly in the case of TNF-α biosynthesis. Both transcription of the TNF-α gene and translation of TNF-α mRNA are down-regulated by glucocorticoid agonists.

The cyclic (often circadian) course followed in many febrile illnesses has not been fully explained. In some instances (e.g., in malaria), a clear relationship to the life cycle of the pathogen has been demonstrated. Cyclicity may, in other cases, follow from the fact that cells constituting the chief source of endogenous pyrogens are rendered refractory by continued exposure to the stimulatory agent and must recover or be replaced.

 Treatment

In the absence of specific knowledge concerning cause in a particular patient, a conservative approach to the treatment of fever is advisable. Core temperatures beneath 105° F are well tolerated by most individuals. Moreover, when its source has been defined, fever often serves as an important indicator of a response to therapy.

Under certain circumstances, aggressive treatment of fever is warranted. Patients with myocardial ischemia, patients predisposed to seizures, and pregnant women may require treatment with antipyretics because elevation of core temperature increases cardiac output and myocardial oxygen demand, increases the likelihood of seizures, and may exert a teratogenic effect. Acetaminophen or nonsteroidal anti-inflammatory agents prove adequate for this purpose in the majority of cases. Physical methods for increasing heat dissipation may also be used.

Temperatures that exceed 106° F may be life threatening and must be lowered immediately. Antipyretics are often ineffective in such instances because pyrexia of this degree may not result from an aberrant hypothalamic set-point. It is advisable, in such cases, to lower the temperature by any means possible; the most effective action to be taken is to immerse the patient in ice water while monitoring core temperature to be certain that a state of hypothermia is not induced. Ice water lavage of the stomach can be employed in extreme circumstances, but fortunately is rarely necessary. The common practice of applying ice packs to the axillae and groin is not particularly effective and can cause unnecessary discomfort. Physiologic doses of hydrocortisone should be given if there is concern about adrenal insufficiency or thyroid storm.

SUGGESTED READINGS

Beutler B: Endotoxin, Toll-like receptor 4, and the afferent limb of innate immunity. Curr Opin Microbiol 2000;3:23–28. *A review of the sensing mechanism used by the innate immune system for the detection of pathogens, and hence, for the generation of fever.*

Moltz H: Fever: Causes and consequences. Neurosci Biobehav Rev 1993;17:237–269. *An excellent review analyzing the neurochemistry and neuroanatomy of fever.*

Rothwell NJ: CNS regulation of thermogenesis. Crit Rev Neurobiol 1994;8:1–10. *A current appraisal of the pyrogenicity of various cytokines.*

297 THE ACUTE PHASE RESPONSE

Charles A. Dinarello
Reuven Porat

Acute Phase Changes

Infections, trauma, inflammatory processes, and some malignant diseases induce a constellation of host responses collectively referred to as the acute phase response. The response is associated with increases in the synthesis of specific proteins by the liver as well as a decrease in hepatic albumin synthesis. On closer examination, changes also occur in several other systems and are responsible for various hematologic, metabolic, endocrinologic, and immunologic dysfunctions. These changes are called "acute" because they can be observed within hours or days following the onset of infection or injury. However, the same changes are also indicative of chronic disease. For example, the serum acute phase protein termed C-reactive protein (CRP) is commonly elevated in patients with rheumatoid arthritis. Patients with coronary artery disease and unstable angina have elevated CRP as well as increased levels of another hepatic acute phase protein called serum amyloid A (SAA); moreover, these two acute phase proteins serve as markers of disease severity. In fact, measurements of CRP can also be used to predict outcomes in asymptomatic patients with coronary artery disease, although these elevated levels of CRP are low compared with those in patients with bacterial infections.

The full spectrum of the acute phase response in patients with infections or chronic inflammatory diseases includes dramatic increases in the synthesis of several unique hepatic proteins that are not produced in health. CRP and SAA are two examples of acute phase proteins that are not produced in healthy subjects. There are other plasma proteins of hepatic origin such as glycoproteins and globulins that are produced in low amounts in health, but with increased synthesis these are responsible for elevated erythrocyte sedimentation rates. Although the liver is producing increasing amounts of a variety of proteins, hepatic albumin synthesis is decreased. Another component of the acute phase response observed in chronic inflammatory diseases is anemia despite adequate stores of iron; thrombocytosis can also be present. Increases in gluconeogenesis, energy expenditure, and muscle proteolysis occur and contribute to weight loss, although anorexia accounts for most of the reduction in weight. Fever may be present. Leukocytosis with increased numbers of circulating immature neutrophils can be present, but is usually observed early in acute infections. Thyroid dysfunction may be present, and glucose tolerance and lipid metabolism are often abnormal. Hypergammaglobulinemia often occurs.

Although the most florid manifestation of the acute phase response is observed in patients with bacterial infections, burns, or multiple injuries, clinicians can search for acute phase changes in patients with occult infections or indolent illnesses, particularly malignant and autoimmune diseases. For example, the presence of acute phase changes can serve as an indicator of renal cell carcinoma and Hodgkin's disease. The acute phase response has the outstanding characteristic of being a generalized host reaction irrespective of the localized or systemic nature of the inciting disease. The various components of the response are remarkably consistent despite the considerable variety of pathologic processes that induce it. For example, plasma levels of CRP are elevated following myocardial infarction, fracture of a bone, or bacterial pneumonia.

Induction of Acute Phase Changes

The initiation of the acute phase response is linked to the production of cytokines. Several cytokines induce acute phase changes:

interleukin-1 (IL-1), tumor necrosis factor (TNF), interferon-γ, IL-6, leukemia inhibitory factor, ciliary neurotropic factor, oncostatin M, and IL-11. The last five cytokines induce hepatic acute phase protein synthesis through glycoprotein cell receptor 130. IL-1 and TNF, two highly inflammatory cytokines, induce IL-6, which in turn stimulates the liver. The ability of microbial products and endogenous inflammatory substances such as activated complement to stimulate the production of cytokines is fundamental to pathologic changes in many diseases. As shown in Figure 297–1, microbial products or cytokines themselves can act on the Kupffer cells of the liver to produce cytokines; alternatively, cytokines produced at distant sites enter the hepatic circulation. Regardless of their origin, cytokines trigger their respective cell receptors on hepatocytes and stimulate the hepatocyte to increase or decrease the expression of specific genes. In the case of positive hepatic proteins such as CRP, there is markedly increased synthesis. The same cytokines acting on the same cell receptor suppress negative protein synthesis, most notably that of albumin.

A patient with a localized bacterial infection represents an excellent example of the acute phase response. At the onset of the infection, blood monocytes, tissue macrophages, and endothelial cells become activated, either by phagocytosis of the invading microbe or by exposure to its products or toxins; the process results in the synthesis and release of various cytokines within 1 to 2 hours. Cytokines enter the circulation and reach the brain, where they initiate fever. Whereas fever is clearly one of the most obvious signs of the acute phase response, other components of the response can be present without apparent clinical manifestations. One of the most sensitive measures of the acute phase response is an increase in the number and immaturity of circulating neutrophils. In human subjects injected with small doses of IL-1 or related cytokines, neutrophilia can be measured in the absence of fever. Although not routinely measured, serum zinc and iron levels are depressed. Low serum iron associated with anemia in the presence of adequate iron stores is characteristic of the acute phase response.

Within 8 to 12 hours after the onset of infection or trauma, the liver increases the synthetic rate of the so-called acute phase proteins. Several plasma proteins found in health increase several-fold during the acute phase response, including haptoglobin, protease inhibitors, complement components, ceruloplasmin, and fibrinogen. However, true acute phase reactants increase several hundredfold. These reactants include SAA, a precursor of the amyloid fibril in secondary amyloidosis, and CRP. CRP was named for its ability to interact with the

Table 297–1 • PLASMA PROTEINS THAT INCREASE DURING THE ACUTE PHASE RESPONSE

C-reactive protein
Serum amyloid A protein
α_1-Glycoprotein
Ceruloplasmin
α-Macroglobulins
Complement components (C1–C4, factor B, C9, C11)
α_1-Antitrypsin
α_1-Antichymotrypsin
Fibrinogen
Prothrombin
Factor VIII
Plasminogen
Haptoglobin
Ferritin
Immunoglobulins
Lipoproteins

C polysaccharide of pneumococci. Table 297–1 lists the characteristic pattern of increased plasma proteins observed during the acute phase response. Note one exception: the plasma concentration of albumin is decreased.

Why the acute phase response? Despite the anabolic processes of the liver, the acute phase response is accompanied by catabolism of muscle protein, loss of body weight, and negative nitrogen balance. Fever increases oxygen and caloric demands (usually 7% per degree F). The negative nitrogen balance results from the oxidation of amino acids from skeletal muscle, which are used for gluconeogenesis. The host requires a large supply of amino acids to synthesize new protein at a time when food intake may be impaired or appetite reduced. Amino acids are required for immunologic and reparative processes such as the clonal expansion of lymphocytes and the repair of tissue. The mechanism of providing ample amino acids for these cellular functions seems to be well orchestrated during the acute phase response. The catabolism during infection and inflammation differs from that of starvation. Unlike a person during starvation, in which large amounts of ketones are spilled into the urine, an individual with an infectious or inflammatory disease excretes protein with small amounts of ketones. IL-1, TNF, and IL-6, the primary mediators of acute phase changes, inhibit lipoprotein lipase and suppress appetite. In addition, these cytokines and interferons directly stimulate hepatic lipogenesis, thereby contributing to the hypertriglyceridemia observed in patients with either acute or chronic disease.

Measurement of Acute Phase Changes in Clinical Medicine

The acute phase response is nonspecific. However, the presence of certain acute phase changes in an otherwise healthy individual can alert the physician to hidden disease. Physicians presented with a patient with vague symptoms of fatigue and other constitutional complaints often seek an objective test for the presence of occult disease. Although there is no single biochemical test with high diagnostic value, the CRP level is perhaps the best indicator of inflammation or occult infection. CRP levels are usually less than 100 µg/L, but increase within hours 10- to 1000-fold. In severe bacterial infections, the serum level can rise from undetectable to over 100 mg/L in 48 hours. The presence of elevated levels of CRP or SAA, even in the absence of fever or neutrophilia, may indicate occult infection or malignant change. Increases in CRP and SAA occur in patients of any age and also in immunocompromised patients with opportunistic infections. In the weeks following an acute illness of infectious origin, particularly viral infections, CRP usually returns to basal levels. Measurement of serum cytokines, such as IL-6 or IL-1 receptor antagonist, can also be used as an indicator of the acute phase response in chronic or acute illness or with ongoing infection, but these are not readily available, whereas CRP can be measured easily in most hospital clinical laboratories. Not all inflammatory diseases are associated with elevated CRP. Autoimmune diseases such as scleroderma, ulcerative colitis, and lupus erythematosus can exist without elevated CRP.

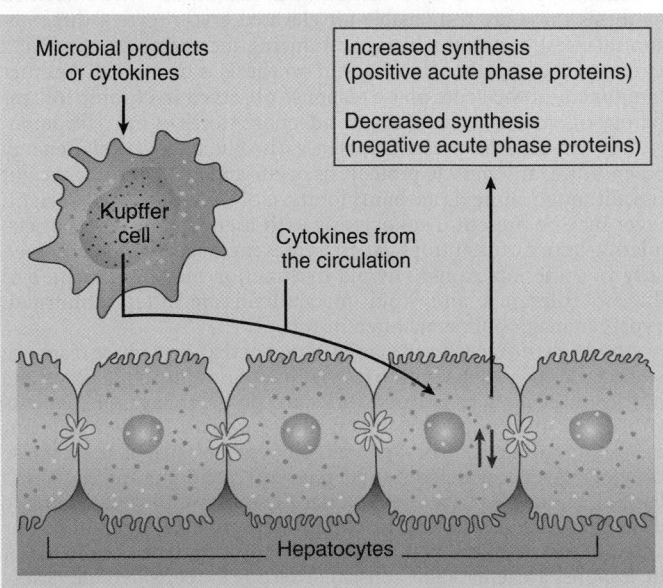

FIGURE 297–1 • Role of cytokines in the hepatic acute phase response. Cytokines, such as interleukin-1 (IL-1), tumor necrosis factor α (TNF-α), IL-6, IL-11, and others, arriving in the liver through the systemic circulation, directly stimulate the hepatocytes to increase the synthesis of acute phase proteins, such as C-reactive protein and serum amyloid A, and suppress the synthesis of albumin. Microbial products or cytokines can also stimulate the hepatic Kupffer cell to release IL-1, TNF-α, and IL-6, which, in turn, activate the nearby hepatocyte.

Labels within figure: Microbial products or cytokines; Increased synthesis (positive acute phase proteins); Decreased synthesis (negative acute phase proteins); Kupffer cell; Cytokines from the circulation; Hepatocytes

℞ Treatment of Acute Phase Responses

Measurements of fever, acute phase plasma proteins, and peripheral leukocyte numbers are well-established procedures for monitoring many disease states. Although nonsteroidal anti-inflammatory agents are used to treat the fever and associated myalgias and arthralgias of acute phase responses, these drugs do not affect the synthesis of acute phase proteins in the liver. Antipyretic blood levels of aspirin and therapeutic concentrations of drugs such as indomethacin or ibuprofen do not reduce the production of cytokines. On the other hand, corticosteroids are highly effective in reducing cytokine synthesis, as well as the effect of these mediators on various tissue targets. Patients receiving therapeutic doses of corticosteroids have blunted acute phase responses with ongoing infections, inflammatory processes, or immunologic reactions. Patients with Crohn's disease or rheumatoid arthritis have elevated serum CRP levels, but treatment with neutralizing antibodies to TNF-α or IL-1 receptor antagonist brings about a rapid reduction in these levels and is used as an indicator of effective treatment.

The role of acute phase proteins in host defense and repair is not entirely clear. Studies suggest that the major role of CRP is to bind serum lipids or opsonize pneumococci, whereas SAA is thought to be immunosuppressive. What is clear, however, is that the production and physical structure of these acute phase proteins have been conserved through 400 million years of evolution, and therefore they have presumably been useful to the host.

SUGGESTED READINGS

Adkis CA, Blaser K: Histamine in the immune regulation of allergic inflammation. J Allergy Clin Immunol 2003;112:15–22. *Histamine regulates the activation, polarization, chemotaxis, and effector functions of immune system cells.*

D'Ambrosio D, Panina-Bordignon P, Sinigaglia F: Chemokine receptors in inflammation: An overview. J Immunol Methods 2003;273:3–13. *A pathophysiologic overview.*

Manson JE, Hsia J, Johnson KC, et al: Women's Health Initiative Investigators: Estrogen plus progestin and the risk of coronary heart disease. N Engl J Med 2003;349:523–534. *Therapy was not beneficial and may even be harmful, perhaps in part because it raises C-reactive protein levels.*

Rhee JS, Santoso S, Herrmann M, et al: New aspects of integrin-mediated leukocyte adhesion in inflammation: Regulation by haemostatic factors and bacterial products. Curr Mol Med 2003;3:387–392. *Overview of integrin-dependent leukocyte adhesion by hemostatic factors and bacterial products.*

Vogeser M, Groetzner J, Kupper C, et al: The serum cortisol:cortisone ratio in the postoperative acute-phase response. Horm Res 2003;59:293–296. *The increase in the cortisol:cortisone ratio is sustained for at least four days and is related to activation of the hypothalamic-pituitary-adrenocortical system by surgical stress and systemic inflammation.*

Yoo JY, Desiderio S: Innate and acquired immunity intersect in a global view of the acute-phase response. Proc Natl Acad Sci U S A 2003;100:1157–1162. *About 7% of genes are mobilized in the acute phase response to endotoxin.*

298 THE COMPROMISED HOST

Nina E. Tolkoff-Rubin
Robert H. Rubin

The last decades of the 20th century bore witness to a remarkable increase in patients whose host defenses against infection were impaired because of disease and/or its therapy. It was recognized that measurable alterations in either or both natural and acquired immunity resulted in an individual who was at constant risk for life-threatening infection; indeed, the nature of these infections provides insight into the nature of the host defense defect or defects present. These individuals are grouped under the rubric of the *compromised host*, which consists of three major categories of patient: those with congenital immunodeficiencies; those with acquired immunodeficiency syndrome (AIDS), a virally induced immunodeficiency characterized by recurrent life-threatening infections caused by pathogens normally controlled by the host defenses that are attenuated by human immunodeficiency virus (HIV) infection; and patients with acquired deficits secondary to disease and, particularly, its therapy.

The last group encompasses a paradox. Many of these patients represent a triumph—in the not so distant past these individuals would have succumbed rapidly to their end-stage liver, heart, and lung disease, to their cancers, or to their collagen vascular disease. Now, because of advances in organ and hematopoietic stem cell transplantation, in the use of immunosuppressive drugs, and in cancer therapy, these patients are being salvaged in increasing numbers and have the potential for years of normal life. The paradox lies in the observation that these individuals are no longer at risk for their primary illness; rather, they are at risk for microbial invasion related to deficits created by their life-saving therapy. Thus, success in the treatment of an increasing number of conditions results in the exponential increase in the compromised hosts that are the subject of this chapter, particularly as these patients are returning to their communities and the care of the primary care physician (HIV infection and AIDS are discussed in Part XXIV).

Approach to the Compromised Host

As the clinician approaches the compromised host, there are a series of challenges that need to be kept in mind:

1. The range of microorganisms causing invasive infection in the compromised host is much broader than that affecting the general population. Thus, the etiology of common clinical syndromes may be far different from that normally observed. For example, cellulitis in a normal host is usually due to *Staphylococcus aureus* or *Streptococcus pyogenes* and rarely requires biopsy before initiating therapy. In the compromised host, a range of organisms including other bacteria and fungi must be considered as well, and biopsy for cultural and pathologic assessment is often required in order to treat effectively.

2. The altered inflammatory response present in the compromised patient changes the clinical presentation in many patients—signs and symptoms are greatly muted, and diagnosis is often unduly delayed. The result is that the infectious process is often further advanced at the time of clinical presentation, the microbial burden is greater, person-to-person transmission is more likely (for conditions such as tuberculosis in which person-to-person spread is the major route of contagion), and biopsies and computed tomographic and magnetic resonance imaging for subtle abnormalities must be used.

3. There is great pressure in the compromised host for early diagnosis and therapy, as early institution of effective therapy is a major factor in determining the prognosis of the patient.

4. Therapy for many of the infections in these patients must be prolonged because of the ongoing host defense abnormalities and the nature of the infections themselves (e.g., fungal infections). This need is further complicated by the toxicities inherent in many of the therapies required.

5. When approaching the effects of a particular infection in the compromised host, both *direct* and *indirect* effects must be considered. The direct effects are the infectious disease syndromes produced by microbial invasion (e.g., pneumonia, bacteremia, pyelonephritis). The indirect effects are due to cytokines, chemokines, and growth factors produced by the host in response to microbial invasion. These include immunomodulating effects, oncogenesis, and, in the case of transplant patients, graft-versus-host disease and acute and chronic allograft injury.

6. Patients who have significant compromise of host defenses have been compared with "sentinel chickens" that monitor microbial activity in particular environments. Any excess trafficking in microbes related to environmental exposures affects these patients far more than normal hosts, so monitoring the quality of the air and potable water that these patients encounter is an essential part of their care.

7. In sum, prevention of infection is the goal in managing compromised patients. This puts even more emphasis on close and continuing surveillance of patients with compromised host defenses.

Definitions

The microbes that cause human disease can be divided into three categories: true pathogens, sometime pathogens, and nonpathogens. *True pathogens* are organisms that possess the genetic capability to invade normal individuals, cross fascial planes, evade *innate* (also called *natural* or *native* immunity) host defense mechanisms, and/or produce potent toxins. The innate defenses have three components: the physical and chemical barriers that are provided by the intact mucocutaneous surfaces, which also produce locally active antimicrobial substances; circulating proteins such as complement components and other mediators of inflammation; and phagocytic cells (neutrophils and macrophages) as well as natural killer (NK) cells. These provide the acute protection against microbial invasion (and provide a level of protection until specific immunity can develop and deal with the invading organisms definitively). True pathogens are characterized at least in part by their ability to evade these initial barriers to invasion. True pathogens are the classic plagues of humankind (e.g., bubonic plague, Shiga dysentery [shigellosis], typhoid fever, and cholera). With these infections, natural immunity is inadequate, and recovery is dependent on the speed at which acquired immunity appears and appropriate antimicrobial therapy is initiated.

Sometime pathogens are organisms that are commonly resident on mucocutaneous surfaces, where they cause no harm. However, with damage to skin, gut, or bronchial tree such that these organisms are introduced into normally sterile tissues or the blood stream, they have sufficient genetically mediated virulence characteristics to cause serious disease in otherwise normal individuals (e.g., peritonitis following gut perforation, staphylococcal sepsis following skin injury, or pneumococcal sepsis following influenza). Although natural immunity may offer some protection against these organisms, acquired immunity, repair of anatomic injuries, and appropriate antimicrobial therapy are critical for survival of the patient.

Nonpathogens are organisms that are controlled by natural immunity augmented by acquired immunity and that have little potential for producing clinical disease in a normal host. Often, these organisms (e.g., *Aspergillus* spp, *Scedosporium*, *Nocardia* spp, *Trichosporon*) are present in the environment and are inhaled or introduced into the skin on a regular basis but do not cause disease in normal individuals.

The term *opportunistic infection*, which is often linked to the compromised host, is used to describe infection of two types: invasive infection caused by nonpathogens and infection of a type and extent unheard of in the normal host, although trivial infections with this organism may occur in normal individuals. For example, candidal vaginitis is a relatively trivial infection in the normal host, but disseminated candidiasis (or hepatosplenic candidiasis) in a patient with leukemia qualifies as an opportunistic infection. Although compromised hosts are uniquely susceptible to opportunistic microbes, it must be recognized that they are also at risk for the more common processes that are caused by true and sometime pathogens. Infections caused by true or sometime pathogens in the compromised host generally progress more rapidly than the same infections in an individual with intact host defenses. Table 298–1 presents a listing of the different infections associated with the different host defense defects.

Table 298–1 • HOST DEFENSE DEFICITS AND PARTICULAR INFECTION PROBLEMS

DEFICIT	INFECTION PROBLEM
Hypogammaglobulinemia	Recurrent sinopulmonary infections and/or otitis media due to encapsulated organisms (*S. pneumoniae, H. influenzae*) *Pseudomas aeruginosa* Recurrent/chronic gastroenteritis (*Giardia*, rotavirus, *Cryptosporidium*) Chronic/progressive enterovirus infection (Including oral polio vaccine)
DiGeorge's syndrome, other T-lymphocyte defects	Candidiasis *Pneumocystis carinii* pneumonia Pneumonia Aspergillosis Salmonellosis Cytomegalovirus infections Severe respiratory viral infections
Complement disorders	Infections by *Neisseria meningitidis, Streptococcus pneumoniae, Haemophilus influenzae*
Phagocytic cells/chemotactic disorders (chronic granulomatous disease)	*Staphylococcus aureus* Gram-negative bacilli *Aspergillus*

It must be emphasized, however, that most adult patients (as opposed to children with congenital immunodeficiencies, who usually have a single defect) have a variety of defects as a consequence of their therapy and their underlying diseases, so a variety of microorganisms are of concern.

Risk of Infection in the Compromised Host

The risk of infection, particularly opportunistic infection, in the compromised host is largely due to the interaction of three factors: the presence of *anatomic-technical abnormalities* that lead directly to invasive infection; excessive *environmental exposures* to contaminated air or potable water or to individuals who have a particular infection and are capable of passing it on to others (e.g., by a cough from an infected respiratory tract or direct transmission from the hands of medical personnel that are contaminated with drug-resistant pathogens); and a function termed the *net state of immunosuppression*.

The anatomic-technical abnormalities that lead to infection in the compromised host are of several types: a surgical misadventure (as during an organ transplant operation) that leads to devitalized tissue or fluid collections (blood, lymph, bile, or urine); mishandling of endotracheal tubes, surgical drains and catheters, and vascular access devices such that the primary mucocutaneous barrier to microbial invasion is compromised; and insufficient attention to protecting the integrity of the skin (such as injury from adhesive tape or water immersion injury), oral mucosa, and gut epithelium (such as maintaining normal bowel habits). Any such anatomic abnormality needs immediate correction, preferably before significant infection develops. Indeed, the optimal therapy for surgical or postoperative infection is to correct the anatomic abnormality under coverage of appropriate antimicrobial therapy. Antimicrobial therapy by itself, leaving the anatomic abnormality uncorrected, not only is associated with a high rate of failure but also has a high probability of inducing antimicrobial resistance.

In the patient who is without anatomic-technical problems, there is a semiquantitative relationship between the intensity of the environmental exposure and the net state of immunosuppression. Thus, if the exposure is great enough, even minimally immunosuppressed individuals are infected; conversely, if the net state of immunosuppression is great enough, minimal exposure can be life-threatening. Environmental problems may be encountered in the community or in the hospital. In the hospital the exposures encountered are of two types: *domiciliary* exposure, which occurs on the ward where the patient is housed and where the cases are clustered in time and space, and *nondomiciliary* exposure, in which the patient encounters the infection while traveling through the hospital for an essential procedure. Nondomiciliary exposures are probably more common than the domiciliary type but are more difficult to detect. The best clue to the presence of this problem is the recognition that the infection occurred at a time when the net state of immunosuppression is, under normal circumstances, not likely to predispose to the current form of infection (Table 298–2).

The net state of immunosuppression is a complex function whose contributing factors are outlined (Table 298–3). Although the nature of the immunosuppressing strategy must be regarded as the prime determinant of the net state of immunosuppression, several other factors make a significant contribution. For example, 90% of opportunistic infections in solid organ transplant recipients occur in patients with immunomodulating viral infection (e.g., with cytomegalovirus [CMV], Epstein-Barr virus, hepatitis B and C, HIV, and, probably, human herpesvirus 6). The 10% of exceptions turned out to have been due to excessive environmental exposures.

A second area contributing to the net state of immunosuppression is the presence of metabolic abnormalities. Of particular importance is protein-calorie malnutrition—for example, if one stratifies organ transplant patients on the basis of a serum albumin level of 2.5 g/dL, those with the lower albumin levels have a 10-fold increase in life-threatening infection. The mechanisms that are responsible for the adverse effects of protein-calorie malnutrition include the following: impaired barrier function of the mucocutaneous tissues related to attenuation of the tissues, low lysozyme concentration, and decreased production of secretory immunoglobulin A (IgA); impairment of both pathways of the complement system, with this in turn impeding both leukocyte chemotaxis and opsonization; and, perhaps most of all, impaired cell-mediated immunity. Practically, these and presumably other mechanisms result in increased occurrence and/or

Table 298–2 • TIMETABLE OF INFECTION FOLLOWING ORGAN TRANSPLANTATION*

First month
1. Infection conveyed with the allograft
2. Persistent infection in the recipient (not eradicated before transplantation)
3. >95% of the infections are due to anatomic technical abnormalities related to the surgery and perioperative care; the same bacterial and candidal infections as in nonimmunosuppressed individuals undergoing comparable surgery
NB: No opportunistic infection unless excessive environmental exposure

One to 6 months after transplantation
1. Viruses—cytomegalovirus (CMV), human herpes virus 6, Epstein-Barr virus, hepatitis, human immunodeficiency virus
2. Opportunistic infection made possible by sustained immunosuppression plus immunomodulating viral infection
NB: CMV dominant; prevention with ganciclovir and trimethoprim-sulfamethoxazole prophylaxis

More than 6 months after transplantation
1. 80% of patients with good results from transplant—good function, minimal immunosuppression; no viruses. Major risk is community-acquired respiratory virus infection
2. 10% chronic hepatitis (B or C)
3. 10% poor results from transplant—poor graft function, too much acute and chronic immunosuppression, chronic viral infection. Major risk for opportunistic infection with *Pneumocystis, Cryptococcus, Listeria,* and others
NB: The last group needs prophylaxis for life.

*A timetable can be constructed for essentially every category of immuno-compromised host; this one was chosen as it is the one that is most generally applicable. This timetable is useful in three ways: differential diagnosis of patients with an infectious disease syndrome (e.g., pneumonia); infection control surveillance—exceptions to timetable suggest a particular hazard; basis of cost-effective preventive strategies.

Table 298–3 • NET STATE OF IMMUNOSUPPRESSION

A complex function determined by interaction of:
Host defense deficits associated with underlying disease
Dose, duration, and temporal sequence of immunosuppressive therapies
Presence of neutropenia
Damage to mucocutaneous barrier
Metabolic abnormalities
Protein-calorie malnutrition
Uremia
Hyperglycemia
Immunomodulating viral infection (cytomegalovirus, Epstein-Barr virus, human herpesvirus 6, hepatitis B or C, human immunodeficiency virus)
Age (two extremes of life)
? Race (blacks have decreased risk of infection and increased risk of allograft rejection)

severity of tuberculosis, bacterial diarrhea, respiratory infection, *Pneumocystis* infection, candidiasis, and aspergillosis.

Other metabolic factors of importance include the following. The presence of increased amounts of particular nutrients results in an increased risk of severe infections of a particular type. Thus, diabetes, corticosteroids, pregnancy, broad-spectrum antimicrobial agents, and so forth (all causing the levels of glucose and glycogen to be increased on mucocutaneous surfaces) result in increased numbers of *Candida* species, primarily at normal sites of colonization. The mobilization of excessive iron stores with desferrioxamine increases the risk of mucormycosis, *Listeria monocytogenes,* and *Yersinia enterocolitica.* Deficiency of such factors as zinc and iron can cause impairment of phagocytic and/or T-cell function, which can increase susceptibility to a wide selection of microorganisms.

The Hierarchy of Host Defenses (the Contribution of Innate Immunity)

The architecture of the body's host defenses is an elegant one, characterized by amplification, redundancy, and levels of increasing complexity. Its design is such that an *emergency response* capability (innate immunity) can be mobilized quickly to preserve life while *adaptive immunity* is being developed over several days to effect the definitive elimination of the invading microbe. Innate immunity is nonspecific in terms of its ability to distinguish one invading microbe from another, with its response being similar whatever the nature of the potential pathogen. The structure of innate immunity consists of three levels of response, with each succeeding level bringing increasing complexity and efficacy to bear (Table 298–4):

1. The first level of innate immunity is the intact mucocutaneous surfaces, where both physical and chemical barriers (e.g., gastric hydrochloric acid and antimicrobial substances produced by the bacteria present on these surfaces) constitute the primary barrier to microbial invasion.
2. Activated leukocytes are the mobile effector cells of this structure. Such cells as NK cells, polymorphonuclear leukocytes (PMNs), and monocytes/macrophages are of critical importance, having two major functions—phagocytosis and the production of key mediators of inflammation.
3. Circulating blood proteins, including components of complement generated by activation of the alternative pathway of complement, as well as such other mediators of inflammation as lysozyme, lactoferrin, and fibronectin, and such proinflammatory cytokines as tumor necrosis factor and interleukin-1, constitute an immediate humoral response to microbial invasion of all types. This function of innate immunity is not limited to the desperately ill situation, as innate immunity also plays several important roles in the induction of a specific immune response. These proteins also serve to augment and amplify the activity of the leukocytes, particularly increasing the efficiency of phagocytosis and intracellular microbicidal function.

MUCOCUTANEOUS SURFACES

The mucocutaneous surfaces of the body constitute the primary barriers to infection, assuming particular importance under conditions where the backup defenses (phagocytes as well as humoral and cellular immunity) are impaired by disease or its therapy. When considering the primary barrier function, two aspects merit review: the normal flora colonizing the surfaces of the skin and mucosal surfaces and the epithelial cells themselves. The normal bacterial flora present on mucocutaneous surfaces is remarkably stable, maintained at least in part by the interaction of specific bacterial surface ligands with specific receptors on the surfaces of the epithelial cells. Other factors that serve to maintain the normal flora include certain blood group glycoproteins as well as major histocompatibility complex (MHC) antigens that are on the surfaces of epithelial cells and serve as receptors for surface ligands of a variety of microbes. An additional positive effect of the normal flora is that the immune system appears to be "primed" by interaction with the normal flora. For example, MHC antigens on macrophages, which are essential for the presentation of antigens to T lymphocytes (a critical step in the initiation of the specific immune response), are expressed at high levels because of

Table 298–4 • HOST DEFENSE MECHANISMS IN INNATE AND SPECIFIC IMMUNITY

LINE OF DEFENSE	NONSPECIFIC	SPECIFIC
Surface defense (skin, mucous membranes)	Mechanical barrier Secretory barrier Ciliary motion Peristalsis	Immunoglobulins (IgG and secretory IgA)
Humoral defense	Lysozyme and lactoferrin Complement system Fibronectin Interferons Interleukins	Immunoglobulins (IgM and, predominantly, IgG)

Cellular defense	Phagocytic cells
	  Neutrophilic granulocytes
	  Eosinophilic granulocytes
	  Mononuclear phagocytes
	Natural killer cells
		Cell-mediated immunity (T lymphocytes and macrophages)

Ig = immunoglobulin.

interactions with the normal flora, resulting in a more effective immune response.

The microorganisms that make up the normal flora provide a significant barrier to colonization, adherence, and invasion by potential pathogens by producing antimicrobial substances called bacteriocins and other products that are antibacterial and by competing successfully for essential nutrients. The totality of these effects of the normal flora is termed *colonization resistance* and is mediated primarily by bowel anaerobes in the gut, diphtheroids in the nose (vs. *S. aureus*) and lactobacilli in the vagina (vs. gram-negative uropathogens). In general, management of the compromised host should include the use of antimicrobial agents that allow colonization resistance to stay intact, particularly bowel anaerobes.

Intact skin is resistant to colonization and invasion by microorganisms. The normal skin surface lipids produced by the sebaceous glands promote the growth of the nonvirulent skin diphtheroids and inhibit the growth of such pathogens as streptococci. However, bacterial and fungal overgrowth occur when the skin is moist and relatively alkaline. In addition, the presence of pathogens in sputum results in an increased microbial burden on the skin of the neck and chest and enhances the chances of vascular access–related infection if the vascular access is placed at these sites.

The intact gastrointestinal tract mucosa (which is attacked by cancer chemotherapy regimens) is augmented by gastric acid, unconjugated bile, and normal intestinal motility as well as immunoglobulins, particularly secretory IgA. Mucosal secretions augment the antimicrobial abilities of these sites: IgG and secretory IgA block the attachment of microorganisms to specific receptors as well as agglutinating these organisms. Iron-binding proteins, present in these secretions, effectively block access of potential pathogens to this critically important growth factor.

Attention to an immunocompromised patient's bowel habits is of great importance as even trivial injury to the gut mucosa can lead to significant infection (e.g., typhlitis, perirectal abscess).

PHAGOCYTES

The most common abnormality noted in innate immunity is that affecting the phagocytes. First, and most common, is a defect in the number of circulating PMNs, usually as a consequence of cytotoxic therapy (often in the treatment of malignant disease).

The consequences of neutropenia are determined by three factors: how low the absolute neutrophil count (ANC) is, the duration of the neutropenia, and the presence of breaks in the integrity of the mucocutaneous surfaces, particularly the gut (the last is particularly important as damage to the gut mucosa is a regular feature of cancer chemotherapy, providing a portal of entry for gut flora to penetrate and enter the blood stream). The incidence of infection begins to rise when the ANC falls below 1000/mm³, becomes a more serious problem below 500 granulocytes/mm³, and is a clinically dominant issue when the ANC is less than 100/mm³. The primary infections that occur in the presence of neutropenia are bacterial and fungal. The more sustained the neutropenia is, the greater the likelihood of these infections.

The nature of these infections has changed over the past 50 years. Initially, the major problem was gram-positive infection, particularly that related to *S. aureus*. This was replaced by gram-negative bacillary infection, entering primarily from the gut and including such organisms as *Escherichia coli, Klebsiella, Enterobacter,* and, most virulent of all gram-negative bacteria in this situation, *Pseudomonas aeruginosa*. With the advent of such preventive strategies as selective bowel decontamination and fluoroquinolone prophylaxis, the nature of these bacterial infections has shifted away from the typical gram-negative infection to gram-positive infection, particularly staphylococcal and streptococcal infection, stemming from either the injured gut or infected vascular access sites.

The importance of vascular access–related infection in the neutropenic patient (especially when the neutropenia is chemotherapy induced) cannot be overemphasized. Such organisms as *Bacillus* species and a particular diphtheroid termed group CDC-JK *Corynebacterium* are not infrequent causes of bacteremia related to line sepsis in the severely neutropenic patient. Methicillin-resistant *S. aureus* and vancomycin-resistant enterococci have become of increasing importance in the neutropenic patient, complicating greatly the antimicrobial management in these patients.

Anaerobes appear to be an uncommon problem in the neutropenic patient unless there is a significant injury to the oral and/or gastrointestinal mucosa that compromises the primary barrier function of the mucosa. When such injury occurs, whatever the cause (e.g., typhlitis, CMV infection, or perforation), *Clostridium* species and *Bacteroides* species (particularly *C. perfringens* and *B. fragilis*) can be virulent pathogens.

Fungal infections during sustained neutropenia are usually due to *Candida* species or *Aspergillus* species, with the risk of such infections being proportional to the extent and the duration of the neutropenia. The range of clinical syndromes produced by these organisms is quite broad. Candidemia is often related to vascular access site infection, mucocutaneous infection, and disseminated disease with metastatic seeding; in the case of *Aspergillus* infection, the cardinal feature is that of angioinvasiveness, accounting for the three major characteristics of this invasive mold—infarction, hemorrhage, and metastatic spread. The predominant candidal species causing disease in this setting are *Candida albicans* and *Candida tropicalis,* which are the most virulent of the *Candida* species but are sensitive to such antifungal drugs as fluconazole. Other species (e.g., *Candida krusei*) appear to be less virulent but are fluconazole resistant. Resistance to fluconazole and the appearance of non-*albicans* strains are, at least in part, related to previous exposure to this drug. Alternatively, azole-resistant *Candida* species can be acquired from the hands of medical personnel. One characteristic of candidemia is its propensity for establishing sites of metastatic infection, with the skin, the eye, the urinary tract, and the liver and spleen being characteristic sites of spread. Often, physical evidence of such metastatic spread is not present during the period of neutropenia, being clearly evident only after the neutropenia resolves weeks to months after the seeding has occurred. It is an absolute rule that any instance of candidal blood stream infection (even a single positive blood culture) requires therapy with such drugs as fluconazole, voriconazole, an amphotericin preparation, or an echinocandin.

Invasive aspergillosis in the compromised host constitutes a medical emergency because of its angioinvasive qualities. *Aspergillus fumigatus* and *Aspergillus flavus* account for the majority of these infections, although other species can cause disease as well. The lungs are the primary site of infection in more than 80% of cases, with the nasal sinuses and skin that has been injured being the other major portals of entry for this organism. Fully 50% of patients with invasive aspergillosis have disseminated disease when first diagnosed.

What have been termed the new and emerging fungi are playing an increasing role in the severely neutropenic or otherwise compromised host. Such organisms as the Mucoraceae, *Trichosporon beigelii, Fusarium,* and *Scedosporium* can produce both local and disseminated infections as virulent as those caused by the traditional fungal pathogens and are far more resistant to such traditional drugs as amphotericin, fluconazole, and itraconazole. Fortunately, newer drugs such as voriconazole appear to offer hope in the management of these infections.

The advent of biologic agents such as granulocyte colony-stimulating factor (G-CSF) and granulocyte-macrophage colony-stimulating factor (GM-CSF) offers an opportunity for shortening periods of chemotherapy-induced neutropenia. In vitro, these compounds can also be shown to stimulate neutrophil functions such as phagocytosis, microbicidal activity, and antibody-dependent cytotoxicity. However, to this point, such in vitro promise has not yet been linked to increased survival of patients or other clinical benefits with the exception of an accelerated rate of return of neutrophils to normal levels.

Whereas neutropenia, particularly that caused by therapy, accounts for more than 90% of the leukocyte disorders observed in adults, there are also functional defects that are uncommon causes of impaired host defense against infection. Thus, patients with acute leukemia, myelodysplastic syndrome, and, probably, chronic myelogenous leukemia have measurable defects in neutrophil function, in addition to any deficit in numbers of circulating cells, that contribute to a further attenuation of phagocytic function and increased risk of infection.

Effective neutrophil mobilization against invading microbes requires a complex, multistep process: (1) the first step in the process is termed *rolling adhesion* and involves marginating neutrophils becoming lightly adherent to endothelial cells through the action of surface structures termed selectins; (2) when these neutrophils encounter inflammatory mediators and activated endothelial cells, tight adhesion is initiated through the action of activated β_2-integrins on the neutrophil; (3) tight adhesion is obtained by the binding of leukocyte function–associated antigen 1 (LFA-1) with intercellular adhesion molecules 1 and 2 (ICAM-1 and ICAM-2); and (4) finally, transmigration across the endothelium and mucosa into inflamed tissue sites occurs. The whole process involves a carefully modulated series of events that are initiated and then maintained by a group of proinflammatory mediators. Perhaps the most important of these mediators are the *chemokines*, which have a major leukocyte-activating function, resulting in adherence, chemotaxis, degranulation, and activation of neutrophil oxidase. Phagocytosis is best accomplished when the microorganism is opsonized by either complement components or IgG. Following phagocytosis, microbial killing is mediated through both an oxidative burst that yields free oxygen radicals and the release of microbicidal proteins from the neutrophilic granules. Particularly potent in this regard is the enzyme myeloperoxidase, which, in combination with hydrogen peroxide produced by the oxidative burst and a halide, results in enhanced microbial killing.

Clinical Syndromes

The importance of this complex series of events is underlined by the gravity of the clinical effects that occur as a consequence of defects in the functioning of the neutrophil. It is fair to say that virtually every step in the processes of microbial phagocytosis and intracellular killing has a corresponding heritable defect that leads to significant infection, which underlines the importance of these individual steps. The most important of these "experiments of nature" include the following.

LEUKOCYTE ADHESION DEFICIENCY SYNDROMES. Leukocyte adhesion deficiency syndromes are characterized by elevated leukocyte counts in the peripheral blood, poor pus formation, and recurrent "cold" abscesses, with *S. aureus* and *P. aeruginosa* infections being particularly prominent.

CHEMOTACTIC DEFECTS. Deficits in the complement system caused by genetic deficiency or certain disease states (e.g., increased protein loss or impaired synthesis), as well as diseases associated with circulating immune complexes (e.g., subacute bacterial endocarditis), can cause impaired chemotaxis. An acquired defect in neutrophil chemotaxis has been described in conjunction with gingival infection with an organism called *Capnocytophaga*, which produced inhibitors of chemotaxis.

CHÉDIAK-HIGASHI SYNDROME. Chédiak-Higashi syndrome is an autosomal recessive disease affecting lysosomes in leukocytes, Schwann cells, melanocytes, renal tubular cells, and thyroid cells. Reflecting these abnormalities, individuals with Chédiak-Higashi syndrome are afflicted with partial oculocutaneous albinism, neuropathy, and recurrent infections. Neutrophils from these patients respond poorly to chemotactic stimuli and exhibit impaired intracellular killing (and degranulation) and depressed T-cell and NK cell killing of microbes. Antimicrobial prophylaxis with trimethoprim-sulfamethoxazole is recommended. Successful bone marrow transplantation cures the hematologic aspects of the disease but has no effect on the neurologic ones.

HYPERIMMUNOGLOBULINEMIA E WITH IMPAIRED CHEMOTAXIS (JOB'S SYNDROME). Features of this syndrome are eczema, "cold" staphylococcal skin abscesses, sinusitis, and otitis media. Originally described in fair-skinned, red-headed women, it has now been described in blacks and males as well. Recurrent pneumonia and mucocutaneous candidiasis are common, as are elevated IgE and eosinophil levels. Levamisole, once touted highly as a treatment, did not work in a well-performed, randomized trial, reducing therapeutic options to symptomatic therapy.

PHAGOCYTIC DEFICITS. Patients with impaired opsonization related to deficits in the complement system (particularly C3) or in antibody formation manifest impaired phagocytosis. Clinically, such individuals are subject to repeated infections with organisms that possess polysaccharide capsules (which, in the absence of opsonins, are antiphagocytic), most commonly *Streptococcus pneumoniae* and *Haemophilus influenzae* type B. Patients with an inherited or acquired deficiency in the terminal components of complement are particularly susceptible to sepsis caused by *Neisseria* species, especially *Neisseria meningitidis*.

DEFICIENT INTRACELLULAR KILLING. The prototype disease in this category is chronic granulomatous disease (CGD), a hereditary disorder characterized by a failure of the respiratory burst that is normally triggered by phagocytosis. This failure results in the generation of inadequate amounts of superoxide anion, which plays a central role in postphagocytic killing. As a consequence of this defect, the patient is subject to recurrent and often severe pyogenic infections as well as a granulomatous tissue reaction to microbial invasion. This hereditary condition can be due to an X-linked inheritance pattern or be transmitted as an autosomal recessive. Because of the absence of the respiratory burst in these cells, no oxygen-derived microbicidal killing (e.g., that related to superoxide, hydrogen peroxide, hydroxyl radical, and hypochlorous acid) can take place. Catalase-negative organisms (e.g., streptococci) can still be killed effectively; in contrast, these patients have a severe problem with catalase-positive organisms (such as *S. aureus, Serratia marcescens, Pseudomonas cepacia,* and *Aspergillus*). Recurrent pneumonia, suppurative lymphadenitis, lung abscess, liver abscess, osteomyelitis, and pyogenic dermatitis related to these and other similar organisms are typical of patients with CGD. Most of these infections are subacute in presentation, are likely to relapse even with extended courses of antibiotics, and exhibit poor wound healing following surgical drainage. The tissue inflammatory response is a mixture of acute inflammation and a granulomatous response to persistent intracellular infection with organisms that usually do not have that capability.

Diagnosis is made by assaying the products of a respiratory burst in vitro, with the nitroblue tetrazolium test being the assay most commonly used to test whether or not superoxide is produced following phagocytosis. Individuals, particularly children, with a history of recurrent infection caused by catalase-positive organisms merit such testing. Treatment of patients with CGD requires a major commitment from the care providers to effect early diagnosis and therapy. Long-term prophylaxis with trimethoprim-sulfamethoxazole is utilized in most CGD patients; if this fails, interferon-γ at a dose of $50\,\mu g/m^2$ three times weekly should be initiated.

Myeloperoxidase (MPO) deficiency of the neutrophils is the most common of the neutrophilic functional disorders, with a frequency of about 1 per 2000 to 4000 individuals. In this condition, intracellular superoxide and its congeners are released much more slowly; eventually, via non-MPO pathways, intracellular killing of microbes occurs. This has a greater consequence for fungal than for bacterial infections.

Role of the Spleen in Host Defense against Microbial Invasion

The normal spleen plays an important role as a bridge between innate and acquired immunity. Because of the abundance of phagocytic macrophages lining its unique sinusoidal bed and the slow percolation of blood through it, the spleen is the most efficient phagocytic structure in the body, requiring only minimal opsonic function to carry out the removal of circulating particles in the blood stream. If splenic function is absent, the importance of opsonic deficiencies is greatly amplified. The liver, with its abundance of macrophages but without the slow percolation of blood seen in the spleen, can take on the role of the absent spleen but only if highly efficient opsonization by specific antibody has taken place—hence the importance of immunizing asplenic individuals against encapsulated organisms. Patients can be asplenic because of surgery or functionally asplenic because of diseases such as sickle cell anemia.

The spleen is the site of the primary immunoglobulin response to an antigen. Thus, subnormal production of IgM has been observed after splenectomy, as has a decreased response to such polysaccharide-based vaccines as the pneumococcal vaccine. Decreased production of properdin, a key factor in the alternative pathway of complement activation, is present after splenectomy, which leads to suboptimal opsonization by complement components, further inhibiting the host's ability to remove particles from the blood stream.

Specific Immunity

Whereas innate immune mechanisms, supplemented by specific humoral immunity (specific antibodies), provide significant protection against extracellular pathogens, the pathogens that are intracellular in location require a different strategy for control. These intracellular pathogens include viruses, some protozoans, fungi, and some bacteria. The major effector mechanisms of the innate immune system, phagocytes (particularly neutrophils) and complement, are ineffective against microorganisms present intracellularly, as are specific humoral responses. The key host defense now is due to a complex interaction between T lymphocytes and antigen-presenting cells that is termed *cell-mediated immunity*. Cell-mediated immunity occurs when peptide antigens derived from the pathogen are processed into a form that can be complexed to MHC antigens on the surface membrane of antigen-presenting cells. Antigen-presenting cells of importance include dendritic cells (Langerhans cells, lymphoid dendritic cells), macrophages, B lymphocytes, and vascular endothelial cells. This MHC-antigen complex is then recognized by T lymphocytes through the T-cell receptor, which initiates and amplifies the cellular immune response.

The T lymphocytes that are engaged in this process can be divided into two functional groups: CD4+ lymphocytes, which are the helper cells that control both T- and B-lymphocyte function, and CD8+ lymphocytes, which have a primary role in killing infected or neoplastic cells and are termed cytotoxic cells. CD4+ lymphocytes produce cytokines that activate and amplify cytotoxic T-cell activity as well as B-lymphocyte activation and the production of specific antibody. CD8+ lymphocytes play a primary role in controlling viral infection (by killing virally infected cells) as well as other intracellular parasites (e.g., bacteria such as *Salmonella* and *Listeria,* mycobacteria, fungi, and protozoa such as *Toxoplasma).*

Deficits in cell-mediated immunity, and the infectious disease consequences of these deficits, are not uncommon and can be divided into three categories:

CONGENITAL IMMUNODEFICIENCY SYNDROMES. A variety of inherited deficiency syndromes have been described in which deficits in T-cell and/or B-cell function are present and clinically important. These include *severe combined immunodeficiency disease* (in which there is a decrease in the number and function of both cell types, a striking immunoglobulin deficiency, anergy, and a failure to respond to immunizations), resulting in recurrent infections with *S. aureus, S. pneumoniae, H. influenzae,* herpes group viruses, *Pneumocystis,* and *Candida.* A variant of this condition is Omenn's syndrome, which is characterized by an eczematoid skin eruption, hepatosplenomegaly, eosinophilia, and histiocytic infiltration of the lymph nodes in addition to the infections listed. Other congenital syndromes affecting cell mediated immunity are outlined in Table 298–5.

HUMAN IMMUNODEFICIENCY VIRUS INFECTION. HIV infects not only CD4+ lymphocytes but also monocytes, follicular dendritic cells, epidermal Langerhans cells, and alveolar macrophages as well as a variety of cell types in the central nervous system (monocytes/macrophages and glial cells being the major target, with occasional infection of oligodendrocytes and astroglial cells). The host defense consequences of this infection are many: impaired regulation of humoral and cellular responses to microbial invasion, a decrease in responsiveness to microbial antigens, impairment of natural killer and cytotoxic T-cell activity, and a decreased humoral response to many pathogens. A wide variety of infections occur as a consequence of these effects, ranging from conditions that result from impaired cell-mediated immunity (e.g., *Pneumocystis carinii, Toxoplasma gondii, Cryptococcus neoformans,* atypical mycobacterial infection, and herpes group viral infections) to those that are due to encapsulated bacterial infection (e.g., *S. pneumoniae).* In addition, simultaneous infection with HIV and the hepatitis viruses leads to an accelerated course for both. The loss of effective surveillance and elimination of cells also has a key role in the pathogenesis of Kaposi's sarcoma (which is initiated by infection with human herpesvirus 8) and post-transplantation lymphoproliferative disorder (which is initiated by Epstein-Barr virus infection of B lymphocytes). The incidence of these infections is determined by the interaction of a number of factors: the degree of immunologic compromise induced by HIV, the environmental exposures to opportunistic pathogens, the HIV viral load and CD4+ count, and whether or not an effective anti-HIV regimen is being administered. A complete description of this problem is presented in Chapter 410.

EXOGENOUS IMMUNOSUPPRESSION. Over the past 2 decades increasing success has been achieved in the deployment of immunosuppressive therapy to control autoimmune disease, prevent and treat allograft rejection and graft-versus-host disease, manage inflammatory bowel disease, and treat a wide variety of other conditions of importance. The consequences of such treatment are many:

1. Rather than a "pure" defect in host defense, such as that seen in the congenital immunodeficiency diseases, the combination of the underlying disease and the immunosuppressive regimen is likely to cause mixed defects in host defense (e.g., combining profound neutropenia with a defect in cell-mediated immunity). Hence, in these patients we recognize the previously discussed net state of immunosuppression and must be prepared to deal with a particularly wide array of microbial invaders.

2. Multiple drugs are usually needed to gain the desired clinical effect while limiting toxicity from any single agent. In particular, steroid-sparing therapy has been a cornerstone of the success being achieved with immunosuppressive therapy today.

3. The anti-inflammatory, as well as the immunosuppressive, effects of these regimens can greatly alter the presentation of infections, complicating the use of these agents—signs and symptoms are blunted, microbial load is usually greater than in the normal host, and therapy needs to be prolonged.

4. The responsible clinician needs to think in terms of the therapeutic prescription as having two components: an immunosuppressive program to control the underlying diseases and an antimicrobial program to make it safe.

Immunosuppressive Drugs and Their Effects

CORTICOSTEROIDS. The clinical impact of corticosteroids includes both anti-inflammatory and immunosuppressive effects, with the former being particularly important. These are predominantly due to steroid-induced inhibition of the production of proinflammatory cytokines. Steroids also have profound inhibitory effects on arachidonic acid

Table 298–5 • HERITABLE CONDITIONS THAT INCLUDE IMPAIRED CELL-MEDIATED IMMUNITY AS PART OF THE SYNDROME		
CONDITION	**IMMUNOLOGIC ABNORMALITY**	**CONSEQUENCE OF DEFICIT**
DiGeorge's anomaly	Thymic hypoplasia	Difficulty with viruses (including live viral vaccines), *Pneumocystis*
Severe combined immunodeficiency disease (SCID)	Severe deficiency in humoral and cell-mediated immunity	Recurrent severe infections with all classes of organisms, *Pneumocystis,* chronic cutaneous candidiasis prominent
Purine pathway enzyme deficiencies (examples: adenosine deaminase deficiency; purine nucleoside phosphorylase deficiency)	Similar to SCID with severe deficiencies of humoral and cell-mediated immunity	Similar to SCID
Common variable immunodeficiency	B- and T-cell deficit, with B-cell dysfunction usually dominant	Recurrent bacterial sinopulmonary infection, but also *Pneumocystis, Mycoplasma,* and herpesviruses
Wiskott-Aldrich syndrome	Combined B- and T-cell deficit, with T-cell abnormality usually later in presentation	Primary problem sinopulmonary infection with *S. pneumoniae* and *H. influenzae*
Cellular immunodeficiency with immunoglobulin G (IgG)	Primary T-cell deficit with variable IgG abnormality particularly with T-dependent antigens	Recurrent infections with all classes of organism; *Pneumocystis carinii*
Chronic mucocutaneous candidiasis	A group of disorders with poor response to *Candida* (chronic cutaneous infection), often with endocrinopathies	Mucocutaneous candidiasis ± hypoparathyroidism, Addison's disease, and diabetes mellitus

pathways that are involved in inflammation (prostaglandins, thromboxane, and leukotrienes, as well as platelet-activating factor). Steroids inhibit microvascular permeability by blocking the production of mediators of vasodilation, particularly through the inhibition of the inducible form of nitric oxide synthase. Steroids, particularly at high doses, inhibit T-cell activation and proliferation through suppression of interleukin-2 (IL-2). Established B-cell responses are resistant to steroids, although primary B-cell responses (as to a vaccine) are significantly attenuated. The net result is that the infections associated with steroid administration reflect a major effect on cell-mediated immunity: herpes group viruses, hepatitis B and C, fungal and nocardial infections, *Pneumocystis*, and a variety of intracellular pathogens.

AZATHIOPRINE. Azathioprine is a prodrug of 6-mercaptopurine, which depletes cellular purine stores and inhibits DNA and RNA stores. Azathioprine has its greatest effect on actively dividing lymphocytes responding to primary antigenic stimulation, with little impact on mature elements of antigenic memory or end-stage lymphocyte function. Azathioprine not uncommonly produces bone marrow toxicity and, less commonly with currently utilized dosages, hepatic toxicity. The effects on infection are of two types: if neutropenia develops, bacterial sepsis may ensue (see earlier); of greater importance is that azathioprine acts to inhibit microbe-specific T-cell responses, thus predisposing to the array of organisms listed previously. It has become clear that there is considerable genetic polymorphism in the rate-limiting enzyme for the metabolism of azathioprine (thiopurine methyltransferase); there are rapid and slow metabolizers of the drug, and it is necessary to make appropriate dosage adjustments in order to get maximal benefit from the use of this drug.

MYCOPHENOLATE MOFETIL. Mycophenolate mofetil (MMF) is a relatively new drug that may be substituted for azathioprine on the basis of greater potency without an apparent increase in infection at recommended doses. It is of interest that whites seem to require only 2 g/day, whereas blacks require 3 g/day to achieve the desired effect (with no increase in infection). The explanation for this finding is unclear, but it is likely to have a genetic base, either affecting the drug's metabolism or its immunosuppressive effects. MMF is a highly selective, noncompetitive, reversible inhibitor of inosine monophosphate dehydrogenase, a crucial enzyme in the synthesis of guanosine. Proliferating lymphocytes require this pathway, whereas other cell types do not. MMF is a potent inhibitor of the proliferative response of both B and T cells. As with azathioprine, the patient immunosuppressed with this agent has particular difficulty dealing with viruses, fungi, mycobacteria, and a variety of other intracellular pathogens.

CYCLOSPORINE. The advent of cyclosporine-based immunosuppression in the early 1980s revolutionized the field. For example, before cyclosporine, 1-year cadaveric renal allograft survival barely reached 50%; since the introduction of cyclosporine-based regimens, the 1-year cadaveric allograft survival rate has become more than 85% at many centers. Cyclosporine exerts its effects through a complex signaling pathway that results in the inhibition of the transcriptional activation of lymphokine and other genes required for T-cell proliferation, activation, and function. The effects of cyclosporine are initiated by binding to receptors known as cyclophilins, which are found on many cells (a factor not only in the efficacy of this agent but also in explaining many of its toxicities). The target of this pathway is the calcium-dependent serine-threonine phosphatase, calcineurin. Calcineurin is a critical factor in the activation of the transcription factor nuclear factor of activated T cells (NF-AT), which is required for the transcription of the genes for the cytokines IL-2, IL-3, IL-4, IL-5, interferon-γ, tumor necrosis factor α (TNF-α), granulocyte-monocyte colony-stimulating factors, and the receptors for IL-2 and IL-7. The most important of these is the inhibition of IL-2, which results in a dose-related inhibition of T-cell function. From the infectious disease point of view, cyclosporine blocks microbe-specific T-cell cytotoxicity, thus enhancing the effects of any replicating herpes group virus but most notably CMV and Epstein-Barr virus.

TACROLIMUS. Tacrolimus is a calcineurin antagonist that is similar to cyclosporine in terms of mechanism of action but is 10 to 100 times more potent. Like cyclosporine, it binds to a family of immunophilins to initiate its effects, but in this case it is a separate group, known as FK506 (the preregistration name for tacrolimus) binding proteins, which initiates a signaling pathway that inhibits the activity of calcineurin. In turn, this blocks the activation of the nuclear transcription factor NF-AT and the activation of cytokine genes, most notably those for IL-2 and its receptor. The final effect is inhibition of T-cell proliferation and of primary or secondary cytotoxic cell proliferation.

Both induced immunoglobulin production by B cells and the proliferation of stimulated B cells are inhibited, thus limiting response to vaccine administration. Tacrolimus, then, has effects similar to those of cyclosporine, particularly on the herpes group viruses. There has been a major increase in interstitial nephritis associated with BK virus, a papovavirus, among kidney transplant recipients being treated with tacrolimus with or without mycophenolate. Optimal management of this entity remains to be determined, although a significant reduction in immunosuppression will undoubtedly be necessary.

RAPAMYCIN (SIROLIMUS). Although bearing a structural resemblance to tacrolimus, rapamycin exerts its effects through an entirely different mechanism—binding to RAFT1/FRAP proteins, which are associated with cell cycle phase G_1. In addition, rapamycin selectively inhibits the synthesis of ribosomal proteins, which prolongs the cell cycle at the G_1/S interface. Finally, there is inhibition of the progression to DNA synthesis and S phase. The clinical effect is that rapamycin can inhibit such cyclosporine- or tacrolimus-resistant immune functions as B-cell immunoglobulin synthesis, antibody-dependent cellular cytotoxicity, and natural killer cell activity. What may be of even greater importance is that rapamycin appears to have a more potent antiproliferative effect than other immunosuppressive agents and holds promise in the prevention of chronic allograft injury. While exploring this possibility, rapamycin is being used in conjunction with other agents as part of a steroid-sparing regimen or as a means of preventing cyclosporine or tacrolimus nephrotoxicity. Whereas the infection risks are generally the same with this agent as with the other drugs, rapamycin use has been associated with a particularly high incidence of *P. carinii* pneumonia.

ANTILYMPHOCYTE ANTIBODY THERAPIES. Three categories of antilymphocyte antibody therapy are available (such therapies should be distinguished from nonspecific immunoglobulin preparations): polyclonal antilymphocyte antibody preparations; the monoclonal antibody OKT3, which is directed against all T cells; and monoclonal antibodies directed against the IL-2 receptor. The polyclonal, pan–T-cell antibody preparations are of equine or rabbit origin and serve to deplete the recipient of T lymphocytes. These, as well as the murine-derived monoclonal OKT3, can be used in two different ways: as induction therapy to prevent rejection and as the most potent therapy available to treat rejection or graft-versus-host disease, particularly that which has not responded to more standard therapies. The big advantage of these therapies is that they allow systemic immunosuppression to be carried out without cyclosporine or tacrolimus and thus avoid the renal toxicity of these drugs at a time when acute renal failure is common. These therapies are usually given for 5 to 14 days, after which an immune response to these foreign proteins limits further efficacy as well as causes an inflammatory response (e.g., fever, chills). The first two or three doses of these agents cause the release of TNF and other proinflammatory cytokines, with possible consequences that are discussed subsequently.

Two antibodies directed against the IL-2 receptor are licensed for the prevention of allograft rejection: daclizumab (Zenapax) and basiliximab (Simulect). These antibodies are nondepleting, non–cytokine-releasing antibodies that have been shown to decrease the incidence of allograft rejection. How best to use them remains to be established.

ANTI–TUMOR NECROSIS FACTOR THERAPIES. TNF is a proinflammatory cytokine that plays an integral role in the response to infection, facilitating cell-to-cell interactions that are essential in the host response to an invasive microbe. At the same time, an overly exuberant TNF response has been linked to the pathogenesis of both localized inflammatory processes (e.g., rheumatoid arthritis, Crohn's disease) and such systemic processes as sepsis and septic shock. The key issue with TNF and, almost assuredly, other cytokines is how to control this response so that infection is not promoted and the desired anti-inflammatory effect is achieved. TNF is synthesized and released predominantly by macrophages in response to inflammatory stimuli. Two TNF-α antagonists, infliximab and etanercept (with a third, adaluminab, still in development), have been licensed and demonstrate significant benefit in the treatment of such idiopathic inflammatory conditions as rheumatoid arthritis, psoriatic arthritis, juvenile rheumatoid arthritis, and Crohn's disease. Not unexpectedly, given the key role of TNF in fighting infection, a wide range of infectious complications have occurred as a consequence of these therapies.

TNF has a wide array of stimulatory effects on host defenses. These include activation of monocytes, macrophages, and cytotoxic T cells and enhancement of NK cell function; increased leukocyte chemotaxis and transmigration; increased phagocytosis by neutrophils;

enhanced production of oxygen free radicals following phagocytosis; stimulation of B cells; and expansion of T-cell clones. Given this array of effects of TNF, there is growing experience in both humans and animal models (particularly knockout mice) with life-threatening infection in individuals receiving TNF antagonists. The range of infections seen in conjunction with the use of these antagonists has been extremely broad. Tuberculosis, with an increase in extrapulmonary and/or disseminated disease (with typical granulomas being absent in biopsy specimens from these patients), has been a particular problem. Although the data are still incomplete, the occurrence of tuberculosis appears to be more common following infliximab therapy as opposed to etanercept therapy and to occur earlier following infliximab therapy (a median of 12 weeks as opposed to 11.5 months with etanercept).

Other infections occurring after the initiation of TNF antagonist therapy include pneumococcal infection, including severe sepsis (reminiscent to that observed after splenectomy), and necrotizing fasciitis. We are aware of at least three such cases of pneumococcal necrotizing fasciitis, a clinical entity that is quite rare in the absence of TNF antagonist therapy. *P. carinii* pneumonia, systemic infection with *Listeria monocytogenes*, invasive aspergillosis, cryptococcosis, and serious infection with both *Histoplasma capsulatum* and *Coccidioides immitis* have been noted as well.

At the same time as these serious complications have occurred, remarkable control of treatment-refractory Crohn's disease and rheumatoid arthritis has been achieved with these novel therapies. Therefore, as with other forms of immunosuppressive or anti-inflammatory therapy, we must develop an antimicrobial strategy that provides protection against infection while continuing to administer this therapy to those who merit it as *therapeutic prescription*. Although the various components of the antimicrobial strategy should be tested, at present the following interventions appear to be warranted in patients receiving TNF antagonist therapy: pretherapy tuberculin testing, with positive tests warranting prophylaxis; pneumococcal and, perhaps, meningococcal immunization; prophylaxis with trimethoprim-sulfamethoxazole; consideration of fluconazole preemptive therapy under circumstances of high risk for coccidioidomycosis and cryptococcosis; and careful education of the patient to avoid potential exposures in the community and to initiate what we term "splenectomy precautions"—the immediate initiation of antibiotic therapy at home with the onset of a rigor (particularly in the setting of an upper respiratory tract infection) and an immediate visit to the emergency ward.

Remarkable strides have been made in the past decade in delineating the roles of cytokines, chemokines, and growth factors in the inflammatory-immunologic response to tissue injury. Both these agents themselves and their antagonists have great potential as disease-modifying agents. The TNF–TNF antagonist story serves as a model for both the challenges and the potential of such treatment. It is clear that future attempts to alter the "cytokine milieu" will need to pay close attention to issues of dosimetry, tissue pharmacokinetics, and the antimicrobial strategies needed to make these innovations as safe as possible.

Principles and Consequences of Immunosuppressive Therapy

The design of an immunosuppressive program to achieve the desired disease-modifying effects while minimizing the consequences, particularly the infectious disease consequences, is a complex process. The following principles should be kept in mind:

1. Immunosuppressive therapy has a narrow therapeutic-to-toxic ratio. The strategy, first worked out with steroids, is to use multiple drugs with different mechanisms of action, and hence different toxicities, at moderate doses to achieve the desired clinical effect. Thus, azathioprine was introduced to allow a decrease in steroid dose; rapamycin and a variety of antilymphocyte antibodies have been introduced to limit the renal toxicity of cyclosporine and tacrolimus.

2. The immunosuppressive programs that have been designed all have a similar effect on the occurrence of infection—the host defense deficit that is created is primarily one in cell-mediated immunity. In particular, the microbe-specific cytotoxic T-cell response is inhibited. This is translated into an increased risk of certain viruses (herpes group viruses, hepatitis viruses, papova

and papillomaviruses, and respiratory viruses), fungi, mycobacteria, *Strongyloides stercoralis*, and such bacteria as *Nocardia* species, *Listeria monocytogenes*, and *Salmonella* species.

3. The infectious disease consequences of immunosuppressive therapy are determined by a number of considerations: (a) Duration of therapy rather than daily dose ("the area under the curve") is the prime factor in determining the direct effects of such therapy. For example, in the first month following organ transplantation, at a time when the daily dose of immunosuppression is at its highest, opportunistic infections are rare unless there is a particularly intense environmental exposure. (b) Infections made possible by immunosuppression, particularly viral infections, can predispose to other infectious processes. Thus, CMV infection increases the risk of Epstein-Barr virus–associated post-transplantation lymphoproliferative disease as well as bacteremia, candidemia, listeriosis, *P. carinii* pneumonia, and invasive aspergillosis. (c) Such commonplace community-acquired infections as respiratory viral infection and bacterial gastroenteritis have very different effects in immunosuppressed patients. In the case of the respiratory viruses, there is a significant increase in viral pneumonia as well as bacterial and/or fungal superinfection. In the case of *Salmonella* infection, and possibly the other causes of bacterial enteritis, the incidence of bacteremia and possible metastatic infection is significantly increased.

4. Proinflammatory cytokines liberated as a consequence of one process can have a profound effect on other processes. For example, the key factor for activating CMV from latency is TNF, which can be elaborated as a consequence of infection, rejection, sepsis, and the administration of the depleting antilymphocyte antibodies. Different immunosuppressive regimens can have disparate effects on the course of CMV and other pathogens. Thus, such drugs as cyclosporine, tacrolimus, rapamycin, or corticosteroids have no ability to reactivate the virus from latency, whereas OKT3 and antilymphocyte antibodies that cause the release of TNF and other proinflammatory cytokines are extremely potent in reactivating latent virus. Once replicating virus is present, cyclosporine, tacrolimus, rapamycin, and steroids are quite potent in terms of amplifying the level of virus present (it is for this reason that cyclosporine and tacrolimus are referred to as in vivo polymerase chain reactions for this and other viruses).

Humoral Immunity

Specific humoral immunity is accomplished by antibodies produced by B lymphocytes responding to presentation of a particular antigen. B lymphocytes function under the control of helper T lymphocytes and such modulating factors as IL-1, IL-2, IL-6, IL-11, and IL-14. The effects of antibodies are accomplished through antigen binding to Fab sites on the immunoglobulin molecule. The functions of these immunoglobulins include complement activation through the classical pathway, neutralization and agglutination of the antigen, prevention of epithelial attachment of the antigen, and, perhaps most important, highly efficient opsonization that facilitates phagocytosis. There are several classes of immunoglobulin molecules that mediate different functions:

1. IgM accounts for approximately 10% of circulating immunoglobulins. This pentameric molecule is the first form of antibody produced on exposure to an antigen and plays a key role in homeostasis, awaiting the production of IgG molecules with greater affinity and specific function.

2. IgD is present in the serum in only trace amounts (<0.2% of serum immunoglobulins) and functions primarily as an antigen receptor on the surface of B cells.

3. IgG accounts for more than 75% of circulating immunoglobulin and is present in bodily secretions on mucosal surfaces. There are four IgG subclasses, with IgG1 and IgG3 particularly important as opsonins and IgG2 and, perhaps, IgG4 playing a key role in the response to organisms with polysaccharide capsules (e.g., *H. influenzae* type B and *S. pneumoniae*).

4. IgA makes up about 15% of circulating immunoglobulin but is the major immunoglobulin present on mucosal surfaces. This form of IgA consists of two subclasses, IgA1 and IgA2, produced locally by lymphoid tissue in the submucosa. Secretory

IgA is a dimer of two IgA molecules joined by a polypeptide termed the J piece, which is produced locally by epithelial cells. Secretory IgA plays several key roles in host defense; it prevents the adherence of bacteria to the mucosa, agglutinates bacteria, and can neutralize both toxins and viruses. IgA1 is cleaved by proteases produced by *Neisseria* species, *H. influenzae, S. pneumoniae,* and *Streptococcus sanguis.* IgA2 is resistant to this effect.

5. IgE plays a role in controlling parasitic infections and in the pathogenesis of acute allergic reactions.

The foregoing brief overview of specific humoral immunity suggests the types of infection that are of concern, whether the deficiency is inborn or acquired. A deficiency of all immunoglobulin classes results in absence of opsonizing, lytic, and neutralizing function. This absence is translated into recurrent respiratory tract infections (sinusitis and otitis as well as pneumonia) with the encapsulated pathogens *H. influenzae* and *S. pneumoniae* as well as *Mycoplasma.* This can lead to progressive bronchiectasis and lung disease, which in turn increases the susceptibility to further infection. Although less common for epidemiologic reasons, there is increased susceptibility to *Salmonella, Campylobacter,* and *Giardia* infection of the gastrointestinal tract. These patients are also subject to enteroviruses and rotavirus. Administration of oral polio vaccine to such patients or their family members can result in a progressive meningoencephalitis. Patients with IgA deficiency may be free of excessive infections or be subject to recurrent respiratory infections. Patients with IgG subclass deficiency, which may be associated with IgA deficiency, are at particular risk for *H. influenzae* infection, and IgM deficiency has been associated with meningococcal infection.

Immunoglobulin and antibody deficiency states can be divided into two major categories: primary disease, usually arising in childhood, and secondary immunodeficiency syndromes related to the acquisition of a major disease. The most severe antibody deficiency syndromes include X-linked agammaglobulinemia, common variable immunodeficiency, and X-linked hyper-IgM syndrome; these may be due to intrinsic defects in the B cells or to abnormalities in helper T-cell function or the communication between T and B cells. Secondary immunoglobulin deficiencies include those caused by such malignant states as chronic lymphocytic leukemia, multiple myeloma, and non-Hodgkin's lymphoma (including Epstein-Barr–related post-transplantation lymphoproliferative disease)—all malignancies involving the B cell. An acquired immunoglobulin deficiency state has been described in organ transplant recipients; although the mechanism is currently unknown, one might hypothesize that an acquired defect in T cell–B cell interaction may be present here, caused by exogenous immunosuppression and the host of viral infections made possible by such immunosuppression. Finally, disorders with increased IgG catabolism—burns, protein-losing enteropathies, and nephrotic syndrome—can result in an acquired hypoglobulinemia that is poorly responsive to immunoglobulin replacement strategies.

Treatment of patients with severe antibody deficiency syndrome has two components: aggressive antimicrobial treatment of acute infection aimed at preventing end-organ damage (particularly of the lungs) and immunoglobulin replacement to aid in the treatment of acute infection, and, more important, the prevention of such infection.

Principles of Antimicrobial Therapy in the Immunocompromised Host

There are four modes in which antimicrobial therapy can be deployed in immunocompromised patients:

THERAPEUTIC MODE. The administration of antimicrobials to treat established infection. Such therapy in this population of patients should be thought of in a somewhat different fashion from that in the normal host. The first question is whether the patient represents a *therapeutic emergency* or a *diagnostic dilemma.* If the first, broad-spectrum, preferably bactericidal therapy is essential, and issues of cost and toxicity are of less importance. When control is achieved and/or an organism is identified, appropriate changes that take into consideration cost and toxicity can be enacted. If the patient represents a diagnostic dilemma, the second level of prescription can be initiated from the start. In general, therapy of greater duration is needed in these patients. Rather than fixed durations of therapy, one must individualize, taking into consideration the net state of immunosuppression and the consequences of too short a course of potentially curative

therapy. We tend to think in terms of eradicating all evidence of infection and then adding a buffer period, with the duration of the buffer depending on the degree of immunosuppression, the nature of the therapy, and the seriousness of the infection.

PROPHYLACTIC MODE. The administration of an antimicrobial to an entire population of individuals before an event to prevent infection that is common enough and important enough to justify such an intervention. Ideally, the intervention is nontoxic and inexpensive. The most successful such strategy is the use of low-dose trimethoprim-sulfamethoxazole, which, in a variety of immunocompromised populations of patients, has resulted in significant prevention of urosepsis, *Pneumocystis* pneumonia, *Listeria* infection, nocardiosis, and toxoplasmosis.

PREEMPTIVE MODE. The administration of an antimicrobial program to individuals who are asymptomatic but are deemed on the basis of a laboratory marker and/or a clinical or epidemiologic characteristic to be at particularly high risk of significant clinical disease. For example, monitoring bone marrow or organ transplant patients by polymerase chain reaction assay for CMV in the blood can allow effective intervention that blocks the development of symptomatic disease. In organ transplant patients who are seropositive for CMV, routine immunosuppression (e.g., cyclosporine, mycophenolate, and prednisone) carries a risk of symptomatic CMV of about 15%; if OKT3 is used to treat refractory rejection, that risk increases to 65%. If one begins ganciclovir therapy with the OKT3 and continues it for 2 to 3 months, the incidence of symptomatic disease approaches zero. Thus, there are two forms of preemptive therapy against CMV in transplant patients. It is likely that such preemptive approaches will increase as better diagnostic techniques become available.

EMPIRICAL MODE. The administration of an antimicrobial program on the basis of a subtle clinical sign to severely neutropenic patients because there is a rather small window of opportunity to intervene effectively. Thus, in these patients (e.g., leukemia patients undergoing chemotherapy, bone marrow transplant recipients), broad-spectrum antimicrobial therapy is initiated on the basis of an unexplained fever, a rigor, unexplained tachypnea or acidosis, hypotension, and so forth. The rationale is not to delay therapy, particularly against early gram-negative infection. The specific approaches taken are many, but the following general principles serve as guidelines.

Initial therapy is aimed at gram-negative organisms, as these progress more rapidly than gram-positive or fungal infections. If the patient is deemed to be a therapeutic emergency, vancomycin is deployed immediately with the gram-negative regimen; if the patient is stable, many experts deploy just the gram-negative therapy (e.g., an advanced spectrum β-lactam with or without an aminoglycoside), reserving the gram-positive coverage for those in whom a gram-positive isolate is identified.

If there is no response at 3 to 5 days, the coverage is broadened to include not only gram-positive coverage but also antifungal therapy (assuming no specific diagnosis such as a perirectal abscess is identified). There are now at least two regimens appropriate for empirical antifungal therapy: a lipid-associated amphotericin preparation and voriconazole. It is likely that one or more of the echinocandins can be similarly deployed as well. When a diagnosis is made, the antimicrobial regimen is modified appropriately. If the patient responds clinically but without microbiologic confirmation, the antimicrobial regimen is continued until the return of the granulocytes or an extended period of afebrility has occurred. If there is no response or diagnosis, appropriate revisions in the program should be contemplated.

An important issue in these patients is the management of central venous access catheters. If the patient is infected with organisms that do not lend themselves to a bactericidal program (e.g., vancomycin-resistant enterococci), early removal is advocated, as it is for candidemia, methicillin-resistant *S. aureus,* and such other virulent pathogens as *P. aeruginosa.* If the patient is stable and responds to therapy for a nonvirulent pathogen, it is reasonable to attempt to treat with the catheter still in place.

It is likely that as better diagnostic techniques with molecular probes are developed, preemptive therapy, based on data, will be increasingly substituted for empirical therapy.

SUGGESTED READINGS
Abbas AK, Lichtman AH, Pober JS: Cellular and Molecular Immunology, 4th ed. Philadelphia, WB Saunders, 2000. *An elegant presentation of modern immunology in a clinically usable format.*

Ellerin T, Rubin RH, Weinblatt M: TNF inhibition and emerging infectious diseases. Arthritis Rheum 2003 (in press). *A critical review of the infectious disease consequences of anti-TNF therapy and possible strategies to limit it.*

Feller-Kopman D, Ernst A: The role of bronchoalveolar lavage in the immunocompromised host. Semin Respir Infect 2003;18:87–94. *Summary of the experience with and efficacy of lavage in different diseases and clinical circumstances.*

Hughes WT, Armstrong D, Bodey GP, et al: 1997 guidelines for the use of antimicrobial agents in neutropenic patients with unexplained fever. Infectious Diseases Society of America. Clin Infect Dis 1997;25:551–573. *Logical guidelines for the management of the patient.*

Rubin RH, Young LS (eds): Clinical Approach to Infection in the Compromised Host, 4th ed. New York, Kluwer/Academic/Plenum Press, 2002. *A complete review of the pathogenesis, diagnosis, and management of infection in the compromised host.*

299 PREVENTION AND CONTROL OF HOSPITAL-ACQUIRED INFECTIONS

Barry M. Farr

Definition

Hospital-acquired infections, often referred to as *nosocomial* (from the Greek word *nosocomium* meaning hospital), are those presenting after hospital admission that were neither present nor incubating at the time of admission. They can sometimes present following hospital discharge. Usually this occurs within days but sometimes it may take months, even years, before such an infection becomes manifest, depending on the incubation period of the particular infection and certain risk factors, such as operative insertion of prosthetic devices that can impair the immune response to infection and allow an insidious infection to continue developing and finally present long after insertion of the device. Likewise, hepatitis B acquired during surgery manifests several months after discharge.

History

The earliest European hospitals were established in the Middle Ages and bore little resemblance to modern hospitals in either form or function. They were thought of as places where patients with intractable disease could be brought to die. Because most patients in that era died of infections, many of which were transmissible, contagion was frequent inside the ancient hospital. As many as eight patients could be required to share the same bed. In some circumstances, crowding was so extreme that hospital beds had to be used in shifts. Such physical proximity allowed for effective exposure to most pathogens and resulted in high rates of infection among those who did not die rapidly of their underlying disease. According to some 19th century reports, surgery was almost always followed by infection, and 60% of limb amputations resulted in fatal infection. These squalid conditions led to early hospitals being called "pest houses."

Originally an outpatient procedure, obstetric delivery provided one of the first clear clues that lethal infections were being spread from one patient to another by their health care providers. In 1843, Dr. Oliver Wendell Holmes published a seminal review on this topic in the *New England Quarterly Journal of Medicine and Surgery*. After reviewing data from many previous publications, Holmes concluded that it was time to end the half century of debate about whether lethal childbed fever was sometimes spread from patient to patient by physicians and midwives. He said that this was obviously true and that it was time to stop talking and start doing something to prevent it.

Just a few years after this publication appeared and apparently unaware of it, Ignaz Philip Semmelweis reached a similar conclusion after investigating the reasons for a consistently higher maternal mortality rate on one obstetric ward than another. In 1846, the first year after being appointed director of the obstetric service of the Allgemeines Krankenhaus (General Hospital) of the University of Vienna, Semmelweis noted that Ward 1 had a maternal mortality rate of 11.4% compared with 2.7% for Ward 2. He investigated a variety of hypotheses involving hospital linen, the hospital kitchen, bell ringing by monks, and even the presence of foreign medical students, all to no avail. One hypothesis was that the deaths were due to differences in socioeconomic conditions of the patients on the two wards, but the two wards took turns admitting all obstetric patients presenting

to the hospital on alternate days and there appeared to be no socioeconomic differences between them. An important clue was then provided when pathology Professor Jakob Kolletchka became ill and died after having his hand nicked by a scalpel during an autopsy on a patient who had died of childbed fever, the usual cause of postpartum death in the hospital. An autopsy was done on Kolletchka's body and Semmelweis reviewed the slides. He wrote in his journal that Kolletchka had died of an illness in many ways pathologically identical "to that form from which I have seen so many hundred puerperal die." He concluded that "not the wound but contamination of the wound with cadaveric material was the cause of death." Because microbiology would not be firmly introduced before the contributions of such pioneers as Pasteur, Koch, and Friedlander several decades later, Semmelweis was derided by many of the leaders of medicine in Europe. As director of the service, however, he required physicians and medical students on Ward 1 to wash their hands with calcium hypochlorite after handling purulent body parts of recently autopsied patients and before examining each obstetric patient. The death rate plummeted on Ward 1 to 1.3% (i.e., a relative 89% decline). He also required handwashing before examination of all obstetric patients on Ward 2, which was staffed by midwives and midwifery students who did not attend autopsies. The death rate on Ward 2 decreased by a relative 52%. Such clear demonstration of the importance of both spread and of the prevention of spread resulted in Semmelweis being considered the "Father of Hospital Epidemiology," a field that focuses on preventing nosocomial infections. The contributions of Holmes and Semmelweis and of Lister, who pioneered the use of antiseptics in surgery, helped decrease the risk of serious infection following childbirth and surgery.

The discovery and clinical application of antibacterial agents during the 1930s and 1940s resulted in still lower rates of surgical infection. These momentous discoveries were followed, however, by the development of a new type of nosocomial infection resistant to antibiotics. Within a relatively short period, some hospitals reached epidemic rates of penicillin-resistant *Staphylococcus aureus* (PRSA), rendering the new wonder drug powerless. It soon became clear that giving penicillin to patients with penicillin-resistant infection had no effect. A pandemic of PRSA nosocomial infections led to national and international meetings, which, in turn, led to a consensus requiring the creation of hospital infection control programs with the rationale that such infections might not always be curable and that prevention might thus be more important than cure.

Other life-saving medical advancements were similarly associated with new types of lethal infection such as catheter-related blood stream infection and ventilator-associated pneumonia. In the 1970s, gram-negative bacillary infections became somewhat more common causes of nosocomial infections, but gram-positive coccal infections resurged again in the 1980s. The latter were largely infections by *S. aureus* and coagulase-negative staphylococci, both of which displayed an increasing frequency of resistance to methicillin and other beta-lactam antibiotics. In the 1990s, vancomycin-resistant enterococci also became frequent causes of infection. Advancements in medical science during these decades allowed prolongation of life for severe trauma and other severe illnesses. Advances in immunosuppression permitted therapy of previously untreatable neoplastic and autoimmune diseases; however, impairment of the immune system and new devices for care of the critically ill also provided new opportunities for nosocomial infection. It became clear that among the extremely immunosuppressed any saprophyte (even baker's yeast) could cause an occasional infection.

Importance of Nosocomial Infections

It was estimated in the 1970s that six to eight nosocomial infections occurred for every 100 patients admitted to hospital. Although the number of patients admitted to hospitals in the United States was reduced by about 10 to 15% during the 1990s in an effort to contain health care costs, the most severely ill patients continued to be admitted. Because these patients had the highest risk for nosocomial infection, the number of infections really did not change much and the rate of infections actually increased (Table 299–1). There were also more antibiotic-resistant infections to be spread. The number of deaths estimated by the Centers for Disease Control and Prevention (CDC) to be directly or indirectly due to nosocomial infections each year also increased during the past decade from 80,000 to 88,000.

Table 299-1 • RATE AND IMPACT OF NOSOCOMIAL INFECTIONS IN ACUTE CARE HOSPITALS

SITE	NO. OF INFs/100 ADMISSIONS	% OF ALL NI	DIRECT COD	EXTRA DAYS	% OF NI EXTRA DAYS
Urinary tract	2.5	30	<1%	1-3	15%
Surgical site	1.4	15	1–2%	7	23%
Lung	1.4	15	5–10%	7	23%
Blood stream					
Primary	1.4	15	3%	7	23%
Secondary	0.3	3	25%	10	5%
Others	2.2	24	<1%	2	11%

COD = cause of death; INFs = infections; NI = nosocomial infection.

Nosocomial infections are important because they cause additional suffering and mortality for patients. For the health care system, for third party payers, and for society, which ultimately pays the bills for health care as health insurance or as taxes, they are also important because they prolong hospitalization and significantly increase the cost of care. This is equally true for the mildest infections (i.e., urinary tract infections) and the most severe infections. Virtually every controlled study has shown this to be the case. Moreover, in the era of prospective payment plans, approximately 95% of the costs of nosocomial infections are not reimbursed by third party payers. It is, therefore, better for the hospital to prevent infections, not only to comply with Hippocrates' admonition "primum, non nocere" ("first, do no harm") and increase patient satisfaction scores, but also to save money.

The attributable costs of nosocomial infections relate in part to prolongation of intensive care unit (ICU) or total hospital stay, both of which are expensive, and in part to specific costs triggered by specific infections such as the need for additional diagnostic tests, antibiotic therapy, and sometimes surgery. For example, nosocomial blood stream infections were shown in one recent study to result in prolongation of stay for 7 days at an extra $40,890 in costs for surviving ICU patients. These results were confirmed in a large follow-up study from a different country. Overall, surgical site infections have resulted in prolongation of hospital stay by about a week. Infections following coronary artery bypass surgery resulted in prolonged stay and extra costs ranging from $14,211 to $20,103 depending on the method used. Nosocomial pneumonia usually occurs in patients on mechanical ventilation and usually results in about an extra week in the hospital, usually in the ICU, resulting in similar increases in extra costs to those found for blood stream infection and surgical site infection. Urinary tract infection, the most frequent and least severe nosocomial infection, has been associated with prolongation of stay for more than 3 days in two large case-control studies from different countries. Cost estimates varied between the two countries, but the study in the United States estimated $3803 (in 1992 U.S. dollars) as a median extra cost. Another recent study estimated that 85 to 97% of all urinary catheter costs were directly due to excess costs of urinary tract infection. The lower end of this range was derived from a 25-year-old CDC estimate from an uncontrolled study (i.e., a sophisticated guess) that urinary tract infections prolonged hospitalization by only 1 day, so even if the controlled studies overestimated the excess costs, a large majority of the costs attributed to urinary catheters relate to the extra costs of the infections rather than the costs of catheters themselves. Although urinary tract infections are generally milder infections, they can cause more severe illness when infection ascends to the kidney or when there is secondary blood stream infection, which has been associated with a crude case-fatality rate of 13 to 30%.

Reservoir and Transmission of Nosocomial Infections

Nosocomial infections occur for a wide variety of reasons due to a wide variety of pathogens. In some cases, the hospitalized patient may be colonized by a microbe that would never otherwise cause an infection until hospitalization provides access to some normally protected part of the body, such as by insertion of a percutaneous catheter into the blood stream. Other nosocomial pathogens are not present in or on the host at the time of hospital admission, but colonize the host after hospital admission and cause infection after a variable period of colonization. Because many patients are colonized or infected with pathogens, spread from one patient to another may occasionally occur by direct contact between patients or, more commonly, indirectly via contamination of environmental surfaces touched by both patients or by contamination of the hands, clothing, or equipment of health care workers who proceed from patient to patient and transmit such microbes, as documented by Holmes and Semmelweis in the 1840s. Transmission is facilitated because health care workers rarely cleanse their hands or disinfect their clothing or equipment when going from one patient to the next. Recent studies have found that health care workers have, on average, cleansed their hands after only 40% of patient contacts. Nurses comply more often than physicians. Poorest compliance has been in areas at highest risk for transmission such as the ICU.

Antibiotic-Resistant Infections

No discussion of nosocomial infections during the last half century would be complete without a prominent focus on antibiotic-resistant infections, which became a significant problem in hospitals within the first few years after the first introduction of antibiotics for clinical therapy. Antibiotic-resistant infections are important because they are, on average, associated with more prolonged illness, longer hospital stay, a higher risk for death, and greater costs to the health care system than infections caused by antibiotic-susceptible strains of the same species. With many antibiotics, resistance has shown up within years of introduction of a particular agent, usually first in the hospital and later in the general community. This was the pattern for penicillin-resistant S. aureus. For other antibiotics such as vancomycin, resistance among enterococci did not appear until 3 decades after its introduction. When vancomycin-resistant enterococci (VRE) first appeared in the mid-1980s, it seemed to be related to clinical use in the United States and to agricultural use of a related compound (avoparcin) in farm animals such as chickens and pigs in Europe.

The two predominant risk factors for patients having antibiotic-resistant pathogens in hospitals have been the volume of antibiotic use and patient-to-patient transmission. The reason that the prevalence of antibiotic-resistant pathogens has grown so rapidly in the hospital was perhaps most clearly explained by Charles Darwin, who noted that nature selects the strain or species most suited to survive within each environment. Because up to half of all patients in U.S. hospitals and almost all patients in ICUs receive antibiotics, a microbe with a mutation for resistance has a selective advantage to survive, proliferate, and spread.

For some combinations of microbe and antibiotic, the probability of a spontaneous mutation to resistance to that particular drug is so high that giving that drug alone for infections by that microbe predictably results in antimicrobial resistance. For example, the risk of mutation to isoniazid resistance among Mycobacterium tuberculosis is so high that monotherapy of active tuberculosis with isoniazid (INH) results in development of INH resistance in 70% of patients; this persists if the drug is stopped and after transmission to other patients. For other combinations of microbes and antibiotics, however, the probability of a spontaneous mutation to resistance is much lower and administration of that drug alone does not result in an increased risk of resistance of that microbe to that drug. The latter pattern is true for combinations such as enterococci and vancomycin or S. aureus and methicillin, which correspond to two of the most frequent antibiotic-resistant infections in U.S. hospitals. The pattern mentioned earlier (i.e., that large proportions of hospital patients are on antibiotics and that microbes are routinely moved from patient to patient) has resulted in a steadily growing prevalence of antibiotic-resistant pathogens like methicillin-resistant Staphylococcus aureus (MRSA) (Fig. 299–1) and vancomycin-resistant Enterococcus (VRE) (Fig. 299–2) inside U.S. hospitals. These facts have led many to believe that antibiotic control must be the most cost-effective means of controlling antibiotic-resistant infections. Although there has been some modest control with this approach, the fact that most hospitals believe they are controlling antibiotics and still failing to control antibiotic-resistant infections raises the question as to whether there are other effective means of control. More than 50 studies have shown that identifying colonized patients (i.e., the reservoir for nosocomial spread) with active surveillance cultures and then implementing CDC guidelines for preventing spread with contact precautions (i.e., gowns and gloves to prevent contamination of the clinician during care of the

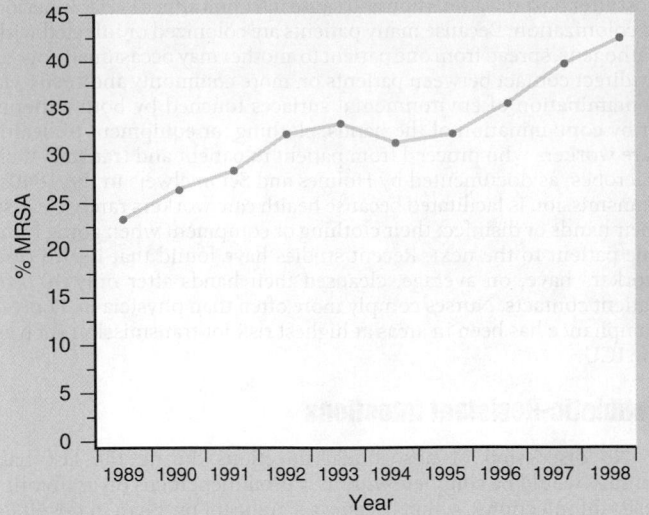

FIGURE 299–1 • Percentage of nosocomial *Staphylococcus aureus* infections reported as resistant to methicillin, by year. (Data from National Nosocomial Infections Surveillance System, 1989–1998.)

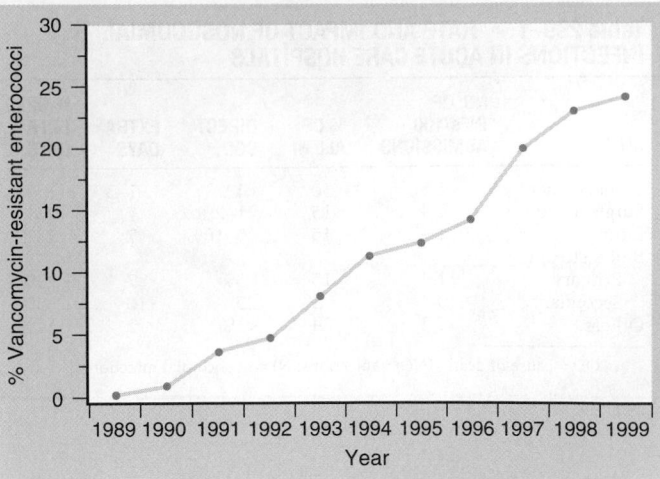

FIGURE 299–2 • Percentage of nosocomial enterococci reported as resistant to vancomycin, by year. (Data from National Nosocomial Infections Surveillance System, 1989–1999.)

colonized patient) can effectively control the problem even in the absence of antibiotic control measures. This has been demonstrated in individual hospital wards, entire hospitals, entire health districts, and even whole countries such as Denmark, Holland, Finland, and Sweden (Fig. 299–3). One of these studies showed that the risk of MRSA spread to other patients was reduced by 15.6-fold when such precautions were used as compared with standard precautions, which rely primarily on hand hygiene between all patient contacts to prevent spread; scores of studies have shown hand hygiene to be frequently forgotten. Another recent study found that clinicians' gowns, gloves, and stethoscopes became contaminated two thirds of the time when examining a patient colonized or infected with VRE.

Many U.S. hospitals have not implemented this approach because of the assumption that the component costs of cultures, gowns, and gloves would result in greater overall costs. However, because the costs of antibiotic-resistant infections are significantly greater and the rates of such infections have been kept very low in countries using this approach (e.g., Denmark), it is likely that the approach employed by those U.S. hospitals, which does not take account of costs to the entire health system, may be wasting more money than it saves. In Denmark, an infection with *S. aureus* is almost always susceptible to beta-lactams and can thus be treated more cheaply with faster response, quicker discharge, and lower total costs. Isolating the minority of colonized patients recognized to have VRE or MRSA through the results of routine clinical microbiology cultures has relatively limited impact on the overall rate of spread and infection with such pathogens because

only about 15% of VRE-colonized and MRSA-colonized patients have been recognized by such routine clinical cultures.

Urinary Tract Infections

Nosocomial urinary tract infection usually follows instrumentation of the urinary tract, most often with a catheter. Infection occurs in about 1% of those with a single in-out catheterization. For those with an indwelling catheter, the risk of infection remains relatively constant at about 3 to 6% per catheter-day, higher for female than for male patients. After 10 to 14 days, about half of catheterized patients have bacteriuria. This means that virtually all patients with a long-dwelling catheter develop infection at some point. Because enteric flora are the usual causes of urinary tract infection and because diarrhea predisposes to contamination of the catheter-urethra interface, diarrhea is an independent risk factor for urinary tract infection.

During a large national study by CDC conducted in the 1970s and 1980s, urinary tract infections accounted for 40% of all nosocomial infections. In recent years, such data have not been available from a national source, but data from individual hospitals conducting hospital-wide surveillance suggest that they remain the most frequent nosocomial infection, accounting for about 30%.

The most frequent microbial agents causing nosocomial urinary tract infection, according to data of the National Nosocomial Infections Surveillance (NNIS) Program of the CDC, have been (in order of decreasing relative frequency) *Escherichia coli*, *Enterococcus* species, *P. aeruginosa*, *Candida* species, *Klebsiella pneumoniae*,

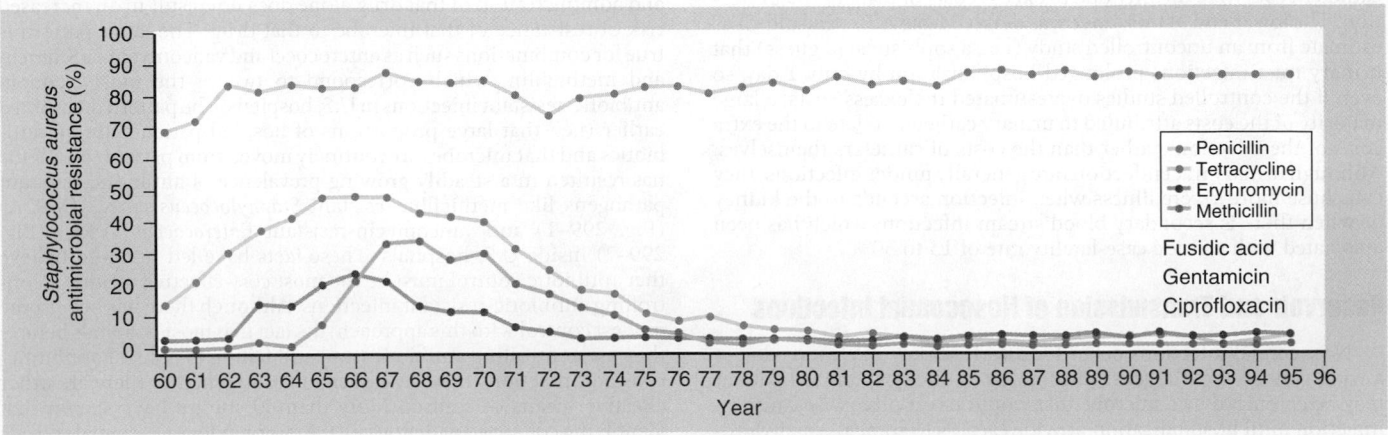

FIGURE 299–3 • Percentage of *Staphylococcus aureus* bacteremias due to strains resistant to antimicrobials in Danish hospitals from 1960 to 1995. (From Bager F [ed]: DANMAP 98—Consumption of antimicrobial agents and occurrence of antimicrobial resistance in bacteria from food animals, food, and humans in Denmark. Copenhagen, Danish Zoonosis Centre, 1999. Available at: *http://www.svs.dk/dk/z/Danmap%201998.pdf*)

Enterobacter species, *Proteus mirabilis*, coagulase-negative staphylococci, other fungi, *Citrobacter* species, and *S. aureus*.

Studies of preventive measures have confirmed the efficacy of closed drainage systems and of a silver alloy urinary catheter for preventing infections.

Pneumonia

Infection of the pulmonary parenchyma can occur after aspiration of microbe-laden secretions from the upper respiratory tract or regurgitated gastric contents. These are believed to be the most common mechanisms in the pathogenesis of nosocomial pneumonia. Infection at a distant site in the body such as *S. aureus* infection of a central venous catheter or arteriovenous fistula used for hemodialysis can sometimes result in septic pulmonary emboli that can, in turn, cause hematogenous pneumonia, often characterized by a different appearance on chest radiography with multiple expanding pneumatoceles at different places in the lungs. Another rare source of pneumonia in the hospital is inhalation of a microbe from the air. Examples of microbes that usually cause pneumonia by inhalation include *M. tuberculosis* and *Aspergillus fumigatus*. The former occurs by contagion via small particle droplet nuclei from a coughing patient that can float in the air for hours and may infect patients several rooms away, although those closer to the coughing patient are at greater risk. The latter occurs by inhalation of a microbe that grows on organic materials and is frequently present in both outdoor and indoor air. *Coxiella burnetii*, the agent of Q fever, has rarely caused pneumonia in medical center employees who inhaled the microbe while working in medical research with parturient sheep. *Legionella*, the cause of Legionnaire's disease, was originally thought to occur primarily by inhalation, but this is now controversial and it may occur more frequently following aspiration of *Legionella*-contaminated potable water.

Most patients acquiring nosocomial pneumonia have been on mechanical ventilators in an ICU. Rates of pneumonia have ranged from 6 to 30% among such populations with a risk of 1 to 3% per day of intubation and mechanical ventilation. The incidence density per 1000 days of mechanical ventilation has ranged from 5 to 34 in different patient populations. Medical and surgical ICU patients have generally had rates in the middle of this range. Abnormal elevation of gastric pH in such patients due to underlying disease, histamine type 2 (H$_2$) blockers or antacid therapy has been a risk factor for infection, apparently because of microbial overgrowth in stomach fluids that may result in higher inocula with regurgitation and aspiration. Use of sucralfate, which does not alter gastric pH, to prevent stress ulceration during mechanical ventilation has been associated with significantly lower rates of nosocomial pneumonia. This finding has been counterbalanced by other studies finding lower overall rates of infection in ICU patients using nasojejunal feeding tubes rather than parenteral nutrition. The lack of nasogastric tubes in such patients in some ICUs has resulted in continuing use of H$_2$ blockers but with acceptably low rates of overall infection. Likewise, selective digestive tract decontamination with antibiotics (e.g., swabbed onto the teeth as a paste and squirted into the stomach via a nasogastric tube) has also resulted in significantly lower pneumonia rates, but is not generally used because of studies showing more rapid development of antibiotic resistance with this approach.

Keeping the intubated patient's torso above the waist elevated to an angle of 45 degrees and using a device for continual subglottic suction to prevent pooling of secretions have been associated with less clinical aspiration and lower rates of pneumonia.

The most frequent microbial agents causing nosocomial pneumonia according to NNIS data have been *S. aureus*, *P. aeruginosa*, *Enterobacter* species, *Klebsiella pneumoniae*, and *E. coli* (in decreasing order of relative frequency).

Surgical Site Infections

As discussed earlier, surgical site infection was almost inevitable in early hospitals. Today, the reverse is true for "clean," elective procedures (e.g., coronary bypass graft or total hip replacement). A large majority of such operations are not complicated by infection because of the use of antiseptic preparation of the surgeon's hands and the patient's skin, sterile aseptic barriers (e.g., surgical gown and gloves), prophylactic antibiotics during the procedure, and sterilization of surgical instruments used for the operation. Despite this major improvement, infections still do occur, more in some hospitals than in others

and more with some surgeons than with others. This can occur despite equal care and provision of preventive measures such as those listed earlier because of systematic differences in the prevalence of risk factors among patients being referred for care (e.g., obesity, diabetes mellitus) or the use of measures shown to increase the risk of infection (e.g., dry shaving to remove hair the day before the operation rather than using clippers within the hour before the operation). Patients with contaminated wounds (e.g., a ruptured appendix) have a much higher risk of intra-abdominal infection despite all of these modern preventive measures because microbial exposure occurs before the surgery. Patients with emergent procedures on organs full of microbes such as the colon also have higher risk for infection because of greater risk of spillage during such procedures. Elective colon surgery with prior antimicrobial prophylaxis and mechanical cleansing are associated with much lower infection rates, because of lower risk of operative spillage of colonic contents. Surgical infection rates can be kept to a minimum by reporting these rates to surgeons, avoiding shaving for hair removal, and ensuring appropriate timing, duration, and choice of antimicrobial prophylactic agents.

The most frequent microbial agents causing surgical site infections according to NNIS data have been *S. aureus*, coagulase-negative staphylococci, enterococci, gram-negative bacilli, such as *E. coli*, *Enterobacter*, *Klebsiella*, and *Enterobacter*, and *Candida* (in decreasing order of relative frequency).

Blood Stream Infections

Blood stream infections can occur as a result of primary infection within the cardiovascular system as when it begins from an infected vascular catheter or secondary to a local infection in another organ (e.g., an *E. coli* infection of the urinary tract). Approximately 80% of nosocomial blood stream infections are primary, most of which are due to vascular catheter infections, and 20% are secondary to infections in other organs. The most frequent causes of primary blood stream infection in the past decade according to NNIS data have been (in decreasing order of frequency) coagulase-negative staphylococci, *S. aureus*, enterococci, *Candida*, and gram-negative bacilli such as *Enterobacter*. It is clear that coagulase-negative staphylococci can cause such infections, but it also appears that a large proportion of patients with blood cultures positive for coagulase-negative staphylococci actually have contaminated blood cultures. In one recent study, 90% of patients with blood cultures positive for coagulase-negative staphylococci appeared to have contaminated blood cultures. By contrast, *S. aureus* and *Candida* are more virulent and are associated with a much higher probability of true blood stream infection.

Catheter-related blood stream infection usually begins with colonization of the catheter with a microbe. Because vascular catheters are usually placed through the patient's skin, most such colonizing microbes come from the patient's own skin. Studies using electron microscopy have shown that microbial contamination of catheters is virtually universal from the first day after insertion. One study cultured the tips of central venous catheters accessed during cardiac surgery (i.e., within 1 to 2 hours of insertion) and showed that the tips of such catheters could be contaminated despite rigorous antiseptic preparation of the skin before insertion. The reason that all vascular catheters do not become clinically infected probably has to do with the body's immune response holding microbial invaders in check. During the first few days after catheter insertion, most significant colonization (as judged by quantitative cultures of catheter segments) and infection seem to occur because of microbes moving through the catheter tract along the external catheter surface. By contrast, after 10 days of placement, ultrastructural studies begin to show an increasing relative frequency of intraluminal contamination and most long-term catheters appear to be infected by the intraluminal route.

Because most colonizing and infecting flora come from the patient's skin, antiseptic preparation before catheter insertion and every few days thereafter has been used to reduce the risk for infection. Chlorhexidine gluconate has been shown to significantly reduce the risk of catheter colonization as compared with alcohol or povidone-iodine preparation of the skin in multiple randomized trials. Although most such trials were designed only to have statistical power to reduce colonization, two trials also showed significant prevention of catheter-related blood stream infection. Other trials have investigated the protective effects of various types of dressings. A meta-analysis of such trials found that cotton gauze covered by tape was associated with significantly lower risk of colonization of catheters than were transparent dressings. Another focus of research for preventing catheter infections has been impregnation with antimicrobial substances such as antiseptics or antibiotics. An antiseptic (chlorhexidine-silver sulfadiazine) impregnated catheter has been shown to reduce both colonization and blood stream infection by about half. Antibiotic-coated catheters may be associated with even greater prevention, although the one available randomized controlled trial (RCT) varied where the antimicrobial was applied as well as type of antimicrobial applied. Antibiotic-coated catheters would also appear to raise the risk of developing clinically significant antibiotic resistance. Although such resistance has not been documented in studies including hundreds of patients, clinical use could involve millions of patients and their usage should thus involve careful observation for development of resistance as was documented for selective digestive tract decontamination with antibiotics.

Other Nosocomial Infections

During a national study of nosocomial infections conducted by CDC in the 1970s, only about 6% of recognized infections did not involve the four main body sites listed earlier; currently about 25% of all infections acquired in hospitals conducting hospital-wide surveillance are of this miscellaneous type. This includes gastrointestinal infections caused by organisms such as *Clostridium difficile*, rotavirus, and *Salmonella*; viral infections caused by varicella, influenza, and respiratory syncytial virus; and candidal infections of the mouth, esophagus, and vagina.

Infection Control Programs

Formal infection control programs did not exist in most hospitals until the 1970s. They were introduced in U.S. hospitals at that time based upon recommendations of the CDC, the American Hospital Association (AHA), and the Joint Commission for Accreditation of Healthcare Organizations (JCAHO). The primary rationale was to control antibiotic-resistant infections, which had soared out of control in most hospitals during the 1950s and 1960s.

As hospitals began to implement such programs, the CDC implemented a national study of the effectiveness of these efforts entitled the Study of the Efficacy of Nosocomial Infection Control (SENIC). The largest study of infection control ever conducted, SENIC used a probability sample of general hospitals nationwide, determined nosocomial infection rates, and assessed predictors in multivariable analysis. The size and intensity of work by the infection control program was found to predict infection rates. The most important predictors in decreasing order of importance were intensity of surveillance, intensity of control measures, ratio of infection control practitioners (ICPs) to number of patient beds, presence of a trained hospital epidemiologist on staff, and provision of SSI rates to surgeons (i.e., so as to influence their behavior). The most effective programs (i.e., those with all of the aforementioned predictors) were associated with a 32% relative reduction in the nosocomial infection rate compared with rates in hospitals with no infection control program. One hospital with an effective program, as defined by the SENIC criteria, calculated that hospital cost savings from investing in such an infection control program had probably exceeded $2 million in 1985, the year in which the SENIC study was published.

The average U.S. hospital at the time of the SENIC study did not have all of these features in place, and the average relative reduction associated with the national effort to control nosocomial infections as measured in SENIC was only 6% when compared with hospitals with no infection control program. The primary reason for creating infection control programs—prevention and control of antibiotic-resistant infections—was not a focus of the SENIC study. This may have been because PRSA infections were still spreading out of control inside and outside of health care facilities and it was not yet clear how such infections could be controlled.

The reason that surveillance for nosocomial infections was likely important in the SENIC study is likely the same reason that surveillance is considered essential in the community for diseases such as syphilis and acquired immunodeficiency syndrome (AIDS). By knowing what is happening, specific control measures can be fashioned to intervene, allowing control of outbreaks and reduction of high endemic rates. When surveillance for surgical site infections was first introduced into some hospitals, infection rates were three to 10 times higher than some surgeons had estimated.

Fads and fashions come and go in health care as in other human enterprises. Initially, many hospitals implemented continual hospital-wide surveillance. Because some infections appeared to be more important than others in analyses from the SENIC database in terms of prolongation of stay and extra costs and because interhospital comparison of crude hospital rates was thought to be difficult given the differences in severity of underlying illness in patients admitted to hospitals of different types in different regions, some advocated targeted surveillance focusing on the biggest problems of a particular hospital. Outbreaks in ICUs were missed for months in hospitals targeting only surgical site infections, however. Likewise, hospitals focusing only on ICU infections have had trouble recognizing high infection rates on regular hospital wards. Many hospitals underwent downsizing of both patient admissions and health care personnel to cut costs, and because infection control programs were not viewed as revenue generating, they were often cut as well. Even when they were not reduced in size, they often underwent relative reduction by having duties added that were not part of their original focus. For example, new Occupational Safety and Health Administration (OSHA) requirements to protect health care workers from infection with blood-borne pathogens required orientation and annual retraining of all health care workers, and development and annual review of exposure control plans for all hospital units and departments. Similar requirements were enacted by OSHA to protect health care workers from nosocomial tuberculosis. These activities clearly relate to infection control and were thus usually assigned to infection control programs. Because they were unfunded mandates, however, the requirements for added work were usually given to infection control programs with no added resources. Infection control programs in U.S. hospitals are often underfunded and undermanned. A recent consensus report from the CDC, the JCAHO, the AHA, and a variety of other agencies and national societies concluded that infection control is more difficult in the hospital now than it was during the 1970s and 1980s when SENIC was conducted. That consensus report also concluded that more than one ICP per every 250 hospital beds (the ratio found to be essential by SENIC) is needed to do an effective job of controlling infections. The consensus report may have been ignored, however, as some hospitals are reportedly reducing their support for infection control activities even further by requiring ICPs to work on other adverse effects of health care such as prescribing errors and patient falls.

Nosocomial Infections of Health Care Workers

Nosocomial infection can affect health care workers as well as patients. Health care workers in facilities taking a "don't ask, don't tell" approach to the rising prevalence of colonization of patients with antibiotic-resistant pathogens such as MRSA become colonized at a higher rate than the general population and have had occasional infections with such microbes. Casually contagious viral infections such as influenza and measles occur more frequently among health care workers because they are exposed to sick people in the community as well as to patients who are not always recognized and placed in appropriate isolation precautions.

OCCUPATIONAL RISK FOR HUMAN IMMUNODEFICIENCY VIRUS INFECTION. Although the risk of acquiring human immunodeficiency virus (HIV) infection from a patient is exceedingly low, it is not zero. This caused great concern among health care workers when first documented. Unlike bubonic plague, which was reported to kill more than half of the health care workers tending the sick during epidemics in Europe during the Middle Ages, HIV has caused less than 100 documented infections among more than 5 million health care workers in the United States during the 2 decades since AIDS and HIV were discovered. This comes to a risk of less than one confirmed HIV infection for each million health care worker-years in the United States during those 2 decades. It is also likely that the risk is now much lower than it was early during that period because of recognition that the virus is spread by exposure to blood and body fluids. Standard precautions require use of barriers such as gowns and gloves to prevent contact with any type of body fluid (except sweat) from all patients.

A multinational case-control study showed that the risk of infection after needlestick increased significantly if the needle had been used in a vein or artery, if there was visible blood on it, if it caused a deep injury, and if the patient had terminal AIDS (i.e., a high viral load). By contrast, the use of postexposure prophylaxis with zidovudine was associated with almost an 80% relative reduction in the risk of infection in multivariable analysis. This finding led to the widespread use of postexposure prophylaxis after occupational exposures to HIV with not one but three highly active antiretroviral drugs. As for most decisions about nosocomial infections, RCTs are not available. On average, about three needlesticks per 1000 involving HIV patients have resulted in HIV infection of the health care worker, but risk is presumably lower now with prophylaxis. Because the long-term consequences of taking such drugs for a month are unknown and because a large majority taking them for postexposure prophylaxis develop adverse effects such as nausea, some hospitals rapidly test the source patient using deemed consent provisions of state law and determine within 1 to 2 hours whether exposure to patients with unknown HIV status will require prophylaxis. This has avoided even brief prophylaxis for a large majority of injured employees in such hospitals.

OCCUPATIONAL RISK FOR HEPATITIS. Although AIDS was the biggest concern among health care workers when it was discovered in the 1980s, studies showed that hepatitis B was paradoxically a much more frequent occupational infection and cause of death among health care workers. Standard precautions and OSHA requirements to offer free hepatitis B vaccine to health care workers have resulted in a dramatic decrease in hepatitis B infections among health care workers. However, about 10% of workers do not respond to vaccine and some workers decline to be vaccinated because of concern about side effects. Studies have shown the vaccine to be safe, and compliance has likely increased with dissemination of this information.

No vaccine is available as yet for hepatitis C, the most common blood-borne viral infection and the most frequent indication for liver transplantation in the United States. A recent open trial of early interferon therapy documented clearly higher cure rates than usually expected with watchful waiting and therapy only for chronic infection. No RCT is available, but this points to early testing and therapy for occupational hepatitis C infection.

OCCUPATIONAL RISK FOR TUBERCULOSIS. After more than a century of declining rates of tuberculosis in the United States, which accelerated in the middle of the last century with discovery of effective antituberculosis therapy, the rate began to increase again in 1985 and continued to do so until 1992. Epidemiologic analysis of the increase suggested that increased immigration of persons with tuberculosis and the expanding pool of patients immunocompromised by AIDS appeared to be the two predominant risk factors. A marked increase in antimicrobial resistance was also observed in isolates during this period as well. All of these influences helped to result not only in the overall increase but also in nosocomial outbreaks in New York, New Jersey, and Miami. The nosocomial outbreaks were found to be related to the lack of negative-pressure ventilation rooms for isolation of patients with possible or known tuberculosis and the lack of administrative control measures (e.g., policies requiring that isolation patients stay in isolation). These outbreaks resulted in new CDC recommendations and OSHA requirements that mandated administrative and engineering controls as well as a program of respirator fit testing, annual or semiannual PPD testing, and regular retraining regarding tuberculosis. The nosocomial outbreaks described herein were controlled before these guidelines were issued and without using HEPA respirators or respirator fit testing, leaving the importance of these measures uncertain. Since 1992, the rate of tuberculosis has steadily decreased in the United States and nosocomial outbreaks have been reported much less frequently.

SUGGESTED READINGS

Booth CM, Matukas LM, Tomlinson GA, et al: Clinical features and short-term outcomes of 144 patients with SARS in the greater Toronto area. JAMA 2003;289:2801–2809. *Of 144 SARS patients in the Toronto epidemic, 111 had acquired SARS as a nosocomial infection in a hospital; 73 (51%) of all SARS patients were health care workers.*

Fridkin SK, Hageman J, McDougal LK, et al: Epidemiological and microbiological characterization of infections caused by Staphylococcus aureus with reduced susceptibility to vancomycin, United States, 1997–2001. Clin Infect Dis 2003;36:429–439. *Patients with infection due to MRSA with reduced susceptibility to vancomycin were more likely to die than patients with MRSA infections and full susceptibility to vancomycin.*

Muto CA, Jernigan JA, Ostrowsky BE, et al: SHEA guideline for preventing nosocomial transmisson of multidrug-resistant strains of Staphylococcus aureus and enterococcus. Infect Control Hosp Epidemiol 2003;24:362–386. *This guideline recommends active identification of the reservoir for spread (often colonized patients) and implementation of contact precautions for preventing spread.*

Ostrowsky BE, Trick WE, Sohn AH, et al: Control of vancomycin-resistant enterococcus in health care facilities in a region. N Engl J Med 2001;344:1427–1433. *Using active surveillance cultures in all health care facilities facilitated control of VRE.*

Seto WH, Tsang D, Yung RW, et al: Effectiveness of precautions against droplets and contact in prevention of nosocomial transmission of severe acute respiratory syndrome (SARS). Lancet 2003:361:1519–1520. *Infection control measures were effective in reducing the risk that health care workers would acquire SARS.*

300 ADVICE TO TRAVELERS
Richard D. Pearson

Millions of North Americans and Europeans travel to developing areas of the world each year. Modern air transportation has brought even the most exotic sites within easy reach. Most travelers go for vacation or business and are away for a few weeks or less, but some spend extended periods abroad. In addition, thousands of American troops are deployed at various times in tropical or developing areas.

The risks associated with international travel depend on the locations visited, the duration of the trip, and the traveler's health status and activities. Persons visiting Australia, Canada, Western Europe, Japan, New Zealand, and the United States require no special prophylactic measures. In contrast, visitors to developing areas, particularly in the tropics, may be exposed to serious infectious and noninfectious risks.

Specific prophylactic health measures should be tailored to the traveler's itinerary and individual needs. They can be separated into the following areas: pretravel health assessment, diseases prevented by immunization, prevention and treatment of traveler's diarrhea, malaria prophylaxis, and behavioral modifications that reduce the risk of infectious or noninfectious hazards. Information about risks and recommendations for travel to specific geographic locations is provided by the Centers for Disease Control and Prevention (CDC) through its publications *Summary of Health Information for International Travel* and *Health Information for International Travel*, Travelers' Hotline (877-FYI-TRIP), and World Wide Web site (*www.cdc.gov/travel*); and by other publications and several commercially available travel information systems.

PRETRAVEL HEALTH ASSESSMENT

It is important to review the past medical history, active medical problems, allergies to antibiotics or vaccine components, and pregnancy status before embarking on prophylactic measures. Special arrangements are often necessary for those with insulin-dependent diabetes, chronic renal failure, or other medical problems. Persons infected with the human immunodeficiency virus (HIV) or who are otherwise immunocompromised also require special attention, as discussed later.

For long-term travelers, it is important to address routine health maintenance issues. Their purified protein derivative (PPD) status should be determined because tuberculosis is prevalent in many developing areas. Some countries require HIV testing before issuing long-term visas. Travelers should check with the appropriate embassies to determine whether it is necessary.

IMMUNIZATIONS

General Considerations

A number of infectious diseases can be prevented by immunization. Vaccines can be grouped into those that everyone should receive, whether they travel or not, those recommended for travelers to tropical or developing areas (see information from the CDC for specific recommendations by location), and those legally required for entrance into a country (Table 300–1). No immunizations are required for American citizens returning to the United States. Some countries require that all visitors be immunized against yellow fever, whereas others require it only for those who have traveled in yellow fever–endemic areas. Countries that require the yellow fever vaccine are listed in the CDC information. Cholera immunization is no longer required to enter any country, but local officials may still request documentation in some areas. Administration of the yellow fever vaccine and other immunizations should be documented in the small booklet "International Certificate of Vaccination," which should be carried during the trip.

Table 300–1 • IMMUNIZATION OF INTERNATIONAL TRAVELERS

ROUTINE VACCINES THAT SHOULD BE UP-TO-DATE IN ALL TRAVELERS
Diphtheria/tetanus
Pertussis (children < 7 yr)
Poliomyelitis
Measles
Mumps
Rubella
Haemophilus influenzae (children)
Hepatitis B
Pneumococcal conjugate vaccine (PCVF)—children 2–23 mo
Varicella

ROUTINE VACCINES INDICATED IN SPECIAL POPULATIONS
Influenza
Pneumococcal-23 valent polysaccharide vaccine (PPV23)—adults > 65 years and persons with underlying conditions that place them at increased risk of pneumococcal disease

VACCINES POTENTIALLY INDICATED FOR TRAVELERS TO DEVELOPING AREAS*
Cholera (not available in the United States)
Hepatitis A (or immune serum globulin)
Influenza
Japanese B encephalitis
Meningococcal
Poliomyelitis
Rabies
Typhoid
Yellow fever[†]

*The choice of specific vaccines depends on the itinerary, activities, and duration of travel, as well as cost, efficacy, and potential side effects of the vaccines.
[†]Required for entry by some countries. See *Health Information for International Travel* and *Summary of Health Information for International Travel* for a listing of countries requiring vaccination for entry.

Before vaccination, persons should be questioned about allergies. A history of hypersensitivity to egg protein is important because many viral vaccines (e.g., yellow fever, mumps, measles, and influenza) are prepared in embryonated eggs or chicken embryo cell cultures. In general, anyone who can eat eggs can tolerate these vaccines. On rare occasion, persons may be hypersensitive to thimerosal, neomycin, or other trace vaccine components.

The precise indications, contraindications, and potential side effects of each vaccine are outlined in the package insert and summarized elsewhere. In general, multiple vaccines can be given simultaneously at different sites without adversely affecting their efficacy. Exceptions include the yellow fever and cholera vaccines, which reciprocally inhibit antibody responses to one another, and immune serum globulin, which inactivates some live vaccines. If used, immune serum globulin should be given at least 3 weeks after or 5 months before most live vaccines are administered. Immune serum globulin has no apparent adverse effect on the efficacy of yellow fever vaccine, but, when possible, it should be given at a separate time. If live viral vaccines are not administered simultaneously, it is recommended that they be spaced 4 weeks apart to avoid immune interference. Vaccination should also be delayed in persons with acute febrile diseases.

Live viral and bacterial vaccines are generally contraindicated in travelers with HIV or who are immunocompromised by chemotherapy, but there are exceptions. The measles vaccine is used when the benefits are deemed to outweigh the risk of vaccine-related infection. It is safe to administer inactivated vaccines to immunocompromised persons, but the immune responses that are elicited may be impaired and may leave the traveler at risk. Live vaccines are also contraindicated during pregnancy. The safety of many inactivated vaccines has not been assessed in pregnant women.

Immunizations to Protect International Travelers

CHOLERA (Chapter 328). Cholera is rare in travelers and the cholera vaccine is no longer available in the United States. Two oral vaccines are available in other countries. Few experts recommend immunization against cholera, but travelers are strongly urged to follow food and water precautions (see later text) and to institute rehydration and antibiotic treatment immediately if diarrhea develops. Cholera immunization is no longer necessary for entrance into any country.

HEPATITIS A (Chapter 151). Hepatitis A constitutes a major risk for travelers to areas where sanitation and hygiene are poor. The likelihood of acquiring hepatitis A has been estimated to be as high as 1 in 1000 travelers per 2- to 3-week trip in some areas. Symptomatic hepatitis A infection can be prevented by immunization with one of the inactivated hepatitis A vaccines. Passive immunization with immune serum globulin, 0.02 mL/kg given intramuscularly for travel less than 3 months and 0.06 mL/kg for travelers going for 3 to 5 months, is effective but seldom used. In some instances, it is cost effective to determine the immune status of travelers who may have been previously infected. The presence of anti–hepatitis A IgG antibodies indicates that the traveler is immune.

HEPATITIS B (Chapter 151). The hepatitis B vaccine is recommended for long-term travelers, health care workers, and others likely to be exposed to blood or body fluids while abroad. It can be argued that everyone should receive the vaccine whether they travel or not.

INFLUENZA (Chapter 363). The influenza vaccine is recommended for travel during influenza season, which includes the months of October to April in the Northern Hemisphere, May to November in the Southern Hemisphere, and all times of the year in the tropics.

JAPANESE B ENCEPHALITIS (Chapter 377). The Japanese B encephalitis vaccine is indicated for travelers who will have intense and/or prolonged (>4 weeks) exposure in endemic areas in China, Korea, Southeast Asia, India, the lowlands of Nepal, Sri Lanka, and, to a limited degree, Japan, eastern areas of Russia, and other areas of Asia and Oceania. This mosquito-borne disease is most common in rural rice and pig farming areas. It occurs from June through September in temperate regions and throughout the year in tropical areas. Travelers to urban sites are usually at low risk of infection.

The Japanese B encephalitis vaccine is not without side effects. Allergic reactions, including rash, urticaria, anaphylaxis, and, rarely, death, occur in approximately 6 per 1000 administrations. Persons with a history of hypersensitivity responses to other allergens seem to be at greatest risk. Vaccine recipients should be observed in the office for 60 minutes after immunization; however, reactions can occur days later. The final dose should be administered at least 10 days before departure so that the recipient may be monitored.

MENINGOCOCCAL DISEASE (Chapter 313). Meningococcal vaccine (A/C/Y/W-135) should be considered for travelers going to Saudi Arabia during the Moslem Hajj, Kenya, Tanzania, Burundi, Nigeria and other countries in sub-Saharan Africa during the dry season, or other sites where travel advisories have been issued. Type A has been the principal cause of meningococcal disease in those areas, but W-135 affected hundreds of pilgrims to Saudi Arabia in 2000 and 2001, who then carried it back to their countries of origin.

POLIOMYELITIS (Chapter 452). Everyone should be immunized against poliomyelitis whether or not they travel. A single booster once in adulthood is recommended for travelers to developing areas, except in those staying in Central and South America, where no cases of wild-type poliomyelitis have been identified since 1991. Despite progress toward eradicating poliomyelitis, there have been recent outbreaks in Haiti, the Dominican Republic, and the Philippines. The inactivated polio vaccine has replaced the oral vaccine, which was associated with a risk of vaccine-related paralytic disease in recipients or their contacts.

RABIES (Chapter 454). Rabies is endemic in many areas. Travelers should be warned about the disease and advised to avoid dogs and other animals. In general, long-term travelers (30 days or more) who live in areas where rabies is a threat should receive pre-exposure immunization. Any short-term traveler who plans to have close contact with dogs, wild animals, or bat-infested caves should also be immunized. Simultaneous administration of chloroquine—and possibly mefloquine—can decrease the immunogenicity of intradermally administered rabies vaccine. Intramuscular administration of vaccine overcomes the interference. The high cost of the rabies vaccine has limited its use for pre-exposure prophylaxis.

All persons, regardless of whether they have received pre-exposure immunization, who are bitten by a potentially rabid animal should be advised to wash the site thoroughly with water and detergent and to seek medical evaluation. Those who have received pre-exposure prophylaxis need two additional doses of the human diploid cell vaccine, but they do not need rabies immune globulin, which is in short supply around the world. Those who have not been previously immunized require full immunization plus human rabies immune globulin.

TYPHOID (Chapter 324). Typhoid is common in developing areas where sanitation is poor. The risk is relatively low among short-term travelers to urban areas who adhere to food and water precautions. Importation accounts for more than 70% of cases in the United States. Even though most cases originate in Mexico, travel to the Indian subcontinent poses the greatest risk. The oral, live Ty21a typhoid vaccine, and the injectable Vi capsular polysaccharide vaccine are well tolerated and have replaced the crude killed vaccine, which was frequently associated with local pain, erythema, and constitutional symptoms. The oral typhoid vaccine should not be given to HIV-infected persons or those taking antibiotics or mefloquine, which can inactivate it. It is recommended that the oral series be repeated at 5-year intervals and the Vi capsular polysaccharide vaccine boosted at 2-year intervals.

YELLOW FEVER (Chapter 375). Yellow fever is endemic in tropical areas of Africa and Latin America in a band ranging from approximately 15 degrees north to 15 degrees south of the equator. The yellow fever vaccine is a live, attenuated strain (17 D). It is available only at licensed centers, which can be identified by calling local or state health offices. The vaccine is boosted at 10-year intervals. The yellow fever vaccine should not be given to HIV-infected or other immunocompromised travelers unless the risk of yellow fever exceeds the risk of vaccine-related disease. If possible, they should avoid travel in endemic areas. If they must travel, they should do all that they can do to minimize mosquito bites and carry with them written evidence of medical exemption. Several cases of multiple organ system failure have recently occurred in recipients of the yellow fever vaccine. Persons age 75 years and older seem to be at increased risk. Although there have been no changes in the recommendations for immunization, care should be taken to give the vaccine only when it is truly indicated.

OTHER VACCINES (Chapter 16). The plague vaccine is no longer available. The use of BCG in long-term travelers, particularly children, is controversial. Currently, PPD skin testing with treatment for those who convert is the approach of choice. Typhus and tick-borne encephalitis vaccines are not available in the United States. Although concerns persist about bioterrorism, the smallpox and anthrax vaccines are not available for civilian travelers. No vaccines are available to protect against a number of other important viral diseases, including dengue, or against parasitic diseases, such as malaria.

TRAVELER'S DIARRHEA

Traveler's diarrhea (Chapter 330) is the most common problem encountered by North Americans who visit developing areas. The incidence is as high as 40 to 60% among short-term travelers if appropriate food and water precautions are not followed.

The risk of traveler's diarrhea can be reduced approximately four-fold by following the commandment "Cook it, boil it, peel it, or forget it" and by eating only foods served "piping hot." Even when these recommendations are followed, diarrhea may occur. The duration and severity can be reduced by early self-treatment. Travelers should be instructed in oral rehydration with solutions containing glucose and electrolytes. They should also have available and take an appropriate antibiotic; ciprofloxacin is widely used in healthy, nonpregnant adults as either a single dose or a short course (3 days). In Asia, *Campylobacter* is prevalent and often resistant to quinolones; azithromycin may be effective in those cases. An antimotility agent such as loperamide can further reduce the duration of secretory diarrhea, but it should not be used in those with bloody diarrhea, high fever, or other evidence of inflammatory colitis.

PREVENTING MALARIA

Malaria (Chapter 392) poses a major health hazard for travelers to endemic tropical areas. The risk of exposure varies greatly throughout the tropics. The frequency of transmission is high in sub-Saharan Africa. Malaria transmission is infrequent in most major urban areas of Latin America and Asia. Country-specific risks and guidelines for prevention are available through the CDC Web site and *Health Information for International Travel*.

Every effort should be made by travelers to minimize contact with *Anopheles* mosquitoes—the vector of malaria—which prefer to feed in the evening, at night, and in the early morning. Travelers who are

---

Table 300–2 • CHEMOPROPHYLAXIS FOR MALARIA*

Travelers to areas with chloroquine-sensitive *Plasmodium* species:
  Chloroquine phosphate, 300-mg base (500 mg salt) orally once a week[†]
Travelers to areas with chloroquine resistance:
  Mefloquine, 250 mg orally once a week[†]
  OR
  Doxycycline, 100 mg orally daily[†]
  OR
  Atovaquone/proguanil (Malarone), 1 adult tablet (250 mg atovaquone/100 mg proguanil) orally daily[†]
Prevention of late relapses with *Plasmodium vivax* and *Plasmodium ovale*[‡]:
  Primaquine phosphate, 15-mg base (26.3 mg salt) orally each day for 14 days

*Insect repellents, insecticide-impregnated bed nets, and proper clothing are important adjuncts for preventing malaria. The potential toxicities and contraindications of antimalarial medications are discussed in Chapter 392 and should be reviewed before use. Chloroquine has been used extensively and safely in pregnancy, but other prophylactic medications are either contraindicated during pregnancy (doxycycline and primaquine) or their safety is uncertain (mefloquine and atovaquone/proguanil). No prophylactic regimen guarantees protection, and travelers should be warned about the possibility of malaria during travel or after return.

[†]Adult dose: start 1 wk before departure with chloroquine and mefloquine, 1–2 days before with doxycycline, continue during travel and for 4 wk after leaving; with atovaquone/proguanil start 1–2 days before departure and continue for 7 days after leaving the malaria risk area.

[‡]Occasional relapses have been reported following this regimen. Some experts prescribe primaquine during the last 2 wk of malaria prophylaxis for travelers with prolonged exposure to *P. vivax* or *P. ovale*. Others avoid primaquine and rely on early detection and treatment of *P. vivax* or *P. ovale* malaria if it occurs. Primaquine is contraindicated in people with G6PD deficiency.

---

outdoors at those times should wear long-sleeved clothing and apply insect repellents that contain N,N-diethylmethyltoluamide (DEET) approximately 30% to exposed skin. DEET should be used cautiously in young children because of the potential for seizures and other neurologic side effects from percutaneous absorption. Clothing and mosquito netting can be treated with permethrin, which confers further protection against mosquitoes for weeks.

Even with these measures, chemoprophylaxis is necessary (Table 300–2). For a full discussion of the efficacy and toxicity of these drugs and alternatives, see Chapter 318.

BEHAVIORAL MODIFICATIONS

Infectious Diseases to Be Avoided

SEXUALLY TRANSMITTED DISEASES (Chapters 151, 345, and Part XXIV). A substantial number of U.S and European travelers have sexual relations with local residents or casual contacts while abroad and therefore are at risk for HIV and other sexually transmitted diseases. These risks must be explicitly discussed with all travelers. Abstinence is the only fully effective way to avoid sexually transmitted diseases. Those who choose to have sex should use latex condoms purchased before departure because condoms manufactured abroad may not be protective. Some countries require HIV testing before granting long-term visas.

ARTHROPOD-BORNE DISEASES (Chapters 375–377 and 391). A number of infectious diseases can be avoided by taking appropriate precautions. Every effort should be made to minimize exposure to arthropod vectors with clothing, insect repellents, and mosquito nets to avoid dengue and other diseases. Travelers to Latin America should not sleep in mud or adobe dwellings in areas where reduviid bugs transmit *Trypanosoma cruzi*, the cause of Chagas' disease.

EMERGING INFECTIOUS DISEASES. The severe acute respiratory syndrome (SARS) has posed a substantial risk for travelers to affected areas and illustrates the potential impact of future emerging and re-emerging infectious diseases. In the case of SARS, for which no treatment or immunoprophylaxis is currently available against the causative coronavirus and evacuation of infected expatriates may be impossible for public health reasons, travelers should be advised to avoid affected sites unless absolutely necessary. The CDC (*www.cdc.gov*) is an excellent source of travel advisories and updated information on SARS and future emerging infectious diseases.

Water and Soil Contact (Chapter 391)

Travelers should not walk barefoot where hookworms and *Strongyloides stercoralis* are endemic. Persons visiting areas where *Schistosoma* species are found should avoid swimming or bathing in fresh or brackish water. People should not lie directly on beaches where dogs may have defecated and left *Ancylostoma braziliense,* the cause of cutaneous larva migrans. Travelers should avoid streams and swamps in areas with leptospirosis.

OTHER IMPORTANT ISSUES

CHRONIC MEDICAL PROBLEMS. Special attention should be directed to patients with preexisting medical problems. They should wear medical alert identification. Travelers requiring medications should always keep these with them because checked luggage may be unavailable, lost, or stolen. It is wise to keep a list of all medications. An extra set of glasses often comes in handy.

LONG-TERM TRAVEL. Those who plan to reside abroad for prolonged periods frequently face special challenges. They should be counseled about the difficulties of adapting to a different language, culture, and climate. Routine health maintenance measures should be addressed before they leave. It is advisable to determine their PPD status and, in selected cases, HIV status, before and after the trip.

JET LAG. When travelers cross multiple time zones, the following few days are frequently disrupted by jet lag. Exposure to bright light after arrival facilitates re-entrainment of the circadian rhythm. Although dietary measures have been proposed, they have not been rigorously evaluated. Short-acting benzodiazepines have been recommended by some to help with the adaptation to new time zones, but they can result in confusion and disorientation.

DEEP VENOUS THROMBOSIS. Long-distance travel is associated with an increased risk of DVT, which has been termed the "economy class syndrome," and pulmonary emboli. Maintaining hydration, exercise, and wearing support stockings may decrease the risk.

MOTION SICKNESS. Travelers with motion sickness may gain relief with short-term, over-the-counter preparations of diphenhydramine. For longer trips or cruises, sustained-release transdermal scopolamine may be preferred.

ALTITUDE SICKNESS. Travelers to high elevations are at risk of acute mountain sickness, particularly if they ascend rapidly to heights greater than 2500 m. Gradual ascent over a period of days is the best way to acclimatize. Acetazolamide, 125 to 250 mg two times a day, beginning 1 to 2 days before and during the first several days of ascent, has been recommended for those who do not have time to acclimatize, but it is a diuretic, causes tingling and paresthesias that may interfere with climbing, and is contraindicated in persons with sulfonamide allergies. If acute mountain sickness develops, the safest course of action is to descend. When descent is not possible, supplemental oxygen, dexamethasone, and portable hyperbaric chambers may be helpful. Anyone going to extreme elevations should seek advice from a mountaineering expert before the trip.

VENOMOUS SNAKES, SPIDERS, AND SCORPIONS. In tropical areas, it is advisable to hike on clear paths, to avoid thick grass or brush, and to check the inside of shoes, closets, and drawers before extending feet or hands into them. Hikers should always wear shoes or boots.

ACCIDENTS AND CRIME. Automobile and other accidents are important causes of morbidity and mortality among travelers. Travelers should wear seat belts and avoid motorcycles. Travelers frequently have a false sense of security. They should inquire about potential risks to their safety before exploring new areas or swimming, particularly in the ocean, where tides may be dangerous. Information about civil unrest, terrorist activities, and political instability can be obtained from the Department of State (888-407-4747; *www.state.gov/travel/*).

ILLNESS ABROAD. Before departure, travelers should review the status of their health and evacuation insurance, and what to do if they become ill. Self-limited traveler's diarrhea and upper respiratory tract infections are common and seldom require medical intervention. Travelers should seek expert medical evaluation if a high temperature develops because it may herald malaria or another life-threatening tropical infection, or if they experience bloody diarrhea or other severe symptoms. Lists of reputable physicians can be obtained from American embassies or consulates or from travel insurance companies. Travelers should beware of previously used needles that might transmit HIV or other viruses. In the United States, physicians with special expertise in tropical diseases are available in traveler's clinics and many academic medical centers.

SUGGESTED READINGS
Centers for Disease Control and Prevention: CDC Health Information for International Travel 2001–2002. Atlanta, U.S. Department of Health and Human Services, Public Health Service, 2001, *http://www.cdc.gov/travel. The publication is for sale by the Public Health Foundation (877-252-1200 or online at http:/bookstore.phf.org). Excellent source of information on health risks in overseas locations, as well as key information on malaria and vaccines. It is updated yearly.*
Centers for Disease Control and Prevention: Summary of Health Information for International Travel. Atlanta, U.S. Department of Health and Human Services, *http://www.cdc.gov/travel/blusheet.htm. Published biweekly, listing countries or areas reporting yellow fever, cholera, and plague.*
Hill DR, Pearson RD: Health advice for international travel. *In* Betts RF, Chapman SW, Penn RL (eds): Reese and Betts' A Practical Approach to Infectious Diseases, 5th ed. Philadelphia, Lippincott Williams & Wilkins, 2003, pp 835–874. *A comprehensive review of health issues related to international travel.*
Keystone JS, Kozarsky PE, Freedman DO: Internet and computer-based resources for travel medicine practitioners. Clin Infect Dis 2001;32:757–765. *Review of available websites and their sometimes contradictory recommendations.*
Ryan ET, Kain KC: Health advice and immunizations for travelers. N Engl J Med 2000;342:1716–1725. *A comprehensive overview.*

301 INTRODUCTION TO BACTERIAL DISEASE

David A. Relman

Approximately 3 billion years ago, and 500 million years following the origins of life, single-cell organisms appeared on our planet with features resembling those of extant bacteria today. They evolved in an anaerobic environment for about 1 billion years until the appearance of oxygenic phototrophic bacteria, such as the cyanobacteria, and the subsequent development of an oxygenated environment. They and the other major prokaryotic lineage, the archaea, encountered the earliest ancestors of modern eukaryotes 1.5 billion years ago. The modern form of *Homo sapiens* did not arise until approximately 100,000 years ago; thus, it is not surprising to find far greater diversity in form and function among the microorganisms as well as evidence of surprisingly sophisticated and intimate adaptation to and co-optation of eukaryotes. For example, ancestors of modern rickettsia and cyanobacteria established a niche within primitive eukaryotic cells and gave rise to today's mitochondria and chloroplasts, respectively. Our body is 10% human cells and 90% bacterial cells! The widespread prevalence of commensal, mutualistic, and endosymbiotic relationships between bacteria and eukaryotes emphasizes the dependence and benefit that result from nearly all of these relationships. In contrast, disease is an uncommon outcome and usually reflects either the deliberate strategy of an unusual microbe or the presence of a host compromised because of biologic or behavioral factors.

Our understanding of bacterial diversity and systematics has been revolutionized over the past 20 years by comparative analyses of molecular features, such as RNA and DNA sequences, and the realization that less than 1% of all bacteria are able to propagate under our laboratory conditions. Among the estimated 36 to 40 major divisions of bacteria, many have no known cultivated representatives despite the cosmopolitan distribution of many of these divisions on the planet and a breadth of diversity comparable to that of the plants (Fig. 301–1). Even though our laboratory conditions are better suited to bacteria that are adapted to the human body, it is now clear that at least one half of the commensal bacterial flora found in healthy humans has not been cultivated ex vivo. Members of approximately 10 divisions have been detected within the human body, including TM7, a highly diverse group with no cultivated members. Among human pathogens such as *Mycobacterium leprae*, *Treponema pallidum*, and *Tropheryma whippelii*, some of the reasons for resistance to cultivation have become revealed by the elucidation of complete genome sequences and include deficiencies in a variety of biosynthetic and energy metabolism pathways—resulting in dependence on the host for these factors. Other reasons may include bacterial codependence and the establishment of consortia and "dormant" states within the host.

Bacteria capable of causing disease (i.e., pathogens) constitute a tiny subset of those that inhabit the human body. For these

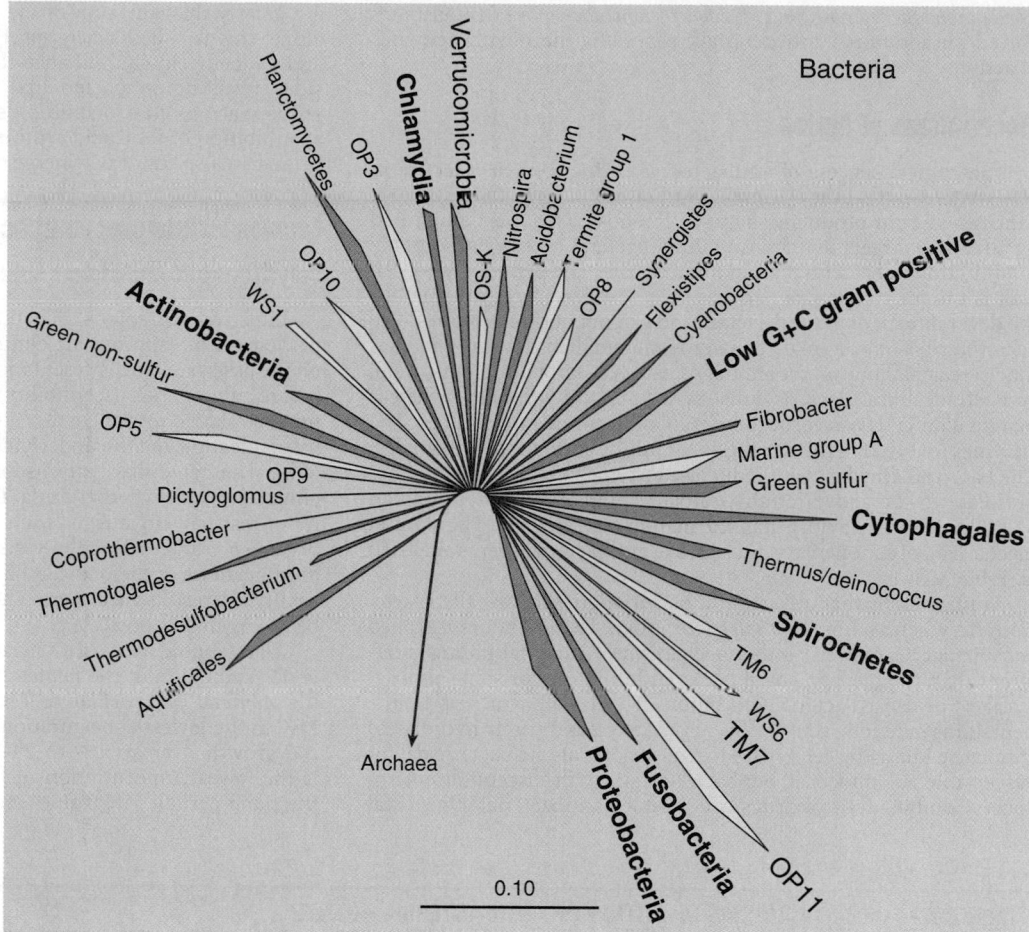

Figure 301–1 • Evolutionary tree of the domain *Bacteria* based upon comparative analysis of 16S ribosomal RNA sequences. The diversity found within each division is proportional to the fan-like breadth of its branch; those that contain at least one cultivated member are shown in red, and those without one are shown in yellow. The names of the 10 divisions that include at least one member found in the human body are in larger type; those that contain pathogens are in bold type. As examples, *Cytophagales* includes the *Bacteroides* spp, *Low G+C gram positive* includes the *Streptococcus* spp and *Staphylococcus* spp, and *Actinobacteria* includes the *Mycobacterium* spp. The scale bar corresponds to 0.10 nucleotide substitution per position.

organisms, strategies for replication, persistence, and transmission entail selection of an anatomic niche or manipulation of a host signaling pathway that necessarily results in host damage, either because of the direct effect of bacterial mechanisms or because of the ensuing host response. In general, virulence can be viewed as the end result of efforts to attach to the host, subvert defenses, multiply, and persist long enough to achieve transmission to a new susceptible host. The molecular basis of virulence is often found in genes that encode adhesins, toxins, and other secreted effector molecules, specialized secretion systems, and regulators that recognize host environmental conditions. Virulence genes are commonly coinherited on a transmissible element such as a plasmid, bacteriophage, or transposable element. As a result, certain clonal populations or strains may be virulent whereas other closely related strains are benign. The modular nature of virulence is apparent in examining the sequence of pathogen genomes in the form of "pathogenicity islands" or "plasticity zones." As larger numbers of pathogens are identified and characterized, new families of virulence genes and nontraditional virulence-associated molecular traits and strategies are certain to be discovered. An example of a nontraditional trait is the absence of a gene that normally blocks virulence, such as a missing gene in *Shigella* that encodes lysine decarboxylase in nonpathogenic close relatives, which would produce cadaverine and in turn inhibit bacterial proinflammatory activity. Vast portions of the domain Bacteria as well as the entire (and immense) domain Archaea are devoid of known pathogens. It remains unclear whether this is due to an actual inability of these organisms to cause disease or to inadequate diagnostic methods.

The foregoing discussion raises questions about the diversity of pathogens, their distribution in nature, and the degree to which unrecognized pathogens and unrecognized infectious diseases remain to be identified. Most physicians can point to cases that appeared to be of infectious or microbial origin but for which a microbiologic diagnosis could not be achieved. As new diagnostic technologies and approaches become available, driven in part by initiatives in biodefense, we may discover that infectious diseases encompass a much broader aspect of clinical medicine than was once thought.

SUGGESTED READINGS

Finlay BB, Falkow S: Common themes in microbial pathogenicity revisited. Microbiol Mol Biol Rev 1997;61:136–169. *Review of the virulence mechanisms and strategies shared by some bacterial pathogens.*

Hornef MW, Wick MJ, Rhen M, et al: Bacterial strategies for overcoming host innate and adaptive immune responses. Nat Immunol 2002;3:1033–1040. *Bacterial pathogens manipulate host immune responses to achieve their goals; by studying these strategies we learn a great deal about the normal functioning of the host immune system.*

Hugenholtz P: Exploring prokaryotic diversity in the genomic era. Genome Biol 2002;3:REVIEWS0003. *Discussion of the bias imposed by cultivation-based approaches on our understanding of bacterial diversity.*

Relman DA: New technologies, human-microbe interactions, and the search for previously unrecognized pathogens. J Infect Dis 2002;186:S254–S258. *Discussion of the evidence for as yet uncharacterized microbial pathogens and the methods that might be used to reveal the nature of these organisms.*

Young D, Hussell T, Dougan G: Chronic bacterial infections: Living with unwanted guests. Nat Immunol 2002;3:1026–1032. *Persistence may be a more common feature of bacterial pathogenesis than we clinicians tend to believe.*

302 ANTIBACTERIAL THERAPY

William A. Craig

In the 60 to 70 years since the introduction of sulfonamides and penicillin, a large array of antibacterial agents has been developed for the treatment and prevention of infectious diseases. This modern era of antibacterial chemotherapy has had a significant impact in reducing the morbidity and mortality of infections. It has also been successful in reducing infectious complications with surgery, trauma, and organ transplantation. The broad use of antibacterials in modern medicine has not been problem free. These drugs or their metabolites can occasionally produce untoward reactions either directly or through interaction with other drugs. They also provide selective pressure for the emergence of antibacterial resistance among bacteria. Despite the availability of a large number of drugs, the emergence of multiply resistant pneumococci, staphylococci, enterococci,

Pseudomonas aeruginosa, and *Mycobacterium tuberculosis* demonstrates a need for additional antibacterials, especially those with new sites of action.

Mechanisms of Action

The clinical success of antibacterials is due to their selective in vivo toxicity in that they primarily kill or inhibit growth of microorganisms without producing harm to the host. This is accomplished by attacking targets that are unique to bacteria or more susceptible to inhibition in bacteria than in human cells. The peptidoglycan cell wall is unique to bacteria and has been a very successful target for the development of many β-lactam and glycopeptide antibiotics. The bacterial ribosome is smaller than the mammalian ribosome and has much greater affinity for the aminoglycosides, macrolides, clindamycin, and tetracyclines. Bacteria must synthesize dihydrofolate whereas mammalian cells can form dihydrofolate from dietary sources. The enzymes involved in this synthesis are inhibited by the sulfonamides. The bacterial dihydrofolate reductase enzyme, which converts dihydrofolate to the active tetrahydrofolate, binds trimethoprim about 55,000 times more avidly than the mammalian enzyme. The site and mechanism of action of major classes of antibacterial agents are listed in Table 302–1.

Antibacterials that only inhibit bacterial growth are called *bacteriostatic*, whereas those that kill bacteria over 18 to 24 hours are called *bactericidal*. Occasionally, the mechanism of bacterial killing is different than the mechanism of bacterial inhibition for some antibacterials. For most bacteria, inhibition of cell wall synthesis by the penicillins indirectly activates bacterial enzymes (murein hydrolases) that cause killing by cell lysis. Most antibacterials are bactericidal for susceptible pneumococci, but bacteriostatic with susceptible enterococci. Combinations of drugs can produce antibacterial effects that

are greater than the sum of the antimicrobial activities when used alone; this is called *synergism*. For example, penicillin, ampicillin, and vancomycin can enhance the bacterial uptake of aminoglycosides resulting in bactericidal synergism with enterococci. The sequential inhibition of multiple steps in a biosynthetic pathway, such as inhibition of folic acid synthesis by a sulfonamide and trimethoprim, can also result in synergism.

Factors Influencing Antibacterial Selection

INFECTING ORGANISM AND SUSCEPTIBILITY TESTING

Effective therapy is dependent on identifying the causative pathogen from appropriate cultures, Gram stains of the cultures, or on the basis of clinical presentation. Because therapy is often required before culture and susceptibility test results are known, the clinician must be able to formulate the likely organisms for the site and severity of infection and the underlying diseases in the patient. Knowledge of local susceptibility patterns for various antibacterials can help the clinician decide whether initial therapy should address the possibility of resistant organisms, such as penicillin-resistant *Streptococcus pneumoniae* and methicillin-resistant *Staphylococcus aureus* (MRSA). Modifications in therapy can be made once the culture and susceptibility test results are known. The final antimicrobial regimen should be as targeted as possible.

The standard method for measuring antimicrobial activity in vitro is determination of the *minimal inhibitory concentration* (MIC) and the *minimal bactericidal concentration* (MBC). By definition, the MIC is the lowest concentration of drug that prevents visible bacterial growth over an 18- to 24-hour incubation period. The MBC is the lowest concentration that kills 99.9% of the organisms over the same period. MIC values and qualitative tests, such as the disc

Table 302–1 • MECHANISMS OF ACTION OF ANTIBACTERIAL AGENTS

AGENT	SITE OF ACTION	EFFECT	CIDAL	STATIC
β-Lactams (penicillins, cephalosporins, carbapenems, and aztreonam)	Cell wall: penicillin-binding proteins (PBPs)	Inhibits cross-linking of peptidoglycan (transpeptidation); impairs cell wall synthesis	+	Occasionally (enterococci)
Vancomycin, teicoplanin	Cell wall: terminal D-alanyl-D-alanine of pentapeptide peptidoglycan precursor	Inhibits polymerization of disaccharide precursors to peptidoglycan (transglycosylation); impairs cell wall synthesis	+	Occasionally (enterococci)
Aminoglycosides	Protein synthesis: 30s ribosome subunit	Inhibits peptide elongation; causes misreading of genetic code; inhibits protein synthesis	+	
Tetracycline	Protein synthesis: 30s ribosome subunit	Inhibits binding of transfer RNA; inhibits protein synthesis	Occasionally	+
Chloramphenicol	Protein synthesis: 50s ribosome subunit	Blocks attachment of amino-acyl transfer RNA; inhibits protein synthesis	Occasionally	+
Macrolides, azalides, and ketolides	Protein synthesis: 50s ribosome subunit	Blocks transfer of amino acids to peptide chain; inhibits protein synthesis	Occasionally	+
Clindamycin	Protein synthesis: 50s ribosome subunit	Blocks transfer of amino acids to peptide chain; inhibits protein synthesis	Occasionally	+
Quinupristin/dalfopristin	Protein synthesis: 50s ribosome subunit	Blocks extrusion of peptide chains; inhibits protein synthesis	+	+ (with quinupristin resistance)
Linezolid	Protein synthesis: 50s ribosome subunit	Blocks formation of the 70s initiation complex; inhibits protein synthesis	Occasionally	+
Rifampin	Nucleic acid synthesis: B subunit of DNA-dependent RNA polymerase	Inhibits RNA synthesis	+	
Metronidazole	Nucleic acid synthesis	Damages nucleic acids; inhibits DNA synthesis	+	
Quinolones	Nucleic acid synthesis: DNA gyrase and topoisomerase IV	Impairs supercoiling of DNA; prevents decatenation of DNA molecules after replication; inhibits DNA synthesis	+	
Sulfonamides	Folic acid synthesis: dihydropteroate synthetase	Competitive inhibition of synthesis of dihydrofolate from *p*-aminobenzoic acid, pteroate and glutamic acid	Occasionally (used with trimethoprim)	+
Trimethoprim	Folic acid synthesis: dihydrofolate reductase	Inhibits reduction of dihydrofolate to tetrahydrofolic acid	Occasionally (used with sulfonamide)	+

diffusion method, are used to classify organisms as *susceptible, intermediate,* or *resistant.* Many laboratories use automated techniques to report MIC values routinely. MBC determinations are reserved for those infections in which bactericidal activity is required. An organism that is not killed by an antibiotic that usually kills that species is said to be tolerant; this usually is defined as an MBC greater than 16 times the MIC.

ANTIMICROBIAL RESISTANCE

Antimicrobial resistance has become a major limitation to the continued success of antibacterial chemotherapy. The mechanisms of resistance are varied and include alteration of the drug's target, decreased permeability of the outer cell membrane, active drug efflux from the bacterial cell, and drug inactivation (Table 302–2). An increasing number of organisms have multiple mechanisms for resistance. The genes that account for these resistance mechanisms are acquired by mutations of existing DNA or acquisition of new DNA. New genes mediating resistance usually are spread from organism to organism by plasmids through conjugation, transduction, or transformation. Some resistance genes are linked to transposons, which can move between plasmids and chromosomes. Resistance genes can be constantly functional or induced with exposure to antimicrobial agents. The ability of bacteria to share various resistance genes accounts for the remarkable speed at which some resistance mechanisms can spread and increase.

Alteration of the target site is a major mechanism of resistance and can occur by different mechanisms. For example, most resistance in mycobacteria to rifampin is due to altered amino acids in the B-subunit of the polymerase enzyme as the result of gene mutations. On the other hand, methicillin resistance in staphylococci is due to acquisition of the chromosomal gene (*mecA*) that encodes for penicillin-binding protein 2a or 2′, which has a very low affinity for penicillins. Last, enzymatic modification of the target site can reduce drug affinity; methylation of the 23s rRNA of the 50s ribosome leads to resistance to macrolides, clindamycin, and streptogramin B.

One of the most common mechanisms of antimicrobial resistance is by enzymatic inactivation of the drug. Enzymatic cleavage of the β-lactam ring by β-lactamases is the primary reason for resistance to the penicillins. The genes for these enzymes can be on the chromosome or on plasmids and transposons. In staphylococci, the enzymes are secreted into the surrounding milieu. In contrast, β-lactamases in gram-negative bacilli are secreted into the periplasmic space between the inner and outer cell membrane. Some of the common enzymes in gram-negative bacilli are TEM-1, TEM-2, SHV-1, and PSE-1. These enzymes inactivate penicillins and some cephalosporins, but not the cephamycins (cefoxitin and cefotetan) and third-generation cephalosporins. However, mutations in the genes of these enzymes have created modified enzymes (ESBLs) primarily in *Klebsiella* species and *E. coli* that are capable of destroying the third-generation cephalosporins. All these enzymes tend to be susceptible to inhibition by the so-called β-lactamase inhibitors (clavulanic acid, sulbactam, and tazobactam), which have been used clinically in combination with various penicillins to treat infections caused by these organisms.

Other β-lactamases are produced at low levels in *P. aeruginosa, Enterobacter* spp., *Citrobacter freundii, Serratia* spp., and some other gram-negative bacilli. However, high levels of these β-lactamases can be induced or stably derepressed, resulting in resistance to penicillin/β-lactamase inhibitor combinations and most cephalosporins. AmpC β-lactamases, which were initially identified in these same bacteria, have also spread to *Klebsiella pneumoniae* and *E. coli.* Carbapenems, on the other hand, are not inactivated by either of these β-lactamases.

Decreased permeability of the outer cell membrane of gram-negative bacilli is a common mechanism of intrinsic resistance to antimicrobials. The permeability of the outer membrane is due to special proteins called *porins,* which form specific channels through the outer membrane. Mutational change of the porin proteins in the channel that carbapenems use to cross the outer cell membrane has resulted in resistance in *P. aeruginosa.* However, much of what was attributed to decreased permeability in the past is now explained by

Table 302–2 • MECHANISMS OF ANTIBACTERIAL RESISTANCE

ANTIBACTERIAL AGENT	MECHANISM	REPRESENTATIVE ORGANISM
β-Lactams (penicillins, cephalosporins, carbapenems, aztreonam)	Altered target (penicillin-binding proteins)	Methicillin-resistant *Staphylococcus aureus* (MRSA); penicillin-resistant *Streptococcus pneumoniae; Enterococcus faecium*
	Reduced permeability	*Enterobacter* species; *Pseudomonas aeruginosa*
	Enhanced efflux	*P. aeruginosa*
	β-Lactamases	*S. aureus;* Enterobacteriaceae (includes ESBLs); *Haemophilus influenzae; Moraxella catarrhalis; Neisseria gonorrhoeae; Enterococcus faecalis*
Aminoglycosides	Inactivating enzymes (acetylation, adenylation, phorylation)	*S. aureus;* enterococci; *P. aeruginosa;* Enterobacteriaceae
	Reduced permeability	Enterobacteriaceae; *P. aeruginosa;* enterococci
	Enhanced efflux	*P. aeruginosa*
	Decreased ribosomal binding	*S. aureus; E. faecalis* and mycobacteria (streptomycin)
Chloramphenicol	Enhanced efflux	*H. influenzae*
	Reduced permeability	Enterobacteriaceae
	Inactivating enzyme (acetylation)	*S. aureus; S. pneumoniae;* enterococci; Enterobacteriaceae
Macrolides, clindamyin, ketolide, quinupristin	Altered target (methylation of ribosomal RNA)	*S. aureus, S. pneumoniae* (not ketolide), streptococci, *Bacteroides fragilis*
	Enhanced efflux (not clindamycin or ketolide)	*S. pneumoniae,* streptococci
	Reduced permeability	Enterobacteriaceae
	Inactivating enzymes	*Escherichia coli, Klebsiella pneumoniae, S. aureus*
Linezolid	Altered target	Enterococci; *S. aureus*
Quinolones	Altered target (DNA gyrase, topoisomerase IV)	Enterobacteriaceae, *S. aureus*
	Reduced permeability	Enterobacteriaceae, *P. aeruginosa*
	Enhanced efflux	*E. coli; P. aeruginosa*
Tetracyclines	Altered target (ribosome)	*N. gonorrhoeae,* streptococci
	Enhanced efflux	*E. coli; S. pneumoniae*
	Reduced permeability	Enterobacteriaceae
	Drug inactivation	*B. fragilis*
Rifampin	Altered target (B-subunit of polymerase)	*E. coli; S. aureus*
Sulfonamides, trimethoprim	Altered target (dihydropteroate synthetase or dihydrofolate reductase)	Enterobacteriaceae; *Moraxella catarrhalis*
	Enhanced para-aminobenzoic acid production	*S. aureus; N. gonorrhoeae*
	Reduced permeability	*P. aeruginosa;* Enterobacteriaceae
Vancomycin	Altered target (peptidoglycan precursor-binding site)	*E. faecium; E. faecalis; S. aureus*

the presence of efflux pumps. Such pumps have been found in an increasing variety of organisms. Efflux is the major mechanism for macrolide resistance in pneumococci in North America.

PHARMACOKINETIC CONSIDERATIONS

The goal of antibacterial activity is to provide adequate but non-toxic concentrations of drug at the site of infection for a sufficient period of time to aid in the eradication of the infecting pathogen. Knowledge of the major pharmacokinetic properties of antibacterial agents (summarized in Table 302–3) is essential for their proper use. Capillaries with pores that readily allow the passage of antibacterials supply most tissues in the body. Thus, therapeutic drug concentrations obtained in serum are usually obtained at most extracellular sites of infection. Antibacterials even penetrate into abscesses, but other factors such as slow bacterial growth and low pH often necessitate surgical drainage for maximum efficacy. Prosthetic joints and other foreign bodies can also provide the environment for biofilm formation that can protect organisms from many antibacterials. Drugs that are eliminated primarily by the kidney provide high urine concentrations for treatment of urinary tract infections. Nitrofurantoin, however, provides low and ineffective urinary concentrations in patients with renal impairment. Biliary excretion can enhance efficacy in biliary tract infections, but bile levels of antibacterials are markedly reduced in the presence of biliary tract obstruction. Penetration of drugs into respiratory secretions, such as epithelial lining fluid, cannot be readily predicted from serum concentrations and may be an important determinant of the outcome of antibacterial therapy in pneumonia.

Antibacterial concentrations inside cells and in tissues that are supplied by capillaries without pores, such as the central nervous system and the vitreous humor of the eye, are dependent more on the lipid solubility of the drug than its pharmacokinetics in serum. For example, rifampin, macrolides, and fluoroquinolones provide high intracellular concentrations and activity against intracellular pathogens, such as mycobacteria and *Legionella pneumophila*. Metronidazole, rifampin, and chloramphenicol are lipid-soluble

drugs that provide adequate cerebrospinal fluid (CSF) penetration in the absence of meningeal inflammation. Inflammation can enhance the influx of many β-lactam antibiotics into the CSF and reduce the active efflux of the same drugs from the CSF by the choroid-plexus pump. The aminoglycosides and the first-generation cephalosporins are examples of drugs with marginal or inadequate CSF penetration even with inflammation.

Parenteral administration is preferred in serious infections and those that require high dosages, such as endocarditis and meningitis. Certain antibacterials with high oral bioavailability make oral dosing an acceptable alternative to parenteral therapy for some moderately severe infections. For example, the fluoroquinolones are effective orally for the treatment of osteomyelitis. With impaired renal function, the dose or frequency of administration of an antimicrobial may need to be reduced. Any drug that is excreted primarily unchanged in the urine requires a downward adjustment in proportion to the decrease in renal function. Similar modifications are necessary in hepatic impairment for antimicrobials with major hepatic metabolism or biliary excretion. The usual dosage regimens for the various antibacterials and the need for dosage modification in patients with renal and hepatic impairment are listed in Table 302–3.

PHARMACODYNAMIC CONSIDERATIONS

Pharmacodynamics is concerned with the relationship between drug concentrations and the time course of antimicrobial activity. The MIC and MBC are good indicators of the potency of an antibiotic, but they provide minimal information about the time course of antimicrobial activity. Parameters such as rate of killing with increasing concentrations and persistent effects (e.g., postantibiotic effect) are much better predictors of the time course of antimicrobial activity. For the aminoglycosides and fluoroquinolones, bacterial killing is concentration dependent. The higher the drug concentration, the faster and more extensive is the rate of killing. Thus, the peak level and the amount of drug, as reflected by the area under the concentration-versus-time curve (AUC) in serum, are important predictors of the efficacy of fluoroquinolones and aminoglycosides. Peak/MIC levels

Table 302–3 • DOSAGE REGIMEN, PHARMACOKINETICS, AND ADJUSTMENT IN HEPATIC AND RENAL FAILURE

CLASS/AGENT	DOSE* SYSTEMIC INFECTION	ORAL FORMULATION	PEAK SERUM CONCENTRATION (µg/mL)	PROTEIN BINDING (%)	NORMAL SERUM HALF-LIFE (hr)	HEPATIC FAILURE	RENAL FAILURE	SERUM LEVELS AFFECTED BY DIALYSIS‡
AMINOGLYCOSIDES								
Amikacin	5 mg/kg/q8h or 15 mg/kg/q24h	—	35	0	2–3	No	Major	Yes (H, P)
Gentamicin	1.7 mg/kg/q8h or 5 mg/kg/q24h	—	7	0	2–3	No	Major	Yes (H, P)
Netilmicin	1.7 mg/kg/q8h or 5 mg/kg/q24h	—	7	0	2–3	No	Major	Yes (H, P)
Tobramycin	1.7 mg/kg/q8h or 5 mg/kg/q24h	—	7	0	2–3	No	Major	Yes (H, P)
ANTITUBERCULOUS AGENTS								
Ethambutol	15 mg/kg/q24h (PO)	Yes	2	10	1.5	No	Major	Yes (H, P)
Isoniazid	5 mg/kg or 300 mg/q24 (PO)	Yes	4.5	10	3	Yes	Major	Yes (H, P)
Pyrazinamide	10 mg/kg/q8h (PO)	Yes	39	—	10	Yes	Yes	Yes (H)
Rifampin	10 mg/kg or 600 mg/q24 (PO)	Yes	7	70	3	Yes	Minor	No (H)
CARBAPENEMS								
Ertapenem	15 mg/kg/q24h	—	115	95	4–5	Unknown	Yes	Yes (H)
Imipenem	7.5 mg/kg/q6h	—	40	15	1	No	Avoid	Yes (H)
Meropenem	15 mg/kg/q8h	—	50	<10	1	No	Yes	Yes (H)
FIRST-GENERATION CEPHALOSPORINS								
Cefadroxil	1000 mg/q12h (PO)	Yes	16	20	1.5	No	Yes	Yes (H)
Cefazolin	15 mg/kg/q8h	—	180	80	2	No	Major	Yes (H) No (P)
Cephalexin	500 mg/q6h	Yes	18	15	1	No	Yes	Yes (H, P)
Cephradine	30 mg/kg/q6h	Yes†	140	10	1.3	No	Yes	Yes (H, P)
SECOND-GENERATION CEPHALOSPORINS								
Cefaclor	500 mg/q8h (PO)	Yes†	10	25	0.8	No	Yes	Yes (H)
Cefditoren pivoxil	400 mg/q12h (PO)	Yes	4	88	1.6	No	Yes	Yes (H)
Cefotetan	30 mg/kg/q12h	—	230	85	3–4	No	Major	Yes (H)

Table 302–3 • DOSAGE REGIMEN, PHARMACOKINETICS, AND ADJUSTMENT IN HEPATIC AND RENAL FAILURE—cont'd

CLASS/AGENT	DOSE* SYSTEMIC INFECTION	ORAL FORMULATION	PEAK SERUM CONCENTRATION (μg/mL)	PROTEIN BINDING (%)	NORMAL SERUM HALF-LIFE (hr)	HEPATIC FAILURE	RENAL FAILURE	SERUM LEVELS AFFECTED BY DIALYSIS‡
Cefoxitin	30 mg/kg/q6h	—	220	70	0.8	No	Yes	Yes (H) No (P)
Cefprozil	500 mg/q12h (PO)	Yes	10	35	1.4	No	Yes	Yes (H)
Cefuroxime	15–20 mg/kg/q8h	—	100	50	1.5	No	Yes	Yes (H, P)
Cefuroxime axetil	500 mg/q12h (PO)	Yes	9	50	1.5	No	Yes	Yes (H, P)
Loracarbef	400 mg/q12h (PO)	Yes†	14	25	1.2	No	Yes	Yes (H)
THIRD-GENERATION CEPHALOSPORINS								
Cefdinir	300 mg/q12h (PO)	Yes	2	65	1.7	Unknown	Minor	Yes (H)
Cefepime	30 mg/kg/q12h	—	193	20	2	No	Yes	Yes (H, P)
Cefixime	500 mg/q24h (PO)	Yes	3–5	67	3	No	Yes	No (H, P)
Cefotaxime	30 mg/kg/q6–8h	—	200	50	1.5	Minor	Minor	Yes (H) No (P)
Cefpodoxime proxetil	200–400 mg/q12h (PO)	Yes	3	25	2.5	No	Yes	Yes (H)
Ceftazidime	30 mg/kg/q8h	—	160	60	2	No	Major	Yes (H, P)
Ceftibuten	400 mg/q24h (PO)	Yes	15	65	2.5	Unknown	Yes	Yes (H)
Ceftizoxime	30 mg/kg/q6–8h	—	130	30	1.3	No	Major	Yes (H) No (P)
Ceftriaxone	30 mg/kg/q12–24h	—	250	90	8	No	No	No (H)
PENICILLINS								
Amoxicillin	500 mg/q8h (PO)	Yes	10	20	1	No	Yes	Yes (H) No (P)
Ampicillin	30 mg/kg/q6h	Yes†	200	20	1	No	Yes	Yes (H) No (P)
Indanyl carbenicillin	500 mg/q6h (PO)	Yes	6	50	1	Minor	Major	Yes (H, P)
Cloxacillin	500 mg/q6 (PO)	Yes†	9	95	0.5	No	No	No (H, P)
Dicloxacillin	500 mg/q6 (PO)	Yes†	10	97	0.5	No	No	No (H, P)
Mezlocillin	50 mg/kg/q6h	—	260	50	1	Yes	Minor	Yes (H) No (P)
Nafcillin	30 mg/kg/q4–6h	—	160	90	0.5	Yes	No	No (H, P)
Oxacillin	30 mg/kg/q4–6h	—	200	90	0.5	Yes	No	Yes (H, P)
Penicillin G	3–4 million units q4–6h	Yes†	60	60	0.5	No	Yes	Yes (H) No (P)
Penicillin V	500 mg/q6 (PO)	Yes	5	80	1	No	No	Yes (H) No (P)
Piperacillin	40 mg/kg/q4–6h	—	240	50	1	Minor	Minor	Yes (H)
Ticarcillin	40 mg/kg/q4–6h	—	220	50	1	Minor	Major	Yes (H, P)
QUINOLONES								
Ciprofloxacin	500–750 mg/q12h (PO)	Yes†	2–3	30	4	No	Minor	No (H, P)
Gatifloxacin	400 mg/q24h (PO)	Yes	4–5	20	7	No	Minor	
Levofloxacin	500–750 mg/q24h (PO)	Yes	6–9	25	7	No	Yes	
Moxifloxacin	400 mg/q24h (PO)	Yes	4–5	50	10	No-Minor	No	Unknown
TETRACYCLINES								
Doxycycline	100 mg/q12–24h (PO)	Yes	1.5–2.1	93	15–20	Avoid	No	No (H, P)
Minocycline	100 mg/q12–24h (PO)	Yes	2.2	75	15	No	Avoid	No (H, P)
Tetracycline	500 mg/q6h (PO)	Yes†	4	50	7	Avoid	Avoid	No (H, P)
SULFONAMIDES								
Sulfadiazine	15 mg/kg/q6h	Yes	30	50	3	Avoid	Avoid	Unknown
Sulfamethoxazole	12 mg/kg/q8h (IV)	Yes	100	50	9	Avoid	Major	Yes (H) No (P)
Trimethoprim (with sulfamethoxazole)	2.3 mg/kg/q8–12h (IV)	Yes	3–9	60	10	No	Avoid	Yes (H) No (P)
MACROLIDES-LINCOSAMIDES-KETOLIDES								
Azithromycin	250 mg/q24h (PO)	Yes†	0.4	25	12–50	Unknown	Unknown	Unknown
Clarithromycin	500 mg/q12h (PO)	Yes	2–3	70	7	No	Minor	Yes (H) No (P)
Clindamycin	8.5 mg/kg/q6h	Yes	15	90	2.5	Minor	No	No (H, P)
Erythromycin	500 mg/q6h (PO)	Yes†	1.8	70	2	Minor	No	No (H, P)
Telithromycin	800 mg/q24h (PO)	Yes	2	65	10	No	No	Unknown
OTHER AGENTS								
Aztreonam	30 mg/kg/q8h	—	250	60	2.0	No	Major	Yes (H, P)
Chloramphenicol	7–15 mg/kg/q6h	Yes	8–14	60	1.5	Minor	No	Yes (H) No (P)
Linezolid	8.5 mg/kg/q12h	Yes	18	30	5	No-minor	No	Yes (H)
Metronidazole	7 mg/kg/q6h	Yes	25	20	8	Yes	No	Yes (H) No (P)
Nitrofurantoin	100 mg/q6h (PO)	Yes	nil	60	0.3	No	Avoid	Yes (H)
Quinupristin/ dalfopristin (30:70)	7.5 mg/kg/q8–12h	—	3.2/8¶	90/30	3/1¶	Minor	No	No (P)
Spectinomycin	30 mg/kg/24h	—	100	0	2	No	Avoid	Unknown
Vancomycin	15 mg/kg/q12h	Yes§	35	10	6	No	Major	No (H, P)

*mg/kg body weight at hour interval and/or mg oral dose in patients with normal renal function; all doses are parenteral unless specified PO.
†Significant decrease or delay in absorption when administered with food.
‡H = hemodialysis, P = peritoneal dialysis.
¶Includes parent compound and active metabolites.
§Oral vancomycin is not absorbed; used for interluminal therapy only.

of 8 to 10 are required for high response rates with aminoglycosides. This has led to once-daily dosing of these drugs. This form of dosing can also lessen the frequency or the rate at which nephrotoxicity develops.

Bacterial killing by β-lactam antibiotics, on the other hand, is slower and shows little dependence on the drug concentration. The duration of time that drug concentrations exceed the MIC is the important predictor of efficacy for these drugs. Serum concentrations need to exceed the MIC for 40 to 50% of the dosing interval to obtain high rates of bacterial eradication in acute otitis media, acute maxillary sinusitis, and pneumococcal pneumonia.

Persistent effects, such as the postantibiotic effect, are potentially important for determining the frequency of dosing regimens. The postantibiotic effect refers to persistent suppression of bacterial growth after antibiotic exposure and when drug concentrations go below the MIC. Antibacterials, such as the aminoglycosides, produce prolonged postantibiotic effects with gram-negative bacilli. This provides additional rationale for the once-daily administration of large doses of these drugs. On the other hand, β-lactam antibiotics produce very short or no postantibiotic effects with most bacteria. The frequency of dosing with these drugs largely depends on the elimination half-life of the drug. For example, ceftriaxone has a half-life of about 8 hours and is usually administered once daily, whereas most of the penicillins have half-lives of 30 to 60 minutes and are administered every 4 to 6 hours. Continuous IV infusion of β-lactam antibiotics, especially those with rapid half-lives, can allow serum concentrations to constantly exceed the MIC even with lower daily total doses of drug.

Protein binding of antibacterials to serum proteins can have important pharmacodynamic effects. First, protein binding reduces the activity of antibacterials; it is only the free drug faction that has antimicrobial activity at any point in time. Thus, it is the free peak concentration, the AUC of free drug, and the time above MIC for free drug that are the important determinants of in vivo antimicrobial activity. Protein binding can also affect the elimination of some antibacterials. For example, the high protein binding of ceftriaxone and ertapenem slows the filtration of these drugs by the kidney and significantly extends the duration of their elimination half-life. Because of their long half-life, ceftriaxone and ertapenem still provide free drug serum concentrations that exceed the MIC of most pneumococci, including many penicillin-resistant strains, with only once-daily dosing.

PATIENT-RELATED CONSIDERATIONS

Antibiotic choice is also dependent on patient characteristics and the site of infection. Recent exposure to an antibiotic, as well as exposure in an intensive care unit, nursing home, or day care center, increases the risk of antimicrobial resistance. Tetracyclines are not used in children because they bind and discolor teeth and bones. Quinolones are currently excluded from children because of the risk of cartilage damage. Both of those drugs are also excreted in breast milk and could pose a risk to neonates and infants. Most antimicrobials administered to pregnant women cross the placenta and expose the fetus. Certain drugs, such as trimethoprim and rifampin, are not recommended in pregnancy because they are teratogens in animals. The recommended antimicrobials in pregnancy are the β-lactams, including penicillin/β-lactamase inhibitor combinations, and erythromycin. There is insufficient safety data in pregnancy on clindamycin, aminoglycosides, and vancomycin.

For many sites of infection, a bacteriostatic antibiotic is as effective as a bactericidal drug, because the body's host defenses (neutrophils, macrophages, antibodies) kill and eliminate the infecting pathogen. However, endocarditis, meningitis, and osteomyelitis are infections that occur in areas of impaired host defenses. Bactericidal drugs are required for effective treatment of these infections. Patients with neutropenia or significant defects in neutrophil function should also receive bactericidal drugs.

Antibacterial Combinations

The major reason for using drugs in combination is to enhance antimicrobial activity. As stated earlier, the addition of an aminoglycoside to penicillin improves the killing effect against most enterococci. This combination also improves efficacy for enterococcal

endocarditis over penicillin monotherapy. Antibacterial combinations also are used to treat mixed infections, to broaden coverage in infections of unknown cause, and to prevent the selection of resistant organisms. Tuberculosis is the primary infection in which drug combinations have successfully prevented the emergence of resistant organisms. Drug combinations have had variable success in preventing resistance in gram-negative bacilli, such as *P. aeruginosa*. The major concerns with antimicrobial combinations are the added cost and increased risk of side effects. In addition, the combination of bacteriostatic and bactericidal drugs can produce antagonism, as was observed with the use of penicillin plus tetracycline for pneumococcal meningitis.

Individual Agents

Table 302–4 lists the agents of choice and some of the alternative antibacterials that are recommended for treatment of infections caused by specific bacteria. Table 302–5 gives more detailed information on the activity of specific antimicrobial agents against multiple pathogenic organisms that commonly cause infections.

β-LACTAMS

The β-lactam antibiotics are the most commonly used antimicrobial agents because of their high potency, low incidence of serious adverse reactions, and proven effectiveness. Penicillin G is still the drug of choice for most streptococcal infections, meningococcal infections, actinomycosis, rat-bite fever, gas gangrene, *Pasteurella multocida* infections, periodontal infections, and syphilis. Although penicillin G is effective in many anaerobic infections of the lung, clindamycin appears to be more effective in cases of lung abscess. Benzathine and procaine salts of penicillin G are relatively insoluble preparations that are absorbed slowly from intramuscular injection sites. However, serum concentrations of benzathine penicillin are so low that this preparation is used only for highly susceptible organisms, as with syphilis and streptococcal pharyngitis, and for prophylaxis against rheumatic fever.

The penicillinase-resistant penicillins (nafcillin and oxacillin and the oral agents cloxacillin and dicloxacillin) remain the drugs of choice for infections caused by methicillin-susceptible *S. aureus* (MSSA). However, the increasing incidence of methicillin-resistant strains (MRSA) has forced many clinicians to use vancomycin for initial empirical therapy until susceptibility results are known. Ampicillin is the preferred agent over penicillin G for enterococcal and *Listeria* infections. Amoxicillin is the most potent β-lactam antibiotic against *S. pneumoniae* and is a common initial choice for therapy of acute otitis media and acute bacterial sinusitis. Ampicillin and amoxicillin are active against certain gram-negative bacteria, including *E. coli, Proteus mirabilis, Shigella, Salmonella,* and *Haemophilus influenzae.* Their use for *Salmonella* infections, *Shigella* infections, and urinary tract infections has been reduced by the appearance of resistant strains.

Even greater activity against gram-negative bacteria, including many strains of *P. aeruginosa*, is obtained with ticarcillin, mezlocillin, and piperacillin. Carbenicillin is available only in an oral form used for urinary tract infections. Piperacillin is more potent than ticarcillin and mezlocillin against *P. aeruginosa*, but this has not resulted in any major increase in clinical efficacy.

Clavulanic acid, sulbactam, and tazobactam are β-lactams with weak antibacterial activity that are potent, irreversible inhibitors of the β-lactamases of staphylococci, *Bacteroides fragilis, Klebsiella,* and most of the common plasmid-mediated enzymes found in *H. influenzae, E. coli,* and other gram-negative bacteria. They do not inhibit the chromosomal β-lactamases produced by *Enterobacter, Citrobacter, Serratia,* and *Pseudomonas.* Sulbactam and tazobactam also have direct activity against *Acinetobacter calcoaceticus.* Amoxicillin plus clavulanic acid and ampicillin plus sulbactam have been useful for upper and lower respiratory tract infections, for staphylococcal and streptococcal skin infections, and in bite wound infections. Ticarcillin plus clavulanic acid and piperacillin plus tazobactam have provided effective therapy in nosocomial pneumonia, intra-abdominal infections, and severe skin and soft tissue infections. The combination of ticarcillin plus clavulanic acid is also active against many *Stenotrophomonas maltophilia* strains.

The first-generation cephalosporins are active against staphylococci, most streptococci, *E. coli, K. pneumoniae,* and *P. mirabilis.* However, these drugs are used primarily as an alternative to

Table 302–4 • ANTIBACTERIAL DRUGS OF CHOICE FOR SELECTED BACTERIA

INFECTING ORGANISM	AGENT OF CHOICE*	ALTERNATIVE AGENT[†]
GRAM-POSITIVE COCCI		
Staphylococcus aureus/coagulase-negative staphylococci		
Nonpenicillinase producing	Penicillin G or V	Cephalosporin,[§] vancomycin, clindamycin, erythromycin
Penicillinase producing	Nafcillin, oxacillin	Cephalosporin,[§] vancomycin, clindamycin, carbapenem, penicillin/β-lactamase inhibitor combination
Methicillin resistant[‡]	Vancomycin	Trimethoprim-sulfamethoxazole, minocycline, daptomycin (investigational), linezolid
β-hemolytic streptococci (groups A, B, C, G)	Penicillin G or V	Cephalosporin,[§] erythromycin, clindamycin, vancomycin
Viridans streptococci, *Streptococcus bovis*	Penicillin G	Cephalosporin, vancomycin, erythromycin
Enterococci[‡]		
Uncomplicated UTI	Ampicillin, amoxicillin	Nitrofurantoin, quinolone[¶]
Moderately severe wound infection	Ampicillin	Penicillin G, vancomycin
Serious infection: endocarditis or meningitis	Ampicillin plus gentamicin or streptomcyin	Vancomycin plus gentamicin or streptomycin (test for high-level aminoglycoside resistance)
Streptococcus pneumoniae[‡]		
Pneumonia, upper respiratory tract infection	Penicillin G, amoxicillin	Cephalosporin, macrolide, clindamycin, quinolone,** vancomycin
Meningitis	Ceftriaxone, cefotaxime	Ceftriaxone plus vancomycin ± rifampin, vancomycin + rifampin, penicillin G if MIC <0.1 µg/mL
GRAM-NEGATIVE COCCI		
Neisseria gonorrhoeae	Ceftriaxone, cefixime	Second- or other third-generation cephalosporin,[††] quinolones, spectinomycin, trimethoprim-sulfamethoxazole, azithromycin
Neisseria meningitidis	Penicillin G	Third-generation cephalosporin,[††] chloramphenicol, sulfonamide (if susceptible)
Moraxella catarrhalis	Trimethoprim-sulfamethoxazole	Amoxicillin/clavulanate, third-generation cephalosporin,[††] cefuroxime, clarithromycin
GRAM-POSITIVE BACILLI		
Bacillus anthracis (anthrax)	Ciprofloxacin, doxycycline	Clindamycin, penicillin G
Corynebacterium diphtheriae	Erythromycin	Clindamycin, penicillin G
Corynebacterium species	Vancomycin	Penicillin G + gentamicin
Listeria monocytogenes	Ampicillin or penicillin G ± gentamicin	Trimethoprim-sulfamethoxazole, vancomycin, doxycycline
Clostridium perfringens	Penicillin G	Metronidazole, doxycycline, chloramphenicol, imipenem
Clostridium difficile	Metronidazole	Vancomycin (oral only), bacitracin
GRAM-NEGATIVE BACILLI[‡]		
Acinetobacter species	Imipenem ± gentamicin	Ureidopenicillin; aminoglycoside
Bordetella pertussis (pertussis)	Erythromycin	Trimethoprim-sulfamethoxazole, ampicillin
Brucella species (brucellosis)	Doxycycline + gentamicin or streptomycin	Rifampin + doxycycline or quinolone, gentamicin + trimethoprim-sulfamethoxazole
Campylobacter fetus spp. *jejuni*	Erythromycin, quinolone[¶]	Tetracycline
Enterobacter species	Carbapenem,[††] cefepime	Quinolone,[¶] third-generation cephalosporin,[††] aminoglycoside, trimethoprim-sulfamethoxazole
Eikenella corrodens	Penicillin G, ampicillin	Trimethoprim-sulfamethoxazole, tetracycline, cefoxitin, third-generation cephalosporin[††]
Escherichia coli		
Uncomplicated UTI	Trimethoprim-sulfamethoxazole	Quinolone, ampicillin, cephalosporins, trimethoprim, tetracycline
Systemic infection	Third-generation cephalosporin[††]	Aminoglycoside, penicillin/β-lactamase inhibitor, aztreonam, trimethoprim-sulfamethoxazole
Helicobacter pylori	Omeprazole + amoxicillin + clarithromycin	Bismuth subsalicylate + metronidazole + tetracycline or amoxicillin; bismuth subsalicylate + tetracycline + clarithromycin
Francisella tularensis (tularemia)	Streptomycin, gentamicin	Doxycycline, ciprofloxacin, chloramphenicol
Haemophilus influenzae		
Meningitis, bacteremia	Ceftriaxone, cefotaxime	Meropenem, ampicillin (if β-lactamase negative)
Other infection	Ampicillin/sulbactam, amoxicillin/clavulanate	Trimethoprim/sulfamethoxazole, cefuroxime, quinolone, third-generation cephalosporin[††]
Haemophilus ducreyi (chancroid)	Ceftriaxone	Azithromycin, erythromycin, amoxicillin/clavulanate, ciprofloxacin
Klebsiella pneumoniae/oxytoca	Third-generation cephalosporin[††]	Quinolone, penicillin/β-lactamase inhibitor; carbapenem, aztreonam, aminoglycosides
Legionella pneumophila	Erythromycin ± rifampin	Quinolone[¶] ± rifampin
Nocardia asteroides	Sulfonamides (high dose)	Trimethoprim-sulfamethoxazole, minocycline, carbapenem
Pasteurella multocida	Penicillin G	Tetracycline, amoxicillin/clavulanate, third-generation cephalosporin[††]
Proteus mirabilis	Ampicillin	Cephalosporin,[†] trimethoprim/sulfamethoxazole
Proteus (indole positive)	Third-generation cephalosporin	Imipenem, aminoglycoside, trimethoprim/sulfamethoxazole, quinolone[¶]
Salmonella spp.	Quinolone, ceftriaxone	Chloramphenicol, trimethoprim-sulfamethoxazole
Serratia marcescens	Third-generation cephalosporin[††]	Carbapenem, quinolone,[¶] aztreonam, aminoglycoside
Shigella spp.	Quinolone[¶]	Trimethoprim-sulfamethoxazole, azithromycin
Stenotrophomonas maltophilia	Trimethoprim-sulfamethoxazole	Ticarcillin/clavulanate, ceftazidime, doxycycline

Continued

Infectious Diseases

Table 302–4 • ANTIBACTERIAL DRUGS OF CHOICE FOR SELECTED BACTERIA—cont'd

INFECTING ORGANISM	AGENT OF CHOICE*	ALTERNATIVE AGENT[†]
P. aeruginosa		
Urinary tract infection	Quinolone,[¶] ureidopenicillin	Aminoglycoside,[††] ceftazidime, carbapenem, aztreonam
Pneumonia, bacteremia	Ceftazidime, cefepime or ureidopenicillin + aminoglycoside[††]	Imipenem, meropenem or aztreonam + aminoglycoside,[††] antipseudomonal β-lactam + ciprofloxacin or levofloxacin
Vibrio vulnificus	Doxycycline + ceftazidime	Cefotaxime, quinolone
Yersinia pestis (plague)	Streptomycin, gentamicin	Doxycycline, chloramphenicol
ANAEROBIC GRAM-NEGATIVE		
Bacteroides fragilis group	Metronidazole	Clindamycin, cefoxitin, cefotetan, carbapenem, penicillin/β-lactamase inhibitor

*Dose and route of administration vary depending on severity and site of infection and host characteristics (organ dysfunction, immune function).
[†]List of alternative agents is not fully inclusive; confirm susceptibility in vitro.
[‡]Must test susceptibility; resistant strains are increasingly frequent.
[§]First-generation cephalosporin preferred (cephalothin, cephapirin, cephradine, cephalexin, cefazolin).
[¶]Ciprofloxacin, gatifloxacin, levofloxacin (or for urinary tract infection, norfloxacin).
[**]Penicillin-resistant *S. pneumoniae* susceptible to gatifloxacin, levofloxacin, and moxifloxacin.
[††]Third-generation cephalosporins for this indication include ceftriaxone, cefotaxime, ceftizoxime.
[‡‡]Aminoglycosides for this indication include gentamicin, tobramycin, netilmicin, amikacin.

Table 302–5 • ACTIVITY OF MAJOR ANTIBACTERIALS AGAINST SELECTED ORGANISMS[a]

	Streptococci	Streptococcus pneumoniae[b]	Enterococci***	Staphylococcus aureus	Staphylococcus aureus	Coagulase-negative staphylococci[e]	Listeria monocytogenes	Neisseria gonorrhoeae	Neisseria meningitidis	Moraxella catarrhalis	Haemophilus influenzae	Escherichia coli	Enterobacter spp.	Klebsiella spp.	Proteus mirabilis
Penicillin G	+	+	+	0	0	0	+	±	+	0	0	0	0	0	±
Oxacillin*	+	±	0	+	0	±	0	0	0	0	0	0	0	0	0
Ampicillin[†]	+	+	+	0	0	0	+	±	+	0	±	±	±	0	+
Ampicillin-sulbactam[†]	+	+	+	+	0	±	+	+	+	+	+	+	±	+	+
Ticarcillin	+	±	+	0	0	0	+	+	+	0	+	±	±	0	+
Ticarcillin-clavulanate	+	±	+	+	0	±	+	+	+	+	+	+	±	+	+
Piperacillin	+	+	+	0	0	±	+	+	+	0	±	+	±	+	+
Piperacillin-tazobactam	+	+	+	+	0	±	+	+	+	+	+	+	±	+	+
Cefazolin[†]	+	±	0	+	0	±	0	±	0	+	0	+	0	+	+
Cefotetan[§]	+	±	0	±	0	±	0	+	+	+	+	+	±	+	+
Cefuroxime	+	+	0	+	0	±	0	+	+	+	+	+	±	+	+
Ceftriaxone	+	+	0	±	0	±	0	+	+	+	+	+	±	+	+
Ceftazidime	+	±	0	±	0	±	0	+	+	+	+	+	±	+	+
Cefepime	+	+	0	+	0	±	0	+	+	+	+	+	+	+	+
Cephalexin[§]	+	±	0	+	0	±	0	0	0	+	±	±	0	+	+
Cefixime	+	+	0	0	0	0	0	+	+	+	+	+	0	+	+
Cefpodoxime proxetil	+	+	0	+	0	±	0	+	+	+	+	+	+	+	+
Imipenem[¶]	+	+	±	+	0	±	+	+	+	+	+	+	+	+	+
Aztreonam	0	0	0	0	0	0	0	+	+	ND	ND	+	+	+	+
Vancomycin	+	+	+	+	+	+	+	0	0	ND	ND	0	0	0	0
Linezolid	+	+	+	+	+	+	+	ND	ND	+	+	0	0	0	0
Gentamicin**	C/S	0	C/S	C/S	±	C/S	C/S	0	0	+	+	+	+	+	+
Ciprofloxacin	±	±	±	±	0	±	±	+	+	+	+	+	+	+	+
Levofloxacin[††]	+	+	±	+	0	±	±	+	+	+	+	+	+	+	+
Clindamycin	+	+	0	+	0	±	0	0	0	0	0	0	0	0	0
Clarithromycin[‡‡]	+	+	0	±	0	±	ND	+	+	+	±	0	0	0	0
Erythromycin	+	+	0	±	0	±	±	±	+	+	±	0	0	0	0
Doxycycline[§§]	±	±	0	±	0	0	±	0	+	+	+	±	0	0	0
Metronidazole	0	0	0	0	0	0	0	0	0	0	0	0	0	0	0
Trimethoprim-sulfamethoxazole	+	+	0	+	±	±	+	±	±	+	+	+	+	+	+
Chloramphenicol	+	+	0	±	0	0	±	+	+	+	+	+	0	±	+
Rifampin[¶¶]	+	C/S	±	C/S	C/S	C/S	C/S	+	+	+	+	0	0	0	0

0 = uniformly or frequently resistant; + = usually susceptible; ± = variable susceptibility; C/S = used in combination or for synergy; ND = insufficient or no data.
[a]Activity estimate is based both on in vitro susceptibility and clinical efficacy, where available. Activity against aerobic gram-negative bacilli can vary markedly between studies.
[b]Full resistance to penicillin increasingly prevalent; resistant to first- and second-generation cephalosporins parallels that to penicillin.
[e]Many nosocomially acquired strains are methicillin resistant.
[¶]Some of the *B. fragilis* group (*B. thetaiotaomicron, B. distasonis, B. ovatus, B. vulgatus*) are more resistant than *B. fragilis*.
*Similar activity for methicillin, nafcillin, cloxacillin, dicloxacillin.
[†]Similar activity for amoxicillin and amoxicillin/clavulanate.
[‡]Similar activity for other first-generation cephalosporins.

Infectious Diseases

penicillin for staphylococcal and streptococcal infections and for surgical prophylaxis. The second-generation cephalosporins can be divided into two groups. The cephamycins (cefoxitin, cefotetan, and cefmetazole) have increased activity against *B. fragilis* and are used primarily for the prevention and treatment of mixed aerobic and anaerobic infections. The remaining second-generation cephalosporins include many oral and parenteral agents with increased activity against *H. influenzae*, including β-lactamase–producing strains. These drugs are used as alternative agents for upper and lower respiratory tract infections. The third-generation cephalosporins are 10 to 100 times more potent against enteric bacteria than are the earlier cephalosporins. Ceftriaxone and cefotaxime provide adequate CSF concentrations in the presence of inflammation and are approved for bacterial meningitis. Cefoperazone and ceftriaxone are excreted extensively into bile. Ceftazidime and cefoperazone also have activity against *P. aeruginosa*. Cefepime, a fourth-generation cephalosporin, combines the activity of first- and third-generation drugs. These drugs are used for a variety of serious gram-negative bacillary infections.

The carbapenems (imipenem, meropenem, and ertapenem) have a broader spectrum of activity than any other antimicrobial agent.

When administered alone, imipenem is inactivated in the kidney by a dehydropeptidase enzyme found along renal tubular cells, resulting in low urine levels and nephrotoxicity. The addition of cilastatin, which blocks the activity of this enzyme, eliminates nephrotoxicity and produces high urine levels. Meropenem and ertapenem are much less susceptible to this inactivation and do not require cilastatin in the commercial product. Aztreonam, the only available monobactam, is active only against aerobic gram-negative bacteria. An advantage of aztreonam is that it does not appear to cause cross-reactivity in patients with allergic reactions to other β-lactams.

AMINOGLYCOSIDES

Streptomycin, kanamycin, neomycin, gentamicin, and tobramycin are naturally occurring aminoglycosides, whereas amikacin and netilmicin are semisynthetic derivatives developed for their activity against resistant strains. The aminoglycosides are active primarily against aerobic gram-negative bacilli. Tobramycin is the most active agent against *P. aeruginosa*, whereas amikacin shows the least resistance. Despite their potential for toxicity, they are recommended for

Salmonella spp.	*Serratia* spp.	*Shigella* spp.	*Acinetobacter* spp.	*Pseudomonas aeruginosa*	*Stenotrophomonas maltophilia*	*Pasteurella multocida*	*Legionella* spp.	*Chlamydia* spp.	*Mycoplasma pneumoniae*	*Rickettsia* spp.	*Bacteroides fragilis group* #	*Clostridium* spp.	*Prevotella*	*Actinomyces* spp.
0	0	0	0	0	0	+	0	0	0	0	0	+	+	+
0	0	0	0	0	0	0	0	0	0	0	0	0	0	0
+	0	±	0	0	0	+	0	0	0	0	0	+	+	+
+	0	±	0	0	0	+	0	0	0	0	+	+	+	+
+	+	+	+	+	0	+	0	0	0	0	0	+	+	+
+	+	+	+	+	±	+	0	0	0	0	+	+	+	+
ǀ	±	ǀ	ǀ	ǀ	±	ǀ	0	0	0	0	†	†	†	+
+	±	+	+	+	±	+	0	0	0	0	+	+	+	+
0	0	0	0	0	0	+	0	0	0	0	0	0	±	+
+	+	+	0	0	0	+	0	0	0	0	±	+	+	+
+	0	+	0	0	0	+	0	0	0	0	0	+	+	+
+	+	+	±	0	0	+	0	0	0	0	0	+	+	+
+	+	+	±	+	±	+	0	0	0	0	0	+	+	+
+	+	+	±	+	ND	0	0	0	0	0	ND	ND	NC
0	0	0	0	0	0	0	0	0	0	0	0	ND	+	+
+	0	+	0	0	0	+	0	0	0	0	0	0	+	ND
+	0	+	0	0	0	ND	0	0	0	0	0	ND	ND	ND
+	+	+	+	+	0	+	ND	0	0	0	+	+	+	+
+	+	+	0	0	+	0	0	0	0	0	0	0	0
0	0	0	0	0	0	0	0	0	0	0	+	±	0
0	0	0	0	0	0	ND	ND	ND	+	ND	0	+	+	ND
0	+	ND	±	+	0	0	0	0	0	0	0	0	0
+	+	+	±	±	0	+	+	+	+	+	0	0	0	ND
+	+	+	±	±	0	+	+	+	ND	0	0	0	ND
0	0	0	0	0	0	0	0	ND	0	0	+	+	+	+
0	0	0	0	0	0	ND	+	+	+	ND	0	+	+	+
0	0	0	0	0	0	0	+	+	+	±	0	+	+	+
0	0	0	0	0	0	+	+	+	+	+	0	±	+	±
0	0	0	0	0	0	0	0	0	0	0	+	+	+	0
+	+	+	0	0	+	±	+	0+	0	0	ND	ND	ND	ND
+	0	0	0	0	+	+	ND	+	+	+	+	+	+	+
ND	0	ND	0	0	ND	ND	C/S	+	ND	±	+	+	+	ND

§Similar activity for cefoxitin and cefmetazole.
¶Similar activity to other carbapenes, except ertapenem is not active against *P. aeruginosa*.
**Similar activity against gram-negative bacilli for tobramycin, netilmicin; resistance of gram-negative bacilli is less frequent to amikacin.
††Similar activity for gatifloxacin and moxifloxacin.
‡‡Similar activity for azithromycin.
§§Similar activity for other tetracyclines.
¶¶Broad spectrum of activity, but resistance emerges rapidly; limit use to combination therapy or eradication of meningococcal and *H. influenzae* pharyngeal carriage.
***E. faecium* intrinsically more resistant than *E. faecalis*; resistance to penicillin, ampicillin, vancomycin, and aminoglycosides (high level) increasingly frequent.

use in combination with broad-spectrum β-lactams in serious gram-negative bacillary infections. In combination with β-lactams, gentamicin and streptomycin exhibit synergism with staphylococci, streptococci, and enterococci unless the bacteria show high-level aminoglycoside resistance. Such combinations have improved the efficacy or shortened the duration of therapy for endocarditis and bacteremia caused by gram-positive cocci.

Streptomycin is still a useful agent for tuberculosis, tularemia, plague, and brucellosis (in combination with a tetracycline). Neomycin

is used orally (to reduce bowel organisms) or topically. Spectinomycin, which is not an aminoglycoside but does contain an aminocyclitol ring, is only occasionally used to treat gonorrhea, especially β-lactamase–producing strains.

QUINOLONES

The quinolones are synthetic compounds consisting of nalidixic acid and its fluorinated derivatives. Several quinolones (enoxacin,

Table 302–6 • ADVERSE EFFECTS OF ANTIBACTERIAL AGENTS*

Agent	General	Skin	GI Tract	Blood Cells	Kidney	Nervous System	Other
				TARGET—MANIFESTATION			
Penicillin	Hypersensitivity; anaphylaxis; serum sickness	Rash; urticaria; erythema multiforme	Diarrhea (ampicillin, amoxicillin/ clavulanate); hepatitis (oxacillin)	Coombs-positive hemolytic anemia; Impaired platelet function (ticarcillin); leukopenia; thrombocytopenia	Nephritis (methicillin); hypokalemia (carboxy- and ureido-penicillins)	Seizures, twitching (high doses, renal failure)	Inactivate aminoglycosides when admixed; possible with concurrent therapy in renal failure
Cephalosporins	Serum sickness (cefaclor); hypersensitivity, anaphylaxis (rare)	Rash; urticaria	Diarrhea (cefoperazone); hepatic dysfunction; precipitates in bile (ceftriaxone); mild increase in LFT	Neutropenia; increase prothrombin time-bleeding (due to MTT side chain); impaired platelet function (moxalactam); positive Coombs test	Enhance amino-glycoside toxicity; acute renal failure (rare); interstitial nephritis		Disulfiram-like reaction with alcohol use (MTT side chain)
Carbapenems	Hypersensitivity	Rash; urticaria, erythema multiforme	Vomiting with rapid infusion (imipenem) Abnormal LFT	Bone marrow suppression; positive Coombs test	Renal dysfunction	Seizures, myoclonus (imipenem)	
Aminoglycosides	Fever	Rash			Reversible renal failure	Irreversible vestibular toxicity and/or auditory damage; muscular blockade (with anesthetics and myasthenia-calcium reverses)	
Vancomycin	Allergy; fever	Rash		Leukopenia; thrombocytopenia	Nephrotoxic with aminoglycoside	Decreased hearing; neuropathy	Histamine release with flushing and hypotension (infusion <1 hr-antihistamines prevent)
Quinolones	Headache; allergy; anaphylaxis (rare)	Rash; urticaria; photosensitivity (lomefloxacin, sparfloxacin)	GI distress; abnormal LFT			Dizziness, insomnia, nervousness, tremors, visual changes, seizures	Tendon rupture; arthropathy in young animals
Sulfonamides	Hypersensitivity, anaphylaxis, serum sickness fever	Rash, Stevens-Johnson syndrome; photosensitivity	Hepatitis	Hemolysis (G6PD deficiency); agranulocytosis; marrow suppression	Crystalluria	Neuropathy	Vasculitis
Trimethoprim with/without sulfamethoxazole	Fever	Rash; erythema multiforme; Stevens-Johnson syndrome, TEN	Hepatitis; pancreatitis	Marrow suppression	Hyperkalemia; acute renal failure		
Chloramphenicol	Fever			Marrow suppression (dose related); aplastic anemia		Optic neuritis; neuropathy	Circulatory collapse (gray baby syndrome-neonate)
Tetracyclines	Hypersensitivity	Photosensitization (doxycycline, demeclocycline)	GI discomfort; hepatotoxicity in azotemia or pregnancy		Antianabolic aggravation of azotemia (except doxycycline)	Vertigo (minocycline)	Deposition in bone (dysplasia) and teeth (staining)
Macrolides	Fever	Rash	GI discomfort; cholestatic jaundice (erythromycin estolate)			Reversible decreased hearing	Phlebitis (IV erythromycin); Metallic taste (clarithromycin)
Metronidazole	Headache; hypersensitivity		Nausea, metallic taste, pancreatitis	Leukopenia		Peripheral neuropathy, ataxia	Mutagenic, carcinogenic in rodents; disulfiram-like reaction with alcohol

*Not all reactions are listed; check other sources for unusual reactions. Reactions to sulfonamides are not repeated.
LFT = liver function tests; MTT = methylthiotetrazole ring; TEN = toxic epidermal necrolysis.

grepafloxacin, lomefloxacin, sparfloxacin, and trovafloxacin) have been withdrawn or are used infrequently because of adverse reactions. Ciprofloxacin is the most potent quinolone against *P. aeruginosa* and other gram-negative bacilli. The newer fluoroquinolones (gatifloxacin, levofloxacin, moxifloxacin) are slightly less active then ciprofloxacin against gram-negative bacilli, but they have increased activity against gram-positive cocci. Moxifloxacin is eliminated primarily by the liver and should not be used for urinary tract infections. Many quinolones are active against intracellular pathogens, such as mycobacteria, *Chlamydia,* and *Legionella*. Their efficacy also

has been documented in a variety of gastrointestinal infections, including traveler's diarrhea and bacterial gastroenteritis.

MACROLIDES, TETRACYCLINES, KETOLIDES, AND CLINDAMYCIN

The macrolides, especially clarithromycin and azithromycin, and the tetracyclines are broad-spectrum agents with activity against many respiratory pathogens. These drugs are recommended for outpatient management of community-acquired pneumonia. However, resistance to macrolides and tetracyclines is increasing in *S. pneumoniae*.

Table 302–7 • IMPORTANT ANTIBACTERIAL-DRUG INTERACTIONS*

ANTIMICROBIAL AGENT	INTERACTING DRUG	EFFECT
Aminoglycosides	Amphotericin B, cyclosporine, vancomycin	Increased nephrotoxicity
	Loop diuretics (bumetanide, furosemide, ethacrynic acid)	Increased ototoxicity
	Ticarcillin or ureidopenicillins	Decreased aminoglycoside activity (renal failure only)
Ampicillin/amoxicillin	Allopurinol	Increased rash
Cephalosporins	Loop diuretics	Nephrotoxicity
Cephalosporins with MTT side chain[†]	Warfarin, dicumarol, heparin, thrombolytics, platelet inhibitors	Increased anticoagulation, bleeding
	Alcohol	Disulfiram-like reaction
Chloramphenicol	Warfarin	Increased anticoagulation
	Phenytoin	Increased phenytoin level, toxicity
	Sulfonylureas	Increased hypoglycemia
Clarithromycin, erythromycin	Carbamazepine	Increased serum carbamazepine (avoid)
	Cyclosporine, tacrolimus	Increased serum tacrolimus and cyclosporine, nephrotoxicity
	Digoxin	Increased serum digoxin, toxicity
	Terfenadine, astemizole, loratadine, cisapride	Increased cisapride or antihistamine level, arrhythmia (avoid)
	Theophylline	Increased theophylline level, toxicity
	Ergot alkaloids	Increased ergot alkaloid
Isoniazid	Warfarin	Increased anticoagulation
	Alfentanil	Prolonged alfentanil activity
	Phenytoin	Increased serum phenytoin, toxicity
	Disulfiram	Psychosis, behavioral change (avoid)
	Carbamazepine	Increased carbamazepine, toxicity (avoid)
	Rifampin	Additive hepatotoxicity
Metronidazole	Alcohol	Disulfiram-like reaction
	Disulfiram	Psychosis (avoid)
	Warfarin, dicumarol	Increased anticoagulation
	Phenobarbital	Decreased metronidazole
Penicillins	Probenecid	Increased serum penicillin
Quinolones	Cimetidine	Increased antibiotic concentration
	Cyclosporine	Increased serum cyclosporine, nephrotoxicity
	Multivalent cations (Ca^{2+}, Mg^{2+}, Fe^{2+}, Zn^{2+}, Al^{3+} orally)	Decreased absorption of quinolones
	Sucralfate, didanosine	Decreased absorption of quinolones
	Warfarin	Increased anticoagulation
	Nonsteroidal anti-inflammatory drugs	Increased central nervous system stimulation
Quinolones (ciprofloxacin, enoxacin)	Theophylline	Increased serum theophylline, toxicity
	Caffeine	Increased serum caffeine, insomnia, restlessness
Rifampin, rifabutin[‡]	Corticosteroids	Decreased corticosteroids
	Cyclosporine, tacrolimus	Decreased cyclosporine, tacrolimus
	Methadone	Decreased serum methadone, withdrawal
	Phenytoin	Decreased serum phenytoin
	Warfarin, dicumarol	Decreased anticoagulation
	Simvastatin	Decreased simvastatin levels
	Oral contraceptives	Decreased contraceptive effect
	Sulfonylureas	Decreased sulfonylurea, hyperglycemia
	Theophylline	Decreased serum theophylline
	Quinidine, β-blocker	Decreased quinidine, beta-blocker
	Protease inhibitors	Uveitis; decreased protease inhibitor levels
	Clarithromycin	Uveitis; decreased clarithromycin levels
Sulfonamides	Cyclosporine	Decreased serum cyclosporine
	Phenytoin	Increased serum phenytoin, toxicity
	Warfarin	Increased anticoagulation
	Sulfonylureas	Increased hypoglycemia
Trimethoprim	Azathioprine, methotrexate	Increased leukopenia
	Dapsone	Increased serum dapsone and trimethoprim; increased methemoglobinemia
	Potassium-sparing diuretics	Increased potassium
Tetracycline	Multivalent cations (Ca^{2+}, Al^{3+}, Mg^{2+}, Bi^{2+}, Zn^{2+}, Fe^{2+})	Decreased tetracycline absorption; reduced efficacy
	Barbiturates, carbamazepine	Decreased doxycycline
	Digoxin	Increased digoxin, toxicity
	Phenytoin	Decreased doxycycline
	Methoxyflurane (Penthrane)	Severe nephrotoxicity (avoid)

*Not all interactions are listed.
[†]MTT = methythiotetrazole ring (cefamandole, cefotetan, cefmetazole, cefoperazone); decreases vitamin K–dependent clotting factors.
[‡]Multiple other rifampin and rifabutin interactions mediated through induction of hepatic P 450 system.

Infectious Diseases

Telithromycin, the first ketolide antibacterial, is active against pneumococci resistant to most other drugs. Clindamycin is used for anaerobic infections and as an alternative agent in mild to moderate streptococcal and staphylococcal infections. The tetracyclines are useful drugs for a variety of sexually transmitted diseases, such as nongonococcal urethritis, granuloma inguinale, and lymphogranuloma venereum, and for rickettsial infections, Lyme disease, and brucellosis (with streptomycin or rifampin).

VANCOMYCIN, QUINUPRISTIN/DALFOPRISTIN, AND LINEZOLID

Vancomycin is active against most gram-positive bacteria, including MRSA and *Staphylococcus epidermidis, Clostridium difficile,* and enterococci. The increased use of vancomycin over the past decade has contributed to the emergence of vancomycin-resistant enterococci. Quinupristin/dalfopristin and linezolid are recently approved drugs with activity against vancomycin-resistant enterococci; quinupristin/dalfopristin is only active against *Enterococcus faecium.* Linezolid, which has high oral bioavailability, is active against staphylococci, including methicillin-resistant strains.

Duration of Therapy

Just like initial antibacterial selection, the optimal duration of therapy depends on a variety of drug, pharmacodynamic, and infection site characteristics. Single doses of ceftriaxone, cefixime, and a fluoroquinolone are highly effective in a superficial mucosal infection such as uncomplicated gonorrhea. Fluoroquinolones and trimethoprim-sulfamethoxazole exhibit optimal efficacy in urinary tract infections with 3 days of therapy. Longer courses are required with nitrofurantoin and β-lactams to provide similar efficacy. Short courses of therapy of around 5 to 7 days are being used with fluoroquinolones in respiratory tract infections because of their concentration-dependent killing. On the other hand, infections in which bacteria are growing slowly, such as endocarditis and osteomyelitis, require longer 4- to 6-week courses of therapy. Patients with impaired host defenses also usually receive longer courses of therapy.

Adverse Reactions and Drug-Drug Interactions

Most adverse reactions with antibacterial therapy are mild and quickly resolve when the causative agent is discontinued. The major adverse reactions observed with various classes of antimicrobials are outlined in Table 302–6. Adverse reactions can also result from interactions between drugs that increase or decrease elimination, alter protein binding, or enhance drug toxicity. Some drugs that are metabolized by the hepatic and intestinal microsomal P-450 (CYP) enzymes are inhibitors of the enzyme as well as substrates. For example, rifabutin induces CYP3A enzymes, which increase the clearance of protease inhibitors used to treat HIV infections. The same protease inhibitors can inhibit the clearance of rifabutin by these enzymes, resulting in higher toxic concentrations of rifabutin. Important drug interactions with antibacterials are shown in Table 302–7.

Failure of Antibacterial Therapy

Persistent fever or symptoms of infection during antibacterial therapy always require reassessment of the initial antibiotic selection and dosage regimen, review of microbiologic data and susceptibility results, and even new culture data to look for emergence of resistance or superinfection. Other causes of antibacterial failure include (1) an obstructed drainage system, (2) an undrained abscess or infected fluid collection, (3) persistence of a foreign body or nonviable tissue (e.g., sequestra), (4) drug fever, and (5) suboptimal drug concentration because of drug interactions or poor oral bioavailability.

SUGGESTED READINGS

Andriole VT (ed): The Quinolones, 2nd ed. San Diego, Academic Press, 1998. *An authoritative monograph on the chemistry, pharmacology, and clinical use of this increasingly used class of antibacterial agents.*

Chang S, Sievert DM, Hageman JC, et al: Brief Report: Infection with vancomycin-resistant *Staphylococcus aureus* containing the vanA resistance gene. N Engl J Med 2003;348:1342–1347. *Reports the first S. aureus isolate fully resistant to vancomycin, which had formerly been uniformly effective against this common pathogen.*

Craig WA: Pharmacokinetic/pharmacodynamic parameters: Rationale for antibacterial dosing of mice and men. Clin Infect Dis 1998;26:1–10. *A detailed explanation of the concepts of pharmacodynamics as applied to antimicrobial therapy and an illustration of the scientific principles that give rise to effective antibiotic dosing.*

Gilbert DN, Moellering RC Jr, Sande MA: The Sanford Guide to Antimicrobial Therapy 2003. Hyde Park, VT, Antimicrobial Therapy, Inc, 2003. *A detailed pocket guide to antimicrobial use that is updated and published annually.*

Gold HS, Moellering RC Jr: Antimicrobial-drug resistance. N Engl J Med 1996;335:1445–1453. *A discussion of selected aspects of antimicrobial resistance, including penicillin resistance in S. pneumoniae, vancomycin resistance in enterococci, and that due to beta-lactamases.*

Kaye KS, Fraimow HS, Abrutyn E: Pathogens resistant to antimicrobial agents. Infect Dis Clin North Am 2000;14:293–319. *A discussion of the epidemiology and molecular mechanisms of antimicrobial resistance.*

Kucers A, Crowe SM, Grayson ML, Hoy JF (eds): The Use of Antibiotics: A Clinical Review of Antibacterial, Antifungal and Antiviral Drugs, 5th ed. Oxford, UK, Butterworth-Heinemann, 1997. *The latest edition of an extensively referenced textbook on antimicrobial agents.*

Nikaido H: Prevention of drug access to bacterial targets: Permeability barriers and active efflux. Science 1994;264:382–388. *A detailed discussion of permeability barriers and active efflux as mechanisms for resistance to antibacterials.*

303 PNEUMOCOCCAL PNEUMONIA

Lionel Mandell

Definition

The term *pneumococcal pneumonia* refers to infection of the pulmonary parenchyma and its associated structures by the microbial pathogen *Streptococcus pneumoniae.* There are an estimated 500,000 cases occurring annually in the United States, resulting in approximately 50,000 deaths. This bacterium has been known by a number of names, including *Microbe septicemique du salive, Micrococcus pasteuri, Diplococcus pneumoniae,* and most recently, *S. pneumoniae.* The pneumococcal appellation was affixed over a century ago because of the strong association of the organism with pulmonary infection. To the family physician, the internist, and certainly the infectious disease specialist, this is one of the most frequently encountered infections and is associated with considerable morbidity and mortality.

Etiology and Epidemiology

THE PATHOGEN. *S. pneumoniae* is a Gram-positive coccus that typically grows in pairs or short chains.

Careful examination of the diplococcal form reveals slightly tapered ends giving rise to the "lancet-shaped" appearance. It is a facultative anaerobe that grows best on blood agar plates in a 5% carbon dioxide–ambient environment. The colonies are typically surrounded by a greenish zone of hemolysis resulting from hemoglobin degradation by a pneumococcal toxin. The organism can be distinguished from other streptococci by its susceptibility to ethylhydrocupreine (optochin) and bile solubility.

The surface of the pneumococcus consists of a capsule and a cell wall. The capsule helps to prevent phagocytosis and is composed of polysaccharides, which define the 90 pneumococcal serotypes. The cell wall is a dynamic structure composed of more than a dozen distinct glycopeptides, but the main components are peptidoglycan and teichoic acid.

The pneumococcus is the single most common cause of community-acquired pneumonia (CAP) but has been reported in hospital-acquired pneumonia patients as well. A meta-analysis of 7000 patients with CAP and proven etiology revealed that *S. pneumoniae* was the etiologic agent in two thirds of cases and was the pathogen in two thirds of the fatalities. Physicians may have the false impression that *S. pneumoniae* is not common because they may not encounter many positive culture results. The reason for this is that at least one third of patients with CAP are unable to produce sputum and, even if they do, often provide an inadequate expectorated sample. Also, if the patient has recently taken just one dose of a drug to which the pneumococcus is susceptible, it may not be possible to isolate the pathogen.

Pneumonia is usually the result of inhalation or aspiration of a pathogen. The former mechanism is more commonly seen with viral infections, whereas the latter is typically associated with bacterial infections such as Gram-negative rods and the pneumococcus. It is important therefore to understand the epidemiology of colonization by *S. pneumoniae* as well as the epidemiology of the disease entity itself.

The ecologic niche of the pneumococcus is the nasopharynx, and up to 80% of infants and 20% of healthy adults may be colonized. This process may begin within the first few days of life and appears to be inversely related to age. Simultaneous colonization with more than one pneumococcal capsular type has been reported, and it appears that asymptomatic colonization is an immunizing experience because homologous anticapsular antibodies may be demonstrated in individuals following colonization with a specific serotype.

A particular serotype may colonize the nasopharynx for varying periods of time, but the average duration in infants is seven weeks. Carriage rates are highest during the late fall winter and early spring. Although each of the 90 serotypes is potentially pathogenic, those most frequently encountered are types 3, 4, 6, 7, 9, 12, 14, 18, 19, and 23.

THE DISEASE. Person-to-person transmission results from close interpersonal contact. Although pneumococcal pneumonia is typically a sporadic illness, epidemics have been reported and usually occur in a setting conducive to crowding such as a barracks, nursing home, or prison. This is also particularly important with young children in a daycare setting. Children are often colonized with high-density populations of pneumococci, and overcrowding facilitates the transmission of resistant strains from colonized to susceptible infants and children and may in turn serve as a source of further transmission to family members and ultimately to the general population.

The disease burden may be expressed as an annual rate of infection per 100,000 of the target population. In one Scandinavian country, the incidence of pneumococcal pneumonia was 18 : 100,000 per year. For those ≤5 years of age and those ≥75 years, the rates were 23 : 100,000 and 35.8 : 100,000, respectively.

Overall pneumococcal bacteremia rates of 7.5 : 100,000 per year have been reported, with case-fatality rates of 21%. The incidence of bacteremia increases with age.

Risk factors for pneumococcal pneumonia are dementia, seizure disorders, congestive heart failure, cerebrovascular disease, chronic obstructive pulmonary disease, human immunodeficiency virus (HIV) infection, prior viral respiratory illness, alcoholism, malnutrition, diabetes, cirrhosis, renal insufficiency and African American race.

Certain subgroups such as Native Americans, particularly those from Alaska and Australian aboriginals, appear to be particularly susceptible to invasive pneumococcal infection. Any individual with a defect in IgG synthesis or phagocyte function and anyone who has undergone splenectomy may be at increased risk of invasive pneumococcal infection as well.

Pathogenesis

Pneumonia is ultimately the result of a breakdown of the interplay between colonizer and host. In the case of pneumococcal pneumonia, the microorganism colonizes the nasopharynx, and if it gains access to the alveoli and incites an inflammatory response, infection may ensue. Typically colonization depends on the lectin-like interaction between bacterial surface proteins and host cell carbohydrate.

Aspiration of small amounts of oropharyngeal contents occurs in deep sleep even in normal individuals, but if the oropharyngeal material includes pneumococcal serotypes associated with invasive infection and if normal clearance mechanisms fail, the colonizers may become pathogens.

The lung has a formidable array of defenses that may be classified in a number of ways, although a functional classification is probably best (i.e., resident or surveillance mechanisms versus augmenting mechanisms). The former are primarily mechanical or anatomic and are operational from the point of air entry to the respiratory bronchioles. They include ciliated and squamous epithelium in the nasopharynx, mechanical barriers such as the larynx and airway angulation, and cough and secretory IgA. Beyond this point, mechanical defenses are ineffective, and resident or surveillance mechanisms that rely on immunoglobulin and phagocytic cells take over. In the region of the alveoli, surveillance mechanisms include opsonic IgG, the alternate complement pathway, and phagocytes such as polymorphonuclear neutrophils (PMNs) and alveolar macrophages.

In response to invasion by pathogens, the augmenting mechanisms that are more specific are recruited and result in the initiation of inflammatory and immune responses.

The risk of infection is increased by any process or condition that exposes the host to pathogens, which allows oropharyngeal secretions to bypass upper airway defenses or interferes with the host's ability to ingest and kill the pneumococci (Table 303-1).

The cellular and molecular mechanisms have not been completely elucidated, but it appears that if the pneumococci are not cleared, they may adhere to type II cells in the alveolus. Attachment to resting cells is mediated by two classes of glycoconjugates, but in the presence of inflammatory mediators, host cell receptors such as those for platelet-activating factor (PAF) are upregulated and provide a site of attachment for the bacteria. This interaction between PAF receptor and pathogen seems to be an important step in the internalization of the bacteria by means of an endocytic vacuole and may promote invasion.

Once in the lung, the pneumococci are able to activate complement and to stimulate the cytokine response. Initially the alveoli fill with fluid exudate (Fig. 303-1), which allows the infection to spread to adjacent uninfected alveoli. In healthy lungs PMNs constitute less than 1 to 2% of alveolar cells and normally reside in the interstitial areas of the lung and in adjacent capillaries. Their recruitment into the alveoli depends on the generation of chemoattractants necessary for the directed migration of neutrophils into the alveoli.

The pneumococcal polysaccharides of the bacterial capsule help the organism to resist phagocytosis, and the absence of anticapsular antibody limits the ability to opsonize and ingest pathogens. Ultimately, the signs and symptoms of disease are due to the pathogens

Table 303-1 • PREDISPOSING FACTORS FOR PNEUMOCOCCAL PNEUMONIA

Increased exposure to *S. pneumoniae*
 Prison
 Military barracks
 Day care centers
 Shelters for the homeless
Decreased host defenses
 Complement deficiency
 Antibody deficiency
 Functional or anatomic asplenia
 Decreased numbers or function of phagocytes
 Specific disease entities
  Multiple myeloma
  Lymphoma
  Chronic lymphocytic leukemia
  Human immunodeficiency virus
Respiratory/pulmonary problems
 Chronic obstructive pulmonary disease
 Smoker
 Allergies
 Prior viral infection

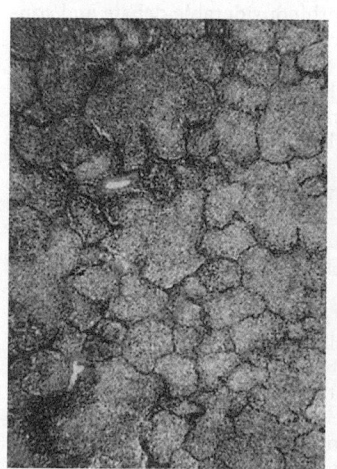 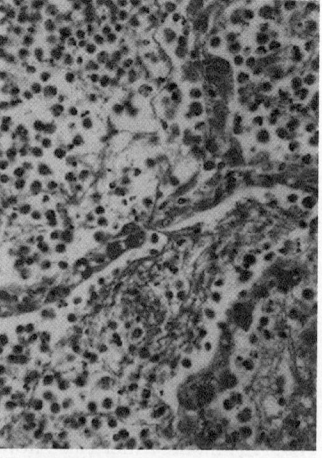

A   B

FIGURE 303-1 • Pneumonia. *A,* Low-power magnification (× 100) of hematoxylin and eosin (H&E) stain of tissue section from left lower lobe of lung. Note intact alveolar walls and alveoli filled with edema and thick cellular exudates. *B,* Higher magnification (× 500) H&E stain of same section shown in A. Note heavy infiltrate of polymorphonuclear cells and intact alveolar walls.

themselves and the body's response to them. The bacterial cytotoxin pneumolysin and various pneumococcal cell wall components such as teichoic acid and peptidoglycan are able to induce a variety of effects that initiate and then enhance the inflammatory response and result in the various signs and symptoms of pneumonia.

The effects of pneumococcal infection are ultimately manifested as changes in lung mechanics secondary to reductions in lung volumes and lung compliance and in gas exchange problems resulting from intrapulmonary shunting and subsequent arterial hypoxemia. If severe enough, this may result in death.

Clinical Manifestations

Until relatively recently, physicians tended to divide patients with CAP into those with typical and atypical pneumonia based on their clinical presentations. This has fallen into disrepute because it is clear that such an approach does not stand up to scrutiny.

The various signs and symptoms include systemic constitutional findings as well as findings limited to the lung and its associated structures. The presentation varies depending on a number of factors such as whether the patient is immunocompetent or immunosuppressed, the severity of illness, and whether the patient has taken antibiotics. Depending on such factors, the patient may have an elevated temperature and particularly in the elderly may be somewhat confused. Temperatures can vary from 101° F to over 103° F (38° C to 39.5° C) and are usually associated with a tachycardic response. Chills and rigors may be seen as well. Gastrointestinal symptoms such as nausea, vomiting, and/or diarrhea may be encountered in 20% of patients. A cough usually productive of purulent and occasionally blood-tinged sputum is often present, and as many as 46% of patients in one series reported the presence of chest pain.

The clinical presentation has frequently been described as being more subtle in the elderly. The reduced prevalence of symptoms is most pronounced in relation to the febrile response (temperature, chills, sweats) and pain, including chest discomfort, headache, and myalgia. Older patients may present with confusion and little else, and the physician must always have a high level of suspicion when dealing with the elderly.

On examination, the patient is often listless and may at times be cyanotic. The respiratory rate is increased, and if pleuritic pain is marked, the patient may be splinting the affected side. Dullness to percussion over a lung segment suggests consolidation, whereas a flat percussion note is typically associated with a pleural effusion. Breath sounds may be "distant" if there is an overlying effusion but are bronchial in nature if the underlying lung is consolidated. Rales may be noted, and if the patient has pleurisy without much accumulation of pleural fluid, a friction rub may be heard as well.

There is no radiographic appearance that is characteristic of pneumococcal pneumonia. Typically, however, involvement is limited to one or more segments within a single lobe. Patients with lobar consolidation are more likely to be bacteremic, but no consistently significant differences in the radiologic manifestations of bacteremic and nonbacteremic pneumococcal pneumonia have been reported, and even patients with a small subsegmental opacity can have bacteremia.

In those who are severely ill, a greater proportion of patients among the pneumococcal cases are bacteremic than among those infected by other pathogens.

Involvement is unilateral approximately 80% of the time, and the presence of cavitation or lung abscess is distinctly uncommon. Forty-five percent of patients have an associated pleural effusion, but only 15% have an effusion of sufficient size to warrant drainage (>10 mm on lateral decubitus view).

The physician must always keep an open mind, and even if the diagnosis of pneumococcal pneumonia seems likely, careful attention must be paid to extrapulmonary involvement by metastatic infection. In the setting of bacteremia, pneumococcal pneumonia may be responsible for seeding of distant sites and the physician must be careful to rule out such entities as meningitis, endocarditis, or septic arthritis.

With sepsis, sepsis syndrome, or septic shock, the patient may be hypotensive and findings of organ failure will vary depending on the target organ involved. For example, oliguria, anuria, and acidosis suggest renal failure; congestive heart failure suggests myocardial impairment; and jaundice is consistent with hepatic failure. Systemic activation of coagulation together with consumption of clotting proteins can result in clotting and bleeding occurring simultaneously in the same patient, and in some cases peripheral gangrene and purpura fulminans may be seen.

Diagnosis

The diagnosis of pneumonia in general and pneumococcal pneumonia in particular is associated with considerable debate and controversy. A detailed discussion of the issues surrounding the diagnosis of pneumonia is beyond the scope of this chapter, but a brief review of this topic is in order. First, it is clear that despite extensive testing even in university medical centers, a specific etiologic agent is not found in half or more of patients. The diagnostic tests used generally fall into two categories: clinical and invasive/quantitative. The former relies on information obtained from the patient history, physical examination, and selected laboratory tests or procedures such as a chest radiograph, a sputum Gram-stain, and blood and sputum cultures. Invasive/quantitative methods include bronchoscopic techniques, pleural fluid aspiration, and, in selected cases, lung biopsy. In general, the clinical method is too sensitive and lacks specificity, whereas the invasive/quantitative method requires special expertise and laboratory support and is more costly. The interested reader is referred to the guidelines for the management of pneumonia published by the Canadian Infectious Disease Society (CIDS) and the Canadian Thoracic Society (CTS), the Infectious Diseases Society of America (IDSA), and the American Thoracic Society (ATS) for a more detailed discussion of this issue.

Once the clinical diagnosis of pneumonia has been made, the next step is to determine the etiologic agent. Clinical and radiographic criteria do not allow the physician to accurately identify the causative pathogen. One must either see the pathogen (staining tests), grow the pathogen (cultures), or identify components of the pathogen (capsular polysaccharide) or responses to the pathogen (antibody).

The sputum Gram-stain is a relatively simple and inexpensive procedure to document the presence of certain pathogens. The adequacy of the specimen is based on the relative number of PMNs and squamous epithelial cells (SECs). Under low-power magnification (×100), there should be hundreds of PMNs and few SECs, whereas under high power (×1000), there should be at least 25 PMNs and less than 10 SECs per high-power field. The sensitivity of the sputum Gram-stain for *S. pneumoniae* is 55%, whereas the specificity is over 80%.

Sputum cultures are neither sensitive nor specific. This is particularly true when dealing with relatively fastidious pathogens such as *S. pneumoniae*.

Approximately 30% of patients overall are unable to produce an appropriate sputum sample. In the elderly, this figure reaches almost 70%. If grading criteria are used to assess the quality of sputum, only 40% at best are rated as being of good quality. This means that overall a maximum of 28% (40% of 70%) are good-quality specimens. If patients have taken a prior dose of antibiotic, this may affect the culture results.

Another method that can be used to demonstrate the pneumococcus is use of the polymerase chain reaction (PCR) in whole blood. This technique appears to be relatively sensitive and very specific but as yet is limited to research laboratories. It is not useful in children, where carriage of pneumococci results in false-positive results.

Large amounts of pneumococcal capsular polysaccharide are apparently excreted in urine and may be detected by a variety of techniques. This may (as for PCR) have a role to play in adults but does not appear to be useful for distinguishing children with pneumococcal pneumonia from those who are merely colonized with *S. pneumoniae*.

Detection of antibody to pneumococcal polysaccharide has not proved useful in identifying patients with pneumococcal pneumonia. The test is neither sensitive nor specific and is further complicated by the fact that those who succumb to pneumococcal infection may be the very patients who are unable to produce adequate amounts of antibody.

 Treatment

The discussion of the treatment of pneumococcal pneumonia or any pneumonia for that matter is complicated by the fact that the physician often does not know the exact identity of the etiologic agent. For this reason, empiric therapy is often used. There are situations, however, when the physician may believe that he or she knows the pathogen and chooses to initiate a course of treatment directed at a specific agent. Rightly or wrongly, this is far too contentious an issue to be settled here. For the sake of completeness and to cover the scenarios encountered in daily practice, treatment is divided into two sections; one dealing with directed therapy and one dealing with empiric therapy. Before doing so, however, there are two issues that have a significant impact on the management of pneumonia that will be dealt with first: (1) site of care decision and (2) antimicrobial resistance.

SITE OF CARE DECISION

This is a relatively new topic that just 5 to 10 years ago would have received little, if any, attention. However, with diminishing health care resources and the rising costs associated with hospital treatment, this has become a topic of considerable importance. The cost of inpatient management exceeds outpatient treatment by a factor of 15 to 20, and it is the cost of hospital treatment that accounts for most of the estimated $4 billion spent annually on CAP in the United States.

Outcome assessment tools are occasionally needed to assist physicians in making the site of care decision. Although it is sometimes obvious that certain patients may be managed at home while others may require treatment in hospital, there are times when it is difficult to decide on the best course of action. Such tools ideally provide an objective means of assessing the risk of adverse outcomes including death. They also serve as quality control tools.

Appropriately designed prediction rules may minimize unnecessary hospital admissions and also help to identify patients who will benefit from care and intervention in the hospital setting. While these were not originally developed as triage tools, they have come to be used in such a manner. The most frequently used assessment tool is the one developed by Michael Fine. This was designed to identify patients at low risk of dying. Patients are assigned to one of five classes based on the total number of points that they accrue. Points are assigned based on age, coexisting illness, and abnormal physical and laboratory findings. The mortality rates for the classes are class 1, 0.1%; class 2, 0.6%; class 3, 2.8%; class 4, 8.2%; and class 5, 29.2%. Based on these mortality rates it has been suggested that patients in classes 1 and 2 be treated outside the hospital while those in classes 4 and 5 be admitted to the hospital. Patients in class 3 should ideally be kept in an observation unit overnight and reassessed the next day if possible.

The rule is accurate as a mortality prediction model and provides a rational basis for decisions about hospitalization. Unfortunately, however, it relies on an inordinately large number of prognostic variables and fails to consider other parameters that may affect patient outcome, such as cognitive impairment and substance abuse, and it may at times oversimplify the interpretation of important predictor variables.

ANTIMICROBIAL RESISTANCE

For years, infectious disease physicians have argued about the dangers associated with the inappropriate use of antimicrobial agents. Now, unfortunately, this has become a reality and affects the way that many infections are managed. S. pneumoniae can be treated with a number of antimicrobials, including various β-lactams, macrolides, and selected fluoroquinolones. Unfortunately, resistance has been described for virtually all of these agents.

The first reported case of infection with penicillin-resistant S. pneumoniae was that of a hypogammaglobulinemic patient from Australia in 1967. In North America, the first reported isolates of penicillin-resistant S. pneumoniae were in 1974 from the United States and in 1983 from Canada. The emergence of resistance to penicillin among S. pneumoniae isolates represents a gradual reduction in in vitro susceptibility. The National Committee Clinical Laboratory Standards (NCCLS) define strains with minimal inhibitory concentrations (MIC) to penicillin of <0.1 μg/mL as sensitive, 0.1 to 1.0 μg/mL as intermediate, and >1.0 μg/mL as resistant. Multidrug-resistant pathogens are those that are resistant to three or more antimicrobial agents having different mechanisms of action. Multidrug-resistant S. pneumoniae, first reported in South Africa in 1977, have now been recovered in a number of countries, including the United States.

The phenotypic expression of resistance corresponds to genetic alterations resulting either from horizontal acquisition of foreign genetic information or from mutations in the microbial genome. In the case of S. pneumoniae, resistance may be acquired by direct DNA incorporation and remodeling from closely related oral commensal bacteria by the process of natural transformation. What seems to happen is that our own microbial flora develop resistance when we are treated unnecessarily or with inappropriate antimicrobial regimens and potential pathogens such as S. pneumoniae may subsequently acquire resistance coding DNA from these bacteria. Pneumococcal resistance to β-lactams such as penicillin is due solely to the presence of low affinity penicillin binding proteins (PBPs).

The PBPs themselves are trans- and carboxypeptidase enzymes involved in bacterial cell wall synthesis and represent the primary sites of action for the penicillins and other β-lactam drugs. Of concern is the propensity for pneumococcal resistance to penicillin to be associated with reduced susceptibility to other drugs such as macrolides, tetracyclines, and trimethoprim-sulfamethoxazole. In the United States, 58.9% of pneumococcal isolates from blood that are penicillin resistant are also macrolide resistant. Risk factors for drug-resistant pneumococcal infection include recent antimicrobial therapy, extremes of age (especially <5 years), attendance at day care center, recent hospitalization, and HIV infection. Resistance to macrolides, in contrast, can occur through multiple mechanisms including target site modification or an efflux pump. Target site modification is caused by a ribosomal methylase encoded by the ermB gene. A change in 23S rRNA mediated by this gene can result in resistance to macrolides, lincosamides, and streptogramin B type antibiotics (MLS$_B$ phenotype). The efflux mechanism is encoded by the mefE gene resulting in an M phenotype. The former is typically associated with high-level resistance with MICs of 64 μg/mL, whereas the latter is usually associated with low-level resistance with MICs of 1 to 32 μg/mL. These two mechanisms account for approximately 45 and 55%, respectively, of resistant isolates. High-level resistance to macrolides is seen more frequently in Europe, whereas low-level resistance seems to predominate in North America. While there have been reports of macrolide failures, these are neither extensive nor consistent, and many experts believe that the macrolides still have a role to play in the management of pneumococcal pneumonia in North America.

For infection with S. pneumoniae with penicillin MICs, up to 1 μg/mL penicillin is still an appropriate agent. For strains with penicillin MICs of 2 to 4 μg/mL, some data suggest that there is no increase in treatment failure, while other data suggest increased mortality or complications. For strains of S. pneumoniae with intermediate levels of resistance to penicillin, higher doses of the drug may be used.

Resistance to fluoroquinolones such as ciprofloxacin and levofloxacin has been reported. Such resistance may be mediated by changes in one or both target sites (topoisomerase II and IV) usually resulting from mutations in the gyrA and parC genes respectively. An efflux pump may have a role as well.

TREATMENT REGIMENS

DIRECTED THERAPY AGAINST KNOWN PATHOGEN. If a good-quality Gram-stain of sputum reveals sheets of PMNs with lancet-shaped Gram-

Continued

positive diplococci as the only organism, some would accept that *S. pneumoniae* is the cause. There is always the possibility that a copathogen such as *Mycoplasma pneumoniae* or *Chlamydia pneumoniae* is also present, but many physicians would accept this as evidence that *S. pneumoniae* is the pathogen requiring treatment.

If the patient has no risk factors for infection with resistant *S. pneumoniae* and is not living in an area endemic for penicillin-resistant *S. pneumoniae*, it is reasonable to initiate treatment with penicillin.

The dose required is only 2.4 million units/day of penicillin G. For those treated as outpatients, oral therapy is usually given in the form of amoxicillin 500 mg PO three times daily. If the patient is allergic to penicillin, a macrolide such as azithromycin (1.5 g over 3 to 5 days) or clarithromycin (500 mg twice daily for 7 to 10 days) may be used.

Approximately 20% of CAP patients are hospitalized; 90% of these patients are treated on a medical ward and 10% in the intensive care unit (ICU). Such figures are not available for the subset of patients with pneumococcal pneumonia. Hospitalized patients are generally more seriously ill and are at greater risk of dying than are those treated on an ambulatory basis; therefore, higher doses of antibiotics are generally used and are given parenterally. Total daily doses of penicillin or ampicillin in the range of 12 million units (2 million every 4 hours) and 4 g (1 g every 6 hours), respectively, are given. Third-generation cephalosporins such as ceftriaxone (1 to 2 g every 24 hours) or cefotaxime (1 to 2 g every 8 hours) may be used as well.

The total duration of therapy is unknown. Generally treatment should be given for a total period of 1 to 2 weeks, but this should be based on the clinical response. An appropriately designed randomized controlled trial has never been done to specifically address the issue of length of treatment. For those initially treated with intravenous therapy, there is no need to continue the parenteral regimen for the entire period of treatment; one can switch to an oral regimen once the patient has stabilized. There are specific criteria to help with this decision: cough and shortness of breath are improving, the patient is afebrile for at least 8 hours, the white blood cell count is normalizing, and oral intake and gastrointestinal tract absorption are adequate.

These specific criteria need not be met. Patients are frequently treated outside the hospital who are febrile; therefore, it does not make sense to always wait until they are afebrile in the hospital to switch to an oral regimen. Obviously the patient must be able to ingest and absorb drugs and the drug must be available in an oral form. Other than that, common sense should prevail when deciding when it is time to switch from intravenous to oral therapy.

EMPIRIC TREATMENT. This is essentially an educated guess; the physician is hoping that the regimen will cover the responsible pathogen. A number of guidelines have been developed in Canada, the United States, the United Kingdom, and Europe to help the physician in selecting an appropriate treatment regimen. Some have suggested that physicians should not rely on guidelines and that each physician should make his or her own decision based on the circumstances of a particular case. However, a look at patterns of practice at several prominent U.S. medical centers before the development of the CAP guidelines showed that a disturbing number and range of antibiotics per patient were used to treat CAP. Several studies that have examined the use of the various guidelines in outpatient community settings as well as in hospitals have shown that their use is associated with a statistically significant reduction in cost, mortality, and length of stay for those requiring admission.

The original guidelines published by the CIDS in 1993 and subsequently by the ATS suggested that macrolides should be used for the management of outpatients. This was not an attempt to deal with pneumococcal resistance to penicillin but rather was meant to address the atypical pathogen issue. It was thought that atypicals such as *M. pneumoniae, C. pneumoniae,* and, occasionally, *Legionella* species were responsible for 20 to 25% of CAP cases. If penicillin was used, it would be the agent of choice for *S. pneumoniae,* but it would be ineffective against any of the atypicals; a macrolide, however, would provide good to excellent coverage for all of these likely pathogens.

The fluoroquinolones have assumed an important role in the management of CAP. This coincides with concerns about pneumococcal resistance to β-lactams and macrolides, the appreciation of the potential importance of Gram-negative rods in selected CAP patients, and the recent appearance of the "respiratory" fluoroquinolones.

There are four sets of guidelines for the initial management of CAP in North America. These have been prepared by the Centers for Disease Control and Prevention (2000), the CIDS and the CTS (2000), the IDSA (2000), and the ATS (2001). The fundamental difference between the CDC document and the other North American guidelines is that the former assumes that the physician knows that he or she is dealing with a pneumococcal infection. The CDC document also suggests that a β-lactam alone might be reasonable coverage for outpatient therapy of CAP and fluoroquinolones are not suggested as initial therapy in any situation. In contrast, the IDSA, ATS, CIDS, and CTS documents assert that the pneumococcus is the single most important pathogen but strongly advocate coverage for the atypicals in the empiric treatment setting. These three documents are remarkably similar in their approach; the Canadian regimen (the CIDS and the CTS) is given in Table 303–2.

For those admitted to a hospital ward, either a β-lactam such as a third-generation cephalosporin plus a macrolide or a fluoroquinolone alone should be used. The fluoroquinolones offer logistic and financial benefits because they permit once-daily dosing with a single drug. There are four randomized controlled trials that have shown a statistically significant benefit in favor of the fluoroquinolones compared with a macrolide, a β-lactam, or both.[1-4] Although such studies have some design flaws, they nevertheless indicate at least a trend in support of such agents. It should be noted, however, that resistance to fluoroquinolones has already been well documented, and misuse of these drugs may result in widespread resistance.

For those treated in the ICU, a fluoroquinolone or macrolide in combination with a β-lactam is suggested if *Pseudomonas aeruginosa* is not a concern. If it is, then an antipseudomonal β-lactam such as ceftazidime or meropenem plus ciprofloxacin is recommended. To date, there are no randomized controlled trials that have specifically addressed the question of monotherapy with a fluoroquinolone for treatment of severe CAP. In fact, a report suggested that monotherapy may be suboptimal for the treatment of severe bacteremic pneumococcal pneumonia. It was found that patients who had received only one agent effective against the pneumococcus did significantly worse than did those who received combination therapy effective against this pathogen. The most commonly used single-drug regimen was levofloxacin, whereas the most common combination regimen was a third-generation cephalosporin plus a macrolide. A number of possible explanations have been invoked, including synergistic effects and differences in cytokine release. It has also been suggested that had fluoroquinolones such as moxifloxacin or gatifloxacin, which are more potent in vitro against *S. pneumoniae,* been used, such a difference might not have been found.

The ATS differs from the IDSA and Canadian guidelines in one important aspect; it suggests that azithromycin alone may be used for hospitalized CAP patients without cardiopulmonary disease and with no modifying factors. Neither the IDSA nor the Canadian guidelines include such a category and neither group suggests monotherapy with azithromycin as an option.

The prompt institution of treatment is important particularly when dealing with elderly patients. A study of older subjects with CAP in emergency departments showed that those who received antibiotics within 4 hours of presentation had a significantly lower mortality rate than did those who waited longer for treatment.

In an otherwise well relatively young patient with no comorbid conditions and with mild to moderate infection, the elevated temperature and white blood cell count usually resolve by days 2 to 4 and 4, respectively. The patient looks and feels better within a few days, but it is important to keep in mind that even in patients younger than 50 years, only 60% will have resolved radiologically by 1 month. In those over 50 years of age or those with more severe infection or chronic obstructive pulmonary disease, only 25% may have cleared radiographically by 1 month.

If the patient fails to respond or deteriorates after initial treatment, a number of possibilities should be entertained. One is that an incorrect diagnosis has been made, and the other is that the initial diagnosis was correct but the situation is complicated by host-, drug-, or pathogen-related issues.

Table 303–2 • **EMPIRICAL ANTIMICROBIAL SELECTION FOR ADULT PATIENTS WITH COMMUNITY-ACQUIRED PNEUMONIA**

TYPE OF PATIENT, FACTOR(S) INVOLVED	TREATMENT REGIMEN	
	First Choice	**Second Choice**
OUTPATIENT		
1. Outpatient without modifying factors	Macrolide*	Doxycycline
2. Outpatient with modifying factors		
a. COLD (no recent antibiotics or PO steroids within past 3 mo)	Newer macrolide†	Doxycycline
b. COLD (recent antibiotics or PO steroids within past 3 mo); *H. influenzae* and enteric Gram-negative rods implicated	"Respiratory" fluoroquinolone‡	Amoxicillin/clavulanate + macrolide or 2G cephalosporin + macrolide
3. Suspected macroaspiration: oral anaerobes	Amoxicillin/clavulanate ± macrolide	"Respiratory" fluoroquinolone (e.g., levofloxacin) + clindamycin or metronidazole
INPATIENT		
1. Hospitalized patient on medical ward *S. pneumoniae, L. pneumophila, C. pneumoniae* implicated	"Respiratory" fluoroquinolone	2G, 3G, or 4G cephalosporin + macrolide
2. Hospitalized patient in ICU		
a. *P. aeruginosa* not suspected; *S. pneumoniae, L. pneumophila,* gram-negative rods	IV respiratory fluoroquinolone + cefotaxime, ceftriaxone or β-lactam/β-lactamase inhibitor	IV macrolide + cefotaxime, ceftriaxone or β-lactam/β-lactamase inhibitor
b. *P. aeruginosa* suspected	Anti–pseudomonal fluoroquinolone (e.g., ciprofloxacin) + anti–pseudomonal β-lactam or aminoglycoside	Triple therapy with pseudomonal β-lactam (e.g., ceftazidine, piperacillin-tazobactam, imipenem, or meropenem) + aminoglycoside (e.g. gentamicin, tobramycin or amikacin) + macrolide
NURSING HOME RESIDENT		
Streptococcus pneumoniae, enteric Gram-negative rods, *H. influenzae* implicated		
1. Treatment in nursing home	"Respiratory" fluoroquinolone alone or amoxicillin/clavulanate + macrolide	2G cephalosporin + macrolide
2. Hospitalized	Identical to treatment for other hospitalized patients (see earlier)	

*Erythromycin, azithromycin, or clarithromycin.
†Azithromycin or clarithromycin.
‡Levofloxacin, gatifloxacin, or moxifloxacin; trovafloxacin is restricted because of potential severe hepatoxicity.
COLD = chronic obstructive lung disease; 2G = second generation; 3G = third generation; 4G = fourth generation.

The patient must be carefully reassessed with a detailed review of the clinical history and treatment course, plus appropriate radiographic studies and cultures. If the diagnosis is incorrect, other infectious causes of pneumonia such as *H. influenzae* or the atypicals must be considered. Noninfectious illnesses that may account for the clinical and radiographic findings must also be ruled out; these include such diverse entities as congestive heart failure, pulmonary embolism, neoplasm, radiation injury, drug reaction, or inflammatory lung disease, to name a few. If the original diagnosis was correct, a number of host-, drug-, and pathogen-related issues may be responsible. Host factors include metastatic infection, lung abscess, or empyema, and drug factors such as errors in selection, dose, or route of administration are possible, as are unsuspected compliance problems in a patient receiving oral medication. The likeliest pathogen-related problem is unsuspected drug resistance. According to current standards of treatment, however, many of these problems are avoided by the use of relatively broad-spectrum empiric therapy as suggested in the IDSA, ATS, and Canadian pneumonia guidelines.

Prevention

The ideal is to prevent pneumococcal disease rather than to treat established pneumonia. This is becoming increasingly important now that resistance looms larger as a problem. Until recently, there has been only one type of pneumococcal vaccine available. This is a polysaccharide vaccine that contains 25 µg of each of 23 capsular polysaccharides. These capsular types account for 90% of invasive infections, but the vaccine could not be used in children under 2 years of age. Polysaccharide vaccines are able to stimulate B-cell responses, resulting in type-specific antibody production that enhances ingestion and killing of the pathogens by phagocytes. The antigens, however, are T-cell independent and therefore do not result in long-lasting immunity. Two types of polysaccharide vaccine have been available—Pneumovax (MERCK) and Pnu-Immune (Lederle). Their use was recommended for adults at risk, but it was recognized that responses were not as good in the elderly and in immunosupressed patients who were at increased risk of infection with *S. pneumoniae.*

A conjugated vaccine also has been approved for use. Unlike its 23-valent predecessor, this is a 7-valent pneumococcal conjugate vaccine (Prevenar; Wyeth-Lederle).

The basis of this newer vaccine is that pneumococcal polysaccharide is conjugated to a carrier protein, thereby producing T-cell–dependent antigens, which results in long-term immunologic memory. In this case, the carrier protein is CRM 197, which is similar to diphtheria toxoid. The seven serotypes (4, 6B, 9V, 14, 18C, 19F, 23F) are found most commonly in children and account for approximately 80% of invasive infections in children younger than 6 years.

The effectiveness of the pneumococcal polysaccharide vaccine ranges from 56 to 81% in case-controlled trials. It is not effective in immunocompromised patients such as those with sickle cell disease, chronic renal failure, immunoglobulin deficiency, Hodgkin's disease, non-Hodgkin's lymphoma, leukemia, and multiple myeloma. It also is not effective in preventing nonbacteremic pneumonia.

The vaccine is recommended for (1) persons aged 65 years or older, (2) persons aged 2 to 64 years having chronic illnesses such as cardiovascular disease, chronic pulmonary disease (not asthma), diabetes mellitus, alcoholism, chronic liver disease, or cerebrospinal fluid leaks, (3) persons aged 2 to 64 years with functional or anatomic asplenia, and (4) persons aged 2 to 64 years living in special environments or social settings (Alaskan natives, certain Native American populations, residents of long-term care facilities).

Although the effectiveness of the vaccine is less in these subgroups, the following immunocompromised patients 2 years of age or older should also be immunized: (1) persons with HIV infection, leukemia,

Infectious Diseases

lymphoma, or Hodgkin's disease and (2) those with multiple myeloma, generalized malignancy, chronic renal failure, nephrotic syndrome, or organ or bone marrow transplantation and individuals on immuno-suppressive chemotherapy, including steroids.

The lack of an anamnestic response with polysaccharide vaccines means that antibody levels decrease over time and revaccination is required. The exact timing, however, is unclear, but most experts in this field suggest revaccination at 5 years. For immunocompetent persons aged 65 years or older, a second dose is suggested if the patient was given the first vaccine 5 years earlier at an age younger than 65 years. For persons aged 2 to 64 years with asplenia, if the patient is older than 10 years of age, a single revaccination is suggested 5 years after the initial dose. However, if the patient is older than 10 years, revaccination should be given 3 years after the first dose. For immuno-compromised patients, revaccination should be given 5 years after the first dose if the patient is older than 10 years and 3 years after the first dose if the patient is younger than 10 years.

The pneumococcal conjugate vaccine should be given to infants at 2, 4, 6, and 12 to 15 months of age. Older, previously unvaccinated infants should receive that vaccine at 7 to 11 months (two doses at least 4 weeks apart) and a third dose at 12 months old or older; second and third doses should be separated by at least 2 months. Children 12 to 23 months old should receive two doses at least 2 months apart. Children 2 to 9 years old should receive one dose. Children in high-risk groups should be given two doses at least 2 months apart.

High-risk groups include patients with HIV infection, immuno-compromized states, chronic illnesses such as nephrotic syndrome, chronic pulmonary conditions and symptomatic heart conditions, and patients with sickle cell disease and anatomic or functional asplenia. At this point, there are no indications for revaccination.

1. Ortqvist A, Valtonen M, Cars O, et al: Oral empiric treatment of community acquired pneumonia: A multicenter, double-blind, randomized study comparing sparfloxacin with roxithromycin. Chest 1996;110:499–506.
2. File TM Jr, Segreti J, Dunbar L, et al: A multicenter, randomized study comparing the efficacy and safety of intravenous and/or oral levofloxacin versus ceftri-axone and/or cefuroxime axetil in treatment of adults with community acquired pneumonia. Antimicrob Agents Chemother 1997;41:965–972.
3. O'Doherty B, Dutchman DA, Pettit R, et al: Randomized, double-blind, comparative study of grepafloxacin and amoxicillin in the treatment of patients with community acquired pneumonia. J Antimicrob Chemother 1997;40(Suppl A):73–81.
4. Tremolieres F, de Kock F, Pluck N, et al: Trovafloxacin versus high-dose amoxicillin (1g three times daily) in the treatment of community acquired bacterial pneumonia. Eur J Clin Microbiol Infect Dis 1998;17:447–453.

SUGGESTED READINGS

American Thoracic Society: Guidelines for the management of adults with community-acquired pneumonia: Diagnosis, assessment of severity, and antimicrobial therapy and prevention. Am J Respir Crit Care Med 2001;163:1730–1754. *A comprehensive guide to diagnosis and initial therapy of patients with community-acquired pneumonia based on treatment setting, underlying diseases, and modifying factors, including risk for resistant organisms.*

Bartlett JG, Dowell LF, Mandell LA, et al: Practice guidelines for the management of community acquired pneumonia in adults. Clin Infect Dis 2000;31:347–382. *Consensus recommendations.*

Centers for Disease Control and Prevention: Severe acute respiratory syndrome (SARS). http://www.cdc.gov/ncidod/sars/ *A regularly updated source of information about this newly recognized syndrome.*

Halm EA, Tiersten AS: Management of community-acquired pneumonia. N Engl J Med 2002;347:2039–2045. *A brief practical review.*

Heffelfinger JD, Dowell SF, Jorgensen JH, et al: Management of community acquired pneumonia in the era of pneumococcal resistance: A report from the Drug-Resistant *Streptococcus pneumoniae* Therapeutic Working Group. Arch Intern Med 2000;160: 1399–1408. *Consensus recommendations.*

Mandell LA, Marrie TJ, Grossman RF, et al: Canadian guidelines for the initial management of community-acquired pneumonia: An evidence-based update by the Canadian Infectious Diseases Society and the Canadian Thoracic Society (The Canadian Community-Acquired Pneumonia Working Group). Clin Infect Dis 2000;31:383–421. *Guidelines for hospitalization and antibiotic therapy.*

304 MYCOPLASMAL INFECTION

David Schlossberg

The mycoplasmas associated with humans include species from the genera *Mycoplasma*, *Ureaplasma*, and *Acholeplasma*. Because these genera all belong to the order Mycoplasmatales in the class Mollicutes, they are collectively called *mollicutes* or, more commonly, *mycoplasmas*. More than 150 species are recognized, and they are found in humans, animals, plants, and insects. Most of these

Table 304–1 • HUMAN MYCOPLASMAS

ESTABLISHED PATHOGENS	OPPORTUNISTS	COMMENSALS
M. pneumoniae	M. salivarium	M. buccale
M. hominis	M. orale	M. faucium
M. fermentans	M. pirum	M. lipophilum
M. urealyticum	M. penetrans	M. primatum
M. genitalium	M. arginini	M. spermatophilum
M. phocacerebrale	M. felis	Acholeplasma
	M. edwardii	laidlawii
		Acholeplasma oculi

organisms are commensals, but some of the human strains are pathogenic; rarely, some of the animal strains infect humans as well.

Mycoplasmas are the smallest free-living organisms. At 200 nm, they approximate the size of the larger viruses. Bound by a triple-layered cell membrane, they have no cell wall (thus the name "mollicute," which is Greek for "soft skin") and are therefore not seen on Gram stain and cannot be treated with cell wall–active antibiotics such as the β-lactams or vancomycin.

Most mycoplasmas are facultative anaerobes. They grow down into agar and produce a dark center with a light periphery on the surface, the so-called fried-egg colonies. Mycoplasmas are distinguished from bacteria in that they lack a cell wall and cannot produce cell wall precursors; they are distinguished from viruses, chlamydiae, and rickettsiae in that the mycoplasmas can grow on cell-free media.

The mycoplasmas of humans are listed in Table 304–1. Some are established pathogens in immunocompetent patients, others infect only the immunocompromised, and some are commensals.

Immunology

Mycoplasmas have a wide range of immunomodulatory effects, including stimulation of T- and B-lymphocyte proliferation, induction of cytolytic activity of macrophages and cytotoxic T cells, stimulation of cytokine production, induction of major histocompatibility complex expression in macrophages and B cells, and production of chemotactic factors, Fc factors, Fc receptors, superantigens, and immunoglobulin proteases. This explosive and varied immunologic activity may contribute to disease expression. It is well known that rheumatoid factor, biologic false-positive tests for syphilis, antinuclear antibodies, and other antibodies sometimes appear in the course of mycoplasmal infection.

MYCOPLASMA PNEUMONIAE

M. pneumoniae accounts for 10 to 20% of all pneumonias and for at least half of all pneumonias in children and young adults. Although most cases occur in the first two decades of life, mycoplasmal infection is seen at all ages. *M. pneumoniae* typically causes community-acquired pneumonia, but rare cases of nosocomial acquisition are reported.

Infection with M. pneumoniae can occur in any season, with a 4-year periodicity for outbreaks. Because epidemics of pneumonia secondary to other agents usually peak in the winter, it is diagnostically helpful when *Mycoplasma* pneumonia occurs in other seasons. College epidemics of *Mycoplasma*, for example, tend to peak in the fall.

The incubation period for *M. pneumoniae* averages 2½ weeks but ranges from 4 days to more than 3 weeks. This longer incubation period furnishes an important diagnostic clue inasmuch as incubation periods for most of the respiratory viruses are measured in days, not weeks. Spread is person to person via droplet nuclei after close and prolonged contact.

The attack rate of *M. pneumoniae* diminishes with age. Second infections can occur (especially if a patient is immunocompromised), but the second case is usually milder than the first. Extremely severe disease is seen in patients who have SS or SC hemoglobinopathy, Down syndrome, or hypogammaglobulinemia. Furthermore, patients with humoral deficiency are more likely to become chronic carriers; most normal patients shed the organism by 6 weeks, although in some it may persist for 3 to 4 months.

Clinical Manifestations

See Figure 304–1. Most patients with *M. pneumoniae* infection are older children, adolescents, and young adults with a minor respiratory illness. In general, 75% of patients have tracheobronchitis, 5% have an atypical pneumonia, and 20% are asymptomatic. Children younger than 5 years tend to have coryza and wheezing, whereas the age of maximum risk for the development of pneumonia is 5 to 15 years. Bronchospasm may develop in asthmatics. In many patients, a sequence of symptoms occurs: The illness begins insidiously over days or a week with constitutional symptoms (e.g., fever, myalgia, headache, and malaise); then upper respiratory signs and symptoms appear, with combinations of sore throat, cervical adenopathy, hoarseness, earache, coryza, and nonproductive cough; less commonly, croup or bronchiolitis may supervene, and in a small percentage, pneumonia ensues. At this point, the cough becomes productive.

Many patients report chilliness but not rigors. Protracted coughing results in tracheal tenderness and a sore chest, but actual pleuritic pain is rare. A prolonged illness with paroxysmal cough followed by vomiting may occur in children and mimic pertussis. Signs include fever, an erythematous pharynx without exudate, and rarely, bullae on the tympanic membrane. The illness is usually self-limited and mild.

The insidious onset is followed by gradual recovery. The upper respiratory symptoms may last for 2 to 3 weeks, and signs of pneumonia may persist for 4 to 6 weeks. Laboratory abnormalities are not specific; a slight leukocytosis (<15,000 per cubic millimeter) is seen in 25% of patients, with a normal differential count. Sputum Gram stain is helpful in demonstrating a suggestive combination of inflammatory cells (polymorphonuclear leukocytes or lymphocytes) but a paucity of bacteria.

Radiographic findings are manifold. Most patients have unilateral lower lobe segmental abnormalities on the right. The earliest signs are an interstitial accentuation of markings with subsequent patchy air space consolidation and thickened bronchial shadows. Additional findings are platelike atelectasis, Kerley B lines, perihilar accentuations of markings, and nodular infiltrates. Hilar adenopathy is seen only occasionally in adults but in 30% of children and

may be unilateral or bilateral. A small effusion (which rarely may be eosinophilic) is seen in one fourth of patients, but even in these patients pleuritic pain is rare. Complications seen on chest radiographs include pneumothorax, pneumatoceles, abscess, and, in the rare case of fulminant disease, changes compatible with respiratory distress syndrome (Chapter 99). In convalescence, an area of hyperlucent lung may persist on chest radiographs (Swyer-James syndrome), but most of the changes resolve. Rarely, bronchiectasis, bronchiolitis obliterans, and progressive fibrosis are permanent sequelae.

Extrapulmonary complications are common and are usually superimposed on pulmonary disease, so a mycoplasmal etiology can be suspected. The most frequent extrapulmonary complication is neurologic.

Neurologic symptoms, seen predominantly in children, occur as early as several days after the onset of respiratory symptoms or 2 weeks or more after the respiratory symptoms subside. Respiratory disease may be absent in as many as 50% of patients at the initial evaluation. Both infectious and immunologic mechanisms seem to be involved, producing peripheral neuropathies or central nervous system (CNS) syndromes. The peripheral neuropathies are either axonal or demyelinating processes and appear to be immunologically mediated. Peripheral neuropathy may involve the peripheral or cranial nerves; it is believed that *M. pneumoniae* accounts for 5% of cases of Guillain-Barré syndrome, and the Miller Fisher variant has been documented. More limited peripheral neuropathies have been manifested as mononeuritis multiplex with brachial plexopathy, as facial nerve palsy, and as acute sensorineural hearing loss.

CNS complications are manifested by meningoencephalitis, CNS vasculitis, and postinfectious leukoencephalitis. The meningoencephalitis represents direct invasion of the CNS and accounts for 10 to 15% of childhood encephalitis.

Encephalitis may result in coma or psychosis or more focal phenomena such as stroke, seizure, ataxia, acute cerebellar dysfunction, choreoathetosis, and nonconvulsive status epilepticus. An acute brain stem syndrome and bilateral striatal necrosis may occur. Patients

Continued

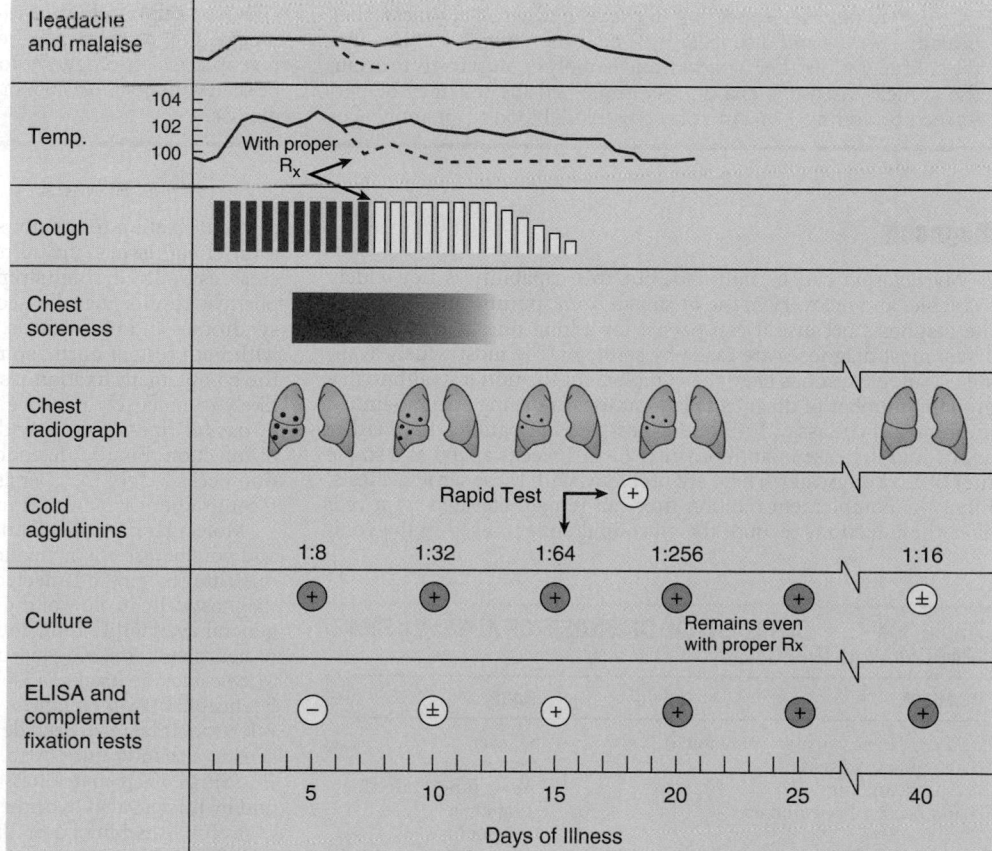

FIGURE 304–1 • Major clinical and laboratory manifestations of mycoplasmal pneumonia. ELISA = enzyme-linked immunosorbent assay.

may also develop clinically characteristic meningitis. A number of types of myelitis are seen, including transverse myelitis and a polio-like syndrome, and a focal CNS vasculitis may supervene, with thrombosis and stroke. Cerebrospinal fluid (CSF) typically displays a small number of lymphocytes (50 to 100) with normal or slightly elevated protein and occasionally lowered glucose levels. Sequelae of CNS involvement range from mental retardation to movement disorders, epilepsy, and Tourette's syndrome. A postinfectious leukoencephalitis that appears immunologically mediated has also been described.

Rashes are seen in 10 to 20% of patients. Most are maculopapular, but they may also be vesicular, petechial, or urticarial, most commonly on the trunk and extremities. Less frequently, the face, buttocks, genitalia, hands, and feet are included. Rash usually begins during the acute illness but may precede or follow it. Most patients have obvious respiratory disease, and some have associated conjunctivitis or an enanthem in the oropharynx. Other exanthemata associated with *M. pneumoniae* infection include pityriasis rosea, leukocytoclastic vasculitis, toxic epidermal necrolysis, erythema nodosum, and erythema multiforme or Stevens-Johnson syndrome. Fifteen percent to 20% of patients with erythema multiforme have been shown to have *M. pneumoniae* infection.

M. pneumoniae is the most common cause of rash and pneumonia, a combination also produced by viruses (herpes simplex, varicella-zoster, Epstein-Barr virus, enterovirus, adenovirus, and measles), *Chlamydia psittaci*, *Mycobacterium tuberculosis*, fungi (*Histoplasma*, *Cryptococcus*, *Coccidioides*), and meningococci.

Hematologic complications are well-known features of mycoplasmal infection. Anemia, hemolytic anemia, thrombocytopenia, disseminated intravascular coagulation, thromboembolism, thrombotic thrombocytopenic purpura, aplastic anemia, Pelger-Huët abnormality (polymorphonuclear leukocytes with a monolobed or bilobed appearance), and hemophagocytic histiocytic syndrome are all described, but the most common hematologic complication is the formation of cold agglutinins. These antibodies agglutinate red blood cells and are seen in a variety of infections (e.g., influenza, mononucleosis, psittacosis, rubella, adenovirus, and measles) but usually occur at higher titer in mycoplasmal infection. If the titer is high enough, they may bind complement and cause hemolysis. These cold agglutinins are IgM antibodies directed against the I antigen of the red blood cell. They are seen in up to 70% of patients, especially those with severe disease. Appearing in the second week of illness, they peak at 4 weeks and disappear by 2 months. Thus at the time that the cold agglutinin titer is highest and hemolysis most likely to occur, the clinical disease is abating. A simple bedside test may be performed by adding 1 to 2 mL of the patient's blood to an anticoagu-lated tube. This tube is placed in a cup of ice water and tilted after 2 to 3 minutes to detect clumping, which represents agglutination of red blood cells. The tube is then warmed by holding it in the hands, and, if the clumps redissolve, the test is positive and correlates with a titer of cold agglutinins of 1 : 64 or greater.

Cardiac complications include pericarditis with occasional hemopericardium, myocarditis with congestive heart failure, complete heart block, or atrioventricular block with atrial tachycardia. A migratory arthritis involving medium-sized joints and occasionally resembling rheumatoid arthritis may be seen, and *M. pneumoniae* has been proposed as a trigger of adult Still's disease. Ophthalmologic complications include uveitis and conjunctivitis, as well as optic neuritis with optic nerve atrophy. On occasion, retinal hemorrhage and exudates are seen. A number of other organ systems may be involved, with resultant bullous myringitis, glomerulonephritis, tubulointerstitial nephritis, hepatitis, pancreatitis, splenomegaly, polymyositis, tubo-ovarian abscess, pediatric priapism, and Raynaud's phenomenon.

The differential diagnosis of *M. pneumoniae* infection includes most causes of the atypical pneumonia syndrome (Table 304–2). This syndrome refers to a generally benign febrile illness with prominent systemic complaints, nonproductive cough, and interstitial abnormalities on chest radiography. The differential diagnosis includes many diseases with clinical or epidemiologic clues. For example, psittacosis should be suspected if a patient has had contact with birds, Q fever follows exposure to farm animals or cats, and *Legionella* tends to infect older men who smoke. *Chlamydia pneumoniae* (Chapter 354) infection often causes a biphasic illness, with sore throat and hoarseness followed by cough. True viruses cause a more fulminant pneumonia. Early in the course of bacterial pneumonia, a cough may be non-productive, but eventually sputum is produced with neutrophils and bacteria on Gram stain, in association with rigors and pleuritic pain. Tularemia follows exposure to an infected animal carcass or arthropod. Other illnesses that rarely mimic *M. pneumoniae* infection include acute fungal infection (such as histoplasmosis) and tuberculosis (particularly primary disease) or reactivation in a compromised host.

Factors suggesting a mycoplasmal etiology are sore throat, headache, fever, rash, an indolent course, a paucity of physical findings on examination, and a chest radiograph more abnormal than the physical examination predicted. Although rare, bullous myringitis is a helpful clue. A fulminant course, extreme leukocytosis, preexisting disease, and recurrent infection suggest against a mycoplasmal etiology. Although both coryza and hoarseness may be seen with mycoplasmal infection, they are more common in viral disease.

Diagnosis

Mycoplasma can be cultured, but this capability is not widely available, and recovery of the organism from sputum does not prove the diagnosis because it can persist for a long time after infection. Thus, most diagnoses are made by serology. The most widely available serologic test has been the complement fixation test, although a growing number of diagnostic laboratories are using enzyme-linked immunosorbent assay. With either test, 90% of patients have either a four-fold increase in antibody titer (2 to 3 weeks apart) or a single titer of 1:32 or greater. There are problems with these serologic tests: First, the complement fixation titer can remain elevated for a year after the infection. Second, the glycolipid antigen used in the com-plement fixation test is not specific for *Mycoplasma* and is found in a variety of tissues, including human heart muscle, brain, and pancreas, as well as in some streptococci and leafy vegetables. Thus false-positive results may be seen, for example, in certain neurologic syndromes and pancreatitis. Third, false-negative reactions are seen with both tests. Fourth, some adults form only IgG antibody. Thus the complement fixation test, which detects primarily IgM, is more likely to be falsely negative. Fifth, antibody appears only after 7 to 10 days of illness, thus providing no diagnostic help early in the course of infection. Finally, detection of IgM does not prove current infection because IgM may persist for months and could thus indicate a recent rather than current infection.

Molecular biologic techniques are increasingly used in diagnosis, and polymerase chain reaction (PCR) has detected *M. pneumoniae* in open lung biopsy and infected bone; detection in sputum is less helpful diagnostically in view of the prolonged carrier state. Cost and lack of general availability limit routine use of these techniques. Diagnosis of neurologic infection has been established by a variety of methods. *M. pneumoniae* has been isolated from CSF in patients with meningoencephalitis, meningitis, and strokes complicating mycoplasmal infection. It has also been detected by CSF-PCR, which appears more sensitive than culture. Also, both IgG and IgM have been identified in CSF. *M. pneumoniae* has been detected in brain tissue by culture and by nucleic acid hybridization. However, for most manifestations of mycoplasmal infection, the diagnosis is made serologically, *proved* by a four-fold increase in antibody titer and strongly *supported* by a

Table 304–2 • DIFFERENTIAL DIAGNOSIS OF *MYCOPLASMA PNEUMONIAE* INFECTION

COMMON	RARE
Chlamydia pneumoniae pneumonia	Q fever
Legionnaires' disease	Psittacosis
Viral pneumonia	Acute fungal infection
Early bacterial pneumonia	Tularemia
	Tuberculosis

single antibody titer of 1:32 or greater, a titer of cold agglutinins of 1:64 or greater, or a single IgM determination.

Rx Treatment

From a practical standpoint, therapy for *M. pneumoniae* infection is empirical because culture takes time and may be misleading, and serologic investigation is not diagnostic early in the course. Thus, a compatible illness in a susceptible patient should be treated on the basis of clinical suspicion. A definite clinical response is seen to tetracycline and erythromycin, although treatment does not influence the carrier state, and the organism may persist in respiratory secretions despite appropriate antibiotic therapy.

Currently, erythromycin or tetracycline is standard therapy (Tables 304–3 and 304–4). Doxycycline and the newer macrolides (azithromycin and clarithromycin) can substitute for tetracycline and erythromycin, respectively, and offer the advantage of greater patient convenience, but at increased cost. Although most recommendations are for 10 to 14 days of therapy, longer courses of treatment (e.g., 2 to 3 weeks) may avoid the relapse that occurs in 5 to 10% of patients. Prophylaxis of contacts does not prevent infection but can prevent clinical disease. Prophylaxis has been effective in household contacts and, as recently demonstrated with azithromycin, in an institutional setting as well. Tetracycline should be avoided in children younger than 8 years and pregnant patients but is preferable if the differential diagnosis includes psittacosis, Q fever, or *Mycoplasma fermentans* (see later text). Correspondingly, erythromycin is preferred if the differential diagnosis includes legionellosis. Fluoroquinolones show good in vitro activity (see Table 304–3), but clinical experience with well-documented cases is limited, and they should be considered alternative therapy only. Fluoroquinolones should be avoided in children and adolescents younger than 18 years and in woman who are nursing or pregnant. Adjunctive therapy with corticosteroids may help ameliorate hemolysis, neurologic complications, and severe lung injury.

Table 304–3 • ANTIBIOTIC SUSCEPTIBILITY

MYCOPLASMA	ERY	TCN	CLN	QUN
M. arginini	res	sens		
M. fermentans	res[†]	sens	sens	sens
M. hominis	res	sens[‡]	sens	sens*
M. penetrans	sens	sens[‡]	sens	sens
M. phocacerebrale	res	sens	res	sens
M. pneumoniae	sens	sens	res	sens*
M. pirum	res[†]	sens[‡]	sens	sens
M. urealyticum	sens[‡]	sens[‡]	res	sens

*Sensitivity to quinolones is adequate for the earlier quinolones (e.g., ciprofloxacin and ofloxacin), but it is greatest for newer agents of this class (e.g., gatifloxacin, levofloxacin, moxifloxacin, and sparfloxacin).
[†]Sensitive to azithromycin and clarithromycin.
[‡]Some resistance seen.
CLN = clindamycin; ERY = erythromycin; QUN = fluoroquinolone; TCN = tetracycline.

Table 304–4 • ANTIBIOTIC REGIMENS FOR ADULTS WITH MYCOPLASMAL INFECTION

DRUG	PO	IV
Doxycycline	200 mg/day 1; then 100 mg/day	Same as PO
Tetracycline	250–500 mg q6h	125–500 mg q6h–12h
Erythromycin	250–500 mg q6h	Same as PO
Azithromycin	500 mg day 1; then 250 mg/day	500 mg/day ×2; then 500 mg PO qd
Clarithromycin	250–500 mg q12h	—
Clindamycin	150–450 mg q6h	150–900 mg q6h–8h
Gatifloxacin	400 mg/day	Same as PO
Levofloxacin	500 mg/day	Same as PO
Moxifloxacin	400 mg/day	—

OTHER MYCOPLASMAS AND UREAPLASMAS

Mycoplasma hominis is a commensal of the genitourinary tract, especially in women. It is seen in up to 50% of sexually active women and 30% of sexually active men. Occasionally it is found in the pharynx. *M. hominis* may produce several different syndromes. A known pathogen of the female urogenital tract, it causes Bartholin's gland abscess, pelvic inflammatory disease, pyelonephritis, and possibly bacterial vaginosis. It also causes postabortal and postpartum fever, wound infection following cesarean section, and postpartum retroperitoneal abscess. *M. hominis* can infect the fetus in utero or during birth and result in neonatal infection and stillbirth. Scalp wound infection may complicate fetal monitoring devices.

M. hominis also causes extragenital infection in adults, often following genitourinary manipulation in an immunosuppressed patient. Some infections caused by *M. hominis* follow trauma (e.g., orbital or retroperitoneal abscess). *M. hominis* pneumonia in organ transplant recipients has resulted both from indigenous and donor *M. hominis*. Infection of surgical wounds should be suspected if a purulent exudate is negative on Gram stain and culture. Other sites of extragenital infection include the brain, lung, prosthetic devices(e.g., vascular grafts), skin, peritoneum, and joints (especially in patients with hypogammaglobulinemia). Although these organisms are not visible on Gram stain, some investigators have identified them in infected joint fluid with acridine orange stain and immunofluorescent staining. The organism may grow on routine media but is easily overlooked, and if it is suspected, the laboratory should be alerted. Because *M. hominis* is resistant to erythromycin, tetracycline is the drug of choice, with clindamycin and the quinolones as alternatives (see Table 304–3).

Another definite pathogen has been recognized in *Mycoplasma fermentans*. This organism has been recovered from the lower genital tract of men and women, the oropharynx, and the lower respiratory tract. Although associated with immunosuppression (leukemia, acquired immune deficiency syndrome [AIDS], and chemotherapy), it has also been described in normal patients in whom a febrile illness with fever, vomiting, and diarrhea developed, with progression to fulminant disease with respiratory distress syndrome, multiple organ failure, and death. *M. fermentans* may also play a role in inflammatory arthritides. This organism is resistant to erythromycin and should be treated with doxycycline or a quinolone (see Table 304–3).

A growing number of other mycoplasmas are thought to possibly cause disease, especially in immunosuppressed patients: *Mycoplasma orale* has been isolated from the blood and marrow of children with leukemia; *Mycoplasma pirum* has been recovered from lymphocytic cells from patients with AIDS; *Mycoplasma genitalium* causes urethritis and arthritis in hypogammaglobulinemic patients and probably is a cause of nongonococcal urethritis; *Mycoplasma penetrans* is strongly associated with homosexual activity and has been isolated from the urine of patients with AIDS; *Mycoplasma felis* has caused septic arthritis in a patient with hypogammaglobulinemia; *Mycoplasma salivarium* causes periodontitis and septic arthritis in hypogammaglobulinemic patients; *Mycoplasma edwardii* has caused septicemia in a patient with AIDS; and *Mycoplasma arginini*, an animal strain of *Mycoplasma*, has caused septicemia and pneumonia in an immunocompromised patient with lymphoma. Like *M. fermentans*, this strain of *Mycoplasma* is resistant to erythromycin and should be treated with tetracycline if suspected (see Table 304–3). Recently, *Mycoplasma phocacerebrale* was isolated from a patient with "seal finger" and from the seal that bit him. The patient responded to therapy with tetracycline. Other human mycoplasmas, as noted in Table 304–1, are currently considered commensals.

Recent interest has focused on the relationship between mycoplasmas and human immunodeficiency virus (HIV) infection. A role of cofactor with HIV has been suggested for several strains of mycoplasmas, including *M. fermentans*, *M. genitalium*, *M. pirum*, and *M. penetrans*, all of which have been isolated from HIV-infected patients and are potent immunomodulators.

Ureaplasma urealyticum colonizes the genital tract of 75% of women and 45% of men who are sexually active (Chapter 345). In an adult, it may cause nongonococcal urethritis, as well as salpingitis and pelvic inflammatory disease; outside the genitourinary tract, it can infect joints (especially in patients with hypogammaglobulinemia), transplant sites, vascular grafts, aneurysms and surgical wounds. In the neonate, it is associated with chorioamnionitis and with chronic lung disease of prematurity, but it is not strongly associated with prematurity, and treatment to eradicate it during pregnancy does not reduce the incidence of premature birth or low birth weight. It may account for some acute respiratory illnesses in children. Tetracycline is the agent of choice, with erythromycin or possibly quinolones as alternatives (see Table 304–3).

SUGGESTED READINGS

Baker AS, Ruoff KL, Madoff S: Isolation of *Mycoplasma* species from a patient with seal finger. Clin Infect Dis 1998;27:1168–1170. *A well-documented instance of the role of* Mycoplasma *in this interesting and mysterious entity.*

Hyde TB, Gilbert M, Schwartz SB, et al: Azithromycin prophylaxis during a hospital outbreak of *Mycoplasma pneumoniae* pneumonia. J Infect Dis 2001;183:907–912. *Excellent demonstration of institutional prophylaxis against* Mycoplasma.

Sotgiu S, Pugliatti M, Rosati G, et al: Neurological disorders associated with *Mycoplasma pneumoniae* infection. Eur J Neurology 2003;10:165–168. *This timely review reports three interesting cases and summarizes our current knowledge about disease spectrum and mechanisms of* M. pneumoniae *neurologic complications.*

305 PNEUMONIA CAUSED BY AEROBIC GRAM-NEGATIVE BACILLI

Lisa L. Dever
Waldemar G. Johanson, Jr.

Gram-negative enteric bacilli (GNB) rarely cause pneumonia in previously healthy hosts. These organisms are not highly virulent respiratory pathogens but instead strike individuals whose defense mechanisms have been diminished by acute or chronic disease. Pneumonia may be community acquired, in which the typical patient would have a chronic underlying disease such as chronic obstructive pulmonary disease, end-stage renal or liver disease, or cancer. More commonly, pneumonias caused by GNB are hospital acquired or nosocomial, in which the typical patient is seriously ill, often intubated and ventilator-dependent.

Pathogenesis

Pneumonias due to GNB are generally caused by aspiration of contaminated oropharyngeal secretions and are preceded by colonization, either of the respiratory or upper gastrointestinal tracts. Colonization of the upper respiratory tract with GNB is present in 10% or fewer of normal persons, but its prevalence is markedly increased among patients with acute or chronic diseases. Colonization increases swiftly among healthy persons undergoing elective surgical procedures from essentially 0% to 35 to 50% within 24 hours after surgery. Similarly, approximately 50% of intensive care unit (ICU) patients become colonized within a few days of admission. This remarkably increased susceptibility for colonization by organisms that are not indigenous to the oropharynx is the key factor underlying these infections.

The sources of the colonizing GNB vary. Most commonly, the patient's fecal flora appears in the oropharynx. Administration of antibiotics creates strong selection pressure so that organisms that colonize the oropharynx are likely to be resistant strains. Transmission of organisms between patients in a hospital has been repeatedly demonstrated, usually on the hands of patient care personnel. Hand-washing after each patient contact is surprisingly effective in limiting this mode of transmission. Contamination of inanimate items in the environment, such as respiratory therapy devices or medications, may serve to colonize many patients with the same organism. Continual vigilance is required to detect such outbreaks promptly and to identify the source. Molecular typing techniques that determine the identity of specific organisms have been used to study the epidemiology of GNB within the ICU. In most recent studies, both transmission from patient to patient and common source outbreaks have been uncommon. Instead, most instances in which multiple patients become infected with similar organisms reflect selection of resistant strains by antimicrobial pressure. By far the most important factor in colonization of ICU patients with multiply resistant GNB is the prior administration of antibiotics.

Of the many species of aerobic GNB that colonize human hosts, only *Haemophilus influenzae* can be classified as a true respiratory pathogen, if the ability of the organism to produce infections in previously normal individuals is accepted as a reasonable criterion of pathogenicity. All the others together, including Enterobacteriaceae (*Escherichia coli, Klebsiella, Enterobacter, Serratia,* and *Proteus*), *Pseudomonas,* and *Acinetobacter,* account for 10 to 20% of community-acquired pneumonias, and these occur almost exclusively in patients with serious underlying disease. The genus *Klebsiella* contains seven species, of which only *Klebsiella pneumoniae* and *Klebsiella oxytoca* cause pneumonia; infections caused by *K. pneumoniae* are by far the most common.

Pneumonia caused by *Klebsiella* has been held separate from that caused by other GNB, largely for historical reasons. It was the first such organism to be recognized as a pulmonary pathogen, and the pneumonia it caused was distinct from that caused by the pneumococcus, especially in its lack of response to early forms of treatment and its predilection to cause upper lobe pneumonias in alcoholic men. However, the classic features of *Klebsiella* pneumonia as described in the earlier literature, such as "currant jelly" sputum (a mixture of blood and mucus), the bulging fissure associated with upper lobe consolidation, and the syndrome of "chronic cavitary pneumonia," are rarely observed today. Although *Klebsiella* remains an important pulmonary pathogen, the illness it causes cannot be clinically differentiated from that caused by other aerobic GNB; thus, the treatment of *Klebsiella* infection is similar to that of infections with other aerobic GNB.

Clinical Manifestations

Pneumonias caused by GNB may be community acquired or hospital acquired (nosocomial). Virtually all patients with community-acquired pneumonias caused by GNB have serious underlying chronic illnesses, especially chronic obstructive pulmonary disease, alcoholism, or malignancy, and the illness produced is typically severe. Nosocomial pneumonias resulting from GNB occur principally in patients with severe, acute illnesses, whether or not they have underlying chronic disease as well. Thus, these infections are most likely to be found in postoperative patients or patients who require intensive care for other reasons. The clinical manifestations of infection are influenced by the nature of the associated processes.

Community-acquired GNB pneumonias share the common features of all bacterial pneumonias-fever, cough productive of purulent sputum, chest pain, and shortness of breath. The illness tends to be abrupt and associated with prominent systemic signs and symptoms, such as mental confusion, vomiting, and hypotension. Physical examination reveals rales in most patients, but the classic findings of dense consolidation are uncommon. Pleural effusion is present in 15 to 20% of patients. Radiographic infiltrates may involve any lobe and are bilateral in about one third of patients. Although cavitation is most likely to occur in pneumonia caused by *Klebsiella*, it also occurs commonly with *Pseudomonas* infections and occasionally with other organisms. Laboratory features include leukocytosis or leukopenia, either of which is characteristically associated with a marked left shift. Leukopenia is a poor prognostic sign.

Nosocomial pneumonia produced by GNB can be an explosive illness similar to the community-acquired form but frequently proceeds with a more indolent but seemingly inexorable course. Often the patient is in respiratory failure, intubated, and receiving mechanical ventilation. GNB are initially found colonizing the oropharynx, and over the subsequent few days appear in tracheal secretions, followed by increasing numbers of neutrophils. Finally, the patient becomes febrile and develops new radiographic infiltrates and worsening hypoxemia. Another common presentation is fever on the second or third postoperative day. Postoperative pneumonias are most common after lateral thoracotomies (especially combined thoracoabdominal procedures) and upper abdominal incisions. When nosocomial GNB pneumonia complicates the course of an already seriously ill patient, it is frequently associated with evidence of multiple organ failure. For a variety of reasons, these patients are usually receiving antibiotics when new GNB appear in the respiratory tract. As a result, the organisms are often resistant to antimicrobial agents used frequently in that particular hospital, reflecting acquisition of nosocomial strains such as *Acinetobacter, Pseudomonas,* and *Stenotrophomonas.* These and other organisms have shown the capacity to develop high-level resistance to virtually all antimicrobial agents in frequent use.

A deteriorating clinical course associated with GNB bacteremia is usually not due to GNB pneumonia. Pulmonary infiltrates in that instance usually represent noncardiogenic pulmonary edema or the adult respiratory distress syndrome (Chapters 99 and 100) and not actual pneumonia, with bacteremia arising from a non-pulmonary source such as the gastrointestinal or urinary tract.

Diagnosis

Confirmation that GNB are responsible for pneumonia is a difficult clinical problem created largely by colonization of proximal airways by these organisms. Thus, GNB are often present in the secretions of ill patients, whether or not they have pneumonia and whether or not the GNB are the cause of pneumonia. Blood cultures are positive in 20 to 30% of patients with community-acquired infections but in as few as 8% of those with nosocomial pneumonias. Nevertheless, because the information gained from a positive blood culture regarding the causative organism and its antimicrobial susceptibility is so important in patient management, blood cultures should always be obtained when GNB pneumonia is suspected. Similarly, although pleural effusion is usually not present, the yield of positive cultures from such fluid when it is present is about 30%, and a diagnostic thoracentesis should be performed if a sufficient volume of fluid is identified radiographically.

Figure 305–1 highlights one diagnostic and therapeutic approach. If GNB pneumonia is suspected on clinical grounds, a decision must be made promptly whether to commence with invasive sampling or empirical therapy. The latter is chosen in most cases of community-acquired pneumonia and in many nosocomial cases because of logistic considerations. If empirical therapy is not successful after 72 hours, invasive sampling should be strongly considered. It is important that an empirically chosen antibiotic regimen be given a chance to prove itself. Continuously changing antibiotics ensures only that microbiologic studies will have little or no value. On the other hand, if invasive studies are done after 72 hours of the same therapy, any organisms persisting are likely to be resistant to the empirical therapy and an informed choice can be made as to a replacement regimen. Invasive sampling consists of performing bronchoalveolar lavage (BAL) and protected specimen brush (PSB) sampling via a fiberoptic bronchoscope. The BAL specimen is centrifuged and the cell pellet stained and examined for phagocytosed bacteria. If more than 7% of cells contain bacteria, it is highly probable that the patient has pneumonia and the Gram stain provides strong evidence of the etiology. Quantitative bacterial counts of 10^4/mL or more for BAL and 10^3/mL or more for the PSB specimen are considered positive and are highly predictive of pneumonia. Among ventilated patients with new onset

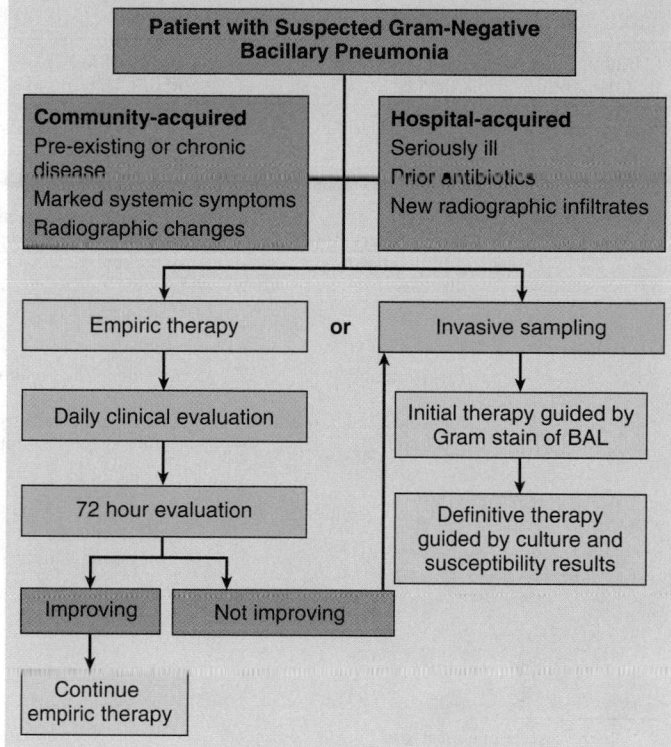

FIGURE 305–1 • Patient with suspected gram-negative bacillary pneumonia.

of fever, leukocytosis, and new radiographic infiltrates, less than one half meet these microbiologic criteria for infection, and antimicrobial therapy can be safely discontinued in those who do not. On the other hand, about one half of patients with positive BAL or PSB cultures demonstrate polymicrobial infections and it is important to treat every organism present in significant concentration. If bronchoscopy is not promptly available, a distal lung sample may be obtained by a blindly placed intratracheal catheter; results of BAL with this approach are almost as reliable as with bronchoscopy.

Attempts to diagnose GNB lung infections with other approaches have not been successful. For example, quantitation of endotoxin in tracheal secretions is no more sensitive than Gram stain of secretions, and the presence of elastic fibers in sputum, although fairly specific for GNB lung infection, are not present in Gram-positive infections.

Rx Treatment

Patients who are susceptible to infection by GNB are at even greater risk of pulmonary infection by more virulent organisms, such as the pneumococci, *Haemophilus,* and *Staphylococcus aureus.* Nosocomial pneumonias are often divided into those occurring early in the hospitalization and those occurring late, after 72 hours, because the causative organisms differ substantially. Early pneumonias are predominantly caused by the usual respiratory pathogens, whereas late pneumonias are caused predominantly by GNB and other antibiotic-resistant organisms. Even though time for exposure to the hospital environment is important in this shift, the selective pressure caused by administration of antibiotics is by far the most important factor. Thus, despite the presence of GNB in sputum, initial treatment of these pneumonias—particularly those acquired outside the hospital or in the absence of antibiotic therapy—should include coverage of the usual respiratory pathogens. Early treatment of nosocomial pneumonia can reduce mortality, so it is important that therapy not be delayed. Table 305–1 provides therapeutic options for the patient with a suspected GNB pneumonia.

Treatment of nosocomial infection is made more difficult by previous antimicrobial therapy, and drug susceptibility studies are critically important. However, empirical therapy usually must be initiated before the results of such studies are available. Factors to consider when selecting appropriate therapy include knowledge of local resistance patterns, previous culture results, and prior treatment. For

example, resistance of *Pseudomonas aeruginosa* to gentamicin may approach 50% in some hospitals. If *P. aeruginosa* is strongly suspected on the basis of previous cultures or the clinical setting (respiratory failure, neutropenia), a β-lactam agent or fluoroquinolone with antipseudomonal activity should be combined with an aminoglycoside (see Table 305–1). Amikacin is often used in this setting because of less frequent resistance to this agent. A single daily dose of an aminoglycoside has been shown to be equally as effective as more frequent dosing and may be less nephrotoxic. Doses must be adjusted in the presence of impaired renal function.

Prospective studies have shown that carefully chosen empirical regimens are inadequate in up to 73% of cases when invasive sampling techniques are used to determine the etiologic organisms. Causes of inadequacy are the presence of resistant organisms singly or in polymicrobial infections; more than 50% of nosocomial pneumonias are polymicrobial. When the pathogenic organisms have been identified and the susceptibility patterns are known, modifications can be made to optimize antibiotic therapy. Ideally, antibiotics with the narrowest spectrum of activity, the least toxicity, and the best lung penetration should be chosen. In neutropenic patients and in seriously ill patients with pneumonia caused by resistant organisms such as *P. aeruginosa, Serratia marcescens,* and *Acinetobacter,* continued combination therapy with an appropriate β-lactam agent and an aminoglycoside is recommended. Duration of therapy should

Continued

Table 305–1 • EMPIRICAL THERAPY OF PNEUMONIA CAUSED BY GRAM-NEGATIVE BACILLI

CLINICAL CIRCUMSTANCE	EXAMPLE	LIKELY GRAM-NEGATIVE PATHOGENS	RECOMMENDED TREATMENT*
Community-acquired	Chronic underlying disease	Enteric gram-negative bacilli, *Haemophilus influenzae* plus usual respiratory pathogens	Ceftriaxone 2 g q24h Levofloxacin 750 mg q24h Ticarcillin/clavulanate 3.1 g q4h Piperacillin/tazobactam 3.375 g q6h
	Alcoholic	*Klebsiella pneumoniae*	Same as above
	Chronic obstructive pulmonary disease, cystic fibrosis	*Pseudomonas aeruginosa, Stenotrophomonas maltophilia, Burkholderia cepacia*	Ceftazidime 2 g q8h Ciprofloxacin 400 mg q8 or 12h Ticarcillin/clavulanate 3.1 g q4h Add trimethoprim/sulfamethoxazole to one of the above if high suspicion of *S. maltophilia* or *B. cepacia*
	Near-drowning	*Aeromonas hydrophilia*	Ciprofloxacin 400 mg q12h Ceftriaxone 2 g q24h
Hospital-acquired	Recent hospital admission (<72 hr)	Enteric gram-negative bacilli, *H. influenzae* plus usual respiratory pathogens	Ceftriaxone 2 g q24h Levofloxacin 750 mg q24h Ticarcillin/clavulanate 3.1 g q4h Piperacillin/tazobactam 3.375 g q6h
	Ventilator-dependent patient	Same as above plus *P. aeruginosa, Acinetobacter* species, and other nonenteric gram-negative bacilli	Cefepime 2 g q8 or 12h Ceftazidime 2 g q8h Piperacillin/tazobactam 4.5 g q6h Imipenem/cilastatin 500 mg q6h Ciprofloxacin 400 mg q8 Combination therapy strongly advised if resistant gram-negative bacilli suspected (e.g., antipseudomonal β-lactam agent[†] plus aminoglycoside[‡] or fluoroquinolone[¶])

*In the absence of normal renal function, dosages must be adjusted for renal failure.
[†]Ceftazidime, cefepime, ticarcillin, piperacillin, aztreonam, imipenem/cilastatin.
[‡]Dosages of 5 mg/kg q24h for gentamicin and tobramycin; 15 mg/kg q24h for amikacin.
[¶]Ciprofloxacin is the most active against *P. aeruginosa*.

be based on clinical response, but a minimum of 1 to 2 weeks is usually required. If invasive sampling has been performed according to the algorithm presented in Figure 305–1 and the results do not indicate significant lung infection, antibiotics should be discontinued unless required for another indication.

Prognosis

Nosocomial pneumonia develops in 17 to 60% of ventilated patients with an overall mortality of more than 50%; the attributable mortality rate is 20 to 30%. Pneumonias caused by multiply resistant organisms, especially *P. aeruginosa, S. maltophilia, Acinetobacter baumanni,* and methicillin-resistant *S. aureus* are associated with significantly increased mortality. A number of studies have compared outcomes of GNB pneumonias when antimicrobial therapy was judged to be either adequate or inadequate; in most, adequate therapy reduced the overall mortality rate. That adequate therapy did not reduce mortality in some studies is explained by the fact that underlying disease is the main predictor of survival for many patients. Early, broad-spectrum therapy that covers all of the organisms present in the lung is important for patients with survivable illnesses.

Complications

Pneumonias caused by GNB are more likely than other pneumonias to be complicated by one or more adverse events. Important complications include empyema, lung necrosis, superinfections, and multiple organ failure; metastatic seeding of infection to other sites is an uncommon complication.

Empyema occurs in perhaps as many as 30% of patients with GNB pneumonias. Criteria for the diagnosis of empyema, besides the presence of gross pus, include the presence of bacteria on Gram stain, pleural fluid pH less than 7.2, or a pleural fluid white blood cell count greater than 30,000/dL. Each of these criteria indicates a condition that is unlikely to respond to antimicrobials alone and that usually requires drainage of the pleural space as well. Thus the term *complicated effusion* has gained favor over *empyema* to identify pleural fluid collections for which drainage needs to be considered. The occur-

rence of a complicated effusion generally prevents the recovery of the patient until it is recognized and effectively treated. Signs and symptoms of continuing illness, such as fever, persistent leukocytosis, and the onset of multiple organ failure, in a patient undergoing treatment for a GNB pneumonia should raise suspicion of a complicated effusion. If pleural fluid is identified on upright posteroanterior and lateral chest radiographs, thoracentesis should be performed; useful studies of the fluid obtained include measurements of pH and glucose, white blood cell count, Gram stain, and cultures for aerobic and anaerobic organisms.

If the fluid qualifies as a complicated effusion, prompt placement of a thoracostomy tube should be considered. Alternative approaches (principally, repeated thoracentesis) are less successful, owing to loculation of the pleural space. Surgical drainage of the pleural space, using localized resection of an overlying rib with creation of a larger drainage tract, is reserved for patients who do not respond to tube drainage and are not candidates for a larger operation. Decortication of the pleura may be necessary if the clinical signs of uncontrolled infection are not ameliorated by simple drainage plus antimicrobial therapy. In such patients, radiographic evidence of effusion persists, along with continued fever and leukocytosis. At surgery, the pleural space is found to contain numerous loculated pockets of pus. The timing of intervention with these techniques requires excellent clinical judgment, because the patients are usually seriously ill and poor candidates for surgical treatment of any kind; on the other hand, they will not recover unless the pleural space is adequately drained.

Extensive lung necrosis has been termed *lung gangrene* because of the rapid occurrence of pulmonary cavitation associated with marked systemic toxicity and the appearance of extensive devitalization of lung tissue at necropsy. Occasionally, an entire lung appears to dissolve within a few days, leaving many cavities with air-fluid levels. This complication occurs with all of the common GNB, although perhaps more commonly in infections produced by *K. pneumoniae* and *P. aeruginosa.* Lung necrosis may be caused by the extracellular products of these organisms. *P. aeruginosa* makes a number of "virulence factors," including exotoxin A, exoenzyme S, elastase, and a neutral protease. However, *K. pneumoniae* makes none of these, and the propensity of this organism to cause lung necrosis remains unexplained. Extensive lung necrosis may be followed by massive hemoptysis, continued suppuration because of inadequate drainage of the massively disrupted lung parenchyma, or bronchopleural fistula caused by extension of the necrotizing process through the pleura. The last must be promptly treated by placing a chest tube because of the attendant pneumothorax. However, the definitive treatment of extensive lung necrosis is surgical resection of the involved lobe or lobes.

Assessment of the patient with multiple organ failure in the context of a serious illness complicated by a GNB pneumonia is always difficult. The major question is usually whether a new complication such as oliguria is due to the underlying disease, to the current treatment, or to the infection. Each of the common manifestations of multiple organ dysfunction—altered liver function, acute renal failure, hematopoietic abnormalities, upper gastrointestinal bleeding, and altered mental state—may be multifactorial, and the antimicrobial agents used to treat GNB pneumonia may cause most of them. The guiding principles are to treat the infection aggressively and to correct life-threatening complications as they occur.

Superinfections may develop during the treatment of GNB pneumonia, just as GNB pneumonia may occur as a superinfection of a previous pneumonia. Treatment of pneumonia does not prevent colonization of the oropharynx and tracheobronchial tree by additional GNB or fungi. Thus, the clinician is often faced with evaluating a new set of microorganisms recovered from the patient's secretions. The guiding principle here is to treat patients, not culture results. If the patient is responding well and appears to be improving, the new culture results can be disregarded for the time being. On the other hand, if the new cultural data correspond to a worsening clinical course, the process of evaluation and revision of treatment must be begun again.

SUGGESTED READINGS
Arancibia F, Torsten TT, Santiago E, et al: Community-acquired pneumonia due to gram-negative bacteria and *Pseudomonas aeruginosa*: Incidence, risk, and prognosis. Arch Intern Med 2002;162:1849–1858. *A large prospective study of patients hospitalized with community-acquired pneumonia. Pneumonia due to GNB occurred in 11% of patients and was independently associated with death.*

Cook D: Ventilator associated pneumonia: Perspectives on the burden of illness. Intensive Care Med 2000;26(Suppl. 1):31–37. *A rigorous overview of much of the clinical literature on nosocomial pneumonia, including risk factors, diagnosis, and outcomes.*

Fiel S: Guidelines and critical pathways for severe hospital-acquired pneumonia. Chest 2001;119(2 Suppl.):412–418. *An updated guideline for nosocomial pneumonia with newer antibiotics. Appropriate emphasis is placed on knowing local microbial resistance patterns to guide empirical therapy.*

306 ASPIRATION PNEUMONIA

Lisa L. Dever
Waldemar G. Johanson, Jr.

Aspiration of foreign materials into the lungs is a key step in the pathophysiology of many pulmonary disorders. Most of the important syndromes are dealt with elsewhere in this volume: gastric acid aspiration (Chapter 92), anaerobic pneumonias and lung abscess (Chapter 93), lipoid pneumonia (Chapter 92), and hydrocarbon aspiration (Chapter 90). Most bacterial pneumonias are initiated by the aspiration of minute quantities of secretions, a process termed *microaspiration*, which occurs in normal individuals during sleep. In this chapter the focus is placed on an infrequent but difficult clinical problem—that of recurrent bacterial pneumonias caused by repeated aspiration of oropharyngeal secretions. These pneumonias are recurring clinical illnesses characterized by fever, purulent sputum, and new radiographic infiltrates in the lungs in a patient with known or suspected chronic aspiration of oropharyngeal contents.

Etiology

Most patients afflicted with this problem have serious problems with swallowing, an altered level of consciousness, or both. Common predisposing conditions are carcinoma of the esophagus with obstruction, tracheobronchial fistula (usually after treatment for cancer), and neurologic diseases affecting deglutition. Strokes are certainly the most common cause of the last condition, but amyotrophic lateral sclerosis (including bulbar palsy), multiple sclerosis, and the myopathies may be responsible. Recurrent nocturnal aspiration of gastric contents by patients with esophageal reflux represents the one situation in which the swallowing mechanism may be intact in this syndrome.

Impaired swallowing due to neural or myopathic causes is most pronounced when the patient attempts to swallow liquids. By contrast, dysphagia caused by obstruction is always worst with solid foods. Thus, it is not surprising that the patient with myoneural deficits of the pharyngeal musculature repeatedly aspirates oropharyngeal secretions. In patients with esophageal obstruction, secretions accumulate proximal to the obstruction, especially at night, and are aspirated. Gastric contents are normally sterile. However, as the patient with reflux aspirates gastric contents, a certain volume of oropharyngeal secretions is necessarily carried along.

Normal individuals aspirate small volumes of oropharyngeal secretions during sleep but do not develop recurrent pneumonias. Patients who do aspirate greater volumes of secretions, often containing lipids and food particulates, and have impaired antibacterial defenses; differences in the bacterial flora of secretions may play a role as well.

Bacteriology

Aspiration pneumonia is frequently polymicrobial and the bacterial etiology is influenced by the setting (e.g., community, nursing home, hospital) and circumstances (e.g., prior antibiotics, poor dentition, underlying diseases). Oropharyngeal secretions are massively contaminated, containing 10^6 to 10^8 aerobic bacteria per milliliter and about 10 times as many anaerobic organisms. Although the majority of these organisms have little invasiveness for the normal host, highly pathogenic organisms, including *Streptococcus pneumoniae*, *Staphylococcus aureus*, and *Haemophilus influenzae*, may be present in the secretions of normal people and result in pneumonia when aspiration occurs. Enteric gram-negative bacilli and *Pseudomonas aeruginosa* are more likely to colonize the upper airways of hospitalized and severely ill patients and therefore be the cause of pneumonias in such patients. The oral anaerobes most frequently involve the anaerobic or microaerophilic streptococci, *Fusobacterium nucleatum*, *Prevotella* species, and *Bacteroides* species. From time to time investigators have questioned the significance of anaerobes in the pathogenesis of aspiration pneumonia, mainly due to the difficulty of recovering these organisms in culture. However, studies that have utilized optimal techniques for the recovery of anaerobes have repeatedly demonstrated the essential role of anaerobic bacteria in these infections. The milieu of the anaerobic infection is a highly specialized environment with contributions by all the bacterial species present. Therapy that is effective against only some of these organisms may successfully treat the patient because of the interdependence of organisms in this environment.

Clinical Manifestations

Episodes of recurrent pneumonia associated with aspiration tend not to be acute fulminant illnesses but rather are characterized by progressive fever, purulent sputum production, shortness of breath, and systemic symptoms (e.g., loss of appetite and malaise) over a period of days.

Physical findings include those related to the underlying illness and the presence of coarse rhonchi over dependent lung zones. Rales and signs of consolidation may or may not be present. Fever and leukocytosis are regularly present. Radiographs of the chest reveal infiltrates of varying intensity, with a preponderance of change in the dependent zones, that is, posterior aspects of the lower lobes and posterior segments of the upper lobes. Pleural effusion is uncommon unless anaerobic infection is present.

Diagnosis

A high index of suspicion, based on the patient's underlying disease, is the first step. Testing the sensitivity of the pharyngeal mucosal and the strength of pharyngeal reflexes is an important part of the physical examination. Important information may be gained by watching the patient swallow water. The presence of food particles in tracheal secretions is clear evidence of aspiration. In patients receiving enteral feedings, the presence of glucose in secretions may be demonstrable by bedside tests. Because glucose cannot be detected in normal secretions, a positive result is highly specific for aspiration. Dietary lipids form large intracellular deposits when ingested by macrophages and it has been suggested that semi-quantitation of such lipid-laden macrophages may be useful in the diagnosis of recurrent aspiration. The sputum is intensely purulent, with a wide spectrum of bacterial forms present on Gram stain. Culture yields upper respiratory flora, with or without additional pathogens. The clinical problem is to discern which of several pathogenic organisms should be treated. Culture may be useful because knowledge of the susceptibility of the organisms present may be needed to guide therapy. Invasive sampling (bronchoalveolar lavage, protected specimen brush) is not routinely required. Blood cultures are rarely positive.

Several techniques may be used when the diagnosis of recurrent aspiration is in doubt (Table 306–1). Cineradiographic studies of the patient swallowing a thin, water-soluble contrast material can demonstrate abnormalities of deglutition and may actually show aspiration. Thick barium should be avoided because aspiration of this material compounds the patient's problems, and a thick solution is less likely to identify the swallowing difficulty. A prolonged pharyngeal transit time may be the best predictor of subsequent pneumonia. Radionuclide salivagrams utilize isotopes for the same purpose and may be particularly useful in children because of lesser radiation exposure. Impaired sensory function in the posterior pharynx and larynx and prolonged transit times can be observed endoscopically and are highly predictive of later aspiration, especially when combined with the aforementioned techniques.

The relationship between esophageal reflux and pneumonia may be difficult to determine. If aspiration is suspected on clinical grounds, monitoring of the pH in the upper esophagus during sleep can confirm it. Reflux into the upper esophagus is marked by a sudden fall in pH, an event that is easily captured on a long-term event recorder for review the next morning. However, prospective studies have shown that it is difficult to predict which patients will experience aspiration pneumonias except in the most obvious situations, indicating that the fact of aspiration does not necessarily lead to clinical pneumonia.

Rx Treatment

Initial antibiotic therapy should provide coverage for the pathogens that are most likely to be involved given the patient's clinical circumstance. This usually requires broad-spectrum coverage with either a single agent or a combination of agents (Table 306–2). Therapy should be modified depending on the results of cultures and susceptibility studies and the clinical response. Supportive care, including aggressive tracheobronchial toilet, is required. Nutrition must not be overlooked despite the difficulties encountered in many of these patients. Failure to address the nutritional deficits of these patients is a common cause of protracted and often lethal complications. Most patients will require a gastrostomy or jejunostomy placed surgically or endoscopically to maintain adequate nutrition.

For many patients with advanced neurologic or malignant disease treatment of one or two episodes of aspiration pneumonia combined with provision for adequate caloric and fluid intake bypassing the mouth is sufficient to maintain quality of life for the patient's remaining few months. The really difficult clinical problem is posed by patients who aspirate their own saliva but are sufficiently stable to live for years if pneumonia can be prevented. Even a cuffed tracheostomy tube fails to prevent pneumonia in these patients because of the milking of secretions around the cuff. A number of surgical techniques have been devised to manage these patients including ligation of the parotid and submaxillary salivary ducts, separation of the larynx and trachea, and surgical closure of the laryngeal apperature, combined with tracheostomy, of course. Only by absolutely preventing the entry of secretions in the larynx can pneumonia be prevented in some of these patients.

Table 306–1 • DIAGNOSTIC TESTS FOR CHRONIC ASPIRATION

TEST	FINDING
Cineradiography	Vallecular and/or pyriform pooling; delayed pharyngeal transit*; laryngeal transit of contrast medium[†]
Radionuclide imaging	Activity over the trachea*; activity over the lungs[†]
Esophageal pH monitoring	Nocturnal decrease of pH in upper esophagus
Bronchoscopy	Bronchial inflammation; lipid-laden macrophages[†]

*Correlated with increased risk of pneumonia.
[†]Confirms a diagnosis of aspiration.

Table 306–2 • EMPIRICAL THERAPY OF ASPIRATION PNEUMONIA

CLINICAL CIRCUMSTANCE	EXAMPLE	LIKELY PATHOGENS	RECOMMENDED TREATMENT
Acute event in a previously healthy individual	Young person with first seizure	Normal oropharyngeal flora including anaerobes	Amoxicillin-clavulanate 875 mg orally q12h (if treatment is begun early) Ampicillin-sulbactam 3 g IV q6h Clindamycin 900 mg IV q8h
Acute event in an individual with chronic underlying disease	An obtunded alcoholic with chronic liver disease who is vomiting	Normal oropharyngeal flora, *Klebsiella pneumoniae*, other enteric bacilli	Ampicillin-sulbactam 3 g IV q6h Cefoxitin 2 g IV q6h Gatifloxacin or moxifloxacin 400 mg IV qd
Acute event in a seriously ill hospitalized patient	Ventilator-dependent patient with copious respiratory secretions	Same as above plus *Staphylococcus aureus, Pseudomonas aeruginosa, Acinetobacter* species, and other nonenteric gram-negative bacilli	Piperacillin-tazobactam 3.375 g IV q6h Ticarcillin–clavulanic acid 3.1 g IV q6h Imipenem 500 mg IV q6h Clindamycin 900 mg IV q8h plus ciprofloxacin 400 mg q12h or aztreonam 1–2 g q8h Consider adding vancomycin 1 g q12h if methicillin-resistant *Staphylococcus aureus* suspected Combination therapy advised if highly resistant gram-negative bacilli suspected, e.g., antipseudomonal β-lactam agent plus aminoglycoside or fluoroquinolone
Recurrent aspiration in an individual with neuromuscular disease or other swallowing disorders	Elderly individual with multiple strokes and absent gag reflex	Any of the above; usually polymicrobial	Same as above; emphasis must be on prevention of subsequent episodes

SUGGESTED READINGS

Hadjikoutis S, Wiles CM: Respiratory complications related to bulbar dysfunction in motor neuron disease. Acta Neurol Scand 2001;103:207–213. *These authors stress the interaction between motor neuron disease and respiratory complications, not only recurrent aspiration pneumonia. Bulbar muscular weakness and local pooling of secretions are strong predictors of respiratory complications.*

Johanson WG, Dever LL: Nosocomial pneumonia. Intensive Care Med 2003;29:23–29. *An overview emphasizing the role of microaspiration.*

McClave S, DeMeo MT, DeLegge MH, et al: North American Summit on aspiration in the critically ill patient: Consensus statement. J Parenter Enteral Nutr 2002;26:S80–S85. *Review and consensus agreement by a panel of experts in critical care nutrition. Notably, they recommend abandoning the use of glucose oxidase strips and blue food coloring as monitors for aspiration of enteral feedings.*

Wang D, Dulguerov P: Laryngeal diversion and tracheotracheal speech fistula for chronic aspiration. Ann Otol Rhinol Laryngol 2000;109:602–604. *Surgical techniques have advanced so that it is not necessary to lose speech altogether when planning to prevent aspiration surgically in carefully selected patients.*

307 LEGIONELLOSIS

Paul H. Edelstein

Definition

Legionellosis is the term used to describe infections caused by bacteria of the genus *Legionella*. The most important of these diseases is pneumonia, called *Legionnaires' disease*. Either as part of Legionnaires' disease or distinct from it, legionellae may cause infections elsewhere in the body, usually in the form of abscesses. Pontiac fever, which is a self-limited mild febrile illness, is assumed to be caused by legionellae, although this assumption is unproven.

History

Legionnaires' disease was initially recognized when it caused epidemic pneumonia among members of the American Legion attending a convention in Philadelphia in 1976; this outbreak resulted in 34 deaths and 221 cases of pneumonia. Charles McDade and William Shepard of the U.S. Centers for Disease Control and Prevention determined that this disease was caused by an ostensibly newly discovered bacterium, which was named *Legionella pneumophila*. Neither the disease nor the bacterium is new. The first documented epidemic of Legionnaires' disease occurred in a meat packing plant in Minnesota in 1957, and the first recorded isolation of the bacterium was in 1943. In fact, three different *Legionella* species had been isolated from humans before 1976, although they were thought to be rickettsia-like agents. Several unsolved epidemics of pneumonia, including one in Philadelphia in 1974, were recognized to have been due to Legionnaires' disease.

Bacteriology

Forty-five *Legionella* species have been recognized to date. About half of them have been isolated from patients with Legionnaires' disease, and about half have been isolated only from the environment. The species that most commonly cause disease are *L. pneumophila*, *L. micdadei*, *L. bozemanii*, *L. dumoffii*, and *L. longbeachae*. Sixteen serogroups are recognized for *L. pneumophila*, whereas several other species contain up to two serogroups. *L. pneumophila* serogroup 1 causes 70 to 90% of cases of Legionnaires' disease in nonimmunocompromised individuals. *L. micdadei* is probably the second most common cause of Legionnaires' disease and frequently causes Legionnaires' disease in immunocompromised patients.

Legionellae are small, Gram-negative, obligately aerobic bacilli. *Legionella* requires complex growth media because of an absolute nutritional requirement for L-cysteine. Optimal growth occurs on a buffered charcoal yeast extract medium supplemented with iron, L-cysteine, and α-ketoglutarate. These bacteria do not grow on conventional bacteriologic media such as trypticase soy broth agar, MacConkey agar, or unsupplemented chocolate agar. Their usual habitat is natural and treated waters such as lakes, ponds, and tap water. Legionellae are found in the highest concentration in warm water, especially in water heaters, hot water plumbing fixtures, and cooling towers. They appear to be obligate or facultative parasites of freshwater amoebae such as *Hartmannella* and *Acanthamoeba*. Humans are very likely accidental hosts of these bacteria.

A large number of bacterial virulence genes have been identified in *L. pneumophila*, almost all of which control the ability of the bacterium to grow within macrophages. The most important of these virulence genes appear to be the *dot/icm* group.

Pathogenesis

Legionnaires' disease is acquired by inhaling aerosolized water containing *Legionella* organisms or possibly by pulmonary aspiration of contaminated water. The contaminated aerosols are derived from humidifiers, shower heads, whirlpool baths, decorative fountains, respiratory therapy equipment, industrial cooling water, cooling towers, and other sources of warm water. Aerosols formed by contaminated water in plumbing systems and in cooling towers are the most common sources of infection. Inhaled organisms undergo phagocytosis by pulmonary alveolar macrophages, which are unable to kill the bacteria. The bacteria multiply within the phagosome. Eventually, the multiplying bacteria kill the macrophage, either by inducing apoptosis or cytotoxicity, and are released extracellularly. The intracellular infection cycle is reinitiated in another macrophage. Continuing bacterial multiplication and consequent lung damage produce symptoms 2 to 10 days after the initiation of infection. Bacterial uptake and multiplication are curtailed by the action of cytokines (e.g., interferon-γ) produced by macrophages and lymphocytes. Natural killer and lymphokine-activated killer cells probably lyse infected macrophages and thereby abort the intracellular infection cycle. The role of polymorphonuclear phagocytes is unclear, although they probably have some part in eliminating bacteria, especially after activation by interleukin-2 and tumor necrosis factor. Antibody appears to have little function in host immunity or defense, whereas T lymphocytes play a major role in the immune process. The actual mechanism of pulmonary damage is not well understood and could be due to bacterial toxins, immune reactions to infection, or both. The bacteria may spread to extrapulmonary sites via the lymphatic system and blood stream; they are probably transported in the blood by infected blood mononuclear cells. The mechanism whereby the pneumonia exerts systemic effects is unknown but could be the result of disseminated bacterial infection, the effect of toxin, or production of host factors such as tumor necrosis factor.

The pathogenesis of Pontiac fever is a mystery. Inhalation of water contaminated with many different types of bacteria, including *Legionella* species, produces the disease. The incubation period of the disease, 12 to 36 hours, is too short to allow for bacterial infection and multiplication. It is possible that bacterial or fungal toxins present in the water produce this illness, as has been hypothesized for a closely related disease, "humidifier fever." Another possibility is an immune response to one or more of the multiple microorganisms found in the water. Antibody to *Legionella* species found in contaminated water is present in most disease victims, but it is unclear what this immune response means.

Epidemiology

Legionnaires' disease occurs worldwide but is primarily a disease found in technically advanced countries. Case reports from underdeveloped countries are rare, perhaps because of limited diagnostic facilities and also perhaps because of the infrequent use of air conditioning and complex plumbing systems. Normal children rarely acquire this disease. Major risk factors for the acquisition of Legionnaires' disease are given (Table 307–1). Legionnaires' disease is an uncommon disease in patients with the acquired immunodeficiency syndrome (AIDS), although they are at increased risk of acquiring the disease. Males get Legionnaires' disease about twice as often as females, although this difference does not hold true for several epidemics of Legionnaires' disease. No good evidence exists for person-to-person spread of Legionnaires' disease.

Legionnaires' disease may occur in epidemics originating in a single building or area. Outbreaks of the disease have occurred among hotel guests, hospital inpatients and outpatients, office building workers, and factory workers. People with occupational water exposure appear to have little, if any increased risk of disease acquisition. About 80% of cases of Legionnaires' disease are nonepidemic. Of these, perhaps 10% may be acquired in the home and the remainder through other exposure.

It is estimated that from 1 to 5% of all pneumonias requiring hospitalization in adults are due to Legionnaires' disease, which

Infectious Diseases

Table 307–1 • RISK FACTORS FOR LEGIONNAIRES' DISEASE

ALTERED LOCAL AND SYSTEMIC HOST DEFENSES
Glucocorticosteroid administration or Cushing's disease (5-10)*
Cytotoxic chemotherapy (5)
Cigarette smoking (2-5)
Diabetes (2)
Male gender or age older than 50 yr (>2)
AIDS (40)
Immune suppressive therapy for solid organ transplantation (>2)
Chronic heart or lung disease (>1)
Renal failure requiring dialysis (20)
Lung or hematologic cancer (especially hairy cell leukemia) (7-20)

INCREASED CHANCE OF EXPOSURE TO ENVIRONMENTAL LEGIONELLA BACTERIA
Recent travel away from home (2)
Use of domestic well water (2)
Recent plumbing work in home or at work (2)
Exposure to poorly maintained hot tub spas
Recent surgical procedure

*Numbers in parentheses represent the approximate relative risk of acquiring Legionnaires' disease over that for someone without the risk, where known.

represents about 10,000 cases of Legionnaires' disease per year in the United States. In some geographic regions, community-acquired Legionnaires' disease is more common, such as in western Pennsylvania and Catalonia, Spain. When the disease occurs in endemic or epidemic nosocomial form, 1 to as many as 20% of hospitalized patients with pneumonia have this disease.

Pontiac fever has been recognized primarily as an epidemic illness, with attack rates in excess of 90%. It has been noted to occur in office and factory workers and in recreational bathers using spa or whirlpool-type baths. The disease very likely has a sporadic form, but the lack of specific diagnostic tests makes diagnosis of this form very difficult.

Pathology

Specific pathologic changes are found only in the lung in the vast majority of fatal cases of Legionnaires' disease. Intense inflammation is present in alveoli, alveolar ducts, respiratory bronchioles, and alveolar septa. The inflammatory process consists of bacteria, polymorphonuclear leukocytes, and macrophages. On occasion, pleuritis, pleural empyema, pericarditis, and cavitary lung disease are found. Very rarely, abscess formation occurs outside the chest cavity.

Clinical Manifestations

Legionnaires' disease is manifested as a febrile systemic illness with pneumonia. Several prospective and retrospective studies of patients with different types of pneumonia have shown that Legionnaires' disease has few, if any characteristic clinical features and that it cannot be clinically distinguished from pneumococcal pneumonia. However, clinical observations during epidemics of Legionnaires' disease have often documented characteristic clinical findings. It is probable that the spectrum of clinical findings is wide, ranging from a "typical" form of Legionnaires' disease to one indistinguishable from other causes of pneumonia. This chapter describes the "typical" form of Legionnaires' disease, which in reality may be present in the minority of patients. A prodromal illness consisting of malaise, low-grade fever, and anorexia may develop several days before the onset of more severe symptoms. Myalgia, extreme fatigue, and high temperature then develop. Gastrointestinal complaints are common, such as generalized or localized abdominal pain, nausea, vomiting, and diarrhea; the diarrhea is generally watery and not dehydrating. Recurrent rigors and prostration may occur. Symptoms referable to the respiratory tract may not develop until later. It is this paucity of respiratory tract symptoms, despite evidence of a systemic febrile illness, that can either be a clue to diagnosis or mislead clinicians. When the patient is pressed for details regarding symptoms, a history of a nonproductive cough or one productive of nonpurulent, sometimes bloody secretions is usually obtained. Production of large amounts of grossly purulent sputum is unusual. Pleuritic chest pain, sometimes in concert with hemoptysis, may occur and can mislead the

clinician into considering pulmonary infarction. Mental confusion is commonly reported in some series; obtundation, seizures, and focal neurologic findings may also occur less frequently.

Fever is almost uniformly present in cases of Legionnaires' disease, although short (days) afebrile periods have been reported in some immunosuppressed patients with L. micdadei pneumonia. Chest examination early in the disease may reveal only scattered rales or evidence of pleural effusion. However, later in the course, most patients have classic findings of consolidating pneumonia. Abdominal examination may reveal generalized or local tenderness and, in rare cases, evidence of peritonitis. Splenomegaly is uncommon. Findings of pericarditis, myocarditis, and focal abscesses are rare. No rash is associated with this disease, except that caused by other factors such as drug therapy.

The fatality rate of untreated Legionnaires' disease is about 3 to 30% in nonimmunosuppressed patients and up to 80% in immunocompromised ones. The majority of previously healthy people recover from untreated Legionnaires' disease after 7 to 10 days of severe illness; those who do not recover die of progressive respiratory and multisystem failure.

Clinically significant extrapulmonary infection in patients with Legionnaires' disease is quite rare (Table 307–2).

Pontiac fever is a nonfatal influenza-like disease, with symptoms of myalgia, fever, headache, and malaise occurring in 60 to 90% of patients. Arthralgia occurs with variable frequency, as do cough, anorexia, and abdominal pain. The illness generally is not sufficiently severe or long in duration to cause most patients to seek medical attention. Not much is known about its physical findings early in the disease; findings after 3 to 5 days of illness are generally normal except for fever and possibly tachypnea. Pneumonia does not occur. The illness lasts about 3 to 5 days, although some patients may have persistent fatigue or nonfocal neurologic complaints for weeks to months afterward.

Chest Radiographic Findings

Legionnaires' disease causes alveolar-filling infiltrates that usually eventuate in consolidation. Interstitial infiltrates are rare, although they may occur early in the course of disease and then progress to consolidating infiltrates. The infiltrates may be unilateral or bilateral and can spread very quickly to involve the entire lung. Pleural effusion, usually small in volume, occurs commonly and may be the sole abnormal radiographic finding in early disease.

Diagnosis

The results of multiple nonspecific laboratory tests may be abnormal in patients with Legionnaires' disease. These abnormal findings include proteinuria, pyuria, hematuria, leukocytosis, leukopenia, and thrombocytopenia. Disseminated intravascular coagulation may be seen in patients with respiratory failure caused by Legionnaires' disease. Hyponatremia, hypophosphatemia, hyperbilirubinemia, and elevated serum alanine transaminase, serum aspartate transaminase, and alkaline phosphatase concentrations may also be found. Elevation of creatine kinase (MM isoenzyme) is common, and myoglobinuria and renal failure develop in some patients. Cerebrospinal fluid is usually normal, although rare patients may have 25 to 100 white blood cells per microliter of cerebrospinal fluid.

Table 307–2 • EXTRAPULMONARY INFECTIONS CAUSED BY *LEGIONELLA*

Dialysis shunt infection
Sinusitis
Pericarditis
Prosthetic valve endocarditis
Peritonitis
Abscesses
  Skin
  Brain
  Bowel
  Rectum
  Kidney
  Myocardium

Table 307–3 • SPECIFIC DIAGNOSTIC TESTS FOR *LEGIONELLA*

TYPE	SUITABLE SPECIMENS	SENSITIVITY* (%)	SPECIFICITY (%)	NOTES
Culture	Sputum, lung, pleural fluid, blood, abscess contents	—	100	Use of special and selective media required; 3 to 5 d required for growth
Immunofluorescent microscopy	Sputum, lung, pleural fluid, abscess contents	25–75	95–99.9	Species-specific monoclonal antibody available; not helpful for diagnosis of all species; highest specificity for *L. pneumophila*; relatively low specificity for other species; 2 to 3 hr required for testing
Urine antigen detection	Urine	90–95	99.9	Useful only for detection of *L. pneumophila* serogroup 1, the most common cause of Legionnaires' disease; 2 to 3 hr required for testing; may be positive despite antimicrobial therapy
Antibody	Serum	60–70	90–99	Requires testing of paired specimens; seroconversion may not occur until 2 to 3 mo after infection; most specific for *L. pneumophila* serogroup 1; cross reactions with antibodies to many other bacteria

*Sensitivity versus culture. Culture is the most sensitive diagnostic technique, but its absolute sensitivity is unknown; reasonable estimates are 80 to 90%. Urinary antigen detection is more sensitive than culture in some circumstances.

Table 307–4 • ANTIMICROBIAL DRUG THERAPY FOR LEGIONNAIRES' DISEASE

PATIENT TYPE	DISEASE SEVERITY*	FIRST CHOICES	DOSAGE	ALTERNATIVES	DOSAGE
Normal host	Mild to moderate	Erythromycin[†]	500 mg to 1 g IV, 500 mg PO each four times daily; 14–21 d	Levofloxacin[‡‡]	500 mg IV or PO once daily; 7–10 d
		or		*or*	
		Doxycycline	200 mg IV or PO once daily; 14–21 d	Azithromycin[†]	500 mg IV or PO once daily; 3 d
	Severe	Levofloxacin[‡‡]	500 mg IV or PO once daily; 7–10 d	Azithromycin[†]	Same dosage as above; 5 d
Immunosuppressed	Any type	Levofloxacin[‡‡]	Same as above	Azithromycin[†]	Same dosage as above; 5 d

*Severe disease is that causing respiratory failure, bilateral pneumonia, or rapidly worsening pulmonary infiltrates, or the presence of at least two of the following three: blood urea nitrogen ≥30 mg/dL (11 mmol/L); diastolic blood pressure <60 mm Hg; respiratory rate >30/min.
[†]Approved by the Food and Drug Administration for the treatment of Legionnaires' disease.
[‡]Acceptable alternatives include ciprofloxacin, 400 mg twice daily IV or 500 mg twice daily PO, and gatifloxacin[†] 400 mg once daily IV or PO, for 7 to 10 days.

Legionnaires' disease can be diagnosed by using specific laboratory tests (Table 307–3). The most sensitive test for *L. pneumophila* serogroup 1 infection is urinary antigen determination. For all other *Legionella* species, the most sensitive and specific test is culture of respiratory tract secretions, such as sputum. Because the infecting type cannot be determined a priori, this means that both urine and culture tests should be performed for maximum sensitivity. Sputum culture for *Legionella* should be performed on every patient suspected of having this disease. Serologic testing is more useful to epidemiologists than to clinicians because of cross-reactions with antibodies to unrelated organisms. No laboratory test currently available is 100% accurate for the diagnosis of Legionnaires' disease. Thus, empirical therapy must be considered in appropriate clinical settings.

The diagnosis of Pontiac fever is based on demonstration of legionellae in water to which the patient was exposed, significant increases in antibody to the isolated *Legionella* species, and a clinical course compatible with this diagnosis. To be certain about the diagnosis of Pontiac fever, it is almost always necessary to perform extensive studies of unaffected people and their environments because recovery of legionellae from water and the elevation of antibodies to *Legionella* are relatively common events. Thus, it is nearly impossible to diagnose nonepidemic cases of Pontiac fever specifically.

The differential diagnosis of Legionnaires' disease is broad because the disease is usually manifested as a nonspecific pneumonia. Mycoplasmal pneumonia is generally much less severe and causes significant respiratory system complaints. Pneumococcal pneumonia, in contrast to Legionnaires' disease, is usually penicillin responsive. Psittacosis and Q fever can have clinical features quite similar to those of Legionnaires' disease.

 Treatment

Azithromycin or levofloxacin is the drug of choice for this disease, except for mild cases in nonimmunocompromised patients, when erythromycin or doxycycline may be used (Table 307–4). Intravenous drug therapy should be given until clinical improvement is seen, which usually occurs in 2 to 4 days. Afterward, oral drug therapy is continued. Mild cases of Legionnaires' disease can be treated with oral therapy exclusively. Quinolone antimicrobials (especially levofloxacin, but also ciprofloxacin or gatifloxacin) and azithromycin are more effective than erythromycin or doxycycline in experimental laboratory studies. Levofloxacin is preferred for organ transplant patients because of its very high activity in experimental Legionnaires' disease and lack of interference with cyclosporine levels. In addition, most immunocompromised patients and most patients with severe Legionnaires' disease should receive levofloxacin or azithromycin rather than erythromycin. Because of its potent activity in experimental Legionnaires' disease, many clinicians add rifampin to an erythromycin or doxycycline regimen for treatment of severe cases of Legionnaires' disease. No clinical data have indicated the superiority of such combination therapy. The availability of newer and more active drugs makes such combination therapy unnecessary; there is no good clinical or laboratory evidence that combinations of levofloxacin and azithromycin are superior to either drug alone, or that addition of rifampin to either drug is of benefit. Penicillins, cephalosporins (first, second, and third generation), and aminoglycosides are ineffective for the treatment of Legionnaires' disease. In fact, failure of pneumonia to respond to these agents should prompt consideration of Legionnaires' disease and perhaps initiation of specific anti-*Legionella* therapy. No effective therapy for Pontiac fever is known.

Most patients with Legionnaires' disease respond within 1 to 4 days to specific antimicrobial therapy. The symptoms clearing most rapidly are rigors, mental confusion, myalgia, anorexia, fatigue, and abdominal complaints. Fever may persist for a week after the initiation of therapy but starts a downward trend within a few days.

Continued

Despite this clinical evidence of improvement, other findings may falsely imply disease progression, such as evidence of increased pulmonary consolidation on physical examination and on radiography. Weeks to months are required for the resolution of pulmonary infiltrates. Patients with respiratory failure have a relatively poor prognosis and tend to have a much slower response to therapy.

SUGGESTED READINGS

Edelstein PH: Chemotherapy of Legionnaires' disease with macrolide or quinolone antimicrobial agents. *In* Marre R, Abu Kwaik Y, Bartlett C, et al (eds): Legionella. Washington, DC, ASM Press, 2001, pp 183–188. *Detailed review of antimicrobial therapy.*

Fang GD, Fine M, Orloff J, et al: New and emerging etiologies for community-acquired pneumonia with implications for therapy: A prospective multicenter study of 359 cases. Medicine (Baltimore) 1990;69:307–316. *Excellent survey of community-acquired pneumonia, including Legionnaires' disease.*

Roig J, Rello J: Legionnaires' disease: a rational approach to therapy. J Antimicrob Chemother 2003;51:1119–1129. *A good review.*

Stout JE, Yu VL: Legionellosis. N Engl J Med 1997;337:682–687. *Good clinical review.*

308 STREPTOCOCCAL INFECTIONS

Dennis L. Stevens

CLASSIFICATION AND IDENTIFICATION OF STREPTOCOCCI

Streptococci are gram-positive globular or coccoid bacteria that grow in chains. Streptococci colonize the skin and mucous membranes of animals, produce catalase, and may be aerobic, anaerobic, or facultative. Streptococci require complex media containing blood products for optimal growth. On blood agar plates, streptococci may cause complete (β), incomplete (α), or no hemolysis (γ). The exhaustive work of Rebecca Lancefield has allowed hemolytic streptococci to be classified into types A through O on the basis of acid-extractable carbohydrate antigens of cell wall material. The availability of rapid latex agglutination kits provides even small clinical laboratories with the means to identify streptococci according to Lancefield group. Bacitracin susceptibility, bile esculin hydrolysis, and the CAMP (Christie-Atkins-Munch-Peterson) test (flame-type synergistic hemolysis on a *Staphylococcus aureus* blood agar streak) are useful presumptive tests for classifying groups A, D, or B streptococci, respectively. Modern schemes of classification of hemolytic and nonhemolytic streptococci use complex biochemical and genetic techniques.

GROUP A STREPTOCOCCAL INFECTIONS

Epidemiology

HOST RANGE. The concept of group A streptococcus as a pure human pathogen is supported by the observations that (1) natural group A streptococcus infection in animals is rare; (2) laboratory animals are not useful models of streptococcal pharyngitis, scarlet fever, erysipelas, rheumatic fever, or poststreptococcal glomerulonephritis; (3) the inoculum needed to cause infection in laboratory animals is orders of magnitude greater than that estimated to cause infection in humans; and (4) streptococci have developed highly sophisticated defensive molecules that bind, inactivate, or destroy human immune response molecules (e.g., immunoglobulin G antibody and complement [C5a]).

AGE-RELATED ATTACK RATES. All group A streptococcal infections have the highest incidence in children younger than 10 years. The asymptomatic prevalence is also higher (15 to 20%) in children than in adults (<5%). Age is not the only factor; crowded conditions in temperate climates during the winter months are also associated with epidemics of pharyngitis in school children as well as in military recruits. Impetigo is most common in children aged 2 to 5 and may occur year-round in tropical areas but largely in the summer in temperate climates. Similarly, 90% of cases of scarlet fever occur in children 2 to 8 years old and, like pharyngitis, it is most common in temperate regions during winter. An experiment of nature in the Faeroe Islands (Denmark) suggested that susceptibility to scarlet fever is not dependent on young age per se. Briefly, scarlet fever had disappeared from that isolated island group for several decades until it was rein-

troduced by a visitor with unsuspected scarlet fever. An epidemic of scarlet fever ensued with significant attack rates in all age groups, suggesting that other factors, such as the lack of protective antibody against scarlatina toxin or the introduction of a new strain, rather than age predisposed those individuals to clinical illness.

In contrast to pharyngitis, impetigo, and scarlet fever, bacteremia has had the highest age-specific attack rate in elderly people and in neonates. However, between 1986 and 1988, the prevalence of bacteremia increased 800 to 1000% in adolescents and adults in Western countries. Although some of this increase is attributable to intravenous drug abuse and puerperal sepsis, most of the increase is due to cases of streptococcal toxic shock syndrome, in which a defined portal of entry is not apparent in 50% of cases.

Transmission

Human mucous membranes and skin serve as the natural reservoirs of *Streptococcus pyogenes*. Pharyngeal and cutaneous acquisition is by person-to-person spread through aerosolized microdroplets or by direct contact, respectively. Epidemics of pharyngitis and scarlet fever have also occurred after the consumption of contaminated, nonpasteurized milk or food. Epidemics of impetigo have been reported, particularly in tropical areas, in daycare centers, and among underprivileged children. Group A streptococcal infections in hospitalized patients occur during childbirth (puerperal sepsis), times of war (epidemic gangrene), and surgical convalescence (surgical wound infection, surgical scarlet fever) or as a result of burns (burn wound sepsis). Thus, in most clinical streptococcal infections, the mode of transmission and portal of entry are easily ascertained. In contrast, among patients with streptococcal toxic shock syndrome, the portal of entry is obvious in only 50% of cases.

Pathogenesis

Adherence of cocci to the mucosal epithelium is necessary but not sufficient to cause disease in all cases inasmuch as prolonged asymptomatic carriage is well documented. Complex interactions between host epithelium and streptococcal factors such as M protein, lipoteichoic acid, and fimbriae are necessary for adherence. Fibronectin binding protein (protein F) also contributes to adherence because protein F–deficient mutants are incapable of binding to epithelial cells. Protein F is upregulated by oxygen and decreased in anaerobic conditions.

Within the tissues, streptococci may evade opsonophagocytosis by virtue of a hyaluronic acid capsule, a C5a peptidase that destroys or inactivates complement-derived chemoattractants and opsonins, or by immunoglobulin binding protein. Expression of M protein, in the absence of type-specific antibody, also protects the organism from phagocytosis by polymorphonuclear leukocytes (PMNs) and monocytes. In tissues, streptolysin O secreted in high concentration destroys approaching phagocytes. Distal to the focus of infection, lower concentrations of streptolysin O stimulate PMN adhesion to endothelial cells, effectively preventing continued granulocyte migration and promoting vascular damage. In a nonimmune host, streptolysin O, streptococcal pyrogenic exotoxins (SPE A, B, C, MF, and SSA), and other streptococcal components stimulate host cells to produce tumor necrosis factor (TNF) and interleukin-1 (IL-1), cytokines that mediate hypotension, stimulate leukostasis, and eventually result in shock, microvascular injury, multiorgan failure, and, if excessive, death. A unique feature of the pyrogenic exotoxins and some M protein fragments is their ability to interact with certain V_β regions of the T-cell receptor in the absence of classical antigen processing by antigen-presenting cells (Fig. 308–1). This interaction results in massive clonal proliferation of T lymphocytes. SPE type B, a cysteine protease, may play a role in the pathogenesis of necrotizing fasciitis and shock through its ability to cleave pre–IL-1β into active IL-1β, activation of endogenous metalloproteases, and cleavage of high-molecular-weight kininogen into bradykinin. Thus, in streptococcal toxic shock syndrome, lymphokines (TNF-β, interferon-γ, and IL-2), monokines (TNF-α, IL-1, and IL-6), and bradykinin may be crucial in the mediation of shock and organ failure.

Bacterial Cell Structure and Extracellular Products

CAPSULE. Some strains of *S. pyogenes* possess capsules of hyaluronic acid and form large mucoid colonies on blood agar. Luxuriant pro-

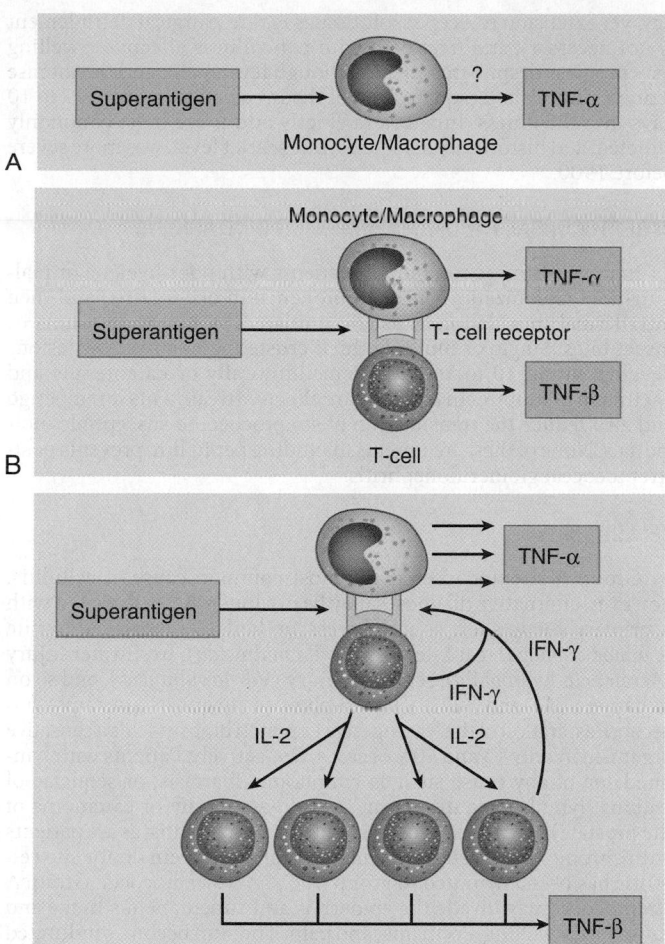

FIGURE 308–1 • Superantigen-induced production of tumor necrosis factor α (TNF-α) and lymphotoxin (TNF-β) by peripheral blood mononuclear cells. *A,* Superantigens induce human monocytes to produce TNF-α; however, it is unclear whether such production results solely from direct stimulation of the monocyte by the superantigen. *B,* In mixed mononuclear cell populations, superantigens stimulate TNF-α synthesis in monocytes and, by binding to specific V_β regions of the T-cell receptor, induce the synthesis of lymphotoxin (TNF-β) from T cells. *C,* The T-cell response to superantigen stimulation includes the production of interleukin-2 (IL-2), which results in clonal proliferation with concordant production of interferon-γ (IFN-γ) and TNF-β. IFN-γ can then amplify monocyte synthesis of TNF-α, IL-1, and IL-6. (From Stevens DL, Bryant AE, Hackett SP: Sepsis syndromes and toxic shock syndromes: Concepts in pathogenesis and a perspective of future strategy. Curr Opin Infect Dis 1993;6:374–383.)

duction of M protein may also impart a mucoid colony morphology, and this trait has been associated with M-18 strains. An operon promoter sequence is the key element in both the constitutive and dynamic regulation of hyaluronic acid synthesis in group A streptococci, and its activity is increased during ideal growth conditions and log-phase growth. It plays an important role in pharyngitis, soft tissue infection, and invasive disease by binding to CD44 on epithelial cells and by serving as an antiphagocytic factor.

CELL WALL. The cell wall is composed of a peptidoglycan backbone with integral lipoteichoic acid components. The function of lipoteichoic acid is not well known, but both peptidoglycan and lipoteichoic acid have important interactions with the host.

M PROTEINS. Over 80 different M protein types of group A streptococci are currently described. The protein is a coil structure consisting of four regions of repeating amino acids (A to D), a proline/glycine-rich region that serves to intercalate the protein into the bacterial cell wall, and a hydrophobic region that acts as a membrane anchor. Region A near the N terminus is highly variable, and antibodies to this region confer type-specific protection. Within the more conserved B to D regions lies an area that binds one of the complement regulatory proteins (factor H), sterically inhibiting antibody binding and complement-derived opsonin deposition and effectively camouflaging the organism against humoral immune surveillance. M protein inhibits the phagocytosis of *S. pyogenes* by PMNs, although this property can be overcome by type-specific antisera. Observations by Lancefield suggest that the quantity of M protein produced decreases with passage on artificial media and conversely increases rapidly with passage through mice. The quantity of M protein produced by an infecting strain progressively decreases during convalescence and during prolonged carriage.

STREPTOLYSIN O. Streptolysin O belongs to a family of oxygen-labile, thiol-activated cytolysins (TACs) and causes the broad zone of β-hemolysis surrounding colonies of *S. pyogenes* on blood agar plates. TAC toxins bind to cholesterol on eukaryotic cell membranes and create toxin-cholesterol aggregates that contribute to cell lysis by a colloid-osmotic mechanism. Cholesterol inhibits toxicity in isolated myocytes and hemolysis of red blood cells in vitro. In situations in which serum cholesterol is high (e.g., nephrotic syndrome), falsely elevated anti-streptolysin O titers may occur because both cholesterol and antistreptolysin O antibody "neutralize" streptolysin O. Striking amino acid homology exists between streptolysin O and other TAC toxins.

STREPTOLYSIN S. Streptolysin S is a cell-associated hemolysin that does not diffuse into agar media. Purification and characterization of this protein have been difficult, and its only role in pathogenesis may be in direct or contact cytotoxicity. Streptolysin S has been cloned and shown to be a lantabiotic whose synthesis is controlled by seven genes.

DEOXYRIBONUCLEASES A, B, C, AND D. Expression of deoxyribonucleases (DNases) in vivo elicits the production of anti-DNase antibody following both pharyngeal and skin infection; this response is most true for DNase B with group A streptococci. DNases may also contribute to cytokine production, although their importance in pathogenesis has not been established.

HYALURONIDASE. This extracellular enzyme hydrolyzes hyaluronic acid in deeper tissues, thereby facilitating the spread of infection along fascial planes. Antihyaluronidase titers rise following *S. pyogenes* infections, especially those involving the skin.

PYROGENIC EXOTOXINS. SPE types A, B, and C, also called scarlatina toxin and erythrogenic toxins, induce lymphocyte blastogenesis, potentiate endotoxin-induced shock, induce fever, suppress antibody synthesis, and act as superantigens. Identification of these three different types of SPEs may in part explain why some individuals may have multiple attacks of scarlet fever. The gene for pyrogenic exotoxin A (*speA*) is transmitted by bacteriophages, and stable production depends on lysogenic conversion in a manner analogous to diphtheria toxin production by *Corynebacterium diphtheriae.* Control of SPE A production is not yet understood, although the quantity of SPE A produced varies dramatically from decade to decade. Historically, SPE A–producing strains have been associated with severe cases of scarlet fever and, more recently, with streptococcal toxic shock syndrome.

Although all strains of group A streptococci are endowed with genes for SPE B (*speB*), as with SPE A, the quantity of toxin produced varies greatly.

Pyrogenic exotoxin type C (SPE C), like SPE A, is bacteriophage mediated, and expression is likewise highly variable. Mild cases of scarlet fever in England and the United States have been associated with SPE C–positive strains. Five other pyrogenic exotoxins, including streptococcal superantigen (SPE SSA) and mitogenic factor (SPE MF), have been described and their roles in pathogenesis are being studied.

NICOTINE ADENINE DINUCLEOTIDASE (NADase). Studies have demonstrated a high association of NADase production among strains isolated from patients with invasive group A streptococcal infections. Interestingly, NADase impairs neutrophil chemotaxis and alters respiratory burst activity.

Clinical Infections

PHARYNGITIS AND THE ASYMPTOMATIC CARRIER

Patients with streptococcal pharyngitis have an abrupt onset of sore throat, submandibular adenopathy, fever, and chilliness but not usually frank rigors. Cough and hoarseness are rare, but pain on swallowing is characteristic. The uvula is edematous, tonsils are hypertrophied, and the pharynx is erythematous with exudate that may be punctate or confluent (Fig. 308–2). Acute pharyngitis is sufficient to induce antibody against M protein, streptolysin O, DNase, hyaluronidase, and, if present, pyrogenic exotoxins. Depending on

Infectious Diseases

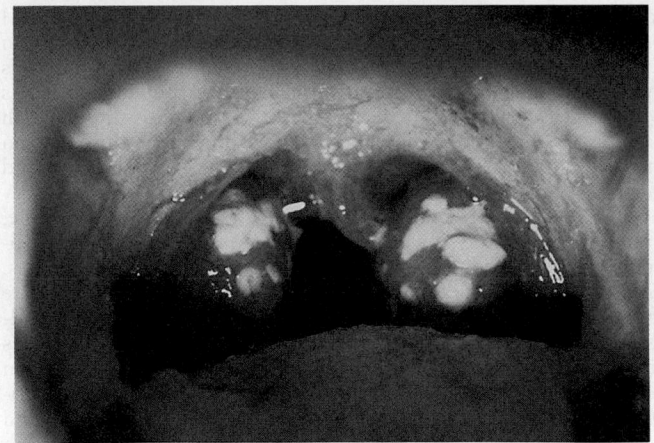

FIGURE 308–2 • Acute streptococcal pharyngitis. There is pus in the tonsillar crypts, and some palatal petechiae are seen. (From Forbes CD, Jackson WF: Color Atlas and Text of Clinical Medicine, 3rd ed. London, Mosby, 2003, with permission.)

the infecting strain, pharyngitis may progress to scarlet fever, bacteremia, suppurative head and neck infections, rheumatic fever, poststreptococcal glomerulonephritis, or streptococcal toxic shock syndrome. Pharyngitis is usually self-limited, and pain, swelling, and fever resolve spontaneously in 3 to 4 days even without treatment.

Definitive diagnosis is difficult when based only on clinical parameters, especially in infants, in whom rhinorrhea may be the dominant manifestation. Even in older children with all the preceding physical findings, the correct clinical diagnosis is made in only 75% of patients. Absence of any one of the classical signs greatly reduces the specificity. Rapid antigen detection tests in the office setting have a sensitivity and specificity of 40 to 90%. A popular approach in clinical practice is to obtain two throat swab samples from the posterior of the pharynx or tonsillar surface. A rapid strep test is performed on the first, and if it is positive, the patient is treated with antibiotics and the second swab discarded. If the rapid strep test is negative, the second sample is sent for culture, and treatment is withheld pending a positive culture.

SCARLET FEVER

During the past 30 to 40 years, outbreaks of scarlet fever in the Western world have been notably mild, and the illness has been referred to as "pharyngitis with a rash" or "benign scarlet fever." In contrast, in the latter half of the 19th century, mortalities of 25 to 35% were common in the United States, Western Europe, and Scandinavia. The fatal or malignant forms of scarlet fever have been described as either septic or toxic. *Septic scarlet fever* refers to the development of local invasion of the soft tissues of the neck and complications such as upper airway obstruction, otitis media with perforation, meningitis, mastoiditis, invasion of the jugular vein or carotid artery, and bronchopneumonia. *Toxic scarlet fever* is rare today, but historically, severe sore throat, marked fever, delirium, skin rash, and painful cervical lymph nodes initially developed. In severe toxic cases, temperatures of 107° F, pulses of 130 to 160 beats per minute, severe headache, delirium, convulsions, little if any skin rash, and death within 24 hours were common. These cases occurred before the advent of antibiotics, antipyretics, and anticonvulsants, and sudden deaths were the result of uncontrolled seizures and hyperpyrexia. In contrast, children with septic scarlet fever had prolonged courses and succumbed 2 to 3 weeks after the onset of pharyngitis. Complications of streptococcal pharyngitis and malignant forms of scarlet fever have been less common in the antibiotic era. Even before antibiotics became available, necrotizing fasciitis and myositis were not described in association with scarlet fever.

ERYSIPELAS

Erysipelas is caused exclusively by *S. pyogenes* and is characterized by an abrupt onset of fiery red swelling of the face or extremities. Distinctive features are well-defined margins, particularly along the nasolabial fold, scarlet or salmon-red rash, rapid progression, and intense pain. Flaccid bullae may develop during the second to third

day, yet extension to deeper soft tissues is rare. Surgical débridement is not necessary, and treatment with penicillin is effective. Swelling may progress despite treatment, although fever, pain, and the intense redness diminish. Desquamation of the involved skin occurs 5 to 10 days into the illness. Infants and elderly adults are most commonly afflicted, and historically erysipelas, like scarlet fever, was more severe before 1900.

STREPTOCOCCAL PYODERMA (IMPETIGO CONTAGIOSA)

Impetigo is most common in patients with poor hygiene or malnutrition. Colonization of the unbroken skin occurs first, and then intradermal inoculation is usually initiated by minor abrasions or insect bites. Single or multiple thick-crusted, golden-yellow lesions develop within 10 to 14 days. Penicillin orally or parenterally and bacitracin or mupirocin topically are effective treatments for impetigo and also reduce the transmission of streptococci to susceptible individuals. None of these treatments, including penicillin, prevents poststreptococcal glomerulonephritis.

CELLULITIS

Group A streptococcus is the most common cause of cellulitis; however, alternative diagnoses may be obvious when associated with a primary focus such as an abscess or boil (*S. aureus*), dog bite (*Capnocytophaga*), cat bite (*Pasteurella multocida*), freshwater injury (*Aeromonas hydrophila*), seawater injury (*Vibrio vulnificus*), and so on (Chapters 311 and 322). Clinical clues to diagnosis are important because aspiration of the leading edge or punch biopsy yields a causative organism in only 15 and 40% of cases, respectively. Patients with lymphedema of any cause such as lymphoma, filariasis, or sequelae of regional lymph node dissection (as in mastectomy or carcinoma of the prostate) are predisposed to streptococcal cellulitis, as are patients with chronic venous stasis. Recurrent saphenous vein donor site cellulitis has been attributed to group A, C, or G streptococci. Group A streptococci may invade the epidermis and subcutaneous tissue and cause local swelling, erythema, and pain. The skin becomes indurated and, unlike the brilliant redness of erysipelas, is pinkish. Streptococcal cellulitis responds quickly to penicillin, although when staphylococcus is of concern, nafcillin or oxacillin may be a better choice. If fever, pain, or swelling increases, if bluish or violet bullae or discoloration appears, or if signs of systemic toxicity develop, a deeper infection such as necrotizing fasciitis or myositis should be considered (see Necrotizing Fasciitis). When an elevated serum creatine phosphokinase level suggests deeper infection, prompt surgical inspection and débridement should be performed.

LYMPHANGITIS

Cutaneous infection with bright red streaks ascending proximally is invariably due to group A streptococcus. Prompt parenteral antibiotic treatment is mandatory because bacteremia and systemic toxicity develop rapidly when streptococci reach the blood stream through the thoracic duct.

NECROTIZING FASCIITIS

Necrotizing fasciitis, originally called "streptococcal gangrene," is a deep-seated infection of the subcutaneous tissue that results in progressive destruction of fascia and fat but may spare the skin itself. Subsequently, *necrotizing fasciitis* has become the preferred term because *Clostridium perfringens*, *Clostridium septicum*, and *S. aureus* can produce a similar pathologic process. Infection may begin at the site of trivial or inapparent trauma. Within the initial 24 hours, swelling, heat, erythema, and tenderness develop and rapidly spread proximally and distally from the original focus. During the next 24 to 48 hours, the erythema darkens, changing from red to purple and then to blue, and blisters and bullae form that contain clear yellow fluid. On the fourth or fifth day, the purple areas become frankly gangrenous. From the seventh to the tenth days, the line of demarcation becomes sharply defined, and the dead skin begins to reveal extensive necrosis of the subcutaneous tissue. Patients become increasingly prostrated and emaciated and may become unresponsive, mentally cloudy, or even delirious. Aggressive fasciotomy and débridement ("bear claw fasciotomy") and irrigations with Dakin's solution achieved mortality rates as low as 20% even before antibiotics were available. Since 1989, the mortality rate of necrotizing fasciitis despite antibiotics, surgical débridement, and intensive care unit treatment has become higher than that reported by Meleney in 1924, probably because of the increased virulence of streptococci (see Streptococcal Toxic Shock Syndrome).

MYOSITIS

Historically, streptococcal myositis has been an extremely uncommon infection, only 21 cases being documented from 1900 to 1985. More recently, the prevalence of streptococcal myositis has increased in the United States, Norway, and Sweden. Translocation of streptococci from the pharynx to the deep site of trauma (muscle) must occur hematogenously. Symptomatic pharyngitis or penetrating trauma is uncommon. Severe pain may be the only symptom, and swelling and erythema may be the only signs of infection. In some cases a single muscle group is involved; however, because patients are frequently bacteremic, multiple sites of myositis or abscess can occur. Distinguishing streptococcal myositis from spontaneous gas gangrene caused by *C. perfringens* or *C. septicum* may be difficult, although the presence of crepitus or gas in the tissue would favor clostridial infection. Myositis is easily distinguished from necrotizing fasciitis anatomically by surgical exploration or incisional biopsy, although the clinical features of both conditions overlap. Many cases of necrotizing fasciitis have associated myositis and myonecrosis. In published reports, the case-fatality rate of necrotizing fasciitis is between 20 and 50%, whereas that of streptococcal myositis is between 80 and 100%. Aggressive surgical débridement is extremely important because of the poor efficacy of penicillin described in human cases as well as in experimental models of streptococcal myositis (see the section on antibiotic efficacy).

PNEUMONIA

Pneumonia caused by group A streptococcus is most common in women in the second and third decades of life and causes large pleural effusions and empyema that develop rapidly. Chest tube drainage is mandatory even though management is complicated by multiple loculations and fibrinous effusions resulting in restrictive lung disease. Prolonged penicillin therapy, thoracoscopy, and decortication of the pleura may be necessary to prevent adhesive pleuritis, fibrosis, and subsequent restrictive lung disease.

STREPTOCOCCAL TOXIC SHOCK SYNDROME

EPIDEMIOLOGY. In the late 1980s, invasive group A streptococcal infections occurred in North America and Europe in previously healthy individuals aged 20 to 50. This illness is associated with bacteremia, deep soft tissue infection, shock, multiorgan failure, and death in 30% of cases. Although streptococcal toxic shock syndrome occurs sporadically, minor epidemics have been reported. Most patients have either a viral-like prodrome, a history of minor trauma, recent surgery, or varicella infection. The prodrome may be due to a viral illness predisposing to toxic shock syndrome, or these vague early symptoms may be related to the evolving infection. In about 50% of cases associated with necrotizing fasciitis, the infection begins deep in the soft tissue at a site of minor trauma that frequently did not result in a break in the skin. Surgical procedures, viral infections such as varicella and influenza, penetrating trauma, insect bites, slivers, and burns may provide portals of entry in the remaining cases.

SYMPTOMS AND PHYSICAL FINDINGS. The abrupt onset of severe pain is a common initial symptom of streptococcal toxic shock syndrome (Table 308–1). The pain most commonly involves an extremity but may also mimic peritonitis, pelvic inflammatory disease, acute myocardial infarction, or pericarditis. Treatment with nonsteroidal anti-inflammatory agents may mask the initial symptoms or predispose to more severe complications such as shock.

Fever is the most common initial sign, although some patients have profound hypothermia secondary to shock (see Table 308–1). Confusion is present in over half the patients and may progress to coma or combativeness. On admission, 80% of patients have tachycardia and over half have systolic blood pressure lower than 110 mm Hg. Of those with normal blood pressure on admission, most become hypotensive within 4 hours. Soft tissue infection evolves to necrotizing fasciitis or myositis in 50 to 70% of patients, and these conditions require emergency surgical débridement, fasciotomy, or amputation. An ominous sign is progression of soft tissue swelling to violaceous or bluish vesicles or bullae. Many other clinical

Table 308–1 • CLINICAL AND LABORATORY FEATURES OF STREPTOCOCCAL TOXIC SHOCK SYNDROME

Symptoms
  Viral-like prodrome
  Severe pain
  Confusion
  Nausea
  Chills
Signs
  Fever
  Soft tissue swelling and tenderness
  Tachycardia
  Tachypnea
  Hypotension
Laboratory Findings
  Hematologic tests
    Marked left shift
    Red cell hemolysis
    Thrombocytopenia
  Chemistry tests
    Azotemia
    Hypocalcemia
    Hypoalbuminemia
    Creatine phosphokinase elevation
  Urinalysis
    Hematuria
  Blood gases
    Hypoxia
    Acidosis
  Radiographic
    ARDS
    Soft tissue swelling
Complications
  Profound hypotension
  ARDS
  Renal failure
  Liver failure
  Necrotizing soft tissue infections
  Bacteremia
  Death (30%)

ARDS = adult respiratory distress syndrome.

pictures may be associated with streptococcal toxic shock syndrome including endophthalmitis, myositis, perihepatitis, peritonitis, myocarditis, meningitis, septic arthritis, and overwhelming sepsis. Patients with shock and multiorgan failure without signs or symptoms of local infections have a worse prognosis because definitive diagnosis and surgical débridement may be delayed.

LABORATORY ABNORMALITIES. Hemoglobinuria is present and serum creatinine is elevated in most patients at the time of admission. Serum albumin concentrations are moderately low (3.3 g/dL) on admission and drop progressively over 48 to 72 hours. Hypocalcemia, including ionized hypocalcemia, is detectable early in the hospital course. The serum creatinine kinase level is a useful test to detect deeper soft tissue infections such as necrotizing fasciitis or myositis.

The initial hematologic studies demonstrate only mild leukocytosis but a dramatic left shift (43% of white blood cells may be band forms, metamyelocytes, and myelocytes). The mean platelet count is normal on admission but may drop rapidly by 48 hours, even in the absence of criteria for disseminated intravascular coagulopathy.

CLINICAL COURSE. Shock is apparent early in the course, and fluid management is complicated by profound capillary leak. Adult respiratory distress syndrome occurs frequently (55%), and renal dysfunction that precedes hypotension in many patients may progress despite treatment. In patients who survive, serum creatinine levels return to normal within 4 to 6 weeks; many require dialysis. Overall, 30% of patients die despite aggressive treatment including intravenous fluids, colloid, pressors, mechanical ventilation, and surgical interventions such as fasciotomy, débridement, exploratory laparotomy, intraocular aspiration, amputation, and hysterectomy.

CHARACTERISTICS OF CLINICAL ISOLATES. Group A streptococcus is isolated from blood in 60% of cases and from deep tissue specimens in 95% of cases. M types 1, 3, 12, and 28 are the most common strains isolated but account for only 60 to 70% of the isolates, the remaining being a wide variety of M typable and nontypable strains. Pyrogenic exotoxin A and/or B has been found in isolates from the majority of

Infectious Diseases

patients with severe infection, although the quantities of these toxins that are produced in vitro vary widely. Infections in Norway, Sweden, and Great Britain have been primarily due to M type 1 strains that produce pyrogenic exotoxin B. Other novel pyrogenic exotoxins are also being described and may explain the recent enhanced virulence of group A streptococcus.

NONSUPPURATIVE COMPLICATIONS

The nonsuppurative complications of streptococcal disease are acute rheumatic fever and acute glomerulonephritis. These conditions are discussed in Chapters 309 and 119, respectively.

Rx Treatment of Group A Infections

PROPHYLAXIS. During epidemics, particularly when rheumatic fever or poststreptococcal glomerulonephritis is prevalent, treatment of asymptomatic carriers may be necessary. Studies by the U.S. military have shown that monthly injections of benzathine penicillin greatly reduce the incidence of streptococcal pharyngitis and rheumatic fever in young soldiers living in crowded conditions.

EMERGENCE OF RESISTANCE. Erythromycin resistance of *S. pyogenes* is currently 4% in Western countries; however, in Japan in 1974 the rate reached 72%, and reports of 100% resistance have emanated from Scandinavia. Sulfonamide resistance is currently reported in fewer than 1% of group A streptococcal isolates.

THERAPEUTIC FAILURE OF PENICILLIN. The recommended antibiotic therapies for group A streptococcal diseases are shown in Table 308–2. Resistance to penicillin has not been described, yet in some settings a lack of in vivo efficacy is seen despite in vitro susceptibility to penicillin. Three mechanisms may explain this lack of efficacy.

1. *β-Lactamase production by coinfecting organisms.* Penicillin failure in pharyngitis, tonsillitis, or mixed infections may be due to inactivation of penicillin in situ by β-lactamases produced by cocolonizing organisms such as *Bacteroides fragilis, Haemophilus influenzae,* or *S. aureus.* For example, the failure rate of penicillin treatment of group A streptococcal pharyngitis may approach 25%, and if such patients are treated with a second course of penicillin, the failure rate may approach 80%, perhaps because of selection of β-lactamase–producing bacteria. In contrast, cure rates of 90% have been achieved when treatment consisted of amoxicillin plus clavulanate or clindamycin.

2. *Genotypic tolerance.* Genotypic tolerance to penicillin may also contribute to penicillin's lack of efficacy in tonsillitis or pharyngitis. In fact, penicillin-tolerant strains have also caused epidemics of pharyngitis. Tolerant strains demonstrate a slower rate of growth, a slower rate of bacterial killing by penicillin, and an absence of β-lactam–induced cell lysis. The role of tolerance in antibiotic treatment failure is not fully understood.

3. *Inoculum effect.* Studies in animals infected with group A streptococcus demonstrate that penicillin is effective only if given early or if small numbers of streptococci are used to initiate infection. It is likely that streptococci are not in a logarithmic phase of growth when the clinical diagnosis of necrotizing fasciitis or myositis is made. Penicillin is most effective against streptococci in log-phase growth, a stage in their life cycle when five penicillin binding proteins are expressed. Conversely, during the stationary phase, the two penicillin binding proteins with the greatest affinity for penicillin are absent.

EFFICACY OF CLINDAMYCIN IN INVASIVE S. PYOGENES INFECTIONS. Clindamycin is superior to penicillin in experimental infections. In addition, retrospective studies in humans have substantiated the greater efficacy of clindamycin compared with penicillin in patients with invasive streptococcal infections. Clindamycin's greater efficacy could be due to its ability to suppress M protein and toxin synthesis, its longer postantibiotic effect, an indifference to the in vivo inoculum effect, or its effects on the host's immune system such as suppression of TNF synthesis.

Table 308–2 • ANTIBIOTIC THERAPY FOR GROUP A STREPTOCOCCAL INFECTIONS

CONDITION	ROUTE	DOSAGES
Pharyngitis and impetigo		
Benzathine penicillin	IM	1.2 million U (>27 kg)
Penicillin G (or V)	PO	200,000 U qid for 10 d
Erythromycin	PO	40 mg/kg/d (up to 1 g/d)
Recurrent streptococcal pharyngitis/tonsillitis		
Same as above, *or*		
Ampicillin plus clavulanic acid	PO	20–40 mg/kg/d
Oral cephalosporin		Check *PDR*
Clindamycin	PO	10 mg/kg/d
Cellulitis and erysipelas		
Penicillin G or V	PO	200,000 U qid for 10 d
Dicloxacillin*	PO	500 mg qid for 10 d (adults)
Necrotizing fasciitis/myositis/ streptococcal toxic shock syndrome		
Clindamycin	IV	1800–2100 mg daily (adults)
Penicillin	IV	2 million U q4h (adults)
Prophylaxis for rheumatic fever (Chapter 309)		

*Alternative to penicillin if *Staphylococcus aureus* is of concern. Cephalosporins could be used; however, most (except ceftriaxone) have less activity than penicillin G against streptococci.
PDR = *Physicians' Desk Reference.*

NON–GROUP A STREPTOCOCCAL INFECTIONS (Table 308–3)

ENTEROCOCCUS FAECALIS AND *ENTEROCOCCUS FAECIUM*

These gram-positive, facultatively anaerobic bacteria are usually nonhemolytic but may demonstrate α- or β-hemolysis. Enterococci were previously classified as group D streptococci because they hydrolyze bile esculin and possess the group D antigen. On the basis of nucleic acid hybridization studies, they are now designated *Enterococcus.* Enterococci are commonly isolated from the stool, urine, and sites of intra-abdominal and lower extremity infection. Enterococci cause subacute bacterial endocarditis and have become an important cause of nosocomial infection, not because of increased virulence but because of antibiotic resistance. First, person-to-person transfer of multidrug-resistant enterococci is a major concern to hospital epidemiologists. Second, superinfections and spontaneous bacteremia from endogenous sites of enterococcal colonization are described in patients receiving quinolone or moxalactam antibiotics. Last, conjugational transfer of plasmids and transposons between enterococci in the presence of intense antibiotic pressure within the hospital milieu has created multidrug-resistant strains, including those with vancomycin and teicoplanin resistance. Acquired resistance to glycopeptide in enterococci is due to the production of peptidoglycan precursors ending in the dipeptide D-alanine-D-lactate (D-ala-D-lac) instead of the dipeptide D-ala-D-ala, which is found in susceptible bacteria. This substitution prevents the formation of complexes between glycopeptides and peptidoglycan precursors at the cell surface that are responsible for inhibition of cell wall synthesis. Acquired glycopeptide resistance by this mechanism is conferred by two classes of genetic elements (Van A or Van B), often carried by mobile elements (transposons), that encode a dehydrogenase (Van H or Van HB) for reduction of pyruvate into D-lactate and a ligase (Van A or Van B) for synthesis of D-ala-D-lac. The majority of enterococci harboring Van B–type gene clusters are inducibly resistant to vancomycin but remain susceptible to teicoplanin because induction occurs only in the presence of vancomycin. Serious enterococcal infections such as endocarditis or bacteremia require a synergistic combination of antimicrobials such as ampicillin or vancomycin, together with an aminoglycoside. Teicoplanin may be substituted for vancomycin if Van B–type resistance is present. Unfortunately, some strains of enterococci are resistant to all known antibiotics. β-Lactamase–positive (nitrocefin disc positive) strains can be treated with ampicillin and sulbactam. Linezolid, a member of the oxazolidinone group of antibiotics, has efficacy against both *E. faecium* and *E. faecalis.*

Table 308–3 • NON–GROUP A STREPTOCOCCAL INFECTIONS

ORGANISM	LANCEFIELD GROUP	TYPE OF INFECTION	THERAPY
S. agalactiae	B	Neonatal sepsis Postpartum sepsis Septic arthritis Soft tissue infection Osteomyelitis	Ampicillin or penicillin
Enterococcus faecalis/ faecium	D	Endocarditis Bacteremia UTI Abscesses, GI	Ampicillin + gentamicin[*]
S. milleri	A, C, F, G, and non-typable	Abscesses Bacteremia	Penicillin
S. bovis	D	Bacteremia Abscesses	Penicillin
S. equi	C	Bacteremia Cellulitis Pharyngitis	Penicillin
S. canis	G	Bacteremia Cellulitis Pharyngitis	Penicillin
"Viridans" S. salivarius	Non-typable	Non-pathogen	
S. mutans		Endocarditis Caries	Penicillin
S. sanguis		Endocarditis	Penicillin
S. mitior		Endocarditis	Penicillin

*Vancomycin-resistant enterococci (VRE) are becoming more common. Linezolid may be a reasonable treatment alternative for VRE infections.
GI = gastrointestinal; UTI = urinary tract infection.

STREPTOCOCCUS BOVIS

S. bovis is also a cause of subacute bacterial endocarditis and bacteremia in patients with underlying gastrointestinal pathology or malignancy. Unlike the enterococcus, it remains highly sensitive to penicillin.

GROUP C AND G STREPTOCOCCI

These organisms may be isolated from the throats of both humans and dogs, produce streptolysin O, and resemble group A in colony morphology and spectrum of clinical disease. Before rapid identification tests were developed, many infections caused by groups C and G were mistakenly attributed to group A, such as pharyngitis, cellulitis, skin and wound infections, endocarditis, meningitis, osteomyelitis, and arthritis. Rheumatic fever following group C or G infection has not been described. These strains also cause recurrent cellulitis at the saphenous vein donor site in patients who have undergone coronary artery bypass graft surgery. Both organisms are susceptible to penicillin, erythromycin, vancomycin, and clindamycin.

STREPTOCOCCUS MILLERI

S. milleri bacteria are usually β-hemolytic but may also be non-hemolytic or α-hemolytic and produce minute colonies on blood agar plates. They normally colonize the oropharynx, upper gastrointestinal tract, and appendix. Infections are most commonly related to contiguous abscess formation such as a tooth abscess or periappendiceal abscess. Primary bacteremia with or without endocarditis and metastatic abscesses of the brain, lung, bone, joints, liver, and spleen are characteristic of S. milleri.

STREPTOCOCCUS AGALACTIAE

S. agalactiae (group B streptococci) colonizes the vagina, gastrointestinal tract, and occasionally the upper respiratory tract of normal humans. These organisms are recognized as gray-white colonies, slightly larger than group A streptococci, but with a narrower zone of hemolysis. They are resistant to bacitracin, do not hydrolyze bile esculin, demonstrate a positive CAMP test, and hydrolyze sodium hippurate. Definitive identification is made with group-specific antiserum or commercial kits that use agglutination

end points. The polysaccharide capsule is the prime virulence factor in group B streptococci and is instrumental in the evasion of phagocytosis. Currently, six different capsular polysaccharide types of group B are recognized and designated Ia, Ib, II, III, IV, and V. Immunity results from the development of opsonic type-specific antibody.

Group B streptococci are the most common cause of neonatal pneumonia, sepsis, and meningitis in the United States and Western Europe, with an incidence of 1.8 to 3.2 cases per 1000 live births. Preterm infants born to mothers with premature rupture of membranes who are colonized with group B streptococci are at highest risk for early-onset pneumonia and sepsis. The mean time of onset is 20 hours, and symptoms are respiratory distress, apnea, fever, and hypothermia. Ascent of the streptococcus from the vagina to the amniotic cavity causes amnionitis. Infants may aspirate streptococci either from the birth canal during parturition or from amniotic fluid in utero. Radiographic evidence of pneumonia and or hyaline membrane disease is present in 40% of neonates with infection, and meningitis occurs in 30 to 40% of cases. Type III group B streptococcus causes most cases of meningitis.

Late-onset neonatal sepsis occurs 7 to 90 days postpartum, with symptoms of fever, poor feeding, lethargy, and irritability. Bacteremia is common, and meningitis occurs in 80% of cases.

Adults with group B infections include postpartum women and patients with peripheral vascular disease, diabetes, or malignancy. Soft tissue infection, septic arthritis, and osteomyelitis are the most common findings. Although penicillin is the treatment of choice, in practice many neonates are treated empirically with ampicillin (300 to 400 mg/kg/day) plus gentamicin. When the diagnosis is established, penicillin at 200 to 500,000 U/kg/day should be given. Adults should receive 10 to 12 million U of penicillin per day for bacteremia, soft tissue infection, or osteomyelitis, but the dose should be increased to 18 to 24 million U/day for meningitis. Vancomycin and a first-generation cephalosporin are alternatives for penicillin-allergic patients. Intrapartum administration of ampicillin to women colonized with group B streptococcus who also had premature labor or prolonged rupture of membranes prevents group B neonatal sepsis. Infants should continue to receive ampicillin for 36 hours postpartum. It is imperative that women during the third trimester be screened for risk factors for premature labor, and those at high risk should undergo culturing for streptococci. Women in labor who have not had such studies could be screened with a rapid antigen detection kit, even though the false-negative rate may be 10 to 30%. Passive immunization with intravenous immune globulin or active immunization with multivalent polysaccharide vaccine shows promise and is probably the best approach to prevent neonatal sepsis as well as postpartum infection of the mother.

SUGGESTED READINGS

Bisno AL, Brito MO, Collins CM: Molecular basis of group A streptococcal virulence. Lancet Infect Dis 2003;3:191–200. *Reviews surface proteins, extracellular toxins, and molecular epidemiology.*

Bisno AL, Gerber MA, Gwaltney JM Jr, et al: Practice guidelines for the diagnosis and management of group A streptococcal pharyngitis. Infectious Diseases Society of America. Clin Infect Dis 2002;35:113–125. *Consensus guidelines.*

Brook I: Antibacterial therapy for acute group a streptococcal pharyngotonsillitis: Short-course versus traditional 10-day oral regimens. Paediatr Drugs 2002;4:747–754. *Six days of amoxicillin, 4 to 5 days of cephalosporins, and 5 days of azithromycin appear to be as or more effective than traditional 10-day penicillin therapy.*

Darenberg J, Ihendyane N, Sjolin J, et al; StreptIg Study Group: Intravenous immunoglobulin G therapy in streptococcal toxic shock syndrome: A European randomized, double-blind, placebo-controlled trial. Clin Infect Dis 2003;37:333–340. *Suggestions but not proof of benefit.*

Kotb M, Norrby-Teglund A, McGeer A, et al: An immunogenetic and molecular basis for differences in outcomes of invasive group A streptococcal infections. Nat Med 2002;8:1398–1404. *Human leukocyte antigen class II allelic variation may contribute to differences in severity through their ability to regulate cytokine responses to streptococcal superantigens.*

Murray BE: Vancomycin-resistant enterococcal infections. N Engl J Med 2000;342:710–721. *This review article outlines the nuances of antibiotic resistance among enterococci and provides the rationale for treatment alternatives.*

Neuner JM, Hamel MB, Phillips RS, et al: Diagnosis and management of adults with pharyngitis. A cost-effectiveness analysis. Ann Intern Med 2003;139:113–122. *Observation, culture, and two rapid antigen test strategies for diagnostic testing and treatment in adults have very similar effectiveness and costs, but culture is the least expensive and most effective strategy when the prevalence of streptococcal pharyngitis is about 10%.*

Nielsen HU, Kolmos HJ, Frimodt-Moller N: Beta-hemolytic streptococcal bacteremia: A review of 241 cases. Scand J Infect Dis 2002;34:483–486. *In bacteremic patients with erysipelas, mortality increased from 8 to 50% when bullae were observed.*

Stevens DL: Streptococcal toxic shock syndrome. Clin Microbiol Infect 2002;8:133–136. *Overview emphasizing that early diagnosis remains a problem, and aggressive surgery often cannot be avoided.*

Infectious Diseases

309 RHEUMATIC FEVER

Alan L. Bisno

Definition

Rheumatic fever is an inflammatory disease that occurs as a delayed, nonsuppurative sequela of upper respiratory infection with group A streptococci. Its clinical manifestations include polyarthritis, carditis, subcutaneous nodules, erythema marginatum, and chorea in varying combinations. In its classic form, the disorder is acute, febrile, and largely self-limited. However, damage to heart valves may be chronic and progressive and cause cardiac disability or death many years after the initial episode.

Etiology

The development of acute rheumatic fever requires antecedent infection with a specific organism—the group A streptococcus—at a specific body site—the upper respiratory tract. Cutaneous streptococcal infection, a precursor of poststreptococcal acute glomerulonephritis, has never been shown to cause rheumatic fever.

A substantial body of evidence indicates that individual strains of group A streptococci vary in their rheumatogenic potential. In discrete epidemics of acute rheumatic fever in the United States, a limited number of group A streptococcal serotypes tend to predominate (e.g., 3, 5, 18, 24), and the infecting organisms are often heavily encapsulated, as evidenced by their growth as mucoid colonies on blood agar plates. Strains of the most common rheumatogenic serotypes share a specific surface-exposed epitope of the M-protein molecule, and elevated levels of IgM antibodies to this epitope are present in most patients with acute rheumatic fever.

Pathogenesis

The mechanism by which group A streptococci elicit the connective tissue inflammatory response that constitutes acute rheumatic fever remains unknown. Various theories have been advanced, including (1) toxic effects of streptococcal products such as streptolysins O and S, (2) inflammation mediated by antigen-antibody complexes and/or streptococcal superantigens, and (3) "autoimmune" phenomena induced by the similarity of certain streptococcal and human tissue antigens ("molecular mimicry").

Efforts to discriminate among these potential pathogenetic mechanisms have been hampered by the lack of an animal model of rheumatic fever. Most authorities currently favor the theory that the tissue damage in acute rheumatic fever is mediated by the host's own immunologic responses to the antecedent streptococcal infection. This theory is rendered more credible by the demonstration of numerous examples of antigenic similarity between somatic constituents of group A streptococci and human tissues, including heart, synovium, and neurons of the basal ganglia of the brain. Taken together, these immunologic cross-reactions could theoretically account for most of the manifestations of acute rheumatic fever. As yet, however, there is no direct evidence that any of these manifestations are pathogenetically significant.

Patients with acute rheumatic fever have, on average, higher titers of antibodies to streptococcal extracellular and somatic antigens than do patients with uncomplicated streptococcal infections. Data relating to cellular immunity are more limited. Patients with acute rheumatic fever exhibit an exaggerated cellular reactivity to streptococcal cell membrane antigens, as demonstrated by in vitro inhibition of migration of peripheral blood lymphocytes. During active rheumatic carditis, both the number of helper (CD4) lymphocytes and the ratio of CD4 to CD8 cells are increased in heart valves and peripheral blood.

Several observations suggest that development of rheumatic fever may be modulated, at least in part, by the specific genetic constitution of the host. These observations include (1) the tendency of rheumatic fever to affect more than one member of a given family, (2) the fact that acute rheumatic fever develops in only a small percentage of all individuals experiencing an immunologically significant streptococcal infection, (3) the tendency of rheumatic individuals to experience recurrent attacks, and (4) the propensity of rheumatic subjects to exhibit exaggerated immunologic responses to streptococcal antigens. To date, however, no consistent associations have been demonstrated between specific class I or class II human leukocyte antigens (HLAs) and susceptibility to acute rheumatic fever. A unique non-HLA alloantigen has been found to be strongly expressed on the B cells of virtually all patients with acute rheumatic fever but in fewer than 20% of controls.

Epidemiology

The epidemiology of acute rheumatic fever mirrors that of streptococcal pharyngitis. The peak age of incidence is 5 to 15 years, but both primary and recurrent cases occur in adults. Acute rheumatic fever is rare in children younger than 4 years, a fact that has led some observers to speculate that repetitive streptococcal infections are necessary to "prime" the host for the disease. No clear-cut gender predilection has been observed, although certain manifestations such as Sydenham's chorea and mitral stenosis are more likely to develop in females.

The frequency with which acute rheumatic fever develops following untreated group A streptococcal upper respiratory infection differs with the prevalence of highly rheumatogenic strains in the population and the epidemiologic circumstances. In the years following World War II, careful prospective studies were conducted among personnel in military camps suffering from exudative tonsillitis or pharyngitis caused by group A streptococci. Under such circumstances, in which cases of streptococcal pharyngitis tend to be clinically severe and to appear in epidemics, acute rheumatic fever developed in approximately 3% of untreated patients. Studies of endemically occurring streptococcal infection among open populations of children are complicated by the difficulties of differentiating cases of streptococcal pharyngitis from viral pharyngitis occurring in streptococcal carriers; nevertheless, the acute rheumatic fever attack rate in such circumstances is clearly lower than in the military experience, with an overall attack rate of less than 1%.

Certain features of the antecedent streptococcal infection are associated with an increased risk of acute rheumatic fever. Among these features are the magnitude of the antistreptolysin O titer increase and the persistence of the infecting organism in the pharynx. Although acute rheumatic fever is more likely to occur following clinically severe exudative pharyngitis than following mild nonexudative illness, one third or more of cases occur after streptococcal infections that are asymptomatic or so mild as to have gone unnoticed by the patient.

Patients with a history of acute rheumatic fever are prone to recurrent attacks following an immunologically significant streptococcal infection. In one long-term prospective study of subjects with a history of rheumatic fever, one of every five documented streptococcal infections gave rise to a recurrence of the disease. The risk of recurrence is greater in patients with preexisting rheumatic heart disease and in those experiencing symptomatic throat infections; the risk declines with advancing age and with increasing interval since the most recent rheumatic attack. Nevertheless, rheumatic patients remain at increased risk well into adult life.

Rheumatic fever occurs in all parts of the world, without any racial predisposition. In temperate climates, acute rheumatic fever peaks in the cooler months of the year, particularly in the winter and early spring. The major environmental factor favoring occurrence appears to be crowding, as in military barracks or similar closed institutions and large households. Crowding favors interpersonal spread of group A streptococci and perhaps enhances streptococcal virulence by frequent human passage.

Acute rheumatic fever remains rampant in developing areas such as the Middle East, the Indian subcontinent, and many nations of Africa. It has been estimated that more than 1 million people have rheumatic heart disease in India. Extremely high acute rheumatic fever attack rates occur among indigenous populations such as the Maoris of New Zealand and the Australian aborigines. In striking contrast, the incidence of acute rheumatic fever and the prevalence of rheumatic heart disease have declined both in North America and in Western Europe during the 20th century. Rates of fewer than 2 per 100,000 school children have been reported from several areas of the United States. The disease has become extremely uncommon in the affluent suburbs of many U.S. cities while persisting among lower socioeconomic groups, particularly in the densely populated core areas of major urban centers. The higher incidence rates reported for blacks than whites appears to be due to socioeconomic rather than genetic factors.

The mid-1980s, however, witnessed some startling developments in the epidemiology of acute rheumatic fever in the United States. Outbreaks of the disease were reported from many communities. The largest outbreak was in Salt Lake City and its environs, where more than 500 cases occurred between 1985 and 2001 (Veasy LG; personal communication). Equally surprising was the fact that, in many of these outbreaks, the victims were predominantly white, middle-class children dwelling in the suburbs. Moreover, epidemics of acute rheumatic fever occurred in military training bases in Missouri and California, a phenomenon that had not been observed for the previous 2 decades. Group A streptococci recovered from patients with acute rheumatic fever, their families, and community and from training camp surveys were generally highly mucoid and belonged to well-established rheumatogenic serotypes (e.g., serotypes 3 and 18). With the exception of the Salt Lake City epidemic, these outbreaks appeared to subside during the 1990s.

Pathology

Acute rheumatic fever is characterized by exudative and proliferative inflammatory lesions in connective tissue, especially connective tissue of the heart, joints, and subcutaneous tissue. The early lesions consist of edema of the ground substance, fragmentation of collagen fibers, cellular infiltration, and fibrinoid degeneration. In the heart, diffuse degeneration and even necrosis of muscle cells may be observed. At a slightly later stage, focal perivascular inflammatory lesions develop. These so-called Aschoff's nodules, considered virtually pathognomonic of rheumatic fever, consist of a central area of fibrinoid surrounded by lymphocytes, plasma cells, and large basophilic cells, some of them multinucleate. Many of these cells have elongated nuclei with a distinctive chromatin pattern, sometimes called "caterpillar" or "owl-eye" nuclei, depending on their orientation in microscopic cross section. Cells containing these nuclei are called "Anichkov's myocytes," even though most authorities believe them to be of mesenchymal origin.

Cardiac findings may include pericarditis, myocarditis, and endocarditis. Foci of coronary arteritis may also be observed. A thickened and roughened area ("MacCallum's patch") is frequently present in the left atrium above the posterior leaflet of the mitral valve. Valvular lesions appear early as small verrucae along the line of closure (Fig. 309-1). Later, as healing occurs, the valves may become thickened and deformed, the chordae shortened, and the commissures fused. These changes result in valvular stenosis or insufficiency. The mitral valve is involved most commonly, followed by the aortic, the tricuspid, and, very rarely, the pulmonic valves.

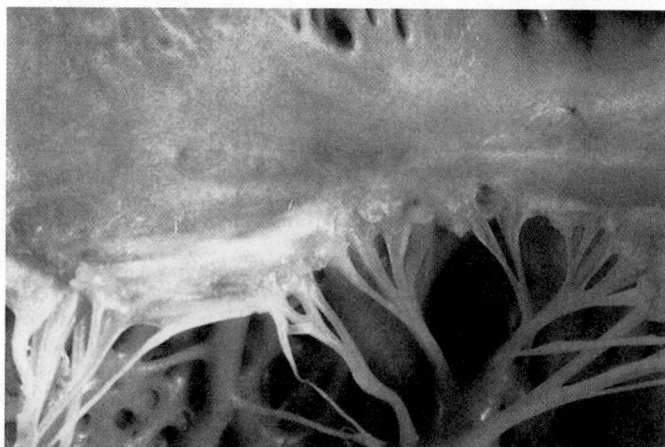

FIGURE 309-1 • Multiple verrucous vegetations along the line of mitral valve closure in a fatal case of acute rheumatic fever. (From Virmani R, Farb A, Burke AP, Narula J: Pathology of acute rheumatic fever. *In* Narula J, Virmani R, Reddy KS, Tandon R, [eds]: Rheumatic Fever. Washington, DC, American Registry of Pathology, 1999.)

Pathologically, the arthritis of acute rheumatic fever is characterized by a fibrinous exudate and sterile effusion without erosion of the joint surfaces or pannus formation. The subcutaneous nodules have many histologic features in common with Aschoff's nodules and consist of central zones of fibrinoid necrosis surrounded by histiocytes, fibroblasts, occasional lymphocytes, and rare polymorphonuclear cells. Inflammation of the smaller arteries and arterioles may occur throughout the body. Despite pathologic evidence of diffuse vasculitis, aneurysms and thrombosis are not typical features of acute rheumatic fever.

Clinical Manifestations

Rheumatic fever may involve a number of different organ systems, most notably the heart, joints, skin, subcutaneous tissue, and central nervous system. The clinical picture of the disease may thus be quite variable (Table 309-1), depending on which systems are attacked, whether they are involved singly or in combination, and the severity of the involvement. Five clinical features of the disease are so characteristic that they are recognized as "major manifestations" according to the revised Jones' criteria (see later text) for the diagnosis of acute rheumatic fever: carditis, polyarthritis, chorea, subcutaneous nodules, and erythema marginatum. Certain other findings, frequently present but nonspecific, have been designated "minor manifestations." These manifestations include arthralgia, fever, and certain laboratory findings (see later discussion).

In cases in which it can be determined, the latent period between the antecedent streptococcal infection and the onset of symptoms of acute rheumatic fever ranges between 1 and 5 weeks. The average latent period is 19 days for both primary and recurrent attacks. When acute polyarthritis is the initial complaint, the onset is often abrupt and may be marked by high fever and toxicity. If isolated carditis is the initial manifestation, the onset may be insidious or even subclinical. Between these two extremes, diverse gradations exist in the initial features of acute rheumatic fever (see Table 309-1). In most attacks, fever and joint involvement are the earliest clinical manifestations, although occasionally they may be preceded by abdominal pain localized to the periumbilical or infraumbilical areas. At times, the location and severity of the pain, as well as fleeting signs of peritoneal inflammation, may lead to a misdiagnosis of acute appendicitis. Carditis, if it is to appear, usually does so within the initial 3 weeks of the illness. In contrast, chorea tends to occur later in the course of the disease, sometimes after all other manifestations have subsided. Chorea and polyarthritis almost never occur simultaneously. Epistaxis may be a feature of acute rheumatic fever occurring both at the onset and throughout the acute phase of the illness; it may be severe.

The incidence of major manifestations varies in reported series. Overall, however, arthritis occurs in approximately 75% of initial attacks of acute rheumatic fever, carditis in 40 to 50%, chorea in 15%, and subcutaneous nodules and erythema marginatum in fewer than 10%. The frequency of individual manifestations varies with age. Carditis is more frequent in the youngest age groups and is relatively uncommon in initial attacks occurring in adults. Chorea occurs primarily in persons between age 5 and puberty. It is seen more frequently in females and virtually never occurs in adult males. Thus, the majority of acute rheumatic fever attacks occurring in adults are manifested primarily by arthritis.

Table 309-1 • THE MANY FACES OF ACUTE RHEUMATIC FEVER: POSSIBLE FEATURES

High fever, prostration, crippling polyarthritis
Lassitude, tachycardia, new cardiac murmurs
Acute pericarditis
Fulminant heart failure
Sydenham's chorea without fever or toxicity
Acute abdominal pain mimicking appendicitis
Varying combinations of the above

ARTHRITIS. Joint involvement ranges from arthralgia alone to acute, disabling arthritis characterized by swelling, warmth, erythema, severe limitation of motion, and exquisite tenderness to pressure. The larger joints of the extremities are usually involved—most frequently the knees and ankles but also the wrists and elbows. The hips and small joints of the hands and feet are affected occasionally. Involvement of shoulders and lumbosacral, cervical, sternoclavicular, and temporomandibular joints occurs in a relatively small percentage of cases. The synovial fluid contains thousands of white blood cells, with a marked preponderance of polymorphonuclear leukocytes; bacterial cultures are sterile. Characteristically, the articular involvement in acute rheumatic fever assumes a pattern of migratory polyarthritis. Migratory does not mean that inflammation in one joint disappears before the next is attacked. Rather, a number of joints are affected in succession, and the periods of involvement overlap. Inflammation in one joint may subside while another is becoming symptomatic, so the process seems to migrate from joint to joint. In untreated cases, as many as 16 joints may be affected, and arthritis develops in more than six joints in about half the patients. This classic migratory pattern is not invariable, however; in some cases, the pattern may be additive, persisting in several joints simultaneously. When effective anti-inflammatory therapy is administered early in the course of the disease, the involvement not infrequently remains monarticular or pauciarticular.

In most instances, inflammation in any one joint begins to subside spontaneously within a week, and the total duration of involvement is no more than 2 or 3 weeks. The entire bout of polyarthritis rarely lasts more than 4 weeks and resolves completely, with no residual joint damage left. Some authors have described the rare occurrence of Jaccoud's arthritis, so-called chronic post-rheumatic fever arthropathy of the metacarpophalangeal joints, following repetitive bouts of rheumatic polyarthritis. This entity is not a true arthritis but a form of periarticular fibrosis; its relationship to rheumatic fever remains unresolved.

CARDITIS. Rheumatic fever may involve the endocardium, myocardium, and pericardium (Table 309–2), and thus the disease is capable of inducing a true pancarditis. Carditis is the most important manifestation of acute rheumatic fever because it is the only one that can cause significant permanent organ damage or death. Although the clinical picture may at times be fulminant, it is more frequently mild or even asymptomatic and may escape notice in the absence of more obvious associated findings such as arthritis or chorea. The diagnosis of carditis requires the presence of one of the following four manifestations: (1) organic cardiac murmurs not previously present, (2) cardiomegaly, (3) pericarditis, or (4) congestive heart failure. In practice, the characteristic murmurs of acute rheumatic fever are almost always present in cases of rheumatic carditis, unless the ability to hear them is obscured (e.g., loud pericardial friction rub, large pericardial effusion, low cardiac output, severe tachycardia). The diagnosis of carditis should be made with caution in the absence of one of the following three murmurs: apical systolic, apical mid-diastolic, and basal diastolic. Such murmurs, if they are destined to develop, do so usually within the first week and almost always within the first 3 weeks of illness. (An exception to this rule may occur in patients with "pure" chorea; see later discussion.) The apical systolic murmur of mitral regurgitation encompasses most of systole. It is blowing, relatively high pitched, and heard best at the apex; it radiates to the axilla and at times to the base of the heart or the back. It must be carefully distinguished by quality, location, and radiation from a variety of functional precordial systolic murmurs heard in normal individuals, especially in children. The apical mid-diastolic (Carey Coombs)

murmur is a low-pitched sound replacing or immediately following the third heart sound and ending distinctly before the first heart sound. It may be heard in a variety of conditions associated with increased flow across the mitral valve and is thus not pathognomonic of acute rheumatic fever. It may be differentiated from the diastolic rumble of mitral stenosis by the absence of an opening snap, presystolic accentuation, or accentuated first sound at the mitral area. The high-pitched, decrescendo basal diastolic murmur of aortic regurgitation is best heard along the upper left sternal border or over the aortic area. It may be brief and faint but is best heard after expiration with the patient leaning forward. Some patients with acute rheumatic fever have echocardiographic evidence of mitral regurgitation in the absence of an audible murmur. This finding is not considered diagnostic of rheumatic carditis for the purpose of fulfilling the Jones' criteria, and its prognostic significance remains uncertain.

Other prominent auscultatory findings in patients with active rheumatic carditis include tachycardia, which persists during sleep; protodiastolic, presystolic, or summation gallops; an indistinct or "mushy" quality to the first heart sound; pericardial friction rub; or muffling of heart tones caused by pericardial effusion. In the early stages of congestive heart failure, rapid distention of the hepatic capsule may lead to right upper quadrant aching and tenderness over the liver. All the usual clinical findings of pericarditis or congestive failure may be observed.

A number of different rhythm disturbances may occur during the course of acute rheumatic fever. By far the most common is first-degree atrioventricular block. Second- and third-degree heart block, nodal rhythm, and premature contractions may also be observed; atrial fibrillation, on the other hand, is usually a feature of chronic rather than acute rheumatic involvement. Conduction disturbances do not in themselves indicate acute carditis, and their presence or absence is unrelated to the subsequent development of rheumatic heart disease.

Echocardiographic studies have demonstrated that, in the absence of preexisting rheumatic valvular disease, patients with acute rheumatic fever and congestive heart failure have preserved left ventricular systolic function but mitral or aortic regurgitation or both. Thus, the etiology of heart failure appears to be valvular dilatation and not myocarditis.

In cases of acute rheumatic fever with severe carditis, areas of patchy pneumonitis are sometimes seen. Many observers believe that these pulmonary infiltrates represent a specific rheumatic pneumonia. The case is difficult to prove, however, because of the confusion induced by such confounding clinical entities as pulmonary edema, pulmonary embolization, superimposed bacterial pneumonia, and acute respiratory distress syndrome in these severely ill and toxic patients.

SYDENHAM'S CHOREA (CHOREA MINOR, "ST. VITUS' DANCE"). This neurologic syndrome occurs after a latent period that is variable but on average longer than that associated with the other manifestations of acute rheumatic fever. It frequently occurs in "pure" form, either unaccompanied by other major manifestations or, after a latent period of several months, at a time when all other evidence of acute rheumatic activity has subsided. In some cases of pure chorea, echocardiographic evidence of subclinical valvular regurgitation may be present. Chorea is characterized by rapid, purposeless, involuntary movements, most noticeable in the extremities and face. The arms and legs flail about in erratic, jerky, uncoordinated movements that may sometimes be unilateral (hemichorea). Facial tics, grimaces, grins, and contortions are evident. The speech is usually slurred or jerky. The tongue, when protruded, retracts involuntarily, and asynchronous contractions of lingual muscles produce a "bag of worms" appearance. The involuntary motions disappear during sleep and may be partially suppressed by rest, sedation, or volition.

Patients with chorea display generalized muscle weakness and an inability to maintain a tetanic muscle contraction. Thus when the patient is asked to squeeze the examiner's fingers, a squeezing and relaxing motion occurs that has been described as "milkmaid's grip." The knee jerk may have a pendular quality. No cranial nerve or pyramidal involvement occurs, and sensory modalities are unaffected. The electroencephalogram may display abnormal slow wave activity.

Emotional lability is characteristic of Sydenham's chorea and may often precede other neurologic manifestations, with teachers and parents left puzzled over apparently inexplicable personality changes.

There is speculation that obsessive-compulsive disorders and/or tic disorders in children may be post-streptococcal sequelae analogous to chorea. Such an association, if it exists, remains to be demonstrated.

Table 309–2 • CLINICAL MANIFESTATIONS OF CARDITIS IN ACUTE RHEUMATIC FEVER

Murmurs*
    Apical systolic
    Apical mid-diastolic (Carey Coombs murmur)
Basal diastolic
Pericarditis
Cardiomegaly
Congestive heart failure

*At least one of the characteristic murmurs is almost always present in acute rheumatic carditis (see text for details).

SUBCUTANEOUS NODULES. These nodules are firm, painless subcutaneous lesions that vary in size from a few millimeters to approximately 2 cm. The skin overlying them is freely movable and not inflamed. The lesions tend to occur in crops over bony surfaces or prominences and over tendons. Sites of predilection include the extensor surfaces of the elbows, knees, and wrists, the occiput, and the spinous processes of the thoracic and lumbar vertebrae (Fig. 309–2). Nodules are virtually never the sole major manifestation of acute rheumatic fever; they almost always appear in association with carditis, and the cardiac involvement in such cases tends to be clinically severe. Nodules ordinarily do not appear until at least 3 weeks after the onset of an attack and persist for several weeks. They may appear in repeated crops in patients with protracted carditis. Similar nodules may be seen in systemic lupus erythematosus (SLE) and in rheumatoid arthritis. Subcutaneous nodules in the latter disease are larger and more persistent than those in rheumatic fever.

ERYTHEMA MARGINATUM. The rash begins as an erythematous macule or papule and then extends outward while the skin in the center returns to normal. Adjacent lesions coalesce and form circinate or serpiginous patterns. The lesions may be raised or flat, are neither pruritic nor indurated, and blanch on pressure. They vary greatly in size and appear mostly on the trunk and proximal parts of the extremities, with the face being spared. The lesions are evanescent, migrating from place to place, at times changing before the observer's eyes, and leaving no residual scarring. The erythema may be brought out by applying heat. Individual lesions may come and go in minutes to hours, but the process may go on intermittently for weeks to months uninfluenced by anti-inflammatory therapy. Its persistence is not necessarily an adverse prognostic sign. In most cases, erythema marginatum is accompanied by carditis; it also tends to be associated with subcutaneous nodules.

Laboratory Findings

No specific laboratory test is diagnostic of acute rheumatic fever. Usually, leukocytosis with an increase in the proportion of polymorphonuclear leukocytes is observed. A mild to moderate normocytic, normochromic anemia is the rule. Evidence of acute inflammation is prominent, including elevated serum levels of C-reactive protein and elevation of the erythrocyte sedimentation rate. An exception is pure chorea, which may appear long after indices of inflammation have returned to normal.

The urine may contain protein, white cells, and red cells. Biopsy studies have revealed a variety of renal abnormalities, but the classic proliferative glomerular abnormalities that characterize post-streptococcal acute glomerulonephritis occur rarely in acute rheumatic fever. Electrocardiographic and radiographic studies may reveal evidence of rhythm disturbances, pericarditis, or congestive heart failure. Two-dimensional echo Doppler and color flow Doppler echocardiography may document valvular dysfunction and pericardial effusion.

The major laboratory contribution to the diagnosis of acute rheumatic fever is the documentation of recent group A streptococcal infection. Throat culture should always be performed but is positive in only a minority of cases. The low rate of culture positivity remains unexplained, although it may be due in part to the time lapse of several weeks between the onset of the pharyngeal infection and the throat culture. The serum titer of antistreptolysin O is elevated in 80% or more of patients with acute rheumatic fever. If two streptococcal antibody tests (e.g., antistreptolysin O plus either anti-DNase B or anti-hyaluronidase) are performed, an elevated titer of at least one is found in 90% of patients with acute rheumatic fever. A battery of three tests establishes the presence of recent, immunologically significant streptococcal infection in more than 95% of individuals experiencing an acute rheumatic attack. The definition of an elevated titer varies, depending on the test used, the patient's age, and the geographic locale. Antistreptolysin O titers of greater than 200 Todd units per milliliter in adults and 320 Todd units in children are generally considered elevated. At times, serial sampling may detect an increasing titer of streptococcal antibodies in patients seen early in the course of a rheumatic attack.

Course and Prognosis

The average duration of an untreated attack of acute rheumatic fever is approximately 3 months. The duration tends to be longer, up to 6 months, in patients with severe carditis. Fewer than 5% of patients have continuing rheumatic activity for longer than 6 months. In a few of these patients, the disease is limited to chorea and is otherwise benign. Other patients exhibit evidence of persistent inflammatory activity, including arthritis, carditis, and subcutaneous nodules. "Chronic rheumatic fever" occurs more frequently in patients who have had one or more previous attacks; cardiac involvement in chronic rheumatic fever tends to be frequent and severe.

Congestive heart failure occurring in patients without preexisting rheumatic heart disease is not due to myocarditis per se but rather to inflammatory valvulitis and annular dilatation, accompanied in more severe cases by chordal elongation and mitral valve leaflet prolapse. Death from intractable congestive failure during the acute phase of acute rheumatic fever is rare. Once the acute attack has subsided, the only long-term sequela is that of rheumatic heart disease, manifested primarily by scarring and/or calcification of the mitral and aortic valves (Chapter 72) and leading to insufficiency and/or stenosis. The prognosis from a cardiac standpoint is related to the clinical findings when the patient is initially seen. In one large study, for example, 347 patients were examined during an acute rheumatic attack and again 10 years later. Among patients who had been free of carditis during their acute attack, only 6% had residual heart disease on follow-up. Patients with mild carditis during their acute attack (i.e., apical systolic murmur without pericarditis or heart failure) had a relatively good prognosis in that only approximately 30% had heart murmurs 10 years later. About 40% of subjects with apical or basal diastolic murmurs and 70% of subjects with heart failure and/or pericarditis during their acute attacks had residual rheumatic heart disease. The prognosis was worse in patients with preexisting rheumatic heart disease and in those who had experienced recurrent attacks of acute rheumatic fever in the 10-year interval.

These data indicate that patients in whom carditis does not develop during an acute attack and who are protected from recurrences of acute rheumatic fever are most unlikely to suffer from rheumatic heart disease. Patients with pure chorea represent an exception to this rule. Some patients who have no evidence of carditis when initially examined may have rheumatic valvular disease on prolonged follow-up. Although the explanation for this phenomenon is unknown, it is conceivable that, in view of the long latent period associated with chorea,

FIGURE 309–2 • Subcutaneous nodules over spinous processes on the back of a patient with acute rheumatic carditis. (Courtesy of S. Levine, MD.)

signs of carditis might have been present earlier but subsided by the time that the neurologic abnormality became evident. Moreover, echocardiographic studies have detected the presence of subclinical valvulitis in some of these patients.

Diagnosis

Although acute rheumatic fever is readily recognized in individuals with multiple major manifestations or in epidemic circumstances, at other times the disease may be extraordinarily difficult to diagnose with confidence because of the variability of its clinical features, the frequency with which only a single major manifestation is detected, and the fact that no definitive diagnostic laboratory test is available. Nevertheless, precise diagnosis is especially important in this disease because of the need to advise the patient regarding prolonged antimicrobial prophylaxis (see later text). The diagnostic criteria of T. Duckett Jones, initially proposed in 1944 and subsequently modified by committees of the American Heart Association, attempt to minimize overdiagnosis and underdiagnosis (Table 309–3). The most recent (1992) revision specifies that the guidelines are designed to assist in the diagnosis of the initial attack of acute rheumatic fever, but they are also applicable to patients presenting with recurrent polyarthritis or chorea. Two major manifestations or one major and two minor manifestations indicate a high probability of acute rheumatic fever if supporting evidence of recent streptococcal infection is present. Although a positive throat culture or rapid antigen test for group A streptococci technically satisfies this requirement, streptococcal carriage rates of 15% are not uncommon among school-aged children during the fall and winter. Elevated titers of antibodies to streptococcal extracellular products, although not diagnostic of acute rheumatic fever, do indicate a recent, immunologically significant streptococcal infection. Conversely, if a battery of streptococcal antibody tests fail to reveal any evidence of recent infection, the diagnosis of acute rheumatic fever must be considered unlikely.

The modified Jones' criteria are only guidelines. They are most difficult to apply confidently when polyarthritis is the single major manifestation. Under such circumstances, the diagnosis of acute rheumatic fever should be made only after excluding other causes of polyarthritis such as rheumatoid arthritis, Still's disease, Lyme disease, viral arthritides (e.g., rubella, hepatitis B), the early prepurpuric phase of Henoch-Schönlein purpura, and septic arthritis, including gonococcal arthritis. As experience grows, the echocardiographic demonstration of valvular insufficiency (using strict criteria to differentiate physiologic regurgitation) may help clarify the diagnosis in some cases. Echocardiography is of established value in the evaluation and management of acute and chronic rheumatic heart disease.

Some patients have been described as manifesting polyarthritis that is atypical in time of onset and duration, does not respond dramatically to salicylate therapy, and is unassociated with other clinical features of acute rheumatic fever. Such individuals have on occasion been categorized as having "post-streptococcal reactive arthritis." The existence of this entity as a distinct syndrome, however, and its relationship to rheumatic fever remain uncertain. Pending further clarification, such individuals should be considered to have acute rheumatic fever if they fulfill the Jones' criteria and alternative diagnoses have been excluded.

Serum sickness is frequently a serious consideration, particularly if the patient has received penicillin or other antibiotics for a preceding respiratory infection. SLE, sickle cell hemoglobinopathies, and infective endocarditis may involve the joints and the heart. Other differential diagnostic considerations include congenital heart lesions, viral and idiopathic forms of myocarditis and pericarditis, and functional heart murmurs. Nonfamilial forms of chorea have been described in SLE, rarely in association with the use of birth control pills, and in patients with neoplasms involving the basal ganglia. The involuntary jerks of Gilles de la Tourette syndrome may be confused with chorea. It remains uncertain how often episodes of chorea occurring during pregnancy ("chorea gravidarum") represent attacks of rheumatic fever. Other disorders that may at times be confused with acute rheumatic fever are gout, sarcoidosis, Hodgkin's disease, and acute leukemia.

In certain circumstances, acute rheumatic fever can be diagnosed even when the guidelines set forth in Table 309–3 have not been met. Patients whose only rheumatic manifestation is Sydenham's chorea may not fulfill the Jones' criteria. Because of the long latent period between the antecedent streptococcal infection and appearance of the neurologic abnormalities, evidence of inflammation encompassed in the minor manifestations may no longer be present, and previously elevated antibody titers may have declined to normal. A similar situation occasionally occurs in patients with indolent carditis, who may not come to medical attention until months after the onset of rheumatic fever. Moreover, it may be difficult to establish evidence of recurrent acute carditis in a patient with preexistent rheumatic heart disease, unless a different valve is affected or pericarditis is present. In such circumstances, particularly common in developing countries, a presumptive diagnosis may be made in the presence of several minor criteria plus evidence of recent streptococcal infection, providing that alternative diagnoses such as infective endocarditis are excluded.

(Rx) Treatment

Antibiotics neither modify the course of a rheumatic attack nor influence the subsequent development of carditis. Nevertheless, it is conventional to give a course of antibiotics designed to eradicate any rheumatogenic group A streptococci remaining in the tonsils and pharynx to prevent spread of the organism to close contacts. The recommended regimens are those conventionally used for the treatment of acute streptococcal pharyngitis (Chapter 308). Benzathine penicillin G is preferred in non–penicillin-allergic patients. Following completion of this therapy, continuous antistreptococcal prophylaxis should commence (see later discussion).

Treatment with anti-inflammatory agents is effective in suppressing many of the signs and symptoms of acute rheumatic fever. These agents do not "cure" the disease, nor do they prevent the subsequent evolution of rheumatic heart disease. They should be avoided in very mild or equivocal cases, because by suppressing the clinical manifestations, they may obscure the diagnosis. The two drugs most widely used are aspirin and corticosteroids. The former is used in patients with acute polyarthritis, as long as carditis is either absent or mild and no evidence of congestive heart failure is found. Aspirin is effective in decreasing fever, toxicity, and joint inflammation. It should be given in a dosage of 90 to 100 mg/kg/day in children and 6 to 8 g/day in adults administered in equally divided doses every 4 hours for the initial 24 to 36 hours; thereafter, it may be given in four doses during waking hours. Maintenance of a salicylate level of 25 mg/dL is usually satisfactory. The incidence of nausea and vomiting may be minimized by starting somewhat below the optimal dosage level and gradually increasing over a few days. The patient should be observed for evidence of significant gastrointestinal bleeding and for signs and symptoms of salicylism (e.g., hyperpnea, tinnitus). After 1 to

---

Table 309–3 • GUIDELINES FOR DIAGNOSIS OF THE INITIAL ATTACK OF RHEUMATIC FEVER (JONES' CRITERIA, UPDATED 1992)*

MAJOR MANIFESTATIONS	MINOR MANIFESTATIONS	SUPPORTING EVIDENCE OF ANTECEDENT GROUP A STREPTOCOCCAL INFECTIONS
Carditis	Clinical findings	Positive throat culture or rapid streptococcal antigen test
Polyarthritis	Arthralgia	
Chorea	Fever	
Erythema marginatum	Laboratory findings	Elevated or rising streptococcal antibody titer
Subcutaneous nodules	↑ Acute-phase reactants	
	↑ Erythrocyte sedimentation rate	
	↑ C-reactive protein	
	Prolonged PR interval	

*If supported by evidence of preceding group A streptococcal infection, the presence of two major manifestations or one major and two minor manifestations indicates a high probability of acute rheumatic fever.

From Special Writing Group of the Committee on Rheumatic Fever, Endocarditis and Kawasaki Disease, American Heart Association: Guidelines for the diagnosis of rheumatic fever: Jones criteria, 1992 update. JAMA 1992;268: 2069–2073, with permission. Copyright, 1992, American Medical Association.

2 weeks, the dosage is reduced to 60 to 70 mg/kg/day for an additional 6 weeks. These dosage schedules represent general guidelines only. The precise aspirin dose must be determined by the patient's clinical response, blood salicylate levels, and tolerance of the drug.

Corticosteroids are generally reserved for patients who have severe carditis manifested by congestive heart failure, who are unable to tolerate large doses of salicylates, or whose signs and symptoms are inadequately suppressed by aspirin. As with aspirin, the dosage must be individualized. Prednisone, 40 to 60 mg/day in divided doses, may be used initially. After 2 to 3 weeks, it should be withdrawn slowly over an additional 3-week period. In cases of fulminating carditis with profound heart failure, intravenous corticosteroids may be used, and at times emergent valve replacement may be life-saving. As for other patients receiving corticosteroids, the physician should be alert to problems such as gastrointestinal bleeding, sodium and water retention, and impaired glucose tolerance. Suppression of the pituitary-adrenal axis or the host immune system is a potential problem but not ordinarily a major one during this relatively short course of treatment. Although nonsteroidal anti-inflammatory drugs appear to be a reasonable alternative to salicylates in patients who do not require corticosteroids, there is a paucity of data on the use of these agents in acute rheumatic fever. Thus, specific regimens remain to be defined.

After cessation of anti-inflammatory therapy, clinical or laboratory evidence of acute rheumatic fever may reappear. Such therapeutic "rebounds" occur more frequently after corticosteroid therapy than after treatment with aspirin. They may be minimized by prolonging salicylate therapy for 9 to 12 weeks and, when corticosteroids have been required, by continuing aspirin for a month after corticosteroid use has been discontinued. Congestive heart failure is managed by conventional measures but with the recognition that, in patients without preexisting rheumatic heart disease, myocardial function is usually well preserved (see earlier discussion). If digitalis is used, the potential risk of drug-induced arrhythmias in patients with active myocarditis must be kept in mind. Patients with Sydenham's chorea require a quiet environment, and sedatives such as phenobarbital or diazepam may be helpful. Trials of plasmapheresis and intravenous immunoglobulin in the management of severe and intractable chorea are currently in progress.

Once the acute attack has subsided completely, the patient's subsequent level of physical activity depends on cardiac status. Patients without residual heart disease may resume full and unrestricted activity. It is important that patients not be subjected to unwarranted invalidism because of either their own inaccurate perceptions of the nature of the rheumatic process or those of parents, teachers, or employers.

Prevention

"Primary prevention" of acute rheumatic fever consists of accurate diagnosis and appropriate treatment of streptococcal sore throat (Chapter 308). Although straightforward in theory, primary prevention is often frustratingly difficult to achieve. In many of the densely populated indigent communities in which the risk of acute rheumatic fever is greatest, children with self-limited illnesses such as sore throats may never come to medical attention, and throat culture services are usually unavailable to aid in diagnosis. Moreover, in one third or more of cases, acute rheumatic fever may arise after a clinically inapparent streptococcal infection.

Perhaps the most effective strategy for avoiding the mortality and chronic cardiac disability associated with acute rheumatic fever is that of "secondary prevention." This strategy focuses on the group of persons who have already suffered a rheumatic attack and who experience a high rate of recurrence following an immunologically significant streptococcal upper respiratory infection. Recurrent attacks tend to be mimetic in nature, so patients who have suffered carditis with their previous attack are likely to have repetitive cardiac involvement and progressive cardiac damage. Because carditis with recurrent attacks of acute rheumatic fever may develop even in patients who experienced only arthritis or chorea, all patients who have experienced a documented attack of acute rheumatic fever should receive continuous antimicrobial prophylaxis to prevent either symptomatic

or asymptomatic streptococcal infections. The specific regimens to be used are indicated in Table 309–4. By far the most effective of these regimens is intramuscular benzathine penicillin G. ■ Rheumatic recurrences are unusual in compliant patients receiving an injection every 4 weeks. In areas of the world where the incidence of acute rheumatic fever and the risk of recurrence are high, however, injections every 3 weeks provide more complete protection.

The total duration of intramuscular or oral rheumatic fever prophylaxis remains unresolved. The risk of rheumatic recurrence is known to diminish with increasing age and increasing interval since the most recent rheumatic attack. Patients who escape carditis during their initial attack are less likely to experience rheumatic recurrences and are less prone to the development of carditis if a recurrence does ensue. These facts suggest that prophylaxis need not be perpetual for all rheumatic subjects. Recommendations of the American Heart Association for the duration of secondary prophylaxis are listed in Table 309–5. The decision to remove a rheumatic subject from continuous prophylaxis should be an individualized one based on the physician's assessment of the risk and probable consequences of recurrence and taken with the patient's informed consent. Particular care should be taken with those at high risk of streptococcal acquisition (e.g., parents of school children, school teachers, military recruits, nurses, pediatricians, or residents of areas with a high incidence of acute rheumatic fever). Patients taken off prophylaxis must be instructed to return immediately for medical follow-up whenever symptoms of pharyngitis occur.

Patients with rheumatic valvular heart disease must receive prophylaxis designed to avoid bacterial endocarditis whenever they undergo dental or surgical procedures likely to evoke bacteremia. Such prophylaxis is not necessary in a rheumatic subject who is free of residual heart disease. Regimens to prevent endocarditis (Chapter

---

Table 309–4 • SECONDARY PREVENTION OF RHEUMATIC FEVER (PREVENTION OF RECURRENT ATTACKS)

AGENT	DOSE	MODE
Benzathine penicillin G	1,200,000 U every 4 wk* *or*	Intramuscular
Penicillin V	250 mg twice daily *or*	Oral
Sulfadiazine	0.5 g once daily for patients ≤27 kg (60 lb)	Oral
	1.0 g once daily for patients >27 kg (60 lb)	
For Individuals Allergic to Penicillin and Sulfadiazine		
Erythromycin	250 mg twice daily	Oral

*In high-risk situations, administration every 3 weeks is justified and recommended.

From Dajani A, Tarbert K, Ferrieri P, et al: Treatment of acute streptococcal pharyngitis and prevention of rheumatic fever: A statement for health professionals. Committee on Rheumatic Fever, Endocarditis and Kawasaki Disease of the council on Cardiovascular. Disease in the Young. Pediatrics 1995; 96: 758, copyright American Academy of Pediatrics.

Table 309–5 • DURATION OF SECONDARY RHEUMATIC FEVER PROPHYLAXIS

CATEGORY	DURATION
Rheumatic fever with carditis and residual heart disease (persistent valvar disease*)	At least 10 yr since last episode and at least until age 40 yr, sometimes lifelong prophylaxis
Rheumatic fever with carditis but no residual heart disease (no valvar disease*)	10 yr or well into adulthood, whichever is longer
Rheumatic fever without carditis	5 yr or until age 21 yr, whichever is longer

*Clinical or echocardiographic evidence.

From Dajani A, Tarbert K, Ferrieri P, et al: Treatment of acute streptococcal pharyngitis and prevention of rheumatic fever: A statement for health professionals. Committee on Rheumatic Fever, Endocarditis and Kawasaki Disease of the council on Cardiovascular. Disease in the Young. Pediatrics 1995; 96: 758, copyright American Academy of Pediatrics.

Infectious Diseases

310) are different from those prescribed for preventing acute rheumatic fever, and the fact that a patient is receiving rheumatic fever prophylaxis does not exempt that patient from endocarditis prophylaxis. This concept is a frequent point of confusion not only among patients but among physicians and dentists as well.

Grade 4
1. Manyemba J, Mayosi BM: Intramuscular penicillin is more effective than oral penicillin in secondary prevention of rheumatic fever—a systematic review. S Afr Med J 2003;93:212–218.

SUGGESTED READINGS

Berrios X, Del Campo E, Guzman B, Bisno AL: Discontinuance of rheumatic fever prophylaxis in selected adolescents and young adults. Ann Intern Med 1993;118:401–406. *A prospective study and literature review of the circumstances under which rheumatic fever prophylaxis might be discontinued.*

Dinkla K, Rohde M, Jansen WT, et al: Rheumatic fever-associated Streptococcus pyogenes isolates aggregate collagen. J Clin Invest 2003;111:1905–1912. *This bacteria can bind collagen, and the presence of collagen-reactive autoantibodies in the serum of rheumatic fever patients may form a basis for post-streptococcal rheumatic disease.*

Gentles TL, Colan SD, Wilson NJ, et al: Left ventricular mechanics before and after acute rheumatic fever: Contractile dysfunction is closely related to valve regurgitation. J Am Coll Cardiol 2001;37:201–207. *A study characterizing left ventricular mechanics in acute rheumatic fever and defining the factors contributing to myocardial damage during and after the acute attack.*

Minich LL, Tani LY, Pagotto LT, et al: Doppler echocardiography distinguishes between physiologic and pathologic "silent" mitral regurgitation in patients with rheumatic fever. Clin Cardiol 1997;20:924–926. *Detailed echocardiologic criteria for differentiation of pathologic from physiologic mitral regurgitation in acute rheumatic fever patients without audible murmurs.*

Marcus RH, Sareli P, Pocock WA, Barlow JB: The spectrum of severe rheumatic mitral valve disease in a developing country. Ann Intern Med 1994;120:177–183. *A detailed analysis of the demographic, pathologic, and hemodynamic profiles of more than 700 South African patients with severe rheumatic valvular disease.*

Veasy LG, Tani LY, Hill HR: Persistence of acute rheumatic fever in the intermountain area of the United States. J Pediatr 1994;124:9–16. *A summary of the demographic and clinical data on 274 patients with acute rheumatic fever hospitalized in Salt Lake City between 1985 and 1992.*

310 INFECTIVE ENDOCARDITIS

Henry F. Chambers

Definition

Infective endocarditis (IE) is defined as an infection, usually bacterial, of the endocardial surface of the heart. IE primarily affects the cardiac valves, although in some cases the septa between the chambers may be involved. Traditionally, IE has been categorized as acute or subacute, depending on the length of symptoms prior to presentation; however, this distinction is somewhat arbitrary. A classification that considers the causative organism and the valve involved is more clinically relevant.

Epidemiology

Estimates of the incidence of IE vary according to the population studied. Most studies have found the incidence of IE in the general population to be 1.7 to 4.9 cases per 100,000 person-years. One recent study in the metropolitan Philadelphia area found the incidence of IE to be 11.6 per 100,000; however, the rate of community-acquired native valve endocarditis in the study was comparable to that from prior data at 4.45 per 100,000, and the higher overall incidence was attributed to the high prevalence of intravenous drug use in the study population. The incidence of IE among intravenous drug users (150 to 2000 cases per 100,000 person-years) is considerably higher than in the general population. IE is most common in middle-aged and elderly persons—a notable change from the preantibiotic era. Men are more frequently affected than women by a ratio of 1.7:1.

Although some patients have no clearly definable risk factor for endocarditis, cardiac conditions that cause turbulent flow at the endocardial surface or across a valve have been found to predispose patients to IE (Table 310–1). Historically, rheumatic heart disease with valvular dysfunction has been the most common underlying condition, although its contribution is diminishing in the antibiotic era—especially in developed countries. Degenerative valvular disease has

Table 310–1 • PREDISPOSING CONDITIONS ASSOCIATED WITH INCREASED RISK OF ENDOCARDITIS

MORE COMMON	LESS COMMON
Mitral valve prolapse	Rheumatic heart disease
Degenerative valvular disease	Idiopathic hypertrophic
Intravenous drug use*	subaortic stenosis
Prosthetic valve*	Pulmonary-systemic shunts*
Congenital abnormalities (valvular or septal defect)	Coarctation of the aorta
	Previous endocarditis*
	Complex cyanotic congenital heart disease*

*Indicates lesions with highest risk for endocarditis.

been associated with IE, particularly in elderly patients; the increasing relevance of senile calcification as a risk factor is reflected in the increasing proportion of aortic valve involvement in IE. Most significant congenital heart defects confer an increased risk of IE, particularly complex cyanotic disease such as single-ventricle states, transposition of the great vessels, and tetralogy of Fallot. Similarly, surgically constructed pulmonary-systemic shunts place patients at high risk for IE.

Mitral valve prolapse (MVP) is currently the most common underlying cardiac condition in IE, a statistic that reflects the high prevalence of MVP in the general population (4%). Notably, only MVP with thickened mitral leaflets and/or regurgitation increases the risk of endocarditis over that of the general population (by about 10-fold). In addition, patients with hypertrophic cardiomyopathy are at increased risk of IE, particularly in the presence of outflow obstruction. Prosthetic cardiac valves constitute a potent risk factor for IE. Older studies suggested a cumulative risk of 3 to 5.7% over the first 5 years after prosthetic valve implantation; newer data reflecting more modern operative techniques demonstrate a 1% cumulative risk over the first 12 months and a 2 to 3% risk at 5 years. Finally, previous endocarditis is a significant risk factor for further episodes of endocarditis.

In addition to these cardiac conditions, several systemic medical conditions predispose patients to the development of IE. Intravenous drug use is a well-known risk factor for IE. In patients who use intravenous drugs, human immunodeficiency virus is an independent risk factor for the development of IE, with increasing risk of IE as the CD4 count decreases. Catheter-related bacteremia is an important risk factor for nosocomial endocarditis. Patients with end-stage renal disease—particularly those receiving long-term hemodialysis—and patients with diabetes mellitus are at increased risk for IE, presumably because of the recurrent vascular access associated with the former and the low-level immunosuppression associated with both conditions.

The mitral valve has classically been the most commonly affected valve in IE, followed by the aortic valve. Although MVP remains the most common underlying condition in IE, the decreasing frequency of rheumatic mitral disease and increasing senescence of the population may account for the increase in aortic valve IE reported in many studies. The next most commonly affected valves in descending order of prevalence are the mitral and aortic valves together, the tricuspid valve, mixed right- and left-sided infection, and the pulmonic valve.

MICROBIOLOGY

Community-acquired, native valve endocarditis is due to staphylococci, streptococci, or enterococci in 90% of cases. These organisms dominate the microbiologic spectrum of IE because they express specific receptors for attachment and adherence to damaged valve surfaces and because they are normal inhabitants of the skin, oropharynx, and urogenital tract with frequent access to the bloodstream. Streptococcal species remain the most common cause of community-acquired IE unless the study population is skewed by patients from referral hospitals or urban areas or by a high number of intravenous drug users, in which case *Staphylococcus aureus* is the most common etiologic agent.

Viridans streptococci (also referred to as α-hemolytic streptococci) are the most common streptococci implicated in native valve IE. This group of organisms that normally inhabit the oropharynx includes species such as *Streptococcus sanguis*, *Streptococcus mutans*, and *Streptococcus mitis*. Group B streptococci, β-hemolytic organisms that are also normal oropharyngeal and urogenital flora, frequently cause IE in patients with cirrhosis or diabetes mellitus and in intravenous drug users. By contrast, group A streptococci, although also β-hemolytic, rarely cause endocarditis. IE related to *Streptococcus bovis*, a group D streptococcus, should prompt endoscopic evaluation for adenocarcinoma of the colon or other malignant lesions of the gastrointestinal tract. Pneumococcal endocarditis is decreasing in incidence but is quite fulminant when present; it may occur as part of Austrian's (or Osler's) triad of endocarditis, meningitis, and pneumonia and is associated with high morbidity and mortality.

S. aureus is the most common pathogen in IE associated with intravenous drug use (60% of cases); it typically causes acute endocarditis with dramatic fevers and a rapid progression over the course of several days. Of note, up to 20 to 25% of patients with community-acquired *S. aureus* bacteremia have endocarditis, and it should be considered whenever multiple blood cultures are positive for this organism. Coagulase-negative staphylococci are an unusual cause of native valve disease but an important pathogen in prosthetic valve endocarditis; presentation is usually subacute.

Enterococcal bacteremia is far more common, particularly in hospitalized patients, than enterococcal endocarditis; however, enterococci are still responsible for a significant number of cases of both community-acquired and nosocomial endocarditis. In most cases, the source of the bacteria is thought to be the genitourinary tract, and the presentation is usually subacute. Enterococcal IE, as opposed to enterococcal bacteremia, is suggested by community acquisition of infection, the absence of a clear source of infection, preexistent valvular heart disease, and the absence of polymicrobial bacteremia. As in most enterococcal infections, the overwhelming majority of cases (over 90%) are due to *Enterococcus faecalis*.

The HACEK group of gram-negative organisms (*Haemophilus* species, *Actinobacillus actinomycetemcomitans*, *Cardiobacterium hominis*, *Eikenella corrodens*, and *Kingella* species) accounts for about 5% of cases of endocarditis. These fastidious organisms usually grow in blood cultures within 7 days; however, 14 to 21 days of incubation may be required to cultivate some strains, and the microbiology laboratory should be notified that these organisms are being sought in order to hold cultures. Many other gram-negative bacilli have been reported to cause IE but are even more unusual.

Fungal endocarditis is difficult to diagnose and treat and is most commonly found in patients with a history of intravenous drug use, recent cardiac surgery, or prolonged use of indwelling vascular catheters, especially those used for total parenteral nutrition. The most common fungi found in IE are *Aspergillus* and *Candida* spp. *Aspergillus* rarely grows in blood cultures and must usually be cultured from a pathologic specimen (either an embolic site or vegetation); by contrast, *Candida* frequently grows out of blood cultures. Mortality is very high and often greater than 50%.

SPECIAL SITUATIONS: NOSOCOMIAL INFECTIVE ENDOCARDITIS AND PROSTHETIC VALVES

Nosocomial endocarditis is endocarditis acquired in the hospital; operationally, it is defined as endocarditis with onset more than 48 hours after admission to the hospital and/or related to a procedure performed in the hospital. Nosocomial endocarditis constitutes 9 to 17% of cases of IE and is most frequently associated with indwelling vascular catheters; as a result, the most common organisms implicated in nosocomial IE are *S. aureus* and coagulase-negative staphy-

Table 310–2 • ETIOLOGY OF PROSTHETIC VALVE ENDOCARDITIS (LISTED IN ORDER OF RELATIVE FREQUENCY)

EARLY (<2 mo POSTOPERATIVELY)	INTERMEDIATE (2–12 mo)	LATE (>12 mo POSTOPERATIVELY)
Coagulase-negative staphylococci	Coagulase-negative staphylococci	Streptococci
S. aureus	*S. aureus*	*S. aureus*
Gram-negative bacilli	Enterococci	Coagulase-negative staphylococci
Enterococci	*S. aureus*	Enterococci
Fungi	Fungi	
Diphtheroids	Streptococci	

lococci. In addition, a significant percentage of cases of nosocomial IE are due to enterococci and fungi.

Prosthetic valve endocarditis can be classified into one of three groups on the basis of time of onset after valve surgery: early (<2 months after surgery), intermediate (2 months to 12 months), and late (>12 months) (Table 310–2). Staphylococci, particularly coagulase-negative staphylococci, predominate during the early period, when most episodes of IE are thought to be related to perioperative infection. Gram-negatives, diphtheroids, and fungi are also relatively common during the early period. The intermediate period has a fairly similar microbiologic spectrum, with unusual gram-negatives and diphtheroids decreasing and streptococci increasing. In the late period, 1 year and more after surgery, the spectrum of organisms becomes more akin to that of community-acquired native valve disease, in which streptococci and *S. aureus* predominate, albeit with a slightly higher proportion of coagulase-negative staphylococci in the prosthetic valve group.

Pathobiology

Experimental models of IE have demonstrated that development of the disease follows a predictable sequence: endocardial damage, aggregation of platelets and fibrin to create a sterile vegetation, transient bacteremia resulting in seeding of the vegetation, and microbial proliferation on and invasion of the endocardial surface.

Most cases of IE, although not all, begin with a damaged endocardial surface. Damage to the endocardium may be caused by a number of factors, ranging from rheumatic disease to senile degeneration and calcification; indeed, any excessive turbulence or high-pressure gradient may cause injury to the nearby endocardium. Next, fibrin-platelet aggregates develop at the site of damage to form sterile vegetations, also termed nonbacterial thrombotic endocarditis (NBTE). NBTE may occur spontaneously in patients with systemic illnesses (for instance, the marantic endocarditis of malignancy or other wasting diseases or Libman-Sacks endocarditis in systemic lupus erythematosus). When transient bacteremia occurs—for instance, as a result of distant infection or gingival disease—the previously sterile vegetation may be seeded. Some bacterial species, such as staphylococci and streptococci, are more avidly adherent than others to vegetations and therefore more frequently cause IE. The bacteria then proliferate within the vegetation and ultimately may achieve an organism load of 10^9 to 10^{11} colony-forming units per gram of tissue. Because the cardiac valves are merely endothelium over fibrous tissue without a dedicated blood supply, vegetations on their surface are similarly avascular, making antibiotic therapy and healing difficult.

Clinical Manifestations

HISTORY. The initial presentation of IE varies enormously from patient to patient, making the diagnosis difficult at times. As previously mentioned, some cases develop acutely, with symptoms progressing rapidly over several days; in these cases, the clinician's index of suspicion for IE must be high because clues to the diagnosis may be masked by overwhelming sepsis. Other cases develop insidiously and present with nonspecific symptoms that have been progressing for weeks or months. In patients suspected of having IE, the initial history should include a complete review of systems, a travel history, and a thorough discussion of health-related behaviors such as illicit

drug use and sexual activity. Most patients with IE complain of fever and nonspecific constitutional symptoms such as fatigue, malaise, or weight loss. Nearly half of patients complain of musculoskeletal symptoms ranging from frank arthritis to diffuse myalgias; 5 to 10% of patients have low back pain as their chief complaint, even in the absence of osteomyelitis or epidural abscess. Many intravenous drug users with endocarditis complain of pleuritic chest pain, as tricuspid valve IE mimics pneumonia. Nosocomial IE more commonly arises with symptoms of congestive heart failure and hypotension but may also develop insidiously.

Continued

Infectious Diseases

Table 310–3 • PHYSICAL EXAMINATION AND LABORATORY FINDINGS IN INFECTIVE ENDOCARDITIS

FINDING	% OF CASES
Fever	80–95
Audible murmur	85
New or changed murmur	15–47
Neurologic abnormalities	20–40
Splenomegaly	0–60
Petechiae	20–40
Splinter hemorrhages	15
Osler's nodes	10–25
Janeway's lesions	<10
Roth's spots	<5
Anemia of chronic disease	50–90
Leukocytosis	20–66
Elevated ESR	90–100
Microscopic hematuria	50–70
Positive rheumatoid factor	40–50
Abnormal CXR (effusion, infiltrate, septic emboli)	67–85 (right-sided IE)

CXR = chest x-ray; ESR = erythrocyte sedimentation rate; IE = infective endocarditis.

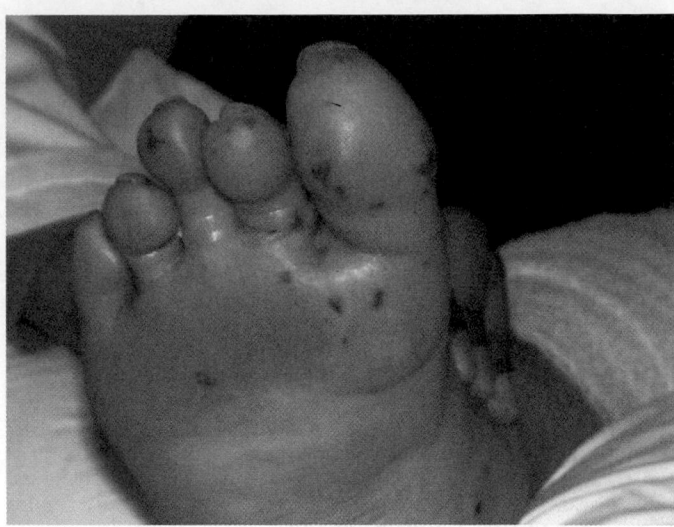

FIGURE 310–1 • Petechiae in infective endocarditis.

PHYSICAL EXAMINATION. A thorough physical examination should be performed, including a search for the peripheral stigmata of IE (Table 310–3). Fever is present in the majority of patients and in most studies approaching 95%; however, elderly patients and patients with renal failure or congestive heart failure may be less likely to mount a febrile response. A widened pulse pressure should alert the clinician to the possibility of acute aortic insufficiency. The skin should be carefully examined for embolic phenomena such as petechiae, Osler's nodes, Janeway's lesions, and splinter hemorrhages. Petechiae are most often found on the conjunctiva, palate, and the extremities; like the other peripheral stigmata of IE, they are a nonspecific but suggestive finding (Fig. 310–1). Osler's nodes are small, painful nodules found most often on the palmar surfaces of the fingers and toes; they frequently wax and wane and are rare in acute IE (Fig. 310–2). Classically considered to be an immunologic phenomenon, Osler's nodes may have an immune complex–mediated component but are most likely initiated by microemboli. Janeway's lesions are hemorrhagic, nonpainful macules most commonly found on the palms and soles; they are embolic in origin and are less frequently noted than the other cutaneous stigmata. Splinter hemorrhages are nonblanching, linear, brownish-red lesions in the nail beds perpendicular to the direction of growth of the nail; they may also be seen as a result of local trauma.

Funduscopic examination should be performed to look for Roth's spots, chorioretinitis, or endophthalmitis, the latter two of which are present in the majority of cases of fungal IE. A careful cardiac examination should be performed to detect any systolic or diastolic murmurs or evidence of congestive heart failure, which is an ominous sign. Of note, intravenous drug users are less likely than nonaddicts to have a pathologic murmur on initial presentation, although a murmur develops in most at some point during their hospitalization. The abdomen should be examined for evidence of splenomegaly. The extremities should be assessed for the presence of peripheral stigmata as mentioned earlier or evidence of congestive heart failure. Finally, a thorough neurologic examination should be performed, both to assess the patient for any focal neurologic deficit and to serve as a baseline during the hospital stay. The neurologic examination may demonstrate evidence of major vessel embolism, cranial nerve palsies, visual field defects, or a generalized toxic-metabolic encephalopathy with altered mental status.

LABORATORY FINDINGS. Initial laboratory tests should include a complete blood count with differential, a set of electrolytes and measurement of renal function, a urinalysis, a chest radiograph, and an electrocardiogram. All patients should receive at least three sets of blood cultures as well, and many require an echocardiogram during their admission (discussed later). Most patients with subacute IE have anemia of chronic disease. The white blood cell count may or may not be elevated; it is more frequently elevated in cases of acute IE, particularly if *S. aureus* or a fungus is the causative organism.

Microscopic hematuria is noted in many cases, as is proteinuria. The chest radiograph is abnormal—demonstrating consolidation, atelectasis, pleural effusion, or clear septic emboli—in the overwhelming majority of patients with right-sided endocarditis; in others, it may provide evidence of congestive heart failure. The electrocardiogram (ECG) should be carefully examined for evidence of conduction blocks, which might suggest an aortic ring abscess or other myocardial involvement, or frank myocardial infarction (MI). Other ancillary tests might include an erythrocyte sedimentation rate, which is elevated in nearly all cases of IE with a mean value of 57 mm/hr. Rheumatoid factor is positive in about half of cases, particularly in subacute IE.

COMPLICATIONS. The complications of IE may be divided into four groups for ease of classification: direct valvular damage and consequences of local invasion, embolic complications, metastatic infections from bacteremia, and immunologic phenomena. Local damage to the endocardium or myocardium can be difficult to diagnose and treat as well as potentially life-threatening. Extension of valvular infection to form a valve ring abscess is a dreaded complication that invariably requires surgical intervention; prosthetic valve infections are particularly prone to this complication. Because of the position of the aortic valve relative to the chest wall, aortic ring abscesses can be ruled out only by transesophageal echocardiography, although a conduction defect on ECG may suggest this diagnosis. Frank myocardial abscess has been found in up to 20% of cases upon autopsy; *Aspergillus* endocarditis invades the myocardium in more than 50% of cases. Pericarditis is rare and is associated with myocardial abscess in most cases. Myocardial infarction, thought to be due to embolism of vegetative material in the coronary arteries, has been found in 40 to 60% of cases upon autopsy, although most cases are clinically silent and without characteristic ECG changes. One study, however, demonstrated that up to 16% of elderly patients present with clinical evidence of MI, with potentially disastrous complications if the MI is thought to be the primary event and the patient is given thrombolytic therapy. Congestive heart failure is the leading cause of death in IE, usually related to direct valvular damage.

Embolic events are less common now than in the preantibiotic era; however, studies consistently demonstrate that 35% of patients have at least one clinically evident embolic event. In fungal endocarditis, the *majority* of patients have at least one embolic event, frequently with a large embolus. The presence of large (>10 to 15 mm) and mobile vegetations on the echocardiogram has been found in many studies to be predictive of a high risk of embolic complications. As previously discussed, most of the classical "peripheral stigmata" of IE are probably embolic in nature; in addition, patients may have frank infarction of cutaneous tissue from emboli. In addition to the skin, emboli most commonly lodge in the lungs (in right-sided IE), the kidneys, the spleen, blood vessels, or the central nervous system (CNS). Vegetations of right-sided endocarditis usually embolize to the lungs, resulting in an abnormality on the chest radiograph.

Renal abscesses are fairly rare in IE, but renal infarction appeared in more than 50% of cases upon autopsy. Similarly, splenic infarction occurs in 44% of cases; it may be silent but may cause left upper quadrant pain radiating to the left shoulder, which in some cases is the presenting symptom of IE. Of note, splenic infarction progressing to abscess may be a cause of persistent fevers in patients with IE. Vascular aneurysms, which frequently occur at bifurcation points, may be clinically silent until they rupture (which may be months to years after apparently successful antibiotic treatment of IE) and have been found in 10 to 15% of cases upon autopsy. When large emboli occlude major vessels, consider fungal or marantic endocarditis or atrial myxoma, as these tend to be associated with large vegetations. Peripheral mycotic aneurysms require surgical resection; intracerebral aneurysms should be resected if they bleed or if they are causing a mass effect.

Finally, many patients have evidence of cerebrovascular emboli, which have a predilection for the middle cerebral artery distribution and may be devastating. Most emboli to the CNS occur early in the course of the disease and are evident at the time of presentation or shortly thereafter. Cerebrovascular accidents related to these emboli are prone to catastrophic hemorrhagic transformation. The

possibility of right-sided endocarditis leading to a paradoxical CNS embolism through a patent foramen ovale should not be neglected. Of note, the majority of patients with fungal endocarditis have a CNS embolic event.

Some complications of endocarditis are a result of bacteremic seeding causing metastatic infection at a distant site. Patients may present with osteomyelitis, septic arthritis, or epidural abscess (particularly common in intravenous drug users); renal abscesses are less common. Purulent meningitis as a result of IE is rare except in cases of pneumococcal endocarditis. Intracranial abscesses are uncommon in bacterial IE but frequent in *Aspergillus* IE; the discovery of such a complication in the setting of IE with sterile blood cultures should prompt consideration of *Aspergillus* as an etiologic agent.

Multiple immunologic phenomena may occur as a result of IE, many of which are directly related to the circulating immune complexes characteristic of the disease. Renal biopsies performed in the setting of active IE show some abnormality in nearly all cases. IE classically causes a hypocomplementemic glomerulonephritis. Histopathologically, the glomerular changes may be focal, diffuse, or membranoproliferative or may be akin to the immune complex disease found in systemic lupus erythematosus. In addition, many of the musculoskeletal conditions associated with IE, including mono- and oligoarticular arthritides, are probably immune mediated.

Diagnosis

The "gold standard" for the diagnosis of IE is culture of a pathologic organism from a valve or other endocardial surface. However, unless the patient undergoes valve replacement or postmortem examination, the diagnosis of IE is made clinically. As a result, various clinical criteria have been proposed over the years to aid in the diagnosis

of IE, the most widely accepted of which are known as the Duke criteria (Tables 310–4 and 310–5). Originally developed in 1994 at Duke University, with modifications proposed in 2000 (Table 310–6), the Duke criteria have been extensively validated in numerous studies with many different populations. The sensitivity of the original Duke criteria has been estimated to be 76 to 100%, and the specificity has been uniformly found to be 88 to 100%, with a negative predictive value of at least 92%.

The Duke criteria rely heavily on the appropriate use of blood cultures and echocardiographic data. At least three sets of blood cultures should be obtained from separate sites, with each set consisting of one aerobic and one anaerobic bottle and with careful attention paid to aseptic technique. Ideally, these sets should be collected at least 1 hour apart in order to document continuous bacteremia; however, in cases in which patients are critically ill, such a leisurely pace may not be feasible.

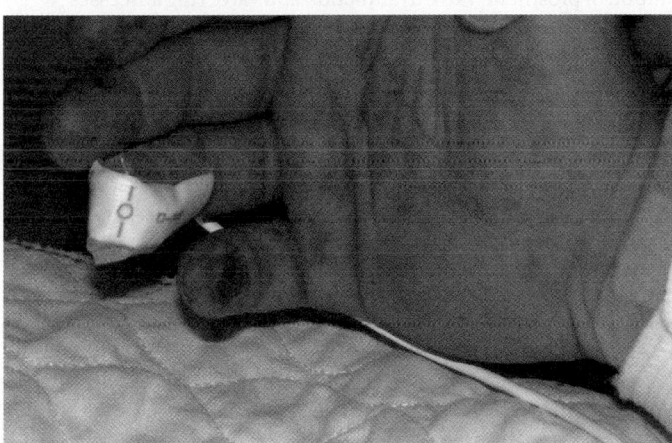

FIGURE 310–2 • Osler's node in infective endocarditis.

Table 310–4 • DUKE CRITERIA FOR THE DIAGNOSIS OF INFECTIVE ENDOCARDITIS

Definite IE	1. Pathologically proven IE
	    OR
	2. Clinical criteria (using terminology as listed in Table 310–5) meeting either
	    a. Two major criteria *or*
	    b. One major and three minor criteria *or*
	    c. Five minor criteria

Possible IE	Findings that fall short of definite IE but not rejected
Rejected IE	1. Firm alternative diagnosis *or* 2. Resolution of IE syndrome with antibiotic therapy of ≤4 days *or* 3. No pathologic evidence of IE at surgery or autopsy with antibiotic therapy of ≤4 days

IE = infective endocarditis.
Adapted from Durack DT, Lukes AS, Bright DK, et al: New criteria for diagnosis of infective endocarditis. Am J Med 1994;96:200–209.

Table 310–5 • TERMINOLOGY USED IN DUKE CRITERIA

Major criteria	1. Blood culture positive:
	    a. Typical organism (α-hemolytic streptococcus, *S. bovis*, HACEK organisms, or community-acquired *S. aureus* or enterococcus without a primary focus) from two separate blood cultures
	    OR
	    b. Persistent bacteremia with any organism (two positive cultures >12 hr apart or three positive cultures or a majority of four or more cultures >1 hr apart)
	2. Evidence of endocardial involvement
	    a. Echocardiographic findings: mobile mass attached to valve or valve apparatus, or abscess, or new partial dehiscence of prosthetic valve
	    b. New valvular regurgitation

Minor criteria	1. Predisposing condition: intravenous drug use or predisposing cardiac condition 2. Fever ≥38.0° C 3. Vascular phenomena: arterial embolism, septic pulmonary emboli, mycotic aneurysm, intracranial hemorrhage, conjunctival hemorrhages, Janeway's lesions 4. Immunologic phenomena: glomerulonephritis, Osler's nodes, Roth's spots, rheumatoid factor 5. Echocardiogram findings consistent with endocarditis but not meeting major criteria 6. Microbiologic evidence: positive blood cultures not meeting major criteria or serologic evidence of active infection consistent with endocarditis

Adapted from Durack DT, Lukes AS, Bright DK, et al: New criteria for diagnosis of infective endocarditis. Am J Med 1994;96:200–209.

Table 310–6 • PROPOSED MODIFICATIONS TO DUKE CRITERIA FOR DIAGNOSIS OF INFECTIVE ENDOCARDITIS

- The category "possible IE" should be defined as at least one major and one minor criterion or three minor criteria
- The minor criterion of echocardiographic findings consistent with endocarditis but not meeting a major criterion should be eliminated because of the widespread use of the more accurate transesophageal echocardiogram
- Bacteremia with *S. aureus* should be considered a major criterion, regardless of whether the bacteremia was nosocomially acquired or whether a removable focus of infection is found
- Positive Q fever serology should be made a major criterion

Adapted from Li JS, Sexton DJ, Mick N, et al: Proposed modifications to the Duke criteria for the diagnosis of infective endocarditis. Clin Infect Dis 2000;30:633–638.

In most cases of endocarditis, in the absence of prior antibiotic therapy, every blood culture is positive because the bacteremia of endocarditis is continuous. Blood cultures are truly negative in less than 5% of cases of endocarditis; however, prior antibiotic administration may decrease the yield of blood cultures by up to 35%. Accordingly, most "culture-negative" cases of endocarditis occur in patients who have recently received antimicrobial agents. These cases are probably caused by the same organisms responsible for most native valve IE; viridans streptococci and the HACEK organisms are the most likely suspects, as they are much more fastidious than staphylococci and enterococci and therefore more likely to be affected by previous antibiotic administration. Ultimately, however, when blood cultures are negative and endocarditis is suspected, especially when a history of recent antimicrobials is lacking, consideration should be given to fastidious organisms, fungi, and noncultivatable organisms (Table 310–7). This possibility should receive particular attention when the patient's history reveals a suggestive exposure: farm animals or unpasteurized milk (*Coxiella burnetii*, *Brucella*), cats (*Bartonella henselae*), body lice (*Bartonella quintana*), or contact with birds or frequent lawn mowing (*Chlamydia psittaci*). As mentioned before, notifying the microbiology laboratory that endocarditis is suspected is an important step in diagnosis, as special culture techniques can increase the yield for the HACEK species, nutritionally variant streptococci (*Abiotrophia* spp.), *Brucella*, *Legionella*, and some fungi. Specific serologic tests can be used to diagnose IE related to *C. burnetii* (the agent of Q fever), *Brucella* spp, *Bartonella*, and *C. psittaci*. *Tropheryma whipplei*, the etiologic agent in Whipple's disease, and multiple other organisms may be diagnosed by PCR. If the search for a causative organism remains fruitless, consider noninfectious etiologies such as marantic or Libman-Sacks endocarditis as well as atrial myxoma.

The Duke criteria are more sensitive than previous guidelines, largely as a result of their inclusion of echocardiographic findings. Both transthoracic (TTE) and transesophageal (TEE) echocardiograms have been found to be highly specific tests (~98%) when used as part of the diagnostic evaluation of suspected endocarditis. By contrast, TEE has a sensitivity of 90 to 95% in this setting, significantly better than the sensitivity of 48 to 63% found in most studies with TTE. Significant controversy still exists over whether the diagnostic approach to suspected IE should begin with a TTE or a TEE echocardiogram. In most cases in which endocarditis is a serious diagnostic consideration, evaluation should begin with TEE because a negative TTE is not sensitive enough to exclude endocarditis. In some cases, however, TEE is unavailable, technically impossible, or considered too invasive by the patient, in which case it is reasonable to begin with TTE. The American Heart Association has proposed an algorithm addressing this decision that hinges on the clinician's index of suspicion for IE (Fig. 310–3).

Some special situations may also dictate whether to begin with TTE or TEE. TEE is the only relatively noninvasive means of detecting perivalvular extension of infection, as the esophageal probe's proximity to the aortic root and basal septal wall of the myocardium allows better visualization of these structures most frequently involved in local spread of infection. For this reason, any patient with a new conduction system abnormality—the only clinical predictor of perivalvular extension—should be initially evaluated with TEE. Likewise, TEE's heightened sensitivity is especially important in the evaluation of suspected prosthetic valve endocarditis, where TEE provides superior definition of prosthetic valve dysfunction and valve ring abscesses.

The combination of negative TTE and negative TEE has a negative predictive value of 95%. Nevertheless, when clinical suspicion of endocarditis is high and the initial TEE is negative, repeating the TEE in 7 to 10 days may reveal the diagnosis.

Table 310–7 • ORGANISMS CAUSING "CULTURE-NEGATIVE" ENDOCARDITIS (LISTED IN APPROXIMATE ORDER OF RELATIVE FREQUENCY)

ORGANISM	EPIDEMIOLOGY	DIAGNOSTIC TESTS
HACEK spp	Mostly oral flora, so often preceded by dental work or history of periodontal disease	Prolonged incubation of standard blood cultures; may need to be subcultured onto blood or chocolate agar
Nutritionally variant streptococci	Slow and indolent course	Supplemented culture media or growth as satellite colonies around *S. aureus* streak
Coxiella burnetii (Q fever)	Worldwide; exposure to raw milk, farm environment, or rural areas	Serologic tests (high titers of antibody to both phase 1 and phase 2 antigens); also PCR on blood or valve tissue
Brucella spp	Ingestion of contaminated milk or milk products; close contact with infected livestock	Bulky vegetations usually seen on echocardiography. Blood cultures positive in 80% of cases with incubation time of 4–6 weeks; lysis-centrifugation technique may expedite growth. Serologic tests are available.
Bartonella spp	*B. henselae*—transmitted by cat scratch or bite or by cat fleas *B. quintane*—transmitted by human body louse; predisposing factors include homelessness and alcohol abuse	Bulky vegetations usually seen on echocardiography. Serologic testing (may cross-react with *Chlamydia* spp). PCR of valve or emboli is best test. Lysis-centrifugation technique may be useful.
Chlamydia psittaci	Exposure to birds; lawnmowing	Serologic tests available, but must exclude *Bartonella* because of cross-reactivity. Monoclonal antibody direct stains on tissue may be useful. PCR now available.
Whipple's disease (*Tropheryma whipplei*)	Systemic symptoms include arthralgias, diarrhea, abdominal pain, lymphadenopathy, weight loss, CNS involvement; however, endocarditis may be present without systemic symptoms.	Histologic examination of valve with PAS stain. Valve cultures may be done using fibroblast cell lines. Also PCR on vegetation material.
Legionella spp	Contaminated water distribution systems; often nosocomial outbreaks. Usually prosthetic valves	Lysis-centrifugation technique; also periodic subcultures onto buffered charcoal yeast extract medium. Serologic tests are available, as is PCR.
Aspergillus and other noncandidal fungi	Prosthetic valve	Lysis-centrifugation technique; also culture and direct examination of any emboli.

CNS = central nervous system; HACEK = *Haemophilus* species, *Actinobacillus actinomycetemcomitans*, *Cardiobacterium hominis*, *Eikenella corrodens*, and *Kingella* species; PAS = periodic acid–Schiff; PCR = polymerase chain reaction.

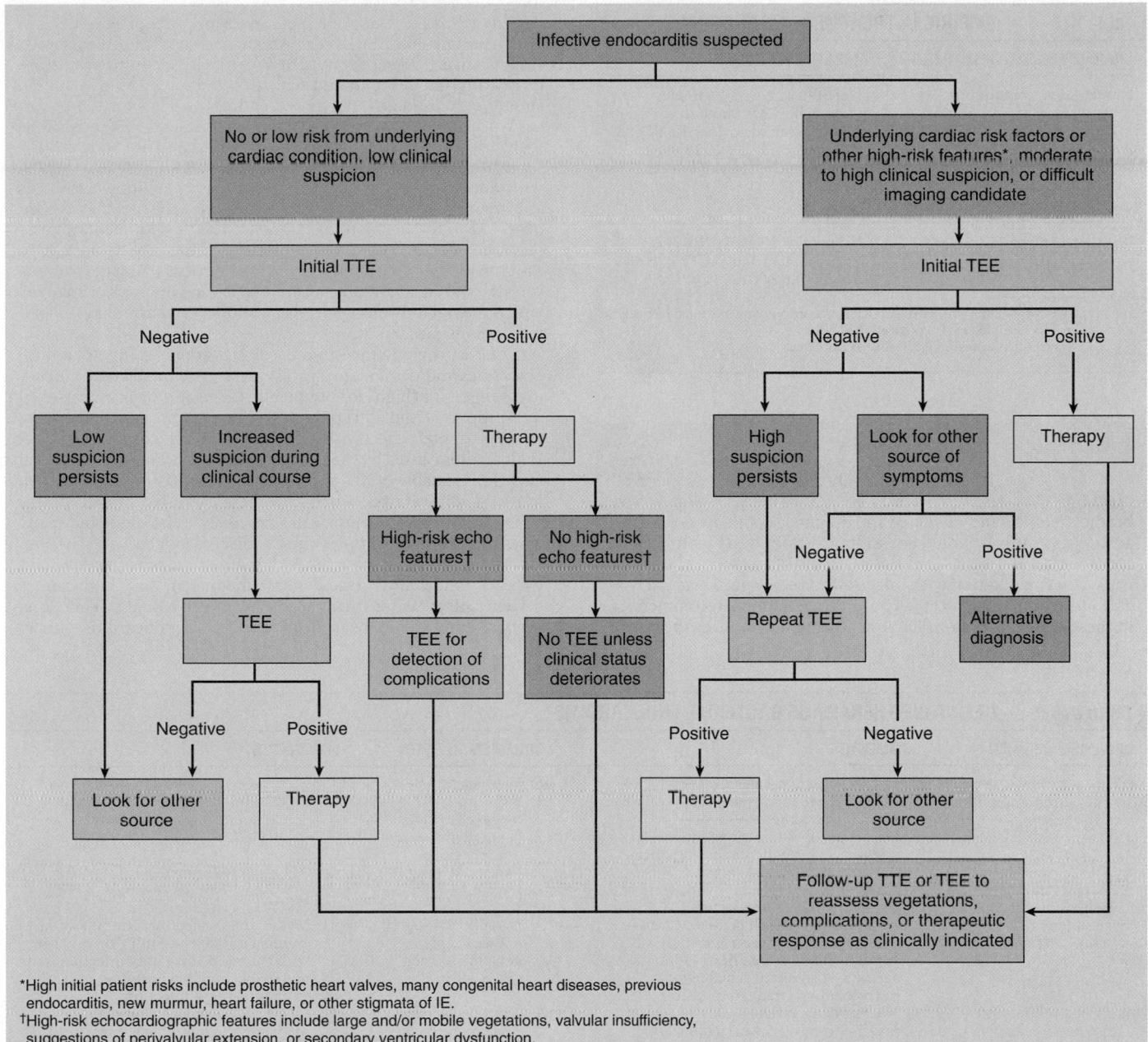

*High initial patient risks include prosthetic heart valves, many congenital heart diseases, previous
 endocarditis, new murmur, heart failure, or other stigmata of IE.
†High-risk echocardiographic features include large and/or mobile vegetations, valvular insufficiency,
 suggestions of perivalvular extension, or secondary ventricular dysfunction.

FIGURE 310–3 • Algorithm for diagnostic use of echocardiography in suspected cases of infective endocarditis. (Adapted from Bayer AS, Bolger AF, Taubert KA, et al: Diagnosis and management of infective endocarditis and its complications. Circulation 1998;98:2936–2948.)

Rx Treatment

Antibiotic treatment of IE must be guided by the isolation of the responsible organism from cultures and susceptibility determinations. Frequently, however, it is advisable to begin empirical treatment before definitive culture results are available. Not all patients admitted to rule out endocarditis need to be empirically treated; patients who are clinically stable, with a subacute presentation of disease and without evidence of congestive heart failure or other end-organ complications, may be closely observed without antibiotics so that serial blood cultures may be obtained. Likewise, stable patients who were empirically started on antibiotics before hospitalization without blood being drawn for cultures may have their antibiotics discontinued so that blood cultures may be obtained, preferably as long after stopping the antibiotics as is feasible. By contrast, acutely ill patients, patients with evidence of sequelae of IE, and patients who are at high risk for IE should be empirically treated with antibiotics pending culture results.

Either of two regimens provides appropriate empirical coverage for patients with suspected native valve endocarditis: nafcillin-penicillin-gentamicin or vancomycin-gentamicin (Table 310–8). Nafcillin-penicillin-gentamicin is suitable in most cases of suspected native valve endocarditis, providing optimal coverage for streptococci, staphylococci, enterococci, and HACEK organisms. If methicillin-resistant *S. aureus* (MRSA) is an important consideration, as it is for patients receiving hemodialysis, intravenous drug users in some cities, and patients with hospital-acquired infection, empirical therapy should be with vancomycin and gentamicin. This regimen is also acceptable for patients with a severe penicillin allergy. Patients with prosthetic valves should be empirically treated with vancomycin, gentamicin, and rifampin for adequate coverage of *S. aureus* (including MRSA), coagulase-negative staphylococci, and gram-negative organisms.

Continued

Table 310–8 • EMPIRICAL TREATMENT OF ENDOCARDITIS*

CHARACTERISTICS OF PATIENTS	TREATMENT REGIMEN
Native valve, community acquisition of infection, MRSA unlikely	Nafcillin 1.5–2 g IV q4h *plus* penicillin 3 million units IV q4h *plus* gentamicin 1 mg/kg IV q8h
Any of the following: Hospital acquisition of infection Hemodialysis patient Other reason to suspect MRSA Severe penicillin allergy	Vancomycin 1 g IV q12h *plus* gentamicin 1 mg/kg IV q8h
Prosthetic valve	Vancomycin 1 g IV q12h *plus* gentamicin 1 mg/kg IV q8h *plus* rifampin 300 mg PO/IV q8h

*Dosages for patients with normal renal function; adjustments must be made for renal insufficiency for all drugs except nafcillin.
MRSA = methicillin-resistant *Staphylococcus aureus*.

TREATMENT OF SPECIFIC ORGANISMS

When the organism is definitively identified, antibiotic treatment must be narrowed accordingly. Standardized regimens have been developed and validated for the most common organisms, and these protocols should be assiduously followed (Table 310–9). More controversy exists over the treatment of more unusual organisms, and consultation with infectious disease specialists is advisable in such circumstances. Of note, the gentamicin recommended in these regimens is so-called low dose, which reduces the risk of

toxicity while providing adequate levels for synergism. In cases in which the risk of aminoglycoside toxicity is significantly increased (for instance, elderly people, patients with preexisting renal disease or hearing impairment, and diabetics), exposure to gentamicin should be minimized or avoided entirely. In fact, for the organisms listed in Table 310–9, gentamicin has been established as truly critical for cure only in cases of enterococcal endocarditis.

In uncomplicated streptococcal endocarditis, outpatient therapy with once-daily dosing of ceftriaxone has been shown to be as effective as more complex regimens, provided the patient has been observed in the hospital for a time for the development of complications.∎ The decision to administer antimicrobial therapy in the outpatient setting must, of course, take into account the patient's social situation, likelihood of compliance, and other risks involved with either an indwelling intravenous line or recurrent peripheral intravenous placement.

Optimal therapy for enterococci that are resistant (to aminoglycosides and/or vancomycin) is not well defined. Some authorities suggest that high-dose ampicillin (20 to 30 g/day, administered by continuous infusion) plus surgical treatment may be effective in cases of enterococci with high-level aminoglycoside resistance. Endocarditis caused by vancomycin-resistant strains of enterococci may be treatable with quinupristin-dalfopristin or linezolid; however, clinical experience with these agents is limited. In this situation, relapse or failure rates are likely to be high, and many cases require surgical intervention (discussed later).

Data suggest that patients with methicillin-sensitive *S. aureus* (MSSA) endocarditis treated with vancomycin have higher rates of bacteriologic failure than those treated with nafcillin. Therefore, every attempt should be made to treat MSSA endocarditis with an

Table 310–9 • DEFINITIVE THERAPY OF BACTERIAL ENDOCARDITIS*

ORGANISM/REGIMEN	COMMENTS	ORGANISM/REGIMEN	COMMENTS
PCN-Susceptible Viridans Streptococci (MIC ≤0.1 μg/mL) and *S. bovis*		***Staphylococcus aureus***	
1. PCN 2 million units IV q4h × 4 weeks	1. Also effective for other PCN-susceptible nonviridans streptococcus	1. Nafcillin 1.5–2 g IV q4h × 4 weeks *plus* gentamicin 1 mg/kg IV q8h × 3–5 days	1. Methicillin-susceptible strain; omit gentamicin if significant renal insufficiency
2. Ceftriaxone 2 g IV qd × 4 weeks	2. Uncomplicated infection with viridans streptococci, candidate for outpatient therapy; also PCN allergy	2. Vancomycin 1 g IV q12h × 4 weeks	2. PCN allergy (immediate hypersensitivity or anaphylaxis) or MRSA
3. PCN 2 million units IV q4h × 2 weeks *plus* gentamicin 1 mg/kg IV q8h × 2 weeks	3. Uncomplicated infection with none of the following features: renal insufficiency, eighth cranial nerve deficit, prosthetic valve infection, CNS complications, severe heart failure, or age >65. Also not acceptable for nutritionally variant streptococci	3. Nafcillin 1.5–2 g IV q4h × 2 weeks *plus* gentamicin 1 mg/kg IV q8h × 2 weeks	3. Methicillin-susceptible strain; 2-week regimen only for use in IV drug abuser with tricuspid valve only infection with no renal insufficiency and no extrapulmonary infection
4. PCN 2 million units IV q4h × 4 weeks *plus* gentamicin 1 mg/kg IV q8h × 2 weeks	4. Nutritionally variant strain; for prosthetic valve, 6 weeks of PCN	4. Nafcillin 1.5–2 g IV q4h × 6 weeks *plus* gentamicin 1 mg/kg IV q8h × 2 weeks *plus* rifampin 300 mg PO/IV q8h × 6 weeks	4. Prosthetic valve infection with methicillin-susceptible strain; use vancomycin instead of nafcillin for MRSA
5. Vancomycin 1 g IV q12h × 4 weeks	5. For PCN allergy	5. Cefazolin 2 g IV q8h for 4-6 weeks	5. PCN allergy other than immediate hypersensitivity
Relatively PCN-Resistant Streptococci (MIC 0.1–1 μg/mL)		**Coagulase-Negative Staphylococci, Prosthetic Valve Infection**	
1. PCN 3 million units IV q4h × 4 weeks *plus* gentamicin 1 mg/kg IV q8h × 2 weeks		Vancomycin 1 g IV q12h × 6 weeks *plus* gentamicin 1 mg/kg IV q8h × 2 weeks *plus* rifamipin 300 mg PO/IV q8h × 6 weeks	Can substitute nafcillin in above doses for vancomycin if isolate is methicillin sensitive
2. Vancomycin 1 g IV q12h × 4 weeks	2. For PCN allergy, or to avoid gentamicin	**HACEK Strains**	
Enterococci† and PCN-Resistant Streptococci (MIC >1 μg/mL)		1. Ceftriaxone 2 g IV qd × 4 weeks; 6 weeks for prosthetic valves	
1. PCN‡ 18–24 million units IV per day in divided doses × 4 weeks *plus* gentamicin 1 mg/kg IV q8h × 4 weeks	1. Increase duration of both drugs to 6 weeks for prosthetic valve infection or symptoms longer than 3 months in enterococcal infection	2. Ampicillin 2 g IV q4h × 4 weeks *plus* gentamicin 1 mg/kg IV q8h; 6 weeks for prosthetic valves	2. Some isolates may produce β-lactamase, making this regimen less effective
2. Vancomycin 1 g IV q12h × 4 weeks *plus* gentamicin 1 mg/kg q8h × 4 weeks§	2. For PCN allergy; PCN desensitization is also an option. High risk of nephrotoxicity with this regimen.		

*Dosages for patients with normal renal function; adjustments must be made for renal insufficiency for all drugs except nafcillin, rifampin, and ceftriaxone. Gentamicin doses should be adjusted to achieve a serum concentration of 3 μg/mL 30 minutes after dosing.
†Enterococci must be tested for antimicrobial susceptibility. These recommendations are for gentamicin- or vancomycin-sensitive enterococci.
‡Ampicillin 12 g/day may be used instead of PCN.
§Need for addition of aminoglycoside has not been demonstrated for PCN-resistant streptococci.
HACEK = *Haemophilus* species, *Actinobacillus actinomycetemcomitans*, *Cardiobacterium hominis*, *Eikenella corrodens*, and *Kingella* species; MIC = minimum inhibitory concentration; MRSA = methicillin-resistant *Staphylococcus aureus*; PCN = penicillin.

antistaphylococcal β-lactam. If vancomycin must be used because of methicillin resistance or severe penicillin allergy and the patient has failed to respond clinically and remains bacteremic a week or more into therapy, the addition of a second antistaphylococcal agent (e.g., rifampin, quinupristin-dalfopristin, or an aminoglycoside) should be considered as this approach has been anecdotally effective.

In cases of presumed culture-negative endocarditis in which unusual organisms (see Table 310–7) and other infections have been reasonably excluded, and when clinical suspicion of endocarditis remains high, an empirical course of treatment for culture-negative endocarditis may be undertaken. In this situation, most authorities recommend a 4- to 6-week regimen of either ceftriaxone alone or vancomycin-gentamicin (if the clinical setting suggests MRSA or enterococcus).

CONTINUING CARE OF THE PATIENT WITH ENDOCARDITIS

In addition to antibiotics, appropriate care of the inpatient with endocarditis requires careful surveillance for the development of any complications of IE. ECGs should be obtained daily for the first several days to look for the development of conduction system disease that might herald perivalvular extension. Widening pulse pressure should alert the clinician to the possible development of acute aortic insufficiency. Similarly, a careful cardiac examination should be performed on a daily basis to assess for new regurgitant murmurs. Any new neurologic findings should prompt a search for cerebrovascular or meningeal complications of IE. Renal function should be closely monitored so that antibiotic dosage may be adjusted if necessary. If gentamicin is to be used for more than a few days, the patient should be alerted to the signs and symptoms of vestibular or otic toxicity. Serum gentamicin trough concentrations should also be assayed at regular intervals (e.g., twice weekly, and more often if renal function is changing) and should be less than 1 μg/mL. Higher concentrations suggest underlying renal insufficiency and accumulation of the drug, indicating that a lower dose should be used. Follow-up blood cultures may be indicated toward the end of the first week of therapy in patients with IE related to organisms that commonly fail first-line treatment, such as *S. aureus* and enterococci. Positive cultures in this setting might suggest the need for a change in therapy or surgical intervention, and negative cultures would be reassuring.

Patients with IE may continue to be febrile for some time after the institution of appropriate antibiotic treatment. About half of patients defervesce within 3 days of starting antibiotics, and 75% have defervesced at 1 week. By 2 weeks, 90% of patients have defervesced. Patients with endocarditis caused by *S. aureus*, gram-negative organisms, or fungi tend to defervesce more slowly than patients with IE related to other organisms. Prolonged fever (>1 week after institution of appropriate antibiotics) should prompt consideration of several possibilities other than treatment failure: perivalvular extension of infection or myocardial abscess, focal metastatic infection, drug fever, nosocomial infection, or other complications of hospitalization such as pulmonary embolism. Appropriate studies might include TEE, computed tomographic scan of the abdomen, bone scan, and urinalysis with microscopy (to elicit evidence of interstitial nephritis). Intravenous line sites should be carefully examined for evidence of infection, and indwelling central lines should be changed. In addition, blood cultures are useful at this point to document the absence of persistent bacteremia and prompt a search for other sources.

Patients who require anticoagulation present a frequent dilemma in the management of endocarditis. Anticoagulation is generally contraindicated in IE because of the increased risk of intracerebral hemorrhage at sites of embolization in patients with IE. Patients with mechanical prosthetic valve endocarditis, for instance, thus pose a management challenge. Current clinical practice, and the recommendation from the American Heart Association, is to continue careful anticoagulation in patients with mechanical valves; some authorities recommend switching from warfarin to heparin on admission so that anticoagulation may be promptly discontinued in the event of a hemorrhagic complication or surgery. The best option for patients with other indications for anticoagulation, such as deep venous thrombosis, major vessel embolization, or atrial fibrillation, is less clear and should be decided in a multidisciplinary fashion that balances the risks and benefits for each individual patient. Patients already receiving therapeutic anticoagulation at the time of admission for IE without any evidence of complications of anticoagulant treatment can probably be continued on anticoagulants. For patients with new indications for anticoagulation, delaying the initiation of anticoagulant treatment until after the first week of antibiotic therapy for IE is complete may be an option because most embolic events that would be susceptible to hemorrhagic conversion occur during this time.

SURGERY

Some patients with IE require surgical treatment, either to establish cure or to prevent death from the complications of IE. The American College of Cardiology and the American Heart Association published an evidence-based set of recommendations for selection of patients for surgical intervention (Table 310–10). Patients with evidence of direct extension of infection to myocardial structures, prosthetic valve dysfunction, or congestive heart failure from IE-induced valvular damage should in most cases undergo surgery. In addition, many cases of endocarditis caused by fungi or by gram-negative or resistant organisms (e.g., vancomycin- or gentamicin-resistant enterococci) require surgical management. Progression of disease or persistence of fever and bacteremia for more than 7 to 10 days in the presence of appro-

Continued

Table 310–10 • INDICATIONS FOR SURGERY IN ENDOCARDITIS*

INDICATION	CLASS
NATIVE VALVE ENDOCARDITIS	
1. Acute aortic insufficiency or mitral regurgitation with heart failure	I
2. Acute aortic insufficiency with tachycardia and early closure of the mitral valve on echocardiogram	I
3. Fungal endocarditis	I
4. Evidence of annular or aortic abscess, sinus or aortic true or false aneurysm	I
5. Evidence of valve dysfunction and persistent infection after a prolonged period (7–10 days) of appropriate therapy, provided there are no noncardiac causes for infection	I
6. Recurrent emboli after appropriate antibiotic therapy	IIa
7. Infection with gram-negative organisms or organisms with a poor response to antibiotics in patients with evidence of valve dysfunction	IIa
8. Mobile vegetations >10 mm	IIb
9. Early infections of the mitral valve that can probably be repaired	III
10. Persistent fever and leukocytosis with negative blood cultures	III
PROSTHETIC VALVE ENDOCARDITIS	
1. Early prosthetic valve endocarditis (<2 months after surgery)	I
2. Heart failure with prosthetic valve dysfunction	I
3. Nonstreptococcal endocarditis	I
4. Evidence of perivalvular leak, annular or aortic abscess, sinus or aortic true or false aneurysm, fistula formation, or new-onset conduction disturbances	I
5. Persistent bacteremia after 7–10 days of appropriate antibiotic therapy without noncardiac causes for bacteremia	IIa
6. Recurrent peripheral embolus despite therapy	IIa
7. Vegetation of any size seen on or near the prosthesis	IIb

*Definitions:
  Class I: Conditions for which there is evidence and/or general agreement that a given procedure or treatment is useful and effective
  Class II: Conditions for which there is conflicting evidence and/or a divergence of opinion about the usefulness/efficacy of a procedure or treatment
    IIa: Weight of evidence/opinion is in favor of usefulness/efficacy
    IIb: Usefulness/efficacy is less well established by evidence/opinion
  Class III: Conditions for which there is evidence and/or general agreement that the procedure/treatment is not useful and in some cases may be harmful
  Adapted with permission from Bonow RO, Carabello B, de Leon AC, et al: Guidelines for the management of patients with valvular heart disease. Circulation 1998;98:1949–1984.

priate antibiotic therapy may indicate the need for surgery; however, a thorough search must be conducted to rule out other foci of infection. Surgical management should also be considered for patients with recurrent (two or more) embolic events or large vegetations (>10 mm) on echocardiography with one embolic event, although the data in these situations are less convincing.

Delaying surgery in patients with deteriorating cardiac function in an attempt to "sterilize" the affected valve is ill advised, as the risk of progressive congestive heart failure or further complications usually outweighs the less than 10% risk of recurrent endocarditis after prosthetic valve implantation. Relative contraindications to valve replacement include recent massive stroke (because of the risk of bleeding in the perioperative period when anticoagulation is required), multiple prior valve replacements (because of the difficulty of sewing a new valve into tissue already weakened from previous surgeries), and ongoing intravenous drug abuse.

After definitive surgical treatment, most patients should receive some amount of further antibiotic therapy unless a full course of antibiotics has been administered before surgery and there is no evidence of ongoing infection. If the patient has received less than 1 week of antibiotics prior to surgery and/or the Gram stain or culture from the operative site is positive, a full 4- to 6-week course of antibiotics after surgery is advised. If the patient has received 2 weeks or more of therapy and the Gram stain and culture of the operative site are negative, 2 more weeks of antibiotic therapy are probably sufficient.

Prevention

Because bacteremia is a critical step in the pathogenesis of IE, logic would dictate that preventing bacteremia in patients at high risk for IE would reduce the incidence of the disease. Thus, the standard of care is to administer prophylactic antibiotics to patients with known risk factors for IE prior to procedures known to cause bacteremia. No large-scale, prospective, randomized controlled trials have been done to address the efficacy of this practice. Several small case-control studies have been performed suggesting that the practice of prescribing prophylactic antibiotics may prevent up to 10% of cases of IE. In addition, animal studies suggest that antibiotic prophylaxis is effective. Retrospective epidemiologic studies, however, have produced conflicting results in attempting to demonstrate an association between prior dental procedures, for instance, and episodes of IE. Nevertheless, in the absence of clear data showing that antibiotic prophylaxis is ineffective and with the high morbidity and mortality associated with endocarditis, antibiotic prophylaxis remains the standard of care.

In 1997, the American Heart Association published practice guidelines on the subject of which patients should receive prophylaxis, which procedures require prophylaxis, and which antibiotics should be used. Predisposing cardiac lesions were stratified on the basis of the relative risk of endocarditis into high risk, moderate risk, and negligible risk, with the first two groups requiring prophylaxis (Table 310–11). Special consideration was given in the creation of these guidelines to the issue of MVP, a highly prevalent condition that confers a small but definitely increased risk of endocarditis. Prophylaxis is recommended only in MVP patients with turbulent flow—that is, patients with MVP with an audible murmur or echocardiographic demonstration of regurgitation and patients with thickened mitral leaflets on echocardiography.

Preprocedure prophylaxis is recommended for procedures that tend to cause bleeding that introduces organisms capable of attachment to the endocardial surface—that is, staphylococci, streptococci, and enterococci (Table 310–12). Thus, many oral and genitourinary

Table 310–11 • CARDIAC LESIONS ASSOCIATED WITH ENDOCARDITIS

Endocarditis Prophylaxis Recommended

High risk	Prosthetic valves
	Previous endocarditis
	Complex cyanotic congenital heart disease, e.g., single ventricle states, transposition of the great vessels, tetralogy of Fallot
	Surgically constructed systemic-pulmonary shunts
Moderate risk	Other congenital heart defects except as below
	Acquired valvular dysfunction as follows: Valvular stenosis, at least mild aortic insufficiency, at least moderate mitral regurgitation or tricuspid regurgitation, and thickened mitral valve with at least mild mitral regurgitation
	Hypertrophic cardiomyopathy
	Mitral valve prolapse with regurgitation and/or thickened leaflets

Prophylaxis Not Recommended

Negligible risk	Isolated secundum atrial septal defect
	Surgical repair of atrial septal defect, ventricular septal defect, or patent ductus arteriosus without residua beyond 6 months
	Previous coronary artery bypass grafting
	Mitral valve prolapse without mitral regurgitation or thickened leaflets
	Physiologic, functional, or innocent heart murmurs
	Previous rheumatic fever without valvular dysfunction
	Pacemakers and implanted defibrillators

Tables 310–11 and 310–12 adapted from Dajani AS, Taubert KA, Wilson W, et al: Prevention of bacterial endocarditis: Recommendations of the American Heart Association. JAMA 1997;277:1794–1801.

Table 310–12 • PROCEDURES AND THE NEED FOR ENDOCARDITIS PROPHYLAXIS

Endocarditis Prophylaxis Recommended*
Dental
  Dental and oral procedures likely to cause significant bleeding, periodontal surgery, scaling, and professional teeth cleaning
  Intraligamentary oral local anesthetic injections
Respiratory tract
  Surgical operations that involve respiratory mucosa
  Bronchoscopy with a rigid bronchoscope
  Tonsillectomy or adenoidectomy
Gastrointestinal tract†
  Sclerotherapy for esophageal varices
  Esophageal stricture dilatation
  Endoscopic retrograde cholangiography with biliary obstruction
  Biliary tract surgery
  Surgical operations that involve intestinal mucosa
Genitourinary tract
  Prostatic surgery
  Cystoscopy
Other
  Incision and drainage of infected tissue

Endocarditis Prophylaxis Not Recommended*
Dental
  Restorative dentistry (including filling cavities and replacement of missing teeth)
  Oral local anesthetic injections
  Placement of removable prosthodontic or orthodontic appliances
  Taking of oral impressions or radiographs
  Orthodontic appliance adjustment
Respiratory tract
  Endotracheal intubation
  Bronchoscopy with flexible bronchoscope, with or without biopsy‡
  Tympanostomy tube insertion
Gastrointestinal tract
  Transesophageal echocardiography‡
  Endoscopy with or without biopsy‡
Genitourinary tract
  Vaginal hysterectomy‡
  Vaginal delivery‡
  Cesarean section
  Uninfected urethral catheterization, uterine dilation and curettage, therapeutic abortion, sterilization procedures, placement or removal of intrauterine devices
Other
  Cardiac catheterization, including angioplasty
  Implanted cardiac pacemakers, implanted defibrillators, and coronary stents
  Incision or biopsy of surgically scrubbed skin
  Circumcision

*Recommendations apply to the previously noted high- and moderate-risk patients only, except where noted.
†Prophylaxis recommended for high-risk patients, optional for moderate-risk patients.
‡Prophylaxis is optional for high-risk patients.

Table 310–13 • SUGGESTED ANTIBIOTICS FOR ENDOCARDITIS PROPHYLAXIS

Dental, Oral, Respiratory Tract, and Esophageal Procedures

Patient able to take oral medications; medication should be administered 1 hour prior to procedure	First-line therapy: amoxicillin 2 g PO For penicillin allergy: cephalexin 2 g PO (not immediate type hypersensitivity) or clindamycin 600 mg PO or azithromycin 500 mg PO or clarithromycin 500 mg PO
Patient unable to take oral medications; medication should be administered within 30 minutes before procedure	First-line therapy: ampicillin 2 g IV/IM For penicillin allergy: cefazolin 1 g IV (not for immediate-type hypersensitivity) or clindamycin 600 mg IV

Genitourinary and Nonesophageal Gastrointestinal Procedures

High-risk patients	First-line therapy: Within 30 minutes of starting procedure: ampicillin 2 g IM/IV PLUS gentamicin 1.5 mg/kg IV/IM, not to exceed 120 mg Six hours after procedure: ampicillin 1 g IM/IV OR amoxicillin 1 g PO For penicillin allergy: Completed within 30 minutes of starting procedure: vancomycin 1 g IV over 1-2 hours PLUS gentamicin 1.5 mg/kg IV/IM, not to exceed 120 mg No postprocedure dose necessary
Moderate-risk patients	First-line therapy: amoxicillin 2 g PO 1 hour prior to procedure For penicillin allergy: vancomycin 1 g IV over 1–2 hours within 30 minutes of starting procedure

Adapted from Dajani AS, Taubert KA, Wilson W, et al: Prevention of bacterial endocarditis: Recommendations of the American Heart Association. JAMA 1997;277:1794–1801.

procedures require prophylaxis, as do most procedures involving infected tissues. As an additional precaution, fastidious oral hygiene should be maintained by patients at high risk for endocarditis, both to decrease the rate of spontaneous bacteremia from gingival disease and to obviate more invasive periodontal work.

The antibiotics chosen for preprocedure prophylaxis should be active against the organisms most likely to be released into the blood stream by the procedure (Table 310–13). For dental, oral, respiratory tract, and esophageal procedures, antibiotics that cover primarily oral flora are recommended. Prophylactic regimens for genitourinary and nonesophageal gastrointestinal procedures need to cover enterococci as well and are therefore more complicated.

Prognosis

Untreated, endocarditis is a uniformly fatal disease. Aggressive medical and surgical management, however, has dramatically improved the outcome. Mortality overall from both native and prosthetic valve endocarditis remains fairly high, ranging from 17 to 36%. Certain subgroups carry a lower risk of death (endocarditis related to viridans streptococci, intravenous drug users), and S. aureus, fungal, and zoonotic endocarditis tend to be more deadly. Congestive heart failure and neurologic events are the most frequent causes of death.

The rate of relapse also varies depending on the causative organism. Easily treated infections, such as those with α-hemolytic streptococci, have a low rate of relapse (<5%), whereas more difficult to eradicate organisms may have significantly higher rates. Prosthetic valve endocarditis is the most potent risk factor for relapse. Endocarditis recurs in 12 to 16% of patients and is more common in patients who use intravenous drugs, elderly people, and those with prosthetic valves.

Future Directions

As cardiac imaging technology continues to improve, the duration of treatment of endocarditis may be dictated in part by the characteristics of visualized vegetations. In addition, now that large vegetations have been demonstrated to cause more embolic events, interventions to remove vegetations prophylactically or to introduce agents that prevent the formation or promote the dissolution of vegetations may be feasible. Finally, novel therapeutic approaches (for instance, antibacterial antibodies and cell wall–specific enzymes) that act as adjuncts to antibiotics in facilitating bacteriologic clearance are currently in development.

1. Sexton DJ, Tenenbaum MJ, Wilson WR, et al: Ceftriaxone once daily for four weeks compared with ceftriaxone plus gentamicin once daily for two weeks for treatment of endocarditis due to penicillin-susceptible streptococci. Endocarditis Treatment Consortium Group. Clin Infect Dis 1998;27:1470–1474.

SUGGESTED READINGS

Bayer AS, Bolger AF, Taubert KA, et al: Diagnosis and management of infective endocarditis and its complications. Circulation 1999;98:2936–2948. *A review of some of the dilemmas that arise in the work-up and treatment of endocarditis.*

Bayer AS, Scheld WM: Endocarditis and intravascular infections. In Mandell GL, Douglas RG, Bennett JE, Dolin R (eds): Mandell, Douglas, and Bennett's Principles and Practice of Infectious Disease, 5th ed. Philadelphia, Churchill Livingstone, 2000, pp 857–902. *An in-depth review of the topic, with emphasis on pathogenesis, microbiology, and antibiotic treatment.*

Blumberg EA, Robbins N, Adimora A, Lowy FD: Persistent fever in association with infective endocarditis. Clin Infect Dis 1992;15:983–990. *Based on case records of patients with persistent fevers; provides a suggested diagnostic algorithm.*

Brouqui P, Raoult D: Endocarditis due to rare and fastidious bacteria. Clin Microbiol Rev 2001;14:177–207. *A comprehensive review of unusual causes of endocarditis, including many "culture-negative" organisms.*

Li JS, Sexton DJ, Mick N, et al: Proposed modifications to the Duke criteria for the diagnosis of infective endocarditis. Clin Infect Dis 2000;30:633–638. *An update to the well-validated Duke criteria from 1994 that suggests modifications more in keeping with recent advances in echocardiography.*

Mylonakis E, Calderwood SB: Infective endocarditis in adults. N Engl J Med 2001; 345:1318–1330. *An excellent and current review; covers topics from epidemiology to treatment.*

Olaison L, Pettersson G: Current best practices and guidelines. Indications for surgical intervention in infective endocarditis. Cardiol Clin 2003;21:235–251. *Heart failure and progressive left-sided valvular dysfunction are the leading indications for surgery, which is required in about 25 to 30% of patients with endocarditis.*

Petti CA, Fowler VG Jr: Staphylococcus aureus bacteremia and endocarditis. Cardiol Clin 2003;21:219–233. *Suggestions for distinguishing the two entities clinically.*

Sexton DJ, Spelman D: Current best practices and guidelines. Assessment and management of complications in infective endocarditis. Cardiol Clin 2003;21:273–282. *Review of how these complications influence clinical management.*

311 STAPHYLOCOCCAL INFECTIONS

Gordon L. Archer

Staphylococcus aureus has been recognized as one of the most important and lethal human bacterial pathogens since the beginning of the 20th century. Until the antibiotic era, more than 80% of patients in whose blood *S. aureus* grew died; most of those who died had been healthy with no underlying disease. Although infections caused by coagulase-positive *S. aureus* were generally known to be potentially lethal, coagulase-negative staphylococci had been dismissed as avirulent skin commensals incapable of causing human disease. However, over the past 20 years, coagulase-negative staphylococcal infections have emerged as one of the major complications of medical progress. They are currently the pathogens most commonly isolated from infections of indwelling foreign devices and are the leading cause of hospital-acquired bacteremias in U.S. hospitals. This ascendancy of staphylococci as preeminent nosocomial pathogens has also been associated with a major increase in the proportion of these isolates that are resistant to multiple antimicrobial agents. If the trend continues, we may be forced to revisit the serious staphylococcal infections of the preantibiotic era that textbooks had long since relegated to medical history.

Bacteriology

The name *Staphylococcus* means "bunch of grapes" and describes the clusters and clumps of gram-positive cocci seen on Gram staining of both infected material and organisms recovered from culture bottles and agar plates. Staphylococci produce catalase, breaking down hydrogen peroxide to H_2O and O_2; streptococci do not. This is the definitive test for separating the two genera of gram-positive cocci. Staphylococci are nonmotile and are facultative anaerobes. The latter characteristic predicts that these organisms should grow equally well in both aerobic and anaerobic media. The coagulase test identifies the exoenzyme produced by *S. aureus* that interacts with a prothrombin-like plasma factor, converting fibrinogen to fibrin and causing plasma to clot. This is the test that traditionally separates the pathogenic species, *S. aureus*, from the numerous nonpathogenic staphylococci, collectively referred to as coagulase-negative staphylococci. However, in current practice, many clinical microbiology laboratories use rapid tests for identifying *S. aureus* that rely on the clumping of latex beads coated with plasma factors that interact with *S. aureus* cell surface components rather than coagulase.

S. aureus is a homogeneous species, as determined by biochemical testing and nucleic acid analysis, whereas coagulase-negative staphylococci are sufficiently varied to be assigned to numerous species. Coagulase-negative staphylococci are found as normal skin flora on all mammals, and 31 different and distinct species are currently recognized. Of these, 15 species are found colonizing the cornified squamous epithelium and mucous membranes of humans. Each species has a unique niche on the body, but *Staphylococcus epidermidis* is the predominant species in terms of numbers and different colonization sites. Many laboratories report specific species of coagulase-negative staphylococci to clinicians, and a list of the most prevalent human pathogenic species is shown in Table 311–1. Because only 60 to 70% of coagulase-negative species identified from specimens processed by the clinical laboratory are *S. epidermidis*, it is clearly improper to refer to coagulase-negative staphylococci as "*S. epidermidis*." However, because no specific pathogenic potential has been recognized for one coagulase-negative staphylococcus versus another, routine species identification of these organisms is useful only for purposes of epidemiology.

The complete DNA sequence of both the *S. aureus* and *S. epidermidis* genomes has been determined and is publicly available. These data should prove to be invaluable for molecular typing, for understanding the virulence of these bacteria, and for devising vaccines for disease prevention.

Epidemiology

S. aureus is carried asymptomatically on the mucous membranes in the anterior nares, nasopharynx, vagina, and/or perianal area in 20 to 40% of normal, healthy adults without underlying diseases. Carriage can be transient, lasting hours to days; intermittent, lasting weeks to months; and recurring or chronic, persisting for months to years despite attempts at eradication. Intact cornified squamous epithelium does not support intermittent or chronic carriage of *S. aureus* for reasons that are not clear but may involve bacteriostatic skin lipids, absence of *S. aureus*–specific receptors, or interference by colonizing coagulase-negative staphylococci. However, transient hand carriage clearly occurs and is an important means of exchange between patients and hospital personnel. Certain conditions have been described, however, that markedly increase skin carriage as well as nasal carriage of *S. aureus*. These include a variety of acute and chronic skin conditions, most prominently burn injuries, atopic dermatitis, eczema, psoriasis, and decubitus ulcers. In addition, needle use by persons with insulin-dependent diabetes and intravenous drug abusers has been associated with increased *S. aureus* carriage, health care workers have been found to have a higher prevalence of nasal colonization

Table 311–1 • STAPHYLOCOCCAL SPECIES FOUND ON HUMAN SKIN AND MUCOUS MEMBRANES

COAGULASE-POSITIVE	COAGULASE-NEGATIVE	
S. aureus	S. epidermidis	S. cohnii
	S. saprophyticus	S. xylosus
	S. haemolyticus	S. auricularis
	S. warneri	S. simulans
	S. capitis	S. schleiferi
	S. hominis	S. lugdanensis
	S. saccharolyticus	S. caprae
		S. pasteuri

than individuals not involved with patients or hospitals, and patients receiving chronic hemodialysis as well as patients with the acquired immunodeficiency syndrome (AIDS) have a higher than expected colonization rate.

S. aureus is extremely hardy and can survive drying, extremes of environmental temperature, wide ranges of pH, and high salt. It can therefore survive in the hospital on inanimate objects such as pillows, sheets, and blood pressure cuffs (called fomites) for some time. However, the major reservoir of *S. aureus*, in both hospitals and nature, is humans (Chapter 299).

S. aureus infections result when patients who are carriers infect themselves (autoinoculation). A study found that 82% of patients who had *S. aureus* bacteremia carried the identical strain, as determined by molecular typing, in both their blood and nares. Autoinoculation has been shown to be true for most hemodialysis shunt and peritoneal dialysis catheter infections, for infective endocarditis in intravenous drug abusers, for both individuals and families who suffer from recurrent staphylococcal furunculosis, and for sternal wound infections after cardiovascular surgery. Eradicating nasal carriage in patients by using topical mupirocin ointment has been shown to reduce the incidence of shunt infections in hemodialysis patients and recurrent furunculosis.

Coagulase-negative staphylococci colonizing the skin and mucous membranes of hospitalized patients and some hospital personnel have been shown to be more resistant to antimicrobial agents than staphylococci found on the skin of outpatients or hospital personnel not working on inpatient units. The alteration in skin flora is associated with antimicrobial use that selects more resistant organisms on patients' skin. This constitutes a huge hospital reservoir for multiple-antibiotic-resistant coagulase-negative staphylococci that can be transferred among patients, can be acquired by hospital personnel, and may eventually be inoculated into wounds in association with implanted, indwelling foreign devices.

Immunity and Pathogenesis of Infections

S. aureus causes disease syndromes by two different mechanisms. The organism can become locally or systemically invasive by producing molecules that thwart host defense mechanisms, or it can elaborate toxins that cause disease without the need for the organism itself to invade tissue (toxinoses).

LOCAL INFECTION. The hallmark of the localized staphylococcal infection is an abscess—a walled-off lesion consisting of central necrosis and liquefaction and containing cellular debris and multiplying bacteria surrounded by a layer of fibrin and intact phagocytic cells. The abscess may be superficial, in skin (furuncle), or deep, in organs (renal carbuncle), as a result of bacteremic dissemination. The factors that result in initial *S. aureus* infections are not clear; normal individuals seem to be fairly resistant to local infection. Intact cornified squamous epithelium is normally a barrier to both colonization and infection by *S. aureus*, and even injecting virulent organisms into the skin causes infection only if a foreign body (e.g., suture) is also present. Furthermore, most adult serum contains both heat-labile and heat-stable opsonins (complement and specific antibody) that are highly efficient at mediating the phagocytosis and killing of *S. aureus* by neutrophils.

Because humoral immunity and opsonophagocytosis are the body's major defense against pyogenic microorganisms such as *S. aureus*, most individuals are well equipped to resist infection. The role of neutrophils and opsonophagocytosis as the primary antistaphylococcal host defense is illustrated by patients with neutrophil defects (Chapters 181 and 298) who have an increase in *S. aureus* infection. These include defects in intracellular killing (chronic granulomatous disease and Chédiak-Higashi syndrome) and impaired neutrophil chemotaxis and humoral immunity (Job's syndrome). When the balance is tipped in favor of the organism, *S. aureus* possesses a number of factors that may produce an abscess and promote the organism's survival inside the lesion. Although no single factor has been shown to be the major abscess-forming virulence factor and mutants deficient in each of the factors have been recovered from full-blown infections, there is a general feeling that, because most of these factors differentiate the pathogenic (*S. aureus*) from nonpathogenic (coagulase-negative staphylococci) members of the genus, they probably play some coordinate role in initiating and maintaining infection. Table 311–2 outlines *S. aureus* factors that may contribute to the establishment of local infections.

Table 311–2 • S. AUREUS FACTORS THAT MAY PROMOTE LOCAL INFECTIONS BY THWARTING HOST DEFENSE

FACTOR	PROPOSED MECHANISMS FOR INTERFERING WITH HOST DEFENSE
Coagulase	Prevents neutrophil access to infection site
Microcapsule	Inhibits phagocytosis
Protein A	Inhibits IgG-mediated opsonization (binds Fc fragment)
Clumping factor (fibrinogen receptor)	Inhibits opsonization (fibrin coating)
Catalase	Interferes with intracellular killing
Proteases, nuclease, lipase, and cytolysins (α, β, and δ)	Liquefaction necrosis and phagocyte dysfunction
Leucocidin and gamma toxin	Neutrophil cytolysis
Fatty acid metabolizing enzyme	Inactivates bactericidal lipids

IgG = immunoglobulin G.

Table 311–3 • INFECTIONS CAUSED BY S. AUREUS

COMMON OR USUAL ETIOLOGIC PATHOGEN	LESS COMMON ETIOLOGIC PATHOGEN	UNCOMMON OR RARE ETIOLOGIC PATHOGEN
Furuncle or skin abscess	Cellulitis	Community-acquired pneumonia
Bullous impetigo	Hospital-acquired pneumonia	Ascending urinary tract infection
Surgical wound infection	Brain abscess	Meningitis
Hospital-acquired bacteremia	Empyema	Enterocolitis
Acute or right-sided bacterial endocarditis		
Hematogenous osteomyelitis		
Septic arthritis		
Pyomyositis		
Renal carbuncle		
Scalded skin syndrome		
Toxic shock syndrome		
Food-borne gastroenteritis (short incubation)		
Botryomycosis		
Paraspinous or epidural abscess		

DISSEMINATED INFECTION. A small percentage of local infections progress to dissemination, in which S. aureus gains access to the blood. Dissemination is characterized by bacteremia and metastatic infection. The factors leading to dissemination and the type and appearance of local infections that are more likely to disseminate are not known.

S. aureus produces such enzymes as staphylokinase (a fibrinolysin), hyaluronidase, and various proteases that may enable it to escape the abscess, invade tissue, and eventually enter the blood. Once it is in the blood, the most lethal immediate consequence is sepsis or septic shock (Chapter 104). This syndrome is mediated chiefly by enterotoxins and toxic shock syndrome toxin (TSST-1), all of which contain similar motifs (superantigens) that enable them to bind to T cells and macrophages, stimulating the production of such sepsis-associated cytokines as interleukin-1, tumor necrosis factor, and interleukin-6. All S. aureus isolates probably contain a gene for one of the many genotypes of enterotoxin or TSST-1.

One of the target cells for bacteremic S. aureus is the endothelial cell. Organisms adhere to and are internalized by endothelial cells, where, by releasing cytolysins, the bacteria can disrupt the endothelial cell layer and invade underlying tissue. S. aureus can also exist inside intact endothelial cells. The ability of the organisms to survive inside phagocytes and endothelial cells may explain their propensity to cause recurrent and refractory bacteremia despite seemingly appropriate therapy.

TOXINOSES. S. aureus produces three toxins, or classes of toxin, that produce specific syndromes without a need for the organism itself to invade and disseminate. Staphylococcal food poisoning occurs when a preformed, heat-stable enterotoxin is ingested and interacts with parasympathetic ganglia in the stomach, producing vomiting. At least 11 closely related toxin genotypes (A through K) can all produce the characteristic symptoms. Staphylococcal scalded skin syndrome results from the production of exfoliative toxin by S. aureus isolates that colonize or infect the skin of newborns. The characteristic exfoliation of the superficial stratum granulosum layer of the epidermis is due to the action of the toxin on desmosomes that hold the cells of this skin layer together. There are two exfoliating serotypes, A and B. The variety of toxic shock syndrome associated with tampon use in young women is due to TSST-1 entering into the blood through the vagina and is produced by one of several closely related clones of S. aureus that colonize the mucosa.

Diagnosis

The diagnosis of staphylococcal infections requires that the organism be seen on Gram staining of an infected specimen and be grown on artificial media, preferably in pure culture. Because coagulase-negative staphylococci are the most common contaminants of any culture obtained by crossing skin, it is important that multiple cultures grow the same organism. This is a major reason for drawing blood culture samples in pairs from two different sites. Although various tests for serum antibody to S. aureus antigens (e.g., teichoic acid antibody) have been evaluated for their ability to differentiate serious, deep-seated infection from trivial infections or self-limited bacteremia, none has proved to have a sensitivity or specificity sufficient to warrant its use as a basis for making clinical decisions.

Clinical Manifestations

S. AUREUS INFECTIONS

SKIN AND SOFT TISSUE INFECTIONS. The most common S. aureus infections are folliculitis and the furuncle, or boil (Table 311–3). These infections involve a single hair follicle or a localized area of the epidermis and dermis. Although most S. aureus furuncles are without systemic symptoms, those on the face should be treated aggressively because of their potential to migrate directly to the brain by means of the venous circulation. Furuncles can coalesce and spread through deeper skin layers or extend down to and along a fascial plane, causing a much more extensive and serious infection called a carbuncle. Carbuncles are most common over the upper back and back of the neck, where they can form multiple draining sinuses; bacteremia occurs in approximately one fourth of patients. A boil or furuncle may also be called a skin abscess if it becomes large but remains circumscribed, confined to one area, and fluctuant. A nonlocalized S. aureus skin infection is called cellulitis and may resemble the skin infections caused by Streptococcus pyogenes, the most common cause of cellulitis (Chapter 308). S. aureus cellulitis can also lead to bacteremia, proving the staphylococcal etiology of some of these infections. S. aureus cellulitis is particularly common in individuals with preexisting chronic skin disease such as stasis dermatitis and diabetic, trophic, or decubitus ulcers. Adults can also develop a form of impetigo called bullous impetigo. The lesions are characterized by erythema with a crusty surface and small or large bullous lesions. The bullae are thought to be the result of the elaboration of exfoliative toxin and are the localized, adult equivalent of the scalded skin syndrome (Ritter's disease) seen in infants.

The most common nosocomial S. aureus skin and soft tissue infection is the wound infection, in which wounds at surgical or catheter exit sites are contaminated with S. aureus and become erythematous, draining purulent or serosanguineous fluid. S. aureus is the most common and most serious cause of hospital-acquired wound infections, leading to local, deep-wound infections and systemic, metastatic infections related to bacteremia.

Continued

Recurrent furunculosis can occur in members of families, usually because of persistent nasal or perineal carriage in family members with autoinoculation of skin by scratching. The infections are commonly superficial and without systemic symptoms but are painful and annoying. Interruption is not possible until the nasal carrier state is eradicated in all family members. Although most individuals with recurrent furunculosis have normal immune systems, a syndrome called Job's syndrome (Chapter 181) is recognized in individuals with recurrent *S. aureus* furunculosis. In addition to recurrent furunculosis, patients have high levels of serum immunoglobulin E, neutrophil chemotactic defects, and a generalized disorder of immunoregulation. Adults with this syndrome usually not only describe a long history of recurrent skin infections since childhood but also often have had recurrent sinopulmonary infections.

PLEUROPULMONARY INFECTIONS. *S. aureus* is an uncommon cause of pneumonia in otherwise healthy, unhospitalized adults, accounting for less than 10% of community-acquired pneumonia. However, following influenza A infections, the incidence of *S. aureus* pneumonia markedly increases. Chest radiographs of patients with community-acquired *S. aureus* pneumonia may show abscesses and thin-walled cysts, resembling the pneumatoceles seen in infants.

In contrast to its role in community-acquired pneumonia, *S. aureus* is a prominent cause of nosocomial pneumonia, particularly in intubated patients receiving mechanical ventilation. Cultures of specimens from intubated patients obtained by techniques designed to minimize contamination of the specimens by organisms colonizing the upper airway have shown *S. aureus* in up to a third of patients. Pneumonia in ventilator-dependent patients is a particularly lethal event, with one fourth to one half of the patients dying as a direct result of their pulmonary infection. There seems to be nothing that distinguishes the radiographic appearance of nosocomial *S. aureus* pneumonia from that of pneumonia caused by other nosocomial pathogens. *S. aureus* bacteremia related solely to nosocomial pneumonia is also uncommon.

Septic pulmonary emboli in patients with right-sided *S. aureus* endocarditis (see later) can also arise as a primary pneumonia. However, these patients all have *S. aureus* bacteremia and usually have discrete lesions in multiple lobes, often accompanied by hemoptysis and chest pain.

S. aureus is cultured from the pleural space in up to 15% of adults with empyema, but it is found in pure culture in fewer than 10%. The incidence of *S. aureus* as a cause of empyema seems to have decreased overall in the past 20 years, but it is still a prominent etiologic pathogen in patients with nosocomial empyema.

ENDOCARDITIS (Chapter 310). There are two different and distinct populations who have endocarditis caused by *S. aureus*; these are compared in Table 311–4. One group consists of older patients with underlying diseases who have primarily left-sided endocarditis and have a high mortality rate (20 to 30%). Approximately half experience heart failure, half have central nervous system (CNS) manifestations, and 40 to 50% have had either a skin infection or an intravenous catheter as the presumed portal of entry. Although it is important to realize that patients with left-sided *S. aureus* endocarditis can present acutely, with symptoms compatible with the sepsis syndrome, and that *S. aureus* can infect previously normal valves, the majority of patients have had more subacute symptoms of fever, malaise, and fatigue for 1 to 2 weeks, and three fourths have evidence by history or echocardiography of previously damaged or abnormal valves. An increasing proportion of patients in this category (almost half in one series) have infected cardiac valves as a result of a hospital-acquired bacteremia (see later). Patients with nosocomial *S. aureus* endocarditis may be infected with methicillin-resistant staphylococci.

The second population in which *S. aureus* endocarditis develops consists of those who inject illicit drugs intravenously. These individuals are younger, are healthier, usually have no known valvular heart disease, and have infections of the tricuspid valve in 80 to 90% of cases. The patient, not the intravenous drug, is the source of the infecting organism. The major presenting symptoms in these patients are those of septic pulmonary emboli. The chest film typically shows multiple nodular infiltrates in various lobes that often cavitate and occasionally form pneumatoceles. Most of these patients have pure right-sided endocarditis and only rarely have any peripheral left-sided manifestations. However, a murmur of tricuspid insufficiency is heard in less than half the cases. The mortality rate is extremely low for these patients, usually only 2 to 5%, but recurrence is relatively common, given the individuals' proclivity for continued drug abuse.

BACTEREMIA. *S. aureus* is second only to coagulase-negative staphylococci as a cause of hospital-acquired bacteremia. The usual source of nosocomial bacteremia is intravenous catheters. The consequences of nosocomial bacteremia are usually only fever and malaise, but they can include endocarditis, osteomyelitis, metastatic abscesses in various organs, and death from overwhelming sepsis. Treatment, therefore, is prolonged in order to eradicate the organism from tissues and organs. Bacteremia caused by *S. aureus* is usually high grade, with the organism grown from all cultures of blood drawn over a period of time even if no endocarditis or infected foreign body is present. Furthermore, bacteremia may persist for several days even with appropriate therapy and removal of an infected catheter. This persistence is believed to be due to the organism's ability to survive host phagocytic defense and to be sequestered inside cells.

In contrast to that of nosocomial *S. aureus* bacteremia, the source of community-acquired bacteremia is often obscure. It may originate from a skin infection, an intravenous injection of illicit drugs, or an infected focus in the heart or at a peripheral site. In all patients with community-acquired *S. aureus* bacteremia, a diligent search should be made for an infected source. If none is found, patients should be treated as if they have endocarditis.

OSTEOMYELITIS (Chapter 315). *S. aureus* is the most common cause of acute hematogenous osteomyelitis. Whereas most cases occur in children, adults are also at risk, particularly those who have had documented *S. aureus* bacteremia. Children have osteomyelitis almost exclusively in long bones, whereas in adults from a third to half of the cases of hematogenous osteomyelitis are in the lumbar or thoracic vertebrae. Vertebral osteomyelitis results when *S. aureus* initially seeds the intervertebral disc space and then spreads from the disc space to involve contiguous vertebrae. A paraspinous or epidural abscess frequently occurs as an extension of the initial intervertebral focus. Patients present with fever and back pain and may have neurologic symptoms from cord compression. Radiographs typically show narrowing of one or more intervertebral disc spaces with collapse of adjacent vertebrae. A magnetic resonance imaging scan is particularly helpful in defining the extent of vertebral osteomyelitis. Long bones may be involved after hematogenous dissemination of *S. aureus*, but osteomyelitis in these locations is more typically the result of contiguous spread from an infected decubitus, trophic ulcer, or traumatic wound. One of the most common causes of *S. aureus* osteomyelitis of the foot bones is infection of ulcers in diabetics with vascular disease. Occasionally, hardware used to repair long-bone fractures becomes infected with *S. aureus*. These infections are particularly refractory to therapy without removal of the foreign body.

SEPTIC ARTHRITIS (Chapter 286). *S. aureus* is a common cause of acute septic arthritis, although spontaneous *S. aureus* septic arthritis in otherwise normal joints is usually seen in children rather than adults. In adults, *S. aureus* septic arthritis typically occurs in joints that have previously been damaged by a chronic inflammatory arthritis or osteoarthritis; that have been violated by needle aspiration, injection, or surgery; or that contain a prosthetic device. Occasionally, an otherwise normal joint is seeded by the hematogenous route or the joint space is invaded from a contiguous focus of osteomyelitis. These infections need to be differentiated from other causes of acute monarticular arthritis in adults such as gout and gonococcal infection. In all cases of septic arthritis, arthrocentesis should be performed before beginning therapy so that a specific cultural diagnosis can be made. *S. aureus* pyarthrosis can be present with relatively little systemic toxicity in patients with chronic inflammatory arthritis taking large doses of anti-inflammatory medication; this may be particularly difficult to diagnose. One unique form of *S. aureus* septic arthritis involves infection of the sternoclavicular joint and is usually seen in intravenous drug users or in patients who have had subclavian intravenous catheters.

GENITOURINARY TRACT INFECTIONS. The only important *S. aureus* infections of the genitourinary tract are those that result from hematogenous dissemination. These include microabscesses, renal carbuncles, and perinephric abscesses. The presence of *S. aureus* in the urine, therefore, is either the result of contamination in individuals asymptomatically colonized in the vagina and/or perianal area or an indication that the kidney has been infected during an episode of *S.*

Table 311–4 • *S. AUREUS* ENDOCARDITIS IN DIFFERENT POPULATIONS OF PATIENTS

CHARACTERISTICS OF PATIENTS AND DISEASE	IV DRUG ABUSERS	NON–IV DRUG ABUSERS
Mean age (yr)	30	50
Underlying disease	No	Yes
Portal of *S. aureus* entry	Skin (IV injection)	Skin (infection or IV catheter)
Valves involved	Tricuspid	Mitral, aortic
Preexisting valve abnormality	No	Yes or no
Presentation	Chest pain. fever, hemoptysis	Fever, fatigue, malaise; sepsis (less common)
Peripheral manifestations	Septic pulmonary emboli	Skin manifestations; central nervous system abnormalities; metastatic infection in bone, kidney, and spleen
Heart failure	Rare	Common
Mortality	<5%	20–30%
Treatment duration	2–3 wk	4–6 wk

IV = intravenous.

Table 311–5 • DIFFERENTIATION OF DESQUAMATING SYNDROMES

FEATURES	STAPHYLOCOCCAL SCALDED SKIN SYNDROME	TOXIC EPIDERMAL NECROLYSIS
Etiology	*S. aureus* exfoliative toxin	During hypersensitivity
Pathology	Intraepidermal cleavage plane: no inflammatory cells	Involvement of entire epidermis; infiltration with inflammatory cells
Clinical appearance	Involvement of epidermis only; positive Nikolsky's sign	Involvement of skin, mucous membranes, and multiple organs; negative Nikolsky's sign
Outcome	Low mortality; heals without scarring	High mortality; often heals with scarring

aureus bacteremia. The absence of cells in the urine should suggest contamination. However, if *S. aureus* is repeatedly cultured from urine or present in the urine together with pyuria or hematuria, the patient should be evaluated for bacteremia, for a deep focus that might have caused disseminated infection, and for an intrarenal or perinephric abscess. The presence of *S. aureus* in the urine should *never* be assumed to be secondary to an ascending urinary tract infection.

CENTRAL NERVOUS SYSTEM (CNS) INFECTIONS. Although brain abscess and meningitis can be caused by *S. aureus,* they are relatively rare. Fewer than 10% of cases of meningitis and 20 to 30% of cases of brain abscess are caused by *S. aureus.* They are usually due to metastatic seeding as a result of bacteremia from an identified focus, to direct inoculation after trauma or a neurosurgical procedure, or to infection of an indwelling foreign body, such as a ventricular shunt. The prognosis of patients infected as a result of metastatic seeding is particularly poor, with a mortality rate of 30 to 50%. The one infection associated with the CNS that is uniquely caused by *S. aureus* is a paraspinous or epidural abscess, usually secondary to vertebral osteomyelitis.

PYOMYOSITIS. Infection of the large skeletal muscles is due to *S. aureus* in more than 80% of cases. It is prevalent in tropical countries, giving it the name "tropical pyomyositis," but it is being increasingly described in temperate climates. Patients in tropical countries are usually adults who have no underlying disease and present with fever, pain, and swelling in the involved muscle, but there is often little evidence of local inflammation. Diagnosis is made by needle aspiration of pus. Because eosinophilia is common in patients in tropical countries who have pyomyositis, parasites are believed to have a role in the pathogenesis of this disease. Pyomyositis in temperate climates arises in much the same manner but more often is seen in children or in adults with underlying diseases, particularly those who have AIDS. It is associated with muscle trauma in more than half of patients and more frequently involves more than one noncontiguous muscle group.

TOXINOSES. *Staphylococcal scalded skin syndrome,* also known as Ritter's or Lyell's syndrome, is usually a disease of neonates and is due to the action of the exfoliative toxins A and B. This syndrome results from *S. aureus* colonization or local infection, usually of the umbilical stump, and causes generalized desquamation of the superficial granulosum cell layer of the epidermis. The adult equivalent is bullous impetigo, associated with localized skin involvement, but adult cases of more generalized desquamation have been described. However, it is important to differentiate staphylococcal scalded skin syndrome from toxic epidermal necrolysis. Table 311–5 contrasts the two syndromes.

The *toxic shock syndrome* was initially described in young, menstruating women and was associated with tampon use in women vaginally colonized with *S. aureus* that produced TSST-I. However, the number of tampon-associated cases has decreased markedly. The majority of cases are now secondary to *S. aureus* infections of skin or other sites, and the etiologic toxin is often one of the enterotoxins rather than TSST-I. The criteria for the diagnosis of staphylococcal toxic shock syndrome are shown in Table 311–6. Staphylococcal toxic shock syndrome is associated with relatively low mortality and is a true toxinosis; bacteremia is rare.

Gastroenteritis or *staphylococcal food poisoning* is due to ingesting preformed staphylococcal enterotoxin. Enterotoxin-producing *S. aureus* are inoculated into food by a colonized or infected food handler. If the food sits at room temperature before being cooked, the organism multiplies and produces toxin. Subsequent cooking does not inactivate the heat-stable toxin, and ingestion produces symptoms predominantly of vomiting after a short (2 to 8 hours) incubation period.

MISCELLANEOUS INFECTIONS. The older literature describes "botryomycosis," a chronic *S. aureus* infection of skin, lung, or bone that produces granules resembling those seen in actinomycosis, and "enterocolitis," a necrotizing infection of bowel in surgical patients associated with sheets of organisms seen on Gram staining of stool. These infections are rarely seen today.

COAGULASE-NEGATIVE STAPHYLOCOCCAL INFECTIONS

The major infections caused by coagulase-negative staphylococci are hospital acquired and involve indwelling foreign devices. Table 311–7 outlines the characteristics of these infections. In general, coagulase-negative staphylococci are of low virulence, rarely causing metastatic infections, even though they are the most common cause of hospital-acquired bacteremia. Bacteremia is usually the result of intravascular catheter infection. However, coagulase-negative staphylococci can be lethal when they infect prosthetic cardiac valves. They are the most common cause of prosthetic valve endocarditis, arising in the first year after surgery, presumably inoculated into the area of the sewing ring during valve implantation. Valve dysfunction results from dehiscence or obstruction of the valve orifice, and most patients require surgery for cure. The exceptions to infections described in Table 311–7 are those caused by *S. saprophyticus*. This organism is second only to *Escherichia coli* as a cause of ascending urinary tract infections in young, sexually active female outpatients, implicated in 15 to 20% of cases in this population. In addition, low colony counts of this staphylococcal species have been recovered from urine obtained by suprapubic aspiration in some women with the anterior urethral syndrome or symptomatic abacteriuria.

Infectious Diseases

Table 311–6 • DIAGNOSTIC CRITERIA FOR STAPHYLOCOCCAL TOXIC SHOCK SYNDROME

1. Fever (usually >38.9° C or 102° F)
2. Rash (diffuse macular erythroderma, sunburn or scarlet fever–like)
3. Desquamation, 1 to 2 weeks after onset of illness, particularly of palms and soles
4. Hypotension (systolic blood pressure <90 mm Hg or orthostatic syncope)
5. Involvement of three or more of the following organ systems: gastrointestinal (nausea and vomiting), muscular (myalgias), mucous membrane (hyperemia), renal, hepatic, hematologic (↓ platelets), central nervous system, or pulmonary (adult respiratory distress syndrome)
6. *S. aureus* infection or mucosal colonization

Table 311–7 • CHARACTERISTICS OF COAGULASE-NEGATIVE STAPHYLOCOCCAL INFECTIONS

1. Hospital acquired
2. Caused by species *S. epidermidis* (70–80%)
3. Resistant to multiple antimicrobial agents (>80% methicillin resistant)
4. Involve indwelling foreign devices (catheters, prosthetic heart valves and joints, vascular grafts)
5. Exhibit a long latent period between device contamination and clinical presentation

Table 311–8 • ANTIMICROBIAL AGENTS EFFECTIVE FOR TREATING *S. AUREUS* INFECTIONS

AGENTS	RESISTANCE* Hospital-Acquired	Community-Acquired
Penicillin G	>90	>90
Antistaphylococcal penicillins and cephalosporins	50	10–30
Erythromycin	60	20
Clindamycin	60	20
Sulfamethoxazole-trimethoprim	20	S
Tetracycline	20	10
Minocycline	S	S
Doxycycline	S	S
Quinupristin (Synercid)	S	S
Linezolid	S	S
Rifampin	S	S
Gentamicin	30	S
Quinolones	40	S
Vancomycin	S	S

*Numbers are percentage of isolates from patients with hospital-acquired or community-acquired infections resistant to each agent; S = >95% susceptible.

Treatment

Antimicrobial agents effective for treating *S. aureus* infections are listed in Table 311–8. Treatment of hospital-acquired infections is limited by resistance to many of these agents. Methicillin-resistant isolates are *cross-resistant* to *all β-lactams* (penicillins, cephalosporins, and carbapenems (imipenem and meropenem) and are usually also resistant to at least three additional classes of antimicrobial agents (multiresistant). However, although only 40 to 50% of nosocomial *S. aureus* isolates are methicillin resistant, more than 70% of nosocomial coagulase-negative staphylococci are methicillin resistant and multiresistant. Thus, whereas the treatment of hospital-acquired *S. aureus* infections should be guided by susceptibility testing, infections caused by nosocomial coagulase-negative staphylococci are usually treated with vancomycin. Vancomycin is the only antimicrobial agent to which some isolates of *S. aureus* and coagulase-negative staphylococci are susceptible, and it is, therefore, the mainstay of therapy for infections caused by methicillin-resistant organisms. However, there have been reports of a few patients in the United States and several other countries who have been infected with *S. aureus* and coagulase-negative staphylococci that have markedly reduced susceptibilities to vancomycin, requiring concentrations of the drug up to eight times that of susceptible isolates for inhibition of bacterial growth to occur. When treatment of these infections with vancomycin is unsuccessful, the appearance of these isolates signals an unfortunate trend toward reduced vancomycin susceptibility among staphylococci, and will have a major impact on chemotherapy.

Another disturbing trend is the increase in outpatient infections caused by methicillin-resistant staphylococci. Many of these infections are in patients who have had recent exposure to a health care or extended care facility, but some infections are truly community acquired, occurring in patients with no obvious health care association.

Treating staphylococcal infections usually consists of administering antimicrobial agents, surgical or catheter drainage of abscesses, and removal of foreign bodies. The duration of therapy is usually 1 to 2 weeks for localized, drained infections not associated with bacteremia or a foreign body. In general, infections can rarely be cured if the foreign material is left in place. Infections requiring more specialized therapeutic decisions are discussed in the following.

BACTEREMIA AND ENDOCARDITIS. For *S. aureus,* all patients with community-acquired bacteremia who have evidence of a metastatic infection or who have no obvious source for bacteremia should be treated as if they have endocarditis. For intravenous drug abusers with right-sided endocarditis, treatment consists of 2 to 3 weeks of an antistaphylococcal penicillin (nafcillin or oxacillin) or vancomycin plus gentamicin for the entire treatment period; for left-sided endocarditis, 4 to 6 weeks of an antistaphylococcal penicillin or vancomycin, with gentamicin for the first week. However, in patients with *S. aureus* bacteremia acquired in the hospital from a removable focus (usually an intravascular catheter), the decision becomes more difficult. The patients whose fever and bacteremia resolve within 3 days after removing the infected focus, those who have no complications or evidence of metastatic infection, and those who have no abnormality of cardiac valves can receive 2 weeks of therapy. All other patients with nosocomial bacteremia who do not meet all the exclusions should be treated as if they have endocarditis (Chapter 310).

OSTEOMYELITIS. Patients with *S. aureus* osteomyelitis require a minimum of 6 weeks of therapy, with the initial 2 to 4 weeks being parenteral. Therapy for osteomyelitis of long bones is often unsuccessful if sequestra are left in place.

Prevention

Preventing hospital-acquired infections is accomplished by paying attention to tenets of infection control. These include handwashing and regloving between patients and strict adherence to aseptic technique when creating or caring for any kind of wound. Patients undergoing procedures that may result in wound or implanted device infections should also receive prophylactic antibiotics before and during the procedure. Patients with recurrent *S. aureus* infections of skin, catheters, or dialysis shunts should have their nares cultured, and if they are *S. aureus* carriers, they should be treated with topical mupirocin ointment. Chronic carriers resistant to topical *S. aureus* eradication may be given oral rifampin plus sulfamethoxazole-trimethoprim, a fluoroquinolone, or minocycline.

SUGGESTED READINGS

Archer GL: *Staphylococcus epidermidis* and other coagulase-negative staphylococci. In Mandell RD, Bennett JE (eds): Principles and Practices of Infectious Diseases, 5th ed. New York, Churchill Livingstone, 2000, pp 2092–2100. *A detailed chapter.*
Chambers HF: Methicillin resistance in staphylococci. Molecular and biochemical basis and clinical implications. Clin Microbiol Rev 1997;10:781–791. *A good review on antistaphylococcal chemotherapy and resistance of staphylococci to the action of therapeutic agents.*

Crossley KB, Archer GL (eds): The Staphylococci in Human Disease. New York, Churchill Livingstone, 1997. *The definitive source for a more detailed discussion of the biology, clinical presentation, and therapy for staphylococcal infections.*

Fowler VG Jr, Olsen MK, Corey GR, et al: Clinical identifiers of complicated *Staphylococcus aureus* bacteremia. Arch Intern Med 2003 (in press). *A helpful scheme for deciding when bacteremia is likely to lead to complications.*

Von Eiff C, Becker K, Machka K, et al: Nasal carriage as a source of *Staphylococcus aureus* bacteremia. N Engl J Med 2001;344:11-16. *The best study done to date documenting the importance of autoinfection in the pathogenesis of serious* S. aureus *infections.*

312 BACTERIAL MENINGITIS

Morton N. Swartz

Meningitis is an inflammation of the arachnoid, the pia mater, and the intervening cerebrospinal fluid (CSF). The inflammatory process extends throughout the subarachnoid space about the brain and spinal cord and regularly involves the ventricles. Pyogenic meningitis, considered in this chapter, is usually an acute infection with bacteria that evoke a polymorphonuclear response in the CSF. One of its major forms, that caused by meningococci, is considered in Chapter 297; less acute forms of bacterial meningitis, characterized by a mononuclear cell response in the CSF, are discussed in Chapters 326 and 448.

Etiology and Incidence

In the 1970s and 1980s about 20,000 cases of bacterial meningitis occurred annually in the United States. This changed dramatically in the 1990s, when the number of cases of community-acquired bacterial meningitis was reduced by 55%. This reduction was the result primarily of the introduction of routine immunization of infants with the *Haemophilus influenzae* type b polysaccharide-protein conjugate vaccines, which effected a 94% decrease in the number of cases of *H. influenzae* meningitis. As a consequence of *H. influenzae* meningitis having been a disease of infancy and childhood, its virtual elimination raised the median age of persons with bacterial meningitis from 15 months in 1986 to 25 years in 1995. In the 1970s and 1980s, data from the Centers for Disease Control indicated that, if all cases were included regardless of the age of patients, *H. influenzae* type b was the most frequent bacterial cause (45%), followed by *Streptococcus pneumoniae* (18%) and *Neisseria meningitidis* (14%); by 1995, *S. pneumoniae* (47%) had become the most common agent, followed by *N. meningitidis* (25%) and group B *Streptococcus (Streptococcus agalactiae)* (12%).

The relative frequencies with which the different bacterial species cause community-acquired meningitis are dependent on age (Fig. 312–1). Currently, in the neonatal period group B *Streptococcus* is the

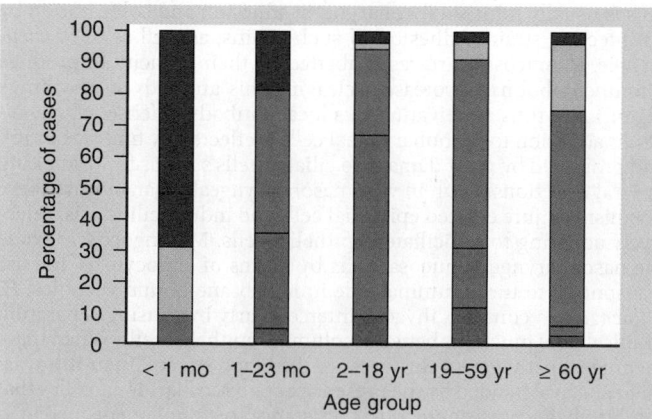

Figure 312–1 • Pathogenic agents of bacterial meningitis by age group: Red = group B *streptococcus;* yellow = *Listeria monocytogenes;* blue = *Streptococcus pneumoniae;* green = *Neisseria meningitidis;* brown = *Haemophilus influenzae.* Meningitis caused by *Escherichia coli* or other enteric pathogens among infants younger than 1 month of age is not included in the surveillance data. (From Schuchat A, Robinson K, Wenger JD, et al: Bacterial meningitis in the United States in 1995. N Engl J Med 1997;337:970–976. Copyright 1997, Massachusetts Medical Society. All rights reserved.)

leading pathogen (almost 70%) followed by *Escherichia coli,* most commonly possessing the K1 envelope antigen, and *Listeria monocytogenes.* Thereafter, up through 23 months of age the principal causes are *S. pneumoniae* (45%) and *N. meningitidis* (31%). In persons 2 to 18 years of age, *N. meningitidis* (59%) is the major cause; and in individuals older than 18 years *S. pneumoniae* (62%) is the most common cause. *L. monocytogenes* accounts for 8% of cases of bacterial meningitis overall but has peak frequencies (about 20%) in the neonatal period and in those 60 years of age and older. Group B *Streptococcus* has been noted as the etiology with increasing frequency of late in adults, commonly those older than 50 years and with comorbid conditions.

Meningococcal meningitis is the only type that occurs in outbreaks; its relative frequency among the meningitides depends on whether statistics have been gathered in a hyperendemic area or during epidemic or interepidemic periods. In about 10% of patients with pyogenic meningitis, the bacterial cause cannot be defined. Simultaneous mixed bacterial meningitis is rare, occurring in the setting of neurosurgical procedures, penetrating head injury, erosion of the skull or vertebrae by adjacent neoplasm, or intraventricular rupture of a cerebral abscess; the isolation of anaerobes should strongly suggest the latter two of these.

Important changes have also occurred in the frequencies of several other types of bacterial meningitis over the past 30 years. Gram-negative bacillary meningitis has doubled in frequency in adults, reflecting more frequent and extensive neurosurgical procedures as well as other nosocomial factors. *L. monocytogenes* has increased 8- to 10-fold as a cause of bacterial meningitis as seen in large urban general hospitals, reflecting the enlarging immunosuppressed population at particular risk. *Listeria* infections appear to be food-borne (dairy products, uncooked vegetables) and involve particularly organ transplant recipients, patients in hemodialysis units, other patients receiving corticosteroids and cytotoxic drugs, patients with liver disease, pregnant women, and neonates. Meningitis caused by coagulase-negative staphylococci, essentially unheard of 30 years ago, now represents about 3% of cases in large urban hospitals. It occurs as a complication of neurosurgical procedures and may present a particular therapeutic problem because of the methicillin resistance of many of the involved strains. Rarely, bacterial meningitis complicates invasive neurodiagnostic (e.g., myelographic) and therapeutic procedures (spinal puncture and rhizotomy). Whereas in the past those infections were usually due to *Pseudomonas aeruginosa,* other gram-negative bacilli, and *Staphylococcus aureus,* currently, viridans streptococci are the agents most often associated with meningitis complicating diagnostic myelography and percutaneous trigeminal rhizotomy.

In large urban tertiary care general hospitals, the distribution of bacterial causes of adult meningitis differs from that in smaller community hospitals, where community-acquired disease predominates. For example, at the Massachusetts General Hospital about 40% of cases of bacterial meningitis in adults are of nosocomial origin. In this category, the leading causes are gram-negative bacilli (primarily *E. coli* and *Klebsiella*), accounting for about 40% of nosocomial episodes, and various streptococci, *S. aureus,* and coagulase-negative staphylococci, each responsible for 10% of nosocomial cases.

Clinical Settings

The clinical setting in which meningitis develops may provide a clue to the specific bacterial cause. Meningococcal disease, including meningitis, may occur sporadically and in cyclic outbreaks. In the past, military recruits were particularly susceptible, but now meningococcal vaccine (polysaccharides of groups A, C, Y, and W135) is employed for their protection. Other high-risk groups include those living in close quarters such as crowded classrooms, jails, or freshman college dormitories (meningococcal vaccine recently advised for the latter). Meningococcal infections occur worldwide in endemic form. In industrialized countries, serogroups C and B (the latter particularly of one clonal complex) have accounted for the majority of infections. In third-world countries, serogroups A and, to a lesser extent, C are dominant. In sub-Saharan Africa, the so-called meningitis belt, recurrent yearly waves of serogroup A meningococcal infections occur. A large epidemic related to serogroup A occurred in 1987 at the hajj in Mecca, and since then pilgrims at this crowded annual gathering have been at increased risk.

Certain predisposing factors are frequently associated with the development of *pneumococcal meningitis. Acute otitis media* (with or without *mastoiditis*) occurs in about 20% of adult patients. *Pneumonia* is present in about 15% of patients with pneumococcal meningitis, a much higher frequency than in meningitis caused by *H. influenzae* or *N. meningitidis*. *Acute pneumococcal sinusitis* is occasionally the initial focus from which infection spreads to the meninges. A significant head injury (recent or remote) has occurred in about 10% of episodes of pneumococcal meningitis. CSF rhinorrhea (usually caused by a defect or fracture in the cribriform plate) is present in about 5% of patients with pneumococcal meningitis. Meningitis occurring in young children with sickle cell anemia is most likely to be caused by *S. pneumoniae*. A variety of defects in host defenses (primary or acquired immunoglobulin deficiencies, the asplenic state, human immunodeficiency virus [HIV] infection) may predispose to severe pneumococcal disease, particularly bacteremia and meningitis. Alcoholism is an underlying problem in 10 to 25% of adults with pneumococcal meningitis in urban hospitals. In one study, the estimated annual incidence of bacterial meningitis (primarily pneumococcal) among HIV-infected patients was 150-fold higher than in the general population.

S. aureus meningitis is seen most commonly as a complication of a neurosurgical procedure, after penetrating skull trauma, or occasionally secondary to staphylococcal bacteremia and endocarditis. Meningitis caused by *gram-negative bacilli* takes one of three forms: neonatal meningitis, meningitis after trauma or neurosurgery, or spontaneous meningitis in adults (e.g., bacteremic *Klebsiella* meningitis in a patient with diabetes mellitus). The most common causes of gram-negative bacillary meningitis in the adult are *E. coli* (about 30%) and *Klebsiella-Enterobacter* (about 40%). The most frequent causes of bacterial meningitis in patients with neoplastic disease are gram-negative bacilli (particularly *P. aeruginosa* and *E. coli*), *L. monocytogenes*, *S. pneumoniae*, and *S. aureus*. Meningitis caused by group A streptococci is uncommon but occasionally occurs after acute otitis media, more often in children than adults.

In the past, the age-related incidence (children younger than 5 years) of *H. influenzae* type b meningitis has been so striking that the occurrence of this disease in an adult has raised, and should still raise, the question of the presence of an underlying anatomic or immunologic defect, circumventing the usual barrier interposed by serum bactericidal mechanisms.

Neonatal Meningitis

The incidence of meningitis is higher in the first month of life than in any other single month. In the newborn, the group B *Streptococcus* can produce either an "early-onset" (occurring within 8 days of delivery and characterized by a fulminant illness with septicemia, severe respiratory distress, and sometimes meningitis) or a "late-onset" (occurring 10 days to 2 months after delivery and presenting a more insidious, slowly progressive illness that usually includes meningitis) infection. The second leading cause, *E. coli* strains containing K1 capsular antigen, is usually acquired by the neonates from their mothers, who carry the organism in their stool.

The clinical signs in neonatal meningitis suggest sepsis but not necessarily central nervous system (CNS) involvement: fever (in only 60%), jaundice, diarrhea, lethargy, poor feeding or vomiting, respiratory distress (including apnea), seizures, irritability, bulging fontanelle (in only 30%), and nuchal rigidity (15%). Frequently, only by examining the CSF can the presence of meningitis be ruled in or out.

Pathology

The purulent exudate is distributed widely in the subarachnoid space, is most abundant in the basal cisterns and about the cerebellum initially, but also extends into the sulci over the cerebrum. There is no direct invasion of cerebral tissue by the infecting organism or the inflammatory exudate, but the subjacent brain becomes congested and edematous. The effectiveness of the pial barrier accounts for the fact that cerebral abscess does not complicate bacterial meningitis. Indeed, when these two processes coexist, the sequence usually has been that of an initial abscess subsequently leaking its contents into the ventricular system, producing meningitis. There are two possible exceptions to the aforementioned generalization: (1) neonatal meningitis caused by *Citrobacter*, in which the organisms appear to invade the brain after producing a necrotizing vasculitis of small penetrating blood vessels, and (2) *Listeria* rhombencephalitis, a rare process

in which brain stem (pons, medulla) infection can occur simultaneously with *Listeria* meningitis (or alone).

Structures adjacent to the meninges may show a variety of pathologic changes secondary to bacterial meningitis. *Cortical thrombophlebitis* results from venous stasis and adjacent meningeal inflammation. Infarction of cerebral tissue may follow. *Involvement of cortical and pial arteries* with peripheral aneurysm formation and vascular occlusion occurs in bacterial meningitis as well as narrowing (related to spasm and/or arteritis) of the supraclinoid portion of the internal carotid artery at the base of the brain. In one prospective study of adults with bacterial meningitis, angiographically documented cerebrovascular involvement was found in 15% (33% in patients with complicated meningitis). Consistent with this has been the relationship of anterior and middle cerebral arteries with markedly increased intracerebral blood flow velocities (an index of stenosis or arterial spasm) on transcranial Doppler ultrasonography to the occurrence of focal cerebral signs. In fulminating cases (particularly meningococcal meningitis), *cerebral edema* may be marked even though the pleocytosis is only moderate. Rarely, such patients develop temporal lobe and cerebellar herniation, resulting in compression of the midbrain and medulla. *Damage to cranial nerves* occurs in areas where dense exudate accumulates; the third and sixth cranial nerves are also vulnerable to damage by increased intracranial pressure. *Ventriculitis* probably occurs in most cases of bacterial meningitis; rarely this progresses to the accumulation of pus, *ventricular empyema*. *Hydrocephalus* can develop during meningitis from obstruction of CSF flow within the ventricular system (obstructive hydrocephalus) or extraventricularly (communicating hydrocephalus). *Subdural effusions* are sterile transudates that develop over the cerebral cortex in about 15% of infants, rarely in adults, with bacterial meningitis. Rarely such effusions become infected, producing a subdural empyema. In the past, the diagnosis was made almost exclusively in infants, in whom abnormal transillumination or increasing head size can be detected. Now, sterile or infected (showing peripheral contrast medium enhancement) subdural collections can be demonstrated readily by computed tomography (CT) as low-density areas about the cerebrum.

Pathogenesis

Bacteria may reach the meninges by several routes: (1) systemic bacteremia, (2) direct ingress from the upper respiratory tract or skin through an anatomic defect (e.g., skull fracture, eroding sequestrum, meningocele), (3) passage intracranially through venules in the nasopharynx, or (4) spread from a contiguous focus of infection (infection of the paranasal sinuses, leakage of a brain abscess). Bacteremic spread to the meninges is probably the most frequent path of infection. However, not all bacteremic organisms have the same likelihood of causing meningitis. Bacteremia with *H. influenzae* and *N. meningitidis* is usually initiated by pharyngeal adhesion and colonization by an infecting strain. Adhesion of such strains, as well as of *S. pneumoniae*, to mucosal surfaces is abetted by their capacity to produce immunoglobulin A proteases (cleaving this antibody in the hinge region) and thus inactivating this local antibody defense. *N. meningitidis* adhesion to nasopharyngeal cells is effected by fimbriae or pili and promoted by prior damage to ciliated cells such as from smoking or viral infections. In an in vitro nasopharyngeal organ culture these organisms injure ciliated epithelial cells and induce ciliostasis, selectively adhering to nonciliated epithelial cells. Meningococci invade the nasopharyngeal mucosal cells by means of endocytosis and are transported to the abluminal side in membrane-bound vacuoles. *H. influenzae*, in contrast, invades intercellularly by causing separation of apical tight junctions between columnar epithelial cells. When these meningeal pathogens gain access to the blood stream, their intravascular survival is aided by the presence of polysaccharide capsules that inhibit phagocytosis and confer resistance to complement-mediated bactericidal activity.

After entry into the blood stream, CNS invasion occurs, but the mechanisms by which and sites at which this occurs are unclear. A high-grade and sustained bacteremia appears necessary. An important role for specific bacterial adhesion to elements of the blood-brain barrier is likely, as indicated by the preferential binding of fimbriated strains of *E. coli* to the endothelial cell surface of cerebral capillaries and the epithelial cell surface of the choroid plexus and ventricles. Evidence from animal models suggests that CNS invasion sites after bacteremia may develop at foci of nonspecific sterile inflammation above the cribriform plate and through the choroid plexus.

Most bacterial species causing meningitis (*H. influenzae* type b, *N. meningitidis*, *S. pneumoniae*, *E. coli* K1, group B *Streptococcus*) are antiphagocytic. Whether the capsular polysaccharide confers some special meningeal tropism, possibly through surface receptors, is not known. Although the primary focus initiating the bacteremia is usually in the upper respiratory tract or lung (pneumonia), it may be in the heart (endocarditis) or the gastrointestinal or urinary tract. Once established in any part of the meninges, infection quickly extends throughout the subarachnoid space. Bacterial replication proceeds relatively unhindered because CSF levels of complement are low early in meningeal inflammation, resulting in minimal opsonic and bactericidal activity (or none), and because surface phagocytosis of unopsonized organisms is meager in such a fluid environment. A secondary bacteremia may follow meningeal infection and itself contribute to continuing further inoculation of the CSF.

Pathophysiology

Current experimental evidence suggests that meningeal inflammation follows bacterial entry and growth in the CSF and that specific bacterial components (e.g., pneumococcal cell walls or lipoteichoic acid, *H. influenzae* lipopolysaccharide) are major elicitors of this response by causing release into the subarachnoid space of various proinflammatory cytokines such as interleukin-1 and tumor necrosis factor from endothelial and meningeal cells, macrophages, and microglia. These cytokines increase adherence and transendothelial movement of neutrophils, as has been shown in endothelial cell monolayers in culture. Cytokines appear to enhance this passage of leukocytes by inducing several families of adhesion molecules that interact with corresponding receptors on leukocytes. The three likely families mediating endothelial-leukocyte adhesion are the (1) immunoglobulin superfamily (e.g., intercellular adhesion molecule 1 and intercellular adhesion molecule 2); (2) integrins (e.g., CD11/CD18 subfamily); and (3) selectins (e.g., endothelial-leukocyte adhesion molecule 1). Cytokines can also act to increase the binding affinity of a leukocyte selectin, leukocyte-adhesion molecule, for its endothelial cell receptor, contributing further to neutrophil trafficking into the subarachnoid space.

Once within the subarachnoid space, neutrophils are further activated to release products such as prostaglandins and toxic oxygen metabolites that increase local vascular permeability and may cause direct neurotoxicity. Evidence of breaching of the blood-brain barrier is found in animal models of meningitis where endothelial intercellular tight junctions are disrupted, increased pinocytotic vesicles appear in endothelial cells, and albumin escapes across postcapillary venules into the subarachnoid space.

The foregoing inflammatory changes can contribute to development of increased intracranial pressure and alterations in cerebral blood flow. Cerebral edema is commonly due to increased permeability of the blood-brain barrier (vasogenic) and may be due to cellular swelling in the brain as a result of toxic molecules released by bacteria and neutrophils (cytotoxic), and sometimes increased CSF pressure may result primarily from obstruction of CSF outflow related to inflammation at the level of the arachnoidal villi (interstitial). Cerebral blood flow appears to be increased in the very early stages of meningitis, but subsequently it decreases, substantially in some patients in whom it may be responsible for ensuing neurologic injury. When cerebral perfusion pressure (intracranial pressure minus mean arterial pressure) is markedly reduced, morbidity and mortality of bacterial meningitis are greatest in children in whom these measurements have been made. Localized regions of marked hypoperfusion (attributable to focal vascular inflammation or thrombosis) can occur in patients with normal blood flow. Impairment of cerebral blood flow autoregulation, as measured by transcranial Doppler ultrasonography of the middle cerebral artery, occurs in the early phase of acute bacterial meningitis, causing cerebral blood flow to correspond directly with mean arterial blood pressure with attendant hyper- or hypoperfusion of the brain. On recovery, the ability of the cerebral vasculature to maintain a constant level of perfusion despite variations in mean arterial pressure is restored. Impairment of autoregulation of cerebral blood flow may be a factor in cerebral edema or ischemia in some patients owing to altered cerebral perfusion pressure.

Clinical Manifestations

HISTORY. An acute onset of fever, generalized headache, vomiting, and stiff neck are common to many types of meningitis. The majority of patients with community-acquired pyogenic meningitis have had an antecedent or accompanying upper respiratory tract infection or nonspecific febrile illness, acute otitis (or mastoiditis), or pneumonia. Myalgias (particularly in meningococcal disease), backache, and generalized weakness are common symptoms. The illness usually progresses rapidly, with development of confusion, obtundation, and loss of consciousness. Occasionally, the onset may be less acute, with meningeal signs present for several days to a week.

GENERAL PHYSICAL FINDINGS. Evidence of meningeal irritation (drowsiness and decreased mentation, stiff neck, Kernig's and Brudzinski's signs) is usually present. In certain patients, the findings of meningitis may be easily overlooked; infants, obtunded patients, or elderly patients with congestive heart failure or pneumonia may have meningitis without prominent meningeal signs. Their lethargy should be investigated carefully, and meningeal signs should be sought; if any doubt exists, examination of the CSF is indicated.

The presence of a petechial, purpuric, or ecchymotic rash in a patient with meningeal findings almost always indicates meningococcal infection and requires prompt treatment because of the rapidity with which this infection can progress (Chapter 297). Rarely, extensive petechial and purpuric lesions occur in meningitis caused by *S. pneumoniae* or *H. influenzae*. Very rarely, skin lesions almost indistinguishable from those of meningococcal bacteremia occur in patients with acute *S. aureus* endocarditis who also have meningeal signs and a pleocytosis (secondary either to staphylococcal meningitis or to embolic cerebral infarction). Usually one or two of the lesions in such a patient are those of purulent purpura; aspiration of material reveals staphylococci on Gram staining. In the summer months, viral aseptic meningitis may produce meningeal signs, macular and petechial skin lesions, and a pleocytosis of several hundred cells, sometimes with neutrophils predominating initially.

NEUROLOGIC FINDINGS AND COMPLICATIONS. Cranial nerve abnormalities, involving principally the third, fourth, sixth, or seventh nerve, occur in 5 to 10% of adults with community-acquired meningitis. These usually disappear shortly after recovery. Persistent sensorineural hearing loss occurs in 10% of children with bacterial meningitis. In another 16% a transient conductive hearing loss develops. The most likely sites of involvement in persistent sensorineural deafness appear to be the inner ear (infection or toxic products possibly spreading from the subarachnoid space along the cochlear aqueduct) and the acoustic nerve. In children, permanent hearing impairment is more common after meningitis caused by *S. pneumoniae* than by *H. influenzae* or *N. meningitidis*.

Seizures (focal or generalized) occur in 20 to 30% of patients. They may result from readily reversible causes (high fever or hypoglycemia in infants; penicillin neurotoxicity when large doses are administered intravenously in the presence of renal failure) or, more commonly, from focal cerebral injury related to arterial hypoperfusion and infarction, cortical venous thrombosis, or focal edema and cerebritis. Seizures can occur during the first few days or can appear with associated focal neurologic deficits caused by vascular inflammation some days after the onset of the meningitis (Table 312-1). In adults with seizures accompanying meningitis, *S. pneumoniae* is more commonly the cause, but alcoholism is a confounding factor.

Brain swelling and increased CSF pressure are associated with seizures, sixth- and third-nerve dysfunction, abnormal reflexes, reduced consciousness or coma, dilated and poorly reactive pupils, decerebrate posturing, hypertension, bradycardia, and irregular respirations. In approximately one fourth of fatal cases of community-acquired meningitis in adults, cerebral edema accompanied by temporal lobe herniation is observed at autopsy.

Continued

Table 312–1 • CENTRAL NERVOUS SYSTEM FINDINGS IN COMMUNITY-ACQUIRED BACTERIAL MENINGITIS IN ADULTS*

	PERCENTAGE OF EPISODES OF MENINGITIS[†]					
TIME OF ONSET OF FINDINGS	Hemiparesis	Aphasia	Visual-Field Defect	Gaze Preference	Seizures	Other[‡]
Early (≤24 hr)	9	6	3	10	15	5
Late (>24 hr)	2	1	0.3	0	8	1
Total[†]	11	7	3.3	10	23	6

*Based on data of Durand ML, Calderwood SB, Weber DJ, et al: Acute bacterial meningitis in adults: A review of 493 episodes. N Engl J Med 1993;328:21–28.
[†]Total percent of 279 episodes in which individual finding occurred (some episodes involved more than one finding).
[‡]Other focal findings include nystagmus, diplopia, ataxia, monoparesis, hemianesthesia, and central seventh nerve palsy.

Papilledema is rare (1%) in bacterial meningitis even with high CSF pressures, probably because the patient is seen early in the process before changes have occurred in the nerve head. Its presence should indicate the possibility of some other associated or independent suppurative intracranial process (subdural empyema, brain abscess). Marked central hyperpnea sometimes occurs in patients with severe bacterial meningitis; CSF acidosis (principally caused by increased lactic acid levels) provides much of the respiratory stimulus.

Focal cerebral signs (principally hemiparesis, dysphasia, visual field defects, and gaze preference) occur in about 25% of adults with community-acquired bacterial meningitis (see Table 312–1). They may develop during early meningitis secondary to occlusive vascular processes or some days later. Also, cerebral blood flow velocity may be decreased in the presence of increased intracranial pressure and lead to temporary or lasting neurologic dysfunction. It is important to distinguish lateralizing findings resulting from postictal changes (Todd's paralysis), which usually persist for no more than several hours.

Prompt treatment of bacterial meningitis usually results in rapid recovery of neurologic function. Persistent or late-onset obtundation and coma without focal findings suggest development of brain swelling, subdural effusion (in the infant), hydrocephalus, loculated ventriculitis, cortical thrombophlebitis, or sagittal sinus thrombosis. The last three are commonly associated with fever and continuing pleocytosis.

Residual neurologic damage remains in 10 to 20% of patients who recover from bacterial meningitis. Developmental delay and speech defects are each observed in about 5% of children. In infants surviving neonatal meningitis, significant sequelae are much more frequent (15 to 50%).

Laboratory Findings

CEREBROSPINAL FLUID EXAMINATION

When the diagnosis of bacterial meningitis is entertained, blood cultures should be obtained, CSF examined and cultured, and antimicrobial therapy instituted promptly. Polymerase chain reaction techniques have been employed in research settings to detect bacterial DNA in CSF of patients with meningitis, but its use in routine diagnostic laboratories has been limited by its time-consuming and technically demanding nature. Circumstances indicating the need for CT (or magnetic resonance imaging, MRI) scanning of the head prior to performance of a lumbar puncture are noted subsequently. Initial CSF pressure is usually moderately elevated (200 to 300 mm H_2O in the adult). Striking elevations (>450 mm H_2O) occur in occasional patients with acute brain swelling complicating meningitis in the absence of an associated mass lesion.

GRAM-STAINED SMEAR. By the time of hospitalization, most patients with pyogenic meningitis have large numbers (at least 10^5/mL) of bacteria in the CSF. Careful examination of the Gram-stained smear of the spun sediment of CSF reveals the etiologic agent in 60 to 80% of cases. In most instances when gram-positive diplococci (or short-chaining cocci) are observed on a stained CSF smear, they are pneumococci. In certain clinical settings it is important to distinguish this organism from the relatively penicillin-resistant *Enterococcus*, an occasional cause of nosocomial meningitis, which would require adding an aminoglycoside to penicillin in treatment. This can be done by identifying pneumococcal polysaccharide in the CSF by latex particle agglutination. Rarely, three species may morphologically mimic *Neisseria* in the CSF or suggest a mixed infection with short gram-negative rods and meningococci: *Acinetobacter baumannii*, *Moraxella* species, and *Pasteurella multocida*. Culture of the CSF reveals the etiologic agent in 80 to 90% of patients with bacterial meningitis.

SPECIAL IMMUNOLOGIC AND SEROLOGIC PROCEDURES. Rapid antigen disclosure by latex agglutination is available for the detection in CSF of the capsular polysaccharides of common meningeal pathogens (*H. influenzae*; *S. pneumoniae*; group B *Streptococcus*; *N. meningitidis* serogroups A, C, Y, W 135; and *N. meningitidis* group B and *E. coli* K1, which share a common antigen). The sensitivity and specificity of these are highest (over 90%) for *H. influenzae*; sensitivity is lower for *S. pneumoniae* and considerably lower for *N. meningitidis*. Antigen testing of urine specimens for diagnosis of specific bacterial causes of meningitis or bacteremia has a high rate of false-positive results owing to the presence of cross-reacting species that may be found in urinary tract colonization or infection. Bacterial antigen testing of CSF as routinely practiced is a low-yield procedure. Gram-stained smears almost invariably show the causative microorganism when the latex agglutination test is a true positive. Latex agglutination testing may be most useful when the CSF cell count is abnormal, the Gram stain is negative, and blood and CSF cultures are unrevealing at 48 hours (at which time a stored sample of the initial CSF specimen can be tested). Occasionally, when only rare organisms of ambiguous morphology or Gram-staining properties are seen, latex agglutination may be helpful in providing a more specific diagnosis.

CELL COUNT. The normal CSF white blood cell count is less than 5 cells/mm³ (all mononuclear). The cell count in untreated meningitis usually ranges between 100 and 10,000/mm³, with polymorphonuclear leukocytes predominating initially (>80%) and lymphocytes appearing subsequently. The cell count in *L. monocytogenes* meningitis tends to be lower (median 585/mm³) than in other types of community-acquired pyogenic meningitis. Extremely high cell counts (>50,000/mm³) may occur rarely in primary bacterial meningitis but also should raise the possibility of intraventricular rupture of a cerebral abscess. Cell counts as low as 10 to 20/mm³ may be observed early in bacterial meningitis (particularly that caused by *N. meningitidis* and *H. influenzae*). Occasionally, in granulocytopenic patients or in elderly persons with overwhelming pneumococcal meningitis, the CSF may contain very few leukocytes and yet may appear grossly turbid because of the presence of a myriad of organisms. Meningitis caused by several bacterial species (*Mycobacterium tuberculosis*, *Borrelia burgdorferi*, *Treponema pallidum*, *Leptospira* spp, *Francisella tularensis*, *Brucella* spp) characteristically produces a lymphocytic pleocytosis. *L. monocytogenes* meningitis in infants may produce a primarily lymphocytic response in the CSF; in the adult there is usually a polymorphonuclear response, but rarely lymphocytes predominate.

GLUCOSE. The CSF glucose is reduced to values of 40 mg/dL or less (or <50% of the simultaneous blood level) in 50% of patients with bacterial meningitis; this finding can be valuable in distinguishing bacterial meningitis from most viral meningitides or parameningeal infections. A normal CSF glucose value does not exclude the diagnosis of bacterial meningitis. The simultaneous blood glucose level should be determined because patients with diabetes mellitus (or those who are receiving intravenous glucose infusions) have an elevated level of glucose in the CSF, and its significance can be appreciated only on comparison with the simultaneous blood level. However, it may take 90 to 120 minutes for equilibration to occur after major shifts in the level of glucose in the circulation. The hypoglycorrhachia characteristic of pyogenic meningitis appears to be due to interference with normal carrier-facilitated diffusion of glucose and to increased utilization of glucose by host cells.

PROTEIN. The level of protein in the CSF is usually elevated above 100 mg/dL, and the higher values are more commonly observed in pneumococcal meningitis. Extreme elevations, 1000 mg/dL or more, indicate subarachnoid block secondary to the meningitis.

OTHER ABNORMALITIES IN THE CSF. Elevated levels of lactic acid occur in pyogenic meningitis. Although lactic dehydrogenase levels are higher in patients with bacterial meningitis than in those with viral infections of the CNS, these alterations are not of help in determining the specific etiologic agent involved. C-reactive protein is increased in about 95% of patients with bacterial meningitis and is not increased in most patients with viral meningitis. However, it does not seem to provide more information than the CSF cell count, is not helpful in diagnosing bacterial meningitis in newborns, and does not provide clues to the bacterial species involved. Models employing a combination of cutoff values for CSF glucose, protein, total leukocyte, and polymorphonuclear counts have been used to discriminate bacterial from viral meningitis, accomplishing statistically what experienced physicians conclude clinically.

BLOOD AND RESPIRATORY TRACT CULTURES

Bacteremia is demonstrable in about 80% of patients with *H. influenzae* meningitis, 50% of those with pneumococcal meningitis, and 30 to 40% of those with meningococcal meningitis. Cultures of the upper respiratory tract are not helpful in establishing an etiologic diagnosis.

Determining serum creatinine and electrolytes is important in view of the gravity of the illness, the occurrence of specific abnormalities secondary to the meningitis (syndrome of inappropriate secretion of antidiuretic hormone), and problems in therapy in the presence of renal dysfunction (seizures and hyperkalemia with high-dose penicillin therapy). In patients with extensive petechial and purpuric skin lesions, evaluation for coagulopathy is indicated. Elevated serum procalcitonin levels have been used to distinguish bacterial meningitis from that of viral origin, but CSF examination (Gram stain, white blood cell count, glucose, culture) usually provides more direct and specific information.

Radiologic Studies

In view of the frequency with which pyogenic meningitis is associated with primary foci of infection in the chest, nasal sinuses, or mastoid, radiographs of these areas should be taken at the appropriate time after antimicrobial therapy begins when clinically indicated. Initial head CT is not indicated in most patients with bacterial meningitis. If a mass lesion (cerebral abscess, subdural empyema) is suspected from the history, clinical setting, or physical findings (papilledema, focal cerebral signs), CT should be performed. *Bacterial meningitis is a medical emergency requiring immediate diagnosis and rapid institution of antimicrobial therapy.* Delay in performing a diagnostic lumbar puncture to obtain a CT scan should be avoided except on the basis of findings indicative of a parameningeal collection or other intracranial mass lesions, and in that case it would be important to initiate antimicrobial therapy aimed at meningitis of unknown etiology or brain abscess before performing CT. Patients with community-acquired meningitis rarely have significant CT abnormalities in the absence of focal neurologic findings.

In a study of 301 adults with suspected meningitis seen in an urban hospital emergency department, 235 underwent head CT prior to lumbar puncture; of the latter, 24% were abnormal but only 5% showed a mass effect. Among baseline clinical features associated with abnormal CT findings were age older than 60 years, history of CNS disease, seizure within the prior week, abnormal level of consciousness, abnormal visual fields, limb drift, and aphasia. In contrast, among the 96 patients with none of these clinical findings who underwent CT scanning, 97% of scans were normal and only one showed a mass effect (mild, with hydrocephalus), indicating that clinical features can be used to identify those who are unlikely to show abnormalities on CT and have no need for this procedure prior to lumbar puncture. Indeed, in this study the mean time from emergency department admission to lumbar puncture was significantly delayed for patients who first underwent CT (5.3 vs. 3.0 hours).

Specific changes that may be observed on CT during meningitis include cerebral edema and enlargement of the subarachnoid spaces, contrast enhancement of the leptomeninges and the ependyma, or patchy areas of diminished density owing to associated cerebritis and necrosis. In the patient with meningitis whose clinical status deteriorates or fails to improve, the CT scan may help demonstrate suspected complications: sterile subdural collections or empyema; ventricular enlargement secondary to communicating or obstructive hydrocephalus; prominent persisting basilar meningitis; extensive areas of cerebral infarction resulting from occlusion of major cerebral arteries, veins, or venous sinuses; or marked ventricular wall enhancement, suggesting ventriculitis or ventricular empyema. Rarely, cerebral hemorrhage, identifiable on CT, may complicate acute bacterial meningitis in adults, occurring much less frequently than thrombotic strokes.

In about 10% of adults with bacterial meningitis, cranial CT findings (mastoid or sinus wall defect, eroding retrobulbar mass, pneumocephalus) are indicative of disruption of the dural barrier.

Diagnosis

Diagnosis of bacterial meningitis is not difficult in a febrile patient with meningeal symptoms and signs developing in the setting of a predisposing illness. The diagnosis may be less obvious in an elderly, obtunded patient with pneumonia or a confused alcoholic patient in impending delirium tremens. Examination of the CSF should be carried out promptly whenever there is any question of meningitis.

Headache, fever, vomiting, stiff neck, and pleocytosis are features of meningeal inflammation and are common to many types of meningitis (e.g., bacterial, fungal, viral) and also to some parameningeal processes. The CSF findings are most helpful in distinguishing among these processes (Chapter 449). Although a lymphocyte-predominant pleocytosis without hypoglycorrhachia is characteristic of viral (usually enteroviral or herpes simplex virus type 2 [HSV-2]) meningitis or meningoencephalitis (HSV-1), the initial CSF finding may be a polymorphonuclear response (of up to 60%) that quickly becomes mononuclear. HSV-1 encephalitis would be suggested by neurologic findings (dysphasia, hemiparesis, olfactory hallucinations and other temporal lobe signs, seizures), MRI abnormalities in the orbitofrontal and medial temporal lobes, and distinctive electroencephalographic changes in the temporal lobe or lobes. The rash, fever, and headache of Rocky Mountain spotted fever might suggest meningococcal infection, but the geographic and seasonal predilections of the former can provide clues. About 10% of patients hospitalized with Rocky Mountain spotted fever have CSF cell counts above 100/mm^3 (>70% polymorphonuclear), and thus the condition may initially be confused with bacterial meningitis. Acute subarachnoid hemorrhage might be confused with bacterial meningitis because of headache, stiff neck, and vomiting. However, the former usually has a more abrupt onset without prodromal fever and with evidence of subarachnoid blood on CT scanning or CSF examination.

In the patient with meningitis whose CSF does not reveal the etiologic agent on a Gram-stained smear, particularly when the CSF glucose is normal and the polymorphonuclear pleocytosis is atypical, certain treatable processes that can mimic bacterial meningitis should be considered in the differential diagnosis:

1. *Parameningeal infections.* The presence of infections (chronic ear or nasal accessory sinus infections, lung abscess) predisposing to brain abscess, epidural (cerebral or spinal) abscess, subdural empyema, or pyogenic venous sinus phlebitis should be sought. Neurologic findings may appear in the course of primary bacterial meningitis, but their presence should alert the physician to the need for close scrutiny for the presence of a space-occupying infectious process in the CNS. Neurologic symptoms or findings antedating the onset of meningeal symptoms should suggest the possibility of a parameningeal infection. The isolation of an anaerobic organism should suggest the possibility of intraventricular leakage of a cerebral abscess.
2. *Bacterial endocarditis.* Bacterial meningitis may occur during bacterial endocarditis caused by pyogenic organisms such as *S. aureus* and enterococci. In subacute bacterial endocarditis, sterile embolic infarctions of the brain may occur and produce meningeal signs and a pleocytosis containing several hundred cells, including polymorphonuclear leukocytes. A history of dental manipulation, fever, and anorexia antedating the meningitis should be sought; careful examination for heart murmurs and peripheral stigmata of endocarditis is indicated.

3. *"Chemical" meningitis.* The clinical and CSF findings (polymorphonuclear pleocytosis and even reduced glucose level) of bacterial meningitis may be produced by chemically induced inflammation. Acute meningitis after a diagnostic lumbar puncture or spinal anesthesia may be due to bacterial or chemical contamination of equipment or anesthetic agent. Chemical meningitis, characterized by a polymorphonuclear pleocytosis, hypoglycorrhachia, and a latent period of 3 to 24 hours, may occur after 1% of metrizamide myelograms. Endogenous chemical meningitis resulting from material from an epidermoid tumor or a craniopharyngioma leaking into the subarachnoid space can produce a polymorphonuclear pleocytosis and hypoglycorrhachia. Birefringent material may be seen on polarizing microscopy of the CSF sediment.

Rarely, a patient experiences meningitis characterized by subacute onset and persistent neutrophilic CSF pleocytosis lasting weeks or months without ready bacteriologic diagnosis. The etiologic agent in such cases of *chronic neutrophilic meningitis* has usually been either a fungus (*Aspergillus, Candida, Blastomyces*) or a bacterium such as *Nocardia* or *Actinomyces* species.

Complications

NON-NEUROLOGIC COMPLICATIONS

SHOCK. When shock occurs in pyogenic meningitis, it is usually a manifestation of an accompanying intense bacteremia, as in fulminant meningococcemia, rather than of the meningitis itself. Management is guided by the principles of septic shock therapy with appropriate modifications for myocardial failure (Chapter 313).

COAGULATION DISORDERS. Coagulopathies are frequently associated with the intense bacteremias (usually meningococcal, occasionally pneumococcal) and hypotension that can accompany meningitis. The changes may be mild, such as thrombocytopenia (with or without prolongation of prothrombin and partial thromboplastin times), or more marked, with clinical evidence of disseminated intravascular coagulation (Chapter 313).

SEPTIC COMPLICATIONS

ENDOCARDITIS. Previously, 5 to 10% of patients with pneumococcal meningitis, particularly those with bacteremia and pneumonia as well, developed acute endocarditis, most commonly on the aortic valve. The incidence is currently much lower as a result of earlier treatment of the initiating infection. In such patients, febrile relapse and a new murmur may appear shortly after completion of antimicrobial therapy for meningitis.

PYOGENIC ARTHRITIS. Septic arthritis may result from the bacteremia associated with meningitis caused by *S. pneumoniae, N. meningitidis,* or *H. influenzae.*

PROLONGED FEVER

With appropriate antimicrobial treatment of community-acquired bacterial meningitis, patients become afebrile within 2 to 5 days. Sometimes fever persists beyond this or recurs after an afebrile period. In the patient with persisting headache, obtundation, and cerebral findings, inadequate drug therapy or neurologic sequelae (cortical venous thrombophlebitis, ventriculitis, subdural collections) are important considerations. Reevaluation of the CSF, particularly Gram-stained smear and culture, is essential under these circumstances. Drug fever may be responsible in the patient who continues to show clinical improvement in all other respects. Metastatic infection (septic arthritis, purulent pericarditis, thoracic empyema, endocarditis) may be the cause of continuing or recurrent fever.

A syndrome consisting of fever, arthritis, and pericarditis 3 to 6 days after initiation of effective antimicrobial therapy of meningococcal meningitis occurs in about 10% of patients (Chapter 313).

Recurrent Meningitis

Repeated episodes of bacterial meningitis generally indicate a host defect, either in local anatomy or in antibacterial and immunologic defenses (e.g., recurrent *N. meningitidis* infections in patients with congenital or acquired deficiencies of complement, particularly

late-acting components). Among episodes of pneumococcal meningitis in adults seen at a large tertiary care general hospital, 11% occurred in patients with recurrent meningitis, but only 0.5% of patients with community-acquired meningitis caused by other microorganisms have had recurrent attacks.

S. pneumoniae is the cause of one third of episodes of community-acquired recurrent meningitis; various streptococci, *H. influenzae,* and *N. meningitidis* are the causes of another one third of episodes. In contrast, in nosocomial recurrent meningitis, gram-negative bacilli and *S. aureus* are the causes of about 60% of episodes. A history of head trauma is much more frequent in patients with recurrent meningitis. Organisms may enter the subarachnoid space directly, through a defect in the cribriform plate (the most common site), in association with the empty sella syndrome, by means of a basilar skull fracture, through an erosive sequestrum of the mastoid, through congenital dermal defects along the craniospinal axis (usually evident before adult life), or as a consequence of penetrating cranial trauma or neurosurgical procedures. The anatomic defect may produce a frank CSF leak (rhinorrhea or, less commonly, otorrhea) or may entrap a vascular cuff of meninges that might subsequently serve as a direct route for organisms to reach the meninges. CSF rhinorrhea may be intermittent, and meningitis may occur months or years after head injury.

Any patient with bacterial meningitis, particularly if meningitis is recurrent, should be evaluated carefully for any congenital or post-traumatic defects. The presence of CSF rhinorrhea should be sought at admission and subsequently (rhinorrhea may clear during active meningitis only to recur when inflammation has resolved). Clinical clues suggesting the presence of a CSF fistula through the cribriform plate, pericranial air sinuses, or temporal bone include (1) salty taste in the throat, (2) positionally dependent rhinorrhea (rhinorrhea only in the lateral recumbent or prone position suggests an otic or sphenoid origin), (3) anosmia (cribriform plate leak), and (4) hearing loss or full feeling in the ear, often with a finding of fluid or bubbles behind the tympanic membrane (leakage into the middle ear). Quantitative determination of glucose and chloride content of nasal secretions and detection by protein electrophoresis of a transferrin band unique to CSF can definitively establish the presence of CSF rhinorrhea.

Recurrent pneumococcal meningitis may occur without apparent predisposing circumstances, and cryptic CSF leaks should be sought actively in such patients by CT scanning of the frontal and mastoid regions and by radioisotope techniques. (Radioiodine-labeled albumin is introduced intrathecally, and pledgets of cotton placed in the nares are subsequently examined for the radionuclide. Radioisotopic cisternography has been used successfully.) Intrathecal introduction of fluorescein as a visual tracer (under ultraviolet light) can be employed similarly to detect active leaks. Surgical closure of CSF fistulas should be carried out to prevent further episodes of meningitis. Newer extracranial approaches through the ethmoidal sinuses to repair cribriform plate or sphenoidal sinus dural defects are successful and avoid the higher morbidity associated with craniotomy.

In most patients with CSF otorrhea and rhinorrhea after an acute head injury, the leak ceases in 1 or 2 weeks. *Persistent rhinorrhea for more than 4 to 6 weeks is an indication for surgical repair.* Prolonged administration of penicillin does not prevent pneumococcal meningitis and may encourage infection with more drug-resistant species.

Rarely, recurrent meningitis of nonbacterial cause may mimic bacterial meningitis. A common cause of recurrent lymphocytic meningitis is infection with HSV-2. *Mollaret's meningitis* consists of repeated febrile episodes of mild meningeal symptomatology, usually without neurologic abnormalities. Initially, large "endothelial" cells may be seen in the CSF along with polymorphonuclear leukocytes, which are subsequently replaced by lymphocytes. *Behçet's syndrome,* characterized by relapsing oral and genital ulcers and ocular lesions (hypopyon), may exhibit a variety of neurologic abnormalities, including recurrent meningitis.

Prognosis

The introduction of antimicrobial agents has converted bacterial meningitis from a disease that was almost always fatal to one that the majority of patients survive without significant neurologic residua. The mortality rate for community-acquired bacterial meningitis in adults varies with the etiologic agent and the clinical circumstances. With current antimicrobial therapy the mortality rate for *H. influenzae* meningitis is below 5% and that for meningococcal meningitis is about 10%. The highest mortality is with pneumococcal and *L. monocytogenes* meningitis, for which the rates are about 20% and 20 to 30%, respectively.

The mortality rate for gram-negative bacillary meningitis, commonly nosocomial in origin, in adults has been 20 to 30%, but it appeared to be decreasing in the past 10 to 15 years. The mortality rate for recurrent community-acquired meningitis in adults (about 5%) is strikingly lower than the 20% rate for nonrecurrent episodes. Poor prognostic factors include advanced age, presence of other foci of infection, underlying diseases (leukemia, alcoholism), obtundation, seizures within the first 24 hours, and delay in instituting appropriate therapy.

 Treatment

ANTIMICROBIAL AGENTS

Antimicrobial therapy should be begun promptly in this life-threatening emergency. Subsequent management should be carried out with close monitoring (as in an intensive care unit). Treatment should be aimed at the most likely causes based on clinical clues (age of the patient, presence of a petechial or purpuric rash, a recent neurosurgical procedure, CSF rhinorrhea). If the infecting organism is observed on examination of the Gram-stained smear of the CSF sediment, specific therapy is initiated. If the etiologic agent is not seen on the smear (and not detected by latex agglutination), treatment of bacterial meningitis of unknown etiology should be carried out (see later).

With the exception of chloramphenicol, the commonly used antimicrobial agents do not readily penetrate the normal blood-brain barrier, but the passage of penicillin and other antimicrobial agents is enhanced in the presence of meningeal inflammation. Antimicrobial drugs should be administered intravenously throughout the treatment period; reducing dosage as the patient improves should be avoided because normalization of the blood-brain barrier during recovery reduces the CSF levels of drug that are achievable. Bactericidal drugs (penicillin, ampicillin, third-generation cephalosporins) are preferred whenever possible in the treatment of meningitis caused by susceptible bacteria. In animal models of bacterial meningitis, CSF levels of antibiotics at least 10 to 20 times the minimal bactericidal concentration appear to be needed for optimal therapy. Several antimicrobial drugs (first- or second-generation cephalosporins, clindamycin) do not provide effective levels in the CSF and should not be used.

MENINGITIS OF SPECIFIC BACTERIAL CAUSE

PNEUMOCOCCAL MENINGITIS. The treatment of choice for pneumococcal meningitis in the adult has been penicillin (Table 312–2). For patients allergic to penicillin, vancomycin (or chloramphenicol) has been a reasonable alternative (see later). However, problems have developed because of the emergence of penicillin resistance in many pneumococcal isolates. Such resistance has arisen as a result of successive stepwise chromosomal mutations in genes for penicillin-binding proteins and is not due to β-lactamase production. Penicillin-resistant isolates are either intermediately resistant (minimal inhibitory concentration [MIC] of 0.1 to 1.0 μg/mL) or highly resistant (MIC > 1.0 μg/mL). Penicillin-resistant pneumococcal strains have been found worldwide: 44% of isolates in parts of Spain, 45% in regions of South Africa, and almost 60% of isolates in Hungary. In the United States, 20 to 25% of clinical isolates overall are penicillin resistant, with higher percentages being noted in some geographic areas such as Tennessee, Georgia, Maryland, and California and lower percentages in others. In a study of bacterial meningitis in the United States in 1995, 35% of *S. pneumoniae* isolates were penicillin resistant (21% intermediately and 14% highly resistant). Thus, initial treatment decisions for pneumococcal meningitis must take into consideration up-to-date data on penicillin susceptibilities of *S. pneumoniae* isolated in a given region.

Antimicrobial susceptibilities should be determined for all pneumococcal isolates from CSF, blood, or sterile body fluids (see Table 312–2). Worrisome has been the appearance of pneumococcal strains resistant to third-generation cephalosporins (9% of isolates from cases of meningitis in the United States showing MIC > 2 μg/ML). If the MIC for cefotaxime or ceftriaxone (<1.0 μg/mL) indicates a susceptible isolate, cefotaxime or ceftriaxone would be the drug of choice. If the isolate is highly penicillin resistant or is resistant to 1.0 μg/mL ceftriaxone or cefotaxime, alternative therapy (vancomycin with or without rifampin intravenously) is indicated. Because of the increasingly wide distribution of highly resistant strains, initial therapy (pending susceptibility testing) with cefotaxime (or ceftriaxone) plus vancomycin intravenously is indicated. When initial adjunctive therapy with dexamethasone is employed (see later) along with vancomycin, it should be borne in mind that vancomycin levels in the CSF may be reduced by the concomitant corticosteroid use.

Although resistance to chloramphenicol is unusual among pneumococcal isolates from the United States, chloramphenicol has shown poor bactericidal activity against penicillin-resistant isolates from children with meningitis in South Africa. The relative chloramphenicol resistance of such strains may not be discerned on usual laboratory testing but is revealed when the minimum bactericidal concentration is determined. For this reason vancomycin is preferred to chloramphenicol for initial treatment of pneumococcal meningitis in the highly penicillin-allergic patient.

The β-lactam antibiotic meropenem has been studied in the treatment of meningitis caused by *S. pneumoniae*, *N. meningitidis*, and *H. influenzae* in children primarily (but also in adults) and has been found comparably effective to cefotaxime. A broad-spectrum fourth-generation cephalosporin, cefepime, has activity against *S. pneumoniae*, *N. meningitidis*, and *H. influenzae* similar to that of ceftriaxone and cefotaxime and achieves comparable penetration into CSF. In addition, it has greater activity than these antibiotics against *Enterobacter* spp and *P. aeruginosa*, but its efficacy in treatment of meningitis related to these organisms is not yet established.

MENINGOCOCCAL MENINGITIS. Penicillin G or ampicillin intravenously, in the dosage used to treat meningitis related to penicillin-susceptible pneumococci, has been used to treat *N. meningitidis* meningitis caused by susceptible strains. Meningococci resistant to penicillin have been isolated occasionally in Spain (up to 50% of strains), South Africa, and Canada but rarely the United States. Most of these isolates have been only intermediately resistant to penicillin (MIC, 0.1 to 1.0 μg/mL), although occasional strains have had high-level resistance related to β-lactamase production. The latter strains require the use of third-generation cephalosporins, but "meningitis dosages" of penicillin or ampicillin may provide CSF levels that are sufficient for infections with some strains of intermediately penicillin-resistant *N. meningitidis*.

H. INFLUENZAE MENINGITIS. At present, 30 to 35% of isolates of *H. influenzae* type b in the United States are β-lactamase producers and ampicillin resistant; cefotaxime is the initial therapy of choice (see Table 312–2). Chloramphenicol combined with ampicillin is an acceptable alternative. If the isolate proves susceptible to ampicillin, the chloramphenicol may be discontinued. Although in areas of Spain more than 50% of isolates are chloramphenicol resistant, less than 1% have been resistant in the United States. Cefuroxime, a second-generation cephalosporin, has been used extensively in the past 10 years, but the third-generation cephalosporins are preferable because of reports indicating slower sterilization of CSF and a higher incidence of sensorineural hearing loss with cefuroxime.

STAPHYLOCOCCAL MENINGITIS. Treatment of adult meningitis caused by methicillin-sensitive *S. aureus* is listed in Table 312–3. For the penicillin-allergic patient, vancomycin is the alternative of choice. Because penetration of vancomycin into the CSF is limited, adjunctive intrathecal (or intraventricular) therapy with vancomycin (without preservative) has occasionally been resorted to when CSF cultures have remained positive after 48 hours of intravenous therapy alone and where CSF levels can be monitored. For adult meningitis caused by methicillin-resistant *S. aureus*, intravenous vancomycin (with adjunctive intrathecal vancomycin as needed) is the treatment of choice. In severe or refractory cases, adding another drug (rifampin or gentamicin) for systemic therapy is warranted.

Continued

Table 312–2 • ANTIMICROBIAL THERAPY OF COMMUNITY-ACQUIRED BACTERIAL MENINGITIS OF KNOWN CAUSE*

ORGANISM	PREFERRED THERAPY			ALTERNATIVE THERAPY		
	Antimicrobial	Adults (24-hr Dose)	Children (24-hr Dose)	Antimicrobial	Adults (24-hr Dose)	Children (24-hr Dose)
S. pneumoniae Penicillin MIC <0.1 µg/mL	Penicillin G or ampicillin	24 million units IV, q4h aliquots 12 g IV, q4h aliquots	300,000 U/kg IV, q4h aliquots 200–300 mg/kg IV, q4h aliquots	Cefotaxime or ceftriaxone† or vancomycin‡ or chloramphenicol	12 g IV, q4h aliquots 4 g IV, q12h aliquots 2 g IV, q8–12h aliquots 4–6 g IV, q6h aliquots	200 mg/kg IV, q4–6h aliquots 80–100 mg/kg IV, q12h aliquots 50 mg/kg IV, q6h aliquots 75–100 mg/kg IV, q6h aliquots
Pencillin MIC 0.1–1.0 µg/mL	Ceftriaxone† or cefotaxime	4 g IV, q12h aliquots 12 g IV, q4h aliquots	100 mg/kg IV, q12h aliquots 200–300 mg/kg IV, q4–6h aliquots	Vancomycin‡ or meropenem§	2 g IV, q8–12h aliquots 6 g IV, q8h aliquots	50 mg/kg IV, q6h aliquots 40 mg/kg q8h IV (each dose)
Penicillin MIC >1.0 µg/mL	Vancomycin† (plus cefotaxime or ceftriaxone as above)¶	2 g IV, q8–12h aliquots	60 mg/kg IV, q6h aliquots	Meropenem§	6 g IV, q8h aliquots	40 mg/kg q8h IV (each dose)
N. meningitidis	Penicillin G or ampicillin	24 million units IV, q4h aliquots 12 g IV, q4h aliquots	300,000 U/kg IV, q4h aliquots 200–400 mg/kg IV, q4h aliquots	Ceftriaxone† or cefotaxime or chloramphenicol	As above 4–6 g IV, q6h aliquots	80–100 mg/kg IV, q12h aliquots 200 mg/kg IV, q4–6h aliquots 100 mg/kg IV, q6h aliquots
H. influenzae β-Lactamase negative	Ampicillin	12 g IV, q4h aliquots	200–400 mg/kg IV, q4h aliquots	Third-generation cephalosporin** or chloramphenicol	As above	Third-generation cephalosporin** or chloramphenicol as above
β-Lactamase positive	Ceftriaxone† or cefotaxime	4 g IV, q12h aliquots 12 g IV, q4h aliquots	80–100 mg/kg IV, q12h aliquots 200 mg/kg IV, q4–6h aliquots	Chloramphenicol	As above	75–100 mg/kg IV, q6h aliquots
L. monocytogenes	Ampicillin‖ or penicillin G‖	12 g IV, q4h aliquots 24 million units IV, q4h aliquots	200–400 mg/kg IV, q4h aliquots 300,000 U/kg IV, q4h aliquots	Trimethoprim-sulfamethoxazole	10–20 mg/kg IV,†† q6–8h aliquots	15–20 mg/kg IV,†† q6h aliquots

*Dosages are those for patients with normal renal and hepatic function.
†4 g maximum daily dose.
‡Monitoring of peak and trough serum levels advisable; may need to monitor CSF levels if patient not responding well and if levels are low, may need to increase daily dose temporarily by 0.5–1.0 g in adults or add adjuvant intrathecal vancomycin as in treatment of methicillin-resistant S. aureus meningitis (see text).
§Use may be associated with seizures, but much less so than with imipenem.
‖Addition of IV gentamicin to be considered.
¶Addition of rifampin should be considered. Consider intrathecal (or intraventricular) vancomycin (5–20 mg/d) if not responding to IV therapy.
**Ceftriaxone or cefotaxime.
††Dosage based on trimethoprim component of the combination.
Modified from Swartz MN: Acute bacterial meningitis. In Gorbach SL, Bartlett OG, Blacklow NR (eds): Infectious Diseases 2nd ed. Philadelphia, WB Saunders, 1998.

Table 312–3 • THERAPY FOR NOSOCOMIAL MENINGITIS OF KNOWN BACTERIAL CAUSE IN ADULTS

ORGANISM	THERAPY OF CHOICE (24-hr DOSE)*	ALTERNATIVE THERAPY (24-hr DOSE)
Staphylococcus aureus Methicillin susceptible	Nafcillin, 10–12 g IV, q4h aliquots; in difficult cases may add rifampin, 600 mg qd IV or PO	Vancomycin, 2 g IV, q8–12h aliquots†
Methicillin-resistant	Vancomycin, 2 g IV, q8–12h aliquots†: in difficult cases may add rifampin as above	
Enterobacteriaceae (susceptible)	Cefotaxime, 12 g IV, q4h aliquots or ceftazidime 6 g IV, q8h aliquots plus aminoglycoside (e.g., gentamicin 5 mg/kg IV, q8h aliquots)†	Meropenem, 6 g IV, q8h aliquots plus an aminoglycoside IV
Pseudomonas aeruginosa	Cefepime, 6 g IV, q6–8h aliquots plus tobramycin, 5 mg/kg, q8h aliquots‡	Meropenem, 6 g IV, q8h aliquots plus tobramycin, 5 mg/kg IV, q8h aliquots†

*All doses are for adults with normal renal function.
†Monitoring of peak and trough levels advisable; may need to monitor CSF levels if patient not responding well and, if levels are low, may need to increase daily dose temporarily by 0.5–1.0 g or add adjunctive intrathecal vancomycin.
‡If no response to initial therapy, consider adding intrathecal gentamicin or tobramycin (free of preservative), 3–5 mg dose q24h for next few days.

GRAM-NEGATIVE BACILLARY MENINGITIS. Cefotaxime (see Table 312–3) is used to treat meningitis known to be due to susceptible gram-negative bacilli (e.g., *E. coli, Klebsiella, Proteus*). It should not be used to treat meningitis caused by less susceptible species such as *P. aeruginosa* and *Acinetobacter*. Initial treatment (on the basis only of findings on a Gram-stained smear of CSF) of adults with gram-negative bacillary meningitis is listed in Table 312–3. After identifying the specific pathogen and determining its drug susceptibilities, alterations in antimicrobial therapy may be indicated. If the organism is *P. aeruginosa*, a third-generation cephalosporin with antipseudomonal activity should be used (see Table 312–3).

BACTERIAL MENINGITIS OF UNKNOWN ETIOLOGY

Initial treatment of meningitis when the etiologic agent cannot be identified on a Gram-stained smear of CSF is based on available clinical clues. *In the neonate*, a wide range of gram-positive (group B streptococci, *Listeria*) and gram-negative (*E. coli, Klebsiella, H. influenzae*) organisms may be the cause, indicating the intravenous use of combined therapy with drugs such as ampicillin with gentamicin (or amikacin) or ampicillin with cefotaxime (the combination favored by most pediatric infectious disease specialists) until results of cultures become available. *In children*, therapy is directed at the three most frequent pathogens: *N. meningitidis, S. pneumoniae*, and *H. influenzae*. Because of the prevalence of penicillin- and cephalosporin-resistant *S. pneumoniae* in some areas, initial treatment includes several doses of vancomycin (until culture results are available) along with ceftriaxone or cefotaxime. *In adults* (Table 312–4), therapy with ampicillin in combination with vancomycin and a third-generation cephalosporin (cefotaxime or ceftriaxone) is employed. This is because of the role of *L. monocytogenes* (susceptible to ampicillin but not to third-generation cephalosporins) in meningitis of older adults and in previously noted high-risk groups, the emergence of infections with intermediately and highly penicillin-resistant pneumococci, and the increased frequency of aerobic gram-negative bacilli in nosocomial meningitis and meningitis in immunocompromised patients. In the penicillin-allergic individual, trimethoprim-sulfamethoxazole is a suitable alternative in the treatment of *Listeria* meningitis. In special settings such as nosocomial meningitis where more resistant species such as methicillin-resistant *S. aureus*, coagulase-negative staphylococci, and *P. aeruginosa* may be responsible, vancomycin plus cefepime is indicated in initial therapy.

DURATION OF THERAPY

The frequency of CSF examinations depends on the clinical course, but a repeated examination should be done in 24 to 48 hours if there has not been satisfactory improvement or if the causative microorganism is a more resistant gram-negative bacillus or a highly penicillin-resistant (or cephalosporin-resistant) *S. pneumoniae*.

Routine "end-of-treatment" CSF examination is unnecessary in most patients with the common types of community-acquired bacterial meningitis. Meningococci are rapidly eliminated from the circulation and CSF with appropriate antimicrobial therapy, which should be continued for 4 to 7 days after the patient becomes afebrile. If the patient has responded well, a follow-up lumbar puncture is not necessary. *H. influenzae* meningitis should be treated for 10 days (at least for 7 days after the patient becomes afebrile). Follow-up CSF examination may be omitted in patients who have responded with rapid clinical resolution of the meningitis. In pneumococcal meningitis, antimicrobial treatment should be continued for 10 to 14 days and follow-up examination of the CSF should be done. More prolonged therapy is indicated with concomitant parameningeal infection. Meningitis caused by *L. monocytogenes* should be treated for 14 to 21 days. Treatment of gram-negative bacillary meningitis with parenteral antimicrobials is prolonged, usually for a minimum of 3 weeks (particularly in patients with a recent neurosurgical procedure) to prevent relapse. Repeated examinations of the CSF are necessary both during and at the conclusion of treatment to determine whether bacteriologic cure has been achieved.

OTHER ASPECTS OF TREATMENT

Occasional patients with acute bacterial meningitis experience marked brain swelling (CSF pressure > 450 mm H_2O), which may lead to temporal lobe or cerebellar herniation after lumbar puncture. To decrease the possibility of this complication when the pressure is noted to be this high, only a small amount of CSF should be removed for analysis (the amount present in the manometer) and a 20% solution of mannitol (0.25 to 0.5 g/kg) infused intravenously over 20 to 30 minutes, monitoring (if possible) the decline of CSF pressure to a lower level before the spinal needle is removed. Continued control of increased intracranial pressure, if needed thereafter, may be effected with mannitol, dexamethasone (10 mg intravenously, followed by 4 mg every 6 hours), or both. Brain swelling is about the only established current indication for the adjunctive use of corticosteroids in treating pyogenic meningitis in adults; they should be employed only when the appropriate antimicrobial drugs are administered.

In the stuporous patient or one with respiratory insufficiency and markedly increased intracranial pressure, use of a ventilator to reduce the arterial carbon dioxide pressure (PCO_2) to between 25 and 32 mm Hg is reasonable and the patient's head should be elevated to 30 to 45 degrees. Intubation should be carried out with minimal stimulation in the patient with increased intracranial pressure because tracheal stimulation can produce an appreciable further rise in pressure. To this end, pharmacologic aids to intubation such as succinyl choline and opioids, with possible use of adjunctive intravenous lidocaine, are employed. Subsequently, transient increases in intracranial pressure associated with hyperactive airway reflexes can be mitigated by intratracheal instillation of lidocaine before vigorous suctioning. With continued marked and fluctuating elevations of intracranial pressure, use of a continuous intracranial monitoring device may be warranted.

Initial hypovolemia or hypotension, if present, should be treated with fluid to prevent significantly decreased cerebral blood flow. Over the next 24 to 48 hours in patients in whom inappropriate antidiuretic hormone secretion, sometimes associated with meningitis, is evident and may contribute to further brain swelling, fluid limitation (1200 to 1500 mL or adjusted replacement volumes daily in adults) is appropriate. One study in children with bacterial meningitis suggests that routine fluid restriction does not improve outcome and that the decrease in extracellular water that can ensue may increase the likelihood of a deleterious outcome.

Four prospective, controlled trials in children of the routine use of dexamethasone to reduce the pathophysiologic CNS consequences

Continued

Table 312–4 • INITIAL THERAPY FOR COMMUNITY-ACQUIRED PURULENT MENINGITIS OF UNKNOWN CAUSE IN ADULTS

AGE	LIKELY PATHOGENS	PREFERRED DRUG	ALTERNATIVE DRUGS
Immunocompetent			
3 mo through 18 yr	*S. pneumoniae; N. meningitidis, H. influenzae*	Cefotaxime or ceftriaxone plus vancomycin	Ampicillin plus chloramphenicol or meropenem
18–50 yr	*S. pneumoniae, N. meningitidis*	Cefotaxime or ceftriaxone plus vancomycin	Meropenem
>50 yr	*S. pneumoniae, N. meningitidis, L. monocytogenes*	Cefotaxime or ceftriaxone plus ampicillin plus vancomycin	Cefotaxime plus trimethoprim-sulfamethoxazole plus vancomycin
Impaired cellular immunity	*L. monocytogenes*, gram-negative bacilli	Ampicillin plus ceftazidime plus vancomycin	Trimethoprim-sulfamethoxazole plus meropenem or chloramphenicol
Cerebrospinal fluid leak, basilar skull fracture	*S. pneumoniae, N. meningitidis, H. influenzae*, various streptococci	Cefotaxime plus vancomycin	Vancomycin plus chloramphenicol or meropenem

of the inflammatory response during bacterial meningitis have been performed. Dexamethasone was administered intravenously (either 0.15 mg/kg every 6 hours for 4 days or 0.4 mg/kg every 12 hours for 2 days) either at the time of or 10 to 20 minutes before initiating antimicrobial therapy (third-generation cephalosporin). Corticosteroid use had no effect on mortality but did reduce the incidence of neurologic sequelae (primarily bilateral sensorineural hearing loss). Complicating gastrointestinal bleeding (usually occult) has been observed rarely but merits caution. On the basis of these studies, by 1992 most pediatric infectious disease programs surveyed used dexamethasone in bacterial meningitis of children older than 2 months. Most of the children in the studies had *H. influenzae* meningitis, the most common type at the time, and the results reflect primarily the effects of dexamethasone on this form. Currently, *H. influenzae* meningitis has been sharply reduced in incidence by the use of protein-conjugate vaccines, but whether dexamethasone would have a similar effect in reducing neurologic sequelae of meningitis caused by *S. pneumoniae* and *N. meningitidis* in children has not yet been established. Use of adjunctive dexamethasone in cases of severe *H. influenzae* meningitis in children seems indicated, but whether adjunctive corticosteroid use would have a similar salutary effect in reducing the incidence of sensorineural hearing loss or neurologic sequelae in adults, in whom *S. pneumoniae* is the leading cause, has not been known. In a recent prospective randomized trial of adjunctive dexamethasone therapy of community-acquired bacterial meningitis in adults,[1] such treatment was associated with reduction in the proportion of patients with an unfavorable outcome (15% vs 25%) and with a smaller proportion of fatal outcomes (7% vs 15%), both statistically significant results. Dexamethasone's beneficial effect was most evident in patients with pneumococcal meningitis, but it did not significantly reduce neu-

rologic sequelae, including hearing loss. It should be noted that this study was done in the Netherlands with amoxicillin as initial antibiotic therapy at a time when rates of penicillin resistance among pneumococci in that country were very low. In the United States the frequency of resistance to penicillin or cephalosporins is sufficiently high to mandate initial therapy to include vancomycin. Despite recommendations for routine use of dexamethasone in bacterial meningitis in adults, caution is warranted in applying the data from the Netherlands to this country in view of the potential reduction by dexamethasone of the concentration of vancomycin in cerebrospinal fluid. As noted earlier, the presence of markedly increased intracranial pressure is an indication for adjunctive corticosteroid use in adults (or children) with community-acquired meningitis related to a bacterial species for which bactericidal antimicrobial therapy is employed.

Patients with acute bacterial meningitis should receive constant nursing attention in an intensive care unit to ensure prompt recognition of seizures and to prevent aspiration. If seizures occur, they should be treated acutely with diazepam (Valium) administered slowly intravenously in a dose of 5 to 10 mg in the adult. Maintenance anticonvulsant therapy can be continued thereafter with intravenous phenytoin (Dilantin) until the medication can be administered orally. Sedation should be avoided because of the danger of respiratory depression and aspiration.

Surgical treatment of an accompanying pyogenic focus such as mastoiditis should be carried out when complete recovery from the meningitis has occurred but under continuing antibiotic administration. Rarely, the mastoid infection (e.g., Bezold's abscess) is so hyperacute that early drainage may be required after 48 hours or so of antibiotic therapy when the acute meningeal process has subsided somewhat.

Chemoprophylaxis

Prompt prophylaxis of close contacts (individuals who frequently slept and ate in the same household with the patient, girlfriend, or boyfriend) is warranted because up to one third of secondary cases of meningococcal disease develop within 2 to 5 days of illness in the initial case. Only hospital personnel who were in close contact with a patient (mouth-to-mouth resuscitation, initial examination prior to institution of respiratory precautions) are at special risk. Commonly, rifampin orally is used for prophylaxis: for adults (other than pregnant women), 600 mg twice daily for 2 days; for children, 10 mg/kg twice daily for 2 days. Alternatively, for adults ciprofloxacin (500 mg), ofloxacin (400 mg), or azithromycin (500 mg), each given orally as a single dose, may be employed. Another choice is ceftriaxone intramuscularly as a single dose for adults (250 mg) or children (125 mg).

Widespread use of *H. influenzae* b polysaccharides protein-conjugate vaccine in developed countries has largely eliminated need for chemoprophylaxis of close childhood contacts of cases of *H. influenzae* meningitis or invasive infection. However, prophylaxis would be indicated for unimmunized close household contacts of an index case (e.g., recent immigrants) younger than 6 years. If two or more cases of invasive *H. influenzae* b disease occur among children at a daycare center, prophylaxis of other unimmunized attendees is warranted. Rifampin (20 mg/kg orally) once daily for 4 days is recommended for such children.

1. De Gans J, Van de Beek D: Dexamethasone in adults with bacterial meningitis. N Engl J Med 2002;347:1549–1556.

SUGGESTED READINGS

Bartt R: *Listeria* and atypical presentations of *Listeria* in the central nervous system. Semin Neurol 2000;20:361–373. *Up-to-date and comprehensive review of CNS infections with Listeria. Clinical and diagnostic features distinguishing the syndromes of meningitis, rhombencephalitis, and brain abscess are well delineated.*

Baty V, Viel JF, Schuhmacher H, et al: Prospective validation of a diagnosis model as an aid to therapeutic decision-making in acute meningitis. Eur J Clin Microbiol Infect Dis 2000;19:422–426. *This study validates an earlier model using the aggregate of various CSF parameters to distinguish bacterial from viral meningitis.*

Beek D, Gans J, McIntyre P, et al: Corticosteroids in acute bacterial meningitis. Cochrane Database Syst Rev 2003;3:CD004305. *Adjuvant corticosteroids are beneficial.*

Durand ML, Calderwood SB, Weber DJ, et al: Acute bacterial meningitis in adults: A review of 493 episodes. N Engl J Med 1993;328:21–28. *A detailed review of an extensive*

experience in adults between 1962 and 1988 in a large urban general hospital. Community-acquired, nosocomial, and recurrent forms of bacterial meningitis are categorized; the bacteriologic, clinical, CSF, and neurologic findings are well described.

Hasbun R, Abrahams J, Jekel J, Quagliarello VJ: Computed tomography of the head before lumbar puncture in adults with suspected meningitis. N Engl J Med 2001;345:1727–1733. *The authors present data strongly supporting the focused use of head CT, prior to lumbar puncture, in patients with suspected meningitis in whom clinical features increase the likelihood of an intracranial mass lesion or effect.*

Pfister H-W, Feiden W, Einhaupl K-M: Spectrum of complications during bacterial meningitis in adults. Arch Neurol 1993;50:575–581. *In this thorough prospective evaluation of 86 adults with bacterial meningitis, neurologic complications (cerebrovascular injury, brain swelling, cerebral herniation, hydrocephalus) are described. This study describes features helpful for identification of these complications and, particularly, their temporal relationships.*

Quagliarello VJ, Scheld WM: Bacterial meningitis: Pathogenesis, pathophysiology, and progress. N Engl J Med 1992;327:864–872. *Comprehensive review, giving particular attention to the role of bacterial components, cytokines and other mediators, and endothelial and leukocyte adhesins in the generation of the inflammatory response in the subarachnoid space.*

Richardson DC, Louie L, Louie M, et al: Evaluation of a rapid PCR assay for diagnosis of meningococcal meningitis. J Clin Microbiol 2003;41:3851–3853. *PCR had a sensitivity of 97% and a specificity of 99.6%; its results were available within 2 hours of the start of the assay.*

Swartz MN, Dodge PR: Bacterial meningitis—A review of selected aspects. N Engl J Med 1965;272:725–731, 779–787, 842–848, 898–902, 954–960, 1003–1010. *Detailed account of Massachusetts General Hospital experience. Particularly good on clinical aspects, neurologic complications, and differential diagnosis.*

313 MENINGOCOCCAL INFECTIONS

Michael A. Apicella

Meningococcal infections are a major cause of mortality and morbidity in developed and developing nations. *Neisseria meningitidis* is the causative agent in meningococcal infections. It has become the most common cause of bacterial meningitis in American children since the use of the *Haemophilus influenzae* type b protein–capsular polysaccharide conjugate vaccine in infants dramatically reduced the incidence of meningitis caused by this organism. Considerable progress has been made in the management and prevention of infections with *N. meningitidis* since the organism was first described in 1887. Because the meningococcal vaccine has limited effectiveness in the group at greatest risk for infection, children younger than 2 years, meningococcal infection is still a major problem worldwide. The devastating nature of systemic meningococcal infection makes it imperative that preventive measures be developed to control this disease fully. In addition, an effective vaccine against meningococcal serogroup B infection has not been developed. Until this goal is realized, it is crucial that the clinician recognize and be able to treat the infection successfully as early as possible in its course to ensure an outcome with minimum mortality and morbidity.

Microbiology and Pathogenesis

N. meningitidis is a gram-negative diplococcus. Meningococci are considered a fastidious species, and media containing appropriate supplementation must be used to ensure reliable growth from clinical samples. The use of selective media such as Thayer-Martin medium has allowed isolation of the organism from sites such as the nasopharynx that contain diverse background flora. The organism grows best between 35 and 37° C in an atmosphere of 5% carbon dioxide. The organism does not grow below 32° C or above 41° C. Laboratory confirmation of the presence of the organism depends on the metabolism of glucose and maltose with production of acid. Gas is not produced during this metabolic process.

The meningococcus has a narrow environmental niche. It is a strict human pathogen that has been isolated only from human mucosal surfaces or body fluids. A number of factors contribute to the ability of the organism to colonize and cause infection. The meningococcus has a typical gram-negative cell wall containing lipopolysaccharide or endotoxin, which is the primary toxin of the meningococcus. Meningococci express pili (attachment organelles), which are important in adhesion to nasopharyngeal epithelial cells. Meningococci can express polysaccharide capsules, and this is probably the most important virulence factor associated with this species. Thirteen serologically distinct encapsulated forms have been implicated in infection. Immunochemical differences in these capsules are the basis for the principal system used to assign encapsulated meningococci to serogroups. Over 98% of cases are caused by five serogroups: A, B, C, W-135, and Y. Meningococci can be cultured that lack capsular polysaccharides. These are called nonencapsulated strains. Nonencapsulated meningococcal strains are frequently identified in nasopharyngeal cultures during screening in endemic periods. They have not been isolated from body fluids of patients with systemic meningococcal disease. In addition to serogrouping on the basis of capsular antigens, meningococci can be serotyped on the basis of antigenic differences in their outer membrane proteins and lipopolysaccharides. These serotypes have become important in studies of the epidemiology of infection and in the development of new vaccines.

The molecular pathogenesis of meningococcal infection is beginning to be understood. Figure 313–1A outlines schematically the process involved in mucosal invasion, and Figure 313–1B shows the factors associated with the generation of the shock state and disseminated intravascular coagulopathy (DIC). The pathogenesis of *N. meningitidis* begins on the nasopharyngeal surface. Colonization of this surface is absolutely necessary for the evolution to systemic infection. The only exceptions are the rare occurrences in which *N. meningitidis* is inoculated parenterally accidentally either in the laboratory or in the clinical setting. Infection of the nasopharynx occurs by inhalation of aerosolized particles containing meningococci. The nasopharynx is a mixed epithelial surface containing ciliated, secretory and nonciliated, nonsecretory cells. There are lymphoid tissues associated with the nasopharynx in the form of adenoidal and tonsillar tissue. These structures have mucosal surfaces that are covered with typical upper airway epithelium. The organism uses adherence factors to adhere to this airway surface. The airway epithelial surface is covered with a mucous layer that the organism must penetrate. How this occurs is not clearly understood. Pili enhance attachment but are not necessary for attachment. The pili act as long-range attachment organelles that bind to CD46 on the human cell surface. As the organisms draws closer to the airway epithelial cell, outer membrane surface proteins such as the class V proteins (opa and opc) play a role in attachment and may be important in defining the tissue specificity of the organism. Lipo-oligosaccharide phase variation appears to play a role in the adherence process. Only unencapsulated meningococci enter epithelial cells, and capsular biosynthesis has been shown to stop as the meningococcus enters the epithelial cell.

On contact with the epithelial cell, the meningococcus initiates cytoskeletal changes within the epithelial cell. These rearrangements are not triggered by nonadherent meningococcal strains. Attachment

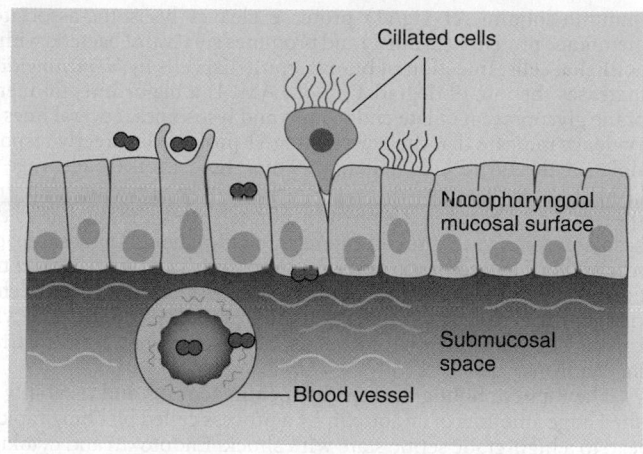

A

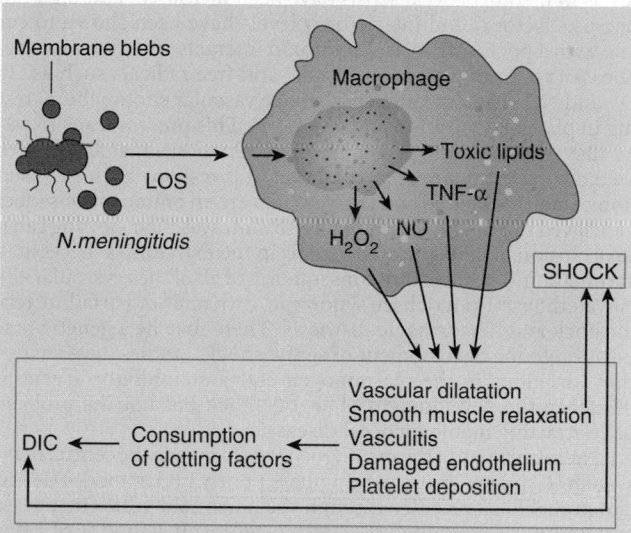

B

FIGURE 313–1 • *A*, Schematic representation of nasopharyngeal invasion by the meningococcus. The process involves attachment to the surface of nonciliated cells by meningococcal pili. Short-range attachment factors (meningococcal surface components) are probably involved in the endocytotic engulfment process as microvilli of the nasopharyngeal cell surround the organism. The nonciliated cells through which the organisms transmigrate do not appear to sustain damage. By contrast, the ciliated mucosal cells die and are extruded from the mucosal surface. Meningococcal lipooligosaccharide, peptidoglycan, and possibly other toxins are thought to be responsible for this cytolytic activity. Organisms in the submucosal space then have access to entry into capillaries and arterioles and can invade the vascular system. *B*, The rapid doubling time of the meningococcus and its ability to shed large amounts of endotoxin by a process called blebbing rapidly lead to a high-grade septic state with shock. Endotoxin (lipooligosaccharide, or LOS) interacts with macrophages to release cytokines, vasoactive lipids (prostaglandins), and free radicals such as H_2O_2, O⁻, and NO. These substances damage vascular endothelium, resulting in platelet deposition and vasculitis. This leads to vascular disruption and the petechiae and ecchymoses that are frequently seen during meningococcal infection. Clotting factors are consumed, and DIC ensues, which is an ominous consequence of delayed treatment. Occasionally, the intravascular clotting can lead to occlusion of major arterial vessels in the extremities, requiring amputation. The most dire consequence of all these vascular effects is Waterhouse-Friderichsen syndrome, which is multiorgan failure caused by shock and hemorrhagic diathesis. (*A*, Data from Stephens DS: Gonococcal and meningococcal pathogenesis as defined by human cell, cell culture, and organ culture assays. Clin Microbiol Rev 1989;2:S104–S111. *B*, Data from Brandtzaeg P, Ovstebo R, Kierulf P: Compartmentalization of lipopolysaccharide production correlates with clinical presentation in meningococcal disease. J Infect Dis 1992;166:650–652.)

of the meningococcus to the epithelial surface is followed by a process that resembles receptor-mediated endocytosis. The bacteria are incorporated into vacuoles.

The factors allowing the survival of the organism within the epithelial cell vacuole are now being elucidated. *Neisseria* type 2 immunoglobulin A1 (IgA1) protease cleaves lysosome-associated membrane protein 1 (LAMP1) and promotes survival of bacteria within epithelial cells. Infection of human epithelial cells by *N. meningitidis* increases the rate of degradation of LAMP1, a major integral membrane glycoprotein of late endosomes and lysosomes. Several lines of evidence indicate that the neisserial IgA1 protease is directly responsible for the LAMP1 degradation. Thus, IgA1 protease cleavage of LAMP1 promotes intracellular survival of pathogenic *Neisseria* species. The meningococci are transported within the vacuole to the basolateral surface of the cell and released into the submucosal space, where they have access to entry into capillaries and arterioles. If the organism can invade the vascular system, the capsular polysaccharide, in the absence of specific antibody, provides an antiphagocytic barrier that protects the organism against normal host clearing mechanisms.

The rapid doubling time of the meningococcus and its ability to shed large amounts of endotoxin by a process called blebbing rapidly lead to a high-grade septic state with shock. Endotoxin and cytokine levels in meningococcal sepsis have been measured, and high tumor necrosis factor α and interferon-γ levels have been shown to correlate with a poor prognosis. Endotoxin interacts with macrophages to release cytokines, vasoactive lipids, and free radicals such as H_2O_2, O^-, and NO. These substances damage vascular endothelium, resulting in platelet deposition and vasculitis. This process leads to vascular disruption and the petechiae and ecchymoses that are frequently seen during meningococcal infection. It is responsible for consumption of clotting factors and DICs, which are an ominous consequence of delayed treatment. Occasionally, the intravascular clotting can lead to occlusion of major arterial vessels in the extremities, necessitating amputation. The most dire consequence of all of these vascular effects is Waterhouse-Friderichsen syndrome, with multiorgan failure related to shock and hemorrhagic diathesis. There may be a genetic predisposition to the development of septic shock. Studies have suggested that variations in the plasminogen activator inhibitor 1 gene may influence the development of septic shock but not the probability of contracting meningococcal disease.

The propensity of the meningococcus to invade the central nervous system (CNS) and cause meningitis is poorly understood. The organism probably gains entry through the arachnoid villi. The release of endotoxin and peptidoglycan in the cerebrospinal fluid (CSF) evokes inflammatory factors that are chemoattractive for polymorphonuclear leukocytes (PMNs). Enzymes released by PMNs intensify the meningeal inflammation, leading to increased cerebrovascular permeability and brain edema.

Epidemiology

N. meningitidis can cause endemic and epidemic infection. At present, meningococcal infection is endemic in the United States, with approximately 2500 cases per year reported to the Centers for Disease Control and Prevention (CDC). This gives a case rate of approximately 1 in 10^5 total population. The case-fatality rate is approximately 12%. Disease rates in children younger than age 2 are approximately 10 times higher than in the overall population. Seasonal variation occurs, with the highest attack rates in February and March and the lowest in September. The male/female ratio of patients is approximately one. The predominant serogroups causing infection in the United States currently are B, C, and Y.

The epidemic form of meningococcal disease was first described in medical journals in Geneva in 1807, 80 years before the causative organism was identified by Weichselbaum. Before World War II, periodic epidemics of meningococcal infection ravaged American cities. These were caused primarily by the serogroup A meningococcus. With increasing standards of living, these epidemics have abated in this country and infection related to the serogroup A has virtually disappeared.

Large-scale epidemics still occur with deadly frequency in Africa, parts of Asia, South America, and the countries of the former Soviet Union. These epidemics are most commonly caused by the serogroup A meningococcus and occasionally by the serogroup C meningococcus. In an area appropriately named the "meningitis belt" because it crosses the waist of sub-Saharan Africa, epidemics of meningococcal infection occur every 7 to 10 years. The case rate during these epidemics can be as high as 1 in 1000 total population. Case rates

in children younger than age 2 can be 1 in 100. In one epidemic in Nairobi, Kenya, which is outside the meningitis belt, the attack rate was 2.5 cases per 10,000 population. Areas that included Nairobi's largest slums had a particularly high attack rate. This epidemic displayed an unusual age distribution, with high attack rates among 20- to 29-year-olds. The case-fatality rate was approximately 10%. Studies of the genetics of the organism causing this epidemic indicate that it was clonally related to group A strains causing epidemics in other parts of Africa. This finding suggests that these epidemics were caused by a particularly virulent clone of group A *N. meningitidis*. In the developed nations of Western Europe, epidemics caused by serogroup B meningococcus have occurred over the past decade. Norway suffered such an epidemic with case rates of 1 in 10,000 individuals. A high attack rate was seen among teenagers in this epidemic.

The reason for the epidemic spread of the meningococcus is not known. The organism is considered a respiratory pathogen, and spread is most likely by the aerosol route. It is clear that the high attack rates seen in the less well-developed countries are in part due to poverty and the consequences of crowding, poor sanitation, and malnutrition. Factors such as herd immunity and specific virulence factors associated with "epidemic strains" have been implicated as factors in the rapid spread of infection in these situations. From studies of an epidemic in central and east Africa, clonal analysis indicated that the epidemic strain had arisen in central Asia almost 7 years before the African epidemic. It had spread through northern India and Pakistan to Saudi Arabia and then with pilgrims from Mecca to Africa. A number of American pilgrims returning from Mecca at that time were found to have nasopharynx colonization with this epidemic strain.

Predisposition to meningococcal infection has been associated with preceding respiratory tract infection, particularly influenza. In one study of an epidemic limited to American schoolchildren traveling on the same school bus, it was shown that school absenteeism was higher during the 3 weeks before the outbreak than at any time in the preceding 3 years. This suggests a particularly severe outbreak of respiratory illness. The five children who developed meningococcal sepsis all complained of influenza-like symptoms before the meningococcal disease. On the basis of serologic analysis, a case-control study revealed that children in this population who complained of respiratory tract symptoms had B/Ann Arbor1/86 influenza. These data add to evidence suggesting that influenzal respiratory infection predisposes to meningococcal disease.

Epidemic infections in American military recruit camps were a major problem before the introduction of vaccination. Throughout the 19th century, the unique susceptibility of military recruits was attested to by the clinical descriptions of this infection that can be found in the records of the Crimean and American civil wars. Since the introduction of vaccination of all recruits in 1972 with a tetravalent vaccine containing serogroup A, C, Y, and W-135 polysaccharides, epidemics have not occurred.

Intimate contacts of cases, including family members, college roommates, and nursery school classmates, are at 100- to 1000-fold increased risk of acquiring meningococcal infection. Such individuals should be told about the increased risk, monitored closely for emergence of coprimary cases (cases that arise within 48 hours of the primary case), and given chemoprophylaxis (see "Treatment") to prevent secondary cases of infection. Hospital personnel who care for patients with meningococcal disease are not at increased risk for acquisition of infection. In the United States, the primary means for prevention of sporadic meningococcal disease is antimicrobial chemoprophylaxis of close contacts of infected persons. The attack rate for household contacts exposed to patients who have sporadic meningococcal disease is 500 to 800 times greater than for the total population. Close contacts include household members, daycare center contacts, and anyone directly exposed to the patient's oral secretions (e.g., through kissing, mouth-to-mouth resuscitation, endotracheal intubation, or endotracheal tube management). Studies have shown that individuals seated in proximity to an index case of meningococcal infection on prolonged airline flights (over 8 hours) may be at high risk for acquiring carriage and possibly disease. The recommendation has been made that antimicrobial chemoprophylaxis should be considered for passengers seated next to an index case patient. Isolation of patients in hospitals is a common practice. It can be limited to respiratory isolation and terminated 24 hours after institution of appropriate antibiotic therapy.

Clinical Syndromes

THE CARRIER STATE. There are several different meningococcal infection syndromes. In the early 20th century, the ability to isolate meningococci from the nasopharynx of otherwise healthy individuals led to the concept of asymptomatic carriage of bacterial pathogens. The observation that increased carriage rates coincided with onset of epidemic among military recruits during World War I first linked the carrier state to disease. The nasopharyngeal carrier state is considered an active infection because some individuals have symptomatic pharyngitis and rises in serologic titers to the infecting organism. It is considered that all cases of acute systemic meningococcal infection are preceded by recent nasopharyngeal colonization. Studies have shown that the carrier state can persist for long periods of time, with about 5% of the population carrying the meningococcus in the nasopharynx during endemic periods. The majority of these isolates are unencapsulated. During epidemics, the carrier rate can rise to over 30% of the population, with the majority of individuals carrying the epidemic strains in the nasopharynx. Generally, most individuals who become carriers are asymptomatic. Evidence exists that the systemic immune system is primed during the period of nasopharyngeal carriage because antibodies to the infecting strains can be shown to evolve concordant with colonization.

In a study of an epidemic among military recruits, it was shown that nasopharyngeal colonization by the meningococcal strain responsible for the epidemic resulted in a 40% incidence of systemic infection if the person colonized also lacked bactericidal antibodies to the epidemic strain. This study confirmed the role of nasopharyngeal carriage as the source of systemic infection and the importance of serum antibody in protection against systemic meningococcal infection.

MENINGITIS AND MENINGOCOCCEMIA. Acute systemic infection can be manifest clinically by three syndromes: meningitis, meningitis with meningococcemia, and meningococcemia without obvious signs of meningitis. Typically, an otherwise healthy patient has sudden onset of fever, nausea, vomiting, headache, decreased ability to concentrate, and myalgia. The patient frequently tells the physician that this is the sickest he or she has ever felt. Many have a feeling of impending death. In children, the infection is rare in those younger than 6 months because of protection by placentally transferred antibodies. Because children younger than 2 cannot relate many symptoms, sudden onset of fever, leukocytosis, and lethargy become important findings. Initially, the physical examination may be unrevealing, with the exception of an acutely ill patient. The preceding symptoms of pharyngitis that may be associated with nasopharyngeal carriage can lead to a preliminary diagnosis of streptococcal infection. This diagnosis frequently results in treatment with low-dose penicillin, which has little effect on the emerging meningococcal sepsis. Alternatively, the diagnosis of influenza is assigned to the patient because of complaints of fever, chills, and myalgia. In general, patients with meningococcal infection are considerably sicker on presentation than the majority of patients with streptococcal or viral infections. The vital signs show a low blood pressure with an elevated pulse rate. Diaphoresis is common. In such patients, an intensive search for petechiae should be mounted (Fig. 313-2). A complete examination of the skin with the patient completely undressed is essential. The physical examination should include provocative tests of meningeal irritability, the Kernig and Brudzinski signs. It must be remembered that patients with meningococcemia may not necessarily have meningeal signs, but 50 to 80% have petechiae on presentation. The mucosal surfaces of the soft palate and ocular and palpebral conjunctiva must be examined for petechiae.

The infection can progress rapidly. Depending on the presentation of the patient, a critical situation can occur quickly. Profound shock with a DIC is the most ominous development in these patients. Coagulopathy defined as a partial thromboplastin time of more than 50 seconds or a fibrinogen concentration less than $150\,\mu g/dL$ is an excellent predictor of a poor prognosis. A number of studies have demonstrated that myocardial dysfunction can occur in meningococcal sepsis. Signs of heart failure including gallop rhythms and congestive heart failure with pulmonary edema are not uncommon. In one large series, 15% of pediatric patients were admitted to intensive care units because of cardiovascular manifestations. Approximately 25% of patients who die of meningococcal sepsis have evidence of myocarditis. Studies of a group of severely ill patients with meningococcal sepsis in France showed low stroke volume indices ($29\,mL/m^2$) and tachycardia (>135 beats per minute), a profile suggesting greater myocardial depression than usually observed in gram-negative sepsis. In infection with meningococcal serogroup C, pericarditis with tamponade can seriously complicate the course of treatment unless recognized and managed. When DIC occurs, persistent bleeding at intravenous sites and sites of arterial punctures can complicate management.

Neurologic complications include signs of meningeal irritation, an encephalopathic state, and coma. Seizures can occur but are less common than in other forms of bacterial meningitis. In general, patients surviving meningococcal CNS infection have remarkably few sequelae, but cerebrovascular accidents secondary to intracranial bleeding can lead to paresis. Cases of posterior pituitary insufficiency have been reported in patients recovering from meningococcal infection.

Prognosis can vary depending on the presentation of the patient, the skill and completeness of the physician, and the nature of the facility. At tertiary care hospitals during endemic periods of infection, mortalities as low as 8% have been reported. Patients who present with meningococcemia alone tend to have a higher mortality (up to 20%). During World War II, when sulfonamides were used, meningococcal mortality rates were as low as 2%. Many of these patients were hospitalized and treated as soon as symptoms began. More recent studies in Norway and Africa have supported the concept that early onset of therapy significantly reduces mortality.

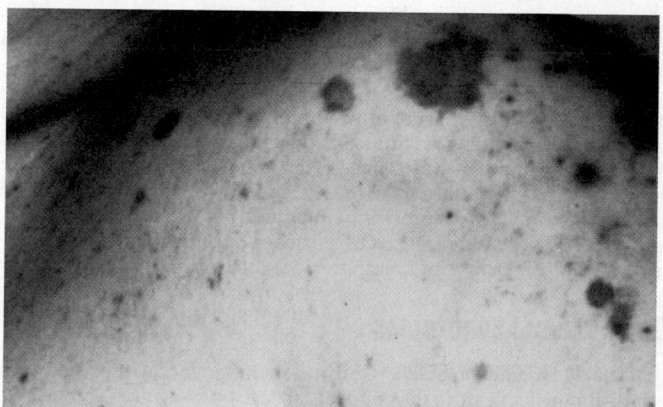

FIGURE 313-2 • A patient with advanced meningococcemia who has multiple petechiae and ecchymoses on the shoulders, chest, and arm.

Laboratory Diagnosis

The laboratory diagnosis is based on the isolation of the *N. meningitidis* from blood cultures or CSF. Blood cultures are positive in 60 to 80% of untreated patients, whereas CSF cultures are positive in 50 to 70%. Gram stain analysis of CSF requires a skilled, patient observer, but it can provide diagnostic results rapidly. Gram staining of the CSF can be useful as a rapid diagnostic tool, especially in patients with meningococcal meningitis. Approximately 50% of these patients have a positive Gram stain. In cases of meningococcemia without overt meningitis, the CSF Gram stain is positive in less than 25% of patients. Studies have suggested that Gram stain analysis of punch biopsy or needle aspiration samples of hemorrhagic skin lesions in meningococcal sepsis without clinical evidence of meningitis can lead to rapid diagnosis. Approximately 70% of such skin lesions were positive. The tinctorial results for punch biopsy specimens were not affected by antibiotics because Gram staining gave positive results up to 45 hours after the start of antibiotic therapy. Cultures of these biopsy specimens or aspirates were also useful diagnostically for as long as 13 hours after the institution of antibiotic therapy. Detection of meningococcal capsular polysaccharide in CSF can also be used as a method for rapid diagnosis. The test is most sensitive for the A and C polysaccharides and considerably less sensitive for serogroup B polysaccharide. In meningococcemia without clinically apparent meningitis, the antigen detection methods can be negative despite profound sepsis. The polymerase chain reaction has been found to be a rapid method for making the diagnosis of CSF infection. Studies in Great Britain during a meningococcal meningitis outbreak indicated its value in establishing the diagnosis in spite of antibiotic therapy prior to hospitalization.

 ## Treatment

In 1933, sulfonamides revolutionized the treatment of meningococcal infection. Before antibiotics, almost all cases resulted in death or profound morbidity with complications. Early administration of appropriate antibiotics is the cornerstone of successful management. As soon as the practitioner seriously considers the diagnosis of systemic meningococcal infection, institution of therapy must follow within 30 minutes. The patient must be considered a medical emergency. Thorough organization and documentation of the patient's management are crucial. Blood should be drawn for cultures immediately, an intravenous line established, and penicillin G (chloramphenicol can be used in penicillin-allergic patients) infused over 15 minutes (Table 313–1). There is no evidence that release of endotoxin that may occur after antibiotic administration adversely effects outcome. This should not be a reason to delay the onset of therapy. Antibiotic administration should not be delayed while waiting for the spinal tap to be done. If the spinal tap is obtained within 45 minutes of the antibiotics, there is limited reduction in positive CSF cultures and no modification of the CSF cytology or hypoglycorrhachia. In two studies in Great Britain, it was shown that the administration, before hospitalization, of high-dose penicillin to patients suspected of having meningococcal infection greatly reduced morbidity and mortality.

Patients with meningococcal sepsis frequently have multisystem involvement. If the patient is not at a tertiary care hospital, transfer of the stabilized patient to such a facility should be considered. The patient should be cared for in an intensive care situation with continuous monitoring and careful management of fluids and electrolytes. Because of fluid loss related to fever and the increased vascular permeability, fluids, electrolytes, and colloid should be administered and blood pressure, urine output, and cardiac function monitored. A number of studies indicate that meningococcal sepsis is associated with cardiac failure; thus, attention must be paid to cardiac status during the sepsis and shock state. Studies measuring release of cardiac troponin as an index of cardiac cell death demonstrated significant increases in 62% of infected children 24 hours after the diagnosis of meningococcal disease. Treatment of heart failure may be indicated. Vasoactive agents such as dopamine may be necessary to maintain blood pressure and tissue perfusion.

Because DIC occurs frequently, monitoring of clotting parameters such as platelets, fibrinogen, and fibrin split products is a crucial part of management. Correction of this problem is a key to survival and reduced morbidity and may require the advice of one skilled in management of bleeding disorders. Studies have shown that the use of fresh frozen plasma may negatively influence outcome in systemic meningococcal disease. Careful consideration should be given before the administration of such products to these patients. Studies have suggested that exchange transfusion may improve the survival rate of patients with fulminant meningococcal sepsis. The beneficial effect is most likely not based on the elimination of endotoxin. Promising results have been obtained in patients with meningococcal sepsis using a truncated version of recombinantly produced bactericidal/permeability-increasing protein (rBPI). This product is undergoing testing in patients and is not available for general use. One of the most serious causes of morbidity in fulminant meningococcal sepsis is skin necrosis with loss of distal digits and limbs. Epidural sympathetic blockade may prove useful in preserving the lower extremities of such patients. Skin necrosis can be managed by débridement, grafting, and nutritional support after the patient's condition has been stabilized.

In the early 1950s, penicillin became the drug of choice for treatment of systemic meningococcal infections. It has remained the cornerstone of therapy since that time. The meningococcus is sensitive to a wide range of antibiotics, including third-generation cephalosporins and quinolones. Ampicillin is equivalent to penicillin G and can be used if there is uncertainty about the etiologic diagnosis at the time when therapy is instituted. Reports from southern Europe (primarily Spain and Greece) of the isolation of penicillin-resistant meningococci could have ominous consequences if epidemics involving these organisms occur. In Spain, the prevalence of *N. meningitidis* isolates that are moderately susceptible to penicillin and ampicillin has increased to almost 50% of isolates. These strains do not produce β-lactamase. In these strains, the basis of meningococcal resistance to penicillin is alterations in a group of inner membrane enzymes, the penicillin-binding proteins (PBPs), which are responsible for cell wall synthesis. Specifically, alterations in PBP-2 result in decreased affinity of binding of penicillin and ampicillin to these enzymes. Third-generation cephalosporins are usually effective against organisms that are resistant on this basis. However, careful antibiotic sensitivity testing should be performed to ensure that this is the case because some third-generation cephalosporins may also not bind efficiently to these modified PBPs. Studies have demonstrated that disc diffusion methods can still be used to analyze such strains, although plate dilution methods are preferred. Sulfonamide-resistant meningococci are still common in the United States; hence, sulfonamides should not be used in treatment of acute infections.

Complement Deficiency and Meningococcal Sepsis

Individuals with deficiencies in complement components appear to be uniquely susceptible to meningococcal infection. In properdin-deficient patients, fulminant meningococcal sepsis is a frequent cause of death. Families of such individuals should be investigated for a history of sudden septic death in relatives. Such families should be observed closely and undergo vaccination with the tetravalent meningococcal vaccine.

In patients with late complement component deficiencies (LCCDs), meningococcal infection occurs in older individuals (mean age, 17 years) and tends to be milder (mortality ~2%) and caused by less common serogroups (serogroup Y and W135) than occur in the general population. Patients with LCCDs respond normally to meningococcal capsular polysaccharide vaccine with the development of antibodies that are functional in both complement-dependent bactericidal assays and opsonophagocytic assays. These patients have a more rapid decline in capsular antibody than is seen in normal individuals. These studies suggest that patients with LCCDs are critically dependent on capsular antibody for protection against meningococcal disease. Vaccination, probably on a recurrent basis, is an important component in the prevention of meningococcal disease in LCCD patients.

Other Clinical Syndromes

CHRONIC MENINGOCOCCEMIA. Chronic meningococcal sepsis, which is indistinguishable from the gonococcal dermatitis-arthritis syndrome, can occur. These patients have typical painful skin lesions usually on the extremities, with migratory polyarthritis and tenosynovitis. This form of meningococcal sepsis can persist for weeks if untreated. It responds promptly to antibiotic therapy.

RESPIRATORY TRACT INFECTION. Pneumonia related to *N. meningitidis* has been reported since the 1930s. In one study of community-acquired infections in Finland, *N. meningitidis* was implicated as the etiologic

Table 313–1 • ANTIBIOTIC MANAGEMENT OF SYSTEMIC MENINGOCOCCAL INFECTION

ANTIBIOTIC	DOSE
Penicillin G	300,000 units/kg/day IV, up to 24 million units/day
Ampicillin	150–200 mg/kg/day IV, up to 12 g/day
Ceftriaxone	2 g/day IV
Chloramphenicol	For use in penicillin-allergic patients, 100 mg/kg/day IV, up to 4 g/day

agent in 6%. Epidemic pneumonia caused by serogroup Y strains has occurred at a military training center. The patients presented with chills, chest pain, and cough. Rales and fever occurred in almost all patients. Infections in these men were frequently multilobar (40%). The incidence of sepsis associated with these infections is quite low, and the diagnosis is usually made with sputum or endotracheal aspirates. There was no mortality in these patients, and all responded well to treatment with penicillin.

MENINGOCOCCAL PERICARDITIS. Pericarditis is usually associated with infections by N. meningitidis serogroup C. It has been associated with meningococcemia and reported as an isolated syndrome. Patients can present with chest pain and signs of tamponade, but relatively asymptomatic disease can occur with detection made by ultrasonography. Treatment with antibiotics and removal of the pericardial fluid usually result in a successful outcome. Pericarditis can occur in patients convalescing from meningococcal sepsis. It should be considered if fever and shortness of breath on minimal exertion occur when the patient is recovering from meningococcal sepsis. Echocardiography provides a rapid diagnosis of this complication of infection. In convalescent patients, antibiotic therapy should be continued and pericardiocentesis may be indicated. There is no evidence that corticosteroids or anti-inflammatory agents have a role in management.

MENINGOCOCCAL URETHRITIS. Meningococci have been isolated from the urethra and can cause clinical urethritis. In one study of more than 5000 urethral cultures from homosexual men, the isolation rate was 0.2% compared with 4.7% for N. gonorrhoeae in the same population. Eight of these patients had symptomatic urethritis. In the same study, there were no isolates among almost 9000 urethral cultures from heterosexual males or almost 16,000 cervical cultures. This study strongly suggested that there is an association between orogenital sex and urethral acquisition of the meningococcus. Meningococcal urethritis has been managed successfully with penicillin and/or tetracycline therapy.

Chemoprophylaxis

The observation that sulfonamides could clear the nasopharynx carriage of meningococci for weeks after a single day of therapy led to the concept of chemoprophylaxis for prevention of secondary infection in hyperepidemic situations. During World War II, using carrier rates to forecast epidemics among recruits, military public health officials were able to abort serious epidemics among military trainees. Because of the profligate use of sulfonamides for chemoprophylaxis in the 1950s, the meningococcus developed resistance to these agents, and in 1963 epidemics were occurring on military bases as the Vietnam military buildup was occurring. These organisms were universally resistant to sulfonamides. This situation led to intensive research by the U.S. Army on vaccines for disease prevention and new agents for chemoprophylaxis. These studies resulted in an effective anticapsular vaccine in 1970 and the application of minocycline and rifampin for chemoprophylaxis. Eradication of the carrier state in intimate contacts of index cases with chemoprophylaxis is an effective way to prevent secondary cases.

The concept behind successful prophylaxis is the use of short-term antibiotic therapy (one to two doses) to achieve long-term (3- to 4-week) eradication of the meningococcus from the nasopharynx. Although physicians realize that prophylaxis is necessary, they fail to appreciate that specific antibiotics must be used for effective management. Penicillin, penicillin derivatives, and first- and second-generation cephalosporins are not effective for prophylaxis because eradication of the meningococcus is not achieved during the short courses of therapy used. Rifampin and ceftriaxone have been shown to be effective agents for prophylaxis (Table 313–2). Quinolone derivatives have also been shown to be effective for chemoprophylaxis.

Prevention

The immunologically different meningococcal serogroups were identified in the early 20th century. This identification led to the use of capsular-specific serotherapy for the management of meningococcal infection before the development of effective chemotherapy. The ability of the meningococcal capsular polysaccharides to evoke a protective immune response is the basis for the meningococcal vaccines. An effective tetravalent capsular polysaccharide vaccine (containing A, C, Y, and W135 polysaccharide) is available for the prevention of meningococcal infections in individuals older than 2 years. Over 100

Table 313–2 • CHEMOPROPHYLAXIS AND IMMUNOPROPHYLAXIS FOR PREVENTION OF MENINGOCOCCAL INFECTION

CHEMOPROPHYLAXIS

Antibiotic	Dose
Rifampin	Adults who are not pregnant, 600 mg PO q12h for 2 days. Children >1 mo, 5 mg/kg PO; <1 mo, 10 mg/kg PO q12h for 2 days
Ceftriaxone	Single 250 mg IM dose for adults, single 125 mg IM dose for children <15 years of age
Ciprofloxacin	Adults who are not pregnant, 500 mg as a single PO dose. Limited experience in children <18

IMMUNOPROPHYLAXIS

Monovalent A, monovalent C, bivalent A-C, or quadrivalent A, C, Y, and W-135 vaccine is administered once by volume according to manufacturer. Amount of polysaccharide delivered is usually 50 µg. Vaccination should be considered an adjunct to antibiotic chemoprophylaxis for household or intimate contacts of meningococcal disease cases when appropriate serogroups are causing disease.

million doses of this vaccine have been given worldwide with no serious side effects reported. Tetravalent vaccine should be administered to all intimate contacts of index cases at the start of chemoprophylaxis. The vaccine has also been used effectively in the U.S. military and in aborting epidemics caused by serogroup strains represented in the vaccine. In addition, because of an elevated risk of meningococcal disease, it is now recommended that college freshmen who live in dormitories be immunized with the tetravalent meningococcal vaccine before starting classes.

A principal drawback of the vaccine is the lack of immunogenicity in children younger than 2 years. This has limited widespread application of the current vaccine in countries with recurrent epidemic infections. Children younger than age 2 respond poorly to polysaccharides for reasons that are not clearly understood. Successes in vaccinating young children with H. influenzae polysaccharide conjugated to proteins suggest that a similar strategy might be useful for meningococcal polysaccharides. A meningococcal serogroup C vaccine has been licensed in Great Britain. This vaccine is immunogenic in young children and produces high-titer bactericidal antibodies against N. meningitidis serogroup C strains. It is anticipated that serogroup A, Y, and W-135 conjugate vaccines will be available shortly.

The lack of an antigen capable of eliciting protection against meningococcal serogroup B infection is a problem. The serogroup B polysaccharide is a poor immunogen even in adults, perhaps because it resembles self-antigens. Vaccine development for serogroup B strains has focused on other meningococcal subcapsular surface antigens (proteins and possibly lipopolysaccharide). These vaccines are based on serotypical protein antigens, and the vaccine must be tailored to the serotype of the specific meningococcal strain causing the epidemic. A noncapsular serogroup B vaccine has been tested in an epidemic in Brazil, and the results indicate that the vaccine was effective in children older than 2 years.

SUGGESTED READINGS

Bruce MG, Rosenstein NE, Capparella JM, et al: Risk factors for meningococcal disease in college students. JAMA 2001;286:688–693. *Analysis of risk of meningococcal disease in college students and recommendations for vaccination.*

Jolly K, Stewart G: Epidemiology and diagnosis of meningitis: Results of a five-year prospective, population-based study. Commun Dis Public Health 2001;4:124–129. *Epidemiologic analysis of the Neisseria meningitidis serogroup C outbreak in Great Britain from 1994 to 1998.*

Kvalsvig AJ, Unsworth DJ: The immunopathogenesis of meningococcal disease. J Clin Pathol 2003;56:417–422. *Description of the immune response to meningococcal disease and how individual variation determines susceptibility.*

Levin M, Quint PA, Goldstein B, et al: Recombinant bactericidal/permeability-increasing protein (rBPI21) as adjunctive treatment for children with severe meningococcal sepsis: A randomised trial. rBPI21 Meningococcal Sepsis Study Group. Lancet 2000;356:954–955. *Description of therapeutic trial with rBPI to reduce mortality in severe meningococcal sepsis.*

Prevention and control of meningococcal disease. Recommendations of the Advisory Committee on Immunization Practices (ACIP). MMWR Recomm Rep 2000;49 (RR-7):1–10. *CDC recommendations for management of meningococcal infections in the community.*

Richardson DC, Louie L, Louie M, et al: Evaluation of a rapid PCR assay for diagnosis of meningococcal meningitis. J Clin Microbiol 2003;41:3851–3853. *Sensitivity was 97% and specificity was 99.6%.*

Rosenstein NE, Perkins BA, Stephens DS, et al: Meningococcal disease. N Engl J Med 2001;344:1378–1388. *Comprehensive review of meningococcal infections.*

Ruggeberg J, Heath PT: Safety and efficacy of meningococcal group C conjugate vaccines. Expert Opin Drug Saf 2003;2:7–19. *The efficacy is about 90% for all age groups, and vaccination programs have been associated with a 90% or more reduction in mortality.*

Welch SB, Nadel S: Treatment of meningococcal infection. Arch Dis Child 2003;88:608–614. *Overview of treatment.*

Westendorp RG, Hottenga JJ, Slagboom PE: Variation in plasminogen-activator-inhibitor-1 gene and risk of meningococcal septic shock. Lancet 1999;354:561–563. *Study demonstrated that severity of sepsis syndrome may have a genetic component.*

314 INFECTIONS CAUSED BY *HAEMOPHILUS* SPECIES

Michael S. Simberkoff

Definition

The name *Haemophilus* is derived from the Greek nouns *haima,* meaning "blood," and *philos,* meaning "lover." *Haemophilus* species primarily infect the respiratory tract, skin, or mucous membranes of humans. From these sites, organisms can invade to cause bacteremia, meningitis, epiglottitis, endocarditis, septic arthritis, or cellulitis.

Microbiology

The *Haemophilus* species are small, nonmotile, aerobic or facultative anaerobic, pleomorphic, gram-negative bacilli. The prototype of this genus, *H. influenzae,* was originally recovered from patients with influenza by Pfeiffer in 1893, and it was considered the cause of that disease for many years. The growth requirements of important *Haemophilus* species are summarized in Table 314–1. Primary isolation of *Haemophilus* species is best accomplished on chocolate agar medium in a CO_2-enriched atmosphere.

INFECTIONS CAUSED BY *H. INFLUENZAE*

General Considerations and Laboratory Characterization

H. influenzae is the most important pathogen in this genus. It can be recovered from sites where it colonizes, such as the nasopharynx and upper respiratory tract, and from sites where it causes disease, such as the blood, cerebrospinal fluid (CSF), sputum, pleura, middle ear, female genital tract, and joints (Table 314–2).

H. influenzae consists of encapsulated (typable) and nonencapsulated (nontypable) strains. The former are responsible for most of the invasive infections in children and acute epiglottitis in both children and adults, whereas the latter cause respiratory mucosal infections, including otitis media, sinusitis, exacerbations of chronic bronchitis, and pneumonia; conjunctivitis; female genital tract infections; as well as invasive disease in adults. The capsules of *H. influenzae* consist of polysaccharide antigens. Six capsular serotypes (a through f) exist in the species.

Table 314–1 • GROWTH REQUIREMENTS AND HEMOLYTIC PROPERTIES OF *HAEMOPHILUS* SPECIES

SPECIES	X	V	CO₂	HEMOLYSIS
H. influenzae	+	+	–	–
H. influenzae, b. *aegyptius*	+	+	–	–
H. parainfluenzae	–	+	–	–
H. aphrophilus	+*	–	+	–
H. paraphrophilus	–	+	+	–
H. haemolyticus	+	+	–	+
H. parahaemolyticus	–	+	–	+
H. ducreyi	+	–	–	+†

*Hematin needed for primary isolation.
†Delayed hemolysis occurs in 11 to 89% of strains.

Table 314–2 • SITES OF COLONIZATION AND INFECTIONS BY *H. INFLUENZAE*

SPECIES	NORMAL FLORA	ASSOCIATED DISEASE(S)
H. influenzae	Nasopharynx Upper respiratory tract	Meningitis Epiglottitis Sinusitis Otitis Pneumonia Cellulitis Arthritis Osteomyelitis Obstetric infections Endocarditis
H. influenzae b. *aegyptius*	No	Purulent conjunctivitis Brazilian purpuric fever

Factors Affecting Virulence

The capsules of *H. influenzae* are important virulence factors that inhibit opsonization, clearance, and intracellular killing of the organisms. *H. influenzae* type b, formerly the most common cause of meningitis in infancy and childhood worldwide, contains a pentose capsular polysaccharide consisting of polyribosyl-ribitol phosphate (PRP). Other serotypes contain hexose polysaccharides. It is believed that *H. influenzae* type b is more virulent than other serotypes because it is highly resistant to clearance once bacteremia has been initiated.

Fimbriae are important virulence factors that enhance the adherence of *H. influenzae* to mucosal surfaces. Both typable and nontypable *H. influenzae* isolates contain fimbriae. The lipo-oligosaccharides (LOSs) of *H. influenzae* also contribute to their virulence. LOSs appear to play a crucial role in facilitating the survival of *H. influenzae* on mucosal surfaces within the nasopharynx and in initiating invasive disease (blood stream invasion) from these sites.

Outer membrane proteins (OMPs) also serve as virulence factors in *H. influenzae* disease. At least 15 different *H. influenzae* OMPs have been identified. One of these (P2, 39 to 40 kD) functions as a porin, and others are associated with iron binding. Successful scavenging of iron within the human host is crucial for *H. influenzae* to multiply.

Host Defenses

Antibodies have been recognized for decades as an important part of the host defenses against *H. influenzae* diseases. The classic studies of Fothergill and Wright, in 1933, demonstrated that most cases of *H. influenzae* meningitis occurred in children during the ages between their losing passively acquired maternal antibodies and developing active humoral immunity to the organism. It is now recognized that these protective antibodies function primarily to opsonize and facilitate *H. influenzae* clearance rather than to directly kill virulent organisms.

Complement is also an essential component of the host defenses against some *H. influenzae* diseases. Children with congenital deficiencies of C2, C3, and factor I have an increased incidence of *H. influenzae* infections. Patients who lack a functional spleen or who have undergone splenectomy also are at risk for developing overwhelming infection with *H. influenzae* type b.

Prevalence, Incidence, and Epidemiology

The precise prevalence and incidence of *H. influenzae* infections are unknown. This organism can be detected frequently in the nasopharynx of both children and adults. Between 3 and 5% of infants harbor *H. influenzae* type b in their nasopharynx. Nontypable *H. influenzae* can be detected in the nasopharyngeal culture of more than 70% of young children. Infections, however, occur in only a small proportion of colonized patients. The risk of infection in nonimmune household contacts of a patient with invasive *H. influenzae* disease is approximately 600-fold greater than the risk in the age-adjusted general population.

H. influenzae type b was the most common cause of meningitis in young children before effective vaccines were introduced in the 1980s. Vaccination dramatically reduced the incidence of this infection in young children. In a population-based study in Atlanta, over a 1-year period, invasive *H. influenzae* disease occurred in only 5.6 per 100,000 children and 1.7 per 100,000 adults. Forty of the 47 strains associated with invasive disease from adult patients in this study were serotyped. Twenty of these isolates (50%) were *H. influenzae* type b, 19 (47.5%) were nontypable, and 1 (2.5%) was a type f.

Patients with human immunodeficiency virus (HIV) infection are at increased risk for *H. influenzae* infection. Rates of invasive *H. influenzae* infection among men aged 20 to 49 with HIV infection and the acquired immunodeficiency syndrome (AIDS) were 14.6 and 79.2 per 100,000, respectively. The majority of these infections were caused by nontypable *H. influenzae* strains, although in a second study, 10 of 15 bacteremic *H. influenzae* type b infections observed in adults occurred in patients at risk for HIV infection, and AIDS was documented in 7 of these patients.

Other factors also increase the risk of *H. influenzae* infections. These include globulin deficiencies, sickle cell disease, splenectomy, malignancy, pregnancy, CSF leaks, head trauma, alcoholism, chronic obstructive pulmonary disease (COPD), and race. Eskimo, Navajo, and Apache children have *H. influenzae* type b infection rates that are significantly greater than those in comparable nonnative populations. In addition, day-care attendance, crowding, presence of siblings, previous hospitalizations, and previous otitis media have been shown to increase the risk of *H. influenzae* type b disease in young children, whereas breastfeeding decreases this risk.

Pathogenesis

H. influenzae is spread from person to person. Colonization of an individual depends on the virulence factors described earlier. When *H. influenzae* translocates across damaged epithelial cells, it invades the bloodstream. Encapsulated organisms, particularly *H. influenzae* type b, are especially resistant to clearance.

The central nervous system (CNS) is primarily invaded through the choroid plexus. *H. influenzae* and its LOSs initiate an inflammatory process within the subarachnoid that is typical of pyogenic meningitis. This process can be transiently accelerated by using antibiotics that liberate LOSs from organisms if corticosteroids are not administered simultaneously.

Clinical Manifestations

MENINGITIS. *H. influenzae* meningitis commonly occurs in children younger than age 5 and in adults with histories of skull trauma or CSF leaks. *H. influenzae* type b strains cause the overwhelming majority of these. A review of 493 episodes of acute bacterial meningitis in adults over a 27-year period showed that 19 cases (4%) were due to *H. influenzae*.

H. influenzae meningitis is clinically indistinguishable from other forms of acute bacterial meningitis. Most patients with *H. influenzae* meningitis have CSF white blood counts of more than 1000/mm³ and hypoglycorrhachia. The CSF Gram stain shows pleomorphic Gram-negative bacilli in 60 to 70% of untreated cases. In some patients, however, the bipolar staining may result in a mistaken diagnosis of pneumococcal meningitis. Thus, Gram stain is neither sensitive nor specific for diagnosing *H. influenzae* meningitis.

A diagnosis of *H. influenzae* type b meningitis can be rapidly and reliably established by detecting PRP capsular antigens in CSF. The diagnosis can be established in most cases even when antibiotics have been given before CSF is obtained. Other serotypes (most commonly type f) can cause meningitis in adults. Therefore, serologic tests for type b antigen in CSF cannot be relied on to rule out *H. influenzae* meningitis in all cases.

EPIGLOTTITIS. *H. influenzae* type b is the most common cause of acute epiglottitis in both children and adults. Epiglottitis is a life-threatening infection in children that usually occurs in patients younger than age 5. The symptoms are fever, drooling, dysphagia, and respiratory distress or stridor, which appear over the course of hours. In adults, fever, sore throat, dysphagia, and odynophagia occur. Cervical tenderness and lymphadenopathy can be found at all ages. Laryngoscopy demonstrates a swollen, cherry-red epiglottis. However, this procedure should be avoided or undertaken only by experts, because it may precipitate an acute airway obstruction and thus make an emergency tracheotomy necessary. The diagnosis of acute epiglottitis is more safely confirmed by a lateral radiograph of the neck. The patient must be maintained in an upright position during this procedure, however, to avoid additional compromise of the airway. The etiology is usually established by blood culture. Cultures of the pharynx and other mucosal surfaces are less useful because *H. influenzae* may be part of the normal flora. One review suggests that although vaccination has effectively reduced the incidence of this disease in children, it is increasingly observed in adults.

PNEUMONIA. *H. influenzae* is a common cause of pneumonia in both children and adults. Nosocomial infections, including ventilator-associated pneumonia, also can be caused by these organisms. The clinical features of *H. influenzae* pneumonia include fever, cough, and signs and radiographic findings of lobar consolidation. Parapneumonic effusions or empyema occur commonly in patients with *H. influenzae* pneumonia. Gram-negative bacilli in sputum suggest the diagnosis, but isolation of *H. influenzae* from sputum culture alone is inadequate to prove an etiology because of the high frequency with which this organism colonizes the respiratory tract. A diagnosis can be established by isolating *H. influenzae* from either the blood or pleural fluid. Most isolates are nontypable.

TRACHEOBRONCHITIS. Tracheobronchitis is a condition characterized by fever, cough, and purulent sputum that occurs in the absence of radiographic infiltrates suggestive of pneumonia. It frequently occurs in patients with known chronic lung disease. Blood cultures are rarely positive. A combination of pleomorphic Gram-negative bacilli predominating in purulent sputum, antibody titers to *H. influenzae* that rise after infection, and the response, at least transiently, to treatment for *H. influenzae* infection strongly suggests this diagnosis.

SINUSITIS. *H. influenzae* and *Streptococcus pneumoniae* are the most frequent bacterial isolates from antral punctures or surgical specimens of patients with acute purulent sinusitis. Most *H. influenzae* isolates are nontypable. Although patients may respond initially to treatment directed against *H. influenzae*, the response is transient if sinus obstruction is not relieved. *H. influenzae* is not an important pathogen in patients with chronic sinusitis.

OTITIS MEDIA. *H. influenzae* is the most frequent cause of otitis media in young children. Approximately 90% of the *H. influenzae* isolates obtained by tympanocentesis are nontypable; *H. influenzae* type b causes most of the remaining 10% of infections. Patients with otitis media may present with ear pain or irritability. Drainage can be present. An inflamed, opaque, bulging, or perforated tympanic membrane is usually demonstrated. The etiology can be proved by Gram stain and culture of purulent fluid obtained by tympanocentesis. Otitis caused by *H. influenzae* type b may occur in association with bacteremia and meningitis.

CELLULITIS. *H. influenzae* type b is the cause of 5 to 15% of the cases of cellulitis in young children. Most of the infections occur on the face or neck. *H. influenzae* cellulitis is often described as causing a distinctive blue or violaceous discoloration of the skin. However, the fever, erythema, and tenderness observed may not be distinguishable from those from other causes. Diagnosis is established by culture of blood and or tissue aspirates from the involved area.

BACTEREMIA WITHOUT A PRIMARY FOCUS OF INFECTION. *H. influenzae* causes primary bacteremia in both children and adults. In infants or children, occult meningitis or epiglottitis can be present. A rigorous clinical and laboratory evaluation is essential to avoid missing diagnoses of life-threatening focal infections in these patients. In adults, primary *H. influenzae* type b bacteremia often occurs in patients with underlying diseases such as lymphoma, leukemia, or alcoholism.

OBSTETRIC AND GYNECOLOGIC INFECTION. Pregnancy is associated with a significant risk for *H. influenzae* infection. In the Atlanta study, 7 of 47 adult *H. influenzae* invasive infections occurred in pregnant women. Nontypable *H. influenzae* is also an important cause of tubo-ovarian abscess and salpingitis in women.

PERICARDITIS. *H. influenzae* type b is an important cause of primary bacterial pericarditis in children. It rarely causes this infection in adults; however, pericarditis can occur in association with pneumonia, probably as a result of contiguous spread of the infection.

Continued

ENDOCARDITIS. *H. influenzae* is a very unusual cause of endocarditis, considering the frequency with which invasive disease occurs. Most infections occur in patients with pre-existing valvular heart disease. Because of its slow initial growth in blood culture media, the diagnosis of this infection may be delayed or missed. Patients with *H. influenzae* endocarditis are at high risk for arterial embolic phenomena.

SEPTIC ARTHRITIS. *H. influenzae* type b is a common cause of septic arthritis in young children; it is rare in adults. *H. influenzae* type b arthritis is clinically indistinguishable from other causes of pyogenic arthritis.

Treatment

Third-generation cephalosporins are considered to be the treatment of choice for serious *H. influenzae* infections, such as meningitis or epiglottitis. Treatment with ceftriaxone (adult dose: 1 to 2 g IV every 12 hours) or cefotaxime (adult dose: 2 g IV every 6 hours) should be started for patients with proven or suspected *H. influenzae* infection, and this should be continued at least until the full susceptibility data are available.

Ampicillin was considered to be the treatment of choice for all *H. influenzae* infections until the mid-1970s. Since the first reports of ampicillin-resistant *H. influenzae* isolates in 1972, however, this problem has been increasing. At present, 39% of *H. influenzae* isolates are resistant to ampicillin. The majority contain a plasmid-mediated, R-factor enzyme (TEM-1), β-lactamase, which can be detected rapidly in the laboratory. A small number of isolates, however, have altered penicillin-binding proteins. These proteins poorly bind penicillin and other β-lactam antibiotics. As a consequence, the isolates may be resistant to some cephalosporins, such as cefaclor, cefamandole, and cefuroxime, in addition to ampicillin. Therefore, patients with proven or suspected *H. influenzae* infections should not be treated with ampicillin or with second-generation cephalosporins until susceptibilities to these antibiotics are proved. Chloramphenicol resistance also occurs in *H. influenzae*; resistance is caused by an inactivating enzyme, chloramphenicol acetyl transferase. A small number of *H. influenzae* isolates are resistant to both ampicillin and chloramphenicol.

Oral antibiotics are commonly used to treat tracheobronchitis in patients with COPD and otitis media in children where *H. influenzae* isolates are common. Because of resistance, ampicillin and amoxicillin cannot be recommended for the more serious of these infections unless the susceptibility of isolates is known. Most *H. influenzae* isolates are susceptible to amoxicillin-clavulanate. They also are susceptible to azithromycin and clarithromycin, the newer macrolide antibiotics. Fluoroquinolones, such as ciprofloxacin, ofloxacin, levofloxacin, and gatifloxacin, are active against these organisms. Bactrim is also effective for most isolates. A combination of erythromycin and sulfisoxazole can be used in patients with documented penicillin allergy.

Prevention

The first *H. influenzae* type b vaccines were licensed for use in the United States in 1985. These contained purified PRP antigens. However, postlicensing studies of PRP vaccines in the United States showed variable efficacy. The PRP vaccines elicit a type 2, thymus-independent B-cell response, generate few (if any) memory B cells, and fail to stimulate a response in neonates and infants.

Protein-conjugated PRP vaccines were developed to overcome the problem of the lack of immune response in the most susceptible infants and some young children. Several are now licensed for use in infants. At present, protein-conjugated PRP vaccines are recommended for use in all infants over age 2 months but not earlier than age 6 weeks. Recent studies have shown that protein-conjugated vaccines are effective in diverse populations. [1,2] True failures after three doses of the protein-conjugated PRP vaccines are quite rare.

Antibiotic prophylaxis should be used for nonimmunized household or day care contacts of a patient with invasive *H. influenzae* type b disease. Rifampin is the treatment of choice. It should be given in a dosage of 10 mg/kg once daily for 4 days to neonates younger than 1 month, 20 mg/kg (up to a maximum of 600 mg) once daily for 4 days to older children, and 600 mg/day for 4 days to adults.

INFECTIONS CAUSED BY *H. INFLUENZAE, BIOGROUP AEGYPTIUS* (PURULENT CONJUNCTIVITIS AND BRAZILIAN PURPURIC FEVER)

H. influenzae, biogroup aegyptius (Koch-Weeks bacillus) causes epidemic purulent conjunctivitis in children. This disease commonly occurs in hot climates or in the summer season. The infection causes conjunctival erythema, edema, mucopurulent exudate, and varying discomfort in the eyes. An unusually virulent clone of *H. influenzae, biogroup aegyptius*, causes an invasive infection called Brazilian purpuric fever, which is characterized by petechial or purpuric skin lesions and vascular collapse, occurring days to weeks after an initial episode of conjunctivitis in infants and children younger than 10 years; this infection is usually fatal.

INFECTIONS CAUSED BY OTHER *HAEMOPHILUS* SPECIES

H. PARAINFLUENZAE. *H. parainfluenzae* can be found as part of the normal flora of the mouth and pharynx (Table 314–3). It is a rare cause of meningitis in children and an even rarer cause of meningitis in adults. It may cause dental infections or dental abscesses. Cases of brain abscess, epidural abscess, liver abscess, osteomyelitis, pneumonia, empyema, epiglottitis, peritonitis, septic arthritis, and septicemia caused by this organism have been reported. *H. parainfluenzae* also causes subacute endocarditis, often in young adults. *Haemophilus* species cause approximately 1% of cases of infective endocarditis in non–drug-abusing patients. *H. parainfluenzae*, *H. aphrophilus*, and *H. paraphrophilus* (see later) are the species most frequently recovered from these patients. *H. parainfluenzae* forms bulky vegetations on heart valves. Arterial embolization is common in patients with *H. parainfluenzae* endocarditis. Most isolates are sensitive to ampicillin, but some produce β-lactamases. Pending sensitivity reports, patients should be treated with a drug that combines a β-lactam antibiotic and a β-lactamase inhibitor (such as ampicillin sulbactam; adult dose: 3 g IV every 6 hours) with ampicillin plus an aminoglycoside or with a third-generation cephalosporin.

H. APHROPHILUS. *H. aphrophilus* can be found as part of the normal oral flora (see Table 314–3). Like *H. parainfluenzae*, *H. aphrophilus* causes endocarditis but grows very slowly on primary isolation from blood cultures. It frequently causes bulky vegetations, and arterial emboli are common. *H. aphrophilus* is also a rare cause of brain abscess, periodontal abscess, meningitis, osteomyelitis, and suppurative pulmonary infections. Ampicillin or ampicillin plus an aminoglycoside should be used to treat infections.

H. PARAPHROPHILUS. *H. paraphrophilus* can be found as part of the normal flora of the mouth and pharynx (see Table 314–3). *H. paraphrophilus* is a cause of endocarditis, and arterial emboli have been observed in 50% of the cases of *H. paraphrophilus* endocarditis. It is also a rare cause of brain abscess and liver abscess. Ampicillin is the treatment of choice for this infection.

Table 314–3 • SITES OF COLONIZATION AND INFECTIONS BY OTHER *HAEMOPHILUS* SPECIES

SPECIES	NORMAL FLORA	ASSOCIATED DISEASE(S)
H. parainfluenzae	Mouth and pharynx	Endocarditis, brain abscess, liver abscess, pneumonia, epiglottitis, arthritis, osteomyelitis
H. aphrophilus	Mouth	Endocarditis, brain abscess, periodontal abscess, osteomyelitis
H. paraphrophilus	Mouth and pharynx	Endocarditis, brain abscess, liver abscess
H. haemolyticus	Nasopharynx	?
H. parahaemolyticus	Mouth and pharynx	Endocarditis, empyema of gallbladder, ? pharyngitis
H. ducreyi	No	Chancroid

H. PARAHAEMOLYTICUS. *H. parahaemolyticus* is an important pathogen in domestic animals, causing porcine pleuropneumonia. The organism can be found in the human mouth and pharynx. It is a rare cause of human subacute endocarditis and of empyema of the gallbladder (see Table 314–3). *H. parahaemolyticus* has been isolated from throat cultures of patients with pharyngitis. Animal isolates of *H. parahaemolyticus* are sensitive to tetracycline and sulfa drugs. There is insufficient information about human isolates to permit recommendations for therapy.

H. DUCREYI. See Chapter 348.

1. Mulholland K, Hilton S, Adegloba R, et al: Randomised trial of *Haemophilus influenzae* type-b tetanus protein conjugate for prevention of pneumonia and meningitis in Gambian infants. Lancet 1997;349:1191–1197.
2. Schuchat A, Robinson K, Wenger JD, et al: Bacterial meningitis in the United States in 1995. N Engl J Med 1997;337:970–976.

SUGGESTED READINGS

Adams WG, Keaver KA, Cochi SL, et al: Decline of childhood *Haemophilus influenzae* type b (Hib) disease in the Hib vaccine era. JAMA 1993;269:264–266. *This report shows that, in children younger than age 5, there was a 71 to 82% reduction in H. influenzae type b meningitis in the year after licensing of the Hib conjugate vaccines in the United States.*

Centers for Disease Control and Prevention: Recommendations for use of the *Haemophilus b* conjugate vaccines and a combined diphtheria, tetanus, pertussis, and *Haemophilus b* vaccine. Recommendations of the Advisory Committee on Immunization Practices (ACIP). MMWR Morb Mort Wkly Rep 1993;42(No.RR-13):1. *Contains recommendations for use of Haemophilus b conjugate vaccines for infants beginning at age 2 months (but not earlier than age 6 weeks); also describes the safety, immunogenicity, efficacy, adverse reactions, contraindications, and precautions for vaccine use.*

Darras-Joly C, Lortholary O, Mainardi JL, et al: Haemophilus endocarditis: Report of 42 cases in adults and review. Clin Infect Dis 1997;24:1087–1094. *This is a report of 42 cases of Haemophilus endocarditis seen in France from 1983 to 1995 and a review of an additional 40 cases reported in the literature. Twenty-six of the 42 cases (62%) were caused by H. parainfluenzae, 9 (21%) by H. aphrophilus, 4 (10%) were caused by H. paraphrophilus, and 3 (7%) were caused by H. influenzae. Arterial embolization occurred in 15 (36%) of the patients.*

Durand ML, Calderwood SB, Weber DJ, et al: Acute bacterial meningitis in adults: A review of 493 episodes. N Engl J Med 1993;328:21–28. *Summarizes data from a large series of adults with acute bacterial meningitis seen over 27 years. H. influenzae caused acute bacterial meningitis in 19 (4%) of the adults. Thirteen of these patients had community-acquired infections and six developed nosocomial H. influenzae meningitis after neurosurgery.*

Farley MM, Stephens DS, Brachman PS, et al: Invasive *Haemophilus influenzae* disease in adults. Ann Intern Med 1992;116:806–812. *A population-based study showing that 47 cases of invasive H. influenzae disease occurred in adults in metropolitan Atlanta from December 1988 through May 1990 (incidence 1.7 per 100,000 adults per year).*

Foxwell A, Cripps A, Dear K: Haemophilus influenzae oral whole cell vaccination for preventing acute exacerbations of chronic bronchitis. Cochrane Database Syst Rev 2003;3:CD001958. *In several small trials, vaccination of patients with recurrent acute exacerbations of chronic bronchitis in the autumn reduced the number and severity of exacerbations over the winter months.*

Sethi S, Evan N, Grant BJ, et al: New strains of bacteria and exacerbations of chronic obstructive pulmonary disease. N Engl J Med 2002;347:465–471. *In 81 patients with chronic obstructive pulmonary disease (COPD), nontypable H. influenzae were the most commonly isolated bacterial pathogens.*

315 OSTEOMYELITIS

Barry D. Brause

Definition

Osteomyelitis is an infection by microorganisms that invade bone. Three pathogenetic routes of infection define the major forms of osteomyelitis, with pathogens reaching osseous tissue by (1) hematogenous seeding, (2) contamination accompanying surgical and nonsurgical trauma (termed *introduced* infection), or (3) spread from infected contiguous tissue.

Etiology

Although virtually all microorganisms can infect bone, bacteria are the usual pathogens and staphylococci are the most prominent etiologic agents. *Staphylococcus aureus* causes approximately 60% of hematogenous and introduced infections and is a principal agent when osseous sepsis spreads by contiguity. *S. epidermidis* has become a major pathogen in bone infections associated with indwelling prosthetic materials, such as joint implants and fracture fixation devices, and is responsible for 30% of these cases. Streptococci, Gram-negative bacilli, anaerobes, mycobacteria, and fungi are etiologic agents in a variety of clinical settings (Table 315–1).

Incidence, Prevalence, and Epidemiology

The anatomic location of hematogenous osteomyelitis is age dependent (see Table 315–1). From birth to puberty the long bones of the extremities are the most frequently involved. In adults, blood-borne osteomyelitis generally affects the spine, because vertebrae become more vascular than other skeletal tissue with maturation. Seventy percent of compound fractures are contaminated, but because of effective débridement and perioperative antibiotic therapy only 2 to 9% develop infection. Osteomyelitis develops by contiguous spread in 30 to 68% of diabetic patients with foot ulcers, and it is notable that more in-hospital days are spent treating foot infections than treating any other complication of diabetes.

Pathogenesis

In childhood, hematogenous osteomyelitis, the initial infective site is the long bone metaphysis, owing to its large blood flow. In adults, bacteremias seed vertebral bodies preferentially at the more vascular anterior end plates. Osteomyelitis commonly involves two adjacent vertebral bodies and the intervertebral disk space. Infection

---

Table 315–1 • PREDISPOSITIONS, ANATOMIC SITES, AND PROMINENT PATHOGENS IN FORMS OF OSTEOMYELITIS

FORM OF OSTEOMYELITIS	PREDISPOSING CONDITION	SITE	PROMINENT PATHOGENS
Hematogenous			
Childhood	None, ? recent blunt trauma	Long bones	*Staphylococcus aureus*, streptococci, *Haemophilus*
	Sickle cell hemoglobinopathy	Multiple	*Salmonella*, *S. aureus*
Adult	Urinary tract infection or instrumentation	Vertebral	Gram-negative bacilli, streptococci
	Skin infection	Vertebral	*S. aureus*, streptococci
	Respiratory infection	Vertebral, hip, knee	Streptococci, *Mycobacterium tuberculosis*
	Intravenous drug abuse or vascular catheters	Vertebral, pelvis, clavicle	Gram-negative bacilli, staphylococci, *Candida*
	Acquired immunodeficiency syndrome	Multiple	Fungi, mycobacteria
	Endocarditis	Vertebral	*S. aureus*, streptococci
Introduced type	Fractures	Fracture site	*S. aureus*, *S. epidermidis*, gram-negative bacilli
	Prosthetic joint	Prosthesis	*S. epidermidis*, *S. aureus*
Contiguous spread	Skin ulcer	Foot, leg	Polymicrobial, staphylococci, streptococci, gram-negative bacilli, anaerobes
	Sinusitis	Skull	Streptococci, anaerobes
	Dental abscess	Mandible, maxilla	Streptococci, anaerobes
	Human or animal bites	Hand	Streptococci, anaerobes, *Pasteurella*
	Felon	Finger	*S. aureus*
	Gardening	Hand	*Sporothrix*
	Puncture wounds	Foot	*Pseudomonas aeruginosa*, anaerobes

compromises the nutrient supply to the intervertebral disk, resulting in disk necrosis and disk space narrowing, which is often the earliest sign of vertebral osteomyelitis (Fig. 315–1). Table 315–1 lists examples of clinical conditions that predispose to the development of blood-borne bone infection.

With the introduced form of osteomyelitis, direct septic trauma breaches all protective tissue around the bone, allowing microorganisms into the osseous matrix. The risk of infection is increased further when metallic fixation devices or prosthetic joints are implanted. Indwelling foreign bodies decrease the quantity of bacteria necessary to establish infection in bone and permit pathogens to persist on the surface of the avascular material, often within host- or pathogen-derived biofilms, sequestered from circulating immune factors and systemic antibiotics.

Osteomyelitis is caused by contiguous extension from infected, adjacent soft tissue when the soft tissue process is sufficiently chronic or uncontrolled (see Table 315–1). Chronic diabetic foot infections reflect persistence of neuropathic and vasculopathic processes that initiate skin ulceration and interfere with healing.

Once infection becomes established in bone, the microorganisms induce local metabolic changes and inflammatory reactions that increase necrosis. As the septic process spreads, local thrombophlebitis develops, further increasing edema and intraosseous pressure, which results in ischemic necrosis of large areas of bone called *sequestra* (Fig. 315–2). When the osseous cortex is breached, subperiosteal abscesses can develop with periosteal inflammation that induces new bone formation in adjacent soft tissue.

Clinical Manifestations

In the classic presentation of childhood hematogenous osteomyelitis, fever, chills, and malaise are present but are frequently absent in the other forms of bone infection. Localized pain is a characteristic feature of osteomyelitis, with overlying erythema, warmth, and swelling variably observed. Limb motion may be limited if infection is near an articulation, and joint effusions can occur but are usually sterile when the epiphyseal cartilage is intact.

Hematogenous vertebral osteomyelitis often presents with back pain, spine tenderness, and low-grade fever after urinary tract instrumentation or infection (30%), skin infection (13%), or respiratory infection (11%). The septic process extending beyond the vertebral column produces suppuration at the particular spinal level of infection such as retropharyngeal abscess, mediastinitis, empyema, subdiaphragmatic and iliopsoas abscesses, as well as meningitis. If paresis, sensory deficits, or bowel or bladder dysfunction develop, spinal epidural abscess—the most feared complication—should be suspected and evaluated immediately. *Mycobacterium tuberculosis* should be considered in relatively indolent infections of vertebrae (as well as at the hip and knee) (see Table 315–1).

Osteomyelitis after trauma or bone surgery is usually associated with persistent or recurrent fevers, increasing pain at the operative site, and poor incisional healing, which is often accompanied by protracted wound drainage or dehiscence. Prosthetic joint infection manifests as joint pain (95%), fever (43%), or cutaneous sinus drainage (32%).

Bone involvement by contiguous spread from an overlying chronic ischemic or neuropathic foot ulcer typically occurs in patients with long-standing insulin-dependent diabetes or other neuropathic or vascular disease and involves the metatarsals or the proximal phalanges. It is characterized by local cellulitis with inflammation and necrosis, but pain is only variably found, owing to the frequent presence of sensory neuropathy. Osseous extension is common when the skin ulcer is more than 2 cm^2 with a depth more than 3 mm or when bone is exposed. Additional examples of osteomyelitis from contiguous spread of infection are listed in Table 315–1.

Diagnosis

Diagnosis requires both confirming the osseous site of involvement and identifying the etiologic microbes. Bone infection must be differentiated from septic arthritis and bursitis, cellulitis and soft tissue abscesses, bone fractures, and neoplasms, as well as bone infarcts seen with sickle cell hemoglobinopathy and Gaucher's disease. Anatomic

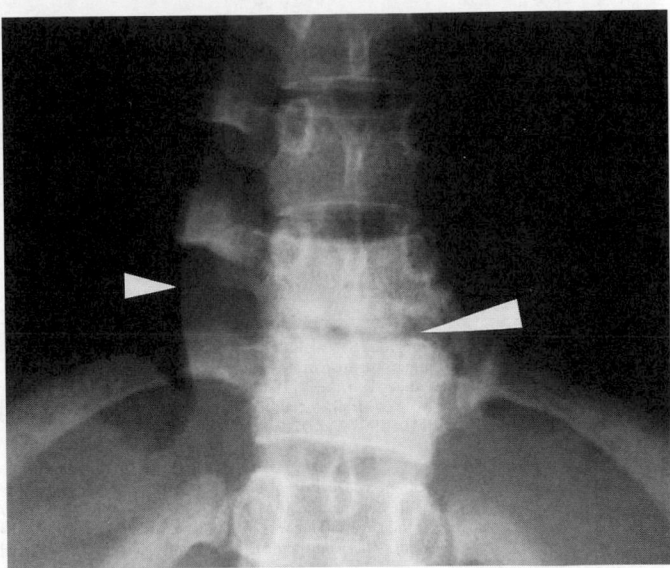

FIGURE 315–1 • Vertebral osteomyelitis. Frontal view of spine illustrates disk space narrowing (large arrowhead) and paraspinal abscess (small arrowhead).

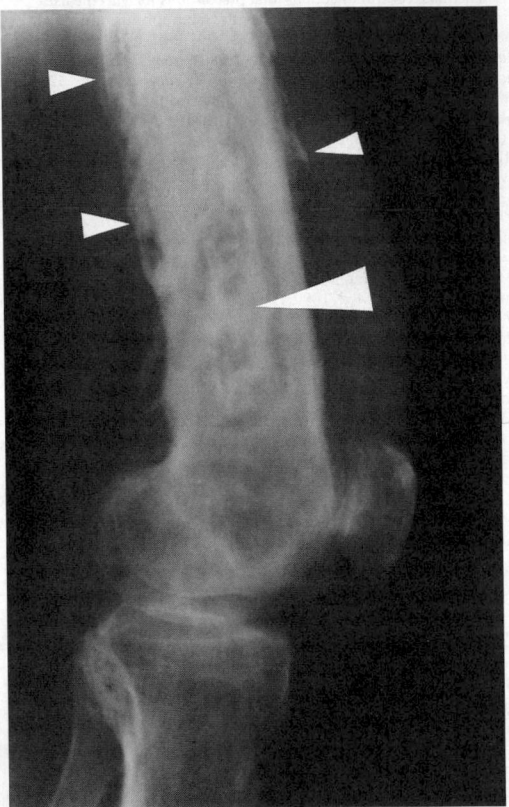

FIGURE 315–2 • Femoral osteomyelitis. Hyperdense central zone is a sequestrum (large arrowhead), and peripheral linear densities are areas of periosteal elevation with periosteal new bone formation (small arrowheads).

delineation of bone infection depends largely on radiologic techniques (Table 315–2). In hematogenous infection, the earliest osseous changes by radiography are osteopenic or lytic intramedullary lesions. They require 30 to 50% decalcification to be seen and take 2 to 4 weeks to develop. With further progression, periosteal elevation, thickening, and new bone formation occur, with sequestra and sclerotic changes occurring in chronic infection (see Fig. 315–2). Vertebral osteomyelitis appears initially as disk space narrowing, followed by cortical destruction at the adjacent end plates (see Fig. 315–1). In the contiguous form of infection the earliest bone defects develop at the cortex.

Table 315–2 • APPROXIMATE SENSITIVITY AND SPECIFICITY OF IMAGING TECHNIQUES FOR OSTEOMYELITIS IN "COMPLICATED CASES" (PATIENTS WITH NEUROPATHY, OVERLYING SOFT-TISSUE INFECTION, OR PRIOR BONE INJURY)

IMAGING TECHNIQUE	SENSITIVITY (%)	SPECIFICITY (%)
X-ray	69	82
Technetium diphosphonate bone scan	77	36
Gallium scan	95	38
Indium leukocyte scan	74	69
Magnetic resonance imaging	83	75

Computed tomography is helpful to identify small osseous alterations and sequestra.

Technetium diphosphonate bone scans, gallium-citrate scans, and indium-labeled leukocyte scintigraphy are far more sensitive than radiography and usually reveal increased radionuclide uptake when symptoms begin (see Table 315–2). However, these techniques are plagued by inadequate specificity and spatial resolution, so they are not conclusively diagnostic. Inflammatory and degenerative processes in adjacent tissues, recent orthopedic surgery, bone fractures, and neoplasms produce abnormal scans in the absence of osteomyelitis. Magnetic resonance imaging can detect the bone edema of osteomyelitis earlier than radiography; however, differentiation from non-specific reactive marrow edema due to adjacent foci of non-osseous infection and other causes of soft-tissue edema is often not possible. Specificity can be as low as 75%, especially in "complicated" cases with neuropathy, overlying soft-tissue infection, or prior bone injury, but magnetic resonance imaging is helpful in identifying paraosseous soft tissue abscesses (see Table 315–2).

The exact microbial cause of osteomyelitis should be determined, because it is never sufficiently predictable to permit routine presumptive therapy (see Table 315–1). Blood cultures are positive in 25 to 50% of acute childhood hematogenous osteomyelitis but are helpful in less than 10% of the other forms of bone infection. When septic arthritis or soft tissue abscess accompanies the osseous process, arthrocentesis or abscess aspiration cultures can be diagnostic. However, superficial cultures of open wounds or skin ulcers and cultures of cutaneous sinus tracts do not delineate the true bone pathogen(s). In patients with deep chronic skin ulcers from which infection has spread to bone, curettage cultures from the base of the ulcer correlate with osseous tissue 75% of the time. Bone aspirate and biopsy cultures are positive in 70 to 93% of cases and should be sought (percutaneously or by operative débridement) when there is no overlying skin ulcer and the microbiologic diagnosis has not been otherwise established. Specimens for mycobacterial, fungal, and anaerobic cultivation should be considered when routine bacterial cultures are negative.

 Treatment

Acute osteomyelitis is curable with adequate antimicrobial therapy and surgical débridement when necessary. Parenterally administered antibiotics are usually used, but oral therapy is also effective when the pathogen is sufficiently susceptible and gastrointestinal absorption is ensured. The exact potency and duration of therapy required to eradicate bone infections are not known. Antibiotics that produce trough serum bactericidal activity at a 1:2 titer have been associated with high cure rates. Treatment should be given for 4 to 6 weeks. Surgery is indicated to drain abscesses, débride necrotic tissues, remove foreign materials, and provide skin closure in patients with chronic unhealed wounds.

Prognosis

Inadequate therapy for acute osteomyelitis results in relapsing infection and progression to chronic osteomyelitis; therefore, definitive treatment of acute infection is obligatory. Because of the presence of gross and microscopic foci of avascular bone, chronic osteomyelitis

is not curable except by radical resection (occasionally amputation). Acute exacerbations of these chronic, recurrent infections can be suppressed successfully by débridement of identifiable sequestra followed by protracted courses of parenteral and oral antimicrobial agents. Very rare complications include pathologic fractures, squamous cell carcinoma at the sinus tract cutaneous orifice, and secondary amyloidosis.

SUGGESTED READINGS

Frykberg RG: Diabetic foot ulcers: Current concepts. J Foot Ankle Surg 1998;37:440–446. *Solid review of the etiology, evaluation, treatment, and prevention of the ulcerations that, if unabated, lead to problematic osteomyelitis.*

Mader JT, Wang J, Calhoun JH: Antibiotic therapy for musculoskeletal infections. Instr Course Lec 2002;51:539–551. *Comprehensive review of antibiotic selection and duration in treating septic arthritis and osteomyelitis.*

McHenry MC, Easley KA, Locker GA: Vertebral osteomyelitis: Long-term outcome for 253 patients from 7 Cleveland-area hospitals. Clin Infect Dis 2002;34:1342–1350. *Current characterization of vertebral osteomyelitis including microbiology, pathogenesis, diagnosis, therapy, complications, and prognosis.*

Stepensky D, Kleinberg I, Hoffman A: Bone as an effect compartment: Models for uptake and release of drugs. Clin Pharmacokinet 2003;42:863–881. *Describes the pharmacokinetic behavior of bone-seeking agents and predicts bone concentrations of these agents for different doses and patient populations.*

Tice AD, Hoaglund PA, Shoultz DA: Outcomes of osteomyelitis among patients treated with outpatient parenteral antimicrobial therapy. Am J Med 2003;114:723–728. *Almost all recurrences occur within 1 year, and diabetes and peripheral vascular disease are important risk factors for outcome.*

316 WHOOPING COUGH (PERTUSSIS)

Richard B. Johnston, Jr.

Definition

Whooping cough (pertussis) is a noninvasive, highly communicable bacterial respiratory illness. It occurs at all ages but is most common and most severe in infants and young children. The etiologic agent of the syndrome is usually *Bordetella pertussis*. The descriptive name derives from a distressing, prolonged inspiratory effort that follows paroxysmal coughing. Whooping cough is estimated to cause 300,000 deaths worldwide yearly, primarily in infants.

Epidemiology

In nonimmune households, the attack rate of pertussis is 80 to 90%. Transmission is by droplet infection. Carriers of *B. pertussis* are found infrequently, but persons previously immunized have been shown during outbreaks of disease to excrete the organism in the absence of clinical symptoms or in the presence of mild or atypical illness.

The mortality rate from whooping cough has fallen since the beginning of the 20th century owing to improved supportive therapy. The incidence of whooping cough, however, did not change until after the 1940s, when immunization of young children became standard practice. In the 1940s, approximately 200,000 cases of pertussis were reported annually in the United States, compared with about 7000 cases annually in recent years. Most deaths occur in children younger than 1 year. The case-fatality rate in infants less than 6 months of age is 1%.

Neither immunization against pertussis nor natural disease provides lifelong protection. In the case of immunization, an attack rate greater than 50% has been reported when the interval after immunization exceeds 12 years. In recent years, almost half of reported cases have occurred in adolescents and adults. This population represents a large reservoir of susceptible persons who can transmit the disease to nonimmunized infants. Pertussis causes about 25% of persistent cough in adults.

Pathobiology

When first isolated, *B. pertussis* is a small, nonmotile, weakly staining, gram-negative coccobacillus that is 0.5 to 1.0 μm in length. Capsules can be demonstrated by special procedures, and bipolar metachromatic granules are present. Regan-Lowe medium or the complex medium containing blood originally used by Bordet and

Gengou is still used (in modified form) for cultivation. *Primary isolates do not grow on conventional laboratory media.*

An estimated 5 to 10% of clinical whooping cough is caused by *B. parapertussis.* The animal pathogen *B. bronchiseptica* is responsible for a minor percentage of cases. These organisms can be differentiated from *B. pertussis* by growth requirements, enzyme production, and presence of species-specific antigens. It has been suggested that adenoviruses, alone or in concert with *B. pertussis,* and *Chlamydia sp.* or *Mycoplasma sp.* may cause some cases of whooping cough syndrome.

B. pertussis adheres to ciliated epithelial cells of the respiratory tract and multiplies there without invading the tissues. Yet this colonization leads to profound changes in tissues that persist long after the responsible bacteria have been cleared. Such observations suggest that a toxin or toxins from the bacteria play an important part in the pathogenesis of the syndrome. A variety of biologic activities have been demonstrated by injecting *B. pertussis* products into experimental animals. An endotoxin and a heat-labile toxin that can cause tissue necrosis have been identified among these bacterial factors, but the exotoxin *pertussis toxin* (PT) clearly constitutes a major virulence factor. Immunization with chemically detoxified PT appears to prevent severe whooping cough. PT is believed to be responsible for the characteristic lymphocytosis of whooping cough.

PT is a protein composed of five noncovalently linked subunits (S1 to S5). The subunits S2 to S5 form a nontoxic unit that binds to the cell membrane; toxicity is mediated by the enzymatically active subunit, S1. Activity of S1 inhibits a subclass of guanosine triphosphate (GTP)-binding proteins (G proteins) that are essential for transmembrane signaling and, thus, certain types of receptor-mediated cell functions.

Adherence of *B. pertussis* to respiratory epithelium is required for the pathogenesis of whooping cough. Adherence appears to involve the bacterial surface proteins pertactin, filamentous hemagglutinin, and fimbriae. An antigenically similar protein to pertactin exists on *B. parapertussis* and *B. bronchiseptica.* Injection of this protein into mice or humans elicits agglutinating antibody to *B. pertussis* and protects the mice against lethal *B. pertussis* respiratory challenge. Synthesis of pertactin is controlled by a regulatory gene at the *vir* (virulence) locus, which modulates synthesis of PT, filamentous hemagglutinin, and other virulence factors.

Lesions caused by *B. pertussis* are found principally in the bronchi and bronchioles, but changes are also seen in the nasopharynx, larynx, and trachea. Masses of bacteria and mucopurulent exudate are intertwined with the cilia of the columnar epithelium. There is necrosis of the midzonal and basilar epithelium with infiltration of polymorphonuclear leukocytes and macrophages. The most frequent findings in the lung are bronchopneumonia, interstitial pneumonitis, and numerous small areas of atelectasis. The brain can show edema and scattered petechiae at autopsy.

Clinical Manifestations

The incubation period lasts 6 to 20 days (rarely >2 weeks). It is customary to divide the clinical course into three stages.

CATARRHAL STAGE. Whooping cough begins with symptoms indistinguishable from those of a mild viral upper respiratory tract infection. Sneezing is frequent, conjunctivae are injected, and a nocturnal cough appears. The temperature may be slightly elevated. Infectivity is greatest at this stage.

PAROXYSMAL STAGE. Seven to 14 days after onset, the cough becomes more frequent, then paroxysmal. In a typical paroxysm there is a series of 5 to 20 short coughs of increasing intensity and then a deep inspiration, making the "whoop." A tenacious mucus plug is usually expelled, and vomiting frequently follows. Paroxysms may occur as often as every half hour and are accompanied by signs of increased venous pressure, including deeply engorged conjunctivae, periorbital edema, petechial hemorrhages, particularly about the forehead, and epistaxis. During the attack, the infant may be cyanotic until the crowing whoop occurs. Between paroxysms, the child usually feels well, although justifiably apprehensive. This phase lasts 2 to 4 weeks.

Physical examination of the chest is often unremarkable except for scattered rhonchi. The chest radiograph sometimes reveals hilar and mediastinal nodal enlargement. The presence of fever should immediately suggest the development of a secondary infectious process.

CONVALESCENT STAGE. Gradually the paroxysms become less frequent and less intense; vomiting ceases, and slow recovery ensues. Convalescence requires 4 to 12 weeks. For many months even a mild, unrelated respiratory infection can induce a return of paroxysmal cough and whoop.

In infants younger than 6 months old, the paroxysms and the whoop are often absent; choking spells and apneic episodes may be the major manifestations. Second attacks of whooping cough as well as disease occurring in previously immunized individuals often present simply as an upper respiratory illness or bronchitis, but may present as protracted, severe coughing.

COMPLICATIONS. Recurrent vomiting can lead to metabolic alkalosis or malnutrition. Central nervous system changes can result from cerebral anoxia or hemorrhages consequent to the elevated venous pressure. Rarely, cortical degeneration occurs, but the exact pathogenesis of the encephalopathy is unknown. A serous meningitis with lymphocytosis of the cerebrospinal fluid has been described. Pneumothorax and interstitial emphysema are infrequently seen. Secondary bacterial otitis media occurs frequently. The major cause of death in whooping cough is pneumonia, either primary or secondary to other bacteria or viruses.

Diagnosis

There is little difficulty in making the clinical diagnosis of whooping cough in a patient who, after a period of coryzal symptoms, develops paroxysmal coughing with a terminal inspiratory whoop. Lymphocytosis often occurs toward the end of the catarrhal stage or early in the spasmodic phase. Characteristically the leukocyte count ranges from 15,000 to 30,000/μL or higher, and 80% of the cells are small lymphocytes. Polymorphonuclear leukocytosis suggests a secondary bacterial complication.

Microbiologic identification of the organisms may be required to make the diagnosis in abortive or mild cases or in young infants or adults. During the early stages, *B. pertussis* can be isolated from approximately 90% of patients. By the third or fourth week, the organism can be recovered in only 50% of cases, and in the convalescent stage, it is unusual to obtain a positive culture.

Specimens for culture are best obtained by nasal swab rather than by the cough plate method. A sterile cotton, Dacron, or calcium alginate swab is passed through the nares, and mucus is obtained from the posterior pharynx. *B. pertussis* is readily killed by desiccation, so the specimen should be quickly inserted into transport medium or plated onto fresh medium, to which antibiotic has been added to prevent overgrowth of adventitious organisms.

A fluorescent antibody staining procedure or analysis by polymerase chain reaction (PCR) can be applied directly to clinical specimens or organisms grown in culture. Of these two, the PCR appears to be more reliable, sensitive, and diagnostic.

Serologic procedures are of little help in diagnosing whooping cough because a rise in titer of most antibodies does not occur until at least the third week of illness. Tests have not been well standardized.

Rx Treatment

SUPPORTIVE THERAPY. Young infants, particularly those younger than 6 months, should be hospitalized. Supportive measures combined with careful nursing care are of paramount importance. Specific attention must be devoted to the maintenance of proper water and electrolyte balance, adequate nutrition, and sufficient oxygenation. Constant alertness for the presence of secondary infectious complications such as pneumonia is required. Mild cases require only supportive treatment.

ANTIMICROBIAL AGENTS. Specific therapy of severe whooping cough has been disappointing despite the in vitro susceptibility of *B. pertussis* to various antimicrobial agents. Antimicrobial agents given in the catarrhal stage may ameliorate the disease. In the established paroxysmal stage, the organisms can be readily eliminated by antimicrobial agents, but the course of the illness is unaltered. Antibiotics may be justified in order to render the patient noninfectious. Erythromycin is the drug of choice. The daily dose is 40 to 50 mg/kg given in four divided doses. The organism is eliminated after a few days of therapy, but because bacteriologic relapse may occur, treatment should be continued for 14 days. Trimethoprim/sulfamethoxazole (8 mg/kg and 40 mg/kg/day in two doses) or the macrolides azithromycin (10 to 12 mg/kg/day PO in one dose for 5 to 7 days) or clarithromycin (15 to 20 mg/kg/day PO in two divided doses; maximum 1 q/day for 5 to 7 days) may be effective alternatives to erythromycin, but their efficacy has not been proved. Corticosteroids, albuterol, and pertussis-specific immunoglobulin each may be effective in reducing coughing paroxysms.

Prevention

Unfortunately, the diagnosis is usually not made until the end of the catarrhal stage, and by then, spread of the disease has already occurred. Exposed susceptibles should receive erythromycin prophylaxis for 14 days, and close (household, day care, classroom) contacts younger than 7 who have been previously immunized should receive a booster dose of vaccine in addition to erythromycin. Booster doses of vaccine or erythromycin chemoprophylaxis have been used to protect adults, such as hospital staff.

ACTIVE IMMUNIZATION. Women of childbearing age generally do not have significant levels of protective antibody in their sera, and most newborns have received no passive protection. Consequently, active immunization is begun as early as is practicable. At the present, it is recommended that the infant receive three injections of pertussis vaccine at 8-week intervals beginning at age 2 months. A fourth injection is given 6 to 12 months after the third dose (15 to 18 months of age), and a booster is given before entering kindergarten. Administration of pertussis vaccine to those older than age 6 has not been recommended as a routine measure, but this practice is being reconsidered in view of the improved vaccine and the severity of the disease in some adults.

Whole cell pertussis vaccine consists of inactive B. pertussis organisms in suspension with alum-precipitated diphtheria and tetanus toxoids (DTP). The newer acellular pertussis vaccines (DTaP) contain various combinations of the B. pertussis products such as pertussis toxin, pertactin, filamentous hemagglutinin, and fimbrial antigen. In the United States, DTaP is preferred for all doses because of the decreased likelihood of vaccine-associated fever and local reactions.

As previously noted, immunization does not confer lifelong protection. Approximately 80% of those vaccinated within 4 years of exposure are protected, whereas 80 to 90% of a matched nonimmunized group with similar exposure contract pertussis. The prophylactic efficacy of pertussis vaccine was clearly demonstrated when epidemics occurred in the United Kingdom in 1977 to 1979 and 1982 after a 3- to 5-year period during which vaccine acceptance had declined to very low levels. More than 170,000 cases of whooping cough were reported, including 42 deaths, principally among children younger than age 5. Similar outbreaks have followed diminished vaccine utilization in Japan and Sweden.

Reactions at the injection site as well as fever and hyperirritability occur commonly after injection of whole-cell pertussis vaccine. The incidence of postinjection acute encephalopathy is uncertain but apparently rare, and it is not clear whether administering DTP vaccine increases the overall risk in children of chronic nervous system dysfunction. It is clear that the risk of neurologic complications from pertussis immunization is far less than the hazards of whooping cough in the young child. Nevertheless, in infants with a personal history of convulsions or other neurologic disorders, pertussis immunization with either vaccine should be deferred until the condition has stabilized.

SUGGESTED READINGS

Cherry JD, Robbins JB (eds): Pertussis in adults: Epidemiology, signs, symptoms, and implications for vaccination. Clin Infect Dis 1999;28:S91–S93. *Symposium presentations on all aspects of the subject by leading investigators in the field.*

Howson CP, Howe CJ, Fineberg HV (eds): Adverse Effects of Pertussis and Rubella Vaccines. Washington, DC, National Academy Press, 1991. *A scientific, fully referenced review by the Institute of Medicine of DTP immunization and possible adverse events.*

Keitel WA, Edwards KM: Acellular pertussis vaccines in adults. Infect Dis Clin North Am 1999;13:83–94. *A review of symptomatology and pertussis vaccine trials in adults.*

Munoz FM, Keitel WA: Progress in the diagnosis, prevention, and treatment of pertussis. Curr Infect Dis Rep 2003;5:213–219. *Review of all aspects of the subject, with emphasis on improved methods for early diagnosis and growing realization of the importance of immunizing adolescents and young adults.*

Pittman M: The concept of pertussis as a toxin-mediated disease. Pediatr Infect Dis J 1984;3:467–486. *A thorough, now classic review of pathogenesis, immunity, and immunization.*

Stratton KR, Howe CJ, Johnston RB Jr (eds): DPT Vaccine and Chronic Nervous System Dysfunction: A New Analysis. Washington, DC, National Academy Press, 1994. *A re-evaluation of this relationship by the Institute of Medicine.*

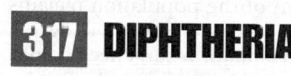

317 DIPHTHERIA

Roland W. Sutter

Definition

Diphtheria is an acute infectious disease caused by *Corynebacterium diphtheriae*, a gram-positive bacillus. The organism primarily infects the respiratory tract, where it causes tonsillopharyngitis and/or laryngitis, typically with a pseudomembrane, and the skin, causing a variety of indolent lesions. If the infecting strain produces exotoxin, myocarditis and neuritis may ensue.

Etiology

C. diphtheriae is an aerobic, nonmotile, unencapsulated, non-sporulating, pleomorphic gram-positive bacillus. Its name comes from the Greek *korynee* (meaning "club"), describing the shape of the organism on stained smears with one end usually being wider, and *diphtheria* (meaning "leather hide"), for the characteristic adherent membrane. Both nontoxigenic and toxigenic strains exist. Toxigenicity is conferred when a nontoxigenic organism is infected by a β-phage carrying the gene for the toxin *(tox)*. *C. diphtheriae* has three biotypes—*gravis*, *mitis*, and *intermedius*—which are distinguished by colonial morphology and varying biochemical and hemolytic reactions. Strains may be distinguished for epidemiologic purposes by molecular techniques. There are a few reports of classic diphtheria, including toxic complications, due to infection with toxigenic *C. ulcerans*.

Epidemiology

Humans are the only natural reservoir of *C. diphtheriae*, although the organism has been isolated occasionally from a variety of domestic and other animals. Spread occurs in close-contact settings through respiratory droplets or by direct contact with respiratory secretions or skin lesions. The organism survives for weeks and possibly months on environmental surfaces and in dust, and fomite transmission may occur. The majority of nasopharyngeal *C. diphtheriae* infection results in asymptomatic carriers, and approximately one in seven individuals develops clinical disease. However, asymptomatic carriers are important in maintaining transmission.

Diphtheria immunization protects against disease but does not prevent carriage. In the prevaccine era, respiratory disease dominated in temperate climates, with a fall/winter peak in incidence, and most individuals developed natural immunity by the mid-teen years. Cutaneous disease is the predominant form of the disease in tropical countries, but over the past two decades, outbreaks of this form of diphtheria have occurred in the United States and Europe, typically among homeless and alcoholic inner-city adults.

Vaccination with diphtheria toxoid (formalin-treated toxin) was introduced in the 1920s and 1930s. Immunization of children in an era when the majority of older individuals had natural immunity resulted in a dramatic drop in diphtheria incidence and an even more rapid decline in the proportion of toxigenic strains isolated, presumably because the selective advantage of the *tox* gene—promotion of greater replication and spread of the organism—is lost in the immune host. In most Western countries, toxigenic *C. diphtheriae* has been virtually eliminated. In the United States, reported cases fell from 147,991 in 1920, to 15,536 in 1940, to a total of 40 cases from 1980 to 1993. Since 1988, all culture—confirmed cases have been caused by imported strains. The absence of reported diphtheria cases in the United States in recent years, however, does not indicate that the circulation of toxigenic *C. diphtheriae* has ceased. Recent investigations among a Northern Plains Indian community in North Dakota and First Nations communities in Ontario, Canada, suggested that *C. diphtheriae* strains may have circulated independently for more than two decades in these communities despite the absence of reported respiratory diphtheria cases.

Vaccine-induced immunity to diphtheria wanes with time, and there is a growing cohort of individuals with no natural diphtheria immunity. Serosurveys indicate that 20 to 60% of adults in industrialized countries have diphtheria antitoxin levels below minimal protective levels. A level of 0.01 IU/mL from an in vitro neutralization assay, the "gold standard" test, is considered the lower limit of protection. As long as a high proportion of the population remains susceptible, the danger of reintroduction or reemergence of toxigenic strains exists. Since 1990 there has been a major resurgence of diphtheria in several countries of the former Soviet Union. In Russia, the number of reported cases rose from 593 in 1989 to 39,582 in 1994, with over two thirds of cases occurring among adults. Large-scale mass campaigns with diphtheria toxoid administered to virtually the entire population in the affected new independent states of the former Soviet Union have since led to significant decreases in the incidence of diphtheria, from a peak of 50,449 cases in 1995 to 7,197 cases in 1997, although pre-resurgence levels of control have not been achieved.

Pathogenesis

In classic respiratory diphtheria, *C. diphtheriae* colonizes the mucosal surface of the nasopharynx and multiplies locally without blood stream invasion. Released toxin causes local tissue necrosis, and a tough, adherent pseudomembrane forms, composed of a mixture of fibrin, dead cells, and bacteria. The membrane usually begins on the tonsils or posterior pharynx. In more severe cases it spreads, extending progressively over the pharyngeal wall, fauces, soft palate, and into the larynx, which may result in respiratory obstruction. Toxin entering the blood stream causes tissue damage at distant sites, particularly the heart (myocarditis), nerves (demyelination), and kidney (tubular necrosis). Nontoxigenic strains may cause mild local respiratory disease, sometimes including a membrane.

Diphtheria toxin is an extremely potent inhibitor of protein synthesis, with an estimated human lethal dose of 0.1 mg/kg. The extent of toxin absorption varies with site of infection, being much less from skin or nose than from the pharynx.

Clinical Manifestations

RESPIRATORY DIPHTHERIA. Infection limited to the anterior nares manifests as a chronic serosanguineous or seropurulent discharge without fever or significant toxicity. A whitish membrane may be observed on the septum. The faucial (pharyngeal) form is most common. After an incubation period of 1 to 7 days, the illness begins with a sore throat, malaise, and mild to moderate fever. There is initial mild pharyngeal erythema, usually followed by progressive formation of a whitish tonsillar exudate, which over 24 to 48 hours changes into a grayish membrane that is tightly adherent and bleeds on attempted removal. In more severe cases, the patient appears toxic and the membrane is more extensive. Cervical adenopathy and soft tissue edema may occur, resulting in the typical bull neck appearance and stridor. Laryngeal involvement, which may occur on its own or as a result of membrane extension from the nasopharynx, presents as hoarseness, stridor, and dyspnea.

The likelihood of toxic complications depends primarily on the interval between disease onset and administration of antitoxin. The severity of disease at initial presentation predicts closely the likelihood of severe clinical course, complications, and death. Myocarditis typically occurs in the first or second week after the onset of respiratory symptoms and presents either suddenly or insidiously with signs of low cardiac output and congestive failure. Conduction disturbances, which may occur without other signs of myocarditis, include ST-T wave abnormalities, arrhythmias, and heart block.

Neurologic impairment manifests as cranial nerve palsies and peripheral neuritis. Palatal and/or pharyngeal paralysis occurs during the acute phase; peripheral neuritis, symmetrical and predominantly motor, occurs from 2 to 12 weeks after disease onset. Motor deficit may range from minor proximal weakness to complete paralysis. Complete recovery is the rule. In fulminant, sometimes called "hypertoxic," diphtheria, toxic circulatory collapse with hemorrhagic features occurs.

Diphtheria, at the end of the 20th century, remains a serious disease, associated with a high case-fatality rate. In the United States, the diphtheria case-fatality rate has remained virtually unchanged between 5 and 10% over recent decades. **CUTANEOUS DIPHTHERIA.** Cutaneous diphtheria lesions are classically indolent, deep, punched-out ulcers, which may have a grayish white membrane. However, the lesions may be indistinguishable from impetigo, or *C. diphtheriae* may infect chronic dermatoses, such as stasis dermatitis. There is frequently coinfection with *Streptococcus pyogenes* and/or *Staphylococcus aureus*. Toxic complications of cutaneous diphtheria are rare. **INVASIVE DISEASE.** Uncommonly, *C. diphtheriae*, both toxigenic and nontoxigenic, may cause invasive disease, including endocarditis, osteomyelitis, septic arthritis, and meningitis. Frequently, these patients have predisposing factors such as a prosthetic cardiac valve or underlying immunosuppression.

Diagnosis

The decision to initiate therapy should be made on clinical grounds, because delayed treatment, especially delays in antitoxin administration, is associated with worse outcomes. A high index of suspicion is required. Cultures should be taken from beneath the membrane, from the nasopharynx, and from any suspicious skin lesions. Because special media are required, the laboratory should be alerted to the concern about diphtheria. *C. diphtheriae* is best isolated on selective media that inhibit the growth of other nasopharyngeal organisms; generally one containing potassium tellurite is used. Based on colonial morphology and Gram stain appearance, a presumptive diagnosis may be possible within 18 to 24 hours. Cultures may be negative if the patient received previous antibiotics. Toxigenicity testing should be performed on all *C. diphtheriae* isolates. Because both nontoxigenic and toxigenic strains may be isolated from the same patient, more than one colony should be tested. Traditional methods include guinea pig inoculation and the Elek test, in which the isolate and appropriate controls are streaked on a culture plate in which a filter strip soaked with antitoxin has been embedded; toxin production is confirmed by an immunoprecipitation line in the agar. A polymerase chain reaction test may allow both detection of the organism and determination of toxigenicity.

The differential diagnosis includes streptococcal and viral tonsillopharyngitis, infectious mononucleosis, Vincent's angina, candidiasis, and acute epiglottitis. A history of travel to a region with endemic diphtheria or of contact with a recent immigrant from such an area increases the possibility of diphtheria, as does a pre-antitoxin treatment serum antitoxin level of less than 0.01 IU/mL.

Rx Treatment

Treatment goals are to rapidly neutralize toxin, eliminate the infecting organism, provide supportive care, and prevent further transmission. The mainstay of therapy is equine diphtheria antitoxin. Because only unbound toxin can be neutralized, treatment should commence as soon as the diagnosis is suspected, and each day of delay in administration increases the likelihood of a fatal outcome. A single dose is given, ranging in quantity from 20,000 units for localized tonsillar diphtheria up to 100,000 units for extensive disease with severe toxicity. Antitoxin may be given intramuscularly or intravenously; particularly for more severe cases, the intravenous route is preferred. Tests for sensitivity to antitoxin should be performed before administering it and desensitization performed if necessary. Antibiotic therapy, by eliminating the organism, halts toxin production, limits local infection, and prevents transmission. Parenteral penicillin (4 to 6 million units/day) and erythromycin (40 mg/kg/day in four divided doses; maximum, 2 g/day, usually orally if the patient can swallow) are the drugs of choice. General supportive care includes ensuring a secure airway, electrocardiographic monitoring for evidence of myocarditis, treating heart failure and arrhythmias, and preventing secondary complications of neurologic impairment such as aspiration pneumonia. The patient should be in strict isolation until follow-up cultures are negative. Convalescing patients should receive diphtheria toxoid.

The local health department must be notified. Close contacts should be cultured and commenced on prophylactic antibiotics. A positive culture in a contact may confirm the diagnosis if the patient is culture negative. All contacts without full primary immunization and a booster within the preceding 5 years should receive diphtheria toxoid.

Because manufacturers in the United States discontinued diphtheria antitoxin production, no licensed product is available. However, diphtheria antitoxin for the therapeutic purposes can be obtained from the Centers for Disease Control and Prevention, which distributes a European-produced antitoxin (Pasteur Merieux, Lyon, France) under an Investigational New Drug protocol. (The antitoxin is comparable to the previous products manufactured in the United States and may be requested by calling 404-639-8255 during working hours or 404-639-2889 at nights or weekends.)

Prevention

Immunization with diphtheria toxoid is the only effective means of primary prevention. The primary series is four doses of diphtheria toxoid (given with tetanus toxoid and pertussis vaccine) at 2, 4, 6, and 15 to 18 months; a preschool booster dose is given at ages 4 to 6 years. Thereafter, Td (tetanus and diphtheria toxoid for adults) boosters should be given as part of the adolescent immunization visit (i.e., between 11 and 13 years of age), followed by doses administered every 10 years.

SUGGESTED READINGS
Dixon JMS, Noble WC, Smith GR: Diphtheria; other corynebacterial and coryneform infections. In Topley WWC, Parker MT, Collier L, et al (eds): Topley and Wilson's Principles of Bacteriology, 8th ed. Philadelphia, BC Decker, 1990, pp 56–75. *A useful review with especially comprehensive epidemiologic data.*

Farizo KM, Strebel PS, Chen RT, et al: Fatal respiratory disease due to *Corynebacterium diphtheriae:* Case report and review of guidelines for management, investigation, and control. Clin Infect Dis 1993;16:59–68. *Includes latest recommendations of the U.S. Centers for Disease Control and Prevention for case and contact management.*
Harnisch JP, Tronca E, Nolan CM, et al: Diphtheria among alcoholic urban adults: A decade of experience in Seattle. Ann Intern Med 1989;111:71–82. *Summary of last major outbreak of diphtheria in the United States.*
Marston CK, Jamieson F, Cahoon F, et al: Persistence of a distinct *Corynebacterium diphtheriae* clonal group within two communities in the United States and Canada where diphtheria is endemic. J Clin Microbiol 2001;39:1586–1590. *Evidence for persistence of endemic transmission of* C. diphtheriae *over two decades in Native American communities in the United States and Canada.*
Pappenheimer AM: Diphtheria: Studies on the Biology of an Infectious Disease. The Harvey Lectures. New York, Academic Press, 1982, series 76, pp 45–73. *Detailed description of the cellular and molecular biology of diphtheria toxin.*
Peter G (ed): 1997 Red Book: Report of the Committee on Infectious Diseases, 24th ed. Elk Grove Village, IL, American Academy of Pediatrics, 1997, pp 191–195. *Description on public health interventions after detection of a suspected case of diphtheria.*
Wharton M, Dittman S, Strebel PM, et al (eds): Control of epidemic diphtheria in the Newly Independent States of the former Soviet Union, 1990–1998. J Infect Dis 2000;181(Suppl 1):S1–S248. *Diphtheria outbreaks (and control measures) in newly independent states are summarized in detail, as well as findings of research studies to understand reasons for these outbreaks.*

318 CLOSTRIDIAL MYONECROSIS AND OTHER CLOSTRIDIAL DISEASES

Dennis L. Stevens

The genus *Clostridium* encompasses over 60 species of grampositive anaerobic spore-forming rods that cause a variety of infections in humans and animals by virtue of a myriad of proteinaceous exotoxins (Table 318–1). *C. tetani* and *C. botulinum* manifest specific clinical disease by elaborating single, but highly potent, toxins. Although botulism is usually the result of ingestion of preformed toxin, tetanus requires the bacteria to proliferate at the site of penetrating injury (Chapters 320 and 321). Frequently, signs of infection are not apparent even with lethal exotoxinemia. In contrast, other strains of clostridia, such as *C. perfringens* and *C. septicum,* cause aggressive necrotizing infections, attributable, in part, to bacterial proteases, phospholipases, and cytotoxins.

MYONECROSIS

Types

Clostridial gas gangrene, or myonecrosis, occurs in three different settings. First, and most commonly, traumatic gas gangrene

Table 318–1 • CLINICAL DISEASES CAUSED BY *CLOSTRIDIA*

ORGANISM	CLINICAL DIAGNOSIS	CLINICAL FEATURES	LABORATORY FEATURES	TOXINS
INVASIVE INFECTIONS				
C. perfringens type a	Traumatic gas gangrene	Pain, necrotizing infection, renal impairment, shock	Renal failure ↑ CK Gas in tissues	α Toxin θ Toxin
C. septicum	Spontaneous gas gangrene	Pain, necrotizing infection, bowel portal	Renal failure ↑ CK Gas in tissues	α Toxin
C. sordellii	Malignant edema	No pain, no fever, massive third spacing	Leukemoid reaction Hemoconcentration	?
C. tertium	Bacteremia in compromised hosts receiving antibiotics	Bacteremia, shock	Positive blood cultures	?
GASTROINTESTINAL				
C. perfringens type a	Food poisoning	Nausea, vomiting, watery diarrhea	None	Enterotoxin
C. perfringens type c	Necrotizing enterocolitis	Bloody diarrhea, ruptured bowel	None	β Toxin
C. septicum	Neutropenic enterocolitis "typhlitis"	Right lower quadrant pain, abdominal distention	Low white blood cell count	Unknown
C. difficile	Pseudomembranous colitis	Watery bloody diarrhea	Stools positive for organism, toxin, blood, and leukocytes	Toxin A Toxin B
NEUROLOGIC				
C. tetanii	Tetanus	Spastic paralysis	None	Tetanospasmin
C. botulinum	Botulism	Flaccid paralysis	None	Botulinum toxin (A, B, E, F, G)

CK = creatine phosphokinase.

develops after deep, penetrating injury that compromises the blood supply (e.g., knife or gunshot wound, crush injury), creating an anaerobic environment ideal for clostridial proliferation. *C. perfringens* accounts for 80% of such infections. The remaining cases are caused by *C. septicum, C. novyi, C. histolyticum, C. bifermentans,* and *C. fallax.* Other conditions associated with traumatic gas gangrene are bowel and biliary tract surgery, criminal abortion, and retained placenta; prolonged rupture of the membranes; and intrauterine fetal demise or missed abortion in postpartum patients. Necrotizing soft tissue infections have been reported in drug abusers who inject black tar heroin intracutaneously (skin popping). *C. perfringens, C. novyi,* and *C. sordellii* have been isolated from such cases. Second, spontaneous or nontraumatic gas gangrene is most commonly caused by the more aerotolerant *C. septicum.* Last, recurrent gas gangrene caused by *C. perfringens* has been described in individuals with nonpenetrating injuries at sites of previous gas gangrene, where spores of *C. perfringens* remain quiescent in tissue for periods of 10 to 20 years and then germinate when minor trauma provides conditions suitable for growth.

Clinical Manifestations

The first symptom is usually sudden and severe pain at the site of surgery or trauma. The mean incubation period is less than 24 hours but ranges from 6 to 8 hours to several days, probably depending on the degree of soil contamination or bowel spillage and degree of vascular compromise. The skin may appear pale initially but quickly changes to bronze and then purplish red and becomes tense and exquisitely tender. Bullae develop that may be clear, red, blue, or purple. Gas present in tissue may be obvious by physical examination, soft tissue radiography, or computed tomography. Signs of systemic toxicity develop rapidly, including tachycardia, low-grade fever, and diaphoresis, followed by shock and multiorgan failure. Bacteremia occurs in 15% of patients and is usually associated with brisk hemolysis. Patients have been described with hematocrits of 0% for as long as 24 hours. Complications include jaundice, renal failure, hypotension, and liver necrosis. Renal failure is largely due to hemoglobinuria and myoglobinuria but complicated by acute tubular necrosis after hypotension. Renal tubular cells are likely directly affected by toxins, but this has not been proved.

Diagnosis

Increasing pain at the site of prior injury or surgery, together with signs of systemic toxicity, fever, and gas in the tissue, supports the diagnosis. Definitive diagnosis rests on demonstrating large, gram-variable rods at the injury site. Note that although clostridia stain gram positive when obtained from bacteriologic media, when visualized from infected tissues, they may appear as either gram positive or gram negative. Surgical exploration is essential and demonstrates muscle that does not bleed or contract when stimulated. Grossly, muscle tissue is edematous and may have a reddish blue to black coloration. Usually, necrotizing fasciitis and cutaneous necrosis are also present. Microscopic evaluation of biopsy material invariably demonstrates organisms among degenerating muscle bundles and, characteristically, an absence of acute inflammatory cells.

Pathogenesis

The initiating trauma introduces organisms (either vegetative forms or spores) into the deep tissues and produces an anaerobic niche with a sufficiently low redox potential and acid pH for optimal clostridial growth. Necrosis progresses within hours. At the junction of necrotic and normal tissues, no polymorphonuclear leukocytes (PMNs) are present, yet pavementing of PMNs is apparent within capillaries and in small arterioles and postcapillary venules, followed later in the course by leukostasis within larger vessels. Thus, the histopathology of clostridial gas gangrene is completely opposite to that seen in soft tissue infections caused by organisms such as *Staphylococcus aureus,* in which an early luxuriant influx of PMNs localizes the infection without adjacent tissue or vascular destruction. In a study in rats, intramuscular injection of α toxin caused a rapid and irreversible

reduction in skeletal muscle perfusion. Unlike the vasoconstrictor phenylephrine, α toxin did not cause a reduction in the vessel diameter. Instead, α toxin induced the formation of intravascular aggregates of platelets, PMNs, and fibrin that were of sufficient size to block blood flow. Interestingly, α toxin-induced formation of these aggregates was mediated by platelet glycoprotein IIb/IIIa.

Studies suggest that θ toxin and α toxin, when elaborated in high concentrations at the site of infection, destroy host tissues and inflammatory cells. As the toxin diffuses into surrounding tissues or enters systemic circulation, it promotes dysregulated PMN–endothelial cell adhesive interactions and primes leukocytes for increased respiratory burst activity. These actions lead to vascular leukostasis, endothelial cell injury, and regional tissue hypoxia. Such perfusion deficits expand the anaerobic environment and contribute to the rapidly advancing margins of tissue destruction that are characteristic of clostridial gangrene.

Shock associated with gas gangrene may be attributable, in part, to direct and indirect effects of toxins. α Toxin directly suppresses myocardial contractility ex vivo and may contribute to profound hypotension by means of a sudden reduction in cardiac output. θ Toxin contributes indirectly by inducing endogenous mediators that cause relaxation of blood vessel wall tension, such as nitric oxide or the lipid autacoids, prostacyclin, or platelet-activating factor. α Toxin also induces platelet-activating factor production by endothelial cells and tumor necrosis factor production by monocytes. In experimental studies, reduced vascular tone develops rapidly due to the effects of platelet activating factor and tumor necrosis factor. In response to a precipitous drop in mean arterial pressure, the normal physiologic response is a compensatory increase in cardiac output. Such a response is characteristic of gram-negative sepsis. However, this does not occur in *C. perfringens*–induced shock, owing to the direct suppression of myocardial contractility by α toxin. Thus, reduced systemic vascular resistance and declining cardiac output are poor prognostic signs and invariable lead to intractable shock.

℞ Treatment

Penicillin, clindamycin, tetracycline, chloramphenicol, metronidazole, and a number of cephalosporins have excellent in vitro activity against *C. perfringens* and other clostridia. No clinical trials have been conducted to compare the efficacy of these agents in humans. Experimental studies in mice suggest that clindamycin has the greatest efficacy, and penicillin, the least. Slightly greater survival was observed in animals receiving both clindamycin and penicillin; in contrast, antagonism was observed with penicillin plus metronidazole. Resistance of some strains to clindamycin suggests a combination of penicillin and clindamycin is warranted. The greater efficacy of clindamycin is in part related to dramatic suppression of bacterial toxin synthesis, to its prolonged post antibiotic effect, and to the absence of an inoculum effect.

Aggressive surgical débridement is mandatory to improve survival and prevent complications. The use of hyperbaric oxygen (HBO) is controversial, although some nonrandomized studies have reported excellent results with HBO therapy when it is combined with antibiotics and surgical débridement. Experimental studies demonstrate slight benefit of HBO when combined with penicillin, although survivals were greater with clindamycin alone.

Therapeutic strategies directed against toxin expression in vivo, such as neutralization with specific antitoxin antibody or inhibiting toxin synthesis with antibiotics such as clindamycin, may be valuable adjuncts to traditional antimicrobial regimens. Future strategies may target endogenous proadhesive molecules such that toxin-induced vascular leukostasis and resultant tissue injury are attenuated.

Prognosis

Patients presenting with gas gangrene of an extremity have a better prognosis than those with truncal or intra-abdominal gas gangrene, in large part because it is difficult to adequately débride such lesions. HBO could be useful in such patients, yet there are little data on this subject. In addition to truncal gangrene, patients with associated bacteremia and intravascular hemolysis have the greatest likelihood of progressing to shock and death.

Prevention

Aggressive débridement of devitalized tissue, as well as rapid repair of compromised vascular supply, greatly reduces the frequency of gas gangrene in contaminated deep wounds. Intramuscular epinephrine, prolonged application of tourniquets, and surgical closure of traumatic, contaminated wounds, particularly those involving fractured bones, should be avoided. Patients with deep contaminated wounds or crush injury should receive prophylactic antibiotics.

SPONTANEOUS, NONTRAUMATIC GAS GANGRENE DUE TO *CLOSTRIDIUM SEPTICUM*

Clinical Manifestations

The onset of disease is abrupt, often with excruciating pain, although the patient may sense only heaviness or numbness. The first symptom may be confusion or malaise. Extremely rapid progression of gangrene follows. Swelling advances, and blisters appear filled with clear, cloudy, hemorrhagic, or purplish fluid. The skin around such bullae also has a purple hue, perhaps reflecting vascular compromise resulting from bacterial toxins diffusing into surrounding tissues. Histopathology of muscle and connective tissues includes cell lysis and gas formation; inflammatory cells are remarkably absent.

Predisposing factors include colonic carcinoma, diverticulitis, gastrointestinal surgery, leukemia, lymphoproliferative disorders, and either chemotherapy or radiation therapy. Cyclic neutropenia is also associated with spontaneous gas gangrene due to *C. septicum*, and, in such cases, necrotizing enterocolitis, cecitis, or distal ileitis is commonly found. These gastrointestinal pathologic processes permit bacterial access to the blood stream; consequently, the aerotolerant *C. septicum* can become established in normal tissues. Patients surviving bacteremia or spontaneous gangrene due to *C. septicum* should have appropriate diagnostic studies of the gastrointestinal tract to rule out pathology in this area.

Diagnosis

Unlike traumatic gas gangrene, transient bacteremia precedes cutaneous manifestations by several hours, causing delays in the appropriate diagnosis and, as a consequence, an increase in the mortality rate.

Pathogenesis

C. septicum produces four toxins—α toxin (lethal, hemolytic, necrotizing activity); β toxin (DNase); γ toxin (hyaluronidase); and δ toxin (septicolysin, an oxygen-labile hemolysin)—as well as a protease and a neuraminidase. This α toxin does not possess phospholipase activity and thus is distinct from the α toxin of *C. perfringens*. Active immunization against α toxin significantly protects against challenge with viable *C. septicum*. The mechanism by which α toxin contributes to *C. septicum* pathogenesis is unknown; however, the cloning and sequencing of this toxin should facilitate studies in this area.

 Treatment

Although no comparative human trials have evaluated the efficacy of antibiotics or HBO for treating clinical cases of spontaneous gas gangrene, in vitro data suggest that *C. septicum* is uniformly susceptible to penicillin, tetracycline, erythromycin, clindamycin, chloramphenicol, and metronidazole. The aerotolerance of *C. septicum* may reduce the efficacy of HBO therapy. It is probable, but not proved, that clindamycin may be more efficacious.

Prognosis

The mortality rate of spontaneous clostridial gangrene ranges from 67 to 100%, with the majority of deaths occurring within 24 hours of onset. Risk factors include underlying malignancy and compromised immune status.

FOOD POISONING (ENTEROTOXEMIA) CAUSED BY *CLOSTRIDIUM PERFRINGENS*

C. perfringens accounts for nearly 20% of all reported cases of food poisoning. Ingesting large numbers of vegetative cells from inadequately prepared and stored food leads to multiplication and sporulation in the intestine. When mature spores are released, enterotoxin is liberated into the lumen of the gastrointestinal tract. The alkaline environment of the proximal small intestine and the presence of trypsin (a pancreatic enzyme found in the gut lumen) cause a 2.5-fold increase in biologic activity of enterotoxin. Histologically, enterotoxin causes bleb formation and desquamation of the microvillus tips of the brush border. Physiologically, such cells are incapable of glucose and ion absorption. The net effect is loss of electrolytes and fluid across the brush border, with resultant diarrhea. Other symptoms that manifest 5 to 24 hours after ingesting contaminated food are nausea, vomiting, and abdominal cramping. The definitive diagnosis rests on demonstrating enterotoxin in stool samples. Reliable biologic tests, radioimmunoassays, and an enzyme-linked immunosorbent assay (ELISA) have been developed, although the ELISA is favored, owing to its sensitivity, cost, and quick results.

NECROTIZING ENTERITIS

Neutropenic enterocolitis is a fulminant form of necrotizing enteritis that occurs in neutropenic patients. Neutropenia is often profound and may be related to cyclic neutropenia, leukemia, aplastic anemia, or chemotherapy. Symptoms include abdominal pain, chills, and malaise. Copious watery diarrhea, abdominal distention, and pain localizing to the right lower quadrant develop, followed rapidly by signs of toxicity, such as tachycardia, fever, and delirium. Radiographic examinations may reveal thickening of the wall of the colon or cecum and, in advanced cases, gas in the wall of the colon. Anecdotal reports suggest that computed tomography may be a superior means of diagnosing this condition. Complications include rupture of the bowel, with peritonitis, bacteremia, and death in 100% of cases. Aggressive supportive measures, surgical intervention, and appropriate antibiotics (see previous section on spontaneous gas gangrene) have reduced the mortality to 25%.

Postmortem examinations reveal that among children dying of leukemia, localized infection of the ileocecal region (typhilitis) is extremely common and may have contributed to death in nearly 40% of cases. *C. septicum* is the most common organism isolated from the blood of such patients, and Gram stain and immunofluorescence studies demonstrate that these bacteria invade the bowel wall in most cases.

Other forms of necrotizing enteritis have occurred endemically in New Guinea (pigbel), in epidemic proportion in Germany after World War II (Darmbrand), and sporadically in Africa, southeast Asia, and the United States. All cases are associated with ingesting meats contaminated with *C. perfringens* type c. Clinical courses vary between abdominal pain, fever, and diarrhea, which resolve spontaneously, to bloody diarrhea, ruptured bowel, and death. β Toxin from *C. perfringens* type c has been implicated as causing these infections. β Toxin paralyzes the intestinal villi and causes friability and necrosis of the bowel wall. Predisposing factors include malnutrition, specifically in those with diets low in protein and rich in trypsin inhibitors such as sweet potato or soybean. In addition, *Ascaris lumbricoides* is found commonly in such patients, and it, too, secretes a trypsin inhibitor. These protease inhibitors protect β toxin from intraluminal proteolysis.

 Treatment

Medical management should include aggressive fluid and electrolyte replacement, bowel decompression, and antibiotic treatment with penicillin or chloramphenicol. Surgical resection of necrotic bowel is necessary in 50% of patients, and mortality rates as high as 40% have been described. If peritonitis develops, broader antibiotic coverage may be necessary. Immunization of children in New Guinea with a β-toxoid vaccine has dramatically reduced the incidence of this disease.

CLOSTRIDIUM SORDELLII INFECTION

Patients with *C. sordellii* infection present with unique clinical features, including edema, absence of fever, leukemoid reaction, hemoconcentration, and later shock and multiorgan failure. Often *C. sordellii* infections develop after childbirth or after gynecologic procedures, although some cases involve sites of minor trauma such as lacerations. Unlike *C. perfringens* and *C. septicum* infections, pain may not be a prominent feature. The absence of fever and paucity of signs and symptoms of local infection make early diagnosis difficult. The mechanisms of diffuse capillary leak, massive edema, and hemoconcentration are not well established but clearly are related to elaboration of a potent toxin. Hematocrits of 75 to 80% have been described, and leukocytosis of 50 to 100,000 cells/mm^3 with a left shift is common.

CLOSTRIDIUM TERTIUM INFECTIONS

C. tertium causes bacteremia in compromised hosts who have received long courses of antibiotics, thus explaining the organism's relative resistance to penicillin, cephalosporins, and clindamycin. *C. tertium* is, however, usually quite sensitive to chloramphenicol, vancomycin, and metronidazole. Because this organism can grow aerobically, it may be mistakenly disregarded as a contaminant such as a diphtheroid or bacillus species.

SUGGESTED READINGS

Asmuth DM, Olson RD, Hackett SP, et al: Effects of *Clostridium perfringens* recombinant and crude phospholipase C and ' toxin on rabbit hemodynamic parameters. J Infect Dis 1995;172:1317–1323. *This study demonstrated a profound drop in mean arterial pressure and cardiac output induced by clostridial exotoxins in an awake rabbit model.*

Bangsberg DR, Rosen JI, Aragon T, et al: Clostridial myonecrosis cluster among injection drug users: A molecular epidemiology investigation. Arch Intern Med 2002;162:517–522. *Showed that some cases of this increasingly frequent complication had a common source.*

Bryant AE, Chen RYZ, Nagata Y, et al: Clostridial Gas Gangrene I: Cellular and molecular mechanisms of microvascular dysfunction induced by exotoxins of *C. perfringens*. J Infect Dis 2000;182:799–807.

Bryant AE, Chen RYZ, Nagata Y, et al: Clostridial Gas Gangrene II: Phosphilipase C-induced activation of platelet gpIIb/IIIa mediates vascular occlusion and myonecrosis in *C. perfringens* gas gangrene. J Infect Dis 2000;182:808–815. *These two papers investigate the mechanism of reduced skeletal muscle blood flow induced by C. perfringens alpha toxin. The authors provide evidence that activation of the platelet fibrinogen receptor may be responsible for intravascular aggregate formation and subsequent ischemic necrosis of tissue.*

MMWR: Update: *Clostridium novyi* and unexplained illness among injecting-drug users—Scotland, Ireland, and England, April–June 2000. *This report indicates that Clostridium species were found in 24% of drug users with soft tissue necrosis and death; half of these were Clostridium novyi.*

Stevens DL, Bryant AE: The role of clostridial toxins in the pathogenesis of gas gangrene. Clin Infect Dis 2002;35(Suppl 1):S93–S100. *Overview emphasizing that radical amputation remains the single best life-saving treatment.*

Stevens DL, Bryant AE, Adams K, et al: Evaluation of therapy with hyperbaric oxygen for experimental infection with *Clostridium perfringens*. Clin Infect Dis 1993;17:231–237. *This study describes the efficacy of hyperbaric oxygen. In the same issue, editorials describe the pros and cons of hyperbaric oxygen treatment.*

Stevens DL, Tweten RK, Awad MM, et al: Clostridial gas gangrene: Evidence that α and θ toxins differentially modulate the immune response and induce acute tissue necrosis. J Infect Dis 1997;176:189–195. *Authors demonstrated that both toxins impede leukocyte infiltration into infected tissues but with differing dynamics.*

319 PSEUDOMEMBRANOUS COLITIS

Theodore Steiner

Definition

Pseudomembranous colitis (PMC) is an inflammatory disease of the colon caused by infection with toxigenic strains of *Clostridium difficile*. PMC most often occurs in patients during or after treatment with antibacterial or antineoplastic drugs. It is characterized clinically by diarrhea, often associated with fever, leukocytosis, and abdominal pain. About 20 to 30% of cases of antibiotic-associated diarrhea (AAD) in adults are due to *C. difficile*, although many of these infections do not become severe enough to produce PMC.

Etiology

PMC was rarely reported in the preantibiotic era and usually followed gastrointestinal surgery. The disease became more common after the introduction of broad-spectrum antibiotics in the 1940s and 1950s. Identification of *Staphylococcus aureus* in biopsy specimens and stool cultures from patients with PMC led to the designation of PMC as "staphylococcal enterocolitis." However, the failure to detect *S. aureus* in modern-day cases of PMC and the clear association of toxigenic *C. difficile* with AAD and PMC suggest that staphylococcal colitis is a disease that has disappeared or perhaps never existed.

C. difficile is an anaerobic, spore-forming, gram-positive rod with a characteristic colony morphology and metabolic signature. Colonization with *C. difficile* is not ordinarily harmful. However, after antibiotic administration or surgery, *C. difficile* can proliferate in the gut, presumably due to the selective removal of competing intestinal flora. Strains that cause diarrhea and PMC always express one or both large *C. difficile* toxins: toxin A (TxA) or toxin B (TxB). It is the expression of these toxins that ultimately causes colitis.

Incidence and Epidemiology

PMC in healthy outpatients is relatively rare, with an incidence of 1 to 3:100,000 among patients receiving antibiotics. It is much more common in hospitalized patients, with an incidence of 1:100 to 1:1000. In addition, there are occasional nosocomial outbreaks associated with a higher incidence. *C. difficile* is clearly spread within the hospital environment between patients and staff. *C. difficile* can be cultured from the hands or shoes of at least half of health care workers caring for patients with PMC. The spores can also persist for months on environmental surfaces such as floors, curtains, and medical equipment. Genetic typing has demonstrated the spread of individual strains from patient to patient.

The epidemiology of *C. difficile* in healthy outpatients is less well understood. Although the organism can be cultured from the stool of 3 to 7% of healthy adults, most of these strains are nontoxigenic. In contrast, 15 to 75% of healthy newborns carry toxigenic *C. difficile*, although they do not develop PMC in the absence of contributing illness. *C. difficile* can also be cultured from vaginal and urethral swabs, from stools of pet cats and dogs, and from sand and soil. Hence, opportunities for acquisition of the organism are plentiful.

Almost any antibacterial agent may precipitate *C. difficile* colitis, although certain classes of drugs are more commonly implicated. These include cephalosporins, aminopenicillins, and clindamycin. In contrast, PMC is significantly less common after the use of mezlocillin, piperacillin, and ticarcillin. In animal models, tetracyclines, chloramphenicol, and sulfonamides are the least likely agents to cause PMC. However, these drugs, and even vancomycin and metronidazole (the agents most commonly used to treat PMC), can precipitate the illness in humans. The reasons for these discrepancies are not presently known.

Pathogenesis

The two *C. difficile* toxins are among the largest natural proteins identified, at 308,000 and 279,000 M_r for TxA and TxB, respectively. Their structure is very similar, although the two toxins demonstrate different activities in various model systems. TxB is 1000-fold more active in cellular cytotoxicity assays, and TxA is significantly more active in producing fluid secretion and tissue damage in animal intestinal loops. These findings led to the suggestion that TxA is primarily responsible for causing disease, although there are many reports of significant clinical disease being caused by TxB-positive, TxA-negative strains. About 75% of *C. difficile* isolates from PMC express both toxins.

The precise mechanisms of disease production by TxA and TxB are still being discovered. Both toxins bind to epithelial cells (most likely through carbohydrate surface receptors as well as nonspecific hydrophobic interactions) and are internalized. The toxins enzymatically transfer a single glucose from UDP-glucose to threonine 37 of Rho family GTPases, inactivating them. This leads to a disruption of many aspects of cell signaling, including cytoskeletal integrity and apoptosis. Other activities of the toxins, which may or may not involve Rho glucosylation, include increasing transcription of proinflammatory genes via nuclear factor-κB, causing mitochondrial damage, and loosening tight junctions. Animal models suggest that TxA triggers an inflammatory cascade that involves prostaglandins, platelet-activating factor, neutrophil migration, mast cell degranulation, and activation of stimulatory pathways in the enteric nervous system. Pharmacologic agents that inhibit these pathways can block TxA effects in vivo, although they have not been tested in patients with *C. difficile* colitis.

Table 319–1 • DIAGNOSTIC TESTING FOR *C. DIFFICILE* COLITIS

TEST	ADVANTAGES	DISADVANTAGES
TESTS FOR *C. DIFFICILE* TOXINS		
Tissue culture cytotoxicity	"Gold standard" test	Expensive, time consuming (24–48 hr), only detects toxin B
Toxin A EIA	Rapid, less expensive, several choices available; high specificity can be obtained	Does not detect clinically important toxin B+/toxin A− strains; maximizing sensitivity will reduce specificity
Toxin A + B EIA	Increased sensitivity versus toxin A alone; can detect both toxins	Remain less sensitive than cytotoxin test
Triage panel (toxin A + *C. difficile* antigen)	Early studies suggest very high negative predictive value; similar to performing toxin A EIA and culture together	Many false-positive results due to detection of nontoxigenic strains; more useful to rule out infection
TESTS FOR *C. DIFFICILE* BACTERIA		
Culture	Highly sensitive; allows for DNA typing of organisms for outbreak investigation; isolates can be grown in laboratory and tested for toxins, increasing sensitivity versus stool assays	Delay in diagnosis; routine culture cannot distinguish nontoxigenic colonizing strains from disease-producing strains, and hence has low specificity for disease
Latex agglutination	Rapid, inexpensive	Less sensitive and specific than toxin testing; detects glutamic dehydrogenase enzyme rather than *C. difficile* or its toxins
Polymerase chain reaction	Can detect toxin A and B genes or bacterial genes	Cannot distinguish colonization and disease
NONSPECIFIC TESTS FOR NOSOCOMIAL DIARRHEA EVALUATION		
Smear for fecal leukocytes	Very rapid and simple; very specific for colitis versus benign diarrheal states	Sensitivity for *C. difficile* <50%; must be performed on fresh sample
Fecal lactoferrin	Rapid; more sensitive than fecal leukocyte examination; can be performed on previously frozen stool samples	Milder cases of *C. difficile* diarrhea likely to be negative; cannot be used to rule out disease
Computed tomography scan	Characteristic appearance of colonic wall thickening with stranding, edema, nodularity, or ascites has high specificity	Expensive, insensitive. Should not be considered part of the *C. difficile* evaluation but can detect unsuspected colitis in hospitalized patients
Radionuclide imaging	Can detect colonic uptake to suggest colitis	Not specific for any particular etiology of colitis
PROCEDURES		
Flexible sigmoidoscopy	Rapid, extremely specific. Biopsy of minor lesions may detect microscopic PMC	Expensive; will miss exclusive right-sided colitis (10–20% of cases)
Colonoscopy	Most sensitive test for PMC, rapid	Expensive; requires sedation; risk of perforation.

EIA = enzyme immunoassay; PMC = pseudomembranous colitis.

Clinical Manifestations

Only about 25% of cases of AAD are due to *C. difficile*. In contrast to *C. difficile* colitis, benign AAD tends to be dose related, usually occurs only while taking the antibiotic, and is seldom associated with cramps or systemic symptoms. In contrast, *C. difficile* colitis is characterized often by fever (usually low grade, but occasionally 40° C or higher), leukocytosis (sometimes >20,000/μL), and abdominal cramps. In fact, fever and leukocytosis may be the only clues to *C. difficile* colitis in a hospitalized patient in whom diarrhea has not developed (due to obstruction or impaired motility caused by opiates or anticholinergic drugs). However, it should be noted that mild cases of *C. difficile* colitis may be clinically indistinguishable from benign AAD.

The diarrhea in PMC may be loose or watery; occasionally it is dysenteric. It may be severe enough to produce hypoalbuminemia, edema, volume depletion, and electrolyte abnormalities. The most severe and dreaded complications are toxic megacolon and perforation, which carry a high mortality rate due to peritonitis and sepsis.

Unusual manifestations of *C. difficile* enterocolitis have been reported. In children, *C. difficile* may cause a nonspecific intestinal syndrome of colic and diarrhea. Rarely, *C. difficile* may infect the small bowel in patients who have undergone total colectomy. As with several other inflammatory enteric pathogens, there are reports of *C. difficile*–associated reactive arthritis after the illness.

The differential diagnosis of *C. difficile* colitis depends on the particular clinical syndrome produced. Diarrhea, fever, and leukocytosis developing in an inpatient after antibiotic treatment should always prompt suspicion of PMC. However, *C. difficile* infection in outpatients may be indistinguishable from many other causes of infectious diarrhea. Therefore, patients presenting with diarrhea should always be questioned for recent antibiotic use, and *C. difficile* testing should be specifically requested in those cases where antibiotics have been taken within the past 6 weeks.

Diagnosis

Table 319–1 describes different methods used to diagnose *C. difficile* colitis. The most rapid and specific means of diagnosis is endoscopy with visualization of pseudomembranes. However, mild cases of PMC may only demonstrate microscopic pseudomembranes, and some cases of *C. difficile* diarrhea may have a normal appearance on colonoscopy. Historically, the "gold standard" test has been the TxB cytotoxicity assay. However, many newer, antibody-based tests are equally specific and rival the cytotoxin assay in sensitivity, and they have the advantage of being more rapid and less costly. Nevertheless, the clinician should be suspicious of a negative result obtained by immunoassay in a patient in whom there is a high clinical suspicion for *C. difficile* colitis, especially if the immunoassay is capable of detecting only TxA.

Treatment

Most cases of PMC resolve with supportive care and discontinuation of antibiotics. However, specific treatment aimed at *C. difficile* is usually used despite the lack of placebo-controlled trials. Clinical experience and numerous comparative trials suggest that oral treatment with either metronidazole 250 to 500 mg three times daily or vancomycin 125 mg four times daily leads to resolution of symptoms after a mean of 2 to 3 days (and within 7 days in most cases). ∎ Treatment is usually continued for 7 to 10 days, at which time the majority of patients will be toxin negative in the stool. However, eradication of *C. difficile* colonization rarely occurs with these regimens, and relapses are common. Metronidazole is far less expensive than vancomycin, and no difference in clinical

Continued

Field M: Intestinal ion transport and the pathophysiology of diarrhea. J Clin Invest 2003;111:931–943. *A superb review of intestinal ion transport physiology and pathophysiology.*

McFarland LV, Mulligan ME, Kwok RY, Stamm WE: Nosocomial acquisition of *Clostridium difficile* infection. N Engl J Med 1989;320:204–210. *Demonstration of spread of* C. difficile *between patients and health care workers, and the impact on diarrheal illness.*

O'Connor D, Hynes P, et al: Evaluation of methods for detection of toxins in specimens of feces submitted for diagnosis of *Clostridium difficile*-associated diarrhea. J Clin Microbiol 2001;39:2846–2849. *A recent study comparing performance characteristics of six diagnostic methods for* C. difficile *colitis.*

Surawicz CM, McFarland LV, Greenberg RN, et al: The search for a better treatment for recurrent *Clostridium difficile* disease: use of high-dose vancomycin combined with *Saccharomyces boulardii*. Clin Infect Dis 2000;31:1012–1017. *A small study demonstrating a reduction in relapses of* C. difficile *colitis with the addition of* Saccharomyces boulardii.

efficacy has been demonstrated, so metronidazole is recommended in most cases. Based on anecdotal data, some physicians choose to treat severe, life-threatening cases with vancomycin 500 mg four times daily. Metronidazole resistance has been found in *C. difficile* isolates from horses but rarely from humans.

In patients unable to take oral medication, intravenous metronidazole is often effective (although intravenous vancomycin is not). However, clinical failures have been reported, and life-threatening cases should be treated by intracecal administration of vancomycin through an endoscopically inserted catheter or even a cecostomy, with enteral treatment initiated as soon as possible. A colectomy may be lifesaving if these methods are unsuccessful.

In patients unable to take metronidazole or vancomycin, alternative agents include bacitracin 20,000 units orally four times daily, fusidic acid 500 mg orally four times daily, and cholestyramine 4 g orally one to three times daily. These agents are probably somewhat less effective than metronidazole or vancomycin, although differences have not been consistently demonstrated statistically. Teicoplanin is highly effective treatment for *C. difficile* colitis, although it is currently not available. There is no evidence that combination treatment is beneficial, and cholestyramine should not be administered with other agents because it may bind them and inhibit activity. Antimotility agents should be avoided in all cases of *C. difficile* colitis.

Treatment with vancomycin or metronidazole may encourage colonization of patients with antibiotic-resistant organisms, particularly vancomycin-resistant enterococcus. Several nonantimicrobial agents, including nonpathogenic yeasts and specific toxin binders, are being investigated. If successful, these agents might supplant the currently preferred treatments.

Relapsing or refractory *C. difficile* colitis remains a difficult problem. Relapses following successful treatment occur in about 20 to 35% of patients, and about 5 to 10% have multiple relapses. There is no standard recommendation for how to treat these cases. Usually, relapses respond to retreatment with metronidazole or vancomycin. Some authorities recommend longer courses, slow tapers, or the addition of rifampin or cholestyramine. A recent retrospective analysis of antibiotic treatment for recurrent *C. difficile* colitis found a reduced rate of subsequent relapse in patients treated with a tapering course of vancomycin (from 500–1000 mg/day orally down to 125 mg/day over 19–25 days) or with vancomycin 125–500 mg orally every two to three days, when compared to standard therapy. Two probiotic agents, *Saccharomyces boulardii* and *Lactobacillus* GG, show promise and are currently being studied in large trials. Intravenous immunoglobulin (400 mg/kg) has been used in refractory cases, based on the observation that patients with relapsing disease have poor antibody responses to TxA and TxB. A highly successful, albeit esthetically distasteful treatment is instillation of feces from healthy donors (usually a spouse or other relative). The usual dose is 50 g stool mixed in 500 mL saline administered as an enema or via a colonoscope.

Prevention

Judicious use of antibiotics is the most prudent way to reduce the incidence of *C. difficile* disease. When antibiotics must be used, small studies suggest that substituting mezlocillin, ticarcillin, or piperacillin (with β-lactamase inhibitors if needed) for cephalosporins or clindamycin will reduce the likelihood of inducing *C. difficile* colitis. Antibiotic control programs aimed at reducing *C. difficile* and other nosocomial infections should be used in concert with solid infection-control practices, such as rigorous handwashing, use of disposable equipment where feasible, and isolation of patients with nosocomial diarrhea or documented toxigenic *C. difficile* carriage.

1. Teasley DG, Olson MM, et al: Prospective randomised trial of metronidazole versus vancomycin for Clostridium difficile-associated diarrhoea and colitis. Lancet 1983;2:1043–1046.

SUGGESTED READINGS
Bartlett JG: Antibiotic-associated diarrhea. N Engl J Med 2002;346:334–339. *A concise, up-to-date review of* C. difficile-*related and unrelated antibiotic-associated diarrheas.*

320 BOTULISM

John G. Bartlett

Definition

Botulism is a severe neuroparalytic disease caused by botulinum toxin produced by clostridial species, usually *Clostridium botulinum*. Four categories of disease are recognized: food-borne botulism, infant botulism, wound botulism, and "other."

Etiology

C. botulinum is a gram-positive, spore-forming obligate anaerobe that is widely distributed in nature and frequently found in soil, marine environments, and agricultural products. Each strain produces one of eight antigenically distinct toxins designated A through H. Human disease is caused by types A, B, E, and (rarely) F. These neurotoxins consist of a dichain peptide of approximately 150,000 D. The toxin is absorbed from the intestine or produced in an infected wound, and it is disseminated by the systemic circulation and then binds to specific receptors, where it blocks acetylcholine release. The result is paralysis reflecting the specific nerves involved, usually expressed as a descending symmetric flaccid paralysis. Botulinum toxin is the most potent poison of humans, with a lethal dose in the systemic circulation estimated to be 10^{-9} mg/kg. Type A botulinum toxin is available for injection as therapy for ocular muscle disorders such as strabismus and blepharospasm, for dystonias such as torticollis and hemifacial spasm, and for cosmetic use. This toxin is also a candidate for bioterrorism because of its extraordinary potency.

Clinical Forms

The frequency of various forms of human botulism in the United States from 1950 to 1993 is summarized in Table 320–1.

FOOD-BORNE BOTULISM. Food-borne botulism, the most common form of botulism in the world, results from the ingestion of preformed toxin in inadequately prepared food. The foods most frequently implicated are home processed. In the United States, an average of 15 "out-

Table 320–1 • INCIDENCE OF BOTULISM IN THE UNITED STATES, 1950–1993

DISEASE FROM	YEARS	TOXIN TYPE* A	B	E	TOTAL	CASE FATALITY (%)
Food-borne	1950–93	436	183	196	1126	17.9
Wound	1950–93	37	15	0	58	10.3
Infant	1975–93	575	603	0	1190	1.1
Other	1978–93	17	6	0	31	29.0

*Nine cases due to type F and 323 cases with unknown toxin type.
Adapted from Hathaway C. *Clostridium botulinum*. In Gorbach SL, Bartlett JG, Blacklow NR (eds): Infectious Diseases, 2nd ed. Philadelphia, WB Saunders, 1997, pp 1919–1925.

breaks" occur annually, and most involve one or two cases. The most frequently implicated source is home canned foods, which usually have a putrefactive odor. Type A is the predominant form in the west, and type B predominates in the east. Alaska had 226 cases of food-borne botulism from 1950 through 2000; this represents 27% of U.S. cases. All followed consumption of food prepared by nontraditional fermentation methods and involved type E, which is associated with fish and marine animals. Meat and meat products are commonly responsible in Europe, and the predominant toxin is type B. In China, the most common vehicle is a vegetable product, and type A toxin predominates.

WOUND BOTULISM. Wound botulism is a relatively unusual form of botulism that was first described in 1943. Toxin types A and B have been implicated in all cases—a reflection of their presence in soil. Most cases result from traumatic wounds; less frequent causes are surgical wounds and illicit drug abuse. Clinical features are identical to those of food-borne botulism except that the incubation period from the time of injury to the onset of symptoms ranges from 4 to 14 days and gastrointestinal symptoms are few.

INFANT BOTULISM. Infant botulism was initially described in 1976 and has subsequently become the most frequently recognized form of botulism in the United States. It results from the production of botulinal neurotoxin in the gastrointestinal tract after colonization in children aged 1 to 9 months. The usual source of C. botulinum is the soil or, less frequently, honey. Nearly all cases are due to type A or type B. The disease spectrum varies considerably, but the most commonly recognized form is the "floppy baby syndrome." Initial symptoms are lethargy, diminished suck, constipation, weakness, feeble cry, and diminished spontaneous activity with loss of head control. These symptoms are followed by extensive flaccid paralysis. The case-fatality rate with or without antitoxin is only 1%.

INHALATIONAL BOTULISM. Botulism is a category A agent, meaning that it is one of the top six agents in terms of desirable properties for use as a bioweapon. The presumed mechanism would be contamination of food or via aerosol release, leading to inhalation. Iraqi officials admitted after the Persian Gulf war to have 10,000 L of concentrated botulism toxin in military weapons. It is estimated that a point source release of the toxin could incapacitate or kill 10% of persons within 0.5 km downwind.

UNDETERMINED CLASSIFICATION. Botulism of undetermined classification applies to isolated cases of botulism that have no plausible food or wound source of C. botulinum.

Clinical Manifestations

All symptoms of botulism reflect absorption of the toxin from the gut, lung, or wound. The toxin does not penetrate intact skin. The incubation period is usually 18 to 36 hours but may be as short as 2 hours or as long as 8 days depending to some extent on the inoculum size, so short incubation periods are associated with more severe disease. The bulbar musculature is usually affected first and results in diplopia, dysphonia, dysarthria, and dysphagia. Involvement of the cholinergic autonomic nervous system may result in decreased salivation with dry mouth and sore throat, ileus, or urinary retention. Neurologic evaluation often shows bilateral paresis of the 6th cranial nerves, ptosis, dilated pupils with sluggish reaction, decreased gag reflex, or medial rectus paresis. These symptoms are followed by descending involvement of motor neurons to peripheral muscles, including the muscles of respiration. The most common cause of death is respiratory failure. The spectrum of disease is quite variable; some patients have mild illness, whereas others have severe paralysis requiring intensive care with mechanical ventilation. Mentation remains clear, patients are afebrile, and neurologic dysfunction is bilateral but not necessarily symmetric. In a review of 272 cases of botulism in adults in the United States, the most frequent symptoms were diplopia and blurred vision (90%), dysphagia (76%), generalized weakness (58%), nausea or vomiting (56%), and dysphonia (55%). The most frequent signs in this series were respiratory impairment (73%), specific muscle paresis or paralysis (46%), and ocular muscle impairment (44%). The clinical features of infant botulism are similar to those described above. Findings in over 80% of reported cases include weakness, hypotonia, constipation, failure with oral feeding, diminished gag or suck reflex, respiratory failure, ptosis, and reduced spontaneous movements.

Diagnosis

Standard laboratory tests in cases of suspected food-borne botulism include analysis of serum, stool, gastric contents, and/or food for botulinum toxin and analysis of stool and/or food for C. botulinum. Toxin assays should be done before treatment with antitoxin. With wound botulism, the diagnosis is established by recovery of C. botulinum from wound cultures or by detection of the toxin in serum. Diagnostic specimens recommended for suspected inhalational botulism are gastric aspirates, stools and serum for toxin assay, and gastric aspirates and stool for culture. Toxin assays are often available only at public health labs and cultures require 7 to 10 days. In all of these adult forms, the lack of positive tests does not exclude this diagnosis. In infants, the recommendation is to test stools by culture and toxin assay; two negative specimens obtained during the acute phase of disease will generally rule out this diagnosis. The classic test for botulinum toxin is the mouse bioassay using intraperitoneal challenge to demonstrate a lethal toxin that is neutralized by type-specific antitoxin. In general, adult patients with clinical evidence of botulism show demonstrable toxin in sera in one third of cases and toxin in stool in one third of cases, and the organism is recovered from stool in 60%.

Botulism should be suspected in patients with acute flaccid paralysis, especially in the presence of bilateral sixth cranial nerve dysfunction, associated neurologic findings, recent ingestion of possibly contaminated food, and/or typical symptoms in other persons who shared this food. The differential diagnosis includes myasthenia gravis, Guillain-Barré syndrome, tick paralysis, cerebrovascular accident involving branches of the basilar artery, trichinosis, Eaton-Lambert syndrome, hypocalcemia, hypermagnesemia, organophosphate poisoning, atropine poisoning, paralytic poisoning caused by shellfish or puffer fish, and psychiatric syndromes. Electromyography using repetitive stimulation at 20 to 50 Hz often distinguishes causes of flaccid paralysis. Electromyography demonstrates a diminished amplitude of muscle action potentials with a single supramaximal stimulus and facilitation of action potentials with paired or repetitive stimuli.

Rx Treatment

Treatment of adults consists of supportive care and passive immunization with botulinum antitoxin. Respiratory failure is the major risk and patients must be monitored carefully with liberal use of ventilatory support. Mechanical ventilation is required and varies from 20% with adults with food-borne disease to 60% with infants. Toxin may be removed from the gastrointestinal tract with gastric lavage, cathartics, and enemas early in the course of disease. The trivalent antitoxin or type-specific antitoxin for types A, B, or E is usually given in a dose of 1 vial (5500 to 8500 IU) delivered by slow IV infusion. There is an experimental heptavalent vaccine (A, B, C, D, E, F, and G) held by the U.S. Army that could be available if there was an unusual type, as may be encountered with bioterrorism. The antitoxin should be given as early as possible. Antitoxin will not reverse paralysis or neutralize toxin bound to nerve endings. The goal is neutralization of unbound toxin in the circulation to prevent further paralysis. The antitoxin is horse serum and was associated with anaphylaxis in 2% and other hypersensitivity reactions in 9% at a time when larger doses were used. Antibiotic treatment is unnecessary except for wound botulism. Infants with botulism should not receive either antibiotics directed against C. botulinum or antitoxin because most do extremely well with supportive care alone and it has been suggested that antibiotics may cause toxin release.

Prognosis

The case-fatality rate for food-borne botulism was formerly 60 to 70%. Improved management, especially with respiratory support, has reduced the case-fatality rate for food-borne botulism in the United States to 6.6%. The mortality rates for other forms of botulism are summarized in Table 320–1. Patients who survive generally have a complete recovery.

Infectious Diseases

Prevention

Food-borne botulism is caused by germination of spores in food, with toxin produced by the vegetative forms of *C. botulinum*; the toxin may also be produced in vivo by ingestion of spores and colonization of the gastrointestinal tract. The disease may be prevented by destruction of spores in the original food source, inhibition of germination, or destruction of preformed toxin. Specific measures are as follows.

1. *Destruction of spores with heat or irradiation.* Spores of types A and B may survive boiling for several hours, especially at high altitudes, such as in Colorado, where the boiling point may be substantially lower. These spores may be destroyed if kept at 120° C for 30 minutes in pressure cookers. Spores of type E are the most heat labile and are killed with heating at 80° C for 30 minutes.
2. *Germination may be inhibited* by reducing the pH, refrigerating, freezing, drying, or adding inhibitory substances such as salt, sugar, or sodium nitrate.
3. *Inactivation of preformed toxin* is accomplished by terminal heating for 20 minutes at 80° C or 10 minutes at 90° C.

The recommendation for persons who are exposed (food-borne or inhalational) but asymptomatic is to follow closely with rapid institution of antitoxin when symptoms occur. This applies to food-borne outbreaks and bioterrorism attacks. With regard to infant botulism, honey has been implicated as a vehicle for spores and should not be fed to infants younger than 1 year.

Special Note

Physicians who suspect food-borne or inhalational botulism or wish to receive botulinal antitoxin should contact their state health department or contact the Centers for Disease Control and Prevention 24-hour hotline [(404) 329-2888] for updated information on prevention (www.cdc.gov/phtn/botulism/default/default.htm).

SUGGESTED READINGS
Arnon SS, Schechter R, Inglesby TV, et al: Botulinum toxin as a biological weapon. JAMA 2001;285:1059–1070. *An updated review of botulism with emphasis on this toxin as one of the five top candidates for bioterrorism. Within this context, the method could be contamination of food or an aerosol release with inhalational botulism.*
Centers for Disease Control and Prevention: Botulism outbreak associated with eating fermented food—Alaska, 2001. Morb Mort Wkly Rep 2001;50:680–682. *This report summarizes an outbreak of botulism type E with three patients who consumed contaminated beaver tail and paw.*
Davis LE: Botulism. Curr Treat Options Neurol 2003;5:23–31. *Overview of diagnosis, management, and prognosis, emphasizing that patients can recover normal muscle strength within weeks to months, but usually complain of fatigue for years.*
Montecucco C, Schiavo G: Mechanism of action of tetanus and botulinum neurotoxins. Mol Microbiol 1994;13:1–8. *The authors review the similar pathophysiologic mechanisms of neurotoxins produced by* Clostridium tetani *and* C. botulinum.
Robinson RF, Nahata MC: Management of botulism. Ann Pharmacother 2003;37:127–131. *Emphasizes the use of antitoxin for food-borne, intestinal, and wound botulism but indicates it remains unproven for inhaled* C. botulinum.
Shapiro RL, Hatheway C, Swerdlow DL: Botulism in the United States. Ann Intern Med 1998;129:221–228. *A review of botulism in the United States from 1973 to 1998. Average annual cases: infant, 71/year; food-borne, 24; wound, 3. Cases of wound botulism increased dramatically with use of black tar heroin in 1994.*

321 TETANUS

John G. Bartlett

Definition

Tetanus is a neurologic syndrome caused by a neurotoxin elaborated at the site of injury by *Clostridium tetani.*

Etiology

C. tetani is an anaerobic, gram-positive, slender, motile bacillus. The sporulated form has a characteristic drumstick or tennis-racket shape with a terminal spore. The vegetative form produces tetanospasmin, which is similar in structure, function and potency to botulinum toxin, although the clinical features of botulism and tetanus are completely different. The vegetative forms of *C. tetani* are highly susceptible to heat, disinfectants, and other adverse environmental conditions, but the spores are highly resistant and can survive in soil for months to years. Killing of spores requires boiling for at least 4 hours or autoclaving for 12 minutes at 121° C.

Epidemiology

C. tetani can be found in 20 to 65% of soil samples, with the highest yields being in cultivated land and the lowest yields being in virgin soil. The organism can also be found in stool from a variety of animals, house dust, operating rooms, and contaminated heroin.

Tetanus is most common in warm climates and in highly cultivated rural areas. The greatest problem globally is neonatal tetanus, which represents an important health problem in developing countries, with about 400,000 deaths annually. The cause is nonimmunized mothers giving birth followed by the tradition of dressing their umbilical cord with animal dung or "dusting powder" that is contaminated with *C. tetani*. In the United States, there are about 50 cases of tetanus annually. Of these, 80% are associated with acute injuries, either punctures or lacerations, 10% are complications of chronic wounds, 5% are complications of injection drug use, and 5% have no clear source. The age of these patients is older than 60 years in about 60% and younger than 20 years in 6%; this age distribution reflects the impact of waning immunity with aging.

Pathogenesis

Clinical tetanus requires a source of the organism, local tissue conditions that promote toxin production, and immunologic naiveté. The usual portals of entry are traumatic wounds, surgical wounds, subcutaneous injection sites, burns, skin ulcers, infected umbilical cords, and otitis media with tympanic membrane perforation. The spores are ubiquitous in the environment, and most cases reflect contamination from exogenous sources, although endogenous infection is conceivable in occasional cases that follow intestinal surgery. Important factors at the site of injury are necrotic tissue, suppuration, and the presence of a foreign body. These are responsible for a reduction in the local oxidation-reduction potential, thus promoting reversion of spores to the vegetative forms that produce tetanospasmin. Tetanospasmin is taken up by the peripheral nerve terminals and carried intra-axonally within membrane-bound vesicles to spinal neurons. Tetanospasmin is a 151-kD protein with heavy and light chains joined by a disulfide bond; the 100-kD heavy chain binds to cell surface receptors and the 50-kD light chain is responsible for presynaptic inhibition of transmitter release. This includes blockage of glycine, which is the neurotransmitter used by group 1A inhibitory afferent motor neurons. Loss of the inhibitory influence results in unrestrained firing with sustained muscular contraction. The result with spinal cord neurons is rigidity. In severe cases, there is also involvement of the sympathetic chain causing autonomic dysfunction. Binding of the toxin is irreversible so that recovery requires generation of new axon terminals.

Clinical Manifestations

Forms of tetanus include generalized, localized, cephalic, and neonatal; these reflect host factors and portal of entry.

Generalized tetanus is the most common, accounting for 85 to 90% of reported cases in the United States. The extent of the associated trauma varies from a rather trivial injury that may be forgotten by the patient to a severe, contaminated crush injury. The usual incubation period is 7 to 21 days, depending in large part on the distance of the site of injury from the central nervous system. The "onset period" refers to the time from the first clinical symptoms of tetanus to the first generalized spasm. Both the incubation period and the period of onset indicate the prognosis. An incubation period of less than 9 days and an onset period of less than 48 hours are associated with more severe symptomatology. Trismus, which is masseter rigidity, or "lockjaw," is the presenting complaint in 75% of cases, so the patient is often initially seen by a dentist or oral surgeon. Other early features include irritability, restlessness, diaphoresis, and dysphagia with hydrophobia and drooling. Sustained trismus may result in a characteristic sardonic smile, or "risus sardonicus," and persistent spasm of the back musculature may cause opisthotonos which resembles decorticate posturing. These early manifestations reflect involvement of the bulbar muscles and paraspinous muscles, possibly because they are innervated by the shortest axons. Waves of opisthotonos are highly characteristic of the disease. With progression, the extremities become involved in episodes characterized by painful flexion and adduction of the arms, clenched fists, and extension of the legs. Noise or tactile stimuli may precipitate spasms and generalized convulsions, although they occur spontaneously as well. Involvement of the autonomic nervous system may result in severe arrhythmias, oscillation in the blood pressure, profound diaphoresis, hyperthermia, rhabdomyolysis, laryngeal spasm, and urinary retention. In most cases the patient remains lucid. The condition may progress for 2 weeks despite antitoxin therapy because of the time required for intraaxonal toxin transport, and recovery usually takes an additional month. The severity may be modified by partial immunity. Complications include fractures from sustained contractions and convulsions, pulmonary emboli, bacterial infections, and dehydration.

Localized tetanus refers to involvement of the extremity with a contaminated wound and shows considerable variation in severity. In mild cases, patients may simply have weakness of the involved extremity, presumably limited by partial immunity. In more severe cases, there are intense, painful spasms that usually progress to generalized tetanus when there is sufficient toxin in the central nervous system. This is a relatively unusual form of tetanus, and the prognosis is excellent providing it remains localized.

Cephalic tetanus generally follows a head injury or occurs with *C. tetani* infection of the middle ear. The clinical symptoms consist of isolated or combined dysfunction of the cranial motor nerves, most frequently the seventh cranial nerve. This may remain localized or progress to generalized tetanus. Again, this is a relatively unusual form of tetanus, the incubation period is only 1 or 2 days, and the prognosis for survival depends on severity.

Tetanus neonatorum refers to generalized tetanus resulting from *C. tetani* infection in neonates primarily in underdeveloped countries, where it accounts for up to half of all neonatal deaths as described above. The usual incubation period after birth is 3 to 10 days, and it is sometimes referred to as "the disease of the seventh day," reflecting the average incubation period. The child typically shows irritability, facial grimacing, and severe spasms with touch. The mortality rate exceeds 70%.

Diagnosis

The diagnosis of tetanus is usually made on the basis of clinical observations. The putative agent, *C. tetani,* is infrequently recovered with cultures of the wound. A confirmed history of immunization or a serum antitoxin level of 0.01 unit/dl or higher makes tetanus unlikely, but exceptions are reported. Cerebrospinal fluid analysis is normal, and the electroencephalogram generally shows a sleep pattern. Diagnostic testing is usually not necessary except in cases lacking an identified portal of entry. The differential diagnosis depends on the dominant clinical features and includes oculogyric crisis secondary to phenothiazine toxicity, meningitis, dental abscess, seizure disorder, subarachnoid hemorrhage, hypocalcemic or alkalotic tetany, alcohol withdrawal, and strychnine poisoning. Strychnine also antagonizes glycine, and strychnine poisoning is the only condition that truly mimics tetanus. Strychnine levels in blood and urine establish the diagnosis. Dystonic reactions may resemble tetanus and are distinguished by rapid response to anticholinergic agents.

 ## Treatment

Patients with tetanus require intensive care with particular attention to respiratory support, benzodiazepines, autonomic nervous system support, passive and active immunization, surgical débridement, and antibiotics directed against *C. tetani.* There may be clinical progression for about 2 weeks despite antitoxin treatment because of the time required to complete transport of toxin. Disease severity may be reduced by partial immunity so that some patients have mild disease with minimal mortality and others show mortality rates as high as 60% despite expert care.

SUPPORTIVE CARE. It is most important to assess airway function. Many patients will require endotracheal intubation with benzodiazepine sedation and neuromuscular blockade; a tracheostomy should be placed if the endotracheal tube causes spasms. A nasal feeding tube is usually required for nutritional support.

CONTROL OF MUSCLE SPASMS. Benzodiazepines have become the mainstay of therapy to control spasms and provide sedation. The most extensively studied is diazepam given in 5-mg increments; lorazepam or midazolam are equally effective. Tetanus patients may have high tolerance for the sedation effects of these drugs, requiring exceptionally high doses. When tetanus symptoms resolve, the drugs must be tapered over at least 2 weeks to prevent withdrawal reactions. If control of spasms cannot be achieved by benzodiazepines, longterm neuromuscular blockade is performed with vecuronium (6 to 8 mg/hr).

PASSIVE IMMUNIZATION. Human Tetanus Immunoglobulin (TIG) should be given in a dose of 500 units intramuscularly as soon as possible to neutralize toxin that has not entered neurons. Higher doses or administration intrathecally does not appear to be more effective. An alternative to TIG is pooled intravenous immunoglobulin, which appears to be equally effective. Equine tetanus immunoglobulin is also effective, but the rate of allergic reactions is high, owing to the equine source. This preparation should no longer be used except in underdeveloped countries where cost dictates such medical decisions.

ACTIVE IMMUNIZATION. The standard three-dose schedule of immunization with tetanus toxoid should be given using an injection site separate from that used for immunoglobulin.

ANTIBIOTIC THERAPY. *C. tetani* is susceptible in vitro to penicillins, cephalosporins, imipenem, macrolides, metronidazole, and tetracyclines. Clinical studies favor the use of metronidazole over penicillin and should be given in a dose of 2 g/day for 7 to 10 days.

AUTONOMIC NERVOUS SYSTEM DYSFUNCTION. This generally reflects excessive catecholamine release and is usually treated with labetalol (0.25 to 1.0 mg/min) for blood pressure control. Other treatments for hypertension include morphine by continuous infusion, magnesium sulfate infusion, or an epidural blockage of the renal nerves. Hypotension may require norepinephrine infusion. Bradycardia may require a pacemaker.

SURGERY. Any wounds should be appropriately débrided.

Prognosis

The overall mortality rate for generalized tetanus is 20 to 25% even in modern medical facilities with extensive resources. Patients with moderate or severe generalized tetanus generally require 3 to 6 weeks for recovery. They may require intensive care during most of this time, but if they survive their recovery is usually complete. The highest mortality rates are at the extremes of age. The most frequent cause of death is pneumonia, but many patients have no obvious findings at autopsy, suggesting that death was directly due to the neurotoxin. Patients who survive generally recover completely except for persisting psychological problems related to the severity and duration of the illness.

Prevention

Nearly all cases of tetanus occur in nonimmunized or inadequately immunized individuals. The Advisory Committee on Immunization Practices recommends active immunization of infants and children with DPT (diphtheria and tetanus toxoids and pertussis adsorbed) at

Infectious Diseases

Table 321–1 • GUIDELINES FOR TETANUS PROPHYLAXIS IN WOUND MANAGEMENT

HISTORY OF ADSORBED TETANUS TOXOID	CLEAN AND MINOR WOUNDS		OTHER WOUNDS*	
No. of Doses	Td	TIG	Td	TIG
Unknown or <3	Yes	No	Yes	Yes
≥3	Yes, if >10 years since last dose	No	Yes, if >5 years since last dose	No

*Included but not limited to wounds contaminated with dirt, feces, soil, saliva, puncture wounds; avulsions; and wounds resulting from missiles, crushing, burns, and frostbite.

2 months, 4 months, 6 months, 15 months, and 4 to 6 years. Tetanus toxoid is a highly effective antigen and protective levels of serum antitoxin in persons who complete the primary series persist for at least 10 years. Td (tetanus and diphtheria toxoids adsorbed for adult use) is recommended every 10 years at mid-decade ages (15 years, 25 years, 35 years, etc.). This is commonly neglected as disclosed by serosurveys showing that 40% of persons over 60 years in the United States lack protective levels of tetanus antitoxin. The recommended primary immunization series for nonimmunized persons over 7 years is Td at time 0, 4 to 8 weeks, 6 to 12 months after the second dose, and then every 10 years. Nearly all states now require DPT immunization for school enrollment. About 95% of tetanus cases in the United States occur in persons who have not received the primary series of tetanus toxoid. Immunized childbearing women confer protection on their infants through transplacental maternal antibody.

Prevention of tetanus after injury requires appropriate wound management, assurance of adequate immunity, and consideration of antibiotic prophylaxis. The aim of surgery is to eliminate necrotic tissue, purulent collections, and foreign bodies that promote the environmental conditions necessary for spore germination. Guidelines for immunoprophylaxis based on immunization status and wound characteristics are summarized in Table 321–1. Passive immunization is recommended only for "tetanus-prone" wounds, using TIG for patients with inadequate or unknown primary immunization status. The definition of *tetanus-prone* depends on the interval between injury and treatment, the degree of contamination, the extent of devitalized tissue or foreign bodies within the site of injury, and the depth of the injury. Antimicrobial agents such as penicillin, erythromycin, or metronidazole may be given to inhibit replication of the vegetative forms of *C. tetani*, but immunization and wound cleansing are considered more important.

SUGGESTED READINGS

Armitage, P, Clifford R: Prognosis in tetanus: Use of data from therapeutic trials. J Infect Dis 1978;138:1–8. *Data for 1385 patients with tetanus in India are reviewed to propose a prognostic classification.*

Bardenheier B, Prevots DR, Khetsuriani N, et al: Tetanus surveillance—United States 1995–1997. MMWR CDC Surveill Summ 1998;47:1–13. *The number of cases of tetanus in the United States has decreased to about 50 annually—about 80% are due to acute injury, 10% to chronic wounds, 5% to injection drug use, and 5% to unknown causes.*

Bizzini B: Tetanus toxin. Microbiol Rev 1979;43:224–240. *An extensive discussion of tetanus toxin.*

Bleck TP: *Clostridium tetani. In* Mandell G, Bennett J, Dolin R (eds): Principles and Practice of Infectious Diseases. Philadelphia, WB Saunders, 2000; pp 2537–2543. *The author, a noted tetanus authority, provides an excellent review of the topic, including a detailed treatment plan.*

Center for Disease Control and Prevention: General recommendations on immunization. MMWR Recomm Rep 2002;51:1–35. *Current recommendations for tetanus immunization in the United States.*

Faust RA, Vickers OR, Cohn L Jr: Tetanus: 2,449 Cases in 68 years at Charity Hospital. J Trauma 1976;16:704–712. *The authors review a large clinical experience with tetanus in a U.S. hospital.*

Griffin JW: Local tetanus. Johns Hopkins Med J 1981;149:84–88. *A good review of local tetanus and the pathophysiology of tetanospasmin.*

McQuillan GM, Kruszon-Moran D, Deforest A, et al: Serologic immunity to diphtheria and tetanus in the United States. Ann Intern Med 2002;136:660–666. *A review of a national cohort of 30,930 persons over 6 years of age; 28% had inadequate levels of tetanus antibodies (<0.15 IU/mL); for persons over 70 years, this rate increased to 69%.*

Schofield F: Selective primary health care: Strategies for control of disease in the developing world, XXII. Tetanus: A preventable problem. Rev Infect Dis 1986;8: 144–156. *The author reviews the tetanus problem in the developing world.*

322 DISEASES CAUSED BY NON–SPORE-FORMING ANAEROBIC BACTERIA

Ellie J. C. Goldstein

Anaerobic bacteria are the predominant indigenous, normal flora of the human body, including the skin and oral, gastrointestinal, and vaginal mucosa (Fig. 322–1; Table 322–1). Although these organisms perform beneficial functions, they are also consummate opportunistic pathogens and can cause serious and lethal infection, often in combination with aerobic bacteria. Their role in disease was first described 100 years ago and has been increasingly appreciated during recent decades. In almost all such infections, anaerobes are mixed with aerobes. Because the flora of these infections is often complex and culture results may be delayed, knowledge of the usual flora at the location of infection is an indispensable guide in selecting and instituting empirical antimicrobial therapy.

Taxonomy

Anaerobic bacteria range from those that die with very brief exposure to oxygen and are usually isolated only in normal flora studies to those that can survive on the surface of a fresh agar plate even in the presence of atmospheric oxygen (e.g., *Bacteroides fragilis*). Most anaerobes require an environment with a low oxidation-reduction potential (eH gradient), which can be accomplished in association with low pH, tissue destruction, byproducts from aerobic bacterial metabolism, or low oxygen content. Although not true anaerobes, some organisms such as microaerophilic streptococci and other capnophilic or hard-to-grow organisms are sometimes lumped together with anaerobes, owing to their fastidious nature. Some genera such as *Lactobacillus* and *Actinomyces* contain both aerobic and anaerobic species.

Taxonomic advances have led to the reclassification of many anaerobic species (Table 322–2). The term "*Bacteroides*" will ultimately be reserved for the 10 species of the *Bacteroides fragilis* group. What were previously considered "oral" *Bacteroides* and "pigmented" *Bacteroides* species have been reclassified as *Prevotella* (*saccharolytic, pigmented species*), *Porphyromonas* (*asaccharolytic species*), and other genera. Those that are capnophilic and not true anaerobes are often more related to *Campylobacter, Capnocytophaga,* and other genera. In addition, many new genera and several new species have been created to accommodate pathogens such as *Bilophila wadsworthia, Sutterella wadsworthensis,* and *Anaerobiospirillum thomasii.*

Virulence Factors

Anaerobic bacteria possess a variety of virulence factors that differ among the species (Table 322–3).

Diseases

BACTEREMIA. Transient anaerobic bacteremia occurs in approximately 85% of patients immediately after dental cleaning or manipulation. More than 220 cases of endocarditis due to anaerobes have been reported and are usually associated with anatomic abnormalities or damaged valves. The majority of anaerobic bacteremias are intermittent and associated with serious intra-abdominal and female genital tract infections. Overall, it has been estimated that 10% of bacteremias are due to anaerobes, and in 80% of those, anaerobes are the sole isolates. *B. fragilis* group bacteremia has been associated with an attributable mortality rate of 19% and a 16-day increase in length of hospital stay.

HEAD AND NECK. Dental infections, including periodontal disease, gingivitis, acute necrotizing ulcerative gingivitis, localized juvenile periodontitis, adult periodontitis, pericoronitis, endodontitis, dental abscess, and postextraction infection, are associated with a variety of oral anaerobic bacteria.

Peritonsillar abscess is a deep-seated and potentially life-threatening complication of acute tonsillitis. It may extend into the

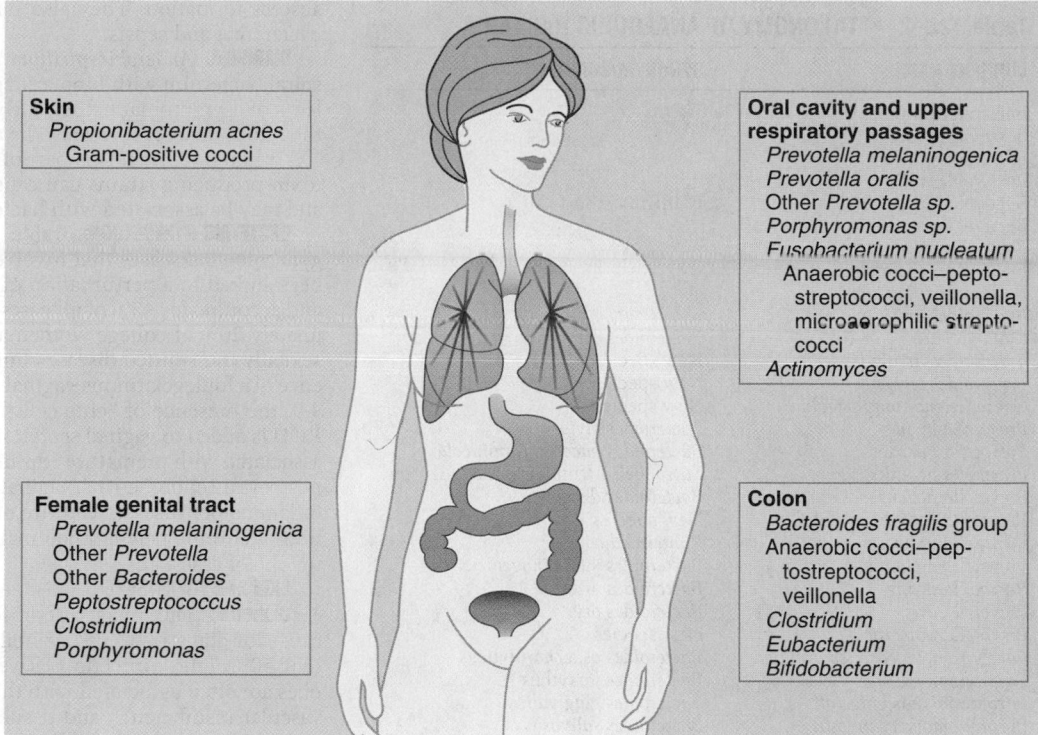

Skin
  Propionibacterium acnes
  Gram-positive cocci

Oral cavity and upper respiratory passages
  Prevotella melaninogenica
  Prevotella oralis
  Other *Prevotella sp.*
  Porphyromonas sp.
  Fusobacterium nucleatum
  Anaerobic cocci–peptostreptococci, veillonella, microaerophilic streptococci
  Actinomyces

Female genital tract
  Prevotella melaninogenica
  Other *Prevotella*
  Other *Bacteroides*
  Peptostreptococcus
  Clostridium
  Porphyromonas

Colon
  Bacteroides fragilis group
  Anaerobic cocci–peptostreptococci, veillonella
  Clostridium
  Eubacterium
  Bifidobacterium

FIGURE 322–1 • Anaerobes as predominant normal microflora of the human body by general anatomic location. (Adapted from Finegold SM, Sutter VL: Diagnosis and Management of Anaerobic Infections. Kalamazoo, MI, Upjohn, 1976. Copyright Dr. Finegold.)

Table 322–1 • LOCATION OF VARIOUS GROUPS OF NONSPORULATING ANAEROBES AS NORMAL MICROFLORA OF HUMANS

ORGANISM	Skin	Oral/Respiratory	Gastrointestinal Tract	Genitourinary Tract
Actinomyces		+		
Bacteroides		+	+	
Eubacterium		+	+	
Fusobacterium		+	+	
Lactobacillus			+	
Peptostreptococcus	+	+	+	+
Porphyromonas		+	+	
Prevotella		+	+	
Propionibacterium	+			
Veillonella		+	+	

various potential spaces of the neck or even the mediastinum and cause jugular vein thrombosis. Anaerobes may be isolated in more than 50% of such cases, usually in mixed culture with aerobes. Other regional infections include cervicofacial actinomycosis, Ludwig's angina, *Fusobacterium necrophorum* sepsis with metastatic infection (Lemiere's syndrome), and neck space infections. Although their acute counterparts are usually infections due to aerobes, chronic sinusitis and chronic otitis media often involve anaerobic bacteria of the normal oral flora.

PULMONARY. Because anaerobic bacteria are the predominant normal flora of the oral cavity and upper respiratory tract and most pneumonias are due to aspiration of indigenous oral flora, it is not surprising that anaerobes are important pulmonary pathogens. They are involved in aspiration pneumonia (both community-acquired and nosocomial), necrotizing pneumonia, empyema, and lung abscess. Aspiration of oral flora may be a result of altered consciousness, dysphagia, or mechanical devices such as intubation. Poor oral hygiene is associated with an increased anaerobic bacterial burden, and the presence of aerobes or tissue necrosis leads to a lowered pH, which in turn facilitates the growth of anaerobes. In community-acquired aspiration pneumonias, anaerobes are involved in 90% of cases, and in many cases they may be the sole pathogens. Anaerobes can be isolated in 35% of nosocomial aspiration pneumonias. If one

forgets to treat a routine aspiration pneumonia for its anaerobic component, then one must remember the propensity for anaerobes to cause abscess.

Management involves good pulmonary toilet and antimicrobial therapy. Because of the increasing resistance of the "oral *Bacteroides* species" (*Prevotella/Porphyromonas* species), penicillin alone is no longer recommended. Alternatives include penicillin plus metronidazole, β-lactamase inhibitor combinations, second-generation cephalosporins such as cefoxitin and cefotetan, carbapenems, and clindamycin plus penicillin. In choosing coverage, one must also consider the microaerophilic streptococci and the aerobic gram-positive and locally prevalent gram-negative components of the oral flora. Nosocomial aspiration frequently is a mixture of all these components.

INTRA-ABDOMINAL. Because anaerobes outnumber aerobes by 1000 : 1 in the large intestine, they play an important role in almost all intra-abdominal infections. Most visceral abscesses (e.g., hepatic), chronic cholecystitis, perforated and gangrenous appendicitis, postoperative wound infections and abscesses, diverticulitis, and any infection associated with fecal contamination of the abdominal cavity involve both aerobes and anaerobes. *B. fragilis* group members are especially important pathogens because they are encapsulated and resist phagocytosis, are often resistant to many commonly used antibiotics, and promote

Table 322–2 • TAXONOMY OF ANAEROBIC BACTERIA

CURRENT NAME	SYNONYM/COMMENT
Bacteroides fragilis	
Bacteroides caccae	
Bacteroides distasonis	
Bacteroides merdae	
Bacteroides eggerthii	B. fragilis group
Bacteroides stercoris	
Bacteroides ovatus	
Bacteroides thetaiotaomicron	
Bacteroides vulgatus	
Bacteroides uniformis	
Campylobacter gracilis	*Bacteroides gracilis*
Bacteroides ureolyticus	New species
Bacteroides tectus	New species
Cholochromatium finegoldii	New species
Prevotella bivia	*Bacteroides bivius*
Prevotella buccae	*Bacteroides buccae (ruminicola)*
Prevotella dentalis	*Mitsuokella dentalis, Hallella sergens*
Prevotella disiens	*Bacteroides disiens*
Prevotella levii–like [PELO]	New species
Prevotella nigrescens	*P. intermedia*
Prevotella melaninogenica	*Bacteroides melaninogenicus*
Prevotella oralis	*Bacteroides oralis*
Prevotella oris	*Bacteroides oris*
Prevotella tancerae	New species
Porphyromonas asancharolytica	*Bacteroides asaccharolyticus*
Porphyromonas forsythus	*Bacteroides forsythus*
Porphyromonas gingivalis	*Bacteroides gingivalis*
Porphyromonas salivosa	*Bacteroides salivosus*
Fusobacterium nucleatum subspecies: nucleatum, polymorphum, fusiforme	New subspecies
Fusobacterium necrophorum	
Fusobacterium ulcerans	New species
Anaerobiospirillum thomasii	New species
Bilophila wadsworthia	New species
Sutterella wadsworthensis	New species
Bacteroides forsythus	New species
Bacteroides tectium	New species
Prevotella tannerae	New species
Bacteroides zoogleoformens	New species

Table 322–3 • POTENTIAL VIRULENCE FACTORS IN VARIOUS ANAEROBES

FACTOR	SPECIES
ADHESION	
Capsule	B. fragilis group, Prevotella melaninogenica
Pili/fimbraie	B. fragilis group P. gingivalis
Hemagglutinin	P. gingivalis
Lectin	F. nucleatum
INVASION/TISSUE DAMAGE	
Proteases	F. necrophorum Bacteroides species Porphyromonas species
Hemolysins	Many species
Fibrinolysin	B. fragilis group Porphyromonas species
Heparinase	B. fragilis group Porphyromonas species
Neuraminidase	B. fragilis group Porphyromonas species
ANTIPHAGOCYTIC	
Capsule	B. fragilis group P. gingivalis
Lipopolysaccharide	B. fragilis group F. necrophorum, P. gingivalis
Metabolic products	Most anaerobes
TOXINS	
Endotoxin	B. fragilis F. necrophorum
Enterotoxin	B. fragilis

Adapted from Duerden BI: Virulence factors in anaerobes. Clin Infect Dis 1994;18(Suppl 4):253.

abscess formation. They also may be associated with concomitant bacteremia and sepsis.

DIARRHEA. *Anaerobiospirillum thomasii* is a motile gram-negative spiral bacterium with bipolar flagellae. It has been isolated from the feces of asymptomatic dogs and cats and has been transmitted from them to humans. It may also be associated with bacteremia.

Although *B. fragilis* is part of the normal intestinal flora, enterotoxin-producing strains can cause diarrhea in animals and humans and may be associated with bacteremia.

OBSTETRIC-GYNECOLOGIC. Table 322–4 lists the various obstetric-gynecologic diseases that involve anaerobes. Bacterial vaginosis has been linked to a perturbation of the normal anaerobic vaginal flora and accounts for 45% of all cases of vaginitis. It is present in approximately 20% of college women and up to 45% of women attending sexually transmitted disease clinics. It can be diagnosed by the presence of a foul, gelatinous vaginal discharge, a vaginal pH greater than 4.5, the presence of "clue cells," and a fishy amine odor after 10% KOH is added to vaginal secretions. Bacterial vaginosis has also been associated with premature rupture of membranes, chorioamnionitis, postpartum endometritis, vaginal cuff cellulitis, and postabortal pelvic inflammatory disease. Culture of tubo-ovarian abscess, a complication of chronic pelvic inflammatory disease, grows anaerobes in up to 85% of cases.

SKIN AND SOFT TISSUE

Diabetes. The infected fetid foot is the most frequent infectious cause for diabetics to be hospitalized. The role of anaerobes in more than 50% of these infections is well established. When present, anaerobes are often associated with the more severe cases, especially with vascular insufficiency and tissue necrosis and those that ultimately require amputation. In addition, the presence of fever, long-standing wounds, crepitus, foul odor, abscess, or prior antimicrobial therapy more often involves anaerobes.

Bites. Anaerobes are present in approximately 65% of animal bite wound infections (Chapter 356), especially those that are more severe or are associated with tissue necrosis or abscess formation. These anaerobes are part of the oral flora of the biting animal. Consequently, the routine bacteriology laboratory may have difficulty in identifying them. Most are penicillin/ampicillin susceptible. Besides anaerobes, *Pasteurella multocida, Staphylococcus intermedius, Staphylococcus aureus,* and streptococci should be considered potential pathogens.

Human bites, both occlusional injuries and clenched fist injuries, tend to be more serious than animal bites. Anaerobes can be isolated from 55% of human bite wounds and are more frequently β-lactamase producing and penicillin resistant. There is also a higher frequency of septic arthritis and osteomyelitis associated with human bite wounds. One must consider anaerobes plus *Eikenella corrodens,* streptococci, *S. aureus,* and *Haemophilus* species as potential pathogens when choosing empirical antimicrobial therapy.

Gangrenes. Gangrene indicates necrosis, most often of skin and subcutaneous tissue, and is often rapidly progressive. Several types of "infectious gangrene" have been described and may sometimes be indistinguishable on a clinical basis. These include the following.

1. *Gas gangrene,* which can incidentally involve other anaerobes besides *C. perfringens* and other clostridia.
2. *Progressive bacterial synergistic gangrene* often involves microaerophilic streptococci and peptostreptococci as well as aerobic bacteria such as *S. aureus* and Enterobacteriaceae.
3. *Synergistic necrotizing cellulitis* involves a mixed aerobic and anaerobic bacteria including *B. fragilis* and peptostreptococci. Diabetic patients may be predisposed. The cellulitis is markedly painful, crepitus may be present, and the discharge has a foul odor.
4. *Fournier's gangrene* is a serious infection of the scrotum or perineum that starts with scrotal pain and erythema and rapidly progresses to necrosis and gangrene, which can lead to sloughing of tissue. It is more often seen in diabetics and can be associated with trauma.

Principles of Diagnosis and Therapy

Clues as to when one should suspect anaerobic infection are listed in Table 322–5. Obtaining an appropriately collected and acceptable specimen (Table 322–6) must be an active process and specified in the orders.

Table 322–4 • OBSTETRIC-GYNECOLOGIC INFECTIONS THAT COMMONLY INVOLVE ANAEROBES

Abscesses
  Pelvic
  Vulvovaginal
  Vaginal cuff
  Tubo-ovarian
  Bartholin's gland
  Skene's gland
Endometritis
Myometritis
Parametritis
Pelvic cellulitis
Pelvic thrombophlebitis
Bacterial vaginosis
Salpingitis
Chorioamnionitis
Intrauterine device–associated infection
Pelvic actinomycosis
Postabortal sepsis

Table 322–5 • CLUES TO THE PRESENCE OF ANAEROBIC INFECTION

Infection in proximity to a mucous membrane
Foul odor to a discharge or wound
Gas or crepitus in a tissue
Infection associated with necrotic tissue or malignancy
Bacteremia with associated jaundice
Gram stain morphology consistent with anaerobes
"Sulfur" granules (actinomycosis)
Infection after human or animal bite
Dental infection
Infection after abdominal or pelvic surgery
No growth on routine bacterial culture (especially if Gram stain shows organisms)
Fistulous tracts
Any abscess
Typical clinical picture of gas gangrene or necrotizing fasciitis
Failure to respond to drugs not active against anaerobes (e.g., trimethoprim/sulfamethoxazole, aminoglycosides, older quinolones)

Adapted from Finegold SM: Anaerobic Bacteria in Human Disease. New York, Academic Press, 1977, p 42.

Table 322–6 • SPECIMENS ACCEPTABLE FOR ANAEROBIC CULTURE

ACCEPTABLE
Any aspirate: abscess, joint, lung, empyema, suprapubic (urine), brain, myringotomy, percutaneous abdominal, or pelvic
Tissue biopsy
Cellulitis after débridement of superficial debris
Bile
Surgical specimen (not contaminated with normal flora)
Transtracheal aspirate of sputum
Culdocentesis fluid
Antral sinus puncture
Deep gingival pocket

UNACCEPTABLE
Sputum
Voided urine
Nasal discharge
Feces/diarrhea
Vaginal discharge
Superficial wounds
Mucous membrane

Table 322–7 • GENERAL PRINCIPLES OF THERAPY FOR ANAEROBIC INFECTIONS

Elimination of dead space
Débridement
Drainage
Irrigation
Provide adequate circulation when possible
Remove foreign body
Antimicrobials
  Activity against most likely pathogen(s): location dependent, normal flora considered
  Absorption, appropriate route of administration
  Penetration into site of infection
  Dosage appropriate for local tissue levels, body mass of patient, renal and liver function
  Duration appropriate for condition
  Susceptibility testing of isolate to guide specific therapy

Table 322–8 • ANTIMICROBIAL SUSCEPTIBILITY PATTERNS FOR ANAEROBIC BACTERIA*

BACTERIA	DRUG							
	Penicillin	β-Lactamase[†]	Cefoxitin	Cefotetan	Imipenem/Meropenem Ertapenem	Moxifloxacin	Clindamycin	Metronidazole
B. fragilis	−	+	+	+	+	+	v	+
B. thetaiotaomicron	−	+	v	v	+	v	v	+
B. fragilis group, other	−	+	v	v	+	+	v	+
Prevotella species	v	+	+	+	+	+	+	+
Fusobacterium nucleatum	v	+	+	+	+	v	+	+
Fusobacterium necrophorum	+	+	+	+	+	v	+	+
Porphyromonas species	+	+	+	+	+	+	+	+
Peptostreptococci	+	+	+	+	+	+	+	v
Propionibacterium acnes	+	+	+	+	+	+	+	−
Veillonella	+	+	+	+	+	+	+	+
Actinomyces	+	+	+	+	+	+	+	−

*Based on a variety of in vitro susceptibility studies from different laboratories and using different techniques.
[†]β-Lactamase inhibitor–β-lactam combination (e.g., ticarcillin/clavulanate, ampicillin/sulbactam, piperacillin/tazobactam).
+ = Susceptible.
− = Resistant.
v = Variable.

General principles of therapy are listed in Table 322–7. In general, appropriate antimicrobial therapy coupled with prompt drainage and surgical débridement are essential for therapeutic success. Table 322–8 notes the susceptibility patterns of the various clinically important anaerobes.

SUGGESTED READINGS
Aldridge KE, Ashcraft D, O'Brien M, et al: Bacteremia due to *Bacteroides fragilis* group: Distribution of species, beta-lactamase production, and antimicrobial susceptibility patterns. Antimicrob Agents Chemother 2003;47: 148–153. *Susceptibilities to metronidazole, beta-lactam-beta-lactamase inhibitor*

combinations, carbapenems, and trovafloxacin were ≥93%, but susceptibility testing is suggested.

Golan Y, McDermott LA, Jacobus NV, et al: Emergence of fluoroquinolone resistance among Bacteroides species. J Antimicrob Chemother 2003;52:208–213. *Documents high rates of resistance among recent blood isolates.*

323 INTRODUCTION TO ENTERIC INFECTIONS

Herbert L. DuPont

Enteric infections are second only to respiratory tract infections as common medical problems. In certain populations, enteric infections are hyperendemic: in poorly nourished children living in developing tropical countries, where the infections are significant causes of pediatric mortality; in infants in day care centers; in residents of custodial institutions for the mentally retarded; in homosexual males; and in those who venture from industrialized to developing regions ("travelers' diarrhea").

In approaching a patient with an enteric infection, epidemiologic (Table 323–1) and clinical (Table 323–2) features are used to determine the proper approach to evaluation and management. One must work through the various considerations to be certain that the proper differential diagnosis and work-up are developed. Recent travel to a mountainous region of North America should raise the possibility of infection by *Giardia lamblia*. Travel to Russia, particularly St. Petersburg, is associated with an increased risk of infection by *Cryptosporidium parvum* and *G. lamblia*. When diarrhea occurs during or after travel to a developing tropical region, a bacterial enteropathogen should be suspected. Infection with *Cyclospora* should be suspected when diarrhea follows travel to Nepal.

A specific food or water vehicle cannot be suspected unless multiple cases of illness with a common exposure occur. In this situation, the incubation period often helps to determine the etiologic diagnosis: less than 8 hours in the case of a *Staphylococcus aureus* or *Bacillus cereus* enterotoxin food poisoning and more than 8 hours in the case of intestinal infection. On evaluation of the clinical expression of the illness (see Table 323–2), a tentative diagnosis may be made. In the patient who is receiving an antimicrobial drug, or who has recently completed a course of therapy, and presents with an enteric infection manifested by diarrhea with or without fever and dysenteric disease, particularly if the patient is hospitalized or was recently hospitalized, *Clostridium difficile* should be suspected. When a person has close contact with an infant or infants attending a day care center, a number of pathogens found in this setting should be suspected. Finally, the homosexual male with an enteric infection may have acquired it through fecal-oral contamination, which is common in this setting (and in this case, multiple pathogens may be found in stool); through receptive anal intercourse; or when intestinal immunity has become depressed as a result of the acquired immune deficiency syndrome (AIDS).

Enteric infection syndromes may be divided into five groups based on the clinical presentation, including febrile systemic disease (enteric fever), acute watery diarrhea (small bowel secretory process), profuse vomiting (gastroenteritis), the passage of many small-volume stools containing blood and mucus (dysenteric disease), and diarrhea lasting longer than 2 weeks (persistent diarrheal disease). Table 323–2 lists the major syndromes along with the expected cause. Norwalk virus has become a major cause of water-borne and food-borne gastroenteritis in the United States. *Campylobacter* is the most common reportable enteric pathogen in industrialized countries and is the most important definable cause of Guillain-Barré syndrome. *Escherichia coli* O157:H7 and other serotypes that produce shiga toxin are important causes of food-borne and water-borne colitis and hemolytic-uremic syndrome in children. In the majority of cases of

Table 323–1 • EPIDEMIOLOGIC FEATURES IMPORTANT IN DETERMINING POTENTIAL CAUSES OF ENTERIC INFECTION

EPIDEMIOLOGIC FEATURE	ETIOLOGIC AGENT TO SUSPECT
Travel to mountainous areas of North America	*Giardia lamblia*
Travel to Russia (especially St. Petersburg)	*Cryptosporidium, G. lamblia*
Travel to Nepal	*Cyclospora*
Travel to the developing tropical/semitropical world from an industrialized region	Enterotoxigenic *Escherichia coli,* enteroaggregative *E. coli, Shigella, Salmonella* (including *S. typhi*), other bacterial causes, *G. lamblia, Cyclospora, Cryptosporidium,* and small round viruses (e.g., Norwalk)
Presence of associated cases (an outbreak)	Use incubation period and clinical features (see Table 323–2) to determine probable cause
Antibiotic use in the past 2 months in hospitalized patient	*Clostridium difficile*
Contact with day care centers	Any enteropathogen, often *G. lamblia, Cryptosporidium, Shigella,* or rotavirus
Homosexual male with diarrhea	Any organism spread by fecal-oral route; with proctitis, suspect *Neisseria gonorrhoeae, Chlamydia trachomatis,* herpes simplex or *Treponema palliium;* with AIDS suspect any agent, especially *Cryptosporidium, Microsporidium, Cyclospora, Isospora, Shigella, Salmonella, C. jejuni, C. difficile, Mycobacterium avium-intracellulare,* and cytomegalovirus

Table 323–2 • CLINICAL FEATURES OF ENTERIC INFECTION

CLINICAL SYNDROME	ETIOLOGIC AGENTS SUSPECTED	SPECIAL CONSIDERATIONS
Enteric or typhoid fever	*Salmonella typhi, S. enteritidis, Campylobacter, Shigella, Yersinia enterocolitica*	Blood cultures, antibiotics generally needed
Acute watery diarrhea	Any agent may be responsible. Consider: *Vibrio cholerae,* enterotoxigenic or enteroaggregative *Escherichia coli, Shigella, Salmonella, C. jejuni*	Fluid and electrolyte therapy crucial for recovery in dehydration
Gastroenteritis with vomiting	Viral agents (rotavirus or small round viruses such as Norwalk virus) or enterotoxin-mediated disease (*Staphylococcus aureus* or *Bacillus cereus*)	In case of an outbreak, incubation period suggests the etiology
Dysentery (bloody diarrhea)	*Shigella, C. jejuni, Salmonella,* enterohemorrhagic (O157:H7 or other shigatoxin producing *E. coli*) or enteroinvasive *E. coli, Aeromonas hydrophilia, Vibrio parahemolyticus, Yersinia enterocolitica, Entamoeba histolytica,* or inflammatory bowel disease	Stool culture and occasionally parasite examination important to determine cause; hemolytic uremic syndrome may complicate diarrheal disease caused by *E. coli* O157:H7 or *S. dysenteriae* 1
Persistent diarrhea (≥2 wk)	*Giardia lamblia,* small bowel bacterial overgrowth, bacterial diarrhea, lactase deficiency, Brainerd diarrhea	Stool culture and parasite examination indicated; empiric anti-*Giardia* therapy may occasionally be useful; milk should not be consumed; a history of raw milk or untreated (well or surface) water consumption or international travel (not responding to antimicrobial therapy) suggests the possibility of Brainerd diarrhea

Table 323–3 • NONINFECTIOUS CAUSES OF DIARRHEA

Running	Bacterial overgrowth
Fecal impaction	Systemic mastocytosis and
Drugs and laxatives	eosinophilic gastroenteritis
Enteral feeding	Tropical sprue
Irradiation	Celiac sprue
Pancreatic insufficiency	Dermatitis herpetiformis
Intestinal lymphangiectasia	Whipple's disease
Foods (especially dietetic)	Thyrotoxicosis
Cirrhosis and biliary obstruction	Adrenal insufficiency
Diabetic diarrhea	Factitious
Alcoholism	Inflammatory bowel disease
Collagenous colitis	Food allergy
VIPoma	Carcinoid
Ischemic bowel disease	Villous adenoma
	Irritable bowel syndrome

enteric infection, it is not possible to determine the cause of illness on clinical grounds. Laboratory tests are often useful, particularly in the more severe or intensely ill patients, to help establish cause and to develop the proper plan of treatment.

In sporadic cases of acute or persistent diarrhea, infectious agents are not always responsible. Table 323–3 offers a partial list of the noninfectious causes of diarrhea that might be considered.

Rx Treatment

Treatment of diarrhea should be tailored to clinical syndrome. Oral rehydration with fluids and electrolytes is used in patients with acute watery diarrhea and gastroenteritis and with all forms of enteric infection when any degree of dehydration occurs. For enteric fever and febrile dysenteric disease, antimicrobial therapy is indicated. For outbreaks of dysenteric diarrhea in children where fever is not important, antibacterial drugs should be withheld to prevent predisposing the patient to hemolytic-uremic syndrome. For pathogen-specific diarrhea, antimicrobial therapy is often advised: shigellosis, salmonellosis (complicated illness), campylobacteriosis, cholera, giardiasis, amebiasis, cyclosporiasis, and isosporiasis. For patients with persistent diarrhea, work-up for cause is indicated before a management plan is developed.

SUGGESTED READINGS

Bartlett JG: Antibiotic-associated diarrhea. N Engl J Med 2002;346:334–339. *A concise, up-to-date review of C.* difficile-*related and unrelated antibiotic-associated diarrheas.*
Field M: Intestinal ion transport and the pathophysiology of diarrhea. J Clin Invest 2003;111: 931–943. *A superb review of intestinal ion transport physiology and pathophysiology.*

324 TYPHOID FEVER

Thomas Butler
W. Michael Scheld

Definition

Typhoid fever is a systemic bacterial disease caused by *Salmonella enterica* serotype *typhi*. It is characterized by prolonged fever, abdominal pain, diarrhea, delirium, rose spots, and splenomegaly and complicated sometimes by intestinal bleeding and perforation. Enteric fever is synonymous with typhoid fever, which is occasionally caused also by *S. enterica* serotype *enteritidis* bioserotype paratyphi A or B.

Etiology

The typhoid bacillus is a motile gram-negative rod in the family Enterobacteriaceae. It possesses a flagellar (H) antigen, a cell wall (O) lipopolysaccharide antigen (09 or 012), and a polysaccharide virulence (Vi) antigen located in the cell capsule. The polysaccharide side chain of the O antigen confers serologic specificity to the organism and is essential in virulence because salmonellae other than *S. enter-*

ica serotype *typhi* and *S. enterica* serotype *enteritidis* bioserotype paratyphi A or B do not produce enteric fever in humans. Recently, the complete genome sequence of a multidrug-resistant strain of *S. enterica* serotype *typhi* (isolated 1993, Vietnam) was determined. The genome is essentially collinear with the genomes of *S. enterica* serotype *typhimurium* and *Escherichia coli*, but unlike *E. coli*, *S. enterica* serotype *typhi* has several large insertions, termed Salmonella *pathogenicity islands of recent horizontal acquisition*. One other noteworthy feature is the presence of 204 pseudogenes, most inactivated by a single frameshift or stop codon, suggesting recent origin facilitating adaption of *S. enterica* serotype *typhi* to its sole host, humans. The strain described in the genome analysis also contains two plasmids: one larger conjugative encoding multidrug resistance and the other with homology with a virulence-associated plasmid in *Yersinia pestis*.

Incidence and Prevalence

Typhoid fever has been almost eliminated from developed countries because of sewage and water treatment facilities but remains a common disease in developing countries. Because most patients with typhoid fever are treated as outpatients presumptively without a confirmed diagnosis in resource-limited regions, reliable data are difficult to obtain, but annual incidence rates rise to 980 per 100,000 in Delhi, India. According to the best estimates from the World Health Organization (1995), at least 16 million new cases of typhoid fever occur annually, with approximately 600,000 deaths. Asia, the Indian subcontinent, followed by Africa, and distantly by Latin America account for most cases. Outbreaks affecting more than 10,000 persons in Tajikistan were reported in 1996 and 1997. About 800 cases are diagnosed each year in the United States, most of these are in recently arrived travelers who contracted their infections abroad.

Epidemiology

Adults and children of all ages and both genders appear equally susceptible to infection. In developing countries, most cases occur in school-age children and young adults, but children younger than 5 years of age are probably under-represented because the illness may be atypical. Although acquired immunity provides some protection, reinfections have been documented. Typhoid fever occurs during all seasons.

Transmission is by the fecal-oral route through contaminated water or food. The main human sources of infection in the community are asymptomatic fecal carriers and cases during either disease or convalescence. Females and older males are prone to become chronic fecal carriers because underlying cholelithiasis enables them to harbor chronic infection in the gallbladder. *S. enterica* serotype *typhi* is resistant to drying and cooling, thus allowing bacteria to survive prolonged periods in dried sewage, water, food, and ice.

Vi-phage typing of *S. typhi* is a useful epidemiologic tool to trace cases of typhoid fever to a carrier or food source. In endemic situations, multiple phage types are present, and several phage types may be responsible for an epidemic. In addition to phage typing, pulse-field gel electrophoresis and ribotyping have been useful in the investigation of outbreaks or tracking strains in circulation in endemic areas.

Pathogenesis and Pathology

After the organism is ingested, the part of the inoculum that survives stomach acid enters the small intestine, where bacteria penetrate the mucosa and enter mononuclear phagocytes of ileal Peyer's patches and mesenteric lymph nodes. Inocula of at least 10^5 bacteria are necessary to initiate disease, and inocula of 10^7 and more cause disease regularly. Survival of the gastric acid barrier is crucial to infection; conditions that produce achlorhydria such as aging, previous gastrectomy, use of histamine H_2-receptor antagonists or proton pump inhibitors, or, most recently, prior infection with *Helicobacter pylori*, enhance *Salmonella* infection by lowering the infectious dose. The incubation period ranges from 8 to 28 days (usually 7 to 14 days), depending on inoculum size and immune status of the host. Bacteria proliferate in mononuclear phagocytes and spread by way of the blood to the spleen, liver, and bone marrow, where further proliferation in macrophages occurs. The earliest symptoms of fever and chills (Table 324–1) are associated with bacteremia. Inflammatory reactions occur

Table 324-1 • EVOLUTION OF TYPICAL SYMPTOMS AND SIGNS OF TYPHOID FEVER

DISEASE PERIOD	SYMPTOMS	SIGNS	PATHOLOGY
First week	Fever, chills gradually increasing and persisting; headache	Abdominal tenderness	Bacteremia
Second week	Rash, abdominal pain, diarrhea or constipation, delirium, prostration	Rose spots, splenomegaly, hepatomegaly	Mononuclear cell vasculitis of skin, hyperplasia of ileal Peyer's patches, typhoid nodules in spleen and liver
Third week	Complications of intestinal bleeding and perforation, shock	Melena, ileus, rigid abdomen, coma	Ulcerations over Peyer's patches, perforation with peritonitis
Fourth week and later	Resolution of symptoms, relapse, weight loss	Reappearance of acute disease, cachexia	Cholecystitis, chronic fecal carriage of bacteria

in the spleen, liver, bone marrow, Peyer's patches mainly in the terminal ileum, and skin, consisting of mononuclear cell infiltration, hyperplasia, and focal necrosis. Focal collections of mononuclear leukocytes are called *typhoid nodules*. Fever and other constitutional symptoms are probably caused by the release of cytokines, including tumor necrosis factor and interleukin-1, from infected mononuclear phagocytes. Intestinal manifestations are caused by hyperplasia of Peyer's patches with ulcerations of overlying mucosa, resulting in pain, diarrhea, bleeding, or perforation.

Although the association of non-*typhi* Salmonella bacteremia with AIDS has been recognized from the early descriptions of the epidemic, the interaction of typhoid fever and human immunodeficiency virus infection is unclear. In contrast, major histocompatibility complex class II and III alleles are definitely associated with typhoid fever in Vietnam: HLA-DRBI* 0301/6/8, HLA-DQBI* 0201-3 and TNFA* 2 (-308) whereas HLA-DRBI* 04, HLA-DQBI* 0401/2 and TNFA*1 (-308) are linked to disease resistance.

Clinical Manifestations

In the first days of illness, the nonspecific symptoms of fever, chills, malaise, dry cough, anorexia, and headache are mild and in the typical case build up in intensity during the first week, resulting in prostration. The evolution of disease syndromes occurs stepwise over 1 to 3 weeks (see Table 324-1) but may be variable in the time of appearance. The early symptoms of fever, abdominal pain, and prostration tend to persist throughout the illness, which in untreated cases lasts a month or longer. Abdominal pain occurs in more than half of patients and is frequently diffuse or located in the right lower quadrant over the terminal ileum. Diarrhea occurs in about a third of patients and consists of either watery stools or semi-solid stools. Melena occurs less commonly. Rose spots occur in more than half of light-skinned individuals but are often not visible in dark-skinned patients (e.g., overall 5 to 30% of cases). The rash is seen most commonly on the shoulders, thorax, and abdomen and rarely affects the extremities. The lesions are erythematous macules or papules about 2 to 4 mm in diameter that typically blanch with pressure but may become hemorrhagic. Many patients display abnormal behavior or altered mental status that may be out of proportion to the severity of the systemic illness. Among the common presentations are "toxic" staring, apathetic appearance, delirium, aphonia, and stupor (although neuropsychiatric manifestations vary geographically). Seizures are common in children. Patients are rarely jaundiced.

In about 5% of patients, intestinal bleeding or intestinal perforation occurs, usually after the second week of illness. Bleeding occurs from ileal ulcers and may present as melena or bright red blood in stools. Brisk bleeding develops rarely but is an occasional cause of death (<2% of cases). Intestinal perforation (~1 to 3% of hospitalized cases) presents as the sudden onset of more severe abdominal pain, distention, and tenderness. Bowel sounds are diminished, and the abdominal radiograph usually reveals free air. Perforation most often occurs unexpectedly after a few days of treatment when a patient has started to improve. Other complications of typhoid fever include pneumonia, which usually develops as a superinfection due to other bacteria, myocarditis, acute cholecystitis shock, and acute meningitis.

Relapses occur in 10 to 20% of patients treated with chloramphenicol (less in patients treated with some other agents; see later). Patients with relapses experience the reappearance of typical symptoms 7 to 14 days after the end of treatment. Relapses tend to be less severe than the initial episode. Although average mortality is less than 1%, especially in "developed" countries, this varies considerably among hospitalized patients from approximately 2% in Pakistan or Vietnam to 30 to 50% in Papua New Guinea and Indonesia.

Diagnosis

The preferred method of diagnosis is isolation of *S. enterica* serotype *typhi* from a blood culture (preferably ≥15 mL in adults), which is positive in most patients during the first 1 to 2 weeks of illness. Urine and stool cultures, and skin snips of rose spots, are positive less frequently but should be obtained to increase the diagnostic yield. The bone marrow culture is the most sensitive test, is positive in nearly 80 to 95% of cases, and can be used when a bacteriologic diagnosis is crucial or in patients who have been pretreated with antibiotics. The duodenal string test to culture bile has also been used with success in typhoid fever.

The Widal test for agglutinating antibodies against the somatic (O) and flagellar (H) antigens of *S. enterica* serotype *typhi* is widely used for serodiagnosis, but sensitivity, specificity, and predictive values vary enormously by geographic region. An O agglutinin titer of 1:80 or more or a fourfold rise supports a diagnosis of typhoid fever, whereas the H agglutinins are more often nonspecifically elevated by immunization or previous infections with other bacteria. Serodiagnosis is of limited value because false-positive results are often obtained in endemic areas and false-negative results occur in some cases of bacteriologically proven typhoid fever. Although DNA probes and polymerase chain reaction tests have been validated to detect *S. enterica* serotype *typhi* in blood, the methods are not widely available for practical reasons. Nevertheless, a Vi agglutination reaction of stool samples may prove useful for the detection of chronic carriers.

Other laboratory findings are anemia of variable severity and a white blood cell count that is normal or decreased with an increased percentage of band forms. Platelets are often diminished, and signs of disseminated intravascular coagulation are present (yet rarely are of clinical significance). Liver function tests frequently show elevated levels of aminotransferases and bilirubin. Renal failure is an infrequent complication. In patients with diarrhea, the stool shows fecal leukocytes.

The differential diagnosis depends on infections that are endemic in the area where an individual contracted the infection. For returned travelers from developing countries, the common possibilities are malaria, hepatitis, typhus, dengue, brucellosis, visceral leishmaniasis, amebic liver abscess, shigellosis, nontyphoid salmonellosis, and leptospirosis. In the United States one must consider septicemias originating from the urinary tract, gastrointestinal tract, or gallbladder as well as influenza, infectious mononucleosis, meningococcemia, miliary tuberculosis toxoplasmosis, noninfectious causes of a fever of unknown origin, and bacterial endocarditis.

Rx. Treatment

Chloramphenicol was the drug of choice, until recently, since its introduction in 1948 because no other drug had been demonstrated to cause more rapid or consistent improvement of disease. Chloramphenicol is given orally in a dose of 50 to 75 mg/kg/day in four equal portions every 6 hours. After defervescence and clinical improvement the dosage can be reduced to 30 mg/kg/day to complete a 14- to 21-day course. In patients unable to take oral medication, the same dosage should be given intravenously until the patient can take capsules.

Unfortunately, multidrug-resistant strains carrying 100,000 to 120,000 kd IncHI plasmids, have emerged worldwide in recent years that confer resistance to chloramphenicol and, most alarmingly, typical back-up drugs such as ampicillin and trimethoprim-sulfamethoxazole. Ceftriaxone-resistance has been described, albeit rare, but the increase in fluoroquinolone-resistant *S. enterica* serotype *typhi* (usually mediated by point mutations in the DNA gyrase enzyme [gyr A] at positions 83 and 87) must be viewed as a major worldwide public health issue, especially in Asia.

Despite this trend, the fluoroquinolones are the most effective agents for the treatment of typhoid fever, even with short courses (e.g., 3 to 7 days). Defervescence of fever usually occurs in 4 days or less, cure rates exceed 96%, and fewer than 2% develop persistent fecal carriage or relapse. Although the issues in children have been largely resolved, and generic drugs may bring quinolones into a favorable (e.g., cost) position in Asia, the concern for the induction of quinolone-resistant *S. enterica* serotype *typhi* is important. Nevertheless, quinolones (e.g., ciprofloxacin or ofloxacin, but not nalidixic acid or norfloxacin), at maximal doses (e.g., ofloxacin 20 mg/kg/day) for 7 to 14 days are now recommended as initial therapy of typhoid fever. In endemic areas with nonresistant strains, chloramphenicol, amoxicillin, or trimethoprim-sulfamethoxazole are still useful. If fluoroquinolone resistance is of concern, azithromycin or a third-generation cephalosporin (e.g., intravenous cefotaxime or oral cefixime) are expensive alternatives. In patients with severe typhoid fever, when parenteral agents are necessary, fluoroquinolones are still the agents of choice followed by cefotaxime or ceftriaxone, both given for 10 to 14 days. Alternatives to all regimens have been published recently.

Patients who are dehydrated, anorectic, or suffering from diarrhea should receive intravenous saline with attention to electrolyte and acid-base disturbances. Patients with brisk intestinal bleeding require blood transfusion, but this is unusual. Patients with suspected perforation should have an abdominal radiograph to look for free air and peritoneal fluid. Laparotomy should be undertaken as early as possible to suture the perforation or make other repairs, as indicated.

In some high-risk patients with delirium, coma, or shock, high-dose dexamethasone in addition to antibiotics reduces mortality. The dose should be 3 mg/kg initially, followed by 1 mg/kg every 6 hours for 48 hours. One must be cautious with this therapy because signs and symptoms of perforation are masked by steroids. Antipyretic drugs such as aspirin should be administered with caution because they occasionally markedly reduce blood pressure.

Patients with relapses of typhoid fever should be treated the same as patients with a first attack. Chronic fecal carriers (asymptomatic excretion for ≥1 year) should be given high doses of ampicillin or amoxicillin, 100 mg/kg/day, plus probenecid, 30 mg/kg/day for 3 months. Trimethoprim-sulfamethoxazole is also effective. Patients with multidrug-resistant infections can be treated with ciprofloxacin (e.g., 750 mg twice daily for 28 days) or other quinolones. Patients with gallstones or cholecystitis may require cholecystectomy to eradicate the carrier state. Chloramphenicol neither prevents nor effectively treats the chronic carrier state.

Prognosis

Typhoid fever carried a case-fatality rate of about 12% in the preantibiotic era, which was reduced to about 4% after chloramphenicol became available. Case-fatality rates of more than 10% continue to be reported in developing countries despite availability of antibiotics, whereas developed countries show case-fatality rates of less than 1%. After treatment with chloramphenicol or other effective drugs, most patients become afebrile in 4 to 7 days. In the preantibiotic era, about 10% of recovered patients had relapses, and chloramphenicol treatment has not reduced this rate; however, relapses appear to be fewer with the other agents (<3%). Intestinal bleeding or perforation occurs in about 5% of patients and may not be prevented by antibiotic treatment. Thus, bleeding or perforation is occasionally detected after patients have defervesced during treatment. Only 1 to 3% of patients become chronic fecal carriers after recovery.

Prevention

Travelers to developing countries should avoid consuming untreated water, ice cream, drinks served with ice, peeled fruits, and other food that is not served hot. American international travelers face an overall risk of developing typhoid fever of fewer than 1 case in 10,000 trips, but travelers to high-risk countries such as India and Pakistan have a probability of about 4 in 10,000 trips of getting typhoid fever. Travelers wishing immune protection should receive either typhoid vaccine live oral Ty21a given as 1 capsule every other day for a total of 4 capsules (e.g., days 1, 3, 5, and 7) or typhoid Vi polysaccharide vaccine given as a single intramuscular injection (0.5 mL or 25 µg), with booster doses given every 2 years if needed. These vaccines give only partial protection, and thus vaccinated persons should still exercise dietary precautions. When polysaccharide antigens are complexed with proteins, vaccines may be effective in infants younger than 2 years of age; this principle has been achieved with a new modified Vi vaccine conjugated with a nontoxic *Pseudomonas aeruginosa* exotoxin A, with 91.5% protective efficacy in recent trials. The traditional method of controlling typhoid is to follow stool cultures of convalescent cases and report positive cultures to the health department. The health department investigates nonimported typhoid cases to identify possible food sources or contact with a chronic carrier. However, the emergence of multidrug-resistant typhoid fever in Asia and Africa is alarming. Improvements in clean water and sanitation, although essential, are difficult to implement in the short term. Strategies to control typhoid fever, including new antimicrobials or combination of agents, or wider use of vaccines in endemic areas, need serious consideration.

SUGGESTED READINGS

Bhan MK, Bahl R, Sazawal S, et al: Association between *Helicobacter pylori* infection and increased risk of typhoid fever. J Infect Dis 2002;186:1857–1860. *Recent or concurrent infection with* Helicobacter pylori, *a common condition in resource-limited settings, by inducing gastric achlorhydria, appears to increase the risk of the acquisition of typhoid fever.*

Frenck RW Jr, Nakhla I, Sultan Y, et al: Azithromycin versus ceftriaxone for the treatment of uncomplicated typhoid fever in children. Clin Infect Dis 2000;31:1134–1138. *Both agents are effective, although expensive, and may be useful in the treatment of quinolone-resistant typhoid fever in children.*

House D, Wain J, Ho VA, et al: Serology of typhoid fever in an area of endemicity and its relevance to diagnosis. J Clin Microbiol 2001;39:1002–1007. *An up-to-date review of the usefulness of serology for detection of typhoid fever in areas where the disease is endemic.*

Lin FYC, Ho VA, Khiem HB, et al: The efficacy of *Salmonella typhi* Vi conjugate vaccine in two- to five-year-old children. N Engl J Med 2001;344:1263–1269. *A new vaccine against typhoid fever consisting of the Vi virulence determinant conjugated to a nontoxic recombinant* Pseudomonas aeruginosa *exotoxin A, was effective in the prevention of typhoid fever in Vietnam. This vaccine has the potential to be immunogenic in infants younger than 2 years of age, a major advantage over currently available vaccines.*

Luxemburger C, Chau MC, Mai NL, et al: Risk factors for typhoid fever in the Mekong Delta, southern Vietnam: A case-controlled study. Trans R Soc Trop Med Hyg 2001;95:19–23. *An excellent overview of risk factors for the development of typhoid fever in a resource-limited setting, including eating food prepared outside the home, eating food prepared by street vendors, drinking contaminated water, poor housing with inadequate facilities for personal hygiene, close contact of a relative with recent typhoid fever, and recent use of antimicrobial drugs.*

Parkhill J, Dougan G, James KD, et al: Complete genome sequence of a multidrug-resistant *Salmonella enterica* serotype *typhi* CT18. Nature 2001;413:848–852. *This paper describes the complete genome sequence of a multidrug-resistant strain of* Salmonella enterica *serotype* typhi (CT18). *The genome harbors 4, 809, 037 base pairs with an estimated 4599 coding sequences. As outlined in this chapter, sequence analysis may provide unique approaches to pathogenesis and management.*

Parry CM, Hien TT, Dougan G, et al: Typhoid fever. N Engl J Med 2002;347:1770–1782. *This is an outstanding, highly recommended recent review of typhoid fever. It contains a thorough discussion of recent trends and antimicrobial resistance of the pathogen and options for antimicrobial management.*

Sinha A, Sazawal S, Kumar R, et al: Typhoid fever in children age less than five years. Lancet 1999;354:734–737. *Typhoid fever in children younger than 5 years of age is probably under-recognized in resource-limited settings.*

325 SALMONELLA INFECTIONS OTHER THAN TYPHOID FEVER

Keith S. Kaye

Donald Kaye

Definition

Salmonella, a genus of the family Enterobacteriaceae, can cause an asymptomatic intestinal carrier state or clinical disease in both humans and animals. One classification system puts all Salmonellae into one species, *Salmonella choleraesuis* (or, as used by some, a species name of *Salmonella enteritica*), which includes more than 2000 serotypes. Each serotype designation then follows the species name (e.g., *S. choleraesuis* serotype *typhimurium*). The more commonly used, less cumbersome system, which is used subsequently in this chapter, defines each serotype as a different species (e.g., *S. typhimurium*).

In humans, the most common clinical manifestation of *Salmonella* infection is enterocolitis, with diarrhea as the major symptom. Some patients develop bacteremia without gastrointestinal manifestations. Bacteremia may result in osteomyelitis, a mycotic aneurysm, or other localized infection. *S. typhi*, a pathogen of humans only, causes enteric fever. Enteric fever produced by *S. typhi* is called typhoid fever, whereas enteric fever caused by other salmonellae is named paratyphoid fever.

An asymptomatic intestinal carrier state of variable duration may follow inapparent or symptomatic infection. Most carriers are transient carriers. A *chronic carrier state,* defined as lasting more than 1 year, is usually permanent and is most often related to persistent infection in the gallbladder. With the exception of *S. typhi, S. paratyphi,* and *S. sendai* in which a human carrier is always implicated, most *Salmonella* infections are acquired from food products derived from infected animals (e.g., eggs, poultry, meat, milk).

Etiology

Salmonellae are motile, Gram-negative, non–spore-forming bacilli. They are differentiated from other Enterobacteriaceae by biochemical tests. They ferment glucose, maltose, and mannitol but not lactose or sucrose. Almost all salmonellae produce acid and gas with fermentation. Exceptions to the rules that are helpful in identification are the following: *S. typhi* does not produce gas, and *S. gallinarum-pullorum* is nonmotile. As another confounding exception, lactose-fermenting strains of salmonellae have been isolated.

Salmonellae can be differentiated into more than 2000 serotypes (serovars) by their somatic (O) antigens, which are composed of lipopolysaccharides and are part of the cell wall, and their flagellar (H) antigens. There are six serogroups based on O antigens: A, B, C_1, C_2, D, and E. Some of the important serovars and their groups are *S. typhi* (group D), *S. choleraesuis* (group C_1), *S. typhimurium* (group B), and *S. enteritidis* (group D).

S. enteritidis and *S. typhimurium* are the most common causes of human disease and together represent almost 50% of human isolates. Other common isolates are *S. heidelberg, S. hadar, S. newport, S. agona, S. montevideo, S. oranienburg, S. meunchen,* and *S. thompson.*

Epidemiology

S. typhi, S. paratyphi A, S. schottmuelleri (S. paratyphi B), S. hirschfeldii (S. paratyphi C), and *S. sendai* are either solely or almost exclusively pathogens in humans, and human-to-human transmission is important.

The remaining serovars of salmonellae are widely spread in the animal kingdom, and salmonellae have been isolated from virtually all species, including birds, poultry, mammals, reptiles, amphibians, and insects. *Salmonella* infection in humans usually occurs from ingesting contaminated animal food products, most often eggs, poultry, and meat. Eggs usually become contaminated from feces on the surface of the egg, with small cracks allowing entry into the egg. However, infection of the ovary allows primary incorporation of salmonellae into the egg. Meat and poultry become widely contaminated at the slaughterhouse with salmonellae spread from carcass to carcass, usually on the surface. *S. choleraesuis* is associated with pig products and *S. dublin* with cattle and consumption of unpasteurized milk from cattle. During the past 25 years, *S. enteritidis* outbreaks related to eggs have increased dramatically. Salmonellae may survive cooking at relatively low temperatures in the center of eggs or cooked turkeys, or food may be contaminated after cooking from kitchen utensils or from the hands of food preparers who handle raw food. Multiplication of organisms can then occur if food is not refrigerated. Any food can become contaminated by feces and outbreaks have occurred from contaminated cheese, ice cream, vegetables, fruits, juice, and alfalfa sprouts.

Salmonella infections have been acquired after contamination of food or water with feces of pet turtles, chicks, ducks, birds, dogs, cats, and many other species. These pets become infected from their food.

Salmonella infection also can be acquired by eating food or, less commonly, drinking water contaminated by a human carrier who has not adequately washed his or her hands. Infection has been spread by the fecal-oral route in children, by contaminated enema and fiberoptic instruments, by diagnostic and therapeutic preparations made from animal or insect products (e.g., pancreatic extract, carmine dye), and from intentional contamination of restaurant salad bars. Homosexual men are prone to fecal-oral infection.

Outbreaks of salmonellosis occur in institutionalized patients, who are probably more prone to develop *Salmonella* infections for three reasons. First, there are more underlying diseases that decrease host defense mechanisms against salmonellae such as disorders of gastric acidity and intestinal motility; second, use of antimicrobial agents reduces the normal, protective intestinal flora; and third, institutional food prepared in bulk is more likely to be contaminated than individually prepared meals. Outbreaks in nurseries and in the elderly in nursing homes have the highest mortality rates (i.e., >5%).

Most cases of *Salmonella* infection occurring in the United States are sporadic rather than related to outbreaks. However, when an infection occurs in a family, other members of the household also tend to have positive stool cultures. It has been estimated that 1 to 2 million cases of *Salmonella* infection occur each year in the United States. A disproportionate number of infections occur in July through October, probably related to the warm weather. *Salmonella* infections are most common in infants and in children younger than 5 years.

Salmonellae have become increasingly resistant to antibiotics, usually by acquiring resistance transfer factors. It is believed that much of the resistance has been related to widespread use of antimicrobial agents in farm animals. A multidrug-resistant strain of *S. typhimurium* (definitive type 104 [DT 104]) has emerged as an important cause of infection in the world and is responsible for about 30% of infections caused by *S. typhimurium* in the United States. These salmonellae are resistant to ampicillin, chloramphenicol, streptomycin, sulfonamides, and tetracycline. In addition, resistance to fluoroquinolones has been reported.

Pathogenesis

After ingestion of organisms, the determinants of whether or not infection results, as well as the severity of infection, are the dose and virulence of the *Salmonella* strain and the status of host defense mechanisms. Large inocula such as 10^7 bacteria are usually required to produce clinical infection in the normal host. Smaller inocula are less likely to result in infection and more likely to produce a transient intestinal carrier state. Gastric acid serves as a host defense mechanism by killing many of the ingested organisms, and intestinal motility is probably a host defense mechanism. In the absence or decrease of gastric acidity (as in the elderly, or after gastrectomy, vagotomy, or gastroenterostomy, or with drugs that reduce gastric acidity) and with decreased intestinal motility (as with antimotility drugs), much smaller inocula can produce infection and the infection tends to be more severe.

Administration of antimicrobial agents before ingestion of salmonellae can markedly reduce the size of inoculum needed to produce infection, presumably by reducing the protective bowel flora.

Although any *Salmonella* serotype can produce any of the *Salmonella* syndromes (transient asymptomatic carrier state, enterocolitis, bacteremia, enteric fever, and chronic carrier state), each serotype tends to produce certain syndromes much more often than others. For example, *S. anatum* usually causes asymptomatic intestinal infection, whereas *S. typhimurium* usually causes enterocolitis. *S. choleraesuis* is more likely to produce bacteremia (often with metastatic infection) than asymptomatic infection or enterocolitis, and some serotypes such as *S. typhi* and *S. paratyphi* are most likely to cause enteric fever as well as the chronic carrier state. Fortunately, most *Salmonella* serotypes are of relatively low pathogenicity for humans; therefore, although food products are commonly contaminated, large outbreaks occur only when more virulent serotypes are involved.

To produce infection, invasion must occur across the mucosa of the intestine. When the organisms reach the lamina propria, an influx of polymorphonuclear leukocytes serves as a defense mechanism to prevent invasion of lymphatics. Certain serotypes seem more able than others to invade lymphatics and subsequently produce bacteremia (e.g., *S. choleraesuis* and *S. dublin,* which commonly produce bacteremia after intestinal infection). Both the small intestine and colon are involved in the inflammatory process. The diarrhea in *Salmonella*

enterocolitis results from the inflammation. In addition, watery stools may occur, apparently the result of secretion of water and electrolytes by small intestinal epithelial cells in response to an enterotoxin secreted by some of the *Salmonella* strains or in response to tissue mediators of inflammation.

Patients with diseases that impair host defense mechanisms seem to have an increased frequency of severe *Salmonella* infection. For many years, a striking association has been recognized between diseases producing hemolysis and *Salmonella* bacteremia. Specifically, *Salmonella* bacteremia is common in patients with sickle cell disorders, malaria, and bartonellosis. In fact, because of the frequency of *Salmonella* bacteremia in sickle cell diseases and the underlying bone disease in these patients to which salmonellae localize, these organisms are the most common cause of osteomyelitis in patients with sickle cell disorders. Prolonged *Salmonella* bacteremia occurs in patients with hepatosplenic schistosomiasis, probably related to localization on and in the intravascular schistosomes. Patients with lymphoma and leukemia also are more prone to develop *Salmonella* bacteremia. Prolonged and recurrent refractory *Salmonella* bacteremia has been observed in patients with the acquired immunodeficiency syndrome (AIDS). Other risk factors that increase the frequency and severity of *Salmonella* infection are extremes of age, immunocompromised state (e.g., from immunosuppressive agents) and probably diabetes.

Clinical Manifestations

ASYMPTOMATIC INTESTINAL CARRIER STATE. The asymptomatic intestinal carrier state may result from inapparent infection, which is the most common form of *Salmonella* infection, or may follow clinical disease (convalescent carrier). The carrier state is usually self-limited to several weeks to months, with the incidence of positive stool cultures rapidly decreasing over time. By 1 year, far less than 1% still have positive stools. The major exception is with *S. typhi*: about 3% of those infected excrete the organism for life. A patient who has had *Salmonella* in the stool for 1 year (chronic carrier) is likely to become a lifelong carrier. Patients with *Schistosoma haematobium* infections are predisposed to become chronic urinary carriers of *Salmonella.*

ENTEROCOLITIS. After an incubation period, which is usually 12 to 48 hours, the illness starts suddenly with crampy abdominal pain and diarrhea. A chill is common. Although occasional patients have nausea and vomit once or twice, vomiting is not persistent. The diarrhea may be watery and of large volume or small volume. The stools may contain mucus and occasionally blood. Polymorphonuclear leukocytes are present in the stool. Diarrhea may be mild or may be severe with up to 20 to 30 stools a day. Fever is present in most patients, whose temperature may reach 40° C (104° F) or higher. The abdomen is tender to palpation. Transient bacteremia may occur and is most likely in infants, the elderly, and patients with impaired host defense mechanisms.

Symptoms usually improve over a period of days, with fever lasting no more than 2 to 3 days and diarrhea no more than 5 to 7 days. However, these symptoms may occasionally persist for up to 14 days. More severe disease is seen with malnutrition, inflammatory bowel disease, and AIDS. Reactive arthritis may follow enterocolitis in up to 7% of cases. It is especially frequent in those with the HLA-B27 phenotype.

ENTERIC FEVER. Paratyphoid fever is an enteric fever syndrome identical to typhoid fever but produced by a serotype other than *S. typhi*

(most often *S. paratyphi A, S. schottmuelleri,* or *S. hirschfeldii*). On occasion, it may immediately follow classic enterocolitis caused by the same organism. The syndrome, characterized by prolonged sustained fever, relative bradycardia, splenomegaly, rose spots, and leukopenia, is described in Chapter 324. Enteric fever produced by serotypes of *Salmonella* other than *S. typhi* is usually milder than typhoid fever, and the chronic carrier state follows less commonly than after typhoid fever.

BACTEREMIA. Patients with the syndrome of *Salmonella* bacteremia usually complain of fever and chills lasting days to weeks. Gastrointestinal symptoms are unusual, but in some patients the syndrome of *Salmonella* bacteremia follows classic enterocolitis. Other symptoms are non-specific, such as malaise, anorexia, and weight loss. Metastatic infection of bones, joints, mycotic aneurysm (particularly of the abdominal aorta), meninges (mainly in infants), pericardium, pleural space, lungs, heart valves, cysts, uterine myomas, malignancies, and other sites is common, and symptoms may be related to the site of metastatic infection. Stool cultures are often negative for *Salmonella,* but blood cultures are positive.

Although any *Salmonella* serotype can produce the syndrome of bacteremia, *S. choleraesuis* and *S. dublin* are most likely to cause this syndrome; over 50% of *S. choleraesuis* infections are bacteremic.

Salmonella bacteremia occurs with increased frequency in infants and the elderly and in patients with diseases associated with hemolysis (e.g., sickle cell diseases, malaria, and bartonellosis), with lymphoma, with leukemia, with disseminated histoplasmosis and perhaps with systemic lupus erythematosus. Localization to bone is common in patients with sickle cell diseases.

Prolonged *Salmonella* bacteremia lasting for months occurs in patients with hepatosplenic schistosomiasis. Patients with AIDS may develop recurrent, relapsing *Salmonella* bacteremia that is difficult to cure with antibiotics.

Diagnosis

The diagnosis of *Salmonella* infection is made by isolating the organism from the stool in enterocolitis, from the blood in bacteremia, from blood and stool in enteric fever, and from the local site in localized infection. Serologic studies are of little clinical value in *Salmonella* infections other than typhoid fever, but they may be of use in epidemiologic studies. A stained smear of the stool usually demonstrates polymorphonuclear leukocytes in patients with *Salmonella* enterocolitis.

The differential diagnosis of *Salmonella* enterocolitis includes all causes of acute diarrhea, including invasive bacteria such as *Campylobacter jejuni, Shigella* species, invasive *Escherichia coli, Yersinia*

enterocolitica, and *Vibrio parahaemolyticus;* toxigenic bacteria such as *V. cholerae,* enterotoxigenic *E. coli, E. coli* O157:H7, *S. aureus, Bacillus cereus, Clostridium perfringens,* and *C. difficile;* viruses; and protozoa such as *Entamoeba histolytica, Giardia lamblia,* and *Cryptosporidium* species. Invasive bacterial causes of diarrhea, *E. coli* O157:H7, and *C. difficile* infection are also associated with polymorphonuclear leukocytes in the stool, whereas bacterial toxigenic causes (other than *C. difficile* and *E. coli* O157:H7), viruses, and protozoa generally are not. The bacterial toxigenic causes of diarrhea other than *C. difficile and E. coli* O157:H7 do not produce fever.

Stool culture is definitive for the diagnosis of *Salmonella* enterocolitis; but by the time the results of the stool culture are available, most patients are recovering.

The differential diagnosis of *Salmonella* bacteremia includes all acute infectious and non-infectious causes of fever, including bacteremia caused by other organisms.

The differential diagnosis of enteric fever is the same as discussed in Chapter 324.

Rx Treatment

ENTEROCOLITIS. The primary approach to treatment of *Salmonella* enterocolitis is fluid and electrolyte replacement. Drugs with antiperistaltic effects such as loperamide or diphenoxylate with atropine can relieve cramps but should be used sparingly because they can prolong the diarrhea.

Salmonella enterocolitis is self-limited, and antimicrobial therapy is not usually indicated. Furthermore, antibiotic therapy has been reported to have little effect on the clinical course and, in some studies, to prolong the period of time salmonellae are excreted in the stool. In addition, most patients are improving by the time that salmonellae or other bacterial pathogens are isolated from the stool. However, infants, the elderly, the immunosuppressed, and those with sickle cell disease, lymphoma, leukemia, or other serious underlying diseases who are severely ill (and may have bacteremia) may benefit from antimicrobial therapy.

The fluoroquinolones are active against virtually all bacterial pathogens that cause diarrhea except for *C. difficile* and many Campylobacter, and it is reasonable to use them empirically in the early therapy of adults with severe diarrhea of presumed bacterial etiology. It is also reasonable to use them for patients with known *Salmonella* enterocolitis who are suspected of being bacteremic. As an example, ciprofloxacin 500 mg every 12 hours orally or 400 mg every 12 hours intravenously for 3 to 5 days or until defervescence, has been widely used. A third generation cephalosporin such as ceftriaxone is an alternative. In the presence of gross bloody diarrhea, antimicrobial therapy should be withheld until the possibility of *E. coli* O157 : H7 infection has been eliminated, because antibiotic therapy may increase the frequency of the development of the hemolytic uremic syndrome.

Other agents, such as amoxicillin and trimethoprim-sulfamethoxazole, have also been widely used in severely ill adults. However, many strains of *Salmonella* are now resistant to these agents.

BACTEREMIA AND ENTERIC FEVER. The agents of choice to treat these disorders are the fluoroquinolones, such as ciprofloxacin and the third-generation cephalosporins, such as ceftriaxone. Typical doses are ciprofloxacin 400 mg every 12 hours intravenously and ceftriaxone 1 to 2 g every 24 hours intravenously. When the salmonellae are known to be susceptible, ampicillin 1 to 2 g IV every 6 hours or trimethoprim-sulfamethoxazole (10 mg/kg/day IV of the trimethoprim component) can be used. Chloramphenicol is an additional option.

Antimicrobial susceptibility testing is necessary, because of the emergence of occasional infections caused by salmonellae resistant to fluoroquinolones or third-generation cephalosporins.

Therapy is continued for 7 to 14 days for enteric fever and bacteremia without localization of organisms and for much longer periods (e.g., 6 weeks) when there is localization to bone, aneurysms, heart valves, and various other sites. Surgical drainage, removal of foreign bodies or resection of an aneurysm is often necessary to cure localized infection.

Curing schistosomiasis in patients with *Salmonella* bacteremia may cure the bacteremia. Patients with AIDS tend to relapse repeatedly after treatment courses for *Salmonella* bacteremia. Long-term suppressive therapy has been recommended by some.

CARRIERS. Chronic carriers (i.e., >1 year) of salmonellae other than *S. typhi* are rare. Stools of convalescent carriers spontaneously become negative over a period of weeks to months, and no therapy should be given. The rare chronic carrier of non-*S. typhi* serotypes (usually infected with *S. paratyphi* A, *S. schottmuelleri*, or *S. hirschfeldii*) may be treated with amoxicillin, trimethoprim-sulfamethoxazole, or a fluoroquinolone for 4 to 6 weeks. Patients who experience relapse usually have gallbladder disease (most often calculi) and will not be cured with antimicrobial therapy alone. Cholecystectomy plus antimicrobial therapy may cure these patients, but it is doubtful that the carrier state per se is a sufficient indication for cholecystectomy.

Prognosis

Mortality in *Salmonella* enterocolitis is rare; infants and the elderly are at greatest risk, with death occurring from dehydration and electrolyte imbalance. Mortality from *Salmonella* bacteremia or enteric fever is not uncommon and is most likely to occur in the very young, the very old, and the immunocompromised. *S. choleraesuis* bacteremia has the highest mortality rate (20 to 30% if untreated) of any *Salmonella* serotype.

Prevention

Salmonella infection is best prevented by properly managing the water supply and sewage disposal, cooking and refrigerating foods made from animal products, pasteurizing milk and milk products, and hand washing before preparing foods and after handling animals and uncooked animal products. Despite these precautions, because of the widespread presence of salmonellae in the animal kingdom, it is unlikely that the frequency of *Salmonella* infections will be significantly diminished.

There is no vaccine for any infection with salmonellae other than that for infection with *S. typhi*.

SUGGESTED READINGS

Centers for Disease Control and Prevention: Outbreaks of *Salmonella* serotype enteritidis infection associated with eating shell eggs—United States, 1999–2001. MMWR Morb Mortal Wkly Rep 2003;51:1149–1152. *A description of the importance of* Salmonella enteritidis *as a cause of infection associated with consumption of egg products.*

Centers for Disease Control and Prevention: Outbreaks of multidrug-resistant *Salmonella typhimurium* associated with veterinary facilities—Idaho, Minnesota, and Washington, 1999. MMWR Morb Mortal Wkly Rep 2001;50:701–703. *A report of 3 outbreaks of multidrug resistant* S. typhimurium *associated with small animal veterinary facilities; two of the three were caused by definitive type 104, a strain that is now responsible for about 30% of* S. typhimurium *infections in the United States.*

Fey PD, Safranek TJ, Rupp ME, et al: Ceftriaxone-resistant salmonella infection acquired by a child from cattle. N Engl J Med 2000;342:1242–1249. *A report of the first documented case of ceftriaxone-resistant salmonella infection acquired in the United States; the source was cattle.*

Molbak K, Baggesen DL, Aarestrup FM, et al: An outbreak of multidrug-resistant, quinolone-resistant *Salmonella enterica* serotype *typhimurium* DT104. N Engl J Med 1999;341:1420–1425. *An outbreak in Denmark due to definitive type 104* S. typhimurium *that was resistant to fluoroquinolones.*

Olsen SJ, DeBess EE, McGivern TE, et al: A nosocomial outbreak of fluoroquinolone-resistant salmonella infection. N Engl J Med 2001;344:1572–1579. *An outbreak of* S. schwarzengrund *resistant to fluoroquinolones in two U.S. nursing homes.*

326 SHIGELLOSIS

Thomas Butler
W. Michael Scheld

Definition

Shigellosis is an acute bacterial infection caused by the genus *Shigella* resulting in colitis affecting predominantly the rectosigmoid colon. "Bacillary dysentery" is synonymous with shigellosis. The disease is characterized by diarrhea, dysentery, fever, abdominal pain, and tenesmus. Shigellosis is usually limited to a few days. Early treatment with antimicrobial drugs results in more rapid recovery.

Etiology

Shigellae are nonmotile gram-negative bacilli belonging to the family Enterobacteriaceae. Four species of shigellae are recognized on the basis of antigenic and biochemical properties: *Shigella dysenteriae* (group A), *Shigella flexneri* (group B), *Shigella boydii* (group C) uncommon, and *Shigella sonnei* (group D). Among these species there are more than 40 serotypes, each of which is designated by the species name followed by a specific Arabic number. *S. dysenteriae* 1 is called the "Shiga bacillus" and causes epidemics with higher mortality than other serotypes and may produce catastrophic pandemics. With the exception of *S. flexneri* 6, they do not ferment lactose.

Serotypes are determined by the O polysaccharide side chain of the lipopolysaccharide (endotoxin) in the cell wall. Endotoxin is

Table 326–1 • EVOLUTION OF CLINICAL SYNDROMES IN SHIGELLOSIS

STAGE	TIME OF APPEARANCE AFTER ONSET OF ILLNESS	SYMPTOMS AND SIGNS	PATHOLOGY
Prodrome	Earliest	Fever, chills, myalgias, anorexia, nausea, vomiting	None or early colitis
Nonspecific diarrhea	0–3 days	Abdominal cramps, loose stools, watery diarrhea	Rectosigmoid colitis with superficial ulceration, fecal leukocytes
Dysentery	1–8 days	Frequent passage of blood and mucus, tenesmus, rectal prolapse, abdominal tenderness	Colitis extending sometimes to proximal colon, crypt abscesses, inflammation in lamina propria
Complications	3–10 days	Dehydration, seizures, septicemia, leukemoid reaction, hemolytic-uremic syndrome, ileus, peritonitis	Severe colitis, terminal ileitis, endotoxemia, intravascular coagulation, toxic megacolon, colonic perforation
Postdysenteric syndromes	1–3 weeks	Arthritis, Reiter's syndrome	Reactive inflammation in HLA-B27 haplotype

detectable in the blood of severely ill patients and may be responsible for the complication of the hemolytic-uremic syndrome. To be virulent, shigellae must be able to invade epithelial cells, as tested in the laboratory by keratoconjunctivitis in the guinea pig (Sereny test) or HeLa cell invasion. Bacterial invasion of cells is genetically governed by three chromosomal regions and a 140-Md plasmid. Shiga toxin is produced by *S. dysenteriae* 1 and in lesser amounts by other serotypes. It inhibits protein synthesis and has enterotoxic activity in animal models, but its role in human disease is uncertain. Many other toxins have been described recently for different *Shigella* species (e.g., ShET1 and ShET2, enterotoxins responsible for watery diarrhea in some *Shigella* infections).

Incidence and Prevalence

In the United States there were more than 14,000 cases reported in 1996 with species distribution of 73% *S. sonnei,* 19% *S. flexneri,* 2% *S. boydii,* and 1% *S. dysenteriae.* Furthermore, shigellosis is on the rise. As an example, the incidence of shigellosis increased from 5.4 to more than 10 per 100,000 in the United States from 1960–1988. Most cases were in young children, women of childbearing age, and low-income minority residents; and a large proportion occurred in population groups living in homes for the mentally ill or in nursing homes. A large outbreak in 1987 in Tennessee affected more than 1000 persons camping under unsanitary conditions at a mass gathering.

Worldwide, most cases of shigellosis occur in children of developing countries, where *S. flexneri* is the predominant species. In 1994, an epidemic in Rwandan refugees caused an estimated 30,000 deaths. The Institute of Medicine estimated that 250 million cases of shigellosis occur annually, with 650,000 deaths worldwide.

Epidemiology

Shigellosis is transmitted by the fecal-oral route. Crowded living conditions, low standards of personal hygiene, poor water supply, and inadequate sewage facilities all contribute to an increased risk of infection. Transmission most often occurs by close person-to-person contact through contaminated hands. During clinical illness and for up to 6 weeks after recovery, organisms are excreted in the feces. Although the organisms are sensitive to desiccation, they may survive several months in food or water, which are occasional vehicles of transmission. Daycare centers, military barracks, and homeless shelters are all high-risk settings for shigellosis.

Children between 1 and 4 years old have the greatest risk of developing shigellosis. Inhabitants of custodial institutions, such as homes for retarded children, are at highest risk. Intrafamilial spread follows often when the initial case has occurred in a preschool child. In young adults, the incidence is higher in women than in men, which probably reflects closer contact of women with children. The male homosexual population in the United States is at increased risk for shigellosis, which is one of the causes of the "gay bowel syndrome."

Humans and higher primates are the only known natural reservoirs of shigellosis. Transmission shows variable seasonal patterns in different regions. In the United States, the peak incidence is in late summer and early autumn.

Pathogenesis and Pathology

Because the microorganisms are relatively resistant to acid, shigellae pass the gastric barrier more readily than other enteric pathogens. In volunteer studies, as few as 10 to 200 ingested bacilli regularly initiate disease in 25% of healthy adults. This contrasts strikingly to the much larger numbers of typhoid or cholera bacilli required to produce disease in normal individuals. During the incubation period (usually 12 to 72 hours), the organisms traverse the small bowel, penetrate colonic epithelial cells, and multiply intracellularly, usually traversing the basolateral surface of intestinal epithelial cells. An acute inflammatory response ensues in the colonic mucosa attended by prodromal symptoms (Table 326–1). Epithelial cells containing bacteria are lysed, resulting in superficial ulcerations and shedding of *Shigella* organisms into stools. Cell death occurs as a result of cell respiration blockage. The mucosa is friable and covered with a layer of polymorphonuclear leukocytes. Biopsy specimens show ulcers and crypt abscesses. Initially, the inflammation is confined to the rectosigmoid colon but after about 4 days of illness may advance to involve the proximal colon and sometimes even the terminal ileum; a pseudomembranous type of colitis may develop. Levels of proinflammatory cytokines are elevated in stool and plasma and correlate with disease severity. Diarrhea results because of impaired absorption of water and electrolytes by the inflamed colon.

Although the colonic inflammation is superficial, bacteremia occurs occasionally, especially in *S. dysenteriae* 1 infections. Susceptibility of organisms to serum complement–mediated bacteriolysis may explain the infrequency of bacteremia and disseminated infection. Colonic perforation is a rare complication during toxic megacolon. Children with severe colitis due to *S. dysenteriae* 1 are prone to develop the hemolytic-uremic syndrome. In this complication, fibrin thrombi are deposited in the renal glomeruli, causing cortical necrosis and fragmentation of red blood cells.

Clinical Manifestations

Most patients with shigellosis begin their illness with a nonspecific prodrome (see Table 326–1). The height of the temperature varies, and children may have febrile convulsions. The initial intestinal symptoms soon follow as cramps, loose stools, and watery diarrhea, which usually precede the onset of dysentery by 1 or more days. The average fecal output is about 600 g/day for adults. The dysentery consists typically of flecks and small clots of bright red blood and mucus in stools that are small in volume. Frequency of passage is often as high as 20 to 40 times a day, with excruciating rectal pain and tenesmus during defecation. Some patients develop rectal prolapse during severe straining. The amount of blood in stools varies widely but usually is small because of the superficial colonic ulcerations. Abdominal tenderness is often most marked in the left lower quadrant over the sigmoid colon but also may be generalized. The fever is likely to abate after a few days of dysentery, making afebrile bloody diarrhea an occasional clinical presentation. After 1 to 2 weeks of untreated disease, spontaneous improvement occurs in most patients. Some patients with mild disease develop only watery diarrhea without dysentery.

Continued

Complications include dehydration, which can cause death, especially in children and the elderly. *Shigella* septicemia occurs mainly in malnourished children with *S. dysenteriae* 1 infections. Meningitis, arthritis, and osteomyelitis due to this organism have been reported but are rare. The leukemoid reaction and hemolytic-uremic syndrome may develop in children late in the course after antimicrobial treatment when the dysentery has started to improve. Neurologic manifestations can be striking and include delirium, seizures (in one recent report, 10% of hospitalized children presented with this manifestation), and nuchal rigidity.

The important postdysenteric syndromes are arthritis and Reiter's triad of arthritis, urethritis, and conjunctivitis (Chapter 279). These are nonsuppurative phenomena that occur in the absence of viable *Shigella* organisms 1 to 3 weeks after resolution of dysentery.

Diagnosis

Shigellosis should be considered in any patient with acute onset of fever and diarrhea. Examination of the stool is essential. Blood and pus are grossly apparent in severe bacillary dysentery; even in milder forms of the disease, microscopic examination of the stool often reveals numerous leukocytes and erythrocytes. The fecal leukocyte examination should be performed with a portion of liquid stool, preferably containing mucus. A drop of stool is placed on a microscopic slide, mixed thoroughly with 2 drops of methylene blue, and overlaid with a coverslip. The presence of abundant polymorphonuclear leukocytes helps distinguish shigellosis from diarrheal syndromes caused by viruses and enterotoxigenic bacteria. The fecal leukocyte examination is not helpful in distinguishing shigellosis from diarrheal illnesses caused by other invasive enteric pathogens (nontyphoidal *Salmonella*, *Campylobacter*, and *Yersinia*). Owing to the inherent limitations of stool leukocyte examination (i.e., negative tests if the specimen is not examined within 30 minutes), stool assay for lactoferrin is gaining favor as the diagnostic test of preference to detect inflammatory diarrhea. Amebic dysentery may be excluded by the absence of trophozoites on a microscopic examination of fresh stool under a coverslip. The peripheral white blood cell count is of little diagnostic value, because it may range from less than 3000 to more than 30,000/mm^3. Sigmoidoscopic examination reveals diffuse erythema with a mucopurulent layer and friable areas of mucosa with shallow ulcers 3 to 7 mm in diameter.

Definitive diagnosis depends on isolating shigellae by selective media. A rectal swab, a swab of a colonic ulcer obtained by sigmoidoscopic examination, or a freshly passed stool specimen should be inoculated immediately on culture plates or into carrying media. Because isolation rates of shigellae from freshly passed stools of patients with shigellosis may be as low as 67%, culturing for 3 successive days is recommended. Stool cultures are generally positive within 24 hours after onset of symptoms and may remain positive for several weeks in the absence of antimicrobial therapy. Appropriate culture media include blood, desoxycholate, and *Salmonella-Shigella* (S-S) agars. Selected colonies should be diagnosed by agglutination with polyvalent *Shigella* antisera. S-S agar is inhibitory for *S. dysenteriae* 1.

Definitive bacteriologic diagnosis becomes critically important for distinguishing the more severe and prolonged cases of shigellosis from ulcerative colitis, with which it may be confused both clinically and on sigmoidoscopic examination. Patients with shigellosis have been subjected to colectomy because of a mistaken diagnosis of ulcerative colitis; a positive culture should prevent such a misadventure.

℞ Treatment

Among diarrheal syndromes, shigellosis always requires specific therapy with antimicrobials. Appropriate antimicrobial therapy instituted early may decrease the duration of symptoms by 50% and decrease the duration of excretion of shigellae (an important epidemiologic factor) by a far greater percentage. Because of the increasing frequency of plasmid-mediated antimicrobial resistance to *Shigella* infections, surveillance of drug susceptibility in an endemic area is important (e.g., ampicillin, cotrimoxazole, and chloramphenicol resistance of 47 to 91% in many endemic

areas). In adults, ciprofloxacin given orally in a dose of 500 mg twice daily for 5 days or 1 g as a single dose is the treatment of choice when the susceptibility of a strain is unknown. In children, treatment should be trimethoprim-sulfamethoxazole, ampicillin, or azithromycin, depending on susceptibilities of *Shigella* in a given location. Cephalosporins, such as cefixime, are not highly effective and should be avoided.

Fluid losses in shigellosis are qualitatively similar to those in other infectious diarrheal diseases, and the patient should be treated with appropriate intravenous or oral electrolyte repletion fluids in quantities adequate to correct clinical signs of saline depletion. The requirement for fluids is generally small, but fluid repletion is lifesaving in exceptional cases.

Agents that decrease intestinal motility should not be used. Such preparations as diphenoxylate and paregoric may exacerbate symptoms, presumably by retarding intestinal clearance of the microorganisms. There is no convincing evidence that pectin- or bismuth-containing preparations are helpful.

Prognosis

The mortality rate in untreated shigellosis depends on the infectious strain and ranges from 10 to 30% in certain outbreaks caused by *S. dysenteriae* 1 to less than 1% in most *S. sonnei* infections. Even with infection caused by *S. dysenteriae* 1, mortality rates should approach zero if appropriate fluid replacement and antimicrobial therapy are initiated early.

About 2% of patients may develop arthritis or Reiter's syndrome weeks or months after recovery from shigellosis.

Prevention

Individuals excreting shigellae should be excluded from all phases of food handling until negative cultures have been obtained from three successive stool specimens collected after completion of antimicrobial therapy. In institutional outbreaks, strict and early isolation of infected individuals is mandatory. Targeted antimicrobial chemoprophylaxis has been disappointing. The most important control measure is rigorous hand washing with soap and water by all individuals involved in handling of food or changing diapers. Reporting of shigellosis cases to health authorities should be mandatory.

For the traveler to countries with major *Shigella* problems, no chemoprophylactic agent is an adequate substitute for good personal hygiene and avoiding contaminated food and water. A variety of vaccines have been developed and tested, but no vaccine is now commercially available. Nevertheless, the following approaches have been pursued recently:

1. Live attenuated *Shigella* strains (especially those with deletion of virulence factor genes or mutations in metabolic pathway genes or expression of virulence factors, e.g., vir G, omp B, iuc, fes-entF)
2. Hybrid anti-*Shigella* vaccines
3. Inactivated vaccines (conjugation of *Shigella* lipopolysaccharide with protein carriers)

It is most probable that a safe and effective vaccine against shigellosis will be available in the not too distant future.

SUGGESTED READINGS

Bogaerts J, Verhaegen J, Munyabikali JP, et al: Antimicrobial resistance and serotypes of *Shigella* isolates in Kigali, Rwanda (1983–1993): Increasing frequency of multiple resistance. Diagn Microbiol Infect Dis 1997;28:165–171. *Emergence of multidrug resistance, including resistance to nalidixic acid in* S. dysenteriae *1, in infected refugees posed threats to effective therapy.*

Gomez HF, Ochoa TJ, Herrera-Insua I, et al: Lactoferrin protects rabbits from *Shigella flexneri*–induced inflammatory enteritis. Infect Immun 2002;70:7050–7053. *Detection of lactoferrin in stool is useful for the diagnosis of inflammatory diarrhea. In addition, lactoferrin at concentrations normally found in human colostrum blocks the development of* S. flexneri–*induced inflammatory enteritis.*

Khan WA, Seas C, Dhar U, et al: Treatment of shigellosis: V. Comparison of azithromycin and ciprofloxacin. Ann Intern Med 1997;126:697–703. *Azithromycin and ciprofloxacin were equally effective against multiresistant infections in Bangladesh.*

Lopez EL, Prado-Jimenez V, O'Ryan-Gallardo M, et al: *Shigella* and shiga toxin-producing *Escherichia coli* causing bloody diarrhea in Latin America. Infect Dis Clin North Am 2000;14:41–65. *A review of Shigellosis and shiga toxin-producing* E. coli *causing bloody* diarrhea with a focus on Latin America. Recent advances in vaccine development are emphasized.

Oldfield EC III, Wallace MR: The role of antibiotics in the treatment of infectious diarrhea. Gastroenterol Clin North Am 2001;30:817–836. *A thorough review of the role of antibiotics in the treatment of diarrhea with consideration of all major bacterial pathogens.*

Radice M, Gonzalez C, Power P, et al: Third-generation cephalosporin resistance in *Shigella sonnei*, Argentina. Emerg Infect Dis 2001;7:442–443. *This paper reports the first detection of a plasmid-encoded extended spectrum β-lactamase (CTX-M-2) in* Shigella sonnei.

Sansonetti PJ: Microbes and microbial toxins: Paradigms for microbial-mucosal interactions: III. Shigellosis: From symptoms to molecular pathogenesis. Am J Physiol Gastrointest Liver Physiol 2001;280:G319–G323. *A masterful review of the molecular pathogenesis of shigellosis by one of the world's leading authorities on the subject.*

Uysal G, Sokmen A, Vidinlisan S: Clinical risk factors for fatal diarrhea in hospitalized children. Indian J Pediatr 2000;67:329–333. *In this study from Turkey, 27 of 100 (6.75%) children with diarrhea died. Shigella infection was strongly associated with death (P = 0.0014). In the multivariant analysis, Shigella infection had an odds ratio of 23 predictive of death. Other risk factors included malnutrition, coexistent sepsis, and various electrolyte abnormalities.*

327 CAMPYLOBACTER ENTERITIS

Richard L. Guerrant

Definition

Enteric infection with a member of the genus *Campylobacter* usually results in an inflammatory, occasionally bloody diarrhea or dysentery syndrome in industrialized, temperate areas. *Campylobacter jejuni* is often the most commonly recognized cause of community-acquired inflammatory enteritis. The diarrhea also may be watery, especially in developing, tropical areas. An enterocolitis or protocolitis syndrome similar to that seen with *C. jejuni* (including the closely related species, *C. coli* in up to 10% of cases) is also seen in homosexual males with several "*Campylobacter*-like organisms," that are now being classified as *Helicobacter* species such as *H. cinaedi*, *H. fennelliae*, and others. Like *C. jejuni*, these *Campylobacter*-like organisms may cause life-threatening bacteremic infections in patients with the acquired immunodeficiency syndrome. The other major *Campylobacter* species that infects humans is *C. fetus*, a relatively uncommon cause of bacteremia and occasional intravascular infection in immunocompromised hosts. *Helicobacter pylori* (the cause of gastritis and peptic ulcers) was once called *Campylobacter pylori* but is now reclassified.

Etiology

Campylobacter (meaning "curved rod") is a curved or spiral, motile, non–spore-forming, gram-negative rod measuring $1.5 \times 3.5\,\mu m$ that is distinguished from Enterobacteriaceae by its inability to ferment or oxidize carbohydrates. It was once called a "vibrio" but is now recognized as a separate genus on the basis of its distinctive DNA content. It is both oxidase and catalase positive and is a microaerophilic organism that requires reduced oxygen (5 to 10%) and increased carbon dioxide (3 to 10%). The organism does not grow at either aerobic or strictly anaerobic conditions. Perhaps reflecting its avian reservoir, *C. jejuni* also requires an increased temperature to 42° C for optimal growth. *C. jejuni* is distinguished from *C. fetus* by its higher growth temperatures, cephalothin resistance, and nalidixic acid sensitivity.

As shown in Table 327–1, the additional *Campylobacter* species that infect humans include *C. lari*, a thermophilic organism commonly found in healthy seagulls that has been reported in children with mild recurrent diarrhea and in an elderly patient with sepsis and terminal multiple myeloma. The weak or non–catalase-producing *C. upsaliensis* may cause diarrhea or bacteremia, and *C. hyointestinalis*, like *C. fetus*, causes occasional bacteremia in compromised hosts. These organisms are also inhibited by cephalothin in some selective culture media. Like *C. fetus*, the *Campylobacter*-like organisms (*H. cinaedi, H. fennelliae*, others) do not grow at 42° C or in the presence of cephalosporin antibiotics (present in some selective media for *C. jejuni*) and may require several days to grow on microaerophilic subcultures on blood agar. *C. jejuni* is further subdivided into over 90 serotypes on the basis of heat-stable somatic lipopolysaccharide O antigens or some 112 heat-labile flagellar and cellular antigens or even additional subtypes based on phage restriction DNA or ribosomal RNA digests—all markers that are helpful in tracing the epidemiology of this common enteric pathogen.

Epidemiology

Although the frequency of other *Campylobacter* infections is either low or unclear, *C. jejuni* infections are extremely common throughout the world. In many studies, the frequency of *Campylobacter* enteritis exceeds that of *Salmonella* or *Shigella* infections, and it has been estimated that as many as 2 million *Campylobacter* enteritis cases occur annually in the United States. The reservoirs of *C. jejuni/coli* include a wide range of mammalian species. Between 30 and 100% of chickens, turkeys, and water fowl may be infected asymptomatically in their intestinal tracts, and commercially prepared poultry in supermarkets is often culture positive. In addition, swine, cattle, sheep, horses, and even household pets and rodents may carry *C. jejuni*, *C. coli*, or *C. fetus*. Dogs and cats are more likely to be infected with *C. upsaliensis*. Enteric symptoms may be found, particularly in puppies, kittens, calves, or lambs, which may have diarrhea when infected. Furthermore, the organisms survive days to weeks in fresh or salt water and in milk and are killed most effectively by pasteurization, chlorination, drying, or freezing.

The transmission of *Campylobacter* infections is likely via the fecal-oral route. Fecal-oral spread may occur by contact among animals, those practicing oral-anal sex, backpackers, travelers, and those in daycare centers. Secondary transmission is relatively infrequent, and the infectious dose appears to vary from 500 to over 1 million organisms. The majority of infections are probably acquired by ingesting contaminated food, water, or milk. Many cases and outbreaks are associated with ingesting inadequately cooked poultry, unpasteurized milk, inadequately treated water, and even cake icing, salads, beef, and clams.

The majority of those infected in well-described outbreaks are symptomatic. Asymptomatic infection appears to be relatively infrequent in temperate climates and in adults. An exception is among young children in certain tropical developing areas such as Bangladesh, where as many as 39% of children younger than 2 years of age may be infected asymptomatically (Table 327–2). These frequent asymptomatic infections in tropical areas raise important questions about possible strain differences in virulence, host susceptibility, and protective immunity against disease that might be acquired very early in developing areas.

Throughout the world, *Campylobacter* infections appear to predominate during the warmer or wet season. As with diarrheal ill-

Table 327–1 • HUMAN *CAMPYLOBACTER* INFECTIONS

SPECIES	GROWTH TEMPERATURE	RESERVOIR	CLINICAL MANIFESTATIONS
C. jejuni/coli	37–42° C	Poultry, mammals	Common cause of dysentery/diarrhea
C. fetus (subsp. *fetus*, old subsp. *intestinalis*)	25–37° C	Cattle, sheep	Uncommon, bacteremia; intravascular infections in debilitated hosts
C. laridis	30–42° C	Sea gulls	Uncommon, childhood diarrhea, one case of sepsis
C. upsaliensis	37–42° C	Dogs	Occasional diarrhea
C. hyointestinalis	37° C	Swine	Occasional bacteremia in compromised hosts
"*Campylobacter*-like organisms": (including *Helicobacter cinaedi, H. fennelliae*)	37° C	?	Proctocolitis, rarely sepsis, in homosexual males

Table 327–2 • CLINICAL PRESENTATIONS OF *CAMPYLOBACTER JEJUNI* INFECTION

	INDUSTRIALIZED COUNTRIES	DEVELOPING COUNTRIES
Percentage of all diarrhea with *C. jejuni*	5–13	2–35
Percentage of *C. jejuni* diarrhea with		
Fecal polymorphonuclear leukocytes	78–93	22–46
Blood in stool	60–65	5–17
Asymptomatic infection rates (%)	<2	0–39*

*Depending on age—39% if <2 years old.

nesses in general, the highest age-specific attack rate is in young children. However, the greatest proportion of positive fecal cultures occurs in older children and young adults. The latter contributes a small peak in the age-specific attack rates during the "second weaning," when young adults leave home and lack experience with cooking poultry and other products. There is little, if any, sexual predominance of recognized *C. jejuni* infections.

Pathogenesis and Pathology

C. jejuni and *C. coli* are reasonably susceptible to gastric acidity. However, the reported variation in infectious dose suggests considerable host or strain variability. After an incubation period of 1 to 7 (median 4) days, symptoms of the enteric infection begin. *C. jejuni* organisms are attracted toward mucus and fucose in bile, and the flagellae may be important in both chemotaxis and adherence to epithelial cells or mucus. Adherence also may involve lipopolysaccharide or other outer membrane components. Several laboratories around the world have documented the production by *C. jejuni* of a cholera-like, heat-labile enterotoxin that binds to ganglioside and is neutralized by anticholera toxin antiserum. However, the genetic code and the role of this toxin in disease remain elusive. Studies from Mexico have shown that antitoxic immunity develops after infection, often with watery diarrhea, suggesting that this toxin is significant in those infections.

However, more characteristic in temperate areas is a diffuse, often bloody exudative enteritis involving the ileum and colon. These pathologic changes may include nonspecific crypt abscesses that on colonoscopy and histopathology may mimic the changes seen with inflammatory bowel disease. Such invasive pathology is also seen in infected rabbits, chicks, mice, dogs, and monkeys. Although *C. jejuni* is negative in the Sereny test for guinea pig conjunctivitis, some studies have reported the production of cytotoxins by certain strains of *C. jejuni* that may be involved in the pathogenesis of the invasive colitis. The relative infrequency of blood stream invasion by *C. jejuni*, compared with *C. fetus*, likely relates to the relative serum sensitivity of most *C. jejuni* strains and to the rapid development of bactericidal antibody with infection in normal individuals. Volunteer studies suggest that effective immunity develops to rechallenge with the homologous strain, and animal studies suggest that protective immunity may be transferred in immune milk to suckling offspring. Additional evidence of effective immunity comes with the decreasing illness-to-infection ratio among children in endemic areas as well as among regular consumers of raw milk.

Once patients are infected, they shed 10^7 to 10^9 organisms per gram of stool for a median duration of 2 to 3 weeks if untreated with effective antibiotics. Although some may continue to excrete the organism for 2 to 3 months, chronic asymptomatic intestinal carriage is rare.

Clinical Manifestations

As noted in Table 327–1, the major recognized disease with human *Campylobacter* infections is the characteristic diarrheal illness seen with *C. jejuni* or *C. coli* infections. Although asymptomatic infections and watery, noninflammatory diarrhea are seen with *C. jejuni* infections in tropical, developing areas as shown in Table 327–2, *C. jejuni* is characteristically associated with an inflammatory, febrile enteritis in industrialized countries throughout the world. After an incubation period of 1 to 7 days, a brief prodrome of fever, headache, and myalgias lasting for 12 to 24 hours is promptly followed in a case of *C. jejuni* enteritis in a child or young adult with the symptoms of acute enteritis. These characteristically include crampy abdominal pain, fever to 39° or 40° C, and diarrhea with up to 10 or more loose, often bloody bowel movements per day. Occasionally, the abdominal pain may predominate as an appendicitis-like syndrome, with mesenteric adenitis or terminal ileitis being the predominant pathology. On physical examination, the abdomen is diffusely tender and may mimic appendicitis. Although the acute febrile enteritis is usually self-limited to 5 to 7 days, 10 to 20% of cases may last longer than 1 week and 5 to 20% of untreated cases may relapse with a similar illness.

Complications, particularly if antimotility agents are used, include toxic megacolon, pseudomembranous colitis, and colonic hemorrhage. In addition, hemolytic-uremic syndrome, postinfectious polyneuritis, or Guillain-Barré (GBS) and Miller Fisher (MFS) syndromes may follow *C. jejuni* enteritis with rates increasing with age. Some suggest that *C. jejuni* (especially O type 19) may be a major recognized predisposing cause of GBS although diverse genetic lineages of GBS/MFS-associated strains are well documented. As in many inflammatory colitis syndromes, reactive arthritis and full-blown Reiter's syndrome may follow weeks after *Campylobacter* enteritis. Bacteremia may occur relatively rarely (usually <2% of cases), particularly in the very young or the elderly, in whom meningitis, endocarditis, cholecystitis, urinary tract infections, and pancreatitis have been described. In patients with hypogammaglobulinemia or human immunodeficiency virus infection, *C. jejuni* infections are more often bacteremic and may be prolonged or severe despite appropriate antimicrobial therapy.

In striking contrast to *C. jejuni*, the slow-growing *C. fetus* is primarily an uncommon cause of bacteremia, often in immunocompromised hosts. Although *C. fetus* would be missed on most routine stool cultures for *C. jejuni*, studies with filtration methods suggest that it is a relatively infrequent cause of diarrhea. Instead, *C. fetus* tends to cause intravascular, meningeal, or localized infections such as arthritis, cellulitis, abscesses, cholecystitis, and urinary, placental, or pleural infections, often in elderly or debilitated hosts. As it does in animals, *C. fetus* may cause stillbirth or septic abortions more often than generally recognized in humans. *C. fetus* infections are often recognized only by astute clinical microbiology technicians who methodically examine or subculture cultured specimens of blood or other body fluids after 1 week in the laboratory. The clinical course of *C. fetus* bacteremia is often related to its recognition and appropriate treatment as well as to the underlying disease.

Diagnosis

The diagnosis of *Campylobacter* infections is related to a careful history for exposure or characteristic clinical syndromes, direct stool examination, and selective culture methods. *C. jejuni* enteritis should be suspected in anyone presenting with a febrile enteritis, especially if there is a history of recent ingestion of inadequately cooked poultry, unpasteurized milk, or untreated water. As suggested in Figure 327–1, such a history should prompt obtaining a fecal specimen in a cup if at all possible and direct microscopic examination using methylene blue or Gram stain for leukocytes or a test for fecal lactoferrin as well as gross and/or occult blood. In many industrialized areas, the presence of blood or fecal leukocytes or lactoferrin with fever strongly suggests the presence of a cultivable enteric pathogen such as *C. jejuni*, *Salmonella*, or *Shigella*, with *C. jejuni* being most common. Additional immediate clues to *C. jejuni* infection may be seen on darkfield or phase microscopy for characteristic darting motility or on a carbolfuchsin-Gram stain of stool for characteristic curved rods or sea gull morphology. However, darkfield and Gram stains, although reasonably specific with trained observers, are each only 50 to 66% sensitive. Patients with febrile enteritis, particularly with blood and leukocytes in the stool, should be cultured for *C. jejuni*.

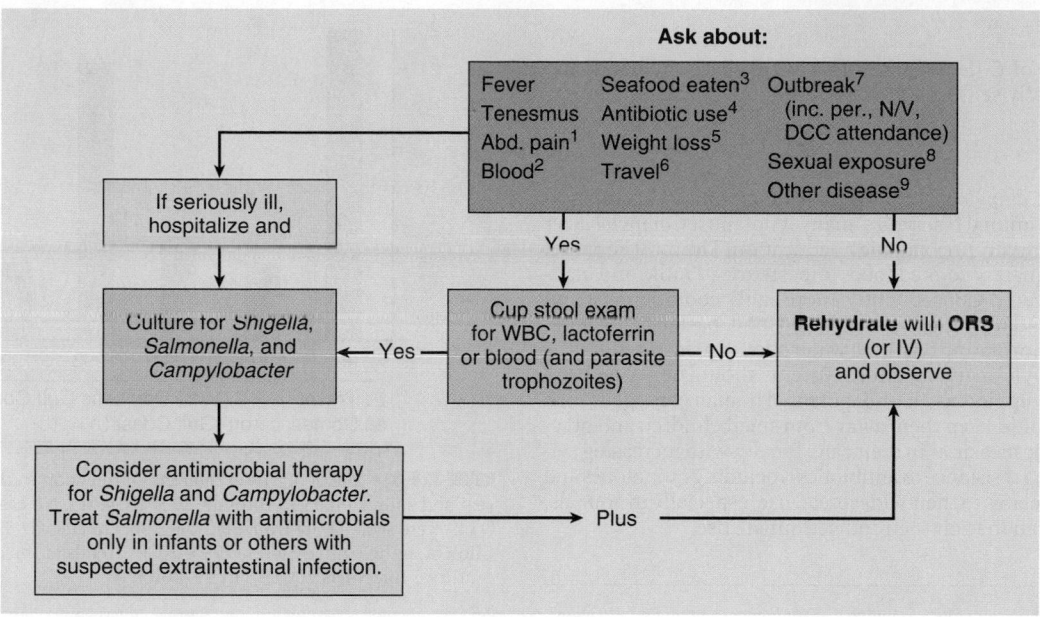

Ask about:

Fever	Seafood eaten[3]	Outbreak[7]
Tenesmus	Antibiotic use[4]	(inc. per., N/V,
Abd. pain[1]	Weight loss[5]	DCC attendance)
Blood[2]	Travel[6]	Sexual exposure[8]
		Other disease[9]

If seriously ill, hospitalize and

Culture for *Shigella*, *Salmonella*, and *Campylobacter*

Cup stool exam for WBC, lactoferrin or blood (and parasite trophozoites)

Rehydrate with ORS (or IV) and observe

Consider antimicrobial therapy for *Shigella* and *Campylobacter*. Treat *Salmonella* with antimicrobials only in infants or others with suspected extraintestinal infection.

Plus

FIGURE 327–1 • Approach to the diagnosis and management of acute infectious diarrhea.

1. If unexplained abdominal pain and fever persist or suggest an appendicitis-like syndrome, culture for *Yersinia enterocolitica*.
2. Bloody diarrhea, especially if without fecal leukocytes, suggests enterohemorrhagic (*Shiga* toxin–producing) *E. coli* O157:H7 or amebiasis (where leukocytes are destroyed by the parasite).
3. Ingestion of inadequately cooked seafood should prompt consideration of *Vibrio* infections or Norwalk-like viruses.
4. Associated antibiotics should be stopped if possible and cytotoxigenic *C. difficile* considered.
5. Persistence (>10 days) with weight loss should prompt consideration of giardiasis or cryptosporidiosis.
6. Travel to tropical areas increases the chance of enterotoxigenic *E. coli* as well as viral (examples, Norwalk-like or rotaviral), parasitic (examples, *Giardia*, *Entamoeba*, *Strongyloides*, *Cryptosporidium*), and, if fecal leukocytes are present, invasive bacterial pathogens as noted in the algorithm.
7. Outbreaks should prompt consideration of *S. aureus*, *B. cereus*, *Anisakis* (incubation period < 6 hours), *C. perfringens*, enterotoxigenic *E. coli*, *Vibrio*, *Salmonella*, *Campylobacter*, *Shigella* or enteroinvasive *E. coli* infection. If unexplained, consider saving *E. coli* for heat-labile and heat-stable toxin testing, invasiveness, adherence testing, and serotyping, and save stool for rotavirus and stool + paired sera for Norwalk-like virus testing.
8. Sigmoidoscopy in symptomatic homosexual males should distinguish proctitis in the distal 15 cm only (caused by herpesvirus, gonococcal, chlamydial, or syphilitic infection) from colitis (*Campylobacter*, *Shigella*, *C. difficile*, or chlamydial [LGV serotypes] infections) or noninflammatory diarrhea (due to giardiasis).
9. Immunocompromised hosts should have a wide range of viral (examples, CMV, HSV, coxsackievirus, rotavirus), bacterial (examples, *Salmonella*, *Mycobacterium avium-intracellular*, *Listeria*), fungal (examples, *Candida*), and parasitic (examples, *Cryptosporidium*, *Strongyloides*, *Entamoeba*, and *Giardia*) agents considered.

(Adapted from Guerrant RL, Shields DS, Thorson SM, et al: Evaluation and diagnosis of acute infectious diarrhea. Am J Med 1985;78:91–98; Guerrant RL, Bobak DA: Bacterial and protozoal gastroenteritis. N Engl J Med 1991;325:327–340; and Choi SW, Park CH, Silva TMJ, et al: To culture or not to culture: Fecal lactoferrin screening for inflammatory diarrhea. J Clin Microbiol 1996;34:928–932.)

Additional differential diagnostic possibilities for febrile inflammatory enteritis include *Salmonella* and *Shigella* infections, for which one should seek a history of an outbreak or contact exposure (such as in daycare centers or among homosexual males, respectively). If the patient has recently taken antibiotics, *C. difficile* colitis or *Salmonella* enteritis should be considered. Recent ingestion of raw seafood should prompt investigation for *Vibrio* infection that may present as either inflammatory or noninflammatory diarrhea. A history of sick pet exposure, persistent abdominal pain, or unexplained inflammatory diarrhea also should prompt consideration of *Yersinia enterocolitica* infections, and travel exposure to tropical areas or residence in an institution where careful hygiene is difficult should prompt an examination of stool and possibly rectal biopsy specimens for *Entamoeba histolytica* (which often destroys fecal leukocytes). Another frequent diagnosis that is considered, especially if *Campylobacter* enteritis has relapsed once or twice, is inflammatory bowel disease. However, it is imperative that anyone who is being considered for that diagnosis have treatable causes such as *Campylobacter* enteritis or amebiasis excluded by appropriate cultures or stains, because treatment with corticosteroids may worsen *Campylobacter* or amebic enteritis, with potentially devastating consequences. Additional noninfectious causes of bloody diarrhea with abdominal pain include intussusception and vascular insufficiency.

 Treatment

The most important treatment for *Campylobacter* enteritis, as with all diarrheal illnesses, is adequate rehydration and maintenance fluid therapy, which can often be accomplished with oral glucose-electrolyte solutions. The effectiveness of specific antimicrobial therapy remains debated. Although most *C. jejuni* strains are sensitive to erythromycin as well as to tetracyclines, chloramphenicol, clindamycin, and aminoglycosides, they are characteristically resistant to penicillin, ampicillin, cephalosporins, and sulfamethoxazole-trimethroprim, and they are increasingly resistant to the quinolones. Indications for antibiotic treatment remain controversial. Several studies have failed to show a significant reduction in the duration of illness with erythromycin treatment despite its prompt eradication of the organism from the stool. Some reserve antimicrobial treatment for those with particularly severe symptoms of high fever, bloody or severe diarrhea, young children in daycare centers, or prolonged or relapsing illnesses. Antimotility agents should be avoided in *Campylobacter* enteritis, as with any inflammatory diarrhea.

Oral erythromycin may not be adequate for systemic *C. jejuni* or *C. fetus* endovascular infections, which probably warrant 2 to 4 weeks of parenteral bactericidal antimicrobial therapy with agents such as ampicillin or third-generation cephalosporins.

Infectious Diseases

Prognosis

The prognosis of *C. jejuni* enteritis is generally quite good, and the disease is usually self-limited with or without specific therapy.

Prevention

Because most *Campylobacter* infections arise from fecal contamination, often from animal reservoirs, many if not most *Campylobacter* infections are potentially preventable by education. The most common sources are inadequately cooked food, unpasteurized milk, and inadequately treated water. Consequently, thoroughly cooking meat and poultry, careful hand washing after preparing food, pasteurizing milk, and adequately chlorinating drinking water should greatly reduce the frequency of *Campylobacter* infections. Parents should be warned that sick pet kittens or puppies may harbor potential human pathogens such as *C. jejuni* and should keep them away from small children and practice careful hygienic measures in their care. Finally, with increasing evidence that emerging resistance to antibiotics (including quinolones and new macrolides) relates to their widespread use, especially in animals, care should be taken to limit their indiscriminate use.

SUGGESTED READINGS

Guerrant RL, Van Gilder T, Steiner T, et al: Practice guidelines for the management of infectious diarrhea. Clin Infect Dis 2001;32:331–350. *Updates age-specific incidence data with guidelines from the Infectious Diseases Society of America for both individual patient care and public health surveillance.*

Guerrant RL, Bobak DA: Bacterial and protozoal gastroenteritis. N Engl J Med 1991;325:327–340. *Update on epidemiology and pathogenesis as well as a practical clinical approach to diagnosis and management of bacterial and other causes of diarrhea.*

Hoge CW, Gambel JM, Srijan A, et al: Trends in antibiotic resistance among diarrheal pathogens isolated in Thailand over 15 years. Clin Infect Dis 1998;26:341–345. *Important report of the alarming increase of ciprofloxacin resistance among* Campylobacter *species from zero before 1991 to 84% in 1995 (with concomitant resistance to the new macrolide azithromycin in 15%).*

Kapperud G, Espeland G, Wahl E, et al: Factors associated with increased and decreased risk of Campylobacter infection: A prospective case-control study in Norway. Am J Epidemiol 2003;158:234–242. *Drinking undisinfected water, eating at barbecues, raw poultry, occupational exposure to animals, and undercooked pork were the leading risk factors.*

Kosek M, Bern C, Guerrant RL: The global burden of diarrhoeal disease, as estimated from studies published between 1992 and 2000. Bull World Health Organ 2003;81:197–204. *Despite reduction in mortality rates, diarrhea accounts for 21% of deaths in children under age 5 years in developing countries and is responsible for 2.5 million deaths per year.*

Randall LP, Ridley AM, Cooles SW, et al: Prevalence of multiple antibiotic resistance in 443 Campylobacter spp. isolated from humans and animals. J Antimicrob Chemother 2003;52:507–510. *Multiple antibiotic resistant* Campylobacter *strains are becoming increasingly prevalent.*

Skirrow MB, Blaser MJ: *Campylobacter jejuni. In* Blaser MJ, Smith PD, Ravdin JI, et al (eds): Infections of the Gastrointestinal Tract, New York, Raven Press, 1995, pp 825–848. *Good review of cultivation methods, epidemiology, pathogenesis, and clinical presentations of* C. jejuni *infections.*

Tam CC, O'Brien SJ, Adak GK, et al: Campylobacter coli—An important foodborne pathogen. J Infect 2003;47:28–32. *Campylobacter coli, the second most common cause of human campylobacteriosis, imposes a considerable health burden.*

Tee W, Mijch A: *Campylobacter jejuni* bacteremia in HIV-infected and nonHIV-infected patients: Comparison of clinical features and review. Clin Infect Dis 1998;26:91–96. *Excellent review of increased risk of* C. jejuni, bacteremia *in AIDS, with extraintestinal involvement such as pneumonitis or cellulitis.*

Walker RI, Caldwell MB, Lee EC, et al: Pathophysiology of Campylobacter enteritis. Microbiol Rev 1986;50:81–94. *Excellent review of the virulence traits, pathogenic mechanisms, and animal models of* C. jejuni *infections.*

328 CHOLERA

William B. Greenough III

Definition

Cholera is an acute-onset, watery diarrheal disease caused by *Vibrio cholerae*, serogroups O1 and O139. The disease occurs sporadically and as large or epidemic outbreaks. Fluid loss may be extreme, exceeding 1 L/hour. The loss of solute-rich body fluids in stools rapidly depletes circulating plasma volume, producing vascular collapse and death in hours. Without treatment, the mortality rate approaches 60% for those severely affected. Mild cases and carriers also occur and participate in the spread of disease.

Etiology

V. cholerae organisms are short, slightly curved, rapidly motile, uniflagellate, gram-negative bacteria that grow aerobically at 37° C

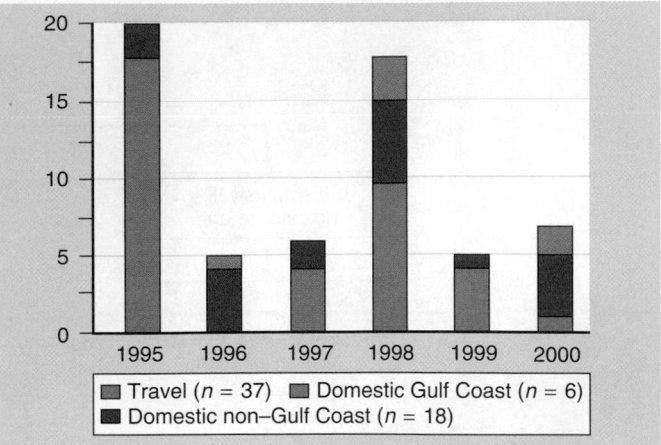

FIGURE 328–1 • Cases of *Vibrio cholerae* O1 infection in the United States by year and source for 1995 through 2000 (N = 61). No cases of *V. cholerae* O139 were seen. (Data from Steinberg EB, Greene KD, Bopp CH, et al: Cholera in the United States, 1995–2000: Trends at the end of the twentieth century. J Infect Dis 2001;184:799–802.)

on relatively simple media. They are classified as Vibrionaceae and are members of a very large group of surface-water organisms distributed in all parts of the world, especially favoring brackish or saltfresh water interfaces. There are many O serogroups of *V. cholerae*, but only serogroups O1 and O139 (Bengal) cause epidemic human disease. Before 1992, two major serotypes, Ogawa and Inaba, and a less common Hikojima variant were observed. Serogroup O1 has two main biotypes: classic and El Tor. The El Tor biotype is recognized by its resistance to polymyxin B, its ability to agglutinate chicken red blood cells, and its characteristic vibriophage susceptibility. These markers are of use epidemiologically. *V. cholerae* produces a potent exotoxin (i.e., cholera toxin) that binds to intestinal epithelium, producing a chloride ion–driven secretion in small intestinal crypts and malabsorption of sodium ion and water at villous tips. Other vibrios and *Escherichia coli* can produce similar exotoxins but do not have other biologic characteristics that lead to epidemic spread as well as endemic disease. However, a new serogroup (O139 Bengal) is responsible for major epidemics.

Epidemiology

Cholera is thought to be a disease of antiquity, with clear descriptions written before 500 BC. The current global spread (i.e., seventh pandemic) has been caused by an El Tor biotype first recognized in 1911 at the El Tor quarantine station in the Persian Gulf. Epidemics due to this organism first appeared in the Celebes in the 1930s, spreading westward through Southeast Asia and reaching the Mediterranean and Africa in the 1970s. In the Ganges delta, epidemics of classic *V. cholerae* were replaced by El Tor late in the 1960s. There have been small but regular outbreaks of cholera in the United States in the Mississippi delta regions since 1973. The El Tor strains isolated have predominated. There has been a decrease since the 1990–1994 period, mainly because of fewer travel-related cases from Latin America (Fig. 328–1). In 1991, *V. cholerae* O1 El Tor caused explosive outbreaks of cholera in Peru and subsequently spread throughout Latin America. *V. cholerae* O139 Bengal is also spreading globally, but it has not yet been reported in the United States.

Clinical Manifestations

Cholera can reduce a perfectly healthy, robust adult to shock and death in 4 to 6 hours, although death usually ensues in 18 or more hours. In rare instances, cholera sicca, shock, and death occur before diarrhea appears, with the voluminous secretions pooling in distended loops of bowel and not escaping as diarrhea or vomiting. Despite the capacity of cholera to cause severe illness, many infected patients have only a mild diarrhea indistinguishable from that of ordinary gastroenteritis. In epidemics, many of those infected have no symptoms or very mild illness.

Without fluid replacement, cholera patients develop signs of severe volume depletion: sunken eyes, poor skin turgor, hoarse voice, extreme thirst, faint heart sounds, weak or absent peripheral pulses, and severe muscle cramps. Patients are oriented but appear apathetic except for thirst. If patients survive and have not received adequate hydration, a reactive phase occurs with fever caused by sepsis and pneumonia. Pulmonary edema can ensue with even modest fluid replacement because of prolonged, severe acidosis.

In children, unconsciousness and/or convulsions may signal hypoglycemia. Initial laboratory values from depleted cholera patients (see Table 328–1) reflect the loss of isotonic fluid without larger molecules such as albumen. This results in increased concentrations of plasma proteins and blood cells. Loss of bicarbonate leads to acidosis with a low arterial pH and bicarbonate. Potassium depletion, which may be severe, is not reflected by low plasma values until acidosis has been corrected.

Diagnosis

Cholera should be considered in any patient with acute onset of watery diarrhea and in those who have traveled or resided in a cholera-endemic area. In clusters of cases of acute-onset watery diarrhea, particularly where sanitation is poor, it is especially important to recognize cholera early to permit advance actions to prevent deaths of large numbers of people.

Treatment does not depend on an etiologic diagnosis. Fluid replacement should be started without delay as soon as watery diarrhea begins for any reason. After initiating treatment, stools should be examined directly for red and white blood cells. Except in cases of mixed infections with invasive organisms, which do occur in cholera outbreaks, fecal red and white cells are not a feature of cholera. If phase or dark-field microscopy is available, the characteristic darting motility of vibrios can be recognized in fresh, wet preparations. To be certain that these motile bacteria are V. cholerae, serogroups O1 and O139 antisera can be applied to wet preparations, immobilizing the organisms in a rapid and specific diagnostic test. For greater sensitivity of this test, a stool sample or rectal swab can be incubated in an enriched medium for vibrios, such as alkaline peptone water, for 12 to 18 hours. Stool culture is best done on a selective medium, because colonies of V. cholerae may be overgrown or are easily missed on standard enteric media. A simple method uses thiosulfate citrate–bile salt–sucrose (TCBS) agar, which is very stable and selective for vibrios. Opaque, flat, yellow colonies form on TCBS agar in 18 hours at 37° C. Confirmation of serogroup and serotype can be done by direct slide agglutination with specific antisera that are available commercially, including those against the O139 Bengal strain. Biotyping requires more elaborate procedures, but resistance to polymyxin B is a quick way to recognize the El Tor biotype. A kit based on a monoclonal antibody against V. Cholerae O1 lipopolysaccharide, called the SMART test, is available for rapid diagnosis. V. cholerae serogroups O1 and O139 can be identified by gene amplification or immunofluorescent methods in many surface waters around the world, and the organisms are often associated with phytoplankton.

Mode of Spread

During epidemics, cholera is mainly a waterborne disease. Large numbers of vibrios enter water sources from the voluminous liquid stools that soak clothing and linens and contaminate the environment. The setting for epidemics is often extreme poverty with a lack of safe water. However, an outbreak in Portugal affected the most careful travelers who used only bottled water, which unfortunately had been supplied from a spring contaminated with V. cholerae. Occasionally, contaminated foods spread disease. Raw or undercooked shellfish or fresh vegetables washed with contaminated water usually are responsible. These sources played an important role in the recent Latin American epidemics. There is a high risk of secondary spread in families or institutions in which water and food are shared. Contamination of household food and water sources is the rule. It is easy to understand how this occurs when an adult patient may produce 30 to 50 L of stool in 2 to 3 days and is usually too weak to use a commode or toilet. Mild cases and convalescent carriers probably spread the disease between communities. True long-term carriers are rare enough to be reportable. During interepidemic periods, V. cholerae lurks in many brackish surface waters in an unculturable form that can be detected by specific gene amplification methods.

Susceptibility to Cholera

In areas where cholera occurs each year, children younger than 5 years have the highest rates. Rates among older children and adults are lower because of local intestinal immunity, which decreases risk. However, older individuals make up a larger part of the population, and many patients present who are older than age 5. Breast-fed infants rarely get cholera because they receive protection from antibodies in their mother's milk. When cholera attacks a population that has not experienced it for many years, as was true during the pandemic in the Philippines and Africa, all ages are attacked equally, but morbidity and mortality are greatest among the very young and very old. Individuals with low gastric acid production, those who are on acid-suppressing medications, and those who have had gastrectomies are especially vulnerable, because V. cholerae is quite sensitive to acid.

Cholera tends to attack persons of blood group O more frequently and with greater severity than other groups, and individuals with AB blood group have less severe disease. People with a safe, piped water supply and effective disinfected waste disposal are at least risk for the disease, regardless of host susceptibility.

Pathogenesis

After V. cholerae is ingested, vomiting and diarrhea may begin as early as 12 hours or not appear for more than a week. Illness occurs when viable organisms reach the duodenum and jejunum, where alkaline pH, nutrients, and bile salts favor rapid multiplication. Actively motile vibrios penetrate mucous layers and attach to the brush border of the intestinal epithelium, where they secrete a potent exotoxin. The toxin is a protein of 84,000 daltons and consists of five B subunits that bind irreversibly to a specific chemical receptor (GM_1 ganglioside) on the cell surfaces. The toxic moiety, or A subunit, is linked to the B aggregate and gains entry after binding occurs. Adenosine diphosphate ribosylates the α subunit of G protein, producing increased adenylate cyclase activity and consequently raised cyclic adenosine monophosphate levels in the enterocytes or any other affected cells. The most visible result in the small intestine is the profuse, watery diarrhea resulting from abolition at the villous tips of the normal absorption of sodium ion and, with it, anions and water, and from stimulation of crypt cells to secrete chloride, drawing with them cations and water from the blood stream into the gut lumen. The resulting solute-rich stream originating in the duodenum and jejunum is profuse, eliciting vomiting as it progresses cephalad and diarrhea as it flushes from small intestine through the colon. The fluid lost in cholera is a slightly fishy-smelling, nonfecal, whitish, mucus-flecked liquid (i.e., rice-water stool). There is no cellular damage and no inflammation or loss of plasma proteins or formed elements of the blood into the gut lumen. There is also increased secretion of hepatic and pancreatic fluids, prostaglandins, and other intestinal hormones.

All signs and symptoms of cholera result from the fluid losses, which approach in composition an ultrafiltrate of plasma enriched in potassium and bicarbonate (Table 328–1). There is no evidence for systemic effects by cholera toxin itself, because V. cholerae does not invade the body and the toxin is not absorbed. The organism exerts all its effects topically by adhering to the intestinal lining and producing toxin that is bound at cell surfaces. Cells at the intestinal surface other than epithelial cells are also affected by the toxin and may contribute to symptoms by the release of cytokines and neural signals.

Table 328–1 • TYPICAL CHEMICAL VALUES IN STOOL AND PLASMA FROM PATIENTS WITH SEVERE CHOLERA

		PLASMA	
	STOOL	Untreated	Treated[†]
Sodium*	138 (105)	141	142
Chloride*	102 (90)	107	106
Potassium*	18 (25)	4.5	3.6
Bicarbonate*	45 (30)	9	21
Arterial pH	—	7.21	7.43
Plasma specific gravity	—	1.040	1.026

*Milliequivalents per liter. Stool values in parentheses are for children younger than 10 years old.
†Four hours after water and electrolyte replacement.

Although the first line of immune defense is local at the intestinal epithelium, circulating antibodies occur to the specific O antigens. Testing for these is of use only as an epidemiologic tool to judge the prevalence of disease in a specific population.

Rx Treatment

Early and complete replacement of fluid loss averts death and all complications. Advanced oral hydration solutions based on rice or other starchy foods hydrate efficiently and reduce diarrhea and vomiting substantially (30 to 50%) compared with intravenous treatment or glucose-based oral rehydration solutions. In all except the most severe cases, oral rehydration therapy alone is sufficient to treat cholera, especially if started as soon as diarrhea begins. All varieties of watery diarrhea lose fluid of similar composition, which varies with the rate of loss. Oral hydration therapy is the treatment of choice in all situations except when a patient is in shock or is comatose. Oral rehydration therapy should be used in hospitals, at home, or in the field, because it entails fewer risks, is much less expensive, does not require trained medical personnel for administration, and is effective. The discovery that absorption of sodium by cotransport pathways in intestinal mucosa is spared during cholera and other diarrheal diseases opened the way for safe, inexpensive, and effective oral replacement solutions. Glucose, amino acids, and small peptides are absorbed by separate cotransport pathways of the intestine and carry with them sodium ions. Water and anions follow down the osmotic and electrochemical gradients from the gut lumen to the blood stream.

Originally, oral rehydration solutions were based only on glucose. These remain very effective but do not diminish diarrheal fluid losses. Advanced oral rehydration solutions based on rice or rice digests hydrate, reduce losses, and shorten illness. The composition of available oral rehydration solutions is listed in Table 328–2, together with some standard intravenous solutions. There is a substantial promise of further improving oral rehydration solutions using the enhanced colonic absorption driven by short-chain fatty acids from nondigestible starches and an optimal amount of protein or peptides.

Intravenous fluid replacement is reserved for patients who have not received early oral replacement and are in shock and for rapidly purging patients who exceed the capacity of oral replacement. In a cholera epidemic, all individuals at risk must be thoroughly familiar with oral rehydration therapy and use it early to minimize deaths and the need for intravenous fluids. Thirst and urination are adequate guides to oral replacement therapy even in small children. This eliminates the need for accurate intake and output measurements and weighings, which even in excellent hospitals are difficult and are out of the question under epidemic conditions. Intravenous replacement with normal saline for patients who are depleted and in shock should be given rapidly through a large-bore needle to ensure infusion rates of 50 to 100 mL/minute until a strong radial pulse has been achieved. Remaining fluid deficits may then be replaced less rapidly over 2 hours. The fluid deficit in a severely depleted patient is about 10% of body weight (e.g., 5 L for a 50-kg patient). As soon as patients are strong enough to drink, oral rehydration therapy should begin, preferably with a rice- or other cereal-based solution of the proper solute composition. If this is done adequately, no further intravenous fluids are needed. In semicomatose patients who are unable to cooperate, nasogastric intubation permits adequate enteral replacement. For intravenous and oral solutions, the composition is crucial and should be within a range to properly replace losses of solutes and water (see Table 328–2). Many drinks ordinarily given to diarrhea patients are not adequate, although they may complement oral rehydration therapy. Vomiting is not a contraindication for oral rehydration therapy; however, fluids of high osmolarity should be avoided.

If a commercial preparation of oral rehydration salts is not available, a home solution can be prepared. The safest and most effective of these is a thick but drinkable suspension prepared from rice or other suitable ground, starchy foods. Precooked products are convenient if available, but they are not essential. To a pint of water with cereal thickly suspended, a one-half level teaspoon (i.e., one three-finger pinch) of salt is added, and the mixture is cooked only long enough to soften the ground cereal powder. The mixture should be used within 6 hours and may be taken warm or cold. This mixture lacks potassium, which can be made up with potassium-rich foods. If hydration is well maintained, the kidney can compensate for stool bicarbonate loss. Patients with cholera may need to drink copious amounts of fluid every hour. The patient must be offered sips every few minutes to minimize overloading the stomach and consequent vomiting. This is labor intensive but does not require medical skills. Especially in epidemics, family members and friends are the backbone of a successful treatment program.

In treating children or adults, fluid therapy should be guided by thirst; observations on the circulation, urine output, and presence of edema; or rales at the lung bases. Feeding is important and should be initiated immediately. Breast-feeding is especially useful in affected infants, although few breast-fed babies contract cholera except in nonendemic areas where maternal milk lacks protective antibodies. Feeding should be achieved with appetizing foods rich in complex carbohydrates and proteins and culturally adapted to the taste of the patient.

Adjunctive antibiotic therapy may be indicated. This varies with the epidemic strain, but tetracyclines, fluoroquinolones, and macrolides have been effective when resistance is not present. However, resistance is common and must be monitored to avoid wasting high-cost antimicrobial agents that are ineffective. Antibiotic prophylaxis has not been useful and encourages the emergence of resistant strains.

Table 328–2 • CHOLERA AND ACUTE DIARRHEA TREATMENT SOLUTIONS (ORAL AND INTRAVENOUS)

TREATMENT SOLUTIONS	SUBSTRATE (g/L)	ELECTROLYTES (MMOL/L)				
		Na$^+$	K†	Base*	Cl$^-$	OSMOLALITY
Oral						
WHO/UNICEF	20 (glucose)	90	20	30	80	330
Pedialyte	25 (glucose)	45	20	30	65	300
Rice solution	80 (rice)	90	20	30	80	240
Infalyte	30 (rice digest)	50	25	34	45	200
Ceralyte†	40 (rice digest)	90	20	30	65	235
Intravenous						
Dhaka solution	0	134	13	48 (bicarbonate)	99	294
Ringer's‡	0	130	4	28 (lactate)	109	271

*Citrate is generally used, but bicarbonate is equally effective, and lactate or acetate is used in intravenous solutions.
†Available as dried powder in packets from Cera Products, LLC, Columbia, Maryland.
‡Also contains calcium, 3.0 mEq/L.

Prevention

Safe water supplies and appropriate disposal of human waste prevent spread of cholera but may not be achievable under conditions of poverty. Rapid loss of large volumes requires the use of special beds (i.e., cholera cots) or fecal conduits that avoid widespread dissemination into surrounding areas. *V. cholerae* is a fragile organism that cannot withstand drying, mild oxidation, or acid conditions. A variety of disinfectants are effective for soiled articles. Bleaching powder is frequently used. Handwashing with soap before handling food is important. Patients suspected to have cholera should be reported to state health authorities by telephone or facsimile machine because of epidemic risks.

The available injected cholera vaccine is not useful, but there are effective killed bacterial and toxoid oral vaccines, as well as very promising genetically altered live vaccines. A single dose of live, attenuated cholera strain CVD 103-HgR oral vaccine is licensed in many countries and is available in Europe under the trade name Orachol and in Canada as Mutachol. This vaccine can be administered in a liquid formulation with Ty 21a oral typhoid vaccine and gives protection beginning in 8 days. An oral vaccine (Dukoral) composed of whole, killed *V. cholerae* plus recombinant cholera toxin is available in Sweden and has been extensively field tested for safety and efficacy.

SUGGESTED READINGS

Barua D, Greenough WB III: Cholera. New York, Plenum Scientific Publishing, 1992. *A broad review of all aspects of cholera.*

Butler TC: New developments in the understanding of cholera. Curr Gastroenterol Rep 2001;3:315–321. *A good current review.*

Field M: Intestinal ion transport and the pathophysiology of diarrhea. J Clin Invest 2003;111:931–943. *A review of the relationships between cholera and other diarrheal diseases for the clinician.*

Ramakrishra BS, Venkataraman S, Srinivasan P, et al: Amylase-resistant starch plus oral rehydration solution for cholera. N Engl J Med 2000;342:308–313. *A new development in oral rehydration therapy.*

Sanchez JL, Taylor DN: Cholera. Lancet 1997;349:1825–1830. *An excellent summary of recent knowledge of microbiology, epidemiology, ecology, treatment, and prevention of cholera, including risks to travelers and in the Western Hemisphere.*

Steinberg EB, Greene KD, Bopp CH, et al: Cholera in the United States: Trends at the end of the twentieth century. J Infect Dis 2001;184:799–802. *Current data on cholera in the United States.*

Wachsmuth IK, Blake PA, Olsvik O: *Vibrio cholerae* and Cholera: Molecular and Global Perspectives. Washington, ASM Press, 1994. *Comprehensive, current review on new epidemic strains, epidemiology, and microbiology of cholera.*

329 ENTERIC *ESCHERICHIA COLI* INFECTIONS

Richard L. Guerrant

Definition

Escherichia coli is the predominant aerobic, coliform species in the normal colon. However, *E. coli* also can be an enteric pathogen and cause intestinal disease, usually diarrhea. Diarrhea caused by *E. coli* may be watery, inflammatory, or bloody, depending on which genetic codes for virulence traits the organism happens to possess. Consequently, diarrheogenic *E. coli* must be defined more specifically according to its virulence traits. Specific virulence traits determine the type of disease the organism causes, such as enterotoxigenic, enteroinvasive, enterohemorrhagic, enteropathogenic, or enteroadherent *E. coli* diarrhea. Each of these categories is being further resolved by the type of enterotoxin (e.g., the cholera-like, heat-labile toxin [LT], or the heat-stable toxin [ST]) or adherence (e.g., localized and effacing, aggregative, or diffuse) it causes. Taken separately, organisms such as enterotoxigenic *E. coli* (ETEC) constitute major bacterial causes of diarrhea morbidity and mortality on a global scale, particularly among children in tropical, developing areas and in travelers. Taken together, the varied types of *E. coli* diarrhea not only constitute the major category of bacterial enteric pathogens but also illustrate the many ways enteric pathogens can cause disease.

As noted in Table 329–1, at least three different types of *E. coli* enterotoxins may cause intestinal secretion (ETEC), others are enteroinvasive (EIEC), and still others cause foodborne hemorrhagic colitis (EHEC) and produce the *Shiga*-like toxin (SLT) (EHEC), whereas the classically recognized enteropathogenic *E. coli* (EPEC) serotypes are neither enterotoxigenic nor invasive but attach and efface the epithelium. Still additional types of enteroadherent *E. coli* exhibit aggregating (EAggEC) or diffuse adherence (DAEC) traits and may be associated with prolonged diarrhea among children in tropical, developing areas and in patients with the acquired immunodeficiency syndrome (AIDS).

Table 329–1 • DIFFERENT TYPES OF ENTERIC *E. COLI* INFECTIONS

TYPE	MECHANISM	PREDOMINANT O SEROGROUPS	GENETIC CODE	DETECTION	CLINICAL SYNDROMES
Enterotoxigenic *E. coli* (ETEC)					
1. Cholera-like, heat-labile toxin (LT)	Activates intestinal adenylate cyclase	6, 8, 11, 15, 20, 25, 27, 63, 80, 85, 139	Plasmid	ELISA, RIA, PIH, CHO, Y1 cells, 18-hr loops, gene probe	Watery diarrhea, travelers' diarrhea
2. Heat-stable toxin (STa: STh or STp)	Activates intestinal guanylate cyclase	12, 78, 115, 148, 149, 153, 155, 166, 167	Plasmid (transposon)	ELISA, RIA, suckling mice, 6-hr loops, gene probes	Watery diarrhea, travelers' diarrhea
3. Heat-stable toxin (STb)	?; Not cyclic adenosine or guanosine monophosphate		Plasmid	Piglet loops, gene probe	?
Enteroinvasive *E. coli*					
4. Enteroinvasive *E. coli*	Cell invasion and spread	11, 28ac, 29, 124, 136, 144, 147, 152, 164, 167	Plasmid (140 Md, pWR110)	Sereny test, gene probe, (lys⁻, NM, often lactose⁻)	Inflammatory dysentery
Enterohemorrhagic *E. coli*					
5. Enterohemorrhagic (EHEC)	Shiga-like toxin(s) (SLT) and adhesin fimbriae	26, 39, 113, 121, 128, 139, 145, 157, occ 55, 111	Phage(s) and adhesin plasmid(s)	ELISA for SLT, serotype, HeLa, Vero cells, sorbitol, agar, SLT or eae gene probes	Bloody noninflammatory diarrhea; hemolytic-uremic syndrome
Enteropathogenic *E. coli*					
6. Focal attaching and effacing (EPEC)	Attach, then efface the mucosa	55, 111, 119, 125, 126, 127, 128, 142, 158,	Plasmid (60 Md, pMAR2) + chromosomal (*esp*, eae, and *tir*)	Serotype, focal HEp2 adhesion, gene probes for EAF or eae	Infantile diarrhea
Enteroadherent *E. coli*					
7. Enteroaggregating *E. coli* (EAggEC)	Colonize? toxins (EAST, EALT)	3, 15, 44, 51, 77, 78, 91	Plasmid	HEp2 cell adherence; AA probe	Persistent diarrhea
8. Diffusely adherent *E. coli* (DAEC)	Colonize (F 1845 fimbriate adhesin)	75 (F 1845), 15 (57-1), ? (189)	Chromosomal/plasmid	HEp2 cell adherence; DA gene probe	Persistent diarrhea in children > 18 mo old

ELISA = enzyme-linked immunosorbent assay; RIA = radioimmunoassay.

Etiology

E. coli is a small, catalase-positive, oxidase-negative, gram-negative bacillus in the family Enterobacteriaceae. It characteristically reduces nitrates, ferments glucose and usually lactose, and is either motile (with peritrichate flagella) or nonmotile. It gives a positive methyl red reaction and negative reactions with Voges-Proskauer, urease, phenylalanine deaminase, and citrate agents. *E. coli* constitutes the predominant facultative gram-negative bacillus in the intestinal tract of humans and other mammals. As with other gram-negative organisms, the lipopolysaccharide cell wall contains lipid A and 2-keto-3-deoxyoctanate (KDO), a core glycolipid that has been used to develop vaccines that provide cross-protection against systemic infections with other gram-negative organisms. Smooth (S) forms of *E. coli* have O-specific carbohydrate chains attached to this core glycolipid to provide 169 O serogroups as well as at least 60 heat-labile protein flagellar (H) antigens by which strains are currently serotyped. Historically, some 80 variably heat-labile capsular (K) antigens also have been described (L, B, and A), not to mention the more recently appreciated numerous adherence, enterotoxin, cytotoxin, and invasiveness factors that may be gained or lost by a particular serotype because they are characteristically encoded on transmissible genetic elements such as plasmids or bacteriophages. Consequently, this common inhabitant of the normal human intestinal tract becomes a pathogen when it houses one or more specific traits contributing to its colonization and virulence in the intestinal tract. Other traits such as O and H serogroup also may be important for certain enteropathogenic and enteroinvasive organisms. For reasons that remain obscure, only a few O serogroups tend to predominate in the normal human colon (O groups 1, 2, 4, 6, 7, 8, 18, 25, 45, 75, and 81), whereas others noted in Table 329–1 tend (albeit not absolutely) to be associated with specific virulence traits and thus different types of pathogenesis in the intestine. The O antigens of invasive *E. coli* often cross-react with various *Shigella* species, suggesting further that, in addition to the 140-Md plasmid, serotype has a role in pathogenesis.

Epidemiology

Enteric *E. coli* infections are essentially acquired by the fecal-oral route, reflecting primarily a human reservoir for most recognized types of *E. coli* enteropathogens. ETEC is also an important veterinary pathogen, especially in calves and piglets. However, the attachment traits of animal strains are different from those that infect humans and likely substantially influence their epidemiology.

The infectious doses of enterotoxigenic, enteroinvasive and enteroaggregative *E. coli* have been determined in volunteers to be 10^6 to 10^{10}, numbers that usually require multiplication in contaminated food or water vehicles for their transmission. Heavy contamination with ETEC has been documented in foods prepared in homes and restaurants and at street vendors as well as in drinking water in many tropical areas, and contaminated water and foods likely represent the major sources of their acquisition, primarily in the warm or wet season. In the United States, major outbreaks of water- or foodborne *E. coli* diarrhea of different types have been documented in the past 3 decades. A large waterborne outbreak of diarrhea at a popular national park was found to be caused by ETEC, and a widespread outbreak of enteroinvasive *E. coli* (EIEC) enteritis was traced to consumption of French Camembert cheese. Bloody, noninflammatory diarrhea has been increasingly associated with enterohemorrhagic *E. coli* (EHEC) (O157:H7 and others) from eating hamburgers from large distributors or several fast-food chains or from ingestion of contaminated unpasteurized apple juice or seed sprouts such as radish or alfalfa sprouts. EHEC infections are especially alarming because they are increasing in frequency and may cause hemolytic-uremic syndrome, which can be fatal despite antimicrobial therapy. Occasional nosocomial outbreaks of ETEC and EPEC serotypes also have occurred in hospitalized infants in the United States and other industrialized countries.

As with most diarrheal illnesses, the highest age-specific attack rates of ETEC infections are in young children, especially at the time of weaning, when ETEC accounts for 15 to 50% of illnesses. Like immunologically inexperienced young children, the traveler visiting tropical areas has a 30 to 50% chance of acquiring travelers' diarrhea over a 2- to 3-week stay unless untreated water or ice and uncooked foods such as salads are strictly avoided. The most commonly recognized pathogen associated with travelers' diarrhea around most tropical areas of the world is ETEC that produces either the STa, LT, or both enterotoxins (Chapter 330).

Of potential immunologic significance is the continued occurrence of symptomatic infections with *E. coli* that produce the less immunogenic STa in adult residents of tropical or other areas endemic for ETEC infections. In contrast, adult residents in endemic areas often carry LT-producing *E. coli* asymptomatically, suggesting that they may be protected from symptoms, if not from colonization.

Limited data on invasive *E. coli* suggest that the infectious doses are relatively high. As with ETEC infections, such large numbers have been readily spread in food with high attack rates. EPEC have been recognized primarily in urban areas, especially among hospitalized infants in their first year of life, with apparent cross-infection in hospital nurseries. Although sporadic cases still occur, nosocomial outbreaks of EPEC diarrhea during the summer appear to have become less common and less severe in industrialized countries in the last few decades. Enteroaggregative *E. coli* increasingly appear to be important causes of persistent diarrhea and malnutrition, especially in children in tropical areas and in patients with AIDS.

Pathogenesis and Pathology

The pathogenesis of enteric *E. coli* infections begins with the ingestion of the organism in contaminated food or water, which then faces the normal gastric acid barrier. Both ETEC and EIEC appear to be sensitive to gastric acid; neutralization by gastric acid reduces the infectious dose by 100- to 1000-fold. This is followed by an incubation period of 2 to 7 days, during which colonization of the involved part of the intestinal tract and toxin production, invasion or other disruption of cell function take place. Best characterized is the colonization by ETEC in the upper small bowel, which involves one of at least five major colonization factor antigen groups (which are fimbriate or fibrillar protein structures on the surface of the organism). The colonization fimbriae bind the organism to cell surface receptors in the upper small bowel where the enterotoxin is delivered to reduce normal absorption and cause net electrolyte and water secretion. LT, with a molecular weight of about 86,000, has a binding and active subunit that, like choleratoxin, binds to a monosialoganglioside (Gm1) receptor. Also like choleratoxin, the active subunit adenosine diphosphate ribosylates the regulatory subunit of adenylate cyclase to activate adenylate cyclase. The consequently increased chloride secretion and reduced sodium absorption combine to cause net isotonic electrolyte loss that must be replaced to prevent severe dehydration and hypotension and its potential consequences. Other strains produce the heat-stable toxin (STa), a much smaller molecule of 18 to 19 amino acids (molecular weight < 2000), which activates intestinal particulate guanylate cyclase. Like cyclic adenosine monophosphate, the cyclic guanosine monophosphate thus formed also causes net secretion. A third type of *E. coli* enterotoxin (STb) causes secretion in porcine intestine without activating adenylate or guanylate cyclase; STb has no known role in human disease. Similarly, the roles of enterotoxins such as LTII, EAST, EIET, and others seen in ETEC, EAggEC, and EIEC, respectively, are unclear at present. Both the colonization traits and enterotoxin production are encoded on transmissible plasmids. Besides the complications of dehydration, the only significant pathologic change is depletion of mucus from intestinal goblet cells.

Other *E. coli*, often of certain serogroups noted in Table 329–1, have the capacity, analogous to *Shigella*, to invade and multiply in epithelial cells, cause conjunctivitis in guinea pigs (Sereny test), and cause inflammatory colitis and dysenteric or bloody diarrhea. As seen with shigellosis, a striking inflammatory response is seen, with sheets of polymorphonuclear leukocytes in the stool. The colon shows patchy, acute inflammation in the mucosa and submucosa with focal denuding of the surface epithelium but usually without deeper invasion or systemic spread. While epithelial cell invasiveness in both EIEC and *Shigella* appears to be encoded on a large 120- to 140-Md plasmid, several chromosomal determinants, including the O antigen, are crucial for full invasive virulence.

Classically recognized EPEC serotypes often fail to produce known enterotoxins or to be invasive. Nevertheless, they are well-established causes of infantile diarrhea and exhibit a remarkable array of chromosomal and plasmid-encoded traits that orchestrate their initial attachment and subsequent effacement of the brush border epithelium. The majority of classically recognized EPEC serotypes such as O55 and O111 exhibit both plasmid-encoded localized adherence to epithelial cells and chromosomally mediated attachment and effacement of the microvilli. There is also villous atrophy, mucosal thinning, inflammation in the lamina propria, and variable crypt cell hyperplasia. These morphologic changes are associated with a reduction in the mucosal brush border enzymes and may contribute to the impaired absorptive function and diarrhea.

Enterohemorrhagic *E. coli*, most notably serotype O157:H7 but also serogroups O26, 39, and others, are associated with foodborne outbreaks of bloody, noninflammatory diarrhea and with the hemolytic-uremic syndrome. These organisms produce SLTs that may be responsible for the characteristic colonic mucosal disruption and hemorrhage, as well as the complication of hemolytic-uremic syndrome. Sigmoidoscopy usually reveals only moderately hyperemic mucosa, and barium enema may reveal a thumbprint pattern of submucosal edema in the ascending and transverse colon. Some patients have superficial ulceration with mild neutrophil infiltration in the edematous submucosa. The mechanisms by which EAggEC (which adhere in an aggregative pattern to the mucosa and produce heat-stable and heat-labile "toxins"), DAEC, or colonization alone may cause diarrhea remain unclear at present.

Clinical Manifestations

The most common clinical manifestation of enteric *E. coli* infections is the watery diarrhea that characterizes ETEC infections, particularly in young children and travelers to tropical or developing areas. This may range from mild to severe, cholera-like diarrhea that may be life threatening, especially in small children and elderly patients, who are particularly prone to have the most severe consequences of dehydration, undernutrition, and electrolyte imbalance (especially hypokalemia and acidosis).

The incubation period (2 to 7 days) varies inversely with the size of the inoculum. Characteristic symptoms include malaise, abdominal cramping, anorexia, and watery diarrhea, occasionally associated with nausea, vomiting, or low-grade fever. The illness is usually self-limited to 1 to 5 days and rarely extends beyond 10 days or 2 weeks. Infections with *E. coli* that produce both ST and LT or ST alone may be more severe than those with only LT-producing *E. coli*. The persistence of impaired mucosal absorptive capacity for 1 to 3 weeks may further compound the cycle of malnutrition that complicates diarrheal illnesses in children in developing, tropical areas.

Infection with EIEC is characterized by inflammatory colitis, often with abdominal pain, high fever, tenesmus, and bloody or dysenteric diarrhea essentially like that seen with *Shigella*, to which this organism is closely related. The incubation period is usually 1 to 3 days with the duration usually self-limited to 7 to 10 days.

Outbreaks of EPEC infections in newborn nurseries have ranged from mild transient diarrhea to severe and rapidly fatal diarrheal illnesses, especially in premature or otherwise compromised infants. The more severe illnesses appear to have been more common in industrialized countries before 1950. However, more recent outbreaks and sporadic cases are well documented.

Hemorrhagic colitis associated with the SLT producing *E. coli* (EHEC) O157:H7, O26:H11, and others is characterized by grossly bloody diarrhea, often with remarkably little fever or inflammatory exudate in the stool. Although the diarrheal illnesses have been self-limited, a significant number of children and adults have subsequently developed a potentially fatal hemolytic-uremic syndrome or thrombotic thrombocytopenic purpura. Outbreaks of hemorrhagic colitis due to EHEC in nursing homes or other institutions may be quite severe and more common than previously appreciated. The incubation period in two outbreaks has been 3 to 4 days (range, 1 to 7 days), and the illness is characteristically self-limited to 5 to 12 days (mean, 7.8 days).

Enteroaggregative *E. coli* have been associated with persistent diarrhea and malnutrition in children in developing areas and in patients with AIDS. Diffusely adherent *E. coli* have also been associated with diarrhea in children older than 18 months.

Diagnosis

With the exception of EHEC, which should be sought by enzyme-linked immunosorbent assay (ELISA), or other testing for the SLT and for sorbitol-negative EHEC O157:H7 in all patients with bloody diarrhea, definitive etiologic diagnosis of *E. coli* diarrhea requires the documentation of a specific virulence trait, such as enterotoxin, invasiveness, enteroadherence, or serotype, which requires specialized immunologic, tissue culture, animal bioassay, or gene probes that are usually available only in research and reference laboratories. Except for EHEC, such tests are rarely cost effective or clinically indicated, except in outbreak or research situations. Fortunately, a likely diagnosis often can be suspected by the clinical and epidemiologic setting. For example, self-limited, noninflammatory diarrhea in tropical, developing areas is most likely due to ETEC, rotaviruses (young children), or Norwalk-like viruses (older children and adults). Noninflammatory diarrhea in winter months in temperate areas in older children or younger adults is more likely to be due to Norwalk-like viruses. Specific tests for the respective virulence traits of different types of *E. coli* are noted in Table 329–1. One should also consider *Vibrio* infections in areas endemic for cholera or in any coastal area where inadequately cooked seafood may be eaten. If noninflammatory diarrhea persists, especially with weight loss, one also should consider *Giardia lamblia* or *Cryptosporidium* infection. In outbreaks of food poisoning, *S. aureus*, *Clostridium perfringens*, and *Bacillus cereus* should be considered.

Inflammatory colitis with high fever, tenesmus, and leukocytes, mucus, and blood in the stool may well be due to EIEC but should prompt a stool culture for more common invasive pathogens such as *Campylobacter jejuni*, *Shigella*, and *Salmonella* or even *Clostridium difficile*, *Yersinia enterocolitica*, or noncholera *Vibrio* (Chapter 327). On the other hand, bloody diarrhea without high fever and few, if any, fecal leukocytes (or minimal or no fecal lactoferrin elevations) should prompt consideration of the SLT-producing EHEC such as strain O157:H7. This organism is often suspected as a sorbitol-negative *E. coli*, which may require further study for serotype or SLT production.

 ## Treatment

As with all diarrheal illnesses, the primary treatment is replacement and maintenance of water and electrolytes. Losses of water and electrolytes may be particularly severe and even life threatening with ETEC and can usually be replaced with a simple oral rehydration solution that uses the intact, sodium-coupled glucose, and/or amino acid absorption to replace fluid losses, as described in Chapter 328. This oral rehydration solution should be given ad libitum with free water and, in breast-fed infants, continued breast-feeding and early refeeding should be done to compensate for the nutritional losses.

Because most *E. coli* diarrhea is self-limited, the role of antimicrobial agents is debated and remains of secondary importance to rehydration. In areas where the ETEC remains sensitive, early initiation of sulfamethoxazole-trimethoprim, tetracycline, or a quinolone antibiotic may reduce a 3- to 5-day illness to a 1- to 2-day illness if the agent is started with the first loose stool in travelers to endemic, tropical areas (Chapter 330). The use of antimotility agents should be tempered by the potential added risk of worsening or prolonging inflammatory diarrheas, increasing the risk of hemolytic-uremic syndrome (HUS) with EHEC infections, and their lack of effectiveness in reducing fluid loss even though abdominal cramping and overt diarrhea may be temporarily reduced. Because of the potential severity of the disease in infants, some pediatricians have used neomycin 100 mg/kg/day orally divided into three or four daily doses for 5 days, for documented EPEC infections in neonates. Bismuth subsalicylate may reduce symptoms in travelers' diarrhea but should be used with caution to avoid toxic doses of salicylate. A number of pharmacologic agents enhance absorption or reduce secretion with experimental diarrhea but remain inadequately studied or too toxic for recommended use to date.

The role of antimicrobial agents in treating EHEC infections or in preventing serious complications remains controversial. The treatment of HUS requires careful supportive care and may require plasma exchange as well.

Prognosis

The overall prognosis in *E. coli* diarrheas of the various types noted, if fully and adequately treated, is generally excellent. However, the impact of *E. coli* and other common diarrheas on mortality and morbidity (particularly with repeated infections compounding malnutrition in young children) remains one of the major health problems on a global scale; this problem may actually be worsening in some transitional areas. The potentially serious complication of hemolytic-uremic syndrome may follow EHEC infection.

Prevention

The prevention of many *E. coli* enteric infections is ultimately related to basic economic development and adequate sanitary facilities and wide availability of sufficient quality and quantity of water. In the interim, especially in areas where adequate water supplies and sanitary facilities are not available, such measures as breast-feeding for at least 6 to 12 months and hygienic measures like hand washing should reduce the likelihood of acquiring *E. coli* enteric infections. Travelers to developing or tropical areas should avoid drinking untreated or unboiled water or ice and should avoid eating uncooked fruits or vegetables that may have been "freshened" with highly contaminated water. Although a number of antimicrobial agents have been documented to be effective over short periods of time when taken prophylactically, their effectiveness is sharply limited by the rapidly emerging resistance to antimicrobial drugs as well as by the potential side effects of their indiscriminate, widespread use. For example, tetracycline resistance among ETEC is common, and combined trimethroprim-sulfamethoxazole and even some quinolone resistance is rapidly emerging around the world. Finally, currently developing toxoid or colonization factor vaccines hold considerable promise for the prevention of ETEC diarrhea. EHEC infections can be largely prevented by adequately cooking beef, especially hamburger, and by careful hand washing and other hygienic measures in daycare centers and nursing homes.

SUGGESTED READINGS

Annual report of the OzFoodNet network, 2002. Foodborne disease in Australia: incidence, notifications and outbreaks. Commun Dis Intell 2003;27:209–243. *Shiga toxin–producing E. coli and the hemolytic uremic syndrome were much less common than campylobacteriosis, salmonellosis, or shigellosis, but about as common as yersiniosis, typhoid, and listeriosis.*

Bhan MK, Raj P, Levine MM, et al: Enteroaggregative *Escherichia coli* associated with persistent diarrhea in a cohort of rural children in India. J Infect Dis 1989; 159:1061–1064. *A first report of a clinical role for new types of enteroadherent E. coli.*

Carter AO, Borczyk AA, Carlson AK, et al: A severe outbreak of *E. coli* O157:H7 associated hemorrhagic colitis in a nursing home. N Engl J Med 1987;317:1496–1500. *A common source outbreak with secondary probable person-to-person spread of this cause of bloody diarrhea and hemolytic-uremic syndrome in the institutionalized elderly.*

Davis KC, Nakatsu CH, Turco R, et al: Analysis of environmental Escherichia coli isolates for virulence genes using the TaqMan(R) PCR system. J Appl Microbiol 2003;95:612–620. *A new approach to screening for the O157:H7 isolates that are especially pathogenic.*

Guerrant RL, Steiner TS, Lima AAM, et al: How intestinal bacteria cause disease. J Infect Dis 1999;179:S331–S337. *Overview of ways that intestinal bacteria disrupt mucosal function using the different types of E. coli as the paradigm.*

Kosek M, Bern C, Guerrant RL: The global burden of diarrhoeal disease, as estimated from studies published between 1992 and 2000. Bull World Health Organ 2003;81:197–204. *Diarrhea accounted for 21% of all deaths of children under age 5 years in developing countries and was responsible for 2.5 million deaths per year.*

Levine MM: *Escherichia coli* that cause diarrhea: Enterotoxigenic, enteropathogenic, enterohemorrhagic, and enteroadherent. J Infect Dis 1987;155:377–389. *A good overview of major pathogenic mechanisms of E. coli diarrhea.*

Molina PM, Parma AE, Sanz ME: Survival in acidic and alcoholic medium of Shiga toxin-producing Escherichia coli O157:H7 and non-O157:H7 isolated in Argentina. BMC Microbiol 2003;3:17. *This bacteria is surprisingly resistant to 6% ethanol and to pH as low as 2.5.*

Nataro JP Kaper JB: Diarrheagenic *Escherichia coli.* Clin Microbiol Rev 1998;11:142–201. *Excellent overview of recent advances regarding the pathogenesis of diarrheagenic E. coli infections.*

Steiner TS, Lima AAM, Nataro JP, et al: Enteroaggregative *Escherichia coli* produce intestinal inflammation and growth impairment and cause interleukin-8 release from intestinal epithelial cells. J Infect Dis 1998;177:88–96. *First report of emerging enteroaggregative E. coli causing inflammation and malnutrition as well as diarrhea in children in the tropics.*

330 THE DIARRHEA OF TRAVELERS

R. Bradley Sack

Definition

Travelers from the developed world who visit the developing world are highly susceptible to an acute infectious diarrheal illness known as "travelers' diarrhea," or by more colorful names that fit the locale in which the travelers find themselves incapacitated. The primary etiologic agents of this syndrome are the same as those that cause endemic diarrheal illness, primarily in children, throughout the areas of the world in which sanitation is less than optimal. Travelers (Chapter 300) from sanitized, developed countries are, in a sense, immunologically naive "children" who are suddenly transported to an endemic area of infection, where they are highly susceptible to the local pathogens. Other than during a common-source outbreak of diarrheal disease (e.g., a gross fecal contamination of a water supply), the attack rates among travelers are the highest known in any identifiable population. From 25 to 50% of travelers experience a diarrheal illness during their first 3 weeks of stay in a developing country; this decreases markedly thereafter as immunity develops.

By way of contrast, travelers from developing countries who visit other developing countries usually have a considerably lower attack rate, owing to their prior exposure and subsequent immunity to these organisms. As expected, these same visitors who visit the developed world do not develop the illness.

Etiology

Multiple studies have described the causes of this syndrome throughout the world, and it is clear that enterotoxigenic *Escherichia coli* is the most common pathogen. Other bacteria, viruses, and protozoa are also involved, but with lesser frequency (Table 330–1). In certain localities and in certain seasons, the prevalence of *Campylobacter* or *Salmonella* may be particularly high. Even now, a considerable proportion of episodes (20 to 30%) cannot be diagnosed microbiologically, and new etiologic organisms continue to be discovered. Contrary to "popular" notions, relatively few cases of travelers' diarrhea are caused by *Entamoeba histolytica* or *Giardia lamblia.*

Clinical Manifestations

The clinical syndrome of travelers' diarrhea is typically that of a nonfebrile, secretory, watery diarrhea that is produced by the enterotoxins of bacteria, particularly *E. coli* (Chapter 329). The watery diarrhea usually lasts 2 to 4 days and, when most severe, may result in 15 to 20 evacuations per day, with significant water and electrolyte loss, leading to clinical signs of dehydration. The vast majority of illnesses are much milder, however, consisting of only three to five diarrheal stools per day, and are important

Table 330–1 • ETIOLOGIC AGENTS OF TRAVELERS' DIARRHEA

AGENT	PERCENTAGE
Enterotoxigenic *Escherichia coli*	20–50
Enteroaggregative *E. coli*	5–15
Shigella	5–10
*Salmonella**	<5
*Campylobacter**	<5
Rotavirus	<5
Giardia lamblia	<3
Entamoeba histolytica	<3
Cryptosporidium	<5
*Cyclospora**	<1
Others[†]	<1
Unknown agents	20–30

*May be higher in certain geographic areas, particularly Thailand.
[†]Includes Shiga toxin–producing *E. coli, Vibrio cholerae,* noncholera vibrios, other viruses, and microsporidia.

primarily because they limit the activities of the traveler. Episodes due to invasive bacteria, such as *Shigella* or *Campylobacter,* may be dysentery-like, with abdominal pain, fever, and blood in the stool (Chapter 326).

Nearly all episodes are self-limited, but a few (<3%) may become persistent and require evaluation after the return home. Some of these prolonged episodes may be due to infection with *E. histolytica, Giardia lamblia,* or *Cyclospora,* an intracellular coccidian protozoan most recently found in the developing world.

Transmission

Transmission of the enteric pathogens occurs almost exclusively through fecally contaminated food and water. Of highest risk to the traveler are foods that are not cooked or peeled, foods obtained from roadside vendors, or foods kept unrefrigerated for long periods of time.

 ## Treatment

Although the diarrhea is usually always self-limited, specific antimicrobials have been shown to significantly shorten the illness and therefore are recommended. Self-treatment is the optimum method for all but the most severe diarrheas. The traveler must therefore be instructed by the physician in the recognition of the illness and when to use the medications that he or she carries. One aim of self-treatment is to avoid visits to local medical practitioners, who may provide less than adequate advice and medications. Treatment includes fluid replacement, specific antimicrobial therapy directed against the most likely causative agents, and, if necessary, symptomatic therapy directed at relieving the frequency of stooling and abdominal cramps.

Fluids may be replaced by increasing the amount of liquids ingested, such as soup and fruit juices, if the diarrhea is mild. For more severe diarrhea, an oral glucose (or rice-based) electrolyte solution, which has been developed to treat all dehydrating diarrheas regardless of etiologic agent or age of the patient, should be taken. This solution is available commercially in packets; the traveler can carry and use them as required by mixing the contents with appropriate volumes of potable water.

In many controlled studies, a short course (1 to 3 days) of appropriate antimicrobial agents has been shown to significantly shorten the disease to 12 to 24 hours. Because the antibacterial spectrum of the fluoroquinolones includes *Campylobacter,* these drugs provide the broadest spectrum of antibacterial coverage against the disease. It should be noted that antimicrobial resistance is, however, now appearing in *Campylobacter* as well. Ciprofloxacin 500 mg twice daily is the most widely used drug, although many of the other fluoroquinolones (e.g., norfloxacin, ofloxacin, fleroxacin), aztreonam, and azithromycin) have been shown to be equally effective. Other antimicrobials drugs that have been used, such as trimethoprim-sulfamethoxazole and doxycycline, are now less effective because of increased antimicrobial resistance.

Additionally, symptomatic therapy with antimotility agents, such as loperamide, given along with the antimicrobials, has been shown to shorten the illness even further and can be recommended, particularly where speed of recovery is important, such as on long bus rides or for critical appointments. Recent studies have shown that a single dose of antimicrobial plus treatment with loperamide is highly effective.

Bismuth subsalicylate (BSS) also has been shown to give significant but less striking symptomatic improvement, although the exact mechanism of action is unknown. Kaolin-pectin preparations are of no significant effect in treatment.

Prevention

Because the modes of transmission are known, prudent attention to the ingestion of uncontaminated food and water should entirely prevent the disease. This has been shown in the military or on board cruise ships, where all food is hygienically prepared and packaged. For the usual traveler, however, food must be obtained from local

sources and contamination cannot be entirely prevented. Even the "best" hotels in the developing world may have unsanitary kitchens, and "first class" travelers are therefore not exempt.

Many studies have now shown that a number of antimicrobials can prevent 80 to 90% of diarrheal episodes when taken daily during short-term travel (<3 weeks). Medication is begun on the day before reaching the locale and discontinued on the day after leaving. The antimicrobial agents that have been well studied and are recommended are also the ones that are used for treatment: norfloxacin and ciprofloxan. Other antimicrobial agents also have been used successfully (i.e., erythromycin, mecillinam, trimethoprim) but have not been tested as extensively. Doxycycline, which was the earliest antimicrobial agent shown to be effective, is no longer recommended because of a marked increase in antibiotic resistance of enterotoxigenic *E. coli.* A nonantimicrobial drug, BSS, taken four times a day, also has given a significant but lesser degree (approximately 60%) of protection.

When to give antimicrobial agents prophylactically and when to rely on early patient-initiated treatment is subject to differing opinions. The decisions should be based on the following considerations. It is known that all persons who travel to developing countries, regardless of whether they are taking antimicrobial agents, have an alteration in their microbial gut flora, which includes acquiring antibiotic-resistant bacteria. Furthermore, antimicrobial agents are widely available without prescription in most developing countries and are used widely; therefore, the contribution of tourists taking antibiotics to the local microbial ecology is probably negligible. The major concern of giving antimicrobial agents prophylactically is the possibility of side effects. Although adverse effects are known to be infrequent, some travelers will experience them. Contraindications to prophylactic antimicrobials include known allergies, pregnancy, and young age. Therefore, the following suggestions are made: travelers should be on short-term visits (<3 weeks), they should request the use of antimicrobial agents, and they should be able to understand and accept the risk of possible side effects. Certain travelers with medical illnesses, for whom an episode of diarrhea would be particularly deleterious, also may be given special consideration for prophylaxis. For the great majority of travelers, the more widely recommended strategy is to have them carry the medicines and self-administer them on recognition of the onset of illness.

The problem of travelers' diarrhea will continue until the general sanitation of the developing world approaches that of industrialized countries or until effective vaccines against the major diarrheal pathogens become available. (Vaccines against both enterotoxigenic *E. coli* and *Shigella* are being field-tested.) However, this common syndrome will need to be addressed for some time to come. Fortunately, this can now be done rationally and effectively based on our knowledge of causes and modes of transmission.

SUGGESTED READINGS

Diemert DJ: Prevention and self-treatment of travelers' diarrhea. Prim Care 2002;29:843–855. *Practical suggestions for patients.*

Ericsson CD, DuPont HL, Steffen R (eds): Travelers' Diarrhea. London, BC Decker, 2003. *A comprehensive text on the subject.*

331 *YERSINIA* INFECTIONS

J. Glenn Morris, Jr.

The genus *Yersinia* contains at least 10 species that have been isolated from humans. *Y. enterocolitica, Y. pseudotuberculosis,* and *Y. pestis* (the causative agent of plague) are well-recognized human pathogens; diseases associated with each of these three species are described in detail in this chapter. Within the past 20 years, DNA hybridization and other studies have resulted in the delineation of seven additional "*Y. enterocolitica*-like" species: *Y. frederiksenii, Y. kristensenii, Y. intermedia, Y. aldovae, Y. mollaretii* (formerly biogroup 3A of *Y. enterocolitica*), *Y. bercovieri* (formerly biogroup 3B of *Y. enterocolitica*), and *Y. rhodei.* These seven species carry antigens that in some instances are identical to those of *Y. enterocolitica* strains (allowing strains to be serotyped with *Y. enterocolitica* typing sera) and may be identified as *Y. enterocolitica* in some laboratory identification systems. It remains controversial as to whether these species do, indeed, cause human

Infectious Diseases

illness, although there are suggestions that they can be pathogenic in AIDS patients and other immunocompromised hosts.

YERSINIA ENTEROCOLITICA

Definition

Y. enterocolitica is a gram-negative bacillus within the family Enterobacteriaceae. It is an enteric pathogen that can cause gastroenteritis, mesenteric adenitis and ileitis ("pseudoappendicitis"), and sepsis. Infection may also trigger a variety of autoimmune phenomena, including reactive arthritis.

Distribution and Epidemiology

Y. enterocolitica is widely distributed in the environment (especially in cooler, temperate regions) and frequently colonizes wild and domestic animals. The organism is a common pharyngeal commensal in swine, with potentially pathogenic strains isolated from 25 to 90% of pork tongues after slaughter. Fifty-eight per cent of Y. enterocolitica infections in Belgium (which has one of the highest rates of Y. enterocolitica disease in the world) have been attributed to eating raw pork; in the United States, illness has been associated with home preparation of chitterlings. Y. enterocolitica outbreaks have also been linked with milk, in which the organism grows at refrigerator temperatures. Y. enterocolitica may be introduced into a household by pets or by symptomatic or asymptomatic human carriers. Once the organism is present within a household, infants and young children appear to be at greatest risk for infection.

In parts of Canada and western Europe, Y. enterocolitica rivals *Salmonella* and surpasses *Shigella* as a cause of acute diarrheal disease. In the United States, isolation rates from diarrheal stool samples are somewhat lower, generally between 5 and 10% of those for *Salmonella*. Isolation rates tend to be much lower in tropical areas. In one study in Bangladesh, Y. enterocolitica was isolated from only 0.06% of diarrheal stool samples from children younger than age 7 years; this very low rate may reflect both the decreased frequency of environmental isolation outside of cold areas and the dietary restrictions limiting pork consumption in Moslem countries.

Pathogenesis

Y. enterocolitica is an intracellular pathogen. It invades and survives within macrophages and may persist and grow within lymph nodes and other lymphoid tissue for extended periods. It can also produce one or more protein enterotoxins, which may contribute to the diarrheal disease caused by the organism. Autoimmune phenomena occurring after Y. enterocolitica infections appear to be due to cross-reactivity between host and bacterial antigens; several putative target antigens are under active investigation, including bacterial antigens that may cross-react with the HLA-B27 antigen.

Human illness is most commonly associated with Y. enterocolitica strains in serogroups (O:3, O:5,27, O:8, O:9, and others) and biogroups (1B, 2, 3, 4) that carry specific plasmid and chromosomal virulence genes.

Clinical Manifestations

The most common clinical manifestation of Y. enterocolitica infection is diarrhea, frequently accompanied by abdominal pain and fever; vomiting occurs in 20 to 40% of cases. Diarrhea is mild to moderate in severity and may last 1 to 2 weeks. As many as 10 to 20% of patients are reported to have bloody diarrhea.

Abdominal pain may be quite severe, mimicking appendicitis, and may occur in the absence of diarrhea. This has resulted in several outbreaks of "pseudoappendicitis" associated with transmission of Y. enterocolitica in a common food item. In one recent U.S. study, 25% of cases of "granulomatous appendicitis" were attributed to *Yersinia* infections, based on polymerase chain reaction (PCR) studies.

Y. enterocolitica can cause pharyngitis (8% of Y. enterocolitica cases identified in one large, multistate outbreak), hepatic and splenic abscesses, peritonitis, and septicemia. Sepsis has been closely linked with iron overload states (and the administration of deferoxamine, used in treating iron overload) and with the presence of underlying conditions such as cirrhosis, chronic renal failure, diabetes, and immunosuppression. Y. enterocolitica sepsis has been reported in association with transfusion of red blood cell units contaminated with the organism. Very young infants (<3 months) with intestinal Y. enterocolitica infections appear to have an increased susceptibility to septicemia; these infants may or may not be febrile and may have protein-losing enteropathy and failure to thrive.

Infection with Y. enterocolitica can trigger myriad autoimmune processes, most notably erythema nodosum and a reactive polyarthritis. Arthritis generally occurs within 1 to 2 weeks of onset of gastrointestinal symptoms, usually in HLA-B27–positive patients. Viable organisms cannot be cultured from involved joints. However, *Yersinia* antigens have been identified in synovial fluid cells and peripheral blood mononuclear cells. Y. enterocolitica infections have also been implicated in the development of Reiter's syndrome, carditis, glomerulonephritis, Graves' disease, and Hashimoto's thyroiditis.

Diagnosis

Diagnosis is based on isolation of the organism from stool, blood, or other clinical specimen. Although not generally available in the United States, serologic diagnosis of Y. enterocolitica infections is widely used in Europe.

Treatment

Available data do not indicate that antimicrobial therapy is efficacious in cases of uncomplicated Y. enterocolitica enteritis, but it is indicated in systemic disease or focal extraintestinal infection. Y. enterocolitica strains are susceptible in vitro to aminoglycosides, chloramphenicol, tetracycline, trimethoprim-sulfamethoxazole, third-generation cephalosporins, and quinolones; isolates are resistant to penicillins and first-generation cephalosporins. Data suggest that fluoroquinolones are the drug of choice for extraintestinal Y. enterocolitica infections, in combination with a third-generation cephalosporin such as cefotaxime in severe cases. There are conflicting data on whether fluoroquinolone therapy has an impact on postinfectious complications.

Prognosis

Most cases of Y. enterocolitica enteritis are self-limited, and recovery is complete. Mortality rates among persons with Y. enterocolitica sepsis were originally reported to exceed 50%. In more recent studies, with aggressive antimicrobial therapy and supportive care, mortality has been approximately 7.5%. Arthritis may persist for a period of months (mean of 3.2 months in one study), with mild residual symptoms occurring in 50% of patients; 1 to 2% develop chronic arthritis.

YERSINIA PSEUDOTUBERCULOSIS

Y. pseudotuberculosis is most commonly recognized as a cause of mesenteric adenitis. Cases of enteritis in children have been reported from Japan (Izumi fever), and septicemia is seen in patients who have underlying liver disease or immunosuppression. The organism is widely distributed in the environment (including water from wells and mountain springs in endemic areas) and is carried by wild and domestic animals. Secondary immunologic complications, such as erythema nodosum, arthritis, and renal insufficiency, have also been observed; in one recent Korean study, 14% of affected children had acute renal failure. Antibiotic use does not appear to influence the occurrence of postinfectious complications.

YERSINIA PESTIS (PLAGUE)

Definition

Y. pestis is the etiologic agent for plague. The most common clinical form is bubonic plague, or acute regional lymphadenitis;

septicemic and pneumonic forms also occur. Epidemics of plague have had a major impact on human history. Whereas cases today are confined largely to isolated endemic foci, recent outbreaks in Madagascar, India, Peru, Ecuador, and East Africa highlight the continued potential for human transmission. The 1994 plague outbreak in India underscored the profound psychological impact that the diagnosis of plague can have on a community, with the early reports of pneumonic plague cases in Surat resulting in over 600,000 of the estimated population of 2 million fleeing the city. Plague has also received increasing recent public and public health attention because of concerns about its potential as a bioterrorism agent.

Distribution and Epidemiology

Among rodent populations, plague is spread by transmission from rodents to fleas and back to rodents (sylvatic plague). Soil can also be contaminated by infected dead fleas and rodents; rodents coming from noninfected areas can become infected when they dig burrows in previously infected areas. This cycle may be relatively stable (enzootic) or may result in periodic epidemics (epizootics) in susceptible rodent populations. Humans are an accidental host in this natural cycle, with cases occurring when infected fleas bite people, or after direct contact or skin inoculation with body fluids of an infected animal (including wild carnivores, rabbits, and cats and dogs). Climatic factors that influence rodent populations may, in turn, have an impact on incidence of human disease in endemic areas.

Direct, person-to-person transmission occurs only in the setting of pneumonic plague. Available data suggest that the risk of person-to-person spread of pneumonic plague is relatively low. Transmission is via respiratory droplet, and appears to require close contact.

In the United States, plague is found west of the 100th meridian, which runs from North Dakota to Texas. Animals most commonly involved have included ground squirrels, rock squirrels, and prairie dogs. From 1947 through 1999, a total of 412 cases of plague were reported to the Centers for Disease Control and Prevention. Approximately one third of recent cases have occurred in Native Americans; this is presumably a function of lifestyle, which may involve herding animals, assisted by dogs, in enzootic areas. Between 1977 and 1998, there were 23 U.S. cases in which cats were implicated as the probable source of infection; it is possible that some of these cases represented pneumonic transmission of the organism from the cat to the affected human.

Clinical Manifestations

Plague presents most commonly as an acute regional lymphadenitis, or bubonic plague. Symptoms generally occur after an incubation period of 2 to 6 days. Illness is marked by the sudden onset of fever, chills, weakness, and headache. Then, or shortly thereafter, patients note an intensely painful swelling in one region of lymph nodes, usually the groin, axilla, or neck. This swelling, or bubo, is typically oval, varying from 1 to 10 cm in length; the overlying skin is elevated and warm and may appear stretched or erythematous. The bubo itself is firm, extremely tender to palpation, and nonfluctuant. Patients with bubonic plague usually do not have skin lesions. However, in studies in Vietnam, about one fourth of patients had pustules, vesicles, eschars, or papules near the bubo or in areas drained by the affected nodes; these were presumed to represent sites of flea bite inoculations.

In the absence of therapy, disease may progress rapidly to a septicemic phase, with marked toxicity, prostration, and shock. The white blood cell count is elevated, and evidence of disseminated intravascular coagulation may appear. Purpura may be seen, associated with vasculitis and thrombosis. Some patients do not develop a bubo and progress directly to septicemia (septicemic plague). Diagnosis in these cases may be particularly difficult, because initial symptoms are relatively nonspecific (fever, headache, sore throat, malaise, myalgia, nausea, diarrhea, vomiting).

One of the feared complications of plague is plague pneumonia. This may occur either as secondary pneumonia, resulting from hematogenous spread of *Y. pestis* to the lung, or as primary plague pneumonia. Patients develop cough and chest pain and may have hemoptysis. Radiographically, there is patchy bronchopneumonia or confluent consolidation. Sputum is purulent and contains the etiologic organism. Plague meningitis is a rarer complication; it typically occurs more than a week after inadequately treated bubonic plague but may be seen as a primary manifestation, without associated lymphadenopathy.

There have been recent concerns about the potential for use of *Y. pestis* as an aerosolized bioterrorism weapon. In such cases, onset of fever, cough, chest pain, and hemoptysis might be expected within 1 to 6 days of exposure, associated with signs of severe pneumonia. Disease might be expected to evolve rapidly within the next 2 to 4 days, leading to septic shock with high mortality in the absence of early treatment.

Diagnosis

Plague can be diagnosed by isolating *Y. pestis* from blood, from an aspirate of a bubo, or from sputum. A presumptive diagnosis can be made in the appropriate clinical setting by demonstrating (by Gram stain or fluorescent antibody) characteristic organisms in sputum or in an aspirate of the bubo. F1 antigen enzyme-linked immunosorbent assay (ELISA) and dipstick assays have been developed, with the F1 dipstick assay for sputum providing a rapid means of diagnosing pneumonic plague.

Rx Treatment and Prognosis

In the absence of therapy, plague has an estimated mortality of more than 50%; untreated primary septicemic or pneumonic plague is almost invariably fatal. Fatality rates of up to 22% continue to be reported in the United States, owing primarily to delays in initiation of appropriate therapy. Because of this, therapy should be started immediately if the diagnosis of plague is suspected.

Streptomycin was the first drug to be shown to have activity against plague, and, in the absence of controlled trials with other agents, it remains the drug of choice. Chloramphenicol and tetracycline are thought to be acceptable alternative therapies. Animal studies suggest that other aminoglycosides and the fluoroquinolones (ciprofloxacin, ofloxacin) may also be effective. Penicillin and first-generation cephalosporins are not effective, are associated with a high mortality, and should not be used. There has been one report from Madagascar of isolation of a *Y. pestis* strain resistant to multiple "first-line" antibiotics (including streptomycin, chloramphenicol, tetracycline, and sulfonamides), emphasizing the need for routine testing of antimicrobial susceptibility of isolates. Aggressive supportive care is essential for patients in shock or with disseminated intravascular coagulation.

Table 331–1 provides recommendations for treatment and for postexposure prophylaxis in both contained and mass casualty settings.

Prevention

All suspected plague cases should be reported immediately to local health authorities. Patients with bubonic plague (with no cough and a normal chest radiograph) should be placed on drainage secretion precautions; if any evidence of pneumonic involvement is present, patients should be placed in respiratory (droplet) isolation. Isolation should be maintained for a minimum of 3 days after starting appropriate antimicrobial therapy. Clinical samples must be carefully handled to minimize the risk of skin contact or aerosolization of the organism. Close contacts of suspected or confirmed plague pneumonia cases (including medical personnel) should be provided with chemoprophylaxis with tetracycline or sulfonamides.

Persons living in endemic areas should be advised to protect themselves against rodents and fleas; this includes measures designed to reduce rodent populations near homes and application of insecticides, as necessary, to control flea populations. Veterinarians should be aware of the potential risk of transmission from infected cats. A formalin-killed vaccine, plague vaccine, is commercially available. Its use is recommended for persons traveling to epidemic areas, for individuals who must live and work in close contact with wild rodents, and for laboratory workers who must handle *Y. pestis* cultures. However, there are data suggesting that the vaccine has limited efficacy in

Table 331–1 • WORKING GROUP RECOMMENDATIONS FOR TREATMENT OF PATIENTS WITH PNEUMONIC PLAGUE IN THE CONTAINED AND MASS CASUALTY SETTINGS AND FOR POSTEXPOSURE PROPHYLAXIS*

PATIENT CATEGORY	RECOMMENDED THERAPY
CONTAINED CASUALTY SETTING	
Adults	Preferred choices
	Streptomycin, 1 g IM twice daily
	Gentamicin, 5 mg/kg IM or IV once daily or 2-mg/kg loading dose followed by 1.7 mg/kg IM or IV 3 times daily[†]
	Alternative choices
	Doxycycline, 100 mg IV twice daily or 200 mg IV once daily
	Ciprofloxacin, 400 mg IV twice daily[‡]
	Chloramphenicol, 25 mg/kg IV 4 times daily[§]
Children[‖]	Preferred choices
	Streptomycin, 15 mg/kg IM twice daily (maximum daily dose, 2 g)
	Gentamicin, 2.5 mg/kg IM or IV 3 times daily[†]
	Alternative choices
	Doxycycline,
	If ≥45 kg, give adult dosage
	If <45 kg, give 2.2 mg/kg IV twice daily (maximum, 200 mg/d)
	Ciprofloxacin, 15 mg/kg IV twice daily[†]
	Chloramphenicol, 25 mg/kg IV 4 times daily[§]
Pregnant women[¶]	Preferred choice
	Gentamicin, 5 mg/kg IM or IV once daily or 2-mg/kg loading dose followed by 1.7 mg/kg IM or IV 3 times daily[†]
	Alternative choices
	Doxycycline, 100 mg IV twice daily or 200 mg IV once daily
	Ciprofloxacin, 400 mg IV twice daily[‡]
MASS CASUALTY SETTING AND POSTEXPOSURE PROPHYLAXIS#	
Adults	Preferred choices
	Doxycycline, 100 mg orally twice daily[††]
	Ciprofloxacin, 500 mg orally twice daily[‡]
	Alternative choice
	Chloramphenicol, 25 mg/kg orally 4 times daily[§**]
Children[‖]	Preferred choices
	Doxycycline,[††]
	If ≥45 kg, give adult dosage
	If <45 kg, then give 2.2 mg/kg orally twice daily
	Ciprofloxacin, 20 mg/kg orally twice daily
	Alternative choices
	Chloramphenicol, 25 mg/kg orally 4 times daily[§**]
Pregnant women[¶]	Preferred choices
	Doxycycline, 100 mg orally twice daily[††]
	Ciprofloxacin, 500 mg orally twice daily
	Alternative choices
	Chloramphenicol, 25 mg/kg orally 4 times daily[§**]

*These are consensus recommendations of the Working Group on Civilian Biodefense and are not necessarily approved by the Food and Drug Administration. One antimicrobial agent should be selected. Therapy should be continued for 10 days. Oral therapy should be substituted when patient's condition improves. IM = intramuscularly; IV = intravenously.

[†]Aminoglycosides must be adjusted according to renal function. Evidence suggests that gentamicin, 5 mg/kg IM or IV once daily, would be efficacious in children, although this is not yet widely accepted in clinical practice. Neonates up to 1 week of age and premature infants should receive gentamicin, 2.5 mg/kg IV twice daily.

[‡]Other fluoroquinolones can be substituted at doses appropriate for age. Ciprofloxacin dosage should not exceed 1 g/d in children.

[§]Concentration should be maintained between 5 and 20 μg/mL. Concentrations greater than 25 μg/mL can cause reversible bone marrow suppression.

[‖]In children, ciprofloxacin dose should not exceed 1 g/d, chloramphenicol should not exceed 4 g/d. Children younger than 2 years should not receive chloramphenicol.

[¶]In neonates, gentamicin loading dose of 4 mg/kg should be given initially.

#Duration of treatment of plague in mass casualty setting is 10 days. Duration of postexposure prophylaxis to prevent plague infection is 7 days.

**Children younger than 2 years should not receive chloramphenicol. Oral formulation available only outside the United States.

[††]Tetracycline could be substituted for doxycycline.

Adapted from Inglesby TV, Dennis DT, Henderson DA, et al: Plague as a biological weapon: Medical and public health management. Working Group on Civilian Biodefense. JAMA 2000;283:2281–2290.

prevention of pneumonic plague. Protection against pneumonic forms may be provided by new, subunit vaccines (based on the F1- and V-antigens) that are under active development.

SUGGESTED READINGS

Abdel-Haq NM, Asmar BI, Abuhammour WM, et al: *Yersinia enterocolitica* infection in children. Pediatr Infect Dis J 2000;19:954–958. *A review of the epidemiology and clinical features of 142 children infected with Y. enterocolitica during a 7-year period.*

Crook LD, Tempest B: Plague: A clinical review of 27 cases. Arch Intern Med 1992;152:1253–1256. *A description of 27 plague cases seen at the Gallup, New Mexico, Indian Medical Center between 1965 and 1989; 19 patients had bubonic plague and 8 had septicemic plague.*

Frean J, Klugman KP, Arntzen L, et al: Susceptibility of Yersinia pestis to novel and conventional antimicrobial agents. J Antimicrob Chemother 2003;52:294–296. *The most active agents were cefditoren and the fluoroquinolones, both conventional and novel.*

Inglesby TV, Dennis DT, Henderson DA, et al: Plague as a biological weapon: Medical and public health management. Working Group on Civilian Biodefense. JAMA 2000;283:2281–2290. *A review of the potential for use of plague in bioterrorism, including recommendations regarding appropriate management of such events.*

Neubauer HK, Sprague LD: Epidemiology and diagnostics of Yersinia infections. Adv Exp Med Biol 2003;529:431–438. *A comprehensive review.*

Ratsitorahina M, Chanteau S, Rahalison L, et al: Epidemiological and diagnostic aspects of the outbreak of pneumonic plague in Madagascar. Lancet 2000;355:111–113.

332 TULAREMIA

William Schaffner

Definition

Tularemia is an infectious zoonosis caused by a small aerobic pleomorphic gram-negative bacillus, *Francisella tularensis*. Many animal species may harbor the organism, most prominently rabbits, squirrels, and muskrats. Humans acquire the infection through various means: direct contact with infected animal tissues, ingestion of contaminated water or meat, from the bite of an infected tick or deer fly, or by breathing an aerosol of bacteria. Although *F. tularensis* is highly infectious and is a well-recognized risk to laboratory personnel manipulating culture plates of the organism, it is something of a paradox that the illness is not communicable from person to person.

The original description of a typhoidal disease following the ingestion of hare meat was made in Japan in 1837. In the United States in 1906 McCoy was alert to the possibility of outbreaks of bubonic plague following the large earthquake in San Francisco when he came on a plague-like illness in ground squirrels. His persistent efforts culminated in the first isolation of the responsible organism that he named *Bacterium tularense* after Tulare County, California, where he had found the ill squirrels. Edward Francis subsequently established that deer flies could transmit the infection from animals to humans and provided detailed descriptions of its clinical manifestations. In recognition, the genus name of the organism was changed to *Francisella* in 1959. Colloquially, the disease often is referred to as "rabbit fever" or "deer fly fever."

Epidemiology

Tularemia occurs only in the Northern Hemisphere; it has been reported from the United States, Canada, Mexico, Japan, and Europe, particularly Scandinavia but not from the United Kingdom. In the United States, reported cases have diminished during the second half of the 20th century from a high of 2291 cases in 1939 to the approximately 125 cases reported annually at present. Tularemia has occurred in all the continental states, but four states account for 56% of reported cases: Arkansas, Missouri, Oklahoma, and South Dakota. The island of Martha's Vineyard off the coast of Massachusetts also is a focus of tularemia.

In the United States, tularemia usually is acquired from tick bites or from contact with infected animals, especially rabbits. Tick-associated cases now constitute the majority and occur during the summer. The most common vectors in the United States are the wood tick (*Dermacentor andersoni*), the dog tick (*D. variabilis*) and the Lone Star tick (*Amblyomma americanum*). A smaller peak of autumn-winter cases is a consequence of rabbit hunting when hunters skin and eviscerate their game. Public health education materials directed at hunters to reduce the hazard of handling wild animals have contributed to the reduction of tularemia among hunters. Mosquitoes are the common vectors in northern Europe. Occasional individuals acquire infection from the bite of an infected animal or, more likely, from the bite of an animal whose mouth was contaminated from recently eating a diseased animal. The latter explains most instances of cat-bite tularemia.

Males experience a higher incidence of disease than females in all age groups, likely as a consequence of their greater exposure to outdoor and animal-related activity and less use of protective measures against tick bites. Persons in all age groups are affected, with children aged 5 to 14 years of age and older adults most prominently represented. In the United States, American Indians/Alaska natives experience the highest annual incidence (0.5 per 100,000); whites have a lower risk (0.04 per 100,000) and African Americans and Asians/Pacific Islanders the lowest occurrence of tularemia (≤ 0.01 per 100,000).

Although tularemia usually is a sporadic infection, outbreaks of disease have been traced to laboratory exposure, contaminated ground water, muskrat handling, lawn mowing, and brush cutting. In the latter, primary pneumonic tularemia apparently occurred when the affected individuals created an environmental aerosol by mowing grass and brush that had been contaminated with *F. tularensis* excreted in the urine and feces of infected rodents. The organism can survive in water, mud, and straw for weeks to months.

Recently, interest in tularemia has been enhanced because of its potential use as a bioterrorist agent. Its high infectivity (as few as 10 organisms have induced pneumonic disease), ease of dissemination, and the difficulty in rapid diagnosis of acute illness have long made it attractive to students of biowarfare. Thus, tularemia is a disease that is reportable immediately to local public health authorities. Unusual patterns of disease will be investigated for both conventional and bioterrorist sources.

Pathobiology

The organism occurs in two major subspecies (biovars). *F. tularensis* biovar *tularensis* (type A) is the more virulent in animals and humans, has distinctive biochemical reactions (it produces acid from glycerol and has citrulline ureidase activity), and is the common North American biovar. In contrast, *F. tularensis* biovar *palaearctica* (type B) is less virulent and occurs commonly in Europe and Asia. Specific virulence factors of *F. tularensis* have not been identified.

F. tularensis can infect humans through several portals of entry including the skin, mucous membranes, and the gastrointestinal and respiratory tracts. It requires intracellular residence and can multiply within macrophages and other cells. After inoculation into the skin and subcutaneous tissues, local bacterial multiplication occurs that evokes a suppurative necrotic reaction characterized by an initial polymorphonuclear response followed by an influx of macrophages and lymphocytes. These suppurative lesions evolve into granulomas. Bacteremia may occur both early and late during this process. The infection may disseminate to the lymph nodes, liver, spleen, lungs, and pleura. Viable *F. tularensis* can persist in tissues for long periods and contribute to the tendency to relapse after treatment.

Clinical Manifestations

Classically, the clinical presentations of tularemia have been separated into six categories: ulceroglandular, glandular, oculoglandular, typhoidal, oropharyngeal, and pneumonic. Although this classification has venerable historic roots, it ought not be employed rigidly; many patients have features of several types. The course of illness is determined by the portal of entry, the degree of systemic involvement, and the dose and virulence of the infecting strain of *F. tularensis*.

The general features of tularemia are similar regardless of the portal of entry. After exposure, the usual incubation period is 3 to 5 days (range, 1 to 21 days). The disease begins abruptly with the onset of fever (≥101° F), chills, malaise, and headache. Myalgia, vomiting, sore throat, and abdominal pain also may occur. Almost half the patients have a pulse rate that is substantially slower than would be anticipated from the height of the fever (a "pulse-temperature dissociation"). The fever may abate somewhat after 1 to 3 days, only to recur and continue along with other symptoms for 2 to 3 weeks. Untreated, weight loss, easy fatigue, and lymphadenopathy may persist for weeks longer.

Ulceroglandular disease is the form of the infection most readily recognized by most physicians. Along with fever and other constitutional symptoms, the patient calls attention to tender, swollen lymph nodes that drain an inoculation site. The nodes are usually axillary or inguinal and a local lesion appears concurrently or just 1 or 2 days before or after the lymphadenopathy. The lesions at the site of inoculation begin as small, red, tender, or painful papules that progress to pustules and then undergo necrosis to produce an ulcer with sharp, somewhat elevated edges and a flat base that becomes black. Untreated, the ulcers heal over weeks, leaving a scar. Tick-induced infections produce lesions on the trunk, about the waist, and in the perineum along with the expected local adenopathy. Children typically have occipital and cervical adenopathy from tick bites on the neck and in the hair. Animal exposures often produce lesions on the hands and forearms. Lesions may be multiple. Because the organisms evoke a localized granulomatous response, frank lymphangitis does not occur in uncomplicated tularemia, but an occasional patient manifests a chain of nodules in "sporotrichoid" fashion along the lymphatic drainage.

Patients with such apparently "localized" disease often have symptoms and findings indicating that they actually have a more widespread infection. Sore throat, with or without an erythematous pharynx, occurs as well as chest radiographic findings of patchy infiltrates in the lower lobes, pleural effusions, and hilar adenopathy.

Glandular disease is essentially the same clinical syndrome but without the local lesion. Thus, the patient presents with fever, constitutional symptoms, and lymphadenopathy. The local lesion may have been on a part of the body where it was not seen or it may have been small and already healed when the patient sought medical care. It accounts only for 3 to 20% of cases. Typhoidal disease does not evidence lymphadenopathy and presents essentially as a fever of unknown etiology. These illnesses evade diagnosis unless the physician specifically considers the possibility of tularemia and inquires about tick or animal exposure. Occasionally the diagnosis is made fortuitously when a positive blood culture is reported.

Oculoglandular disease is rare (<5% of cases) and occurs when the conjunctival sac is the portal of entry via an aerosol, splash, or contaminated fingers. It is almost always unilateral and can have a dramatic presentation with inflamed, swollen eyelids, chemosis, and painful conjunctivitis. The palpebral conjunctiva often shows small yellow nodules and ulcers, counterparts to the skin lesions of ulceroglandular disease. The affected regional lymph nodes are those of the head and neck.

Oropharyngeal disease also is uncommon in the United States and occurs when the mucous membranes of the mouth and pharynx are the portal of entry. Contaminated water or food (inadequately cooked game meats) is the source. Painful exudative pharyngitis and tonsillitis, pharyngeal ulcers, and swollen retropharyngeal and cervical lymph nodes are seen.

Although other tularemic syndromes may have pneumonia as an aspect of the total illness, *pneumonic tularemia* refers to an illness that presents as a distinctive pneumonia. It accounts for about 10% of reported cases and occurs from an inhalational exposure. It is the form of the disease that would be the consequence of a bioterrorist event. In addition to fever and malaise, patients may have a dry cough, substernal discomfort, pleural pain, dyspnea, and sore throat. These pulmonary symptoms may not be very prominent in the context of the systemic illness. Hemoptysis is unlikely. The results of physical examination reflect the extent and distribution of the pneumonic process that may range from barely evident to frank consolidation with pleural effusion. The radiographic findings range from modest peribronchial infiltrates early in the illness to distinctive bronchopneumonia with effusion. Hilar adenopathy is present in more than a third of cases. Sputum examination is not helpful. Pleural effusions usually contain more than 1000 lymphocytes per cubic millimeter. Gram stains are negative and pleural biopsies may occasionally contain granuloma, inviting confusion with tuberculosis. Without a suggestive history of tick or animal exposure, patients with tularemic pneumonia may be considered to have poorly responding community-acquired pneumonia. The common use of fluoroquinolone antibiotics as empirical therapy in this circumstance undoubtedly has treated some patients with undiagnosed tularemia pneumonia.

Infectious Diseases

Diagnosis

The differential diagnosis of patients with tularemia is substantial. The local lesions can be confused with cat-scratch disease, brown recluse spider bites, *Mycobacterium marinum* infections, herpes simplex infections, and even syphilis and chancroid when the lesions are in the perineum or on the penis. Pneumonic tularemia resembles common community-acquired pneumonia as well as less common infections such as psittacosis, legionellosis, and Q fever. The glandular and typhoidal forms can resemble typhoid fever, brucellosis, ehrlichiosis, and other illnesses that present as nonspecific fevers.

Routine laboratory studies do not provide specific results. Leukocyte counts may be within normal limits or elevated; thrombocytopenia, elevated liver enzymes, and sterile pyuria occur with some frequency. *F. tularensis* may be isolated from blood cultures and tissue specimens when media containing cysteine are employed. Laboratory personnel should be notified when tularemia is suspected so that appropriate media can be employed and also to ensure that safeguards are in place to protect against the production of hazardous aerosols.

The diagnosis of tularemia usually employs serologic testing using tube agglutination or microagglutination techniques. Antibody levels do not reach diagnostic levels until after the 11th day of illness. A single acute titer of 1:160 is considered presumptive; a confirmed diagnosis requires a fourfold rise in titer between acute and convalescent specimens. Titers of both IgM and IgG antibodies may remain elevated for many years after the illness.

Rx Treatment

Because tularemia is a relatively uncommon disease, therapeutic recommendations are based on a combination of in vitro studies and accumulated clinical experience. The preferred antimicrobials are streptomycin or gentamicin, either for 10 days. Streptomycin is given as 1 g intramuscularly (IM) twice daily. Gentamicin may be more readily available and is administered 5 mg/kg IM or intravenously (IV) once daily. Both chloramphenicol and the tetracyclines have been used in the past to treat tularemia; however, use of both of these bacteriostatic agents has resulted in higher rates of relapse than with streptomycin or gentamicin treatment. Because chloramphenicol may produce bone marrow toxicity, it is rarely used today. Doxycycline is administered 100 mg IV twice daily for 14 days. In recent years ciprofloxacin has been used successfully in a growing number of patients; it is given 400 mg IV twice daily for 10 days. Both these drugs may be switched to oral administration in the same doses as soon as tolerated by the patient.

Prevention

The prevention of tularemia entails minimizing exposure to ticks and avoidance of direct exposure to wild animals. Tick protection includes clothing that extends to the wrists and ankles, regular inspection for attached ticks, and the use of insect repellents containing diethyltoluamide (DEET). Gloves should be worn when skinning and dressing game animals, especially rabbits, and all wild rabbit and other game meats should be cooked thoroughly.

A live, attenuated vaccine has been used in the past to provide some protection to researchers working with *F. tularensis*. The vaccine is not available commercially.

Prognosis

Before treatment became available, acute tularemia often lasted as long as a month with several subsequent months of debility. Mortality approached 10%. When appropriately diagnosed and treated, the mortality from tularemia is now 1% or less.

Future Directions

The current awareness of tularemia as a possible bioweapon has stimulated new research into this disease and its pathogenesis. Emphasis will be placed on developing rapid diagnostic tests and a new vaccine and identifying virulence factors.

SUGGESTED READINGS

Dennis DT, Inglesby TV, Henderson DA, et al: Tularemia as a biological weapon: Medical and public health management. JAMA 2001;285:2763–2773. *Tularemia in an ominous new light.*

Ellis J, Oyston PCF, Green M, Titball RW: Tularemia. Clin Microbiol Rev 2002;15:631–646. *A comprehensive introduction to pathogenesis.*

Evans ME, Gregory DW, Schaffner W, McGee ZA: Tularemia: A 30-year experience with 88 cases. Medicine 1985;64:251–269. *A comprehensive summary of the clinical presentations of tularemia.*

Feldman KA, Enscore RE, Lathrop SL, et al: An outbreak of primary pneumonic tularemia on Martha's Vineyard. N Engl J Med 2001;345:1601–1606. *A clever and rigorous public health investigation of an unexpected outbreak of a rare disease.*

Haristoy X, Lozniewski A, Tram C, et al: *Francisella tularensis* bacteremia. J Clin Microbiol 2003;41:2774–2776. *An excellent example of the precision of modern molecular diagnostic methods.*

333 ANTHRAX

Jonas A. Shulman
Henry M. Blumberg

Definition

Anthrax is a zoonotic disease caused by *Bacillus anthracis*, a large, gram-positive, spore-forming bacillus transmitted to humans by contact with infected animals or contaminated animal products. Other names for anthrax include woolsorter's disease, Siberian ulcer, malignant pustule, charbon, malignant edema, and ragsorter's disease. In 1877, Koch described *B. anthracis* as one of the first microbes identified as a cause of specific disease, making anthrax the prototype for Koch's postulates and the first disease to satisfy them. Anthrax had all but disappeared from North America, Western Europe, and Australia until the 2001–2002 outbreak of inhalational anthrax that occurred as a result of a major episode of bioterrorism in the United States. This outbreak is described further in other portions of this chapter.

Anthrax had been nearly eradicated in livestock in North America and Western Europe by extensive veterinary programs, including vaccination. The disease remains prevalent in many developing countries, especially Asia, Africa, and Central America, where livestock are only marginally subjected to veterinary control and where environmental conditions are favorable for an animal-to-soil-to-animal cycle.

Anthrax occurs primarily in herbivorous animals, especially cattle, goats, and sheep, but many other animals, including pigs, buffalo, and elephants have also been infected. Cattle are particularly susceptible to the systemic form of anthrax, which clinically progresses to death in 24 to 48 hours. The large numbers of organisms found in infected cattle may contaminate the animal and its products and environs, thereby allowing infection to occur in animals more resistant to anthrax, such as humans.

The primary forms of anthrax in humans are cutaneous, inhalation, gastrointestinal, and oropharyngeal. Septicemia and meningitis may occur from any of these primary foci. Until the 2001–2002 outbreak, by far the most common form of the disease in the United States was the cutaneous lesion, which accounted for more than 95% of clinical cases. Inhalation anthrax had occurred only rarely in the United States during the 25 years before the 2001–2002 episode, and gastrointestinal anthrax had never been reported in this country. In the 2001–2002 outbreak, 23 cases of human anthrax were reported in the United States, and all were the result of bioterrorism. Eleven of these cases were of the inhalational type, 12 were cutaneous. Many other individuals in the United States were affected by this outbreak, including large groups of people that requested evaluation for colonization or disease and placement on antibiotic prophylaxis and others affected because of spore contamination of their working environments.

Etiology

Bacillus anthracis is a large (1 to 1.3 × 3 to 8 μm), gram-positive, nonmotile, aerobic, spore-forming bacillus. Although spores of *B. anthracis* do not form in living tissue, they are induced by aerobic conditions in the external environment and may persist for years in the soil, in animal products, or in an appropriate industrial setting. The organism grows well aerobically on ordinary laboratory media at 35° to 37°C. The colonies produced are especially sticky (i.e., positive tenacity test and positive strand of pearls test results), and they have a tendency to stand up in stalagmite fashion when lifted with a bacteriologic loop. The gray-white colonies are nonhemolytic, rough, and flat, with many comma-shaped outgrowths on blood agar. Microscopic examination of organisms growing on artificial media shows long, parallel chains of organisms that are frequently described as having a rather characteristic boxcar appearance. Spores are oval and occur centrally or paracentrally but cause no swelling of the bacillus. Material from fresh lesions contains single or short chains of two or three bacilli, which may appear encapsulated with slightly rounded ends.

Anthrax organisms can be differentiated from the saprophytic *Bacillus* species by fluorescent antibody staining, antibiotic sensitivity testing, lysis with a specific γ bacteriophage, and virulence in mice, guinea pigs, and rabbits. Parenteral inoculation into these species results in death in 1 to 3 days.

Incidence and Prevalence

B. anthracis is a soil organism that has worldwide distribution. Animal anthrax is endemic in some areas of Asia, Africa, and Latin America, especially in rural regions that have inadequate animal vaccination programs and inadequate animal husbandry. These areas also are more likely to have a number of human cases. Certain areas within the United States and other parts of the world may provide a particularly favorable environment for large numbers of resistant spores to survive in the soil for many years. Several epizootics related to focal regions of heavily contaminated soil have occurred.

Because no reliable reporting of anthrax exists and the diagnosis may never by made in many instances, the worldwide incidence of anthrax is unknown. Estimates in the past have ranged between 20,000 and 100,000 human cases per year, but the rate has more recently been estimated at 2000 to 20,000 cases per annum. In the United States, approximately one case of human anthrax per year was reported between 1970 and 1985 and zero to one cases per year from 1985 until 2001, with only three cases documented between 1984 and 2000. Reports of human anthrax during that time demonstrated that anthrax had been seen frequently in Turkey, Pakistan, Iran, Haiti, and several Asian and African countries. There are probably many parts of the world with significant endemic problems but from which data are not available.

Apart from the possible use of anthrax as a bioterrorist's weapon, the potential for large outbreaks among animals and humans continues to exist, especially where economic or political upheaval is present. One of the largest epidemics of anthrax was reported in Zimbabwe between 1978 and 1980, when nearly 10,000 human cases of cutaneous anthrax and a few cases of gastrointestinal anthrax occurred, resulting in approximately 100 deaths. This outbreak was related to an extensive epizootic infection in cattle. Another major outbreak of anthrax occurred in Sverdlovsk, USSR, in 1979. It was initially thought by some to be related to the ingestion and handling of infected "black market" meat. The source of anthrax in the cattle in this Soviet epidemic was initially reported to be a single 29-ton lot of bone meal used as animal feed. The bone meal was thought to have been made from the bones of animals that had died of anthrax in the previous year. Later data suggest that this outbreak was not related to contaminated meat but was related to inhalational anthrax contracted by the airborne spread of anthrax spores that were being developed for biological warfare in a nearby Soviet biologic warfare facility where an explosion occurred. This Siberian inhalation outbreak accounted for approximately 96 cases and 64 deaths. Later polymerase chain reaction (PCR) analysis of tissue samples from 11 victims of this outbreak identified multiple strains of *B. anthracis* in each sample, consistent with infection by a manufactured preparation of bacterial spores.

Rare cases of inhalation anthrax have developed in workers exposed to aerosolized anthrax spores generated during the processing of contaminated materials such as woolens, hides, or bone meal and even more uncommonly in people who have been in the vicinity of a wool-processing mill or tannery but who were not directly involved in the processing of the product. Cases have even been reported in home weavers, such as those using contaminated goat yarn, or in individuals working with contaminated bone meal fertilizer.

Before the recent outbreak in the United States, the average annual occurrence of human anthrax had become negligible. From 1977 to 1988, the average number of cases was only 0.8, compared with the 127 cases reported to occur annually between 1916 and 1925. The case-fatality rate of the 221 U.S. cases of cutaneous anthrax from 1955 through 1986 was approximately 5.0% (11 of 221), whereas the case-fatality rate was 82% (9 of 11) among patients with inhalation anthrax. The overall mortality rate for the 232 American cases of anthrax was 8.6%.

In the 2001–2002 outbreak, 23 cases of inhalational (11) and cutaneous anthrax (12) occurred. These cases were related to weapons-grade anthrax spores that had been sent through the United States Postal Service and handled by a variety of postal workers, individuals opening the mail, and individuals in their working environments. These cases occurred in clusters and could not be ascribed to any of the usual sources of acquisition of anthrax. Although the individual or group responsible for the bioterrorism episode has not been identified, there was no doubt that bioterrorism was the source of this epidemic.

Epidemiology

Cases of anthrax are classified generally as agricultural or industrial. Bioterrorism probably represents a new epidemiologic classification. Most of the agricultural cases of human anthrax result from direct contact with discharges from infected animals. Occasionally, human cases have been transmitted by bites of flies that have fed on the carcasses of animals that died of anthrax. Others have been caused by ingestion of poorly cooked or raw infected meat. Industrial cases usually result from contact with anthrax spores contaminating animal products, such as goat hair, wool, hides, and skin, and with animal bones, especially those imported from areas of high endemicity. Transmission usually occurs during the processing of these animal products by direct contact with the contaminated raw material or by indirect contact with a contaminated environment; rarely, transmission may occur from airborne particles produced during the manufacturing process. Because the *B. anthracis* spores can survive for long periods, a wide variety of unusual products have been associated with human infection, such as imported bongo drums made with goat skins, shaving brushes, various leather or woolen blankets, and ivory piano keys. Laboratory-acquired infections have been reported; however, human-to-human transmission of anthrax is not thought to occur.

Before the 2001–2002 outbreak, most cases of anthrax in the United States were sporadic, but epidemics had been reported occasionally. In 1957, a large and serious epidemic of inhalational anthrax occurred in New Hampshire, where nine employees of a textile mill acquired anthrax while processing a batch of contaminated goat hair imported from Asia. This outbreak included four cutaneous cases and five inhalation cases, with four fatalities reported in the later group. The 23 cases in the 2001–2002 episode constituted the largest epidemic seen in a century in the United States. The mortality rates were 45% for 11 inhalational cases and 0% for the 12 cutaneous cases.

Pathogenesis

The major virulence factors of *B. anthracis* are encoded on two plasmids, pXO1 and pXO2. Both plasmids are required for full virulence of *B. anthracis*. The small capsule-bearing plasmid, pXO2, is 95 kilobase pairs and is responsible for the synthesis of a polyglutamyl capsule that interferes with phagocytosis. The toxin-bearing plasmid, pXO1, is 184 kilobase pairs and codes for the genes that make up the excreted exotoxins. The toxin gene complex is composed of protective antigen (PA), lethal factor (LF), and edema factor (EF). PA can bind to host cell receptor sites, allowing the complexes (PB-LF and PF-EF) to enter cells and create a sequence of events that has deadly consequences.

The combination of PA and EF causes local edema, whereas the combination of PA and LF can cause overwhelming toxemia and death in as little as 60 minutes in some animal models. None of these toxins, when administered alone without PA, has any biologic effect in experimental animals. The edema produced by EF is related to the factor's ability to increase the level of cyclic AMP and thereby affect water homeostasis. EF is a calmodulin-dependent adenylate cyclase. LT is a zinc metalloprotease that cleaves specific kinases, which may then induce cell lysis. LT stimulates the production of interleukin-β and tumor necrosis factor-α, as well as superoxides and a variety of other cytokines. Strains of *B. anthracis* must contain both plasmids, pXO1 and pXO2, to be virulent.

In cutaneous anthrax, the organism is introduced through a wound or by means of infected animal fibers that disrupt the skin. The organism is not known to penetrate intact skin. Once in the subcutaneous tissue, the anthrax spore is thought to germinate, multiply, and produce its exotoxin and the antiphagocytic capsular material. The toxins are capable of provoking a marked edematous response and tissue necrosis with a paucity of neutrophil invasion. Phagocytosis of the organisms by local macrophages occurs, and the bacilli are then spread to regional lymph nodes, where further production of toxins produces a hemorrhagic, necrotic, and edematous lymphadenitis. Bacilli may enter the circulation, sometimes producing meningitis, pneumonia, and systemic toxicity. The macrophages seem to play a particularly important role in the potential spread of the organism to other sources and in the production of a variety of cytokines that are capable of causing severe local and systemic inflammatory responses.

In the past, a person presenting with inhalation anthrax has been an uncommon event. In an era in which bioterrorism exists, anthrax spores may be manipulated to be more readily spread by the airborne route and be made more antibiotic resistant. In the past, the mortality rate for inhalation anthrax was between 90 and 100% in most clinical descriptions. In the most recent U.S. outbreak, the mortality rate was 45% for the inhalation anthrax cases. Before the 2001–2002 outbreak, inhalation anthrax was considered essentially obsolete in the United States, although this form of the disease still is considered significant in many parts of the world because of traditional, nonterrorist epidemiologic sources. The recent epidemic in the United States has heightened concerns about the use of *B. anthracis* as a biological weapon for the production of inhalation anthrax with its attendant high mortality rate and demands that physicians recognize the disease promptly.

Inhalation anthrax, also known as woolsorter's disease, usually occurs by inhalation of an aerosol of spores with a particle size less than 5 μm, not as a result of direct contact with infected animals. These aerosols, unless produced specifically for purposes of bioterrorism, usually occur during processing of contaminated material. In humans, spores are inhaled, reach the alveoli, and may eventually be phagocytized by macrophages and carried by these cells to the mediastinal lymph nodes. Germination, growth, and toxin formation at this site can produce severe, massive hemorrhagic lymphadenitis and mediastinitis. *B. anthracis* may also directly affect the pulmonary capillary endothelium, causing thrombosis and respiratory failure. Pleural effusion, which may become hemorrhagic, is common. Anthrax does not cause a primary pneumonia, but secondary bacterial pneumonia may complicate inhalation anthrax. *B. anthracis* may also enter the blood stream from this site, with the evolution of intense bacteremia. In some instances, the number of organisms per milliliter of blood may be so great that the organism may be seen on smears of the peripheral blood. Hemorrhagic meningitis may ensue and was seen in one of the inhala-

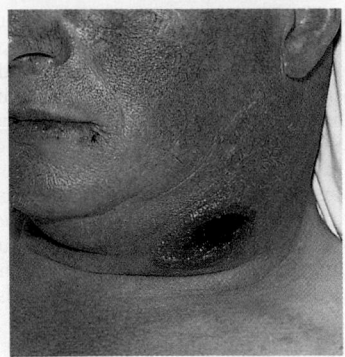

FIGURE 333–1 • Anthrax. A single, malignant pustule in a typical position on the neck. The patient was a porter who carried animal hides over his shoulders. (From Forbes CD, Jackson WF: Color Atlas and Text of Clinical Medicine, 3rd ed. London, Mosby, 2003.)

tion cases in the recent U.S. epidemic. Respiratory failure, shock, and pulmonary edema are frequent causes of death. Autopsy usually reveals hemorrhagic necrosis of the thoracic lymph nodes, drainage from the lungs, and hemorrhagic mediastinitis.

Ingestion of markedly contaminated, poorly cooked meat may result in the oropharyngeal or the gastrointestinal form of infection. When oropharyngeal anthrax occurs, there is localized swelling of the pharynx, sometimes causing tracheal obstruction, and marked cervical adenopathy with overlying brawny edema. Similarly, the organism may reach the small and large intestines and cause a gastrointestinal syndrome. In this case, the spores that are deposited in the submucosa of the intestinal tract may germinate, multiply, and produce toxin, resulting in marked edema, hemorrhage, and necrosis. Regional mesenteric lymphadenopathy is common, and findings associated with the syndrome include fever, vomiting, abdominal pain and distention, massive bloody diarrhea, mesenteric adenitis, hemorrhagic ascites, and septicemia. Gastrointestinal anthrax is a very severe form of the disease, has a high mortality rate (25 to 75%), and is rarely diagnosed during life except in the setting of an epidemic.

Although antimicrobial agents may rapidly eradicate the organism, the persistence of the toxin that has been produced may result in continued development of the disease process until the toxin is metabolized. Although the mortality rate may be somewhat diminished by appropriate antibiotic therapy, especially in the cutaneous form of the disease, the clinical process may continue to progress even after the institution of antimicrobial therapy. Antitoxins have been tried in the past, but such antitoxins are currently unavailable. Newer efforts to block toxin production or to affect its entry into cells or its action are being actively investigated.

Clinical Manifestations

Forms of the disease include cutaneous anthrax, gastrointestinal and oropharyngeal anthrax, inhalational anthrax, and anthrax meningitis, which may occur as a result of bacteremia after inhalational or cutaneous anthrax.

CUTANEOUS ANTHRAX. Cutaneous anthrax accounts for more than 95% of naturally occurring disease due to *B. anthracis*; the naturally occurring cases are primarily caused by occupational exposure, such as to goats, cows, or sheep or their products. In the bioterrorism-related anthrax cases that occurred in the United States in October and November 2001, 12 (50%) of the 23 cases were cutaneous anthrax (7 confirmed and 4 suspected); all were associated with contaminated mail with the exception of one case that occured in a laboratory worker. Cutaneous anthrax occurs as a result of direct contact with *B. anthracis*. After an incubation period of 1 to 12 days, the infection usually begins with a small, somewhat pruritic papule at the site of an abrasion, which over the next several days develops into a vesicle containing serosanguineous fluid teeming with organisms (Fig. 333–1). For naturally occurring disease, the lesion generally occurs on the upper extremities, especially the arms and hands, or on the face, neck, or other areas that are likely to be exposed to the contaminated animal product or infected soil. As the lesion progresses, ulceration occurs, with formation of a necrotic ulcer base that is frequently surrounded by smaller vesicles. The characteristic black

eschar evolves over several weeks to a size of several centimeters, gradually separating and leaving a scar (Fig. 333–2). This black eschar accounts for the name *anthrax*, which comes from the Greek word for coal. The edema is frequently nonpitting, gelatinous, and brawny and is quite striking. It may be extensive, spreading over a wide area in severe cases. With involvement near the eye, periorbital swelling may be especially intense. The edema may be so dramatic that hypotension occurs in part because of the loss of intravascular volume as fluid enters the subcutaneous tissues. This edema, in combination with the vesicle progressing to the necrotic, black eschar, forms the lesion that is highly characteristic of anthrax. Despite the dramatic appearance of the lesion, it is frequently painless. Most patients with the localized cutaneous lesion have minimal constitutional findings, such as fever, malaise, myalgias, and headaches. In those with extensive edema, the systemic symptoms may be more severe. Localized lymphadenopathy may occur and may be complicated by bacteremia and meningitis. Bacteremia is a rare complication of cutaneous anthrax, and death is rare if appropriate antimicrobial therapy is instituted; in untreated cases of cutaneous anthrax, however, the mortality rate can be as high as 20 to 25%.

The differential diagnosis for cutaneous anthrax includes the bite of a brown recluse spider, erysipelas, cellulitis, rickettsialpox, cat scratch disease, ecthyma gangrenosum, localized herpesvirus

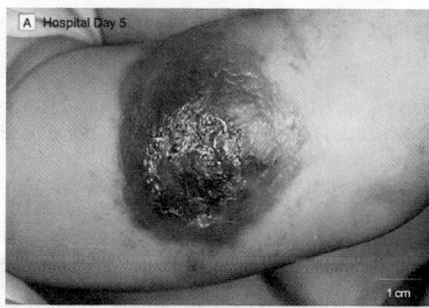
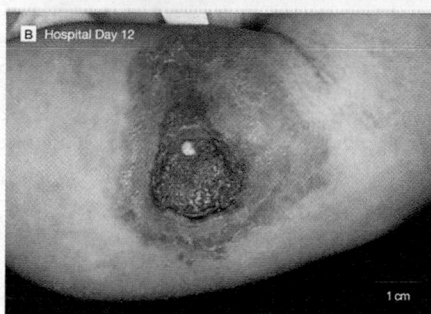
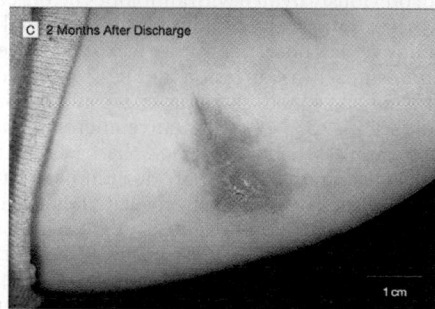

FIGURE 333–2 • The lesion of cutaneous anthrax. (From Freedman A, Freedman A, Afonja O, et al: Cutaneous anthrax associated with micro-angiopathic hemolytic anemia and coagulopathy in a 7-month-old infant. JAMA 2002;287:869–874.)

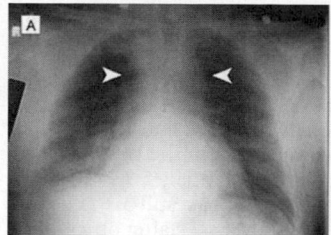
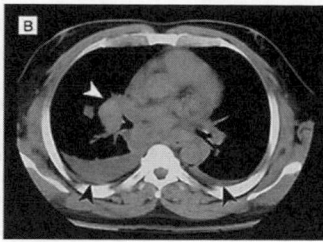

FIGURE 333–3 • *A*, Portable chest radiograph of 56-year-old man with inhalational anthrax depicts a widened mediastinum (white arrowheads), bilateral hilar fullness, a right pleural effusion, and bilateral perihilar airspace disease. *B*, Noncontrast spiral CT scan depicts an enlarged and hyperdense right hilar lymph node (white arrowhead), bilateral pleural effusions (black arrowheads), and edema of the mediastinal fat. (From Mayer TA, Bersoff-Matcha S, et al: Clinical presentation of inhalational anthrax following bioterrorism exposure. JAMA 2001;286:2549–2543.)

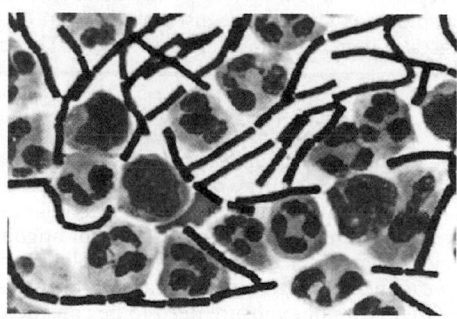

FIGURE 333–4 • Gram stain of cerebrospinal fluid shows *Bacillus anthracis*. (From Jernigan JA, Stephens DS, Ashford DA, et al: Bioterrorism-related inhalational anthrax: The first 10 cases reported in the United States. Emerg Infect Dis 2001;7:933–944.)

infection, bacterial adenitis due to staphylococci and streptococci, plague, and ulceroglandular tularemia.

The diagnosis of cutaneous anthrax is rarely be missed if the disease is considered in any patient who has had exposure to an appropriate animal or animal product and who develops a painless ulcer surrounded by small vesicles, along with marked edema and eschar formation. Given the anthrax attacks in the United States that followed the events of September 11, 2001, bioterrorism-related cases (with anthrax spore contaminates on letters or other inanimate sources) also should be considered. If prior antibiotic therapy has not been given, Gram stains of the vesicular fluid and lesion usually readily demonstrate the characteristic gram-positive bacilli, because the organisms are present in large numbers in these lesions and are readily isolated by culture. Informing the bacteriology laboratory of the possibility of the diagnosis of anthrax is important to prevent the organism from being discarded as merely a probable contaminant or other *Bacillus* species, which is frequently not fully characterized. Alternative tests that are suggested in the event of a negative culture and when there is clinical suspicion include biopsy for silver stain and specialized immunohistochemical testing and serologic tests.

INHALATIONAL ANTHRAX. Historically, inhalation anthrax had been a rare, usually fatal, occupational disease in the United States. Before October 2001, there had only been 18 reported cases in the United States in the past 100 years, and the most recent case had occurred in 1976. Between October and November 2001, there were 11 bioterrorism-related cases of inhalational anthrax in the United States. Based on data from the Sverdlovsk outbreak in the former Soviet Union caused by the accidental release of anthrax spores from a bioweapons facility, the incubation period was 2 to 42 days. For 9 of the 11 U.S. bioterrorism-related inhalational anthrax patients for whom the time

of exposure is known, the incubation period was 4 to 6 days. The illness is generally biphasic in its presentation, although the two phases can blend and be indistinguishable. Initially, a brief, nonspecific, influenza-like illness occurs, manifested by fever, fatigue, myalgias, malaise, a nonproductive cough, drenching sweats, and possibly some chest discomfort. Few physical findings are identified at this time; however, within several days after a short period of clinical improvement, the patient becomes much more ill. The second phase is manifested by severe dyspnea, fever, and shock; other manifestations can include cyanosis, hypoxia, hemoptysis, stridor, chest pain, and diaphoresis. Physical examination may reveal some crepitant rales and evidence of pleural effusions. Some subcutaneous, brawny edema of the chest wall and neck may be noticed. The median leukocyte count of U.S. bioterrorism-related patients was 9800 cells/mm³, and the peak white blood cell count was 26,400 cells/mm³. The chest radiographs of these patients revealed characteristic mediastinal widening (Fig. 333–3); pulmonary infiltrates may or may not be present and were identified in 7 of the 10 U.S. patients. Pleural effusions usually occur and characteristically are hemorrhagic. Computed tomography (CT) findings include hyperdense (hemorrhagic) mediastinal and hilar lymph nodes, mediastinal edema, and pleural effusions. Blood cultures are almost always positive if obtained before the initiation of antibiotic therapy. Factors that may be useful in distinguishing inhalational anthrax from other infections include the link to an epidemiologic source (e.g., mail exposure in the 2001 outbreak) with a short incubation period (4 to 6 days); clinical features that include a lack of coryza, presence of drenching sweats and gastrointestinal symptoms, chest radiograph and CT showing typical mediastinal changes and pleural effusions; fulminant progression to shock in a previously healthy person; and established

Continued

Infectious Diseases

or suspected isolation of *B. anthracis* in cultures of patients with a clinical syndrome consistent with inhalational anthrax.

Historically mortality for this disease has been extremely high even with the use of effective therapy; 16 (89%) of the 18 patients reported with inhalational anthrax between 1900 and 1976 died. In the 2001–2002 bioterrorism-related outbreak in the United States, mortality was notably lower but still substantial; 5 (45%) of 11 patients died. Anthrax meningitis may occur as a result of bacteremia after inhalational anthrax and is almost never seen after other forms of anthrax. With meningitis, cerebral spinal fluid is frequently hemorrhagic, and there is a polymorphonuclear pleocytosis. Numerous, large, encapsulated, gram-positive bacilli are present (Fig. 333–4). Anthrax meningitis is usually fatal.

In the past, inhalation anthrax could be considered in patients with appropriate exposure to an animal product, as in a weaver using imported goat hair or a textile mill worker. However, such occupational exposure to animals or animal products resulting in inhalational anthrax has not been seen in more than 25 years in the United States. The finding of inhalational anthrax in the United States is almost diagnostic of a bioterrorism event. Suspected or proven cases should be reported immediately to public health officials. A high index of suspicion is critical, because any delay in diagnosis and treatment greatly increases the likelihood of a fatal outcome.

GASTROINTESTINAL ANTHRAX. Gastrointestinal anthrax is a rare disease that occurs 2 to 5 days after the ingestion of undercooked meat that contains anthrax spores; there are some cases in which a more prolonged incubation period has been postulated. The diagnosis is rarely suspected before death, except in areas where anthrax is highly endemic and in which multiple human cases are occurring. The symptoms include severe abdominal pain, hematemesis, melena, rapid onset of ascites, and occasionally, marked diarrhea. Paracentesis may reveal hemorrhagic ascites, and these cases sometimes simulate an acute or surgical abdomen. Mesenteric lymphadenitis usually occurs with gastrointestinal anthrax. The primary lesions are ulcerative and occur most frequently in the terminal ileum or cecum. The disease usually progresses to bacteremia, toxemia, shock, and eventually death in more than 50% of patients. No cases of intestinal anthrax have been reported in the United States. The deposition and germination of spores in the oropharynx can result in oropharyngeal anthrax, which manifests as severe sore throat with neck swelling, adenopathy, dysphagia, and sometimes with tracheal compression and dyspnea. Cervical and submandibular lymphadenopathy is common, and oral or pharyngeal ulcers covered with a pseudomembrane may be seen. Bacteremia and its complications may ensue.

Diagnosis

In the past, the diagnosis of anthrax was made on the basis of clinical findings and the history of exposure to animal products, especially those that originated outside of the United States. After the 2001 bioterrorism-related episode and because of ongoing concern about biologic warfare or a terrorist attack involving the airborne delivery of weaponized anthrax spores capable of widespread dissemination, other types of exposure need to be considered by clinicians when patients present with signs or symptoms suggesting anthrax. Suspected or proven cases of anthrax should be reported immediately to the institution's hospital epidemiologist and infection control department, as well as to local and state public health officials. The differential diagnosis for cutaneous anthrax was previously discussed. Inhalation anthrax should be considered in the differential diagnosis in a patient with a widened mediastinum, hemorrhagic pleural effusions, or associated hemorrhagic meningitis.

Ordinarily, Gram stains of sputum and sputum cultures do not demonstrate *B. anthracis*; however, these patients frequently do develop bacteremia, and the organism can be readily isolated from blood (if the patient was not previously treated with antibiotics before cultures were obtained) and sometimes seen on stains of the peripheral blood.

The presumptive diagnosis of anthrax is based on the finding on the gram-positive smear of a skin lesion (i.e., vesicular fluid or eschar), cerebrospinal fluid, or blood showing encapsulated, large, gram-positive bacilli (see Fig. 333–4). A tentative microbial diagnosis can be made in most clinical laboratories on the basis of the recovery of gram-positive bacilli that are spore forming, nonmotile, nonhemolytic, penicillin sensitive, and encapsulated. Specialized testing such as phage γ lysis, detection of capsule and cell-wall antigens by direct fluorescent antibody, *B. anthracis*–specific PCR, or serologic tests can be used to make a definitive diagnosis; these tests are generally only available at state public health laboratories in the Laboratory Response Network or the Centers for Disease Control and Prevention (CDC).

Antibody detection in the serum may also be helpful as a diagnostic test, especially in patients who have received antibiotics before obtaining specimens for culture. A CDC report mentioned the utility of an enzyme-linked immunosorbent assay (ELISA) for IgG antibodies to *B. anthracis* PA in human serum in patients with cutaneous and inhalational anthrax.

Rx Treatment

There are no controlled trials for the treatment of inhalational anthrax. After the anthrax attacks of 2001, the CDC published guidelines recommending the use of two or three antibiotics in combination in persons with inhalational anthrax. It is unclear whether the use of two or more antibiotics improves survival, but combination therapy is not an unreasonable approach given the extremely high mortality rate associated with the disease. Another factor supporting the use of multiple drugs is the concern about genetically manipulated strains of *B. anthracis* that could be engineered to be drug resistant.

Essential components of care for patients with inhalational anthrax include the rapid institution of antibiotic therapy and supportive care (i.e., intravascular volume repletion, vasopressors if indicated, and ventilatory support); drainage of large pleural effusions by chest tubes was required in most of the inhalational anthrax cases that occurred in 2001. Adjunctive corticosteroid therapy is a consideration for patients with meningitis and for patients who have severe mediastinal adenopathy and edema.

Ciprofloxacin (initial dose of 400 mg IV every 12 hours) is recommended in combination with one or two additional antimicrobial agents (e.g., doxycycline, rifampin, penicillin, vancomycin, chloramphenicol, imipenem, clindamycin, clarithromycin). Ciprofloxacin has been recommended based on data from animal models suggesting excellent efficacy. Other fluoroquinolones (e.g., levofloxacin, moxifloxacin, gatifloxacin) all have good activity but have not been as well studied. Current drugs that have U.S. Food and Drug Administration (FDA) approval for the treatment of anthrax include ciprofloxacin, doxycycline, and penicillin. In the past, penicillin G was the drug of choice, but its use as a single agent is not recommended because of concerns about activation of an inducible penicillinase in the face of treatment with β-lactams (e.g., penicillin, ampicillin) and because of concerns about poor penetration of β-lactam drugs into macrophages, the site where *B. anthracis* spores germinate. The recommendation for duration of therapy is 60 days; initial intravenous therapy is followed by oral therapy after clinical improvement and resolution of symptoms.

Patients with severe cutaneous disease (e.g., systemic involvement, extensive edema, lesions of the head and neck, age younger than 2 years) should be treated with the regimens described for inhalational anthrax, including the use of intravenous antibiotics and combination therapy. Severe neck swelling may require intubation or tracheostomy. Corticosteroid therapy is sometimes recommended for patients with extensive edema. For patients with localized cutaneous disease without the complications mentioned, oral therapy with ciprofloxacin (500 mg twice daily) or doxycycline (100 mg twice daily) is recommended. Amoxicillin may be used in patients unable to take these two first-line agents. In children and pregnant women, ciprofloxacin or doxycycline are recommended, at least as initial therapy, even though these agents have not typically been used in these patient populations. Previous guidelines had suggested only short courses of therapy for cutaneous anthrax (e.g., 7 to 10 days of penicillin), but much longer courses of therapy have been recommended by the CDC. Concerns about the use of penicillin were described previously. The duration of therapy for cutaneous anthrax related to bioterrorism attacks is recommended to be 60 days because of the likelihood of exposure to aerosolized *B. anthracis* in the persons who developed cutaneous anthrax.

Prevention

Anthrax vaccine adsorbed (AVA) (Bioport Corporation, Lansing, MI), an inactivated, cell-free product, is the only licensed anthrax vaccine in the United States. The vaccine is licensed to be given in a six-dose series (i.e., subcutaneous injections at 0, 2, and 4 weeks; then at 6, 12, and 18 months). Annual booster injections are required if immunity is to be maintained. In 1997, it was mandated that all U.S. military active- and reserve-duty personnel receive the vaccine. The principal antigen responsible for induction of immunity is the PA. Pre-exposure vaccination with AVA has been shown to have efficacy in animal models, including nonhuman primates. The safety of the vaccine has been the subject of much debate and study. An Institute of Medicine (IOM) report in 2002 concluded that AVA is acceptably safe and effective against inhalational anthrax. If given with appropriate antibiotic therapy, the IOM panel reported that AVA might help prevent the development of disease after exposure. The most frequent side effects of the vaccine include local and injection-site reactions (3.6%). Current vaccine supplies are limited, and U.S. production is modest. Because of the complexity of a six-dose primary vaccination schedule and frequency of local or injection-site reactions, studies are under way to assess the immunogenicity of schedules with a reduced number of doses and with intramuscular administration rather than subcutaneous administration. The vaccine has not been approved by the FDA for use as postexposure prophylaxis, but when administered in conjunction with antimicrobial prophylaxis, it is one of three options recommended by the CDC for postexposure prophylaxis in persons thought to have been exposed to anthrax spores.

Postexposure prophylaxis with antibiotics is recommended for persons exposed to aerosolized *B. anthracis* spores. Such exposure could occur after inadvertent exposure in a laboratory setting or a terrorist using biological weapons. Potential exposure to aerosols include inside a laboratory while working with large volumes of *B. anthracis*, textile mills while working with heavily contaminated animal products, or after a terrorism or biological warfare attack. After naturally occurring anthrax among livestock, cutaneous and rare gastrointestinal exposures among humans are possible, but inhalation anthrax has not been reported in these settings. After likely exposure to anthrax spores, the CDC has recommended the use of ciprofloxacin (500 mg every 12 hours for adults) for postexposure prophylaxis; doxycycline (100 mg every 12 hours) can be used if the source strain has been proved to be susceptible. Amoxicillin (500 mg PO every 8 hours) is recommended only after 14 days of initial therapy with ciprofloxacin or doxycycline and only if there is a contraindication to the continued use of the preferred agents such as pregnancy, lactation, age younger than 18 years, or intolerance of other antibiotics. The optimal duration of prophylaxis is uncertain, but 60 days is recommended primarily on the basis of animal studies of anthrax. The CDC recommended three options for postexposure prophylaxis to spores of *B. anthracis*—60 days of antibiotic prophylaxis; 100 days of antibiotic prophylaxis, or 100 days of antibiotic prophylaxis—plus anthrax vaccine as investigational postexposure treatment (i.e., three AVA doses over a 4-week period). Patients exposed to *B. anthracis* also should be washed with soap and water, and personal items should be decontaminated with a 1:10 dilution of household bleach.

Infection control guidelines recommend the use of standard barrier precautions. There are no data to suggest person-to-person transmission of anthrax, and no such cases occurred after the 2001–2002 anthrax attacks. There is no need to immunize or provide prophylaxis to patient contacts (e.g., household contacts, coworkers, health care workers) unless these contacts, like the patient, were exposed to the aerosol or surface contamination at the time of the attack. The hospital epidemiologist and local and state public health officials should be immediately contacted when suspected (or proven) anthrax cases are seen. The clinical microbiology laboratory should also be notified so safe specimen processing can occur under biosafety level 2 conditions. A number of standard hospital disinfectants, including hypochlorite, are effective in cleaning environmental surfaces contaminated with infected body fluids. Proper burial or cremation of humans or animals that have died from anthrax is important in preventing further transmission of disease. If autopsies are preformed, all related instruments and materials should be autoclaved or incinerated. State and local health departments and/or the CDC can provide advice on postmortem procedures in anthrax cases.

SUGGESTED READINGS

Bartlett JG, Inglesby TV Jr, Borio L: Management of anthrax. Clin Infect Dis 2002;35:851–858. *Updated summary of the management of anthrax including the bioterrorism-related outbreak that occurred in 2001.*

Bush LM, Abrams BH, Beall A, Johnson CC: Index case of fatal inhalational anthrax due to bioterrorism in the United States. N Engl J Med 2001;345:1607–1610. *Excellent clinical description of inhalational anthrax with meaningful case histories.*

Centers for Disease Control and Prevention: Use of anthrax vaccine in the United States: Recommendations of the Advisory Committee on Immunization Practices (ACIP). MMWR Morb Mortal Wkly Rep 2000;9(RR-15):1–20. *Current use should be updated by review of CDC website.*

Farrar F: Anthrax: Virulence and vaccines. Ann Intern Med 1994;121:379–380. *Excellent editorial outlining newer molecular biologic features of B. anthracis, the role of virulence factors in pathogenesis of the disease, and new approaches to vaccine development.*

Inglesby TV, O'Toole T, Henderson DA, et al: Anthrax as a biological weapon, 2002: Updated recommendations for management. JAMA 2002;287:2236–2262. *A consensus statement.*

Jernigan DB, Raghunathan PL, Bell BP, et al: Investigation of bioterrorism-related anthrax, United States, 2001: Epidemiologic findings. Emerg Infect Dis 2002;8:1019–1028. Available at: http://www.cdc.gov/ncidod/EID/vol8no10/02–0353.htm. *Excellent review of the U.S. epidemic.*

Joellenbeck LM, Zwanziger LL, Durch JS, Strom BL (eds): The Anthrax Vaccine: Is It Safe? Does It Work? Committee to Assess the Safety and Efficacy of the Anthrax Vaccine. Washington, D.C., Institute of Medicine: National Academy Press, 2002. *Review of currently available anthrax vaccine status.*

Meselson M, Guillemin J, Hugh-Jones M, et al: The Sverdlovsk anthrax outbreak of 1979. Science 1994;266:1202–1208. *An outbreak of inhalational anthrax related to accidental expulsion from a mishap in a biologic warfare facility.*

Quinn CP, Semenova VA, Elie CM, et al: Specific, sensitive, and quantitative enzyme-linked immunosorbent assay for human immunoglobulin G antibodies to anthrax toxin protective antigen. Emerg Infect Dis 2002;8:1103–1110. Available at: http://www.cdc.gov/ncidod/EID/vol8no10/02–0380.htm. *A serologic test of use especially in previously treated potential cases of anthrax or cases with no definitive microbiologic identification of the organism.*

Swartz MN: Recognition and management of anthrax—an update. N Engl J Med 2001;345:1621–1626. *Excellent review article for use by clinicians.*

334 DISEASES CAUSED BY PSEUDOMONADS

Stephen C. Schimpff

The pseudomonads are gram-negative aerobic bacilli that prefer moist environments and are relatively noninvasive yet can cause serious and often fatal infection when host defense mechanisms are damaged or deficient. Many organisms once considered in the genus *Pseudomonas* have been reclassified on the basis of contemporary genetic standards (Table 334–1). *Pseudomonas maltophilia* (RNA group V) became *Xanthomonas maltophilia* over a decade ago and now is known as *Stenotrophomonas maltophilia*, and the RNA group II organisms became *Burkholderia mallei*, *Burkholderia pseudomallei*, *Burkholderia cepacia*, and *Ralstonia pickettii*, respectively. A number of newly appreciated human pathogens are also listed in the table. For convenience, old and new nomenclatures are used here. Each organism is different in its pathogenic properties, each causes somewhat different types of infection, and each invades as a result of different host defense defects; but with each, the environmental source is usually water, moist soil, or a contaminated medical device, infusion, or injection.

Pseudomonads are divided into five major groups on the basis of RNA homology (see Table 334–1). Most human infections are caused by members of groups I, II, and V. For purposes of discussion, this chapter considers *Burkholderia* (*Pseudomonas*) *pseudomallei* (the cause of melioidosis), *Burkholderia mallei* (the cause of glanders), *Pseudomonas aeruginosa* (which principally causes bacteremia, endocarditis, pneumonia, keratitis, and urinary tract infections), and *Burkholderia cepacia*, *Ralstonia pickettii*, and *Stenotrophomonas* (*Pseudomonas*) *maltophilia* (which cause bacteremia, pseudobacteremia, endocarditis, and urinary tract infections).

PSEUDOMONAS AERUGINOSA

The name *aeruginosa* comes from the fluorescent blue-green pigment pyocyanin produced by many, but not all, strains. Like other pseudomonads, *P. aeruginosa* grows well in multiple moist settings with limited nutrients. Found in soil, in water, and on plants, it can also be a normal commensal in animals and humans. Colonization in humans usually takes place in moist areas, such as the perineum, auditory canal, axillae, and the lower alimentary canal. It is commonly found in faucet aerators, sink traps, ice machines, and kitchen

Table 334–1 • **CLASSIFICATION OF PSEUDOMONADS THAT HAVE BEEN ISOLATED FROM CLINICAL SPECIMENS**

GROUP/SUBGROUP	GENUS AND SPECIES
RNA group I	
Pseudomonas	
Fluorescens	*P. aeruginosa*
	P. fluorescens
	P. putida
Others	*P. stutzeri*
	P. alcaligenes
	P. pseudoalcaligenes
	P. mendocina
	Pseudomonas CDC group 1
	P. luteola
	P. oryzihabitans
RNA group II	
Burkholderia	*B.* (formerly *Pseudomonas*) *mallei*
	B. (formerly *Pseudomonas*) *pseudomallei*
	B. gladioli
	B. thailandensis
	Burkholderia (formerly *Pseudomonas*) *cepacia* complex with eight species
Ralstonia	*Ralstonia* (formerly *Pseudomonas* and formerly *Burkholderia*) *pickettii*
	R. mannitolytica
RNA group III	
Comamonas	*P. acidovorans*
	P. testosteroni
Acidovorax	*A. delafieldii*
	A. facilis
RNA group IV	
Brevundimonas	*B.* (formerly *Pseudomonas*) *diminuta*
	B. (formerly *Pseudomonas*) *vesicularis*
RNA group V	
Stenotrophomonas	*S.* (formerly *Xanthomonas* and formerly *Pseudomonas*) *maltophilia*
	R. africana

From Sanford JP: *Pseudomonas* species (including melioidosis and glanders). *In* Mandell GL, Dolin R, Bennett JE (eds): Principles and Practice of Infectious Diseases, 4th ed. New York, Churchill Livingstone, 1995, pp 2003–2009. extensively modified to recognized newly observed clinical pathogens and new nomenclatures of RNA groups II, IV, and V.

settings in the hospital; it can become a particular problem when it contaminates medications or medical devices with a moist environment, such as ventilators, endoscopes, or pressure monitors. It can withstand many disinfectants and is resistant to a broad variety of antimicrobial agents. In the nonhospital setting, infections have been related to growth in swimming pools, contact lens solutions, and hot tubs.

Infection with *P. aeruginosa* has become, to a large degree, a byproduct of medical advances in technology. In the 20 years before 1960 at the Johns Hopkins Hospital, only 91 cases of *P. aeruginosa* bacteremia occurred. More recently, *P. aeruginosa* has been the fourth most common cause of primary nosocomial gram-negative bacteremia and the fourth most frequently isolated nosocomial pathogen, causing about 10% of all hospital-acquired infections nationwide.

The most common infections caused by *P. aeruginosa* include nosocomial bacteremia, nosocomial pneumonia, nosocomial urinary tract infection, surgical wound infection, endocarditis related to intravenous drug abuse or placement of artificial heart valves, respiratory tract infection associated with cystic fibrosis, external otitis (including "malignant" external otitis), corneal keratitis, uncommon occurrences of spinal osteomyelitis in heroin addicts (Chapter 315), and rare cases of meningitis or brain abscess. A common origin of bacteremia in the granulocytopenic patient is infection along the alimentary canal, especially perianal cellulitis, colonic lesions, and, occasionally, pharyngitis or esophagitis. Finally, extensive burns are commonly colonized by *P. aeruginosa*, with progression to sepsis and death.

P. aeruginosa almost never causes infection in the absence of (1) damage to a normal host defense mechanism (e.g., cancer chemotherapy–induced mucosal damage to the alimentary canal, granulocytopenia, or extensive third-degree burns), (2) deficiency or alteration of a defense mechanism (e.g., the progressive respiratory tract changes of cystic fibrosis), or (3) bypass of a normal defense mechanism (e.g.,

respiratory assist device directly inoculating organisms into the bronchial tree while concurrently limiting or damaging the mucociliary mechanism or insertion of an indwelling urinary catheter, circumventing the normal bladder clearance mechanism). Thus, infections with *P. aeruginosa* are seen most commonly in patients with a chronic urinary catheter; those neutropenic from disease, chemotherapy, or both; those with cystic fibrosis; those with extensive thermal injuries; those in the intensive care unit who are subjected to any number of invasive procedures; those with head trauma, allowing entry either directly or by means of a pressure-monitoring device; those with artificial heart valves or damaged endocardium from contaminants in illicit drugs; and those who have had extensive surgery, particularly when there is consequent need for open drainage. Pulmonary infection late in the course of the acquired immunodeficiency syndrome may arise as an acute infection or as an indolent, frequently recurrent infection mimicking that seen with cystic fibrosis.

Pollack has pointed out three distinct stages of *Pseudomonas* infection: stage I, bacterial attachment and colonization; stage II, local invasion; and stage III, blood stream dissemination and systemic disease. Stage I is a prerequisite to stage II, which, in turn, is a prerequisite to stage III, although obviously not all colonized individuals have local invasion and not all those with local invasion progress to dissemination or systemic disease. The three stages relate to the fact that this organism is both invasive and toxigenic. Colonization in a normal person is relatively uncommon at most sites, although, over time, a fair proportion of the population have transient colonization of the colon. Hospitalized patients have a much higher frequency of colonization, related in part to changes in host defenses, as discussed earlier, and in part to the frequency of hospital reservoirs of this organism. In addition, broad-spectrum antimicrobial therapy suppresses other normal microbial flora, especially along the alimentary canal. This suppression reduces the body's normal mechanism of colonization resistance so that an organism such as *P. aeruginosa* or other species resistant to the antibiotics used can more readily colonize multiple locations in high concentration.

Additional specific factors further predispose to colonization by *P. aeruginosa*. These include the presence of pili for attachment, flagella for motility, and exoproducts, especially proteinases. Also involved is the secretory protease–induced loss of fibronectin from epithelial cells during serious illness (among patients hospitalized or not), which in turn allows the pili or fimbriae to adhere to the oral, pharyngeal, and respiratory epithelium. Thus, the illness determinants of protease production are major modulators of the oral flora. This colonization in turn can be accentuated by local damage caused by an endotracheal tube, by viral infection (such as influenza), by thermal injury, or by cancer chemotherapy and is exacerbated by antibiotics. *P. aeruginosa*, in some settings, can help protect itself from defense mechanisms by producing a glycocalyx, a carbohydrate produced by many bacteria, which, by surrounding the cell and anchoring it to epithelial cells or invasive devices such as an intravascular or urinary catheter, protects the bacterium from antibody, complement, and polymorphonuclear leukocytes or macrophages.

After colonization, *P. aeruginosa* can invade in the appropriate setting through the effect of extracellular enzymes, which can act as cellular toxins. These include elastase, alkaline protease, cytotoxin, and hemolysins. Elastase and protease have been demonstrated to cause necrotizing lesions in the skin, lung, and cornea, along with small vessel necrotizing lesions, which cause the characteristic skin finding known as ecthyma gangrenosum. It is this combination of local necrosis and blood vessel destruction that is the essence of the initial invasion characteristic of *P. aeruginosa*. Cytotoxin damages granulocytes and may be involved in initial adult respiratory distress syndrome. Hemolysins are cytotoxic as well, thus augmenting tissue invasion.

The third stage of *Pseudomonas* infection, dissemination and systemic disease, is due, in the first case, to the same extracellular enzymes and, in the second case, to *Pseudomonas* liposaccharide (endotoxin) and exotoxin A. As with other septicemias caused by gram-negative bacilli, endotoxin is thought to be a critical factor in the activation of the clotting, fibrinolytic, kinin, and complement systems, along with the production of prostaglandins and leukotrienes, the release of β-endorphins, and the release of cytokines, including tumor necrosis factor. Some interaction of many or all of these factors results in fever, shock, disseminated intravascular coagulation (which is relatively uncommon with *Pseudomonas* bacteremia), and the adult respiratory distress syndrome. The other factor, exotoxin A, is similar to diphtheria toxin in that it inhibits protein synthesis. It causes local necrosis and encourages bacterial dissemination to the systemic circulation and, in itself, has been shown to produce shock in animal models.

BACTEREMIA

Pseudomonas bacteremia occurs most commonly in cancer patients who are receiving intensive chemotherapy that produces granulocytopenia, in patients with extensive third-degree burns, and occasionally in patients with immunoglobulin or hypocomplementemia states. It is also a common cause of bacteremia in the patient with urinary catheterization. Sepsis in burn patients arises from the thermally damaged skin. Bacteremia in neutropenic patients arises principally from the lower intestinal tract and occasionally from primary pneumonia. Granulocytopenic patients frequently become colonized, and bacteremia develops in nearly all colonized patients if profound (<100 cells/µL) granulocytopenia persists for more than a few days. Ecthyma gangrenosum, usually a sign of fairly advanced systemic infection, is not pathognomonic but is most frequently associated with *P. aeruginosa* bacteremia. These skin lesions at first are small and indurated and then rapidly enlarge, become necrotic, and may ulcerate. Bacteria, on histologic section, are seen to be invading small arteries and veins, with remarkably minimal evidence of inflammation. A histologically similar lesion can be found in the lungs as a secondary consequence of bacteremia. The mortality associated with *Pseudomonas* sepsis is high, with the underlying status of the patient's host defenses and the promptness of instituting empirical antibiotic therapy being the two critical factors affecting survival. The presence of septic shock, the evidence of septic metastases, or both when antibiotics are started are usually considered adverse prognostic signs but, in reality, represent another measure of late institution of therapy.

Treatment

> The standard approach to suspected gram-negative sepsis, including that caused by *P. aeruginosa*, is a combination of an antipseudomonal β-lactam (e.g., piperacillin, ceftazidime, cefepime, imipenem) with an aminoglycoside. An antipseudomonal quinolone (e.g., ciprofloxacin) in combination with an aminoglycoside may also be effective. In the febrile neutropenic patient, monotherapy has been recommended with agents such as ceftazidime or imipenem; however, mortality with either single agents or combinations remains high. Studies suggest that survival is improved when two antibiotics to which the organism is susceptible are given immediately and that survival is further improved if the two agents prove to be synergistic in activity. For example, in a study of 200 episodes of *P. aeruginosa* bacteremia, most not neutropenic, the mortality with combination therapy was 27%, whereas the mortality with monotherapy was 47%. The author's recommendation is to focus on prompt initiation of antimicrobial therapy. If a combination is chosen initially, the aminoglycoside can be discontinued when the patient is stable and susceptibility results have returned.

RESPIRATORY TRACT INFECTIONS

Respiratory tract infections (Chapter 305) can take the form of a primary pneumonia, a secondary pneumonia related to bacteremia, or a chronic infection with intermittent exacerbations. Primary pneumonia occurs almost exclusively in hospitalized patients whose oropharynx or tracheobronchial tree is colonized by *P. aeruginosa*, the latter as a result of intubation. Frequently, *Pseudomonas* pneumonia occurs in the setting of additional pulmonary damage, such as blunt trauma, substantial atelectasis, or hemothorax. Atelectasis appears to be a key contributing pathogenic factor. Early, aggressive physiotherapy for the chest sometimes clears what appears to be a pneumonia but, in fact, is atelectasis that has resulted in fever, purulent sputum production, and a positive chest radiograph. However, once actual pneumonia has begun, the prognosis is poor and early empirical therapy is crucial.

The pneumonia that follows bacteremia is usually fulminant, with multiple areas of hemorrhage around small and medium-sized pulmonary arteries and lesions caused by necrosis of the small muscular arteries and veins in a fashion similar to that in ecthyma gangrenosum. Survival is limited even with prompt, aggressive therapy.

Chronic *Pseudomonas* respiratory tract infections are largely limited to patients with cystic fibrosis (Chapter 86), with the frequency of this infection increasing with age so that, ultimately, almost all patients have significant *Pseudomonas* pulmonary infection. The age differential is probably related to the progressive development of airway obstruction, a crucial factor in development of *Pseudomonas* infection. This chronic infection is associated with chronic cough, nutritional losses, and progressive loss of pulmonary function.

Treatment

> The standard treatment has been an antipseudomonal penicillin plus an aminoglycoside. Development of resistance is common, so therapy must be based on susceptibility patterns. Ceftazidime, imipenem, or a quinolone may also be considered. Acute exacerbations may be reduced or even prevented with intermittent therapy a number of times each year, irrespective of whether the infection is currently quiescent.

BURKHOLDERIA (PSEUDOMONAS) CEPACIA

B. cepacia is a complex of eight related genomovars, five designated as species and three (genomovars I, III, and VI) currently unnamed. Genomovars are phenotypically the same but genotypically distinct. Genomovar III and *Burkholderia multivorans* (genomovar II) are responsible for most human infections among this complex. These organisms can grow as well in distilled water as they can in trypticase soy broth, they are resistant to many of the commonly used hospital disinfectants, they can use penicillin as a carbon source, and they are resistant to many of the commonly used antimicrobials. The virulence properties are not understood.

B. cepacia has become a significant pathogen for immunocompromised patients and those hospitalized with serious underlying diseases. Often, patients have been hospitalized for a month or more before infection develops. Community-acquired infections are rare. Certain hosts are at substantially increased risk: endocarditis has occurred among intravenous drug abusers; skin infections related to extensive burns have occurred; a necrotizing, occasionally recurrent pneumonia has occurred among patients with the phagocytic dysfunction of chronic granulomatous disease; and an emerging problem for cystic fibrosis patients has been a relentless, often fulminating pneumonia caused by *B.(P.) cepacia*. Indeed, after *P. aeruginosa*, *B.(P.) cepacia* has become the second leading cause of chronic progressive lung infection among cystic fibrosis patients, in whom it causes major pulmonary deterioration. Patients may acquire this organism in the clinic or at home from various foods such as unpasteurized milk products (e.g., cheeses). Of interest, some strains are being considered as biopesticides or to degrade environmental pollutants; this is causing some concern within the cystic fibrosis community.

Nosocomial infections and pseudoinfections are considered together because of a common origin and because it can be difficult to distinguish between the two. The source of hospital *B.(P.) cepacia* is usually a moist or water-based reservoir, which, given the technologic advances of medicine, suggests that *B.(P.) cepacia* has the potential to become a not infrequent cause of infection and pseudoinfection in the high-technology or intensive care setting. *B.(P.) cepacia* has been found to cause pneumonitis, endocarditis, wound infections, and urinary tract infections, along with primary bacteremia. The origins of iatrogenic bacteremia can be conveniently divided into those related to contaminated solutions, injectables, and medical devices. Among the contaminated solutions implicated in bacteremia or pseudobacteremia have been multidose albuterol used with ventilators, disinfectant solutions, heparinized flushing solutions, distilled water, topical anesthetics, and intravenous infusates, including human serum albumin and cryoprecipitate. Contaminated injectables have included saline, methylprednisolone, and fentanyl. The implicated devices all include a moist environment where the organism can multiply; pressure-monitoring devices, respiratory assist devices, peritoneal dialysis machines, reusable hemodialysis coils, and blood gas analyzers have been documented as point sources. Dental equipment contamination may be one source of colonization among cystic fibrosis patients.

Figure 334–1 shows an epidemic of *B.(P.) cepacia* bacteremia among patients at the Clinical Center of the National Institutes of Health. The figure indicates that *B.(P.) cepacia*–positive blood cultures were uncommon in the years preceding this outbreak and that the majority during the epidemic occurred within the medical intensive care unit. A blood gas analyzer in an adjoining laboratory was found to be contaminated, and it served as the point source for this series of bacteremias. Although some were apparently pseudobacteremias (i.e., the blood culture became positive owing to contamination by skin or other sources), others were true bacteremias with significant morbidity. Indeed, among the highly compromised patients, many with cancer and significant immune suppression, the mortality resulting from the *B.(P.) cepacia* infection itself was 38%. Respiratory colonization in an appropriately predisposed host can progress to pneumonia, as evidenced by 14 of 37 patients with colonization and hematologic malignancies who developed pneumonia during an 18-month outbreak. In another outbreak of 14 bacteremias among cancer patients, all had central venous lines flushed with a contaminated heparin solution.

B.(P.) cepacia is resistant to many of the commonly used broad-spectrum antibiotics but is usually susceptible to trimethoprim-sulfamethoxazole and ceftazidime. Mortality rates are high in compromised patients.

RALSTONIA (PSEUDOMONAS, BURKHOLDERIA) PICKETTII

This is an uncommon cause of infection. In the past 30 years, 49 cases of bacteremia were reported. Thirty-eight of the 49 were caused by contaminated injected solutions; 7 more were related to contaminated ventilators or dialysis equipment. Four patients had bacteremia related to indwelling intravenous catheters; all were treated at one institution over a 2-year period. *R. (P., B.) pickettii* is usually resistant to aminoglycosides but susceptible to cephalosporins and antipseudomonal penicillins.

COMAMONAS (PSEUDOMONAS) TESTOSTERONI

C. (P.) testosteroni is an uncommon cause of human infection but may not be rare. For example, 10 cases were identified over a 3-year period at one Texas hospital. Most were associated with gastrointestinal tract anatomic abnormalities such as appendiceal perforation (5 of the 10), and most were polymicrobial with other fecal organisms.

BURKHOLDERIA (PSEUDOMONAS) PSEUDOMALLEI

This organism causes melioidosis. It was first described in Rangoon among debilitated morphine addicts. The term *melioidosis* means "a similarity to distemper of asses." Despite the clinical resemblance to glanders (see later), it has a totally different epidemiology. Melioidosis occurs in animals and humans in endemic areas of Southeast Asia and northern Australia and has now been recognized to occur in epidemic-like form in specific areas, given the combination of the environment (an appropriate rainy season with water-covered rice paddies) and a susceptible host (abraded skin in barefoot farmers who have a high prevalence of diabetes mellitus, renal disease, or both). It is the leading cause of community-acquired sepsis in Thailand during the June-to-November rainy season. Melioidosis has been detected in a few patients in India (who had not traveled to known endemic areas) and occasionally in Central America and South America. The organism has also been isolated in multiple areas of southern and coastal China. There is speculation that it could become an agent of bioterrorism.

B.(P.) pseudomallei is a gram-negative, motile, aerobic bacillus that is small and may grow in filamentous chains. Staining with methylene blue or Wright stain shows a bipolar "safety pin" pattern. *B. pseudomallei* has a characteristic wrinkling appearance of the colonies on agar if held long enough. The organism, like most pseudomonads, can be isolated from soil; water, particularly streams, rice paddies, and ponds of the endemic areas; and plants, including commonly consumed vegetables. Most human infection probably occurs through skin abrasions. In endemic areas, the organism is easy to culture from soil samples of flooded rice paddies and is still detectable during dry seasons from deep soil samples that are moist. However, laboratory animals have been found to become infected by the respiratory route, so inhalation may be a possible human route of acquisition, which would explain the occurrence of primary pneumonia. Both this pathogen and *B.(P.) mallei* have a polysaccharide biopolymer capsule that adversely affects phagocytosis. This organism may also be found as a biofilm in the water supply in endemic regions. But not all *B. pseudomallei* are equally virulent; it appears that those that infect are differentiated by the inability to assimilate arabinose (Ara biotype).

At the conclusion of U.S. involvement in the Vietnam War, 343 cases had been reported, with 36 deaths; however, serologic surveys suggest that either mild or inapparent infection may have been fairly common, with positive serologies found in 1 to 2% of healthy, non-wounded Army troops returning to the United States. This would suggest that as many as 225,000 military personnel may have had subclinical infection with *B.(P.) pseudomallei*. The importance of this observation is that recrudescence of disease, usually as cavitary pneumonia, has been observed many years after primary infection. That said, reports of such reactivation have been exceedingly rare in the United States.

In addition to inapparent infection or asymptomatic pulmonary infection, the frequently observed forms of melioidosis are an acute, localized, suppurative soft tissue infection, an acute pulmonary infection, and an acute septicemic presentation. The localized infections are probably related to skin abrasion, with development of a nodule with secondary lymphangitis and regional lymphadenitis. An apparent primary pulmonary infection ranges from bronchitis to necrotizing pneumonia. The patient with pneumonia usually has a high fever

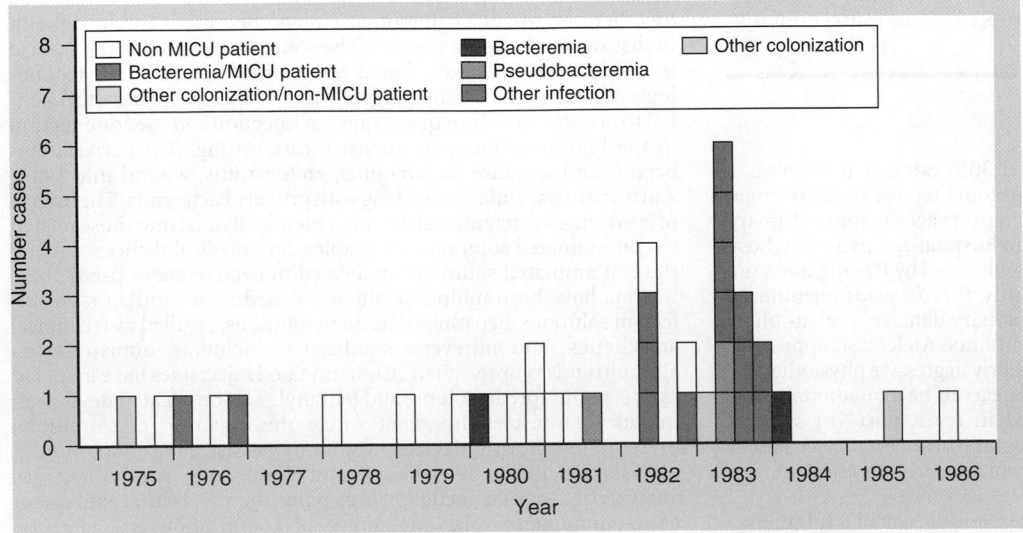

FIGURE 334–1 • An epidemic of *Burkholderia (Pseudomonas) cepacia* bacteremia among patients at the Clinical Center of the National Institutes of Health. Note that the epidemic in 1982 to 1983 within the medical intensive-care unit was caused by a contaminated nearby blood gas analyzer. (From Henderson DK, Baptiste R, Parillo J, et al: Indolent epidemic of *Burkholderia (Pseudomonas) cepacia* bacteremia and pseudobacteremia in an intensive care unit traced to a contaminated blood gas analyzer. Am J Med 1988;84:75–81.)

Infectious Diseases

and signs and symptoms of consolidation, ordinarily in an upper lobe. It is an acute pyogenic process, frequently leading to early cavitation and giving a pulmonary appearance consistent with tuberculosis. Progression to bacteremia is rare. In Singapore, *B.(P.) pseudomallei* is the cause of a small but important percentage of the severe community-acquired pneumonia cases that require hospitalization.

Patients with the acute septic form characteristically present with a short history of fever and no clinical evidence of focal infection, although skin abrasion is the presumed site of origin. Most are profoundly ill, with signs of sepsis, such as tachypnea or Kussmaul's breathing, and occasional evidence of septic shock. Clinical and radiologic evidence frequently demonstrates progression to diffuse bilateral and patchy pulmonary infiltrates, which progresses to abscess and cavity formation if the patient survives. Subcutaneous abscesses are relatively uncommon but can occur at multiple sites. Liver abscess, usually multiple, is not uncommon and is accompanied in more than 50% by multiple splenic abscesses, a combination unlikely for most other causes of liver abscess. Neurologic involvement may be seen with the septic form.

The diagnosis should be considered in any patient living in an endemic area who has a febrile illness, especially one occupationally at risk and, perhaps, at further risk of sepsis because of diabetes or renal disease. The diagnosis is highly suggested in such an individual with a rapidly progressive, extensive pulmonary process if subcutaneous lesions are present or in one whose condition progresses to a cavitary form indistinguishable from tuberculosis. Although frequently negative, Gram staining of pulmonary or abscess exudate may show small gram-negative bacilli, and methylene blue staining shows the characteristic bipolar safety pin. The organism grows on standard media and is usually detected in blood cultures within 48 hours. Efforts are under way to create rapid immunoassays to detect antigen in urine or antibody in serum or to identify the organism in specimens or early cultures.

In northeast Thailand, a report from a hospital serving a population of nearly 2 million rural rice farming families determined that about 20% of all community-acquired bacteremias were caused by *B.(P.) pseudomallei* and that during the rainy season, when the paddy fields are under water (from June to September), *B.(P.) pseudomallei* was the single most common organism isolated from blood culture, representing nearly one half of all documented cases of community-acquired bacteremia in the month of August (Fig. 334–2). An interesting observation was the higher than expected frequency of both diabetes mellitus and renal calculi in patients with sepsis who are from this region, where both diabetes and calculi are common.

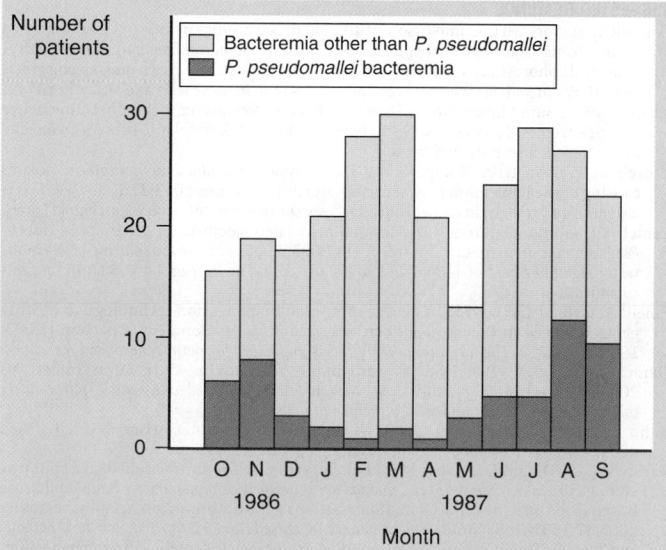

FIGURE 334–2 • Number of persons with community-acquired bacteremia caused by *P. (B.) pseudomallei* and other organisms in northeast Thailand from October 1986 to September 1987. (From Chaowagul W, White NJ, Dance DAB, et al: Melioidosis: A major cause of community-acquired septicemia in northeastern Thailand. J Infect Dis 1989;159:890–899.)

Rx Treatment

Pulmonary and septic diseases are associated with very high mortality and hence, when suspected, should be treated aggressively with intravenous ceftazidime (imipenem or piperacillin are acceptable substitutes; meropenem and ciprofloxacin may be acceptable but have had limited usage). Surgery may be necessary for abscesses. Treatment must be prolonged, including intravenous therapy for 2 to 4 weeks followed by oral therapy (perhaps amoxicillin–clavulanic acid or, possibly, ciprofloxacin) for 6 months or longer to prevent recrudescence. Trimethoprim-sulfamethoxazole appears to be more active in vivo than in vitro. The susceptibility of this organism to ciprofloxacin is variable.

The prognosis for patients with localized disease should be excellent with appropriate therapy. However, those with the septicemic form are often gravely ill at the time of admission, and the mortality rate, even with current therapy given promptly, is about 40%. Patients with the highest mortality include those who are hypothermic, azotemic, or unable to produce a leukocytosis. Relapses are common, perhaps 25% overall, with clinical severity and initial therapy the crucial risk factors (Fig. 334–3). Long-term oral treatment with amoxicillin–clavulanic acid appears logical to reduce relapses because recurrence carries a high mortality rate.

BURKHOLDERIA (PSEUDOMONAS) MALLEI

B.(P.) mallei can cause an infection in horses, mules, and donkeys that has occasionally been transmitted to humans. The name "glanders" comes from the prominent pulmonary involvement, although the infection can, instead, be characterized by subcutaneous ulcerative lesions or lymphatic thickening with nodules (known as farcy).

Glanders was never a common human infection, and with the decline in the use of horses for day-to-day activities and with aggressive veterinary control measures (skin testing animals and immediate slaughtering of infected animals with proper carcass disposal), glanders has become a rare disease. Apparently, there had been no naturally acquired infections in the United States since 1938 until the report of a microbiologist working with the organism at Fort Detrick, Maryland, in 2001. Glanders was used as a form of biologic warfare in World War I with deliberate infection of animals near the front lines. There is some concern that it could be utilized by bioterrorists.

Like melioidosis, glanders tends to occur as an acute localized suppurative infection, an acute pulmonary infection, an acute septicemic infection, or a chronic suppurative infection. An abraded area of skin may lead to a local nodule with acute lymphangitis. Inoculation into an abraded mucous membrane can lead to extensive ulcerating granulomatous lesions. These forms of infection seem to have an incu-

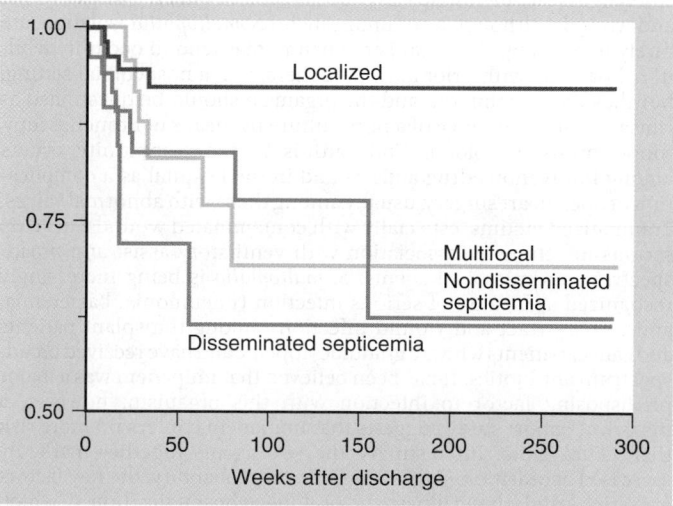

FIGURE 334–3 • Relapse-free probability in survivors of acute melioidosis stratified by clinical severity on first admission. (From Chaowagul, W, Suputtamongkol Y, Dance DAB, et al: Relapse in melioidosis: Incidence and risk factors. J Infect Dis 1993;168:1181–1185.)

Infectious Diseases

bation period of 1 to 5 days; in contrast, after inhalation, a primary pneumonia tends to develop 10 to 14 days later. Symptoms are relatively nonspecific and include fever, occasional rigors, malaise, fatigue, and headache. Examination findings depend on the form of infection. Leukocytosis is common. Chest radiographs of the acute pulmonary form usually show densities consistent with early lung abscess; however, lobar or bronchopneumonia-type infiltrates are common. Chronic suppurative disease involves multiple subcutaneous and intramuscular abscesses, especially on the extremities, with lymphatic involvement and, in many, a nasal discharge with or without ulceration.

The organism is usually difficult to find in exudates but when seen with a Gram stain or methylene blue appears similar to *B.(P.) pseudomallei*. It is reasonably easy to cultivate.

℞ Treatment

The treatment of glanders is uncertain because of its rarity, hence the inability to carry out clinical trials. A reasonable recommendation is to initiate therapy with regimens found effective for melioidosis, recognizing that the acute septicemic form has been uniformly fatal and suggesting that full dosages of intravenous combinations of agents be given initially. The recent (2001) patient was treated successfully with meropenem and doxycycline intravenously followed by 6 months of azithromycin and doxycycline orally.

STENOTROPHOMONAS (XANTHOMONAS, PSEUDOMONAS) MALTOPHILIA

S. maltophilia is atypical of the other pseudomonads in that the oxidase test is negative or equivocal. It is probably a fairly common commensal and a part of the transient flora, especially of hospitalized patients. In hospitals it is not infrequently found in moist or wet settings. The organism is resistant to most of the cephalosporins, semisynthetic penicillins, and aminoglycosides, although it has variable susceptibility to the antipseudomonal penicillins. It is generally susceptible to trimethoprim-sulfamethoxazole, ticarcillin-clavulanate, many fluoroquinolones, and rifampin. Synergy has been noted with trimethoprim-sulfamethoxazole plus carbenicillin and with the triple regimen of trimethoprim-sulfamethoxazole plus carbenicillin and rifampin.

S. maltophilia is an uncommon cause of a wide spectrum of diseases that, in general, are less severe than infections caused by other gram-negative bacilli in similar locations. Most infections occur after long hospitalizations, antibiotic exposure, and after a central venous line has been in place. Polymicrobial infections are not uncommon. The most common types of infection are pneumonia, endocarditis, urinary tract infection, and iatrogenic bacteremia or pseudobacteremia. Cholangitis and meningitis have been reported but are quite unusual, and wounds, although a common site for *S. maltophilia* isolation, are rarely infected by this organism. Pneumonias tend to occur in debilitated patients with prior antibiotic therapy in a nosocomial setting, but they are uncommon, and the organism should be questioned as causative in the absence of a pure culture by means of bronchoscopy, thoracentesis, or blood. Endocarditis in the community occurs among intravenous drug abusers and in the hospital as a complication of open heart surgery, usually among those with abnormal valves. Traumatized victims, especially with contaminated wounds, develop serious infections in association with ventilatory assist and broad-spectrum antimicrobial agents. *S. maltophilia* is being increasingly recognized as a cause of serious infection (pneumonia, bacteremia, and urinary tract and wound infection) among transplant patients and cancer patients who are granulocytopenic and have received broad-spectrum antibiotics. It has been believed that imipenem was a major predisposing factor to infection with this organism; however, a historical cohort study suggests that imipenem confers no more risk than ceftazidime. Interestingly, the two agents together markedly increased acquisition (Fig. 334–4). In all probability, the key factors are serious underlying illness and prolonged hospitalization, to which antibiotic administration is an added pressure toward colonization.

S. maltophilia bacteriuria is found occasionally in patients with indwelling long-term catheters; however, only rarely has the organism been shown to cause clinical infection. When infection has occurred, it has usually been in association with significant

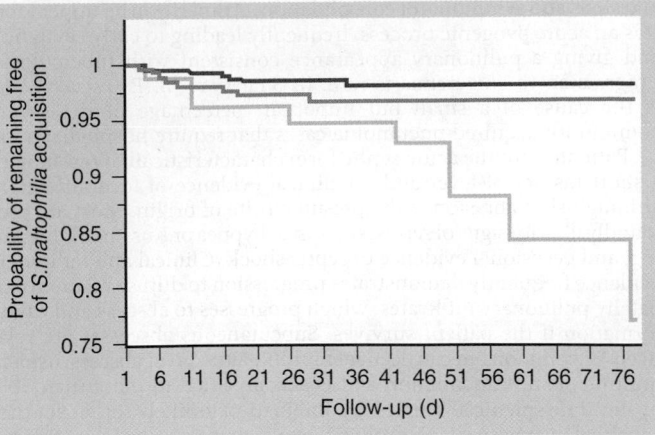

FIGURE 334–4 • Kaplan-Meier curve showing the probability of remaining free of *S. maltophilia* acquisition in each of the three treatment groups: ceftazidime (dashed line), imipenem (solid line), and both agents (dotted line). This probability did not differ significantly between the imipenem and ceftazidime groups (log-rank test; $P = .19$). The probability of acquisition was higher for patients treated with both agents ($P = .0017$). (From Carmeli Y, Samore MH: Comparison of treatment with imipenem vs. ceftazidime as a predisposing factor for nosocomial acquisition of *Stenotrophomonas maltophilia*: A historical cohort study. Clin Infect Dis 1997;24:1131–1134.)

instrumentation, genitourinary surgery, or both. The morbidity has tended to be low, and therapy, especially with trimethoprim-sulfamethoxazole, has frequently been effective.

Iatrogenic bacteremia and pseudobacteremia caused by this organism have often been reported. In one epidemic among 25 patients with positive blood cultures, it was determined that these cases were pseudobacteremias caused by contaminated blood collection tubes. In another setting, eight children were found to have bacteremia after open heart surgery, apparently as a result of contamination of the monitoring transducers in the intensive care unit. *S. maltophilia* has been found to contaminate the deionized water used for diluting disinfectants, and the organism can even survive in the diluted disinfectant. It is important to emphasize that not all of these bacteremias have been pseudobacteremias; for example, two fatal cases of endocarditis have been noted as a result of bacteremia caused by a contaminated device or solution. Permanent indwelling vascular catheters are a major source of bacteremias.

SUGGESTED READINGS

Carmeli Y, Samore MH: Comparison of treatment with imipenem vs. ceftazidime as a predisposing factor for nosocomial acquisition of *Stenotrophomonas maltophilia*: A historical cohort study. Clin Infect Dis 1997;24:1131–1134. *Nosocomial infection rates were higher in patients who received both agents than in those who received either alone.*

Chaowagul W, Suputtamongkol Y, Dance DAB, et al: Relapse in melioidosis: Incidence and risk factors. J Infect Dis 1993;168:1181–1185. *A 23% relapse rate was related to initial infection severity and therapy.*

Cowell BA, Weissman BA, Yeung KK, et al: Phenotype of *Pseudomonas aeruginosa* isolates causing corneal infection between 1997 and 2000. Cornea 2003;22:131–134. *This is a significant pathogen in corneal infection, especially in patients who wear contact lenses.*

Crnich CJ, Gordon B, Andes D: Hot tub-associated necrotizing pneumonia due to *Pseudomonas aeruginosa*. Clin Infect Dis 2003;36:e55–e57. *Free chlorine levels in the water should be kept at 1–3 mg/L, and the pH should be kept at 7.2–7.8 to prevent this complication.*

Finelli A, Gallant CV, Jarvi K, et al: Use of in-biofilm expression technology to identify genes involved in *Pseudomonas aeruginosa* biofilm development. J Bacteriol 2003;185:2700–2710. *The formation of biofilms is important for pathogenesis and resistance.*

Garau J, Gomez L: *Pseudomonas aeruginosa* pneumonia. Curr Opin Infect Dis 2003;16:135–143. *A practical overview including inhaled antibiotics, particularly tobramycin, to prevent and treat patients with cystic fibrosis.*

Kahn AS, Ashford DA: Ready or not—Preparedness for bioterrorism. N Engl J Med 2001;345:287–289. *An overview, including Pseudomonas spp.*

Karlowsky JA, Draghi DC, Jones ME, et al: Surveillance for antimicrobial susceptibility among clinical isolates of *Pseudomonas aeruginosa* and *Acinetobacter baumannii* from hospitalized patients in the United States, 1998 to 2001. Antimicrob Agents Chemother 2003;47:1681–1688. *Multidrug resistance increased from 5.5 to 7% in non-ICU patients and 7.4 to 9.1% in ICU patients, but >90% were susceptible to amikacin and piperacillin-tazobactam; 80 to 90% to cefepime, ceftazidime, imipenem, and meropenem; and 70 to 80% to ciprofloxacin, gentamicin, levofloxacin, and ticarcillin-clavulanate.*

Pirnay JP, De Vos D, Cochez C, et al: Molecular epidemiology of *Pseudomonas aeruginosa* colonization in a burn unit: Persistence of a multidrug-resistant clone and a silver sulfadiazine-resistant clone. J Clin Microbiol 2003;41:1192–1202. *A common problem in burn units.*

Pollack M: *Pseudomonas aeruginosa*. In Mandell GL, Bennett JE, Dolin R (eds): Principles and Practice of Infectious Diseases, 5th ed. New York, Churchill Livingstone, 2000, pp 2310–2334. *A very thorough discussion of the microbiology, epidemiology, pathogenic factors, and clinical syndromes of* P. aeruginosa.

Raveh D, Simhon A, Gimmon Z, et al: Infections caused by *Pseudomonas pickettii* in association with permanent indwelling intravenous devices: Four cases and a review. Clin Infect Dis 1993;17:877–880. *A review of the few reported cases of bacteremia caused by this organism.*

Spencer DH, Kas A, Smith EE, et al: Whole-genome sequence variation among multiple isolates of *Pseudomonas aeruginosa*. J Bacteriol 2003;185:1316–1325. *Approximately 10% of the genome varies among different isolates.*

Srinivasan A, Kraus CN, DeShazer D, et al: Glanders in a military research microbiologist. N Engl J Med 2001;345:256–258. *Example of unusual human infection.*

Srinivasan A, Wolfenden LL, Song X, et al: An outbreak of *Pseudomonas aeruginosa* infections associated with flexible bronchoscopes. N Engl J Med 2003;348:221–227. *Emphasizes the infectivity and epidemic potential.*

Thuong M, Arvaniti K, Ruimy R, et al: Epidemiology of *Pseudomonas aeruginosa* and risk factors for carriage acquisition in an intensive care unit. J Hosp Infect 2003;53:274–282. *Endogenous sources may account for the majority of infections, but exogenous sources occur and warrant reinforced barrier precautions.*

335 LISTERIOSIS

Bennett Lorber

Definition

Listeriosis is a food-borne infection caused by the bacterium *Listeria monocytogenes*. Most patients have impaired cell-mediated immunity and present with life-threatening bacteremia or meningitis, although a mild, self-limited, febrile gastroenteritis in healthy persons is also recognized.

Epidemiology

Widely distributed in nature, *L. monocytogenes* may be found in soil, on vegetation, and in the stool of healthy mammals, including humans ($\approx$5%). It causes disease in animals, especially herd animals, and in humans. The organism has been isolated commonly from foods, including raw vegetables, raw milk, fish, poultry, and meat. Ingestion of contaminated foods appears to be the source of most human infection. Outbreaks have been documented in association with coleslaw, milk, soft cheeses, pâté, ready-to-eat pork products, deli-counter meats, smoked fish, and butter. Sporadic cases have been traced to contaminated cheese, milk, deli-counter meats, turkey frankfurters, and alfalfa tablets.

Listeriosis is not a reportable disease in each of the United States; information on annual incidence comes from active surveillance studies performed by the Centers for Disease Control and Prevention. Although the annual incidence of listeriosis decreased by 44% between 1989 and 1993, possibly related to more stringent regulations in the food processing industry; it has remained stable since at approximately 5 cases per million population, accounting for 1500 to 2500 cases per year in the United States and about 400 deaths. Neonates and adults over the age of 50 years have the highest infection rates. Pregnant women make up 30% of all cases. Adults at increased risk for invasive listeriosis include those who have hematologic malignancy, advanced acquired immunodeficiency syndrome (AIDS), a solid organ transplant, or anyone treated with corticosteroids. However, as many as one fourth of all invasive listeriosis cases occur in apparently healthy persons, particularly those over age 60.

Pathogenesis

L. monocytogenes enters the human body through the intestine, most often after ingestion of a contaminated food. The bacterium induces its own uptake by gastrointestinal cells and macrophages. Within the host cell the bacterium is enclosed in a phagolysosome, but through the production of an exotoxin called listeriolysin O, it destroys the phagolysosome membrane and gains access to the cytoplasm. All pathogenic strains of *L. monocytogenes* produce listeriolysin O, the major virulence factor. Listeriae actively divide in the cytoplasm, then migrate to the periphery of the cell, using polymerization of host cell actin, and push out the cell membrane, forming pseudopods that are taken up by adjacent host cells. The bacteria move from cell to cell in this fashion, repeating their life cycle.

After invasion through the gastrointestinal tract, listeriae may disseminate hematogenously to any body site but show a particular tropism for the central nervous system.

Immunity to listerial infection is handled through the cell-mediated arm of the immune system; persons with abnormalities solely of humoral immunity or leukocytes are not at increased risk of infection.

Clinical Manifestations

The incubation period for invasive listeriosis (time from ingestion of contaminated food to illness) averages about 30 days. Invasive listeriosis in the immunocompromised adult most often manifests as bacteremia without an obvious focus. In such cases, patients have nonspecific complaints such as fever, malaise, myalgias, and back pain. Bacteremia is the form of invasive listeriosis that complicates pregnancy; central nervous system (CNS) infection is extremely rare in the absence of other risk factors. Listeriosis during pregnancy may lead to spontaneous abortion or neonatal sepsis, but early antimicrobial therapy may lead to birth of a healthy child. Endocarditis with *L. monocytogenes* can occur on both native and prosthetic valves, and carries a high rate of septic complications. Endocarditis, but not bacteremia per se, may be a clue to underlying colon cancer; colonoscopy should be considered in all cases of listerial endocarditis.

Persons who develop bacteremia with *L. monocytogenes* may progress to CNS infection, most commonly manifested as meningitis. Listeria has a predilection for infecting brain tissue as well as the meninges, and unlike other common bacterial causes of meningitis, such as *H. influenzae*, *S. pneumoniae*, *N. meningitidis*, and group B streptococcus, not infrequently causes encephalitis or brain abscess. Brain abscess due to *L. monocytogenes* exhibits unusual features when compared with other bacteria: listerial brain abscess coexists with bacteremia in nearly all cases, and with meningitis in one fourth; in addition, abscesses are often subcortical.

L. monocytogenes is the most common cause of bacterial meningitis in patients with lymphomas, organ transplant recipients, and patients treated with corticosteroids for any reason. Affected persons usually present with the classic acute symptoms of meningitis but may also have a subacute disease course more characteristic of tuberculous meningitis. Most have stiff neck, but 15 to 20% may not. Focal neurologic findings, including ataxia, tremors, myoclonus, and seizures, may be seen consistent with listeria's tropism for brain parenchyma. Cerebrospinal fluid (CSF) glucose is normal in over 60% of cases. Gram stain of CSF reveals *L. monocytogenes* in only about 40% of cases, and even when seen, the organisms may be mistaken for pneumococci.

Listerial rhombencephalitis is an unusual form of listerial encephalitis involving the brain stem, similar to the unique zoonotic listerial infection known as circling disease of sheep. Unlike other listerial CNS infections, rhombencephalitis usually occurs in healthy adults. The typical clinical picture is one of a biphasic illness with a prodrome of fever, headache, nausea, and vomiting lasting about 4 days followed by the abrupt onset of asymmetric cranial nerve deficits, cerebellar signs, and hemiparesis or hemisensory deficits, or both. About 40% of patients develop respiratory failure. Nuchal rigidity is present in about half, and CSF findings are only mildly abnormal with a positive CSF culture in about 40%. Almost two thirds of patients are bacteremic. Magnetic resonance imaging is superior to computed tomography for demonstrating rhombencephalitis. Mortality is high, and serious sequelae are common in survivors.

Localized infection may occur after hematogenous seeding (e.g., liver abscess, septic arthritis) or, rarely, following direct inoculation (e.g., conjunctivitis, cellulitis).

Well-documented reports of foodborne outbreaks have demonstrated that ingestion of *L. monocytogenes* in a sufficiently large inoculum can result in a self-limited illness consisting of fever, chills, diarrhea, abdominal cramps, and sometimes nausea and vomiting. Symptoms follow exposure by 1 to 2 days and last for about 2 days.

Diagnosis

Clinical situations in which a diagnosis of listeriosis should be considered include (1) neonatal sepsis or meningitis, (2) meningitis or parenchymal brain infection in patients with hematological malignancies, AIDS, organ transplantation, or corticosteroid immuno-suppression, (3) meningitis or parenchymal brain infection in adults older than 50 years, (4) simultaneous infection of the meninges and brain parenchyma, (5) subcortical brain abscess, (6) fever during pregnancy, particularly in the third trimester, (7) blood, CSF, or other normally sterile specimen reported to have "diphtheroids," on Gram stain or culture, and (8) food-borne outbreak of febrile gastroenteritis when routine cultures fail to identify a pathogen. Differential diagnosis of listerial CNS infection includes the more common causes of bacterial meningitis and brain abscess; indolent listerial meningitis or rhombencephalitis may mimic CNS tuberculosis.

Diagnosis of listeriosis is best made by routine bacterial culture of specimens from usually sterile sites such as blood or CSF. The laboratory must exercise caution because *L. monocytogenes* may be mistaken for diphtheroids, streptococci, enterococci, or *H. influenzae*. Stool culture is recommended only when routine stool cultures are negative in the setting of an outbreak of gastroenteritis; many people have enteric colonization with *L. monocytogenes* without invasive disease. The laboratory must be advised that listerial infection is suspected because the organism is unlikely to be identified with routine stool culture media.

Serologic testing (antibody to listeriolysin O) is not useful in invasive disease but may be helpful in retrospective identification of outbreaks of foodborne febrile gastroenteritis when routine cultures are negative.

Rx Treatment and Prevention

Guidelines for preventing listeriosis are similar to those for preventing other foodborne illnesses. In general, one should thoroughly cook raw food from animal sources, wash raw vegetables thoroughly before eating, keep uncooked meats separate from vegetables and from cooked foods and ready-to-eat foods, avoid raw (unpasteurized) milk or foods made from raw milk, and wash hands, knives, and cutting boards after each handling of uncooked foods.

People at high risk for listeriosis may choose to avoid soft cheeses such as feta, Brie, Camembert, blue-veined, and Mexican-style cheese such as queso fresco. Hard cheeses, processed cheeses, cream cheese, cottage cheese, and yogurt are safe. Leftover foods or ready-to-eat foods, such as hot dogs, should be cooked until steaming hot. It is best to avoid foods from deli counters, such as prepared salads, meats, and cheeses, or at least to thoroughly reheat cold cuts until they are steaming hot before eating.

Listeriosis is effectively prevented by trimethoprim-sulfamethoxazole given as *Pneumocystis* prophylaxis to organ transplant recipients or to individuals with HIV infection. In areas with a high prevalence of AIDS, the widespread use of trimethoprim-sulfamethoxazole for *Pneumocystis* prophylaxis appears to have resulted in a marked decline in nonperinatal listeriosis.

Second episodes of neonatal listerial infection are virtually unheard of, and intrapartum antibiotics are not recommended for women with a history of perinatal listeriosis.

Except from infected mother to fetus, human-to-human transmission of listeriosis does not occur; patients do not need to be isolated.

Recommendations for the treatment of infections with *L. monocytogenes* derive from in vitro data, animal models, and clinical experience with small numbers of patients; no controlled trials have been performed to prove the efficacy of one drug compared with another. Many antimicrobials show in vitro activity against *L. monocytogenes*. One should be careful to equate susceptibility with clinical utility since some drugs that show excellent in vitro activity are inadequate to treat infection; cephalosporins serve as examples.

Twenty percent of bacterial meningitis in those over age 50 is due to *L. monocytogenes*. Therefore, empirical therapy for bacterial meningitis in all adults older than 50 years should include either ampicillin or trimethoprim-sulfamethoxazole, especially in the absence of associated pneumonia, otitis, sinusitis, or endocarditis that would suggest a cause other than *L. monocytogenes*. Cephalosporins, commonly used in the treatment of bacterial meningitis, have limited activity against listeria.

Ampicillin is generally considered the drug of choice for treating confirmed cases of listeriosis. In cases of meningitis and endocarditis and in patients with severely impaired T-cell function, most authorities recommend the addition of gentamicin to ampicillin for synergy, based on in vitro testing and animal models. For meningitis, therapy should be continued for at least 3 weeks; bacteremic patients without CNS involvement may be treated for 2 weeks. Endocarditis and brain abscess should be treated for at least 6 weeks. Meningitis doses should be used to treat all cases of invasive listeriosis, even in the absence of CNS or CSF abnormalities.

In case of penicillin hypersensitivity, trimethoprim-sulfamethoxazole is the preferred agent. It is bactericidal and appears to be as effective as the combination of ampicillin and gentamicin. Drugs that should be avoided due to treatment failures and relapses include cephalosporins, chloramphenicol, tetracycline, and erythromycin.

Corticosteroids appear to be important adjunctive agents in treating the most common forms of bacterial meningitis. Their role in the treatment of listerial CNS infection is unknown.

Iron is a virulence factor for *L. monocytogenes*, and clinically, iron overload states are risk factors for listerial infection. Therefore, in patients with listeriosis and iron deficiency, it seems prudent to withhold iron replacement until antimicrobial therapy is complete.

Prognosis

Listeria meningitis carries a mortality of about 25%; mortality is higher in those with underlying malignancy. Mortality from brain abscess and endocarditis is about 50%; survivors of brain abscess commonly have significant neurological residua.

SUGGESTED READINGS

Aureli P, Fiorucci GC, Caroli D, et al: An outbreak of febrile gastroenteritis associated with corn contaminated by *Listeria monocytogenes*. N Engl J Med 2000;342:1235–1241. *Description of an investigation of a large food-borne outbreak of fever and diarrheal disease in healthy school children citing clinical manifestations and the role of molecular epidemiology in defining the outbreak.*

Bucholz U, Mascola L: Transmission, pathogenesis, and epidemiology of *Listeria monocytogenes*. Infect Dis Clin Pract 2001;10:34–41. *A concise overview of human listeriosis.*

Mylonakis E, Hohmann EL, Calderwood SB: Central nervous system infection with *Listeria monocytogenes*. 33 Years' experience at a general hospital and review of 776 episodes from the literature. Medicine 1998;77:313–336. *The largest and most detailed review of the most commonly recognized clinical syndromes caused by L. monocytogenes. Well-referenced.*

Slifman NR, Gershon SK, Lee JH, et al: *Listeria monocytogenes* infection as a complication of treatment with tumor necrosis factor alpha-neutralizing agents. Arth rheum 2003;48:319–324. *Anti–tumor necrosis factor alpha agents are increasingly used for treatment of rheumatoid arthritis and Crohn's disease. Listeriosis can complicate this treatment.*

Vazquez-Boland JA, Kuhn M, Berche P, et al: *Listeria* pathogenesis and molecular virulence determinants. Clin Microbiol Rev 2001;14:584–640. *A detailed discussion of the molecular biology of this unique intracellular pathogen.*

Wing EJ, Gregory SH: *Listeria monocytogenes*: Clinical and experimental update. J Infect Dis 2002;185(suppl):S18–S24. *A concise review of clinical listeriosis and lessons about host defenses learned from animal models.*

336 ERYSIPELOID

Annette C. Reboli

Definition

Erysipelothrix rhusiopathiae causes three well-defined patterns of human infection: (1) erysipeloid, a cellulitis of the fingers and hands (also known as whale finger or pork finger), which is the most common manifestation of infection with *E. rhusiopathiae*; (2) a diffuse cutaneous form; and (3) a bacteremic form, with or without cutaneous involvement, usually complicated by endocarditis.

Epidemiology

E. rhusiopathiae is found worldwide as a commensal or a pathogen in a variety of animals, including swine, sheep, cattle, horses, dogs, and rodents; fowl, including chickens, ducks, turkeys, and parrots; and flies, ticks, mites, and lice. The greatest commercial impact of *E.*

rhusiopathiae infection is due to disease in swine, but infection of sheep and poultry is also important economically. Although the organism colonizes the mucoid surface slime of fish, it does not appear to cause disease in these animals. Environmental surfaces in contact with infected animals or their products are potential sources of *E. rhusiopathiae*. It can persist for prolonged periods in contaminated soil. Although *E. rhusiopathiae* is resistant to smoking, salting, and pickling, it is killed within 15 minutes by heating to 55° C.

While the incidence of infection in humans seems to be decreasing because of technological advances in animal industries, human infection still occurs in specific settings. Infection in humans is usually the result of contact with infected animals or their products. Persons at greatest risk for infection include fishermen, fishmongers, butchers, slaughterhouse workers, and veterinarians. The organism gains entry through cuts and abrasions on the skin. The seasonal incidence of erysipeloid parallels that of swine erysipelas and is highest in the summer and early fall. The rare instances of systemic infection that do not have an occupation link suggest that oropharyngeal or gastrointestinal colonization with the organism may occur. Erysipeloid and erysipeloid with bacteremia have been reported rarely following cat and dog bites, suggesting that *E. rhusiopathiae* may be part of the oral flora of these animals.

Pathobiology

Virulence of *E. rhusiopathiae* is associated, at least in part, with resistance to phagocytosis by polymorphonuclear leukocytes. This antiphagocytic ability results from its possession of a capsule. In the absence of specific antibodies, *E. rhusiopathiae* evades phagocytosis, but even if phagocytized, it is able to replicate intracellularly in these cells.

Clinical Manifestations

Because of its mode of acquisition (contact with infected animals or their products, with organisms inoculating abrasions on the skin), lesions are usually confined to the fingers and hands. A well-defined, slightly elevated, violaceous lesion, accompanied by a very painful, throbbing, burning, or itching sensation, develops within 2 to 7 days of traumatic dermal inoculation. The infected area is swollen. Vesicles may be present, but suppuration is absent. The lesion spreads slowly to other fingers but rarely involves the fingertips or the skin above the wrist. As the lesion spreads peripherally, the central area clears. Systemic signs and symptoms are rare. There may be sterile arthritis of an adjacent joint. Regional lymphadenopathy or lymphadenitis occurs in about 20% of cases, and low-grade fevers occur in approximately 10%. Lesions usually resolve within 3 weeks without treatment. Relapse occurs in 1% of cases.

The diffuse cutaneous form is rare. The cutaneous lesion progresses proximally from the site of inoculation or appears at remote areas. The patients often have fever and arthralgias, but blood cultures are usually negative.

Systemic infection with *Erysipelothrix* is uncommon. Approximately 60 cases of bacteremia have been reported; 90% of the patients had endocarditis. All but two cases involved native valves. In 60% of cases, infection developed on apparently normal heart valves. One third of patients had an antecedent or concurrent skin lesion of erysipeloid. Clinical manifestations of endocarditis due to *E. rhusiopathiae* and other microorganisms are similar. *E. rhusiopathiae* endocarditis correlates highly with occupation, exhibits a tropism for the aortic valve, affects more males than females, and is associated with a high mortality. Cases of *E. rhusiopathiae* endocarditis have been complicated by paravalvular and myocardial abscess formation and acute renal failure. Very few cases of systemic infection have occurred in immunocompromised hosts, although one third had a history of ethanol abuse. There has been a suggestion that bacteremia due to *E. rhusiopathiae* without endocarditis occurs more frequently than was previously believed and that bacteremia may be occurring with increased frequency in immunocompromised patients, while endocarditis usually occurs in immunocompetent patients. Focal infections including brain abscess, osteomyelitis, septic arthritis, and peritonitis have been reported.

Diagnosis

E. rhusiopathiae is a thin, pleomorphic, non-sporulating, microaerophilic, gram-positive rod. It may be confused with other gram-positive bacillary organisms, in particular *Listeria monocytogenes* and *Corynebacterium* species. It can be differentiated from *L. monocytogenes* by its lack of motility, lack of catalase and coagulase production, and resistance to neomycin. Most strains of *E. rhusiopathiae* produce hydrogen sulfide on triple sugar iron agar slants, a feature that distinguishes *E. rhusiopathiae* from *L. monocytogenes* and from corynebacteria. Because a-hemolysis may be seen after 48 hours of incubation of *E. rhusiopathiae*, confusion with streptococci also may occur. The term *erysipeloid* refers to cutaneous infection caused by *E. rhusiopathiae* and should not be confused with erysipelas, which is a superficial cellulitis due to streptococci or staphylococci.

E. rhusiopathiae grows on routine laboratory media. Because *E. rhusiopathiae* is located only in deeper parts of the skin in cases of erysipeloid, biopsy of the entire thickness of the dermis from the edge of the lesion yields maximum recovery of the organism. Routine blood culture techniques are adequate for growth and isolation of the organism in suspected cases of bacteremia or endocarditis. Two PCR assays have been described for the rapid diagnosis of swine erysipelas, one of which has been applied successfully to human samples.

Rx Treatment and Prevention

Most isolates of *E. rhusiopathiae* are susceptible to penicillin, cephalosporins, imipenem, clindamycin, ciprofloxacin, and ofloxacin. Some resistance has been observed with erythromycin, tetracycline, and chloramphenicol. *E. rhusiopathiae* is resistant to vancomycin, aminoglycosides, trimethoprim/sulfamethoxazole, and sulfonamides. Penicillin G is the treatment of choice. Uncomplicated cutaneous lesions usually respond well to a 5- to 7-day course of oral penicillin. Treatment hastens healing, although relapse may still occur. Bacteremia should be treated with intravenous penicillin; cases of endocarditis should be treated with 12 to 20 million units of penicillin G daily for 4 to 6 weeks. Cephalosporins are an alternative for the penicillin-allergic patient. Use of quinolones, in particular, ofloxacin or ciprofloxacin, may be considered in *Erysipelothrix* infections when the patient is allergic to β-lactams. Valve replacement may be necessary in patients with endocarditis. Vaccines are available for commercial use in animals only.

SUGGESTED READINGS

Brooke CJ, Riley TV: *Erysipelothrix rhusiopathiae*: bacteriology, epidemiology and clinical manifestations of an occupational pathogen. J Med Microbiol 1999;48:789–799. *A comprehensive review including recent advances in molecular approaches to diagnosis and understanding of taxonomy and pathogenesis.*

Dunbar SA, Clarridge JE. Potential errors in recognition of *Erysipelothrix rhusiopathiae*. J Clin Microbiol 2000;38:1302–1304. *Reviews laboratory diagnosis.*

Reboli AC, Farrar WE: *Erysipelothrix rhusiopathiae*: An occupational pathogen. Clin Microbiol Rev 1989;4:354–359. *Reviews epidemiology, clinical features, and bacteriology.*

Robson JM, McDougall R, van der Valk S, Waite SD, Sullivan JJ: *Erysipelothrix rhusiopathiae*: An uncommon but ever present zoonosis. Pathology 1998;30:391–394. *Clinical manifestations, pathological findings, and treatment are reviewed.*

Shimoji Y: Pathogenicity of *Erysipelothrix rhusiopathiae*: virulence factors and protective immunity. Microbes Infect 2000;2:965–972. *Recent advances in our understanding of pathogenicity and protective immunity are discussed.*

337 ACTINOMYCOSIS

Itzhak Brook

Definition

Actinomycosis is an uncommon, chronic bacterial infection that induces both suppurative and granulomatous inflammation. Localized swelling with suppuration, abscess formation, tissue fibrosis, and draining sinuses characterize this disease. The infection spreads contiguously forming often draining sinuses that extrude characteristic but not pathognomonic "sulfur granules." Infections of the oral and cervicofacial regions are most common; however, any site in the body can be infected. Other regions that are often affected are the thoracic region, abdominopelvic region, and the central nervous system (CNS). Musculoskeletal and disseminated disease can also be rarely seen.

Etiology

Actinomyces israelli is the most common species causing human disease. Other species include *Actinomyces naeslundii, Actinomyces odontolyticus, Actinomyces viscosus, Actinomyces meyeri,* and *Propionibacterium propionicum* (formerly *Arachnia propionica*). The organisms are filamentous, branching, gram-positive, pleomorphic non–spore-forming, non–acid-fast anaerobic or microaerophilic bacilli. It takes 3 to 10 or more days to grow them in culture. They are prokaryotes with cell walls that contain both muramic acid and diaminopimelic acid. Most actinomycotic infections are polymicrobial, involving other aerobic and anaerobic bacteria. The most commom co-isolates depend on the infection site and are *Actinobacillus actinomycetemcomitans, Eikenella corrodens, Bacteroides, Fusobacterium, Capnocytophaga, Staphylococcus, Streptococcus,* and members of the family Enterobacteriaceae.

Epidemiology

The agents of actinomycosis are members of the endogenous mucous membrane flora in the oral cavity, gastrointestinal tract, bronchi, and female genital tract. Infection can occur in all age groups; however, it is rarely seen in children or in patients older than 60 years. Most cases are encountered in individuals in the middle decades of life. A male-to-female infection ratio of 3:1 is reported in most series. The explanation for this ratio is the poorer oral hygiene and augmented oral trauma in males. The annual reported incidence in the United States is fewer than 100 cases. However, because of the fastidious nature of the organism, the true incidence is likely much higher.

Pathogenesis and Pathology

Actinomyces species are agents of low pathogenicity that require disruption of the mucosal barrier to cause disease. Oral and cervicofacial diseases commonly are associated with dental procedures, oral surgery, trauma, or dental sepsis. Pulmonary infections usually arise after aspiration of oropharyngeal or gastrointestinal secretions. Gastrointestinal infection frequently follows loss of mucosal integrity, such as with surgery, appendicitis, diverticulitis, trauma, or foreign bodies. The use of intrauterine contraceptive devices (IUDs) was linked to the development of actinomycosis of the female genital tract. The presence of a foreign body in this setting appears to trigger infection. Other predisposing factors are steroid use, immunosuppression, and human immunodeficiency virus infections.

Other bacterial species that often are co-pathogens to *Actinomyces* species may assist in the spread of infection by inhibiting host defenses and reducing local oxygen tension. Once the organism is established locally, it spreads to surrounding tissues in a progressive manner that ignores tissue planes, leading to a chronic, indurated, suppurative infection often with draining sinuses and fibrosis, especially in pelvic and abdominal infection. The fibrotic walls of the mass before suppuration are "wooden" in nature and may be confused with a neoplasm. Hematogenous spread can be fulminant but is rare.

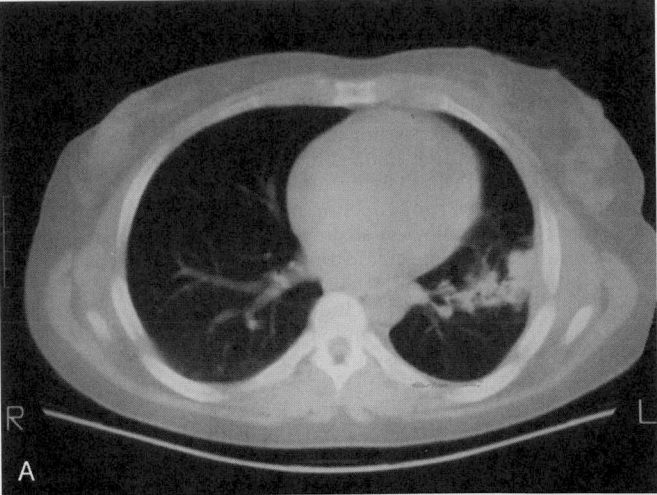

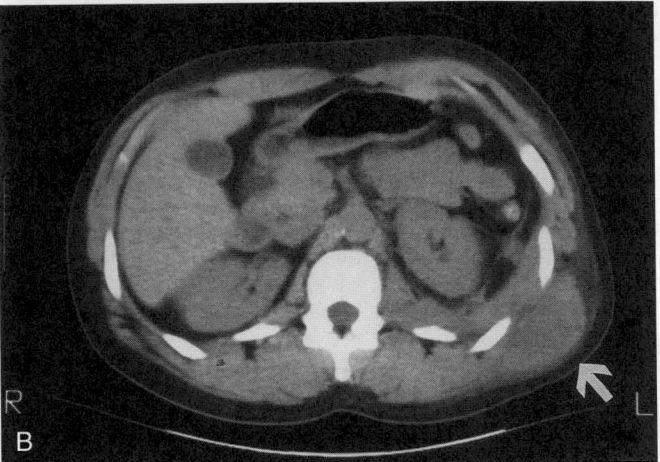

FIGURE 337–1 • Thoracic computed tomographic scan of a 43-year-old woman with pulmonary actinomycosis. There is consolidation of the lung with pleural thickening adjacent to the parenchymal disease (*A*). Abscess extended into the left breast and inferiorly to the costophrenic sulcus, to the retroperitoneum, and into the lateral abdominal wall (*B*) (arrow).

Actinomycetes grow in microscopic or macroscopic clusters of tangled filaments surrounded by neutrophils. Plasma cells and multinucleated giant cells often are observed with lesions, as may be large macrophages with foamy cytoplasm around purulent centers. When visible, these clusters are pale yellow and exude through sinus tracts; they are called sulfur granules. These granules (1 to 2 mm in diameter) are made of aggregates of organisms and contain calcium phosphate. A central purulent loculation surrounds the granules. Their centers have a basophilic staining property, with eosinophilic rays terminating in pear-shaped "clubs." One to six granules can be present per loculation, and up to 50 loculations can be present in a lesion. Multicenter giant cells can be seen.

Clinical Manifestations

CERVICOFACIAL. This is the most common and recognized infection and is usually observed in a setting of poor oral hygiene with tooth decay, periodontal disease, or gingivitis, in which mucosal integrity is disrupted by dental manipulations or other injury. Chronic tonsillitis, mastoiditis, and otitis also are important risk factors.

The infection generally evolves as a chronic or subacute painless or painful soft-tissue swelling or mass involving the submandibular or paramandibular region. However, the submental and retromandibular spaces, tempomandibular joint, and cheek can be involved. The swelling may have ligneous consistency caused by tissue fibrosis. More rapidly developing lesions often simulate pyogenic infections. Periapical infection can also occur. Trismus may be present, and advanced lesions may discharge odorless pus-containing sulfur

granules through one or more sinuses. Fever, pain, and leukocytosis may be present. The infection can extend to the carotid artery, tongue, sinuses, ears, mastoid orbit, salivary glands, pharynx, larynx, trachea, or thorax. Bone (most commonly the mandible) may be invaded from the adjacent soft tissue. Cervical spine or cranial bone infection may lead to subdural empyema and invasion of the CNS. The differential diagnosis includes tuberculosis (scrofula), fungal infections, nocardiosis, suppurative infections by other organisms, and neoplasms.

THORACIC. This is an indolent, slow process involving the pulmonary parenchyma and pleural space. This form accounts for 15 to 30% of actinomycosis cases and often results from aspiration of infective material from the oropharynx, and rarely following esophageal perforation, by extension into the mediastinum from

Infectious Diseses

the neck, or by spread from an abdominal site, and hematogenous spread to the lung. It often spreads from pneumonic focus across lung fissures to involve the pleura and the chest wall, with eventual fistula formation and drainage containing sulfur granules (Fig. 337–1). The mediastinum, pericardium, and myocardium can also rarely be affected. Granules rarely are present in the sputum. The incidence of this complication, as well as the destruction of thoracic vertebrae and adjacent ribs, has declined in the antibiotic era.

The complaints of patients with thoracic actinomycosis are nonspecific. The most common are chest pain, a productive cough, dyspnea, weight loss, and fever. Anemia, mild leukocytosis, and an elevated sedimentation rate are relatively common. There often is a history of underlying lung disease, and patients rarely present in an early stage of infection. The pulmonary lesion is either a mass lesion or pneumonitis and may resemble tuberculosis, especially when cavity formation occurs, and blastomycosis, which may destroy ribs posteriorly but rarely forms sinuses. Nocardiosis, bronchogenic carcinoma, cryptococcosis, aspiration pneumonia, pulmonary infection, and lymphoma can also mimic thoracic actinomycosis. Pleural thickening, effusion, and emphysema are common.

ABDOMINAL. This is a chronic, localized, inflammatory process that often is preceded weeks, months, or years after the integrity of the gastrointestinal mucosa is broken by surgery for acute appendicitis with perforation, or for perforated colonic diverticulitis, or by emergency surgery on the lower intestinal tract after trauma. Occasionally, abdominal actinomycosis may manifest without identifiable predisposing factors. The ileocecal region is involved most frequently (usually following appendicitis with perforation), with the formation of a mass lesion. The infection extends slowly to contiguous organs, especially the liver, and may involve retroperitoneal tissues, the spine, or the abdominal wall. Hepatic, renal, and splenic disseminations are uncommon complications. Persistent draining sinuses may form, and those involving the perianal region can sim-

ulate Crohn's disease or tuberculosis. The extensive fibrosis of actinomycotic lesions, presenting to the examiner as a mass, often suggests tumor. A frequent finding on computed tomography (CT) is an infiltrative mass with dense inhomogeneous contrast medium enhancement. Constitutional symptoms and signs are nonspecific; the most common are fever, diarrhea or constipation, weight loss, nausea, vomiting, pain, and sensation of mass.

PELVIC. This condition is observed in patients who present with prolonged use of IUDs, usually for longer than 2 years. Pelvic actinomycosis may also occur from extension of intestinal infection, commonly from indolent ileocecal disease. Manifestations of infection may range from a chronic vaginal discharge to pelvic inflammatory disease with tubo-ovarian abscesses or pseudomalignant masses. Patients generally present with abnormal vaginal bleeding or discharge, abdominal or pelvic pain, menorrhagia, fever, and weight loss.

Endometritis is the earlier form of the infection, followed by tubo-ovarian abscesses. Extension to the uterus, bladder, rectal area, abdominal wall, peritoneum, pelvic bones, thorax, and systemic can also occur.

CENTRAL NERVOUS SYSTEM. Infections of the CNS are very rare and generally manifest as single or multiple encapsulated brain abscesses that appear as ring-enhancing lesions with a thick wall that may be irregular or nodular on CT with intravenous contrast material and are indistinguishable from those caused by other organisms. Rarely, solid nodular or mass lesions termed actinomycetomas or actinomycotic granulomas are found. Headache and focal neurological signs are the most common findings. Most actinomycotic infections of the CNS are thought to be seeded hematogenously from a distant primary site; however, direct extension of cervicofacial disease is well recognized. Sinus formation is not a characteristic of CNS disease. The rare meningitis caused by *Actinomyces* is chronic and basilar in location, and the pleocy-tosis usually is lymphocytic. Thus, it may be misdiagnosed as tuberculous meningitis.

Diagnosis

A combination of appropriate microbiologic and pathologic studies are essential for proper diagnosis. A high index of suspicion should be communicated to the microbiology diagnostic laboratory, along with material from draining sinuses, from deep-needle aspiration, or from biopsy specimens. It is important to avoid antimicrobial therapy prior to obtaining a specimen. Anaerobic culture is required, and no selective media are available to restrict overgrowth of the slow-growing *Actinomyces* by associated microflora. The presence, in pus or tissue specimens, of non–acid-fast, gram-positive organisms with filamentous branching is very suggestive of the diagnosis.

The characteristic morphology of sulfur granules and the presence of gram-positive organisms within are helpful. However, the granules must be distinguished from similar structures that are sometimes produced in infections and that are caused by *Nocardia, Monosporium, Cephalosporium, Staphylococcus* (botryomycosis), and others. *Actinomyces* and *Arachnia* generally can be differentiated from other gram-positive anaerobes by means of growth rate (slow), by catalase production (negative, except *A. viscosus*), and by gas-liquid chromatographic detection of acetic, lactic, and succinic acids produced in peptone-yeast-glucose broth. Direct fluorescent antibody conjugates and immunofluorescence testing can be used but are not readily available to clinical microbiology laboratories.

Treatment

Penicillin G is the drug of choice for treating an infection caused by any of the *Actinomyces*. It is given in high dosage over a prolonged period, because the infection has a tendency to recur. Most deep-seated infections can be expected to respond to intravenous penicillin G 10 to 20 million units/day given for 2 to 6 weeks, followed by an oral phenoxypenicillin in a dosage of 2 to 4 g/day. A few additional weeks of oral penicillin therapy may suffice for uncomplicated cervicofacial disease; complicated cases and extensive pulmonary or abdominal disease may require treatment for 12 to 18 months. Little evidence exists of acquired resistance to penicillin G by *Actinomyces* during prolonged therapy. Alternative first-line antibiotics include tetracycline, erythromycin, and clindamycin. First-generation cephalosporins, ceftriaxone, and imipenem also have been used successfully. Metronidazole, aminoglycosides, and antifungal drugs are not active against these organisms. In vitro antibi-

otic sensitivity testing of *Actinomyces* is difficult, and the results may not be predictive of antibiotic activity in vivo.

The need to use combination antibiotic therapy to attack microorganisms that are isolated in association with *Actinomyces* has not been established. However, because many of these organisms are known pathogens, coverage is desirable for them as well. This is especially important in lower-abdominal infections. Surgical removal of infected tissue may also be necessary in some cases, especially if extensive necrotic tissue or fistulas are present, if malignancy cannot be excluded, and if large abscesses cannot be drained by percutaneous aspiration. When well-defined IUD-related symptoms and Papanicolaou smears demonstrate *Actinomyces* by specific fluorescence-labeled antibody, the IUD should be removed. Antibiotic administration for a 2-week period may be indicated. More serious infections require prolonged therapy.

Prognosis

The availability of antibiotics has greatly improved the prognosis for all forms of actinomycosis. At present, cure rates are high and neither deformity nor death is common.

SUGGESTED READINGS

De Feiter PW, Soeters PB: Gastrointestinal actinomycosis: An unusual presentation with obstructive uropathy: Report of a case and review of the literature. Dis Colon Rectum 2001;44:1521–1525. *Actinomycosis can cause recurrent retroperitoneal infection.*

Hamid D, Baldauf JJ, Cuenin C, Ritter J: Treatment strategy for pelvic actinomycosis: Case report and review of the literature. Eur J Obstet Gynecol Reprod Biol 2000;89:197–200. *Emphasizes its association with intrauterine devices and difficulty in diagnosis.*

Mabeza GF, Macfarlane J: Pulmonary actinomycosis. Eur Respir J 2003;21:545–551. *Review of the clinical presentation, radiographic changes, and treatment options for these three different sites of infection.*

338 NOCARDIOSIS

Richard J. Wallace, Jr.

Definition

Nocardiosis is a localized or systemic infection produced by multiple species of the genus *Nocardia*. It characteristically manifests as pneumonia in a patient on chronic corticosteroid therapy, but it may also produce post-traumatic, localized skin infections and disseminated disease with abscesses of the skin and brain. It is named for Alfred Nocard, who first described the disease in cattle in 1889.

Epidemiology

Nocardia infection is a nonreportable disease, and there are no recent, large, population-based studies of its incidence. It is a rare disease in general, and it occurs worldwide, with no localized geographic distribution. The presumed reservoir is environmental, with no human-to-human transmission. The usual risk factors for pulmonary or central nervous system (CNS) disease are chronic, high-dose corticosteroid use; organ transplantation; chemotherapy for solid tumor malignancy; and advanced human immunodeficiency virus (HIV) disease. Less common risk factors include alcoholism, bronchiectasis, pulmonary alveolar proteinosis, and local, invasive trauma (for primary cutaneous disease).

The *Nocardia* species usually involved with pulmonary or disseminated disease are *Nocardia nova*, *Nocardia farcinica*, *Nocardia abscessus*, and *Nocardia asteroides* complex. For *N. farcinica*, the rate of associated disseminated disease is especially high, exceeding 50%. Less common species include *Nocardia transvalensis*, *Nocardia pseudobrasiliensis*, and *Nocardia otitidis-caviarum*.

Patients with primary cutaneous disease usually have no underlying systemic disease. Infection follows penetrating trauma, which usually occurs in the lower extremities in adults. In young children, the face is the most common site of disease. More than 80% of cases of primary cutaneous disease are caused by *Nocardia brasiliensis*.

Rarely, other forms of nocardiosis are seen. They include post-traumatic ocular infections (e.g., keratitis), catheter-related infections, endocarditis, surgical wound infections, and a chronic form of cellulitis or osteomyelitis of the foot known as Madura foot (i.e., mycetoma), which occurs in underdeveloped countries where laborers often go barefoot.

Etiology

The taxonomy of clinical nocardiosis has expanded dramatically in recent years. The exact biology and clinical features of individual species are just being assessed. Differences between species may affect therapy, because each species has its own susceptibility pattern. For example, isolates of *N. farcinica* are resistant to third-generation cephalosporins such as ceftriaxone, whereas isolates of *N. transvalensis* are resistant to amikacin. The major taxonomic changes have been the recognition that *N. asteroides*, as it was once known, consisted of multiple species, including *N. nova*, *N. farcinica*, *N. transvalensis*, *N. abscessus*, and *Nocardia cyriacigeorgici*. It is now often referred to as *N. asteroides* complex because many laboratories do not identify the newer species. The other recent taxonomic change is the recognition that most pulmonary or CNS diseases due to organisms identified as *N. brasiliensis* are caused by the much more virulent species *N. pseudobrasiliensis*.

Pathobiology

Nocardia infection occurs in the setting of systemic immuno-compromise of the cell-mediated type. Chronic, high-dose steroid therapy seems especially to facilitate disease. It also occurs with local immunocompromise, as with bronchiectasis in the lung and local trauma of the skin. The immune response is pyogenic, with local collections of acute inflammatory cells that may form microabscesses or macroabscesses. No specific virulence factors or toxins are recognized for *Nocardia*.

Clinical Manifestations

Patients with pulmonary nocardiosis present with the usual clinical signs of subacute pneumonia. Fever is an almost universal sign, along with cough and purulent sputum production, even in patients on corticosteroids or other immune system–suppressing agents. Less common signs or symptoms include pleurisy, hemoptysis, and an abnormal chest radiograph for a patient with signs of skin or brain abscesses. This presentation is not specific, and numerous other fungal and bacterial pathogens can manifest similarly.

CNS *Nocardia* usually manifests with the typical signs of a brain abscess or, rarely, meningitis. Fever, headache, confusion, or altered mental status and grand mal seizures are most common. Some patients are asymptomatic, with one or multiple brain abscesses detected only by computed tomography (CT) or magnetic resonance imaging (Fig. 338–1). Approximately one third of patients with CNS disease present with a brain abscess alone, approximately one third present with a brain abscess and pneumonia simultaneously, and approximately one third develop the brain abscess up to 3 months after starting therapy for pulmonary disease. The differential diagnosis of combined lung and brain lesions in an immunosuppressed individual includes disseminated aspergillosis and toxoplasmosis.

Primary cutaneous disease manifests with a suppurative, draining lesion or ulcer after local trauma. Enlarged regional adenopathy may occur, especially with facial lesions in young children. Ascending, proximal, linear lymphangitic disease (i.e., lymphocutaneous disease or sporotrichoid disease) is relatively common. Dissemination from a primary skin infection is rare. The major differential diagnoses include cat-scratch disease, tularemia (i.e., ulceroglandular fever), mycobacterial pathogens such as *Mycobacterium marinum*, and sporotrichosis.

Diagnosis

For pulmonary nocardiosis, the diagnosis depends on a high index of suspicion, recognition of the somewhat unique radiographic features, and quality evaluation by Gram stain of sputum or bronchoalveolar lavage. The obvious high-risk patient is one on chronically administered corticosteroids who presents with a subacute, necrotizing pneumonia with purulent sputum. *Nocardia* may produce almost any pneumonic radiographic picture, but one or more rounded masses that enlarge fairly rapidly are typical (Fig. 338–2). Most undergo central cavitation with liquefied necrosis, and air-fluid levels are common findings. The usual presumptive diagnosis results from recognition of typical clumps of beaded, branched, gram-positive rods in a purulent respiratory specimen without other bacteria present. The

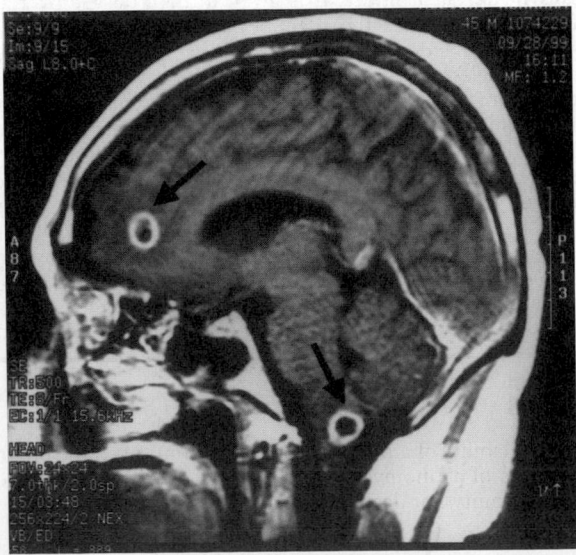

FIGURE 338–1 • Multiple, gadolinium-enhanced brain lesions (arrows) caused by *Nocardia* infection.

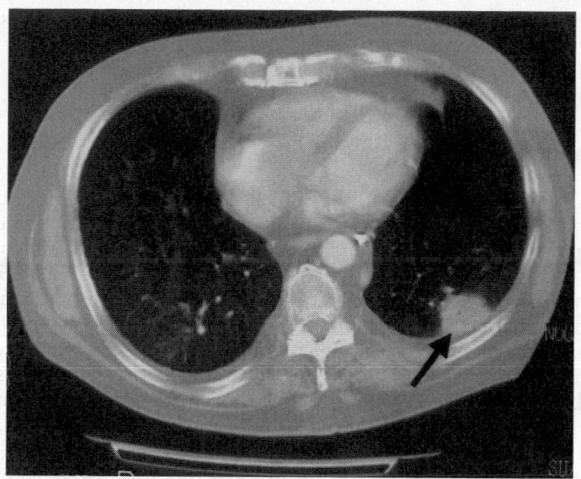

FIGURE 338–2 • Chest CT shows a peripheral nodular lung lesion (arrow) caused by *Nocardia* infection.

major Gram stain differential diagnosis is actinomycosis, but the causative organism is not seen in sputum and, when present in clinical specimens, is always present with other anaerobes or *Actinobacillus*. The clinical settings of the two organisms also are different.

Bronchoscopy or a fine-needle aspirate sometimes is needed to diagnose *Nocardia* disease. The organisms grow readily on routine blood agar in 3 to 5 days as small, fuzzy, white colonies. Because the organism's growth is inhibited by most gram-negative bacteria such as *Pseudomonas*, the culture plates should be examined carefully with a stereoscopic microscope and the microbiology laboratory should be alerted about the clinical suspicion of *Nocardia*. There are no commercial serologic or molecular tests to diagnose *Nocardia* from clinical specimens. Positive blood cultures are rare, but Gram stain and culture of associated cutaneous or brain abscess material may produce a diagnosis.

Nocardia often produces multiple brain abscesses. Isolated CNS disease requires a brain biopsy or aspirate for Gram stain and culture. The diagnosis can be presumptive in patients in whom *Nocardia* infection is diagnosed from respiratory secretions or cutaneous abscesses.

For primary cutaneous disease, clinical suspicion combined with Gram stain and culture of purulent drainage provides the basis of the diagnosis.

Susceptibility Testing

Susceptibility testing of clinical isolates is generally required, because *Nocardia* infection is caused by numerous species, each of which has a specific susceptibility pattern. Correct identification of the organism invariable takes a long time. The National Committee for Clinical Laboratory Standards (NCCLS) published the first guidelines for susceptibility testing of *Nocardia* in 2000. Overall, the most active agents against all species of *Nocardia* are sulfonamides, amikacin, imipenem, ceftriaxone, and linezolid.

Rx Treatment

Sulfonamides have been the treatment of choice for nocardiosis since the late 1940s. They are active against all species of *Nocardia* and generally perform well against localized cutaneous or pulmonary disease. The most commonly used drug is trimethoprim/sulfamethoxazole (TMP/SMX), given orally at a dose of 160/800 mg (one double strength) three times daily (adults).

Noncontrolled clinical studies have shown that the survival of patients with disseminated nocardiosis or CNS *Nocardia* infection is less than 50% when treated with a sulfonamide preparation alone. In these settings, one or more additional agents are given early in the treatment course. For severe disease, the most common adult regimen is amikacin (10 mg/kg/day in divided doses), ceftriaxone (2 g twice daily), and TMP/SMX at the dosage previously described. Alternative agents are imipenem, given as 500 mg every 6 hours, and linezolid, administered as 600 mg twice daily. These

combination agents may need to be modified when susceptibility results are available, and are usually continued until there is marked clinical and radiographic improvement (usually 4 to 6 weeks), and the therapy then is continued with the sulfonamide combination alone. The usual length of therapy is 6 to 12 weeks for primary cutaneous disease, 6 months for pulmonary disease, and 12 months for CNS disease. There are no treatment trials of these therapies because of the rarity of the diseases, but published case reports and series support this approach.

Surgical drainage is usually required for *Nocardia* abscesses of the skin or large brain abscesses. A patient with a pleural effusion or empyema requires a chest tube. Patients with small brain abscesses can usually be treated medically.

Prognosis

Left untreated, pulmonary nocardiosis is a uniformly fatal disease. Survival with the long-term use of sulfonamides was first reported in the late 1940s. With treatment, survival rates for uncomplicated pneumonia approach 90%. Most fatalities result from undiagnosed or overwhelming disease. The mortality rate of *Nocardia* brain abscesses or meningitis exceeded 50% when sulfonamides alone were used, but it is much better with the use of combination therapy. Non-CNS disseminated disease is also a highly fatal disease when treated with sulfonamide monotherapy, and survival is markedly improved with the use of combination therapy. Primary cutaneous disease can be a self-limited disease, and fatalities are rare.

Future Directions

The major changes expected in the near future include a more complicated list of *Nocardia* species that cause disease and greater availability of standardized susceptibility tests. Linezolid is the only drug with activity against all strains and species of *Nocardia*, and it may be used increasingly in complicated cases or until susceptibility studies are available.

SUGGESTED READINGS

Fergie JE, Purcell K: Nocardiosis in South Texas children. Pediatr Infect Dis J 2001;20:711–714. *A good review of the presentation and management of disease due to N. brasiliensis in children.*

Pintado V, Gomez-Mampaso E, Fortun J, et al: Infection with Nocardia species: Clinical spectrum of disease and species distribution in Madrid, Spain, 1978–2001. Infection 2002;30:338–340. *Treatment with sulfonamides was usually effective.*

Torres HA, Reddy BT, Raad II, et al: Nocardiosis in cancer patients. Medicine (Baltimore) 2002;81:388–397. *Emphasizes role of timely diagnosis and the adverse consequences of cytomegalovirus coinfection.*

339 BRUCELLOSIS

Robert A. Salata

Definition

Bacteria of the genus *Brucella* cause disease with protean manifestations. Infection is transmitted to humans from animals as a consequence of occupational exposure or ingestion of contaminated milk products. Despite the attempt to institute effective control measures, brucellosis remains a significant health and economic burden in many countries.

Etiology

Brucellae are slow-growing, small, aerobic, nonmotile, nonencapsulated, non–spore-forming, gram-negative coccobacilli. *B. abortus, B. suis, B. melitensis,* and *B. canis* are known to infect humans and are typed on the basis of biochemical, metabolic, and immunologic criteria. DNA hybridization analysis shows a high degree of homology between strains. There are differences in virulence among these four species. *B. abortus,* with a reservoir in cattle, usually is associated with mild to moderate sporadic disease; suppurative or disabling complications are rare. *B. suis* infection, resulting from swine contact, is often associated with destructive, suppurative lesions and may have a prolonged course. *B. melitensis,* with a reservoir in sheep and goats, may cause severe, acute disease and disabling complications. *B. canis,* spread to humans from infected dogs, causes disease with an insidious onset, frequent relapse, and a chronic course that is indistinguishable from infection related to *B. abortus.*

Epidemiology

More than 500,000 cases of brucellosis are reported yearly to the World Health Organization from 100 countries. *B. melitensis* infection, distributed primarily in the Mediterranean region (particularly Spain and Greece), Latin America, the Arabian Gulf, and the Indian subcontinent, accounts for the majority of cases. *B. abortus* infection occurs worldwide but has been effectively eradicated in several European countries, Japan, and Israel. *B. suis* occurs mainly in the midwestern United States, South America, and southeast Asia, whereas *B. canis* infection is most common in North and South America, Japan, and Central Europe. Identification of the *Brucella* species recovered in humans can provide clues to the likely source of infection.

In animals, brucellosis is a chronic infection that persists for life. In association with effective control programs in animals, human brucellosis has decreased dramatically in the United States, from over 6000 cases in 1947 to fewer than 200 cases per year since 1980. States reporting the greatest number of cases include Texas, California, Virginia, and Florida. In North America, brucellosis occurs mainly in spring and summer and is most common in men, usually related to occupational exposure.

Brucella infection in the United States most frequently occurs in high-risk groups, including slaughterhouse workers, farmers and dairymen, veterinarians, travelers to endemic areas, and laboratory workers handling the organisms. More than one half of reported cases occur in the meat-processing industry, particularly in the kill areas, where infection is spread through abraded or lacerated skin and the conjunctiva, possibly by aerosolization, and rarely by ingestion of infected tissue. Many cases of *B. abortus* infection in veterinarians have accidentally occurred from the strain 19 vaccine used to immunize cattle. *B. melitensis* infection, transmitted through the ingestion of goat's milk cheese, has been seen in U.S. travelers to and immigrants from Mexico. Brucellosis contracted abroad may not become symptomatic until the patient returns to the United States. Although persons with HIV infection are at risk for intracellular pathogens, the clinical manifestations of brucellosis in HIV-infected and noninfected individuals are similar.

Brucellosis in children accounts for only 3 to 10% of all reported cases worldwide, is common in endemic areas (may account for 20 to 25% of cases), and is often a mild, self-limited process. Infection occurs most frequently in school-age children and in familial outbreaks. No convincing evidence exists to associate *Brucella* infection with abortion in humans.

Pathogenesis and Immunity

After penetrating the epithelial cells of human skin, conjunctiva, pharynx, or lung, *Brucella* organisms initially induce an exuberant polymorphonuclear neutrophil response in the submucosa. After ingestion of organisms by neutrophils and tissue macrophages, spread to regional lymph nodes occurs. If host defenses within the lymph nodes are overwhelmed, bacteremia follows. The usual incubation period between infection and bacteremia is 1½ to 3 weeks. Bacteremia is accompanied by phagocytosis of free *Brucella* organisms by neutrophils and localization of bacteria primarily to the spleen, liver, and bone marrow, with the formation of granulomas.

If the inoculum is large and the patient receives no treatment, large granulomas may form, suppurate, and serve as a source of persistent bacteremia with the potential for multiorgan spread. The primary virulence factor of *Brucella* appears to be cell wall lipopolysaccharide.

Both virulent and attenuated strains of *Brucella* are readily phagocytized by neutrophils after opsonization with normal human serum. Whole bacteria and extracts of *Brucella* species may inhibit neutrophil oxidative burst activity and degranulation. Intracellular killing of ingested bacteria has been demonstrated with *B. abortus* but not *B. melitensis;* this may explain differences in pathogenicity between these species. The major cell wall antigen and virulence factor of *Brucella* is the S-LPS, containing A and M antigens, which also dominates antibody production.

Humoral factors may be important in the host defense against *Brucella.* Even in the absence of specific agglutinating antibody, normal human serum is bactericidal for *Brucella* organisms; *B. abortus* is more susceptible to serum lysis than is *B. melitensis.* The intracellular location within macrophages of the organism may provide a means for the bacteria to escape the lethal effects of serum. Specific serum agglutinating antibody has opsonic activity but does not correlate with the development of protective immunity.

A role for mononuclear phagocytes and cell-mediated immunity in brucellosis has been demonstrated. Protection against *Brucella* infection in animals is associated with preceding infection with *Listeria monocytogenes* or *Mycobacterium tuberculosis,* both of which stimulate cell-mediated immune mechanisms. Skin testing with *Brucella* proteins elicits a typical delayed hypersensitivity response in infected individuals. Macrophages, activated with Th I-type cytokines (e.g., interferon-γ and tumor necrosis factor-α, interleukin-1 and -12), kill *Brucella.*

Clinical Manifestations

Clinically, human brucellosis may be conveniently, but arbitrarily, divided into subclinical illness, acute/subacute disease, localized disease and complications, relapsing infection, and chronic disease (Table 339–1).

SUBCLINICAL ILLNESS. Detected only by serologic testing, asymptomatic or clinically unrecognized human brucellosis often occurs in high-risk groups, including slaughterhouse workers, farmers, and veterinarians. More than 50% of abattoir workers and up to 33% of veterinarians have high anti-*Brucella* antibody titers but no history of recognized clinical infection. Children in endemic areas frequently have subclinical illness.

ACUTE AND SUBACUTE DISEASE. After an incubation period of several weeks or months, acute brucellosis may occur as a mild, transient illness (with *B. abortus* or *B. canis*) or as an explosive, toxic illness with the potential for multiple complications (with *B. melitensis*). Approximately 50% of patients have an abrupt onset over days, whereas the remainder have an insidious onset over weeks. Symptoms in brucellosis are protean and nonspecific. More than 90% of patients experience malaise, chills, sweats, fatigue, and weakness. More than 50% of patients have myalgias, anorexia, and weight loss. Fewer patients complain of arthralgias, cough, testicular pain, dysuria, ocular pain, or visual blurring. Likewise, few localizing physical signs are apparent. Fever, often greater than 39.4° C (103° F), occurs in 95%. An undulating or intermittent fever pattern is unusual. A relative pulse-temperature deficit may occur. Splenomegaly is present in 10 to 15%, and lymphadenopathy occurs in up to 14% (axillary, cervical, and supraclavicular locations are most frequent, related to hand-wound or oropharyngeal routes of infection); hepatomegaly is less frequent. Other laboratory findings in acute or subacute disease may include mild anemia, lymphopenia or neutropenia (especially with bacteremia), lymphocytosis, thrombocytopenia, or (rarely) pancytopenia. The majority of infected individuals recover completely without sequelae if the diagnosis is appropriately made and prompt therapy is initiated.

LOCALIZED DISEASE AND COMPLICATIONS. *Brucella* organisms may localize in almost any organ but most commonly localize in bone, joints, central nervous system (CNS), heart, lung, spleen, testes, liver, gallbladder, kidney, prostate, and skin. Localized disease may occur simultaneously at multiple sites. Localized complications most often appear in association with a more chronic course of illness, although complications may occur with acute disease due to *B. melitensis* or *B. suis.* In the United States, localized disease is most frequently related to *B. suis.*

RELAPSING INFECTION. Up to 10% of patients with brucellosis relapse after antimicrobial therapy. This probably results from the intracellular location of the organisms, which protects the bacteria from certain antibiotics and host defense mechanisms. Relapses occur most frequently within months after initial infection but may occur

Table 339–1 • CLINICAL CLASSIFICATION OF HUMAN BRUCELLOSIS

	DURATION OF SYMPTOMS BEFORE DIAGNOSIS	MAJOR SYMPTOMS AND SIGNS	DIAGNOSIS	COMMENTS
Subclinical		Asymptomatic	Positive (low titer) serology, negative cultures	Occurs in abattoir workers, farmers, and veterinarians
Acute and subacute	Up to 2–3 mo and 3 mo to 1 yr	Malaise, chills, sweats, fatigue, headache, anorexia, arthralgias, fever, splenomegaly, lymphadenopathy, hepatomegaly	Positive serology, positive blood or bone marrow cultures	Presentation can be mild, self-limited (*B. abortus*), or fulminant with severe complications (*B. melitensis*)
Localized	Occurs with acute or chronic untreated disease	Related to involved organs	Positive serology, positive cultures in specific tissues	Bone/joint, genitourinary, hepatosplenic involvement most common
Relapsing	2–3 mo after initial episode	Same as acute illness but may have higher fever, more fatigue, weakness, chills, and sweats	Positive serology, positive cultures	May be extremely difficult to distinguish relapse from reinfection
Chronic	Longer than 1 yr	Nonspecific presentation but neuropsychiatric symptoms and low-grade fever most common	Low titer or negative serology, negative cultures	Most controversial classification; localized disease may be associated

as long as 2 years after apparently successful treatment. Relapsing infection is difficult to distinguish from reinfection in high-risk groups with continued exposure. Recent studies have shown that relapses are associated with inappropriate or insufficient antimicrobial therapy, positive blood cultures on initial presentation, and an acute onset of disease.

CHRONIC DISEASE. Disease with a duration of more than 1 year has been called chronic brucellosis. A majority of patients classified as having chronic brucellosis really have persistent disease caused by inadequate treatment of the initial episode, or they have focal disease in bone, liver, or spleen. About 20% of patients diagnosed as having chronic brucellosis complain of persistent fatigue, malaise, and depression; in many aspects this condition resembles the chronic fatigue syndrome. These symptoms frequently are not associated with clinical, microbiologic, or serologic evidence of active infection and may represent a preexisting psychoneurosis.

Diagnosis

Many more common illnesses mimic the clinical presentation of brucellosis. The most conclusive means of establishing the diagnosis of brucellosis is by positive cultures from normally sterile body fluids or tissues. Isolation of the organism can be enhanced by use of special media. The culture of *Brucella* organisms is potentially hazardous to laboratory personnel. Therefore, most cases of brucellosis are diagnosed by serologic testing.

In acute brucellosis, positive blood cultures are obtained in 10 to 30% of cases (as high as 85% with *B. melitensis*). Blood culture positivity decreases with increasing duration of illness. With *B. melitensis* infection, bone marrow cultures are of higher yield than are blood cultures. Blood cultures processed in radiometric detection or isolator systems may yield positive cultures in less than 10 days. With localized brucellosis (e.g., lymph nodes, spleen, liver, or skeletal system), cultures of purulent material or tissues usually yield *Brucella* organisms. Culture of cerebrospinal fluid is positive in 45% of patients with meningitis. Antibody against *Brucella* may be demonstrated in cerebrospinal fluid by enzyme-linked immunosorbent assay (ELISA).

Most patients mount significant serologic responses to *Brucella* infections. The most frequently used test is the standard tube agglutination (STA) test, measuring antibody to *B. abortus* antigen. A four-fold or greater rise in titer to 1:160 or higher is considered significant. A presumptive case is one in which the agglutination titer is positive (>1:160) in single or serial specimens, with symptoms consistent with brucellosis. By 3 weeks of illness, more than 97% of patients demonstrate serologic evidence of infection. This test equally detects antibodies to *B. abortus, B. suis,* and *B. melitensis* but not to *B. canis*. Serologic confirmation of *B. canis* infection requires *B. canis* or *B. ovis* antigen. Despite adequate antibiotic treatment, significant STA titers can persist for up to 2 years in 5 to 7% of cases. Because the STA titer may remain elevated, it is not useful in differentiating relapsing infection from other febrile illnesses in patients with past *Brucella* infections. Individuals with subclinical infection may demonstrate significant STA titers. In chronic localized brucellosis, STA titers may appear absent or low owing to a prozone phenomenon. This prozone effect appears to be related to the presence of immunoglobulin G (IgG) or immunoglobulin A (IgA) blocking antibodies; it can be eliminated if dilutions are carried out to at least 1:1280. False-positive STA titers due to immunologic cross-reactivity have been associated with *Brucella* skin testing, cholera vaccination, or infections due to *Vibrio cholerae, Francisella tularensis,* or *Yersinia enterocolitica*.

Immunoglobulin M (IgM) is the major agglutinating antibody formed in the first few weeks after infection with *Brucella* organisms; thereafter, IgG levels also rise. The STA test measures both IgM and IgG. With prompt and adequate therapy, IgG antibody levels usually become undetectable after 6 to 12 months. If therapy is given, those patients who develop persistent *Brucella* infection usually maintain elevated IgG agglutinins. In the absence of rising STA titers, a single elevated 2-ME *Brucella* agglutination titer (>1:160) suggests either current or recent infection. Certain newer antibody tests, including an ELISA and radioimmunoassay, are more sensitive than the STA; these methods are becoming more widely employed. Preliminary studies for diagnosis of brucellosis using the polymerase chain reaction with random or selected primers have been very promising, but additional evaluation is necessary and access to this diagnostic technology is still limited.

Rx Treatment

Effective treatment of *Brucella* infection requires antibiotics that can penetrate intracellularly, are available for prolonged therapy to prevent relapse, and are bactericidal in order to treat CNS infection and endocarditis. Debate is still considerable regarding which antibiotic regimen is superior due to the lack of controlled, randomized, double-blind studies comparing different antimicrobial regimens. However, recommendations are available and are given in Table 339–2.

Prognosis

Brucellosis appropriately treated within the first month of symptom onset is curable. Acute brucellosis often produces severe weakness and fatigue, and patients are frequently unable to work for up to 2 months. Immunity to reinfection follows initial *Brucella* infection in the majority of individuals. With early antimicrobial therapy, cases

Infectious Diseases

Table 339–2 • TREATMENT FOR BRUCELLOSIS

	TREATMENT	COMMENTS
Acute		
With no endocarditis or central nervous system involvement	Doxycycline (200 mg/day) plus rifampin (600 to 900 mg/day) for 6 wk	Treatment of choice by World Health Organization; widely used; low rate of relapse; intramuscular administration of streptomycin may be difficult
	or	
	Tetracycline (2 g/day) for 6 weeks plus streptomycin (1 g/day) or gentamicin for 3 weeks. *Alternative agents:* chloramphenicol, fluoroquinolones, trimethoprim/sulfamethoxazole, imipenem	Combination therapy still preferred
In children	Trimethoprim/sulfamethoxazole	
Central nervous system	Doxycycline plus rifampin and trimethoprim/sulfamethoxazole	Third-generation cephalosporin can be substituted if susceptible in vitro
Localized	Surgically drain abscesses plus antimicrobial therapy for ≥6 wk	
Brucella endocarditis	Bactericidal drugs; early valve replacement may be necessary	Possible aortic valve destruction and/or major arterial emboli

of chronic brucellosis or localized disease and complications are rare. Of patients who die of brucellosis, 84% have endocarditis involving a previously abnormal aortic valve, often associated with severe congestive heart failure.

Prevention

The control of human brucellosis relates directly to prevention programs in domestic animals and avoiding unpasteurized milk and milk products. In slaughterhouses, important means of prevention include careful wound dressing, protective glasses and clothing, prohibition of raw meat ingestion, and the use of previously infected (immune) individuals in high-risk areas.

SUGGESTED READINGS

Ko J, Splitter GA: Molecular host-pathogen interaction in brucellosis: Current understanding and future approaches to vaccine development for mice and humans. Clin Microbiol Rev 2003;16(1):65–78. *A good summary of current research.*

Solera J, Lozano E, Martinez-Alfaro, et al: Brucellar spondylitis: Review of 35 cases and literature survey. Clin Infect Dis 1999;29:1440–1449. *Stresses that spondylitis related to brucellosis causes significant morbidity but a favorable long-term prognosis.*

Solera J, Martinez-Alfaro E, Espinosa E: Recognition and optimal treatment of brucellosis. Drugs 1997;53:245–256. *A thorough analysis of current treatment options for human brucellosis stressing prolonged combined antibiotic therapy in conjunction with surgery where clinically indicated.*

Young EJ: An overview of human brucellosis. Clin Infect Dis 1995;21:283–289. *General review of epidemiology, clinical presentations, and approaches to diagnosis and management of human brucellosis.*

340 DISEASE CAUSED BY *BARTONELLA* SPECIES

Craig J. Hoesley
David A. Relman

The genus *Bartonella* includes at least 19 species or subspecies, but only 9 (*Bartonella henselae, Bartonella quintana, Bartonella bacilliformis, Bartonella elizabethae, Bartonella clarridgeiae, Bartonella vinsonii* subsp. *berkhoffii, Bartonella vinsonii* subsp. *arupensis, Bartonella washoensis,* and *Bartonella grahamii*) have been implicated in human disease. During recent years, an increasing number of distinct *Bartonella* taxa have been identified, particularly in animals, and members of this genus, extended by unification with the genera *Rochalimaea* and *Grahamella*, are considered emerging pathogens in humans.

Three major histologic varieties of disease are attributed to *Bartonella* infection: (1) vasculoproliferative disease, (2) endovascular disease with primary bacteremia, and (3) granulomatous disease. Examples of vasculoproliferative disease include bacillary angiomatosis and peliosis caused by *B. henselae* or *B. quintana*, and verruga peruana, which is a manifestation of chronic *B. bacilliformis* infection. Bacteremia may occur during any form of bartonellosis; however, it is convenient to consider separately the specific disorders of the endovascular compartment in which bacteremia is a dominant feature: trench fever (caused by *B. quintana*), infective endocarditis (caused by *B.*

henselae, B. quintana, B. elizabethae, B. vinsonii subsp. *berkhoffii*), and Oroya fever (caused by *B. bacilliformis*). *B. henselae* also causes the granulomatous disorder known as cat-scratch disease, which primarily affects lymph nodes but can sometimes cause systemic complications. *B. clarridgeiae* has been implicated as a cause of cat-scratch disease in a small number of individuals, and *B. grahamii* DNA was detected in the aqueous humor of a single patient with neuroretinitis.

The state of host immune competence plays an important role in determining which of these disparate forms of pathology become manifest during *Bartonella* infection. For example, *B. henselae* usually causes bacillary angiomatosis in immunocompromised individuals and cat-scratch disease in immunocompetent hosts. Genetic differences between *Bartonella* species or strains may also account for differences in pathogenicity and host response. *B. quintana* and *B. henselae* are equally likely to cause cutaneous lesions of bacillary angiomatosis, but *B. quintana* is more likely to induce subcutaneous or osseous lesions whereas *B. henselae* is almost exclusively implicated in disease of the liver, spleen, and lymph nodes.

Etiology

VASCULOPROLIFERATIVE DISEASE. Bacillary angiomatosis (epithelioid angiomatosis) was first described in 1983 in a person infected with human immunodeficiency virus (HIV). It was not until 1990 that a visualized but uncultivated bacillus was identified from tissues affected by this disease using molecular methods. In a serendipitous development, the same organism was cultivated for the first time in that same year; it was subsequently named *Rochalimaea henselae*. The close evolutionary relationships between this organism, *Rochalimaea quintana,* and *B. bacilliformis* led to the reclassification of all of these species within the *Bartonella* genus in 1993 (Fig. 340–1). *B. henselae* and *B. quintana* have each been cultivated directly from and detected in tissues affected by bacillary angiomatosis, as well as a variant form of pathology, bacillary peliosis. *B. henselae* is responsible for cases of bacillary angiomatosis-peliosis associated with cat exposure, and *B. quintana* is responsible for cases in impoverished, homeless individuals who are louse infested. Certain *B. henselae* genotypes appear to be more capable than others of causing hepatosplenic disease.

Classic bartonellosis (*B. bacilliformis* infection; Carrión's disease) is an insect-borne disorder characterized by two well-defined clinical stages: Oroya fever and verruga peruana, the second of which is characterized by vascular proliferative lesions similar to those of bacillary angiomatosis. The link between the two stages was established in 1885 by Daniel Carrión, a Peruvian medical student, when he developed acute hemolytic anemia (Oroya fever) 39 days after self-inoculation with material from a verruga lesion. In 1909, Barton named the causative agent Bartonella bacilliformis.

BACTEREMIC DISEASE. Trench fever was first described during World War I when more than 1 million military personnel were affected by this disorder. Trench fever has also been called 5-day or *quintan fever, shinbone fever, shank fever,* and *His-Werner disease* and has primarily been recognized during war-related epidemics. The etiologic agent was initially considered to be a member of the *Rickettsia* genus, but in 1961 the organism was isolated from infected lice and human blood and assigned to the genus *Rochalimaea* as *R. quintana*. In 1964, Koch's

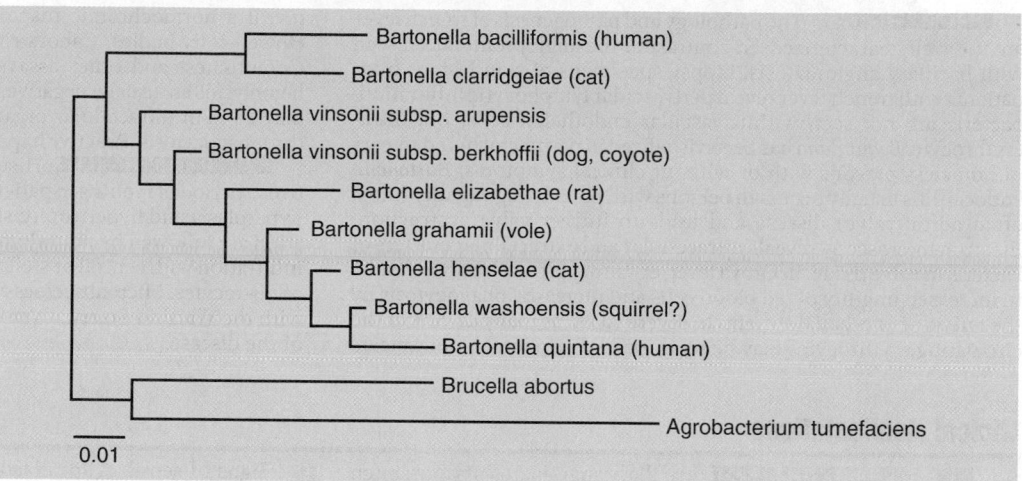

FIGURE 340–1 • Phylogenetic relationships among some of the α-proteobacteria, including the *Bartonella* species pathogenic for humans, based on small subunit ribosomal RNA sequence analysis. Many of these organisms are endosymbiotic and may have evolved in close association with insects or plants. The primary reservoirs for the *Bartonella* species are indicated in parentheses after their names, if known. The scale bar indicates 0.01 nucleotide substitutions.

postulates were fulfilled when trench fever was experimentally induced in human volunteers after inoculation with *R. quintana* organisms isolated from patients with trench fever. The agent was renamed *B. quintana* in 1993. *B. quintana, B. henselae, B. elizabethae,* and *B. vinsonii* subsp. *berkhoffii* all have been associated with endocarditis in humans. *B. vinsonii* subsp. *arupensis* was recently identified in a cattle rancher with fever and bacteremia; the reservoir for this pathogen has not been elucidated.

GRANULOMATOUS DISEASE. In 1983, small pleomorphic weakly gramnegative but strongly argyrophilic bacilli were first described in cat-scratch disease tissues. A variety of data now indicate that *B. henselae* is the cause of this syndrome in the vast majority of cases. Eighty-four to 88% of patients who meet traditional diagnostic criteria for cat-scratch disease (see later) demonstrate a significant elevation of serum IgG antibodies directed against *B. henselae,* whereas approximately 20% of asymptomatic cat owners and 4 to 6% of the general population have elevated titers. In addition, *B. henselae* DNA and antigens can be detected in tissues from these patients with the polymerase chain reaction (PCR) and in situ immunohistochemistry. *B. henselae* has also been cultivated from blood and tissues of patients with cat-scratch disease. However, Koch's postulates have not been fulfilled for this organism. In a small number of cases, *B. clarridgeiae* is believed to be the causative agent.

Epidemiology

VASCULOPROLIFERATIVE DISEASE. Cats and other felids are reservoirs for *B. henselae* in many regions of the world. In one study, 41% of cats were bacteremic with this organism. Bacteremia is more common in cats that are younger than 1 year of age, free ranging, and seropositive. Feline *B. henselae* infection is usually asymptomatic and may persist for the lifetime of the animal. Thus, it is not surprising that cat ownership and cat bites or scratches are the strongest risk factors for *B. henselae*–associated bacillary angiomatosis. Cat fleas transmit this species between cats, but fleas do not play a major role in transmission to humans. *B. quintana* has not been detected in cats, and cat exposure is uncommon among patients with *B. quintana*–associated bacillary angiomatosis. Humans appear to be the sole reservoir of *B. quintana,* and the human body louse, *Pediculus humanus,* serves as the transmission vector. The microorganism has been found in saliva, feces, and material regurgitated by lice. Direct human-to-human transmission has not been demonstrated. Risk factors for *B. quintana*–associated disease include homelessness, low economic status, and louse infestation. Approximately 90% of patients with bacillary angiomatosis-peliosis are coinfected with HIV or are immunocompromised by another mechanism.

B. bacilliformis infection is restricted to the habitat of its principal vector, the sandfly, *Phlebotomus verrucarum.* The sandfly breeds and transmits the infection in river valleys of the Andes Mountains at altitudes between 2500 and 9000 feet. Humans are the only known reservoir of the microorganism. Convalescent individuals may have low-grade bacteremia for months to years after infection, and *B. bacilliformis* may be recovered from 5 to 10% of apparently healthy persons in an endemic area. These carriers represent the greatest epidemiologic threat.

BACTEREMIC DISEASE. Trench fever and *B. quintana* have a worldwide distribution; disease occurs sporadically in endemic sites, such as eastern Europe, Russia, and Mexico. Epidemic disease was described during World Wars I and II in Europe. In the 1990s, temporal and geographic clusters of endemic disease were recognized for the first time among urban homeless populations in the United States and western Europe. In one study, 20% of attendees at an inner-city clinic in Seattle had elevated antibody titers to *B. quintana.* In a separate study in France, 30% of homeless persons seeking care in hospital emergency departments were seropositive for *B. quintana* and 14% were bacteremic.

Bartonella species account for approximately 3% of all cases of infective endocarditis and a significant portion of "culture-negative" endocarditis cases in both immunocompetent and immunocompromised hosts. *B. henselae* has been incriminated in 5% of cases of fever of unknown origin in children.

GRANULOMATOUS DISEASE. Cat-scratch disease affects approximately 22,000 persons in the United States per year. The highest incidence of the disease occurs in the 5- to 14-year-old age group and in the South, where cat fleas are most prevalent and *B. henselae* infection of cats is most common. The disease usually occurs in the summer and autumn. A history of cat scratch or bite is elicited in approximately 75% of patients. Fewer than 5% of cases of cat-scratch disease belong to a family cluster; however, small clusters of disease with neurologic complications have been noted.

Pathology and Pathogenesis

VASCULOPROLIFERATIVE DISEASE. The lesions of bacillary angiomatosis assume diverse macroscopic appearances, including an erythematous, polypoid or papular, cutaneous or mucosal pattern; deeply erythematous and indurated dermal plaques; and subcutaneous or visceral nodules. In all of these lesions, a distinctive lobular proliferation of capillaries is seen within a fibrous stroma. Hematoxylin and eosin staining reveals granular amphophilic material in the interstitium between vessels. This and other microscopic features distinguish bacillary angiomatosis from Kaposi's sarcoma. The amphophilic material corresponds to clumps of extracellular bacteria, as viewed with the Warthin-Starry silver stain or with electron microscopy. Bacillary peliosis is a histologically variant form of bacillary angiomatosis that is characterized by blood-filled cystic spaces, fibromyxoid stroma, and inflammatory cells; it is almost always associated with *B. henselae* and occurs most often within the liver and spleen. The pathogenesis of bacillary angiomatosis includes early blood-borne dissemination of organisms throughout the body. The bartonellae attach readily to and may enter erythrocytes; persistence within the intravascular compartment suggests bacterial mechanisms for avoidance of opsonization and host phagocytosis.

After inoculation by the sandfly, *B. bacilliformis* invades erythrocytes and endothelial cells. Most untreated patients who survive the acute hemolytic anemia go on to develop the chronic cutaneous lesions of verruga peruana. These hemangiomatous nodules consist of proliferating small vessels infiltrated by lymphocytes and macrophages. Verruga may also occur in the viscera, bone, and central nervous system.

BACTEREMIC DISEASE. The pathology and pathogenesis of trench fever are not well characterized. In contrast to the angioproliferation seen with bacillary angiomatosis, biopsy specimens of skin lesions from patients with trench fever reveal perivascular lymphocytic infiltration; bacteria are not seen within vascular endothelial cells, but intra-erythrocytic *B. quintana* has been visualized in peripheral blood smears of homeless persons with or without clinical symptoms. *Bartonella* endocarditis usually occurs in persons with preexisting valvular (most often aortic valve) disease and leads to further valve destruction. Electron microscopy reveals intracellular and extracellular clusters of bacteria in valve tissue. In Oroya fever, erythrocyte parasitization results in increased fragility of red blood cells and increased phagocytosis by the reticuloendothelial system. In severe cases, as many as 90% of the circulating erythrocytes may be parasitized. Peripheral blood smears reveal a normochromic macrocytosis and striking polychromasia, Howell-Jolly bodies, Cabot's rings, and nucleated erythrocytes. The Coombs test and other assays for red blood cell agglutinins and hemolysins are usually negative. Cells of the reticuloendothelial system may contain intracellular organisms, presumably as a result of erythrophagocytosis. Reactive hyperplasia of lymphatic tissue is common.

GRANULOMATOUS DISEASE. Histologic changes in lymph nodes evolve over a period of months in patients with cat-scratch disease. Follicular hyperplasia and hypertrophy, sinus histiocytosis, and B-cell proliferation are followed by granuloma formation and later by neutrophilic infiltration with central or stellate necrosis and surrounding palisades of histiocytes. Microabscesses are common. Bacilli are best visualized with the Warthin-Starry silver impregnation stain early in the course of the disease.

Clinical Manifestations

VASCULOPROLIFERATIVE DISEASE. Bacillary angiomatosis is most often associated with tender cutaneous or subcutaneous lesions. Mucosal lesions are also common. Lesions of bacillary angiomatosis may be indistinguishable from those of Kaposi's sarcoma. The lesions may be solitary or multiple, red, purple, or flesh-colored dome-shaped papules, nodules, polypoid tumors, or plaques. With age the lesions may ulcerate, form a crust, or develop a collarette of scale. Subcutaneous lesions sometimes erode underlying bone; this finding should raise suspicion of bacillary angiomatosis. In an undetermined percentage of cases, visceral bacillary angiomatosis-peliosis occurs, sometimes in the absence of cutaneous disease. Visceral involvement may be asymptomatic or, as in disseminated cutaneous disease, may be associated with fever, chills, malaise, and anorexia. Liver, spleen, and internal lymph nodes appear to be the most frequent sites of extracutaneous disease. Biliary obstruction has resulted from external compression of periportal lymph nodes. Other sites affected by bacillary angiomatosis include bone marrow, lung, and brain. In general, cases of bacillary angiomatosis and peliosis are less frequent in the current era of more potent HIV-specific therapies.

Verruga peruana develops after a latent period of weeks to months following the resolution of acute *B. bacilliformis* infection in untreated patients. This disorder is characterized by 1- to 2-cm hemangiomatous nodules that typically evolve over a period of 1 to 2 months in crops on exposed skin but also on mucous membranes and within internal organs. The lesions are usually nontender and may vary morphologically, appearing sometimes as ulcers or as secondarily infected pustules. The verruga may persist for months to years in untreated patients.

BACTEREMIC DISEASE. The incubation period for trench fever ranges from 4 to 35 days. In human volunteers the average duration is 22 days. Clinical manifestations vary from a febrile illness of 4 to 5 days' duration in some patients to a severe illness with prolonged fever in others. In the classic descriptions of more severe disease, infected persons experience three to five febrile paroxysms, each lasting approximately 5 days (quintan or 5-day fever). A syndrome of continuous fever lasting 2 to 6 weeks has also been noted. In addition to fever and chills, symptoms of trench fever include malaise, anorexia, night sweats, headache with retro-orbital pain, and severe bone pain in the neck, back, and lower extremities, especially the tibia (shinbone fever). Conjunctival injection, hepatosplenomegaly, mild to moderate leukocytosis, and an erythematous maculopapular truncal rash occur in most patients. Symptoms and signs are typically most severe during the initial febrile period. Subsequent attacks are milder, with the exception of persistent, severe bone pain. Irregular episodes of remission and late relapses have been reported. Specific antibodies to *B. quintana* appear within several weeks of primary infection, but they are not fully protective, because reinfection has been documented within 3 to 6 months of the initial illness.

The clinical manifestations of *Bartonella* endocarditis are similar to those of more typical forms of infective endocarditis. In a retrospective analysis of 22 patients, the majority presented with fever with a temperature higher than 38° C and approximately 40% manifested embolic phenomena. Echocardiography revealed a valvular (predominantly aortic) vegetation in 86% of patients. Approximately 90% required valve surgery; despite antibiotic therapy, the mortality rate was close to 30%. *B. henselae*, *B. quintana*, *B. elizabethae*, and *B. vinsonii* subsp. *berkhoffii* all have been reported to cause infective endocarditis.

Signs of sepsis or localized (granulomatous or angioproliferative) disease are uncommon in cases of *B. henselae* or *B. quintana* bacteremia. Fever, headache, myalgias, and arthralgias may persist or recur over a period of weeks to months despite therapy. Homeless persons with *B. quintana* bacteremia are more likely to have been exposed to lice, have headaches and severe leg pain, and have lower platelet counts than homeless people who have no serologic evidence of exposure to *B. quintana* and no bacteremia. In some cases, *B. henselae* bacteremia has been associated with a lymphocytic meningitis.

Within 2 to 6 weeks after the bite of an infected sandfly, the nonimmune host develops Oroya fever. It is characterized by the insidious onset of myalgias and low-grade fever, followed by high fever, headache, and painful muscles and joints. Tender lymphadenopathy is common; splenomegaly is rare. Erythrocyte counts decrease rapidly within a few days and many fall as low as 1 million/mm³. In some patients there is a febrile crisis, followed by rapid resolution of symptoms and signs, increased erythropoiesis, and gradual reduction of fever. Recurrence of fever after initial improvement suggests secondary infection. Salmonellosis is an especially important complication of acute *B. bacilliformis*–associated disease in South America and may reflect transient immunosuppression. In addition, malaria, amebiasis, and tuberculosis also appear to be more common in these patients. Historically, mortality in untreated Oroya fever approached 50% as a result of both acute hemolytic anemia and secondary infections. In a recent report of 68 persons with Oroya fever, the most common symptoms were fever, malaise, anorexia, and headache whereas the most common signs were pallor, hepatomegaly, cardiac murmur, and jaundice. The mortality rate in this case series was only 9%. After resolution of the febrile hemolytic anemia, immunity develops; relapses or reinfections are unusual.

GRANULOMATOUS DISEASE. After an incubation period of 3 to 10 days, an erythematous papule develops at the inoculation site in more than half of those later diagnosed with cat-scratch disease. These lesions may form a crust or become pustular; they resolve spontaneously in 1 to 3 weeks. Within a few weeks of inoculation, regional lymphadenopathy becomes apparent; usually a lymph node in the axillary or neck regions is found to be enlarged and tender (Table 340-1). Low-grade fever, malaise, anorexia, and nausea each occur in a minority of patients. In a typical case of cat-scratch disease, lymph nodes remain enlarged for at least 2 to 4 months. Infrequently, inoculation of the eye results in a granulomatous lesion of the conjunctiva and in preauricular adenopathy, a condition known as *oculoglandular syndrome of Parinaud* (affecting 4 to 6% of cat-scratch disease patients).

Severe or systemic, non-neurologic manifestations are reported in 2% of cat-scratch disease patients. These include persistent fever, weight loss, splenomegaly, diffuse papular rash, erythema nodosum, pleuritis, splenic abscess, central lymphadenopathy, osteolytic lesions, hepatitis, and thrombocytopenic purpura. An additional 2% of patients with cat-scratch disease develop neurologic complications. Encephalopathy or encephalitis are most common and are manifested by seizures and confusion; other presentations include radiculitis, meningitis, cranial neuritis, neuroretinitis, and cerebral arteritis. Neurologic complications occur 2 to 3 weeks after onset of the initial illness. Spontaneous, complete resolution is the rule in these cases.

Table 340–1 • SELECTED CLINICAL FEATURES OF CLASSIC CAT-SCRATCH DISEASE

FEATURE	PERCENTAGE OF CASES
Site of lymphadenopathy	
Axilla	25–52
Neck	26–39
Groin	7–18
Elbow	2–13
Preauricular region	5–7
Single node involvement	43–85
Lymphadenopathy only	48–51
Fever	31–48
Splenomegaly	11–12
Hospitalization	9–17

Table 340–2 • TREATMENT SUGGESTIONS

Severe Cat-Scratch Disease*	
Doxycycline, plus	100 mg bid
rifampin	300 mg bid
or azithromycin	500 mg qd × 1 d, then 250 mg qd ×4 d
Bacillary Angiomatosis-Peliosis or *Bartonella* Bacteremia[†]	
Erythromycin or	250–500 mg qid
doxycycline	100 mg bid
plus rifampin (severe disease)	300 mg bid
Consider addition of an aminoglycoside	

*Therapy should be continued for at least 14 days.
[†]Treat patients with bacillary angiomatosis-peliosis for at least 3–4 months, patients with *Bartonella* bacteremia for 2–4 weeks, and patients with *Bartonella* endocarditis for at least 6 weeks.

Diagnosis

VASCULOPROLIFERATIVE DISEASE. *B. henselae* is a slightly curved, small (0.5×1 to 2 μm), self-aggregating, gram-negative bacillus that is capable of twitching motility. Optimal growth occurs on enriched media supplemented with 5% sheep or rabbit blood at 35° C in a 5 to 10% CO_2-humidified atmosphere. Colonies become visible after 9 to 21 days of primary culture (two different morphologies) and after 3 to 5 days on subsequent laboratory passage. *B. quintana* grows under similar conditions, especially after cocultivation with endothelial cell monolayers. *B. bacilliformis* grows preferentially at 25 to 30° C. Species identification requires specific antisera, cellular fatty acid analysis, or DNA polymorphism or sequence analysis.

The diagnosis of both bacillary angiomatosis and cat-scratch disease rests on tissue examination and serologic tests in a compatible clinical setting. Histology typical of bacillary angiomatosis in hematoxylin and eosin—stained tissue is suggestive of the diagnosis. Warthin-Starry stains usually confirm this diagnosis (i.e., revealing clumps of small, pleomorphic bacilli). Commercial laboratories, as well as the Centers for Disease Control and Prevention, offer an immunofluorescent or enzyme-linked immunosorbent assay for serum IgG antibodies directed against *B. henselae*, *B. quintana*, and *B. elizabethae*. Most assays cannot distinguish reliably among humoral responses to each of these species. Cultivation of *Bartonella* species and detection of specific genetic sequences by PCR or antigens by immunohistochemical methods are more specialized procedures and are not available at most clinical microbiology laboratories. Kaposi's sarcoma is the most important entity confused with bacillary angiomatosis. Visual detection of bacilli distinguishes the latter from the former. Lytic bone lesions in an HIV-infected individual should raise the possibility of bacillary angiomatosis.

BACTEREMIC DISEASE. *Bartonella* species are slow growing and fastidious, but they can be cultivated on blood-enriched media or in the presence of endothelial cells (see earlier). Formation of colonies on an agar surface directly from an infected clinical specimen may require more than 21 days of incubation and subculturing on freshly prepared media. Acridine orange staining procedures and lysis centrifugation culture methods enhance the detection and recovery, respectively, of *Bartonella* species from blood specimens. Serologic methods may aid in the diagnosis of *Bartonella* bacteremic disease. The serologic cross-reactivity of *Chlamydia* and *Bartonella* species may present a diagnostic problem because both groups of microorganisms must be considered in cases of culture-negative endocarditis. PCR assays have also proven successful in detecting *Bartonella* species on resected heart valve tissue.

The differential diagnosis of trench fever includes epidemic (louseborne) typhus, which occurs under similar demographic circumstances and shares the same vector (*P. humanus*) as trench fever, endemic (murine) typhus, ehrlichiosis, Q fever, Rocky Mountain spotted fever, relapsing fever, Lyme disease, malaria, and plague. Local disease endemicity or history of body louse infestation should raise the clinical suspicion of trench fever.

The diagnosis of Oroya fever is made by examining a peripheral blood smear or by serology. Bacilli may be seen within red blood cells as single organisms or in pairs or clusters. With Giemsa staining, the bacilli appear as 0.3- to 1.5-μm pleomorphic red-purple rods.

GRANULOMATOUS DISEASE. Cat-scratch disease is diagnosed most often by examination of Warthin-Starry silver–stained tissue or by using serologic methods. The differential diagnosis for localized cat-scratch disease may include pyogenic lymphadenitis, mycobacterial infection, tularemia, brucellosis, lymphogranuloma venereum, syphilis, fungal disease, toxoplasmosis, and Epstein-Barr virus or cytomegalovirus infection.

 Treatment

There are few data from prospective randomized studies from which to choose an antimicrobial regimen for *Bartonella*-associated disease. Antibiotic susceptibility testing has demonstrated that *Bartonella* species are frequently susceptible in vitro to a variety of classes of antimicrobial agents, including β-lactams, tetracyclines, macrolides, aminoglycosides, rifampin, and ciprofloxacin. Unfortunately, the minimum inhibitory concentrations derived in laboratory testing do not consistently correlate with in vivo efficacy. Retrospective or empirical clinical observations offer the primary basis for the suggested approaches in Table 340–2. Corticosteroids are not recommended for any of these diseases.

VASCULOPROLIFERATIVE DISEASE. All forms of *Bartonella*-associated vasculoproliferative disease warrant antimicrobial treatment. As stated earlier, in vitro antibiotic susceptibility testing has not consistently correlated with clinical experience in the treatment of bacillary angiomatosis-peliosis. In particular, there are well-documented instances of clinical failure with β-lactam agents. Based on empirical observations, the treatment of choice for bacillary angiomatosis-peliosis is either erythromycin, 500 mg every 6 hours, or doxycycline, 100 mg every 12 hours. Azithromycin is an alternative. Patients who are severely ill or unable to absorb oral medications should be treated with intravenous formulations. Rifampin should be added to the regimen for patients in the former category. Because disease relapse is otherwise so common in these immunocompromised hosts, patients should be treated for at least 3 months. Verruga lesions do not respond consistently to antimicrobial agents, but a recent review of 77 patients with the eruptive phase of bartonellosis reported a good response to rifampin (46 [84%] of 55 patients) and a modest response to streptomycin (5 [56%] of 9 patients). Verruga lesions refractory to antimicrobial therapy may require surgical resection.

BACTEREMIC DISEASE. *Bartonella* bacteremia also warrants antimicrobial treatment, despite the fact that some immunocompetent hosts with *B. quintana* bacteremia clear their infection spontaneously. The same drugs and doses listed earlier for treatment of bacillary angiomatosis-peliosis are recommended for primary bacteremias. All patients should be evaluated for endocarditis. Treatment should be administered for at least 6 weeks and for 2 to 4 weeks in patients with and without endocarditis, respectively.

Continued

Rifampin should be added to the regimen for treatment of endocarditis. A recent retrospective study has concluded that aminoglycoside administration for at least 2 weeks is an important component of antibiotic treatment regimens. Close monitoring of hemodynamics is essential because historically the majority of endocarditis patients have ultimately required valve repair or replacement, perhaps related to delay in diagnosis in many instances. Patients with trench fever usually respond rapidly to antibiotic therapy with resolution of fever and other symptoms within 1 to 2 days. Relapses in treated patients have been well described.

In patients with Oroya fever, clinical observations suggest that penicillin, chloramphenicol, tetracycline, and streptomycin are effective. Chloramphenicol at a dose of 2 to 4 g/day for 7 or more days is the therapy of choice because of the frequent association of *Salmonella* infection in endemic regions. After the institution of therapy, fever generally disappears within 2 to 3 days, although blood smears may remain positive for some time.

GRANULOMATOUS DISEASE. Most patients with cat-scratch disease do not require more than symptomatic support. A fluctuant or suppurative lymph node may benefit from needle aspiration. Antibiotic therapy should be reserved for immunocompromised individuals or those with evidence of severe or systemic disease. It remains unclear what constitutes the most useful agents in this setting. Doxycycline plus rifampin may be effective, but well-controlled data are lacking. One published randomized, placebo-controlled study suggests that a 5-day course of azithromycin speeds resolution of cat-scratch lymphadenopathy.■

1. Bass JW, Freitas BC, Freitas AD, et al: Prospective randomized double-blind placebo-controlled evaluation of azithromycin for treatment of cat-scratch disease. Pediatr Infect Dis J 1998;17:447–452.

SUGGESTED READINGS

Anderson BE, Neuman MA: *Bartonella* spp. as emerging human pathogens. Clin Microbiol Rev 1997;10:203–219. *Useful review of the biology of the bartonellae. Emphasizes diagnostic approaches.*

Capo C, Amirayan-Chevillard N, Brouqui P, et al: *Bartonella quintana* bacteremia and overproduction of interleukin-10: Model of bacterial persistence in homeless people. J Infect Dis 2003;187:837–844. *Recent findings.*

Kerkjoff FT, Bergmans AM, van Der Zee A, Rothova A: Demonstration of *Bartonella grahamii* DNA in ocular fluids of a patient with neuroretinitis. J Clin Microbiol 1999;37:4034–4038. *Bartonella caused an inflammatory retinitis in a nonimmunocompromised patient.*

Koehler JE, Glaser CA, Tappero JW: *Rochalimaea henselae* infection: A new zoonosis with the domestic cat as reservoir. JAMA 1994;271:531–555. *The first definitive demonstration that B. henselae bacteremia is common in asymptomatic domestic cats! Even though cat fleas were implicated, the mechanism(s) of B. henselae transmission from the cat reservoir to humans is believed to be direct inoculation.*

Koehler JE, Sanchez MA, Garrido CS, et al: Molecular epidemiology of *Bartonella* infections in patients with bacillary angiomatosis-peliosis. N Engl J Med 1997;337:1876–1883. *Defines the different epidemiologic settings for B. henselae– and B. quintana–associated disease.*

Maguina C, Garcia PJ, Gotuzzo E, et al: Bartonellosis (Carrión's disease) in the modern era. Clin Infect Dis 2001;33:772–779. *Describes the clinical manifestations and treatment of acute (Oroya fever) and chronic (eruptive) bartonellosis in 145 symptomatic patients.*

Relman DA, Loutit JS, Schmidt TM, et al: The agent of bacillary angiomatosis: An approach to the identification of uncultured pathogens. N Engl J Med 1990;323:1573–1580. *Describes the first clinical application of a molecular approach for identifying previously uncharacterized fastidious or uncultivated microbial pathogens directly from infected host tissue.*

Spach DH, Kanter AS, Dougherty MJ, et al: *Bartonella (Rochalimaea) quintana* bacteremia in inner-city patients with chronic alcoholism. N Engl J Med 1995;332:424–428. *The first description of urban trench fever in the United States. These unexpected findings occurred after the institution of a more sensitive blood culture protocol at a major public hospital in Seattle.*

341 TUBERCULOSIS

Michael D. Iseman

Definition

Tuberculosis is an infectious disease caused by *Mycobacterium tuberculosis*. Characteristic features include a prolonged latency period between the initial infection and overt disease, prominent pulmonary disease (although other organs can be involved), and a granulomatous response associated with intense tissue inflammation and damage.

Etiology

Mycobacteria are small, rod-shaped, aerobic, non–spore-forming bacilli. The genus *Mycobacterium* contains a group of organisms so closely related that they are referred to as the "tuberculosis complex": *M. tuberculosis*, *Mycobacterium bovis*, *Mycobacterium africanum*, and *Mycobacterium microti*. However, given the singular epidemiologic, clinical, public health, and therapeutic considerations associated with *M. tuberculosis*, the term *tuberculosis* should be reserved exclusively for infection or disease caused by this organism. Disease caused by other organisms of this genus should be referred to as "mycobacteriosis due to *M. x*" and not as "atypical tuberculosis" or "tuberculosis due to . . ." (Chapter 342).

The mycobacteria are environmental organisms found extensively in water and soil. However, *M. tuberculosis* has become so adapted to the human body that it has no natural reservoirs in nature other than infected/diseased persons. Although disease due to strain identified as *M. tuberculosis* has been reported rarely in primates, elephants, and other mammals, the presumption is that the animals usually acquired the infection from humans.

Mycobacterial cell walls contain high concentrations of lipids or waxes, making them resistant to standard staining techniques. They can be induced to take up a dye such as carbol fuchsin by imposing alkalinity or by heating. After dye absorption, they are resistant to acid-alcohol, a potent decolorizing agent, which provides the basis of the reference to acid-fast bacilli (AFB).

M. tuberculosis and most of the other mycobacteria grow quite slowly; their doubling time in most media is approximately 18 to 24 hours. Readily discernible colonies typically do not appear on solid media for 2.5 to 5 weeks; because of this, culture confirmation, speciation, and drug susceptibility testing done by conventional techniques have been clinically problematic. Hence, there has been great interest in rapid, novel techniques to indicate the presence, species, and drug-susceptibility of mycobacteria, including *M. tuberculosis*.

M. tuberculosis is an aerobic, facultative, intracellular parasite. The ability to invade and spread throughout the human body largely results from the capacity of tubercle bacilli to survive and proliferate within mononuclear phagocytes.

Transmission

Infection is spread almost exclusively by aerosolization of contaminated respiratory secretions. Patients with *cavitary* lung disease are particularly infectious because their sputum usually contains 1 to 100 million bacilli/mL, and they cough frequently.

However, the intact respiratory mucous membranes are quite resistant to invasion. For infection to occur, bacilli must be delivered to the distal air spaces of the lung, the alveoli, where they are not subject to mucociliary clearance. Once deposited in alveoli, bacilli are adapted to promote uptake by alveolar macrophages. Depending on innate, genetically determined properties, the macrophages may be more or less permissive to bacillary proliferation.

To reach the alveoli, the bacilli must be suspended in very fine units that behave as the air itself. These units are the dehydrated residuals of the tinier particles generated by high-velocity exhalational maneuvers; cough-inducing procedures such as bronchoscopy or endotracheal intubation are particularly likely to generate infectious aerosols. These droplet nuclei are calculated to be 0.5 to 3 µm in diameter, may remain suspended in room air for many hours, and when inhaled, can traverse the airways to reach the alveoli.

Although patients with cavitary tuberculosis expectorate massive numbers of bacilli, the probability of generating infectious particles is relatively low. Household contacts of patients with extensive pulmonary disease who have had productive coughs for weeks or months before diagnosis have, on average, less than a 50% chance of being infected. The usual case of pulmonary tuberculosis is of a low order of infectiousness compared with an airborne disease such as measles. However, uncommon cases demonstrate extremely high rates of transmission; specific factors in these instances have not been clearly elucidated.

The preponderance of transmission occurs as described earlier, but other mechanisms have been identified. Aerosols generated by débridement or by dressing changes of skin or soft tissue abscesses due to *M. tuberculosis* are highly infectious. Tissue agitation associated with autopsies and direct inoculation into soft tissues from contaminated instruments or bone fragments also have been reported. Fomites do not play a significant role in transmission.

Pathogenesis and Immunity

The natural history and various clinical syndromes of tuberculosis are intimately related to the hosts' defenses. Tubercle bacilli do not elaborate classic toxins; rather, the inflammatory illness and tissue destruction are mediated by products elaborated by the host during the immune response to infection (Part XXI).

When an immunologically naive alveolar macrophage engulfs a tubercle bacillus, it initially provides a nurturing environment within its phagosome in which the bacilli survive and replicate. However, the infected phagocytic cells release substances that attract T lymphocytes; the dendritic cells then present antigens from bacilli to lymphocytes, initiating a series of committed immune effector cells. The lymphocytes elaborate cytokines that activate macrophages, enhancing their antimicrobial capacity and producing a delicately balanced struggle between the host and the parasite.

Among normal, otherwise healthy adults, the host initially prevails in more than 95% of cases. However, this initial encounter typically extends over a few weeks to several months, during which the bacillary population has proliferated massively and undergone various degrees of dissemination. Tissues that are most heavily seeded during this bacillemia, such as the apices of the lungs, the kidneys, bones, meninges, or other extrapulmonary sites, are the common foci for subsequent *reactivation tuberculosis*. Through complex interactions involving mononuclear phagocytes and various T-cell subsets, host defenses are enhanced. This *cell-mediated immunity* (CMI) is related to but not identical with *delayed-type hypersensitivity* (DTH). DTH is associated with the development of the tuberculin reaction, an indurated response 48 to 72 hours after the intradermal injection of tuberculosis protein antigens (e.g., purified protein derivative [PPD]). Skin test reactivity typically develops 4 to 6 weeks after infection, although intervals up to 20 weeks have been reported.

As these defenses gain momentum, involution of the numerous disseminated granulomatous foci occurs in the lungs, lymph nodes, and scattered sites. Typically, all that remains to overtly mark this encounter is the tuberculin skin test reactivity. In a minority of cases, a small, single, residual site of the primary infection (i.e., Ghon focus) appears in the lung parenchyma; occasionally, this is accompanied by calcifications of the ipsilateral hilar nodes. Some patients also develop fibronodular shadowing in one or both lung apices (i.e., Simon foci); the foci presumably are the residua of subclinical disease at these sites.

Most tuberculosis cases occur because of late reactivation of the vestigial lesions of the primary infection in the lungs or in extrapulmonary sites. Rapid progression to overt disease occurs in a minority of newly infected persons who cannot mount sufficient immune responses. Groups at high risk include children from infancy through 4 years of age, the infirm elderly, and immunocompromised subjects, including those with human immunodeficiency virus (HIV) infection or acquired immunodeficiency syndrome (AIDS), organ transplant recipients, and those with other immunosuppressive illnesses or on chemotherapy.

Epidemiology

Globally, tuberculosis is one of the leading infectious causes of adult mortality. However, in the more industrialized nations, the disease has retreated from the general populations, afflicting selected groups. Recognition of these high-risk groups is vital in terms of diagnosis, prevention, and control programs.

WORLDWIDE. The World Health Organization (WHO) estimates that approximately one third of the world's population is latently infected with *M. tuberculosis*. From this pool, 8 to 10 million new active cases emerge per year, and the WHO estimates that roughly 50% of these are communicable forms of pulmonary disease. Regions in the world

Table 341–1 • TUBERCULOSIS MORBIDITY IN THE UNITED STATES, 1993 TO 1997

YEAR	CASES	CASE RATE (per 100,000)
1993	25,287	9.8
1994	24,361	9.4
1995	22,860	8.7
1996	21,337	8.0
1997	19,851	7.4

where the infection and disease are most prevalent include the Pacific Rim nations (excluding Japan), Asia, the Indian subcontinent, sub-Saharan Africa, and Latin America. Because of delayed, inadequate, or unavailable therapy, 2 to 3 million persons die annually; WHO estimates that more than one fourth of preventable deaths in the developing nations are attributable to tuberculosis.

UNITED STATES. The United States has a considerably lower prevalence of infection; recent Centers for Disease Control and Prevention (CDC) estimates suggest that only 4 to 6% of the population (10 to 15 million persons) harbor latent infections. Case rates in the United States had fallen consistently from 1953 to 1984; however, from 1985 to 1992, there was a substantial upsurge, resulting in more than 75,000 surplus cases in this period. Elements feeding this increase included HIV, immigration, and especially deterioration of the public health infrastructure in America's larger cities. In response to this pattern, treatment programs were strengthened, and measures were taken to reduce nosocomial transmission; from 1992 to 2001, case rates dropped substantially, with an all-time low of 15,989 cases in 2001. This represents a 40% reduction from 1992; case rates fell from 10.5 to 5.2 per 100,000 per year in this period.

U.S. morbidity entails remarkable disparities according to race, age, and national origins. Among nonwhite Americans, tuberculosis is largely a disease of young adults, with the peak incidence between the ages of 25 and 44 years; the peak age among whites is 70 years and older, presumably because of latent early infections (Table 341–1). In 2001, 79% of U.S. tuberculosis cases occurred among minorities. Compared with the case rate for the white population in the United States (1.6 cases/100,000 persons/year), the relative risk is 9 for blacks, 7 for Hispanic Americans, 20 for Asians, and 7 for American Indians.

Immigration has contributed significantly to the increased morbidity rates. In 2001, roughly 50% of cases occurred among foreign-born persons (up from 27% in 1992). Major sources of these cases include Mexico, the Philippines, Southeast Asia, the Caribbean, and Latin America, with most cases occurring within 5 years of arrival in the United States. This rising percentage reflects declining case rates among the indigenous population and relatively high rates among immigrants. In 2001, the case rate (26.6) for foreign-born persons was ninefold higher than for persons born in the United States.

HIV INFECTION AND AIDS. HIV infection and AIDS have contributed to the rising case rates of tuberculosis through three broad pathways. First, individuals with latent tuberculosis infection who acquire HIV infection are at much greater risk of reactivation as their immune capacity diminishes. Second, persons with HIV infection or AIDS may well be at higher risk of acquiring new tuberculosis infections, probably because of biologic factors (e.g., impaired defenses) and situational factors (e.g., more time spent in high-risk, congregate environments, including hospitals). Third, young adults with HIV infection and active tuberculosis transmit tuberculosis to people with whom they reside (Part XXIII). The upsurge in tuberculosis cases since 1985 has been linked to the HIV epidemic, although full quantification of the association is not possible because of incomplete serologic testing. In 1993, only 30% of U.S. tuberculosis patients had HIV testing, and 15% of these had positive results; among those 25 to 44 years of age, 29% were HIV positive. By 2001, 49% of the total cases had HIV testing, and 9% were positive; among those 25 to 44 years of age, 17% were HIV infected.

Clinical Manifestations

Because the primary infection results in bacillemic dissemination, tuberculosis entails disease in extrathoracic as well as pulmonary or pleural sites. Hosts with more competent immunity tend to have disease limited to their lungs or other single sites, whereas those with less robust defenses have multifocal or disseminated disease.

NORMAL ADULTS

Overall, excluding the influence of HIV infection, about 80% of adults present with exclusively pulmonary parenchymal disease, 15% with disease at extrapulmonary sites, and approximately 5% with simultaneously active disease at intrathoracic and extrathoracic locations.

In normal adults, the tuberculin skin test result is falsely negative for 20 to 25% at the time of diagnosis, and although most complain of feeling "feverish," a substantial proportion do not have fever when measured. The clinician should not be diverted from considering the diagnosis by nonreactive tuberculin skin test results or lack of fever in patients with other typical features of tuberculosis.

PULMONARY DISEASE. Classic symptoms include cough, fever, and sweating. Cough is nearly universal; typically, it is initially dry but then progresses with increasing volumes of purulent secretions and the variable appearance of blood streaking or gross hemoptysis. Feverishness is common as the disease advances; actual temperatures range from subnormal to extreme elevations. Sweating, including drenching night sweats, is typical. Other common complaints include malaise, fatigue, weight loss, nonpleuritic chest pain, and dyspnea.

Signs may be limited until the disease is in advanced stages. Fever with peaks as high as 40 to 41° C, typically occurring in the evening, occurs in patients with various forms and stages of tuberculosis. Localized rales are early findings; coarse rhonchi evolve as secretions become more voluminous and tenacious; and signs of lung consolidation are rarely heard. Wheezing and/or regionally diminished breath sounds may be heard in patients with peribronchial or endobronchial airway narrowing.

The chest radiograph is central to the diagnosis. Upper lung zone fibronodular shadowing involving one or both apices is seen in most cases. As these lesions advance, they enlarge and become fluffy or softly marginated; the lesions coalesce, and cavitation devolves as intense local inflammation produces necrosis and sloughing of lung tissue. The most common sites involved in reactivation adult tuberculosis are, in descending order, the posterior and apical segments of the right upper lobe, the apical-posterior segment of the left upper lobe, and the superior segments of the lower lobes. Lower zone disease is seen at presentation of less than 15% of HIV-negative adults; it is seen somewhat more commonly in diabetics and patients with prominent peribronchial and endobronchial involvement. Pleural effusions are uncommon in adults with reactivation-type pulmonary disease.

Sputum smears and cultures are the most specific components of diagnosis. Some contemporary laboratories still use the classic acid-fast stains (i.e., Ziehl-Neelsen or Kinyoun); however, most use a modified acid-fast method, auramine-O, a dye that fluoresces when excited by ultraviolet light. With this fluorochrome technique, the mycobacteria are more easily discernible (i.e., bright yellow contrasted to an inky black background) than with the older methods (i.e., red on a blue and white background). AFB found on microscopic examination of respiratory secretions associated with suitable clinical, epidemiologic, and radiographic findings is highly suggestive of tuberculosis. However, microscopy is not specific, because other mycobacteria may be found in sputum. The test is not very sensitive; the likelihood of positive smears depends heavily on the extent of pulmonary involvement. With readily visible cavities and no prior treatment, it is rare to have negative sputum results on microscopy. However, with noncavitary fibronodular or miliary patterns on chest films, negative microscopic results are common. Overall, 50 to 60% of patients with active pulmonary tuberculosis yield AFB smear–positive sputum. Cultures are the "gold standard" for diagnosis; however, current methods typically entail 3 to 6 weeks to cultivate and identify species. More rapid cultivation and identification techniques that use liquid media and/or radiometric, molecular biologic, or chromatographic methods have reduced the required time substantially. Nucleic acid amplification techniques potentially offer a

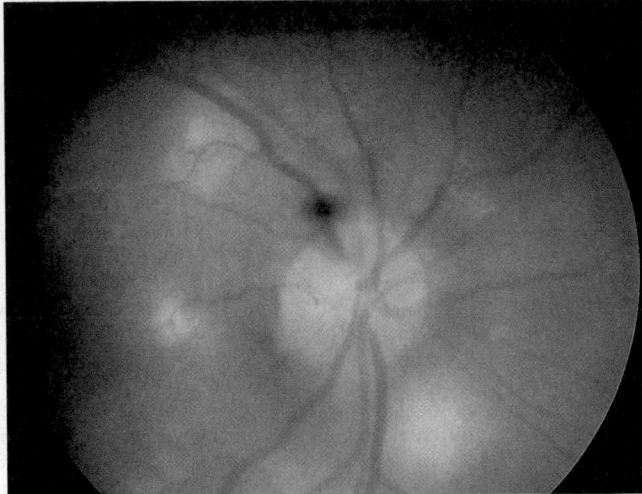

FIGURE 341–1 • Choroidal tubercles in acute miliary tuberculosis. This appearance is virtually diagnostic, so it is essential to examine the fundi of any patient in whom miliary tuberculosis is a possibility. (From Forbes CD, Jackson WF: Color Atlas and Text of Clinical Medicine, 3rd ed. London, Mosby, 2003, with permission.)

diagnosis in 1 to 2 days; these tests are particularly useful in differentiating tuberculosis from environmental mycobacterioses such as *Mycobacterium avium* complex. The diagnosis is occasionally made on the basis of symptoms, radiographic findings, and response to empirical therapy *without* culture confirmation. Because of the clinical importance of resistance to the first-line drugs, susceptibility testing on all initial *M. tuberculosis* isolates is recommended.

The tuberculin skin test is falsely negative in 20 to 25% of HIV-negative adults with pulmonary tuberculosis. Anergy panel testing has not been useful in identifying tuberculosis infection.

EXTRAPULMONARY TUBERCULOSIS. Extrapulmonary tuberculosis occurs in roughly one sixth of HIV-negative adults in the United States with active disease. The most common sites and relevant features are provided in Table 341–2 (Fig. 341–1).

The severe wasting seen with advanced pulmonary diseases (i.e., consumption) is rarely seen with extrapulmonary tuberculosis. Feverishness occurs with more extensive disease, prominently including miliary, pleural, and genitourinary disease.

Diagnosis is problematic in most forms of extrapulmonary tuberculosis because of the relative paucity of bacilli. Histopathologic analysis of involved tissues typically shows giant cell granulomas with caseating necrosis and few, if any, demonstrable AFB. Analysis of mesothelial effusions (i.e., pleural, peritoneal, or pericardial) characteristically reveals a lymphocyte-rich exudate with low concentrations of glucose; however, the *initial* inflammatory responses in these spaces may be polymorphonuclear leukocyte predominant. Cerebrospinal fluid (CSF) changes in meningitis begin with a modest leukocytosis, shifting from polymorphonuclear to lymphocyte dominance; leukocyte counts typically range from 50 to 300 cells/mL. The CSF protein concentration is typically moderately elevated. Glucose levels are progressively depressed in relation to the degree of leukocytosis.

PERSONS WITH HIV INFECTION OR AIDS

Early in the course of HIV infection, the clinical manifestations of tuberculosis are quite similar to those in normal hosts. However, with the progressive reduction in the CD4-lymphocyte population, several major changes ensue: (1) a steady reduction in the proportion who react significantly to tuberculin skin testing, reaching a nadir of 10 to 20% of reactors among those with advanced AIDS; (2) substantially greater extrapulmonary involvement, reaching 60 to 80% prevalence of extrapulmonary tuberculosis, including exotic presentations such as diffuse lymphadenitis, cutaneous disease, or disseminated multiorgan involvement; and (3) changing patterns of disease on chest radiography, evolving from classic upper zone fibronodular, cavitary disease to lower zone, nondescript pneumonic patterns, infrequent cavity formation, interstitial or miliary shadowing, very prominent hilar or paratracheal adenopathy, and substantial pleural effusions.

Table 341–2 • COMMON FORMS OF EXTRAPULMONARY TUBERCULOSIS IN PATIENTS WITHOUT HIV INFECTION

ORGAN SYSTEM*	RELATIVELY HIGH-RISK GROUPS	COMMON CLINICAL MANIFESTATIONS	DIAGNOSIS	MANAGEMENT
Lymphatic	Youngsters and young adults; F > M, Asian and Indian females at higher risk	Unilateral, cervical; painless; sinus tracts late	Excisional biopsy with culture; PPD usually positive	May respond slowly to medication; rarely may require excision
Pleural	Young adults with primary infection; older adults with reactivation disease	May be acute *or* indolent; severe pleurisy or asymptomatic	Lymphatic exudate; AFB smear usually negative; biopsy with culture gives best yield	Usually responds well to medication; do not drain with tube thoracostomy
Genitourinary	Rare in young; more frequent among females, foreign born, and Native Americans	May involve kidneys, ureters, bladder, testes, epididymis, uterus, fallopian tubes	Culture urine; biopsy and culture masses and uterine scrapings	Usually responds well to medication; beware of early or late obstructive uropathy
Bone or joint	More common in elderly, although seen in all ages	Lumbar and low dorsal spine common in older patients; high dorsal in young; weight-bearing bones and joints	Needle biopsy and aspirate for spinal lesions; synovial biopsy and culture for joints	Débride and stabilize spine; try to avoid fusing joints
Disseminated	Most frequent in very young or old; blacks and Native Americans	Chest x-ray film abnormalities may lag; progressive fever and inanition; PPD negative in 50%	Smears and cultures of involved fluids, organs, and mesothelia; smear and culture urine	Early therapy vital; corticosteroids of uncertain value
Meninges or CNS	Most common among infants/children with XPTB; higher risk for Hispanic Americans, blacks, and Native Americans	Three stages; early fever, headache, and malaise; later confusion, obtundation, seizures, and coma	Lumbar puncture: ↑ protein and cells; ↓ glucose, ↑ pressure; smears rarely positive; special tests (see text)	Prognosis related to stage; corticosteroids indicated in most cases; drugs must penetrate CNS
Peritoneal or gastrointestinal	Increases with age; higher risk among minorities	Mainly mesothelial, but ileal involvement may resemble Crohn's; abdominal swelling and vague pain common	Laparoscopic biopsy ideal; smear and culture ascites; stool cultures may be useful	Beware of adhesions and obstruction; corticosteroids may be useful
Pericardial	Rare in children; more common in blacks	Acute pain rare; cough, dyspnea, and vague discomfort	Widened cardiac silhouette; left pleural effusion; ECG low voltage and chronic ST/T wave changes; ↓ heart sounds, rubs rare	Corticosteroids: ↓ effusion, improve performance; may reduce late adhesive complications; pericardiectomy for tamponade

*Among persons without HIV infection, roughly 15 to 16% of tuberculosis manifests as extrapulmonary involvement. Lymphatic and pleural diseases are the most common forms.

AFB = acid-fast bacilli; CNS = central nervous system; ECG = electrocardiogram; PPD = purified protein derivative test; XPTB = extrapulmonary tuberculosis.

 Treatment

A unique aspect to the care of tuberculosis patients merits emphasis. Because of the hazard of casual, airborne transmission of infection and of the potentially morbid or lethal consequences for the recipients, there is a singular public health mandate that *persons with communicable tuberculosis must be treated or quarantined.* The 2001 recommendations of the American Thoracic Society, CDC, and Infectious Disease Society of America explicitly state that "the responsibility for successful treatment is clearly assigned to the public health program or private provider, *not* the patient. It is strongly recommended that the initial treatment strategy utilize patient-centered case management with an adherence plan that emphasizes direct observation of therapy." U.S. public health policy throughout the 20th century empowered governmental representatives to quarantine patients with potentially lethal infectious diseases. In the case of tuberculosis, modern chemotherapy has effectively become a chemical quarantine; nonadherence to treatment may be seen as breaching this quarantine. Because of the consequences of inadequate or incomplete treatment, directly observed therapy (DOT) to prevent noncompliance has become a standard rather than an exceptional or punitive protocol (see later section on nonadherence).

INDICATIONS FOR COMMENCING TREATMENT

Because it often takes 3 to 8 weeks to culture and identify species, treatment for most patients is initiated before a definitive diagnosis is established. The diagnosis usually is based on an amalgam of historical and epidemiologic features, radiographic, tissue, or fluid analysis, and microscopic findings. Beginning empirical therapy for patients with potentially rapid, life-threatening conditions such as central nervous system or miliary disease usually entails a low threshold of suspicion; however, care should be taken to obtain optimal diagnostic specimens before commencing medication to avoid suppression of growth from paucibacillary material by the chemotherapy.

PRINCIPLES OF MULTIDRUG TREATMENT

Patients with active tuberculosis should receive multiple agents to accelerate bacterial clearance and, more crucially, to prevent the emergence of drug-resistant mutants, which can significantly and permanently compromise the treatment outcome.

Tubercle bacilli undergo spontaneous mutations that confer resistance to the various antituberculosis medications. These mutations occur at predictable frequencies, usually in the range of 1 in 10^5 to 10^8 replications, and they are unlinked, resulting in resistance to only one drug or drug category. In cavitary tuberculosis, the population of bacilli is so numerous that small numbers of mycobacteria exist that are resistant to each of the standard medications. However, because the mutations are unlinked, there is an extremely low probability of spontaneous resistance to two or more drugs by a single bacillus. According to the principle of multidrug therapy, isoniazid (INH)-resistant mutants are killed by rifampin (RIF), and the rifampin-resistant mutants are killed by INH. Early in treatment, when the mycobacterial burden is greatest, at least two effective agents must be employed.

Continued

Infectious Diseases

If patients are nonadherent and stop one of their medications without the knowledge of the clinician, the unopposed mutants may proliferate, resulting in treatment failures or relapses associated with acquired drug resistance. When this happens serially, multidrug resistance is created. Such organisms can be transmitted to other persons, giving rise to initial drug-resistant tuberculosis.

In addition to combating drug resistance, multidrug regimens can shorten the required duration of treatment through unique contributions by the various agents. A regimen of INH and ethambutol (EMB) requires 18 months to cure the typical case of pulmonary tuberculosis. Adding RIF to INH reduces the duration to 9 months, and when an initial 2-month phase of pyrazinamide (PZA) is added to INH and RIF, cure occurs in 6 months.

CHOICE OF REGIMEN

Because of concern over the prevalence of drug resistance, current recommendations advocate a four-drug regimen for most cases of known or suspected tuberculosis (Table 341–3). INH and RIF are the central agents of any regimen based on their superior bactericidal activity and low toxicity. PZA has special utility in promoting rapid, early reduction of the bacillary burden; in drug-susceptible cases, PZA needs to be given only for the initial 2 months to produce this effect. EMB is useful primarily to protect against the emergence of drug resistance in cases with unknown initial susceptibility patterns and large mycobacterial burdens; EMB may be terminated if susceptibility is reported or be continued throughout the duration of treatment if resistance occurs. Streptomycin, a parenteral agent, has found a diminishing role in modern therapy because of problems with regularly administering intramuscular injections; however, for patients with very extensive tuberculosis, streptomycin may accelerate initial bactericidal activity. Rifapentine is a long-acting, potent form of rifamycin. It has been employed mainly in once-weekly, continuation-phase regimens. Recent trials employing INH and rifapentine in once-weekly schedules during the continuation phase of treatment (months 3 to 6) demonstrated overall failure and relapse rates slightly higher than INH and RIF comparator arms given twice or thrice weekly. Hence, INH and rifapentine in the continuation phase of therapy is advocated only for patients with noncavitary lung disease whose sputum smears are negative after 8 to 9 weeks of treatment. Because of the possible risk of acquired resistance to

the rifamycins, rifapentine is not indicated for patients with AIDS. Rifabutin is also a long-acting rifamycin. Its primary asset is that it does not induce the hepatic cytochrome P-450 pathways in the manner of rifampin, and it is therefore useful for simultaneous treatment of tuberculosis and antiretroviral therapy for AIDS. Dosage and toxicity for these agents are provided in Table 341–4.

Does every patient need to receive a four-drug regimen? In practice, clinicians should review every proven or suspected case and consider individual modifications or exemptions of this standard program. For example, an elderly patient with remote exposure to tuberculosis in the era before chemotherapy, with no recent contacts, and with no history of tuberculosis medical treatment may reasonably be started on a three-drug (i.e., INH, RIF, and EMB) regimen because of the very low likelihood of drug resistance, poor tolerance of PZA in the elderly, and a low risk of absconding or abandoning treatment. In contrast, an individual who gives a history of prior antituberculosis therapy or comes from a household in which there has been prior multidrug-resistant (MDR) tuberculosis may receive an empirically expanded regimen, including the standard four oral agents plus a fluoroquinolone and amikacin.

Common factors that may influence the initial choice of drugs are included in Tables 341–3 and 341–4. Additional considerations in selecting therapy are addressed in the following sections.

AIDS. Treatment of tuberculosis in persons with AIDS is similar to standard therapy. Particular issues of concern are drug-drug interactions between the antituberculosis agents and the various antiretroviral medications or drugs given for other opportunistic infections, the immune-reconstitution syndrome when antiretroviral therapy restores the host's capacity to mount an inflammatory response, and the potential for malabsorption of medications secondary to various AIDS-related enteropathies.

Drug-drug interactions are the most significant element of the treatment of tuberculosis in persons with AIDS. RIF, by inducing hepatic cytochrome P-450 pathways, causes accelerated elimination of most protease inhibitors and non-nucleoside reverse-transcriptase inhibitors, as well as antifungal azoles and other drugs (see 2003 ATS/CDC/IDSA Guidelines for the extensive list of drug-drug interactions). Conversely, the various antiretroviral drugs may result in accelerated elimination or retarded catabolism of the antituberculosis agents. Given the potentially severe consequences of these interactions, including treatment failure, acquired drug resistance,

Table 341–3 • RECOMMENDED TREATMENT REGIMENS FOR TUBERCULOSIS IN THE UNITED STATES

REGIMEN	MEDICATIONS	TOTAL DURATION	COMMENTS
ATS/CDC*	INH and RIF daily for 6 mo PZA and SM or EMB daily for 2 mo	6 mo	Add SM or EMB in areas or patients at risk for initial drug resistance. Stop PZA, EMB, or SM after 2 mo if strain susceptible; continue or modify regimen if resistance present.
Denver	INH, RIF, PZA, and SM daily for 2 wk; then twice weekly for 6 wk. Follow with INH and RIF twice weekly for 18 wk. Note: All intermittent regimens must be given as DOT.	6 mo	EMB has replaced SM in most cases. Stop PZA and EMB at 8 wk if strain is susceptible; continue through 6 mo if there is initial INH resistance; 24 wk of twice-weekly therapy facilitates directly observed therapy.
Hong Kong	INH, RIF, PZA, and SM or EMB thrice weekly for 6 mo (may stop PZA, SM, or EMB after 2 mo). Note: All intermittent regimens must be given as DOT.	6 mo	All-intermittent. If strain is susceptible, may stop PZA and SM or EMB after 2 mo. If there is INH resistance, stop INH and add the fourth drug (EMB or SM).
Arkansas	INH and RIF daily for 1 mo; then INH and RIF twice weekly for 8 mo	9 mo	This regimen should only be employed in populations with a very low prevalence of drug resistance. Initial therapy probably should include a third drug until drug susceptibility is reported. Although this regimen is self-administered in Arkansas, authorities strongly recommend DOT for all intermittent regimens.
CDC trial 22	INH, RIF, PZA, and EMB for 2 mo; may be given daily, per the Denver regimen or per the Hong Kong regimen; then INH and rifapentine once weekly for 4 mo (not for persons with AIDS)	6 mo	Rifapentine is a potent and long-acting rifamycin. In trials comparing once-weekly INH and rifapentine with twice-weekly INH and RIF, the rifapentine regimen performed slightly less well and hence is recommended only for patients with noncavitary lung disease and negative sputum smears at 2 mo of therapy.

*The ATS and CDC advocate initial four-drug therapy for cases in communities with a background prevalence of initial drug resistance of 4% or greater. If susceptibility has been demonstrated or if resistance is deemed very unlikely, initial three-drug regimens may be used.

ATS = American Thoracic Society; CDC = Centers for Disease Control and Prevention; DOT = directly observed therapy; EMB = ethambutal; INH = isoniazid; PZA = pyrazinamide; RIF = rifampin; SM = streptomycin.

Table 341-4 • **DOSAGE, TOXICITY, AND SPECIAL CONSIDERATIONS FOR STANDARD ANTITUBERCULOSIS MEDICATIONS**

DRUG	DAILY DOSAGE	USUAL ADULT DOSE THRICE II TWICE WEEKLY	TOXICITY	SPECIAL CONSIDERATIONS	COMMENTS
Isoniazid (INH)	300 mg PO	600 mg II 900 mg	Hepatitis, neuritis, mood/cognition, lupus reaction	Pregnancy: safe Liver disease: caution Renal impairment: ↓ dose if severe	Monitor liver function tests monthly in most patients; clinically significant interactions with phenytoin and antifungal agents (azols)
Rifampin (RIF)*	600 mg PO 450 mg in persons <50 kg body weight	600 mg II (same)	Hepatitis, thrombopenia, nephritis, flu syndrome	Pregnancy: acceptable Liver disease: caution Renal impairment: safe	Key: multiple, profound drug interactions possible (see later); turns urine and fluids red
Rifapentine (RPT)	Not recommended	Not recommended (600 mg PO once weekly)	Similar to RIF	Similar to RIF	The primary role for RPT is in *once-weekly* continuation therapy given with INH. Not indicated for persons with AIDS.
Rifabutin (RBU)	150–300 mg/kg PO	300 mg II (same)	Similar to RIF; modestly more neutropenia and thrombopenia than RIF	Similar to RIF	The primary role for RBU is for tuberculosis in persons with AIDS to lessen drug-drug interactions.
Pyrazinamide (PZA)	20–30 mg/kg PO	30–40 mg/kg II 40–50 mg/kg	Hepatitis, arthralgias and arthritis from hyperuricemia, gastrointestinal distress, rash	Pregnancy: unknown (avoid) Liver disease: caution Renal impairment: caution	Urate levels always rise; do not treat or stop PZA unless unmanageable gout develops
Ethambutol (EMB)	15–20 mg/kg PO	30–35 mg/kg II 40–50 mg/kg	Optic neuritis; gastrointestinal distress; rare peripheral neuritis	Pregnancy: safe Liver disease: safe Renal impairment: ↓ dose/frequency	Monitor visual acuity and color vision regularly
Streptomycin (SM)	12–15 mg/kg IM	15 mg/kg II (same)	Vestibular and auditory, cation depletion	Pregnancy: high-risk (avoid) Liver disease: safe Renal impairment: ↓ dose/frequency	Reduce dose and/or frequency in case of renal impairment

*Rifampin drug interactions have been reported with antiretroviral agents, including protease inhibitors and non-nucleoside reverse transcriptase inhibitors, oral contraceptives, anticoagulants, methadone, corticosteroids, estrogen replacement, calcium channel blockers, β-blockers, cyclosporine, antifungal agents (azols), phenytoin, theophylline, sulfonylureas, haloperidol, and others (see *Physicians' Desk Reference*).

and toxicity related to both categories of therapy, simultaneous antituberculosis and antiretroviral therapy should only be undertaken in specialized centers or with skilled consultative support. Contemporary information is available on the Internet (www.atsjournals.org).

As antiretroviral therapy restores CD4 lymphocyte levels and reconstitutes immune function, patients may experience increased symptoms or other manifestations from preexisting infections such as tuberculosis. Examples include increased fever, worsening of infiltrates or effusions seen on chest radiographs, and enlarging lymph nodes. Patients may be particularly troubled by enlarging central nervous system lesions or pericardial disease, in which deterioration may be lethal. Up to one third of patients with AIDS and tuberculosis who receive antiretroviral therapy experience such paradoxical worsening. Delaying the initiation of antiretroviral therapy until several months of tuberculosis treatment have been completed lessens the likelihood and severity of the reactions but does not obviate the risk. Most patients can be guided through the reactions, but in severe cases, antiretroviral therapy may be terminated and/or steroids given for several weeks to lessen the inflammatory reaction.

Contemporary antituberculous regimens involving INH and RIF for 6 months and PZA for the initial 2 months result in 96 to 99% durable cure rates for HIV-negative patients with drug-susceptible tuberculosis. Although current guidelines espouse this standard therapy for persons with AIDS and tuberculosis, they point out that therapy should be extended for those who are slow to respond. Sputum cultures after 2 months of therapy are a useful marker of slow response by patients at higher risk of failure or relapse. In such patients, therapy should be extended to 9 months' total duration. Reassessment to rule out malabsorption or cryptic noncompliance also is appropriate, and persons with AIDS should be given high priority for DOT.

CENTRAL NERVOUS SYSTEM DISEASE. Smaller, nonionized molecules such as INH and PZA cross the blood-brain barrier well, even in the absence of gross inflammation. RIF crosses less well, although therapeutic effects are seen. EMB CSF levels are significantly lower than those in serum, and its use in meningitis is less well established. Streptomycin and the other aminoglycoside antibiotics are large, complex, and ionically charged molecules; they are active early in the presence of inflammation but lose their efficacy as it subsides.

TREATMENT ISSUES

COMBATING NONADHERENCE WITH DIRECTLY OBSERVED INTERMITTENT CHEMOTHERAPY. Treatment given intermittently, thrice or twice weekly, is generally comparable in efficacy to daily treatment. These intermittent schedules make it practical for patients to come to treatment centers or have visits by outreach workers at home or in shelters, schools, or work sites to observe ingestion or to administer medications. Most reported regimens have begun with a daily phase of therapy and switched to an intermittent schedule after 1 or 2 months. However, effective treatment can entail a brief (2-week) initial daily phase or be intermittent (thrice weekly) throughout. Formerly, DOT was regarded as a selective strategy to be employed for those with demonstrated nonadherence or for extremely high-risk individuals. However, the ATS/CDC Guidelines regard DOT as standard practice. Clinicians may elect to have patients self-administer treatment, but in so doing, the clinician assumes responsibility for any consequences of nonadherence. Implicit in this policy is that DOT should be available in all communities or regions of the United States.

CLINICIANS' ERRORS CONTRIBUTING TO ACQUIRED DRUG RESISTANCE. Among the more common errors that contribute to the evolution of mul-

Continued

tidrug resistance are failure to recognize and cope with nonadherence in a timely manner, failure to identify an individual at high risk for preexisting drug resistance that results in the use of an inadequate initial regimen, and adding a single drug to a failing regimen.

MONITORING FOR AND COPING WITH DRUG TOXICITY. In the general population, significant reactions requiring transient or permanent discontinuation of one or more drugs occur in about 5% of those receiving a typical three- or four-drug regimen. Common drug toxicities are listed in Table 341–4. Vague gastrointestinal complaints are relatively common in association with all the first-line oral drugs. However, with coaching and encouragement, most patients can be persuaded to tolerate these drugs. In an effort to diminish gastrointestinal intolerance, patients must not take their oral medications directly with meals, antacids, or H_2-receptor blockers, any of which may substantially reduce absorption of certain of these agents.

Adults receiving the regimens listed in Table 341–3 should have baseline measurements of liver functions; complete blood counts, including platelets; uric acid (if PZA is included); and vision, including acuity and color discrimination (if EMB is included). These tests can identify preexisting problems and enable comparison with data from subsequent testing. Monitoring during therapy is generally done by clinical assessment. Patients receiving DOT should be queried regularly for any perceived adverse effects, and those self-administering drugs should be seen monthly and instructed regarding the more likely complications, including prompt reporting of adverse effects.

DURATION OF TREATMENT AND POST-TREATMENT SURVEILLANCE

A 6-month regimen consisting of INH and RIF supplemented by an initial 2-month phase of PZA is regarded as sufficient and curative for most cases caused by drug-susceptible strains. However, a major change in the 2003 Guidelines is emphasis on the importance of sputum cultures obtained after the first 2 months of therapy because of significantly higher risks for failure and relapse. Patients with cavitary disease whose 2-month culture is still positive are to be treated for a total of 9 months. If these three agents cannot be used, the duration of treatment may be prolonged (see Table 341–4). Other situations in which therapy may be extended beyond 6 months include the following:

HIV infection or AIDS. Although no well-controlled studies have demonstrated the superiority of longer therapy, some clinicians fear that impaired immunity may place these patients at higher risk for relapse.

Far-advanced, cavitary lung disease with delayed clinical response or sputum conversion. About 85 to 90% of patients become culture negative by 2 months of treatment; for those who remain positive longer than this, treatment for a total of 9 months is recommended.

Irregular, interrupted therapy. If patients fail to attend 10% or more of DOT encounters or are otherwise deemed to have been significantly noncompliant with treatment, extended treatment is prudent. A semiquantitative model to calculate the need for extended therapy is described in the 2003 ATS/CDC/IDSA Guidelines.

Miliary or meningeal cases. Because of the concern that such patients may be less competent hosts and the implications of disease recurrence, therapy may be extended to 9 to 12 months.

A low and unavoidable risk of relapse exists after treatment; for the regimens described previously in the usual populations, the probability is less than 5%. Most such patients have recurrences within 2 years that are usually associated with the same drug susceptibility profile as before treatment began. Current guidelines do not compel post-treatment surveillance. Patients instead should be instructed to return after treatment when there are changes in their clinical status; suitable tests, including sputum analyses, chest radiographs, or other studies should be obtained if symptoms or signs appear.

INDICATIONS FOR CORTICOSTEROID THERAPY

Corticosteroids may be used to reduce acute inflammation and limit delayed fibrotic complications. Acute reductions in inflammation with significant benefits in outcome have been demonstrated in meningitis and pericarditis cases treated with corticosteroids. Prednisone at a dose of 1 mg/kg is usual. Less well proved are the benefits of such therapy in pleural, peritoneal, miliary, or extensive pulmonary disease, although salutary effects may occur in individual cases. High-dose corticosteroids may impair immune responses, but there is no evidence that they adversely affect the outcome of treatment when given for 4 to 8 weeks to patients who are receiving adequate chemotherapy.

Adrenal insufficiency due to tuberculous destruction is uncommon in this era. However, among patients with marginal cortisol production, RIF may precipitate hypocortisolism by accelerating catabolism of endogenous steroids.

DRUG-RESISTANT TUBERCULOSIS

During the past decade, drug resistance in the United States has dropped considerably. In 1991, the overall prevalence of drug resistance was 14.2%. INH resistance was most common, occurring in 8.2% of new cases and in 21.5% of previously treated cases. Resistance to INH and RIF (i.e., MDR tuberculosis) occurred in 3.5% of cases. By the year 2001, for those not previously treated, the rate of drug resistance to INH was 7.1% overall, with rates of 4.5% for American-born and 9.6% for foreign-born patients. The rate of resistance to both INH and RIF was 1.0% overall, with rates of 0.6% for American-born and 1.4% for foreign-born patients. Among those previously treated, resistance rates in 2001 were considerably higher. In this group, the rate of resistance to INH was 13.0% overall, with rates of 7.4% for American-born and 19.3% for foreign-born patients. The multidrug resistance rate was 4.7% overall, with rates of 1.6% for American-born and 8.1% for foreign-born patients.

MDR tuberculosis is of particular importance because of the profoundly increased risk of treatment failure and further acquired resistance. MDR tuberculosis may be associated with resistance to other first-line drugs, which further compromises treatment prospects. The most significant aspect of MDR tuberculosis is resistance to rifampin, because it is this drug, not INH, that is central to short-duration therapy.

Patients with suspected MDR tuberculosis (i.e., those with prior treatment, with recent exposure to an MDR case, or from extremely high-risk areas) should be considered for initially extended empirical regimens, especially if they have extensive lung disease or perilous extrapulmonary forms such as miliary or meningeal disease. For those with proven MDR tuberculosis, it is important to employ at least four drugs to which the organisms are susceptible, usually three oral and one injectable agent. Patients should receive prompt, expert consultation and have the highest priority for DOT. Preventive therapy or treatment of latent infection for contacts of persons with MDR tuberculosis is problematic, because the only agents widely regarded as appropriate are INH and RIF.

Contact Investigation

Clinicians must realize that their responsibilities are not complete when they have established the diagnosis and initiated chemotherapy for a patient. Tuberculosis is a reportable disease in all U.S. communities and states; clinicians are obligated to promptly notify public health authorities of all cases of proven or suspected tuberculosis. Contact investigation of the home, workplace, school, or other congregate facilities may reveal other active cases or newly infected persons who are at substantial risk for tuberculosis. Priority must be given to investigations in which infants or AIDS patients have been exposed because of their compressed incubation periods for potentially lethal forms of tuberculosis. Preventive chemotherapy for infected contacts is a highly efficient means of curtailing tuberculosis morbidity.

Prevention

Multiple modalities are involved in the effort to control tuberculosis. In the United States over the past 35 years, INH preventive chemotherapy (IPT) has been relied upon. For the remainder of the world, vaccination with bacille Calmette-Guérin (BCG) has been the central element.

TREATMENT OF LATENT INFECTION: PREVENTIVE THERAPY

Because most U.S. tuberculosis cases arise from endogenous reactivation of latent infection acquired remotely in time, authorities reasoned that chemotherapy given to persons harboring such infections might be an efficient prevention strategy. In a series of randomized, placebo-controlled studies, IPT demonstrated 75% reduction of morbidity in the year of treatment and 54% protection in the post-treatment years; even higher rates of protection were shown in a large trial in Eastern Europe, ranging from 70 to 90% with 6- and 12-month treatment of latent infection (TLI), respectively. In the 2000 ATS/CDC Guidelines, the terminology was changed from preventive therapy to treatment of latent infection (TLI), and regimen options were added, as subsequently discussed.

INDICATIONS FOR TREATMENT OF LATENT INFECTION. The recommendations focus on persons who are deemed to be at relatively higher risk for active disease. Specific groups or conditions that are regarded at high risk and considered to be candidates for IPT are described in Table 341-5.

In most instances, the tuberculin skin test is the central modality used to identify latent infection. Interpretation of the tuberculin skin test, however, is influenced by circumstances, and in some instances, therapy would be recommended despite nonreactivity, whereas in other cases, 15 mm or more of induration is required for significance.

SPECIAL CONSIDERATIONS IN TREATMENT OF LATENT INFECTION. HIV infection is the most potent risk factor for endogenous reactivation. Persons with positive HIV serologic results or strong epidemiologic or clinical markers for HIV risk should be assigned very high priority for TLI. In addition to protecting the individual patient from tuberculosis, such treatment may extend survival by ameliorating the accelerated progression of HIV infection seen with active tuberculosis and may prevent transmission to other, very vulnerable HIV-infected persons (e.g., in shared health care, social, or residential facilities).

Others requiring particular attention are foreign-born persons from high-risk nations, notably Mexico, the Philippines, Vietnam, India, China, Haiti, and Korea. Immigrants from these and other endemic regions, particularly newly arrived immigrants, should be screened and, if found to be infected, considered for TLI.

REGIMEN OPTIONS FOR TREATMENT OF LATENT INFECTION. The 2000 ATS/CDC Guidelines identified a variety of drug regimens for TLI (see Table 341-3). Unlike earlier recommendations, which advised 6 months of INH for all except those with HIV infection or fibrotic lesions (who were to receive 12 months), the 2000 ATS/CDC Guidelines identify 9 months of INH as the standard for all subjects, with 6 months as an acceptable alternative. Also new were recommendations for a 4-month RIF regimen or 2 to 3 months of RIF plus PZA. These short-duration regimens were explicitly designed to combat nonadherence and to overcome INH resistance. Unfortunately, early experience with the RIF-PZA regimen resulted in more than 30 cases of severe hepatitis and seven deaths in the initial cohort of more than 7000. Because of the apparent lethality of this combination, it is no longer recommended.

MONITORING FOR COMPLIANCE AND TOXICITY. Patients receiving TLI should be seen periodically to promote adherence to the treatment regimen and survey for signs or symptoms of drug toxicity. Intermittent DOT is not widely feasible; however, it may be applicable in selected circumstances such as for prisoners, especially those with HIV infection, or for recently infected infants or children in households where reliable treatment is unlikely.

The major toxicity of INH, RIF, and PZA is hepatitis, which may prove fatal if therapy is continued into the period of symptoms and gross chemical derangements. It is therefore important that initial education alert the patient and/or responsible family members to the early manifestations of liver injury (i.e., anorexia, nausea, malaise, loss of taste for cigarettes, and dark urine) and provide instructions to stop therapy and report promptly for evaluation. Patients also should have monthly communication with a health care worker, directly if

possible but by telephone as an alternative, to inquire regarding their health and to reiterate the education. Biochemical monitoring of liver chemistry is not routinely indicated. For those reporting symptoms, liver function tests should be obtained. Among symptomatic patients, even modest derangements are grounds for halting therapy. Unless there was major toxicity, the same drug may be reinstituted later or an alternative regimen can be attempted.

BACILLE CALMETTE-GUÉRIN VACCINATION

BCG is a live vaccine prepared from an attenuated strain of *M. bovis*. It has been used widely around the world, but its efficacy and utility are debated. The performance of various strains of BCG given to different populations over time has ranged from 80% protection to detrimental effects (i.e., more tuberculosis in those receiving the

---

Table 341-5 • HIGH-RISK CANDIDATES FOR INFECTION PREVENTIVE THERAPY

Candidates for treatment of latent infection or preventive therapy are persons at high risk for tuberculosis. Some persons with latent tuberculosis infection are at relatively great risk of developing active disease. The degree of tuberculin skin test reactivity used to identify such persons varies based on epidemiologic and biologic factors. The recommended duration of therapy is 9 months of isoniazid for most candidates. The American Thoracic Society and Centers for Disease Control and Prevention guidelines identify various alternative regimens, including 6 months of INH, 4 months of rifampin (RIF), 2 or 3 months of RIF and pyrazinamide (PZA) twice weekly or daily. [Note: Because of the risk of severe, even lethal, hepatitis, I do not recommend the RIF/PZA regimen.]

Certain groups within the infected population are at greater risk than others and should receive high priority for preventive therapy. In the United States, persons with any of the following six risk factors should be considered candidates for preventive therapy, regardless of age, if they have not previously been treated:

1. Persons (≥5 mm tuberculin skin test reaction) with human immunodeficiency virus (HIV) infection and persons with risk factors for HIV infection whose HIV infection status is unknown but who are suspected of having HIV infection
2. Close contacts of persons with newly diagnosed infectious tuberculosis (≥5 mm) and tuberculin-negative (<5 mm) children and adolescents who have been close contacts of infectious persons within the past 3 months are candidates for preventive therapy until a repeat tuberculin skin test is done 12 weeks after contact with the infectious source.
3. Recent converters, as indicated by a tuberculin skin test (≥10 mm increase within a 2-year period)
4. Persons (≥5mm) with abnormal chest radiographs showing fibrotic lesions that probably represent old healed tuberculosis
5. Intravenous drug users (≥10mm) known to be HIV seronegative
6. Persons (≥10mm) with medical conditions that have been reported to increase the risk of tuberculosis

In the absence of any of the previous risk factors, persons younger than 35 years of age in the following high-incidence groups are appropriate candidates for preventive therapy if their reaction to a tuberculin skin test is ≥10mm:

1. Foreign-born persons from high-prevalence countries
2. Medically underserved, low-income populations, including high-risk racial or ethnic minority populations, especially blacks, Hispanic Americans, and Native Americans
3. Residents of facilities for long-term care (e.g., correctional institutions, nursing homes, mental institutions)

Public health officials should be alert for additional high-risk populations in their communities. For example, through a review of cases reported in the community over several years, health officials may use geographic or sociodemographic factors to identify groups that should be targeted for intervention. Screening and preventive therapy programs should be initiated and promoted within these populations based on an analysis of cases and infection in the community. To the extent possible, members of high-risk groups and their health care providers should be involved in the design, implementation, and evaluation of these programs. Staff of facilities in which an individual with disease would pose a risk to large numbers of susceptible persons (e.g., correctional institutions, nursing homes, mental institutions, other health care facilities, schools, child-care facilities) may also be considered for preventive therapy if the tuberculin reaction is a ≥10-mm induration.

vaccine). A meta-analysis of published BCG studies indicated that vaccinations offered an overall 50% protective effect, with higher levels of protection against meningeal or disseminated tuberculosis. This study revealed that the efficacy of BCG diminished in countries near the equator. Although the calculated protection in this meta-analysis reached statistical significance, no explanation was offered for the failure to show efficacy in two large trials conducted in India and Malawi.

Because BCG is presumed to work by conferring tuberculosis immunity in those not previously infected, it is not appropriate for widespread use in the United States, where most cases arise among those already infected with *M. tuberculosis*. Some have called for BCG vaccinations for health care workers at high risk for tuberculosis infection. However, given the disputable protection afforded by the vaccines and the loss of utility of the tuberculin skin test (i.e., reactivity is induced by BCG) as a tool to mark recent infection and to qualify for preventive chemotherapy, which does have proven efficacy, this seems to be a dubious proposition.

LIMITING NOSOCOMIAL TRANSMISSION

Substantial microepidemics of tuberculosis have been documented recently in various institutions, including hospitals, clinics, residential facilities, and prisons. To prevent institutional transmission, the CDC has advocated a three-tiered system: administrative measures, environmental programs, and personal respiratory protection. *Administrative measures* include educational programs to alert staff about how to recognize and isolate possible active cases early. Staff tuberculin skin testing is required to assess the risks of intra-institutional transmission. *Engineering or environmental programs* are intended to effectively isolate proven or suspected cases by placing them in negative-pressure rooms and diluting the air in the patients' environment through six or more air changes per hour, with the options of decontamination by the adjunctive use of HEPA filtration or ultraviolet germicidal irradiation. *Personal respiratory protection* entails the use of respirators or masks that theoretically can filter out the infectious droplet nuclei. A National Institute for Occupational Safety and Health (NIOSH) category N95 personal respiratory device meets federal guidelines, providing there is fit testing. The optimal role for personal respirators is controversial. Perhaps the most suitable role is to protect health care workers who have unavoidable exposure to smear-positive cases during cough-inducing procedures such as bronchoscopy or intubation. Use in other circumstances depends on the source case and environmental factors. The regulations regarding mandated use of these devices are under review. For considerations of public health concerns and regulatory oversight, all institutions that may be involved with caring for tuberculosis patients should have an active program to limit the hazard of nosocomial transmission to health care workers and other patients or clients.

SUGGESTED READINGS

Blumberg HM, Burman WJ, Chaisson RE, et al; American Thoracic Society, Centers for Disease Control and Prevention and the Infectious Diseases Society: American Thoracic Society/Centers for Disease Control and Prevention/Infectious Diseases Society of America: Treatment of tuberculosis. Am J Respir Crit Care Med 2003;167:603–662. *Most recent guidelines for treatment of adults, children, and infants. Excellent overview of contemporary issues, including practical approaches to compliance and to drug-resistant infections.*

Centers for Disease Control and Prevention: Reported tuberculosis in the United States, 2002. Atlanta, GA, US Department of Health and Human Services, Centers for Disease Control and Prevention, August 2003. *A comprehensive review of tuberculosis case numbers and epidemiologic profiles by state and city.*

Centers for Disease Control and Prevention: Update: Fatal and severe liver injuries associated with rifampin and pyrazinamide for latent tuberculosis infection, and revisions in the American Thoracic Society/CDC recommendations—United States, 2001. Am J Respir Crit Care Med 2001;164:1319–1320. *Documents 20 cases of severe hepatitis and five deaths associated with the rifampin and pyrazinamide regimen for treatment of latent infection. It calls for more limited use of the regimen and stricter monitoring, although I would be very reluctant to employ this regimen in light of the lethal outcomes.*

Greco S, Girardi E, Masciangelo R, et al: Adenosine deaminase and interferon gamma measurements for the diagnosis of tuberculous pleurisy: A meta-analysis. Int J Tuberc Lung Dis 2003;7:777–786. *Both had sensitivities and specificities estimated to be about 95%.*

Iseman MD: A Clinician's Guide to Tuberculosis. Baltimore, Lippincott Williams & Wilkins, 1999. *Textbook focuses on the diagnosis, treatment, and prevention of tuberculosis and expands on the issues addressed in the chapter.*

342 OTHER MYCOBACTERIOSES

Laurel C. Preheim

Microbiology

Among the mycobacteria, *M. tuberculosis*, *M. bovis*, and *M. leprae* have caused most human infections. In the 1950s, however, Timpe and Runyon established that other mycobacteria could cause disease in humans and classified these organisms based on pigment production, growth rate, and colonial characteristics. Photochromogens (group I) grow slowly on culture media (>7 days). Their colonies change from a buff shade to bright yellow or orange after exposure to light. Scotochromogens (group II) also grow slowly but demonstrate pigmented colonies when incubated in the dark or the light. Group III mycobacteria grow slowly and lack pigment in the dark or light. Rapid growers (group IV) also lack pigment, but they grow in culture within 3 to 5 days. Collectively, these four groups have been called the "atypical mycobacteria," nontuberculous mycobacteria (NTM), mycobacteria other than tubercle bacilli (MOTT), and "potentially pathogenic environmental mycobacteria" (PPEM).

Epidemiology

The rate of isolation of NTM is increasing and has surpassed that for *M. tuberculosis* in some areas. Ubiquitous in nature, many have been isolated from ground or tap water, soil, house dust, domestic and wild animals, and birds. Despite their wide distribution, some species are more common in certain geographic locations. Most infections, including those that are hospital acquired, result from inhalation or direct inoculation from environmental sources. Ingestion may be the source of infection for children with NTM cervical adenopathy and for patients with the acquired immunodeficiency syndrome (AIDS) whose disseminated infection may begin in the gastrointestinal tract. Because person-to-person transmission is extremely rare, infected patients do not require isolation.

Pathophysiology

The pathogenic potential for human disease varies among NTM. As a group, these organisms are less virulent for humans than *M. tuberculosis* and may colonize body surfaces or secretions without causing disease. Tissue invasion is most likely to occur in individuals with predisposing conditions associated with impaired local or systemic host defenses. In general, disease is slowly progressive, and histopathologic findings resemble those seen in tuberculosis.

Diagnosis

The steps taken to diagnose tuberculosis generally apply to NTM infections. Standardized, specific skin test antigens for NTM, however, are unavailable. In addition, colonization of asymptomatic individuals and environmental contamination of specimens can yield positive cultures in the absence of clinical disease. The diagnosis of pulmonary disease must meet clinical, radiographic, and bacteriologic criteria. Patients must exhibit compatible signs/symptoms (cough and fatigue are most common; fever, weight loss, hemoptysis, and dyspnea may be present) and reasonable exclusion of other disease (e.g., tuberculosis, cancer, histoplasmosis). Radiographic criteria include (1) chest radiographic findings of infiltrates with or without nodules (persistent for at least 2 months or progressive), cavitation, or one or more nodules, or (2) high-resolution computed tomography findings of multiple small nodules or multifocal bronchiectasis with or without small lung nodules. Bacteriologic criteria require (1) at least three available sputum/bronchial wash samples within 1 year, including three positive cultures with negative AFB smears, or two positive cultures and one positive AFB smear; or (2) if sputum samples are unavailable, a single bronchial wash culture with 2+, 3+, or 4+ growth (≥1+ growth in immunocompromised patients), or a positive culture with a 2+, 3+, or 4+ AFB smear; or (3) any growth on bronchopulmonary tissue biopsy, or granuloma and/or AFB on lung biopsy with one or more positive cultures from sputum/bronchial wash.

Extrapulmonary or disseminated disease is confirmed by isolation of the organism from normally sterile body fluids, closed sites, or lesions and when environmental contamination of specimens is excluded. A variety of new culture systems, DNA probes, and polymerase chain reaction assays have increased the speed and accuracy of laboratory diagnosis of pulmonary and extrapulmonary infections.

CLINICAL DISEASE

NTM cause a broad spectrum of diseases (Table 342–1). The following discussion includes infections caused by selected species most likely to be encountered in clinical settings. Therapeutic approaches continue to evolve and therefore remain controversial. Most conventional antituberculous agents have little or no activity against the majority of these organisms. Most treatment regimens are based on expert opinion rather than randomized, controlled trials. Therapeutic decisions must weigh all potential drug toxicities and interactions. Routine testing of all NTM isolates is not recommended. However, in some instances, baseline susceptibility data are helpful, especially if patients fail to respond to therapy, or when relapses occur.

MYCOBACTERIUM AVIUM-INTRACELLULARE. M. avium and M. intracellulare are closely related and commonly grouped as M. avium-intracellulare (MAI) or M. avium complex (MAC). Distributed worldwide, they rank first among NTM isolates in the United States. MAI causes about 80% of NTM lymphadenitis cases. M. scrofulaceum is responsible for most of the rest. Excisional therapy without chemotherapy is curative in about 95% of cervical adenopathy cases. Pulmonary infection usually occurs in individuals with underlying lung disease and generally follows an indolent or slowly progressive course. Differentiation between colonization and true infection may be difficult initially. Extrapulmonary or disseminated disease, infrequently seen in immunocompetent patients, occurs in up to 40% of individuals with AIDS. It usually affects patients with advanced human immunodeficiency virus infection. Therefore, prophylaxis with clarithromycin (500 mg twice daily) or azithromycin (1200 mg once weekly) is recommended for patients with CD4+ T-lymphocyte counts of less than 50 cells/μL. Suggestive symptoms of disseminated MAI include fever, weight loss, anorexia, abdominal pain, and diarrhea. Findings may include hepatosplenomegaly and generalized lymphadenopathy, including mediastinal adenopathy. Diagnosis of disseminated disease is commonly made by culture of the organism from blood, bone marrow, stool, or tissue biopsy.

Adult HIV-negative patients who require therapy for MAI infections should receive an initial regimen of at least three drugs, including either azithromycin (600 mg once daily) or clarithromycin (500 mg twice daily), rifabutin (300 mg once daily) or rifampin (600 mg once daily), and ethambutol (25 mg/kg once daily for 2 months followed by 15 mg/kg once daily). One or more of the following may be added as needed: ciprofloxacin (750 mg twice daily) or ofloxacin (400 mg twice daily) and, in severe illness, amikacin (7.5 to 15 mg/kg/day). Isoniazid and pyrazinamide are not effective. No specific regimen has emerged as being superior for pulmonary or disseminated disease, and the optimal duration of therapy remains unknown. Immunocompetent patients with pulmonary infection should be treated until culture negative on therapy for at least 1 year. Patients with disseminated MAI disease probably should be treated indefinitely until more data become available.

MYCOBACTERIUM KANSASII. M. kansasii, the most important photochromogen, often appears beaded or cross-barred on acid-fast stain. It ranks second among NTM in causing human infections. Most disease occurs in the midwest and southern United States. Pulmonary infection resembling tuberculosis is the usual clinical presentation. Although adult white men are most commonly affected, infection can occur in individuals of any age, sex, or race. Extrapulmonary disease can involve any organ system, and risks of dissemination are increased in immunocompromised patients.

Standard treatment is with isoniazid (300 mg), rifampin (600 mg), and ethambutol (25 mg/kg for the first 2 months and then 15 mg/kg) given daily for 18 months. This regimen applies to patients with pulmonary or extrapulmonary infection and has been used with some success in individuals with AIDS. Clarithromycin (500 mg twice daily) can be used as a substitute in patients who are unable to tolerate one of these three drugs and as a replacement for rifampin in patients receiving a protease inhibitor for HIV infection. The optimal agents or duration of therapy for disseminated disease in patients with AIDS is unknown. Clarithromycin or trimethoprim-sulfamethoxazole (160/800 mg two or three times daily), amikacin, or newer fluoroquinolones may be effective against M. kansasii strains that are resistant to first-line antimicrobial agents.

RAPIDLY GROWING MYCOBACTERIA. Rapidly growing mycobacteria are acid-fast rods that resemble diphtheroids on Gram stain. Growth is rapid on subculture to solid media (<7 days), but primary isolation from clinical specimens may require 2 to 30 days. Unlike other mycobacteria, they grow well on most routine laboratory media. Sporadic, community-acquired infections have been reported from most areas of the United States. The spectrum of diseases ranges from localized to disseminated, with cutaneous involvement being most common. Most infections are acquired by inoculation after accidental trauma, surgery, or injection. Nosocomial epidemics or clusters have been reported in numerous settings, including augmentation mammaplasty, hemodialysis, plastic surgery, long-term venous catheters, cardiac surgery, and jet injector use.

These NTM are highly resistant to conventional antituberculous drugs but may be sensitive to traditional or newer antibiotics. Susceptibility testing of individual isolates is important because resistance patterns vary by and within species subgroups. The newer macrolides, clarithromycin and azithromycin, are highly effective against most strains of rapidly growing mycobacteria. They may be successful as monotherapy for minor infections. Extensive disease, however, often requires combination therapy. M. fortuitum and M. peregrinum are usually also susceptible to amikacin, fluoroquinolones, sulfonamides, cefoxitin, and imipenem and occasionally to doxycycline. M. abscessus is generally also susceptible to amikacin, imipenem, and cefoxitin. In contrast, M. chelonei is most likely to be susceptible to tobramycin or imipenem. In addition to the new macrolides, therapeutic options for M. mucogenicum may include trimethoprim-sulfamethoxazole, tetracyclines, fluoroquinolones, amikacin, imipenem, or cefoxitin.

Treatment duration should be a minimum of 3 months for serious disease and 6 months for bone infections. Any regimen should include surgical debridement of infected wounds or excision of infected foreign bodies.

OTHER NONTUBERCULOUS MYCOBACTERIA. M. marinum cutaneous infections commonly follow aquatic-related inoculation. Papules on an extremity, especially on the elbows, knees, and dorsum of feet and hands, may progress to shallow ulceration and scar formation.

Table 342–1 • NONTUBERCULOUS MYCOBACTERIAL DISEASES AND ETIOLOGIC SPECIES

CLINICAL DISEASE	ETIOLOGIC SPECIES (RUNYAN GROUP)*	
	Common	Less Common
Pulmonary	M. avium complex (III)	M. simiae (I)
	M. kansasii (I)	M. szulgai (II)
	M. abscessus (IV)	M. malmoense (III)
	M. xenopi (II)	M. fortuitum (IV)
		M. chelonei (IV)
Lymphadenitis	M. avium complex (III)	M. fortuitum (IV)
	M. scrofulaceum (II)	M. chelonei (IV)
		M. abscessus (IV)
		M. kansasii (I)
Cutaneous	M. marinum (I)	M. avium complex (III)
	M. fortuitum (IV)	M. kansasii (I)
	M. chelonei (IV)	M. terrae (III)
	M. abscessus (IV)	M. smegmatis (IV)
	M. ulcerans (III)	M. haemophilum (III)
Disseminated	M. avium complex (III)	M. fortuitum (IV)
	M. kansasii (I)	M. xenopi (II)
	M. chelonei (IV)	M. simiae (I)
	M. abscessus (IV)	M. gordonae (II)
	M. haemophilum (III)	M. terrae complex (III)
		M. neoarum (II)
		M. celatum (III)
		M. genavense (?III)

*I = photochromogen; II = scotochromogen; III = nonpigmented; IV = rapid grower.

Therapeutic approaches have included simple observation for minor lesions, surgical excision, and the use of antimicrobial agents. Acceptable regimens include clarithromycin (500 mg twice daily), doxycycline (100 mg twice daily), trimethoprim-sulfamethoxazole (160/800 mg twice daily), or rifampin (600 mg) plus ethambutol (15 mg/kg) daily. Therapy should continue for a minimum of 3 months.

M. gordonae, a scotochromogen, is also known as the "tap water bacillus." This organism has been associated with nosocomial pseudo-outbreaks, and its isolation is commonly due to environmental contamination of a clinical specimen. *M. gordonae* has been reported to cause pulmonary or disseminated infections in patients with AIDS.

M. xenopi, M. malmoense, M. szulgai, M. simiae, M. haemophilum, M. terrae, M. neoarum, M. celatum, and *M. genavense* are being reported with increasing frequency as causes of pulmonary or disseminated infections in Europe, England, Canada, and the United States. Patients with AIDS appear particularly prone to disseminated disease. Initial therapy for these infections should probably consist of clarithromycin, rifabutin, ethambutol, with or without streptomycin or amikacin pending results of antimicrobial susceptibility testing. Optimal duration of therapy is unknown, but at least 18 to 24 months is recommended.

A growing number of uncommon NTM, including *M. shimoidei, M. branderi, M. asiaticum, M. gastri, M. phlei, M. thermoresistible, M. flavescens,* and *M. intermedium,* are being implicated as rare causes of pulmonary, extrapulmonary, or disseminated infections. The clinical significance of these NTM is likely to increase among patients with AIDS or other immunocompromising conditions.

SUGGESTED READINGS

American Thoracic Society: Diagnosis and treatment of disease caused by nontuberculous mycobacteria. Am J Respir Crit Care Med 1997;156(2 Pt 2):S1–S25. *Benchmark guidelines for the diagnosis and therapy of nontuberculous mycobacteria infections.*

Holland SM: Nontuberculous mycobacteria. Am J Med Sci 2001;321:49–55. *Includes an excellent discussion on the immunopathogenesis of nontuberculous mycobacteria infections.*

Phillips MS, Fordham von Reyn C: Nosocomial infections due to nontuberculous mycobacteria. Clin Infect Dis 2001;33:1363–1274. *Good information on nontuberculous mycobacteria infections and pseudo-outbreaks in health care settings.*

343 LEPROSY (HANSEN'S DISEASE)

Gilla Kaplan
Victoria H. Freedman

Definition

Leprosy is a worldwide disease of great chronicity but low transmissibility that is caused by infection with *Mycobacterium leprae*. The infecting bacilli accumulate largely in the skin and peripheral nerves, leading to a variety of cutaneous lesions and loss of nerve conduction. Secondary to nerve damage, loss of digits and serious disfigurement may occur, giving rise to the typical stigmata of this biblical disease. The varied ability of infected hosts to mount a cell-mediated immune (CMI) response to the infecting bacilli and their antigens results in the wide range of clinical manifestations. In patients who are unable to generate a CMI response, bacterial growth is essentially unrestricted, and widely distributed skin lesions of the lepromatous type develop (lepromatous leprosy). In contrast, a moderate to vigorous CMI response leads to reduced numbers of bacteria and localized cutaneous lesions of the tuberculoid type (tuberculoid leprosy). In addition to these polar forms of the disease, there are intermediate forms resulting from gradations in CMI. Spontaneous changes in the type of disease toward either polar form can occur and are usually associated with tissue damage via humoral (immune complex formation) or cellular (CMI) immune mechanisms. Multidrug therapy promptly reduces viable organisms but must be maintained for long periods of time (6 to 12 months) to achieve clearance of the bacilli and resolution of skin lesions.

Transmission

Little detailed information is available about how the bacillus is transmitted from one individual to another. This deficit in our understanding is related to the long incubation period (6 months to 10 years) and the absence of adequate information about the life of the organism in the environment. Other than in humans, the disease has been discovered in feral armadillos studied in Louisiana and Texas. When infected, these animals contain large numbers of acid-fast bacilli in parenchymatous organs, which have been shown to be identical to bacilli obtained from humans by DNA hybridization and restriction fragment length polymorphism analysis techniques. The sooty mangabey, a New World monkey, can become infected naturally in the wild or when injected with human bacilli. In both armadillos and monkeys, it takes 18 to 24 months for the injected bacilli to reach high numbers. These infections are quite unlike the spectrum of human disease.

The initial route of infection of humans may be through broken skin or through the respiratory or gastrointestinal tract. Direct inoculation via trauma or puncture wounds might result in an initial lesion containing a focus of bacilli. Whatever the source and route of infection, at some point hematogenous spread occurs, with wide bacterial seeding of the body. In the absence of CMI, this seeding leads to lepromatous leprosy with generalized cutaneous distribution of the bacilli. In the presence of CMI, all but a few foci of infection are probably eliminated. The remaining foci give rise to the localized skin lesions characteristic of tuberculoid leprosy.

Lepromatous patients with lesions in the nasal mucosa discharge large numbers of organisms. Bacilli recovered from dry nasal discharges retain some viability for up to 7 to 10 days, with somewhat greater viability under conditions of higher humidity. Transmission of disease from an untreated, infected mother to an infant is not uncommon and should always be considered. The incidence of disease within a household containing an infected tuberculoid or lepromatous patient may be 4 to 8 times that of the general population. Nevertheless, accumulated clinical wisdom suggests that disease transmission takes place only after years of exposure. Therefore, there is little likelihood of transmission in a ward or hospital setting. Consequently, leprosy patients are now cared for on an outpatient basis with a minimum of infection-control precautions.

Susceptibility

Leprosy occurs worldwide and in individuals of all ages. It appears more frequently in young adults, but this may be related to a parental index case and the long period of incubation. A number of studies suggest, but do not prove, that the overall susceptibility to leprosy may be controlled by immune response genes including those of the major histocompatibility complex (class II). Analyses of the disease incidence and susceptibility in identical twins have not been conclusive. More recent studies suggest that the type of leprosy rather than overall disease susceptibility may be controlled by HLA determinants and other genes regulating the immune response. Environmental factors such as nutrition and coincident microbial and parasitic infections may also contribute to susceptibility. The AIDS pandemic has been associated with a rise in the incidence of other mycobacterial diseases, but association has not yet been observed in leprosy.

Epidemiology

The worldwide number of new cases reported by the World Health Organization for 1999 was 678,758 for a prevalence of 1.25 per 100,000 total population. However, in the top 11 endemic countries with 92% of the reported cases, detection rates of 41.7 per 100,000 were seen. In many countries, valid statistics are not available, and the incidence in outlying rural areas is poorly documented. The highest prevalence rates are in Asia and Africa, followed by Central and South America and Oceania. With effective chemotherapy and advanced diagnostic and public health methods the worldwide prevalence is dropping. However, the incidence does not appear to be changing and the number of new cases detected worldwide per year since 1985 has increased from about 550,000 to about 700,000 in 1999. In addition, it is estimated that 1 to 2 million people with irreversible and visible disabilities live in endemic areas and require ongoing care. The majority of leprosy cases are found in tropical areas. Socioeconomic conditions, availability of health care, and body exposure to the environment may all contribute to this. However, the disease also occurs in the colder climates of Tibet, Nepal, Korea, and Siberia. In

Table 343–1 • **IMMUNOLOGIC FEATURES OF LEPROSY PATIENTS**

	TUBERCULOID	BORDERLINE TUBERCULOID	MID- BORDERLINE	BORDERLINE LEPROMATOUS
Acid-fast bacilli in skin lesions	–	–/+	+	+++
Lepromin (Mitsuda) reaction	+++	+++	–	–
Lymphocyte transformation test	95%	40%	10%	1–2%
Anti–*M. leprae* antibodies	–/+	–/++	++	+++
CD4+/CD8+ T-cell ratio in lesions	1.35	1.11	NT	0.48

previous centuries, the disease also occurred in Scandinavia and the countries bordering the North Sea. Small numbers (300 to 500 per year) of leprosy cases currently occur in the United States. The majority of these are seen in immigrant groups from Asia and South America, although occasional cases are seen in individuals who have never left the United States or have lived in the United States for decades. The nature of the disease varies considerably with geographic distribution. In African and Asian countries there is a predominance of tuberculoid leprosy, and 20% or fewer of the reported cases are of the lepromatous type. In contrast, larger numbers of lepromatous cases are reported in Mexico, Brazil, and Venezuela. Early infection and or sensitization with cross-reacting antigens of other environmental mycobacteria have been considered as an explanation for the geographic variation in leprosy type at presentation.

Etiologic Agent

Mycobacterium leprae, discovered by G. A. Hansen in 1873, is the causative agent of leprosy. It has never been successfully cultivated in laboratory culture media. The organism is acid-alcohol fast when stained by the Ziehl-Neelsen method. *M. leprae* is an obligate intracellular parasite that resides in the phagolysosomes of macrophages and in vacuoles of endothelial cells and Schwann cells. *M. leprae* appears to selectively infect Schwann cells of the peripheral nerves. This affinity may be explained by the observation that *M. leprae* binds specifically to extracellular components on the Schwann cell surface, which then presumably leads to internalization of the bacilli. *M. leprae* is classified as a mycobacterium and contains mycolic acid, arabinogalactan, and phenolic glycolipid in the cell wall. The latter molecule is the only *M. leprae*-specific component. No evidence of strain variation has been noted by DNA-DNA hybridization or restriction fragment length polymorphism. The *M. leprae* genome has recently been fully sequenced, providing many new insights into the physiology of the organism. The analysis of the 3.27-mb genome sequence reveals that less than half of the genome contains functional genes. It appears that gene deletion and decay have eliminated many important metabolic activities found in other mycobacteria such as *M. tuberculosis*. For example, siderophore production, parts of the oxidative and anaerobic respiratory pathways, and many catabolic systems and their regulatory pathways are all missing. Thus, many of the metabolic activities of *M. leprae* appear to be low compared with other mycobacteria. A major effort to identify the greater than 300 proteins of *M. leprae* has resulted in the detection of proteins preferentially found in either the cytosol, the bacterial membrane, and the cell wall. How these components contribute to the pathogenicity and immunogenecity of *M. leprae* infection in humans remains to be elucidated.

The absence of an in vitro culture system for *M. leprae* has complicated any investigations of the physiology and pathogenicity of the organism. However, the armadillo has been used successfully to grow large numbers of the mycobacteria. Eighteen to 24 months after inoculation, 10^9 bacilli per gram can be purified from liver and spleen of infected animals; these serve as a source for genetic, chemical, and antigenic analysis. *M. leprae* replicates very slowly within host cells and has a doubling time of approximately 13 days. The organism prefers ambient temperatures below 37° C and grows selectively in cooler portions of the body such as skin, testes, and nasal mucosa. Determination of bacillary viability and resistance to chemotherapeutic agents depends on slow bacillary growth in the footpads of mice—a bioassay taking about 12 months. Accelerated bacillary growth occurs in the athymic nude mouse but still requires 6 or more months. These properties impose severe restrictions on determination of viability and antibiotic sensitivity. Radiorespirometric assays have been developed to assess metabolic activity and drug

sensitivity of *M. leprae* in vitro. For these assays, *M. leprae* is grown in nude mouse footpads and then inoculated into axenic media, and the rate of $^{14}CO_2$ evolution from ^{14}C-palmitic acid is used to measure the metabolic activity. Use of polymerase chain reaction–based technology, in which selected DNA sequences are amplified a million fold, may facilitate more efficient analyses of mycobacterial physiology and drug sensitivity.

Immunologic Considerations

A specific defect in CMI occurs in patients with lepromatous leprosy. This is expressed as a selective unresponsiveness of T cells to *M. leprae* and is evident in skin test (Mitsuda) anergy and lack of responsiveness to *M. leprae* antigens in the in vitro lymphocyte transformation assay (Table 343–1). Lepromatous patients, although unresponsive to *M. leprae* antigen, develop adequate reactions to other antigens to which they have been sensitized, including skin test antigens such as purified protein derivative of tuberculin (PPD), mumps, *Candida*, trichophytin, and tetanus toxoid. In contrast, T cells from patients with the tuberculoid form of the disease respond normally to *M. leprae* antigens. In neither form of the disease are there abnormalities in humoral immunity. The association between cell-mediated cutaneous responses, T-cell accumulation in lesions, and the number of *M. leprae* in the tissues is shown in Table 343–1. These parameters are inversely related. In the absence of *M. leprae*–specific T-cell reactivity, Th1-type cytokine production is depressed or absent and tissue macrophages fail to be activated to an antimicrobial state. Thus, bacilli taken up by the macrophages are able to multiply intracellularly, leading to multibacillary vacuoles in the skin of lepromatous leprosy patients. In tuberculoid leprosy patients, the T-cell response to *M. leprae* results in the release of interferon-γ (IFN-γ), a T-cell cytokine that activates macrophages, thereby enhancing the production of toxic oxygen intermediates in these cells. In these patients, the bacilli are largely destroyed.

Clinical Manifestations

Patients with leprosy are first seen and followed by dermatologists because the anesthetic cutaneous lesions are often the presenting complaint. The range in immune response to *M. leprae* is reflected clinically by a wide variation of skin lesions and peripheral nerve involvement. In this section, we review the characteristics of the major polar and borderline forms.

POLAR TUBERCULOID LEPROSY (TT). This form presents as one to a few asymmetric plaques or macules defined by a sharp, raised border. In dark-skinned patients, the lesions are often centrally hypopigmented with a more erythematous border. The central area of the lesion is frequently scaly, lacks hair, and is anesthetic. Nerves leading to the ear, elbow, and knee may be palpably enlarged. Almost any area of the skin may be affected except for the warmer regions of the scalp, axilla, and perineum. Only very few bacilli are found in affected lesions giving rise to the term paucibacillary. The disease is stable.

BORDERLINE TUBERCULOID (BT) AND BORDERLINE LEPROMATOUS (BL) LEPROSY. As the burden of bacilli in the body increases, in association with a partial reduction in immunity, the number, distribution, and nature of the cutaneous lesions increase in complexity. The skin exhibits a polymorphic array of macular, erythematous, hypopigmented lesions involving the trunk, extremities, and face. These vary randomly in number and distribution. The widely dispersed lesions suggest hematogenous spread of *M. leprae* and

Continued

indicate a cell-mediated immune reaction that is not capable of controlling bacillary growth. Larger nerve trunks are infiltrated with a granulomatous reaction, leading to nerve damage resulting in foot drop, flexion contractions of the digits, and corneal abrasions. The anesthesia of hands and feet and the resulting damage from burns, trauma, and secondary infection leads to loss of digits, plantar ulcerations, and blindness. The disease is unstable and may evolve toward either of the polar forms. Reactional states (see below) are common.

LEPROMATOUS LEPROSY (LL). In these patients, there is little or no CMI to *M. leprae*, and tremendous numbers of organisms are dispersed throughout the skin, giving rise to the term multibacillary. Again, the lesions are pleomorphic but often are less "angry" or erythematous than in borderline disease. Macules, papules, and nodules may cover wide areas of the trunk and extremities, and lesion distribution is often symmetric. Almost any area of affected or even normal-looking skin contains bacilli. Often there are no obvious lesions, but the skin looks shiny and full, as the dermis is expanded with macrophages containing the bacilli. This is particularly prominent on the ears, eyebrows, and face, resulting in the characteristic appearance termed "leonine facies." Eyebrow loss is frequent; a saddle nose deformity may result from cartilage destruction; gynecomastia from reduced testosterone levels secondary to testicular damage may be present; and blindness and iridocyclitis, laryngeal stenosis, loss of incisor teeth, and loss of digits may occur. Rigid, swollen nerves are palpable in many locations. Nerve damage in lepromatous leprosy is more slowly progressive but is eventually severe and diffuse and leads to a sensory polyneuropathy. The disease is stable. The deformities associated with long-term untreated lepromatous leprosy are the stigmata that lead to the ostracism of the leper from his or her community and necessitate custodial care. However, today patients undergoing chemotherapy often remain members of their households.

Reactional States

ERYTHEMA NODOSUM LEPROSUM (ENL). Patients with BL and LL disease maintain high levels of circulating anti–*M. leprae* antibodies as well as high antigen levels. After effective chemotherapy, a prompt and extensive killing of bacilli takes place, and large amounts of soluble antigens are liberated extracellularly. More than 30% of such treated patients develop ENL and present with painful subcutaneous erythematous nodules that arise diffusely and may eventually lead to necrosis and suppuration. These symptoms, accompanied by fever and malaise, can continue for months, are extremely debilitating, and are often accompanied by acute inflammation of the eyes, testes, nerves, lymph nodes, and joints. Some patients develop glomerulonephritis with the deposition of complement and immune complexes in the glomeruli. Enhanced production of the cytokine tumor necrosis factor-α (TNF-α) has been associated with ENL. This serious complication of leprosy requires prompt diagnosis and therapy.

REVERSAL REACTIONS. This reactional state also may occur after chemotherapy but differs from ENL in that either increase or decrease of the local CMI may be observed, accompanied by widespread erythema and induration of preexisting lesions as well as systemic symptoms, e.g., pyrexia. The onset of this state is slower than that of ENL (weeks to months), and it may persist for many months if not properly treated. Rapid progression of preexisting peripheral nerve damage may take place. Any deterioration in nerve conduction should be considered a medical emergency and treated accordingly. Both ENL and reversal reactions as well as progressive nerve damage can occur or recur even after completion of the course of therapy and bacteriologic cure.

Laboratory Findings

In addition to clinical manifestations, the primary method for diagnosis of leprosy is by identification of acid-fast bacilli in the skin. The slit smear technique is used throughout the world. The skin is incised with a scalpel, squeezing the area to maintain a bloodless field. The edges of the slit are scraped with the edge of the scalpel, smeared on a slide, fixed, and stained by the Ziehl-Neelsen method. A microscopic logarithmic score (1+ to 6+; 5+ equals 100 to 1000 acid-fast bacilli per high-power field) is used to quantify the bacterial load.

Usually six sites on the earlobes, elbow, knee, and a lesion are prepared. This simple method, when skillfully employed, is as sensitive as other diagnostic procedures. A more definitive estimate of bacillary numbers in the skin may be obtained from biopsy material. A logarithmic score is derived from counting the number of bacilli in high-power microscopic fields. This score or bacteriologic index ranges from 1+ to 6+ and is a useful index in following the response of patients to therapy in terms of bacillary numbers and histopathologic classification. (Bacterial index: no bacilli in 100 microscopic fields [×100]; 1+ = 1 to 10 bacilli in 100 fields; 2+ = 1 to 10 bacilli in 10 fields; 3+ = 1 to 10 bacilli per field; 4+ = 10 to 100 bacilli per field; 5+ = 100 to 1000 bacilli per field; and 6+ = many 1000s per field.)

A skin test is often used to distinguish the immunologically reactive (tuberculoid) and nonreactive (lepromatous) poles of the disease. A crude antigen consisting of heat-killed bacilli prepared from infected armadillos is injected into the skin and induces local induration and the formation of granulomas in 3 to 4 weeks in most tuberculoid patients. Patients with lepromatous leprosy fail to react to the antigen and may remain unresponsive long after effective chemotherapy. Serologic tests are useful in assaying the level of anti–*M. leprae* antibodies in multibacillary lepromatous but not in the paucibacillary tuberculoid patients. However, the many cross-reactive antigenic epitopes shared with other mycobacteria complicate interpretation and the differential diagnosis. ELISA tests, which recognize antibodies against the carbohydrate moieties of the phenolic glycolipids, the only molecules that are *M. leprae* specific, are positive in patients with lepromatous but not tuberculoid disease and decline after chemotherapy is initiated. Patients with lepromatous leprosy have a polyclonal hypergammaglobulinemia, as well as acute phase reactants such as C-reactive protein, and immune complexes in the circulation. Ten percent of lepromatous patients give false-positive tests for syphilis and 30% have cryoglobulinemia.

Histopathology and Immunopathology

Microscopic analysis of tissue plays a primary role in diagnosing and classifying the various clinical forms of leprosy. A standardized classification described by Ridley and Jopling is used. Five histologic groups have been defined, spanning the spectrum from polar tuberculoid (TT) to polar lepromatous (LL) and including borderline (BB) as well as borderline tuberculoid (BT) and borderline lepromatous (BL). Our discussion focuses on the polar forms; the details pertaining to the intermediate manifestations can be found in more specialized texts.

LESIONS OF THE SKIN

Tuberculoid Leprosy. Microscopic examination of hematoxylin and eosin–stained sections of biopsies obtained from a TT macular plaque reveals infiltration of the dermis by mononuclear leukocytes organized in well-developed granulomas. These granulomas contain large numbers of lymphocytes scattered between and surrounding macrophage-derived epithelioid cells and Langhans-type multinucleated giant cells (Fig. 343–1). Occasional plasma cells but few granulocytes are found. Langerhans (dendritic) cells are found within the dermal infiltrate in significant numbers. Staining with monoclonal antibodies shows that the majority of lymphocytes are T cells and that the CD4+ T helper–type phenotype predominates over CD8+ T suppressor/cytotoxic cells. The epidermis overlying the dermal infiltrate is thickened (two- to three-fold), and individual keratinocytes are enlarged. The keratinocytes display large amounts of MHC class II determinants on their surface. This is a response to the local production of IFN-γ in the dermis and is accompanied by the expression of other IFN-γ induced molecules by keratinocytes and other cell types. Acid-fast staining of sections reveals an occasional bacillus or bacillary remnants within macrophages. BT lesions are similar except that the lesions are more numerous and acid-fast bacilli are more easily seen.

Lepromatous Leprosy. In contrast to TT lesions, the lepromatous lesion contains only small numbers of lymphocytes, predominantly of the CD8+ T-cell phenotype, scattered through a background of loosely organized dermal macrophages and collagen (Fig. 343–2). The macrophages often have a pale, foamy cytoplasm and may contain large clumps of *M. leprae* called globi (Fig. 343–3). By electron microscopy, these organisms are observed within large cytoplasmic vacuoles, embedded in a lucent matrix that contains phenolic glycolipid. Remnants of the osmiophilic bacilli are present along with structurally intact organisms (see Fig. 343–3). A gram of skin may

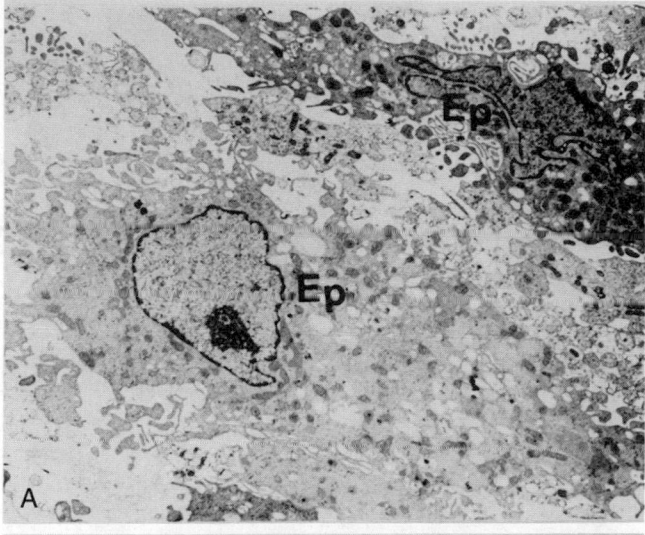

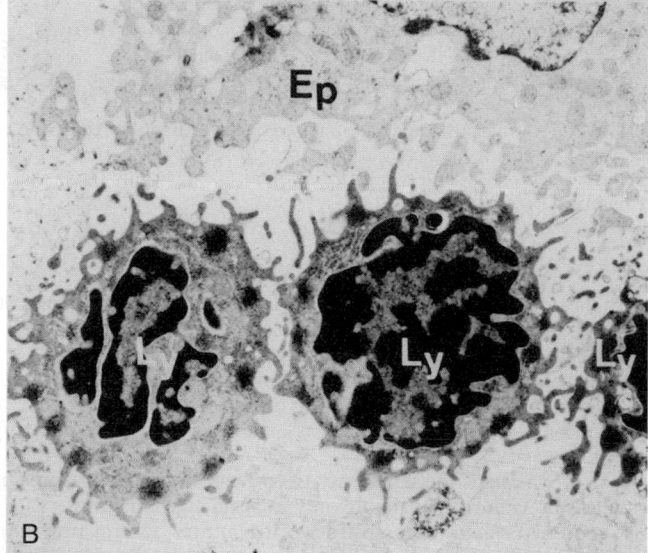

FIGURE 343-1 • Transmission electron photomicrographs of cutaneous granulomas from a patient with tuberculoid leprosy. *A*, the granuloma contains large epithelioid cells (Ep) with multiple cytoplasmic organelles (×4500). *B*, Three T lymphocytes (Ly) and an epithelioid cell are observed (×9000).

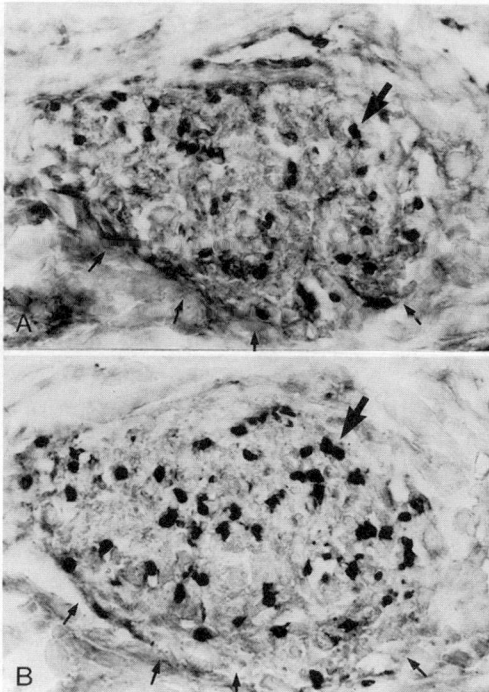

FIGURE 343-2 • Lepromatous leprosy—cutaneous lesion. Frozen serial sections stained with Leu 3 (anti-CD4–helper T-cell subset) (*A*) and with Leu 2 (anti-CD8–suppressor/cytotoxic T-cell subset) (*B*). The inflammatory infiltrates (*small arrows*) contain few T cells. Cells of the CD4+ subset (*large arrow in A*) are less numerous than those of the CD8+ subset (*large arrow in B*). Immunoperoxidase, counterstained with hematoxylin (×200).

contain 10^9 bacilli. Neither Langhans giant cells nor Langerhans dendritic cells are seen in the dermis. The overlying epidermis is thin and atrophic and the cells fail to show surface MHC class II antigens. The loose bacilli-rich infiltrates of LL are present in almost every area of the skin.

LESIONS OF PERIPHERAL NERVE

Tuberculoid Leprosy. The paucibacillary granulomatous response is associated with significant destruction of peripheral nerve fascicles and late in the disease may lead to caseous necrosis of nerve trunks. Large numbers of T cells and mononuclear phagocytes breach the perineurium and lead to destruction of Schwann cells and axons alike. By the time the skin lesion is apparent, nerve damage and sensory loss have occurred. The mechanism of the nerve damage in TT is unclear but is related to CMI and the granulomatous response.

Lepromatous Leprosy. In the majority of subcutaneous nerve trunks many bacilli are observed within macrophages outside the perineural sheath as well as in Schwann cells and macrophages within the perineural sheath (Fig. 343–4). Nerve damage is relatively slow as compared with TT but is more extensive and insidious. Few, if any, lymphocytes are part of the nerve lesion. Schwann cells are capable of taking up *M. leprae* and serve as permissive hosts for their replication (see Fig. 343–4).

OTHER ORGANS. Lepromatous lesions can be found in the lymph nodes, liver, spleen, bone marrow, endocrine organs, and eye. These lesions contain macrophages infected with bacilli but are not considered to be an important site of infection. Patients with untreated

multibacillary disease can have a constant bacteremia of 10^5 AFB per milliliter, all of which are present within monocytes. The total body burden of *M. leprae* can reach 10^{12} bacilli.

LESIONS OF REACTIONAL STATES

Erythema Nodosum Leprosum (ENL). Examination of the skin nodules of ENL shows extensive mixed leukocyte infiltration consisting of neutrophils and mononuclear cells and tissue necrosis. Immune complexes are evident, and there is a panvasculitis of dermal arteries and veins. These are all hallmarks of an extensive acute inflammatory response resulting in tissue damage. TNF-α–induced and other cytokine-induced cell surface antigens can be demonstrated.

Reversal Reactions. Patients with BT, BB, or BL leprosy, who are partially responsive to *M. leprae* antigens, occasionally undergo an upgrading reaction after several months of therapy. This differs from ENL in that there is migration of a predominantly T-cell infiltrate into preexisting affected sites. Many of the T cells are of the helper CD4+ phenotype and secrete cytokines into their environment. T-cell migration into skin lesions is associated with mononuclear phagocyte differentiation and the formation of the organized granuloma and is often associated with the rapid progression of peripheral nerve damage. This enhancement of CMI leads to limited bacillary destruction. A downgrading or reduction in CMI also may occur. Such reactions may continue for weeks or months and are associated with severe morbidity leading to serious sequelae.

Pathogenesis

Recovery from infections with obligate intracellular parasites such as *M. leprae* requires the host to mount an effective CMI response. Antigen-presenting cells must recognize and cluster with appropriate T cells, leading to T-cell stimulation, differentiation, and replication. T helper cells synthesize and secrete a variety of hormone-like lymphokines that enhance the microbicidal activity of monocytes and macrophages as well as stimulating other cells in the environment, such as keratinocytes, endothelial cells, and fibroblasts. This leads to the development of T cells that are antigen specific and MHC class II or class I restricted. Along with natural killer (NK) and lymphokine-activated killer (LAK) cells, they serve as potent specific and nonspecific cytotoxic effector cells. In lepromatous leprosy, in the absence

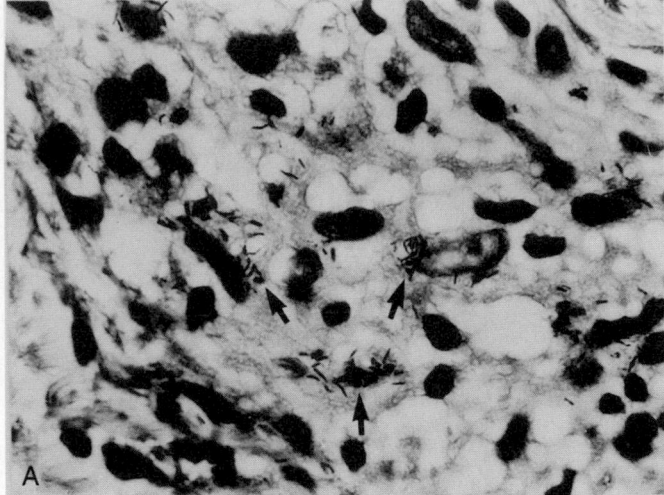

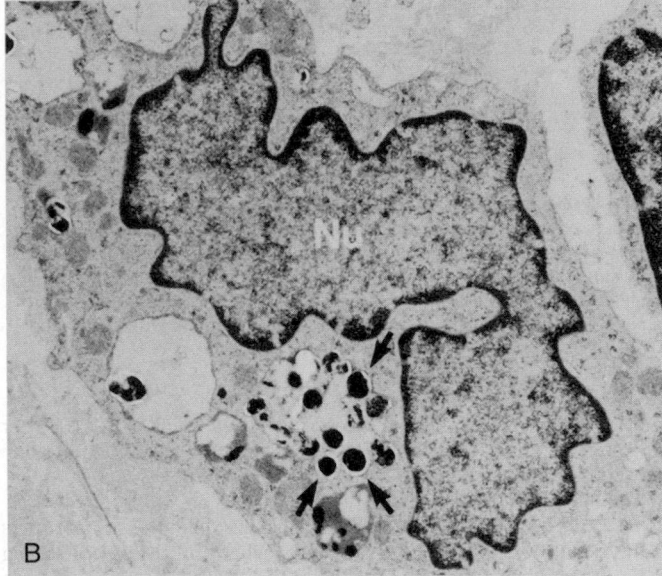

FIGURE 343–3 • Lepromatous leprosy—cutaneous lesions. Acid-fast staining of histologic section (*A*) and transmission electron photomicrograph (*B*) of *M. leprae*—parasitized foamy macrophages (*arrows*). The phagocytes have large nuclei and many light and electron lucent vacuoles containing darkly staining bacteria (A, ×500; B, ×9000). Nu = nucleus.

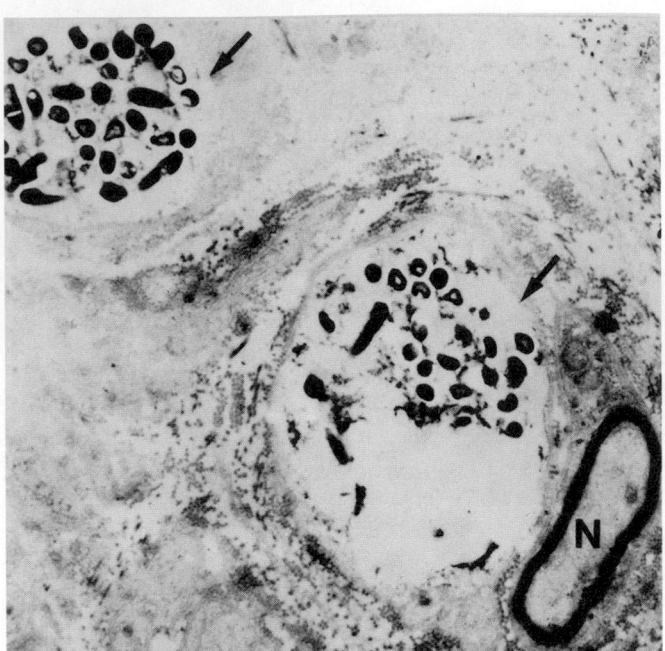

FIGURE 343–4 • Transmission electron micrograph of an infiltrated peripheral nerve of a cutaneous lesion from a lepromatous leprosy patient. The myelinated neuron (N) and two *M. leprae*–infected Schwann cells (*arrows*) are observed (× 9000).

of local lymphokine production, the mycobacteria multiply in macrophages that have neither the capacity to kill the organism nor the capability to be activated by lymphokines. To modify this fertile intracellular environment, the host must destroy the heavily parasitized macrophage, liberating its contents into the extracellular milieu. Here, newly emigrated monocytes ingest, kill, and degrade *M. leprae* with the help of a lymphokine stimulus. This is the situation that occurs in the tuberculoid form of the disease and is lacking in the lepromatous state.

Recommended Treatment Schedules

The most commonly used drug in the therapy of leprosy is 4,4-diamino-diphenylsulfone (Dapsone, DDS). Because of the widespread emergence of Dapsone-resistant strains of *M. leprae*, all patients now receive multidrug therapy. The components and schedules vary depending on the presence of Dapsone-sensitive strains and the part of the world in which the patient resides.

In the United States, the following recently modified regimens are used.

1. Paucibacillary disease of the TT and BT categories.
   a. Dapsone-sensitive *M. leprae:* Dapsone is given in a daily dose of 100 mg and rifampin at a daily dose of 600 mg for 1 year.

b. Dapsone-resistant *M. leprae:* Clofazimine at a daily dose of 50 to 100 mg is substituted for Dapsone.
2. Multibacillary disease of the BB, BL, and LL categories.
   a. Dapsone-sensitive or Dapsone-resistant *M. leprae:* Dapsone is given in a daily dose of 100 mg, rifampin is given in a dose of 600 mg/day, and clofazimine is given in a daily dose of 50 mg for 2 years.

To evaluate the Dapsone sensitivity, the mouse footpad assay must be used; this procedure is available only in specialized facilities.

A modified schedule for third world country control programs was issued by the World Health Organization (WHO) in 1982 and is based on practical considerations, including the availability of slit smear facilities and financial constraints:

1. *Paucibacillary disease defined as a bacillary index of 0 at all six skin sites:* Dapsone is given daily at a dose of 100 mg, unsupervised. Rifampin is given at a dose of 600 mg once a month, supervised. Treatment is given for 6 months and is then discontinued.
2. *Multibacillary disease defined as a bacillary index of 1+ or more at any one of six skin sites:* Dapsone is given daily at 100 mg with clofazimine 50 mg daily, unsupervised. Rifampin 600 mg and clofazimine 300 mg are given once monthly, supervised. This therapy is continued for 1 year.

The WHO schedule for intermittent rifampin therapy is based in part on its expense and on clinical and laboratory trials. It should be noted, however, that many leprologists use rifampin at 450 to 600 mg daily for 2 to 3 years. Relapses under the WHO schedule are infrequent. Rifampin is the most rapidly effective bactericidal agent and kills the majority of *M. leprae* within 2 to 3 weeks, according to mouse foot pad assays. Resistance to rifampin is well known in the therapy of *M. tuberculosis* and is now becoming evident with *M. leprae*. Therapy with clofazimine, a phenazine derivative, has certain unpleasant side effects based on its lipophilicity. The compound is a red-purple dye taken up and concentrated by macrophages of the skin, causing increased skin pigmentation. This is distressing to certain light-skinned patients. Clofazimine is also deposited in the small intestine, where at high concentrations it causes segmental thickening associated with crampy pain and diarrhea. If clofazimine is unacceptable to patients, the physician should consider substitution with 100 mg daily of minocycline or 400 mg daily of ofloxacin.

Children with leprosy should receive appropriately reduced doses of the above mentioned drugs.

Rx Treatment of Reaction

ERYTHEMA NODOSUM LEPROSUM. The acute onset of ENL may be mild enough to require only salicylates or other cyclooxygenase inhibitors. With severe episodes, high doses of corticosteroids (prednisone 60 to 80 mg/day) are necessary and should be tapered off as soon as feasible. However, exacerbations occur frequently, and repeated dosing is necessary. A particularly useful drug in severe ENL is thalidomide, a selective inhibitor of TNF-α production. It is given initially at 200 mg twice a day and then tapered to levels of 50 to 100 mg/day. Thalidomide is a potent teratogen and should be assiduously avoided if pregnancy is possible. Clofazimine also has been found useful in ENL but requires 4 to 6 weeks to achieve therapeutic effects. In some patients ENL responds poorly to thalidomide, and prednisone and/or clofazimine are used.

REVERSAL REACTIONS. The chronicity and potential nerve damage of this CMI reaction require high-dose steroids and careful evaluation of peripheral nerve conduction. Thalidomide is not used in this condition. The use of clofazimine together with steroids allows for a more rapid withdrawal of prednisone.

OTHER COMPLICATIONS. A number of surgical procedures are available at specialized leprosy hospitals to help correct foot drop, hand deformities, madarosis, and lagophthalmos. Plastic surgical procedures can replace nasal septa and help close large plantar ulcerations. On occasion, patients with gynecomastia request the removal of glandular tissue. The presence of a cold abscess of a peripheral nerve with sudden increase in pain and functional loss requires immediate decompression by surgical drainage.

Prognosis

Tuberculoid leprosy may be self-limited and usually responds well to chemotherapy. Nerve damage is, however, irreversible. In lepromatous disease, prolonged courses of multiple drugs arrest the progression of the illness when compliance is good. It is the ability of the public health infrastructure to monitor compliance that is central to effective therapy. However, even in bacteriologically cured patients, ENL and progressive nerve damage can occur. Recurrences due to poor maintenance therapy are not infrequent.

Prevention and Prophylaxis

Education of the general public plays an important role in sensitizing individuals to the nature of leprosy as an infectious disease and the ability to cure the illness with medication. Once a case has been identified in a household, careful physical examination of all contacts accompanied by the biopsy of suspicious lesions should be carried out. The threat of contagion is much higher in children younger than age 16. In this adolescent category, the prophylactic use of Dapsone should be considered. Vaccine trials have been carried out sponsored by WHO. These have used BCG vaccine with and without heat-killed *M. leprae* or other mycobacteria in highly endemic areas of Africa, Asia, and India. There is evidence that BCG vaccination alone may reduce the incidence of disease.

SUGGESTED READINGS

Cole ST, Eiglmeier K, Parkhill J, et al: Massive gene decay in the leprosy bacillus. Nature 2001;409:1007–1011. *Analysis of the* M. leprae *genome and its implications for the lifestyle of the organism.*

Hatta M: Epidemiology of leprosy. Molecular, biological, and immunological approach. Adv Exp Med Biol 2003;531:269–278. *Contact with a leprosy patient is the major determinant in the incidence of leprosy.*

Jardim MR, Antunes SL, Santos AR, et al: Criteria for diagnosis of pure neural leprosy. J Neurol 2003;250:806–809. *Polymerase chain reaction testing, in conjunction with clinical and neurological examination results, can identify and confirm the diagnosis.*

Pessolani MCV, Brennan PJ: Molecular definition and identification of new proteins of Mycobacterium leprae. Infect Immunol 1996;64:5425–5427. *Discussion of* M. leprae *proteins and their properties.*

Rambukkana A. Yamada H, Zanazzi G, et al: Role of alpha-dystroglycan as a Schwann cell receptor for Mycobacterium leprae. Science 1998;282:2076–2079. *How M. leprae infects peripheral nerves.*

Smith WC: International Leprosy Congress 2002—lessons learned. Lepr Rev 2003;74: 7–10. *A recent overview.*

344 URINARY TRACT INFECTIONS

Ragnar Norrby

Definition

This chapter deals with infections characterized by colonization of the normally sterile urine by bacteria or fungi. Urinary tract infections (UTIs) included are asymptomatic bacteriuria, cystitis, pyelonephritis, and urosepsis. Urethritis caused by *Chlamydia trachomatis, Ureaplasma urealyticum,* or *Neisseria gonorrhoeae,* and prostatitis are not dealt with here and renal tuberculosis is mentioned only as a differential diagnosis.

Definitions and Classifications

In the 1950s, Kass studied patients with or without bacterial colonization of the bladder urine (defined as bacterial growth in a urine sample obtained by catheterization of the bladder). He defined *significant bacteriuria* as $\geq 10^5$ colony-forming units (CFUs, where 1 CFU = one or more bacterial cells forming a colony when growing on an agar plate) per mL in two consecutive samples of midstream urine (i.e., urine obtained during voiding discarding the first and last urine portions). Later this definition has been revisited, and *significant bacteriuria* has been redefined to optimize the sensitivity and specificity of the diagnostic procedures. In women with symptoms of uncomplicated cystitis (see later), significant bacteriuria is today defined as $\geq 10^2$ CFU/mL midstream urine plus pyuria (≥ 5 leukocytes/mm^3 of urine). In women with uncomplicated pyelonephritis and men with UTIs, significant bacteriuria is defined as $\geq 10^4$ CFU/mL plus pyuria, and in patients with complicated UTIs the definition is $\geq 10^5$ CFU/mL with or without pyuria.

It is clinically important to classify UTIs by type of infection, presence or absence of symptoms, tendency to recur, and presence or absence of complicating factors (Table 344–1). Recurrent infections can be subdivided into reinfections caused by new bacterial strains and relapses caused by the same strains that caused the preceding infections. Complicating factors are host factors facilitating establishment and maintenance of bacteriuria or worsening the prognosis of UTIs engaging the kidneys. The most common ones are listed in Table 344–2.

Pathogenesis

In a majority of patients, UTIs are the result of colonization of the urine with fecal bacteria, which grow aerobically. Growth of anaerobic bacteria, such as *Bacteroides fragilis,* in the urine indicates a communication between the intestines and the urinary tract. That is seen in rare cases of fistulas between the intestines and the renal tract and following reconstructive surgery in the urinary tract, which involves the intestines. Growth of fungi in the urine may be seen in patients with bladder catheters and in immunocompromised patients with hematologic dissemination of *Candida* spp. from infections at other sites.

In women, bacteria colonize the periurethral area, from where they reach the distal part of the urethra. Atrophic vaginal mucosa after

Table 344–1 • CLASSIFICATION OF URINARY TRACT INFECTIONS (UTIs)

CLASSIFICATION BY	TYPES OF UTIs
Type of UTI	Cystitis
	Pyelonephritis
	Asymptomatic bacteriuria
Symptoms	Symptomatic
	Asymptomatic
Recurrences	Sporadic (≤ 1 UTI/6 mo and ≤ 2 UTIs/yr)
	Recurrent (≥ 2 UTIs/6 mo or ≥ 3 UTIs/yr)
	Relapse
	Reinfection
Complicating factors	Uncomplicated
	Complicated (see text)

Table 344–2 • **HOST FACTORS COMPLICATING BACTERIURIA**

OUTCOME	FACTORS

Facilitated establishment and maintenance of bacteriuria	Residual bladder urine after voiding
	   Physiologic
	   Neurogenic bladder
	   Prostate hyperplasia/tumor
	Turbulent urethral urine flow
	   Strictures
	Foreign bodies
	   Catheters
	   Calculi
	   Tumors
	Atrophic vaginal mucosa postmenopause
	Vesicoureteral reflux
	   Anatomic defects
	   Pregnancy

Worse prognosis of UTIs involving the kidneys	Childhood pyelonephritis Diabetic nephropathy Malignant hypertension Chronic pyelonephritis

menopause with altered vaginal flora, and diaphragms and spermicides in sexually active women are factors that increase the risk of colonization with large amounts of uropathogenic bacteria. Sexual intercourse results in increased numbers of bacteria in the periurethral area of the vagina and the distal part of the urethra, increasing the risk of bacteriuria.

In the normal male urethra, the distance between the end of the urethra and the bladder is too long to allow ascending transport of bacteria to the bladder. Therefore, bacteriuria in men should always be considered an abnormal finding, and men cannot have uncomplicated infections. However, transport of bacteria to the bladder urine through the male urethra is possible when there is a turbulent urine flow, such as the result of a stricture or obstruction of the urethra, as occurs as a result of prostatic hyperplasia, and when the patient has a bladder catheter.

The female urethra is short and allows transport of bacteria to the bladder also in healthy individuals. With many uropathogens such transport is facilitated by adherence of the bacteria to urethral epithelial cells. Bacterial cells, such as *Escherichia coli* strains causing uncomplicated pyelonephritis, have fimbriae that adhere to α-D-Gal-4)-β-D-Gal receptors (the P blood group) on the mucosal cells in the urethra and the ureters, thus facilitating establishment of bacteriuria and further transport to the kidneys. Such adhesion is important also in that it stimulates mucosal cells to release cytokines such as interleukin-6 and interleukin-8, causing fever plus increase of C-reactive protein in blood and mobilization of leukocytes, respectively. Individuals who lack the receptors for the bacterial adhesions, that is, those who do not have the P blood group, seem to be less prone to have acute pyelonephritis. In patients with complicated UTIs, bacterial adhesion seems to be of less importance.

The role in the pathogenesis of UTIs of other bacterial virulence factors, such as the O- and K-antigens of *E. coli*, is less well known.

When bacteria have reached the bladder, establishment of bacteriuria is facilitated by incomplete bladder emptying, that is, if there is residual urine. Already at residual urine volumes of 10 mL, which are not uncommon in healthy individuals, bacterial growth in the urine may be established since the reproduction time is 20 minutes for *E. coli* and normal diuresis is 60 mL/min.

Pyelonephritis results from ascending bacteriuria from the bladder via the ureter to the renal pelvis and the renal parenchyma. This transport may be facilitated by host factors such as anatomic defects of the ureters or the kidneys, vesicoureteral reflux, or, in patients without anatomic defects, adhesion to the ureter mucosa. In about one third of patients with pyelonephritis there also is bacteremia.

In rare cases, bacteriuria and funguria may result from hematogenous dissemination of bacteria to the kidneys causing a renal abscess. The focus of the infection is then an infection at a site outside the renal tract, such as endocarditis.

Patients with asymptomatic bacteriuria frequently harbor organisms, which are less virulent than those causing symptomatic infections. Such organisms are often killed by normal human plasma or serum ("serum bactericidal effect"). It has been demonstrated that patients with persistent asymptomatic bacteriuria may be protected from symptomatic UTIs by large numbers of less virulent bacteria ($\geq 10^6$ CFU/mL) in the urine. However, in pregnant women and in patients with type 2 diabetes, there are studies showing that asymptomatic bacteriuria is a strong predictor of subsequent symptomatic infections. In pregnancy, pyelonephritis is common because these women frequently have a vesicoureteral reflux during the last two trimesters. In children as well as in adults, asymptomatic bacteriuria may be a sign of underlying urinary tract malformations.

Bladder catheterization leads to bacteriuria or funguria in all patients who have had their catheters for more than 1 week. Formation of a biofilm on the catheter surfaces facilitates growth of microorganisms. Urosepsis, resulting from dissemination of bacteria from the urine to the blood in a patient with bacteriuria, is often the consequence of removal or change of a bladder catheter during the preceding 24 to 48 hours. This risk is further increased if the catheter has been in place for more than 1 week when the softener in the plastic material of the catheter is eluted, rendering the catheter stiff. Damage to the urethral mucosa is often also caused by crystals on the catheter surface.

Etiology

The microbiologic etiology of a UTI depends on several factors. Table 344–3 summarizes the most common findings. In all types of UTI, *E. coli* is the dominating bacterial species causing up to 85% of all symptomatic UTIs in women with community-acquired, sporadic, uncomplicated infections. In most countries, the second most common species causing such infections is *Staphylococcus saprophyticus* (sometimes called micrococci), which, at least in North Europe, has a pronounced seasonal pattern, accounting for up to 40% of all uncomplicated cases of cystitis and pyelonephritis in July and August and virtually no infections in January and February. In patients with recurrent infections, species such as *Enterococcus faecalis, Enterococcus faecium, Klebsiella* spp., *Proteus* spp., *Providencia stuartii,* and *Morganella morganii* become more common. In patients with very frequent recurrences and/or bladder catheters, especially in hospital and nursing home settings where antibiotics are frequently used, *Pseudomonas aeruginosa, Acinetobacter baumanii, Serratia marcescens,* and *Stenotrophomonas maltophilia* are important organisms. In such patients, *E. coli* accounts for less than 50% of the infections. Findings of *Proteus mirabilis* or other *Proteus* spp. may indicate that the patient

Table 344–3 • **MICROBIAL ETIOLOGY OF URINARY TRACT INFECTIONS**

ORGANISMS	CLINICAL CHARACTERISTICS
GRAM-NEGATIVE BACTERIA	
Escherichia coli	Typical
Klebsiella pneumoniae	Often reinfection
Enterobacter spp.	Often reinfection and/or nosocomial infection*
Proteus spp.	May indicate tumor or calculi
Providencia stuartii	Often reinfection and/or nosocomial infection*
Morganella morganii	Often reinfection and/or nosocomial infection*
Serratia marcescens	Often nosocomial infection*
Acinetobacter baumanii	Often nosocomial infection*
Burkholderia spp.	Often nosocomial infection*
Pseudomonas aeruginosa	Often nosocomial infection*
Stenotrophomonas maltophilia	Often nosocomial infection*
GRAM-POSITIVE BACTERIA	
Staphylococcus saprophyticus	Most common during summer
Staphylococcus aureus	May indicate focus outside the genitourinary tract
Enterococcus spp.	Often reinfection
Other Gram-positive bacteria	In most cases contaminants
FUNGI	
Candida spp.	May indicate focus outside the genitourinary tract

*Includes hospital and nursing home care.

Table 344–4 • CLINICAL SYMPTOMS OF URINARY TRACT INFECTIONS

TYPE OF URINARY TRACT INFECTION	TYPICAL SYMPTOMS
Cystitis	Frequent voiding
	Burning during and after voiding
	Suprapubic pain
	Hematuria and/or cloudy urine
Pyelonephritis	Fever
	Chills
	Flank pains
	Cystitis symptoms (may be absent)
Urosepsis	Fever
	Chills
	Septic shock

has renal calculi or a tumor, because these organisms grow in an alkaline environment. Calculi in the renal pelvis, the ureter, or the bladder may also be formed as a result of growth of ammonia-producing organisms such as *Proteus* spp. Because *Proteus* spp. are common in the male preputial flora, the finding of such organisms in a voided urine sample from uncircumcised men or young boys should be interpreted with caution.

Epidemiology

It has been calculated that worldwide there are at least 150 million cases of symptomatic UTIs each year. Because many UTI patients have recurrent infections, the number of individuals who have UTIs each year is lower than the number of cases.

In an unselected material, 90% of the patients will have cystitis and 10% pyelonephritis. The infections will be sporadic in about 75% of the patients and recurrent in 25%. About 2% will have complicated infections due to factors that increase the risk of establishment and maintenance of bacteriuria. These patients typically have frequently recurring UTIs. If factors that may increase the severity of a renal infection are included, the frequency of complicated infections is about 8%.

During life, UTIs are somewhat more common in very young boys than in very young girls; that is due to the higher frequency of urethral malformations in boys. Later in childhood, symptomatic UTI is more common in girls, who also more frequently have asymptomatic bacteriuria. This is in most cases due to the short urethra but may also be the result of sexual abuse. Symptomatic UTIs are by far most common in sexually active women. In young men, bacterial UTIs are rare and often the result of underlying infections of the prostate. In the elderly, both symptomatic UTIs and asymptomatic bacteriuria are common. In women, that is often the result of an atrophic vaginal mucosa, and in men, to prostate hyperplasia or prostate cancer.

UTI is the most common type of hospital-acquired infection, because of the frequent use of bladder catheters.

Clinical Manifestations

Typical symptoms of cystitis, pyelonephritis, and urosepsis are listed in Table 344–4.

Onset of cystitis is rapid, and symptoms develop over less than 24 hours. It is clinically often impossible to differentiate between cystitis and urethritis caused by chlamydia, ureaplasma, or gonococci, especially when urethritis patients do not present with a urethral discharge. There is normally no or very low fever in cystitis. In sexually active women, cystitis commonly occurs 24 to 48 hours after intercourse, especially if the practice of postcoital bladder emptying (see later) has not been followed. Cystitis patients normally have symptoms for 3 to 5 days. Antibiotic treatment does not markedly reduce the duration, and bacteriuria may persist after treatment.

Pyelonephritis also has a rapid onset with or without preceding cystitis symptoms. About one third of the patients develop bacteremia. The typical loin pain, resulting from inflammation and edema of the renal parenchyma, may be masked by intake of analgesic drugs such as acetaminophen, which also may reduce

the fever. An important differential diagnosis is renal calculi, which may give a similar location of the pain but normally without fever. Also, appendicitis and cholecystitis can present with loin pains similar to those in a patient with right-sided pyelonephritis.

Urosepsis is a life-threatening condition caused by dissemination of bacteria, which normally are Gram-negative, from the urine in a patient with bacteriuria. As mentioned earlier, the most common reason for urosepsis is insertion or, especially, withdrawal of a bladder catheter. Thus, urosepsis patients do not always have renal involvement of their infections.

The prognoses of uncomplicated cystitis and pyelonephritis are generally good, and there are no deaths unless a patient with pyelonephritis is left untreated, in which case sepsis may develop and lead to death. Also, secondary complications are rare in these patients. In patients with complications such as renal scars from childhood pyelonephritis, chronic pyelonephritis or glomerulonephritis, or other chronic renal diseases, acute pyelonephritis may lead to further reduction of renal function. As mentioned above, infections with *Proteus* spp. or other ammonia-producing organisms may lead to formation of calculi or aggravation of existing ones.

Patients with urosepsis have a poor prognosis with fatality rates of about 30% or higher.

Factors increasing the risk of death are high age and underlying diseases but also inadequate choice of antibiotic treatment. It has been demonstrated that in patients with sepsis caused by Gram-negative bacteria, the death rate increases drastically if the organisms are resistant to the empirical treatment given.

Diagnosis

The hallmark of the types of UTIs dealt with here is demonstration of bacteriuria in a urine sample that has been incubated in the bladder for at least 2 hours to allow growth of bacteria. The most reliable result is obtained if the sample is taken via suprapubic aspiration, a technique frequently used in infants but rarely in older children and adults. It is superior to sampling by bladder catheterization, which carries a risk of about 2% for introduction of bacteria into the bladder and subsequent iatrogenic bacteriuria. The normal procedure for quantitative cultures is to collect a midstream urine sample. This requires that the patient is well informed about the sampling procedures. Men should withdraw the foreskin and women should keep the labia apart. Washing of the genital tract before sampling is not recommended. During voiding, the first and the last parts of the urine should not be sampled. After sampling, the urine should be chilled (but not frozen) to prevent growth during transportation to the laboratory. At the laboratory, the sample is streaked onto agar plates using a loop, which delivers a known amount of urine. The result is obtained after incubation overnight and allows determination of the bacterial species present in the sample and the number of organisms per milliliter of urine. The presence of more than one species in a sample is a strong indication of defective sampling procedures and contamination.

A simplified quantitative urine culture can be obtained outside of the microbiologic laboratory by using a dip-slide. With that technique, the sample is inoculated by dipping a plastic slide with agar on both surfaces in the urine sample or pouring the sample over the surfaces. After overnight culture in room temperature or in a simple incubator, the culture allows a highly reliable quantification of bacteriuria. Because Gram-negative bacteria grow on both sides of the slide but Gram-positive ones grow on only one of them, the method also allows a classification into Gram-positive or Gram-negative etiology. However, if determination of the species or the antibiotic sensitivity pattern is required, the dip-slide must be transported to a regular laboratory. The dip-slide is most suitable for use in outpatient settings, especially when distances to laboratories are long.

All culture techniques require overnight incubation. For screening of bacteriuria, a nitrite test can be used. It is a stick test, which demonstrates presence of nitrite in the urine. Gram-negative bacteria, with the exception of *P. aeruginosa*, metabolize nitrate to nitrite, which can be demonstrated by a color reaction on a paper stick. Gram-positive bacteria and fungi do not metabolize nitrate. The technique is rapid (<1 minute) and inexpensive. It has a high degree of

Infectious Diseases

specificity but is rather insensitive because it does not detect infections caused by Gram-positive organisms. Thus, it is not suitable for use in patients with recurrent infections (in whom enterococcal etiology is common) or when the frequency of *S. saprophyticus* infections is high.

Using modern definitions of bacteriuria, pyuria should be demonstrated in patients with symptomatic UTIs. This is best done by staining uncentrifuged urine and counting leukocytes in a Bürker chamber. The second best technique is to use a leukocyte esterase stick test, which is highly sensitive and allows a crude quantification of pyuria. The previously used routine technique, to count leukocytes in the sediment obtained after centrifugation of a urine sample, is very imprecise and is not recommended. Persistent pyuria with negative routine bacteriologic cultures should lead to a suspicion of renal tuberculosis, and a sample should be obtained for direct microscopy and culture for *Mycobacterium tuberculosis*.

Blood cultures should be obtained in all patients with suspected pyelonephritis or urosepsis. It is recommended that at least two cultures are taken in each patient.

Radiography and ultrasound examination are normally not helpful in the acute phase of a suspected pyelonephritis. An exception is if there is a suspicion of a blockage of the urine flow in a patient with pyelonephritis, which may indicate formation of a renal abscess. When the patient has recovered, such investigations are recommended in patients with recurrent infections to exclude complicating factors. Normally a simple pyelography or ultrasound examination is performed. For diagnosis of vesicoureteral reflux, special radiographic techniques are used.

Although the clinical manifestations should lead to a relatively clear differentiation of acute cystitis and acute pyelonephritis, it is often difficult to diagnose the latter. Laboratory tests may offer some help and should be used. Patients with acute pyelonephritis but not those with acute cystitis have increased values of C-reactive protein (CRP) in blood. That acute phase parameter increases rapidly in patients with acute pyelonephritis. It is also a useful test for determination of response to therapy and diagnosis of recurrences. Erythrocyte sedimentation rate, on the other hand, is a less useful test because it takes several days to increase in a patient with acute pyelonephritis. In patients with acute pyelonephritis, leukocyte casts

can often be demonstrated in urine sediment. When a patient with suspected acute pyelonephritis has become afebrile, the diagnosis can be supported by testing urine osmolality, which is markedly reduced for at least 1 month after the onset of symptoms. Practically the test can be done on urine obtained after 12 hours of fasting and no fluid intake or, easier, by intramuscular or subcutaneous injection of a small dose of desmopressin, a vasopressin analogue. Urine is then collected 1 to 8 hours after the injection. Urine osmolality in individuals with normal renal concentration ability is 850 to 1000 mOsm/L, varying with age. Previously demonstration of antibody-coated bacteria in the urine as a sign of pyelonephritis was used in scientific studies. The technique had problems with specificity and sensitivity and is not recommended.

Table 344–5 • ANTIBIOTICS USED FOR TREATMENT OF CYSTITIS

ANTIBIOTIC	DOSE AND DURATION
Trimethoprim	100–150 mg q12h for 3 days
Trimethoprim/sulfamethoxazole	80/400 mg q12h for 3 days or 320/1600 mg single dose
Nitrofurantoin	50 mg q8h for 5–7 days
Amoxicillin/clavulanic acid	250 mg (amoxicillin dose) q8h for 5–7 days
Cefuroxime axetil	250 mg q8h for 5–7 days
Cefpodoxime proxetil	200 mg q8h for 5–7 days
Cefixime	400 mg qd for 5–7 days
Ceftibuten	400 mg qd for 5–7 days
Cefprozil	250 mg qd for 5–7 days
Norfloxacin*	200 mg q12h for 7 days
Ciprofloxacin*	100 mg q12h for 7 days
Levofloxacin*	250 mg qd for 7 days
Fosfomycin	400 mg single dose

*Should be reserved for recurrent and/or complicated cystitis.
NOTE: Doses are those for adults with normal renal function. The need for dose reductions made necessary by renal impairment due to infections in the kidneys, other renal diseases, or high age should always be considered.

Rx Treatment

ANTIBIOTIC THERAPY. All types of symptomatic UTIs should be treated. The purpose of early treatment of cystitis is to reduce the risk of progression to a pyelonephritis. Cystitis patients gain little from antibiotic treatment in terms of duration of symptoms, which is 3 to 4 days irrespective of whether bacteriuria persists. In patients with pyelonephritis, early treatment aims at reducing the duration of symptoms, eliminating microorganisms from the renal parenchyma, and reducing the risk of dissemination to the blood.

Because verification of the microbial etiology and determination of the susceptibility to antimicrobial drugs take at least 1 and often more than 2 days, treatment is in most cases started empirically. For choice of antibiotics, it is therefore of utmost importance that the responsible physician is aware of the antibiotic susceptibility pattern. Such information must be based on recent, local surveillances of urinary bacterial isolates from relevant patients. If the patient is a woman with a sporadic uncomplicated cystitis or pyelonephritis, surveillance data must be generated in outpatients with sporadic UTIs. If, on the other hand, the patient is hospitalized and has a nosocomially acquired pyelonephritis, surveillance data must be generated from samples collected in the hospital environment, and preferably at the department where the patient acquired the infection. Large national or international surveillance studies have limited value for decisions on choice of antibiotic treatment in the individual patient. It is also important to realize that antibiotic resistance surveillances are often based on results obtained in routine samples investigated at various laboratories. In times of economic restrictions in most health care systems, such samples are often taken only when something is abnormal in the course of the patients' infections, such as when there are treatment failures or recurrences. Therefore, it is not unusual that the large surveillances give resistance rates, which are falsely high.

Table 344–5 lists possible choices for antibiotic treatment of cystitis. Such antibiotics should be excreted renally to achieve high concentrations in the renal parenchyma and in the urine. Because this infection is extremely common and not associated with mortality, the drugs used must have a very high degree of safety. The treatment time varies with type of antibiotic. Trimethoprim, trimethoprim-sulfamethoxazole, and fluoroquinolones markedly affect the periurethral flora and the fecal flora reducing the numbers of uropathogenic bacteria. As a result these antibiotics are not more effective for treatment of sporadic cystitis if used for 5 to 7 days than for 3 days. β-Lactam antibiotics and nitrofurantoin generally have shorter elimination times and do not affect the normal periurethral and fecal flora to the same extent. Therefore, higher frequencies of elimination of bacteriuria are achieved if they are given for 5 to 7 days. Single-dose treatment is recommended only for a high dose of trimethoprim-sulfamethoxazole and for fosfomycin (which is licensed only for single-dose treatment). Such treatment may seem preferable to treatment for several days, but because the patients normally have symptoms for 3 days, 3-day regimens seem to have the best acceptance among the patients. When the patients have recurrent or complicated cystitis, treatment time should be at least 7 days.

Fluoroquinolones are not recommended for routine use in sporadic cystitis, although many of them have well documented efficacy when used at relatively low doses for 3 days or even as a high single dose. The reason for that is that a widespread use in cystitis patients is likely to lead to overuse and emergence of resistance.

Patients with frequently recurring cystitis can sometimes, if they are well informed and compliant, benefit from early self-treatment. If treatment is started very shortly after the onset of symptoms, it seems likely that a short course or even a single dose of antibiotics will give fast relief of symptoms.

Table 344–6 • ANTIBIOTICS USED FOR TREATMENT OF PYELONEPHRITIS

ROUTE OF ADMINISTRATION AND ANTIBIOTIC	DOSAGE	COMMENTS
INJECTABLE		
Cefipime	2 g q12h	Nosocomial infections*
Cefotaxime	1 g q12h	Community acquired infections
Ceftazidime	1 g q12h	Nosocomial infections*
Ceftriaxone	2 g qd	Community acquired infections
Cefuroxime	750 mg q8h	Community acquired infections
Amikacin	15 mg/kg qd	Monitor renal function
Gentamicin	4.5 mg/kg qd	Monitor renal function
Netilmicin	4.5 mg/kg qd	Monitor renal function
Tobramycin	4.5 mg/kg qd	Monitor renal function
Ciprofloxacin	200 mg q12h	
Levofloxacin	250 mg qd	
Trimethoprim/ sulfamethoxazole	160/800 mg q12h	Community-acquired infections
ORAL		
Amoxicillin/clavulanic acid	500 mg (amoxicillin dose) q8h	Only step-down therapy
Cefuroxime axetil	250 mg q12h	Only step-down therapy
Cefpodoxime proxetil	200 mg q8h	Only step-down therapy
Cefixime	400 mg qd	Only step-down therapy
Ceftibuten	400 mg qd	Only step-down therapy
Cefprozil	250 mg qd	Only step-down therapy
Norfloxacin	400 mg q12h	
Ciprofloxacin	100 mg q12h	
Levofloxacin	250 mg qd	

*Includes hospital and nursing home care.
NOTE: Doses are those for adults with normal renal function. The need for dose reductions made necessary by renal impairment due to infections in the kidneys, other renal diseases, or high age should always be considered.

Table 344–7 • FOLLOW-UP PROCEDURES IN PATIENTS WITH URINARY TRACT INFECTIONS OTHER THAN SPORADIC CYSTITIS

PROCEDURE	RECOMMENDATION
Urine culture	All patients with pyelonephritis, complicated infections, or frequent recurrences; 4–5 days and 3–4 weeks after treatment
Pyuria test	Always together with urine cultures
C-reactive protein	4–5 Days and 3–4 weeks after treatment of pyelonephritis
Radiography or ultrasonography	After pyelonephritis to exclude scars from childhood infections in patients with recurrent infections to exclude complications
Serum creatinine	Before treatment in elderly; 3–4 weeks posttreatment in patients with pyelonephritis
Urine osmolality	Verification of suspected pyelonephritis

For antibiotic treatment of pyelonephritis, the primary decision should be if the patient needs initial treatment with an injectable antibiotic or if she or he is in a general condition, which allows oral treatment throughout the course. Table 344–6 lists antibiotics suitable for treatment of pyelonephritis. Oral formulations of penicillins or cephalosporins should never be used for other purposes than follow-up to injectable antibiotics. When treatment is started with an injectable drug, step-down to oral treatment is normally possible after 24 to 48 hours. The recommended treatment time is still 14 days, although recent information indicates that in patients with uncomplicated pyelonephritis, treatment for 7 days should suffice.

Only fluroquinolones and trimethoprim-sulfamethoxazole can be used for initial oral treatment of pyelonephritis if the patient's general condition allows it. Because both of these alternatives are unsuitable for use in pregnant women, pyelonephritis during pregnancy should be treated with an injectable antibiotic, preferably a cephalosporin, followed by oral step-down therapy.

Bacteriuria in patients with catheters should not be treated unless there are symptoms of systemic infections, that is, fever. Administration of antibiotics to catheterized patients with asymptomatic bacteriuria inevitably results in selection of multiresistant and difficult-to-treat organisms.

In patients with suspected urosepsis, antibiotic treatment must start as early as possible. Antibiotics should be given intravenously. Antibiotics recommended for injectable treatment of pyelonephritis should be used. Previous antibiotic treatment should always be sought in patients with urosepsis because such treatment may have resulted in selection of resistant organisms.

Funguria can be treated with fluconazole 400 mg once daily for 1 day followed by 200 mg once daily for 7 to 14 days. Funguria in catheterized patients should be treated only when there is a symptomatic UTI.

ADVICE TO THE PATIENT. There are well known measures that markedly reduce the risk of recurrences of UTIs. The most important one is to recommend that sexually active women urinate shortly after sexual intercourse. In doing so, they wash out the increased number of bacteria in the distal urethra. Another useful suggestion is to recommend double or triple voiding to patients with recurrent UTIs. This means that the patient should make extra efforts to empty the bladder at each urination. The volume of residual urine is then decreased. Increased fluid intake was previously advocated, probably based on the risk of crystalluria with older sulfonamides. There are no obvious benefits with excessive diuresis.

PROPHYLAXIS. Antibiotic prophylaxis of UTIs is today used with considerable restrictions. One group in which it is still recommended is pregnant women with asymptomatic bacteriuria. As a consequence of that, screening for bacteriuria at regular intervals during pregnancy is recommended. Another group in which screening of bacteriuria and prophylaxis have been proposed is patients with diabetes mellitus, especially those with type 2.

Prophylaxis is sometimes used in patients with frequently recurring UTIs, especially when there are no defined, treatable complications. In such patients, one daily dose of nitrofurantoin 50 to 100 mg or trimethoprim 150 to 200 mg, taken at bedtime, is recommended.

Antibiotic prophylaxis should not be used in catheterized patients because it will only result in selection of microbes resistant to the antibiotic used.

In postmenopausal women with atrophic vaginal mucosa and recurrent symptomatic UTIs, replacement therapy with estriol orally or vaginally should be considered. Such treatment restores a premenopausal vaginal and periurethral normal microbial flora and, subsequently, reduces the incidence of symptomatic UTIs.

FOLLOW-UP. Patients with sporadic uncomplicated cystitis need not be followed up. Patients with symptomatic recurrences, pyelonephritis or complicated UTI should be followed. Table 344–7 lists some examinations that may be considered. Follow-up cultures are important because bacteriuria may persist and cause renal damage in afebrile pyelonephritis patients.

SUGGESTED READINGS

Fihn SD: Clinical practice. Acute uncomplicated urinary tract infection in women. N Engl J Med 2003;349:259–266. *A practical overview.*

Hooton TM, Scholes D, Stapleton AE, et al: A prospective study of asymptomatic bacteriuria in sexually active young women. N Engl J Med 2000;343:992–997. *Asymptomatic bacteriuria in young women is common, rarely persistent, but predictive of subsequent symptomatic infection.*

Kvieger JN: Urinary tract infections: What's new? J Urol 2002;168:2351–2358. *A recent review.*

Stamm WE, Norrby SR: Urinary tract infections: Disease panorama and challenges. J Infect Dis 2001;183(Suppl 1):S1–S4. *Review of epidemiology, diagnosis, and management.*

Infectious Diseases

345 INTRODUCTION TO SEXUALLY TRANSMITTED DISEASES AND COMMON SYNDROMES

Michael F. Rein

Definition

The sexually transmitted diseases (STDs) are a diverse group of infections caused by biologically dissimilar microbial agents. They are grouped together because sexual contact plays a statistically and clinically significant role in their overall epidemiology. The precise contribution of sexual transmission varies among these infections, playing a major role in the transmission of, for example, gonorrhea and chlamydial infection; a far less significant role for hepatitis C; and a largely insignificant role in vulvovaginal candidiasis. For some conditions, such as bacterial vaginosis, the precise role of sexual transmission remains incompletely defined.

These microorganisms depend on sexual contact for transmission because: (1) many of these organisms, such as *Treponema pallidum* and *Trichomonas vaginalis,* have limited environmental survival and are susceptible to drying; (2) only limited sites can be infected by some of these agents (e.g., *Neisseria gonorrhoeae* and *Chlamydia trachomatis* can produce primary infection at only certain mucosal surfaces in the adult: urethra, endocervix, rectum, pharynx, and conjunctivae); and (3) lesions containing microorganisms in numbers adequate to transmit disease frequently occur at those anatomic sites used for sexual contact.

Although sexual contact is not the exclusive means of transmission for any of these agents, recognizing an infection as sexually transmitted has profound clinical significance. First, one can immediately identify a population at very high risk for an STD, namely the population of sexual partners of patients in whom a diagnosis has been made. Obviously, not all sexual partners are at equal risk. Some will have had only a single sexual contact, whereas others may be in a regular sexual relationship. Specific sexual practices, including anatomic sites of contact and the use of various contraceptives, influence the likelihood of transmission. Transmission is also influenced by the concentration of microorganisms in lesions or body fluids, which varies during the course of most infections. Finally, there are individual variations in susceptibility that remain incompletely defined. It does appear, for example, that prior infection with herpes simplex virus type 1 (HSV-1) reduces the likelihood that an exposed individual becomes infected with HSV-2. It is therefore very treacherous to extrapolate from group statistics to individual cases; however, many of the classic STDs are found in approximately one to two thirds of the heterosexual partners of patients in whom a diagnosis has been made.

The high prevalence of some conditions among sexual partners has led to the principle of *epidemiologic treatment,* which is a cornerstone of the management of STDs. Epidemiologic treatment is provided on the basis of statistical risk rather than on the basis of a specific diagnosis. Sexual partners of patients with some infections (denoted by an asterisk in Table 345–1) should be treated at the time of initial presentation.

A second consequence of sexual transmissibility is *coprevalence.* High-risk sexual behaviors increase the likelihood of acquiring each of the STDs and, thus, the STDs appear to travel together. A patient presenting with one sexually transmitted condition should be screened carefully for others, including infection with human immunodeficiency virus (HIV). The coprevalence of gonococcal and chlamydial infection is so high that patients diagnosed with gonorrhea routinely are treated for chlamydial infection as well. In addition to epidemiologic coprevalence, a number of STDs have been shown to increase the risk of acquiring HIV. Genital inflammation appears to increase the rate of HIV synthesis, and ulcerative or inflammatory processes may serve as a portal of entry for the virus.

Finally, STDs are best managed when sexual partners are treated simultaneously, meaning that all have completed treatment before unprotected sexual contact is resumed. When one cares for a patient with an STD, one is always obliged to consider other people, who may be either the source of the patient's infection or secondary cases, to whom the infection has been spread.

Table 345–1 • SEXUALLY TRANSMITTED AGENTS AND THEIR SYNDROMES

MICROORGANISM	SYNDROMES
BACTERIA	
*Neisseria gonorrhoeae**	Urethritis, cervicitis, bartholinitis, proctitis, pharyngitis, salpingitis, epididymitis, conjunctivitis, perihepatitis, arthritis, dermatitis, endocarditis, meningitis, amniotic infection syndrome
Mobiluncus species and *Gardnerella vaginalis*	Bacterial vaginosis
*Treponema pallidum**	Syphilis (multiple clinical syndromes)
*Haemophilus ducreyi**	Chancroid
Calymmatobacterium granulomatis	Granuloma inguinale
Shigella species	Enteritis in homosexual men
Campylobacter species	Enteritis in homosexual men
Group B *Streptococcus*	Neonatal sepsis and meningitis
CHLAMYDIAE	
*Chlamydia trachomatis**	Nongonococcal urethritis, purulent hypertrophic cervicitis, epididymitis, salpingitis, conjunctivitis, trachoma, pneumonia, perihepatitis, lymphogranuloma venereum, Reiter's syndrome
MYCOPLASMAS	
*Ureaplasma urealyticum**	Nongonococcal urethritis, ? premature rupture of membranes and abortion
Mycoplasma hominis	Postpartum fever, pelvic inflammatory disease
Mycoplasma genitalium	Nongonococcal urethritis
VIRUSES	
Herpes simplex virus (HSV)	Genital herpes, proctitis, meningitis, disseminated infection in neonates
Hepatitis A virus	Hepatitis in homosexual men
Hepatitis B virus	Hepatitis, periarteritis nodosa, hepatoma; especially prevalent in homosexual men
Hepatitis C virus	Hepatitis, cryoglobulinemia
Cytomegalovirus	Congenital infection (birth defects, infant mortality, mental deficiency, hearing loss), mononucleosis syndrome
Human papillomavirus (HPV)	Condyloma acuminatum, cervical and perianal
Molluscum contagiosum virus	Molluscum contagiosum
Human immunodeficiency virus (HIV)	Acquired immunodeficiency syndrome (AIDS) and related illnesses
PROTOZOA	
*Trichomonas vaginalis**	Trichomonal vaginitis, occasional urethritis
Entamoeba histolytica	Enteritis in homosexual men
Giardia lamblia	Enteritis in homosexual men
FUNGI	
Candida albicans	Vaginitis, balanitis
ECTOPARASITES	
*Phthirus pubis**	Pubic lice infestation
*Sarcoptes scabiei**	Scabies

*Epidemiologic treatment of sexual partners is recommended.

Sexual contact includes the full range of heterosexual or homosexual behavior, including genital, oral-genital, oral-anal, and genital-anal contact. The anatomic sites in which one should seek evidence of infection will be guided by the sexual practices involved, and a complete, nonjudgmental sexual history is an essential part of the work-up.

The STDs remain common infections. Many of the most important are not reported, and so their incidence and prevalence are poorly defined. Even among the reportable STDs (e.g., gonorrhea, chancroid, syphilis, lymphogranuloma venereum), there is considerable underreporting. Chancroid is principally seen in major urban areas, often in the setting of prostitute contact, and syphilis is seen most commonly in the rural southeast, often along major truck routes. Its overall incidence declined to 2.2 : 100,000 in the United States in 2000, which is so low that the U.S. Public Health Service has planned a campaign to "eliminate" syphilis in the United States, meaning an annual incidence of less than 1000 cases. This campaign can succeed, however, only if individual practitioners remain aware of the presence of syphilis and contribute to its early recognition and treatment. Seroepidemiologic studies suggest that approximately 20% of young people in this country are infected with HSV-2.

Management of sexually transmitted infections is complicated by the frequent lack of symptoms. Most women with gonococcal or chlamydial infection are asymptomatic or have symptoms that do not persuade them to seek medical attention. Only about 20% of patients with genital herpes have classic clinical findings.

COMMON SYNDROMES

Urethritis

Urethritis, presenting as some combination of urethral discharge and dysuria, is usually sexually transmitted. Nonsexually transmitted urethritis is seen most commonly in men with underlying diseases such as diabetes (Table 345–2). Urethritis is traditionally termed either gonococcal (GCU) or nongonococcal (NGU). Differential diagnosis is usually based on the urethral Gram stain. If discharge can be expressed from the meatus by stripping the urethra, it should be transferred to a microscope slide, Gram-strained, and examined at ×1000 for the presence of polymorphonuclear neutrophils (PMNs) and perinuclear clusters of classic Gram-negative diplococci (Chapter 346). The presence of these organisms identifies a case of gonorrhea but does not rule out the possibility of coincidental infection with one of the agents of NGU. In the absence of identifiable gonococci, the diagnosis of NGU is reliably made. If no discharge is expressed from the meatus, urethral material must be sought by inserting a calcium-alginate swab into the urethra to the depth of about 4 to 5 cm. The swab may be rotated during removal, and the material thus collected is transferred to a microscope slide by rolling the swab along the glass.

Unfortunately, N. gonorrhoeae has become resistant to many of the traditional regimens. Current therapy is described in Chapter 346 and in the Centers for Disease Control and Prevention Guidelines. The Gram stain does not provide specific etiologic information for NGU, and the condition is treated syndromically. Appropriate treatments for NGU are listed in Table 345–3. The diagnosis of either GCU or NGU calls for the epidemiologic treatment of female or gay male sexual partners. It is a mistake for female partners of men with NGU to be denied treatment on the basis of a negative test for C. trachomatis. Because this agent is now responsible for only about 25% of cases of NGU, its absence in a sexual partner does not obviate the need for treatment.

Treatment is usually highly effective, but some men return with persistent symptoms. The clinician must first document the persistence of urethritis by identifying PMN on the Gram stain of urethral material. Careful history must rule out the possibility of reinfection. Treatment failure is managed through an understanding of those organisms that might be resistant to the initial therapy. Treatment with doxycycline, minocycline, or azithromycin is successful in about 80% of patients. [1,2] Many infections that are resistant to the tetracy-

Table 345–3 • SYNDROMIC TREATMENT OF NONGONOCOCCAL URETHRITIS [1-5]

DRUG	DOSE	COMMENTS
Doxycycline	100 mg PO bid for 7 days	
Azithromycin	1000 mg as a single oral dose	
Minocycline	100 mg qhs for 7 nights	
Ofloxacin	300 mg PO bid for 7 days	
Erythromycin	500 mg PO qid ×7	
Tetracycline hydrochloride	500 mg PO qid ×7 *or* 250 mg PO qid ×14 days	
Clindamycin	450 mg PO tid for 10 days	If known to be chlamydial
Sulfisoxazole	500 mg PO qid for 10 days	If known to be chlamydial Trimethoprim-sulfamethoxazole has no advantage

clines are susceptible to the macrolides/azalides (MA) or the fluoroquinolones (FQ). T. vaginalis resists all of the standard antibacterial therapies for NGU but is usually susceptible to metronidazole. NGU that has failed to respond to a tetracycline should be treated with metronidazole in combination with either an MA or an FQ. Patients failing initial treatment with an MA or an FQ should be treated with metronidazole. A small number of patients respond to initial therapy but relapse without sexual reexposure. Such patients are unlikely to be infected either with C. trachomatis or Ureaplasma urealyticum and are sometimes cured by 4 to 6 weeks of therapy with a standard antimicrobial agent. On rare occasions, one can only provide long-term suppression with a low dose of an antimicrobial agent.

Women with GCU or NGU usually present with some combination of dysuria and pyuria. As such, the condition must be differentiated from standard lower urinary tract infection. Because the symptoms of sexually transmitted urethritis often respond to therapies directed against classic uropathogens, the clinician must maintain a high index of suspicion for STD, especially in the setting of frequently recurring lower urinary tract symptoms, which may result from reinfection by an untreated sexual partner. Clindamycin is an effective therapy for chlamydial infections in women. [3] Amoxicillin (500 mg tid for 7 days) is an acceptable alternative in pregnant women. [4]

Genital Ulcers

The differential diagnosis of genital ulcer disease is difficult, and the relative frequency of specific etiologies varies geographically. Genital infection with herpes simplex virus (HSV) is the most common cause of genital ulcer disease in the United States, but chancroid becomes relatively more common in Africa and Asia. When confronted with a classic presentation, differential diagnosis often can be made clinically. Genital herpes usually develops after an incubation period of 3 to 13 days and presents initially as grouped vesicles on an erythematous base. The vesicles become somewhat pustular and then rupture to form shallow, painful ulcers, which may coalesce. The ulcers heal by crusting over, and the process is usually completed in about 2 to 3 weeks with initial infection. Recurrences proceed through the same progression but generally last only about 5 to 7 days. Local paraesthesias may precede the appearance of recurrent lesions. Only about 20% of infected individuals manifest the classic presentation. Approximately 60% of people with genital herpes have relatively atypical symptoms that do not suggest the diagnosis. Some 20% of infected individuals remain completely asymptomatic, although they shed the virus intermittently. Most people acquiring genital herpes do so from individuals who do not realize they are infected. The treatment of genital herpes is described in Chapter 369. Patients with frequent, symptomatic recurrences may elect long-term suppressive therapy. Asymptomatic individuals and those with recurrence who are currently asymptomatic appear to shed virus approximately 3 to 4% of the time, and so they pose a risk to sexual partners.

Chancroid, infection with Hemophilus ducreyi, produces ragged, dirty ulcers and tender inguinal lymphadenopathy, which may be fluctuant. Unlike the lesions of HSV, these are likely to vary in size.

The primary ulcerative lesion of syphilis, the chancre, is palpably indurated and is usually painless.

Table 345–2 • CAUSES OF NONGONOCOCCAL URETHRITIS

SEXUALLY TRANSMITTED
Chlamydia trachomatis (15–50%)
Ureaplasma urealyticum (10–40%)
Mycoplasma genitalium (~30%??)
Trichomonas vaginalis (1–17%)
Herpes simplex virus (Primary) (?%)

NOT SEXUALLY TRANSMITTED
Gram-negative rods
Adenovirus
Microsporidia (AIDS)
Neisseria meningitidis
Streptococcus pneumoniae
Staphylococcus saprophyticus??
Haemophilus species??
Bacteroides ureolyticus??

Infectious Diseases

In several studies in the developing world, multiple organisms have been identified in a single ulcerative lesion. Molecular techniques have superseded cultures for diagnosis.

Lower Genital Tract Infections in Women

Infections of the female genitourinary tract produce several syndromes with overlapping symptoms (dysuria, vaginal discharge, vulvar irritation). Differential diagnosis can usually be made on relatively simple clinical and laboratory grounds, and a precise microbial cause often can be established. One must first determine the primary anatomic site of infection: urinary tract, endocervix, or vagina. In the adult, the columnar epithelium of the endocervix is susceptible to infection with *N. gonorrhoeae, C. trachomatis,* or HSV. The mature vagina, however, is susceptible to infection with *Candida albicans, Trichomonas vaginalis,* or the syndrome of bacterial vaginosis. Dysuria is often recognized as "internal" by women with urethritis or cystitis, whereas it is often perceived as "external" in women with vulvovaginitis. Cervicitis is diagnosed on physical examination; the cervix may be red or friable, and cervical discharge, normally clear, may be mucopurulent. The cervix may, however, appear completely normal in women with cervical infection. Vaginitis is associated with an increased vaginal discharge that may differ from its normal microfloccular appearance.

VAGINAL INFECTIONS. Although there is considerable clinical overlap, a specific diagnosis can be made in most women with vaginal infections. Bacterial vaginosis (BV) is now the most common vaginal infection in the United States. Affected women are often minimally symptomatic but may complain of mild vaginal discharge, vaginal odor (often increased after coitus), and a relative absence of vaginal discomfort. The resulting discharge is homogeneous and may contain bubbles. Vaginal pH is elevated above the normal 4.0 to 4.5. Adding 10% KOH to the vaginal discharge on the microscope slide or in the speculum elicits an amine-like, fishy odor, yielding a positive "whiff test." Examination of vaginal material as a wet mount reveals the absence of the normal flora of rods and its replacement with clumps of coccobacilli. Some vaginal epithelial cells are coated with coccobacilli, which may obscure their edges ("clue" cells). Relatively few PMNs are observed, and large numbers of PMNs in the wet mount of a woman with BV suggest a coincident infection, possibly trichomoniasis or cervicitis.

The process begins with the disappearance of the normal vaginal flora of hydrogen-peroxide producing lactobacilli and their replacement with *Gardnerella vaginalis,* several species of anaerobic bacteria, and mycoplasmas. The precise mechanism causing this shift in vaginal flora is poorly understood. The odor and positive whiff test result from the elaboration of amines by the anaerobic flora. BV is not a benign infection. It is associated with an increased rate of upper tract infection (endometritis, salpingitis) and with several complications of pregnancy, including premature rupture of the membranes and premature delivery. Treatment is generally directed against the anaerobic flora and consists of metronidazole 500 mg orally twice daily for 7 days or clindamycin 300 mg orally twice daily for 7 days. Vaginal preparations of these two medications are also available and equally effective. Unfortunately, the relapse rate, even in the absence of sexual exposure, is about 30%. There is no advantage to treating male sexual partners, who are always asymptomatic, simultaneously; however, some women with frequently recurring disease may benefit if sexual partners are treated. Recurrence is common even in the absence of sexual exposure, and the precise contribution of sexual contact is unclear.

Vulvovaginal candidiasis (VC) is also common and is seen more frequently in women taking antibiotics or using oral contraceptives. The role of sexual transmission is quite limited. Affected women usually complain of vulvar itching and discomfort and may or may not notice an accompanying discharge. The vagina usually contains normal numbers of lactobacilli, and the vaginal pH is therefore usually normal, which is very helpful in discriminating between candidiasis and other vaginal infections. The labia and vaginal walls may be quite erythematous. Although classically described as "curdy," the discharge of candidiasis is frequently loose and distinguished from other discharges only with difficulty. Vaginal material may be treated with 10% KOH to destroy other cellular elements and make the fungi easier to observe. Wet mount, however, has a sensitivity of only about 50%, and a woman with classic presentation should not be denied treatment on the basis of a failure to observe fungal elements.

A wide range of topical antifungal medications is available, and these drugs are approximately equally effective. The cure rate with some single-dose therapies appears lower than that with longer regimens. Fluconazole administered as a single oral dose of 150 mg is also highly effective.

Recurrent VC is a problem for many women. Optimal management has not been defined. Elimination of predisposing factors is important. Some women with frequently recurring disease benefit from long-term suppression with oral fluconazole administered weekly.

Vaginal infection with *T. vaginalis* is becoming far less common, possibly because of the amount of metronidazole now used in the sexually active population to treat BV. Infected women usually complain of discharge, which may be yellow or green, and vulvar irritation. There may be internal or external dysuria. The vaginal walls are red, and the vagina contains an excessive yellow or green discharge displaying large bubbles. The exocervix may also be inflamed. Vaginal pH is elevated, but the whiff test is often negative. Wet mount reveals large numbers of PMNs, and motile protozoa, about the same size as PMNs, are recognized in about two thirds of cases. Therapy for trichomoniasis is described in Chapter 400. Organisms resistant to metronidazole are encountered with increasing frequency.

Upper Genital Tract Disease in Women

Salpingitis is an important clinical problem, resulting in considerable morbidity to the estimated 250,000 to 500,000 women affected annually in the United States.

N. gonorrhoeae or *C. trachomatis* can ascend from the cervix into the uterine cavity, producing endometritis, and thence to the fallopian tubes causing salpingitis. Chlamydial salpingitis may be mild, and patients may not seek medical attention. Some intrauterine devices have been associated with an increased risk of salpingitis, and some data support douching as a predisposing factor. Anaerobic bacteria and mycoplasmas are also thought to play a role, particularly in chronic or recurrent disease.

The clinical diagnosis of salpingitis is made by finding adnexal tenderness on bimanual examination. Cervical tenderness, fever, leukocytosis, and an elevated sedimentation rate are sometimes observed. The clinical diagnosis is confirmed laparoscopically in only about 70% of cases. Vaginal ultrasonography or computed tomography is often helpful in defining the cause of pelvic pain syndromes.

Involuntary infertility complicates approximately 15% of initial attacks of salpingitis and about 75% after three or more attacks. Ectopic pregnancy and tubo-ovarian abscess are additional complications.

1. Stamm WE, et al: Azithromycin for empirical treatment of the nongonococcal urethritis syndrome in men: A randomized double-blind study. JAMA 1995;274:545–549.
2. Romanowski B, et al: Minocycline compared with doxycycline in the treatment of nongonococcal urethritis and mucopurulent cervicitis. Ann Intern Med 1993;119:16–22.
3. Campbell WF, Dodson MG: Clindamycin therapy for Chlamydia trachomatis in women. Am J Obstet Gynecol 1990;162:343–347.
4. Crombleholme WR, et al: Amoxicillin therapy for Chlamydia trachomatis infections in pregnancy. Obstet Gynecol 1990;75:752–756.

SUGGESTED READINGS

Burstein GR, Zenilman JM: Nongonococcal urethritis—a new paradigm. Clin Infect Dis 1999;28(Suppl 1):S66–S73. *Information on a common syndrome.*

Centers for Disease Control: 2002 Sexually transmitted disease treatment guidelines. Morb Mortal Wkly Rep 2002;51(RR-6):1–80. *The classic reference on management, updated frequently.*

DiCarlo RP, Martin DH: The clinical diagnosis of genital ulcer disease in men. Clin Infect Dis 1997;25:292–298. *Clinical and laboratory aspects of diagnosis.*

LaMontagne DS, Fine DN, Marrazzo JM: Chlamydia trachomatis infection in asymptomatic men. Am J Prev Med 2003;24:36–42. *Among 43,000 men seen in STD clinics, 10% were positive, 91% of whom had symptoms or a known positive partner.*

Leitich H, Brunbauer M, Bodner-Adler B, et al: Antibiotic treatment of bacterial vaginosis in pregnancy: A meta-analysis. Am J Obstet Gynecol 2003;188:752–758. *Data support screening and treating pregnant women with bacterial vaginosis; if they have a previous preterm delivery, an oral regimen of longer duration can be justified on the basis of current evidence.*

Rottengin J-A, Cameron DW, Garnett GP: A systematic review of the epidemiologic interactions between classic sexually transmitted diseases and HIV: How much is really known? Sexual Transm Dis 2001;28:579–87. *A careful analysis of the quality of epidemiologic data for this important interaction.*

Totten PA, Schwartz MA, Sjostrom KE, et al: Association of Mycoplasma genitalium with nongonococcal urethritis in heterosexual men. J Infect Dis 2001;183:269–276. *The latest organism to be associated with this common condition.*

346 GONOCOCCAL INFECTIONS

H. Hunter Handsfield
P. Frederick Sparling

Definition

Neisseria gonorrhoeae is a sexually transmitted organism that primarily infects the columnar epithelia of mucosal surfaces, causing urethritis in men and endocervicitis and urethritis in women. Other sites of primary infection include the rectum, pharynx, and conjunctiva, and vulvovaginitis can occur in prepubertal girls. The most common complication is acute salpingitis, or pelvic inflammatory disease, in turn leading to infertility and ectopic pregnancy. Other complications are epididymitis, posterior urethritis, urethral stricture, Bartholin gland abscess, and perihepatitis. Bacteremia may occur, with production of characteristic cutaneous lesions, arthritis, and rarely endocarditis or meningitis. Neonatal conjunctivitis (ophthalmia neonatorum) formerly was a common cause of blindness.

Epidemiology

Gonorrhea is the second most commonly reported infectious disease in the United States, following genital infection with *Chlamydia trachomatis*. In 2001, 362,000 cases were reported, an incidence of 129 cases per 100,000 population, but the true incidence is probably twice as high. The incidence declined dramatically in most industrialized countries from the 1970s to the mid-1990s, but the rate remained stable in the United States from 1997 to 2001. The incidence of gonorrhea is lowest in western Europe, but the disease remains epidemic in eastern Europe, much of Africa, the Indian subcontinent, and parts of Asia and South America.

The epidemiology of gonorrhea varies greatly between geographic areas and populations. In the United States, as many as 5% of persons at risk, or up to 20% of persons attending some public sexually transmitted disease (STD) clinics, may be infected at any time, but the prevalence is under 1% in most clinical venues. A population-based study in Baltimore, Maryland, found a prevalence of 5.3%, but during the years the study was conducted (1997 and 1998), public health STD services had been sharply curtailed, and Baltimore had the highest rate of reported gonorrhea nationwide. It is unlikely that prevalences are that high in most geographic areas.

The highest incidences occur in young (ages 15 to 30 years), single persons of low socioeconomic and educational attainment, in inner city residents, and in some rural settings, especially in the southeast. The incidence of reported gonorrhea is 30-fold higher in African Americans than in whites or persons of Asian or Pacific Island ancestry; the rates in those of Hispanic or Native American ethnicity are 3-fold and 4-fold higher than in whites, respectively. The differences between racial and ethnic groups are reflections of differing sex partner network structures, socioeconomic attainment, education, and access to health care. Persons of lower socioeconomic status selectively attend public clinics, where reporting is more complete than in the private sector, but this bias accounts for only a small part of the observed differences between racial and ethnic groups. The incidence of gonorrhea is several times higher in men who have sex with men (MSM) than in heterosexuals. Rates of gonorrhea and other STDs rose dramatically among MSM in the United States and other industrialized countries from 1997 to 2002, in association with improved therapy and survival of persons with human immunodeficiency virus (HIV) infection.

The likelihood that a woman will acquire gonorrhea from a man with urethral infection approximates 50% per episode of unprotected vaginal intercourse, whereas the transmission risk from female to male averages 20 to 30% per exposure. The difference likely reflects the size of the inoculum of *N. gonorrhoeae* deposited on a susceptible mucosal surface, as well as the inherent efficiency of internal deposition of infective secretions. Transmission rates for other exposures have not been quantified, but anal intercourse clearly is a relatively efficient mode of transmission. Urethral-to-pharyngeal transmission by fellatio also occurs frequently, and pharyngeal gonococcal infection is especially common among MSM. Conflicting data exist on the efficiency of transmission of pharyngeal infection to the urethra by fellatio. Both transmission and acquisition of gonorrhea by cunnilingus appear to be very rare. Gonococci die rapidly on drying, so that transmission by fomites is rare. Perinatal transmission, with neonatal ophthalmitis or pharyngeal infection, now is rare. Gonorrhea in prepubertal children older than 1 year almost always results from sexual abuse.

At least 50% and perhaps as many as 70% of infections in females cause no symptoms or mild ones that do not lead to a health care visit. By contrast, the large majority of urethral infections in men cause overt, symptomatic urethritis, with no more than a few percent asymptomatic infections. The proportion of men with urethral infection who remain asymptomatic depends in large part on the local prevalence of particular strains of *N. gonorrhoeae*, which selectively cause subclinical infection. In addition, some men deny symptoms and continue to be sexually active despite overt urethral discharge on examination, perhaps especially in settings of socioeconomic deprivation and poor education. Whether truly asymptomatic or with ignored symptoms, persons with subclinical infection are the primary transmitters of gonorrhea and other STDs, because those with prominent symptoms usually cease sexual activity and seek treatment.

The Organism

Neisseria gonorrhoeae is a Gram-negative, aerobic diplococcus that produces cytochrome oxidase. Many strains require an atmosphere containing 3 to 10% CO_2 for optimal growth, and the organism grows best on media with added starch, which blocks the inhibitory effect of fatty acids present in agar. Growth is less rapid than that of most bacteria that compose the normal flora of the genitourinary tract, rectum, or pharynx, so that selective media, which incorporate antibiotics to inhibit the growth of competing bacteria, are required for optimal isolation by culture. The gonococcus metabolizes glucose but not maltose, sucrose, or lactose, the historic basis for differentiation from *N. meningitidis*, *Branhamella* (*Moraxella*) sp., and nonpathogenic *Neisseria* spp.

When propagated on agar-containing media, *N. gonorrhoeae* forms colonies of varied morphology, known as *phase variation*. Small, cohesive colonies dominate in the first one or two passages, contain organisms with pili (hairlike projections of the organism's outer membrane), and retain virulence when inoculated into human volunteers. The larger colonies that come to predominate after unselective passage contain nonpiliated gonococci and have limited infectivity for human volunteers. Gonococci propagated in the laboratory also undergo rapid variation in the antigenic type of pilus expressed, which probably contributes to prolonged infections without treatment and to the ability of persons to acquire repeat infections. The importance of these and other surface components of the gonococcus in the pathogenesis of infection and as the potential basis for a future vaccine are important research themes.

Gonococci can be serotyped on the basis of antigenic differences in outer membrane proteins and can be auxotyped on the basis of genetically determined nutritional requirements of the organism for specific amino acids and nucleotides. Auxotyping and serotyping often are performed simultaneously for enhanced strain discrimination, an approach that has been useful in studying the dynamics of introduction and spread of *N. gonorrhoeae* in communities and other aspects of the epidemiology of gonorrhea. In addition, some auxotype/serotype classes of *N. gonorrhoeae* are associated with enhanced antimicrobial susceptibility, with asymptomatic urethral or cervical infection, and with resistance to the bactericidal properties of normal (nonimmune) serum and a resulting propensity for bacteremic dissemination. Other methods for strain typing have had few clinical or epidemiologic applications and are not widely used, but analysis of gonococcal DNA by pulsed-field gel electrophoresis (PFGE) is a promising new method.

Pathogenesis

Pili help gonococci attach to mucosal surfaces by binding to the host cell receptor CD46. Attachment is also mediated by a family of outer membrane proteins designated opacity proteins, which bind either to CD66 or heparin-like molecules on host cells. Attachment and invasion of host epithelium are influenced by antigenic variations of pili and opacity proteins and by variations in the core sugars of lipooligosaccharide components of the organism's outer membrane.

These variations also help the organism evade the immune response. Typical urethral infections result in moderately severe inflammation, probably due to release of toxic lipopolysaccharide and peptidoglycan fragments and to chemotactic factors that attract neutrophilic leukocytes. The reasons that some gonococcal strains selectively cause asymptomatic genital infection are poorly understood, but this propensity may be related to differences in the ability of the organism to bind complement-regulatory proteins that downregulate the production of chemotactic peptides.

In the preantibiotic era, gonorrhea usually persisted for 2 to 3 months before host defenses finally eradicated the infection. These defenses include serum opsonic and bactericidal antibodies, as well as mucosal antibodies of the IgG and IgA classes. All gonococci produce IgA1 protease, an enzyme that inactivates the major class of secretory IgA, perhaps contributing to persistence of mucosal infection. Gonococcal opacity proteins also appear to downregulate the immune response, perhaps accounting for the observed paucity of mucosal antibodies after natural infection.

Serum bactericidal antibodies are important in preventing bacteremia, as indicated by the increased likelihood of disseminated infection in persons infected with strains resistant to normal serum bactericidal activity. In addition, persons with homozygous deficiency of one of the complement components C6, C7, C8, or C9, which results in diminished serum bactericidal activity without alteration in serum opsonic activity, are particularly prone to gonococcemia and to meningococcal meningitis and bacteremia.

Clinical Manifestations

UROGENITAL GONORRHEA IN MALES. Gonococcal urethritis in men ("clap") typically is characterized by purulent urethral discharge and dysuria. The usual incubation period is 2 to 6 days. Only a small minority of men who acquire urethral infection, generally estimated at 1 to 10% and varying with the auxotype/serotype class of the infecting strain, remain asymptomatic. Physical examination typically reveals purulent (yellowish) urethral exudate, usually apparent spontaneously but sometimes only expressed by compression of the urethra. Erythema of the meatus sometimes is present. Nongonococcal urethritis (NGU) typically presents with less copious and less purulent discharge and meatal erythema is rare. The diagnosis of gonococcal urethritis usually is suspected clinically, confirmed preliminarily by a Gram-stained smear showing leukocytes with intracellular Gram-negative diplococci, and made definitively when N. gonorrhoeae is identified by culture or other specific test. The differential diagnosis of urethritis is discussed in Chapter 345.

Urethral stricture formerly was a common complication but now is rare. Even in the preantibiotic era, more strictures may have resulted from the use of caustic treatment regimens, such as urethral irrigation with antiseptic solutions like silver nitrate or potassium permanganate, than from gonorrhea itself. Acute epididymitis, although uncommon, is the most frequent complication of gonococcal urethritis today, but more common causes are C. trachomatis or, in men over 35 years old, Escherichia coli and other uropathogens. Epididymitis usually presents with unilateral testicular pain and swelling, often with fever. Posterior urethritis, typically presenting with pelvic or perineal pain and urinary retention (suggesting acute prostatitis), once was fairly common; it is uncertain whether true gonococcal prostatitis also occurred, but in any case the clinical syndrome now is rare.

LOWER GENITAL TRACT GONORRHEA IN FEMALES. The primary site of infection in women is the endocervical canal, and N. gonorrhoeae is isolated from the cervix in 85 to 90% of women with gonorrhea. When symptoms are present, the dominant ones are vaginal discharge and abnormal vaginal bleeding, typically with scant intermenstrual bleeding, often following intercourse, or enhanced bleeding during menses (metrorrhagia). Dysuria also is frequent, and N. gonorrhoeae can be isolated from the urethra in up to 80% of women with gonorrhea, although it rarely is the only infected site except in women who have had hysterectomies.

The physical examination may be normal, but many women have evidence of cervicitis, with purulent or mucopurulent exudate and often with edema and easily induced bleeding (e.g., with gentle swabbing, sometimes mistakenly called "friability") in an area of endocervical ectopy. Many women with gonorrhea have simultaneous bacterial vaginosis or trichomonal vaginitis, with abnormal vaginal discharge. However, gonorrhea itself does not cause vaginitis, because N. gonorrhoeae does not infect the estrogen-influenced, glycogen-rich squamous epithelium of sexually mature women. As discussed later, microbiologic diagnosis usually rests on identification of N. gonorrhoeae in cervical secretions by culture or other specific test; the Gram stained smear is insensitive. The differential diagnosis of cervicitis, vaginal infection, and urethritis in women is discussed in Chapter 345.

In uncomplicated infection, purulent exudate sometimes can be expressed from a Bartholin gland duct, near the vaginal introitus laterally, or from Skene's glands, adjacent to the urethral meatus.

Bartholin gland abscess is an uncommon complication, presenting with a tender introital mass, and may involve superinfection with facultative and anaerobic bacteria. Gonococcal ophthalmia occasionally is seen in adults, usually as a result of autoinoculation in persons with anogenital gonorrhea. It presents with acute, purulent conjunctivitis that can result in corneal ulceration if not treated promptly.

PELVIC INFLAMMATORY DISEASE. The most common complication of gonorrhea is acute salpingitis, often accompanied by endometritis, collectively termed *pelvic inflammatory disease* (PID), which is estimated to occur in 10 to 20% of infected women. Chlamydia trachomatis is the dominant cause of PID in the United States, but gonorrhea remains a frequent cause; the proportion of cases due to either organism is directly related to their relative prevalences in the local population. Neither organism can be implicated in a substantial minority of patients; Mycoplasma genitalium may cause some cases. Regardless of the initiating infection, several other vaginal organisms, such as Mycoplasma hominis and various facultative and anaerobic Gram-positive and Gram-negative bacteria, often are implicated as co-pathogens. Low abdominal pain is the dominant symptom and often begins in proximity to a menstrual period; fever and other systemic manifestations such as malaise and anorexia are common. Often there are symptoms of lower genital tract infection, but their absence does not exclude the diagnosis of PID.

Examination usually discloses low abdominal tenderness, cervical motion tenderness, and bilateral adnexal tenderness, sometimes with a palpable mass. Most women have signs of cervicitis or vaginal infection. In a small proportion of cases, the abdominal or adnexal signs may be unilateral, causing confusion with appendicitis, ectopic pregnancy, and other conditions. Right upper quadrant abdominal tenderness sometimes is present due to Fitz-Hugh-Curtis syndrome, in which intra-abdominal extension of infection results in perihepatitis, which can mimic acute cholecystitis or viral hepatitis. Although Fitz-Hugh-Curtis syndrome usually is seen in conjunction with overt PID, sometimes perihepatitis occurs in the absence of other abdominal or pelvic findings, perhaps especially when caused by C. trachomatis. Severe PID may present with signs of generalized peritonitis. Laboratory studies often show elevation of the white blood cell count and erythrocyte sedimentation rate or C-reactive protein. However, these tests often are normal, and they are more useful in judging clinical severity than as diagnostic criteria.

The clinical diagnosis of PID is inexact. When laparoscopy showing visible salpingitis is used as the definitive test, the clinical diagnosis of PID is both insensitive and nonspecific; that is, many cases of PID lack classic signs and symptoms, and some women with clinically typical PID have no laparoscopic abnormality. The finding of plasma cells on endocervical biopsy, which can be performed by an aspiration technique with little pain or morbidity, has been used as a research tool and promoted as a useful aid to clinical diagnosis but is not yet in widespread use. Because the consequences of untreated PID may be severe, the U.S. Centers for Disease Control and Prevention (CDC) recommends that all sexually active women with uterine or adnexal tenderness and cervical motion tenderness be treated for PID if no other cause is readily apparent.

Fallopian tube scarring due to PID often results in infertility or ectopic pregnancy, and prior gonococcal and chlamydial infections probably are the most common antecedents of both complications.

The incidence of tubal infertility has been estimated at 15% after one episode of PID and up to 50% after three attacks. The incidence of ectopic pregnancy is increased up to tenfold in women with previous salpingitis. However, most cases of tubal infertility and ectopic pregnancy attributable to STDs occur in women with neither a prior diagnosis of PID nor past symptoms suggestive of pelvic infection, indicating that subclinical infection—usually with *C. trachomatis* but perhaps with *N. gonorrhoeae* as well—can result in tubal scarring. Chronic pelvic pain, sometimes of disabling severity, also is a common consequence of PID. Each episode of PID, whether due to *N. gonorrhoeae*, *C. trachomatis*, or neither of these, significantly increases the risk of recurrent salpingitis. Many recurrent cases are associated with neither gonococcal nor chlamydial infection, suggesting that initial infection alters tubal clearance mechanisms or other defenses against ascending infection with vaginal bacteria.

RECTAL INFECTION. Gonococcal infection of the rectum is common in women and in MSM. In women, most infections probably are acquired through perineal contamination with cervicovaginal secretions, but MSM and some women acquire infection by anal intercourse. In women with cervical gonorrhea, and among MSM with gonorrhea of any anatomic site, about 40% have rectal infection. Most infections are subclinical, but symptomatic proctitis occasionally occurs, presenting with anal pruritus, mucopurulent discharge (often recognized by the patient as exudate coating feces), and sometimes pain, tenesmus, and bleeding. Symptomatic proctitis seems to be more common among MSM than in women with rectal gonorrhea, suggesting that the size of the infecting inoculum or the trauma of anal intercourse may contribute to the clinical manifestations.

Diagnosis of rectal infection depends on isolation of *N. gonorrhoeae* by culture. The Gram-stained smear is insensitive and, in most examiners' hands, nonspecific. No other test is approved for diagnosis of rectal gonorrhea, although preliminary data suggest that some DNA amplification tests may give accurate results. The differential diagnosis of symptomatic proctitis includes other traditional STDs, especially herpes, syphilis, and chlamydial infection, including lymphogranuloma venereum, as well as ulcerative colitis, Crohn's colitis, anal fissure, rectal lacerations, and proctocolitis due to *Shigella, Campylobacter, Yersinia enterocolitica*, and other enteric pathogens.

PHARYNGEAL INFECTION. Pharyngeal gonococcal infection results from orogenital exposure, is more efficiently acquired by fellatio than cunnilingus, and is found in about 5% of heterosexual men, 5 to 10% of women, and 10 to 20% of MSM with gonorrhea. Asymptomatic infection is the rule, although rare cases present with exudative pharyngitis and cervical lymphadenopathy. Isolated pharyngeal infection is rare, complications occur infrequently if ever, and most cases resolve spontaneously within a few weeks or in response to therapy for genital or rectal infection. In addition, transmission of pharyngeal infection to other sites is inefficient. For these reasons, testing persons at risk for pharyngeal gonococcal infection is optional, although most providers routinely test MSM. Culture is the only approved test.

GONORRHEA IN CHILDREN. Infants born to mothers with gonorrhea may develop gonococcal conjunctivitis, or ophthalmia neonatorum. Formerly a common cause of blindness, gonococcal ophthalmia now is rare in industrialized countries, owing both to improved gonorrhea control and to routine use of neonatal ocular prophylaxis with topical antibiotics or 1% silver nitrate. Neonates also may acquire pharyngeal or rectal infection and, rarely, gonococcal pneumonia or sepsis. Neonatal vaginal infection is uncommon, because under the influence of maternal estrogen, the glycogen-rich squamous epithelium of the neonatal vagina is resistant to gonococcal infection, just as *N. gonorrhoeae* does not cause vaginitis in sexually mature women. From the neonatal period through 1 year of age, most cases present with conjunctivitis or vaginitis resulting from accidental contamination from an adult. After age 1, almost all childhood gonorrhea is the result of sexual abuse by an adult. Beyond the neonatal period, purulent vaginitis is the most common manifestation of gonorrhea or chlamydial infection in girls, and rectal or pharyngeal infection is the most common manifestation in prepubertal boys. Culture is the test of choice for all childhood gonorrhea, because nonculture tests have not been validated and because forensic considerations may dictate preservation of an isolate.

DISSEMINATED GONOCOCCAL INFECTION. Disseminated gonococcal infection (DGI) usually is manifested by various combinations of polyarticular tenosynovitis, dermatitis due to focal septic embolization, and septic arthritis. DGI has been estimated to occur in 1 to 3% of adults with gonorrhea, but the risk depends on the likelihood of infection with particular strains of *N. gonorrhoeae* and probably is well under 1% in most geographic areas. Women may be somewhat more susceptible to DGI than men, and onset often occurs in association with menstruation. Severity varies from a mild illness with slight joint discomfort, few skin lesions, and little or no fever, to a fulminant illness with overt polyarthritis, high fever, and prostration. Most women and many men with DGI have no symptoms of genital gonorrhea, because the same auxotype/serotype classes of *N. gonorrhoeae* are associated with both resistance to serum bactericidal activity and the propensity to cause subclinical genital infection.

The early stage of DGI is sometimes called the arthritis-dermatitis syndrome, the main symptoms of which are polyarthralgias, skin lesions, and fever. Physical examination usually reveals tenosynovitis of two or more joints, most commonly the wrists, ankles, hands, and feet and less commonly the knees or elbows. Axial skeletal involvement is rare, a feature that can help differentiate DGI from Reiter's syndrome and other kinds of reactive arthritis. Skin lesions are few in number (usually <30) and normally are limited to the extremities. The individual lesions tend to evolve over several days from papules to pustules, often with a hemorrhagic component, so that lesions at various stages typically are present simultaneously. Bullae, petechiae, or overtly necrotic lesions that mimic ecthyma gangrenosum occasionally are seen. Although other conditions (e.g., bacterial endocarditis, meningococcemia) can cause similar lesions, the rash is sufficiently typical that it should strongly suggest DGI when seen in a sexually active young person.

Blood cultures are often positive for *N. gonorrhoeae*, but they are insensitive and bacteremia is intermittent, so that several cultures should be obtained to maximize the likelihood of isolation. All or most of the clinical manifestations appear to be related directly to bacteremic dissemination of the organism, even though it often cannot be isolated from blood, skin lesions, or synovial fluid. The leukocyte count usually is elevated but may be normal. The leukocyte count in synovial fluid, when obtained, usually is less than 20,000/mm^3. Liver function tests often show transaminase elevations suggestive of mild hepatitis. Circulating immune complexes sometimes are present, but it is uncertain whether they contribute to the clinical manifestations.

The arthritis-dermatitis syndrome often subsides spontaneously, or it may evolve over several days into a second stage of septic arthritis, usually involving only one or two joints, with positive synovial fluid culture for *N. gonorrhoeae*. Skin lesions often have resolved by this time, and blood cultures nearly always are negative. However, sequential evolution from the arthritis-dermatitis syndrome to septic arthritis often is not observed, so that some patients present with one or two inflamed joints, most commonly the elbow, wrist, knee, or ankle, without prior symptoms. The physical examination and laboratory findings are typical for septic arthritis. The involved joint is swollen and warm, often with overlying erythema, with an overt synovial effusion that usually contains more than 40,000 leukocytes/mm^3. Degenerative arthritis or frank joint destruction can result if treatment is delayed, and contiguous osteomyelitis can occur. Other manifestations of DGI are bacterial endocarditis and, very rarely, meningitis or myocarditis. In the preantibiotic era, *N. gonorrhoeae* caused up to 10% of all bacterial endocarditis but is now a rare cause. Gonococcal endocarditis usually involves the aortic valve and often progresses rapidly with valve destruction and congestive heart failure.

Young, sexually active persons with arthritis, tenosynovitis, or papulopustular skin lesions should be tested for *N. gonorrhoeae* at all potentially exposed anatomic sites. The diagnosis of DGI is secure when gonococci are recovered from the blood, a skin lesion, or synovial fluid but often is made presumptively when anogenital or pharyngeal gonorrhea is present in a patient with a typical clinical syndrome that responds promptly to antibiotics. The differential diagnosis includes Reiter's syndrome and other forms of reactive arthritis, meningococcemia, other kinds of septic arthritis, rheumatoid arthritis, systemic lupus erythematosus, and other rheumatologic conditions and infectious diseases. Reiter's syndrome, which usually is triggered by sexually acquired chlamydial infection, is the principal consideration in young adults. The skin lesions of the two conditions, when present, usually are distinct, and conjunctivitis and spinal involvement both are rare in DGI.

Laboratory Findings

GRAM-STAINED SMEARS. The Gram-stained smear is positive when polymorphonuclear neutrophils are observed to contain intracellular Gram-negative diplococci of typical morphology. Methylene blue and other stains are standard in some countries and probably have performance characteristics similar to those of the Gram stain but are rarely used in the United States. The Gram-stained smear is 90 to 98% sensitive in the diagnosis of symptomatic gonococcal urethritis in men and the specificity is greater than 95%, so that confirmation by culture or another test is optional. However, the sensitivity is only around 50% for cervical or rectal infection and for asymptomatic urethral gonorrhea. Although the test is often considered highly specific for such infections, the actual performance varies with the skill and experience of the examiner, and rectal and cervical smears are unreliable in many clinical settings. Smears are both insensitive and nonspecific for pharyngeal gonococcal infection and are not recommended.

CULTURE. Isolation of *N. gonorrhoeae* by culture, usually using antibiotic-containing selective media, is the historic mainstay of gonorrhea diagnosis. Ideally, growth media should be inoculated directly and placed promptly into a humid atmosphere with increased carbon dioxide, such as a candle-extinction jar. However, standard transport systems (e.g., Culturette) are acceptable if specimens are kept moist, not refrigerated, and processed within 6 hours. When testing specimens not likely to be colonized by competing flora (e.g., synovial fluid), nonselective chocolate agar should be used.

NUCLEIC ACID AMPLIFICATION TESTS. In many laboratories, culture is rapidly being supplanted by nucleic acid amplification tests (NAATs), including ligase or polymerase chain reaction, transcription-mediated amplification, and the DNA strand displacement assay. The NAATs for *N. gonorrhoeae* are only slightly more sensitive than culture, but they are more expensive, do not preserve an isolate for antimicrobial susceptibility testing, and have not been validated for rectal or pharyngeal specimens. In addition, even a highly specific nonculture test may have a low positive predictive value when used in a population with a low prevalence of infection, so that many results will be falsely positive when persons at low risk are tested. This may be a particular problem when an NAAT for *N. gonorrhoeae* is "bundled" with a test for *C. trachomatis* for a single price and used to test persons at substantial risk for chlamydial infection but at low risk for gonorrhea, a common occurrence. On the other hand, the NAATs retain excellent sensitivity when used to test voided urine or self-obtained vaginal swabs and offer more convenient specimen management than culture, and the combination assays for *N. gonorrhoeae* and *C. trachomatis* may facilitate screening for both STDs in some settings.

Other nonculture tests, based on nonamplified DNA probe technology or immunochemical detection of gonococcal antigens, are substantially less sensitive and probably are less specific than culture or the NAATs, and they cannot be used to test urine or anatomic sites other than the urethra or cervix. Although some such tests have been used commonly in recent years, they have little clinical use today and are not recommended.

Rx Treatment

ANTIMICROBIAL SUSCEPTIBILITY. At first exquisitely susceptible to most antimicrobial agents, *N. gonorrhoeae* strains with clinically significant antimicrobial resistance began to evolve almost immediately after the introduction of treatment with the sulfonamides and then penicillin. Today, gonococci with chromosomal or plasmid-borne mutations that confer relative or absolute resistance to the penicillins, tetracyclines, and sulfonamides—to which all strains initially were susceptible—are prevalent worldwide, and none of these drugs remains acceptable as empirical therapy anywhere in the world. However, the prevalences of specific kinds of resistance vary widely between geographic areas and populations. For example, compared with heterosexual men and women, MSM more commonly are infected with relatively resistant gonococci. Infection of the rectum is required for propagation of gonorrhea among MSM, and the rectal environment selects for mutations that reduce permeability of the organism's outer membrane to toxic fecal bile salts and fatty acids, and the same membrane changes also reduce permeability to β-lactam antibiotics, tetracyclines, and macrolides. The prevalence of β-lactamase (penicillinase) plasmids, conferring absolute resistance to penicillin and ampicillin—formerly the worldwide mainstays of therapy—varies from around 10% of gonococci in the United States and western Europe to almost 50% in some developing countries.

Despite these trends, virtually all gonococci remain susceptible to the newer cephalosporins, and until recently the fluoroquinolones were uniformly active. However, *N. gonorrhoeae* strains with clinically significant resistance to the fluoroquinolones began to emerge in the late 1980s, primarily in east Asia and Pacific island nations, and by the mid-1990s, these drugs had lost their utility for gonorrhea in the Philippines, Japan, and parts of southeast Asia. For several years, fluoroquinolone-resistant strains were isolated only sporadically in North America and Europe. However, by 2002 such strains accounted for 20% of all gonorrhea in Hawaii, in 2001 they appeared in rapidly rising numbers in California, and sporadic cases have been reported elsewhere. Thus, the fluoroquinolones no longer are recommended for empiric treatment of gonorrhea in California and Hawaii, and soon they probably will be unacceptable as routine therapy throughout North America. Clinicians who treat patients for gonorrhea and other STDs should keep abreast of regional trends in resistance and therapeutic recommendations.

PRINCIPLES OF TREATMENT. Unlike most bacterial infections, uncomplicated gonorrhea infection almost always responds to single dose treatment with an appropriate antibiotic. Because of the need to immediately curtail transmission, therapy usually is selected before the diagnosis is confirmed, and even when *N. gonorrhoeae* is isolated by culture, antimicrobial susceptibility testing usually is not done. Accordingly, treatment is determined solely by local or regional patterns of gonococcal antimicrobial susceptibility. (However,

susceptibility testing should be used to guide the treatment of gonococcal endocarditis or meningitis.) Five to 10% of MSM, 10 to 20% of heterosexual men, and 20 to 40% of women with gonorrhea also are infected with *C. trachomatis*, so that routine treatment for chlamydial infection is advised in addition to specific therapy for gonorrhea. At one time it was considered important that gonorrhea therapy be effective against syphilis, but incubating or active syphilis now is rare in persons with gonorrhea, and data show that the use of antibiotics without activity against *Treponema pallidum* does not influence the incidence of syphilis.

TREATMENT REGIMENS. Regimens for treating uncomplicated gonorrhea in adults are summarized in Table 346–1. In most settings, ceftriaxone 125 mg intramuscularly or an oral cephalosporin, such as cefpodoxime 400 mg, should be given. Cefixime 400 mg, heretofore the oral treatment of choice, is no longer available in the United States. Cefuroxime 1.0 g also is an option, but might be slightly less effective than other regimens for gonococcal urethritis. Cefpodoxime and cefuroxime may be less effective for pharyngeal gonococcal infection than ceftriaxone or cefixime. Single-dose oral therapy with ciprofloxacin, ofloxacin, or levofloxacin is highly effective for genital, rectal, or pharyngeal infection due to susceptible strains, but should not be used for gonorrhea acquired in geographic areas where fluoroquinolone-resistant strains are prevalent. Other fluoroquinolones have no advantage over the recommended ones. Spectinomycin can be used in the rare circumstance when neither a cephalosporin nor a fluoroquinolone can be given (e.g., a pregnant woman with severe allergy to penicillin or other β-lactam antibiotics). Another option is azithromycin 2 g orally in a single dose; 1 g is insufficient. The patient always should be directly observed taking single-dose oral therapy; studies show that when persons with bacterial STDs are given prescriptions, many fail to take the drug properly or even to fill the prescription.

All persons with gonorrhea should be routinely treated with an oral regimen active against *C. trachomatis*, usually azithromycin in a single dose of 1 g or doxycycline 100 mg twice daily for 7 days. Some experts and the CDC advise that co-therapy may be deleted if chlamydial infection has been excluded by specific testing. However, no test for *C. trachomatis* is 100% sensitive, and co-treatment often is warranted regardless of such testing. Also, even though neither doxycycline nor 1 g of azithromycin is sufficiently effective for use as sole therapy for gonorrhea, in most settings either regimen will cure about 90% of patients, perhaps further reducing the small chance of treatment failure and diminishing selection pressure for antibiotic-resistant *N. gonorrhoeae*. Indeed, one reason that fluoroquinolone-resistant gonococci have spread from Asia to North America more slowly than did β-lactamase–producing strains 15 years earlier may be that co-therapy was less commonly used in the early 1980s than in the 1990s.

Women with acute PID should be treated with antibiotics active against *N. gonorrhoeae*, *C. trachomatis*, and a broad range of facultative and anaerobic pathogens, regardless of whether gonococcal or chlamydial infection is documented. Recommended oral regimens are ofloxacin (400 mg twice daily) or levofloxacin (500 mg once daily), plus metronidazole (500 mg twice daily), for 14 days; or a single dose of one of the parenteral cephalosporins, such as ceftriaxone (250 mg IM), followed by doxycycline (100 mg twice daily), with or without metronidazole (500 mg twice daily), for 14 days. For hospitalized patients or others who require parenteral therapy, the CDC recommends cefoxitin or cefotetan plus doxycycline; or clindamycin plus gentamicin. Other options include ofloxacin or levofloxacin, with or without metronidazole; and ampicillin/sulbactam plus doxycycline. For all of these regimens, parenteral therapy is continued until improvement is observed, after which oral therapy is prescribed to complete 14 days total treatment.

Most persons with DGI should be hospitalized and treated with a parenteral third-generation cephalosporin, such as ceftriaxone, cefotaxime, or ceftizoxime, or with ciprofloxacin, ofloxacin, or levofloxacin if antimicrobial susceptibility testing shows the infecting strain to be sensitive. Joint irrigation or drainage appears not to be necessary for septic arthritis, although repeated aspiration of synovial fluid may speed improvement. Oral treatment (e.g., cefixime or a fluoroquinolone) usually can be substituted after improvement begins, then continued to complete 7 days' therapy. More prolonged parenteral treatment and higher doses are indicated for treatment of gonococcal meningitis or endocarditis. Gonococcal epididymitis, bartholinitis, and other localized complications usually should be treated for 7 to 14 days with drugs active against both *N. gonorrhoeae* and *C. trachomatis*. Gonococcal conjunctivitis in adults can be managed with a single dose of ceftriaxone 1 g intramuscularly, optionally with saline lavage.

MANAGEMENT OF SEX PARTNERS. Failure to ensure treatment of patients' sex partners contributes to continued transmission of gonorrhea and often results in reinfection of the index case. Most persons with genital discharge, lesions, or dysuria cease sexual activity and seek treatment; therefore, gonorrhea and other STDs are selectively transmitted by persons with subclinical infection or with ignored symptoms. Accordingly, most patients' source contacts—the partners from whom they acquired infection—do not spontaneously seek health care, and active efforts are necessary to bring them to treatment. For some gonorrhea patients, such as those with PID, DGI, or childhood infection resulting from sexual abuse, the local or state health departments may assist with partner management. However, contrary to many clinicians' expectations, few health departments in the U.S. attempt to contact patients with uncomplicated gonorrhea or chlamydial infection or their sex partners, even when cases are promptly reported. Thus, the clinician must take active steps to assure partner treatment. Often this can be accomplished by simply advising the patient to refer his or her partners, who should be tested for both *N. gonorrhoeae* and *C. trachomatis* (and usually screened for syphilis and HIV infection) and treated as if infected, without awaiting test results. Often it is necessary and appropriate to arrange for treatment of partners who have not been examined, by writing a prescription for the partner or giving the patient extra drug to share with one or more partners. The efficacy of such expedited partner management in preventing recurrent gonorrhea and chlamydial infection recently was demonstrated in a large, community-based randomized controlled trial.

FOLLOW-UP. The recommended regimens cure 96 to 100% of uncomplicated genital or rectal gonorrhea due to susceptible strains. Accordingly, retesting of infected patients to assure cure is not recommended, unless therapeutic compliance is unlikely or circumstances require treatment with a suboptimal regimen. If an NAAT is used for test of cure, testing should be delayed until at least 2 weeks after treatment, to reduce the likelihood of detecting persistent gonococcal DNA despite eradication of viable organisms.

Although test of cure usually is unnecessary, *rescreening* may be warranted. Rescreening is retesting 3 to 6 months after treatment to detect reinfection. Studies show that 10 to 20% of both men and women with gonorrhea or chlamydial infection once again have positive tests within a few months, regardless of whether they believe their sex partners received treatment. Although rescreening of women for gonorrhea was first recommended in the 1970s, it was rarely implemented because of the need for a vaginal speculum examination, a barrier that has been eliminated by NAAT testing of urine and self-obtained vaginal swabs. Rescreening of women is well established as a chlamydia prevention strategy, and recent research suggests an important role for all persons with either gonorrhea or chlamydial infection. Using urine or vaginal swab testing by NAAT, rescreening can be accomplished without directly examining the patient, and even without an office visit if specimen transport can be arranged.

Table 346–1 • ANTIBIOTIC REGIMENS RECOMMENDED FOR UNCOMPLICATED GONORRHEA IN ADULTS IN THE U.S.

REGIMENS OF CHOICE	ALTERNATIVE REGIMENS
INITIAL SINGLE-DOSE THERAPY	
Ceftriaxone 125 mg IM[†]	Cefixime 400 mg PO[§]
Cefpodoxime 400 mg PO**	Cefuroxime 1 g PO[††]
Ciprofloxacin 500 mg PO[‡]	Ceftizoxime 500 mg IM
Ofloxacin 400 mg PO[‡]	Cefotaxime 500 mg IM
Levofloxacin 250 mg PO[†]	Gatifloxacin 400 mg PO[‡]
	Lomefloxacin 400 mg PO[‡]
	Spectinomycin 2 g IM*
	Azithromycin 2 g PO
FOLLOW-UP THERAPY	
Azithromycin 1 g PO in a single dose	
or	
Doxycycline 100 mg PO twice daily for 7 days[‖]	

*Spectinomycin is ineffective against pharyngeal gonococcal infection.
[†]The smallest marketed dose of ceftriaxone is 250 mg; therefore some clinicians administer the entire 250 mg. May be reconstituted in 1% lidocaine to reduce injection pain.
[‡]The fluoroquinolones should not be used to treat patients whose gonorrhea was acquired in Asia, Pacific islands including Hawaii, California, or other areas where fluoroquinolone-resistant *Neisseria gonorrhoeae* strains are prevalent.
[§]Oral regimen of choice, but not available in the U.S.
[‖]Another tetracycline may be substituted in therapeutically equivalent dosage, such as tetracycline HCl 500 mg 4 times daily or minocycline 100 mg PO twice daily.
**A 200 mg dose is approved by the U.S. FDA, but confirmatory data have not been published and efficacy for rectal and pharyngeal infections is uncertain. Pharmacokinetic considerations favor the 400 mg dose.
[††]May have lower efficacy for male urethral infection than for cervical gonorrhea in women.
Author's recommendations, modified from the CDC's Sexually Transmitted Diseases Treatment Guidelines, 2002.

Prevention and Control

Control of gonorrhea depends on prompt diagnosis and effective treatment of infected persons, screening sexually active women in settings where gonorrhea is prevalent, treatment of patients' partners, and rescreening. Asymptomatic MSM in many settings, including many HIV-infected men, remain sexually active and at high risk for gonorrhea and other STDs and should be tested periodically for rectal and perhaps pharyngeal gonococcal infection, and for other STDs. The prevention value of screening asymptomatic heterosexual men or MSM for urethral infection (by NAAT testing of urine) is unknown. Public education and personal counseling of persons with gonorrhea or at risk should emphasize the effectiveness of mutual monogamy, selection of partners at low risk, and, except in committed relationships, the use of condoms or other barrier methods. Every patient with gonorrhea should be counseled about the risks of HIV acquisition or transmission and should be routinely tested for *C. trachomatis*, HIV, syphilis, and perhaps infection with type 2 herpes simplex virus. Because accurate epidemiologic data are essential to maintain and generate resources for STD prevention and control, all cases of gonorrhea, chlamydial infection, syphilis, and HIV infection should be promptly reported to the health department in accordance with local laws. Ultimate control of gonorrhea may require immunization, but despite intensive research for two decades, no effective vaccine is on the horizon.

SUGGESTED READINGS

Centers for Disease Control and Prevention: Sexually transmitted diseases treatment guidelines, 2002. MMWR Recomm Rep 2002;51:1–78. *CDC's latest STD management recommendations, with substantial information about diagnosis and prevention as well as treatment; also available at http://www.cdc.gov/std/treatment/default.htm*

Cohen MS, Cannon JG: Human experimentation with *Neisseria gonorrhoeae*: progress and goals. J Infect Dis 1999;179:S375–S379. *A review of pathogenesis in humans as tested in experimental male volunteers.*

Fenton KA, Ison C, Johnson AP, et al; GRASP collaboration: Ciprofloxacin resistance in *Neisseria gonorrhoeae* in England and Wales in 2002. Lancet 2003;361:1867–1869. *Documents resistance to cipro, a problem that is widespread in the U.S. as well.*

Handsfield HH: Color Atlas and Synopsis of Sexually Transmitted Diseases, 2nd ed. New York, McGraw-Hill, 2001. *A heavily illustrated, clinically oriented guide to clinical recognition, diagnosis, and treatment of STDs.*

Moran JS, Handsfield HH: *Neisseria gonorrhoeae. In* Yu VL, Merigan TC JR, Barriere SL (eds): Antimicrobial Therapy and Vaccines, 2nd ed. Baltimore, Williams & Wilkins, 2002. *A detailed review of antimicrobial susceptibility of* N. gonorrhoeae *and treatment of gonorrhea.*

Smith KR, Ching S, Lee H, et al: Evaluation of ligase chain reaction for use with urine for identification of *Neisseria gonorrhoeae* in females attending a sexually transmitted disease clinic. J Clin Microbiol 1995;33:455–457. *One of many papers showing the urine-based nucleic acid amplification tests are simple, sensitive, and specific.*

Sparling PF, Handsfield HH: *Neisseria gonorrhoeae. In* Mandell GF, Bennett JE, Dolin R (eds): Principles and Practice of Infectious Diseases, 5th ed. New York, Churchill Livingstone, 2000, pp 2242–2258. *Highly referenced overview of pathogenesis, epidemiology, clinical presentation, diagnosis, and treatment.*

347 GRANULOMA INGUINALE (DONOVANOSIS)

Edward W. Hook III

Definition

Granuloma inguinale, also known as donovanosis, is a slowly progressive ulcerative disease involving principally the skin and subcutaneous tissues of the genital, inguinal, and anal regions. It is primarily transmitted sexually but probably can be transmitted by nonsexual contact as well. Multiple sexual contacts with an infected partner seem necessary for transmission of infection. The disease is uncommon in the United States, with fewer than 100 recorded cases annually. It is quite common, however, in certain other areas of the world, especially Papua New Guinea, South Africa, and parts of Australia.

Etiology

The causative organism is *Calymmatobacterium granulomatis*, a Gram-negative bacterium related to certain *Klebsiella* strains. Current evidence suggests that *C. granulomatis* is a member of the *Klebsiella-Enterobacter-Serratia* family. The organism can be grown in yolk sacs, and successful cell culture has been reported from laboratories in South Africa and Australia. Successful culture has in turn permitted development of polymerase chain reaction (PCR) assays for research purposes. It is apparently a facultative intracellular parasite because in infected lesions it is found primarily in histiocytes or other mononuclear cells.

Clinical Manifestations

The initial lesion usually appears as a subcutaneous nodule that erodes through the surface and develops into a beefy, elevated granulomatous lesion. This usually is painless and unassociated with systemic symptoms. Secondary bacterial infection may cause a necrotic painful ulcerative lesion that may be rapidly destructive. A cicatricial form may also occur with a depigmented elevated area of keloid-like scar containing scattered islands of granulomatous tissue. Lesions in the genital area are commonly associated with pseudobuboes in the inguinal region; these swellings are usually not due to involvement of the inguinal lymph nodes but rather to granulomatous involvement of the subcutaneous tissues. Metastatic infection of bones or other viscera is occasionally seen. Clinical experience suggests that secondary carcinomas may be a complication of granuloma inguinale.

Differential Diagnosis

The differential diagnosis includes tumor, lymphogranuloma venereum, chancroid, syphilis, and other ulcerative granulomatous diseases. Chancroid is usually differentiated by its irregular undermined borders, which are not seen in the usual cases of granuloma inguinale. Darkfield examination and serologic tests should help to distinguish syphilis. Biopsy of lesions may be necessary to distinguish granuloma inguinale from certain tumors.

Diagnosis

Diagnosis is made by demonstrating intracellular "Donovan bodies" in histiocytes or other mononuclear cells from lesion scrapings or biopsies. Wright stain and Giemsa stain of fresh impression smears or unfixed biopsy samples usually demonstrate the bacilli relatively easily, although multiple biopsies may be necessary in chronic cases. Cell culture and PCR methods have been described but are primarily research tools. A serologic test has been devised but is not clinically available. Histologic examination of biopsy specimens shows mononuclear cells with some infiltration by polymorphonuclear leukocytes but no giant cells.

Rx Treatment

Recommended treatment consists of azithromycin 1.0 g weekly or 500 mg daily, supplanting previously recommended regimens of trimethoprim/sulfamethoxazole one double-strength tablet twice daily or doxycycline 100 mg twice daily for at least 3 weeks. Other regimens that have proved effective include ciprofloxacin, erythromycin, or gentamicin. Patients should be followed for at least several weeks after treatment is discontinued because of the possibility of relapse. Although the risk of communicability appears to be low, sexual contacts should also be examined; at present, treatment of contacts is not indicated in the absence of clinically evident disease.

Prevention

No effective prevention is known.

SUGGESTED READINGS

Carter J, Bowden FJ, Sriprakash KS, et al: Diagnostic polymerase chain reaction for donovanosis. Clin Infect Dis 1999;28:1168–1169.

Clinical Effectiveness Group: National guideline for the management of donovanosis. Sex Transm Inf 1999;75(Suppl 1):S38–S39.

Rosen T, Tschen JA, Ramsdell W, et al: Granuloma inguinale. J Am Acad Dermatol 1984;11:433–437. *An American epidemic of this relatively rare disease is described.*

348 CHANCROID

Edward W. Hook III

Chancroid is a sexually transmitted infection caused by the gram-negative bacillus *Haemophilus ducreyi*. Although originally thought to be closely related to other *Haemophilus* species, rRNA studies suggest it is a member of the genus *Pasteurellaceae*.

Epidemiology

Worldwide, chancroid is considerably more common than syphilis, and in parts of Africa and in Southeast Asia it is nearly as great a problem as gonorrhea. The World Health Organization estimates the annual global incidence of the infection to be about 6 million cases. In the United States it is an uncommon disease. In the mid 1980s, chancroid rates increased more than fivefold, peaking at 4986 cases in 1987. Since then, rates have steadily, concomitant with a rising crack cocaine use, declined to 42 cases in 2001, with 15 of these cases occurring in a single state. Worldwide there are strong epidemiologic links between chancroid and prostitution. As for other genital ulcer diseases, chancroid is associated with increased risk for human immunodeficiency virus (HIV) acquisition. The majority of reported cases occur in men. An outbreak in Greenland was exceptional in that about 40% of cases were noted in women. It is quite likely that there has been significant underdiagnosis of chancroid in women in the past.

Clinical Manifestations

The usual incubation period is 2 to 5 days, but it may be up to 14 days. In the Greenland outbreak the incubation period averaged nearly 2 weeks in women. The clinical manifestations of chancroid are quite variable. Classically, the initial manifestation is an inflammatory macule that then becomes a vesicle-pustule and finally a sharply circumscribed, somewhat ragged, and undermined painful ulcer. The base is moist and may be covered with a grayish necrotic exudate. Removal of the exudate reveals purulent granulation tissue. There is usually surrounding cutaneous erythema. Lesions typically are single but may be multiple, possibly owing to autoinoculation of nearby tissues. There are rarely systemic symptoms. Inguinal adenopathy is noted in one half of patients, approximately two thirds of whom have unilateral adenopathy. Lesions are usually noted on the penile shaft or glans. In women, lesions may occur on the cervix, vagina, vulva, or perianal area. Lesions may occasionally occur primarily on or spread to the abdomen, thigh, breast, fingers, or lips. Intraoral lesions are uncommon.

There are reports of a transient genital ulcer, followed by significant inguinal adenopathy. This may be difficult to distinguish from lymphogranuloma venereum. Other uncommon clinical variants include the *phagedenic* type of ulcer with secondary superinfection and rapid tissue destruction; *giant chancroid,* which is characterized by a very large single ulcer; *serpiginous ulcer,* which is characterized by rapidly spreading, indolent, shallow ulcers on the groin or the thigh; and a *follicular* type with multiple small ulcers in a perifollicular distribution.

Differential Diagnosis

The differential diagnosis includes syphilis, herpes genitalis, lymphogranuloma venereum, traumatic ulcers, and granuloma inguinale. Of these, the most commonly confused are syphilis and genital herpes. Multiple infections are relatively common. Outpatients with suspected chancroid should have a serologic test for syphilis and preferably a darkfield examination as well.

Diagnosis

The diagnosis of chancroid is most often made on the basis of the clinical appearance of the lesions plus either morphologic demonstration of typical organisms in the lesions or demonstration of *H. ducreyi* by culture or polymerase chain reaction (PCR) assays. PCR assays for chancroid diagnosis have been developed and found to be more sensitive than culture but are not currently commercially available. Culture is the preferred method in nonresearch settings, but selective culture media are often not available. Under optimal conditions, positive cultures can be obtained in more than 80% of cases. Best culture results seem to be obtained with supplemented chocolate agar media containing 3 µg/mL of vancomycin and incubated at 33° C. For culture of lesions, necrotic debris should be removed from the ulcer with physiologic saline. The base and edges of the ulcer should be swabbed with a cotton-tipped swab and inoculated directly onto the culture plate if possible; swabs may be put into Amies transport medium if culture plates are not immediately available. Smears obtained from the undermined edges should be gently rolled onto a slide. *H. ducreyi* is a small gram-negative bacillus with rounded ends that typically forms chains or parallel aggregates in lesions. Typical organisms are seen in 50 to 80% of cases. Organisms may also be obtained by aspirating inguinal nodes. Nodes should be aspirated by placing the needle through normal skin to avoid formation of fistulous tracts. Nodes should not be incised. There is no commercially available serologic test for chancroid.

Rx Treatment

The drug of choice is a single intramuscular dose of ceftriaxone, 250 mg, or a single 1-g dose of azithromycin, given orally. Erythromycin, 500 mg orally four times daily for 7 days, is also usually curative. Another effective agent is ciprofloxacin, 500 mg orally twice daily for 3 days. Ampicillin should not be used because some strains of *H. ducreyi* produce a typical TEM-type β-lactamase and are quite ampicillin resistant. The plasmids containing the gene for production of β-lactamase are closely related to the penicillinase plasmids present in *H. influenzae* and *Neisseria gonorrhoeae.* Tetracycline resistance is common. Serologic testing for HIV is recommended for all patients treated for possible chancroid. All regular sexual partners should be examined and epidemiologically treated with a similar regimen.

Prevention

No vaccine is available. Use of a condom is presumably helpful. There are no data regarding the efficacy of antibiotic prophylaxis; however, most experts recommend prophylactic therapy for persons sexually exposed to chancroid in the preceding 10 days.

SUGGESTED READINGS
Blackmore CA, Limpakarnjanarat K, Rigau-Perez JG, et al: An outbreak of chancroid in Orange County, California: Descriptive epidemiology and disease-control measures. J Infect Dis 1985;151:840–844. *A large continental U.S. outbreak is described. Sulfa and tetracycline resistance was common, but erythromycin and co-trimoxazole were effective.*
Centers for Disease Control and Prevention: Sexually transmitted diseases, treatment guidelines 2002. MMWR 2002;51(RR-6):11–12. *Current treatment and management recommendations for chancroid.*
Sehgal VN, Srivastava G: Chancroid: Contemporary appraisal. Int J Dermatol 2003;42: 182–190. *A current review.*

349 SYPHILIS

Edward W. Hook III

Definition

Syphilis is a chronic infectious disease caused by the bacterium *Treponema pallidum.* It is usually acquired by sexual contact with another infected individual. Syphilis is relatively remarkable among infectious diseases in its large variety of clinical presentations. It progresses, if untreated, through primary, secondary, and tertiary stages. The early stages (i.e., primary and secondary) are infectious. Spontaneous healing of early lesions occurs, followed by a long latent period. In about 30% of untreated patients, late disease of the heart, central nervous system (CNS), or other organs may develop years after initial infection. At one time, this disease was called the great imitator. Although the disease is less common now than previously, it remains a challenge to the clinician because of its protean manifestations, and it is of interest to biologists because of the long and tenuous balance between the host and the invading spirochete.

Etiology

The cause of syphilis was discovered by Schaudinn and Hoffman in 1905, when they visualized spirochetal organisms in early infectious lesions. The causative agent of syphilis, *T. pallidum,* is closely related to other pathogenic spirochetes, including those causing yaws (*Treponema pallidum* subspecies *pertenue)* and pinta (*Treponema carateum).*

T. pallidum is a thin, helical bacterium approximately 0.15 µm wide and 6 to 50 µm long. Ordinarily, there are 6 to 14 spirals. The organism is tapered on either end. It is too thin to be seen by ordinary Gram stain but can be visualized in wet mounts by darkfield microscopy or by silver stain or fluorescent antibody methods.

Studies have described several unusual characteristics of the organism's outer membrane that may provide clues to the pathogenesis of syphilis. Unlike most bacteria having protein-rich outer membranes, the outer membrane of *T. pallidum* appears to be predominantly made up of phospholipids with few surface-exposed proteins. It has been hypothesized that, because of this structure, syphilis can progress despite a brisk antibody response to non–surface-exposed, internal antigens. Between the outer membrane and the peptidoglycan cell wall are six axial fibrils. The axial fibrils are attached three at each end and overlap in the center of the organism. They are structurally and biochemically similar to flagella and are in part responsible for the motility of the organism.

It is possible to culture *T. pallidum* in vitro, but sustained in vitro cultivation is not yet possible and yields are very low. Culture is of limited use in research but of no use in clinical practice. *T. pallidum* can be maintained by serial passage in rabbits without loss of virulence. Only a few strains have been isolated in rabbits and carefully studied, and little evidence is available regarding the genetic diversity of the organism. All studied isolates have been susceptible to penicillin and are similar antigenically. Immunity to the homologous strain develops after prolonged, untreated infection in rabbits. The only known natural hosts for *T. pallidum* are humans and certain monkeys and higher apes.

Pathogenesis and Host Response

T. pallidum may penetrate through normal mucosal membranes and through minor abrasions of epithelial surfaces. In experimental rabbit syphilis, spirochetes can be found in the lymphatic system within 30 minutes of inoculation and are found in blood shortly thereafter. There have been a few instances of transfusion syphilis in humans resulting from use of blood from a donor who was in the incubation stage of the disease. It therefore seems clear that syphilis is a systemic disease from the onset in humans.

The first lesions appear at the site of primary inoculation, presumably because of the large numbers of treponemes implanted at this site. In laboratory animals, there is an inverse relationship between number of treponemes inoculated and time required for development of the primary cutaneous lesion. The minimal number of treponemes required to establish infection is not known but may be as low as one treponeme. Multiplication of organisms is very slow, with a division time in rabbits of approximately 33 hours. Similarly, slow growth of treponemes in humans probably accounts in part for the protracted nature of the illness and for the relatively long incubation period.

T. pallidum is not known to produce toxins. Treponemes are capable of specific attachment to host cells, but it is not known whether attachment results in damage to host cells. Most treponemes are found in intercellular spaces, but treponemes occasionally are seen within phagocytic cells. However, there is no evidence for prolonged intracellular survival of treponemes.

The primary pathologic lesion of syphilis is a focal endarteritis with an increase in adventitial cells, endothelial proliferation, and presence of an inflammatory cuff around affected vessels. Lymphocytes, plasma cells, and monocytes predominate in the inflammatory lesion, and polymorphonuclear cells are seen in some cases. The vessel lumen is frequently obliterated. With healing, there is considerable fibrosis. Treponemes may be seen in most early lesions of syphilis and in some of the late lesions, such as the meningoencephalitis of general paresis.

Granulomatous reaction is common in secondary syphilis and in late syphilis. The granuloma is histologically nonspecific, and cases of syphilis have been incorrectly diagnosed as sarcoidosis or other granulomatous diseases. Human inoculation studies suggest that the pathogenesis of the gumma, which is a granulomatous lesion, involves hypersensitivity to small numbers of virulent treponemes introduced into a previously sensitized host.

Intracutaneous inoculation of patients with syphilis in various stages with partially purified antigens of *T. pallidum* showed that delayed cellular hypersensitivity developed only late in secondary syphilis but was uniformly present in latent syphilis. There may be temporary hyporesponsiveness of lymphocytes from patients with primary and secondary syphilis to treponemal antigens. It is possible that the unusual waxing and waning of lesions in early syphilis depend on the balance between development of effective cellular immunity and suppression of thymus-derived lymphocyte function.

The host also responds to infection with production of numerous antibodies, and in some instances, circulating immune complexes may be formed. The nephrotic syndrome has been recognized occasionally in secondary syphilis, and renal biopsy specimens from such cases have shown membranous glomerulonephritis characterized by focal subepithelial basement membrane deposits. The deposits contain IgG, C3, and treponemal antibody. Antibodies useful for diagnosis are discussed in the Serologic Tests section.

Epidemiology

Syphilis, with the exception of congenital syphilis, is acquired almost exclusively by intimate contact with the infectious lesions of primary or secondary syphilis (e.g., chancre, mucous patches, condylomata lata). This disease is usually acquired through sexual intercourse, including anogenital and orogenital intercourse. Health care workers have sometimes been infected during unsuspecting examination of patients with infectious lesions. Infection by contact with fomites is extremely uncommon.

Syphilis is most common in large cities and in young, sexually active individuals. The highest rate is in men between the ages 35 and 39 years, which is considerably older than for gonorrhea and chlamydial infection. In 2001, 2520 (80%) of 3139 U.S. counties reported no cases of primary or secondary syphilis, and 20 (<1%) of counties accounted for about 50% of all reported infections. The disease is most prevalent in the Southeast.

Syphilis spares no class, race, or group but is more prevalent in the United States among the poorly educated and economically deprived than among more prosperous groups. In 2001, U.S. syphilis rates were 16-fold greater among African Americans than among non-Hispanic whites (11 versus 0.7 cases per 100,000 people). Increased numbers of different sexual partners and perhaps indiscriminate choice of partners increase the risk of acquiring sexually transmitted disease. Patients with primary and secondary syphilis name on average nearly three different sexual contacts within the previous 90 days. A traditional cornerstone of syphilis control has been epidemiologic investigation and treatment of sexual contacts of patients with primary or secondary lesions and of patients with early latent disease. As syphilis has become associated with drug use and anonymous sex, epidemiologic investigations have become less efficacious.

In the 1970s and 1980s, male homosexuals accounted for a disproportionate number of the total cases of infectious syphilis. The ratio of male-to-female cases of primary and secondary syphilis in the United States rose from 1.6 : 1.0 in 1965 to 2.5 : 1.0 in 1975 and to about 3 : 1 in the mid-1980s. Similar trends occurred in other countries. From 1986 to 1990, U.S. syphilis rates nearly doubled, reaching 50,578 cases in 1990. This epidemic disproportionately affected multiracial heterosexual men and women and occurred contemporaneously with an epidemic of crack cocaine use. Many cases were related to the exchange of sex for drugs or money to buy drugs. After 1990, syphilis rates again declined, and in 2001, there were 6103 cases of primary and secondary syphilis reported, one of the lowest numbers since 1959. The epidemic of the late 1980s probably also contributed to the spread of human immunodeficiency virus (HIV) infection (see Syphilis-HIV Interactions) and to dramatic increases in the rate of congenital syphilis.

The annual incidence of syphilis has generally declined worldwide for approximately 100 years, with the exception of periods of war or social upheaval. With the introduction of penicillin, there was a rapid decline in primary and secondary syphilis after World War II to annual rates of approximately 4 cases per 100,000 people in 1957. This was followed by declining federal expenditure for syphilis control, and there was a subsequent resurgence in infectious primary and secondary syphilis in the United States, reaching peaks of more than 12 cases per 100,000 people several times in the period from 1965 through 1983. Because many cases of syphilis are not reported, the true incidence is much higher.

Reported deaths from syphilis declined from 2434 in 1965 to 200 in 1976. Infant deaths from syphilis fell by 98 to 99% by 1980 but rose sharply in 1988 through 1990. Patients with clinically evident late syphilis, particularly those with cardiovascular or gummatous syphilis, are becoming less common, perhaps as a result of the effectiveness of penicillin therapy for early syphilis. However, surveys indicate that there still are significant numbers of patients with untreated neurologic syphilis, especially among older age groups. Evidence suggests that neurosyphilis may manifest with a wide of variety of clinical features and therefore may not be easily recognized.

Natural Course of Untreated Syphilis

The incubation period from the time of exposure to development of the primary lesion at the place of initial inoculation of treponemes averages approximately 21 days (range, 10 to 90 days). A painless papule develops and soon breaks down to form a clean-based ulcer, the chancre, with raised, indurated margins. The chancre persists for 2 to 6 weeks and then heals spontaneously. Several weeks later, the patient characteristically develops a secondary stage characterized by low-grade fever, headache, malaise, generalized lymphadenopathy, and a mucocutaneous rash. There may be involvement of visceral organs. The secondary eruption may occur while the primary chancre is still healing or several months after the disappearance of the chancre. The secondary lesions also heal spontaneously within 2 to 6 weeks, and the infection then enters latency. More than 20% of untreated patients later develop relapsing lesions similar to those of the secondary stage; rarely, the relapse takes the form of recurrence of the primary chancre. In the era before antibiotics, about one third of untreated patients eventually developed late, destructive tertiary lesions involving one or more of the eyes, central nervous system, heart, or other organs, including skin. These lesions may occur in a few years to as late as 25 years after infection.

The incidence of late complications of untreated syphilis is unknown but seems less than seen previously. Cases of gumma are now so rare as to be reportable.

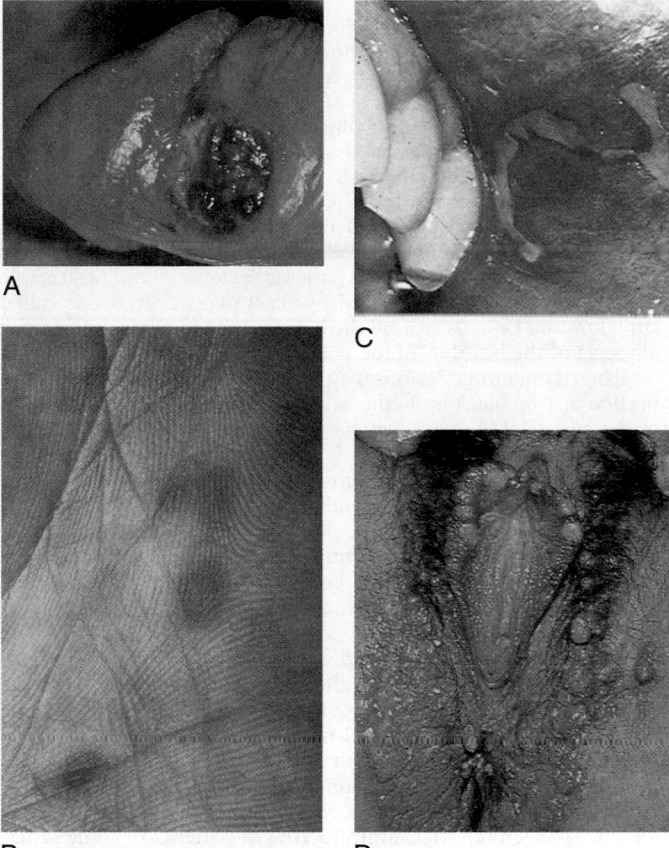

FIGURE 349–1 • *A*, Chancre in primary syphilis. *B*, Palmar lesions of a coppery color in secondary syphilis. *C*, Mucous patch in secondary syphilis. *D*, Condylomata lata in secondary syphilis. (*A*, *C*, and *D* from Forbes CD, Jackson WF: Color Atlas and Text of Clinical Medicine, 3rd ed. London, Mosby, 2003; *B* from Habif TP, Cambell JI, Quitadamo MJ, et al: Skin Disease: Diagnosis and Treatment. St. Louis, Mosby, 2001.)

Clinical Manifestations

PRIMARY SYPHILIS

The typical lesion of primary syphilis, the chancre, is a painless, clean-based, indurated ulcer (Fig. 349–1*A*). The chancre starts as a papule, but then superficial erosion occurs, resulting in the typical ulcer. The borders of the ulcer are raised, firm, and indurated. Occasionally, secondary infections change the appearance, resulting in a painful lesion. Most chancres are single, but multiple ulcers are sometimes seen, particularly when skin folds are apposed (i.e., kissing chancres). The untreated chancre heals in several weeks, leaving a faint scar. The chancre is usually associated with regional adenopathy, which may be unilateral or bilateral. The regional nodes are movable, discrete, and rubbery. If the chancre occurs in the cervix or in the rectum, the affected regional iliac nodes are not palpable.

Chancres may occur at any site of potential inoculation by direct contact. Most chancres occur in anogenital locations. Chancres may also be seen in the pharynx, on the tongue, around the lips, on the fingers, on the nipples, or in other, diverse areas. The morphology depends in part on the area of the body in which they occur and on the host's immune response. Chancres in previously infected individuals may be small and may remain papular. Chancres of the finger may appear more erosive and may be quite painful.

The *differential diagnosis* of a genital ulcer should include genital herpes. Classically, herpetic ulcers are multiple, painful, superficial, and if seen early, vesicular. However, atypical presentations may be indistinguishable from a syphilitic chancre. Genital herpes is orders of magnitude more common than syphilis. Genital herpes is now the most common cause of a "typical chancre" in North America. Herpetic ulcers, unlike syphilitic ulcers, may yield positive findings on the Tzanck test (i.e., multinucleated giant cells in the base of the ulcer). The ulcers of chancroid are usually painful, often multiple, and frequently exudative and nonindurated. Lymphogranuloma

venereum may produce a small, papular lesion associated with a regional adenopathy. Other conditions that must be distinguished include granuloma inguinale, drug eruptions, carcinoma, superficial fungal infections, traumatic lesions, and lichen planus. Final distinction in most cases is made on the basis of darkfield examination, which is positive only in syphilis.

SECONDARY SYPHILIS

Between 4 and 8 weeks after the appearance of the primary chancre, patients typically develop lesions of secondary syphilis. They may complain of malaise, fever, headache, sore throat, and other systemic symptoms. Most patients have generalized lymphadenopathy, including the epitrochlear nodes. Approximately 30% of patients have evidence of the healing chancre, although many patients, including male homosexuals and women, give no history of a primary lesion.

At least 80% of patients with secondary syphilis have cutaneous lesions or lesions of the mucocutaneous junctions at some point in their illness. The diagnosis is usually first suspected on the basis of the cutaneous eruption. The rash is often minimally symptomatic, and many patients with late syphilis do not recall primary or secondary lesions. The rashes are quite varied in their appearance but have certain characteristic features. The lesions are usually widespread, are symmetric in distribution, and often are pink, coppery, or dusky red (particularly the earliest macular lesions). They usually are nonpruritic, although occasional exceptions have been reported, and they are almost never vesicular or bullous in adults. They are indurated, except for the very earliest macular lesions, and frequently have a superficial scale (i.e., papulosquamous lesions). They tend to be polymorphic and rounded, and on healing, they may leave residual pigmentation or depigmentation. The lesions may be quite faint and difficult to visualize, particularly on dark-skinned individuals.

Continued

The earliest pink macular lesions typically are seen on the margins of the ribs or the sides of the trunk, with later spread to the rest of the body. The face is often spared, except around the mouth. Subsequently, a papular rash appears, which is usually generalized but is quite marked on the palms and soles (Fig. 349–1B). These rashes frequently are associated with a superficial scale and may be hyperpigmented. When the rash occurs on the face, it may be pustular, resembling acne vulgaris. Occasionally, the scale may be so great as to resemble psoriasis. Deep nodular lesions may cause confusion. Ulceration may occur, producing lesions resembling ecthyma. In malnourished or debilitated patients, extensive and destructive ulcerative lesions with a heaped-up crust may occur, the so-called rupial lesion. Lesions around the hair follicles may result in patchy alopecia of the beard or of the scalp.

Ringed or annular lesions may occur, especially around the face, particularly on black individuals. A lesion at the angle of the mouth or the corner of the nose may have a central linear erosion, the so-called split papule.

In warm, moist areas such as the perineum, large, pale, flat-topped papules may coalesce to form condylomata lata (Fig. 349–1D). These papules may also be seen in the axilla and occur rarely in a generalized form. They are extremely infectious. They are not to be confused with the common venereal warts (i.e., condylomata acuminata), which are small, often multiple, and more sharply raised than condylomata lata.

Other lesions of the mucous membranes are common. The palate and pharynx may be inflamed. Approximately 30% of secondary syphilis patients develop the so-called mucous patch (Fig. 349–1C). It is a slightly raised, oval area covered by a grayish white membrane, which when raised reveals a pink base that does not bleed. These lesions may be seen on the genitalia, in the mouth, or on the tongue and, like condylomata lata, are highly infectious.

Other manifestations of secondary syphilis include hepatitis, which has been reported in up to 10% of patients in some series. Jaundice is rare, but an elevated alkaline phosphatase level is common. Liver biopsy reveals small areas of focal necrosis and mononuclear infiltrate or periportal vasculitis. Spirochetes can often be visualized with silver stains. Periostitis with widespread lytic lesions of bone has been reported occasionally; bone scanning appears to be a sensitive test for early syphilitic osteitis. An immune complex type of nephropathy with transient nephrotic syndrome has been rarely documented. There may be iritis or an anterior uveitis. Between 10 and 30% of patients have pleocytosis in the cerebrospinal fluid (CSF), but symptomatic meningitis is seen in less than 1% of patients. Symptomatic gastritis may occur.

Differential diagnosis of secondary syphilis includes a large number of diseases. The cutaneous eruptions may be mimicked by pityriasis rosea, which can be differentiated by the occurrence of lesions along lines of skin cleavage and frequently by the presence of a herald patch. Drug eruptions, acute febrile exanthems, psoriasis, lichen planus, scabies, and other diseases must also be considered in some cases. The mucous patch may superficially resemble oral candidiasis (i.e., thrush). Infectious mononucleosis may appear very similar to secondary syphilis, with sore throat, generalized adenopathy, hepatitis, and a generalized rash. Infectious hepatitis may also cause confusion. A high index of suspicion is required to make the diagnosis of syphilis in some cases. Unfortunately, even classic cases with widespread, hyperpigmented, papulosquamous lesions involving the palms and the soles can be misdiagnosed. Fortunately, if the serologic tests for syphilis are obtained, results are positive in 99% of syphilis patients. The condylomata lata and mucous patches contain large numbers of treponemes that are seen on darkfield examination. Aspiration of lymph nodes may occasionally reveal motile *T. pallidum* organisms.

RELAPSING SYPHILIS

After resolution of primary or secondary syphilis skin lesions, 20 to 30% of patients experience cutaneous recurrences. Recurrent lesions may be fewer or more firmly indurated than initial lesions and, like typical lesions of primary or secondary syphilis, are infectious for exposed sexual partners.

LATENT SYPHILIS

By definition, latent syphilis is that stage in which there are no clinical signs of syphilis and the CSF is normal. Latency begins with the passing of the first attack of secondary syphilis and may last for a lifetime thereafter. It is usually detected by reactive serologic tests for syphilis. The test must be shown to be reactive on more than one occasion to rule out technical errors. Diseases known to cause occasional false-positive nontreponemal test reactions for syphilis, such as systemic lupus erythematosus (SLE), must be excluded. Congenital syphilis also must be excluded before the diagnosis of latent syphilis can be made. Patients may or may not have a history of earlier primary or secondary syphilis, although such history is obviously helpful in making a firm diagnosis of latent syphilis.

Latency has been divided into two stages: early and late latency. Evidence suggests that most infectious relapses occur in the first year, and epidemiologic evidence shows that the most infectious spread of syphilis occurs during the first year of infection. Early latency in the United States therefore is defined as the first year after the resolution of primary or secondary lesions or as a newly reactive serologic test for syphilis in an otherwise asymptomatic individual who has had a negative serologic test within the preceding year. Late latent syphilis is ordinarily not infectious, except for the pregnant woman, who may transmit infection to her fetus after many years.

LATE SYPHILIS

Late, or tertiary, syphilis is the destructive stage of the disease and can be crippling. Late syphilitic complications are still important medical problems, but newly recognized cases of late syphilis have been declining steadily in the United States since World War II. Although the incidence of late syphilis is unknown, the prevalence of various types of late syphilis has been approximated (Table 349–1).

Late syphilis is usually very slowly progressive, although certain neurologic syndromes may have sudden onset because of endarteritis and thrombosis in the CNS. Late syphilis is noninfectious. Any organ of the body may be involved, but three main types of disease may be distinguished: late benign (gummatous), cardiovascular, and neurosyphilis.

LATE BENIGN SYPHILIS. Late benign syphilis, or gumma, was the most common complication of late syphilis in the Oslo Study of untreated patients (1891 to 1951). In the penicillin era, gummas are rare. They typically develop 1 to 10 years after the initial infection and may involve any part of the body. Although they may be very destructive, they respond rapidly to treatment and therefore are relatively benign. Histologically, the gumma is a granuloma. The histologic findings are nonspecific and may be associated with central necrosis surrounded by epithelioid and fibroblastic cells and occasionally by giant cells. Patients sometimes have vasculitis. *T. pallidum* is ordinarily not demonstrable by silver stain but can sometimes be recovered by inoculation of rabbits.

Gummas may be solitary or multiple. They are usually asymmetrical and are often grouped. They may start as a superficial nodule or as a deeper lesion that breaks down to form punched-out ulcers. They are ordinarily indolent, slowly progressive, and indurated on palpation. There often is central healing with an atrophic scar surrounded by hyperpigmented borders. Cutaneous gummas may resemble other chronic granulomatous ulcerative lesions caused by tuberculosis, sarcoidosis, leprosy, and other deep fungal infections. Precise histologic diagnosis may not be possible. However, the syphilitic gumma is the only such lesion to heal dramatically with penicillin therapy. Another form of gumma is the papulosquamous type, which may mimic psoriasis.

Gummas may also involve deep visceral organs, particularly the respiratory tract, gastrointestinal tract, and bones. In earlier centuries, gummas of the nose and palate commonly resulted in septal perforations and disfiguring facial lesions. Gummas may also involve the larynx or the pulmonary parenchyma. Gummas of the stomach may masquerade as carcinoma of the stomach or lymphoma. Gummas of the liver were once the most common form of visceral syphilis, manifesting often with hepatosplenomegaly and anemia and occasionally with fever and jaundice. Skeletal gummas typically produce lesions in the long bones, skull, and clavicle. A characteristic symptom is nocturnal pain. Radiologic abnormalities, when present, include periostitis and lytic or sclerotic, destructive osteitis.

CARDIOVASCULAR SYPHILIS. The primary cardiovascular complications of syphilis are aortic insufficiency and aortic aneurysm, usually

Infectious Diseases

Table 349–1 • NEWLY DIAGNOSED TERTIARY SYPHILIS IN 105 PATIENTS IN DENMARK, 1961–1970

TYPE OF TERTIARY SYPHILIS	NO. OBSERVED*
Neurosyphilis	72
Asymptomatic	45
Tabes dorsalis	11
General paresis	13
Meningovascular	1
Optic atrophy	2
Cardiovascular syphilis	44
Aortic insufficiency	16
Aortic aneurysm	13
Uncomplicated aortitis†	15
Late benign syphilis (gumma)	4

*Some patients had more than one form of late syphilis.
†Autopsy diagnoses only.

Table 349–2 • SEROLOGIC TESTS FOR SYPHILIS

TYPE	USE
Nontreponemal (anticardiolipin) antibodies	
VDRL (slide flocculation)	Screening, quantitation, after response to treatment
RPR (circle-card) (agglutination)	Screening
Specific treponemal antibodies	
FTA-ABS (immunofluorescence with absorbed serum)	Confirmatory, diagnostic, not for routine screening
MHA-TP (microhemagglutination)	Similar to FTA-ABS but can be quantified and automated

FTA-ABS = fluorescent treponemal antibody absorption test; MHA-TP = microhemagglutination assay for *Treponema pallidum*; RPR = rapid plasma reagin test; VDRL = Venereal Disease Research Laboratories test.

of the ascending aorta. Less commonly, other large arteries may be involved, and involvement of the coronary ostia rarely results in coronary insufficiency. All of these complications are caused by obliterative endarteritis of the vasa vasorum with resultant damage to the intima and media of the great vessels. This damage results in dilatation of the ascending aorta and eventually results in stretching of the ring of the aortic valve, producing aortic insufficiency. The valve cusps remain normal. Death may eventually result from congestive heart failure. There has been some success with placing prosthetic heart valves in patients with syphilitic aortic insufficiency. An aneurysm occasionally manifests as a pulsating mass bulging through the anterior chest wall. Syphilitic aortitis may involve the descending aorta, but this is usually proximal to the renal arteries, unlike atherosclerotic aneurysms, which typically involve the descending aorta below the renal arteries.

The disease usually begins within 5 to 10 years after initial infection but may not manifest clinically until 20 to 30 years after infection. Cardiovascular syphilis is thought to be more common in men than in women and possibly in blacks than in whites. Cardiovascular syphilis does not occur after congenital infection—a phenomenon that remains unexplained.

Asymptomatic aortitis is best diagnosed by visualizing linear calcifications in the wall of the ascending aorta by radiography. The signs of syphilitic aortic insufficiency are the same as for aortic insufficiency of other causes. In aortic insufficiency resulting from dilatation of the aortic ring, the decrescendo murmur is often loudest along the right sternal margin. Syphilitic aneurysms may be fusiform but are more typically saccular and do not lead to aortic dissection. Between 10 and 20% of patients with cardiovascular syphilis have coexistent neurosyphilis.

Syphilis is a relatively more common cause of aortic insufficiency among the elderly than among younger patients. This pattern reflects the progressively decreasing incidence of new cases of late cardiovascular syphilis.

NEUROSYPHILIS. Neurosyphilis may be divided into five groups: asymptomatic, syphilitic meningitis, meningovascular syphilis, tabes dorsalis, and general paresis. These are more fully described in Chapter 474. Division is not absolute, and overlap between syndromes is typical. Current cases of neurosyphilis are more likely than heretofore to be variants of the classic syndromes, possibly as a result of use of antimicrobial agents for other diseases.

Asymptomatic Neurosyphilis. Asymptomatic neurosyphilis is diagnosed when there are CSF abnormalities, such as pleocytosis, protein elevation, or a reactive Venereal Disease Research Laboratories [VDRL] test result (Table 349–2 and see Serologic Tests) in a syphilis patient in the absence of signs and symptoms of neurologic disease. Although numerous other processes may cause CSF pleocytosis or protein elevations, false-positive VDRL test results are rare for CSF in the absence of a traumatic tap. The CSF usually shows an increased total protein concentration and lymphocytic pleocytosis. If the CSF is normal 2 or more years after the initial infection, the patient is not likely to develop a positive CSF finding later. Although up to 50% of patients with untreated secondary syphilis have an abnormal CSF test result, recommended therapy

with 2.4 million units of benzathine penicillin given intramuscularly apparently prevents progression to late symptomatic neurosyphilis. Because of this, routine lumbar punctures for examining CSF are not indicated in early syphilis unless the patient is known to have HIV infection. Unfortunately, it has become common practice to avoid lumbar punctures in later stages of syphilis as well. Instead, patients are treated with doses of penicillin thought to be effective for neurosyphilis, if present. As a result, there are few data on the current frequency and course of asymptomatic neurosyphilis.

Some laboratories perform a fluorescent treponemal antibody absorption (FTA-ABS) test (see Serologic Tests and Table 349–2) on CSF. Interest in tests such as this has been prompted by good evidence that patients with untreated neurosyphilis may have a nonreactive VDRL test result for CSF. Reports were published of positive FTA-ABS test results for the CSF of patients with otherwise normal CSF and for whom there were clinical signs and symptoms compatible with neurosyphilis. However, the CSF FTA-ABS test has not been standardized, and some evidence exists that reactive CSF test results are caused by passive transfer of serum antibody into CSF. Although a nonreactive CSF FTA-ABS may be useful to rule out the diagnosis, no diagnosis of asymptomatic (or symptomatic) neurosyphilis should be based solely on the CSF FTA-ABS test (see Table 349–2 and Serologic Tests).

Syphilitic Meningitis. An acute to subacute, aseptic meningitis may occur at any time after the primary stage but usually within the first year of infection. It frequently involves the base of the brain and may result in unilateral or bilateral cranial nerve palsies. In about 10% of cases, the onset of meningitis coincides with the rash of secondary syphilis. The CSF shows a lymphocytic pleocytosis with increased protein and usually normal glucose concentrations. The CSF-VDRL test is nearly always reactive. Rarely, the CSF glucose concentration is decreased. Without treatment, syphilitic meningitis usually resolves, following the course of other manifestations of early syphilis. This syndrome can mimic tuberculous or fungal meningitis or nonpurulent meningitis of various causes.

Meningovascular Syphilis. Some patients have sufficient endarteritis and perivascular inflammation to result in cerebrovascular thrombosis and infarction. This usually occurs 5 to 10 years after the initial infection and is more common in men. Patients often have associated aseptic meningitis. Most cerebrovascular accidents are not caused by syphilitic arteritis, even in patients with a reactive serologic test result for syphilis. However, syphilis should be considered as the cause in young patients with a history of syphilis and without other causes for cerebrovascular accidents.

Tabes Dorsalis. Tabes dorsalis is a slowly progressive, degenerative disease involving the posterior columns and posterior roots of the spinal cord, resulting in progressive loss of peripheral reflexes, impairment of vibration and position sense, and progressive ataxia. There may be chronic destructive changes in the large joints of the affected limbs in far-advanced cases (i.e., Charcot's joints). Incontinence of the bladder and impotence are common. Sudden and severely painful crises of uncertain origin are a characteristic part of the syndrome. These features most typically involve the lower extremities but may occur at any site. Severe, sharp abdominal pains may lead to ex-

Continued

ploratory surgery. These attacks may be triggered by exposure to cold or other stresses or may arise with no obvious precipitating cause.

Optic atrophy is seen in 20% of cases. The pupils are abnormal in 90% of cases; they are bilaterally small and fail to constrict further in response to light but do constrict normally to accommodation (i.e., Argyll Robertson pupils).

The cause of tabes dorsalis is unclear. Spirochetes cannot be demonstrated in the posterior column or dorsal root.

Onset of the disease is usually delayed and often first noticed 20 to 30 years after the initial infection. It is thought to be more common in whites and in men. Typical cases of patients presenting with lightning pains, ataxia, Argyll Robertson pupils, absent deep tendon reflexes, and loss of posterior column function are easy to diagnose. Atypical cases may be more troublesome, particularly because the VDRL test result for the serum is normal in as many as 30 to 40% of patients, and 10 to 20% of patients (even before the advent of penicillin) have normal CSF-VDRL results. The FTA-ABS test for serum is nearly always reactive.

Treatment is unsatisfactory. Penicillin usually arrests progression but does not reverse the symptoms. Carbamazepine in doses of 400 to 800 mg/day has been reported to effectively treat the lightning pains.

Tabes dorsalis is thought to be uncommon, although a survey of newly diagnosed late syphilis cases in Denmark between 1961 and 1970 showed that approximately 10% of all persons with late syphilis and 40% of all persons with clinical neurosyphilis had evidence of tabes dorsalis.

General Paresis. This form of neurosyphilis is a chronic meningoencephalitis resulting in gradually progressive loss of cortical function. It typically occurs 10 to 20 years after the initial infection. Pathologically, there is a perivascular and meningeal chronic inflammatory reaction with thickening of the meninges, granular ependymitis, degeneration of the cortical parenchyma, and abundant spirochetes in the tissues.

The most devastating effect of general paresis is on the mind. With effective penicillin therapy, this disease has become much less common; in the United States, first admissions to mental hospitals because of syphilitic psychosis declined from 7694 in 1940 to 154 in 1968, the last year for which definite figures are available.

In its early stages, general paresis results in nonspecific symptoms such as irritability, fatigability, headaches, forgetfulness, and personality changes. Later, there is impaired memory, defective judgment, lack of insight, confusion, and often depression or marked elation. The patients may be delusional, and seizures sometimes occur. There may also be loss of other cortical functions, including paralysis or aphasia.

Physical signs are primarily those of the altered mental status. Cranial nerve palsies are uncommon. Optic atrophy is rare. The complete Argyll Robertson pupil is also uncommon, but irregular or otherwise abnormal pupils are not infrequent. Peripheral reflexes are often somewhat increased.

The CSF is nearly always abnormal, with lymphocytic pleocytosis and an increased total protein concentration. The VDRL test is usually reactive for CSF and serum. The disease responds well to penicillin therapy if administered early, although as many as one third of treated patients may develop progressive neurologic decline in later years. Fever therapy induced with malaria was formerly an effective adjunct to treatment with arsenicals, but it has been abandoned.

Even though classic general paresis is now infrequent, it remains reasonable to suspect syphilis as the cause of undiagnosed neurologic illness.

Syphilis-HIV Interactions. Syphilis and HIV infection interact on multiple levels. Clinicians evaluating patients with newly diagnosed syphilis should consider whether coexistent HIV infection is present and how the two diseases may be interacting. Clinicians seeing patients with newly diagnosed HIV should be attuned to the possible existence of previously undiagnosed syphilis.

Syphilis, like other genital ulcer diseases, is associated with a three-fold to five-fold increased risk for HIV acquisition. Presumably, genital ulcers act as portals of entry through which HIV may more readily infect exposed individuals. In individuals with HIV infec-

tion who acquire syphilis, the natural history of the infection may be modified. HIV-infected syphilis patients are somewhat more likely to present with secondary syphilis than are non–HIV-infected patients. HIV-infected, secondary syphilis patients are more likely to have coexistent chancres than are HIV-negative, secondary syphilis patients, suggesting that the healing of chancres is delayed or the appearance of secondary manifestations is accelerated in the presence of HIV co-infection.

Several reports have suggested that neurosyphilis may be more common in patients with HIV infection; however, no large or carefully controlled studies document this association. In HIV-infected syphilis patients in whom therapy fails, neurosyphilis may be a more common presenting feature than in patients without HIV infection.

Most experts agree that failure of treatment using currently recommended regimens for syphilis therapy is more common in patients with coexistent HIV infection. The magnitude of this increase, however, is small, and as a result, alternate treatment regimens are not recommended. Rather, closer and longer follow-up is suggested to permit early detection of treatment failure and to help prevent disease progression or transmission of infection to others.

CONGENITAL SYPHILIS. Congenital syphilis results from transplacental, hematogenous spread of syphilis from the mother to the fetus. The incidence of congenital syphilis diagnoses in the United States fell below 1000 per year for the first time in 1975, and fewer than 500 cases occurred per year until 1988, when the epidemic of syphilis in adults led to similar epidemic increases in congenital infections. From 1990 through 1993, more than 3000 new cases of congenital syphilis were reported each year. Each case of congenital syphilis represents a tragedy that could have been prevented by better case reporting and by proper prenatal care. A VDRL test should be obtained in all expectant mothers at the beginning and near the end of pregnancy.

Spirochetes can be found in abortuses of as little as 9 to 10 weeks' gestation. The risk of fetal infection is greatest in the early stages of untreated maternal syphilis and declines slowly thereafter, but the mother may infect her fetus during at least the first 5 years of her infection. Adequate treatment of the mother before the 16th week of pregnancy usually prevents clinical illness in the neonate. Later treatment may not prevent late sequelae of the disease in the child. Untreated maternal infection may result in stillbirth, neonatal death, prematurity, or syndromes of early or late congenital syphilis among surviving infants.

Manifestations of early congenital syphilis are often seen in the perinatal period but may not develop until the infant has been discharged from the hospital. The disease resembles secondary syphilis of the adult except that the rash may be vesicular or bullous, which is rare in adults. The child often has rhinitis, hepatosplenomegaly, hemolytic anemia, jaundice, and pseudoparalysis (i.e., immobility of one or more extremities) resulting from painful osteochondritis. There may be thrombocytopenia and leukocytosis. The early stages of congenital syphilis must be differentiated from congenital rubella, cytomegalovirus infection, toxoplasmosis, bacterial sepsis, and other diseases.

Late congenital syphilis is defined as congenital syphilis of more than 2 years' duration. The disease may remain latent with no manifestation of late damage. Cardiovascular alterations have not been observed in patients with congenital syphilis. Neurologic manifestations are common, and there may be eighth cranial nerve deafness and interstitial keratitis. The latter occurs in more than 10% of patients but may not be apparent until the 10th year of life or later. Periostitis may result in prominent frontal bones, depression of the bridge of the nose (i.e., saddle nose), poor development of the maxilla, and anterior bowing of the tibias (i.e., saber shins). There may be late-onset arthritis of the knees (i.e., Clutton's joints). The permanent dentition may show characteristic abnormalities known as Hutchinson's teeth; the upper central incisors are widely spaced, centrally notched, and tapered in the manner of a screwdriver. The molars may show multiple, poorly developed cusps (i.e., mulberry molars). Some of the late manifestations such as interstitial keratitis and Clutton's joints may be caused by hypersensitivity responses and are benefited by corticosteroids in some cases.

part XVI

Metabolic Diseases

211 THE HYPERLIPOPROTEINEMIAS

Joseph L. Witztum
Daniel Steinberg

Hyperlipidemia, abnormal elevation of plasma cholesterol and/or triglyceride levels, is one of the most common clinical problems that confronts the physician in daily practice. Much attention has been focused on these disorders because there is a strong association of hyperlipidemia—especially hypercholesterolemia—with development of atherosclerosis, and of hypertriglyceridemia with pancreatitis. Hyperlipidemia may occur because of a primary genetic disorder or as a result of environmental influences secondary to other medical conditions, or any combination of these factors. Because lipids are transported in plasma as components of lipoprotein complexes, understanding lipoprotein physiology is necessary for informed diagnosis and therapeutic planning.

PHYSIOLOGY OF LIPOPROTEIN TRANSPORT

Lipoproteins are complex macromolecules that transport nonpolar lipids through the aqueous environment of plasma. The more nonpolar lipids—triglycerides and cholesteryl esters—are carried almost exclusively in the central core of the spherical lipoprotein particles. The more polar lipids (such as phospholipids and free cholesterol), together with amphipathic apolipoproteins, form a surface monolayer that serves to "solubilize" the particles and allows them to remain in stable solution in the aqueous plasma.

Each lipoprotein particle contains on its surface one or more apolipoproteins that have a variety of functional and structural roles. Some apolipoproteins provide structural stability to the lipoprotein, serve as ligands for cellular lipoprotein receptors that help determine the metabolic fate of individual particles, and act as cofactors for plasma enzymes involved in plasma lipid and lipoprotein metabolism. Other apolipoproteins play several roles; for example, apolipoprotein B (apo B) is the major structural apolipoprotein of the triglyceride-rich lipoproteins secreted by the liver (very low density lipoproteins [VLDL]), but it also serves as the ligand for binding of low-density lipoproteins (LDL) (formed from VLDL) to cellular LDL receptors. Table 211–1 lists major apoproteins, lipoproteins on which they reside, and known or postulated functions.

The most widely used classification of lipoproteins is based on their different densities, which determine their behavior during preparative equilibrium ultracentrifugation. The fact that lipoprotein particles exist as relatively discrete species when separated this way led to the currently used density classification system outlined in Table 211–2. A second classification system originally proposed many years ago assigns priority to the apoprotein content of the lipoproteins. For example, in the high-density lipoprotein (HDL) density class, there are lipoprotein particles that contain mainly apo A-I and others that contain both apo A-I and apo A-II; these are designated LpA-I and LpA-I, A-II, respectively. Current research suggests that it is primarily LpA-I that confers the antiatherogenic properties of HDL. Thus, in the future, full evaluation may include this type of analysis, but for now more research is needed to determine its clinical value.

An older classification system of the lipoproteins, based on their electrophoretic patterns (lipoprotein pattern typing), while important historically for the development of our understanding of lipid transport disorders, is not used commonly today. However, for the sake of completeness, the electrophoretic mobility of each lipoprotein class is also given in Table 211–2.

SYNTHESIS AND TRANSPORT OF ENDOGENOUS LIPIDS. The endogenous lipid transport system can be divided into two major classes: the apo B-100 lipoprotein system (VLDL, intermediate-density lipoproteins [IDL], and LDL) and the apo A-I lipoprotein system (HDL).

Metabolism of VLDL. Between meals, free fatty acids are mobilized from the adipose tissue and serve as a major source for hepatic triglyceride synthesis. Lipogenesis, the synthesis of fatty acids de novo from carbohydrate or protein, also can occur in the liver. Fatty acids can either enter mitochondria (where β-oxidation occurs) or they can undergo esterification to form triglycerides in the cytosol. Control of triglyceride synthesis is a complex process that appears to be regulated in part by changes in insulin and glucagon that occur with feeding. Glucagon enhances fatty acid oxidation, whereas insulin inhibits it. In addition, insulin may induce lipogenic enzymes in the liver. Triglycerides, together with cholesterol synthesized de novo in the liver or delivered to the liver by chylomicron remnants, are packaged together with apo B and phospholipids and form a nascent VLDL (Fig. 211–1).

The details of the packaging process are still being worked out, but it is known that a microsomal triglyceride transfer protein (MTP) is essential for normal VLDL assembly and secretion from the hepatocyte. When mutations in MTP occur, the newly synthesized apo B is not lipidated within the lumen of the endoplasmic reticulum, and as a result the apo B is degraded, leading to abetalipoproteinemia, even though the apo B gene is normal. This results in a serious clinical syndrome in which patients lack any apo B-containing lipoproteins in their plasma. However, partial inhibition of MTP activity by drugs might be an effective way to decrease VLDL secretion.

Plasma VLDL also contains other apolipoproteins, including the C apoproteins and apo E. Apo B is found as a full-length protein termed *apo B-100* (or *apo B*), which is made by the liver, or as a shortened form termed *apo B-48*, which is made in humans only by the intestine. Apo B is an obligatory component for nascent VLDL assembly and secretion from the hepatocyte; other apoproteins are added to VLDL after their entry into plasma. The size of the VLDL particle released depends on the availability of triglycerides in the liver. Very large triglyceride-rich VLDLs are secreted when excess hepatic triglyceride synthesis is occurring, as in cases of obesity, non-insulin dependent diabetes, and excess alcohol consumption. In contrast, small VLDLs are secreted when the availability of triglyceride, but not cholesterol,

Table 211–1 • APOLIPOPROTEIN CHARACTERISTICS

APOPROTEIN	LIPOPROTEINS	FUNCTION
Apo B-100	VLDL, IDL, LDL	Secretion of VLDL from liver. Structural protein of VLDL IDL, and LDL. Ligand for the LDL receptor
Apo B-48	Chylomicrons, remnants	Secretion of chylomicrons from intestine
Apo E	Chylomicrons, VLDL, IDL, HDL	Ligand for binding of IDL and remnants to LDL receptor and LRP
Apo A-I	HDL, chylomicrons	Structural protein of HDL Activator of LCAT
Apo A-II	HDL, chylomicrons	Unknown
Apo C-II	Chylomicrons, VLDL, IDL, HDL	Activator of LPL
Apo C-III	Chylomicrons, VLDL, IDL, HDL	Inhibitor of LPL activity

HDL = high-density lipoprotein; IDL = intermediate-density lipoprotein; LCAT = lecithin cholesterol acyl transferase; LDL = low-density lipoprotein; LPL = lipoprotein lipase; VLDL = very low-density lipoprotein.

Table 211–2 • CHARACTERISTICS OF MAJOR LIPOPROTEIN CLASSES

LIPOPROTEIN CLASS	DENSITY (g/mL)	DIAMETER (nm)	MAJOR LIPID	ELECTROPHORETIC MOBILITY
Chylomicron and remnants	<<1.006	500–80	Dietary triglycerides	Remains at origin
Very low-density lipoprotein	<1.006	80–30	Endogenous triglycerides	Pre-β
Intermediate-density lipoprotein	1.006–1.019	35–25	Cholesteryl esters, triglycerides	Slow pre-β
Low-density lipoprotein	1.019–1.063	25–18	Cholesteryl esters	β
High-density lipoprotein	1.063–1.210	5–12	Cholesteryl esters, phospholipids	α
Lp(a)	1.055–1.085	30	Cholesteryl esters	Slow pre-β

Diagnosis

DARKFIELD EXAMINATION. The most definitive means of making a diagnosis is finding spirochetes of typical morphology and motility in lesions of early acquired or congenital syphilis. The darkfield examination result is often positive in cases of primary syphilis and for the moist mucosal lesions of secondary and congenital syphilis. The result may occasionally be positive for aspirates of lymph nodes in secondary syphilis. Problems arise, however, because of false-negative results in primary syphilis because of application by the patient of soaps or other toxic compounds to the lesions. A single negative result is therefore insufficient to exclude syphilis. Optimally, patients with suspicious lesions but with an initially negative darkfield examination result should be instructed to avoid washing the lesion and to return daily for two successive examinations. In practice, however, for high-risk individuals (e.g., drug users, homosexually active men), it may be more appropriate to treat patients with suspicious lesions presumptively after obtaining serologic tests. Confusion may also arise because of the presence of spirochetes that are morphologically indistinguishable from *T. pallidum* organisms in the mouth, particularly around the gingival margins. For lesions in these areas, diagnosis often depends on clinical appearance, history, and serologic testing.

To perform the darkfield examination, the surface of the suspected ulcerative lesion should be cleaned with saline solution and gauze without producing bleeding. The presence of red blood cells in the specimen makes it difficult to visualize small numbers of *T. pallidum*. Squeezing of the lesion (with gloves on) may help produce serous fluid, which is picked up on a glass slide, covered with a coverslip, and examined with the darkfield microscope. Living *T. pallidum* organisms demonstrate gradual motion to and fro, rotational movement around the long axis, and rather sudden 90-degree bending near the center of the organism. Because most physicians do not have the proper equipment and are not familiar with the techniques of darkfield microscopy, public health authorities can be called for assistance. *T. pallidum* may also be demonstrated in biopsy or pathologic specimens by fluorescent antibody stains or by silver stains.

SEROLOGIC TESTS. Two basic types of serologic tests for humoral antibody are widely used to diagnose infection with *T. pallidum*: (1) nontreponemal tests that detect antibodies reactive with diphosphatidylglycerol (cardiolipin), which is a normal component of many tissues, and (2) specific treponemal antibodies. Nonspecific antibodies against cardiolipin were formerly designated *reagin,* a term that should be discarded to avoid confusion with another reagin, IgE. The kinds of tests used in syphilis are summarized in Table 349–2.

Nontreponemal Tests. Anticardiolipin antibodies were first discovered by Wassermann in 1907, using extracts of congenitally infected syphilitic livers as the antigen for a complement fixation test. Subsequently, it was shown that normal livers contained the same antigen as many other tissues; the antigen for this class of test is now extracted from beef heart. There is no convincing explanation for why patients infected with *T. pallidum* develop increasing titers of antibody against a normal tissue component.

The Wassermann test has been replaced by related tests. The standard test in use today to detect anticardiolipin antibody is the VDRL test, which is an easily quantified slide flocculation test. Many similar tests, including the rapid plasma reagin (RPR) test and the unheated serum reagin (USR) test, are frequently used for screening for syphilis.

The VDRL and related tests are simple, well standardized, and inexpensive and are the screening tests of choice. Because the VDRL and RPR are readily quantified, they are the tests of choice for following the response of patients to treatment. Because the VDRL and RPR detect antibody against a normal tissue component, results may be falsely positive in a significant number of conditions. The relative proportion of patients with a false-positive VDRL results depends on the prevalence of syphilis in the community; the lower the prevalence of syphilis, the higher is the proportion of reactive VDRL test results from nonsyphilitic causes.

The VDRL test begins to turn positive about 1 week after the onset of the chancre. In a large series of patients with primary syphilis, approximately two thirds had a positive VDRL test result. A nonreactive VDRL test does not exclude primary syphilis, particularly if the lesion is less than 1 week old. The VDRL test result is positive for 99% of patients with secondary syphilis. The only exceptions are patients with such high titers of antibody that they are in antibody excess; dilution of the serum then paradoxically results in conversion of a negative test to a positive test result. In patients with

coexistent HIV infection, the serologic responses to syphilis may be modified. In large groups of syphilis patients, nontreponemal test titers tend to be higher than for comparison groups of patients without HIV infection. There are case reports of patients with advanced HIV infection in whom development of a serologic response was delayed or absent and infection could be diagnosed only by biopsy of typical lesions. For most patients with HIV infection, however, serologic tests for syphilis remain useful for diagnosis and management. VDRL reactivity tends to diminish in later stages of the disease, and only about 70% of patients with cardiovascular or neurosyphilis have positive VDRL test results.

The *quantitative titer* of the VDRL or RPR test is somewhat useful in diagnosis and quite useful in following therapeutic response. The titer is reported as the highest dilution that gives a positive response. Most patients with secondary syphilis have titers of at least 1 : 16. Most patients with false-positive VDRL test results have titers of less than 1:8. No single titer is in itself diagnostic. Significant rises (fourfold or greater) in paired sera, however, strongly indicate acute syphilis.

Treponemal Tests. There are many varieties of specific treponemal antibody tests. Among the most widely used is the FTA-ABS test. Patient serum is absorbed with extracts of nonpathogenic cultivable treponemes to remove cross-reacting a group of treponemal antibody. Agglutination of red blood cells to which *T. pallidum* antigens have been fixed is the basis of the microhemagglutination assay for *T. pallidum* (i.e., MHA-TP test).

The precise nature of the antigens involved in these tests is not known. Characterization of the antigens of *T. pallidum* has been greatly hindered by the inability to grow the organism in cell-free culture. Recent success in cloning *T. pallidum* antigens into *Escherichia coli* may circumvent this problem. Antibodies reactive in the various tests are found in all major immunoglobulin classes (e.g., IgG, IgM, IgA). A modification of the FTA-ABS test has been developed using fluorescein-labeled anti-human IgM (IgM FTA-ABS). The IgM FTA-ABS test is of some use in the diagnosis of early congenital syphilis but is of no use in distinguishing acute disease from old infections in adults.

The FTA-ABS test is best used as a confirmatory test. It is somewhat more difficult to perform than the VDRL test and cannot be easily quantified. It is sensitive and has a high degree of specificity, being reactive in only approximately 1% of normal individuals. It is reactive in 85% of patients with primary syphilis, 99% with secondary syphilis, and at least 95% with late syphilis. It may therefore be the only test with a positive result for patients with cardiovascular or neurologic syphilis. For patients with late syphilis, the FTA-ABS test often remains reactive for life despite adequate therapy. It (and the MHA-TP test) is positive in other treponemal diseases, such as pinta, yaws, and endemic syphilis (formerly bejel) (Chapter 350).

The FTA-ABS test is reported in terms of relative brilliance of fluorescence, from borderline to 4+. Borderline reactivity has the same meaning as nonreactive for clinical purposes. Most laboratories report 1+ positive results as borderline because some studies have shown that such tests may be difficult to reproduce. Most laboratories therefore report as positive only tests with 2+ or greater reactivity. For patients lacking historical or clinical evidence of syphilis but with a reactive FTA-ABS test result, the FTA-ABS test should be repeated. Use of another treponemal test such as the MHA-TP test may be helpful in problem cases.

The MHA-TP test is less sensitive than the VDRL or the FTA-ABS test in primary syphilis. Its sensitivity and specificity otherwise are nearly identical to those of the FTA-ABS test, being reactive in nearly all patients with secondary syphilis and in more than 95% of patients with late syphilis. The reactivity of serologic tests for syphilis in various stages of disease is shown in Table 349–3.

Table 349–3 • FREQUENCY OF POSITIVE SEROLOGIC TESTS IN UNTREATED SYPHILIS

STAGE	VDRL (%)	FTA-ABS (%)	MHA-TP (%)
Primary	70	85	50–60
Secondary	99	100	100
Latent or late	70	98	98

FTA-ABS = fluorescent treponemal antibody absorption test; MHA-TP = microhemagglutination assay for *Treponema pallidum*; VDRL = Venereal Disease Research Laboratories test.

Table 349–4 • PENICILLIN TREATMENT PRACTICE FOR SYPHILIS AS RECOMMENDED BY UNITED STATES PUBLIC HEALTH SERVICE

INDICATIONS FOR SYPHILIS THERAPY[†]	DOSAGE AND ADMINISTRATION*	
	Benzathine Penicillin G	Aqueous Benzyl Penicillin G or Procaine Penicillin G
Primary, secondary, and early latent syphilis (<1 year); epidemiologic treatment	Total of 2.4 million units; single IM dose of two injections of 1.2 million units in one session	Total of 4.8 million units IM in doses of 600,000 units daily for 8 consecutive days
Late latent (>1 year) or when CSF was not examined in "latency"; cardiovascular syphilis, late benign (cutaneous, osseous, visceral gumma)	Total of 7.2 million units IM in doses of 2.4 million units at 7-day intervals, over 21 days	Total of 9 million units IM in doses of 600,000 units daily over 15 days
Symptomatic or asymptomatic neurosyphilis	2 to 4 million units of aqueous (crystalline) penicillin G IV every 4 hours for at least 10 days	2 to 4 million units procaine penicillin IM daily and probenecid, 500 mg orally four times daily for 10–14 days
Congenital Infants	CSF normal: Total of 500,000 units/kg IM in a single or divided dose at one session	CSF abnormal: Total of 50,000 units/kg IM per day for 10 consecutive days[‡]
Older children	CSF normal: Same as for early congenital syphilis, up to 2.4 million units	CSF abnormal: 200,000–300,000 units/kg/day IV aqueous crystalline penicillin for 10–14 days

CSF = cerebrospinal fluid.
*Individual doses can be divided for injection in each buttock to minimize discomfort.
[†]In *pregnancy*, treatment depends on the stage of syphilis.
[‡]For aqueous penicillin, give in two divided IV doses per day; for procaine penicillin, give as one daily dose IM.

FALSE-POSITIVE SEROLOGIC TEST RESULTS FOR SYPHILIS. The VDRL or RPR test may be reactive in a variety of diseases other than syphilis. A false-positive result is defined as a reproducible positive test in a patient with no clinical or historical evidence of syphilis and whose serum FTA-ABS or MHA-TP test result is negative.

Acute (<6 months) false-positive VDRL test results occur with low frequency in atypical pneumonia, malaria, and other bacterial or viral infections and may occur after smallpox or other vaccinations as well. Chronic false-positive VDRL tests (>6 months) are relatively common in autoimmune disorders such as SLE, in parenteral drug users, in HIV infection, in leprosy, and in aged persons. Between 8 and 20% of patients with SLE have false-positive VDRL test results, and the false-positive result may develop many years before the onset of other manifestations of the disease. A chronic false-positive VDRL test result for female patients 20 years old or younger carries a significant risk of future development of SLE, thyroiditis, or other autoimmune disorders, and such patients should be followed carefully for a considerable period of time. As many as one third of parenteral drug users have false-positive VDRL test results. More than 1% of patients 70 years old and 10% of patients older than 80 years have low-titer, false-positive VDRL test results. Most false-positive VDRL tests have a titer of less than 1:8, although a few patients with lymphoma and other diseases have been described with very-high-titer, false-positive VDRL test results.

A reactive FTA-ABS result is usually indicative of recent or past syphilis. However, there is an increased incidence of false-positive FTA-ABS results in SLE and in other chronic inflammatory diseases associated with hyperglobulinemia, including rheumatoid arthritis, biliary cirrhosis, and others.

Occasionally, reproducible positive FTA-ABS results are obtained for patients with no clinical or historical evidence of syphilis and in whom there is no evidence of diseases associated with false-positive FTA-ABS results. It may be wise to obtain CSF for examination of total protein, cells, and VDRL reactivity to rule out neurosyphilis. If in doubt and if the patient is not allergic to penicillin, it is often prudent to treat such patients for possible syphilis.

IgM FTA-ABS TEST FOR CONGENITAL SYPHILIS. Mothers with a reactive VDRL or FTA-ABS test result are delivered of infants with a reactive VDRL or FTA-ABS result because of passive transfer of the IgG antibodies that are reactive in these tests. Because many infants with congenital syphilis are clinically normal at birth but develop serious, symptomatic disease some weeks later, it is important to determine whether a newborn with a reactive VDRL or FTA-ABS test result has passively transferred maternal antibody or is actively infected. Because maternal IgM antibodies are not passively transferred to the fetus, an IgM FTA-ABS test has been developed to detect syphilis in the newborn. Unfortunately, there is an approximately 35% incidence of false-negative IgM FTA-ABS test results for cases of delayed-onset congenital syphilis, and there is a false-positive rate of approximately 10%. For these reasons, the IgM FTA-ABS test is of limited use for diagnosing neonatal syphilis.

If the mother has been adequately treated for syphilis during pregnancy and the infant is clinically normal at birth, the physician may elect to follow the infant carefully by serial examinations and VDRL titers. If the reactive VDRL result for the infant is caused by passively transferred maternal antibody, the titer of reactivity falls markedly in the first 2 months of life. A rising titer indicates active disease and the need for treatment. Many physicians are unwilling to risk failure of proper follow-up of VDRL-positive but clinically normal neonates and instead administer effective therapy immediately. The risk of penicillin allergy in neonates is very low.

Rx Treatment

T. pallidum is highly susceptible to penicillin; it is inhibited by less than 0.01 µg/mL of penicillin G. Because treponemes divide slowly and because penicillin acts only on dividing cells, it is necessary to maintain serum levels of penicillin for many days. Studies in animals and in humans show that more therapy is required as the length of infection increases. The recommendations for treatment of syphilis are summarized in Table 349–4.

EARLY INFECTIOUS SYPHILIS. Early syphilis (<1 year) may be treated with a single injection of 2.4 million units of benzathine penicillin G, which provides low but effective serum levels for more than 2 weeks. Extensive studies in the 1940s and 1950s with regimens that provided similar serum levels and duration of therapy showed that approximately 95% of patients were cured by such treatment. Some of the remaining 5% who had clinical or serologic evidence of relapse may have been reinfected. It is not necessary to examine the CSF at this stage because penicillin prevents development of later neurosyphilis. Motile treponemes disappear from primary lesions in 24 hours after treatment.

A single injection of 2.4 million units of aqueous procaine penicillin, which provides relatively high serum levels for a brief period, is ineffective in established early syphilis but is curative if the disease is still in the incubating stage. The ceftriaxone regimen useful for gonorrhea probably is curative for incubating syphilis, but data are few, and careful follow-up is indicated if there is reason to suspect exposure to syphilis in a patient treated for gonorrhea with ceftriaxone. The incidence of incubating syphilis in gonorrhea patients is 2% or more in several older series.

For patients allergic to penicillin, 100 mg of doxycycline, given twice daily for 14 days, is recommended. Particularly careful follow-up is necessary for patients treated with drugs other than penicillin, because patients may not be fully compliant with these prolonged courses of oral therapy and these regimens have been less fully evaluated clinically. Azithromycin, given as a single dose of 2.0 g, and ceftriaxone, with 2 g given intramuscularly daily for 10 days, may be effective, but these agents have not been well studied. Spectinomycin and quinolone antibiotics have essentially no effect on syphilis. Erythromycin is of questionable efficacy.

SYPHILIS OF MORE THAN 1 YEAR'S DURATION. Larger doses of penicillin are recommended for neurosyphilis (Chapter 474) than for syphilis of less than 1 year's duration. Patients with general paresis usually respond better to treatment than patients with tabes dorsalis, although patients with paresis should be expected to show residual effects of the infection. This is particularly true in advanced cases. Meningovascular syphilis usually responds well, except for residual damage resulting from ischemic infarcts. Published studies show that a total of 6.0 to 9.0 million units of penicillin G results in a satisfactory clinical response in approximately 90% of patients with neurosyphilis who do not have HIV infection.

Benzathine penicillin regimens for neurosyphilis have received relatively little study but were previously recommended. Benzathine penicillin does not provide measurable levels of penicillin in the CSF or aqueous humor of the eye. There are anecdotal reports of increased treatment failures in patients with concomitant HIV infection, and there is considerable rationale to treat with intravenous penicillin G (20 million units/day for at least 10 days). Therapy for neurosyphilis can result in increased CSF pleocytosis for 7 to 10 days after starting treatment and may transiently convert a normal CSF to abnormal.

Limited evidence suggests that treating latent syphilis with a total dose of 7.2 million units of benzathine penicillin (administered as three successive weekly injections of 2.4 million units) is curative, even if the patient has asymptomatic neurosyphilis. However, because of the possible lack of the efficacy of benzathine penicillin in some patients with CNS syphilis, it is preferable to examine CSF in patients with latent syphilis to exclude asymptomatic neurosyphilis. This is particularly important for HIV positive patients. Alternatively, a lumbar puncture may be performed at the conclusion of the follow-up period (2 years); if the CSF is normal, the patient can be reassured that neurosyphilis will not develop.

There is no evidence that therapy with antimicrobial drugs is clinically beneficial to patients with cardiovascular syphilis. Nevertheless, treatment of cardiovascular syphilis is recommended to prevent further progression of disease and because approximately 15% of patients with cardiovascular syphilis have associated neurosyphilis.

There is no evidence regarding the efficacy of other antimicrobial agents in the treatment of later syphilis. If patients are allergic to penicillin, it is mandatory that the CSF be examined before therapy is undertaken. Tetracycline or doxycycline taken for 4 weeks is probably effective.

SYPHILIS IN PREGNANCY. All pregnant women should be examined with a VDRL or RPR test during pregnancy, and if they are at high risk for syphilis, a second test should be obtained before delivery. Because of the risk to the fetus, evaluation and treatment of the VDRL-positive patient should be done as rapidly as possible, particularly for patients first seen in the later stages of pregnancy. If a confirmatory FTA-ABS test is positive and the patient has not been treated, penicillin should be administered in doses appropriate for early or late syphilis, as outlined earlier. Penicillin-allergic patients should not be treated with tetracycline or erythromycin because of toxicity (tetracycline) or lack of efficacy (erythromycin). Penicillin desensitization may be considered but also carries risks. For patients who are VDRL positive but FTA-ABS negative and who have no clinical signs of syphilis, treatment may be withheld. For such patients, a quantitative VDRL test and another FTA-ABS test should be repeated in 4 weeks. If the VDRL titer has risen by four-fold or more or if clinical signs of syphilis have developed, the patient should be treated. If after repeat examination the diagnosis remains equivocal, the patient should be treated to prevent possible disease in the neonate. After treatment, a quantitative VDRL titer should be followed monthly; if it rises four-fold, the patient should be treated a second time.

CONGENITAL SYPHILIS. Proper treatment of the mother usually prevents active congenital syphilis in the neonate. However, infected infants may be clinically normal at birth, and the infant may be seronegative if the mother's infection was acquired late in pregnancy. The infant should be treated at birth if the mother has received no or inadequate treatment or has been treated with drugs other than penicillin, if the mother has not yet responded to possibly effective therapy, or if the infant cannot be carefully followed for several months after birth. The CSF should be examined before the infant is treated. If the CSF is normal, the mother may be treated with a single injection of 50,000 U/kg of benzathine penicillin G. If the CSF is abnormal, she should be treated with 50,000 U/kg of aqueous penicillin G, given intramuscularly or intravenously twice daily for a minimum of 10 days. Alternatively, a single daily intramuscular injection of 50,000 U/kg of procaine penicillin may be given for 10 days. These recommendations are based on the failure of benzathine penicillin to provide adequate treponemicidal levels in CSF and on evidence that aqueous or procaine penicillin does provide adequate CSF levels of penicillin. Many experts believe that all syphilis in infected infants should be treated with procaine or aqueous penicillin to ensure adequate CSF levels. Tetracycline should not be used to treat children younger than 8 years. Antimicrobial agents other than penicillin are not recommended for treating congenital syphilis.

FOLLOW-UP EXAMINATIONS. All HIV-seronegative patients with early syphilis or congenital syphilis should return for quantitative VDRL titers and clinical examination 6 and 12 months after treatment. Treatment failure is somewhat more common in patients with HIV infection, and although more aggressive therapy is usually not required, more aggressive follow-up is suggested. Serologic tests should be repeated at 1, 2, 3, 6, 9, and 12 months. Patients with late latent syphilis should be examined also at 24 months after therapy; if CSF was not examined before therapy, a lumbar puncture should be done before discharge to rule out inadequately treated asymptomatic neurosyphilis.

In about 85% of patients with early (i.e., primary, secondary, or early latent) syphilis, quantitative VDRL titers become nonreactive in 12 to 24 months after therapy. Prolonged reactive VDRL test results are associated with higher initial VDRL titers, prolonged infection, more advanced stage (primary < secondary < early latent), or repeated infection. In a small percentage of patients with early syphilis, the VDRL result remains reactive in low titers for long periods. Chronic, low-titer VDRL reactivity after therapy is much more common in cases of late syphilis and should not be viewed with alarm. The FTA-ABS test may remain positive for years despite adequate therapy. A four-fold or greater rise of VDRL titer after therapy is sufficient evidence for repeat treatment. Patients with treated early syphilis are susceptible to reinfection, and many clinical and serologic relapses after therapy are probably reinfections. As such, they represent failures of proper epidemiologic case finding and of preventive therapy of the patient's sexual contacts.

Patients with neurosyphilis should be followed with serologic tests for at least 3 years and with repeat examinations of CSF at 6-month intervals. CSF pleocytosis is the first abnormality to disappear, but cell counts may not be normal for 1 to 2 years. The elevated CSF protein level falls more slowly, followed by a change in the positive CSF-VDRL test, which may take years to become negative. It is not known whether high-dose intravenous penicillin therapy accelerates the return of CSF to normal. Rising CSF cell counts, protein, and VDRL titer obtained at follow-up are an indication for repeat treatment.

EPIDEMIOLOGIC INVESTIGATION AND TREATMENT. All patients with syphilis should be reported to public health authorities. In the absence of an effective vaccine, control of syphilis depends on finding and treating persons with infectious lesions of primary and secondary syphilis before they can further transmit the disease and on finding and treating persons with incubating syphilis before they develop infectious lesions. All patients with early syphilis (<1 year) should be carefully interviewed by qualified persons to determine the nature of their recent sex contacts. Approximately 16% of the named recent contacts of patients with early syphilis are found to have active, untreated syphilis on examination, and a similar proportion of individuals named as suspects or associates also have active syphilis.

Most authorities, particularly in the United States, recommend treating sexual contacts of patients with early syphilis even if the contacts are clinically and serologically normal on examination. This is justifiable, because 30% of clinically normal individuals named as contacts of persons with infectious lesions of syphilis within the previous 30 days go on to develop syphilis if untreated. In general, preventive treatment is given to all sexual contacts of the past 90 days, although nearly all cases of syphilis in contacts develop within 60 days of exposure.

JARISCH-HERXHEIMER REACTIONS. Up to 60% of patients with early syphilis and a significant proportion of patients with later stages of

Continued

syphilis experience a transient febrile reaction after therapy for syphilis. This usually occurs in the first few hours after therapy, peaks at 6 to 8 hours, and disappears within 12 to 24 hours of therapy. Temperature elevation is usually low grade, and there is often associated myalgia, headache, and malaise. The skin lesions of secondary syphilis are often exacerbated during the Herxheimer reaction, and cutaneous lesions that were not visible may become visible. It is usually of no clinical significance and may be treated with salicylates in most cases. In patients with syphilis of the coronary ostia or of the optic nerve, there is a theoretical risk that local inflammation coincident with the Herxheimer reaction could precipitate serious damage. This is the subject of much discussion in the older literature, but there is little current evidence that "local Herxheimer reactions" constitute a significant risk to the patient. Corticosteroids have been used to prevent adverse effects of the Herxheimer reaction, but there is no evidence that they are clinically beneficial (other than reducing fever) or necessary. Institution of treatment with small doses of penicillin does not prevent the Herxheimer reaction.

The pathogenesis of the Herxheimer reaction is unclear. It may be caused by liberation of antigens from the spirochetes. There is evidence that the complement cascade (Chapter 45) is activated, including transient consumption of C3, C4, C6, and C7, and of transient decrease in treponemal antibodies coincident with the Herxheimer reaction. There is also evidence for endotoxemia, obtained by positive limulus amebocyte gelatin tests, at the time of the Herxheimer reaction, although *T. pallidum* does not contain biologically active endotoxin. These seemingly contradictory observations could be explained if the reaction resulted in release of endogenous endotoxin from the gut.

PERSISTENCE OF TREPONEMES AFTER TREATMENT. Studies of syphilis in humans and in rabbits have shown that spiral forms of the organism may be visualized by silver stains in lymph nodes after effective treatment. Living, virulent treponemes have occasionally been recovered by rabbit inoculation from lymph nodes, CSF, or ocular fluids after effective treatment has been given. These documented cases of treponemal persistence are rare, and there is little reason to worry about persistence of virulent treponemes after therapy with penicillin, with the possible exception of CNS syphilis, which needs further evaluation. No evidence exists for selection of penicillin-resistant mutants of *T. pallidum*.

Prevention

Solid immunity develops in rabbits after prolonged infection with virulent *T. pallidum*. It has not yet been possible to transfer immunity passively in laboratory animals by immune serum or immune lymphocytes alone, suggesting that both cellular and humoral systems are necessary for immunity. Rabbits have been effectively immunized with multiple injections of treponemes that have been rendered avirulent by irradiation or by exposure to cold. However, a very large number of injections and a large mass of treponemes are necessary to effect immunity in the laboratory animal. For this reason and because *T. pallidum* cannot yet be grown in a virulent state in cell-free medium, there is no immediate prospect for a vaccine. However, significant immunity does develop in humans after prolonged infection. Control currently depends entirely on clinical awareness on the part of physicians, adequate reporting to public health authorities, and vigorous application of epidemiologic investigation and preventive treatment of sexual contacts.

SUGGESTED READINGS

Cox DL, Chang P, McDowell A, Radolf JD: The outer membrane, not a coat of host proteins, limits the antigenicity of virulent *Treponema pallidum*. Infect Immun 1992;60:1076–1083. *Data regarding the causative agent of syphilis and the reasons humoral antibody does not control or prevent infection.*

Hook EW 3rd, Marra CM: Acquired syphilis in adults. N Engl J Med 1992;326:1060–1069. *A review of syphilis in the 1990s, including syphilis-HIV interactions.*

Kassutto S, Sax PE: HIV and syphilis coinfection: Trends and interactions. AIDS Clin Care 2003;15:9–15. *A review of this frequent problem.*

Macaron NC, Cohen C, Chen SC, et al: Cutaneous lesions of secondary syphilis are highly angiogenic. J Am Acad Dermatol 2003;48:878–881. *There is increased angiogenesis in secondary syphilis, perhaps due to vascular endothelial growth factor and epidermal growth factor.*

Rolfs RT, Joesoef MR, Hendershot EF, et al: A randomized trial of enhanced therapy for early syphilis in patients with and without human immunodeficiency virus infection. N Engl J Med 1997;337:307–314. *The addition of amoxicillin and probenecid to benzathine penicillin did not provide incremental benefit.*

350 NONSYPHILITIC TREPONEMATOSES

Edward W. Hook III

Definition

The nonsyphilitic treponematoses (yaws, endemic syphilis [previously known as bejel], and pinta) are the spirochetal diseases caused by *Treponema pallidum* subspecies (yaws and endemic syphilis) or a closely related organism, *T. carateum* (pinta). Like syphilis, the nonsyphilitic treponematoses are usually transmitted through direct contact with an infectious cutaneous or mucosal lesion. The natural history of the nonsyphilitic treponematoses is likewise similar to syphilis. Primary nodular or ulcerative lesions typically develop at sites of inoculation after an incubation period of several weeks. Untreated primary lesions serve as a source for local spread through scratching or for hematogenous dissemination, which gives rise to the secondary stage of infection characterized by development of widespread manifestations involving skin, lymph nodes, and bone or cartilage. Without therapy the primary and secondary manifestations of infections resolve and the infection becomes latent, although periodic recurrent secondary manifestations may occur for several years. Persons with long-standing untreated infections are at risk for late sequelae, which may include bony deformity, destruction of nasal cartilage, or chronic skin changes.

Unlike syphilis, the nonsyphilitic treponematoses are primarily diseases of children, are not congenitally transmitted across the placenta, and do not invade the central nervous system. Treatment with benzathine penicillin G is effective, and the World Health Organization (WHO) has carried out extensive treatment campaigns in endemic areas.

Etiology

Yaws is caused by *Treponema pallidum* subspecies *pertenue*, pinta is caused by *T. carateum*, and endemic syphilis is caused by *T. pallidum* subspecies *endemicum*. The *T. pallidum* subspecies causing nonsyphilitic treponematoses is closely related to *T. pallidum* subspecies *pallidum*, which causes venereal syphilis; there is a high degree of DNA homology, and they share unique, pathogen-restricted antigens. Like *T. pallidum*, these treponemes are spirochetal bacteria with helical structures and measure about 0.2 µm in diameter and 10 µm in length. They are visible by darkfield microscopy but cannot be cultivated for prolonged periods in vitro.

Distribution and Epidemiology

Yaws is prevalent in moist, humid regions including rural areas of tropical Africa, the Americas, southeast Asia, and Oceania. The highest incidence is in children between ages 2 and 5 years. Endemic syphilis occurs in more arid climates including Africa, in eastern Mediterranean countries, on the Arabian peninsula, in Central Asia, and in Australia. Pinta occurs in rural areas of tropical Central and South America and affects mostly older children and adolescents. Humans are the only known carriers of the nonsyphilitic treponematoses. The spirochete enters the skin only after it is broken, as by a scratch or insect bite. Transmission is believed to occur by contacting the skin directly or indirectly by contaminated hands or fomites and is facilitated by conditions of poor personal hygiene and crowding.

Clinical Manifestations

Yaws, the most common nonsyphilitic treponematosis, produces a skin papule at the inoculation site after an incubation period of 3 to 4 weeks. The most common sites are the legs and buttocks. The papule enlarges, ulcerates, and develops a serous crust from which treponemes can be recovered. Regional lymphadenitis may accompany the papule, which will heal spontaneously within 6 months.

A generalized secondary rash will occur before or after the initial lesion heals, and these rashes are also papular and often covered with brown crusts. Relapsing crops of lesions can occur. Papillomas may result, and the plantar surfaces of the feet are involved with hyperkeratotic lesions. Periostitis of long bones leads to tender bones, and fever may be present. Relapsing lesions of early yaws may occur over several years, resulting in chronic ulcerations and destructive gummatous lesions affecting the skin and bones.

Endemic syphilis produces patches on the mucous membranes of the oral cavity and pharynx and can cause split papules at the mucocutaneous junction of the oral angles. Anal, genital, and other intertriginous skin areas can be affected by lesions that resemble secondary syphilis. Regional lymphadenitis is common, and generalized rashes are rare. Healing of these early lesions is followed by latency manifested by seropositivity or by late lesions that resemble tertiary syphilis. These include nodular ulcers of skin, deformities of bones, and ulcerative lesions that can perforate the palate.

Pinta starts similarly as a cutaneous papule with regional lymphadenitis that is followed by a generalized maculopapular eruption. One to 3 years after healing of the initial lesion, large hyperpigmented macules that are brown or blue develop and subsequently lose their pigment and become white. The time required for lesions to pass through these stages varies, so that the same patient may have coexisting areas of increased pigment and loss of pigment.

Diagnosis

Clinical diagnosis is difficult, with skin lesions of the endemic treponematoses resembling other cutaneous processes including impetigo, cutaneous fungal infections, etc. By darkfield microscopy, the causative spirochetes from early skin lesions can be observed directly. Spirochetes have been demonstrated also in lymph node aspirates. There is no specific test for any of the nonsyphilitic treponematoses. Serologic tests for syphilis detect cross-reacting antibodies in these diseases. The Venereal Disease Research Laboratories (VDRL) test, the serologic test for syphilis, and the fluorescent treponemal antibody absorption test each give positive results if serum is obtained at least 2 weeks after the lesions initially appear.

Rx Treatment and Prognosis

Long-acting benzathine penicillin G given as 1.2 million units intramuscularly is the preferred treatment for patients with early lesions. For patients with late manifestations, this therapy should be repeated twice at approximately 7-day intervals. The early lesions heal rapidly, and most seropositive cases convert to seronegative status. Late destructive lesions take longer to show improvement.

Prevention

The prevalence of these diseases was reduced in the 1950s by mass treatment campaigns using penicillin. The WHO treated about 53 million cases of yaws and 350,000 cases of pinta in the 1950s with good results. These campaigns, however, were not adequate to eradicate the disease, and in recent years the prevalence of yaws has again increased. Current estimates suggest that worldwide as many as 2.5 million persons are infected, 75% of whom are less than 15 years of age. It has been suggested that reduction in transmission requires improvements in the sanitation and economic standards of people living in endemic areas.

SUGGESTED READINGS

Antal GM, Lukehart SA, Meheus AZ: The endemic treponematoses. Microbes Infect 2002;4:83–94. *An excellent review article with good clinical descriptions and an up-to-date discussion of genetic differences between the* T. pallidum *subspecies.*

Koff AB, Rosen T: Nonvenereal treponematoses: Yaws, endemic syphilis, and pinta. J Am Acad Dermatol 1993;29:519–535. *With worldwide travel, there is a need to consider diagnosis of nonvenereal treponematoses in appropriate clinical and historical situations.*

Vorst FA: Clinical diagnosis and changing manifestations of treponemal infection. Rev Infect Dis 1985;7Suppl 2:S327–S331. *This report shows that yaws in populations after mass treatment with penicillin assumes attenuated forms characterized by shorter duration of papillomas and lower antibody titers.*

351 RELAPSING FEVER

Molly A. Hughes
William A. Petri, Jr.

Definition

Relapsing fever is a spirochetal infection with bacteria of the genus *Borrelia*. There are two modes of transmission: epidemic louse-borne and endemic tick-borne relapsing fever.

Etiology

Borrelia are motile spirochetes that measure $0.5\,\mu m$ in diameter and 5 to $40\,\mu m$ in length. They are aerophilic and require long-chain fatty acids for growth. Louse-borne relapsing fever is caused by *B. recurrentis*. Tick-borne relapsing fever organisms are named after their tick vector and include the closely related species *B. duttonii* (Old World) and *B. hermsii*, *B. turicate*, and *B. parkeri* (North America).

Epidemiology

Louse-borne epidemic relapsing fever is caused by *Borrelia recurrentis* and is carried from person to person by the human body louse (*Pediculus humanus*). There is no animal reservoir. The spirochete lives in the louse hemolymph; infection is transmitted to humans when the louse is crushed on human skin, and infective spirochetes penetrate the skin or mucous membranes. Epidemics have occurred during famines and at wartime when breakdown in sanitation favors transmission of body lice. Louse-borne disease remains endemic in central and east Africa (Ethiopia, Somalia, Chad, and the Sudan) and in the South American Andes (Bolivia and Peru).

Tick-borne endemic relapsing fever is transmitted to humans by *Ornithodoros* soft ticks. The ticks become infected by feeding on wild rodents (including mice, rats, squirrels, chipmunks), which serve as the natural reservoirs for the organisms. In the United States, relapsing fever is limited to humid, mountainous areas of the West at altitudes of 1500 to 8000 feet where the tick vector *O. hermsii* resides in forests of Ponderosa pine and Douglas fir trees. A key diagnostic clue has been a history of sleeping in rodent-infested rustic cabins in western U.S. national parks.

Pathology and Pathogenesis

Borrelia infection begins in the skin at the site of the louse or tick bite and is followed by rapid dissemination of the spirochetes through the bloodstream. Spirochetes are visible on Wright's stained peripheral blood smears during the initial febrile episode and during each relapse in most patients. Clearance of spirochetes from the blood is associated with the production of serotype-specific immune sera; anti-*Borrelia* antibodies have been shown in animal models to be the major mechanism of immune clearance of infection.

Relapses are associated with cyclic antigenic variation in the variable major proteins (VMPs), which are the abundant outer-membrane proteins of the spirochete that carry the serotype-specific epitopes. Antigenic variation is the consequence of recombination events occurring between VMP genes at silent and expression sites on linear plasmids. A single bacterium of *B. hermsii* may produce as many as 40 antigenically distinct serotypes. Because spirochetes undergo one or several antigenic phases during infection, no specific or standard procedure has been developed for routine serodiagnosis of relapsing fever.

Clinical Manifestations

An abrupt onset of fever to $38.5°$ to $40°$ C ($>39°$ C in most patients), headache, myalgias, and shaking chills characterize the onset of illness. Cough, nausea and vomiting, and fatigue are less frequent complaints. Signs include fever, tachycardia, lethargy or confusion, conjunctival injection, and epistaxis. Hepatosplenomegaly, jaundice, and often a truncal petechial rash

Continued

are common signs in louse-borne relapsing fever. Untreated louse-borne disease lasts 6 days and relapses occur once after an afebrile period of 9 days. Tick-borne relapsing fever lasts about 4 days without antibiotic treatment, and an average of two relapses occur after a 10-day afebrile period.

Relapsing fever in pregnancy results in miscarriage in one third of patients. Neonatal infection presents in both the tick- and louse-borne forms with jaundice, hepatosplenomegaly, and often sepsis and hemorrhage. Fever and hepatosplenomegaly are also common signs in children.

Laboratory Findings

Spirochetes can be demonstrated in the Wright's stained peripheral blood smear of most patients. The degree of spirochetemia can often reach 100,000 organisms/mm^3 on peripheral blood smear. Due to their characteristic locomotion, spirochetes can be readily detected by direct visualization of thick blood films under low power microscopy. The white blood cell count is usually normal, but platelet counts less than 50,000/mm^3 occur in up to 90% of cases of louse-borne disease. Prothrombin and partial thromboplastin times are often prolonged. In louse-borne disease, elevations in liver function tests (serum transaminases and bilirubin) and blood urea nitrogen are common. Urinalysis may reveal proteinuria and microscopic hematuria.

Diagnosis

Spirochetes can be demonstrated on peripheral blood smears taken during the febrile episodes in 70% of patients. With an average incubation period of 1 week, relapsing fever is often diagnosed in nonendemic areas after a patient has returned from a stay in the Rocky Mountains. Only a few patients will remember tick exposure because *O. hermsii* is a night feeder, has a painless bite, and remains attached for only 15 minutes. Culture of the organism requires a special medium and is not practical in a clinical laboratory setting. Because the number of organisms in blood is extremely high, the diagnosis is most often made by direct visualization of the organism on a blood smear.

Prognosis

Epidemics of louse-borne relapsing fever have been reported, with mortality rates approaching 40%. With antibiotic treatment, mortality is less than 5% in all recent series, with complete recovery expected. Autopsies of patients with louse-borne disease have documented intracranial hemorrhage, brain edema, bronchopneumonia, hepatic necrosis, and splenic infarcts.

Rx Treatment

A single 500-mg dose of tetracycline may be as effective as longer treatments in clearing spirochetemia of louse-borne disease, although many physicians still treat with 500 mg tetracycline every 6 hours for 5 to 10 days. Erythromycin is also effective and should be used in pregnant women and in children younger than age 7 (in whom tetracyclines can stain the permanent teeth). Penicillin treatment has been reported to clear the spirochetemia more slowly than tetracycline.

The Jarisch-Herxheimer reaction (typically characterized by a rise in body temperature of 1° C, rigors, a slight fall followed by a rise in blood pressure, and transient leukopenia) occurs 2 to 3 hours after treatment in many patients with louse-borne disease, less commonly in tick-borne disease, and should be anticipated and managed supportively. Deaths due to shock from the Jarisch-Herxheimer reaction occur rarely. The Jarisch-Herxheimer reaction has been associated with accelerated phagocytosis of spirochetes by neutrophils and transient elevations of tumor necrosis factor α (TNF–α), interleukin-6, and interleukin-8.

SUGGESTED READINGS

Barbour AG, Carter CJ, Sohaskey CD: Surface protein variation by expression site switching in the relapsing fever agent *Borrelia hermsii.* Infect Immun 2000;68:7114–7121. *Expression of* B. hermsii *variable surface protein 33 (Vsp33) occurs at the level of transcription. When the vsp33 expression site is active, an expression site for other variable surface proteins is silent, showing that* B. hermsii *can change its major surface protein by switching between expression sites.*

Coxon RE, Fekade D, Knox K, et al: The effect of antibody against TNFα on cytokine response in Jarisch-Herxheimer reactions of louse-borne relapsing fever. QJM 1997;90:213–221. *In a small trial, this antibody was effective in reducing peak IL-6 and IL-8 levels and the incidence of the Jarisch-Herxheimer reaction.*

Dworkin MS, Anderson DE Jr, Schwan TG, et al: Tick-borne relapsing fever in the Northwestern United States and Southwestern Canada. Clin Infect Dis 1998; 26:122–131. *One hundred-eighty cases of tick-borne relapsing fever from 1980 through 1995 in the Northwest are reviewed with an emphasis on clinical complications, serodiagnosis, epidemiology, entomology, and geographic distribution.*

Raoult D, Roux V: The body louse as a vector of reemerging human diseases. Clin Infect Dis 1999;29:888–911. *The physiology and epidemiology of the body louse, louse control and eradication methods, and the spectrum of reemerging louse-associated diseases including relapsing fever (Borrelia recurrentis) are reviewed.*

Schwan TG, Hinnebusch BJ: Bloodstream- versus tick-associated variants of a relapsing fever bacterium. Science 1998;280:1938–1940. *The authors show that alternating serotype-specific variable major proteins (Vmps) of Borrelia hermsii rapidly cycle between the mammalian bloodstream (mouse-associated serotype 7) and arthropod vector (tick-associated serotype 33), which suggests reciprocal changes in two different Vmp expression sites.*

352 LYME DISEASE

Stephen E. Malawista

Definition

Lyme disease is a tick-borne, inflammatory disorder caused by the spirochete *Borrelia burgdorferi.* Its clinical hallmark is an early expanding skin lesion, called *erythema migrans* (EM) and previously called *erythema chronicum migrans.* EM may be followed weeks to months later by neurologic, cardiac, or joint abnormalities. Symptoms may refer to any of these four systems alone or in combination. All stages of Lyme disease may respond to antibiotics, but treatment of early disease is the most efficient. Although cases of the illness are concentrated in certain endemic areas, foci of Lyme disease are widely distributed within the United States, Europe, and Asia.

Lyme arthritis was recognized in November 1975 because of unusual geographic clustering of children with inflammatory arthropathy in the region of Lyme, Connecticut. It soon became clear that this was a multisystem disorder (*Lyme disease*) occurring at any age, in both sexes, and often preceded by a characteristic expanding skin lesion, EM. In Europe, EM had been associated with the bite of the sheep tick, *Ixodes ricinus,* and with tick-borne meningopolyneuritis. In the Lyme region, a closely related deer tick, *Ixodes scapularis* (thought until recently to represent a new species, called *Ixodes dammini*), was implicated as the principal disease vector on epidemiologic grounds. In 1982, Burgdorfer and associates isolated a spirochete, now called *B. burgdorferi,* from *I. scapularis* and linked it serologically to patients with Lyme disease. It was soon recovered from patient specimens.

Distribution and Epidemiology

Lyme disease is widespread. In the United States, there are three distinct foci: the Northeast from southern Maine to Maryland, the upper Midwest, and the West in northern California and Oregon. More than 90% of reported cases come from just 10 states: Connecticut, Rhode Island, New York, New Jersey, Delaware, Pennsylvania, Wisconsin, Maryland, and Massachusetts. However, the illness has been reported in 49 states, as well as across Europe and Asia. The earliest known cases in the United States occurred on Cape Cod, Massachusetts, in 1962 and in Lyme, Connecticut, in 1965; annual cases now number about 15,000. Disease can occur at any age and in either gender. Onset of illness is generally between May 1 and November 30, with the peak in June and July.

Lyme disease accounts for more than 90% of reported vector-borne infectious diseases in the United States. Its primary vectors are tiny ixodid ticks. Major foci of disease correspond to the distribution of *I. scapularis* (Northeast, Midwest), *Ixodes pacificus* (West), *I. ricinus* (Europe), and *Ixodes persulcatus* (Eurasia, Asia). In one U.S. study, 31% of 314 patients recalled a tick bite at the skin site where EM developed days to weeks later. The six ticks that were saved were invariably nymphal *I. scapularis,* whose peak questing period is May through July; the nymphal stage is primarily responsible for transmission of disease. Preferred hosts for *I. scapularis* nymphs are white-footed mice and, for adults, white-tailed deer, in whose fur they mate. A less successful transmission cycle involving the dusky footed woodrat has been described in California.

The rising incidence of Lyme disease in the United States may be explained by multiple factors, including an increase in the numbers of ixodid ticks, the outward migration of residential areas into previously rural woodlands (habitats favored by ixodid ticks and their hosts), an exploding deer population, and increased recognition.

In areas endemic for Lyme disease, the prevalence of *B. burgdorferi* in nymphal *I. scapularis* ranges from about 20% to more than 60% (for *I. pacificus,* 1 to 2%), but rates of human infection by engorged ticks are much less. The organism has been isolated or a specific antibody found in the blood and tissues of a wide variety of large and small animals, including domestic dogs and birds. Indiscriminate feeding on a variety of animals by immature *I. scapularis* may favor the spread of infection.

Pathogenesis

Recovery of *B. burgdorferi* is straightforward from the tick but difficult from patients—except from EM lesions, in which case the clinical diagnosis is usually obvious—in part because of a relative paucity of organisms in specimens of tissue and fluids from the latter. Nevertheless, rare positive cultures are reported at all stages of the illness—from blood (early), secondary annular lesions, meningitic cerebrospinal fluid (CSF), heart, joint fluid, ligament, and even a late skin lesion, *acrodermatitis chronica atrophicans,* that had been present for 10 years. Spirochetes have been identified by silver stain or by immunofluorescence in some histologic sections of EM and rarely in secondary annular lesions, synovium, brain, eye, heart, striated muscle, ligament, liver, spleen, kidney, and bone marrow.

From these data, combined with the clinical and epidemiologic features of Lyme disease, the following pathogenetic sequence is likely. *B. burgdorferi* is transmitted to the skin of the host by the tick vector but usually only after about 48 hours of engorgement. Within 3 to 32 days, the organism migrates outward in the skin (EM), spreads in lymph (i.e., regional adenopathy), or disseminates in blood to organs (i.e., central nervous system [CNS], joints, heart, and presumably liver and spleen) or other skin sites (i.e., secondary annular lesions). Maternal-fetal transmission is distinctly uncommon. Although organisms are hard to find in later stages of Lyme disease, it is entirely possible that persistent live spirochetes or their undegraded antigens are driving the illness throughout its course. Evidence for this interpretation includes the responsiveness of most patients to antibiotics, the rare sightings of spirochetes in affected tissues, the variable recovery from affected tissues and fluids of spirochetal DNA amplified by the polymerase chain reaction (PCR), and an expansion of the antibody response to additional spirochetal antigens over time. If live spirochetes are invariably present, it is not clear how they occasionally remain out of harm's way in the face of antibiotic therapy and the body's usual phagocytic and other immune clearance mechanisms. Antigenic variation, particularly as mediated by *VlsE* genes, is currently a prime suspect in immune evasion. Autoimmune mechanisms have been proposed, although not proved, in the propagation of prolonged (i.e., chronic) Lyme arthritis, which in any case generally resolves within 4 years.

In the clinical laboratory, characteristic immune abnormalities are found. At disease onset (i.e., EM), almost all patients have evidence of circulating immune complexes. At that time, the findings of elevated serum immunoglobulin M (IgM) levels and cryoglobulins containing IgM predict subsequent nervous system, heart, or joint involvement; the early humoral findings have prognostic significance. These abnormalities tend to persist during neurologic or cardiac

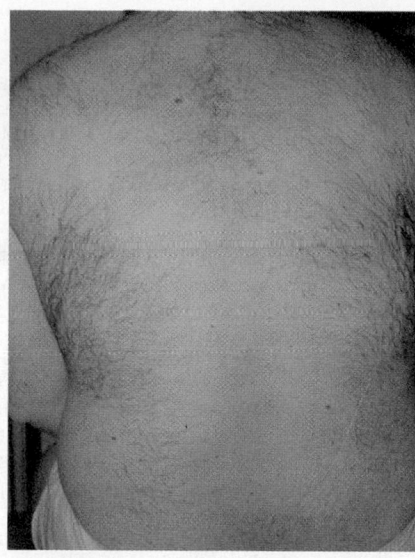

FIGURE 352–1 • Erythema migrans (EM) is the major dermatologic manifestation of Lyme disease. Four days after onset of EM, this patient developed secondary annular lesions, and some of their borders have merged. (From Steere AC, Bartenhagen NH, Craft JE, et al: The early clinical manifestations of Lyme disease. Ann Intern Med 1983;99:76–82.)

involvement. Later in the illness, when arthritis is present, serum IgM levels are more often normal. By then, immune complexes are usually lacking in serum but are present uniformly in joint fluid, where their titers correlate positively with the local concentration of polymorphonuclear leukocytes. Mononuclear cells from peripheral blood increase their antigen-specific proliferative response as the disease progresses, but the greatest reactivity to antigen is seen in cells from inflamed joints. On biopsy, adjacent to that joint fluid is seen a proliferative synovium, often replete with lymphocytes and plasma cells that are presumably capable of producing immunoglobulin locally. An initially disseminated, immune-mediated inflammatory disorder becomes in some patients localized and propagated in joints.

B. burgdorferi does not destroy tissue directly. During the innate immune response (i.e., before antibodies have developed), the spirochete's surface lipoproteins can mediate inflammation via Toll-like receptors and activate monocytes, macrophages, synovial lining cells, natural killer cells, B cells, and complement, resulting in the elaboration of a host of proinflammatory materials. The spirochetes adhere to extracellular matrix proteins, to endothelial cells (and penetrate endothelial monolayers), and to neural glycolipid. They can induce the production of cross-reactive antibodies and of specific immune B and T lymphocytes that may be associated histologically with endarteritic, microvascular occlusive changes (e.g., in nervous tissue, hearts, joints), but it is not clear that these phenomena persist in the absence of live spirochetes or their antigens.

In addition to factors related to the pathogenicity of specific isolates of *B. burgdorferi,* immunogenetic makeup may play a role in whether infected individuals can rid themselves of spirochetes, their antigens, or their effects. Patients with treatment-resistant chronic arthritis have been reported to have an increased frequency of *HLA-DRB1*0401* or related alleles.

Clinical Manifestations

Lyme disease is conveniently divided into three clinical stages, but the stages may overlap. Most patients do not exhibit all of them, and seroconversion can occur in asymptomatic individuals. The illness usually begins with EM and associated symptoms (stage 1), sometimes followed weeks to months later by neurologic or cardiac abnormalities (stage 2) and weeks to years later by arthritis (stage 3). Chronic neurologic and skin involvement also may occur years after onset.

EARLY MANIFESTATIONS

EM, the unique clinical marker for Lyme disease, is recognized in 90% or more of patients. It begins as a red macule or papule at the site where the tick vector, usually long gone, had engorged. As the area of redness expands to about 15 cm (range, 3 to 68 cm), there is often partial central clearing (Fig. 352–1). The outer borders are red, generally flat, and without scaling. The centers are occasionally red and indurated, even vesicular or necrotic. Variations may occur, such as multiple rings. The thigh, groin, and axilla are particularly common sites. The lesion is warm to touch but not often sore, and it is easily missed if out of sight. Routine histologic findings are nonspecific: a heavy dermal infiltrate of mononuclear cells, without epidermal change except at the site of the tick bite.

Within days of onset of EM, one fourth or fewer patients in the United States develop multiple annular secondary lesions (more did

Continued

so in the initial study) (Table 352–1). These lesions, from which spirochetes have been cultured, represent clear evidence of dissemination. They resemble EM itself but are generally smaller, migrate less, and lack indurated centers. Individual lesions may come and go, and their borders sometimes merge. Other occasional skin lesions are mentioned in Table 352–1. Benign lymphocytoma cutis has been reported in Europe. In the United States, EM and secondary lesions fade in 3 to 4 weeks (range, 1 day to 14 months) but take longer on average in Europe. They may recur.

Skin involvement is often accompanied by musculoskeletal flulike symptoms: malaise and fatigue, headache, fever and chills, myalgia, and arthralgia (Table 352–2). Even without EM, this syndrome in summer and in an endemic area for Lyme disease is grounds for treatment. Some patients have evidence of meningeal irritation or mild encephalopathy (e.g., episodic attacks of excruciating headache and neck pain, stiffness, or pressure) that typically lasts only for hours at this stage of the illness and has no CSF pleocytosis or objective neurologic deficit. Except for fatigue and lethargy, which are often constant, the early signs and symptoms are typically intermittent and changing. For example, a patient may have meningitic attacks for several days, a few days of improvement, and then the onset of migratory musculoskeletal pain. The pain may involve joints (generally without swelling), tendons, bursa, muscle, and bone. The pain tends to affect only one or two sites at a time and to last a few hours to several days in a given location. The various associated symptoms may occur several days before EM (or without it) and last for months (especially fatigue and lethargy) after the skin lesions have disappeared.

LATER MANIFESTATIONS

NEUROLOGIC INVOLVEMENT. Within several weeks to months of the onset of illness, about 15% of untreated patients develop frank neurologic abnormalities, including meningitis, encephalitis, chorea, cranial neuritis (including bilateral facial palsy), motor and sensory radiculoneuritis, or mononeuritis multiplex, occurring in various combinations. The usual pattern is fluctuating meningoencephalitis with superimposed cranial nerve (particularly facial) palsy and peripheral radiculoneuropathy, but Bell's-like palsy may occur alone. At this point, patients with meningitic symptoms have a lymphocytic pleocytosis (about 100 cells/mm^3) in the CSF and sometimes diffuse slowing on an electroencephalogram. However, the neck is rarely stiff except in extreme flexion; Kernig's and Brudzinski's signs are absent. Neurologic abnormalities typically last for months but usually resolve completely.

CARDIAC INVOLVEMENT. Weeks to months after onset, about 8% of patients develop cardiac involvement. The most common abnormality is fluctuating degrees of atrioventricular block (i.e., first-degree, Wenckebach, or complete heart block). Some patients have evidence of more diffuse cardiac involvement, including electrocardiographic changes compatible with acute myopericarditis, radionuclide evidence of mild left ventricular dysfunction, or rarely, cardiomegaly. None has had heart murmurs. Cardiac involvement is usually brief (3 days to 6 weeks), but it may recur.

ARTHRITIS. Weeks to as long as 2 years after the onset of illness, about 60% of patients develop frank arthritis, usually characterized by intermittent attacks of asymmetrical joint swelling and pain primarily in large joints, especially the knee, one or two joints at a time. Affected knees are commonly more swollen than painful, often hot, and rarely red; Baker's cysts may form and rupture early. Large and small joints may be affected, and a few patients have had symmetrical polyarthritis. Attacks of arthritis, which generally last weeks to months, typically recur for several years and decrease in frequency with time. Fatigue is common with active joint involvement, but fever or other systemic symptoms at this stage are unusual. Joint fluid white blood cell counts vary from 500 to 110,000 cells/mm^3, with an average of about 25,000 cells/mm^3, mostly polymorphonuclear leukocytes. Total protein ranges from 3 to 8 g/dL. The C3 and C4 levels are generally greater than one third and glucose levels usually more than two thirds that of serum. Rheumatoid factor and antinuclear antibody are absent.

In about 10% of patients with arthritis, involvement in large joints may be prolonged (>1 year), occasionally with pannus formation and erosion of cartilage and bone. Synovial biopsy findings may mimic those of rheumatoid arthritis: surface deposits of fibrin, villous hypertrophy, vascular proliferation, and a heavy infiltration of mononuclear cells. There may be an obliterative endarteritis and (rarely) demonstrable spirochetes. B. burgdorferi stimulates mononuclear cells to produce cytokines (e.g., interleukin-1, tumor necrosis factor-α, interleukin-6), and elevated concentrations of inflammatory cytokines have been found in synovial fluid. In one patient with chronic Lyme arthritis, synovium grown in tissue culture produced large amounts of collagenase and prostaglandin E$_2$. In Lyme disease, the joint fluid cell counts, immune reactants (except for rheumatoid factor), synovial histology, amounts of synovial enzymes released, and occasionally, the destruction of cartilage and bone may be similar to those in rheumatoid arthritis. The major difference is that prolonged Lyme arthritis typically resolves in time.

Other late findings (years) associated with this infection include a chronic skin lesion—acrodermatitis chronica atrophicans—well known in Europe but still rare in the United States. The examiner sees violaceous infiltrated plaques or nodules, especially on extensor surfaces, that eventually become atrophic. Uncommon, late, chronic neurologic disease includes transverse myelitis, diffuse sensory axonal neuropathy, and demyelinating lesions of the CNS. Mild memory impairment, subtle mood changes, and chronic fatigue states may also occur.

Table 352–1 • EARLY SIGNS OF LYME DISEASE IN A STUDY OF 314 PATIENTS

SIGNS	NO. OF PATIENTS (%)
Erythema migrans	314 (100)*
Multiple annular lesions	150 (48)
Lymphadenopathy	
Regional	128 (41)
Generalized	63 (20)
Pain on neck flexion	52 (17)
Malar rash	41 (13)
Erythematous throat	38 (12)
Conjunctivitis	35 (11)
Right upper quadrant tenderness	24 (8)
Splenomegaly	18 (6)
Hepatomegaly	16 (5)
Muscle tenderness	12 (4)
Periorbital edema	10 (3)
Evanescent skin lesions	8 (3)
Abdominal tenderness	6 (2)
Testicular swelling	2 (1)

*Erythema migrans was required for inclusion in this study.

From Steere AC, Bartenhagen NH, Craft JE, et al: The early clinical manifestations of Lyme disease. Ann Intern Med 1983; 99:76–82.

Table 352–2 • EARLY SYMPTOMS OF LYME DISEASE IN A STUDY OF 314 PATIENTS

SYMPTOMS	NO. OF PATIENTS (%)
Malaise, fatigue, and lethargy	251 (80)
Headache	200 (64)
Fever and chills	185 (59)
Stiff neck	151 (48)
Arthralgias	150 (48)
Myalgias	135 (43)
Backache	81 (26)
Anorexia	73 (23)
Sore throat	53 (17)
Nausea	53 (17)
Dysesthesia	35 (11)
Vomiting	32 (10)
Abdominal pain	24 (8)
Photophobia	19 (6)
Hand stiffness	16 (5)
Dizziness	15 (5)
Cough	15 (5)
Chest pain	12 (4)
Ear pain	12 (4)
Diarrhea	6 (2)

From Steere AC, Bartenhagen NH, Craft JE, et al: The early clinical manifestations of Lyme disease. Ann Intern Med 1983;99:76–82.

Laboratory Test Results

The diagnosis of Lyme disease is based on recognizing clinical features of the illness in a patient with a history of possible exposure to the causative organism. Culture of *B. burgdorferi* from patients is definitive but has rarely been successful, except from skin biopsy specimens. The organism can be isolated from blood in a significant minority of patients with systemic manifestations of early disease; it grows very slowly. Special tissue staining techniques generally have a low yield and are not readily available. Determination of specific antibody titers, usually performed by enzyme-linked immunosorbent assay (ELISA), is the most helpful adjunctive diagnostic test for Lyme disease. In serum, specific IgM antibody titers against *B. burgdorferi* usually reach a peak between the third and sixth weeks after the onset of disease; specific immunoglobulin G (IgG) antibody titers rise more slowly and are generally highest months later when arthritis is present (Fig. 352–2). Individuals with untreated Lyme disease of more than 6 weeks' duration can be expected to have elevated levels of specific anti-bodies. However, the tests employed are not standardized, and results from different commercial laboratories may vary, especially for borderline elevations. Most individuals with established Lyme arthritis have elevated specific IgG titers. This finding makes antibody titers against *B. burgdorferi* particularly useful in differentiating Lyme disease from other rheumatic syndromes, especially when EM is missed, forgotten, or absent. Antibodies may cross-react with other spirochetes, including *Treponema pallidum*, but patients with Lyme disease do not have positive VDRL test results. Western blots are important for confirmation of positive ELISA results.

Another test of diagnostic interest uses the PCR to detect spirochetal DNA in host material. Although this powerful tool is notorious for false-positive results when not performed under the most stringent conditions, it can be very useful when properly done, particularly in cases of Lyme arthritis, in which synovial fluid from most untreated patients is positive.

The most common nonspecific laboratory abnormalities, particularly early in the illness, are a high erythrocyte sedimentation rate, an elevated serum IgM level, and increased serum levels of aspartate transaminase (AST). The enzyme levels generally return to normal within several weeks. Patients may be mildly anemic early in the illness and occasionally have elevated white blood cell counts with shifts to the left in the differential count. A few patients have had microscopic hematuria, sometimes with mild proteinuria (dipstick); values for creatinine and blood urea nitrogen have been normal. Throughout the illness, serum C3 and C4 levels are generally normal or elevated. Rheumatoid factor and antinuclear antibodies are usually absent.

Differential Diagnosis

EM is the unique herald lesion of Lyme disease. When present in its classic form, there is little else that may be confused with it. However, some patients are not aware of having had EM, and in others, its appearance is not always characteristic. Secondary lesions may suggest *erythema multiforme,* but blistering, mucosal lesions, and involvement of the palms and soles are not features of Lyme disease. Malar rash may suggest systemic lupus erythematosus; an urticarial rash suggests hepatitis B infection or serum sickness. Evanescent blotches and circles may resemble *erythema marginatum,* but those of Lyme disease do not expand.

Early musculoskeletal flulike symptoms may be misinterpreted, especially when EM is absent or missed or is not the first manifestation. In patients with particularly severe constitutional symptoms, the physician should consider possible concomitant infection with two other illnesses whose causative agents are transmitted by the same tick: the rickettsia-like disorder, human granulocytic ehrlichiosis (watch for leukopenia, thrombocytopenia, elevated transaminases, occasional inclusions in granulocytes) (Chapter 355) or the malaria-like disorder, babesiosis (occasional inclusions in erythrocytes) (Chapter 400).

Severe headache and stiff neck may resemble symptoms of other aseptic meningitis; abdominal symptoms, those of hepatitis; and generalized tender lymphadenopathy and splenomegaly, those of infectious mononucleosis. As in mononucleosis, fatigue in Lyme disease may be a major and persistent complaint. However, initial presentations of an isolated chronic fatigue syndrome or of fibromyalgia-like complaints (e.g., diffuse aching, trigger points, sleep disturbance) are not characteristic of Lyme disease.

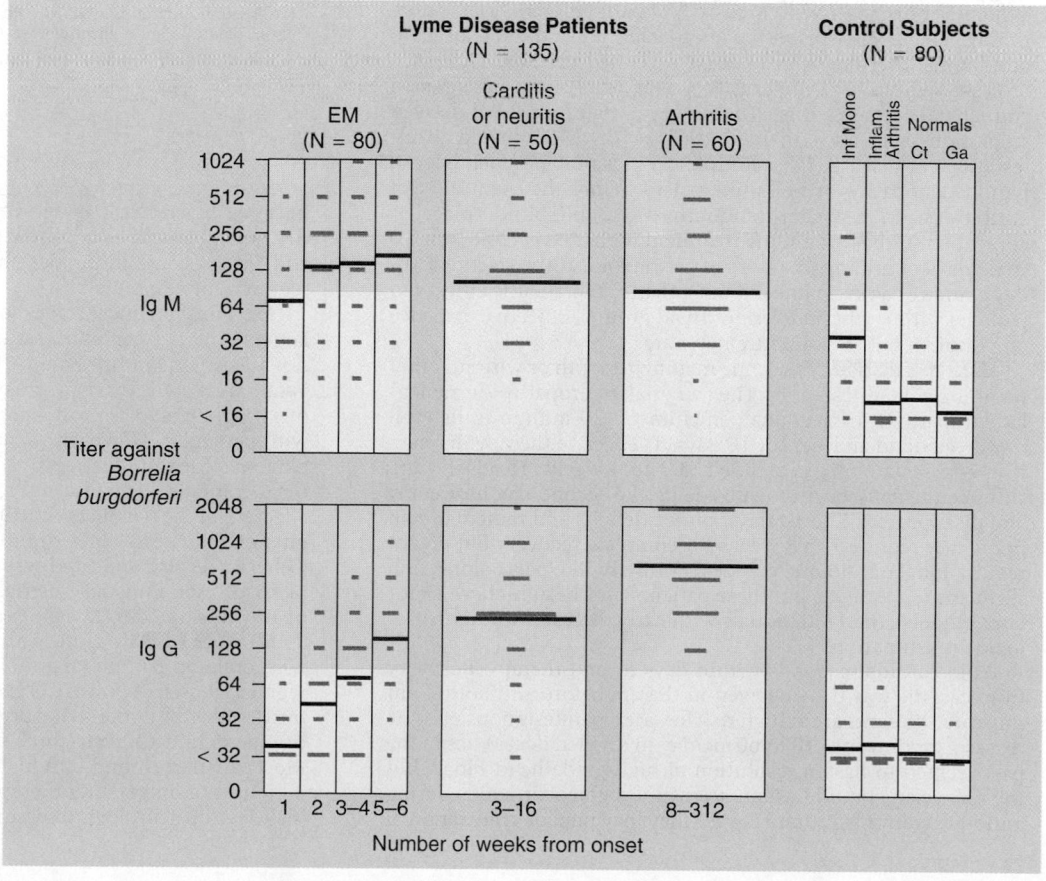

FIGURE 352–2 • Antibody titers against *Borrelia burgdorferi* are shown in serum samples from 135 patients with different clinical manifestations of Lyme disease and from 80 control subjects with infectious mononucleosis, inflammatory arthritis, or no disease (titers determined by indirect immunofluorescence). The black bar shows the geometric mean titer for each group; the pink shaded areas indicate the range of values generally observed in control subjects. Notice that all patients with Lyme arthritis have elevated IgG antibody titers. (Adapted from Steere AC, Grodzicki RL, Komblatt AN, et al: The spirochetal etiology of Lyme disease. N Engl J Med 1983;308: 733–740. Copyright 1983 Massachusetts Medical Society.)

In later stages, Lyme disease may mimic other immune-mediated disorders. Like rheumatic fever, Lyme disease may be associated with sore throat followed by migratory polyarthritis (more often, polyarthralgias) and carditis but have no evidence of valvular involvement or of a preceding streptococcal infection. Migratory pain in tendons and joints may also suggest disseminated gonococcal disease. An isolated facial weakness may mimic Bell's-like palsy of other causes. Late neurologic involvement may suggest multiple sclerosis (i.e., transverse myelitis), Guillain-Barré syndrome (i.e., symmetrical peripheral neuropathy), primary psychosis, or brain tumor. In adults with Lyme arthritis, the large knee effusions can resemble those in Reiter's syndrome, and the occasional symmetrical polyarthritis may mimic rheumatoid arthritis. In children, the attacks of arthritis, although generally shorter, may be identical to those seen in the oligoarticular form of juvenile rheumatoid arthritis but without iridocyclitis.

Treatment

The major goal of therapy in Lyme disease is to eradicate the causative organism. Like other spirochetal diseases, Lyme disease is most responsive to antibiotics early in its course. Treatment regimens have evolved over time based on controlled clinical data and on clinical experience. Because of the difficulty in proving that bacteria have been eradicated and the common persistence of some symptoms long after treatment, the end point of antibiotic therapy is not always clear. The treatment regimens presented here represent guidelines that will no doubt be further refined in time (Table 352–3).

EARLY LYME DISEASE. If patients are treated early with oral antibiotics, EM typically resolves promptly, and major later sequelae (i.e., myocarditis, meningoencephalitis, or recurrent arthritis) usually do not occur. Prompt treatment is therefore important, even though such patients may be susceptible to reinfection. Antibiotic choices and doses are listed in Table 352–3; doxycycline or amoxicillin is favored. Doxycycline is the drug of choice if concomitant human granulocytic ehrlichiosis, which does not respond to the penicillins, is suspected.

About 10% of patients with early Lyme disease experience a Jarisch-Herxheimer–like reaction (i.e., higher fever, redder rash, or greater pain) during the first 24 hours of antibiotic therapy. Whichever drug is given, 30 to 50% of patients have brief (hours to days) recurrent episodes of headache, musculoskeletal pain, and fatigue that may continue for extended periods. The cause of these symptoms is unclear; they may result from undegraded spirochetal antigens. It is clear, however, that the risk of delayed resolution is greatest in individuals with disseminated manifestations of disease (i.e., multiple skin lesions, headache, fever, lymphadenopathy, or Bell's-like palsy) before the institution of antibiotics. In a recent randomized, double-blind, placebo-controlled study,[1] extending treatment with doxycycline from 10 to 20 days or adding one dose of ceftriaxone at the start of a 10-day course of doxycycline did not enhance therapeutic efficacy in patients with *erythema migrans*. In all groups, objective evidence of treatment failure was extremely rare.

LATER LYME DISEASE. For Lyme meningitis, with or without other neurologic manifestations (i.e., cranial neuropathy or radiculoneuropathy), intravenous penicillin G (20 million units each day in six divided doses for 10 days) is effective therapy; in practice, courses are often extended to 3 to 4 weeks. Headache and stiff neck usually begin to subside by the second day of therapy and disappear by 7 to 10 days; motor deficits and radicular pain frequently require 7 to 8 weeks for complete recovery but do not require longer antibiotic courses. For Bell's-like palsy alone, oral regimens may suffice, but these patients may be at higher risk for later sequelae than individuals with early disease without neurologic dissemination.

Mild carditis responds within days to oral therapy. Recovery from carditis was the rule even in the era before antibiotics, but untreated patients are at high risk for later manifestations of Lyme disease. Prednisone (40 to 60 mg/day in divided doses) has in the past seemed to hasten resolution of high-grade heart block, but the physician should hesitate to institute glucocorticoids during antibiotic administration because they may impede eradication of

infecting organisms. If second- or third-degree heart block is present, the patient should be admitted to hospital for cardiac monitoring and intravenous antibiotics; temporary pacing is occasionally required for complete heart block.

In clinical practice, ceftriaxone (2 g daily for 14 to 28 days) has largely replaced penicillin for the therapy of disseminated Lyme disease. Arguments in favor of this practice are a once-daily administration schedule that is amenable to outpatient intravenous antibiotic programs and improved penetration of the CSF in comparison with penicillin. However, in one study, 3 weeks of oral doxycycline was equally effective for acute disseminated disease, excluding meningitis. Penicillin and cefotaxime have been found equally effective for the treatment of acute neurologic Lyme disease (meningitis or radiculitis) in a group of patients studied in Germany. Ceftriaxone also appeared responsible for the complete recovery of six of nine unusual Austrian patients with dilated cardiomyopathy attributed to Lyme disease.

LATE LYME DISEASE. Lyme arthritis has been successfully treated with oral and parenteral antibiotics, but failures occur with any regimen chosen.[2] Unless CNS involvement coexists, first-line treatment with 1 or 2 months of doxycycline (100 mg twice each day) or amoxicillin (500 mg three times each day) is recommended. Most patients respond, although complete response can be delayed 3 months or longer after therapy is completed, and some patients may develop neurologic disease later. During treatment, the affected

---

Table 352–3 • RECOMMENDATIONS FOR ANTIBIOTIC TREATMENT OF LYME DISEASE IN ADULTS*

EARLY LYME DISEASE[†]
Doxycycline, 100 mg, PO twice daily for 14–21 days
Amoxicillin, 500 mg, PO three times daily for 14–21 days
Cefuroxime axetil, 500 mg, PO twice daily for 21 days
If intolerant to all of the above drugs: erythromycin, 250 mg, PO four
    times daily for 14–28 days

NEUROLOGIC MANIFESTATIONS
Bell's-like palsy alone
    Oral regimens of doxycycline or amoxicillin may suffice
Other neurologic abnormalities
    Ceftriaxone, 2 g, IV daily for 14–28 days
    Cefotaxime, 2 g, IV every 8 hours for 14–28 days
    Penicillin G, 20 million units, IV daily (in six divided doses) for 14–
        28 days
If intolerant to all of the above drugs: doxycycline, 100–200 mg, PO
    twice daily (oral or intravenous) for 30 days[‡]

ARTHRITIS[§]
Doxycycline, 100 mg, PO twice daily for 30–60 days
Amoxicillin, 500 mg, PO three times daily for 30–60 days
Ceftriaxone, 2 g, daily for 14–28 days
Penicillin G, 20 million units, daily for 14–28 days

CARDITIS[¶]
Ceftriaxone, 2 g, IV daily for 14 days
Penicillin G, 20 million units, IV daily for 14 days
Amoxicillin, 500 mg, three times daily for 21 days
Doxycycline, 100 mg, PO twice daily for 21 days

PREGNANCY
Standard therapy for a given stage of disease, but avoid doxycycline

TICK BITES
Rarely employ a single dose of doxycycline, 200 mg

*These are guidelines to be modified by new findings and to be applied always with close attention to the clinical context of individual patients.
[†]Without neurologic, cardiac, or joint involvement. For early Lyme disease, limited to a single erythema migrans lesion, 10 days is sufficient.
[‡]No published experience in the United States; may be ineffective for late neuroborreliosis.
[§]An oral regimen should be selected if there is no neurologic involvement.
[¶]Oral regimens have been reserved for mild carditis limited to first-degree heart block with PR ≤ 0.30 seconds and normal ventricular function.
Adapted from Wormser GP, Nadelman RB, Dattwyler RJ, et al: Practice guidelines for the treatment of Lyme disease. Clin Infect Dis 2000;31 (suppl 1):S1–S14.

joint should be kept at rest and effusions drained by needle aspiration as for any infected joint. In patients who fail one or more courses of antibiotics, arthroscopic synovectomy appears to cure most patients. Even without antibiotic or surgical treatment, persistent Lyme arthritis tends to resolve within several years.

Recommended therapy for the later neurologic complications of Lyme disease is like that for earlier neurologic disease but generally for the full 28 days (see Table 352–3). Recovery of chronic involvement may be slow. The frequency of subtle, chronic encephalopathy and peripheral neuropathy is debated. These entities, when suspected, should be carefully documented through neurologic, neuropsychological, and electrophysiologic testing before antibiotic therapy is instituted. The infiltrative lesions of acrodermatitis chronica atrophicans are usually cured by 30 days of penicillin V (1 g three times each day) or of doxycycline (100 mg twice each day).

PREGNANCY. Recommended therapy for a given stage of disease during pregnancy differs from that of nonpregnant patients only in the avoidance of doxycycline. Because the spirochetes that cause relapsing fever and syphilis can cross the placenta, there has been concern regarding this possibility in Lyme disease. Maternal-fetal transmission of *B. burgdorferi* resulting in neonatal death or stillbirth has been reported in rare instances in which symptomatic, early Lyme disease occurred early in pregnancy and was untreated or inadequately treated. In follow-up studies conducted by the Centers for Disease Control and Prevention, maternal Lyme disease was not directly implicated as a cause of fetal malformations. There have been no cases of fetal infection occurring when the recommended antibiotic regimens for Lyme disease have been used during pregnancy. Women acquiring the illness during pregnancy should be reassured that most infants born to women in these circumstances have been entirely well.

POST-LYME SYNDROME. After recommended courses of antibiotics for Lyme disease, some patients have persistent fatigue, myalgias, arthralgias without arthritis, dysesthesias or paresthesias, or mood and memory disturbances, with or without seropositive results for *B. burgdorferi*. Some of these individuals have been treated with extended courses of antibiotics, sometimes with reported relief during their administration. However, in a placebo-controlled study of such individuals, those who received intravenous ceftriaxone (2 g daily for 30 days) followed by oral doxycycline (200 mg daily for 60 days) did no better symptomatically than the placebo control group. Prolonged treatment with antibiotics is not benign and cannot be recommended in patients without objective evidence of persistent infection. Supportive therapy is indicated.

Prevention

TICK BITES. A single 200-mg dose of doxycycline given within 72 hours of a bite by *I. scapularis* can prevent the development of Lyme disease. However, the attack rate among bitten but untreated controls in the hyperendemic area where the relevant study was done was only 3.2% (i.e., 96.8% of untreated subjects did not develop Lyme disease). Prophylaxis may be most reasonable when the tick is a nymphal deer tick that is at least partially engorged with blood, with flat ticks not having had time to transmit disease, and in a region where the incidence of Lyme disease is high. Otherwise, tick bites may be observed for development of EM and patients cautioned regarding the common associated symptoms of early Lyme disease. A watched tick bite allows for very early treatment of EM in the few patients in whom it will develop, and this is the stage of disease most amenable to therapy.

VACCINATION. A marketed vaccine against Lyme disease based on one of the outer surface proteins (OspA) of *B. burgdorferi* appeared to be safe and effective, but was withdrawn by the manufacturer because of limited demand.

1. Wormser GP, Ramanathan R, Nowakowski JM, et al: duration of antibiotic therapy for early Lyme disease. Ann Intern Med 2003;138:769–704.
2. Klempner MS, Hu LT, Evans J, et al: Two controlled trials of antibiotic treatment in patients with persistent symptoms and a history of Lyme disease. N Engl J Med 2001;345:85–92.

SUGGESTED READINGS
Hayes EB, Piesman J: How can we prevent Lyme disease? N Engl J Med 2003;348: 2424–2430. *A comprehensive overview of prevention strategies in light of the demise of the Lyme disease vaccine.*
Krupp LB, Hyman LG, Grimson R, et al: Study and treatment of post Lyme disease (STOP-LD): A randomized double masked clinical trial. Neurology 2003;60:1923–1930. *There was no benefit from additional antibiotic therapy in post-treatment, persistently fatigued patients.*
Nowakowski J, Nadelman RB, Sell R, et al: Long-term follow-up of patients with culture-confirmed Lyme disease. Am J Med 2003;115:91–96. *Long-term outcome after antibiotic therapy was excellent, but patients from endemic areas remained at high risk of reinfection.*

353 LEPTOSPIROSIS

Christopher D. Huston
William A. Petri, Jr.

Definition

Leptospirosis is a spirochetal infection with bacteria of the genus *Leptospira*. The severe icteric form of infection is called Weil's disease, after the investigator who in 1886 described four men with an acute but self-limited infectious illness characterized by fever, jaundice, nephritis, hepatomegaly, and a biphasic course, with fever recurring 1 to 7 days into convalescence.

Etiology

There are two species of *Leptospira: L. interrogans*, which is pathogenic in humans and animals, and *L. biflexa*, which is free-living. *L. interrogans* is divided into more than 200 serovars grouped into 19 serogroups based on shared major agglutinins. Virulence does not in general correlate with serovars, although serovar classifications can be useful epidemiologically to identify common-source outbreaks. *Leptospira* are motile spirochetes 6 to 20 μm in length and 0.1 to 0.2 μm in diameter. They are obligate aerobes with unique nutritional requirements for long chain fatty acids.

Epidemiology

Leptospirosis is one of the most common, widespread, and underdiagnosed infections transmitted from animals to humans. *L. interrogans* can survive for months in the proximal convoluted tubules of the kidney in asymptomatically infected animals and upon excretion in urine survives in the environment for as long as 6 months. The most common source of exposure in the United States is dogs, followed by livestock, rodents, and other wild animals. Humans become infected through recreational (e.g., windsurfing, kayaking, swimming) or occupational exposure to animal urine or urine-contaminated water and soil. Both sporadic cases and epidemics occur. In developing countries, epidemics are associated with exposure to flood waters during rainy season. In the United States, outbreaks affecting as many as 11% of triathlon participants have occurred, presumably related to freshwater swimming events. Similarly, 45% of U.S. athletes participating in an "EcoChallenge" event in Malaysia became infected. Occupations with the greatest documented risks include New Zealand dairy farmers (incidence of 1.1 infections per 10 person-years), Glasgow sewer workers (3.7 infections per 10 person-years), and U.S. Army soldiers undergoing jungle warfare training in Panama (4.1 infections per 10 person-years). Approximately 15% of veterinarians and abattoir workers have serologic evidence of infection. Leptospirosis is up to 10 times more frequent in rural than in urban dwellers and three times more frequent in men, with a peak incidence in men at ages 30 to 39.

Pathology and Pathogenesis

Leptospira bacteria penetrate intact mucous membranes and abraded skin and disseminate widely through the blood stream. In the first week to 10 days of illness, spirochetes can be cultured with special media from blood and cerebrospinal fluid (CSF). Leptospirosis is an infectious vasculitis, with damage to capillary endothelial cells responsible for the major clinical manifestations of disease, including renal tubular and hepatic dysfunction, myocarditis, and pulmonary hemorrhage. Intravascular to extravascular fluid shifts secondary to endothelial damage lead to hypovolemia, which complicates renal dysfunction and can lead to shock. Fatal cases are associated with widespread hemorrhage of mucosal, skin, and serosal surfaces. Examination of the kidneys from autopsies has revealed ischemic damage, including epithelial cell necrosis in the distal convoluted tubules and the ascending loop of Henle, and interstitial nephritis but only rarely glomerular damage. Liver pathology includes disorganization of liver cell plates, marked variation in the size and shape of parenchymal cells, mitotic figures, and evidence of cholestasis but not necrosis. Muscle biopsies have demonstrated focal necrotic changes with a mild mononuclear infiltrate. Only rarely is the spirochete visualized in the infected tissue. Hemorrhagic myocarditis has been observed frequently in autopsies. The secondary "immune" phase of leptospirosis is associated with the clearance of the organism from blood and CSF and the appearance of agglutinating anti-*Leptospira* antibodies.

Clinical Manifestations

Symptoms develop 7 to 12 days after exposure. Most patients have an abrupt onset of a self-limited 4- to 7-day anicteric illness characterized by the sudden onset of fever, mild to severe headache, myalgias, chills, cough, chest pain, neck stiffness, and/or prostration. An estimated 10% of patients will present with jaundice, hemorrhage, renal failure, and/or neurologic dysfunction (Weil's disease). Signs of leptospirosis include fever of 38° to 40° C (97 to 100% of patients), conjunctival suffusion (40 to 100%), hepatomegaly (80% of icteric cases), splenomegaly (15 to 25%), diffuse abdominal tenderness (5 to 30%), muscle tenderness (40 to 80%), meningeal signs (12 to 40%), disturbances in sensorium (50% of icteric cases), jaundice (10%), and a truncal rash that can be macular, urticarial, or purpuric (7 to 9%). Abdominal pain may be prominent and can mimic acute cholecystitis. Pretibial, raised, 1- to 5-cm erythematous lesions are seen characteristically in a form of leptospirosis called "Fort Bragg fever."

Classically, leptospirosis has been considered a biphasic illness, although many patients with mild disease do not have symptoms of the secondary "immune" phase of illness, and patients with very severe disease have a relentless progression from onset of illness to jaundice, renal failure, hemorrhage, hypotension, and coma. Overall, about half the patients with leptospirosis have a relapse. Typically 1 week after the initial fever resolves, fever, headache, and meningeal signs return. This immune phase of the illness can last several days to a month. A late complication is anterior uveitis, which may be seen in 10% of patients during the months to years after convalescence. Leptospirosis in pregnancy is associated with spontaneous abortion; children born with congenitally acquired leptospirosis have not been described to have congenital anomalies and have been treated successfully with antibiotics.

Laboratory Findings

Leptospira can be cultured with special media from blood and CSF early in the illness, but incubation of the cultures for 5 to 6 weeks at 28° to 30° C is often required. Mild proteinuria is seen in most patients and may be accompanied by pyuria, casts, and microscopic hematuria. In patients with renal failure, the blood urea nitrogen level rarely exceeds 100 mg/dL and the creatinine concentration is usually less than 8 mg/dL. Liver function test results are usually abnormal only in icteric patients, where two- to three-fold elevations in aminotransferases and alkaline phosphatase are observed (lower than the elevations commonly seen in acute viral hepatitis), and a predominantly conjugated bilirubinemia is seen. Myositis with elevated serum creatine phosphokinase (MM band) occurs in about half of patients. Thrombocytopenia (usually >50,000/μL), anemia, and leukocytosis are commonly seen. Thrombocytopenia is seen most commonly in patients with renal failure. CSF examination shows a pleocytosis (<500 cells/mm^3) with an early neutrophilic and late mononuclear cell predominance, a normal glucose level, and mildly elevated protein level (50 to 110 mg/dL). Chest radiographs were abnormal in the majority of patients in one study, with small nodular densities showing a tendency to consolidate. First-degree atrioventricular block and changes consistent with acute pericarditis have been documented in one third of patients.

Diagnosis

The presentation of the illness in anicteric cases is nonspecific. It is important to search for an exposure history to animal urine in a patient with a flulike illness, respiratory illness, aseptic meningitis, acute hepatitis, acute renal failure, pericarditis, atrioventricular block, or anterior uveitis. In some developing countries, leptospirosis is more common than hepatitis A as a cause of acute hepatitis. Useful means to distinguish icteric leptospirosis from acute viral hepatitis include the prominent myalgias, conjunctival suffusion, elevated serum creatine phosphokinase, and the only two- to three-fold elevations in aminotransferases seen in leptospirosis. The diagnosis is usually made retrospectively by a four-fold rise in agglutinating antibody titer. The microscopic agglutination test (MAT) detects serum antibodies against the 21 most common serovars of *Leptospira*. The MAT is the most reliable test and is available from the Centers for Disease Control and Prevention. Agglutinins characteristically appear within the first 1 to 2 weeks of illness and peak at 3 to 4 weeks. It is possible to grow the organism from blood and CSF collected during the first week of illness or from urine collected late in disease, but it may take 4 to 6 weeks for the cultures to become positive.

Prognosis

Case-fatality rates for leptospirosis are less than 1% in studies in which aggressive surveillance has been conducted (increasing the proportion of mild cases). The illness is usually self-limited. Liver and renal dysfunction are for the most part reversible, with return to normal function over 1 to 2 months. The mortality rate for icteric disease has been reported in different studies to be 2.4 to 11.3%, with deaths occurring secondary to renal failure, gastrointestinal and pulmonary hemorrhage, and the acute respiratory distress syndrome.

 Treatment

Antibiotic treatment is most beneficial when started within 4 days of illness; unfortunately, the diagnosis of leptospirosis is rarely made this rapidly. Doxycycline, 100 mg orally twice a day for 7 days, started within 48 hours of illness, decreased the duration of illness by 2 days in one study; penicillin at a dosage of 2.4 to 3.6 million units/day also has been successful early treatment. A beneficial effect of antibiotic therapy later in disease has not been uniformly seen. While a randomized, double-blinded trial of penicillin treatment (1.5 million units intravenously every 6 hours for 7 days) started on average 9 days into illness showed a decrease in fever duration from 11.6 to 4.7 days and in elevated serum creatinine level from 8.3 to 2.7 days, a second randomized trial of penicillin in patients with icteric leptospirosis and a median duration of illness of 1 week demonstrated no beneficial effect. Jarisch-Herxheimer reactions (fever, rigors, hypotension, and tachycardia) following intravenous antibiotic treatment have been reported but appear to occur less often than in other spirochete diseases. Ceftriaxone yields results equivalent to those of penicillin. Supportive care and treatment of the hypotension, renal failure (including rehydration and dialysis), and hemorrhage, which can complicate leptospirosis, are crucial for a good outcome.

Prevention

Immunization of animals is not necessarily effective at preventing human disease, because leptospiruria can still occur in immunized animals. Because asymptomatically infected wild animals can chronically excrete large numbers of spirochetes in their urine, controlling environmental sources of leptospirosis is difficult if not impossible. Occupationally exposed individuals (abattoir workers, veterinarians) should wear protective clothing to prevent exposure of skin and mucous membranes to potentially infected urine. Bodies of water associated with recreational exposures to leptospirosis may need to be placed off limits. Doxycycline, 200 mg orally once a week, has been 95% effective at preventing leptospirosis in U.S. troops undergoing training in the jungle warfare school in Panama and has a place in the short-term prevention of the disease in high-risk settings (e.g., participants in EcoChallenge events). No licensed vaccine is available in the United States for humans.

1. Panphut T, Domrongkitchaipom S, Vibhagool A, et al: Ceftriaxone compared with sodium penicillin G for treatment of severe leptospirosis. Clin Infect Dis 2003;36:1507–1513.

SUGGESTED READINGS
Centers for Disease Control and Prevention: Outbreak of acute febrile illness among participants in EcoChallenge Sabah 2000-Malaysia, 2000. Morb Mortal Wkly Rep 2000;49:816–817. *Thirty-seven (45%) of evaluable U.S. participants developed leptospirosis, prompting the CDC to recommend weekly doxycycline prophylaxis for high-risk individuals and consideration of single-dose postexposure prophylaxis during known outbreaks. Postexposure prophylaxis is of unproved benefit.*

Centers for Disease Control and Prevention: Leptospirosis and unexplained acute febrile illness among athletes participating in Triathlons—Illinois and Wisconsin, 1998. Morb Mortal Wkly Rep 1998;47:673–676. *An outbreak of leptospirosis in which 110 athletes (9% overall) from 44 states and seven countries became ill after participation in Illinois and/or Wisconsin triathlons.*

Guarner J, Wun-Ju S, Morgan J, et al: Leptospirosis mimicking acute cholecystitis among athletes participating in a triathlon. Human Pathol 2001;32:750–752. *Two patients had their gallbladders removed because of acute abdominal pain and a clinical suspicion of acute cholecystitis. Immunohistochemistry demonstrated leptospira antigens in the gallbladder wall.*

354 DISEASES CAUSED BY CHLAMYDIAE

Robert C. Brunham

Chlamydiae are obligate intracellular bacteria whose extreme biosynthetic defects in intermediate metabolism and energy generation cause them to be absolutely dependent on a host cell to grow and replicate. They are among the most common of all human infectious agents and produce much disability, although little mortality.

CHLAMYDIAE AS ORGANISMS

Genome analysis demonstrates that chlamydiae are a unique monophyletic bacterial group distantly related to cyanobacteria. Radical revision to chlamydia taxonomy has been proposed but not yet widely accepted; currently chlamydiae are composed of four species (Table 354–1).

The chlamydial bacterial cell has a gram-negative cell wall structure consisting of an outer membrane and an inner cytoplasmic membrane. However, no peptidoglycan layer is found within the periplasmic space separating these two layers. The outer membrane is protein-rich, composed of a single major outer membrane protein (MOMP; 40 kD) and two minor outer membrane proteins (60 and 12.5 kD). All three proteins are extraordinarily rich in the amino acid cysteine, and intermolecular and intramolecular disulfide bonding produces a supramolecular protein complex that confers structural rigidity on the bacterial cell analogous to the role played by peptidoglycan in other bacteria. Within *Chlamydia trachomatis*, MOMP variation determines the serologic types that characterize the individual serovars.

Polymorphic membrane proteins have also been recently identified on the surface of the chlamydial cell. Their role in pathogenesis is undefined. As with other gram-negative bacteria, the chlamydial outer membrane also contains lipopolysaccharide (LPS). Chlamydial LPS is a rough type without O-saccharides and is composed of a trisaccharide of 3-deoxy-D-manno-octulosonic acid (KDO). Although the core KDO sequences are shared by LPS from many other gram-negative bacteria, the chlamydial LPS is unique because two of the three KDOs are bonded through a 2.8 instead of a 2.4 linkage. Thus, antibodies to chlamydial LPS are specific. Because all four species of chlamydiae share the same LPS structure, antibodies to chlamydial LPS are genus specific.

Chlamydiae share a common and distinctive developmental cycle. Figure 354–1 shows the distinctive developmental cycle typical for all chlamydiae. The size of the chlamydial genome is small with *C. trachomatis* containing 894 protein-coding genes and *C. pneumoniae* containing 1052 genes. Most strains of *C. trachomatis* also contain a 7-kb cryptic plasmid; some strains of *C. pneumoniae* contain a 4-kb phage. Chlamydiae absolutely depend on host cells to obtain nutrients from the extracellular environment and convert them into forms they can use. In comparison with other bacteria, chlamydiae are virtually unique in being able to transport phosphorylated compounds found in the host cell cytoplasm, and this undoubtedly represents their premiere adaptation to the intracellular environment.

CHLAMYDIAE AS PATHOGENS

Depending on the species of chlamydiae, macrophage or non-macrophage host cells support the organisms' replication. Macrophages appear to be the principal target cell for *C. psittaci* and *C. trachomatis* lymphogranuloma venereum (LGV) biovars. Columnar epithelial cells found in mucous membranes are the usual host cells for trachoma biovar and for *C. pneumoniae* replication. Host cell trophism correlates with the type of inflammation elicited by chlamydiae. LGV biovar and *C. psittaci,* which infect macrophages, produce granulomatous inflammation characteristic of delayed hypersensitivity reactions. Trachoma biovar, which infects epithelial cells, produces neutrophilic exudate during acute infection and submucosal mononuclear infiltration with lymphoid follicle formation during later stages of infection.

Chlamydiae elicit both humoral and cellular immune responses. *C. trachomatis* elicits secretory IgA and circulatory IgM and IgG antibodies. Serum antibodies commonly recognize the chlamydial LPS as detected in the complement-fixation assay. *C. trachomatis* infection also elicits antibodies to the MOMP detected by the microimmunofluorescence assay. Women with reproductive sequelae such as tubal infertility or ectopic pregnancy due to *C. trachomatis* infection often have antibody responses to the heat shock protein 60 of chlamydiae.

Because chlamydiae produce intracellular infection, T-cell–mediated immune responses are prominent. HLA-restricted CD4 and CD8 T-cell responses occur. CD4 TH1 activation with interferon-γ (IFN-γ) secretion correlates with immunity and CD4 TH2 activation correlates with persistent infection. CD8 T-cell responses are detectable, but their role in resistance or immunopathogenesis is unclear.

PATHOGENESIS AND MECHANISM OF HOST INJURY

Most animal model studies of chlamydial infection demonstrate an acute self-limited course. However, case reports of human LGV biovar and *C. psittaci* infections that last 10 to 20 years and observations from a longitudinal follow-up study of untreated cervical *C. trachomatis* infection showing that infection can last 15 months or more suggest that chlamydiae also can produce chronic persistent infection. Chronic persistent infection or repeated episodes of acute infection appear to elicit the immune mechanisms that cause host injury. Infection of a previously exposed host results in an accelerated and intensified inflammatory response, and tissue destruction appears to be directly correlated with the intensity of inflammation. This is best elucidated for *C. trachomatis* ocular infection. Inflammatory and scarring (cicatricial) trachoma are diseases of reinfection, and the more intense the inflammatory response, the more prominent is the late fibrotic response. Thus, the mechanism for host injury with *C. trachomatis* infection is thought to be mediated by cellular immune

Table 354–1 • CLASSIFICATION OF BIOLOGIC VARIANTS (BIOVARS) AND SEROLOGIC VARIANTS (SEROVARS) OF THE GENUS *CHLAMYDIA*

	BIOVAR	SEROVAR
C. trachomatis	Trachoma	12
	Lymphogranuloma venereum	3
	Mouse pneumonitis	1
C. pneumoniae	TWAR	1
C. psittaci	Birds, mammals	Unknown, multiple
C. pecorum	Ruminants	Unknown, multiple

TWAR = Taiwan Acute Respiratory strain of *C. pneumoniae.*

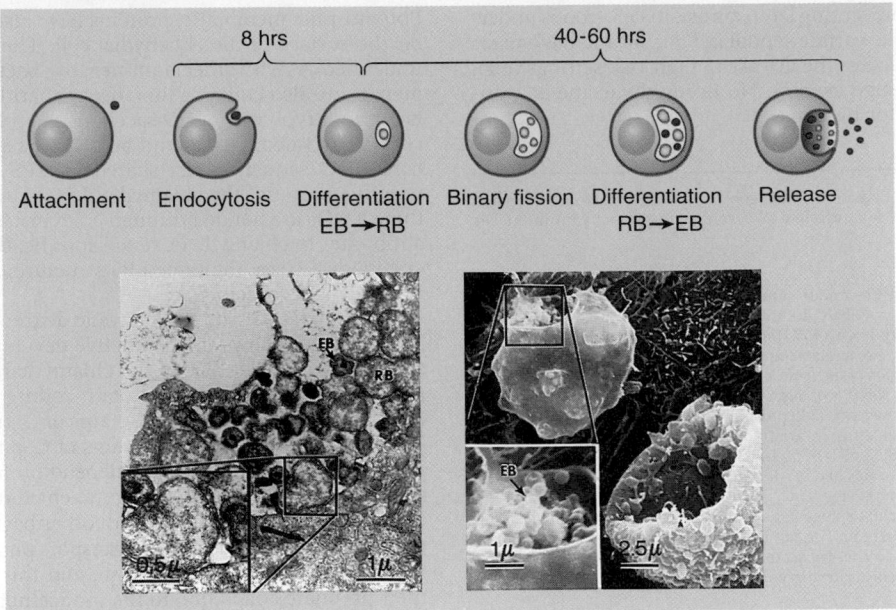

FIGURE 354–1 • The top panel schematically shows the developmental cycle common to all chlamydiae. The red circles represent elementary bodies (EBs), and the open circles represent reticulate bodies (RBs). Chlamydiae infect eukaryotic cells through multiple attachment mechanisms, best understood for *C. trachomatis*. A trimolecular complex with a secreted heparan sulfate–like glycosaminoglycan synthesized by *C. trachomatis* acts as a bridge between ligands on the chlamydial EB and the eukaryotic cell surface. Different mechanisms exist among different chlamydial species and may explain their distinct trophism. After attachment, EBs enter the cell within a membrane-bound vacuole that remains unfused with lysosomes. EBs reorganize into RBs and asynchronously replicate 8 to 12 times with a doubling time of 2 to 3 hours. At the conclusion of the growth cycle, RBs differentiate back to EBs, and each inclusion yields 100 to 1000 new infectious EBs. The bottom left panel is a transmission electron micrograph at 40 hours after infection showing the large RBs and the smaller EBs, which have a condensed nucleoid structure within their cytoplasm. The bottom right panel is a scanning electron micrograph at 60 hours after infection showing a membrane-bound vacuole containing many EBs exiting from an infected HeLa cell.

responses. Additionally, host cells infected by chlamydiae release proinflammatory chemokines and cytokines, which may cause tissue damage during chronic persistent infection.

CHLAMYDIAL DISEASES

Table 354–2 lists the most frequent chlamydial diseases.

CHLAMYDIA TRACHOMATIS

The major diseases caused by *C. trachomatis* are trachoma produced by serovars A, B, Ba, and C; sexually and perinatally transmitted diseases caused by serovars D through K; and sexually transmitted lymphogranuloma venereum caused by serovars L_1, L_2, and L_3. Trachoma and lymphogranuloma venereum are essentially restricted to developing areas of the world, whereas sexually and perinatally transmitted chlamydial infections are distributed globally. Trachoma and sexually/perinatally transmitted chlamydial infections are restricted to the mucosal surfaces of the body, and lymphogranuloma venereum causes systemic infection, principally of the lymphoid system.

TRACHOMA

Epidemiology

Trachoma is a distinctive ocular disease from infection by specific serovars of *C. trachomatis*. An estimated 150 million people worldwide, most of whom are young children, are afflicted with trachoma. Trachoma is especially common in poor areas of sub-Saharan Africa. Trachoma is a major public health problem because 1 to 5% of infected individuals later develop scarring, which deforms the eyelid, causes inward turning of the eyelashes (entropion), and results in corneal abrasion (trichiasis). Corneal damage results in blindness. Trachoma is the most common preventable cause of blindness; an estimated 6 million people are blind as a result of trachoma. Most of these individuals are middle-aged and elderly adults. Active trachoma often occurs within the first 1 to 2 years of life but after the first month. Recurrences of active disease are common during childhood and spontaneously cease by age 10 to 15. Among children, the frequency of face washing, access to water, sharing a sleeping room with an affected individual, and intensity of eye-seeking fly exposure are important risk factors for trachoma. Active trachoma also can occur in adults, especially in mothers caring for young children with active disease.

Table 354–2 • MAJOR DISEASES CAUSED BY CHLAMYDIA AND CARDINAL EPIDEMIOLOGIC FEATURES

	DISEASE	HOST RESERVOIR	TRANSMISSION ROUTE	EPIDEMIOLOGIC PERIODICITY
C. trachomatis	Trachoma	Children	Fomites/flies	Endemic
	Urethritis/cervicitis	Sexually active teenagers and adults	Direct sexual contact	
	Epididymitis/salpingitis	Sexually active teenagers and adults	Direct sexual contact	
	Lymphogranuloma venereum	Sexually active teenagers and adults	Direct sexual contact	
	Inclusion conjunctivitis	Infected pregnant mothers	Direct perinatal contact	
	Infant pneumonia			
C. psittaci	Atypical pneumonia	Birds	Aerosol	Epidemic
	Culture-negative endocarditis			
C. pneumoniae	Bronchitis	Humans	Respiratory droplet	Epidemic and endemic
	Atypical pneumonia			

Trichiasis is related to repeated intense trachoma episodes in childhood, is more common in women than in men, and preferentially occurs in families.

The *C. trachomatis* serovars that produce trachoma are spread by direct contact with contaminated fomites such as washcloths or eye-seeking flies. Perinatal exposure to *C. trachomatis* from maternal genital tract infection is not important in transmitting trachoma.

Clinical Manifestations

Trachoma is a chronic follicular conjunctivitis that causes macroscopically visible lymphoid follicles to form in the submucosa. These are especially apparent along the upper tarsal plate. The bulbar conjunctiva is minimally involved. Limited mucoid ocular discharge occurs; preauricular lymphadenopathy is rare and, if present, suggests other diagnoses such as adenovirus infection. The cornea may be involved with superficial vascularization and lymphocytic infiltration (pannus). Epidemic bacterial conjunctivitis due to *Haemophilus influenzae* can supervene on trachoma and cause a marked purulent conjunctivitis involving the bulbar conjunctiva. Bacterial conjunctivitis worsens the trachoma inflammatory damage. Tarsal conjunctival scarring deforms the eyelid structure and produces entropion and trichiasis in adulthood. Eventually, the corneal epithelium is eroded, and bacterial keratitis occurs. The cornea subsequently heals with opacification, resulting in blindness.

Diagnosis

Trachoma is most often a clinical diagnosis and is made if two of the following findings are observed: lymphoid follicles along the upper tarsal plate, lymphoid follicles (or Herbert's pits) along the corneal limbus, linear conjunctival scarring, and corneal pannus. Because most cases of trachoma occur in remote areas of the developing world without access to laboratory testing, most cases are diagnosed clinically. When laboratories are available, isolating *C. trachomatis* in cell culture provides definitive proof of the diagnosis. Culture is most often positive in young children with active disease and is rarely positive in adults with late scarring disease. Even in young children with active disease, culture is positive in only one third to one half of cases. Nonculture tests such as the direct immunofluorescent detection of elementary bodies (EBs) with monoclonal antibody or detecting chlamydial antigen by enzyme-linked immunosorbent assay (ELISA) are more frequently positive than are cultures. Detecting chlamydial DNA by polymerase chain reaction (PCR) is the most sensitive diagnostic test, with about 70 to 80% of children with active trachoma testing positive. Few adults with late cicatricial disease are found to have positive tests for chlamydial EBs, antigen, or DNA.

 Treatment

Active trachoma in children can be treated with the topical ocular application of tetracycline or erythromycin ointment for 21 to 60 days. Because extraocular *C. trachomatis* infection of the nasopharynx and gastrointestinal tract is relatively common during childhood trachoma, oral antibiotics such as erythromycin may be preferred. Single-dose oral azithromycin (20 mg/kg) seems as effective as 6 weeks of topical tetracycline. Trichiasis can be alleviated by depilation.

Prevention

The prevalence of trachoma in a community responds dramatically to socioeconomic development. Mass chemotherapy for young school-aged children has a temporary impact on trachoma prevalence. Control of fly exposure also assists in trachoma control. No vaccine is available.

SEXUALLY AND PERINATALLY TRANSMITTED CHLAMYDIAL INFECTIONS

Epidemiology

C. trachomatis is the most prevalent sexually transmitted bacterial infection in the United States. More than 3 million chlamydial infections occur annually, and prevalence rates are highest (>10%) among sexually active adolescent females. Prevalence is higher in inner-city areas among individuals of lower socioeconomic status and among minority ethnic groups such as African-Americans in the United States and Native Americans in Canada. Importantly, although prevalence rates are higher in these subgroups, with few exceptions, prevalences are 5% or more irrespective of geographic region, urban location, or ethnicity. In the United States, the direct and indirect costs of chlamydial disease exceed $2.4 billion annually. From a global perspective, sexually transmitted chlamydial infections are a major cause of total disease burden and morbidity because of effects on the reproductive health of women and because they facilitate the transmission of human immunodeficiency virus.

Clinical Manifestations

URETHRITIS. *C. trachomatis* causes 30 to 40% of cases of non-gonococcal urethritis (NGU) in men, and an estimated 40 to 60% of urethral chlamydial infections are symptomatic with NGU. NGU is characterized by complaints of mild urethral discharge, urethral discomfort, and mild dysuria. On examination, a mild to moderate clear or cloudy urethral exudate can be detected. Often this is best observed in the morning before voiding. Sometimes, urethral discharge is apparent only on "milking" the urethra from the base of the penis to the glans. Gram stain of urethral exudate demonstrates 5 or more polymorphonuclear leukocytes per ×1000 field and no gram-negative intracellular diplococci. Asymptomatic urethral infection is common with *C. trachomatis* infection and can be recognized by the urinary leukocyte esterase test on unspun first-void urine.

C. trachomatis urethral infection also occurs in women, in whom it produces the acute urethral syndrome. In such cases, the individual complains of dysuria, and pyuria (>5 white blood cells per ×1000 field) is found on urinalysis, but culture for uropathogens is negative. Urinary frequency and urgency are usually absent. Mild urethral exudate may be observed during pelvic examination when the urethra is compressed against the pubic ramus.

EPIDIDYMITIS. In some men with urethral chlamydial infection (an estimated 1 to 3%), infection spreads from the urethra to the epididymis. This results in unilateral testicular pain, scrotal erythema and tenderness, or swelling over the epididymis. Epididymitis associated with urethritis is most commonly due to *C. trachomatis* or *Neisseria gonorrhoeae* (Chapter 346). Among men younger than 35 years, *C. trachomatis* is the principal cause of epididymitis. Among men older than 35 years, complicated urinary tract infection with uropathogens is more commonly the cause of epididymitis.

REITER'S SYNDROME. Reactive arthritis can complicate chlamydial infection (Chapter 279). About 50% of men with non-diarrheal Reiter's syndrome have urethral *C. trachomatis* infection. It is estimated that approximately 1% of men with chlamydial urethritis develop Reiter's syndrome.

MUCOPURULENT CERVICITIS. Mucopurulent cervicitis in women is the clinical counterpart of NGU in men. As with NGU, *C. trachomatis* causes 40 to 50% of cases of mucopurulent cervicitis. Twenty to 50% of women with cervical chlamydial infection have mucopurulent cervicitis. Women with mucopurulent cervicitis may complain of mucoid vaginal discharge. Unless concurrent infection with other pathogens is present, the vaginal discharge lacks odor, and vulvar pruritus does not occur. Mucopurulent cervicitis is best recognized during vaginal speculum examination with the cervix fully exposed and well illuminated. There is a yellow or cloudy mucoid discharge from the cervix, although the color may be better appreciated on the tip of a cotton swab than in situ. Gram stain of endocervical mucus shows more than 10 polymorphonuclear leukocytes per ×1000 field. Often, a red area of columnar epithelium is visible on the face

Continued

of the cervix (ectopy). The area is erythematous, is edematous, and bleeds easily when touched with a cotton-tipped swab.

ENDOMETRITIS AND SALPINGITIS.

C. trachomatis infection can spread from the cervix to the endometrium to produce endometritis and to the fallopian tubes to produce salpingitis. Spread occurs in 10 to 40% of women with cervical chlamydial infection. If *C. trachomatis* spreads to the endometrium after therapeutic or postvaginal delivery, it can produce late onset postpartum or postabortal endometritis. More commonly, chlamydial infection spreads spontaneously to the upper reproductive tract. Although endometritis and salpingitis can occur subclinically, clinically patent disease includes the following features: subacute onset of low abdominal pain during menses or during the first 2 weeks of the menstrual cycle, pain on sexual intercourse (dyspareunia), and prolonged menses or intermenstrual vaginal bleeding. Fever is not a common feature of *C. trachomatis* endometritis or salpingitis.

INFANT INCLUSION CONJUNCTIVITIS AND PNEUMONIA.

Perinatally transmitted *C. trachomatis* infection is an important health problem for infants. Approximately two of three infants perinatally exposed to *C. trachomatis* acquire infection. Clinically patent disease occurs in about 75% of infected infants, and 25% are subclinically infected. Inclusion conjunctivitis of the newborn develops in one in three exposed infants and a distinctive pneumonia syndrome in about one in six. Because 5 to 20% of pregnant women in the United States have *C. trachomatis* cervical infection, morbidity due to perinatally transmitted chlamydial infection is substantial.

The distinctive pneumonia syndrome has a subacute onset in infants between ages 1 and 4 months. The natural history of illness is protracted and, importantly, fever is absent. The cardinal clinical characteristic is a distinctive staccato cough reminiscent of pertussis but without the whoop or post-tussive vomiting. Hematologic examination consistently shows eosinophilia and hypergammaglobulinemia.

LYMPHOGRANULOMA VENEREUM.

LGV is the result of sexually transmitted infection with *C. trachomatis* serovars L_1, L_2, or L_3. This is a systemic infection that involves lymphoid tissue. LGV is most common in sub-Saharan Africa, although accurate statistics are lacking. LGV is rare in the United States, with a few hundred cases reported annually.

The *C. trachomatis* serovars that produce LGV are much more invasive than are other *C. trachomatis* serovars. Similar to diseases due to other *C. trachomatis* serovars, LGV produces acute disease and late fibrotic complications. Among heterosexuals, primary LGV infection produces an evanescent and rarely observed genital ulcer 2 to 3 weeks after exposure. The ulcer spontaneously heals, and 2 to 4 weeks later painful bilateral inguinal lymphadenopathy develops, often associated with signs of systemic infection such as fever, headache, arthralgias, leukocytosis, and hypergammaglobulinemia. In the absence of treatment, LGV spontaneously heals, sometimes leaving lymphatic scarring. Late fibrotic complications of LGV include genital elephantiasis, strictures, and fistulas of the penis, urethra, and rectum.

In women and homosexual men, rectal infection with *C. trachomatis* L_1, L_2, or L_3 strains produces a severe febrile proctocolitis illness. Patients complain of frequent painful defecation (tenesmus) with urgency and, less commonly, mucopurulent bloody discharge in stool. Biopsy of rectal mucosa shows submucosal granulomas, crypt abscesses, and diffuse mononuclear cell inflammation. The clinical, endoscopic, and histopathologic findings can mimic Crohn's disease of the rectum.

Laboratory Findings

Empirical treatment for *C. trachomatis* infection should be initiated when a specific chlamydial syndrome is recognized. However, definitive diagnosis of *C. trachomatis* infection depends on laboratory identification of the organism. Laboratory diagnosis confirms the clinical diagnosis, assists in managing contacts of infected cases, and detects asymptomatic but infectious individuals. Screening women for *C. trachomatis* has been demonstrated to reduce the incidence of acute salpingitis as well as prevention of pelvic inflammatory disease.

The "gold standard" for diagnosing *C. trachomatis* infection is isolating the organism in cell culture. The development of culture-independent technologies to identify *C. trachomatis* infection was an important advancement. Culture-independent tests detect (1) *C. trachomatis* EBs in mucosal exudate by fluorescent-labeled monoclonal antibody, (2) antigen (mainly lipopolysaccharide) in extracted mucosal exudate by ELISA, (3) plasmid DNA by direct probing, and (4) chlamydial DNA by PCR amplification. The relative sensitivity of these tests is as follows: cell culture or PCR (capable of detecting a single EB) > LPS antigen detection by ELISA (lower limit of detection, ≈10^3 EBs) > chromosomal or plasmid DNA probe detection (lower limit of detection, ≈10^3 to 10^4 EBs). Because many chlamydial infections such as NGU, salpingitis, and trachoma are characterized by low numbers of organisms, amplification-based tests are preferred. At present, the higher costs of these tests limit their widespread use, and antigen- or probe-based tests remain the most commonly used tests. Interpreting a positive ELISA test for chlamydia antigen can be difficult in situations in which the prevalence of *C. trachomatis* is low (<5%) because such tests typically have false-positive rates of 1 to 3%. For example, when an antigen-ELISA has a specificity of 98%, has a sensitivity of 80%, and is used to screen 1000 individuals from a high-risk population with a *C. trachomatis* prevalence of 15%, the predictive value of a positive test is 88%. When the same test is used to screen 1000 individuals from a low-risk population with a *C. trachomatis* prevalence of 2%, the predictive value of positive tests falls to 44%. Clinicians should verify positive antigen-ELISA tests with a second *C. trachomatis* diagnostic test based on a different method if the risk of false-positive tests results in adverse medical, social, or legal consequences.

Serology is infrequently used to diagnose *C. trachomatis* infection except in two circumstances: Specific *C. trachomatis* IgM antibody at a titer of 1:32 or more is useful to diagnose the infant pneumonia syndrome, and a complement-fixation antibody titer of 1:64 or more suggests LGV.

Rx Treatment

C. trachomatis is uniformly susceptible to tetracyclines, macrolides, and sulfonamides. Recent data also suggest that selected quinolones (ofloxacin) are useful to treat *C. trachomatis* infection.

The recommended treatment for uncomplicated *C. trachomatis* urethritis and mucopurulent cervicitis is doxycycline (100 mg orally twice daily for 7 days) or azithromycin (1 g orally in a single dose), although azithromycin is substantially more expensive than doxycycline. Alternate treatment regimens include erythromycin base (500 mg orally four times a day for 7 days) or ofloxacin (300 mg orally twice daily for 7 days). *C. trachomatis* epididymitis and endometritis/salpingitis should be treated for 10 to 14 days. LGV should be treated for 3 weeks.

Sexual partners and parents of infants infected with *C. trachomatis* should be evaluated, tested, and empirically treated. Sexual contacts within the preceding 30 to 60 days should be seen.

CHLAMYDIA PNEUMONIAE

In 1986, a new chlamydial pathogen was recognized—*C. pneumoniae*—that causes respiratory illness. Although initially confused with *C. psittaci*, genome analysis demonstrates that *C. pneumoniae* is a separate species more closely related to *C. psittaci* than to *C. trachomatis*. Pneumonia and bronchitis are the most frequently identified illnesses caused by *C. pneumoniae*. Emerging evidence suggests that *C. pneumoniae* may cause atherosclerosis.

Epidemiology

More than 50% of adults in the United States and from other developed countries are seropositive. Most seroconversion occurs during childhood with rates of 6 to 9% per year for the age group 5 to 14. Many seroconversions occur subclinically. *C. pneumoniae* causes both endemic and epidemic atypical pneumonia syndromes. In Seattle, the average annual endemic incidence of *C. pneumoniae* pneumonia was

1.2 per 1000 population. Approximately 10% of pneumonia illnesses were attributed to *C. pneumoniae*. Periods of increased incidence were observed at 3- to 4-year cycles. This organism also produces epidemics of atypical pneumonia in closed populations such as military recruits, university students, and the institutionalized elderly. Case-to-case transmission appears to involve respiratory droplet spread with an average case-to-case interval of 1 month. Both diseased and asymptomatically infected individuals transmit infection.

Clinical Manifestations

Even though most acute infections occur in children, most *C. pneumoniae* disease occurs in adults, especially the elderly. It causes an afebrile, usually relatively mild pneumonia. Extrapulmonary findings are not prominent. Nonproductive cough with sore throat and hoarseness is characteristic. The time from onset of illness to clinical presentation is long. On auscultation, localized crackles are often heard. Chest radiography shows a pneumonitis, most often evident as a single subsegmental lesion. Hematologic studies show a normal leukocyte count but a high erythrocyte sedimentation rate.

C. pneumoniae also causes bronchitis and sinusitis. Bronchitis is often subacute in onset, lasting several days or weeks. Some patients with bronchitis unexpectedly have pneumonia on radiography. Sinusitis is often demonstrated by sinus percussion tenderness. Isolated pharyngitis is rarely attributable to *C. pneumoniae* infection, but when pharyngitis, sinusitis, and bronchitis are observed in association with pneumonia, *C. pneumoniae* is a likely cause.

Laboratory Findings

Serology, isolation, and nonculture detection are the primary methods for laboratory diagnosis of *C. pneumoniae* infection. The indirect microimmunofluorescent test for *C. pneumoniae* antibodies remains the best method for laboratory diagnosis. Isolating *C. pneumoniae* in cell culture (HL cell line) is successful in 50 to 75% of cases of serologically confirmed infections but is technically demanding. PCR of *C. pneumoniae*–specific DNA is about 25% more sensitive than culture and likely will become the diagnostic test of choice. At present, no effective diagnostic method for *C. pneumoniae* is commercially available.

 Treatment

C. pneumoniae is susceptible to tetracycline and macrolides but not sulfonamides. Antimicrobial therapy for *C. pneumoniae* infection can be difficult, and clinical response is not dramatic. Recommended treatment includes tetracycline or erythromycin base 500 mg orally four times a day for 10 to 14 days.

Association with Atherosclerosis

Four lines of evidence suggest that *C. pneumoniae* may cause atherosclerosis and plaque instability. Seroepidemiologic studies have shown a constant excess prevalence of *C. pneumoniae* antibodies among atherosclerosis cases compared with controls. *C. pneumoniae* has been isolated from atherosclerotic plaques on several occasions and has been identified in plaques by nonculture tests in over 50% of cases. *C. pneumoniae* infection in animal models causes atherosclerosis. Preliminary intervention trials have shown that antibiotic treatment substantially reduces coronary events among individuals presenting with ischemic heart disease, and additional large-scale antibiotic intervention trials are under way.

CHLAMYDIA PSITTACI

Epidemiology

Strangely, *C. psittaci* is the least common but the only reportable chlamydial infection. *C. psittaci* is reportable because it produces common-source outbreaks of serious disease often related to infected imported birds. *C. psittaci* is a heterogeneous chlamydial species that

naturally infects a variety of nonhuman mammals and birds. *C. psittaci* strains appear to be host specific, and most human psittacosis infections are linked to bird and not mammal exposure. One hundred to 200 cases of psittacosis are reported annually in the United States with no apparent periodicity. The annual incidence has been stable for the past 15 years. Psittacine birds (parrots, parakeets, budgerigars) are most commonly implicated as source contacts, although human cases have been traced to contact with pigeons, ducks, turkeys, chickens, and other birds. Among infected birds, *C. psittaci* is present in nasal and cloacal secretions, guano, and feathers. Psittacosis in birds is a mild illness manifested by ruffled feathers and anorexia. Recovered and asymptomatically infected birds can shed the organism for months.

Transmission to humans is by the aerosol route to the respiratory tract. The infectious inoculum is likely very small, and brief contact with a contaminated environment can result in transmission. Person-to-person spread of *C. psittaci* rarely occurs.

Clinical Manifestations

Psittacosis is a systemic infection of the reticuloendothelial system and of the interstitium and alveoli of the lung. Seven to 14 days after aerosol exposure, an abrupt febrile illness begins with shaking chills and a fever as high as 40° C. Headache, myalgias, and arthralgias can be disabling. Cough appears early in the illness but is usually nonproductive. Auscultation may be normal or show bilateral crackles. Chest radiograph shows single or multiple localized bronchopneumonic patches. Clinically, psittacosis can resemble legionnaires' disease. In distinction to *C. pneumoniae* pneumonia, psittacosis is more severe with high fever and absent or minimal upper respiratory complaints.

Extrapulmonary findings are usual with psittacosis, and myalgias can mislead the clinician to suspect meningitis or pyelonephritis. Fulminant psittacosis can produce meningoencephalitis, hepatitis, and a faint macular rash (Horder's spots) resembling the rose spots of typhoid fever. Like typhoid fever, psittacosis may cause abdominal pain, diarrhea, constipation, and splenomegaly. Occasional patients, especially with underlying valvular heart disease, develop endocarditis, and *C. psittaci* is a recognized, if rare, cause of culture-negative endocarditis. Untreated psittacosis can be fatal, but most patients recover slowly after an illness lasting 10 to 21 days.

Laboratory Findings

The diagnosis can be established by isolating the organism in cell culture or by serology. Because laboratory-acquired *C. psittaci* infections are well documented, cell culture isolation is discouraged and serology is the preferred test method. If culture is attempted, it is essential to contain the specimen in a biosafety cabinet for processing. Blood and respiratory secretions can be used to isolate the organism during acute disease. Psittacosis is most readily diagnosed by demonstrating a rising titer of complement-fixing antibody in the serum. Acute and 3- to 6-week convalescent sera should be tested.

 Treatment

C. psittaci is susceptible to tetracyclines and macrolides but resistant to sulfonamides. Tetracycline has had the greatest clinical use. Psittacosis is the most gratifying of all chlamydial diseases to treat. Defervescence and marked symptomatic relief of systemic signs occur within 24 to 48 hours after starting tetracycline 500 mg four times a day or doxycycline 100 mg twice a day. Treatment should be continued for 10 to 21 days.

Prevention

Epidemic psittacosis is preventable by quarantining and giving all imported psittacine birds tetracycline. Preventing psittacosis acquired from nonpsittacine birds is more problematic and will remain a continuing source for human infection. No vaccine is commercially available.

1. Scholes D, Stergachis A, Heidrich FE, et al: Prevention of pelvic inflammatory disease by screening for cervical chlamydial infection. N Engl J Med 1996;334:1362–1366.

SUGGESTED READINGS

Bachmaier K, Neu N, de la Maza LM, et al: Chlamydia infections and heart disease linked through antigenic mimicry. Science 1999;283:1335–1339. *An animal model demonstrating that chlamydia-initiated heart disease is immune-mediated.*

Grayston JT: Background and current knowledge of Chlamydia pneumoniae and atherosclerosis. J Infect Dis 2000;181(Suppl 3):S402–S410. *A masterly review of evidence linking chlamydia to heart disease.*

Parish WL, Laumann EO, Cohen MS, et al: Population-based study of chlamydial infections in China: A hidden epidemic. JAMA 2003;289:1303–1305. *Emphasizes the importance of chlamydia in developing countries.*

Stamm WE: *Chlamydia trachomatis* infections: Progress and problems. J Infect Dis 1999;179(Suppl 2):S380–S383. *Succinct review of the tremendous progress in understanding and control of chlamydia infection.*

Stephens RS, Kalman S, Lammel C, et al: Genome sequence of an obligate intracellular pathogen of humans: Chlamydia trachomatis. Science 1998;282:754–759. *The first publication of the entire genetic blueprint for a chlamydia.*

355 RICKETTSIOSES

Didier Raoult

Rickettsioses are emerging infectious diseases. Because of better diagnostic tools and, maybe, changes in tick exposure, many new rickettsial diseases have been described in the past 15 years. Three families of diseases are grouped under this name: Q fever, ehrlichioses (4 out of 5 currently identified have been described since 1987), and diseases caused by rickettsiae (9 of 18 described since 1990).

The agents of rickettsial diseases (formerly grouped in the family Rickettsiales) are small gram-negative bacteria that grow within eukaryotic cells. They have never been grown in axenic media and require, for culture, living hosts such as cell cultures, embryonated eggs, or susceptible animals. With the exception of *Rickettsia prowazekii*, the agent of epidemic typhus, these bacteria infect humans incidentally and are mainly agents of zoonoses. On the basis of molecular phylogeny, the bacteria causing rickettsial diseases have been reclassified in three phyla (Table 355–1).

Coxiella burnetii, the agent of Q fever, belongs to the γ proteobacteria phylum, related to *Legionella pneumophila* and *Francisella tularensis*. It causes a zoonosis infecting many species, including ungulates and pets, and is excreted in birth products and milk. Human beings are usually contaminated by aerosols and experience an acute primary infection eventually followed by a chronic disease when predisposing factors are present.

Rickettsia species and *Orientia tsutsugamushi* belong to the α1 subgroup of proteobacteria. These bacteria live free in the cytoplasm of their infected hosts. Many pathogenic bacteria belong to this branch of bacteria. The main pathogenic mechanism of *Rickettsia* is a vasculitis following infection of vascular endothelial cells. These bacteria are transmitted through arthropods. Medically and epidemiologically, it is possible to classify rickettsioses on the basis of their vectors as tick-borne, louse-borne, flea-borne, and mite-borne rickettsioses. The arthropod host determines the epidemiology of the disease, including its geographic distribution. On the basis of antigenic divergence and phylogenic studies, *Rickettsia* sp were divided into three taxonomic groups:

The spotted fever group includes the tick-transmitted diseases, Rocky Mountain spotted fever (caused by *R. rickettsii*), Mediterranean spotted fever (*Rickettsia conorii*), and African tick bite fever (*Rickettsia africae*); one mite-transmitted disease, rickettsialpox (*Rickettsia akari*); and the flea-borne spotted fever caused by *Rickettsia felis*.

The typhus group comprises *R. prowazekii*, causing louse-borne epidemic typhus, and *Rickettsia typhi*, the agent of the flea-borne murine typhus.

The scrub typhus group includes *O. tsutsugamushi*, causing a mite (chigger)-borne disease.

Ehrlichioses are zoonoses caused by bacteria constituting another branch of the α1 subgroup of proteobacteria. The bacteria grow in cells in a cytoplasmic vacuole, forming clusters or morulae. This large group of bacteria are increasingly recognized as potential human pathogens, and their current taxonomy has been changed to match current phylogenic knowledge. Four genera are described. One, which is apparently associated with helminths, is named *Neorickettsia* and comprises one identified human pathogen recognized only in Japan (*Neorickettsia sennetsu*). Two are associated with ticks: *Ehrlichia* (including *Ehrlichia chaffeensis*, *Ehrlichia canis*, and *Ehrlichia ewingii*, three human pathogens) and *Anaplasma* (with *Anaplasma phagocytophila* being the only currently identified pathogen). The fourth genus, *Wolbachia*, with one species, *Wolbachia pipientis*, is associated with either arthropods or nematodes. In this case, when associated with filaria, it appears to be a pathogenic factor and a treatment target in human filariasis.

Because of the difficult growth in vitro, the main diagnostic tool for rickettsioses has been serology for years. Serology is frequently

Table 355–1 • GENETIC CLASSIFICATION OF RICKETTSIALES

	GENUS	GROUP	SPECIES	SEROTYPE	FIRST YEAR OF ISOLATION OR DISCOVERY
Rickettsiae		Typhus	R. prowazekii	1916	
			R. typhi	1920	
	Rickettsia				
		Spotted fever	R. conorii	Malish	1932
				Israel	1974
				Astrakhan	1991
				Indian	2001
			R. rickettsii		1919
			R. sibirica		1946
			R. mongolotimonae		1996
			R. slovaca		1997
			R. honei		1991
			R. japonica		1992
			R. heilonjanghensis		1998
			R. aeschlimannii		2001
			R. helvetica		2000
			R. australis		1950
			R. felis		2001
			R. akari		1946
	Orientia				
		Scrub typhus	O. tsutsugamushi		1920
Ehrlichiae	*Ehrlichia*		E. chaffeensis		1991
			E. ewingii		1999
			E. canis		1996
	Anaplasma		A. phagocytophilum		1992
	Neorickettsia		N. sennetsu		1957
	Wolbachia		W. pipientis		2001
	Coxiella		C. burnetii		1931

hampered by late positivity and cross-reactivity. The development of direct staining in blood smears or skin biopsies as well as polymerase chain reaction (PCR) amplification of blood samples or biopsy specimens has considerably helped identification at the species level and description of emerging pathogens. Finally, rickettsial diseases have a common treatment, which is currently based mainly on doxycycline in adults and children.

RICKETTSIOSES (DISEASES CAUSED BY *RICKETTSIA* SP AND *ORIENTIA* SP)

Bacteriology and Pathophysiology

Rickettsia sp are small gram-negative bacteria that multiply in the cytoplasm of their host cells. The target cells in humans are endothelial. The genome of *Rickettsia* is small, between 1.1 and 1.6 Mb, and they do not possess mobile genetic elements. These bacteria have four (typhus group) or five outer membrane proteins of the surface cell antigen (SCA) family; two are also known as specific protein antigens, that is, rOmpA (lacking in typhus group) and rOmpB. These proteins are major antigens that help identify the rickettsial species, and their encoding genes are used for amplification and sequencing for diagnostic or taxonomic purposes. These bacteria invade cells by phagocytosis and escape the phagosome vacuole. Among rickettsiae, two subgroups, typhus group (TG) and spotted fever group (SFG), were identified on the basis of growth conditions and antigenicity. A specific group antigen, determined by lipopolysaccharide, has been identified. Optimal growth temperature is 37° C for TG and 32 to 35° C for SFG. TG lacks one of the major surface proteins (rOmpA). TG rickettsiae are unable to move intracellularly, but SFG rickettsiae show actin-based mobility. TG rickettsiae have a smaller genome. The complete genome sequencing of *R. prowazekii* (from the typhus group) showed that it is mainly a subset of *R. conorii* (a member of the spotted fever group).

There is no clear relationship between the bacteriologic grouping of *Rickettsia* and their specific arthropod host; rickettsiae from both groups could have as vector an insect (louse or flea) or an acarid (tick or mite). The species definition among *Rickettsia* has mainly been based on serotype. Many rickettsial species were identified first in their arthropod vectors; however, it is misleading to refer to these as "nonpathogenic" unless they have been inoculated in human beings. Many bacteria earlier classified as nonpathogenic *Rickettsia* are currently recognized pathogens: *L. pneumophila*, *C. burnetii*, and *R. africae*.

ROCKY MOUNTAIN SPOTTED FEVER

Epidemiology

Rocky Mountain spotted fever (RMSF), the most severe of the rickettsioses, is caused by *R. rickettsii* (Table 355–2). It is currently the only tick-transmitted rickettsiosis recognized in America (with *R. africae* in the French West Indies). It was described first in the 19th century in the western United States. It is prevalent in 44 states in the United States (Fig. 355 1) and in Central and South America (Argentina, Brazil, Colombia, Costa Rica, Mexico, and Panama).

Rickettsia is transmitted transovarially to the tick progeny from one generation to the next. The infecting ticks are mainly *Dermacentor andersoni* (a wood tick) in the western United States and *Dermacentor variabilis* (the American dog tick) in the East, the Middle West, and the South. In Central and South America, *Amblyomma cajennense* is the major vector. Humans are infected, after tick bite, through infected saliva. The duration of attachment is critical in any tick-borne rickettsiosis, and transmission is unlikely when the tick feeds for less than 20 hours. However, the tick bite is painless and frequently unnoticed. Rarely, an eschar at the site of the tick bite is observed in RMSF. The epidemiology of RMSF undergoes largely unexplained yearly variations. This temporal repartition is determined by tick activity and human encounter. There are 500 to 1000 cases annually, with a majority of cases diagnosed during late spring and summer, as over 90% of cases are reported from April to September. The disease is more prevalent in children younger than 10 years.

Clinical Manifestations

Two to 14 days after the tick bite, the disease starts with fever and headaches. Fever is high (temperature greater than 102° F) and associated with unspecific symptoms including malaise, myalgias, nausea, vomiting, anorexia, and diarrhea. At this stage, RMSF is not frequently diagnosed, but during the "tick season" patients with high fever who live in or have a history of travel to an endemic location and, possibly, a history of tick bite should be considered as possible RMSF cases.

The diagnostic clue, clinically, is a rash. However, the classical triad of fever, headache, and rash is present in only 44% of confirmed cases. The untreated patient worsens progressively. Rash is found in 14% of cases in the first day of disease and in less than 50% in the first 3 days. The rash is macular; it appears first on

Continued

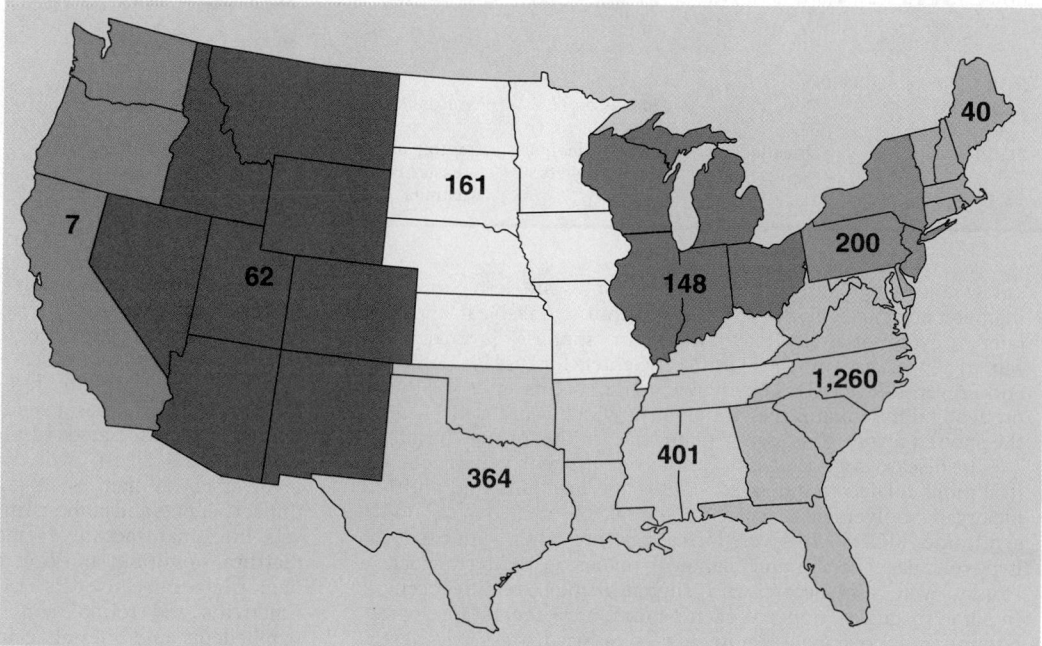

FIGURE 355–1 • Number of reported cases of Rocky Mountain spotted fever by region, 1994 to 1998.

Infectious Diseases

Table 355–2 • RICKETTSIAL DISEASES IN HUMAN BEINGS

DISEASE	ORGANISM	ARTHROPOD HOST	GEOGRAPHIC AREA	RASH	ESCHAR TACHE NOIRE	REGIONAL LYMPH NODE	HIGH FEVER	FATALITY RATE
TICK-TRANSMITTED SPOTTED FEVERS								
Rocky Moutain spotted fever	R. rickettsii	Dermacentor andersoni Dermacentor variabilis Amblyomma cajennense	America (north, central, and south)	Yes, may be purpuric	Very rare	No	Yes	High
Mediterranean spotted fever Astrachan fever, Israeli spotted fever	R. conorii complex	Rhipicephalus sanguineus	Mediterranean, India, Caspian Sea, Africa	Yes, papular may be purpuric	Yes	No	Yes	Moderate
African tick bite fever	R. africae	Amblyomma hebraum Amblyomma variegatum	Sub-Sahara, Africa, West Indies	Yes, (half of cases) may be vesicular	Yes (frequently multiple)	Yes	No	Low
Queensland tick typhus	R. australis	Ixodes holocyclus	Eastern Australia	Yes, may be vesicular	Yes	?	Yes	Moderate
Siberian tick typhus	R. sibirica	Dermacentor nuttallii	Siberia, China, Mongolia	Yes	Yes	No	Yes	Low
Tick-borne lymphadenopathy (TIBOLA)	R. slovaca	Dermacentor marginatus Dermacentor reticulatus	Europe, Pakistan	Very rare	Yes, may be erythematous	Yes (painful)	No	Low
Unnamed	R. mongolo-timonae	Hyalomma asiaticum	Mongolia, Africa	Yes	Yes	Yes	Yes	Low
Unnamed	R. aeschlimannii	Hyalomma marginatum	Mediterranean, Africa	Yes	Yes	Yes	Yes	Unknown
Flinders Island spotted fever	R. honei	Ixodes granulosus	Flinder's Island, eastern Australia	Yes	Yes	Yes	Yes	Low
Japanese spotted fever	R. japonica	Ixodes ricinus	Japan (China?)	Yes	Yes	No	Yes	Low
Unnamed	R. helvetica	Ixodes ricinus	Europe, Asia	No	Yes	No	No	? Sudden death reported
FLEA-TRANSMITTED DISEASES								
Murine typhus	R. typhi	Xenopsylla cheopis Ctenocephalides felis	Worldwide	Yes	No	No	Yes	Low
Flea-borne spotted fever	R. felis	Ctenocephalides felis	Worldwide	Sometimes	Sometimes	Unknown	Yes	Unknown
LOUSE-TRANSMITTED DISEASE								
Epidemic typhus	R. prowazekii	Pediculus humanus corporis	Wordwide	Yes	No	No	Yes	High
American sylvatic typhus	R. prowazekii	Flying squirrel ectoparasites	United States	Yes	No	No	Yes	Low
Brill-Zinsser disease (relapse of epidemic typhus)	R. prowazekii		Worldwide	Yes, could lack	No	No	No	Low
MITE-TRANSMITTED DISEASE								
Rickettsial pox	R. akari	Liponyssoides sanguineus	Worldwide	Yes vesicular	Yes	Yes	Yes	Low
Scrub typhus	Orientia tsutsugamushi	Leptotrombidium sp (chiggers)	Central and eastern Asia Australia	Yes	Yes	Yes	Yes	High, may relapse

ankles and wrists and then generalizes. Spots are 1 to 5 mm in diameter and can evolve from pink to purpuric. A rash can appear later or even not at all; Rocky Mountain "spotless" fever represented 34% of cases in a series from the Centers for Disease Control and Prevention (CDC). The involvement of palms and soles theoretically differentiates the typhuses (in which it is absent) from the spotted fevers. This sign is frequently lacking or may be late.

The disease is associated in various degrees with general manifestations related to increased vascular permeability and multiple organ involvement that can lead to multiple organ dysfunction syndrome (MODS). In severe forms, patients suffer from edema, hypovolemia, hypoalbuminemia, and hypotension leading to shock. In very severe cases, necrosis and gangrene of the extremities occur. In some instances, noncardiogenic pulmonary edema develops; pulmonary involvement leading to respiratory distress can cause

death. Renal failure can result either from hypovolemia and shock and be reversible or from acute tubular necrosis and require hemodialysis. Usual neurologic symptoms are confusion, lethargy, and stupor. In severe cases, delirium, coma, and seizures are observed. Cerebrospinal fluid (CSF) sampling exhibits meningitis in one third of cases; usually a few monocyte cells (10 to 100) are observed, associated with increased protein levels but normal glucose levels. Heart involvement can cause dysrhythmia. Liver involvement is manifest as an increase in transaminases in one third of patients and jaundice in 8%. Jaundice can also reflect hemolysis. Intestinal tract involvement is manifest as abdominal pain, diarrhea, vomiting, and severe bleeding (upper gastrointestinal hemorrhage can cause death). Ocular involvement consists of conjunctivitis and retinal abnormalities including hemorrhages, papilledema, and arterial occlusion.

Biologically, the blood cell count shows a normal number of white blood cells but often immature myeloid cells. Thrombocytopenia is observed in 30 to 50% of cases and may be marked in severe cases. Anemia develops in 30% of patients. Coagulopathy with decreases in clotting factors (including fibrinogen) and prolonged coagulation times may contribute to bleeding; albuminemia may be low and proteins of the acute phase response increased (C-reactive protein, ferritin, fibrinogen). Hyponatremia and hypocalcemia can be noted and correlated with severity, as with an increase in creatininemia. Increased concentrations of serum enzymes such as aminotransferases (aspartate and alanine aminotransferases, AST and ALT), lactate dehydrogenase (LDH), and creatine phosphokinase usually reflect the severity of organ involvement including lung, heart, and liver and multifocal rhabdomyolysis.

The evolution of RMSF depends strongly on the timing of diagnosis and of antibiotic treatment. Spontaneous evolution of RMSF is frequently fatal; the current fatality rate is 2.4% on the basis of a 4-year national survey in the United States (27 deaths were attributable to RMSF during this period). No significant statistical difference in the outcome was observed between blacks and whites, but the case fatality rate was highest among people older than 70 years (9%). The survey found cases of fulminant infection. Patients with glucose-6-phosphate dehydrogenase (G6PD) deficiency were more susceptible. Chloramphenicol is associated with a poorer outcome than doxycycline. Usually, recovery from RMSF is complete but neurologic sequelae can remain, and amputation of extremities may be necessary after gangrene.

Diagnosis of RMSF should be based on clinical and epidemiologic findings, leading to early use of doxycycline. The most important clue is unexplained fever in a patient with a history of tick exposure in an endemic area. When a rash is present, RMSF should be suspected and the patient treated accordingly unless another cause is demonstrated. The differential diagnosis includes other rickettsioses, meningococcemia, enterovirus infections, typhoid, leptospirosis, ehrlichiosis, gonococcemia, toxic shock syndrome, syphilis, rubella, measles, and Kawasaki syndrome. The major cause of error when a rash appears after inappropriate antibiotic prescription in a febrile patient is drug hypersensitivity.

Diagnosis

Criteria for laboratory confirmation include a fourfold or greater change in antibody titers determined by serology (measured by immunofluorescence assay [IFA], complement fixation, or latex agglutination) or direct detection of the bacterium by demonstration of specific antigens by immunodetection, genomic amplification by PCR, or culture. A biopsy specimen of a skin lesion is the best sample for this purpose. Culture of *Rickettsia* takes 3 to 7 days and is restricted to specialized laboratories. It is performed on cell lines such as Vero, L929, or HEL cells. For this purpose, the shell vial device, also used in virology for cytomegalovirus isolation but avoiding the addition of antibiotics, is efficient. Immunodetection by immunofluorescence or immunohistochemistry is sensitive and specific. It can be performed with frozen or fixed and paraffin-embedded material and allows retrospective diagnosis. PCR amplification and identification give promising results in rickettsioses in general but have not been properly evaluated in RMSF. For this purpose, skin biopsy and direct detection in removed ticks give the best results as blood contains inhibitors and few copies of rickettsial DNA.

Currently, the diagnosis is based mainly on serology. Two serum samples should be tested (early and convalescent). The early serum is usually negative as patients seroconvert between the 7th and the 15th day. IFA is highly sensitive and specific. A cutoff value of 1/64 for total

Clinical Manifestations

R. conorii comprises different but closely related serotypes. The type strain is Malish, and the other regional serotypes are Israel (in Israel and Southern Europe), Astrakhan (in Russia), and Indian tick typhus *Rickettsia* (in India). Many names are given to the infection caused by *R. conorii*: Mediterranean spotted fever (MSF), boutonneuse fever, Marseilles fever, Astrakhan fever, Israeli spotted fever,

immunoglobulin (Ig) and 1/32 for IgM antibodies is required for diagnosis. The latex agglutination cutoff is 64 or 128. Cross-reactive antibodies have been reported with infections caused by other rickettsioses, *Ehrlichia*, *Bartonella*, *Legionella*, and *Proteus*. False positives including IgM may be observed when rheumatoid factor is present in the serum and in patients with viral infection generating unspecific lymphocyte B proliferation (cytomegalovirus, Epstein-Barr virus). Complement fixation (which lacks sensitivity) and the Weil-Felix test (using antibodies that cross-react with *Proteus* strains) should not be used. In conclusion, the main diagnostic test is serology, and appropriate treatment should be prescribed without biologic confirmation.

Rx Treatment

The prognosis for RMSF is based on early antibiotic treatment. Doxycycline saves patients with RMSF. It should be prescribed in any suspected cases in both children and adults but not in pregnant women and allergic patients. In other rickettsioses a single-day treatment with doxycycline (200 mg) is efficient, but this has not been studied so far for RMSF. The treatment should be given orally except in patients with gastric intolerance or coma, for whom it should be given intravenously. The usual dosage is 200 mg daily in two doses. The treatment duration is not fully determined but, because of the lack of relapse, it can be stopped 3 days after apyrexia. For pregnant women, chloramphenicol is the only available alternative to doxycycline. Several antibiotics are efficient in vitro against *R. rickettsii*, including fluoroquinolones, rifampin, and new macrolide antibiotics (but not erythromycin), but the lack of clinical experience precludes their use in RMSF. β-Lactam antibodies, aminoglycosides, and cotrimoxazole are inefficient in vitro and in patients.

Severely ill patients should be treated in intensive care units and fluid administration carefully monitored. Mechanical ventilation is used in case of respiratory distress, hemodialysis in patients with renal insufficiency, and antiseizure drugs in patients with seizures. Anemia and coagulation abnormalities may also be corrected. For patients with gangrene of the extremities, amputation may be necessary. Glucocorticoids have not proved useful.

Prevention is based on avoidance of tick bites by using repellents and/or protective garments. It is also useful to check for ticks after exposure. Careful examination of scalp, groin, and axillae is recommended. The tick can be removed by forceps and the skin should be disinfected.

OTHER TICK-BORNE RICKETTSIOSES

Epidemiology

As with other tick-transmitted diseases, rickettsioses have a limited geographic distribution that is determined mainly by the tick vector ecology (Fig. 355–2). Many of the rickettsiae obtained first in ticks were demonstrated to cause diseases in patients. In Europe, *R. conorii* is found around the Mediterranean and Caspian seas (Astrakhan serotype), *Rickettsia slovaca* and possibly *Rickettsia helvetica* in Western and Central Europe, and *Rickettsia mongolotimonae* in France. In Asia, *R. conorii* is prevalent in the Middle East (*R. conorii* Israel serotype) and in central Asia (Indian tick typhus) and *R. slovaca* has been isolated in Pakistan. *Rickettsia sibirica* is prevalent in eastern Russia, Mongolia, and China, "*Rickettsia mongolotimonae*" and "*Rickettsia heilongjanghensis*" in China, *Rickettsia japonica* and *R. helvetica* in Japan, and *Rickettsia honei* in Thailand. In Australia, *Rickettsia australis* and *R. honei* are prevalent. In Africa, *R. conorii* and *Rickettsia aeschlimannii* are found in North and South Africa, *R. africae* is prevalent in sub-Saharan Africa, and *Rickettsia mongolotimonae* is found in Mali (see Table 355–2).

Indian tick typhus, and Kenya tick typhus. It is closely related to *R. rickettsii*, with which it shares many common antigens that generate cross-reactive antibodies. MSF resembles RMSF but has several specificities. The spontaneous evolution is milder, but a fatality rate of 1.5 to 2.5% of hospitalized patients is still observed. A malignant form of the disease including purpuric rash, shock, and MODS has been

Continued

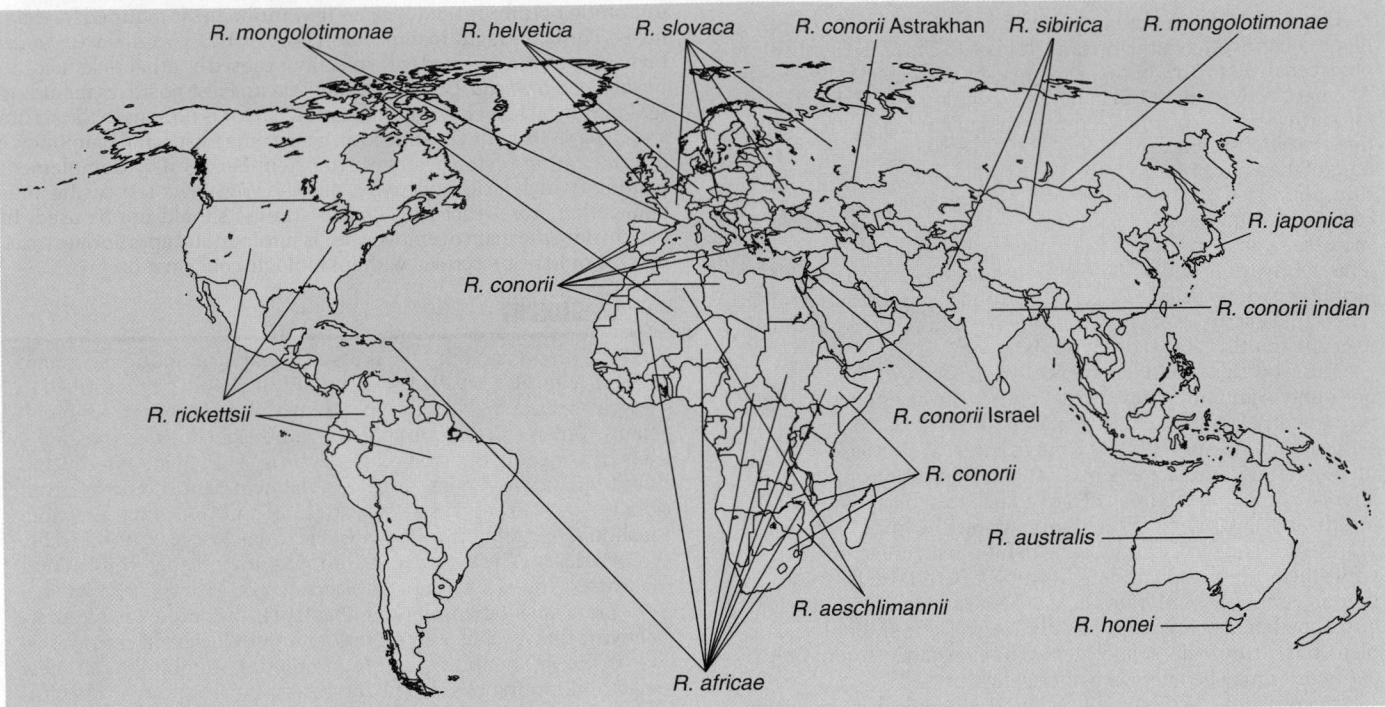

FIGURE 355-2 • Geographic repartition of tick-borne rickettsioses.

described in alcoholic, diabetic, human immunodeficiency virus (HIV)–infected, and old or debilitated patients. The typical clinical presentation is that of a patient with fever, a rash, and a tache noire (i.e., a black eschar at the site of the tick bite). The tache noire is found in 50 to 80% of cases, but there is only one, as *Rhipicephalus sanguineus*, the dog tick, seldom bites humans, and several bites by infected ticks in the same time period are highly unusual. The rash is frequently clearly papular, which led to one of the names of the disease (boutonneuse fever). Israel tick bite fever and Astrakhan fever appear milder than typical MSF, and tache noire is frequently lacking.

R. africae, which determines African tick bite fever, may be responsible for most of the rickettsioses worldwide. It is transmitted by African ticks, *Amblyomma hebraeum* and *Amblyomma africanum*. These ticks are often infected; as many as 60% can harbor *R. africae*. They usually feed on ungulates but attack human beings in groups and cause a high prevalence of infection in rural Africa (60% of tested patients exhibit antibodies) and in travelers. The tick attacks typically generate grouped cases in Safari tourists or visitors; hence, in more than half of cases patients exhibit more than one tache noire. The disease differs from MSF in that it is much milder, fever is frequently absent, a rash is observed in only half of the patients, and the rash may be vesicular (which has never been reported in confirmed MSF) in half of the cases. Moreover, several taches noires

are frequently observed. They are prevalently found on lower limbs and frequently associated with a draining lymphadenopathy in the groin.

Japanese spotted fever (caused by *R. japonica*) and Siberian tick typhus (caused by *R. sibirica*) resemble MSF. Infections caused by *R. mongolotimonae* resemble MSF but in some cases exhibit specific clinical features including a tache noire, a groin lymphadenopathy, and a lymphangitis joining these two lesions. *R. australis* (Queensland tick typhus) and *R. honei* (Flinders Island spotted fever) cause diseases resembling MSF, but their rash can be vesicular.

R. slovaca causes a disease apparently common in Europe (Hungary, France, Spain). Its tick vectors, *Dermacentor marginatus* and *D. reticulatus*, bite preferentially in cold months and bite the scalp as they prefer hairy prey. In contrast to other tick-borne rickettsioses, the disease is more prevalent in children and women. It is rarely exanthematic; the typical clinical picture consists of an erythematous skin lesion at the site of the tick bite on the scalp, ranging from 2 to 8 cm in diameter, and a draining neck lymphadenopathy (that may be painful). Patients may exhibit, rarely, fever and a rash. Deep postinfectious asthenia and residual alopecia at the site of the tick bite can be observed. The occurrence of this rickettsiosis without rash may stimulate research on other new rickettsial diseases with only localized manifestations.

Diagnosis

The diagnosis of other tick-borne rickettsioses is similar to that of RMSF, using mainly serology (IFA; see earlier). An exception is *R. slovaca* infection, in which the serologic response is weak, possibly because of its lack of general infection; in this case PCR of a skin lesion or a lymph node aspirate is the best solution. In *R. africae* infection, the serologic response is later than in RMSF and MSF and late serum samples are recommended.

 Treatment

The treatment of tick-borne rickettsioses is based on doxycycline. A single-day treatment is efficient in children; in adults with a severe form, it is prescribed until the patient is afebrile for 24 hours. In pregnant women josamycin, a macrolide antibiotic, has proved efficient at a dose of 3 g daily for 7 days; quinolones and newer macrolide antibiotics give results comparable to those of doxycycline but with longer regimens.

FLEA-TRANSMITTED DISEASES

Fleas can harbor two rickettsial species. *R. typhi*, the agent of murine typhus, and *R. felis*, the agent of flea-borne spotted fever. Both rickettsiae can be transmitted transovarially in the flea. Vectors are *Xenopsylla cheopis* and *Pulex irritans* but also *Ctenocephalides felis*, a cat flea. Rats, cats, opossums, and dogs can propagate infected fleas. As their reservoirs and vectors are distributed worldwide, these diseases are prevalent in different continents. Fleas are usually infected by *R. typhi* when feeding on apparently healthy rats with infected blood. Mammals are infected by autoinoculation by scratching a lesion contaminated by infected flea feces. *R. felis* is mainly transmitted transovarially. Fleas can be infected by both species at the same time. The two flea-transmitted rickettsiae belong, antigenically, genetically, and according to antibiotic susceptibility, to the two different groups, TG and SFG. Initial confusion, probably caused by dual infections of fleas, led practitioners to believe that *R. felis* shares common antigens with *R. typhi*, but this was not confirmed. A main difference between the two bacteria is the temperature of growth; *R. typhi* grows at 37° C whereas *R. felis* grows under 30° C and requires specific cell lines (XTC2).

MURINE TYPHUS. Murine typhus, or endemic typhus, was suggested to be a disease distinct from epidemic typhus by Maxcey in 1926, with rats and fleas as reservoirs and vectors. Human beings are contaminated by rat fleas, usually by scratching contaminated pruritic lesions, following flea bites. Murine typhus, because of its cycle, is more prevalent in hot and humid areas, specifically when rats proliferate. In the United States 50 to 100 cases are reported yearly, mainly in southern California and southern Texas. In California a transmission cycle involving opossums and cat fleas was demonstrated. Elsewhere in the world, murine typhus was reported in Mexico, Indonesia, Southern Europe, and Africa.

The incubation period ranged from 8 to 16 days in infected volunteers. The disease begins with abrupt fever, nausea, vomiting, myalgias, arthralgias, and headache. A rash is observed in 40 to 50% of patients 6 days on average after the onset. It is detected even less frequently in patients with dark skin. The rash consists of pink maculae that can evolve to maculopapular. It is often discrete, starting in the axilla; it generalizes to the trunk but usually does not involve the face, palms, and soles. In severe cases, it can become purpuric. The most frequently involved organ is the lung. One third of patients have a cough and one fourth an unspecific interstitial pneumonia sometimes associated with pleural effusion. In severe forms, respiratory distress can lead to intubation and artificial ventilation. Neurologic symptoms range from confusion and stupor to coma and seizures in severe forms. Cerebral hemorrhages may occur. Digestive involvement can be manifest as vomiting, abdominal pains, jaundice, and, in severe cases, hematemesis.

Biologically, the white blood cell count shows a leukopenia, and then a hyperleukocytosis. A thrombocytopenia can be noted as well as anemia, specifically when hemolysis is observed (frequently in patients with G6PD deficiency). A moderate increase in serum liver enzymes is common. In patients with severe diseases, hyponatremia and hypoalbuminemia are observed.

Prognosis is usually favorable, but 10% of patients require intensive care and 1% die. Older patients and those with G6PD deficiency or debilitating conditions are at risk.

Diagnosis is based mainly on serology (IFA) with titers similar to those of RMSF. Serologically, *R. typhi* cross-reacts with *R. prowazekii*; it can be differentiated either by comparing titers (two dilutions or more if IgG and IgM titers are discriminative) or by cross-adsorption. With this technique, the serum is absorbed with either antigen and then retested, and the causative agent is that removing antibodies to both bacteria. Skin biopsies and blood samples for culture and PCR may be valuable. Treatment is similar to that of RMSF.

FLEA-BORNE SPOTTED FEVER CAUSED BY R. FELIS. This is a new, incompletely defined disease. The bacterium is found in fleas in the United States, Peru, Europe, and Africa. Seven cases were reported from Texas, Mexico, Brazil, France, and Germany. Reported cases all exhibited fever, a rash in six of seven cases, and inoculation eschar in some cases. The diagnosis can be based on serology using specific *R. felis* antigen or PCR of blood or skin biopsies. The treatment is not established, but the bacterium is highly susceptible to doxycycline and resistant to erythromycin.

EPIDEMIC LOUSE-BORNE TYPHUS

Epidemiology

The human body louse lives in clothes and multiplies rapidly when cold weather and lack of hygiene allow it to. Its prevalence reflects the low socioeconomic status of certain members of a society. It is prevalent during war, in poor countries, and in the homeless population of rich countries, including the United States and Europe. A 100,000-person outbreak of typhus was reported during the civil war in Burundi in 1997, and cases were reported in Russia, Peru, the United States, Algeria, and France in the 1990s. The body louse transmits three bacterial diseases: trench fever (caused by *Bartonella quintana*), relapsing fever (caused by *Borrelia recurrentis*), and exanthematic typhus (caused by *R. prowazekii*). The name *typhus* is derived from the Greek *tuphos*, which describes the neurologic condition associated with this disease and with typhoid. The two diseases were distinguished at the end of the 19th century by Gerhard on the basis of the existence of a rash (exanthematic) in typhus. The role of the louse in the transmission was demonstrated in 1909 by Ch. Nicolle, who received the Nobel prize for this discovery. Louse-transmitted diseases killed more people than did weapons during central and eastern European wars in the 19th and 20th centuries.

The epidemiology of *R. prowazekii* is mainly related to humans as reservoirs and lice as vectors. However, flying squirrels in the United States constitute a sylvatic reservoir and generate a few cases of typhus in this country. The louse is infected when feeding on blood, which it does five times a day. *R. prowazekii* multiplies in the gut of the louse and is released in feces; after a few days, it destroys intestinal epithelium, causing bright red blood to spread from the gut (typhus was also named the red louse disease). The patient is usually contaminated by infected feces (in which *R. prowazekii* survives for weeks), through aerosols, or by skin autoinoculation after scratching. Patients who recover from typhus may keep the bacterium in a dormant form. They may suffer relapses under stressing conditions years later; the relapsing form is called Brill-Zinsser disease. During the relapse, a bacteremia occurs that may allow the start of a new outbreak if the patient is bitten by lice. In the United States, the eastern flying squirrel (*Glaucomys volans volans*) and its fleas, lice, and mites can be infected.

Clinical Manifestations

Typhus begins abruptly with fever, headaches, and myalgias, which may lead to a crouched, crowding attitude termed "sutama" in the largest recent outbreak in Burundi. Cough and neurologic involvement, reflected as stupor, confusion, or coma, are common. A rash is observed in 20 to 80% of the patients, depending on the population studied; it is more rarely observed on dark skin. It usually starts in the axilla and then spreads. It is usually macular but can be papular or purpuric in severe cases. In some cases, diarrhea and jaundice are reported. A splenomegaly is infrequently found. In severe cases, shock and MODS are observed; the spontaneous fatality rate is 20 to 30%. Biologically, leukopenia, thrombocytopenia, and anemia may be noted as well as an increase in serum hepatic enzymes.

This diagnosis should be considered when grouped cases of high fever with confusion are observed in patients exposed to lice. The most common diagnostic error is typhoid, which can have fatal consequences because the currently prescribed treatments for typhoid (β-lactams, cotrimoxazole, and quinolones) are inefficient for typhus. In tropical countries, it is frequently confused with malaria, hemorrhagic fever, and dengue. In people with lice, it can be confused with trench fever and relapsing fever, but a treatment for both can be prescribed.

Brill-Zinsser disease is a late relapsing form of typhus. It is frequently undiagnosed as the rash as well as recent exposure to lice can be lacking. Interviewing the patient may reveal previous exposure to lice, associated or not with a diagnosis of typhus, in previous years. The disease is mild and the prognosis is good.

Sylvatic typhus in the United States is caused by an *R. prowazekii* variant and is a milder disease. The most prominent clinical features are neurologic. Few cases have been described and nearly all occurred in areas where the eastern flying squirrel is found, east of the Mississippi.

Diagnosis

The diagnosis of typhus should be clinical because the fatality rate is high and the treatment safe and efficient. Any brutal outbreak of unexplained fever in unhygienic environments may suggest typhus, including outbreaks during civil wars (such as in Algeria, Rwanda, and Burundi), during social collapses (such as in Russia and Ukraine), in jails (such as in Rwanda and Burundi), and in chronically poor and cold countries. Biologically, the diagnosis is based mainly on serology, in which there is cross-reaction with *R. typhi* (see earlier). When the investigation is performed under difficult field conditions, a drop of blood applied on filter paper and sent to a reference laboratory is valuable for serologic testing. Culture and PCR are valuable and can be performed with a skin biopsy sample or blood. Lice are good diagnostic tools as they can be PCR tested even when dry and can be sent in closed containers without specific temperature conditions.

Treatment

The treatment of typhus is extremely simple, cheap, and effective as a single prescription of two pills of 100 mg of doxycycline saves the patients. Comatose patients should be treated parenterally. In allergic patients, chloramphenicol is the only known alternative, prescribed at a dose of 2 g/day for 10 days. There is no current vaccination, and the fight against lice is the major prevention strategy. Because lice are fragile, changing and boiling clothes are efficient. When this is not possible, insecticide (primarily permethrin) should be used.

SCRUB TYPHUS (*ORIENTIA TSUTSUGAMUSHI*)

Epidemiology

Scrub typhus is transmitted by the bite of trombiculid mite larvae infected by *O. tsutsugamushi*. These mites, also named chiggers, are vertically infected through their mother. Scrub typhus distribution is limited in a triangle extending between northern Japan, eastern Australia, and eastern Russia and including the Far East, China, and the Indian subcontinent. All together, 1 million people may be exposed. Seasonality is determined by emergence of larvae. In temperate zones, it occurs mainly in autumn and to a lesser extent in spring. *O. tsutsugamushi* species have a wide heterogenicity that may allow the definition of several species, but currently a single species is recognized with many serotypes. The more frequent are Kato, Karp, Gilliam, and Kawasaki.

Clinical Manifestations

The disease occurs in patients exposed to rural or urban foci of scrub typhus after a delay of 10 or more days. The onset is usually sudden and includes fever, headache, and myalgias. Attentive examination may reveal an inoculation eschar at the site of the mite bite and tender draining lymph nodes. Generalized lymphadenopathies and rash may be observed. The symptoms vary according to organ involvement. Neuromeningeal symptoms are relatively common. Severe forms can present as septic shock with MODS.

Biologically, leukopenia, thrombocytopenia, and increased levels of hepatic enzymes can occur. Evolution depends on hosts and strains, and the fatality rate ranges from 0 to 30%. Interestingly, scrub typhus is not more severe in HIV-infected patients and, surprisingly, HIV suppressive factors appear to be produced during infection. Relapses may occur in this disease.

Diagnosis

Diagnosis may be difficult. As the clinical presentation is frequently not specific, epidemiologic factors are critical. A diagnosis of infectious mononucleosis has been frequently considered in patients with scrub typhus. The bacterium can be detected by culture (in cells or mice) or PCR in blood and biopsies. Serologically, the technique first used was agglutination of *Proteus mirabilis* serotype OXK in the Weil-Felix reaction. This test lacks sensitivity and specificity and should be replaced by IFA or enzyme-linked immunosorbent assay tests using the three or four major serotypes.

 Treatment

Treatment was based on chloramphenicol for years and then doxycycline was recommended. Single-day treatment with 200 mg of doxycycline was followed by relapses, as was a regimen with treatment for 2 days at a 7-day interval. The currently recommended regimen is doxycycline 200 mg daily for 7 days. In Thailand, cases resistant to doxycycline were reported; rifampin (600 mg daily) gave good results and should be recommended in this country. It should also be recommended in pregnant women. Prophylaxis is based on the use of repellents.

RICKETTSIALPOX (*RICKETTSIA AKARI*)

Epidemiology

Rickettsialpox was first described in New York City, where it is still prevalent, by a general practitioner in 1946. *R. akari*, the causal agent, is an SFG rickettsia transmitted by the bite of the mouse mite (*Liponyssoides sanguineus*). Serologically, it cross-reacts with other SFG rickettsia. Prevalence is probably underestimated; an active search revealed 13 cases in a New York hospital in the 1980s. Cases were reported in Arizona, Utah, and Ohio. A high seroprevalence was reported in intravenous drug users in Baltimore. Cases were diagnosed in Russia, Ukraine, Slovenia, and Korea.

Clinical Manifestations

Ten days after the mite bite, the beginning of the illness is marked by fever, headache, and myalgia. A careful examination reveals an inoculation eschar and a draining lymphadenopathy. Two to 6 days later, a rash appears and comprises 5 to 40 macular then papular and vesicular spots. This aspect led to the name of the disease. It is frequently mistaken for chickenpox. The disease is usually mild. The diagnosis can be made by serology using IFA. Specific antigens react with high titers, but antibodies to other SFG rickettsia may be detected. Diagnosis may also be made on skin biopsies by culture, immunodetection, or PCR. The prescription of doxycycline is highly efficient in these patients. Prevention is based on the control of mice.

EHRLICHIOSES

The first ehrlichial infection diagnosed in human beings was reported in Japan in the late 1950s in patients with mononucleosis. It apparently then disappeared and has been retrospectively attributed to the ingestion of local raw fish (gray mullet) parasitized by *Ehrlichia*-infected worms. This mode of contamination was demonstrated for *Neorickettsia helminthoeca* in bears and dogs eating wild salmon.

The index case of modern ehrlichioses was reported in the United States in 1987. The patient died of fever, presumably acquired after a tick bite in Arkansas, despite receiving chloramphenicol. The patient had, on blood smears, morulae in polymorphonuclear (PMN) cells and antibodies to *E. canis*, a pathogen of dogs. This patient was considered to have an *E. canis* infection, but *E. canis* was not demonstrated later to be a human pathogen. He was then assumed to be infected by the first agent of ehrlichiosis identified in the United States, *E. chaffeensis*. This bacterium, however, infects monocytes and in this patient morulae were in PMN cells. Then it was thought that the causal agent was *Anaplasma phagocytophila* (or human granulocytic *Ehrlichia*, HGE), the second American ehrlichial pathogen that infects PMN, but the tick vector of this disease is absent in Arkansas. Currently it is believed to have been caused by *E. ewingii*, an agent transmitted by *Amblyomma americanum* and prevalent in Arkansas that infects PMN cells and cross-reacts with *E. canis*, but it infects mainly immunocompromised hosts. This case illustrates the progress in knowledge on ehrlichioses and how difficult it is to conclude definitively the etiology of an atypical infection on the basis of serology only.

Bacteriology and Pathophysiology

All *Ehrlichia* pathogenic for humans are currently cultured with the exception of *E. ewingii*. The *Ehrlichia* have been reclassified into four genera, mainly on the basis of 16S ribosomal RNA–derived phylogenetic analysis. Two are the tick-associated genera *Ehrlichia* and *Anaplasma* (consisting of the species *A. phagocytophila*, formerly named *Ehrlichia phagocytophila*, or HGE agent). One is a helminth-associated genus, *Neorickettsia*, including *N. sennetsu* (formerly *Rickettsia sennetsu*, then *Ehrlichia sennetsu*). The fourth is *Wolbachia pipientis*, a bacterium associated with fertility bias in arthropods (insects, crustaceans, and acarids) and in helminth worms (mainly filaria). There are large serologic cross-reactions among *Ehrlichia*.

Ehrlichieae multiply exclusively in vacuoles of their eukaryotic cell host, where they form clusters also termed morulae. These vacuoles are phagosome derived, and Ehrlichieae avoid bactericidal lysosomal fusion. Their target cells differ among species; Ehrlichieae are associated in human beings with monocytes (*E. chaffeensis, E. canis, N. sennetsu*) or PMN cells (*A. phagocytophila, E. ewingii*). In the helminth-borne ehrlichioses, *W. pipientis* lives mainly in the body of the infected worm. In animals, *Ehrlichia ruminantium* infects endothelial cells, *Anaplasma marginale* bovine red blood cells, and *Ehrlichia platys* canine platelets.

Two main routes of inoculation described for ehrlichioses are tick bite and, surprisingly, infected nematode worms. These may be ingested in contaminated water or animals (fish, snails) or infected during filariasis.

AMERICAN HUMAN MONOCYTIC EHRLICHIOSIS (HME) (*EHRLICHIA CHAFFEENSIS*)

Epidemiology

E. chaffeensis has been isolated or identified by PCR only in the United States, mainly in southeastern, south central, and mid-Atlantic states and California (Table 355–3). Many publications report the presence of antibodies to *E. chaffeensis* in Europe, Asia, and Africa. However, because of the cross-reactions among *Ehrlichia*, these findings do not allow one to infer an extension of the distribution of *E. chaffeensis*. In the United States, it is associated with an American tick, *A. americanum* (Lone Star tick), as the vector and mainly the white-tailed deer as the mammalian reservoir. Immature ticks are infected by blood while feeding on persistently bacteremic reservoirs. *E. chaffeensis* is transmitted transtadially in the tick and infects its next host (deer or human) during its next blood meal. The disease epidemiology reflects the tick habitat and activity as most cases are contracted in the southern United States, in rural areas, and from April to September. In highly endemic areas, the incidence can reach 100 cases per 100,000 inhabitants. The severity is age dependent, which may explain the lower incidence reported for children. Males are more often affected than females, with a sex ratio of 4.

Clinical Manifestations

The incubation lasts for 7 to 10 days following an identified tick exposure in 80% of cases. Patients present with fever, headache, malaise, nausea, and anorexia. Untreated patients worsen and may require intensive care. Digestive tract involvement is common with nausea, vomiting, diarrhea, and abdominal pains. Neurologic central system infection is manifest in many forms from confusion to coma. A rash is observed in one third of the cases and lymphadenopathies in one fourth. In severe forms, sepsis and MODS may be observed, including hypotension, tachycardia, respiratory distress, seizures and coma, renal insufficiency, and myocardial failure.

Biologically, the white blood cell count typically shows leukopenia, caused by both lymphopenia and neutropenia. Thrombocytopenia is also frequently noticed; anemia may appear later. Coagulopathy may be observed in severe forms. Increases in serum enzymes including AST, ALT, and LDH may reflect organ involvement, as does creatininemia. CSF examination in patients with neurologic symptoms reveals pleocytosis and increased protein levels. Cells may be monocytic or polymorphonuclear. The prognosis in HME depends on early antibiotic treatment, but the fatality rate is still high at 2.5%. In persons coinfected with HIV, it may be most severe; in one series 6 of 13 patients died.

Diagnosis

The diagnosis of HME should be invoked in patients with a history of tick exposure with unexplained fever. HME resembles RMSF, but rash is less frequent. Later in the disease it can be misdiagnosed with any cause of severe sepsis with MODS.

Leukopenia associated with thrombocytopenia and increase in liver enzyme level may establish the etiology. Careful examination of blood smears and CSF smears may help to identify typical morulae. Treatment should be started in any suspected case. Diagnosis can be biologically confirmed by culture in specialized laboratories using a canine cell line, DH82. However, PCR is more practical; a confirmatory PCR using a second target gene is useful. Most cases are currently diagnosed serologically by a fourfold or greater increase in antibody titers or by seroconversion. The reference technique is IFA. A single titer of 25 is indicative of the diagnosis. There are cross-reactive antibodies among *Ehrlichia* species and with *A. phagocytophila*. Western blotting may be valuable to distinguish among these bacteria.

Rx Treatment

Treatment is based upon doxycycline; *E. chaffeensis*, like *Rickettsia*, is resistant to β-lactam antibiotics, aminoglycosides, and macrolides but also to chloramphenicol and fluoroquinolones. Only rifampin shows in vitro activity; it has, however, been tested only in a few pregnant patients. The treatment is usually prescribed for 2 weeks.

HUMAN GRANULOCYTIC EHRLICHIOSIS (HGE) (*ANAPLASMA PHAGOCYTOPHILA*)

Epidemiology

A. phagocytophila was identified in ungulates in the 1930s as an agent causing chronic neutropenia and consequent superinfections. The first human case was recognized in 1990. The disease is found in America and in Europe (Fig. 355–3). It is transmitted by *Ixodes scapularis* (eastern North America), *Ixodes pacificus* (western North America), *Ixodes ricinus* (Europe), and *Ixodes persulcatus* (Asia), the vectors of Lyme disease, and its epidemiology should be similar. Coinfection with the two diseases may occur. The temporal distribution of the disease parallels that of nymph tick activity, with two peaks in spring and autumn. Ticks are born free of *Ehrlichia* and are infected while feeding on bacteremic small mammals. Deer play a major role as hosts of adult ticks and reservoirs. In highly endemic areas, the incidence can reach 50 per 100,000 inhabitants per year. The mean age of diagnosed patients is high, and males are more infected than females, with a sex ratio of 3.

Clinical Manifestations

The incubation time is usually between 7 and 10 days, and 80% of patients report a history of tick exposure. Many infections may be asymptomatic or too mild to require a diagnostic procedure. The disease frequently begins abruptly, including fever, headache, malaise, and myalgias that may be particularly severe. Rash is found in less than 10% of cases. Visceral involvement may be observed and includes digestive symptoms such as nausea, vomiting, and diarrhea. Neurologic symptoms may include confusion, meningitis, and meningoencephalitis.

Continued

Table 355–3 • EHRLICHIOSES

DISEASE	AGENT	VECTOR	GEOGRAPHIC REPARTITION
American monocytic ehrlichiosis	E. chaffeensis	Amblyomma americanum	South central, southeastern, mid-Atlantic coastal states
Human granulocytic ehrlichiosis	A. phagocytophilum	Ixodes ricinus	Europe
		Ixodes scapularis	Northeast, upper midwest, northern California
E. ewingii	E. ewingii	A. americanum	South central, southeastern, mid-Atlantic coastal states
Japanese monocytic ehrlichiosis	N. sennetsu	Helminth of the gray mullet?	Japan
E. canis	E. canis	Rhipicephalus sanguineus	Venezuela (one case)

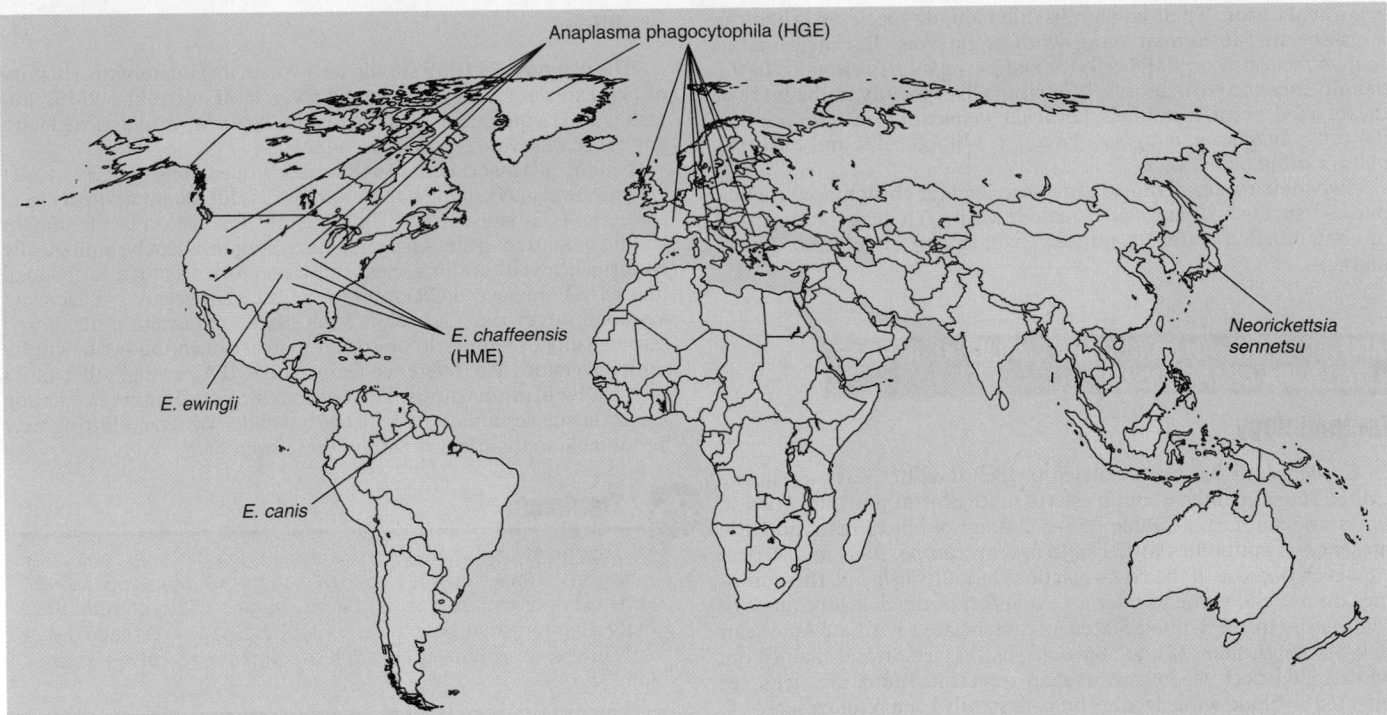

FIGURE 355–3 • Geographic repartition of ehrlichioses. HGE = human granulocytic ehrlichiosis; HME = human monocytic ehrlichiosis.

The evolution of the disease is favorable in most cases, even without specific therapy, but in some patients the disease may evolve to septic shock and MODS. Patients with underlying diseases are more at risk of dying. Most deaths are the consequence of *Ehrlichia*-induced immunosuppression, and patients may experience invasive aspergillosis, candidiasis, cryptococcosis, and herpes esophagitis.

Diagnosis and Treatment

Laboratory findings consist of the association of thrombocytopenia and leukopenia (lymphopenia and/or neutropenia). Increase in serum transaminases is also frequent. The diagnosis can be made by careful examination of blood smears for morulae within PMN cells. Culture from blood is possible in appropriate cells (HL-60), and PCR is useful as for HME. Most cases are diagnosed by serology using IFA, which is comparable to that in HME (see earlier). Treatment is also similar to that of HME except that *A. phagocytophila* is susceptible to fluoroquinolones in vitro, but these have not been tested in patients.

EHRLICHIA EWINGII

Canine granulocytic ehrlichiosis, reported in the United States in 1972, is caused by uncultured *E. ewingii*. This bacterium was characterized by amplification and sequencing of the 16S ribosomal RNA gene. The vector of *E. ewingii* is *A. americanum*, which also transmits *E. chaffeensis*. Among 60 cases of ehrlichioses in Missouri in 1999, 4 were caused by *E. ewingii*; 4 other cases have been reported since by the CDC. The disease was prevalent in immunocompromised hosts (seven of eight) coinfected with HIV or receiving immunosuppressive drugs. Patients, who report tick exposure, present with fever, thrombocytopenia, leukopenia, and various symptoms including meningitis. Morulae may be seen on blood smears in PMNs. The evolution in reported cases was good; patients responded dramatically to doxycycline. Patients have antibodies to *E. chaffeensis*, and PCR has been shown to be useful when applied to blood samples. This diagnosis should be considered in ehrlichioses suspected in immunocompromised patients exposed to *A. americanum* ticks.

EHRLICHIA CANIS

Canine monocytic ehrlichiosis was reported first in Algeria in the 1930s. It is caused by *E. canis* and transmitted by the dog tick *Rhipicephalus sanguineus*. This tick is found worldwide and is prevalent in temperate and hot areas. In 1996, a single case of infection was reported in an asymptomatic man from Venezuela who owned an infected dog.

WOLBACHIA SPECIES

Wolbachia bacteria are endosymbionts of arthropods and nematodes. They were known to be present in filarial worms, but it was later shown that they may play a role in human diseases. These bacteria manipulate the fertility of their host. The eradication of *Wolbachia* in filaria may lead to infertility and stop the microfilaria from spreading. This effect was demonstrated by field treatment of patients with onchocerciasis with doxycycline. The patients improved when treated with this drug, which is effective on *Wolbachia* and subsequently on the worm's fertility but not on the worm itself. In 2001 it was shown that the adverse reactions observed after the treatment of lymphatic filariasis may be caused by the release of *Wolbachia* from destroyed worms and specifically by its lipopolysaccharide. Some authors suggested that eradicating *Wolbachia* prior to the antihelminth prescription would avoid these reactions.

Q FEVER

Q fever is a worldwide zoonosis caused by *Coxiella burnetii*. The name Q fever is derived from "query" to emphasize the surprising aspect of the disease first described in Queensland, Australia in 1935 by Derrick. The infection in humans is variable in its severity, clinical expression, and natural course (i.e., acute or chronic). Ungulates and pets are the major reservoirs.

Bacteriology and Pathophysiology

C. burnetii is a gram-negative bacterium that naturally infects its host's monocytes. It multiplies in an acidic vacuole. Strains are heterogeneous genetically and antigenically, but no clear relationship is established between strains and pathology. *C. burnetii* in vitro generates a deleted, avirulent mutant also named phase II. This mutant exhibits diagnostic antigens that are useful as they are more reactive during acute infection.

C. burnetii is incompletely eliminated after acute infection in immunocompromised hosts and patients with cardiac valve lesions. *C. burnetii* continues to multiply despite high levels of antibodies and causes chronic infection. In patients with endocarditis, the level of interleukin-10 (an immunosuppressive cytokine) is elevated and monocytes are unable to control *C. burnetii* growth. The control of the disease in acute Q fever is associated with the constitution of a granuloma.

Epidemiology

C. burnetii infects a wide range of animals, including mammals, birds, and ticks. Ungulates and pets (cats and dogs) are the most common source of the disease. Mammals are infected through aerosols and may shed *Coxiella* in feces, urine, milk, and birth products. Humans are usually infected by aerosols or less frequently by milk products. Interhuman infections through sexual intercourse, during delivery, or by blood transfusion have been reported. *Coxiella* survive in the environment and can be spread far by the wind. In the past few years, major outbreaks were related to sheep and goats. The disease is partly seasonal and related to lambing time. The current geographic repartition is largely unknown. *C. burnetii* is considered a potential bioterrorism agent. Males are more sick but not more exposed to Q fever, and middle-aged people are more frequently affected and hospitalized.

Clinical Manifestations

After contamination by *C. burnetii*, 60% of patients seroconvert without apparent disease, 38% experience a self-limited disease, and only 2% require an exhaustive diagnostic procedure. Following this primary infection, after months to years, 0.2 to 0.5% of patients develop a chronic infection associated with an immunocompromised situation, a cardiac valve lesion, or a vascular prosthesis or aneurysm.

Patients with diagnosed acute infection present with a variety of symptoms (Table 355–4). Isolated prolonged fever was observed in 14% of more than 1000 patients. Pneumonia was found in 37% and was the only symptom in 17%. This percentage may vary according to the place of study and reach 90% of diagnosed cases. Some cases may be associated with respiratory distress. Hepatitis is found in 60% of cases, isolated in 40%. It is usually diagnosed by the association of fever and moderate increase in transaminases. Some hepatitides, specifically in middle-aged men, are associated with an inflammatory syndrome and autoantibodies and may be resistant to antibiotic treatment. Liver biopsy, when performed, exhibits granulomas that may be typified by a lipid vacuole and surrounded by a fibrinoid ring in the form of a doughnut. Less frequently, in 1.5% of cases, the patients exhibit a rash. Patients can have specific neurologic manifestations such as meningitis, encephalitis, meningoencephalitis, or peripheral neuropathy. In 1 to 2% of cases, patients have cardiovascular manifestation such as pericarditis or more rarely myocarditis.

Evolution is usually favorable even without treatment except in special hosts. In pregnant women, symptomatic or not, Q fever compromises the pregnancy. When infected during the first trimester, the patient usually aborts spontaneously. When the patient is infected later, the disease can result in fetal death or prematurity or the outcome may be normal. Half of patients infected during pregnancy may develop chronic uterine infection and may later experience multiple spontaneous abortions. Thirty to 50% of patients with heart valve lesions or vascular lesions may experience chronic endocarditis within 2 years. This evolution is not prevented by regular treatment.

Patients with Q fever endocarditis have a chronic infection with low-grade fever, progressive degradation of valve function, and progressive heart failure. Fever is intermittent, and vegetations are frequently absent on cardiac echocardiography. Endocarditis, therefore, is not frequently considered. If not diagnosed, the disease progressively worsens and emboli (mainly cerebral) may be observed, associated with renal insufficiency, splenomegaly, and hepatomegaly. Digital clubbing may also be observed. The main clue to the diagnosis in a patient with a valvulopathy is unexplained sickness (unexplained fatigue, weight loss, fever), a biologic abnormality (leukopenia, increased erythrocyte sedimentation rate, thrombocytopenia, increase in hepatic enzymes), or rapid degradation of a prosthetic valve. Some cases of chronic osteomyelitis, hepatitis, and infection of aneurysm and vascular prosthesis have been reported.

Biologically, a leukopenia may be observed; thrombocytopenia is frequent, as are increases in hepatic enzymes. Circulating anticoagulant associated with antiphospholipid may be observed, as may anti–smooth muscle antibodies. During endocarditis, antinuclear antibodies, microhematuria, and rheumatoid factor are frequently found.

Diagnosis

Diagnosis is based mainly on serology, which must be prescribed in all kinds of situations (see Table 355–4). The main diagnostic tools are direct detection by culture and PCR or immunochemistry in valve, liver, or blood samples, but serology with IFA is the best method. Two antigens (phase I and phase II) can be tested. Acute Q fever is diagnosed when seroconversion or a fourfold increase is obtained using phase II antigen. A single serum test exhibiting IgG antibodies of 200 or greater and IgM of 50 or greater against phase II is also diagnostic. During chronic Q fever, antibodies are at higher titers and directed against both phase I and phase II. IgG at phase I at a titer of 800 or 1600 is diagnostic of chronic infection, as is IgA at 100 or greater.

Serology is useful for follow-up of patients with acute Q fever and underlying disease and those with treated chronic Q fever.

Treatment

Treatment is easy during acute Q fever. Doxycycline is the most efficient antibiotic, and it should be prescribed for 2 weeks. Some patients with hepatitis do not respond well because of an excessive immune response. They are rapidly improved by a short course of glucocorticoids. In pregnant women, it was shown that taking cotrimoxazole during the entire pregnancy avoided an unfavor-

Continued

Table 355–4 • SITUATIONS THAT SHOULD PROMPT SEROLOGIC TESTING FOR Q FEVER

ACUTE Q FEVER (PHASE II ANTIGEN AND IgG ≥ 200 AND IgM ≥ 50)

Fever in a patient in contact with ungulates	Fever in a patient in contact with parturient pet
Unexplained prolonged fever (>7 days)	Unexplained atypical pneumonia
Granulomatous hepatitis	Fever and increase in transaminases (2 to 5 times the normal level)
Fever and thrombocytopenia	
Meningoencephalitis	Aseptic meningitis
Myocarditis	Guillain-Barré syndrome
Erythema nodosum	Pericarditis
Fever during pregnancy	Spontaneous abortion

CHRONIC Q FEVER (PHASE I ANTIGEN AND IgG ≥ 800 AND IgA ≥ 100)
Blood culture–negative endocarditis
Patient with a valvulopathy and unexplained
    Fever
    Weight loss
    Fatigue
    Increased ESR
    Increased transaminases
    Thrombocytopenia
Patient with unusually rapid degradation of a prosthetic valve
Fever in a patient with vascular aneurysm or prosthesis
Aseptic osteomyelitis
Chronic pericarditis
Multiple spontaneous abortions

ESR = erythrocyte sedimentation rate; Ig = immunoglobulin.

able outcome. As for endocarditis, a bactericidal treatment is necessary. In vitro, antibiotic efficacy is impaired by the low pH of the vacuole in which *C. burnetii* reside. Hydroxychloroquine increases the pH of this vacuole and restores the bactericidal effect of doxycycline. In patients with endocarditis, the recommended treatment is a combination of doxycycline (200 mg daily) and hydroxychloroquine (600 mg/day, then adjusted to reach a 1 mg/mL plasma concentration). This regimen is prescribed for 18 to 36 months according to serologic results. The major problem with this treatment is photosensitivity; sun exposure should be avoided. An alternative treatment is a combination of doxycycline and ofloxacin for 3 years or more. Prevention is based on veterinary control in animals. A vaccine is currently available in Australia.

SUGGESTED READINGS

Cross HF, Haarbrink M, Egerton G, et al: Severe reactions to filarial chemotherapy and release of Wolbachia endosymbionts into blood. Lancet 2001;358:1873–1875. *The first description of Wolbachia as a human pathogen.*

Masters EJ, Olson GS, Weiner SJ, et al: Rocky Mountain spotted fever: A clinician's dilemma. Arch Intern Med 2003;163:769–774. *Treatment with doxycycline must be based on clinical suspicion even in the absence of a petechial rash or history of a known tick bite.*

Maurin M, Bakken JS, Dumler JS: Antibiotic susceptibilities of Anaplasma (Ehrlichia) phagocytophilum strains from various geographic areas in the United States. Antimicrob Agents Chemother 2003;47:413–415. *Doxycycline, rifampin, and levofloxacin are recommended.*

Parola P, Raoult D: Ticks and tickborne bacterial diseases in humans: An emerging infectious threat. Clin Infect Dis 2001;32:897–928. *A review of ticks as reservoirs and vectors of infectious diseases.*

Sampere M, Font B, Font J, et al: Q fever in adults: Review of 66 clinical cases. Eur J Clin Microbiol Infect Dis 2003;22:108–110. *About 50% presented with pneumonia; all cases were successfully treated.*

Treadwell TA, Holman RC, Clarke MJ, et al: Rocky Mountain spotted fever in the United States, 1993–1996. Am J Trop Med Hyg 2000;63:21–26. *A review of the disease in the United States.*

356 ZOONOSES

Stuart Levin
Jeffrey Nelson

Zoonoses are most simply defined as human infections derived from animals. Approximately 200 different infectious agents, many of them rare, cause disease in humans and fulfill the definition of zoonoses. There are more than 50 million dogs in the United States, and they have been targeted as facilitating the transmission of more than 50 infectious agents while being credited with more than 1 million bite injuries each year. There is an even greater number of cats in the

United States, and more than 40 infectious diseases have been transmitted by them. In addition, the list of exotic pets, including ferrets, monkeys, and reptiles, continues to grow. Almost all arthropod-transmitted infectious agents in the United States are due to either ticks or mosquitos, with ticks being the more common villain and Lyme disease being the most common arthropod-transmitted infectious disease in the United States. New threats from mosquito bites transmitting the West Nile virus, which causes central nervous system disease, have emerged.

The risk of contracting a zoonosis is increased by direct animal contact, outdoor activities, exposure to and inhalation of infectious air particles, insect bites, contact with previously infected human blood products, and contact with and ingestion of infectious agents transmitted by animal-contaminated water and insufficiently cooked meat, eggs, dairy products, fish, and shellfish. Raw shellfish are the "garbage filters" of the ocean and can transmit at least 25 different infectious or toxic illnesses to humans. Ticks not infrequently introduce more than one pathogen while feeding. In addition, the farmer, pet owner, hunter, laboratory researcher, cave explorer, hiker, and veterinarian, among others, are at higher risk for a zoonosis than the general population. Infectious agents transmitted by these routes from animal sources essentially include members of all microbial classes: viruses, bacteria, fungi, and parasites. Immunocompromised hosts such as splenectomized patients, transplant recipients, patients with the acquired immunodeficiency syndrome (AIDS), and pregnant women and their fetuses are at higher risk of clinical disease when exposed to these various infectious agents. New emerging infectious diseases seem inevitable because of increased interest in xenotransplantation, global warming trends, human intrusion in previously underexplored or never-explored sites, and an increasing threat of biologic terrorism or warfare. Reviews have begun to address this last threat. Preventive measures to decrease infection in the compromised host include utilizing routine pet care immunization, neutering pets, using caution when handling pet fomites, rigorous handwashing practices, and avoiding ingestion of undercooked meat, fish, and eggs.

Massive warming changes and human entry into previously inaccessible geographic areas both increase the potential to encounter known zoonoses on a more frequent basis as well as new emerging pathogens. Despite the increased risk of acquisition of zoonoses, zoonoses remain less frequent as a cause of fever in travelers than the usual gastrointestinal and pulmonary pathogens.

Non–animal-associated environment- or travel-related infectious diseases can be confused with zoonoses. The vast majority of clinical diseases caused by *Legionella pneumophila, Plasmodium falciparum, Entamoeba histolytica, Giardia lamblia, Pseudomonas pseudomallei, Chromobacterium violaceum, Aeromonas hydrophila,* and airborne fungi such as *Blastomyces dermatitidis, Coccidioides immitis,* and *Histoplasma capsulatum* are acquired through environmental exposure and are only

Table 356–1 • RESPIRATORY TRACT ZOONOSES

DISEASE*	MICROORGANISM[†]	CLINICAL SYNDROME	RESERVOIR AND/OR VECTOR
Psittacosis[‡]	*Chlamydia psittaci*	Pneumonia, often severe	Aerosols from parrots, ducks, turkeys
Q fever	*Coxiella burnetii*	Pneumonia, hepatitis, or myocarditis	Airborne from soil contaminated by sheep, goats, and cats, particularly if parturient
Tularemia	*Francisella tularensis*	Cutaneous ulcer and regional node, pneumonia and hilar node; pleural effusion	Rabbit contact (winter) and tick bites
Plague	*Yersinia pestis*	Inguinal nodes, bubonic plague (10% develop basilar pneumonia); hilar node enlargement	Fleas from prairie dogs, rock squirrels, rats
Hantavirus syndrome	*Hantavirus*	Upper respiratory to lower respiratory to adult respiratory distress syndrome to death	Deer mouse fomites: urine, feces, saliva
Rhodococcus pneumonia	*Rhodococcus equi*	Pneumonia, often cavitates, in patients with acquired immunodeficiency syndrome and other immunosuppressed patients	Horse manure, soil
Mycoplasma arginini pneumonia	*Mycoplasma arginini*	Pneumonia, sepsis, neutropenia	Sheep, goats
Foot-and-mouth disease	*Aphthovirus*	Nonspecific upper respiratory tract infection, oral vesicles	Cloven-footed mammals
Bordetella bronchoseptica		Pneumonia, bronchitis, whooping cough	Dogs
Histoplasmosis	*Histoplasma capsulatum*	Pneumonia or fever of unknown origin	Bats
Anthrax	*Bacillus anthracis*	Mediastinal widening, no pneumonia	Herbivores

*See table of contents and index to locate a more detailed discussion of each disease.
[†]Because of the fastidious nature of some organisms, the rapid development of diagnostic tools, and the risk that some agents pose to laboratory workers, we recommend that a clinical microbiologist be consulted if these agents are considered in a patient's differential diagnosis.
[‡]Occurs in more than 1000 animal species.

rarely related to animal hosts. *Sporothrichosis schenckii,* typically an environment-acquired pathogen stemming from vegetation injuries, has also been transmitted from draining cutaneous ulcers of cats to owners and animal handlers. Histoplasmosis has been acquired by explorers (spelunkers) in caves contaminated by bat guano. Other noninfectious diseases acquired from animals and insects, such as tick paralysis and the fish toxin illnesses, do not represent zoonoses.

Unfortunately, some descriptive disease titles can be misleading to clinicians and thus can interfere with correctly considering the possible diagnosis. The transmission of tick-borne Rocky Mountain spotted fever actually occurs more commonly in the southeastern United States than in the Rocky Mountains and has even occurred in the middle of New York City. Vegetarians and other strict non–pork-eating persons have been seriously infected with the pig tapeworm *Taenia solium* as a result of fecal contamination of food from unsuspected infected human sources. Human influenza A is not typically considered a zoonosis; however, interspecies spread of swine, avian, and human influenzaviruses can occur in unique geographic areas, such as southern China, where dense concentrations of ducks, pigs, and people cohabit. Viral incubation of the three influenza species in the pig with reassortment of antigens and subsequent spread to humans of virulent "new" influenza strains can lead to influenza pandemics that in sheer number (billions) surpass any past epidemics of smallpox or plague. In a similar way, the initial infections with human immunodeficiency virus type 1 (HIV-1) (AIDS) almost definitely began as zoonoses transmitted as simian immunodeficiency viruses from chimpanzees and mangabey primates to humans. As with influenza, the subsequent 60 million and counting cases of HIV no longer require an animal reservoir for continuing transmission.

Leprosy, a human-to-human–transmitted illness of biblical notoriety, is endemic in at least three animal species, including the armadillo. This animal has rarely been implicated in the transmission of this disease to humans in the United States.

Table 356–2 • CENTRAL NERVOUS SYSTEM INFECTION: ZOONOSES

DISEASE*	ORGANISM	CLINICAL SYNDROME AND DIAGNOSIS	ACQUISITION
Listeriosis	*Listeria monocytogenes*	Purulent meningitis during pregnancy, over 65, and in neonate; immunosuppressed	Unpasteurized cheese and other dairy products; cattle; goats
Leptospirosis	*Leptospira interrogans*	Aseptic meningitis, hepatorenal syndrome	Asymptomatic dogs, cattle, common water source
Herpes B encephalitis	*Herpes simiae*	Diffuse, progressive encephalitis	*Macaca* monkey bites or scratches
Lyme disease	*Borrelia burgdorferi*	Lymphocytic meningitis, motor-sensory neuropathy, facial palsy	Acquired from tick bites
Lymphocytic choriomeningitis	Lymphocytic choriomeningitis virus	Lymphocytic meningitis occasionally with pneumonia	Inhalation of mouse secretions, urine, feces, saliva
Mosquito-borne encephalitis, United States	Eastern, Western equine encephalitis; St. Louis, California encephalitis; West Nile virus	Diffuse encephalitis, least severe; California encephalitis, most severe; Eastern equine encephalitis	Mosquito-borne from horses, birds
Rabies encephalitis	Rabies virus	Almost always fatal; encephalitis	Bites from dogs, skunks, bats, raccoons, foxes
Toxoplasmosis	*Toxoplasma gondii*	CNS, multiple brain masses, AIDS patient	Cat feces or ingestion of undercooked lamb or pork
Cerebral cysticercosis	*Taenia solium*	Epilepsy, CNS cysts, eosinophilic meningitis, hydrocephalus	Fecal-oral; contamination of food with pork tapeworm eggs
New variant: Creutzfeldt-Jakob disease	Prion (proteinaceous infectious particle)	Dementia, ataxia, and myoclonus	Beef from cattle fed scraps from contaminated sheep carcasses

*See table of contents and index to locate a more detailed discussion of each disease.
AIDS = acquired immunodeficiency syndrome; CNS = central nervous system.

Table 356–3 • RASHES: ZOONOSES

DISEASE*	MICROORGANISM†	CLINICAL INFORMATION AND DIAGNOSIS	RESERVOIR AND/OR VECTOR
Ehrlichiosis	*Ehrlichia chaffeensis* (monocytic)	Macular rash (seen in less than one third of patients), central distribution; in south central United States	Tick bite
Leptospirosis	*Leptospira interrogans*	Central macular rash in 20%, with occasional enanthem	Urine-contaminated water, dogs, cattle
Lyme disease	*Borrelia burgdorferi*	Primary lesion is erythema migrans; 40% have multiple lesions	Mouse reservoir—tick bite
Rocky Mountain spotted fever	*Rickettsia rickettsii*	Acral or peripheral distribution of macular papular to hemorrhagic rash to gangrenous lesions	Tick bite
Typhus (endemic)	*Rickettsia prowazeckii*	Central distribution, macular rash (can be hemorrhagic)	Flying squirrel fleas or fomites
Scabies	*Sarcoptes scabiei*	Pruritic macules on trunk; skin burrow	Dogs—close contact. Up to one third of asymptomatic dogs have mite infection.
Flea bite dermatitis	*Pulex irritans*	Pruritic papules, urticarial vesicles; fleas found on pets or in the environment	Fleas on dogs
Cat-scratch disease	*Bartonella* species	Bacillary angiomatosis, peliosis hepatitis, cervical adenopathy, subacute bacterial endocarditis and fever of unknown origin	Cat scratch or bite
Tularemia	*Francisella tularensis*	Ulcer and node	Rabbit contact and tick bite
Anthrax	*Bacillus anthracis*	Painless, edematous, nonpurulent ulcer	Herbivore, infected animal product
"Spotted fever Rickettsia"	*Rickettsia conorii, Rickettsia africae*	Tache noire (eschar)	Tick

*See table of contents and index to locate a more detailed discussion of each disease.
†Because of the fastidious nature of some organisms, the rapid development of diagnostic tools, and the risk that some agents pose to laboratory workers, we recommend that a clinical microbiologist be consulted if these agents are considered in a patient's differential diagnosis.

Despite the large number of zoonoses described, clinicians evaluating an individual patient usually need consider only a limited number of historical details to arrive at an appropriate differential diagnosis:

1. Questions regarding direct contact with animals or animal products, animal bites, arthropod exposures, and food ingestion may offer clues to the correct etiology.
2. Consideration must be given to a patient's travel history; a number of zoonoses are quite limited in geographic distribution.
3. Details about occupational and recreational high-risk activities must be ascertained.
4. The patient's clinical presentation (course and organ involvement) is used to focus simultaneously on the most likely cause and disease considerations. Tables 356–1 through 356–5 take advantage of this "syndrome" approach. Additional lists of zoonotic agents can be generated for the differential diagnoses of arthritis, jaundice, diarrhea, sepsis and shock, renal failure, fever of unknown origin, and endocarditis.

Guidelines have been published to prevent nosocomial transmission of zoonotic diseases. These have included special isolation for anthrax, Andes Hantavirus disease, herpes B virus infections, hemorrhagic fevers, plague, and rabies.

Table 356–4 • HIGHLY FATAL ZOONOSES

DISEASE*	FATALITY RATE (%)
Creutzfeldt-Jakob disease (new variant)	100
Rabies	100
Anthrax inhalational	80–90
Herpes simiae[†]	50–75
Ebola virus	70
Eastern equine encephalitis	50–70
Hantavirus pulmonary syndrome, United States[†]	60
Yellow fever[§]	20–50
Lassa fever[§]	15–25
Plague[†]	50–80
Rocky Mountain spotted fever[†]	20–60
East African sleeping sickness[†]	20–30
Anthrax[†]—cutaneous	20
Tularemia—pneumonic[†]	30–60
Tularemia—cutaneous	2–10
Visceral leishmaniasis[†]	5–25
Louse-borne relapsing fever[†]	5–40

*See table of contents and index to locate a more detailed discussion of each disease.
[†]Fatality rate if untreated.
[‡]Case mortality of hospitalized patients.
[§]If jaundiced.

Table 356–5 • NEWER ZOONOSES

DISEASE*	INFECTIOUS AGENT	CLINICAL INFORMATION	VECTOR/ACQUISITION
Ehrlichiosis, monocytic	*Ehrlichia chaffeensis*	Fever, myalgia, leukopenia, monocyte inclusions not often seen	*Amblyomma* (Lone Star) tick bite
Ehrlichiosis, granulocytic	Human granulocytic *Ehrlichia* (HGE)	Fever, myalgia, leukopenia, granulocyte inclusions often seen on blood smear	*Ixodes* (deer) tick bite
	Ehrlichia ewingii		*Amblyomma*
Cat-scratch disease	*Bartonella* species	Cervical lymphadenopathy in normal hosts and cutaneous and hepatic angiomatosis in AIDS patients	Cat scratch or bite
Hemorrhagic diarrhea	Enterohemorrhagic *Escherichia coli* O157:H7 (other species)	Rectal bleeding, dysentery, hemolytic-uremic syndrome	Contaminated, undercooked meat
Hantavirus pulmonary syndrome (HPV)	Hantavirus—Sin Nombre	Adult respiratory distress syndrome, elevated hematocrit	Fomites of rodents
Cryptosporidium diarrhea	*Cryptosporidium parvum* (?)	Prolonged watery diarrhea	Contaminated water
Dysentery	*Campylobacter jejuni*	Dysentery, Reiter's syndrome, Guillain-Barré syndrome	Contaminated chicken
Pyogenic skin ulcer	*Capnocytophaga canimorsus*	Sepsis, skin infection	Dog bites

*See table of contents and index to locate a more detailed discussion of each disease.

SUGGESTED READINGS

Craven RB, Roehrig JT: West Nile virus. JAMA 2001;286:651–653. *The first large review of this disease in the U.S.*

Inglesby TV, Dennis DT, Henderson DA, et al: Plague as a biological weapon: Medical and public health management. Working Group on Civilian Biodefense. JAMA 2000;283:2281–2290. *Emphasizes the risks of aerosolized plague, as well as approaches to treatment and prophylaxis.*

O'Brien D, Tobin S, Brown GV, Torresi J: Fever in returned travelers: Review of hospital admissions for a 3-year period. Clin Infect Dis 2001;33:603–609. *Malaria, respiratory tract infections, gastroenteritis, and dengue fever are leading causes.*

Rosen T, Jablon J: Infectious threats from exotic pets: Dermatological implications. Dermatol Clin 2003;21:229–236. *An updated review.*

Weber DJ, Rutala WA: Risks and prevention of nosocomial transmission of rare zoonotic diseases. Clin Infect Dis 2001;32:446–456. *Guidelines for isolation and prevention.*

357 INTRODUCTION TO VIRAL DISEASES

Richard J. Whitley

Viral diseases have become the domain of molecular biologists, geneticists, pharmacologists, microbiologists, vaccinologists, immunologists, practitioners of public health, epidemiologists, and clinicians, both pediatric and adult. This principle can be illustrated by several examples. Striking advances have been achieved in antiviral therapy for human immunodeficiency virus (HIV) and hepatitis C, vaccination for influenza, and viral diagnostics with the use of polymerase chain reaction. Nevertheless, morbidity and mortality related to chronic virus infections, especially HIV and chronic hepatitis B and C viruses, are being increasingly documented. New viral agents have resulted in epidemics caused by Nipah virus and several New World arenaviruses. Ebola has reappeared in Africa and is a significant cause of mortality. The epidemiology of viral diseases is changing, as illustrated by the transoceanic spread of West Nile virus. Organ transplantation continues to increase and xenotransplantation looms on the horizon—both being associated with predicted and unpredicted virus infections. Lastly, the threat of viruses as weapons of bioterrorism, particularly smallpox, cannot be ignored.

In order to better understand the relationship between virus and disease, a taxonomic chart provides guidance. Historically, classification reflected the information available from general descriptive biology. Viruses were thus classified by host (e.g., plant, insect, murine, avian), by disease or target organ (e.g., respiratory, hepatitis, enteric), or by vector (e.g., arboviruses). These classifications were often overlapping and inconsistent. Molecular biology now permits us to classify by genomic and biophysical structure, which can be quantitative and evolutionarily meaningful. The accompanying table of the taxonomy of human viruses is derived from the comprehensive Seventh Report of the International Committee on Taxonomy of Viruses.

Table 357–1 represents viruses known to infect humans. Many of the agents are primarily animal viruses that accidentally infect humans: herpesvirus B, rabies, the Arenaviridae, the Filoviridae, the Bunyaviridae, and the arthropod-borne viruses. The role of intraspecies

Table 357–1 • TAXONOMY OF HUMAN VIRUSES

FAMILY	SUBFAMILY GENUS	TYPE SPECIES OR EXAMPLE	MORPHOLOGY	ENVELOPE
THE DNA VIRUSES				
The dsDNA Viruses				
Poxviridae			Brick shaped or ovoid	+
	Chordopoxvirinae			
	Orthopoxvirus	Vaccinia virus, variola		
	Parapoxvirus	Orf virus		
	Molluscipoxvirus	Molluscum contagiosum virus		
	Yatapoxvirus	Yaba monkey tumor virus		
Herpesviridae			Icosahedral	+
	Alphaherpesvirinae			
	Simplexvirus	Human herpesvirus (HSV) 1 and 2		
		Cercopithecine herpesvirus 1 (herpesvirus B)		
	Varicellovirus	Human herpesvirus 3 (VZV)		
	Betaherpesvirinae			
	Cytomegalovirus	Human herpesvirus 5 (CMV)		
	Roseolovirus	Human herpesvirus 6 and 7		
	Gammaherpesvirinae			
	Lymphocryptovirus	Human herpesvirus 4 (EBV)		
	Rhadinovirus	Human herpesvirus 8 (KSHV)		
Adenoviridae	*Mastadenovirus*	Human adenoviruses	Icosahedral	–
Polyomaviridae	*Polyomavirus*	JC virus	Icosahedral	–
Papillomaviridae	*Papillomavirus*	Human papillomaviruses	Icosahedral	–
The ssDNA Viruses				
Parvoviridae			Icosahedral	
	Parvovirinae			
	Erythrovirus	B19 virus		
	Dependovirus	Adeno-associated virus 2*		
Circoviridae (proposed)		TTV	Icosahedral	–
THE DNA AND RNA REVERSE TRANSCRIBING VIRUSES				
Hepadnaviridae	*Orthohepadnavirus*	Hepatitis B virus	Icosahedral	+
Retroviridae			Spherical	+
	Delta retrovirus	HTLV 1 and 2		
	Lentivirus	Human immunodeficiency virus 1 and 2		
	Spumavirus	Spumavirus (foamy virus)*		
THE RNA VIRUSES				
The dsRNA Viruses				
Reoviridae			Icosahedral	
	Orthoreovirus	Reovirus 3*		
	Orbivirus	Kemerovo viruses		
	Rotavirus	Human rotaviruses		
	Coltivirus	Colorado tick fever virus		
The Negative-Stranded ssRNA Viruses				
Paramyxoviridae			Spherical	+
	Paramyxovirinae			
	Respirovirus	Human parainfluenza viruses		
	Morbillivirus	Measles virus		
	Rubulavirus	Mumps virus		
	Zoonotic paramyxovirus	Nipah virus		
	Pneumoniavirinae			
	Pneumovirus	Human respiratory syncytial virus		
Rhabdoviridae			Bacilliform	+
	Vesiculovirus	Vesicular stomatitis virus		
	Lyssavirus	Rabies virus		
Filoviridae	*Filovirus*	Ebola virus	Bacilliform	+
Orthomyxoviridae			Spherical	+
	Influenzavirus A	Influenza A virus		
	Influenzavirus B	Influenza B virus		
	Influenzavirus C	Influenza C virus		
Bunyaviridae			Amorphic	?
	Bunyavirus	Bunyamwera virus, LaCrosse virus		
	Hantavirus	Hantaan virus, Sin Nombre virus		
	Nairovirus	Congo-Crimean hemorrhagic fever virus		
	Phlebovirus	Rift Valley fever virus		
Arenaviridae	*Arenavirus*	Lymphocytic choriomeningitis virus	Spherical	+
The Positive-Stranded ssRNA Viruses				
Picornaviridae			Icosahedral	–
	Enterovirus	Polioviruses		
	Rhinovirus	Human rhinoviruses		
	Hepatovirus	Hepatitis A virus		
Caliciviridae	*Calicivirus*		Icosahedral	–
		Norwalk virus		
		Hepatitis E virus		

Continued

Table 357–1 • TAXONOMY OF HUMAN VIRUSES—cont'd

FAMILY	SUBFAMILY GENUS	TYPE SPECIES OR EXAMPLE	MORPHOLOGY	ENVELOPE
Astroviridae	*Astrovirus*	Human astrovirus 1	Icosahedral	–
Coronaviridae	*Coronavirus*	Human coronavirus	Pleomorphic	+
Flaviviridae			Spherical	+
	Flavivirus	Yellow fever virus		
	Hepacivirus	Hepatitis C virus		
Togaviridae			Spherical	+
	Alphavirus	Western equine encephalitis virus		
	Rubivirus	Rubella virus		
THE SUBVIRAL AGENTS: SATELLITES, VIROIDS, AND AGENTS OF SPONGIFORM ENCEPHALOPATHIES				
Satellites (single-stranded RNA)	*Deltavirus*	Hepatitis delta (D) virus	Spherical	+
Prion protein agents		Creutzfeldt-Jakob agent	?	–

*Human virus with no recognized human disease.
CMV = cytomegalovirus; EBV = Epstein-Barr virus; HTLV = human T-cell lymphotropic virus; KSHV = Kaposi's sarcoma herpes virus; TTV = transfusion-transmitted virus; VZV = varicella-zoster virus.
Derived from van Regenmortel MHV, Fauquet CM, Bishop DHL, et al (eds): Virus Taxonomy: Classification and Nomenclature of Viruses: Seventh Report of the International Committee on Taxonomy of Viruses. San Diego, Academic Press, 2000.

transmission of viruses is becoming increasingly appreciated. Although its contribution to antigenic shift of influenza A virus is well documented, the role of intraspecies transmission is a major consideration in the "emerging" diseases caused by Sin Nombre virus and Nipah virus.

The following chapters summarize our knowledge of these viral infections with emphasis on the natural history, epidemiology, diagnosis, and treatment.

358 ANTIVIRAL THERAPY (NON–AIDS)

Richard J. Whitley

Advances in the chemotherapy of viral diseases are increasingly common. With the exception of human immunodeficiency virus (HIV) infection, only a few antiviral agents of proven clinical value are available and for a limited number of indications.

ANTIVIRALS FOR HERPESVIRUS INFECTIONS

Acyclovir

MECHANISM OF ACTION. Acyclovir is an acyclic analogue of guanosine. Virus-specified thymidine kinase (TK) phosphorylates acyclovir to its monophosphate derivative, an event that does not occur in uninfected cells to a significant extent. Acyclovir is then further phosphorylated by cellular enzymes to its triphosphate derivative. Acyclovir triphosphate binds viral DNA polymerase, acting as a DNA chain terminator. Because acyclovir is taken up selectively by virus-infected cells, the concentration of acyclovir triphosphate is 40 to 100 times higher in infected than in uninfected cells. Furthermore, viral DNA polymerase exhibits a 10- to 30-fold greater affinity for acyclovir triphosphate than cellular DNA polymerases. The higher concentration in infected cells plus the affinity for viral polymerases results in the low toxicity of acyclovir for normal host cells. Although Epstein-Barr virus (EBV) and cytomegalovirus (CMV) do not have virus-specific TKs, acyclovir does have minimal activity against these viruses.

LICENSED USES. Acyclovir is available in ointment, capsule, and intravenous formulations. In the topical form, acyclovir is licensed for managing primary herpes genitalis in both immunocompetent and immunocompromised hosts as well as in limited, non–life-threatening mucocutaneous herpes simplex virus (HSV) infections in immunocompromised hosts. It is less active topically than when delivered by other routes, and its use by this route should be discouraged.

Oral acyclovir is indicated in the management of most cases of primary or initial genital herpes in all populations of patients and as suppressive therapy in normal hosts with frequently recurrent genital herpes (six or more recurrences a year). It can reduce viral shedding in late pregnancy and at the time of delivery.■ Oral acyclovir is also used as prophylaxis and treatment in immunocompromised patients with a history of HSV infections (e.g., herpes labialis or genital herpes). High-dose oral acyclovir (i.e., 800 mg five times per day) has been approved for use in immunocompetent patients with localized herpes zoster.

Intravenous acyclovir is indicated in severe initial herpes genitalis of immunocompetent patients and in the treatment of some initial and recurrent mucocutaneous infections in immunocompromised patients as well as in the treatment of herpes simplex encephalitis (HSE). Intravenous acyclovir is approved for treatment of varicella-zoster virus (VZV) infections in immunocompromised hosts.

TOXICITY. Acyclovir has an excellent safety profile and is well tolerated. The major adverse effect of acyclovir is that it alters renal function. High-dose bolus injection of acyclovir can cause crystallization in renal tubules and subsequent acute tubular necrosis or simply a reversible elevation of serum creatinine. Dehydration, preexisting renal insufficiency, and higher doses of acyclovir are risk factors for renal toxicity. Dosage alterations are required with renal impairment (Table 358–1). In addition, there have been a few brief reports suggesting central nervous system (CNS) toxicity after intravenous administration of acyclovir. Oral acyclovir has not been associated with renal toxicity, even when given in high doses (800 mg five times a day).

Because acyclovir is a nucleoside analogue that can be incorporated into both viral and host cell DNA, it has been studied extensively for its potential as a carcinogen, teratogen, and mutagen. There is no significant evidence that acyclovir is a carcinogen in humans, and animal studies indicate that acyclovir is not a significant teratogen in clinically used doses. Acyclovir is not a significant mutagen in vitro but seems to be able to induce chromosomal events as does caffeine. Because of the many possible indications for acyclovir during pregnancy, as well as the likelihood of frequent first-trimester exposures to drug before pregnancy is established, it

Table 358–1 • DOSAGE ADJUSTMENTS FOR INTRAVENOUS ACYCLOVIR IN PATIENTS WITH IMPAIRED RENAL FUNCTION

CREATININE CLEARANCE (mL/min/1.73 m²)	PERCENTAGE OF STANDARD DOSE	DOSING INTERVAL (hr)
>50	100	8
25–50	100	12
10–25	100	24
0–10*	50	24

*Administered after hemodialysis.

is extremely important to define its risk. The safety of acyclovir in pregnancy, therefore, has not been unequivocally established. Because acyclovir crosses the placenta and can concentrate in amniotic fluid, there is valid concern about the potential for renal toxicity in the fetus.

RESISTANCE TO ACYCLOVIR. Resistance to acyclovir develops through mutations in one of two HSV genes, namely those specifying viral TK or DNA polymerase. Clinical isolates resistant to acyclovir are almost uniformly deficient in TK. Until recently, such resistance has been rare; all such mutants had reduced neurovirulence and did not readily establish latency. However, acyclovir-resistant HSV mutants are being reported more frequently in immunocompromised patients and in one normal host. These mutants are deficient in viral TK and sensitive to vidarabine and foscarnet, drugs that do not require viral TK for activation. Some isolates are fully neurovirulent and able to establish latency in a murine model. With the growing population of immunocompromised patients (related to both HIV infection and ther-apeutic immunosuppression) who suffer from frequent and severe herpesvirus infections, acyclovir resistance is expected to become more prevalent.

Valaciclovir

MECHANISM OF ACTION. Valaciclovir is the L-valyl ester of acyclovir that, after oral administration, is cleaved in the gastrointestinal tract and liver by an enzyme identified as valaciclovir hydrolase. The end product is acyclovir and the natural amino acid L-valine. The mechanism of action and disposition of acyclovir have been described previously.

LICENSED USES. Valaciclovir is licensed for the treatment of primary, recurrent, and suppressive therapy of genital HSV infections. In comparative studies, valaciclovir has been as effective as treatment with acyclovir; however, dosing frequency can be decreased in many patients to once daily (Table 358–2).

Table 358–2 • INDICATIONS FOR THE USE OF AVAILABLE ANTIVIRAL AGENTS

INDICATION	ANTIVIRAL AGENT	ROUTE	DOSE	COMMENTS
Respiratory syncytial virus infection (infants)	Ribavirin	Aerosol	Diluted in sterile water to a concentration of 20 mg/mL, then delivered via aerosol for 12–18 hr/day for 3–7 days	Only for infants at high risk
Life- or sight-threatening cytomegalovirus (CMV) infections in immunocompromised hosts	Ganciclovir	IV	5.0 mg/kg q12 h × 14–21 days	Maintenance therapy at 5.0 mg/kg/day recommended for AIDS patients. Leukopenia is a frequent complication; in bone marrow transplant patients with CMV pneumonia, CMV immune globulin may be a useful adjunct
	or Valganciclovir		900 mg bid × 21 days followed by 900 mg once a day	
	or Foscarnet	IV	60 mg/kg q8 h or 90 mg/kg q12 h × 14–21 days followed by 90–120 mg/kg q2 wk	
	or Cidofovir	IV	5 mg/kg once weekly × 2 then 5 mg/kg q2 wk	Induction therapy Maintenance therapy
	or Fomivirsen	Intravitreally	330 μg q2 wk × 2 then 1 x/mo	
Condyloma acuminatum	Interferon-α	Intralesional	1.0 million units injected into the base of each lesion up to 3 times per week for 3 weeks	Influenza-type symptoms may occur with administrations
Influenza A infection	Amantadine	Oral	Adults: 100–200 mg/day for 5–7 days Children ≤ 9 years: 4.4–8.8 mg/kg/day for 5–7 days not to exceed 150 mg/day	Normal person > 65 years should receive
Prophylaxis against influenza A virus infection	Amantadine	Oral	Adults: 100–200 mg/day Children < 9 years: 4.4–8.8 mg/kg/day (not to exceed 150 mg/day)	Continued for the duration of the epidemic or for 2 wk in conjunction with influenza vaccination (until vaccine-induced immunity develops); normal persons > 65 years should receive 100 mg/day
	or Zanamivir	Aerosol	10 mg bid × 5 days	
	or Oseltamivir	Oral	75 mg bid × 5 days	
	or Rimantadine	Oral	100 mg PO bid × season	
Herpes simplex virus (HSV) encephalitis	Acyclovir	IV	10–15 mg/kg (1-hr infusion) every 8 hr for 14–21 days	Morbidity and mortality are significantly lower in patients treated with acyclovir than with vidarabine
Neonatal herpes	Acyclovir	IV	20 mg/kg (1-hr infusion) every 8 hr for 14–21 days	Efficacy of vidarabine is established; vidarabine and acyclovir show equal efficacy
Mucocutaneous HSV in immunocompromised hosts	Acyclovir or	IV	5.0 mg/kg (1-hr infusion) every 8 hr for 7 days	Choice of topical, oral, or intravenous preparation depends on clinical severity and setting; topical acyclovir is appropriate only when it can be applied to all lesions; it does not affect untreated lesions or systemic symptoms
	Acyclovir	Oral	400 mg 3 times/day for 7–14 days	
	Valaciclovir	Oral	500 mg bid	10 days
	Famciclovir	Oral	500 mg tid	10 days

Continued

Infectious Diseases

Table 358–2 • **INDICATIONS FOR THE USE OF AVAILABLE ANTIVIRAL AGENTS—cont'd**

INDICATION	ANTIVIRAL AGENT	ROUTE	DOSE	COMMENTS
Prophylaxis against mucocutaneous HSV during intense immunosuppression	Acyclovir or Acyclovir	Oral IV	200 mg 3–4 times/day 5 mg/kg/q8 h	Oral therapy most convenient; lesions recur when therapy stops Lesions recur when therapy stops
Treatment of initial genital HSV infections	Acyclovir or Acyclovir	Oral IV	200 mg 5 times/day for 10 days or 400 mg tid × 10 days 5 mg/kg (1-hr infusion) every 8 hr for 5–7 days	Drug of choice in most clinical settings; treatment has no effect on subsequent recurrence rates For patients requiring hospitalization or with neurologic or other visceral complications
	Valaciclovir Famciclovir	Oral Oral	1 g bid 250 mg tid	7–10 days 5–10 days
Recurrent genital herpes	Acyclovir	Oral	400 mg tid/d for 5 days	No effect on subsequent recurrence rates; efficacy greater if used early in attack
	Valaciclovir Famciclovir	Oral Oral	500 mg qd × 3 days 125 mg tid × 5 days	
Prophylaxis against frequently recurring genital herpes	Acyclovir	Oral	400 mg × 5 days bid	Occasional "breaking through" attacks and/or asymptomatic virus shedding during treatment; reevaluation every 6 mo recommended
	Valaciclovir Famciclovir	Oral Oral	500-1000 mg bid or 1 g/day 250 mg bid	
Treatment of HSV keratitis	Trifluorothymidine	Topical	One drop of 0.1% ophthalmic solution every 2 hr while awake (up to 9 drops/day)	3% acyclovir ointment (ophthalmic) is equal or superior to idoxuridine, vidarabine, and trifluridine for treatment of HSV keratitis but is not available in the United States
	or Vidarabine	Topical ½-inch ribbon of 3% ophthalmic ointment 5 times/day		
	or Idoxuridine	Topical ½-inch ribbon of 0.5% ophthalmic ointment 5 times/day		
Localized herpes zoster in immunocompetent hosts	Acyclovir or Famciclovir or Valaciclovir	Oral	800 mg 5 times/day for 7–10 days 250 mg tid × 5–7 days 1 g tid × 5–7 days	Shortens time to lesion healing but not shown to decrease the incidence of postherpetic neuralgia
Chickenpox in immunocompromised hosts	Acyclovir	IV	500 mg/m² (1-hr infusion) every 8 hr for 7 days	In the absence of comparative data, acyclovir is preferred because of its lower toxicity
Treatment of severe localized or disseminated herpes zoster in immunocompromised hosts	Acyclovir or	IV	10 mg/kg q8 h × 7 days	Comparative trials in severe localized and disseminated herpes zoster are under way; pending results, acyclovir is preferred because of its ease of administration and lower toxicity
	Valaciclovir Famciclovir	Oral Oral	1 g tid 500 mg tid	7–10 days 7–10 days
Chronic hepatitis B	Interferon-α	SQ	10 × 10⁶ units tiw for 16 wk or 5 × 10⁶ units daily for 16 wk	Patients must have compensated liver disease
	Lamivudine	Oral	100 mg 1 ×/day × 1–3 years	
Chronic hepatitis C liver disease	Interferon-α	SQ	3 × 10⁶ units tiw for 24 wk	Must have compensated liver disease
	Pegylated interferon-α-2b plus ribavirin	Oral	1 μg/kg once a week 1000–1200 mg × 48 wk	

IV = intravenous; SQ = subcutaneous

Valaciclovir is also licensed for the treatment of herpes zoster in the immunocompetent host (see Table 358–2). In a clinical trial that directly compared valaciclovir and acyclovir therapy, valaciclovir significantly accelerated the resolution of zoster-associated pain and therefore is the medication of preference. A dosing interval of three times a day provides an advantage over acyclovir.

TOXICITY. In general, valaciclovir is well tolerated because it is metabolized to acyclovir. However, in HIV-infected individuals who were exposed to high doses of valaciclovir for prolonged periods of time, a thrombotic thrombocytopenic purpuric syndrome was reported. On detailed analysis, other concomitantly administered drugs were associated with greater risk ratios for this syndrome.

Valaciclovir is under investigation for suppression of reactivation of CMV infections in transplant recipients.

Penciclovir and Famciclovir

MECHANISM OF ACTION. Penciclovir is another nucleoside analogue in which the base, guanine, is normal but the sugar moiety has a structural modification. The structural similarity to acyclovir is apparent; however, there is no oxygen atom in the acyclic sugar moiety, although an OH group exists in the position equivalent to that of the 3′ OH group in the normal nucleoside, guanosine. Like acyclovir, penciclovir is converted to its monophosphate by HSV or VZV TK. Penciclovir triphosphate inhibits viral DNA polymerase, but it is not a DNA chain terminator; therefore, there is potential for internal incorporation of penciclovir residues into viral DNA and further DNA elongation. The initial conversion of penciclovir to its monophosphate is more efficient than the phosphorylation of acyclovir; however, the penciclovir triphosphate formed in infected cells is less active than acyclovir triphosphate as an inhibitor of HSV and VZV DNA polymerase.

The triphosphate of penciclovir has a significantly longer intracellular half-life than acyclovir triphosphate. The full implication of this observation remains to be elucidated. The oral bioavailability of penciclovir is poor (<5%).

Famciclovir is the diacetyl ester of penciclovir. When administered orally, the compound undergoes a two-step modification to penciclovir. Penciclovir, then, behaves as noted earlier.

LICENSED USES. Famciclovir is licensed for the treatment of primary, recurrent, and suppressive therapy of genital HSV infections (see Table 358–2). In addition, famciclovir has been shown to be equivalent to acyclovir for suppression of HSV reactivation in immunocompromised hosts.

Famciclovir is also licensed for the treatment of herpes zoster in the normal host (see Table 358–2).

Penciclovir is licensed only in its topical formulation (Denavir) for the treatment of herpes simplex labialis.

TOXICITY. Famciclovir and penciclovir (applied topically) have excellent safety profiles and are well tolerated. The most commonly reported adverse events are headache, nausea, and diarrhea; however, these event rates have occurred at no greater frequency than either background or concomitant acyclovir administration. The long-term toxicity of penciclovir has not been well established, although carcinogenicity in animal models has been demonstrated. The relevance of the latter finding is unknown.

Ganciclovir

MECHANISM OF ACTION. Ganciclovir, also known as dihydroxy propoxymethyl guanine (DHPG), is an acyclic nucleoside analogue of acyclovir that has increased in vitro activity against all herpesviruses compared with acyclovir, including 8 to 20 times greater antiviral activity against CMV. As with acyclovir, the activity of ganciclovir in HSV-infected cells depends on phosphorylation by virus-specific TK. Also as with acyclovir, ganciclovir monophosphate is further converted to its diphosphate and triphosphate derivatives by cellular kinases. In cells infected by HSV-1 or HSV-2, the triphosphate (DHPG-TP) competitively inhibits the incorporation of guanosine triphosphate into viral DNA and terminates chain synthesis. The mode of action of ganciclovir against CMV and EBV (which do not produce virus-specific TK) is not entirely known, but it has been suggested that these viruses may induce a cellular TK or viral kinase that efficiently promotes the obligatory initial phosphorylation of ganciclovir to its monophosphate.

LICENSED USES. Ganciclovir has been licensed by the U.S. Food and Drug Administration for treating CMV retinitis and life-threatening CMV diseases in patients with acquired immunodeficiency syndrome (AIDS) and other immunocompromised patients.

TOXICITY. The most important side effects of ganciclovir are neutropenia and thrombocytopenia. Neutropenia occurs in approximately 35% of patients and is usually (but not always) reversible with dose adjustment or discontinuation. Thrombocytopenia occurs in about 20% of patients. Numerous other side effects possibly related to ganciclovir, such as nausea, vomiting, dizziness, and headache, are usually not of clinical significance. Agents with significant myelotoxicity, such as antimetabolites or alkylating agents, cannot be used concomitantly with ganciclovir. Zidovudine (azidothymidine or AZT) may be used cautiously in low doses in patients receiving ganciclovir, but hematologic parameters must be monitored closely.

Ganciclovir also has significant gonadal toxicity in animal screening systems, most notably as a potent inhibitor of spermatogenesis. As an agent affecting DNA synthesis, ganciclovir has carcinogenic potential.

CLINICAL USE. Ganciclovir has been the most widely tested drug for the treatment of CMV infections. There is support for clinical benefit in immunocompromised patients with CMV retinitis[2] and gastrointestinal infection. Benefit is suggested but has been less dramatic for CMV pneumonia in AIDS patients and organ transplant recipients. Ganciclovir has effectively suppressed the reactivation of CMV infections in organ transplant recipients.

Valganciclovir

MECHANISM OF ACTION. Valganciclovir is the L-valyl ester of ganciclovir that, after oral administration, is cleaved in the gastrointestinal tract to ganciclovir. The end products are ganciclovir and L-valine. The mechanism of action and disposition of ganciclovir have been described previously.

LICENSED USES. Valganciclovir is licensed for the therapy of CMV retinitis in patients with AIDS. The high plasma levels achieved with oral therapy obviate the need for intravenous administration. This drug is under investigation in organ transplant recipients.

TOXICITY. Because plasma levels of ganciclovir after oral valganciclovir administration are similar to that determined by the intravenous route, the toxicity is virtually identical to that of the parent compound.

Cidofovir

MECHANISM OF ACTION. Cidofovir (hydroxyphosphonylmethoxycytosine) is unlike nucleoside analogues. Cidofovir does not require specific conversion to the monophosphate derivative to initiate its inhibitory effects. Although the mechanism of action has not been completely elucidated, the essential target is virus-specific DNA polymerase. Cidofovir has an additionally important feature, namely a very prolonged tissue half-life. In humans, a dose of once weekly for induction and biweekly thereafter for maintenance has been established for the treatment of CMV retinitis in patients with AIDS.

LICENSED USES. Cidofovir is licensed only for the treatment of CMV retinitis in patients with AIDS (see Table 358–2). Cidofovir provides an alternative to ganciclovir or foscarnet therapy for retinitis in this population of patients.

TOXICITY. Cidofovir is directly associated with nephrotoxicity. In the presence of proteinuria or elevated serum levels of creatinine, significant risk of renal failure exists. As a consequence, pretreatment hydration and concomitant administration with probenecid are mandatory before the use of this medication.

Idoxuridine and Trifluorothymidine

Idoxuridine and trifluorothymidine are analogues of thymidine. When administered systemically, these nucleosides are phosphorylated by both viral and cellular TK to active triphosphorylate derivatives that inhibit both viral and cellular DNA synthesis. The result is antiviral activity but also sufficient host cytotoxicity to prevent the systemic use of these drugs. Toxicity of these compounds is not significant, however, when applied topically to the eye in the treatment of HSV keratitis. Both idoxuridine and trifluorothymidine, as well as vidarabine, ophthalmic ointments are effective and licensed for such treatment. Acyclovir as an ophthalmic preparation also appears to be effective but is not yet licensed. Trifluorothymidine appears to be the most efficacious of these compounds. Although these agents are not of proven value in the treatment of stromal keratitis and uveitis, trifluorothymidine is more likely to penetrate the cornea. Some forms of stromal keratitis and uveitis are thought to be caused by immune mechanisms and thus would not respond to antiviral drugs. The ophthalmic preparations of idoxuridine, vidarabine, and trifluorothymidine may cause local irritation, photophobia, edema of the eyelids and cornea, punctal occlusion, and superficial punctate keratopathy.

Infectious Diseases

Vidarabine

Vidarabine has been shown to be effective when administered parenterally for HSE, neonatal herpes, and VZV infections in the immunocompromised host. Because of a lower therapeutic index than acyclovir, it is available only as an ophthalmic preparation for therapy of HSV keratitis.

Foscarnet

Foscarnet, a pyrophosphate analogue of phosphonoacetic acid, has potent in vitro and in vivo activity against herpesviruses. Foscarnet inhibits the DNA polymerase of all human herpesviruses by blocking the pyrophosphate binding site and preventing chain elongation. Unlike acyclovir, which requires activation by a virus-specific TK, foscarnet acts directly on the virus DNA polymerase. TK-deficient, acyclovir-resistant herpesviruses remain sensitive to foscarnet.

Foscarnet was approved for the treatment of CMV retinitis in HIV-infected patients. Data collected from the Soka clinical trial indicate equal effectiveness of foscarnet and ganciclovir therapy for retinitis in this population. However, use of foscarnet in combination with zidovudine resulted in enhanced survival. These findings remain to be confirmed in a larger study population. Foscarnet has been used for induction therapy of retinitis as well as when ganciclovir is not tolerated. However, administration of foscarnet is not without toxicity. Renal toxicity has been documented as well as hypocalcemia and altered levels of serum magnesium. Foscarnet's lack of bone marrow toxicity offers an advantage over ganciclovir. In addition, foscarnet has been used to treat acyclovir-resistant herpes simplex genital disease.

ANTIVIRALS FOR RESPIRATORY VIRAL INFECTIONS

It is difficult to overestimate the impact of respiratory viral illnesses on human health. Almost 90% of the population experience one of these illnesses each year, resulting in a staggering number of days lost from work and school as well as significant potential for serious morbidity and even death. Nonetheless, because these conditions in most populations of patients are self-limited and rarely fatal, the requirements for new drugs are stringent: an extreme degree of safety, moderate to high effectiveness, ease of administration, and low cost. Accordingly, only two such antiviral agents are approved for use in the United States, each with fairly limited indications. Because of the number of developmental programs identifying new antiviral agents for treatment of respiratory viruses, it seems likely that an expanded armamentarium will be forthcoming.

Amantadine and Rimantadine

MECHANISM OF ACTION. Amantadine and rimantadine have a narrow spectrum of activity and at concentrations achievable in humans are useful only against influenza A infections. Although amantadine was the first antiviral agent to be approved in the United States, its mechanism of action is not yet completely understood. Influenza A viruses differ in their susceptibility to amantadine, and the drug may have different actions depending on the concentration and virus strain. Early studies indicated that amantadine acted by preventing the penetration and/or uncoating the virus. Subsequently, low concentrations of the drug were shown to inhibit virus assembly by interacting with hemagglutinin; high concentrations appear to inhibit an early stage of the infection involving fusion between the virus envelope and the membrane of secondary lysosomes. Rimantadine has a similar mechanism of action.

LICENSED USES. As antiviral agents, amantadine and rimantadine are licensed for both the chemoprophylaxis and the treatment of influenza A infections. Both drugs can be used for any unimmunized member of the general population who wishes to avoid influenza A, but prophylaxis is especially recommended to control presumed influenza outbreaks in institutions housing high-risk persons. High-risk individuals include adults and children with chronic disorders of the cardiovascular or pulmonary systems requiring regular follow-up or hospitalization during the preceding year as well as residents of nursing homes and other chronic-care facilities. In these instances, drugs should be administered to all residents of the institution, whether or not they received influenza vaccination the previous fall. To reduce spread of virus and to minimize disruption of patients' care, it is also recommended that amantadine prophylaxis be offered to unvaccinated staff who care for high-risk patients. Amantadine prophylaxis is also recommended in the following situations:

1. As an adjunct to late immunization of high-risk individuals. Amantadine does not interfere with antibody response to the vaccine.
2. For persons who have not been immunized and who care for high-risk persons in home settings, both to reduce spread of virus and to allow persons to maintain care for high-risk persons in the home setting.
3. For immunodeficient persons, who may be expected to have a poor antibody response to vaccine.
4. For persons for whom influenza vaccine is contraindicated (e.g., for persons hypersensitive to egg protein).

Both drugs are also indicated in the treatment of uncomplicated respiratory illness caused by influenza A. Studies have shown a beneficial effect on the signs and symptoms of acute influenza as well as a significant reduction in quantity of virus in respiratory secretions. Because of the short duration of disease, amantadine must be administered within 48 hours of symptom onset to show benefit. The effect of amantadine on the prevention of complications in high-risk groups is under evaluation.

Rimantadine is a structural analogue of amantadine with the same spectrum of activity, mechanism of action, and clinical indications. Rimantadine is somewhat more effective than amantadine against influenza type A viruses at equal concentrations. Absorption of rimantadine is delayed compared with that of amantadine, and, furthermore, equivalent doses of rimantadine produce lower plasma levels than does amantadine. The lower plasma levels may explain the lower incidence of side effects at similar doses. Rimantadine has similar CNS side effects even though, unlike amantadine, this drug does not affect CNS catecholamine release and is not effective in the treatment of Parkinson's disease. The efficacy of rimantadine in both the prophylaxis and treatment of influenza A infections is similar to that of amantadine. There has been a report of rimantadine-resistant strains of influenza isolated from patients treated for acute influenza A.

TOXICITY. Amantadine is reported to cause side effects in 5 to 10% of healthy young adults taking the standard adult dose of 200 mg/day. These side effects are usually mild, cease soon after amantadine is discontinued, and often disappear even with continued use of the drug. CNS side effects are most common and include difficulty in thinking, confusion, lightheadedness, hallucinations, anxiety, and insomnia. Activities requiring mental alertness (e.g., driving) should be avoided until it is reasonable to assume that these symptoms will not occur. More severe adverse effects (e.g., mental depression and psychosis) are usually associated with doses exceeding 200 mg daily. About 5% of patients complain of nausea, vomiting, or anorexia. Older individuals are more likely to experience side effects. Rimantadine appears to be somewhat better tolerated.

Patients with renal disease should receive doses based on their creatinine clearance (Table 358–3). Doses for older people and children are usually lower as well. Persons with an active seizure disorder may be at increased risk for seizures when amantadine is given at standard doses.

Table 358–3 • DOSAGE ADJUSTMENT FOR ORAL AMANTADINE IN PATIENTS WITH IMPAIRED RENAL FUNCTION

CREATININE CLEARANCE mL/min/1.73 m²	SUGGESTED ORAL MAINTENANCE REGIMEN AFTER 200 mg (100 mg bid) ON THE FIRST DAY
>80	100 mg bid
60–80	100 mg bid alternating with 100 mg daily
40–60	100 mg daily
30–40	200 mg (100 mg bid) twice weekly
20–30	100 mg three times each week
10–20	200 mg (100 mg bid) alternating with 100 mg every 7 days
<10	100 mg every 7 days

Zanamivir

MECHANISM OF ACTION. Zanamivir is a novel sialic acid analogue inhibitor of the neuraminidases of influenza A and B. The design of the molecule was based on the characterization of crystallographic structure of influenza viral neuraminidase that has been shown to be essential for viral replication in vitro. This viral enzyme cleaves terminal sialic acid residues from cellular and viral glycoproteins and glycolipids to allow release of virus from infected cells, preventing viral aggregation and possibly preventing binding and inactivation by respiratory mucus. Zanamivir is a highly specific and potent inhibitor of influenza viral neuraminidase with little activity against mammalian or bacterial neuraminidase. It is inhibitory for a range of influenza A and B viruses in cell culture and in explants of human respiratory epithelium. Of note, the oral bioavailability of zanamivir is poor, and, as a consequence, the compound can be delivered only topically to mucosal surfaces.

LICENSED USES. Zanamivir is licensed for aerosol administration for both the prevention and treatment of influenza infections. Zanamivir administration is highly protective against infection with febrile illness after intranasal challenge with influenza virus. In patients older than 7 years with uncomplicated illness less than 48 hours in duration, zanamivir therapy accelerated resolution of disease significantly.

TOXICITY. The only reported toxicity is the induction of bronchospasm in a limited number of patients.

Oseltamivir

MECHANISM OF ACTION. Oseltamivir inhibits both influenza A and B virus at concentrations of 2 nM. The drug inhibits viral replication by targeting the neuraminidase protein through binding in a competitive fashion to the enzyme, rendering the virus incapable of reproducing. Because it has activity against influenza B, like zanamivir, it has an advantage over the adamantadines. It has no activity against any other virus.

Oseltamivir is converted by oseltamivir carboxylate, the active compound, through hydrolysis by hepatic esterases. Oral bioavailability is about 75%. The active metabolite appears in the plasma in 30 minutes and peaks at 350 to 550 ng/mL within 4 hours of a standard dose. Drug is excreted as the carboxylate derivative in the urine. Bronchoalveolar fluid drug levels are approximately 50% that of the plasma. The active metabolite is cleared by active tubular excretion—unchanged—in the urine. The plasma half-life is 8 to 10 hours in healthy adults.

LICENSED USES. The drug is licensed for the treatment and prevention of influenza A and B infections. In the United States it is licensed for individuals 2 years of age and older. Clinical trials indicate 30% acceleration in resolution of clinical symptoms. Of note, in pediatric studies, treatment accelerated disease resolution and was associated with a significantly decreased incidence of otitis media and antibiotic usage by 30 to 40%. Prophylactic efficacy is reported to be between 75 and 85%.

TOXICITY. Oseltamivir is generally well tolerated. Adverse events are related to the gastrointestinal tract; the most common is nausea with or without vomiting in 10% of patients. Food alleviates side effects. Because of its oral bioavailability, oseltamivir is the choice for prevention and treatment of both influenza A and B viruses.

Ribavirin

MECHANISM OF ACTION. Ribavirin is a nucleoside analogue whose mechanisms of action are poorly understood and probably not the same for all viruses; however, its ability to alter nucleotide pools and the packaging of messenger RNA (mRNA) appears to be important. This process is not totally virus specific, but there is a certain selectivity in that infected cells produce more mRNA than noninfected cells. The capacity of viral mRNA to support protein synthesis is markedly reduced by ribavirin. High concentrations also inhibit cellular protein synthesis.

LICENSED USES. Ribavirin is licensed for the treatment of respiratory syncytial virus (RSV) infections of children. Drug must be delivered by aerosol. Because the vast majority of infants and children with RSV infection have disease that is mild and self-limited, ribavirin is rarely used. Ribavirin was licensed for cotherapy of hepatitis C with either interferon-α or pegylated interferon. Therapy results in approximately 40% sustained virologic response.

TOXICITY AND CLINICAL PROBLEMS. No adverse effect has been clearly attributable to aerosol therapy with ribavirin, although reports of adverse effects during or after therapy in infants with RSV have included bronchospasm, pulmonary function test changes, pneumothorax in ventilated patients, apnea, cardiac arrest, hypotension, and concomitant digitalis toxicity. Precipitation of drug within the ventilatory apparatus of patients receiving mechanical ventilation can be a serious problem. When proper precautions are taken, such as frequent changes in ventilator tubing, safe delivery of ribavirin to ventilated patients can be accomplished. Reticulocytosis, rash, and conjunctivitis have been associated with the use of ribavirin aerosol. Although there are no pertinent human data, ribavirin has been found to be teratogenic and mutagenic in nearly all species in which it has been tested. This drug is therefore contraindicated in women who are or may become pregnant. Some concern has been expressed about the risk to persons in the room with infants being treated with ribavirin aerosol, particularly females of childbearing age. Although this risk seems to be minimal with limited exposure, awareness and caution are warranted.

OTHER LICENSED AND PROMISING COMPOUNDS

Lamivudine

MECHANISM OF ACTION. Lamivudine is a nucleoside analogue that is an inhibitor of reverse transcriptase. Its activity in the treatment of individuals with HIV infection is described elsewhere.

LICENSED USES. Lamivudine is licensed for the therapy of chronic hepatitis B virus (HBV) infection. Treatment for 1 year normalizes serum alanine aminotransferase and improves histologic inflammatory scores in 50 to 70% of patients. Loss of hepatitis B early antigen (HBeAg) occurs in 30% of treated patients. Its use is limited by the rapid emergence of resistance to medication. Within 1 year as many as 25% of patients develop resistance to medication. It is undergoing extensive evaluation as combination therapy in the treatment of chronic hepatitis B.

TOXICITY. The toxicity profile of lamivudine for therapy of hepatitis B is excellent. Nausea and vomiting occur at low incidences.

Fomivirsen

MECHANISM OF ACTION. Fomivirsen is the first antisense oligonucleotide licensed for the treatment of a viral disease. The 50% inhibitory concentration against laboratory strains of CMV is about 0.37 μM. Drug binds to the mRNA of the immediate early 2 gene of CMV. Fomivirsen can be administered only by intravitreal injection. The pharmacokinetics of drug administration to the rabbit eye indicate a half-life of 62 hours.

LICENSED USES. Fomivirsen delays progression of CMV retinitis when administered at a dosage of 330 mg every other week on three occasions and followed by the same dose monthly. Drug is approved for patients intolerant of other medications.

TOXICITY. Increased intraocular pressure and inflammation have been reported as the major side effects of fomivirsen therapy, occurring in as many as 20% of patients.

Pleconaril

Pleconaril is a broad-spectrum antipicornaviral agent. It is currently being assessed for the treatment of rhinovirus infections in phase III trials. This medication binds to the hydrophobic pocket of the virus capsid protein VP1. By binding to this pocket, pleconaril induces conformational changes in the viral capsid that lead to altered receptor binding and viral uncoating. It is active against most enteroviruses and rhinoviruses. The current regulatory applications demonstrate antiviral activity for rhinovirus colds and chronic enterovirus infections of the CNS in patients with agammaglobulinemia.

Adefovir

Adefovir dipivoxil is the orally bioavailable prodrug of adefovir. This drug has activity against both herpes and hepadnaviruses. It is in the nucleotide class of medications. Treatment of chronic hepatitis B at 10 mg daily significantly decreases HBV DNA polymerase (3.56 logs compared with 0.55 in placebo recipients), improves hepatitic histopathology scores, and induces loss of HBeAg.

Entecavir

Entecavir is a nucleoside analogue that is orally bioavailable for the treatment of chronic hepatitis B. Phase III trials are in progress.

INTERFERONS

History and Introduction

Interferons (IFNs) are glycoprotein cytokines (intracellular messengers) with a complex array of immunomodulating, antineoplastic, and antiviral properties. The name *interferon* was derived from landmark experiments by Isaacs and Lindemann in 1957 demonstrating the existence of a biologic substance that "interfered" with viral replication in infected cells. IFNs are currently classified as α, β, or γ, with natural sources of these classes, in general, being leukocytes, fibroblasts, and lymphocytes, respectively. Each type of IFN can now be produced through recombinant DNA technology. The complexity of the response to IFN, including the variability of dose response, duration of therapy, and combination with other treatments, creates enormous challenges to determine appropriate clinical scenarios in which IFN might be a worthwhile therapeutic agent.

Mechanism of Action

Binding of IFN to the intact cell membrane is the first step in establishing an antiviral effect. IFN binds to specific cell surface receptors; IFN-γ appears to have a different receptor from either IFN-α or IFN-β, which may explain the purported synergistic antiviral and antitumor effects sometimes observed when IFN-γ is given with either of the other two IFN species.

A long-acting, slow-release formulation of IFN has been licensed; IFN is combined with polyethylene glycol. In contrast to the usual three times weekly administration, pegylated IFN is given once weekly.

A prevalent view of IFN action is that after binding there is synthesis of new cellular RNAs and proteins that mediate the antiviral effect. The antiviral state is not fully expressed until these primed cells are infected with virus. In addition to their antiviral effect, IFNs have a number of other biologic activities, including inhibition of cell proliferation and enhancement of the cytotoxic activities of lymphocytes, the expression of cell surface antigens, and the phagocytic and tumoricidal activities of macrophages. These properties may play an important role in the in vivo antiviral and antitumor effects of the IFNs.

Licensed Uses

Although promising for a number of viral infections and HIV-associated conditions, the only licensed use of IFN as an antiviral agent is its intralesional administration in the treatment of condyloma acuminatum, or genital wart, which is caused by human papillomaviruses, and therapy for chronic hepatitis B and C. Only IFN-α is licensed.

Toxicity and Clinical Problems

Side effects are frequent with IFN administration and are usually dose limiting. Influenza-like symptoms (i.e., fever, chills, headache, and malaise) commonly occur, but these symptoms usually become less severe with repeated treatments. At doses used in the treatment of condyloma acuminatum, these side effects rarely cause termination of treatment and may be reduced in severity by pretreatment with acetaminophen. For local treatment (intralesional injection), pain at the injection site does not differ significantly from that in placebo-treated patients and is short lived. Leukopenia is the most common hematologic abnormality, occurring in up to 26% of patients treated for condyloma. Leukopenia is usually modest, not clinically relevant, and reversible when therapy is discontinued. Increased alanine aminotransferase levels may also occur, as well as nausea, vomiting, and diarrhea.

At higher doses of IFN, neurotoxicity is encountered, as manifested by personality changes, confusion, loss of attention, disorientation, and paranoid ideation. Early studies with IFN-γ showed side effects similar to those of treatment with IFN-α and IFN-β but with the additional side effects of dose-limiting hypotension and a marked increase in triglyceride levels.

Clinical Trials

IFN has potential use against virtually all viral infections. Its ultimate utility depends on a number of factors, including the acceptability of side effects, cost, and the availability of other antiviral agents. Of the many viral infections in which IFN has been tested, treatment of condyloma acuminatum, chronic hepatitis B, chronic hepatitis C, and recurrent respiratory papillomatosis and prophylaxis of rhinovirus and coronavirus upper respiratory tract infection have been promising.

CONDYLOMA ACUMINATUM. Several large controlled trials have demonstrated the clinical benefit of IFN-α therapy for condyloma acuminatum. [3] These studies have demonstrated clearance rates of treated lesions from 36 to 62%. Up to one third of lesions treated with IFN recur. Much research remains to be done to examine the effects of different routes of administration, prolonged therapy, repeated courses of treatment, and combined treatment with other therapeutic modalities (i.e., cryotherapy, podophyllin, and laser ablation).

RESPIRATORY PAPILLOMATOSIS. Recurrent respiratory papillomatosis is a disease in which squamous papillomas relentlessly recur within the larynx and trachea of both children and young adults. Standard management consists of careful microendoscopic excision, usually with a CO_2 laser. There have been numerous case reports and uncontrolled studies supporting benefit from IFN as an adjunct to surgery. Results of placebo-controlled trials have suggested benefit.

HEPATITIS. The inhibitory effect of human leukocyte IFN-α on HBV replication was first reported more than 10 years ago. Treatment with IFN-α in chronic hepatitis B has subsequently been investigated in several large, randomized, controlled trials. The earlier studies were encouraging, but the response rate was low at approximately 30%.

In an attempt to enhance the efficacy of antiviral therapy, combinations of IFN with other agents have also been studied. Vidarabine and acyclovir have been used in such studies with little success. It has been observed, however, that a short course of corticosteroids before treatment with IFN-α results in immunologic "rebound" after prednisone withdrawal. This phenomenon, which seems to be directed at virus-infected hepatocytes, is characterized by an acute hepatitis-like elevation of serum aminotransferases and a transient decline in levels of HBV DNA polymerase and HBV DNA.

A large multicenter trial comparing patients randomly assigned to receive one of two doses of IFN-α versus prednisone followed by IFN-α or no treatment showed that a 4-month treatment regimen of subcutaneous IFN-α in a dose of 5 million units daily resulted in a complete response (loss of serum HBeAg and HBV DNA) in nearly 40% of patients and that reactivation of infection within 6 months after treatment was no greater than 2%. The beneficial effect of pretreatment with a tapering dose of prednisone was limited to patients with low baseline levels of alanine aminotransferase (<100 units/L). The best predictor of response in this study was the HBV DNA level before treatment, with approximately half of the patients who had levels less than 100 pg/mL experiencing a complete response. Long-term follow-up studies are required to determine the duration of antiviral effect and the impact on survival.

The efficacy of IFN for treating chronic hepatitis C (non-A, non-B hepatitis) has been established. The use of the licensed pegylated IFNs for administration with ribavirin results in 50% response rates.

RESPIRATORY INFECTIONS. The upper respiratory tract infection known as the "common cold" has a multitude of possible viral causes (Chapter 359). It has been demonstrated that nasal spray or drops of IFN-α provide prophylaxis against the common cold caused by rhinovirus or coronavirus infection. Although clinical benefit was demonstrated in these studies, administration of IFN-α for 2 to 3 weeks led to hemorrhage of nasal mucosa.

IMMUNOGLOBULIN THERAPY

Efficacy has been established for prophylactic immunoglobulin administration for several viral infections, but the use of immunoglobulin alone for therapy for established disease has not been proved unequivocally beneficial for any viral infection. Benefit has been shown for the administration of intravenous immunoglobulin or CMV hyperimmune globulin when combined with ganciclovir in the treatment of CMV pneumonia in bone marrow transplant recipients. Survival was increased to 52 to 79%, which is significantly better than that of historical controls treated with either agent alone. Currently active areas of research include the efficacy of CMV hyperimmune globulin for prevention and treatment of disease in bone marrow, kidney, and heart transplant patients and that of CMV monoclonal antibody in the treatment of established CMV disease in AIDS patients.

Although relatively few antiviral drugs are licensed for use at this time, there is significant interest in the development of antiviral compounds. Table 358–3 summarizes the use of currently available antivirals for indications other than therapy of HIV infections. Systematic approaches have revealed a number of promising new drugs and biologic agents in various stages of evaluation. A better understanding of the molecular biology of virus replication and pathogenesis should elucidate agents with enhanced virus-specific activity.

1. Watts DH, Brown ZA, Money D, et al: A double-blind, randomized, placebo-controlled trial of acyclovir in late pregnancy for the reduction of herpes simplex virus shedding and cesarean delivery. Am J Obstet Gynecol 2003;188:836–843.
2. Martin DF, Kuppermann BD, Wolitz RA, et al: Oral ganciclovir for patients with cytomegalovirus retinitis treated with a ganciclovir implant. Roche Ganciclovir Study Group. N Engl J Med 1999;340:1063–1070.
3. Reichman RC, Oakes D, Bonnez W, et al: Treatment of condyloma acuminatum with three different interferons administered intralesionally. A double-blind, placebo-controlled trial. Ann Intern Med 1988;108:657–659.

SUGGESTED READINGS

Karayiannis P: Hepatitis B virus: Old, new and future approaches to antiviral treatment. J Antimicrob Chemother 2003;51:761–785. *A current review.*
Komarova NL, Barnes E, Klenerman P, et al: Boosting immunity by antiviral drug therapy: A simple relationship among timing, efficacy, and success. Proc Natl Acad Sci U S A 2003;100:1855–1860. *Drug therapy can result in sustained immunity.*
Stiver G: The treatment of influenza with antiviral drugs. CMAJ 2003;168:49–56. *Recommends treatment within 30–36 hours in high-risk patients and immunosuppressed patients with influenza-like illness.*

 **THE COMMON COLD**

J. Owen Hendley

Definition

The common cold, also known as upper respiratory infection, is an acute, self-limited illness caused by a virus. Nasal symptoms including rhinorrhea and nasal obstruction are invariably present; sore or scratchy throat and/or cough may be present. Many myths surround the source of the virus causing colds. There are no normal viral flora of the respiratory tract in humans (two possible exceptions are human herpesvirus type 6 in saliva and adenovirus, which can be recovered from adenoid tissue of otherwise healthy children by cocultivation with susceptible cells). In sharp contrast, luxuriant normal bacterial flora occur in the upper respiratory tract and mouth. Because viruses are not part of normal flora, the viruses that cause colds are not present in the host ready to be activated because "resistance" has been lowered by chilling, loss of sleep, or bad diet. Instead, the virus must be *passed* from another human to produce the cold.

Etiology

Colds are common because the viruses with few serotypes reinfect many times and the viruses that infect an individual only once have multiple serotypes (Table 359–1). Rhinoviruses (*rhino* = "nose") cause at least 50% of colds in adults; coronaviruses (corona = "crown") and respiratory syncytial virus (RSV) are each responsible for about 10%. Each of the other virus groups listed in Table 359–1 causes less than 5% of colds. Adults are susceptible to RSV and parainfluenza virus, but the illness in adults is usually a cold rather than the more severe involvement seen in infants. Some of the viruses that cause colds are characteristically associated with other syndromes. Influenza viruses cause febrile respiratory disease with lower tract involvement,

Table 359–1 • IMMUNITY TO COMMON COLD VIRUSES

VIRUS	NUMBER OF SEROTYPES
Solid immunity not produced by infection (repeated infection with same serotype usual)	
Respiratory syncytial virus	1
Parainfluenza virus	4
Coronavirus	4
Immunity produced by infection (reinfection with same serotype uncommon)	
Rhinovirus	>100
Adenovirus	>33
Influenza	3 (type A subtypes change)
Echovirus	31
Coxsackievirus	
Group A	23
Group B	6

From Hendley JO: Immunology of viral colds. *In* Veldman JE, McCabe BF, Huizing EH, Mygind N (eds.): Immunobiology, Autoimmunity, Transplantation in Otorhinolaryngology. Amsterdam, Kugler Publications, 1985, pp 257–260.

adenoviruses cause pharyngoconjunctival fever or acute undifferentiated febrile illness, echoviruses and other enteroviruses are an important cause of aseptic meningitis, and coxsackievirus A causes herpangina.

Epidemiology and Transmission

Colds are the most frequent disease of humans and the single most common cause of absenteeism from school and work. Frequency of colds varies with age. Even before widespread daycare attendance, colds were particularly common in children younger than age 6. In the Cleveland family study in the 1950s, infants younger than age 1 had an average of 6.7 colds per year, 1- to 5-year olds had 7.4 to 8.3 colds per year, and teenagers averaged about 4.5 colds per year. Mothers reported 4.5 colds and fathers 3.5 colds per year. The wider exposure to other preschoolers in daycare has increased the frequency of colds in children younger than 6 even more. The number of colds in adults may increase for several years because of exposure to young children, which highlights the fact that children commonly introduce new viruses to their families. At least with rhinovirus, the home setting is the primary site for viral transmission. Coworkers in an insurance company office with simultaneous rhinovirus colds were usually infected with different serotypes of virus, but each worker's serotype was found in his or her family contacts.

In temperate climates, colds are epidemic in the winter months (Fig. 359–1). The epidemic starts with a sharp rise in frequency in September after children have returned to school; the incidence then remains at an almost constant level until spring. This epidemic curve is produced by successive waves of different viruses moving through the community. Although rhinovirus infections occur year-round, the epidemic is initiated by a sharp rise of rhinovirus infections in early fall. Parainfluenza viruses move through in October and November, followed by RSV and coronaviruses in winter months. Influenza viruses appear later in winter; then rhinovirus has a resurgence in spring. Summer colds are usually caused by rhinovirus or one of the enteroviruses. The wave of each virus moving through is not sharp, and many times two or three viruses may be overlapping. Adenovirus and parainfluenza virus type 3 contribute to the burden of illness throughout the epidemic.

Determinants of this yearly epidemic of colds are not established but certainly include human behavior, with more virus transmitted by higher indoor contact in colder months. Another determinant might be attributes of the viruses. Enveloped viruses, including RSV, parainfluenza virus, influenza virus, and coronavirus, may survive outside the host for longer periods in winter when the relative humidity of indoor (but not outdoor) air is low.

Transmission of viruses causing colds can occur by one or more of three mechanisms: (1) small-particle (<5 μm in diameter) aerosol in which virus may be suspended in air for an hour and infect by inhalation, (2) large-particle (>10 μm in diameter) airborne droplets that travel less than 1 m and infect by landing on a mucosal surface such as conjunctiva or nasal mucosa, and (3) direct transfer of virus in secretions through hand contact from a person with a cold to a

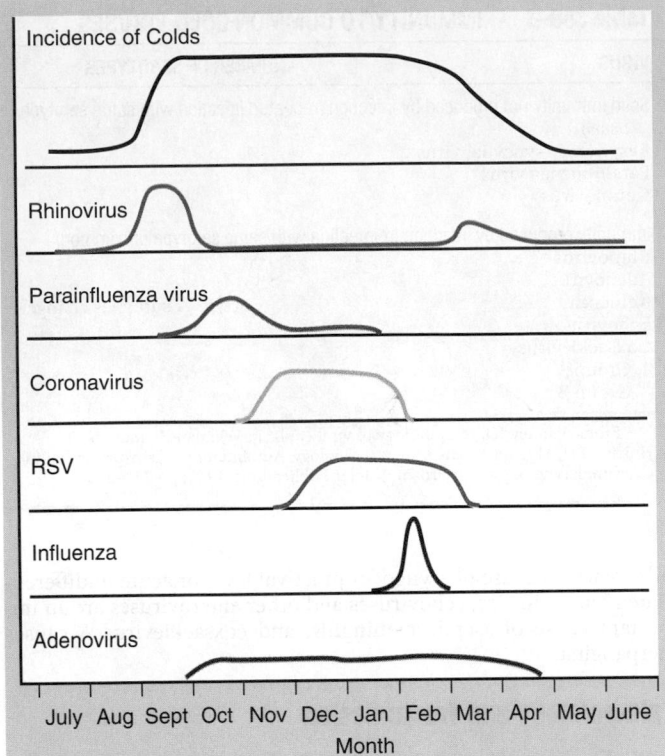

FIGURE 359–1 • Schematic diagram of the incidence of colds and frequency of the causative viruses.

well person, who inoculates the virus onto his or her own conjunctival or nasal mucosa. Oral inoculation of rhinovirus or RSV does not result in infection, presumably because the stratified squamous epithelium of the mouth and oropharynx is not susceptible. The transmission route under natural conditions in the home has not been definitely established for any of the viruses. However, the importance of spread of colds in the home favors direct contact and/or large-droplet spread as being most likely. Influenza virus clearly can be transmitted by small-particle aerosol in some circumstances.

Pathogenesis

It had been assumed that the symptoms of colds were produced by a viral cytopathic effect destroying the nasal mucosa. However, in a study of natural colds the histologic appearance of the nasal mucosa in biopsy specimens taken during illness could not be distinguished from that of biopsy specimens taken 2 weeks after illness except for an increased number of polymorphonuclear leukocytes (PMNs) during illness. The infiltration of PMNs in the nose in uncomplicated colds, which was unexpected, was confirmed in another study; the number of PMNs in nasal secretions increased coincidently when symptoms appeared in experimentally induced rhinovirus colds. Rhinovirus and coronavirus, in contrast to influenza virus and adenovirus, were not found to be destructive of nasal epithelium in organ cultures in vitro.

Because mucosal damage by the virus during colds does not adequately explain the symptoms, the hypothesis that the viral infection of the nose triggers a cascade of inflammatory mediators that results in the symptoms is being explored. Initial support for this hypothesis was provided in volunteers with experimentally induced rhinovirus colds. Kinins (primarily bradykinin) and PMNs appeared in nasal secretions of infected volunteers at the time that they became ill, and their presence paralleled cold symptoms. Subsequent work has suggested that viral infection of individual epithelial cells in the mucosa of the nose and nasopharynx can lead to elaboration of cytokines that effect the symptomatic illness and influx of PMNs. Infected cells have been shown to elaborate interleukin-8 (IL-8), which is a chemoattractant for PMNs. Increased levels of IL-1β, IL-6, and IL-8 have been detected in nasal secretions during colds. Whether the release of proinflammatory cytokines from the host cells induced by the viral infection can be interrupted has not been ascertained. However, the concept

that it might be possible to ablate cold symptoms by blocking the mediators of the host response without having to kill the virus is exciting.

Clinical Manifestations

The clinical manifestations of colds, which are familiar to all, are predominately subjective. In adults, rhinorrhea, nasal obstruction, and scratchy or sore throat are usually noted. The rhinorrhea is usually clear early in illness and may become white or yellow-green. Some malaise and nonproductive cough are common; sneezing is noted in some colds. Other common symptoms include sinus fullness and a "nasal" quality to the voice. Hoarseness is sometimes present. Objective findings in an adult with a cold are usually minimal. The nasal mucosa may be red but not to a degree that differs from normal. Mild erythema of the pharynx and redness around the external nares from nose blowing may be noted. Fever (temperature > 38° C) is uncommon in a cold in an adult; the presence of fever would suggest influenza or a bacterial complication of the cold. The symptoms of the cold usually abate in 5 to 7 days.

Colds in infants and children may be associated with more objective signs than those in adults. In addition to rhinorrhea and nasal obstruction, moderate enlargement of the anterior cervical lymph nodes is frequent. Fever during the first 2 to 3 days of a cold in young children is not unusual, even when the child's parent or older sibling does not have an elevated temperature during the cold caused by the same virus. In contrast to that in adults, the usual duration of cold symptoms in children is 10 to 14 days.

Diagnosis

Self-diagnosis of a cold by the patient is usually accurate. Laboratory tests including white blood cell count and differential are not helpful. Sloughed ciliated cells may be present, and PMNs would be expected in nasal secretions during viral colds. The differential diagnosis of a cold includes an intranasal foreign body in a child and allergic or vasomotor rhinitis in adults and children. Examination of the nose should exclude a foreign body; the chronicity of symptoms with allergic or vasomotor rhinitis should differentiate these conditions from an acute cold.

Etiologic (virologic) diagnosis of a cold can be attempted by inoculation of a sample of nasal secretions into tissue cell cultures, but this is rarely needed or useful. Rhinovirus can be grown in human embryonic lung fibroblast cultures. Influenza and parainfluenza viruses can be grown in primary rhesus monkey kidney cell culture, and adenoviruses grow in human embryonic kidney cells. Coronaviruses cannot be detected accurately in cell culture. Assays using polymerase chain reaction (PCR) for detection of respiratory viruses have been developed that will facilitate diagnosis of these infections. Rapid tests for RSV antigen in nasal secretions are not reliable in adults. Detection of nucleoprotein of both A and B influenza may be useful to screen for these viruses.

Rx Treatment

Given the self-limited nature of colds, any treatment should be completely safe. Antibiotics have no place in therapy for uncomplicated colds because they neither hasten nor delay recovery from the cold, nor do they reduce the frequency of bacterial complications.

Because the subjective symptoms of a cold disappear in 7 days without intervention, a variety of actually ineffective treatments have been reported to be effective because of inadequate "blinding" of placebo recipients. One example of this phenomenon was a study of large doses of vitamin C to prevent colds, in which many placebo recipients dropped out of the study because they could tell by tasting the medication that they were not receiving the vitamin C. Another example was the use of zinc gluconate lozenges as an antiviral treatment for colds. In the blinded trial, the only appropriate placebo that could be found to match the noxious taste of the zinc was denatonium benzoate, which is so bitter that it has been painted on the thumbs of children to discourage them from thumb-sucking.

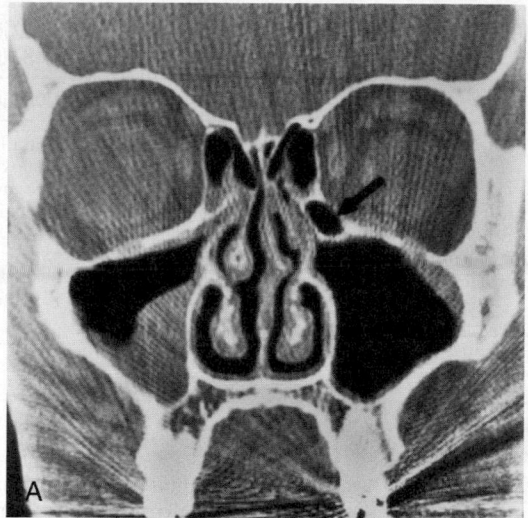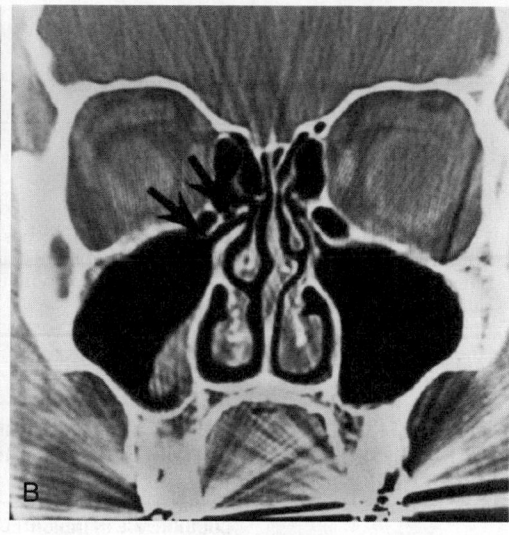

FIGURE 359–2 • Sinus computed tomographic scan of adult during symptomatic cold (left) and 2 weeks later (right). Arrow in the left panel denotes an infraorbital air cell (Haller cell). Bilateral abnormalities were observed in the ethmoid and maxillary sinuses during the cold, with an air-fluid interface in the right maxillary sinus. Two weeks later, all abnormalities had cleared except for a residual density in the right maxillary sinus. The infundibulum (two arrows) draining the maxillary antrum was now open. (Courtesy of Dr. Jack M. Gwaltney, Jr., Department of Internal Medicine, University of Virginia School of Medicine, Charlottesville, VA.)

No antiviral agents are currently available for treating colds, except those caused by influenza virus. Individual symptoms may be treated. Malaise may be relieved by analgesics (e.g., aspirin, acetaminophen, ibuprofen). Nasal congestion may be relieved by decongestants by mouth (pseudoephedrine, 60 mg, three times a day) or by topical application (oxymetazoline 0.05%, two sprays to each nostril twice daily). Oral first-generation antihistamines (e.g., brompheniramine, chlorpheniramine, clemastine) may provide modest relief of sneezing and rhinorrhea in colds.

Complications

Secondary bacterial infection may complicate viral colds. The most common is bacterial suppurative otitis media, which occurs in some 5% of colds in preschool-aged children. Otitis media may be heralded by a secondary fever with associated ear pain. Bacterial sinusitis is estimated to occur in 0.5% of colds, primarily in adults. Sinusitis would be suggested by the presence of fever and/or facial pain (Chapter 468). Bacterial pneumonia is thought to complicate colds, but it is uncommon.

Clinical differentiation between primary viral and secondary bacterial infection of the respiratory tract is a challenge because respiratory viruses may involve the middle ear or paranasal sinuses in the absence of bacterial infection. Tympanocentesis or maxillary sinus puncture provides definitive information on viral versus bacterial infection, but these are too invasive for routine use. Coronal computed tomography (CT) is an accurate noninvasive method for imaging the paranasal sinuses. Work using CT has demonstrated that abnormalities in the sinuses may occur in colds not complicated by secondary bacterial infection. Coronal CT in 27 (87%) of 31 young adults during uncomplicated colds showed abnormalities in one or more sinuses (Fig. 359–2). In 11 (79%) of the 14 subjects who had repeated scans 2 weeks later, the abnormalities had cleared or were markedly improved without antibiotic therapy.

An important complication of viral colds occurs in adults and children with underlying reactive airways disease or asthma. Wheezing occurs in 30 to 50% of episodes of viral colds in prospective studies of patients with asthma. Colds in these patients produce a large burden of illness because up to 50% of asthma exacerbations in children and up to 20% of exacerbations in adults have been associated with an identified virus.

Prevention

Vaccines to prevent common colds are unlikely to be useful given the multiplicity of immunotypes of some of the viruses and the lack of solid immunity to reinfection with the other viruses (see Table 359–1). Prophylaxis with topical interferon applied intranasally for 5 days after one family member appears with a cold has been shown to be moderately effective in preventing other family members from acquiring a cold, particularly colds caused by rhinovirus. The

practicality of this preventive approach may be argued, particularly in view of the fact that prolonged use of intranasal interferon is complicated by alteration or damage of the nasal mucosa.

Probably the only practical, albeit imperfect, means of preventing colds available is to prevent virus from reaching the nasal or conjunctival mucosa by way of one's own hands. If transmission occurs by inhalation of airborne small particles or by adherence of large droplets to a mucosal surface, infection is inevitable for those who enjoy contact with other humans. However, if transmission occurs by self-inoculation with virus on contaminated fingertips, the simple measure of ridding the fingers of viable virus before touching one's eye or nose might be helpful. The virus can be removed physically by rinsing the hands. Applying a virucide to the hands might be another approach.

SUGGESTED READINGS

Anzueto A, Niederman MS: Diagnosis and treatment of rhinovirus respiratory infections. Chest 2003;123:1664–1672. *The diagnosis is usually empiric, and no active antiviral agents are available.*

Falsey AR, Formica MA, Walsh EE: Diagnosis of respiratory syncytial virus infection: Comparison of reverse transcription–PCR to viral culture and serology in adults with respiratory illness. J Clin Microbiol 2002;40;817–820. *PCR and/or serology detected more than twice as many RSV infections as viral culture in ill adults.*

Greenberg SB: Respiratory consequences of rhinovirus infection. Arch Intern Med 2003;163:278–279. *A practical overview.*

Musher DM: How contagious are common respiratory tract infections? N Engl J Med 2003;348:1256–1266. *Reviews all the relevant viruses.*

360 VIRAL PHARYNGITIS, LARYNGITIS, CROUP, AND BRONCHITIS

Maurice A. Mufson

Definition

Viral infections that localize to the upper and middle respiratory tract passages produce an acute inflammatory response and, depending on the anatomic site involved, evoke the clinical manifestations of pharyngitis, laryngitis, croup (i.e., laryngotracheobronchitis), and bronchitis. Ordinarily, these infections do not involve the pulmonary alveoli. Pharyngitis, laryngitis, and bronchitis occur in persons of any age, but croup occurs characteristically in children and rarely in adults. Usually, these viral illnesses begin abruptly with predominant upper respiratory tract signs and symptoms and limited systemic findings. Mainly uncomplicated illnesses, they abate after 5 to 10 days.

Etiology

The viral pathogens of the respiratory tract that cause pharyngitis, laryngitis, croup, and bronchitis include the influenza and

Table 360–1 • VIRUSES THAT CAUSE PHARYNGITIS, LARYNGITIS, CROUP, AND BRONCHITIS

VIRUS	SEROTYPE
Influenza virus	Types A, B
Parainfluenza virus	Types 1, 2, 3
Respiratory syncytial virus	Subgroups A, B1, B2
Adenovirus	Types 1, 2, 3, 4, 5, 6, 7 (also others)
Coronavirus	Types 229E, OC43 (also others)
Rhinovirus	Most or all of more than 110 serotypes
Enterovirus	At least some of more than 75 serotypes
Herpes simplex virus	Type 1

Table 360–3 • EPIDEMIOLOGY OF VIRUSES THAT CAUSE PHARYNGITIS, LARYNGITIS, CROUP, AND BRONCHITIS

EPIDEMIC	ENDEMIC	SPORADIC
Parainfluenza virus 1*	Parainfluenza virus 3	Parainfluenza virus 2
Influenza virus A†	Adenovirus	Herpes simplex virus
Influenza virus B	Coronavirus	
Respiratory syncytial virus‡	Rhinovirus	
	Enterovirus	

*Epidemics occur in alternate years.
†Epidemics usually occur annually, and pandemics occur at about 10-year intervals.
‡Epidemics occur annually.

Table 360–2 • RELATIVE IMPORTANCE OF VIRUSES CAUSING PHARYNGITIS, LARYNGITIS, CROUP, AND BRONCHITIS

VIRUS	OCCURRENCE IN INDICATED ILLNESS*			
	Pharyngitis	**Laryngitis**	**Croup**	**Bronchitis**
Influenza virus A	++++	++++	+	++++
Influenza virus B	++	++		++
Parainfluenza virus 1	++	++	++++	++
Parainfluenza virus 2	+	+	+++	+
Parainfluenza virus 3	++	++	++++	++
Respiratory syncytial virus	+		+	+++
Adenovirus	++++	++		++
Coronavirus	+	+		+++
Rhinovirus	++	+		+
Enterovirus	+			
Herpes simplex virus	+	±	±	±

*Graded as ±, uncommon occurrence; +, minimal, to ++++, major importance; blank, very unlikely occurrence.

parainfluenza viruses, respiratory syncytial virus, adenoviruses, coronaviruses, rhinoviruses, enteroviruses, and herpesviruses (Table 360–1). However, they differ in their propensity to cause these illnesses (Table 360–2). An etiologic diagnosis requires either isolation of virus or detection of viral antigen or demonstration of a rise in antibody during convalescence. Such diagnostic studies are done infrequently for the management of these viral illnesses, except for influenza virus because specific anti-influenza drugs are available that preferably should be begun in persons with laboratory-confirmed infection.

Pharyngitis also can occur as part of systemic viral illnesses associated with Epstein-Barr virus (Chapter 371) or cytomegalovirus (Chapter 370) infection or of the acute retroviral syndrome caused by human immunodeficiency virus (Chapter 409). Laryngitis and bronchitis can occur in measles *virus* infection (Chapter 365). When coryza is the dominant feature of an upper respiratory infection, the term *common cold* (Chapter 359) prevails. When influenza virus is the infecting virus, the designation *influenza* describes an acute respiratory tract infection with fever and systemic features (Chapter 363).

Incidence and Prevalence

Most children and adults experience three to five viral infections of the upper respiratory tract each year. In infants and children, croup is a serious illness that peaks in the second year of life, with as many as 47 cases per 1000 children per year, and by 4 to 5 years of age, the rate declines to less than 15 cases per 1000 children per year.

Epidemiology

Viral pharyngitis, laryngitis, croup, and bronchitis occur during all months of the year, in parallel with the occurrence of individual viruses. Respiratory syncytial virus, influenza A and B viruses, and parainfluenza virus type 1 occur in epidemics, mainly in the late fall, winter, and spring (Table 360–3). The other viral pathogens occur endemically or sporadically. Virus infections of the respiratory tract spread mainly by direct person-to-person contact and less commonly by infectious aerosols and fomites.

Clinical Manifestations

VIRAL PHARYNGITIS. Acute viral pharyngitis is characterized by a scratchy and sore throat, but pain on swallowing is not a prominent or constant feature. Dysphagia occurs infrequently and cough is not a feature. Fever and malaise often accompany influenza and adenovirus infections; they infrequently occur with the other respiratory virus infections. Pharyngeal erythema and enlarged tender lymph nodes may be the only physical findings. Adenovirus pharyngitis may be associated with conjunctivitis. Exudative tonsillitis occurs in adenovirus infections, infectious mononucleosis associated with Epstein-Barr virus infection, and herpetic pharyngitis (with or without vesicles or small ulcers), as well as streptococcal pharyngitis. Bronchospasm occurs as a feature of herpes simplex virus tracheobronchitis in elderly persons.

VIRAL LARYNGITIS. In acute viral laryngitis, hoarseness predominates, associated with difficulty in talking, with pain on clearing respiratory secretions, and often with fever, depending on the infecting virus. Cough and pharyngitis may be present. The larynx appears erythematous and edematous, and the regional lymph nodes show slight enlargement and tenderness. Wheezes may be audible on auscultation.

VIRAL CROUP. The clinical picture of croup characteristically includes inspiratory stridor, hoarseness, and a brassy cough. This distinctive triad of symptoms reflects the acute and intense edema and mucoid exudative secretions of the larynx and associated obstruction of the subglottic portion of the upper airway. These symptoms develop acutely, accompanied by fever, cough, tachypnea, and wheezing. Retractions of the chest wall occur. Hemoptysis does not occur. Rhonchi, rales, or wheezes, alone or in combination, may be audible on auscultation of the lungs. Radiographic examination of the neck can demonstrate subglottic narrowing, and views of the chest can show hyperinflation of the lungs. In the uncomplicated case, the findings resolve in several days, but some children develop respiratory failure and pneumonia. A child who experiences multiple episodes of croup may as an adolescent or adult manifest bronchial hyperreactivity and peripheral airways obstruction.

VIRAL BRONCHITIS. In acute viral bronchitis, cough, with or without sputum production, and fever are the main features. The sputum is slightly mucoid or watery and white. Other symptoms and signs include hoarseness, nonpleuritic substernal chest pain, malaise, rhonchi, and rales. The chest roentgenogram may show increased intensity of the vascular pattern but not pulmonary infiltrates. Acute bronchitis associated with influenza or coronavirus infection occurs often as an exacerbation of chronic bronchitis. Persons with chronic respiratory disease suffer more severe exacerbations.

Infectious Diseases

Table 360–4 • ANTIVIRAL DRUG THERAPY OF VIRUSES THAT CAUSE PHARYNGITIS, LARYNGITIS, CROUP, AND BRONCHITIS			
VIRUS	**DRUG**	**DOSE (DURATION)**	**ROUTE**
Influenza viruses A and B	Zanamivir (Relenza)	10 mg q12h by inhalation for 5 days	Inhalation
	Oseltamivir (Tamiflu)	75 mg PO bid for 5 days	Oral
Respiratory syncytial virus	Ribavirin (Virazole)	20 mg/mL solution (administered over 12–18 hr for 3–7 days)	Aerosol
Herpes simplex virus* Acyclovir (Zovirax)	8 mg/kg q8h (7–10 days)	IV	

*Herpes simplex virus laryngotracheobronchitis treated with intravenous acyclovir.

 Treatment

ANTIVIRAL DRUGS. Antiviral drug therapy is available for influenza A and B and herpes simplex virus infections, but not any of the other viruses (Table 360–4). Influenza A and B virus infections of the upper respiratory tract respond to treatment with one of the neuraminidase inhibitors administered within 48 hours of the onset of symptoms, either zanamivir (Relenza), 10 mg every 12 hours by inhalation for 5 days, or oseltamivir (Tamiflu), 75 mg orally twice daily for 5 days. Influenza A virus only responds to treatment with two other antivirals, rimantadine (Flumadine) and amantadine (Symmetrel). The dose for each is 100 mg orally twice daily for 5 days. The frequent central nervous system side effects associated with amantadine make it less desirable. Preferably, they should be given when influenza virus infection is confirmed by laboratory tests. Serious herpes simplex virus laryngitis and laryngotracheobronchitis can be treated with a course of intravenous acyclovir (Zovirax) (see Table 360–4). Although no controlled studies exist for oral acyclovir treatment of acute herpes simplex virus pharyngitis, acyclovir may be considered in adults whose symptoms are particularly distressing, at a dose of 400 mg given three times daily for 7 days or until severe symptoms subside.

TREATMENT OF SYMPTOMS. The symptoms of these illnesses should be treated with analgesics, fluids, and rest. Persistent cough can be treated with suppressant preparations. Pharyngeal pain or dysphagia of pharyngitis should be treated with analgesics and fluids. Less serious cases of croup can be managed by having the child rest in bed at home and use a room vaporizer. Children with moderately severe croup who can be managed at home may benefit from a single intramuscular injection of dexamethasone (0.6 mg/kg) administered before they leave the emergency department; this treatment usually reduces the severity of illness within 24 hours.■ Oral dexamethasone appears to be as efficacious as intramuscular.❷ However, children with severe croup require hospitalization, supportive treatment, dexamethasone, and constant monitoring for the development of respiratory distress. If hypoxemia develops, oxygen therapy is essential; hypoxemia requiring oxygen can develop even before cyanosis becomes evident. Subglottic edema may be reduced by the administration of racemic epinephrine.

ANTIBIOTICS. Because viruses cause most cases of acute pharyngitis, laryngitis, croup, and acute bronchitis, antibiotics are not indicated for these illnesses. Antibiotic use in viral respiratory tract illnesses should be avoided because they are ineffective and to minimize the emergence of antibiotic-resistant bacteria. However, when secondary bacterial infection complicates one of these viral illnesses, which is more likely in influenza virus infection than in the other virus infections of the respiratory tract, treatment with appropriate antibiotics is indicated.

Prevention

An efficacious and safe vaccine is available only for influenza A and B viruses. It should be administered annually to persons in high-risk groups (unless contraindicated because of allergy to eggs) to reduce their chances of acquiring this infection. The dose in adults is 0.5 mL administered intramuscularly in the deltoid muscle. The vaccine, which is reformulated each year, comprises only the hemagglutinin (designated as subvirion, split, or purified vaccine) of two recent influenza A strains and one influenza B strain. It is recommended for persons older than 65 years, all persons with underlying heart and lung diseases, persons who reside in long-term care facilities, persons living with acquired immunodeficiency syndrome (AIDS), and persons whose public position requires their protection, such as physicians, nurses, police officers, and fire fighters.

Prognosis

Acute pharyngitis, laryngitis, and bronchitis due to respiratory viruses, except the influenza viruses, are moderate, self-limited illnesses. Influenza infections associated with pharyngitis, laryngitis, and bronchitis more often can be severe and complicated by bacterial superinfection. Although herpes simplex virus pharyngitis and laryngotracheobronchitis illnesses can be severe, they are rarely fatal. The rare cases of croup in adults are not fatal. Viral respiratory tract infections in adults with underlying cardiopulmonary or other chronic diseases place them at higher risk for hospitalization and fatal outcome.

Future Directions

Rapid and cost-effective (inexpensive and highly specific and sensitive) diagnostic procedures can answer the questions of physicians concerning the possible infecting virus in patients with pharyngitis, laryngitis, croup, and bronchitis. Such procedures are available for influenza and parainfluenza viruses, respiratory syncytial virus, and herpesviruses. Urgently needed are more effective antiviral drugs for these infections. Because influenza and respiratory syncytial virus infections predominate among the viral respiratory tract infections, the development of new antiviral drugs for these viruses holds first priority. A vaccine for respiratory syncytial virus still must be developed. It also has the highest priority; however, it has been an elusive goal for the past three decades.

1. Cruz MN, Stewart G, Rosenberg N: Use of dexamethasone in the outpatient management of acute laryngotracheitis. Pediatrics 1995;96:220–223.
2. Donaldson D, Poleski D, Knipple E, et al: Intramuscular versus oral dexamethasone for the treatment of moderate-to-severe croup: A randomized, double-blind trial. Acad Emerg Med 2003;10:16–21.

SUGGESTED READINGS
Glezen WP, Greenberg SB, Atmar RL, et al: Impact of respiratory virus infections on persons with chronic underlying conditions. JAMA 2000;283:499–505. *Viral infections can trigger serious complications in these patients.*
McGinn TG, Deluca J, Ahlawat SK, et al: Validation and modification of streptococcal pharyngitis clinical prediction rules. Mayo Clin Proc 2003;78:289–293. *These rules generally are accurate.*
Vabret A, Mourez T, Gouarin S, et al: An outbreak of coronavirus OC43 respiratory infection in Normandy, France. Clin Infect Dis 2003;36:985–989. *Of 501 patients with acute respiratory tract disease, 40 had coronavirus infection detected by RT-PCR and one-third of these positive patients had pharyngitis.*
Woo PC, Young K, Tsang KWT, et al: Adult croup: A rare but more severe condition. Respiration 2000;67:684–688. *Non-fatal croup due to parainfluenza virus 3 in an adult and a review of adult croup.*

361 RESPIRATORY SYNCYTIAL VIRUS

Edward E. Walsh

Definition

Respiratory syncytial virus (RSV) causes yearly outbreaks of illness during the fall, winter, and early spring. Since its discovery in 1957,

RSV has been found to be the single most important cause of bronchiolitis and pneumonia in young infants and is a common cause of upper respiratory illness in older children and young adults. In addition, RSV is a cause of serious respiratory infection in elderly people, adults with underlying cardiopulmonary disease, and those who are severely immunocompromised.

Etiology

RSV is an enveloped virus of the family Paramyxoviridae, genus *Pneumovirus*. The single-stranded negative-polarity RNA encodes 11 proteins, of which 8 are found in purified virions. Three transmembrane glycoproteins (G, attachment protein; F, fusion protein; SH protein) protrude from a lipid bilayer encompassing three nucleocapsid proteins (N, P, polymerase) complexed with the genome. Two additional proteins (M, M2) are associated with the viral envelope. Two nonstructural proteins (NS1 and NS2) block the antiviral activity of interferon-α. Neutralizing antibodies are directed at F and G glycoproteins, whereas F, N, and M2 are primary targets for cytotoxic T cells. Two major virus groups (A and B), each with four to five subgroups, are distinguishable by antigenically divergent G proteins.

Epidemiology

As with influenza, worldwide RSV outbreaks occur annually. In the United States, epidemics generally begin in the southern states in late fall, move steadily north, and peak in February and March in colder climates. RSV causes approximately 90,000 hospitalizations and accounts for 60% of bronchiolitis and 25% of pneumonia cases in infants in the United States. In the first year of life, over half of all infants become infected, with the remainder infected the following year. Family studies suggest that schoolchildren introduce RSV into the home with subsequent spread to parents and younger siblings, with infection rates of 43 and 62%, respectively. Like rhinovirus (see Chapter 359), RSV is transmitted principally by direct contact with large-particle fomites from respiratory secretions, in contrast to the primary mode of spread of influenzavirus, aerosolization.

Approximately 0.5% of infected infants require hospitalization, but underlying prematurity, congenital cardiac abnormalities, bronchopulmonary dysplasia, and immunosuppression significantly increase the risk of serious disease. Hospitalization is most frequent between the ages of 1 and 6 months, with a median age of 2 months. Maternally derived antibody appears to protect in the first month of life, when serious lower respiratory symptoms are infrequent, but this benefit is rather brief. Reinfection occurs frequently throughout life, although illness is less severe and hospitalization infrequent except for those with underlying cardiac or pulmonary conditions.

Although often not considered in adults, RSV infection is frequent and, in certain populations, may be severe. In a British study, RSV accounted for 17% of medically attended respiratory illnesses in those older than 45. RSV has been identified as a relatively common cause of community-acquired pneumonia in adults, ranking third behind pneumococcus and influenza in one large study. Elderly persons appear to be at highest risk, and nosocomial outbreaks in nursing homes are common. In addition, RSV infection has been associated with about 10% of hospitalizations for cardiopulmonary deterioration in the winter among community-dwelling elderly persons. RSV infection in severely immunocompromised adults, such as bone marrow transplant recipients and those with acute leukemia undergoing cytotoxic chemotherapy, is associated with 60% mortality rates when pneumonia develops.

Both RSV groups usually cocirculate during outbreaks, although group A strains usually dominate. Within groups, the dominant genotypes shift annually and may reflect immune pressure in the susceptible population. Partial immunity to RSV develops over time, as indicated by the resistance to both infection and illness. Experimental studies suggest that immunopathologic mechanisms, principally mediated by T helper cells and their cytokines, contribute to disease manifestations.

Clinical Manifestations

After an incubation period of 2 to 8 days, previously uninfected infants experience upper respiratory symptoms. Conjunctival injection, mucopurulent nasal discharge, cough, and low-grade fever (38° C) are typical and indistinguishable from those in other respiratory infections. Otitis media occurs commonly, generally in association with bacteria. After several days, lower respiratory tract symptoms develop in 25 to 50% of infants. Cough, wheezing, increased respiratory rate, accessory muscle use, intercostal retractions, and cyanosis are seen as the disease progresses. Expiratory wheezes, rhonchi, and fine rales are the most common findings on lung examination. Sudden apnea may develop in the youngest infants. Mortality for otherwise healthy children is about 1% in hospitalized infants but can reach 37% in infants with cardiac disorders. Hyperinflation and diffuse interstitial pneumonitis are the most frequent radiographic findings. Infiltrates are usually diffuse, but consolidation is seen in up to one fourth.

Virus shedding lasts 7 to 10 days, although immunocompromised infants may excrete virus for a month or longer. Interestingly, clinical symptoms may not correlate with prolonged shedding. Coinfection with other respiratory viruses is not uncommon but is not clinically discernible. Should bacterial superinfection develop, with *Streptococcus pneumoniae* and *Haemophilus influenzae* the most frequent organisms isolated, treatment with antibiotics is indicated. Lower respiratory tract infection has been linked to childhood asthma, although the precise contributions of RSV infection and allergic predisposition are unknown.

Illness in normal adults typically lasts for 9 days, manifested by nasal discharge, pharyngitis, and low-grade fever. Virus is shed at low titer for approximately 3 days. Elderly persons with RSV infection may experience cough, dyspnea, fever, wheezing, and, in some cases, respiratory failure. Adults most at risk of severe infection are frail elderly persons, those with underlying chronic obstructive pulmonary disease or congestive heart failure, and those with severe immunocompromise. Attack rates are variable in nosocomial outbreaks in nursing homes, averaging 10 to 15%. Rales and wheezes are evident in one third of patients, and radiographically confirmed pneumonia is noted in approximately 10%. Annual attack rates are 5 to 10% among community-dwelling elderly people, and infection can lead to pneumonia, exacerbation of underlying congestive heart failure, or chronic bronchitis.

RSV infection has been documented in up to 10% of bone marrow transplant recipients and those with acute leukemia during the winter months. The illness begins with upper respiratory symptoms but frequently spreads to the lower respiratory tract. If RSV infection occurs before marrow engraftment, pneumonia develops in half with an attendant mortality of 90%. Notably, this figure is somewhat higher than the mortality with influenzavirus pneumonia in this population. Chest radiographs demonstrate diffuse interstitial and alveolar infiltrates. A useful clinical clue to the presence of RSV is the almost universal presence of radiographically proven sinusitis. The presence of upper respiratory tract symptoms distinguishes this illness from cytomegalovirus pneumonia.

Diagnosis

In the pediatric setting, a presumptive diagnosis is suggested by typical symptoms occurring during the epidemic season. In adults, the diagnosis is often never considered. Because the clinical picture of RSV is indistinguishable from that of illness caused by other infectious agents of respiratory disease, laboratory confirmation of RSV infection is required, especially if antiviral therapy is contemplated. In infants the sensitivity of viral culture is about 75%. Rapid diagnostic tests rely on detecting viral antigen or RNA in respiratory secretions. Immunofluorescence (IF) has a sensitivity of about 80%, whereas commercial enzyme immunoassay (EIA) is less sensitive and less specific than IF. Reverse transcription–polymerase chain reaction (RT-PCR) is considerably more sensitive than culture. In normal adults, diagnostic tests are significantly less sensitive: approximately 50% for virus culture and 10% or less for IF and EIA antigen detection. RT-PCR is very sensitive for detection of RSV in adults, detecting infection in a high proportion of culture-negative cases. In immunocompromised adults, detection of RSV antigen in throat swabs by EIA is only 15% sensitive, but it is 90% sensitive when bronchoalveolar lavage specimens are used.

Rx Treatment

Therapy for hospitalized infants includes hydration, oxygen, bronchodilators, and specific antiviral medication. Severely ill infants are commonly dehydrated and require intravenous fluid. Supplemental oxygen should be given to all infants with hypoxia. The effectiveness of nebulized bronchodilators, such as salbutamol, is variable, but a subset of infants respond. Glucocorticosteroids have not been shown to have benefit. Specific antiviral therapy is currently limited to inhaled ribavirin (1-β-D-ribafuranosyl-1,2,4-triazole-3-carboxamide), a nucleoside analogue with activity against several RNA viruses. Ribavirin is administered by aerosol, typically for 4 hours three times a day for 3 to 5 days, although longer therapy has been used. High-dose, short-duration (2 hours three times daily) treatment is considered equivalent. Some placebo-controlled clinical trials demonstrated more rapid resolution of respiratory symptoms and hypoxia. The majority of infants do not require therapy, but ribavirin treatment may be indicated for infants at high risk of serious disease and those who are severely ill. There are no placebo-controlled studies of the effect of ribavirin in adults with severe RSV disease, although anecdotal data suggest benefit in immunocompromised adults with RSV pneumonia, especially if therapy is begun before respiratory failure develops. Finally, intramuscular humanized RSV monoclonal antibody has demonstrated benefit when administered prophylactically to high-risk infants with underlying cardiopulmonary disease or prematurity. Studies using monoclonal antibody, in combination with inhaled ribavirin, suggest benefit in treatment of RSV pneumonia in immunosuppressed adults.

Prevention

Adherence to standard infection-control principles (e.g., gloves, gowns, and frequent handwashing) can substantially reduce nosocomial spread. A vaccine for prevention of RSV is not available, although both inactivated purified subunit and live attenuated vaccines are in clinical trials.

SUGGESTED READINGS

Committee on Infectious Diseases and Committee on Fetus and Newborn. Prevention of respiratory syncytial virus infections: Indications for the use of palivizumab and update on the use of RSV-IVIG. Pediatrics 1998;102:1211–1216. *Recommendations for the use of immunoglobulin prophylaxis for high-risk infants.*

Dowell SF, Anderson LJ, Gary HE, et al: Respiratory syncytial virus is an important cause of community-acquired lower respiratory infection among hospitalized adults. J Infect Dis 1996;174:456–462. *Clinical epidemiology of RSV as a cause of community-acquired pneumonia in adults.*

Englund JA, Piedra PA, Whimbey E: Prevention and treatment of respiratory syncytial virus and parainfluenza viruses in immunocompromised patients. Am J Med 1997;104:61–70. *Review of studies describing RSV infection and treatment in immunocompromised adults.*

Falsey AR, Cunningham CK, Barker WH, et al: Respiratory syncytial virus and influenza A infections in the hospitalized elderly. J Infect Dis 1995;172:389–394. *Prospective description of RSV and influenzavirus infection in elderly persons hospitalized with cardiopulmonary deterioration.*

Falsey AR, Walsh EE: Respiratory syncytial virus infection in adults. Clin Microbiol Rev 2000;13:371–384. *A detailed review of RSV infection in adults, including the epidemiology, clinical disease, immunology, therapy, and prospects for vaccines.*

Thompson WW, Shay DK, Weintranb E, et al: Mortality associated with respiratory syncytial virus in the United States. JAMA 2003;289:179–186. *A recent epidemiologic study of influenza and RSV.*

362 PARAINFLUENZA VIRAL DISEASE

Edward E. Walsh

Definition

Parainfluenza viruses are important causes of a wide spectrum of respiratory illness in infants and young children, producing syndromes ranging from the common cold and otitis media to severe croup,

bronchiolitis, and pneumonia. In older children and adults, illness is usually limited to the upper respiratory tract, although immunocompromised individuals may have fatal respiratory failure.

Etiology

The parainfluenza viruses are enveloped, single-stranded, nonsegmented RNA viruses and belong to the family Paramyxoviridae, which also includes measles, mumps, and respiratory syncytial viruses (RSVs). The genome encodes six structural proteins, of which the hemagglutinin neuraminidase (HN) and fusion (F) proteins are exposed on the bilayered lipid envelope that surrounds a helical nucleocapsid-RNA complex. The two surface proteins, which mediate attachment and penetration of the virus into susceptible mammalian cells, have retained antigenic stability for more than 30 years.

There are four serotypes of human parainfluenza viruses, types 1 through 4, with two subgroups (A and B) of type 4 virus. In addition, numerous animal strains of parainfluenza viruses exist, including shipping fever virus of cattle and Newcastle disease virus of chickens, important causes of lost income for the livestock industry. These viruses do not cause human illness.

Epidemiology

The parainfluenza viruses are ubiquitous and have a worldwide geographic distribution. Spread principally by large-particle fomites and close person-to-person contact, each of the four serotypes displays somewhat different epidemiologic features.

Over the years, parainfluenza virus activity has displayed both endemic and epidemic patterns (Table 362-1). Primary infection with parainfluenza viruses begins soon after birth, with each serotype favoring different age groups and distinct clinical syndromes. Significant overlap exists in this regard, thus precluding a specific diagnosis based on clinical and epidemiologic grounds. Among the parainfluenza viruses, type 3 infects infants first, with more than 50% showing serologic evidence of infection in the first year of life. Parainfluenza virus type 3 is second only to RSV as a cause of bronchiolitis and pneumonia in this youngest age group. Parainfluenza virus type 1, which exhibits characteristic epidemiology with biennial outbreaks in the fall of odd-numbered years, and type 2 infections occur later in childhood between ages 2 through 6. The peak incidence of infection with parainfluenza virus 1, manifest principally as croup, occurs between ages 1 and 2. The lower infection rate with parainfluenza type 1 and 2 viruses in very young infants suggests that maternally derived antibody is protective, in contrast to parainfluenza virus type 3 infection, in which maternal antibody has only limited benefit. After primary infection, a relatively brief period of immunity against homotypic reinfection develops; however, the fact that reinfections are common later in childhood highlights the lack of durable immunity.

Clinical Manifestations

Illness associated with primary parainfluenza virus infection varies by age and the virus serotype, although substantial overlap occurs. Underlying medical conditions, such as cardiopulmonary or immune disorders, also influence the severity of disease. In general, parainfluenza virus types 1 and 2 are associated with croup, whereas parainfluenza virus type 3 causes bronchiolitis and pneumonia. Other causes of croup include influenza A and RSV.

Infection typically starts with upper respiratory signs and symptoms, notably coryza, rhinorrhea, pharyngitis without cervical adenopathy, and low-grade fever. In 15%, signs of lower respiratory tract disease develop. If croup evolves, the child manifests a raspy, barking cough with notable inspiratory stridor, dyspnea, and respiratory distress. The latter symptoms, which may be spasmodic, are due to subglottic inflammation and edema. Typically, in mild to moderate illness symptoms last 3 to 5 days but may be quite unpredictable and result in sudden respiratory failure. In hospitalized infants, hypoxia is universal and hypercarbia is present in half. In severe stridor, differentiation from epiglottitis related to *Haemophilus influenzae* type b (see Chapter 314) may be suggested by lateral neck radiography, which can show subglottic edema and narrowing in contrast to epiglottic swelling. Although also a cause of croup, parainfluenza virus type 3 more commonly

Continued

Table 362–1 • PARAINFLUENZA PATTERNS

TYPE	MANIFESTATION	SEASON	COMMENTS
1	Epidemic croup	Fall of odd-numbered years	Since 1970
2	Epidemic croup	Fall or early winter	Less predictable than type 1; less widespread
3	Epidemic bronchitis and pneumonia	Late winter, early spring	Recently epidemic; often following influenza season; low levels of virus year-round
4	Unknown	?	Mild illness; frequently unrecognized

causes disease indistinguishable from that caused by RSV: tracheobronchitis, bronchiolitis, and pneumonia. Cough, rales, and wheezing associated with hypoxia and air trapping on radiography are common.

Reinfection with the parainfluenza viruses is less severe and typically causes cold symptoms in normal children and adults. However, as with RSV, some adults may develop severe disease. Nursing home outbreaks with a high incidence of pneumonia have been reported, and parainfluenza viruses have been implicated in severe pneumonia in immunocompromised children and adults. In a report of more than 1000 bone marrow transplant recipients, 61 parainfluenza virus infections were documented; of these patients 44% developed pneumonia and 27% died, with most having had preceding upper respiratory symptoms. The latter finding is clinically useful in distinguishing parainfluenza virus pneumonia from cytomegalovirus pneumonia in this group. Many of the parainfluenza infections in immunosuppressed persons are acquired nosocomially. As with RSV infection, the most severe illnesses and 90% of the deaths related to parainfluenza virus pneumonia occur in the first 100 days after transplantation when lymphopenia is most pronounced. Fever, cough, shortness of breath, and sputum production are the most common symptoms, and bilateral pulmonary infiltrates are the most common radiographic finding.

Diagnosis

Although the clinician may suspect parainfluenza virus on clinical and epidemiologic grounds, specific diagnosis requires isolating the virus or detecting viral antigen in respiratory secretions. Monkey kidney or human embryonic kidney cell cultures are optimal for virus recovery, generally in 5 to 10 days, with the exception of type 4 virus, which requires up to 3 weeks in culture. Indirect immunofluorescence tests are also available for rapid antigen detection and, although specific, are less sensitive than culture. Diagnosis of parainfluenza infection in adults may be more difficult than in children, but virus can usually be recovered from the nasal or pharyngeal secretions of bone marrow transplant recipients with pneumonia and also generally from bronchoalveolar specimens in this group.

Rx Treatment and Prevention

Specific antiviral treatment for parainfluenza virus is currently unavailable. Aerosolized ribavirin, approved for use in RSV infection, has in vitro activity against the parainfluenza viruses. Uncontrolled studies of ribavirin therapy of immunocompromised children and adults with severe parainfluenza virus pneumonia suggest possible benefit when administered at a dose of 20 mg/mL for 12 to 20 hours per day for 7 to 14 days.

Treatment of croup in children, under usual circumstances, includes mist and supplemental oxygen. Aerosolized bronchodilators (racemic epinephrine) have definite but only transient benefit, whereas corticosteroid use is controversial. Antibiotics are indicated only when bacterial superinfection is documented, an uncommon occurrence. Immunization to prevent parainfluenza virus infection with live attenuated vaccines is under study.

SUGGESTED READINGS

Hall CB: Respiratory syncytial virus and parainfluenza virus. N Engl J Med 2001;344:1917–1928. *This review article describes the epidemiology and clinical diseases of parainfluenza viruses.*

Henrickson KJ: Parainfluenza viruses. Clinical Microbiology Reviews 2003;16:242–264. *A practical review.*

Lewis VA, Champlin R, Englund J, et al: Respiratory disease due to parainfluenza virus in adult bone marrow transplant recipients. Clin Infect Dis 1996;23:1033–1037. *Clinical description of parainfluenza virus infections in bone marrow transplant patients.*

Marx A, Gary HE, Marston BJ, et al: Parainfluenza virus infection among adults hospitalized for lower respiratory tract infection. Clin Infect Dis 1999;29:134–140. *This article describes the epidemiology and clinical characteristics of serious parainfluenza virus in nonimmunocompromised adults.*

Marx A, Torok TJ, Holman RC, et al: Pediatric hospitalizations for croup (laryngotracheobronchitis): Biennial increases associated with human parainfluenza virus 1 epidemics. J Infect Dis 1997;176:1423–1427. *Describes the epidemiology of and clinical illness associated with parainfluenza virus infections in the United States from 1979 to 1993.*

Reed G, Jewett PH, Thompson J, et al: Epidemiology and clinical impact of parainfluenza virus infections in otherwise healthy infants and young children < 5 years old. J Infect Dis 1997;175:807–813. *This report describes the epidemiology and clinical characteristics of parainfluenza virus infection among outpatient infants and children during a 20-year period at a single center.*

363 INFLUENZA

Frederick G. Hayden

Influenza is an acute febrile respiratory illness that occurs in annual outbreaks of varying severity. The causative virus infects the respiratory tract, is highly contagious, and typically produces prominent systemic symptoms early in the illness. Influenza virus infection can produce various clinical syndromes in adults, including common colds, pharyngitis, tracheobronchitis, and pneumonia. Conversely, infections with other respiratory viruses, such as respiratory syncytial virus or adenovirus, may produce influenza-like illness. Influenza A viruses can cause worldwide epidemics (pandemics) and did so four times in the 20th century (Table 363–1). The pandemic of 1918 to 1919 caused at least 500,000 deaths in the United States and over 40 million worldwide. Influenza epidemics are associated with enormous morbidity, economic loss, and often substantial mortality. Recent epidemics have caused on average over 36,000 respiratory and circulatory deaths and about 114,000 hospitalizations in the United States alone.

Etiology

Influenza viruses belong to the family Orthomyxoviridae and are divided into three types (A, B, and C) distinguished by the antigenicity of their internal and external proteins (Table 363–2). The virion (Fig. 363–1) is a medium-sized enveloped pleomorphic particle covered with two types of surface glycoprotein spikes, hemagglutinin (H or HA) and neuraminidase (N or NA). The envelope is composed of a lipid bilayer overlying the matrix (M1) protein that surrounds the segmented viral genome. The genome comprises eight segments of single-stranded RNA. Influenza C viruses have seven segments and only a single surface glycoprotein. Whereas influenza B and C viruses are human pathogens, influenza A viruses infect diverse animal species, including birds, horses, swine, and marine mammals. Influenza A viruses are further classified into subtypes on the basis of their HA and NA glycoproteins. Each strain within a subtype is identified by site, sample number, and year of isolation. Three hemagglutinins (H1, H2, and H3) and two neuraminidases (N1 and N2) have been recognized in epidemic human influenza A viruses. In addition zoonotic infections occur rarely from swine, poultry, or other animals. An avian H5N1 subtype virus caused a cluster of severe illnesses in humans in Hong Kong in 1997 and again in 2003 in southern China.

Table 363–1 • ANTIGENIC SUBTYPES OF INFLUENZA A VIRUS ASSOCIATED WITH PANDEMIC INFLUENZA

YEAR	INTERVAL (YEARS)	DESIGNATION	EXTENT OF ANTIGENIC CHANGE IN INDICATED SURFACE PROTEIN*	SEVERITY OF PANDEMIC (MORTALITY)
1889	?	H3N?	H+++N?	Severe
1918	18	H1N1[†]	H+++N+++	Very severe
1957	39	H2N2	H+++N+++	Severe
1968	11	H3N2	H+++N−	Moderate[‡]
1977	9	H1N1	H+++N+++	Negligible[§]

*Compared with antecedent or cocirculating virus: + = minor change; ++ = moderate change; +++ = major change; − = no change.
[†]Formerly designated as H0N1 (swine virus prototype) or Hsw1N1.
[‡]Population had some immunity to the N2 neuraminidase.
[§]Most of population immune because of prior infection with earlier circulating antigenically identical virus. Primarily affected those born after 1957.

Table 363–2 • INFLUENZA VIRUS PROTEINS

DESIGNATION	LOCATION (APPROXIMATE NO. PER VIRION)	FUNCTION	OTHER
Hemagglutinin (HA)	Surface (500)	Cell attachment and penetration; fusion activity	Subtype- and strain-specific antigens
Neuraminidase (NA)	Surface (100)	Virus release; enzymatic activity	Subtype- and strain-specific antigens; site of action of zanamivir, oseltamivir carboxylate
Membrane or M1 matrix	Internal (3000)	Major structural envelope protein; virus assembly	Type-specific antigen
M2	Surface (20–60)	Virus uncoating and assembly; ion channel	Site of action of amantadine/ rimantadine
Nucleoprotein (NP)	Internal (1000)	Associated with RNA and polymerase proteins	Type-specific antigen
Polymerases (PB1, PB2, PA)	Internal (30–60)	RNA replication and transcription	Probable site of action of ribavirin
NS1	Nonstructural (infected cells)	Regulation of virus replication	Interferon antagonist
NEP	Internal (130–200)	Nuclear export factor	Formerly NS2

Adapted from Lamb RA, King RM: Orthomyxoviridae. *In* Fields BN, Knipe DM, Howley PM (eds): Fields Virology, 3rd ed. Philadelphia, Lippincott–Raven, 1996, p. 1355.

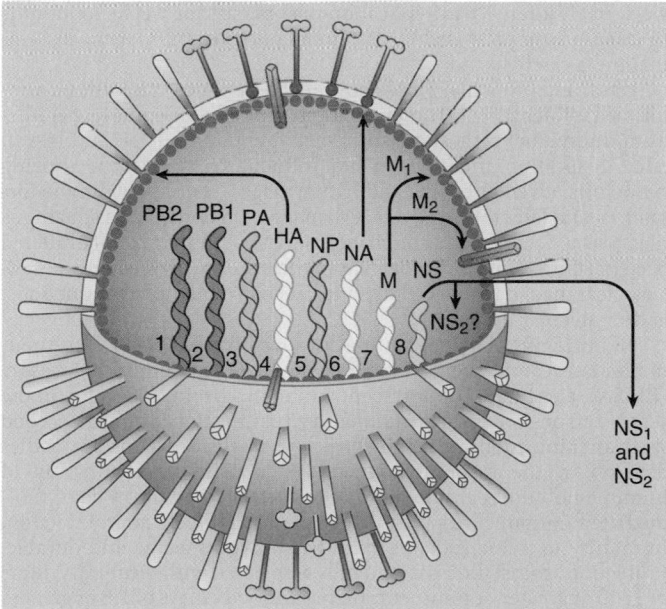

FIGURE 363–1 • Diagram of influenza virus structure. Eight segments of viral RNA are contained within the envelope and matrix (M1) shell. Each codes for one or two proteins that form the virus or regulate its intracellular replication. The presumed functions of each are listed in Table 363–2. (Courtesy of Dr. Robert G. Webster.)

Epidemiology

ANTIGENIC VARIATION. Influenza viruses are unique among the respiratory viruses with regard to their extent of antigenic variation, epidemic behavior, and association with excess mortality during community outbreaks. The changing antigenicity of the surface glycoproteins accounts in part for the continuing epidemics of influenza in humans. Antibody to the HA neutralizes viral infectivity and thus is the major determinant of immunity. Anti-NA antibody limits viral replication and therefore the severity of infection. Variation involves either relatively minor (antigenic drift) or major (antigenic shift) changes in antigenicity. Significant antigenic variation is much less frequent with influenza B than with influenza A and may not occur with influenza C.

Antigenic drift refers to small changes that occur frequently (every year or every few years) within an influenza A or B virus. For example, the original H3N2 variant, A/Aichi/68, has undergone successive drifts resulting in epidemic strains that include the recent circulation of A/Fujian/411/2002-like viruses. Antigenic drift results from an accumulation of point mutations in the RNA segment coding for the HA that cause amino acid substitutions in at least one of five antigenic sites on the HA. Immunologic selection favors the new variant over the old for transmission because of the less frequent presence in the population of antibody to the new virus.

Antigenic shift results from the appearance of an influenza A virus with HA or with HA and NA glycoproteins new to humans or possible reappearance of virus after decades of absence. Because of the lack of immunity to the new strain within the human population, a virulent new strain can cause pandemic disease (see Table 363–1). Infection by one subtype does not provide cross-protection against another. The origin of new pandemic strains and the basis for their apparent recirculation remain incompletely defined. Reassortment of gene segments may occur when two influenza viruses simultaneously infect a single cell. Because swine can support replication of both human and avian viruses, they have been postulated to serve as a mixing vessel for generation of new strains or the host in which avian viruses can adapt to mammals. At least 15 HA and 9 NA subtypes exist in animal influenza A viruses, particularly in aquatic birds, and these serve as the reservoir of new genes for human pandemic strains. Although avian influenza viruses generally do not cause infections directly in humans, bird-to-human transmission of avian H5N1, H9N2, and H7N7, subtype viruses has been documented in recent years. In addition, the HA and NA genes of the 1918 virus were projected to enter human or swine viruses from an avian source shortly before the pandemic.

EPIDEMIC OR INTERPANDEMIC INFLUENZA. An *epidemic* is an outbreak of influenza confined to one geographic location. In a given community, epidemics of influenza A virus infection often have a characteristic pattern. They usually begin rather abruptly, reach a sharp peak in 2 or 3 weeks, and last 6 to 10 weeks. Increased numbers of schoolchildren with febrile respiratory illness are often the first indication of influenza in a community. This indication is soon followed by illnesses among adults and about a week later by increased hospital admissions of patients with influenza-related complications. Hospitalization rates in high-risk persons increase two- to fivefold during major epidemics (Table 363–3). School and employment absenteeism increases, as does mortality from pneumonia and influenza, especially in older persons (see Table 363–3). The latter finding is a highly specific indicator of influenza activity.

Epidemics occur almost exclusively during the winter months in temperate areas, but influenza activity may continue year-round in the tropics. Outbreaks may occur in tour groups (land or ship) and in facilities during summer months, particularly after the appearance of a drift variant. Regional differences in the time and magnitude of occurrence of influenza outbreaks are common. During epidemics, the overall attack rates typically average 5 to 20% in adults. Attack rates of 40 to 50% are not uncommon in closed populations, including those in hospitals and nursing homes, and in certain highly susceptible age groups. Two different strains within a single subtype, two different influenza A subtypes (H1N1 and H3N2), or both influenza A and B viruses may cocirculate. In addition, simultaneous outbreaks of influenza A and respiratory syncytial viruses have been found. Strains circulating at the end of one season's epidemic are sometimes responsible for the next season's outbreak (the so-called herald wave phenomenon). Furthermore, other than the association of influenza outbreaks with colder seasons, the factors that allow an epidemic to develop or those responsible for the tapering off of an epidemic when only some susceptible persons have been infected are unknown.

Pneumonia and influenza (P + I)–related deaths fluctuate annually, with peaks in the winter months. When such P + I deaths exceed the predicted number, it is due to influenza A or occasionally to influenza B virus or respiratory syncytial virus activity. Although mortality is greatest during pandemics, substantial total mortality occurs with epidemics. Over 85% of P + I deaths occur among persons aged 65 and older (see Table 363–3). Other cardiopulmonary and chronic diseases also result in increased mortality after influenza epidemics, so that overall influenza-associated mortality is about two- to fourfold higher than P + I deaths.

PANDEMIC INFLUENZA. *Pandemics* of influenza A result from the emergence of a new virus capable of sustained person-to-person transmission and to which the population contains no or limited immunity. The virus spreads worldwide and infects persons of all ages (see Table 363–1). The pandemics of 1957, 1968, and 1977 all began in mainland China, and Southeast Asia has been postulated to be the epicenter for such strains. The interval between pandemics is variable and unpredictable. The most severe pandemics have resulted when there were major antigenic alterations in both major surface antigens. Furthermore, it appears that virulence is a multigenic characteristic that also varies among strains. The intrinsic virulence of recent H1N1 viruses appears to be milder than that of H3N2 viruses. Although the 1918 pandemic strain has been partially sequenced through molecular techniques, the reasons for its unique virulence remain uncertain. After one or more waves of pandemic influenza, the level of immunity in the population increases. Repeated epidemics caused by strains showing antigenic drift within the subtype occur in subsequent years. After 10 to 40 years of circulation of variants within this given subtype, the population's immunity to all variants within the subtype is very high and the conditions for the emergence of a new virus are favorable.

Pathogenesis and Pathology

Influenza virus infection is transmitted from person to person by virus-containing respiratory secretions. Small-particle aerosols appear most important, but transmission by other routes, including fomites, may be possible. Virtually all cells lining the respiratory tract can support viral replication. Once the virus initiates infection of the respiratory tract epithelium, successive cycles of viral replication infect large numbers of cells and result in destruction of ciliated epithelium. The incubation period averages 2 days and varies from 1 to 4 days. The quantity of virus in respiratory tract specimens correlates with the severity of illness, which suggests that a major mechanism in producing illness is virally mediated cell death. Elevations of proinflammatory cytokines such as interferon-α, interleukin-6, and tumor necrosis factor α occur in blood and respiratory secretions and probably contribute to systemic symptoms and fever. The pathogenicity of the H5N1 Hong Kong virus for humans is linked to a nonstructural gene variant (NS1) that both mediates resistance to interferons and tumor necrosis factor α and fosters pro-inflammatory cytokine elaboration. The duration of viral shedding depends on age, and shedding generally lasts for 3 to 5 days in adults and often into the second week in children. Virus replication may persist for weeks to months in immunocompromised hosts. Viremia or extrapulmonary dissemination is rarely found.

Nasal and bronchial biopsy specimens from persons with uncomplicated influenza reveal desquamation of the ciliated columnar epithelium. Individual cells show shrinkage, pyknotic nuclei, and loss of cilia. In addition, the lungs in fatal influenza may show necrotizing bronchitis, alveolar edema and hemorrhage, hyaline membrane formation, and later diffuse alveolar damage with fibrosis and squamous metaplasia. Secondary bacterial infections develop as a result of altered bacterial flora, damage to bronchial epithelium with depressed mucociliary clearance, decreased PMN and alveolar macrophage functions, and/or alveolar fluid.

Neutralizing, hemagglutination-inhibiting (HAI), antineuraminidase, complement-fixing, enzyme-linked immunosorbent assay (ELISA), and immunofluorescent antibodies begin to develop in the sera of persons with primary influenza virus infection during the second week after infection and reach a peak by 4 weeks. Secretory antibodies develop in the respiratory tract and consist predominantly of immunoglobulin A antibodies that reach peak titers in 14 days. Cell-mediated immune responses develop by 1 week after infection. Immunity to influenza appears to be subtype specific and durable. Protection against illness is generally associated with serum HAI titers of 1 : 40 or greater, serum-neutralizing antibody titers of 1:8 or greater, or nasal neutralizing antibody titers of 1 : 4 or greater.

Clinical Manifestations

INFLUENZA SYNDROME. The abrupt onset of feverishness, chilliness, frank rigors, headache, myalgia, and malaise is characteristic of influenza. Systemic symptoms predominate initially, and prostration occurs in more severe cases. Usually myalgia or headaches are the most troublesome early symptoms, and their severity is related to the level of fever. Arthralgia is common, and less often

---

Table 363–3 · AGE-SPECIFIC RATES FOR ILLNESS AND MORTALITY DURING URBAN INFLUENZA EPIDEMICS

AGE (YEARS)	PHYSICIAN VISITS PER 100	ARD HOSPITALIZATIONS PER 10,000	P + I MORTALITY PER 100,000
<5	28	43	3
5–14	14	5	1
15–44	10	8	1
45–54	9	13	10
55–64	10	21	10
≥65	—	73	104

ARD = acute respiratory disease; P + I = pneumonia and influenza; – = not stated.
Adapted from Glezen WP: Anatomy of an urban influenza epidemic. *In* Hannoun C, Kendal AP, Klenk HD, et al (eds): Options for the Control of Influenza II. Amsterdam, Elsevier Science, 1993, p 12.

Infectious Diseases

ocular symptoms, photophobia, tearing, burning, and pain on moving the eyes, are helpful diagnostically. Respiratory symptoms, particularly dry cough and nasal discharge, are usually also present at the onset but are overshadowed by the systemic symptoms. Nasal obstruction, hoarseness, and sore throat are also common. As systemic illness diminishes, respiratory complaints and findings become more apparent. Cough is the most frequent and troublesome and may be accompanied by substernal discomfort or burning. Cough, lassitude, and malaise may persist for several weeks before full recovery.

Fever is the most important initial physical finding. The temperature usually rises rapidly to a peak of 38 to 40° C within 12 hours of onset, concurrently with systemic symptoms. Fever is usually continuous but may be intermittent, especially if antipyretics are administered. As fever subsides, the systemic symptoms diminish. Typically, the duration of fever is 3 days, but it may last from 1 to 5 or more days. Uncommonly, a biphasic fever course occurs. Early in the course of illness, the patient appears toxic, the face is flushed, and the skin is hot and moist. The eyes are watery and reddened. Clear nasal discharge is common. The mucosa of the nose and throat is hyperemic, but exudate is not observed. Small, tender cervical lymph nodes are often present. Transient scattered rhonchi or localized areas of rales are found in less than 20% of cases.

The pattern of illness just described occurs with any strain of influenza A or B virus. Illness is more frequent and severe in smokers, and attack rates are higher in children than in adults. Maximum temperatures are higher in children, cervical adenopathy may be more frequent, and gastrointestinal symptoms of nausea, emesis, or abdominal pain more common. Women experience increased complications of influenza during the second and third trimesters of pregnancy. Symptoms may be protracted for some persons infected with human immunodeficiency virus (HIV), and they are also at higher risk of complications. Older adults (older than 60 years) experience muscle aches, sore throat, and headache less often but have higher rates of pulmonary complications. Influenza C virus generally causes sporadic upper respiratory tract illness or bronchitis.

RESPIRATORY COMPLICATIONS. Three kinds of pneumonic syndromes have been described: primary influenza viral pneumonia, secondary bacterial pneumonia, and mixed viral and bacterial pneumonia. Influenza A and B virus infections may be associated with other respiratory tract complications, including exacerbations of chronic bronchitis, asthma, or cystic fibrosis; croup and bronchiolitis in young children; and otitis media, sinusitis, and rarely parotitis or bacterial tracheitis. Apparently uncomplicated influenza is often accompanied by abnormal tracheobronchial clearance, airway hyperactivity, and small airways dysfunction lasting weeks. A syndrome mimicking pulmonary embolism with transiently altered perfusion scans has also been described.

Primary influenza viral pneumonia occurs predominantly among persons with underlying pulmonary and cardiac disorders, pregnancy, or immunodeficiency states, although up to 40% of reported cases have no recognized underlying disease. Following a typical onset of influenza, there is rapid progression of fever, cough, dyspnea, and cyanosis. Physical examination and chest radiographs reveal bilateral findings consistent with the adult respiratory distress syndrome. Blood gas studies show marked hypoxia. Gram staining of the sputum may show abundant PMNs but scant bacterial flora. Sputum may be bloody. Viral cultures of sputum or tracheal aspirates usually yield high titers of influenza virus. Antibiotics are not helpful, and the value of antiviral therapy is uncertain.

Bacterial superinfection is often clinically distinguishable from primary viral pneumonia. The patients are most often elderly or have chronic pulmonary, cardiac, metabolic, or other diseases. After a typical influenza illness, a period of improvement lasting from 1 to 4 days may occur. Recrudescence of fever is associated with symptoms and signs of bacterial pneumonia, such as cough, sputum production, pleuritic chest pain, and a localized area of consolidation apparent on physical and chest radiographic examination. Gram staining and culture of sputum most often reveal *Streptococcus pneumoniae*, *Staphylococcus aureus*, or *Haemophilus influenzae* (see relevant chapters for specific bacterial diseases). Such patients usually respond to specific antibiotic therapy, although staphylococcal infections may be particularly virulent and cause destructive pulmonary lesions. Invasive aspergillosis occurs rarely after influenza.

In addition, during an outbreak of influenza, many less distinct cases are observed that do not clearly fit into either of these categories. These patients may have viral tracheobronchitis, milder forms of localized viral pneumonia, or mixed viral and bacterial infection. Many respond to antibiotics. Immunocompromised hosts, including transplant recipients and acute leukemia patients undergoing chemotherapy, have high rates of pneumonia and mortality after influenza.

NONPULMONIC COMPLICATIONS. Reye's syndrome is a well-recognized hepatic and central nervous system (CNS) complication of influenza A and B virus infections that arises typically in children but rarely in adults and is associated with salicylate use. Toxic shock syndrome caused by respiratory tract infection with toxin-bearing S. *aureus* has been reported. Outbreaks of meningococcal infections have been associated with both influenza A and B virus infections. Myositis with tender leg muscles and elevated serum creatine kinase levels may develop uncommonly, more often in children. Disseminated intravascular coagulation (DIC) develops rarely, as does renal failure related to DIC or myoglobinuria. Myocarditis or pericarditis has been described uncommonly. Aseptic meningitis, myelitis, encephalopathy associated with acute illness, and postinfluenzal encephalitis also occur.

Diagnosis

In an individual case, influenza often cannot be distinguished from infection with a number of other viruses (and occasionally streptococcal pharyngitis) that produce headache, muscle aches, fever, and/or cough. In summer, enteroviruses produce a similar clinical picture, and the acute manifestations of many other infections, including those of respiratory syncytial viruses, parainfluenza viruses, and adenoviruses, may mimic influenza. On the other hand, when public health authorities report an epidemic of influenza A and B virus infection in a given community and a patient is seen with typical illness, it is highly likely that these symptoms are caused by an influenza virus infection. Under such circumstances, the presence of fever and cough has a positive predictive value of about 80% for laboratory-proven influenza in adults.

Influenza virus is readily isolated from throat or nasal specimens, sputum, or tracheal secretion specimens in the first 2 or 3 days of illness. Usually, infectivity is detected within 48 to 72 hours in cell cultures. Immunofluorescence testing of respiratory cells or of inoculated cell cultures (shell vials) can reduce time to detection. Commercially available enzyme immunoassays or neuraminidase detection–based assay can document influenza virus infection rapidly but may have limited sensitivity (50 to 70%) in adults; some do not distinguish between influenza A and B. The limited specificity of some assays makes their predictive value low outside the influenza season. Detection of viral RNA by reverse transcription–polymerase chain reaction appears highly sensitive and specific. Serologic methods are less useful clinically because they require a convalescent serum obtained 14 to 21 days after the onset of infection.

 Treatment

Oral rimantadine or amantadine therapy shortens the duration of fever and of systemic and respiratory symptoms in uncomplicated influenza A by 1 to 2 days and speeds functional recovery. The possible effectiveness of these drugs in preventing or treating pulmonary complications of influenza is unknown. The usual dosage is 100 mg twice daily for 5 days. A daily dose of 100 mg should be used in older adults. Rimantadine involves a lower risk of the CNS side effects that occur with amantadine; both may cause gastrointestinal upset. Because amantadine is excreted unchanged in the urine, dose adjustments are needed for those with renal impairment. These agents are ineffective for influenza B infections. Treated persons sometimes transmit drug-resistant virus to close

Continued

contacts. Inhaled zanamivir (10 mg twice daily) and oral oseltamivir (75 mg twice daily), neuraminidase inhibitors active against influenza A and B viruses, are also effective in treating acute influenza and reduce the risk of lower respiratory complications, particularly bronchitis, and with oseltamivir the risk of hospitalization. Zanamivir may be infrequently associated with bronchospasm, sometimes severe, and oseltamivir with nausea or emesis.

Other symptomatic measures include antipyretics and cough suppressants. Many authorities recommend that aspirin not be used, especially for children younger than age 16, because of its association with Reye's syndrome.

Influenza viral pneumonia in its severe form requires intensive respiratory monitoring and support. Oral amantadine or rimantadine, intravenous ribavirin, aerosolized ribavirin, nebulized zanamivir, and oral oseltamivir have been used with uncertain benefit. Secondary bacterial pneumonia should be treated with appropriate antibiotics. When studies of the sputum do not clearly indicate an infecting bacterium, antibiotics that are effective against the likely pathogens, including *S. aureus*, should be used.

Prevention

The mainstay of prevention is using inactivated influenza virus vaccines. These vaccines provide 70 to 90% protection against influenzal illness when the vaccine matches the epidemic strain. Immunogenicity and hence protection rates are often lower in elderly persons, particularly in infirm nursing home residents, and immunosuppressed patients, including those with advanced HIV infection or receiving chemotherapy. In institutionalized elderly people, immunization is 50 to 60% effective in preventing hospitalization and pneumonia and reduces influenza-related mortality by 70 to 80%. In ambulatory elderly patients, immunization reduces hospitilizations for pneumonia or influenza by 20 to 40% and all-cause mortality by 30 to 50%. Immunization also appears cost-effective in working adults depending on the size of the epidemic. Immunization of school-aged children appears to reduce respiratory illness in household contacts and in one Japanese study excess deaths in the elderly. Immunization is essential for health care providers to reduce the risk of transmission to patients. The antigenic composition is reviewed annually so that the vaccine contains the most recently circulating strains, usually one or more subtypes of influenza A and an influenza B virus. Fever and systemic symptoms occur at rates comparable to those of placebo in adults but are more common in young children. In adults 25% or more may have mild local reactions at the site of injection. Persons with malignant disease should receive vaccine between chemotherapy courses.

The priority groups for vaccine include those at highest risk for influenza complications and their immediate contacts (Table 363–4), although vaccine can be safely administered to anyone trying to avoid influenza. Vaccine should be given each year in the fall, preferably October or November, before the influenza season. The vaccine is contraindicated in persons with chicken egg anaphylactic hypersensitivity. Inactivated vaccine does not cause asthma exacerbation but may rarely be associated with Guillain-Barré syndrome in older adults. Intranasal cold-adapted live-attenuated vaccines are highly protective in children, appear effective in adults younger than 65 years, but are not adequately immunogenic in elderly persons. They may be associated with coryza and sore throat and are investigational at present.

Rimantadine and amantadine are 70 to 90% effective in preventing influenza A illness and can be used to supplement vaccine programs. The neuraminidase inhibitors, inhaled zanamivir (investigational for this indication) and oral oseltamivir (75 mg once daily) are highly effective for chemoprophylaxis of both influenza A and B virus infections. Persons who are not vaccinated in the fall should be given prophylaxis when an outbreak occurs or throughout the influenza season for the highest risk group. If vaccine is available, persons may be vaccinated simultaneously and drug therapy stopped after 14 days. Alternatively, if vaccine is not available or is a poor match, administration may be continued for the duration of the outbreak. When given to patients and staff alike, these drugs may be helpful in managing nosocomial outbreaks. Postexposure prophylaxis in households is also effective. Hospitalized patients should be placed in respiratory isolation.

Table 363–4 • RECOMMENDED TARGET GROUPS FOR INFLUENZA IMMUNIZATION

GROUPS AT INCREASED RISK OF COMPLICATIONS
Persons aged 50 and older
Residents of nursing homes and other chronic care facilities
Patients with chronic pulmonary (including asthma) or cardiac disorder
Patients with chronic metabolic disease (including diabetes), renal dysfunction, hemoglobinopathies, or immunosuppression (including HIV infection)
Children and teens receiving long-term aspirin
Pregnant women who will be in second or third trimester during influenza season
Children aged 6–23 months (encouraged)

GROUPS IN CONTACT WITH HIGH-RISK PERSONS
Physicians, nurses, and other health care providers
Employees of nursing homes and chronic care and assisted-living facilities
Providers of home care to high-risk persons
Household members of high-risk persons (including children aged 0–23 months)

OTHER GROUPS
Providers of essential community services (e.g., police, fire)
Travelers (including to the tropics, large organized groups, or to the southern hemisphere in summer)
Students, dormitory residents
Anyone wishing to reduce risk of influenza

HIV = human immunodeficiency virus.
Adapted from Advisory Committee on Immunization Practices, Centers for Disease Control and Prevention. MMWR 2003;52(RR-8):1–35.

SUGGESTED READINGS

Centers for Disease Control and Prevention: Prevention and control of influenza: Recommendations of the Advisory Committee on Immunization Practices (ACIP). MMWR Morb Mortal Wkly Rep 2003;52(RR-8):1–34. *Recommendations for influenza immunization and antiviral use that are updated on an annual basis.*

Centers for Disease Control Influenza Website. (Available at: *http://www.cdc.gov/cnidod/diseases/flu/weekly.htm*) *Updated information on influenza surveillance, prevention, detection and control measures.*

Cheung CY, Poon LLM, Lau AS, et al: Induction of proinflammatory cytokines in human macrophages by influenza A (H5N1) viruses: A mechanism for the unusual severity of human disease? Lancet 2002;360:1831–1837. *Hypercytokinemia as explanation for unusual severity of human H5N1 disease.*

Kaiser L, Hayden FG: Hospitalizing influenza in adults. *In* Remington JS, Swartz MN (eds): Current Clinical Topics in Infectious Diseases, vol 19. Malden, MA, Blackwell Science, 1999, pp 112–134. *Summary of clinical presentation, diagnosis, and management of influenza in hospitalized adults.*

Nichol KL, Nordin J, Mullooly J, et al: Influenza vaccination and reduction in hospitalizations for cardiac disease and stroke among the elderly. N Engl J Med 2003;348:1322–1332. *Large cohort study showing that in ambulatory elderly patients, immunization reduces hospitalization for influenza and pneumonia (29–32%), cardiac disease (19%), stroke (16–23%), and all-cause mortality (48–50%).*

Nicholson KG, Webster RG, Hay AJ (eds): Textbook of Influenza. Malden, MA, Blackwell Science, 1998, p 578. *Multiauthored, authoritative text covering all aspects of influenza virus infections.*

Osterhaus AD, Cox N, Hampson A: Options for the Control of Influenza IV: Proceedings of the World Congress held in Crete, Greece, September 23–28, 2000, 1st ed. Atlanta, Elsevier Science, 2001. *Compilation of review articles and papers from an international conference covering developments in influenza, including epidemiology, pathogenesis, newer antivirals, and vaccines.*

---

364 ADENOVIRUS DISEASES

John J. Treanor

Virology

The adenoviruses are found in a variety of animal species, including humans, simians, horses, pigs, goats, and dogs. The virus is nonenveloped and has a double-stranded DNA genome. The human adenoviruses are grouped into six subgenera (A-F) on the basis of differences in genome content, pattern of hemagglutination, and ability to cause tumors in experimental animals. In addition, at least 49 distinct serotypes are defined on the basis of neutralization tests. Specific disease syndromes or hosts are often associated with specific adenovirus serotypes (Table 364–1).

Table 364–1 • ADENOVIRUS SEROTYPES AND ASSOCIATED SYNDROMES

HOST AND DISEASE CATEGORY	EPIDEMIOLOGIC FEATURES	ASSOCIATED ADENOVIRUS SEROTYPES
IMMUNOCOMPETENT HOSTS		
Pharyngoconjunctival fever	Epidemics in schools, families, and military personnel; associated with swimming pools	3, 7
Epidemic keratoconjunctivitis	Sporadic epidemics in schools, families, and industrial sites; may cause nosocomial outbreaks; more common in fall and winter	8, 19, 37
Endemic upper respiratory disease	Seen predominantly in children, families, and daycare settings	1, 2, 5
Acute respiratory disease of military recruits		3, 4, 7, 14, 21
Acute hemorrhagic cystitis	Male predominance	7, 11, 21, 35
Gastroenteritis	Predominant in children <2 yr	40, 41
IMMUNOCOMPROMISED HOSTS		
Transplantation		7, 11, 31, 34, 35
Acquired immunodeficiency syndrome		Multiple, 35, 42–47

Clinical Manifestations

DISEASE IN NORMAL HOSTS

The adenoviruses can infect and cause disease in a variety of human epithelial tissues, including those of the eye, respiratory tract, gastrointestinal tract, and urinary bladder. Most infections in immunologically competent individuals are subclinical. Virus may be shed for months after infection from either the gastrointestinal or respiratory tract. Adenoviruses appear to utilize multiple mechanisms to circumvent the host immune response, including inhibition of the antiviral effects of interferons, downregulation of the expression of human leukocyte antigen molecules on the surface of infected cells, and antagonism of the effects of tumor necrosis factor α.

Eye Disease

PHARYNGOCONJUNCTIVAL FEVER. The syndrome of pharyngoconjunctival fever (Chapter 360) is seen predominantly in children and is characterized by bilateral conjunctivitis accompanied by mild pharyngitis without exudate. Fever, myalgias, and malaise may also be present. The eyes are itchy but not painful, with a boggy, hyperemic conjunctiva and watery discharge. Occasionally, the syndrome may be complicated by punctate keratitis.

Pharyngoconjunctival fever is highly contagious (see Table 364–1) and can be spread by contact with the eyes and mouth for 8 to 10 days after the onset of symptoms. The incubation period is 5 to 8 days. The illness is self-limited, with a duration of a few days to as long as 3 weeks. There is no specific therapy.

EPIDEMIC KERATOCONJUNCTIVITIS. In contrast to pharyngoconjunctival fever, epidemic keratoconjunctivitis occurs as unilateral disease in the majority of cases and is generally not accompanied by sore throat, fever, or systemic symptoms. The patient may complain of a mild foreign body sensation with watery tearing but is not in significant discomfort. Physical findings include a swollen eyelid, conjunctival hyperemia with edema and chemosis, and tender preauricular adenopathy. Keratitis eventually develops in about 80% of patients and is usually noted on about the eighth day of illness with the onset of pain, photophobia, lacrimation, and blepharospasm. Visual acuity may be temporarily reduced during the height of illness. Subepithelial corneal infiltrates can be detected in about one third of patients and may take weeks or months to resolve.

Many outbreaks of epidemic keratoconjunctivitis (see Table 364–1) have been attributed to contamination of ophthalmologic equipment, such as tonometers. Sterilization of such equipment between patients, good handwashing, segregation of patients, and other infection control procedures are critical in terminating nosocomial outbreaks.

Respiratory Disease

UPPER RESPIRATORY TRACT ILLNESS. Acute pharyngitis is the most common respiratory syndrome attributed to the adenoviruses (Chapter 360). Adenoviruses can cause an exudative tonsillitis similar to that caused by group A streptococci. In children, common associated syndromes include otitis media, coryza, and undifferentiated fever. Overall, adenoviruses are associated with about 7% of acute febrile illnesses in children, with a peak age of incidence between 6 months and 2 years. High secondary attack rates are seen in families or in the daycare setting.

LOWER RESPIRATORY TRACT ILLNESS. Adenoviruses have been implicated as causing approximately 10% of childhood pneumonias. Clinical features are nondescript, and chest radiographs are similar to those in other forms of viral pneumonia with the exception that hilar adenopathy is more common in children with adenoviral pneumonia than with other forms of viral pneumonia. Mixed bacterial-viral pneumonia is often present and may be suggested by elevations in band forms in peripheral blood.

Military recruits generally present with the atypical pneumonia syndrome (see Table 364–1), and illness clinically resembles that caused by *Mycoplasma pneumoniae*. Although the illness is typically mild, more severe disseminated infections and deaths have been reported. Multiple radiographic patterns are noted; there may be large pleural effusions. Prodromal symptoms of upper respiratory tract infection are reported by most patients, and pharyngitis is often found on presentation. Bacterial superinfection, particularly with *Neisseria meningitidis*, may occur. The disease is classically seen in military recruits and appears to be associated with the special conditions of fatigue and crowding found in military barracks. Formerly well controlled by vaccination, adenovirus type 4 (Ad4) has reemerged as an important cause of acute respiratory illness in recruits with the discontinuation of adenovirus vaccine. Outbreaks have also been reported among young adults in psychiatric hospitals. However, this syndrome does not commonly occur in similarly crowded situations such as college dormitories.

Because adenoviruses rarely cause pneumonia in otherwise healthy adults (Fig. 364–1) but are frequently shed asymptomatically, isolation of adenovirus from stool or respiratory secretions in normal adults with pulmonary infiltrates should be interpreted with caution.

Urinary Disease: Hemorrhagic Cystitis

Acute hemorrhagic cystitis may be caused by adenoviruses (see Table 364–1). The patient complains of gross hematuria and dysuria. The presentation may be confused with that of glomerulonephritis, but laboratory tests of renal function remain normal and fever and hypertension do not occur. Acute hemorrhagic cystitis is generally self-limited.

Gastrointestinal Disease: Gastroenteritis

Although multiple adenovirus serotypes may be shed in the stool, only the so-called enteric adenoviruses (i.e., types 40 and 41) have been convincingly associated with acute gastroenteritis (Chapter 374). These adenovirus types belong to subgroup F and differ from other adenoviruses in being highly restricted in their ability to replicate in conventional cell culture.

Gastroenteritis caused by enteric adenovirus is a disease predominantly of children younger than age 2. Clinical features include watery diarrhea and vomiting similar to those seen with infection

Continued

Infectious Diseases

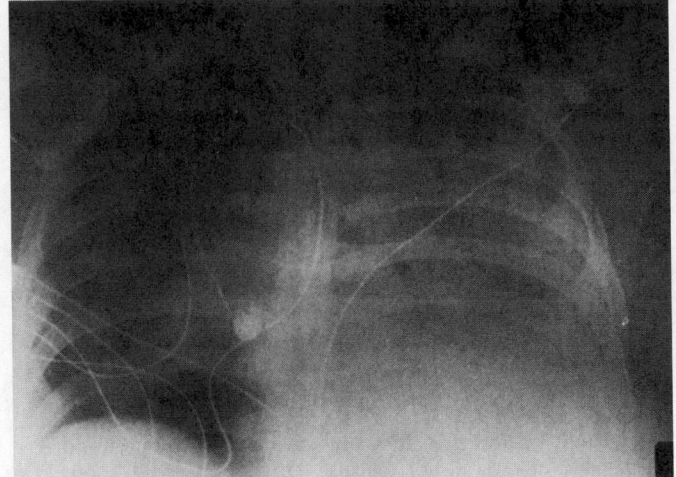

FIGURE 364–1 • Portable upright chest film of a previously healthy 36-year-old woman with adenovirus pneumonia showing consolidation of the left lower lobe and lingula as well as left-sided pleural effusion. (From Klinger JR, Sanchez MP, Curtin LA, et al: Multiple cases of life-threatening adenovirus pneumonia in a mental health care center. Am J Respir Crit Care Med 1998;157:645–649.)

with group A rotavirus. In contrast to gastroenteritis associated with the rotaviruses and astroviruses, adenoviral gastroenteritis shows no significant seasonal variability. The frequency of illness is about 5 to 10% of that caused by rotavirus in the same age group. Adenoviruses are rarely causes of acute gastroenteritis in adults.

Other Syndromes Associated with Adenoviruses in Immunocompetent Hosts

Adenoviruses are often isolated in cases of pertussis-like syndrome, but there is no evidence that adenoviruses by themselves are important causes of whooping cough. A toxic shock–like presentation of disseminated adenovirus infection in a normal host has been reported. Adenoviruses have occasionally been isolated from cerebrospinal fluid in immunocompetent individuals with meningitis or meningoencephalitis. These viruses have also been implicated in sudden infant death syndrome. Adenoviruses may be detected in mesenteric lymph nodes at the time of surgery for intussusception, and it is postulated that viral infection causes an acute mesenteric lymphadenitis that leads to the development of this condition.

DISEASE IN IMMUNOCOMPROMISED HOSTS

TRANSPLANTATION. Adenoviruses are causes of morbidity and mortality in immunocompromised patients, particularly after transplantation. In contrast to infection in normal hosts, infection in immunocompromised subjects tends to be disseminated, with virus isolated from multiple body sites, including lung, liver, and gastrointestinal tract, and urine. In addition, the spectrum of serotypes includes those found in immunocompetent individuals and a markedly increased frequency of higher numbered serotypes found rarely in immunologically normal subjects (see Table 364–1). The source of infection may be reactivation of latent virus; nosocomial infection has also been documented.

Adenoviruses may cause hemorrhagic cystitis in bone marrow transplant recipients, which may be confused with that related to cyclophosphamide. Differentiation between these two possibilities is generally made by virus culture and by the timing of cystitis in relationship to drug administration. Individuals with cystitis may develop pneumonia, hepatic necrosis, gastroenteritis, and encephalitis. The case-fatality rate of disseminated infection can be as high as 60%. Disseminated disease after liver transplantation can be seen and frequently leads to loss of the transplanted liver. However, this occurrence does not appear to preclude successful transplantation of a new liver if one is available. Adenovirus disease in renal transplant recipients is generally not as severe as

that seen with other transplants. Hemorrhagic cystitis is the most common problem, with pneumonia seen more rarely. In cardiac transplant recipients, adenovirus infection has been associated with rejection of the transplanted organ.

ACQUIRED IMMUNODEFICIENCY SYNDROME. Adenoviruses have also been isolated frequently from the stool and urine of individuals with the acquired immunodeficiency syndrome (AIDS), particularly those with relatively low CD4+ lymphocyte counts. The most remarkable aspect of this situation is the isolation of a wide variety of serotypes in these patients (see Table 364–1), including new, higher-numbered serotypes isolated for the first time in these subjects. In addition, antigenically intermediate types have been isolated that possibly reflect recombination events made possible by prolonged virus replication in these hosts.

Because adenoviruses are often isolated in these patients in conjunction with multiple other opportunistic pathogens, it is difficult to ascribe specific clinical syndromes to them. Described associations include pneumonia, meningoencephalitis, hepatitis, gastroenteritis, and colitis. Adenoviruses have been detected in the large bowel of such patients in association with chronic diarrhea, but generally these have not been the enteric adenoviruses most commonly associated with gastroenteritis in immunologically normal hosts.

Diagnosis

Virus can be isolated efficiently from conjunctival swabs, respiratory secretions, urine, or stool in primary cells of human epithelial origin, such as human embryonic kidney cells. However, diagnosis is complicated by the prolonged time required for isolation. Other means of directly detecting viral antigen or nucleic acid in clinical specimens are therefore widely used, including enzyme immunoassays, immunofluorescence tests, and polymerase chain reaction techniques. In addition, the time required to detect virus in cell culture can be shortened to as little as 2 days by applying centrifugation culture systems coupled with detection of early virus replication in culture using immunofluorescent or other means.

℞ Treatment

CONJUNCTIVITIS. Therapy is generally supportive. Corticosteroids should be avoided in mild cases of conjunctivitis because symptoms usually recur when these agents are discontinued. In more severe cases of keratitis, mild topical corticosteroids may be used with cycloplegics as needed for iritis. Topical antibiotics may be administered to prevent bacterial superinfection. Topical use of cidofovir has been reported to decrease the frequency of severe corneal opacities but is associated with significant local toxicity.

SYSTEMIC INFECTIONS. No antiviral therapy has been proved to be effective in any systemic adenoviral syndrome. Both intravenous ribavirin and cidofovir have been used to treat disseminated disease in immunosuppressed individuals, with some reports of success. In one report, cidofovir appeared to be more effective for treatment but was associated with severe nephrotoxicity.

Prevention

Live adenovirus vaccines administered orally in enteric-coated capsules were developed for serotypes 4 and 7. These vaccines provided effective serotype-specific protection against adenovirus respiratory disease in high-risk military recruits but are no longer in production. Adenovirus vaccines have not been used in civilian populations because of the plethora of additional serotypes causing severe disease in these populations.

Because relatively large portions of the adenovirus genome can be replaced without affecting viral viability, adenoviruses have received considerable attention in constructing recombinant vaccines for other infectious diseases and as a vector for the delivery of gene therapy.

SUGGESTED READINGS
Bordigoni P, Carret A-S, Venard V, et al: Treatment of adenovirus infections in patients undergoing allogeneic hematopoietic stem cell transplantation. Clin Infect Dis 2001;32:1290–1297. *In this retrospective analysis of patients with disseminated aden-*

ovirus infection, 3 of 13 subjects treated with ribavirin and 2 of 3 subjects treated with cidofovir survived.

Kolavic-Gray SA, Binn LN, Sanchez JL, et al: Large epidemic of adenovirus type 4 infection among military trainees: Epidemiological, clinical, and laboratory studies. Clin Infect Dis 2002;35:808–818. *Adenovirus type 4 has reemerged as an important cause of acute respiratory illness in military recruits with the discontinuation of adenovirus vaccination.*

Ruuskanen O, Meurman O, Akusjarvi G: Adenoviruses. *In* Richman DD, Whitley RJ, Hayden FG (eds): Clinical Virology, 2nd ed. Washington, DC, ASM Press, 2002, pp 515–537. *Excellent, clinically oriented review of the biology, immunology, and clinical features of adenovirus infection in humans.*

365 MEASLES

Philip A. Brunell

Definition

Measles is an acute, highly contagious disease characterized by fever, coryza, cough, conjunctivitis, and both an enanthem and an exanthem.

Etiology

The virus is an enveloped, negative-stranded RNA paramyxovirus (genus Morbillivirus) that is 120 to 250 mm in diameter, similar to other members of the Paramyxovirus family but lacking neuraminidase. Its single antigenic serotype has been remarkably stable throughout the world for many years; however, sequencing has revealed geographic strain differences. The virus contains six major polypeptides, which are responsible for a number of structural and functional properties, including hemagglutination (of primate erythrocytes), hemolysis, cell fusion, and others. Isolation of virus from clinical specimens is most successful with primary kidney cell cultures of human or simian origin, but newer cell lines may be equally sensitive.

Epidemiology

Before the advent of measles vaccine, almost every child got measles, most before entering school. With the introduction of routine immunization against measles in the United States in 1963, the incidence of the disease has decreased to less than 100 cases in the last reporting period, and indigenous transmission was interrupted at times. Most isolated strains appear to be of foreign origin.

Smaller outbreaks have occurred at increasing intervals in 1971, 1976, and 1989. During the 1989–1990 epidemic in the United States, the highest attack rates were in infants, followed by preschool children. The largest number of measles deaths (89) in more than a decade was reported in 1990. Of those who died, about 30% were older than 20 years, and many were immunocompromised. Almost all the remaining deaths occurred in those younger than 5 years, most of whom were unimmunized and otherwise normal.

In developing countries, where measles in the very young is common, it is estimated that there are 1 to 2 million deaths annually worldwide. As a result of eradication efforts, the number of cases globally has fallen, particularly in Latin America.

Communicability. Measles is one of the most highly contagious infections. Almost all unprotected household contacts are infected. Demonstration of virus in nasopharyngeal secretions during the prodromal, pre-eruptive phase and in the first days of rash is in accord with epidemiologic evidence of contagiousness. Close physical proximity or direct person-to-person respiratory droplet contact is the usual requisite for infection, although airborne transmission has been documented.

IMMUNITY. An unmodified attack of measles is followed by lifelong immunity. Passively transferred maternal antibody protects the young infant during the early months of life.

Pathology and Physiologic Responses

Pathologic changes in fatal measles usually represent the compound effect of viral and secondary bacterial infection. Pneumonia is almost invariably present, and it is most frequently interstitial. More representative are changes of the uncomplicated viral disease within the tonsillar, nasopharyngeal, and appendiceal tissues examined during the prodrome. These changes consist of round cell infiltration and the presence of multinucleated giant cells. Giant cells also are observed in tissue cultures infected with measles virus. The skin and mucous membranes contain perivascular round cell infiltrates, with congestion and edema. Koplik's spots are inflammatory lesions of the submucous glands with similar microscopic features.

Simultaneous with the onset of rash, measles-specific antibodies are detectable in serum. Leukopenia is observed on the first day of rash, mainly because of a decrease in lymphocytes; subsequently, granulocytopenia ensues. Measles virus replicates in lymphoid tissues (e.g., spleen, thymus, lymph nodes) and can be isolated from monocytes and other mononuclear cells during acute infection. The virus can be propagated in a suspension of leukocytes in vitro.

IMMUNOSUPPRESSIVE EFFECTS OF MEASLES. Cell-mediated immunity is impaired during measles. There is transient suppression of the tuberculin reaction (observed also with measles vaccines); improvement in eczema and allergic asthma and the induction of remission in nephrosis have been described. In severe disease, the magnitude of depression of the total lymphocytes has been positively correlated with a lessened chance of recovery.

Clinical Manifestations

After an incubation period that averages 11 days, measles clinically manifests with symptoms of fever, malaise, myalgia, and headache. Within hours, the ocular symptoms of photophobia and conjunctival injection occur. The palpebral and, to a lesser extent, the bulbar conjunctivae are involved. There is usually no exudate. Sneezing, coughing, and nasal discharge occur almost simultaneously. Less commonly, hoarseness and aphonia may reflect laryngeal involvement. In this prodromal stage of 1 to 4 days' duration, tiny white spots on the buccal mucosa may herald the appearance of rash. The white lesions described by Koplik characteristically occur lateral to the molar teeth and typically are mounted on a bluish red areola of injected mucosa, superimposed on a diffuse red background. They generally appear a day or so before the rash and disappear within 2 days after its appearance. They constitute a pathognomonic, diagnostic sign. The enanthem may involve other mucous membranes such as the palpebral conjunctiva and vaginal lining.

The rash of measles follows the prodromal symptoms by 2 to 4 days, occasionally occurring as late as 7 days. It first appears behind the ears or on the face and neck as a blotchy erythema, spreads downward to cover the trunk, and finally involves the extremities. The hands and feet may escape involvement. Initially, the eruption consists of discrete red macules that blanch with pressure. Subsequently, these lesions become papular, tend to coalesce, and may develop a red, nonblanching component. In adults, the rash generally is more extensive, with a greater tendency to become confluent and slightly more raised and redder than in children. This is particularly true on the face. The rash fades in the order of its appearance; its disappearance about 5 days after onset may be attended by a fine, powdery desquamation that spares the hands and feet. In adults, malaise may continue for 1 to 2 weeks.

The fever of measles may persist for about 6 days and frequently reaches 40 or 41° C. Throughout the febrile period, productive cough and auscultatory evidence of bronchitis may be evident. These manifestations may persist after defervescence, and cough is often the last symptom to disappear. Bronchopulmonary symptoms are an integral part of the primary viral infection; roentgenographic evidence of pulmonary involvement is frequently seen in the uncomplicated disease in the absence of leukocytosis and obvious bacterial infection. Generalized lymphadenopathy accompanies the acute febrile illness and may persist for several weeks thereafter. Nausea and, less commonly, emesis appear to affect adults more often than children and are usually accompanied by slightly elevated serum aminotransferase levels.

Complications

The persistence or recurrence of fever and development of leukocytosis are presumptive evidence of the common bacterial sequela of otitis media or pneumonia. Laryngitis of sufficient severity to embarrass respiration has been observed. Keratoconjunctivitis is part of the acute phase. Electroencephalographic abnormalities have been described in about one half of children with measles. Severe measles has been described in pregnant women along with hepatitis and pneumonia; the latter is sometimes fatal. Premature labor has resulted in prematurity and stillbirths.

ENCEPHALOMYELITIS. A rare (0.1%) but serious consequence of measles is a demyelinating encephalomyelitis that may appear 1 to 14 days after the onset of rash. This complication is associated with recurrence of fever and headache, vomiting, and stiff neck. Stupor and convulsions usually follow. Death ensues in about 10% of patients; more than one half of survivors suffer permanent residuals of varying severity.

Infection of brain cells results in an incomplete viral replicative cycle with production of defective virions lacking the matrix (M) measles virus protein. Studies of patients with acute measles encephalomyelitis and those with late-onset, subacute sclerosing panencephalitis show high titers in serum and cerebrospinal fluid of antibodies to all the measles virus proteins except M.

Other late sequelae of measles are thrombocytopenic purpura and exacerbation or activation of preexisting pulmonary tuberculosis. The late complications of subacute sclerosing panencephalitis are discussed in Chapter 451.

GIANT-CELL PNEUMONIA. In patients who are immunocompromised (e.g., those with the acquired immunodeficiency syndrome [AIDS]), measles virus may induce an interstitial pneumonia characterized by giant cells and intracellular inclusion bodies that is often fatal. This reaction also has been reported in a human immunodeficiency virus (HIV)–positive measles vaccine recipient.

MEASLES MODIFIED BY ADMINISTERING ANTIBODIES. Attenuation of the natural disease by antibody prophylaxis may result in an illness of lessened severity, comparable with the milder infection seen in infants with illness modified by maternally acquired antibody. Fever alone may be observed, but some degree of exanthem is usually apparent. Koplik's spots may not appear. In general, the course is truncated and relatively uncomplicated. Lasting immunity is uncertain, and later routine immunization of these individuals is probably indicated.

ATYPICAL MEASLES. From 1963 to 1967, two types of measles vaccine, one live attenuated and the other inactivated or "killed," were available in the United States. The live attenuated vaccine has been the sole product licensed and used in this country since 1967. A severe illness was reported in killed vaccine recipients after exposure to natural measles. These patients had high fever, pneumonia with pleural effusion, obtundation, and an unusual rash. The exanthem was hemorrhagic and was most marked on the extremities. In some instances, vesicular, macular, or maculopapular phases have been observed. The rash is sometimes accompanied by edema of hands and feet. The patients' sera revealed extraordinarily high titers of measles-specific antibodies.

Subsequent investigations showed that patients who had received inactivated measles vaccines failed to develop antibodies to the fusion (F) protein of the virus. Lack of antibodies to the cell fusion factor is believed to have permitted the patients to support measles infection. The atypical measles syndrome may be caused by an anamnestic antibody response in the face of an abundance of measles antigens.

In addition to the rash and pulmonary findings, these patients may have elevated liver enzymes, disseminated intravascular coagulation, and marked myalgia. Nodular pulmonary changes have persisted in some patients. Some cases of pneumonia occurred in the absence of rash. Initial diagnoses on presentation have included Rocky Mountain spotted fever and meningococcemia because of the similarities of rash and toxicity. Because inactivated vaccines were available only from 1963 through 1967 in the United States, the past recipients are now adults. This atypical measles syndrome is of increasing importance to the internist. Atypical measles has been reported in some patients who received live vaccine alone or after killed vaccine. Recipients of killed vaccine who later received live vaccine may have severe local and systemic reactions to reimmunization.

Diagnosis

The diagnosis of measles should be suspected during an epidemic or in a patient with a history of exposure or foreign travel. Before the appearance of rash, the diagnosis may be difficult unless Koplik's spots are present. Finding an uncomfortable patient in a darkened room who has conjunctivitis, coryza, and cough should make the physician suspect measles. The rash in adults may be more violaceous, confluent, slightly raised, and more extensive than in children. A history of having received measles vaccine does not preclude the diagnosis, because most individuals with measles of school age or older have had the vaccine.

The differential diagnosis (Table 365–1) includes consideration of rubella, scarlet fever, infectious mononucleosis, secondary syphilis, drug eruptions, toxic shock syndrome, and Kawasaki's disease. Of value in excluding these possibilities are the milder course, postauricular nodes, and pinker rash of rubella; the sore throat, eventual desquamation, strawberry tongue, and leukocytosis of scarlet fever; and serologic test results for infectious mononucleosis. Fever, enanthem, and catarrh are uncommon with the cutaneous manifestations of drug hypersensitivity. Erythema infectiosum is usually an afebrile illness with rash on the cheeks, arms, and legs. There is little or no prodrome or accompanying respiratory tract involvement. Kawasaki's disease is rare in adults.

SPECIFIC DIAGNOSIS. Virus isolation is technically difficult. Increased levels of a specific antibody may be detected as early as the first or second day of rash. Acute and convalescent sera usually are required. Demonstration of measles IgM is available in some laboratories. A presumptive diagnosis may be made if giant cells are detected in stained smears of nasal exudate in the pre-eruptive period.

Prognosis

Uncomplicated measles is rarely fatal, and complete recovery is the rule. Fatalities are almost always the result of pneumonia, occurring in adults or children younger than 1 year. Congestive cardiac failure is a common cause of death in patients older than 50 years. The prognosis is particularly poor for patients with AIDS and other immunocompromised patients (Chapter 410).

Antimicrobial drugs effective against the usual secondary invaders have reduced the case-fatality rate of measles sharply. They have proved effective in therapy of bacterial complications but not in prophylaxis.

Encephalitis occurs as frequently in mild as in severe measles (about 1 case per 1000). Subacute sclerosing panencephalitis occurs about 7 years after measles and has essentially disappeared with widespread vaccine use.

Table 365–1 • A GUIDE TO THE DIFFERENTIAL DIAGNOSIS OF MEASLES

	CONJUNCTIVITIS	RHINITIS	SORE THROAT	ENANTHEM	LEUKOCYTOSIS	SPECIFIC LABORATORY TESTS AVAILABLE
Measles	++	++	0	+	0	+
Rubella	0	0	0	0	0	+
Exanthem subitum	0	0	0	0	0	+
Enterovirus infection	0	0	±	0	0	+
Adenovirus infection	+	+	+	0	0	+
Scarlet fever	0	0	++	±	+	+
Infectious mononucleosis	0	0	++	±	±	+
Drug rash	0	0	0	0	0	0

0 Not usually present or no test available.
± Variable in occurrence.
+ Present: test available (virus or bacterial culture, serology)
++ Present and severe.

Rx Treatment

There is no specific antiviral therapy with demonstrated efficacy for measles, although ribavirin has been used in some cases. **SYMPTOMATIC THERAPY.** In the absence of complications, bedrest is the essence of treatment of this self-limited disease. Codeine sulfate may be useful to ameliorate headache and myalgia and for cough. Analgesics and antipyretics may be useful. Fluids should be encouraged. Bright light is not an ocular hazard, but photophobia may require darkening the patient's room.
ANTIMICROBIAL PROPHYLAXIS. The course of uncomplicated measles is not influenced by antimicrobial drugs, and their use during the acute illness has resulted in no decrease of secondary bacterial complications such as otitis, sinusitis, and pneumonia. Instead, the same rates of complications (10 to 15%) have been observed, although with organisms resistant to the antibiotics used during the viral illness. If careful observation of the patient is possible, rational therapy is based on promptly recognizing and defining the cause of complications, followed by starting the appropriate antimicrobial drug in proper dosage.

Prevention

VACCINATION. A highly effective vaccine available for preventing measles is derived from the Edmonston strain of virus, which was isolated originally in the laboratory of Dr. John Enders. This live virus vaccine produces immunity by infection. A second dose now is recommended routinely. In children older than 1 year, the rate of sero conversion after vaccination in recent years is 98 to 99%. Measles vaccine usually is given as a single preparation of the measles, mumps, and rubella (MMR) vaccine. Failure of measles immunization was much more common before 1980. The reasons for this are unclear but may include poor recall or faulty documentation of immunization, age of immunization, use of immune globulin with the vaccine, receipt of killed rather than live vaccine, and the type of live vaccine.

Vaccine recommendations depend on the measles experience in the community (Chapter 16). The first dose of MMR is recommended at the age of 12 months. During epidemics, it may be given as monovalent measles vaccine to infants as young as 6 months, in which case it should be repeated in combination with mumps and rubella (MMR) after the first birthday. A second routine dose of MMR at school entry is recommended. All entering college students and beginning health care workers born after 1956 should show evidence of measles immunity: positive serologic test, physician-documented measles, or receipt of two doses of measles vaccine or, preferably, MMR. The immune status of those contemplating foreign travel should be reviewed. A large number of military personnel have been reimmunized without significant side effects. Measles vaccine may be given at the same time as other live or killed vaccines.
CONTRAINDICATIONS. Pregnancy, immunodeficiency, leukemia, other systemic malignant diseases, active tuberculosis, and administration of resistance-depressing drugs such as corticosteroids and antimetabolites are contraindications to live virus vaccine. Measles immunization of HIV-infected children is recommended, with the caveat to avoid severely immunocompromised individuals.

SUGGESTED READINGS

Annunziato D, Kaplan MH, Hall WW, et al: Atypical measles syndrome: Pathologic and serologic findings. Pediatrics 1982;70:203–209. *Excellent clinical description and explanation of a syndrome seen in young adults.*

Atmar RL, Englund JA, Hammill H: Complications of measles during pregnancy. Clin Infect Dis 1992;14:217–226. *A review of the complications and the treatment of measles in pregnancy.*

Centers for Disease Control and Prevention: Measles prevention: Recommendations of the Immunization Practices Advisory Committee (ACIP). MMWR Morb Mortal Wkly Rep 1989;38:1–18. *Everything you want to know about the use of measles vaccine.*

Giladi M, Schulman A, Kedem R, Danon YL: Measles in adults: A prospective study of 291 consecutive cases. BMJ 1987;295:1313–1314. *A brief summary of findings in a large number of adults.*

Gremillioin DH, Crawford GE: Measles pneumonia in young adults. Am J Med 1981;71:539–542. *A large series of cases of measles pneumonia in young adults and other features of measles in this group.*

Gustafson TL, Brunell PA, Lievens AW, et al: Measles outbreak in a "fully-immunized" secondary school population. N Engl J Med 1987;316:771–774. *School outbreaks are described in a presumably well-immunized population.*

Global Measles Control and Mortality Reduction—Worldwide, 1991–2001. MMWR Morb Mortal Wkly Rep 2003;52:471–475. *Nearly all deaths occur in the 75 poorest countries.*

Measles Evaluation: Recommendations from a meeting co-sponsored by the World Health Organization, the Pan American Health Organization and CDC. MMWR Morb Mortal Wkly Rep 1997;46(RR-1):1–20. *A progress report and recommendations for the worldwide eradication of measles.*

Panum PL: Observations Made During the Epidemic of Measles on the Faroe Islands. New York, Delta Omega Society, 1940. *A classic clinical epidemiologic description of measles introduced into an isolated population, with disease occurring among all susceptibles born since the previous epidemic 65 years earlier.*

366 RUBELLA (GERMAN MEASLES)

Philip A. Brunell

Definition

Rubella is an acute, usually benign infectious disease characterized by a 3-day rash, generalized lymphadenopathy, and minimal or no prodromal symptoms. Since 1941, it has been known to cause congenital malformations when infection occurs during the early months of pregnancy.

Etiology

Rubella is a small, spherical, enveloped virus containing single-stranded RNA of positive polarity. Structural proteins include two envelope glycoproteins and a nucleocapsid protein. The virus is classified as a togavirus, genus *Rubivirus*. It multiplies slowly in a variety of primary cell culture systems and in some continuous cell lines in most systems without detectable cytopathic effects.

Epidemiology

Before rubella vaccines were available, the disease was worldwide in distribution, produced major epidemics at 6- to 9-year intervals, and was recognized mainly in school-age children; it also produced outbreaks in settings such as military recruit bases and college campuses where large numbers of susceptible young adults gathered in relatively crowded conditions. Since licensure in 1969 of the vaccine in the United States, there has been strikingly altered epidemiology. There has been no major epidemic since 1964–1965. In other nations where rubella vaccine has not been widely used the epidemiology has remained unchanged. Because the disease may be quite nonspecific clinically, with nearly one third of adults undergoing infection without rash, epidemiologic reporting tends to underestimate its prevalence. Since 1966, congenital rubella has been a reportable disease.

It is probable that rubella is spread by the respiratory route and by close and sustained personal contact. The incubation period in experimentally infected individuals was found to be 12 to 19 days, with most cases occurring 14 to 15 days after exposure. Although virus was isolated as early as 7 days before and as late as 21 days after the onset of rash, infectivity is probably greatest throughout the period of prodromal symptoms and for as long as 7 days after the appearance of rash. Infants with congenitally acquired infection may excrete virus in respiratory secretions and in urine for months after birth and are contagious during this time. In hospital environments, especially in nurseries, the newborn with congenital rubella had been a source of nosocomial infection of personnel involved in his or her care.

Immunity is lifelong after initial infection. Authenticated second attacks are exceedingly rare and require serologic documentation because of the nonspecific nature of the clinical syndrome. Subclinical reinfection demonstrated by increase in immunoglobulin G (IgG) serum antibody has been documented. Such reinfections are not associated with viremia and thus pose little threat to pregnant women. IgM response has been used to distinguish primary infection from reinfection. Immunity that follows artificial immunization with live virus vaccine is apparently of equal duration even though the antibody titers induced may be somewhat lower.

Pathology

Death from postnatal rubella is usually due to encephalitis. Thus, most autopsies describe only the brain findings. Since 1962, it has been possible to investigate the pathogenesis and to correlate clinical findings with virologic events. After initial invasion of the upper respiratory tract, virus spreads to local lymphoid tissue, where it multiplies and initiates a viremia of approximately 7 days' duration. Respiratory tract shedding of virus and the viremia rise to peak levels until the onset of rash, at which time the latter becomes undetectable, whereas respiratory secretions contain diminishing quantities of virus over the succeeding 5 to 15 days. Specific serum antibodies can be demonstrated with the onset of rash, and circulating immune complexes are detectable soon thereafter.

Clinical Manifestations

POSTNATALLY ACQUIRED RUBELLA. Twelve to 19 days after exposure, the onset of rubella is manifested by the appearance of a rash with mild accompanying constitutional symptoms of malaise and occasionally mild sore throat. Enlargement of the postauricular and suboccipital nodes generally appears about a week before the rash. Moderate fever may accompany or precede the rash. Generalized peripheral lymphadenopathy and, more rarely, splenomegaly may occur.

The exanthem of rubella is usually apparent within 24 hours of the first symptoms as a faint macular erythema that first involves the face and neck. Characterized by its brevity and evanescence, it spreads rapidly to the trunk and extremities, sometimes leaving one site even as it appears at the next. The pink macules that constitute the rash blanch with pressure and rarely stain the skin. Rubella virus has been isolated from the skin lesions as well as from uninvolved sites. The truncal rash may coalesce, but the lesions on the extremities remain discrete. The eruption usually vanishes by the third day. Rubella may occur without rash. In the absence of an epidemic and of serologic or virologic confirmation, the clinical diagnosis of rubella is not reliable.

COMPLICATIONS. Recovery is almost always prompt and uneventful. In contrast to those in measles, secondary bacterial infections are not encountered in rubella. Transient polyarthralgia and polyarthritis are more common among adolescents and adults with rubella, particularly females. They appear 3 or more days after onset of rash and may last 5 to 10 days. The knees and joints of the hands and wrists are most often involved. Surveys during urban epidemics have revealed rates of 5 to 15% in males and 10 to 35% in females.

Thrombocytopenia, when sought by serial platelet counts, is common but rarely of clinical consequence. A meningoencephalitis of short duration may occur 1 to 6 days after the appearance of rash. Its incidence is estimated at 1 in 5000 cases, and it is fatal in approximately 20% of those afflicted. Rubella encephalopathy is not associated with demyelinization, in contrast to other postviral encephalitides. Survivors may have electroencephalographic abnormalities, but intellectual function seems to be preserved.

CONGENITAL RUBELLA. Necropsies of fetal and neonatal victims of intrauterine infection have shown a variety of embryonal defects related to developmental arrest involving all three germ layers.

The virus establishes chronic persistent infection of many tissues, with resultant intrauterine growth retardation. Delayed and disordered organogenesis produces embryopathic structural defects of the eye, brain, heart, and large arteries; continued viral infection during the fetal and postnatal period causes organ and tissue damage (e.g., hepatitis, nephritis, myocarditis, pneumonia, osteitis, meningitis, cochlear degeneration, and pancreatitis with the development of diabetes).

CONGENITAL RUBELLA. Congenital transplacental infection of the fetus occurs as a consequence of maternal infection, usually in the first 4 months of pregnancy. Virus is demonstrable in placental and fetal tissues obtained by therapeutic abortion at that time. If pregnancy is not interrupted, fetal infection persists, and on delivery of the infant, virus is recoverable from the throat, urine, conjunctivae, bone marrow, and cerebrospinal fluid of the living infant and from most organs at autopsy. From 20 to 80% of infants born to mothers infected in the first trimester of pregnancy have stigmata of infection readily recognizable in the first year of life. These include cardiac lesions (most commonly patent ductus and peripheral pulmonic stenosis) and eye defects (e.g., cataracts, glaucoma, retinitis, microphthalmia). Most infants in whom virus is detectable do not have evidence of disease at birth or may simply have intrauterine growth retardation. In others, more severe disease occurs. Most prominent of these manifestations is hemorrhagic skin lesions related to extramedullary erythropoiesis, which disappears soon after birth. Hepatosplenomegaly with active hepatitis may persist for months. Other involvement includes interstitial pneumonia, meningoencephalitis, hearing loss of varying extent, and lesions of the long bones. A progressive panencephalitis simulating subacute sclerosing panencephalitis has been observed in the second decade after congenital infection. The long-term sequelae for infants with congenital rubella include psychomotor retardation, hearing loss, retinopathy, and diabetes.

A striking finding has been the persistence of virus in the pharynx, urine, and cerebrospinal fluid for as long as 1 year after birth in 7% of infants. Infective virus was found in a congenital cataract after 3 years. This evidence of continuing viral synthesis occurs coincidentally with circulating antibody. The character of the antibody changes during the first months from maternal IgG to IgM, indicating a primary response of the infant to the persisting viral antigen. Studies of older infants and children with stigmata of congenital rubella show them to be free of demonstrable virus and to possess the IgG immunoglobulins that characteristically persist after other viral infections.

Diagnosis

Rubella may be diagnosed clinically with assurance only during an epidemic. Distinction from measles may be made on the basis of a fainter, nonstaining rash, the milder course, and the minimal or absent systemic complaints. Sore throat is a more prominent complaint in scarlet fever; the course of infectious mononucleosis is often more protracted, and splenomegaly is more frequent than in rubella. Specific diagnosis of rubella is made by isolating the virus in any of several cell culture systems or by demonstrating a rise by latex agglutination, hemagglutination inhibition, enzyme-linked immunosorbent assay, or complement fixation.

Prognosis

Complete recovery from postnatally acquired rubella is almost invariable. The rare deaths attributable to rubella follow the infrequent complication of meningoencephalitis. Infection in pregnancy constitutes a grave hazard to the fetus but not to the mother.

Treatment

There is no specific antiviral therapy. Few patients suffer discomfort severe enough to warrant symptomatic medication. Headache and myalgia or arthritis may be controlled by analgesics.

Prevention

PASSIVE IMMUNIZATION. Administration of gamma globulin to the pregnant woman may only mask her symptoms of infection and not protect the fetus from viral invasions. Thus, its use may only obscure the picture and confound decision about the need to terminate the pregnancy.

ACTIVE IMMUNIZATION. Rubella may be prevented in children and adults by parenteral attenuated live virus vaccines produced in cell cultures. Seroconversion rates after immunization are at least 98% with the current RA 27/3 vaccine. Joint symptoms are less common than with the older HPV 77-DE strain, occurring in about 2.5% of adults. Arthritis occurs 13 to 19 days after immunization and lasts 2 to 11 days. The fingers are most often affected, with the wrists and knees less commonly involved. Arthralgias generally begin 10 to 25 days after vaccination and last 1 to 9 days. Joint symptoms are less common in men than in women. In children, vaccination is attended by little or no reaction. Although rubella vaccine has allegedly been the cause of chronic arthritis, evidence has been accumulating that there is no etiologic relationship.

It was initially recommended in the United States that immunization be carried out principally in childhood. There is now a more aggressive attempt to immunize the remaining susceptible women and adolescent girls. Current policy recommends vaccinating all such persons who have no history of previous rubella immunizations. Postpartum immunization of those found to be seronegative during pregnancy is encouraged. Although occasionally vaccine virus has been transmitted to the newborn by breast milk, it has proved to be of little consequence. Only nonpregnant individuals should be immunized, and contraception, when appropriate, should be carried out for at least 3 months after vaccination. Inadvertent administration of vaccine to pregnant women has occasionally resulted in attenuated vaccine virus infection of the fetus. In more than 500 such cases studied, no infant has been observed with congenital malformations as a result. The frequency of fetal infection with the RA 27/3 vaccine currently used is less than with the previous rubella vaccine. Use of vaccine in the United States prevented a large epidemic of rubella expected in the early 1970s and has reduced the reported annual occurrence from more than 50,000 cases, with epidemic peaks of 200,000 to 500,000, to an all-time low in 2002 of 14 cases. A slight increase in cases of rubella accompanied by cases of congenital rubella syndrome occurred in 1990. Rubella is still endemic in many countries, and imported cases have occurred.

SUGGESTED READINGS

Gregg NM. Congenital cataract following German measles in the mother. Trans Ophthalmol Soc Aust 1941;3:35–46. *The original "classic" report associating rubella in pregnancy with congenital malformations.*

Hanon FX, Spika John J, Wassilak Steven S, et al: WHO European Region's strategy for elimination of measles and congenital rubella infection. Euro Surveill 2003;8:129–138. *An overview of surveillance and immunization strategies.*

Sherman FE, Michaels RH, Kenny FM: Acute encephalopathy (encephalitis) complicating rubella. JAMA 1965;192:675–681. *A clinical, pathologic, and epidemiologic study of rubella encephalitis.*

Spika JS, Wassilak S, Pebody R, et al: Measles and rubella in the World Health Organization European region: Diversity creates challenges. J Infect Dis 2003;187(Suppl 1): S191–S197. *Rubella will become part of the measles-mumps vaccine in most European countries.*

Townsend JJ, Stroop WG, Baringer JR, et al: Neuropathology of progressive rubella panencephalitis after childhood rubella. Neurology 1982;32:185–190. *A review of the clinical and neuropathologic findings.*

367 VARICELLA (CHICKENPOX, SHINGLES)

Philip A. Brunell

Definition

Varicella, or chickenpox, is an acute communicable disease characterized by a generalized vesicular rash. Because it is highly contagious, most individuals contract it in childhood. Herpes zoster, caused by reactivation of varicella-zoster virus (VZV), is a dermatomal cutaneous eruption.

Etiology

Varicella is caused by VZV, which is a member of the alpha Herpesviridae subfamily. It has the characteristic structure of a herpesvirus with an envelope, a tegument, a capsid, and a core of double-stranded DNA. The DNA is organized with terminal and internal repeats flanking unique short and long segments containing about 125,000 base pairs coding for approximately 70 genes. There are at least six glycoproteins. Its thymidine kinase has been a target for antiviral agents. There is some diversity in the restriction enzyme patterns among isolates; there is only a single serotype. Although the human is the only known natural host, a closely related virus has been identified in a simian species.

Epidemiology

Varicella is a highly contagious disease. After continuing household exposure, as would occur in a family, almost all susceptible persons are infected. The subclinical attack rate is believed to be no more than 4%. The results of nonhousehold exposure are less predictable. Chickenpox may be most contagious the day before the onset of rash. The period of contagiousness lasts for no more than 5 days after the appearance of the first lesion. Children may return to school at this time or earlier if the lesions are crusted. The incubation period is usually about 14 days. Ninety-nine per cent of the cases occur 10 to 20 days after exposure. The disease is known to be spread by direct contact. Airborne spread has also been demonstrated, most notably in hospitals.

Nosocomial spread of varicella has been well documented. It has occurred from room to room by airborne spread as well as between patients and staff. Adults with herpes zoster who are hospitalized are less likely to cause secondary cases of chickenpox than are children. The reason is that hospitalized children are more likely to be susceptible to chickenpox than hospitalized adults. Strict isolation is recommended for hospitalized patients with varicella and for children or immunocompromised adults with herpes zoster. Adults with localized herpes zoster require less stringent isolation procedures.

Most cases of chickenpox occur in childhood. Most children contract chickenpox prior to school entry, often in out-of-home care. Fewer than 2% of the cases occur after the second decade. Less than 10% of hospital workers with a negative history are seronegative. Almost all individuals with a positive history are seropositive. A single attack of chickenpox usually confers lifetime immunity.

There appears to be more efficient transmission of disease in temperate than in tropical climates. The reason for this is uncertain, but it may be due to temperature rather than urbanization. Varicella occurs most commonly during the late winter and spring months, the peak being in about March. Sporadic cases occur into the early summer and start in late fall.

Varicella is more common than other childhood diseases during the early months of life. After the first 2 weeks of life, the disease is generally mild. Maternal antibody transferred across the placenta may not be as effective in protecting infants against this disease as are antibodies against other viruses. However, nursery outbreaks have been rare. Children who have varicella during the early months of life or are exposed in utero have a greater risk of herpes zoster in childhood.

Pathogenesis

Replication of virus is believed to occur initially in the epithelial cells of the mucosa of the upper respiratory tract. Because VZV produces a disseminated rash, one can assume that blood stream distribution must have occurred. Virus can be isolated from white blood cells from 5 days before to 2 days after the appearance of rash. After clinical recovery, the virus persists in the absence of clinical symptoms in a latent phase. During this time, DNA and some species of messenger RNA can be demonstrated in neurons in dorsal root ganglia. The segmental distribution of herpes zoster, which usually occurs decades after the initial VZV infection, is consistent with a dorsal root ganglion site for the latent virus. In uncomplicated chickenpox, rises in serum aminotransferase levels have been demonstrated. This observation suggests that there is visceral involvement in the normal course of this disease.

The vesicular lesions of varicella contain a predominance of polymorphonuclear leukocytes even during the early phase of vesicle formation. Multinuclear giant cells are occasionally found in the base of the lesions, often containing eosinophilic intranuclear (Cowdry type A) inclusions. Large amounts of virus can be demonstrated in vesicular fluid by electron microscopy, and virus can be isolated.

Postmortem descriptions of patients with varicella have usually involved immunocompromised subjects. In these cases, inflammatory changes are usually found in multiple organs, including the lung, liver, spleen, and skin, together with anoxic changes in the brain. Similar involvement is found in the newborn. Focal areas of necrosis and intranuclear eosinophilic inclusions are common. Changes in otherwise normal individuals usually include myocardial and pulmonary lesions. On microscopic examination, the brain has demonstrated edema with some lymphocyte cuffing around the cerebral vessels.

Infectious Diseases

Infectious Diseases

Clinical Manifestations

Varicella is characterized by a generalized eruption that is centripetal in distribution; erythematous macules, papules, vesicles, and scabbed lesions may be present at the same time. The vesicles are superficial, with varying amounts of erythema at their bases. Adults tend to have considerably more erythema than children. During the early phase of the eruption, lesions are found on the face, scalp, and trunk. Often, lesions can be detected in the scalp before their appearance on the skin by running the fingers through the hair. Later, new lesions appear on the extremities. By this time, the earlier lesions have dried and crusted. Excoriations are common, attesting to the pruritic nature of the lesions. Mucous membranes of the conjunctiva and oropharynx are more frequently involved in adults than in children. New lesions continue to appear over a 3- or 4-day period, after which the rate of their appearance decelerates markedly.

There is a striking variation in the extent of systemic symptoms associated with varicella. Most children have a mild illness with few systemic complaints and an average maximal temperature of about 38.3° C. It is more common for adults to have considerable malaise, muscle ache, arthralgia, and headache. These may precede the first skin lesions by 24 to 48 hours.

In the immunocompromised subject, the disease is often severe. Approximately 30% of children with leukemia or lymphoma who contract varicella and receive no prophylaxis or treatment develop progressive varicella. Vesicles continue to erupt into the second week of illness, accompanied by high fever. Lesions tend to be deep seated rather than superficial. Toward the end of the first week and the beginning of the second week, the lesions are more common on the extremities than on the trunk. Indeed, the distribution and appearance may resemble those with smallpox. Visceral involvement occurs in about 30% of these patients. The lung, liver, pancreas, and brain may be involved. Death occurs in about 9% of immunocompromised patients who contract varicella. The death is usually due to pulmonary involvement. Patients with human immunodeficiency virus (HIV) infections may have recurrent attacks of varicella in the absence of exposure or a persistent eruption that may continue for months, the latter usually in severely immunocompromised patients.

Varicella in pregnant women is believed to be more serious than in nongravid females; fatalities have been reported. The rate of fetal wastage is not increased. About 1% of infants born to mothers who have had varicella early in pregnancy, however, have been found at birth to have varicella embryopathy. Risk appears to be greatest during midpregnancy. The infants are born with cerebral damage and a variety of ocular findings, and characteristically they have a scarred, atrophic limb. The children are generally small for gestational age and may have other abnormalities as well. When mothers develop chickenpox within a few days of delivery, varicella of the newborn may occur. If maternal onset of varicella is between 5 and 10 days prior to birth, it is associated with a higher risk of serious disease and even death of the newborn.

Bacterial infections of the skin are the most common complication of chickenpox in childhood. The frequency of invasive streptococcal superinfection has increased. The rate of complications is much higher in adults than in children. Although fewer than 2% of the reported cases occur after the second decade, almost 35% of the deaths occur in this group. A disproportionate rate of hospitalization is also found in adults. The major complications of varicella in adults are encephalitis and pneumonia.

Approximately 1 in 400 adults with chickenpox are hospitalized for pneumonia. In a prospective study, however, it was found that only 6% of young adults with chickenpox had respiratory symptoms, whereas 16% had roentgenographic evidence of pulmonary involvement.

Infection produces a diffuse interstitial type of pneumonia with hypoxia resulting from poor diffusion of gases. Diffuse calcification of the lung parenchyma may be found years after recovery.

Encephalitis in childhood is most commonly manifested by a cerebellitis, which usually occurs at the end of the first week or during the second week after the onset of rash. This complication is almost always self-limited. In contrast, an acute form of encephalitis usually occurring soon after the onset of rash often has a fulminating course; it is characterized by severe brain swelling. When Reye's syndrome was prevalent, as many as 20% of cases were preceded by chickenpox. A variety of other neurologic complications, including optic neuritis, transverse myelitis, and Guillain-Barré syndrome, may be associated with chickenpox. Hemorrhagic complications of chickenpox include thrombocytopenic purpura and purpura fulminans. Nephritis, myocarditis, hepatitis, and arthritis have also been described.

Diagnosis

There is usually little difficulty in recognizing typical forms of chickenpox, particularly if there has been a history of exposure. The diagnosis may be more difficult in immunocompromised hosts because they may have features of progressive varicella with visceral involvement. The umbilicated lesions in a peripheral distribution late in the course in these patients may be mistaken for smallpox. In the latter infection, all the lesions appear simultaneously rather than in crops.

Modified cases of chickenpox may occur after passive or active immunization. These cases may require laboratory confirmation. The most common sources of confusion are insect bites, generalized herpes in the immunocompromised host, rickettsialpox, or "hand, foot, and mouth disease" caused by an enterovirus. The differentiation of disseminated herpes zoster from chickenpox may be difficult. The former usually has dermatomal involvement initially. Generalization usually does not occur until 3 to 5 days after onset of the zosteriform rash. In severely immunocompromised patients (e.g., bone marrow recipients), generalization may occur earlier and the clinical differentiation may be difficult.

Fluorescence microscopy is a rapid and accurate method of confirming the diagnosis from vesicular scrapings. Virus can usually be isolated during the first 3 or 4 days after the onset of lesions. The virus is quite labile; it must be stored at −70° C if cultures cannot be inoculated immediately. My preference is to collect vesicular fluid in unheparinized capillary tubes and put the specimen directly into human embryonic lung fibroblasts at the bedside. Specimens from throat, urine, or stool are of little value for isolation of virus. Polymerase chain reaction can be used to demonstrate the presence of virus in vesicular fluid and throat swabs. This technique is particularly useful when viable virus cannot be obtained. It can also be used to distinguish vaccine from wild strains of virus.

Serologic confirmation of diagnosis can be made using a variety of techniques. The enzyme-linked immunosorbent assay (ELISA) and the latex agglutination assay are the most generally available. The laboratory director should be consulted regarding appropriate time of collection of specimens as well as interpretation of data.

The immune status of contacts can be determined most reliably with the latex agglutination test. Because complement-fixing antibody is lost rapidly after infection, it cannot be used for determining susceptibility. Fluorescence antibody testing using fixed cells sometimes yields false-positive results. Commercial ELISAs have been unpredictable. A number of laboratories have developed tests for VZV immunoglobulin M (IgM). It was hoped that these might differentiate varicella from herpes zoster in cases in which this was unclear. Unfortunately, these tests have not been very useful because VZV IgM is present in the sera of many patients with acute herpes zoster.

Rx Treatment

Major therapeutic objectives are the prevention of superinfection and relief of pruritus. The latter can be accomplished frequently by application of calamine lotion. Occasionally this does not suffice, and a systemic antipruritic agent such as trimeprazine may be necessary. It is advisable to trim and file nails to reduce the damage from scratching. Bacterial superinfection can best be prevented by encouraging daily bathing with an antibacterial soap. Following this with a colloidal starch bath may also be useful for relieving pruritus.

Relief of systemic symptoms may require additional medication such as acetaminophen, although this may increase pruritus. Salicylates are contraindicated because there is an association between their use and development of Reye's syndrome in children. Special care should be taken to be certain that over-the-counter medications containing salicylates are avoided. Necrotizing fasciitis caused by group A Streptococcus has been associated with the use of ibuprofen. The increased frequency has been shown in some studies to be due to the selection of more severe disease for treatment with this drug.

Some patients, particularly those who are immunocompromised, may require antiviral therapy. Intravenous acyclovir has been shown to be effective in immunocompromised children with varicella. A dose of 500 mg/m² repeated every 8 hours has been used. VZV is generally less sensitive to acyclovir than herpes simplex. For this reason, larger doses are probably required. Studies of the use of oral acyclovir in the treatment of varicella have demonstrated some efficacy. Newer drugs (e.g., valacyclovir and famciclovir) have been effective in treating zoster with less frequent dosing. Although oral therapy may be useful in adolescents and adults, immunocompromised patients who are sick enough to require antiviral therapy probably should be treated with parenteral rather than oral medication.

Patients receiving high doses of corticosteroids or other immunosuppressive drugs who have been exposed to chickenpox are at high risk of developing progressive varicella. Corticosteroids appear to be most deleterious when given during the incubation period. They have been used in the treatment of pneumonia after the eruption has occurred without any obvious deleterious effects.

Prevention

Live attenuated varicella vaccine is recommended for all children aged 1 through 12 years and for certain adults. A single dose is recommended for children, and two doses at least 2 months apart are given to adults. Most adults, including those with a negative history, are immune to varicella. Assuring the immunity of child care or institution workers, those traveling abroad, military personnel, and postpartum women is highly desirable. Immunization during pregnancy should be avoided, but if it occurs it should be reported by calling 1-800-986-8999. Immunity of health care workers should be ensured.

The vaccine is quite safe and effective. Breakthrough cases are generally mild. Some vaccinees have developed a rash after immunization and may spread vaccine virus to contacts. Caution is advised when immunizing those who may come in contact with pregnant women or immunocompromised individuals. Except for relatively immunocompetent HIV-infected individuals, the latter should not be immunized.

Increased immunization of health care workers and increased use of the vaccine in the general population would be expected to decrease the risk of nosocomial infection. However, cases occurring after exposure to zoster continue to be a problem. Some immunized staff may contract varicella and have the potential to infect others. Patients in whom varicella develops should have strict isolation precautions in a negative-pressure room if possible. Those who are susceptible and cannot be discharged should be isolated from the 10th to the 20th day after exposure. Screening for susceptibility with the latex agglutination test may be useful in grouping patients. This test is not as reliable for predicting protection of vaccinees. Some susceptible persons, especially those who are immunocompromised, should be passively immunized with varicella-zoster immune globulin (VZIG). Consideration should be given to administration of acyclovir orally from the seventh day after exposure for 7 days. This approach was found to be effective in preventing disease in exposed children. Administration of vaccine up to 3 days after exposure may prevent infection.

Immune serum globulin does not prevent varicella. Massive doses are required to produce measurable modification. If prevention or modification is indicated, VZIG should be given. Candidates are those who (1) are susceptible, (2) are at high risk of developing complicated varicella, and (3) have had a significant exposure to the disease. Any individuals fulfilling the first two criteria who have had a household exposure should receive prophylaxis. It is often difficult to judge the degree of intimacy in other types of exposure. Reference to guidelines published by the Academy of Pediatrics or Centers for Disease Control and Prevention may be helpful.

Patients considered at high risk are (1) those who are immunocompromised by virtue of either disease or immunosuppressive therapy, (2) infants born to mothers who have had varicella less than 5 days before or 2 days after delivery, (3) certain premature infants, (4) bone marrow transplant recipients regardless of susceptibility, and (5) certain adults.

A history of varicella is usually reliable in both adults and children. Children who have a negative history are usually susceptible. Serologic testing of adults with the latex agglutination test who have a negative history is useful if it does not delay administration of VZIG. VZIG should be given as soon as possible after exposure and has not been shown to be effective if delayed more than 96 hours.

SUGGESTED READINGS

American Academy of Pediatrics, Committee on Infectious Processes: Recommendations for the use of the live attenuated varicella vaccine. Pediatrics 2000;105:136–141. *Vaccine update.*

Arvin AM, Gerston AA (eds): Varicella Zoster Virus. Cambridge, UK, Cambridge University Press, 2000. *Everything you ever wanted to know about V-Z.*

Galil K, Lee B, Strine T, et al: Outbreak of varicella at a day-care center despite vaccination. N Engl J Med 2002;347:1909–1915. *Emphasizes that the vaccine is not 100% effective.*

Gnann JW Jr, Whitley RJ: Clinical practice. Herpes zoster. N Engl J Med 2002;347:340–346. *A practical overview of diagnosis and treatment.*

Johnson RW, Dworkin RH: Treatment of herpes zoster and postherpetic neuralgia. BMJ 2003;326:748–750. *Emphasizes how appropriate treatment of herpes zoster can control acute symptoms and reduce the risk of longer term complications.*

Varicella-related deaths—United States, 2002. MMWR Morb Mortal Wkly Rep 2003;52:545–547. *There were nine fatal cases in 2002.*

Varicella-Zoster Infections. Report of the Committee on Infectious Diseases, 26th ed. Evanston, IL, American Academy of Pediatrics, 2003. *A useful guide to management for patients exposed to varicella, including control of nosocomial infection.*

Vazquez M, LaRussa PS, Gershon AA, et al: The effectiveness of the varicella vaccine in clinical practice. N Engl J Med 2001;344:955–960. *The vaccine was 85% effective overall, 97% effective against severe disease.*

368 MUMPS

John W. Gnann, Jr.

Mumps is an acute systemic viral infection that occurs most commonly in children, is usually self-limited, and is clinically characterized by nonsuppurative parotitis.

Virology

Mumps virus is a member of the Paramyxovirus family. Mumps virions are pleomorphic, roughly spherical, enveloped particles with an average diameter of 200 nm. Glycoprotein spikes project from the surface of the envelope, which encloses a helical nucleo capsid composed of nucleoproteins and linear, nonsegmented, single-stranded, negative-sense RNA. Humans are the only natural hosts for mumps virus, although infection can be induced experimentally in a variety of mammalian species. In vitro, mumps virus can be cultured in many mammalian cell lines and in embryonated hens' eggs.

Epidemiology

In unvaccinated urban populations, mumps is a disease of school-aged children (5 to 9 years), and more than 90% have mumps antibodies by age 15 years. Before the mumps vaccine was released in the United States in 1967, mumps was an endemic disease with a seasonal peak of activity occurring between January and May. The largest number of cases reported in the United States was in 1941, when the incidence of mumps was 250 cases per 100,000 population. In 1968, when the mumps vaccine was first entering clinical use, the incidence of mumps was 76 cases per 100,000 population. In 1985, only 2982 cases of mumps were reported, an incidence of 1.1 per 100,000 population, representing a 98% decline from the number of cases reported in 1967. Between 1985 and 1987, the incidence of mumps in the United States increased five-fold to 5.2 cases per 100,000 population. More than one third of the cases reported between 1985 and 1989 occurred in adolescents and young adults, reflecting the slow acceptance of universal mumps vaccination during the 1970s. Epidemiologic studies of mumps epidemics in high schools, colleges, and military units during the 1980s demonstrated that outbreaks were due principally to failure to vaccinate. Renewed emphasis on vaccination resulted in a further decline in the annual incidence of mumps. More recent studies have attributed smaller mumps outbreaks in the 1990s to primary vaccine failure and possibly to waning vaccine-induced immunity. In 1999, the Centers for Disease Control and Prevention reported only 387 cases of mumps in the United States, the lowest annual total ever recorded.

Pathogenesis

Mumps is highly contagious and can be transmitted experimentally by inoculation of virus onto the nasal or buccal mucosa, suggesting that most natural infections result from droplet spread of upper respiratory secretions. The average incubation period for mumps is 18 days. Primary viral replication takes place in epithelial cells of the upper respiratory tract, followed by spread of virus to regional lymph nodes and subsequent viremia and systemic dissemination. Virus can be isolated from saliva for 5 to 7 days before and up to 9 days after the onset of clinical symptoms, meaning that an infected individual is potentially able to transmit mumps for a period of about 2 weeks. An estimated 30% of mumps infections in children are subclinical or associated only with nonspecific upper respiratory infection symptoms. Transient immunoglobulin M (IgM) antibody responses are detected early in the course of mumps infection, followed by the appearance of IgG antibody and cytotoxic T lymphocytes. Mumps-specific IgG can be detected during the first week of acute infection, peaks at 3 to 4 weeks, and persists for decades. Lifelong immunity follows natural infection. Patients who report more than one episode of mumps probably had parotitis of another cause.

Clinical Manifestations

PAROTITIS. Mumps usually begins with a short prodromal phase of low-grade fever, malaise, headache, and anorexia. Young children may complain initially of ear pain. Patients then develop the characteristic parotid tenderness and enlargement, which lifts the earlobe forward and obscures the angle of the mandible. The parotid glands are involved most commonly, although other salivary glands may occasionally be enlarged. Parotitis may initially be unilateral, with swelling of the contralateral parotid gland occurring 2 to 3 days later; bilateral parotitis eventually develops in 70% of patients with symptomatic salivary gland involvement. Painful parotid gland enlargement progresses over about 3 days, followed by defervescence and resolution of parotid pain and swelling within about 7 days. Long-term sequelae of mumps parotitis are uncommon.

ASEPTIC MENINGITIS. Symptomatic meningitis occurs in 15% of cases and is the second most common manifestation of mumps. About 50% of patients with mumps parotitis have cerebrospinal fluid (CSF) pleocytosis, although many have no clinical evidence of meningitis. Signs and symptoms of meningeal inflammation (headache, neck stiffness, vomiting, and lethargy) plus high fever usually develop 4 to 5 days after the onset of parotitis, although the meningitis may occasionally precede the parotitis. Indeed, 40 to 50% of all cases of documented mumps meningitis occur in patients who never have clinical parotitis. For unexplained reasons, symptomatic central nervous system (CNS) involvement with mumps is two to three times more common in males than in females. Examination of the CSF usually reveals normal opening pressure and a mononuclear cell pleocytosis with an average cell count of 450/mm³. A polymorphonuclear leukocyte predominance may be seen in some patients early during the course of mumps meningitis. The CSF protein is usually normal or mildly elevated (<100 mg/dL). Hypoglycorrhachia, which is not usually seen in viral meningitis, may be present in 10 to 30% of patients with mumps meningitis. Mumps virus can be recovered from CSF. Whereas the symptoms of mumps meningitis usually resolve within 7 to 10 days, the CSF abnormalities may persist for up to 5 weeks. Mumps meningitis is usually benign, and significant neurologic complications are rare.

ENCEPHALITIS. The spectrum of mumps-induced CNS disease ranges from mild "aseptic" meningitis (which is common) to severe encephalitis (which is rare). Some cases of encephalitis develop concurrently with the parotitis and are thought to result from direct extension of viral infection from the choroid plexus ependyma into parenchymal neurons. Other cases of mumps encephalitis occur 1 to 2 weeks after the onset of parotitis and may represent a demyelinating postinfectious encephalitis. Clinical findings in mumps encephalitis include obtundation (and less commonly delirium), generalized seizures, and high fever. Other neurologic findings can include focal seizures, aphasia, paresis, and involuntary movements. Recovery from mumps encephalitis is usually complete, although complications such as aqueductal stenosis with hydrocephalus, seizure disorders, and psychomotor retardation have been reported. The overall mortality from mumps encephalitis is 0.5 to 2.3%.

ORCHITIS. Epididymo-orchitis is rare in boys with mumps but occurs in 15 to 35% of postpubertal men with mumps. Orchitis is most often unilateral (bilateral involvement occurs in 17 to 38% of cases) and results from replication of mumps virus in seminiferous tubules with resulting lymphocytic infiltration and edema. Orchitis typically develops within 1 week of the onset of parotitis, although orchitis (like mumps meningitis) can develop before or even in the absence of parotitis. Mumps orchitis is characterized by marked testicular swelling and severe pain accompanied by fever, nausea, and headache. The pain and swelling resolve within 5 to 7 days, although residual testicular tenderness can persist for weeks. Testicular atrophy may follow orchitis in 35 to 50% of cases, but sterility is an uncommon complication even among men with bilateral orchitis.

OTHER MANIFESTATIONS. Mumps can cause inflammation of other glandular tissues, including pancreatitis and thyroiditis. Oophoritis and mastitis have been reported in postpubertal women with mumps. Transient renal function abnormalities are common in mumps, and virus can be isolated readily from urine; significant renal damage is rare, however. Other infrequent manifestations of mumps include sensorineural deafness (either transient or permanent), arthritis, myocarditis, and thrombocytopenia. Maternal mumps infection during the first trimester of pregnancy results in an increased frequency of spontaneous abortions, but no clear association between congenital malformations and maternal mumps has been demonstrated.

Diagnosis

The diagnosis of mumps is usually based on clinical findings in a child who presents with fever and parotitis, particularly if the individual is known to be susceptible and has been exposed to mumps during the preceding 2 to 3 weeks. An atypical clinical presentation (e.g., meningitis or orchitis without parotitis) requires laboratory confirmation. Culturing for mumps virus is definitive but not universally available. Testing of acute and convalescent sera should demonstrate a diagnostic four-fold rise in mumps antibody titer. Alternatively, finding mumps IgM antibody provides good evidence of recent infection. About 30% of patients have an elevated serum amylase level that may be due to parotitis or pancreatitis.

The differential diagnosis of parotitis includes infections caused by other viruses such as influenza A, parainfluenza virus, coxsackievirus, or lymphocytic choriomeningitis virus or bacteria such as *Staphylococcus aureus*. Parotid gland enlargement can also be associated with Sjögren's syndrome, sarcoidosis, amyloidosis, thiazide ingestion, iodine sensitivity, tumor, or salivary duct obstruction. A careful examination should distinguish parotitis from lymphadenopathy.

Treatment

Management of the patient with mumps consists of conservative measures to provide symptomatic relief and to ensure adequate hydration and nutrition. Treatment of orchitis includes bedrest, scrotal support, analgesics, and ice packs. Patients with significant CNS involvement require hospitalization for observation and supportive care. There is currently no established role for antiviral drugs, corticosteroids, or passive immunotherapy in treatment of mumps.

Prevention

The cornerstone of mumps prevention is active immunization using the live attenuated mumps vaccine. In the United States, mumps vaccine is administered in combination with the measles and rubella vaccines (MMR) to children at age 12 to 15 months and produces protective antibody levels in more than 95% of recipients. A second dose of MMR is recommended for children at age 4 to 6 years. The mumps vaccine is also indicated for susceptible adults.

The Jeryl-Lynn strain of attenuated mumps virus used in the United States since 1967 is a very well tolerated vaccine, although rare instances of fever, parotitis, and possibly aseptic meningitis have been reported after immunization. In recent years, an increased frequency of cases of vaccine-related mumps meningitis has been recognized in other countries. These cases occurred after administration of an MMR vaccine that contained the Urabe AM9 mumps virus. In several cases, the vaccine virus was isolated from CSF and positively identified by nucleotide sequencing. This problem has not been recognized in the United States, where the Jeryl-Lynn mumps vaccine continues to be used.

Questions regarding prevention often arise when an individual with no history of mumps (typically an adult male) is exposed to a patient with active mumps. The immune status of the exposed individual can be determined by serologic testing, although this may involve some delay. A variety of serologic tests are available to determine susceptibility to mumps. The neutralizing antibody assay has been considered the "gold standard" test but is technically demanding. The hemagglutination inhibition assay is simple to perform but less specific because of cross-reactivity with other paramyxoviruses. Detection of complement-fixing antibodies against V (hemagglutinin-neuraminidase) and S (nucleocapsid) antigens was previously the routine method for determining immune status but has been replaced by more sensitive and specific enzyme-linked immunosorbent assays. The mumps skin test is not a reliable indicator of immune status. The vast majority of adults born in the United States before 1957 were naturally infected and are therefore immune. Mumps vaccine can be safely administered to an individual of unknown immune status, although vaccine given to a susceptible individual after exposure to mumps may not provide protection.

Highly controversial reports have been published that suggest an etiologic association between administration of MMR vaccine and development of autism. Parental concerns generated by the adverse publicity resulted in lower rates of immunization. However, subsequent large-scale epidemiologic studies conducted in the United States and the United Kingdom have failed to demonstrate any link between the MMR vaccine and childhood autistic disorders.

SUGGESTED READINGS

Centers for Disease Control and Prevention: Measles, mumps, and rubella—Vaccine use and strategies for measles, rubella, and congenital rubella syndrome elimination and mumps control: Recommendations of the Advisory Committee for Immunization Practices (ACIP). MMWR Recomm Rep 1998;47(RR-08):1–57. *Recommendations for mumps vaccination.*

Dales L, Hammer SJ, Smith NJ: Time trends in autism and in MMR immunization coverage in California. JAMA 2001;285:1183–1185. *Study found no association between MMR immunization and increased risk of autism in children.*

369 HERPES SIMPLEX VIRUS INFECTIONS

Richard J. Whitley

Herpes simplex virus (HSV), a member of the family Herpesviridae, has been implicated in human infections since descriptions of cutaneous-spreading lesions in ancient Greek times. Scholars of Greek civilization define the word *herpes* to mean "to creep or crawl," in reference to the spreading nature of the observed skin lesions. More recently, infection has been defined by the spectrum of illnesses caused by HSV. In 1968, well-defined antigenic and biologic differences were demonstrated between HSV type 1 (HSV-1) and HSV type 2 (HSV-2). HSV-1 was more frequently associated with nongenital infection and HSV-2 with genital disease. Further study has revealed that, of all the herpesviruses, HSV-1 and HSV-2 are closely related, with approximately 60% genomic homology. These two viruses can be distinguished most reliably by DNA restriction enzyme analyses; however, differences in antigen expression and biologic properties also serve as methods for differentiation.

Structure

Membership in the family Herpesviridae is based on the structure of the virion (Fig. 369–1). HSV contains double-stranded DNA at the

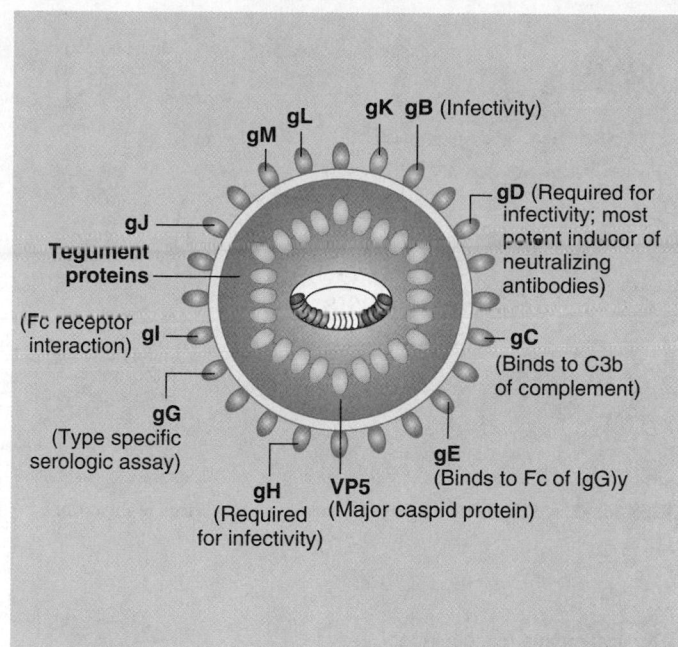

FIGURE 369–1 • Schematic diagram of the herpes simplex virus virion.

central core, has a molecular weight of approximately 100 million, and encodes at least 80 polypeptides. The DNA core is surrounded by a capsid that consists of 162 capsomers, arranged in icosapenta-hedral symmetry. The capsid is 100 to 110 nm in diameter. Tightly adherent to the capsid is the tegument, consisting of amorphous material. Loosely surrounding the capsid and tegument is a lipid bilayer envelope derived from host cell membranes. The envelope consists of polyamines, lipids, and glycoproteins. These glycoproteins confer distinctive properties to the virus and provide unique antigens to which the host is capable of responding. Notably, glycoprotein G (gG) provides antigenic specificity to HSV and therefore results in an antibody response that allows for the distinction between HSV-1 (gG-1) and HSV-2 (gG-2).

A unique feature of HSV DNA is its genomic sequence arrangement. The genome consists of two components, L (long) and S (short), each of which contains unique sequences that can invert on themselves, leading to four isomers. Viral DNA extracted from virions of infected cells consists of four equimolar populations, differing only with respect to the relative orientation of the two unique components. Biologic relevance of this phenomenon is unknown.

Replication

Replication of HSV is a multistep process (Fig. 369–2). After the onset of infection, DNA is uncoated and transported to the nucleus of the host cell. This is followed by transcription of immediate-early genes, which encode for the regulatory proteins, and is followed by the expression of proteins encoded by early and then late genes. These proteins include enzymes necessary for viral replication and structural proteins.

Assembly of the viral core and capsid takes place within the nucleus. Envelopment at the nuclear membrane and transport out of the nucleus occur through the endoplasmic reticulum and the Golgi apparatus. Glycosylation of the viral membrane occurs in the Golgi. Mature virions are transported to the outer membrane of the host cell inside vesicles. Release of progeny virus is accompanied by cell death. Replication for all herpesviruses is considered inefficient, with a high ratio of noninfectious to infectious viral particles.

Pathogenesis and Latency

A critical factor for transmission of HSV, regardless of virus type, is intimate contact between a person who is shedding virus and a susceptible host. With inoculation onto the skin or mucous membrane, HSV replicates in epithelial cells; the incubation period is 4 to 6

Infectious Diseases

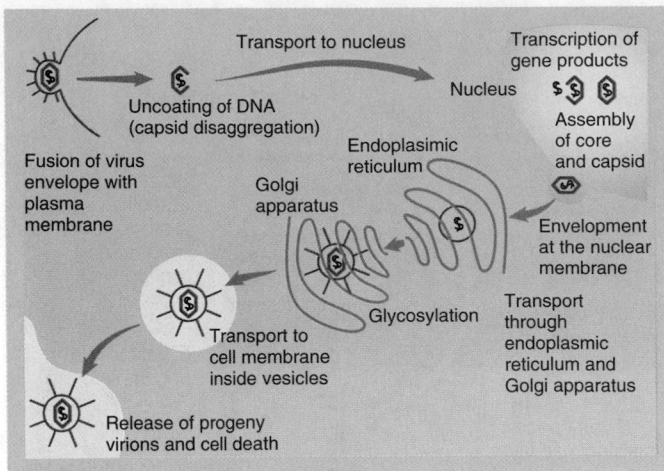

FIGURE 369–2 • Schematic diagram of herpes simplex virus replication.

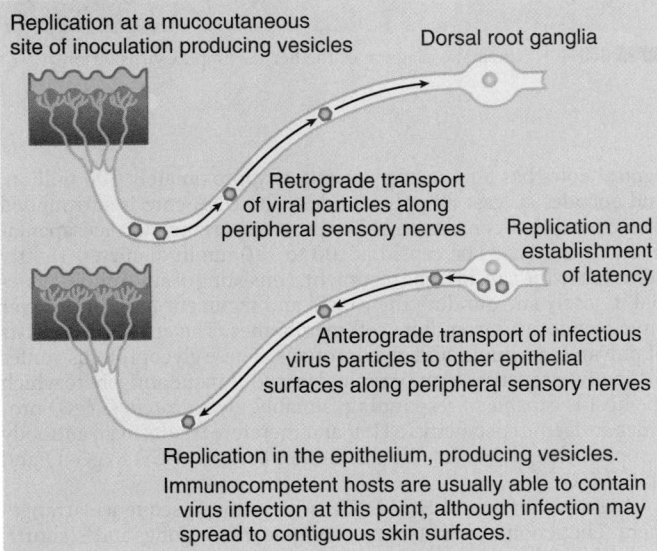

FIGURE 369–3 • Schematic diagram of primary herpes simplex virus infection.

days (Fig. 369–3). As replication continues, cell lysis and local inflammation ensue, resulting in characteristic vesicles on an erythematous base. Regional lymphatics and lymph nodes become involved with the draining of infected secretions from the area of viral replication. Viremia and visceral dissemination may develop depending on the immunologic competence of the host. In all hosts, the virus generally ascends peripheral sensory nerves to reach the dorsal root ganglia. Replication of HSV within neural tissue is followed by spread of the virus to other mucosal and skin surfaces by means of the peripheral sensory nerves. Virus replicates further in epithelial cells, reproducing the lesions of the initial infection, until infection is contained through host immunity.

The histopathologic changes induced by HSV replication are similar for both primary and recurrent infection. Changes induced by viral infection include ballooning of infected cells and the appearance of condensed chromatin within the nuclei of cells, followed by subsequent degeneration of the cellular nuclei. Cells lose intact plasma membranes and form multinucleated giant cells. They also may demonstrate the intranuclear inclusion bodies known as Cowdry type A bodies, which are suggestive but not diagnostic of HSV infection. With cell lysis, a clear vesicular fluid containing large quantities of virus forms between the epidermis and dermal layer. The dermis reveals an intense inflammatory response, more so with primary infection than with recurrent disease. As healing progresses, the clear vesicu-

lar fluid becomes pustular with the recruitment of inflammatory cells. The pustule then forms a scab, with scarring being uncommon.

The vascular changes in the area of infection include perivascular cuffing and hemorrhagic necrosis. These changes are particularly prominent when organs other than skin are involved, as is the case with herpes simplex encephalitis or disseminated neonatal HSV infection. Local lymphatics can show evidence of infection with intrusion of inflammatory cells due to the draining of infected secretions from the area of viral replication. As host defenses are mounted, an influx of mononuclear cells can be detected in infected tissue.

A unique characteristic of the herpesviruses is their ability to establish latent infection, persist in an apparently inactive state for varying amounts of time, and then be reactivated (Fig. 369–4). The latent viral genome may be either extrachromosomal or integrated into host cell DNA.

Latency is established when HSV reaches the dorsal root ganglia after retrograde transmission through sensory nerve pathways. Latent virus may be reactivated and enter a replicative cycle at any point in time. The reactivation of latent virus is a well-recognized biologic phenomenon but not one that is understood from a molecular standpoint. Stimuli that have been observed to be associated with the reactivation of latent HSV have included stress, menstruation, and exposure to ultraviolet light. Precisely how these factors interact at the level of the ganglia remains to be defined. Reactivation may be clinically asymptomatic, or it may produce life-threatening disease.

Diagnosis

The definitive diagnosis of HSV infection requires isolation of virus. Swabs of clinical specimens or other body fluids can be inoculated into susceptible cell lines and observed for the development of characteristic cytopathic effects. This technique is useful for the diagnosis of HSV-1 and HSV-2 infection because of the short replicative cycles.

In the absence of diagnostic virology facilities, cytologic examination of cells scraped from a clinical lesion may be useful in making a presumptive diagnosis of HSV infection. Material obtained from scraping the base of a lesion should be smeared on a glass slide and promptly fixed in cold ethanol. The slide can be stained according to the methods of Papanicolaou, Giemsa, or Wright. The presence of intranuclear inclusions and multinucleated giant cells is indicative, but not diagnostic, of HSV infection. This method has a sensitivity of only 60 to 70% and should not be the sole diagnostic method used.

Additional diagnostic techniques of clinical utility include in situ and dot-blot hybridization and DNA amplification by polymerase chain reaction (PCR). DNA amplification has become the diagnostic method of choice in assessing cerebrospinal fluid (CSF) specimens for evidence of HSV infection of the central nervous system.

In addition to new tests for virus gene products and viral DNA, improved serologic assays are also becoming available. However, these tests are useful only for making a diagnosis in retrospect.

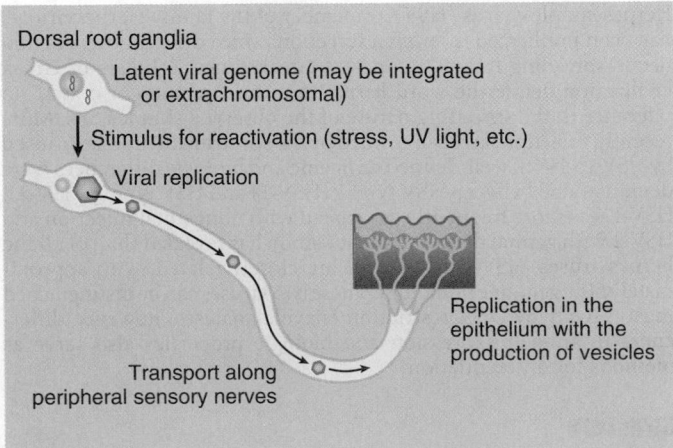

FIGURE 369–4 • Schematic diagram of herpes simplex virus latency and reactivation. UV = ultraviolet.

Clinical Manifestations

MUCOCUTANEOUS INFECTIONS

GINGIVOSTOMATITIS. Gingivostomatitis (usually caused by HSV-1) occurs most frequently in children younger than 5 years of age. Illness is characterized by fever, sore throat, pharyngeal edema, and erythema, followed by the development of vesicular or ulcerative lesions on the oral and pharyngeal mucosa. Recurrent HSV-1 infections of the oropharynx are most frequently manifest as herpes simplex labialis (cold sores) and usually appear on the vermilion border of the lip (Fig. 369–5). Recurrences are triggered by fever, stress, and exposure to ultraviolet light, as well as other factors. Intraoral lesions as a manifestation of recurrent disease are uncommon.

GENITAL HERPES. Genital herpes is most frequently caused by HSV-2. Primary infection in women usually involves the vulva, vagina, and cervix. In men, initial infection is most often associated with lesions on the glans penis, prepuce, or penile shaft. In individuals of either gender, primary disease is associated with fever, malaise, anorexia, and bilateral inguinal adenopathy. Women frequently have dysuria and urinary retention due to urethral involvement. As many as 10% of individuals develop an aseptic meningitis with primary infection. Sacral radiculomyelitis may occur in both men and women, resulting in neuralgias, urinary retention, or obstipation. The complete healing of primary infection may take several weeks. The first episode of genital infection is less severe in individuals who have had previous HSV-1 infections at other sites. Antibodies to HSV-1 appear to ameliorate the expression of HSV-2 clinical disease.

Recurrent genital infections in either men or women can be particularly distressing. The frequency of recurrence varies significantly from one individual to another. Of note, viral DNA can be detected by PCR in genital secretions three- to fourfold more frequently than symptomatic recurrences. One third of infected individuals have virtually no or few recurrences, one third have approximately three recurrences per year, and another third have more than three per year. Seroepidemiologic studies have found that between 25 and 65% of individuals in the United States in 1988 had antibodies to HSV-2 and that seroprevalence is correlated with the number of sexual partners.

HERPETIC KERATITIS. Herpes simplex keratitis is usually caused by HSV-1 and is accompanied by conjunctivitis in many cases. It is considered the most common infectious cause of blindness in the United States. The characteristic lesions of HSV keratoconjunctivitis are dendritic ulcers best detected by fluorescein staining. Deep stromal involvement also has been reported and may result in visual impairment.

OTHER CUTANEOUS MANIFESTATIONS. HSV infections can occur at any skin site. Common among health care workers are lesions on abraded skin or the fingers, known as *herpetic whitlows*. Similarly, wrestlers, because of physical contact, may develop disseminated cutaneous lesions known as *herpes gladiatorum*.

NEONATAL HERPES SIMPLEX VIRUS INFECTION

Neonatal HSV infection is estimated to occur in approximately 1 in 3500 deliveries in the United States each year. Approximately 70% of cases are caused by HSV-2 and usually result from contact of the fetus with infected maternal genital secretions at the time of delivery. Manifestations of neonatal HSV infection can be divided into three categories: (1) skin, eye, and mouth disease; (2) encephalitis; and (3) disseminated infection. As the name implies, skin, eye, and mouth disease consists of cutaneous lesions and does not involve other organ systems. Involvement of the central nervous system may occur with encephalitis or disseminated infection and generally results in a diffuse encephalitis. The CSF formula characteristically reveals an elevated protein and a mononuclear pleocytosis. Disseminated infection involves multiorgan systems and can produce disseminated intravascular coagulation, hemorrhagic pneumonitis, encephalitis, and cutaneous lesions. Diagnosis can be particularly difficult in the absence of skin lesions, which occurs in as many as 36% of cases. The mortality rate for each disease classification varies from zero for skin, eye, and mouth disease to 5% for encephalitis and 25% for neonates with disseminated infection, even with appropriate antiviral treatment. In addition to the high mortality associated with these infections, morbidity is significant in that children with encephalitis or disseminated disease develop normally in only 40% of cases, even with appropriate antiviral therapy.

HERPES SIMPLEX ENCEPHALITIS

Herpes simplex encephalitis is characterized by hemorrhagic necrosis of the temporal lobe. Disease begins unilaterally, spreads to the contralateral temporal lobe, and is characterized by hemorrhagic necrosis (Fig. 369–6). It is the most common cause of focal, sporadic encephalitis in the United States today and occurs in approximately 1 in 150,000 individuals. Most cases are caused by HSV-1.

Continued

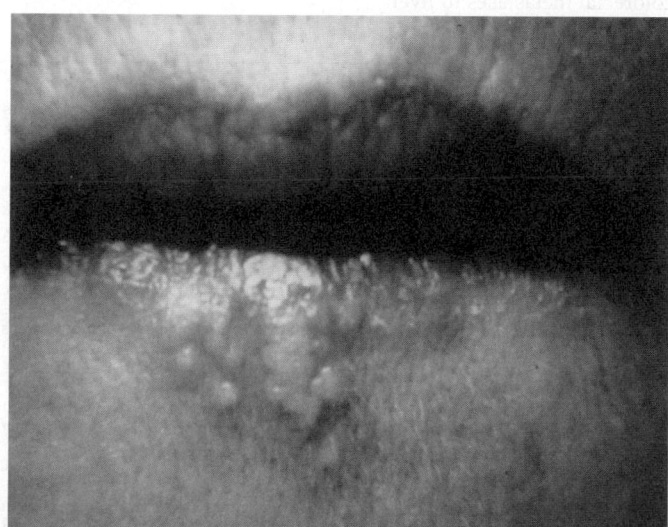

FIGURE 369–5 • Herpes simplex labialis.

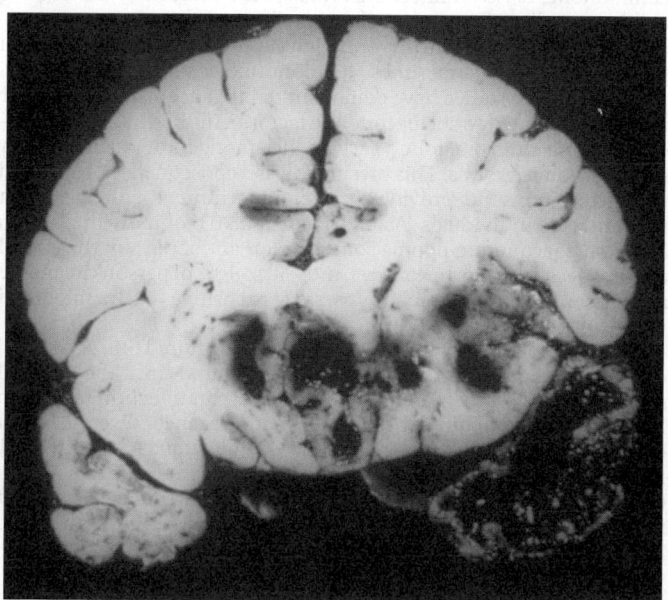

FIGURE 369–6 • Hemorrhagic necrosis in herpes simplex encephalitis.

The actual pathogenesis of herpes simplex encephalitis requires further clarification, although it has been speculated that primary or recurrent virus can reach the temporal lobe by ascending neural pathways, such as the trigeminal tracts or the olfactory nerves.

Clinical manifestations of herpes simplex encephalitis include headache, fever, altered consciousness, and abnormalities of speech and behavior, findings characteristic of temporal lobe involvement. Focal seizures also may occur. The CSF formula for these patients is variable but usually consists of a pleocytosis with both polymorphonuclear leukocytes and monocytes present. The protein concentration is characteristically elevated, and glucose level is usually normal. Diagnosis can be achieved by PCR evaluation of CSF in experienced laboratories. The mortality and morbidity are high, even with appropriate antiviral therapy. At present, the mortality rate is approximately 30% 1 year after treatment. In addition, approximately 50% of survivors have moderate or severe neurologic impairment.

HERPES SIMPLEX VIRUS INFECTIONS IN THE IMMUNOCOMPROMISED HOST

HSV infections in the immunocompromised host, including patients with acquired immunodeficiency syndrome, are usually due to reactivation of latent infection and are clinically more severe, may be progressive, and require a longer time to heal. Manifestations of HSV infections in this patient population include pneumonitis, esophagitis, hepatitis, colitis, and disseminated cutaneous disease. Individuals suffering from human immunodeficiency virus (HIV) infection may have extensive perineal or orofacial ulcerations. HSV infections are also noted to be of increased severity in individuals with extensive burns.

Epidemiology

HSV infections are distributed worldwide and have been reported in both developed and underdeveloped countries. Animal vectors for human HSV infections have not been described, and there is no seasonal variation in the incidence of HSV infections. The virus is transmitted from infected to susceptible individuals during close personal contact, and virus must come in contact with mucosal surfaces or abraded skin for infection to be initiated. Because approximately one third of the world's population has recurrent HSV infections, and because infection is rarely fatal, a large reservoir of HSV exists in the community.

Although HSV-1 and HSV-2 are usually transmitted by different routes and involve different areas of the body, there is a great deal of overlap between the epidemiology and clinical manifestations of infections caused by these viruses. The mouth and lips are clearly the most common sites of HSV-1 infection. Primary HSV-1 infection in the young child is usually asymptomatic but may be manifest as gingivostomatitis. Primary infection in young adults has been associated with pharyngitis and sometimes a mononucleosis-like syndrome. Seroprevalence studies have demonstrated that acquisition of HSV-1 infection is related to socioeconomic factors. Antibodies, which indicate past infection, are found early in life among individuals of lower socioeconomic groups. This presumably is a consequence of crowded living conditions that provide a greater opportunity for direct contact with infected individuals. As many as 75 to 90% of individuals from lower socioeconomic populations develop antibodies by the end of the first decade of life. In contrast, only 30 to 40% of persons in middle and upper socioeconomic groups are seropositive by the middle of the second decade of life.

Because infections with HSV-2 are usually acquired through sexual contact, antibodies to this virus are rarely found until the onset of sexual activity. There is a progressive increase in infection rates with HSV-2 in all populations beginning in adolescence. Overall, about one in five Americans has genital HSV-2 infection. As with HSV-1 infections, the rate of acquisition of HSV-2 infection appears related to socioeconomic factors. The number of sexual contacts is also an important risk factor for the acquisition of HSV-2. Genital herpes infection has been found to be a risk factor for another sexually transmitted virus: HIV.

Localized, recurrent HSV-2 infection is the most common form of HSV infection during gestation. Transmission of infection to the fetus is most frequently related to the shedding of virus at the time of delivery. Because HSV infection of the fetus is usually the consequence of contact with infected maternal genital secretions at the time of delivery, the determination of viral excretion at this time is of utmost importance. The incidence of cervical shedding in pregnant women with asymptomatic HSV infection is approximately 1%. Most infants who develop neonatal disease are born to women who are completely asymptomatic for genital HSV infections at the time of delivery and who have neither a past history of genital herpes nor a sexual partner reporting a genital vesicular rash. These women account for 60 to 80% of all women whose children develop neonatal HSV infection.

Prevention

At present, there are no licensed vaccines directed against HSV. Experimental vaccines for HSV-1 and HSV-2 have not been proved efficacious; nevertheless, they remain under investigation. Acyclovir, valaciclovir, and famciclovir are being given to recipients of solid organ and bone marrow transplants in the immediate post-transplant period in an effort to prevent reactivation of latent disease.

 Treatment

Infections caused by HSV-1 and HSV-2 are amenable to therapy with antiviral drugs (see Chapter 358). At present, acyclovir is the treatment of choice for mucocutaneous HSV infections in the immunocompromised host, herpes simplex encephalitis, herpes simplex in women near-term, and neonatal HSV infections. Intravenous administration is preferred for therapy for life-threatening disease. Intravenous acyclovir is also recommended for clinically severe initial genital herpes in the immunocompetent host. This includes patients with complications such as urinary retention or aseptic meningitis, and they should receive 5 mg/kg of intravenous acyclovir every 8 hours for 5 to 7 days. Caution must be exercised when acyclovir is used intravenously because it may crystallize in the renal tubules when given too rapidly or to dehydrated patients.

Immunocompromised individuals with mucocutaneous HSV infections that are not life threatening may be given oral acyclovir, valaciclovir, or famciclovir. Any of the three aforementioned drugs is also useful in treating initial genital herpes. Recurrent episodes, however, are not as responsive to acyclovir.

Other Considerations

Herpes simplex virus has been used for experimental gene therapy. By removing the $\lambda_1 34.5$ gene, both neurovirulence and the propensity to establish latency are ablated. These engineered viruses are being experimentally tested in patients with glioblastoma multiforme and colorectal metastases to liver.

Grade A

1. Watts DH, Brown ZA, Money D, et al: A double-blind, randomized, placebo-controlled trial of acyclovir in late pregnancy for the reduction of herpes simplex virus shedding and cesarean delivery. Am J Obstet Gynecol 2003;188: 836–843.

SUGGESTED READINGS

Engelberg R, Carrell D, Krantz E, et al: Natural history of genital herpes simplex virus type 1 infection. Sex Transm Dis 2003;30:174–177. *Genital HSV-1 recurs infrequently, and the rate decreases further over time.*

Kleymann G: Novel agents and strategies to treat herpes simplex virus infections. Expert Opin Investig Drugs 2003;12:165–183. *Summary of the current therapeutic options, as well as investigational drugs.*

Weidmann M, Meyer-Konig U, Hufert FT: Rapid detection of herpes simplex virus and varicella-zoster virus infections by real-time PCR. J Clin Microbiol 2003; 41:1565–1568. *Sensitivities of new assays are above 95% with nearly 100% specificity.*

Whitley RJ, Roizman B: Herpes simplex virus: Is a vaccine tenable? J Clin Invest 2002;110:145–151. *An optimistic viewpoint for preventing primary but not recurrent infection in the future.*

Whitley RJ, Roizman B: Herpes simplex viruses infections. Lancet 2001;357:1513–1518. *A comprehensive overview.*

Wolf R, Wolf D, Orion E, et al: Long-term prophylactic antiviral therapy for recurrent herpes simplex: The controversy goes on. Clin Dermatol 2003;21:164–167. *Reviews literature and generally does not support long-term use.*

Yeung-Yue KA, Brentjens MH, Lee PC, et al: Herpes simplex viruses 1 and 2. Dermatol Clin 2002;20:249–266. *Overview of the pathogenesis and transmission of HSV infections, type-specific diagnostic tests, and new treatments, such as cidofovir gel and resiquimod.*

William J. Britt

Human cytomegalovirus (HCMV) is the largest and most structurally complex human herpesvirus. Its linear double-stranded DNA genome consists of 250,000 base pairs that can potentially encode over 200 different proteins; however, comparison of DNA sequences of different primate CMVs has suggested that the number of proteins encoded by HCMV is approximately 160. Two different types of infections have been defined: primary and nonprimary. Because HCMV infection is persistent for the life of the host, nonprimary infection may follow reactivation of previous infection or reinfection by a superinfecting viral strain. Host immunity is thought to protect from disease because clinical symptoms of infection rarely develop in the immunocompetent host. Immunosuppression caused by corticosteroids and other immunosuppressive drugs used after allotransplantation, lymphocyte depletion in patients with human immunodeficiency virus (HIV) infection, or developmental immune dysfunction in the fetus predispose these unique populations to HCMV-induced disease.

Epidemiology

HCMV circulates within the population, and there is no evidence of epidemics or seasonal dependence. In most underdeveloped countries, HCMV is acquired early in childhood, probably as a result of either breast-feeding or crowded living conditions. In these populations, seropositivity reaches nearly 100% before childbearing age. In contrast, the seroprevalence in the United States is related to both age and socioeconomic status. By childbearing age, the seroprevalence often exceeds 90% in lower socioeconomic groups. Of individuals in higher socioeconomic groups, approximately 50% are seropositive by early adulthood.

Several routes of community acquisition of HCMV have been documented. Previous studies have documented large amounts of virus within semen and cervical secretions, and epidemiologic studies have demonstrated a correlation between a history of sexually transmitted disease and HCMV seropositivity. Together, these findings have indicated that HCMV is a sexually transmitted infection. Transmission from young children represents another important source of HCMV infection. Careful epidemiologic studies in child care centers demonstrated virus transmission between young children as well as transmission to adult caretakers and susceptible parents. The importance of children as a major source of virus can be appreciated if one considers that approximately 1% of all infants are born with HCMV infection (congenital) and that 30 to 70% of breast-fed infants of seropositive mothers become infected. Because these infants often excrete large amounts of virus in their saliva and urine for months to years after infection, they provide an important reservoir of infectious HCMV. Finally, studies have documented that previously infected women of childbearing age can be reinfected by a new strain of virus, suggesting that HCMV is readily transmitted between individuals even in seroimmune populations.

Major sources of virus exposure among hospitalized patients include blood products and transplanted organs. Transfusion-acquired HCMV infection, before routine serologic screening of donor blood products, occurred at a rate of approximately 2.5% per unit of transfused blood. Numerous studies have demonstrated that leukocytes present within various blood products were responsible for the majority of transfusion-acquired HCMV infections. Measures that reduce leukocyte contamination of blood products, such as filtration or, alterna-

tively, screening blood donors and matching the HCMV serologic status of donor and recipient, have nearly eliminated transfusion-associated HCMV infection. Nosocomial transmission of HCMV to health workers is uncommon, even in personnel caring for patients who excrete large amounts of HCMV, such as congenitally infected infants.

Pathology

Although HCMV can be consistently propagated in vitro only in human fibroblast cells, it can be isolated from a myriad of organs and cell types from infected humans. HCMV has been demonstrated in the endothelium and in blood monocytes, epithelium of almost every organ (including endocrine and exocrine organs), and resident cells of the central nervous system (CNS). Histopathologic findings range from extensive tissue destruction to isolated cytomegalic cells. The histologic appearance of the typical cytomegalic cell consists of an enlarged cell with scant to reduced cytoplasm containing a large nucleus with prominent nucleoli and intranuclear inclusions, a finding characteristic of HCMV infection. Often, the extent of organ dysfunction far exceeds the frequency of virus-infected cells detected in the diseased tissue.

Pathogenesis

Cellular and antibody- and cytokine-mediated immune responses have been proposed to limit HCMV infection in vivo, although in most cases direct evidence is lacking. A number of studies in bone marrow and solid organ allograft recipients have provided a strong correlation between the depression of HCMV-specific T-lymphocyte responses and susceptibility to HCMV-associated infection and, more important, clinical disease. These responses have included both major histocompatibility complex class II–restricted CD4+ T lymphocytes and class I–restricted CD8+ cytotoxic T lymphocytes (CTLs). Findings from several laboratories have suggested that a limited number of virion structural proteins (pp65 and pp150) are major targets of protective cellular immune responses. Reconstitution of protective immunity following transfer of autologous HCMV-specific CTLs to bone marrow allograft recipients has provided direct evidence for the role of HCMV-specific CTLs in protective immunity.

Several studies have shown that passively transferred antiviral antibodies failed to prevent HCMV infection in susceptible patients but modulated clinical disease associated with HCMV infection. The importance of natural killer (NK) cell responses and cytokines to the course of HCMV infection is unknown, but on the basis of findings in animal models of HCMV infection it is assumed that these responses play an important role in resistance to HCMV disease. Lastly, HCMV has been shown to encode several viral functions that (1) reduce class I and class II major histocompatibility antigen expression on virus-infected cells and subsequently interfere with antigen presentation and recognition by HCMV-specific T cells, (2) prevent NK recognition of virus-infected cells, and (3) encode anti-inflammatory cytokines as well as functional chemokine receptor molecules that can inhibit the activity of inflammatory cytokines and chemokines. Together, these viral gene products are postulated to act as immune evasion functions, which in turn allow persistence of HCMV in the presence of an effective host immune response. However, it should be stressed that the importance of these immune evasion functions to the clinical course of HCMV infection is not known.

As yet poorly defined nonlytic effects of the virus may contribute to disease syndromes associated with HCMV infection. Clinical syndromes of bacterial and fungal infections after HCMV infection in allograft recipients are consistent with an immunomodulatory activity of the virus; however, specific mechanisms accounting for this immunosuppressive activity of HCMV remain inadequately defined.

Clinical Manifestations

The clinical manifestations of acute HCMV infections in immunocompromised patients are well described; however, the clinical findings of diseases associated with chronic or persistent infection are less well defined. The latter may include inflammatory vasculature disease such as atherosclerotic coronary artery disease and transplant vasculature sclerosis. A substantial number of studies have linked HCMV to coronary artery atherosclerotic disease, and both

studies in animal models of allograft rejection and clinical studies of cardiac allograft recipients point to a potential role of persistent HCMV infection in vascular disease of the heart. It remains to be shown whether HCMV in concert with host inflammatory responses is directly responsible for disease progression or whether HCMV acts as a cofactor with other infectious agents in the pathogenesis of these diseases.

Continued

IMMUNOCOMPETENT PATIENTS. Although infection in the immunocompetent host rarely results in clinically apparent disease, acute infection in the normal individual can infrequently result in a mononucleosis-like syndrome. Approximately 8% of cases of infectious mononucleosis may be caused by HCMV. Clinically, this infection is indistinguishable from mononucleosis caused by Epstein-Barr virus with the exception that it is heterophile negative. Nonspecific constitutional symptoms predominate, including malaise, decreased appetite, and low-grade fever. Laboratory abnormalities include atypical lymphocytosis, chemical hepatitis and cholestasis, and, less frequently, thrombocytopenia. Similar but often exaggerated findings have been associated with transfusion-acquired HCMV, including the previously described postperfusion syndrome that followed cardiopulmonary bypass.

NEWBORNS. Congenital HCMV infection (present at birth) is common, occurring in approximately 1% of all live births in the United States. Some 10% of these suffer signs and symptoms of cytomegalic inclusion disease, which include petechiae, hepatosplenomegaly, jaundice, and microcephaly. Thrombocytopenia, cholestasis, and evidence of hepatocellular damage are consistent laboratory findings. Although almost all end-organ disease is self-limited, CNS damage associated with congenital HCMV infection is permanent and can result in significant developmental delays, seizure activity, gross neurologic impairment, and, most frequently, hearing loss. Subclinical congenital HCMV infection is less commonly associated with permanent CNS sequelae; however, between 8 and 15% of infants with subclinical infection may exhibit evidence of CNS damage, such as sensorineural hearing loss. Either type of congenital HCMV infection is characterized by chronic virus excretion that may persist for years, providing an important source of HCMV exposure in the community.

TRANSPLANT RECIPIENTS. HCMV is one of the most common opportunistic infections in the post-transplantation period. An estimated 50 to 100% of seropositive renal transplant recipients excrete HCMV after transplantation. Although the vast majority of patients do not exhibit evidence of end-organ disease associated with-HCMV infection, HCMV is a major cause of disease in heart, heart-lung, liver, and bone marrow transplant recipients. In bone marrow transplant recipients, HCMV pneumonia has been the leading infection-related cause of death, with mortality rates approaching 50 to 60%. Sources of HCMV infection in the allograft recipient include (1) reactivated infection in the HCMV-seropositive recipient, (2) exogenous blood products given in the post-transplantation period, and (3) most commonly, the transplanted organ obtained from an HCMV-seropositive donor. The highest risk for infection and disease is observed in the HCMV-seronegative recipient of an allograft from a HCMV-seropositive allograft donor (Chapter 298). Other factors associated with clinically significant HCMV infections in solid organ allograft recipients include the use of cadaveric grafts, leukocyte-containing blood products, and immunosuppressive agents that deplete T lymphocytes such as antithymocyte globulin or anti-CD8 monoclonal antibodies. Several studies have indicated that the HCMV viral burden in transplant recipients is most predictive of invasive disease, irrespective of donor-recipient status. In bone marrow allograft recipients, the severity of HCMV infection often parallels the development of graft-versus-host disease.

Clinical evidence of HCMV infection usually develops 4 to 6 weeks after transplantation and can be manifest as a variety of end-organ diseases such as pneumonitis or hepatitis and more commonly as a syndrome similar to HCMV mononucleosis, which can include fever, leukopenia, thrombocytopenia, and hepatitis. Virus can be isolated from the urine in almost all infected patients and from the blood in a subset of patients. The latter finding may presage the development of invasive multiorgan disease. Potentially fatal invasive infections include pneumonitis, severe gastrointestinal ulcerative disease with perforation, and life-threatening hepatitis. HCMV pneumonitis most commonly arises insidiously as a diffuse interstitial pneumonia and progressive hypoxemia. Acute allograft loss may accompany HCMV disease either as a direct result of graft involvement, as seen with hepatic transplants, or secondary to the reduction in immunosuppression that may be necessary during treatment of invasive HCMV disease. Long-term allograft survival also appears to be reduced as a result of HCMV infection. In cardiac allografts this reduction of survival has been proposed to result from virus-associated acceleration of coronary artery atherosclerosis (transplant vasculature sclerosis) of the allograft, whereas in hepatic allografts it has been suggested that HCMV causes enhanced immunologic recognition of the graft, leading to loss of intrahepatic biliary structures as well as vascular sclerosis.

AIDS PATIENTS. HCMV has been a major cause of morbidity and mortality in patients with acquired immunodeficiency syndrome (AIDS) (see Part XXIV). Because of the importance of sexual transmission in the spread of HCMV in adult populations, it is not surprising that the rate of HCMV seropositivity approaches 100% in populations at high risk for HIV infection. Thus, endogenous virus and frequent sexual exposure to reinfecting viral strains are likely sources of HCMV in these populations. The importance of HCMV coinfection in the progression of AIDS remains controversial even though in vitro findings have suggested a potential role of HCMV in enhanced replication of HIV. Risk factors for the development of invasive HCMV disease include a CD4+ lymphocyte count of less than $50/mm^3$. In the recent past, the development of invasive HCMV disease was a grave prognostic sign because overall survival was significantly shortened in patients with documented HCMV end-organ disease.

Clinical manifestations of invasive HCMV infections in patients with AIDS have included end-organ disease in almost all organ systems, with three systems being more frequently involved: the CNS, gastrointestinal system, and pulmonary system. Before the introduction of newer antiretroviral agents, it was estimated that between 8 and 25% of long-lived patients with AIDS developed invasive HCMV infections. The most common and important disease associated with HCMV in this population is retinitis. Although uncommon in allograft recipients, encephalopathies, both diffuse and focal, as well as myelopathies and neuropathies have been ascribed to HCMV in HIV-infected patients. Gastrointestinal involvement includes both colitis and esophagitis and less frequently gastritis. Clinical and laboratory evidence of HCMV colitis is often found in association with other gastrointestinal pathogens, raising questions about the importance of HCMV as a primary pathogen. Likewise, most investigators do not view HCMV as a significant cause of pneumonitis in AIDS patients. With the advent of highly active antiretroviral therapy, the incidence of invasive HCMV disease has decreased significantly in patients with AIDS. Immune restoration or reconstitution has been proposed as a mechanism for the declining rate of invasive HCMV disease in this population. Resolution of disease and clearance of viral DNA from the plasma have been correlated with increased numbers of CD4+ lymphocytes.

Diagnosis

The diagnosis of HCMV has traditionally relied on isolating the virus from urine, saliva, blood, or biopsy specimens obtained from patients exhibiting symptoms compatible with HCMV infection. Adaptation of immunocytochemistry and centrifugation-enhanced culture techniques has shortened the time required to identify HCMV in clinical specimens to less than 24 hours. There is no convenient method to distinguish acute, invasive infection from peripheral shedding after reactivation of a preexisting infection. In the allograft recipient and patients with AIDS, this has prompted diagnostic approaches for measuring viral burden, including HCMV blood cultures, cultures from biopsy specimens, and quantitative polymerase chain reaction (PCR) assays, all of which more closely correlate with invasive disease as compared with qualitative assays of viruria.

Serologic determination of HCMV is valuable when both immunoglobulin G (IgG) and IgM virus-specific antibodies are measured but usually only in normal hosts. Measurement of IgG alone is of limited value because of the high seroprevalence of HCMV in the population and the persistence of antibody responses to the virus. Although HCMV-specific IgM antibodies persist for up to 4 months in most normal individuals, their predictive value in the diagnosis of invasive infection in immunocompromised hosts is often limited because of their low positive and negative predictive value for invasive disease. Several investigators have demonstrated a correlation between affinity maturation of HCMV-specific IgG antibodies and the duration of primary HCMV infection in pregnant women. This assay has allowed the clinician to estimate the chronicity of an infection in a patient with a single positive IgG antibody titer. Larger studies with adequate follow-up are necessary before widespread use of this assay in the evaluation of pregnant women with presumed acute HCMV infection.

Newer methods of diagnosis include analysis of body fluids as well as biopsy material by PCR. PCR has been used successfully to detect viremia and plasma HCMV DNA. Quantifying PCR results has defined a threshold of viral burden that is associated with an increased likelihood of the development of invasive infection. Similarly, a semiquantitative assay of viral burden that utilizes a monoclonal antibody to detect virus-encoded protein in polymorphonuclear leukocytes, the antigenemia assay, appears predictive of invasive disease in allograft recipients and patients with AIDS. This assay is less sensitive than PCR, but its predictive value for invasive disease is similar to that of quantitative PCR and it is technically more straightforward.

Rx Treatment

Until recently, effective antiviral therapy was not available for HCMV infection. Two agents, ganciclovir and foscarnet, have been shown to be virostatic in vitro and in vivo. Clinical trials have documented efficacy of these agents in treating invasive HCMV disease in both transplant and AIDS patients. Both have significant toxicity, which often precludes their long-term administration. Ganciclovir causes dose-limiting hematopoietic toxicity, often resulting in clinically significant neutropenia. The most significant recent advance in therapy for CMV infections has been the licensing of an oral formulation of valganciclovir, the valine ester of ganciclovir, for treatment of invasive CMV infections. Early studies suggested that the poor oral bioavailability of ganciclovir could be overcome by increasing the oral dosage significantly and this therapeutic option appeared to offer similar therapeutic efficacy to intravenously administered ganciclovir. A simple chemical modification of ganciclovir produced valganciclovir, a drug with favorable oral bioavailability. Pharmacokinetic studies demonstrated that serum levels of the active drug could be obtained that were comparable to parenterally administered ganciclovit.**1** Clinical trials have documented similar efficacy and toxicity between the oral and intravenous formulations of the ganciclovir.**2** Foscarnet has significant nephrotoxicity, which limits its use in patients with azotemia. In addition, long-term therapy in immunocompromised patients has resulted in the development of viral resistance to both agents. Local therapy for HCMV retinitis has included intraocular injection of cidofovir and antisense oligonucleotides. Both therapies are well tolerated and lack systemic toxicity.

Perhaps the most beneficial use of these agents has been as prophylaxis in the immediate transplant period. Both foscarnet and ganciclovir have been used successfully to reduce the incidence of HCMV disease in the post-transplant period in both solid organ and bone marrow transplant recipients. More recent protocols include the use of quantitative assays of viral burden and so-called preemptive therapy in those patients at risk for developing invasive disease. This approach not only is more cost-effective but also will limit the development of resistance by reducing the indiscriminate use of these agents.

Immunoprophylaxis of HCMV infection has included passive transfer of antibody and limited clinical trials of live-virus vaccine. The use of intravenous immunoglobulin containing anti-HCMV antibodies remains controversial, although clinical trials in solid organ allograft recipients have provided evidence of its efficacy. Its use in bone marrow transplantation is contentious, but accumulating evidence suggests that any beneficial effects may result from poorly understood immunomodulatory properties that influence the severity of GVHD. Active immunization with a replicating HCMV virus as a means of inducing protective immunity has been attempted on a limited scale in renal transplant recipients. The results of this trial remain controversial, although there was some evidence suggesting that protective immunity was induced by the vaccine virus.

1. Lalezari J, Lindley J, Walmsley S, et al: A safety study of oral valganciclovir maintenance treatment of cytomegalovirus retinitis. J Acquir Immune Defic Syndr 2002;30:392–400.
2. Martin DF, Sierra-Madero J, Walmsley S, et al: A controlled trial of valgancyclovir as induction therapy for cytomegalovirus retinitis. N Engl J Med 2002; 346:1119–1126 [erratum appears in N Engl J Med 2002;347:862].

SUGGESTED READINGS

Cope AV, Sabin C, Burroughs A, et al: Interrelationships among quantity of human cytomegalovirus (HCMV) DNA in blood, donor-recipient serostatus, and administration of methylprednisolone as risk factors for HCMV disease following liver transplantation. J Infect Dis 1997;176:1484–1490. *A very complete study of the relationship between virus load and disease in solid organ allograft recipients. This article also demonstrates that viral load is predictive of disease development, independent of donor-recipient serologic matching.*

Flint SJ, Enquist LW, Krug RM, Skalka AM: Principles of Virology: Molecular Biology, Pathogenesis, and Control. Washington, DC, ASM Press, 1999. *An excellent text that includes basic principles of virology and discussions of aspects of the molecular biology of herpesviruses.*

Hart GD, Paya CV: Prophylaxis for CMV should now replace pre-emptive therapy in solid organ transplantation. Rev Med Virol 2001;11:73–81. *Review of benefits of ganciclovir prophylaxis in solid organ allograft recipients.*

Limaye AP, Raghu G, Koelle DM, et al: High incidence of ganciclovir-resistant cytomegalovirus infection among lung transplant recipients receiving preemptive therapy. Infect Dis 2002;185:20–27. *Report of emerging problem of antiviral drug resistance in CMV infection solid organ transplant recipients.*

Ljungman P. Prophylaxis against herpesvirus infections in transplant recipients. Drugs 2001;61:187–196. *Discussion of antiviral agents used for treatment of herpesvirus infections in transplant recipients.*

Ljungman P: Larsson K, Kumlien G, et al: Leukocyte depleted, unscreened blood products give a low risk for CMV infection and disease in CMV seronegative allogeneic stem cell transplant recipients with seronegative stem cell donors. Scand Infect Dis 2002;34:347–350. *The use of unscreened blood products for transplant recipients from a blood donor population with an increased rate of CMV seropositivity.*

Singh N: Preemptive therapy versus universal prophylaxis with ganciclovir for cytomegalovirus in solid organ transplant recipients. Clin Infect Dis 2001;32:742–751. *Discussion comparing merits of preemptive therapy and prophylaxis with ganciclovir in transplant recipients.*

Singh N, Paterson DL, Gayowski T, et al: Cytomegalovirus antigenemia directed preemptive prophylaxis with oral versus I.V. ganciclovir for the prevention of cytomegalovirus disease in liver transplant recipients: A randomized, controlled trial. Transplantation 2000;70:717–722. *Study of the use of preemptive therapy for treatment of CMV infections in solid organ allograft recipients.*

Soderberg Naucler C, Nelson JA. Cytomegalovirus. In Ahmed R, Chen I (eds): Persistent Viral Infections. New York. John Wiley & Sons. 1999. *Monograph providing an up-to-date discussion of the pathogenesis and persistence of human cytomegalovirus.*

371 INFECTIOUS MONONUCLEOSIS: EPSTEIN-BARR VIRUS INFECTION

Elliott D. Kieff

Definition

Infectious mononucleosis (IM) is a clinical syndrome characterized by malaise, headache, fever, pharyngitis, pharyngeal lymphatic hyperplasia, lymphadenopathy, atypical lymphocytosis, heterophile antibody, and transient mild hepatitis. The syndrome occurs most commonly in adolescents and young adults but can occur in older adults or in preadolescent children.

Etiology

Primary infection with the Epstein-Barr herpesvirus (EBV) during adolescence is the usual cause of heterophile-positive IM. Many adolescents and most adults are EBV infected and excrete EBV in their saliva. In primary infection, EBV replicates in oropharyngeal epithelial cells and establishes a nonreplicative, "latent," infection in subepithelial, tonsil, and systemic B lymphocytes, causing their proliferation. EBV infection induces strong natural killer (NK) cell responses followed by uniquely expansive T-cell responses. Most clinical manifestations of IM are due to cytotoxic T-cell eradication of the proliferating EBV-infected B lymphocytes and the associated release of inflammatory cytokines. After several weeks of primary EBV infection, EBV establishes long-term latent infection in nonproliferating B lymphocytes. Reactivation of lytic EBV infection in these latently infected B lymphocytes when they traffic near oropharyngeal surfaces seeds the oropharyngeal epithelium with virus that is amplified through lytic infection of epithelial cells and then excreted in saliva.

Much of the medical significance of EBV derives from the unusual strategy with which EBV establishes latent persistence in normal humans by initially causing massive proliferation of latently infected B lymphocytes. EBV and the closely related Kaposi's sarcoma herpesvirus are a subgroup of potentially oncogenic human herpesviruses. For example, in primary infection, EBV can cause malignant EBV-infected B-cell lymphoproliferative disease (LPD) in immunosuppressed organ transplant recipients, those infected with human immunodeficiency virus (HIV), or genetically susceptible people, who are unable to mount an effective T-cell response to the B-cell proliferative phase of EBV infection. After primary infection, EBV is etiologically implicated in LPD of immunocompromised people, in Burkitt's lymphoma, Reed-Sternberg–positive Hodgkin's disease, some T-cell lymphomas, lymphomatoid granulomatosis, anaplastic nasopharyngeal carcinoma, a small fraction of gastric carcinomas, and leiomyomas of immunocompromised people.

Two EBV types (EBV types I and II) and many closely related strains or variants persist in most human populations. EBV types I and II differ in the primary amino acid sequence of only a few EBV-encoded nuclear proteins that are expressed in latent proliferative B-lymphocyte infection. The nuclear proteins are critical for EBV-driven B-cell proliferation and distinguish EBV from Kaposi's sarcoma herpesvirus.

Epidemiology

EBV infection is usually communicated by direct contact of saliva from a previously infected person with the oropharyngeal epithelium of a nonimmune person. Almost all adults are EBV infected, harbor EBV in various states of latent infection in their B lymphocytes, and frequently excrete EBV in their saliva. Vertical transmission from mother to fetus is rare. Although EBV DNA can be detected in breast milk, neonatal or infant infection from breast milk is unusual and not well documented. After 6 months of age, infant feeding with premasticated food is presumed to account for the high level of asymptomatic early childhood infection in non-Western countries. Spread among young children sharing toys has not been studied. Infection in childhood, adolescence, and young adulthood is usually due to salivary transfer during food sharing or kissing. Virus survival in expectorated saliva is probably brief because infection does not usually spread among susceptible college roommates. The epidemiology of classical IM has been studied at elite American or Western European colleges that are largely populated with students from middle and upper socioeconomic classes, many or most of whom have not been previously EBV infected. In these late adolescents and young adults, the acquisition of primary EBV infection is frequently associated with "deep kissing"; as many as 30 to 50% of the primary infections lead to classical IM.

Although the amount of EBV in saliva is highest during primary infection and for months thereafter, virus replication in the oropharynx persists at a low level for many years, possibly for life. In the course of primary oropharyngeal infection, EBV infects B lymphocytes, initially causes their proliferation, and persists indefinitely in a small fraction of mature B lymphocytes, particularly in tonsils. Transfusion of whole blood, bone marrow, blood fractions, or organs containing viable B lymphocytes to susceptible, nonimmune, people can result in symptomatic primary infection, which may be indistinguishable from IM or from the post-transfusion syndrome related to cytomegalovirus. After bone marrow transplantation, the donor's virus may predominate in the recipient and may emerge as the dominant virus in the oropharynx of the recipient, indicating that a donor bone marrow– or blood-derived cell such as the B lymphocyte is the site of persistent latent infection and the source of virus for continuing infection of the epithelium. EBV has also been found in salivary gland and cervical secretions, indicating that latently infected B lymphocytes can transmit virus to other epithelial tissues. More than 90% of adults in all human populations have serologic evidence of previous primary EBV infection and are carriers of the virus.

Previously infected normal people are almost always immune to the development of significant secondary EBV-related IM. Second

Table 371–1 • CLINICAL MANIFESTATIONS OF INFECTIOUS MONONUCLEOSIS

COMMON MANIFESTATIONS
Splenomegaly (50%)
Vomiting (20%)
Hepatitis (20-50%)
Jaundice (5%)
Palatal petechiae
Rash (4%)
Albuminuria (10%)

LESS FREQUENT MANIFESTATIONS (0.5-1%)
Cough
Pneumonitis
Neck stiffness
Aseptic meningitis
Cerebritis
Cerebellar dysfunction
Mononeuritis or polyneuritis
Transverse myelitis
Guillain-Barré syndrome
Uveitis
Subcapsular splenic hemorrhage or rupture
Myocarditis
Pericarditis
Cardiac conduction abnormalities
Nephrotic syndrome
Renal dysfunction
Diarrhea
Hemolytic anemia with anti-i antibody
Thrombocytopenia
Agranulocytosis
Pancytopenia
Hemophagocytic syndrome

instances of IM related to EBV are rare and may be a harbinger of intermittent or persistent symptomatic EBV infection, rare entities, which can have a familial and presumably genetic basis. Transient or even long-term oropharyngeal carriage with a second, third, or multiple EBV strains is more frequent, particularly in HIV-infected or otherwise immunocompromised people. Sexually active, HIV-infected people are particularly likely to have simultaneous oropharyngeal colonization with several EBV strains or types. Usually, only a single EBV strain predominates in their latently infected peripheral blood B lymphocytes.

EBV type I is dominant in the B-cell compartment of most people in all populations. A significant fraction of people in sub-Saharan Africa have EBV type II instead of type I, whereas type II EBV is rarely found in B lymphocytes elsewhere except among people of African decent. Considering the predominance of EBV type I infection in B lymphocytes of people outside Africa, the frequent oropharyngeal colonization with type II EBV in sexually active HIV-infected people outside Africa is somewhat surprising.

EBV infection is limited to humans. However, closely related viruses are endemic in most Old World and some New World primate species. The primate viruses are so closely related to EBV that infected animals are frequently protected against EBV infection. Cells of some Old World and New World primates are readily EBV infected. Experimental infection of uninfected primates with EBV or their natural EBV-related virus is the only orthologous experimental model for human EBV infection.

Clinical Manifestations

The syndrome of IM was a distinctive clinical entity for at least 40 years before the discovery of EBV. After a 2- to 3-week incubation period, most infected nonimmune adolescents and young adults develop malaise, headache, fever, pharyngitis, and lymphadenopathy lasting from several days to several weeks. Temperatures may reach 40° C, with daily spikes for a week or more. Tonsils or cervical lymph nodes may be quite enlarged, painful, and tender. Laboratory findings include relative or absolute lymphocytosis and a high titer of antibody to horse or ox red blood cells, referred to as a heterophile antibody. Up to 40% of the peripheral lymphocytes may be atypical large cells with unusually abundant cytoplasm and a large pale pleomorphic nucleus. Other common manifestations, which may be the presenting clinical problem, are listed in Table 371–1. Malaise or weakness may recur over several months. Rashes are significantly more common in patients with primary EBV infection receiving penicillin or ampicillin treatment than in untreated patients or patients with other diseases who are treated with penicillin. Almost all normal people recover completely from acute IM within 1 to 4 months. Persistent systemic, hematologic, neurologic, or cardiac abnormalities are rare. Outside adolescent and young adult populations, primary EBV infection less frequently results in the full IM syndrome. In younger children, fever and pharyngitis resulting from primary EBV infection may be clinically indistinguishable from those associated with upper respiratory tract infections caused by other viruses, mycoplasmas, or streptococci.

At any age, inflammation of the cerebrum, cerebellum, or meninges; Guillain-Barré syndrome; pneumonitis; hepatitis; car-ditis; autoimmune hemolytic anemia; thrombocytopenia; or hemophagocytic syndrome may be the predominant clinical manifestation. Atypical lymphocytosis or heterophile antibody may be less prominent or absent.

Severe, progressive, and sometimes fatal primary EBV infections occur in children with X-linked LPD, X-linked lymphoproliferative (XLP) syndrome, or Duncan's syndrome. Non–X-linked, sporadic cases also occur. Although the children with XLP syndrome have no obvious preexisting immune deficiency and respond normally to infection with other herpesviruses, primary EBV infection leads to fulminant hepatic necrosis, acute LPD, anemia, pancytopenia, hypo- or agammaglobulinemia, or other B-cell disorders. Oligoclonal or uniclonal EBV-infected B-cell lymphomas may occur after recovery from severe primary EBV infection in these individuals. Formal molecular genetic analysis of XLP families has led to the identification of a locus that encodes a small protein consisting of little more than a phosphotyrosine binding domain. The protein can modulate phosphotyrosine signaling in T, NK, and B cells. Most likely, disordered T or NK cell responses to the unusual challenge of EBV-driven B-cell proliferation that occurs with primary EBV infection is responsible for the various XLP phenotypes.

Similar, less severe, familial or sporadic, chronic persistent EBV infections occur rarely in otherwise normal adolescents or young adults. These patients may have severe acute mononucleosis that persists with intermittent or sustained episodes of abnormal lymphadenopathy or visceral organ involvement. They frequently have strikingly high antibody titers to EBV antigens; their titers are characteristically at least 10- to 100-fold higher than those in normal persons after primary EBV infection. Some of these patients lack antibody to EBV nuclear antigens. Most patients eventually recover without specific treatment. In one patient, acyclovir treatment produced a clinical remission.

Administration of high-dose cyclosporin or FK-506 as part of immunosuppressive regimens for heart, lung, liver, or bone marrow transplantation and HIV infection has been associated with severe EBV infection and polyclonal LPD. The LPD may involve cervical, abdominal, or gastrointestinal lymphatics. Children or adults with HIV infection are also at risk for severe EBV infection and LPD (Chapter 419). The proliferation of EBV-infected lymphocytes is the usual cause of the central nervous system lymphomas that occur late in the course of acquired immunodeficiency syndrome (AIDS) or in organ transplant recipients. In AIDS patients, EBV replication is implicated in the etiology of oral hairy leukoplakia of the tongue, a proliferative epithelial lesion.

EBV infection has been proposed to be the cause of *chronic fatigue syndrome*. This syndrome is characterized by recurrent episodes of malaise and weakness, sometimes accompanied by report of myalgias, arthralgias, pharyngitis, lymphadenitis, or mild fever. The persistent lack of significant objectively abnormal clinical or laboratory data operationally differentiates the large number of patients with this mostly symptomatically defined clinical syndrome from the few

patients with underlying identifiable infectious, autoimmune, oncologic, metabolic, or neurologic diseases that can occur in patients with chronic fatigue. EBV specific antibody titers in patients with the chronic fatigue syndrome do not differ significantly from those of normal infected adults (see later). Thus, there is little to support the initial hypothesis that EBV is a frequent cause of this syndrome.

Latent EBV infection is associated with B-cell lymphomas in immunosuppressed patients, with Burkitt's lymphoma in African children, with approximately 20% of sporadic Burkitt's lymphoma in developed societies, with about 50% of Hodgkin's disease, with some T-cell lymphomas in adolescents or young adults, and with almost all nasopharyngeal carcinoma. These malignancies are associated with statistically significantly higher titers of EBV antibodies. In many patients, EBV antibody titers have been useful in following treatment or in the detection of recurrent disease. The association with EBV is established by the presence of EBV DNA in every tumor cell. Furthermore, each of these malignancies has usually been found to have the same EBV genome in every tumor cell by using repeat DNA markers of postreplicative EBV genome diversity. Thus, the tumor appears to have evolved from a single EBV-infected cell. EBV gene expression probably provided an initial or an ongoing stimulus for cell proliferation and survival. Malignant conversion to Burkitt's lymphoma, Hodgkin's disease, or nasopharyngeal carcinoma requires additional cellular genetic changes. For example, Burkitt's lymphoma is uniformly characterized by the presence of a reciprocal chromosome translocation between an immunoglobulin and the *c-myc* locus that enhances *c-myc* oncogene expression. In a prospective study of African children, a correlation was noted between children with higher EBV antibody responses in the years after primary infection and tumor occurrence, suggesting that the extent of EBV replication is an important parameter in tumor induction.

In regions of southern China, nasopharyngeal carcinoma is the most common or second most common malignancy. EBV antibody titers have been clinically useful in high-risk ethnic southern Chinese populations to identify individuals who are most likely to develop nasopharyngeal carcinoma over the ensuing years. In retrospective and prospective clinical studies, high levels of immunoglobulin A (IgA) antibody to EBV early or late lytic replication-associated antigens (EA or VCA) have been closely associated with the subsequent diagnosis of nasopharyngeal carcinoma. EBV DNA has usually been uniformly present in each tumor cell. The uniclonality of the virus genomes in these tumor cells indicates that the tumors arise in a single virus-infected cell. EBV is therefore necessary for early oncogenic conversion to nasopharyngeal carcinoma. Given the uniquely high occurrence of nasopharyngeal carcinoma in southern Chinese, Aleuts, North Africans, and other defined populations, genetic factors are likely to be important determinants of tumor incidence. Specific genetic factors have not yet been defined.

EBV is also an etiologic agent in Hodgkin's disease (Chapter 194). EBV DNA is present in about 50% of patients with Hodgkin's disease, with the highest incidence of EBV positivity in younger patients, in Hispanic patients, and in patients with the mixed cellularity or Reed-Sternberg–rich forms of Hodgkin's disease. When present, EBV DNA is in all of the Hodgkin's disease "tumor" cells, and the cells are uniclonal with regard to EBV infection, indicating that infection did not occur after the onset of Hodgkin's disease.

Pathology and Pathogenesis

EBV first infects pharyngeal epithelial cells and then spreads to subepithelial circulating B lymphocytes. The virus carries a gene similar to the human interleukin-10 (IL-10) gene, and the expression of this protein in cells with lytic EBV infection partially blocks the initial interferon, NK, and T-cytotoxic responses. Infection may be confined to epithelial and B-lymphocyte tissues because only these cells have EBV receptors. The B-cell EBV receptor is also the receptor for the C3d fragment of complement. Tonsils and regional and systemic lymph nodes enlarge because of follicular hyperplasia owing in part to virus-infected B lymphocytes and infiltration of sinuses and paracortex with reactive, atypical T lymphocytes. Loss of normal architecture and the presence of Reed-Sternberg–like cells may make EBV infection difficult to distinguish from Hodgkin's disease. Similar changes occur in the spleen. In patients with significant hepatitis, hepatic lobules or portal areas may be infiltrated with mononuclear cells. The bone

marrow is usually unaffected. Early in the illness, 1 to 2% or more of the circulating leukocytes may be EBV-infected B lymphocytes.

At this early stage of primary EBV infection, EBV expresses six nuclear proteins (EBV nuclear antigens [EBNAs]), two integral membrane proteins (latent membrane proteins [LMPs]), and two small RNAs, thereby causing infected B-lymphocyte proliferation from within the infected cell. This type of latency, in which six EBNAs, LMP1 and LMP2, and EBV-encoded RNAs (EBERs) are expressed, is termed latency III. The EBV-encoded nuclear proteins are transactivators of virus and cell gene expression, and four of the nuclear proteins are critical for infected B-cell proliferation. EBV LMP1 is also an activator of cell gene transcription and is essential for survival of proliferating infected cells. One of the EBNAs, LMP2, and the EBERs are not critical for EBV-driven lymphoproliferation in vitro. EBV infection of B lymphocytes stimulates both B-cell proliferation and immunoglobulin, particularly IgM, secretion. Heterophile antibody may be produced by EBV-infected B lymphocytes or may be an effect of B-cell lymphokines produced by EBV-infected or reactive lymphocytes, such as viral and cellular IL-10 and cellular IL-6. In immunosuppressed people after organ transplantation or with HIV infection, EBV latency III infected B lymphocytes can cause an acute LPD.

Latency III EBV infection with B-cell proliferation is a transient phenomenon in primary EBV infection of normal people because of the overwhelming T-cell responses that result in the death of the vast majority of EBV latency III infected B cells. Some of these T lymphocytes suppress both B-lymphocyte proliferation and immunoglobulin secretion. Other peripheral blood T lymphocytes from patients with IM are cytotoxic to autologous EBV-infected B cells. Most cytotoxic T lymphocytes are CD8+ and recognize EBNA or LMP epitopes in the context of class I major histocompatibility complex (MHC). CD4+ T lymphocytes augment the T- and B-lymphocyte immune responses and have also been implicated in cytotoxic responses. The magnitude of the CD8+ T-cell response to primary and persistent EBV infection is larger than that to almost all other infections, probably because of the extent of B-cell infection, the complexity of EBV gene expression in type III latency, and the capacity of B cells to express high levels of class I and II MHC as well as adhesion molecules. In primary EBV infection, as many as 10% of the circulating CD8+ T cells may be committed to an epitope in an EBNA or EBV lytic replication protein. EBV types I and II differ in their EBNA proteins, and some EBNA-specific cytotoxic T lymphocytes recognize an EBNA protein epitope that is specific to EBV type I or II.

After recovery from acute IM, the proportion of circulating EBV-infected B lymphocytes is 1 in 10^5 to 10^6. Most of these lymphocytes express only EBNA1 and EBERs. This is the simplest form of EBV latency in human cells and is known as latency I. EBNA1 is necessary for maintaining the EBV episome in dividing cells but has no effect on cell growth or survival. EBNA1 is not processed through cellular proteasomes, and cells that express EBNA1 are not recognized by immune cytotoxic T lymphocytes. Consequently, latently infected B lymphocytes that express only EBNA1 are likely to be the principal site of long-term EBV persistence. Another piece of evidence for the role of latently infected B cells in EBV reactivation and persistence is that suppression of virus replication in the oropharynx with antiviral chemotherapy blocks virus secretion but does not decrease the number of circulating EBV-infected B lymphocytes. After treatment cessation, EBV rapidly returns to the oropharyngeal epithelium. Also, as noted earlier, after bone marrow transplantation, the donor's rather than the recipient's virus frequently persists in the oropharynx of the recipient.

Long after primary EBV infection, substantial numbers of T lymphocytes, which can suppress or kill cells that express EBNAs and LMPs, continue to circulate in the peripheral blood, indicative of continued expression of these proteins at some sites. Effective immune surveillance remains necessary because immune suppression of EBV-infected people at levels necessary for liver, pancreas, lung, heart, bowel, or bone marrow transplantation or as occurs as a consequence of AIDS is associated with as much as a 10% risk of LPD.

Not all LPD in immunocompromised patients is associated with EBV latency III or even EBV. Analysis of tissue with EBNA- or LMP1-specific antibodies can be used to clarify the role of EBV. Some EBV-associated LPDs that occur after transplantation or in people with HIV or AIDS evolve into or arise as EBV-associated Burkitt's lymphoma and are usually EBV latency I in their phenotype.

Other EBV-associated malignancies that occur long after EBV infection and without overt immune suppression, such as Hodgkin's disease and nasopharyngeal carcinoma, are frequently EBV latency II in their phenotype. EBV latency II is characterized by the expression of EBNA1, LMP1 and LMP2, and EBERs. LMP1 and LMP2 may both contribute to the survival of Hodgkin's disease and nasopharyngeal carcinoma cells.

Diagnosis

In normal adolescents the diagnosis of acute IM can usually be made on clinical grounds and confirmed by the laboratory findings of atypical lymphocytosis and heterophile antibody to ox or horse erythrocytes. Bacterial throat culture should be obtained in patients with significant pharyngitis to exclude concomitant β-hemolytic streptococcal infection. Rapid heterophile tests are more than 95% sensitive and more than 95% specific in an adolescent or young adult population. Titers are substantially diminished by 3 months after primary infection and undetectable by 6 months. In patients with

absent or equivocal heterophile antibodies, EBV-specific serologic testing should be done. Depending on the clinical situation, the differential diagnosis may include HIV; cytomegalovirus; human herpesvirus 6; adenovirus; paramyxovirus; hepatitis B, C, or A; streptococcal or gonococcal pharyngitis; *Toxoplasma* infection; drug reaction; leukemia; lymphoma; and Hodgkin's disease. EBV is also a frequent cause of heterophile-negative IM with pharyngitis. In the absence of pharyngitis or significant heterophile antibody, non-EBV causes need to be considered more seriously at the outset. In some populations of patients, acute HIV infection is a significant cause of typical or atypical IM syndromes. HIV antigen or nucleotide sequence-specific detection may be necessary to diagnose HIV infection early in the illness. Months later, seroconversion may establish the diagnosis.

Specific serologic testing for EBV infection involves determining antibody titers to latently infected (anti-EBNA), early replication cycle (anti-EA), or late replication cycle (anti-VCA) viral proteins (Fig. 371–1). This is usually done by indirect immunofluorescence microscopy or by enzyme-linked immunoassay. Antibodies to EBNA1 tend to appear later than antibodies to EA or VCA (Table 371–2). Serologic diagnosis may be misleading in immunosuppressed patients, including children with X-linked immunodeficiency. These infected children may have high or low antibody titers. EBV serologic studies are helpful in screening for early detection of nasopharyngeal carcinoma in high-risk populations or in observing patients with nasopharyngeal carcinoma for therapeutic response or recurrence. Patients at risk for primary anaplastic nasopharyngeal carcinoma or for

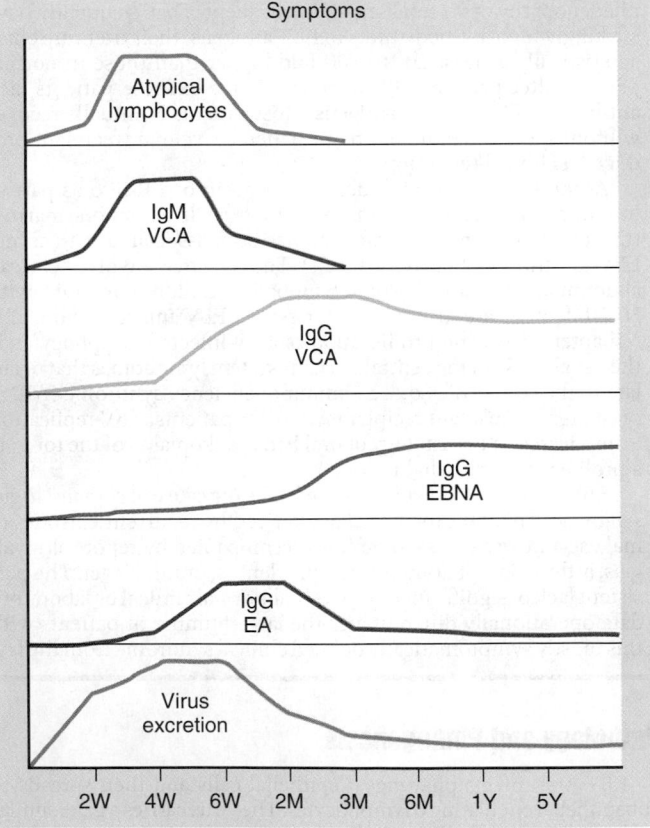

FIGURE 371–1 • The usual incubation period after Epstein-Barr virus (EBV) infection is 10 days to 2 weeks. By the time headache, malaise, and fever develop there are usually a few atypical lymphocytes and the monospot or heterophile test may be slightly positive. By 4 weeks, symptoms, monospot test, atypical lymphocytosis, and immunoglobulin M (IgM) antibody against EBV viral capsid antigen (VCA) are usually at their maximum. They may persist for another 2 to 3 weeks. IgG anti-EBV early antigen (EA) and anti-VCA are frequently detectable at 4 weeks but reach their maximum at 6 to 8 weeks. Anti-EBV nuclear protein (EBNA) IgG is usually not detectable until symptoms begin to resolve. Malaise may persist for 8 to 12 weeks. By 3 months, patients are usually fully recovered. IgG anti-VCA and EBNA titers persist at a high level for many years thereafter. EBV infection in normal humans is persistent but asymptomatic.

Hislop AD, Annels NE, Gudgeon NH, et al: Epitope-specific evolution of human CD8(+) T cell responses from primary to persistent phases of Epstein-Barr virus infection. J Exp Med 2002;195:893–905. *Demonstrates the evolution of phenotypic changes.*
Timms JM, Bell A, Flavell JR, et al: Target cells of Epstein-Barr virus (EBV)-positive post-transplant lymphoproliferative disease: Similarities to EBV-positive Hodgkin's lymphoma. Lancet 2003;361:217–223. *These two types of tumors share a similar pathogenesis.*

Table 371–2 • ANTIBODY TESTS FOR EPSTEIN-BARR VIRUS

TESTS	TITERS
ACUTE PRIMARY INFECTION	
IgM EA and VCA	High
IgG VCA and EBNA	Low
RECOVERING FROM PRIMARY INFECTION	
IgM EA or VCA	Lower
IgG VCA	Rising
EBNA	Low
AFTER SEVERAL MONTHS	
IgM EA and VCA	Low or absent
IgG VCA and EBNA	Persist at high for several years

EA = early antigen; EBNA = Epstein-Barr virus nuclear antigen; IgM = immunoglobulin M; VCA = viral capsid antigen.

recurrences have high IgG or IgA EA antibody titers. EBV specific serology may also be useful in immunosuppressed patients who are a risk for LPD. Previously seronegative patients are at greater risk for LPD than seropositive patients. Rising titers to EBV can be an early indication of LPD in previously seronegative or seropositive patients. However, immunosuppressed patients may not have increasing EBV antibody titers. Monitoring blood for rising EBV DNA levels may provide an early indication of increased risk of LPD.

Rx Treatment

No treatment is necessary for most EBV infections. Rest during the period of acute symptoms and slow return to normal activity are commonly advised, although the therapeutic efficacy of this regimen has not been firmly established. Patients with primary EBV infections and splenomegaly should restrict their involvement in sports to avoid traumatic rupture. Acetaminophen or aspirin may be used to reduce temperature and pharyngeal pain in most patients who have normal or only slightly abnormal liver function. Brief courses of glucocorticoid treatment (e.g., 30–60 mg of prednisone per day for 4 days followed by rapidly decreasing doses) have been effective in shrinking obstructing tonsils or markedly enlarged spleens, probably by ameliorating an overactive T-cell response. Autoimmune hemolytic anemia, granulocytopenia, and thrombocytopenia usually respond to longer courses of glucocorticoid therapy. The use of glucocorticoids for other manifestations of EBV infection is less certain to be beneficial. Glucocorticoids have no antiviral activity and are contraindicated in most herpesvirus infections.

A few patients with severe hemorrhagic thrombocytopenia refractory to glucocorticoids have responded to intravenous immunoglobulin. Early plasmapheresis is indicated in patients with Guillain-Barré syndrome. Acyclovir and its derivatives have activity against EBV in vitro and in vivo at doses that are used for varicella-zoster virus infection but are not approved for use against EBV. Acyclovir is not effective in altering the length or severity of IM, consistent with the prevailing view that IM is primarily a manifestation of the immune response to EBV infection. Acyclovir can be used for AIDS patients with oral hairy leukoplakia or for patients with well-documented chronically progressive EBV infection. Acyclovir has not affected the outcome of EBV-associated LPD in immunosuppressed patients. For LPD, partial restoration of immune function by lowering immune suppression is beneficial. Studies also support the use of anti-B cell antibodies or of autologous, human leukocyte antigen–compatible, EBV-specific T cells.

SUGGESTED READINGS
Bickham K, Munz C, Tsang ML, et al: EBNA1-specific CD4+ T cells in healthy carriers of Epstein-Barr virus are primarily Th1 in function. J Clin Invest 2001;107:121–130. *These cells contribute to resistance to EBV and EBV-associated malignancies.*
Chien YC, Chen JY, Liu MY, et al: Serologic markers of Epstein-Barr virus infection and nasopharyngeal carcinoma in Taiwanese men. N Engl J Med 2001;345:1877–1882. *IgA antibodies against EBV capsid antigen and neutralizing antibodies against EBV-DNase predicted nasopharyngeal carcinoma.*

372 RETROVIRUSES OTHER THAN HIV

William A. Blattner

The discovery of human T-lymphotropic virus type I (HTLV-I) in 1979 by Poiesz and Gallo opened the field of human retrovirology, culminating a search for a human retrovirus dating back to the turn of the 20th century. HTLV-I has been linked causally to adult T-cell leukemia/lymphoma (ATL) and to several chronic degenerative conditions, most notably HTLV-I–associated myelopathy/tropical spastic paraparesis (HAM/TSP). The techniques employed to isolate and characterize HTLV-I provided the intellectual and technical basis for the discovery of the human immunodeficiency virus (HIV), the etiologic agent of acquired immunodeficiency syndrome (AIDS). This chapter focuses on the virologic, epidemiologic, and clinical correlates of the HTLV class of viruses; it reviews the distribution of HTLV-I and HTLV-II and presents the known and possible disease associations and summarizes treatment approaches (see also Chapter 191 concerning cancer chemotherapy).

Virology

The HTLV viruses are classified in the taxa of DNA and RNA reverse-transcribing viruses within the subfamily Retroviridae in the genus *Deltaretrovirus*. They are single-stranded RNA viruses that contain a diploid genome which replicates through a DNA intermediary that integrates into the genome of the target T cell as a provirus, resulting in lifelong infection. HTLV-I is approximately 100 nm in diameter with a thin, electron-dense outer envelope and an electron-dense, roughly spherical core. The genomic structure of HTLV-I is shown in Figure 372–1. The total provirus genome contains 9032 nucleotides with two identical sequences termed *long terminal repeats* (LTRs) at the 5′ and 3′ ends of the genome, which contain regulatory elements that control virus expression and virion production. Retroviral structural genes generally code for large overlapping polyproteins that are later processed into functional peptide products by virally encoded protease and cellular proteases. The encoding genes of the virus are *gag* (group-specific antigen), *pol* (polymerase/integrase/protease), *env* (envelope), and a series of regulatory genes, *tax* and *rex*, that regulate virus expression. The Gag proteins function as structural proteins of the matrix, capsid, and nucleocapsid. The *pol* gene encodes for several enzymes—reverse transcriptase (involved in RNA to DNA transcription), endonuclease (ribonuclease-H), protease (overlapping *gag* and *pol*), and integrase, which functions for viral integration. The *env* gene encodes the major components of the viral coat: the surface

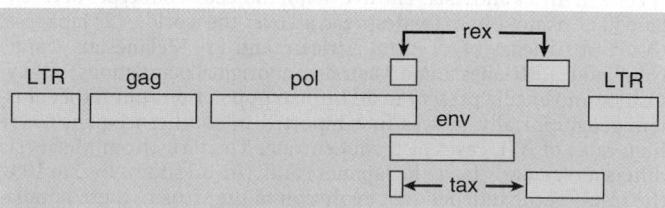

FIGURE 372–1 • Genomic structure of human T-lymphotropic viruses. LTR = long terminal repeat, which is organized into three regions—U5, R, and U3—that house the polyadenylation site; and the rev = response element, and the transactivating response element, which are involved in controlling virus expression. *env* = envelope gene; *gag* = group-specific antigen, whose products form the skeleton of the virion (matrix, capsid, nucleocapsid, nucleic acid–binding protein); *pol* = gene for reverse transcriptase, integrase, and protease; *rex* = viral regulatory gene involved in promoting genomic RNA production; *tax* = transactivator gene. (Courtesy of Dr. Robert C. Gallo.)

Infectious Diseases

glycoprotein (gp) of 46,000 molecular weight (MW) (gp46) and the transmembrane 21,000 MW (gp21). The pX region expresses Tax, a viral regulatory protein that enhances transcription of viral and cellular gene products by modifying the clearance of the $p53$ suppressor gene and through stimulation of the nuclear factor (NF)-$\kappa\beta$ pathway, pathogenic mechanisms thought to play a crucial role in leukemogenesis. Rex (regulator of expression of virion proteins for HTLV) modulates the pattern of viral RNA production and transport of virion components in the production of virus particles. Another open reading frame from the pX region, ORF I codes for p12^{I}, a viral protein that targets cellular pathways involved in T-cell proliferation through the STAT5 pathway, thus contributing along with Tax to T-cell activation. p12^{I} also interferes with trafficking of the heavy chain of MHC I to the cell surface of T cells, thus contributing to persistence of infected cells by blocking immune recognition. ORF II, p30^{II} functions in the cell cycle to abrogate p53 suppressor cell function as well as other cell cycle regulators. The function of these accessory and regulatory genes is thought to play a key role in disease pathogenesis.

The initial step in the life cycle of HTLV is attachment of the virus envelope glycoprotein to an unknown cell surface receptor. Recent data suggest that postattachment interactions between virus and target cell result in preferential infection of CD4 T-helper cells for HTLV-I, and both CD4 and CD8 cells for HTLV-II. Following uptake and uncoating, viral RNA is transcribed by *reverse transcriptase,* an RNA-dependent DNA polymerase complexed to the RNA in the core of the virus particle into double-stranded DNA. This double-stranded viral DNA is integrated into the host cell nucleus by the virally encoded integrase, resulting in lifelong cell infection.

The viral LTR elements are essential to the integration and regulation of viral genome expression. They form the sites for covalent attachment of the provirus to cellular DNA and contain important regulatory elements such as the U3 region, where viral Tax exerts its upregulatory effects through interactions with the AFT/CREB family of DNA-binding proteins whose active complexes are enhanced by a stabilizing effect of Tax. The virus may remain "hidden" (unexpressed, not replicated) in cells for long periods. This may contribute to the long interval (sometimes many years to decades) between the time of infection and disease.

HTLV-I and -II are routinely detected through blood bank screening assays and confirmed by Western blotting. The current generation of assays uses whole-virus lysates and recombinant viral antigens to ensure sensitivity for detecting both HTLV-I and -II and for distinguishing these subtypes. Polymerase chain reaction (PCR) is another technique that is useful in research settings for detecting and distinguishing virus type and, more recently, in quantifying cell-associated virus as a marker in disease.

Distribution of HTLV

The number of persons worldwide infected with HTLV-I is estimated to be 10 million; among these, 2 to 3% develop an aggressive T-cell malignancy ATL, and another 2 to 3% chronic inflammatory diseases, mainly HAM/TSP, in their lifetime. Similar to HIV, HTLV-I is thought to have entered humans through contact with primate retroviruses (STLV) that have been isolated from several Old World primate species in Africa and Asia. The five major molecular subtypes of HTLV-I are (1) Cosmopolitan (widespread all over the world), (2) Japanese, (3) West African, (4) Central African, and (5) Melanesian (Papua New Guinea, Melanesia, and Australian aboriginal populations). HTLV-I is not universally present in all human populations but rather clusters geographically, as was first reported in southern Japan, where high rates of ATL cases also concentrate. The virus from Melanesia differs molecularly from the Japanese and African strains by 5 to 10%, the result of the independent evolution of the virus in these populations separated for tens of thousands of years. A concentration of HTLV-I in northeastern Iran may have resulted from the cross-cultural migrations occurring along the trade routes from the Far East to the Middle East and Europe. HTLV-II is found among Native American people throughout North, Central, and South America. An Asian focus of HTLV-II in remote areas of Mongolia is found among people who share genetic links with Native American populations, whose ancestors emigrated from this region during the Ice Age. HTLV-II has also been detected in Africa, mainly in West Africa. Most infections in the United States and Europe occur among injection drug

users, where the virus is spread by needle sharing and other injection practices.

Routes of Transmission

Table 372–1 summarizes the routes, cofactors, and viral characteristics associated with HTLV-I transmission; the basic modes of transmission for HTLV-I and HIV-1 are similar.

SEXUAL TRANSMISSION. Sexual transmission of HTLV-I from male to female and female to male as well as from male to male has been documented. HTLV-I transmission is cell-associated and appears to be at least an order of magnitude less infectious than HIV-1. Coincidental infection with other sexually transmitted diseases, particularly those associated with ulcerative genital lesions in men and inflammatory lesions in women, amplify the risk of transmission. For HTLV-I, elevated antibody titer, which appears to correlate with elevated virus load, is linked to heightened transmission. In viral endemic regions there is a characteristic age-dependent rise in HTLV-I seroprevalence. This increase first becomes evident in the adolescent years; it is steeper in women than in men and continues in women after age 40, whereas rates in men plateau around age 40. This pattern reflects more efficient male-to-female transmission. For HTLV-II the pattern differs; here, the rates for both genders are equal. This finding suggests that there may be differences between the two viruses in the kinetics of transmission.

PERINATAL TRANSMISSION. The second major route of transmission is from mother to child. For HTLV-I, transmission through breast feeding is more efficient than in utero or perinatal transmission. On average, 20% of infants breast-fed by HTLV-I–positive mothers seroconvert to HTLV-I, whereas only 1 to 2% of bottle-fed infants of HTLV-I–positive mothers become infected. In this regard HTLV-I differs significantly from HIV-1; in utero and perinatal transmission accounts for virtually all HIV-1 transmission in the West, whereas breast feeding accounts for 15% of infant infection in Africa. HTLV-II has been detected in breast milk and, similar to HTLV-I, accounts for many childhood infections.

TRANSFUSION AND INJECTION DRUG USE. Parenteral transmission either through transfusion or injection drug use is a major source of HTLV infection. Among blood donors in the United States, more than half of the HTLV infections are due to HTLV-II. Among injection drug users the vast majority of infections are due to HTLV-II; it is projected that HTLV-II is more efficiently transmitted by this route than is HTLV-I.

Prospective studies of transfusion transmission indicate that both HTLV-I and -II are transmitted in association with cellular components. This is in sharp contrast to HIV-1, which is transmitted by cells, plasma, or plasma products. Approximately one half of the recipients of HTLV-I/II–positive blood seroconvert; the percentage for HIV-1 is greater than 95%.

Table 372–1 • **TRANSMISSION OF HTLV-I AND HTLV-II**		
MODES OF TRANSMISSION	**HTLV-I**	**HTLV-II**
Mother to infant		
Transplacental	Yes	Not known
Breast milk	Yes	Probable
Sexual		
Male to female	Yes	Yes
Female to male	Yes	Yes
Male to male	Yes	Not known
Parenteral		
Blood transfusion	Yes	Yes
Intravenous drug use	Yes	Yes
Cofactors		
Elevated virus load		
Mother to infant	Yes	Not known
Heterosexual	Yes	Not known
Ulcerative genital lesions	Yes	Not known
Cellular transfusion products	Yes	Yes
Sharing of "works"*	Yes	Yes

*Intravenous paraphernalia, e.g., needles.
HTLV-I/II = human T-lymphotropic virus type I, II.

The only documented illness linked to HTLV-I or -II transfusion transmission is the HTLV-associated demyelinating neurologic syndrome, HAM/TSP. Leukemia has not been associated with transfusion of HTLV-positive blood. Among U.S. blood donors who are confirmed HTLV positive in the United States (slightly less than half are HTLV-I and the others are HTLV-II), the major risk factors are intravenous drug use, birthplace in a viral endemic area in the Caribbean or Japan, or sexual contact with a person with this profile.

Coinfection with HTLV-I and HIV-1 appears to increase the progression to AIDS through unexplained mechanisms, possibly related to the cell-proliferative effects of HTLV-I on HIV-1–infected T cells. Such a relationship has not been shown for HTLV-II. Other modes of transmission involving "casual contact," mosquito vector transmission, and so on are not a source of infection. Health care and laboratory workers who experience a needle stick, skin, or mucous membrane exposure in the absence of protective barriers have little or no risk for infection; a single case of such infection has been documented following exposure to a "microtransfusion" from a syringe.

HTLV-ASSOCIATED DISEASES

ADULT T-CELL LEUKEMIA/LYMPHOMA

HTLV-I–associated diseases are listed in Table 372–2. The most common malignancy caused by HTLV-I is ATL: a form of peripheral T-cell lymphoma, often with spread in the peripheral blood. The subtypes of ATL (acute, chronic, smoldering, and lymphoma) have different clinical features and prognoses (Fig. 372–2). These tumors represent high-grade lymphomas, usually of large, medium, and/or

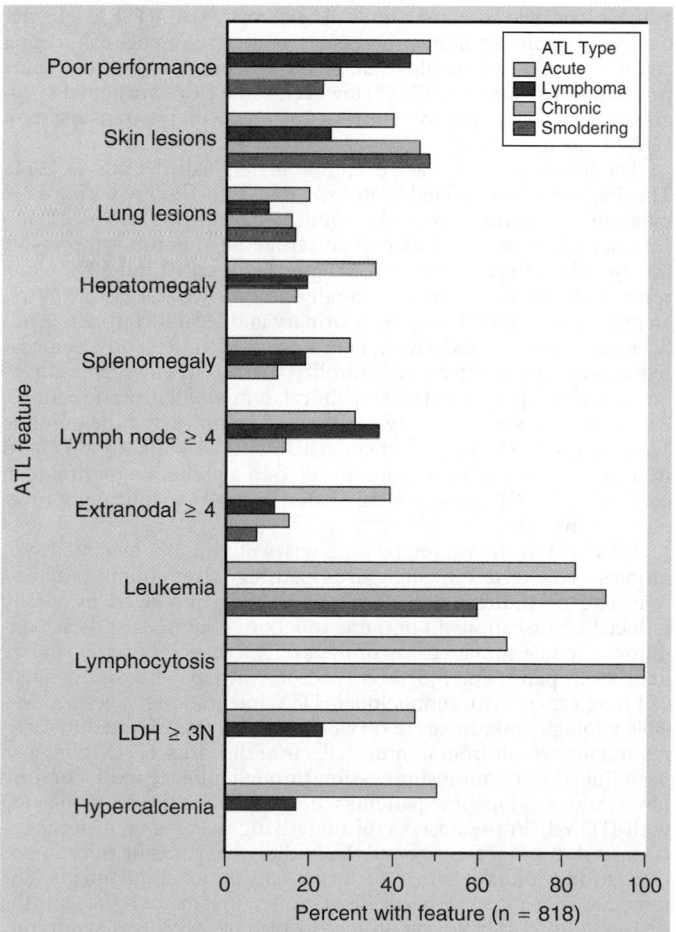

FIGURE 372–2 • Features of adult T-cell leukemia/lymphoma (ATL) in Japan. A combination of clinical and laboratory features is involved in defining the various subtypes of ATL (see text for details). LDH = lactate dehydrogenase. (From Blattner W: Human T-cell lymphotropic viruses and cancer causation. *In* Devita VT, Hellman S, Rosenberg SA [eds]: Cancer Prevention, Update. Philadelphia, JB Lippincott, 1993, p 1.)

Table 372–2 • HTLV-ASSOCIATED DISEASES

DIAGNOSIS	NATURE OF SYNDROME	STRENGTH OF ASSOCIATION
HTLV-I–Associated Diseases		
Adult T-cell leukemia/lymphoma	Aggressive lymphoproliferative malignancy of mature T lymphocytes	Strong
B-cell chronic lymphocytic leukemia	Tumor-associated immunoglobulin reacts to HTLV antigen	Two cases reported
HTLV-associated myelopathy/tropical spastic paraparesis (HAM/TSP)	Chronic progressive demyelinating syndrome of long motor tracks of spinal cord	Strong
Polymyositis	Degenerative inflammatory syndrome of skeletal muscles	Probable
Infective dermatitis	Chronic generalized eczema of skin in children; potential for preleukemia and immunodeficiency	Strong
Uveitis	Inflammatory infiltration of the uvea of the eye	Strong
HTLV-associated arthritis	Large-joint polyarthropathy; rheumatoid factor positive with HTLV-I–positive cells infiltrating the synovia	Probable
Immunodeficiency	Anecdotal reports of AIDS-like illness in HTLV-I positive patients; subclinical (e.g., decreased PPD response) or clinical (e.g., poor response to therapy for symptomatic strongyloidiasis)	Possible
Miscellaneous clinical conditions	Case reports or case series of Sjögren's syndrome, interstitial pneumonitis, small cell lung cancer with monoclonal HTLV-I integration, and invasive cervical cancer	Uncertain
HTLV-II–Associated Diseases		
T-hairy cell/large granulocytic leukemia	Case reports of T-cell/NK-cell malignancy with either monoclonal or polyclonal integration	Possible
HTLV-associated myelopathy	Increased numbers of cases among blood donors	Definite but rare

AIDS = acquired immunodeficiency syndrome; HTLV-I/II = human T-lymphotropic virus type I, II; NK = natural killer; PPD = purified protein derivative.

pleiotropic morphology and advanced clinical stage and are associated with a poor prognosis.

The incidence of ATL is approximately 1 per 1000 carriers per year, and thus the number of cases varies by the underlying prevalence of infection. Among the approximately 10 million infected persons worldwide, there are approximately 2500 to 3000 cases per year. In the United States, with a low prevalence of infection, it is estimated that there are approximately 30 cases per year. In HTLV-I endemic areas such as southern Japan and the Caribbean Islands, ATL accounts for half or more of adult lymphoid malignancies. The chance of an infected individual developing a malignancy over a lifetime is approximately 3 to 5%; studies of mothers of ATL cases emphasize that early life exposure is associated with the greatest risk for subsequent disease.

The age group of cases ranges from adolescence to a peak in middle-aged (40s in the Caribbean and 50s in Japan) adults. The diagnosis should be considered in an adult with mature T-cell lymphoma and hypercalcemia and/or cutaneous involvement, particularly if the individual is from a known risk group or endemic region. The diagnosis is established by testing serum for HTLV-I antibodies. Occasionally cases are antibody negative but provirus is detectable in the blood or in biopsy specimens.

The acute form of ATL is characterized by an aggressive, mature T-cell lymphoma whose clinical course is often associated with high white blood cell count, hypercalcemia, and cutaneous involvement. Other cases resemble T-prolymphocytic leukemia and are termed *chronic ATL*. Smoldering ATL may clinically resemble mycosis fungoides/Sézary syndrome, with cutaneous involvement presenting as erythema or as infiltrative plaques or tumors. Sometimes a long prodrome of signs (e.g., cutaneous rashes) and symptoms (e.g., fevers) are noted before transformation to an acute, rapidly fatal form of disease occurs. In addition to differences in clinical presentation, the different forms of ATL—acute, chronic and smoldering—have distinctive morphologic features. A particularly distinctive morphology includes the so-called flower cells, which represent a sine qua non of HTLV-I associated leukemia. Interestingly, cells with this morphology are also seen in healthy carriers. Sometimes ATL presents as a T-cell non-Hodgkin's lymphoma with many of the signs and symptoms of acute ATL, such as hypercalcemia and monoclonal integration of HTLV-I proviral DNA in the tumor cells, but without the characteristic peripheral blood involvement of acute ATL. Patients with acute and lymphoma-type ATL have a poor prognosis, especially when hypercalcemia is present, and death within 6 months of diagnosis is common. The cause of death is usually an explosive growth of tumor cells, hypercalcemia, and various opportunistic infections, including *Pneumocystis* pneumonia and other infections observed in AIDS patients.

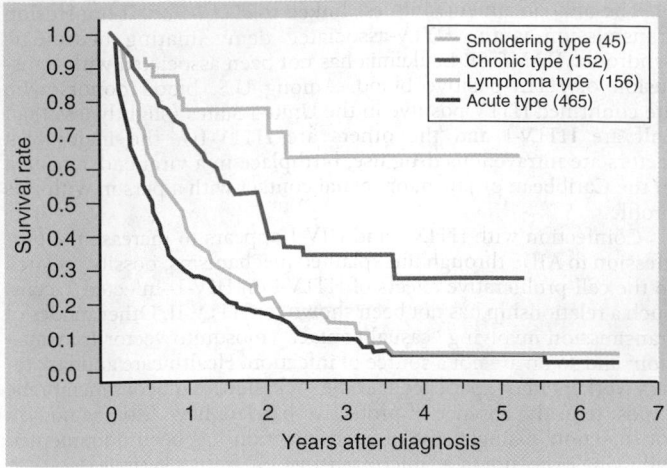

FIGURE 372–3 • Survival by adult T-cell leukemia/lymphoma (ATL) subtype after polychemotherapy in Japan. Poorest survival is observed in patients with acute and lymphoma-type ATL. (From Tsukasaki K, Ikeda S, Murata K, et al: Characteristics of chemotherapy-induced clinical remission in long survivors with aggressive adult T-cell leukemia/lymphoma. Leuk Res 1993;17:157–166.)

Rx Treatment

ATL has proven refractory to most conventional and experimental chemotherapeutic regimens (Fig. 372–3). Patients with chronic and smoldering ATL are generally monitored for progression to a more aggressive type. Treatment with prednisone, with or without cyclophosphamide, has not been proven effective but may provide a benefit in some patients. However, it is well established that when patients with these more indolent forms of ATL are treated with aggressive therapy, they experience a high rate of complicating infections due to the damaging effects of therapy on the bone marrow. The acute and lymphoma types of ATL should be managed as aggressive high-grade lymphomas. As such they generally have a poor prognosis, but some cases do respond with prolonged remission to multidrug regimens. Among Japanese patients, a variety of multidrug regimens such as VEPA or VEPA-M (vincristine, cyclophosphamide, prednisolone, and doxorubicin, plus or minus methotrexate) and other complex 9- and 10-drug regimens achieve initial complete (20%) and partial remissions (50%). However, these are generally of short duration, and long-term survival is poor. Approximately 15% of such cases experience prolonged remissions (>2 years), predicted by initial complete remission and total doxorubicin dose administered. Prognostic factors include poor performance status at diagnosis, age older than 40 years, extensive disease, hypercalcemia, and high serum lactate dehydrogenase level. Relapses often occur in the central nervous system (CNS) and are refractory to subsequent therapy.

Experimental approaches that use monoclonal antibodies to interleukin-2 receptor (IL-2R) linked with cell toxins selectively targeted to the leukemic cells are being tested, with some evidence of at least partial responses. A number of small phase I trials using a combination of zidovudine and interferon have resulted in remission in some cases, sometimes with prolonged remission, and an initial trial with this regimen may be indicated prior to attempting more cytotoxic multidrug regimens. The mechanism of action of this therapy is not understood since the regimen does not induce direct cytotoxic killing of the leukemia cells, nor does it counteract viral-specific pathways of leukemogenesis. Allogeneic bone marrow transplantation and autologous stem cell transplants are being employed for high-grade T-cell lymphomas and have shown similar success in the context of ATL.

HTLV-ASSOCIATED MYELOPATHY/TROPICAL SPASTIC PARAPARESIS

HTLV-I is linked to a neurologic syndrome known as *HAM/TSP*. This disease is characterized by a chronic, slowly progressive devel-

opment of spastic paraparesis resulting from the demyelination of the long motor neurons of the spinal cord. Symptoms often begin with a stiff gait, progressing (usually slowly) to increasing spasticity and weakness, with incontinence and impotence developing later in the course of the illness. Sometimes ataxia develops. In some cases, isolated lesions of the CNS are detected on a nuclear magnetic resonance scan. In contrast to classic multiple sclerosis, HAM/TSP is characterized by a generally slow, progressive course, the absence of a waxing and waning symptomatology, and demyelination of the long motor neurons rather than the CNS. However, some cases are acutely progressive; such cases are sometimes associated with the transfusion of HTLV-I–positive blood.

The incidence of disease is approximately half the rate for ATL. The diagnosis is suspected in unexplained CNS disease with loss of pyramidal tract functions and is confirmed by testing sera for HTLV-I antibodies. Treatment with corticosteroids and immunosuppressive therapies benefit some patients, ranging between 30 and 50% in one series, particularly those with rapidly progressive disease. Danazol, an androgenic steroid, improves urinary and fecal incontinence but does not affect the underlying neurologic deficit. Recently, pentoxifylline was reported in an uncontrolled trial to have favorable effects on clinical symptoms and on subclinical immunologic perturbations. Based on the association between the IL-2 complex and the immune activation in HAM/TSP, a humanized anti-IL-2R antibody was used in treatment of seven cases and resulted in a reduction of viral load confirmed by PCR, clinical stabilization in six, and clinical improvement in one case.

HAM/TSP is the prototype for a series of immune-mediated syndromes characterized by high virus load, significant immune activation, and an indirect pathogenic mechanism produced by virally induced perturbations in immune function. Examples of these conditions include polymyositis of the skeletal muscle, uveitis, a large joint arthropathy, and Sjögren's syndrome. A Japanese case of small cell lung cancer with monoclonal HTLV integration suggests a possible etiologic link. Invasive cervical cancer is also elevated in carriers and may result from immune effects of the virus. HTLV-I has also been linked to immunosuppression through clinical and laboratory observations of Japanese patients with AIDS-like illnesses associated with HTLV-I (in the absence of underlying malignancy), perturbations in skin test reactivity, and the finding that parasitic infestations (e.g., strongyloidiasis) are refractory to conventional treatments. The infective dermatitis syndrome first reported in Jamaica represents the first childhood HTLV-I syndrome. In patients with this syndrome, refractory bacterial infections develop with saprophytic skin organisms, which respond to antibiotic therapy but relapse when therapy is stopped. It is hypothesized that these symptoms result from immunosuppressive effects of HTLV-I. Long-term follow-up of some patients have documented the subsequent development of ATL and HAM/TSP in patients originally diagnosed with infective dermatitis.

HTLV-II

HTLV-II continues to be an "orphan" virus with no true disease association. Although HTLV-II was originally isolated from a patient with hairy T-cell leukemia, which on reanalysis was thought to represent large granulocytic cell leukemia, a malignancy with a natural killer cell phenotype, there has been no consistent evidence of an association of HTLV-II with this or any lymphoid malignancy.

More than a dozen HAM/TSP cases associated with HTLV-II have been reported. In some instances the clinical pattern had features of the ataxic form, but most had the more typical spastic paraparesis. Preliminary data suggest that this syndrome is infrequent compared to its occurrence in HTLV-I carriers.

HTLV Disease Pathogenesis

A great deal has been learned about the pathogenesis of HTLV-I–associated leukemia. Early in infection, HTLV-I infects only a small number of T lymphocytes and probably the monocyte/macrophage. The DNA provirus randomly integrates into the DNA of infected cells. Although HTLV-I may exist as a latent virus, the virus genes promote cell proliferation by direct and indirect mechanisms, including various lymphokine and cell regulatory pathways. In particular, Tax directly binds to essential elements of the NF-$\kappa\beta$ pathway, which plays a central role in controlling cellular transcription and immune activation pathways. In this way, Tax promotes the expression of additional activated target cells and thereby amplifies virus spread. Viral genes are reported to modify the clearance of the *p53* suppressor gene and, via Tax, stimulate the NF-$\kappa\beta$ pathway. In addition, ORF I, p12^I targets cellular pathways involved in T-cell proliferation through the STAT5 pathway, contributing along with Tax to T-cell activation. p12^I also interferes with trafficking of the heavy chain of MHC I to the cell surface of T cells, thus contributing to the persistence of infected cells by blocking immune recognition. ORF II, p30^{II} functions in the cell cycle to abrogate *p53* suppressor cell function as well as other cell cycle regulators. The function of these accessory and regulatory genes is thought to play a key role in disease pathogenesis. Immunosuppressive events may also play a role, since transforming growth factor-β is upregulated in ATL. The explanation for why only a small percentage of infected individuals develop malignancy (3 to 5% lifetime risk), why the latency from infection to disease is so prolonged, and why CD4 cells are selectively transformed (although CD8 cells can also be infected) remains unknown. Early in the infection phase, host immune responses to the virus are activated, producing viral antibodies and cytotoxic T lymphocytes (CTLs) targeted at viral antigens. In particular, CTLs targeted at viral antigens play an essential role in the regulation of viral expression, as suggested by the finding that up to 1% of CD8+ CTLs recognize at least one epitope of the HTLV virus. In particular the CTL response to Tax suggests that this is an important target of the cell-mediated immune response. As a consequence of ongoing viral-associated Tax proliferation, there is a cell-associated expansion of HTLV-I genome containing CD4+ cells, and a compensatory expansion of CD8+ CTL. As CD4 cells containing the HTLV-I genome expand, HTLV-I antigens are expressed on the cell surface and become targets for CD8-mediated cytotoxic killing. The blunting of cell-mediated immune responses by virally induced immunosuppression may dampen the host capacity to clear virus infection and contribute to pathogenesis of ATL and other associated diseases.

In some cases persons with documented exposure (e.g., via blood transfusion) do not seroconvert, but some express cell-mediated responses that are thought to represent an immune response involved in clearance of infection. Some healthy carriers develop T-cell polyclonal and oligoclonal proliferations that can later progress to malignancy or may disappear spontaneously. Morphologically distinct flower cells, representing T cells with deeply lobulated nuclei resembling ATL leukemic cells, are seen on peripheral blood smears of healthy carriers but do not presage risk for subsequent disease. In ATL, the HTLV-I provirus is found integrated in the DNA of the leukemic cells in a clonal fashion with one (or occasionally two) copy of the provirus integrated in the same chromosomal location in each cell. This would indicate that ATL is tumor derived from a single transformed cell that sprouted from a virus infection before transformation and clonal expansion rather than afterward as a passenger virus. Tumors from different patients have proviral integration in different locations. This

indicates that *cis*-activation of a nearby cellular gene by the LTR of the virus, as occurs with some animal leukemia viruses, is not the mechanism for transformation in ATL. However, the tumor cells of ATL patients do not have detectable actively replicating virus, suggesting that HTLV-I is not actively involved in maintaining the leukemic state but rather in promoting transformation.

The latent period for this process is years to several decades; it involves an interaction between viral expression and oncogenic mutations. For example, recent studies have identified abnormalities in the clearance of the *p53* suppressor gene in HTLV-I infected cells; other studies demonstrate the binding of viral *tax* to a receptor on NF-$\kappa\beta$. Other cell-suppressive pathways are also perturbed by HTLV-I Tax. Immunosuppressive events may also play a role because the tumor necrosis factor-β is turned on in ATL. Evidence is growing that at some stage, transformation involves the expression of the Tax protein encoded by the *px* gene of HTLV-I. Because the Tax protein induces expression of cellular genes critical for T-cell proliferation, including IL-2 and IL-2R, an autocrine mechanism may be involved, particularly in the first steps of leukemogenesis, which involves polyclonal expansions of T cells. For malignancy to develop, additional genetic changes most probably take place (e.g., cytogenetic changes, oncogene alterations). Because *tax* gene expression is detectable in tumor samples, even in some cases of antibody-negative ATL, this viral gene may be crucial in oncogenesis. However, the *tax* gene is not widely expressed in the tumor cells.

HAM/TSP occurs with a latency from infection to disease of months to years, which contrasts with the years-to-decades incubation for ATL. Current data suggest an indirect mechanism of pathogenesis involving immune-mediated responses that appear to cause local damage in the myelin sheath of the long motor neuron.

Prevention

A major issue confronting practicing physicians is what to tell patients identified as HTLV positive based on blood bank screening. First and foremost, they must emphasize that disease complications related to HTLV-I are rare and that for HTLV-II no specific disease has been verified. Second, it should be emphasized that the viruses are not easily transmitted. Third, the patient should be clearly counseled concerning the distinction between the HTLV and the HIV viruses because the greatest fear the patient may have is that he or she has the "AIDS virus." Guidelines for prevention and counseling have been developed for HTLV-I and -II by a Centers for Disease Control and Prevention Working Group:

1. Blood for donation should be screened prior to transfusion, and positive donors should be deferred from donating.
2. HTLV-I/II–positive mothers should be discouraged from breast feeding when practicable to prevent mother-to-infant transmission (except in particular settings, such as in the tropics, where diarrheal disease in non–breast-fed infants presents a high risk for morbidity and mortality).
3. Condoms should be used by discordant couples, but, given the relatively low frequency of sexual transmission per sexual encounter, couples who desire a pregnancy could time unprotected sexual intercourse to coincide with periods of maximal fertility. (Such decisions require careful discussion between physician and patient; there are no absolute guidelines in this area.)

Vaccines containing whole virus and recombinant HTLV-I envelope antigens have successfully prevented HTLV-I infection in monkeys and in a rabbit model; however, a vaccine for humans is unlikely to ever be developed for disease prevention owing to the relatively low incidence of disease.

SUGGESTED READINGS

Bazarbachi A, Hermine O: Treatment of adult T-cell leukemia/lymphoma: Current strategy and future perspectives. Virus Res 2001;78:79–92. *Provides an up-to-date perspective on current treatment options and management strategies.*

Blattner WA: Human T-lymphotropic viruses: HTLV-1 and HTLV-2. *In* Richmann DD, Whitley RJ, Hayden FG (eds): Clinical Virology. Washington DC: ASM Press, 2002, pp 659–685. *An in-depth review of HTLV epidemiology, clinical disease, and treatment.*

Centers for Disease Control and Prevention, U.S. Public Health Service Working Group: Guidelines for counseling persons infected with human T-lymphotropic virus type I (HTLV-I) and type II (HTLV-II). Ann Intern Med 1993;118:448–454. *Presents impor-*

tant information to clinicians confronted with counseling persons referred with HTLV infection.

Knipe DM, Howley PM, Griffin DE, et al (eds): Fields Virology. Philadelphia, Lippincott Williams & Wilkins, 2001. *Provides a detailed review of molecular virology of human retroviruses and HTLV.*

Maloney EM, Blattner WA: HTLV-1 Worldwide Patterns and Disease Associations. Gann Monogr Cancer Res 2003;50:339–361. In Uchiyama T, Matsuoka M, Kannagi M (eds): 2 decades of adult T-cell leukemia and HTLV-1 research. Japan Scientific Societies Press and Karger. *Progress in basic research and its implications in clinical advances.*

373 ENTEROVIRUSES

Michael N. Oxman

Definitions

Enteroviruses, so named because they generally infect the alimentary tract and are shed in the feces, cause a variety of diseases in humans and lower animals. They comprise one of the six major subgroups, or genera of the *Picornaviridae* (the Picornavirus [*pico*, small; *rna*, ribonucleic acid] family). The other Picornavirus genera are: *Rhinoviruses*, which inhabit the upper respiratory tract and include the principal recognized etiologic agents of the common cold (see Chapter 359); *Cardioviruses*, recovered chiefly from rodents and only very rarely implicated in human disease; *Aphthoviruses*, named for the vesicular lesions that they produce in cloven-footed animals; and two newly designated genera, *Hepatovirus*, a genus with human hepatitis A virus as its only currently recognized member, and *Parechovirus*, which contains two serotypes that were previously classified as *echoviruses* types 22 and 23.

Enteroviruses are differentiated from rhinoviruses primarily by their resistance to acid; they are fully infectious at pH 3 or even lower. Consequently, enteroviruses that have undergone limited replication in the oropharynx survive passage through the stomach and implant in the lower intestinal tract, where they undergo more extensive multiplication. In contrast, rhinoviruses are acid labile; they begin to lose infectivity at pH 6 and are completely inactivated at pH 3. They are further distinguished from enteroviruses by their lower optimal temperature of replication (33° versus 37° C for enteroviruses) and higher buoyant density in cesium chloride. Because rhinoviruses inhabit the nasopharynx, they have no obvious need for acid stability, and preferential replication at lower than body temperature probably reflects their adaptation to the cooler nasal passages.

Hepatitis A virus was originally classified as an enterovirus and designated enterovirus 72. However, it is more resistant to inactivation by heat than enteroviruses, and its genome has relatively little nucleotide sequence homology with members of the enterovirus genus. In contrast to enteroviruses, hepatitis A virus does not cause a rapid shut-off of host cell protein synthesis, and the infected cells are not lysed. Because of these important differences, hepatitis A virus has been accorded its own genus, Hepatovirus, within the Picornavirus family. Hepatitis A virus is discussed in Chapter 151.

Within the Enterovirus genus, species are distinguished immunologically by the ability of specific antisera to neutralize only the homotypic virus. There are 65 recognized human enterovirus species (i.e., serotypes or immunotypes), as well as numerous enteroviruses of lower animals. Humans appear to be the only natural host for the human enteroviruses, and in general, the enteroviruses of lower animals are not natural pathogens for humans.

Historically, human enteroviruses have been subclassified into *Polioviruses*, group A and group B *Coxsackieviruses*, and *Echoviruses* on the basis of antigenic relationships, differences in host range, and types of disease produced (Table 373–1). By 1969, 67 species (serotypes) of human enteroviruses had been identified and classified according to these criteria, although reclassification and redundancy have reduced this number to 61. The distinguishing characteristics of these enterovirus subgroups are outlined here.

POLIOVIRUSES. The first human enteroviruses to be recognized, polioviruses, produce characteristic lesions when inoculated into the central nervous system (CNS) of primates. Clinical isolates replicate only in primates and in primate cell cultures (Chapter 452). There are three poliovirus serotypes.

COXSACKIEVIRUSES. In contrast to polioviruses, coxsackieviruses produce paralysis and death when inoculated into suckling mice. This property was responsible for their detection and differentiation from polioviruses when they were first recovered in 1948 from the feces of two children in the village of Coxsackie, New York, who were suffering from a poliomyelitis-like paralytic illness. With the isolation of additional serotypes, it was recognized that, when inoculated into suckling mice, some coxsackieviruses, designated group A coxsackieviruses, produced generalized myositis of skeletal muscles that resulted in flaccid paralysis, whereas others, designated group B coxsackieviruses, produced only focal myositis but caused an encephalitis that resulted in spastic paralysis, and a generalized infection that involved the myocardium, brown fat, pancreas, and other organs. Moreover, group B coxsackieviruses could be readily propagated in primate cell cultures, whereas group A coxsackieviruses grew poorly or not at all. Twenty-three group A and six group B coxsackievirus serotypes have been identified.

ECHOVIRUSES. Use of the cell culture techniques developed by Enders and colleagues led to the recovery, from the feces of healthy children, of additional enteroviruses that produced cytopathic effects in primate cell cultures but failed to produce disease in suckling mice or in the CNS of primates. These agents, initially considered "orphan" viruses because they were unrelated to any disease, were called *Echoviruses* (enteric cytopathic human orphan). However, in the half century since their discovery, echoviruses have been shown to cause a variety of clinical syndromes (see Table 373–1), and 31 serotypes have been identified. Most echoviruses are readily propagated in primate cell cultures. Recently, echoviruses types 22 and 23 were found to differ substantially in nucleotide and amino acid sequence from other enteroviruses and to have three, rather than four, capsid proteins. Consequently, they have been reclassified as *parechoviruses* 1 and 2, the first members of a new *Parechovirus* genus within the Picornavirus family. Epidemiologic and clinical features of these two parechoviruses are similar to those of the echoviruses.

Table 373–1 • CLASSIFICATION OF HUMAN ENTEROVIRUSES*

ENTEROVIRUS GROUP	NUMBER OF SEROTYPES	NUMERIC DESIGNATION	GROWTH IN PRIMATE CELL CULTURE	PATHOGENICITY FOR SUCKLING MICE	PATHOGENICITY FOR MONKEYS
Poliovirus	3	1–3	+	−	+
Coxsackievirus, group A	23	A1–22, A24†	±‡	+	−§
Coxsackievirus, group B	6	B1–6	+	+	−
Echovirus	29	1–9, 11–21, 24–27, 29–33¶	+	−	−
Enterovirus	4	68–71**	+	Variable††	Variable‡‡

*Many enterovirus strains have been isolated that do not conform to these criteria.

†Coxsackievirus A23 has been reclassified as echovirus 9.

‡Except for a few serotypes (e.g., A7, A9, A16), primary isolates of group A coxsackieviruses grow poorly or not at all in cell culture; virus isolation requires inoculation of suckling mice.

§Coxsackievirus A7 is neurovirulent in monkeys.

¶Echovirus 10 has been reclassified as reovirus type 1; echovirus 28 has been reclassified as rhinovirus 1A; echovirus [22] and echovirus [23] have been reclassified as parechovirus 1 and parechovirus 2, respectively, members of a new *Parechovirus genus*; echovirus 34 has been reclassified as a variant of coxsackievirus A24.

**Hepatitis A virus, formally classified as human enterovirus 72, is now classified as a member of the hepatovirus genus.

††Enteroviruses 70 and 71 are pathogenic for suckling mice.

‡‡Enteroviruses 70 and 71 are neurovirulent in monkeys.

SIMPLIFIED TAXONOMIC SCHEME. The detailed comparison of enterovirus genomes supports the validity of this classification scheme. Different serotypes within the same human enterovirus subgroup (e.g., group B coxsackieviruses) generally have 30 to 50% of their nucleotide sequences in common, whereas serotypes from different subgroups generally share less than 20% of their nucleotide sequences. About 5% of the nucleotide sequences are conserved among all human enteroviruses.

Over the years, however, an increasing number of enterovirus isolates were identified that could not be subclassified unambiguously by these criteria, for example, viruses serologically related to known echoviruses but with a host range characteristic of coxsackieviruses. Consequently, in 1970, it was agreed that newly recognized human enteroviruses would be classified simply as "enteroviruses" and numbered sequentially, beginning with enterovirus 68. To avoid confusion with the older literature, the original classification (i.e., poliovirus, group A and group B coxsackieviruses, and echovirus) has been retained for the first 61 serotypes. Since adoption of this simplified taxonomic scheme, four new human enteroviruses, enteroviruses 68 to 71, have been recognized.

ENTEROVIRUSES 68 TO 71. Enterovirus 68 was initially isolated from the throat of an infant with bronchiolitis and pneumonia. Few isolates have since been reported, and the agent is little studied. Enterovirus 69 was recovered from the feces of an asymptomatic child, and this serotype has not yet been associated with disease. Enterovirus 70 is the principal cause of acute hemorrhagic conjunctivitis, a disease first recognized in 1969, which has subsequently affected tens of millions of persons throughout the world. Enterovirus 70 has an unusually broad host range; it causes meningoencephalitis in humans and in experimentally infected monkeys, and it infects both primate and nonprimate cell cultures. Genome analysis and serologic surveys raise the possibility that enterovirus 70 may be a zoonotic enterovirus that has recently extended its host range to include humans. Enterovirus 71, first recognized as the cause of an outbreak of aseptic meningitis and encephalitis in California between 1969 and 1972, is neurovirulent in monkeys and produces a myositis in suckling mice that is typical of that produced by group A coxsackieviruses. Enterovirus 71 has been recovered throughout the world in association with a variety of clinical syndromes and many fatal infections. These syndromes include respiratory infections, aseptic meningitis, cerebellar ataxia, encephalitis, hand-foot-and-mouth disease, and maculopapular exanthems. In addition, enterovirus 71 has been responsible for epidemics of acute paralytic disease (acute flaccid paralysis) indistinguishable from poliomyelitis, and for a syndrome of brainstem encephalitis with neurogenic pulmonary edema and hemorrhage.

Reverse transcription-polymerase chain reaction (RT-PCR) amplification and sequencing has provided a new and powerful approach to enterovirus identification and classification. The most variable regions of the enterovirus genome are within the genes encoding capsid proteins VP1, VP2 and VP3, which are partially exposed on the virus surface. VP1 contains major antigenic and receptor binding sites. Thus the VP1 nucleotide sequence is most representative of the enterovirus serotype, and sequence comparisons and phylogenetic analyses indicate that the VP1 nucleotide sequence contains serotype-specific information that can be used for virus identification. Sequence analysis of the VP1 region has proven extremely useful in epidemiologic studies of enteroviral disease outbreaks, and comparable analyses of other regions of the enterovirus genome should lead to the identification of viral genetic determinants of enterovirus pathogenicity. In addition, the human enteroviruses have been recently classified into 5 groups on the basis of a phylogenetic analysis of the nucleotide sequence of the region of the genome encoding capsid protein VP1. These groups are: (1) Poliovirus types 1–3; (2) Human Enterovirus A (HEV-A): 11 group A coxsackieviruses and enterovirus 71; (3) HEV-B: all group B coxsackieviruses, all echoviruses, coxsackievirus A9 and enterovirus 69; (4) HEV-C: 11 group A coxsackieviruses; and (5) HEV-D: enteroviruses 68 and 70. Phylogenetic analysis of the region of the genome encoding the 3D polymerase has confirmed this classification.

The discovery of the enteroviruses, as well as the origins of modern virology, closely associated with efforts to control poliomyelitis. Poliovirus type 1 is the prototype for the enterovirus genus and for the Picornavirus family. It is one of the most extensively studied and thoroughly characterized agents of disease. Although a number of nonpolio enteroviruses have also been well characterized and the genomes of many have been cloned and sequenced, much of our understanding of enterovirus structure, replication, genetics, pathogenesis, and immunology is derived from studies carried out with wild-type and vaccine strains of poliovirus.

The enteroviruses have many features in common, and they are discussed here as a group before considering the special features of individual members. Because polioviruses are the subject of Chapter 452 this discussion is limited to the nonpolio enteroviruses.

Physical and Biochemical Characteristics of Enteroviruses

The enteroviruses share with all picornaviruses certain important physical and biochemical characteristics. They are small, spherical, nonenveloped viruses approximately 30 nm in diameter. Their genome consists of a linear, single-stranded, unsegmented molecule of RNA with a molecular mass of about 2.6×10^6 D (approximately 7500 nucleotides) that has the same polarity as messenger RNA; it is plus (+) stranded and is infectious. Purified enterovirus RNA can initiate the synthesis of complete infectious virions in vitro in cell-free extracts from susceptible cells. The viral genome has a small, virus-encoded polypeptide (VPg) covalently bound to its 5′ end and a poly-A tail at its 3′ end. It contains a single open reading frame of about 6620 nucleotides flanked by 5′ (740 to 750 nucleotide) and 3′ (70 to 90 nucleotide) nontranslated regions. These nontranslated regions are highly conserved among enteroviruses and are involved in the regulation of viral RNA translation and replication. The viral genome is tightly packed within an icosahedral protein shell, or capsid, composed of 60 identical subunits, or protomers, each of which has a molecular mass of 90,000 to 100,000 D and is itself composed of four nonidentical virus-encoded polypeptides (VP1, VP2, VP3, and VP4). VP1, VP2, and VP3 are exposed on the virion surface, whereas VP4 lies buried in association with the RNA core. Like all picornaviruses, enteroviruses exhibit a unique pattern of replication in which the viral genome binds host cell ribosomes directly to an internal ribosome entry site (IRES) in the 5′ nontranslated region (5′-NTR) and is translated into a single giant polyprotein of about 250,000 D. This polyprotein is then cleaved by endogenous viral proteinases into the individual viral structural and nonstructural proteins.

Enteroviruses are stable over a wide range of pH (pH 3 to 10) and retain infectivity for days at room temperature, weeks at refrigerator temperature, and indefinitely when frozen at −20° C or lower. They are readily inactivated at temperatures above 50° C, but this inactivation is inhibited by molar magnesium chloride, which greatly enhances the stability of enteroviruses at all environmental temperatures. Magnesium chloride is widely used as a stabilizer for oral poliovirus vaccines.

Enteroviruses are resistant to proteolytic enzymes and to inactivation by organic solvents, deoxycholate, and various detergents that destroy lipid-containing enveloped viruses such as herpesviruses, orthomyxoviruses, and paramyxoviruses. Enteroviruses are inactivated by formaldehyde, chlorination, and ultraviolet light but are protected from inactivation by dissolved organic matter, the formation of virus aggregates, and adsorption to particulate matter. Consequently, enteroviruses may survive secondary sewage treatment and chlorination as generally practiced, and are abundant in urban sewage and treated wastewater. The agricultural use of treated sewage and recycled wastewater may contaminate food and water supplies. Because sewage treatment that destroys fecal coliform bacteria does not eliminate enteroviruses, the use of fecal coliform counts to assess the sanitary quality of water is inadequate with respect to its potential for transmission of enteroviral diseases. Enteroviruses are often detectable in samples of recreational water judged acceptable on the basis of fecal coliform counts. Although person-to-person (fecal-oral) spread is the dominant mode of transmission and water-borne outbreaks of enterovirus infection have rarely been documented, the hazard associated with the discharge of virus-laden sewage into coastal waters is demonstrated by the occurrence of shellfish-associated outbreaks of hepatitis A. Clams, mussels, and oysters are filter-feeders that concentrate virus and function as passive virus carriers. Most of the enteroviruses in sewage are associated with suspended solids, and virus adsorbed to sediment remains infectious for long periods in the marine environment. The reintroduction of specific enteroviruses into coastal populations when marine sediments are disturbed by storms or dredging may explain the sudden occurrence of epidemics and the reappearance of certain enterovirus serotypes after years of absence from the human population.

Epidemiology

Human enteroviruses have worldwide distribution, and humans are their only known reservoir. The prevalence of enterovirus infection varies markedly with season and climate, and with the age and socioeconomic status of the population studied. In tropical and semitropical regions, enterovirus infections occur frequently throughout the year. In temperate climates, the incidence of infection is markedly increased in the summer and early fall; in Europe and North America, 80 to 90% of enterovirus isolates are recovered from June through October, with peak recovery in August. Even within the United States, climatic and socioeconomic factors affect the prevalence of enterovirus infections. Enterovirus isolation rates from young children are twofold to threefold higher in southern than in northern cities, and threefold to sixfold higher in lower than in middle and upper socioeconomic districts. In developed countries, usually only one to three enterovirus serotypes are highly prevalent in a given community each year, with different serotypes predominating in different years, and isolation rates in young children rarely exceed 10%. In developing countries with poor sanitation, a greater number of enterovirus serotypes circulate simultaneously, and isolation rates in children are regularly more than 75%, with many fecal specimens yielding three or more enterovirus serotypes.

Some enteroviruses appear to be endemic, being isolated at low frequency in the same locality each year, whereas others produce local or regional epidemics and then disappear, only to return again years later. Occasionally, an enterovirus spreads worldwide, infecting tens of millions of persons and producing pandemic disease. This pattern was observed with echovirus 9 in the late 1950s; with enterovirus 70, which caused a pandemic of acute hemorrhagic conjunctivitis beginning in 1969; and with enterovirus 71, which has caused large epidemics of hand-foot-and-mouth disease with severe neurologic complications in East and Southeast Asia and Australia beginning in 1997.

With the elimination of wild-type polioviruses by immunization, nonpolio enteroviruses account for virtually all of the 10 to 30 million symptomatic enterovirus infections observed annually in the United States. However, except for paralytic polio (acute flaccid paralysis), diseases associated with enterovirus infections are not nationally notifiable. The National Enterovirus Surveillance System (NESS) collects information on enteroviruses isolated from human specimens submitted for testing to participating laboratories and the CDC, and monitors temporal and geographic trends. NESS identifies some 2,000 enterovirus isolates each year, a very small sample of the total number of symptomatic enterovirus infections. In addition, these data may be biased by the inability to isolate certain enterovirus serotypes in tissue culture, particularly group A coxsackieviruses, and by the submission of specimens primarily from patients with more serious diseases.

Two or 3 serotypes regularly account for 50% or more of the enterovirus isolates identified in any given year, and a single serotype will often account for more than 30%. The 15 most frequently detected serotypes account for more than 90% of all isolates identified in a given year. While the predominant serotypes vary from year to year, certain serotypes are regularly among the 15 most frequently detected. During the past decade these have included coxsackieviruses A9, B2, B4 and B5, and echoviruses 6, 9, 11, 18 and 30. In some years one or two of these endemic enteroviruses have predominated (e.g., echovirus 30 in 1998, echovirus 11 in 1999 and coxsackievirus B5 in 2000) whereas in other years enteroviruses that previously were rarely reported emerged as the predominant serotype (e.g., echovirus 13 in 2001). Discontinuation of the use of oral polio vaccine in the United States has resulted in the virtual disappearance of vaccine-related poliovirus isolates since 2000.

The age-related incidence of enterovirus infection is determined, in part, by local patterns of serotype prevalence. Endemic serotypes that occur with significant incidence every year are likely to infect only the youngest children, since older children and adults are immune as a result of prior infection. In contrast, older children and adults are lilkely to predominant in outbreaks of infection with serotypes that have not been present in the community for a number of years.

Enteroviruses exhibit a high rate of mutation during replication in the human gastrointestinal tract, and this can lead to the appearance of antigenic variants and virus strains with altered tissue tropism and virulence. Such mutations are readily detected within days after administration of attenuated poliovirus vaccines to normal children. They have also been observed in a number of nonpolio enteroviruses. Recently isolated strains of several coxsackieviruses, echoviruses, and enteroviruses 70 and 71 have been found to differ in many epitopes from the corresponding prototype strains isolated more than a decade earlier, a pattern of "*antigenic drift*" not unlike that seen with influenzaviruses. This antigenic variation has been demonstrated using panels of monoclonal antibodies. However, there is no evidence that "antigenic drift" has resulted in "escape mutants" resistant to neutralization by human convalescent serum.

Recombination between the genomes of different enterovirus serotypes can be observed in multiply infected individuals (e.g., young children in developing countries) and in recipients of trivalent oral poliovirus vaccines. Genetic changes acquired by mutation or recombination may result in antigenic changes, alterations in host range and cell tropism (e.g., the emergence of a zoonotic enterovirus as a cause of epidemics of acute hemorrhagic conjunctivitis in humans) or the acquisition of new pathogenic properties (e.g., the induction of brainstem encephalitis and rapidly fatal neurogenic pulmonary edema by enterovirus 71). These changes may help to account for the ability of individual enteroviruses to persist in nature and to cause a variety of clinical syndromes. The broader application of genomic sequencing can be expected to reveal the genetic determinants of specific enterovirus pathogenic properties. For example, specific nucleotide sequence changes in the 5'-NTR appear to be responsible for attenuation of neurovirulence in vaccine strains of poliovirus, and sequence differences in the same region correlate with differences in the neurovirulence of certain nonpolio enteroviruses, as well.

Transmission of human enteroviruses is chiefly by the fecal-oral route directly from person to person or through fomites; spread by respiratory secretions plays a lesser role. After infection by most serotypes, virus can be recovered from the oropharynx and intestine of symptomatic and asymptomatic individuals, but virus is shed in greater amounts and for a longer period (a month or more) in the feces. Young children have the highest rates of infection, and enteroviruses are most efficiently disseminated by infected children younger than 2 years of age. Spread is from child to child, and then within family groups, and it is facilitated by crowding and poor hygiene. Secondary attack rates of approximately 90% for polioviruses, 75% for coxsackieviruses, and 50% for echoviruses are observed in families. Middle-class parents with children in daycare centers are at particular risk. Reared in circumstances that minimized their childhood exposure, they are likely to be susceptible to infection by many of the enteroviruses brought home from daycare centers by their asymptomatically infected toddlers.

Although the epidemiology of most enteroviruses is similar, patterns of infection with some serotypes are distinctive. Enterovirus 70 and coxsackievirus A24, etiologic agents of acute hemorrhagic conjunctivitis, are transmitted by direct inoculation of the conjunctivae by fingers and fomites contaminated with infected tears. Replication of these viruses in the alimentary tract, if it occurs at all, is limited. Coxsackievirus A21 is shed primarily from the upper respiratory tract, where it produces a rhinovirus-like illness. It is transmitted by respiratory secretions.

The incubation period for illnesses caused by enteroviruses may vary from less than 1 day to more than 3 weeks, but it is usually 2 to 7 days. It is shortest when symptoms are the direct result of virus replication at the portal of entry (e.g., acute hemorrhagic conjunctivitis caused by enterovirus 70 or coxsackievirus A24) and longest when they reflect tissue injury that involves immunopathology in target organs infected after viremia (e.g., some forms of coxsackievirus myocarditis).

Pathogenesis

The pathogenesis of enterovirus infections is understood best for polioviruses, which have been extensively studied in experimentally infected primates and in humans infected with attenuated vaccine strains. The pathogenesis of most nonpolio enterovirus infections appears to be similar, except for the principal target organs affected.

After ingestion of fecally contaminated material, virus implants in susceptible tissues of the pharynx and distal small intestine. Whereas some replication occurs in the pharynx, the primary site of infection is the distal small intestine; virus traverses the intestinal lining cells without causing detectable cytopathology, and reaches Peyer's patches in the lamina propria where significant replication occurs. Within a day or two virus spreads to regional lymph nodes, and on about the third day small quantities escape into the blood stream (the "minor viremia") and are disseminated throughout the reticuloendothelial system and to other receptor-bearing target tissues. In most cases, infection is contained at this stage by host defense mechanisms with no further progression, resulting in *asymptomatic infection*. In a minority of infected persons, replication continues in reticuloendothelial tissues producing, by about the fifth day, heavy sustained viremia (the "major viremia") that coincides with the "minor illness" of poliovirus infection (Chapter 452) and with the "nonspecific febrile illness" caused by other human enteroviruses.

The major viremia disseminates large amounts of virus to target organs, such as the spinal cord, brain, meninges, heart, and skin, where further virus replication results in inflammatory lesions and cell necrosis. In most such patients, host defense mechanisms quickly terminate the major viremia and halt virus replication in target organs; only rarely is virus replication in target organs extensive enough to be manifest clinically. Although other host defense mechanisms (e.g., macrophages, natural killer [NK] cells, interferon production) are doubtless involved, neutralizing antibodies play a major role in terminating viremia and limiting enterovirus multiplication in target tissues. Serotype-specific neutralizing antibodies may be detected in the serum within 4 or 5 days of the infection, and they generally persist for life. Evidence for the critical role of antibodies in terminating infection is provided by the occurrence of chronic persistent enterovirus infections in agammaglobulinemic children. Host defenses do not, however, terminate virus replication in the intestine, and fecal shedding continues for weeks after symptomatic and asymptomatic enterovirus infections. Reinfection (i.e., virus excretion by a person with preexisting homotypic antibodies) is relatively uncommon. When it occurs, infection is confined to the alimentary tract and is not associated with illness, and the duration of virus shedding is markedly reduced.

The clinical syndromes caused by a given enterovirus reflect the particular target organs and tissues that it infects (i.e., its *cell tropism*). All of the determinants of cell tropism have not been elucidated, but a major factor is the presence on the cell surface of specific *receptor* molecules to which the virus attaches. Different groups of enteroviruses use different receptors, many of which are encoded by genes on human chromosome 19. A number of distinct receptors, each shared by multiple enterovirus serotypes, have been identified. The receptor used by all three polioviruses (PVR) and a receptor used by a subset of group A coxsackieviruses and by most human rhinoviruses (ICAM-1) are both members of the immunoglobulin superfamily. A receptor used by a subset of the echoviruses (VLA-2) and another used by coxsackievirus A9 are members of the integrin family. Decay-accelerating factor (DAF), a surface glycoprotein that protects cells from complement-mediated lysis, is used as a receptor by another group of echoviruses and by enterovirus 70. All six group B coxsackieviruses share the same receptor (CAD), a 46-kD cell-surface glycoprotein that is also used as a receptor by a number of human adenoviruses. Many of the enteroviruses that bind to DAF must also bind to a co-receptor (e.g., ICAM-1 or β2-microglobulin) to initiate infection.

Because cells in tissue culture exhibit different patterns of receptor expression than comparable cells in vivo, serial passage in tissue culture may select for viruses with altered receptor utilization. Such changes may contribute to the attenuation of virulence often associated with serial passage of a virus in tissue culture.

Enterovirus receptors bind to specific sites on the floor of a canyon at the junction of capsid proteins VP1 and VP3. This binding is followed by a conformational change in the enterovirus capsid that leads to the entry of the viral RNA into the cell cytoplasm. Neutralizing antibodies bind to sites on the canyon wall, blocking entry of the receptor into the canyon.

Clinical Manifestations

Between 50 and 80% of nonpolio enterovirus infections are asymptomatic. Most symptomatic infections consist of *undifferentiated febrile illnesses* (i.e., *summer grippe*), often accompanied by upper respiratory symptoms. These infections are generally mild and last only a few days. This syndrome is totally nonspecific; it can be caused by virtually any enterovirus serotype as well as by members of a number of other virus families (e.g., adenoviruses, paramyxoviruses, orthomyxoviruses). The so-called characteristic enterovirus syndromes, such as aseptic meningitis, hand-foot-and-mouth disease, and pleurodynia, are unusual manifestations of enterovirus infection. They represent the very small tip of a very large iceberg.

Some clinical syndromes are highly associated with certain enterovirus serotypes or subgroups (e.g., hand-foot-and-mouth disease with coxsackievirus A16, and enterovirus 71; myopericarditis with group B coxsackieviruses; acute hemorrhagic conjunctivitis with enterovirus 70 and coxsackievirus A24, but even these associations are not specific. The same syndrome may also be caused by a number of other enterovirus serotypes. Conversely, a single enterovirus serotype may cause several different syndromes, even within the same outbreak (Table 373–2). The more important syndromes are discussed next.

CENTRAL NERVOUS SYSTEM SYNDROMES

Aseptic Meningitis

Aseptic meningitis is the most common significant illness caused by nonpolio enteroviruses, and these viruses are responsible for more than 80% of the cases of aseptic meningitis in developing countries in which an etiologic agent is identified. Almost every enterovirus serotype has been implicated, but those most frequently associated include coxsackieviruses A2, A4, A5, A7, A9, A10, A16, and B1-5; echoviruses 3, 4, 6, 9, 11, 14, 16, 17, 18, 19, 25, 30, and 33; and enteroviruses 70 and 71, all of which have been responsible for outbreaks and sporadic cases. Although attack rates are generally highest in children, cases also occur in adults, especially during larger outbreaks. Initial symptoms, which are typical of the *undifferentiated febrile illness* (e.g., fever, headache, malaise, myalgias, and sore throat), are followed, usually within a day, by signs and symptoms of meningitis, including a more severe headache that is often retrobulbar, photophobia, meningismus, stiffness of the neck and back, and nausea and vomiting, especially in children. The illness is sometimes biphasic like poliomyelitis. The cerebrospinal fluid (CSF) is clear and under slightly increased pressure. The total cell count, which can vary from less than 10 cells/mm^3 to more than 3000 cells/mm^3, averages 50 to 500 cells/mm^3. Initially, neutrophils may predominate (although they rarely exceed 90%), but they are quickly replaced by mononuclear cells. The glucose concentration is usually normal, although levels less than 40 mg/dL are occasionally observed. The protein concentration is normal or slightly elevated, but it rarely exceeds 100 mg/dL. Fever and signs of meningeal inflammation subside in 3 to 7 days, although CSF pleocytosis may persist for an additional week or more. Most children and adults recover fully without sequelae. However, enteroviral meningitis during the first year of life may result in permanent neurologic damage in up to 10% of affected infants, as evidenced by paresis, reduced head circumference, spasticity, and impaired intellectual function.

In some cases, especially those caused by echoviruses, coxsackieviruses A9 and A16, and enterovirus 71, meningitis may be accompanied by a rash, which, if petechial, may raise the specter of meningococcemia. It is frequently necessary to distinguish enteroviral meningitis from partially treated bacterial meningitis. In bacterial meningitis, even when treated with appropriate antibiotics, the polymorphonuclear pleocytosis in the CSF is usually more persistent, the protein concentration is higher, and the glucose concentration is lower. Aseptic meningitis may be caused by a number of other infectious and noninfectious agents, including mumps virus, arthropod-borne viruses (e.g., Eastern, Western and Venezuelan equine encephalitis viruses; Powassan, Japanese and Saint Louis Encephalitis viruses; California, LaCrosse and West Nile viruses), lymphocytic choriomeningitis virus (LCM), human

Infectious Diseases

Table 373–2 • CLINICAL MANIFESTATIONS OF NON-POLIO ENTEROVIRUS INFECTIONS*

CLINICAL SYNDROME	GROUP A COXSACKIEVIRUSES†	GROUP B COXSACKIEVIRUSES	ECHOVIRUSES§	ENTEROVIRUSES
Asymptomatic infection	All serotypes	All serotypes	All serotypes	All serotypes
Undifferentiated febrile illness ("summer grippe") with or without respiratory symptoms	All serotypes	All serotypes	All serotypes	68, 70, 71
Aseptic meningitis (often associated with an exanthem)	1, 2, 3, 4, 5, 6, 7, 8, 9, 10, 11, 14, 16, 17, 18, 22, 24	1, 2, 3, 4, 5, 6	1, 2, 3, 4, 5, 6, 7, 8, 9, 10, 11, 12, 14, 16, 17, 18, 19, 20, 21, [22], [23], 25, 30, 31, 33	70, 71
Encephalitis	2, 4, 5, 6, 7, 9, 10, 16	1, 2, 3, 4, 5	2, 3, 4, 6, 7, 9, 11, 14, 17, 18, 19, [22], 25, 30, 33	70, 71
Paralytic disease (poliomyelitis-like)	4, 5, 6, 7, 9, 10, 11, 14, 16, 21, 24	1, 2, 3, 4, 5, 6	1, 2, 4, 6, 7, 9, 11, 14, 16, 17, 18, 19, 30	70, 71
Myopericarditis	1, 2, 4, 5, 7, 8, 9, 14, 16	1, 2, 3, 4, 5, 6	1, 2, 3, 4, 6, 7, 8, 9, 11, 14, 16, 17, 19, [22], 25, 30	
Pleurodynia	1, 2, 4, 6, 9, 10, 16	1, 2, 3, 4, 5, 6	1, 2, 3, 6, 7, 8, 9, 11, 12, 14, 16, 19, [23], 25, 30	
Herpangina	1, 2, 3, 4, 5, 6, 7, 8, 9, 10, 16, 22	1, 2, 3, 4, 5	6, 9, 11, 16, 17, [22], 25	71
Hand-foot-and-mouth disease	4, 5, 7, 9, 10, 16	2, 5	7	71
Exanthems	2, 4, 5, 6, 7, 9, 10, 16	1, 2, 3, 4, 5	2, 4, 5, 6, 9, 11, 16, 18, 25	71
Common cold	2, 10, 21, 24	1, 2, 3, 4, 5	2, 4, 8, 9, 11, 20, 25	
Lower respiratory tract infections (broncheolitis, pneumonia)	7, 9, 16	1, 2, 3, 4, 5	4, 8, 9, 11, 12, 14, 19, 20, 21, 25, 30	68, 71
Acute hemorrhagic conjunctivitis‡	24			70
Generalized disease of the newborn	3, 9, 16	1, 2, 3, 4, 5	3, 4, 6, 7, 9, 11, 12, 14, 17, 18, 19, 20, 21, [22], 30	

*A great many enterovirus serotypes have been implicated in most of these syndromes, at least in sporadic cases. The serotypes listed are those that have been clearly and/or frequently implicated. Serotypes with a strong association are underlined, and those with the strongest association are double underlined.

†Because isolation of many of the group A coxsackieviruses requires suckling mouse inoculation, they are likely to be underreported as causes of illness.

‡Conjunctivitis without hemorrhage is frequently seen in association with other manifestations in patients infected with many group A and group B coxsackieviruses and echoviruses, especially coxsackieviruses A9, A16, B1–5 and echoviruses 2, 7, 9, 11, 16, and 30.

§Echovirus types [22] and [23] were found to differ substantially in nucleotide and amino acid sequence from other enteroviruses and to have three, rather than four, capsid proteins. Consequently, they have been reclassified as parechoviruses 1 and 2, the first members of a new genus, *Parechovirus*, within the Picornavirus family. Epidemiologic and clinical features of these two parechoviruses are similar to those of the echoviruses.

immunodeficiency virus (HIV), herpes simplex virus, Lyme borreliosis, and leptospirosis. Differential diagnosis is aided by the distinct epidemiologic features and characteristic signs and symptoms of these other diseases.

Paralytic Disease

Paralytic disease may occur in the course of many nonpolio enterovirus infections. It is similar, but generally less severe, than that caused by polioviruses. Muscle weakness is far more common than frank paralysis, and recovery is usually complete, although occasional patients suffer cranial nerve palsies or severe, sometimes fatal, bulbar involvement. Frequently implicated serotypes include coxsackieviruses A7, A9, and B2 through B5; echoviruses 2, 4, 6, 9, 11, and 30; and enteroviruses 70 and 71. In contrast to paralytic poliomyelitis, which in the prevaccine era occurred in epidemics, cases of paralysis associated with nonpolio enteroviruses are generally sporadic. However, several nonpolio enteroviruses produce paralytic disease with sufficient frequency to cause local outbreaks and epidemics. A variant of coxsackievirus A7 has caused outbreaks and numerous sporadic cases of paralytic disease. In fact, coxsackievirus A7 was once thought to be a fourth serotype of poliovirus. Paralytic disease resembling poliomyelitis, with a significant incidence of residual paralysis and muscle atrophy, has been observed in patients with acute hemorrhagic conjunctivitis caused by enterovirus 70. Since its discovery in California in 1969, enterovirus 71 has been recognized as a highly neurotropic virus associated with a variety of CNS syndromes, including aseptic meningitis, encephalitis, acute cerebellar ataxia, Bell's palsy, acute flaccid paralysis and bulbar poliomyelitis. These neurologic syndromes have frequently occurred during epidemics of hand-foot-and-mouth disease and herpangina caused by enterovirus 71. Beginning in 1997, there has been a large increase in enterovirus 71 epidemic acitivity throughout the Asia-Pacific region, with the result that enterovirus 71 is emerging as the most important virulent neurotropic enterovirus.

Encephalitis

Encephalitis is a well recognized but uncommon manifestation of enterovirus infection. Thus, despite their prevalence, enteroviruses account for only 10 to 20% of the cases of encephalitis of proven viral origin in the United States. The most frequently implicated serotypes include coxsackieviruses A9, B2, and B5; echoviruses 4, 6, 9, 11, and 30; and enterovirus 71. In most cases, encephalitis complicates the course of aseptic meningitis; parenchymal involvement is indicated by the onset of confusion, coma, abnormalities of motor function, hemiparesis, vasomotor instability, cranial nerve palsies, cerebellar ataxia, and focal or generalized seizures, singly or in various combinations. Cerebral involvement is usually generalized, but focal encephalitis does occur and may be clinically indistinguishable from herpes simplex encephalitis. In one series, enteroviruses were demonstrated by brain biopsy in 13% of patients suspected of having herpes simplex encephalitis. Recovery from enteroviral encephalitis is usually complete, although neurologic sequelae and deaths do occur, especially in young infants and during enterovirus 71 epidemics. The large epidemics of enterovirus 71 hand-foot-and-mouth disease in the Asia-Pacific region that began in 1997 have been associated with a syndrome of brainstem encephalitis and rapidly fatal pulmonary edema and hemorrhage that was previously described in only a single case of enterovirus 71 infection in 1995. A similar syndrome was, however, frequently described in the 1950s in patients with acute bulbar poliomyelitis caused by polioviruses.

Other Reported Neurologic Complications

Enteroviruses, particularly group A coxsackieviruses, appear to be an important cause of febrile seizures in children during enterovirus season. Other neurologic complications, including Guillain-Barré syndrome, transverse myelitis, and Reye's syndrome, have been reported in patients with enterovirus infections. However, no clear epidemiologic or etiologic linkage to enteroviruses has been established. Given the high prevalence of asymptomatic enterovirus infections, these associations may be coincidental.

EPIDEMIC PLEURODYNIA (BORNHOLM DISEASE)

Epidemic pleurodynia is an acute febrile viral illness characterized by the sudden onset of intense paroxysmal lower thoracic or abdominal pain. Synonyms include Bornholm disease; devil's grip; epidemic myalgia; epidemic benign dry pleurisy; and Sylvest's disease. The name, pleurodynia (*pleura*, side; *odyne*, pain) reflects the characteristic intercostal location of the pain and does not connote disease of the pleura. Pleurodynia is usually an epidemic disease, but sporadic cases do occur.

Etiology

The enteroviral etiology of epidemic pleurodynia was established in 1949. Group B coxsackieviruses, especially B3 and B5, are the principal cause. Other viruses associated with epidemic disease include echoviruses 1 and 6. Sporadic cases have also been associated with these viruses, as well as with many other enteroviruses, including coxsackieviruses A1, A2, A4, A6, A9, A10, and A16; echoviruses 2, 3, 7, 8, 9, 11, 12, 14, 16, 19, 25, and 30; and parechovirus 1.

Epidemiology

Epidemics of pleurodynia have been recognized in Scandinavian countries for more than 2 centuries, but the disease was little known elsewhere until 1933, when the Danish physician Ejnar Sylvest described an epidemic on Bornholm, a Danish island in the Baltic Sea. Since then, epidemics and sporadic cases have been recognized in many parts of the world. As with other enteroviral infections, most illnesses occur in summer and early fall. However, in contrast to the annual outbreaks of enteroviral aseptic meningitis, epidemics of pleurodynia are much less frequent, generally occurring at intervals of 10 to 20 years.

Transmission is primarily from person to person, and multiple family members may be attacked almost simultaneously or in rapid succession at intervals of 2 to 5 days. In epidemics, disease is observed in children and adults of both genders. Although the peak age of incidence is somewhat older than with other enterovirus syndromes, most cases occur in persons younger than 30 years of age. The incubation period is usually 2 to 5 days.

Pathogenesis

Pleurodynia is a disease of skeletal muscle, not of the pleura or peritoneum. As in most enteroviral diseases, infection is initiated in the alimentary tract. Skeletal muscle is probably most often infected during the primary (minor) viremia, although it may be infected later, during the major viremia in the minority of patients in whom pleurodynia is preceded by a prodromal illness. Host immune responses terminate viremia and halt virus replication in the tissues, but they also contribute to the severity of local inflammation. Histopathologic data in humans are lacking because of the benign nature of the disease, but studies in murine models of coxsackievirus infection suggest that the myositis results from a combination of direct virus-induced cytolysis and immunopathology mediated by sensitized T lymphocytes.

Clinical Manifestations

Pleurodynia is characterized by the abrupt onset of fever and sharp, paroxysmal pain over the lower ribs or upper abdomen. In about 25% of patients, this is preceded by a 1- or 2-day prodrome of headache, malaise, anorexia, sore throat, and diffuse myalgia. The pain varies in intensity but is often severe. It is accentuated, sometimes elicited, by deep breathing, coughing, and movement. The pain of pleurodynia has been described as catching (i.e., a "stitch" in the side), stabbing, knifelike, lancinating, crushing, or viselike. In adults, the pain is primarily in muscles of the thorax, especially the intercostals. In children, abdominal muscles are more often involved. Occasionally, pleurodynia may involve muscles in the neck or limbs. The pain is often unilateral, and it is generally experienced in only one or two locations. Muscle tenderness and, occasionally, swelling can be detected at the site of pain, and characteristic paroxysms of pain can often be elicited by pressure on the affected muscles. Pleural friction rubs are uncommon, and peritonitis generally has not been observed in patients who have come to laparotomy. The level of creatine kinase in the serum may be elevated, reflecting injury to striated muscle. Other laboratory values are usually normal, although some patients may have mild leukopenia.

During paroxysms of severe pain, the patient lies still in bed, sweating profusely and appearing acutely ill and apprehensive. Respiration, limited by pain, is shallow, rapid and grunting, suggesting pneumonia or pleural inflammation. A temperature of 38° to 40° C is present at the onset of pain, reaches its peak during the episode, and resolves between paroxysms. Multiple paroxysms of pain occur, each lasting from a few minutes to several hours. The initial paroxysm is usually the most severe, and patients frequently appear relatively well between paroxysms.

The acute illness may last for 2 to 6 days, with a range of 12 hours to 3 weeks. The disease is often biphasic; the initial pain and fever resolve, and the patient is asymptomatic for a day or more, but then the pain and fever recur, frequently at the same site. Rarely, patient will have several recurrences over a period of several weeks or will have a late recurrence after being symptom free for a month or more.

Differential Diagnosis

The most useful distinguishing feature of pleurodynia is the intermittent, paroxysmal character of the pain. Epidemiologic information, such as the occurrence of similar illnesses in family members or in the community, may also suggest the diagnosis. Nevertheless, depending on the location of the pain, pleurodynia may be confused with any of a number of more serious diseases. When the pain is thoracic, these include pneumonia, pulmonary infarction, rib fracture, costochondritis, and myocardial infarction. The absence of physical and roentgenographic evidence of fracture, costochondritis, or pulmonary parenchymal disease; lack of sputum production; absence of leukocytosis; and normal electrocardiographic (ECG) findings help to exclude these diagnoses. When the pain is abdominal, it can be difficult to differentiate pleurodynia from serious causes of acute abdominal pain, such as peritonitis, cholecystitis, appendicitis, perforated peptic ulcer, and acute intestinal obstruction. During epidemics of pleurodynia, it is common to have as many children with the disease admitted to surgical wards as to medical wards, and in one epidemic, 9 of 49 of these children underwent laparotomy with normal findings before the nature of their disease was recognized. The absence of signs of peritonitis and the normal white blood cell count are helpful in excluding these diagnoses, as are normal ultrasound and roentgenographic studies. Pleurodynia may also be confused with the pain of pre-eruptive herpes zoster, herniated intervertebral disk, and renal colic. However, the pain of pre-eruptive herpes zoster is usually more constant, and the localization of pain and tenderness to the affected muscle, normal roentgenographic and neurologic examinations (except perhaps for a local area of hyperesthesia over the affected muscle), and the absence of hematuria help to exclude the other two diagnoses.

Rx Treatment and Prognosis

Treatment of pleurodynia is symptomatic. Episodes of pain can usually be controlled with salicylates or other mild analgesics, but opiate analgesics are recommended for severe pain once serious intra-abdominal processes have been excluded. Heat applied to affected muscles may also be useful. Despite the tendency of the disease to relapse, patients with epidemic pleurodynia eventually recover completely. Occasionally, convalescence may be prolonged, with malaise or asthenia persisting for several months. Complications, which reflect dissemination of virus to other tissues, are relatively uncommon. When they do occur, they generally become apparent within several days after the onset of the disease. Aseptic meningitis is observed in approximately 5% of cases and orchitis in a similar proportion of postpubertal males. Pericarditis and myocarditis are rare complications of epidemic pleurodynia.

MYOCARDITIS AND PERICARDITIS CAUSED BY ENTEROVIRUSES

Myocarditis and pericarditis have long been known to occur in association with epidemic viral diseases, including measles, mumps, rubella, varicella, influenza, poliomyelitis, and pleurodynia. Because many of these diseases have been controlled with vaccines, enteroviruses have emerged as the major recognized infectious cause of myocarditis and pericarditis in North America and Western Europe. The pathogenesis, clinical manifestations, and outcome of enteroviral infections of the heart vary markedly, depending on properties of the virus and characteristics of the host, especially age. Neonatal infections frequently result in severe myocarditis, widespread involvement of other organs and high mortality, whereas in older children and adults, pericarditis often predominates and the disease is generally benign and self-limited. In fact, the clinical manifestations are frequently so subtle that cardiac involvement during enteroviral infections is often unrecognized. However, idiopathic dilated cardiomyopathy may, in many cases, be a late sequela of both recognized and unrecognized enteroviral myocarditis.

Etiology

The evidence linking specific enteroviruses with myocarditis or pericarditis varies markedly. Proof of causation requires isolation of virus from, or demonstration of viral proteins or nucleic acids in, the myocardium, pericardium, or pericardial fluid. Except in neonatal myopericarditis, virus is rarely isolated from cardiac tissue or pericardial fluid, and detection of viral proteins has been difficult, primarily because lack of specificity has led to false-positive results. However, increasing use of endomyocardial biopsy and application of new techniques such as in situ hybridization and, especially, RT-PCR for detection and amplification of enteroviral nucleic acid have substantially improved our ability to establish the etiology in cases of myocarditis and pericarditis. Although these techniques are only now becoming widely available, their limited application has already demonstrated the presence of enteroviral RNA in 20 to 30% of myocardial specimens from patients with acute myocarditis. In most instances, however, the association of a particular enterovirus with myocarditis or pericarditis is based only on isolation of virus from noncardiac sources (e.g., feces) and/or serologic evidence of recent or concurrent enterovirus infection. These associations may often be coincidental rather than causal.

Coxsackieviruses B1 through B6, A4 and A16, and echoviruses 9, 11, and 22 have been proven to cause myopericarditis in children and adults. Coxsackieviruses A1, A2, A5, A8, A9 and A14, and echoviruses 1, 2, 3, 4, 6, 7, 8, 14, 16, 19, 25 and 30 have also been implicated. The group B coxsackieviruses are the most common etiologic agents of myocarditis and pericarditis. They appear to account for approximately 50% of sporadic cases of acute myocarditis and for virtually all cases that have occurred in epidemics. Group B coxsackieviruses also appear to account for 30% or more of sporadic cases of acute nonbacterial pericarditis.

Epidemiology

Enteroviral myocarditis and pericarditis occur most frequently in the summer and early fall. Idiopathic myopericarditis also peaks during this period of maximum enteroviral prevalence; this is consistent with the notion that most cases of idiopathic myopericarditis are caused by enteroviruses.

The incidence of myopericarditis during enteroviral infections depends on the virus and characteristics of the host, especially age. Myopericarditis has been the predominant manifestation in only about 3% of group B coxsackievirus infections. However, 5 to 10% of infected adults and children older than 9 who have sought medical care during coxsackievirus B5 epidemics have had evidence of acute myopericarditis. The incidence of myocarditis and disseminated disease during group B coxsackievirus infection is very high during the neonatal period. It drops to a minimum (e.g., approximately 1% of symptomatic coxsackievirus B5 infections) in children 1 to 9 years of age and then increases again in older children and adults. Thus, despite the higher frequency of enterovirus infections in younger children, enterovirus myopericarditis is primarily a disease of adolescents and young adults. At least two thirds of the cases occur in males, and the risk of cardiac involvement also appears to be increased during pregnancy and immediately postpartum. Enterovirus transmission associated with myocarditis and pericarditis is the same as that of enteroviruses in general: It is primarily fecal-oral transmission.

Pathogenesis

When enteroviral infections involve the heart, they almost always cause an inflammatory response in both the myocardium (i.e., myocarditis) and the pericardium (i.e., pericarditis). Although one or the other usually predominates, the term *myopericarditis* best describes the pathologic process. The hallmark of enteroviral myopericarditis is injury to myocytes with an adjacent inflammatory infiltrate. Cardiac myocytes, which bear a receptor used by all six group B coxsackieviruses, are infected and lysed. The acute process may resolve completely or progress. Healing and progression are reflected by the development of interstitial fibrosis and loss of myocytes. Enteroviral pericarditis is almost always accompanied by focal subepicardial myocarditis, which has these same pathologic characteristics.

In neonatal enteroviral myopericarditis, the relatively short incubation period, the widely disseminated infection, and the presence of high titers of virus in the heart and other organs indicate that the primary pathogenic mechanism is direct cytolytic virus infection of the tissues involved. In myopericarditis in older children and adults, the longer incubation period, the presence of virus-specific antibodies and T lymphocytes at clinical presentation, the low frequency of virus isolation from the heart and pericardial fluid, and the later occurrence of relapses all suggest that immunopathologic mechanisms are involved. Patients with myocarditis have been found to have cytotoxic T lymphocytes that react with normal cardiac myocytes and high titers of antimyocyte antibodies. The role of host immune responses in enterovirus myopericarditis is complex and poorly understood.

Idiopathic dilated cardiomyopathy (IDC) (Chapter 64) may in many instances represent the end stage of an immunologically mediated disease initiated by an episode of enteroviral myocarditis. This notion is supported by the development of chronic cardiomyopathy in approximately 10% of patients observed long-term after group B coxsackievirus myocarditis, and by the demonstration of progressive fibrosis in such patients by serial endomyocardial biopsies. It is also supported by the demonstration of molecular mimicry of cardiac antigens by group B coxsackievirus epitopes. The 2A protease of group B coxsackieviruses has been shown to cleave dystrophin, a key protein in cardiac myocytes that is the target of mutations associated with inherited forms of dilated cardiomyopathy. Thus virus-mediated destruction of dystrophin is another possible mechanism for the development of dilated cardiomyopathy following acute enterovirus myocarditis.

The question of whether enteroviruses persist in IDC and contribute directly to the chronic inflammatory process has yet to be answered. The failure to isolate enteroviruses from myocardial biopsy specimens, and the failure of several groups to detect enterovirus RNA with extremely sensitive nested PCR assays in cardiac tissue obtained from cases of end-stage IDC at the time of heart transplantation, suggest that enteroviruses do not persist after acute myocarditis. However, there are also reports of the detection of enterovirus RNA in cardiac tissue from patients with IDC by in situ hybridization and PCR assays, and thus the question of enteroviral persistence in IDC is still unresolved.

Clinical Manifestations

Although the term *myopericarditis* best describes the pathologic process observed in enteroviral infections of the heart, *myocarditis* or *pericarditis* usually predominates, and the two syndromes are sufficiently distinct in clinical presentation and pathophysiology to warrant separate consideration. They are discussed in detail in Chapters 64 and 65.

NEONATAL MYOCARDITIS. Most severe neonatal enterovirus infections begin during the first week of life; the infant's mother has frequently been infected shortly before delivery and has transmitted the virus transplacentally or by contact during or soon after delivery without also transferring virus-specific neutralizing antibodies. The disease can be present at birth or may occur at any time during the first 3 months of life following a 2- to 8-day incubation period. It is usually a manifestation of generalized enterovirus disease of the newborn.

MYOCARDITIS AND PERICARDITIS IN OLDER CHILDREN AND ADULTS. In contrast to the neonate, enteroviral infections of the heart in older children and adults often present clinically as pericarditis rather than myocarditis, although the myocardium is almost always involved to some degree. Approximately 60% of older children and adults with symptomatic group B coxsackievirus-associated heart disease have a clinical diagnosis of pericarditis; approximately 40% have a clinical diagnosis of myocarditis. More than two thirds of the patients are male.

Treatment and Prognosis

Enterovirus replication in cardiac tissues plays a central role in the pathogenesis of neonatal myocarditis and acute myopericarditis in older children and adults. Thus, antiviral therapy with drugs that inhibit enterovirus replication would be highly desirable. Until such drugs are available, treatment is supportive. Infants with neonatal myocarditis are unlikely to have received transplacental antibodies to the causative virus from their mothers. Thus, it seems reasonable to administer human immune serum globulin, which contains high titers of neutralizing antibodies to a number of enterovirus serotypes, in an attempt to terminate viremia and limit further virus replication in infected tissues. This approach is supported by anecdotal experience, but results of randomized clinical trials involving adequate numbers of patients are not available.

Treatment of enteroviral myopericarditis in older children and adults is also primarily supportive. It should include control of pain with analgesics; careful monitoring for arrhythmias, heart failure, and hemodynamic compromise; and prompt treatment of these complications if they arise. Bedrest is an important component of therapy because of clear evidence in mice with coxsackievirus B3 myocarditis that exercise markedly increases the extent of myocardial necrosis and mortality during the acute phase of the disease. Adequate oxygenation should be ensured and fluid overload avoided and promptly treated if it develops. In severe cases, cardiac assist devices may be life-saving.

Corticosteroids should not be administered to patients with suspected enteroviral myocarditis or pericarditis. Their use during the acute phase of viral myocarditis has been associated with rapid clinical deterioration.

Clinical trials are assessing the efficacy of a class of antienteroviral drugs (Pleconari capsid and other binding inhibitors) that bind within a hydrophobic pocket under the floor of the receptor-binding canyon in the enterovirus capsid. This binding inhibits virus replication by blocking receptor attachment and/or virus penetration and uncoating. When available, these antiviral drugs would be recommended for the early treatment of neonatal enteroviral infections and acute myopericarditis in children and adults.

Most children and adults with enteroviral myopericarditis recover without obvious sequelae. Acute mortality is low (0 to 5%), and deaths occur as a result of arrhythmias or congestive heart failure in patients with myocarditis; cardiac tamponade is rare in enteroviral pericarditis.

Approximately 20% of patients experience one or more episodes of recurrent myopericarditis within 1 year of their initial illness, and persistent ECG abnormalities are observed in 10 to 20% of patients. Cardiomegaly persists in 5 to 10% of patients, and long-term follow-up suggests that 10% or more may develop chronic cardiomyopathy. Constrictive pericarditis rarely occurs following enteroviral pericarditis.

TYPE I DIABETES MELLITUS

Epidemiologic evidence suggests a role for enteroviruses, especially group B coxsackieviruses, in the etiology of type I diabetes mellitus (IDDM) (Chapter 242). Several serologic studies have found evidence of a higher frequency of group B coxsackievirus infection in children with new-onset type I diabetes than in matched controls, and maternal enterovirus infections during pregnancy have been associated with the subsequent development of type I diabetes in offspring during early childhood. Moreover, enteroviral RNA has been identified by RT-PCR at a higher frequency in children with new-onset type I diabetes than in matched controls. Studies in mouse models suggest several potential mechanisms by which enteroviruses might be involved in the genesis of type I diabetes. Enteroviruses could initiate type I diabetes directly by infecting and destroying pancreatic β cells. Enteroviral infection might also initiate autoimmune responses to pancreatic β cells in genetically susceptible individuals as a consequence of direct cytolytic infection or by molecular mimicry. For example, there are homologous domains on group B coxsackievirus protein 2C and a pancreatic β cell autoantigen, glutamic acid decarboxylase (GAD_{65}), that induce cross-reactive humoral and cellular immune responses. Alternatively, enterovirus infection might accelerate an already ongoing process of immunologically mediated β-cell damage or precipitate symptomatic type I diabetes when most β cells have already been destroyed. These mechanisms are not mutually exclusive, and their relative importance may vary depending on the properties of the inciting enterovirus and the age and genetic susceptibility of the host.

MUCOCUTANEOUS SYNDROMES CAUSED BY ENTEROVIRUSES

Enteroviruses are the leading cause of exanthematous disease in the United States and most other developed countries. Almost all enteroviruses can cause maculopapular eruptions, and most serotypes are occasionally responsible for petechial or papulovesicular exanthems and enanthems. Moreover, a given enterovirus may cause more than one pattern of mucocutaneous disease, even within a single infected household. Consequently, except for hand-foot-and-mouth disease, which is usually caused by coxsackievirus A16 or enterovirus 71, there are no clinical or epidemiologic characteristics of any given enteroviral rash that point to a specific enterovirus as its cause.

Epidemiology

The epidemiology of enteroviral exanthems and enanthems is the epidemiology of enteroviral infections in general. Most occur during the summer and early fall. The incidence of enanthems and exanthems in enterovirus-infected persons varies among different enteroviruses and even among different strains of the same enterovirus. For example, enanthems and exanthems are often seen in more than 50% of infected children during outbreaks of infection caused by echovirus 9 or coxsackievirus A16, but they are rare during outbreaks caused by echovirus 6 or coxsackievirus A7. Host factors, especially age, are also important; infants and young children are more likely to develop mucocutaneous lesions, whereas other manifestations of enterovirus infection, such as aseptic meningitis, are more likely in older children and adults. During outbreaks of echovirus 9 infection, rash is often seen in the majority of infected children younger than 5 years of age, but in less than 5% of infected adults, and it is not uncommon when evaluating an adult with aseptic meningitis and no rash to find that a child in the same household is convalescing from an illness characterized by a maculopapular rash.

Enteroviral exanthems and enanthems occur in outbreaks and as sporadic cases. Asymptomatic infections are common and are often the source of virus-causing symptomatic infections. Attack rates are highest in young children, who frequently introduce the virus into households where several members may become infected simultaneously or sequentially, with an incubation period of 3 to 10 days.

Pathogenesis

Enteroviral lesions in the oropharyngeal mucosa and skin are manifestations of a systemic virus infection. They result from the secondary infection of endothelial cells of small vessels in the underlying lamina propria and dermis, which occurs during the viremia that regularly follows enteroviral infection and replication in the alimentary tract. Their pathogenesis resembles that of the mucocutaneous lesions of measles, rubella and varicella, and contrasts with the pathogenesis of the lesions of acute herpetic gingivostomatitis, human papillomavirus infections (i.e., warts), and acute hemorrhagic conjunctivitis, which are the direct result of exogenous virus infection and replication in epithelial cells at the portal of entry.

The obligatory occurrence of alimentary tract replication and viremia before mucocutaneous lesions develop explains the 3- to 10-day incubation period and the frequent occurrence of prodromal signs and symptoms. Moreover, simultaneous dissemination of virus to a number of target organs explains the concurrent appearance of other manifestations of enterovirus infection, such as aseptic meningitis and myopericarditis.

Clinical Manifestations

ENANTHEMS. The oropharyngeal mucosa is involved to some degree during most symptomatic enteroviral infections. This is usually manifested by mild pharyngitis and mucosal erythema, but it may also result in a variety of enanthems. They may consist of macules, papules, vesicles, petechiae or ulcers, and they may occur alone or in association with exanthems and other manifestations of systemic enteroviral infection. They are often transient and frequently unrecognized, but they occasionally lead to diagnostic confusion, such as when they resemble Koplik's spots and accompany a morbilliform exanthem in a child infected by echovirus 9. Two enanthems, herpangina and hand-foot-and-mouth direase, are sufficiently unique to warrant separate description.

Herpangina. Herpangina (*herpes*, vesicular eruption; *angina*, inflammation of the throat) is a syndrome characterized by sudden onset of fever, sore throat, pain on swallowing, and a vesicular enanthem of the posterior pharynx. It is seen primarily in children between the ages of 3 and 10 years. The disease begins abruptly, after a 3- to 10-day incubation period, with fever ranging from 38° to 41° C, sore throat, and pain on swallowing. There may also be anorexia, vomiting, and abdominal pain. Fever tends to be higher in younger children, who may suffer febrile convulsions; older children and adults frequently complain of headache and myalgia. On examination, there is pharyngeal erythema but little or no tonsillar exudate. The characteristic lesions are discrete, 1- to 2-mm vesicles and ulcers surrounded by 1- to 5-mm zones of erythema. Lesions are few, averaging four to five per patient, with a range of 1 to 20. They occur most frequently on the anterior tonsillar pillars, the posterior edge of the soft palate, and the uvula, and less frequently on the tonsils, the posterior pharyngeal wall, and the posterior buccal mucosa. They begin as small papules, progress to vesicles, and ulcerate within 24 hours. The shallow ulcers, which are moderately painful, may enlarge over the next day or two to a diameter of 3 to 4 mm. Symptoms generally disappear in 3 or 4 days, but the ulcers may persist for up to a week. Most cases are mild and resolve without complications, but herpangina is occasionally associated with exanthems, aseptic meningitis, or other serious manifestations of systemic enterovirus infection.

Outbreaks of herpangina are common during the summer, and sporadic cases are also observed. Group A coxsackieviruses (A1 through A6, A8, A10 and A22) account for most outbreaks, but outbreaks have also been caused by other enteroviruses, including coxsackievirus B1 and echoviruses 16 and 25. These viruses, as well as coxsackieviruses A7, A9, A16, and B2 through B5 echoviruses 6, 9, 11 and 17, and parechovirus 1, have been isolated from sporadic cases.

Acute Lymphonodular Pharyngitis. Acute lymphonodular pharyngitis is a variant of herpangina that has been described in children infected with coxsackievirus A10. The lesions have the same distribution as typical cases of herpangina, but instead of evolving into vesicles and ulcers, they remain papular and are infiltrated with lymphocytes to form 2- to 3-mm, gray-white nodules surrounded by narrow zones of erythema. The disease is otherwise indistinguishable from herpangina.

Hand-Foot-and-Mouth Disease. Hand-foot-and-mouth disease (i.e., vesicular stomatitis with exanthem) is a mild enteroviral disease characterized by a vesicular eruption in the mouth and over the extremities. It occurs most frequently in children younger than 5 years of age. After an incubation period of 3 to 6 days, the disease begins with mild fever ranging from 38° to 39° C, anorexia, malaise, and often, a sore mouth. Within 1 or 2 days vesicular lesions appear in the oral cavity, most frequently on the anterior buccal mucosa and the tongue, but also on the labial mucosa, gingivae, and hard palate. In most preschool children, but in only about 10% of infected adults, the oral lesions are accompanied by vesicular skin lesions, most often on the dorsal or lateral surfaces of the hands and feet and on the fingers and toes, but not infrequently on the palms and soles. Less often, lesions occur on the buttocks or more proximally on the extremities, and rarely on the genitalia. The lesions are 3 to 7 mm in diameter and surrounded by a narrow zone of erythema. They range in number from 2 to 30 or more, and consist of subepidermal vesicles containing a mixed inflammatory infiltrate of lymphocytes, monocytes and neutrophils, with acantholysis and cellular degeneration in the overlying epidermis.

Hand-foot-and-mouth disease is caused most frequently by coxsackievirus A16 and enterovirus 71, less frequently by coxsackieviruses A5, A9 and A10; and occasionally by coxsackieviruses A4, A7, B2 and B5. Outbreaks and sporadic cases occur primarily in the summer and early fall. The disease may be accompanied by more serious manifestations, especially when caused by enterovirus 71.

EXANTHEMS. Enterovirus exanthems themselves are benign, but they are clinically important for at least three reasons. First, they constitute direct evidence of enterovirus dissemination and thus provide a clue to the presence and the etiology of coexistent disease referable to other infected target organs, such as the heart and the CNS. Second, they represent the "tip of the iceberg" of enterovirus infection in the community. Third, they are often confused with other infectious exanthems, some of which have more serious consequences, require specific control measures, or are amenable to specific anti-infective therapy. Misdiagnosis of enteroviral rashes assumes added significance as we prepare to deal with the threat of bioterrorism involving the use of smallpox. Because enteroviral rashes are not sufficiently distinctive to permit an etiologic diagnosis to be made on clinical grounds, laboratory testing is required. However, the problem of confusing enteroviral rashes with other infectious exanthems can be approached by comparing the enterovirus rashes to the nonenterovirus rashes that they resemble.

The most common cutaneous manifestation of enterovirus infection is an erythematous maculopapular rash that appears together with fever and other manifestations of systemic infection. This is also a common manifestation of infection by a variety of other organisms, but it is more often caused by enteroviruses. Only certain enteroviruses (e.g., echovirus 9) cause this syndrome with high frequency, but almost all can produce it at least occasionally. The rash begins on the face and quickly spreads to the neck, trunk, and extremities. It consists of 1- to 3-mm erythematous macules and papules that may be discrete (*rubelliform*, resembling rubella) or confluent (*morbilliform*, resembling measles). It usually lasts for 2 to 5 days and does not itch or desquamate. Enteroviral exanthems usually are not accompanied by significant posterior cervical, suboccipital, or postauricular lymphadenopathy, but there are many exceptions. For example, posterior cervical and suboccipital lymphadenopathy similar to that seen in rubella has been observed in many children with exanthems caused by coxsackievirus A9.

Enteroviral rashes are sometimes petechial and occasionally purpuric. Although this pattern is seen most frequently in echovirus 9 and coxsackievirus A9 infections, it is observed occasionally with many other enterovirus serotypes.

Vesicular exanthems are most often seen as a component of hand-foot-and-mouth disease (see earlier), but several enteroviruses, including echovirus 11, coxsackievirus A9 and enterovirus 71, may cause vesicular exanthems without an associated enanthem. The lesions resemble those caused by varicella-zoster and herpes simplex viruses. In contrast to varicella, however, vesicular rashes caused by enteroviruses are usually peripheral in distribution and consist of relatively few lesions that heal without crusting. When they are not associated with hand-foot-and-mouth disease, vesicular lesions caused by enteroviruses are often confused with insect bites or poison ivy. Echovirus 11 and several coxsackievirus serotypes have been associated with skin lesions resembling papular urticaria, lesions that usually result from insect bites.

Enteroviral rashes are generally accompanied by fever, and they develop at or within 1 or 2 days of its onset. In some cases, however, the rash does not develop until the fever subsides, a pattern resembling that of *roseola infantum* (exanthem subitum), a benign sporadic disease of infants 6 to 24 months of age now known to be caused by human herpesvirus 6. These roseola-like enterovirus infections are typified by the *Boston exanthem*, caused by echovirus 16 and first described during an epidemic in Boston in 1951. It is characterized by fever (to 38° or 39° C) lasting 2 to 4 days, followed by defervescence and then by the appearance of a salmon-pink maculopapular rash on the face and upper chest. The rash resolves in 1 to 5 days without sequelae. Frequently, multiple cases occur sequentially in households. The illness is mild in children and more severe in adults, who often develop high fever and aseptic meningitis without rash. In addition to echovirus 16, a number of other enterovirus serotypes have occasionally been associated with roseola-like illnesses.

Differential Diagnosis

Herpangina is most often confused with bacterial pharyngitis or tonsillitis, or with pharyngitis caused by other viruses. Other considerations include hand-foot-and-mouth disease; primary herpes simplex virus infections, particularly acute herpetic pharyngotonsillitis; and herpes zoster involving the palate.

The vesicular lesions of hand-foot-and-mouth disease resemble those caused by herpes simplex and varicella-zoster viruses. Patients with primary herpetic gingivostomatitis usually have more toxicity, cervical lymphadenopathy, and more prominent gingivitis. Their cutaneous lesions are usually perioral, but they may occasionally involve a finger that has been in the mouth. Recurrent herpes simplex (herpes labialis) usually involves the vermilion border of the lip or the adjacent skin, is rarely accompanied by lesions on the hands or feet, often has a neuralgic prodrome, and frequently has a history of recurrent episodes. The cutaneous lesions of varicella are generally more extensive and are centrally distributed, sparing the palms and soles. Oral lesions are far less prominent in varicella, and its prevalence in winter and spring further distinguishes it from hand-foot-and-mouth disease. Like vesicular lesions caused by herpes simplex and varicella-zoster virus, enteroviral vesicles are generally more superficial and evolve more rapidly than those caused by variola and vaccinia viruses. Aphthous stomatitis is distinguished from hand-foot-and-mouth disease by the absence of fever and other signs of systemic illness, by the absence of cutaneous lesions, and often by a history of recurrence.

Maculopapular exanthems caused by enteroviruses are distinguished from measles and rubella by their summertime occurrence, by the usual absence of posterior cervical, suboccipital, and postauricular lymphadenopathy, and by their relatively short incubation period. The absence of significant coryza and conjunctivitis further distinguishes the typical enteroviral exanthems from measles. In addition, the probability of measles and rubella is markedly reduced in persons with a well-documented history of adequate immunization.

When enteroviral rashes are maculopapular they may be confused with drug reactions; when they are petechial, they may be confused with bacterial or rickettsial rashes. When enteroviral rashes are petechial or purpuric, it is impossible to rule out meningococcemia on clinical grounds alone, and when the rash is associated with aseptic meningitis (as is often the case in echovirus 9 and coxsackievirus A9 infections), it is clinically indistinguishable from meningococcal meningitis. Laboratory investigation is required, even during proven outbreaks of enteroviral disease, because concurrent enteroviral and meningococcal infections can occur.

Rx Treatment and Prognosis

Enteroviral enanthems and exanthems are generally benign, self-limited illnesses that require only symptomatic therapy for headache and sore throat. However, the severe neurologic manifestations of hand-foot-and-mouth disease and herpangina caused by enterovirus 71, as well as the serious consequences of neonatal enterovirus infections, will warrant consideration of antiviral therapy when it becomes available. When illness mimics meningococcemia or meningococcal meningitis, antimicrobial chemotherapy should be initiated until bacterial infection is ruled out by appropriate cultures and antigen-detection assays.

RESPIRATORY TRACT DISEASE CAUSED BY ENTEROVIRUSES

A number of enteroviruses have been associated with mild upper respiratory tract illness in children and adults, especially coxsackieviruses A21, A24, and B1 through B5, and echoviruses 9 and 11, as well as echoviruses 2, 4, 8, 20, and 25. Many of the enteroviruses, most notably coxsackievirus A21, produce illnesses that resemble the common cold, except for a higher incidence of fever. In contrast to most other enteroviruses, coxsackievirus A21 is shed primarily from the upper respiratory tract, rather than in feces. Enteroviruses have also been associated with lower respiratory tract illnesses in infants and children, although rarely in adults. These illnesses include tracheitis, bronchitis, croup, bronchiolitis, and pneumonia. Frequently implicated serotypes include coxsackieviruses A7, A9, A16, and B1 through B5; echoviruses 4, 8, 9, 11, 12, 14, 19, 20, 21, 25, and 30; and enterovirus 68. In addition, respiratory tract symptoms frequently accompany the undifferentiated febrile illnesses (i.e., summer grippe) caused by most enteroviruses. Surveillance data indicate that enteroviruses account for 2 to 10% of viral respiratory disease, and that 1 to 15% of symptomatic enterovirus infections are associated with respiratory symptoms. The respiratory illnesses caused by enteroviruses are clinically indistinguishable from similar illnesses caused by viruses more commonly considered to be respiratory tract pathogens, such as rhinoviruses, influenzaviruses, parainfluenza viruses, respiratory syncytial virus, and adenoviruses. However, infections with these viruses occur most frequently during the winter, whereas enterovirus infections occur primarily in the summer and early fall. Viral respiratory tract infections are discussed in Chapters 357 through 373.

ACUTE HEMORRHAGIC CONJUNCTIVITIS

Acute hemorrhagic conjunctivitis (AHC) is an acute, highly contagious, self-limited disease of the eye characterized by sudden onset of pain, photophobia, conjunctivitis, swelling of the eyelids, and prominent subconjunctival hemorrhages. Since its first appearance in 1969, AHC has occurred in explosive epidemics throughout the world. The disease was initially nicknamed Apollo 11 disease because its appearance in Ghana coincided with the Apollo 11 moon landing.

Etiology

Enterovirus 70, a new enterovirus isolated from patients during the initial pandemic of AHC that began in Ghana in 1969, has been responsible for tens of millions of cases that have occurred in widespread epidemics during the past 25 years. A variant of coxsackievirus A24, which first appeared at about the same time as enterovirus 70, has been responsible for hundreds of thousands of cases of the disease that have occurred in a number of more circumscribed epidemics during the same period. Both viruses have been involved concurrently in some epidemics. Coxsackievirus A24 has been responsible for fewer cases of epidemic conjunctivitis than enterovirus 70, and it does not cause subconjunctival hemorrhages in as high a proportion of patients. Nucleic acid hybridization and serologic studies have shown that the two viruses are genetically and antigenically unrelated.

Enterovirus 70 is a most unusual enterovirus. In addition to being a naturally occurring, temperature-sensitive enterovirus that causes disease at its portal of entry and is not transmitted by the fecal-oral route, it has an exceptionally broad host range. Oligonucleotide mapping of a series of epidemic strains suggests that they all evolved from a hypothetical ancestor strain that did not exist before 1967. Serologic studies have reinforced the notion that enterovirus 70 has only recently emerged as a human pathogen; neutralizing antibodies to enterovirus 70 have generally not been found in human sera collected before 1969, even sera from elderly persons. Neutralizing antibodies to enterovirus 70 have been detected in animal sera from Japan and West Africa collected before 1969, indicating that enterovirus 70 or a very similar virus was circulating in animals before the first appearance of AHC in humans. These observations suggest that enterovirus 70 may represent a zoonotic picornavirus that extended its host range to humans, perhaps as a consequence of recombination with poliovirus type 3.

Epidemiology

Although mild conjunctivitis may occur as a minor manifestation of infection by many enteroviruses, especially in children, its occurrence as the major clinical manifestation of enterovirus infection was not observed until 1969, when explosive epidemics of AHC occurred in Ghana and almost simultaneously in Indonesia. Over the next 2 years, the disease assumed pandemic proportions, with large epidemics occurring in many areas of Africa, Southeast Asia, the Far East, India, and Japan and involving tens of millions of people. A number of smaller outbreaks also occurred in Europe. Scattered epidemics of AHC continued to occur in these same areas during the remainder of the decade, and the recurrence of epidemics in the same geographic areas suggests that immunity to AHC may be short-lived.

AHC is a highly contagious disease. In contrast to most enteroviral infections, it is transmitted by direct inoculation of the conjunctivae with virus-contaminated fingers or fomites (i.e., transmission is eye-to-finger or fomite-to-eye). Enterovirus 70 and the coxsackievirus

A24 variant are both naturally occurring, temperature-sensitive viruses that replicate optimally at 33° to 35° C, the temperature of the conjunctivae. There appears to be little or no virus replication in the alimentary tract. Virus is abundant in the conjunctivae and in the ocular exudate, from which it can be readily isolated early in infection. During epidemics, all age groups are affected; attack rates of clinical illness are highest in young adults, but infection rates are highest in children younger than 10 years of age, many of whom experience mild or inapparent infections. Infection rates are also substantially higher among the poor than in middle and upper socioeconomic groups. School-age children are most likely to introduce infection into households, where secondary attack rates are often more than 50%.

Pathogenesis

In contrast to other enterovirus infections, AHC is transmitted by direct inoculation of the conjunctivae with virus on contaminated fingers or fomites (e.g., ophthalmologic instruments, shared towels). Disease results from local virus replication at the portal of entry; prior replication in the alimentary tract and viremia are not required to disseminate virus to ocular tissues. This explains the unusually short incubation period, usually 24 hours or less (range, 12 to 72 hours).

The major complication of AHC is poliomyelitis-like flaccid paralysis, which occurs in a very small proportion of patients with AHC caused by enterovirus 70 but apparently not at all in patients with AHC caused by coxsackievirus A24. The pathogenesis of this AHC-associated paralytic disease is not clear, but infections and destruction of motor neurons appear to reflect axonal rather than viremic spread of enterovirus 70 to the CNS.

Clinical Manifestations

AHC begins with the sudden onset of eye pain and foreign body sensation, lacrimation, photophobia, blurred vision, and bulbar conjunctivitis. Signs and symptoms rapidly increase in severity with the development of palpebral conjunctivitis, conjunctival edema, swelling of the eyelids, subconjunctival hemorrhages in the bulbar conjunctivae, and a serous or seromucoid ocular discharge containing large numbers of polymorphonuclear leukocytes. The subconjunctival hemorrhages, which are the hallmark of the disease, range from discrete petechiae to confluent hemorrhages that occupy virtually the entire bulbar conjunctiva. They are present, usually within 24 hours of onset, in 70 to 90% of patients with AHC caused by enterovirus 70, but they are much less frequent in AHC caused by coxsackievirus A24. AHC often begins unilaterally, but it rapidly spreads to the other eye. Signs and symptoms peak within 24 to 36 hours of onset, by which time most patients have also developed hypertrophy of palpebral follicles and papillae, preauricular lymphadenopathy, and punctate epithelial keratitis with tiny corneal erosions that are often seen only by slit lamp examination after fluorescein staining. Clinical improvement usually begins by the second or third day, and recovery is generally complete without sequelae within 7 to 10 days. Constitutional symptoms, including headache, low-grade fever, and malaise, occur in a minority of patients.

Poliomyelitis-like motor paralysis occurs as a rare complication of AHC caused by enterovirus 70, but not in AHC caused by coxsackievirus A24. It occurs predominantly in adult males. The neurologic disease generally does not begin until 2 to 5 weeks after AHC (range, 5 to 60 days or more), and its relationship to the conjunctivitis is often overlooked by physicians and by the patients themselves. Radicular pain and paresthesia, usually accompanied by headache, fever, and malaise, are followed in 1 to 3 days by acute asymmetrical areflexic paresis or paralysis of one or more limbs. Proximal muscles are usually affected more than distal muscles and lower limbs more than upper limbs. Bulbar involvement, as evidenced by paralysis of one or more cranial nerves, is observed in one third or more of affected patients. The CSF is characterized by mononuclear pleocytosis and elevated protein concentration. Permanent paralysis and muscular atrophy occur in approximately 25% of affected patients. More than 200 cases have been reported to date, and the long interval between AHC and paralysis almost certainly accentuates underreporting. Nevertheless, in view of the many tens of millions of cases of AHC that have occurred since 1969, the incidence of this neurologic complication is probably less than 1 in 10,000 cases of AHC.

Differential Diagnosis

During major epidemics, AHC is unlikely to be confused with other eye infections. However, small outbreaks and sporadic cases may be mistaken for adenovirus infections, either acute follicular conjunctivitis or the more severe epidemic keratoconjunctivitis. A variety of noninfectious conditions can produce the signs and symptoms of conjunctivitis.

 ## Treatment and Prognosis

AHC almost always resolves spontaneously without sequelae, and treatment is symptomatic. Topical application of antihistamine or decongestant eye drops and cold compresses may be used to reduce discomfort. Corticosteroids, a component of many topical ophthalmic preparations, are contraindicated. Transmission of AHC can be prevented by careful handwashing, avoidance of contaminated washcloths and towels, and sterilization of all ophthalmologic instruments. These practices should be routine in eye clinics.

CHRONIC MENINGOENCEPHALITIS IN AGAMMAGLOBULINEMIC PATIENTS

Enteroviruses, primarily echoviruses, have been responsible for a syndrome of chronic meningoencephalitis in patients with inherited or acquired defects in B lymphocyte function, most often children with X-linked agammaglobulinemia. Most of these patients also have a dermatomyositis-like syndrome, and many have chronic hepatitis. Surprisingly, despite the presence in their CSF of abundant virus, an increased number of lymphocytes, and elevated protein concentration, these patients generally exhibit few or no clinical signs of meningitis. Enteroviruses have been recovered from many sites in addition to the CSF, including cardiac and skeletal muscle. However, the pathogenesis remains to be elucidated. Some of these patients have improved after treatment with immune serum globulin containing high titers of neutralizing antibody to the responsible virus. Anecdotal experience indicates that these patients may benefit from prolonged treatment with Pleconaril.

DIAGNOSIS

The enteroviral etiology of a disease may be suspected on clinical and epidemiologic grounds, but the multiplicity of agents capable of causing most clinical syndromes associated with enterovirus infections makes it impossible to establish a specific etiologic diagnosis on the basis of such information alone. Virus isolation from the site of pathology (e.g., CSF in aseptic meningitis; brain biopsy in encephalitis, myocardial tissue and pericardial fluid in myopericarditis, vesicle fluid in hand-foot-and-mouth disease, eye swabs or tears in acute hemorrhagic conjunctivitis) has been the "gold standard" of enteroviral diagnosis. Isolation of an enterovirus from the nasopharynx or feces is less definitive, because isolation of an enterovirus from these sites may reflect an intercurrent asymptomatic enterovirus infection or prolonged virus shedding from an earlier enterovirus infection and be etiologically unrelated to the observed illness.

The development and commercialization of methods for the detection and identification of enterovirus RNA that employ reverse transcription and amplification by polymerase chain reaction (RT–PCR) make it possible to provide an accurate diagnosis of enterovirus infection in less than a day with a sensitivity substantially greater than virus isolation and a specificity of 100%.

The use of universal primers that are targeted to highly conserved regions of the 5'-NTR and detect virtually every enterovirus serotype has revolutionized the laboratory diagnosis of enterovirus infections. Their application to CSF has accelerated the diagnosis of enterovirus aseptic meningitis, thereby significantly reducing the duration and cost of hospitalization and the unnecessary use of antibiotics. The addition of primers targeted to type-specific sequences in the region of the enterovirus genome encoding VP1 permits the detection and identification of specific enterovirus serotypes (e.g., enterovirus 71) and the discrimination of polioviruses (wild type and vaccine strains) from nonpolio enteroviruses. This is important for the diagnosis of enterovirus infections in young children vaccinated with live attenuated polio vaccine, who regularly shed vaccine virus for weeks after immunization. These assays also play an important role in monitoring progress toward the eradication of polio. Serologic testing has a very limited role in the diagnosis of enteroviral infections because of the great diversity of serotypes and the lack of a common antigen.

TREATMENT AND PREVENTION

Specific antiviral chemotherapy and chemoprophylaxis are currently unavailable for enterovirus infections. Treatment is symptomatic and, in severe disease, supportive. Corticosteroids, which have a deleterious effect on coxsackievirus-infected mice, should not be administered during acute enterovirus infections. Strenuous exercise and intramuscular injections, both of which may precipitate paralysis of the involved muscles during enterovirus viremia, should also be avoided during the acute, presumably viremic phase of symptomatic enterovirus infections. Intravenous immunoglobulin (IVIG), which contains high titers of neutralizing antibodies to many enteroviruses, appears to have been useful in some agammaglobulinemic patients with chronic enteroviral meningoencephalitis. IVIG may also have a role in the treatment of enteroviral infections in other patients with severely compromised B-lymphocyte function. Infants with generalized neonatal enterovirus infections are unlikely to have received transplacental antibodies to the causative virus from their mothers. Consequently, it would seem reasonable to administer IVIG to such infants in an attempt to terminate their viremia and limit virus replication in infected tissues. Prophylactic IVIG should also be considered for patients with severely compromised B-lymphocyte function, including bone marrow transplant recipients. Several promising inhibitors of enterovirus replication are undergoing clinical evaluation. They belong to a class of antienterovirus drugs known as capsid-binding inhibitors or WIN compounds that bind within a hydrophobic pocket under the floor of the receptor-binding canyon in the enterovirus capsid. This binding inhibits enterovirus replication by blocking receptor attachment and/or virus penetration and uncoating. One of these compounds, Pleconaril, has broad and potent anti-enterovirus activity, excellent bioavailability, and a very favorable safety profile. Clinical trials have demonstrated benefit in children and adults with enterovirus meningitis, and in adults with respiratory infections caused by enteroviruses and rhinoviruses. Anecdotal data from compassionate use in severe enterovirus diseases also suggest benefit, and a multi-center, placebo-controlled trial in neonates with severe enterovirus infections is currently underway. If proven effective, Pleconaril and similar compounds would be very useful for the treatment of a number of serious enterovirus diseases. Unfortunately, however, enterovirus 71 is resistant to Pleconaril.

Live attenuated and inactivated poliovirus vaccines have been remarkably successful in preventing paralytic poliomyelitis. Although inactivated vaccines could be produced for nonpolio enteroviruses as well, the large number of antigenically distinct serotypes and the benign nature of most nonpolio enterovirus infections have discouraged their development. However, the emergence of specific enterovirus serotypes (e.g., enterovirus 71) as important causes of neurologic disease and mortality may warrant the development of inactivated vaccines for these enteroviruses comparable to the inactivated polio vaccines.

Preexposure administration of immune serum globulin reduces the risk of paralytic poliomyelitis. Because immune serum globulin also contains neutralizing antibodies to many nonpolio enteroviruses, it would probably prevent many nonpolio enteroviral diseases as well. This approach has proved effective for pre-exposure and postexposure prophylaxis of hepatitis A and probably reduces the frequency of severe enteroviral infections in agammaglobulinemic patients receiving replacement therapy. However, the benign nature of most enterovirus infections, the fact that exposures are rarely recognized (i.e., most result from contact with an asymptomatically infected person), and the relatively short half-life of exogenous immune serum globulin make this approach to prevention impractical in most situations. Nursery outbreaks of severe enteroviral disease provide an exception. The administration of IVIG to all infants in the nursery offers protection to infants without transplacentally acquired neutralizing antibody who have not yet been infected.

SUGGESTED READINGS

Abzug MJ, Cloud G, Bradley J, et al; National Institute of Allergy and Infectious Diseases Collaborative Antiviral Study Group: Double blind placebo-controlled trial of pleconaril in infants with enterovirus meningitis. Pediatr Infect Dis J 2003; 22:335–341. *This medication is probably effective, but drug accumulation is a potential concern.*

Bergelson JM, Cunningham JA, Droguett G, et al: Isolation of a common receptor for coxsackie B viruses and adenoviruses 2 and 5. Science 1997;275:1320–1323. *Isolation and characterization of the receptor for coxsackie B viruses and adenoviruses.*
Centers for Disease Control and Prevention (CDC): Outbreaks of aseptic meningitis associated with echoviruses 9 and 30 and preliminary surveillance reports on enterovirus activity—United States, 2003. MMWR Morb Mortal Wkly Rep 2003;52:761–764. *Enteroviruses, especially E9 and E30, are part of the differential diagnosis of aseptic meningitis.*
Ho M: Enterovirus 71: The virus, its infections and outbreaks. J Microbiol Immunol Infect 2000;33:205–216. *A comprehensive review of the nature, evolution, epidemiology and clinical manifestations of enterovirus 71.*
Modlin JF: Coxsackieviruses, echoviruses, and newer enteroviruses. In Mandell GL, Bennett JE, Dolin R (eds): Principles and Practice of Infectious Diseases, 5th ed. New York, Churchill Livingstone, 2000, pp 1904–1919. *Extensive review of epidemiology and clinical manifestations of nonpolio enterovirus infections with excellent bibliography.*
Pallansch MA, Roos RR: Enteroviruses: polioviruses, coxsackieviruses, echoviruses and newer enteroviruses. In Knipe DM, Howley PM (eds): Fields Virology, 4th ed. Philadelphia, Lippincott Williams & Wilkins, 2001, pp 723–775. *Authoritative and comprehensive summary of current knowledge of enterovirus structure, molecular biology, pathogenesis, epidemiology and clinical manifestation.*
Rotbart HA: Enteroviruses. In Richman DD, Whitley RJ, Hayden FG (eds): Clinical Virology, 2nd ed. Washington DC, ASM Press, 2002, pp 971–994. *Authoritative review of all aspects of enterovirus infections by a leader in the application of PCR technology to enteroviral diagnosis.*
Savoia MC, Oxman MN: Myocarditis and pericarditis. In Mandell GL, Bennett JE, Dolin R (eds): Principles and Practice of Infectious Diseases, 5th ed. New York, Churchill Livingstone, 2000, pp 925–941. *Well-referenced review of etiology, pathogenesis, clinical manifestations, and diagnosis of myocarditis and pericarditis.*
Vuorinen T, Vainionpaa R, Hyypia T: Five years' experience of reverse-transcriptase polymerase chain reaction in daily diagnosis of enterovirus and rhinovirus infections. Clin Infect Dis 2003;37:452–455. *RT-PCR is more rapid and sensitive than virus isolation and is recommended as the primary diagnostic tool for enterovirus infections.*

374 VIRAL GASTROENTERITIS

Albert Z. Kapikian

Definition

Viral gastroenteritis (i.e., acute infectious nonbacterial gastroenteritis, epidemic diarrhea, winter vomiting disease, or sporadic infantile gastroenteritis) is a common acute infectious disease of all age groups, characterized by vomiting or watery diarrhea, or both, that may be accompanied by fever, nausea, anorexia, and malaise. It ranges from a mild, self-limited illness of short duration to life-threatening dehydration, especially in infants and young children.

The importance of this disease in a developed country was highlighted in the Cleveland Family Study, in which infectious gastroenteritis, presumably nonbacterial, was the second most common disease experienced, accounting for 16% of approximately 25,000 illnesses in a period of almost 10 years and averaging 1.5 episodes per person per year, an incidence that was remarkably similar in two family studies completed up to 20 years later. In developing countries, the impact of diarrheal illnesses is staggering: in the under 5-year age group in Africa, Asia (excluding China), and Latin America, estimates indicated that 1 billion episodes of diarrheal illness and 3.3 million diarrhea-associated deaths occurred annually, with an incidence of 2.6 episodes per child per year. More recently, the total number of diarrheal deaths was placed at about 2 million for all World Health Organization (WHO) member states combined for 2001. Although this indicated a downward trend in mortality, diarrheal illnesses were ranked as the seventh leading cause of death from any disease or condition, and the fifth leading cause of disability-adjusted life years (DALYs) lost, wherein one DALY equals a single lost year of healthy life (behind perinatal conditions, lower respiratory infections, HIV/AIDS, and unipolar depressive disorders).

Despite major discoveries in bacteriology and parasitology in the past century, the cause of most acute diarrheal illnesses remained elusive for many years. In the 1940s and 1950s, oral administration of bacteria-free stool filtrates from patients with acute diarrhea induced illness in volunteers, but the suspected viral etiologic agent could not be identified. In 1972, Kapikian and colleagues, employing immune electron microscopy (IEM), discovered the first virus-like particles that could be implicated as an important cause of acute gastroenteritis in a stool suspension derived from a gastroenteritis outbreak in Norwalk, Ohio. In 1973, Bishop and associates, using electron microscopy (EM), discovered rotavirus particles in duodenal biopsies from infants and young children hospitalized with acute gastroenteritis. Rotaviruses have emerged as the major known cause of severe diarrhea of infants and young children worldwide.

Etiology

NORWALK VIRUS GROUP (NOROVIRUS). The 27-nm Norwalk virus is the prototype strain of a group of fastidious, nonenveloped, 27- to 40-nm particles usually named after the geographic location of the gastroenteritis outbreak from which they were first derived. They share these common characteristics: (1) they are detected in feces of patients with gastroenteritis; (2) they lack a distinctive morphologic appearance by EM; (3) they have not been grown in cell culture; (4) they possess a positive-sense, single-stranded RNA genome; (5) they have a buoyant density of 1.33 to 1.41 g/cm^3 in cesium chloride; (6) they possess a single, primary, virion-associated protein with a molecular mass of approximately 60,000 D.

The Norwalk virus group includes at least four serotypes by IEM: Norwalk, Hawaii, Snow Mountain, and Taunton viruses, but a unified serotyping system is not yet available. Related viruses include the Montgomery County (MC), Southampton, Lorsdale, Desert Shield, Toronto (formerly minireovirus), Otofuke, and other small, round-structured viruses. Although lacking the distinctive cuplike surface indentations of the "classical" caliciviruses (Latin *calix,* cup), the Norwalk virus group, provisionally named "Norwalk-like" caliciviruses, is now classified in a separate genus, named norovirus, in the family Caliciviridae. Previously, other noncultivatable human enteric viruses, which were associated with gastroenteritis in infants and young children or with outbreaks in the elderly, were considered to be "classical" caliciviruses morphologically. These classical caliciviruses (provisionally named the "Sapporo-like" caliciviruses) have also been classified into a separate genus, named sapovirus, in the Caliciviridae; they have been associated primarily with pediatric gastroenteritis, and their role in causing severe diarrhea requiring hospitalization appears to be relatively minor (Table 374–1).

ROTAVIRUS. Rotaviruses are classified as a genus in the family Reoviridae and are etiologic agents of diarrhea in humans and in numerous animal and a few avian species. They are 70 nm in diameter, are nonenveloped, and possess a distinctive double-layered capsid that surrounds a third layer, the core, which contains the genome consisting of 11 segments of double-stranded RNA (Fig. 374–1). The name rotavirus (*rota,* wheel) was adopted because the sharply defined circular outline of the outer capsid was reminiscent of the rim of a wheel placed on short spokes radiating from a wide hub. The virions have a density of 1.36 g/cm^3 in cesium chloride. Rotaviruses possess three important antigenic specificities—group, subgroup, and serotype—that are mediated by different proteins: group specificity prominently by VP6 and subgroup by VP6 alone (encoded by RNA segment 6). Serotype specificity has been defined by VP7, a glycoprotein that is one of the two major neutralization antigens located on the outer capsid (encoded by RNA segment 7, 8, or 9). The other outer capsid protein, VP4, which is encoded by RNA segment 4 and which protrudes from the smooth outer surface as a series of 60 short spikes about 12 nm long, also induces neutralizing antibodies. VP4 is the hemagglutinin in certain strains. Antibodies to both VP4 and VP7 are associated with protection against rotavirus illness. There are 10 human rotavirus serotypes as defined by VP7 (also designated as

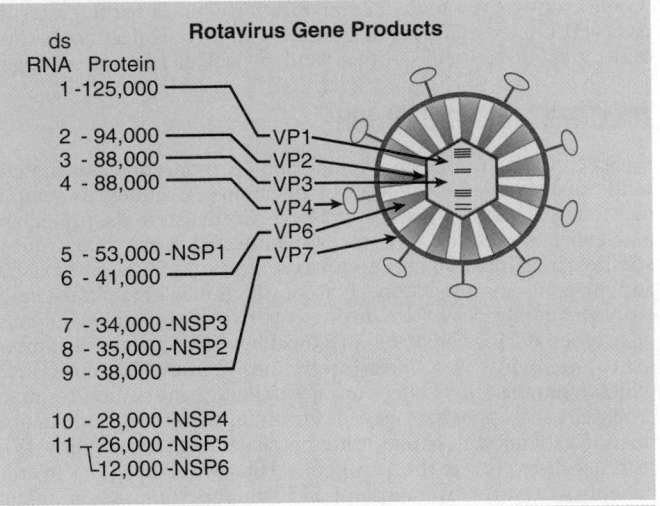

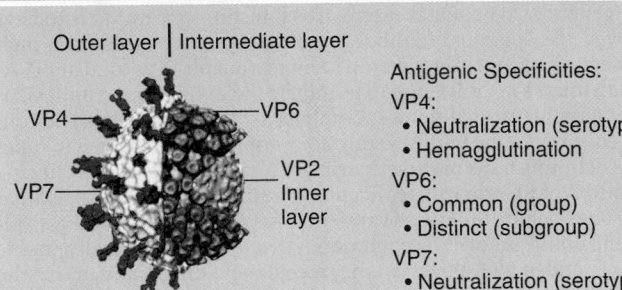

FIGURE 374–1 • *Top,* Schematic representation of the rotavirus particle. *Bottom,* Surface representations of the three-dimensional structures of the outer layer of the complete particle (left) and a particle (right) in which the outer layer and a small triangular portion of the intermediate layer have been removed, exposing the inner layer. (*Bottom,* Courtesy of B.V.V. Prasad. Modified from Kapikian AZ, Hoshino Chanock RM: Rotaviruses. *In* Knipe DM, Howley PM, Griffin DE, et al [eds]: Field's Virology, 4th ed. Philadelphia, Lippincott Williams & Wilkins, 2001; modified from Kapikian AZ: Overview of viral gastroenteritis. *In* Chiba S, Estes MK, Nakata S, Calisher CH [eds]: Viral gastroenteritis. Arch Virol 1996;12[Suppl]:7–19.)

"G" [for glycoprotein] serotypes), of which only four (numbers 1, 2, 3, or 4) are of epidemiologic importance worldwide, although serotype G9 appears to have a wide distribution, whereas G serotypes 5, 8, and 10 have been found more focally. Many human and animal rotavirus strains share VP7 serotype specificity. Most animal and human rotaviruses share the common group antigen and are classified as group A rotaviruses, and these are further divided into subgroups. A

Table 374–1 • VIRUSES ASSOCIATED WITH ACUTE GASTROENTERITIS IN HUMANS

VIRUS	SIZE (nm)	EPIDEMIOLOGY	IMPORTANT AS A CAUSE OF HOSPITALIZATION
Rotavirus			
Group A	70	Single most important cause (viral or bacterial) of endemic severe diarrheal illness in infants and young children worldwide (in cooler months in temperate climates)	Yes
Group B	70	Outbreaks of diarrheal illness predominantly in China in adults (mostly) and children	No
Group C	70	Sporadic cases and occasional outbreaks of diarrheal illness in children	
Enteric adenovirus	70–80	Endemic diarrheal illness of infants and young children.	No
Norovirus (Norwalk-like viruses of caliciviruses)	27–32	Most important cause of outbreaks of nonbacterial gastroenteritis in older children and adults in families, communities, and institutions; frequently associated with ingestion of food Also implicated in diarrheal illnesses of infants and young children using recently developed sensitive assays	No
Sapovirus (Sapporo-like viruses of caliciviruses)	28–40	Sporadic cases and occasional outbreaks of diarrheal illness in infants and young children primarily, and in the elderly	No
Astrovirus	28	Sporadic cases and occasional outbreaks of diarrheal illness in infants, young children, and the elderly	No

Adapted from Kapikian AZ: Viral gastroenteritis. JAMA 1993;269:627–630.

serotyping scheme based on neutralization of VP4 (also designated "P" [for protease sensitive]) has been developed. The VP4 genotype of various strains has also been described, based on sequence analysis or nucleic acid hybridization of VP4. The human rotaviruses have been grown efficiently in cell culture. Several human and animal rotavirus strains have been discovered that do not share the common group antigen and are classified as non–group A rotaviruses (groups B to G). In this chapter, when the term *rotavirus* is used, it is meant to describe only rotaviruses belonging to group A, unless specified otherwise.

OTHER AGENTS. Other viral agents have been associated with gastroenteritis and include enteric adenoviruses belonging to types 40 and 41 (70 to 80 nm in diameter); astroviruses (28 to 30 nm); small, round viruses other than the Norwalk virus group (20 to 30 nm); putative coronavirus-like particles (100 to 150 nm); the pleomorphic, fringed toroviruses (100 to 140 nm); 35-nm "picobirnaviruses;" and a pestivirus antigen. The role of these agents in the etiology of severe infantile diarrhea requiring hospitalization appears to be relatively minor, although the enteric adenoviruses and astroviruses have been established firmly as etiologic agents of acute gastroenteritis. The role of these other agents in epidemic viral gastroenteritis appears to be minor. Additional systematic studies are needed to assess the role of these agents in gastroenteritis. About one third of severe gastroenteritis episodes in developed countries have yet to be associated with an etiologic agent.

Epidemiology

NOROVIRUS. The noroviruses are the major etiologic agents of acute nonbacterial gastroenteritis, which typically occurs as a sharp outbreak affecting adults, school-age children, and family contacts. The location or source of contamination responsible for these outbreaks includes various settings such as schools, camps, recreational areas, nursing homes, hospitals, swimming facilities, cruise ships, and restaurants or events with catered meals. For example, the Norwalk virus was derived from an outbreak in an elementary school in Norwalk, Ohio, in which 50% of the students and teachers developed gastroenteritis within a 2-day period. The Norwalk group of viruses (i.e., noroviruses) have been detected in 217 (93%) of 233 nonbacterial gastroenteritis outbreaks that occurred in the United States between July 1997 and June 2000 that were submitted to the Centers for Disease Control and Prevention (CDC). In another CDC study, the noroviruses were the leading cause of both the total number of cases of gastroenteritis annually in the United States and the number of cases that were foodborne, accounting for an estimated 23 million total cases, 40% of which were foodborne. In addition, noroviruses were estimated to cause 50,000 hospitalizations and 310 deaths in the United States annually. Studies of acute gastroenteritis in general practices in the Netherlands indicated that bacterial and viral agents were detected with near equal frequency (and norovirus in 5% and rotavirus in 5%), whereas in a population-based cohort study of gastroenteritis, viral agents were detected more frequently than bacterial agents with the noroviruses being the leading pathogens (11%). In the United States, antibody to the Norwalk virus is acquired gradually in childhood and somewhat more rapidly in the adult years, so that by the age of 50 years, at least 50% of individuals have serum antibody. In developing countries, infants and young children acquire Norwalk virus antibody at an earlier age, and the virus had been associated with mild gastroenteritis in this age group. Although infants and young children can undergo infection with the noroviruses, the contribution of these agents to the etiology of severe diarrhea in this young age group has appeared to be quite low or infrequent until recently. However, with new sensitive assays, the noroviruses have been detected more frequently in this age group, indicating that additional studies are needed to examine their role as agents of severe diarrhea in infants and young children requiring hospitalization.

Noroviruses are most likely transmitted by the fecal-oral route; however, Norwalk virus has also been detected in vomitus. Although sporadic cases attributed to person-to-person transmission may occur, the explosive nature of outbreaks associated with the noroviruses often suggests a common source of infection, such as water or food. Common-source outbreaks have been attributed to contamination of community and noncommunity public water systems, stored water on cruise ships, or recreational swimming water and to ingestion of various foods, such as tainted oysters, lettuce, potato salad, cole

slaw, or cake frosting. Secondary person-to-person transmission to contacts is relatively common. The incubation period in Norwalk virus challenge studies ranges from 10 to 51 hours, with means ranging from 24–37 hours, and illnesses last characteristically approximately 24 to 48 hours. Norovirus outbreaks occur throughout the year without a peak season.

Norwalk virus infections have been detected in individuals with travelers' diarrhea. However, this agent is not considered to be an important cause of this disease. The Norwalk virus or related agents have been shown to be important agents of acute gastroenteritis in military personnel deployed to different parts of the world.

ROTAVIRUS. Rotaviruses are the major known etiologic agents of severe diarrhea in infants and young children in most areas of the world and are usually associated with sporadic or endemic infantile gastroenteritis, which differs from epidemic viral gastroenteritis associated with the noroviruses in the following characteristics: (1) it usually does not occur in sharp outbreaks; (2) it is consistently the most important cause of severe diarrheal illness in infants and young children; (3) it does not usually cause illness in adults; and (4) the attack rate among family contacts of index cases is low, although subclinical infections occur frequently in contacts. In contrast to Norwalk virus infections, about 90% of infants and young children in developed and developing countries experience a rotavirus infection (as determined from antibody prevalence) by about 3 years of age.

The most compelling evidence for the importance of rotaviruses in severe infantile gastroenteritis has emerged from numerous cross-sectional studies in developed and developing countries. In developed countries, rotaviruses are associated with approximately 35 to 52% of acute diarrheal illness requiring hospitalization of infants and young children. It is estimated that annually in the United States in infants and young children under 5 years of age, rotaviruses are responsible for 2.7 million episodes of diarrheal illness, 410,000 visits to a physician, 160,000 emergency room visits, 50,000 hospitalizations, and 20 deaths. The contribution of other enteric pathogens is consistently relatively minor. A similar pattern is also usually observed in developing countries, where rotaviruses are the most frequently detected pathogens in children younger than 2 years who have severe gastroenteritis; however, bacterial agents also play an important role in such areas. It is estimated that predominantly in developing countries, up to 592,000 infants and young children younger than 5 years die from rotavirus diarrhea each year (i.e., up to more than 1600 deaths each day). In developing countries, during longitudinal studies in infants and young children in a community setting where all diarrheal episodes are monitored, the incidence of rotavirus diarrhea is lower than that of diarrhea caused by various other pathogens, but characteristically dehydration is more often associated with rotavirus disease than with illness caused by other agents.

In temperate climates, rotavirus gastroenteritis has a characteristic seasonal occurrence during the cooler months of the year, with a peak prevalence in the winter months. In tropical countries, it occurs throughout the year, with less pronounced peaks. Rotavirus diarrhea occurs most frequently in children between age 6 months and 24 months. Infants younger than 6 months have the next highest incidence, although in certain studies, the highest frequency is observed in this age group. The low frequency of clinical illness in neonates who undergo rotavirus infection is an unusual paradox that has not been explained, although the protective role of maternal antibodies is considered to be of prime importance. Rotavirus gastroenteritis occurs infrequently in adults, but subclinical infections are common.

Rotaviruses probably are transmitted by the fecal-oral route, although respiratory transmission remains a possibility, because there is such a rapid acquisition of serum antibody during the first 2 years of life, regardless of hygienic conditions. Nosocomial rotavirus infections occur frequently. The incubation period of rotavirus illness is approximately 2 to 4 days. There are 10 recognized group A human rotavirus serotypes, of which those numbered 1 to 4 appear to be consistently clinically important, although serotypes G5, G8, G9, and G10 have also been detected as described earlier. Group B rotavirus has been responsible for widespread outbreaks of gastroenteritis in adults in China, and a relatively small number of group C rotaviruses have been recovered from individuals with gastroenteritis in various countries. With the exception of the group B rotaviruses in China, the role of the non–group A rotaviruses in other regions of the world appears to be relatively minor at this time.

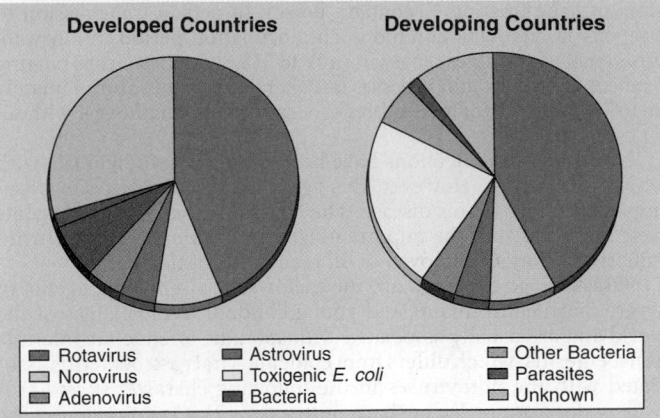

Developed Countries   **Developing Countries**

Legend:
- Rotavirus
- Norovirus
- Adenovirus
- Astrovirus
- Toxigenic *E. coli*
- Bacteria
- Other Bacteria
- Parasites
- Unknown

FIGURE 374–2 • Estimates of the roles of etiologic agents in severe diarrheal illnesses requiring hospitalization of infants and young children in developed and developing countries. (Adapted from Kapikian AZ: Viral gastroenteritis. JAMA 1993;269:627–630.)

Rotavirus infections have been observed in individuals with travelers' diarrhea. However, rotaviruses are not considered to be an important cause of this illness.

An estimate of the role of rotaviruses and other microbial agents as the cause of severe diarrhea of infants and young children requiring hospitalization is shown in Figure 374–2. A summary of key findings regarding the epidemiology and importance of various viruses associated with acute gastroenteritis is shown in Table 374–1.

Pathology and Pathogenesis

NOROVIRUS. Histopathologic lesions after Norwalk or Hawaii virus infection are characterized by a reversible involvement of the upper jejunum. The jejunal mucosa remains intact, with marked broadening and blunting of the villi and shortening of the microvilli, along with mononuclear cell infiltration and cytoplasmic vacuolization. Functional alterations may include a transient malabsorption of fat, D-xylose, and lactose and a significant decrease in levels of small intestinal brush border enzymes (i.e., alkaline phosphatase and trehalase). Adenylate cyclase activity in the jejunum is not elevated. Delay in gastric emptying may be responsible for the nausea and vomiting associated with these agents.

The nature of immunity to Norwalk virus is perplexing, because about 50% of adults are susceptible to natural and experimental illnesses. Although immunity has been observed in approximately 50% of adults, it appears to correlate inversely with the level of serum or local jejunal antibody. In recent volunteer studies with the Norwalk virus, innate genetic resistance appeared to be an important protective factor against Norwalk virus infection.

ROTAVIRUS. The major histopathologic lesions are characterized by reversible involvement of the proximal small intestine. The mucosa remains intact, with shortening of the villi, mononuclear cell infiltration in the lamina propria, distended cisternae of the endoplasmic reticulum, mitochondrial swelling, and sparse, irregular microvilli. Functional alterations may include impaired D-xylose absorption and depressed levels of disaccharidases (i.e., maltase, sucrase, and lactase). The nonstructural protein NSP4, with enterotoxin activity (encoded by gene 10), has been shown to induce diarrhea in a mouse model by its effect on calcium regulation. Its role in humans awaits further study.

The mechanism of immunity to human rotaviruses is not clear. Although significant levels of serum antibodies correlate with resistance to illness, the role of local intestinal immunity has not been evaluated as extensively. Animal studies indicate that antibody in the small intestine is the major determinant of resistance to illness. A high rate of subclinical infection in neonates is well documented and may be related to passively acquired maternal antibody, host factors, or naturally attenuated rotaviruses that are able to persist in newborn nurseries.

Clinical Manifestations

NOROVIRUS. Clinical characteristics of illness induced by the noroviruses include nausea, vomiting, diarrhea, anorexia, abdominal discomfort, or any combination. Accompanying clinical manifestations may also include myalgias, low-grade fever, headache, and chills. In children, vomiting occurs more often than diarrhea, whereas in adults, the opposite pattern is observed. The onset of illness may be abrupt, marked by vomiting or diarrhea, or both. The illness is usually mild and characteristically lasts about 24 to 48 hours in volunteer challenge studies. In addition, the mean (or median) duration of illness was between 12–60 hours in 26 of 28 naturally-occurring Norwalk virus out-breaks. However, severe gastroenteritis has been observed in middle-aged patients and has contributed to the death of elderly, debilitated individuals. The stools are characteristically loose and watery; blood, mucus, and leukocytes are not typically present. A transient decrease in the T-, B-, and null-cell lymphocyte subpopulations has been observed. The role of Norwalk virus in the etiology of gastroenteritis in human immunodeficiency virus (HIV)–positive individuals appears to be similar to that observed in non–HIV-infected controls.

ROTAVIRUS. Rotavirus infection can produce a variety of responses in infants and young children, ranging from subclinical infection and mild diarrhea to a severe and occasionally fatal dehydrating illness. Clinical characteristics include vomiting, diarrhea, abdominal discomfort, fever, or any combination. Fever and vomiting often develop before the diarrhea. Accompanying clinical manifestations may include dehydration, irritability, and pharyngeal or tympanic membrane erythema. For hospitalized patients, the mean duration of confinement is 4 days (range, 2 to 14 days). The stools are characteristically loose and watery and only infrequently contain blood or leukocytes.

Although rotaviruses can cause severe or fatal dehydrating illnesses in developing countries, deaths have also been documented in developed countries. In a study in Canada, rotavirus gastroenteritis was implicated in the deaths of 21 children 4 to 30 months old (mean, 11 months) over a period of about 5 years. Twenty children were dead or moribund on arrival at hospitals, and one child was infected nosocomially. With the exception of the latter patient and one other, each child was considered healthy before the rotavirus illness. Death occurred within 1 to 3 days of onset of symptoms. Dehydration and electrolyte imbalance leading to cardiac arrest were believed to be the major cause of death in 16 patients; aspiration of vomitus was the cause of death in 3 patients; and seizures were a contributing factor in the remaining 2 patients.

Rotavirus can also induce chronic symptomatic diarrhea with prolonged fecal shedding of the virus and antigenemia in patients with primary immunodeficiency diseases. Infections with rotaviruses or other viral and bacterial enteric pathogens may be especially severe in individuals who are immunosuppressed for bone marrow transplantation. In one study, 8 of 78 such patients (average age of the entire group, 20.5 years) shed rotavirus in stools, and 5 of the 8 died. Nosocomial rotavirus infection has been associated with severe diarrhea in adult renal transplant recipients; and a non–group A rotavirus was associated with severe gastroenteritis in an 8-year-old bone marrow transplant recipient. Rotavirus infections have also been persistent and severe in children with severe combined immunodeficiency. Rotavirus infections have been associated with necrotizing enterocolitis and hemorrhagic gastroenteritis in neonates. Outbreaks of rotavirus gastroenteritis have occurred among elderly individuals in nursing homes, with several fatalities. Rotaviruses do not appear to have an important role as etiologic agents of acute diarrhea in HIV-positive adults. Studies evaluating the role of rotavirus infection with intussusception have yielded conflicting results that need to be resolved by controlled epidemiologic investigations.

Diagnosis

NOROVIRUS. Because a specific diagnosis of infection with noroviruses cannot be made by clinical observation, the diagnosis must be made in the laboratory and relies on detection of virus in the stool or a serologic response to a virus-specific antigen. These tests include IEM (for the entire group) and enzyme-linked immunosorbent assay

(ELISA). Molecular biologic advances—notably the cloning and sequencing of Norwalk and related viruses and expression of their capsids in baculovirus, which also resulted in a ready source of recombinant virus-like particles—have led to a proliferation of diagnostic assays such as PCR-based and ELISA procedures for research use. By IEM, shedding of the Norwalk virus is maximal at or shortly after onset of illness and minimal at 72 hours after onset. However, by PCR, the peak of virus shedding in volunteers was 25 to 72 hours after challenge, with virus detection for at least 7 days. The characteristic absence of fecal leukocytes in Norwalk infection may be helpful for differentiation from *Shigella* or *Salmonella* enteritis.

Although a specific clinical diagnosis of infection with noroviruses cannot be made in the individual patient, a tentative diagnosis of infection can be made during an outbreak if certain criteria are met: (1) bacterial or parasitic pathogens are not detected; (2) vomiting is present in at least 50% of cases; (3) incubation period is 24 to 48 hours; and (4) mean or median duration of illness is 12 to 60 hours.

ROTAVIRUS. The clinical manifestations of rotavirus gastroenteritis are not distinctive enough to enable diagnosis. The diagnosis requires detection of the virus or demonstration of a significant serologic response to rotavirus in paired, acute and convalescent sera. The epidemiologic pattern relating to the age of the patient, the temporal occurrence of illness, and the signs and symptoms of illness, however, may suggest the diagnosis. The usual absence of fecal leukocytes in rotavirus diarrhea may help in early differentiation from *Shigella* or *Salmonella* enteritis.

By conventional assays such as EM and ELISA, stools obtained from the first to fourth day of illness are optimal for detecting rotavirus, but virus shedding may continue up to 21 days. Virus is characteristically present in stools during the early phase of diarrhea, but diarrhea may continue for 2 to 3 days after virus shedding has ceased. However, by a PCR-based assay, the duration of virus shedding ranged from 4 to 57 days after onset of diarrhea, with 30% of the children shedding virus for 25 to 57 days.

More than 25 assays have been developed to detect rotavirus in stools. The most rapid method is still direct EM because in negatively stained preparations these agents have a distinctive morphologic appearance and are present in large amounts. The non–group A rotaviruses, which do not share the common group antigen, can also be detected by EM. However, an electron microscope may not be readily available, and its use may be impractical when evaluating a large number of specimens. Other rapid and highly effective methods for virus detection of group A rotaviruses have been developed, including ELISA, counterimmunoelectro-osmophoresis, radioimmunoassay, reverse passive hemagglutination assay (RPHA), latex agglutination (LA), RNA electrophoresis (electropherotyping), dot hybridization, and PCR. Commercial kits are available for the ELISA and LA assays. A popular method is the confirmatory ELISA because it is simple to perform, is sensitive, does not require specialized equipment, and has a negative serum antibody control for detecting nonspecific reactions. An ELISA using monoclonal anti-VP7 antibody is also available. An ELISA for group B or group C rotavirus has been developed. Diagnosis of group A rotavirus infection by growth in cell cultures is not practical. Serotyping by ELISA or PCR remains a research tool.

There are many methods for measuring a serologic response to rotavirus infection, including IEM, complement fixation, immunofluorescence, immune adherence hemagglutination assay, ELISA, neutralization, hemagglutination-inhibition, inhibition of RPHA, and a competition solid-phase immunoassay that measures epitope-specific immune responses to individual rotavirus serotypes. Complement fixation is an efficient assay for detecting a serologic response to rotavirus in patients between the ages of 6 and 24 months but is not as effective in adults or infants younger than 6 months. Detection of rotavirus or demonstration of a serologic response does not necessarily establish an etiologic association with the patient's illness, especially in newborns and adults, who frequently undergo subclinical infection.

Rx Treatment

NOROVIRUS. Because the noroviruses characteristically cause mild, self-limited gastroenteritis, replacement of fluid and electrolyte loss with orally administered isotonic fluids is usually sufficient However, if severe vomiting or diarrhea occurs, parenteral fluid replacement may be necessary. The principles for fluid replacement for noroviruses are similar to those outlined for rotavirus below. In volunteer studies with Norwalk virus, oral administration of bismuth subsalicylate following the onset of symptoms, significantly reduced the severity and duration of abdominal cramps, and significantly decreased the median duration of gastrointestinal symptoms from 20 hours to 14 hours. However, the number, weight, and water content of stools and the level of virus excretion were not affected significantly. The American Academy of Pediatrics did not recommend the use of bismuth subsalicylate for treatment of acute diarrhea of infants and young children because of concerns about toxic effects.

ROTAVIRUS. Because rotavirus gastroenteritis may lead to severe dehydration in infants and young children, the early replacement of fluids and electrolytes is essential. Intravenous fluids have been used effectively in treating dehydration. However, in various parts of the world where such treatment is not feasible, efforts have been made to evaluate the effectiveness of an oral rehydration solution (ORS), and oral rehydration therapy with ORS has been shown to be safe and effective in the treatment of mild to moderate dehydration secondary to diarrhea of varying etiology. In a double-blind study comparing ORS with intravenous fluids in infants and young children with uncomplicated rotavirus watery diarrhea, ORS containing glucose (20 g/L) or sucrose (40 g/L) plus electrolytes was found to be as effective as intravenous therapy for rehydration. Glucose electrolyte solutions were recommended for optimal results. The recommended WHO ORS is composed of the following: sodium, 90 mmol/L; chloride, 80 mmol/L; potassium, 20 mmol/L; trisodium citrate dihydrate, 10 mmol/L; and glucose, 111 mmol/L, for an overall osmolarity of 311 mOsm/L. Sodium bicarbonate, 30 mmol/L, may be substituted for the trisodium citrate, dihydrate. The efficacy of oral glucose-electrolyte solutions that contained 90 mmol of sodium per liter (as in the WHO formula described above) or an ORS with a reduced sodium concentration (i.e., reduced-osmolarity ORS) was compared in infants and young children with watery diarrhea of various causes, including rotavirus. The reduced-osmolarity ORS was composed of the following: sodium, 75 mmol/L; chloride, 65 mmol/L; potassium, 20 mmol/L; citrate, 10 mmol/L; and glucose, 75 mmol/L, for an overall osmolarity of 245 mOsm/L. The proportion of infants and young children requiring unscheduled intravenous therapy was found to be significantly lower among those who were given the reduced-osmolarity ORS (required in 10%) than in those who were given the WHO ORS (required in 15%). After the initial calculated fluid deficit is corrected by the ORS, ongoing diarrheal or vomiting fluid losses should be replaced with ORS, volume for volume, until the diarrhea or vomiting stops. The infant's usual diet should be resumed when the rehydration therapy is completed. If oral rehydration fails to correct the fluid and electrolyte loss, if the patient has severe persistent vomiting and is unable to drink, or if the patient is severely dehydrated or in a state of shock or near shock or has depressed consciousness (see later), intravenous therapy must be given immediately. In patients with severe dehydration, intravenous therapy should be used until the patient is able to drink fluids, as needed. Beverages containing high concentrations of simple sugars such as commercial carbonated drinks should be avoided during a diarrheal illness.

Rice-based ORS is effective in rehydrating infants and young children hospitalized with mild to moderate dehydration caused by diarrhea associated with various pathogens, including rotavirus. Glucose-based or rice-based ORS was effective in rehydration and maintenance therapy. Patients with vomiting usually may be treated with ORS if it is administered in frequent, small amounts (e.g., 5 mL/minute). Oral rehydration therapy should not be given to infants and young children with depressed consciousness because of the possibility of fluid aspiration.

With regard to antidiarrheal compounds for treatment of acute diarrhea of infants and young children, the American Academy of

Continued

Pediatrics did not recommend the use of loperamide, anticholinergic agents, bismuth subsalicylate, adsorbents, or lactobacillus-containing compounds; they also stated that the use of opiates as well as opiate and atropine combination drugs for the treatment of acute diarrhea in infants and young children was contraindicated.

In a limited study, chronic rotavirus illness in immunodeficient children has been treated effectively by oral feeding of pooled human milk that contained rotavirus antibody. Oral administration of preparations containing rotavirus antibody has produced conflicting results regarding their efficacy for treatment of normal children during episodes of rotavirus gastroenteritis.

Prevention

NOROVIRUS. There are no specific methods for preventing illness by the noroviruses. However, because of the extremely infectious nature of these agents, careful handwashing and proper disposal of contaminated material should minimize transmission. Hygienic preparation of food and measures to decrease contamination of drinking water or swimming facilities should limit the frequency of Norwalk virus outbreaks. Active immunization against this group of viruses is not yet feasible.

ROTAVIRUS. Epidemiologic studies indicate the global need for a rotavirus vaccine to prevent rotavirus diarrhea in the first 2 years of life, when illness is most severe. Efforts have focused on developing a live, attenuated oral vaccine that is effective against all important serotypes. A promising initial strategy involved the Jennerian approach, in which a related rotavirus from a nonhuman host (i.e., bovine or rhesus rotavirus strain) was used as the immunizing agent. Efficacy trials of several such candidate rotavirus vaccines gave variable results, and it soon became apparent that these vaccines did not induce satisfactory heterotypic immunity in infants not primed by previous rotavirus infection. The rhesus rotavirus vaccine (a VP7 serotype 3 strain) induced protection against rotavirus diarrhea in the 1- to 4-month age group in a study in which VP7 serotype 3 was predominant, but in other studies it failed to protect unprimed infants against illnesses caused by rotaviruses other than those of serotype 3. Thus, the Jennerian approach was modified, with the goal being a quadrivalent vaccine composed of rhesus rotavirus (serotype 3) and three reassortant rotaviruses, each containing 10 rhesus rotavirus genes, and a single human rotavirus gene that encodes VP7 serotype 1, 2, or 4 specificity. Field trials of the quadrivalent vaccine in infants and young children have shown that three oral doses of live, attenuated quadrivalent (or tetravalent) rotavirus vaccine are highly effective in preventing severe rotavirus diarrhea, achieving an efficacy of 80% in a U.S. multicenter trial (100% against dehydration), 91% in Finland (97% against dehydration and 100% against hospitalization), 88% in Venezuela (75% against dehydration), and 69% in Native Americans (too few cases of dehydration to evaluate). Efficacy against any rotavirus-caused diarrhea ranged from 48 to 68%, which is consistent with the goal of the rotavirus vaccine to prevent severe (but not any) rotavirus diarrhea, because reinfections also occur commonly after natural rotavirus infection. In these trials, up to 29% of vaccinees developed a characteristically low-grade transient fever of 38.1° C or higher (rectal) within 5 days of the first dose of vaccine. In February and June 1998, the U.S. Advisory Committee on Immunization Practices (ACIP) recommended routine immunization with three oral doses at 2, 4, and 6 months of age. In August 1998, this quadrivalent rotavirus vaccine (RotaShield) was licensed by the U.S. Food and Drug Administration for the immunization of infants at 2, 4, and 6 months of age.

However, in July 1999, after more than 1 million doses of vaccine had been given, the CDC recommended suspending further vaccination because postlicensure surveillance suggested that the vaccine was linked with cases of intussusception. In October 1999, the ACIP withdrew its recommendation because of additional data that supported the association, notably in the first 2 weeks after vaccination and predominantly after the first dose. In conjunction with these events, the manufacturer (Wyeth Laboratories) withdrew the vaccine from the market. The population-attributable risk of the vaccine with intussusception is estimated to be approximately 1 in 10,000 vaccinated infants from CDC case-control and cohort studies. However, NIH ARHQ population-based analyses for intussusception place the risk at 1 excess case per ≅32,000 in the target population of 45–210-day-old infants, the age group that was given practically all first doses of Rotashield. A decrease in hospitalization for intussusception was observed in the <1 year age group overall. The fate of this vaccine has aroused considerable national and international interest and controversy.

Breast milk is considered to confer some degree of protection against clinically significant rotavirus diarrhea during infancy. Prophylactic oral administration of human serum globulin containing rotavirus antibody to low-birth-weight neonates provides significant protection against rotavirus diarrhea. Passive oral immunization of infants and young children with bovine colostrum that contains antibodies to human rotavirus is effective in preventing rotavirus illness when compared with a control group.

---

1. Choice Study Group: Multicenter, randomized, double-blind clinical trial to evaluate the efficacy and safety of a reduced osmolarity oral rehydration salts solution in children with acute watery diarrhea. Pediatrics 2001;107:613–618.

SUGGESTED READINGS

Cunliffe NA, Bresee JS, Hart CA: Rotavirus vaccines: Development, current issues and future prospects. J Infect 2002;45:1–9. *A review of the development of rotavirus vaccines, of the events leading to the withdrawal of the licensed vaccine and of vaccines under development.*

Fankhouser RL, Monroe SS, Noel JS, et al. Epidemiologic and molecular trends of "Norwalk-like" viruses associated with outbreaks of gastroenteritis in the United States. J Infect Dis 2002;186:1–7. *Describes the role of noroviruses in outbreaks of nonbacterial gastroenteritis in the United States.*

Green KY, Chanock RM, Kapikian AZ: Human caliciviruses. In Knipe DM, Howley PM, Griffin DE, et al (eds): Fields Virology, 4th ed. Philadelphia, Lippincott, Williams & Wilkins, 2001, pp 841–874. *A comprehensive review of the human caliciviruses from a virologic, epidemiologic, and clinical perspective (375 references).*

Kapikian AZ, Hoshino Y, Chanock RM: Rotaviruses. In Knipe DM, Howley PM, Griffin DE, et al (eds): Fields Virology, 4th ed. Philadelphia, Lippincott, Williams & Wilkins, 2001, pp 1787–1833. *A comprehensive review of the human rotaviruses from a virologic, epidemiologic, and clinical perspective (549 references).*

Murphy BR, Morens DM, Simonsen L, et al: Reappraisal of the association of intussusception with the licensed live rotavirus vaccine challenges initial conclusions. J Infect Dis 2003;187:1301–1308. *A perspective reappraising the withdrawal of the vaccine and offering various hypotheses that illustrate the major issues.*

Murphy TV, Smith PJ, Gargiullo PM, Schwartz B: The first rotavirus vaccine and intussusception: Epidemiologic studies and policy decisions. J Infect Dis 2003;187:1309–1313. *A response to the perspective regarding withdrawal of this vaccine.*

Parashar VD, Hummelman EG, Bresee JS, et al: Global illness and deaths caused by rotavirus disease in children. Emerging Inf Dis 2003;9:565–571. *Provides recent estimates on the importance of rotavirus disease.*

Provisional Committee on Quality Improvement, Subcommittee on Acute Gastroenteritis: Practice parameter: The management of acute gastroenteritis in young children. Pediatrics 1996;97:424–433. *A comprehensive examination of issues in the management of acute gastroenteritis in young children 1 month to 5 years of age, from the American Academy of Pediatrics. Important reading for the clinician.*

375 INTRODUCTION TO HEMORRHAGIC FEVER VIRUSES

Robert E. Shope

The viral hemorrhagic fevers encompass syndromes that vary from febrile hemorrhagic disease with capillary fragility to acute severe shock leading rapidly to death. The causative agents include arthropod-borne and rodent-associated viruses. The rodent-associated viruses do not require an arthropod vector but are transmitted directly to vertebrates by aerosol spread or contact with infected excreta or body secretions of the rodent. The reservoir and natural mode of transmission for the African hemorrhagic fever viruses, Marburg and Ebola, are not known.

At least 18 viruses cause human hemorrhagic fevers (Table 375–1). They are in the families Flaviviridae, Bunyaviridae, Arenaviridae, and Filoviridae. All contain RNA, and nearly all are zoonoses.

The hemorrhagic fevers form a special group of diseases characterized by viral replication in lymphoid cells, followed by fever and myalgia and leading to hemorrhagic manifestations and hypovolemic shock. The basic physiologic defect in most is capillary leakage. In some, such as yellow fever, hepatocellular damage is prominent. In others, such as hantavirus disease, renal or pulmonary lesions are striking. The case-fatality rates may be high, and the pathogenesis is poorly understood. Disseminated intravascular coagulopathy (DIC) is a feature in some cases but probably not all. Antigen-antibody complexes may lead to release of mediators of shock in some cases, and

Table 375–1 • CLINICAL PARAMETERS OF VIRAL HEMORRHAGIC FEVERS

DISEASE	VIRAL AGENT	INCUBATION PERIOD (DAYS)	Hemorrhage	Hepatitis	Encephalitis	Nephropathy	ARDS	CASE-FATALITY RATE (%)
			CLINICAL SYNDROMES					
Yellow fever	Yellow fever	3–6	Major	Major	Absent	Moderate	Absent	2–20
Dengue hemorrhagic fever	Dengue 1-4	5–8	Moderate	Moderate	Absent	Absent	Absent	2–10
Rift Valley fever	Rift Valley fever	3–6	Major	Major	Moderate	Absent	Absent	0.2–10
Crimean-Congo hemorrhagic fever	Crimean-Congo hemorrhagic fever	2–9	Major	Major	Minor	Absent	Absent	30–50
Kyasanur Forest disease	Kyasanur Forest disease	3–8	Minor	Minor	Moderate	Absent	Absent	5–10
Omsk hemorrhagic fever	Omsk hemorrhagic fever	3–8	Minor	Minor	Moderate	Absent	Absent	0.4–2.5
Hemorrhagic fever with renal syndrome	Hantaan, Puumala, Dobrava, Seoul	2–42	Moderate	Rare	Minor	Major	Absent	2–5
Hantavirus pulmonary syndrome	Sin Nombre	12–16	Minor	Minor	Absent	Minor	Major	40–50
Venezuelan hemorrhagic fever	Guanarito	7–14	Moderate	Rare	Rare	Minor	Absent	33
Brazilian hemorrhagic fever	Sabiá	8–12	Major	Minor	Minor	Minor	Absent	33
Argentine hemorrhagic fever	Junin	10–14	Minor	Rare	Moderate	Minor	Absent	10–20
Bolivian hemorrhagic fever	Machupo	7–14	Moderate	Rare	Moderate	Minor	Absent	15–30
Lassa fever	Lassa	3–16	Minor	Major	Minor	Minor	Absent	15
African hemorrhagic fever	Marburg	3–9	Major	Major	Minor	Absent	Absent	20–30
	Ebola	3–18	Major	Major	Minor	Absent	Absent	53–88

ARDS = adult respiratory distress syndrome.

direct effects of viral replication on capillary permeability in some have not been ruled out. It is important to understand the pathogenetic mechanism to manage these infections, but our knowledge is sparse at present.

Control can be achieved by interrupting the cycle of infection, including peridomestic rodent control (Bolivian hemorrhagic fever) and, for arboviruses, vaccination of reservoir animals (Rift Valley fever), vector control, and education on methods to avoid the vector (dengue) or rodent reservoir (hantavirus pulmonary syndrome). Vaccines are available or are under development for some of the agents, such as Rift Valley fever, yellow fever, dengue, and Junin viruses. For others such as Lassa virus, we now have an antiviral drug, and for still another (Junin) preexposure and postexposure protection is afforded by human immune plasma.

YELLOW FEVER

Definition

Yellow fever is an acute viral disease caused by infection with yellow fever virus. The disease is exemplary of the viral hemorrhagic fevers described in the following sections (see Table 375–1). The infection is often subclinical, but it may lead to disease whose severity varies from mild and self-limited to fulminant with a fatal outcome. Classical yellow fever is characterized by sudden onset, moderately high fever, nausea, bradycardia, prostration, vomiting of altered blood, jaundice, oliguria, and albuminuria. Natural cycles of the infection occur periodically in mosquitoes and primates of tropical South America as far north as Panama and in tropical west, central, and east Africa.

Etiology

Yellow fever virus is in the genus *Flavivirus* of the family Flaviviridae. Members of the family are single-stranded, negative-sense RNA viruses, spherical, and approximately 40 nm in diameter. Particles form in the cytoplasm in close association with endoplasmic reticulum. They contain a lipid envelope and replicate in both arthropod and vertebrate cells. Other members of the Flaviviridae, including dengue, West Nile, and St. Louis encephalitis, cross-react with yellow fever virus in serologic tests and may confound the diagnosis. Minor antigenic differences exist between strains of yellow fever virus from Africa and South America and among strains from different regions of Africa; however, the 17D yellow fever vaccine protects against all strains. The virus can be isolated in mosquito, arthropod, and vertebrate tissue cultures; baby mice; and several monkey species. Rhesus monkeys regularly succumb after experimental inoculation, and their disease mimics severe human disease.

Epidemiology

Two epidemiologic types of yellow fever are distinguished: the urban and the sylvan (jungle) forms. Urban yellow fever is transmitted by *Aedes aegypti* mosquitoes from person to person, whereas sylvan yellow fever is maintained in a forest cycle of monkeys and forest canopy mosquitoes; humans are infected when they enter the forest or when infected monkeys exit and establish transmission in mosquitoes at the forest fringe. The two types do not differ clinically.

A. aegypti is a domiciliary mosquito that breeds in abandoned tires, jars, cans, water storage containers, roof catchments, and drains in and around houses. Urban yellow fever was a major killer until the early 1900s, when mosquito control in Havana, Rio de Janeiro, Guayaquil, and other large urban centers eliminated the disease. The last recorded urban epidemic case in the Americas was in Trinidad in 1954. *A. aegypti* continues to be prevalent in African cities, and *A. aegypti*–transmitted outbreaks still occur there. Major epidemics were recorded in Ethiopia, 1960 to 1962; Nigeria, 1969; Senegal, 1965 and 1979; Gambia, 1978; Ghana and Burkina Faso, 1983; and Kenya, 1993. In 1986, an epidemic involving at least 3000 persons occurred in Nigeria, in Benue and Cross River States, and it extended into Oyo and Niger States in 1987. An estimated 39,000 cases, with 8400 deaths, were recorded.

Yellow fever virus in Africa is transmitted by *A. aegypti* not only in the cities but also in semirural areas. In addition, some African epidemics are maintained by other *Aedes* species, such as *Aedes bromeliae* and the tree hole–breeding *Aedes africanus*, *Aedes luteocephalus*, and *Aedes furcifer-taylori*, which transmit the virus in savannah and the transition forest–savannah zones of west Africa.

Sylvan yellow fever was recognized initially in Brazil in 1932. After urban yellow fever had been controlled in the Americas, sporadic cases continued to occur in persons exposed to mosquitoes in the jungles of South America and Africa. This sylvan form is maintained in tropical America by *Haemagogus* mosquitoes and forest primates and sometimes by other sylvan animals. Evidence favors the hypothesis that the virus moves through the forest, cycling in one place until the monkeys are immune, then dying out and moving to areas where susceptible monkeys live. People entering the forest are at risk. Sylvan yellow fever extends periodically outside the enzootic zone into forests such as those in Panama and Central America. The virus can be maintained over dry periods by transovarial transmission in mosquitoes, although it remains to be shown whether maintenance in mosquito eggs is more than a temporary mechanism.

The sylvan cycle in Africa is more complicated than in the Americas; in tropical Africa, the virus cycles between *A. africanus* and monkeys. Another African mosquito, *A. bromeliae*, which feeds on both humans and monkeys, serves in some areas as a link between primates in the deep forest and people in the African villages.

A. aegypti was once carried on sailing ships between tropical ports and into temperate zone cities. Modern oceangoing ships no longer harbor mosquito breeding sites, but the mosquito continues to travel by small boats, airplanes, and cars and especially in the form of dried eggs transported by used tires. Cities such as Rio de Janeiro, which were once freed of the mosquito, are now reinfested, as are most tropical Latin American cities. Dengue fever, which is also spread by *A. aegypti*, reappeared in Rio de Janeiro in 1986 and subsequently spread widely. To control the mosquito again in the Americas will be difficult because of insecticide resistance, population growth, and the high price of labor and materials. Jungle yellow fever continues to cycle, reappearing in the same locale every 5 to 40 years. The scene is thus set again for emergence of the virus from the jungle to reinitiate the urban cycle in the Americas.

A. aegypti is easily identified. It has white thoracic scales in the shape of a lyre and black legs with white bands. Mosquitoes that have fed on a viremic vertebrate become infective after an extrinsic incubation period of 9 to 30 days, the shorter periods correlating with higher ambient temperatures. This extrinsic incubation period in the mosquito accounts for the delay from the first human infection in an urban outbreak to subsequent clusters of infection.

Yellow fever is not found in Asia, although large areas harbor *A. aegypti* that are capable of transmitting the virus should it be introduced. India and other Asian nations require vaccination of travelers from regions in which yellow fever is endemic.

All age groups and races are susceptible. However, sylvan yellow fever is found almost always in young males because they are the individuals who venture into the forest. Immunity following vaccination or infection is long lasting. During an epidemic, the population at risk may therefore be limited to age groups not covered by prior immunization or those born since a prior outbreak. There is also some evidence that persons may be protected by antibody to heterologous flaviviruses.

During the 24-year period from 1965 to 1988, 3324 cases of yellow fever were reported in the Americas and 7701 in Africa. The numbers of cases are greatly underestimated; the World Health Organization (WHO) estimates that 200,000 yellow fever cases and 30,000 deaths occur annually. Case-fatality rates are usually about 20%, but they are higher in some epidemics. Ratios of apparent to inapparent infection, estimated at 1:10, may vary greatly.

Pathology and Pathogenesis

The lesions of yellow fever involve primarily the liver, heart, kidneys, and lymphoid tissues. Grossly, the skin is icteric, and there may be multiple hemorrhages or petechiae of the skin, mucous membranes, and multiple organs. The liver is normal in size, icteric, and fatty. The heart is soft and flabby, and the kidneys are swollen and a pink-gray color. Small peritoneal and pleural effusions are sometimes observed.

Histologic findings are often characteristic in patients who die before the ninth day of illness, but the lesions are not always pathognomonic. The most striking lesion is the eosinophilic degeneration and coagulation of hepatocytes (Councilman's bodies). Hepatocyte destruction is most marked in the midzone of the lobule, with relative sparing of the central vein and portal areas. Intranuclear eosinophilic granular inclusions or enlarged nucleoli (Torres bodies) are also described. Both microvacuolar and multivacuolar fatty changes are prominent, especially after the first week of illness. Inflammation is uncommon, and the reticulum framework is unaffected, probably accounting for the absence of postnecrotic fibrosis in convalescence and the regeneration of hepatocytes in recovered patients. The kidneys show cloudy swelling of tubular epithelium leading to acute tubular necrosis. The glomeruli are not obviously affected, but special stains indicate Schiff-positive alterations in the basal membranes, and proteinaceous material accumulates in the capsular spaces and lumina of the proximal tubules. The myocardium is characterized by granular or fatty infiltration of muscle fibers and of the atrioventricular conduction system and cloudy swelling and degeneration of myocytes without inflammation. Large monocytes replace lymphocytic cells in the splenic follicles and lymph nodes. Encephalitis is rare, although petechial hemorrhage in the brain stem and cerebral edema are observed.

Knowledge of the pathogenesis of yellow fever is sparse. Yellow fever cases occur in remote areas, and pathophysiologic studies of yellow fever patients are usually done with only rudimentary laboratory facilities. The virus replicates in the hepatocytes and myocytes, and it is presumed that lesions in these target cells are a direct effect of the virus. Jaundice and prolonged prothrombin time can be explained by hepatocellular damage; bradycardia and arrhythmias are explained by myocyte and atrioventricular node perturbation. The etiology of renal tubular necrosis is not clear, but it may be secondary to hepatic changes. Some, but not all, fatal cases are associated with thrombocytopenia; increased prothrombin, partial thromboplastin, and thrombin times; diminished factor VIII and fibrinogen levels; and the presence of fibrin split products. The bleeding in these cases may be secondary to DIC, but this is not generally accepted by all investigators. Hypoglycemia, metabolic acidosis, and hyperkalemia characterize the terminal stage and are probably the result of multiple organ system failure.

Clinical Manifestations

Severe yellow fever is a fulminant febrile illness with 50% or greater case fatality. A great deal of variation occurs, however; most cases are mild with a better prognosis, and only about 10 to 20% are in the severe category. The intrinsic incubation period is 3 to 6 days and in exceptional cases as long as 10 days.

The clinical syndrome is classified as very mild, mild, moderately severe, or malignant. Patients with very mild cases have fever and headache and recover in 48 hours or less. Those with mild cases have sudden fever and headache with nausea, sometimes bleeding of the gums or epistaxis, bradycardia, or albuminuria. These patients recover in 2 or 3 days. Those with moderately severe cases have more marked manifestations of bleeding, definite bradycardia in relation to the fever, nausea and vomiting, jaundice, and striking albuminuria. The illness may be aborted after 3 to 4 days or serious hemorrhagic manifestations may develop, such as black vomit, melena, and metrorrhagia. Moderately severe yellow fever may last 1 week or even longer.

Classical yellow fever is characterized as malignant and is divided into three periods: infection, remission, and intoxication. The period of infection involves sudden onset of fever and headache, with initial rapid pulse, but by day 2 the pulse slows despite continued fever (Faget's sign). Headache, backache, and muscle pain may be severe, blood oozes from the gums, and other signs of bleeding become prominent. The face is flushed, the tongue is reddened (strawberry tongue), and the conjunctivae are injected; the patient is irritable, unable to sleep, and frequently constipated. The temperature is often 40° C or higher. On the third day of illness, nausea, vomiting of coffee-ground material, and notable albuminuria are characteristic. The bleeding is usually gastric, not lower intestinal, in origin. In the period of remission, often on day 4, the patient feels better, the fever drops, and headache and nausea subside. Remission lasts a few hours to 2 days. It is followed by the period of intoxication, in which the classical signs of fever, epigastric tenderness with vomiting of altered blood, nosebleeds, and albuminuria leading to oliguria or anuria occur. Dehydration may predispose to suppurative parotitis; the lungs are usually normal, but bacterial pneumonia may complicate the disease. Intoxication lasts from 3 days to 2 weeks and may be accompanied by heart failure with drop in blood pressure, hiccup, coma, and death. Sometimes the patient is lucid until the end.

The clinical syndrome may be predominantly one of hepatic, renal, or cardiac failure. Meningoencephalitis has also been recorded. Death usually occurs between the seventh and the tenth day of illness. Patients who survive generally recover completely, although the convalescence may be prolonged, and late death from cardiac failure or arrhythmias is a rare complication.

Laboratory Findings

Early in the course of disease, the following may be present: leukopenia with relative neutropenia (but sometimes with normal or elevated leukocyte count), decreased prothrombin time, and elevation of serum bilirubin level. After the third day of illness, full-blown yellow fever is associated with abnormalities referable to the liver, kidneys, and heart. The total and conjugated bilirubin concentration values are elevated and rise together. The mean bilirubin value is 9 to 10 mg/dL, but it averages 15 to 20 mg/dL in severe cases and may be much higher. Prothrombin and partial thromboplastin times are increased, and platelets, blood glucose, and clotting factors II, V, VII, IX, and X are decreased. Alkaline phosphatase levels are normal. Aminotransferase levels are of prognostic value; serum aspartate aminotransferase and alanine aminotransferase levels are consistently elevated in jaundiced patients.

Albuminuria usually appears on the fourth day, reaching levels of 3 to 5 mg/L (much higher in severe cases). Blood urea averages 109 mg/dL, and creatinine averages 5.9 mg/dL in fatal cases; the averages are much lower in nonfatal yellow fever. The urine may contain bile and casts. Electrocardiogram abnormalities are sometimes present, including abnormal ST-T waves and prolonged PR and QT intervals. The cerebrospinal fluid (CSF) is under increased pressure and may contain increased protein with normal cell counts.

Diagnosis

Diagnosis can be made by histopathologic examination of the liver, by isolation of yellow fever virus from blood during life and from liver and other tissues after death, by demonstration of specific nucleic acid, or by serologic tests. Yellow fever should be suspected in any febrile patient from endemic zones of Africa and the Americas and in areas of high *A. aegypti* prevalence where yellow fever may be introduced. Postmortem diagnosis by examination of liver taken by a viscerotome was successfully used in South America routinely for many years, and postmortem immunohistochemistry of liver is sensitive and relatively specific. Liver biopsy should not be attempted because of the danger of uncontrolled bleeding.

Yellow fever virus can be isolated from serum and blood during the first 4 days of fever by inoculation intracerebrally into baby mice or onto mammalian or mosquito cell cultures. Mice are observed for death; the virus causes cytopathic effect in Vero cells and is detected by immunofluorescence tests in mosquito cells 3 to 6 days after inoculation. The most rapid methods of diagnosis are identification of RNA by reverse transcription–polymerase chain reaction (RT-PCR) and detection of antigen in acute phase blood by the antigen capture enzyme-linked immunosorbent assay (ELISA). The tests can be completed in a few hours, although detection of antigen by ELISA is less sensitive than virus isolation.

Serologic diagnosis is made by demonstrating immunoglobulin M (IgM) by the antibody capture ELISA. Because IgM is relatively specific and is detectable in high titer for only a short time after infection, this technique is reliable using a single convalescent serum specimen. Alternatively, tests of sera collected during the acute and convalescent phases are diagnostic if they show a fourfold or greater rise (or fall) of yellow fever antibody. The neutralization test is highly specific, but the complement fixation, hemagglutination inhibition, and ELISA tests are usually used because they are quicker and lend themselves to field laboratory use. The laboratory must also rule out cross-reacting antibody by related viruses such as dengue. A radiolabeled RNA probe was able to detect yellow fever RNA in fixed human liver that had been stored for more than 20 years.

Differential Diagnosis

The mild form of yellow fever is not clinically distinguishable from other tropical fevers. Severe yellow fever simulates viral hepatitis, including hepatitis D; other hemorrhagic fevers; leptospirosis; rickettsial fevers; malignant malaria; and drug- and toxin-related conditions.

Prognosis

Two to 20% of patients with clinically evident yellow fever die, although as many as 50% of severely ill patients die. It is not clear whether these patients would survive if they received the most modern supportive treatment because most cases are treated in primitive clinics in Africa and South America. Patients who enter the period of intoxication have a guarded prognosis, especially if they develop anuria, high levels of albuminuria and bilirubinemia, a prothrombin time prolonged beyond 25% of normal, a rapid and weak pulse, uncontrolled bleeding, persistent hiccup, delirium, hypotension, or coma.

 Treatment

Treatment consists of complete bedrest, fluid and blood replacement, and supportive care, including monitoring of vital signs. Analgesics and antiemetics may be useful, but aspirin is contraindicated because it may exacerbate bleeding. Patients are placed under bed nets to prevent possible mosquito transmission to other patients and to hospital personnel. Malaria and bacterial complications should be treated if diagnosed. Electrolyte imbalance should be corrected. Dialysis has not been used in cases of renal tubular damage, but on theoretical grounds it may benefit patients with renal failure. If DIC is evident from laboratory tests, heparin may be used cautiously, although experience to date is insufficient to predict its efficacy. Interferon and other antiviral substances have not been tried in patients with yellow fever.

Prevention and Control

Yellow fever can be prevented by inoculation of 17D attenuated vaccine. This vaccine is safe, although rare severe and fatal illnesses have been recorded following administration. It induces antibody that persists at least 10 years in more than 90% of vaccinees, usually for life. The vaccine is produced in eggs and should not be given to persons with egg allergies. Travelers should be vaccinated at least 10 days before arrival in yellow fever–endemic areas. Because the presence of yellow fever often goes undetected and unreported in tropical Africa and South America, the vaccine should be given to travelers whether or not there is known active transmission. Human immunodeficiency virus infection is not a contraindication to vaccination. Unless the risk of exposure to yellow fever is great, vaccine is not recommended during pregnancy; however, it is not known to have caused fetal damage. In an epidemic, mosquito control measures and personal protection with repellents are recommended until vaccine can be obtained. An urban epidemic may represent an international emergency and should trigger immediate public health measures, both locally and abroad.

HEMORRHAGIC FEVER CAUSED BY DENGUE VIRUSES

Definition

Dengue hemorrhagic fever (DHF) is an acute febrile illness characterized by decreased platelet counts and hemoconcentration in patients infected with any one of the four serotypes of dengue virus. The disease in highly endemic areas affects primarily children and in other areas including the Americas affects all ages. Capillary permeability and coagulation defects lead to hemorrhagic manifestations and, in the more severe cases, to hypovolemic shock (dengue shock syndrome), with death in 40 to 50% of untreated shock syndrome patients. The disease has been endoepidemic in Southeast Asia since 1953 and is increasing in prevalence. It was restricted to Asia and the Pacific until 1981, when epidemic DHF appeared in Cuba. WHO estimated that 500,000 cases of DHF occur each year with at least 12,000 deaths.

Etiology

DHF is caused by infection with dengue viruses, but it is not yet established why hemorrhagic fever develops in one patient and classical dengue fever develops in another. Initially, it was hypothesized that strains of dengue virus that caused DHF were more virulent than others; this may still be true, but overwhelming evidence indicates that infection is enhanced and disease is more severe when the host has been sensitized by a prior dengue infection of different serotype.

Epidemiology

The epidemiology of DHF is that described for dengue fever with some added features. Epidemics of DHF are most common in Southeast Asia, the Pacific Islands, and, since 1981, the Caribbean and South America. It is estimated that fewer than 7% of individuals with dengue develop DHF. The attack rate in Thailand is highest in children, with a minor peak in infants, when maternal antibody is waning, and a major peak at ages 4 to 12 years, when second dengue infections are most common; adults as well as children develop DHF in some outbreaks, such as those in Cuba in 1981 and 1997. Well-nourished children in Southeast Asia appeared to be at higher risk than the undernourished, and blacks in the 1981 Cuban epidemic had milder illness than whites; well-controlled studies are needed to substantiate these observations.

Pathology

Postmortem focal hemorrhages, vascular congestion, and edema are evident in multiple organs. The spleen and lymphoid tissues show marked lymphocytolysis and phagocytosis of lymphocytes, primarily in the T cell–dependent zones. Proliferation of lymphoblasts and young plasma cells is also noted. Monocytic and lymphocytic nonnecrotizing perivascular infiltration is found in skin lesions, resembling an antibody-dependent Arthus reaction.

Pathogenesis

Dengue virus infects the macrophages, lymphocytes, and endothelial cells. On rare occasions, DHF occurs in primary dengue, indicating that direct infection of these cells with the virus can lead to the syndrome; however, the vast majority of cases consist of secondary infections. In these cases, the anamnestic antibody response is rapid, with formation of antigen-antibody complexes. Experimentally, formation of complexes enhances infectivity of the virus for monocytes through attachment of complexes at the Fc receptor site and entry of virus into the cell. Between 0.05 and 0.1% of monocytes in the peripheral blood can be visualized carrying dengue antigen. The replication of dengue virus in the monocyte is postulated to be the effector pathway leading to vascular permeability. Monocyte infection is presumably responsible for the observed complement activation and consumption by the classical and perhaps the alternative pathway. This process may result in formation of C3a and C5a, which are anaphylatoxins, or some other as yet unknown mediator of vascular permeability may be activated. Another effector pathway leads to coagulation defects, including thrombocytopenia and abnormal clotting. The entire process is rapid. It may evolve in a few hours to shock and death or, if managed effectively, to complete recovery. Although the pathogenesis is incompletely understood, the pathophysiologic events are known and can be treated rationally.

Clinical Manifestations

DHF usually starts with sudden onset of high fever and the signs and symptoms of dengue fever, which include facial flush, anorexia, headache, nausea, and pains in the muscles and joints. Hepatic tenderness, epigastric or generalized abdominal pain, and sore throat are frequent. The liver is usually palpable in children, and the spleen is characteristically prominent on radiographs. A high temperature continues for 2 days to a week. A positive tourniquet test result, easy bruising, and fine petechiae on the face, soft palate, and extremities indicate a hemorrhagic disorder. Sometimes gum bleeding and epistaxis are noted. The majority of cases are moderately severe or mild, and the patients recover after lysis of fever. The lysis may be associated with sweating, coolness of extremities, and transient lowering of blood pressure.

More severe cases are associated with shock. The fall in blood pressure occurs suddenly on the third to the seventh day of illness and is accompanied by cool, blotchy skin, circumoral cyanosis, and tachycardia. The patient becomes restless and may complain of acute abdominal pain. The pulse pressure drops to 20 mm Hg or less, and in severe cases blood pressure and pulse may not be detectable. Uncorrected shock may lead to metabolic acidosis and severe bleeding from the gastrointestinal tract and other sites. Death or recovery usually occurs in 12 to 24 hours. Surviving patients do not usually have sequelae. The white blood cell count is normal or slightly elevated, with lymphocytosis and atypical lymphocytes commonly seen. Hemoconcentration and elevated serum aspartate aminotransferase and blood urea nitrogen levels are noted.

Diagnosis

The laboratory diagnosis is that of dengue fever (Chapter 360); RT-PCR provides the possibility of rapid diagnosis. DHF with shock syndrome is a medical emergency, and therefore early clinical diagnosis is essential. Patients with DHF present with (1) acute onset of fever, which is high, continuous, and lasts 2 days or more; (2) positive tourniquet test result with spontaneous petechiae or ecchymoses, bleeding from gums or nose, hematemesis, or melena; (3) hepatomegaly, observed in more than 90% of pediatric Asian patients; (4) hypotension with cold, clammy skin, restlessness, and pulse pressure less than 20 mm Hg; (5) thrombocytopenia; (6) hematocrit increased 20% over the convalescent value; and (7) radiographic or ultrasound evidence of pleural and peritoneal effusion. Fever, hemorrhagic phenomena, thrombocytopenia, and hemoconcentration are the hallmarks of DHF, and, with hypotension or narrow pulse pressure, of dengue shock syndrome (DSS). Hepatoencephalopathy sometimes develops as a late manifestation. Bacterial endotoxic shock and meningococcemia can mimic DHF-DSS.

Rx Treatment

No specific treatment has been established. The object of therapy is to maintain hydration, to combat acidosis, and to correct coagulation abnormalities. Salicylates may contribute to bleeding and acidosis, and they are contraindicated. Paracetamol may be used. Steroids should not be used. Hematocrit should be determined frequently, at least daily, to measure the degree of plasma loss and the need for intravenous fluid. Fluid should be started at 20 mL/kg of body weight. One third to one half of fluid should be physiologic saline, and the remainder should be 5% glucose in water. If acidosis is present, one quarter of fluid should be 0.167 mol/L sodium bicarbonate. In shock cases, one should use Ringer's lactate solution, 5% glucose in physiologic saline, 5% glucose in one-half physiologic saline, 5% glucose in one-half Ringer's solution, or 5% glucose in one-third physiologic saline (depending on degree of dehydration and age). One should monitor for signs of cardiac failure during rapid fluid administration.

In case of shock, one should administer fluid rapidly and under pressure if necessary. Plasma or another volume expander should be given if shock persists, and the vital signs and hematocrit should be followed. The hematocrit should decline with fluid therapy, which is continued until the hematocrit is less than 40%, urine output is adequate, and the appetite returns. If levels of electrolytes and blood gases indicate acidosis, sodium bicarbonate should be administered. Heparin for intravascular coagulopathy (prolonged prothrombin and partial thromboplastin times) is usually not needed, but it may be used cautiously in refractory cases. Chloral hydrate should be given for sedation, oxygen should be administered for shock, and blood should be administered as needed.

Prognosis

Case fatality from DHF is 2 to 10%; deaths occur in patients with shock. Most patients survive when treated early by experienced health care workers. Recovery is rapid and without sequelae.

Prevention

Prevention is as described for dengue fever (Chapter 360).

TICK-BORNE FLAVIVIRUS DISEASES: KYASANUR FOREST DISEASE AND OMSK HEMORRHAGIC FEVER

Definition

Kyasanur Forest disease (KFD) of India and Omsk hemorrhagic fever (OHF) of western Siberia are tick-transmitted flavivirus fevers characterized by hemorrhage or encephalitis. Some patients manifest both syndromes.

Etiology

KFD and OHF viruses belong to the tick-borne complex of flaviviruses, which also encompasses the closely related viruses of central European tick-borne encephalitis, Russian spring-summer encephalitis, and Powassan encephalitis of North America and Asia.

Epidemiology

KFD was originally limited to the forests of Shimoga District of Karnataka State, India, but since its discovery in 1957 it has spread in an unpredictable fashion to three other neighboring forested districts. The largest outbreak occurred during 1982 to 1983 in a new focus in Nidle Forest. Many tick species are involved in transmission, especially nymphal *Haemaphysalis spinigera*. Small terrestrial mammals, as well as birds and bats, are infected in nature. When the forest is felled for plantations, the ecology is upset. Cattle brought in to graze at the forest fringe are not infected but serve as hosts that greatly increase the numbers of ticks. Infected ticks feed on black-faced langur monkeys and South Indian bonnet macaques, which become viremic, serve as amplifiers of infection, and often die. At the same time, epidemics occur in persons with forest occupations. People are infected incidentally and do not form part of the transmission cycle.

OHF occurs in the forest-steppe areas of the lake region of western Siberia. Epidemics of as many as 600 cases were recorded in the 1940s, but the disease has now become uncommon. Numbers of cases peak in May and again in August and September. The virus is transmitted by *Dermacentor pictus* ticks and is maintained in small-mammal populations. Muskrats, which were introduced for hunting in the 1920s, are susceptible and apparently transmit OHF virus to other muskrats and to hunters by direct contact. Lake water contaminated by dead muskrats is said to be responsible for water-borne disease. Both KFD and OHF are transmitted transovarially and trans-stadially in ticks.

Clinical Manifestations and Pathology

The incubation period is 3 to 8 days. Onset is sudden, with temperature up to 40° C, headache, papulovesicular lesions of the soft palate, myalgia, and prostration lasting 1 to 2 weeks. In more severe cases, nasal, enteric, uterine, or pulmonary hemorrhage may be evident. Leukopenia, thrombocytopenia, and albuminuria are found. Some patients have a diphasic course, with a more severe illness and meningoencephalitis after a 1- or 2-week afebrile period. The second phase is characterized by fever, severe headache, meningismus, mental disturbances, and tremors. Hemorrhagic manifestations or pneumonia may also be prominent in the second phase. The case-fatality rate of KFD is 5 to 10%; that of OHF is 0.4 to 2.5%. There are no sequelae. Infections in laboratory workers are common but are usually mild. Histopathologic findings are minor in comparison with the gravity of the clinical disease. Findings include extravasation of red blood cells, edema, and thrombi in the small vessels.

Diagnosis and Treatment

Diagnosis is by isolation of virus or detection of RNA in the blood during the first 10 days of illness and by demonstration of antibody rise or presence of specific IgM during convalescence. There is no specific treatment, but fluid and electrolyte balance should be maintained and blood transfused if needed. Analgesics other than aspirin may be indicated.

Prevention

Tick repellents, protective clothing, and spraying of forest tracts with acaricides are the only measures available for prevention.

CRIMEAN-CONGO HEMORRHAGIC FEVER

Definition

Crimean-Congo hemorrhagic fever (CCHF) is an acute febrile hemorrhagic tick-borne disease of Asia, Europe, and Africa. Mortality is high and hospital-based outbreaks are common.

Etiology

The disease is caused by CCHF virus of the *Nairovirus* genus, family Bunyaviridae. The virus kills baby mice and replicates in CER cells and several other cell culture systems.

Epidemiology

CCHF virus is transmitted in nature principally by hard ticks of the genus *Hyalomma* but also by ticks in the genera *Rhipicephalus, Boophilus,* and *Amblyomma*. The virus is maintained by transovarial and trans-stadial passage in the tick and is amplified by hares and possibly hedgehogs, sheep, and cattle. The giraffe, rhinoceros, eland, buffalo, kudu, zebra, and dogs in southern Africa carry antibodies to CCHF virus.

The virus or its antibody is found in the distribution of *Hyalomma* ticks. Foci occur in the former Soviet Union, the Balkan nations, Iraq, Iran, Pakistan, Afghanistan, western China, the Middle East, and most of sub-Saharan Africa, including South Africa. Outbreaks occur among military personnel, campers, and persons tending sheep and cattle. Medical workers are at high risk because of frequent spread in hospitals from infected human blood and tissue.

Clinical Manifestations

The incubation period is usually between 2 and 9 days. Onset is sudden, with severe headache, fever, chills, myalgia (especially in the back and legs), sore throat, abdominal pain, nausea, vomiting, diarrhea, photophobia, and conjunctival injection. The fever is constant but may be remitting. The patient is often confused or aggressive, with a marked mood change. Leukopenia and thrombocytopenia are usually observed. On days 3 to 6, hemorrhagic manifestations and a petechial rash on the trunk, limbs, and oral cavity appear. Epistaxis, hematemesis, melena, and uterine bleeding may be severe and require transfusion. The liver is sometimes enlarged and tender. In severe cases, hepatorenal failure or multiple organ system failure leads to death, usually on days 6 to 14 of illness. Death may also result from blood loss, cerebral hemorrhage, dehydration after diarrhea, or pulmonary edema. Patients recover gradually, starting on day 10 when the rash fades. Asthenia may last for a month or more. Recovery is usually complete, although neuritis may persist for months. Liver function tests are abnormal, especially the aspartate aminotransferase test, and serum bilirubin levels are often elevated late in the illness. Abnormal prothrombin, activated partial thromboplastin, and thrombin times as well as increased fibrin degradation products are indicative of DIC.

Diagnosis

Virus or nucleic acid is easily detected during the first 8 days of illness. Antibodies are detectable by immunofluorescence and ELISA in surviving patients. Specific IgM and IgG are present by days 7 to 9 of illness.

 ## Treatment and Prognosis

Patients suspected of having CCHF should be housed in an isolation facility with needle and blood precautions. Health care personnel who work with them should use respirators and protective clothing. Treatment is supportive, including monitoring and correcting fluid and electrolyte imbalance and treating DIC. The vital signs and hematocrit should be tested frequently, and blood should be replaced by transfusion. Case-fatality rates range from 30 to 50%.

Prevention

Protection from tick bites and care in handling blood and tissue of sick sheep and cattle are the only preventive measures available in the case of exposure in natural foci.

HEMORRHAGIC DISEASES CAUSED BY ARENAVIRUSES (ARGENTINE, BOLIVIAN, VENEZUELAN, AND BRAZILIAN HEMORRHAGIC FEVERS AND LASSA FEVER)

Definition

Argentine, Bolivian, Venezuelan, and Brazilian hemorrhagic fevers and Lassa fever are acute febrile diseases characterized by hemorrhagic diatheses, marked myalgia, and, in severe cases, shock. Case-fatality rates are between 5 and 33%.

Etiology

The diseases are caused by the viruses Junin (Argentina), Machupo (Bolivia), Guanarito (Venezuela), Sabiá (Brazil), and Lassa (West Africa) of the family Arenaviridae.

Epidemiology

The reservoirs are rodents that excrete virus in urine and possibly other body fluids. The viruses involved with various rodents are Junin virus, *Calomys musculinus, Calomys laucha,* and *Akodon arenicola;* Machupo virus, *Calomys callosus;* Guanarito virus, *Zygodontomys brevicauda;* Sabiá virus, not known; and Lassa virus, *Mastomys natalensis.* People are believed to be infected by inhaling or eating contaminated excreta or by passage of virus through abraded skin or mucous membranes. In Argentina, exposure to Junin virus occurs primarily in workers harvesting corn in Cordoba and Buenos Aires provinces in the north. In Bolivia, domestic and peridomestic exposure to Machupo virus occurs in Beni province, and in Venezuela, exposure occurs to Guanarito virus in agricultural settings in Portugesa and Barinas states. The site of exposure to Sabiá virus in Sao Paulo State, Brazil, is not known. Lassa virus is endemic in west and central Africa, especially in Liberia, Sierra Leone, and parts of Nigeria, where it is transmitted in and around homes that have an abundance of its host, *M. natalensis.*

Argentine hemorrhagic fever epidemics involving hundreds of farm workers were recorded annually until vaccination was carried out starting in 1988. Bolivian hemorrhagic fever epidemics were common in the 1960s, but after institution of rodent control measures the disease was not reported after 1974 until it reappeared in 1994. Lassa fever was recognized first in 1969 in a nosocomial outbreak in Nigeria. Several other nosocomial outbreaks were subsequently diagnosed, but studies in Sierra Leone established the basic endemic nature of the disease. In the eastern province, 8 to 52% of the population have antibody, and the annual seroconversion rate in susceptible subjects ranges between 5 and 22%. It is estimated that 5 to 14% of all fevers are due to Lassa virus infections and that Lassa fever accounts for 10 to 16% of the adult hospital admissions.

Pathogenesis and Pathology

The diseases are characterized by multiple organ impairment, yet specific lesions are absent. The prominent findings are focal diapedesis and capillary hemorrhage, but inflammation is minimal. Focal areas of liver necrosis in Lassa fever are not sufficient to account for the profound shock and death. It is postulated that the virus infects cells of the reticuloendothelial system, including the B and T cells. It causes temporary inhibition of immune cell function, leading to prolonged and high-titered viremia. It is not known whether subsequent capillary damage and parenchymal edema are direct or indirect effects of the virus.

Clinical Manifestations

The five diseases have many similarities. The incubation period of Lassa fever is 3 to 16 days; of Argentine hemorrhagic fever, 10 to 14 days; and of Bolivian hemorrhagic fever, 7 to 14 days. Onset is insidious, initially with fever, chills, malaise, asthenia, headache, retro-ocular pain, anorexia, nausea, vomiting, and muscle pain (especially at the costovertebral angle in the South American forms and in the legs in Lassa fever). Fever, between 39 and 40.5° C, is nonremitting. Sore throat is not prominent in the Argentine, Venezuelan, and Bolivian diseases, but purulent pharyngitis and aphthous ulcers are common in Lassa fever.

Signs include conjunctivitis; facial edema; enanthem with pharyngeal vesicles; exanthem of the face, neck, and upper thorax; tenderness of thighs; laterocervical and other polyadenopathy; and petechiae (especially in the axillae). No jaundice or hepatosplenomegaly is present. Leukopenia, thrombocytopenia, and albuminuria with casts are characteristic.

Late in the first week of illness, the signs and symptoms become more pronounced. Signs of dehydration, decreased blood pressure, and relative bradycardia are prominent. Hemorrhage from the gums, nose, stomach, intestines, uterus, and urinary tract indicates a severe hemorrhagic diathesis. Bleeding was observed commonly in the South American forms but in only 17% of Lassa fever cases. Blood loss is not massive enough to account for the shock. The acute phase usually lasts 7 to 15 days. Death is the result of uremia or hypovolemic shock, usually in the second week of illness. Recovery is heralded by lysis of fever; there is usually a prolonged convalescence marked by periods of sweating, flush, and postural hypotension, but patients suffer no permanent non-neurologic sequelae.

Neurologic signs are prominent in Bolivian hemorrhagic fever; nearly 50% of patients have an intention tremor of the tongue and hands at about the fifth day of illness, and in 25% symptoms progress to more serious encephalopathy with delirium and convulsions. The CSF is normal in these patients. A similar syndrome is occasionally seen in Lassa fever, and about 5% of patients develop unilateral or bilateral eighth cranial nerve damage, which may be permanent. Other transient complications are loss of hair and Beau's lines of the nails.

Most patients have leukopenia with depression of both lymphocytes and neutrophils; however, some Lassa fever patients have markedly elevated white blood cell counts. Thrombocytopenia is present during the first week of illness.

Diagnosis

The diagnosis can be made definitively only with laboratory tests. Fever, muscle pain, and diminished white blood cell count in the endemic areas should alert the physician to the diagnosis. RT-PCR is used to detect and identify specific RNA. Virus can be isolated in Vero cells from blood, CSF, and throat washings during life and from most tissues at necropsy. Virus is recoverable even in the presence of antibody. Isolation of virus from Bolivian hemorrhagic fever cases is more difficult than from the Argentine or West African form. Virus isolation should be attempted only in laboratories with high biosecurity containment equipment because of the risk of infection of laboratory workers. Serologic diagnosis is made by the immunofluorescence test or ELISA. IgG is present in 53% of Lassa fever patients on admission to hospital, and IgM is present in 67%. The IgM test is useful for early and rapid diagnosis.

 ## Treatment

Supportive therapy, including attention to electrolyte and fluid balance, is essential. Hematocrit and urine protein measurements aid in detection of hypovolemic shock. Plasma expanders are effective if used early but may precipitate pulmonary edema late in the clinical course.

Specific Junin virus–immune human plasma given during the first 8 days of Argentine hemorrhagic fever reduced the case-fatality rate from 16 to 1%. A neurologic illness was observed about 3 weeks after the acute attack in some patients receiving this therapy. Most of these persons recovered completely.

Ribavirin given to Lassa fever patients early in the illness significantly reduced mortality. The drug was administered intravenously, 60 mg/kg/day for the first 4 days, and then orally, 30 mg/kg/day for 6 days more. Immune plasma was not effective in Lassa fever patients in controlled trials.

Prognosis

In Lassa fever, bleeding manifestations, high levels of circulating virus in the blood, and elevated aspartate aminotransferase levels in serum are predictive of death. There are no such predictors for the South American arenavirus hemorrhagic fevers. Shock or abnormal neurologic findings indicate a poor prognosis.

Prevention and Control

Environmental sanitation, including rodent-proofing of homes and proper storage of grains and other foods to diminish rodent populations, are the only community control measures now available. A live attenuated vaccine for Junin virus has proved efficacious in Argentina. Barrier nursing, with use of gloves and gowns, should be instituted in suspected cases of arenaviral hemorrhagic fevers. Blood and other tissue are infective and should be decontaminated.

AFRICAN HEMORRHAGIC FEVER (MARBURG-EBOLA DISEASE)

Definition

African hemorrhagic fever is an acute, often fatal, hemorrhagic disease. Fever, rash, hemorrhage, hepatic and pancreatic inflammation, and prostration are hallmarks of the illness.

Etiology

The disease is caused by Marburg and Ebola viruses of the family Filoviridae. The two viruses are distinct antigenically but are of very similar morphology.

Epidemiology

African hemorrhagic fever caused by Marburg virus was described in 1967 in Germany and Yugoslavia, where workers in vaccine manufacturing facilities sickened and died after they were exposed to infected tissue of African green monkeys from Uganda. Where the monkeys became infected is not known, although Marburg virus is indigenous to Africa. (Additional isolated cases in South Africa and Kenya have been recorded.) Ebola virus epidemics in Sudan and Zaire in 1976 were traced to contact with infected patients and, in Zaire, to spread by needle. The disease recurred in Sudan in 1979, and there was an isolated case in Kenya in 1980. The outbreak in Kikwit, Zaire, in 1995 involved 315 cases, and a single case in Ivory Coast followed exposure of a Swiss ethologist during necropsy of a naturally infected chimpanzee in 1994. (The ethologist recovered.) In 1996, an Ebola outbreak in Gabon involved 54 cases and 41 deaths. A physician infected in Gabon flew to South Africa and fatally infected a nurse there. The source of the outbreaks is unknown, and the natural history remains a mystery. A third filovirus, most closely related to Ebola virus, was isolated in 1989 from sick cynomolgus monkeys recently imported to the United States from the Philippines. Animal handlers in the United States experienced seroconversion to the virus without associated illness.

Pathology

African hemorrhagic fever is a systemic disease with multiple organ involvement, most prominently the lymphatic system, testes, ovaries, and liver. Liver cell necrosis with eosinophilic inclusions, unlike that in yellow fever, is random and focal. Fibrin deposits are found in the renal glomeruli, consistent with DIC. There are edema and diffuse inflammation in the brain.

Clinical Manifestations

The incubation period is 3 to 9 days for Marburg virus infection and 3 to 18 days for Ebola virus. Onset is abrupt, with severe headache, backache, muscle pains, and, sometimes, abdominal pain. At this stage, the disease is not readily differentiated from malaria, typhoid fever, and other bacterial, rickettsial, or viral illnesses. On about the third day, nausea, vomiting, and profuse watery diarrhea with mucus and blood commence. Diarrhea may continue for several days. A maculopapular rash appears on the trunk and spreads to the rest of the body. On day 4 or 5, the patient's status becomes critical, with high, unremitting fever and an altered mental state, including confusion, aggression, or lethargy. Spontaneous bleeding from injection sites is seen, as are hematemesis, melena, hemoptysis, and, in pregnant patients, abortion, often with massive blood loss. Renal failure may be a terminal event. Death occurs from day 8 to 17, often on day 8 or 9. Recovery is marked by fatigue, anorexia, weight loss, hair loss, and, sometimes, psychological problems.

The pathophysiology is characterized by leukopenia, thrombocytopenia, increased prothrombin time, and other abnormalities in the liver function tests; increased serum amylase; proteinuria; and electrocardiographic changes indicative of myocardial disease. DIC has been documented in some cases.

Diagnosis

Antigen is detected in acute phase blood by antigen capture ELISA. Alternatively, virus is isolated from acute phase blood, liver, and other organs by inoculation into guinea pigs or cell culture. Antibody is detected by immunofluorescence and ELISA during the second week of illness.

℞ Treatment and Prognosis

No specific treatment is available. Supportive therapy consists of maintenance of fluid and electrolyte balance and administration of blood, platelets, or fresh frozen plasma to control bleeding. Peritoneal dialysis for renal failure and heparin for DIC have been recommended, but their value in African hemorrhagic fever has not been established. Convalescent blood transfusion appeared to be beneficial in an uncontrolled study in Kikwit, Zaire. The presence of bleeding indicates a poor prognosis. The case-fatality rate under relatively sophisticated hospital conditions in Marburg, Germany, was 22% in 1967 and under Third World conditions in Zaire was 90% in 1976 and 78% in 1995.

Prevention

Control activities are not carried out because the natural reservoir is unknown. Nosocomial spread can be minimized by barrier nursing and handling of blood and tissue in isolator laboratory units with proper decontamination.

HEMORRHAGIC FEVER WITH RENAL SYNDROME

Definition

Hemorrhagic fever with renal syndrome (HFRS) is a disease of Europe and Asia characterized by fevers, capillary dilatation, leakage of blood leading to hemorrhagic manifestations, and, in severe cases, shock and renal tubular disease.

Etiology

HFRS is caused by any one of several closely related viruses of the genus *Hantavirus,* family Bunyaviridae. The prototype is Hantaan virus, originally isolated from *Apodemus agrarius* field mice in the endemic region of Korea.

Epidemiology

The virus is transmitted from rodents. *A. agrarius* in Korea and other parts of Asia, *Clethrionomys glareolus* in Finland and west of the Ural Mountains, and *Rattus rattus* and *Rattus norvegicus* in cities of Japan, Korea, and Belgium serve as reservoirs. The rodent excretes virus in urine, saliva, and feces for weeks, and sometimes for months, after infection. Transmission is presumably by respiratory spread or direct contact with fomites contaminated by rodent excreta. Persons at risk include soldiers in field operations, campers, farmers, people who work in the woods, and, especially in the winter, family groups in houses that harbor field rodents seeking shelter from the cold. Outbreaks have also occurred in laboratories housing field rodents or laboratory rats that carry the virus as an inapparent infection. Nosocomial infections have not been reported.

Pathology

Patients who die of shock in the early stages demonstrate retroperitoneal gelatinous edema. Macroscopic hemorrhages are seen in the pituitary and right atrium. The renal medulla is congested and hyperemic, and patients who die later in the course of the disease have marked renal tubular necrosis. Petechial hemorrhages found in the skin and in multiple organs indicate widespread capillary fragility.

Clinical Manifestations and Pathologic Physiology

The incubation period ranges from 2 to 42 days but is usually about 2 weeks. Eighty per cent of cases are mild (demonstrating only fever, facial flush, backache, and muscle ache) or moderate (fever plus proteinuria and petechial hemorrhages). The remaining 20% are severe. They progress through five characteristic phases: febrile, hypotensive, oliguric, diuretic, and convalescent. The febrile phase lasts about 5 days, during which fever, facial flush, conjunctival injection, and backache precede the appearance of petechial hemorrhages and albuminuria. In the hypotensive phase, the temperature returns to baseline, and the patient manifests nausea, vomiting, abdominal pain, and about 3 days of capillary leakage with a rising hematocrit, heavy proteinuria, leukocytosis, thrombocytopenia, and decreased renal clearance. This phase is followed for about 4 days by the oliguric phase, when extravascular fluid is resorbed, leading to relative hypervolemia, hypertension, metabolic acidosis, and, sometimes, pulmonary edema and/or acute renal failure. The diuretic phase is accompanied by return of renal clearance to normal but with marked electrolyte and fluid imbalance, which may lead to death if it is not adequately managed. The convalescent phase may last 1 to 3 months, with slowly recovering renal function. The clinical diagnosis may be reliable during an outbreak with classical severe cases but not with mild infections; serologic confirmation is obtained by immunofluorescence, ELISA, and neutralization tests, which become positive at the end of the first week of illness. Antibody titers peak at 2 weeks and antibody lasts for many years.

℞ Treatment and Prognosis

Management includes careful monitoring of electrolytes and fluid intake and output with correction, especially during the oliguric and diuretic phases. Plasma expanders can be used for shock, and hemodialysis can be undertaken in cases of renal failure with hyperkalemia. Ribavirin improves survival if given within 5 days of onset. The case-fatality rate in Korea is about 5% with hospital management; the disease in northern Europe is milder with a more favorable prognosis.

Prevention

Rodent control should be practiced where feasible, especially in urban settings.

HANTAVIRUS PULMONARY SYNDROME

Definition

Hantavirus pulmonary syndrome (HPS) is a disease of North America and South America first recognized in the Four Corners region of New Mexico in 1993 and characterized by fever, muscle pain, and gastrointestinal symptoms, progressing to acute respiratory failure and shock. The case-fatality rate approaches 50%.

Etiology

HPS is caused by any one of several closely related viruses of the genus *Hantavirus,* family Bunyaviridae. The prototype is Sin Nombre virus, originally characterized from human lung by RT-PCR analysis of its RNA.

Epidemiology

The viruses are transmitted from cricetid rodent excreta, presumably by inhalation and percutaneous contamination. *Peromyscus maniculatus* (Sin Nombre virus) in New Mexico and neighboring states, *Peromyscus leucopus* (New York virus) in New York, *Oryzomys palustris* (Bayou virus) in Texas and Louisiana, and *Sigmodon hispidus* (Black Creek Canal virus) in Florida serve as reservoirs of different but related viruses in North America. Transmission, seasonality, and risk factors are very similar to those of hantaviruses in Europe and Asia. No person-to-person transmission has been documented in North America. Patients range in age from 12 to 69 years, with a median age of 35 years. The disease has not been recognized in young children. Fifty-four per cent of patients are male and 62% are white. Subclinical infections are rare.

HPS was first recognized in South America in 1995. Disease in Argentina and Chile caused by Andes virus resembled that in North America except that person-to-person transmission was documented for the first time and disease was recognized in children. As in North America, HPS is caused by genetically different hantaviruses, each with a different rodent reservoir.

Pathology

Pleural effusions and lung edema are found at autopsy. Microscopically, alveolar edema and pulmonary interstitial infiltrates of T cells and macrophages are evident in the absence of necrosis. Splenomegaly may be present, but lymph nodes and other organs appear grossly normal. Infiltrates of atypical mononuclear cells are found in the spleen, liver, and lymph nodes. The hemorrhage, retroperitoneal effusions, and kidney lesions of HFRS are usually absent.

Clinical Manifestations and Pathologic Physiology

A prodrome of fever and myalgia, sometimes with abdominal pain, nausea, vomiting, and dizziness, lasts 3 to 6 days. A cardiopulmonary phase follows in which the patient has fever, cough, dyspnea, hypoxia, noncardiogenic pulmonary edema, and shock. Surviving patients recover completely, usually within a week after onset of respiratory signs, although fever may continue. The partial thromboplastin and prothrombin times are prolonged, and thrombocytopenia and hemoconcentration are common, as are increased levels of aspartate aminotransferase and serum lactate dehydrogenase. Leukocytosis, atypical lymphocytes, and immature granulocytes are noted in the peripheral blood. Metabolic acidosis develops in severe cases. Signs of renal involvement in Sin Nombre virus infections are minimal; however, Bayou and other New World hantaviruses may cause renal insufficiency and elevated creatine kinase levels. Viral antigen has been found in capillary endothelium of several organs. Diagnosis depends on demonstration of specific antibodies by immunofluorescence, ELISA, and Western blot. IgM detected with hantavirus antigens is usually present on admission to the hospital. RT-PCR and immunohistochemistry of lung or other tissues have also been used for diagnosis.

℞ Treatment and Prognosis

Management includes adequate oxygenation and monitoring of hemodynamic status. Mechanical ventilation may be needed. Invasive monitoring is required in hypotensive patients and guides therapy with pressors and/or inotropic agents. Crystalloids are recommended instead of colloids for volume replacement because of the increased pulmonary capillary permeability. Overhydration should be avoided. Ribavirin efficacy in HPS is not established, but it is available for intravenous administration to HPS patients under an investigational protocol.

SUGGESTED READINGS

Arthur RR: Ebola in Africa—discoveries in the past decade. Euro Surveill 2002;7:33–36. *Highlights of recent discoveries.*

Bausch DG, Ksiazek TG: Viral hemorrhagic fevers including hantavirus pulmonary syndrome in the Americas. Clin Lab Med 2002;22:981–1020. *Reviews diagnoses and emphasizes that treatment is largely supportive.*

Castleberry JS, Mahon CR: Dengue fever in the Western Hemisphere. Clin Lab Sci 2003;16:34–38. *Current overview with emphasis on recent serologic testing.*

de Manzione N, Salas RA, Paredes H, et al: Venezuelan hemorrhagic fever: Clinical and epidemiological studies of 165 cases. Clin Infect Dis 1998;26:308–313. *Clinical and epidemiologic description of Venezuelan hemorrhagic fever.*

Schnittler HJ, Feldmann H: Viral hemorrhagic fever—a vascular disease? Thromb Haemost 2003;89:967–972. *Discusses how these viruses infect and destroy endothelial cells.*

376 ARTHROPOD-BORNE VIRUSES CAUSING FEVER AND RASH SYNDROMES

Stanley J. Naides

COLORADO TICK FEVER

Colorado tick fever is an acute, often self-limited, typically biphasic febrile illness common in Canadian Rocky Mountain areas and in the U.S. Sierra Nevada and Wasatch ranges and the Black Hills. The causative agent, the Colorado tick fever virus, is a member of the Coltivirus genus, family Reoviridae. The coltiviruses constitute a recently recognized genus whose members were previously included in the Orbivirus genus. Coltiviruses have a genome consisting of 12 double-stranded RNA segments. Colorado tick fever virus is the prototype member. The virus is transmitted through the bite of the hard-shelled tick, *Dermacentor andersoni,* and the disease range corresponds to vector range. Other coltiviruses, such as the Salmon River, Eyach, Banna, Beijing, and Gansu viruses, also have been implicated in human disease.

Epidemiology

D. andersoni is found at elevations of 4000 to 10,000 feet. Seasonal temperatures tend to influence the range, with the vector being found at higher elevations in warmer seasons and lower elevations in colder seasons. Human exposures usually occur during outdoor recreational activities in these areas. Occasional exposure occurs in nonendemic areas from ticks exported out of the endemic region in clothes, hiking equipment, or baggage. Infections usually occur between March and September, when the adult tick is most plentiful. Ticks are most abundant in south-facing dry and rocky slope habitats that favor small rodent hosts (e.g., chipmunks, ground squirrels, marmosets), with underbrush cover, burrows, and humidity for the ticks. Colorado tick fever virus overwinters in nymphal and adult ticks that feed on the rodent host, in which viremia persists for weeks to months. As many as 14% of *D. andersoni* ticks in the endemic area carry Colorado tick fever virus. Humans are an accidental host, and patients report a tick bite or exposure in 90% of cases. There were 1992 cases reported in the endemic area from 1990 to 1996. The actual number of cases is probably significantly larger and includes subclinical, mild, and unreported cases.

The geographic range of Colorado tick fever may be larger than the well-recognized endemic mountain areas. Serologically confirmed cases in California have been attributed to the Colorado tick fever–related virus S1-14-03, which is transmitted by *Dermacentor variabilis.* Salmon River virus causes a Colorado tick fever–like illness in rafters on the Salmon River in Idaho. Another similar virus, Eyach virus, has been implicated in neurologic illness in Europe and has been isolated from the deer ticks *Ixodes ricinus* and *Ixodes ventalloi.*

Pathobiology

Colorado tick fever virus replicates in bone marrow CD34-positive stem cells, leading to mild to moderate leukopenia and thrombocytopenia. The virus also replicates in committed erythrocyte precursors and may be detected in circulating erythrocytes up to 4 weeks after infection.

Clinical Manifestations

There is no notable local reaction to the tick bite. After a mean incubation of 3 to 4 days (range, 0 to 14 days), patients develop sudden-onset fever associated with malaise, chills, myalgia, weakness, headache, photophobia, retro-orbital pain, and cutaneous hyperesthesia. Conjunctival and oropharyngeal injection, palatal enanthem, lymphadenopathy, and splenomegaly may be present. The absence of prominent respiratory and gastrointestinal symptoms helps exclude other febrile illnesses. A petechial or maculopapular exanthem in 15% of patients may be confused with the rash of Rocky Mountain spotted fever. Initial fever resolves within 1 week but recrudesces after a 2- to 3-day hiatus, giving a "saddleback" fever pattern. A third fever episode may occur. Leukopenia occurs 5 to 6 days after onset of illness. Mild thrombocytopenia and anemia may occur. Myocarditis, pneumonitis, hepatitis, orchitis, and epididymitis may complicate adult infection, and aseptic meningitis or encephalitis may occur in up to 10% of childhood infections. Extreme weakness and malaise may persist for weeks to months after the final resolution of fever. Older patients have a prolonged recovery, and 70% of patients older than 30 years of age may still have fatigue 3 weeks after the fever, whereas children and adolescents may recover completely within a week. Rare instances of maternal-fetal transmission have been reported.

Diagnosis

Clinical diagnosis is confirmed by demonstration of the Colorado tick fever viral genome or specific acute phase IgM antibody. The viral genome may be detected up to 6 weeks after infection by nucleic acid based methods such as reverse transcriptase–polymerase chain reaction (RT-PCR) using blood or stored blood clots. Virions in circulating erythrocytes may be detected by immunofluorescent antibody labeling. Anti-Colorado tick fever virus IgM antibody is detected by antibody-capture enzyme-linked immunosorbent assay (ELISA) or complement fixation. Neutralization assays using Vero or BHK 21 cells have been helpful. Differentiating Colorado tick fever from Rocky Mountain spotted fever may be difficult before the appearance of the typical rash of the latter. However, Rocky Mountain spotted fever does not have a saddleback fever pattern and is 20 times less common than Colorado tick fever in the western endemic area.

Rx Treatment and Prognosis

Treatment is supportive. Aspirin is contraindicated to avoid complicating thrombocytopenia. Full recovery eventually occurs, except when complicated by neurologic insult. Patients should refrain from donating blood for 6 months.

DENGUE

Dengue is an acute febrile illness characterized by severe muscle and joint pain, rash, malaise, and lymphadenopathy. The severity of the musculoskeletal complaints gave rise to the sobriquet *break bone fever.* Dengue occurs in the tropical climes of the Caribbean, Central and South America, Asia, and Africa. The mosquito range extends into the southeastern United States, where dengue re-emerged in the 1980s. After World War II, a global pandemic has been associated with erosion of mosquito control programs, human populations that have spread into rural settings, travel by airplane that has accelerated population movements, and large areas that have experienced deterioration in public health infrastructure. Tens of millions of individuals are infected annually.

Dengue is a member of the Flaviviridae family, consisting of single-stranded RNA viruses with a lipid envelope approximately 50 nm in diameter. There are four serotypes of dengue: DEN-1, DEN-2, DEN-3, and DEN-4. There is no cross-protection between the serotypes, allowing individuals to experience dengue after infection with another serotype, and infection with a second serotype places the individual at risk for developing a hemorrhagic fever.

Epidemiology

Dengue is transmitted to humans by the bite of the female mosquitoes *Aedes aegypti* and *Aedes albopictus.* The latter, also known as the tiger mosquito, was introduced into the United States from Japan in Houston, Texas, in 1981. *A. albopictus* has become the dominant pest mosquito in many urban centers. Members of the two mosquito species acquire dengue virus by biting humans, typically during the day. Zoonotic life cycles involving nonhuman primates (i.e., chimpanzees, gibbons, and macaques) and canopy dwelling forest *Aedes* species have been demonstrated in West Africa and Malaysia. The mosquitoes nest in stagnant water around human dwellings. They are not typically encountered in the forest. Dengue virus may reach a titer of greater than 10^8/mL mean infective dose (MID_{50}) in the human host. The mosquito becomes infected when taking its meal during viremia. The virus maintains replication in the midgut epithelium and salivary glands of the female mosquito, which remain infectious for life. Within 8 to 12 days of the initial infection, the mosquito's salivary glands become infected, and the virus is shed with the saliva during the next blood meal. A given mosquito may infect multiple individuals, especially in view of its skittishness during feeding, interrupting its meal with slight movement of the host then returning to the original or another host.

The incubation period is typically 4 to 7 days but may range from 3 to 14 days. During outbreaks in the southeastern United States and Puerto Rico, infection risk may be as high as 79% in naïve hosts and clinical attack rates as high as 20%. Immunity against the infecting serotype is probably lifelong, but individuals remain susceptible to the remaining serotypes. Peak transmission occurs after increased rainfall, when collected rainwater in household containers allows expansion of mosquito populations. Epidemics tend to occur in 3- to 5-year cycles, but interepidemic cases occur regularly. Dengue is a particular risk to visitors to the tropics.

Pathobiology

Dengue hemorrhagic fever (DHF) and dengue shock syndrome (DSS) are hemorrhagic forms of dengue reinfection. They are characterized by capillary leakage. Prior infection with an alternative serotype allows antibody to the previously encountered serotype to combine with the newly infecting serotype. Although the antibody is not neutralizing, it does allow enhanced antibody-mediated macrophage uptake, leading to a macrophage activation state. Macrophage excretion of vasoactive inflammatory mediators results in vascular leak. Shock results when the leak is severe. Endothelial cell swelling and perivascular edema may occur. Rarely, DSS may occur in primary infection. Variation in a strain's ability to generate enhancing antibody, as well as differences in virulence, may account for differences in clinical behavior. For example, variation in the severity of clinical disease was documented between islands during the reintroduction of DEN-1 and DEN-2 in the Pacific in the 1970s. Hemorrhage is often widespread but variable in severity and associated with pleural effusions and ascites. Focal hepatic necrosis, immune complex–mediated glomerulonephritis, and transient bone marrow suppression may be seen. The skin demonstrates perivascular monocytic cell inflammatory infiltrates with edema.

Clinical Manifestations

Dengue infection is often subclinical. When symptomatic, dengue may manifest as classic dengue, DHF, or DSS. Patients may present with mild illness characterized by nonspecific fever, anorexia, and headache.

Classic dengue occurs in older children and adults who are usually nonindigenous, and it is characterized by sudden-onset fever, severe frontal headache, retroorbital pain, myalgias, and in many cases, nausea, vomiting, rash, lymphadenopathy, and arthralgias. Generalized weakness, altered taste, rigors, and cutaneous hyperesthesia may occur. Examination demonstrates fever, relative bradycardia, scleral injection, ocular pressure tenderness, and pharyngeal injection. A macular rash appears transiently on days 1 or 2 of illness. On days 2 and 3 of illness, fever and other symptoms may improve. Fever is typically but not consistently biphasic. After a hiatus of typically 2 days, fever and other symptoms recrudesce, although less severely. Generalized, nontender lymphadenopathy of the posterior cervical, epitrochlear, and inguinal regions may occur. Rash also recurs, taking on the appearance of 2- to 5-mm speckles of pallor surrounded by erythema and occasionally accompanied by burning dysesthesias of the palms and soles. The rash may desquamate. Illness resolves abruptly in 5 to 7 days, but fatigue and depression may linger for weeks.

In cases of DHF, the tourniquet test result may be positive, and epistaxis, petechiae, purpura, ecchymoses, and bleeding of the gums may occur. In severe cases, DSS occurs with hypotension, narrowed pulse pressure, and shock.

Diagnosis

Adequate travel history and knowledge of community disease occurrence may allow consideration of dengue in the differential diagnosis. Viremia is of adequate intensity in infections with DEN-1, DEN-2, and DEN-3 to allow viral isolation. Viremia in DEN-4 infections is often less intense and the viremia more difficult to detect through inoculation of mosquito cells in vitro. Detection of IgM antibody confirms recent infection but cross-reactivity with other flaviviruses prevents serotype-specific diagnosis. Neutralization testing is more specific with hemagglutination inhibition, and complement fixation testing for immunoglobulin G (IgG) in paired sera is more helpful.

Leukopenia occurs by the second day of fever and is 2000 to 4000 cells/µL by day 4 or 5 and associated with granulocytopenia. A positive tourniquet test result for a patient with DHF, thrombocytopenia of less than 100,000 cells/µL, and a prolonged prothrombin time are characteristic. Mild to moderate proteinuria and few casts may be detected. Aspartate transaminase levels may be increased.

Rx Treatment and Prognosis

Treatment is supportive. Survival is uniform in classic dengue. The prognosis for DHF and DSS patients depends on early diagnosis and introduction of supportive measures.

WEST NILE FEVER VIRUS

West Nile fever is an acute febrile illness associated with malaise, rash, headache, myalgia, and lymphadenopathy. West Nile fever virus is a flavivirus transmitted by a variety of mosquito species, including *Culex pipiens*, *Culex univittatus*, and *Culex molestus* in the Middle East; *Culex tritaeniorhynchus* in Asia; and *Mansonia metallicus* in Uganda. Infection involves a bird-mosquito-human cycle. All varieties of birds develop viremia. Bats, cats, chipmunks, domestic rabbits, horses, skunks, and squirrels may be infected.

Epidemiology

Most cases remain asymptomatic, but aseptic meningitis or encephalitis may occur in the elderly and, less commonly, in the very young. Infection rates may be as high as 6% of school children and more than 60% of adults. Between 0.5 and 1% of infected individuals develop a more severe illness. In a Romanian outbreak in 1996, the case fatality rate was 10%. Incubation is 3 to 14 days, but may be as short as 1 day. West Nile virus emerged in the United States in New York in the summer of 1999 and has spread through the eastern United States. By 2002, it was reported present (not imported) in all the states of the United States except Alaska, Arizona, Hawaii, Nevada, Oregon, and Utah. In the American outbreak, birds of the Corvidae family (e.g., crows, jackdaws, ravens) were often affected, and recognition of increased death in crow populations continues to serve as a sentinel for West Nile virus presence. *C. pipiens* is the major vector in the United States. In addition to mosquito transmission, the virus has been transmitted by a transplanted organ, through blood transfusion, transplacentally, and in the laboratory.

Pathobiology

Individuals developing encephalitis show evidence of diffuse brain inflammation and neuronal degeneration.

Clinical Manifestations

Most symptomatic cases are mild, with fever, malaise, headache, nausea, anorexia, generalized lymphadenopathy, and myalgia. Like Colorado tick fever and dengue, fever may be biphasic. Nonpruritic, maculopapular, or roseolar rash occurs in one half of cases on the chest, back, and arms, beginning during or with resolution of fever. Rash persists up to 1 week and then resolves with desquamation. Vomiting, diarrhea, abdominal pain, and pharyngitis may occur. Anterior myelitis, meningoencephalitis, or hepatitis may occur. Illness persists 3 to 6 days before rapid recovery. Disease in children is usually milder than in adults.

Diagnosis

West Nile virus grows in a variety of cells in vitro and produces cytopathic effects in *A. albopictus* cells. West Nile virus may be isolated from up to 77% of infected patients on the first day of illness. Low-titer viremia may persist for the first 5 days of illness. Tests for virus-specific antibody using ELISA or immunofluorescence are available. RT-PCR may detect viral RNA in human samples and in avian and insect specimens.

 Treatment and Prognosis

Treatment is supportive. The prognosis is good in the absence of encephalitis.

PHLEBOTOMUS FEVER

Phlebotomus fever (i.e., sandfly fever, pappataci, and 3-day fever) is an acute, mild, self-limiting, febrile illness transmitted through the bite of *Phlebotomus* flies. Phlebotomus fever is caused by a member of the sandfly fever group of viruses of the genus Phlebovirus, family Bunyaviridae. The latter consists of a group of single-stranded RNA viruses that are 80 to 120 nm in diameter, possess a lipid envelope, and have three segments in the genome. A related virus, the Toscana virus hosted by *Phlebotomus perniciosus*, causes a similar illness in central Italy, Cyprus, Spain, and Portugal.

Epidemiology

Sandfly fever Sicilian and Naples viruses were first isolated in Italy in the 1940s. The virus's distribution parallels the distribution of *Phlebotomus* flies that are found throughout the Mediterranean basin, Middle East, and western India and Pakistan. In Central America, *Lutzomyia* fly species may transmit the virus. These tiny sandflies pass through mosquito netting to feed in the early evenings. Virus is maintained by transovarial and transstadial transmission. During outbreaks, humans may serve as a reservoir. Human infection is more common in rural areas during the summer months. The incubation period is 2 to 6 days.

Clinical Manifestations

Sandfly fever virus causes an acute febrile illness associated with malaise, headache, photophobia, ocular pain, altered taste, myalgias, and arthralgias. Myalgias may be localized to specific regions (e.g., chest) and simulate regional syndromes such as pleurodynia. A macular or urticarial rash may appear. Examination may show relative bradycardia after the first day, conjunctival injection, mild papilledema, or small palatal vesicles. Fever lasts 2 to 4 days then subsides. Weakness and malaise may persist during convalescence. About 15% of patients experience a recrudescence in 2 to 12 weeks. Aseptic meningitis may occur with mild cerebrospinal fluid pleocytosis. Peripheral leukopenia and lymphopenia may occur early in the illness. However, leukopenia may be delayed in some patients until the third day of illness, and rebound relative lymphocytosis may be encountered.

Diagnosis

Diagnosis is confirmed by viral isolation after intracerebral inoculation of suckling mice or by detecting the presence of specific IgM antibody with ELISA.

 Treatment and Prognosis

Treatment is supportive, and recovery is complete. Ribavirin has been proposed as a therapeutic option. Sandflies spread by hopping, limiting their travel range. Use of insect sprays locally is effective in decreasing risk.

RIFT VALLEY FEVER

Rift Valley fever (RVF) is an acute-onset, febrile illness in humans that is often associated with epizootic waves of spontaneous abortion in livestock. The RVF virus is a member of the family Bunyaviridae, genus Phlebovirus, but unlike other members of the genus, it is transmitted by *Aedes* mosquitoes.

Epidemiology

RVF occurs throughout most of Africa, with most epizootic outbreaks occurring in east and southern Africa. RVF was first documented in Saudi Arabia and Yemen in 2000. The principal initial vectors are likely the *Aedes* species associated with flooding. Shallow pools along rivers and streams play an important role as mosquito breeding sites. These mosquito species are the earliest to hatch after flooding. Feeding on nearby livestock allows a local epizootic outbreak and amplification of the virus in local mosquito populations. These have included *C. pipiens* in Egypt and *Culex theileri* in east Africa. Hemorrhagic fever in humans is typically seen 1 to 2 weeks after a wave of abortion in livestock. Initial human cases are usually among those with close contact with livestock. RVF virus is highly transmissible through aerosolization. Those at risk are involved with animal birth or handling aborted materials, including farmers, abattoir workers, veterinarians, butchers, and laboratory personnel. Although the risk of severe human infections is less than 1%, the extensive exposures associated with outbreaks can lead to significant morbidity and mortality. For example, in the 1977–1978 Egyptian outbreak, an estimated 200,000 people were infected, with 600 deaths. Movement of camels from Sudan was associated with this outbreak in Egypt. Zinga virus, isolated in central Africa and Madagascar and shown to be responsible for mild human illness, was demonstrated to be a strain of RVF virus.

Pathobiology

RVF virus grows well in a variety of cell cultures and has cytopathic effects. After infection by mosquito bite, virus is transported through the lymphatics to regional lymph nodes, where replication allows amplification of the input inoculum and development of viremia with systemic spread. RVF virus replication in liver, spleen, lymph node, adrenals, lung, and kidney tissues is highly cytopathic. In severe cases, hepatic necrosis and, rarely, focal brain necrosis may occur. Although spontaneous abortion is common in livestock, RVF virus infection in humans is not clearly correlated with fetal loss.

Clinical Manifestations

Most human infection is mild, with abrupt-onset fever, chills, and malaise. However, about 0.5% of infections cause a severe hemorrhagic fever associated with hepatic necrosis and disseminated intravascular coagulopathy. Recovery is complicated by retinal vasculitis or encephalitis in less than 0.5% of patients. This occurs at 1 to 4 weeks after recovery and is associated with recurrent fever. In severe cases, focal brain necrosis and encephalitis may be associated with hallucination, stupor, coma, and death. Encephalitis is not associated with viremia, suggesting that this sequela is immune mediated rather than a direct viral effect. Inflammatory cell infiltration is associated with focal necrosis in the brain.

Diagnosis

Intense viremia allows detection of virus through inoculation of suckling mouse brain or a variety of cells in culture. Specific IgM and IgG are detectable by ELISA using acute and convalescent (after 1 to 2 weeks) paired sera.

 Treatment and Prognosis

Treatment is supportive. Ribavirin has been proposed as a therapeutic option. The prognosis is good in the absence of retinitis or encephalitis. In endemic areas, livestock vaccination is the most effective preventive.

CHIKUNGUNYA FEVER

Chikungunya fever is a febrile arthritis occurring in sporadic cases and in epidemics. *Chikungunya* is derived from the Swahili word for "that which twists or bends up." Chikungunya is a member of the family Togaviridae, genus Alphavirus, consisting of enveloped, single-stranded RNA viruses that are 60 to 70 nm in diameter. Chikungunya virus is transmitted by mosquitoes, principally *Aedes* species, but also *Mansonia africana* and other genera. Known animal reservoirs are monkeys, baboons, and in Senegal, *Scotophilus* bat species. During outbreaks, humans are the major reservoir.

Epidemiology

Chikungunya is endemic in sub-Sahara Africa, India, the Philippines, and Southeast Asia. Outbreaks typically occur after heavy rains. In urban settings, outbreaks are explosive. In a 1964 epidemic in Bangkok, Thailand, an estimated 40,000 patients of an urban area of 2 million were infected. In endemic areas, seroprevalence rates may be as high as 90%, suggesting that time required for loss of herd immunity is the reason for prolonged absence of cases in a region after an outbreak. Globalization may contribute to increasing risk of spread. An outbreak in Malaysia from 1998 to 1999 was attributed to migrant workers from endemic areas. After inoculation, the incubation period is typically 2 to 3 days but ranges from 1 to 12 days.

Pathobiology

Intense viremia occurs within 48 hours of the mosquito bite and wanes 2 to 3 days later. Onset of hemagglutination inhibition and neutralizing antibodies clears the viremia. Superficial capillaries in rash-involved skin demonstrate erythrocyte extravasation and perivascular cuffing. The virus adsorbs to human platelets, causing aggregation. Synovitis probably results from direct Chikungunya viral infection of synovium.

Clinical Manifestations

Chikungunya fever is characterized by explosive onset of fever and severe arthralgia. Constitutional symptoms, fever to 40° C, rigors, headache, photophobia, retro-orbital pain, conjunctival injection, pharyngitis, anorexia, nausea, vomiting, abdominal pain, tense lymphadenopathy, and myalgias are common. Facial flushing is common initially. A maculopapular rash located on the torso, extremities, and occasionally the face, palms, and soles occurs in most patients 1 to 10 days after onset of illness. However, the appearance of rash is often associated temporally with initial defervescence, and rash may recur with fever and may be pruritic. Isolated petechiae and mucosal bleeding may occur, but significant hemorrhage is rare. Desquamation may occur with rash resolution. The initial acute illness may last 2 to 3 days (range, 1 to 7 days). Fever may recrudesce after a 1- to 2-day hiatus. Polyarthralgia is migratory and predominantly affects the small joints of the hands, wrists, feet, and ankles, with less prominent involvement of the large joints. Previously injured joints may be more severely affected. Stiffness and swelling may occur, but large effusions are uncommon. In most cases, mild joint symptoms may last months. Destructive arthropathy is rare and may be associated with low-titer rheumatoid factor, suggesting an unrelated, underlying inflammatory arthritis. Approximately 10% of patients have joint symptoms 1 year after infection. Symptoms in children tend to be milder; arthralgia and arthritis are milder and briefer in duration. Synovial fluid shows decreased viscosity with poor mucin clot and 2000 to 5000 white blood cells/mm³.

Diagnosis

Chikungunya fever must be differentiated from dengue and O'nyong-nyong fever. Chikungunya virus may be isolated from blood during the initial 2 to 4 days of illness. In some patients, viral antigen may be detected in acute sera by hemagglutination assay due to the intensity of the viremia. Specific IgM antibody tests are available; specific IgM may be detected for 6 months or longer. Hemagglutination inhibition and neutralization antibodies develop as viremia is cleared. Complement fixation antibodies are positive by the third week and slowly decrease over the subsequent year. RT-PCR offers an approach to diagnosis more rapidly than viral culture or antibody testing.

 Treatment and Prognosis

Treatment is supportive. During the acute arthritis, range of motion exercises lessen stiffness. Nonsteroidal anti-inflammatory agents are useful. Chloroquine phosphate (250 mg/day) has been used when nonsteroidal anti-inflammatory agents failed.

O'NYONG-NYONG FEVER

O'nyong-nyong means "joint breaker" in the Acholi dialect of northwestern Uganda, where O'nyong-nyong fever first appeared in February 1959. O'nyong-nyong fever is clinically similar to Chikungunya fever, and the viruses share antigenic similarity. O'nyong-nyong virus is also a member of the family Togaviridae, genus Alphavirus.

Epidemiology

Within 2 years of its appearance in 1959, the O'nyong-nyong fever virus spread through Uganda and the surrounding region, affecting 2 million people. Serologically determined attack rates ranged from 50 to 60%, with case rates of 9 to 78%. Disease spread at a rate of 2 to 3 km daily. After the epidemic, the virus was not detected again until it was isolated from *Anopheles funestus* mosquitoes in Kenya in 1978. *Anopheles gambiae* also serves as a vector. Serologic surveys suggested that O'nyong-nyong virus is endogenous, but cases were not detected again until 1996 to 1997, during an outbreak in south-central Uganda. The nonhuman vertebrate reservoir for O'nyong-nyong virus is not known. The incubation period lasts at least 8 days.

Igbo Ora (meaning "the disease that breaks your wings") virus is serologically similar to Chikungunya and O'nyong-nyong viruses. In 1984, an epidemic of fever, rash, arthralgia, and myalgia occurred in four villages in the Ivory Coast. The virus was isolated from *A. funestus* and *A. gambiae* mosquitoes and from affected individuals.

Pathobiology

Little is known about the pathobiology of O'nyong-nyong fever.

Clinical Manifestations

Illness begins with sudden onset of polyarthralgia and polyarthritis. Between 4 and 7 days later, rash begins with improvement in joint symptoms. The rash is uniform in nature, begins on the face, and then spreads to the torso and extremities and occasionally to the palms. The rash lasts 4 to 7 days before fading. Fever is not prominent, but postcervical lymphadenopathy may be marked. Arthralgia is incapacitating in most patients for up to a week, but residual joint pain may persist for months.

Diagnosis

O'nyong-nyong fever is difficult to differentiate from Chikungunya fever. Viral isolation by intracerebral injection into suckling mice produces rash, alopecia, and runting. Specific hemagglutination inhibition and complement fixation tests are available. Mouse antisera raised against Chikungunya virus reacts equally well with O'nyong-nyong virus, but O'nyong-nyong antisera does not react well with Chikungunya virus.

 Treatment and Prognosis

Treatment is symptomatic. Although residual joint pain often persists, there appear to be no long-term sequelae.

MAYARO FEVER

Mayaro fever is an acute febrile illness characterized by fever, rash, arthralgia, and arthritis. Mayaro virus was first recognized in Trinidad in 1954. It has caused recorded outbreaks in Bolivia and Brazil, and its endemicity in the rain forest region where Bolivia, Brazil, and Peru share borders has been recognized. Mayaro virus has a monkey reservoir and is transmitted to humans by *Haemagogus* mosquitoes dwelling in the tropical rain forest canopy. Mayaro virus is a member of the family Togaviridae, genus Alphavirus.

Epidemiology

Mayaro virus was responsible for an outbreak in Belterra, Brazil in 1988. Eight hundred of 4000 exposed latex gatherers became infected, with a clinical attack rate of 80%. Cases of imported Mayaro virus infection have been documented in the United States after travel from the endemic Brazil-Bolivia-Peru interborder region. Mayaro virus has been isolated from a bird in Louisiana, raising the specter of emergence of Mayaro virus in North America.

Pathobiology

Viremia occurs during the first 1 to 2 days of illness.

Clinical Manifestations

Illness is characterized by sudden onset of fever, headache, dizziness, chills, and arthralgia in the small joints of the hands and feet. About 20% of patients have joint swelling. Unilateral inguinal lymphadenopathy is occasionally seen. Leukopenia is common. After 2 to 5 days, fever resolves, but a maculopapular rash on the trunk and extremities appears. The rash lasts about 3 days.

Diagnosis

Mayaro virus may be isolated from blood by growth in Vero or C6/36 cells. A specific IgM-capture enzyme immunosorbent assay is available.

 Treatment and Prognosis

Recovery is complete, although some patients have persistent arthralgia at the 2-month follow-up assessment.

ROSS RIVER FEVER VIRUS (EPIDEMIC FEBRILE POLYARTHRITIS)

Ross River fever virus causes an acute-onset, febrile illness characterized by rash and arthralgia. Ross River virus is a member of the family Togaviridae, genus Alphavirus.

Epidemiology

Epidemics of fever and rash have been observed in Australia since 1928. Isolation of Ross River virus from mosquitoes, its serologic association with epidemic polyarthritis, and the isolation of the virus from epidemic polyarthritis patients in Australia confirmed Ross River virus as the etiologic agent of epidemic polyarthritis. Seroprevalence has been observed in endogenous populations in Papua New Guinea, West New Guinea, the Bismarck Archipelago, Rossel Island, and the Solomon Islands. An outbreak in the Fiji Islands occurred in 1979 to 1980, affecting more than 40,000 individuals. A similar epidemic occurred in the Cook Islands early in 1980. Weber's line is a hypothetical line separating the Australian geographic zone from the Asiatic zone. West of Weber's line, antibodies to Ross River virus are not found. Endemic cases and epidemics occur in tropical and temperate regions in Australia. Queensland and New South Wales have particularly high annual incidences associated with higher rainfall. High rainfall usually precedes epidemic periods, with cases subsequently occurring from the spring through the fall. Seroprevalence may reach only 6 to 15% in temperate coastal zones but is 27 to 39% in the plains of the Murray Valley river system. In Queensland, annual rates of disease range from 31.5 to 288.3 per 100,000 person years.

Aedes vigilax is the major vector on the eastern coast of Australia and *Aedes camptorhynchus* in salt marshes of southern Australia, where the mosquitoes breed in salt marshes. *Culex annulirostris* is a freshwater breeding vector. Other Australian *Aedes* species and *Mansonia*

uniformis may also serve as vectors. In outbreaks in the Pacific islands, *Aedes polynesiensis*, *A. aegypti*, *A. vigilax*, and *C. annulirostris* may have contributed to transmission. Domestic animals, rodents, and marsupials may serve as intermediate hosts.

Most of those infected become symptomatic. Although male and female infection rates are similar, there is a predominance of women among presenting cases. Children have a case–attack rate ratio lower than adults. The incubation period is 7 to 11 days.

Barmah Forest virus, another alphavirus found in Australia in 1986, may manifest in a fashion similar to epidemic febrile polyarthritis.

Pathobiology

Ross River viral antigen may be detected in monocytes and macrophages early in infection, but intact virus is not identifiable by electron microscopy or cell culture. Dermal vessels show mild perivascular mononuclear cell, mostly T-lymphocytic, infiltrates in erythematous and purpuric areas. Vessels in purpuric areas also show erythrocyte extravasation. Antigen can be demonstrated in epithelial cells in the erythematous or purpuric skin and in the perivascular zone in the erythematous skin. However, viral antigens have not been found in the skin. Synovium undergoes lining cell hypertrophy and sublining vascular proliferation and mononuclear cell infiltration. Viral RNA can be identified by RT-PCR. Synovial fluid cell counts range from 1500 to 13,800 cells/mm^3, consisting of monocytes, vacuolated macrophages, and a few neutrophils.

Clinical Manifestations

Arthralgia typically occurs abruptly, followed in 1 to 2 days by a macular, papular, or maculopapular rash that may be pruritic. Most patients have severe, incapacitating arthralgia in an asymmetric and migratory distribution and that commonly affects the metacarpophalangeal joints, finger interphalangeal joints, wrists, knees, and ankles. Shoulders, elbows, toes, spine, hips, and temporomandibular joint also may be affected. Arthralgias are worse in the morning and after periods of inactivity. One third of patients have synovitis. Polyarticular swelling and tenosynovitis are common. Up to one third of patients have paraesthesias or have palm or sole pain. Classic carpal tunnel syndrome may occur. One half of all patients return to activities of daily living within 4 weeks despite residual polyarthralgia. Joint symptoms may recur, but episodes gradually resolve. In a few, joint symptoms may persist for up to 3 years.

In some individuals, rash may precede or follow joint symptoms by 11 or 15 days, respectively. Occasionally, vesicles, papules, or petechiae are seen. The trunk and extremities are typically involved, but the palms, soles, and face also may be involved. Rash resolves by fading to a brownish discoloration or by desquamation. Fever tends to be mild to moderate and lasts 1 to 3 days. Headache, nausea, and myalgia are common. Mild photophobia, respiratory symptoms, and lymphadenopathy may occur.

Diagnosis

Ross River virus is detectable in seronegative serum by inoculation of C6/36 cells and subsequent fluorescent antibody staining. A specific IgM-capture enzyme immunoassay is available, but antibody may be detectable up to 2 years. In the Australian epidemics before 1979, patients were antibody positive at the time of presentation. However, in the Pacific island epidemics of 1979 to 1980, patients remained viremic and serologically negative for up to a week after onset of symptoms. Virus in serum is stable for up to a month at 0 to −10°C.

 Treatment and Prognosis

Treatment is supportive. Nonsteroidal anti-inflammatory drugs provide relief for joint pain. The prognosis is good, with full recovery the usual outcome, but a few patients develop more persistent joint symptoms. Mild exercise tends to improve joint symptoms.

Infectious Diseases

SINDBIS

Sindbis virus causes a sudden-onset, febrile illness associated with arthralgia and rash. It is known as Ockelbo disease in Sweden, Pogosta disease in Finland, and Karelian fever in the Karelian Isthmus of Russia. *Aedes*, *Culex*, and *Culiseta* mosquitoes transmit the virus to humans through birds serving as intermediate hosts. Sindbis virus is the prototype alphavirus used for molecular virology studies of its genus.

Epidemiology

The virus was first isolated from *Culex* mosquitoes in the Egyptian village of Sindbis in 1952. Infection is confined predominately to forested areas. Outbreaks frequently occur in the forested areas of Sweden, Finland, and the Karelian Isthmus, but sporadic cases and small outbreaks have occurred in Uganda, South Africa, Zimbabwe, Central Africa, and Australia. Individuals involved in outdoor activities or occupations are at greatest risk.

Pathobiology

Skin lesions show perivascular hemorrhage, lymphocytic infiltrates, edema, and areas of necrosis. Virus has been isolated from a skin vesicle in the absence of viremia. Antiviral IgM may persist for years, raising the possibility that Sindbis virus arthritis is associated with viral persistence and a direct viral effect on the synovium.

Clinical Manifestations

Arthralgia and rash are the initial symptoms, although one may precede the other by a few days. Arthralgia and arthritis involve the small joints of the hands and feet, wrists, elbows, ankles and knees. Occasionally, arthralgia involves the spine. Tendinitis is common, often involving the Achilles tendons and hand extensor tendons. Fever may be present, but it tends to be mild to moderate. Constitutional symptoms, headache, fatigue, malaise, nausea, vomiting, pharyngitis, and paresthesias may be present but are usually not severe. Macular rash typically begins on the torso and then involves the arms, legs, palms, soles, and occasionally, head. Macules evolve to papules that have a tendency to vesiculate. Vesiculation is prominent on pressure points, including the palms and soles. As the eruption fades, a brownish discoloration is left. Vesicles on the palms and soles may become hemorrhagic. Rash may recur during convalescence.

Diagnosis

Hemagglutination inhibition and complement fixation tests may detect antibodies that appear during the first week of illness.

℞ Treatment and Prognosis

Treatment is supportive. Nonerosive chronic arthropathy is common in Sweden and Finland, with up to one half of all patients having joint symptoms 2.5 years after infection. In a few, symptoms may persist for up to 6 years.

SUGGESTED READINGS

Doggett SL, Russell RC, Clancey J, et al: Barmah Forest virus epidemic on the south coast of New South Wales, Australia, 1994–1995: Viruses, vectors, human cases, and environmental factors. J Med Entomol 1999;36:861–868. *A major contribution to the description of an emerging viral infection.*

Knipe DM, Howley PM, Griffin DE, et al: Fields Virology, 4th ed. Philadelphia, Lippincott Williams & Wilkins, 2001. *The bible for review of molecular virology, epidemiology, and clinical manifestations of human viral diseases.*

Petersen LR, Marfin AA: West Nile virus: A primer for the clinician. Ann Intern Med 2002;137:173–179. *A concise, lucid review of this virus emerging in the United States.*

Tesh RB: Arthritides caused by mosquito-borne viruses. Ann Rev Med 1982;33:31–40. *Somewhat dated but a good review of mosquito-transmitted viral arthritis.*

Tesh RB, Watts DM, Russell KL, et al: Mayaro virus disease: An emerging mosquito-borne zoonosis in tropical South America. Clin Infect Dis 1999;28:67–73. *Report highlighting the epidemiology and clinical presentation of this emerging American infection.*

377 ARTHROPOD-BORNE VIRUSES AFFECTING THE CENTRAL NERVOUS SYSTEM

Thomas P. Bleck

Viruses affecting the central nervous system (CNS) that are transmitted by arthropod vectors share a number of clinical and epidemiologic similarities and are presented together even though they do not form a formal virologic taxonomic group. These viruses generally share avian or small mammalian reservoirs and are transmitted to humans and other large mammals incidentally when an infected mosquito or other arthropod obtains a blood meal. Most human disease is subclinical; a few patients have a brief febrile illness resembling influenza, and a small percentage, usually at the extremes of age, suffer meningitis or encephalitis. The diseases reflect the quotidian and seasonal characteristics of their insect vectors, but the clinician must remember to elicit a travel history to match the epidemiology to the patient.

The viruses considered here do not constitute a genetic family, despite all having an RNA genome, but are united by their mode of transmission and their similar clinical manifestations. Several other members of their genera cause hemorrhagic fevers and are considered in Chapter 376. Those discussed here are summarized in Table 377–1; many other arboviruses are capable of producing encephalitis but are less frequently encountered. Within each family (e.g., Togaviridae) they are classified predominantly by serologic complexes as well as according to their insect vector.

Many of these agents cause notifiable diseases in the United States; the clinician diagnosing them should be certain to report them appropriately. Currently, these include St. Louis (SLEn), West Nile (WN), Powassan, eastern equine (EEE), western equine (WEE), and the California serogroup encephalitides. Case definitions and additional information are available at http://www.cdc.gov/epo/dphsi/casedef/encephalitis_arboviral_current.htm.

The diseases described here are zoonoses (i.e., illnesses caused by viruses transmitted from animals to humans). They are more prevalent in the tropics and subtropics and are usually localized because of ecologic restrictions on their transmission. Diagnosis depends on a careful history encompassing exposure to vertebrate animals and arthropod vectors, age, season, and travel, including geographic site of exposure. Laboratory confirmation of infection is essential. The virus may be isolated from acute-phase serum or whole blood in laboratory animals or in tissue culture. Neutralization, complement-fixation (CF), hemagglutination-inhibition (HI), fluorescent antibody, and enzyme-linked immunosorbent assay (ELISA) tests of acute and 3-week convalescent sera can also produce the correct diagnosis. Antigen detection and IgM-capture ELISA often permit diagnosis on initial presentation and at least within a week of illness onset in most cases. Treatment is symptomatic and may include bedrest, antipyretics, and analgesics.

Control can be achieved by interrupting the cycle, including vaccination of reservoir animals, vector control, and education on vector avoidance. Vaccines are currently available for Japanese encephalitis.

Pathology and Pathogenesis

Two pathologic processes are common to the arboviral encephalitides: (1) neuronal and glial damage mediated by intracellular viral infection and (2) migration of immunologically active cells into the perivascular space and brain parenchyma. Endothelial cell swelling and proliferation, destruction of myelin sheaths in deep white matter areas, and vasculitis are present in some arboviral encephalitides.

After a bite by an infected arthropod, viral replication occurs in local tissues and in regional lymph nodes. Viremia, which seeds extraneural tissues, occurs and persists depending on the extent of replication in extraneural sites, the rate of viral clearance by the reticuloendothelial system, and the appearance of humoral antibodies. The sites of extraneural infection vary among the viruses. Many alphaviruses and flaviviruses involve striated muscle and endothelium, whereas Venezuelan encephalitis virus is associated with myeloid and lymphoid tissue invasion. During viremia, the neural parenchyma

Table 377–1 • ARTHROPOD-BORNE VIRUSES ASSOCIATED WITH HUMAN ENCEPHALITIS

VIRUS	INSECT VECTOR	COMMON VERTEBRATE HOSTS	GEOGRAPHIC DISTRIBUTION
Togaviridae			
Alphaviruses	Mosquitoes		
Eastern equine encephalitis (EEE)	*Culiseta* spp., *Aedes* spp., *Coquillettidia* spp.		Eastern United States and Gulf Coast; Caribbean region; South America
Western equine encephalitis (WEE)	*Culiseta* spp., *Culex* spp.		Western United States, Canada
Venezuelan equine encephalitis (VEE)	*Aedes* spp., *Culex* spp., *Psorophora* spp., and *Mansonia* spp.		South America; Central America; Florida and southwestern United States
Flaviviridae			
Japanese serocluster	Mosquitoes		
Japanese encephalitis (JE)	*Culex* and *Aedes* spp.		East and Southeast Asia, India, Australia
West Nile encephalitis (WNE)	*Aedes* spp., *Culex* spp., and others		Africa, Middle East, North America
St. Louis encephalitis (SLEn)	*Culex* spp.		Western hemisphere
Murray Valley encephalitis	*Culex* spp.		Australia
Tick-borne encephalitis complex			
Central European encephalitis	*Ixodes* spp.	Goats, sheep	Europe, Russia
Russian spring-summer encephalitis	*Ixodes* spp.		Europe, Northern and Central Asia
Kyasanur Forest disease	*Haemaphysalis spinigera*	Rodents, insectivores	India
Omsk hemorrhagic fever	*Dermacentor reticulatus*	Rodents	Central Asia
Powassan	*Ixodes* spp.	Squirrels, groundhogs	North America, Russia
Louping ill	*Ixodes ricinus*	Small mammals, sheep, and birds	British Isles
Langat	*Ixodes* spp.	Rodents	Malaysia, Thailand, parts of former Soviet Union
Rocio	*Aedes* spp.		
Bunyaviridae			
Bunyaviruses			
California encephalitis	*Aedes malanimon, Aedes dorsalis*	Rodents, rabbits	California
LaCrosse encephalitis	*Aedes triseriatus*	Chipmunks, squirrels	Eastern and Midwestern United States

may be invaded, but the mode of penetration of virus across the blood-brain barrier is not completely understood. Possible mechanisms include passive movement of virus across vascular membranes and viral replication in the cerebral capillary endothelium. Factors increasing vascular permeability promote nervous system invasion. In experimental animal infection, flaviviruses enter the CNS via the olfactory epithelium.

The immature brain is more susceptible to damage by WEE, Venezuelan equine, and California serogroup encephalitis viruses (Table 377–2). SLEn principally affects the elderly, whereas Japanese encephalitis and EEE have a bimodal incidence, striking both children and elderly persons. In endemic areas, immunity accumulated with increasing age may reduce the incidence of disease in older persons for some viruses; however, the reasons for increased severity of illness with other viruses remain unknown.

Differential Diagnosis

The most important initial consideration is to differentiate arboviral encephalitides from acute CNS infection due to treatable organisms. The early prodrome resembles influenza. Bacterial meningitis (especially early or partially treated), infective bacterial endocarditis, brain abscess, subdural empyema, and cerebral thrombophlebitis may mimic viral encephalitis, and the cerebrospinal fluid (CSF) profile is sometimes similar. Other infections that occasionally cause meningoencephalitis resembling arthropod-borne viral encephalitis include tuberculosis, cryptococcosis, histoplasmosis, coccidioidomycosis, Rocky Mountain spotted fever, leptospirosis, falciparum malaria, trichinosis, *Naegleria* meningitis, typhoid fever, Lyme disease, and *Mycoplasma* pneumonia.

Acute meningoencephalitis may result from infections with other viruses, including herpesviruses, human immunodeficiency virus (HIV), mumps virus, enteroviruses, lymphocytic choriomeningitis virus, rabies, influenza, and the exanthematous viral infections of childhood. The exposure history, the presence of similar disease in the community, and summer-fall occurrence are principal clues to an arboviral etiology. Enteroviruses also cause summer-fall outbreaks, but the predominant syndrome is aseptic meningitis, and the occurrence of rash or pleurodynia is a helpful clue. Herpes simplex encephalitis presents an important diagnostic challenge because effective therapy

Table 377–2 • FEATURES OF ARBOVIRAL ENCEPHALITIDES IMPORTANT IN THE UNITED STATES

	EASTERN EQUINE ENCEPHALITIS	WESTERN EQUINE ENCEPHALITIS	VENEZUELAN EQUINE ENCEPHALITIS	WEST NILE ENCEPHALITIS	ST. LOUIS ENCEPHALITIS	CALIFORNIA SEROGROUP ENCEPHALITIS
Annual U.S. cases of symptomatic disease	10	0–2 cases; mostly infants and children	Rare; mostly children	Up to 3000; mostly >40 yr	0–2000; mostly >50 yr	10–50; mostly children
Time of year	Late summer, early fall	Early and mid-summer	Summer	Summer, fall	Mid to late summer	July–September
Case-fatality rate	50–70%, highest in children <15 yr and adults >55 yr	3–5% in children	35% in children; <10% in older persons	14–19%; 30% in adults >70 yr	9% overall; 0% <20 yr, 30% >65 yr	<1%
Residual damage	30–50%, especially in children	33% in infants	Frequent in children	50%, more frequent in elderly in elderly	Frequent in elderly	Probably rare
Cerebrospinal fluid findings	500–2000 cells, predominantly neutrophils	<500 cells, predominantly lymphocytes	<500 cells, predominantly lymphocytes	<500 cells, predominantly lymphocytes	<500 cells, predominantly lymphocytes	<500 cells, predominantly lymphocytes

is available and should be started quickly. The presence of localizing neurologic signs, localizing findings on computed tomography (CT) or magnetic resonance imaging (MRI) scans, or the detection of herpes simplex DNA in CSF by polymerase chain reaction (PCR) help to distinguish herpes simplex encephalitis from the arboviral encephalitides.

Noninfectious diseases of the CNS such as stroke may rarely be confused with viral encephalitis. Subarachnoid hemorrhage produces meningismus, fever, headache, and neurologic signs that mimic an infectious etiology. Metabolic encephalopathies occasionally present features suggesting infectious encephalitis. Neoplastic or granulomatous diseases involving the CNS, and a variety of diseases of uncertain etiology (e.g., cat-scratch disease, Behçet's disease, Reye's syndrome, acute multiple sclerosis, and systemic lupus erythematosus) must be considered in the differential diagnosis as well.

EASTERN EQUINE ENCEPHALITIS (EEE)

EPIDEMIOLOGY

INCIDENCE AND PREVALENCE. Human disease is relatively rare, with fewer than 10 cases occurring each year in the Gulf Coast and Atlantic states, usually in association with an equine epizootic involving 100 to 300 animals. Outbreaks usually occur during the late summer and early fall. The occurrence of equine cases or outbreaks of fatal encephalitis in penned exotic birds precedes the appearance of human cases by several weeks or more. Epizootics of EEE have been reported in the Caribbean (Hispaniola) and South America.

Despite the small size of EEE epidemics, the severity is high. The case-fatality rate is 50 to 70%. Incidence and mortality are highest in children younger than 15 years of age and in persons older than 55 years, with no gender predilection.

TRANSMISSION. In temperate areas, EEE virus circulates between wild birds and *Culiseta melanura* mosquitoes in a freshwater swamp habitat. Equine epizootics and associated human cases result from extension of the transmission cycle to involve *Aedes* and *Coquillettidia* mosquitoes, which feed on horses and humans.

Clinical Manifestations and Pathology

The disease is more acute and rapidly progressive than the other arboviral encephalitides. Onset is abrupt, with high fever, vomiting, and somnolence. Stupor, coma, myoclonus, and generalized convulsions appear within 24 to 48 hours. Autonomic disturbances (sialorrhea) may be prominent, and respiratory difficulty and cyanosis are frequent. In children, facial, periorbital, or generalized edema may be present. Death usually occurs during the first week; in surviving patients, recovery begins during the second week and may progress rapidly. Good functional recovery is associated with a long prodromal course and absence of coma. Residual damage, found in 30 to 50% of the patients, is often severe, especially in children, and is characterized by mental retardation, spastic paralyses, and radiographic evidence of brain atrophy.

A striking peripheral leukocytosis with immature neutrophils occurs frequently in patients with EEE. The CSF reveals 500 to 2000 white blood cells/mm³ (predominantly neutrophils). As the total cell count falls, the neutrophils persist as a significant fraction. Red blood cells may be present, the protein is elevated, and glucose level is normal.

In contrast to SLEn and WEE, the brain is grossly edematous and congested, and the inflammatory response is predominantly polymorphonuclear. The areas most affected are the basal ganglia, thalamus, hippocampus, and frontal and occipital cortices. Focal vasculitis, endothelial cell swelling, intravenous and arteriolar thrombus formation, demyelination, necrosis, neuronolysis, and neuronophagia are prominent.

Diagnosis

Isolating the virus from blood and CSF is rarely successful. Serologic diagnosis by demonstrating a rise in antibody titer using appropriately timed paired sera is the most practical and available test. Because of the rapid course of the clinical disease, sera should be obtained at 2- to 3-day intervals during the acute phase of illness.

Brain CT scans and MRIs are frequently abnormal, revealing lesions in the basal ganglia, thalami, and brain stem.

 ## Treatment, Prevention, and Control

Treatment is supportive. Control of fever, intracranial pressure, seizures, fluid and electrolyte disturbances, and the airway is critical. Although attempts at immunologic therapy have been reported, no controlled data are available. An experimental formalin-inactivated chick embryo cell culture vaccine is used to protect laboratory and field workers. Reduction of mosquito populations by appropriate use of insecticides may be effective in threatened or established outbreaks.

WESTERN EQUINE ENCEPHALITIS (WEE)

Epidemiology

INCIDENCE AND PREVALENCE. Few cases of WEE have been reported in the past decade; the most recent epidemic occurred in Colorado in 1987. Epidemics occur in early or midsummer and may follow heavy snow melt or flooding, conditions favorable for breeding of mosquitoes. Cases of encephalitis in equines often precede the appearance of human disease. The illness principally affects residents of rural communities, and the incidence is higher in males than in females. WEE is most severe in infants and young children. The case-fatality rate is between 3 and 5%. The ratio of inapparent to apparent infection is also age dependent, ranging from about 1:1 in infants younger than 1 year of age, to 58:1 in children aged 1 to 4 years, to more than 1000:1 in persons older than 14 years of age. WEE virus also occurs in South America. Equine epizootics in Argentina have been associated with human cases.

TRANSMISSION. WEE virus circulates between wild birds and *Culex tarsalis* mosquitoes. *C. tarsalis* is responsible for infection of humans and equines, which develop low or undetectable viremia and do not perpetuate the chain of transmission. In temperate areas, transmission ceases during the winter months.

Clinical Manifestations and Pathology

The disease usually begins with an influenza-like illness of fever, headache, malaise, and myalgia lasting 1 to 4 days. Somnolence, lethargy, photophobia, vomiting, and neck stiffness may follow; neurologic involvement may rapidly progress to stupor, coma, and seizures. Pareses, cranial nerve deficits, tremors, and abnormal reflexes may be present. In fatal cases, patients die 1 to 2 days after coma develops. Survivors generally experience a sudden and rapid recovery. However, about one third of surviving infants suffer mental retardation, cerebellar damage, choreoathetosis, and spastic paralysis. Children with protracted illnesses who develop convulsions during the acute stage are more likely to suffer long-term neurologic sequelae. Adults may have a prolonged convalescent syndrome, but objective residua are rare. Congenital infections are documented and result in severe and progressive neurologic deterioration.

Leukocytosis and shift to the left are common. The CSF contains less than 500 white blood cells/mm³ (at first polymorphonuclear, then mononuclear) and elevated protein concentration (usually 90 to 110 mg/dL).

Pathologic examination of the brains of infants reveals massive parenchymal destruction; children dying months or years after the acute insult often have large cystic lesions in many areas of the brain. In older children and adults, acute WEE is characterized by focal necrosis and perivascular cuffing, predominantly in the basal ganglia and thalami but also in deep cerebral white matter.

Diagnosis

Viral isolation from blood or CSF is almost never successful. Diagnosis is achieved by demonstrating a rise in HI, fluorescent, CF, ELISA, or neutralizing-antibody titers in appropriately timed (10 to 14 days apart) paired sera. IgM antibodies demonstrated in serum or CSF by ELISA provides a presumptive diagnosis.

Rx Treatment, Prevention, and Control

There is no specific therapy for WEE. Supportive therapy is similar to that discussed earlier for EEE. An experimental formalin-inactivated vaccine grown in chick embryo cell cultures has been used to protect laboratory workers but is not indicated for others. In threatened or ongoing epidemics, residents should be advised to use protective clothing, insect repellents, and window screens and to restrict outdoor activity in the early morning, late afternoon, and evening (times of greatest mosquito activity). Public health measures include spraying insecticides aimed at the adult *C. tarsalis* vector.

VENEZUELAN EQUINE ENCEPHALITIS (VEE)

Six antigenic subtypes of VEE (I to VI) with several antigenic variants of subtypes I and III are recognized serologically. Subtypes IAB and IC are responsible for epidemics involving humans and equines. In Florida, subtype II is enzootic and produces sporadic human disease. Methods of transmitting the VEE virus as a biological warfare agent were developed in the 1960s; an epidemic of VEE, especially if humans and horses become ill simultaneously, could represent an attack rather than naturally occurring illness.

Epidemiology

INCIDENCE AND PREVALENCE. Before 1973, large equine epizootics occurred at 5- to 10-year intervals in Venezuela, Colombia, Ecuador, and Peru, involving many thousands of animals and incurring mortality rates as high as 40%. Associated human morbidity also was great (up to 32,000 clinical cases). The disease was quiescent for several years but has re-emerged in the past decade. The last major outbreak occurred in Venezuela and Colombia in 1995, with more than 85,000 human cases.

The predominant syndrome is a self-limited influenza-like illness; only about 4% of infected persons, principally children younger than 15 years of age, develop encephalitis. Subclinical infections are rare. The case-fatality rate in children 5 years old or younger with encephalitis is approximately 35%, but in older persons it is less than 10%. Laboratory infections are common in unvaccinated persons working with the virus or infected animals.

TRANSMISSION. A large variety of mosquito vectors, including species of the genera *Aedes*, *Psorophora*, and *Mansonia*, transmit subtypes IAB and IC during epizootic epidemics. Equines are the principal viremic hosts. Virus may be present in pharyngeal excretions of human patients; contact or aerosol person-to-person spread, although possible, is not epidemiologically important.

The other members of the VEE viral complex, including subtype II in Florida, have enzootic transmission cycles involving *Culex* species mosquitoes and small forest rodents and marsupials. Human disease is sporadic and relatively uncommon.

Clinical Manifestations and Pathology

After an incubation period of 2 to 5 days, there is sudden onset of fever, chills, malaise, and headache, followed by myalgias, nausea, vomiting, and occasionally diarrhea. Physical examination reveals fever, tachycardia, conjunctival injection, and, in some cases, non-exudative pharyngitis. The acute illness generally subsides in 4 to 6 days, and convalescent symptoms may last up to 3 weeks. A biphasic course has sometimes been noted; acute symptoms reappear after a brief remission, within a week after the initial onset.

Some patients exhibit evidence of mild CNS involvement (photophobia, somnolence, confusion) during the otherwise typical influenza-like illness. When it occurs, severe encephalitis is characterized by meningeal signs, seizures, tremor, stupor, coma, spastic paralysis, abnormal reflexes, cranial nerve palsies, and central respiratory failure. Residual neurologic damage occurs in severe cases. Infections of pregnant women acquired during the first and second trimesters may result in fetal encephalitis and death.

The peripheral leukocyte count is often low, with decrease in both lymphocytes and neutrophils, or normal with relative lymphopenia. In patients with CNS signs, the CSF contains up to 500 cells/mm^3, predominantly lymphocytes. The serum lactate dehydrogenase and aspartate aminotransferase concentrations may be elevated.

Pathologic changes in the CNS include edema, congestion, meningeal and perivascular inflammation, intracerebral hemorrhage, neuronal degeneration, and vasculitis. In addition, hepatocellular degeneration and necrosis, widespread lymphoid depletion and follicular necrosis, and interstitial pneumonitis are frequent. The congenitally infected fetus demonstrates massive and widespread necrosis of brain tissue, hemorrhage, and resorption of brain material, resulting in hydranencephaly.

Diagnosis

In contrast with the other arboviral encephalitides, VEE virus can be isolated from the blood or from throat swabs or washings during the first 3 or 4 days of illness. Serodiagnosis is usually more practical and is achieved by testing appropriately timed paired sera by HI, CF, ELISA, neutralization, or IgM immunoassay.

Rx Treatment, Prevention, and Control

No specific therapy is available, and treatment of encephalitis cases is supportive. An experimental live, attenuated vaccine made from subtype IAB is used for adult laboratory personnel. It provides solid immunity to subtype IAB and its closest relative (IC) but incomplete protection against other heterologous VEE viruses. Epidemics and epizootics can be prevented by effective vaccination of equines. Spraying insecticides to reduce adult (infective) mosquito populations is the only means of immediate control in the face of an ongoing epidemic. Individual protection against mosquitoes is advised.

JAPANESE ENCEPHALITIS (JE)

Etiology and Epidemiology

JE virus causes epizootics of clinical encephalitis in equines. The disease occurs throughout Asia, including Japan, the Korean peninsula, Taiwan, the People's Republic of China, Okinawa, Vietnam, the Philippines, Burma, Malaysia, Bangladesh, east and south India, Sri Lanka, Thailand, and Indonesia. More than 30,000 clinical cases occur annually. JE is a summertime disease in temperate areas but occurs sporadically year-round in the tropics. Epidemics are most frequent at the northern fringe of the tropical zone. JE is a predominantly rural disease, and the incidence in males is often higher than in females. In hyperendemic areas, more than 70% of adult populations surveyed have antibodies, and children younger than 15 years of age are principally affected by the disease. In areas without a high prevalence of background immunity (e.g., northern India), however, all age groups are affected. In Japan, where schoolchildren have been protected by vaccination campaigns targeted at this age group, encephalitis has become prominent in the elderly. The ratio of clinically inapparent to apparent infection is higher than 500:1 in children and decreases with age; in Korea, the ratio among American servicemen was estimated at 25:1. The case-fatality rate probably is about 25%.

Clinical Manifestations and Pathology

Manifestations of JE include abrupt fever, headache, and gastrointestinal symptoms. Meningeal irritation develops within 24 hours and is followed on the second or third day by the appearance of irritability, impaired consciousness, seizures (especially in children), muscular rigidity, parkinsonian findings, ataxia, coarse tremor, involuntary movements, cranial nerve deficits, paresis, hyperactive deep tendon reflexes, and pathologic reflexes. Weight loss and dehydration are often striking findings. In mild cases, fever subsides after the first week and neurologic signs resolve by the end of the second week after onset. In severe cases, hyperpyrexia, progressive neurologic dysfunction, and coma result in death, usually between the 7th and 10th days. About

Continued

Infectious Diseases

25% of patients undergo a prolonged recovery, often leaving permanent sequelae. Cardiorespiratory complications are frequent during the acute stage in these patients. A poor prognosis is associated with protracted high fever, frequent or prolonged seizures, high protein content in the CSF, Babinski's sign, and early respiratory depression. Fetal death due to transplacental JE infection have been reported.

The occurrence of sequelae correlates with severity of the acute stage of illness. Young children are most susceptible, and sequelae such as mental impairment, emotional lability, choreoathetosis, tremor, parkinsonism, autonomic disturbances, paralysis, and psychiatric disturbances have been reported in up to 75% of patients.

A moderate peripheral leukocytosis and neutrophilia occur early in the disease. Pleocytosis, protein elevation, and normal glucose in the CSF are usual findings.

Neuropathologic changes and distribution of lesions are similar to those described for SLEn (see subsequent discussion of SLEn).

Diagnosis

Isolating JE virus from blood is uncommon; virus may be recovered from the CSF of a third of those progressing to death but rarely from patients who live. HI and neutralizing antibodies appear during the first and CF antibodies during the second week after onset. Cross-reactions with other flaviviruses make serodiagnosis difficult. Specific IgM antibodies in the serum or CSF are detectable by immunoassays in more than three fourths of patients at the time of hospital admission.

MRI in JE reveals edema in the basal ganglia, thalami, and focal area of the cerebral cortex; evidence of hemorrhage in these areas may also be present. Meningeal enhancement may also be noted.

Rx Treatment, Prevention, and Control

Treatment is supportive (see EEE). Uncontrolled trials of interferon-alfa suggested an effect, but a randomized trial showed no benefit. Inactivated, partially purified mouse brain vaccines produced in Japan are safe and effective in preschool- and school-aged children. A vaccine produced in Japan is available to U.S. citizens traveling to high-risk areas. Because three doses of the inactivated vaccine are used and approximately 1 month is required to confer protection, vaccination is not a practical measure in the face of an ongoing epidemic. Reduction of vector mosquito populations by applying insecticides may help abort outbreaks. Immunization of swine is an ancillary control strategy.

WEST NILE (WN) FEVER AND ENCEPHALITIS

Prior to 1999, WN virus was confined to the Old World. First isolated in 1937 in Uganda, the virus is closely related to the agents of JE and SLEn. It emerged in North America unexpectedly and spread rapidly throughout much of the continent; more than 3000 cases were reported in 2002 (Figs. 377–1 and 377–2). Also unexpected is a shift in the clinical spectrum of disease; prior to 1996, WN was predominantly a brief influenza-like illness, sometimes with a rash but with only infrequent neurologic manifestations. Epidemics since then in Romania, Israel, and North America have added meningitis, meningoencephalitis, and myelitis to the list of disorders attributable to the virus. Sequence analysis of various isolates of the virus indicate two lineages. The first includes viruses from North America, Europe, Israel, west Africa, India, Russia, and Australia and the second those from sub-Saharan Africa and Madagascar.

Virus transmission involves mosquitoes and wild birds, with mammals, including humans, as incidental end-stage hosts. The mosquito vector species varies: *Culex univittatus*, *Culex pipiens*, and *Culex molestus* in the Middle East and Africa, *Mansonia metallicus* in Uganda, and *Culex tritaeniorhynchus* in Asia. *C. pipiens*, *Culex quinquefasciatus*, *Culex nigripalpus*, and *C. tarsalis* are likely vectors in North America, although at least 25 other mosquito species carry the virus. In endemic areas, human infections are common, with more than 60% of young adults having antibodies; this suggests a high prevalence of inapparent or undifferentiated febrile illness in children. There is no gender predominance. Recent studies document transmission by blood transfusion and by organ transplantation.

Clinical Manifestations

Following an incubation period of 1 to 6 days, the onset is usually abrupt without prodromal symptoms. The temperature rises quickly to 38.3° to 40° C, with rigors in one third of patients. Symptoms include drowsiness, severe frontal headache, ocular pain, myalgia, and pain in the abdomen and back. A small number of patients have dryness of the throat, anorexia, and nausea. Cough is common. Examination shows facial flushing, conjunctival injection, and coating of the tongue. Generalized lymphadenopathy had been a prominent feature in past epidemics but is no longer commonly reported. The spleen and liver are occasionally slightly enlarged. The temperature curve may be biphasic. A pale roseolar maculopapular rash, predominantly on the trunk and upper arms, may appear from the second to fifth day, but this is now less common as well; it may be evanescent (several hours) or persist until defervescence; and it does not desquamate. Vesicular lesions occur rarely. The illness lasts 3 to 5 days in 80% of patients.

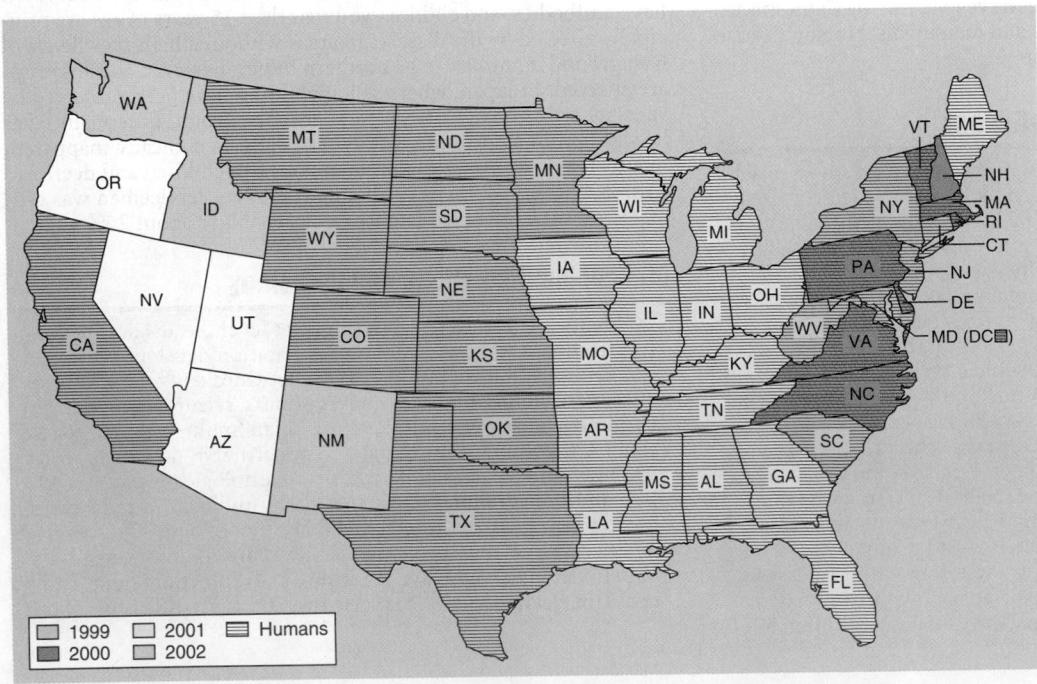

FIGURE 377–1 • Spread of West Nile virus activity in the United States by year, 1999–2002. (From the Division of Vector-Borne Infectious Diseases, Centers for Disease Control and Prevention. http://www.cdc.gov/ncidod/dvbid/westnile/surv&control.htm#map1.)

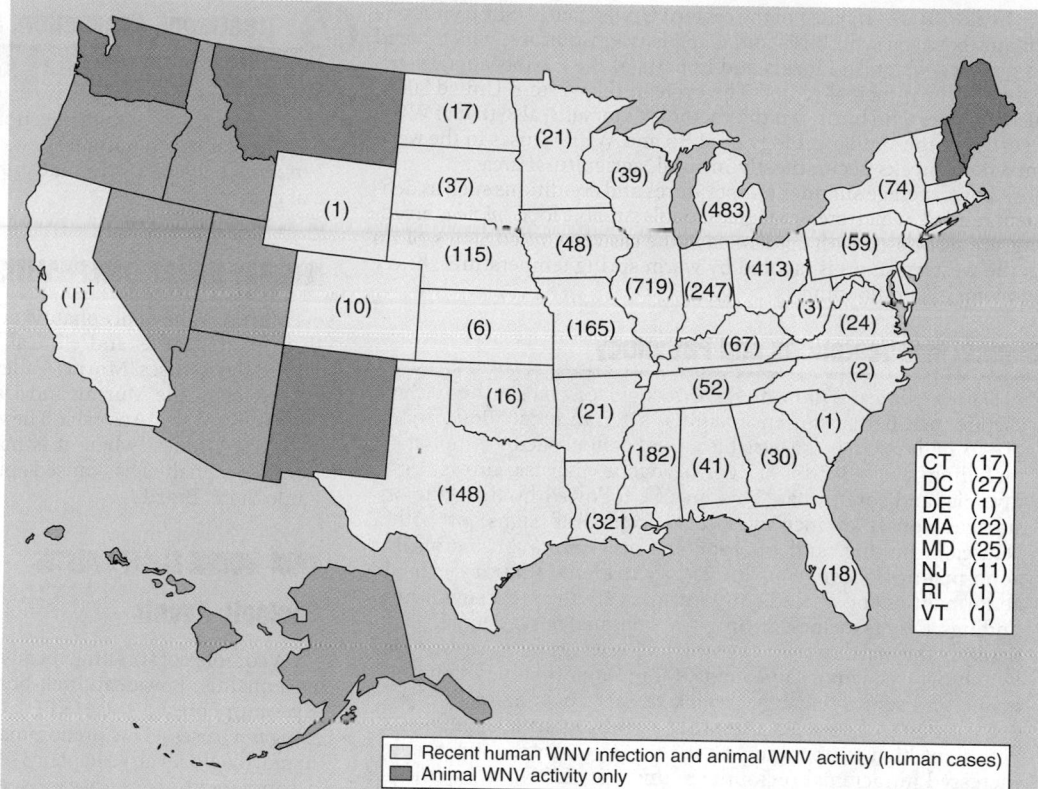

FIGURE 377–2 • U.S. West Nile (WN) virus activity in 2002. †California reported only human WN activity. (From Centers for Disease Control and Prevention: West Nile virus activity—United States, October 31–November 6, 2002. MMWR 2002;51:999–1000.)

CT (17)
DC (27)
DE (1)
MA (22)
MD (25)
NJ (11)
RI (1)
VT (1)

☐ Recent human WNV infection and animal WNV activity (human cases)
■ Animal WNV activity only

Infection also may result in aseptic meningitis or meningoencephalitis, especially in the elderly. In the past decade the incidence of CNS disease has increased in several epidemics; this appears to be a true increase in the invasiveness and neurovirulence of the virus. CSF examinations may reveal a lymphocytic pleocytosis (<1800 cells/mm^3) with some increase in protein concentration. WN virus causes a syndrome resembling poliomyelitis, with prominent lower motor neuron dysfunction, which may be seen independently or with signs of meningoencephalitis. Some of these patients developed prolonged, possibly permanent, ventilatory failure requiring mechanical ventilation. A parkinsonian syndrome has also been noted, usually remitting after months. Acute inflammatory polyneuropathy (AIPN; Guillain-Barré syndrome) has also been reported. Other rare complications include myocarditis, pancreatitis, and hepatitis. Convalescence is often prolonged, lasting several weeks with prominent symptoms of fatigue. Lymph node enlargement requires several months to regress. Laboratory findings often include leukocytosis; in contrast, the classically described leukopenia has become less frequent (now seen in 10 to 15% of patients).

WN virus may be isolated from the blood of three fourths of patients with WN fever on the first day, with viremia persisting but decreasing over 5 days. However, patients with WN encephalitis appear less likely to be viremic, and isolation of virus from the CSF is infrequent. Viral RNA is detected in CSF by reverse transcriptase (RT)-PCR in about half of cases. Serologic diagnosis is possible using a number of tests; however, cross-reactions with other flaviviruses, particularly SLEn virus, complicate interpretation. IgM antibody-capture immunoassay is the test of choice, but IgM antibody may remain detectable for up to 500 days after infection.

Rx Treatment and Prognosis

Treatment is symptomatic and is similar to that suggested for EEE. Patients may require prolonged mechanical ventilation for either the polio-like syndrome or AIPN. The latter does not appear to respond to plasma exchange or intravenous immunoglobulin (IVIg), in contrast to other forms of AIPN. Ribavirin has activity against WN fever virus, but its clinical utility is unknown. Interferon, and IVIg collected from populations with a high incidence of WN exposure, are the subjects of proposed randomized trials.

The prognosis for neurologic recovery is guarded, with about half of WNE patients still reporting difficulties 1 year after the illness.

ST. LOUIS ENCEPHALITIS (SLEn)

Etiology

SLEn virus, a member of the family Flaviviridae, shares close antigenic relationships with JE, Murray Valley encephalitis, and WN viruses and is related to yellow fever and dengue viruses. Strains associated with *C. pipiens*–borne epidemics in the eastern United States are distinct from endemic strains transmitted by *C. tarsalis* in the western states.

Epidemiology

INCIDENCE AND PREVALENCE. The virus is present in all parts of the Western Hemisphere, but epidemics occur only in North America and some Caribbean islands. During epidemic years, the virus has been responsible for up to 80% of all reported cases of encephalitis of known etiology in the United States. Epidemics of up to 2000 cases have taken place, the last in 1990, mainly in urban-suburban localities of the Ohio–Mississippi River basin and in eastern and central Texas and Florida. Small outbreaks also have occurred in the western United States. Epidemics usually transpire between July and September but may arise later in the year in warm areas such as Florida. Prior exposure and immunity to dengue may provide a degree of cross-protection against clinical SLEn.

The overall case-fatality rate is approximately 9%. Mortality is negligible in persons younger than 20 years of age but rises steeply after age 55 years to approximately 30% in patients older than 65 years of age. The inapparent to apparent infection ratio is 800:1 in children up to age 9 years, 400:1 in persons aged 10 to 49 years, and 85:1 in persons older than 60 years.

TRANSMISSION. In most of the eastern United States, SLEn virus circulates between wild birds and *C. pipiens* mosquitoes, which breed in polluted water. In Florida and in parts of the Caribbean, *C. nigripalpus* is the principal vector. The cycle in the western United States also involves wild birds, but the vector is *C. tarsalis*, also that of WEE. Because of the similar ecology of SLEn and WEE viruses in the west, mixed outbreaks occur, mostly in rural, agricultural areas.

Above-average summer temperatures and conditions such as deficient rainfall, which create stagnant pools suitable for *C. pipiens* breeding, are associated with epidemics in the eastern United States. SLEn in the western states is favored by warm spring temperatures, heavy snow melt, and flooding.

Clinical Manifestations and Pathology

Three clinical syndromes are recognized: febrile headache, aseptic meningitis, and encephalitis. After an incubation period of 4 to 21 days, there is a variable period of nonspecific symptoms, including fever (38° to 41° C), headache, malaise, drowsiness, myalgia, and sore throat. This may be followed by the acute or subacute onset of meningeal or encephalitic signs, or both. Nausea, vomiting, and photophobia are common. Neurologic abnormalities occur in up to 25% of patients. Extrapyramidal abnormalities and altered consciousness are the most significant findings. Others include meningismus, cranial nerve deficits (particularly the facial nerve), abnormal reflexes, tremors, myoclonic twitching, nystagmus, and ataxia. Motor abnormalities are infrequent, and sensory changes are extremely uncommon. Seizures occur in 10% of patients and are a poor prognostic sign, as is a persistent high temperature of 40° to 41° C. Signs of markedly increased intracranial pressure are unusual. AIPN has occasionally been associated with SLEn, both as an acute presentation and during the convalescent period. Approximately half the patients with fatal outcome succumb during the first week and 80% die within 2 weeks after onset.

In uncomplicated cases of SLEn, a moderate peripheral neutrophilic leukocytosis and shift to the left are noted. CSF pressure is elevated, protein is mildly elevated, and sugar is normal. A pleocytosis up to 500 cells/mm^3 is present, with an early neutrophilia predominance changing to lymphocytes within days. Serum creatine kinase, aspartate aminotransferase, and aldolase levels are frequently elevated. The electroencephalogram typically shows polymorphic delta activity, most prominently in the frontal and temporal regions; electrographic seizures are common. CT scans are normal, but MRI may show edema involving deep structures such as the substantia nigra. Hypo-osmolality, presumably due to syndrome of inappropriate antidiuretic hormone, is noted in one third of patients.

Genitourinary tract symptoms (urgency, frequency, incontinence, and retention), microscopic hematuria, pyuria, proteinuria, and elevated blood urea nitrogen are frequent. SLEn viral antigen in cells of the urinary sediment has been detected by fluorescent techniques and virus-like particles in urine by immunoelectron microscopy.

A convalescent syndrome characterized by weakness, fatigue, nervousness, tremulousness, sleeplessness, irritability, depression, difficulty in concentrating, and headaches occurs in 30 to 50% of older persons and clears in 80% of these within 3 years.

Pathologic changes in fatal cases are limited to microscopic findings. Leptomeningitis is characterized by lymphocytic inflammation. Parenchymal changes consist of lymphocytic perivascular cuffing, cellular nodule formation, and neuronal degeneration.

Diagnosis

SLEn virus is rarely isolated from blood or CSF obtained during the acute phase of illness. Serologic diagnosis is achieved by demonstrating changing antibody titers; the HI, fluorescent, ELISA, and neutralizing tests demonstrate antibody within the first week after onset, and titers rise during the ensuing 2 weeks. CF antibodies appear 10 to 20 days after onset. Rapid, early diagnosis is possible by detecting IgM antibodies by ELISA in serum and CSF. Serologic cross-reactions may occur in persons with prior exposures to dengue, WN, and other related flaviviruses. RT-PCR provides a more specific diagnosis, but its sensitivity is uncertain.

 Treatment, Prevention, and Control

Treatment is supportive. No vaccine is available for SLEn. Surveillance of viral activity in vectors and avian hosts is used to define the risk of human infection and initiate vector control efforts. In an established outbreak, avoiding mosquito bites and spraying to reduce infected adult mosquitoes are the only effective means of control.

MURRAY VALLEY ENCEPHALITIS AND ROCIO ENCEPHALITIS

Murray Valley encephalitis and Rocio encephalitis are similar to JE in pathogenesis and clinical features and are caused by closely related flaviviruses. Murray Valley encephalitis has occurred in small epidemics in the Murray and Darling River valleys of Victoria and New South Wales, Australia. The virus is endemic in northern Australia and New Guinea, where it is maintained in a bird-mosquito cycle. Rocio encephalitis has caused epidemics of 1000 or more cases in Saõ Paulo State, Brazil.

TICK-BORNE ENCEPHALITIS

Etiologic Agents

A complex of six antigenically related tick-borne flaviviruses cause encephalitis: Powassan, tick-borne encephalitis (TBE), Louping ill, Kyasanur Forest disease (KFD), Omsk hemorrhagic fever (OHF), and Langat viruses. The predominant syndrome in KFD and OHF is hemorrhagic fever (Chapter 376), but meningoencephalitis may be a component of the disease spectrum. Two subtypes of TBE virus (Central European encephalitis and Russian spring-summer encephalitis) are distinguished by serologic tests, are ecologically distinct, and differ in virulence for humans. Powassan and Louping ill viruses are rare causes of encephalitis in North America and the British Isles, respectively. These viruses are serologically easily distinguished from mosquito-borne flaviviruses but induce cross-reactions within the complex.

Tick-Borne Encephalitis (TBE)

TBE occurs in Europe (including Eastern Europe and Ukraine), southern Scandinavia, and far eastern Russia during summer months, corresponding to peak tick vector populations. Several hundred to more than 2000 cases are reported annually, with morbidity rates of up to 20 per 100,000 inhabitants. Inapparent infections are common. Adults older than 20 years of age are mainly affected, and persons frequenting wooded areas that are heavily tick-infested are at highest risk. In Europe, the disease is relatively mild (case-fatality rate 1 to 2%), but in the Far East, it is severe (20 to 25%).

In Europe, the vector of TBE is *Ixodes ricinus*, and in the Far East, *Ixodes persulcatus*. The tick vector also serves as a reservoir of the virus. Larval ticks parasitize small rodents, which serve as amplifying viremic hosts during the spring and summer. Large vertebrates (goats, sheep, cattle) are hosts for nymphal and adult ticks. Outbreaks have occurred in families or groups of individuals ingesting unpasteurized milk or cheese from goats or sheep.

TBE in Europe typically (but not invariably) has a biphasic course, beginning 7 to 14 days after exposure with an influenza-like illness lasting 1 week, followed by a period of clinical remission for several days, and then the abrupt onset of aseptic meningitis or meningoencephalitis. The latter is usually benign, although severe paralytic illness, myelitis, myeloradiculitis, and bulbar forms may occur. Convalescence is often prolonged, and residual paralysis may follow in severe cases.

In the Far East, TBE begins suddenly with fever, headache, and gastrointestinal symptoms, followed rapidly by the appearance of depressed sensorium, coma, convulsions, and paralysis. Bulbar paralysis and cervical myelitis are frequent findings. In fatal cases, death occurs in the first week after onset. Survivors frequently manifest residual paralyses, especially lower motor neuron paralysis of the upper extremities or shoulder girdle, reflecting spinal cord involvement. Aseptic meningitis and milder forms of encephalitis also occur. Chronic forms of TBE have been described, with active clinical and pathologic abnormalities a year or more after onset.

Brain MRI of patients with TBE shows evidence of edema in the basal ganglia, thalami, and brain stem in about 20% of cases. MRI of the spinal cord may show anterior horn cell lesions corresponding to lower motor neuron weakness on examination.

In TBE, virus isolation from blood is also possible during the early phase of illness. Serologic diagnosis is achieved by the HI, CF, N, or ELISA techniques.

Treatment is supportive (see EEE). In eastern Europe and the former Union of Soviet Socialist Republics (U.S.S.R.), TBE vaccines are used in high-risk groups (forestry and agricultural workers, military personnel). In Austria, immunization of the general population has resulted in a marked decline in incidence. Avoiding tick exposure by wearing protective clothing and using repellents may be recommended in areas of high TBE activity.

Louping III Encephalitis

Louping ill causes encephalitis in sheep (rarely in cattle, horses, and swine) in Scotland and in northern England and Ireland. Sporadic human cases have been recognized. Louping ill virus is maintained in nature by *I. ricinus* ticks and a variety of hosts, including small mammals, ground-dwelling birds (grouse), and probably sheep. The clinical features of Louping ill resemble the European form of TBE.

Powassan Virus Encephalitis

Powassan virus encephalitis has been documented in a small number of cases in the northeastern United States and eastern Canada, with a case-fatality rate of about 50%. The virus is not associated with animal disease. The transmission cycle of Powassan virus involves *Ixodes cookei, Ixodes marxi*, and possibly other tick species, along with mammals, particular rodents and carnivores. Powassan encephalitis is characterized by fever and nonspecific symptoms, followed by encephalitic signs, which are frequently severe. Residual paralysis may occur. Peripheral blood and CSF changes are similar to those described in other forms of flaviviral encephalitis.

CALIFORNIA SEROGROUP ENCEPHALITIS

Etiology

At least four members of the California serogroup of the Bunyaviridae family (*Bunyavirus* genus)—LaCrosse, California encephalitis, Jamestown Canyon, and snowshoe hare virus—cause encephalitis. California encephalitis virus occurs in the western United States (California, New Mexico, Utah, Texas) and has been implicated in only three human cases. In contrast, LaCrosse virus, distributed more widely in the eastern half of the United States and southern Canada, is a major human pathogen. Jamestown Canyon and snowshoe hare viruses have also been implicated in sporadic human encephalitis cases in the north central United States and Canada. California serogroup viruses have been implicated in human disease in the People's Republic of China and the former U.S.S.R.

Epidemiology

INCIDENCE AND PREVALENCE. California serogroup encephalitis occurs as an endemic rather than an epidemic disease, with individual or small clusters of cases scattered across the affected areas. Seventy to 115 cases are reported each year, generally occurring between July and September, with peak incidence in August. The virus primarily affects persons younger than 15 years of age living in rural and suburban areas characterized by deciduous hardwood forests. It is most prevalent in the north central states, where it is responsible for as many as 20% of cases of acute CNS infection in children. Focal "hot spots" (communities, even backyards) of recurrent summertime viral activity are recognized. The case-fatality rate is less than 1%. The inapparent/apparent infection ratio has been estimated variably at between 26:1 and 157:1.

TRANSMISSION. The vector of LaCrosse virus is *Aedes triseriatus*, which breeds both in forest tree holes and in artificial containers, notably discarded tires. The vector also serves as a reservoir of LaCrosse virus. Wild rodents (squirrels, chipmunks) contribute to the cycle of transmission as viremic hosts. Humans acquire the disease by being bitten by an infected mosquito.

Aedes communis, Aedes stimulans, A. triseriatus, and possibly anopheline mosquitoes are involved in transmitting Jamestown Canyon virus, and deer are the principal vertebrate hosts.

Clinical Manifestations

The clinical spectrum of California serogroup virus infection includes nonspecific febrile illness, aseptic meningitis, and meningoencephalitis. The disease begins with fever, headache, sore throat, and gastrointestinal symptoms, with appearance of the neurologic disorder within 1 to 3 days. In mild cases, CNS signs appear on the third day after onset and subside within 7 to 8 days. In the more severe form, neurologic signs appear within 24 to 48 hours of onset, usually in the form of generalized seizures, elevated intracranial pressure, and altered consciousness, and persist longer. Encephalitis may be quite severe in the acute stage, but the disease is almost always self-limited; death is extremely rare. The question of permanent sequelae is unsettled. Many researchers believe LaCrosse virus infection is responsible for residual psychological problems, emotional lability, hyperkinesis, infantilism, compulsive behavior, and auditory and visual perceptual problems. Cases of hemiparesis and persistent seizure disorders have been reported.

The peripheral white blood cell count is elevated, with a predominance of polymorphonuclear cells and a shift to the left. The CSF contains up to 500 lymphocytes/mm^3, normal or mildly elevated protein, and normal glucose concentrations. The electroencephalogram reveals generalized slowing in the delta and theta range. Focal delta wave activity related to cortical destruction or focal seizures are also common findings.

Histopathologic features in the CNS are qualitatively similar to those of other viral encephalitides; however, absence of inflammatory lesions in cerebellum, medulla, and spinal cord may be a distinguishing feature of LaCrosse infection.

Diagnosis

The virus cannot be recovered from blood or CSF obtained during the acute phase. Diagnosis is best achieved by tests for antibody in paired acute and convalescent sera using counterimmunoelectrophoresis, HI, CF, fluorescent, ELISA, and neutralization tests. The most practical, sensitive, and reliable methods are the HI test using the LaCrosse viral antigen and IgM antibody-capture ELISA. Viral RNA can be detected in CSF or brain tissue by RT-PCR, although the sensitivity of the test remains to be determined.

In contrast to the other arboviral encephalitides, the brain MRI of patients with California serogroup encephalitides may show lesions involving the temporal lobe in a pattern similar to herpes simplex encephalitis.

Rx Treatment, Prevention, and Control

Treatment is supportive. There is no vaccine for California encephalitis, although research into DNA-based vaccines appears promising. Vector control methods are of uncertain usefulness in this disease. In defined "hot spots" of recurrent viral activity, breeding sites for *A. triseriatus* should be eliminated, particularly by draining or eliminating standing water (e.g., discarded tires or birdbaths), and filling holes in trees. Parents should protect children by limiting exposure and using mosquito repellents.

SUGGESTED READINGS
Campbell GL, Marfin AA, Lanciotti RS, Gubler DJ: West Nile virus. Lancet Infect Dis 2002;2: 519–529. *An excellent summary of current understanding of the virus and the disease.*
Mertz GJ: Bunyaviridae: Bunyaviruses, phleboviruses, nairoviruses, and hantaviruses. *In* Richman DD, Whitley RJ, Hayden FG (eds): Clinical Virology, 2nd ed. Washington DC, ASM Press, 2002, pp 921–948.
Monath TP, Tsai TF: Flaviviruses. *In* Richman DD, Whitley RJ, Hayden FG (eds): Clinical Virology, 2nd ed. Washington DC, ASM Press, 2002, pp 1097–1152. *A comprehensive chapter.*
Shlim DR, Solomon T: Japanese encephalitis vaccine for travelers: Exploring the limits of risk. Clin Infect Dis 2002;35:183–188. *A useful discussion of the variables for making a decision about the vaccine.*

Infectious Diseases

Solomon T, Dung NM, Wills B, et al: Interferon alfa-2a in Japanese encephalitis: A double-blind placebo-controlled trial. Lancet 2003;361:821–826. *Interferon has been used frequently in JE; this study shows it is no more useful than placebo.*

Solomon T, Vaughn DW: Pathogenesis and clinical features of Japanese encephalitis and West Nile virus infections. Curr Top Microbiol Immunol 2002;267:171–194. *Explores the many similarities between these diseases.*

Tsai TF, Weaver SC, Monath TP: Alpha-viruses. In Richman DD, Whitley RJ, Hayden FG (eds): Clinical Virology, 2nd ed. Washington DC, ASM Press, 2002, pp 1177–1210. *A detailed chapter.*

Wurtz R, Paleologos N: LaCrosse encephalitis presenting like herpes simplex encephalitis in an immunocompromised adult. Clin Infect Dis 2000;31:1113–1114. *Medial temporal lobe focal encephalitis is not always due to herpes simplex virus.*

378 INTRODUCTION TO THE MYCOSES

Carol A. Kauffman

Overview

Fungi constitute a kingdom characterized by nonmotile, mostly aerobic, organisms that lack chlorophyll and that reproduce by spores. Within this huge kingdom, less than 0.1% actually cause disease in mammals. Fungi are eukaryotes; thus, they are more complex in structure and physiology than bacteria and treatment is more difficult. The primary component of the cell membrane of pathogenic fungi is ergosterol, which is similar to cholesterol in the cell membrane of human cells. Most antifungal agents target the cell membrane and, not surprisingly, have toxicities and drug interactions that create serious side effects. In contrast to mammalian cells, fungi also have cell walls that are usually composed of chitin, glucans, and mannoproteins. The cell wall is an attractive target for antifungal agents; toxicity should be expected to be much less.

Fungi cause a broad spectrum of infection in humans—from superficial infection of the stratum corneum to life-threatening invasion of viscera. The superficial mycoses include the dermatophytes that cause tinea infections, such as tinea pedis (athlete's foot) and tinea corporis (ringworm), and yeast-like organisms that cause tinea versicolor. Subcutaneous mycoses are those that are inoculated and generally cause only local invasion of tissue; the best known example is sporotrichosis. Rarely these organisms can disseminate in an immunosuppressed host. The invasive mycoses can be separated into the endemic mycoses that can cause disease in healthy hosts who are exposed to them in the environment and the opportunistic mycoses that cause serious infection almost entirely in immunosuppressed hosts (Table 378–1).

THE ENDEMIC MYCOSES

The endemic mycoses (histoplasmosis, blastomycosis, coccidioidomycosis, and paracoccidioidomycosis) are caused by a diverse group of fungi that share several important characteristics but differ greatly in other respects. These fungi are all dimorphic, existing as molds in the environment and as either yeasts or spherules in tissues. Each organism occupies a different ecological niche; infection is directly related to exposure to the mycelial or mold phase of the organism in the environment. They are true pathogens in that they are capable of causing infection in normal hosts. The severity of infection is determined both by the extent of the exposure to the organism and by the immune status of the host. These organisms are inhaled, have the propensity to disseminate hematogenously, and can be reactivated years later. Although many of the disease manifestations overlap, each of the four has its own distinctive characteristics.

The endemic mycoses mimic many common bacterial infections involving lungs, skin, and other organs; frequently, especially in the nonendemic setting, the diagnosis of infection with an endemic mycosis is not entertained. With increased travel and leisure time activities in the past several decades, patients often present with illness outside the endemic area. When presented with an elderly retiree who winters in Arizona and who has fever, headache, and visual complaints, a physician who works in Ohio and who may never have seen coccidioidomycosis must remember that this fungal infection causes chronic meningitis. Similarly, a patient with the acquired immunodeficiency syndrome (AIDS) who lives in Seattle but who spent his or her childhood in Arkansas and has not returned there for the last 20 years might well have reactivation disseminated histoplasmosis causing fever, hepatosplenomegaly, and pancytopenia.

THE OPPORTUNISTIC MYCOSES

Increasingly, fungal infections are a major cause of morbidity and mortality in hospitalized and immunocompromised patients. Almost all of these infections are caused by fungi that do not cause serious disease in the normal host. These so-called opportunistic fungi include both yeast-like organisms and filamentous fungi.

The most common opportunistic infection is candidiasis. *Candida* species are part of the normal human flora in the gastrointestinal and genitourinary tracts and the skin. Most other opportunistic fungi are normally found in the environment, and infection occurs after inhalation or inoculation of the infectious form. The most common non-*Candida* pathogens include the filamentous fungi belonging to the genus *Aspergillus* and the class Zygomycetes and the yeast *Cryptococcus neoformans*. Increasingly, however, many previously nonpathogenic fungi are reported as causing infection in the markedly immunosuppressed host. These include the dematiaceous or pigmented molds, such as *Bipolaris, Curvularia, Exophiala,* and *Phialophora,* and the nonpigmented molds, including *Paecilomyces, Fusarium,* and *Pseudallescheria*. In the immunosuppressed host, widespread dissemination is typically seen with angioinvasive fungi such as *Aspergillus, Pseudallescheria,* the Zygomycetes, and *Fusarium; C. neoformans* is neurotropic and causes predominantly meningitis with or without dissemination to other organs.

Diagnosis of Fungal Infections

The most useful diagnostic tests differ for each endemic mycosis, but, as a general rule, histopathologic demonstration of the fungi in biopsy specimens is the most expeditious way to make a diagnosis, especially in a severely ill patient; growth of the organism in vitro is definitive. Serologic assays are useful in the diagnosis of histoplasmosis and coccidioidomycosis, and an enzyme immunoassay for *Histoplasma* antigen is especially helpful in the diagnosis of disseminated histoplasmosis in AIDS patients.

For opportunistic fungi, diagnosis of invasive infection is often difficult. On the one hand, *Candida* species are part of the normal flora, and growth in nonsterile sites, such as sputum, usually reflects only colonization. On the other hand, growth in blood cultures, even in the presence of widespread dissemination, occurs in only about 50% of patients. Assays for *Candida* antibodies, antigens, or metabolites have proved to be neither sensitive nor specific enough for clinical use. Similarly, growth of filamentous fungi that are ubiquitous in the environment may reflect only contamination, and samples from patients with disseminated infection often show no growth. Other than a very specific and sensitive latex agglutination assay for the polysaccharide capsule of *C. neoformans,* there are no antigen or antibody assays currently available to help with the diagnosis of infection caused by the opportunistic fungi. Histopathologic demonstration of tissue invasion by opportunistic fungi is an important diagnostic test, especially in those who are desperately ill.

Table 378–1 • MOST COMMON SYSTEMIC MYCOSES AND CAUSATIVE FUNGAL ORGANISMS

DISEASE	CAUSATIVE FUNGUS
ENDEMIC MYCOSES	
Blastomycosis	*Blastomyces dermatitidis*
Coccidioidomycosis	*Coccidioides immitis*
Histoplasmosis	*Histoplasma capsulatum*
Paracoccidioidomycosis	*Paracoccidioides brasiliensis*
Sporotrichosis (usually subcutaneous but can be systemic)	*Sporothrix schenckii*
OPPORTUNISTIC MYCOSES	
Aspergillosis	*Aspergillus* species
Candidiasis	*Candida* species
Cryptococcosis	*Cryptococcus neoformans*
Zygomycosis (mucormycosis)	*Rhizopus, Mucor,* and others

Antifungal Agents

Currently available classes of antifungal agents include those that target ergosterol in the cell membrane of fungi (polyenes, azoles, allylamines), glucans in the fungal cell wall (echinocandins), and fungal DNA and RNA synthesis (flucytosine) (Table 378–2). With the approval of several new agents, including those in an entirely new class, future studies will revolve around investigations concerning the use of possibly synergistic combinations of drugs that act at different targets on the fungal cell.

For years, amphotericin B has been considered the "gold standard" against which all other agents have been compared. However, the toxicity of amphotericin B continues to be a major drawback to its use. Nephrotoxicity occurs to some degree in most patients who receive the drug, and infusion-related reactions are quite common and can be severe. Lipid formulations of amphotericin B were developed specifically to decrease the toxicity of the parent compound. Three formulations are currently available: liposomal amphotericin B, amphotericin B lipid complex, and amphotericin B colloidal dispersion. Each differs from the others and from standard amphotericin B with respect to composition, pharmacologic parameters, recommended dosages, and toxicity. Because of their high cost, these preparations are often used only after initial therapy with standard amphotericin B or for patients with preexisting renal insufficiency. Increasingly, however, when a higher dosage of amphotericin B is required for difficult-to-treat infections and when amphotericin B is required in certain groups, such as bone marrow transplant recipients, in whom other nephrotoxic drugs are routinely given, a lipid formulation is used.

Four azole agents are currently available for systemic use: ketoconazole, itraconazole, fluconazole, and voriconazole. The azoles have classically been considered to be fungistatic, but the newest agents are fungicidal for certain filamentous fungi. The toxicity of the azoles varies with the specificity of binding to ergosterol in fungal cells compared with cholesterol in mammalian cells. Because of its greater toxicity, poor absorption, and modest spectrum of activity, ketoconazole is now used infrequently. Itraconazole is the azole of choice for most endemic mycoses; it is also used for infections caused by several opportunistic fungi and for many superficial cutaneous fungal infections. Poor absorption of itraconazole capsules, the initial formulation, has been a major drawback to the use of this drug; the newer oral suspension and intravenous formulation have helped to solve this problem.

Fluconazole, available as oral and intravenous formulations, is used frequently for treatment of a variety of different infections by *Candida* species, *C. neoformans*, *Coccidioides immitis*, and several other opportunistic fungi. The pharmacologic characteristics of fluconazole are excellent, but the spectrum of activity is the narrowest among the azoles. It has no *Aspergillus* activity, for example.

Voriconazole, available in both oral and intravenous formulations, is the newest azole agent. It has a broad spectrum of activity, including all *Candida* species and *C. neoformans*, and has fungicidal activity against *Aspergillus* and several other filamentous fungi. Voriconazole also has excellent pharmacologic characteristics.

All azoles interact with different cytochrome P-450 enzymes to varying degrees and thus have major drug interactions. The potential for drug interactions must always be considered before prescribing one of these agents. All azoles also have the potential to cause hepatotoxicity, and liver enzyme tests should be followed to assess this possibility.

Another agent that interferes with ergosterol synthesis is the allylamine terbinafine. This agent is used primarily for dermatophyte infections but on occasion has proved useful in combination with other agents for serious opportunistic fungal infections.

Caspofungin is the first echinocandin approved for use in humans. The echinocandins act to inhibit β-glucan synthesis in the fungal cell wall, are fungicidal against *Candida* species and probably *Aspergillus* species, but are not active against *C. neoformans*. Caspofungin is available only as an intravenous formulation and, as predicted, appears to have little toxicity.

Flucytosine (5-fluorocytosine) is an oral fluorinated pyrimidine that is converted to 5-fluorouracil and acts to interfere with fungal DNA and RNA synthesis. It has been used primarily in treating cryptococcosis and candidiasis. However, it must be used with another agent because of the rapid development of resistance, and serum levels must be monitored because of dose-related bone marrow suppression.

SUGGESTED READINGS
Dismukes WE, Pappas PG, Sobel JD: Clinical Mycology. New York, Oxford University Press, 2003. *An authoritative, updated text.*

379 HISTOPLASMOSIS

Carol A. Kauffman

Definition

Histoplasmosis is the most common endemic mycosis in the United States. Most infections are self-limited, but the organism has the ability to cause severe acute pulmonary and disseminated infection, as well as chronic pulmonary and disseminated infection. *Histoplasma capsulatum* var. *capsulatum* is a thermally dimorphic fungus. In the environment and at temperatures lower than 35° C, it exists as a mold that produces conidia, both tuberculate macroconidia, that are helpful for identification purposes in the laboratory, and microconidia, that are likely the infectious form. In tissues and at 35° to 37° C, *H. capsulatum* transforms into tiny 2- to 4-μm oval yeasts that reproduce by budding and parasitize macrophages. African histoplasmosis is caused by a different subspecies of *H. capsulatum* (var. *duboisii*) and has different disease manifestations.

Epidemiology

Histoplasmosis, although found worldwide, is primarily a disease of North and Central America. *H. capsulatum* is endemic in the Mississippi and Ohio River valleys, extending into the St. Lawrence basin; microfoci exist in discrete isolated areas in several eastern states. Soil, caves, and abandoned buildings containing high concentrations of bird or bat guano support the luxuriant growth of the organism. Every year, hundreds of thousands of individuals who live in areas endemic for *H. capsulatum* are infected. Most cases are sporadic and the exact source of exposure is unknown. Point-source outbreaks that have included as few as four or five persons and as many as 100,000 persons have been well-described in association with disruption of

Table 378–2 • ANTIFUNGAL AGENTS USED FOR THE TREATMENT OF SYSTEMIC MYCOSES

AGENT	MECHANISMS OF ACTION	MAJOR SIDE EFFECTS
Polyenes AmB deoxycholate Liposomal AmB AmB colloidal dispersion AmB lipid complex	Bind to ergosterol, increase cell membrane permeability causing leakage of cell contents and cell death	Nephrotoxicity, anemia, chills, fever, nausea; lipid formulations less nephrotoxic and most have less infusion toxicity
Azoles Ketoconazole Itraconazole Fluconazole Voriconazole	Block ergosterol synthesis via demethylase in cell membrane (cytochrome P-450 dependent)	Hepatotoxicity, nausea, drug-drug interactions Suppress testosterone and adrenal steroids (mostly ketoconazole)
Allylamines Terbinafine	Block ergosterol synthesis via squalene epoxidase inhibition	Nausea, hepatotoxicity, rash
Fluorinated pyrimidines Flucytosine	Converted to 5-fluorouracil; inhibit RNA and DNA synthesis	Bone marrow suppression, hepatotoxicity, nausea
Echinocandins Caspofungin	Block β-glucan synthesis in cell wall	Flushing with infusion

AmB = amphotericin B.

soil, cleaning attics, bridges, or barns, tearing down old structures laden with guano, and spelunking.

Pathogenesis

After inhalation of the microconidia into the alveoli, a localized pulmonary infection ensues. Neutrophils and macrophages phagocytize the organism, now in the yeast phase; the organism is able to survive and travel within macrophages to the hilar and mediastinal lymph nodes and throughout the reticuloendothelial system by hematogenous dissemination. This dissemination probably occurs in most persons who are infected and in normal hosts is associated with no symptoms. After several weeks, T cells specifically sensitized by *H. capsulatum* antigens activate macrophages, which then are able to kill the intracellular fungi. Histoplasmosis is a classic example of the pivotal importance of the cell-mediated immune system in containing intracellular pathogens. Not surprisingly, most patients with severe infection are those who have cellular immunodeficiencies.

The extent of disease is determined by both the number of conidia inhaled and the immune response of the host. A small inoculum can cause severe pulmonary infection or progress to acute symptomatic disseminated histoplasmosis in a patient with advanced human immunodeficiency virus infection, whose cell-mediated immune system is unable to contain the organism. Conversely, a healthy individual may develop severe life-threatening pulmonary infection if a large number of conidia are inhaled, as might occur during demolition activities on old buildings or while spelunking in a heavily infested cave.

Reinfection occurs in persons who previously had histoplasmosis; this is almost always in the setting of a heavy exposure. Reinfection histoplasmosis is usually less severe than primary infection because of residual immunity induced by the initial episode. Reactivation of latent infection occurs in patients who have deficient cell-mediated immunity as evidenced by the occurrence of histoplasmosis in persons who grew up in the endemic area but have not been back in that area for years.

Clinical Manifestations

ACUTE PULMONARY HISTOPLASMOSIS. Infection is asymptomatic in most people infected with *H. capsulatum*. Those who do have symptomatic pulmonary infection usually have a self-limited illness that begins several weeks after exposure and is characterized by fever, chills, fatigue, nonproductive cough, anterior chest discomfort, and myalgias. Arthritis or arthralgia, often accompanied by erythema nodosum, occurs in 5 to 10% of patients with acute pulmonary histoplasmosis. A patchy lobar or multilobe nodular infiltrate is noted on chest radiograph.

The differential diagnosis of acute pulmonary histoplasmosis includes pneumonia due to *Blastomyces dermatitidis*, *Mycoplasma pneumoniae*, *Legionella* spp., and *Chlamydia pneumoniae*. When enlarged hilar or mediastinal lymph nodes are present, histoplasmosis should be strongly considered. The most difficult to differentiate is acute pulmonary blastomycosis because the endemic areas overlap, a similar history of outdoor activities is often obtained, and the radiographs show similar findings.

In patients who have had a heavy exposure to *H. capsulatum* and in those who are immunosuppressed, acute pulmonary histoplasmosis can be life threatening. High spiking fevers, chills, prostration, dyspnea, and cough are prominent. Chest radiographs show diffuse reticulonodular pulmonary infiltrates, and respiratory failure can occur rapidly.

CHRONIC PULMONARY HISTOPLASMOSIS. Chronic cavitary pulmonary histoplasmosis is a progressive, fatal form of histoplasmosis that develops almost exclusively in older patients who have chronic obstructive pulmonary disease. Symptoms include fever, fatigue, anorexia, weight loss, cough productive of purulent sputum, and hemoptysis. On chest radiograph, the usual findings are unilateral or bilateral upper lobe infiltrates with multiple cavities and extensive fibrosis in the lower lobes. Bronchopleural fistula formation and pneumothorax can occur. Chronic pulmonary histoplasmosis mimics tuberculosis, other fungal pneumonias (especially blastomycosis and sporotrichosis), and nontuberculous mycobacterial infections in regard to symptoms, signs, and radiographic findings.

COMPLICATIONS OF PULMONARY HISTOPLASMOSIS. Mediastinal and hilar lymph nodes often calcify as the infection resolves; years later they can erode into bronchi, causing hemoptysis and expectoration of broncholiths. Granulomatous mediastinitis is an uncommon syndrome characterized by continuing inflammation and necrosis in the mediastinal lymph nodes. The enlarged nodes are readily apparent on chest radiographs, and computed tomographic (CT) scans show central necrosis and impingement on adjacent structures, including the esophagus, the airways, and blood vessels. Although symptoms usually resolve without treatment, obstructive syndromes can be severe and the nodes can persist for years.

Fibrosing mediastinitis is a rare but fatal complication of histoplasmosis in which the host responds to the infection with an inappropriate excessive fibrotic response. Obstruction of the esophagus, the airways, the superior vena cava, or the pulmonary arteries and veins can occur with resultant progressive right heart failure and respiratory insufficiency. Mediastinal widening is seen on chest radiographs, and CT scans define the extent of invasion and obstruction of mediastinal structures.

Pericarditis is a manifestation of a local inflammatory reaction to adjacent histoplasmosis. Patients respond promptly to anti-inflammatory medications without antifungal therapy. Hemodynamic compromise, although unusual, requires drainage of pericardial fluid; only rarely has progression to constrictive pericarditis been documented.

DISSEMINATED HISTOPLASMOSIS. Symptomatic disseminated histoplasmosis occurs mostly in immunosuppressed patients. Patients with acquired immunodeficiency syndrome (AIDS) with CD4 counts less than 150/μL, infants, and those who have a hematologic malignancy, have received an organ transplant, or are on corticosteroid therapy are at greatest risk for acute disseminated histoplasmosis. Symptoms and signs include chills, fever, anorexia, weight loss, hypotension, dyspnea, hepatosplenomegaly, and skin and mucous membrane lesions. Pancytopenia, diffuse pulmonary infiltrates on chest radiograph, findings of disseminated intravascular coagulation, and acute respiratory failure are common. This syndrome is indistinguishable from sepsis due to any bacterial or viral etiology. In AIDS patients, the differential diagnosis includes cytomegalovirus, disseminated *Mycobacterium avium* complex infection, and tuberculosis.

Chronic progressive disseminated histoplasmosis is a fatal form of histoplasmosis that occurs mostly in middle-aged to elderly men who have no known immunosuppressive illness. The illness is characterized by fever, night sweats, weight loss, anorexia, and fatigue. Patients appear chronically ill, hepatosplenomegaly and mucocutaneous ulcerations are common, and a small proportion have signs of adrenal insufficiency. Increased erythrocyte sedimentation rate, elevated alkaline phosphatase, pancytopenia, and diffuse reticulonodular infiltrates on chest radiographs are typical. Patients with this form of histoplasmosis often present with fever of unknown origin. Miliary tuberculosis, lymphoma, and sarcoidosis must be excluded.

Involvement of almost every organ system has been reported with disseminated infection. Adrenal insufficiency must be sought in any patient who has unexplained hypotension, hyponatremia, and hyperkalemia. Abdominal CT scan shows markedly enlarged adrenal glands. Central nervous system involvement is manifest either as meningitis or as focal lesions seen on magnetic resonance imaging and is more common in patients with AIDS. Skin lesions, also more common in patients with AIDS, can be papular, pustular, or ulcerated. *Histoplasma* endocarditis is a rare form of disseminated infection.

PRESUMED OCULAR HISTOPLASMOSIS. Choroiditis causing visual loss has been attributed to histoplasmosis based on residence in an area endemic for histoplasmosis and histoplasmin skin test reactivity rather than demonstration of the organism in the eye. So-called histo spots are not a manifestation of active infection of the eye with *H. capsulatum* and should not be treated with antifungal agents.

Diagnosis

The definitive diagnostic test for histoplasmosis is growth of the organism in culture. Unfortunately, *H. capsulatum* may take as long as 6 weeks to grow in vitro. Tissue samples, bronchoalveolar lavage fluid, sputum, and blood are appropriate for culture. For those patients who have evidence of dissemination, blood cultures are best performed using the lysis-centrifugation (Isolator tube) system; bone marrow and liver biopsy material often yield *H. capsulatum* in the setting of dissemination. If pulmonary histoplasmosis is a diagnostic consideration, the laboratory should be informed so that a special medium that decreases the growth of commensal fungi can be used for the culture of pulmonary samples. As soon as growth of a mold has been detected, highly specific DNA probes for *H. capsulatum* allow the rapid identification of the organism.

For an acutely ill patient, tissue biopsy should be done to search for the distinctive 2- to 4-μm oval budding yeasts that allow a tentative diagnosis to be made as quickly as possible. Routine tissue stains do not show the tiny yeasts; biopsy material must be stained with methenamine silver or periodic acid–Schiff stains. In patients with disseminated disease, bone marrow, liver, skin, and mucocutaneous lesions usually reveal many organisms. The organisms can also be seen in Wright's stain of peripheral blood in patients with acute disseminated infection. For patients with chronic pulmonary histoplasmosis or granulomatous mediastinitis, biopsy of lung or lymph nodes may reveal the organism. It is unusual to find the small yeasts of *H. capsulatum* on cytologic examination of sputum or bronchoalveolar lavage fluid.

Serology plays an important role in the diagnosis of some forms of histoplasmosis. Complement-fixation (CF) assays that utilize two different antigens, mycelial and yeast, and immunodiffusion (ID) tests are available. The ID test is more specific than the CF test, but the CF tests are more sensitive. CF antibody titers frequently remain positive at a low titer for years after the infection. Serology is often the most important diagnostic test for establishing the diagnosis of acute pulmonary histoplasmosis. In this form of histoplasmosis cultures often are negative. The diagnosis can be made by a fourfold rise in CF titer, a CF titer higher than 1 : 32, or the appearance of an M precipitin band by ID assay. These tests also are quite useful for patients with chronic forms of pulmonary or disseminated histoplasmosis, but they are rarely useful in immunosuppressed patients, who cannot mount an antibody response. Serologic tests are less definitive in patients who have mediastinal lymphadenopathy and should always be confirmed by tissue biopsy. False-positive CF tests occur in patients with lymphoma, tuberculosis, sarcoidosis, and other fungal infections, all of which may present as mediastinal masses.

An enzyme immunoassay for *H. capsulatum* polysaccharide antigen in urine and serum is extremely helpful in AIDS patients with disseminated infection. The sensitivity for antigen detection is higher in urine than in serum. Antigen levels should become undetectable with successful therapy; the persistence of antigen implies active infection. Antigen assays are less useful for pulmonary histoplasmosis; only about 20% of patients with pulmonary histoplasmosis have antigen detected in urine or serum. The assay is fairly specific with cross-reactivity shown in only a small number of cases of blastomycosis, paracoccidioidomycosis, and penicilliosis.

Skin testing with histoplasmin antigen is not useful. In the endemic area, most adults are skin-test positive because of prior exposure to *H. capsulatum*. Cross-reactions occur in other fungal infections, especially blastomycosis; negative skin tests are the rule in patients who have severe histoplasmosis; and the skin test antigens can falsely elevate CF antibody titers.

Treatment

Guidelines for the treatment of histoplasmosis have been published by the Mycoses Study Group and the Infectious Diseases Society of America. Itraconazole is the drug of choice for mild to moderate histoplasmosis, and amphotericin B is for severe, life-threatening infection. Fluconazole is less active and should be considered a second-line agent, and ketoconazole has become a second-line agent because of increased toxicity when compared with itraconazole.

PULMONARY HISTOPLASMOSIS. Treatment is usually not given for acute pulmonary histoplasmosis, many times the diagnosis is not made until after symptoms have resolved. However, if the patient remains symptomatic after 4 weeks, therapy with itraconazole 200 mg daily for 6 to 12 weeks can be given. Patients who have severe outbreak-associated histoplasmosis and all immunosuppressed patients should be treated. Initial therapy with amphotericin B, 0.7 to 1 mg/kg daily can be followed with oral itraconazole after a favorable response is noted. Antifungal therapy should be given to all patients with chronic pulmonary histoplasmosis. Itraconazole, 200 mg once or twice daily for 12 to 24 months, is preferred; if amphotericin B is used, the total dosage should be 30 to 35 mg/kg.

A trial of itraconazole for 6 to 12 months is recommended for patients with symptomatic granulomatous mediastinitis, although there are no data proving this to be effective. Surgical resection of nodes causing obstructive symptoms may be beneficial. Antifungal therapy probably offers no benefit for patients with fibrosing mediastinitis. However, because of the inexorable downhill course of this illness, a several-month course of itraconazole is often tried. Surgery for this condition carries a high operative mortality rate. Intravascular stents may be helpful in some patients with vascular obstruction.

DISSEMINATED HISTOPLASMOSIS. All patients with symptomatic disseminated histoplasmosis should receive antifungal therapy. Patients who have only mild to moderate symptoms with acute disseminated disease and most patients with chronic progressive disseminated histoplasmosis can be treated with itraconazole, 200 mg twice daily. A total of 12 months of therapy is usually adequate, but for those with chronic progressive disease this should be determined by the patient's clinical course. Patients who have AIDS should be maintained on chronic suppressive itraconazole therapy, 200 mg daily, after they receive an initial course of 12 weeks of twice-daily itraconazole.

Immunosuppressed patients with moderately severe to severe symptoms should be treated with amphotericin B, 0.7 to 1 mg/kg daily. For most patients, therapy can be changed to itraconazole after their condition has improved and they are able to take oral medications. If it is elected to treat only with amphotericin B, the total dosage should be 35 mg/kg. For certain patients, including stem cell and solid organ transplant recipients and those on nephrotoxic drugs or with preexisting renal failure, a lipid formulation of amphotericin B should be used.

Prognosis

Acute pulmonary histoplasmosis is usually a self-limited disease. Patients who require treatment usually respond promptly to antifungal agents. However, the response of patients with chronic cavitary pulmonary histoplasmosis is often poor, primarily because of their severe underlying pulmonary disease. Patients with disseminated histoplasmosis, even those with advanced AIDS, usually respond promptly to antifungal therapy. Older patients with chronic progressive disseminated histoplasmosis have a slower but usually complete response to therapy.

1. Wheat J, Sarosi G, McKinsey D, et al: Practice guidelines for the management of patients with histoplasmosis. Clin Infect Dis 2000;30:688–695.

SUGGESTED READINGS

Cano M, Hajjeh RA: The epidemiology of histoplasmosis: A review. Semin Respir Infect 2001;16:109–118. *Excellent overview of the epidemiology of histoplasmosis.*

Wheat LJ: Laboratory diagnosis of histoplasmosis: A review. Semin Respir Infect 2001;16:131–140. *In-depth review of the utility of various diagnostic tests for histoplasmosis.*

Wheat LJ, Connolly-Stringfield PA, Baker RL, et al: Disseminated histoplasmosis in the acquired immune deficiency syndrome: Clinical findings, diagnosis and treatment, and review of the literature. Medicine (Balt) 1990;69:361–374. *Details the clinical findings of histoplasmosis in this high-risk population.*

Wheat LJ, Kauffman CA: Histoplasmosis. Infect Dis Clin North Am 2003;17:1–19. *Recent review of clinical aspects of histoplasmosis.*

380 COCCIDIOIDOMYCOSIS

John N. Galgiani

Definition

Coccidioidomycosis is a systemic fungal infection due to *Coccidioides spp.* endemic to some deserts of the Western Hemisphere (Table 380–1).

Etiology

C. immitis and *C. posadasii* are dimorphic fungi that are classified as ascomycetes by ribosomal gene homology. In their vegetative state, mycelia with true septations mature to produce arthroconidia, single cells approximately 2 to 5 mm in diameter. After infection, an arthroconidium enlarges to as much as 75 mm in diameter as a spherule, undergoing internal septation to produce scores of endospores. When spherules rupture, packets of endospores are released, and these produce more spherules in infected tissue or revert to mycelia if removed from the body.

Epidemiology

Coccidioides spp. can be recovered from the soil of the low deserts of Arizona; the Central Valley of California; parts of other states, including New Mexico and Texas; and parts of Central and South America. Endemic regions follow the climatologic Sonoran life zone, which is characterized by modest rainfall, mild winters, and low humidity. Mycelia bloom beneath the surface during periods of rain, and arthroconidia develop as the earth dries. Rates of infection are highest during dry months and are accentuated when soil is disturbed by windstorms or construction equipment. Exposure to contaminated bales of cotton or other fomites can result in infection beyond the endemic regions, but this is rare. Person-to-person transmission of pulmonary infection has not been reported, and isolation precautions are unnecessary. *C. immitis* is listed by the Centers for Disease Control and Prevention as a possible agent for bioterrorism.

Incidence and Prevalence

In general, the annual risk of infection within the most strongly endemic areas is 3% and results in approximately 150,000 new infections. With unusually intense exposure, such as at archeology sites or during military maneuvers within endemic regions, infections can

Table 380–1 • COCCIDIOIDOMYCOSIS: CLINICAL CHARACTERISTICS AND TREATMENT

CHARACTERISTIC	DESCRIPTION
Causative fungus	*Coccidioides immitis* and *Coccidioides posadasii*
Primary geographic distribution	Lower Sonoran deserts of the Western Hemisphere, including parts of Arizona, California, New Mexico, western Texas, and parts of Central and South America
Primary route of acquisition	Respiratory (inhalation of arthroconidia)
Principal site of disease	Lungs most common; spread to skin, bones, meninges, and other viscera, uncommon but serious
Opportunistic infection in compromised hosts	Diffuse pneumonia and widespread infections common in patients with T-lymphocyte defects or during high-dose corticosteroid therapy
Drug of choice for most patients	No antifungal is required for uncomplicated pneumonia; fluconazole or itraconazole for progressive forms of infection
Alternative therapy	Amphotericin B (especially with diffuse pneumonia or rapidly progressive infections); ketoconazole; voriconazole

develop in the majority of persons exposed for only a matter of days. More than 60% of new infections are likely to occur in Arizona because of the rapid growth of populations in the Phoenix and Tucson areas.

Pathogenesis and Pathology

Inhaling an arthroconidium to the level of the terminal bronchiole initiates virtually all coccidioidal infections. Fungal proliferation engenders both granulomatous inflammation, which is associated with intact spherules, and acute inflammation including eosinophils, which is associated with spherule rupture. Focal pneumonia is often associated with ipsilateral hilar adenopathy, and, less frequently, infection enlarges peritracheal, supraclavicular, and cervical nodes. Lesions occurring elsewhere are the result of hematogenous dissemination and most become apparent within 2 years of the initial infection. Although progressive dissemination results from fewer than 1% of infections, as many as 8% of persons with self-limited infection manifest asymptomatic chorioretinal scars, suggesting that subclinical hematogenous spread may be frequent. Within weeks after infection, durable T-cell immunity normally arrests fungal proliferation, allowing inflammation to resolve and preventing reinfection in the future. However, control of the infection may occur without sterilizing lesions, and reactivation of dormant infection or second infections is possible in patients whose cell-mediated immunity becomes deficient.

Clinical Manifestations

At least two of every three infections are detected only by finding dermal hypersensitivity to coccidioidal antigens. Those who become ill usually experience self-limited pulmonary syndromes. However, a few patients develop complications or progressive forms of infection that display a broad variety of manifestations and pose difficult problems in management for the clinician.

PRIMARY PULMONARY INFECTIONS. Symptoms develop within 5 to 21 days after exposure. Fever, weight loss, fatigue, a dry cough, and pleuritic chest pain are common but not specific complaints. Arthralgia of multiple joints without significant effusions is also frequent and is referred to as "desert rheumatism." Occasionally skin manifestations develop, including a short-lived nonpruritic maculopapular rash, *erythema multiforme,* or *erythema nodosum.* These arthritic and dermatologic manifestations are mediated by circulating immune complexes or other immunologic phenomena rather than fungal dissemination. Radiographs of the chest may show no abnormalities or may demonstrate pulmonary infiltrates, either segmental or lobar. Hilar adenopathy is often a distinctive finding. Peripneumonic pleural effusions may occur and usually resolve without intervention, although cultures of pleural biopsies usually yield *Coccidioides spp.* Eosinophilia is frequently a prominent finding in differential leukocyte counts of peripheral blood, and the erythrocyte sedimentation rate is usually elevated. Symptoms may persist for several weeks before improvement is clearly under way, and the illness, especially lassitude, may persist for months.

The primary pulmonary process produces a variety of sequelae. The most frequent is the development of a pulmonary nodule (Fig. 380–1), typically measuring 1 to 4 cm and lying within 5 cm of the hilus. Despite their harmless nature, coccidioidal nodules may engender concern because of their similarity to a malignant mass. For this reason, management usually requires percutaneous needle aspiration or resection. Another consequence of pulmonary coccidioidomycosis is cavitation of the infiltrate, which occurs in approximately 5% of cases of pneumonia. Most cavities are solitary and thin walled, residing in an upper lobe close to the pleura. Occasionally they produce pain, hemoptysis, or adjacent infiltrates. Cavities may acquire mycetomas either from *C. immitis* itself or some other colonizing mould. Infrequently a cavity ruptures, forming a pyopneumothorax. This usually is the first symptom of coccidioidal infection and typically occurs in otherwise healthy young men. An air-fluid level in the pleural space, detectable by roentgenography, often helps differentiate this problem from a spontaneous pneumothorax. Surgical resection of the cavity is the preferred treatment for this complication. The least common pulmonary complication is persistent fibrocavitary infection that progresses to involvement of both lungs.

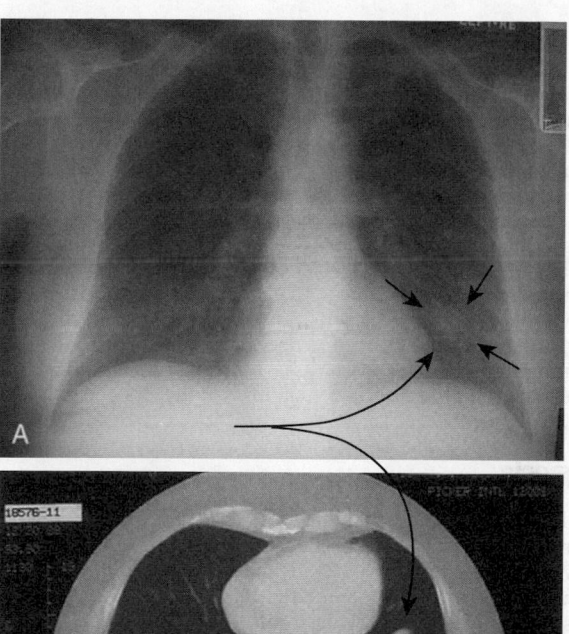

FIGURE 380–1 • *A,* Benign nodule due to coccidioidomycosis (arrows). *B,* CT image of the nodule shown in *A* (arrows).

EXTRAPULMONARY DISSEMINATION. Coccidioidomycosis in immuno-suppressed patients, such as organ recipients, those with acquired immunodeficiency syndrome (AIDS) or lymphoma, or women during their third trimester of pregnancy, usually results in dissemination beyond the lungs. However, disseminated infection also occurs in some patients who have no underlying disease and do not manifest heightened susceptibility to other infections. The most common locations for disseminated lesions are skin (cutaneous papules or subcutaneous abscesses); joints (especially the knee); bones, including vertebrae; and the basilar meninges. Such infections may produce one or many lesions and frequently are subacute or chronic in their presentation. In broadly immuno-suppressed patients, coccidioidal infections may be more fulminant, with fungemia detectable with blood cultures and diffuse reticulonodular embolic pulmonary infiltrates. Although the kidneys and the urinary bladder are rarely involved, *C. immitis* may be recovered from concentrated specimens of urine because of either transient fungemia or focal dissemination to the prostate. In contrast with histoplasmosis, the gastrointestinal tract is rarely involved in coccidioidomycosis.

Diagnosis

The diagnosis is firmly established by recovering *Coccidioides spp.* from clinical specimens. On direct examination of respiratory specimens or tissue, spherules can be seen as large structures with refractile walls and internal organization; these are also seen on hematoxylin-eosin, silver, or periodic acid–Schiff stains of histologic preparations. The Gram stain does not detect spherules. In culture, mycelial growth is often evident within the first week of incubation, and DNA probing with commercially available kits allows rapid species identification. Recovery of *Coccidioides spp.* may be difficult in patients who have only scant respiratory secretions associated with the initial

pneumonia and from the cerebrospinal fluid (CSF) of patients with meningitis.

A presumptive diagnosis of coccidioidal infection is often based on detecting specific antibodies in serum. Within the first weeks of initial infections, a precipitin-type antibody is detected, usually by immunodiffusion techniques. Later, complement-fixation (CF)–type antibodies usually appear. When reported quantitatively, CF antibodies generally are found to be highest in the most extensive infections and to decrease in concentration in patients whose infections are controlled. An important means of diagnosing coccidioidal meningitis is by detection of CF antibodies in the CSF, along with other abnormalities, such as leukocytosis, elevated protein concentration, or low glucose concentration.

Rx Treatment

The role of antifungal therapy for primary uncomplicated infections is controversial because clinical trials have not been performed to determine if treatment either shortens the course of symptoms or diminishes the chances of complications. However, the value of treatment is clear for patients with progressive illness. Because many coccidioidal infections are chronic in nature, treatment with oral azole antifungal agents, such as ketoconazole, fluconazole, and itraconazole, is often used for initial therapy. Doses of these azoles are 400 mg/day or higher and treatment is usually continued for a year or more. Responses with these agents are satisfactory in approximately two thirds of patients. Fluconazole is effective therapy for coccidioidal meningitis and has greatly reduced the number of patients treated with intrathecal amphotericin B. Unfortunately, cessation of azole therapy, especially of therapy for coccidioidal meningitis, often is followed by recurrence of symptoms. Therefore, many patients may need protracted or even life-long therapy to maintain control of disease activity. Amphotericin B remains a rational choice in cases in which treatment with azole antifungals has failed. Daily doses range from 0.4 to 1 mg/kg and cumulative therapy ranges from 0.5 to 3 g. Occasionally, in a patient in whom disease progression is rapid, amphotericin B may produce a more rapid therapeutic response and therefore is preferred initial therapy. Delivery of amphotericin B in liposomes or lipid complexes is being explored as a means of reducing its well-recognized toxic effects. In addition to selection of antifungal agents, surgical removal of necrotic tissue is often essential to control the damage from specific lesions.

Prognosis

After resolution of the initial infection, most patients maintain lifelong immunity, and infections after re-exposure are rare. However, cessation of symptoms is often accomplished without eradicating *Coccidioides spp.* completely, and recurrence of the original infection up to many years after the original episode is a well-recognized risk of intercurrent profound immunosuppression. For patients in whom the initial infection cannot be resolved, the disease typically follows a protracted course. Although infection is more often debilitating than fatal, fulminant respiratory failure can occur and, if untreated, coccidioidal meningitis is nearly always fatal within 2 years.

SUGGESTED READINGS
Centers for Disease Control and Prevention: Increase in coccidioidomycosis Arizona, 1998–2001. MMWR 2003;52(16):109–112.
Galgiani JN: Coccidioidomycosis: A regional disease of national importance. Ann Intern Med 1999;130:293–300. *Emphasis on the primary care aspects of Valley fever.*
Galgiani JN, Ampel NM, Catanzaro A, et al: Treatment guidelines for coccidioidomycosis. Clin Infect Dis 2000;30:658–661. *Consensus statement regarding current therapy of coccidioidomycosis. Accessible online at http://www.idsociety.org.*
Galgiani JN, Catanzaro A, Cloud GA, et al: Comparison of oral fluconazole and itraconazole for progressive nonmeningeal coccidioidomycosis: A randomized, double-blind trial. Mycoses Study Group. Ann Intern Med 2000;133:676–686. *Similar response rates for all patients except those with skeletal infection, in whom itraconazole appeared more potent.*
McNeil MM, Ampel NM: Opportunistic coccidioidomycosis in patients infected with human immunodeficiency virus: Prevention issues and priorities. Clin Infect Dis 1995;21(Suppl 1):S111–S113. *An important finding from this study is that 46% of all coccidioidal infections in patients with AIDS occurred outside of the endemic regions, indicating the increased importance of this disease as a national problem.*
Pappagianis D, Zimmer BL: Serology of coccidioidomycosis. Clin Microbiol Rev 1990; 3:247–268. *Comprehensive review of diagnostic tests for coccidioidomycosis.*
Stevens DA: Current concepts: Coccidioidomycosis. N Engl J Med 1995;332:1077–1082. *Review of coccidioidomycosis with more detailed discussion of its pathogenesis.*

Infectious Diseases

381 BLASTOMYCOSIS

Carol A. Kauffman

Definition

Blastomycosis (North American blastomycosis) is an endemic mycosis that primarily causes infection of the lungs and skin and, less commonly, of the osteoarticular and genitourinary systems. *Blastomyces dermatitidis* is a thermally dimorphic fungus. In the environment in the mold phase, the organism produces conidia, which when aerosolized and inhaled cause infection. At 37° C on culture media and in tissues, the organism is a yeast that is 5 to 20 μm in diameter, has a thick refractile cell wall, and produces single broad-based buds.

Epidemiology

B. dermatitidis exists in many diverse geographic areas world-wide, but most cases of blastomycosis are reported from the south central and north central United States. The ecology of *B. dermatitidis* is not well defined, but it is likely that the natural niche is soil and decaying vegetation. Although most cases occur sporadically, several well-described outbreaks have helped define the natural habitat. The largest outbreak traced the source of *B. dermatitidis* to decaying wood and a beaver lodge on a pond in Wisconsin. The typical patient who develops blastomycosis is a middle-aged man who has an outdoor occupation or hobby.

Pathogenesis

Following inhalation of conidia, *B. dermatitidis* transforms into the yeast phase and causes pulmonary infection. Although many patients manifest only pulmonary symptoms, others present with cutaneous lesions in the absence of other organ involvement or with disseminated infection. It is likely that most patients have asymptomatic hematogenous dissemination following the initial pulmonary infection. Thus, cutaneous lesions should be viewed as a manifestation of hematogenous spread of the organism. Except in rare instances, blastomycosis is not acquired by inoculation. Cellular immunity involving T lymphocytes and macrophages is an important component of the host response to infection with *B. dermatitidis*, but neutrophils probably also play a role. Most patients with blastomycosis are healthy hosts. Patients who are immunosuppressed are more likely to have severe disease. Infection in the immunosuppressed host can occur after new exposure to *B. dermatitidis* or from reactivation of a latent focus of infection acquired years earlier.

Clinical Manifestations

PULMONARY. Most patients with acute pulmonary blastomycosis are asymptomatic or diagnosed as having a "viral syndrome." Patients with acute pneumonia have fever, malaise, a nonproductive cough, and a pulmonary infiltrate that shows lobar or multilobar patchy or nodular infiltrates on chest radiograph. Development of skin lesions is a strong clue for blastomycosis. Chronic pulmonary blastomycosis must be differentiated from tuberculosis, other fungal infections, and lung cancer. Fever, night sweats, weight loss, fatigue, cough, sputum production, hemoptysis, and dyspnea are commonly noted. On chest radiograph, the lesions are cavitary, nodular, fibrotic, or masslike in appearance. Hilar and mediastinal lymphadenopathy and pleural effusions are uncommonly seen. Rarely, overwhelming pulmonary disease with acute respiratory distress syndrome occurs; this appears to be more common in older adults and immunosuppressed patients.

DISSEMINATED INFECTION. Cutaneous lesions are the most common manifestation of disseminated blastomycosis. The lesions are usually well-circumscribed, painless papules, nodules, or plaques that become verrucous and develop multiple punctate draining areas in the center. Cutaneous lesions, sometimes single but more often multiple, are most common on the face and extremities but can appear anywhere. The skin lesions of blastomycosis clinically mimic those due to nontuberculous mycobacteria, other fungal infections, mycosis fungoides, and the lesions associated with bromide use. An uncommon manifestation, seen more often in immunocompromised patients, is the appearance of hundreds of pustular lesions that readily reveal the organism when aspirated.

Another manifestation of disseminated blastomycosis is osteoarticular involvement. Osteomyelitis can be associated with contiguous skin lesions or can appear at sites distant from cutaneous lesions. It is helpful to obtain a bone scan on all patients with disseminated blastomycosis because of the propensity of the organism to infect bone. Genitourinary involvement may be asymptomatic or associated with signs of prostatism and presence of a nodule on digital examination. Laryngeal and oropharyngeal nodules, ocular lesions, central nervous system involvement, either meningitis or intracerebral mass lesions, and dissemination to liver, spleen, and lymph nodes occur infrequently.

Diagnosis

The definitive diagnostic test for blastomycosis is growth of the organism from an aspirate, tissue biopsy, sputum, or body fluid. Urine obtained before and after prostatic massage should be sent for fungal culture in those with disseminated blastomycosis. The mold phase takes several weeks to grow at room temperature. Once growth has occurred, the organism can be rapidly identified as *B. dermatitidis* with highly specific and sensitive DNA probes. Histopathologic examination of cutaneous or pulmonary lesions; cytologic examination of sputum, bronchoalveolar lavage fluid, or other tissue fluids; and KOH smears of sputum or purulent material from pustular lesions should be performed to look for the distinctive large, thick-walled yeast with a single broad-based bud. Identification of characteristic organisms allows a tentative diagnosis of blastomycosis and initiation of antifungal therapy before culture results are known. Standard serologic assays for blastomycosis are neither sensitive nor specific. Although several different enzyme immunoassays have been developed to enhance specificity and sensitivity, none of these are currently available.

Treatment

Guidelines for the treatment of blastomycosis have been published by the Mycoses Study Group under the auspices of the Infectious Diseases Society of America.▉ Many patients with acute pulmonary blastomycosis are better before the diagnosis is established and do not need antifungal therapy. All patients with skin lesions or other manifestations of dissemination should receive systemic antifungal therapy to prevent progression of disease. Patients who have mild-to-moderate pulmonary or disseminated blastomycosis should be treated with itraconazole, 200 mg once or twice daily. The length of treatment is 6 to 12 months to achieve a mycologic cure and to prevent relapse. Fluconazole is not as effective as itraconazole. However, if the patient is unable to take itraconazole, fluconazole can be used, but the dosage should be 400 to 800 mg daily for 6 to 12 months.

Patients who have severe pulmonary or disseminated blastomycosis, all patients who have central nervous system infection, and most immunosuppressed patients should be treated initially with amphotericin B. The daily dosage is 0.7 to 1 mg/kg daily. A total of 1 to 2 g can be given, or after clinical improvement has occurred, therapy can be changed to itraconazole, 200 mg twice daily, for a total of 6 to 12 months of therapy.

Prognosis

The prognosis for patients with pulmonary or disseminated blastomycosis treated with itraconazole is excellent; more than 90% are cured. If relapse does occur, a second course of itraconazole is usually successful. Most reported deaths occur in those patients who present with overwhelming pneumonia and acute respiratory distress syndrome.

1. Chapman SW, Bradsher RW, Campbell GD, et al: Practice guidelines for the management of patients with blastomycosis. Clin Infect Dis 2000;30:679–683.

SUGGESTED READINGS

Areno JP, Campbell GD, George RB: Diagnosis of blastomycosis. Semin Respir Infect 1997;12:252–262. *Nice review of available methods for the diagnosis of blastomycosis.*

Baumgardner DJ, Buggy BP, Mattson BJ, et al: Epidemiology of blastomycosis in a region of high endemicity in north central Wisconsin. Clin Infect Dis 1992;15:629–635. *Gives insight into the epidemiologic features of blastomycosis in a highly endemic region.*

Bradshev RW, Chapman SW, Pappas PG: Blastomycosis. Infect Dis Clin North Am 2003;17:21–40. *Up-to-date review of blastomycosis.*

Pappas PG, Threlkeld MG, Bedsole GD, et al: Blastomycosis in immunocompromised patients. Medicine (Balt) 1993;72:311–325. *Excellent review of blastomycosis in immuno-suppressed patients.*

382 PARACOCCIDIOIDOMYCOSIS

Carol A. Kauffman

Definition

Paracoccidioidomycosis (South American blastomycosis) is a subacute to chronic mycosis that is endemic in Central and South America. The disease is characterized primarily by pulmonary, mucous membrane, and cutaneous lesions, but disseminated disease also occurs. *Paracoccidioides brasiliensis* is a thermally dimorphic fungus. In the environment and at temperatures below 35° C, the organism is a mold that produces conidia (spores). In tissues and at 37° C, the organism assumes the yeast form with multiple narrow-based buds.

Epidemiology

P. brasiliensis exists only in humid areas of Central and South America. The presumed ecological niche is in soil, but the exact conditions that favor growth of the organism have not been elucidated. The disease is most prevalent in middle-aged to elderly men from rural areas. The reason for the sexual imbalance (male-to-female ratio of 13:1) is possibly related to inhibitory effects of estrogens on the growth of the organism rather than solely to environmental exposure. Although the disease classically presents later in life, it is likely that initial exposure occurs in childhood in the endemic areas. Cases seen in areas outside of Central and South America all have been linked to prior residence in the endemic area.

Pathogenesis

Paracoccidioidomycosis develops following inhalation of aerosolized conidia encountered in the environment. Once in the alveoli, the mycelial phase converts to the yeast phase, a transformation noted to be inhibited by estrogens. The infection may remain localized to the lungs, although it is likely that asymptomatic hematogenous dissemination occurs during most infections. The primary host defense mechanism against *P. brasiliensis* appears to be cell-mediated immunity, but neutrophils also may play a role in host defense. The histopathologic picture shows both neutrophilic and granulomatous responses. There have been increasing reports of paracoccidioidomycosis in patients with acquired immunodeficiency syndrome (AIDS) and in other immunosuppressed patients; in these patients, there is widespread dissemination, and histopathology shows poorly formed granulomas. Reactivation of latent infection acquired in childhood is the presumed pathogenesis of most cases of the chronic adult form of paracoccidioidomycosis and of those cases that appear years after the patient has left the endemic area.

Clinical Manifestations

ACUTE-SUBACUTE (JUVENILE) PARACOCCIDIOIDOMYCOSIS. This form of paracoccidioidomycosis occurs in less than 10% of patients. It should be considered a disease of the reticuloendothelial system with widespread dissemination to liver, spleen, lymph nodes, and bone marrow. Patients younger than 30 years of age typically have this manifestation of paracoccidioidomycosis; however, older adults, especially those who are immunosuppressed, can also manifest this type of rapidly progressive disease. In the most severe involvement, as seen in those who have AIDS, cutaneous lesions are common and pulmonary involvement often progresses to respiratory failure.

CHRONIC (ADULT) PARACOCCIDIOIDOMYCOSIS. This form of paracoccidioidomycosis is seen in more than 90% of patients, most of whom are older men. The disease progresses slowly over years. Pulmonary involvement is prominent and clinically mimics tuberculosis and other chronic fungal pneumonias. Radiographically, nodular, interstitial, or cavitary lesions are seen but differ from tuberculosis and histoplasmosis in that the infiltrates tend to be in the middle and lower lung fields rather than the apices. Most patients with the adult form of paracoccidioidomycosis also have ulcerative or nodular mucous membrane lesions, primarily in the anterior nares and oral cavity. Cutaneous lesions, particularly on the face, are also common and may be papular, nodular, ulcerative, or plaquelike. The mucocutaneous lesions must be differentiated from mucocutaneous leishmaniasis and from squamous cell carcinoma. Adrenal involvement has been noted frequently in several, but not all, series of the adult form of paracoccidioidomycosis.

Diagnosis

The diagnosis of paracoccidioidomycosis is definitively made by growth of *P. brasiliensis*. The organism may take as long as 4 weeks to grow. For seriously ill patients, direct examination of body fluids, sputum, or purulent material treated with KOH or histopathologic examination of tissue biopsy samples can provide a tentative diagnosis while awaiting culture results. A presumptive diagnosis can be made and therapy initiated if the characteristic yeast forms with multiple small, circumferentially attached, narrow-based daughter buds creating a distinctive morphologic picture likened to a ship's steering wheel are seen.

There are several serologic assays that are routinely used in the endemic area: both immunodiffusion (ID) and counterimmunoelectrophoresis assays for precipitin antibodies and a complement fixation (CF) assay, but there continue to be problems with sensitivity and specificity. In the United States, CF and ID assays for paracoccidioidomycosis are available through the Centers for Disease Control and Prevention.

Rx Treatment

The drug of choice for the treatment of paracoccidioidomycosis is itraconazole, 100 mg daily, for 6 to 12 months. Although ketoconazole, at a dosage of 200 to 400 mg daily for 1 year, is effective and certainly less expensive than itraconazole, the incidence of side effects is greater and there appear to be more relapses than with itraconazole. There is little experience with fluconazole, which should remain as a second-line agent. Sulfonamides had been used for years for treating paracoccidioidomycosis but are less effective than the azoles. Amphotericin B is effective but rarely required except in immunosuppressed patients with life-threatening disseminated disease. Most AIDS patients with paracoccidioidomycosis have been treated with amphotericin B as initial therapy followed by lifelong suppressive therapy either with itraconazole or trimethoprim-sulfamethoxazole. The latter is preferred in AIDS patients because it also prevents infections with *Pneumocystis carinii* and *Toxoplasma gondii*.

Prognosis

Patients with paracoccidioidomycosis have an excellent prognosis when appropriate therapy is given. The response in patients with AIDS appears to be less successful.

SUGGESTED READINGS

Goldani LZ, Sugar AM: Paracoccidioidomycosis and AIDS: An overview. Clin Infect Dis 1995;21:1275–1281. *Excellent overview of this disease in AIDS patients.*

Manns BJ, Baylis BW, Urbanski SJ, et al: Paracoccidioidomycosis: Case report and review. Clin Infect Dis 1996;23:1026–1032. *Well-written review of paracoccidioidomycosis as seen in North America.*

Restrepo A: Paracoccidioidomycosis. In Dismakes WE, Pappas PG, Sobel JD (eds): Clinical mycology. New York, Oxford University Press, 2003. *Extensive review of clinical and laboratory aspects of paracoccidioidomycosis.*

383 CRYPTOCOCCOSIS

Carol A. Kauffman

Definition

Cryptococcosis occurs most often in persons who are immuno-suppressed, especially those with human immunodeficiency virus (HIV) infection. Meningitis is the most common clinical presentation, but pulmonary and other organ involvement also occur. *Cryptococcus neoformans* is a yeast in both the environment and in tissues. In tissues, the organism is enveloped by a large polysaccharide capsule that is a major virulence factor. In the environment, *C. neoformans* yeast cells are smaller and less encapsulated and thus more easily aerosolized and inhaled.

Epidemiology

There are two varieties of the species: *C. neoformans* var. *neoformans* and *C. neoformans* var. *gatti*. Both varieties are pathogenic and cause similar disease manifestations. *C. neoformans* var. *neoformans* accounts for most cases of human disease throughout the world. This organism has been linked to pigeons; the birds do not become infected but rather the organism grows luxuriantly in dried pigeon excreta because of its high nitrogen content. *C. neoformans* var. *gatti* is more restricted, found mostly in subtropical and tropical areas of Australia, Southeast Asia, Africa, and the Americas. In the United States most infections with this variety occur in California. The ecologic niche of the *gatti* variety is the eucalyptus tree. There are at least 38 other species of *Cryptococcus*, and only rarely have these non-*neoformans* isolates (*Cryptococcus laurentii* and *Cryptococcus albidus*, primarily) caused disease.

Prior to highly active antiretroviral therapy (HAART), cryptococcosis occurred in 5 to 10% of patients with acquired immunodeficiency syndrome (AIDS). The patients at highest risk were those with less than 50 CD4 cells/μL. Although less commonly seen now, cryptococcosis remains extremely common among AIDS patients in Africa and in the United States is seen almost entirely in those who have not received medical therapy or who refuse HAART. In the non-AIDS population, cryptococcosis is a frequent opportunistic infection in patients who have received an organ transplant; have been treated with corticosteroids; or have diabetes mellitus, renal failure, liver dysfunction, or chronic pulmonary disease. For some patients, the only risk factor appears to be older age. In every reported series, approximately 20% of patients have no known underlying illness.

Pathogenesis

The organism is inhaled from the environment, causing pulmonary infection initially. The primary host defense at this stage is complement-dependent macrophage and neutrophil phagocytosis and killing. Natural killer cells also have the ability to kill the organism. Ultimately, however, T-cell immunity is the most important host determinant in limiting the replication of *C. neoformans*. In normal hosts, the infection remains localized to the lungs and does not cause symptomatic infection. It is likely that a few organisms exist as walled-off subpleural granulomas in many who have had pulmonary infection. If the host becomes immunosuppressed, the organism then can reactivate and disseminate to other sites. *C. neoformans* clearly is neurotropic, and the primary disease manifestation is meningoencephalitis. However, dissemination to many organs is likely, especially in those with deficient T-cell immunity.

Virulence factors for *C. neoformans* include the capsule, which requires opsonization for efficient phagocytosis, and the production of melanin, which has been shown to occur in vivo and which enables the organism to resist intracellular killing. Both of these factors may help explain the virulence of the organism once it has reached the central nervous system. Antibody and complement levels are low in the brain and thus phagocytosis of the organism is minimal. Brain tissue provides high concentrations of substrates, such as catecholamines, for the phenol oxidase enzyme systems of *C. neoformans* that produce melanin, aiding survival of the organism.

Clinical Manifestations

CENTRAL NERVOUS SYSTEM INFECTION. This is the most common manifestation of cryptococcosis. The typical picture is that of a subacute to chronic meningoencephalitis. Patients usually have increasingly severe headache over several weeks. Other symptoms and signs include nuchal rigidity, lethargy, personality changes, confusion, visual abnormalities (photophobia, diplopia, decreased visual acuity, papilledema, extraocular nerve palsies), and nausea and vomiting. Less commonly, hearing loss, ataxia, and seizures occur. Fever is present in only approximately half of the patients. Elderly persons with cryptococcal meningitis can present only with dementia, without other neurologic findings. AIDS patients often have subtle central nervous system symptoms but usually have fever and other constitutional symptoms and rapidly manifest signs of dissemination.

PULMONARY INFECTION. In non-HIV infected patients, the most common underlying risk factor for pulmonary cryptococcal infection is chronic obstructive pulmonary disease, followed by corticosteroid use and receipt of a solid-organ transplant. *C. neoformans* may merely be an airway colonizer in some patients; in others symptomatic infection, mostly manifested by fever, cough, and dyspnea, requires treatment with an antifungal agent. The typical lesion noted with pulmonary cryptococcosis is a pleural-based nodular lesion. However, patchy pneumonitis, multiple nodular lesions, cavitary lesions, masslike lesions, and diffuse pulmonary infiltrates all have been noted with pulmonary cryptococcosis. Patients with advanced HIV infection are likely to have diffuse interstitial infiltrates that can progress rapidly to acute respiratory insufficiency. Given the proclivity of *C. neoformans* to invade the central nervous system, all patients who have pulmonary cryptococcosis should have a lumbar puncture to be certain that meningitis is not present.

OTHER ORGAN INVOLVEMENT. *C. neoformans* has been reported to infect most organs during the course of disseminated infection, especially in AIDS patients. Skin lesions are a prominent clue to dissemination. Papules that resemble molluscum contagiosum or an acneiform rash, nodules, ulcers, plaques, draining sinuses, and cellulitis all have been reported. Focal involvement can occur in prostate and other genitourinary tract organs, osteoarticular structures, eye, breast, larynx, and other head and neck structures. The prostate, in particular, has been noted as a sanctuary from which persisting organisms can later disseminate.

Diagnosis

The diagnosis of cryptococcosis is established when the yeast is grown in culture. Appropriate specimens for culture include cerebrospinal fluid (CSF), blood, sputum, material from skin lesions, and other body fluids or tissues that appear to be infected. The organism grows in several days on most standard agar media. Most automated blood culture systems, as well as the lysis-centrifugation (Isolator tube) system allow rapid growth of *C. neoformans*. Visualization of the capsule and performance of a few simple tests differentiate *C. neoformans* from other yeasts. Tissue biopsy shows the 5- to 10-μm yeast surrounded by the acellular capsule. A definitive diagnosis of cryptococcosis can be made with a mucicarmine stain, which selectively stains the polysaccharide capsule a deep rose color. In CSF or other body fluids, an India ink preparation allows visualization of the budding yeast cells surrounded by the large capsule.

The latex agglutination assay for cryptococcal polysaccharide antigen (CRAG) is a highly sensitive and specific diagnostic test. Of patients with meningitis, the CSF CRAG is positive in almost 100% and the serum CRAG in about 75%. In AIDS patients, the serum CRAG is almost always positive and is an excellent screening tool; the titers in both CSF and serum are exceptionally high, reflecting the enormous burden of organisms. In non-AIDS, nonmeningeal, pulmonary cryptococcosis, the CRAG assay is positive in only 25 to 50% of cases. False-positive results with the CRAG assay are uncommon, generally low titer (≤1:4), are more likely with serum than CSF, and can be caused by interference with the assay by rheumatoid factor. Most laboratories correct for false-positive reactions by pretreating the serum to eliminate nonspecific agglutination reactions. The rare patient with *Trichosporon aschii* infection can have a positive CRAG test because of cross-reacting antigens shared by both fungi.

The CSF formula typical for cryptococcal meningitis shows an increased number of white blood cells (but rarely >500/µL); a predominance of lymphocytes (although neutrophils sometimes are prominent early in the course); elevated protein; and decreased glucose. AIDS patients most often have normal or only mildly abnormal findings, reflecting their markedly defective immune response. In spite of normal CSF findings in regard to cells, protein, and glucose, every AIDS patient with a headache must have a CRAG, India ink preparation, and culture performed on CSF. It is extremely important that an opening pressure be obtained when the lumbar puncture is performed. Especially in AIDS patients, extremely high intracranial pressures (>350 mm H₂O) have been associated with poor outcomes and must be aggressively lowered.

All patients with cryptococcal meningitis should have a computed tomographic (CT) or magnetic resonance imaging (MRI) study of the brain to look for mass lesions (cryptococcomas) and to assess ventricular size. Obstructive hydrocephalus is uncommon but requires a shunting procedure to decrease the pressure. More commonly, increased intracranial pressure associated with cryptococcal infection is associated with normal-sized ventricles and is due to blockage at the arachnoid villi and/or increased brain edema, perhaps related to the osmotic effect of the polysaccharide capsule. Different methods for reducing pressure are employed in this situation.

 Treatment

Guidelines for the treatment of cryptococcal infection have been published by the Mycoses Study Group and the Infectious Diseases Society of America. All recent controlled treatment trials have been carried out in AIDS patients; most recommendations for treatment of non-AIDS patients have used the results obtained in AIDS patients.

CENTRAL NERVOUS SYSTEM INFECTION. Early multicenter randomized trials in non-AIDS patients showed the superiority of the combination of amphotericin B and flucytosine for 6 weeks over amphotericin B alone for 10 weeks.[1] Subsequent randomized trials in the azole era have been performed only in the AIDS population. They have confirmed the benefit of flucytosine added to amphotericin B for induction therapy[2] and have shown that initial therapy with fluconazole is not as effective as amphotericin B.[3] Itraconazole is not as effective but can be used if for some reason fluconazole cannot be given.[4] Current recommendations are to give intravenous amphotericin B (0.7 to 1 mg/kg daily) combined with oral flucytosine (100 mg/kg daily, given in four divided doses) for a minimum of 2 weeks or longer if required, until the CSF cultures become negative and the patient has begun to improve. Note that the dosage of flucytosine should *not* be 150 mg/kg daily as described in the package insert, because of its dose-related marrow toxicity. Therapy can then be switched to oral fluconazole (400 mg daily) for a minimum of 8 to 10 weeks. AIDS patients should be placed on lifelong suppression with 200 mg fluconazole daily, although patients responding to HAART ultimately can stop maintenance azole therapy.[5] Suppressive therapy with fluconazole for non-AIDS patients has not been studied, but an additional 6 to 12 months of fluconazole, 200 mg daily, for immunosuppressed patients is recommended. Whether suppressive therapy should be used in "normal" hosts with cryptococcal meningitis is not clear and is left to the clinician's judgment.

Open-label studies with lipid formulations of amphotericin B have been performed in AIDS patients. It appears that these agents are at least as effective as amphotericin B and could be used in those patients who have preexisting renal insufficiency and those at high risk for nephrotoxicity. Liposomal amphotericin B (AmBisome) is the only lipid formulation that is approved by the U.S. Food and Drug Administration for treatment of cryptococcosis.

A significant observation that grew out of the AIDS treatment trials was the role of increased intracranial pressure as a cause of early death from cryptococcal meningitis. An aggressive approach to the diagnosis and treatment of increased intracranial pressure in both AIDS and non-AIDS patients is mandatory. This should include daily lumbar punctures or placement of a temporary lumbar drain or ventriculostomy until the opening pressure remains lower than 190 mm H₂O. Treatment with corticosteroids, acetazolamide, or mannitol has not proved efficacious in this setting.

PULMONARY AND OTHER NONMENINGEAL INFECTIONS. The treatment of nonmeningeal cryptococcosis depends on the severity of the infection. Many patients with isolated pulmonary or other focal infections are not severely ill, and an oral azole can be used. The preferred therapy is oral fluconazole, 400 mg daily for 6 to 12 months. Itraconazole, 200 mg twice daily, is a second-line choice. For patients who are severely ill, initial therapy with IV amphotericin B, 0.7 mg/kg daily, and oral flucytosine, 100 mg/kg daily, is warranted for the first few weeks, before switching to oral fluconazole after clinical improvement has occurred. AIDS patients who have isolated pulmonary or focal infection can be treated as noted earlier. However, most often pulmonary or other organ involvement is only one manifestation of disseminated infection in patients with AIDS, and initial therapy should be with amphotericin B and flucytosine for several weeks before switching to fluconazole. For AIDS patients, lifelong maintenance therapy with fluconazole, 200 mg daily, is recommended, but with effective HAART, it may ultimately be shown that lifelong suppression is not needed.

Prognosis

The outcome for both AIDS and non-AIDS patients with cryptococcal meningitis has improved markedly over the last decade. In the last randomized treatment trial of AIDS patients, the overall mortality was less than 10%.[3] In non-AIDS patients, a recent large, retrospective review noted a mortality rate due to cryptococcosis of 12%. Dementia in older patients may not be reversed even though a mycologic cure is achieved.

Grade A

1. Bennett JE, Dismukes WE, Dumas RRJ, et al: A comparison of amphotericin B alone and combined with flucytosine in the treatment of cryptococcal meningitis. N Engl J Med 1979;301:126–131.
2. Van der Horst CM, Saag MS, Cloud GA, et al: Treatment of cryptococcal meningitis associated with the acquired immunodeficiency syndrome. N Engl J Med 1997;337:15–21.
3. Saag MS, Powderly WG, Cloud GA, et al: Comparison of amphotericin B with fluconazole in the treatment of acute AIDS-associated cryptococcal meningitis. N Engl J Med 1992;326:83–89.
4. Saag MS, Cloud GA, Graybill JR, et al: A comparison of itraconazole versus fluconazole as maintenance therapy for AIDS-associated cryptococcal meningitis. Clin Infect Dis 1999;28.291–296.
5. Vibhagool A, Sungkanuparph S, Mootsikapun P, et al: Discontinuation of secondary prophylaxis for cryptococcal meningitis in human immunodeficiency virus infected patients treated with highly active antiretroviral therapy: A prospective, multicenter, randomized study. Clin Infect Dis 2003;36:1329–1331.

SUGGESTED READINGS
Graybill JR, Sobel J, Saag M, et al: Diagnosis and management of increased intracranial pressure in patients with AIDS and cryptococcal meningitis. Clin Infect Dis 2000;30:47–54. *An important paper that puts forth the evidence that increased intracranial pressure is a major variable determining outcome of cryptococcal meningitis in AIDS patients.*
Pappas PG, Perfect JR, Cloud GA, et al: Cryptococcosis in human immunodeficiency virus–negative patients in the era of effective azole therapy. Clin Infect Dis 2001;33:690–699. *Report on the largest series of non-AIDS patients with cryptococcosis.*
Saag MS, Graybill JR, Larsen RA, et al: Practice guidelines for the management of cryptococcal disease. Clin Infect Dis 2000;30:710–718. *Guidelines for the clinician.*
Sorrell TC: *Cryptococcus neoformans* variety gatti. Med Mycol 2001;39:155–168. *This review from Australia focuses on the mycology, epidemiology, and clinical aspects of the less common gatti variety of C. neoformans.*

 # 384 SPOROTRICHOSIS

Carol A. Kauffman

Definition

Sporotrichosis is a subacute or chronic infection that is usually localized to cutaneous and lymphocutaneous structures, but pulmonary, osteoarticular, and disseminated infection can occur in patients who have certain underlying diseases. *Sporothrix schenckii* is a thermally dimorphic fungus. In the environment at temperatures lower than 35° to 37° C, the organism is a mold and produces conidia, the infectious form. In tissues and at 35° to 37° C, *S. schenckii* transforms into the yeast phase; the yeasts are 4 to 6 µm in diameter; cigar shaped, round, or oval; and reproduce by budding.

Epidemiology

S. schenckii is found worldwide in climates ranging from temperate to tropical. The organism exists in a variety of environmental niches that include soil, sphagnum moss, hay, decaying wood, and other vegetation. Infection is seen almost entirely in persons whose vocation, avocation, or living condition brings them into contact with the organism in the environment. Landscaping activities, gardening, farming, and motor vehicle accidents have been associated with sporotrichosis. Most cases of sporotrichosis are sporadic, but outbreaks have been described. Sporotrichosis also occurs as a zoonotic infection acquired directly from infected animals, especially cats, or passively from soil by scratches or bites from animals. Inhalation of *S. schenckii* conidia occurs less commonly and results in pulmonary and rarely disseminated sporotrichosis.

Pathogenesis

Infection is almost always acquired by inoculation of the conidia and remains localized to the immediate and contiguous cutaneous, subcutaneous, and lymphatic structures. Some strains of *S. schenckii* grow poorly at temperatures above 35° C; these strains usually cause fixed cutaneous lesions without lymphatic spread. The typical host response to infection with *S. schenckii* is a mixed neutrophilic and granulomatous reaction. Antibody is not protective; T lymphocytes are important in containing infection. In individuals who have underlying illnesses that include alcoholism, diabetes mellitus, and chronic obstructive pulmonary disease, *S. schenckii* is more likely to involve osteoarticular structures and lungs. Persons with human immunodeficiency virus (HIV) infection develop widespread dissemination, a distinctly unusual event in normal hosts.

Clinical Manifestations

LYMPHOCUTANEOUS. Days to weeks after inoculation of *S. schenckii* conidia, a papular lesion develops at the inoculation site; the lesion becomes nodular and often ulcerates. Drainage is not grossly purulent, and the lesion is not terribly painful. Similar lesions occur along the lymphatic channels proximal to the primary lesion. Verrucous or ulcerative fixed cutaneous lesions do not have lymphatic extension. The differential diagnosis of lymphocutaneous sporotrichosis includes *Nocardia* infections, particularly *Nocardia brasiliensis*; atypical mycobacterial infections, especially *Mycobacterium marinum*; *Leishmania brasiliensis* infections; and tularemia.

VISCERAL AND OSTEOARTICULAR. Pulmonary sporotrichosis occurs most often in middle-aged men who have chronic pulmonary disease and abuse alcohol. Fever, night sweats, weight loss, fatigue, dyspnea, cough, purulent sputum, and hemoptysis are common. Chest radiographs show unilateral or bilateral upper lobe cavities with variable amounts of fibrosis and nodular lesions. The disease mimics tuberculosis in almost all aspects. Osteoarticular sporotrichosis is found most often in middle-aged men and occurs more frequently in alcoholics. Infection may involve one or multiple joints; the joints most commonly affected are the knee, elbow, wrist, and ankle. Isolated bursitis, tenosynovitis, and nerve entrapment syndromes have been reported. Osteoarticular infection can follow local inoculation, but most patients likely have had hematogenous spread. Isolated case reports document sporotrichosis involving the pericardium, eye, perirectal tissues, larynx, breast, epididymis, spleen, liver, bone marrow, lymph nodes, and meninges. Disseminated sporotrichosis, manifested as widespread ulcerative cutaneous lesions with or without visceral involvement, is uncommon; most cases have been reported in patients with advanced HIV infection.

Diagnosis

Growth of *S. schenckii* from material aspirated from a lesion, a tissue biopsy specimen, sputum, or body fluid is the most effective method of establishing the diagnosis of sporotrichosis. Growth of the mold phase of the organism is usually evident within a few days. Histopathologic examination of biopsy material shows a mixed granulomatous and pyogenic process; however, the organisms are often present in small numbers and frequently are not visualized. Serology is not very useful in the diagnosis of sporotrichosis. A tube agglutination test is available at the Centers for Disease Control and Prevention, but sensitivity and specificity have not been established.

Treatment

Because sporotrichosis is usually a localized subacute to chronic infection, oral antifungal agents are preferred; amphotericin B is reserved for severe visceral infections. Guidelines for the management of sporotrichosis have been published by the Mycoses Study Group and the Infectious Diseases Society of America. Itraconazole is the drug of choice for lymphocutaneous sporotrichosis. The usual dosage is 200 mg daily, and treatment should continue for several weeks after all lesions have disappeared, usually a total of 3 to 6 months. Saturated solution of potassium iodide (SSKI) has been used to treat sporotrichosis for more than a century. The initial dose is 5 to 10 drops three times daily in water or juice, increasing over several weeks to a maximum of 40 to 50 drops three times daily. SSKI has many side effects, including salivary gland swelling, metallic taste, rash, and fever; the only advantage is that it is inexpensive. Fluconazole is less effective than itraconazole but for occasional patients can be used at a dosage of 400 mg daily. Terbinafine appears to be effective for sporotrichosis, but few patients have been treated to date. Local hyperthermia, induced by a variety of different warming devices or baths, has been shown effective in some patients who have fixed cutaneous lesions.

Osteoarticular and pulmonary sporotrichosis are usually treated with itraconazole, 200 mg twice daily, for 1 to 2 years. Other azoles are less effective, and SSKI is ineffective. For a seriously ill patient with pulmonary sporotrichosis, amphotericin B, 0.7 to 1 mg/kg daily, should be used as initial therapy. After the patient has shown improvement, therapy can be changed to itraconazole. Amphotericin B is the drug of choice for disseminated sporotrichosis. Therapy can be changed to itraconazole, 200 mg twice daily, once the patient has stabilized. Patients with acquired immunodeficiency syndrome with disseminated sporotrichosis should remain on lifelong maintenance therapy with itraconazole, 200 mg daily.

Prognosis

The prognosis for cutaneous and lymphocutaneous sporotrichosis is excellent. Almost all patients are cured with one course of therapy; relapses occur in only a small proportion of patients. Extracutaneous forms of sporotrichosis do not respond well to therapy. This is related partly to delays in diagnosis and partly to the underlying diseases that are frequently found in those who have extracutaneous sporotrichosis. The outcome of disseminated sporotrichosis in patients with HIV infection has been especially poor.

SUGGESTED READINGS

Bolao F, Podzamczer D, Ventin M: Efficacy of acute-phase and maintenance therapy with itraconazole in an AIDS patient with sporotrichosis. Eur J Clin Microbiol Infect Dis 1994;13:609–612. *Good review of disease manifestations and treatment options for sporotrichosis in patients with HIV infection.*

Coles FB, Schuchat A, Hibbs JR, et al: A multistate outbreak of sporotrichosis associated with sphagnum moss. Am J Epidemiol 1992;136:475–487. *Describes the epidemiology of the largest outbreak of sporotrichosis.*

Kauffman CA, Hajjeh R, Chapman SW: Practice guidelines for the management of patients with sporotrichosis. Clin Infect Dis 2000;30:684–687. *A consensus statement.*

Kauffman CA: Sporotrichosis (state of the art). Clin Infect Dis 1999;29:231–236. *Overview of all clinical aspects of sporotrichosis.*

Pappas PG: Sporotrichosis. *In* Dismukes WE, Pappas PG, Sobel JD (eds): Clinical mycology. New York, Oxford University Press, 2003. *In-depth overview of sporotrichosis.*

Reed KD, Moore FM, Geiger G, et al: Zoonotic transmission of sporotrichosis: Case report and review. Clin Infect Dis 1993;16:384–387. *Nice review of animal-associated sporotrichosis.*

385 CANDIDIASIS

Carol A. Kauffman

Definition

Candidiasis encompasses a wide variety of clinical syndromes that are caused by yeasts of the genus *Candida*. Of the species that cause infection in humans, *Candida albicans* is the most common; *Candida glabrata*, *Candida parapsilosis*, and *Candida tropicalis* are responsible for most of the remaining infections. Organisms such as *Candida krusei*, *Candida lusitaniae*, *Candida guilliermondii*, and many others cause infection in the occasional patient. All *Candida* species are 4- to 6-μm yeast-like organisms that reproduce by budding. Most species, with the exception of *C. glabrata*, form pseudohyphae (elongated buds that remain attached to the mother cell) and hyphae in tissues.

Clinical disease due to *Candida* species varies from localized mucous membrane infection to life-threatening disseminated disease. The major determinant of the extent of infection is the host response. Local infections are often related to local overgrowth of *Candida* due to changes in the normal flora. Invasive infections that remain within an organ system, such as urinary tract infections, often occur because of local anatomic abnormalities. In the immunosuppressed host, especially the patient with neutropenia, widespread visceral dissemination is common.

Epidemiology

Candida species are part of the normal human flora of the gastrointestinal and genitourinary tracts and skin. As colonizers, *Candida* species do not cause infection unless there is a defect in host defense mechanisms or exogenous factors, such as antibiotic use, have upset the ecology of the normal flora. *C. albicans* is the species found most commonly colonizing humans; *C. glabrata* is the second most common species and *C. tropicalis*, *C. parapsilosis*, and others are found less often. Changes in the species of *Candida* colonizing patients occur with hospitalization and use of antifungal agents. *C. glabrata* and *C. krusei*, species known to be relatively and totally resistant to fluconazole, respectively, are associated with increased use of this agent in the hospital setting.

Although uncommon, acquisition of *Candida* from health care workers or from environmental sources has been noted. Most often the *Candida* species associated with transmission from contaminated fluids or devices, especially central intravenous catheters, has been *C. parapsilosis*. This species also is the most common colonizer of the hands of health care workers.

Candidiasis is the most common opportunistic fungal infection. This is related to both the ubiquity of the organisms and the increasing number of patients with risk factors for infection with these organisms. The classic immunosuppressed host who is at risk for serious *Candida* infections is a patient who has a hematologic malignancy, is neutropenic, and has received cytotoxic agents and corticosteroids. Increasingly, however, candidiasis is an infection seen in patients who are in intensive care units (ICUs). The risk factors for development of serious *Candida* infections among ICU patients include broad-spectrum antibiotics, indwelling intravenous and urethral catheters, prior surgical procedures, renal failure, parenteral nutrition, and high Apache score. Certain ICU populations, especially very-low-birthweight neonates and burn victims, are at even higher risk of *Candida* infection than the typical ICU patient.

The acquired immunodeficiency syndrome (AIDS) epidemic has led to a marked increase in *Candida* infections. However, in contrast to candidiasis in the hospital setting, the primary manifestation of *Candida* infection in AIDS patients is mucocutaneous infection, especially oropharyngeal candidiasis. The development of *Candida* infection is directly related to deficient T-cell immunity as reflected in a low CD4 count. With appropriate antiretroviral therapy, oropharyngeal candidiasis has become an uncommon opportunistic infection that is seen almost entirely in patients whose human immunodeficiency virus (HIV) infection is refractory to therapy or in patients who have not received medical care and at initial presentation have advanced HIV infection and oropharyngeal candidiasis.

Pathogenesis

The usual mode of infection with *Candida* is egress from its normal niche into the blood stream or other tissues; most times the source is the gastrointestinal tract, but the skin and the genitourinary tract are other sources. The primary host defense in response to this event is phagocytosis and killing by neutrophils, monocytes, and macrophages. Phagocytosis is enhanced in the presence of specific anti-*Candida* antibody and complement. Several different mechanisms are operative within neutrophils and macrophages that allow killing of yeasts. Thus, patients who are neutropenic, and especially those with chemotherapy-induced disruption of the gut mucosa, are at the greatest risk for invasion with *Candida* species. Once *Candida* gain access to the blood stream, widespread hematogenous dissemination is the rule. Biopsy of many different organs usually shows multiple microabscesses composed of neutrophils (in the host who has these cells), budding yeasts, and often pseudohyphae or hyphae; over time, the lesions show a mixed neutrophilic and granulomatous response.

T-cell immunity is also an important host defense against infection with *Candida*. T-cell immunity controls *Candida* at mucosal surfaces. In contrast to those with neutropenia, patients with deficient T-cell immunity are at risk for persistent and recurrent mucocutaneous candidiasis but rarely develop invasive infection.

Clinical Manifestations

MUCOCUTANEOUS CANDIDIASIS

Oropharyngeal Candidiasis. Local mucous membrane and cutaneous lesions are the most common forms of *Candida* infection. Oropharyngeal candidiasis or thrush can be due either to local mechanical factors or to T-cell dysfunction. Local factors include the use of broad-spectrum antibiotics, inhaled corticosteroids, xerostomia, and radiation to the head and neck. Chronic atrophic candidosis, also called *denture stomatitis*, occurs frequently in persons who wear full upper dentures and especially in those who do not remove their dentures at night.

Thrush due to T-cell dysfunction is most commonly seen in patients with HIV infection and is the most common opportunistic infection noted in patients with AIDS. The appearance of thrush in a previously healthy individual with no known risk factors should immediately raise the suspicion for HIV infection.

Thrush is manifested by white plaques on the buccal mucosa, palate, oropharynx, or tongue. Scraping the lesions with a tongue depressor reveals an erythematous, nonulcerated mucosa under the plaques. Denture stomatitis is almost always manifested as a painful erythematous palate without plaques. Angular cheilitis or perlèche, painful cracks at the corners of the mouth, can occur with or without thrush.

Esophagitis. Esophagitis may accompany oropharyngeal candidiasis or may occur independently of lesions in the oropharynx. Almost always the development of *Candida* esophagitis is related to immune dysfunction and not simply to local factors. Although seen most often in AIDS patients with low CD4 counts, esophagitis also occurs in patients with leukemia and others on immunosuppressive agents. The classic symptom of *Candida* esophagitis is odynophagia localized to a discrete substernal area; in AIDS patients the differential diagnosis includes herpes simplex, cytomegalovirus, and idiopathic ulcers seen with advanced AIDS.

Vulvovaginitis. *Candida* vulvovaginitis is a common infection in women of childbearing age and the most common mucocutaneous manifestation of *Candida* infection. Risk factors include conditions associated with increased estrogen levels, such as oral contraceptives and pregnancy, diabetes mellitus, therapy with corticosteroids or broad-spectrum antibiotics, and HIV infection. Symptoms include vaginal discomfort, discharge, and vulvar pruritus. The discharge is usually curdlike, but it can also be thin and watery. The labia are erythematous and swollen, and the vaginal walls show erythema and white plaques. Although most women have only a few episodes throughout their life, a minority has frequent recurrences; in most

Continued

of these patients no discrete risk factor is found, and they are presumed to have local immune dysregulation as the cause.

Cutaneous Candidiasis. *Candida* infection of the skin occurs mostly in the intertriginous areas or under a large pannus or pendulous breasts. The lesions are erythematous, pruritic, frequently pustular, have a distinct border, and are almost always associated with smaller satellite lesions. The presence of satellite lesions helps distinguish candidiasis from tinea cruris or corporis. *Candida* onychomycosis results in thickened, opaque, and onycholytic nails. *Candida* can also cause paronychia, especially in those whose occupation involves frequent immersion of their hands in water.

Chronic Mucocutaneous Candidiasis. This is an uncommon syndrome that usually begins in childhood and is characterized by recalcitrant and relapsing thrush, vaginitis, onychomycosis, and hyperkeratotic skin lesions on the face, scalp, and hands. It is thought to be due to a specific defect in the T-cell response to *Candida* antigens. Some patients have associated endocrinop-athies, such as hypoparathyroidism, hypothyroidism, and hypoadrenalism.

DISSEMINATED INFECTIONS

Candidemia. The most common manifestation of disseminated *Candida* infection is candidemia. However, candidemia merely implies the presence of *Candida* in the blood but does not define the extent of visceral involvement. *Candida* obtained from a blood culture should never be considered a contaminant and always should prompt a search for the likely source and the extent of infection. Risk factors for candidemia include broad-spectrum antibiotics, central intravenous catheters, parenteral nutrition, renal failure, surgical procedures involving the gastrointestinal tract, neutropenia, and corticosteroid therapy. The attributable mortality from candidemia approaches 40%, and overall mortality is higher in the elderly and neonates.

Although candidemia is the most obvious manifestation of serious infection with *Candida* species, patients can have septic shock and invasion of multiple viscera without positive blood cultures. The clinical picture of disseminated candidiasis is indistinguishable from that due to bacterial infection. The histologic picture characteristic of disseminated candidiasis is that of multiple microabscesses in many organs. The eyes, kidneys, liver, spleen, and brain are the most commonly infected sites, but virtually all organs have been noted to show microabscesses due to *Candida*. Clinical clues to the diagnosis of candidemia include the appearance of skin and retinal lesions. The nonpainful, nonpruritic skin lesions are papular to pustular and surrounded by a zone of erythema. The eye lesions appear as distinctive white exudates in the retina; with extension into the vitreous body, the retina becomes obscured.

Endocarditis. *Candida* endocarditis is an uncommon and often fatal complication of candidemia. It occurs most often in intravenous drug users, patients who have prosthetic cardiac valves, and patients who have central venous catheters in place. Blood cultures are usually persistently positive, and echocardiography usually reveals large vegetations, which readily embolize to major vessels.

Chronic Disseminated Candidiasis (Hepatosplenic Candidiasis). This is a specific syndrome that occurs almost entirely in leukemic patients who have had an episode of neutropenia. After the neutrophil count returns to normal, the patient develops fevers that are often quite high, right upper quadrant tenderness, and nausea. The alkaline phosphatase level usually is elevated, and distinctive punched-out lesions are seen in liver, spleen, and sometimes kidneys on computed tomographic (CT) scan. Biopsy of these lesions shows microabscesses that contain budding yeasts.

FOCAL INVASIVE INFECTIONS

These forms of candidiasis result from local inoculation, contiguous spread, or hematogenous spread. Hematogenous spread, which often goes undetected, is probably the most common pathogenetic mechanism. Although *Candida* infection of all organs has been reported, the most common focal infections are urinary tract infections, osteoarticular infections, endophthalmitis, peritonitis, and meningitis.

Urinary Tract Infections. Urinary tract infections are the most common locally invasive *Candida* infection. Candiduria is a common finding in patients in the hospital. Factors predisposing to candiduria include diabetes mellitus, broad-spectrum antibiotics, indwelling urinary devices, and genitourinary tract structural abnormalities. Most patients with candiduria have only bladder colonization and not infection, and most have no urinary tract symptoms. Patients with actual *Candida* infection of the bladder may have symptoms indistinguishable from those of bacterial cystitis. Those who have upper urinary tract infection may have fever, flank pain, nausea, and vomiting, similar to those seen with acute bacterial pyelonephritis. A fungus ball composed of fungal hyphae can develop at any level of the collecting system and lead to obstruction with subsequent infection.

Osteoarticular Infections. Osteoarticular infections arise secondary to hematogenous seeding or to exogenous inoculation that occurs during intra-articular injection, a surgical procedure, or trauma. Vertebral osteomyelitis is probably the most common manifestation of osteoarticular candidiasis. The symptoms of back pain and fever may occur weeks after an episode of fungemia. A unique triad of face, scalp, and upper chest folliculitis, endophthalmitis, and sternoclavicular or costochondral septic arthritis has been reported due to *C. albicans* in drug users who inject brown heroin intravenously.

Endophthalmitis. Exogenous endophthalmitis occurs secondary to trauma or ophthalmic surgery. Most often, the procedure involved is cataract extraction with or without lens implantation, and the most common infecting species is *C. parapsilosis*. Primary infection is in the anterior chamber, but ultimately the posterior chamber is also involved. Endogenous *Candida* endophthalmitis results from hematogenous seeding of the choroid and the retina. This is one of the most serious complications of candidemia. Characteristic white exudates are visible in the retina, and with progression of the infection, vitritis occurs and the risk of loss of vision is quite high.

Peritonitis. *Candida* peritonitis can follow bowel surgery or perforation. Symptoms are the same as those noted in bacterial peritonitis. Usually this type of infection is polymicrobial, and abscess formation is common. Patients on continuous ambulatory peritoneal dialysis generally develop *Candida* peritonitis as a late infection after prior episodes of bacterial peritonitis. A cloudy dialysate, abdominal pain, and fever are typically noted.

Meningitis. Acute *Candida* meningitis occurs as a part of disseminated infection, especially in low-birthweight neonates. Chronic meningitis, an uncommon manifestation of candidiasis, resembles cryptococcal or tuberculous meningitis in regard to symptoms and cerebrospinal fluid findings.

Diagnosis

The diagnosis of mucocutaneous candidiasis is often made clinically. Culture is rarely indicated. Confirmation can be sought by scraping the lesions and doing either a KOH preparation or a Gram stain to look for budding yeast and pseudohyphae. Pseudohyphae are not always noted and are never seen in infection due to *C. glabrata*. In circumstances in which disease is recurrent or unresponsive to standard therapy, culture should be done to establish whether a more resistant species, such as *C. glabrata* or *C. krusei*, is the causative agent. In the case of suspected esophagitis, endoscopy should be performed; biopsy of the plaquelike lesions or ulcerations will show mucosal invasion with budding yeasts and pseudohyphae.

The diagnosis of invasive or disseminated candidiasis is more difficult. Evidence for dissemination is usually sought by culturing blood or other sterile body sites. Automated blood culture systems (BacT/Alert, BACTEC, and ESP) are as sensitive as the lysis-centrifugation system for growing *Candida* from blood. However, no system is sensitive enough for clinicians to rely on blood cultures to always establish the diagnosis of invasive candidiasis or to rule out candidiasis as a diagnostic possibility. In addition, 1 to 4 days are required for growth to occur; in a desperately ill patient, this is problematic.

The tip of intravenous catheters that have been removed should be sent for culture. No studies have evaluated the number of yeast that are indicative of infection, and many physicians accept the growth of any yeast as affirming infection that requires treatment. Because osteomyelitis and other focal forms of candidiasis are generally indistinguishable from bacterial infection, biopsy should be done for histopathologic and culture studies.

For the seriously ill patient suspected of having candidiasis, the development of pustular skin lesions or typical retinal lesions can be helpful. Budding yeasts typical for *Candida* species should be sought by smearing material from a pustule on a slide and staining with Gram stain or by performing a biopsy of a lesion and staining the tissue section with a silver stain. All patients who are candidemic or suspected of having disseminated *Candida* infection should have an ophthalmologic examination to look for typical retinal lesions.

Imaging studies are invaluable for certain forms of candidiasis, especially chronic disseminated candidiasis, and can be of major help in defining the extent of infection in other types of *Candida* infections, such as urinary tract infections and endocarditis.

Candida antibody tests have proved to be neither sensitive nor specific and are of no benefit in the diagnosis of *Candida* infections.

Cell wall or cytoplasmic antigen tests and metabolite detection systems also have not been proved useful in the clinical setting. Although it is hoped that a polymerase chain reaction–based assay for *Candida* species will prove to be both sensitive and specific, this has not yet occurred; for current assays, the sensitivity is similar to that of standard blood culture methods.

Treatment

Guidelines for the treatment of the various forms of candidiasis have recently been published by the Mycoses Study Group under the auspices of the Infectious Diseases Society of America.[1] Mucocutaneous disease is obviously treated in a much different fashion than disseminated life-threatening illness. Treatment of the latter depends on the ability of the host to tolerate standard amphotericin B, the species of *Candida* causing infection, the organs involved, and the immune status of the host. Since diagnostic tests are not terribly sensitive, empirical therapy is indicated in some circumstances, and for patients at the highest risk of infection, antifungal prophylaxis can be used to decrease the risk of *Candida* infections.

MUCOCUTANEOUS INFECTIONS. Most mucocutaneous infections should be initially treated with local creams, solutions, troches, or suspensions. For thrush, clotrimazole troches (10 mg four or five times daily) are preferred to nystatin suspension (commonly given as "swish and swallow" four times daily). AIDS patients may not respond to local therapy, especially when their CD4 counts are low; in that situation, oral fluconazole, 100 mg daily, or itraconazole solution, 200 mg daily, should be used. For vaginitis, a variety of creams and vaginal tablets (miconazole, clotrimazole, and others) are effective, but many women prefer to take a single oral 150-mg fluconazole tablet. Recurrent vaginitis is a more complicated therapeutic issue and often requires chronic suppressive therapy with an oral azole. Esophagitis should always be treated with a systemically absorbed agent; the usual treatment is either 100 mg fluconazole or 200 mg itraconazole solution (not capsules) daily for 14 days.

Patients who have advanced AIDS and low CD4 counts and who are often on chronic suppressive therapy with fluconazole to prevent recurrent candidiasis may develop fluconazole-refractory disease. For these patients, increasing the dosage of fluconazole or switching to itraconazole suspension or oral voriconazole should be effective. If oral tablets and solutions are no longer effective, then intravenous amphotericin B or caspofungin are alternative agents that can be used. Patients with the syndrome of chronic mucocutaneous candidiasis require lifelong suppressive therapy with oral azole agents.

CANDIDEMIA AND OTHER DISSEMINATED INFECTIONS. All patients with candidemia should be treated with an antifungal agent; this includes patients who have only one blood culture that yields *Candida* and those with a vascular catheter tip that yields *Candida*. The rationale for this recommendation relates to the high rate of metastatic foci in major organs associated with hematogenously disseminated candidiasis. Amphotericin B, 0.7 mg/kg daily, fluconazole, 400 mg daily, or caspofungin, 50 mg daily, can be used.[2,3] Fluconazole is preferred because it is less toxic; however, if the patient has received prior fluconazole or if *C. glabrata* has historically been a common infection, then amphotericin B is the drug of choice. Caspofungin will likely assume an expanded role as clinical experience increases. Lipid formulations of amphotericin B can be used for those patients who have renal insufficiency or who cannot tolerate standard amphotericin B. All vascular catheters should be removed if at all possible because this has been shown to help clear *Candida* from the blood more quickly. Repeated blood cultures should be obtained to be certain that fungemia has resolved, and treatment should continue for 2 weeks after the date of the first negative blood culture.

Because diagnostic tests are not sensitive enough, seriously ill patients who could have disseminated candidiasis may need to be treated prior to culture confirmation. This approach is used frequently in neutropenic patients for whom outcomes are poor if

disseminated fungal infection goes untreated. The agent used most often is amphotericin B or a lipid-based formulation of amphotericin B so that filamentous fungi as well as *Candida* species are covered. The other group of patients for whom this approach has been used are those in the ICU. However, the risk factors for candidiasis are less well defined in this group compared with neutropenics, and recommendations for empiric treatment have not been defined. Fluconazole is usually used in this setting, and the combined use of fluconazole and amphotericin B provides more rapid clearing of bloodstream infections than fluconazole alone in non-neutropenic patients.[4] The new antifungal agents, caspofungin and voriconazole, may have a role to play in empirical treatment in the future.

Endocarditis should be treated with either standard amphotericin B for a total amount of 2 g or a lipid formulation of amphotericin B (total amount not known). Flucytosine is often added to enhance killing. The valve should be replaced. A few patients have been reported for whom valve replacement was not an option and for whom lifelong suppression with fluconazole appeared to be effective.

Chronic disseminated candidiasis generally requires months of therapy for cure. Most patients begin therapy with amphotericin B, usually a lipid formulation, and then are switched to fluconazole and treated until the lesions disappear on CT scan.

FOCAL INVASIVE INFECTIONS. The treatment of focal infections depends very much on the organ system involved. Perhaps the simplest to treat are urinary tract infections. Most patients with candiduria are not infected and are merely colonized; removing the selective pressure of antibiotics and indwelling catheters eliminates candiduria in many of these patients. For those who have an infection, oral fluconazole is the preferred treatment. Treatment should continue long enough to allow eradication of upper tract as well as lower tract infection; 2 weeks of 200 mg fluconazole daily is an appropriate regimen.[5] Bladder irrigation with amphotericin B eradicates only bladder colonization, requires that a catheter be placed into the bladder, and is associated with a high recurrence rate.

Osteoarticular infections often require months of therapy; frequently amphotericin B is given initially followed by long-term therapy with fluconazole for susceptible organisms. Peritonitis associated with chronic ambulatory peritoneal dialysis can be treated with amphotericin B, fluconazole, or caspofungin, depending on the species of *Candida* causing infection. Intraperitoneal administration of amphotericin B can be extremely irritating and should not be attempted. The catheter should be removed. Meningitis should be treated initially with amphotericin B and flucytosine; some patients with a more chronic form of the disease have been able to be switched to fluconazole for a longer duration of therapy.

Treatment of *Candida* eye infections varies with the extent of ocular involvement. Lesions that are discovered early at the stage of choroidal or retinal involvement can probably be treated effectively with systemic antifungal agents (amphotericin B, caspofungin, or fluconazole) alone. Lesions that have extended into the vitreous body require more aggressive therapy. The best results have been obtained with pars plana vitrectomy, which also provides material for culture, injection of amphotericin B into the vitreous, and a systemic antifungal agent, either amphotericin B or fluconazole. Clearly management must be individualized and done in concert with an ophthalmologist experienced with treatment of this infection. Treatment of endophthalmitis associated with an intraocular lens implant requires removal of the implant, vitrectomy, and local amphotericin B injections. The use of systemic antifungal therapy is debated, but fluconazole has proved useful.

Prevention

For certain populations at highest risk of invasive fungal infections, prophylactic antifungal agents have been shown to prevent infections.[6,7] The prophylactic use of fluconazole has become standard

in the bone marrow transplant population, but in leukemic patients with neutropenia, efficacy is not as clear-cut. Controversy surrounds the use of prophylactic fluconazole in ICU patients. Although one study has shown the efficacy of prophylactic fluconazole in a surgical ICU, it is not clear that this ICU is typical of most others. Restricting the use of prophylaxis to those at the highest risk for disseminated candidiasis is essential to prevent widespread use of azoles with subsequent selection for resistant species. The role of new antifungal agents for prophylaxis has yet to be defined.

Prognosis

The prognosis for mucocutaneous infections is excellent. The major problem occurs in AIDS patients who continue to have recurrent infections unless their CD4 counts revert toward normal with antiretroviral therapy. The prognosis for focal invasive infections depends on the organ involved and the immune state of the patient. For example, although pyelonephritis may respond well to antifungal therapy, meningitis is more difficult to treat and has a poor outcome. Disseminated infection has a high mortality rate. The immune state of the host is the primary determinant of outcome. If the risk factors that led to candidemia and widespread visceral dissemination, especially neutropenia, are not corrected, the outcome is poor.

1. Rex JH, Pappas PG, Sobel JD, et al: Treatment guidelines for candidiasis. Clin Infect Dis 2003 (in press).
2. Rex JH, Bennett JE, Sugar AM, et al: A randomized trial comparing fluconazole with amphotericin B for the treatment of candidemia in patients without neutropenia. N Engl J Med 1994;331:1325–1330.
3. Mora-Duarte J, Betts R, Rotstein C et al: Comparison of caspofungin and amphotericin B for invasive candidiasis. N Engl J Med 2002;347:2020–2029.
4. Rex JH, Pappas PG, Karchmer AW, et al: A randomized and blinded multicenter trial of high-dose fluconazole plus placebo versus fluconazole plus amphotericin B as therapy for candidemia and its consequences in nonneutropenic subjects. Clin Infect Dis 2003;36:1221–1228.
5. Sobel JD, Kauffman CA, McKinsey D, et al: Candiduria: A randomized, double-blind study of treatment with fluconazole and placebo. Clin Infect Dis 2000;30:19–24.
6. Goodman JL, Winston DJ, Greenfield RA, et al: A controlled trial of fluconazole to prevent fungal infections in patients undergoing bone marrow transplantation. N Engl J Med 1992;326:845–851.
7. Pelz RK, Hendrix CW, Swoboda SM, et al: Double-blind, placebo-controlled trial of fluconazole to prevent candidal infections in critically ill surgical patients. Ann Surg 2001;233:542–548.

SUGGESTED READINGS

Fidel PL Jr, Vazquez JA, Sobel JD: *Candida glabrata*: Review of epidemiology, pathogenesis, and clinical disease with comparison to *C. albicans*. Clin Microbiol Rev 1999;12:80–96. *Extensive review of* C. glabrata *infections that is especially pertinent as the number of infections due to this organism increases.*

Kauffman CA, Vazquez JA, Sobel JD, et al: Prospective multicenter surveillance study of funguria in hospitalized patients. Clin Infect Dis 2000;30:14–18. *Large multicenter surveillance study defining the natural history of funguria.*

Martinez-Vazquez, C, Fernandez-Ulloa, J, Bordon, J, et al: *Candida albicans* endophthalmitis in brown heroin addicts: Response to early vitrectomy preceded and followed by antifungal therapy. Clin Infect Dis 1998;27:1130–1133. *Gives insight into this syndrome seen in heroin addicts and provides a useful approach to the treatment of endogenous* Candida *endophthalmitis.*

Rex JH, Walsh TJ, Sobel JD, et al: Practice guidelines for the treatment of candidiasis. Clin Infect Dis 2000;30:662–678. *Consensus guidelines.*

Rex JH, Sobel JD: Prophylactic antifungal therapy in the intensive care unit. Clin Infect Dis 2001;32:1191–1200. *Thoughtful review of the use of antifungal agents to prevent fungal infections in high-risk ICU patients.*

386 ASPERGILLOSIS

David A. Stevens

Definition

Aspergillosis refers to infection with any of the species of the genus *Aspergillus*. They are in mould form in the environment, on artificial media, and when invading tissues. Clinical characteristics of aspergillosis and its treatment are summarized in Table 386–1.

Etiology and Epidemiology

Aspergilli are ubiquitous in the environment and have been isolated with ease from soil and air and even from swimming pools and saunas. They are associated with decaying matter and may grow in temperatures of 40 to 50° C (e.g., self-heating organic compost). The ease with which they are isolated from composting materials, silos, and the cooling canals of nuclear power plants has been an environmental and industrial concern. They are easily isolated from houses, particularly from basements, crawl spaces, bedding, humidifiers, ventilation ducts, potted plants, wicker or straw material, and house dust;

Table 386–1 • ASPERGILLOSIS: CLINICAL SUMMARY

Causative fungus	*Aspergillus* species: *A. fumigatus, A. flavus, A. niger, A. terreus,* other species
Primary geographic distribution	Ubiquitous: human habitat, soil, water, air
Primary route of acquisition	Inhaling spores
Principal site of disease	Lung
Opportunistic infection in compromised hosts	Invasive form, pulmonary
Drug of choice for most patients	Amphotericin, itraconazole, voriconazole
Alternative therapy	None

Table 386–2 • ASPERGILLOSIS SYNDROMES

Invasive disease	Asthma
Aspergilloma (fungus ball)	Invasive airways disease
Superficial bronchial disease	Bronchocentric granulomatosis
Extrinsic allergic alveolitis	Pleural disease
Mixed forms	Local disease
Allergic bronchopulmonary disease	Endocarditis

in surveys they have been found in, for example, condiments, pasta, and marijuana samples. This pervasiveness should not make it surprising that they are sometimes found in normal expectorated sputa. They are important pathogens of insects (of economic importance to beekeepers) and birds, both domesticated and wild, and they cause abortion in cattle. As they grow, they produce toxins, such as aflatoxin—one of the most potent carcinogens known—which contaminates the food chain, posing a risk to animals and humans. Their threat to hospitalized patients has been revealed in outbreaks of infection, particularly pulmonary infection in immunocompromised hosts, associated with building renovation and new construction. The suspected vector has been unfiltered air, as from inlets contaminated with bird excreta and fireproofing materials. Hospital water, which may become aerosolized during activities such as patient showering, is a newly described possible source.

The most common species infecting humans are *Aspergillus fumigatus, Aspergillus flavus, Aspergillus niger,* and *Aspergillus terreus.* Some are speciated by the clinical laboratory only with difficulty, and they may be reported only as "*Aspergillus* species." In tissues, they may be seen as septate hyphae, dichotomously branched (resembling the divergence of fingers from one another), and they may produce their characteristic conidia in tissues or artificial media, which is one way to differentiate them. If the septation can be seen, they can be differentiated from organisms of the class Zygomycetes; they may be confused with *Pseudallescheria boydii,* however, unless the characteristic terminal spores of the latter are seen.

Aspergillosis usually results from airborne conidia and is not contagious.

Clinical Manifestations

The main forms of clinical aspergillosis are shown in Table 386–2. *Invasive disease* is generally a problem of immunocompromised hosts (Chapter 298), and more aggressive immunosuppression and anticancer therapy are the most important factors contributing to the rise of *Aspergillus* infections. Series have reported an incidence as high as 41% in those with acute leukemia at autopsy, and in 89% of these cases, *Aspergillus* played a significant role in the death of the patient. In 97%, pulmonary involvement was present, and in 25%, the infection was disseminated widely to various organs. Similarly, in a group of heart transplant recipients, the incidence of infection was 28%. The incidence in bone marrow transplant recipients has ranged from 5 to 20%, with a higher frequency in certain groups, such as patients with graft-versus-host disease, and mortality is 68% to more than 95% in various series. *Aspergillus* is also common in lung and liver transplant recipients and other steroid-treated patients. It is is also a problem in patients with the neutrophil defect of chronic granulomatous disease. Diagnosis is difficult because aspergilli frequently are contaminants in sputum and in other cultures during handling. In patients with leukemia, *Aspergillus* is particularly associated with relapses of the malignancy, and usually three or four of the following factors are present: leukopenia, glucocorticoid therapy, cytotoxic chemotherapy, and broad-spectrum antibacterials. The classic picture is that of fever and pulmonary infiltrates or nodules, especially progressing to a cavity (usually when granulocytopenia is reversed), or wedge-shaped densities resembling infarcts. The pulmonary pathology in all these entities is that of hemorrhagic infarction and pneumonia. Pulmonary emboli are common because of the organism's tendency to invade blood vessel walls. These processes often combine to produce a "target lesion," consisting of a necrotic center surrounded by a ring of hemorrhage.

Targets of *disseminated disease* include the central nervous system, where abscesses are characteristic. The cerebrospinal fluid (CSF) glucose level is normal, and cultures of the CSF are negative. Mycelia invading blood vessels may produce a microangiopathic hemolytic anemia. Dissemination can result in Budd-Chiari syndrome, myocardial infarction, gastrointestinal disease, or skin lesions. Esophageal ulcers may produce gastrointestinal bleeding. Abscesses are common in the kidney, liver, and myocardium.

Endocarditis is associated with cardiac surgery and particularly with prostheses or intravenous drug abuse. Major arterial emboli occur in 83% of patients, and neurologic presentations are common. Only 8% have positive blood cultures, and this positivity usually is delayed 14 to 20 days, contributing to the poor record of diagnosis antemortem, which is usually made on histologic examination of an embolus. Overall, the survival rate is about 5%, and these individuals have had valve replacement. The disease should be suspected in any patient who presents after cardiac surgery with endocarditis or emboli and negative blood cultures.

The typical picture of an aspergilloma is a fungus ball (i.e., matted hyphae and debris) in a cavity in an upper lobe (Fig. 386–1). This has been reported as a complication in as many as 11% of old tuberculous cavities. The patients present with cough (87%), hemoptysis (81%), dyspnea (61%), weight loss (61%), fatigue (61%), chest pain (31%), or fever (25%). The sputum culture is positive in most. Patients with marked underlying lung disease, large or numerous aspergillomas, rising anti-*Aspergillus* antibody, or sarcoidosis, or those who are immunocompromised, do particularly poorly.

Pleural disease is associated with tuberculosis and bronchopleural fistulas. It may occur after surgery or spontaneously.

Allergic bronchopulmonary aspergillosis is usually superimposed on a background of chronic asthma or cystic fibrosis. The disease appears to be triggered in genetically susceptible individuals by specific *Aspergillus* antigens. It is characterized by episodic airway obstruction, fever, eosinophilia, mucous plugs, positive sputum cultures, and the presence of grossly visible brown flecks in the sputum (hyphae), transient infiltrates and parallel "tram-line" or ring markings on chest radiographs, proximal bronchiectasis, upper lobe contraction, and elevated levels of total immunoglobulin E (IgE), especially when the patient is symptomatic. It is more common in agricultural areas and in the winter, presumably representing an association with stored agricultural products (especially moldy hay) and spore production. The eosinophilia is present in blood, sputum, and the lung on biopsy. The mucous plugs contain mycelia, and the

plugs may be the cause of the infiltrates, with collapse and inflammation occurring peripherally, or inflammatory edema may be responsible. The parallel or ring markings are caused by thickened ectatic bronchi, and the upper lobe changes are a result of progressive apical fibrosis. The infiltrates may be nonsegmental and transient, with a clinical presentation of "eosinophilic pneumonia" and asthma, with eosinophils in blood and sputum; alternatively, they may be segmental, associated with the blocking of bronchi by plugs, and asthma and eosinophilia may be absent. A biphasic skin test response may assist in the diagnosis. A scratch test with *Aspergillus* antigens produces an immediate wheal and flare reaction, mediated by IgE and blocked by antihistamines but not by corticosteroids. An intracutaneous test with the antigens produces a later (6 to 8 hours) reaction, mediated by IgG antibody and complement and blocked by steroids. Similarly, bronchial challenge with the antigens can produce a biphasic response.

Extrinsic allergic alveolitis is an unusual form of *Aspergillus* lung disease and has been most associated with *Aspergillus clavatus* in malt workers. The patients develop a hypersensitivity pneumonitis with dyspnea and fever 4 hours after exposure. Diffuse micronodular infiltrates may be present at the time of symptoms. The patients have IgG precipitins and cell-mediated immune reactions against *Aspergillus* antigens, and granulomas are identified on biopsy. Eosinophilia is not a feature. The scratch test is negative, although an intradermal test produces a reaction in 4 hours, with immunoglobulins and complement present on biopsy. Bronchial challenge produces a reaction in 4 hours, with systemic symptoms and a restrictive defect but without airway resistance. The entity can progress to irreversible fibrosis. The same pathophysiology may be involved in episodes after massive inhalation of spores, usually occurring in farm environments. Symptoms are present within 24 hours, and granulomas are found on biopsy.

Superficial bronchial disease, an acute or chronic bronchitis with brown-flecked sputum, *extrinsic asthma* due to airborne conidia, and *bronchocentric granulomatosis,* a peribronchial destructive disease with wheezing or fever and weight loss, are other important pulmonary diseases. The aspergilloma, allergic, alveolitis, and superficial forms rarely progress to invasive disease. However, more *invasive airway disease* with ulcerative, pseudomembranous, or plaquelike tracheobronchitis occurs, particularly in immunocompromised hosts, and may presage parenchymal invasion. *Chronic necrotizing pulmonary aspergillosis* is a poorly defined entity that usually occurs in patients with underlying lung disease, often with features of invasive disease and aspergilloma.

Examples of *locally invasive disease* abound and are usually severe. They include invasion of burn wounds, keratitis, external otitis (particularly in the tropics), focal rhinitis (particularly in immunosuppressed or granulocytopenic hosts), sinusitis (in these hosts or after dental procedures) and osteomyelitis or endophthalmitis (after fungemia, trauma, or surgery). Cutaneous ulcers have been associated with the use of adhesive tape. Bloodborne disease in addicts can produce foci of dissemination that are similar to those associated with the invasive pulmonary form of the disease. A noninvasive form of sinus disease has a predominantly allergic component and eosinophilia. It is responsive to drainage and corticosteroids.

Diagnosis

Some of the modalities of diagnosis have been mentioned in connection with specific syndromes. Antibody to *Aspergillus* has been detected by a variety of techniques and with a variety of antigen preparations. Data from the more commonly reported techniques suggest a high degree of sensitivity in allergic disease or aspergillomas but a low degree of sensitivity in invasive disease. Because the frequency of false-positive reactions, even in the presence of other mycoses, is low, a positive test result in cases of invasive disease may be useful. IgE and IgG antibody specific to *Aspergillus* antigens is another serodiagnostic adjunct in allergic disease. The sputum culture, although having good positive predictive value in the appropriate setting (especially a neutropenic patient, particularly if febrile), is positive in only 8 to 34% of cases, and tissue must be obtained to make the diagnosis. Prospective culturing of the nose of granulocytopenic patients has been of some value, because a positive nasal culture (particularly the presence of nasal *Aspergillus* lesions) has led to the early diagnosis of concurrent

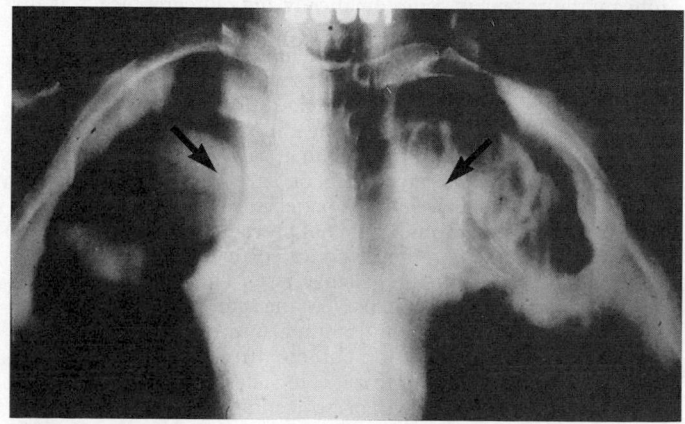

FIGURE 386–1 • Tomogram of pulmonary aspergillomas (arrows).

pulmonary or sinus disease. However, negative nasal cultures are common in pulmonary aspergillosis. Detection of a galactomannan antigen in serum, initially studied by latex agglutination methods and later by enzyme-linked immunosorbent assay (ELISA), has been useful in identifying invasive disease, particularly with repeatedly positive results and serial monitoring, and in following responses to therapy. In some laboratories, detection of *Aspergillus* DNA in blood by polymerase chain reaction (PCR) has demonstrated high specificity and sensitivity, and in a few laboratories, detection of glucan in serum is promising. Culture or cytology of bronchoalveolar lavage fluid also is useful in diagnosis of invasive disease. The problem with all serodiagnostic modalities is the lack of a generally available, standardized technique in the United States. The physician should know the background data (i.e., the sensitivity and specificity of the assay in the various syndromes) for the laboratory to which the specimens may be sent.

In severe disease, an aggressive, invasive approach, as well as making a tissue diagnosis early in the illness, appears to be a key to survival. In the appropriate clinical setting, such as an immunocompromised host with fever and a pulmonary infiltrate, repeated isolation of the same species in culture, particularly a bronchial lavage or other endobronchial culture, correlates with invasive disease; sometimes, even a single sputum culture (especially with heavy growth) may have to be the stimulus for therapy if invasive procedures cannot be done. Negative culture results do not rule out invasive disease. Blood cultures are rarely helpful. Computed tomographic scanning of the chest done at the earliest suspicion of this diagnosis initially may reveal a lesion with peripheral haziness (i.e., halo sign) or later reveal a lesion with an air crescent; both lesions are highly predictive of this diagnosis. These are radiographic correlates of edema or hemorrhage and of infarction that are related to the organism's vasculotropism. In these situations, a positive galactomannan assay, PCR, or glucan test is particularly helpful in prompting therapy, even if a specific microbiologic diagnosis from tissue is not possible.

Rx Treatment

In invasive disease, prompt, aggressive chemotherapy has produced superior survival statistics at some institutions, although recovery from neutropenia is a necessary accompaniment of recovery in almost every success. The role of granulocyte transfusions, colony-stimulating factors, or proinflammatory cytokines is unclear. In endocarditis, in addition to prompt, aggressive chemotherapy, valve replacement appears to be necessary. Locally invasive disease in other sites also requires systemic or local chemotherapy, particularly intravitreal therapy or nephrostomy irrigation in renal disease. Surgical excision has an important role in the invasion of bone, burn wounds, epidural abscesses, vitreal disease, sinus disease of nonimmunocompromised hosts, endocarditis, and removal of catheters for peritonitis and of silk sutures in bronchial stump (postpneumonectomy) aspergillosis. Surgery may have a function in invasive pulmonary disease for which chemotherapy has failed or when disease impinges on major vascular structures. In pleural disease, local installation of nystatin or amphotericin has been helpful.

In cases involving aspergilloma, there is evidence that patients with fever, cough, weight loss, malaise, and hemoptysis have an element of allergy, which can be demonstrated by bronchial challenge or the presence of specific IgG and IgE. These patients symptomatically improve if given glucocorticoids. Intravenous amphotericin B therapy of patients with aspergilloma produces results no better than those with routine pulmonary toilet. Intracavitary antifungals, instilled through a catheter, are a heroic form of therapy that has been attempted in some patients.

The role of surgery for aspergilloma is controversial. Between 7 and 15% of mycetomas undergo spontaneous lysis. The overall operative mortality rate aggregated from several series is 7%, but it may be as high as 14% in some large series. The frequency of various operative complications aggregated from several series is 22%, with a range of 7 to 60%. New aspergillomas have developed after surgical successes. On the other hand, in various series, 18 to 26% of patients with adequate follow-up treated without surgery died of disease complications, usually hemoptysis, whereas 50% had significant improvement symptomatically and radiographically. If any consensus exists, it is that surgical resection has a role in treating patients with recurrent, significant hemoptysis. An alternative temporary therapy, particularly for the nonsurgical patient, is selective bronchial arterial embolization to the bleeding vessel. Oral itraconazole may have a role in treating chronic aspergilloma.

In allergic disease, measures that have *not* worked include hyposensitization and avoidance of sites in the environment. Cromolyn is inadequate in most patients. Aerosolized antifungals have produced remissions but do not prevent recurrences. Treating the clinical disease is more complicated than the effects of drug blockade demonstrable in challenge tests. The continuous use of systemic glucocorticoids can prevent the acute infiltrates and some accompanying symptoms. Intermittent use of glucocorticoids or raising the dose in patients on chronic therapy can produce rapid resolution of marked symptomatic episodes; this is also indicated in patients with rising IgE or worsening spirometry readings.

Bronchodilators ameliorate acute exacerbations, and leukotriene modifiers may be of benefit. The long-term beneficial effects of glucocorticoids are less clear; they are not so useful in arresting dyspnea or wheezing in the long term, and they do not prevent the development of the accompanying bronchiectasis. A randomized study using oral itraconazole indicated amelioration of disease and a steroid-sparing effect. The proper approach to extrinsic alveolitis is to avoid the stimulus.

When systemic chemotherapy has been indicated, most clinical experience has been with amphotericin B in deoxycholate. Its track record is generally poor in invasive or disseminated disease in immunocompromised hosts, especially in those with cerebral or hepatic disease and in bone marrow transplant recipients. In the immunocompromised host, the drug should be used aggressively, with prompt progression to a full therapeutic dose, which should be more than 1 mg/kg/day, if tolerated. Some species, such as *A. terreus*, may be more resistant to amphotericin. Prophylactic therapy may have a role in patients who have survived invasive disease and will become neutropenic again. Rifampin almost always potentiates the activity of amphotericin in vitro against aspergilli, whereas results with flucytosine are unpredictable. Animal models have shown an enhanced effect of combinations of these drugs over that with amphotericin alone. Clinical data to support combination therapy are limited, but given the poor record of amphotericin alone in invasive disease, combination therapy appears a logical avenue to explore, particularly if synergy in vitro can be demonstrated. Among the azole drugs, itraconazole as sole therapy has produced similar response rates in invasive disease and is an alternative if the patient is reliable, can be shown to absorb the drug adequately (by monitoring serum concentrations), and is not receiving other drugs that interact with itraconazole and present management difficulties. Oral itraconazole as a continuation therapy after amphotericin is logical and appears safe. A new oral solution in cyclodextrin lessens absorption problems, and an intravenous formulation is available for patients who cannot take or absorb oral preparations. A new triazole, voriconazole, proved superior to conventional chemotherapy in a randomized trial. Lipid-complexed amphotericin B given in higher doses than deoxycholate amphotericin has also produced similar response rates in historical comparisons and is less nephrotoxic but more expensive. A new class of antifungals (echinocandins) that inhibits glucan synthesis has shown activity against *Aspergillus* in vivo, and capsofungin has been licensed on the basis of data showing responsiveness of cases refractory to conventional chemotherapy. Combinations of polyenes, azoles, and/or echinocandins are being explored. A recent clinical trial found favorable results with voriconazole therapy,◼ but more clinical trials are needed to assess all alternative forms of systemic therapy. Therapy should be continued after lesions are resolving, cultures are negative, and reversible underlying predispositions have abated. Reinstating therapy in patients who have previously responded should be considered if immunosuppression is reinstituted or if neutropenia recurs.

Prevention

Prophylaxis of susceptible patients, such as immunocompromised hosts, using intranasal, inhaled, or systemic antifungals, or of allergic patients using inhaled or systemic antifungals, is an approach to avoid disease and the need for therapy. Reducing airborne spores, such as by filtering hospital air, reducing activities such as room maintenance that increase spore counts when the patient is in the room, preventing dust, and restricting contaminated materials (e.g., potted plants), is believed to be a worthwhile effort for patients who will be transiently immunosuppressed or neutropenic.

1. Herbrecht R, Denning DW, Patterson TF, et al: Voriconazole versus amphotericin B for primary therapy of invasive aspergillosis. N Engl J Med 2002;347:408–415.

SUGGESTED READINGS

Patterson TF, Kirkpatrick WR, White M, et al.: Invasive aspergillosis. Disease spectrum, treatment practices, and outcomes. Medicine 2000;79:250–260. *Reviews sites and treatment outcomes in 595 nonrandom invasive aspergillosis cases.*

Stevens DA, Kan VL, Judson MA, et al.: Practice guidelines for diseases caused by *Aspergillus.* Clin Infect Dis 2000;30:696–709. *Infectious Disease Society of America consensus guidelines for patient management.*

Torres HA, Rivero GA, Lewis RE, et al: Aspergillosis caused by non-fumigatus *Aspergillus* species: Risk factors and in vitro susceptibility compared with *Aspergillus fumigatus.* Diagn Microbiol Infect Dis 2003;46:25–28. *Invasive aspergillosis was more likely to be resistant to antifungal agents and to be caused by non-*fumigatus Aspergillus spp.

387 *PNEUMOCYSTIS CARINII* PNEUMONIA

Judith E. Feinberg
Fred R. Sattler

Pneumocystis carinii pneumonia remains the most frequent case-defining infection in acquired immunodeficiency syndrome (AIDS), despite an almost 50% decrease in the number of first episodes (see Chapter 415) recently reported to the Centers for Disease Control and Prevention. A large number of second or third episodes also occur annually in AIDS patients, although these are less well reported.

Moderate to severe episodes cause appreciable morbidity, and even with effective therapy, up to 20% of cases are fatal. For mild episodes, the fatality rate is less than 5%, but the diagnosis can be challenging because signs and symptoms may mimic community-acquired bacterial infections and the presentation may be atypical in patients receiving prophylaxis. It is therefore imperative that episodes be detected when alteration of gas exchange is mild and lung damage minimal if hospitalization and mortality are to be minimized. Clinicians caring for human immunodeficiency virus (HIV)–infected patients must be aware of various manifestations of *P. carinii* infection so that therapy can be initiated as early as possible.

Etiology

P. carinii is a eukaryotic microbe with morphologic features similar to those of protozoa. Lack of growth on fungal culture media and lack of response to antiprotozoan agents have also supported the notion that it is a protozoan. However, *P. carinii* has an affinity for fungal stains, is ultrastructurally similar to fungi, and is phylogenetically closely related to the Ascomycetes yeasts by molecular analysis of its 16S ribosomal RNA and mitochondrial DNA. The base pair sequence of its mitochondrial DNA contains genes of NADH dehydrogenase subunits and cytochrome oxidase subunits, which show 60% homology with fungi but only 20% with protozoa. The dihydrofolate reductase (DHFR) of *P. carinii*, like that of fungi, is a single enzyme with a lower molecular weight than the dual thymidylate synthetase–DHFR enzyme found in protozoa.

This is not a purely academic issue. Although *P. carinii* does not respond to antifungal drugs such as amphotericin or azoles, β-glucan synthesis in the cyst wall is inhibited by newer antifungal agents, such as echinocandins and papulocandins. These agents are active against the cyst and trophozoite forms in experimental infections, whereas traditional anti-*Pneumocystis* therapies affect only the trophozoite. Novel therapeutic approaches that affect both stages of

the life cycle are being developed in an attempt to improve response rates.

Epidemiology and Transmission

Within the first few years of life, nearly all children have serologic evidence of exposure to *P. carinii*. The most accepted hypothesis for pathogenesis has been that *P. carinii* remains latent in the lung and that active disease is caused by reactivation during severe immune system depression. However, few data support chronic carriage, because the organism is detected neither in lung sections at autopsy of previously healthy individuals nor by polymerase chain reaction (PCR) in bronchoalveolar lavage (BAL) fluid of immunocompetent adults.

P. carinii may be found incidentally in lungs of immunocompromised patients, and genetic sequences have been detected in the absence of histologic evidence of infection. Case clusters and familial spread have been reported, and in one natural history study of HIV-infected patients, upper respiratory infections peaked in winter months, followed by *P. carinii* pneumonia 4 months later, suggesting that *P. carinii* may have been acquired by prior exposure to infected aerosols when community respiratory infections were common. These data suggest that *P. carinii* may be acquired by person-to-person spread.

Pathogenesis and Pathophysiology

In cortisone-treated rats, inhaled *P. carinii* adheres to type 1 alveolar cells through fibronectin. After several weeks, small clusters of *P. carinii* can be detected in alveolar spaces. Later, air sacs become filled with organisms, indicating that replication is slow, but proliferation is extensive. Two morphologic forms are readily detected. Most are small, pleomorphic trophozoites. A more mature, larger, thick-walled cyst containing up to eight intracystic bodies is less common. Histologic analysis typically shows foamy alveolar exudates consisting of degenerative *P. carinii* cell membranes, surfactant, host proteins, and a modest number of alveolar macrophages. As infection progresses, septal hypertrophy occurs, and interstitial edema is evident. Mononuclear cells accumulate and similar abnormalities occur in humans.

These abnormalities result in increased alveolar-capillary permeability, which is associated with physiologic alterations: impaired gas exchange and decreased membrane diffusing capacity, compliance, total lung capacity, and vital capacity. Soon after anti-*Pneumocystis* therapy begins, lung function is further impaired by an inflammatory response, as evidenced by a rapid decline in oxygenation that reaches its nadir after 3 to 4 days. This inflammatory reaction appears to be mediated by tumor necrosis factor-α (TNF-α) and interleukin-1, -6, and -8 released by alveolar macrophages. TNF-α is modulated by the β-glucan component of the cell wall, providing further evidence that *P. carinii* is a fungus.

Risk for Infection

In the rat model, depletion of T lymphocytes is the critical determinant in the development of *P. carinii* pneumonia. In humans, *Pneumocystis* occurs in association with lymphoreticular malignancy, certain congenital immune disorders, solid organ transplantation (recipients), and therapy with cyclosporine or corticosteroids, which have in common variable defects in T-cell function. In patients with HIV, the risk of developing *P. carinii* pneumonia is related to a decrease in T lymphocytes with the CD4 surface phenotype. The median CD4+ T-cell count is typically 50 to 70 at the time of a first episode. That *P. carinii* pneumonia may occur with transient declines in CD4+ T-cell counts to less than 100 during primary HIV infection suggests it is the absolute number of CD4+ T cells and not the stage of HIV infection that is important in determining risk for infection. Although more than 90% of episodes occur at total counts less than 200, *P. carinii* pneumonia may occur at higher counts in individuals whose CD4+ T cells are declining rapidly and those with thrush and unexplained fever (>100° F for more than 2 weeks).

Histopathology

Microscopic analysis of lung tissue from AIDS patients with *P. carinii* pneumonia shows a prominent eosinophilic, foamy, intra-alveolar exudate and proliferation of type II pneumocytes but only mild interstitial inflammation. Detection of *P. carinii* requires special stains. The cysts are uniformly 5 to 7mm in diameter and collapse easily, which gives them a helmet or banana shape. Trophozoites are smaller, measuring 1 to 4mm in diameter, and, unlike the cysts, are pleomorphic.

Diffuse alveolar damage is common. Interstitial fibrosis is present in approximately 6% of cases, and intraluminal fibrosis occurs in almost 40%; fibrosis appears to be related to the severity of the inflammatory response and duration of therapy. In contrast, acute exudative alveolar damage is unusual, and hyaline membranes have been detected in less than 5% of lung biopsies, but they may occasionally be so prominent that they obscure the typical eosinophilic alveolar material. Other less common histologic abnormalities include pneumatoceles and cavities, granulomas, lymphocytic interstitial infiltrates, microcalcifications, vasculitis, and alveolar proteinosis. In patients with cavitation and pneumothorax, *P. carinii* invades the interstitium, and unlike typical cases, greater proportions of trophozoites are present.

Clinical Manifestations

Early recognition and treatment are imperative. Figure 387–1 shows that the risk of a fatal outcome increases progressively for patients whose room air arterial oxygen partial pressure (PaO_2) values are less than 75 and alveolar-arterial oxygen differences (A-a DO_2) are 35 mm Hg or more at presentation. Clinicians must therefore be familiar with the typical manifestations and the unusual presentations of *P. carinii* pneumonia.

TYPICAL PRESENTATIONS

The onset of *P. carinii* pneumonia in AIDS patients is usually insidious. The cardinal manifestation is a hacking, typically nonproductive cough that might have been present for weeks. Retrosternal chest tightness, intensified by coughing and inspiration, is also common. Fever occurs in 80 to 90% of these patients. Dyspnea occurs later, when oxygenation is moderately to severely impaired. In contrast, *P. carinii* pneumonia in HIV-seronegative patients is typically acute in onset, with high fever and chest x-ray abnormalities.

Physical findings are often limited and nonspecific. No tachypnea usually occurs with mild episodes, whereas respiratory distress and use of accessory respiratory muscles may be seen in severe episodes. Auscultation of the lungs is frequently normal because rales occur in only 30 to 40% of cases and are usually a late finding, indicating greater severity. Occasionally, patients have wheezing or overt bronchospasm. In one report, 84% of patients had peak expiratory flow rates (PEFR) less than 80% of predicted, with 54% of these responding to bronchodilator therapy compared with those without *Pneumocystis*, of whom only 23% had low PEFR and 3% had a response to bronchodilator therapy.

Physical findings outside the lung may be helpful. Oral thrush is a nearly universal finding in patients not taking antifungals. Facial seborrheic dermatitis is also common. Generalized adenopathy with lymph nodes larger than 1 cm is rare because patients with *P. carinii* generally have severe immunodeficiency with hypoplastic lymph nodes.

In one study of 2526 men and 544 women, women were more likely to be hospitalized for their first episode of *P. carinii* pneumonia, were less likely to be white, and were more likely to die in the hospital. These differences in clinical course suggest that *P. carinii* pneumonia has been less frequently diagnosed early in HIV-infected women.

ATYPICAL PRESENTATIONS

PNEUMOTHORAX AND CAVITATION. Pneumothoraces that may be associated with refractory bronchopleural fistulas and chronic lung cavitation are an increasingly frequent presentation and may occur in up to 10% of episodes. Pneumothoraces occurred spontaneously in 20 (2%) of 1030 patients with AIDS at one medical center; 50 to 95% of episodes are associated with active *P. carinii* pneumonia. HIV-positive patients with spontaneous pneumothorax should undergo work-up and treatment for *P. carinii* pneumonia along with lung re-expansion.

Lung destruction and cavitation may appear as solitary, thin-walled cavities; regional honeycombing; blebs; or bullae; these findings are often bilateral, and they usually occur in the upper lobes and precede the development of pneumothorax. Although cavitation and pneumothorax were initially associated with aerosol pentamidine prophylaxis, these complications may occur in the absence of aerosol therapy, in nonsmokers, and in first episodes, as well as in patients with prior bronchoscopy or mechanical ventilation and barotrauma.

FEVER OF UNKNOWN ORIGIN. In some AIDS patients, *P. carinii* pneumonia may present as an occult febrile illness, with few or no respiratory symptoms. Nonspecific complaints of high fever, night sweats, fatigue, and malaise are prominent. Other causes of fever of unknown origin in this population, such as occult sinusitis, cytomegalovirus retinitis, disseminated *Mycobacterium avium* infection, and endocarditis, must be excluded, and oxygen desaturation with exercise and histologic evidence of *P. carinii* should be sought.

EXTRAPULMONARY *P. CARINII* INFECTION. Infection with *P. carinii* may occur outside the lung in 0.5 to 3.0% of patients with *P. carinii* pneumonia. At the time at which extrapulmonary *Pneumocystis* infection is diagnosed, more than 50% of patients have concurrent *P. carinii* pneumonia. Nucleotide sequences of the *P. carinii* DHFR gene have been detected by PCR in blood of 5 of 11 patients with acute *P. carinii* pneumonia, which suggests that hematogenous dissemination occurs.

Clinical presentations have included external auditory polyps, mastoiditis, choroiditis, cutaneous lesions or digital necrosis from vasculitis, small bowel obstruction, ascites with gross nodules in the stomach and duodenum, hepatic or splenic infiltration, hilar or mediastinal lymphadenopathy, thyroiditis, thymic involvement, and cytopenia due to bone marrow infection. At autopsy, disseminated infection has been documented in other organs, including abdominal lymph nodes, pancreas, gastric mucosa, adrenal glands, myocardium, kidneys, and central nervous system. Lymph nodes, liver, spleen, and bone marrow are the most commonly affected organs.

Histologic analysis of affected organs shows foci of eosinophilic frothy exudates, and special stains reveal *P. carinii*. Unlike the lung, these lesions are often calcified (punctate or rimlike) and show vasculitis with frank invasion of vessel walls.

Nonspecific complaints of fever and sweats predominate. Two extrapulmonary sites are associated with specific symptoms or signs. Thyroid involvement may present with neck pain, hyperthyroidism or hypothyroidism, and goiter, which may be multinodular or a solitary neck mass. The thyroid is usually "cold" on ^{125}I scanning, and the diagnosis is made by fine-needle aspiration. Choroiditis appears as slightly elevated, yellow-white plaques, and it is generally limited to the choroid without involvement of retinal vessels (unlike cytomegalovirus retinitis) or evidence of intraocular inflammation. Identification of typical choroidal lesions may provide the first clue of disseminated infection. Although the lung is involved in nearly 90% of cases, choroiditis may be the only evidence of extrapulmonary disease.

Extensive extrapulmonary infection portends a poor prognosis, frequently associated with organ failure and death, but involvement of a single extrapulmonary site often responds favorably to anti-*Pneumocystis* therapy.

Laboratory Abnormalities

PULMONARY FUNCTION TESTS

Hypoxemia is the most useful marker of *Pneumocystis* pneumonia and is highly predictive of outcome. At presentation, PaO_2 less than 80 mm Hg or A-a DO_2 greater than 15 on room air occurs in more than 80% of episodes.

In patients with normal or nearly normal PaO_2, A-a DO_2, and chest radiographs, graded exercise testing results in increases in the A-a DO_2, and oxygen desaturation can be readily demonstrated with pulse oximetry. The carbon monoxide diffusing capacity (DL_{CO}) is also a sensitive but nonspecific marker. Despite the lack of specificity, DL_{CO} values greater than 80% make *Pneumocystis* unlikely (i.e., negative predictive values are >98%). In AIDS patients with asthma who have

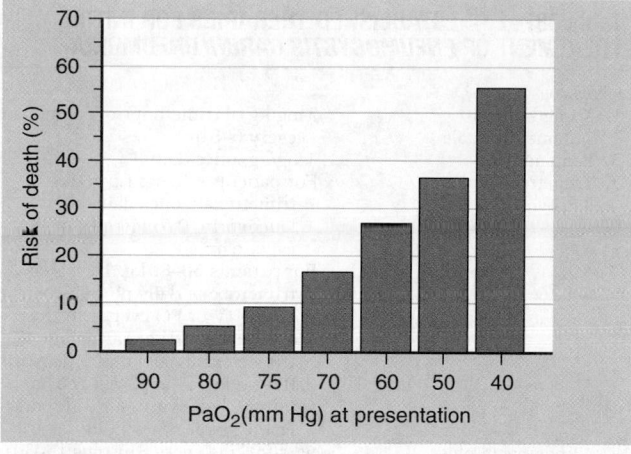

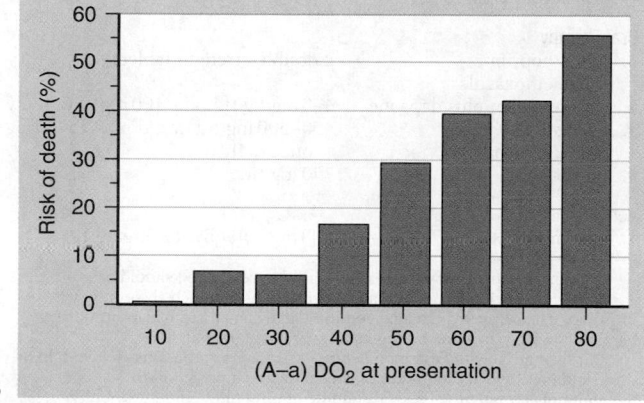

FIGURE 387-1 • *A,* Risk of death according to the partial pressure (PaO₂) of oxygen on room air at the time of admission to the hospital for patients receiving conventional therapies without adjunctive corticosteroids. *B,* Risk of death according to alveolar-arterial oxygen difference (A-a Do₂) on room air at the time of admission to the hospital for patients receiving conventional therapies without adjunctive corticosteroids. (Adapted from the U.S. Public Health Service: Consensus Statement on the Use of Corticosteroids as Adjunctive Therapy for *Pneumocystis* Pneumonia in the Acquired Immunodeficiency Syndrome. www.cdc.gov)

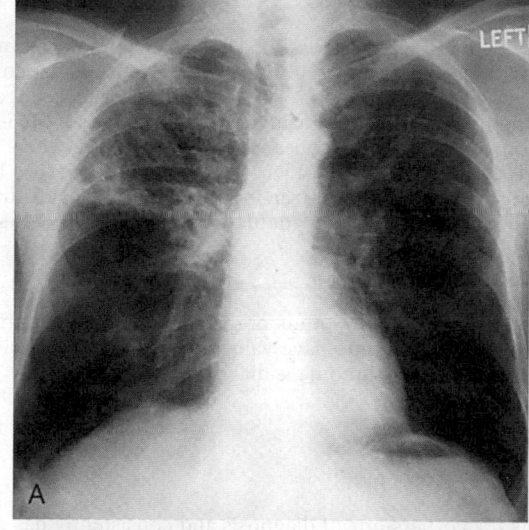

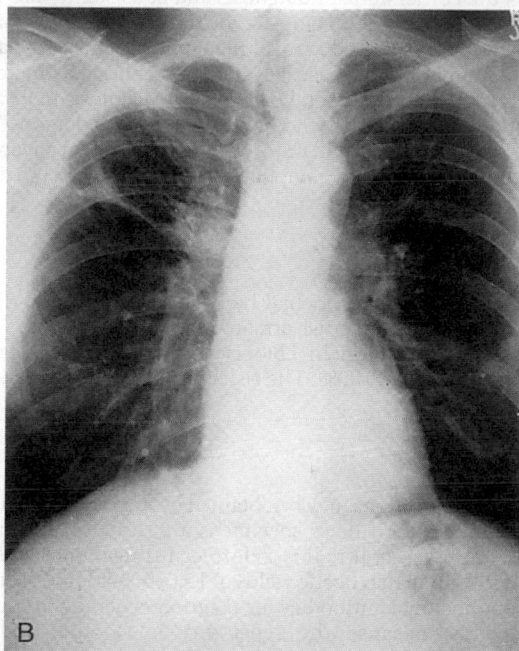

FIGURE 387-2 • *A,* This chest radiograph was obtained from a 42-year-old homosexual man who presented with a 14-month history of chronic cough, dyspnea with minimal exertion, and 25-lb weight loss. He was treated for 8 weeks with four standard antituberculous drugs plus intravenous amikacin, but cultures for *Mycobacterium tuberculosis* remained negative. A repeat induced sputum at that time showed large numbers of *P. carinii* organisms. *B,* Chest radiographs from the same patient after a 3-week course of therapy with oral trimethoprim-sulfamethoxazole (15 mg/kg/day of the trimethoprim component). At the completion of therapy, cough and dyspnea had completely subsided.

cough and hypoxemia, results of DL_CO should be normal when hypoxemia is due solely to bronchospasm.

RADIOGRAPHIC PROCEDURES

ROUTINE RADIOLOGY. Routine chest radiographs typically show interstitial infiltrates, beginning in perihilar areas and spreading to the lower and finally to upper lung fields in a butterfly pattern. The apices are usually spared. Alveolar patterns with air bronchograms may be superimposed on the interstitial process in more advanced infection, although alveolar infiltrates may be the initial presentation in up to 10% of cases. Because *P. carinii* pneumonia is so common, the range of radiographic findings is wide. In 10 to 30% of cases, the radiograph is atypical, with asymmetrical or predominantly upper lobe infiltration, especially in patients receiving aerosol pentamidine prophylaxis. Other atypical abnormalities include cysts, pneumatoceles, cavitation, honeycombing, pneumothorax, adenopathy (with or without calcifications), pleural effusions, abscesses, lobar or segmental consolidation, solitary parenchymal nodules, or postobstructive infiltration from endobronchial nodules. In one series of 100 patients with *P. carinii* pneumonia, cysts were documented in 34%, and of these, 32 had multiple cysts measuring 1.0 to 5.0 cm in diameter that occurred predominantly in the upper lobes. Cysts resolved partially or completely in most cases with specific therapy for *Pneumocystis* infection, but 12 (35%) of the 34 patients developed pneumothoraces, compared with only 2 of 30 patients without cysts. These cystic cavitary lesions may mimic those of tuberculosis (Fig. 387–2). Chest radiographs may be normal at presentation for 10 to 20% of patients with documented *Pneumocystis* infection.

COMPUTED TOMOGRAPHY. Computed tomography (CT) typically shows fine, diffuse alveolar consolidation with bronchial wall thickening, even when chest radiographs are normal, and less often, CT shows regional consolidation or cystic air spaces. Low-attenuation lesions and calcifications of lymph nodes, spleen, liver, and kidneys may be present in patients with extrapulmonary involvement. CT is primarily valuable in patients who have normal chest radiographs or unsuspected extrapulmonary *Pneumocystis* infection.

NUCLEAR IMAGING. Nuclear imaging may be of ancillary value in some cases, such as in patients with chronic lung disease, abnormal radiographs, and worsening respiratory symptoms. Gallium 67 accumulates in activated macrophages through transferrin receptors in areas of lung inflammation, but pulmonary uptake is not specific for *Pneumocystis.* Specificity is improved when scans are reported as positive only if gallium uptake in lung equals or exceeds uptake in liver; images are read at 48 to 72 hours after injection.

LACTATE DEHYDROGENASE

Serum lactate dehydrogenase (LDH) level is more elevated in patients with *Pneumocystis* pneumonia than in matched patients with other pulmonary complications of HIV. Although serum levels of LDH are not highly specific, the sensitivity was greater than 90% in one study of patients with dyspnea and *Pneumocystis* when values exceeded 220 IU/L. However, LDH values greater than 500 IU/L at presentation are associated with an increased risk for a fatal outcome. Equally important, serial tests gradually improve in survivors.

CD4+ T-CELL COUNTS

Typically, CD4+ T-cell counts are less than 100 cells/mm³, and more than 90% of patients have values of less than 200 cells/mm³ when *Pneumocystis* pneumonia is diagnosed.

Diagnosis

BRONCHOALVEOLAR LAVAGE

BAL is the cornerstone of diagnosis and consistently has a sensitivity of 86 to 96%. The diagnostic yield is lower—only 62%—for patients who have received aerosol pentamidine and who have predominantly upper lobe disease. Several approaches may increase the yield for such patients. Bilateral BAL yields a diagnosis in 94%, compared with 84% in patients who have previously undergone BAL on one side. Because several-fold more organisms may be recovered from upper than from lower lobes, sampling involved sites is likely to increase the yield.

TRANSBRONCHIAL BIOPSY

The yield from transbronchial biopsy approaches that of BAL if tissue is obtained without crush artifact and contains at least 25 alveoli. If both BAL and transbronchial biopsies are obtained, the diagnostic sensitivity approaches 100%. The risk of pneumothorax makes BAL more attractive.

SPUTUM INDUCTION

Pulmonary secretions may be obtained by ultrasonic nebulization of hypertonic saline. If these specimens are treated with mucolytic agents to solubilize oral debris before centrifugation, cytostaining procedures result in diagnostic yields of 15 to 90%. Fluorescent staining with monoclonal antibodies for *P. carinii* generally produces the highest yields. Because the sensitivity is variable and yields greater than 80% have been consistently achieved in only a few centers, a negative result for induced sputum does not exclude the diagnosis.

IDENTIFICATION OF *PNEUMOCYSTIS CARINII*

CYST WALL STAINS. The standard staining procedure for identifying *P. carinii* in clinical specimens has used Gomori's methenamine silver

Table 387–1 • ESTABLISHED THERAPIES FOR INITIAL TREATMENT OF *PNEUMOCYSTIS CARINII* PNEUMONIA

Intravenous Therapy	
1. Trimethoprim-sulfamethoxazole	5 mg/kg of trimethoprim component every 6–8 hr
2. Pentamidine*	4 mg/kg, once daily
3. Trimetrexate plus leucovorin	For patients <50 kg: 1.5 mg/kg trimetrexate once daily plus leucovorin, 0.5 mg/kg IV or PO every 6 hr
	For patients 50–80 kg: 1.2 mg/kg trimetrexate daily plus leucovorin, 0.5/kg IV or PO every 6 hr
	For patients >80 kg: 1.0 mg/kg trimetrexate daily plus leucovorin, 0.8 mg/kg IV or PO every 6 hr
	Continue leucovorin for 72 hr after last dose of trimetrexate
4. Clindamycin plus primaquine base (oral)†	600–900 mg every 8 hr plus 15–30 mg PO, once daily
Oral Therapy	
1. Trimethoprim-sulfamethoxazole	2 double-strength tablets tid
2. Trimethoprim plus dapsone	4–5 mg/kg tid plus 100 mg once daily
3. Clindamycin plus primaquine base†	450–600 mg tid or qid plus 15–30 mg once daily
4. Atovaquone‡	750 mg tid
Aerosol Therapy	
1. Pentamidine	600 mg daily by Respirgard II§

*Intramuscular therapy may cause sterile abscesses and should be avoided.
†The combination is not advisable in situations in which absorption may be impaired (e.g., severe hypoxemia, vomiting, diarrhea, ileus, malabsorption) because clindamycin alone has no activity against *P. carinii*.
‡Must be given with fatty food because serum concentrations are two-fold or three-fold lower when drug is administered on an empty stomach.
§Administered at 50 psi and 8 L/minute of oxygen.

because the sensitivity is generally greater than 95%. Toluidine blue O also stains the cyst, is more rapid, and is comparably reliable.

NONCYST WALL STAINS. Wright-Giemsa and Diff-Quik stains are commonly used. They stain trophozoites, nuclei of cysts, and intermediate forms, and they can be completed within 30 minutes. However, organisms may be missed in 10 to 15% of cases. Papanicolaou silver stains the nonspecific foam surrounding large clusters of *P. carinii*, but organisms are not readily identified. The methodology is quick and useful for screening.

IMMUNOCHEMICAL STAINS. Immunofluorescent staining with monoclonal antibody results in yields greater than 90% for BAL specimens and appears to be more sensitive for sputum samples than silver or Wright-Giemsa stains.

MOLECULAR IDENTIFICATION. Oligonucleotide probes and PCR are promising methodologies that may increase the diagnostic yield in identifying *P. carinii*, especially in induced sputum specimens.

℞ Treatment

INITIATING THERAPY

The key to successful treatment is prompt suspicion of the diagnosis and early initiation of therapy when episodes are mild. Because sputum induction and bronchoscopies are generally not done after hours and results of special stains may not be immediately available, patients with typical clinical features of *Pneumocystis* pneumonia and moderate to severe hypoxemia should be treated empirically. This does not impair the ability to make a diagnosis, because large numbers of *P. carinii* are detectable in lung tissue and secretions for weeks after therapy is begun.

SEVERE EPISODES

PARENTERAL THERAPY. Initial therapy should be given parenterally for patients with moderate to severe impairment in oxygen exchange determined by PaO₂ less than 70 mm Hg or A-a DO₂ greater than 35 (Table 387–1). Drugs with high oral bioavailability, such as trimethoprim-sulfamethoxazole (TMP-SMX), may be erratically absorbed from the gut in subjects with severe hypoxemia. AIDS patients may have enteropathy and malabsorption even in the absence of diarrhea; consequently, drug concentrations may be subtherapeutic.

TRIMETHOPRIM-SULFAMETHOXAZOLE. The antifolate combination of TMP-SMX is the "gold standard" for severe episodes (Chapters 415 and 421). Prospective, double-blind studies, each involving more than 300 patients, confirmed that TMP-SMX was more effective than trimetrexate, atovaquone, or aerosolized pentamidine in AIDS patients with *Pneumocystis*. Although no comparably rigorous studies have compared TMP-SMX with parenteral pentamidine, TMP-SMX is associated with less serious toxic effects.

The most frequent potentially serious toxic effect with TMP-SMX is neutropenia (Table 387–2). Because this reaction is dose

Table 387–2 • TOXICITIES ASSOCIATED WITH STANDARD THERAPIES FOR *PNEUMOCYSTIS CARINII* PNEUMONIA

DRUG	FREQUENT CAUSES OF DRUG MORBIDITY	INFREQUENT CAUSES OF MORBIDITY
Trimethoprim-sulfamethoxazole	Fever Morbilliform rash Nausea and vomiting Neutropenia* Thrombocytopenia† Anemia‡	Stevens-Johnson syndrome Exfoliative dermatitis Diarrhea Liver test abnormalities Elevated serum creatinine Hyperkalemia Hyponatremia Renal impairment Hallucinations or agitation
Parenteral pentamidine	Fever Morbilliform rash Nausea and vomiting Renal impairment Hypoglycemia Hypotension Pancreatitis	Hypocalcemia Ventricular tachycardia/fibrillation Torsades de pointes Neutropenia Thrombocytopenia Liver test abnormalities Ketoacidosis and diabetes Hypomagnesemia Myoglobinuria Hematuria
Trimetrexate plus leucovorin	Fever Neutropenia	Liver test abnormalities Morbilliform rash Thrombocytopenia Mucositis
Dapsone	Fever Morbilliform rash Nausea and vomiting	Methemoglobinemia Hemolytic anemia Sulfone syndrome
Clindamycin	Fever Morbilliform rash Diarrhea	Liver test abnormalities *Clostridium difficile* colitis
Primaquine	Nausea Abdominal distress Neutropenia	Methemoglobinemia Hemolytic anemia Hypertension Arrhythmias
Atovaquone	Rash	Fever Nausea and vomiting Liver test abnormalities
Aerosolized pentamidine	Cough Bronchospasm Metallic taste	Contact dermatitis Morbilliform rash Hypoglycemia Pancreatitis Renal impairment

*Reduced to <1000 cells/μl
†Reduced to <50,000 cells/μL.
‡>2 g/dL decline.

Table 387–3 • ADJUNCTIVE CORTICOSTEROIDS* FOR PATIENTS WITH *PNEUMOCYSTIS CARINII* PNEUMONIA AND A-a DO$_2$ ≥ 35 mm Hg OR Pao$_2$ ≤ 70 mm Hg

DRUG	DOSE	TREATMENT DAYS
Oral		
Prednisone	40 mg bid	1–5
	40 mg once daily	6–10
	20 mg once daily	11–21
Intravenous		
Methylprednisolone	30 mg bid	1–5
	30 mg once daily	6–10
	15 mg once daily	11–21

*Efficacy established only when adjunctive corticosteroids are initiated within 72 hours of starting specific treatment for *P. carinii*.

TRIMETREXATE. Trimetrexate (NeuTrexin) is a powerful antifolate drug that binds to the DHFR of *P. carinii* nearly 1500 times more avidly than trimethoprim, and it is concentrated in *P. carinii*. Leucovorin (folinic acid) must be co-administered to protect against bone marrow toxicity. In a comparative study, trimetrexate was effective but inferior to TMP-SMX for moderate to severe episodes. [1] Treatment-limiting toxicity, particularly critical neutropenia, thrombocytopenia, and anemia, occurred significantly more often with TMP-SMX than with trimetrexate.

ADJUNCTIVE CORTICOSTEROIDS. The major breakthrough in the search for more effective therapies for *Pneumocystis* has been the irrefutable evidence that mortality for severe episodes can be reduced nearly twofold by use of corticosteroids within 72 hours after beginning specific anti-*Pneumocystis* therapy (Table 387–3). With adjunctive corticosteroids, oxygen desaturation occurs less often, and fewer patients require mechanical ventilation. [2] Serious adverse consequences are uncommon, perhaps because the course is limited (21 days) and the tapering period is rapid; an increase in mucocutaneous herpes infections was seen in the largest study. However, adjunctive corticosteroids can be deleterious if given with empiric anti-*Pneumocystis* therapy for patients who have pulmonary fungal infection or tuberculosis, because these patients may show initial improvement, which could thereby delay diagnosis and specific antimicrobial therapy. Corticosteroids can also aggravate and accelerate the progression of cutaneous and pulmonary Kaposi's sarcoma.

SALVAGE THERAPY. After respiratory failure has developed, prognosis is poor. Parenteral TMP-SMX, pentamidine, trimetrexate, and clindamycin-primaquine have all been evaluated for salvage in uncontrolled studies and appear to provide limited benefit. Little reason has been put forward to favor any of these, and no data are available to support the use of multiple concurrent therapies.

MILD EPISODES

For mild episodes (Pao$_2$ > 70 mm Hg or A-a DO$_2$ < 35), management should focus on tolerable oral agents that can be used in an ambulatory setting, because mortality rates are low (see Table 387–1). TMP-SMX is inexpensive and can be conveniently given orally, but it causes substantial toxic effects.

TRIMETHOPRIM-DAPSONE. Trimethoprim-dapsone, like TMP-SMX, results in sequential blockade of folate synthesis in *P. carinii*. Dapsone, a sulfone, binds to dihydropteroate synthetase two-fold more avidly than sulfamethoxazole. Treatment-limiting neutropenia and transaminase elevations occur less frequently than with TMP-SMX.

CLINDAMYCIN-PRIMAQUINE. Clindamycin and the antimalarial drug primaquine together have excellent activity against *P. carinii* in a limited cell culture system and in the murine model, but neither agent alone is effective, and the mechanism of action is unclear. The combination has been effective for *Pneumocystis* as initial therapy, with response rates in the range of 90%, regardless of whether clindamycin is given intravenously or orally and whether the dose of primaquine base is 15 or 30 mg/day. Controlled trials

dependent, a lower dose (15 mg/kg/day of trimethoprim) is preferred. Several controlled trials have indicated that this dose results in survival rates greater than or equal to 88% for severe episodes, suggesting that it does not compromise outcome.

PARENTERAL PENTAMIDINE. Parenteral pentamidine is also highly effective. As with TMP-SMX, toxic reactions are common (see Table 387–2). In one study in which patients received a minimum of 14 days of therapy, nephrotoxicity (>1 mg/L rise in serum creatinine) occurred in 64% of patients, hypotension in 27%, and hypoglycemia in 21%. Impaired renal function and hypoglycemia are dose dependent and more likely to be seen after 2 weeks of therapy or a total dosage of more than 4 g. Hypotension generally occurs during or shortly after intravenous infusion and may last several hours, although low blood pressures may persist for several months.

Hypoglycemia is the most treacherous reaction and occurs in 10 to 20% of AIDS patients treated with pentamidine; this results from sudden increases in serum insulin caused by lysis of pancreatic β cells. Because of the prolonged binding of pentamidine to tissue, precipitous hypoglycemia may occur after the drug is discontinued, with fatal reactions occurring up to 2 weeks after the last dose. When hypoglycemia is detected, pentamidine should be discontinued, and patients should be monitored closely with daily capillary glucose measurements for several weeks.

Continued

Infectious Diseases

have not established whether trimethoprim-dapsone and clindamycin-primaquine are as effective as TMP-SMX. **3.4** In a comparative study of these three oral regimens for mild to moderate disease, the frequency of treatment-limiting toxicity effects was not significantly different among the arms of the study, although the specific types of adverse effects were not evenly distributed. Clindamycin-primaquine was the most common cause of severe rash and anemia, whereas TMP-SMX more frequently caused hepatitis, and trimethoprim-dapsone caused nausea and vomiting. Awareness of the potential problems with each of these regimens permits better matching of *Pneumocystis* therapy to the patient's clinical status at diagnosis. The U.S. Public Health Service has not recommended adjunctive corticosteroids for mild episodes because the mortality rate is very low. However, one study indicated that there was less desaturation, better exercise tolerance, and a quicker return of elevated LDH levels to baseline with adjunctive corticosteroids in episodes of mild or moderate severity.

ATOVAQUONE. Atovaquone (Mepron) is an oral hydroxynaphthoquinone originally developed as an antimalarial, and it is well tolerated. The drug inhibits mitochondrial electron transport necessary for the biosynthesis of pyrimidines in protozoa, but its mode of action against *P. carinii* is unknown. In a comparative study of atovaquone for 322 patients with mild to moderate (A-a $DO_2 < 45$) *Pneumocystis* pneumonia, failures due to inadequate therapeutic response occurred in 31% of patients receiving atovaquone and in 16% receiving TMP-SMX ($P = .002$). Mortality rates were also imbalanced, with 1 death in the TMP-SMX group and 11 in the atovaquone arm. Patients in whom atovaquone failed were more likely to have low plasma concentrations (<15 mg/mm) and diarrhea. Atovaquone must be given with fatty foods, because blood levels are two-fold to three-fold lower when it is taken on an empty stomach.

Outcome and Prognosis

Clinical parameters at presentation that are associated with an increased risk for fatal outcome include an elevated serum LDH of more than 500 IU/dL, PaO_2 less than 70 mm Hg or A-a DO_2 more than 35, BAL neutrophils greater than 5%, and low triiodothyronine (T_3) and reverse-T_3 hormone concentrations.

CHANGING THERAPY. It can be difficult to know when therapy is failing in a specific patient. Persistence of fever or lack of improvement on chest radiographs is common, especially during the first several days of treatment. Unchanged or progressive infiltrates frequently occur even in patients who show an ultimate response. Oxygenation reaches its nadir 3 to 4 days after beginning treatment. A sustained respiratory rate greater than 35 per minute and absolute increase in room air A-a DO_2 of more than 20 above baseline have proved to be reproducible end points for failure in clinical trials. These signs provide objective justification for changing therapy and for evaluating other possible complications in the lung. It is important to remember that another concurrent pulmonary diagnosis exists for up to 15% of AIDS patients with *Pneumocystis* pneumonia.

SUPPORTIVE CARE. Evidence suggests that the degree of alveolar damage is the most important determinant of outcome. As with adult respiratory distress syndrome (ARDS), which has histologic features similar to those of severe *Pneumocystis* infection, supportive care is crucial for severely ill patients. Continuous positive airway pressure by facemask improves oxygenation in patients with tachypnea and refractory desaturation with standard masks and may mitigate the need for mechanical ventilation.

MECHANICAL VENTILATION AND INTENSIVE CARE UNIT CARE. The mortality rate for AIDS patients on mechanical ventilators in intensive care units (ICUs) has ranged from 30 to 50% in recent reports, supporting the value of aggressive measures in selected patients. A low albumin level, arterial pH less than 7.35, or need for positive end-expiratory pressure greater than 10 cm H_2O after 96 hours in the ICU portends a several-fold greater risk for a fatal outcome. Patients with better nutritional status and those who have less severe alveolar damage and a normal pH may benefit most from ventilatory support.

Prophylaxis

The U.S. Public Health Service recommends prophylaxis for *Pneumocystis* in patients at high risk for infection (Table 387–4). Those at highest risk include patients with prior *Pneumocystis* infection, those

Table 387–4 • PROPHYLACTIC THERAPIES FOR PREVENTION OF *PNEUMOCYSTIS CARINII* PNEUMONIA

DRUG*	DOSE OR REGIMEN	ALTERNATE DOSE OR REGIMEN
Antifolate Regimens		
Trimethoprim-sulfamethoxazole	1 double-strength tablet daily	1 double-strength tablet 3 times weekly 1 single-strength tablet daily
Dapsone	100-mg tablet daily	50-mg tablet once or twice daily
Dapsone-pyrimethamine	50-mg tablet dapsone daily 50-mg tablet pyrimethamine weekly	None
Aerosolized pentamidine	300 mg monthly by Respirgard II jet nebulizer	None established
Other Regimens		
Atovaquone	1500 mg once daily	None
Primaquine-clindamycin	Unknown	None

*Patients receiving therapy for toxoplasmosis are unlikely to need additional prophylaxis for *Pneumocystis* because pyrimethamine-sulfadiazine has been used successfully to treat *Pneumocystis* pneumonia, and the alternative combination of pyrimethamine-clindamycin is similar to the regimen of primaquine-clindamycin, which is also an effective treatment for *Pneumocystis*.

with fewer than 200 CD4+ T cells, and patients with thrush and a fever higher than 100° F for at least 2 weeks; a prior AIDS-defining illness may also increase the risk of *Pneumocystis* infection. TMP-SMX is the most effective form of prophylaxis. **5** In several studies, the relative hazard of developing *Pneumocystis* was approximately three to four times less with TMP-SMX than with aerosolized pentamidine. In controlled trials, dapsone has been comparable to aerosolized pentamidine but somewhat inferior to TMP-SMX. When combined with pyrimethamine (usually 50 mg given once weekly), this approach is also effective in preventing toxoplasmosis. Atovaquone and dapsone appear equally useful in the sulfa-intolerant patient.

Significant immune recovery in AIDS patients is possible with potent combination antiretroviral therapy. Several studies have demonstrated that *Pneumocystis* prophylaxis may be safely discontinued in patients whose total CD4+ T-cell count has increased above 200 for at least 3 months **6**; prophylaxis should be reintroduced if the cell count falls below 200. An "immune reconstitution syndrome," manifested by a marked inflammatory response and clinical worsening due to a sharp increase in CD4+ T cells during the subclinical phase of *Pneumocystis* infection, has not yet been convincingly demonstrated, as it has for other AIDS-associated opportunistic infections such as cytomegalovirus retinitis or disseminated *Mycobacterium avium* complex infection.

1. Sattler FR, Frame P, Davis R, et al: Trimetrexate with leucovorin versus trimethoprim-sulfamethoxazole for moderate to severe episodes of *Pneumocystis carinii* pneumonia in patients with AIDS: A prospective, controlled multicenter investigation of the AIDS Clinical Trials Protocol 029/031. J Infect Dis 1994;170:165–172.
2. Bozzette SA, Sattler FR, Chui J, et al: A controlled trial of early adjunctive treatment with corticosteroids for *Pneumocystis carinii* pneumonia in the acquired immunodeficiency syndrome. N Engl J Med 1990;323:1451–1457.
3. Safrin S, Finkelstein DM, Feinberg J, et al: Comparison of three regimens for treatment of mild to moderate *Pneumocystis carinii* pneumonia in patients with AIDS: A double-blind, randomized trial of oral trimethoprim-sulfamethoxazole, dapsone-trimethoprim, and clindamycin-primaquine. Ann Intern Med 1996;124:792–802.
4. Toma E, Fournier S, Dumont M, et al: Clindamycin-primaquine versus trimethoprim-sulfamethoxazole as primary therapy for *Pneumocystis carinii* pneumonia in AIDS: A randomized, double blind pilot trial. Clin Infect Dis 1993;17:178–184.
5. Hardy DW, Feinberg J, Finkelstein DM, et al: A controlled trial of trimethoprim-sulfamethoxazole or aerosolized pentamidine for secondary prophylaxis of *Pneumocystis carinii* pneumonia in patients with the acquired immunodeficiency syndrome: AIDS Clinical Trials Group Protocol 021. N Engl J Med 1992;327:1842–1848.
6. Lopez JC, Miro JM, Pena JM, Podzamczer D, and the GESIDA 04/98 Study Group: A randomized trial of the discontinuation of primary and secondary prophylaxis against *Pneumocystis carinii* pneumonia after HAART in patients with HIV infection. N Engl J Med 2001;344:159–167.

SUGGESTED READINGS
Mussini C, Pezzotti P, Antinori A, et al: Discontinuation of secondary prophylaxis for *Pneumocystis carinii* pneumonia in human immunodeficiency virus-infected patients: A randomized trial by the CIOP Study Group. Clin Infect Dis 2003;36:645–

651. Patients who present with symptoms after discontinuation of secondary prophylaxis should be evaluated for PCP despite a high CD4 count and complete virus suppression.

Roblot F, Le Moal G, Godet C, et al: Pneumocystis carinii pneumonia in patients with hematologic malignancies: A descriptive study. J Infect 2003;47:19–27. *PCP can occur with various hematologic malignancies, and its prognosis remains poor.*

Stringer JR, Beard CB, Miller RF, et al: A new name (*Pneumocystis jiroveci*) for pneumocystis from humans. Emerg Infect Dis 2002;8:891–896. *The organism that causes human PCP has been renamed.*

388 MUCORMYCOSIS

David A. Stevens

Definition

Mucormycosis is an acute and rapidly developing fungal infection caused by fungi of the class Zygomycetes. In healthy hosts, these organisms seldom cause infection. However, in debilitated or immunosuppressed hosts, they produce a fulminant opportunistic infection, resulting in marked tissue destruction. Several predisposing conditions have been identified. The infection is most commonly associated with diabetic ketoacidosis. Prolonged treatment with antibiotics, corticosteroids, and cytotoxic drugs and, most recently, with the use of deferoxamine in dialysis patients also has been associated with mucormycosis, as have severe malnutrition, hematologic malignancies, and extensive burns.

The clinical characteristics of mucormycosis and its treatment are summarized in Table 388–1.

Pathogens

The pathogenic zygomycetes are largely in the order Mucorales, which is related to the term for this infection, mucormycosis. Zygomycosis has also been used to refer to the disease caused by organisms of the class, but that term would include diseases due to fungi of the order Entomophthorales. The latter diseases usually are different from those caused by Mucorales organisms (i.e., largely superficial infections) and are rare in North America. The Mucorales pathogens are morphologically distinct. Their hyphae are nonseptated, broad, and variable in size and shape. Branching of the hyphae usually is at right angles. Species of the genera *Rhizopus* and *Mucor* are the common pathogens of this group. Other genera, including *Absidia, Cunninghamella, Rhizomucor,* and *Apophysomyces,* have also been reported to cause disease. These fungi cannot be differentiated histopathologically. Further speciation requires culturing the pathogen and characterizing the isolates by their morphologic and physiologic features.

Epidemiology

The Mucorales organisms are ubiquitous saprophytic fungi and are abundant in nature. They have been recovered from bread, fruits, vegetables, soil, and manure. These fungi have been isolated from the

Table 388–1 • MUCORMYCOSIS: CLINICAL CHARACTERISTICS AND TREATMENT

Causative fungus	The order Mucorales; *Rhizopus, Mucor* species most common
Primary geographic distribution	Ubiquitous: air, bread, fruit, vegetables, soil, manure
Primary route of acquisition	Inhaling spores
Principal sites of disease	Rhinocerebral, pulmonary, cutaneous, gastrointestinal, disseminated, central nervous system (CNS)
Opportunistic infection in compromised hosts	Pulmonary, rhinocerebral
Drug of choice for most patients	Amphotericin B
Alternative therapy	Amphotericin combined with rifampin, azoles, flucytosine

Table 388–2 • CLINICAL MANIFESTATIONS OF MUCORMYCOSIS

Rhinocerebral	Gastrointestinal
Pulmonary	Widely disseminated
Cutaneous	Central nervous system

nose, stool, and sputum of healthy individuals. Despite their widespread distribution, they cause disease infrequently. Fortunately, even in the severely immunocompromised hosts, mucormycosis remains a rare opportunistic infection. The disease is not contagious.

Pathogenesis and Pathology

There is no unifying concept of the pathogenesis of mucormycosis. In diseases of the airways (e.g., sinus, lung), the infection is presumed to originate from inhaled spores, although the lung may also be involved because of bloodstream invasion. Diabetic patients appear to be more frequently colonized. Whereas normal human serum can inhibit their growth, serum obtained from patients with diabetic ketoacidosis is not inhibitory and may even promote fungal growth. Undefined defects of macrophages and neutrophils contribute to the loss of immunity against this infection in the susceptible host. Corticosteroids weaken normal inhibitors of spore germination in tissue. Unlike most pathogenic fungi, these can grow in the absence of oxygen.

Invasion, thrombosis, and necrosis are the characteristic findings in this disease. After the fungal spores have germinated at the site of infection, the hyphal elements are very aggressive and tend to invade blood vessels, nerves, lymphatics, and tissues. The infarction leads to further tissue hypoxia and acidosis, resulting in a vicious cycle that enhances rapid growth and infection. The paucity of a granulomatous reaction is quite characteristic. The fungal hyphae sometimes have little or no inflammation around them.

Clinical Manifestations

Mucormycosis can manifest as at least six distinct clinical entities, depending on the types of predisposing factors of the patient and the portal of entry of the organism (Table 388–2).

Rhinocerebral mucormycosis is the most common presentation, accounting for more than 75% of the cases in the literature. It frequently affects the poorly controlled diabetic patient who is also in ketoacidosis. It has also been reported in patients with hematologic malignancies who have been neutropenic for an extended period and who have received broad-spectrum antibacterial drugs or immunosuppressive therapy, in other acidotic patients, and in those with azotemia. This can be one of the most rapidly fatal fungal diseases if left undiagnosed. Hyphae invade the paranasal sinuses and palate from the oronasal cavity. From the sinuses, especially the ethmoid

sinus, the infection spreads to involve the retro-orbital region or the central nervous system (CNS). Epistaxis, severe unilateral headache, alteration in mental status, and eye symptoms such as lacrimation, irritation, or periorbital anesthesia are common symptoms. Examination of the nose may reveal the classic black necrotic turbinates (too often mistaken for dried blood) or nasal septum perforation. However, at the early stage of infection, the nasal mucosa may appear only inflamed and friable. Facial cellulitis and palatal necrosis may be seen. The early eye findings include mild proptosis, periorbital edema, decreased visual acuity, or lid swelling. In more advanced orbital involvement, exophthalmos, complete ophthalmoplegia, conjunctival hemorrhage, blindness, fixed and dilated pupil, and corneal anesthesia may be found. These conditions result

Continued

from fungal invasion of the roof of the orbit, affecting the nerves (i.e., third, fourth, and sixth cranial nerves and the ophthalmic branch of the fifth cranial nerve), muscles, and orbital vessels, a condition also known as the *orbital apex syndrome*. The infection can spread through the superior orbital fissure or the cribriform plate to involve the brain. Cavernous sinus thrombosis is a frequent complication, usually resulting from hematogenous spread from the ophthalmic veins.

This spread results in additional cranial nerve involvement outside the orbital apex, specifically the trigeminal nerve ganglion and the root of the facial nerve, leading to ipsilateral paresthesia of the face or peripheral facial palsy. Internal carotid artery thrombosis, resulting from retrograde spread from the ophthalmic artery or invasion from the cavernous sinus, is another late complication, leading to cerebral infarction. The middle ear may be involved by means of the blood, cerebrospinal fluid (CSF), or eustachian tube.

The radiographic manifestations are nonspecific. Plain roentgenograms of the sinuses and orbits may reveal nodular thickening of the mucosa of multiple sinuses, usually without air-fluid levels, or spotty destruction of the bone through the walls of the sinuses or into the orbit. Computed tomography (CT) or magnetic resonance imaging (MRI) is useful in better defining the bone destruction and soft tissue involvement, which may be important in guiding subsequent surgical intervention. The CSF findings are usually nonspecific and often normal even in the presence of CNS involvement. The common findings are pleocytosis, with about 50% polymorphonuclear cells and slight protein elevation; hypoglycorrhachia is rare. Results of smear and culture of CSF are usually negative for fungus, even in cases with documented meningeal involvement. Several infectious diseases can produce a similar picture. Black necrotic lesions may also be seen with invasive aspergillosis and with infections by *Pseudomonas aeruginosa* or *Pseudallescheria boydii*. The only definitive method of differentiating these possibilities is by examination of tissue. Cavernous sinus thrombosis due to *Staphylococcus aureus*, as well as rhinoscleroma, aggressive orbital tumor, midline granuloma, and other fungal infections, can mimic the disease.

Pulmonary mucormycosis usually occurs in patients with hematologic malignancies or diabetes. The presentation usually is acute, and the patients are often profoundly ill, with variable complaints of cough and fever. No pathognomonic clinical or radiographic findings exist. Sputum culture usually is negative. Antemortem diagnosis is often missed because of the acuteness of the illness, the lack of consideration of the diagnosis, and the need for tissue to establish the diagnosis. Renal insufficiency, metabolic acidosis, or neutropenia are associated with a worse outcome.

Invasive pulmonary aspergillosis or other mycoses, nocardiosis, other bacterial infections such as *Pseudomonas* infection, malignant invasion, hemorrhage, and pulmonary embolism or infarction may mimic the presentation of pulmonary mucormycosis.

Cutaneous mucormycosis is rare and is primarily a nosocomial infection in burn and blunt trauma victims. Local infection has resulted from using contaminated elastic bandages. The involved area is erythematous and painful, with various degrees of central necrosis that can progress to gangrenous cellulitis. Cutaneous infection can also occur as a result of dissemination from another site of involvement. Skin and subcutaneous infections can occur in diabetics.

Gastrointestinal mucormycosis is the least common form of infection. It is seen primarily in patients suffering from intrinsic abnormalities of the gastrointestinal tract or severe malnutrition. The infection is thought to arise from fungi entering the body with food. Any part of the gastrointestinal tract is susceptible to infection, with the stomach, terminal ileum, and colon being the most common sites. Wall invasion, ischemic infarction, and ulceration are characteristic. The diagnosis is frequently made at autopsy. Gastrointestinal zygomycosis, an entity similar to that caused by *Basidiobolus ranarum*, usually occurs in otherwise healthy individuals and responds to surgery.

Disseminated mucormycosis is defined as infection occurring in two or more noncontiguous organ systems. The distant sites are infected by blood stream invasion from a local site. Although any organ can be affected, the lungs and CNS are the two common sites. The outcome of this infection is almost invariably fatal.

Isolated CNS mucormycosis results from hematogenous spread and is seen primarily in intravenous drug addicts.

Diagnosis

The diagnosis of any form of mucormycosis depends on direct and histologic examinations of scrapings and biopsies of necrotic material. In contrast to most fungi, these organisms are readily seen in hematoxylin and eosin-stained tissue. The Gomori methenamine silver stain usually is adequate, but some special fungus stains, such as periodic acid–Schiff, do not demonstrate the organism well. However, a more rapid but preliminary diagnosis can sometimes be made by demonstrating hyphal elements after potassium hydroxide digestion of a fresh tissue scraping. The alkali digests some of the tissue debris but not the fungus, which makes identifying the fungi easier. Swabs of discharge or abnormal tissue are not adequate and can give erroneous information. Fungal cultures are occasionally positive, but a negative culture result does not exclude the diagnosis nor make it less likely. Teasing rather than homogenization of the tissue may increase the yield of cultures. The media used for culturing these fungi should not contain cycloheximide. No skin tests or serologic methods are adequate for diagnosing mucormycosis, and blood cultures are not helpful.

 ## Treatment

Successful outcome in treating this aggressive infection relies on early diagnosis by invasive procedures, immediate correction of the underlying predisposing condition, aggressive surgical débridement, and early systemic amphotericin therapy. Endoscopic surgery has a role in early rhinocerebral cases. Amphotericin B is the only drug with proven clinical efficacy, and a high therapeutic dosage (e.g., 1.0 to 1.5 mg/kg/day, if tolerated) should be achieved as soon as possible. This may be reduced to alternate-day dosing after the patient is stabilized. Typically, a cumulative dose of 2 to 5 g may be needed to achieve cure. Lipid-complexed amphotericin could enable continued aggressive therapy in the nephrotoxic patient. Although local irrigation of infected sites with amphotericin is an unproven adjunct, given the difficulties in perfusion of infected areas because of the tendency to thrombosis, this measure seems logical. Similarly, potentiation of amphotericin with other drugs (e.g., rifampin, azoles, flucytosine) is of unproven benefit, but given the poor results with conventional therapy, this approach should be considered if susceptibility testing can be done in vitro with the patient's isolate to show synergy and exclude antagonism. The azoles appear to be of little benefit, except itraconazole for basidiobolomycosis. Improvement of survival may necessitate repeated major surgical débridement of necrotic tissue, resulting in significant disfiguring. Hyperbaric oxygen therapy may be of some value in deterring progression. Colony-stimulating factors may accelerate neutrophil return in neutropenic patients. If the patient survives, major reconstructive surgery may be needed. Pulmonary lesions may be amenable to surgical removal.

Prognosis

Mucormycosis remains a disease with guarded prognosis. It is difficult to ascertain accurately the effectiveness of any therapeutic approach because the disease is uncommon and there is a general bias toward reporting cases only if therapy is effective. With the introduction of amphotericin B in 1961, it is generally accepted that the survival rate significantly improved. Rhinocerebral mucormycosis is the most common form of infection and is thought to have an overall mortality rate of about 50%. Patients who develop hemiplegia or nasal deformity have higher mortality rates. Pulmonary or disseminated mucormycosis frequently escapes antemortem diagnosis, and only a handful of patients have been reported to recover from these conditions. Superficial infections, particularly in immunocompetent patients, can be successfully treated with débridement and antifungal therapy. Deeper cutaneous infections of the extremities usually require amputation, and when the head or trunk is involved, the condition is commonly fatal.

The most aggressive approach we can take toward this lethal disease is rapid diagnosis and immediate institution of surgical débridement plus systemic and local chemotherapy.

SUGGESTED READINGS

Lee FY, Mossad SB, Adal KA: Pulmonary mucormycosis: The last 30 years. Arch Intern Med 1999;159:1301–1309. *Emphasizes improved survival in recent years.*

Ribes JA, Vanover-Sams CL, Baker DJ: Zygomycetes in human disease. Clin Microbiol Rev 2000;13:236–301. *Comprehensive, 65-page review with 522 references. Particularly good details on the less common Mucorales, the differential microbiologic diagnosis of the pathogens, and the Entomophthorales.*

Yohai RA, Bullock JD, Aziz AA, Markert RJ: Survival factors in rhino-orbital-cerebral mucormycosis. Surv Ophthalmol 1994;39:3–22. *Comprehensive review of 208 cases in the literature since 1970. Factors are identified that help determine prognosis. Standard treatment is discussed, as well as data on hyperbaric oxygen.*

389 MYCETOMA

D. P. Kontoyiannis

Definition

Mycetoma (a tumor produced by fungi) was first described in 1842 in the Madura district of India, hence the terms "Madura foot," "maduromycosis," and "maduromycetoma." However, there is evidence of its existence from as far back as the Byzantine era.

Mycetoma is a chronic, slowly progressive infection that starts in the subcutaneous tissue and spreads across tissue planes to contiguous structures. The disease has diverse etiology; also, the offending organism is inoculated into the subcutaneous tissues by trauma typically associated with soil contamination. The hallmarks of mycetoma are the presence of "grains" that consist of colonies of the infectious organism and chronically draining sinus tracts. There is some confusion in the literature, however, because the term *pulmonary mycetoma* is used inappropriately to describe fungus balls typically caused by *Aspergillus* species that colonize a preexisting lung cavity; the term aspergilloma is more appropriate for this entity, the pathogenesis of which is distinctly different from that of true mycetoma.

Etiology

Two groups of pathogens, each of which accounts for approximately 50% of the cases, cause mycetoma: (1) the filamentous aerobic actinomycetes, hence the term actinomycetoma, and (2) a wide range of saprophytic soil and woody plant fungi, hence the term eumycetoma. A variety of *Nocardia* species (e.g., *Nocardia brasiliensis, Nocardia asteroides*), *Actinomadura* species (e.g., *Actinomadura pelletierii, Actinomadura madurae*), and *Streptomyces* species (e.g., *Streptomyces somaliensis*) have been reported to cause actinomycetoma. Even more numerous are the agents that cause eumycetoma, such as *Madurella* species (e.g., *Madurella mycetomatis, Madurella grisea*), which are probably the most prevalent mycetoma-causative fungal species worldwide, as well as *Fusarium* species, *Acremonium* species, *Pseudallescheria boydii, Exophiala* species, and *Curvularia* species. There is controversy about whether the various dermatophytes and *Aspergillus* species can cause mycetoma. Eumycetoma is often further characterized on the basis of the color of the grains; specifically, white to yellow grain mycetomas (white piedra) are typically caused by hyalohyphomycetes (e.g., *P. boydii, Fusarium* species, *Acremonium* species), and black grain eumycetomas (black piedra) are caused by *Madurella* species and other less common fungi. However, the geographic distribution of the fungi that cause black grain eumycetoma is variable.

Epidemiology

Although mycetoma has a broad worldwide distribution, it occurs primarily in the tropical and, to a lesser extent, the temperate zones. More specifically, the infection is quite prevalent in India, Mexico, Central America, South America, the Middle East, and especially sub-Saharan Africa (the "mycetoma belt"); mycetoma is more sporadic in North America and Europe. In addition, eumycetoma is more common in India and Africa, and actinomycetoma is more common in Latin America. Furthermore, the causative agents of mycetoma differ in their geographic distribution. For example, *P. boydii* is the most common agent of mycetoma in North America, and *Actinomadura* and *Nocardia* species are predominant in Central America and South America. Finally, *S. somaliensis* and *M. mycetomatis* are predominant in sub-Saharan Africa and India.

Pathogenesis

Local trauma introduces a mycetoma-causative organism into the skin and subcutaneous tissues and initiates a chain of events that leads to chronic, suppurative granulomatous inflammation, tumefaction, formation of multiple fistulous tracts and sinuses, deep abscesses, fibrosis and scar formation, and extension to adjacent connective tissue across the lines of least resistance (fascia) and ultimately to bones, muscles, nerves, and tendon sheaths, leading to gross anatomic distortion of the affected site. In addition, a chronic suppurative granuloma featuring reactive fibrosis and grains (sclerotia), which is a matrix consisting of vegetative aggregates of the etiologic agents and host-derived inflammatory response, is characteristic of mycetoma in histologic sections. This infection is not contagious, however. Even though the genetics and immunopathogenesis of mycetoma are not well defined, it appears that some affected persons have impaired or delayed hypersensitivity reactions.

Clinical Manifestations and Natural History

The clinical manifestations and natural history of mycetoma are variable and, to some degree, related to the pathogenic agent involved. For example, the progression of eumycetoma tends to be slower than that of actinomycetoma. In addition, eumycetoma lesions tend to be more confined and have less inflammation and fewer granulomas and fistulas but more fibrosis when compared with actinomycetoma lesions. Furthermore, male mycetoma patients predominate (5:1 over female patients), and the disease is typically seen in rural areas and in persons susceptible to local trauma and contamination from soil (e.g., thorns). Hence, farmers, gardeners, wood cutters, herders, and people who work outside while barefoot are more susceptible to this infection. Not surprisingly, the foot is the most common site involved in mycetoma (Fig. 389–1), but any other part of the body, such as the hands, thighs, torso, and back of the head, may become involved. Painless nodular and/or papular swelling is the most common early manifestation of mycetoma, which is followed by a slow evolution to painless woody induration. This infection typically runs a chronic, relentless course, sometimes spanning several decades. It is characterized by recurring, vicious cycles of suppuration, draining sinuses, bacterial superinfection, and scar formation. Old sinuses may close up, but new ones may occur, and satellite lesions may be seen. Constitutional symptoms are surprisingly rare. In particular, the presence of fever indicates bacterial superinfection. Bone involvement mimicking clinically chronic osteomyelitis with osteolytic cavitary bone lesions (seen in x-ray, computed tomography [CT], or magnetic resonance imaging [MRI] studies), osteoporosis, and reactive periosteal bone formation may occur; such involvement can be substantial. However, because nerves are relatively spared from involvement, neuropathic manifestations are uncommon. Inexorable limb deformity and misuse because of destruction of deeper tissues may be seen in chronic, refractory, and advanced cases. Finally, because mycetoma does not spread hematogenously, visceral dissemination is not seen. However, because lymphatic spread may occur (typical incidence of 1 to 3% but more common with actinomycetoma and especially after surgery), regional lymphadenitis may develop.

Infectious Diseases

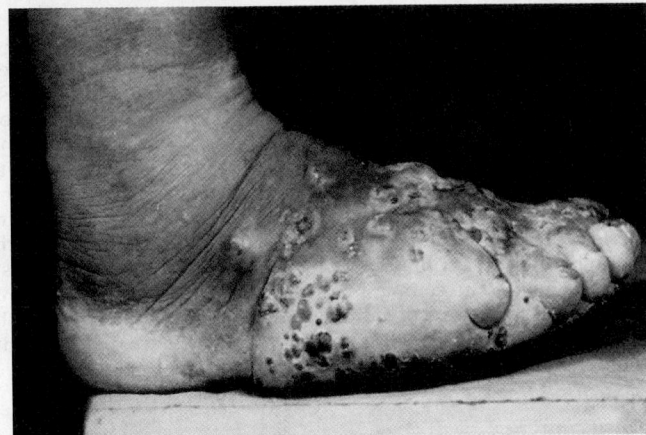

FIGURE 389–1 • A 40-year-old farmer from rural Venezuela with a 10-year history of foot edema and slowly progressive deformity following an injury caused by being struck by a hammer presented with chronic crusted plaques, multiple confluent tender abscesses with fistulization, and release of black grains. The range of motion of the patient's ankle and foot joints was limited, but the joints were not painful. A deep skin biopsy with hematoxylin and eosin staining, periodic acid–Schiff staining, foot radiography, sampling of black grain smears, and a mycology culture were performed. The foot radiograph showed osteofibrosis, destruction of articular surfaces, osteoporosis, and ankylosis, and *Madurella* spp grew in the culture. (Courtesy of Dr. M. Mendoza, Instituto De Biomedicina, Laboratorio de Micología, San Jose Caracas, Venezuela.)

Diagnosis

Mycetoma, especially in its advanced forms, has a rather characteristic presentation that facilitates diagnosis with a high degree of accuracy, especially in endemic areas. For instance, the macroscopic and microscopic appearance of grains in pus-filled draining sinuses frequently allows presumptive diagnosis of the offending pathogen. However, basing the diagnosis on the presence of grains in tissue may be difficult. Furthermore, grains may be contaminated by surface bacteria or fungi. Therefore, a deep-tissue biopsy specimen is ideal for staining with hematoxylin and eosin, and appropriate selective bacterial (e.g., Löwenstein-Jensen culture medium) and fungal (e.g., blood agar and modified Sabouraud dextrose agar with antibiotics) cultures and stains (Gram stain, modified Ziehl-Neelsen stain, Gomori methenamine silver, periodic acid–Schiff stain) are preferable for primary detection. The culture should be maintained for several weeks, as some of the causative agents of mycetoma (e.g., *Nocardia* and *Streptomyces* spp) can take 4 to 6 weeks to grow. Serologic tests for diagnosis and follow-up after therapy remain limited to only certain institutions.

Differential Diagnosis

The specific manifestations of mycetoma are sometimes confused with other rare entities. For example, mycetoma must occasionally be distinguished from chronic cutaneous fungal infections such as sporotrichosis (mycetomatous lymphatic sporotrichosis) and dermatophytic mycetoma. The latter infection, which is typically seen in Africans and sometimes called pseudomycetoma, is a painless granulomatous induration of the skin and subcutaneous tissues caused by ringworm that may be associated with grains consisting of fungi. However, unlike mycetoma, dermatophytic mycetoma is confined to the skin and subcutaneous tissue and does not spread to fasciae or bone. Similarly, chronic severe botryomycosis (typically caused by gram-positive cocci) with purulent exudates, grains, and draining sinus tracts may be confused with mycetoma; however, the presence of visceral dissemination supports a diagnosis of (severe) botryomycosis. Actinomycosis, which is caused by endogenous microaerophilic actinomycetes (part of normal mucosa flora), also has a propensity for grains and formation of draining sinus tracts, but unlike mycetoma, its location (e.g., neck, chest, pelvis) is rather characteristic. In addition, differentiation between mycetomas with bone involvement and chronic osteomyelitis may be difficult. Finally, in cases of mycetoma without draining sinus tracts, benign or malignant skin tumors, chronic granulomatous lesions (e.g., thorn granuloma, cutaneous tuberculosis), chromomycosis, and verrucous leishmaniasis are diagnoses that should be excluded.

Rx Treatment

Therapy for mycetoma should be individualized. Optimal management has not been well defined, however, because the literature consists of rather heterogeneous and uncontrolled studies. No single agent is effective against all causative agents of mycetoma. Hence, successful treatment necessitates a reliable diagnosis, differentiation between actinomycetoma and mycetoma, and identification of the causative agent. Also, the degree of tissue invasion, especially bone involvement, site affected, and specific etiologic diagnosis determine the type and intensity of therapy; in general, considering the refractoriness of eumycetoma to medical therapy, surgery plays a more prominent role. In contrast, considering the satisfactory response of actinomycetoma to medical therapy (success rate of up to 90%) and recognized risk of lymphatic spread following surgery, chronic antibiotic administration is the mainstay of actinomycetoma management.

For actinomycetoma, treatment consists primarily of chronic antibiotic therapy (for at least 9 to 12 months) in conjunction with limited debulking surgery in selected cases; combination therapy designed for potential synergy is preferred. A variety of drugs (trimethoprim-sulfamethoxazole, tetracyclines, dapsone, streptomycin) have been used in different sequences and combinations according to the specific cause of actinomycetoma (e.g., trimethoprim-sulfamethoxazole with or without dapsone for *Nocardia* spp or *S. somaliensis*, streptomycin with dapsone for *A. madurae*). Parenteral streptomycin is usually reserved for cases that do not respond to oral therapy. Responses to these drugs tend to occur slowly (within at least 1 month). Also, relapse is not uncommon, and multiple cycles of therapy may be needed for chronically recurrent disease. Side effects and compliance issues after prolonged administration of antibiotics are common problems.

For eumycetoma, however, medical therapy has produced mixed results. The best results were obtained with prolonged (9 to 12 months) use of oral imidazoles (e.g., 200 mg of ketoconazole given twice a day for *M. mycetomatis*). The experience using newer triazoles (e.g., 200 mg of itraconazole given twice a day) is not as extensive or encouraging, however. Also, intravenous amphotericin B and its lipid formulations have been used for refractory cases with rather disappointing results. This is not surprising because most eumycetoma-causative agents are resistant to amphotericin B in vitro.

The need for and extent of surgery for mycetoma depend on the etiologic agent and, more important, extent of the lesion. Early wide-margin surgery for early localized lesions is curative. Although it is potentially curative, major disfiguring or mutilating surgery (e.g., amputation) is reserved for very advanced or refractory cases. Furthermore, primary reliance on surgery could result in recurrence or even spreading of the disease because of incomplete excision.

Finally, the prognosis for mycetoma depends on the site and degree of tissue involvement (e.g., worse with involvement of the back because of poor healing or in the presence of bone destruction) and, more important, the timeliness of the diagnosis and monitoring of recurrence and extension to other tissues, especially bone. CT and MRI are important modalities for early detection of bone involvement. Finally, education of persons at risk for mycetoma in endemic areas is crucial for prompt recognition and a better outcome of this difficult-to-manage, chronic infection.

SUGGESTED READINGS

Maiti PK, Ray A, Bandyopadhay S: Epidemiological aspects of mycetoma from a retrospective study of 264 cases in West Bengal. Trop Med Int Health 2002;7:788–792. *This large recent study describes key epidemiologic features of actinomycetomas and eumycetomas from an endemic area.*

390 DEMATIACEOUS FUNGAL INFECTIONS

Peter G. Pappas

Definition

Dematiaceous fungi represent a large group of fungal organisms characterized by the presence of abundant melanin in the cell wall, giving rise to a brown-black coloration on artificial culture media. A related term, *phaeohyphomycosis,* refers broadly to infection by these pigmented fungi. The two items are often used interchangeably, but when dematiaceous fungal infections are reviewed, three distinct clinical conditions are encountered: eumycetoma (e.g., Madura foot), chromomycosis (i.e., chromoblastomycosis), and phaeohyphomycosis. This chapter focuses on the latter two entities.

Etiology

More than 100 dematiaceous fungi causing colonization or disease have been isolated from humans. The more common organisms and their related conditions are listed in Table 390–1. The taxonomy of the dematiaceous fungi is somewhat confusing because these agents belong to different classes, including Hyphomycetes, Ascomycetes, Basidiomycetes, Coelomycetes, and Zygomycetes. The most common agents of phaeohyphomycosis include species in the following genera: *Bipolaris, Curvularia, Exophiala, Cladophialophora, Alternaria, Exserohilum, Dactylaria, Wangiella, Phialophora,* and *Phaeoacromonium.* These agents are ubiquitous saprophytes of soil and decaying matter, and some are important plant pathogens. In tissue, these organisms exist as yeastlike cells, septated hyphae, or a combination of yeast and hyphae. Many have a histologic appearance similar to *Aspergillus* and *Fusarium* species, but they may be distinguished on the basis of positive melanin staining using the Fontana-Masson procedure.

Chromomycosis is a chronic skin and soft tissue infection that is observed most frequently in the tropics. Virtually all cases of chromomycosis are caused by three species: *Fonsecaea pedrosoi, Cladophialophora carrionii,* and *Phialophora verrucosa.* The distinctive histologic appearance is characterized by the presence of thick-walled, dark brown bodies known as *sclerotic cells* or *copper pennies,* which represent individual organisms and may be seen in clusters or as single cells. The etiologic fungi are indistinguishable on histologic examination of tissue.

Table 390–1 • DEMATIACEOUS FUNGI AND ASSOCIATED CONDITIONS

CLINICAL CONDITION	COMMON ETIOLOGIC AGENTS
Chromomycosis	*Fonsecaea pedrosi*
	Cladophialophora carrionii
	Phialophora verrucosa
Cutaneous or subcutaneous condition	*Exophiala jeanselmei*
	Wangiella dermatitidis
	Phialophora spp.
	Bipolaris spp.
	Alternaria spp.
Sinusitis	*Bipolaris* spp.
	Curvularia spp.
	Exserohilum spp.
	Alternaria spp.
Central nervous system	*Cladophialophora bantiana*
	Dactylaria gallopava
	Ramichloridium spp.
Disseminated	*Wangiella dermatitidis*
	Exophiala jeanselmei
	Bipolaris spp.
	Dactylaria gallopava
	Phialophora spp.

Epidemiology and Pathogenesis

The agents of chromomycosis and phaeohyphomycosis are found worldwide. While there is no unique endemic area for most of these infections, some observations are relevant. Allergic fungal sinusitis associated with dematiaceous fungi appears to be more common in the southern United States. Chronic infections of the lower extremities are more commonly seen in men and in tropical areas. Chromomycosis is more prevalent in rural populations in the tropics and is hyperendemic in certain geographic areas such as Madagascar, where most infection is caused by *Cladophialophora carrionii.*

Most cutaneous infections occur as a result of minor skin trauma and direct inoculation of the organism. In the nosocomial setting, infection due to contaminated intravascular catheters and intravenous fluids are reported. Other risk factors include intravenous drug abuse, chronic sinusitis, fresh water immersion, and chronic corticosteroid therapy.

In the developed world, phaeohyphomycosis is an important emerging fungal infection, particularly among immunocompromised patients such as solid organ transplant and hematopoietic stem cell transplant recipients, patients with prolonged neutropenia, and other chronically immunocompromised individuals. Phaeohyphomycosis is reported among human immunodeficiency virus (HIV)–infected patients but is far less common than other opportunistic fungi. Extracutaneous invasive disease occurs in otherwise normal patients but is much less common.

Clinical Manifestations

Chromomycosis manifests as a cutaneous or subcutaneous lesion that may range in size from a small papule to a large plaque. Lesions may remain unchanged in size and consistency for months or years, although most tend to progress in the absence of specific therapy. Single or multiple lesions may be seen, and ulceration may occur. Chronic lesions may become dry and crusted with a raised border, which may be smooth or irregular. Multiple lesions can coalesce to form larger plaques that develop central scarring. Occasionally, lesions develop a verrucous, warty appearance. The differential diagnosis includes other fungal infections such as blastomycosis, coccidioidomycosis, sporotrichosis, histoplasmosis, and paracoccidioidomycosis. Nocardiosis and cutaneous mycobacteriosis also can mimic the lesions of chromomycosis. Cutaneous lesions usually remain confined to one anatomic site, although nodular lymphangitis and autoinoculation resulting in multifocal cutaneous disease may occur. Disseminated disease involving visceral organs is rare.

Phaeohyphomycosis is associated with several well-described clinical syndromes. *Superficial* infection is characterized by tinea nigra and black piedra. Tinea nigra is a darkening of the skin caused by growth in the stratum corneum of *Phaeoannellomyces werneckii.* Black piedra is associated with the development of focal thickening on the hair shaft and results from colonization of the shaft by *Piedraia hortae. Cutaneous* phaeohyphomycosis involves deeper skin structures, resulting in dermatomycosis and onychomycosis, and is frequently due to agents such as *Scytalidium* and *Phyllosticta* species.

Subcutaneous phaeohyphomycosis is relatively common and may be confused with chromomycosis. Patients present with discrete subcutaneous nodules or cysts that result from direct inoculation or penetrating trauma. The most common organisms are *Exophiala jeanselmei, Wangiella dermatitidis, and Phialophora* spp. *Mycotic keratitis* due to *Curvularia, Exophiala,* and *Exserohilum* species has occurred after corneal trauma or surgery.

Foreign body–related infections are seen in patients receiving chronic ambulatory peritoneal dialysis who develop fungal peritonitis and among patients with indwelling intravenous catheters.

Fungal sinusitis is commonly associated with dematiaceous fungi and can manifest as allergic fungal sinusitis, a fungus ball (eumycetoma) in a sinus cavity, and invasive fungal sinusitis associated with extension into the bone, soft tissue, and central nervous system. This latter manifestation is indistinguishable from rhinocerebral zygomycosis or invasive aspergillus sinusitis. *Bipolaris, Curvularia,* and *Alternaria* species are the most common organisms causing invasive fungal sinusitis.

Continued

Systemic phaeohyphomycosis may result from direct extension from a colonized area or dissemination from a distant source. Most patients with systemic disease have significant underlying immunosuppression, and the organisms have a proclivity for involvement of the brain, lungs, endocardium, and other visceral organs. Among patients with central nervous system disease, *Cladophialophora bantiana, Dactylaria gallopava,* and *Ramichloridium* spp. are the most common etiologic agents.

Diagnosis

The diagnosis of phaeohyphomycosis is suggested by direct examination of a clinical specimen using a 10% potassium hydroxide preparation or special stains to demonstrate pigmentation in the cell walls of these organisms. For patients with chromomycosis, the finding of sclerotic bodies or copper pennies on skin biopsy is characteristic, and special stains are usually unnecessary. For patients with other forms of phaeohyphomycosis, the Fontana-Masson stain is useful in distinguishing organisms with significant melanin content. Culture remains the "gold standard" by which a specific etiologic diagnosis is established, and the identity of the organism is largely based on colonial and microscopic morphology. Serologic studies and molecular diagnostics usually are not available for these organisms.

Rx Treatment

For patients with localized disease, surgical excision is important in the management of chromomycosis and phaeohyphomycosis. In many instances, surgical excision of a cutaneous or subcutaneous lesion is curative, although antifungal therapy is usually given in conjunction with surgery. There are limited clinical studies that assess the efficacy of antifungal therapy for these conditions. Historically, 5-flucytosine (5-FC, 150 mg/kg/day) has been advocated for the oral therapy of chromomycosis based on moderate in vitro activity and clinical experience. Because of limited availability, the need for prolonged therapy, and the necessity of monitoring serum levels, 5-FC is uncommonly used for this purpose. Amphotericin B has only modest in vitro activity against most of the dematiaceous fungi and is most often reserved for patients with life-threatening or disseminated disease. The triazoles, including itraconazole (200 mg PO twice daily) and voriconazole (200 mg PO twice daily), demonstrate the best in vitro activity, although clinical studies with these agents are limited. Terbinafine (500 mg, PO twice daily) has also been used successfully in the treatment of chromomycosis and is an effective alternative to azole therapy. Investigational triazoles, including posaconazole and ravuconazole, demonstrate excellent in vitro activity against the dematiaceous fungi and will likely be effective agents in the clinical setting. The length of therapy with any of the oral antifungal agents for dematiaceous fungal infections is unclear, but treatment should probably be continued for at least 6 months or 1 month after resolution of all signs and symptoms of disease.

SUGGESTED READINGS

Adam RD, Paquin ML, Peterson EA: Phaeohyphomycosis caused by the fungal genera *Bipolaris* and *Exserohilum*: A report of 9 cases and review of the literature. Medicine (Baltimore) 1986;65:203–217. *One of the earliest and most comprehensive reviews of human phaeohyphomycosis, this paper serves as an excellent review.*

Clancy CJ, Wingard JR, Nguyen MH: Subcutaneous phaeohyphomycosis in transplant recipients: Review of the literature and demonstration of *in vitro* synergy between antifungal agents. Med Mycol 2000;38:169–175. *A case report and review of* Exophiala *spp. subcutaneous infections in transplant recipients, this report focuses on the need for surgical resection and antifungal susceptibility testing to select the best therapy.*

Dixon DM, Walsh TJ, Merz WG, et al: Infections due to *Xylohypha bantiana* (*Cladosporium trichoides*). Rev Infect Dis 1989;11:515–525. *This review emphasizes the proclivity of this organism, currently classified as* Cladophialophora bantiana, *to invade the central nervous system in normal and immunocompromised patients.*

Morrison VA, Weisdorf DJ: *Alternaria*: A sinonasal pathogen of immunocompromised hosts. Clin Infect Dis 1993;16:265–270. *Six cases of invasive sinonasal disease due to* Alternaria *spp. in bone marrow transplant recipients are reviewed. All but one patient survived with a combined surgical and antifungal approach.*

Revankar SG, Patterson JE, Sutton DA, et al: Disseminated phaeohyphomycosis: Review of an emerging mycosis. Clin Infect Dis 2002;34:467–476. *Review of disseminated disease in immunocompromised patients, this report emphasizes central nervous system, pulmonary, and other visceral involvement.*

Rossman SN, Cernoch PL, Davis JR: Dematiaceous fungi are an increasing cause of human disease. Clin Infect Dis 1996;22:73–80. *The report of five cases from one institution and a review of the literature is very well referenced.*

Singh N, Chang FY, Gayowski T, Marino IR: Infections due to dematiaceous fungi in organ transplant recipients: Case report and review. Clin Infect Dis 1997;24:369–374. *A comprehensive review of 35 cases of dematiaceous fungal infections in solid organ transplant recipients with emphasis on skin, articular, and brain infections.*

391 INTRODUCTION TO PROTOZOAN AND HELMINTHIC DISEASES

Keith A. Joiner

Interactions between microorganisms and their hosts can be classified as mutualistic, commensalistic, or parasitic. Only in a parasitic relationship does the organism flourish at the expense of host fitness. By this definition, all human pathogens are parasites. By convention, however, the term *parasitic infection* is used to describe infestations with protozoa and helminths. These two categories of organisms are typically distinguished from other human pathogens by having complex life cycles, often involving sequential developmental stages in different hosts or in a free-living state; by causing chronic infections; and by expression of highly evolved immune system–evasion mechanisms.

There are several essential distinctions between protozoan and metazoan (helminthic) pathogens and the infections they cause. Protozoa are unicellular, are typically microscopic, and replicate within their mammalian hosts. Disease from protozoans can result even when the initial parasite inoculum to which the host is exposed is small and the time of exposure is short. In contrast, helminths are generally macroscopic, multicellular organisms that do not multiply within their mammalian hosts. Helminthic disease typically requires repeated exposure to infective forms to increase the organism's burden to a level sufficient to cause disease. This usually necessitates prolonged residence in the endemic area. Sexual reproduction does occur in the host, but the eggs or larvae that are generated must be passed from the host into the environment for development of a stage infective for humans to occur.

Biology of Parasites

MOLECULAR PARASITOLOGY. The field of molecular parasitology has undergone revolutionary advances in the past 15 years. Many fundamental new paradigms in eukaryotic molecular and cellular biology, such as trans-splicing of mRNA and anchoring of membrane proteins by glycosylphosphatidylinositol anchors, were first revealed in parasites. DNA for endogenous or foreign genes can be introduced into most pathogenic protozoan parasites, and gene function can be further assessed after gene knockout or downregulation of gene expression by RNA interference. Reverse genetics can be used to identify genes encoding critical parasite functions. This has stimulated the interest of the scientific community at large and induced investigators from other fields to begin working in parasite systems.

The nucleotide sequence of entire genomes is available for most major protozoan pathogens of humans and for selected helminths. The hope, still largely unrealized, is that these advances, coupled with new bioinformatics tools, will lead to the identification of new diagnostic methods, new targets for chemotherapy, and new candidates for successful vaccine development. A striking example of this promise is the identification in *Plasmodium* and *Toxoplasma* of unusual plant-like biosynthetic pathways within the apicoplast organelle, a chloroplast remnant.

IMMUNITY AND VACCINE DEVELOPMENT. Protozoa and helminths exhibit elaborate strategies for evading the host response, which contributes to their chronicity and latency. Antigenic variation, in which the major antigen on the microbial surface undergoes periodic and spontaneous switching, thereby precluding effective antibody-mediated clearance by the host, was first described in *Trypanosoma brucei*. This phenomenon is now known to occur in some form or another with many other pathogenic protozoans, including plasmodia, giardia, and *Trypanosoma cruzi*. The relevance of the observation that immunologic effector functions could be divided into two categories based on lymphokine expression by CD4+ T cells (the T_H1-T_H2 paradigm) was first demonstrated with *Leishmania major* and is now commonly recognized with a wide variety of parasitic diseases. Parasites have proved instrumental in defining effector mechanisms of host resistance that are critical for effective vaccine development. Studies in this area have focused on the role of antigen-presenting cells (e.g., dendritic cells, macrophages) in determining the character of antiparasitic responses. Disappointingly, after decades of research, there is still no commercially available vaccine for any parasitic infection of humans.

Epidemiology

The magnitude of parasitic infections worldwide is staggering. One billion individuals are infected with ascariasis or trichuriasis, and 600 million are infected with malaria and schistosomiasis or filariasis.

One of the most important changes in the epidemiology of protozoal diseases is the association of selected infections with human immunodeficiency virus (HIV) infection. Some infections, such as *Toxoplasma* and *Cryptosporidia*, occur to an equal extent in the developed and the underdeveloped world. In contrast, more than 90% of the approximately 41 million individuals infected with HIV live in tropical and subtropical countries, where malaria, leishmaniasis, and trypanosomiasis are endemic. HIV-positive pregnant women are more likely to become infected with malaria and to have higher levels of parasitemia, resulting in greater perinatal morbidity and mortality. The risk of developing visceral leishmaniasis is increased by as much as 500-fold, and the resultant disease is more severe and difficult to treat. HIV-infected individuals with chronic *T. cruzi* infection have an increased incidence of central nervous system disease. Strongyloidiasis is more likely to disseminate in the presence of concomitant human T-cell leukemia virus type 1 (HTLV-1) infection than HIV infection.

Diagnosis

Probably nowhere else in clinical medicine is the question "Where have you been?" more important than in the diagnosis of parasitic and helminthic disease. A precise accounting of the places visited in chronologic order, extent of rural travel, and exposure to water and vegetation is essential. The answers to these questions lead the clinician to a consideration of the geographic distribution and the major modes of clinical presentation of various parasitic diseases. Adjunctive laboratory data, most notably peripheral blood eosinophilia, may provide an additional clue to the presence of infection with a tissue-invasive helminth.

 Treatment

There are a limited number of effective agents for protozoal and helminthic infections. Fortunately, most parasites remain susceptible to the limited armamentarium of available agents. Unfortunately, some are toxic, such as melarsoprol for African sleeping sickness, but replacements such as eflornithine (DMSO) remain out of reach of those who need it. The situation is decidedly different with malaria, for which chloroquine resistance is worldwide. Alternative agents with good activity, such as artemesin, are available, but concerns about toxicity may ultimately limit use.

SUGGESTED READINGS

Centers for Disease Control and Prevention (CDC): Health Information for International Travel, 2001–2002. (Available at: http://www.cdc.gov/travel/yb/index.htm) *A review of the recommendations for prophylaxis and vaccination for international travel by destination. Frequently updated.*

Drugs for parasitic infections. Med Lett April 2002. (Available at: http://www.medletter.com/html/prm.htm#Parasitic) *Review of drugs for parasitic infections, providing dose, adverse reactions, and alternative agents. Published and updated annually.*

Guerrant RL, Walker DN, Weller PF: Tropical Infectious Diseases: Principles, Pathogens and Practice. New York, Churchill Livingstone, 1999. *A comprehensive text.*

Sher A, Wynn T, Sacks D: The immune response to parasites. *In* Paul WE (ed): Fundamental Immunology, 6th ed. New York, Lippincott Williams & Wilkins (in press). *A detailed review of the immune response to parasitic infection and of the current status of vaccine development.*

Wilson ME: A Worldwide Guide to Infections: Diseases, Distribution, Diagnosis. New York, Oxford University Press, 1991, p 769. *A description of the manifestations and diagnosis of diseases worldwide, grouped by geographic distribution.*

392 MALARIA

Donald J. Krogstad

Definition

Malaria is characterized by recurrent fever and chills associated with the synchronous lysis of parasitized red blood cells. Its name is derived from the belief of the ancient Romans that malaria was caused by the bad air of the marshes surrounding Rome.

Etiology

Malaria is produced by intraerythrocytic parasites of the genus *Plasmodium*. Four plasmodia produce malaria in humans: *Plasmodium falciparum*, *Plasmodium vivax*, *Plasmodium ovale*, and *Plasmodium malariae*. The severity and characteristic manifestations of malaria are governed by the infecting species, the magnitude of the parasitemia, the metabolic effects of the parasite, and the cytokines released as a result of the infection.

Incidence, Prevalence, and Resurgence

INCIDENCE. Although precise data are difficult to obtain, malaria is one of the most common infectious diseases worldwide. At least 200 to 300 million cases of malaria occur each year, with 1 to 2 million deaths. Most deaths are caused by *P. falciparum* infection and occur among children younger than 5 years who live in sub-Saharan Africa. One of the major unanswered questions about malaria is how plasmodia produce repetitive infections without stimulating an effective (protective) immune response.

PREVALENCE. The prevalence of malaria varies widely. It may reach 70 to 80% or more among children in hyperendemic areas during the transmission season. Its impact on the health of the developing world is enormous.

RESURGENCE. The major factors responsible for the resurgence of malaria are drug resistances: the widespread resistance of the anopheline vector to economical insecticides such as chlorophenothane (DDT) and the increasing prevalence of resistance to chloroquine and pyrimethamine-sulfadoxine (Fansidar) in *P. falciparum*, which is established in South America, Southeast Asia, and Africa.

Life Cycle and Epidemiology

LIFE CYCLE. The life cycle can be viewed as beginning with the synchronous asexual replication of the erythrocytic stage of the parasite (Fig. 392–1). During the asexual erythrocytic cycle, parasites mature from rings to trophozoites and ultimately to schizonts, which rupture the red blood cell and release merozoites that enter uninfected red blood cells through receptors such as Duffy factor in *P. vivax* infections; they then repeat the asexual cycle. In contrast, some erythrocytic parasites mature to sexual forms (gametocytes) that are ingested by the female anopheline mosquito. Within the mosquito intermediate host, male and female gametocytes mature to gametes and fuse to form ookinetes that mature to zygotes, which produce the sporozoites that are infectious for humans. When an infected mosquito bites a human, sporozoites travel through the blood stream to the liver, where they enter hepatocytes and mature to tissue schizonts. Tissue schizonts then release merozoites that are infectious for red blood cells and produce the asexual erythrocytic cycle. Two of the four species that infect humans (*P. vivax* and *P. ovale*) produce dormant (hypnozoite) forms in the liver, which may mature 2 to 11 months or more after the initial infection and produce relapsing malaria.

Two characteristics of the life cycle are essential for the long-term survival of the parasite: multiplicity of infection and antigenic variability. *Multiplicity of infection* is apparent at each stage of the life cycle. The mature asexual erythrocytic schizont releases 8 to 32 merozoites when it ruptures its host red blood cell, up to 10,000 sporozoites result from one zygote, and 10,000 to 30,000 merozoites are released from each tissue (exoerythrocytic) schizont in the liver. This multiplicity of infection provides a redundancy that protects the parasite against losses from immune and nonimmune host factors.

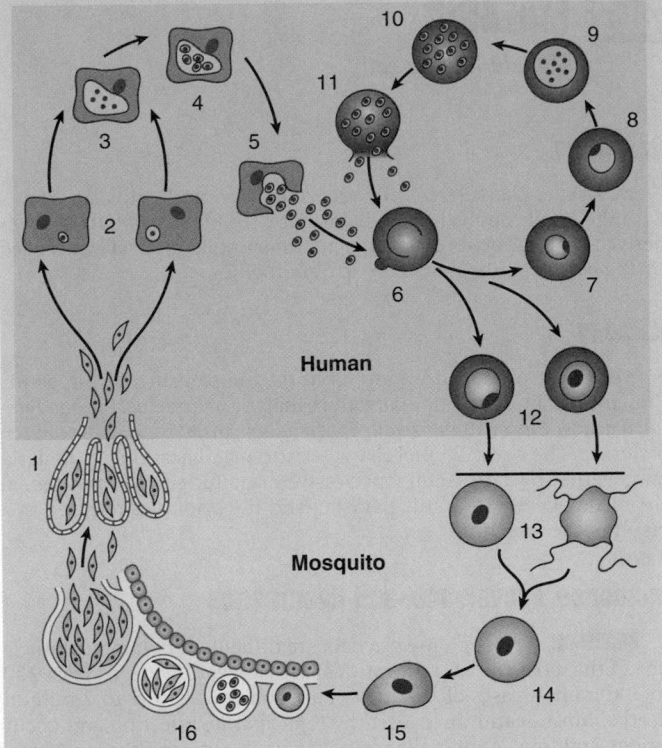

FIGURE 392–1 • Life cycle of the malaria parasite. The upper and lower halves of the diagram indicate the human and anopheline mosquito parts of the cycle, respectively. Sporozoites from the salivary gland of a female *Anopheles* mosquito are injected under the skin (1). They then travel through the blood stream to the liver (2) and mature within hepatocytes to become tissue *schizonts* (4). Up to 30,000 parasites are then released into the blood stream as *merozoites* (5) and produce symptomatic infection as they invade and destroy red blood cells. However, some parasites remain dormant in the liver as *hypnozoites* (2, dashed lines from 1 to 3). They are the parasites that cause relapsing malaria (in *P. vivax* or *P. ovale* infection). Once within the blood stream, merozoites (5) invade red blood cells (6) and mature to the *ring* (7,8), *trophozoite* (9), and *schizont* (10) asexual stages. Schizonts lyse their host red blood cells as they mature and release the next generation of merozoites (11), which invade previously uninfected red blood cells. Within the red blood cell, some parasites differentiate to sexual forms (male and female *gametocytes*) (12). When taken up by a female *Anopheles* mosquito, the gametocytes mature to *male and female gametes*, which produce *zygotes* (14). The zygote invades the gut of the mosquito (15) and develops into an *oocyst* (16). Mature oocysts produce *sporozoites*, which migrate to the salivary gland of the mosquito (1) and repeat the cycle. The dashed line between 12 and 13 indicates that an absence of the mosquito vector prevents natural transmission by means of this cycle. Infection by the injection of contaminated blood bypasses this constraint and permits transmission among intravenous drug addicts or to recipients of blood transfusions. (From Krogstad DJ: Blood and tissue protozoa. *In* Schaechter M, Medoff G, Eisenstein BI [eds]: Mechanisms of Microbial Diseases, 2nd ed. Baltimore, Williams & Wilkins, 1993, p 600.)

Antigenic variability is associated with the different stages of the parasite's life cycle, with variability among strains within species and with the expression of *var* genes in *P. falciparum*. For example, antibodies against sporozoites are ineffective against asexual erythrocytic and sexual (gametocyte) stages of the parasite. There is also antigenic variability between species and among strains within the species that infect humans. The *var* genes encode parasite molecules on the red blood cell surface that permit the parasite to evade the immune response because of their variable regions. This variability is a major challenge in the development of a malaria vaccine, discussed below.

EPIDEMIOLOGY. The epidemiology of malaria is determined by the distributions of the anopheline mosquito vectors required for natural transmission and of the infected human reservoir. Both factors are present in endemic areas of the tropics. Important determinants of transmission include the vector population (e.g., vectors such as *Anopheles gambiae* in Africa may be more efficient), temperature (i.e., elevated temperature shortens the life of the vector and hastens the maturation of the parasite), and control programs that reduce the prevalence of human infection and contact between humans and the vector population.

Competent mosquito vectors are present in the United States: *Anopheles albimanus* in the east and *Anopheles freeborni* in the west. Although transmission in the United States is limited by the absence of infected humans, natural mosquito-borne transmission can and does occur with the importation of infected humans (e.g., soldiers returning after exposure to infected mosquitoes in endemic areas). Mosquito-borne transmission (i.e., *introduced malaria*) occurred in the United States after World War II, the Korean War, the Vietnam War, and the arrival of refugees from Southeast Asia.

Pathogenesis

SPECIES-DEPENDENT FACTORS. Malaria is a multifactorial disease that can be explained in part by the magnitude of the parasitemia. *P. falciparum* is the most lethal parasite because it can invade red blood cells of any age and can produce unrestricted parasitemias involving 10^6 or more parasitized red blood cells per cubic millimeter of blood (>20% of circulating red blood cells). Conversely, *P. vivax* and *P. ovale*, which invade only young red blood cells, are limited to parasitemias less than 25,000/mm³, and *P. malariae*, which invades only older red blood cells, is limited to parasitemias of less than 10,000/mm³.

HOST IMMUNE RESPONSE. Because millions of people experience repetitive episodes of malaria throughout their lives in the tropics, the immune response to natural infection is inadequate by definition. The term *semi-immune* is used for residents of endemic areas who are reinfected regularly but are at reduced risk of severe or complicated malaria. The reasons for this incomplete host immune response (i.e., protection against severe disease but not against infection) are not clear, but they are likely to be key for the development of a successful vaccine. For example, cell-mediated responses may be essential for effective immunity, although virtually all exposed persons make antibodies against the repetitive epitopes on the surface of the sporozoite, and antibodies to asexual stages reduce the magnitude of the parasitemia in children. Factors potentially responsible for poor cell-mediated responses to sporozoite antigen include host immune restriction related to HLA haplotype and the dependence of cellular responses on hypervariable regions downstream from the coding region.

PERIPHERAL SEQUESTRATION OF PARASITIZED RED BLOOD CELLS. With maturation, red blood cells containing *P. falciparum* parasites develop knobs that contain histidine-rich proteins. In vivo, these knobs adhere to

Table 392–1 • MALARIA PARASITES THAT INFECT HUMANS			
			MORPHOLOGY
PLASMODIUM SPECIES	**PARASITEMIA (per µL blood)**	**COMPLICATIONS**	**Red Blood Cell Stage**
P. falciparum Hypoglycemia	$\geq 10^6$	Coma (cerebral malaria)	No RBC enlargement
		Pulmonary edema, renal failure Severe malarial anemia (<5 g Hb/dL)	
P. vivax	≤25,000	Late splenic rupture (2–3 mo)	Enlarged host RBCs
P. ovale	≤25,000	—	Enlarged host RBCs
P. malariae	≤10,000	Immune complex nephritic syndrome	No RBC enlargement

endothelial cells in the peripheral microvasculature by means of receptors such as intercellular adhesion molecule type 1 (ICAM-1), thrombospondin, or CD36. This phenomenon has at least two consequences. First, it exacerbates the microvascular pathology produced by the parasite, and second, it removes mature *P. falciparum* parasites from the circulation, so that only early asexual erythrocytic stages, such as rings, are seen on peripheral blood smears.

CYTOKINES IN THE PATHOGENESIS OF MALARIA. Studies suggest that cytokine release is a central factor in the pathogenesis of severe disease. Cytokines shown to be important include tumor necrosis factor (TNF). Serum levels of TNF are elevated in severe *P. falciparum* infection and correlate with complications such as cerebral malaria and death. Interferon-γ has antiparasitic activity against the exoerythrocytic stages of the parasite in the liver.

Pathology

The pathology of severe malaria is that of a microvascular disease involving the brain, lung, and kidney. Postmortem examination after fatal *P. falciparum* infection demonstrates parasitized red blood cells in the capillaries and venules of the brain and other affected organs. In severe cases, acute tubular necrosis may be present, and the liver, spleen, and other sites in the reticuloendothelial system may be filled with malarial pigment from the phagocytosis of parasitized red blood cells. This predominantly microvascular pathology is consistent with the roles of sequestration and cytokine release in the pathogenesis of severe disease. In contrast, the other malarias that infect humans produce lower parasitemias, do not sequester, and are rarely fatal.

Clinical Manifestations

FEVER AND CHILLS. Most patients with malaria have recurrent fever and chills at 48-hour intervals for *P. vivax* and *P. ovale* and at 72-hour intervals for *P. malariae*. Patients with *P. falciparum* infection typically have irregular fever and chills and rarely present with a regular 48-hour cycle of symptoms despite the 48-hour erythrocytic cycle of the asexual parasite.

COMA. Coma (i.e., cerebral malaria) is the most feared complication of *P. falciparum* infection and has a substantial fatality rate. Although it has been attributed to the blockage of capillaries with parasitized red blood cells, hypoglycemia and the effects of cytokines such as TNF are important factors. Hypoglycemia in *P. falciparum* malaria may have at least three causes: (1) glucose consumption by the massive numbers of parasites present in the blood, (2) liver glycogen depletion in persons who have not eaten for several days before seeking medical care because they were ill with malaria, and (3) insulin released from the pancreatic β-cell by quinine or quinidine during treatment. Hypoglycemia is particularly important because it is readily treatable. Although the effects of TNF contribute to cerebral malaria, it is difficult to separate them from the magnitude of the parasitemia because the concentration of TNF correlates with the magnitude of the parasitemia.

RENAL FAILURE. Patients with massive parasitemias may have dark urine from the free hemoglobin produced by hemolysis (black-water fever) and may develop renal failure subsequently. Although most patients recover uneventfully, acute renal failure may occur and may require dialysis similar to other causes of acute tubular necrosis.

PULMONARY EDEMA. Pulmonary edema also occurs in patients with high *P. falciparum* parasitemias (>5% of circulating red blood cells). Hemodynamic measurements indicate that this is a noncardiogenic form of pulmonary edema with normal pulmonary arterial and capillary pressures. These findings and the association with high TNF levels suggest that the pathogenesis of pulmonary edema is similar in severe malaria and bacterial septicemia.

GASTROINTESTINAL MANIFESTATIONS. Diarrhea is common among children with *P. falciparum* infection. The pathogenesis of this complication is unclear, although postmortem studies of children with diarrhea have revealed parasitized red blood cells in the microvasculature of the intestine.

Diagnosis

GIEMSA-STAINED THICK AND THIN SMEARS. The most direct way to diagnose malaria is to examine Giemsa-stained, thick or thin smears using oil immersion magnification (×1000). Giemsa stain is preferable to Wright's stain, especially for persons with *P. vivax* or *P. ovale* infection, because the Schüffner's dots characteristic of those infections may not be visible with Wright's stain. Thick smears are more sensitive than thin smears because the red blood cells have been lysed. As a result, approximately 10 times as much blood can be examined per field and therefore per unit of time. However, because the red blood cells have been lysed, it is not possible to determine the effect of the parasite on red blood cell size or the position of the parasite within the red blood cell on a thick smear (Table 392–1). Persons without previous experience in reading thick smears should consider using thin smears to identify the infecting parasites. A common mistake is to require characteristic gametocytes for a diagnosis of *P. falciparum* infection. Because gametocytes require longer to develop than asexual parasites (7 to 10 days versus 2 days), they are usually not present in the peripheral blood when nonimmune tourists or expatriates first become ill. Conversely, gametocytes are frequently present in the blood of semi-immune residents of endemic areas with few or no symptoms or asexual parasites. A second common mistake is to assume that the patient can have only one parasite species; approximately 5% of persons with malaria are infected with more than one parasite species.

ANTIGEN DETECTION. Testing for parasite antigen (e.g., parasite lactate dehydrogenase) is a potential alternative to microscopy for the diagnosis of *P. falciparum* infections, especially in nonendemic areas where skilled microscopists are rare. Potential advantages of this approach include the ability to distinguish between *P. falciparum* and *P. vivax*.

FLUORESCENT STAINING WITH ACRIDINE ORANGE (QBC SYSTEM). Because parasitized red blood cells are less dense, they are at the top of the red blood cell layer after centrifugation. However, parasites of all species are visualized with fluorescence microscopy, because all species stain with acridine orange. For this reason, it can be difficult to distinguish among species with this technique.

DNA PROBES AND POLYMERASE CHAIN REACTION. DNA probes and polymerase chain reaction (PCR) methods may both achieve the sensitivity of a thick smear. However, obstacles to the routine use of these

	MORPHOLOGY			
Schüffner's Dots	Stages on Smear	RELAPSE FROM HYPNOZOITES	ANTIMALARIAL RESISTANCE
Absent	Rings, occasional gametocytes	No	Chloroquine, mefloquine, halofantrine, pyrimethamine-sulfadoxine, plus partial resistance to quinine and quinidine
Present	All stages	Yes	Chloroquine
Present	All stages	Yes	None known
Absent	All stages	No	None known

Table 392–2 • TREATMENT OF MALARIA

CHLOROQUINE-RESISTANT *P. FALCIPARUM*
For Patients Able To Take Oral Medications

PO Quinine plus	650 mg quinine sulfate q8h × 3–7 days
Doxycyline (Vibramycin) or plus	100 mg bid × 7 days
Tetracycline or plus	250 mg qid × 7 days
Pyrimethamine-sulfadoxine or	3 tablets (1500 mg sulfadoxine, 75 mg pyrimethamine) as a single dose on the last day of treatment
Clindamycin or	900 mg tid × 5 days
PO Atovaquone (Malarone) plus	1000 mg/day (2 Malarone tablets bid) × 3 days
Proguanil (Malarone) or	400 mg/day × 3 days (2 Malarone tablets per day)
*PO Mefloquine** or	1250 mg (1140 mg base) once as 750 mg, followed by 500 mg in 8–12 hr
PO Halofantrine[†] or	500 mg q6h × 3 doses and repeat in 1 wk
PO Artesunate[†] plus	4 mg/kg/day × 3 days[‡]
PO Mefloquine	1250 mg (1140 mg base) once as 750 mg, followed by 500 mg in 8–12 hr

For Patients Unable To Tolerate Oral Medications

IV Quinidine or	6.25 mg base/kg (10 mg gluconate salt/kg, maximum of 600 mg salt) in normal saline over 1–2 hr, followed by 0.0125 mg base/kg (0.02 mg gluconate salt/kg)/min until parasitemia is <1% or patient tolerates oral medications
IV Quinine or	16.7 mg/kg base (20 mg dihydrochloride salt/kg) loading dose in D5W over 4 hr, followed by 8.3 mg base/kg over 2–4 hr, q8h until patient tolerates oral medications
IM Quinine or	8.3 mg base/kg (10 mg dihydrochloride salt/kg) q8h until able to take oral medications; may begin with 16.7 mg base/kg (20 mg quinine dihydrochloride salt/kg) loading dose
IM Artemether[†]	3.2 mg/kg initially on day 0, followed by 1.6 mg/kg/day × 5–7 days[‡]

FOR MULTIPLY RESISTANT *P. FALCIPARUM*

PR Artesunate[†] or	1200–1600 mg PR × 3 days[‡]
PO Artesunate[†] plus	As above[‡]
PO Mefloquine	750 mg, followed by 500 mg 12 hr later

CHLOROQUINE-RESISTANT *P. VIVAX*

PO Quinine plus	650 mg quinine sulfate q8h × 3–7 days
Doxycyline (Vibramycin) or	100 mg bid × 7 days
PO Mefloquine or	750 mg, followed by 500 mg in 8–12 hr
PO Halofantrine or	500 mg q6h × 3 over 24 hr for a total dose of 1500 mg
PO Chloroquine plus	25 mg base/kg × 3 days
PO Primaquine	2.5 mg base/kg in 3 doses × 48 hr

P. VIVAX, P. OVALE, P. MALARIAE*, AND CHLOROQUINE-SUSCEPTIBLE *P. FALCIPARUM
For Patients Able To Take Oral Medications

PO Chloroquine	10 mg base/kg = 600 mg base, followed by an additional 300 mg base after 6 hr and 300 mg base again on days 2 and 3 (1500 mg base total = 2500 mg chloroquine phosphate salt)

For Patients Unable To Take Oral Medications

IM Chloroquine	2.5 mg base/kg IM q4h or 3.5 mg/kg q6h (total dose not to exceed 25 mg/kg base)
IV Chloroquine	10 mg base/kg over 4 hr, followed by 5 mg/kg base q12h (given in a 2-hr infusion; total dose not to exceed 25 mg base/kg)

TO PREVENT RELAPSE IN *P. VIVAX* OR *P. OVALE* INFECTION

PO Primaquine[§]	15 mg primaquine base (26.3 mg primaquine phosphate) daily × 14 days

*For areas without mefloquine resistance.
[†]Not yet available in the United States.
[‡]Doses used vary among investigators for IM artemether on subsequent days of treatment (after the initial 3.2 mg/kg dose) from 0.8 to 1.6 mg/kg for 4 to 7 days; for PO artesunate as 12 mg/kg over 3 to 7 days; for PR artesunate, the information available suggests that effective PR doses are likely to be approximately four times greater than PO doses.
[§]To prevent potentially severe hemolysis, patients should be tested for glucose-6-phosphate dehydrogenase deficiency before treatment with primaquine.

methods in endemic areas include the need for nonisotopic labeling of probes and the cost of a thermocycler and consumable reagents for PCR. For these reasons, neither DNA probes nor PCR is used routinely in malaria-endemic areas.

SEROLOGY (ANTIBODY TESTING). Testing for antibodies to plasmodia is of limited value in individual patients. This is because the decision to treat must be made in the first few hours of evaluation, although 3 to 4 weeks may be required to develop a diagnostic rise in antibody titer. In endemic areas, most persons have antibody titers from previous infections whether they have been infected recently or not. Serology may be of value retrospectively in nonimmune persons (e.g., expatriate tourists) who have been treated empirically for malaria without a microscopic diagnosis. For example, a high titer of antibodies to *P. vivax* suggests that the patient had a *P. vivax* infection recently and should receive primaquine to prevent relapse, if primaquine has not been given previously.

Rx Treatment

Successful treatment of patients with malaria depends primarily on effective antimalarial drugs, but it also depends on ancillary measures as diverse as the infusion of glucose and dialysis. Monitoring of the blood glucose level is important because hypoglycemia is a common cause of coma and because both quinine and quinidine stimulate the release of insulin directly from the pancreatic β-cell. Steroids are contraindicated in cerebral malaria because they prolong the duration of coma.

The treatment of chloroquine-susceptible malaria (*P. vivax, P. ovale,* or *P. malariae* malaria and chloroquine-susceptible *P. falciparum* malaria) is satisfactory (Table 392–2) because chloroquine is a safe and effective antimalarial in those situations. Patients with chloroquine-resistant *P. vivax* have been treated successfully with mefloquine or halofantrine. However, the treatment of chloroquine-resistant *P. falciparum* infection is unsatisfactory. Patients able to tolerate oral medications may be treated with mefloquine alone in areas without mefloquine resistance. In areas with mefloquine resistance, treatments include quinine plus pyrimethamine-sulfadoxine, doxycycline, or clindamycin; atovaquone plus proguanil; and doxycycline (see Table 392–2). For patients who cannot tolerate oral medications, potential strategies include intravenous quinidine, intravenous quinine, intramuscular quinine, and intramuscular artemether or artesunate, which are reported to be effective without detectable neurologic toxicity, although they have not yet been approved by the U.S. Food and Drug Administration. The general principle of parenteral treatment is to stabilize patients until they can tolerate oral medications. Oral regimens are available for multiply resistant *P. falciparum*.

Patients with *P. vivax* or *P. ovale* infection should be tested for glucose-6-phosphate dehydrogenase deficiency before treatment with primaquine, which is used to eradicate persistent hypnozoites in the liver to prevent relapse.

Prevention

Exposed nonimmune persons may reduce their risk of malaria by taking antimalarials prospectively (i.e., chemoprophylaxis); by using insect repellents and insecticide-impregnated bed nets to reduce contact with the anopheline vector; and possibly in the future, by a malaria vaccine (i.e., immunoprophylaxis).

CHEMOPROPHYLAXIS. Drugs used for chemoprophylaxis must be safe because they are given to healthy persons for long periods. Several have been chosen for their long serum half-lives so that they can be given infrequently. On the basis of these criteria, chloroquine is an excellent drug for chemoprophylaxis in areas without chloroquine-resistant *P. falciparum* (Table 392–3). It is the only chemoprophylactic agent known to be safe for pregnant women and does not produce retinal toxicity at the doses used for antimalarial chemoprophylaxis. Unfortunately, strains of *P. falciparum* resistant to chloroquine and to pyrimethamine-sulfadoxine are established in Southeast Asia, South America, and Africa. For areas with chloroquine-resistant *P. falciparum*, mefloquine is the recommended chemoprophylactic agent, although resistance to mefloquine is developing in Southeast Asia and South America. Doxycycline and atovaquone-proguanil are alternatives. The advantage of doxycycline is that it reduces the frequency of traveler's diarrhea; its disadvantages include the need for daily dosing, photosensitivity reactions, and yeast vaginitis. The major disadvantage of atovaquone-proguanil is its cost. Because of hypersensitivity reactions to pyrimethamine-sulfadoxine and because of agranulocytosis and hepatitis with amodiaquine, neither agent is recommended for chemoprophylaxis.

VECTOR CONTROL. Because of widespread drug resistance by *P. falciparum*, increasing emphasis has been placed on reducing exposure to the anopheline vector, especially in areas with intense transmission such as Africa. Strategies that are successful and should be considered include DEET-containing insect repellents and pyrethrin (insecticide)-impregnated bed nets. DDT is no longer effective in most regions of the world because of widespread resistance.

Table 392–3 • CHEMOPROPHYLAXIS OF MALARIA*

FOR AREAS WITH CHLOROQUINE-RESISTANT *PLASMODIUM FALCIPARUM*:

Mefloquine (Lariam)	250 mg/wk during exposure and for 4 wk after leaving the endemic area
Doxycycline	100 mg/day during exposure and for 4 wk after leaving the endemic area
Atovaquone-Proguanil (Malarone)	250 mg and 100 mg (1 tablet) daily during exposure, and for 1 wk after leaving endemic area
Primaquine	30 mg daily during exposure and for 1 wk after leaving endemic area

FOR AREAS WITHOUT CHLOROQUINE-RESISTANT *PLASMODIUM FALCIPARUM*:

Chloroquine phosphate (Aralen)	500 mg/wk (300 mg chloroquine base) during exposure and for 4 wk after leaving the endemic area

*Alternatives for areas with chloroquine-resistant *P. falciparum* include weekly chloroquine plus daily proguanil (200 mg/day; note that the chloroquine + proguanil regimen has not been approved by the FDA and that breakthroughs occur with some frequency in areas with chloroquine-resistant *P. falciparum*) and weekly chloroquine plus single-dose presumptive treatment as needed with pyrimethamine-sulfadoxine (Fansidar) for presumed breakthrough infection with 75 and 1500 mg of pyrimethamine and sulfadoxine (3 tablets), respectively. Updated information on malaria chemoprophylaxis may be obtained from the CDC Hot Lines at 404-223-4559 and 404-332-4565 and from the CDC and Medical Letter WEB Sites at *www.cdc.gov* and *www.medletter.com*, respectively; see also Med Lett Drugs Ther 2002;44:1–4.

IMMUNOPROPHYLAXIS—DEVELOPMENT OF A MALARIA VACCINE. Although a malaria vaccine is not available, it is hoped that this goal will ultimately be achievable. Because the three major parasite stages in humans are antigenically distinct, a successful vaccine will likely need to contain at least three parasite antigens (e.g., sporozoite, merozoite, gametocyte). However, a vaccine need not be 100% effective to be valuable. For example, a vaccine that requires boosting could be quite effective for residents of endemic areas because of repetitive exposure to natural infection. Alternatively, a vaccine that limited the magnitude of the parasitemia could improve the survival of nonimmune persons even if it had no effect on the incidence of infection, because high parasitemias produce severe morbidity and death in nonimmune persons.

Prognosis

Most patients with *P. vivax*, *P. ovale*, or *P. malariae* infection respond well to chloroquine and make an uneventful recovery. The reported chloroquine-resistant strains of *P. vivax* have responded to treatment with mefloquine or halofantrine. For patients with *P. falciparum* infection, the quantitative parasite count is the best predictor of the outcome. Patients with more than 5% parasitemia (>250,000 parasites/μL of blood) are at increased risk for severe and complicated malaria, including death. In addition to the standard antimalarial treatment directed at the parasite (see Table 392–2), such patients may require glucose for hypoglycemia, treatment of acidosis, dialysis for renal failure, and respiratory support. The role of exchange transfusion is controversial, in part because there have been no controlled clinical trials. Oral treatment, including nasogastric administration, may be successful even in patients with severe or cerebral malaria.

SUGGESTED READINGS

Baird JK, Lacy MD, Basri H, et al: Randomized, parallel placebo-controlled trial of primaquine for malaria prophylaxis in Papua, Indonesia. Clin Infect Dis 2001;33:1990–1997. *The protective efficacy of primaquine against malaria was 93%, with good tolerance in G6PD-normal travelers.*

Garner P, Gulmezoglu AM: Drugs for preventing malaria-related illness in pregnant women and death in the newborn. Cochrane Database Syst Rev 2003;1:CD000169. *Drugs for malaria reduce severe anemia in the mother, and are associated with higher birthweight and probably reduced perinatal mortality.*

Graves P, Gelband H: Vaccines for preventing malaria. Cochrane Database Syst Rev 2003;1:CD000129. *No convincing evidence of their efficacy.*

Olliaro P, Mussano P: Amodiaquine for treating malaria. Cochrane Database Syst Rev 2003;2:CD000016. *Amodiaquine was more effective than chloroquine but not as effective as sulfadoxine/pyrimethamine for treating malaria.*

Parola P, Ranque S, Badiaga S, et al: Controlled trial of 3-day quinine clindamycin treatment versus 7-day quinine treatment for adult travelers with uncomplicated falciparum malaria imported from the tropics. Antimicrob Agents Chemother 2001;45:932–935. *Three days of quinine-clindamycin was as good as seven days of quinine for the treatment of imported uncomplicated P. falciparum malaria in travelers returning from the tropics.*

Stoppacher R, Adams SP: Malaria deaths in the United States: Case report and review of deaths, 1979–1998. J Forensic Sci 2003;48:404–408. *There were a total of 118 deaths due to malaria in the United States between 1979 and 1998, with an average of 5.9 deaths per year.*

Wilson JF: Advancing the war on malaria. Ann Intern Med 2003;138:693–696. *An overview, including guidelines for prophylaxis in travelers.*

393 AFRICAN TRYPANOSOMIASIS (SLEEPING SICKNESS)

Thomas C. Quinn

Definition

Known widely as sleeping sickness, African trypanosomiasis is an acute and chronic disease caused by *Trypanosoma brucei*. The parasites are transmitted to humans through the bite of tsetse flies located in 36 countries of Africa between 15 degrees north and 15 degrees south latitude. In humans, there are two distinct forms of the disease: East African trypanosomiasis caused by *T. brucei rhodesiense* and West African trypanosomiasis caused by *T. brucei gambiense*. Although there is some clinical overlap, East African trypanosomiasis primarily causes

Infectious Diseases

an acute febrile illness with myocarditis and meningoencephalitis that is rapidly fatal if not treated, whereas West African trypanosomiasis is characterized as a chronic debilitating disease with mental deterioration and physical wasting (Table 393–1). A closely related variant, *T. brucei brucei*, is noninfectious for humans but causes a chronic wasting illness in cattle, called *nagana*, which has a considerable indirect effect on human nutrition in sub-Saharan Africa.

Etiology and Life Cycle

Trypanosomes are motile hemoflagellates with a single undulating membrane that passes along the length of the parasite, terminating in an anterior flagellum (Fig. 393–1). Located anteriorly is a kinetoplast, an organelle containing topologically interlocked circular DNA molecules and mitochondria. In the peripheral blood of humans, trypanosomes vary in length from 10 to 40 μm. Both short, stumpy and long, slender forms can be present in a patient at the same time. The different variants of *T. brucei* cannot be distinguished morphologically but can be identified by differences in pathogenicity for certain animals, as well as in biochemical requirements, electrophoretic pattern of component enzymes, and DNA hybridization.

T. brucei is transmitted by the tsetse fly *Glossina*, within which it undergoes several developmental changes. When biting an infected host, trypanosomes are ingested and within the insect midgut rapidly differentiate into procyclic forms with loss of their dense surface coat, composed of variant surface glycoprotein. After 2 to 3 weeks of multiplication in the midgut, the procyclic trypanosomes migrate to the insect's salivary glands, where they change morphologically into epimastigotes. These forms further undergo multiplication and

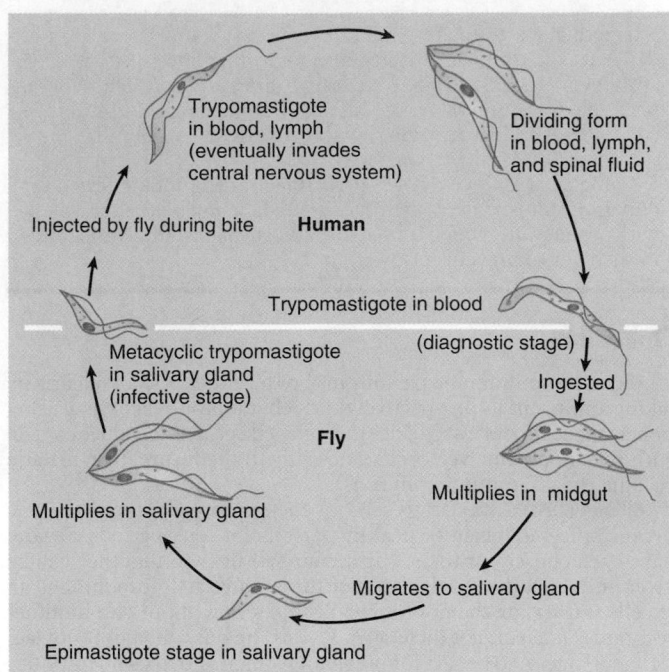

FIGURE 393–2 • Life cycle of *Trypanosoma (Trypanozoon) brucei*, *Trypanosoma (Trypanozoon) brucei gambiense*, and *Trypanosoma (Trypanozoon) brucei rhodesiense*.

ultimately differentiate into metacyclic trypanosomes that are coated with characteristic variant surface glycoprotein and are infectious to mammalian hosts. When a new host is bitten by the tsetse fly, the trypanosomes present in the salivary glands are injected into the connective tissue and blood. Within the human host they divide by binary fission and undergo antigen variation, a process by which they continually change their variable surface glycoproteins (VSGs) and evade the immune system of the host. With the bite of another tsetse fly, ingestion of the parasite occurs, and the life cycle of the organism is completed (Fig. 393–2). Mechanical transmission can theoretically also occur via blood transfusion or by interrupted biting of a tsetse fly feeding on an infectious person and directly thereafter biting an uninfected individual.

Table 393–1 • COMPARISON OF GAMBIAN AND RHODESIAN SLEEPING SICKNESS

	GAMBIAN (WEST AFRICAN)	RHODESIAN (EAST AFRICAN)
Etiologic agent	*Trypanosoma brucei gambiense*	*Trypanosoma brucei rhodesiense*
Vector	*Glossina palpalis or tachinoides* (riverine tsetse)	*Glossina morsitans* (savanna tsetse)
Distribution	West and Central Africa	East Africa
Reservoir	Humans (domestic animals)	Wild game
Course of infection	Slow (months–years)	Rapid (<1 yr)
Clinical features		
Lymphadenopathy	++ (Winterbottom's sign)	±
Myocarditis, heart failure	–	++
Neurologic symptoms	++	+
Disseminated intravascular coagulation	–	+
Parasitemia	Low	High

Epidemiology

It is estimated that 400,000 people are currently suffering from African trypanosomiasis, that more than 40,000 Africans become infected annually, and that 25,000 people die from it each year. Approximately 50 million people in 36 African countries live at risk of acquiring trypanosomiasis because of the presence of the disease and its vector. Within recent years, there has been a resurgence in African trypanosomiasis, particularly in central African countries, due to decreased surveillance, prophylaxis, and treatment as a consequence of war and civil unrest. In some areas the prevalence of African trypanosomiasis has increased 10-fold over the past decade. Approximately 4 million square miles in Africa remain unpopulated because of the presence of *T. brucei brucei* infection, which results in the loss of domestic and wild animals, including cattle, waterbuck, bushbuck, and buffalo.

T. brucei gambiense occurs primarily in the west and central regions of sub-Saharan Africa. Although it primarily infects humans, there may be animal reservoirs, such as pigs, dogs, and sheep. Gambian sleeping sickness is spread mainly by three species of tsetse fly: *Glossina palpalis, Glossina tachinoides*, and *Glossina fuscipes*. Distribution of these flies includes shaded areas along rivers and streams, where the conditions of temperature, darkness, and moisture are optimum.

T. brucei rhodesiense differs from *T. brucei gambiense* in that it is primarily a parasite of wild game, with humans serving only as occasional hosts. The geographic distribution of *T. brucei rhodesiense* is primarily East Africa from Ethiopia and eastern Uganda south to Zambia and Botswana. Rhodesian sleeping sickness is spread by tsetse flies of the *Glossina morsitans* group, including *Glossina pallidipes* and *Glossina swynnertoni*. These flies can survive in the open savanna,

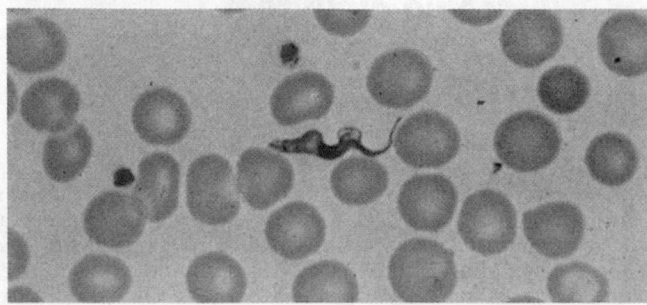

FIGURE 393–1 • *Trypanosoma rhodesiense* in the peripheral blood. It has a nucleus, posterior kinetoplast, undulating membrane, and flagellum (× 1500).

and Rhodesian sleeping sickness usually occurs among individuals visiting or traveling through an endemic area. Consequently, hunters, fishermen, and tourists are at risk, exposing themselves to vectors that usually feed on wild animals.

Imported African trypanosomiasis is a rare disease. Most cases were due to *T. brucei rhodesiense* acquired by Americans who had been on safari in East Africa for a brief period. Nearly all of these cases were initially misdiagnosed because of the unfamiliarity of U.S. physicians with this disease. With an increase in international travel, 20,000 Americans are now estimated to visit endemic areas yearly, and approximately 10,000 aliens enter the United States each year from countries in Africa where the infection is endemic.

Pathogenesis and Pathology

Following the bite of the tsetse fly, trypanosomes accumulate in the connective tissue, where they multiply to produce a local chancre (trypanoma). The organisms subsequently spread through the lymphatics, resulting in enlargement of lymph nodes secondary to reactive plasma cell and macrophage infiltration. The trypanosomes eventually disseminate to the circulatory system, where the parasitemia usually remains at low intensity and the organisms multiply by binary fission. Systemic African trypanosomiasis without central nervous system (CNS) involvement is generally referred to as *stage I disease*.

The host immune response plays an integral role in the pathogenesis of African sleeping sickness, although the exact nature of the immunopathogenic reactions has not been clearly defined. Trypanosomes survive by periodically altering their surface antigenic coat, avoiding successful eradication by the host. Any single parasite may contain some 1000 genes for VSG that can be activated in a variety of ways and selected by the host antibody response. Consequently, trypanosomes occur in the peripheral blood of infected individuals in waves, with each parasite wave consisting of a serologically distinct organism.

Tissue damage is induced by either toxin production or immune complex reaction with release of proteolytic enzymes. Immune complexes consisting of variant antigens of the organism and complement-fixing antibodies have been demonstrated in both the circulation and the target organs of infected patients. The production of autoantibodies is a prominent feature, and they are frequently directed against antigen components of red blood cells, brain, and heart. Thus the host-parasite interaction can result in generalized febrile episodes, lymphadenopathy, and myocardial and pericardial inflammation, along with anemia, thrombocytopenia, disseminated intravascular coagulation, and renal disease primarily during the acute stage of the disease.

Stage II of human African trypanosomiasis involves invasion of the CNS, which occurs during the period of circulatory dissemination when trypanosomes localize in the small vessels of the CNS. Pathologic changes in the CNS are most prominent in chronic cases of Gambian sleeping sickness. The meninges are thickened and infiltrated with lymphocytes, plasma cells, and morular cells. Morular cells are modified plasma cells ($\leq$20 mm in diameter) with large granular inclusions that have been shown to consist of immunoglobulin. These cells may play an important role in the local production of immunoglobulin M (IgM) in the cerebrospinal fluid (CSF). Edema, hemorrhages, and granulomatous lesions are frequently present, along with thrombosis as a result of endarteritis and with neuronal degeneration.

African trypanosomes appear to induce a state of B-cell polyclonal activation caused either by interference with host T-cell control of antibody production or by a B-cell mitogen released by the parasite. Polyclonal hypergammaglobulinemia, with very high levels of IgM, is commonly seen. High levels of nonspecific heterophile antibody, rheumatoid factor, and autoantibodies are also produced. In patients with late-stage *T. brucei gambiense*, circulating levels of tumor necrosis factor-α and interleukin-10 are markedly elevated, which decline following effective treatment.

Clinical Manifestations

The signs and symptoms of sleeping sickness differ according to the infecting organism (see Table 393–1). Rhodesian sleeping sickness, due to *T. brucei rhodesiense*, causes a rapid, progressive disease often resulting in cardiac failure and acute neurologic manifestations. Gambian sleeping sickness, caused by *T. brucei gambiense*, is typically a more chronic illness with primarily neurologic features. However, this difference is not absolute; in some cases Gambian sleeping sickness can progress rapidly, and occasionally Rhodesian sleeping sickness may follow a more chronic course.

GAMBIAN SLEEPING SICKNESS. Within several days following the bite by an infected tsetse fly, a trypanosomal nodule or chancre develops, typically on the exposed parts of the body. Within a week the lesion becomes a hard, painful nodule surrounded by erythema and swelling, which persists for 1 to 2 weeks. After this incubation period, clinical features develop after systemic, lymphatic, and circulatory invasion of the trypanosomes. Fever, headache, dizziness, and weakness occur in the majority of these patients. Febrile episodes may last 1 to 6 days, alternating with afebrile periods. Lymphadenopathy with prominent supraclavicular and posterior cervical enlargement is seen in more than 80% of infected individuals. Known as *Winterbottom's sign*, these enlarged lymph nodes are usually discrete, rubbery, and painless. Moderate splenomegaly may occur, and urticaria and erythematous rashes have also been observed. Electrocardiograms are often abnormal, but clinical signs of heart disease are unusual.

Six months to several years after symptoms first appear, the clinical features of this early hemolymphatic stage progress to a late meningoencephalitic stage. Behavioral and personality changes are often the first signs of CNS involvement. Later, more florid psychological changes may occur, with hallucinations and delusions. Reversion of sleep rhythm is characteristic, with drowsiness during the day, a feature from which the disease derives its name. Other

nervous symptoms include tremor, most characteristically of the face and lips, and hyperesthesia, causing some patients to avoid common practices such as closing (Kerandel's sign) or locking doors (key sign). Without treatment, the patient's level of consciousness progressively deteriorates until there is lapse into stupor. Alterations in thermoregulation may lead to hypothermia or hyperthermia, and progressive neurologic alterations lead to convulsions, chorea, and athetosis. Adrenal insufficiency, hypothyroidism, and hypogonadism are frequently observed, and pituitary function tests suggest an unusual combined central (hypothalamic/pituitary) and peripheral defect in hormone secretion. The CSF shows an increase in cells and protein, much of which is IgM. Free immunoglobulin light chains may be present. Most of the cells are lymphocytes, but a few are plasma cells and morula cells. Trypanosomes may also be evident within the CSF.

RHODESIAN SLEEPING SICKNESS. This disease is more acute than Gambian sleeping sickness, and symptoms usually occur a few days after the victim has been bitten by the tsetse fly. Alternating periods of high fever, malaise, and headache, followed by several days of well-being, are often misinterpreted as acute malaria infection. Lymphadenopathy is not prominent in this variety of the disease, and Winterbottom's sign is usually absent. Tachycardia with arrhythmias and extrasystoles is common. Anemia, thrombocytopenia, and disseminated intravascular coagulation are usually evident within the first several weeks of infection. Liver enzyme values are often elevated, and electrocardiograms are abnormal, usually reflecting underlying myocarditis. Neurologic features are similar to those described for Gambian sleeping sickness, but they occur much earlier and with more rapid deterioration. Without treatment, the disease may result in death within a matter of weeks to months, without clear distinction into an early and late phase, as described for Gambian trypanosomiasis.

Diagnosis

Although a presumptive diagnosis of trypanosomiasis is based on clinical suspicion, history of travel to areas where this disease is

endemic, and tsetse fly exposure, confirmation of the diagnosis is based solely on the demonstration of trypanosomes. These organisms may be found in the blood (see Fig. 393–1), bone marrow, centrifuged CSF, lymph node aspirates, and scrapings from the chancre. Giemsa or Wright's stain of the buffy coat of centrifuged heparinized blood makes identification easier because the trypanosomes are often concentrated in the buffy coat. In one technique, referred to as the *quantitative buffy coat*, 60 μL of blood obtained by a fingerprick is drawn up in a glass hematocrit tube precoated with acridine orange and anticoagulant. Following centrifugation, the buffy coat can be examined and trypanosomes fluoresce greenish yellow, remain motile, and are easily identified. In patients with Gambian sleeping sickness, in which trypanosomes are found less frequently in the blood, concentration methods such as anion exchange chromatography, diethylaminoethyl filtration, culture, or animal inoculation should be used.

All patients should have a lumbar puncture prior to and following therapy to determine whether CNS involvement is present. Documentation of CNS involvement is imperative because suramin, a drug effective against the hemolymphatic stage of *T. brucei*, does not penetrate the spinal fluid. CNS disease is manifested by pleocytosis (>5 polymorphonuclear leukocytes per milliliter) and elevation of spinal fluid total protein and IgM levels. Trypanosomes can be found in most patients, provided that the CSF is examined immediately after collection and that clean glassware is used. For those patients in whom trypanosomes cannot be found, measuring the CSF IgM is often of great diagnostic help. A high CSF IgM value and a modest increase in total protein are almost pathognomonic of sleeping sickness.

Several immunodiagnostic tests and molecular diagnostic assays have been developed for African trypanosomiasis, including an indirect hemagglutination test, indirect fluorescent antibody test, and enzyme-linked immunosorbent assay, which are useful for epidemiologic surveys. A card agglutination trypanosome test (CATT) with pre-fixed trypanosomes is frequently used for rapid serodiagnosis. Although highly sensitive, CATT may remain positive for several years after successful treatment, thereby decreasing its ability to differentiate between acute infection and a previous, treated infection. A polymerase chain reaction assay for African trypanosomiasis has recently been developed for detection of trypanosomal DNA in blood and CSF. Although the test is highly sensitive, specificity for detection of active disease still needs to be more accurately determined in large clinical trials.

Rx Treatment

Suramin* is the drug of choice for the early hemolymphatic stage of both *T. brucei gambiense* and *T. brucei rhodesiense* infections before CNS invasion has occurred. Suramin does not cross the blood-brain barrier in increased amounts, and it does not cure the disease once CNS invasion has occurred. The dose is 20 mg/kg of body weight given intravenously up to a maximum single dose of 1 g. Suramin is freshly prepared as a 10% aqueous solution. Intramuscular injection is not advised because of local irritation and pain. Suramin binds to plasma proteins and may persist in the circulation at low concentrations for as long as 3 months. A test dose of 200 mg is given initially; if no adverse side effects are noted, then full doses of the drug may be given on days 1, 3, 7, 14, and 21. A single course for an adult is usually 5 g; it should not exceed 7 g.

Suramin is a toxic drug that may result in idiosyncratic reactions in some individuals (1 in 20,000). The drug is excreted entirely by the kidneys; renal damage may result because the drug is deposited in the renal tubules. The urine should be examined before administering each dose of suramin, and if proteinuria or casts are present, treatment should be stopped. Other side effects include a papular eruption, photophobia, arthralgias, peripheral neuritis, fever, and agranulocytosis.

Pentamidine isethionate* is an alternative drug for treating early hemolymphatic African trypanosomiasis, but it is much less active against *T. brucei rhodesiense* than is suramin. The dose is 4 mg/kg of body weight; it is given every other day by intramuscular injection for a total of 10 injections. Pentamidine is also ineffective for treating CNS trypanosomiasis.

The arsenical melarsoprol* (Mel B) is the treatment of choice for both Gambian and Rhodesian sleeping sickness once involvement of the CNS has occurred. The drug is given in three courses of 3 days each. The recommended dosage is 2 to 3.6 mg/kg per day given intravenously in three divided doses for 3 days, followed 1 week later by 3.6 mg/kg per day in three divided doses for 3 days. This latter course is then repeated 10 to 21 days later. A recent trial showed similar efficacy with 10 daily injections of 2.2 mg/kg of melarsoprol compared to the standard 26-day course, although additional studies are required to examine long-term effects from either treatment regimen. Melarsoprol is a highly toxic drug and should be administered with great care. If signs of arsenical toxicity occur, the drug should be discontinued. The most important side effects involve the CNS. A reactive encephalopathy, probably due to release of trypanosomal antigens, may occur early in the course of treatment, and its incidence has been reported to be as high as 18%. It may develop very rapidly or insidiously, and its mortality is about 50%. Clinical indications of reactive encephalopathy include high fever, headache, tremor, seizures, and finally coma. It has been suggested that corticosteroids protect patients from melarsoprol encephalopathy, but this assertion has not been clearly documented.

An alternative drug for both systemic and CNS involvement is difluoromethylornithine (eflornithine, DFMO), a specific, irreversible inhibitor of orboxylase. In one large trial of 207 patients with late-stage *T. brucei gambiense* sleeping sickness, eflornithine was highly effective in successful treatment of both hemolymphatic and CNS stages of infection. Eflornithine dramatically reduced symptoms and rapidly cleared parasites from blood and CSF, even in those patients who had relapsed after melarsoprol therapy. The recommended dosage is 400 mg/kg per day given intravenously in four divided doses for 2 weeks, followed by 300 mg/kg per day given orally in four doses for 30 days. In a multicenter, randomized, controlled trial of 321 patients, a 7-day course of eflornithine was effective in the treatment of relapsing cases of Gambian trypanosomiasis but was inferior to the 14-day course for treatment of new cases. Frequent side effects include diarrhea and anemia. Unfortunately, its efficacy in *T. brucei rhodesiense* has been quite variable, and its cost and long duration of therapy have limited its usefulness in the field. In addition, immunocompromised patients such as those with HIV infection do not respond to treatment as effectively with any of the earlier mentioned agents because a normal immune response is necessary for a cure. Regular follow-up with clinical examination and a lumbar puncture is necessary for all patients for at least a year after treatment.

Prognosis

Untreated African sleeping sickness is almost invariably fatal. Many patients with early Gambian sleeping sickness may remain relatively well for months to years without treatment, but once CNS involvement has occurred, death is inevitable unless treatment is given. Death frequently results from pneumonia in Gambian sleeping sickness and from heart failure in Rhodesian sleeping sickness. Treatment with suramin in the early phase of sleeping sickness results in a cure rate of more than 90%. A few patients may subsequently develop CNS involvement and require further treatment. Mel B achieves a parasitologic cure in at least 90% of cases of advanced disease, and many patients may recover completely. Unfortunately, some patients are left with irreversible neurologic damage. Approximately 5% of patients may die during the course of Mel B therapy.

Control and Prevention

Measures to prevent and control African trypanosomiasis can be instituted at three different levels: surveillance and treatment, chemoprophylaxis, and vector control. Surveillance with treatment is necessary to reduce the human reservoir of infection, particularly in areas where epidemics have occurred in the past. Pentamidine has been successfully used as a chemoprophylactic in Gambian sleeping sickness following mass screening and treatment of seropositive and trypanosomal-positive individuals regardless of symptoms. Pentamidine is given as a single intramuscular injection of 4 mg/kg every 3 to 6

---

*Available from the Centers for Disease Control and Prevention, Atlanta, GA.

months. However, the drug is generally not recommended for mass use, and it appears to be ineffective against Rhodesian trypanosomiasis.

Vector control requires destruction of tsetse fly habitats by selective clearing of vegetation and spraying with insecticides, which are effective only temporarily. Because of the wide range of the tsetse fly, these vector control measures are not economically feasible except when it is necessary to break transmission in epidemics. For individual protection, avoidance of contact with infected tsetse flies is best achieved by the use of repellents and protective clothing.

A vaccine is not currently available because of the occurrence of antigenic variation. However, the potential for development of a vaccine has increased with the progress in cultivation of *T. brucei* in vitro and analysis of the chemical structure of its variant antigens.

SUGGESTED READINGS

Burri C, Nkunku S, Merolle A, et al: Efficacy of new, concise schedule for melarsoprol in treatment of sleeping sickness caused by *Trypanosoma brucei gambiense*: A randomised trial. Lancet 2000;355:1419–1425. *A trial that showed similar efficacy with 10 daily injections of 2.2 mg/kg of melarsoprol compared to the standard 26-day course.*

Hutchinson OC, Fevre EM, Carrington M, et al: Lessons learned from the emergence of a new *Trypanosoma brucei rhodesiense* sleeping sickness focus in Uganda. Lancet Infect Dis 2003;1:42–45. *Describes the evolution of a new epidemic of trypanosomiasis in Uganda and efforts to control it utilizing new molecular biology techniques and successful disease control management.*

Legros D, Ollivier G, Gastellu-Etchegorry M, et al: Treatment of human African trypanosomiasis—present situation and needs for research and development. Lancet Infect Dis 2002;2:437–440. *An excellent review of the current treatment regimens, with a discussion of their pros and cons.*

Pepin J, Khonde N, Maiso F, et al: Short-course eflornithine in Gambian trypanosomiasis: A multicentre randomized controlled trial. Bull World Health Organ 2000;78:1284–1295. *The largest trial to date comparing a 7-day regimen versus the standard 14-day regimen of eflornithine. The 14-day regimen was found to be superior for acute disease.*

Pepin J, Meda IIA. The epidemiology and control of human African trypanosomiasis. Adv Parasitol 2001;49:71–132. *The most recent review of the resurgence in African trypanosomiasis in sub-Saharan Africa.*

394 AMERICAN TRYPANOSOMIASIS (CHAGAS' DISEASE)

Franklin A. Neva

Definition

Chagas' disease, resulting from infection with the protozoan parasite *Trypanosoma cruzi*, is named after the Brazilian physician Carlos Chagas, who discovered the parasite. Distinction should be made between infection by the parasite (i.e., positive serology only) and presence of clinical disease. Chronic disease manifestations develop years after initial infection in the form of chronic cardiomyopathy with conduction defects or with dysfunction of the esophagus or colon (i.e., megadisease syndromes).

Life Cycle of the Causative Agent

The causative agent, *T. cruzi*, is usually transmitted by various species of blood-sucking reduviid bugs. The bugs become infected when they take a blood meal from animals or humans who have circulating parasites, trypomastigotes, in the blood. The ingested parasites transform into epimastigotes and multiply in the midgut of the insect vector, where they later transform again into metacyclic trypomastigotes in the hindgut of the bug. When the infected bug takes a subsequent blood meal, it frequently defecates during or after feeding, so that the infective metacyclic forms are deposited on the skin. Transmission to a second vertebrate host occurs when the feeding puncture site or a mucous membrane is inadvertently contaminated with infective bug feces. The parasites can penetrate a variety of host cell types, within which they transform into intracellular amastigote forms. In contrast to certain other intracellular organisms, amastigotes of *T. cruzi* are not enclosed in phagolysosomes. They multiply in the cytoplasm, elongate, transform into motile trypomastigotes, and rupture out of the cells. Liberated organisms penetrate new cells or are carried into the blood stream to initiate further cycles of multiplication, preferentially in muscle cells, or are ingested by new vectors to maintain the cycle (Fig. 394–1).

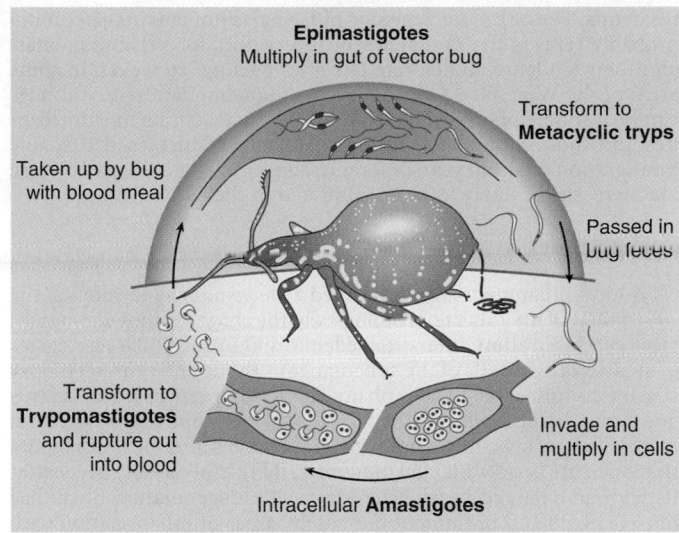

Epimastigotes
Multiply in gut of vector bug

Transform to **Metacyclic tryps**

Taken up by bug with blood meal

Passed in bug feces

Transform to **Trypomastigotes** and rupture out into blood

Invade and multiply in cells

Intracellular **Amastigotes**

FIGURE 394–1 • Life cycle of *Trypanosoma cruzi*.

Asymptomatic infected individuals with low-level parasitemia can transmit *T. cruzi* through blood transfusion. Another route of transmission of the parasite is congenital infection.

Epidemiology

T. cruzi and its arthropod vectors are widely distributed from the southern United States through Mexico and Central America into South America down to central Argentina and Chile. The parasite is restricted to the Western Hemisphere. In most countries where it occurs, the parasite cycle is sylvatic (i.e., it takes place in wild animals and their associated vector bugs). A peridomestic cycle occurs under conditions in which infected animals, such as opossums and rats, live close to human habitations, and vector bugs may invade houses to seek a blood meal. Certain species of triatomine bugs, such as *Triatoma infestans* and *Rhodnius prolixus*, have a great propensity to invade and breed in houses if suitable microenvironments are present. Cracks and holes in adobe mud huts or in crude wooden walls, thatched roofs, and household rubble provide hiding and breeding places for the bugs, which venture out at night to feed on sleeping inhabitants. Under these conditions *T. cruzi* is transmitted from person to person—a domiciliary cycle—and the infection becomes a public health problem. Human trypanosomiasis in Latin America is primarily an infection of rural poor people living in substandard housing.

The prevalence of antibodies to the parasite in human populations varies widely in different countries and within regions of a country. It is not unusual for up to one half of all inhabitants in selected villages to be antibody positive. However, since 1984, the overall prevalence of seropositivity in Brazil, for example, has decreased greatly from about 4% to less than 0.5%. Countries with the highest incidences of infection and disease due to *T. cruzi* include Brazil, Argentina, Chile, Bolivia, and Venezuela. It is estimated that, in all of the Americas, a total of 15 million people are infected. In many Latin American countries, positive serology for *T. cruzi* constitutes a social stigma; a lower socioeconomic background is implied, and employers are reluctant to hire someone who may later develop chronic Chagas' disease.

Considerable geographic variation exists in the prevalence and the type of chronic disease manifestations. In Brazil, for example, cardiomyopathy and megadisease are common, and some patients may have both types of involvement. However, chagasic megaesophagus and megacolon are virtually unknown in Venezuela, Colombia, and Panama, whereas the prevalence of cardiomyopathy is relatively high, moderate, and low, respectively. In general, the frequency of cardiac disease in Central America and Mexico in seropositive persons is low, even though rates of seropositivity may be substantial. In these countries, heart disease tends to develop later in life than in Brazil, Bolivia, or Argentina.

The situation regarding Chagas' disease in the United States is interesting because only four autochthonous acute cases have been recognized despite the presence of *T. cruzi* in vector bugs and in animal reservoirs. The lack of transmission of *T. cruzi* to humans in this country probably reflects the preference of the vectors for sylvatic habitats and their tendency to defecate late after feeding. However, in some areas of the West, bites from aggressive and abundant reduviid bugs can be a source of annoyance to and allergic reactions in suburbanites and those frequently outdoors. Because of increased Hispanic immigration in recent years, sporadic cases of chronic Chagas' disease are increasingly likely to be encountered in the United States.

Pathology

A local inflammatory lesion called a *chagoma* may develop at the site of entry of the parasite. Histologically, the chagoma shows mononuclear cell infiltration, interstitial edema, and intracellular aggregates of amastigotes in cells of the subcutaneous tissue and muscle. Biopsy specimens from enlarged lymph nodes show hyperplasia, and amastigotes may be present in reticular cells. Skeletal muscle tissue from muscle biopsy specimens has shown organisms and focal inflammation. In acute cases with fatal outcomes, there is invariably myocarditis with an enlarged heart. Microscopically, degeneration of cardiac muscle fibers and prominent but patchy areas of inflammation with nests of amastigotes in the muscles are observed. The brain and meninges may also be parasitized in acute Chagas' disease. Virtually all organs and cell types can be invaded by *T. cruzi.*

The organs primarily affected in *chronic Chagas' disease* are the heart and hollow viscera, especially the esophagus and colon. Surprisingly, the intracellular *T. cruzi* usually cannot be found in the affected organs, or a few may be demonstrable after protracted search of many tissue sections. The size of the heart in patients with chronic disease who die suddenly, presumably of ventricular arrhythmias or heart block, may be normal or only moderately enlarged. Other patients with chronic chagasic cardiomyopathy experience cardiomegaly and die of intractable failure. The hearts are hypertrophied and dilated, with thinning, especially at the apex, to form a characteristic apical aneurysm. Mural thrombi, with subsequent embolization of the lungs and peripheral organs, are frequently seen. The coronary arteries usually are normal.

Microscopic findings in the heart are not specific, consisting of focal mononuclear cell infiltrates, hypertrophy of cardiac fibers with patchy areas of necrosis, variable fibrosis, and edema. The components of the conduction system of the heart most often involved by inflammatory changes are the sinoatrial and atrioventricular nodes, as well as the right branch and left anterior branches of the bundle of His. Andrade's detailed studies of these pathologic changes indicated that they correlated well with electrocardiographic (ECG) changes during life but were diffusely scattered without specific localization to the conducting system.

When the esophagus or the colon is affected in chronic Chagas' disease, the gross appearance is of dilation and hypertrophy of the affected organ. The microscopic pathologic changes are disappointingly similar to those in the heart, with no or very few organisms identified. However, myenteric ganglion cells are strikingly reduced in number. This type of parasympathetic denervation may also be found in other hollow viscera, such as the duodenum, ureters, or biliary tree.

The significant pathologic characteristic of *congenital Chagas' disease* is chronic placentitis, with inflammatory changes and focal necrosis in the chorionic villi. Amastigotes of *T. cruzi* are present in the lesions. The presence of lesions and organisms in the placenta may be associated with abortion, stillbirth, or acute disease in the fetus. However, pregnancy may result in a normal fetus, even though placental lesions are present.

Individuals with antibodies to *T. cruzi* but without evidence of clinical disease are considered to represent the *indeterminate* form. Some of these patients maintain a low-level parasitemia demonstrable only with very sensitive techniques. One point of view is that indeterminate cases have a smoldering disease process that will become evident later. However, there are no tests that can predict whether or when evidence of chronic disease will develop. Even in areas where chronic disease is common, one half or more of those with positive serologic findings eventually die of causes other than Chagas' disease. In countries of lower endemicity, the risk of chronic disease is correspondingly less.

The pathologic characteristics of acute Chagas' disease are straightforward, but the pathogenesis of chronic cardiomyopathy or megadisease is still poorly understood. Key features of the chronic disease that must be explained include the following: (1) a latent period of up to 20 years from presumed initial infection with *T. cruzi* before manifestations of cardiomyopathy or megadisease appear; (2) no or very few intracellular parasites in the affected organs, in contrast to abundant parasites in tissues in acute cases; (3) destruction of autonomic parasympathetic ganglia (i.e., Auerbach's plexus) of the esophagus and colon; and (4) great geographic variation in the frequency and type of chronic Chagas' disease. Genetic diversity in parasite strains, including variation in animal virulence, may explain geographic differences in disease. The autoimmunity concept for pathogenesis of chronic disease has been losing favor to increasing evidence by polymerase chain reaction (PCR) and immunohistochemical staining that focal inflammatory lesions containing mainly CD8+ T cells in affected tissues contain a few persisting parasites. However, this does not preclude a concomitant autoimmune reaction to parasite antigens that have been shown to share antigenic epitopes with neural tissues.

The indeterminate latent stage of infection with *T. cruzi* may be activated into a state of acute disease under conditions of severe immunosuppression. This can occur in seropositive recipients of organ transplantation. Reports of activation of disease are increasing, especially with brain involvement similar to that produced by *Toxoplasma* species, in patients with acquired immunodeficiency syndrome (AIDS) who also have latent *T. cruzi* infection.

Clinical Manifestations

In endemic areas, first exposure to *T. cruzi* generally is subclinical and unnoticed. When those initially exposed do have clinical manifestations, the disease is an acute systemic infection. Chronic Chagas' disease evolves as a later sequela with specific organ involvement and no systemic features.

ACUTE CHAGAS' DISEASE. Although acute Chagas' disease is most commonly seen in children in endemic areas, it can occur at any age, depending on epidemiologic circumstances. The incubation period under natural conditions cannot be established accurately but is probably at least a week. A local area of erythema and induration (i.e., chagoma) may develop in the skin at the site of parasite entry. When infection takes place by the conjunctival route, as it frequently does, the local periorbital swelling is referred to as Romaña's sign. The chagoma is often accompanied by regional adenopathy and persists for several weeks. Other signs of acute Chagas' disease include fever, generalized lymphadenopathy, hepatosplenomegaly, and transient skin rashes.

Myocarditis, accompanied by tachycardia and nonspecific ECG changes, can occur in the acute stage. Meningoencephalitis is another serious complication, particularly in very young patients. The fact that trypanosomes may be found in the spinal fluid of some acute cases who show no obvious meningeal signs helps explain the frequent involvement of the brain in latent infections activated by human immunodeficiency virus (HIV) infection or AIDS. Fatal outcomes are rare, but when death does occur, it is caused by myocarditis and congestive failure or by meningoencephalitis.

Signs and symptoms of acute disease gradually subside within a few weeks to several months even without treatment. Trypanosomes, which have been demonstrable by direct microscopy in the peripheral blood during the acute phase, become more difficult to find and then disappear. The patient then enters the *indeterminate phase*. This state of apparent complete recovery with positive serologic findings may continue indefinitely without further evidence of disease or sequelae. However, a variable proportion of indeterminate cases, years to a decade or more later, develops signs and symptoms of chronic Chagas' disease. Except for epidemiologic experience from a particular geographic region, there are no laboratory or clinical indicators to predict the likelihood of future chronic disease.

CHRONIC CHAGAS' DISEASE. Cardiac signs and symptoms are the most common manifestations of chronic disease and are likely to begin with palpitations, dizziness, precordial discomfort, and even syncope. These reflect a variety of arrhythmias, including ventricular extrasystoles, bouts of tachycardia, and various degrees of heart block. Sudden death due to ventricular tachycardia in an otherwise healthy young adult is not unusual. Symptoms due to arrhythmias may be present for a long time before cardiomegaly or evidence of cardiac failure appears. When congestive failure develops, it is predominantly right sided and is likely to lead to a fatal outcome within a few years. Peripheral emboli to the brain or other organs are common.

Physical examination reveals only an irregular pulse, distant heart sounds, and perhaps a gallop rhythm. With failure, the heart can be very large, functional regurgitant murmurs may be heard, and there are often congestive hepatomegaly and peripheral edema.

The second most common chronic manifestation is megadisease of the esophagus or colon, most frequently the former. The symptoms are indistinguishable from those of idiopathic achalasia and include dysphagia, feeling of fullness after eating or drinking only small amounts, chest pain, and regurgitation. Aspiration with secondary pneumonia is a common complication in advanced cases, as are weight loss and cachexia. Salivary gland hypertrophy from hypersalivation is sometimes seen. Esophageal cancer is reported to be more common in patients with chagasic megaesophagus, as with idiopathic achalasia.

Patients with chagasic megacolon suffer from chronic constipation and abdominal pain. Volvulus, obstruction, and perforation of the bowel may occur. An astonishing history of an interval of several weeks between bowel movements has been obtained from some patients with severe megacolon. Megaesophagus and megacolon may both be present in the same patient, and cardiomyopathy can occur with either form of megadisease.

Diagnosis

For acute and chronic Chagas' disease, a history of possible exposure to *T. cruzi* should be sought. Usual tourist travel to endemic areas is not likely to provide sufficient exposure to infected vectors. Blood transfusion from a chronically infected donor can be a source of infection.

For *acute Chagas' disease,* direct microscopic examination of anticoagulated blood or a buffy coat preparation for motile trypanosomes is the most important procedure. Organisms are more difficult to find on stained thin or thick blood films, but the morphologic features of organisms seen on direct microscopy should be confirmed in a stained preparation. Red cells may be lysed, using a 0.083% solution of ammonium chloride (NH_4Cl) to concentrate parasites by centrifugation. If parasites cannot be found in the peripheral blood and acute disease is still suspected, blood can be cultured on Novy, MacNeal, and Nicolle's medium (NNN) or other suitable media. Inoculation of mice with the patient's blood may sometimes result in recovery of the parasite. Biopsy of an enlarged lymph node or of skeletal muscle for culture or histologic examination is another possibility.

A time-honored, labor-intensive, but very sensitive technique for recovering trypanosomes from the blood is a procedure referred to as *xenodiagnosis.* It is a form of blood culture using the insect vector, by allowing up to 40 normal, laboratory-reared reduviid bugs to feed directly on the patient or on the patient's blood through a membrane. Circulating parasites ingested by the bugs multiply in the gut and can be detected when the intestinal contents are examined 30 days later. PCR detection of *T. cruzi* DNA from the blood has been demonstrated and will likely replace other methods in terms of sensitivity and convenience.

Serologic testing is generally not needed to diagnose acute disease. Parasite-specific immunoglobulin M (IgM) antibodies detected by immunofluorescence or direct agglutination do not become positive until 20 to 40 days after the onset of symptoms. In certain situations, this delayed antibody response permits the demonstration of seroconversion. Other laboratory tests often show nonspecific changes, such as a lymphocytic leukocytosis, elevated sedimentation rate, or transient ECG abnormalities. Reversible cardiomegaly and even pericardial effusion may occur.

The diagnosis of *chronic Chagas' disease* requires demonstration of antibodies to *T. cruzi* in the presence of the characteristic cardiac abnormalities or megadisease. Except for the positive serologic findings, the diagnosis relies heavily on clinical judgment to exclude other causes of heart disease or gastrointestinal dysfunction. A positive xenodiagnosis or PCR result is strongly supportive but is not in itself diagnostic of chronic disease, because patients in the indeterminate phase may have low-level parasitemia. A variety of assays for specific antibody are available, and the results of different tests generally are comparable. However, there are cross-reactions in some tests with sera from patients with leishmaniasis or syphilis, for example. In individual cases, it may be helpful to confirm the presence of antibody to specific antigens of *T. cruzi* with more sophisticated tests, such as immunoblots.

Symptomatic heart involvement in the chronic disease manifests with characteristic ECG abnormalities, often without cardiomegaly. The most common of these is complete right bundle branch block. Other frequent ECG findings are left anterior hemiblock, ventricular extrasystoles, and complete heart block. If heart failure occurs, radiographs and echocardiograms show generalized cardiomegaly with a reduced ejection fraction (Fig. 394-2).

Chagasic megaesophagus in the early stages shows only delayed emptying and minimal dilation on studies after a barium swallow. With more advanced disease, retention of swallowed material and esophageal dilation are progressively increased. Manometric studies show spasm of the esophageal sphincter and uncoordinated peristaltic movements. Endoscopy should be performed to rule out malignant

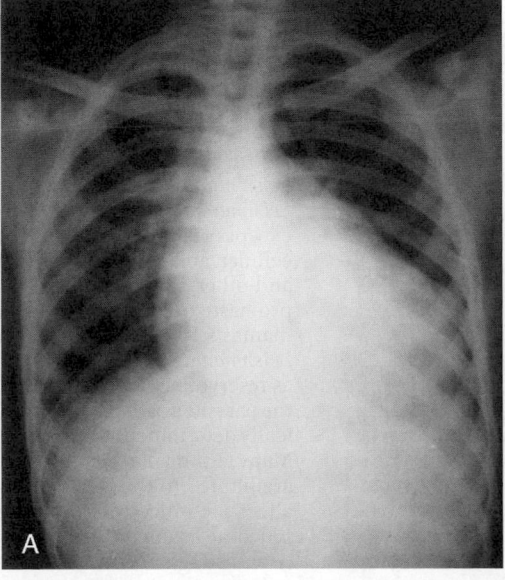
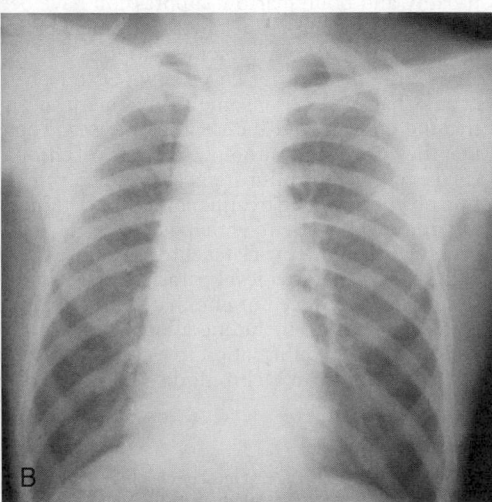

FIGURE 394–2 • *A,* Cardiac silhouette in a patient with chronic chagasic cardiomyopathy and heart failure. *B,* Chest radiograph shows a widened mediastinum due to a greatly dilated megaesophagus of chronic Chagas' disease.

disease. All of these findings, however, are indistinguishable from those of idiopathic achalasia. Barium enema with air contrast shows the dilated colon with impaired peristalsis, but other causes of colonic obstruction must be ruled out.

Differential Diagnosis

When acute Chagas' disease is symptomatic and severe, it can resemble a variety of acute systemic infections. Romaña's sign must be distinguished from other causes of unilateral orbital edema, such as the reaction to an insect bite, trauma, or orbital cellulitis. Congenital infections are virtually indistinguishable from congenital toxoplasmosis, cytomegalic inclusion disease, and syphilis.

Various cardiomyopathies, such as postpartum, alcoholic, and endomyocardial fibrosis, can resemble chronic Chagas' heart disease. Routine endomyocardial biopsy is of limited diagnostic value. However, substantial yields for PCR-positive biopsy specimens have been reported when the procedure is guided by imaging techniques to sites of myocardial inflammation and when multiple biopsies are taken. The characteristic heart murmurs of rheumatic valvular disease are helpful in differentiating this entity from chagasic cardiomyopathy. The value of positive serologic findings for *T. cruzi* in the differential diagnosis of heart disease and megadisease depends on the background prevalence of antibodies in the general population.

Rx Treatment

Two drugs with reasonable antitrypanosomal activity are currently in use for treating Chagas' disease. One of these is a nitrofuran derivative, nifurtimox,* which has been extensively evaluated. Nifurtimox is the only drug available in the United States for treating Chagas' disease; it is used in a dose of 8 to 10 mg/kg/day. The second drug, benznidazole, is a nitroimidazole derivative that appears to be equal to nifurtimox in efficacy, although there is less experience with its use. The exact mechanism of antitrypanosomal action of both of these drugs is unknown.

There is considerable evidence that, if patients with acute Chagas' disease are treated with nifurtimox or benznidazole, the extent of disease and parasitemia usually is reduced. More importantly, in many patients treated in the acute phase, antibodies to *T. cruzi* never develop or do so only transiently. From this observation, plus the fact that xenodiagnosis in such treated patients often has negative findings, it is assumed that parasites can be eliminated and the patient cured if treated in the acute stage. However, nifurtimox is not uniformly effective in producing these results, and parasite strains from certain geographic areas (e.g., Brazil) appear to be less responsive to treatment than do strains from other countries (e.g., Argentina, Chile).

The frequency of side effects from nifurtimox and benznidazole is high; because they are administered for 90 to 120 days, drug toxicity is a serious problem. The most common adverse effect with nifurtimox is gastrointestinal intolerance, with anorexia, nausea, vomiting, and abdominal pain. Neurologic symptoms include restlessness, insomnia, disorientation, paresthesias, polyneuritis, and seizures. Rashes can also occur. Peripheral neuropathy and bone marrow suppression have been reported with benznidazole. These side effects subside when the dosage of the drugs is reduced or treatment is stopped.

Because these drugs have shown effectiveness in treatment of acute Chagas' disease, some Latin American physicians are also treating chronic and indeterminate cases. There is no evidence that the established pathologic changes of chronic Chagas' disease can be reversed by nifurtimox or benznidazole therapy. The question of whether drug treatment in the indeterminate case (i.e., the asymptomatic patient with positive serologic findings) would prevent development of later chronic disease is controversial. Some data suggest that low-level parasitemia, as assessed by xenodiagnosis, can be reduced or eliminated after treatment with antitrypanosomal drugs, including allopurinol. However, such studies require critical confirmation to establish their ultimate influence on the development of chronic disease, as well as risk versus benefit evaluation.

*An investigational drug that must be obtained from the Centers for Disease Control and Prevention Drug Service (404-639-3670).

The treatment of patients with established chronic heart disease is supportive. Patients with frequent ventricular premature beats can benefit from antiarrhythmic drugs such as amiodarone. Cardiac pacemakers can prolong survival of those with complete heart block. The congestive failure of chagasic cardiomyopathy is disappointingly refractory to the usual cardiotropic drugs.

More options are open for managing and treating megadisease. In the early stages of megaesophagus, pneumatic dilation of the sphincter is probably more effective than bougienage. For more advanced cases, various surgical procedures involving myotomy of the sphincter or partial resection are necessary. Early stages of megacolon can be managed by manipulating diet and using laxatives and occasionally using enemas. Sometimes, an aperistaltic section of the colon can be resected in more severe cases.

Prevention

Chagas' disease could be eliminated as a serious health problem for the rural poor of Latin America by adequate housing and education. However, stark socioeconomic realities dictate another approach to control. It consists mainly of the use of residual insecticides directed at domiciliary vectors and sprayed once or twice each year. With this measure, plus screening in blood banks to exclude seropositive donors, the transmission of *T. cruzi* in several South American countries has been greatly reduced.

Serologic testing in blood banks to prevent use of seropositive donors is carried out in endemic areas. Another precaution is to add a 1 : 4000 dilution of gentian violet to blood 24 hours before use to kill trypanosomes that may be present. With the occurrence of several transfusion-associated cases of acute Chagas' disease in North America, the question of serologic screening of blood donors has been raised for areas of the country with large Latin American populations. The development of vaccines is still in the research stage.

SUGGESTED READINGS

Coura JR, de Castro SI: A critical review on Chagas' disease chemotherapy. Mem Inst Oswaldo Cruz 2002;97:3–24. *This review, which concentrates mainly on chemotherapy for Chagas' disease, also touches on other aspects of the subject.*

Gomes JA, Bahia-Oliveira LM, Rocha MO, et al: Evidence that development of severe cardiomyopathy in human Chagas' disease is due to a Th1-specific immune response. Infect Immun 2003;71:1185–1193. *Data to suggest that an exacerbated production of IFN-gamma against Trypanosoma cruzi antigens favors the development of a strong Th1 response, which leads to progression of heart disease.*

Kirchhoff LV: Changing epidemiology and approaches to therapy for Chagas disease. Curr Infect Dis Rep 2003;5:59–65. *Blood screening programs and vector control have reduced incidence, but nifurtimox and benznidazole, both of which have limited efficacy and often cause severe side effects, remain the only treatment options.*

Salles G, Xavier S, Sousa A, et al: Prognostic value of QT interval parameters for mortality risk stratification in Chagas' disease: Results of a long-term follow-up study. Circulation 2003;108:305–312. *The QT interval and echocardiographic LV end-systolic dimension were the most important predictors of mortality.*

395 LEISHMANIASIS

Selma M. B. Jeronimo
Anastacio de Queiroz Sousa
Richard D. Pearson

Leishmaniasis refers to the spectrum of clinical disease produced by *Leishmania* species, which are endemic in areas of every continent except Australia and Antarctica. *Leishmania* are found in their intracellular, amastigote form within mononuclear phagocytes in humans and other mammals. The parasite is transmitted in its extracellular, promastigote form by phlebotomine sand flies. In many areas leishmaniasis is a zoonosis. Depending on the geographic location and *Leishmania* spp., various wild or domestic animals or humans serve as reservoirs. The clinical manifestations of leishmaniasis depend on the parasite's pathogenicity, which differs among species, and the genetically determined cell-mediated immune responses of its human host. Many leishmanial infections are asymptomatic and self-resolving. Some are limited to the skin resulting in cutaneous leishmaniasis, or they affect the mucosa of the nose, mouth, or oral pharynx resulting in mucosal leishmaniasis. In visceral leishmaniasis parasites disseminate throughout the reticuloendothelial system.

An estimated 350 million people are at risk of acquiring infection in focally endemic regions scattered throughout the world. The incidence of cutaneous leishmaniasis is estimated to be 1 million to 1.5 million cases a year and the incidence of visceral leishmaniasis to be 500,000 cases per year. Cutaneous leishmaniasis poses a substantial problem for settlers, residents, military personnel, and expatriates working or traveling in endemic areas of Latin America, the Middle East, and Asia. Mucosal leishmaniasis due to *Leishmania braziliensis* and related species is a serious problem in Latin American countries. Visceral leishmaniasis is endemic in eastern India and Bangladesh, the Sudan where a major epidemic has occurred over the past decade among refugees, and in Latin American countries. It has emerged as a major urban pathogen in northeastern Brazil. Visceral leishmaniasis is an important opportunistic disease among persons with acquired immunodeficiency syndrome (AIDS) in Southern Europe. In the United States sporadic cases of leishmaniasis are diagnosed in returning travelers or immigrants.

Classification and Life Cycle

The *Leishmania* species that cause human disease, their geographic locations, and the clinical syndromes that they produce are summarized in Table 395–1. They are divided into two subgenera, *Leishmania* and *Viannia*. Although there are slight ultrastructural differences among species, they cannot be used to differentiate one from another. Isoenzyme analysis is available at World Health Organization reference laboratories for speciation. Species-specific monoclonal antibodies and polymerase chain reaction (PCR)–based assays are available in research settings and may emerge as the method of choice for both speciation and diagnosis. Further refinement of the current classification system is likely in the future.

The life cycle is depicted in Figure 395–1. *Leishmania* are digenetic parasites with two basic forms. In humans and other mammals, *Leishmania* are found within mononuclear phagocytes as intracellular amastigotes that are oval or round in shape and 2 to 3 μm in

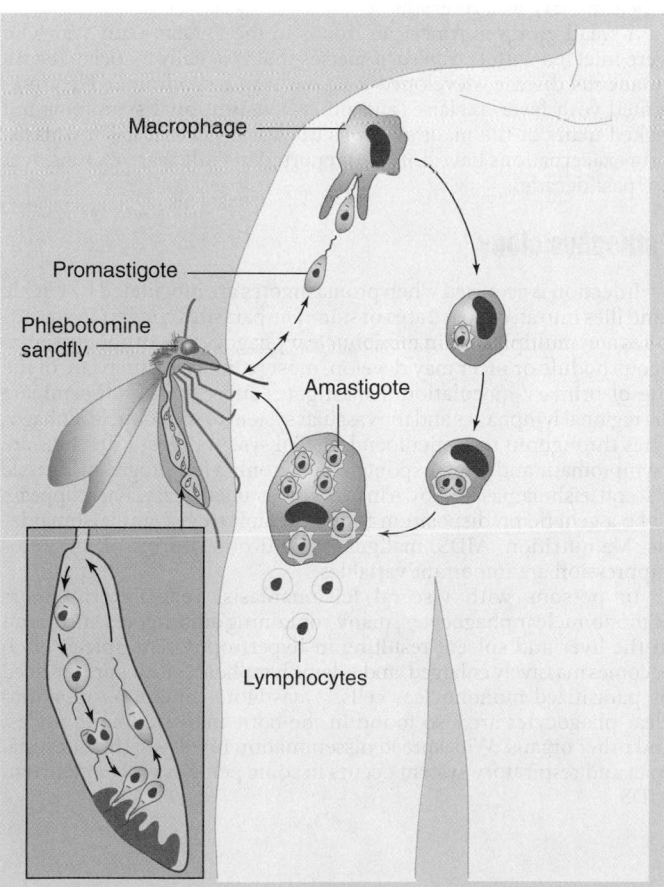

FIGURE 395–1 • Life cycle of *Leishmania*. Humans serve as the reservoir for *Leishmania donovani* in India, as depicted here. In most settings leishmaniasis is a zoonosis with rodents or canines as reservoirs.

Table 395–1 • GEOGRAPHIC DISTRIBUTION AND CLINICAL SYNDROMES CAUSED BY *LEISHMANIA* SPECIES

CLINICAL SYNDROMES	*LEISHMANIA* SPECIES	LOCATION
Visceral Leishmaniasis		
Kala-azar: generalized involvement of the reticuloendothelial system (e.g., spleen, bone marrow, liver)	L. donovani	Indian subcontinent, North and East China, Pakistan, Nepal
	L. donovani	Sudan, Kenya, Ethiopia
	L. infantum*	Middle East, Mediterranean littoral (e.g., Spain, southern France, Italy), Balkans, Central and Southwest Asia, North and Northwestern China, North and sub-Saharan Africa, Latin America
	L. chagasi*	
	L. amazonensis	Brazil (Bahia State)
	L. tropica	Israel, India, and "viscerotropic" disease in Saudi Arabia (U.S. troops)
Post–kala-azar dermal leishmaniasis	L. donovani	Indian subcontinent
	L. donovani	Sudan, Kenya, Ethiopia, Somalia
Old World Cutaneous Leishmaniasis		
Single or limited number of skin lesions	L. major	Middle East, Northwest China, Northwest India, Pakistan, Africa
	L. tropica	Mediterranean littoral, Middle East, western Asiatic area, Indian subcontinent, Kenya
	L. aethiopica	Ethiopian highlands, Kenya, Yemen
	L. infantum*	Mediterranean basin
	L. donovani	Sudan, Kenya, Ethiopia, Somalia
Diffuse cutaneous leishmaniasis	L. aethiopica	Ethiopian highlands, Kenya, Yemen
New World Cutaneous Leishmaniasis		
Single or limited number of skin lesions	L. mexicana (Chiclero's ulcer)	Central America, Mexico, Texas
	L. amazonensis	Amazon basin, including Brazil and neighboring countries
	L. braziliensis	Multiple areas of Central and South America
	L. guyanensis† (forest yaws)	Guyana, Surinam, northern Amazon basin
	L. panamensis†	Panama, Costa Rica, Colombia
	L. peruviana (uta)	Peru (western Andes), Argentinean highlands
	L. lainsoni	Peru, South America
	L. pifanoi	Venezuela
	L. garnhami	Venezuela
	L. venezuelensis	Venezuela
	L. chagasi*	Central and South America
Diffuse cutaneous leishmaniasis	L. amazonensis	Amazon basin, neighboring areas, Bahia and other states in Brazil
	L. pifanoi	Venezuela
	L. mexicana	Mexico, Central America
	Leishmania spp.	Dominican Republic
American mucosal leishmaniasis	L. braziliensis (Espundia)	Multiple areas in Latin America

*Recent evidence suggests that *L. infantum* and *L. chagasi* are the same species.
†*L. guyanensis* and *L. panamensis* are closely related.
Adapted from Pearson RD, Sousa AQ: Clinical spectrum of leishmaniasis. Clin Infect Dis 1996; 22:1. Data from Lainson R, Shaw JJ: Evolution, classification, and geographic distribution. *In* Peters W, Killick-Kendrick R (eds): The Leishmaniases in Biology and Medicine, vol. 1. London, Academic Press, 1987, pp 1–20.

diameter. They have a relatively large, eccentrically located nucleus; an internalized flagellum; and a rod-shaped specialized mitochondrial structure, the kinetoplast, that contains extranuclear DNA in catenated mini- and maxicircles. Amastigotes are adapted for survival in phagolysosomes in macrophages at mammalian body temperature.

Female sand flies serve as vectors. *Lutzomyia* species predominate in Latin America, and *Phlebotomus* species transmit *Leishmania* elsewhere in the world. Some are peridomestic and live in rubble and debris near houses or farm buildings; others thrive in thick vegetation in forest areas. Sand flies are modified pool feeders and tend to bite at night. They ingest amastigote-containing macrophages when they take a blood meal.

Leishmania convert to flagellated, extracellular promastigotes in the gut of the female sand fly. Promastigotes are 15 to 26 μm in length and 2 to 3 μm in width. They develop from amastigotes and multiply at ambient temperatures of 22° to 26° C. They differentiate through multiple steps to become infectious metacyclic promastigotes, which migrate to the proboscis and are inoculated when the sand fly attempts to take its next blood meal.

Rodents, dogs, humans, or occasionally other animals serve as reservoirs depending on the *Leishmania* species and the geographic location. Promastigotes are phagocytosed by macrophages in the skin and convert to amastigotes within them. Sand fly saliva contains factors such as maxadilan that enhance the infectivity of promastigotes.

Immunologic Characteristics

The outcome of leishmanial infection depends on the virulence characteristics of the infecting species and the genetically determined, cell-mediated immune responses of its human hosts. There appears to be a tenuous balance between the development of protection and disease-permissive immune elements. Animal models of experimental leishmaniasis and humans with naturally acquired infection have been studied in an attempt to identify the cell populations and cytokines involved. Resolution of infection and protection against reinfection correlate with the expansion of CD4+ lymphocytes of the T-helper 1 ($T_H 1$) type (see Chapter 270) and with the secretion of interleukin-12 and interferon-γ in response to leishmanial antigens. Exposure to interferon-γ produced by $T_H 1$ or CD8+ lymphocytes, or direct contact with *Leishmania*-specific CD4+ T cells, can activate macrophages to kill intracellular amastigotes. The production of nitric oxide following induction of nitric oxide synthase in concert with oxygen intermediates is responsible for the microbicidal effect. Tumor necrosis factor-α (TNF-α) appears to contribute to the protective response. Once infection has resolved, humans are typically resistant to disease with the infecting *Leishmania* species unless they become immunocompromised.

The development of protective $T_H 1$ responses is delayed or inhibited in persons with clinically apparent leishmaniasis. In the case of cutaneous leishmaniasis, this occurs locally at the site of the lesion in the skin. In those with progressive visceral leishmaniasis it is generalized. Two cytokines, interleukin-10 and transforming growth factor-β, are thought to be important in interfering with the development of protective $T_H 1$ responses. Antileishmanial antibodies are produced during infection, but they are not protective. The highest titers are observed in persons with progressive visceral leishmaniasis and large parasite burdens.

There is evidence that both $T_H 1$ and $T_H 2$ cells are present early in human infection. Despite intensive study, the precise interactions among infected macrophages, dendritic cells, and lymphocyte populations and the cytokines that they produce have not yet been fully characterized. A number of factors may be involved. There is evidence to suggest that the size of the infecting inoculum, the natural macrophage resistance factors, the sequence of the initial cytokine response, and the manner in which leishmanial antigens are presented affect the immune response and outcome of infection.

VISCERAL LEISHMANIASIS

Epidemiology (see Table 395-1)

Most cases of visceral leishmaniasis are caused by *Leishmania donovani* or *Leishmania infantum/Leishmania chagasi*. The latter two species are closely related if not identical. On occasion *Leishmania* species predominantly associated with cutaneous disease, such as *Leishmania tropica* or *Leishmania amazonensis,* are isolated from patients with classic visceral leishmaniasis. Transmission is dependent on an appropriate reservoir and sand fly vector. Rarely transmission is congenital, through transfusion of contaminated blood, or by accidental needle stick in the laboratory. Recent data from Spain suggest that sharing of needles by *Leishmania*-infected addicts may also be important.

L. donovani remains an important cause of morbidity and mortality in eastern India and Bangladesh, where as many as half of the world's cases of visceral leishmaniasis occur. The number of cases decreased with the widespread use of residual chlorophenothane spraying for malaria following World War II, but there was a dramatic increase in incidence when spraying was discontinued. Humans are the reservoir of infection for *L. donovani* in India; the disease is transmitted by anthropophilic sand flies that become infected when they feed on persons with visceral leishmaniasis or post–kala-azar dermal leishmaniasis. Disease occurs in persons of all ages. *L. donovani* is also endemic in focal areas of eastern Africa in Kenya, Ethiopia, Somalia, and the Sudan, where a very large epidemic has occurred among refugees during the past decade. The reservoirs include rodents and small carnivores. Humans may serve as a reservoir during epidemics.

Visceral leishmaniasis due to *L. infantum* occurs sporadically among infants, children, and immunocompromised persons in Southern Europe, North Africa, the Middle East, Central Asia, and China, although cases are now rare in the latter. Canines including domestic dogs are reservoirs. Visceral leishmaniasis has emerged as an important opportunistic infection among persons with AIDS in Spain, southern France, and Italy. *L. chagasi* is responsible for visceral leishmaniasis in Brazil, Colombia, Venezuela, and other countries in Latin America. It occurs sporadically in endemic rural areas, but large urban epidemics have emerged over the past decade in northeastern Brazil. Most cases are in children younger than 10 years of age. The gender distribution is approximately equal in those younger than 5 years, but males predominate later in life. Domestic dogs and foxes have been incriminated as reservoirs. Family clustering suggests that humans may also serve as a reservoir.

A small group of American troops in the Persian Gulf War who were infected with *L. tropica,* a species that is usually associated with cutaneous disease, developed a viscerotropic syndrome. They presented with fever, malaise, and other constitutional symptoms but lacked many of the manifestations of classic visceral leishmaniasis. Late exacerbations have not been reported in Gulf War veterans over the past decade.

Pathophysiology

Infection is acquired when promastigotes are inoculated by female sand flies into an exposed area of skin. The parasites convert to amastigotes and multiply within mononuclear phagocytes. Although a cutaneous nodule or ulcer may develop, most patients are unaware of the site of primary inoculation. Amastigotes subsequently disseminate via regional lymphatics and the vascular system to mononuclear phagocytes throughout the reticuloendothelial system. Most infections are asymptomatic and resolve spontaneously; only a few progress to classic visceral leishmaniasis, known in many areas as kala-azar. There appears to be a genetic predisposition to progression to visceral leishmaniasis. Malnutrition, AIDS, malignancy, and other forms of immunosuppression are important variables.

In persons with visceral leishmaniasis, increased numbers of mononuclear phagocytes, many containing amastigotes, are found in the liver and spleen, resulting in hypertrophy. The spleen often becomes massively enlarged, and splenic lymphoid follicles are replaced by parasitized mononuclear cells. Amastigote-containing mononuclear phagocytes are also found in the bone marrow, lymph nodes, and other organs. Widespread dissemination involving the intestinal tract and respiratory system occurs in some persons with concurrent AIDS.

Clinical Manifestations

The incubation period for visceral leishmaniasis is quite variable but typically ranges from 2 to 8 months. The onset is often insidious and difficult to date. The disease usually has a subacute or chronic course, but in some cases, there is a more abrupt onset. Symptoms include fever, malaise, anorexia, weight loss, and enlargement of the abdomen. Fever may be intermittent, remittent with twice-daily temperature spikes to 38° to 40° C, or less commonly, continuous. It is usually well tolerated. Visceral leishmaniasis has developed in former residents of endemic areas who have become immunocompromised years after leaving an endemic area.

Splenomegaly and hepatomegaly are hallmarks of classic visceral leishmaniasis. The spleen is firm and nontender and frequently becomes massively enlarged (Fig. 395–2). Lymphadenopathy is common in some sites, such as the Sudan, and rare in others, such as Latin America. Wasting can be pronounced in chronic infection. Patients in India may develop hyperpigmentation, which led to the name *kala-azar*, meaning "black fever" in Hindi. Jaundice is occasionally present. Late in visceral leishmaniasis patients may have epistaxis, gingival bleeding, and petechiae. They may also develop edema and ascites due to hypoalbuminemia.

On laboratory examination, anemia, thrombocytopenia, neutropenia, and hypergammaglobulinemia are common. The anemia is usually normocytic and normochromic unless complicated by blood loss. The white blood cell count may be as low as 1000/mm^3; eosinopenia is common. Thrombocytopenia may be associated with evidence of bleeding. Hemophagocytosis has been observed in bone marrow specimens. The erythrocyte sedimentation rate and C-reactive protein are elevated. The levels of gamma globulin are markedly increased, at times in the range of 9 to 10 g/dL, as a consequence of polyclonal B-cell activation. Circulating immune complexes, autoantibodies, and rheumatoid factors are present in many patients. Glomerulonephritis may develop, but renal failure is rare. Liver enzyme and bilirubin levels are elevated in some. Hypertriglyceridemia and hypofibrinogenemia have also been reported.

Persons who develop classic visceral leishmaniasis typically have a progressive course unless treated. Severe cachexia may result. They evidence neutropenia as well as anergy to *Leishmania* and eventually other antigens. Concomitant bacterial pneumonia, measles, dysentery, tuberculosis, and other secondary or nosocomial infections are common and frequently lead to death. Overall, the fatality rate in developing areas approaches 5 to 10% even with antileishmanial chemotherapy.

VISCERAL LEISHMANIASIS IN PERSONS WITH HUMAN IMMUNODEFICIENCY VIRUS (HIV). Visceral leishmaniasis can occur as an opportunistic infection in persons with AIDS, usually in those with CD4+ counts lower than 100/mm^3. It is not clear whether this is due to recrudescence of previously asymptomatic infection or acquisition of infection or both. Most cases present in the classic manner with fever and hepatosplenomegaly, but organomegaly may be absent, and atypical presentations with involvement of the lungs, pleura, oral mucosa, esophagus, stomach, small intestine, or skin have been reported. Some have presented with aplastic anemia. Asymptomatic leishmanial infections have also been diagnosed in persons with concomitant HIV. The prevalence of visceral leishmaniasis in patients with AIDS in southern Europe has decreased since the introduction of highly active antiretroviral therapy.

VISCEROTROPIC LEISHMANIASIS. In the *L. tropica*–related "viscerotropic" syndrome observed in American military personnel during Operation Desert Storm during the Persian Gulf War, symptoms included chronic, low-grade fever, malaise, fatigue, and, in some instances, diarrhea. The troops did not experience massive splenomegaly or the progressive wasting associated with classic visceral leishmaniasis. No new cases have been identified in veterans over a 10-year period of follow-up.

POST–KALA-AZAR DERMAL LEISHMANIASIS. A subset of persons infected with *L. donovani* in India and up to 50% of those in the Sudan who are treated for visceral leishmaniasis develop post–kala-azar dermal leishmaniasis. In Africa the lesions appear during or shortly after treatment and persist for several months. In India they appear up to 2 years after treatment and persist for months to as long as 20 years. The skin lesions vary from hyperpigmented macules or maculopapules to nodules. Lesions are frequently found on the face, trunk, and extremities and may be confused with leprosy. Amastigotes are found in them, and they may serve as a reservoir of infection, particularly in areas where humans are a reservoir of infection and transmission is by anthroponotic sand flies. Post–kala-azar dermal leishmaniasis is not typically a feature of *L. infantum/L. chagasi* infection, but it has been reported after treatment of persons with concurrent AIDS.

Diagnosis

A presumptive diagnosis of visceral leishmaniasis is often made on the basis of the classic clinical presentation of fever, splenomegaly, hepatomegaly, and hematologic abnormalities in endemic areas. The diagnosis may be delayed or missed in early infection, in an immigrant or traveler returning to a nonendemic country, and in persons with concurrent AIDS who present in an atypical manner. The diagnosis is confirmed by identifying amastigotes in tissue or by growing promastigotes in culture. Splenic aspiration results in a diagnosis in 96 to 98% of cases. It is relatively safe when performed by an experienced physician, but significant hemorrhage can occur, particularly in patients with clotting abnormalities. Bone marrow aspiration for examination and culture is safer but less sensitive. Alternative sites for aspiration and/or biopsy include the liver or lymph nodes if they are enlarged. Culture of the buffy coat can also be performed. PCR-based assays applied to blood, bone marrow, or other samples appear promising, but they are not widely available. In patients with concurrent AIDS, amastigotes may be observed in macrophages in unexpected sites such as bronchoalveolar lavage fluid, pleural effusions, or lesions in the oral pharynx, larynx, stomach, or intestine.

Antileishmanial antibodies are present in high titer in immunocompetent persons with visceral leishmaniasis. An enzyme-linked immunosorbent assay (ELISA) using rK39, a recombinant kinesin-related antigen, is both sensitive and specific. ELISAs using other antigens, indirect immunofluorescence assays, and direct agglutination assays are also available. The sensitivity and specificity vary depending on the antigen used and the methodology. Persons with concurrent AIDS may have low titers or undetectable antileishmanial antibodies. The leishmanin skin test, also known as the *Montenegro test*, is nonreactive in persons with visceral leishmaniasis. It eventually becomes positive in those with spontaneous, self-resolving infections and most patients who undergo successful chemotherapy. The leishmanin skin test is not approved for use in the United States.

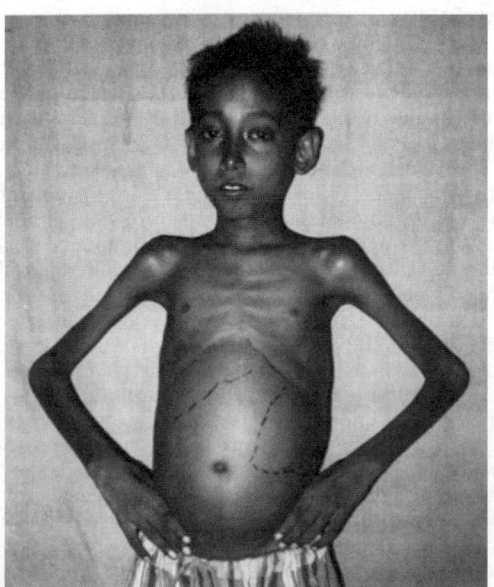

FIGURE 395–2 • Indian patient with kala-azar. Note wasting of the thorax and shoulder girdle and hepatosplenomegaly as outlined.

Rx Treatment

For many years pentavalent antimonials, sodium stibogluconate (Pentostam) and meglumine antimoniate (Glucantime), were the mainstays of therapy for visceral leishmaniasis. They are still used in many areas, but antimony resistance is now prevalent in India, where the anthroponotic nature of transmission may facilitate its spread, and emerging in some other areas. In addition pentavalent antimonials are associated with a number of untoward effects. Short-course therapy with liposomal amphotericin B is highly effective and relatively well tolerated. It is the only drug licensed for the treatment of visceral leishmaniasis in the United States. Liposomal amphotericin B, 3 mg/kg of body weight daily on days 1 through 5, 14, and 21, is recommended for immunocompetent persons. A higher dose and longer duration of therapy are recommended for immunocompromised patients. Liposomal amphotericin B is theoretically attractive because the drug is targeted to macrophages, the site of leishmanial infection. Other forms of lipid-associated amphotericin B, although less well studied, also appear to be effective. The high costs of liposomal and lipid-associated amphotericin limit their use in developing areas. Amphotericin B deoxycholate is also effective but more toxic.

In Latin American and other areas where *Leishmania* species remain sensitive to pentavalent antimony, stibogluconate sodium or meglumine antimoniate continues to be used. The two agents appear to be of comparable efficacy and toxicity and are administered on the basis of their pentavalent antimony content. The recommended treatment course of pentavalent antimony is 20 mg/kg of body weight daily for 28 days. Relapses occur and patients should be monitored closely for at least 6 months after therapy. A second and longer course of pentavalent antimony is frequently used in patients who relapse. The

mechanism of action of pentavalent antimony is not known, but the therapeutic effect appears to depend on the endogenous production of interferon-γ. This may explain the frequent therapeutic failures observed in persons with concurrent HIV infection. Side effects are common and more severe in the elderly. They include pancreatitis, arthralgias, myalgias, nausea, vomiting, headache, liver enzyme abnormalities, leukopenia, skin rash, and cardiac toxicity. ST-T wave changes are common. Sudden death has occurred in patients who have received more than the recommended dose.

Conventional amphotericin B deoxycholate (0.5 to 1 mg/kg intravenously daily for 20 days) or pentamidine are alternative drugs, but both have important side effects (see Chapter 393). Amphotericin B deoxycholate is associated with renal insufficiency, electrolyte disorders, fever, weight loss, and constitutional symptoms. Pentamidine can produce hypotension, pancreatic β-cell damage, hypoglycemia followed later by hyperglycemia, renal toxicity, and bone marrow suppression. Resistance to pentamidine has been reported from India. Recent reports from India suggest that miltefosine (hexadecylphosphocholine), a phosphocholine analogue that is administered orally, is highly effective in the treatment of visceral leishmaniasis in an area where antimony resistance is prevalent. Studies now underway should determine whether it will emerge as the treatment of choice.

Unfortunately, persons with concurrent AIDS frequently relapse after initially successful chemotherapy. Secondary suppressive therapy should be considered, although the optimal drug and regimen have yet to be defined. Highly active antiretroviral therapy should be instituted in persons coinfected with visceral leishmaniasis and AIDS.

CUTANEOUS AND MUCOSAL LEISHMANIASIS

Epidemiology (see Table 395-1)

Leishmania species produce a spectrum of cutaneous disease. Most common are chronic, localized, ulcerative lesions (Fig. 395–3A). In the Americas cutaneous leishmaniasis is caused by *Leishmania mexicana*, *L. amazonensis*, *L. braziliensis*, *Leishmania panamensis*, *Leishmania guyanensis*, *Leishmania peruviana*, *Leishmania lainsoni*, and several other species including dermatotropic strains of *L. chagasi*. Except for *L. peruviana* and *L. chagasi*, which are found in dogs and other canines, the reservoirs are forest rodents. The vectors are ground-dwelling or arboreal sand flies. Humans become infected when they live in or enter endemic forested areas for work, recreation, or military activities. A number of cases of cutaneous leishmaniasis occur each year among American travelers with rural exposure in Belize

and other areas of Latin America. *L. mexicana* is found in focal areas extending from Texas to Argentina. *L. braziliensis* is endemic throughout Latin America and produces mucosal disease in a small subset of those infected. Dermatotropic *L. chagasi* has been reported from Central America.

Most cases of cutaneous leishmaniasis outside Latin America are caused by three *Leishmania* species. *Leishmania major* is an important problem among settlers, visitors, and troops in endemic rural areas of the Middle East, Central Asia, and North Africa. Rodents are the principal reservoir. *L. tropica* is found primarily in urban areas of the Middle East, the Mediterranean littoral, India, Pakistan, and Central Asia. The reservoirs are dogs and humans. *Leishmania aethiopica* is endemic in Ethiopia, Kenya, and southwest Africa, where hyrax are reservoirs. On occasion *L. donovani* or *L. infantum/L. chagasi* are isolated from cutaneous lesions.

Pathophysiology

A cutaneous lesion develops at the site where promastigotes are inoculated by sand flies. Amastigote-infected macrophages are the predominant histologic finding early in infection as circulating monocytes home to the site. Over time, a granulomatous response develops with increasing numbers of lymphocytes, decreasing numbers of parasites, and necrosis of the skin resulting in ulceration. The histopathology usually reveals acute and chronic inflammation with granulomatous changes. Peripheral blood mononuclear cells from persons with typical cutaneous leishmaniasis proliferate and produce interferon-γ in response to leishmanial antigens in vitro, and patients evidence delayed-type hypersensitivity responses in vivo. In the lesion there seems to be a stalemate between protective and disease-enhancing cell-mediated immune responses. Eventually T_H1 cells dominate and the lesion heals, leaving an atrophic scar.

The spectrum of cutaneous leishmaniasis includes several variants. One extreme is diffuse cutaneous leishmaniasis, a relatively infrequent, anergic condition characterized by disseminated nodular skin lesions containing large numbers of amastigote-infected macrophages. These lesions do not ulcerate, protective T_H1 responses do not develop, and the syndrome persists indefinitely. Another extreme is represented by the chronic, destructive lesions observed in patients with mucosal leishmaniasis. There is evidence of a vigorous T_H1 response, the leishmanin skin test is positive, and amastigotes are usually scant, but the lesions persist.

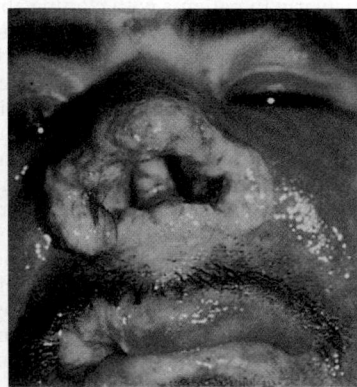

FIGURE 395–3 • *A,* Cutaneous leishmaniasis due to *Leishmania braziliensis*. *B,* Brazilian patient with mucosal leishmaniasis due to *L. braziliensis*. Note the destructive lesions involving the nose, nasal septum, and lips. (*A,* From Jeronimo SM, Pearson RD: The *Leishmania*: Protozoans adapted for extracellular and intracellular survival. Subcell Biochem 1992;18:1; *B,* From Pearson RD, Wheeler DA, Harrison LH, et al: The immunobiology of leishmaniasis. Rev Infect Dis 1983;5:907.)

Clinical Manifestations

CUTANEOUS LEISHMANIASIS. Cutaneous leishmaniasis may involve single or multiple lesions. They are relatively heterogeneous and vary as a function of the infecting *Leishmania* species and the host's immune response. Lesions are found on exposed areas of the skin. They typically start as erythematous papules at sites where promastigotes are inoculated, slowly increase in size, become nodular, and eventually ulcerate. "Wet" lesions are covered with exudate and have raised borders (see Fig. 395–3). They are frequently associated with superficial, secondary bacterial or fungal infections. Other lesions are "dry" with a central crust. Satellite lesions may be found at or near the edges of the primary site of infection. Wet lesions are commonly associated with *L. braziliensis* and *L. major* and dry ones with *L. mexicana* and *L. tropica*, but the morphology of lesions varies widely, and substantial overlap occurs. Sometimes lesions are nodular, suggesting neoplasms. On occasion cutaneous leishmaniasis due to *L. braziliensis, L. guyanensis*, or other species involves local lymphatics mimicking sporotrichosis. Cutaneous lesions persist for months, and in some cases years, before they spontaneously heal, leaving flat, hypopigmented, atrophic scars.

Observations in Brazil indicate that *L. braziliensis* can cause regional lymphadenopathy, fever, and constitutional symptoms before the primary cutaneous lesion becomes apparent. Splenomegaly occurs in some patients. These findings resolve as the skin lesion develops. It is thought that *L. braziliensis* may disseminate to distant mucosal sites during this early phase of infection.

DISSEMINATED CUTANEOUS LEISHMANIASIS. Disseminated cutaneous leishmaniasis with a large number of skin lesions has been reported in a small subset of persons. Some have been apparently immunocompetent; others have had AIDS.

DIFFUSE CUTANEOUS LEISHMANIASIS. Diffuse cutaneous leishmaniasis is a rare anergic variant. It starts as a localized papule that does not ulcerate. Satellite lesions develop (Fig. 395–4), and eventually multiple cutaneous nodules form on the face and extremities. Large numbers of amastigotes are present in macrophages. The disease progresses slowly and may persist for decades. The syndrome is most frequently associated with *L. aethiopica* infection in Africa and *L. amazonensis* in Latin America

LEISHMANIASIS RECIDIVA. Leishmaniasis recidiva, typically associated with *L. tropica* infection in the Middle East, is a chronic syndrome. Skin lesions on the face or exposed extremities enlarge slowly, tend to heal in the center, and persist for many years. Biopsy findings reveal chronic inflammatory changes; amastigotes are sparse.

AMERICAN MUCOSAL LEISHMANIASIS (ESPUNDIA). A small percentage of persons infected with *L. braziliensis* or related *Viannia* species in Latin America develop mucosal lesions of the nose, mouth, pharynx, or larynx months to years after the primary skin ulcer heals (see Fig. 395–3B). The disease typically begins with nasal inflammation and stuffiness, followed by ulceration of the mucosa. The lesions are characterized by a chronic granulomatous response. There is destruction of the mucosa and eventually of the underlying cartilage of the nasal septum or palate. The differential diagnosis of American mucosal leishmaniasis includes paracoccidioidomycosis, histoplasmosis, tertiary syphilis, tertiary yaws, sarcoidosis, Wegener's granulomatosis, angiocentric T-cell lymphoma, rhinoscleroma, and carcinoma. Mucosal involvement is occasionally observed in persons with visceral leishmaniasis, particularly those with concurrent AIDS. Involvement of the mucosa also occurs in persons with post–kala-azar dermal leishmaniasis or with contiguous extension of simple cutaneous leishmaniasis or leishmaniasis recidiva.

Diagnosis

Cutaneous leishmaniasis should be considered in the differential diagnosis of any chronic, localized skin lesion(s) in persons who have been exposed in an endemic area. The diagnosis is confirmed by identifying amastigotes in tissue or by growing promastigotes in culture. A biopsy and aspirate should be obtained from the margin of the lesion after it has been meticulously cleaned. Touch preparations are stained with a Wright-Giemsa preparation. The remaining tissue should be divided and used for culture and histopathologic analysis. Species-specific PCR-based diagnostic assays are under development. Serologic tests are not diagnostic. Antileishmanial antibodies are detectable in the serum of some patients with cutaneous leishmaniasis, but the titers are usually low and cross-reactions occur. The leishmanin skin test, which is not available in the United States, is positive in simple cutaneous leishmaniasis, leishmaniasis recidiva, and mucosal leishmaniasis. It is negative in patients with diffuse cutaneous leishmaniasis.

Parasites are usually scant in mucosal lesions due to *L. braziliensis*. A positive leishmanin skin test, the presence of antileishmanial antibodies, a history of exposure in an endemic area, and evidence of a healed cutaneous lesion allow for a presumptive diagnosis.

Rx Treatment

Cutaneous lesions that are large or located in cosmetically important sites and those that are caused by *L. braziliensis* or other *Leishmania* species associated with mucosal disease should be treated. Small, inconspicuous, or healing skin lesions caused by *Leishmania* species that are not associated with mucosal disease can be followed expectantly. The pentavalent antimonials, stibogluconate sodium and meglumine antimoniate, are used for the treatment of cutaneous leishmaniasis in many situations. In the United States stibogluconate sodium is available from the Centers for Disease Control and Prevention Drug Service. Full doses of 20 mg/kg pentavalent antimony per kg of body weight/day are recommended for 20 days; lower doses may favor the development of antimony resistance. Cutaneous lesions heal slowly during antimony therapy. As described earlier, pentavalent antimonials are frequently associated with toxicity, and clinical failure occurs. They are particularly common in persons infected with *L. aethiopica*.

A number of other drugs and therapeutic approaches, including immunotherapy with killed promastigotes inoculated with bacille Calmette-Guérin, have been studied and shown to have some activity. Direct injection of pentavalent antimony into cutaneous lesions is used in some areas. The administration of intralesional human granulocyte macrophage colony-stimulating factor with systemic pentavalent antimony improved the cure rate in a recent study. A topical formulation of paromomycin

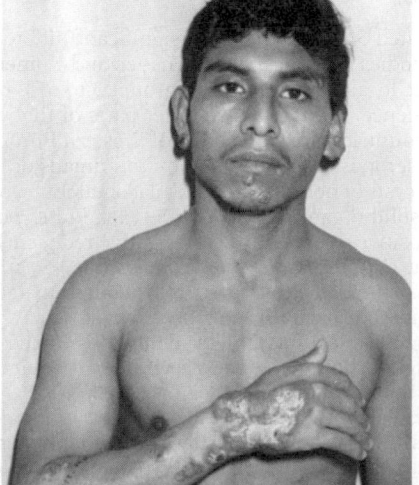

FIGURE 395–4 • Patient with diffuse cutaneous leishmaniasis of 5 years' duration. Note the nonulcerative lesions of the chin, ear lobes, and right arm and hand.

Continued

Infectious Diseases

sulfate, methylbenzethonium chloride, and white paraffin has been used successfully to treat skin lesions caused by *L. major* in the Middle East and, to a limited degree, cutaneous disease in Latin America. Oral itraconazole or ketoconazole has activity, but failures are common in persons infected with *L. braziliensis*.

The treatment of persons with mucosal leishmaniasis and diffuse cutaneous leishmaniasis is more challenging. Therapeutic failures and relapses are common after treatment with pentavalent antimony, and longer courses of therapy are often used. The concurrent administration of pentoxifylline, which decreases TNF-α production, with pentavalent antimony has been reported to improve the response in patients with refractory mucosal disease. Amphotericin B and pentamidine are potentially effective but toxic alternatives. Lipid-encapsulated amphotericin B and miltefosine have not yet been evaluated. The combination of recombinant interferon-γ administered with pentavalent antimony has been used effectively in a limited number of persons. When necessary, reconstructive surgery in persons with mucosal disease should be delayed for 6 to 12 months after chemotherapy since relapses are associated with poor cosmetic outcomes.

PROPHYLAXIS

The transmission of *Leishmania* species depends on the presence of appropriate sand fly vectors and reservoirs. Residual insecticide spraying has been used successfully to limit disease where transmission is due to peridomestic sand flies, but it is seldom widely employed because of emerging insect resistance and environmental concerns. Personal protective measures including insecticide-impregnated, fine-mesh netting for sleep, insect repellents containing diethyltoluamide (DEET) applied to the skin and permethrin-impregnated clothing reduce the frequency of sand fly bites and the likelihood of transmission. Unfortunately, these measures are often not available for residents of endemic areas. Large-scale control programs have been carried out in areas of South America where domestic dogs are a reservoir, but their efficacy is debated. Clinical observations in humans and studies of experimental animal models suggest that immunoprophylaxis should be possible. Experience with killed-promastigote vaccines is mixed. Recent studies have focused on the development of DNA, recombinant, and live-attenuated vaccines, but none is currently available for human use.

SUGGESTED READINGS

Davies CR, Kaye P, Croft SL, et al: Leishmaniasis: New approaches to disease control. BMJ 2003;326:377–382. *An overview emphasizing that simple and rapid diagnostic tools as well as affordable and effective treatments may soon be available.*

Murray HW: Clinical and experimental advances in treatment of visceral leishmaniasis. Antimicrob Agents Chemother 2001;45:2185–2197. *The emergence of pentavalent-antimony resistance, the development of liposomal and lipid-associated amphotericin B, and recent experimental advances with miltefosine and other drugs for the treatment of visceral leishmaniasis are reviewed.*

Zijlstra EE, el-Hassan AM: Leishmaniasis in Sudan: Visceral leishmaniasis. Trans R Soc Trop Med Hyg 2001;95(Suppl 1):27–58. *Visceral leishmaniasis has claimed more than 100,000 lives in the Sudan since 1988. The epidemiology and manifestations of disease in the epidemic are described in detail.*

396 TOXOPLASMOSIS

Oliver Liesenfeld

Definition

Toxoplasma gondii is a protozoan parasite that is ubiquitous in nature and infects a variety of mammals and birds throughout the world. The *acute acquired* infection in humans is usually asymptomatic. However, clinical or pathologic evidence of disease (i.e., toxoplasmosis) may occur, particularly in the immunocompromised patient, the congenitally infected fetus and child, and those in whom chorioretinitis develops during the acute acquired infection. Infection is characterized by two stages: acute (i.e., recently acquired) and chronic (i.e., latent). More information on congenital toxoplasmosis is provided in the book by Remington and Klein.

Life Cycle

There are three forms of the parasite: the tachyzoite, which is the asexual invasive form; the tissue cyst, containing bradyzoites, which persists in tissues of infected hosts during the chronic phase of the infection; and the oocyst, containing sporozoites, which is produced during the sexual cycle in the intestine of members of the cat family, the definitive host. The extraintestinal asexual cycle occurs in all incidental hosts and in cats. After ingestion of tissue cysts or oocysts, bradyzoites or sporozoites, respectively, are released into the intestinal lumen, where they invade surrounding cells, become tachyzoites, and disseminate throughout the body through the blood. The *tachyzoite* has a crescent shape, measures approximately $3 \times 7\,\mu m$, requires an intracellular habitat for survival, and can infect all mammalian cells. Continued multiplication ultimately results in destruction of the host cell and release of tachyzoites, which can then infect other cells. Tachyzoites are found in tissues during the acute stage of the infection or during reactivation of the chronic infection. Freezing and thawing, desiccation, and gastric secretions kill tachyzoites. Development of immunity is associated with disappearance of tachyzoites and formation of tissue cysts containing bradyzoites.

Tissue cysts are 10 to 200 μm in diameter and may contain up to several thousand bradyzoites, which are indiscernible from tachyzoites by light microscopy. *Bradyzoites* can be found in all organs and are most readily observed in the central nervous system (CNS) and in myocardial, skeletal, and smooth muscle. In humans, they appear to persist for life. Unlike tachyzoites, bradyzoites released from tissue cysts are relatively resistant to the digestive process of the gastrointestinal tract. The enteroepithelial sexual cycle results in the formation of oocysts in the cat's intestine. *Oocysts* containing sporozoites are 10 to 12 μm in diameter, are excreted in the feces 3 to 34 days after the cat becomes infected, and continue to be excreted for 7 to 20 days, after which excretion rarely recurs. They become infectious only after they are excreted and sporulation occurs; the duration of this process depends on environmental conditions but usually is 2 to 5 days. They may remain infectious in the environment for more than 1 year. Transmission is primarily by the oral route through ingestion of raw or undercooked meat containing *T. gondii* cysts or through accidental ingestion of food or water contaminated with oocysts.

Virulence in laboratory mice, isoenzyme pattern analysis, and restriction-fragment length polymorphisms have been used to differentiate virulent and avirulent strains of *T. gondii*. *T. gondii* strains can be divided into three clonal lineages, designated I, II, and III. They appear to be derived from two genetically distinct ancestries by sexual recombination. Whereas most strains isolated from acquired immunodeficiency syndrome (AIDS) patients are type III, type I strains are commonly found in cases of congenital disease.

Epidemiology

In the United States, there is no significant difference in prevalence of antibodies to *T. gondii* between men and women. Depending on geographic locale and population group, 3 to 67% of adults have serologic evidence of infection. In other parts of the world, including tropical countries and some areas of Western Europe, up to 75% of adults are seropositive. Transmission to humans occurs by ingestion of tissue cysts or oocysts, the transplacental route, blood product transfusion, solid organ transplantation (i.e., kidney, heart, or liver from a seropositive donor into a seronegative recipient), and laboratory accident. Outbreaks of toxoplasmosis due to eating of undercooked meat or exposure to oocysts (e.g., contaminated water) have occurred. Commercial cuts of lamb, beef, and pork may contain tissue cysts that remain infectious unless the meat is frozen to −20° C or heated throughout to 66° C. The percentage of commercial cuts of meat containing tissue cysts has declined to below 5% in industrialized countries. Whether transmission by eating undercooked or raw meat containing tissue cysts or vegetables or other food products contaminated with oocysts is more common than transmission by contact with cat feces in the United States is unknown.

The estimated incidence of congenital toxoplasmosis in the United States is 1 case in 1000 to 8000 live births. Transplacental infection resulting in congenital infection can occur in immunocompetent pregnant women with recently acquired *T. gondii* infection and in immunocompromised pregnant women with reactivation of their chronic infection. The frequency of transmission to the fetus probably depends on maternal parasitemia, maturity of placenta, and competency of

Table 396–1 · INCIDENCE OF CONGENITAL *TOXOPLASMA GONDII* INFECTION ACCORDING TO GESTATIONAL AGE AT TIME OF INFECTION OF THE MOTHER

WEEKS OF GESTATION*	NO. OF INFECTED FETUSES/ TOTAL NO. OF FETUSES (%)
0–2	0/100 (0)
3–6	6/384 (1.6)
7–10	9/503 (1.8)
11–14	37/511 (7.2)
15–18	49/392 (13)
19–22	44/237 (19)
23–26	30/116 (26)
27–30	7/32 (22)
31–34	4/6 (67)
Unknown	8/351
Total	194/2632 (7.4)

*Patients were treated with spiramycin.
From Hohlfeld P, Daffos F, Costa J-M, et al: Prenatal diagnosis of congenital toxoplasmosis with a polymerase-chain-reaction test on amniotic fluid. N Engl J Med 1994;331:695–699.

the maternal immune response to *T. gondii*. Congenital transmission has been shown to vary considerably, depending on the time during gestation the mother acquired her infection (Table 396–1). Approximately 85% of infants with congenital infection appear normal at birth. However, if untreated, as many as 85% of these children will later have signs and symptoms of the disease, in most cases chorioretinitis or delays in development. Maternal infection acquired around the time of conception and within the first 2 weeks of gestation usually does not result in transmission. Maternal infection acquired weeks or a few months before gestation rarely has been reported to result in fetal infection. The earlier the transmission to the fetus, the more severe is the outcome. Toxoplasmic encephalitis (TE) in AIDS patients (and in Hodgkin's disease patients and bone marrow transplantation recipients) in the United States is almost always caused by reactivation of a chronic infection. The incidence of this disease therefore is proportional to the prevalence of *T. gondii* antibodies (i.e., latent infection) in a given population and the stage of human immunodeficiency virus (HIV) infection in the respective patients (usually a CD4 T-cell count <200 cells/μL). In the United States, *T. gondii* seroprevalence in HIV-infected individuals varies from 10 to 45%. It is estimated that 20 to 47% of HIV-infected, *T. gondii*–seropositive patients ultimately develop TE if they are not receiving appropriate antiparasitic prophylaxis or highly active antiretroviral therapy (HAART).

Pathogenesis

After infection by the oral route, tachyzoites disseminate from the gastrointestinal tract and can invade virtually any cell or tissue, where they proliferate, infect adjoining cells, and produce necrotic foci surrounded by inflammation. In immunocompromised individuals, acute infection may result in severe damage to multiple organs. Cell-mediated immunity and humoral immunity play a crucial role in resistance against *T. gondii*. Immune mechanisms that contribute to control of the acute infection and termination of continued tissue destruction by the proliferating parasite include local and systemic activation of the cytokine system, especially the helper T-cell type 1 (T_H1) response. *T. gondii* infection triggers production of immunoglobulin IgG, IgM, IgA, and IgE antibodies against multiple *T. gondii* proteins. Activation of the monocyte-macrophage system after phagocytosis of parasites leads to death of the parasite. The αβ and γδ T cells are activated, and sensitized CD4+ and CD8+ T cells are cytotoxic for *T. gondii*–infected cells. Upregulatory (e.g., interferon-γ, interleukin-12, tumor necrosis factor-α) and downregulatory (e.g., interleukin-10, transforming growth factor-β) cytokines affect the response; Interferon-γ plays the pivotal role in this immunity. Despite a normal immune response, tissue cysts form in multiple organs. Although disruption of cysts or "leakage" of bradyzoites from cysts appears to occur in normal hosts without causing disease, it can result in life-threatening disease in immunocompromised patients. Immunocompetent children or adults with congenital *T. gondii* infection can have a localized reactivation that usually manifests clinically as recurrent retinochoroiditis.

Genetic regulation of susceptibility to infection has been reported in murine models of the disease. In AIDS patients, the human leukocyte antigen DQ3 (HLA-DQ3) was found to be a genetic marker of susceptibility to development of TE, whereas HLA-DQ1 was found to be a genetic marker of resistance to development of TE.

Pathology

Pathologic changes vary, depending on the immune status of the individual. Histologic preparations of tissues of normal individuals rarely reveal the presence of tissue cysts; when present, they do not have a surrounding inflammatory response. The exception occurs in immunocompetent adults suffering from toxoplasmic retinochoroiditis, who may have tachyzoites, necrosis, and mononuclear cell infiltrates in their retinas and choroids.

Histopathologic changes of toxoplasmic lymphadenitis in immunocompetent patients consist of a distinctive and usually diagnostic triad of reactive follicular hyperplasia, irregular clusters of epithelioid histiocytes that encroach on and blur the margins of germinal centers, and focal distention of sinuses with monocytoid cells. These findings reflect an immune response to infection rather than the presence of the organism, which is rarely observed.

Tissues of immunocompromised patients with toxoplasmosis exhibit, in addition to tissue cysts, foci of intracellular tachyzoite proliferation with resultant cell death, tissue necrosis, and inflammation. The inflammatory response can occur in multiple tissues and consists of lymphocytes, plasma cells, mononuclear phagocytes, and few neutrophils. This occurs most commonly in the brain, lung, heart, and gastrointestinal tract but has also been observed in the liver, spleen, pancreas, kidney, seminiferous tubules, prostate, adrenals, bone marrow, and skeletal muscle. The most frequently clinically apparent site of involvement in these patients is the CNS, which may have acute focal or diffuse meningoencephalitis with necrosis, microglial nodules, and perivascular mononuclear inflammation. These lesions are usually multiple and diffusely distributed. Tachyzoites and tissue cysts are usually found at the periphery of necrotic areas. TE has a predilection for the subcortical area of the cerebral hemispheres, basal ganglia, cerebellum, and brain stem. Some patients have a diffuse form of TE with widespread microglial nodules without abscess formation that involves the gray matter of the cerebrum, cerebellum, and brain stem. Spinal cord involvement can occur and mimic tumor. Pulmonary involvement is second in frequency only to TE in AIDS patients and is characterized by interstitial or necrotizing pneumonitis and areas of consolidation.

Clinical Manifestations

ACUTE INFECTION IN IMMUNOCOMPETENT PATIENTS. *T. gondii* infection is symptomatic in only approximately 10% of immunocompetent individuals. In these patients, toxoplasmosis most often manifests as lymphadenopathy. Although any or all lymph node groups may be involved, cervical lymphadenopathy is most common; nodes are usually discrete, nontender, nonsuppurative, and asymptomatic. However, some patients may experience fever, myalgias, arthralgias, fatigue, headache, visual disturbances (due to chorioretinitis), sore throat, maculopapular rash, urticaria, hepatosplenomegaly, small numbers (<10%) of atypical lymphocytes, and rarely, myocarditis. Involvement of retroperitoneal or mesenteric nodes may be associated with abdominal pain. Toxoplasmic lymphadenopathy is a self-limited disease, although fatigue or lymphadenopathy, or both, may persist or recur for months. Clinical illness due to reinfection from an exogenous source has not been reported.

OCULAR TOXOPLASMOSIS IN IMMUNOCOMPETENT PATIENTS. *T. gondii* infection has been reported to be responsible for approximately 35% of retinochoroiditis in older children and adults in the United States. *T. gondii* retinochoroiditis usually is a late manifestation of congenital infection. These patients are usually asymptomatic until ado-

Continued

lescence or adulthood. Reactivation is uncommon after the age of 40 years. Uncommonly, individuals with recently acquired infection experience ocular involvement. Adults diagnosed as having toxoplasmic chorioretinitis should be studied serologically to define whether the chorioretinitis is caused by a recently acquired infection. Patients may have blurred vision, scotoma, pain, photophobia, or epiphora. Macular involvement may impair central vision. Systemic symptoms usually do not accompany ocular involvement. Ophthalmologic examination reveals multiple, yellow-white, cottonlike patches with indistinct margins, located in small clusters in the posterior pole. Flare-up of congenitally acquired chorioretinitis is often associated with scarred lesions juxtaposed to the fresh lesion. Chorioretinitis in the context of congenital infection is often bilateral, whereas retinochoroiditis in patients with recently acquired infection is typically unilateral. Retinochoroiditis may be part of a syndrome of panuveitis; isolated anterior uveitis has not been associated with *T. gondii*.

Lesions may heal spontaneously, in which case they become atrophic with whitish gray plaques with distinct margins surrounded by areas of black choroidal pigment. Lesions at different stages of development may occur simultaneously. Multiple relapses may occur and may result in glaucoma and loss of vision.

TOXOPLASMOSIS IN IMMUNOCOMPROMISED PATIENTS. Toxoplasmosis in the immunocompromised patient in most cases is the result of reactivation of the latent infection. Numerous conditions that compromise the immune system have been associated with toxoplasmosis, with the highest frequencies in patients with AIDS, Hodgkin's disease, or other lymphoma and in other patients who are on high-dose corticosteroids or other immunosuppressive agents for the treatment of malignancies, collagen-vascular disorders, or prevention of organ transplant rejection. In patients with these conditions, toxoplasmosis may also be caused by exogenous acquisition of infection, especially in seronegative recipients of organ transplants from seropositive donors. If untreated, toxoplasmosis in immunocompromised patients is often rapidly progressive and fatal.

Clinical manifestations most commonly reflect involvement of the CNS, lungs, eyes, and heart. In 30 to 50% of HIV-infected, toxoplasma-seropositive individuals, TE will develop if they are not receiving appropriate antiparasitic prophylaxis or HAART. TE traditionally has been the most common manifestation and along with lymphoma has been the most frequent cause of intracerebral mass lesions in patients with AIDS (Chapter 414); the relative incidence of TE may be decreasing. As a result of multifocal involvement of the CNS, clinical findings vary widely; they include alterations in mental status, seizures, motor weakness, cranial nerve disorders, sensory abnormalities, cerebellar signs, meningismus, movement disorders, and neuropsychiatric manifestations. Typically, TE is characterized by focal neurologic abnormalities of subacute onset, frequently accompanied by nonfocal signs and symptoms such as headache, altered mental status, and fever. The most common focal neurologic sign is motor weakness, but patients may also experience cranial nerve abnormalities, cognitive disorders, speech disturbances, visual field defects, sensory disturbances, cerebellar signs, focal seizures, and movement disorders. Meningeal signs may be present. Analysis of cerebrospinal fluid (CSF) may detect slight mononuclear pleocytosis, increased protein level, and normal glucose level. Although radiologic findings are not pathognomonic, the presence of multiple focal lesions in AIDS patients strongly favors the diagnosis of TE, whereas the presence of a single lesion makes TE less likely and lymphoma more likely. Results of computed tomographic (CT) scans usually show multiple bilateral cerebral lesions, which tend to be located at the corticomedullary junction and the basal ganglia. Lesions are surrounded by edema, are generally hypodense, and show ring enhancement after intravenous contrast. CT scans tend to underestimate the number of lesions and may show a single lesion when magnetic resonance imaging (MRI) reveals two or more lesions. Because MRI is more sensitive for detecting the lesions of TE, it is the preferred radiologic method for patients with suspected TE and is of particular importance in patients with only a single lesion indicated on CT scans. The differential diagnosis of TE includes CNS lymphoma, progressive multifocal leukoencephalopathy, and infections due to other pathogens, including viruses, fungi, and bacteria.

Toxoplasmic pneumonitis may develop in the absence of extrapulmonary disease and is associated with a high mortality rate of 35% even when treated. Its clinical and radiologic features are nonspecific and may mimic those of *Pneumocystis carinii* pneumonia. Patients experience fever, dyspnea, and nonproductive cough, and the chest radiograph finding usually shows bilateral interstitial infiltrates. Disseminated toxoplasmosis in AIDS patients has been reported to present a picture of septic shock and adult respiratory distress syndrome. Although ocular toxoplasmosis is uncommon in patients with AIDS, it is still the second most common cause of retinal infection in these individuals (Chapter 418). Toxoplasmic chorioretinitis in AIDS patients is characterized by yellow-white areas of retinitis with fluffy borders. It should be distinguished from ocular involvement due to cytomegalovirus (CMV), syphilis, herpes simplex, varicella zoster, *P. carinii*, fungi, and lymphoma. When compared with those of CMV retinitis, lesions of toxoplasmic chorioretinitis usually occur at the posterior pole, are more fluffy and edematous, have ill-defined margins, and are nonhemorrhagic. Clinical manifestations from cardiac involvement occur but are unusual. In non-AIDS immunocompromised patients, congestive heart failure, arrhythmias, and pericarditis have been identified. Toxoplasmic myocarditis can mimic heart transplant rejection.

Diagnosis

Toxoplasmosis can be diagnosed by isolation of the organism, polymerase chain reaction (PCR) methods, demonstration of tachyzoites in tissues or body fluids by histologic or cytologic analysis, and serologic testing. Whereas direct demonstration of the parasite is often used for diagnosis of the infection in immunocompromised patients, serologic analysis is most commonly used for diagnosis in immunocompetent patients. Serologic tests for detection of *Toxoplasma* IgG and IgM antibodies are most commonly used for diagnosis of *T. gondii* infection and toxoplasmosis in the immunocompetent patient. Many commercial serologic testing kits to detect *T. gondii* IgM antibodies are not adequate and give unacceptable numbers of false-positive results. IgG antibodies can be detected with the Sabin-Feldman dye test (considered the "gold standard"), indirect fluorescent antibody (IFA), agglutination, or enzyme-linked immunosorbent assay (ELISA) test. IgG antibodies measured by the dye test and IFA test usually appear 1 to 2 weeks after infection, peak in 6 to 8 weeks, and gradually decline thereafter; low titers usually persist for life. The agglutination test is a sensitive and inexpensive method to screen for IgG antibodies.

Detection of IgM antibodies is frequently useful when attempting to diagnose the acute infection. IgM antibodies are demonstrable as early as 5 days after infection and usually decrease after a few weeks or months. However, because IgM antibodies may persist for 1 year or longer after infection, a positive IgM antibody titer finding does not necessarily mean that the patient has recently been infected. The greatest value of an IgM antibody test lies in determining whether an otherwise normal individual has *not* been infected recently. A negative IgM serologic test result in immunocompetent patients virtually rules out recently acquired infection unless sera are tested so early that an antibody response has not yet developed or is not yet detectable. Correct interpretation of serologic test results is of utmost importance for the diagnosis of infection in pregnant women. For example, pregnant women may choose abortion when informed of a positive IgM test result; a negative IgM test result late in gestation may reflect that the patient had not recently acquired the infection or that IgM antibodies, because of *T. gondii* infection acquired early in pregnancy, may have disappeared by that time. Testing of avidity (i.e., functional affinity) of *Toxoplasma* IgG antibodies has proved an excellent tool to distinguish recent and distant infection in patients with positive IgM antibodies; the presence of high-avidity antibodies in the first trimester excludes an infection acquired during pregnancy. Appropriate diagnosis and interpretation of results in pregnant women often require that a panel of tests be performed and evaluated in a reference laboratory to assist in discriminating between recent and more distant infection. Results of confirmatory testing in a reference laboratory revealed that recently acquired infections had occurred in only 40% of those women who had positive results in tests for IgM antibodies in commercial laboratories; 17% of these women had their pregnancies terminated when informed of the results. Communication of the results and their correct interpretation by an expert in *Toxoplasma* serologic characteristics decreased the rate of unnecessary abortions by 50% among those women with positive IgM *Toxoplasma* antibody test results by commercial laboratories.

A definitive serologic diagnosis of acute infection requires the demonstration of seroconversion (i.e., from seronegative to seropositive). Recent infection is likely when serial specimens obtained at least 3 weeks apart and tested in parallel show a significant rise in IgG antibody titers and when IgM, IgA, or IgE antibody titers are present in conjunction with an "acute" pattern in an avidity test result.

Serologic testing in HIV-infected patients is mainly useful for identifying those at risk for development of toxoplasmosis and in assisting the physician faced with the problem of diagnosing the cause of CNS lesions in such individuals. All HIV-positive patients should be tested for the presence of IgG antibodies. In AIDS patients with CD4+ T-cell counts less than 200/μL, high IgG *Toxoplasma* antibody titers are associated with a greater likelihood of development of TE. Serologic test findings may be misleading in chronically infected patients who receive heart or other organ transplants, because these patients can show rising titers of IgG and IgM antibodies without clinical evidence of active *T. gondii* infection. Definitive diagnosis of toxoplasmosis in immunodeficient patients ultimately relies on histologic studies, isolation of the parasite, or identification of *T. gondii* DNA in body fluids or tissues. However, a presumptive diagnosis of TE in AIDS patients can be made when a compatible clinical presentation, multiple ring-enhancing lesions on CT or MRI scans, and IgG *Toxoplasma*

antibodies are present. HIV-infected patients who have a single lesion on MRI, are seronegative for *T. gondii* antibodies, or are not responding to specific treatment should be considered for brain biopsy.

Isolation of *T. gondii* is accomplished by inoculating blood, CSF, bronchoalveolar lavage (BAL) fluid, vitreous fluid, amniotic fluid, or tissue specimens into mice or cell culture. Mouse inoculation is more sensitive but less rapid than cell culture. Positive results obtained in isolation studies from tissue samples do not necessarily indicate acute infection because a positive result may be caused by the presence of bradyzoites (cysts), indicating latent infection.

PCR has been used successfully on CSF, amniotic fluid, samples from BAL, and blood to diagnose toxoplasmosis. The sensitivity of PCR on CSF ranges from 11 to 77%; PCR on blood has been successfully used primarily in patients with disseminated disease due to *T. gondii*. PCR on amniotic fluid has been successfully used for the diagnosis of fetal infection at 18 weeks' gestation. Because of its greater sensitivity and specificity, which approach approximately 100% rapid performance and safety, PCR on amniotic fluid has replaced conventional prenatal diagnostic techniques, including fetal blood sampling. Routine histologic and cytologic staining may not allow tachyzoites to be identified in tissue sections. An immunohistochemical method (e.g., immunoperoxidase staining) should be used to confirm their presence. The presence of multiple cysts in tissue sections near an area of inflammation and necrosis is highly suggestive of active infection. The characteristic lymph node histologic findings are in most cases sufficient to make the diagnosis of toxoplasmic lymphadenitis.

 Treatment

The need for and duration of therapy depend on the clinical manifestations of toxoplasmosis and the immune status of the patient. The drug combination of pyrimethamine and sulfadiazine (P+S) is considered the regimen of choice and is synergistic against tachyzoites. It is not active against the tissue cyst form. In adults, a loading dose of 200 mg of pyrimethamine is administered orally in two divided doses on the first day. Thereafter, patients receive 25 to 100 mg/day orally; the dosage depends on the severity of the disease and the immunologic status of the patient. Sulfadiazine is administered as a loading dose of 75 mg/kg (up to 4 g) orally, followed by a daily dose of 100 mg/kg (up to 6 g) divided into two doses. Other sulfonamides have less activity against *T. gondii*. Treatment is usually continued for 1 to 2 weeks after resolution of signs or symptoms of the infection in other than the most severely immunocompromised patients such as those with AIDS. Thereafter, careful follow-up observation is indicated. Because pyrimethamine is a folate antagonist, the most common side effect is dose-related bone marrow suppression. Patients receiving pyrimethamine should be placed on an oral dose of 5 to 20 mg/day of folinic acid (not folic acid) and have complete blood cell and platelet counts measured twice weekly. Patients receiving sulfonamides should maintain high urinary flow to prevent crystal-induced nephrotoxicity. Other important side effects of sulfonamides are fever, rash, leukopenia, and hepatitis.

ACUTE INFECTION IN IMMUNOCOMPETENT PATIENTS. Patients with toxoplasmic lymphadenitis do not require antimicrobial therapy unless symptoms are severe and persistent. Infections acquired after a blood transfusion or laboratory accident may be severe and therefore should be treated. Patients with toxoplasmic retinochoroiditis should be treated with P+S. The recommended dose of pyrimethamine in these cases is 50 mg/day as a single dose. Clindamycin, alone or in combination with pyrimethamine or sulfadiazine, has also been effective. Systemic corticosteroids are added to the regimen when chorioretinitis involves the macula, optic nerve head, or papillomacular bundle.

ACUTE INFECTION IN PREGNANT WOMEN. Spiramycin at a dose of 3 g/day (obtained from the U.S. Food and Drug Administration; 301-827-2335) has been stated to reduce the incidence of fetal infection by about 60%. If prenatal diagnosis reveals infection in the fetus, the pregnant patient should receive P+S plus folinic acid to treat the

fetus. Because of potential teratogenicity, pyrimethamine should not be administered in the first trimester. If necessary, sulfadiazine may be used, but its efficacy when used alone for this purpose has not been studied.

TOXOPLASMOSIS IN IMMUNOCOMPROMISED PATIENTS. Immunodeficient patients with toxoplasmosis or with serologic evidence of an acute *T. gondii* infection should be treated. Chronic asymptomatic infection does not require treatment. In non-AIDS immunodeficient patients, therapy is usually administered until 4 to 6 weeks after all clinical evidence of toxoplasmosis resolves. Treatment is usually based on the presumptive diagnosis of TE. Treatment of toxoplasmosis in AIDS patients has two phases: acute-stage therapy and maintenance treatment. Acute therapy should be administered for at least 3 weeks; 6 weeks is recommended in patients with severe illness or no significant clinical or neuroradiologic response. P+S and pyrimethamine plus clindamycin (P+C) have been used with comparable results (Table 396–2). Most patients respond to these regimens, and neurologic improvement usually occurs within the first 7 days. Brain biopsy should be considered if clinical improvement does not occur during the first 10 days of treatment or if deterioration occurs during the first 7 days. Brain biopsy should also be considered at initial presentation in AIDS patients who are seronegative for IgG antibodies to *T. gondii* and those compliant with primary prophylaxis against toxoplasmosis who have focal lesions indicated by neuroimaging study results (see Prevention). Many AIDS patients do not tolerate one or the other regimen because of rash (P+S), rash and diarrhea (P+C), or bone marrow suppression (P+S, P+C). Short courses of corticosteroids can be administered to treat cerebral edema and intracranial hypertension.

The mortality rate for treated patients ranges from approximately 1 to 25%. Because most AIDS patients relapse when treatment is discontinued, maintenance therapy is necessary. The optimal regimen has not been identified. Usually, the same drugs used for acute therapy are continued but at lower doses (see Table 396–2). For patients who do not tolerate any of these regimens for acute-stage or maintenance therapy, the alternatives listed in Table 396–3 can be tried in combination with pyrimethamine. Recommendations regarding discontinuation of secondary prophylaxis are given in the next section.

Prevention

Preventing the infection is particularly important for seronegative immunocompromised patients and pregnant women. Because the

infection is acquired primarily through the oral route—through ingestion of undercooked meat or food contaminated with oocysts—it is in most cases preventable. It is the responsibility of the physician to instruct patients on how to prevent infection. Recommendations

Table 396–2 • GUIDELINES FOR ACUTE AND MAINTENANCE THERAPY OF TOXOPLASMIC ENCEPHALITIS IN AIDS PATIENTS

	ACUTE THERAPY	MAINTENANCE THERAPY*
SUGGESTED REGIMENS (GRADE A EVIDENCE)		
Pyrimethamine plus	Oral 200 mg loading dose, then 50 to 75 mg qd	25 to 50 mg qd
Folinic acid (leucovorin) plus one of the following:	Oral, IV, or IM 10 to 20 mg qd (up to 50 mg qd)	10 to 20 mg qd
Sulfadiazine or	Oral 1 to 1.5 g q6h	0.5 g q6h
Clindamycin	Oral or IV 600 mg q6h (up to IV 1200 mg q6h)	450 to 600 mg q6h
ALTERNATIVE REGIMENS†		
Trimethoprim-sulfamethoxazole	Oral or IV 5 mg (trimethoprim component)/kg q6h	No adequate data
Pyrimethamine plus	No adequate data	50 mg qd
Folinic acid		10 to 20 mg qd
Pyrimethamine and folinic acid plus one of the following:	As in suggested regimens	As in suggested regimens
Clarithromycin or	Oral 1 g q12h	1 g q12h
Azithromycin or	Oral 1200 to 1500 mg qd	1200 to 1500 mg qd
Atovaquone or	Oral 750 mg q6h	750 mg q6h
Dapsone	Oral 100 mg qd	100 mg biw

*Drugs administered orally.
†Data inadequate for definitive recommendation.
Adapted from Liesenfeld O, Wong SY, Remington JS: Toxoplasmosis in the setting of AIDS. In Merigan TC Jr, Bartlett JG, Bolognesi D (eds): Textbook of AIDS Medicine. Baltimore, Williams & Wilkins, 1999, pp 225–259; and from 2001 U.S. Public Health Service Infectious Disease Society of America Guidelines for the prevention of opportunistic infections on persons infected with HIV, Nov 28, 2001. (www.hivatis.org/guidelines/other/OIs/).

Table 396–3 • PRIMARY PROPHYLAXIS FOR TOXOPLASMOSIS IN AIDS PATIENTS*

FOR THE *T. GONDII*–SEROPOSITIVE HIV-INFECTED INDIVIDUAL†	
Trimethoprim-sulfamethoxazole	1 DS tab qd
	2 DS tab biw
Pyrimethamine-dapsone	Pyrimethamine, 50 mg once each week, plus dapsone, 50 mg qd, plus folinic acid (leucovorin), 25 mg qd.
	Pyrimethamine, 25 mg biw, plus dapsone, 100 mg biw, plus folinic acid (leucovorin), 25 mg qd
	Pyrimethamine, 75 mg once each week, plus dapsone, 200 mg once each week, plus folinic acid (leucovorin), 25 mg qd
Pyrimethamine-sulfadoxine (Fansidar)	3 tablets every 2 weeks
	1 tablet biw

FOR PREVENTION OF CONGENITAL TRANSMISSION OF *T. GONDII* IN SEROPOSITIVE, HIV-INFECTED PREGNANT WOMEN‡	
Spiramycin	1 g q8h

*Drugs are administered orally.
†These regimens have been reported to be effective for primary prophylaxis of toxoplasmic encephalitis in AIDS patients.
‡Although no data are available on the efficacy of prophylaxis against congenital transmission in this group of patients, we consider it prudent to recommend spiramycin because preliminary studies suggest that the transmission rate for congenital toxoplasmosis in these women is remarkably and significantly higher than in non–HIV-infected, *T. gondii*–seropositive women.
AIDS = acquired immunodeficiency syndrome; DS = double strength; HIV = human immunodeficiency syndrome.
Adapted from Liesenfeld O, Wong SY, Remington JS: Toxoplasmosis in the setting of AIDS. In Merigan TC Jr, Bartlett JG, Bolognesi D (eds): Textbook of AIDS Medicine. Baltimore, Williams & Wilkins, 1999, pp 225–259; and from 2001 U.S. Public Health Service and Infectious Disease Society of America Guidelines for the prevention of opportunistic infections in persons infected with HIV, November 28, 2001 (www.hivatis.org/guidelines/other/OIs/).

include eating meat (i.e., lamb, pork, beef, and venison) only if it is well cooked throughout, washing hands after touching raw meat, washing fruits and vegetables, and avoiding contact with cat feces. To attempt to prevent congenital toxoplasmosis, routine serologic screening of pregnant women has been performed to identify fetuses at risk of becoming infected. Mandatory screening programs have been successfully implemented in France and Austria. If serologic testing should be chosen, the serologic status of pregnant women should be evaluated no later than the 10th or 12th week of gestation. Those who are seronegative should be retested at the 20th to 22nd week and then again near term.

Administering spiramycin to acutely infected pregnant women (see section on treatment) appears to reduce the incidence of congenital infection by approximately 60%. In Massachusetts, a secondary screening program consisting of screening of all newborns for IgM antibodies has been implemented because of the lack of feasibility of screening all pregnant women. Compared with initial clinical examination, neonatal screening showed a dramatically higher sensitivity for diagnosis of congenital infection. However, because detection of IgM antibodies in newborns is only 25 to 75% sensitive, this program will miss a significant number of subclinically infected infants or infants infected in the late third trimester. Moreover, a secondary prevention program does not allow for prenatal diagnosis and subsequent treatment of the fetus.

It seems prudent to avoid transfusions of blood products from a seropositive donor to a seronegative, immunocompromised patient when feasible. If possible, seronegative recipients should receive transplanted organs from seronegative donors. If that is not feasible, seronegative patients who receive organs from seropositive donors should be treated with pyrimethamine (25 mg/day) for 6 weeks.

For primary prophylaxis in *T. gondii*–seropositive, HIV-infected patients with a CD4+ T-cell count of less than 200 cells/μL, administering trimethoprim-sulfamethoxazole, pyrimethamine-dapsone, or pyrimethamine-sulfadoxine (Fansidar) is indicated to prevent development of toxoplasmosis (see Table 396–3). Secondary prophylaxis (i.e., maintenance therapy) in AIDS patients was found to be effective in the prevention of relapse of TE (see Table 396–2). Discontinuation of primary prophylaxis against TE has proven safe in AIDS patients on HAART with an increase in their CD4+ T-cell counts to at least 200 cells/μL for at least 12 weeks. At this time, it appears reasonable to consider discontinuation of secondary prophylaxis in patients with sustained increases in their CD4+ T-cell counts to more than 200 cells/μL after HAART (e.g., for 6 months).

SUGGESTED READINGS

Hohlfeld P, Daffos F, Costa J-M, et al: Prenatal diagnosis of congenital toxoplasmosis with a polymerase-chain-reaction test on amniotic fluid. N Engl J Med 1994;331:695–699. *Definitive study reporting the greater sensitivity of PCR on amniotic fluid than of conventional prenatal diagnostic methods for the diagnosis of congenital infection with Toxoplasma gondii.*

Liesenfeld O, Wong SY, Remington JS: Toxoplasmosis in the setting of AIDS. In Broder S, Merigan TC, Bolognesi D (eds): Textbook of AIDS Medicine, 2nd ed. Baltimore, Williams & Wilkins, 1998. *A comprehensive overview of the clinical presentation, diagnosis, management, and prevention of toxoplasmosis in AIDS patients.*

Liesenfeld O, Montoya JG, Kinney S, et al: Effect of testing for IgG avidity in the diagnosis of infection with Toxoplasma gondii in pregnant women: Experience in a United States reference laboratory. J Infect Dis 2001;183:1248–1253. *An overview of the value of testing for avidity of IgG toxoplasma antibodies to distinguish between recent and distant infection.*

Remington JS, McLeod R, Desmonts G: Toxoplasmosis. In Remington JS, Klein KO (eds): Infectious Diseases of the Fetus and Newborn Infant, 5th ed. Philadelphia, WB Saunders, 2000. *A comprehensive discussion of congenital toxoplasmosis and the diagnosis and management of acute T. gondii infection during pregnancy.*

Su C, Evans D, Cole RH, et al: Recent expansion of Toxoplasma through enhuaced oral transmission. Science 2003;299:414–416. *Explanation of how this organism has evolved and enhanced its oral infectivity.*

397 CRYPTOSPORIDIOSIS

Beth D. Kirkpatrick
Cynthia L. Sears

Definition

Cryptosporidiosis is a leading cause of endemic and epidemic diarrheal disease worldwide. *Cryptosporidium parvum*, the agent of human cryptosporidiosis, is an intestinal protozoan parasite of the phylum Apicomplexa and is related to *Toxoplasma* and *Cyclospora*.

C. parvum was first described by Tyzzer in 1912, in the intestinal tract of mice. Human disease was recognized in 1976 and attracted interest in the early 1980s, when it was identified as a cause of chronic diarrhea in patients with AIDS. Cryptosporidiosis came to public attention in 1993 as a result of the Milwaukee *C. parvum* outbreak, which affected 403,000 people, the largest recorded diarrheal disease outbreak from a public water supply in U.S. history. The impact of *C. parvum* infections on public health led to its classification as an "emerging infectious disease" in the landmark 1992 Institute of Medicine report entitled *Emerging Infections: Microbial Threats to Health in the United States*. There is increasing recognition of outbreaks due to contamination of food and water with *Cryptosporidium* oocysts. Fortunately, widespread use of highly active antiretroviral therapy in patients with acquired immunodeficiency syndrome (AIDS) has decreased the impact of cryptosporidiosis in this population.

Epidemiology

Transmission of *C. parvum* occurs through the fecal-oral route by ingestion of oocysts, which are shed in very high numbers in the feces of many mammals, including humans. For example, AIDS patients with symptomatic cryptosporidiosis may shed up to 1.2 billion oocysts per day. Originally thought to be predominantly a zoonosis, *C. parvum* transmission is now thought to occur primarily through person-to-person contact or contaminated water. Transmission from environmental sources, such as food, fomites, and animals, also occurs. Data from genotyping studies suggest that two major genotypes of *C. parvum* (i.e., "human-adapted," type 1 and "animal-adapted," type 2) and several novel non-*parvum Cryptosporidium* species have been identified. All genotypes cause human disease. Initial studies indicate that isolates may vary in their ability to produce disease.

The oocysts of *C. parvum* are ubiquitous and highly infectious. Thick-walled cysts survive well in the environment and are extremely resistant to sterilizing agents, including iodine and chlorine. In the United States, it is estimated that 80% of surface water and up to 26% of treated drinking water contain *C. parvum* oocysts, although in most studies the viability of oocysts has not been assessed. Studies of human volunteers have demonstrated that clinical disease may result from ingestion of less than 10 to 500 oocysts, depending on the *C. parvum* isolate. Because of the high infectivity, secondary transmission occurs, ranging from 5% if an adult is the index case to 20% if a child is the index case. The secondary transmission rate of *C. parvum* parallels that of other highly infectious enteric organisms, such as *Shigella*.

Water-borne outbreaks of cryptosporidiosis have highlighted its epidemic potential. Attack rates during epidemics of cryptosporidiosis are as high as 62%. In addition to the magnitude of the 1993 Milwaukee outbreak, a notable 1994 Las Vegas outbreak occurred with a state-of-the-art water filtration system without signs of malfunction, indicating that current water treatment regulations do not prevent *C. parvum* water contamination. Swimming pools and lakes have been the sources of recreational water-borne outbreaks. Food-borne outbreaks are infrequently recognized but occur because of fecal contamination of food. In 1993, 160 cases of cryptosporidiosis resulted from contamination of unpasteurized apple cider by cattle feces. Eighty-eight persons were infected in a University outbreak traced to an infected food handler. Multiple outbreaks also have been reported as a result of direct person-to-person transmission; these include daycare settings and nosocomial spread. Inapparent fecal contamination of objects has also caused nosocomial disease, including one outbreak from a contaminated ice machine on a psychiatric ward. With the use of appropriate infection control precautions, however, transmission of *C. parvum* from hospitalized patients with human immunodeficiency virus (HIV) infection to uninfected HIV-positive roommates can be prevented. Because of the technical difficulty of identifying oocysts in stool specimens and faulty commercial assays, false outbreaks have also been reported.

C. parvum is responsible for endemic acute and persistent diarrheal disease in the normal host domestically and abroad. Prevalence of infection varies greatly from industrialized to developing countries. Among immunocompetent adults in industrialized nations, the prevalence of *C. parvum* in stool is approximately 2 to 6% and

seroprevalence to oocyst antigens is 17 to 32%. In less developed countries, however, cryptosporidiosis is primarily a disease of childhood; for example, in Brazil, more than 95% of children are seropositive by 5 years. Populations at increased risk of exposure and infection include veterinary workers, caregivers of infected patients, daycare workers, and travelers. In immunocompromised patients, particularly those with primary T-cell defects, infection is typically much more serious than in normal hosts. Before the use of highly active antiretroviral therapy in patients with AIDS, *C. parvum* was the cause of up to 14 to 24% of cases of chronic diarrhea.

Life Cycle, Pathogenesis, and Immunology

C. parvum has a complex life cycle and completes its entire life cycle in a single host (i.e., is monoxenous). After oocysts are ingested, excystation occurs in the upper small intestine after contact with gastric acid and proteolytic enzymes. Four crescentic sporozoites per oocyst are released. Sporozoites penetrate the brush border membrane of the enterocyte to reside in a distinctive intracellular but extracytoplasmic position. Sporozoites develop into trophozoites intracellularly and divide asexually to form a schizont with four to eight merozoites, which are released by rupture of the enterocyte. Some merozoites invade adjacent cells, expanding the infection asexually. Others form sexual stages in host cells to produce male and female gametocytes that result in oocyst formation. It appears that 80% of oocysts are thick walled and excreted into the environment, whereas 20% are thin walled and capable of initiating cycles of autoinfection. Autoinfection expands and augments infection and, if uncontrolled by host defenses, is presumed to cause persistent disease in immunocompromised hosts. The intracellular position of *C. parvum* may protect the organism from host immune defenses.

All structures contiguous to the intestine that are lined with polarized epithelial cells are at risk of infection. Infection is typically concentrated in the small bowel with lesser colonic involvement. The biliary and pancreatic tracts and, rarely, the respiratory tree may also be infected. Intestinal infection results in villous atrophy and crypt hyperplasia, causing a malabsorptive or secretory diarrhea. Combined small and large bowel infection correlates with the severity of clinical disease in AIDS patients. A variable inflammatory infiltrate of neutrophils and mononuclear cells is found in the lamina propria.

Piglet studies of the pathophysiology of *C. parvum* infection indicate that impaired glucose-stimulated sodium and water absorption in the jejunum and ileum contributes to the occurrence of malabsorptive diarrhea. Cholera-like (20-L) stool losses in some AIDS patients infected with *C. parvum* have prompted the search for a possible enterotoxin. Although no specific toxin has been found, animal models show a net increase in chloride secretion, mediated by prostaglandin E_2, which may be responsible in part for secretory diarrhea. The secretory response may be further augmented by epithelial cell secretion of proinflammatory cytokines, including tumor necrosis factor-α and interleukin-8. Disruption of the intestinal epithelial barrier due to impairment of tight junctions by *C. parvum* infection also increases membrane permeability to the back diffusion of water and ions into the gut lumen.

The specific immune response to *C. parvum* in humans is poorly understood. Severe cryptosporidiosis is found in patients with cellular or humoral immune defects, and both arms of the immune response are thought necessary to control infection. In humans, specific serum antibodies (IgG, IgM, and IgA) and intestinal secretory IgA (sIgA) are found in response to infection but have not been shown to be protective. The presence of IgG antibodies in healthy adults with previous infection confers a relative resistance to reinfection only at low oocyst doses. After reinfection of healthy adults, diarrhea recurs at the same frequency as primary infection, although the diarrheal illness is less severe and fewer oocysts are shed. Epidemiologic data suggest that maternal antibodies may be an important defense against primary infection; breast-fed children appear to have less *C. parvum* infection before 6 months of age. Studies of cell-mediated immune responses have demonstrated a role for systemic and intraepithelial CD4+ helper T cells and interferon-γ, but not CD8+ cytotoxic T cells or natural killer cells, in preventing and recovering from disease. However, high levels of interferon-γ are not helpful in controlling infection in AIDS patients and interferon-γ is not found in fecal analysis of children with cryptosporidiosis.

Clinical Manifestations

Clinical manifestations of infection vary with age and immune status. Diarrhea is the predominant symptom in all groups. In otherwise healthy adults, the incubation period is 2 to 14 days, followed by the onset of noninflammatory (i.e., watery and nonbloody) diarrhea, which may be copious, as seen in other infectious diarrheal diseases. Diarrhea is frequently associated with abdominal cramping, nausea, flatulence, and vomiting. Symptoms are usually self-limited, with recovery in 10 to 14 days. Relapse of diarrhea after 1 to 2 days of apparent recovery can occur. Fever and other systemic signs of infection are uncommon, but weight loss may be prominent. In the Milwaukee outbreak, approximately 75% of otherwise healthy people with diarrhea lost a median of 10 lb. Infection with *C. parvum* may also be asymptomatic.

In developing nations, cryptosporidiosis is predominately a childhood disease and is recognized as a major cause of persistent diarrhea in these populations. As found in Peru and Brazil, children younger than 1 year of age appear to be at greater risk for persistent diarrhea and may suffer enhanced morbidity from other enteric infections and growth stunting after *C. parvum* infection. Malnutrition and vitamin A deficiency preceding infection are found in Haitian children with acute cryptosporidiosis. Brazilian children with cryptosporidiosis before 2 years of age have impaired functional status (i.e., physical fitness and cognitive function) 4 to 7 years after the initial infection.

In the immunocompromised host, the severity and duration of infection are directly related to the type and degree of immunosuppression. Disease is more likely to become fulminant, persistent, and life-threatening. Excessive fluid and electrolyte losses with malabsorption can cause progressive weight loss, dehydration, and malnutrition. Although most data are from patients with AIDS, severe, chronic cryptosporidiosis has been found in almost all immunocompromised populations, including patients with common variable immunodeficiency, hematologic malignancies, hypogammaglobulinemia, and during chemotherapy and steroid use. Most have primary T-cell defects. Reversal of the immune compromise often results in rapid cessation of symptoms of cryptosporidiosis.

In HIV-positive patients with chronic diarrhea, intestinal cryptosporidiosis is an AIDS-defining illness. Up to 30% of this group may also have a second intestinal coinfection. Uncontrolled, persistent diarrhea is directly related to the CD4+ T-cell count; patients with CD4 levels higher than 180 are able to recover from *C. parvum* infection, whereas patients with lower CD4 counts often have chronic diarrhea with an associated poor survival of approximately 6 months. In this population, the disease fits one of four patterns: cholera-like (31%), chronic diarrhea (37%), relapsing (14%), or resolved (17%). Acalculous cholecystitis and, less frequently, sclerosing cholangitis are found in 10 to 15% of AIDS patients with cryptosporidiosis, causing symptoms of fever, right upper quadrant pain, and nausea. Pancreatitis and respiratory tract involvement have also been reported, although the clinical significance of the latter is unknown.

Diagnosis

C. parvum enteric infection is diagnosed by stool examination. The classic acid-fast stain of the stool with modified Ziehl-Nielsen stain demonstrates bright pink, 4- to 6-μm-diameter oocysts. Sensitivity is diminished with formed stool but is increased by techniques to concentrate oocysts. Direct immunofluorescence stains, including acridine orange and auramine-rhodamine, are often used to screen stool samples in clinical laboratories and are more sensitive than acid-fast staining, but they may not distinguish oocysts from yeast forms. Monoclonal and polyclonal antibodies to *Cryptosporidium* antigens are used in commercial ELISA and immunofluorescent assays. These assays are costly but are rapid and easier to interpret than acid-fast-stained smears. Their use is often favored in clinical laboratories that infrequently diagnose *Cryptosporidium*. Sensitivity of these commercially available assays is variable (66 to 100%), but specificity is generally high (>93%). Important to all assays, *Cryptosporidium* must be differentiated from yeast and the oocysts of *Cyclospora*, which are 8 to 10 μm in diameter and, unlike *C. parvum*, glow with ultraviolet light. Serologic methods are not useful in the diagnosis of

acute disease. Diagnostic polymerase chain reaction (PCR) techniques are being developed. Rarely, intestinal biopsy is necessary for diagnosis. Histologic samples are stained by hematoxylin and eosin and demonstrate *C. parvum* in the brush border of intestinal epithelial cells.

Other laboratory findings are nonspecific. Signs of malabsorption may be found by measuring serum B_{12}, stool fat, or D-xylose absorption. In biliary disease, the alkaline phosphate, γ-glutamyl transferase, and bilirubin levels may be increased; transaminase levels are usually normal. Ultrasound and CT scans may show dilation of the biliary ducts. Endoscopic retrograde cholangiopancreatography to obtain bile or tissue is the most sensitive method of diagnosing biliary disease.

Acute diarrhea with *C. parvum* has no distinguishing features, and the differential diagnosis varies with the patient population and the clinical setting. In patients with AIDS and persistent diarrhea, other parasitic infections such as *Microsporidia, Isospora,* and *Cyclospora* should be considered, as well as cytomegalovirus and *Mycobacterium avium*. Cryptosporidiosis should be included in the differential of persistent diarrhea in all hosts, particularly in children of developing nations, travelers, and immunocompromised populations, and as a cause of any epidemic of diarrheal disease.

Rx Treatment

The cornerstone of therapy is fluid replacement and, in immunocompromised patients, an attempt to reverse the immunodeficiency. Since 1996, the use of highly active antiretroviral therapy (HAART) has dramatically decreased clinically apparent cryptosporidiosis in patients with AIDS. Complete resolution of established cryptosporidial diarrhea in AIDS patients has been shown after initiation of effective HAART therapy. *Mycobacterium avium* chemoprophylaxis with rifampin and the macrolide clarithromycin in AIDS patients may also be protective against the development of cryptosporidiosis. In patients with AIDS and low CD4+ T-cell counts, there is no clearly demonstrated specific drug therapy once infection is established. In case reports, the nonabsorbable aminoglycoside paromomycin temporarily decreased oocyst excretion and stool frequency in infected AIDS patients. However, in a controlled clinical trial (ACTG 192), paromomycin treatment of cryptosporidiosis in patients with advanced AIDS was no more effective than placebo. Paromomycin used with azithromycin to treat chronic cryptosporidiosis in patients with AIDS (CD4+ T cells < 100) dramatically reduced oocyst excretion, but not volume of diarrheal stools. In a placebo-controlled trial, treatment of AIDS patients with nitazoxanide, an antiparasitic agent, at 500 or 1000 mg daily led to parasitologic cure in 63% and 67% of patients, respectively. However, in the same study, parasitologic cure rates were predominantly limited to patients with CD4+ T-cell counts above 50 μL, and "seriously ill" patients were excluded from the study. Passive oral transfer of antibody through hyperimmune bovine colostrum has had limited success in diminishing symptoms in AIDS patients with cryptosporidiosis. Future rational drug development for cryptosporidiosis will be enhanced by the growing knowledge of basic parasite biology.

For immunocompetent patients, one Egyptian placebo-controlled trial of nitazoxanide led to significantly faster resolution of diarrhea in children, with a less clear benefit in adolescents and adults. All individuals appeared to benefit parasitologically (i.e., decreased oocyst excretion) from nitazoxanide treatment.

Prevention

Eliminating exposure to *C. parvum* oocysts is the cornerstone of preventing infection. Specific guidelines for the prevention of cryptosporidiosis in persons infected with HIV are published by the U.S. Public Health Service. Avoidance of contact with human and animal feces in water, food, and through sexual practices is essential for all hosts, but particularly for immunocompromised patients. Contact with newborn animals and patients with diarrhea should be minimized and handwashing emphasized.

The difficulty of eliminating *C. parvum* from public drinking water remains an important public health problem. In outbreak settings, drinking water can be considered safe when boiled for 1 minute or if purified with ozone, an absolute less than 1-μm filter, or by reverse osmosis. Filters should meet the National Sanitation Foundation standard #53 criterion for cyst removal. Because sources differ, bottled water should not be assumed to be free of oocysts. The risk of acquiring cryptosporidiosis in tap water in nonoutbreak settings is unknown. No special tap water precautions are recommended for HIV and immunocompromised patients.

SUGGESTED READINGS

Goodgame RW: Understanding intestinal spore forming protozoa: Cryptosporidia, microsporidia, isospora and cyclospora. Ann Intern Med 1996;124:429–441. *An excellent review, comprehensively referenced.*

Guerrant RL: Cryptosporidiosis: An emerging highly infectious threat. Emerg Infect Dis 1997;3:51–57 *A synopsis, with an emphasis on prevalence and the public health impact of outbreaks.*

Leav BA, Mackay M, Ward HD: *Cryptosporidium* species: New insights and old challenges. Clin Infect Dis 2003;36:903–908. *A succinct review of the taxonomy, pathogenesis and immunology of Cryptosporidium species.*

USPHS/IDSA Guidelines for the Prevention of Opportunistic Infections in persons with HIV: Available at http://aidsinfo.nih.gov/guidelines/op_infections/OI_112801.pdf *Consensus guidelines.*

398 GIARDIASIS

Cynthia L. Sears

Etiology

Giardia lamblia, also known as *Giardia intestinalis* or *Giardia duodenalis*, is the most common human protozoan enteric pathogen worldwide. It causes endemic and epidemic diarrheal illnesses, but the parasite is most often carried asymptomatically by humans. Discovered in 1681, it is among the most primitive eukaryotes known and has a simple life cycle alternating between trophozoite and cyst stages. The pear-shaped, flagellated trophozoites (10 to 20 µm long × 5 to 15 µm wide) contain two nuclei and resemble a "face" microscopically. Trophozoites proliferate in the small bowel and may be identified in the liquid stools of symptomatic patients. Encystation in the jejunum yields the infective cyst stage (12 µm long × 7 to 10 µm wide) that is identified in the formed stools of asymptomatic carriers and in the liquid stools of symptomatic patients. The oval cysts are resistant to chlorine and can survive in water for up to 3 months.

These features facilitate spread of infection and make this parasite one of the most frequently identified water-borne pathogens in the United States. Importantly, the parasite is genetically heterogeneous with two major genotypes (A and B). Some strains appear more biologically fit than others, a factor potentially important in disease pathogenesis. Recent work indicates that *G. lamblia* undergoes surface antigenic variation that is most likely stimulated by the host immune response or the intestinal microenvironment. Sequential presentation of different surface antigens to elude the host immune response may increase the parasite's chances of a successful reinfection or development of a persistent initial infection.

Epidemiology

Transmission of *G. lamblia* infection occurs directly person to person or indirectly by ingestion of contaminated water or, less often, food. Person-to-person, fecal-oral transmission and small-scale water contamination results in endemic infection, whereas epidemic disease is recognized when food or large-scale drinking water contamination occurs. The infection is transmitted by ingestion of as few as 10 to 100 *G. lamblia* cysts. Persons of all age groups are susceptible to this infection, although exclusive breast-feeding may lower the risk of infection in young children. In the developing world, infection is nearly universal by the age of 5 years, but recurrent infections are not uncommon, indicating that the primary immune response to infection is incompletely protective. In the United States, infection is usually sporadic, with certain groups of individuals at higher risk, including children (particularly those attending daycare centers), male homosexuals engaging in oral-anal sexual behavior, campers and hikers (from ingestion of untreated surface water), and international travelers. A notable

association of travel to Russia (particularly St. Petersburg) with acquisition of *G. lamblia* infection is amply documented.

Although both T- and B-cell–mediated immune mechanisms appear necessary to eradicate infection, immunocompromised patients with hypogammaglobulinemia (e.g., common variable immunodeficiency, X-linked hypogammaglobulinemia) are primarily those at increased risk for prolonged, sometimes intractable, infections. *G. lamblia* does not clearly exhibit enhanced virulence in patients with human immunodeficiency virus infection or selective IgA deficiency. Similar to other enteric infections, achlorhydria or hypochlorhydria enhances the likelihood of infection. Although humans are the main reservoir of *G. lamblia* infection, genetically related species infect humans, beavers, guinea pigs, cats, and dogs, strongly suggesting that *G. lamblia* infection is a zoonosis. Surface water (e.g., streams) contaminated with cysts excreted by beavers has been linked to human infection.

Pathogenesis

G. lamblia is strictly a small bowel, noninvasive enteric pathogen. Infection is initiated by the ingestion of the cyst form of the parasite, which releases two trophozoites aided by the pH and protease conditions of the upper small bowel. Trophozoites firmly attach by means of a ventral surface disc-shaped sucker to the small bowel mucosa, aided initially by a surface lectin and subsequently by contractile parasitic proteins and the negative pressure created by the parasite's beating flagella. Attachment is most often patchy and imprints the mucosa, creating localized microvillus damage. A well-established sequel to this pathology is inhibition of mucosal digestive enzyme activities. In some patients, these events culminate in onset of symptoms after an incubation period of 6 to 15 days. As trophozoites migrate distally in the small bowel, the higher bile concentrations stimulate encystation, resulting in excretion of the environmentally resistant, but immediately infective, cyst form of the parasite.

The histopathologic response to *G. lamblia* infection varies and imperfectly correlates with the clinical findings. In asymptomatic patients, no abnormalities may be identified on histopathologic examination of a small bowel biopsy by light microscopy, but electron microscopy often reveals evidence of ultrastructural changes in the microvilli. Biopsies of symptomatic patients may reveal villous atrophy and crypt hyperplasia with an inflammatory lamina propria infiltrate consisting of polymorphonuclear leukocytes, plasma cells, and lymphocytes. Lymphoid nodular hyperplasia has been associated with giardiasis and hypogammaglobulinemia.

One of the unresolved puzzles is how *G. lamblia* causes a broad spectrum of disease, ranging from asymptomatic infection to acute and sometimes chronic diarrhea. Two major postulates accounting for disease variability exist. First, *G. lamblia* strains may vary in virulence, as suggested by experimental animal and human infections. However, specific genes essential to the virulence of the parasite have yet to be identified. Second, the host response, particularly the mucosal immune response, to the parasite may vary. These postulates for disease pathogenesis are not mutually exclusive. Clarification of the host-parasite relationship will require further characterization of infecting strains by molecular approaches and correlation of these results with the clinical disease observed.

The mechanisms by which *G. lamblia* results in diarrhea appear to be multifactorial. First, documented disaccharidase deficiencies and the ultrastructural and histopathologic changes observed in association with some *G. lamblia* infections are consistent with the clinical observation of malabsorption in infected patients. Experimental animal and in vitro duodenal epithelial cell infections also reveal increased intestinal permeability, impaired glucose and amino acid–dependent sodium absorption, and in some instances, net sodium and chloride secretion. Second, the patchy distribution of *G. lamblia* infection in contrast to the large surface area of the small bowel and the absence of overt abnormalities in gut architecture in some symptomatic individuals have suggested that the parasite may secrete a factor (e.g., enterotoxin) that alters intestinal transport. Only limited experimental data support this hypothesis. Third, the mucosal immune response probably contributes to intestinal secretion, given that certain cytokines released by host inflammatory cells in the lamina propria are known to stimulate chloride secretion by intestinal epithelial cells.

Clinical Manifestations

Giardiasis manifests in one of three clinical forms: the asymptomatic carrier state (accounting for most infections); acute, self-limited diarrheal illnesses; and persistent (>2 weeks) or chronic (>30 days), sometimes relapsing, diarrhea associated with malabsorption and, in young children in the developing world, growth retardation (i.e., stunting). Data suggest that recurrent *G. lamblia* infection in the first years of life is associated with poor cognitive function years later. Although disease chronicity may be associated with certain immunodeficient conditions (see Epidemiology), immunocompetent hosts are also susceptible to protracted illnesses caused by *G. lamblia*. Between 40 and 50% of infected persons develop diarrhea. Symptomatic patients experience anorexia and nausea combined with, most characteristically, explosive, watery, foul-smelling diarrhea with increased passage of gas. Only low-grade fever occurs. Leukocytes and blood are not present in feces, and even mucus in the stool is rare. Nevertheless, the diarrheal illness caused by *G. lamblia* is indistinguishable from that caused by other small bowel enteric pathogens. In some, the infection may clear spontaneously. Experimental studies suggest intestinal secretory IgA and helper T lymphocytes (CD4) contribute to infection resolution. In those with persistent or chronic illnesses, malabsorption may be associated with foul-smelling, oily stools that float and prominent weight loss. Between 20 and 40% of patients with diarrhea and *G. lamblia* infection experience lactose intolerance that may last for several weeks after successful therapy. Rare associations with *G. lamblia* infection include urticaria, cholecystitis, pancreatitis, arthritis, retinal arteritis, and iridocyclitis. The white blood cell count is normal in cases of *G. lamblia* infection.

Diagnosis

Demonstration of the cysts or, rarely, trophozoites of *G. lamblia* in fecal specimens is most often essential for diagnosis. However, diagnosis can be elusive because cyst excretion may be erratic and symptoms may begin before the organism is detectable in stool. Examination of two concentrated stools using a trichrome stain, a more sensitive direct immunofluorescence assay, or one of the newer enzyme-linked immunosorbent assay (ELISA) techniques that detect giardial antigens in stool generally yields the diagnosis for more than 90% of infected individuals. Although use of an "enterotest" (i.e., gelatin capsule-string test) or endoscopy can improve detection of trophozoites in the upper small bowel, these examinations are rarely necessary for patient management.

℞ Treatment

Three major drugs are used for the therapy of giardiasis based on clinical experience. Treatment failures may occur with any of these standard therapies consistent with in vivo and in vitro data, suggesting that strain-dependent drug resistance exists and may be induced during therapy. The nitroimidazoles, metronidazole and tinidazole (not yet available in the United States), are most often the drugs of choice and are more than 90% effective. Notable side effects include a metallic taste and gastrointestinal and central nervous system (e.g., headache, vertigo) symptoms. Quinacrine (mepacrine), the second major drug used in therapy, appears to be about equal in efficacy to the nitroimidazoles but is no longer available in the United States. Among other side effects, this drug causes gastrointestinal upset, skin discoloration, and rarely, a toxic psychosis.

Furazolidone, which is approximately 80% effective and the only drug approved by the U.S. Food and Drug Administration for giardiasis, is often used in children, in part because of its availability as a suspension. Furazolidone may precipitate hemolysis in patients with glucose-6-phosphate deficiency and is contraindicated in patients on monoamine oxidase inhibitors.

Each of these medications inhibits aldehyde dehydrogenase and may precipitate a disulfiram-like reaction if taken with alcohol. None of these therapeutic alternatives is clearly safe in pregnancy, for which the poorly absorbed oral aminoglycoside paromomycin has been suggested. Nitazoxanide or albendazole are potential alternative therapies for *G. lamblia* infection. Limited clinical data suggest that dual drug therapy offers benefit in recalcitrant infections.

Prevention

Because *G. lamblia* is a zoonosis transmitted by environmentally resistant cysts and does not stimulate complete protective immunity, prevention of infection requires public health measures to ensure the availability of clean water and education to promote excellent personal hygiene to interrupt the infection cycle. Boiling of water for 1 minute or treatment with two to four drops of household bleach or 0.5 mL of a 2% tincture of iodine per liter for at least 60 minutes (overnight if the water is cold) before drinking renders the parasite noninfective. Although a commercial vaccine for cats and dogs is available, the antigenic variability of *G. lamblia* and the ill-defined correlates of protective immunity hinder human vaccine development for this infection.

SUGGESTED READINGS

Eckmann L, Gillin FD: Pathophysiological aspects of enteric infections with the lumen-dwelling protozoan pathogen *Giardia lamblia.* Am J Physiol Gastrointest Liver Physiol 2001;280:G1–G6. *Reviews the genetics, pathophysiology, and host defenses of* G. lamblia *infections.*

Farthing MJG: Giardiasis. Gastroenterol Clin North Am 1996;25:493–515. *This article provides a comprehensive overview of the epidemiology, mechanisms of disease, and clinical illnesses resulting from* G. lamblia *infection.*

Gardner TB, Hill DR: Treatment of giardiasis. Clin Microbiol Rev 2001;14:114–128. *A comprehensive review of therapeutic approaches to* G. lamblia *infection.*

399 AMEBIASIS

Jonathan I. Ravdin

Human amebiasis is caused by infection with the enteric protozoan *Entamoeba histolytica*. This parasite infects 1% of the world's population, with the disease burden highest in poor, developing areas. To manage patients with amebiasis appropriately, physicians must know the biology of the organism; risk factors for infection; mechanisms of disease, pathogenesis, and host immunity; the presenting manifestations of the invasive syndrome; the correct diagnostic approach; alternative therapeutic drug regimens; and strategies for preventing infection.

Biology and Epidemiology

E. histolytica infection results from ingestion of the excreted acid-resistant cysts in fecally contaminated water or food. Excystation occurs in the small bowel, leading to colonization of the colon with trophozoites. Transmission of infection may also result from direct fecal-oral contact because of poor hygiene or anal-oral sexual practices. Epidemiologic and molecular biology studies indicate that there are two morphologically identical but distinct species, the pathogenic *E. histolytica* and the nonpathogenic *Entamoeba dispar*. Infection with the latter is more common but does not result in systemic invasive disease or a humoral immune response. Approximately 10% of those with *E. histolytica* present clinically with invasive amebiasis, although all manifest a serum antiamebic antibody response.

The relative frequency of *E. histolytica* and *E. dispar* infection varies, depending on geographic area. Regions of the world with a high incidence of invasive amebiasis include Mexico, parts of South America, West and South Africa, the Indian subcontinent, the Middle East, and Southeast Asia. High-risk groups in the United States include institutionalized and mentally challenged populations and travelers or emigrants (especially Mexican Americans) from areas of high prevalence. Although amebiasis is one of the causes of diarrhea in individuals with acquired immunodeficiency syndrome (AIDS), in the United States, it is uncommon unless the patients are men having sex with men or emigrants from Latin America. Groups that experience an increased severity of invasive amebiasis when infected are the very young (<2 years), pregnant women, malnourished individuals, and patients receiving corticosteroids.

Pathogenesis and Host Immunity

E. histolytica trophozoites cause disease by sequentially adhering to colonic mucins, disrupting mucosal barriers with proteolytic enzymes, and contact-dependent lysis of host cells, including responding inflammatory cells. Trophozoite adherence to colonic mucins is mediated by a galactose-binding surface lectin; attachment by this lectin is the first step in the amebic lysis of human cells. Intestinal infection with *E. dispar* usually clears within 8 to 12 months without evidence of a systemic immune response. Cure of invasive amebiasis is associated with some resistance to recurrent disease and immunity

for a year or more to asymptomatic intestinal infection. Protective immunity is apparently mediated by development of a serum antibody and an amebicidal cell-mediated immune response with lymphokine-activated macrophages and a CD8 subset of cytotoxic lymphocytes serving as effector cells. Acute amebiasis is associated with the occurrence of antigen-specific suppression of cell-mediated responses to *E. histolytica,* facilitating parasite survival in tissues. A mucosal secretory IgA antiamebic antibody response to the galactose-binding lectin develops after *E. histolytica* infection and appears to have a protective role against recurrent intestinal infection.

Clinical Manifestations

The disease syndromes caused by *E. histolytica* are summarized in Table 399–1. It is unknown whether health is impaired by asymptomatic infection with *E. histolytica*. Occasionally, infected patients present with nonspecific gastrointestinal complaints, such as bloating and cramps, without evidence of invasive colitis. Amebic rectocolitis is characterized by the subacute onset of bloody diarrhea over days, abdominal tenderness, and weight loss. Fever occurs in only one third of cases. Fulminant colitis with perforation is uncommon; patients are in a toxic state, are acutely ill, and have a rigid, tender abdomen. Toxic megacolon is an unusual complication that is associated with the inappropriate use of corticosteroids, such as when amebic colitis is mistaken for idiopathic inflammatory bowel disease. Chronic, nondysenteric amebic colitis can manifest with years of intermittent bloody diarrhea, a syndrome symptomatically indistinguishable from ulcerative colitis. Ameboma is a rare, segmental form of chronic amebic colitis commonly found in the cecum and ascending colon; it manifests as a tender abdominal mass and can be confused with colonic carcinoma.

Extraintestinal disease consists mainly of amebic liver abscess, which can occur up to 5 months after the onset of intestinal infection. This is overwhelmingly a disease of men (9:1), except for prepubetory or postmenopausal women, when the male-to-female ratio is only 2:1. The presentation may be acute, with fewer than 10 days of high fever and marked right upper quadrant tenderness. Alternatively, with more than 10 days of symptoms, fever is less frequent, and pain and weight loss predominate. Less than one third of patients have concurrent diarrhea. Studies suggest that, in highly endemic areas, up to one half of amebic liver abscesses can be self-limited. Extension of an amebic liver abscess into the peritoneum or pericardium is a very acute clinical presentation that is more likely with a left lobe abscess. Disease can extend to the pleura, causing empyema, or less likely, disseminate hematogenously to the lung and brain.

Differential Diagnosis

Algorithms for the diagnosis of amebic colitis and liver abscess are provided in Figures 399–1 and 399–2, respectively. The differential diagnosis of acute amebic colitis includes infection due to *Shigella, Campylobacter, Salmonella, Yersinia,* and invasive *Escherichia coli* species or *Clostridium difficile* toxin-mediated disease. Amebiasis is one cause of inflammatory colitis in which fecal leukocytes may be absent because of the ability of trophozoites to lyse human neutrophils. Several research groups succeeded in correctly diagnosing *E. histolytica* and *E. dispar* intestinal infections by directly detecting amebic antigen in feces and serum. These diagnostic tests are commercially available and can be useful as complementary diagnostic tools; however, in clinical practice, the diagnosis of intestinal amebiasis still rests on the morphologic identification of trophozoites in fecal specimens. At least three stool samples are necessary to reach a 90% yield; samples should be refrigerated or placed in fixative if they cannot be processed

immediately. Laboratories in the United States frequently falsely identify fecal leukocytes as trophozoites; careful study with skilled microscopy is necessary.

Serology for antiamebic antibodies is positive in more than 90% of patients with amebic colitis having at least 1 week of symptoms and is very helpful in making a correct diagnosis. Interpretation of results can be difficult in highly endemic areas, where up to 25% of the population is seropositive because of the persistence of serum antibodies for years after asymptomatic *E. histolytica* infection. Use

Table 399–1 • CLINICAL SYNDROMES ASSOCIATED WITH *ENTAMOEBA HISTOLYTICA* INFECTION

Asymptomatic infection
Acute rectocolitis (dysentery)
Fulminant colitis with perforation
Toxic megacolon
Chronic nondysenteric colitis
Ameboma
Liver abscess
Liver abscess complicated by
   Peritonitis
   Empyema
   Pericarditis
   Lung abscess
   Brain abscess
   Genitourinary disease

*From Ravdin JI, Mandell GL, *Entamoeba histolytica* (amebiasis). *In* Bennett JE, Dolin R (eds): Principles and Practice of Infectious Disease, 5th ed. New York, Churchill Livingstone, 2000.

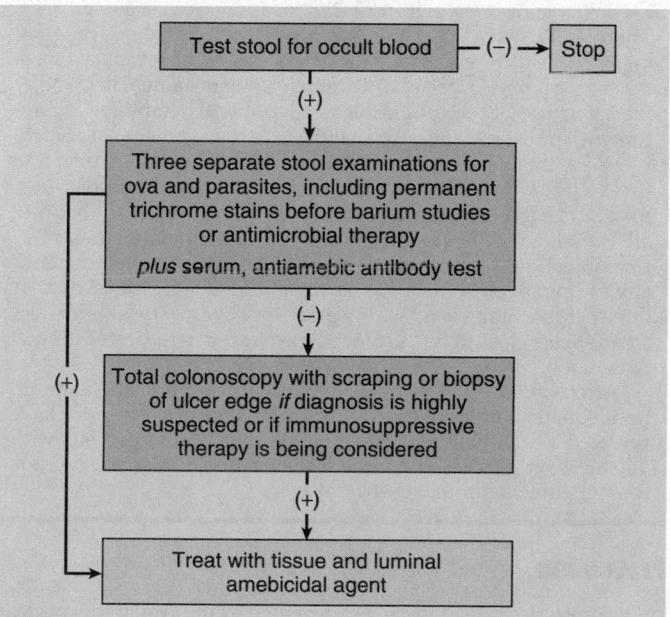

FIGURE 399–1 • Diagnostic evaluation for acute amebic rectocolitis in a patient with suggestive epidemiology and clinical manifestations. (From Kass EH, Platt R [eds]: Current Therapy in Infectious Disease—3. Philadelphia, BC Decker, 1990.)

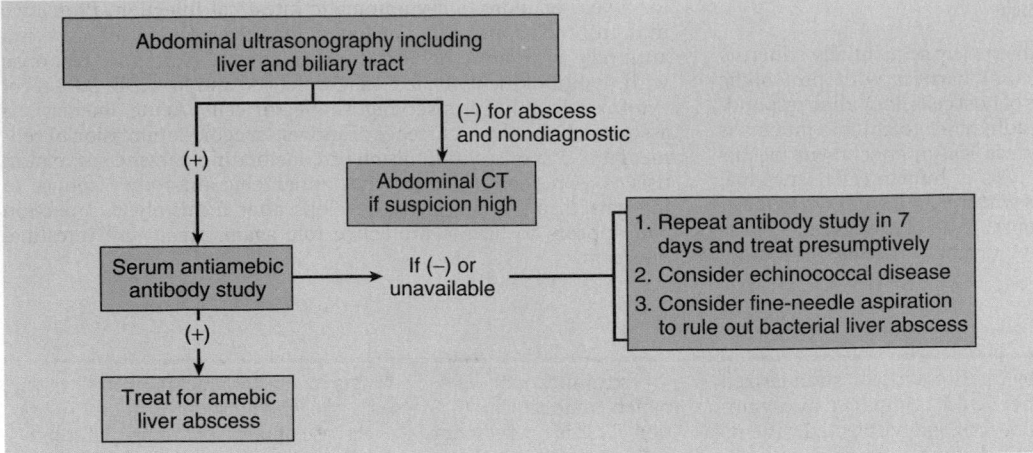

FIGURE 399–2 • Diagnostic evaluation for amebic liver abscess in a patient with suggestive epidemiology and clinical manifestations. (From Kass EH, Platt R [eds]: Current Therapy in Infectious Disease—3. Philadelphia, BC Decker, 1990.)

of polymerase chain reaction (PCR) methods to detect *E. histolytica* or *E. dispar* DNA in feces appears to be very sensitive and specific, having great promise for future application as a diagnostic tool. Endoscopy with biopsies of the ulcer edge is diagnostic in 90% of cases; this is helpful in differentiating amebiasis from idiopathic inflammatory bowel disease.

The key study for detecting an amebic liver abscess is abdominal ultrasonography, a rapid, noninvasive procedure that differentiates biliary tract disease from a nonhomogeneous cavitary defect in the liver. The differential diagnosis can then be narrowed to amebic liver abscess, pyogenic bacterial abscess, echinococcal cyst, and hepatocellular carcinoma. Attention to epidemiologic risk factors and detecting serum antiamebic antibodies are usually sufficient to establish the diagnosis, with the caveat that serology may be negative in patients with fewer than 7 days of symptoms. However, if there is sufficient risk for a bacterial abscess and a serologic study is not immediately available, a "skinny-needle" aspiration, guided by ultrasonography or computed tomography (CT), can be performed. This procedure with culture can diagnose and assist with therapy of a bacterial abscess; aspiration of an amebic abscess yields a yellow, proteinaceous fluid, often without white blood cells or amebas. The trophozoites are found in tissue at the periphery of the liver lesion.

Rx Treatment

Regimens for treating amebiasis are summarized in Table 399–2. Therapy for invasive amebiasis requires a tissue-active agent followed by a drug effective in the bowel lumen. In pregnant women, the use of nonabsorbable agents (e.g., paromomycin) or the judicious use of metronidazole is advisable. Therapy for asymptomatic intestinal infection with *E. dispar* is not indicated; however, it is advisable for asymptomatic *E. histolytica* infection in which serology for serum antiamebic antibodies should be positive. Careful follow-up stool examinations are necessary, because all available agents are not always effective in eradicating intestinal infection. Patients with amebic liver abscess respond gradually to therapy, with decreased pain and fever over 3 to 5 days. A few do not respond at all within 3 days or have a very large abscess that appears close to rupture; needle aspiration is indicated in such patients.

After aspiration, continued therapy with metronidazole should be adequate. Studies of stool culture or PCR for *E. histolytica* have revealed a high incidence of intestinal infection in patients with amebic liver abscess. To avoid a recurrence of disease, therapy must include a luminal cysticidal agent.

Prevention

E. histolytica infection can be prevented by the availability of clean water, adequate sanitation, and avoidance of sexual practices or living conditions that facilitate direct fecal-oral contamination. Boiling is the only reliable way of killing cysts; halide solutions are not reliable. In endemic areas, uncooked foods such as salads and vegetables should

Table 399–2 • **THERAPEUTIC REGIMENS FOR AMEBIASIS***

CYST PASSERS
Diloxanide furoate, 500 mg twice daily × 10 days, or
Paromomycin, 30 mg/kg/day in three divided doses × 5–10 days, or
Tetracycline, 250 mg, four times daily × 10 days, then diiodohydroxyquin, 650 mg, three times daily × 20 days

INVASIVE RECTOCOLITIS
Metronidazole, 750 mg, three times daily × 5–10 days
or 2.4 g/days × 2–3 days
or 50 mg/kg × 1 dose
plus diloxanide furoate or paromomycin or if metronidazole not tolerated
Dehydroemetine, 1–1.5 mg/kg/day × 5 days plus diloxanide furoate or paromomycin

LIVER ABSCESS
Metronidazole, 750 mg, three times daily × 5–10 days or 2.4 g/day × 1–2 days plus diloxanide furoate or paromomycin or if metronidazole not tolerated
Dehydroemetine, 1–1.5 mg/kg/day × 5 days plus diloxanide furoate or paromomycin

*All dosages are for oral administration except dehydroemetine, which is given intramuscularly; metronidazole can be used intravenously.
Adapted from Ravdin JJ, *Entamaeba histolytica* (amebiasis). In Mandell GL, Bennett JE, Dolin R (eds): Principles and Practice of Infectious Diseases, 5th ed. New York, Churchill Livingstone, 2000.

be avoided. No vaccine or acceptable form of chemoprophylaxis is available; however, research on the pathogenesis of amebiasis and the host immune response has led to the production of multiple, recombinant *E. histolytica* antigens that are effective as subunit vaccines in experimental models of amebic liver abscess. •

AMEBIC MENINGOENCEPHALITIS

Amebic meningoencephalitis is a rare clinical syndrome caused by the free-living amebas *Naegleria fowleri, Acanthamoeba* species, and *Balamuthia mandrillaris*. *N. fowleri* causes a primary amebic meningoencephalitis (PAM), whereas *Acanthamoeba* produces a subacute granulomatous amebic encephalitis (GAE).

N. fowleri in trophozoite or flagellate form grows best at high temperatures (46° C); encystment occurs at low temperatures. *Acanthamoeba* species, which have a trophozoite and cyst form, grow at normal ambient temperatures (25° to 35° C). PAM is a highly uncommon disease despite the massive exposure of populations to warm fresh water. GAE is usually restricted to immunosuppressed populations, such as those with AIDS or those with organ transplants. *B. mandrillaris* is a free-living ameba from soil that causes meningoencephalitis in immunocompetent and immunocompromised patients. *N. fowleri* enters the central nervous system (CNS) by penetrating the nasal mucosa and cribriform plate and is highly cytolytic.

GAE probably results from hematogenous dissemination and can be distinguished from PAM by the presence of cysts in tissue.

Clinical Manifestations

PAM is characterized by the abrupt onset of headache, fever, and meningismus, with rapid development of focal neurologic findings, including olfactory loss. CT demonstrates nonspecific edema. A neutrophilic cerebrospinal fluid (CSF) pleocytosis is frequently associated with increased CSF protein and hypoglycorrhachia. A negative CSF Gram stain result, India ink preparation, culture for bacteria, and cryptococcal antigen study in a patient with acute meningitis who has a history of exposure to fresh water suggests the need to examine the CSF for motile trophozoites (10 to 30 μm), a finding that is diagnostic. *Acanthamoeba* and *B. mandrillaris* can be cultured from brain tissue. PCR and DNA probes specific for *N. fowleri* have been developed but are not yet clinically appropriate.

GAE manifests subacutely over weeks with focal CNS signs, headache, fever, and depressed mental status and is often complicated by seizures. The presence of *Acanthamoeba* organisms in a nodular or ulcerative skin lesion is helpful, and study of the CSF usually reveals a nonspecific lymphocytosis with abnormally elevated protein levels. A brain biopsy is necessary to differentiate GAE from toxoplasmosis, pyogenic brain abscess, and other causes of focal CNS disease.

 Treatment

There is no treatment known to be efficacious for PAM or GAE. Treatment with systemic and intrathecal amphotericin B, which is effective in a mouse model, resulted in survival in a handful of patients with PAM. *Acanthamoeba* organisms are usually susceptible in vitro to ketoconazole, miconazole, 5-flucytosine, and pentamidine. One report indicated that trimethoprim-sulfamethoxazole might be useful in treating GAE. Pentamidine isethionate has some activity against *B. mandrillaris*. After determination of susceptibility of the patient's isolate in vitro, these agents and amphotericin B can be considered. These are rare disorders, and the risk of PAM from diving or water skiing in warm fresh water cannot be quantified. Other opportunistic infections are much more common than those caused by *Acanthamoeba* in immunosuppressed patients.

SUGGESTED READINGS

Denney CF, Iragui VJ, Uber-Zak LD, et al: Amebic meningoencephalitis caused by *Balamuthia mandrillaris*: Case report and review. Clin Infect Dis 1997;25:1354–1358. *The third genus of ameba to cause meningoencephalitis.*

Haque R, Huston CD, Hughes M, et al: Current concepts: Amebiasis. N Engl J Med 2003;348:1565–1573. *A recent review.*

Lowther SA, Dworkin MS, Hanson DL, et al: *Entamoeba histolytica/Entamoeba dispar* infections in human immunodeficiency virus–infected patients in the United States. Clin Infec Dis 2000;30:955–959. *Only 111 of 34,063 HIV-infected patients followed from 1990 through 1998 were infected with E. dispar or E. histolytica.*

Marciano-Cabral F, Puffenbarger R, Cabral G: The increasing importance of *Acanthamoeba* infections. J Eukaryot Microbiol 2000;47:29–36. *An interesting study of* Acanthamoeba *infections.*

Martinez AJ, Visvesvara GS: Free-living, amphozoic and opportunistic amebas. Brain Pathol 1997;7:583–598. *An authoritative review.*

Ravdi JI (ed): *Amebiasis.* Singapore, World Scientific Publishing, 2000. *A monograph with excellent reviews of all clinical and research aspects of amebiasis.*

Stanely SL Jr: Protective immunity to amebiasis: New insights and new challenges. J Infect Dis 2001;184:504–506. *Current review of immunity in amebiasis.*

400 OTHER PROTOZOAN DISEASES

Richard D. Pearson

CYCLOSPORIASIS

Cyclospora cayetanensis, a coccidian parasite, has emerged as an important cause of gastroenteritis in many areas throughout the world, including Peru, Mexico, Haiti, Caribbean countries, and Nepal. It is acquired through ingestion of contaminated food or water and lives within enterocytes in the small bowel. Cyclosporiasis has been reported among international travelers and has caused outbreaks among North Americans who have eaten raspberries imported from Guatemala or ingested fresh basil or mesclun. *C. cayetanensis* produces watery diarrhea, anorexia, fatigue, and abdominal pain. Symptoms can be prolonged and associated with substantial weight loss, particularly in persons with acquired immunodeficiency syndrome (AIDS).

The diagnosis is confirmed by identifying the cyclospora in stool samples. They stain with modified acid-fast or modified safranin preparations and appear autofluorescent in stool specimens examined by ultraviolet microscopy. Polymerase chain reaction (PCR) assays have proved to be sensitive in research settings.

 Treatment

C. cayetanensis responds to treatment with 160 mg of trimethoprim and 800 mg of sulfamethoxazole taken twice daily for 7 to 10 days. Although ciprofloxacin is not as effective, it is acceptable as an alternative in persons who cannot tolerate trimethoprim-sulfamethoxazole. Chronic suppressive therapy is often necessary in HIV-infected patients.

OTHER ENTERIC PROTOZOANS

Other protozoa can cause enteric disease (Table 400–1). They are acquired through ingestion of contaminated food or water. Some reside in the lumen of the bowel, and others invade and multiply within enterocytes. Enteric protozoa should be considered in the differential diagnosis of patients with persistent diarrhea and abdominal symptoms, particularly those with a history of recent international travel. Along with *Cryptosporidium parvum* and *C. cayetanensis*, *Isospora belli* and microsporidia can cause chronic diarrhea and weight loss in persons with AIDS.

The diagnosis is typically made by identifying ova or parasites in the stool. PCR-based diagnostic assays are under development for some of these pathogens. Microscopic examination should be performed by an expert, because these parasites may be confused with fecal debris. Pathogenic protozoa must also be differentiated from nonpathogens such as *Entamoeba coli*, *Endolimax nana*, *Iodamoeba butschlii*, *Trichomonas hominis*, and *Chilomastix mesnili*.

 Treatment

Therapy includes rehydration and administration of the appropriate antiprotozoal drug (see Table 400–1).

BABESIOSIS

Babesiosis is a tickborne, malaria-like disease. It is caused by *Babesia* species that infect erythrocytes. They are important pathogens of animals around the world and occasionally infect people. Most human infections in North America are caused by *Babesia microti*, which is found in areas of coastal New England, including the barrier islands of Nantucket, Martha's Vineyard, Long Island, Block Island, and Shelter Island; New Jersey; the upper Midwest, particularly Wisconsin; and occasionally elsewhere. Sporadic human cases due to *Babesia WA-1* have been reported from Washington and northern California. Babesiosis has been reported from other sites around the world. *Babesia divergens* is responsible for most of the European cases.

In the northeastern United States, the major reservoir is the white-footed deer mouse, *Peromyscus leucopus*, but other rodents may be involved. The vector is the deer tick, *Ixodes scapularis*, the same tick that transmits *Borrelia burgdorferi*, the cause of Lyme disease (Chapter 352) and human granulocytic ehrlichiosis. Concurrent cases of babesiosis and Lyme disease or ehrlichiosis have been reported. *Babesia* organisms are transmitted to humans by the nymph stage of the tick, which is 1.5 to 2.5 mm long and easily missed, or less commonly by adult ticks that are somewhat larger. Adult *I. scapularis* feeds on deer, but the deer do not become infected. The convergence of mice, deer, and humans is necessary for tickborne transmission. Blood transfusions have also been implicated in some cases. Congenital infection can occur but is rare. *B. divergens* in Europe is transmitted by *Ixodes ricinus*.

Infectious Diseases

Table 400–1 • OTHER ENTERIC PROTOZOA

ORGANISM	EPIDEMIOLOGY	MANIFESTATIONS	THERAPY*
Balantidium coli	Primarily an infection of animals, especially pigs, but also affects humans	Asymptomatic or mild and self-resolving; a few cases are more severe with abdominal pain, blood, and mucus in the stool	Tetracycline (500 mg qid for 10 days) *Alternative:* metronidazole (750 mg tid for 5 days) *or* Iodoquinol (650 mg tid for 20 days)
Blastocystis hominis	Probably worldwide, including North America; often found concomitantly with *Giardia lamblia*	Pathogenicity is debated	The need for treatment is debated, but efficacy has been reported with metronidazole (750 mg tid for 10 days) *or* iodoquinol (650 mg tid for 20 days)
Cyclospora cayetanensis[†]	Distribution appears to be worldwide; associated with imported raspberries from Guatemala	Can produce severe, watery diarrhea; anorexia; fatigue; weight loss lasting weeks; and prolonged disease in those with AIDS	Trimethoprim, 160 mg, and sulfamethoxazole, 800 mg, bid for 7 to 10 days; HIV-infected patients may require higher doses and long-term suppressive therapy. Ciprofloxacin, 500 mg bid for 7 days is an alternative.
Dientamoeba fragilis	Worldwide distribution; frequently found concomitantly with the pinworm *Enterobius vermicularis*	Often asymptomatic; diarrhea reported	Iodoquinol (650 mg tid for 20 days) *or* paromomycin (25–30 mg/kg body weight/day in 3 doses for 7 days) *or* tetracycline (500 mg qid for 10 days) *or* metronidazole (500–750 mg tid for 10 days)
Entamoeba polecki	Most cases reported from Papua New Guinea, but probably worldwide distribution; primarily found in pigs and monkeys; human infections are rare	Often asymptomatic; some have symptoms similar to those of *Entamoeba histolytica* colitis	Metronidazole (750 mg tid for 10 days)
Isospora belli[†]	Worldwide distribution, most prevalent in Latin America and Africa	Self-limited diarrhea in immunocompetent residents and travelers, but persistent, severe diarrhea in patients with AIDS	Trimethoprim, 160 mg, plus sulfamethoxazole, 800 mg, bid, for 7–10 days; HIV-infected patients may require higher doses and long-term suppressive therapy. Ciprofloxacin, 500 mg bid for 7 days is an alternative.
Microsporidia[†] (*Enterocytozoon bieneusi* and *Encephalitozoon intestinalis*)	Apparent worldwide distribution	AIDS patients with persistent diarrhea and wasting; self-limited cases in immunocompetent persons	Oral fumagillin (60 mg daily for 14 days) has been effective for *E. bieneusi*, but it has been associated with thrombocytopenia. Albendazole (400 mg bid for 21 days) has been effective for *E. intestinalis*. Treatment with highly active antiretroviral therapy (HAART) may lead to clinical response in HIV-intected patients with microsporidial diarrhea.
Sarcocystis species	Common pathogens of animals; rare in humans; acquired by ingesting contaminated beef or pork	Often asymptomatic; nausea, vomiting, abdominal pain, and diarrhea may occur; eosinophilic necrotizing enteritis has been reported	No specific therapy

*Recommendations are based on Drugs for Parasitic Infections (Med Lett Drugs Ther April 2002;1–12 (www. medletter.com). The dosages and durations are for adults.
[†]Associated with persistent, severe diarrhea in persons with AIDS.

Clinical Manifestations

Babesia infections are frequently subclinical or mild and self-limited in immunocompetent persons, but they can be severe in splenectomized persons, the elderly, or those with AIDS or other comorbid conditions. The incubation period varies from 1 to 6 weeks after tick transmission and up to 9 weeks after blood transfusion. Most of those infected by ticks are unaware of the bite. Symptomatic patients experience irregular fever, sweats, chills, headache, myalgia, fatigue, and other constitutional symptoms. Unlike malaria, there is no periodicity to the disease. Fever is frequently the only abnormality identified on physical examination, but hepatomegaly or splenomegaly may be present. Erythema migrans may be observed in persons with concurrent *B. burgdorferi* infection.

Diagnosis

There is frequently evidence of hemolytic anemia of varying severity. The white blood count may be normal or decreased, and the platelet count is often low. Liver enzymes and bilirubin levels can be elevated. Severe cases may be associated with gross hemoglobinuria, jaundice, pancytopenia, or acute respiratory distress syndrome. Parasitemia persists for a few weeks to several months in untreated persons. In Europe, *B. divergens* has been associated with the sudden onset of fulminant disease that can progress to death. Most cases are in splenectomized individuals.

Babesiosis is diagnosed by identifying intraerythrocytic parasites in Giemsa-stained or Wright-stained blood smears. They must be differentiated from *Plasmodium falciparum* and other *Plasmodium* species. Occasionally, dividing babesia make up a tetrad of merozoites that appears as the characteristic "Maltese cross." In contrast to malaria, *Babesia* species do not form hemoglobin-derived pigment. Results of blood smears may be negative in patients with low parasitemia. Antibodies to *B. microti* can be detected by indirect immunofluorescent assay, but the test does not differentiate persons with prior exposure from those with acute infection. Inoculation of Syrian hamsters and PCR-based assays have been used to diagnose cases in which parasites were not seen in blood smears.

Rx **Treatment**

Many cases of babesiosis in North America occur in immuno-competent persons and resolve spontaneously. In adult patients who have symptoms, particularly those who are asplenic, elderly, or have comorbid conditions, babesiosis has been treated with 650 mg of quinine sulfate taken orally three times daily plus 600 mg of clindamycin taken three or four times daily for 7 to 10 days. Combination therapy with azithromycin 600 mg daily plus ato-vaquone 750 mg twice daily for 7 to 10 days appears to be as effective and better tolerated. Exchange transfusion has been used in severily ill patients and those with high parasitemia. Consideration should be given to treating patients diagnosed with babesiosis for Lyme disease because of the prevalence of coinfection in North America. Therapy should be initiated early in persons infected with *B. divergens* in Europe, particularly those who have been splenectomized, because rapidly increasing parasitemia can result in massive hemolysis, renal failure, and death.

TRICHOMONIASIS

Trichomonas vaginalis is among the most prevalent of all pathogenic protozoa and an important cause of vaginitis around the world. The organism is oval, approximately 10 by 15 μm wide, and has four free flagella at its anterior pole and a fifth in an undulating membrane that runs along one side of the body. *T. vaginalis* is usually spread by sexual contact. The highest incidence of infection is among women with multiple sexual partners and those with other sexually transmitted diseases (Chapter 345). *T. vaginalis* can also be passed from infected mothers to their newborn daughters, but it is seldom symptomatic in girls before menarche. The parasite is able to survive for some time in moist environments, and nonvenereal transmission, although uncommon, can occur. Trichomoniasis, like other sexually transmitted diseases, may be a cofactor in the transmission of human immunodeficiency virus (HIV).

Clinical Manifestations

The incubation period for trichomoniasis is 5 to 28 days. Symptoms include vaginal discharge, vulvovaginal irritation, dyspareunia, and dysuria. The discharge tends to be watery and copious, but it may be thick, yellow or green, and frothy. Patients may notice an odor, but that is more common with bacterial vaginosis. Symptoms may worsen during menstruation. Population-based studies indicate that as many as one half of *T. vaginalis* infections in women are asymptomatic. On pelvic examination, there is typically inflammation of the vaginal walls. Punctate hemorrhages on the exocervix, colpitis macularis, or "strawberry cervix" are seldom visible on gross inspection, but they are observed in approximately one half of all cases if colposcopy is performed. The pH of the vaginal contents is typically elevated above the normal level of 4.5, as it is in bacterial vaginosis.

T. vaginalis can frequently be isolated from the male partners of infected women. Although most men are asymptomatic, *T. vaginalis* can produce symptomatic urethritis (Chapter 354). Urethral discharge is usually scant in those cases. Rarely, *T. vaginalis* is associated with epididymitis; superficial penile ulcerations, which are usually located under the prepuce; or involvement of the prostate.

Diagnosis

T. vaginalis is seen in wet mounts of vaginal secretions in approximately 60% of infected women, confirming the diagnosis. The organisms have a twitching motion with active flagella. Polymorphonuclear leukocytes are usually present. Culture is a more sensitive method of diagnosis, and commercial kits are available. *T. vaginalis* is occasionally identified in Papanicolaou-stained smears. PCR-based assays of vaginal specimens have been sensitive and specific in preliminary studies. For men, a wet mount of material from a platinum loop scraping of the anterior urethra reveals the organism in approximately one half of cases. Prostatic massage before collecting urine for trichomonas culture is a more sensitive diagnostic approach. Serologic studies lack sensitivity and specificity.

Rx **Treatment**

Metronidazole is the treatment of choice; a single dose of 2 g is effective in women. Sexual partners should be treated concurrently to prevent reinfection. Metronidazole, 500 mg two times daily for 7 days, is an alternative. Single-dose therapy ensures patient compliance, but the higher dose can produce nausea and a metallic taste. Metronidazole also has a disulfiram-like effect, and patients consuming it with alcohol may experience severe nausea, vomiting, and flushing. The use of metronidazole is relatively contraindicated during pregnancy. Treatment failures with metronidazole are uncommon but well documented. Some result from reinfection and others from poor compliance, but some are caused by metronidazole resistance. In such cases, high doses of metronidazole have been administered for longer periods. Tinidazole, which is not licensed for use in the United States, is also effective for trichomoniasis when administered as a single 2-g dose. It has been used effectively in some persons with metronidazole-resistant isolates.

SUGGESTED READINGS
Cyclosporiasis
Herwaldt BL: *Cyclospora cayetanensis*: A review, focusing on the outbreaks of cyclosporiasis in the 1990s. Clin Infect Dis 2000;31:1040–1057. *Reviews food and waterborne outbreaks of cyclosporiasis in the 1990s and the manifestations of disease.*

Verdier RI, Fitzgerald DW, Johnson WD Jr, Pape JW: Trimethoprim-sulfamethoxazole compared with ciprofloxacin for treatment and prophylaxis of *Isospora belli* and *Cyclospora cayetanensis* infection in HIV-infected patients: A randomized, controlled trial. Ann Intern Med 2000;132:885–888. *Trimethoprim-sulfamethoxazole is the treatment of choice for C. cayetanensis; ciprofloxacin is an alternative.*

Other Enteric Protozoans
Drugs for parasitic diseases. Med Lett Drugs Ther April 2002;1–12 (www.medletter.com). *Consensus recommendations for the treatment of parasitic diseases are provided. Key articles are referenced.*

Gillespie SH, Pearson RD: Principles and Practice of Clinical Parasitology. Chichester, UK, John Wiley & Sons, 2001. *The epidemiology, clinical manifestations, and treatment of enteric protozoa and other parasitic infections are reviewed.*

Babesiosis
Hatcher JC, Greenberg PD, Antique J, Jimenez-Lucho VE: Severe babesiosis in Long Island: Review of 34 cases and their complications. Clin Infect Dis 2001;32:1117–1125. *Series of cases characterizes the manifestations, complications, and treatment of severe B. microti infection.*

Herwaldt BL, McGovern PC, Gerwel MP, et al: Endemic babesiosis in another eastern state: New Jersey. Emerg Infect Dis 2003;9:184–188. *The authors provide composite data on 40 cases of babesiosis acquired in New Jersey, illustrating that Babesia microti is endemic there.*

Homer MJ, Aguilar-Delfin I, Telford SR 3d, et al: Babesiosis. Clin Microbiol Rev 2000;13:451–469. *The life cycle, epidemiology, clinical manifestations, and diagnosis of babesiosis are reviewed.*

Trichomoniasis
Forna F, Gulmezoglu AM: Interventions for treating trichomoniasis in women. Cochrane Database Syst Rev 2003;2:CD000218. *A single oral dose of nitroimidazole is curative.*

Krieger JN: Consider diagnosis and treatment of trichomoniasis in men. Sex Transm Dis 2000;27:241–242. *An excellent summary of the clinical manifestations of trichomoniasis in men.*

Wendel KA: Trichomoniasis: What's New? Curr Infect Dis Rep 2003;5:129–134. *An overview of diagnosis and treatment.*

401 CESTODE INFECTIONS

Charles H. King

The eight cestode species that most commonly cause human infection are listed in Table 401–1. Although this class of parasites is often referred to collectively as tapeworms, not all cestode parasites develop into tapeworms in the human host. The key to understanding the rather broad spectrum of cestode-associated illness is to recall that these parasites divide their life cycle between two or more different animal hosts, called *intermediate* and *definitive* hosts. The intermediate host harbors the immature parasite as a tissue cyst, whereas the subsequent definitive host harbors the mature parasite as a tapeworm.

Table 401-1 • COMMON HUMAN CESTODE INFECTIONS

SPECIES	STAGE FOUND IN HUMANS	COMMON NAME	PATHOLOGY	THERAPY
Diphyllobothrium latum	Adult	Fish tapeworm	Pernicious anemia	Niclosamide Praziquantel
Hymenolepis nana	Adult	Dwarf tapeworm	Rarely symptomatic	Niclosamide Praziquantel
Taenia saginata	Adult	Beef tapeworm	Rarely symptomatic	
Taenia solium	Adult	Pork tapeworm	Rarely symptomatic	Niclosamide Praziquantel
	Larva	Cysticercosis	Brain and tissue cysts	Albendazole Praziquantel Surgery
Echinococcus granulosus	Larva	Hydatid cyst disease	Solitary tissue cysts	Surgery Albendazole
Echinococcus multilocularis	Larva	Alveolar cyst disease	Multilocular cysts	Surgery Albendazole
Taenia multiceps	Larva	Bladderworm, coenurosis	Brain and eye cysts	Surgery
Spirometra mansonoides	Larva	Sparganosis	Subcutaneous larvae	Surgery

For a given cestode species, humans may serve as intermediate or definitive hosts.

The intermediate host is typically an insect or herbivorous (omnivorous) vertebrate that ingests parasite eggs in fecally contaminated food or water. The cestode eggs hatch into invasive oncospheres in this primary host's intestinal tract and then migrate into the host viscera or muscles to develop into immature cystic forms, called cysticerci or cysticercoids (for Cyclophyllidea cestodes such as *Taenia* and *Hymenolepis*) or procercoid and plerocercoid larvae (for Pseudophyllidea cestodes such as *Diphyllobothrium*). Humans become intermediate hosts for cestode species by ingesting parasite eggs in food or water, as in echinococcosis, or rarely by direct transfer of plerocercoid larvae from animal tissues, as in sparganosis.

The *definitive* host for a cestode species is a carnivorous or omnivorous mammal that acquires infection by consuming larval cysts in the uncooked tissues of an intermediate host. On exposure to stomach acid and bile salts in the digestive tract, the larvae excyst and develop into mature tapeworms within the intestinal lumen. Adult tapeworms contain two sections: a *scolex* (or head), used to adhere to the wall of the intestine, and a *strobila*, a tapelike chain of developing segments called proglottides. The hermaphroditic proglottides produce large numbers of fertile, infectious parasite eggs that reach the environment free or enclosed within parasite segments in the host's feces. Carnivorous humans become definitive hosts by ingesting cyst-infested meat of intermediate hosts (e.g., fish, pork, beef), after which the cysts develop into intraluminal, intestinal tapeworms.

Humans are strictly definitive hosts for the cestodes *Diphyllobothrium latum* (i.e., fish tapeworm), and *Taenia saginata* (i.e., beef tapeworm). These adult tapeworms do not enter the tissues of the human body and cause only minimal clinical symptoms. In contrast, humans are solely intermediate hosts for *Echinococcus granulosus* (hydatid cyst disease), *Echinococcus multilocularis* (alveolar cyst disease), *Taenia multiceps* (coenurosis), and *Spirometra* species. In the human body, these parasites develop as larval cysts and cause significant symptomatic tissue damage.

There are two exceptions to this rule. First, patients with *Taenia solium* infection may be infected with larval cysts (cysticercosis), adult tapeworms (i.e., pork tapeworm), or both. Second, in the case of the dwarf tapeworm, *Hymenolepis nana,* complete egg-to-tapeworm development can take place within a single human host. *H. nana* can be transmitted directly from person to person, and internal autoinfection may substantially increase the tapeworm burden of an infected individual. For all other cestode infections, increases in parasite burden occur only by means of continued exposure to egg-contaminated or larvae-infested foods and water.

INTESTINAL CESTODE (TAPEWORM) INFECTIONS

DIPHYLLOBOTHRIUM LATUM

D. latum tapeworms are the largest parasites that infect humans, ranging up to 10 m long. Infection is acquired by ingestion of parasite cysts in the tissues of smoked or uncooked freshwater fish (e.g., sushi, sashimi, ceviche). Tapeworms develop to maturity within 3 to 6 weeks after exposure and may survive for up to 20 years. Infection is prevalent (up to 2% of local residents) in many parts of the world, and endemic foci are found in lake or delta regions of Scandinavia, Russia, Japan, Europe, Chile, and North America. Contamination of freshwater bodies by raw sewage increases the risk for *D. latum* infection, but stable transmission may also occur because of local infection of alternate definitive hosts, such as foxes, wolves, minks, and bears.

Clinical Manifestations

For most patients, *D. latum* infection produces few or no symptoms. These are typically limited to nonspecific complaints of weakness, dizziness, craving for salt, diarrhea, and intermittent abdominal discomfort. Some patients may experience vomiting, severe abdominal pain, and weight loss. In cases of multiple infections, biliary or intestinal obstruction may occur. Between 1 and 2% of patients with *D. latum* infection develop significant vitamin B_{12} deficiency, resulting in megaloblastic anemia or neurologic disease. Folate deficiency may also occur. Vitamin B_{12} deficiency is a product of extensive vitamin uptake by the worm and worm-induced interference with gastrointestinal uptake by the host despite normal gastric acidity and intrinsic factor production. Vitamin B_{12} deficiency is most common among older patients and is more likely to occur in patients with low dietary intake of vitamins, multiple tapeworms, or a tapeworm in the proximal jejunum. In the debilitated host, nervous system complications can be quite extensive and can range from peripheral neuropathy to the syndrome of severe combined degeneration (Chapter 458).

Diagnosis

The diagnosis of *D. latum* infection is made by stool examination for characteristic operculated eggs that are 65 by 45 μm in diameter. Recovery of proglottides is uncommon because of segment degeneration during intestinal transit.

℞ Treatment

D. latum infection is treated with niclosamide or praziquantel, as summarized in Table 401–2. Severe vitamin B_{12} deficiency can be rapidly treated by parenteral vitamin injections.

Prevention

Fish tapeworm infection is prevented by avoiding consumption of raw, smoked, or salted fish from endemic areas. Parasite cysts may be killed by cooking (above 56° C for 5 minutes) or by freezing (−20° C for 24 hours).

Table 401–2 • THERAPY FOR INTESTINAL CESTODE (TAPEWORM) INFECTION

TREATMENT	NICLOSAMIDE	PRAZIQUANTEL
Dosage		
Adults	2 g (4 tablets)	10–12 mg/kg for all age groups (25 mg/kg for *H. nana*)
Children >34 kg	1.5 g (3 tablets)	
Children 11–34 kg	1 g (2 tablets)	
Administration	For most tapeworm species, taken as a single dose; tablets must be thoroughly chewed before swallowing to obtain complete therapeutic effect; a 7-day course of drugs used for *H. nana*, with reduced pediatric doses on days 2–7	Taken as a single dose for all species; may repeat after 7 days for heavy *H. nana* infections
Side effects	Nausea, vomiting, abdominal pain, diarrhea, drowsiness, dizziness, headache, pruritus	Mild but frequent, including dizziness, myalgias, nausea, vomiting, diarrhea, abdominal pain
Pregnancy	No known mutagenic effects; considered safe if indicated; because of risk of cysticercosis by autoinfection in *T. solium* tapeworm infection, therapy should not be delayed	

HYMENOLEPIS NANA

H. nana, or dwarf tapeworm, is found frequently in warm, dry climates and is prevalent in Southern and Eastern Europe, Asia, Africa, Central and South America, and Australia. It is the only human tapeworm that does not require an intermediate host. In the small intestine, hatching eggs release oncospheres that penetrate the villi of the mucosa. Four to 5 days later, the developed cysticercoid ruptures out of the villus, and a parasite scolex attaches to the lining of the ileum, maturing in 10 to 12 days. Mature worms are small, measuring 25 to 40 mm long and 1 mm wide. Autoinfection can occur internally (i.e., within the small bowel) or externally through the fecal-oral route, resulting in heavy infection. With time, however, a regulatory immunity to infection may develop, so that *H. nana* infection can be spontaneously cleared. Intensive infection is more common in institutionalized, malnourished, or immunodeficient individuals.

Clinical Manifestations

The clinical manifestations of *H. nana* vary with intensity and may include diarrhea, anorexia, abdominal pain, and pallor. A statistical association with phlyctenular keratoconjunctivitis has been observed and has been tentatively ascribed to the immune response to infection.

Diagnosis

The diagnosis of *H. nana* infection is made by examining stool for eggs 30 to 47 μm in diameter that have a characteristic double membrane. Proglottides are usually not seen in the stool.

℞ Treatment

H. nana infection is treated with niclosamide or praziquantel, as outlined in Table 401–2. Compared with the treatment of other tapeworm infections, longer courses of niclosamide and higher doses of praziquantel are recommended for the treatment of *H. nana* infection because of the relative resistance of larval cysticercoids to drug therapy. Because of the potential for late emergence of worms from viable cysticercoids remaining in the ileum, heavily infected individuals should be retested for infection and retreated 10 to 14 days after initial therapy.

Prevention

Because *H. nana* is easily transmitted from person to person, sanitation and handwashing are essential to control this parasite. Mass chemotherapy may also be used to suppress endemic transmission, particularly within closed institutions.

TAENIA SAGINATA

T. saginata, or beef tapeworm, is widespread in cattle-breeding areas of the world. Endemic foci (defined as prevalence >10%) are found in the southern Russian republics, in the Near East, and in central and eastern Africa. Infection is less common in other parts of the world but is found at prevalence rates of 0.1 to 5% in Europe, Southeast Asia, and South America. Infection is acquired by consuming cysticerci in the muscle tissue of infected cattle. The consumption of dishes such as steak tartare, "bleu" or rare steak, and undercooked shish kebabs is associated with infection in North American travelers to endemic areas.

Clinical Manifestations

T. saginata infection may cause nonspecific complaints of weakness and mild abdominal discomfort in up to one third of patients. Because *T. saginata* proglottides are motile, they may cause acute abdominal symptoms by migrating into and obstructing the appendix or the pancreatic and biliary ducts. A psychologically distressing feature of infection (and often the first symptom reported by the patient) occurs when motile proglottides migrate out of the anus onto skin or clothing or when they are observed moving in the feces.

Diagnosis

The diagnosis of taeniasis is most readily established by stool examination and perianal inspection for parasite proglottides and eggs. It is not possible, however, to distinguish *T. saginata* eggs from those of *T. solium* morphologically, and the definitive diagnosis of *T. saginata* infection requires pathologic examination of proglottid features or DNA hybridization studies. In practice, because patients with *T. solium* are at risk for self-infection with cysticercosis and because medical therapy for taeniasis is both safe and highly effective, treatment of an undetermined *Taenia* species infection should not be delayed pending speciation of the infecting tapeworm.

℞ Treatment

Beef tapeworm infection is treated with praziquantel or niclosamide, as outlined in Table 401–2. Both medications are highly effective in eliminating infection, and no special preparation or purgation is required. After therapy, the parasite scolex is digested within the gastrointestinal tract before it is passed in the feces. Although with the highly effective medications in use it is no longer necessary to collect the scolex to be assured that the parasite head has been expelled, digestive destruction of the head limits the ability to establish a species-specific clinical diagnosis for individual *Taenia* infections.

Prevention

T. saginata infection is prevented by avoiding foods containing undercooked or raw beef. As for the fish tapeworm, cooking to 56° C for 5 minutes or freezing at −20° C for 7 to 10 days destroys the infective larvae.

TAENIA SOLIUM

T. solium, also known as pork tapeworm, causes human infection in two different forms. Individuals who consume undercooked pork containing intermediate parasite cysts develop intestinal *T. solium* tapeworms. Individuals who consume parasite eggs may develop intermediate parasite cysts within the tissues of the body. (This condition, called *cysticercosis*, is described in more detail in the section on tissue cestode infections.) Autoinfection, most likely through the fecal-oral route, is possible, and a single patient may harbor an adult tapeworm and tissue cysticerci. *T. solium* infection is prevalent in Mexico, Central and South America, Africa, the Cape Verde Islands, southern Europe, Southeast Asia, and the Philippines. Most infections seen in the United States and Canada are found in immigrants from these endemic foci.

Clinical Manifestations

T. solium tapeworms are relatively short (3 m) but may survive for several decades once established in the human jejunum. Generally, tapeworm infections with *T. solium* produce no or minimal symptoms, which are limited to mild, nonspecific abdominal complaints. Unlike *T. saginata* proglottides, the segments of *T. solium* are nonmotile and are unlikely to cause obstruction.

Diagnosis

The diagnosis of intestinal infection with *T. solium* tapeworm is made by examining the stool for eggs and proglottides. Because the eggs are morphologically indistinguishable from those of *T. saginata*, study of the proglottid or head of the tapeworms is required for species identification. Stool samples and proglottides should be handled with care because of the risk of acquiring cysticercosis by accidental ingestion of *T. solium* eggs.

Rx Treatment

T. solium tapeworm infection is treated with niclosamide or praziquantel, as outlined in Table 401-2. After the diagnosis is established and concurrent central nervous system (CNS) and ocular cysticercosis have been excluded, therapy should be instituted as soon as possible because of the risk of autoinfection with cysticercosis. Therapy of concurrent cysticercosis is substantially longer and more intensive than that for intestinal infection and is described later in the section on tissue cestode infections.

OTHER INTESTINAL CESTODES

Other tapeworms that occasionally infect humans include the dog tapeworm, *Dipylidium caninum*, and the rodent tapeworm, *Hymenolepis diminuta*. These are most common in children and are acquired by inadvertently ingesting the intermediate larval forms of these parasites in the bodies of fleas or other insects. Usually, *D. caninum* and *H. diminuta* infections produce minimal symptoms. Diagnosis is established by stool examination, and infections are readily treated with standard doses of niclosamide or praziquantel.

TISSUE CESTODE (CYST) INFECTION

ECHINOCOCCOSIS

Human echinococcosis causes significant morbidity and mortality in livestock-raising regions in all parts of the world. The causative agents of "hydatid" and "alveolar" cyst disease in humans are the intermediate larval forms of the tapeworms *Echinococcus granulosus* and *Echinococcus multilocularis*, respectively.

Like other cestodes, *Echinococcus* tapeworms have intermediate and definitive hosts. For *Echinococcus* species, dogs and other canines are the definitive hosts. Tapeworm-infected animals pass eggs in their feces, which contaminate the local environment. Contamination of grazing areas and foodstuffs results in egg ingestion by intermediate hosts such as humans, sheep, goats, camels, and horses for *E. granulosus* and mice or other small rodents for *E. multilocularis*. Life-cycle transmission is completed when the definitive carnivore host consumes meat or offal

of the intermediate host that contains hydatid or alveolar cysts. Protoscolices within the cysts mature in the lumen of the canine gut to become adult, egg-bearing tapeworms. Because the cysts of *Echinococcus* contain a germinal layer that can produce multiple internal "daughter" cysts by asexual budding, an individual dog may develop infection with dozens of tapeworms after consuming a single, large cyst. After the tapeworms mature, a heavily infected dog may contaminate 10 or more hectares of ground with infectious eggs in a week.

In most areas of the world, burial practices make humans a "dead-end" host for *Echinococcus*; human infection does not perpetuate transmission in the local ecosystem. Nevertheless, the "inadvertent" hydatid cyst disease caused by *E. granulosus* and the more aggressive alveolar cyst disease caused by *E. multilocularis* are severe or even fatal illnesses for a significant minority of infected individuals.

Epidemiology

E. granulosus is common in livestock-raising areas of developed and developing countries. Sheep- and goat-herding populations that keep dogs as pets or work animals are at highest risk for hydatid cyst disease. Until recently, hydatid disease was common in Australia, New Zealand, Argentina, Chile, Ireland, Scotland, the Basque country, the Mediterranean basin, and throughout middle Europe. Currently, the area with the highest prevalence in the world is the Turkana and Samburu region of northwestern Kenya, where domestic and feral transmission of *E. granulosus* is perpetuated among nomadic farmers by poor hygienic practices. Occasional hydatid disease transmission is also found in central Asia, Mexico, the United States, and South America.

Alveolar cyst disease due to *E. multilocularis* is usually transmitted by wild animals, such as foxes and bush dogs, and is found in the arctic regions of the United States, Canada, and the former Soviet Union, as well as in rural areas of Europe and Turkey.

Clinical Manifestations

Human disease caused by *Echinococcus* species results from blood-borne invasion of the liver (50 to 70% of patients), lungs (20 to 30%), or other organs by developing parasite oncospheres. As these mature, they grow within tissues by concentric enlargement (*E. granulosus*) or by extension through adjacent host tissues (*E. multilocularis*). At any given time, most infected individuals are asymptomatic, and it may take 5 to 20 years for a cyst to grow to sufficient size (3 to 15 cm) to cause symptoms. When present, symptoms and findings refer to the anatomic site of involvement and derive from local inflammation, secondary bacterial infection, obstruction, or local mass effect. In hydatid cyst disease, the growing cyst becomes surrounded by a fibrous capsule formed by host immune reaction. Within this primary unilocular cyst, multiple daughter cysts, each containing an infective protoscolex, develop by asexual budding of the germinal layer. In alveolar cyst disease, the parasite cyst is not well separated from surrounding tissues, and lateral budding and malignancy-like growth (including distant metastasis of daughter cysts) may occur.

Patients with symptomatic hydatid liver cysts may complain of abdominal discomfort or mass in the right upper quadrant. Cyst leakage into the peritoneal cavity or pleural space may be associated with fever, urticaria, or a severe anaphylactoid reaction. Invasion of the biliary system often leads to the passage of daughter cysts into the common bile duct, with clinical and chemical evidence of intermittent obstruction resembling choledocholithiasis. Individuals with symptomatic hydatid involvement of the lungs present with cough, hemoptysis, and pleurisy. Spontaneous rupture of the cyst may lead to intrathoracic spread or to evacuation of daughter cysts through the bronchus. At lung or liver sites, bacterial superinfection may cause an acute presentation with symptoms of sepsis. Hydatid involvement of the brain is marked by slow-onset mass effect, hydrocephalus, and often by seizures. Cysts of the bone frequently fail to form a discrete capsule but rather cause local erosion of the cortex, resulting in pathologic fracture.

Symptomatic alveolar cyst disease most frequently refers to liver involvement and manifests as vague, mild upper quadrant and epigastric pain. Signs of hepatomegaly or obstructive jaundice may be present. Occasionally, metastatic lesions in the lung or brain are the first to cause symptoms by local inflammation or mass effect.

Diagnosis

Laboratory evaluation may show marked eosinophilia, but this finding is inconstant (30% prevalence). In hydatid cyst disease, radiographic and ultrasonographic studies typically show characteristic large, avascular cysts containing internal structures consistent with daughter cysts. Detection of mural calcification strongly favors the diagnosis of hydatid cyst. The differential diagnosis includes hemangioma, metastatic carcinoma, and remote bacterial or amebic liver abscess. Confirmatory evidence of infection may be obtained by serology (sensitivity of 60 to 90%, depending on the test used). Serologic testing is available commercially or from the Centers for Disease Control and Prevention (CDC, Atlanta, GA) through local state health departments. Until recently, it has not been recommended to perform closed aspiration on the cyst for diagnosis, because cyst leakage has the potential to initiate a severe allergic reaction and may result in the metastatic spread of daughter cysts. However, clinical series have reported successful computed tomography (CT)–guided or ultrasound-guided thin-needle aspiration of hydatid cysts for diagnosis. This procedure, when followed by immediate instillation of ethanol to kill viable protoscoleces, is rarely associated with side effects and is usually followed by regression of cysts on follow-up scans.

With alveolar cyst disease due to *E. multilocularis,* the organism's appearance on radiographic and sonographic imaging often mimics that of hepatic carcinoma. A definitive diagnosis may require angiography or open biopsy at surgery. Precautions must be taken to prevent metastatic dissemination of daughter cysts at the time of surgery.

Rx Treatment

Stable, asymptomatic, calcified cysts do not require specific therapy but should be monitored by serial imaging over several years to ensure a benign resolution. When technically feasible, expanding, symptomatic, or infected cysts are best removed in toto at surgery, with care taken to isolate the cyst to avoid secondary spread during the procedure. Controversy has developed over the practice of intraoperative instillation of cysticidal agents, because some patients have developed sclerosing cholangitis as a late complication of surgery when hepatic cysts communicate with the biliary system. Perioperative drug therapy alone is likely to be sufficient to prevent spread of daughter cysts at the time of surgery. If a cysticidal agent is used during surgery, hypertonic (25 to 30%) saline or 95% ethanol appears to pose the least risk to the patient, whereas iodophor and formalin instillation should definitely be avoided. Surgical resection should include careful closure of biliary and enteric fistulas and extensive postoperative drainage of the cyst bed to prevent fluid accumulation and secondary bacterial infection. Alveolar cyst disease may require wide resection (i.e., total lobectomy of liver or lung or even organ transplantation) to remove all cyst material.

In many cases, symptomatic echinococcal cysts are not amenable to resection. In such cases, oral drug therapy with the anthelminthics, either long-term mebendazole (40 mg/kg of body weight per day in three divided doses for 6 to 12 months) or albendazole (400 mg twice daily for one to eight periods of 28 days each, separated by drug-free rest intervals of 14 to 28 days), has been recommended for cure or palliation. ■ Cure rates, particularly for difficult cases with recurrent or extrahepatic or extrapulmonary cysts, have been low (<33%), although most patients show some improvement. Because the efficacy of drug therapy is limited, it is usually necessary to tailor a combined medical-surgical approach for each patient.

A minimally invasive option, *percutaneous aspiration, injection, and reaspiration* (PAIR procedure), performed under ultrasound or CT guidance, has been successful in controlling hydatid disease in many patients with inoperable intra-abdominal or bone cysts, although it has been less successful in patients with lung cysts. During PAIR, risk of parasite spread should be minimized by concurrent anthelminthic therapy and immediate treatment should be available for possible allergic reaction during the procedure.

CYSTICERCOSIS

Cysticercosis represents human tissue infection with the intermediate cyst forms of the pork tapeworm *T. solium.* Cysticercosis is acquired by ingestion of *T. solium* eggs in contaminated foods. Infection prevalence is approximately 5 to 25% in endemic areas of Latin America, India, Asia, Indonesia, and parts of Africa. Because of its potentially life-threatening complications, cysticercosis has greater clinical significance than does intestinal *T. solium* tapeworm infection, particularly if cyst disease involves the CNS, eyes, heart, or other vital organs.

Clinical Manifestations

Clinical manifestations depend on the location and number of infecting cysts. Cysticerci are bladder-like, fluid-filled cysts containing an invaginated protoscolex. They are often surrounded by a dense, fibrous capsule of host origin. In infected humans, cysticerci are usually multiple, 0.5 to 2 cm in diameter, and distributed widely throughout the body. Many patients have minimal or no symptoms of infection. However, symptomatic *neurocysticercosis* (e.g., cerebral cysticercosis, eye or spinal cord involvement) requires medical attention. Because this condition may prove lethal, any neurologic, cognitive, or personality disorder in an individual from an endemic area should be considered a possible manifestation of undiagnosed neurocysticercosis. Diagnosis has been facilitated by CT and magnetic resonance imaging (MRI), both of which are highly sensitive in detecting CNS cysticerci. Patients with CNS involvement have an average of 10 cysts distributed throughout the brain and spinal cord. These cysts may be in different stages of development, with symptoms commonly arising when older cysts begin to die, lose osmoregulation, and release antigenic material that provokes significant host inflammatory response.

In practice, neurocysticercosis may be divided into six discrete syndromes for management. In the *acute invasive* stage of cysticercosis, immediately after infection, the patient may experience fevers, headache, and myalgias associated with significant peripheral eosinophilia. Heavy infection at this stage may result in a clinical picture of "cysticercal encephalitis" associated with coma and rapid deterioration. This presentation should be treated aggressively with anti-inflammatory drugs. After cysticerci become established, *parenchymal CNS cysticercosis* (50% of cases) may be associated with seizures, intellectual impairment, and personality changes. Compression due to swelling or inflammation around the cysts may result in focal deficits, signs of cerebral edema, and hydrocephalus. Seizures may be focal (jacksonian), referring to the specific cortical locus of involvement, or may be generalized. *Subarachnoid cysticercosis* (30% of cases) is frequently associated with obstruction of cerebrospinal fluid (CSF) flow. Intracranial hypertension may manifest as vomiting, headache, and visual disturbances. Sensorial changes may include apathy, amnesia, dementia, hallucination, and emotional disturbance. Like other forms of basilar meningitis, pericysticercal inflammation at the base of the brain may cause obstruction or vasculitis of the cerebral arteries, leading to intermittent ischemia or stroke. *Intraventricular cysticercosis* (15% of cases) is, because of its location, the most difficult to diagnose and treat. Symptomatic cysts are most frequent in the fourth ventricle, where they cause outflow obstruction and increased intracranial pressure without localizing signs. An aggressive variant of ventricular neurocysticercosis involves the basal cisterns. This form of cysticercosis occurs most often in young women and involves multiple, rapidly spreading cysts in the cerebrum and around the base of the brain. Whereas symptoms due to isolated cysts may remit, cisternal cysticercosis usually has a progressive, deteriorating course if therapy is not given. Those with *spinal cysticercosis* may present with cord compression, radiculopathy, transverse myelitis, or signs of meningitis, depending on the location of involvement. *Ocular cysticercosis* is a distinct syndrome that manifests as eye pain, scotomata, and decreasing vision due to iridocyclitis, clouding of the vitreous, and retinal inflammation or detachment.

Diagnosis

A definitive diagnosis of cysticercosis requires examination of biopsy material obtained from a tissue cyst. However, a presumptive diagnosis may be made on the basis of a history of residence in an endemic area, the presence of characteristic radiographic findings on plain films (i.e., calcified cysts in soft tissues) or scans (i.e., low-density, enhanced, and unenhanced lesions on CT or MRI) and suggestive laboratory findings. Concomitant infection with *T. solium* tapeworm is present in about 25% of neurocysticercosis cases. In patients with neurocysticercosis, lumbar puncture is contraindicated in the presence of increased intracranial pressure. When obtainable, CSF may show hypoglycorrhachia, elevated total protein levels, and lymphocytic and eosinophilic pleocytosis (5 to 500 cells/μL). Although serum enzyme-linked immunosorbent assay (ELISA) and immunoblot assays may prove insensitive for detection of infection (as low as 50% in some MRI series of symptomatic patients), the CSF ELISA and immunoblot tests for specific immunoglobulin M (IgM) and IgG anti-cysticercal antibodies have a sensitivity of 75 to 100%. These tests are available through commercial laboratories or from the CDC (samples should be sent through state health departments). However, antiparasite antibodies may persist long after infection, and positive IgG serology may indicate only prior *Taenia* exposure, not necessarily active disease. The differential diagnosis of neurocysticercosis includes tumor, hydatid cyst disease, vasculitis, and chronic fungal and mycobacterial infection.

Rx Treatment

Given the high prevalence of cysticercosis in some areas of the world, it is evident that most cysticerci do not cause significant symptoms. For *symptomatic cysts outside the CNS,* the optimal therapy is surgical removal, because this ensures complete elimination of the cyst.

Inactive, asymptomatic neurocysticercosis does not need to be treated and should be followed prospectively. In cases of *active neurocysticercosis,* symptomatic therapy is definitely indicated, but surgery may be risky or technically unfeasible. For most intraparenchymal brain cysts, the optimal therapy involves control of seizures with anticonvulsants and reduction of cerebral inflammation with anti-inflammatory doses of corticosteroids, as needed. As shown in placebo-controlled randomized trials,[2,3] specific antiparasitic therapy is generally not helpful in speeding symptom resolution in these patients. For patients with extraparenchymal neurocysticercosis (i.e., ventricular or subarachnoid disease), antiparasite therapy may limit extension of the infection and reduce the number of complications. For such patients, antiparasite therapy must be combined with relief of hydrocephalus through shunting, along with control of local inflammation with the use of corticosteroids. When anthelminthics are to be used, therapy with praziquantel (50 to 100 mg/kg/day in three divided doses for 30 days) or albendazole (10 to 15 mg/kg/day for 8 days) is recommended. Recommendations for drug therapy continue to evolve, however, and it is appropriate to review the latest literature before embarking on a course of drug treatment. Follow-up tomographic scanning should be repeated 1 to 3 months after therapy is stopped to ensure adequate response. In cases of progressive disease, a repeat course of drug therapy with the alternate antiparasitic agent may be given to improve response.

Before institution of antiparasitic therapy, a careful examination should be made for eye involvement. In about 20% of treated cases, starting drug therapy is associated with an increased inflammatory response at the site of the cyst. Because parasite-induced ocular inflammation does not respond well to systemic anti-inflammatory agents, patients with cysticercosis of the eye (20% of cases of neurocysticercosis) should not receive drug therapy until the eye disease has been controlled surgically.

COENUROSIS

A different and less common form of tissue cysticercosis may be caused by larval stages of the dog tapeworms *T. multiceps* and *T. serialis*. Lesions tend to be solitary and are distinguished pathologically from *T. solium* cysticerci on biopsy. Ocular involvement is common, and surgical resection is the only effective mode of therapy.

SPARGANOSIS

Sparganosis is a tissue cestode infection caused by the plerocercoid larval stages of *Spirometra* species tapeworms of cats and other carnivores. Humans may become infected by ingesting infected water fleas (*Cyclops*), by ingesting uncooked meat from infected animals (i.e., reptiles, birds, or mammals), or by cutaneous exposure (i.e., traditional skin or eye poultices) to uncooked, infected meat. Usually, the larva encysts within the intestinal submucosa or skin. In some cases, however, parasites may invade the eye or CNS and cause significant inflammatory pathology at the site of encystment. Occasionally, proliferation into surrounding tissues occurs by lateral budding of the parasite, called *sparganum proliferum.* The treatment of choice for sparganosis is ethanol injection and/or surgical removal, because limited experience with medical anthelminthic therapy has shown no beneficial effect.

1. Keshmiri M, Baharvahdat H, Fattahi SH, et al: Albendazole versus placebo in treatment of echinococcosis. Trans R Soc Trop Med Hyg 2001;95:190–194.
2. Carpio A, Santillan F, Leon P, et al: Is the course of neurocysticercosis modified by treatment with antihelminthic agents? Arch Intern Med 1995;155:1982–1988.
3. Salinas R, Counsell C, Prasad K, et al: Treating neurocysticercosis medically: A systematic review of randomized, controlled trials. Trop Med Int Health 1999;4:713–718.

SUGGESTED READINGS

Carpio A: Neurocysticercosis: An update. Lancet Infect Dis 2002;2:751–762. *Update of recent findings.*

Koch S, Bresson-Hadni S, Miguet JP, et al: For the European Collaborating Clinicians: Experience of liver transplantation for incurable alveolar echinococcosis: A 45-case European collaborative report. Transplantation 2003;75:856–863. *A recent report.*

Schantz PM: Echinococcosis. *In* Guerrant RL, Walker DH, Weller PF (eds): Tropical Infectious Diseases: Principles, Pathogens, & Practice. Philadelphia, Churchill Livingstone, 1999, pp 1005–1025. *Summary of* Echinococcus *biology and infections in humans by a leading expert.*

White AC: Neurocysticercosis: Updates on epidemiology, pathogenesis, diagnosis, and management. Annu Rev Med 2000;51:187–206. *State-of-the-art article discussing the different presentations of CNS cysticercosis and their management.*

World Health Organization: Guidelines for treatment of cystic and alveolar echinococcosis in humans. Bull World Health Organ 1996;74:231–242. *Summary of multicenter experience in the treatment of human echinococcosis.*

402 SCHISTOSOMIASIS (BILHARZIASIS)

Edgar M. Carvalho
Aldo A. M. Lima

Definition

Schistosomiasis is one of the most important parasitic diseases of humans. Schistosomiasis is a global public health problem in the developing world. The disease is caused by trematodes of the genus *Schistosoma,* and it is estimated that 200 million people are infected and that 20 million have debilitating disease.

Epidemiology

There are five major species of *Schistosoma* affecting humans: *Schistosoma mansoni, Schistosoma haematobium, Schistosoma japonicum, Schistosoma intercalatum,* and *Schistosoma mekongi.* Other species that occasionally infect humans include *Schistosoma bovis, Schistosoma mathei,* and some avian schistosomes. These species differ biologically from one another and in their geographic distribution and in the type of disease they produce. Schistosomiasis occurs mainly in rural agriculture and periurban areas. *S. mansoni* is found in 55 countries, including the Arabian peninsula, Egypt, Libya, Sudan, most countries in sub-Saharan Africa, Brazil, some Caribbean islands, Suriname, and Venezuela. *S. hematobium* is endemic in 53 countries in the Middle East and most of the African continent, including the island of Madagascar and Mauritius. *S. japonicum* is endemic in China, Indonesia, and the Philippines and has been reported from Thailand. *S. intercalatum* has been reported from 10 countries in Africa. *S. mekongi* is found in Cambodia and Laos.

The endemicity of schistosomiasis depends on the urban disposal of urine (*S. haematobium*) and feces (*S. mansoni, S. japonicum, S. intercalatum, S. mekongi*), the presence of suitable snail hosts, and human exposure to cercariae. The freshwater snail intermediate hosts are *Biomphalaria* in Africa and *Biomphalaria glabrata* (*Australorbis*) and

Tropicarbis in South America and the West Indies. In some cases, the endemicity of schistosomiasis may be maintained by animal reservoirs. This is the case with *S. japonicum*, which infects dogs and cows. Rodents, monkeys, and baboons have been found infected in nature, but the role of these animals as reservoirs does not seem to be epidemiologically important.

Etiology and Life Cycle

The schistosomes are digenetic parasitic trematodes (Fig. 402–1). Although they are morphologically distinct, the species of *Schistosoma* that infect humans share some common factors. The large male (0.6 to 2.2 cm × 2 to 4 mm) has a ventral gynecophoric canal in which the female (1.2 to 2.6 cm × 1 to 2 mm) is held during copulation. Adult worms live in the mesenteric veins (*S. mansoni*, *S. japonicum*, *S. mekongi*, and *S. intercalatum*) or in the venous plexus around the lower ends of the ureters and the urinary bladder (*S. haematobium*). In these sites, they start their sexual reproduction by releasing eggs. Once deposited in the host, eggs may stay in the mesenteric vein, be trapped in the intestines, escape to intestinal lumen, and migrate by portal blood to the liver (*S. mansoni*, *S. japonicum*). Eggs of *S. haematobium* may be trapped in the intestines and bladder and may escape to the intestinal or bladder lumen. After being excreted by feces or urine into fresh water, the eggs hatch and release ciliated motile miracidia that penetrate into excreted to the snail intermediate host. After asexual multiplication the snail, the development of cercariae, the infective forms for humans, takes 4 to 7 weeks. After leaving the snails, the cercariae can survive in fresh water for almost 72 hours. When penetration of the skin in the human host occurs, the cercariae lose their

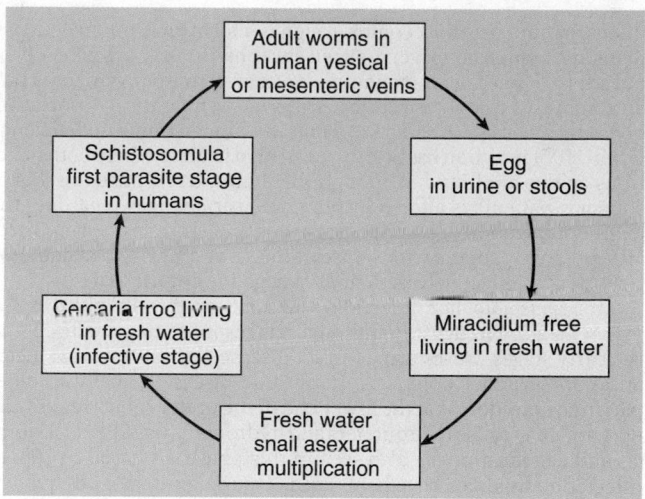

FIGURE 402–1 • Schistosome life cycle.

tails and change into schistosomula. The schistosomula migrate to the lungs and, in about 6 weeks, mature to adult worms and descend to their final habitat. Viable eggs can be seen in the excretions (i.e., stool or urine) 5 to 9 weeks after cercarial penetration. The lifespan of the worms ranges from 5 to 10 years.

Pathogenesis and Clinical Manifestations

Clinical manifestations of schistosomiasis are divided into schistosome dermatitis, acute schistosomiasis, and chronic schistosomiasis. Schistosome dermatitis or swimmer's itch is seen mainly when avian cercariae penetrate the skin and are destroyed. Although this manifestation is not common in human schistosomiasis, recognition of this clinical entity is gradually expanding. Schistosome dermatitis is a sensitization phenomena, because it occurs in previously exposed persons. The cercariae are destroyed in the epithelial layers of the skin. They evoke an acute inflammatory response with edema, early infiltration of neutrophils and lymphocytes, and later invasion of eosinophils. A pruritic papular rash occurs within 24 hours after penetration of cercariae, reaching maximal intensity in 2 to 3 days.

The pathogenesis of human schistosomiasis is mainly related to egg deposition and liberation of antigens of adult worms and eggs. Acute schistosomiasis occurs with the beginning of oviposition, usually 20 to 50 days after primary exposure. Although asymptomatic in endemic areas, acute schistosomiasis is becoming a frequent and major clinical problem in nonimmune individuals from urban regions who are exposed for the first time to a heavy infection in an endemic area. A strong inflammatory response characterized by high levels of pro-inflammatory cytokines such as interleukin-1 (IL-1), IL-6, and tumor necrosis factor-α (TNF-α) and circulating immune complexes participate in the pathogenesis of the disease. The absence of this clinical picture in individuals living in endemic areas is related to a modulation of the immune response in such case by antigens or idiotypes transferred from mother or child. The clinical syndrome (i.e., fever, chills, liver and spleen enlargement and marked eosinophilia) originally described for *S. japonicum* infection and still common for this species, is being increasingly diagnosed in Brazil in individuals with *S. mansoni* infection. Malaise, diarrhea, weight loss, cough, dyspnea, chest pain, restrictive respiratory insufficiency, and pericarditis are important findings in this phase. High levels of TNF-α and circulating immune complexes are found in patient's serum in this phase of illness, and they correlate with the presence of abdominal pain, diarrhea, and weight loss and with respiratory and pericardial manifestations, respectively. Acute disease is more frequently observed in individuals living outside the endemic areas of schistosomiasis, because modulation of the immune response by antigens or idiotypes transferred from mother to child decreases the frequency of this manifestation in subjects living in endemic areas.

In chronic schistosomiasis, tissue injury is mediated by egg-induced granulomas and subsequent appearance of fibrosis. Because the habitat of *S. mansoni*, *S. japonicum*, *S. mekongi*, and *S. intercalatum* worms are the mesenteric blood vessels, the intestines are involved primarily, and egg embolism results in secondary involvement of the liver. Abdominal pain, irregular bowel movements, and blood in the stool are the main symptoms of intestinal involvement. Colonic polyposis may occur, especially in Egypt.

Hepatosplenic involvement is the most important cause of morbidity in *S. mansoni* and *S. japonicum* infections. Patients may remain asymptomatic until the manifestation of hepatic fibrosis and portal hypertension. Hepatic fibrosis is caused by a granulomatous reaction to *Schistosoma* eggs that have been carried to the liver. Hepatic fibrosis in *S. mansoni* infection has been associated with intensity of infection, genetic background, and immunologic response. Although the severity of infection is clearly linked with liver disease, the immune response, collagen deposition, and genetic factors potentiate disease in some individuals with only moderate infections or inhibit disease in others with heavy infections. Both T_H1 and T_H2 cytokines are involved in the granulomatous response. An association between the human leukocyte antigen (HLA) class II allele DQ B1*0201 and a greater chance for hepatosplenism has been demonstrated.

Enzymes and antigens released from eggs sensitize the host lymphocytes, which migrate to areas of egg deposition and recruit other cell types, such as macrophages, eosinophils, and fibroblasts. The size of these granulomas and the resulting fibrosis lead to most of the chronic fibro-obstructive lesions in schistosomiasis. In the liver, the granulomas result in perisinusoidal obstruction of portal blood flow, portal hypertension, splenomegaly, esophageal varices, and portosystemic collateral circulation. Liver cell perfusion is not reduced; consequently, liver function test results remain normal for a long time. Hematemesis from bleeding esophageal or gastric varices may occur. In such cases, anemia and decreasing levels of serum albumin are observed. A few patients have a severe hepatosplenic disease with decompensated liver disease. Jaundice, ascites, and liver failure are then observed. Concomitant infection by *Salmonella* species and, less extensively, gram-negative bacteria with *S. mansoni* or *S. haematobium* leads to a picture of prolonged fever, hepatosplenomegaly, and mild leukocytosis with eosinophilia. Other complications associated with hepatosplenic schistosomiasis include pulmonary hypertension, glomerulonephritis, infantilism, and hypersplenism. In adult hospitalized patients with *S. japonicum* infection, cerebral schistosomiasis occurs in 1.7 to 4.3%. It may occur as early as 6 weeks after

Continued

infection, and the most common sign is a focal jacksonian epilepsy. Signs and symptoms of generalized encephalitis may occasionally be found. In *S. mansoni* infection, nervous system involvement is rare and mainly characterized by transverse myelitis. Association between *S. mansoni* or *S. hematobium* and human immunodeficiency virus (HIV) infection has been documented in areas where both infectious agents are found. Although the immune response of schistosomiasis patients is altered by HIV, no clear changes regarding the degree of infection or severity of schistosomiasis have been reported. HIV-positive patients with schistosomiasis respond to praziquantel treatment as effectively as their HIV-negative counterparts.

In *S. haematobium* infection, the main system involved is the urinary tract. The acute granulomatous response to parasite eggs in the early stages causes urinary tract disease, such as urethral ulceration and bladder polyposis. In chronic disease, usually in older patients, granulomas at the lower end of the ureters obstruct urinary flow and may cause hydroureters and hydronephrosis. Bladder fibrosis and calcification are also seen in this phase. Up to 50 to 70% of infected individuals have hematuria, dysuria, or urinary frequency. Urine examination reveals proteinuria and hematuria. Radiologic findings include hydronephrosis, hydroureter, ureteral strictures, dilation or distortion, ureteral calcifications, ureterolithiasis, calcified bladder, polyps, reduction in bladder capacity, irregular contraction of the bladder wall, or dilated bladder due to bladder neck fibrosis. An increased incidence of squamous cell carcinoma of the bladder has been reported in endemic areas of *S. haematobium* infection, but the mechanism of carcinogenesis is unknown. *S. haematobium* eggs have occasionally been found in the lungs with subsequent focal pulmonary arteritis and pulmonary hypertension.

In schistosome-infected populations, intensity of infection increases during the first 2 decades of life as children accumulate worms and then declines. The susceptibility of younger children to infection is even more evident when intensities of reinfection are studied after the elimination of existing worms by chemotherapy. Although there is a decrease in exposure with age, the lower intensities of infection in older individuals are due in part to an acquired resistance. Both T_H1 (interferon-γ) and T_H2 types of immune response, mediated by IgE, may participate in resistance to reinfection. In the *S. haematobium*–infected population, IgE increases progressively with age, and IgE antibodies directed against adult worm antigens are associated with subsequent low intensities of reinfection. Similar associations between high IgE levels or high IgE/IgG_4 ratio and resistance to reinfection have been found among Brazilian and Kenyan subjects exposed to *S. mansoni*. Evidence that a T_H1-type immune response may also be involved in the protection against *S. mansoni* comes from the immunologic studies in subjects who are highly exposed to contaminated water but have negative stool examination results. In these subjects, there is evidence of higher interferon-γ production in response to *S. mansoni* membrane extract. The existence of a major codominant gene, called *SM1*, controlling the intensity of infection by *S. mansoni* has been demonstrated. The localization of *SM1* on chromosome 5q31-q33, close to several genes involved in the regulation of immune response, including those for colony-stimulating factor-1 receptor, granulocyte-macrophage colony-stimulating factor, IL-3, IL-4, IL-5, IL-13, and immune regulatory factor-1 and a locus regulating IgE levels, indicates that genetic factors are probably critical to susceptibility and resistance to schistosome infection.

Diagnosis

A definitive diagnosis of schistosomiasis can be made only by finding schistosome eggs in feces, urine, or a biopsy specimen, usually from the rectum (Table 402–1). The history of contact with contaminated water and clinical manifestations are important steps in establishing the diagnosis. Because schistosome eggs may be few, concentration by sedimentation should be employed. All eggs from the feces, urine, or tissues should be examined under high power to determine their viability by the activity of the cilia of the excretory flame cell of the enclosed miracidium. Dead eggs may persist for a long time after successful therapy or natural death of the worms. The presence of only dead eggs does not necessarily require treatment. Because intensity of infection is associated with morbidity, quantitative techniques are recommended. For *S. mansoni* and *S. japonicum* the Kato-Katz thick smear method is used. Rectal biopsy may be used for those with light infection. In patients with chronic *S. mansoni* and *S. japonicum* infection and liver disease, diagnosis is sometimes made by the documentation of eggs in liver specimens. Ultrasonography allows determination of the degree of liver fibrosis. Diagnosis of *S. mekongi* and *S. intercalatum* infections is performed by examining the stool for eggs.

Urine examination for *S. haematobium* eggs can be performed by direct or concentration methods. Samples should be obtained at midday, when excretion of the eggs is maximal. Rectal biopsy may be done in patients with light infection and negative urine results. After *S. haematobium* infection is diagnosed, assessment of urinary tract pathology by ultrasonography is recommended. Because of an increased incidence of carcinoma of the bladder, cancer surveillance should be performed in patients with *S. haematobium* infection.

Several serologic tests with detection of IgM, IgG, and IgA antibodies to *Schistosoma* antigens are available. Serologic tests are important in the diagnosis of acute infection because the symptoms are not specific and the finding of eggs in the stool may refelct chronic infection. High levels of IgA anti-egg antigen and IgM and IgG antibodies to keyhole limpet hemocyanin (KLH) are predominantly observed during the acute phase. The KLH from the murine mollusk *Megathura crenulata* shares carbohydrate epitopes with the surface of schistosomula.

Quantification of circulating antigens in serum and urine is an alternative for the diagnosis of schistosome infection. However, the sensitivity of the method decreases in cases of light infection (<100 eggs per gram of feces). This test has also been used to monitor efficacy of schistosome chemotherapy. Significant decrease in antigen

Table 402–1 • DIAGNOSIS OF SCHISTOSOMIASIS

SCHISTOSOME	EGGS	DIAGNOSIS
S. haematobium	Mainly found in urine but may be found in stools or rectal biopsy Eggs: $143 \times 50\,\mu m$; spindle shaped: rounded anterior, conical posterior, tapering to a terminal delicate spine	Obtain urine sample at midday (when eggs are excreted); more than one sample may be needed Examine urine directly or by filtering 10 mL of urine through Nuclepore membrane Rectal biopsy in suspected cases with normal urine Serologic testing to diagnose early or light infection
S. mansoni	Eggs: $155 \times 66\,\mu m$; oval with lateral, long spine	Examine stool for eggs Use Kato-Katz thick smear method for quantification purposes Rectal biopsy or serologic testing to diagnose stool-negative cases, particularly in lightly infected patients
S. japonicum	Found in stool; eggs: $89 \times 67\,\mu m$; oval or rounded with lateral, short, sometimes curved spine	Examine stool for eggs Kato-Katz thick smear (for quantitative assessment) Rectal biopsy for those with light infections, especially with less common manifestation (i.e., cerebral schistosomiasis)
S. mekongi	Found in stool; eggs: $60 \times 32\,\mu m$; smaller than eggs of *S. japonicum*	Examine stool for eggs
S. intercalatum	Found in stool; eggs: $180 \times 65\,\mu m$; terminal spine	Examine stool for eggs

levels or negativation of the test is observed as early as 10 days after therapy.

 Treatment

Chemotherapy is by far the major tool for the control and cure of schistosomiasis. Three compounds are in use—metrifonate, oxamniquine, and praziquantel—and all three are included in the World Health Organization's list of essential drugs. Praziquantel, a pyrazinoisoquinoline derivative, is the drug of choice for the treatment of schistosomiasis for four reasons: high efficacy against all schistosome species and against cestodes, lack of serious short-term and long-term side effects, administration as a single oral dose, and competitive cost.

The standard recommended treatment consists of a single dose of 40 mg/kg for *S. mansoni, S. hematobium,* and *S. intercalatum* infection. In *S. japonicum* infection, a total dose of 60 mg/kg is recommended, split into two or three doses in a single day. *S. mekongi* may require two treatments at 60 mg/kg of body weight. Using these dosages, recorded cure rates are 75 to 85% for *S. hematobium*, 63 to 85% for *S. mansoni*, 80 to 90% for *S. japonicum*, 89% for *S. intercalatum*, and 60 to 80% for double infections with *S. mansoni* and *S. hematobium*.

Praziquantel is well tolerated and effective in patients of all ages and in different clinical forms of schistosomiasis, including advanced hepatosplenic cases (*S. mansoni*), cerebral schistosomiasis (*S. japonicum*), and neurologic syndromes (*S. mansoni* and *S. hematobium*), possibly in association with corticosteroids. However, praziquantel has low prophylactic effect, which reduces its efficacy in areas of high transmission. There have been several reports of persistent schistosome egg shedding after treatment, posing concerns about emergence of drug resistance.

The effects of praziquantel on schistosomes can be summarized under three headings: muscular contraction, tegumental damage (i.e., vacuolization and blebbing), and metabolic alterations (i.e., decreased glucose uptake, lactate excretion, and glycogen content). The praziquantel activity also depends on the immune system. Several studies have reported that praziquantel induces the exposure of worm surface antigens that may function as targets to immune responses.

The most common side effects observed with praziquantel or oxamniquine administration are related to the gastrointestinal tract: abdominal pain or discomfort, nausea, vomiting, anorexia, and diarrhea. These symptoms can be observed in up to 50% of patients but are usually well tolerated. Other side effects are related to the central nervous system (e.g., headache, dizziness, drowsiness) and the skin (e.g., pruritus, eruptions) or may be nonspecific (e.g., fever, fatigue). Toxicity is very low in animal studies with praziquantel, and no genotoxic risk has been reported. In general, the cumulative experience from a large number of studies allows the conclusion that praziquantel is an extremely well-tolerated drug, requiring minimal medical supervision, and is therefore particularly suitable for mass chemotherapy programs.

Although a reduction of intensity of infection and morbidity has been documented with mass chemotherapy, provision for clean water, use of molluscicides, and adequate sanitation should be combined to control the disease.

SUGGESTED READINGS

Appleton CC, Mbaye A: Praziquantel—quality, dosages and markers of resistance. Trends Parasitol 2001;17:356–357. *Highlights the new findings on the quality of generic drugs, an initiative to promote the Africa-wide distribution of praziquantel, and new results in the search for markers of praziquantel-resistant schistosomes.*

Barsoum RS: Schistosomiasis and the kidney. Semin Nephrol;23:34–41. *Schistosomiasis can cause glomerulonephritis, fibrosis, calcification in the lower urinary tract, and precancerous bladder lesions.*

de Jesus AR, Silva A, Santana LB, et al: Clinical and immunologic evaluation of 31 patients with acute *Schistosomiasis mansoni.* J Infect Dis 2002;185:98–105. *Some immune markers were associated with specific clinical manifestations.*

Magnussen P: Acta Trop 2003;86:243–254. Treatment and re-treatment strategies for schistosomiasis control in different epidemiological settings: A review of 10 years' experiences. *Cheap and simple screening of urine and stool specimens can lead to effective therapy with praziquantel.*

Pearce EJ: Progress towards a vaccine for schistosomiasis. Acta Trop 2003;86:309–313. *One vaccine is in phase II trials.*

Richter J: The impact of chemotherapy on morbidity due to schistosomiasis. Acta Trop 2003;86:161–183. *Earlier chemotherapy increases the chances of reversing schistosomal pathology.*

Stephenson I, Wiselka M: Drug treatment of tropical parasitic infections: Recent achievements and developments. Drugs 2000;60:985–995. *General review of drug development solutions to a number of tropical health diseases, including schistosomiasis. For this disease, the report focuses on the widespread use of praziquantel and concerns about the emergence of drug resistance.*

Utzinger J, Keiser J, Shuhua X, et al: Combination chemotherapy of schistosomiasis in laboratory studies and clinical trials. Antimicrob Agents Chemother 2003;47:1487–1495. *An overview of drug therapy.*

World Health Organization: The Control of Schistosomiasis. Technical report series 728. Geneva, World Health Organization, 1993, pp 1–86. *Description of the epidemiology, morbidity, and methods of control of schistosomiasis. This report also includes a summary of control programs in endemic areas and outline for strategy of morbidity control.*

403 LIVER, INTESTINAL, AND LUNG FLUKE INFECTIONS

Adel A. F. Mahmoud

Parasitic flukes belong to the phylum Platyhelminthes. These organisms are dorsoventrally flattened and are typically bilaterally symmetrical. With the exception of the schistosomes, all flat worms of clinical significance are hermaphroditic. Morphologically, the body of adult worms is leaf shaped and possesses two prominent suckers, one located anteriorly and the other ventrally. These are attachment organs that help anchor adult worms in their habitat within the organs of the definitive host. During the typical life cycle of a flat worm, the organism uses two, three, or more hosts; one is the definitive host, and the others are intermediate hosts. Fluke infections challenge the protective mechanisms of the definitive hosts because of their size, complex anatomic and antigenic structure, and remarkable abilities to evade expulsion. Clinically relevant flukes are usually grouped according to the main location of adult worms in infected humans. These include liver, intestinal, and lung flukes (Table 403–1). Blood flukes or schistosomes are discussed in Chapter 402.

The geographic distribution of liver, intestinal, or lung flukes (Table 403–2) is global. The liver flukes *Clonorchis sinensis, Opisthorchis felineus,* and *Opisthorchis viverrini* are the most prevalent. Liver, intestinal, and lung flukes vary in size from 1 mm to 7 cm long. The pattern of life cycle of these flukes is similar. Eggs are passed in the feces or sputum of infected individuals. Eggs hatch in the aquatic outside environment, releasing miracidia that seek specific snail intermediate hosts, where they undergo several asexual multiplication steps, resulting finally in the release of cercariae. This stage is free living but has a limited lifespan; it has to encyst on vegetation or in the tissues of fish or crabs, where it changes into the metacercarial stage, which is infective to humans. Human acquisition of infection depends on ingestion of metacercariae in raw or improperly cooked aquatic plants or animals.

Diagnosis of a specific tissue fluke is a significant clinical challenge. Knowing the geographic distribution of infection, the specific symptoms and signs, and the proper identification of eggs in feces or sputum samples is necessary. The specificity and sensitivity of serologic tests have progressed to being helpful in diagnosis with a certain degree of confidence.

LIVER FLUKES

Several species of liver flukes are capable of inducing significant morbidity and mortality in humans. Opisthorchiasis and clonorchiasis are the most common of these infections.

OPISTHORCHIASIS

Human infection is caused by *O. viverrini* or *O. felineus,* parasitic flukes of cats, dogs, and other fish-eating mammals. Human infection is acquired by ingestion of metacercariae found in the second intermediate host (e.g., cyprinoid fish, carp). The metacercariae excyst in the duodenum and migrate through the ampulla of Vater to reach their final habitat in the bile ducts. *O. viverrini* is endemic in Thailand, Laos, and Cambodia, and *O. felineus* is distributed widely in Russia and Eastern and Central Europe (see Table 403–2). The incidence of *O. viverrini* in northeastern Thailand has been increasing, reaching 90% of the population in specific foci.

Table 403–1 • MAJOR LIVER, INTESTINAL, AND LUNG FLUKE INFECTIONS IN HUMANS

INFECTION	CAUSATIVE ORGANISMS	SECOND INTERMEDIATE HOST	SIZE OF ADULT FLUKE (mm)	FINAL HABITAT IN HUMANS	SIZE OF EGGS (µm)
Opisthorchiasis	O. viverrini O. felineus	Cyprinoid fish	5–10 × 1–2	Distal bile ducts, gallbladder	28 × 16 Operculated
Clonorchiasis	C. sinensis	Carp fish	10–24 × 3–5	Bile and pancreatic ducts	29 × 16 Operculated
Fascioliasis	F. hepatica F. gigantica	Aquatic vegetation or water	20–30 × 13 75 × 20	Large biliary ducts	140 × 75 Inconspicuous operculum 175 × 80
Fasciolopsiasis	F. buski	Aquatic plants	50–75 × 8–20	Small intestine	135 × 35 Small operculum
Paragonimiasis	P. westermani	Freshwater and brackish water crabs	7–16 × 4–8	Lungs, brain, or abdominal organs	100 × 60 Operculated

Table 403–2 • GEOGRAPHIC DISTRIBUTION OF FLUKES

FLUKE	DISTRIBUTION
Liver	
Opisthorchis viverrini	Thailand, Laos, Cambodia
O. felineus	Russia, Eastern and Central Europe
Clonorchis sinensis	China, Japan, Korea, Taiwan, Vietnam, Hong Kong (imported fish from China)
Fasciola hepatica	United States, Europe, Africa, Asia
F. gigantica	Less common: Africa, Asia, Hawaii
Dicrocoelium sp.	Europe, Africa, Asia, North America
Intestinal	
Fasciolopsis sp.	Taiwan, Thailand, Bangladesh, India, plus other Asian and Western countries
Echinostoma sp.	Indonesia, Philippines, Thailand, Taiwan
Heterophyes heterophyes	Egypt, Iran, Far East, Southeast Asia
Metagonimus yokogawai	China, Japan, Korea, Taiwan
Gastrodiscoides hominis	India, Southeast Asia, Russia
Lung	
Paragonimus sp.	Asia, West Africa, Central and South America

Pathogenesis and Clinical Features

Adult flukes inhabit the distal bile ducts and may occasionally be seen in the gallbladder. Most infected individuals are asymptomatic. Lesions have been demonstrated in the biliary system, varying from hyperplasia of ductal epithelium to obstruction and bile retention. There is significant correlation between intensity of infection and severity of observed lesions. Because very few controlled studies have been performed in infected and uninfected populations of endemic areas, the specificity of symptoms and signs is questionable. Symptomatic infections are associated with right upper quadrant discomfort, dyspepsia, and change in bowel habits. Generalized symptoms such as decrease of appetite and weight loss have also been observed. In severe cases, relapsing cholangitis and cholecystitis may occur. Associations between *O. viverrini* and cholangiocarcinoma, gallstones, and obstructive jaundice have been reported. Liver enlargement is demonstrated in most symptomatic individuals along with imaging evidence for biliary tree disease.

Infection with *O. felineus* has a characteristic clinical course. In its acute phase (2 to 3 weeks after infection), the clinical features include irregular fever, lymphadenopathy, myalgia, and eosinophilia. In chronic infections, symptoms and signs of biliary disease resemble those of *O. viverrini* infection; however, the worms may also be found in the pancreatic duct, causing manifestations related to this organ.

CLONORCHIASIS

C. sinensis also is frequently referred to as the Chinese or oriental liver fluke. Carnivorous animals such as dogs, cats, and rats are probably the reservoir hosts in nature. Human infection is acquired by ingestion of the second intermediate host, a freshwater carp of the family Cyprinidae. In endemic areas (see Table 403–2), many species of this family are parasitized with *C. sinensis* metacercariae. Clonorchiasis is also seen in many countries, including the United States among immigrants from endemic areas. Importation of *C. sinensis* is a risk in the international food trade.

Pathogenesis and Clinical Features

The life cycle, pathologic features, and clinical manifestations of clonorchiasis are similar to those of opisthorchiasis. Adult flukes reside in the medium-sized and small bile ducts. They may also be found in the gallbladder, common bile duct, and pancreatic duct. In early infection, the pathologic features consist of edema and epithelial desquamation in bile ducts associated with an inflammatory response. Later, metaplasia and glandular proliferation occur with dilatation and thickening of bile ducts. The final pathologic insult is related to marked periductal fibrosis. The specificity of symptoms due to clonorchiasis such as anorexia, epigastric pain, or diarrhea has been questioned in studies performed on immigrants to the United States from the Far East. In chronic infection as seen in endemic areas, the association with cholangitis, gallstones, and cholangiocarcinoma has been reported repeatedly. Sonography or computed tomography (CT) demonstrates the pathologic changes in the liver: flukes within dilated bile ducts and periductal changes.

FASCIOLIASIS

Human infection with the zoonotic flukes *Fasciola hepatica* and *Fasciola gigantica* is acquired by ingestion of metacercariae that are attached to various aquatic plants or through drinking of water contaminated with the infective stage of the organisms. The natural hosts of fascioliasis include sheep, goats, cattle, and horses; endemic regions occur in all five continents (see Table 403–2). After the infective metacercariae are consumed, they excyst in the duodenum, penetrate its wall, and travel through the peritoneal cavity to enter the liver through its capsule. The organisms migrate into the liver parenchyma to reach their final habitat in large bile ducts.

Pathogenesis and Clinical Features

Human fascioliasis is usually associated with mild clinical features. The resulting syndromes may be conveniently divided into the *acute migratory phase*, while the organisms are finding their way through the peritoneal cavity to the liver capsule and parenchyma, and the *established phase*, which is associated with the mature flukes' taking residence in the bile ducts. The acute phase is marked with fever, right upper quadrant or epigastric pain, and eosinophilia. The clinical presentation may last 4 to 8 weeks after ingestion of metacercariae and is usually self-limited. Stool examination during this phase usually yields negative findings for parasite eggs. During the established phase, most infected individuals are asymptomatic. Some may complain of abdominal pain and dyspepsia. Hepatomegaly and jaundice may occur, as well as significant peripheral blood eosinophilia. Borderline changes in liver function test results have also been reported. CT of the liver may help in demonstrating hepatic lesions, including the nodular or the more characteristic linear hypodense tracks, particularly if they are located subcapsularly. In the *biliary stage,* ultrasonography may demonstrate the adult flukes in the bile ducts or gallbladder.

DICROCELIASIS

Human infection with *Dicrocoelium dendriticum* or *Dicrocoelium hospes* is rare (see Table 403–2). Dicroceliasis is a zoonosis in sheep, goats, deer, and other herbivores. Its life cycle is similar to that of other liver flukes, except that metacercariae encyst in ants, the second intermediate host. Humans are infected by eating metacercariae-containing ants. Most cases of dicroceliasis are asymptomatic. In those with heavy infection, vague abdominal complaints—vomiting, diarrhea or constipation, and biliary colic—have been observed.

INTESTINAL FLUKES

Human infection with one of more than 50 species of intestinal trematodes has been reported from the Far East, Middle East, and North Africa. Clinically significant disease may be encountered in infection with only few species.

FASCIOLOPSIASIS

The giant intestinal fluke, *Fasciolopsis buski,* inhabits the small intestine of pigs. Humans are infected by ingestion of raw stems, leaves, and pods of aquatic plants with encysted metacercariae. The geographic distribution is given in Table 403–2. Endemicity depends on close contact among water plants, pigs, and populations that consume raw aquatic plants.

F. buski flukes attach to the mucosa of small intestine, particularly the duodenum and jejunum. Most infected individuals are asymptomatic. The site of attachment, however, becomes ulcerated, and a local inflammatory response follows. In cases of heavy infection, intestinal obstruction and protein-losing enteropathy have been reported. With heavy infection, abdominal pain and diarrhea may be observed along with edema and anasarca caused by hypoalbuminemia.

ECHINOSTOMIASIS

Humans can be infected with any of several genera of the family Echinostomatidae (see Table 403–2). The common species are *Echinostoma ilocanum, Echinostoma malayanum,* and *Echinostoma revolutum.* Adult flukes are parasites of the small intestine of birds and mammals. Humans are occasionally infected after eating undercooked pila, other fish, and tadpoles. Mature adult worms attach to intestinal mucosa, causing ulceration and subsequent inflammatory response. Little morbidity has been reported in association with echinostomiasis. High-intensity infection may be associated with abdominal pain and diarrhea.

HETEROPHYIASIS

Heterophyes heterophyes infects humans, cats, dogs, and other fish-eating mammals. Infection is acquired by ingestion of the fish second intermediate host, which contains the fluke metacercariae. The common fish hosts include mullet and minnow and the brackish-water fish *Mugil capito.* They are usually consumed raw or salted. Metacercariae can live in salted fish for approximately 1 week. Adult *H. heterophyes* attach to the mucosa of the jejunum and upper ileum, producing shallow ulcers and a mild inflammatory response. Symptomatic patients complain of gastroenterocolitis with diarrhea and tenesmus. Stools characteristically contain abundant mucus and occasionally contain blood.

OTHER INTESTINAL FLUKES

Several other species may cause disease limited to defined geographic areas (see Table 403–2). The *Metagonimus yokogawai* life cycle and the associated disease syndromes are similar to those in *H. heterophyes* infection, but *M. yokogawai* may invade the mucosa of small intestine, resulting in ulceration and granuloma formation. Another intestinal fluke, *Gastrodiscoides hominis* (see Table 403–2), has its final habitat in humans in the cecum. Clinically, it is believed to produce mucous diarrhea.

LUNG FLUKES: PARAGONIMIASIS

Human infection by species of *Paragonimus* may cause considerable pulmonary or extrapulmonary morbidity in several endemic areas (see Table 403–2). *Paragonimus* infection exists in nature in humans and carnivores. There are at least 10 species of *Paragonimus* known to cause human disease; of these *Paragonimus westermani* is most common. Infection is acquired by ingestion of metacercariae encysted in freshwater and brackish-water crabs or crayfish (raw or undercooked). Infection may also be transmitted to humans through contaminated utensils used to prepare crabs or crayfish. Rarely, consumption of wild boar meat may result in transmission of immature flukes to humans, in whom they complete their development into adult worms.

Pathogenesis and Clinical Features

Disease in infected humans is related to migration of young flukes from the gastrointestinal tract to their final habitat (i.e., early or acute stage) and more characteristically results when adult worms become established in the lungs or at extrapulmonary sites (i.e., late or chronic stage).

Acute paragonimiasis occurs during the 3-week period after infection. It passes unnoticed in most infected individuals. Symptoms include diarrhea, abdominal pain, fever, and malaise associated with cough, dyspnea, and night sweats. Pulmonary paragonimiasis results from invasion of the host lungs and establishment of adult worms in cysts or abscess cavities. The lung parenchyma demonstrates hemorrhage and an inflammatory response of predominantly eosinophils. Worm cysts are 1 to 2 cm in diameter and usually contain one or two worms. Pathologic changes in the remaining lung tissues may result in bronchopneumonia, bronchiectasis, fibrosis, and pleural thickening. The established pulmonary stage of paragonimiasis results usually in mild chronic cough with production of mucoid, rusty brown sputum. Hemoptysis that may be severe and life-threatening occurs rarely.

Microscopic examination of sputum demonstrates necrotic tissue and parasite eggs. Results of physical examination of patients with pulmonary paragonimiasis are usually within normal limits. Chest radiography findings may be normal in 10 to 20% of cases. Typical changes in the lungs include pathway infiltrate and ring shadow with a crescent-shaped "corona." Cystic and nodular lesions are also commonly seen. Pleural lesions, including effusion, pneumothorax, and thickening, may be encountered in approximately two thirds of infected individuals. Other imaging methods, such as CT, may define better the pulmonary abnormalities, including worm migration tracks.

Extrapulmonary paragonimiasis occurs because maturing flukes migrate to tissues other than the lungs or because adult flukes migrate from the lungs to other tissues. It is believed that extrapulmonary paragonimiasis may be mainly caused by *Paragonimus* flukes other than *P. westermani.* The tissues most commonly affected are the brain, abdominal organs, and skin. In cerebral paragonimiasis, the clinical presentation may be acute or chronic. Acute cerebral paragonimiasis manifests as fever, headache, visual disturbances, paralysis, and generalized or focal convulsions. Evidence for an intracranial inflammatory process may be demonstrated as papilledema, high cerebrospinal fluid pressure, and eosinophilic pleocytosis. Chronic cerebral paragonimiasis is characterized by space-occupying lesions that cause epilepsy or paralysis. Abdominal or cutaneous paragonimiasis results from invasion of liver, spleen, or skin by maturing or adult flukes. This results in space-occupying lesions, abscesses, or migratory swellings.

MANAGEMENT OF LIVER, INTESTINAL, AND LUNG FLUKE INFECTIONS

Diagnosis

Diagnosis of human infection with liver, intestinal, or lung flukes requires knowledge of the geographic distribution of these infections, a high degree of clinical correlation of mainly nonspecific symptoms and signs with history of possible exposure, and demonstration of peripheral blood eosinophilia. Definitive diagnosis is established by finding the characteristically shaped fluke eggs in fecal samples or sputum. In general, the sensitivity of fecal or sputum examination is enhanced by examining two or three separate specimens.

Seroimmunodiagnostic tests are available for fascioliasis and paragonimiasis. They are particularly helpful in cases of early infection, for which parasitologic diagnosis usually yields negative results.

 Treatment

> Chemotherapy for fluke infections has become a more effective management strategy with the introduction of praziquantel. This anthelminthic agent is orally administered for 1 day. It results in cure rates of 70 to 90% and an even more remarkable decrease in egg counts. Its administration is associated with few side effects. The recommended dose of praziquantel is 75 mg/kg of body weight divided into three doses and given in 1 day. A 2-day course of praziquantel is necessary for treatment of paragonimiasis. For fascioliasis, the drug of choice is triclabendazole, which is given orally as 10 mg/kg once.

Prevention

Prevention of infection with any of these parasitic trematodes depends on proper medical advice given to individuals traveling or planning to reside in endemic areas (Chapter 300). Avoidance of ingestion of suspected intermediate hosts and the proper washing, cooking, or preservation methods of such food items constitute the most effective strategy. Engaging in some of the local dietary habits in endemic areas should be discouraged. Water for drinking must be properly purified to prevent the possible transmission of *F. hepatica*. Control of parasitic trematodes in endemic areas is a much more complex challenge. It involves changing long-established cultural, dietary, and sanitary habits.

With the availability of a safe broad-spectrum anthelminthic (praziquantel), chemotherapy may play a significant role in controlling infection and disease. As a long-term strategy, vaccines and socioeconomic development will be needed.

SUGGESTED READINGS

Chan HH, Lai KH, Lo GH, et al: The clinical and cholangiographic picture of hepatic clonorchiasis. J Clin Gastroenterol 2002;34:183–186. *Clinical and imaging features of clonorchiasis in the endemic areas.*

Drugs for Parasitic Infections: Med Lett Drugs Ther 2002;1. *Yearly update of drugs of choice and alternatives.*

Harinasuta T, Bunnag D: Liver, lung and intestinal trematodiasis. *In* Warren KS, Mahmoud AAF (eds): Tropical and Geographical Medicine, 2nd ed. New York, McGraw-Hill, 1990, pp 473–489. *An authoritative description of the causative agents, clinical syndromes, and management strategies.*

Hurtrez-Bousses S, Meunier C, Durad P, Renaud F: Dynamics of host parasite interactions: The example of population biology of the liver fluke (*Fasciola hepatica*). Microbes Infect 2001;3:841–849. *Description of the dynamic relationships between the liver fluke and its intermediate and definitive hosts.*

Guoqing L, Xiaozhu H, Kanu S: Epidemiology and control of *Clonorchiasis sinensis* in China. Southeast Asian J Trop Med Public Health 2001;32 Suppl 2:8–11. *A brief summary of the situation in China.*

Im JG, Whang HY, Kim WS, et al: Pleuropulmonary paragonimiasis: Radiologic findings in 71 patients. AJR Am J Roentgenol 1992;159:39–43. *Retrospective evaluation of 71 individuals with evidence of pleuropulmonary paragonimiasis. Details frequency of specific radiographic and CT findings.*

King S, Scholz T: Trematodes of the family Opisthorchiidae: A mini review. Korean J Parasitol 2001;39:209–221. *Up-to-date review of parasites and their intermediate hosts.*

Millan JC, Mull R, Freise S, Richter J: The efficacy and tolerability of triclabendazole in Cuban patients with latent and chronic *Fasciola hepatica* infection. Am J Trop Med Hyg 2000;63:264–269. *Detailed clinical laboratory and ultrasonographic evaluation of 82 patients treated with triclabendazole.*

Velez ID, Ortega JE, Velasquez LE: Paragonimiasis: A view from Colombia. Clin Chest Med 2002;23:421–431. *A recent review of Paragonimus species and their spectrum of infection and disease in humans.*

404 NEMATODE INFECTIONS

James W. Kazura

Nematodes (phylum Nematoda), or roundworms, include a vast number of species of free-living and parasitic helminths. These multicellular organisms differ from unicellular bacteria and protozoa in that they have organ systems with specialized nervous, muscular, gastrointestinal, and reproductive functions. Parasitic nematodes vary in length from several millimeters to approximately 2 m and have four larval stages and adult worms of both sexes. With the exception of *Strongyloides* and a few other helminths of medical importance, larvae are produced after mating of sexually mature adult worms, which by themselves are incapable of multiplying in the mammalian host. The inability of adult worms to replicate has important implications for the propensity of this class of organism to establish an infection and cause disease. Unlike the situation pertaining to bacterial, viral, or protozoan infections, casual or a low degree of exposure to infective stages of parasitic helminths generally does not result in patent infection or pathologic manifestations. Repeated or intense exposure to a large number of infective larvae is required for infection to be established and disease to develop.

Nematode infections are endemic in temperate and tropical climates. They are transmitted by the fecal-oral route or by inoculation of infective larvae into the skin, primarily by blood-feeding intermediate insect vectors. The prevalence of infection is greatest in circumstances conducive to the development and transmission of infective forms of the parasites, such as the overcrowded, perennially warm geographic areas with poor sanitation in many developing countries of Africa, Asia, and Latin America and economically poor areas of North America and Europe.

The epidemiology of human nematode, as well as trematode and cestode, infections has several unique features. The infection in an endemic area generally has a negative binomial distribution; most individuals have low parasite burdens, and a few harbor relatively high burdens. Persons in the latter group are important from an epidemiologic perspective in that they contribute most substantially to transmission and are most likely to develop pathologic manifestations. This characteristic implies that transmission in an endemic area may be decreased or interrupted by reduction of the parasite burden in a small proportion of the population. Because total worm load correlates directly with the propensity to develop disease, treatment of lightly infected persons may not be indicated or may be unnecessary, especially if the available chemotherapy has major side effects.

Nematode infections of medical importance may be broadly classified into those in which the route of infection, larval migration, and disease manifestations are primarily gastrointestinal and those that affect other tissues. The former group includes hookworms (*Ancylostoma duodenale, Necator americanus*), the roundworm *Ascaris lumbricoides*, the pinworm *Enterobius vermicularis*, and the whipworm *Trichuris trichiura*. Animal intestinal nematodes such as *Trichostrongylus* and *Anisakis* species also occasionally infect and cause disease in humans. *Trichinella spiralis, Strongyloides stercoralis,* and *Angiostrongylus cantonensis* infect humans by the oral route, but disease manifestations primarily result from migration in other tissues. Tissue-invasive nematodes include lymphatic filariae (*Wuchereria bancrofti, Brugia malayi,* and *Brugia timori*), skin-dwelling *Onchocerca volvulus* and *Loa loa,* and the guinea worm, *Dracunculus medinensis*.

INTESTINAL NEMATODES

Intestinal nematode infections include hookworm disease, ascariasis, enterobiasis, trichuriasis, and rarely, animal nematodiases. They are prevalent in temperate and tropical areas of the world, especially those with overcrowding and poor sanitation. Intestinal nematode infections have little morbidity in most cases, except when children in developing countries experience repeated and chronic infections. They are easily treated with mebendazole or albendazole, although the latter has not been officially approved for use in the United States by the U.S. Food and Drug Administration.

HOOKWORM DISEASE

Etiology and Epidemiology

The major hookworms that infect humans are *A. duodenale* and *N. americanus. Ancylostoma ceylanicum* infection is less common and occurs primarily in the South Pacific. Animal hookworms such as *Ancylostoma braziliense* and *Uncinaria stenocephala* do not undergo full development in incidentally exposed humans. Infection occurs when exposed skin maintains contact for several minutes with soil contaminated with parasite eggs containing viable larvae. Larvae penetrate the skin and subsequently migrate to and mature in the lungs. The parasites then break into the air spaces, ascend the trachea, and are swallowed. Adult worms mature in the upper small intestine and attach to the mucosa. Female worms release more than 10,000 eggs per day, which are passed in the stools and deposited in the soil. The prepatent period (i.e., time between infection and passing of eggs in the feces) is 40 to 105 days. Adult hookworms have a lifespan of 2 to 5 years.

Hookworms infect more than 1 billion persons worldwide. The highest prevalences of infection (80 to 100%) occur in tropical and less developed countries, where environmental and socioeconomic conditions are especially favorable to transmission. These factors include warm, moist soil; lack of public sewage disposal systems; and the habit of walking barefoot. The higher prevalence of hookworm infection in children than adults results from more frequent exposure of skin to larvae in soil. Acquired resistance is minimal or does not appear to develop as a consequence of previous infection.

Pathogenesis and Clinical Manifestations

Hookworm disease primarily is caused by gastrointestinal blood loss and attendant iron deficiency anemia. The latter correlates directly with the total worm burden. Adult worms attached to the mucosa of the upper small intestine digest ingested blood and cause focal bleeding. *A. duodenale* is estimated to cause a blood loss of 0.3 mL/day per worm; *N. americanus* induces loss of approximately 0.03 mL/day. Light infections (<400 eggs/g of feces) do not cause blood loss sufficient to induce iron deficiency. Nutritional deficiencies from coexisting conditions that result in low iron stores (i.e., malabsorption or insufficient dietary intake in children and multiparous women) contribute significantly to morbidity. Hypoproteinemia has been reported in children with hookworm disease in less developed countries. This complication most likely results from coexisting malnutrition rather than gastrointestinal disease caused by hookworm infestation. Abdominal signs or symptoms are not caused by hookworm infection.

Pruritus at the site of larval skin penetration ("ground itch") occurs occasionally. In the case of primary exposure, local itching and erythematous papules develop and last 1 week. More intense pruritus, vesiculation, and edema of 2 to 3 weeks' duration may occur after repeated exposure to infective larvae. Hookworm larvae migrating through the lungs rarely cause pulmonary symptoms.

Diagnosis

Hookworm infection is diagnosed by identification of the characteristic round eggs containing convoluted larvae. Direct smears of freshly passed stool using the Kato or other techniques are satisfactory for the diagnosis of moderately to heavily infected cases (>400 eggs/g of feces).

 ## Treatment and Prevention

Mebendazole is the treatment of choice, although albendazole is equally effective and may have fewer side effects (Table 404–1). The ideal method for preventing hookworm infection is improvement of hygienic conditions. Use of footwear, especially by children, is the only practical means of avoiding infection.

ASCARIASIS

Etiology and Epidemiology

A. lumbricoides are roundworms that are 2 to 3 cm long and that reside in the lumen of the jejunum and in the midileum. Infection occurs by the oral route when soil containing embryonated eggs is ingested. Larvae are released from eggs in the small intestine, penetrate the gut, and migrate to the liver and then lungs through the blood or lymphatic circulation. After maturation in the lungs over a 4-week period, the parasites ascend the respiratory tract and are swallowed. Adult worms reach sexual maturity (i.e., female worms release eggs that are detectable in feces) approximately 60 days after infection.

Ascariasis affects approximately one fourth of the world's population and probably is the most prevalent helminthiasis of humans. Infection is common in Africa, Asia, and Latin America, especially in areas of high population density and poor sanitary conditions. The

Table 404–1 • TREATMENT FOR INTESTINAL NEMATODES

NEMATODE	TREATMENT
Hookworms	Mebendazole, 100 mg orally bid for 3 days. Do not give to pregnant women; iron supplementation (if warranted by anemia and complicating illnesses). Alternatives: albendazole, 400 mg one time, or pyrantel pamoate, 11 mg/kg for 3 days; maximum daily dose not to exceed 1 g
Ascaris	Mebendazole, 100 mg orally bid for 3 days, or albendazole, 400 mg one time. Children with heavy infections, biliary tract obstruction: piperazine, 50–75 mg/kg for 2 days
Enterobius	Pyrantel pamoate, 11 mg/kg once, with a repeated dose 2 weeks later; maximum single dose, 1 g. Several treatments may be required (every 3–4 months) if exposure continues (e.g., institutional setting). Alternatives include mebendazole, 100 mg, or albendazole 400 mg once, and repeat in 2 weeks.
Trichuris	Mebendazole or albendazole, at same dosages as for ascariasis
Trichostrongylus	Pyrantel pamoate, 11 mg/kg once; maximum dose of 1 g
Anisakis	Thiabendazole, 25 mg/kg bid for 3 days or surgical or endoscopic removal of worm from gastrointestinal tract
Capillaria	Mebendazole, 200 mg bid for 20 days. Alternative: albendazole, 400 mg once daily for 10 days. Supportive care: replace fluid and electrolytes, high-protein diet
Gnathostoma	For subcutaneous lesions: surgical removal. For CNS infection: albendazole, 400 qd for 21 days, or ivermectin, 200 µg/kg qd for 2 days

use of human feces as fertilizer, defecation in soil, and hand-to-mouth contact with contaminated soil are major factors that contribute to the spread of *Ascaris*. The ability of *Ascaris* eggs to remain viable in harsh environmental conditions (i.e., embryonated eggs remain infectious after exposure to freezing temperatures and desiccation for several weeks) also facilitates transmission.

Pathogenesis and Clinical Manifestations

Disease caused by *A. lumbricoides* is infrequent and generally correlates with the intensity of infection. Most infected individuals are asymptomatic.

Symptomatic cases can be divided into two broad categories based on the phase of infection and site of pathology (i.e., pulmonary or gastrointestinal tract). Pulmonary disease is caused by the migration of larvae in the small vessels of the lung and their subsequent rupture into alveoli. Tissue damage is thought to result from the host immune response, which includes production of immunoglobulin E (IgE) and eosinophilia. Transient pulmonary infiltrates, fever, cough, dyspnea, and eosinophilia lasting 1 to several weeks are the major clinical manifestations. This complex of symptoms and signs is frequently seasonal and coincidental with environmental changes that favor development of infective-stage larvae in eggs (e.g., spring rains that follow cold and dry periods). Intestinal signs and symptoms result from obstruction caused by the presence of an exceptionally large number of parasites in the small intestine or migration of adult worms to unusual sites, such as the biliary tree or pancreatic duct. Intestinal obstruction almost always occurs in children younger than 6 years. The onset is sudden and characterized by colicky abdominal pain and vomiting. Heavily infected children are also prone to biliary disease or pancreatitis secondary to *Ascaris* lodging in the ducts draining these organs. A malabsorption syndrome characterized by steatorrhea and low vitamin A levels has been reported in Latin American children with ascariasis.

Diagnosis

Intestinal infection is diagnosed by the presence of the typical oval, thick-shelled *Ascaris* eggs in thick smears of fecal specimens. The existence of adult worms in pancreatic or biliary ducts should be suspected in children who have high egg outputs in conjunction with jaundice or pancreatitis. Treatment of the latter cases is with piperazine citrate, which causes neuromuscular paralysis of the worms. Pulmonary ascariasis cannot be diagnosed on the basis of identification of ova in feces because adult worms have not yet matured and reached the intestinal tract. Biopsy of the lung is unlikely to demonstrate larvae and is not recommended.

 Treatment and Prevention

> Treatment for uncomplicated intestinal ascariasis is listed in Table 404–1. No specific treatment is recommended for pulmonary ascariasis because the condition is self-limited.
>
> The major means of preventing *Ascaris* infection is improvement of hygienic and socioeconomic conditions. Mass chemotherapy successfully reduces worm loads but requires frequent treatment.

ENTEROBIASIS

E. vermicularis or pinworm infection is cosmopolitan in its distribution. It is common in overcrowded settings and spreads rapidly in conditions in which person-to-person contact is frequent, such as in institutions for children.

Infection occurs by the fecal-oral route. Embryonated eggs carried on the fingernails, bed clothing, or bedding are ingested and hatch in the upper small intestine. Larvae develop in the large bowel into adult worms that are 2 to 5 mm long. Female worms migrate nightly out of the rectum and deposit large numbers of ova (11,000 per worm) in the perianal and perineal areas. Larvae in the deposited eggs become infective within several hours of exposure to ambient oxygen. Infectivity is usually maintained for 1 to 2 days.

Most pinworm infections are asymptomatic or associated with perianal pruritus and consequent sleep deprivation. *E. vermicularis* is a rare cause of appendicitis and, when the adult worms follow an aberrant path of migration, vulvovaginitis, urethritis, or peritonitis.

The diagnosis of pinworm infection is easily made by identifying ova on a piece of cellophane tape applied to the perirectal area in the morning. *E. vermicularis* eggs are oval and slightly flattened on one side. It is unusual to find eggs in feces or adult worms in the perianal area. Repeated examinations may be necessary.

Treatment

> Treatment (see Table 404–1) is mebendazole or albendazole given to affected individuals and to close associates, such as family members. Although personal cleanliness is recommended as a means of limiting transmission, there is no clear-cut demonstration that it prevents infection.

TRICHURIASIS

T. trichiura or whipworm infection is similar to pinworm infection in that it is limited to the gastrointestinal tract and does not have a tissue migratory phase. Eggs containing infective larvae mature in warm, moist soil over a 2-week period. Ingested eggs hatch in the small bowel and subsequently develop in epithelial cells of the cecum and ascending colon into adult worms that are 40 mm in length. The body of the parasite protrudes into the colonic lumen. Its anterior portion has a whiplike shape.

As is the case with most intestinal nematode infections, trichuriasis is most common in overcrowded areas with poor sanitation. The estimated prevalence worldwide is 800 million, with approximately 2 million cases in the southern United States. Children are more frequently infected than adults and more likely to have higher worm burdens.

Adults with trichuriasis are usually asymptomatic. In children with heavy infections (>10,000 eggs/g of feces), a syndrome of dysentery, growth retardation, and rectal prolapse has been described. The pathologic manifestations include infiltrates of eosinophils and neutrophils accompanied by epithelial denudation. Complicating diseases such as shigellosis and amebiasis may contribute to this condition in children.

Whipworm infection is diagnosed by identification of football-shaped eggs in direct smears of fecal specimens. Mebendazole or albendazole at the same dosage indicated for ascariasis is satisfactory treatment, as listed in Table 404–1.

OTHER ANIMAL NEMATODIASES

Humans may serve as paratenic hosts for several nematodes that ordinarily parasitize the intestine of other mammals. These helminths are incapable of completing their life cycle in humans and display aberrant migration patterns in both intestinal and nonintestinal tissues.

Several species of the genus *Trichostrongylus* infect humans and domestic ruminants. The infection is found widely in the Middle and Far East and Australia. Ova are passed in the stool of ruminants and hatch in the soil. Humans are incidentally infected when larvae are ingested with leafy vegetables. The adult worms live in the intestines and suck small amounts of blood; heavy infections result in anemia. Diagnosis is made by identifying ova, which resemble those of hookworm, in the stool. Treatment is explained in Table 404–1.

Anisakis is an intestinal nematode of marine mammals. Several species of saltwater fish are intermediate hosts. Human infection occurs when raw fish is eaten. The larvae of *Anisakis* and *Phocanema decipiens* have been implicated. Most cases have been reported in Japan or Western Europe, particularly in Scandinavia. The larvae invade the wall of the small intestine or stomach, causing pain and, rarely, intestinal obstruction or perforation. Intestinal anisakiasis often resembles an acute abdomen, leading to laparotomy. Thiabendazole treatment is detailed in Table 404–1. The treatment of choice is surgical or endoscopic removal of worms. Infection is prevented by cooking or freezing fish before eating.

Capillaria philippinensis infection has been reported from the Philippines and Thailand. This nematode is thought to parasitize birds, with fish and crustaceans serving as intermediate hosts. Humans are infected by eating the raw intermediate hosts. The ingested larvae mature and live in the crypts of the small intestine, where they reproduce. The result is often a heavy infection; up to 40,000 adult worms have been recovered at one autopsy. The clinical syndrome includes severe malabsorption and protein-losing enteropathy. The diagnosis is made by finding eggs or larvae in the stool; an intradermal test is also available. The treatment of choice is mebendazole or albendazole (see Table 404–1).

Gnathostoma spinigerum is an intestinal nematode of dogs and cats; fish are intermediate hosts. The infection is endemic in rodents in the Far East and Thailand. Human infection has also been reported in South America. Infective larvae are ingested by humans in raw or undercooked fish. The larvae do not complete their life cycle in humans but migrate through the body. The most frequent site is subcutaneous tissue, where larvae are found in eosinophilic granulomas. A few weeks after infection, pruritic or painful subcutaneous nodules and swellings appear. These may be migratory and develop into abscesses. In central nervous system (CNS) gnathostomiasis, hemorrhagic tracts may be found in the brain. Fever, vomiting, and abdominal pain occur a few days after larvae are ingested. Paralysis of the extremities, encephalitis, and subarachnoid hemorrhage has been reported. Eye involvement with uveitis and orbital cellulitis represents a third variety.

Peripheral eosinophilia is usual in cutaneous gnathostomiasis; the diagnosis may be established by biopsy. In CNS infection, blood eosinophilia is an inconstant feature, but eosinophils are present in the cerebrospinal fluid (CSF), as in the case of angiostrongyliasis. Treatments are explained in Table 404–1. The infection may be prevented by thorough cooking of fish.

Several nematodes that ordinarily parasitize the intestine of monkeys occasionally infect humans. *Oesophagostomum* has been reported from Africa, Asia, and Brazil; it is responsible for the formation of granulomas in the intestinal wall. *Ternidens deminutus* is sometimes found in the human colon in Africa and Asia; a heavy infection may cause anemia. *Physaloptera mordens*, also reported from Africa, may attach itself to the esophagus, stomach, or small intestine of humans. The definitive host of *Lagochilascaris minor* is unknown. About 30 human cases have been reported from Central and South America, usually with worms invading the soft tissues of the neck, throat, and sinuses.

TOXOCARIASIS

Definition

Visceral larva migrans (VLM) and ocular larva migrans (OLM) are caused by ingestion and subsequent development and migration of embryonated eggs of the canine roundworm *Toxocara canis*. Roundworms of cats (*Toxocara cati*) and raccoons (*Baylisascaris procyonis*) also rarely cause VLM.

Etiology

In its normal canine host, *T. canis* organisms follow a route of migration similar to that described for *Ascaris*. Ingested larvae penetrate the small intestine, migrate to the lungs, are reswallowed, and develop into adult worms in the small intestine; the adult worms lodge there and release eggs that are passed in the feces. When embryonated *T. canis* eggs are ingested by humans, larvae also migrate throughout the body (i.e., lung, liver, brain, muscles, and occasionally eyes) but fail to complete development to the adult stage. Tissue necrosis caused by penetrating larvae and associated host inflammatory reactions, such as eosinophil-rich granulomas, are the underlying cause of disease.

Epidemiology

Toxocariasis is endemic in temperate and tropical areas of the world. Most symptomatic cases occur in young children. This age group is most likely to be infected by virtue of frequent and intimate handling of dogs (especially newborn puppies that may be hyperinfected), playing in areas where dogs and cats defecate (e.g., public sandboxes), and the habit of geophagia. The potential of exposure to embryonated eggs is high in that *T. canis* infection is common in dogs (a 20% infection rate in dogs in the United States).

Clinical Manifestations

Most children who ingest *T. canis* eggs are asymptomatic. VLM is the most common clinically defined entity attributable to *T. canis*. It occurs most frequently in children younger than 5 years (there are no published series of adults with VLM) and is characterized by fever less than 39° C; pulmonary symptoms, including wheezing and cough; and less frequently, pain in the right upper quadrant. These symptoms have a gradual onset and resolve over 4 to 8 weeks. Physical signs include wheezing and hepatomegaly in about one fourth of cases. Larvae less commonly migrate to the brain and heart and cause focal neurologic defects and heart failure.

OLM has an incidence approximately one tenth that of VLM and affects children older than 8 to 10 years. Visual disturbances due to VLM are not distinguishable from other causes of focal intraretinal granulomas or space-occupying lesions, such as tuberculosis and retinoblastoma. *T. canis* larvae may migrate intraretinally and produce transient and recurrent impairment of vision.

Rx Diagnosis and Treatment

VLM is diagnosed on the basis of suspicion of ingestion of *T. canis* eggs in a child with the symptoms previously described. Eosinophilia, elevated erythrocyte sedimentation rate, and generalized hypergammaglobulinemia are also consistent with the diagnosis. Biopsy to document the presence of larvae is insensitive and not recommended. An enzyme-linked immunosorbent assay (ELISA) for measuring anti-*Toxocara* antibodies is helpful if elevated immunoglobulin M (IgM) antibodies and a rise in titer between acute and convalescent phases are documented.

Most cases of VLM are not life-threatening and are self-limited. Treatment is therefore not required. In persons with severe pulmonary, cardiac, or neurologic involvement and high-grade eosinophilia (>10,000/mm³ of blood), albendazole (400 mg given twice daily for 5 days), and corticosteroids may be used to reduce symptoms and shorten the course of the illness. No controlled studies, however, demonstrate the efficacy of chemotherapy.

OLM represents a diagnostic dilemma in that it must be distinguished from intraretinal neoplasms and infections. Expert ophthalmologic consultation is necessary. Computed tomography and fluorescein angiography are helpful in diagnosis. Elevated anti-*Toxocara* antibody titers in aqueous fluid relative to serum values are consistent with OLM. It is unclear whether anthelmintics are useful for the treatment of OLM.

VLM and OLM may be prevented by periodic deworming of dogs, especially puppies, and limiting their defecation in public places.

CUTANEOUS LARVA MIGRANS

Animal hookworms, most frequently the dog parasite *A. braziliense* and less commonly *U. stenocephala* and *Bunostomum phlebotomum*, are the major causative agents of cutaneous larva migrans, or creeping eruption. *A. duodenale, N. americanus*, and *S. stercoralis* may produce a similar syndrome during the phase of infection that involves penetration of the skin.

The disease occurs when skin comes into direct and prolonged contact with hookworm larvae contained in the feces of dogs, cats, or humans. Moist areas visited by animals, such as vegetation near beaches and exposed soil covered by porches, are common sites in which humans may be infected. Cutaneous larva migrans in the United States is most prevalent in southern coastal regions.

Clinical manifestations result from penetration and migration of larvae in the epidermal-dermal junction of the skin. Within several hours of contact with exposed skin, the patient notices pruritus and raised erythematous serpiginous lesions. The lesions migrate approximately 1 cm each day and evolve into bullae. Multiple lesions may appear if large areas of the body have been exposed, as in sunbathing.

Creeping eruption may be treated with 400 mg of albendazole per day for 3 days. If untreated, cutaneous larva migrans is self-limited; signs and symptoms resolve in several weeks to 2 months.

ANGIOSTRONGYLIASIS

A. cantonensis is a cause of eosinophilic meningitis in Asia and the South Pacific. Small numbers of cases have also been reported in Cuba and Africa. *Angiostrongylus costaricensis* is a rare cause of gastrointestinal bleeding. The nematode is limited in its distribution to Central and South America. Humans are infected with these rodent (primarily rat) nematodes after ingesting poorly cooked or raw intermediate mollusk hosts, such as snails, slugs, and prawns. Fresh vegetables may also be contaminated with infective larvae and serve as a vehicle of infection.

In the case of *A. cantonensis* infection, ingested infective larvae penetrate the gut wall and migrate to small vessels of the meninges and, less commonly, the spinal cord and eye. An intense local inflammatory reaction ensues within 1 week. Fever, meningismus, and headache develop in association with eosinophilic pleocytosis of the CSF. Strabismus, paresthesias, and vomiting have been observed in a minority of cases. Diagnosis is based on a history of ingesting potentially contaminated foodstuffs and the presence of eosinophils in CSF. Larvae are usually not found in CSF. Other infectious causes of eosinophilic meningitis include *T. spiralis, Taenia solium, T. canis, G. spinigerum*, and *Paragonimus westermani*.

Symptomatic *A. cantonensis* infection resolves over a 2-week period. The value of anthelmintic therapy has not been established. Analgesics and corticosteroids have been suggested to relieve symptoms.

A. costaricensis larvae penetrate the mucosa of the terminal ileum, appendix, and ascending colon. The larvae subsequently develop into adult worms in the local lymphatics and mesenteric arterioles. Eggs released by the female worms elicit multiple eosinophil-rich granulomatous reactions that cause edematous, thickened bowel and necrosis from mesenteric blood vessel obstruction. Clinical presentations typically include right-sided abdominal pain, vomiting, and fever. Abnormal laboratory findings include leukocytosis with eosinophilia. Parasite larvae and eggs are not present in stools. A palpable mass derived from granulomatous lesions may be present and cause intestinal obstruction. Less frequently, gastrointestinal bleeding is the principal manifestation.

Treatment is surgical. There is no demonstrated benefit of specific anthelmintic chemotherapy of human infection.

TRICHINOSIS

Definition

Infection by *T. spiralis* occurs when infective larvae are eaten in undercooked pork or other meats. Most infected individuals are asymptomatic. Clinical manifestations in heavily infected persons include diarrhea, myalgias, fever, and less commonly, myocarditis and neurologic disease. Trichinosis occurs in all areas of the world, including the Arctic and temperate regions. The incidence of trichinosis in the United States has decreased markedly over the past several decades.

Etiology

Infection is initiated by ingesting infective larvae encysted in striated muscle. Excystment occurs in the acid-pepsin environment of the stomach, and parasites develop into sexually mature adult worms in the upper to middle small intestine of the human host. Completion of the enteric phase of the parasite life cycle takes about 1 week, with adult worms remaining viable and productive of larval offspring for an additional 3 to 5 weeks. The systemic phase commences 1 week after infection, when larvae released by female worms migrate through blood vessels and lymphatics and invade multiple organ systems. Mature, third-stage larvae develop in host-derived nurse cells in striated skeletal and cardiac muscle, where they become encysted and remain viable for years.

As is the case with most helminthiases, the severity of symptoms is related to the total parasite load. Because adult worms are incapable of reproducing themselves, the number of infective larvae ingested is the most important determinant of worm load (i.e., number of larvae that invade muscle and other tissues).

Epidemiology

T. spiralis infection is enzootic in omnivorous and carnivorous animal populations, including rats, bears, and aquatic mammals of the Arctic. The nematode is introduced into domestic animals such as pigs and horses by feeding them garbage containing carcasses of these animals, most commonly rats. Human infection usually occurs in two settings: first, when undercooked or smoked pork products or beef contaminated with nematodes is eaten, and second, when flesh of poorly cooked wild game, such as bear or boar meat, is ingested. An important source of infection in Alaskan and Canadian Arctic native populations is uncooked walrus meat.

The annual incidence of human trichinosis in the United States has decreased dramatically over the past 60 years. This decline is primarily due to fewer cases related to ingestion of commercial pork products. Recent cases in the United States occur in point-source outbreaks associated with eating game or noncommercial pork products.

Pathogenesis and Clinical Manifestations

Tissue-invasive *T. spiralis* larvae elicit an eosinophilic granulomatous reaction that may result in significant end-organ tissue damage and dysfunction. Skeletal muscle is the most frequent site involved. Myocardial damage, pulmonary infiltration, and focal neurologic damage caused by CNS invasion by larvae are seen in only the most heavily infected persons. The systemic phase of infection usually occurs 2 to 3 weeks after ingestion of infective larvae and may last for 2 months. Clinical manifestations typically include myalgias (especially of the gastrocnemius and masseter), periorbital edema, and fever. Myocardial damage may manifest as heart failure or dysrhythmias.

The enteric phase of infection may cause gastrointestinal signs and symptoms, such as diarrhea and abdominal cramps. These typically occur within 1 week of eating contaminated meat and last less than 2 weeks. Reports from the Canadian Arctic suggest that the *T. spiralis* larvae that infect walrus meat may cause diarrhea of 1 to 3 months' duration.

Diagnosis

A diagnosis of trichinosis should be considered in individuals with generalized myalgias and eosinophilia (>600 eosinophils/mm³).

Serologic testing for *T. spiralis* antibodies is available at the Centers for Disease Control and Prevention. Elevation of IgM antibodies or a more than fourfold rise in titer between acute and convalescent phases of infection is helpful in making the diagnosis. The levels of creatine phosphate kinase and of serum immunoglobulins and the erythrocyte sedimentation rate are also increased for several weeks after infection. Muscle biopsy (e.g., gastrocnemius) may demonstrate larvae, although their absence does not exclude the diagnosis.

Rx Treatment and Prevention

If patients present at a time when adult parasites are in the intestine (i.e., during the initial 1 to 2 weeks after infection, when gastrointestinal symptoms are prominent), albendazole is recommended at a dosage of 400 mg given twice daily for 8 to 14 days. It is not clear whether larvae in muscle are killed by this drug, and treatment is primarily symptomatic with antipyretics and analgesics. Although there are too few recent cases to establish a possible beneficial effect of corticosteroids, they may be useful to diminish the severity of inflammation when signs of myocarditis, neurologic disease (e.g., seizures, focal weakness), or pulmonary insufficiency develop.

T. spiralis infection is prevented by killing larvae in meat products. This is achieved by heating until no trace of pink flesh remains. Freezing, smoking, or exposure to microwaves does not reliably kill the helminth.

STRONGYLOIDIASIS

Definition

S. stercoralis infection is endemic in warm climates worldwide, including the southern United States. In immunologically normal individuals, infection is usually asymptomatic or causes gastrointestinal dysfunction, manifested as abdominal pain, bloating, or bleeding. Persons who have deficient cell-mediated immunity can develop an autoinfective and hyperinfective life cycle of the nematode that markedly increases the total worm load. Life-threatening acute pulmonary disease and organ dysfunction due to dissemination of larvae to aberrant sites such as the brain, pancreas, and kidneys may result in immunocompromised hosts.

Etiology

S. stercoralis infection occurs when skin contacts free-living filariform larvae in the soil. After penetrating the skin, the parasite embolizes to the small vessels of the lungs through the venous circulation. Rhabditiform larvae then break into the alveolar spaces, ascend the respiratory tree, and are swallowed. Further development to adult worms occurs in the duodenum and upper jejunum, where egg-laying parasites live in the mucosa and submucosa. Rhabditiform larvae are released from eggs and are passed from the body in stools. Infective filariform larvae develop in the soil by direct transformation from rhabditiform larvae or indirectly from free-living intermediate forms.

Several unusual features of the life cycle of *S. stercoralis* are crucial to understanding how this parasitic nematode causes life-threatening disease. First, unlike most human helminthic parasites, adult worms reproduce parthogenetically in the gastrointestinal tract. The total worm burden in the host may therefore be greatly increased in the absence of repeated exposure to infective larvae in the environment. Second, rhabditiform larvae may develop into infective filariform larvae in the gastrointestinal tract and after passage in feces. Occurrence of the former process in immunocompromised hosts allows autoinfection, whereby larvae pass directly through the bowel (i.e., internal autoinfection) or perianal skin (i.e., external autoinfection) to reinitiate migration and development in the lungs. When this event is frequent, a hyperinfection syndrome ensues. Disseminated strongyloidiasis refers to a situation of hyperinfection in which the organisms also migrate to and cause pathology in organs not usually traversed by larvae, such as the CNS.

Epidemiology

S. stercoralis infection is endemic in Africa, Asia, Latin America, and areas of Eastern and Southern Europe. Prevalence rates based on stools examined for rhabditiform larvae vary from more than 40% in areas of sub-Saharan Africa to 1 to 7% in rural Eastern Europe. In the United States, the infection is endemic in rural Appalachia and other parts of the South. Prevalences range from 0.4 to 3% in the United States. Refugees from Asia have a higher prevalence of infection than do indigenous Americans. Surveys of homosexual men indicate a frequency of infection of 3.9%. It is likely that most studies of prevalence underestimate infection because they are based on examination of a single stool specimen, which is less sensitive than multiple examinations performed over days or weeks.

Strongyloidiasis is especially common in overcrowded situations in which sanitation and personal hygiene are poor, such as in institutions for retarded children and POW camps. An unusually high frequency of *S. stercoralis* infection has also been reported in persons with asymptomatic human T-cell lymphotropic virus type 1 (HTLV-1) infection.

Pathogenesis

Adult worms and larvae penetrating the upper small bowel cause enteritis characterized histopathologically by eosinophil and mononuclear cell infiltration of the lamina propria. Edema and mucosal atrophy are present on gross examination. Ulcerative lesions with hemorrhages are present in the most severe cases. Filariform larvae in the lungs elicit an inflammatory response in the alveoli consisting of mononuclear cells and eosinophils. In hyperinfection syndrome, these may coalesce and result in alveolar hemorrhage.

Autoinfection leading to exceptionally high worm loads (i.e., hyperinfection) and disseminated strongyloidiasis occur in persons with deficient cell-mediated immunity. Groups at risk include persons who are chronically taking corticosteroids, renal transplant recipients, patients with Hodgkin's disease and other lymphomas, and leukemic patients. Because *S. stercoralis* may persist and remain asymptomatic for decades after exposure, it is important to keep in mind that a change in immune status may convert a previously asymptomatic infection to hyperinfection. In this regard, there is a suspected association between acquired immunodeficiency syndrome (AIDS) and disseminated strongyloidiasis.

Clinical Manifestations

More than 50% of immunocompetent infected persons are asymptomatic. The frequency of clinical manifestations among infected immunocompromised subjects is unknown.

Signs and symptoms of *S. stercoralis* infection are attributable to the presence of adult worms in the upper gastrointestinal tract and larval invasion and to attendant host pathologic responses in the lung, skin, and aberrant sites of migration, such as the brain, eyes, pancreas, and kidney. Immunocompetent individuals rarely develop signs or symptoms attributable to larval migration outside the gut.

Gastrointestinal disease usually manifests as abdominal bloating, vague epigastric pain, and diarrhea with nausea. Symptoms are exacerbated by eating. Hematochezia and melena occur in less than 20% of subjects with intestinal strongyloidiasis. Major causes of morbidity related to *S. stercoralis* infection of the intestine are paralytic ileus, small bowel obstruction, and a malabsorption syndrome.

Pulmonary signs and symptoms in immunocompromised persons with hyperinfection syndrome are similar to those seen in the adult respiratory distress syndrome (i.e., acute onset of dyspnea, productive cough, and hemoptysis). These are accompanied by fever, tachypnea, hypoxemia, and respiratory alkalosis. *Strongyloides* larvae may also invade the CNS, pancreas, and eye and cause signs and symptoms attributable to tissue destruction in these sites.

Dermatologic manifestations include self-limited creeping eruption and, more commonly, larva currens, which results from migration of filariform larvae produced by a process of external autoinfection as described previously. The larvae elicit serpiginous erythematous papules and occasionally cause urticaria around the buttocks, upper thigh, and lower abdomen. Larva currens has been identified in former prisoners of war in the South Pacific.

Diagnosis

The unequivocal diagnosis of *S. stercoralis* infection depends on identifying larvae in host tissues or gastrointestinal and pulmonary secretions. The existence of filariform larvae in stools implies active autoinfection.

Intestinal strongyloidiasis is most easily diagnosed by identification of parasites in direct smears of freshly passed stools. Rhabditiform larvae are 225 to 380 mm long. Repeated examinations and concentration of stools increase the sensitivity of this method from approximately 25 to 80%. Examination of fluid obtained by duodenal aspiration or passage of a swallowed string into the upper small bowel may also be used if stool examination results are negative. Serologic tests are sensitive but not generally available. The differential diagnosis of intestinal *S. stercoralis* infection includes sprue, peptic ulcer, regional enteritis, and ulcerative colitis.

Hyperinfection syndrome and disseminated strongyloidiasis are diagnosed by identification of filariform larvae (500 to 600 mm long) in gastrointestinal secretions, as described previously, or in pulmonary tissues, secretions, or washings, such as those obtained by bronchoalveolar lavage or in sputum. Larvae have also been recovered from CSF, peritoneal washings, kidneys, urine, skin, and brains of immunocompromised persons.

Accompanying laboratory abnormalities frequently include eosinophilia. However, eosinophilia may not develop in immunocompromised hosts. Lack of eosinophilia is therefore not helpful in excluding strongyloidiasis in the differential diagnosis. The differential diagnosis of hyperinfection and disseminated strongyloidiasis includes overwhelming bacterial or fungal sepsis.

Complications

Disseminated strongyloidiasis is frequently accompanied by fungal or bacterial sepsis. Gram-negative enterococcal and polymicrobial septicemia has been observed. These infections likely result from translocation of gut organisms by migrating larvae.

Treatment

Uncomplicated intestinal strongyloidiasis should be treated with ivermectin (200 μg/kg of body weight given daily for 1 to 2 days). Parasitologic cure rates are higher than 90%. Therapy may need to be extended for several more days in immunocompromised individuals, who should be closely monitored. Symptomatic improvement and failure to detect larvae in gastrointestinal secretions or other sites is indicative of cure. Corticosteroids and other immunosuppressive agents should be discontinued when possible.

Prevention

Infection is preventable by avoiding skin contact with contaminated soil. Immunocompromised patients in endemic areas should be advised to avoid walking barefoot. Persons residing in endemic areas who are to become immunosuppressed (e.g., for renal transplantation) should have their stools examined three times for the presence of larvae, and they should be treated if the examination result is positive. Because infected individuals may be incorrectly categorized as uninfected by this test, it is suggested by some authorities that prophylactic thiabendazole (50 mg/kg of body weight given twice daily for 2 days, maximum of 3 g/day) or ivermectin be given in the month preceding iatrogenic immunosuppression. Positive serology for *S. stercoralis* is also an indication for treatment before immunosuppression.

SUGGESTED READINGS

Crompton DWT: Ascaris and ascariasis. Adv Parasitol 2001;48:285–375. *A complete review of the topic of ascariasis.*

DeVault GA Jr, King JW, Rohr MS, et al: Opportunistic infection with *Strongyloides stercoralis* in renal transplantation. Rev Infect Dis 1990;12:653–671. *Excellent discussion of clinical presentation and management of hyperinfection in immunocompromised hosts.*

Drugs for parasitic infections. Med Lett 2002;1127:1. *An updated summary of drugs used to treat worm infections of humans.*

Glickman LT, Magnaval JF: Zoonotic roundworm infections. Infect Dis Clin North Am 1994;7:717–732. *A good review of VLM and OLM.*

Hall A, Holland C: Geographical variation in Ascaris lumbricoides fecundity and its implication for helminth control. Parasitol Today 2000;16:540–544. *Discussion of the public health significance and transmission dynamics of ascariasis.*

MacLean JD, Viallet J, Law C, et al: Trichinosis in the Canadian Arctic: Report of five outbreaks and a new clinical syndrome. J Infect Dis 1989;160:513–520. *Excellent description of severe gastrointestinal manifestations of T. spiralis in a population in which the prevalence of trichinosis is among the highest in the world.*

Mahmoud AAF: Strongyloidiasis. Clin Infect Dis 1996;23:949–952. *A concise review of this disease.*

Moorhead A, Grunenwald PI, Dietz VJ, Schantz P: Trichinellosis in the United States, 1991–1996: Declining but not gone. Am J Trop Med Hyg 1999;60:66–69. *Recent trends in the incidence and transmission patterns of trichinosis in the United States.*

Robinson PD, Lindo JF, Neva FA, et al: Immunoepidemiologic studies of *Strongyloides stercoralis* and human T lymphotropic virus type I infection in Jamaica. J Infect Dis 1994;169:692–696. *Describes the association between HTLV-I infection and strongyloidiasis.*

Sarangarajan R, Ranganathan A, Belmonte AH, Tchertkoff V: *Strongyloides stercoralis* infection in AIDS. AIDS Patient Care STDS 1997;11:407–414. *Discussion of disseminated strongyloidiasis in AIDS patients.*

Tsai HC, Liu YC, Kunin CM, Lee SJ, et al: Eosinophilic meningitis caused by Angiostrongylus cantonensis: Report of 17 cases. Am J Med 2001;111:109–114. *An excellent discussion of this agent as a cause of meningitis.*

Woolhouse ME, Taylor LH, Haydon DT: Population biology of multihost pathogens. Science 2001;292:1109–1112. *A good overview of the population biology of helminthiases of human and veterinary importance.*

405 FILARIASIS

David O. Freedman

Definition

The filariases are a group of arthropod-borne parasitic diseases of humans caused by threadlike nematodes that in their mature adult stage reside in the lymphatics or in connective tissue. Eight filarial species infect humans (Table 405–1): *Wuchereria bancrofti, Brugia malayi, Brugia timori, Onchocerca volvulus, Loa loa, Mansonella streptocerca, Mansonella perstans,* and *Mansonella ozzardi.* Three species, *W. bancrofti, B. malayi,* and *O. volvulus,* which infect approximately 150 million individuals, are responsible for most human filarial disease in the world. Loiasis, however, is a relatively common affliction of returned travelers and expatriates.

Infection of the human host begins with the bite of an infected arthropod vector (see Table 405–1). Infective larvae are deposited into the skin or blood of a new host, where at least 3 to 12 months are required for the development of the mature adult female capable of producing larvae called *microfilariae.* To complete the life cycle, microfilariae, which circulate in the blood or migrate through the skin, are ingested by another arthropod vector to develop into new infective larvae ready to be passed to the next human host in a blood meal. Generally, infection is only established with repeated and prolonged exposure to infective larvae. After successful infection, no multiplication of the adult worms occurs in the human host. Because adult worms live for 5 to 15 years, these are chronic diseases. Microfilariae live for approximately 5 to 15 months. The long asymptomatic incubation period significantly lessens the chance that the relevant travel history will be elicited in an individual who has the nonspecific symptoms that occur with many of the filarial infections.

Disease expression varies. The adult parasite itself may provoke chronic inflammatory reactions in tissues; whereas in other filariases, reaction to microfilariae migrating through tissue may incite the abnormality observed. Newly exposed individuals characteristically have manifestations of acute symptoms that are exaggerated compared with those of chronically infected natives of the endemic area.

Definitive diagnosis of any of the filarial infections usually depends on the parasitologic demonstration of 170- to 300-µm-long and 5- to 9-µm-wide microfilariae in blood or in skin snips. The presence or absence of a sheath, the arrangement of the nuclei in the tail, and the tissue of origin are usually sufficient to differentiate the species. Diagnostic blood sampling must be timed during the day to account for the periodicity of every filarial parasite that is epidemiologically possible in the particular patient. Available serologic methods use crude heterologous antigen preparations. A positive result is not species specific, and individuals resident in endemic areas have antibodies whether they are currently infected or not. A positive result may be helpful in individuals infected with filarial parasites who are originally from nonendemic areas and were presumably seronegative initially.

Diethylcarbamazine and ivermectin are the backbone of antifilarial treatment. Diethylcarbamazine has substantial adulticidal effects against *L. loa* and the lymphatic filariases. Curative efforts with repeated courses of adulticidal therapy are more important in nonendemic individuals who will not be subsequently re-exposed to the parasite. Diethylcarbamazine is microfilaricidal to all species of human filaria except *M. ozzardi* and *M. perstans.* Ivermectin is not an adulticide and is microfilaricidal to *O. volvulus, W. bancrofti, Brugia* sp., *L. loa, M. ozzardi,* and *M. streptocerca.* Suppression of microfilaremia may vary from weeks to months. Treatment regimens differ according to whether the ultimate aim is treatment and cure of an individual patient or widespread, single-dose, community-based interruption of transmission by suppression of microfilariae available to vectors. Albendazole has significant antifilarial activity, but lack of data precludes its use as first-line therapy of individual patients.

LYMPHATIC FILARIASIS

Etiology

W. bancrofti, B. malayi, and *B. timori* adults are threadlike worms that are convoluted in lymph nodes but have been shown by ultrasound to be extended into afferent lymph vessels. The females, which are about twice the size (80 to 100 mm long × 0.2 to 0.3 mm wide) of the males, produce microfilariae that circulate in the peripheral blood until ingestion by mosquito intermediate hosts. After a 1- to 3-week incubation, mosquitoes take a second blood meal, and infective larvae penetrate the skin at the puncture wound. An additional 4 to 12 months elapses for development into mature adults in the lymphatics of the new host.

Epidemiology

An estimated 120 million people are affected by lymphatic filariasis—90% with bancroftian and 10% with brugian filariasis. Humans are the only definitive host for *W. bancrofti,* which has no animal

Table 405–1 • THE COMMON FILARIAL PARASITES OF HUMANS

SPECIES	DISTRIBUTION	VECTOR	PRIMARY PATHOLOGY	MICROFILARIAE Primary Location	Periodicity	Presence of Sheath
Wuchereria bancrofti	Tropics worldwide	Mosquitose	Lymphatic, pulmonary	Blood, hydrocele fluid	Nocturnal, subperiodic	+
Brugia malayi	Southeast Asia, West Pacific	Mosquitoes	Lymphatic, pulmonary	Blood	Nocturnal, subperiodic	+
Brugia rimori	Indonesia	Mosquitoes	Lymphatic	Blood	Nocturnal	+
Onchocerca volvulus	Africa, Central and South America	Black fly	Skin, eye, lymphatic	Skin, eye	None or minimal	–
Loa loa	Africa	Deer fly	Allergic	Blood	Diurnal	+
Mansonella perstans	Africa, South America	Midge	? Allergic	Blood	None	–
Mansonella streptocerca	Africa	Midge	Skin	Skin	None	–
Mansonella ozzardi	Central and South America	Midge	Vague	Blood	None	–

reservoir. *W. bancrofti* is found in 76 countries throughout the tropics and subtropics, encompassing areas of South America, the Caribbean, Africa, Asia, and the South Pacific. Two forms of the parasite are distinguished by the periodicity of their circulating microfilariae. Nocturnally periodic forms of the parasite, found in most endemic areas, have microfilariae detectable in blood primarily at night, peaking between 10:00 PM and 2:00 AM. Subperiodic bancroftian filariasis is found only in the Pacific islands, with microfilariae circulating at all hours but with peak levels in the late afternoon. The natural vectors are *Culex quinquefasciatus* in urban settings and usually anopheline or aedean mosquitoes in rural areas.

B. malayi is restricted to an area of Asia from India in the west to Korea in the northeast. Foci also exist in Indonesia, Vietnam, Malaysia, China, and the Philippines. Two forms of *B. malayi* are distinguished. The nocturnally periodic form, which has no animal reservoir, is transmitted by *Mansonia* and *Anopheles* species in India, Sulawesi, Vietnam, and China. The nocturnally subperiodic form is transmitted by *Mansonia* species and coexists with periodic forms in Malaysia and Indonesia. Subperiodic *B. malayi* can produce a natural infection of cats. *B. timori*, transmitted by anophelines, has been described from only two Indonesian islands.

Pathology

Microfilariae in blood are not associated with any disorder. The mature adult lymphatic-dwelling parasite induces a parasite-specific local inflammatory reaction, with cell-mediated and humoral components leading to hypertrophy of the vessel walls. The worm itself does not seem to cause blockage of the vessel. Endothelial and connective tissue proliferation leads to vessel dilatation and intraluminal polyposis that diminish normal lymphatic function. The resulting lymphedema is reversible in its early stages. Worm death leads to necrosis and a granulomatous reaction with infiltration of plasma cells, eosinophils, and giant cells. Over time, fibrosis and obstruction of lymph flow within the lumen lead to irreversible elephantiasis of the affected part. Although some recanalization and collateralization of lymph vessels take place, lymphatic function remains compromised.

At least two other components play clear-cut roles at different stages of disease. First, mechanical damage to lymph vessels due to the whip-like action of the constantly motile adult worms and toxic effects of parasite excretory and secretory products are important early in the clinically asymptomatic noninflammatory stage of infection. Second, at an uncertain point during the clinical evolution of the lymphatic insufficiency, repeated limb bacterial infections in previously damaged vessels may become superimposed on other processes. The relative contribution to disease evolution of each of the components and the degree of interindividual variability are incompletely defined.

Until recently, entirely asymptomatic individuals with microfilaremia but no overt clinical manifestations of filarial infection had been thought to have infection but not disease. Imaging of the lymphatic system with ultrasound and radionuclide lymphoscintigraphy and biopsy of affected tissue have demonstrated that lymphatic structural and functional abnormalities are often far advanced even before overt lymphatic insufficiency manifests clinically.

Endosymbiotic *Wolbachia* bacteria have been found within *W. bancrofii, B. malayi,* and *O. volvulus* adult worms. Necessary for these worms' development, viability, and fertility, *Wolbachia* bacteria trigger inflammatory host responses as well as adverse reactions after standard antiparasitic drug regimens. The use of antibacterial agents in filariasis treatment is under investigation.

Clinical Manifestations

The common clinical outcomes of lymphatic filariasis are asymptomatic microfilaremia, acute episodic adenolymphangitis (also called *filarial fever*), and chronic lymphatic obstruction. Clinically asymptomatic microfilaremia is the most common outcome of lymphatic filariasis. These individuals, however, almost uniformly have underlying lymphatic damage with impaired lymphatic function. Microscopic hematuria and low-grade proteinuria are common but of uncertain clinical significance.

Acute attacks of retrograde adenolymphangitis, accompanied by fever, chills, and malaise, each lasting 3 to 15 days, can occur up to 10 times per year and are often presenting manifestations of progressive filarial disease. Patients usually give a clear history of pain, erythema, and tenderness in the affected lymph node region for hours or a day before onset of the lymphangitis. Some individuals may have only one or a few attacks in a lifetime. Adenolymphangitis most often affects the groin and, in male patients, the lymphatics of the genitalia, leading to funiculitis, orchitis, and epididymitis, but essentially any lymph node group and any body part may be involved. Patients with filarial fevers may be microfilaremic but often are not.

After months to years of acute episodes ranging from very insidious to severe, transient then chronic obstructive disease due to lymphatic insufficiency develops. Pitting edema progresses to brawny edema, and thickening of subcutaneous tissue and hyperkeratosis develop. Fissuring of the skin develops along with nodular and papillomatous hyperplasia. Bacterial superinfection of limbs with such loss of integrity of skin surfaces manifests as a typical cellulitis type of presentation with a warm edematous extremity and anterograde lymphangitis. In many areas, the most common chronic manifestation is hydrocele, and scrotal lymphedema is seen in more advanced cases. Many patients give no history of earlier acute attacks, emphasizing the need for disrobing of all male patients to carry out a genital examination. Female patients occasionally have lymphedema of the vulva. If retroperitoneal lymphatics are obstructed, the rupture of renal lymphatics leads to the development of intermittent chyluria. In endemic areas, the prevalence of chronic manifestations increases with age. Patients with chronic disease may be microfilaremic but most often are not. Attacks of acute adenolymphangitis often continue even in those with advanced disease.

Newly exposed individuals (e.g., long-term visitors, military personnel, migrants) characteristically have manifestations of typical acute inflammatory symptoms with more rapid progression to chronic or irreversible abnormality than those born in the endemic area. Prolonged, severe episodes of adenolymphangitis, often with genital involvement, may lead to the relatively rapid development of lymphedema and elephantiasis within 6 to 12 months of arrival. Disease abates quickly with removal of the patient from the endemic area. These individuals are uniformly amicrofilaremic.

Brugian filariasis differs in several respects from bancroftian filariasis. In *B. malayi* infection, only the lower leg is affected, whereas in *W. bancrofti* infection, the thigh and lower leg are involved. In brugian filariasis, infected superficial nodes, usually inguinal, may suppurate and form sterile abscesses that heal with a characteristic scar. In general, brugian filariasis is more clinically dramatic. Insidious onset of chronic lymphedema, as may occur in bancroftian filariasis, is uncommon. Urogenital disease and chyluria do not occur.

Diagnosis

Definitive diagnosis often depends on the parasitologic demonstration of the 250- to 320-μm-long microfilariae in blood. Diagnostic sampling must take into account the periodicity of the microfilariae in the area of exposure. A Giemsa-stained thick blood smear, performed as for the diagnosis of malaria, can detect heavily infected individuals but is relatively insensitive. Parasites may be concentrated by passage through a polycarbonate membrane filter (3-μm pore size) or by centrifugation of 1 mL of anticoagulated blood in a conical tube with 9 mL of 2% formalin. The filter itself or the sediment is then stained and examined. Microfilariae of *W. bancrofti* have occasionally been found in urine but are usually not present in chyluric patients. Only an experienced pathologist can identify the sections of adult worms that are found incidentally in specimens of diverse human body tissues. Lymph node biopsy is not indicated in suspected filariasis unless neoplasia is also a diagnostic concern.

Serologic measurement of antifilarial antibodies is often not useful because existing assays cannot distinguish among the eight human filarial parasites. The assays cannot distinguish actively infected patients from those previously infected, and those merely exposed but not infected may also have positive findings. Cross-reactivity occurs with other helminth infections. A rapid card test assay sensitive enough to detect circulating *W. bancrofti*–specific antigen liberated by adult worms (and present in the blood both day and night) has dramatically advanced the serologic approach to diagnosing filariasis. The card test is commercially available but is not U.S. Food and Drug Administration (FDA) approved.

Ultrasound techniques have been used to visualize rapidly moving ("dancing") adult worms in the dilated scrotal lymphatics of infected men. Such findings are pathognomonic of filarial parasites, but the technique is less sensitive than other modalities. Abnormalities detected by lymphoscintigraphy are not specific for filarial disease.

Bacterial infection, thrombophlebitis, or trauma may be mistaken for acute filarial adenolymphangitis. Filarial lymphangitis is retrograde, a characteristic that helps differentiate it from bacterial lymphangitis. In cases of orchitis and epididymitis, sexually transmitted diseases must be considered. Chronic lymphedema may be caused by malignancy, postoperative changes, congenital malformations, and renal or cardiac failure. Physical examination cannot distinguish a filarial from a nonfilarial cause of lymphedema or elephantiasis. A foreign body reaction to silica dust introduced into traumatized legs accounts for elephantiasis in some parts of the world. Patients with filarial lymphedema are often amicrofilaremic, and diagnosis therefore depends on the clinical history, epidemiologic features, and physical examination results and may be supported by a positive serologic or antigen assay result.

Rx Treatment

Individual patients, whether symptomatic or asymptomatic, with lymphatic filariasis should be treated with diethylcarbamazine (6 mg/kg/day in three divided doses for 2 to 3 weeks). FDA-approved diethylcarbamazine is available only through the Centers for Disease Control (CDC) Drug Service (404-639-3670). Side effects are caused by dying parasites, not to direct drug toxicity, and are directly proportional to the number of circulating microfilariae. They include fever, chills, headache, dizziness, nausea, vomiting, and arthralgias, all usually occurring in the first 24 to 36 hours and then subsiding even with continued therapy. For highly parasitemic persons, the physician can initiate treatment with single doses of 50 to 100 mg of diethylcarbamazine on the first 2 days or premedicate the patients with steroids. Some patients may experience adenolymphangitis due to dying adult worms. A single dose of diethylcarbamazine is microfilaricidal and is used in control programs in which the aim is to break transmission by suppression of microfilariae available to vectors. In individual patients who will not be returning to endemic areas, adulticidal therapy, which requires a prolonged course of diethylcarbamazine, is necessary. If the patient remains microfilaremic, at least two repeat courses at several-month intervals should be considered. Patients with lymphedema or elephantiasis should receive low-dose diethylcarbamazine daily for at least a year in an attempt to determine whether there is any reversible component of the chronic disease. Limb elevation, massage, use of elastic stockings, and prevention of superficial bacterial and fungal infection through meticulous hygiene are important in the care of a lymphedematous extremity. Suspected bacterial superinfection should receive antibiotic therapy. In ongoing trials, albendazole alone or in combination with diethylcarbamazine has adulticidal and microfilaricidal activity in lymphatic filariasis, but appropriate dosing regimens for the treatment of individual patients have yet to be developed.

Single doses of diethylcarbamazine, ivermectin, or albendazole, alone or in combination, are effectively microfilaricidal for periods of up to a year. These regimens are well tolerated and therefore are ideally suited for mass treatment as part of control programs.

Prognosis

Though the psychosocial morbidity associated with this deforming disease is profound, there is little mortality associated with lymphatic filariasis. It is likely that some untreated asymptomatic microfilaremic individuals become symptomatic, but factors determining such clinical changes are unknown. The determinants of which patients with chronic manifestations have a component that is reversible with therapy are not defined. Disease should not progress in those removed from an endemic area and adequately treated.

Prevention

Diethylcarbamazine has some value as a prophylactic agent in humans in a dose of 10 mg/kg on 2 consecutive days each month. Yearly mass treatment with a single dose of diethylcarbamazine significantly reduces the prevalence of infection within a community. Diethylcarbamazine-supplemented table salt can reduce the number of blood-borne microfilariae in the community to levels so low that transmission is interrupted. Vector control in endemic areas has proved difficult but bednet programs may have some efficacy.

TROPICAL EOSINOPHILIA

Tropical pulmonary eosinophilia is a syndrome that develops in a small percentage of individuals infected with lymphatic filarial parasites. The characteristic patient is a male (4:1 male-to-female ratio) in his teens or 20s who is a resident of India, Pakistan, Sri Lanka, Brazil, or Southeast Asia. Characteristic clinical findings include paroxysmal cough and wheezing that occur almost exclusively at night, weight loss, low-grade fever, adenopathy, and extreme blood eosinophilia. Chest radiograph results generally show diffusely increased bronchovascular markings or mottled opacities in middle and lower lung fields. Restrictive and obstructive abnormalities are found through pulmonary function tests. Total serum immunoglobulin E (IgE) level and antifilarial antibody levels are extremely elevated.

Tropical pulmonary eosinophilia is thought to occur as a result of unusually rapid immune-mediated clearance of blood microfilariae with trapping in the lung. The pulmonary symptoms result from allergic (IgE-mediated) and inflammatory reactions to the cleared parasites (*W. bancrofti* or *B. malayi*). Several reports have described microfilariae or their degenerating remnants in lung biopsy specimens, and eosinophils are present in bronchial lavage fluid. Untreated disease can progress to interstitial fibrosis.

The differential diagnosis of tropical pulmonary eosinophilia includes asthma, Löffler's syndrome (which can be caused by migrating larval forms of other helminths), allergic bronchopulmonary aspergillosis, Churg-Strauss syndrome or other systemic vasculitides, chronic eosinophilic pneumonia, and idiopathic hypereosinophilic syndrome. Diagnosis of tropical pulmonary eosinophilia is usually confirmed by the coexistence of nocturnal wheezing, very high antifilarial titers, and rapid initial response to diethylcarbamazine therapy in a patient with the right geographic exposure. Diethylcarbamazine at a dose of 6 mg/kg/day for 14 to 21 days is the treatment of choice. Ivermectin is not useful for tropical pulmonary eosinophilia. Symptoms typically respond within a week but may relapse even after an interval of years in 25%, necessitating repeat treatment.

ONCHOCERCIASIS (RIVER BLINDNESS)

Etiology

Transmission of *O. volvulus* occurs through the bites of black flies (*Simulium* species) that ingest microfilariae from the skin of an infected person. After development in the vector, infective larvae are transmitted to a new human host. Over a period of several months, the larvae develop into adult worms that are coiled within fibrotic subcutaneous nodules. Nine to 18 months after infection, each mature female worm begins to produce up to 2000 microfilariae per day, which migrate primarily through the skin and ocular tissues.

Adult female worms are 23 to 70 cm long, and the males are 3 to 6 cm long. Microfilariae are unsheathed and 200 to 300 μm long and 6 to 9 μm wide. The average lifespan of the adult worm is 8 to 10 years, and that of the microfilariae is 13 to 14 months. Two distinct strains or biotypes of *O. volvulus* are present in West Africa. The blinding or savanna strain is associated with the development of ocular disorders, whereas the nonblinding or forest strain is generally not associated with ocular disease.

Epidemiology

Onchocerciasis is endemic in 34 countries, 27 in equatorial Africa in a broad belt extending from the Atlantic coast to the Red Sea and more focally in 6 Latin American countries (i.e., Guatemala, Mexico, Venezuela, Brazil, Colombia, and Ecuador) and in the Arabian peninsula (i.e., Yemen and Saudi Arabia). Current estimates are that approximately 18 million people are infected, 270,000 of whom are blind and another 500,000 of whom have severe visual disability. More than 99% of the cases occur in sub-Saharan Africa, with almost one half of these in Nigeria and Zaire. Because the black flies depend on well-oxygenated, fast-flowing waterways for egg laying and reproduction, the vectors and the disease are concentrated around streams and rivers, often in the most fertile farming areas.

O. volvulus–induced blindness is associated with a life expectancy that is decreased by at least 10 years over that of nonblinded individuals in the same area. However, more than the blinding disease, which affects only a small proportion of those infected, the pervasiveness of the chronic skin lesions and intense pruritus caused by onchodermatitis make it a leading cause of morbidity in infected areas.

Pathology

Onchocerciasis predominantly affects the skin, the eyes, and the lymph nodes. The inflammatory reaction is elicited by the microfilariae and not the adult worms, whose encapsulation seems to protect them from the immune response. Tissue damage results primarily from the host response to the secretion of toxic products by granulocytes, particularly granular proteins from eosinophils that adhere to microfilariae. Sclerosing keratitis, the major cause of blindness, is caused by a parasite antigen–specific, lymphocytic inflammatory reaction to dying intraocular microfilariae that appears dependent on T_H2 cytokines. With time, neovascularization and scarring of the cornea lead to loss of transparency and to blindness. Ongoing low-grade inflammation in the skin eventually leads to loss of elastic fibers and atrophy. Chronic inflammatory changes and fibrosis are seen in lymph nodes.

Clinical Manifestations

DERMATITIS. The pruritus of onchocerciasis is often intractable and unresponsive to antipruritis medication. In heavily infected individuals in endemic areas, scratching and excoriation occur to the point of bleeding and even suicide. Episodes of localized rash, erythema, and angioedema may be superimposed on the ongoing dermatologic manifestations at any stage of disease. The five categories used to classify onchodermatitis are not mutually exclusive in a given patient, and the clinical findings are not necessarily specific for onchodermatitis. In type 1, acute papular onchodermatitis, the small, pruritic papules may be scattered on the limbs, shoulders, and trunk. Lesions may progress to become vesicular or pustular. In type 2, chronic papular onchodermatitis, the often flat-topped papules are larger but more variable in size and height than in the acute papular eruption. Lesions are less pruritic than in the acute eruption. In type 3, lichenified dermatitis (i.e., Sowda), an intensely pruritic eruption is limited to one limb, usually the leg, and consists of hyperpigmented papules and plaques with accompanying edema of the entire limb. In type 4, atrophy-premature atrophy, one or more of the structural elements of the skin degenerate, pruritus is uncommon, and fine wrinkles appear on the skin after pushing along the surface with one finger. Loss of elasticity can be demonstrated by a slow return to the original position of skin pinched between two fingers. In type 5, depigmentation, areas of complete depigmentation occur over the anterior shin, with islands of normally pigmented skin, also called "leopard skin." In short-term residents of endemic areas, an evanescent acute papular dermatitis is almost always the sole manifestation of infection.

EYE. Involvement of all tissues of the eye has been described. Inflammation due to microfilariae of *O. volvulus* as they migrate through the eye initially manifests as a punctate keratitis or as snowflake corneal opacities. Free microfilariae may be visible by slit lamp examination in the anterior chamber or aqueous humor but are rarely found in infected short-term visitors, who are typically very lightly infected. Long-standing infection with savanna strain *O. volvulus* leads to sclerosing keratitis characterized by a fibrovascular pannus. Iridocyclitis with flare and cells in the anterior chamber leads to development of synechiae, raised intraocular pressure, and secondary glaucoma. Chorioretinitis and chorioretinal atrophy are the common manifestations of posterior ocular disease. Optic neuritis and optic atrophy occur in

savannah regions. Infected short-term visitors do not have ocular involvement.

SUBCUTANEOUS NODULES. Asymptomatic 0.5- to 3.0-cm subcutaneous onchocercomas, occurring most often over bony prominences, are freely movable encapsulated nodules that contain coiled masses of adult worms. In Latin America, the nodules are often located on the head and upper body, whereas in Africa, the nodules are most often over the hips and lower limbs. More than 80% of nodules are not palpable and, in lightly infected expatriates, are rarely detectable.

LYMPHADENOPATHY. Lymphadenopathy is frequently found in inguinal and femoral areas. When it occurs in inguinofemoral nodes in a sling of stretched-out atrophic abdominal skin, the so-called hanging groin results. Lymph nodes are nontender and fibrotic.

Diagnosis

Definitive diagnosis depends on the demonstration of motile microfilariae in superficial, bloodless skin snips. This type of skin biopsy employs a razor blade to slice a thin piece of skin that has been tented up with a needle or a corneoscleral biopsy instrument to obtain 1 to 2 mg of skin bloodlessly. Six snips, one from over each scapula, iliac crest, and lateral aspect of each calf, are incubated with saline solution in microplate wells and examined microscopically. Deep punch biopsy of the skin is not necessary, and multiple skin snips have a higher yield than one random traumatic deep biopsy. When available, polymerase chain reaction (PCR) amplification of parasite DNA directly from skin snips is far more sensitive than direct visualization. Blood contamination of a skin snip may cause one of the blood-borne microfilaria to escape into the specimen. If the patient has been in an area endemic for *M. streptocerca*, it is necessary to fix the skin and to stain the microfilariae for identification. In well-equipped clinical settings, biopsy or ultrasound demonstration of adult parasites in any nodules that are present can be diagnostic. Elevated titers of antifilarial antibodies may support the diagnosis of onchocerciasis but should not be used alone. The total eosinophil count is unhelpful diagnostically because it is often but inconstantly elevated in onchocerciasis.

Scabies, insect bites, hypersensitivity reactions, miliaria rubra, and atopic or contact dermatitis enter the differential diagnosis of acute pruritic disease. In expatriates, Calabar swellings (see the discussion of loiasis), clinically similar episodes of localized rash and mild angioedema, can mimic onchodermatitis. Tuberculoid leprosy, streptocerciasis, and eczema should be considered if there are chronic skin changes. Dermatomycoses, previous trauma, and yaws can also cause hypopigmented skin lesions. The posterior eye lesions are not at all specific for onchocerciasis.

 Treatment

No available nontoxic agent is able to kill the long-lived adult worms of *O. volvulus*. Repeated microfilaricidal therapy with ivermectin (150 µg/kg) in a single dose every 6 to 12 months is effective in ameliorating symptoms. For unclear reasons, pruritus in lightly infected expatriates may be refractory to 6-monthly therapy, and many clinicians find it necessary to treat more aggressively for the first 2 years or so. Appropriate duration of therapy in those without further exposure is unknown, but it probably should be offered for at least 10 years. In *L. loa* co-infected individuals with high levels of circulating microfilaremia, ivermectin therapy may precipitate a toxic encephalopathy. In areas endemic for loiasis, high microfilaremia should be ruled out before ivermectin administration for onchocerciasis. Because of frequent unacceptable reactions to dying microfilariae, ranging from urticaria and angioedema to hypotension and death, diethylcarbamazine should never be used for microfilaricidal treatment of onchocerciasis. Suramin (available from the CDC drug service) is adulticidal, but because of toxicity and even potentially life-threatening effects, it should be used only in extreme situations. Surgical removal of palpable nodules in order to reduce the microfilarial load and the ensuing disorder has been successful in some areas. Nodulectomy is appropriate for cosmetic reasons but cannot be expected to cure infection because most nodules are impalpable.

Prognosis

Ivermectin is effective in reversing existing early skin and ocular abnormalities but must be given repeatedly because adult parasites begin producing microfilariae again with time. The atrophic skin changes, sclerosing keratitis, and established lesions in the posterior segment of the eye are not helped by therapy.

Prevention

There are no effective vaccines or chemoprophylactic drugs. For expatriates or others with sufficient resources, personal mosquito protection using repellents is likely of benefit. The Onchocerciasis Control Program has been ongoing in West Africa since 1974 and involves vector control in 11 countries and 50,000 km of rivers. It is estimated that 30 million people have been protected from infection, 10 million children have been born into areas that are free of disease transmission, and blindness has been prevented in 125,000 to 200,000 others. Building a sustainable infrastructure for the mass community-based distribution of the microfilaricide ivermectin has now become the primary global control strategy. Annual mass treatment of an affected community with ivermectin, which is available free through a remarkable donation program of Merck, should break the transmission cycle within 10 to 15 years by eliminating microfilariae available to vectors from the skin of infected individuals. There is no nonhuman reservoir of *O. volvulus.*

LOIASIS

Etiology and Epidemiology

L. loa, the African eye worm, is restricted to the rain forest area of Central and West Africa. Prevalence and endemicity are imprecisely defined, but loiasis appears to be most prevalent in Gabon, Cameroon, Congo, Nigeria, and the Central African Republic. Adult parasites (females are 50 to 70 mm long; males are 25 to 35 mm long) live a constantly migratory existence in subcutaneous tissues. Blood-borne microfilariae have a diurnal periodicity peaking between noon and 4:00 PM. Tabanid flies of *Chrysops* species are the vectors. In temporary residents, a shorter period of exposure appears necessary to acquire infection compared with that of other filarial parasites.

Pathology

The pathogenesis of the angioedematous reaction that occurs in response to the adult worm is poorly understood. The extremely elevated serum IgE level and eosinophilia seen in newly infected individuals prone to Calabar swellings indicate a hypersensitivity reaction to adult worms or worm products.

Clinical Manifestations

More so than with the other filarial infections, clinical manifestations are much exaggerated in short-term residents or visitors to endemic areas compared with those of natives. Nonendemic persons, who are usually amicrofilaremic, have severe allergic symptoms with frequent and incapacitating Calabar swellings, pruritus, and urticaria. Calabar swellings are localized areas of evanescent erythema and angioedema (up to 5 to 10 cm in diameter) that occur primarily on the extremities and last 1 to 3 days. The subcutaneous adult organisms, which are large enough to be visible, only rarely migrate across the conjunctiva. Among endemic individuals, infection is most often asymptomatic with microfilaremia and has a much lower incidence of Calabar swellings and allergic manifestations. Eye worm occurs in up to 50% of these individuals. In chronically infected individuals, nephropathy and cardiomyopathy occur only rarely.

Diagnosis

Definitive diagnosis depends on the demonstration of characteristic sheathed microfilariae on an afternoon blood film. Nonendemic individuals are usually amicrofilaremic, and the diagnosis often cannot be made parasitologically and must be based on the characteristic history, clinical presentation, blood eosinophilia, and elevated antifilarial antibody titers. *O. volvulus, M. perstans, M. ozzardi,* and *M. streptocerca* all cause overlapping syndromes and must, if epidemiologically possible, be ruled out by a complete search for microfilariae in blood and skin. Occasionally, an adult *L. loa* is excised while crawling across the conjunctiva or under the skin. Definitive diagnosis sometimes occurs after initiation of diethylcarbamazine therapy and subcutaneous biopsy of a swelling developing at the site of a dying adult worm.

Treatment And Prognosis

Diethylcarbamazine (6 to 10 mg/kg/day for 21 days) has both microfilaricidal and adulticidal effects. Decisions about retreatment should be based on clinical resolution, and multiple courses of diethylcarbamazine may be required before signs and symptoms completely resolve. One course of therapy cures about one half those infected, and a second course cures one half of the remaining infected individuals. Eosinophilia and antifilarial titers resolve slowly even with effective therapy and therefore should not be closely followed as a test of cure. However, an antifilarial titer or an eosinophilia that is increasing or unchanged after 6 months should prompt suspicion of failure of treatment given up until that time.

In patients with any microfilaremia, diethylcarbamazine therapy should be initiated with low doses of drug (50 mg/day) on the first few days, and pretreatment with corticosteroids should be considered. With microfilaremia levels greater than a few hundred microfilariae per milliliter of blood, diethylcarbamazine-induced inflammatory reactions to dying microfilariae may progress to encephalopathy and death. If available, apheresis to remove circulating microfilariae can be performed before initiating diethylcarbamazine therapy in these individuals. If this latter option is not available for highly microfilaremic individuals, limited data support the use of albendazole (200 mg twice daily for 21 days) because it appears to be moderately adulticidal without effects on the microfilariae. Ivermectin is microfilaricidal but has no adulticidal effect and may cause toxic encephalopathy in highly microfilaremic individuals. If epidemiologically appropriate, onchocerciasis must be carefully ruled out before the initiation of diethylcarbamazine therapy for loiasis to prevent toxicity due to dying *O. volvulus* microfilariae.

Prevention

Diethylcarbamazine is effective in preventing loiasis when taken in prophylactic doses of 300 mg/week.

DRACUNCULIASIS

Dracunculiasis, or guinea worm disease, is caused by the helminth *Dracunculus medinensis* and is close to eradication. A global effort reduced incidence from 3.5 million cases in 20 countries in 1986 to 63,000 cases in 2001, of which 78% were in Sudan. The infection has been eradicated from the Indian subcontinent and remains in only 13 countries of sub-Saharan Africa.

Transmission to humans occurs through drinking water contaminated with tiny crustaceans called *copepods* that carry larval forms of the parasite. A year or so later, adult female worms up to 1 m long emerge through the skin, usually of the lower leg or foot. Transmission is perpetuated when the female releases thousands of larvae into the water if the human host immerses that part of the body in a source of drinking water. Emergence of the worm is accompanied by a painful blister that ruptures and ulcerates. Fever and allergic symptoms, including wheezing and urticaria, often precede rupture of the blister. Affected persons may be incapacitated for weeks or months, often coinciding with major planting or harvesting seasons. Secondary bacterial infection of the ulcer with abscess formation is common.

Emerging worms can be extracted by winding of a few more centimeters on a stick each day. Chemotherapy is ineffective. Worms may be removed surgically. Prevention is achieved through the provision of safe drinking water.

OTHER FILARIASES

PERSTANS FILARIASIS. *M. perstans* infection occurs commonly throughout Central Africa and in northeast South America, but exact numbers are unknown. The blood-borne microfilariae circulate without periodicity, and adults reside in serous body cavities (i.e., pleural, peritoneal, and pericardial) and in the mesenteric, perirenal, and retroperitoneal tissues. Most individuals are asymptomatic or at most mildly symptomatic, but a distribution that overlaps with several other human filariids has hampered definition of distinct clinical features. Reported manifestations include transient angioedematous swellings, pruritus, fever, headache, arthralgias, abdominal pain, and neurologic syndromes. Pericarditis and hepatitis have been reported. Eosinophilia and elevated antifilarial antibody titers are often present. No reliable therapy exists. Diethylcarbamazine and ivermectin are clearly ineffective. Some success with albendazole (two 400 mg/day doses) or mebendazole (two 100 mg/day doses) for at least 1 month has been reported.

STREPTOCERCIASIS. *M. streptocerca*, transmitted by midges, was thought to be restricted to the tropical forest zone of Africa from Ghana to Zaire, but it has recently been described as far east as Uganda. The adult worms are subcutaneous, and the microfilariae, which have characteristic hooked tails, are found in the skin, most often on the upper body. Ocular involvement does not occur. Infection is usually asymptomatic, but pruritus and acute or chronic papular dermatitis similar to that of onchodermatitis can affect the trunk and upper extremities of up to 24% of those infected. Inguinal adenopathy is common. In areas of epidemiologic overlap, skin snips must be stained to differentiate *M. streptocerca* from *O. volvulus*. Adult worms and microfilariae are killed by diethylcarbamazine (6 mg/kg/day for 2 weeks). Ivermectin, in a single dose of 150 µg/kg, is microfilaricidal.

MANSONELLA OZZARDI INFECTION. *M. ozzardi* is found only in Central and South America and certain islands of the Caribbean. The blood-borne microfilariae circulate without periodicity, and the location of adults is unclear. Adult worms have been recovered only twice, both times from the peritoneal cavity. Although it is generally considered nonpathogenic, articular pain, headache, fever, pulmonary symptoms, adenopathy, hepatomegaly, and pruritic skin eruptions are reported. Ivermectin in a single dose of 150 µg/kg appears to suppress microfilaremia reliably for at least several months but probably is not adulticidal. Diethylcarbamazine is ineffective.

ZOONOTIC FILARIAL INFECTIONS. Uncommonly, several animal filariae, including *Dirofilaria immitis* and *Dirofilaria repens* in dogs, as well as *Dirofilaria tenuis* in raccoons, can infect humans. Distribution is worldwide, and the organisms are found in nontropical and tropical climates. The parasites die in the larval stages before reaching maturity and cause few symptoms. Localization is to the lungs in *D. immitis* infection (appearing as coin lesions) or to the subcutaneous tissues and lymph nodes in the other *Dirofilaria* species. Subcutaneous lesions may be migratory. Zoonotic *Brugia* species infection localizes to lymph nodes. Eosinophilia and positive antifilarial antibody titers are unusual. Surgical removal of lesions is diagnostic and curative. Chemotherapy is uniformly ineffective.

SUGGESTED READINGS

Boussinesq M, Gardon J: Prevalences of *Loa loa* microfilaremia throughout the area endemic for the infection. Ann Trop Med Parasitol 1997;91:573–589. *Extensive graphical material on infection prevalence down to the village level.*

Burnham G: Onchocerciasis. Lancet 1998;351:1341–1346. *Concise review of clinical, parasitologic, and epidemiologic aspects of onchocerciasis with very up-to-date references.*

Fischer P, Bamuhiiga J, Buttner DW: Occurrence and diagnosis of *Mansonella streptocerca* in Uganda. Acta Trop 1997;63:43–55. *First large clinical study of an underinvestigated infection in more than 25 years.*

Hoerauf A, Mand S, Volkmann L, et al: Doxycycline in the treatment of human onchocerciasis: Kinetics of *Wolbachia* endobacteria reduction and of inhibition of embryogenesis in female *Onchocerca* worms. Microbes Infect 2003;5:26–73. *Perspective on a role for doxycycline as an adjunct treatment for filariasis.*

Michael E, Bundy DAP, Grenfell BT: Re-assessing the global prevalence and distribution of lymphatic filariasis. Parasitology 1996;112:409–428. *Most comprehensive review of infection prevalence ever done, extensively referenced.*

Pani S, Subramanyam Reddy G, Das L, et al: Tolerability and efficacy of single dose albendazole, diethylcarbamazine citrate (DEC) or co-administration of albendazole with DEC in the clearance of *Wuchereria bancrofti* in asymptomatic microfilaraemic volunteers in Pondicherry, South India: A hospital-based study. Filaria J 2002;1:1. *Albendazole alone or in combination with DEC may be optimal for treatment of bancroftian filariasis.*

406 ARTHROPODS AND LEECHES

David Schlossberg

Arthropods are bilaterally symmetrical invertebrates with an exoskeleton, segmented bodies, and jointed appendages. In the phylum Arthropoda, six classes are important sources of disease in humans: Arachnida, Pentastomida, Chilopoda, Diplopoda, Crustacea, and Insecta. Table 406–1 lists these classes, and their members are discussed in this chapter.

Arthropods cause disease in humans directly and indirectly. They bite, sting, envenomate, and evoke hypersensitivity reactions; they also serve as vectors for infectious pathogens. Arthropods are the link between humans and age-old scourges such as plague, typhus, and malaria.

Infections spread by arthropod vectors are listed in Table 406–2. They are each described in greater detail elsewhere in this text and are not reviewed further here.

SCABIES

Mites are small arachnids, about the size of a grain of sand. They have a single apparent body region, with a fused cephalothorax and abdomen. The best-known mite, *Sarcoptes scabiei*, is the cause of scabies. It has a worldwide distribution and is associated with war,

Table 406–1 • MEDICALLY IMPORTANT ARTHROPODS

1. Arachnida (four pairs of legs)
   A. Acari—mites, ticks
   B. Araneida—spiders
   C. Scorpionida
2. Pentostomida—tongue worms
3. Chilopoda—centipedes
4. Diplopoda—millipedes
5. Crustacea
   A. Copepoda—cyclops, diptomus
   B. Decapoda—shrimp, lobster, crayfish, crab
6. Insecta (three pairs of legs)
   A. Anoplura—lice
   B. Coleoptera—beetles
   C. Diptera—flies (mosquitoes, black flies, midges, horse flies, deer flies, greenheads, tsetse flies, stable flies, sand flies, houseflies, bluebottle flies, cockroaches; myiasis)
   D. Hemiptera—bed bugs, cone-nose bugs
   E. Hymenoptera—ants, bees, wasps
   F. Lepidoptera—moths, caterpillars
   G. Siphonoptera—fleas

Table 406–2 • ARTHROPOD VECTORS OF INFECTION

Mites	Rickettsialpox, scrub typhus
Ticks	Colorado tick fever, viral encephalitides (e.g., Powassan encephalitis, louping-ill), viral hemorrhagic fevers (e.g., Crimean-Congo hemorrhagic fever, Omsk hemorrhagic fever), tick-borne rickettsioses (e.g., Rocky Mountain spotted fever, Mediterranean tick fever), ehrlichiosis, relapsing fever, Lyme disease, babesiosis, tularemia
Crustaceans	Dracunculosis, nematode and cestode infestation, paragonimiasis
Lice	Typhus, trench fever, relapsing fever
Mosquitoes	Malaria, filariasis, viral encephalitides (e.g., West Nile virus, Eastern equine encephalitis), dengue, yellow fever
Deer flies	Loiasis, tularemia
Black flies	Onchocerciasis
Tsetse flies	Trypanosomiasis
Sand flies	Leishmaniasis, bartonellosis, sand fly fever
Cone-nose bugs	Chagas' disease
Fleas	Plague, murine typhus, ?*Bartonella henselae*, *Rickettsia felis*, *Dipylidium caninum*, *Hymenolepis diminuta*

poverty, malnutrition, and sexual promiscuity. Although it causes dramatic skin manifestations, the scabies mite is not a vector for other infectious diseases.

Scabies is spread by skin-to-skin contact, such as shaking hands, sharing a bed, and having sexual relations. It is also spread by fomites, because the mite is able to survive for 2 to 3 days away from human skin and may infect clothing, towels, and bed linen. Activated by warmth, the mite burrows under the skin to the bottom of the stratum corneum in 2.5 minutes. The female moves at a rate of 2 to 3 mm/day and lays eggs as she tunnels. The male (seldom seen, because it is smaller than the female and dies a day or two after copulation) makes side chambers or branches in the female's burrows. Burrows contain mites, fecal pellets, and eggs. In 2 to 3 days, a larva is born, and it eventually molts through nymphal stages to an adult. This cycles takes 10 to 17 days. During the female's lifespan of 4 to 5 weeks, she lays a total of 40 to 50 eggs.

Clinical Manifestations

Typical lesions are small papules over the female mite, with wavy or linear burrows indicating her path. Typical locations of lesions are the interdigital webs, wrist folds, elbows, axillae, feet, thigh, nipples in women, genitalia, buttocks, and belt line. Crusted, excoriated, pruritic papules on the penis or buttock are almost pathognomonic for scabies. Infants may have involvement of head, neck, palms, and soles, areas typically spared in the adult, although geriatric and immunosuppressed adults (e.g., acquired immunodeficiency syndrome [AIDS] patients) may also have head and neck involvement.

These lesions cause severe itching, especially at night. A generalized rash may occur separate from the burrows. Other secondary local phenomena include urticaria, eczematous plaques, excoriation, and impetigo. Superimposed streptococcal infection occasionally results in post-streptococcal glomerulonephritis.

Many of the clinical phenomena result from sensitization. The incubation period for the initial infection is 2 weeks to 2 months, because time is required for sensitization. With subsequent infection, however, itching may begin in 1 to 4 days. During the prolonged incubation period patients may be entirely asymptomatic even though they can transmit the disease. A clue to the presence of scabies is the appearance of typical lesions and pruritus in multiple family members.

In elderly and immunosuppressed patients, the skin reaction may be muted, with pruritus but minimal inflammation. Outbreaks in nursing homes and early disease in AIDS patients may go undetected. Scabies may also be asymptomatic (i.e., *scabies incognito*) in patients receiving topical or systemic corticosteroids. Diagnosis is made by skin scrapings of burrows or papules. Burrows may be enhanced by applying washable ink or tetracycline (which fluoresces under Wood's light) to an area of suspected involvement. When the area is washed off, remaining ink or tetracycline may indicate the presence of burrows. For microscopic diagnosis, mineral oil is applied to a scalpel blade and allowed to flow onto a burrow or papule, which is then scraped gently (until pinpoint bleeding occurs). Then the oil and tissue mixture is microscopically examined for mites, eggs, or fecal pellets.

Scabies may take other forms. Nodular scabies forms red brown papules and nodules in the groin, axillae, and genitalia. Histopathologically, these lesions may mimic Hodgkin's disease because of multinucleated cells that resemble Reed-Sternberg cells. Bullous scabies is seen in infants and children and mimics bullous impetigo and pemphigus. In the adult, vesicular scabetic lesions mimic dermatitis herpetiformis, especially when in a sacral and gluteal location. The mites that cause scabies in animals (i.e., mange) are transmissible to humans after direct contact with horses, dogs, and other infested species. These mites are unable to propagate in humans, although they may cause papules or vesicles. *Norwegian or crusted scabies* is seen in patients with altered cell-mediated immunity or in the elderly. It occurs as local or generalized dermatitis with scaling and crusting and may mimic psoriasis. When the extremities are involved, there may be heavy involvement of the nails. Itching is often minimal. In this disease, thousands of mites are present, rather than the 3 to 50 organisms in normal scabies. It is extremely contagious. The diagnosis is relatively easy because there are so many mites, and scrapings should demonstrate their presence. This form of scabies may be complicated by bacteremia.

Treatment

The treatment of choice is 5% permethrin (Elimite). This cream is applied from the neck to the feet and washed off 8 to 14 hours later. One application is usually adequate. In infants, the scalp, temple, and forehead are included. Crotamiton (Eurax) is also effective. It is applied from the neck down and repeated in 24 hours. The patient bathes and washes off the crotamiton 48 hours later. In infants, it is applied to the entire body. Lindane (Kwell) had been the mainstay of treatment for years, but it is limited in application as a result of toxicity; excessive absorption of lindane may result in central nervous system (CNS) toxicity. It should not be used in individuals who have Norwegian scabies, premature infants, young children, pregnant or lactating mothers, or patients with a history of seizure disorder. In treating Norwegian scabies, the patient should take a bath first, apply permethrin, and repeat after 12 hours. It should again be repeated in a week, and an additional scraping should be done afterward in case additional therapy is necessary.

The literature supports the usefulness of ivermectin—alone or in combination with other topical preparations—in the treatment of scabies, although ivermectin is not approved for this indication in the United States, and safety in pregnancy and in pediatric patients weighing less than 15 kg is not established. Administered as a single oral dose of 200 μg/kg, ivermectin has been especially helpful in treating Norwegian scabies, because topical agents may have difficulty penetrating the crusts. Ivermectin has also been used in institutional outbreaks of scabies, providing single-dose convenience in the therapy or prophylaxis of large numbers of patients. Some authorities recommend a second dose in cases of severe infection or therapeutic failure.

Nodular scabies may be treated by intralesional steroids. Antiscabietic medication is not effective in nodular scabies because there are no mites at this stage of the disease. Fortunately, its natural history is resolution with time.

In all of the therapies discussed, it is important to follow the manufacturer's instructions. Patients should trim their nails and scrub under their nails with a toothbrush that is then discarded. Close contacts and family members who have had skin-to-skin contact should also be treated without waiting for lesions to appear. It is not necessary to clean furniture or carpets, but bed covers, pillow cases, sheets, outer clothes, and underwear, if used in the previous 48 hours, should be put in a hot water cycle or dry cleaned.

After one course of treatment, scabies is no longer contagious. In the hospital, patients should have contact isolation for 24 hours after the start of therapy. Clothes and linens should be placed in plastic laundry bags and handled only by personnel wearing gloves. Particular care should be taken for patients with Norwegian scabies because it is highly contagious, and these patients should be isolated.

After therapy for scabies, pruritus may persist for 1 to 2 weeks. Most of the time, this does not indicate treatment failure. Symptomatic therapy with antipruritics is indicated. Treatment of scabies is summarized in Table 406–3.

Table 406–3 • TREATMENT OF LICE AND SCABIES

	TREATMENT	ALTERNATIVES
Lice		
Head lice	1% Permethrin (Nix), clean clothing and headwear	5% permethrin (Elimite) Pyrethrins (RID) Malathion (ovide) Lindane (Kwell) Ivermectin*
Crab lice	1% Permethrin (Nix) Clean clothing and bedding	Pyrethrins (RID) Lindane
Body lice	Clean clothing	
Eyelashes	Petrolatum	Yellow oxide of mercury
Contacts	Treat if evidence of lice	
Scabies		
Typical	5% Permethrin (Elimite) Clean clothes and bedding	Crotamiton (Eurax) Lindane (Kwell) Ivermectin*†
Norwegian	5% Permethrin (Elimite) Clean clothes and bedding	Crotamiton (Eurax) Lindane (Kwell) Ivermectin*†
Nodular	Intralesional steroids	
Contacts	Treat for typical scabies	

*Ivermectin is not approved for this indication in the United States, and safety in pregnancy and in pediatric patients weighing less than 15 kg has not been established.

†Manufacturers' instructions should be followed carefully with these products.

OTHER MITES

Mites other than scabies generally do not cause permanent infestation. Most of them can bite and produce pruritic or allergic reactions. However, because their involvement with humans is transitory, treatment is symptomatic and involves elimination of the mite from a pet or the local environment. Topical therapy with corticosteroids and oral antihistamines are useful.

The follicle mite (*Demodex*) is an elongated, wormlike mite that occurs on the face, living in hair follicles or sebaceous glands. It rarely causes discomfort or needs therapy although some patients with rosacea or chronic blepharitis appear to respond to topical therapy. Dust mites do not bite, but exposure to them may result in rhinitis, asthma, and childhood eczema. Infestation with these organisms requires treating the house by cleaning carpets, mattresses, and blankets and by minimizing household humidity. Fowl mites infest humans in association with birds such as pigeons, and they are capable of biting and may cause a local dermatitis. Some of them are occasionally important vectors. For example, the fowl mite *Ornithonyssus sylviarum* can transmit the western equine encephalitis virus, and the viruses of St. Louis encephalitis and western equine encephalitis have been isolated from the chicken mite *Dermanyssus gallinae*.

A variety of food mites (e.g., *Pyemotes ventricosus*) are associated with cheeses, cereals, sugar, flour, grain, dried vegetable products, eggs, and other foodstuffs. These mites penetrate the superficial epithelium and cause a papulovesicular or urticarial eruption. Occasionally, exposure to them results in fever, diarrhea, and anorexia. More commonly, it causes a chronic dermatitis; it has been held responsible for "grocer's itch," "copra itch," "dried fruit dermatitis," and "vanillism" (in those who work with vanilla pods). When inhaled, some of the food mites cause pulmonary infiltrates and peripheral eosinophilia, called *acariasis*.

The best known of the nonscabies mites is the harvest mite, chigger, or "red bug." These are *Trombicula* species and are the bane of picnickers and campers. They are bright orange to red and attach where clothing fits snugly, especially at the ankles, groin, and waist. They do not burrow but feed at a sweat pore or the base of a hair follicle for several days. It is the larva stage, not the adult, that attacks humans. Chigger larvae are tiny, about 0.2 mm long, in contrast to the 1-mm adults. The initial reaction to their bite is itching within 3 to 6 hours. Some patients experience a papular, urticarial, or vesicular rash, occasionally with fever and adenopathy. Treatment is a warm soapy bath or shower plus antipruritic lotions; topical corticosteroids or anesthetic ointments are also used. These mites are the vector for *Rickettsia tsutsugamushi* (scrub typhus) in Central and Eastern Asia.

An important mite associated with rats is *Ornithonyssus bacoti*, a vector of murine or endemic typhus (*Rickettsia typhi*). Another medically important vector is *Liponyssoides sanguineus*, the mouse mite, which transmits rickettsialpox (*Rickettsia akari*) to humans. This mite is capable of biting and is seen on rats and other rodents as well as mice. Cheyletiellid mites are parasites of dogs, cats, rabbits, and other small mammals and are the cause of "walking dandruff" in these animals. They do not burrow, but live on the keratin layer of the epidermis, producing a mange-like dermatitis in the animal. Humans, often pet owners, experience transient pruritus and a rash, typically papulovesicles on the flexor side of the arms, breasts, or abdomen. Cure in humans follows treatment of the pet.

The straw itch mite is also capable of biting; it is acquired by handling grain or sleeping on straw mattresses. The clover mite, associated with ivy, grass, clover, and fruit trees, may infest humans but does not bite.

TICKS

Like mites, ticks have a single, disc-shaped body region with a fused cephalothorax and abdomen. They are larger than mites, about the size of a pea. However, after feeding, engorged ticks may appear much larger. Conversely, the larvae of some species may be extremely small, resembling a sesame seed. Ticks are divided into soft and hard varieties based on a dorsal plate, or scutum. Most infections transmitted to humans are from hard ticks.

Ticks cause disease in a variety of ways. They transmit microorganisms that cause infection; they cause toxic and hypersensitivity reactions to their salivary secretions; and they directly inject toxin into a human host.

Most tick bites occur in the spring and summer. The bites are usually not painful or even symptomatic. Local swelling and erythema may result, and occasionally blistering or ecchymosis follows, sometimes followed by necrosis and ulceration. In some cases, a chronic granulomatous reaction may develop and persist for years.

Ticks do not fly, jump, or swim. They quest for host animals by waiting on low-lying vegetation and waving their legs or moving around on the plant, responding to nearby vibrations or carbon dioxide. After they contact their host, they move around to find a suitable location, often for 1 to 2 hours, before attaching to feed.

Ticks need time to transmit disease. For example, to transmit Rocky Mountain spotted fever, the tick has to feed for at least 8 to 14 hours before rickettsiae are released from salivary glands. For Lyme disease, the tick needs at least 24 hours of feeding and possibly 72 hours to transmit disease efficiently. A tick removed while it is still wandering in search of a location for feeding or before it has had an adequate chance to feed is not likely to have spread disease to its human host.

Tick paralysis is not an infection but intoxication. Worldwide, 50 species of ticks cause paralysis in humans or animals. In North America, there are six, including the species that also transmit Lyme disease, tularemia, Rocky Mountain spotted fever, ehrlichiosis, Colorado tick fever, and babesiosis; some ticks harbor more than one infectious agent, so that it is possible to acquire multiple infections or both infection and tick paralysis simultaneously. The paralysis begins 5 to 7 days after attachment of the tick. It occurs most frequently in small girls. The child becomes irritable and lethargic, and leg weakness, which may progress to complete paralysis, develops. The weakness can ascend and cause bulbar paralysis. Cranial nerve involvement includes the face and extraocular muscles. Eventually, respiratory paralysis supervenes, and death may occur. The patient remains afebrile. Characteristic features of this disease are its symmetry, the flaccid nature of the paralysis, normal pupils, intact sensory examination findings, clear sensorium, preservation of sphincter tone, lack of fever, and normal cerebrospinal fluid. Unusual presentations can be extremely misleading and have included unilateral Bell's palsy, ataxia, chorea, and localized weakness of one arm or leg. These unilateral localized presentations are attributed to the nearby location of the tick. Facial weakness has resulted from a paralytic tick in the ipsilateral ear. The differential diagnosis for tick paralysis is extensive, and tick paralysis has been misdiagnosed as Guillain-Barré syndrome, botulism, poliomyelitis, spinal cord compression, myasthenia gravis, and transverse myelitis. It is important to consider tick paralysis in a susceptible host; without removal the process may be fatal, but after the tick is removed, most patients improve within a few hours.

Tick removal has acquired an elaborate folklore. The safest and most efficient method is to grab the tick at the skin surface with tweezers or blunt forceps. The tick is then pulled steadily and gently out of the skin. None of the mouthparts should be left in the skin. The tick itself should be incinerated and the site disinfected. The best ways to prevent tick attachment are to keep pant legs tucked in boots or socks and to use an effective repellent.

SPIDERS

Spider bites cause secondary infection, allergic reactions, and envenomation. Approximately 50 species bite humans, but a limited number cause severe disease in the United States: the widow (*Latrodectus*), the brown recluse (*Loxosceles*), the hobo spider (*Tegenaria*), the wolf spider (*Lycosa*), the fishing spider (*Dolomedes*), the green lynx spider (*Peucetia*), the jumping spider (*Phidippus*), and the yellow sac spider (*Cheiracanthium*), a greenish gray garden dweller that is the most common domestic spider in many areas of the United States. All of these spiders except the widow may cause necrotic arachnidism. Bites from other spiders may be painful but are not dangerous. It is important for a bite victim to save the spider for identification.

The brown recluse, or *Loxosceles*, is the best known cause of necrotic arachnidism in the United States. Those spiders have a 2- to 4-cm leg span. There is a violin-shaped marking from the eyes to the abdomen, with the base pointing forward. The brown recluse is not aggressive but hides in clothing and in the bathroom, attic, and closets. It bites only when threatened. Bites are painless until 3 to 8 hours afterward; then the lesion ranges from a local urticarial reaction to full-thickness skin necrosis. Redness, swelling, and tenderness develop; slough, ulceration, and scabbing may follow. Some lesions show central blistering with ecchymosis surrounded by blanched skin, which in turn is surrounded by erythema. This is called the *red, white, and blue sign*. The lesion tends to extend downward gravitationally, "to flow downhill." Systemic reactions include fever, arthralgias, maculopapular rash, nausea, and vomiting. Treatment includes antibiotics, which help prevent abscess formation and secondary infection; rest; elevation; and ice packs. Some advocate use of dapsone for its leukocyte-inhibiting qualities. The use of antivenin is controversial. Additional modalities reported anecdotally include hyperbaric oxygen, corticosteroids, aspirin, heparin, nitroglycerin, and even stun guns. If used at all, surgical excision should be postponed until later in the course, when the venom is less likely to impair wound healing. Eventually, many patients require extensive plastic surgical repair. The differential diagnosis for necrotic arachnidism includes arthropod stings and bites, pyogenic infection, pyoderma gangrenosum, Sweet's Syndrome, vasculitis, and cutaneous anthrax.

The widow spider, also known as the hourglass, shoe-button, or po-ko-moo spider, does not cause necrotic arachnidism but injects a neurotoxin (α-latrotoxin) into its victims. This toxin results in acetylcholine depletion at neuromuscular junctions. The bite causes pain at the bite site, which then spreads to local and regional muscle groups as a dull aching and sometimes numbness. This is followed by sweating, nausea, tremor, myalgias, muscle spasm, boardlike abdomen, chest pain, paralysis, bradycardia, seizures, and rarely, death. Fortunately, less than 1% of bites are fatal.

The female spider (males do not bite humans) has a leg span of 3 to 4 cm. There is a red-orange hourglass on the ventral side of the abdomen; however, some species have red markings on the dorsal side, and in some, the hourglass is incomplete, appearing more like hatch marks. The wound should be cleaned and ice packs applied. Systemic therapy is undertaken with intravenous calcium gluconate, muscle relaxants, and tetanus toxoid. Antivenin is given if the envenomation is severe.

SCORPIONS

In the United States, the only dangerous species of scorpions is *Centruroides exilicauda*, found in Arizona and New Mexico. Otherwise, scorpion bites in the United States are not serious unless patients have a severe allergic reaction to them.

Scorpions inject a neurotoxic venom when they sting. The sting produces local swelling, pain, and numbness. Systemic signs may be neurologic (e.g., coma, tremor, paralysis of respiratory muscles, seizures), cardiac (e.g., hypertension, arrhythmias, pulmonary edema), and pancreatic. Scorpion bite is a common cause of pancreatitis in Brazil. Death may ensue within hours.

Therapy for bites includes ice packs and antihistamines. Some advocate applying a tourniquet and removing the venom from the wound by suction. Antivenin use is controversial. It has been suggested that patients receive nonopiate analgesics, because opiates may have a synergistic effect with the venom of some scorpions.

TONGUE WORM (PENTASTOMIASIS)

Pentastomiasis is human infection by two genera of Pentastomids, *Armillifer* and *Linguatula*. These wormlike arthropods are found principally in Asia and Africa and reside in the respiratory tract of birds, reptiles, dogs, and other mammals. Animals such as sheep or goats may also serve as intermediate hosts to the parasite, and when humans eat uncooked viscera or lymph nodes of these animals, gastric juices liberate the nymphs, which are encapsulated in the viscera, and they ascend the esophagus and anchor themselves in the upper respiratory tract. This produces severe inflammation with violent coughing and occasionally causes asphyxiation. This syndrome is known as *halzoun* or *marrara syndrome*, referring to suffocation. Other symptoms include hemoptysis, sneezing, lacrimation, aural pruritus, coryza, facial edema, and vomiting.

Visceral infection is acquired by ingesting eggs in water contaminated with the sputum of animals harboring the pentastome in their upper respiratory tract. These eggs then hatch and develop into larvae that spread hematogenously through the body. This infection is usually asymptomatic and is discovered incidentally by the pathologist or radiologist as comma-shaped pleural or peritoneal calcifications. However, fatal infections do occur rarely.

CENTIPEDES AND MILLIPEDES

Chilopods (i.e., centipedes) and diplopods (i.e., millipedes) are elongated, multisegmented arthropods. The centipede, or "hundred legger," has one pair of legs per segment and is a carnivore. Its bite produces a painful wound, and the larger species seen in the tropics and subtropics are also capable of secreting venom through their claws while holding their victim. The site of this envenomation may become ulcerated and necrotic, and patients may experience nausea, vomiting, and headache. Secondary infection is common. The wounds should be washed and cool compresses applied; antibiotics should be given for secondary infection, and some patients have required administration of corticosteroids and local injection of anesthetic for the extreme pain.

The millipede, or "thousand legger," has two pairs of legs per body segment. This arthropod is a vegetarian and does not bite or sting. However, some tropical species emit a toxic fluid from glands on each segment when they are threatened. This fluid may cause local skin discoloration and burning, with the formation of blisters. If the eyes are contaminated, conjunctivitis or keratitis results, rarely causing blindness. Some species are able to squirt these secretions as far as 80 cm. Treatment includes washing the involved area of skin, and some advocate the application of solvents such as ether or alcohol to help remove the toxic fluid. If the eyes are involved, they should be irrigated copiously with water.

CRUSTACEANS

The crustaceans may function as intermediate hosts of parasites that infect humans. Copepods are tiny aquatic arthropods that may be intermediate hosts of the guinea worm *Dracunculus medinensis*, the nematode *Gnathostoma spinigerum*, and the cestodes *Spirometra mansonoides* and *Diphyllobothrium latum*. The decapods include shrimp, lobster, crab, prawn, and crayfish. Land crabs and freshwater prawns may be host to the rat lungworm *Angiostrongylus* species; the lung fluke *Paragonimus westermani* is an occasional parasite of freshwater crabs and crayfish.

LICE

Lice are small (2 to 4 mm), dorsoventrally flattened, wingless insects that have mouthparts modified for piercing and sucking blood. They are parasites exclusively of humans and are seen in three varieties: *Pediculus humanus* var *capitis* (i.e., head louse), *Pediculus humanus* var *humanus* (i.e., body louse), and *Phthirus pubis* (i.e., crab louse).

HEAD LICE

The head louse ("motorized dandruff") is usually transmitted by direct contact but can be spread by fomites such as combs, hats, brushes, headgear, earphones, bedding, upholstered furniture, and rugs. It is seen under circumstances of crowding and poor hygiene and is particularly common among schoolchildren, the elderly, and the senile. The organisms live for approximately 1 month on the scalp but are able to live only a few days (as long as a week) if removed from the warmth and blood meals available on the scalp.

Infestation of scalp hairs can produce severe itching (although many cases are asymptomatic) and occasionally secondary pyogenic infection and cervical lymphadenopathy. Head lice favor hair in the back of the head. Lice may be visible crawling on hair shafts, and they may move quite rapidly, approximately 23 cm/minute. However, they are few in number (<10), and it is much easier to identify the nits, the gray-white, glistening, oval eggs, 0.6 to 0.8 mm in diameter, that the lice attach to the base of scalp hairs. These nits are cemented securely to the hair shafts and are difficult to remove. They fluoresce under ultraviolet light (e.g., Wood's light), facilitating diagnosis, especially when large numbers of patients are screened.

 Treatment

Patients should be treated with 1% permethrin (Nix), which has some ovicidal activity. It is available over the counter. The patient should shampoo, rinse, and dry the hair and then apply it to the hair and scalp. After 10 minutes, it is rinsed off. Repetition in 1 week is necessary only if lice are again seen. As a result of growing resistance, there may be treatment failures with 1% permethrin, in which case 5% permethrin (Elimite) may be used. Other alternatives include pyrethrins with piperonyl butoxide (RID), Lindane (Kwell), (see precautions for Lindane under Treatment for Scabies) Malathion (Ovide) [contraindicated in neonates & infants], or a single oral dose of ivermectin (200 μg/kg). Ivermectin is not approved for this indication in the United States, and safety in pregnancy and in pediatric patients weighing less than 15 kg has not been established. Because ivermectin has no ovicidal activity, a second dose may be necessary to kill nymphs that hatch subsequently from nits. The manufacturers' instructions should be followed carefully with all of these products. When the patient is treated, all infested family members should be treated simultaneously. Combing the nits reduces the number of viable ova and decreases the chance of relapse and treatment failure. Clothing that had contact with the patient's head should be washed and dried in a dryer or dry cleaned.

BODY LICE

Body lice ("cooties") look like head lice but are slightly larger and have a different clinical behavior. Body lice are seen in cold climates (because of heavy clothing) and under conditions of crowding and poor sanitation. They are most common in jails and crowded tenements and among military personnel. Unlike head lice, body lice are uncommon among affluent members of our society.

Lice and eggs are found in the seams of clothing, and very few lice are seen on the body of patients. The lice favor clothing fibers, especially wool, and live in the clothing, visiting the body only to feed. Clinically, the major manifestation is itching. Small red spots are produced, especially on the back and under the arm. Ultimately, excoriations, urticaria, pigmentary changes, and secondary infection may occur. "Vagabonds' disease" refers to the hyperpigmentation and thickening of the skin seen in chronic, untreated infestation. Body lice are also a vector for serious diseases of humanity, including typhus (*Rickettsia prowazekii*), trench fever (*Bartonella quintana*), and relapsing fever (*Borrelia recurrentis*).

 Treatment

Treatment of body lice requires only improved hygiene and cleaned clothing in mild cases. Heat kills both ova and lice in clothing. In severe cases and in epidemics, topical pediculicidal agents may be used.

CRAB LICE

Crab lice are transmitted predominantly by sexual contact, clothes, or infected hairs. During coitus, adult lice and nits are transmitted on broken hairs. Less frequently, they are transmitted by toilet seats or bedding. Although typically found on pubic hair, crab lice occasionally infect other short hairs of the body, including eyebrows, eyelashes, the edge of the scalp, moustache, and axilla.

Symptoms may not begin for 30 days after infection. On close inspection, nits are visible, and the louse may be seen clinging to one or two hairs. Also evident in these infestations are dried serous fluid, blood, and louse feces. The combination of louse saliva and blood produces a blue-gray macule known as *macula caerulea*. The crab louse dies after 24 to 48 hours off the host.

Treatment

Treatment is similar to that for pediculosis capitis. It is important to clean bedding and clothing, which should be washed in hot water. Treatment failure often results from not treating other involved areas of the body. Infestation of the eyelid can be treated with petrolatum occlusions, yellow oxide of mercury ointment, or mechanical removal of nits. Sexual partners and intimate contacts should be treated when they have evidence of lice. One third of patients with pubic lice have other sexually transmitted diseases, including human immunodeficiency virus (HIV) infection, and should be screened for them. Children with pubic lice infestation in facial hair or eyes should be evaluated for the possibility of sexual abuse.

Symptomatic treatment of pruritus in all types of lice infestation consists of antihistamines, and in some cases, topical corticosteroids may be applied to affected areas for additional symptomatic relief. Treatment of lice infestation is summarized in Table 406–3.

BEETLES

Of the 250,000 species of beetles, some are injurious to humans. The most common beetle injury is not from a bite or sting but from the formation of blisters. The best known blister beetle is *Lytta vesicatoria*, the Spanish fly. This beetle fills its breathing tube with air and closes its breathing pores to elevate body pressure. This forces the toxin cantharidin out through its leg joints. On human skin, cantharidin forms blisters within hours. Some of the blistering may evolve to ulceration and secondary infection. Clues to this cause of blisters are the presence of multiple blisters in the same stage of development and the lack of an accompanying rash. Sometimes, the blisters form a line, reflecting the path of the beetle as it crossed the skin. When ingested, cantharidin causes nausea and abdominal pain. Cantharidin has been prepared commercially and used as a diuretic, aphrodisiac, and rubefacient. Other beetles, such as the carpet beetle, cause papulovesicular dermatitis.

Treatment of these beetle-related skin injuries is soap and water and wet compresses. Occasionally, topical or systemic corticosteroids are used.

FLIES

The order Diptera contains the true flies, which transmit more disease than any other arthropod order. Prominent among the flies is the mosquito, a slender delicate insect that is a vector for disease throughout the world. *Anopheles* mosquitoes transmit malaria and filariasis; *Aedes* mosquitoes transmit viral encephalitis, dengue, yellow fever, and filariasis; and *Culex* mosquitoes transmit filariasis and viral encephalitis, including the West Nile virus, established in the United States in 1999. In addition to functioning as vectors, mosquito bites are irritating. The female mosquito lacerates human skin with her jaws and inserts a blood tube. Her salivary secretions contain an anticoagulant and cause local inflammation, pruritus, and urticaria. Mosquitoes prefer blacks to whites, young to old, warmth, strong scents, bright colors, and carbon dioxide, which is an effective attractant when humans and animals are grouped. Mosquito bites may be prevented by netting, protective clothing, and repellents.

Black flies (i.e., buffalo gnats) are bloodsucking flies that are small (2 to 3 mm) and humpbacked. This fly injects an anesthetic compound into the wound so that the initial bite is not painful. Subsequently, the bitten area becomes pruritic, red, and swollen. Black flies transmit onchocerciasis in the tropics. Biting midges (i.e., punkies, gnats, no seeums, flying teeth) are tiny (1 to 1.5 mm). They cause immediate pain and erythema and eventually cause papulovesicles, with a nodular reaction that may last for months. These flies are small enough to pass through screens. Tabanid flies are large and colorful and include the horse flies, deer flies, and greenheads. They cause painful bites that often bleed because of the relatively large size of the fly and its bladelike mouthparts. Only the Chrysops (i.e., deer fly) is a vector of human disease in this group; it transmits loiasis in Africa and tularemia in the United States.

The Muscidae include *Glossina* species (e.g., tsetse flies), the vector of trypanosomiasis, and *Stomoxys* species (e.g., stable flies, storm flies, stinging flies, dog flies). The *Stomoxys* fly is slightly larger than the common housefly, and its resemblance has misled some patients into thinking they were bitten by a housefly (which does not bite). The Phlebotomid sand flies cause a painful bite and also transmit leishmania, *Bartonella bacilliformis*, and sandfly fever, a nonfatal viral disease. The bites of all of these flies are treated symptomatically by cleaning with soap and water, treating secondary infection with antibiotics, and applying soothing topical ointments or corticosteroids. Nonbiting flies such as houseflies, flesh flies, and blowflies (i.e., bluebottle flies) can transmit disease, particularly that caused by gastrointestinal pathogens, by acting as mechanical vectors. They are also occasional causes of myiasis. Eye gnats do not bite but may transmit bacterial conjunctivitis and yaws.

Other than biting and acting as vectors of disease, flies may affect humans by causing *myiasis*, infestation of the skin or a body orifice with fly larvae. A well-known example is the botfly found in the American tropics, which glues its eggs to a bloodsucking fly like the mosquito; when the mosquito bites humans, the larvae leave the mosquito, hatch, and penetrate the skin of their new host. A similar form of myiasis is caused by the tumbu or mango fly in Africa, which lays its eggs on the ground or on soiled clothing. On direct contact with humans, the larvae penetrate the skin. The screwworm lays its eggs at the edge of wounds and may infect nose, eyes, ears, and other body orifices. This larva often travels through tissues. Sarcophagid flies deposit their living larvae on the hosts. Some larvae migrate in tortuous channels and produce a type of larva migrans (i.e., hypoderma). Other flies that feed on decaying tissue occasionally cause myiasis in humans; the larvae enter living tissue after feeding on necrotic wounds. Although usually confined to the skin or superficial wounds, myiasis can involve the genitourinary tract and the intestine; the larvae are usually passed spontaneously, although urethral involvement sometimes requires cystoscopy. Areas of cutaneous myiasis are frequently misdiagnosed as pyogenic infection, and this diagnosis should be kept in mind for a "boil" that is refractory to medical therapy if a patient has visited an endemic area. Treatment for the cutaneous form requires mechanical removal with tweezers or by excision. This may be facilitated by covering the embedded larvae with petrolatum or strips of raw bacon fat, both of which encourage them to move upward, where they are grasped more easily.

Cockroaches are important pests. They are able to consume any human or animal food, dead plant or animal material, leather, glue, fabrics, grease, hair, wallpaper, and bookbindings. They may function as mechanical vectors of pathogens and are sometimes intermediate hosts of helminths. Cockroaches can bite, but these bites are not particularly painful. Their glandular secretions can cause asthma when ingested, and cockroaches may be an important cause of asthma in children, in which group sensitization to cockroach allergens is commonly demonstrable.

HEMIPTERA: BUGS

Hemiptera are the true bugs, comprising bed bugs, cone-nose bugs, and wheel bugs. Bed bugs are 5-mm-long, flat, oval insects that resemble large ticks or small cockroaches. The most common species in temperate climates is *Cimex*. Bed bugs are not an important vector of disease, but their bites cause inflammation and occasionally produce hemorrhagic bullae. They are nocturnal feeders, have a distinct odor, and are capable of hiding successfully in the seams of mattresses, in couches, behind loose wallpaper, and under baseboards.

The cone-nose bugs are members of the Reduviid family. They are 1 to 3 cm long and can fly. The best known of these are the assassin bug (so named because it kills other insects) and the "kissing" bug (because it often bites around the lips and face). The kissing bug may transmit Chagas' disease, caused by *Trypanosoma cruzi*. Although some species of Reduviid bugs produce painful bites that occasionally ulcerate and resemble necrotic arachnidism, the vectors of Chagas' disease produce painless bites. The bug defecates after eating, and it is the human host who scratches the trypanosomes into the skin. Although some species of cone-nose bugs are found throughout the United States, those that transmit Chagas' disease are found in Mexico, Central and South America, and only rarely in the U.S. Southwest.

The bites of all these bugs are treated symptomatically, with topical antipruritic ointments and corticosteroids when needed, antihistamines for allergic reactions, and antibiotics for secondary infections.

HYMENOPTERA

The Hymenoptera include bees, wasps, and ants. These insects have an ovipositor, designed to deposit eggs; however, the ovipositor has been modified to a stinging apparatus that injects venom, causing severe local inflammation and sometimes producing hypersensitivity. The familiar honeybee is yellow and black striped and has an ovipositor that is barbed; after the honeybee stings, the stinger and venom sacs are left in its victim, and the bee dies. During stinging, the honeybee releases pheromones that attract other bees to attack. "Killer bees" are Africanized honeybees imported to South America to improve honey production. However, multiple swarms escaped from experimental colonies, and they have spread northward to Central America and the southern United States. The sting of the killer bee is not more toxic or allergenic than that of the domesticated honeybee, but the killer bee is more aggressive; it attacks with less provocation and exhibits massive stinging behavior in defense of the colony. Up to 50% of the bees in a killer bee colony are guard bees that respond to perceived threats. The bumble bee is not as aggressive as the honeybee but otherwise exhibits similar behavior.

Wasps include yellowjackets, hornets, and paper wasps. The yellowjackets are usually 1.5 to 2 cm long and are attracted to bright colors, perfumes, and human foods, especially those with high sugar content. They have familiar black bands and produce a large, honeycombed nest with a paper envelope. Hornets are larger than yellowjackets, 2.5 to 3.5 cm, and are brown, orange, and red. Paper wasps are the same size as yellowjackets but may be black, brown, red, or yellow. Their nest is a single open comb of gray paper, usually attached to a building or tree.

Of the 15 species of ants capable of stinging humans, 8 are found in the United States. The imported fire ants are the most troublesome; found in the southeastern states, they bite and sting. They attach to the skin with their jaws and then pivot around their head, stinging multiple times. The harvester ant, found in the western and southeastern states, stings its victim, and like that of the honeybee, its stinger may be torn off after envenomation. Velvet ants (i.e., wooly ants, cow killers, or mutilid wasps) look like ants but are wingless female wasps. They are red, orange, or yellow and achieve a size of 0.75 to 2.5 cm. Found in the western and southeastern states, they are capable of a painful sting.

The Hymenoptera produce local and systemic reactions. The local reaction is an area of inflammation that involves the immediate area of the sting, appears within 2 to 3 minutes, and abates within hours. Fire ant stings often develop into pustules, and lymphangitis may complicate harvester ant bites. Patients who have extensive local reactions have a slightly increased risk for future anaphylaxis. Local reactions themselves are not life-threatening except for instances of multiple stings (50 to 100 or more), which may be fatal as a result of toxicity rather than hypersensitivity. The effects of multiple stings suggest excessive histamine release; antihistamines may be appropriate in this setting. Otherwise, local reactions are treated with ice, elevation, local analgesics, corticosteroid creams, and lotions such as calamine. If a stinging apparatus remains in the skin, it should be removed. Systemic anaphylactic reactions are treated with epinephrine, corticosteroids, and antihistamines (Chapter 265). Patients with severe Hymenoptera allergies should consider venom immunotherapy.

LEPIDOPTERA

Lepidoptera insects cause dermatologic and systemic disease through the hairs of caterpillars and moths. The caterpillars of several moth and butterfly families secrete venom from a gland at the base of specialized hairs or from cells lining the lower part of sharp spines. These hairs and spines can be irritating and allergenic when touched. An immediate burning sensation develops, followed by swelling, numbness, urticaria, extreme pain referred to regional lymph nodes, and rarely, headache, nausea, paralysis, and seizures. In the United States, the most bothersome varieties are the caterpillars of the io, browntail, saddleback, and gypsy moths, and the puss caterpillar. The puss caterpillar is a particular problem in the southern United States; it does not look like a caterpillar, but rather like a teardrop-shaped tuft of yellow cotton. Some caterpillars, such as the gypsy moth larvae, do not sting, but contact with their hair causes dermatitis, which has occurred in outbreak form in the northeastern United States. Some moths have scales or hairs that become airborne and cause urticaria, skin irritation, upper respiratory symptoms, and conjunctivitis. When occurring in great numbers, such airborne spread has caused epidemics on land or onboard ship. Treatment of caterpillar stings includes repeated stripping of the sting site with cellophane or adhesive tape to remove spines, in addition to local application of ice, antihistamines, calamine lotion, and corticosteroids; zinc oxide and lime water have been helpful as well. Some advocate use of meperidol, codeine, or intravenous calcium gluconate for pain in view of the poor analgesic effect of aspirin for these lesions. Systemic symptoms are treated with epinephrine, antihistamines, and corticosteroids.

FLEAS

Fleas are small, brown, wingless insects that are flattened laterally. Human and animal (e.g., cat, dog, bird, rat) species may bite humans. Animal fleas can live for months without a host. If humans are available and their natural host is not accessible, they will bite. Their ability to jump several inches increases humans' vulnerability. Flea bites produce a punctate, hemorrhagic area initially, followed by a maculopapular, pruritic dermatitis; typically the papules are linear or clustered. The dermatitis may be more severe in previously sensitized patients. Most fleas feed on humans only transiently, but the chigoe flea (i.e., jigger, nigua, chica, pico, pique, or suthi), *Tunga penetrans*, burrows into the dermis, lays her eggs, and remains embedded in the skin. The chigoe is found in tropical America, Africa, the Near East, and India; lesions are most commonly seen between the toes and under the toenails. If it is found within the first 48 hours, a sterile needle can remove the flea; later, surgical removal is usually necessary.

The term *sand flea* is used loosely by the lay public to indicate chigoes, cat fleas, dog fleas, human fleas, and tiny crustaceans found in seaweed along coastal beaches.

Other than the minor discomfort of bites or the focal persistence of the chigoe, fleas are vectors. The rat flea *Xenopsylla cheopis* is the most efficient vector of plague (*Yersinia pestis*) and murine typhus (*Rickettsia typhi*). In the southwestern United States, a natural reservoir of plague exists among wild rodents, especially ground squirrels; domestic pets may then carry these infected fleas to their owner's home. Recent observations associate *Bartonella henselae*, which causes cat scratch disease, bacillary angiomatosis, and peliosis hepatis, with exposure to flea-infested cats. A newly described rickettsial agent, *Rickettsia felis,* is maintained in cat fleas by transovarian passage and uses the opossum as a reservoir host. It has caused a murine typhus—like illness in humans. Fleas may also act as mechanical vectors for numerous bacterial and viral infections by contaminated wind-borne feces that reach humans' mucous membranes. Several flea species act as intermediate hosts of the dog tapeworm *Dipylidium caninum* and the rat tapeworm *Hymenolepis diminuta*, infecting humans when fleas are accidentally ingested.

DELUSORY PARASITOSIS

The psychiatric disorder delusory parasitosis can torture both patient and physician. Typically, patients are elderly, white women who have seen many physicians and then present the examining physician with a container or small bag containing the suspected "bugs." Often, they claim that these bugs are in their vagina or rectum and emerge at night. Some patients have skin lesions from excoriation. After excluding true parasitosis and somatic disease, physicians should refer patients for psychiatric evaluation. Some patients have responded to therapy with psychoactive agents such as pimozide or haloperidol.

LEECHES

Leeches are members of the phylum Annelida, class Hirudinea. They are segmented worms found in fresh water and salt water and on land. Aquatic leeches are found in temperate and tropical climates. They attach to their swimming or wading hosts to acquire a blood meal. The bite of saltwater leeches is painful, whereas the attachment of the freshwater variety may be asymptomatic. Smaller leeches may invade the upper respiratory or gastrointestinal tract, eye, nose, vagina, urethra, and anus.

Bites of leeches often bleed freely after the leech has stopped feeding, because the leech injects hirudin, an anticoagulant that inhibits thrombin. Other allergens the leech introduces may elicit anaphylaxis or a local hypersensitivity response, including bullae, urticaria, or necrotic ulceration.

In the Far East, land leeches attach themselves to travelers in tropical forests, often crawling between boot and sock and feeding by penetrating the material of the sock. Treatment is removal, often facilitated by local anesthetic, salt solutions, alcohol, vinegar, or a lighted match. No mouthparts should be left behind. The wound is then cleaned and disinfected; residual bleeding can be stemmed by a styptic pencil. Leeches have been used in plastic surgery to reduce vascular congestion in tissue flaps. They have also been applied to sites of cutaneous ischemia in patients with purpura fulminans. Medicinal leech therapy has been associated with infection (usually due to *Aeromonas*) in as many as 20% of patients, although infection is not common after leech bites in the wild.

Other marine annelids related to the leech can bite or envenomate. The bloodworm, used as fish bait in North America, causes a painful bite that takes days to resolve. The bristle worm, found in Asia and the Gulf of Mexico and California, has chitinous spines filled with venom. A sting from one of these spines causes pain, rash, swelling, and occasionally skin necrosis. It is important to remove the spines in addition to applying topical soothing creams and ice.

SUGGESTED READINGS

Clark NM, Femino JE, Chenoweth CE: *Aeromonas* infection after medicinal leech therapy: Case reports and review of the literature. Infect Dis Clin Pract 2001;10:211–218. *A thorough review of infectious complications of leeches, both iatrogenic and naturally acquired.*

Goddard J: Infectious Diseases and Arthropods. Totowa, NJ, Humana Press, 2000. *A thorough compendium of the biologic characteristics, classification, and behavior of medically important arthropods.*

Jones KN, English JC: Review of common therapeutic options in the United States for the treatment of pediculosis capitis. Clin Infect Dis 2003;36:1355–1361. *This is a thorough literature review of the various treatment modalities currently available for pediculosis capitis.*

Parola P, Roault D: Ticks and tickborne bacterial diseases in humans: An emerging infectious threat. Clin Infect Dis 2001;32:897–928. *A thorough review of the biology of ticks and the pathogenesis of tick-borne bacterial diseases.*

Sams HH, Dunnick CA, Smith ML, King LE: Necrotic arachnidism. J Am Acad Dermatol 2001;44:561–573. *A practical and current review of clinical presentation and management of necrotic arachnidism.*

407 VENOMOUS SNAKE BITES

Ralph Corey
James O. Armitage

Although most of the 3500 species of snakes are harmless, there remain more than 200 that have caused fatal envenomation in humans. Throughout the world, an estimated 20,000 to 50,000 deaths occur annually, and hundreds of thousands suffer serious morbidity.

Epidemiology

The incidence of venomous snake bites varies enormously throughout the world. Snake-free areas consist primarily of islands, and Europe continues to be the continent with the lowest venomous snake bite incidence. In the United States, more than 8000 bites occur each year. Fortunately, the number of fatalities, primarily caused by rattlesnakes, is below 20 per year.

Unprovoked attacks by venomous snakes are extremely unusual, because humans are not seen as prey. Most bites occur on extremities when snakes are threatened by being trod on, by someone reaching where they did not look, or by intentional handling of poisonous snakes. Prevention of snake bite is much better than therapy.

Etiology

Poisonous snakes belong to one of five families: Viperidae with its two subfamilies—Viperinae or Old World vipers and Crotalinae or pit vipers, including rattlesnakes, copperheads, and water moccasins; Elapidae, including cobras, mambas and coral snakes; Hydrophidae (e.g., sea snakes); Atractaspididae (e.g., asps); and Colubridae, including boomslangs. Although all five categories are important, the two families responsible for more than 90% of venomous bites are Viperidae and Elapidae. In North America pit vipers, named for the heat-sensitive organ between the eyes and nostrils that is used for hunting warm-blooded prey, have tubular retractable fangs and account for most bites. The coral snake, a member of the Elapidae, which have fixed front fangs, is the only other endemic venomous snake in the United States.

Pathogenesis

Snake venoms are complex and are highly variable poisons created to immobilize and digest prey. As a result of their heterogenous composition, exact classification as neurotoxic, cardiotoxic, hemotoxic, or myotoxic is impossible.

Local swelling and bruising after a bite is caused by increased vascular permeability as a result of endothelial cell damage and is mediated by hydrolases, proteases, phospholipase A_2, polypeptide toxins, metalloproteinases and the release of endogenous autocoids such as bradykinin and histamine. Snakes from the Viperidae and Elapidae families are primarily responsible for these effects.

Hemostatic abnormalities are frequent and varied. Procoagulants activate factors V, IX, X; protein C (Russell's viper); and prothrombin (vipers) and cleave fibrinopeptide A from fibrinogen. Fibrinolytic activators result in a disseminated intravascular coagulation (DIC)–like picture without elevation of D-dimer (rattlesnakes). Snake venom hemorrhagins damage endothelium and increase the potential for serious bleeding, especially after viper bites. Intravascular hemolysis can occur after bites by *Bothrops* (e.g., fer-de-lance) and other species resulting in severe anemia and acute renal failure.

Paralysis is the primary function of many types of venom of the Elapidae, Viperidae, and Hydrophidae families. Presynaptic neurotoxins (i.e., β-bungarotoxins, crotoxin, and taipoxin) prevent acetylcholine release, and postsynaptic toxins (i.e., α-bungarotoxins and cobrotoxin) bind to acetylcholine receptors on the motor end plate.

Rhabdomyolysis is caused primarily by the presynaptic neurotoxins of sea snakes, Australasian elapids, Russell's viper, and selected rattlesnakes. Patients often develop acute renal failure, hyperkalemia, and death. Other mechanisms for renal failure after these envenomations include a direct renal toxin, hemoglobinuria after massive intravascular hemolysis, hypotension, and DIC.

Toxins that do not immobilize prey through neurotoxins may immobilize by causing hypotension. Some snakes (primarily vipers) cause an acute hypotensive syndrome just minutes after envenomation through the release of vasodilating autocoids. *Bothrops* species inhibit bradykinin and angiotensinogen (ACE inhibitors) breakdown. Vasodilation, diffuse vascular permeability, myocardial depression, and atrioventricular block all play roles in the hypotension caused by crotalids and elapids.

Clinical Manifestations

PIT VIPER ENVENOMATION. Swelling and pain are the first and most important signs of early envenomation. These often occur within 10 minutes and are followed by progressive swelling and ecchymoses. The development of systemic symptoms such as nausea, diaphoresis, and dizziness indicate more severe envenomation. Hypotension, bleeding manifestations (i.e., gingival), and paresthesias followed by oliguria and coma indicate a life-threatening state. During this period, the white blood cell count often is rising, blood is becoming hypocoagulable, red blood cells are lysing, acidosis is progressing, and acute renal failure is supervening. Local necrosis develops with the potential for compartment syndrome and infection.

CORAL SNAKE ENVENOMATION. Unlike the pit vipers, local symptoms after coral snake bites are confined to paresthesias around

the bite. Systemic symptoms are often delayed for 1 to 6 hours. With severe envenomation, perioral paresthesias, nausea, vomiting, hypersalivation, and euphoria give way to cranial nerve paralysis (e.g., ptosis, diplopia, dysphagia) and respiratory failure.

Treatment

The immediate care of someone bitten by a venomous snake has been a point of contention. Popular approaches such as tourniquets, incision, suction, and electric shock are not helpful and can be harmful. Appropriate care consists of immobilization of a bitten extremity, perhaps wrapping of a bitten extremity (e.g., with elastic wrap), and most importantly, rapid transit to a hospital or clinic where definitive care is possible.

On arrival in the emergency facility, the first issue is to assess the likelihood of envenomation. The chance of a bite resulting in envenomation varies from 70 to 95% for Viperidae to about 20% for Hydrophidae. The symptoms of pit viper envenomation are quickly obvious, whereas the seriousness of bites by Elapidae snakes can be easily underestimated early after the bite.

When envenomation is apparent, only one specific therapy is available. Snake antivenom consists of antibodies to specific components of venom that usually were raised in horses or sheep. It is most likely to be effective if the snake causing the bite was the species used to inoculate the horse or sheep, although cross-reactivity, particularly with closely related species, is common. In the United States, equine polyvalent antivenom for pit viper bites, ovine polyvalent Fab antibody fragment antivenom for pit viper bites, and monovalent antivenom for coral snake bites have been available. However, it appears that the Fab antibody fragment preparation will soon be the only product available for pit viper envenomation in the United States.

Because antivenom contains foreign proteins, severe adverse reactions, including fatal anaphylaxis, are possible. It appears that the Fab antibody fragment preparation is less likely to cause serious reactions than the preparations with intact antibodies. Cutaneous sensitivity testing is not always accurate and not recommended, but the treatments for anaphylaxis must be immediately available. Antivenom should always be given for envenomation by large rattlesnakes, cobras, mambas, coral snakes, and for severe envenomation by other snakes. In some countries, antivenom is withheld if possible because of concerns about toxicity or cost. The initial dose of antivenom is determined by the package insert, but repeated dosing may be necessary to control life-threatening manifestations of envenomation, and a second dose is routine using the Fab antibody fragment preparation. If envenomation is determined to be life-threatening, anaphylaxis, if it occurs, should be treated and administration of antivenom reinstituted cautiously.

Supportive care is an important component of management. This might include intravenous fluids, blood components, tetanus toxoid, antibiotics, mechanical ventilation, pressors, pain medications, and surgical treatment of compartment syndrome.

SUGGESTED READINGS

Dart RC, McNally J: Efficacy, safety, and use of snake antivenoms in the United States. Ann Emerg Med 2001;37:181–188. *Overview of the various antivenoms.*

Gold BS, Dart RC, Barish RA: Bites of venomous snakes. N Engl J Med 2002;347:347–355. *A comprehensive review of snakes, venoms, and treatments.*

McKinney MD: Out-of-hospital and interhospital management of crotaline snakebite. Ann Emerg Med 2001;37:168–174. *Suction and appropriate antivenom can be used in the prehospital setting to reduce morbidity.*

408 VENOMS AND POISONS FROM MARINE ORGANISMS

Jay W. Fox

The term *envenomation* implies penetration by an organism for delivery of a venom containing one or more toxins. In contrast, poisons are toxins acquired from the environment by mechanisms such as absorption, inhalation, and ingestion. In the marine environment, both forms of intoxication occur with effects ranging from mild irritation and discomfort to death. Previously, most clinically relevant intoxications were envenomations from marine organisms found primarily in tropical and subtropical waters. However, severe outbreaks of poisoning from ingesting marine organisms containing toxins have occurred recently. This is probably caused by increased microorganism growth in coastal waters as a result of eutrophication. Encroachment on the marine environment for recreation, living

space, and food sources may be expected to increase the frequency of adverse encounters with venomous and poisonous marine organisms.

This chapter discusses the marine organisms responsible for most clinically significant intoxications, with emphasis on the pharmacologic and symptomatic properties of the toxins. Table 408–1 lists venomous and poisonous marine organisms that can produce severe intoxication or death and indicates whether antivenin is available. The sites of action of some marine neurotoxins are depicted in Figure 408–1.

Table 408–1 • SIGNIFICANT VENOMOUS AND POISONOUS MARINE ORGANISMS

ORGANISM	TYPE OF ENVENOMATION (POISONING)	PRIMARY TOXINS	ANTIVENOM AVAILABLE
Sea snakes (Hydrophiidae)	Bite	Postsynaptic neurotoxin	Yes
Blue-ringed octopus (Octopodidae)	Bite	Postsynaptic neurotoxin (tetrodotoxin)	No
Cone shell (Conidae)	Bite	Presynaptic and postsynaptic neurotoxins	No
Box jellyfish (*Chironex fleckeri*, *Chiropsolmus quadrigatus*)	Sting	Hemolysins, proteinases, cardiotoxin, necrotoxins	Yes
Portuguese man-o-war (*Physalia physalis*)	Sting	Hemolysins, proteinases, cardiotoxin, necrotoxins	No; may be needed
Sea nettles (*Chrysaora quinquecirrha;Cyanea capillata*)	Sting	Hemolysins, proteinases, cardiotoxin, necrotoxins	No; generally no need
Sea anemone (*Anemonia sulcata*)	Sting	Neurotoxins	No; generally no need
Scorpionfish (Scorpaenidae)	Sting puncture	Hemolysins, necrotoxins?	Yes
Lionfish (Scorpaenidae)	Sting puncture	Hemolysins, necrotoxins?	No
Stonefish (Scorpaenidae)	Sting puncture	Hemolysins, necrotoxins?	Yes
Weeverfish (Trachinidae)	Sting puncture	Hemolysins, necrotoxins?	No
Stingrays (Rajiformes)	Sting puncture	?	No
Dinoflagellates		Ciguatera poisoning, ciguatoxins, maitotoxin (neurotoxins)	
Gambierdiscus toxicus	Poisonous (found in fish)		
Ptychodiscus brevis	Poisonous (found in shellfish)	Neurotoxic shellfish poisoning, neurotoxins	
Gonyaulax species	Poisonous (found in shellfish)	Paralytic shellfish poisoning	
Pyrodinium species	Poisonous (found in shellfish)	Saxitoxin, neosaxitoxin, and gonyautoxin	
Jania species	Poisonous (found in shellfish)	Okadaic acid (phosphatase inhibitors)	
Pufferfish (Tetraodontiformes)	Poisonous	Tetrodotoxin (neurotoxin)	No
Porcupinefish (Tetraodontiformes)	Poisonous	Tetrodotoxin (neurotoxin)	
Sunfish (*Mola* species)	Poisonous	Tetrodotoxin	

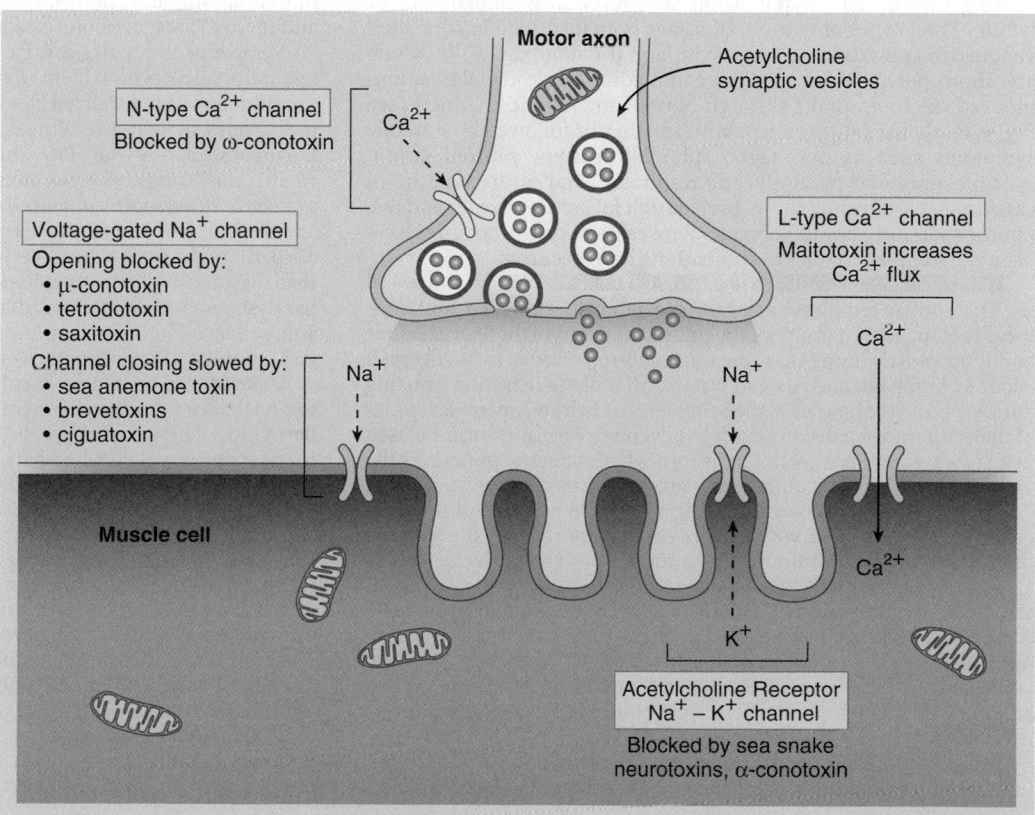

FIGURE 408–1 • Schematic representation of a motor axon synapse and the sites of action of various marine neurotoxins.

VENOMOUS MARINE ORGANISMS

Venomous marine organisms deliver their venoms by biting and stinging (see Table 408–1). Envenomation involves penetration of the skin. Consideration must be given to the potential of infection by microorganisms, especially in situations involving deep puncture wounds and bites, as well as to the treatment of the toxicologic effects of the venom.

SEA SNAKES. Sea snakes are members of the family Hydrophiidae and are generally found in tropical and subtropical waters. Sea snakes are very common in the coastal waters of Thailand, Indonesia, the Persian Gulf, Australia, and India. One species of sea snake, *Pelaramis platurus,* the yellow-bellied sea snake, is found in the Pacific coastal waters of Central America. These snakes are very capable swimmers but do not come ashore and are relatively immobile on land. They inject their venom with two small maxillary fangs (2 to 4 mm long) containing ducts connected to venom glands located posterior and ventral to the maxillary bone. The relatively short aspect of the fangs prevents effective envenomation through most protective clothing such as dive suits. In the case of human envenomation, if the subject reacts by violent retraction, the fangs are often dislodged from the maxillary bone of the snake and may remain in the site.

Because of the nature of the venom and the size of the fangs, the sea snake bite itself is generally not painful. One or two small prick marks are present at the envenomation site, as occasionally are additional marks from the other teeth in the snake's mouth. The primary toxin in sea snake venom is a postsynaptic peptide neurotoxin that functions by blocking the acetylcholine receptor at neuromuscular junctions (see Fig. 408–1). The symptoms of sea snake envenomation are mainly neurologic and typically appear within 30 minutes to 2 hours after the bite. Ptosis, dysphagia, and nonrigid paralysis occur. In severe cases, respiratory failure may occur, and respiratory intervention may be necessary.

MOLLUSKS

Blue-Ringed and Spotted Octopus. The blue-ringed and spotted octopuses (*Hapalochlaena maculosa* and *Hapalochlaena lunulata*), found in Australian waters, inject their venom by a relatively painless bite, producing two small puncture wounds. Hemorrhage at the site may occur. The major toxic component in the venom is tetrodotoxin, a postsynaptic neurotoxin that causes perioral and intraoral paresthesias, dysphagia, nausea, ataxia, aphonia, flaccid muscular paralysis, and respiratory distress or failure. Fatal envenomations have occurred.

Cone Shells. Cone shell venoms are injected into victims through a hollow, harpoon-like tooth. The venom is primarily neurotoxic, causing paresthesias, hypotension, and respiratory impairment or failure. Three types of neurotoxins have been identified in cone shell venoms: ω-conotoxin, α-conotoxin, and μ-conotoxin, all of which are short polypeptides. The ω-conotoxins block depolarization-induced calcium uptake through N-type presynaptic channels (see Fig. 408–1). The bite is very painful and may be followed by systemic symptoms such as dysphagia, aphonia, pruritus, blurred vision, syncope, muscular paralysis, and respiratory and cardiac failure. In cases of severe envenomation, preparation for cardiovascular and respiratory support should be made. Rare cases of coagulopathies have been reported, and fatal envenomations have occurred.

WEEVERFISH, SCORPIONFISH, STONEFISH, AND LIONFISH. Weeverfish are of the Trachinidae family, whereas the scorpionfish, stonefish, and lionfish all belong to the family Scorpaenidae. Members of the Scorpaenidae family are mostly found in tropical and subtropical waters. Weeverfish occur in European and African waters. All of these fish sting by using dorsal spines. Anal spines of the Scorpaenidae fish and opercular spines of the Trachinidae fish can also deliver venom. The spines are encased in an integumentary sheath that is torn when the spine punctures the victim's skin. Venom glands are located at the base of the spine.

Few details are known regarding the biochemistry and pharmacology of the toxins in weeverfish venom. The sting of the weeverfish is extremely painful and may produce systemic effects such as aphonia, fever, chills, dyspnea, cyanosis, nausea, syncope, hypotension, and arrhythmias. The wound is edematous, erythematous, and ecchymotic. Bacterial infection is typical, and gangrene has developed in severe cases of infection. The venom may be somewhat heat labile, and soaking in tolerably hot water may relieve some pain and attenuate the effects of the venom. Death from a weeverfish sting is rare.

Scorpionfish (*Scorpaena*) are primarily found in tropical and subtropical waters and the Mediterranean. The stings of these fishes have

been described to be very similar to those of the weeverfish. Lionfish (*Pterois*) dwell in tropical waters; their stings generally are the most severe of all of the fish stings and occasionally cause death from hypotension. Because the venom is heat labile, soaking in hot water is recommended.

The stonefish (*Synanceja*) group is found throughout the Indo-Pacific area, China, Australia, and the Indian Ocean and is considered to be the most venomous fish. Symptoms are similar to those from the stings of members of the other groups. Similar high-molecular-weight toxins—verrucotoxin from *Synanceja verrucosa,* stonustoxin from *Synanceja horrida,* and cytolysin from *Synanceja trachynis*—have been isolated and characterized. They are multimeric, heat-labile protein toxins composed of α- and β-subunits and are the toxins that are primarily responsible for many of the symptoms associated with the sting from these fish. A lethal toxin, stonustoxin, has been isolated in the venom of *S. horrida* and has been shown to cause muscle relaxation by production of nitric oxide and activation of potassium ion channels. Soaking of the wound site in hot water (45° C) is recommended. In cases of severe blistering, the blisters should be excised to flush residual active venom from the blister fluid to ameliorate dermal necrosis. As with all fish stings, care should be taken to ensure that no broken portions of the spines remain in the wound; vigilance against bacterial infections should be observed.

COELENTERATES

Jellyfish and Anemones. Jellyfish and anemones belong to the Cnidaria phylum, so named because of their venomous organelles, called *cnidae.* The cnidae found in jellyfish and anemones (called *nematocysts* and *spirocysts,* respectively) are located on exposed tentacles. On tactile stimulation, the tentacles send forth a tethered projectile to deliver venom through the dermis. As the victim's surrounding musculature contracts, the venom is disseminated. The toxins contained in the venom from these organisms have not been fully documented. Hemolysins, DNases, and histamine releasers have been identified in some venoms. Several peptide toxins have been characterized from the sea anemone, *Anemonia sulcata,* which act similarly to α-scorpion toxins by inactivating the sodium channel.

Stings by jellyfish and anemones typically produce immediate pain at the site of envenomation, followed by erythematous and urticarial lesions. Anaphylaxis is not common in most situations unless previous sensitization has occurred. Depending on the severity of the sting, wheals and whiplike patterns at the sites of envenomation may appear within a few minutes or be delayed by several hours, followed in some cases by dermal necrosis. Recurrence of eruptions days after the envenomation has been reported. Systemic reactions may include muscle spasms and cramps, vomiting, nausea, diarrhea, diaphoresis, and in rare cases, cardiorespiratory failure.

Verapamil eliminates cardiac arrhythmia but does not ameliorate respiratory depression. Unfired nematocysts on tentacles adhering to the skin may be neutralized by vinegar or baking soda, depending on the species of jellyfish. Vinegar seems to be most useful for the Portuguese man-of-war (*Physalia physalis*) and Australian blue bottle (*P. utriculus*) stings, whereas baking soda appears more efficacious for sea nettle (*Chrysaora quinquecirrha*) stings.

The box jellyfish (*Chironex fleckeri*) found in Australian waters are perhaps the most venomous jellyfish, producing very severe stings that may cause death from hypotension, muscular and respiratory paralysis, and ultimately, cardiac arrest. Treatment of box jellyfish stings must include consideration of the option of respiratory support and administration of an antivenin.

Sponges. Some sponges colonized by coelenterates elaborate toxins that can produce a pruritic, allergenic dermatitis or an irritant dermatitis. These toxins are delivered by the sharp spicules present in the sponges, which when handled penetrate the dermis. The toxins can cause the typical sponge diver's disease, characterized by local burning and itching, which in severe cases may be accompanied by soft tissue edema and purulent vesiculation. Serious illness is rare.

Corals. Fire coral (*Millepora alcicornis*) is found in shallow tropical waters. Stings are a common consequence of brushing or rubbing against the coral. Envenomation produces a burning or stinging sensation, followed by severe pruritus. Edematous wheals may occur but generally dissipate over the course of several days. The site of envenomation should be soaked in dilute acetic acid or isopropanol to relieve pain.

BRISTLEWORMS. Bristleworms (Annelida) are segmented invertebrates found in tropical Pacific waters and the Gulf of Mexico. The bristles present on the segments of the organism are capable of penetrating the skin and producing a severely painful envenomation with pruritus and burning that may persist for several days. Local paresthesia is likely and may linger for weeks. Treatment is symptomatic, with consideration of possible tetanus infection. Little is known regarding the chemistry of bristleworm venoms.

SEA URCHINS. Of the echinoderms, sea urchins and sea stars are responsible for most stings to humans. The venom is delivered by the long spines and pedicellariae protruding from the sea urchin body. The spines are covered at the tips with a venom sac that is broken when it penetrates the skin. The pedicellariae, present on some species of sea urchins, are pincer-like appendages carrying venom glands. The toxins of sea urchin venoms are not well characterized. Stings can produce pain, hemorrhage, aphonia, paresthesias, paralysis, hypotension, nausea, syncope, and respiratory distress. Immersion in hot water helps inactivate heat-labile toxins in the venoms. Attached pedicellariae and embedded spines must be removed to prevent additional envenomation.

STINGRAYS. Stingrays (order Rajiformes) are found in most seas but are predominant in the Indo-Pacific area. Venom is delivered by stings from spines (one or more) on the tail of the stingray. Stingray spines are retroserrated on the margins and are covered by an integumentary sheath. Venomous glandular tissue is located at the base of the spines. On puncture of the skin, the sheath is torn by the serrated spine and venom flows along the two ventrolateral grooves of the spine into the surrounding tissue. One of the identified toxins in the venom is serotonin. The spines are often deeply embedded in the tissue and difficult to extract due to the retroserration. Care must be taken to remove all spine and sheath fragments. A sting produces severe pain and edema, which in extreme cases is accompanied by hemorrhage, syncope, vomiting, hypotension, and cardiac arrhythmia. In rare cases, death can occur, especially if the pericardial, peritoneal, or pleural cavities are penetrated. Soaking the wound in hot water inactivates some of the heat-labile toxins in the venom.

POISONOUS MARINE ORGANISMS

Marine poisoning nearly always results from consumption of a fish or shellfish harboring various toxins. The causes of three types of marine poisoning are fish or shellfish containing toxins produced by dinoflagellates (i.e., ciguatera, neurotoxic shellfish, paralytic shellfish, and diarrhetic shellfish poisoning); fish that produce their own toxin (i.e., Tetraodontiformes fish); and fish containing significant levels of bacteria that have metabolized histidine to histamine, resulting in pseudoallergic reactions.

CIGUATERA POISONING. Ciguatera toxins have been identified in more than 400 species of fish. During blooms of the dinoflagellate *Gambierdiscus toxicus,* toxins produced by these organisms concentrate in the fish to levels that are toxic to humans when ingested. The primary toxins responsible for ciguatera poisoning are ciguatoxins, which are cyclic polyethers and act as excitatory agents by binding to sodium channels. Maitotoxin, from the same dinoflagellate, is a water-soluble polyether and acts by enhancing calcium entry through L-type calcium channels. Symptoms of ciguatera poisoning generally appear within 2 to 12 hours after ingestion of contaminated fish. Gastrointestinal symptoms including diarrhea, abdominal pain, nausea, and vomiting appear first, followed by neurologic and cardiovascular symptoms. Neurologic symptoms include aphonia, dental dysesthesias, fatigue, tremor, ataxia, pruritus, extremity and perioral dysesthesia, vertigo, headache, myalgias, arthralgias, temperature reversal, and hyporeflexia. Cardiovascular symptoms, such as bradycardia and hypotension, occur least often. There is no specific treatment for ciguatera poisoning; supportive, symptom-based therapy is indicated. Death from ciguatera poisoning has occurred but is rare.

NEUROTOXIC SHELLFISH POISONING. Neurotoxic shellfish poisoning is caused by eating shellfish that contain brevetoxins produced by the dinoflagellate *Ptychodiscus brevis.* Brevetoxins are cyclic polyethers that function similarly to the ciguatoxins. Gastrointestinal and neurologic symptoms of intoxication appear within 3 hours after toxic shellfish is eaten and are similar to those of ciguatera poisoning. Treatment is supportive. No deaths have been reported for neurotoxic shellfish poisoning.

PARALYTIC SHELLFISH POISONING. Paralytic shellfish poisoning is significantly more severe than neurotoxic shellfish poisoning and predominantly involves neurologic symptoms with less pronounced gastrointestinal symptoms such as nausea, vomiting, and diarrhea. The toxins responsible for paralytic shellfish poisoning are from the dinoflagellate genera *Gonyaulax, Pyrodinium,* and *Jania* and are harbored in a variety of shellfish. The primary paralytic shellfish poisoning toxins—saxitoxin, neosaxitoxin, and gonyautoxin—are heterocyclic compounds that block nerve and muscle action potentials by binding to sodium channels. The site of binding overlaps with tetrodotoxin, resulting in paralysis. Symptoms appear soon after consumption of contaminated shellfish (minutes to hours), beginning with circumoral and extremity paresthesias. Additional neurologic symptoms, such as ataxia, arthralgia, dysphagia, dysmetria, diaphoresis, and tachycardia, soon follow the initial paresthesias. Respiratory depression or failure can occur and may result in death, usually within 12 hours of the onset of symptoms. As with other shellfish poisoning, therapy is supportive, with close attention given to potential respiratory distress or failure.

DIARRHETIC SHELLFISH POISONING. Diarrhetic shellfish poisoning is also caused by eating shellfish that are contaminated by dinoflagellate toxins. The two primary toxins associated with diarrhetic shellfish poisoning are okadaic acids and pectenotoxins. Okadaic acid is a polyether derivative of a 38-carbon fatty acid. It functions as an inhibitor of protein phosphatase-1 and -2A and causes smooth and cardiac muscle contraction. Symptoms of diarrhetic shellfish poisoning begin with abdominal cramps and nausea and progress to diarrhea. Additional, delayed symptoms occurring approximately 35 hours after ingestion may appear and include vomiting, vertigo, diarrhea, cramps, and headache. Treatment is supportive.

TETRAODONTIFORMES (PUFFERFISH, PORCUPINEFISH, AND SUNFISH) POISONING. Pufferfish (i.e., blowfish, balloonfish, and toadfish), porcupinefish, and sunfish (*Mola* species) have a very potent toxin, tetrodotoxin, in their livers, gonads, intestines, and skin. The flesh of the fish (fugu) is a delicacy in Japan and is prepared by specially trained chefs to avoid serving significant amounts of toxins. Tetrodotoxin is a heterocyclic compound that binds at voltage-sensitive sodium channels (at an overlapping site with saxitoxin) to block sodium passage, preventing nerve and muscle action potentials, thus resulting in paralysis. Symptoms occur rapidly (several minutes to several hours) beginning with circumoral paresthesias and progressing to widespread paresthesias. After the initial paresthesias, additional symptoms soon follow, including ataxia, weakness, aphonia, diaphoresis, excess salivation, dyspnea, dysphagia, weakness, and respiratory distress or failure. Gastrointestinal symptoms include nausea, vomiting, and diarrhea. Coagulopathies have been associated with tetrodotoxin intoxication. Respiratory intervention is crucial in light of the potential for complete flaccid paralysis. Without respiratory assistance, death is not unusual in cases of severe intoxication.

SCOMBROID FISH POISONING. Scombroid poisoning is a pseudoallergic fish poisoning caused by consumption of certain types of fish that have been improperly stored, including the scombroid fish (e.g., tuna, mackerel, wahoo, bonito, albacore, skipjack) and nonscombroid fish (e.g., mahi-mahi, amberjack, sardines, and herring). The poisoning results from high levels of histamine and saurine present in the fish because of bacterial catabolism of histidine. Presentation of symptoms from intoxication is rapid (within minutes to hours), beginning with a flushing of the skin, oral paresthesias, pruritus, urticaria, nausea, vomiting, diarrhea, vertigo, headache, bronchospasm, dysphagia, tachycardia, and hypotension. Therapy should follow a course for allergic reaction and anaphylaxis. Symptoms usually resolve in several hours.

SUGGESTED READINGS

Adams ME: Neurotoxins. Trends Neurosci 1994;17(Suppl):151–155. *This issue is a concise tabulation of neurotoxins, their biologic sources, and pharmacologic activities.*

Auerbach PS: Marine envenomations. N Engl J Med 1991;325:486–493. *A thorough guide to the types of marine envenomations and symptoms that they cause.*

Burnett JW: Human injuries following jellyfish stings. Md Med J 1992;41:509–513. *Describes the mechanism of jellyfish stings and therapy.*

Gwee MCE: A review of stonefish venoms and toxins. Pharmacol Ther 1994;64:509–528. *Review article that describes the biological, clinical, and biochemical properties of stonefish venom and envenomation.*

Hamilton B, Hurbungs M, Vernoux JP, et al: Isolation and characterisation of Indian Ocean ciguatoxin. Toxicon 2002;40:685–693. *Identification of a new, distinct ciguatoxin.*

Khoo HE: Bioactive proteins from stonefish venom. Clin Exp Pharmacol Physiol 2002;29: 802–806. *Review of one of the most common venomous fish.*

Schnorf H, Taurarii M, Cundy T: Ciguatera fish poisoning: A double-blind randomized trial of mannitol therapy. Neurology 2002;58:873–880. *Mannitol was no better than normal saline.*

Trevino J: Fish and shellfish poisoning. Clin Lab Sci 1998;11:309–314. *Overview of scombroid and ciguatera.*

Tu AT (ed): Handbook of Natural Toxins, vol 3. Marine Toxins and Venoms. New York, Marcel Dekker, 1988. *Discusses many types of marine toxins and provides a section on treatment.*

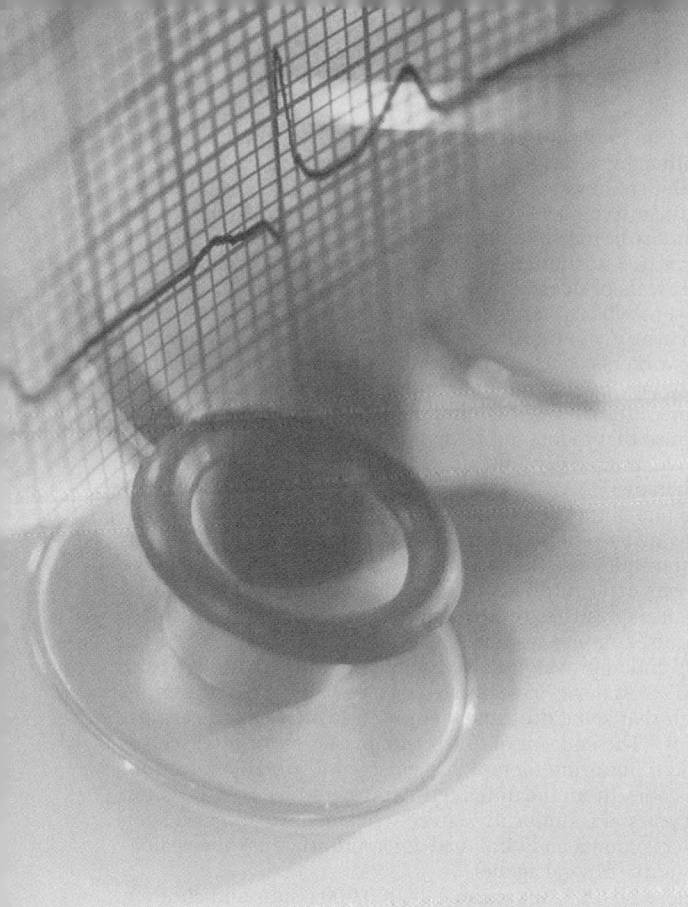

part XXIV

HIV and the Acquired Immunodeficiency Syndrome

409 INTRODUCTION TO HIV AND ASSOCIATED DISORDERS

W. Michael Scheld

The acquired immunodeficiency syndrome (AIDS) caused by the human immunodeficiency virus (HIV) has profoundly changed medical practice, contemporary society, and public health initiatives worldwide. HIV infection and AIDS constitute a global health crisis of unprecedented magnitude. Since the first cluster of cases was described in 1981, HIV has infected approximately 67 million people, and 25 million people have died (about 3 million deaths in 2002 alone), eclipsing the Black Death of 14th century Europe and the influenza pandemic of 1918 and 1919 as the most lethal pandemic in human history. The development gains of three decades have been reversed in many resource-limited settings in the world, with an economic decline of 10 to 40%, health system chaos, political instability, a rapidly increasing number of orphans, and an immense humanitarian concern.

The chapters in this section enable the physician to understand the virus, the immunopathogenesis of HIV infection and the development of AIDS, the natural history of untreated infection, the dynamic epidemiology of HIV infection and AIDS on a worldwide scale, and the protean manifestations of HIV infection with its attendant associated opportunistic infections and malignancies. The treatment of HIV and of the associated opportunistic infections and malignancies is considered in some depth.

At the end of 2002, about 42 million adults and children were living with HIV infection or AIDS worldwide, and the annual number of new infections with HIV eclipsed 5 million per year, as calculated by the Joint United Nations Programme on HIV/AIDS (UNAIDS). More than 16,000 HIV infections were acquired daily, 95% in developing countries. Of these new infections, about 2000 occurred in children younger than 14 years of age, and about 14,000 occurred in adults; almost 50% were women, and about 50% were between 15 and 24 years old. By the end of 2002, more than 16 million children had been orphaned by AIDS, and one report suggests that this number may exceed 40 million in sub-Saharan Africa alone by the year 2010.

Sub-Saharan Africa has been particularly hard hit by the AIDS epidemic. The epidemic began in this region and has blossomed; two thirds of the world's total infections occur in this area (about 29.4 million by the end of 2002). Seventeen million HIV deaths have occurred in sub-Saharan Africa, representing 83% of the deaths from AIDS in the world, and AIDS is now the leading cause of death in Africa. At least 10% of the population is infected in 16 African countries, and in some urban areas, 75 of the hospital beds are occupied by AIDS patients. The life expectancy in Botswana, Malawi, Mozambique, and Swaziland is now less than 40 years, erasing more than 3 decades of progressive improvement. The annual per capita growth in many countries is falling by 0.5 to 1.2%, and by 2020, the gross domestic product should drop by more than 20% in several areas. As a very graphic statistic, a 15-year-old boy in Botswana at the current level of seroprevalence (about 35%) has a 90% chance of dying of AIDS.

AIDS is a substantial threat to human security, not in terms of armed conflict, but rather in the fundamental conditions necessary for people to lead safe, productive lives. AIDS is the only disease to receive attention at a special session of the United Nations (June 25–27, 2001).

There is some glimmer of hope in this heart of darkness. For example, the seroprevalence of HIV infection in Uganda has been reduced from one of the highest in the world in the late 1980s (about 30%) to the current level of 8%. Similarly, some countries in Africa (e.g., Senegal) have arrested the epidemic and continue to have a low prevalence. Prevention remains the cornerstone of any approach to HIV infection and AIDS in resource-limited settings. However, in recent years, many groups have made progress in developing infrastructure, capacity building, and with attendant reduction in drug prices, delivering HIV care, including antiretroviral therapy in developing countries.

The first cluster of cases of AIDS was described in 1981. The causative agent, HIV, was described in 1983, and a blood test to detect HIV to reduce the risk of transmission by blood products was developed in 1985. The first antiretroviral drug with activity against HIV was licensed in 1987, but early enthusiasm led to disappointment with monotherapy. Nearly all of the early identified cases were in homosexual men; however, it is now apparent that HIV is transmitted predominantly by heterosexual contact in resource-limited settings and can also be transmitted by blood transfer. There is no evidence that HIV can be transmitted by casual contact or by an arthropod vector. Early fears of transmission to health care workers have given way to the somewhat reassuring situation in which a needlestick or other sharp instrument transmittal of blood from infected patients to health care workers occurs at a rate of about 3 cases per 1000 people, and this rate may be reduced further by postexposure prophylaxis. Universal precautions were introduced in the early AIDS era based on the premise that blood and body fluids from all patients should be considered potentially infectious. Effective highly active antiretroviral therapy (HAART), with a reduction in viral load, markedly reduces the rate of transmission.

AIDS has had a profound impact on the public health approach to sexually transmitted diseases worldwide. A therapeutic or preventive vaccine is years in the future despite decades of progress. Educational efforts to reduce spread have been highly effective where implemented, but they require complex resources and political will. The process for drug testing and approval has also been altered dramatically by the advent of AIDS. Activists have insisted on a reevaluation of the entire process such that some drugs now enjoy "fast track" status against certain agents. The concept of "surrogate markers" for disease progression and monitoring therapy has emerged. With HIV infection, the natural course from the initial retroviral syndrome to AIDS often exceeds 10 years; it is uniformly agreed that surrogate markers such as CD4+ T-cell counts and viral load are appropriate for the evaluation of new antiretroviral agents.

At the close of 2002, approximately 980,000 adults and children were living with HIV infection or AIDS in North America, with another approximately 570,000 in Western Europe. In addition to the calamity unfolding in Africa, the AIDS epidemic continues to explode in India, China, Russia, and Eastern Europe and may be more destabilizing than international terrorism. Despite nearly 2 decades of spectacular progress in understanding the virus, the immunopathogenesis of disease, and the myriad manifestations, neither a cure nor an effective vaccine is within reach.

Modern antiretroviral therapy entered a new era in 1995, coincident with the introduction of protease inhibitors. Since then, survival has improved with a reduction in the annual number of AIDS deaths in the United States. On a more sober note, this trend has plateaued and may even be reversing. Nevertheless, documented benefits of antiretroviral therapy are many and varied and include an increase in survival, a decrease in opportunistic infections, a decrease in hospitalizations, a decrease in the incidence of AIDS, a decrease in perinatal transmission, and importantly, a restoration of hope.

The care of patients with AIDS can be complex and is often frustrating. Care typically is directed by a physician, but it includes multiple other health care workers, including counselors, social workers, addiction counselors, and public health employees. Although there has been some agreement in recent years on when to initiate HAART and the initial selection of individual antiretroviral agents in a combination regimen, this is a dynamic area requiring constant updating. Care of an AIDS patient who is failing therapy after exposure to multiple antiretroviral agents is complex and challenging. Care often requires review of extensive genotypic or phenotypic resistance profiles and the use of agents with multiple drug-drug interactions. In some respects, the care of patients with HIV and AIDS has evolved into a sub-subspecialty. Recently, the HIV Medicine Association of the Infectious Diseases Society of America has approached the American Board of Internal Medicine regarding the development of a certificate of added qualification in HIV medicine, similar to efforts in geriatrics and critical care medicine in the past.

Despite the complexity, all practicing physicians in this era must know the basics of AIDS pathogenesis, routes of disease transmission, the manifestations of the mononucleosis-like acute retroviral syndrome, and principles of management of HIV and its associated complications. At the dawn of the 20th century, Sir William Osler said, "To know syphilis is to know medicine," and AIDS appears to be the modern equivalent of syphilis as we enter the new millennium. Practicing physicians should routinely screen for HIV risk factors and consider HIV as the underlying process in numerous clinical scenarios, given the protean manifestations of HIV infection itself and the associated opportunistic infections and malignancies.

SUGGESTED READINGS

Hogg R, Cahn P, Katabira ET, et al: Time to act: Global apathy towards HIV/AIDS is a crime against humanity. Lancet 2002;360:1710–1711. *This commentary by an international consortium of leading AIDS researchers raises many of the points considered in this chapter and concludes in part with "Inaction against HIV/AIDS is a crime against humanity that cannot be tolerated any longer." Although there are multiple public health concerns worldwide, the Global Fund to fight AIDS, Tuberculosis, and Malaria received pledges of less than 4% of those requested as of December 2002. For those interested in the early studies leading to the identification of HIV as the cause of AIDS and, more importantly, suggestions for future protocols, consult a series of papers by Prusiner, Montagnier, and Gallo published in Science 2002;298:1726–1731.*

Jost S, Bernard M-C, Kaiser L, et al: A patient with HIV-superinfection. N Engl J Med 2002;347:731–736. *A patient, initially infected with an AE clade virus, was superinjected more than 2 years later with a B clade virus that accelerated disease progression. The implications to disease pathogenesis and vaccine development are amply covered in an accompanying editorial by Goulder and Walker*

Kilby JM, Eron JJ: Novel therapies based on mechanisms of HIV-1 cell entry. N Engl J Med 2003;348:2228–2238. *An excellent review of novel drug targets for HIV as the first fusion inhibitor is released in the United States.*

Mbulaiteye SM, Mahe C, Whitworth JAG, et al: Declining HIV-1 incidence and associated prevalence over 10 years in a rural population in south-west Uganda: A cohort study. Lancet 2002;360:41–46. *Documents a decline in incidence of about 35% from 1989 to 1999.*

Schreibman T, Friedland G: Human immunodeficiency virus infection prevention: Stategies for clinicians. Clin Infect Dis 2003;36:1171–1176. *Cogent quidelines for care providers.*

410 IMMUNOLOGY RELATED TO AIDS

Paul E. Sax

Bruce D. Walker

The clinical consequences of human immunodeficiency virus (HIV) infection are due to the ability of this retrovirus to infect crucial cells of the immune system. This infection occurs because the primary target for the virus is lymphocytes expressing the cell surface marker CD4, which serves as a receptor that binds the envelope protein of the virus. These lymphocytes, also called *help-inducer lymphocytes,* act as the pivotal orchestrator of a myriad of immune functions. HIV-1 infection can be considered a disease of the immune system, characterized by the progressive loss of CD4+ lymphocytes. Immunodeficiency results not only from a lack of effective immunity against HIV itself, but also because the virus damages CD4 cell subsets that are crucial for containing other pathogens—explaining the problems encountered with so-called opportunistic pathogens that are not a problem for persons with intact immunity.

Although the immune system ultimately fails to control HIV-1 infection, emerging data indicate that at least partially effective virus-specific immune responses are generated after acute HIV-1 infection. These responses contribute to the long, asymptomatic phase that typically follows infection by keeping the virus at least partially contained, but in most infected persons the immune system ultimately fails to contain the virus, and disease progression ensues. There are notable exceptions, however. With the epidemic now entering its third decade, a small group of persons has been identified who seem to be able to control HIV-1 infection for 20 or more years without the need for antiviral drug therapy. These persons, likely representing much less than 1% of infected persons, suggest that persistent immune control can be achieved against HIV. Understanding of the immunology related to HIV provides insight not only into the clinical sequelae of infection, but also into the prospects for development of effective therapeutic and prophylactic vaccines against HIV.

Evidence That the Immune System Achieves Partial Control of HIV Infection

The acute phase of HIV infection is associated with nonspecific symptoms common to many viral infections, including fever, sore throat, malaise, swollen lymph nodes, and a transient maculopapular rash. The symptoms are likely a result not only of the virus replication, but also the immune response that is being generated. The adaptive immune response consists of humoral (antibody-mediated) and cellular (cell-mediated) immunity, both of which are generated against the virus. It is the antibody response to HIV that is the basis for detection of infection by enzyme-linked immunosorbent assay (ELISA).

During acute infection, viral load reaches levels by standard assays currently available in most clinics of more than 10 million viral RNA

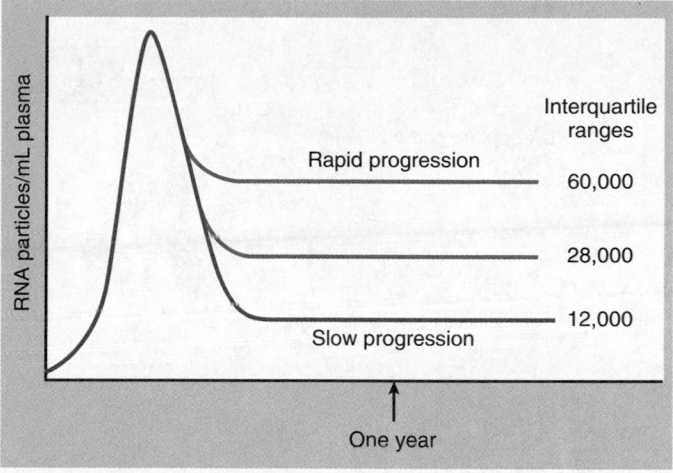

FIGURE 410-1 • Steady-state viral load after acute HIV-1 infection. Plasma viremia reaches a mean peak of greater than 10 million viral particles/mL plasma during acute HIV infection, then drops precipitously coincident with the appearance of virus-specific immune responses. The differences in steady-state viral load relate to, among other things, differences in immune selection pressure, viral attenuation, HLA type of the infected person, and differences in viral coreceptors needed for viral entry

particles per milliliter of plasma. The initial peak in viremia is brought to an average steady-state level of about 30,000 copies within 6 months of infection (Fig. 410–1), and this decrease in viremia is thought to be due to generation of antiviral immune responses. Among these responses is the generation of virus-specific CD4 T-helper cells, which orchestrate a coordinated humoral and cellular immune response. Because CD4 is a receptor for the virus, and HIV has the unique ability to preferentially infect activated CD4 cells, these cells that are attempting to orchestrate an effective immune response against the virus are infected and likely partially deleted in the early phase of infection when viral load is so high. This leaves most infected persons with an impaired ability to fight HIV-1 infection.

Lymphocytes bearing the CD8 cell surface marker, called *cytotoxic T lymphocytes* (CTLs), are generated, and their appearance correlates with the initial dramatic decrease in plasma viral load. The functioning of these cells is impaired in the absence of an adequate virus-specific CD4 T-helper cell response, however, explaining the lack of effective long-term control of infection. The difficulty with immune control is augmented further by the continued evolution of the virus within an infected person. Infidelity of the viral reverse transcriptase allows for the generation of multiple, closely related yet distinct viruses within a given person. In the same way that partial antiviral drug pressure allows for the generation of drug resistance mutations, partial antiviral immune pressure allows for the gradual development of mutations within key sites targeted by the immune responses that have been generated.

In contrast to the rapid generation of cellular immune responses, the antibody response to HIV is slower to develop, presenting a clinical problem with using the standard ELISA for diagnosis of acute infection. Antibodies generally are detected within a few weeks of infection, and these are mostly antibodies that bind to virion debris but are not functional in terms of being able to neutralize infectious virus. The lack of induction of strong neutralizing antibodies is one of the major problems with HIV infection and represents a major hurdle for vaccine development. The reasons these antibodies are only weakly neutralizing include the impressive ability of HIV to mutate its outer envelope protein, the major target for neutralizing antibodies, and the heavy sugar coating on the envelope of the virus that keeps crucial neutralization sites masked from the immune system. Figure 410–2 provides an overview of immune responses to HIV.

CLINICAL IMPLICATIONS OF HIV-RELATED IMMUNOLOGY

Absolute CD4 Cell Count: Measurement and Interpretation

To the practicing clinician, the most important application of HIV-related immunology is the measurement and interpretation of the

HIV and AIDS

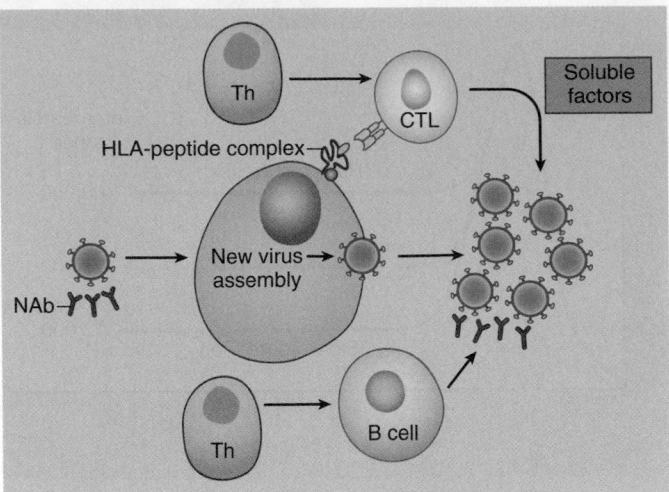

FIGURE 410–2 • Immune responses to HIV. Virus-infected cells produce progeny virions within approximately 2 days. After viral entry, virion proteins are presented at the cell surface in the groove of an HLA class I molecule. This complex is recognized by cytotoxic T lymphocytes (CTLs), which can directly lyse infected cells and secrete soluble factors that inhibit viruses that may have been released already. B cells produce neutralizing antibodies that directly neutralize free virions. B-cell function and CTL function are critically dependent on signals received from CD4 T-helper cells.

absolute CD4 cell count. This value is derived from multiplying the number of lymphocytes on a complete blood count by the percentage of CD4+ lymphocytes, the latter determined by flow cytometry. CD4 cells are composed of many different specificities—not only those that are specific for HIV, but also those that are specific for other pathogens, including opportunistic pathogens. The CD4 cell count does not provide any indication of the specific function of the CD4 cells, but only a cumulative number of cells present. It currently is recommended that patients have this test done at the time of HIV diagnosis, then repeated approximately every 3 to 4 months, usually in conjunction with an HIV RNA (viral load) test.

The risk of HIV-related complications correlates strongly with the absolute count and the CD4 percentage, although presently only the absolute count is formally incorporated into guidelines for initiation of antiretroviral therapy (ART) or prevention of opportunistic infections. This relationship is due to the fact that as more CD4 cell decline occurs, the individual subsets that orchestrate effective immunity against a variety of pathogens drops below a crucial threshold. From an epidemiologic perspective, patients with CD4 cell counts less than 200 cells/mm³ or CD4 percentage less than 14% meet the Centers for Disease Control and Prevention case definition of AIDS even in the absence of an HIV-related opportunistic infection. Some clinicians make a further distinction of 50 cells/mm³ as another important threshold (often called *advanced HIV disease*) because these patients are at particularly high risk for opportunistic infections and HIV-related death.

CD4 Cell Counts, Immune Responses, and Antiretroviral Therapy

For treatment-naive patients, potent ART with at least three active agents has a rapid, predictable effect on lowering HIV RNA levels, with a corresponding (albeit slower) increase in the CD4 cell count. The CD4 cell count recovery in response to ART has important clinical implications and has been shown to be the most important predictor of clinical outcome, even more so than the virologic response.

After introduction of potent ART in the mid-1990s, the most immediate evidence of improved immunologic function secondary to ART was the improvement or resolution of opportunistic processes for which specific therapy either did not exist or was only marginally effective. These processes included progressive multifocal leukoencephalopathy, cryptosporidiosis, azole-resistant *Candida* esophagitis, and Kaposi's sarcoma. These clinical improvements provided persuasive evidence that the immune system recovery resulting from ART was

of a considerable qualitative and not just quantitative (as measured by absolute CD4 cell count) nature. The incidence of common HIV-related opportunistic infections, such as *Pneumocystis carinii* pneumonia, disseminated *Mycobacterium avium* complex (MAC) infection, and invasive cytomegalovirus (CMV) disease, decreased dramatically after the introduction of protease inhibitor–based therapy, even without an increase in the use of specific opportunistic infection prophylaxis.

Recognition of this markedly reduced risk of opportunistic infections with ART-associated increases in CD4 cell counts led to clinical studies of withdrawing specific prophylaxis for patients who have experienced ART-induced increases in CD4 numbers above certain thresholds. These studies so far uniformly have shown that this strategy is safe, and as a result recent guidelines for prevention of opportunistic infections have incorporated stopping strategies for prophylaxis of most conditions. Because antibody responses to vaccinations are improved with higher CD4 cell counts, these guidelines now recommend deferring certain vaccinations (e.g., the pneumococcal vaccine) until CD4 has risen to greater than 200 cells/mm³.

Discordant CD4/HIV RNA Responses

ART-induced increases in the CD4 cell count are much more variable from patient to patient than HIV RNA reduction. Although most patients experience at least a 100 cell/mm³ increase after 12 months of therapy, some have an even more robust response, with others having hardly any increase at all. Factors found in some studies to be associated with poor CD4 responses include older age, high baseline HIV RNA levels and low CD4 cell counts, hepatitis C coinfection, and receipt of a non–protease inhibitor–containing regimen. Some genetic factors are involved as well, including the patient's chemokine-receptor CCR5 and multidrug-resistance (MDR1) transporter genotype. These genetic tests are not currently available to clinicians on a routine basis, however.

Because some patients do not experience a sustained significant increase in CD4 cell counts, there has been considerable interest in using interleukin (IL)-2 to boost this response. Several studies have shown that patients with HIV given IL-2 plus ART in a variety of different dosing strategies have a significantly greater CD4 response than patients receiving ART alone. Further studies of IL-2 are ongoing to establish whether this increase in CD4 cells translates into clinical benefit because the therapy has a high rate of subjective adverse effects (mostly flulike symptoms) and is costly.

A different form of discordant HIV RNA and CD4 response is seen when there is a continued increase or stability in the CD4 cell count despite a rebounding HIV RNA level. This situation has been observed most commonly in patients treated with a protease inhibitor–containing regimen and accounts for in part the ongoing excellent short-term prognosis of HIV patients on therapy despite the high rates of virologic breakthrough seen in clinical practice. Several possible explanations for this HIV RNA-CD4 "disconnect" phenomenon have been proposed, not mutually exclusive. They include (1) emergence of antiviral-resistant HIV strains with impaired virulence ("fitness") compared with wild-type virus; (2) reduced CD4 cell turnover compared with untreated controls; and (3) the prolonged time that the HIV RNA level remains below the pretreatment baseline, even after clear emergence of drug resistance. The duration of this immunologic benefit from ART despite virologic rebound varies among patients but in one study persisted for 72 weeks.

Immune Reconstitution Syndromes

Improvements in immune function after starting ART sometimes can lead to dramatic worsening of preexisting opportunistic infections, either infections that have been diagnosed previously (e.g., CMV retinitis) or that were clinically inapparent (most commonly disseminated MAC). These *immune reconstitution* syndromes likely result from eliciting a previously weak or absent host inflammatory response, which becomes much stronger as a result of ART. In a typical case, a patient with a severely depleted CD4 cell count (usually <50 cells/mm³) starts a potent ART regimen and has a prompt HIV RNA decline and CD4 cell count increase. Several weeks to months later, the patient may present with fevers, night sweats, and on computed tomography scan, dramatic focal lymphadenitis—any or all of the mesenteric, thoracic, inguinal, cervical, and axillary sites may be involved. On biopsy, pathology reveals acid-fast organisms

HIV and AIDS

Table 410–1 • IMMUNOTHERAPEUTIC APPROACHES BEING TESTED FOR TREATMENT OF HIV INFECTION
Recombinant virus vaccines
Interleukin-2 therapy
Whole inactivated viral vaccines
Antigen-pulsed dendritic cells
CD4 and/or CD8 T-cell infusions
Passive antibody infusions

and granulomatous inflammation. In the United States, this most commonly would be MAC disease, but an identical presentation has been reported with tuberculosis. With CMV retinitis, a patient with indolent retinal disease suddenly may develop a brisk vitritis, a response that was distinctly unusual in the pre-ART era. Analogous immune reconstitution syndromes have been described for several common HIV-related opportunistic infections, including *P. carinii* pneumonia, cryptococcosis, toxoplasmosis, and progressive multifocal leukoencephalopathy.

Optimal management of these syndromes is still being defined. ∎ Targeted treatment of the underlying opportunistic infection and continuation of ART are desirable. If symptoms are particularly prolonged or severe, palliative corticosteroids may be required, although only when the risk of further immunosuppression is warranted based on the severity of the syndrome.

Prospects for Immune Augmentation as a Treatment for HIV Infection

The increases in CD4 cell counts that accompany treatment with ART are associated with significant increases in immunity to opportunistic infections, but similar increases in immunity to HIV itself rarely are observed. The major exception is when persons are treated with highly active antiretroviral therapy (HAART) in the earliest stages of acute HIV infection. HAART has been shown to result not only in dramatic increases in CD4 cell count, but also increases in the subset of CD4 cells that are directed specifically against HIV, which function to orchestrate effective immunity during the chronic phase of infection. The ART likely protects these activated HIV-specific CD4 cells from becoming infected. These persons, when exposed to limited amounts of their own virus through brief treatment interruptions—called *structured treatment interruption*—have been shown to develop stronger HIV-specific CD4 and CD8 T-cell responses, and many have been able to go on to prolonged periods of immune control in the absence of ongoing therapy. Later development of mutations that occur when the virus continues to replicate at low levels has led to viral breakthrough, however. Although the transient augmentation in immune control is encouraging, the prospects for long-term control are unclear. Structured treatment interruption in chronic infection has been less successful as a means of boosting immunity to HIV. This situation likely relates to a greater viral quasispecies present later in infection, more immune escape variants, and the lack of HIV-specific T-helper cell responses when therapy is started in chronic infection.

Many other approaches are being undertaken to augment immunity in HIV-infected persons (Table 410–1). Prominent among these is therapeutic immunization, in which persons already infected are immunized to boost immune responses. The hypothesis that increasing or broadening the HIV-specific CD4 and CD8 T-cell responses would allow for better immune control has yet to be proved in humans, but encouraging data have been generated in animal models of AIDS virus infection, and numerous studies of this approach are likely to be seen in the next few years.

1. Currier JS, Williams PL, Koletar SL, et al: Discontinuation of *Mycobacterium avium* complex prophylaxis in patients with antiretroviral therapy–induced increases in CD4+ cell count: A randomized, double-blind, placebo-controlled trial. AIDS Clinical Trials Group 362 Study Team. Ann Intern Med 2000;133:493–503.

SUGGESTED READINGS

Altfeld M, Allen TM, Yu XG, et al: HIV-1 superinfection despite broad CD8+ T-cell responses containing replication of the primary virus. Nature 2002;420:434–439. *This study in a single patient provides the first clear evidence of superinfection with a second strain of HIV of the same clade, in this case clade B. This superinfection occurred despite broadly directed and strong CTL responses to the initial virus, half of which were cross-reactive with the second strain.*

Barouch DH, Kunstman J, Kuroda MJ, et al: Eventual AIDS vaccine failure in a rhesus monkey by viral escape from cytotoxic T lymphocytes. Nature 2002;415:335–339. *In a cohort of rhesus monkeys that were vaccinated and subsequently infected with a pathogenic hybrid simian human immunodeficiency virus, excellent initial control of viremia was achieved. A single mutation within an immunodominant CTL epitope in an animal with undetectable plasma viral RNA resulted, however, in viral escape from CTLs, a burst of viral replication, clinical disease progression, and death from AIDS-related complications.*

Deeks SG, Barbour JD, Martin JN, et al: Sustained CD4+ T cell response after virologic failure of protease inhibitor–based regimens in patients with human immunodeficiency virus infection. J Infect Dis 2000;181:946–953. *Even after experiencing virologic rebound on protease inhibitor–containing ART, patients in this observational cohort had stable or increasing CD4 cell counts. Their HIV RNA levels remained below their pretreatment baseline, suggesting possible attenuation of viral fitness in drug-resistant viruses.*

DeSimone JA, Pomerantz RJ, Babinchak TJ: Inflammatory reactions in HIV-1-infected persons after initiation of highly active antiretroviral therapy. Ann Intern Med 2000;133:447–454. *A review of the clinical manifestations and management of the paradoxical worsening of opportunistic infections that may occur shortly after starting ART.*

Fellay J, Marzolini C, Meaden ER, et al: Response to antiretroviral treatment in HIV-1-infected individuals with allelic variants of the multidrug resistance transporter 1: A pharmacogenetics study. Lancet 2002;359:30–36. *Despite having lower blood levels of antiretroviral agents, patients with lower expression of MDR1 had a greater increase in their CD4 cell counts after achieving virologic suppression; the likely explanation is that they had higher intracellular concentrations of active drugs. This raises the question of whether knowledge of patient MDR1 genotype can help predict response to ART.*

Grabar S, Le Moing V, Goujard C, et al: Clinical outcome of patients with HIV-1 infection according to immunologic and virologic response after 6 months of highly active antiretroviral therapy. Ann Intern Med 2000;133:401–410. *The lowest risk for opportunistic infections after starting ART was seen in patients who experienced virologic suppression and a significant CD4 cell count increase. Patients with CD4 increases who did not have virologic suppression also had an excellent prognosis, which was better than patients who had virologic suppression without CD4 increases.*

Lalezari JP, Beal JA, Ruane PJ, et al: Low-dose daily subcutaneous interleukin-2 in combination with highly active antiretroviral therapy in HIV+ patients: A randomized controlled trial. HIV Clin Trials 2000;1:1–15. *IL-2 increases CD4 cell count numbers in patients on ART; although the study was not powered for clinical end points, no difference in clinical outcomes was observed.*

Ledergerber B, Egger M, Opravil M, et al: Clinical progression and virological failure on highly active antiretroviral therapy in HIV-1 patients: A prospective cohort study. Swiss HIV Cohort Study. Lancet 1999;353:863–868. *The risk of HIV disease progression in this prospective cohort study was extremely low for patients receiving ART, even with relatively high rates of virologic failure.*

Lyles RH, Munoz A, Yamashita TE, et al: Natural history of human immunodeficiency virus type 1 viremia after seroconversion and proximal to AIDS in a large cohort of homosexual men. Multicenter AIDS Cohort Study. J Infect Dis 2000;181:872–880. *This study of 269 untreated persons with documented acute HIV infection indicates that the decline in CD4 lymphocyte counts was associated strongly with initial HIV RNA measurements. Initial HIV RNA levels and slopes were associated with AIDS-free times.*

Palella FJ Jr et al: Survival benefit of initiating antiretroviral therapy in HIV-infected persons in different CD4+ cell strata. Ann Intern Med 2003;138:620–626. *Patients who begin antiretroviral therapy before their CD4 cell count falls below 200 have a survival benefit compared with those who defer until counts are below 200. This study and others suggest an irreversible loss of immune function after moderate-severe CD4 depletion.*

Parren PW, Moore JP, Burton DR, Sattentau QJ: The neutralizing antibody response to HIV-1: Viral evasion and escape from humoral immunity. AIDS 1999;13(Suppl A):S137–S162. *An excellent review of neutralizing antibodies in HIV infection.*

Rosenberg ES, Altfeld M, Poon SH, et al: Immune control of HIV-1 after early treatment of acute infection. Nature 2000;407:523–526. *In this study, eight persons with acute HIV infection underwent treatment with HAART, followed by one or two treatment interruptions. Despite rebound in viremia, all were able to achieve at least transient control of viremia less than 5000 RNA copies/mL plasma.*

Viard JP, Mocroft A, Chiesi A, et al: Influence of age on CD4 cell recovery in human immunodeficiency virus-infected patients receiving highly active antiretroviral therapy: Evidence from the EuroSIDA study. J Infect Dis 2001;183:1290–1294. *Older age was an independent predictor of a less robust CD4 response to ART. The authors postulate that this may be due to preserved thymic function in younger patients.*

411 BIOLOGY OF HUMAN IMMUNODEFICIENCY VIRUSES

George M. Shaw

Discovery of Human Immunodeficiency Viruses

Identification of human immunodeficiency virus type 1 (HIV-1) as the causative agent of acquired immunodeficiency syndrome (AIDS) just 3 years after the clinical syndrome initially was described represents a remarkable scientific achievement that had its roots in earlier discoveries of animal and human retroviruses (Chapter 372). The selective loss of CD4+ helper T lymphocytes in patients with the disease implicated an agent with T-lymphocyte tropism. As expected for an etiologic agent, HIV-1 was shown to be uniformly present in subjects with AIDS and to reproduce the hallmark of disease, destruction of T lymphocytes, in tissue culture.

HUMAN IMMUNODEFICIENCY VIRUS TYPE 1

General Biologic Properties

Soon after its discovery, HIV-1 was shown to be biologically, structurally, and genetically distinct from human T-lymphotrophic virus type 1 (HTLV-1) and type 2 (HTLV-2) and more like members of the lentivirus subfamily of retroviruses (Chapter 372). Unlike the leukemia viruses, which lead to immortalization of lymphocytes in vitro and in vivo, HIV-1 exhibits pronounced cytopathic properties for lymphocytes, causing syncytia formation and cell death. Morphologically, HIV-1 differs from HTLV-1 and other type C oncogenic retroviruses in exhibiting a dense, cylindrical core surrounded by a lipid envelope typical of lentiviruses (Fig. 411–1).

The structural organization of HIV-1 is shown diagrammatically in Figure 411–2. Like all retroviruses, HIV-1 is a single-stranded, plus-sense RNA virus. The RNA-dependent DNA polymerase, or reverse transcriptase, is packaged within the virion core and is responsible for replicating the single-stranded RNA genome through a double-stranded DNA intermediate, which serves as the precursor molecule for proviral integration within the host cell genome. The major structural core proteins of HIV-1 are the p24 capsid protein and the p18 matrix protein. Surrounding the viral core protein structures is a bilayered lipid envelope that is derived from the outer limiting membrane of the host cell as the virus buds from the cell surface during replication. Studding this outer viral membrane are the envelope glycoproteins, gp120 and gp41, which are encoded by virus-specific genes and are responsible for cell attachment and entry.

The life cycle of HIV-1 is shown diagrammatically in Figure 411–3. Features of this life cycle distinguish retroviruses from all other viruses. The cell-free virion first attaches to the target cell through a specific interaction between the viral envelope and the host cell membrane. The specificity of this interaction between virus and cell results from a high-affinity interaction between the viral gp120 envelope glycoprotein and the target cell–associated CD4 molecule, leading to a conformational change in gp120 and a subsequent interaction with a member of the cellular chemokine receptor family (CCR5 or CXCR4). These highly specific interactions among gp120, CD4, and CCR5/CXCR4 lead to fusion of viral and cellular membranes and internalization of the nucleoprotein viral complex. Reverse transcription catalyzed by the viral reverse transcriptase generates a double-stranded DNA copy of the viral RNA within the nucleoprotein complex, and this migrates to the nucleus, where covalent integration of viral DNA into the host chromosomes leads to formation of the provirus. Subsequent expression of viral DNA is controlled by a combination of viral and host cellular proteins that interact with viral DNA and RNA regulatory elements. Transcribed viral mRNA is translated into viral proteins, and new virions are assembled at the cell surface, where genomic-length viral RNA, reverse transcriptase, structural and regulatory proteins, and envelope glycoproteins are assembled. Because the HIV-1 provirus is covalently integrated within the host cell chromosome, it represents a stable component of the host genome. Relevant to subsequent discussions of viral pathogenesis, the integrated provirus may remain transcriptionally latent or may exhibit high levels of gene expression with explosive production of progeny virus.

Molecular Structure and Function of HIV-1

The genomic organization of HIV-1 is shown diagrammatically in Figure 411–4. The HIV-1 genome, like other retroviral genomes, is diploid, consisting of two identical viral RNA molecules assembled in a hydrogen-bonded 70S complex. These genomic subunits are plus strands of viral RNA in that they have the same chemical polarity as the mRNA from which viral products are translated. Like eukaryotic mRNAs, the genomic viral RNA contains a 5'-methyl-G nucleotide, a poly(A) tract of 100 to 200 nucleotides at its 3' end, and a number of methylated(A) residues. Host cell-derived tRNA incorporated within the virion is base paired over a stretch of 18 nucleotides to the primer-binding site of the genomic viral RNA near its 5' terminus and serves to prime the synthesis of minus-strand DNA during the initial stages of viral replication after infection.

The HIV-1 genome is bounded by long terminal repeat (LTR) elements and contains genes encoding structural and enzymatic proteins (gag, pol, and env) found in all other replication-competent retroviruses. In addition to these, HIV-1 contains genes encoding other viral functions unique to this family of viruses that are responsible for their biologic behavior. The LTR sequences of HIV-1 direct and regulate expression of the viral genome (Fig. 411–5).

The *gag* gene encodes a precursor protein (p55) of 55 kD, which is cleaved into four smaller products with the linear order of NH_2-p18-p24-p9-p7-COOH. These proteins constitute the core protein structure of the virus and subserve nucleic acid and lipid membrane binding functions. The gag proteins of HIV-1, like those of other retroviruses, are synthesized as a polyprotein precursor that subsequently is cleaved during the viral maturation process. This facilitates the assembly of the different components of the virus core structure into a three-dimensional configuration that, when cleaved by a specific virus-derived protease, acquires the specialized functions characteristic of the mature virion. The polymerase gene products are translated from the same genomic RNA message as the gag proteins but in a different, overlapping reading frame as a result of ribosomal frame shifting. The *pol* gene encodes three proteins that are cleaved from a larger precursor polypeptide. These genes include NH_2-protease

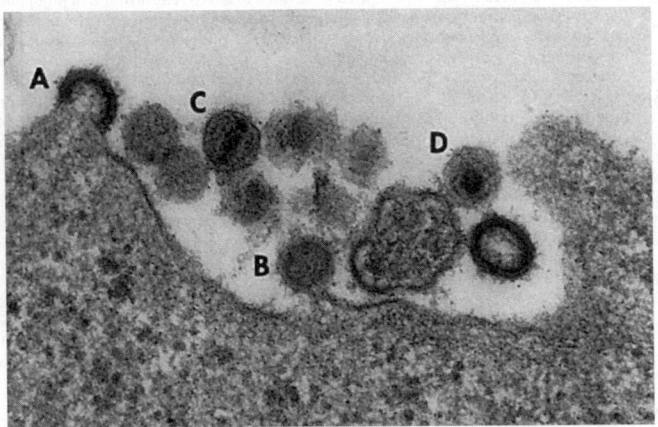

FIGURE 411–1 • Transmission electron micrograph of HIV-1. Virions are shown at all stages of morphogenesis: early (*A*) and late (*B*) budding forms, and cell-free mature virions (*C* and *D*) with condensed central cores. The virion diameter is approximately 110 nm.

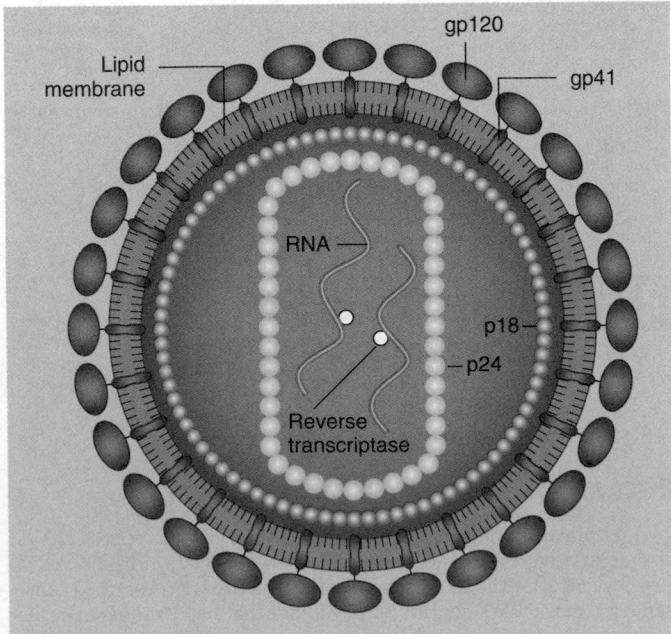

FIGURE 411–2 • Structure of HIV-1. (Adapted from RC Gallo. Copyright © 1987 by Scientific American, Inc., and George V. Kelvin.)

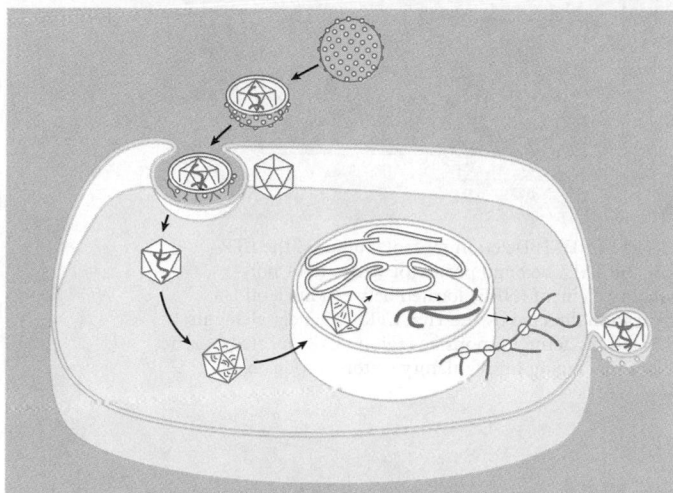

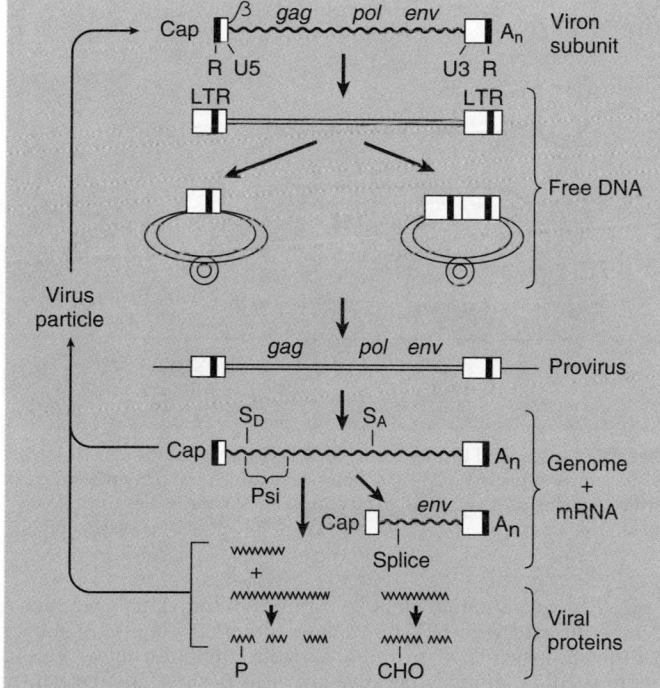

FIGURE 411–3 • Different representations of the HIV-1 life cycle. *A*, Thick arrows denote amplification of viral products that may occur in the latter half of the replication cycle. *B*, A pictorial overview of the virus life cycle outlined in *A*. *C*, Major transformations of retroviral genetic information during the life cycle. A$_n$ = poly(A) tract; Cap = 5′-methyl-G nucleotide; CHO = glycosylation site; S$_A$ = splice acceptor site; S$_D$ = splice donor site; P = phosphorylation site; Psi = viral packaging signal sequence. (From Varmus H, Brown P: Retroviruses. *In* Berg DE, Howe MM [eds]: Mobile DNA. Washington, DC, American Society for Microbiology, 1989, p 53.)

(p13)–reverse transcriptase (p66/p51)–integrase (p31)–COOH. The HIV-1 protease plays a critical role in virus biology, acting specifically to cleave gag and pol precursor polypeptides into functionally active proteins. The reverse transcriptase of HIV-1 is a magnesium-requiring, RNA-dependent DNA polymerase responsible for replicating the RNA viral genome. The integrase protein is required for proviral integration into the host cell genome.

The envelope gene *(env)* encodes a glycosylated polypeptide precursor (gp160), which is processed to form the exterior envelope glycoprotein (gp120), and the transmembrane glycoprotein (gp41), which anchors the envelope complex to the virus surface. In recent years, much has been learned about the structure and function of the HIV-1 envelope. The gp120/gp41 heterodimer exists as a trimeric spike complex on the virion surface and must serve two separate but essential functions: mediation of virus entry into cells and avoidance of immunologic detection by antibodies. The former task is accomplished by sequential gp120 binding of CD4 and a chemokine receptor, which triggers a gp41-mediated fusion event. The latter function results from a combination of carbohydrate cloaking and variation on exposed surfaces of gp120 along with mutational escape at variable envelope surface loop sequences and conformational masking at conserved receptor surfaces.

Within the HIV-1 genome, additional genes serve important viral functions and distinguish HIV-1 from oncogenic retroviruses. They include the *vif, vpr,* and *vpu* genes located between *pol* and *env;* the *nef* gene located 3′ to the *env* and extending into the U3 region of the viral LTR; and the *tat* and *rev* genes, both of which exist as bipartite coding exons in the central and 3′ end of the virus. The *tat* gene encodes a 14-kD protein that is essential for HIV-1 replication, upregulating HIV-1 expression at transcriptional and post-transcriptional levels. The target sequence for *tat*-mediated upregulation of HIV-1 expression is the *trans*-acting responsive region (TAR) of the LTR, which interacts with cellular factors to bind and activate TAR (see Fig. 411–5). The *rev* gene is absolutely required for HIV-1 replication, facilitating transport of unspliced viral mRNA from the nucleus to cytoplasm. In the absence of *rev* genes, gag and env mRNA transcripts are multiply spliced such that gag and env proteins are not made. The *vif* gene encodes a protein product of 23 kD, which is required for the production of virions that are fully infectious. The *vpr* gene encodes a protein of 15 kD that is involved in transport of the viral preintegration complex (see Fig. 411–3) to the nucleus and arrests activated and dividing cells in the G$_2$ phase of the cell cycle. The latter is believed to enhance HIV-1 production. The *vpu* gene encodes a 16-kD protein that is involved in virus assembly and release. The *nef* gene encodes a 27-kD protein that decreases CD4 expression in virally infected cells and, by this or other means, accentuates viral pathogenesis in vivo.

In summary, HIV-1 encodes the usual structural and enzymatic proteins typical of other replication-competent retroviruses, including gag, pol, and env, but it also encodes a group of at least six regulatory or auxiliary proteins (vif, vpr, vpu, tat, rev, and nef) whose activities are critically important in regulating the life cycle and pathogenesis of the virus.

Cell Tropism

The hallmark of AIDS is a selective depletion of CD4+ helper-inducer T lymphocytes. This defect is believed to result largely from the selective tropism of HIV-1 for this population of cells based on the high affinity of the viral gp120 envelope protein for the CD4 molecule ($k_m = 4 \times 10^{-9}$ M). CD4 normally serves as a ligand for major histocompatibility complex type II (MHC II) interaction, but in HIV-1 infection, it is used as the primary receptor molecule for HIV-1 targeting. This has been shown conclusively by studies demonstrating (1) direct complexing of gp120 and CD4 during viral infection; (2) viral attachment and infection inhibition by anti-CD4 monoclonal antibodies that prevent gp120 binding; and (3) the ability of recombinant CD4 to confer susceptibility to HIV-1 infection to transfected human cells that normally do not express CD4 (e.g., HeLa cells).

CD4 expression alone is not sufficient to mediate HIV-1 entry. Coreceptors essential for virus entry include members of the chemokine receptor family, which are G-protein–coupled receptors for pro-inflammatory chemokines. They include CCR5, which normally responds to the chemokines RANTES, MIP-1α, and MIP-1β, and CXCR4, which normally binds SDF-1. CCR5 and CXCR4 are

HIV and AIDS

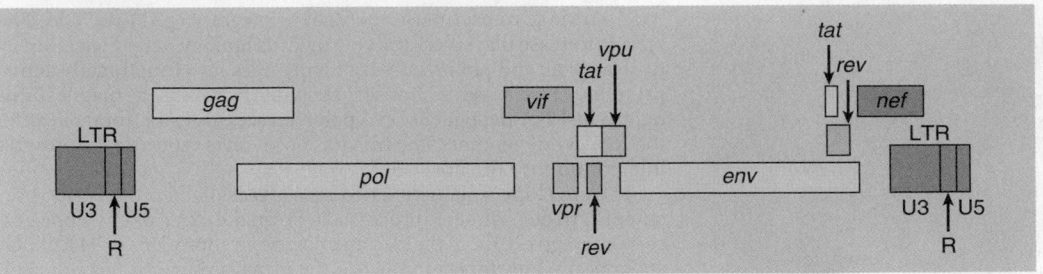

FIGURE 411–4 • Genomic organization of HIV-1.

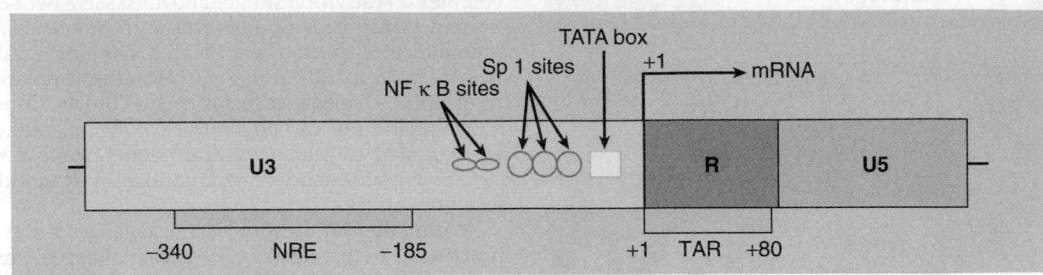

FIGURE 411–5 • Regulatory regions in the long terminal repeat (LTR) of HIV-1. Deletion mutant studies of the LTR have identified at least five regions for gene expression, including the TATA box and promotor where RNA polymerase binds and transcription is initiated (+1); a negative regulatory element (NRE) located between nucleotides −340 and −185, deletion of which increases the level of gene expression directed by the viral LTR; enhancer elements (NFκB and Sp-1) located between nucleotides −137 and −17; and a *trans*-acting responsive region (TAR) located between nucleotides +1 and +80, which represents the putative binding region for regulatory factors responsible for tat-mediated transcriptional activation.

differentially expressed on normal human cells that serve as targets of HIV-1 infection and are importantly involved in cellular and tissue tropism of HIV-1 and in virus transmission and pathogenesis.

A variety of cell types other than helper-inducer T lymphocytes are known to express CD4 on their surface and are capable of replicating HIV-1. They include blood monocytes, tissue macrophages, Langerhans cells in skin, and microglial and multinucleated giant cells in the central nervous system (CNS). These cells generally express smaller amounts of CD4 on their cell surface, but in each case, they express one or more coreceptor molecules. Infection of such cells is believed to play an important role in the pathogenesis of AIDS. Other cell types, including neurons, glial cells, gastrointestinal epithelial cells, and kidney epithelium, can support HIV-1 infection, but the pathophysiologic significance of such findings in regard to viral pathogenesis in vivo is uncertain.

Viral Pathogenesis

Retroviral diseases are typically characterized by restricted viral gene expression, latency, and lifelong persistence of virus in the face of substantial host immune responses. From cohort studies of individuals infected with HIV-1 before the era of highly active antiretroviral therapy (HAART), it was estimated that between 26 and 36% of infected individuals develop AIDS within 7 years of infection and that an additional 40% develop lesser signs of immune dysfunction. This protracted clinical course suggested that expression of the HIV-1 genome in vivo was to some degree downregulated compared with in vitro infection of lymphocytes by HIV-1, which is characterized by explosive lytic viral infection.

Figure 411–6 depicts the natural history of HIV-1 infection of humans in relation to clinical symptoms, immune function, and viral replication. Initial infection with HIV-1 frequently causes an acute viral syndrome with protean manifestations typically characterized by fever, lymphadenopathy, pharyngitis, and rash. Other symptoms and signs that may occur with acute HIV-1 infection include myalgias and arthralgias, leukopenia, thrombocytopenia, nausea, diarrhea, headache, and encephalopathy. During this primary phase of infection, symptoms are accompanied by high-level HIV-1 plasma viremia, with peak titers reaching 10^8 virions/mL. Viremia is also accompanied by high levels of circulating HIV-1 p24 antigen, only part of which is virion associated, with the remainder circulating alone or

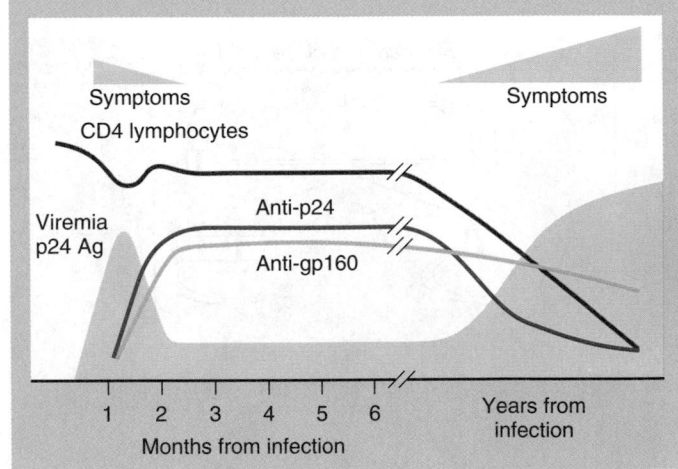

FIGURE 411–6 • Natural history model for HIV-1 infection. Viremia denotes cell-free virus in plasma, p24 Ag denotes circulating viral p24 antigen in plasma, and anti-p24 and anti-gp160 correspond to antibodies to viral core and envelope proteins.

complexed with immunoglobulin. Studies of individuals who have become infected with HIV-1 at defined points in time have shown that there is a "window" period of variable length during which the patient is HIV-1 antibody negative but virus positive and frequently highly infectious. This antibody-negative, virus-positive period generally ranges from 2 to 6 weeks from initial exposure (and infection), but rare cases have been documented in which antibody seroconversion has occurred as long as 6 months after infection. During this time, patients may or may not have symptoms of acute infection prompting medical attention. Plasma virus RNA is the first serologic indicator of HIV-1 infection in the setting of acute infection. Positive tests for plasma viral RNA, followed by plasma virus p24 antigen, and HIV-1 antibodies by ELISA and then immunoblot analysis, indicate recent exposure and infection by HIV-1.

Although HIV-1 replication is to some degree downregulated by host defense mechanisms and resolution of the acute pro-inflammatory infectious state, virus replication is not contained. Even during the clinically quiescent stages of infection, substantial viral replication ensues, leading to progressive CD4+ cell destruction. This serves as the rationale for clinical studies examining the utility or cost-benefit ratio of antiviral therapy initiated at the earliest stages of infection.

The protracted clinical course of HIV-1 infection and the demonstrated benefits and toxicities of HAART raise clinically relevant questions regarding viral pathogenesis. What are the mechanisms responsible for CD4+ cell loss in vivo? What are the viral and host interactions that underlie the chronicity of HIV-1 infection, and how can they be manipulated? What is the relation between plasma viral load set point, CD4+ lymphocyte count, immunologic competence, irreversible immunologic decline, and clinical outcome?

The precise biologic mechanisms responsible for the cytopathic effects of HIV-1 in vivo are unknown. Molecularly cloned HIV-1 proviral DNA, transfected into human cells, has been shown in cell culture experiments to contain all necessary information to generate infectious and cytopathic virus. Expression of HIV-1 proteins in activated lymphocytes leads to cell cycle arrest in G_2 and cell death within approximately 2 days. There is no question that HIV-1 alone exerts direct cytopathic activity against CD4+ lymphocytes in vitro and in vivo. Expression of only the HIV-1 envelope on lymphocytes is sufficient for inducing fusion of cells with normal uninfected CD4+ bystander cells, suggesting that syncytium formation mediated by gp120-CD4 interaction may also contribute to cell loss in vivo. Other mechanisms of CD4 cell loss may also be operative. Cell-free HIV-1 gp120 envelope protein adsorbs to CD4+ cells and may serve as an antigen for mediating antibody-dependent cell-mediated cytotoxicity and, when processed by antigen-presenting cells, to constitute a target for direct T-cell cytotoxicity. The relative importance of these processes to CD4 cell loss in vivo remains to be determined. Similarly, in the CNS of infected individuals, in which the predominant cell types infected with HIV-1 are cells of the monocyte-macrophage lineage, additional mechanisms of cellular and organ dysfunction probably are involved. Possibilities include the elaboration of cytotoxic factors from infected cells and interference with neurotropic factors leading to the clinically recognized AIDS dementia complex.

Despite uncertainties regarding the actual mechanisms of CD4+ lymphocyte destruction and immune dysfunction, the magnitude of ongoing HIV-1 replication in the absence of effective antiretroviral therapy and its relation to disease outcome are clear. Based on kinetic analyses of plasma virus decay curves after the initiation of HAART, it is known that the lifespan of HIV-1 in plasma is less than 6 hours; that the lifespan of activated, virus-producing CD4+ lymphocytes is less than 1.2 days; and that as many as 10 billion HIV-1 virions are produced and released into the circulation daily. Productively infected macrophages also produce HIV-1, have somewhat longer lifespans (measured in weeks), but nonetheless suffer the same fate of viral or immune-mediated elimination. Plasma virus load measurements in patients directly reflect this extraordinary degree and incessant reiteration of virus production, infected cell turnover, and de novo infection. It is not surprising that clinical outcome as measured by time to AIDS diagnosis or time to AIDS death is significantly related to the steady-state plasma virus load. Ironically, de novo virus infection and more than 99.9% of virus production can almost be eliminated by HAART therapy, but the residual latently infected CD4+ memory T-lymphocyte population (with a lifespan measured in years) remains the major obstacle to therapeutic success.

Because of the balance between the benefits of virus suppression from HAART and its toxicities, host factors responsible for the partial downregulation of HIV-1 replication after initial infection are of particular interest. A strong humoral and cellular immune response to HIV-1 has been documented on the basis of ELISA, immunoblot, and radioimmunoprecipitation assays of patient sera and cell-mediated cytotoxicity to target cells displaying viral antigens. Neutralizing antibodies, antibody-dependent cell-mediated cytotoxicity, antibody-dependent complement-mediated cytotoxicity, MHC-restricted virus-specific cytotoxic T-lymphocyte–mediated cytotoxicity, and natural killer (NK) cell–mediated cytotoxicity all have activity against HIV-1 in vitro and may play an important role in the downmodulation of viral replication. The most convincing evidence for a significant role for cytotoxic T cells in virus containment comes from human studies in which virus escape mutants have been detected and primate studies in which plasma virus loads increased dramatically after elimination of CD8+ cells by monoclonal antibody administration. A major research effort is searching for ways to maintain immunologic

competence in infected individuals and to prevent infection by means of vaccination.

Genetic variability is a hallmark of HIV-1. The variability of the HIV-1 genome is characteristic of retroviruses in general because reverse transcription of viral RNA into proviral DNA and transcription of proviral DNA into genomic viral RNA are not subject to cellular proofreading mechanisms. The rate of nucleotide misincorporation by the viral reverse transcriptase is on the order of 10^{-4} per nucleotide per replication cycle. Because the HIV-1 genome is 10^4 nucleotides long, this high rate of nucleotide misincorporation means that virtually no two viruses are identical and that HIV-1 isolates must, by definition, be described in terms of a "quasi-species" composed of populations highly related by distinct viral genomes. Direct nucleotide sequence analysis of uncultured, virally infected human tissues using polymerase chain reaction amplification has confirmed these findings. At a population level, the variability in HIV-1 can be recognized in the phylogenetic relationships between and among virus strains. HIV-1 viruses globally are composed of three distinct groups: M, N, and O. Group M is present globally and is responsible for 95% of infections worldwide. Groups N and O are largely restricted to west-central Africa. It is believed that HIV-1 groups M, N, and O represent separate introductions of virus into the human population sometime early in the 20th century. Group M viruses can be further subdivided by phylogeny into subtypes A through K. Although these phylogenetic distinctions allow molecular epidemiologic tracking of HIV-1 at a population level, there is little evidence to suggest that the different virus groups and subtypes differ in any clinically meaningful manner. All are pathogenic in humans. However, this is not to say that HIV-1 genetic variability is not clinically important. To the contrary, there is evidence that mutations in the HIV-1 genome lead to viral resistance to reverse transcriptase, protease, and entry inhibitors, thereby limiting their effectiveness. Antigenic properties of the virus may also vary. Studies have shown that HIV-1 commonly escapes from the cellular and humoral arms of the immune system as a result of viral mutation. Genetic variability leads to biologic changes in the virus over time, frequently resulting in the accumulation of virus strains with altered cellular tropism. Patients who develop predominant virus strains that use the CXCR4 coreceptor and display a syncytium-inducing phenotype in vitro have a poor clinical prognosis.

HUMAN IMMUNODEFICIENCY VIRUS TYPE 2

After the discovery of HIV-1 as the cause of epidemic AIDS in the United States, Europe, and Asia, patients in West Africa with AIDS-like symptoms were identified whose sera reacted more strongly with a simian immunodeficiency virus (SIV$_{MAC}$) isolated from captive rhesus macaques in U.S. primate centers than with HIV-1. The identification of patients with serologic reactivity for SIV$_{MAC}$ raised the possibility that certain African human and simian populations could be infected with immunodeficiency viruses related to but distinct from HIV-1. An extensive survey of African primate species for such viruses led initially to the identification of distinct SIV viruses in African green monkeys (SIV$_{AGM}$), mandrills (SIV$_{MND}$), sooty mangabeys (SIV$_{SM}$), and chimpanzees (SIV$_{CPZ}$) (Fig. 411–7). At least 31 naturally infected primate species in Africa are recognized to harbor HIV-like viruses.

West African patients with AIDS-like symptoms and healthy individuals at risk for AIDS were identified who were infected with a virus closely related to SIV$_{SM}$. This virus was isolated, molecularly cloned, and shown through sequence analysis to represent a second major class of human immunodeficiency viruses called HIV-2. Although originally limited geographically to West Africa, HIV-2 has now been identified in patients in Europe, the United States, South America, and India. HIV-2 is approximately 40 to 50% similar to HIV-1 in overall nucleotide sequence homology. There are two major differences in the genomic organization of HIV-1 and HIV-2. The *vpu* gene of HIV-1 is not present in HIV-2, and HIV-2 contains an additional gene, *vpx*, in its central region that is not present in HIV-1. Interestingly, vpx is involved in nuclear transport of the HIV-1 preintegration complex, whereas vpu is responsible for G_2 cell cycle arrest. Antigenically, HIV-2 and HIV-1 are distinct, with greatest cross-reactivity in structural proteins and least in envelope proteins. Licensed ELISA tests to detect HIV-1 infection include HIV-2 antigens as well.

Like HIV-1, HIV-2 selectively infects CD4+ cells. Although HIV-2 can cause profound immunodeficiency and an AIDS syndrome

HIV and AIDS

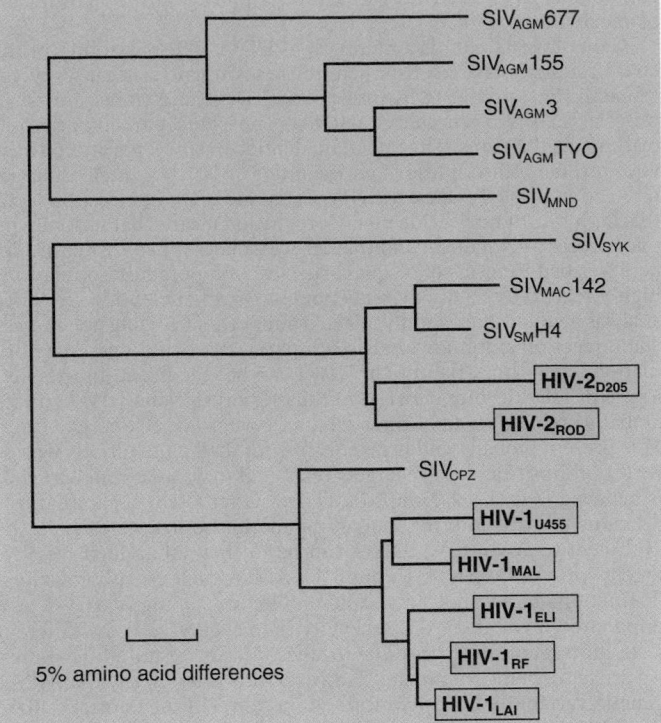

FIGURE 411–7 • Phylogenetic relationships among primate lentiviruses, inferred from pol protein sequences. Independent isolates of simian immunodeficiency viruses (SIVs) obtained from African green monkeys (AGM), mandrill (MND), Sykes (SYK), rhesus macaque (MAC), sooty mangabey (SM), and chimpanzee (CPZ) are depicted along with representative isolates of HIV-1 and HIV-2 (boxed). The horizontal branch lengths are drawn to scale and can be used to determine the percentage difference in pol protein sequences between the different virus strains. There are five major and roughly equidistant phylogenetic lineages of viruses: SIV $_{AGM}$; SIV $_{MND}$; SIV $_{SYK}$; SIV $_{MAC}$/SIV $_{SM}$/HIV-2; and SIV $_{CPZ}$/HIV-1. HIV-1 and HIV-2 appear as members of larger viral lineages composed of simian- and human-derived viruses. Such relationships are indicative of cross-species transmission. (Adapted from Hahn BH: Viral genes and their products. *In* Broder S, Merigan TC, Bolognesi D [eds]: Textbook of AIDS Medicine. Baltimore, Williams & Wilkins, 1994, p 21.)

indistinguishable from that caused by HIV-1, evidence suggests that HIV-2 may be somewhat less virulent than HIV-1 and cause disease over a more prolonged period.

The discovery of two distinct types of human immunodeficiency viruses (HIV-1 and HIV-2) having closely related counterparts in African primates (SIV $_{CPZ}$ in chimpanzees and SIV $_{SM}$ in sooty mangabeys, respectively), along with epidemiologic findings revealing Africa as the geographic source of all human and SIVs, suggested a cross-species (zoonotic) origin for HIV-1 and HIV-2. This conclusion has been confirmed by additional molecular epidemiologic studies that have identified unequivocally the chimpanzee subspecies *Pan troglodytes troglodytes* in west-central Africa as the source of the HIV-1 pandemic and the sooty mangabey (*Cercocebus atys*) in west Africa as the source of HIV-2.

SUGGESTED READINGS

Bailes E, Chaudhuri RR, Santiago ML, et al: The evolution of primate lentiviruses and the origins of AIDS. *In* Leitner T(ed): The Molecular Epidemiology of Human Viruses. Boston, Kluwer Academic Publishers, 2002, p 65. *Comprehensive review of human and primate lentiviral evolution.*

Gallo RC, Salahuddin SZ, Popovic M, et al: Frequent detection and isolation of cytopathic retroviruses (HTLV-III) from patients with AIDS and at risk for AIDS. Science 1984;224:500–503. *Initial report conclusively identifying HIV-1 as the etiologic agent responsible for AIDS.*

Gao F, Bailes E, Robertson DL, et al: Origin of HIV-1 in the chimpanzee *Pan troglodytes troglodytes.* Nature 1999;397:436–441. *Discovery of the origin of HIV-1 in chimpanzees.*

Perelson AS, Essunger P, Cao Y, et al: Decay characteristics of HIV-1 infected compartments during combination therapy. Nature 1997;387:188–191. *Dynamic analysis of HIV-1 production and infected cell turnover in humans.*

Persaud D, Zhou Y, Siliciano JM, Siliciano RF: Latency in human immunodeficiency virus type 1 infection: No easy answers. J Virol 2003;77:1659–1665. *Comprehensive review of HIV-1 latency and implications for therapy.*

Wei X, Ghosh SK, Taylor ME, et al: Viral dynamics in human immunodeficiency virus type 1 infection. Nature 1995;373:117–122. *First description of viral and cellular dynamics underlying HIV-1 pathogenesis.*

412 EPIDEMIOLOGY OF HIV INFECTION AND AIDS

Thomas C. Quinn

Historical Perspective

Two decades after the first recognition of the acquired immunodeficiency syndrome (AIDS) in the United States, the disease has become epidemic in every country of the world. Initially reported as a disease primarily among homosexual men, the disease was rapidly identified among many other risk groups, and it became evident that it was caused by an infectious agent transmitted through sexual activities, parentally through blood transfusions and injecting drug use, and perinatally from mother to infant. Early investigations in the 1980s demonstrated that the etiologic agent of AIDS was the human immunodeficiency virus (HIV), which existed in two types, HIV-1 and HIV-2 (Fig. 412–1). After the development of diagnostic assays for HIV antibody, it became possible to track and monitor the escalating spread of HIV throughout the world, definitively define the modes and probabilities of transmission, and to study the natural history of HIV. Twenty years after the discovery of HIV, it is recognized that HIV disseminated rapidly throughout the world, causing a massive epidemic and becoming one of the leading causes of death worldwide. Prevention efforts and treatment with antiretroviral drugs have tempered the spread and decreased the fatality rate in some countries, but in developing countries where the social, demographic, cultural, and economic impact of the AIDS epidemic has been the greatest, these gains have been too limited and too slow to reverse the escalating trends of the epidemic.

Global Statistics

By December 2002, 67 million people had become infected with HIV since the beginning of the epidemic in 1981 (Table 412–1). Of these individuals, more than 25 million people had already died from AIDS, and it became ranked as one of the leading causes of death throughout the world. According to estimates by Joint United Nations Programme on HIV/AIDS (UNAIDS), 42 million people are living with HIV, representing the human reservoir of HIV infection (Fig. 412–2). In 2002 alone, 5 million people became newly infected, one half of whom were young individuals between the ages of 15 and 24. Nearly 95% of all new infections occurred in developing countries; 50% occurred among women; and the major mode of transmission was heterosexual transmission, although infections continue to spread at high rates among men who have sex with men (MSM). Injecting drug use remains the second leading mode of transmission responsible for rapid spread of HIV throughout Asia, Eastern Europe, and in other developed countries of the world. Perinatal transmission also continues to occur in developing countries, where access to antiretroviral drugs to prevent mother-to-infant transmission is limited or nonexistent. In 2002, 800,000 children became newly infected, and 14 million children have been orphaned by the premature deaths of their parents from AIDS. In 2002, 3.1 million people died of AIDS, including 610,000 children.

From these epidemiologic trends, it is projected that, within the next 8 years, an additional 45 million people will become infected with HIV in 126 low- and middle-income countries, which have the most concentrated or generalized epidemics, unless the world succeeds in mounting a drastically expanded global prevention and treatment effort. It is anticipated that more than 40% of these new infections will occur in Asia and Pacific, although it is apparent that the epidemic will continue to devastate nearly all of the countries of the African continent. During the next decade, without treatment and care in many countries, millions of individuals will join the ranks of the more than 25 million people who have already died.

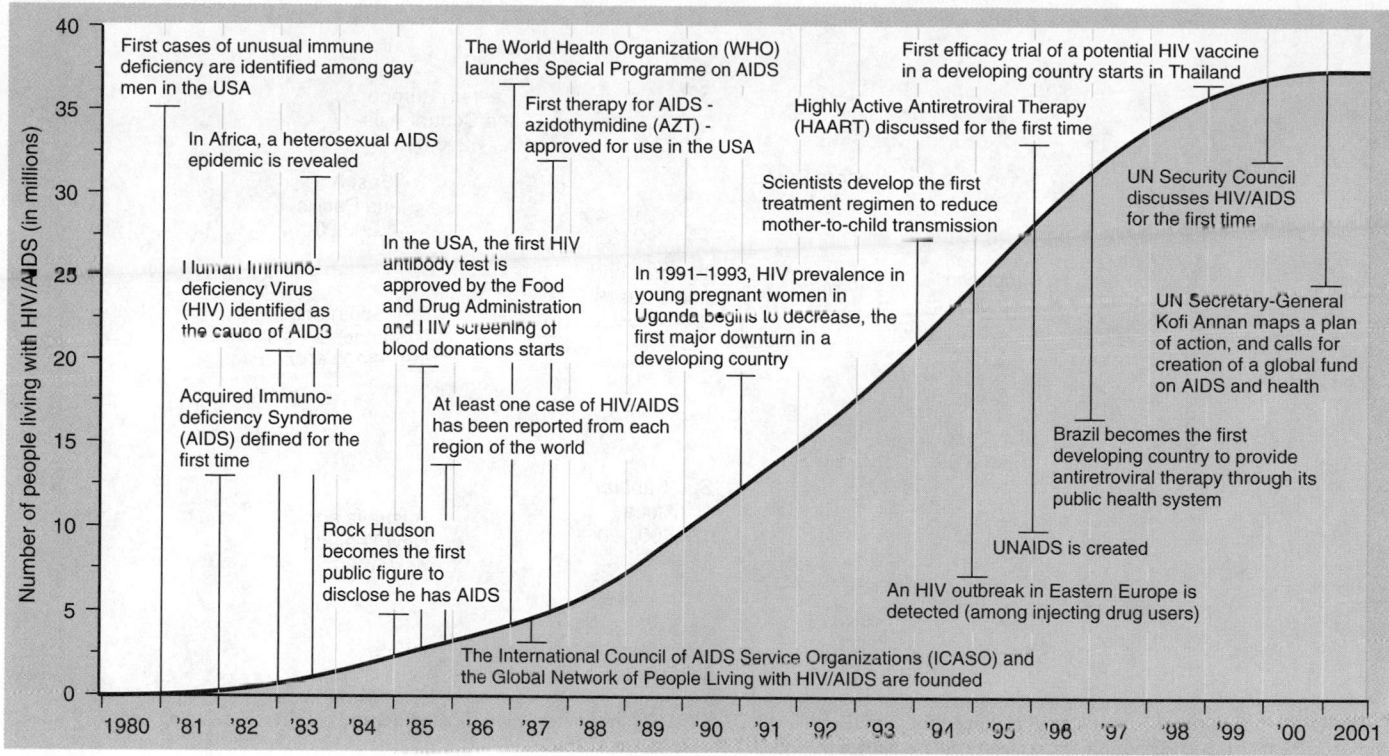

FIGURE 412–1 • Historical perspective on the timeline of HIV infection and AIDS as shown by the epidemic increase in the number of people living with this disease worldwide.

Table 412–1 • REGIONAL HIV AND AIDS STATISTICS AND FEATURES AT THE END OF 2002

REGION	ADULTS AND CHILDREN LIVING WITH HIV/AIDS	ADULTS AND CHILDREN NEWLY INFECTED WITH HIV	ADULT PREVALENCE RATE*	MAIN MODES OF TRANSMISSION FOR ADULTS LIVING WITH HIV/AIDS
Sub-Saharan Africa	29,400,000	3,500,000	8.8%	Hetero
North Africa and Middle East	550,000	83,000	0.3%	Hetero, IDU
South and Southeast Asia	6,000,000	700,000	0.6%	Hetero, IDU
East Asia and Pacific	1,200,000	270,000	0.1%	IDU, hetero, MSM
Latin America	1,500,000	150,000	0.6%	MSM, IDU, hetero
Caribbean	440,000	60,000	2.4%	Hetero, MSM
Eastern Europe and Central Asia	1,200,000	250,000	0.6%	IDU
Western Europe	570,000	30,000	0.3%	MSM, IDU
North America	980,000	45,000	0.6%	MSM, IDU, hetero
Australia and New Zealand	15,000	500	0.1%	MSM
Total	42,000,000	5,000,000	1.2%	

*The proportion of adults (15 to 49 years of age) living with HIV infection or AIDS in 2002, using 2002 population numbers.
Hetero = heterosexual transmission; IDU = transmission through injecting drug use; MSM = sexual transmission among men who have sex with men.

Demographic, Social, and Economic Impact of HIV and AIDS

AIDS is the leading cause of death in sub-Saharan Africa and the fourth largest killer worldwide. Average life expectancy in sub-Saharan Africa is now 47 years; it would have been 62 years of age without AIDS. Life expectancy at birth in Botswana has dropped to a level not seen in that country since the 1950s. Even in Haiti, life expectancy is nearly 6 years less than it would have been in the absence of AIDS. In Asia, Cambodia has experienced the reduction in life expectancy of 4 years. Current HIV prevalence levels merely hint at the greater lifetime probability of being infected with AIDS. In Lesotho, it is estimated that a person who is 15 years old has a 74% chance of being infected with HIV by his or her 50th birthday.

According to one report, AIDS is expected to cause a decline in life expectancy in 51 countries over the next 20 years. Seven nations in sub-Saharan Africa now have life expectancies less than 40 years, and this number will increase by 11 countries over the next 7 years. The declining life expectancies will soon reach levels that have not existed since the 19th century. In Zimbabwe and South Africa, the

infant mortality rate is higher than it was in 1990. Five African nations will experience more deaths than births by 2010, with the resultant decrease in population size. Life expectancy will drop to just 27 years in Botswana and Mozambique in the next 8 years, and Swaziland will have an estimated life expectancy of 33. In Zimbabwe, Zambia, and Namibia, the expected lifespan will be 34 years. In contrast, the overall life expectancy in an African without AIDS would be 70 years by 2010.

REGIONAL EPIDEMICS

HIV and AIDS in Sub-Saharan Africa

Sub-Saharan Africa represents the epicenter of the global HIV/AIDS pandemic. Studies in the late 1990s and in early 2000 support the theory that HIV originated in Africa, and humans probably became infected sometime in the mid-20th century from a similar, related retrovirus in chimpanzees and sooty mangaby monkeys. For years, the infection remained limited in remote rural regions of Africa, but with urbanization, infected individuals migrated to major urban

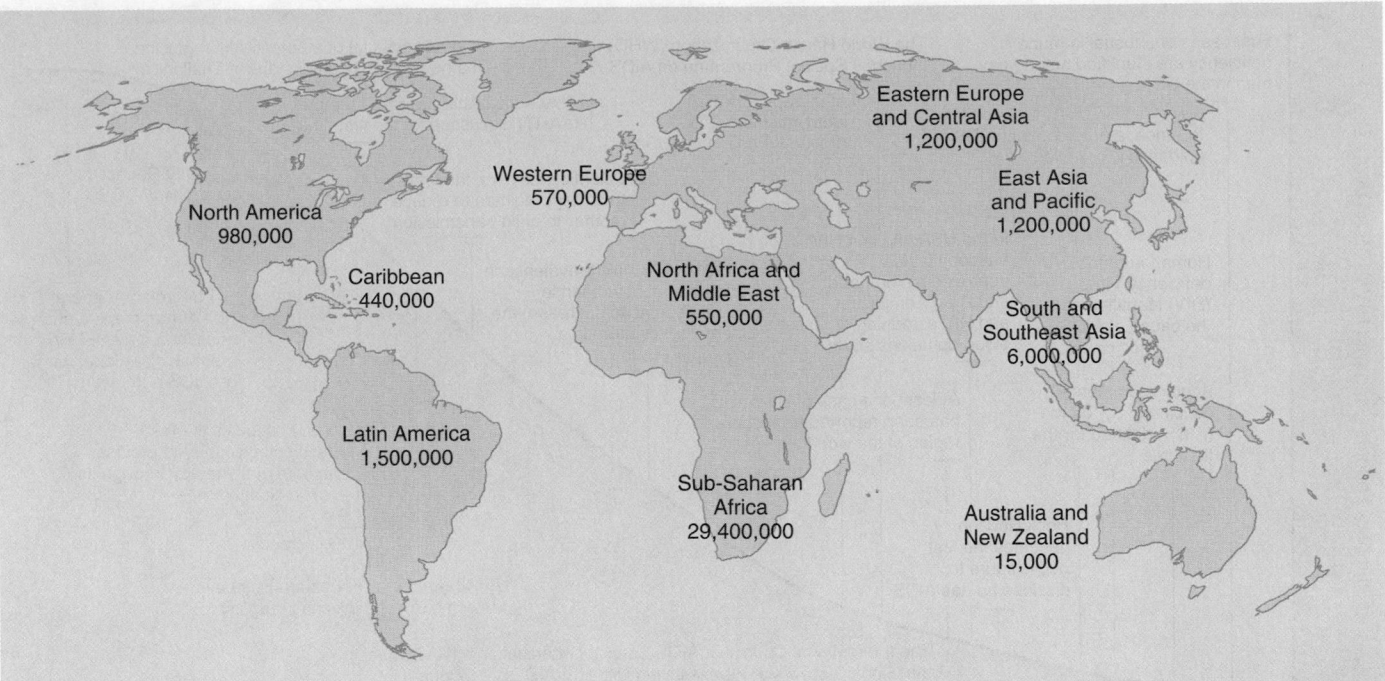

FIGURE 412-2 • According to Joint United Nations Programme on HIV/AIDS (UNAIDS) estimates, 42 million adults and children were living with HIV infection or AIDS in 2002. Distribution of infected people is shown by region. (Data from UNAIDS.)

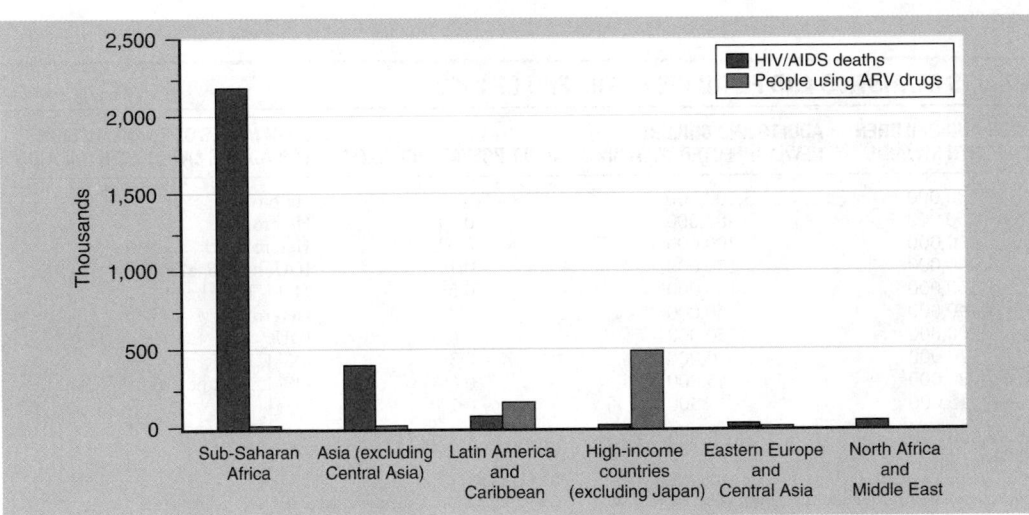

FIGURE 412-3 • Distribution of HIV- and AIDS-related deaths in 2001 and the number of people using antiretroviral drugs during the same time period by region. Notice the extraordinarily large number of deaths in sub-Saharan Africa in contrast to the small number of people accessing antiretroviral drugs. (Data from UNAIDS.)

centers, where transmission was amplified and spread to thousands of individuals within a relatively short period.

Most HIV transmissions in sub-Saharan Africa occur through sexual intercourse, with unsafe blood transfusions and unsafe injections accounting for a smaller fraction. Although sexual behavior is the most important factor influencing the spread of HIV in Africa, that behavior varies greatly across cultures, age groups, socioeconomic class, and gender. The interplay of multiple factors, biologic and behavioral, determines the spread of HIV. One study of four African cities (Cotonou, Kisumu, Ndola, and Yaounde) revealed that the most common behavioral and biologic factors in those cities with the highest HIV prevalence were young age at women's first sexual intercourse, young age at first marriage, age difference between spouses, the presence of herpes simplex type 2 infection and trichomoniasis, and lack of male circumcision. There is substantial evidence that sexually transmitted diseases (STDs) enhance the risk of sexual transmission of HIV, that the level of HIV viral load in an individual enhances the probability of infectiousness, and that male circumcision may be associated with reduced risk of transmission. Although the complex interplay of factors makes it difficult to estimate the likely growth of the epidemic within the region, evidence from the past 2 decades demonstrates that HIV can spread rapidly and widely from very low seroprevalence levels.

Africa is by far the worst affected region in the world for AIDS. It is estimated that nearly 30 million people in sub-Saharan Africa are living with HIV. In 2002, 2.4 million Africans died, and 3.5 million became newly infected. Ten million people younger than 25 years and 3 million children younger than 15 years of age are now living with HIV. In contrast to the developed world, where up to 30% of all infected people receive antiretroviral therapy, fewer than 30,000 people (0.1%) of the 29.4 million infected Africans were estimated to have received antiretroviral therapy in 2002 (Fig. 412–3). Of the 14 million children orphaned by AIDS worldwide, 11 million live in sub-Saharan Africa.

Approximately 50 to 65% of HIV infections in Africa have occurred in east and central Africa, an area that accounts for only 15% of the total population of sub-Saharan Africa. However, studies indicate that the pandemic has continued to evolve, particularly in western and southern Africa. At least 10% of those between the ages of 15 and 49 years are infected in 12 African countries. Seven countries, all in southern Africa, have prevalence rates higher than 20%. Women account for most of the persons living with HIV in sub-Saharan Africa (58%), with the disease primarily obtained through heterosexual transmission. With increasing rates among women, HIV prevalence rates among pregnant women also appear to be increasing across the continent.

Although the general population in Africa is at risk, specific population groups are disproportionately affected by the epidemic. Men and women between the ages of 15 and 40 years, people with STDs, and people in certain occupational groups such as long-distance truck drivers, military personnel, and women employed in commercial sex have had the highest prevalence of infection. HIV prevalence of up to 80 to 90% has been reported for female sex workers in east and central Africa. In Nigeria, a country with more than 117 million inhabitants (20% of sub-Saharan Africa's population), HIV is rapidly spreading among female sex workers and their clients and now in the general population. In some urban populations, more than 10% of the adults are infected, and the annual incidence is estimated to be 3%.

The highest HIV prevalence worldwide for pregnant women stands at 45% in Botswana. In neighboring countries, HIV prevalence rates continue to rise among pregnant women. In Zimbabwe, the prevalence rose from 29% in 1997 to 35% in 2000; in Namibia, it rose from 26% in 1998 to 30% in 2000. Prevalence rates are even higher among specific age groups. For example, in Botswana, among 25- to 29-year-old women attending antenatal clinics in urban areas, 55.6% of pregnant women were infected with HIV. In Swaziland, the corresponding prevalence was 33.9%, and in Zimbabwe, it was 40.1%. For the Republic of South Africa, HIV prevalence rapidly escalated during the 1990s to a rate of 25%. Increasing HIV prevalence is also being reported from West Africa. The relatively low adult HIV prevalence in Senegal and Mali (<2%) are shadowed by the more ominous patterns of growth in neighboring countries. HIV prevalence is estimated to exceed 5% in 0 countries of west and central Africa, including Cameroon (11.8%), Central African Republic (12.9%), and Cote d'Ivoire (9.7%). In Nigeria, the most populous country in sub-Saharan Africa, an increase in prevalence in the general population was reported from 1.9% in 1993 to 6% in 2002. More than 3 million Nigerians are estimated to be living with HIV infection or AIDS. These statistics serve as reminders that no country or region is safe or protected from this epidemic.

Over the past decade, AIDS has become the leading cause of death and years of productive life lost throughout the continent. Excess deaths attributable to HIV are highest in the 25- to 34-year-old group, usually a group with low mortality. Nearly 90% of deaths in this age group are in excess of background rates and were attributable to HIV. Because AIDS deaths are concentrated in childhood and young adult age groups, their effects are substantial, reducing life expectancy by more than 20 years in several countries. Demographic projections have estimated that population growth will decline more rapidly than expected and that the size of the African population in 2005 will be smaller than it would have been without AIDS. HIV or AIDS cases will put an increasing strain on the health care systems, which are already overburdened, and on individual households that are trying to manage with limited economic resources. Care and support for children orphaned by AIDS will become a growing concern throughout the region.

In contrast to the escalation in several areas of Africa, prevention efforts have had substantial dividends in some countries. Treatment and prevention programs in Ethiopia, Uganda, Senegal, Zambia, and Cote d'Ivoire demonstrate that HIV incidence can be stabilized and, in some cases, can even be reduced over time. HIV prevalence levels among young women in Addis Ababa declined by more than one third between 1995 and 2001. In Uganda, HIV prevalence has declined by more than 50% over the past 8 years. In South Africa, HIV prevalence levels decreased among teenagers by 25% between 1998 and 2001. Although prevalence remains unacceptably high in many countries, the positive trends confirm the value of investing in prevention programs aimed at youth and the introduction of treatment programs.

HIV and AIDS in Asia and the Pacific

After sub-Saharan Africa, Asia and the Pacific have the second largest number of HIV-infected individuals in the world, estimated at 7.2 million people. In 2002, 1 million adults and children became newly infected in part because of the explosive growth of the HIV epidemic in China, India, and several other countries in Southeast Asia. With the exception of Cambodia, Myanmar, and Thailand, national HIV prevalence levels remain comparatively low in most countries of Asia and the Pacific, in part because of their large population

base. For example, in China, Indonesia, and India, where large numbers of people are infected, national HIV prevalence rates in these highly populous countries do not provide the full impact of the epidemic. India's national adult HIV prevalence rate of 1% offers little indication of the serious situation facing the country. An estimated 4 million people were living with HIV at the end of 2001—the second highest figure in the world after South Africa. HIV prevalence among women attending antenatal clinics was higher than 1% in Andhra Pradesh, Karnataka, Maharashtra, Manipur, Nagaland, and Tamil Nadu.

Throughout the region, injecting drug use remains one of the most prominent modes of transmission of HIV. More than 50% of injecting drug users (IDUs) have already acquired HIV in Malaysia, Myanmar, Nepal, Thailand, Indonesia, Manipur, and southern China. Very high rates of needle sharing have been documented among users in Bangladesh and Vietnam, along with evidence that a considerable proportion of sex workers in Vietnam also inject drugs. China, with a fifth of the world's population, has also witnessed a dramatic escalation of the HIV epidemic in the past 3 years, with a 67% increase in reported HIV in 2001. One million Chinese individuals are estimated to be living with HIV. The HIV epidemic is particularly severe among IDUs in at least seven provinces, with prevalence rates higher than 70% among IDUs in areas such as Yili prefecture in Xinjiang and Ruili county in Yunnan province. Another nine provinces in China are on the brink of similar HIV epidemics because of the very high rates of needle sharing. To compound the tragedy of the epidemic in China, reports from Henan province in central China demonstrate that tens of thousands and possibly more rural villagers became infected by selling their blood to collecting centers that did not follow basic blood donation safety procedures. It has been estimated that 150,000 people have been infected through these practices. There are new signs of heterosexually transmitted HIV epidemics in at least three provinces—Guangdong, Guangxi, and Yunnan—where HIV prevalence rates have been documented at 11 to 15% among sentinel sex workers in 2000. Several other factors highlight the swift escalation of HIV in China. STDs quadrupled between 1997 and 2002, suggesting that unprotected sex with nonmonogamous partners is increasing in China. There is massive population mobility. Approximately 100 million Chinese are temporarily or permanently away from their registered addresses, and increasing socioeconomic disparities add to the likelihood of HIV spread.

Indonesia, the world's fourth most populous country, is another example of how quickly the AIDS epidemic can emerge. After more than 10 years of negligible HIV prevalence, the infection rate among IDUs, sex workers, and blood donors in some regions are rapidly increasing. In one drug treatment center in Jakarta, HIV prevalence rose from 15.4% in 2000 to more than 40% by 2002. Papua New Guinea has also reported the highest HIV infection rates among the Pacific Island countries and territories. The results of studies in the capital of Port Moresby show high HIV prevalence levels among female sex workers (17%) and attendees of STD clinics (7%) in 1999. Even though the Philippines have maintained a low HIV prevalence, higher rates of STDs among Filipino sex workers, their clients, and MSM indicate low levels of condom use and the potential for rapid spread of HIV.

In some countries of Southeast Asia where HIV rose rapidly in the 1990s, strong prevention programs have limited the spread more recently. In Thailand, the number of new HIV infections has declined from 143,000 in 1991 to 29,000 in 2001. Similarly, in Cambodia, HIV prevalence fell by more than 4% between 1999 and 2001 as a result of a multifaceted response that included a 100% condom use program and steps to counter stigma. Despite these advances, AIDS is still a leading cause of death in Thailand, and 1% of the country's 63.6 million people are infected with HIV. Although STDs and heterosexual transmission have declined as a result of the government's prevention programs, HIV continues to spread rapidly among IDUs and MSM.

HIV and AIDS in Eastern Europe and Central Asia

The HIV epidemic has increased faster in Eastern Europe and Central Asia between 2000 and 2003 than in any other area of the world. In 2002, there were an estimated 250,000 new infections, bringing to 1.2 million the number of people living with HIV. In recent years, the Russian Federation has experienced an exceptional steep rise in reported HIV infections, 90% of which have been attributed to injecting drug use. It is estimated that nearly 1% of the young people in Eastern Europe and central Asia are injecting drugs, which places these individuals and their sex partners at high risk for being infected with HIV. In one study in Moscow, secondary school students acknowledged that 4% injected drugs. In countries such as Azerbaijan, Georgia, Tajikistan, and Uzbekistan, HIV has experienced explosive growth. In the first 6 months of 2002, there were as many new HIV infections in these countries as has been reported in the whole of the previous decade. In the Baltic countries, similar explosive high rates of HIV are being documented among IDUs and heterosexuals at risk for STDs.

Similar to the situation in China, very high rates of STDs are being found in Eastern Europe and Central Asia, increasing the odds of HIV being transmitted through unprotected sex. In 2000, the number of newly reported cases of syphilis in the Russian Federation was 157 per 100,000 persons, dramatically higher than the 4.2 per 100,000 persons in 1987. Similar trends have been reported in other countries of the Commonwealth of Independent States, in the Baltic states, and in Romania. In Estonia, Latvia, and Lithuania, major HIV outbreaks are also occurring in selected populations such as prison inmates. In one prison in Lithuania, 15% of inmates were HIV positive, confirming the role of prisons in the spread of HIV in many countries of the region. The concentration of large numbers of young people in overcrowded prisons or juvenile justice facilities, often marked by the abundance of drugs but a scarcity of HIV information, clean needles, or condoms, provides fertile ground for the rapid spread of HIV among inmates and, on their eventual release, into the wider population.

Initially driven by injecting drug use among young people, heterosexual transmission of HIV has become the prominent mode of spread in Belarus and Ukraine. With an estimated adult HIV prevalence rate of 1%, the Ukraine is the most affected country in the region and in all of Europe. Three fourths of HIV infections in the Ukraine are related to injecting drug use, but the proportion of sexually transmitted infection is increasing. New diagnoses of HIV and persons infected through heterosexual intercourse accounted for 28% of all new cases reported in the first 6 months of 2002, up from 15.3% in 1998. Although many of these infections may occur in sex partners of IDUs, the trend may also indicate spread into the wider population of these countries. Studies in Donesk, Moscow, and St. Petersburg revealed HIV prevalence rates of 13 to 17% among sex workers. In the Russian Federation in the Ukraine, up to 30% of female IDUs are also involved in commercial sex work. The public health efforts to stem the tide of these epidemics in these countries are limited and, in some cases, nonexistent. In contrast, prevalence for HIV remains low in Poland, the Czech Republic, Hungary, and Slovenia, where well-designed national HIV/AIDS programs are in operation. If effective interventions are not implemented in the more severely affected countries, it is likely that the situation will become dramatically worse over the next 5 years.

HIV and AIDS in Latin America and the Caribbean

An estimated 1.9 million adults and children are living with HIV in Latin America and the Caribbean. Twelve countries in this region have an estimated HIV prevalence of 1% or greater among pregnant women. In several Caribbean countries, adult HIV prevalence rates are surpassed only by the rates experienced in sub-Saharan Africa, making this the second most affected region in the world. Haiti remains the worst affected, with an estimated national prevalence of more than 6%, along with the Bahamas, where the prevalence is 3.5%.

AIDS is the leading cause of death in some countries of the Caribbean basin. In Haiti, the Bahamas, and Guyana, the number of deaths among 15 to 34 year olds is 2.5 times higher than it would have been in the absence of AIDS. The estimated 100,000 AIDS deaths in 2001 have further increased the ranks of children orphaned by epidemics in this region. About 330,000 of the orphans are living in Latin America (130,000 of them in Brazil) and 250,000 in the Caribbean (200,000 in Haiti alone).

Homosexual and heterosexual transmission continues to be the major modes of transmission throughout the region, although there is evidence that spread of HIV is increasing through sharing of infected drug equipment. Population mobility, spurred by high rates of unemployment and poverty, is emerging as a significant factor in the epidemic's growth in this region. Central America's geographic position also makes it an important transit zone for people moving between the rest of the region and North American countries. Appropriately,

protecting vulnerable populations on the move, including adolescent girls and young women, is now the focus of a regional prevention program in Central America. In Mexico, adult HIV prevalence in the wider population is still well under 1%, but prevalence rates are higher in specific population groups—6% among IDUs and 15% among MSM. There is significant overlap between IDUs and MSM, especially in Brazil and the southern Latin American countries where injecting drug use is a growing social phenomenon. Injecting drug use is also a major route of HIV transmission in Argentina, Chile, and Uruguay.

Despite many constraints, the region has made progress in provision of treatment and care. An estimated 170,000 people, primarily in Brazil, were receiving state-sponsored treatment by the end of 2001. By reducing HIV-related morbidity through treatment, Brazil's treatment and care program is estimated to have avoided 234,000 hospitalizations in 1996 through 2000, thereby demonstrating the cost-effective approach to care. Argentina, Costa Rica, Uruguay, and Cuba now guarantee free and universal access to drugs through the public sector, and sharp reductions recently have been secured in Honduras and Panama. Unfortunately, access to antiretrovirals remains unequal across the region, largely because of discrepancies in drug prices in different countries. Unless overcome, economic difficulties within some countries will continue to plague the region, facilitating further economic decline and the spread of HIV.

HIV and AIDS in Western Europe

More than 500,000 HIV-infected individuals reside in Western Europe, and in 2002, 30,000 became newly infected, with trends similar to those witnessed in the United States, Australia, and New Zealand. The introduction of combination antiretroviral therapy in 1996 to 1998 has dramatically reduced HIV-related mortality, although this trend has begun to level off in the past 2 years. Approximately 500,000 people received antiretroviral drugs in high-income countries by 2002. Longer survival of people living with HIV has led to a steady increase in the number of people living with the virus in high-income countries.

The HIV epidemic in Western Europe is a result of a multitude of epidemics that differ in their timing, scale, and effects on populations. A larger proportion of new HIV diagnoses (59% overall between 1997 and 2001) in Western European countries occurred through heterosexual intercourse. More than one half of the new HIV infections in the United Kingdom resulted through heterosexual sex, compared with 33% in 1998. In Ireland, a similar trend is visible, with the numbers of heterosexually transmitted HIV infections increasing fourfold between 1998 and 2001. Injecting drug use remains the main mode of transmission in Spain, but about one fourth of all HIV infections are now heterosexually transmitted. Reported HIV prevalence among IDUs in Spain in 2002 was 30% nationwide, whereas in France, prevalence rates range from 10 to 23%. Portugal's serious epidemic among IDUs accounted for more than half of the newly diagnosed infections in 2000 and 2001, although the number of reported HIV infections declined in 2001.

Most of the data from the high-income countries demonstrate that the epidemic has shifted into the poor and marginalized sections of society. Underscoring the need for renewed prevention efforts, especially among young people, are findings of increases in high-risk behaviors, less frequent condom use, and higher rates of STDs in several countries. In the United Kingdom, for example, rates of gonorrhea, syphilis, and chlamydial infections have more than doubled since 1995, and increases have been found in other Western European countries.

HIV and AIDS in the United States

By 2002, the United States had reported the highest number of AIDS cases in the world, with more than 800,000 cases and nearly 500,000 fatalities. Estimates from the Centers for Disease Control and Prevention (CDC) suggest that 900,000 people were living with HIV in the United States in 2002, of whom 360,000 had AIDS. Since the use of antiretroviral drugs began, sharp declines in AIDS incidence have occurred from 1996 through 1999 (Fig. 412–4). Since then, AIDS incidence has leveled off, and essentially no changes have occurred in incidence through 2002. Similarly, from 1996 through 1997, the number of deaths among persons with AIDS also declined sharply. As a result, HIV/AIDS prevalence has increased steadily over time

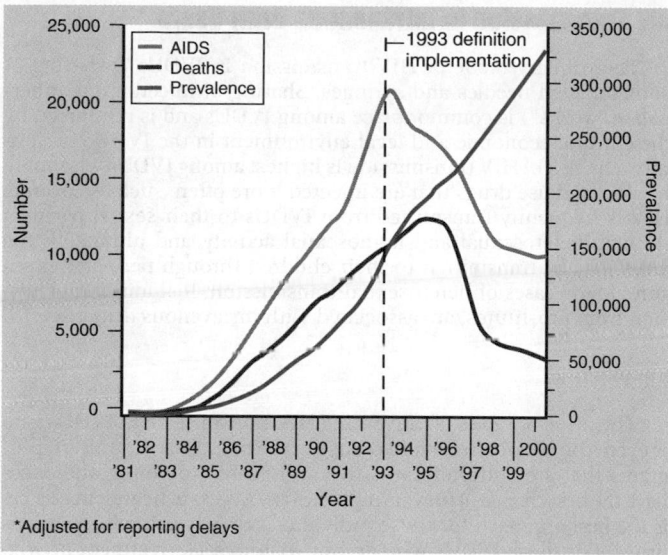

FIGURE 412–4 • Estimated AIDS incidence, deaths, and prevalence by year of diagnosis or death for the United States, 1981 through 2000. (Data from Centers for Disease Control and Prevention.)

because of prolonged survival. In 2002, 39% of persons living with AIDS lived in the South, 29% in the Northeast, 19% in the West, 10% in the Midwest, and 3% in U.S. territories. Of persons living with AIDS, 42% were African American, 37% were white, 20% were Hispanic, and 1% were Asian Pacific Islander, and less than 1% were American Indian or Alaskan native. Of the reported AIDS cases, 57% were MSM, 24% were IDUs, 9% were exposed through heterosexual contact, and 8% were MSM and IDU. Of the 76,000 women with AIDS reported in 2001, 59% were infected through heterosexual contact and 38% through injecting drug use.

The number of pediatric AIDS cases has markedly declined since the advent of antiretroviral drug use during pregnancy to prevent HIV perinatal transmission. In 2001, only 175 new cases of AIDS were diagnosed in children, of which 86% were attributed to perinatal exposure.

The impact of AIDS in the African American community has been particularly severe. Representing only an estimated 12% of the U.S. population, African Americans make up 38% of all reported AIDS cases. It is estimated that almost 129,000 African Americans are living with AIDS. In 2000, more African Americans were reported with AIDS than any other racial or ethnic group. Nearly half of all reported AIDS cases in 2000 were among African Americans. Almost two thirds (63%) of all women reported with AIDS were African American, and African American children represented two thirds of all reported pediatric cases.

The AIDS epidemic in the United States evolved from a small outbreak among homosexual men in a few cities to a major killer of young adults. The epidemic continues to evolve. During the 1990s, transmission had markedly decreased among MSM, but later data suggest that new infections are increasing in this population, particularly among younger men. Similarly, heterosexual transmission is becoming an increasingly important part of the U.S. epidemic, with certain groups at disproportionately high risk. Those at greatest risk are the young, disadvantaged minority populations, particularly women living in the inner cities of the Northeast and in parts of the rural South. A major source of infection for these women has been male IDUs. Transmission occurs particularly among women with multiple sex partners and those who exchange sex for drugs or money.

With an epidemic that is nearly into its third decade, complacency has increased, and prevention efforts have dwindled as a result of declining mortality. Multiple studies illustrate that prevention efforts are not reaching the large number of at-risk individuals who engage in unsafe sex. The rates of sexually transmitted infections among MSM have been documented in the United States, Australia, Great Britain, Canada, and other developed countries. Rates of gonorrhea, syphilis, and chlamydia have more than doubled in the past 5 years among MSM in selected U.S. and European cities. Renewed efforts to enhance

prevention efforts, particularly in HIV care clinics, are being echoed throughout all of these countries.

SUGGESTED READINGS

Centers for Disease Control and Prevention: HIV and AIDS—United States, 1981–2000. MMWR Morb Mortal Wkly Rep 2001;50:430–434. *This document reviews the course of the epidemic over 2 decades in the United States underscoring important differences over time in epidemiologic trends.*

Centers for Disease Control and Prevention: USPHS Task Force recommendations for use of antiretroviral drugs in pregnant HIV-1-infected women for maternal health and interventions to reduce perinatal HIV-1 transmission in the United States. MMWR Morb Mortal Wkly Rep 2002;51(RR-18):1. *The definitive set of recommendations from the USPHS on how to prevent mother-to-infant transmission of HIV through counseling, testing, and treatment with antiretroviral drugs.*

Corbett EL, Watt CJ, Walker N, et al: The growing burden of tuberculosis: Global trends and interactions with the HIV epidemic. Arch Intern Med 2003;163:1009–1021. *Describes the increasing global burden of tuberculosis with HIV infection.*

DeCock KM, Mbori-Ngacha D, Marum E: Shadow on the continent: Public health and HIV/AIDS in Africa in the 21st century. Lancet 2002;360:67–72. *An excellent review of the AIDS crisis in Africa that details the statistics of the epidemic and outlines steps needed in efforts to slow the spread of the disease.*

Fleming DT, Wasserheit JN: From epidemiological synergy to public health policy and practice: The contribution of other sexually transmitted diseases to sexual transmission of HIV infection. Sex Transm Infect 1999;75:3–17. *A review article that discusses the importance of STDs in potentiating the spread of HIV and how STD control can be used to limit transmission of HIV and other STDs.*

Quinn TC, Wawer MJ, Sewankambo N, et al: Viral load and heterosexual transmission of human immunodeficiency virus type 1. Rakai Project Study Group. N Engl J Med 2000;342:921–929. *A report from Uganda that definitively demonstrates that the level of viral load of HIV is one of the most important biologic factors involved in sexual transmission of HIV.*

UNAIDS/WHO: Report on the Global HIV/AIDS Epidemic, 2002. Geneva, UNAIDS and WHO, July, 2002, p 1. *Referred to as the Barcelona Report this detailed publication reviews the HIV/AIDS epidemic globally with emphasis on successful prevention and treatment programs.*

UNAIDS/WHO: AIDS: Epidemic Update, December 2002. Geneva, UNAIDS and WHO, 2002, p 1. *This report published at the end of 2002 provides the most up-to-date statistics and trends in the course of the epidemic globally.*

413 PREVENTION OF HIV INFECTION

Michael S. Saag

Prevention of human immunodeficiency virus (HIV) infection requires a thorough understanding of the modes of viral transmission, the populations at risk, and the established guidelines to avoid high-risk exposures. HIV has been identified in virtually every body fluid and tissue, including blood, semen, vaginal secretions, saliva, tears, breast milk, cerebrospinal fluid, amniotic fluid, urine, and fluid obtained from bronchoalveolar lavage. In most instances, the virus resides in lymphocytes present within body fluids; therefore, any fluid that contains lymphocytes could be implicated theoretically in the spread of the virus. Nonetheless, no cases of HIV transmission have been documented through any body fluids except blood and fluids grossly contaminated with blood, semen, vaginal secretions, and breast milk. HIV has been transmitted through transplanted organs, including kidney, liver, heart, pancreas, and bone.

MODES OF HIV TRANSMISSION AND PREVENTION

Sexual Transmission

HIV infection is a sexually transmitted disease (STD). Like other STDs, HIV spreads bidirectionally and appears to be transmitted from male to female and female to male with roughly the same efficiency. Historically, most sexually transmitted cases reported in the United States have occurred through male homosexual activity, but heterosexual transmission is becoming the leading mode of transmission in the United States and is the primary mode of disease acquisition in many African countries.

Certain cofactors are associated with an increased risk of acquiring HIV infection. Receptive anal intercourse and contact with a large number of different sexual partners are the most important risk factors. Activities that may lead to damage of the rectal mucosa, such as rectal douching, manual penetration of the rectum ("fisting"), and concomitant ulcerative STDs, increase the likelihood of disease acquisition. In order of relative risk, insertive rectal intercourse, sexual practices that damage vaginal mucosa, vaginal intercourse, fellatio, and ingestion of semen are all associated with HIV transmission. The

HIV and AIDS

likelihood of disease acquisition increases with exposure to sexual partners with higher risk of infection, such as prostitutes, intravenous drug users (IVDUs), and individuals with a previous history of other STDs. A single case report of female-to-female transmission has been reported through orogenital contact.

PREVENTION

Abstinence is the only absolute way of preventing sexual acquisition of HIV infection. Persons who have been engaged in a mutually monogamous relationship since the mid-1970s are at extremely low risk of acquiring disease; however, the assurance that both partners have remained "faithful" is sometimes difficult to confirm. For most sexually active individuals, it should be assumed that the partner is seropositive until demonstrated otherwise. Verbal claims of seronegativity should be viewed with skepticism. When a couple, heterosexual or homosexual, is establishing a long-term relationship, it is recommended that they undergo serologic testing to determine their HIV status. However, the decision to be tested should be of mutual consent and viewed in the context that exposures outside the relationship may lead to seropositivity in the future.

In situations in which a decision to engage in sexual activity has been made and the HIV status of the partner is unknown or in doubt, safe sexual practices ("safe sex") should be implemented (Table 413–1). Mutual masturbation is considered "safe," assuming it is nontraumatic and not followed by ingestion of body fluids such as semen or vaginal secretions. Transmission of HIV has never been documented to occur through saliva; however, no group of patients has ever been studied who engage in deep "French" kissing as their sole means of sexual activity. Because HIV exists in saliva, albeit in very low titers, deep French kissing cannot be considered absolutely safe even though the likelihood of HIV transmission is extremely low. Condom use is the most effective means of preventing HIV infection among individuals who engage in oral, vaginal, or anal intercourse. To be effective, however, the condom should be made of latex and must be used properly. Natural skin condoms have been shown to leak in laboratory studies, whereas latex condoms maintain their integrity and are more durable. Nonoxynol-9, a spermicide with some antiviral activity, enhances the protective effects of condoms and should be used in conjunction with condoms as a spermicidal jelly or impregnated into the latex condom itself. Petroleum-based lubricants enhance the likelihood of latex condom rupture and should be avoided. If needed, water-based lubricants such as K-Y Jelly should be used.

Both partners should be knowledgeable about the correct use of condoms. Discussions regarding condom use should occur before the need arises, and ideally, condom placement should be practiced in advance. A new condom should be used for each act of intercourse, and each condom should be used only one time. Even under the best of circumstances, a 5 to 15% failure rate has been documented among couples using condoms as their sole means of contraception, and HIV transmission has been reported in discordant couples using condoms. Condom ineffectiveness most often is caused by improper placement, falling off during intercourse, and rupture. Although condom use during intercourse is considered "safer" sex, it is not absolutely safe.

Table 413–1 • SAFE AND UNSAFE SEXUAL PRACTICES IN ORDER OF "SURENESS" OF SAFETY

SAFE
Abstinence
Monogamous relationship with confirmed seronegative partner
Manual sex (manual masturbation)
Kissing
Intercourse with latex condom (used in combination with
  nonoxynol-9)

UNSAFE
Intercourse with "natural skin" condom
Intercourse with latex condom lubricated with petroleum-based
  lubricants
Unprotected orogenital sex
Unprotected vaginal intercourse
Unprotected anal intercourse

HIV Transmission in Intravenous Drug Users

The primary mode of HIV transmission in IVDUs is sharing of contaminated needles and syringes. Sharing of injection paraphernalia ("works") is commonplace among IVDUs and is reinforced by the cultural economic and legal environment in the IVDU community. The risk of HIV transmission is highest among IVDUs who share needles and use drugs that are injected more often, such as cocaine. HIV is frequently transmitted from IVDUs to their sexual partners through heterosexual and homosexual activity, and ultimately, the virus may be transmitted to their children through perinatal exposure. Many cases of heterosexual transmission, including transmission from prostitutes, are associated with intravenous drug use.

PREVENTION

The primary mode of preventing HIV transmission in IVDUs is to prevent the use of intravenous drugs in the first place. Education programs that are culturally sensitive and geared to young audiences have the best chance of preventing drug use. Access to treatment centers is the best approach for those individuals already using intravenous drugs. For those IVDUs who do not wish to seek treatment or who are unable to gain access to treatment, the most effective way to prevent HIV infection is to avoid sharing needles and works. Where works are in short supply, needles and syringes should be cleaned after each use, preferably with readily accessible virucidal cleansers such as chlorine bleach (diluted 1 : 100). Some communities have adopted programs that provide free needles and syringes for IVDUs, and there is strong evidence that these programs, when implemented properly, are effective in reducing HIV transmission. Voluntary HIV testing and outreach programs that rigorously maintain confidentiality can be effective in reducing transmission to sexual partners of IVDUs. To be effective, antibody testing should be combined with intensive pretest and post-test counseling.

The efficacy of many community programs is limited, however, by cultural barriers, including lack of trust, fear of prosecution, misconceptions regarding the prevalence of HIV infection within the local drug-using population, and the use of ineffective language in delivering anti-HIV messages by program staff. When combined with the relative paucity of intravenous drug treatment resources, HIV education among IVDUs that ultimately results in behavioral changes remains a challenging HIV prevention goal.

Transmission of HIV Through Blood Products

HIV has been transmitted through transfusion of single-donor blood and blood products, including whole blood, fresh-frozen plasma, packed red blood cells, cryoprecipitate, clotting factors, and platelets. Before May 1985, when the Red Cross began testing the blood supply for evidence of HIV antibodies, an estimated 10,000 to 12,000 individuals received blood products from HIV-infected donors. Most recipients develop infection after transfusion with HIV-tainted blood products, and the time to development of advanced disease is generally shorter among transfusion recipients than among those who acquired their disease through sexual contact.

Since 1985, the rate of HIV transmission through transfusion has dropped precipitously. The estimated rate of transmission is 1 in 40,000 to 200,000 units of blood, depending on the prevalence of HIV infection in the community where the blood was collected. Pooled plasma components often require 2000 to 30,000 donors per lot and represent a higher potential risk of transmission than single-donor blood products if the pooled product is not treated to eliminate the infectious virus.

PREVENTION

Aggressive efforts by the American Red Cross have greatly reduced the risk of HIV transmission through transfusion in the United States. Voluntary self-deferral of donors at risk for HIV acquisition in the community was initiated in 1983. The effectiveness of self-deferral is limited, however, by social pressures. Some high-risk individuals view blood donation as a means of being tested for HIV and provide erroneous screening information to receive free, confidential evaluation of their HIV status. Other at-risk individuals may be coerced to participate in blood donation drives at work. Potentially infected donors may feel uncomfortable excusing themselves from donation and provide false information on screening to avoid possible disclosure of a high-risk lifestyle to their coworkers. Self-deferral programs are most effective when free, voluntary testing centers are readily available elsewhere in the community and when blood drives encourage potential donors to come to donation centers by themselves and not in groups.

The institution of HIV antibody testing of donated blood and blood products in 1985 has had the most dramatic effect on lowering the incidence of transfusion-related transmission. When combined with voluntary self-deferral, the blood supply has become relatively free of HIV. Heat inactivation processes for cryoprecipitate and clotting factor concentrates have virtually eliminated transmission of HIV through use of these products. Other products, such as immune globulin preparations and hepatitis B vaccines, are produced by methods that inactivate HIV and have never been associated with transmission of HIV.

Transmission of HIV to Health Care Workers

Transmission of HIV in the health care delivery setting has been the subject of intense investigation throughout the course of the epidemic. The percentage of health care workers with AIDS who have "no identified risk" for HIV infection has remained low (<10%) and has not increased over time, despite the dramatic increase in the number of AIDS cases and concomitant exposure of health care workers to patients with HIV disease. More importantly, detailed studies examining the risk of specific exposures, such as needlestick injuries and mucous membrane exposures, have demonstrated very low risk of disease acquisition in the workplace. More than 3628 health care workers have been examined prospectively in carefully designed surveillance studies at 10 high-incidence medical centers. The overall risk of seroconversion after a percutaneous needlestick from a known HIV-positive source is 0.3% per exposure. Although mucous membrane exposures to HIV-positive blood have resulted in seroconversion in at least five health care workers, prospective studies of more than 900 splash exposures have failed to identify any seroconverters, implying that the risk of infection is even lower after mucous membrane exposure (estimated to be 0.1 to 0.3%). No transmission has occurred after exposure to body fluids other than blood or fluids heavily contaminated with blood. Although the potential for HIV transmission to health care providers clearly exists, the risk of infection is inherently low and can be further minimized by following routine precautions to prevent transmission.

PREVENTION

In August 1987, the Centers for Disease Control and Prevention (CDC) published guidelines designed to minimize health care worker exposure to blood and body fluids that may be infected with blood-borne pathogens such as HIV. The guidelines, updated in June 2001 (http://www.aidsinfo.nih.gov/guidelines/), remain the principal mode of HIV prevention among health care workers today. These so-called universal precautions are based on the premise that any patient may be infected with blood-borne infectious agents and it may be difficult, if not impossible, to differentiate those with infection from their uninfected counterparts. All specimens containing blood or blood-tinged fluids obtained from *any* patient should be considered hazardous and handled as such (Table 413-2).

Handwashing is the cornerstone of universal precautions, as it is with all infection control practices. Gloves should be worn when spillage of blood or body fluids is likely. Gloves should *never* be washed and should be changed after soiling or after gross contamination, with handwashing immediately after the gloves are removed. Handwashing may be performed using soap and water or with the use of commercially available alcohol-based cleansing gels. Gowns, protective eyewear, and masks usually are not needed except in circumstances in which splattering or splashing of blood-containing fluids is likely to occur. Masks should always be worn in situations in which eyewear is required. Reusable equipment should be cleaned of visible organic material, placed in an impervious bag, and returned to central supply for decontamination. Although heat is the single best decontamination method, chemical agents that possess mycobactericidal activity are effective against hepatitis B and HIV and are acceptable alternatives when heat inactivation is impractical. Blood spills should be

Table 413–2 • SUMMARY OF UNIVERSAL PRECAUTIONS

Specimens, including blood, blood products, and body fluids, obtained from all patients should be considered hazardous and potentially infected with transmissible agents.

Handwashing should be performed before and after patient contact, after removing gloves, and immediately if hands are grossly contaminated with blood.

Gloves should be worn when hands are likely to come in contact with blood or body fluids.

Gowns, protective eyewear, and masks should be worn when splashing, splattering, or aerosolization of blood or body fluids is likely to occur.

Sharp objects ("sharps") should be handled with great care and disposed of in impervious receptacles.

Needles should never be manipulated, bent, broken, or recapped.

Blood spills should be handled by initial absorption of spill with disposable towels, cleaning area with soap and water, followed by disinfecting area with 1:10 solution of household bleach.

Contaminated reusable equipment should be decontaminated using heat sterilization or, when heat is impractical, using a mycobactericidal cleanser.

Pocket masks or mechanical ventilation devices should be available in areas where cardiopulmonary resuscitation procedures are likely.

Health care workers with open lesions or weeping dermatitis should avoid direct patient contact and should not handle contaminated equipment.

Private rooms are not required for routine care; select circumstances, however, such as the presence of concomitant transmissible opportunistic disease, may warrant respiratory, enteric, or contact isolation.

cleaned with appropriate caution. After placing gloves and other appropriate barrier precautions, excess blood should be removed with absorbent materials (e.g., paper towels), the area then cleaned with soap and water, and the area disinfected with a 1:10 solution of sodium hypochlorite (i.e., household bleach) and water. Health care workers with denuded skin, open lesions, or active dermatitis should avoid direct patient contact and should not process contaminated equipment or materials. Private rooms generally are not required for patients known to be HIV infected unless a concomitant opportunistic disease is present that requires respiratory, enteric, or contact isolation. Food service should be provided as usual on reusable dishware.

Because *all* blood and body fluids should be handled as potentially hazardous and *all* patients presumed to be infected, it makes little sense to identify infected patients or their specimens with "blood and body fluid" labels. The use of such labels on known infected patients implies that unlabeled specimens or specimens from patients of unknown status are less hazardous and may be handled with less care. Studies have shown that more than one half of the specimens containing antibodies to HBsAg or HIV went to the laboratory unlabeled.

The handling of sharp instruments ("sharps") represents the greatest risk of HIV transmission to health care workers. Although sharp injuries cannot be entirely eliminated, the number of exposures can be reduced substantially by adhering to guidelines put forth in universal precautions. Before a sharp instrument is used, thought should be given to where the instrument will be disposed after use. Impervious containers should be readily available in all patient care areas and identified by the health care worker *before* sharp use. The containers should be checked frequently and should not be allowed to overfill. Used needles should never be manipulated, bent, broken, or recapped. Recapping of needles is the single most common activity that results in needlestick injuries.

Despite their logical basis and relative ease of implementation, universal precautions have not been used routinely by many health care providers. Studies have shown that more than 50% of health care workers engage in inadequate infection control practices, even in high-impact AIDS centers, and up to 40% of the needlestick exposures were judged to be preventable. Although lack of adequate education may partly explain these findings, implementation of infection control practices has been generally poor historically. Between 200 and 400 health care workers die each year as a result of hepatitis B infection acquired on the job. The use of universal precautions helps minimize the transmission of many transmissible diseases in addition to HIV.

Even in the best of circumstances, accidental mucous membrane and percutaneous exposures to blood from HIV-infected patients do occur. Each institution and health care facility should adopt procedures for managing these exposures based on guidelines published by the CDC (see References). The essential elements of management after needlestick or mucous membrane exposure include defining the type of exposure, appropriately evaluating the donor (patient) and recipient (health care worker) at the time of exposure, and follow-up of the health care worker for at least 1 year after exposure.

Proposed definitions of the types of exposure are summarized in Table 413–3. Health care workers with any kind of parenteral exposure should be counseled and evaluated for possible acquisition of HIV and receive routine prophylaxis against hepatitis B. The source patient (donor) should be evaluated for HIV infection; if the donor's HIV status is unknown, the donor should be informed about the incident and encouraged to allow voluntary, confidential screening of his or her blood for HIV and hepatitis B antibody. If the patient refuses or cannot give consent, he or she should be considered to be infected. In cases where exposure to HIV is documented or presumed to have occurred, the health care worker should be evaluated serologically for the presence of HIV as soon as possible after the exposure (baseline) and again at 6 weeks, 12 weeks, 24 weeks, and 1 year after the exposure to determine whether HIV transmission has occurred. The health care worker should report any acute illnesses that occur during the follow-up period, especially during the first 6 to 12 weeks after exposure. Exposed workers should follow the recommended guidelines for preventing HIV transmission, including using safe sexual practices; refraining from blood, semen, and organ donation; and avoiding breast-feeding. If the source patient is seronegative for HIV and has no clinical manifestations of HIV disease, no further follow-up of the exposed health care workers is necessary, although some workers prefer follow-up for their own peace of mind. Serologic testing should be made available to all health care workers who are concerned about potential on-the-job exposure.

The use of chemoprophylaxis after parenteral exposure to HIV is routinely recommended for all health care workers who experience a massive or definite parenteral exposure. Many clinicians favor using prophylactic antiretroviral therapy after possible parenteral exposures, although this practice remains controversial. The firm recommendation to administer routine chemoprophylaxis in cases of massive or definite exposure is based on increasing evidence of the beneficial protective effects from its use in animal and human studies. In some animal models of retroviral infection, zidovudine (ZDV), when given early after inoculation, modifies the course of disease. Reports from the CDC indicate an 80% reduction in anticipated transmission rates of HIV to parenterally exposed health care workers who had received ZDV prophylaxis. With the introduction of more potent antiretroviral therapy, even more reduction in HIV transmission in the health care worker setting is anticipated. In most medical centers, multidrug chemoprophylaxis has become a standard of practice. The CDC recommends use of at least a dual nucleoside regimen (e.g., zidovudine with lamivudine), with or without the addition of a third agent, usually a potent protease inhibitor or a non-nucleoside reverse transcriptase inhibitor. Health care workers with doubtful parenteral or nonparenteral exposures generally should not take chemoprophylaxis.

The optimal timing and dosage of chemoprophylaxis are unknown; however, animal studies suggest that higher doses given as soon as possible after exposure have the best chance of being effective. Most centers that offer chemoprophylaxis to their employees have established mechanisms whereby the health care worker can be evaluated and the drugs administered within 2 to 4 hours after the exposure. Standard doses of the antiretroviral agents are administered for 4 to 6 weeks. The U.S. Public Health Service has established a National Clinicians' Post-Exposure Prophylaxis Hotline (PEPLINE) to provide expert consultation about the management of health care workers with potential HIV exposures. The PEPLINE can be accessed at 1-888-448-4911 or through the Internet at http://pepline.ucsf.edu/pepline.

Transmission from Infected Health Care Workers to their Patients

In July 1990, the first case of possible transmission of HIV from an infected health care worker, a dentist, to his patients was reported. Six patients are believed to have acquired infection from the dentist based on the absence of other risk factors among the patients and the high degree of homology between the viruses isolated from the dentist and those isolated from the patients. Although each patient underwent an invasive procedure in the dental office, the precise mode of transmission remains unknown.

Based on the known transmission of other blood-borne pathogens from health care providers to their patients (e.g., hepatitis B), it was anticipated that HIV might also be transmitted in this fashion. Remarkably, despite the prolonged duration of the epidemic, the dentist described previously remains the only documented case of transmission to patients in the health care setting. Several "look-back" studies of more than 4000 patients who underwent invasive surgical procedures performed by HIV-infected physicians have failed to identify any additional cases of nosocomial transmission. The risk of transmission from infected health care workers to patients is thought to be very low (1 case in 42,000 to 420,000 encounters). Routine use of universal precautions should minimize the risk of transmission from HIV-infected patients to health care providers and vice versa.

VACCINE DEVELOPMENT

Education is the only means of HIV prevention available. During the past few years, significant efforts have been directed toward the development of an effective vaccine against HIV. Although

---

Table 413–3 • CDC RECOMMENDATIONS FOR POSTEXPOSURE PROPHYLAXIS (PEP) FOR PERCUTANEOUS AND MUCOUS MEMBRANE EXPOSURES TO HIV

EXPOSURE TYPE	HIV POSITIVE, CLASS 1*	HIV POSITIVE, CLASS 2†	HIV STATUS OR SOURCE UNKNOWN	HIV NEGATIVE
Percutaneous exposure: less severe (e.g., solid needlestick)	Recommend basic PEP‡	Recommend expanded PEP	No PEP, but should consider PEP if source has HIV risk factors	No PEP
Percutaneous exposure: more severe (e.g., large-bore hollow needlestick)	Recommend expanded PEP‡	Recommend basic PEP	No PEP, but should consider PEP if source has HIV risk factors	No PEP
Mucous membrane exposure: small volume (e.g., few droplets)‖	Consider basic PEP§	Recommend basic PEP	No PEP, but should consider PEP if source has HIV risk factors	No PEP
Mucous membrane exposure: large volume (e.g., major blood splash or prolonged contact)	Recommend expanded PEP	Recommend basic PEP	No PEP, but should consider PEP if source has HIV risk factors	No PEP

*Asymptomatic patient with HIV infection; low viral load (<1500 copies/mL). If drug resistance suspected, obtain expert consultation regarding choice of antiretroviral regimen. Postexposure prophylaxis (PEP) should not be delayed while awaiting consultation.

†Symptomatic patient with HIV, high viral load (>1500 c/mL), AIDS, or acute seroconversion syndrome.

‡Basic postexposure prophylaxis (PEP) refers to dual nucleoside therapy (e.g., zidovudine plus lamivudine); expanded PEP includes dual nucleosides combined with a potent protease inhibitor or non-nucleoside reverse transcriptase inhibitor (NNRTI). PEP should be discontinued if the source patient is later determined to be HIV negative.

§Consider PEP indicates that PEP is optional and should be individualized for each situation based on the nature of the exposure and the opinion of the exposed health care worker and the treating clinician.

‖Body fluids considered to be potentially infectious include blood, blood products, cerebrospinal fluid, amniotic fluid, menstrual discharge, inflammatory exudates, pleural fluid, peritoneal fluid, pericardial fluid, and any fluid visibly contaminated with blood. All other fluids are considered noninfectious.

Adapted from Henderson D, Gerberding J: Occupational and Nonoccupational Exposure Management. In Dolin R, Masur H, Saag M (eds): AIDS Therapy, 2nd ed. New York, Churchill-Livingstone, 2003, pp 327–346.

substantial progress has been achieved, several obstacles remain. Despite enormous advances in understanding the immunopathogenesis of HIV infection, the precise mechanism of protective immunity remains unknown. Without such knowledge, it is difficult to develop vaccines that ensure targeting the appropriate arm of the immune system that confers long-term protective immunity. Another obstacle is the lack of correlation of data from animal models to the potential protective effects of vaccines in humans. Even if a vaccine were available, it would take years of human testing to demonstrate its effectiveness. Moreover, after a candidate vaccine is in human trials, the relatively low rate of HIV transmission and, in some cases, the difficulty in determining whether HIV infection has actually occurred will complicate the evaluation process. Despite the enormous progress made in vaccine development over the past few years, it will take several more years before protective efficacy can be established. Even if an effective vaccine is established, education will remain the primary mode of HIV prevention because of the difficulty in knowing how long the protective immune effect will last. Complicating this issue is the documented increased risk behavior among some vaccine recipients in clinical trials. Never before has so much been known about an epidemic during the time it was occurring. The challenge is to disseminate the knowledge to populations at risk in language they can understand and ultimately to modify activities so that the risk of transmission is minimized.

SUGGESTED READINGS

Bell DM: Occupational risk of human immunodeficiency virus infection in healthcare workers: An overview. Am J Med 1997;102(Suppl 5B):9–15. *A thorough overview of risks of HIV transmission; part of a supplement to the American Journal of Medicine dedicated to this subject.*

Centers for Disease Control: Updated U.S. Public Health Service guidelines for the management of occupational exposures to HBV, HCV, and HIV and recommendations for postexposure prophylaxis. MMWR Morb Mortal Wkly Rep 2001;50(RR-11):1–52. *A comprehensive summary of guidelines for management of HCW exposure to HIV. A "must" for employee health and infection control counselors. Extensive reference list.*

Gray RH, Wawer MJ, Brookmeyer R, et al: Probability of HIV-1 transmission per coital act in monogamous, heterosexual, HIV-1-discordant couples in Rakai, Uganda. Lancet 2001;357:1149–1153. *A carefully performed study demonstrating the likelihood of transmission to be 0.01 to 0.2% per coital act, depending on plasma viral load.*

Koblin BA, Chesney MA, Husnik MJ, et al, for the EXPLORE Study Team: High-risk behaviors among men who have sex with men in 6 US cities: Baseline data from the EXPLORE Study. Am J Public Health 2003;93:926–932. *About half of the men reported unprotected receptive and insertive anal sex in the previous 6 months, with alcohol and drug use being associated with these risky behaviors.*

Lo B, Steinbrook R: Health care workers infected with the human immunodeficiency virus: The next steps. JAMA 1992;267:1100–1105. *Thoughtful review of the medical, epidemiologic, and ethical issues surrounding the practice of HIV-infected health care providers.*

McCarthy M: HIV vaccine fails in phase 3 trial. Lancet 2003;361:735–756. *A commentary on a yet-to-be-published, negative trial.*

Pradier C, Bentz L, Spire B, et al: Efficacy of an educational and counseling intervention on adherence to highly active antiretroviral therapy: French prospective controlled study. HIV Clin Trials 2003;4:121–131. *This simple program improved adherence to HAART.*

414 NEUROLOGIC COMPLICATIONS OF HIV TYPE 1 INFECTION

Richard W. Price

The neurologic complications of human immunodeficiency virus type 1 (HIV-1) infection may be common and varied. It is unusual for the central and peripheral nervous systems of HIV-infected patients to remain unaffected through the course of untreated disease. However, the incidence of these neurologic complications has been markedly reduced by combination antiretroviral treatment. By preventing or delaying immunosuppression, the burden of neurologic disease in those with HIV has been greatly alleviated. However, the preventative effect of this treatment sometimes paradoxically makes the diagnostic approach to neurologic disease in those with HIV infection more difficult. Because of the overwhelming effect of HIV-mediated immunosuppression in rendering the nervous system vulnerable to a circumscribed constellation of diseases, diagnosis of the neurologic complications of acquired immunodeficiency syndrome (AIDS), or late-stage systemic HIV infection, was generally easy and formulaic in the pretreatment era. This is still the case for those who are not being treated or "fail" antiviral therapy, and most of this chapter is devoted to the approach to neurologic disease in this setting.

The revolutionary effect of potent antiretroviral therapy has altered the natural history of HIV infection and with it the neurologic disease vulnerability profile of the population infected. In the developed world, HIV infection is a chronic condition affecting a longer-lived infected population with relatively preserved immune defenses. In the past, a physician could often presume that neurologic disease was HIV related, but this is often no longer the case, and it is frequently necessary to consider a broader differential diagnosis that includes non–HIV-related conditions (e.g., stroke, degenerative diseases). Other background vulnerabilities now more prominently compete with those of helper T-cell depletion; examples include infections related to intravenous drug injection (i.e., endocarditis or spinal epidural abscess), intoxications or acute complications of alcohol or cocaine (e.g., stroke), neurosyphilis, and the more general ravages of drug use and neglected nutrition. Those with progressive T-cell loss may have other underlying conditions, such as psychiatric disease, that contribute to their remaining outside the therapeutic domain and make neurologic diagnosis more difficult. Antiviral therapy itself may also complicate presentation and management indirectly by increasing the vulnerability to cerebrovascular disease or by metabolically interacting with other drugs (e.g., with several of the anticonvulsant drugs) or as a result of more direct neurotoxic effects, the most notable example being peripheral neuropathy caused by some of the nucleosides.

In approaching neurologic diagnosis in the HIV-infected patient, it is critical to consider the broader array of probabilities in differential diagnosis conferred by the stage of their HIV infection and immune compromise, other disease vulnerabilities and treatment. The range of the non-HIV disorders that increasingly enter into neurologic diagnosis is far beyond the scope of this chapter, which focuses on those that more directly relate to HIV infection. Because most of the individual HIV-related neurologic diseases are discussed in more detail elsewhere in this volume, the major purpose of this chapter is to provide an overview and a general guide to diagnosis and management.

EARLY HIV-1 INFECTION

Although most of the HIV-related conditions complicate its late phase, there are several, less common, disorders that occur during the earlier phase.

Individual reports have described examples of focal or diffuse encephalopathy, ataxia, myelopathy, and meningitis presenting within the context of primary HIV infection and seroconversion. Peripheral nervous system disorders, including mononeuropathy involving cranial or segmental nerves, brachial plexopathy, and polyneuropathy, have also been reported during this phase, and sometimes, these peripheral and central nervous system (CNS) conditions occur together. These rare disorders evolve acutely or subacutely, pursue a monophasic course, and are generally followed by good recovery.

Several neurologic conditions have also been reported to occur during the asymptomatic phase of infection (with CD4+ T-cells above 150 cells/μL). Among these are the Guillain-Barré syndrome and its more protracted counterpart, chronic idiopathic demyelinating polyneuropathy (CIDP), both of which are clinically indistinguishable from demyelinating polyneuropathies affecting non–HIV-infected individuals, except for higher cerebrospinal fluid (CSF) cell counts and perhaps a poorer prognosis. Responses to treatment with plasma exchange and intravenous immunoglobulin have been noted, supporting an autoimmune pathogenesis. Although the epidemiology has not been precisely defined, the incidence of the demyelinating neuropathies may be lower than noted early in the epidemic, despite the higher number of individuals sustaining CD4 counts in this vulnerable range. The reason for this seeming decline is not clear, but possibly could relate to an effect of antiviral treatment and of consequent reduced antigenic stimulation. Isolated cases of a multiple sclerosis-like demyelinating CNS disease have also been reported in this stage of HIV infection, but this appears to be rare.

An additional important aspect of HIV infection, with diagnostic and pathogenetic implications, is the common finding of cerebrospinal fluid (CSF) abnormalities, most notably CSF pleocytosis, as a result of early and continued infection of the CNS. This begins during primary systemic infection and continues chronically in viremic patients in whom it is common to find HIV RNA in CSF, usually at levels 10- to 100-fold below those in plasma but sometimes equal to or even exceeding plasma levels. Lymphocytic pleocytosis is also common (usually about 6 to 12 cells/μL, but occasionally in the range of 30 to 60 cells/μL or even higher); this resolves with effective antiviral therapy and, conversely, may appear when therapy is stopped. The CSF pleocytosis is almost always asymptomatic. CSF protein is also often mildly elevated, and IgG antibody levels may be increased as well. Early CSF HIV infection and related reactive changes do not clearly predict the subsequent development of AIDS dementia complex, at least in the short term. However, it is important to take these background findings into account when interpreting diagnostic lumbar puncture in the HIV-infected patient being evaluated for other infections, such as neurosyphilis.

LATE HIV-1 INFECTION

The evolving and eventually severe impairment of immune defenses caused by untreated HIV renders the nervous system highly vulnerable to a broad spectrum of disorders. The following overview emphasizes general principles of pathogenesis and approach to diagnosis in this late phase of infection.

Pathophysiology

A number of pathophysiologic processes may lead to neurologic dysfunction in the late phase of HIV infection (Table 414–1). These include diseases that distinguish the AIDS patient from other groups, such as certain *opportunistic infections, opportunistic neoplasms,* and several conditions that appear to relate to more *direct effects of HIV* itself. AIDS patients are also susceptible to the neurologic conditions that affect other acute and chronically ill populations, including metabolic brain disease resulting from systemic organ dysfunction, stroke related to nonbacterial thrombotic endocarditis or coagulopathies, toxic effects of medications, and primary psychiatric disturbances. We focus on disorders that particularly distinguish AIDS patients.

OPPORTUNISTIC NERVOUS SYSTEM INFECTIONS

As with other organ systems, the spectrum of opportunistic infections of the nervous system results from the intrinsic vulnerabilities of the tissue (fertile soil) and the pattern of immunosuppression—in this case, circumscribed impairment of T-cell and macrophage defenses. The patient's long-term history of exposure to particular organisms is also important because most of the opportunistic infections result from reactivation of latent infections rather than from new encounters with pathogens. An important implication of the preeminence of reactivated infection is related to serologic testing, which is most useful for assessing prior exposure to an organism and hence susceptibility to clinically important reactivation, but not for defining active infection. For example, patients with cerebral toxoplasmosis usually exhibit antecedent positive *Toxoplasma gondii* blood

serology result, and a negative serum IgG antibody titer therefore militates against this diagnosis. However, these serum antibody titers very often do not rise before or during the course of disease, and a four-fold increase cannot be relied on to establish disease activity. Moreover, as long as immunosuppression persists and therapy still cannot eliminate latent infection, suppressive antibiotic therapy must be maintained for the remainder of the patient's life or until immune defenses can be restored by antiretroviral therapy. Prophylaxis also influences vulnerability to some infections and therefore their diagnostic probability. If a patient is taking trimethoprim-sulfamethoxazole, the likelihood of cerebral toxoplasmosis is much reduced.

The reason for the intrinsic vulnerability of the nervous system to certain infections (e.g., *T. gondii*) and not others (e.g., *Pneumocystis carinii*) in many cases remains uncertain. However, in some instances, susceptibility is related to the capacity of local cells to support intracellular replication. The virus causing progressive multifocal leukoencephalopathy (PML), JC virus, causes a productive and lytic infection of oligodendrocytes and leads to spreading infection and demyelination as the processes of these myelin-producing cells disappear. In the case of HIV, productive infection appears to involve monocyte-derived perivascular and parenchymal macrophages and perhaps local microglial cells.

The circumscribed nature of the immunologic defect in AIDS determines the range of opportunistic infections, which therefore differs somewhat from that of other immunosuppressed states. For example, AIDS patients are particularly susceptible to cerebral toxoplasmosis but, unlike patients with organ transplants, are much less likely to develop cerebral *Candida* or *Aspergillus* infections unless additional defenses are also compromised by medications or other factors. For this reason, AIDS patients present a characteristic set of disease probabilities.

OPPORTUNISTIC NEOPLASMS

The major consideration in the category of opportunistic neoplasms is primary brain lymphoma. These B-cell lymphomas arise in the CNS, usually are multicentric (at least microscopically), and rarely metastasize systemically. Characteristically, they develop late in HIV infection when blood CD4+ T lymphocytes are low (i.e., in the same setting as major opportunistic infections). The tumor cells are nearly always positive for Epstein-Barr virus (EBV), which likely plays an important role in their genesis. This association has been exploited diagnostically using polymerase chain reaction (PCR) DNA amplification to detect EBV sequences in CSF. Before the advent of antiretroviral therapy, this was a relatively common disorder with a very poor prognosis. Although radiation therapy usually induced tumor regression, the prognosis was poor, principally because other complications developed. In the current treatment era, this disease is far less common and may even regress when antiretroviral therapy restores immunity; the prognosis is now generally better. Systemic lymphoma can also spread to the CNS, although usually to the leptomeninges rather than brain parenchyma. Although Kaposi's sarcoma has been reported to metastasize to brain, this is rare.

EFFECTS OF HIV ON THE NERVOUS SYSTEM

Several disorders appear to be associated in a more direct or fundamental way with HIV infection, including the AIDS dementia complex and predominantly distal sensory polyneuropathy. Although uncertainty still exists regarding the detailed mechanisms of their pathogenesis, the uniqueness of these conditions in HIV-infected compared with other immunosuppressed patients, as well as more direct evidence of brain virus infection in some patients with the AIDS dementia complex, lends support to this contention. Uncertainty regarding the mechanisms of brain injury is related to the fact that, although HIV exposure of the brain occurs early in systemic infection, AIDS dementia complex is generally a late complication that develops in the same setting of compromised immunity as opportunistic infections (i.e., generally <200 CD4+ T cells/μL and often at much lower levels). Productive brain HIV infection is confined to macrophages and related cells but does not involve the "functional elements" of the brain such as neurons, oligodendrocytes, or astrocytes (although the latter may support incomplete viral infection with synthesis of regulatory proteins). These puzzling features appear to relate to (1) the general necessity for the host immune system to be altered to allow advanced brain infection and a "pathogenic" profile of host

---

Table 414–1 • PATHOPHYSIOLOGIC CLASSIFICATION OF SOME COMMON NEUROLOGIC COMPLICATIONS OF LATE HIV-1 INFECTION

UNDERLYING PROCESS	EXAMPLES
Opportunistic infections	Cerebral toxoplasmosis
	Cryptococcal meningitis
	Progressive multifocal leukoencephalopathy
	Cytomegalovirus encephalitis, polyradiculitis
Opportunistic neoplasms	Primary central nervous system lymphoma
	Metastatic lymphoma
Conditions possibly related to HIV-1 itself	AIDS dementia complex
	Aseptic meningitis and asymptomatic CSF pleocytosis
	HIV-related distal sensory polyneuropathy
Metabolic and vascular complications of systemic disease	Hypoxic, sepsis-related encephalopathies
	Stroke (nonbacterial thrombotic endocarditis, coagulopathies)
Toxic reactions	Deoxynucleoside neuropathies
	Zidovudine myopathy
Functional (psychiatric) disorders	Anxiety disorders
	Psychotic depression

reactions to infection; (2) the presence of neuropathic or neurovirulent viral quasi-species, including CCR5 coreceptor use and other viral genetic factors; and (3) a pathogenic cascade of events leading to "indirect" virus-initiated injury. Infection in macrophages appears to lead to production of an array of host toxins, including nitric oxide, quinolinic acid, and other toxins released by cytokine-mediated pathways, with several of these converging on the N-methyl-D-aspartate glutamine receptor, along with certain viral products with signaling or toxic properties (most attention has centered on these effects mediated by gp120 and the *tat* gene product). The combination of these events leads to an amplified pathogenic process that eventuates in neural cell dysfunction and death by apoptosis.

Diagnosis: Neuroanatomic Approach

As with other neurologic disease, diagnosis in AIDS patients begins with localization of symptoms and signs and therefore involves neuroanatomic classification (Table 414–2).

Table 414-2 • NEUROANATOMIC CLASSIFICATION OF THE LATE COMPLICATIONS OF HIV-1 INFECTION

Meningitis and headache
  Cryptococcal meningitis
  Aseptic meningitis (HIV-1)
  Idiopathic, "HIV-1-related" headache
  Tuberculous meningitis (*Mycobacterium tuberculosis*)
  Syphilitic meningitis
  Lymphomatous meningitis (metastatic)
Diffuse brain diseases
  With preservation of consciousness
    AIDS dementia complex
  With concomitant depression of arousal
    Metabolic encephalopathies (alone or as an exacerbating influence)
    Toxoplasmosis ("encephalitic" form)
    Cytomegalovirus encephalitis
    Herpes encephalitis
Focal brain diseases
  Subacute
    Cerebral toxoplasmosis
    Primary CNS lymphoma
    Progressive multifocal leukoencephalopathy
    Tuberculous brain abscess (*M tuberculosis*)
    Cryptococcoma
    Varicella-zoster virus (VZV) encephalitis
    Herpes encephalitis
  Acute
    Vascular disorders (VZV vasculitis)
Myelopathies
  Subacute/chronic, progressive and "diffuse"
    Vacuolar myelopathy
    HTLV-1/2-associated myelopathies
  Acute/subacute and segmental
    Transverse myelitis
      Varicella-zoster virus (herpes zoster)
      Spinal epidural or intradural lymphoma
    With polyradiculopathy
      Cytomegalovirus
Peripheral neuropathies
  Polyneuropathies
    HIV-1–related distal sensory polyneuropathy
    Nucleoside toxic neuropathies
    Autonomic neuropathy
    CD8 cell neuropathy associated with diffuse infiltrative lymphocytosis syndrome
  Focal neuropathies and radiculopathies
    CMV polyradiculopathy
    Mononeuritis multiplex
      CMV-related malignant type
      Early, benign vasculopathic form
    Mononeuropathy associated with aseptic meningitis
    Neuropathy related to lymphomatous meningitis or epidural compression
Myopathies
  Inflammatory
  Noninflammatory
  Zidovudine toxic myopathy

MENINGITIS AND HEADACHE

Several disorders may involve the leptomeninges in patients with advanced HIV disease. The most important of these is infection by *Cryptococcus neoformans* (Chapter 383). This condition may manifest subacutely with headache, nausea, vomiting, and confusion, just as in non-AIDS patients. However, in some patients, initial symptoms can be remarkably mild, with only low-grade headache or fever. The CSF findings may be bland, with few or no cells and little or no perturbation in glucose or protein levels. For this reason, the clinician should have a low threshold for obtaining a lumbar puncture and should routinely examine CSF for *Cryptococcus* (e.g., India ink stain, cryptococcal antigen determination, culture). Initial treatment is usually gratifying, although continued chronic therapy is required, at least until systemic immunity is restored by antiretroviral therapy.

A syndrome of aseptic meningitis was described earlier in the epidemic, manifesting acutely or pursuing a more chronic course. This was presumed to result from direct HIV infection of the leptomeninges. However, the frequency of detection of HIV in CSF and of asymptomatic lymphocytic pleocytosis raises questions regarding the identity of this syndrome. The background CSF abnormalities discussed earlier make it difficult to automatically classify patients with headache and pleocytosis as suffering from a distinct syndrome; there may be another cause of pleocytosis, or this finding may be coincidental. Because CSF pleocytosis above 10 cells/μL is uncommon in patients taking combination antiretroviral therapy, therapy status may help in the diagnosis. In those not taking antiretrovirals, a trial of therapy may also be undertaken to see if the pleocytosis responds; in most subjects, the high cell count should substantially diminish or resolve within a few weeks.

Other, less common meningeal disorders (e.g., meningeal lymphoma, tuberculous meningitis, meningovascular syphilis) resemble their counterparts in the non-AIDS patient. A number of other conditions may produce symptoms resembling meningitis; for example, parenchymal brain diseases such as toxoplasmosis and primary CNS lymphoma may initially manifest with headache as an important symptom. More common is the development of headache of uncertain cause. Although not well understood, this headache occurs in late HIV infection and sometimes can be a severe, debilitating problem. In some patients, this headache may be related to systemic infection, but in others, the explanation is elusive, and for this reason, it has been referred to as *HIV headache*.

PREDOMINANTLY FOCAL BRAIN DISORDERS

In approaching diagnosis of parenchymal brain disease, it is useful to separate the conditions that cause predominantly focal symptoms and signs from those producing more generalized brain dysfunction. Patients in the former group present with hemiparesis, aphasia, apraxia, hemisensory abnormalities, visual field loss, and ataxia as a result of focal macroscopic lesions in cortical or subcortical brain regions. In the pretreatment era, the most important of the focal brain diseases were cerebral toxoplasmosis, primary CNS lymphoma, and PML, in that order. However, with the widespread use of antiretroviral therapy, all of these disorders are far less common, and their relative frequency has changed. At least in part because of the use of trimethoprim-sulfamethoxazole prophylaxis in addition to antiviral therapy, cerebral toxoplasmosis is now quite uncommon in the United States, although it is still common in Europe, where exposure is greater. Primary CNS lymphoma is also much less common than a decade ago in those with HIV infection. Both of these focal brain diseases still develop in patients who have not been on antiretroviral therapy; these patients are most often receiving no medical care. In contrast, PML, although also less common, is still seen with regularity even in some subjects on antiretroviral therapy. One reason for this may be that PML can develop at higher CD4+ counts than the other disorders, and patients can present with this infection with counts above 200 CD4+ T cells/μL.

Although these three major focal disorders characteristically have a subacute onset and may be clinically indistinguishable, they tend to have somewhat different temporal profiles (Table 414–3). Cerebral toxoplasmosis typically progresses most rapidly (over a few days), and PML evolves most slowly (over a few weeks), with primary CNS lymphoma somewhere in between. Each may cause similar

Table 414-3 • COMPARATIVE CLINICAL AND RADIOLOGIC FEATURES OF CEREBRAL TOXOPLASMOSIS, PRIMARY CNS LYMPHOMA, AND PROGRESSIVE MULTIFOCAL LEUKOENCEPHALOPATHY

	CLINICAL ONSET			NEURORADIOLOGIC FEATURES		
	Temporal Profile	Level of Alertness	Fever	Number of Lesions	Type of Lesions	Location of Lesions
Cerebral toxoplasmosis	Days	Reduced	Common	Multiple	Spherical, ring-enhancing	Basal ganglia, cortex
Primary CNS lymphoma	Days to weeks	Variable	Absent	One or few	Irregular, weakly enhancing	Periventricular white matter
Progressive multifocal leukoencephalopathy	Weeks	Preserved	Absent	Multiple	Nonenhancing, no mass effect	White matter

neurologic deficits, but there are often differences in the associated findings. Toxoplasmosis commonly manifests with a combination of focal deficit and generalized encephalopathy with confusion or clouding of consciousness; the patient may also have fever and headache. This contrasts with PML, in which focal neurologic deficits are unaccompanied by diffuse brain dysfunction or evidence of a systemic toxic state. CNS lymphoma, when accompanied by significant mass effect or when deep in the frontal or periventricular region, may cause more global mental dysfunction, but these patients are usually afebrile without constitutional symptoms or signs.

After the focal nature of the patient's symptoms and signs is recognized, neuroimaging, including computed tomography (CT) or preferably magnetic resonance imaging (MRI), is critical to confirm the presence of macroscopic focal disease and to determine the nature of the abnormalities (see Table 412–3). Multiple lesions involving the cortex or deep brain nuclei (e.g., thalamus, basal ganglia) surrounded by edema strongly favor cerebral toxoplasmosis. In most cases *Toxoplasma* abscesses exhibit ringlike contrast enhancement. Cerebral lymphoma may produce a similar neuroimaging appearance, although the lesions of lymphoma are usually less numerous (one or two definable lesions), commonly exhibit more diffuse or less clear-cut contrast enhancement, and are more often located in the white matter adjacent to the ventricles. Spread beneath the ependymal lining or across the corpus callosum is also characteristic. PML characteristically involves the white matter, most often adjacent to the cortex, and has no mass effect or contrast enhancement. Magnetic resonance spectroscopy promises to enhance diagnosis, although it is still an evolving methodology.

The approach to diagnosis of focal brain lesions has evolved as the definition of their neuroimaging characteristics has improved, as the value of toxoplasma serology has been fully appreciated, and as CSF PCR detection of pathogens has been introduced. The first step in diagnosing patients with focal neurologic symptoms and signs involves neuroimaging. When mass lesions are present, the next step usually is distinguishing primary brain lymphoma from toxoplasmosis. If the blood toxoplasma serology is negative and MRI shows lesions characteristic of lymphoma, EBV DNA sequences should be sought in CSF or a brain biopsy undertaken without delay so that therapy can begin quickly. If the brain lesions appear more characteristic of toxoplasmosis and the serology is positive, a trial of antitoxoplasma therapy is undertaken with expectation of clinical improvement within several days and neuroimaging improvement within 1 to 2 weeks. Unless brain herniation threatens, corticosteroids should be avoided because their effect on lymphoma and brain edema can obscure the more specific influence of antitoxoplasma treatment. Lack of improvement or suspicion of another diagnosis should signal the need for brain biopsy or other diagnostic measures. PML can usually be identified by the combination of steadily progressive focal neurologic dysfunction and the characteristic white matter lesions on MRI. When further confirmation is needed, CSF PCR for JC virus (about 70% sensitive and more than 95% specific in this setting) or brain biopsy can be used.

Other focal CNS disorders are uncommon but include some treatable lesions such as cryptococcal invasion of brain, which usually develops in the setting of meningitis. Varicella-zoster virus (VZV) can cause a demyelinating focal disease resembling PML and a cerebral vasculitis with stroke. Cytomegalovirus (CMV) may rarely cause macroscopic lesions accompanied by focal clinical deficit. Herpes simplex viruses have also been reported to cause focal deficits. All of these except VZV-related stroke evolve subacutely, as do the more common opportunistic problems.

PREDOMINANTLY NONFOCAL BRAIN DISORDERS

The disorders presenting with more general or diffuse brain dysfunction and without focal features can be further divided into those in which consciousness remains fully preserved and those accompanied by a concomitant decrease in alertness. Most important among the former is the *AIDS dementia complex,* a clinical syndrome characterized by cognitive, motor, and sometimes, behavioral dysfunction.

The incidence and severity of the AIDS dementia complex increase with advancing immunosuppression, although combination antiviral therapy has a strong preventative influence. Its early, mild form is usually characterized by impaired concentration and attention along with reduced mental agility, resulting in complaints of forgetfulness and slowness in performing complex mental tasks. With more severe involvement, cognitive dysfunction worsens and involves other domains, and motor dysfunction is manifested clinically with gait unsteadiness and difficulty with rapid, fine movements of the hands. Personality change with apathy, lack of initiative, or hyperactivity and agitation may be part of the syndrome. In its most severe form, global dementia, paraplegia, and virtual mutism may evolve with resultant incapacity. Although it is in part a diagnosis of exclusion, the symptoms and signs of the AIDS dementia complex are sufficiently distinct to allow bedside diagnosis in most patients on the basis of their stereotypy. Neuroimaging characteristically reveals cerebral atrophy, and MRI may demonstrate increased signal in the central white matter in a diffuse or patchy pattern and sometimes in the basal ganglia.

Individual case experience clearly shows that AIDS dementia complex can be altered by antiretroviral therapy. Outcomes depend on the time course of its evolution and therapeutic intervention. Treatment of subacute disease is more likely to reverse, whereas more indolent or chronic disease may only stop progressing with some improvement but leave residual impairment. Because of the limited experience, there is no agreement on the optimal treatment regimen for AIDS dementia complex. In the absence of clear guidelines, we suggest that priority be given to use of a potent combination regimen (usually four or more drugs); if there is evidence of or history suggesting likely drug resistance, the regimen is tailored to ensure maximum susceptibility; and if not contraindicated, one or more of the drugs with better CNS penetration should be included. Among the antiretrovirals with better penetration are several nucleoside reverse transcriptase inhibitors (e.g., stavudine, zidovudine, abacavir), nonnucleoside inhibitors (e.g., nevirapine, efavirenz), and indinavir with ritonavir metabolic boosting. These considerations are offered with the caveat that most information regarding CNS penetration comes from studies of CSF, which may not fully reflect brain penetration or intracellular effectiveness within the infected brain cells (chiefly macrophages).

Because of the indirect pathways mediating brain injury, consideration has been given to an additional approach to treating the AIDS dementia complex, to use of so-called *adjuvant* therapies. This approach targets the secondary toxic mechanisms leading to neuronal dysfunction or death. At this time, none of these efforts have clearly established the utility of this approach, although additional trials are ongoing. Fortunately, because HIV infection is the driver of the pathology, eliminating viral replication is likely to mitigate these processes.

In patients with AIDS dementia complex, there is relative preservation of alertness in relation to cognitive loss. This contrasts with most metabolic encephalopathies developing as sequelae of the systemic diseases suffered by AIDS patients; for example, hypoxia and sepsis are characteristically accompanied by a degree of lethargy and confusion which parallels the decline in cognition. Likewise, CNS-active drugs often cloud mentation and alertness together. Although such metabolic and toxic disorders may present alone, they may also have an exacerbating or unmasking influence on the AIDS dementia complex, resulting in a mixture of the two conditions. HIV-infected patients may also be more sensitive to neuroleptics and manifest parkinsonian or other movement disorders as side effects at low doses.

Brain infections may produce diffuse brain dysfunction. The most important cause is CMV, which can be difficult to diagnose. Clinical features that raise suspicion include clouded consciousness, ataxia and nystagmus, or seizures, whereas MRI findings of contrast enhancement or increased attenuation of the ventricular ependyma also support this diagnosis. CSF PCR detection of CMV nucleic acid sequences provides diagnostic confirmation in this setting; CMV encephalitis is usually preceded by CMV disease in other locations and develops in the setting of markedly compromised immunity. Although CNS toxoplasmosis characteristically causes focal neurologic symptoms and signs, in some patients, generalized encephalopathy predominates. Similarly, CNS lymphoma may infiltrate deep structures and impair cognition and motor function without prominent focal symptoms or signs. Herpes simplex virus types 1 and 2 may also cause subacute nonfocal encephalitis.

As antiviral therapy has reduced the incidence of the major brain disorders discussed previously, some clinicians have raised the question whether treated patients might be manifesting brain diseases not recognized during the early part of the epidemic, related to atypical presentations of the disorders discussed previously or to the advent of new disorders. One mechanism that may lead to atypical presentations is the effect of immune reconstitution after initiation of antiretroviral therapy. In this situation, the host may mount a particularly robust and subacute immune response to the pathogen that otherwise incited little reaction, thereby causing severe inflammatory brain dysfunction. Although this type of response has been well documented in other settings and might develop in the CNS, it is likely to be a rare occurrence, particularly now that patients are more often treated early in the course of their disease. However, the clinician should still be alert for this type of reaction, which may benefit from judicious use of corticosteroids along with specific antimicrobial therapy.

MYELOPATHIES

The most common spinal cord affliction in AIDS patients is the pathologically defined vacuolar myelopathy, which has been included within the broader clinical designation of the AIDS dementia complex because it is often accompanied by evidence of concomitant brain dysfunction. The disorder is generally of subacute or gradual onset and progression, with painless gait disturbance characterized by ataxia and spasticity. Bladder and bowel difficulty usually follow deterioration of gait, and sensory symptoms and signs are less prominent than gait dysfunction unless there is concomitant neuropathy. Patients do not manifest a distinct sensory or motor "level" as in transverse myelopathies, but rather distal loss of large-fiber modalities is accompanied by increased deep tendon reflexes (in the absence of neuropathy) and Babinski signs. The efficacy of antiretroviral therapy in this subgroup of AIDS dementia complex patients is uncertain, but personal experience suggests that some respond and others do not.

Infections by two other retroviruses, human T-lymphotropic viruses types 1 and 2 (HTLV-1 and HTLV-2), can cause similar myelopathies and coexist in the same population at risk for HIV or even co-infect the same patient. Diagnosis of these infections is established by serology, and other than the overlap in epidemiology related to sexual or intravenous inoculation, they do not appear to interact in causing CNS disease. HTLV-1/2 myelopathy diagnosis may be aided by detection of antiviral IgG antibodies in the CSF; PCR diagnosis may prove helpful in the future. Spinal MRI is not helpful in distinguishing these from vacuolar myelopathy, and results usually are negative or show only spinal cord atrophy in long-standing disease. MRI is most useful in detecting and characterizing the segmental myelopathies listed in Table 412–2. Chief among the latter is the common myelopathy developing after herpes zoster, usually centered on or near the spinal cord level corresponding to the infected dermatome. The focal diseases affecting the brain also may cause focal myelopathy.

PERIPHERAL NEUROPATHIES

HIV infection can be complicated by several neuropathies, including polyneuropathies and focal neuropathies (see Table 412–2). The most common of these, sometimes called HIV-related distal sensory polyneuropathy (DSPN), is a distal, predominantly sensory polyneuropathy that usually manifests in late HIV infection, though may have onset at higher CD4 counts than AIDS dementia complex. In this axonal neuropathy, sensory symptoms exceed sensory and motor dysfunction, and severity ranges from asymptomatic increase in sensory thresholds to paresthesias and numbness to severe neuropathic pain. The latter begins with distal burning of the toes or bottoms of the feet and may ascend subacutely or more indolently to the ankles or beyond. Although associated with HIV infection, its pathogenesis is unknown and, like the AIDS dementia complex, is thought to result from cytokine-mediated injury. Unlike the CNS disease, however, antiretroviral therapy does not dramatically reverse the condition. Treatment is directed at relief of pain, using gabapentin or some of the newer anticonvulsants, tricyclic antidepressants, or when necessary, narcotic analgesics.

A second and clinically very similar sensory polyneuropathy is caused by some of the nucleoside antiretroviral drugs, including zalcitabine, didanosine, and stavudine. The underlying mechanism appears related to an effect on mitochondria metabolism, and the syndrome may be associated with lactic acidosis, although this has not proved a reliable diagnostic finding. Clinical differentiation of this dose-related neuropathy from HIV-related polyneuropathy is difficult and relies on temporal linking of onset with drug therapy or its alleviation, after a delay of several weeks, when the drug is stopped. Electromyography or other laboratory studies are not helpful in separating these conditions. Other than stopping therapy, treatment is the same as that of HIV-related DSPN.

Among the focal neuropathies, CMV can cause an uncommon but severe polyradiculopathy that usually begins with pain, weakness, and sensory loss in the lumbosacral roots and progresses over days in ascending fashion to affect thoracic and cervical roots. The CSF usually has a characteristic polymorphonuclear cell-predominant pleocytosis. Rapid institution of combination-drug anti-CMV treatment is paramount in halting its progression, which may otherwise be fatal. CMV can also cause a severe mononeuritis multiplex, often involving proximal nerves. This occurs in the setting of low CD4+ T lymphocyte counts and mandates rapid treatment, even without laboratory proof of its cause. It should be distinguished from a more benign and limited mononeuritis multiplex that can occur with higher CD4 counts and likely has an immunopathologic basis.

MYOPATHIES

Several types of myopathy may complicate HIV infection. Inflammatory and noninflammatory myopathies have been described, ranging in severity from asymptomatic creatine kinase elevation in blood to severe proximal weakness. Patients with inflammatory, polymyositis-like illnesses have improved with corticosteroid therapy. These syndromes appear far less common in the antiretroviral therapy era than they were earlier in the epidemic.

Zidovudine can also cause proximal weakness and loss of muscle mass. This toxic myopathy appears to develop only after prolonged use and perhaps relates to the drug's effect on mitochondria; muscle biopsy may reveal excessive or abnormal mitochondria. This is also far less common than earlier, probably because of the lower doses of this nucleoside drug used. Discontinuing the drug usually results in clinical improvement.

SUGGESTED READINGS

Berenguer J, Miralles P, Arrizabalaga J, et al, for the GESIDA 11/99 Study Group: Clinical course and prognostic factors of progressive multifocal leukoencephalopathy in patients treated with highly active antiretroviral therapy. Clin Infect Dis 2003;36:1047–1052. *One third died, but neurologic function improved in half of the survivors.*

Brew BJ: HIV Neurology. New York, Oxford University Press, 2001. *A comprehensive review of the neurologic complications of HIV infection with a clinical emphasis.*

Dore GJ, McDonald A, Li Y, et al, for the National HIV Surveillance Committee: Marked improvement in survival following AIDS dementia complex in the era of highly active antiretroviral therapy. AIDS 2003;17:1539–1545. *Median survival has increased from 11.9 months to 48.2 months.*

Gray F, Chretien F, Vallat-Decouvelaere AV, et al: The changing pattern of HIV neuropathology in the HAART era. J Neuropathol Exp Neurol 2003;62:429–440. *Toxoplasmosis, cytomegalovirus encephalitis, and HIV encephalitis have decreased; progressive multifocal leukoencephalopathy and non-Hodgkin lymphomas have remained stable, but herpes zoster encephalitis and herpes simplex virus encephalitis have increased in frequency.*

Keswani SC, Pardo CA, Cherry CL, et al: HIV-associated sensory neuropathies. AIDS 2002;16:2105–2117. *A review of the sensory neuropathies with more general background discussion.*

Price RW: Neurologic disease. *In* Dolin R, Masur H, Saag MS (eds): AIDS Therapy, 2nd ed. Philadelphia, Churchill-Livingston, 2003, pp 737–757. *A review that emphasizes diagnosis and includes a series of algorithms.*

415 PULMONARY MANIFESTATIONS OF HIV/AIDS

Laurence Huang

Respiratory symptoms are common in persons with human immunodeficiency virus (HIV) infection, and HIV-infected persons are subject to a wide spectrum of pulmonary diseases, both HIV-associated and non–HIV-associated (Table 415–1). The spectrum of HIV-associated pulmonary diseases encompasses opportunistic infections, neoplasms, and other pulmonary disorders. Table 415–1 lists the most frequent pulmonary diseases seen in HIV-infected persons in the United States. In other parts of the world, these frequencies may be strikingly different. Although each pulmonary disease has a characteristic clinical and radiographic presentation, the presentations can vary and often overlap. This chapter describes a basic diagnostic approach to pulmonary disease in HIV-infected persons.

Initial Diagnostic Approach

The frequency of HIV-associated opportunistic infections and the need for prompt therapy of these infections often focuses the initial diagnostic approach and management on identifying and treating possible infectious etiologies. However, HIV-infected persons may present with HIV-associated neoplasms or other disorders. In addition, risk factors for HIV infection such as injection drug use (IDU) may also contribute to pulmonary disease (e.g., endocarditis with septic pulmonary emboli). Finally, HIV-infected persons may have preexisting pulmonary disease (e.g., asthma) or may develop pulmonary disease unrelated to their HIV infection (e.g., pulmonary embolism) that is the cause of their symptoms. Therefore, in the proper clinical context, clinicians must also consider noninfectious HIV-associated pulmonary diseases and non–HIV-associated pulmonary disorders before embarking on an exhaustive search for HIV-associated opportunistic infections.

CLINICAL SETTING

The clinical setting where the patient presents and is evaluated impacts upon the relative frequency of pulmonary diseases seen (Table

415–2). This point has been established by several different studies. The Pulmonary Complications of HIV Infection Study, an observational cohort study that followed more than 1150 HIV-infected subjects for 5 years at six sites across the United States, found that patients presenting to an outpatient clinic with respiratory illness more often had upper respiratory tract infections and acute bronchitis than pneumonias due to bacteria or *Pneumocystis jiroveci* (formerly *Pneumocystis carinii*). However, neither of the former conditions typically necessitates hospitalization, whereas a significant number of patients with

---

Table 415–2 • DIAGNOSTIC APPROACH TO PULMONARY DISEASE IN HIV-INFECTED PERSONS: CLUES

Clinical Setting
  Ambulatory care/outpatient clinic: URI > acute bronchitis > bacterial pneumonia > *Pneumocystis* pneumonia
  Hospital: bacterial pneumonia > *Pneumocystis* pneumonia > tuberculosis > pulmonary Kaposi's sarcoma
  Intensive care unit: *Pneumocystis* pneumonia > bacterial pneumonia
CD4+ Cell Count (see Table 415–3)
Patient Background
  HIV transmission category: MSM: ↑ incidence Kaposi's sarcoma; IDU: ↑ incidence bacterial pneumonia, tuberculosis
  Habits: cigarettes: ↑ incidence bacterial bronchitis, bacterial pneumonia, COPD, RB-ILD, bronchogenic carcinoma
  Travel and residence: assess risk for endemic fungal diseases, tuberculosis
Medical Background and Use of Prophylaxis
  Prior disease ↑ incidence of recurrence: bacterial pneumonia, *Pneumocystis* pneumonia, fungal pneumonias
  Prophylaxis/maintenance ↓ incidence of disease: *Pneumocystis* pneumonia, fungal pneumonias, tuberculosis (if PPD+)
Symptoms and Signs
  Respiratory symptoms: especially cough (productive or nonproductive) and symptom duration
  Symptoms suggesting extrapulmonary or disseminated disease
  Physical examination of chest: focal or nonfocal
  Signs suggesting extrapulmonary or disseminated disease
Laboratory Tests
  White blood cell count: elevated or if normal, elevated relative to baseline: bacterial pneumonia
  Serum lactate dehydrogenase: elevated: nonspecific but classically seen in *Pneumocystis* pneumonia
  Arterial blood gas: nonspecific but useful for prognosis, management decisions (e.g., admit and whether corticosteroids are indicated for *Pneumocystis* pneumonia)
Chest Radiograph (see Table 415–4)

COPD = chronic obstructive pulmonary disease; IDU = injection drug users; MSM = men who have sex with men; PPD = purified protein derivative (in HIV-infected person, PPD considered positive if ≥5-mm induration); RB-ILD = respiratory bronchiolitis-interstitial lung disease; URI = upper respiratory tract infection.

Table 415–1 • HIV-ASSOCIATED PULMONARY DISEASES

OPPORTUNISTIC INFECTIONS

BACTERIAL	MYCOBACTERIAL	FUNGAL	VIRAL/PARASITIC
Streptococcus pneumoniae	*Mycobacterium tuberculosis*	*Pneumocystis jiroveci**	Cytomegalovirus
Haemophilus species	*Mycobacterium kansasii*	*Cryptococcus neoformans*	*Toxoplasma gondii*
Pseudomonas aeruginosa	*Mycobacterium avium* complex	*Histoplasma capsulatum*	
Staphylococcus aureus		*Coccidioides immitis*	
Klebsiella pneumoniae		*Aspergillus* species (esp. *fumigatus*)	

NEOPLASMS AND SELECTED NONINFECTIOUS DISEASES

NEOPLASM	LYMPHOPROLIFERATIVE DISORDERS	MISCELLANEOUS DISORDERS
Kaposi's sarcoma	Nonspecific interstitial pneumonitis	Pulmonary hypertension
Non-Hodgkin's lymphoma	Lymphocytic interstitial pneumonitis	Chronic obstructive pulmonary disease
		Sarcoidosis
		Immune reconstitution syndromes

*The form of *Pneumocystis* that infects humans is *Pneumocystis jiroveci* (formerly *Pneumocystis carinii*).

the latter diseases require hospitalization. At San Francisco General Hospital, the most common pulmonary diseases among hospitalized HIV-infected patients are bacterial pneumonia, followed by *Pneumocystis* pneumonia, both of which are significantly more common than the next most common diagnoses: tuberculosis, pulmonary Kaposi's sarcoma (KS), and *Cryptococcus neoformans* pneumonia. Among patients requiring critical care, the Pulmonary Complications of HIV Infection Study found that the most common pulmonary disease was *Pneumocystis* pneumonia, followed by bacterial pneumonia.

The geographic location of the clinic or hospital may also influence the frequency of different diagnoses. In specific populations or particular geographic regions, mycobacterial and endemic fungal pneumonias become important considerations. In endemic areas, disease due to *Histoplasma capsulatum* or *Coccidioides immitis* are among the most frequent infections seen, whereas neither is encountered more than a few times a year at San Francisco General Hospital.

CD4+ CELL COUNT

The CD4+ cell count remains an excellent indicator of an HIV-infected patient's risk of developing a specific opportunistic infection or particular neoplasm, and it is an essential component of the diagnostic approach. Many of the HIV-associated pulmonary diseases primarily manifest themselves once a patient's CD4+ cell count has declined to less than a characteristic CD4+ count range, and these diseases only occasionally occur in a patient whose CD4+ cell count is greater than that range (Table 415–3). The exceptions are diseases that can present in persons without underlying immunodeficiency such as bacterial pneumonia, tuberculosis, and non-Hodgkin's lymphoma. These diseases can present at any CD4+ cell count in HIV-infected patients. However, their incidence increases as the CD4+ cell count declines. One study found that the risk of bacterial pneumonia among HIV-infected subjects with a CD4+ cell count less than 200 cells/μL was more than 5½ times greater than that for subjects whose CD4+ count was more than 500 cells/μL. In addition, as the CD4+ cell count declines, the incidence of bacterial pneumonia accompanied by bacteremia (especially *Streptococcus pneumoniae*) and the incidence of *Mycobacterium tuberculosis* infection accompanied by extrapulmonary or disseminated disease increases, features that have important implications for diagnosis.

At CD4+ cell counts of less than 200 cells/μL, *Pneumocystis* and *C. neoformans* pneumonias both become significant diagnoses to consider. A review from the Clinical Center of the National Institutes of Health found that 46 of 49 patients (94%) diagnosed with *Pneumocystis* pneumonia had a CD4+ cell count less than 200 cells/μL. The Multicenter AIDS Cohort Study demonstrated that HIV-infected subjects with a CD4+ cell count less than 200 cells/μL at study entry had a nearly five-fold greater risk of developing *Pneumocystis* pneumonia compared to subjects who had a CD4+ cell count greater than 200 cells/μL at entry. Finally, the Pulmonary Complications of HIV Infection Study reported that 95% of 145 cases of *Pneumocystis* pneumonia occurred in subjects whose CD4+ cell count was less than 200 cells/μL (median CD4+ cell count = 29 cells/μL).

At CD4 cell counts less than 100 cells/μL, pneumonias due to *Pseudomonas aeruginosa*, *Staphylococcus aureus*, and *Toxoplasma gondii* and lung involvement from KS are increasingly diagnosed. One study of 64 HIV-infected patients with pulmonary toxoplasmosis diagnosed by bronchoalveolar lavage (BAL) reported a mean CD4+ cell count of 40 cells/μL; 82% had a CD4+ count of less than 50 cells/μL, and only 4% had a count greater than 200 cells/μL. A series of 168 consecutive HIV-infected patients with pulmonary KS diagnosed by bronchoscopy reported a median CD4+ cell count of 19 cells/μL; 68% had a CD4+ count less than 50 cells/μL, and only 4% had a count greater than 200 cells/μL.

Finally, at CD4+ cell counts less than 50 cells/μL, diseases caused by nontuberculous mycobacteria (*Mycobacterium avium* complex), endemic (*H. capsulatum, C. immitis*) and nonendemic (*Aspergillus* species) fungi, and cytomegalovirus increasingly become important diagnoses to consider. These diseases usually present with extrapulmonary or disseminated disease that can dominate the clinical presentation. In many of these presentations, the patient may have minimal or no respiratory complaints and the chest radiograph is often normal. One review of 72 HIV-infected patients with disseminated histoplasmosis noted respiratory complaints in 53% and a normal chest radiograph in 43%.

PATIENT BACKGROUND

A number of important diagnostic clues are contained in a patient's personal and medical background that may help suggest specific diagnoses (see Table 415–2).

HIV TRANSMISSION CATEGORY AND HABITS. A patient's HIV transmission category and health-related habits influence the relative frequency of various HIV-related and non–HIV-related pulmonary diseases. HIV-associated KS is seen almost exclusively in men who report having sexual relations with other men (MSM). Bacterial pneumonia and tuberculosis are more common in HIV-infected patients who are injection drug users than in HIV-infected patients without a history of IDU. Furthermore, IDU or other illicit drug use can cause a variety of non–HIV-related pulmonary diseases such as endocarditis-related septic pulmonary emboli, pulmonary talcosis-interstitial lung disease, aspiration pneumonia secondary to respiratory depression, and drug-induced pulmonary edema.

Perhaps more so than in the general population, HIV-infected patients who are cigarette smokers are at an increased risk for a variety of smoking-related respiratory illnesses and diseases. Both bacterial bronchitis and bacterial pneumonia are more common in HIV-infected cigarette smokers than in HIV-infected nonsmokers or former smokers. This is especially the case among persons with a CD4+ cell count of less than 200 cells/μL. In addition, HIV-infected patients who report a long history of cigarette use may present with manifestations of chronic obstructive pulmonary disease (COPD) or with respiratory bronchiolitis—interstitial lung disease as the cause of their symptoms. Although it is currently debated whether HIV infection itself is associated with an increased risk of lung carcinoma, most cases of lung cancer reported in HIV-infected patients have developed in persons with a history of cigarette smoking.

TRAVEL AND RESIDENCE. Travel to or residence in a geographic region that is endemic for fungi such as *C. immitis, H. capsulatum*, or *Penicillium marneffei* is a strong determinant of the risk of exposure, infection, and, ultimately, disease. HIV-infected patients without such a history are unlikely to have been exposed and infected and, therefore, are unlikely to develop these diseases. However, clinicians caring for patients in nonendemic areas would be wise to query their patients for details on their residence and travel history if the presentation is suggestive of an endemic fungal infection.

Tuberculosis is more common in certain geographic areas and in certain populations. HIV-infected patients who were born in or have traveled to a country with a high prevalence of tuberculosis and patients who are homeless or previously incarcerated are at higher risk for exposure to *M. tuberculosis*. Patients who have a positive tuberculin skin test (defined as ≥ 5-mm induration in HIV-infected persons),

---

Table 415–3 • CD4+ CELL COUNT RANGES FOR HIV-ASSOCIATED PULMONARY DISEASES

Any CD4+ cell count
Bacterial pneumonia (most often *Streptococcus pneumoniae*, *Haemophilus* species)
Mycobacterium tuberculosis pneumonia
Non-Hodgkin's lymphoma
Nonspecific interstitial pneumonitis
Pulmonary hypertension
Chronic obstructive lung disease

CD4+ cell count <200 cells/μL
Pneumocystis pneumonia
Cryptococcus neoformans pneumonia

CD4+ cell count <100 cells/μL
Bacterial pneumonia due to *Pseudomonas aeruginosa*, *Staphylococcus aureus*
Toxoplasma gondii pneumonia
Pulmonary Kaposi's sarcoma

CD4+ cell count <50 cells/μL
Mycobacterium avium complex—usually associated with disseminated disease
Histoplasma capsulatum—usually associated with disseminated disease
Coccidioides immitis—usually associated with disseminated disease
Aspergillus species (most often *A. fumigatus*) pneumonia
Cytomegalovirus pneumonia—usually associated with disseminated disease

especially if recent converters, are at an increased risk for developing tuberculosis.

MEDICAL BACKGROUND AND USE OF PROPHYLAXIS

Many of the HIV-related opportunistic infections recur, and the current presentation may be due to a recurrence or relapse of a prior pulmonary disease (see Table 415–2). Bacterial infections are often recurrent, and recognition that bacterial pneumonias are common in HIV-infected patients and frequently recur led to the inclusion of recurrent pneumonia (≥2 episodes within a 12-month period) as an AIDS-defining condition. In addition, patients with recurrent episodes of bacterial pneumonia can develop airway damage or bronchiectasis, which, in turn, predisposes them to further bacterial infections. Patients with prior *Pneumocystis* pneumonia are at high risk for recurrence, especially if their CD4+ cell count remains less than 200 cells/µL. If the count rises to greater than 200 cells/µL with therapy, prophylaxis against *Pneumocystis* is discontinued.[1,2] Similarly, patients with previous cryptococcosis, coccidioidomycosis, or histoplasmosis are at high risk for relapse. Patients with a positive purified protein derivative (PPD) and no evidence of active tuberculosis should receive treatment for latent tuberculosis infection; failure to do so places the patient at high risk of developing tuberculosis. In HIV-infected patients, adherence to the prescribed regimen lessens the probability of disease, whereas failure to adhere to the regimen frequently results in recurrent and/or relapsed disease.

Symptoms and Signs of Diagnostic Use (see Table 415–2)

SYMPTOMS

The Pulmonary Complications of HIV Infection Study demonstrated that respiratory symptoms are a frequent complaint in HIV-infected persons and that symptoms increase in frequency as the CD4+ cell count declines. In this study, subjects reported cough at 27%, dyspnea at 23%, and fever at 9% of more than 12,000 routine visits. Of note, these symptoms increased in frequency in the subset of subjects with a CD4+ cell count of less than 200 cells/µL.

In general, respiratory symptoms are nonspecific. All of the HIV-associated pulmonary diseases may present with cough, dyspnea, and/or pleuritic chest pain. However, each pulmonary disease has a characteristic presentation and particular aspects of these symptoms may be useful in suggesting a specific diagnosis. For example, in patients who complain of a cough, it is important to elucidate whether the cough is productive of purulent sputum or nonproductive. The two most common HIV-associated pulmonary diseases encountered in many hospital settings are bacterial pneumonia and *Pneumocystis* pneumonia; most patients with bacterial pneumonia present with a cough productive of purulent sputum, whereas most patients with *Pneumocystis* pneumonia note a nonproductive cough. In one study, subjects presenting with a productive cough were 2½ times more likely to have bacterial pneumonia than those without such complaints. Similarly in this study, subjects presenting with a nonproductive cough were more than two times as likely to have *Pneumocystis* pneumonia than those without such complaints. The duration of symptoms may also be useful. Bacterial pneumonias due to *S. pneumoniae* and *Haemophilus* species characteristically present with an acute onset and a symptom duration of 3 to 5 days. In contrast, *Pneumocystis* pneumonia usually presents with a subacute onset and a typical symptom duration of 2 to 4 weeks. One early study found a median symptom duration of 28 days among 49 HIV-infected patients with *Pneumocystis* pneumonia. Thus, in an HIV-infected patient with a CD4+ cell count of less than 200 cells/µL (and hence at risk for both pneumonias), the presence of cough productive of purulent sputum and a symptom duration of a few days favors the diagnosis of bacterial pneumonia. In contrast, the absence of purulent sputum and a symptom duration of a few weeks strongly favor the diagnosis of *Pneumocystis* pneumonia. Patients with mixed clinical findings may well have dual infections (*Pneumocystis* and bacterial pneumonias).

Constitutional symptoms such as fever, night sweats, and weight loss may suggest the presence of a systemic or disseminated disease. Fever and weight loss may be the sole complaints associated with disseminated disease due to mycobacteria or fungi, or they may be "B" symptoms associated with non-Hodgkin's lymphoma.

Extrapulmonary symptoms, when present, are often useful in suggesting a specific diagnosis. Although HIV-infected patients can present with multiple concurrent illnesses, many of the HIV-associated pulmonary diseases have important extrapulmonary manifestations that account for their nonpulmonary findings. For example, the presence of respiratory symptoms and headache in a patient with a CD4+ cell count less than 200 cells/µL should suggest the possibility of *C. neoformans* pneumonia and meningitis. In fact, although the lungs are the portal of entry for *Cryptococcus*, many patients present with asymptomatic or minimally symptomatic pulmonary disease and the diagnosis is only suggested by the presence of extrapulmonary symptoms. In one series, 84% of 106 patients with *C. neoformans* infection presented with meningitis; cough or dyspnea was present in less than one third of these patients (31%).

SIGNS

In general, HIV-infected patients with pneumonia may be febrile, tachycardic, and tachypneic. The presence of systemic hypotension often suggests a fulminant disease process (e.g., bacterial septicemia). Pulse oximetry often reveals a decrease in the oxygen saturation and provides an estimate of the severity of the disease. The presence of exercise-induced oxygen desaturation is reported to be a sensitive indicator of *Pneumocystis* pneumonia.

Examination of the lungs may suggest an etiology for the respiratory symptoms. Patients with bacterial pneumonia often have focal lung examinations suggestive of consolidation and/or pleural effusion. In contrast, patients with *Pneumocystis* pneumonia most often have a normal lung examination and only a minority have inspiratory crackles. Wheezing in a patient with a history of asthma suggests an exacerbation of that condition, whereas diminished breath sounds in a longtime smoker may indicate emphysema. Finally, abnormal findings on lung examination may be the result of a nonpulmonary disease. For example, rales in association with an S3 cardiac gallop and an elevated jugular venous pressure suggest a cardiac etiology.

The remainder of the physical examination may also suggest an etiology for the respiratory symptoms. Altered mental status in an HIV-infected patient with pulmonary disease whose CD4+ cell count is less than 200 cells/µL suggests *C. neoformans* with neurologic involvement. A patient with a focal neurologic examination and pulmonary disease may have concurrent *T. gondii* encephalitis and pneumonitis. The presence of mucocutaneous KS lesions may point to pulmonary involvement with Kaposi's. However, the absence of KS lesions on the skin and mucous membranes does not preclude the possibility of significant visceral disease, including the lung. One series found that 15% of 168 patients with pulmonary KS diagnosed by bronchoscopy had no evidence of concurrent or preexisting mucocutaneous Kaposi's. Patients with new cutaneous lesions may have disseminated fungal disease. An abdominal examination revealing hepatosplenomegaly suggests either disseminated mycobacterial or fungal disease or non-Hodgkin's lymphoma.

Laboratory Tests

Laboratory tests may provide important clues to the diagnosis of pulmonary disease (see Table 415–2). In general, however, HIV-infected patients typically have a host of laboratory abnormalities that are nonspecific or due to conditions unrelated to the pulmonary disease. Laboratory tests that may be useful include complete blood count with white blood cell count (WBC) and differential, serum lactate dehydrogenase (LDH), and arterial blood gas (ABG). These tests also serve as prognostic markers and as baseline values for subsequent measurements. Serial measurements are useful in any patient who fails to exhibit a clinical response or who worsens despite appropriate therapy.

WHITE BLOOD CELL COUNT. The WBC is frequently elevated and a left shift is present as well in persons with bacterial pneumonia. This elevation may be relative to the baseline value in a patient whose baseline WBC is less than the normal laboratory range. HIV-infected patients with neutropenia are at higher risk for bacterial and certain fungal infections such as those due to *Aspergillus* species.

SERUM LACTATE DEHYDROGENASE. The serum LDH is often elevated in patients with *Pneumocystis* pneumonia. However, it may be elevated in other pulmonary (including bacterial pneumonia and tuberculosis) and nonpulmonary conditions. Most of the published studies reporting a high sensitivity of serum LDH for *Pneumocystis* pneumonia consisted of hospitalized patients, some of whom had acute respiratory failure and were mechanically ventilated. The study that reported the lowest sensitivity examined outpatients presenting to an urgent care clinic. These findings suggest that the severity of *Pneumocystis* pneumonia and the patient population studied affect the diagnostic sensitivity of the test. Despite its diagnostic limitations, the degree of LDH elevation has been shown to correlate with prognosis and response to therapy. Patients with *Pneumocystis* pneumonia and an initial markedly elevated serum LDH or an increasing serum LDH despite *Pneumocystis* pneumonia treatment have a poor prognosis.

ARTERIAL BLOOD GASES. As in any population, ABGs are frequently abnormal in HIV-infected patients with significant pulmonary disease. The findings of hypoxemia, an increased alveolar-arterial oxygen difference, and hypocarbia with respiratory alkalosis are nonspecific. However, ABG analysis is useful for prognosis as well as clinical decisions regarding whether to admit the patient and whether adjunctive corticosteroids are indicated in those patients with *Pneumocystis* pneumonia.

Radiographic Data and Pulmonary Function Tests

CHEST RADIOGRAPH

The chest radiograph is the cornerstone of the evaluation of pulmonary diseases in HIV-infected patients. Because each of these diseases has a characteristic radiographic presentation, the radiograph can narrow the diagnostic possibilities and suggest a diagnostic approach (Table 415–4).

Bacterial pneumonia is currently the most common pulmonary disease seen among HIV-infected persons at many institutions in the United States. Three large series of HIV-associated bacterial pneumonia have yielded similar results in that the most frequently identified pathogens are *S. pneumoniae*, *Haemophilus* species, and *P. aeruginosa*. Classically, the chest radiographic presentation of bacterial pneumonia in HIV-infected patients demonstrates focal, segmental, or lobar consolidation, similar to the presentation observed in non–HIV-infected persons (Fig. 415–1). However, this presentation may be more frequent in pneumonias due to *S. pneumoniae* and to a lesser

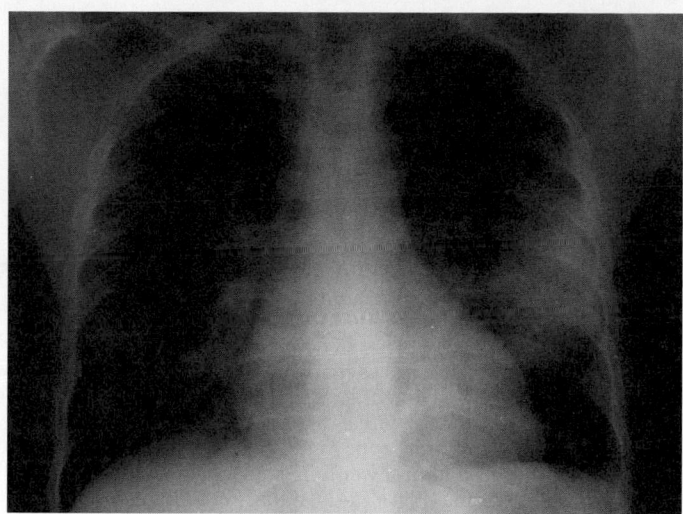

FIGURE 415–1 • Chest radiograph of an HIV-infected person, CD4+ cell count greater than 200 cells/μL, revealing left lingular consolidation. Sputum and blood cultures were positive for *Streptococcus pneumoniae*. (Courtesy of Laurence Huang, MD, and Chin Tang Huang, MD.)

extent *Haemophilus* species than community-acquired *P. aeruginosa*. A review of all English-language published articles and abstracts from 1981 to 1990 on HIV-infected persons with *S. pneumoniae* disease found that three fourths of bacterial pneumonias presented with segmental, lobar, or multilobar consolidation on chest radiograph. One study reported that a classic lobar alveolar pattern was seen in 67% and a diffuse alveolar pattern in 10% of 21 HIV-infected patients with *S. pneumoniae* pneumonia. Another study found similar proportions in 34 HIV-infected patients with *H. influenzae* pneumonia; in this study, focal or diffuse lobar infiltrates were noted in 74%. However, a

Table 415–4 • CHARACTERISTIC CHEST RADIOGRAPH FINDINGS FOR SELECTED PULMONARY DISEASES*

PULMONARY DISEASE	AUTHOR (YEAR), PATIENTS	DISTRIBUTION (%)	PATTERN (%)	ASSOCIATED FINDINGS (%)
Bacteria[†]	Selwyn (1998), 99	Focal (71%) Diffuse (29%)	Lobar (54%) Interstitial (17%) Nodular (10%)	Cavitation (1%) Pleural effusion (7%) Adenopathy (2%)
Mycobacterium tuberculosis, CD4+ ≥400 cells/μL	Abouya (1995), 30	Miliary (0%)	Cavitary (63%) Noncavitary (33%)	Pleural effusion (3%) Adenopathy (0%)
M. tuberculosis, CD4+ 200-399 cells/μL	Abouya (1995), 36	Miliary (6%)	Cavitary (44%) Noncavitary (44%)	Pleural effusion (11%) Adenopathy (14%)
M. tuberculosis, CD4+ <200 cells/μL	Abouya (1995), 45	Miliary (9%)	Cavitary (29%) Noncavitary (58%)	Pleural effusion (11%) Adenopathy (20%)
Pneumocystis jiroveci	DeLorenzo (1987), 104	Bilateral (95%) Diffuse (48%)	Interstitial or mixed (88%) Alveolar (12%)	Cysts (7%) Honeycomb lesions (4%)
Cryptococcus neoformans	Batungwanayo (1994), 37	Diffuse (76%)	Interstitial or mixed (76%) Alveolar (19%) Nodular/nodules (5%)	Cavitation (11%) Adenopathy (11%) Pleural effusion (5%)
Cytomegalovirus	Salomon (1997), 18	Normal (33%)	Reticular-granular (33%) Alveolar (22%) Nodular (11%)	Cavitation (11%) Cyst (6%) Pleural effusion (33%) Adenopathy (11%)
Cytomegalovirus	Rodriguez-Barradas (1996), 17	Bilateral (71%) Unilateral (29%)	Interstitial (82%) Alveolar (18%)	Pleural effusion (12%)
Toxoplasma gondii	Rabaud (1996), 43	Normal (23%) Bilateral (58%)	Interstitial (53%) Nodular (16%)	Pleural effusion (7%) Pneumothorax (2%)
Kaposi's sarcoma	Gruden (1995), 76	Normal (3%) Bilateral (96%) Diffuse or mid-lower lung zones (92%)	Bronchial wall thickening +/– coalescence (95%) Nodules (78%)	Kerley B lines (71%) Pleural effusion (53%) Adenopathy (16%)
Non-Hodgkin's lymphoma	Eisner (1996), 38	Normal (3%)	Nodules (40%) or mass (24%) Lobar (40%) Reticular (24%)	Cavitation (3%) Pleural effusion (44%) Adenopathy (21%)

*Chest radiograph presentations can vary significantly depending on a number of factors, including severity of disease and use of prophylaxis.
[†]The characteristic chest radiograph presentation is influenced by the specific bacteria (see text).

different series of 12 HIV-infected patients with *H. influenzae* pneumonia reported that the presentation may be clinically and radiographically indistinguishable from *Pneumocystis* pneumonia. The patients complained of nonproductive cough and dyspnea with a median symptom duration of 4 weeks. All presented with bilateral interstitial or mixed interstitial-alveolar infiltrates similar to *Pneumocystis* pneumonia. In contrast, a study of 16 HIV-infected patients with *P. aeruginosa* pneumonia found that the pneumonia was community acquired in 15 (94%). Chest radiographs revealed cavitary infiltrates on admission in 50% and an additional 19% presented with pulmonary infiltrates that subsequently cavitated. The frequency of cavitary infiltrates in *P. aeruginosa* pneumonia was also noted in a study of 58 HIV-infected patients with *P. aeruginosa* infection, 25 of whom had pneumonia. Of these 25 patients, 24% had cavitary pneumonia. Thus, the presence of a cavitary pneumonia may be more suggestive of *Pseudomonas* than either *Streptococcus* or *Haemophilus*.

Tuberculosis can present with a variety of chest radiographic findings, including upper lung zone infiltrates, often with cavitation (Fig. 415–2), middle and/or lower lung zone consolidation mimicking bacterial pneumonia (Fig. 415–3), miliary or nodular disease, and pleural effusions and/or intrathoracic adenopathy. The frequency that each of these specific findings is seen is influenced by the patient's CD4+ cell count. In general, patients with a CD4+ cell count well above 200 cells/μL are more likely to present with a radiograph that has upper lung zone infiltrates and cavitation than patients with a CD4+ cell count of less than 200 cells/μL. In this latter group, patients are as likely or more likely to present with a radiograph that has mid and/or lower lung zone involvement or diffuse involvement and are more likely to have associated intrathoracic adenopathy. One study reviewed the chest radiographic presentation of 111 HIV-infected patients with tuberculosis. The proportion of patients with cavitary infiltrates declined significantly as the CD4+ cell count declined from 400 cells/μL or more to less than 200 cells/μL, whereas the proportions with noncavitary infiltrates and with intrathoracic adenopathy increased significantly as the CD4+ count declined. Thus, the radiographic key to the diagnosis of tuberculosis is knowledge of the patient's CD4+ cell count and understanding which patterns are more common at that CD4+ count.

Classically, *Pneumocystis* pneumonia presents with bilateral interstitial-reticular or granular opacities (Fig. 415–4). Often the opacities are symmetrical, and they are diffuse when the disease is severe. One large study of 104 HIV-infected patients with *Pneumocystis* pneumonia revealed that 87.5% presented with either an interstitial pattern (75%) or a mixed interstitial-alveolar pattern (12.5%), whereas the remaining patients had an alveolar pattern. In addition, 7% had thin-walled cysts (pneumatoceles) and 4% had honeycomb lesions.

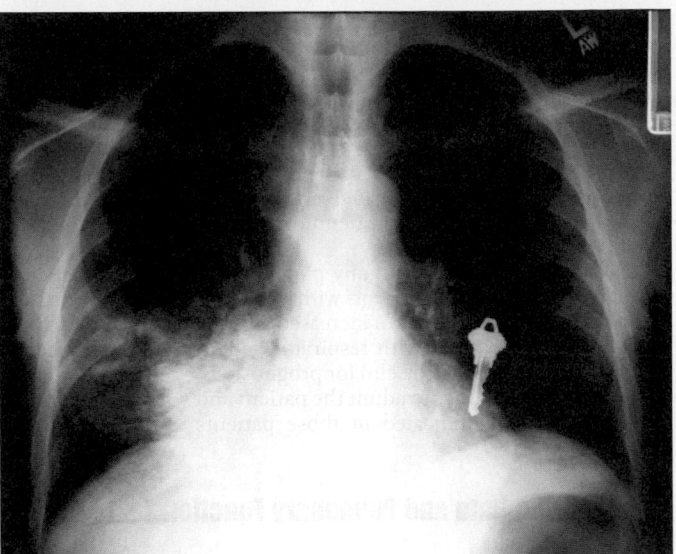

FIGURE 415–3 • Chest radiograph of an HIV-infected person, CD4+ cell count less than 200 cells/μL, revealing right lower lung consolidation with air bronchograms. Sputum culture grew *Mycobacterium tuberculosis* that was monorifampin resistant. In this case, the key to the diagnosis of tuberculosis was knowledge of the patient's CD4+ cell count and an understanding that tuberculosis can present in this manner in such an individual.

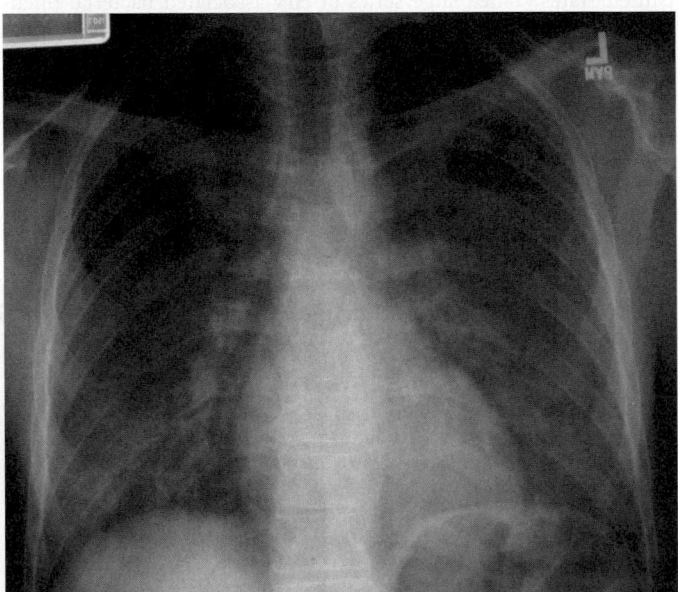

FIGURE 415–4 • Chest radiograph of an HIV-infected person, CD4+ cell count less than 200 cells/μL, demonstrating the characteristic bilateral, reticular-granular opacities of *Pneumocystis* pneumonia. Bronchoscopy with bronchoalveolar lavage fluid examination revealed *Pneumocystis jiroveci*.

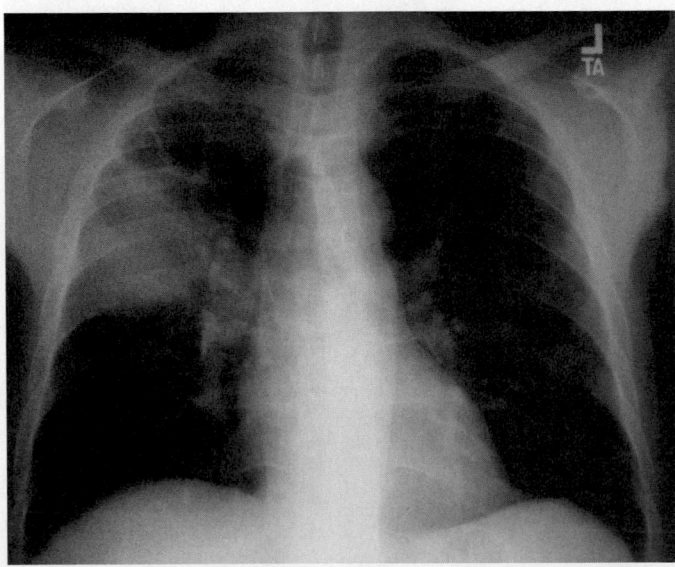

FIGURE 415–2 • Chest radiograph of an HIV-infected person, CD4+ cell count greater than 200 cells/μL, revealing right upper lobe infiltrate, with areas of cavitation. Sputum acid-fast bacillus stain was positive, and multiple sputum cultures grew *Mycobacterium tuberculosis*.

Infiltrates were bilateral in 95% and involved the entire lung in 48%. Importantly, this study predates the widespread use of *Pneumocystis* prophylaxis. Several reports have described the radiographic findings in patients receiving aerosolized pentamidine prophylaxis; these radiographs characteristically reveal an upper lung zone predominance mimicking mycobacterial disease. However, this upper lung zone predominance can also be seen in patients who never received aerosolized pentamidine and the pattern seen (reticular, granular) is more important than the distribution in suggesting the diagnosis of *Pneumocystis* pneumonia.

Similar to tuberculosis, *C. neoformans* pneumonia can present with a variety of chest radiographic findings. Although bilateral interstitial-reticular infiltrates appear to be the most common radiographic presentation (mimicking *Pneumocystis* pneumonia), pulmonary involvement due to *Cryptococcus* can also present with an alveolar or nodular pattern, thin-walled cysts or cavities, nodules, masses, intrathoracic adenopathy, and pleural effusions.

Pulmonary KS characteristically presents with bilateral opacities in a central or perihilar distribution (Fig. 415–5). Linear densities, nodules, and pleural effusions are all common findings. One study of 76 HIV-infected patients with pulmonary KS diagnosed by bronchoscopy (where a BAL was negative for infectious organisms) found that 95% of the chest radiographs had peribronchial cuffing and tram track opacities with (45%) or without (50%) more extensive perihilar coalescent opacities. Small nodules (50%) or nodular opacities (28%) were seen in 78%, Kerley B lines in 71%, and pleural effusions in 53% of the radiographs. No patient presented with either Kerley B lines or pleural effusions without concurrent parenchymal findings. Sixteen per cent of these patients had hilar or mediastinal lymph node enlargement, a finding that is often better appreciated on chest computed tomography (CT).

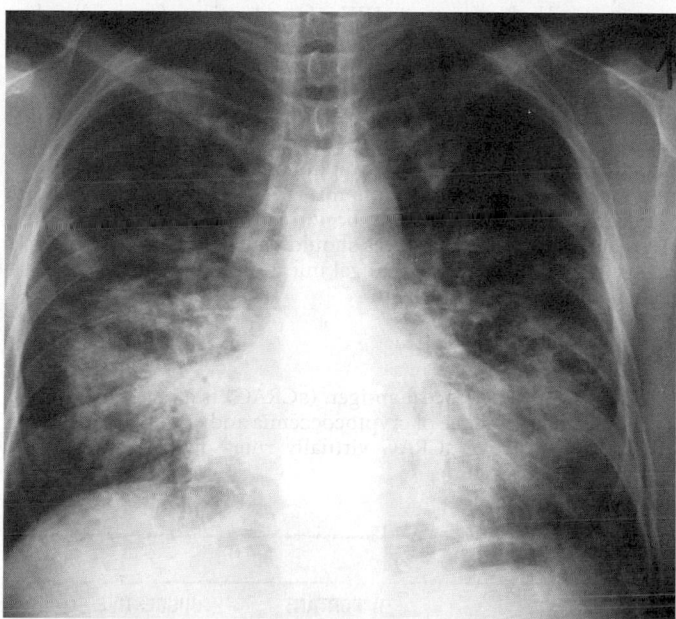

FIGURE 415–5 • Chest radiograph of an HIV-infected person, CD4+ cell count less than 100 cells/µL, with the characteristic bilateral, middle and lower lung zone, predominantly central distribution of abnormalities of pulmonary Kaposi's sarcoma. The patient had no evidence of mucocutaneous Kaposi's sarcoma, and the diagnosis of pulmonary disease was made by bronchoscopy with visualization of the characteristic erythematous-violaceous Kaposi's lesions throughout the visible airway (see Fig. 415–7).

CHEST COMPUTED TOMOGRAPHY

Chest CT scans are more sensitive than chest radiographs for detecting the presence and defining the characteristics and extent of pulmonary disease. However, a CT scan is unnecessary in most evaluations because the clinical and chest radiographic presentation often suggest a single diagnosis or a few diagnoses to consider primarily. There are a number of specific clinical scenarios where chest CT scans may be of particular use in HIV-infected patients. In the author's experience, a high-resolution CT (HRCT) is extremely useful in cases of clinically suspected *Pneumocystis* pneumonia in which the chest radiograph is normal or unchanged, a phenomenon that occurs in up to 39% of reported series. When there is a clinical suspicion for *Pneumocystis* pneumonia, dismissing the possibility of the disease based on a normal or unchanged radiograph could have catastrophic consequences. Nevertheless, the majority of patients with symptoms suggestive of *Pneumocystis* pneumonia whose radiograph is normal or unchanged do not have the disease. Subjecting these patients to diagnostic procedures such as bronchoscopy or to empirical *Pneumocystis* treatment with its associated toxicities is also ill advised. In these cases, a sensitive follow-up test is needed to select which patients require either diagnostic procedures or empirical therapy and, as importantly, which patients require neither invasive procedure nor *Pneumocystis* treatment. Chest HRCT scan is one such test because patients with *Pneumocystis* pneumonia and a normal chest radiograph have patchy areas of ground-glass opacity (GGO) on HRCT scan (Fig. 415–6). Although the presence of GGO is nonspecific and may be seen in a number of pulmonary disorders, its absence strongly argues against the presence of *Pneumocystis* pneumonia.

Chest CT can also be useful in suggesting a diagnosis in cases in which the chest radiograph reveals multiple pulmonary nodules. Finding a predominance of nodules less than 1 cm in diameter in a centrilobular distribution strongly suggests the presence of an opportunistic infection, whereas a predominance of nodules greater than 1 cm in diameter is suggestive of neoplasm. When the nodules are mostly less than 1 cm in diameter, the presence of intrathoracic adenopathy, especially if low attenuation (another use for CT), indicates that mycobacterial (or fungal) disease is probable. When the nodules are mostly greater than 1 cm, the finding of associated peribronchovascular thickening inevitably results in a diagnosis of pulmonary KS.

HIV-infected patients may present with disseminated mycobacterial or fungal disease. In these patients, the chest radiograph may reveal little or no parenchymal lung involvement. However, chest CT may reveal intrathoracic adenopathy, which, if low attenuation, strongly suggests these infections. Finally, chest CT scans are useful in guiding diagnostic procedures such as bronchoscopy, CT-guided transthoracic needle aspiration, and surgical procedures.

GALLIUM-67

Gallium-67 scanning has been the most frequently used nuclear medicine study in the evaluation of HIV-associated pulmonary disease.

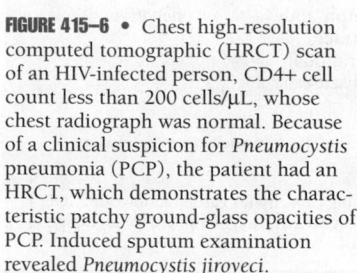

FIGURE 415–6 • Chest high-resolution computed tomographic (HRCT) scan of an HIV-infected person, CD4+ cell count less than 200 cells/µL, whose chest radiograph was normal. Because of a clinical suspicion for *Pneumocystis* pneumonia (PCP), the patient had an HRCT, which demonstrates the characteristic patchy ground-glass opacities of PCP. Induced sputum examination revealed *Pneumocystis jiroveci*.

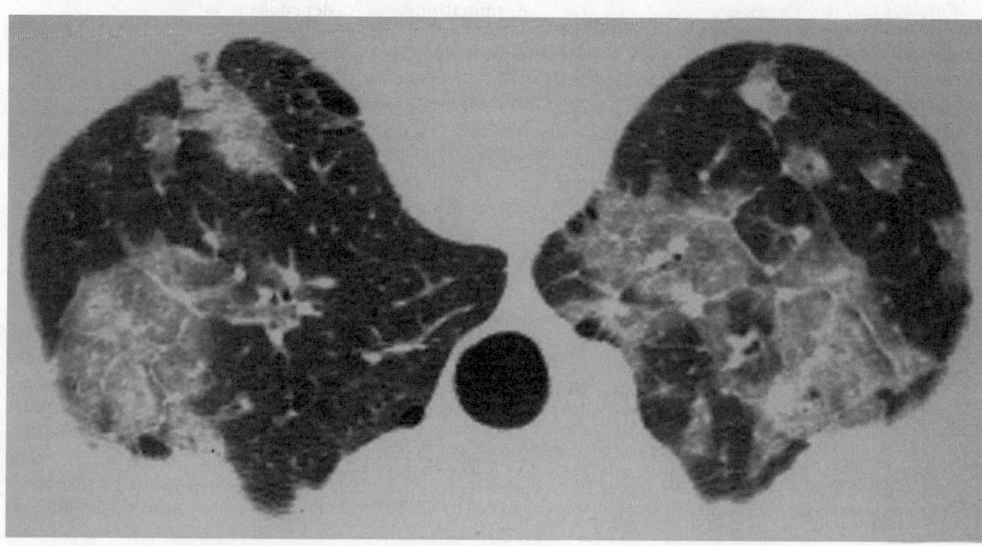

Gallium scans can be extremely useful in the evaluation of patients with suspected pulmonary KS in which bronchoscopy is unavailable or fails to document endobronchial KS lesions, because KS, unlike opportunistic infections, non-Hodgkin's lymphoma, and lymphocytic interstitial pneumonitis (LIP), is gallium negative. Thus, in an HIV-infected MSM patient with mucocutaneous KS and a chest radiograph suggestive of pulmonary KS, a negative gallium scan is indicative of pulmonary Kaposi's alone. In a patient with known pulmonary KS who develops progressive respiratory complaints and a worsening chest radiograph, a gallium scan with increased uptake over the lungs suggests a superimposed opportunistic infection that warrants prompt evaluation and management.

PULMONARY FUNCTION TESTS

Pulmonary function testing can be useful in the evaluation of respiratory complaints in HIV-infected patients. In patients complaining of dry cough and/or dyspnea whose chest radiograph is normal, spirometry may diagnose airflow obstruction that is often responsive to bronchodilators. Pulmonary function testing often reveals a restrictive ventilatory defect with decreased lung volumes and increased airflow in patients with *Pneumocystis* pneumonia. In addition, the diffusing capacity for carbon monoxide (DLco) is a sensitive but nonspecific indicator of *Pneumocystis* pneumonia and a normal DLco makes the diagnosis of *Pneumocystis* pneumonia extremely unlikely. One study demonstrated that the combination of a chest radiograph followed by a DLco if the radiograph was normal or unchanged identified greater than 97% of the 80 cases of *Pneumocystis* pneumonia. Importantly, the sensitivity of a DLco less than or equal to 75% of predicted after a normal or unchanged radiograph was 90% (specificity was 53%).

Although the DLco can be useful in the evaluation of symptomatic patients, it has no role as a screening test to detect, for example, early *Pneumocystis* pneumonia in asymptomatic individuals. In an evaluation of 64 patients who experienced a 20% decline or greater in their DLco from a baseline value in the absence of new respiratory symptoms or new chest radiographic findings, none of the patients had *Pneumocystis* pneumonia or any other opportunistic infection on sputum induction, bronchoscopy, or clinical follow-up. Finally, as in

any patient, but perhaps more so in HIV-infected patients given the varied clinical and radiographic presentations, care should be exercised to exclude a diagnosis of tuberculosis before pulmonary function testing.

Diagnostic Tests

The approach to the evaluation of HIV-infected patients with suspected pulmonary disease begins with consideration of the spectrum of pulmonary diseases outlined in Table 415–1. After a careful history and physical examination supplemented by selected laboratory tests and a chest radiograph, the goal is to arrive at a probable diagnosis (or at most a few diagnoses) in which specific diagnostic tests can be ordered and appropriate treatment initiated. The next section provides a brief discussion of selected diagnostic tests (Table 415–5).

BLOOD CULTURES

Blood cultures can be obtained for bacteria, fungi, and mycobacteria assays. Because *S. pneumoniae* is the most frequent cause of bacterial pneumonia, and because pneumococcal pneumonia is often accompanied by bacteremia in HIV-infected patients (especially when the CD4+ cell count is less than 200 cells/μL), blood cultures should always be obtained in cases of suspected bacterial pneumonia. When positive, blood cultures are specific for the diagnosis and, in an era of increasing antibiotic resistance, the utility of drug susceptibility testing cannot be overemphasized. Tuberculosis and many of the fungal pneumonias may present with extrapulmonary or disseminated disease in which respiratory complaints may be minimal or absent and in which the chest radiographs may be normal. For this reason, mycobacterial and fungal blood cultures should usually be obtained in cases of suspected tuberculous or fungal infection, especially if the CD4+ cell count is below 200 cells/μL.

SEROLOGIES

The serum cryptococcal antigen (sCRAG) is an extremely sensitive test for the presence of cryptococcemia and cryptococcal meningitis, and a negative sCRAG virtually rules out the diagnosis of

---

Table 415–5 • DIAGNOSTIC TESTS FOR SELECTED PULMONARY DISEASES*

PULMONARY DISEASE	SEROLOGY OR BLOOD CULTURES	SPUTUM	BAL AND/OR TBBX	PLEURAL FLUID	IMPORTANT OTHER SITES[†]	SUGGESTIVE TESTS
Bacteria	Blood cultures (esp. *Streptococcus pneumoniae*)	Gram stain and culture	Rarely quantitative cultures	Consider (esp. if concern for empyema)		WBC ↑ (may be relative to patient baseline)
Mycobacterium tuberculosis	Blood cultures	AFB smear and culture ×3	Occasionally BAL and TBBX	Consider (w/ biopsy)	Lymph node Liver Spleen Bone marrow	
Pneumocystis jiroveci	No	Induced sputum examination	BAL +/– TBBX (depends on respective sensitivities at institution)	Rarely		HRCT-GGO, PFTs- ↓ DLco, Gallium- ↑ uptake, O₂ sat- ↓ w/exercise
Cryptococcus neoformans	Serum CRAG[‡] Blood cultures	Occasionally	BAL	Rarely	Cerebrospinal fluid Skin	
Cytomegalovirus	? CMV-PCR	No	TBBX	No	Retina GI tract	
Toxoplasma gondii	T. gondii IgG IgM	Occasionally	BAL	Rarely	Central nervous system	Head CT/MRI w/multiple lesions
Kaposi's sarcoma	? HHV-8	No	Visualization of lesions +/– TBBX	No	Mucocutaneous Lymph node GI tract	Gallium-negative
Non-Hodgkin's lymphoma	No	No	TBBX, Wang needle biopsy	Cytology	Extranodal disease	

*Tests in **BOLD** are usual diagnostic tests of choice. Other tests should be considered if tests of choice are nondiagnostic.
[†]Many of the pulmonary diseases present with important extrapulmonary sites of involvement that may dominate the clinical presentation. In such cases, pulmonary disease (if classic presentation) may be presumed in selected patients if the diagnosis is established from another site.
[‡]The serum CRAG may be negative in isolated cryptococcal pneumonia.
AFB = acid-fast bacilli; BAL = bronchoalveolar lavage; CRAG = cryptococcal antigen; CT = computed tomography; DLco = diffusing capacity for carbon monoxide; GGO = ground-glass opacities; GI = gastrointestinal; HHV-8 = human herpes virus-8 (Kaposi's sarcoma herpes virus, KS-HV); HRCT = chest high-resolution computed tomography; MRI = magnetic resonance imaging; PFTs = pulmonary function tests; TBBX = Transbronchial biopsies; WBC = White blood cell count.

cryptococcal meningitis. However, the sCRAG may be negative in HIV-infected patients who have isolated cryptococcal pneumonia. In a study of 37 HIV-infected patients with cryptococcal pneumonia, the sCRAG was only positive in 8 of 26 patients (31%) in whom it was obtained. However, the sCRAG is extremely specific for cryptococcal infection; false-positive tests are rare but may result from infection with *Trichosporon beigelii*. Therefore, an sCRAG should be obtained in all patients with suspected cryptococcal disease; patients with a positive sCRAG should have an evaluation to determine the extent of disease (i.e., lumbar puncture for possible meningitis), whereas those with a negative sCRAG but respiratory complaints or chest radiograph findings should undergo further pulmonary evaluation (i.e., bronchoscopy with BAL). In patients with cryptococcal disease, there appears to be little to no utility in measuring serial sCRAG titers.

Similar to the sCRAG, the *Histoplasma capsulatum* polysaccharide antigen (HPA) is a sensitive test for the presence of disseminated histoplasmosis. However, the HPA test may be negative in patients with mild or localized disease. The antigen, which can be measured in blood and other fluids (including BAL) but is most commonly assayed from urine, should be obtained in patients with suspected histoplasmosis. In the proper clinical context, a positive result indicates *H. capsulatum* infection. However, patients with a positive HPA test should have appropriate fungal cultures (i.e., blood) sent because fungal pathogens such as *P. marneffei, Blastomyces dermatitidis,* and *Paracoccidioides braziliensis* may cause a false-positive result. One final important benefit of serial HPA testing is its use in diagnosing relapsed disease where a two-unit increase is associated with relapsed disease.

Most cases of HIV-associated *T. gondii* encephalitis result from reactivation of latent infection. In studies of central nervous system toxoplasmosis, up to 97% of patients had a positive *Toxoplasma* IgG and a smaller percentage had a positive *Toxoplasma* IgM result. In one study of 64 HIV-infected patients with pulmonary toxoplasmosis, the *Toxoplasma* IgG was positive in 92% in which prior serology results were available and an additional 5% in this study seroconverted (IgA, IgM, and IgG all detected after previous negative results) at the time that toxoplasmosis was diagnosed. Thus, while a positive *Toxoplasma* IgG merely indicates prior infection and cannot be taken as proof of acute toxoplasmosis, a negative *Toxoplasma* IgG, especially if accompanied by a negative IgM, makes the diagnosis of toxoplasmosis unlikely.

SPUTUM

Most patients with bacterial pneumonia have a productive cough. In these patients, a Gram stain of an appropriate expectorated sputum specimen can provide a presumptive diagnosis of bacterial pneumonia and suggest a probable specific etiology. Although neither the American Thoracic Society nor the Infectious Diseases Society of America guidelines for the management of patients with community-acquired pneumonia specifically addressed HIV-infected patients with bacterial pneumonia, there is no evidence to support a different diagnostic approach concerning sputum examination and culture. Thus, the recommendation that a sputum Gram stain and culture be obtained in all patients with suspected community-acquired bacterial pneumonia is entirely appropriate for HIV-infected patients as well.

Sputum acid-fast bacilli (AFB) smear and culture are the foundations for the diagnosis of pulmonary tuberculosis and other nontuberculous mycobacterial pneumonias. Sputum AFB specimens—either spontaneous or induced—should ideally be obtained on 3 consecutive days, preferably in the morning. Several studies report that the sensitivity of sputum AFB smears and cultures for tuberculosis in HIV-infected patients is similar to that seen in the overall population. The sensitivity of sputum AFB smears for *M. tuberculosis* ranged from 50 to 60% in two large series; the sensitivity of sputum AFB smears in persons presenting with disseminated disease was significantly higher (90%). In one of these studies, the proportion of patients who were sputum AFB smear positive was no different in patients with a normal chest radiograph compared with those with an abnormal radiograph. Thus, all patients with suspected tuberculosis, even if respiratory complaints and chest radiograph findings are absent, should have three sputum specimens sent for AFB smear and culture. Patients with a positive AFB smear must be presumed to have tuberculosis and appropriate measures must be instituted while awaiting either culture or direct DNA amplification probe results. Patients with three negative sputum AFB smear results may still have tuberculosis detected on culture or determined by clinical and radiographic response but

are at reasonably low likelihood for transmission so that discontinuation of respiratory isolation (if hospitalized) can be done. Whereas a single positive sputum AFB culture result for *M. tuberculosis* is diagnostic of tuberculosis, the same cannot be said for a sputum specimen positive for a nontuberculous mycobacteria (i.e., *Mycobacterium kansasii, M. avium* complex). In these patients, a positive sputum culture result can be due to colonization, and the determination of when these mycobacteria are causing pulmonary disease relies on a constellation of clinical, radiographic, and microbiologic criteria.

Most patients with *Pneumocystis* pneumonia have a dry, nonproductive cough and sputum must be induced. Sputum induction should be performed in a properly engineered room to minimize transmission of infectious microorganisms. Sputum induction is a sensitive diagnostic test for *Pneumocystis* pneumonia with a reported sensitivity ranging from 55% in early studies to 95% with fluorescent antibody testing. The published studies were conducted in a number of different cities throughout the world and used a number of different staining techniques. Three studies also examined the impact of aerosolized pentamidine prophylaxis on induced sputum; two of the three concluded that there was no difference in the sensitivity of induced sputum examination for *Pneumocystis* pneumonia between patients on aerosolized pentamidine prophylaxis and those on no prophylaxis. In addition, one study found that there was no difference in the sensitivity of induced sputum examination whether the *Pneumocystis* pneumonia episode was a first or second episode. These results imply that sputum induction can be used in a number of different clinical settings and that its success is not limited to a few select institutions, a specific staining technique, absence of prophylaxis, or a particular clinical situation. At institutions where sputum induction is used, this procedure decreases the need for bronchoscopy. In one study of 992 HIV-associated diagnoses of *Pneumocystis* pneumonia over a 4-year period, sputum induction accounted for 800 of the 992 (80%) diagnoses; the remainder were diagnosed by bronchoscopy. In addition, induced sputum diagnosed cases of certain bacterial, mycobacterial, fungal, and parasitic pneumonias, and suggested the presence of bacterial bronchitis/bronchopneumonia. Recent studies have examined the utility of polymerase chain reaction (PCR)-based assays applied to noninvasive respiratory specimens (i.e., oropharyngeal washing or oral gargle) and have reported encouraging results. These PCR-based assays appear to be sensitive diagnostic tests, but they are less specific than standard microscopy in that patients without clinical *Pneumocystis* pneumonia have been demonstrated to have positive assay results. Nevertheless, these assays are typically available only in a research setting. Thus, sputum induction should be the initial diagnostic test for patients with suspected *Pneumocystis* pneumonia at institutions where it is available.

Although the experience is limited compared with that for tuberculosis and *Pneumocystis* pneumonia, sputum examination and/or culture can occasionally diagnose fungal pneumonias, including *C. neoformans, H. capsulatum,* and *C. immitis* but not invasive *Aspergillus* disease, nontuberculous mycobacterial pneumonia (e.g., *M. kansasii*), and *T. gondii* and other parasitic pneumonias (e.g., *Strongyloides stercoralis*).

BRONCHOSCOPY

Bronchoscopy is a mainstay in the diagnosis of HIV-associated pulmonary disease. In general, bronchoscopy should be considered for any patient with pulmonary disease whose severity warrants a prompt and accurate diagnosis, for patients with suspected pulmonary KS, for patients in whom the diagnosis is unclear despite less invasive diagnostic tests (e.g., sputum), and for patients who are failing empirical therapy for a presumed pathogen.

Bronchoscopy with BAL is the "gold standard" diagnostic test for *Pneumocystis* pneumonia, and it is the initial test of choice at institutions where sputum induction is either unavailable or its sensitivity is low. Numerous studies report that the sensitivity of BAL alone for *Pneumocystis* pneumonia is 95 to 98% or greater. At San Francisco General Hospital, we perform bronchoscopy with BAL for patients with suspected *Pneumocystis* pneumonia whose induced sputum examination is negative. In a study of 992 cases of *Pneumocystis* pneumonia diagnosed over a 4-year period, only 2 of the 992 episodes (0.2%) were diagnosed *solely* by transbronchial biopsy (TBBX). This is not to imply that TBBX is an insensitive test for *Pneumocystis* pneumonia but to demonstrate that most cases of *Pneumocystis* pneumonia can be diagnosed by other, less invasive (sputum induction) or risky (BAL) procedures. However, there can be institutional differences in the sensitivity of BAL and both BAL and TBBX are warranted at institutions where the yields of these two procedures are complementary.

Bronchoscopy is an important test to diagnose cryptococcal pneumonia, especially if the disease is limited to the lungs. One study reported that BAL fluid culture was positive in 27 of 33 HIV-infected patients (82%) with cryptococcal pneumonia in whom it was performed. These results are similar to another study in which 23 of 27 HIV-infected patients (85%) with pulmonary cryptococcosis had a positive BAL fluid culture. In this study, two of the patients with a negative BAL fluid culture had a positive BAL CRAG and the remaining two had pleural cryptococcosis that was diagnosed by pleural fluid culture as well as pleural fluid CRAG.

Bronchoscopy with a thorough visual inspection of the airways is the procedure of choice for the diagnosis of pulmonary KS. In these patients, neither endobronchial nor transbronchial biopsies add to the yield when the characteristic KS lesions are seen (Fig. 415–7). However, the absence of visible KS lesions does not preclude their presence in more distal airways nor does it preclude the possibility of parenchymal Kaposi's involvement. In these select patients, TBBX can occasionally establish the diagnosis.

Bronchoscopy with BAL may diagnose *M. tuberculosis* (although diagnostic yield improved with addition of TBBX), *H. capsulatum, C. immitis,* and *T. gondii* pneumonias. Bronchoscopy with TBBX (or other biopsy specimen) is required to establish the definitive diagnosis of *Aspergillus* species and cytomegalovirus pneumonias. Similarly, biopsy is an important tool in the diagnosis of non-Hodgkin's lymphoma pulmonary disease.

OTHER PROCEDURES

A diagnostic thoracentesis should be considered for any HIV-infected patient with evidence of pleural effusion in whom other tests are nondiagnostic or in whom there is a concern for empyema. In most situations, pleural fluid culture or cytology in the case of non-Hodgkin's lymphoma can establish the diagnosis. However, in patients with pleural effusion and suspected tuberculosis, the diagnostic yield is improved with the addition of pleural biopsies.

CT-guided transthoracic needle aspiration is an important and useful diagnostic procedure for selected patients. HIV-infected patients with focal parenchymal lesions, most often peripheral lung nodules or masses that may be beyond the reach of a bronchoscope, are ideal candidates for CT-guided aspiration. In one study of 32 HIV-infected patients undergoing this procedure, a diagnosis was established in 27. Mediastinoscopy should be considered for patients with mediastinal mass and/or adenopathy. Video-assisted thoracoscopic surgery can be an important procedure in selected patients.

Occasionally, despite all of these efforts, HIV-infected patients with pulmonary disease may elude definitive diagnosis. In such patients,

consideration should be given to open lung biopsy although results have been mixed. Often, open lung biopsy provides important new information. However, frequently patients who undergo this procedure are already so ill that this new information fails to translate into improved survival.

NONINFECTIOUS COMPLICATIONS

The focus of the evaluation and management of respiratory symptoms in an HIV-infected patient is frequently placed on opportunistic infections and their prompt diagnosis and treatment. However, there are several noninfectious complications associated with HIV-infection that warrant discussion.

Kaposi's Sarcoma

The overwhelming majority of HIV-infected patients with KS are MSM. Clinically symptomatic pulmonary KS presents at the lower range of CD4+ cell counts but tracheobronchial lesions may be seen in patients with higher CD4+ cell counts who are undergoing bronchoscopy for other reasons. Most patients with pulmonary KS have mucocutaneous disease.

Pulmonary KS characteristically presents with nonproductive cough, dyspnea, and occasionally fever. Chest pain and hemoptysis are less frequently noted. Symptoms are usually present for weeks or months but may also progress rapidly in a manner indistinguishable from opportunistic infection. As described previously, pulmonary KS characteristically presents with bilateral middle-lower lung zone opacities in a central or perihilar distribution. Typical chest radiograph findings include linear densities (bronchial wall thickening), nodules or nodular opacities of varying size, Kerley B lines, pleural effusions, and intrathoracic adenopathy. Chest CT scans often demonstrate the characteristic peribronchovascular distribution with associated nodules.

The diagnosis of pulmonary KS is usually established by bronchoscopy. The finding of characteristic endobronchial, reddish-purplish, flat or slightly raised lesions is sufficient to diagnose pulmonary disease in the proper clinical context (see Fig. 415–7). Most patients with chest radiograph findings suggestive of pulmonary KS have endobronchial KS lesions seen below the level of the carina. However, the absence of lesions in the observable airway does not preclude more distal airway disease or parenchymal, pleural, or nodal involvement. When there is a strong clinical suspicion for pulmonary KS but no endobronchial lesions are seen, TBBX should be considered to establish the diagnosis. A significant proportion of patients with pulmonary KS have concurrent opportunistic infection, and patients undergoing an evaluation for pulmonary KS should have a concomitant evaluation for opportunistic infection.

Non-Hodgkin's Lymphoma

Most HIV-infected patients with non-Hodgkin's lymphoma present with widely disseminated disease and extranodal involvement. Frequent extranodal sites include the liver, spleen, bone marrow, meninges, and gastrointestinal tract, whereas intrathoracic involvement is seen in a smaller proportion. Occasionally, the lung is the only site involved. Non-Hodgkin's lymphoma can present at a wide range of CD4+ cell counts. The median CD4+ cell count is approximately 100 cells/μL, and 75% of patients have a CD4+ cell count of less than 50 cells/μL.

When the lungs are involved, the most common symptoms are cough and dyspnea, with pleuritic chest pain and hemoptysis occurring less frequently. Classic B symptoms such as fever, sweats, and weight loss are also common features. The most common chest radiograph parenchymal findings are multiple nodular opacities or masses, lobar infiltrates, and diffuse interstitial infiltrates. Occasionally, a solitary nodule or mass is seen. Pleural effusions are the most common radiographic abnormality, occurring in 40 to 70% of cases and may occur in the absence of parenchymal disease. Hilar and mediastinal adenopathy is found in up to 60% of these patients.

The diagnosis of non-Hodgkin's lymphoma requires demonstration of malignant lymphocytes on cytology or biopsy specimens. Persons presenting with isolated intrathoracic involvement should undergo bronchoscopy with biopsies or CT-guided fine-needle aspiration. Other options include mediastinoscopy, thoracoscopy, and open

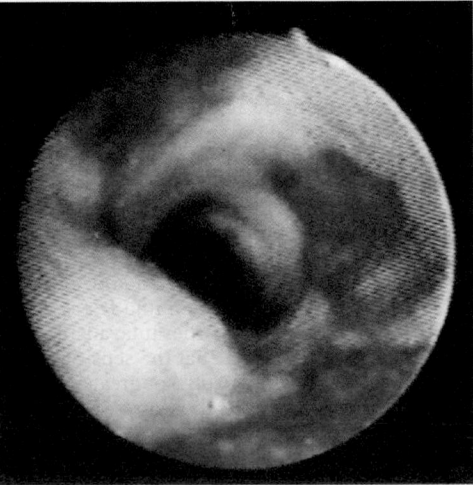

FIGURE 415–7 • Characteristic Kaposi's sarcoma lesions located in the trachea in an HIV-infected person, CD4+ cell count less than 100 cells/μL. Concurrent bronchoalveolar lavage also revealed *Pneumocystis* pneumonia.

lung biopsy. For patients with effusions, pleural fluid cytology and/or biopsy is often diagnostic.

Nonspecific Interstitial Pneumonitis

Nonspecific interstitial pneumonitis (NSIP) has been reported with various frequencies in HIV-infected patients. Because it is a histologic diagnosis, its incidence depends on the frequency that biopsy is performed during the diagnostic evaluation. The symptoms of NSIP include dyspnea, nonproductive cough, and fever. These clinical features are indistinguishable from *Pneumocystis* pneumonia. However, NSIP may present at CD4+ cell counts greater than 200 cells/μL, whereas *Pneumocystis* pneumonia rarely does. The chest radiograph presentation of NSIP is nonspecific and usually indistinguishable from *Pneumocystis* pneumonia and, as with *Pneumocystis* pneumonia, NSIP can present with a normal radiograph. One study of patients with NSIP found that 44% of 36 patients had a normal radiograph. The most common radiographic abnormality seen was a diffuse interstitial pattern. Other abnormalities include pleural effusions, alveolar infiltrates, and nodules. Pulmonary function tests often reveal a mildly decreased diffusing capacity. The diagnosis of NSIP requires histologic confirmation and exclusion of other etiologies.

Lymphocytic Interstitial Pneumonitis

The most striking feature of HIV-associated LIP is the effect of age on its incidence. LIP has been a frequent AIDS-defining diagnosis in children but is rare in adults. The symptoms of LIP include slowly progressive dyspnea, nonproductive cough, and fever indistinguishable from opportunistic infection. The chest radiograph presentation of LIP is nonspecific and characteristically shows bilateral reticulonodular "interstitial" infiltrates with a lower lung zone predominance. Hilar or mediastinal adenopathy is occasionally seen and potentially can be used to distinguish LIP from *Pneumocystis* pneumonia. Pulmonary function tests often reveal a restrictive ventilatory defect and a decreased diffusing capacity. Chest CT scans may reveal small (2 to 4 mm) nodules often in a peribronchovascular distribution or diffuse areas of GGO (Fig. 415–8). Gallium scan may note diffuse pulmonary uptake, indistinguishable from *Pneumocystis* pneumonia. The diagnosis of LIP requires histologic confirmation by biopsy.

Pulmonary Hypertension

Numerous reports of primary pulmonary hypertension in HIV-infected patients are scattered throughout the literature. The characteristic clinical presentation is one of progressive dyspnea, with nonproductive cough, chest pain, and syncope or near-syncope seen in a minority. Chest radiograph findings include cardiomegaly and prominence of the pulmonary arteries. Most often, chest radiograph

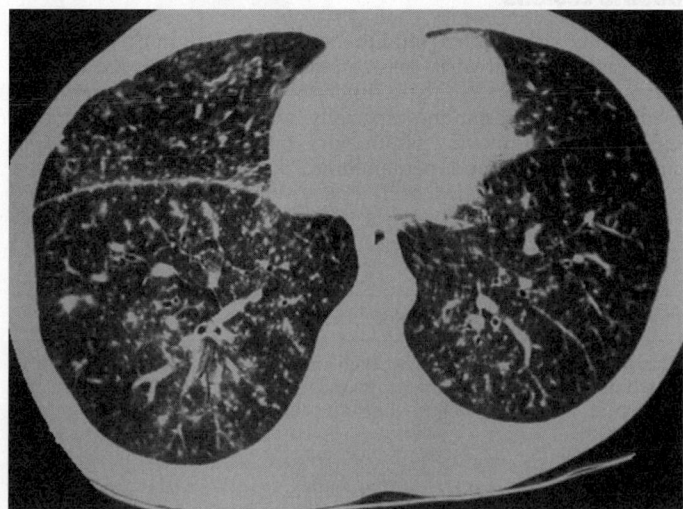

FIGURE 415–8 • Chest high-resolution computed tomographic scan of an HIV-infected person, CD4+ cell count less than 200 cells/μL, with lymphocytic interstitial pneumonitis diagnosed by transbronchial biopsy.

or electrocardiogram with evidence of right ventricular hypertrophy first suggests the diagnosis of pulmonary hypertension. Patients diagnosed with pulmonary hypertension should undergo thorough evaluation for secondary causes, including underlying cardiac (i.e., left ventricular failure, valvular disease) and pulmonary diseases (i.e., COPD, recurrent pulmonary emboli).

Chronic Obstructive Pulmonary Disease

HIV infected patients are subject to the entire spectrum of pulmonary disease, including the obstructive lung diseases. Reports and studies have suggested that HIV-infected cigarette smokers may be at greater risk for development of emphysema than HIV-infected nonsmokers or nonimmunocompromised cigarette smokers. In addition to cigarette smoking, repeated opportunistic pulmonary infections may eventually result in the development of chronic bronchitis and bronchiectasis. The clinical and radiographic presentation, diagnosis, and management of obstructive lung disease in HIV-infected patients are identical to that in immunocompetent patients, including the use of inhaled corticosteroids, when indicated.

Sarcoidosis

Several cases of sarcoidosis in HIV-infected patients have been reported. In these cases, the clinical and radiographic presentation, diagnosis, and clinical course with corticosteroid therapy were similar to cases of sarcoidosis in non–HIV-infected persons.

Immune Reconstitution Syndromes

The initiation of combinations of potent antiretroviral therapies and the subsequent improvement in immune function have also resulted in several syndromes that have important clinical implications. Interestingly, in some of the examples provided, the use of antiretroviral therapy serves to transiently exacerbate the disease, whereas in others, its use is seemingly solely responsible for the reported improvements. Finally, in some cases, the use of antiretroviral therapy has been associated with the development of pulmonary disease that is host-mediated.

The transient worsening of clinical symptoms and signs and chest radiograph findings of tuberculosis after the initiation of appropriate antituberculosis therapy have been well recognized. These paradoxical reactions are thought to represent an enhanced antituberculous immune response, and they usually resolve with continued therapy alone. HIV-infected patients who develop tuberculosis and receive concurrent antiretroviral and antituberculous therapies appear to have an increased incidence of paradoxical worsening. One study found that 36% of HIV-infected tuberculosis patients receiving these dual therapies developed a paradoxical reaction compared to 7% of HIV-infected tuberculosis patients who received tuberculosis therapy alone and 2% of tuberculosis patients without concomitant HIV infection. Another study noted transient worsening on serial chest radiographs in 45% of HIV-infected tuberculosis patients receiving dual HIV and TB therapies. The radiographic worsening consisted of new or worsening parenchymal disease in 32%, new or worsening intrathoracic lymphadenopathy in 23%, and new or worsening pleural effusion in 19%. The diagnosis of paradoxical reaction must be one of exclusion. HIV-infected tuberculosis patients with suspected paradoxical reactions must also be thoroughly evaluated for progressive tuberculosis resulting from drug resistance or patient nonadherence and for the presence of a concurrent, superimposed opportunistic infection.

Similar to tuberculosis, paradoxical reactions in HIV-infected patients have been reported in patients receiving concurrent therapy for HIV and for opportunistic infection, including important pulmonary pathogens such as *Pneumocystis* and *Cryptococcus*.

In contrast to the paradoxical reactions observed in the setting of opportunistic infection, the use of antiretroviral therapy, often in the absence of specific chemotherapy, has resulted in clinical regression and, occasionally, complete resolution of KS (including pulmonary KS) lesions.

Whether the addition of antiretroviral therapy to standard opportunistic infection treatment is beneficial—or potentially harmful if paradoxical reactions develop—in patients with opportunistic infections is a largely unanswered question. Recent retrospective studies have suggested that the use of potent antiretroviral therapy in critically ill HIV-infected patients may be associated with an improved survival. Given the still significant mortality associated with respiratory failure due to opportunistic infections, this question is particularly important to HIV-associated pneumonias.

Improved immune function may also play a role in the development of host-mediated pulmonary disease. There are several reports of sarcoidosis or a sarcoidosis-like disease that developed after the initiation of antiretroviral therapy. In addition, hypersensitivity pneumonitis to avian antigen that only developed once the patient's immune function improved on antiretroviral therapy has been described. Diseases in which host immune response plays an essential role in pathogenesis can be expected to become more prevalent as more HIV-infected patients receive potent antiretroviral therapies.

1. Ledergerber B, Mocroft A, Reiss P, et al: Discontinuation of secondary prophylaxis against *Pneumocystis carinii* pneumonia in patients with HIV infection who have a response to antiretroviral therapy. Eight European Study Groups. N Engl J Med 2001;344:168–174.
2. Lopez Bernaldo de Quiros JC, Miro JM, Pena JM, et al: A randomized trial of the discontinuation of primary and secondary prophylaxis against *Pneumocystis carinii* pneumonia after highly active antiretroviral therapy in patients with HIV infection. N Engl J Med 2001;344:159–167.

SUGGESTED READINGS

Beck JM, Rosen MJ, Peavy HH: Pulmonary complications of HIV infection. Report of the Fourth NHLBI Workshop. Am J Respir Crit Care Med 2001;164:2120–2126. *A consensus overview.*

Jasmer RM, Gotway MB, Creasman JM, et al: Clinical and radiographic predictors of the etiology of computed tomography-diagnosed intrathoracic lymphadenopathy in HIV-infected patients. J Acquir Immune Defic Syndr 2002;31:291–298. *Opportunistic infections and lymphoma are the most common causes.*

Kaplan JE, Masur H, Holmes KK: Guidelines for preventing opportunistic infections among HIV-infected persons—2002. Recommendations of the U.S. Public Health Service and the Infectious Diseases Society of America. MMWR Recomm Rep 2002;51:1–52. *Consensus guidelines.*

Morris A, Creasman J, Turner J, et al: Intensive care of human immunodeficiency virus-infected patients during the era of highly active antiretroviral therapy. Am J Respir Crit Care Med 2002;166:262–267. *Improved survival is in part due to the increased percentage of admissions for non-AIDS associated causes.*

Morris A, Wachter RM, Luce J, et al: Improved survival with highly active antiretroviral therapy in HIV-infected patients with severe *Pneumocystis carinii* pneumonia. AIDS 2003;17:73–80. *Use of HAART is associated with better outcomes.*

Rimland D, Navin TR, Lennox JL, et al: Prospective study of etiologic agents of community-acquired pneumonia in patients with HIV infection. AIDS 2002;16:85–95. *P. carinii remains common, but in many patients a causative organism cannot be identified.*

416 GASTROINTESTINAL MANIFESTATIONS OF AIDS

John G. Bartlett

The gastrointestinal tract is an especially common site for clinical expression of human immunodeficiency virus (HIV) infection and is an important factor in both morbidity from opportunistic infections in late-stage disease and gastrointestinal complications from antiretroviral agents or other drugs. Nearly all opportunistic infections occur when the CD4+ T-cell count is less than 200/mm³, and almost all seem to respond well to immune reconstitution when achieved with antiretroviral therapy.

Oral Lesions

Oral candidiasis ("thrush") is encountered at some time in 80 to 90% of all patients with advanced stages of HIV infection. The usual finding is white patches that show yeast forms and pseudohyphae on potassium hydroxide (KOH) preparation. Thrush is often asymptomatic, or it may cause mouth pain, dysphagia, and taste change. The diagnosis is usually made by visual appearance. Treatment consists of topical agents (e.g., nystatin, clotrimazole troches), oral therapy with azoles, or in severe refractory cases, intravenous amphotericin. Because relapse rates are high, continuous therapy with topical agents or azoles is often necessary.

Oral hairy leukoplakia is characterized by white patches consisting of white fibrillar projections that are usually located on the tongue and are often confused with thrush. Oral hairy leukoplakia is usually asymptomatic, but some patients complain of pain or voice changes; symptomatic patients usually respond to treatment with acyclovir. Herpes simplex virus (HSV) often causes painful oral lesions that show typical vesicles on an erythematous base that break down to form ulcers. Herpetic oral lesions are common in the general population, but they tend to be more severe and prolonged in patients with advanced HIV infection. The usual treatment is acyclovir, famciclovir, or valacyclovir given orally; severe cases may require intravenous acyclovir or, for acyclovir-resistant strains, foscarnet given parenterally. The major source of confusion is aphthous ulcers of unknown origin, which seem to respond best to thalidomide or to corticosteroids given topically or systemically.

Patients with Kaposi's sarcoma may have involvement of the oral cavity, most frequently with typical purplish raised lesions on the palate, although any site in the oral cavity may be involved. Most are asymptomatic; symptomatic lesions generally respond to irradiation, laser treatments, or vinblastine injections.

Periodontal disease, with gingivitis or periodontitis, is relatively common. Treatment consists of topical chlorhexidine (Peridex) or systemically administered metronidazole.

Esophagitis

Dysphagia or odynophagia in a patient with advanced HIV infection and thrush generally indicates *Candida* esophagitis, and most patients are treated empirically with fluconazole. Alternative causes of esophagitis include esophageal ulcers most commonly due to cytomegalovirus (CMV) or aphthous ulceration and infrequently caused by *H. simplex* (Table 416–1). Endoscopy is recommended for patients with atypical symptoms and those who fail to respond to fluconazole. Some cases are caused by fluconazole-resistant *Candida* species and require intravenous amphotericin B. Herpes simplex may be treated with acyclovir, CMV responds to ganciclovir, and aphthous ulcers are optimally treated with systemic corticosteroids or thalidomide.

Gastric Lesions

Patients with acquired immunodeficiency syndrome (AIDS) often have gastric achlorhydria; less common gastric lesions are Kaposi's sarcoma and opportunistic infections. Gastric intolerance to medications is common, especially with zidovudine, ritonavir, didanosine, indinavir, saquinavir, macrolides, trimethoprim-sulfamethoxazole, and pentamidine. Symptoms include nausea,

Table 416–1 • ESOPHAGEAL COMPLICATIONS OF HIV INFECTION

AGENT	FREQUENCY* (%)	CD4 COUNT	CLINICAL FEATURES	DIAGNOSIS	TREATMENT
Candida	50–70	<200/mm³	Odynophagia, thrush, diffuse pain, usually afebrile	Usually treated empirically; endoscopy shows plaques	Fluconazole
Cytomegalovirus (CMV)	10–20	<50/mm³	Odynophagia, focal pain, usually febrile	Biopsy of ulcer to show CMV inclusions	Ganciclovir or valganciclovir
Herpes simplex virus (HSV)	2–5	<200/mm³	Odynophagia, oral HSV lesions common, usually afebrile	Biopsy of ulcer to show HSV inclusions	Acyclovir
Idiopathic	10–20	<300/mm³	Odynophagia, focal pain, usually afebrile	Negative biopsy of ulcer	Prednisone or thalidomide

*Approximate frequency in HIV-infected patients with odynophagia.

vomiting, anorexia, and epigastric pain and usually resolve promptly when use of the implicated drug is discontinued.

Small Bowel and Colon Lesions

Acute or chronic diarrhea is a frequent complication and may be caused by medications, opportunistic infections, or common sources occurring in the general population such as viral gastroenteritis or irritable bowel syndrome. The antiretroviral agents that most commonly cause diarrhea are lopinavir, nelfinavir, didanosine, and saquinavir. Treatment with bacterial agents may be complicated by *Clostridium difficile*–associated diarrhea or colitis, but the frequency and severity do not appear to be increased by immunosuppression.

Diagnostic Evaluation

The differential diagnosis must include consideration of medication effects, CD4 count, acute versus chronic diarrhea, and clinical features of inflammatory (colonic) versus secretory (small bowel) diarrhea. The duration that separates acute and chronic diarrhea is 3 weeks. Characteristic features of inflammatory diarrhea are colitis, clinical symptoms of cramps and fever with small volume "fractions" stools, and stool examinations showing leukocytes and/or blood. Secretory diarrhea is usually caused by small bowel pathology; the diarrhea is watery and large volume, and stool studies are negative for fecal leucocytes and blood. The CD4 count that generally defines vulnerability to opportunistic enteric pathogens is 200/mm³, although the common forms (i.e., CMV colitis, microsporidiosis, chronic cryptosporidiosis, and disseminated *Mycobacterium avium*) are usually seen only with CD4 counts less than 50/mm³.

The most common infectious causes of acute diarrhea in HIV-infected patients are salmonellosis, *C. difficile*, and enteric viruses (Table 416–2). When the CD4 count is greater than 200/mm³, the differential diagnosis includes the same pathogens seen with immunocompetent patients. HIV-infected patients do not appear uniquely susceptible to *C. difficile*, but this complication is relatively common because they often take antibiotics. The only enteric pathogen responsible for acute diarrhea to which HIV-infected patients are uniquely susceptible is salmonella. The diagnostic evaluation is the same as for immunocompetent patients based on the severity of the symptoms, the epidemiology, and the probability of inflammatory diarrhea because these enteric pathogens (i.e., *Salmonella*, *Shigella*, *Campylobacter jejuni*, *C. difficile*, and *Escherichia coli* O157) are more likely to be serious and treatable. Treatment is the same as for persons without HIV infection, except salmonellosis is usually treated with antibiotics and treated for a longer period. With CD4 counts less than 200/mm³, especially if less than 50/mm³, acute diarrhea may represent the early stages of enteric infection caused by pathogens more commonly associated with chronic diarrhea.

Opportunistic pathogens that cause chronic diarrhea are much more tightly associated with the CD4 count. With counts greater than 200/mm³, the usual causes are medications, idiopathic or functional bowel disease, inflammatory bowel disease, and occasionally, chronic parasitic infections such as cryptosporidiosis, giardia, or amebiasis. With CD4 counts less than 200/mm³, the "big four" enteric pathogens are *Cryptosporidia parvum*, microsporidia (*Enterocytozoon bieneusi* and *Encephalitozoon intestinalis*), M. avium, and CMV; less common is *Isospora belli*.

The diagnostic evaluation is dictated by the symptoms and CD4 count. Standard screening tests for HIV-infected patients who have diarrhea that is severe, chronic, and not medication-associated includes a stool culture for enteric pathogens, ova and parasite exam times two with acid-fast stain (to detect cryptosporidia, isospora, and cyclospora), stool stain and microscopy for microsporidia (×1000 magnification with trichrome stain), *C. difficile* toxin assay (especially with recent antibiotic use), and stool analysis for fecal leukocytes and red blood cells. Endoscopy is usually reserved for patients with severe or persistent symptoms and a negative evaluation using noninvasive studies. Endoscopy is often necessary to establish the diagnosis of CMV colitis or enteritis.

Treatment of chronic infectious diarrhea in the HIV-infected patient is determined by the severity of symptoms and pathogen. In nearly all cases, the most important facet of care is immune reconstitution with antiretroviral agents. With chronic cryptosporidiosis and most cases of CMV colitis and microsporidiosis, this is the only intervention that is likely to be effective. Nonspecific interventions that are commonly used and are effective include antiperistaltic agents such as loperamide and diet modification including small, frequent, bland feedings without caffeine, fat, milk, or milk products. Antimicrobial recommendations are summarized in Table 416–2: cryptosporidiosis is commonly treated with paromomycin, but evidence of benefit by this or other antimicrobials is sparse. *E. intestinalis* responds to albendazole, but *E. bieneusi* causes 80% of microsporidia cases and cannot be treated with antimicrobials. CMV is usually treated with intravenous ganciclovir or oral valganciclovir, but response is modest and recurrence rates are high. M. avium usually responds to standard treatment, but therapy must be lifelong unless there is immune reconstitution.

Adverse Reactions to Antiretroviral Agents

The gastrointestinal complications of antiretroviral agents are common and important—important because they often interfere

Table 416–2 • AGENTS OF ACUTE AND CHRONIC DIARRHEA

AGENT	FREQUENCY* (%)	CD4 COUNT	CLINICAL FEATURES	DIAGNOSIS	TREATMENT
ACUTE DIARRHEA					
Salmonella	5–15	Any	Watery diarrhea, fever	Stool and blood culture	Fluoroquinolone
Clostridium difficile	10–15	Any	Cramps, watery diarrhea, fever	Stool toxin assay	Metronidazole
Enteric viruses	15–30	Any	Watery diarrhea, usually afebrile	None	Symptomatic
Idiopathic	25–40	Any	Variable	Negative culture, O&P exam, and *C. difficile* toxin	Symptomatic
CHRONIC DIARRHEA					
Cryptosporidia	10–30	<100/mm³	Watery diarrhea, fever variable, may have devastating fluid losses	Stool O&P with AFB	(Antiretrovirals)
Microsporidia	15–30	<100/mm³	Watery diarrhea, afebrile	Stool trichrome stain	Albendazole (*Encephalitozoon intestinalis* only)
Isospora belli	1–3	<100/mm³	Watery diarrhea	Stool O&P with AFB	TMP-SMX
Mycobacterium avium	10–20	<50/mm³	Watery diarrhea, fever, wasting	Blood culture	Clarithromycin and ethambutol
Cytomegalovirus	15–40	<50/mm³	Watery or bloody diarrhea; fever, fecal WBCs	Colon biopsy	Ganciclovir or valganciclovir
Idiopathic	20–30	Any	Watery diarrhea	Negative culture, O&P, *C. difficile* toxin, endoscopy	Symptomatic

*Frequency among HIV-infected patients with acute or chronic diarrhea; with chronic diarrhea, frequency is CD4 count <200/mm³.
AFB = acid-fast bacillus; O&P = ova and parasites; TMP-SMX = trimethoprim-sulfamethoxazole; WBCs = white blood cells.

with adherence that is critical for virologic control and response and because they may represent potentially life-threatening complications. Gastrointestinal intolerance with nausea, vomiting, and abdominal pain may occur with all antiretrovirals, but is especially common with zidovudine, didanosine, ritonavir, amprenavir, and indinavir. All are dose related, and tolerance to protease inhibitors may be improved with the use of ritonavir boosting. Diarrhea is also common, but secretory diarrhea is especially common with nelfinavir and lopinavir; this can usually be controlled with loperamide or calcium. Life-threatening complications attributed to antiretroviral agents include pancreatitis (i.e., didanosine and stavudine) and lactic acidosis and hepatotoxicity (i.e., nevirapine). Pancreatitis occurs in 1 to 9% of didanosine recipients, is more common in patients with other risk factors for pancreatitis, and presents with the typical symptoms of severe abdominal pain with elevated amylase and lipase. Lactic acidosis results from mitochondrial toxicity caused by nucleoside analogues, primarily stavudine and/or didanosine, although any nucleoside may do this. The usual presentation is prolonged nucleoside exposure, gastrointestinal symptoms, including weight loss, and an elevated blood lactate level, usually greater than 5 mmol/mL. Treatment of pancreatitis and lactic acidosis is largely supportive, recovery is often prolonged, and the inducing agent should be avoided.

Tumors

Tumors of the gastrointestinal tract associated with HIV infection include Kaposi's sarcoma, non-Hodgkin's lymphoma, cloacogenic carcinoma of the rectum, and squamous cell carcinoma of the rectum and anus. The most common of these is Kaposi's sarcoma, which has been found in gut tissue at autopsy in 40 to 50% of persons with typical cutaneous lesions. Endoscopy typically shows raised red nodules, but histologic confirmation is difficult owing to the depth of pathologic changes. Most are asymptomatic; less common manifestations include diarrhea, subacute intestinal obstruction, protein-losing enteropathy, and rectal ulcer. The lymphomas associated with HIV infection are usually high-grade B-cell lymphomas that are extranodal in origin. The gastrointestinal tract is affected in up to 20% of patients, and any site may be involved from the oral cavity to the rectum.

AIDS Enteropathy

Endoscopy in patients with advanced AIDS often shows morphologic changes in the small bowel in the absence of evidence of a superimposed opportunistic infection. Characteristic features are villous blunting, a reduced villus-crypt ratio, and an inappropriately low number of mitotic figures. In the absence of an enteric pathogen, the findings are sometimes referred to as *AIDS enteropathy*. Studies of gastrointestinal function in the presence of AIDS enteropathy usually show malabsorption with abnormal D-xylose and ^{14}C-glycerol-tripalmitin absorption tests. The cause of these changes is unknown, but the major considerations include direct invasion by HIV, an opportunistic infection that has not been detected, or a consequence of immune suppression.

Malnutrition and Wasting

The average patient with late-stage AIDS loses 15 to 20% of baseline weight. Protein-calorie malnutrition is a common and important sequela that may accelerate progressive immunosuppression. Factors contributing to malnutrition include a hypermetabolic state associated with chronic infection (especially with fever), oral lesions causing pain, esophageal lesions resulting in dysphagia, reduced taste sensation, depression, HIV-associated subcortical dementia, gastrointestinal side effects of medications, hypogonadism, and AIDS enteropathy. Many patients lose weight with sequential opportunistic infections that is not regained during asymptomatic intervals. Therapy for wasting depends on the severity, cause, patient gender, and response. Immune reconstitution with antiretroviral therapy has been associated with remarkable weight gain. Prevention of opportunistic infections is an important factor in stabilizing weight. A number of pharmacologic agents are in common use, with variable responses in terms of the amount and the quality of the weight gained (fat versus muscle). The most commonly used agents for wasting are appetite stimulants (e.g.,

megestrol acetate, dronabinol), testosterone, or synthetic anabolic steroids (e.g., oxandrolone, nandrolone).

Hepatobiliary Disease

The prevalence of markers for hepatitis B (i.e., hepatitis B surface antigen [HBsAg], antibody to HBsAg, or antibody to hepatitis B core antigen) is 35 to 80% in AIDS patients, which is a reflection of their prevalence among homosexual men, intravenous drug abusers, and hemophiliacs. HBsAg is found in 5 to 10% of patients. Hepatitis C virus (HCV) infection is found in up to 90% of injection drug users and patients with hemophilia. It is clear that the course of HCV is accelerated by HIV coinfection, but evidence for the reverse is less impressive.

The preferred treatment for chronic HCV is pegylated interferon plus ribavirin, but indications are confounded by drug interactions and toxicity when used with antiretroviral agents, the uncertain natural history of HCV, and high rates of intolerance to HCV drugs. Patients co-infected with hepatitis B (HBVsAg positive) may be treated with lamivudine, which is active against both viruses. Granulomatous hepatitis is most often caused by M. *avium*; less common are histoplasmosis, cryptococcosis, and tuberculosis. Hepatotoxic drugs commonly taken by HIV-infected patients include all antiretroviral agents as well as azoles, sulfonamides, isoniazid, and rifampin. With nucleosides, lactic acidosis with steatosis may develop; the presentation is typical findings of lactic acidosis (e.g., nausea, vomiting, abdominal pain, weight loss) combined with elevated transaminase levels and characteristic features on liver scans. The non-nucleoside reverse transcriptase inhibitors may cause hepatotoxicity; nevirapine is particularly problematic, with occasional cases of fulminant hepatic necrosis, usually during the first 12 weeks of therapy when hepatic function should be carefully monitored. All protease inhibitors may cause hepatotoxicity; rates are highest with ritonavir. This is usually a dose-related toxicity, and therapy should be changed when the transaminase levels exceed five times the upper limits of normal.

Cholestasis from papillary stenosis and sclerosing cholangitis are most often caused by *Cryptosporidium*, *Microsporida*, or CMV or are idiopathic. The usual presentation is right upper quadrant pain and laboratory evidence of cholestasis in patients with late-stage AIDS. The diagnosis and treatment is usually established with endoscopic retrograde cholangiopancreatography. Treatment directed against an identified pathogen is usually unsuccessful.

SUGGESTED READINGS

Centers for Disease Control and Prevention: Serious adverse events attributed to nevirapine regimens for postexposure prophylaxis after HIV exposures—worldwide, 1997–2000. MMWR 2001;49:1153–1156. *A CDC review of 12 cases of severe hepatotoxicity after nevirapine use for occupational exposure to HIV including one healthcare worker who required a hepatic transplant.*

Corcoran C, Grinspoon S: Treatments for wasting in patients with the acquired immunodeficiency syndrome. N Engl J Med 1999;340:1740–1750. *A review of the assessment and treatment of HIV-associated wasting including nutrition, megestrol, dronabid, testosterone, oxandrolone, nandrolone, growth hormone, thalidomide, and exercise.*

Dassopoulos T, Ehrempreis E: Acute pancreatitis in human immunodeficiency virus-infected patients: A review. Am J Med 1999;107:78–84. *The review includes three categories—drug related, opportunistic infections of the pancreas (primarily CMV), and causes in the general population such as alcoholism and biliary tract disease.*

Dworkin MS, Williamson JM, for the Adult/Adolescent Spectrum of HIV Disease Project. AIDS wasting syndrome: Trends, influence on opportunistic infections, and survival. J Acquir Immune Defic Syndr 2003;33:267–273. *The incidence is declining.*

Falco V, Rodriguez D, Ribera E, et al: Severe nucleoside-associated lactic acidosis in human immunodeficiency virus-infected patients. Clin Infect Dis 2002;34:838–846. *A review of 60 reported cases that show the most common presentation is GI symptoms with weight loss, the most commonly implicated NRTI is stavudine, and the mortality rate is directly related to the lactic acid level.*

Gan I, May G, Raboud J, et al: Pancreatitis in HIV infection: Predictors of severity. Am J Gastroenterol 2003;98:1278–1283. *Outcomes are similar to those in non-HIV infected patients.*

Leav BA, Mackay M, Ward HD: Cryptosporidium species: New insights and old challenges. Clin Infect Dis 2003;36:903–908. *The authors provide a comprehensive review of the most common enteric pathogen associated with HIV infection; they emphasize the lack of any good antimicrobial treatment except immune reconstitution.*

Sherman DS, Fish DN: Management of protease inhibitor-associated diarrhea. Clin Infect Dis 2000;30:908–914. *The authors summarize methods to manage PI-associated diarrhea including use of loperamide, calcium, oat bran, and psyllium—all over-the-counter and inexpensive.*

Weber R, Ledergerber R, Zbinden R, et al: Enteric infections and diarrhea in human immunodeficiency virus-infected patients. Arch Intern Med 1999;159:1473–1480. *The results are from the Swiss Cohort Study based on the experience with 1, 933 patients with 590 episodes of diarrhea; major causes of chronic diarrhea were cryptosporidiosis, C. difficile, Salmonella, and microsporidia.*

Holmes RB, Martins C, Horn T: The histopathology of folliculitis in HIV-infected patients. J Cutan Pathol 2002;29:93–95. *Detailed descriptions of histopathology in HIV infected patients.*
Sande M, Volberding P: The Medical Management of AIDS, 6th ed. Philadelphia, WB Saunders, 1999.

417 SKIN DISEASE IN PATIENTS WITH HIV INFECTION

Timothy Berger

Cutaneous manifestations seen in patients with human immunodeficiency virus (HIV) infection can be categorized as infectious, neoplastic, and inflammatory.

Infectious Conditions

Herpes zoster occurs 25 times more frequently in HIV infection, but it usually responds well to standard treatment. It can be disseminated, multidermatomal, and involve the eye, in which case intravenous antiviral treatment may be required. Anogenital ulceration in HIV disease is herpes simplex until proven otherwise. In persons with T-cell counts below 200, treatment of herpes simplex may require doses of antivirals similar to zoster treatment, and acyclovir resistance may occur. The pearly, umbilicated papules of molluscum contagiosum on the face of an adult strongly suggest advanced HIV infection. Disseminated cryptococcosis, histoplasmosis, or penicilliosis can mimic molluscum. HIV patients with scabies may have more mites, in the extreme resulting in hyperkeratotic (crusted) lesions that are highly infectious and treatment resistant. Ivermectin (2 doses of 200 µg/kg orally, 15 days apart) is useful in this setting along with topical treatment. Disseminated bartonellosis, caused by *Bartonella henselae* or *Bartonella quintana,* presents with red, friable, vascular papules and may be associated with bacteremia and visceral involvement. It is easily diagnosed by skin biopsy and sequelae are prevented by antibiotic treatment.

Neoplastic Conditions

Kaposi's sarcoma (KS) is caused by human herpesvirus 8 (HHV8). Highly active antiretroviral therapy (HAART) has dramatically reduced the prevalence of this neoplasm, and alone often results in gradual clearing of the skin lesions. Non-Hodgkin's lymphoma, cutaneous T-cell lymphoma, basal and squamous cell carcinomas (especially superficial basal cell carcinomas), and melanoma are seen in HIV infection. Squamous cell carcinoma and melanoma may behave more aggressively.

Inflammatory Conditions

Psoriasis, Reiter's syndrome, atopic dermatitis, and seborrheic dermatitis can worsen or appear de novo as CD4 counts drop. Eosinophilic folliculitis presents as multiple, severely pruritic, urticarial, red papules involving the head, neck, upper arms, chest, and back, with most lesions occurring above the nipple line. Enhanced reactions to arthropod assaults are common in acquired immunodeficiency syndrome (AIDS) patients. Ultraviolet phototherapy is safe and beneficial for most pruritic HIV patients.

Drug Eruptions

In patients on HAART, the most common cutaneous complications are adverse drug reactions, human papillomavirus infection (i.e., warts), and the fat redistribution syndrome. Fat redistribution can be accompanied by hyperlipidemia and glucose intolerance. Drug eruptions, from morbilliform to Stevens-Johnson syndrome have been reported with antiretrovirals. These eruptions can appear alone or in the context of a hypersensitivity syndrome (i.e., with fever and internal organ dysfunction). Human papillomavirus infection is common in immune-reconstituted patients, and the incidence of warts in patients on HAART may be increased. Infection with high-risk human papillomavirus types may result in mucocutaneous squamous cell carcinoma cancer of the anogenital region and nail fold.

SUGGESTED READINGS
HIV Lipodystrophy Case Definition Study Group. An objective case definition in HIV infected adults: A case-control study. Lancet 2003;361:726–734. *Identifies a case definition of HIV lipidystrophy.*

418 OPHTHALMOLOGIC MANIFESTATIONS OF AIDS

Mark A. Jacobson

Infectious or noninfectious ocular disorders, some of which may lead to severe visual impairment, have been reported in 40 to 90% of patients with acquired immunodeficiency syndrome (AIDS) referred for formal ophthalmoscopy. In prospective observational cohort studies conducted before the clinical availability of the new, more potent generation of antiretroviral agents for the treatment of human immunodeficiency virus (HIV) disease, the incidence of cytomegalovirus (CMV) retinitis (the most common ophthalmologic complication of AIDS) was reported to be in the range of 20 to 40% in patients with an AIDS diagnosis. In the first 18 months since highly active antiretroviral therapy (HAART) became widely available in the United States and Europe, the incidence of new CMV retinitis diagnoses decreased markedly. Since then, the number of new CMV retinitis cases seen at referral centers has stabilized at about 25% the rate observed in the pre-HAART era.

The differential diagnosis of HIV-associated ocular disease is best considered by its anatomic location.

DISEASES OF THE CHOROID, RETINA, AND VITREOUS

RETINAL MICROVASCULAR DISEASE

The most common ophthalmologic complication observed in patients with HIV infection is retinal microvascular disease, which usually manifests as asymptomatic cotton-wool spots or small retinal hemorrhages. Cotton-wool spots have been reported in up to half of patients with advanced HIV disease. Histopathologically, these lesions represent areas of retinal ischemia. Immune complex deposition and direct HIV retinal infection have been implicated in the pathogenesis of cotton-wool spot lesions. On funduscopic examination, they typically appear as white spots with feathered edges on the surface of the retina. A common location is near major posterior retinal vessels, and these lesions can have small associated retinal hemorrhages. It may be difficult to differentiate between cotton-wool spots and early lesions of CMV retinitis, which can have a very similar appearance. Sometimes, the distinction can be made only by serial ophthalmoscopic examination. Cotton-wool spots remain stationary or resolve, whereas the lesion of CMV retinitis increases in size. Because cotton-wool spots virtually never cause symptomatic loss of vision and often spontaneously resolve, no treatment is indicated.

Small retinal hemorrhages and other microvascular abnormalities have been reported in up to 40% of patients with AIDS. These lesions also are asymptomatic, except in the rare case where perifoveal involvement may result in visual blurring.

CYTOMEGALOVIRUS RETINITIS

CMV retinitis is the most common sight-threatening ocular opportunistic infection in patients with AIDS. It usually occurs only in patients with a history of an absolute CD4+ T (helper) lymphocyte count of less than 50 cells/µL. The typical appearance is a white, cottage cheese–like retinal exudate, often associated with hemorrhage and frequently located adjacent to major retinal vessels. In tissue sections, full-thickness retinal necrosis and swollen retinal cells containing intranuclear and intracytoplasmic inclusions are observed.

Patients with CMV retinitis typically present with complaints of painless visual impairment—"floaters," blurred vision, decreased visual acuity, or visual field defects—almost always affecting one eye more than the other. Several studies of untreated CMV retinitis have demonstrated a natural history of progressive retinal destruction caused by new retinal lesions or increasing size of previous lesions usually evident within weeks by serial ophthalmoscopy.

CMV retinitis is diagnosed primarily by its typical clinical appearance. The differential diagnosis includes cotton-wool spots, retinal hemorrhages, choroidal granulomas, acute retinal necrosis syndrome, and toxoplasmic and syphilitic retinitis. Because differentiating between these entities may be difficult and the therapy of CMV retinitis is expensive, time-consuming, and toxic, the diagnosis of CMV retinitis must be confirmed by an experienced ophthalmologist. Because of poor specificity and sensitivity, CMV cultures of blood or urine are not clinically useful diagnostic tests. However, studies of more sensitive techniques of detecting CMV viremia (e.g., CMV DNA amplification by polymerase chain reaction [PCR] or staining peripheral blood leukocytes for CMV antigen) appear to have better predictive value for identifying patients at high risk for developing CMV retinitis. It is not yet clear whether these more sensitive tests have clinical utility in screening.

Rx Treatment

Treatment options for CMV retinitis include daily treatment with ganciclovir or foscarnet, intermittent therapy with cidofovir, or surgical placement of an intraocular device that releases ganciclovir intravitreally (Table 418–1). Ganciclovir is a nucleoside analogue prodrug that is preferentially phosphorylated within CMV-infected cells to an active drug, ganciclovir triphosphate, which inhibits CMV replication. Systemic ganciclovir therapy can be administered intravenously as a ganciclovir infusion or orally as valganciclovir, a valine ester of ganciclovir. The short-term efficacy of local therapy with the ganciclovir intraocular device in preventing retinitis progression is greater than that of systemic intravenous ganciclovir,[1] although the device must be surgically replaced after 8 months and concomitant systemic anti-CMV therapy (e.g., oral valganciclovir) must be given to prevent CMV disease in the contralateral eye and other organs.[2] The efficacy of intravenous ganciclovir and oral valganciclovir appear to be the same.[3] Foscarnet is a pyrophosphate analogue that does not require phosphorylation for its anti-CMV activity. It can only be administered intravenously and has efficacy similar to ganciclovir.[4] Cidofovir is a very potent anti-CMV nucleotide analogue that does not require phosphorylation by CMV-encoded enzymes. It is administered intravenously every 1 to 2 weeks. The efficacy of cidofovir has not been compared with that of other agents in randomized controlled trials. Ganciclovir- and foscarnet-resistant strains of CMV have emerged and have been associated with therapeutic failure. In such cases, use of these agents in combination or of cidofovir may be effective in controlling retinitis progression. To minimize further irreversible retinal loss, anti-CMV therapy must be given indefinitely, unless immune reconstitution in response to HAART occurs. Many patients who have had sustained increases in absolute CD4+ T lymphocyte counts to more than 100 cells/μL for at least 3 to 6 months have discontinued anti-CMV therapy without further retinitis reactivation.

Because atrophy occurs in areas of active CMV retinitis, patients are susceptible to rhegmatogenous retinal detachment (resulting from a scar in a thinned portion of the retina), even when active retinitis has been controlled with antiviral therapy. Immune reconstitution after HAART actually increases the risk of this and other complications in patients with healed CMV retinitis.

TOXOPLASMIC CHORIORETINITIS

Toxoplasmic chorioretinitis is rare compared with CMV retinitis, but it may complicate up to 20% of cases of AIDS-associated toxoplasmic encephalitis (Table 418–2). Unlike toxoplasmic retinitis in immunocompetent individuals, which typically results from reactivation of congenitally acquired cysts latent in the retina, AIDS-associated toxoplasmic chorioretinitis does not appear to originate in preexisting retinochoroidal scars but from dissemination of organisms from nonocular sites of disease. Necrotizing retinal lesions are often bilateral and multifocal and, as in CMV retinitis, may result in rhegmatogenous retinal detachment. Vitreous inflammation and anterior uveitis are more common and associated hemorrhage less common than in CMV retinitis. Because nearly all cases of toxoplasmic chorioretinitis are associated with toxoplasmic encephalitis, a computed tomographic (CT) or magnetic resonance (MR) scan of the brain should be done whenever this diagnosis is considered. Specific antiparasitic therapy (i.e., pyrimethamine and sulfadiazine or pyrimethamine and clindamycin, in the same doses used to treat toxoplasmic encephalitis) usually is effective in preventing further retinal necrosis, but chronic maintenance therapy must be continued to prevent relapse.

Table 418–1 • THERAPY FOR CYTOMEGALOVIRUS RETINITIS

Ganciclovir	Induction therapy: 5 mg/kg IV ganciclovir or 900 mg PO valganciclovir q12 h × 14 days
	Chronic maintenance therapy: 5-6 mg/kg IV ganciclovir qd or 5 days/wk, or 900 mg PO valganciclovir qd
	Intraocular device: must replace after 8 mo
Efficacy	Intraocular device > systemic drug
Adverse effects	Systemic therapy can cause granulocytopenia, thrombocytopenia, azoospermia. Intraocular device placement can be complicated by retinal detachment, bleeding, or endophthalmitis. High risk of contralateral or extraocular CMV disease with intraocular device as sole therapy; should have PO valganciclovir coadministered.
Foscarnet	Induction therapy: 90 mg/kg IV q12 h × 14 days
	Chronic maintenance therapy: 90-120 mg/kg IV qd
Efficacy	Equivalent to IV ganciclovir
Adverse effects	Nephrotoxicity, ionized hypocalcemia (seizure or arrhythmia with overdose), hypomagnesemia, hypophosphatemia, hypocalcemia, hypokalemia, genital ulcers, nephrogenic diabetes insipidus
Cidofovir	Induction therapy: 5 mg/kg IV q wk × 2
	Chronic maintenance therapy: 5 mg/kg IV q 2 weeks
	Concomitant saline hydration and oral probenecid must be coadministered to decrease risk of nephrotoxicity
Efficacy	Has not been compared with other anti-CMV treatments
Adverse effects	Nephrotoxicity, neutropenia, probenecid-induced hypersensitivity reaction or nausea, neuropathy, anterior uveitis, hypotony, increased risk of ocular toxicity with concomitant HAART

Table 418–2 • DIAGNOSTIC FEATURES OF IMPORTANT CAUSES OF HIV-ASSOCIATED RETINITIS

FEATURE	CYTOMEGALOVIRUS	ACUTE RETINAL NECROSIS (VZV, HSV)	TOXOPLASMOSIS	SYPHILIS
Ocular symptoms	Floaters, visual field defect or decreased visual acuity	Same	Same	Same
	Painless	Pain common	±Photophobia	±Photophobia
Associated clinical findings	AIDS	Orolabial herpes, trigeminal zoster	AIDS, encephalitis	Rash, hearing loss
Typical retinal lesion	Cottage-cheese exudate with hemorrhage	Confluent, gray or pale retina	White or yellow exudate	Variable
Typical retinal location	Adjacent to major vessel	Peripheral	Multifocal	Focal or posterior
Risk of retinal detachment	+++	++++	++	+
Serology, culture	Not helpful	Viral culture of skin lesion	*T. gondii* IgG titer	VDRL, FTA-ABS

Modified from Culbertson WW: Infection of the retina in AIDS. Int Ophthalmol Clin 1989;29:108.

ACUTE RETINAL NECROSIS SYNDROME

Widespread, often bilateral, necrotizing retinitis caused by herpes simplex or varicella-zoster virus is a well-characterized, although rare, AIDS-associated condition. Unlike CMV retinitis, this disease often is associated with ocular pain and concomitant keratitis or iritis. Many individuals have had recent or concurrent trigeminal zoster or orolabial herpes simplex infection, and evidence of concurrent viral meningoencephalitis may be present. On funduscopic examination, widespread, pale or gray, peripheral retinal lesions are observed. Although intravenous acyclovir or oral valacyclovir may be effective in preventing further retinal necrosis, subsequent retinal detachment is a frequent, sight-threatening complication.

PROGRESSIVE OUTER RETINAL NECROSIS SYNDROME

Progressive outer retinal necrosis is a clinical variant of varicella-zoster retinitis that occurs in patients with CD4+ lymphocyte counts less than 100 cells/μL and is characterized by multifocal, deep retinal lesions that rapidly progress to confluence. Less inflammatory cell response is observed in this condition than in acute retinal necrosis. The clinical response to available antiviral therapies is poor unless immune reconstitution occurs.

OTHER CAUSES OF CHORIORETINITIS AND VITRITIS

Cases of syphilitic retinitis have been reported in individuals with AIDS and asymptomatic HIV infection. There is no characteristic ophthalmologic appearance, but nearly all reported cases have had markedly positive serologic tests for active syphilis and dermatologic or central nervous system manifestations of secondary syphilis. Generally, response to intravenous penicillin therapy has been good. Disseminated pneumocystosis (associated with use of inhaled pentamidine prophylaxis against *Pneumocystis carinii* pneumonia), *Mycobacterium tuberculosis,* and *Mycobacterium avium* complex infection with choroidal infiltrates have been described, but these lesions generally have not been sight threatening. Rare cases of indolently progressive retinitis have been attributed to endogenous bacterial infection on the basis of retinal histopathology and response to broad-spectrum antibiotics.

Vitritis (i.e., endophthalmitis) due to disseminated candidiasis may occur in parenteral drug users who are HIV infected or AIDS patients with indwelling central venous catheters. An immune-mediated vitritis has been observed in some AIDS patients diagnosed with CMV retinitis soon after they initiated HAART. This CMV retinitis–associated vitritis resolves with continued anti-CMV treatment and HAART.

OPTIC NEUROPATHY

Opportunistic infectious diseases affecting the optic nerve of patients with advanced HIV disease may result in visual impairment or blindness. The most common cause of optic neuropathy is CMV infection. When CMV retinitis involves the optic disc, swelling of the optic nerve head (i.e., papillitis) leads to decreased visual acuity. This may occur in the presence or absence of other areas of retinitis and may affect the intraorbital optic nerve (i.e., optic neuritis) or retrobulbar nerve (i.e., retrobulbar neuritis). The acute retinal necrosis syndrome caused by herpes simplex or varicella-zoster virus infection may cause papillitis; syphilis may cause papillitis, optic neuritis, or retrobulbar neuritis in patients at any stage of HIV disease. The most serious ocular complication of cryptococcal meningitis is an arachnoiditis that compresses the retrobulbar optic nerve, occasionally causing blindness. The cause of optic neuropathy usually can be established by seeking the other characteristic features of the specific infection. However, specific antimicrobial therapy for the cause of optic neuropathy often fails to improve vision after significant visual loss has occurred.

UVEITIS

Severe anterior uveitis is uncommon in patients with HIV disease, but when such cases occur, syphilis or varicella-zoster virus infection are the most common causes. Mild, asymptomatic anterior uveitis commonly is observed in patients with CMV retinitis, but inflammation severe enough to cause symptoms is rare. Occasional cases of toxoplasmic anterior uveitis have been reported.

Uveitis, sometimes leading to macular edema and epiretinal membrane formation, can occur as a complication of cidofovir therapy for CMV retinitis (particularly among patients receiving concomitant HAART) or as an immune reconstitution reaction in AIDS patients with CMV retinitis whose absolute CD4+ T lymphocyte counts have increased to more than 100 cells/μL in response to HAART.

KERATITIS

Inflammatory disease of the cornea (keratitis) is most frequently caused by varicella zoster or herpes simplex virus, and the clinical features usually make diagnosis relatively simple. Patients with advanced HIV disease who develop this complication may require intravenous acyclovir therapy in addition to topical trifluridine. Microsporida infection has also been reported to cause keratitis in HIV-infected patients.

DISEASES OF THE CONJUNCTIVA AND ADNEXA

Kaposi's sarcoma (KS) has a predilection to involve ocular structures. Conjunctival KS lesions appear as bright red subepithelial nodules, and small lesions may be mistaken for subconjunctival hemorrhages. Periorbital edema may be caused by lymphangitic KS, even in the absence of apparent ocular or cutaneous lesions. Most ocular lesions respond to local irradiation.

Nonspecific, nonpurulent conjunctivitis that often is self-limited has been reported in up to 10% of AIDS patients. Topical steroid and sulfa drug therapy may be beneficial for this condition. Other rare causes of conjunctivitis include syphilis and molluscum contagiosum infection. Orbital KS or Burkitt's lymphoma may manifest with ptosis and diplopia.

 1. Musch DC, Martin DF, Gordon JF, et al: Treatment of cytomegalovirus retinitis with a sustained-release ganciclovir implant. The Ganciclovir Implant Study Group. N Engl J Med 1997;337:83–90.
2. Martin DF, Kuppermann BD, Wolitz RA, et al: Oral ganciclovir for patients with cytomegalovirus retinitis treated with a ganciclovir implant. Roche Ganciclovir Study Group. N Engl J Med 1999;340:1063–1070.
3. Martin DF, Sierra-Madero J, Walmsley S, et al: A controlled trial of valganciclovir as induction therapy for cytomegalovirus retinitis. N Engl J Med 2002;346:1119–1126.
4. Studies of Ocular Complications of AIDS Research Group: Mortality in patients with the acquired immunodeficiency syndrome treated with foscarnet or ganciclovir for cytomegalovirus retinitis. N Engl J Med 1992;326:213–220.

SUGGESTED READINGS

Goldberg DE, Wang H, Azen SP, et al: Long term visual outcome of patients with cytomegalovirus retinitis treated with highly active antiretroviral therapy. Br J Ophthalmol 2003;87:853–855. *HAART-related immune reconstitution is associated with complications that induce loss of vision in AIDS patients with healed CMV retinitis.*

Jacobson MA: Treatment of cytomegalovirus retinitis in patients with the acquired immunodeficiency syndrome. N Engl J Med 1997;337:105–114. *Reviews and compares advantages and disadvantages of available treatments for CMV retinitis.*

Margolis TP, Lowder CY, Holland GN, et al: Varicella-zoster virus retinitis in patients with the acquired immunodeficiency syndrome. Am J Ophthalmol 1991;112:119–131. *Detailed description of unique clinical characteristics of varicella-zoster virus retinitis.*

419 HEMATOLOGY AND ONCOLOGY IN AIDS

David T. Scadden
Jerome E. Groopman

A signature abnormality of human immunodeficiency virus (HIV) infection is the decline in the number of CD4+ T lymphocytes over time. However, other cytopenias also are seen in advanced disease, with anemia reported in 60%, thrombocytopenia in 40%, and neutropenia in 50% of patients with acquired immunodeficiency syndrome (AIDS). These cytopenias occur in conjunction with progressive deterioration of immune function and are less common in the earlier stages of HIV infection or in patients responding to antiretroviral medications. Thrombocytopenia is the exception and may constitute a manifestation of HIV infection during the asymptomatic phases. Multiple contributing factors frequently are operative in the cytopenia in advanced HIV infection, including direct and indirect effects of HIV, opportunistic infections, neoplasms, and toxic anti-retroviral, antimicrobial, or antitumor chemotherapy.

Evaluation of patients with low blood cell counts should focus on infectious processes and attendant myelotoxic effects of therapy. In addition to the usual laboratory approaches to cytopenia based on impaired production, excess consumption, or sequestration, other diagnostic studies should be considered, including blood isolator cultures for fungi and mycobacteria and serum assessment for cytomegalovirus (CMV) antigen or IgM antibody to parvovirus.

Although the utility of bone marrow aspirate and biopsy in an HIV-infected patient with low blood cell counts has been debated, morphologic changes such as giant pronormoblasts in parvovirus infection and special stains for mycobacteria and fungi may hasten identification of a reversible cause of myelosuppression. Marrow sampling is not more sensitive, however, than routine microbiologic tests in diagnosing these abnormalities.

Morphologic abnormalities of myeloid and erythroid lineages often are present in the bone marrow of patients with HIV disease in the absence of infection or neoplasm. These changes are nonspecific and include hypercellularity, dysplasia with frequent megaloblastosis, lymphoid aggregates, and increased plasma cells and reticulin. The pathogenetic mechanisms for these morphologic abnormalities and the associated impaired hematopoiesis are not well defined. Laboratory studies of hematopoiesis in HIV infection have yielded variable and differing results. The bulk of evidence suggests that HIV does not directly infect early progenitors but may alter the proliferative capacity of progenitors by two possible mechanisms: induction of inhibitory factors in the marrow microenvironment or interaction with the progenitor cell surface and induction of cell death (i.e., apoptosis) without infecting stem cells. Regardless of the mechanism, it has become clear that suppression of HIV replication using highly active antiretroviral therapy (HAART) permits repair of the defect and improvement in blood cell counts.

THROMBOCYTOPENIA

Thrombocytopenia (Chapter 177) may be a presenting laboratory finding in an otherwise asymptomatic HIV-infected person. HIV infection should be considered in the differential diagnosis of thrombocytopenia, and the history should include questions regarding risk factors for infection. Clinically asymptomatic but thrombocytopenic HIV-infected patients have a rate of progression to AIDS similar to that of asymptomatic HIV-seropositive persons without thrombocytopenia. Thrombocytopenia is not a criterion for more advanced HIV disease according to the staging system developed by the Centers for Disease Control and Prevention (CDC). Multiple causes need to be considered in evaluating thrombocytopenia in HIV infection. Immune-mediated destruction and ineffective hematopoiesis usually are identified. Cases of AIDS with apparent hemolytic-uremic syndrome or thrombotic thrombocytopenic purpura have been described but are rare. Isolated thrombocytopenia is most often clinically similar to classic autoimmune thrombocytopenic purpura (ITP). Bone marrow examination reveals an increased number of megakaryocytes, and there are elevated levels of bound immunoglobulin on the platelet surface. However, distinct from ITP, the immunoglobulin is generally immune complexes often involving anti-HIV antibodies, and splenomegaly is common. Detection of antibody on platelet surfaces does not correlate with thrombocytopenia, possibly because reticuloendothelial cell dysfunction often occurs in AIDS and may reduce platelet clearance. In addition to peripheral destruction of platelets, reduced production appears to be common in HIV disease. Even in patients with an ITP-like presentation, production is reduced. This mechanism predominates in patients with thrombocytopenia in the setting of AIDS.

The thrombocytopenia in HIV-infected patients has sequelae similar to classic immune thrombocytopenia, but special attention to the issue of thrombocytopenia should be given in HIV-infected hemophiliacs. Complications from thrombocytopenia may be more severe in hemophiliacs, and therapy should be considered at a higher platelet count than in HIV-infected patients without other coagulation defects. An important observation has been the improvement in platelet count from treatment with zidovudine (AZT) in HIV-infected patients with significant thrombocytopenia, regardless of risk group. Nearly two thirds of such patients may respond to AZT therapy and increase their platelet counts, with a mean threefold increase, within 12 weeks of

initiating treatment. If AZT is an unacceptable option, there have been several anecdotal reports of responses to other antiretroviral agents. If there is no response to AZT, several treatment modalities may be considered, including corticosteroids, dapsone, interferon-α, splenectomy, and danazol; for rapid, temporary reversal of severe thrombocytopenia, intravenous gamma globulin and anti-RhD preparations are quite active.

There are possible risks of using steroids in HIV-infected individuals, including exacerbation of fungal infection, Kaposi's sarcoma (KS), and the replicative activity of HIV itself. Nonetheless, most patients have tolerated corticosteroids for short intervals. Their long-term use in HIV-associated thrombocytopenia cannot be recommended.

ANEMIA

The incidence of anemia increases among HIV-infected patients as their degree of immune dysfunction worsens. The anemia is usually normochromic and normocytic, with iron study results that are normal or indicative of chronic disease. Occasionally, the vitamin B_{12} level is decreased, but true vitamin B_{12} deficiency is uncommon; rather, transcobalamin transport may be altered, and therapy with the vitamin does not lead to improved erythropoiesis. If a low vitamin B_{12} level is found, a true deficiency should be ruled out by a Schilling test and other studies (Chapter 175).

The Coombs' test (i.e., antiglobulin) may be positive for most patients with AIDS and for about one third of asymptomatic, HIV-infected individuals. Although anti-i or other specific antibodies may occur, nonspecific binding of antiphospholipid antibodies or immune complexes to erythrocytes is more common. Immune-mediated hemolysis is unusual in HIV-infected patients as a cause of anemia.

Impaired erythropoiesis accounts for anemia in most HIV-infected individuals. Serum erythropoietin levels are often low for the degree of anemia in the patient without renal abnormalities and are of unclear origin. Parvovirus infection has been reported in HIV-infected patients and may result in red cell aplasia. Gamma globulin therapy has been reported to reverse this unusual cause of severe anemia.

AZT is associated with dose-related and idiosyncratic suppression of erythropoiesis, whereas other antiretroviral drugs generally are not associated with anemia. Macrocytic changes occur in the erythrocytes with AZT therapy. The mechanism of impaired erythropoiesis due to the drug appears to be impairment of DNA synthesis in developing progenitors.

Recombinant erythropoietin therapy may decrease the transfusion requirement and increase the hemoglobin in anemic AIDS patients on AZT. The response to recombinant erythropoietin treatment is most clearly seen in patients with pretreatment serum erythropoietin levels less than 500 mU/mL. Some anemic AIDS patients receiving AZT have developed red cell aplasia that does not improve with recombinant erythropoietin therapy.

NEUTROPENIA

Neutropenia occurs in the HIV-infected patient in concert with decreases in other cell counts with progressive deterioration of the immune system. In addition to neutropenia, neutrophil dysfunction has been reported in AIDS. The extent to which neutrophil defects, particularly microbial killing, contribute to host immune impairment is unknown.

Neutropenia is most commonly caused by myelosuppressive therapy in AIDS patients. AZT treatment is sometimes limited by neutropenia, although other antiretrovirals do not seem to cause this problem. Other therapies, including trimethoprim-sulfamethoxazole for *Pneumocystis carinii* pneumonia, pyrimethamine-sulfadiazine for central nervous system (CNS) toxoplasmosis, acyclovir for disseminated herpes simplex or herpes zoster, and most prominently, ganciclovir for CMV retinitis may be myelotoxic and result in neutropenia.

HEMATOPOIETIC GROWTH FACTORS

Suppression of leukocyte or erythrocyte production can be a limiting factor in treating HIV infection or its complications. This problem has become less restrictive with newer antiretroviral therapies and better control of HIV-1. However, for patients who do develop severe cytopenia, hematopoietic growth factors are useful in raising cell counts. In most patients with anemia due to HIV infection or concomitant AZT therapy who have baseline serum erythropoietin concentrations of less than 500 mU/mL, recombinant erythropoietin increases the hemoglobin concentration and reduces the transfusion requirement. Use of the myeloid growth factors—granulocyte colony-stimulating factor (G-CSF) or granulocyte macrophage colony-stimulating factor (GM-CSF)—has been successful in ameliorating leukopenia due to HIV infection or treatment with AZT, interferon-α, ganciclovir, or cancer chemotherapy. Use of G-CSF modestly reduces bacterial infection rates in HIV-infected individuals with neutrophil counts between 750 and 1000/mm³.

The major issue in the safety profile of the myeloid growth factors is their potential effect on the replication of HIV. In vitro data indicate that HIV replication is stimulated by GM-CSF but not G-CSF. The data conflict about whether this phenomenon occurs in vivo, but some data indicate that GM-CSF combined with AZT does not result in an increased HIV-1 viral load. Increases in circulating levels of virus have occurred with G-CSF used to mobilize stem cells, but this phenomenon is transient and seen in only about 50% of patients.

Clinical trials have indicated that the lymphopoietic cytokine interleukin-2 (IL-2) may be used to enhance lymphoid cell numbers, particularly CD4+ T lymphocytes. Intermittent use of this cytokine has been shown to raise CD4 counts with tolerable toxicity in patients whose baseline CD4 count is greater than 200 cells/mm³. Use of concurrent antiretroviral therapy is necessary to prevent enhanced virus replication. Whether this cytokine results in any clinical benefit remains controversial, and this approach should still be regarded as experimental pending data on clinical outcomes. Similarly, adoptive transfer of T cells or gene-modified T cells have been shown to alter immune parameters but with unclear clinical effect.

Neoplasms that occur with increased frequency in the setting of HIV disease are KS, B-cell lymphoma, and squamous cell neoplasia of the anogenital region. Smaller, but statistically meaningful increases have also been documented for Hodgkin's disease, leiomyosarcoma (in children only), seminoma, and plasmacytoma. Clinical management of AIDS-associated neoplasia must balance therapy directed at HIV-1, opportunistic infections, and tumors.

KAPOSI'S SARCOMA

KS (Chapters 164, 190, and 417) is the most frequent neoplastic manifestation of HIV infection and is one of the CDC criteria that define an HIV-infected individual as having AIDS. AIDS-associated KS more frequently is seen among homosexual or bisexual men with HIV than in other HIV-transmission risk groups. This epidemiologic observation led to a search for a second transmissible factor, which resulted in the identification of a new member of the gamma herpesvirus family, KS herpesvirus (KSHV) or human herpesvirus 8 (HHV-8). This virus is associated with KS, a subset of B-cell lymphomas (discussed later), and Castleman's disease. The epidemiologic data indicate that exposure to this virus is more common in promiscuous homosexual men and in populations with higher frequencies of classic or endemic KS not associated with HIV-1, such as those in the Mediterranean basin and sub-Saharan Africa.

The virus is found in KS tissue regardless of the epidemiologic background, but the mechanism by which the virus participates in tumor development is unclear. There are a number of KSHV genes with human homologues that suggest possible direct effects of the virus (i.e., cyclin D, BCL-2, and activated G protein–coupled receptor homologues) or effects at a distance (i.e., interleukin-6, chemokine, and Ox-2 homologues). Hypotheses for how this virus is oncogenic are wide ranging, and the mechanisms involved may be quite distinct from those of other tumor viruses.

The nature of the immunologic response to KSHV remains ill defined, but it clearly plays an important role in the control of KSHV-related tumors. KS in the setting of organ transplantation often regresses with reduction of immunosuppressive medication. Similarly, AIDS patients treated with potent antiretroviral drug combinations have a markedly reduced incidence of KS, and preexisting KS often regresses.

Histopathologically, KS lesions are a mixture of different cell types. Endothelial cells are present within the KS lesions, as is a prominent spindle-cell proliferation surrounded by extravasated erythrocytes and macrophages. The cell of origin of the neoplasm is still debated, as is the clonality of the disease. Some patients have multiple, independent clones of tumor cells, whereas a subset of patients appear to have metastatic lesions derived from a single clone. In general, however,

aggressive treatment of the original lesion has not had substantial impact on the ultimate development of other lesions.

KS often is a cutaneous, nonblanching, red macule. As lesions increase in size, they often have surrounding ecchymoses and acquire more of a violet hue. Sometimes, the lesions may become nodular, and with advanced disease, the lesions may become confluent, with large plaques developing, particularly on the legs. There is no orderly pattern of tumor progression, and patients may present with lesions at multiple sites. The rate of growth of the primary lesions, as well as the appearance of new lesions, is quite variable. The lesions may occur on any cutaneous site and on mucous membranes. Lymphatic involvement is not unusual, and KS may present as lymphadenopathy. Visceral involvement, particularly of the trachea, lungs, and gastrointestinal tract, occurs commonly and may be seen in the absence of cutaneous disease. The most striking morbidity associated with KS is that of lymph node involvement and consequent lymphedema involving the lower extremities, groin, and head and neck. Extensive parenchymal or pleural involvement of the lung may result in life-threatening respiratory compromise.

The diagnosis of KS is relatively straightforward in HIV-infected individuals presenting with an erythematous or violaceous cutaneous or mucosal lesion. However, bacillary angiomatosis caused by *Bartonella* species (Chapter 340) may result in similar lesions. This process, which is treatable with antibiotics, should be excluded by Warthin-Starry staining of biopsy material. After diagnosis, an assessment should be made of the distribution of the lesions. Because the presence of visceral disease does not necessarily correlate with poor response of lesions to therapy, an extensive evaluation for gastrointestinal or lymphadenopathic KS is not indicated unless there are specific symptoms referable to such involvement.

Rx Treatment

In patients with symptomatic visceral disease, lesions associated with edema, or rapidly evolving extensive cutaneous disease, chemotherapy can often provide symptomatic relief (Table 419–1). The most active chemotherapeutic drugs appear to be paclitaxel, liposomal anthracyclines, or combinations of vincristine and bleomycin or doxorubicin, vincristine, and bleomycin. Liposomal doxorubicin or liposomal daunorubicin have been shown to be active with reduced toxicity compared with standard agents and often are used as a first-line approach. For patients who fail liposomal agents (common after 10 weeks), low-dose paclitaxel is highly active, desirable, and well tolerated. Response to chemotherapy usually occurs within the first few weeks of treatment. Unfortunately, the lesions regrow when the chemotherapy is stopped, and treatment usually is chronic.

Patients with KS who do not have rapidly progressive disease and therefore do not require immediate intervention may be treated with several other approaches. The most important among these is aggressive antiretroviral therapy. Regression of KS is common among patients treated with combinations of antiretroviral drugs and occurs 2 to 4 months after control of viremia has been achieved. For patients whose KS persists despite antiretrovirals, options include observation, single-agent interferon-α, local irradiation, intralesional chemotherapy, local cryotherapy, topical retinoid (9-cis-retinoic acid), or combinations of these. Selecting the optimal therapeutic approach involves determining the clinical status of the patient, particularly using the staging classification (Table 419–2), as well as lifestyle issues. Patients who are categorized as "good risk" by the TIS staging system are also good candidates for response to interferon-α, but toxicity is common. Several agents currently in clinical trials appear to have potential for this patient group. Among these are thalidomide, 9-cis-retinoic acid, and angiogenesis inhibitors.

NON-HODGKIN'S LYMPHOMA

B-cell lymphoma frequently occurs in immunosuppressed individuals. Genetic disorders of the immune system such as Wiskott-Aldrich syndrome and the immunosuppressive therapy used in organ transplantation are associated with malignant transformation of B cells and an oligoclonal or monoclonal lymphoma. Non-Hodgkin's B-cell lymphoma is a frequent manifestation of HIV infection, occurring in

Table 419–1 • TREATMENT OF KAPOSI'S SARCOMA

Chemotherapy single agent	Liposomal doxorubicin	20 mg/m² IV every 3 weeks
	Liposomal daunorubicin	40 mg/m² IV every 2 weeks
	Paclitaxel	100 mg/m² IV every 2 weeks
Combined therapy	Bleomycin/vincristine	Bleomycin 15 U IV Vincristine 2 mg IV every 2–3 weeks
	Doxorubicin-bleomycin-vincristine	Doxorubicin 20 mg/m² Bleomycin 15 μm² IV Vincristine 2 mg IV every 3 weeks

Table 419–2 • KAPOSI'S SARCOMA (KS): RECOMMENDED STAGING CLASSIFICATION

	GOOD RISK (0) (ALL OF THE FOLLOWING)	POOR RISK (1) (ANY OF THE FOLLOWING)
Tumor (T)	Confined to skin and/or lymph nodes and/or minimal oral disease*	Tumor-associated edema or ulceration, extensive oral KS, gastrointestinal KS, or KS in other non-nodal viscera
Immune system (I)	CD4 cells ≥200/μL	CD4 cells <200/μL
Systemic illness (S)	No history of opportunistic infection (OI) or thrush No B symptoms† Performance status ≥70 (Karnofsky)	History of OI and/or thrush, B symptoms present Performance status <70 Other HIV-related illness (e.g., neurologic disease, lymphoma)

*Minimal oral disease is non-nodular KS confined to the palate.
†"B" symptoms are unexplained fever, night sweats, >10% involuntary weight loss, or diarrhea persisting more than 2 weeks.
Modified from Krown SE, Metroka C, Wernz J: Kaposi's sarcoma in the acquired immune deficiency syndrome: A proposal for uniform evaluation, response, and staging criteria. J Clin Oncol 1989,7:1201–1207.

approximately 1.6% of the affected population per year in patients with advanced HIV disease. The relative risk of lymphoma in HIV-infected individuals compared with matched uninfected controls is 60- to 100-fold. The incidence of B-cell lymphoma in this population appears to be reduced in the setting of HAART. Systemic lymphoma is estimated to be reduced in incidence by 50% compared with the pre-HAART era, and primary CNS lymphoma has become a rare complication, generally occurring only among those who have failed HAART therapy.

Causative factors operative in the development of lymphoma in AIDS are likely to be multiple. HIV provides a permissive environment in which lymphoma develops. Lymphoma in this setting may be regarded as an opportunistic neoplasm and is considered an AIDS-defining illness. Proliferative signals to B cells, whether from dysfunctional T cells, aberrant cytokine production, or infections (such as Epstein-Barr virus or HIV-1 itself), may induce polyclonal expansion of the B-cell population (Chapter 371). This expanded population may provide targets for genetic abnormalities that lead to malignant transformation and emergence of several dominant clones. The oligoclonal populations of malignant B cells seen in some HIV-infected individuals with lymphoma support such a model. Ultimately, a single malignant clone may emerge, leading to a monoclonal neoplasm. The chromosomal abnormalities frequently seen in B-cell lymphoma involve translocation of loci encoding the immunoglobulin genes with the *MYC* oncogene. More than 75% of AIDS-related lymphomas have alterations in at least one proto-oncogene, and a large fraction also have alterations in at least one tumor-suppressor gene. Genetic evidence of Epstein-Barr virus (EBV) is found in about one half of B-cell lymphomas and virtually all primary CNS lymphomas in AIDS patients.

A number of interacting factors are likely to be important in the pathogenesis of lymphoma in patients with HIV infection united by the disorganization of immune function induced by HIV. KSHV or HHV-8 infection has been associated with a distinct subset of B-cell lymphomas that presents with body cavity effusions. These aggressive lymphomas frequently have genomic material from Epstein-Barr virus.

Clinically, B-cell lymphoma in AIDS patients tends to have a high-grade histologic pattern and to follow an aggressive clinical course. Small, noncleaved or large cell histologies account for nearly all lymphomas in this setting. The low-grade lymphomas are uncommon and may represent background rather than a neoplasm directly associated with immunosuppression. Rarely, B-cell acute lymphoblastic leukemia or T-cell neoplasms have been reported.

Most patients have extranodular disease involving the gastrointestinal tract, CNS, liver, soft tissues, or bone marrow. In one large series, nearly 80% of patients diagnosed with B-cell lymphoma in AIDS had extranodal involvement. Lymphoma strictly confined to lymph nodes is uncommon. Gastrointestinal lymphoma may occur anywhere from the esophagus to the anus. Primary CNS lymphoma is usually immunoblastic in histologic type (Chapter 414). Such patients generally have solitary mass lesions in the parenchyma of the brain, whereas CNS involvement in conjunction with systemic lymphoma is more often meningeal in location. All AIDS patients diagnosed with systemic non-Hodgkin's lymphoma should be considered for careful CNS assessment.

Most AIDS patients with B-cell lymphoma are classified as having stage III (i.e., involving both sides of the diaphragm without visceral involvement) or stage IV (i.e., visceral involvement). Systemic B symptoms are common, but fever should not be immediately ascribed to lymphoma in AIDS patients, and secondary infectious causes should be ruled out. Staging for these patients should follow the approach used in other settings of non-Hodgkin's lymphoma, with particular attention to the gastrointestinal tract, bone marrow, and CNS.

The major differential diagnosis to be considered with primary CNS lymphoma is *Toxoplasma gondii* infection or progressive multifocal leukoencephalopathy (PML) (Chapter 414). PML usually can be distinguished from CNS lymphoma by its lack of enhancement with gadolinium on MRI. CNS lesions due to lymphoma may be isodense or hypodense and contrast enhancing on CT, and they may enhance on MRI, thereby resembling toxoplasmosis. Nonetheless, toxoplasmosis usually manifests with multiple lesions throughout the neuraxis, whereas primary CNS lymphoma tends to be a single lesion located in a paraventricular site. Accessible lesions should be biopsied to distinguish between lymphoma and toxoplasmosis; an alternative to tumor biopsy is analysis by polymerase chain reaction (PCR) for EBV. Primary CNS lymphoma is uniformly associated with EBV in the tumor, and the specificity and sensitivity of PCR amplification of EBV in cerebrospinal fluid for diagnosing a lymphomatous mass lesion is more than 95% and 80 to 100%, respectively.

Rx Treatment

Treatment for primary CNS lymphoma is radiation therapy and steroids, with taper of the steroids as rapidly as tolerated. Approaches are currently in clinical trial for those patients who relapse with reasonable underlying immune function and performance status.

The treatment of AIDS-related B-cell lymphoma has in the past pivoted on a balance between the poor prognosis associated with the neoplasm and the limited tolerance to aggressive chemotherapy. Opportunistic infection and bone marrow suppression often limited the delivery of high doses of chemotherapy before the advent of HAART. With the availability of potent antiviral medications, patients often have sufficient immune reconstitution to mitigate these issues. Before the era of HAART, prognostic factors defined as negatively affecting outcome included a CD4+ T-cell count of less than 100 cells/mm³, age older than 35 years, intravenous drug use, and stage III or IV disease. Some studies have also identified poor performance status and prior opportunistic infection as negative prognostic factors.

For "good prognosis" patients with relatively intact immune function and those responding to HAART, aggressive therapy with combination regimens is indicated. The combination of cyclophosphamide, doxorubicin, vincristine, and prednisone (CHOP regimen) is most often used, although infusional regimens with etoposide, vincristine, prednisone, doxorubicin, and cyclophosphamide also have had good results. Hematopoietic growth factors to ameliorate cytopenias generally are needed. Antiretroviral therapy generally can be sustained, but systematic pharmacokinetic studies are limited, and significant drug-drug interactions may occur. No undue toxicity when using indinavir, 3TC, and d4T in conjunction with CHOP was observed in one multicenter study, and clearance of indinavir and Adriamycin was not affected, but cyclophosphamide clearance was reduced by one half without clinical effect. For patients who do not have CNS involvement at the time of presentation, prophylactic therapy often is given to prevent CNS relapse. This may be particularly important for patients with small, noncleaved cell histology or bone marrow, testicular, or paranasal sinus involvement. Data have also indicated that EBV in the tumor at diagnosis may predict a higher risk for CNS involvement, and CNS prophylaxis for this subgroup is recommended. The complete response rate for patients undergoing systemic chemotherapy is 50 to 70%, with long-term lymphoma-free survival achievable in a subfraction of these. The potential for eradication of the non-Hodgkin's lymphoma is real and should be pursued. For those failing initial therapy, no clear second-line approach has been defined, but there is a growing experience with infusional therapies or stem cell transplantation. Patients with this disorder should be treated in clinical trial settings whenever possible.

Patients with severe immune suppression or complicating opportunistic infections who have failed HAART pose a particularly complex treatment dilemma. Some patients have opted for palliative therapy with corticosteroids because intensive chemotherapy may lead to further immune compromise and infection. However, lymphoma usually is rapidly growing and fatal for patients who are not aggressively treated. The clinician needs to pursue therapy in such patients only with an informed discussion of the risks and benefits of treatment, honestly emphasizing the poor prognosis with or without chemotherapy.

OTHER MALIGNANCIES

The incidence of Hodgkin's disease has been estimated to be approximately fivefold greater in HIV-infected individuals compared with the HIV-seronegative population. In patients with HIV infection and Hodgkin's disease, the clinical presentation usually includes B symptoms (i.e., fever, night sweats, anorexia, and weight loss), stage III or IV disease, and extranodular disease. The histopathology is often mixed cellularity. HIV-infected individuals with Hodgkin's disease appear to tolerate chemotherapy less well and may have a higher incidence of tumor relapse than do those without HIV infection, although the outlook with HAART is expected to be much improved.

Hodgkin's disease therapy among HIV-infected patients should be according to guidelines for non–HIV-positive individuals (Chapter 298). The major difference is to incorporate prophylaxis against opportunistic infections, particularly *P. carinii* pneumonia; to be particularly alert to infectious complications during therapy; and to anticipate needing growth factor support given the frequent cytopenias in HIV-infected hosts. We generally continue antiretroviral therapy, but drug interactions are possible and poorly defined.

There is a high prevalence of papillomavirus infection in groups at risk for HIV (Chapter 345) and the dysplasia associated with it. Whether the incidence of squamous cell cancer of those sites is increased is controversial. Although the rate of anal cancer is higher among homosexual men, it is not clear whether it is higher among HIV-infected individuals, and no increase in invasive cervical cancer is apparent. However, because of a concern about the potential premalignant nature of the dysplastic lesions often seen, frequent cervical examinations, including colposcopy, are recommended for HIV-infected women to detect early malignant change. Anal Papanicolaou tests (Pap smears) are being evaluated for their diagnostic and prognostic significance in men and women with HIV who may be at risk for carcinoma.

Although anecdotal reports abound of other malignancies in HIV-infected individuals, it is unclear whether these occur above that of the background prevalence in the general population. Nonetheless, consideration should be given to the significance of the HIV infection in clinical management. Vigilance should be maintained regarding possible interactions with antiretroviral drugs, opportunistic infections, and the often increased sensitivity to bone marrow and mucosal injury caused by cytotoxic therapies.

SUGGESTED READINGS

Allardice GM, Hole DJ, Brewster DH, et al: Incidence of malignant neoplasms among HIV-infected persons in Scotland. Br J Cancer 2003;89:505–507. *The incidence of cancer was 11-fold higher than in the general population.*

Glaser SL, Clarke CA, Gulley ML, et al: Population-based patterns of human immunodeficiency virus-related Hodgkin lymphoma in the Greater San Francisco Bay Area, 1988–1998. Cancer 2003;98:300–309. *Emphasizes the aggressiveness of these lymphomas but the fact that HAART has resulted in less aggressive disease and better survival.*

Kirk O, Pedersen C, Cozzi-Lepri A, et al: Non-Hodgkin lymphoma in HIV-infected patients in the era of highly active antiretroviral therapy. Blood 2001;98:3406–3412. *Defines the impact of HAART on AIDS-related lymphoma.*

Knowles DM: Etiology and pathogenesis of AIDS-related non-Hodgkin's lymphoma. Hematol Oncol Clin North Am 2003;17:785–820. *The variations in genetics suggest more than one pathogenetic mechanism.*

Levine AM, Tulpule A: Clinical aspects and management of AIDS-related Kaposi's sarcoma. Eur J Cancer 2001;37:1288–1295. *An excellent review of presentation, staging and treatment.*

Little RF, Pittaluga S, Grant N, et al: Highly effective treatment of acquired immunodeficiency syndrome–related lymphoma with dose-adjusted EPOCH: Impact of antiretroviral therapy suspension and tumor biology. Blood 2003;101:4653–4659. *This report provides information on the evolving nature of AIDS lymphomas in the setting of HAART and introduces an infusional therapy that may be particularly potent if multi-institutional trials support its conclusions.*

Martin JN, Ganem DE, Osmond DH, et al: Sexual transmission and the natural history of human herpesvirus 8 infection. N Engl J Med 1998;338:948–954. *A seroepidemiologic study of the virus associated with Kaposi's sarcoma.*

Moses A, Nelson J, Bagby GC Jr: The influence of human immunodeficiency virus-1 on hematopoiesis. Blood 1998;91:1479–1495. *An excellent review of hematopoietic abnormalities associated with HIV.*

Schmidt-Wolf IG, Rockstroh JK, Schlegel U, et al: Treatment options of AIDS-related lymphoma. Expert Opin Pharmacother 2003;4:1331–1343. *A comprehensive review.*

Sparano JA: Clinical aspects and management of AIDS-related lymphoma. Eur J Cancer 2001;37:1296–1305. *An excellent review of presentation, staging, and treatment.*

420 RENAL, CARDIAC, ENDOCRINE, AND RHEUMATOLOGIC MANIFESTATIONS OF HIV INFECTION

Michael S. Saag

Infection with human immunodeficiency virus type 1 (HIV) is a multisystem disease. Manifestations of pulmonary, gastrointestinal, neurologic, hematologic, and oncologic disease are well described in the literature, owing mainly to their high prevalence and often dramatic modes of presentation. In contrast, HIV-related renal, cardiac, endocrine, and rheumatologic diseases are more insidious in presentation. As overall survival of HIV-infected individuals continues to improve and therapeutic regimens become more sophisticated, clinicians have begun to encounter disorders of the latter organ systems with increasing frequency.

RENAL DISEASE

Renal disease associated with HIV infection may present as fluid-electrolyte and acid-base abnormalities, acute renal failure, coincidental renal disorders, or a glomerulopathy directly related to underlying HIV infection, called *HIV-associated nephropathy* (HIVAN). Originally observed in patients with acquired immunodeficiency syndrome (AIDS) and called *AIDS-associated nephropathy,* more recent studies have described the characteristic renal changes of HIVAN in asymptomatic HIV-infected individuals and patients with early symptomatic HIV disease, broadening the definition to include all HIV-infected patients. With the advent of the potent protease inhibitor indinavir, renal stones have been reported with increasing frequency. Of indinavir recipients, 10% experience flank pain, with or without hematuria, while on therapy. Crystallization of drug in the renal collecting system leads to development of "sludge," or frank stones, resulting in renal colic.

FLUID-ELECTROLYTE AND ACID-BASE DISORDERS

Fluid-electrolyte disorders are common in patients with advanced HIV infection. Hyponatremia is noted in 40% of hospitalized AIDS patients and occurs with hypovolemia and euvolemia. Hypovolemia, most often caused by gastrointestinal fluid losses, is the most common cause of hyponatremia among this group of patients. The syndrome of inappropriate antidiuretic hormone release is responsible for most cases of euvolemic hyponatremia and is most often due to underlying *Pneumocystis carinii* infection, malignancy, or central nervous system disease. Hyponatremia is associated with increased morbidity and mortality, especially in conjunction with certain opportunistic infections, such as cryptococcosis.

Adrenal insufficiency is a less frequent cause of hyponatremia. Although abnormalities of the adrenal glands frequently are reported at autopsy, overt adrenal insufficiency occurs in less than 5% of patients. The typical findings of hyponatremia, hyperkalemia, non–anion gap metabolic acidosis, hypovolemia, renal salt wasting, and mild renal insufficiency are usually present in some combination.

Drugs are an important cause of fluid and electrolyte disorders in HIV-infected patients and can mimic the abnormalities associated with adrenal dysfunction. Hyperkalemia and non–anion gap metabolic acidosis have been noted in patients receiving parenteral pentamidine. Amphotericin B is associated with hypokalemia, hypomagnesemia, renal tubular acidosis, and renal insufficiency. Foscarnet therapy is associated with decreased levels of ionized calcium and, on occasion, renal insufficiency. Nucleotide analogues, such as cidofovir and adefovir, are associated with renal insufficiency and electrolyte disorders. A Fanconi-like proximal renal tubule disorder (Chapter 122), characterized by hypophosphatemia and creatinine elevation, has been observed frequently in patients receiving adefovir; the incidence of this disorder increases dramatically after 24 weeks of adefovir therapy. These abnormalities are rarely described, however, with tenofovir. Chemotherapeutic agents used to treat AIDS-associated malignancies may lead to fluid-electrolyte disturbances through direct nephrotoxicity or gastrointestinal losses associated with prolonged vomiting or diarrhea.

ACUTE RENAL FAILURE

As with most chronic illnesses, acute renal dysfunction may develop as a complication in the management of HIV-infected patients. Prerenal azotemia often results from hypovolemia secondary to poor fluid intake, increased gastrointestinal losses, or both. Acute tubular necrosis can be ischemic in origin, usually secondary to hypotension or sepsis, or due to nephrotoxic agents. Acute interstitial nephritis is another complication associated with drugs used to treat HIV-related diseases. Table 420–1 lists agents with nephrotoxic potential commonly used in HIV-infected patients.

Opportunistic infections, invasion of renal parenchyma with lymphoma or Kaposi's sarcoma, and amyloidosis, which occurs as a complication of subcutaneous narcotic abuse, all may result in interstitial nephritis. Other renal lesions such as hepatitis B–induced membranous glomerulonephritis, IgA nephropathy, acute glomerulonephritis secondary to bacterial infection, direct infection of the renal parenchyma with cytomegalovirus (CMV), fungi, or mycobacteria, and hemolytic uremic syndrome all have been associated with renal dysfunction in HIV-infected individuals. The diagnosis and management of acute renal failure are no different in HIV-infected patients than in their uninfected counterparts (Chapter 116).

HIV-ASSOCIATED NEPHROPATHY

Definition

HIVAN first was established as a unique clinical entity in 1984. Originally called *AIDS-associated nephropathy* (AAN), many investigators questioned whether AAN was a unique manifestation of AIDS or simply represented heroin-associated nephropathy (HAN) occurring in intravenous drug users (IVDUs) who also happened to be infected with HIV. Although the lesions and clinical manifestations of HAN are similar to those of AAN, further studies have established clear distinctions between the two entities. AAN occurs in individuals, including children, who have never used intravenous drugs. Nearly half of the cases presenting with the manifestations of AAN have early (asymptomatic or minimally symptomatic) HIV disease. HIVAN has replaced AAN as the most appropriate name for this entity.

Epidemiology

The first cases of HIVAN were described in major urban centers, such as New York and Miami, which also had many IVDUs among the HIV patient population. In contrast, centers whose HIV population consisted primarily of white homosexual and bisexual men, such as San Francisco and the National Institutes of Health, were not observing the renal changes of HIVAN in patients, implying that HIVAN was a manifestation of HAN. More recent epidemiologic data indicate that 50% of patients with HIVAN are IVDUs, with the remaining cases occurring in homosexual and bisexual men, immigrants from Haiti, women who have acquired HIV from heterosexual contacts, and children born to infected mothers, many of whom did not use intravenous drugs.

More than 90% of patients with HIVAN are black. No explanation regarding the high prevalence of cases among blacks has been established, although many investigators have speculated that cofactors such as superimposed infections or specific immune response genes may be responsible.

Pathology and Pathogenesis

Focal and segmental glomerulosclerosis (FSGS) is the characteristic renal lesion identified in patients with HIVAN, occurring in 80 to 90% of patients. On gross inspection, the kidneys usually are enlarged, and the cortical surface is smooth, even in advanced uremia. Microscopic examination of early lesions reveals diffuse mesangial hyperplasia with minimal glomerular sclerosis over time. A variable number of glomeruli develop segmental sclerosis characterized by hyperplastic visceral epithelial cells with coarse cytoplasmic vacuoles, collapsed capillary walls or capillaries obliterated by protein deposits (hyalinosis), and foam cells (lipid-filled monocytes) in the lumens (Fig. 420–1). Bowman's spaces are usually dilated, and tubular damage is universal. Microcystic dilation of tubules is a unique feature of HIVAN not reported in the FSGS of HAN (Fig. 420–2). Interstitial changes consisting of mild edema with scattered mononuclear cells are usually evident in HIVAN kidneys but not nearly to the degree noted in HAN. Similarly, although interstitial fibrosis may be present in advanced HIVAN disease, it is not nearly as prominent as the marked interstitial fibrosis noted in HAN disease.

The cause of HIVAN seems to be related to direct infection of renal epithelial cells by HIV. Ultrastructural studies have shown tuboloreticular structures in vascular endothelium and in circulating and tissue lymphocytes. Other findings, such as many nuclear bodies existing as budding forms in renal and lymphoid tissues, have been interpreted by some investigators to suggest a viral etiology. Proviral HIV DNA has been detected in microdissected glomeruli. In situ hybridization studies have shown viral mRNA in podocytes, renal tubular epithelial cells, and infiltrating mononuclear cells, implicating HIV as the causative agent. The predominance of HIVAN in blacks and the relative paucity of cases among white homosexual men suggest, however, that other factors not yet identified must play a role in the pathogenesis of HIVAN.

Table 420–1 • DRUGS WITH NEPHROTOXIC POTENTIAL COMMONLY USED IN THE TREATMENT OF HIV-RELATED DISEASE

Acyclovir	Ganciclovir
Adefovir	Nonsteroidal anti-inflammatory agents
Aminoglycosides	Penicillins
Amphotericin B	Pentamidine
Aspirin	Phenytoin
Cephalosporins	Rifabutin
Cidofovir	Rifampin
Cimetidine	Spiramycin
Cisplatin	Sulfonamides
Dapsone	Tetracyclines
Ethambutol	Thiazides
Foscarnet	Trimethoprim

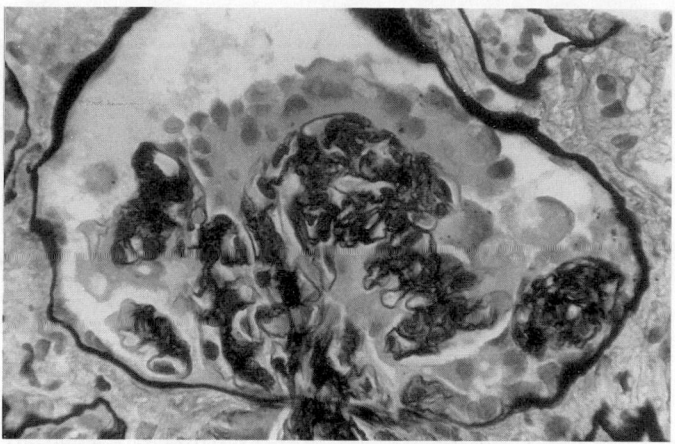

FIGURE 420–1 • Glomerulus from a patient with HIV-associated nephropathy showing global collapse of the glomerular capillaries, increased mesangial sclerosis, and a proliferative "cap" of visceral epithelial cells (silver methenamine, × 400). (Courtesy of Dr. William L. Clapp.)

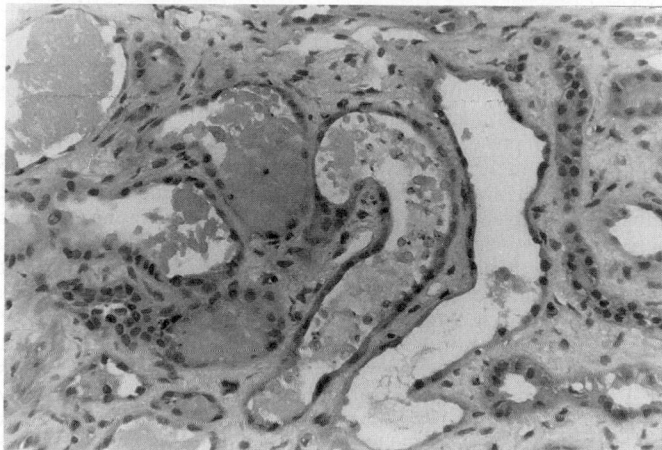

FIGURE 420–2 • Dilated degenerated tubules showing flattened epithelium and loss of nuclei and containing proteinaceous casts from a patient with HIV-associated nephropathy (hematoxylin-eosin, ×200). (Courtesy of Dr. William L. Clapp.)

Clinical Manifestations

HIVAN is characterized by the development of proteinuria, nephrotic syndrome, and rapidly progressive irreversible azotemia. The proteinuria is typically heavy and presents as an early manifestation. Untreated, the time to the development of end-stage renal disease from the initial diagnosis of proteinuria is 4 to 16 weeks in patients with HIVAN compared with 20 to 40 months among patients with HAN. Another clinical distinction between HIVAN and HAN is the relative absence of significant hypertension among patients with HIVAN. Accelerated hypertension is a hallmark of HAN. Peripheral edema and anasarca are conspicuously absent in many HIVAN patients with high-grade proteinuria and hypoalbuminemia.

Nephropathy has been documented in patients months to years before the onset of clinical symptoms of early symptomatic HIV disease or AIDS. HIVAN is being reported with increasing frequency among HIV-infected children and seems to be independent of the risk factors for HIV infection in the mothers. It is anticipated that the incidence of HIVAN will continue to grow and should be considered as a diagnostic possibility in any HIV-infected patient who presents with unexplained proteinuria regardless of the stage of disease.

Diagnosis

Quantitative measurement of the amount of protein excreted in the urine along with estimation of the creatinine clearance via a 24-hour urine collection should be performed early in the evaluation. Other reversible causes of renal insufficiency, such as bacterial infection, crystalluria, and obstructive uropathy, should be ruled out using urine culture, urinalysis, and ultrasonography. The kidneys are enlarged early in HIVAN and remain enlarged throughout the course of disease. Because a variety of other renal lesions, such as membranous nephropathy related to hepatitis B, membranoproliferative disease, and immune complex–related glomerular damage, also may present as nephrotic syndrome in HIV-infected patients, renal biopsy should be performed to determine a precise diagnosis. The presence of the typical features of FSGS with tubular involvement as described previously establishes the diagnosis of HIVAN when renal tissue is obtained.

Rx Treatment

Improved outcome, including reversal of renal insufficiency and marked reduction in proteinuria, has been reported with many interventions. The use of highly active antiretroviral therapy (HAART), usually consisting of a regimen containing a potent protein inhibitor, in combination with other modalities (e.g., corticosteroids or angiotensin-converting enzyme [ACE] inhibitor therapy) is the cornerstone of therapy. In the pre-HAART era, corticosteroids (60 mg prednisone daily over 2 to 6 weeks) were shown to reverse partially the progressive azotemia and prevent the need for dialysis in a subgroup of patients. Several uncontrolled studies have shown benefit of ACE inhibitors, either captopril or fosinopril, in the treatment of biopsy-proven HIVAN. Outcomes were better among patients receiving ACE inhibitors along with potent antiretroviral therapy.

Nutritional support in the form of high-protein, high-calorie diets along with appropriate dosage adjustments of nephrotoxic drugs is crucial. Hemodialysis is of marginal benefit in prolonging survival of patients with advanced HIV disease when they have reached end-stage renal disease. Among patients with AIDS, hemodialysis provides significant prolongation of life. Patients who are asymptomatic or have early symptomatic HIV disease survive longer, with some patients living more than 6 years on long-term hemodialysis. Peritoneal dialysis should be considered in patients who are suitable candidates. Continuous ambulatory peritoneal dialysis may offer several advantages over hemodialysis, including avoiding leukopenia caused by the hemodialysis membranes, fewer problems with anemia, and theoretical advantages of less stimulation of HIV-infected T lymphocytes via membrane-induced cytokine release. A potential disadvantage of continuous ambulatory peritoneal dialysis is the higher incidence of peritonitis. Renal transplantation is a viable option for selected HIV-infected patients. Studies are under way to evaluate the effects of the intensive immunosuppressive regimens required to prevent rejection.

CARDIAC DISEASE

A wide variety of cardiac abnormalities have been reported in HIV-infected patients, including ventricular dysfunction, myocarditis, pericarditis, endocarditis, and arrhythmias. Most often, cardiac involvement is clinically silent and is noted as an incidental finding at autopsy. When clinical symptoms are present, however, disease manifestations can be debilitating and, in many cases, life-threatening. In contrast to HIV-associated renal disease, no specific cardiac syndrome or disease state has been described.

Epidemiology

Cardiac abnormalities have been observed in 25 to 75% of HIV-infected patients studied at autopsy. Myocardial disease is noted most frequently, occurring in 90% of subjects with cardiac findings. Pericardial disease, often with adjacent myocardial involvement, is observed in more than 20% of cases with cardiac abnormalities. Endocarditis is evident histologically in 3 to 5% of cases reported in autopsy series. No characteristic epidemiologic factor, such as age, gender, race, or means of acquiring HIV infection, has been identified that predisposes patients to cardiac disease. Although cardiac abnormalities are observed more frequently in AIDS patients, 30% of patients with early symptomatic HIV disease are noted to have abnormal findings on echocardiograms and electrocardiograms. As more patients experience hyperlipidemia as a complication of antiretroviral therapy, the incidence of ischemic cardiac disease is expected to rise over the next decade.

Pathology and Pathogenesis

HIV-related heart disease may result from metastatic extension of a concomitant opportunistic infection or malignancy but most often is seen as lymphocytic infiltration of the myocardium or as an unspecified myocarditis. The mechanism responsible for the myocarditis is unknown, although many investigators believe that HIV itself may be directly responsible. Other viruses, such as CMV, may be responsible for the development of myocarditis, although the typical "owl's eye" inclusion bodies rarely are seen in patients with HIV-associated cardiomyopathy. Additional mechanisms, such as postviral myocarditis or catecholamine-induced myocarditis, have been postulated, but little evidence exists to support their role.

A broad range of opportunistic infections and malignant diseases has been described in cardiac tissue examined at autopsy. Among the infectious disorders, fungal and viral pathogens are identified most often, followed by bacterial and protozoal infections (Table 420–2). Although the invading pathogen frequently is diagnosed at another primary site antemortem, cardiac involvement is rarely (<2%) identified before autopsy. This situation is largely due to the clinically silent nature of cardiac disease in HIV infection and a low index of suspicion by clinicians. Kaposi's sarcoma and metastatic lymphoma are the most common neoplastic diseases reported that invade the heart. Primary cardiac lymphoma has been reported rarely.

Pericardial disease almost invariably is associated with adjacent myocardial involvement. Pericarditis is usually nonspecific in origin, but when an etiologic process is identified, Kaposi's sarcoma or a pathogen, such as *Mycobacterium tuberculosis* or *Cryptococcus neoformans*, is responsible most often. Drugs used to treat HIV-associated disorders, such as doxorubicin for Kaposi's sarcoma, may cause myocardial damage. Other toxins, vitamin deficiencies, or metabolic abnormalities (e.g., hypothyroidism) also may result in myocardial dysfunction or pericardial disease.

Endocardial disease has been described in 3% of cases studied at autopsy and usually presents as either nonbacterial thrombotic (marantic) endocarditis or healed bacterial endocarditis. The precise cause of marantic endocarditis is unknown, but it has been reported in other long-term wasting illnesses and malignant diseases. Vegetations usually are located on the mitral valve, although lesions on the tricuspid valve have been noted in 29% of AIDS patients with this disorder. Significant embolization to the spleen and brain was noted in greater than 50% of patients with marantic endocarditis studied at autopsy. Bacterial endocarditis is reported rarely in AIDS patients. Healed lesions from previous bouts of bacterial endocarditis have been reported in autopsy series but are of little clinical significance.

Table 420–2 • INFECTIOUS CAUSES OF CARDIAC DISEASE IN HIV-INFECTED PATIENTS

BACTERIA	VIRUSES
Bacteria (endocarditis)	Cytomegalovirus
Mycobacterium tuberculosis	Herpes simplex virus
Mycobacterium avium-intracellulare	HIV
Nocardia asteroides	
Actinomyces	PROTOZOA
	Toxoplasma gondii
FUNGI	*Pneumocystis carinii*
Cryptococcus neoformans	
Histoplasma capsulatum	
Coccidioides immitis	
Candida	
Aspergillus	

Clinical Manifestations

Most cardiac disease in HIV-infected patients is clinically silent. When symptoms are present, they usually consist of the ordinary findings noted in non–HIV-infected patients with myocarditis or pericarditis, such as fever, dyspnea, chest pain, fatigue, cough, and orthopnea. Hepatomegaly and jugular venous distention are the most common signs noted on physical examination, followed by rales, systolic murmurs, and the presence of an S_3 gallop. Signs of advanced pericardial disease with impending tamponade are among the most common clinical manifestations observed in patients who present with clinical symptoms of cardiac disease.

Diagnosis

Demonstrated cardiomegaly on a chest radiograph is an important marker of underlying cardiac disease in HIV-infected patients. Right ventricular enlargement is usually the result of pulmonary artery hypertension, which in AIDS patients is often due to severe or recurrent opportunistic pneumonia. Left ventricular or biventricular enlargement is a characteristic finding of congestive cardiomyopathy resulting from any cause. Elevation of serum cardiac troponin, a marker of myocardial injury, may help identify myocarditis, unstable angina, or acute myocardial infarction. Assessment of brain natriuretic peptides in the serum is useful in determining the presence of left ventricular dysfunction and may be used as a screening test in the setting of suspected congestive cardiomyopathy. Echocardiography is a more sensitive and specific noninvasive test that is used to assess the degree of ventricular dysfunction and to characterize the extent of pericardial effusion, if present. Several series have shown echocardiographic abnormalities in 50% of HIV-infected patients who had no cardiac symptoms at the time of study. Ventricular enlargement, pericardial effusion, and ventricular hypokinesis were the abnormalities noted most frequently. In view of the overall silent nature of cardiac disease, the high likelihood that infiltrative processes will be evident and diagnosed at another site, and the often limited therapeutic options available for treating cardiac disease in HIV-infected patients, routine echocardiography should be discouraged in patients without cardiac symptoms. The experience with endomyocardial biopsies in HIV-infected patients is limited; however, in patients who show signs of cardiac disease and have not had a specific diagnosis established, endomyocardial biopsy is a viable option for a definitive diagnosis.

Treatment

Supportive treatment consisting of diuretic therapy, reducing preload and afterload when appropriate, and correcting cardiac arrhythmias is the initial approach to treating myocardial disease. Pericardial disease requires careful volume management with avoidance of aggressive diuresis or preload reduction. In the case of pericardial tamponade, surgical intervention is warranted. When the underlying cause of the cardiac disease is known, appropriate therapy directed at the specific infectious agent or malignancy is indicated.

ENDOCRINE DISORDERS

Overt endocrine dysfunction has not been prominent in HIV infection. Nonetheless, all glands of the endocrine system may be infiltrated with opportunistic infections or malignancies or may be affected by drugs used to treat HIV-related disorders. Hyperlipidemia and lipodystrophy have been associated with the use of HAART, especially with certain protease inhibitors. The specific cause of these disorders is unclear. The subtle presentations of endocrine diseases create difficult diagnostic challenges.

Adrenal Gland Dysfunction

The adrenal gland is the endocrine gland most commonly affected in AIDS patients examined at autopsy, although clinical evidence of adrenal insufficiency is observed in less than 8% of AIDS patients.

Widespread lipid depletion and varying degrees of adrenal necrosis are the most prevalent pathologic findings in postmortem examinations. Adrenal invasion by CMV is noted in 50% of patients with adrenal pathology. *Mycobacterium avium* complex, Kaposi's sarcoma, *C. neoformans,* and *Histoplasma capsulatum* involve the adrenal glands in 5 to 12% of cases. Drug therapy, with agents such as ketoconazole (adrenal dysfunction) or rifampin (increased clearance of cortisol) also may result in adrenal insufficiency. Megestrol acetate can suppress the hypothalamic-adrenal axis and result in adrenal insufficiency when the drug is discontinued. Fatigue, anorexia, nausea, vomiting, orthostatic hypotension, and hyponatremia are symptoms frequently noted in many HIV-infected patients; however, only a few of these patients are adrenal insufficient when evaluated using standard laboratory criteria.

Basal 8 AM plasma cortisol levels are usually higher in patients with advanced HIV disease than in asymptomatic patients and uninfected healthy controls. Other adrenocorticotropin hormone (ACTH)–dependent steroids, such as deoxycorticosterone (DOC), compound B, and 18-hydroxy-DOC, are not elevated, however, and show a blunted response to ACTH stimulation, implying subnormal adrenal reserves. Patients who fail to achieve plasma cortisol levels greater than $20\,\mu g/dL$ 60 minutes after ACTH stimulation should be considered to have, or be at high risk of developing, adrenal insufficiency. Plasma ACTH levels are frequently normal or subnormal even when plasma cortisol levels are depressed, suggesting that adrenal insufficiency in some HIV-infected patients is due to a primary pituitary or central nervous system disorder. Treatment of adrenal insufficiency in HIV-infected patients is the same as in other individuals with abnormal adrenal function (Chapter 240).

Hypogonadism

The most common abnormality of endocrine function noted clinically is hypogonadism. Decreased libido occurs in more than half of men with AIDS, and impotence, usually associated with low serum testosterone levels, is reported in 30% of AIDS patients. Serum gonadotropin levels may be below normal or inappropriately within normal limits in hypogonadal men with AIDS. When pituitary responsiveness to gonadotropin-releasing hormone is assessed in these hypogonadotropic men, normal release of luteinizing hormone and follicle-stimulating hormone has been observed, suggesting a hypothalamic basis for the central hypogonadotropism. Other studies have shown appropriately elevated levels of luteinizing hormone and follicle-stimulating hormone in hypogonadal men, implying primary testicular dysfunction. Drugs, such as ketoconazole, ganciclovir, and acyclovir, have been associated with low testosterone levels or decreased spermatogenesis. Long-term use of megesterol acetate is invariably associated with suppression of testosterone levels in men. Studies of gonadal function in women are limited, although menstrual irregularities are common in women with advanced HIV disease.

Thyroid Disease

Thyroid function remains remarkably normal throughout the course of HIV disease. Low levels of thyroxine (T_4), triiodothyronine (T_3), and free thyroxine index (FTI) in the setting of low concentrations of thyrotropin, the so-called euthyroid sick syndrome, are remarkably uncommon among ambulatory HIV-infected patients. Decreased levels of T_3 resin uptake and elevated levels of T_4-binding globulin are noted frequently in ambulatory patients with advanced disease; however, concentrations of T_3 and T_4 are most often within normal limits. Invasive disease secondary to CMV, *P. carinii, C. neoformans,* Kaposi's sarcoma, and lymphoma has been described in the thyroid. Even patients with infiltrating opportunistic diseases of the thyroid gland usually remain euthyroid throughout the course of their disease. Nonetheless, despite the relative infrequency of clinical disease, hypothyroidism is a potentially reversible cause of fatigue, malaise, altered mental status, and "failure to thrive" in HIV-infected patients and should be evaluated routinely.

Less common causes of hypothyroidism in HIV-infected patients include adverse effects of medications. Ketoconazole rarely has been associated with primary hypothyroidism. Drugs that are strong inducers of hepatic microsomal enzymes, such as rifampin, may lead to increased clearance of T_4.

Metabolic Abnormalities

Hyponatremia is the most common electrolyte disturbance noted in HIV-infected individuals (see discussion in renal section). Disorders of carbohydrate metabolism have been reported in association with direct pancreatic invasion by opportunistic processes and with drug therapy. Pancreatic lesions caused by CMV, toxoplasmosis, Kaposi's sarcoma, and lymphoma are noted in 35% of cases at autopsy. The development of type I diabetes mellitus has been reported in only a few instances, however. Hypoglycemia is often the result of direct toxic effects of drugs and leads to premature release of insulin by β cells, resulting in hypoglycemic episodes that may be severe and prolonged. Pentamidine isothionate is the most common cause of hypoglycemia, occurring in 4% to 33% of treated patients. Renal insufficiency is a predisposing factor in the development of pentamidine-induced hypoglycemia. Although most hypoglycemic episodes result from parenteral administration of pentamidine, several cases have been reported in patients receiving aerosolized drug. Of more concern is the development of insulin resistance, occurring in 50% of patients receiving protease-containing HAART regimens. The management of insulin resistance in HIV patients seems to be similar to non-HIV patients, although formal studies comparing the effectiveness of metformin versus the thiazolidinediones or a combination of both have not been completed. Exercise and nutrition are the mainstays of therapy for insulin resistance.

Disorders of calcium metabolism are relatively uncommon but do occur. Hypercalcemia is associated with HIV-related leukemia and lymphoma. Hypocalcemia usually is the result of drug therapy with agents such as amphotericin B and foscarnet, which induce magnesium wasting and decrease levels of ionized calcium. CMV has been observed in parathyroid tissue, but CMV-induced hypoparathyroidism is extremely rare.

Hyperlipidemia is noted commonly in HIV-infected patients. Isolated elevation of triglycerides is reported in 50% of patients with either asymptomatic HIV disease or AIDS. Although hypertriglyceridemia is noted routinely among patients with HIV wasting syndrome, no relationship has been noted between the serum triglyceride level and the degree of wasting. Elevation of cachectin (tumor necrosis factor), inhibition of lipoprotein lipase, and decreased clearance of circulating lipoproteins all have been proposed as potential mechanisms of hypertriglyceridemia, but no clear association of any of these factors has been established.

In the HAART era, patients receiving protease inhibitor therapy have been noted to have elevated plasma triglyceride and cholesterol levels. Initial reports identified ritonavir as the most likely cause of these metabolic abnormalities, but more recently, indinavir, nelfinavir, and saquinavir also have been implicated. Sporadic reports of non-protease inhibitor–containing regimens causing this syndrome also have appeared. Abnormalities in body fat distribution have been observed in some individuals on HAART regimens. Loss of peripheral body fat (lipoatrophy) in the extremities and excess accumulation of fat in the abdominal region (so-called protease paunch) and breasts have been reported, to some degree, in many patients on HAART; severe manifestations are observed in 10% of patients. Dorsocervical fat pad enlargement (buffalo hump) among HAART recipients has been reported commonly, although a cohort study comparing the incidence of buffalo humps among HIV-infected patients versus age-matched non–HIV-infected individuals showed no difference between the two groups. Patients with buffalo humps have normal cortisol levels and varying degrees of hypertriglyceridemia or lipoatrophy. No specific therapeutic approaches for this syndrome have been elucidated, although intense exercise programs seem to have the most benefit. In severe cases, the HAART regimen must be modified.

RHEUMATOLOGIC DISEASE

Rheumatologic manifestations of HIV disease are being recognized with increased frequency. Musculoskeletal complaints are reported in 33 to 75% of HIV-infected patients and may present as a variety of rheumatologic disorders (Table 420–3). The severity of disease ranges from intermittent arthralgias to debilitating arthritis and vasculitis. An array of autoimmune antibodies, including antinuclear, antiplatelet, antilymphocyte, antigranulocyte, and antiphospholipid

HIV and AIDS

Table 420–3 • RHEUMATOLOGIC DISEASES ASSOCIATED WITH HIV INFECTION

AUTOIMMUNE PHENOMENA	**MYOPATHIES**
Anticardiolipin antibodies	Infectious (septic) myositis
Antigranulocyte antibodies	Myalgias
Antilymphocyte antibodies	Idiopathic
Antinuclear antibodies	Zidovudine-associated
Antiplatelet antibodies	Necrotizing, noninflammatory
Circulating immune complexes	myopathy
Cryoglobulins	Nemaline rod polymyositis
Rheumatoid factor	Polymyositis
	Pyomyositis
DERMATOLOGIC	
Dermatomyositis	**SJÖGREN'S SYNDROME**
Malar flush	Sicca complex
Psoriasis	
	VASCULITIS
JOINT DISEASE	Central nervous system angiitis
Arthralgias	Eosinophilic vasculitis
Arthritis	Henoch-Schönlein purpura
Enthesopathies	Hypersensitivity (drug-induced)
HIV-associated arthritis	Leukocytoclastic vasculitis
"Painful articular syndrome"	Polyarteritis nodosa
Psoriatic arthritis	Unspecified vasculitis
Reactive arthropathy	
Reiter's disease	
Septic arthritis	
Systemic lupus erythematosus	
(lupus-like syndrome)	

(anticardiolipin and lupus anticoagulant) antibodies are associated with HIV infection along with circulating immune complexes, rheumatoid factor, and cryoglobulins. Despite the presence of these antibodies in some patients, the precise mechanisms by which the rheumatologic abnormalities develop have not been elucidated and most likely are different for each particular disorder.

Arthralgias

Arthralgia is a common manifestation of acute HIV seroconversion, in addition to fever, myalgia, headache, sore throat, abdominal cramps, and lymphadenopathy. Generalized arthralgias are reported in one third of HIV-infected patients with minimally symptomatic disease. Some patients develop arthralgias and myalgias when zidovudine therapy is initiated; however, these symptoms are usually self-limited and abate within 4 to 6 weeks after starting treatment. The "painful articular syndrome" is characterized by severe articular pain of 2 to 24 hours' duration. Although uncommon, this disorder is incapacitating and usually unresponsive to oral nonsteroidal anti-inflammatory drugs (NSAIDs) or narcotic analgesics. Its cause is unknown. With the exception of the painful articular syndrome, most of the arthralgias associated with HIV disease are treated with NSAIDs.

Myopathies

Polymyositis-like illnesses, characterized by myalgias, proximal muscle weakness, and wasting, have been reported in several HIV-infected patients and have been the initial HIV-defining presentation in a few. The findings of creatinine phosphokinase elevation (greater than five times normal) and abnormal electromyography are indistinguishable from idiopathic polymyositis. Muscle biopsy specimens reveal necrosis, fibrosis, and inflammation, but usually to a lesser extent than is noted in non–HIV-infected individuals. The presence of nemaline rods, often noted in muscle biopsy specimens of older adults with myositis, suggests the likelihood of underlying HIV infection when noted in biopsy specimens obtained from younger adults, especially in the absence of inflammation.

Although virus-like particles have been shown rarely in synovial tissue, and HIV p24 antigen has been noted in the cytoplasm of degenerating muscle cells, no specific viral cause has been determined. All attempts to culture HIV-1 from muscle tissue of patients with myositis have been unsuccessful.

Patients receiving long-term zidovudine therapy may develop myositis characterized by muscle weakness, elevated creatinine phosphokinase levels, myalgias, and evidence of myopathy with a paucity of inflammatory cells on biopsy. Zidovudine-associated myositis usually responds to drug discontinuation and may recur on rechallenge. No definitive therapy exists for HIV-associated polymyositis, although corticosteroid therapy has been successful in reversing symptoms in some patients. If corticosteroid therapy is contemplated, the potential risks of superimposing immunosuppressive therapy on an immunocompromised host must be considered.

Reiter's Syndrome

Reiter's syndrome (Chapter 279) is noted in 10% of HIV-infected patients who develop arthritis, and an additional 10 to 20% of patients are classified as having "reactive arthritis" because they lack the non-articular features of Reiter's syndrome. Severe, persistent oligoarticular arthritis associated with urethritis, conjunctivitis, painless oral ulcerations, keratoderma blennorrhagicum, or circinate balanitis is the hallmark of Reiter's disease in HIV-infected and noninfected individuals. Clinical manifestations of Reiter's syndrome may precede or occur at the time of the initial diagnosis of HIV infection but most often follow the onset of immunodeficiency. HLA-B27 positivity is noted in 65 to 75% of HIV-infected patients with Reiter's syndrome. Studies of African HIV patients with Reiter's disease or reactive arthritis revealed no increased incidence of HLA-B27, however, suggesting involvement of other gene markers in this group. *Shigella, Campylobacter, Ureaplasma,* and other bacterial species associated with the development of reactive arthropathies rarely are described in HIV patients with Reiter's syndrome. Underlying concomitant sexually transmitted diseases may prove to be an important etiologic factor, however.

Treatment options for HIV patients with Reiter's disease are limited. Responses to NSAIDs are minimal, and more potent immunosuppressive agents, such as methotrexate and azathioprine, have led to opportunistic diseases and Kaposi's sarcoma shortly after initiation of therapy in the pre-HAART era. It is not known if these diseases will occur as readily in the HAART era when these agents are employed.

Sjögren's Syndrome

Xerophthalmia and xerostomia, the characteristic symptoms of Sjögren's syndrome (Chapter 282), have been reported with increasing frequency in AIDS patients. Features that closely resemble idiopathic Sjögren's syndrome, including sicca symptoms, a positive Schirmer test, abnormal salivary gland emptying, and abnormal salivary gland biopsies, have been reported in HIV-infected patients. As a result, it has been suggested that AIDS be an exclusionary disease for the diagnosis of idiopathic Sjögren's syndrome. The predominance of male patients; the absence of anti-Ro/SS-A and anti-La/SS-B antibodies; the absence of a well-defined connective tissue disease; the presence of HLA-DR52 and HLA-DR5 alleles instead of the characteristic A1, B8, DR3, DR2, and DQ1/DQ2 antigens; and a predominance of CD8+ lymphocytes instead of CD4+ cells infiltrating salivary tissue are the characteristic features of AIDS-associated Sjögren's syndrome, which differs from classic idiopathic Sjögren's syndrome. Treatment is primarily symptomatic.

Septic Arthritis

Joint space infection is uncommon in HIV-infected patients. Sporadic case reports have been published of septic arthritis resulting from fungal pathogens, such as *C. neoformans, H. capsulatum,* and *S. schenkii;* mycobacteria; and routine pyogenic organisms. The approach to diagnosis and treatment of septic arthritis is the same for HIV-infected patients as non–HIV-infected individuals.

HIV-Associated Arthropathy

A relatively uncommon arthritis has been described in patients with moderately advanced HIV disease who show no other signs of any recognizable rheumatologic disease. So-called HIV-associated arthropathy (HIVAA) presents as a monarticular or pauciarticular arthritis. The arthritis is usually severe, affects primarily the knees and ankles, and lasts 1 week to 6 months. No extra-articular manifestations have been noted. The synovial fluid is noninflammatory in nature, although a mild synovitis consisting of a chronic mononuclear cell infiltrate is noted on biopsy. Rheumatoid factor, antinuclear antibodies, anti-DNA antibodies, and antibodies against RNP, Sm, Ro/SS-A, and La/SS-B are negative. No predominant HLA pattern has been described. NSAIDs are of some benefit, but some patients require intra-articular steroid injections.

Vasculitis

Several varieties of vasculitis (Chapter 284) have been reported in association with HIV infection. Necrotizing vasculitis of the polyarteritis nodosa type is reported most commonly and presents as a peripheral sensory or sensorimotor neuropathy. The vasculitis involves the medium-sized vessels of the nerves, skin, and muscle. None of the reported patients with HIV-related polyarteritis nodosa were hepatitis B surface antigen positive. Primary angiitis of the central nervous system has been noted in two patients, one of whom had persistent varicella-zoster virus infection. Lymphomatoid granulomatosis also has been reported in HIV-infected patients. Henoch-Schönlein purpura has been reported rarely; however, no distinct cause has been elucidated. Drug-induced hypersensitivity vasculitis, usually presenting as cutaneous disease, has been reported associated with penicillin, trimethoprim-sulfamethoxazole, amitriptyline, and griseofulvin. Several cases of uveitis have been reported with rifabutin therapy, especially when this drug is administered with fluconazole and clarithromycin.

It is unclear whether HIV-associated vasculitis is the result of direct HIV invasion of the vessels, an immunologic reaction to an underlying viral infection, or a response to an opportunistic viral pathogen that invades vascular tissue. As with other serious rheumatologic manifestations of HIV disease, treatment options are limited by the underlying immunodeficiency of the host.

SUGGESTED READINGS
Cotter BR: Epidemiology of HIV cardiac disease. Prog Cardiovasc Dis 2003;45:319–326. *A useful overview emphasizing that increased insulin resistance, dyslipidemia, and lipodystrophy syndrome may accelerate atherosclerosis.*
Etzel JV, Brocavich JM, Torre M: Endocrine complications associated with human immunodeficiency virus infection. Clin Pharm 1992;11:705–713. *A practical, easy-to-read overview of the endocrine abnormalities seen in HIV-infected patients.*
Munoz Fernandez S, Cardenal A, Balsa A, et al: Rheumatic manifestations in 556 patients with human immunodeficiency virus infection. Semin Arthritis Rheum 1991;21:30–39. *One of the largest published reports on the rheumatologic manifestations of HIV infection. Numerous tables, charts, and figures are included.*
Gherardi R, Belec L, Mhiri C, et al: The spectrum of vasculitis in human immunodeficiency virus–infected patients. Arthritis Rheum 1993;36:1164–1174. *A thorough review of an uncommon, yet diverse complication of HIV disease.*
Huang JS, Wilke SJ, Dolan S, et al: Reduced testosterone levels in HIV-infected women with weight loss and low weight. Clin Inf Dis 2003;36:499–506. *A study of HIV-infected women versus age- and weight-matched controls that demonstrates a high degree (up to 50%) of low testosterone levels.*
Kimmel PL, Barisoni L, Kopp JB: Pathogenesis and treatment of HIV-associated renal diseases: Lessons from clinical and animal studies, molecular pathologic correlations, and genetic investigations. Ann Intern Med 2003;139:214–226. *A comprehensive overview indicating the benefits of HAART and possible roles for steroids and ACE inhibitors.*
Klotman PE: HIV-associated nephropathy. Kidney Int 1999;56:1161–1176. *An overview of the etiology, presentation, and treatment of HIVAN.*
Moroni M, Antinori S: HIV and direct damage of organs: Disease spectrum before and during the highly active antiretroviral therapy era. AIDS 2003;17(Suppl 1):S51–64. *Overview including cardiac, renal, and hematologic abnormalities.*
Rao TK: Acute renal failure syndromes in human immunodeficiency virus infection. Semin Nephrol 1998;18:378–395. *Succinct review of the renal complications of HIV disease, with special focus on HIV-associated nephropathy.*
Schambelan M, Benson C, Carr A, et al: Management of metabolic complications associated with antiretroviral therapy for HIV-1 infection: Recommendations of an International AIDS Society–USA Panel. J Acquir Immune Defic Syndr 2002;31:257–275. *A comprehensive overview of the emerging metabolic complications associated with HIV therapy and the current approaches to management of these disorders.*
Smith MC, Austen JL, Carey JT, et al: Prednisone improves renal function and proteinuria in HIV associated nephropathy. Am J Med 1996;101:41–48. *A case series of successful outcomes using steroid therapy for HIVAN.*

421 TREATMENT OF HIV INFECTION AND AIDS

Henry Masur

When the first cases of acquired immunodeficiency syndrome (AIDS) were recognized in the United States in the late 1970s, strategies for

patient management focused on prompt diagnosis and therapy of opportunistic infections. Clinicians recognized that this strategy resulted in a short survival. The median time to death after the first AIDS-defining opportunistic process was about 9 months, and most patients were dead within 2 years of this initial opportunistic process. By the mid-1980s, there was growing enthusiasm for chemoprophylaxis against the most common opportunistic infections, although at that time, trimethoprim-sulfamethoxazole (TMP-SMX) was the only agent marketed that seemed to be useful. TMP-SMX prophylaxis was found to be protective against *Pneumocystis jiroveci* pneumonia (PCP) and against toxoplasmosis and certain bacterial infections. TMP-SMX chemoprophylaxis was highly effective in preventing opportunistic complications and in prolonging survival. Chemoprophylaxis against *Mycobacterium avium* complex and improved survival became feasible when rifabutin, then clarithromycin and azithromycin were developed. Chemoprophylaxis against *Mycobacterium tuberculosis* also was shown to prolong survival.

With the licensing of zidovudine in 1987, treatment of the underlying retroviral cause of immunosuppression became possible for the first time. Monotherapy with nucleosides in that era (zidovudine, didanosine, zalcitabine, and stavudine) slowed the immunologic decline caused by human immunodeficiency virus (HIV), reduced the number of HIV-related opportunistic infections, and prolonged survival. The combination of anti-infective chemoprophylaxis and nucleoside antiretroviral therapy (ART) represented a multifaceted approach to improving the quality and duration of survival. The antiviral and immunologic enhancing effects of these nucleoside agents were modest in potency, however, and lacked durability. Within 6 to 18 months, many patients developed nucleoside resistant virus. As patients' viral loads returned to their pre–nucleoside therapy levels, CD4+ T-lymphocyte counts began to decline, and patients again became susceptible to opportunistic processes.

The development of more potent ART agents in the mid-1990s and the recognition that combination therapy was more effective than monotherapy led to regimens that provided more potent and durable virologic and immunologic effects and better clinical benefit. These regimens have been a major advance in the management of patients with HIV who have access to medical care and who are capable and willing to take these drugs. Taking these drugs, given their toxicities and their inconvenience, has been no small challenge for patients in every social and economic stratum. For many patients who can tolerate and adhere to these regimens, quality and duration of survival have improved dramatically.

Current strategies focus on determining how to develop a regimen for an individual patient that has durable efficacy (i.e., how to maximize the likelihood that the patient will have a prolonged survival free of disease-related or drug-related complications). These strategies depend on early recognition of HIV infection (i.e., recognition of HIV before the occurrence of severe immunosuppression or devastating clinical events) and on access to a full range of adequate medical services. These strategies require determination of which drug regimens are proven to be durably safe and effective. These approaches also require individualization of regimens to maximize the likelihood of long-term patient adherence and minimize the likelihood that drug toxicities or drug interactions will affect adversely the quality or duration of the patient's survival.

The treatment of HIV and AIDS can be organized into three major areas: (1) ART, (2) prophylaxis for opportunistic infections, and (3) treatment of HIV-related complications. These treatments need to be used with the goal of preventing HIV-related complications with as little disruption as possible for the patient's lifestyle and treating complications when they occur expeditiously, before they become debilitating or life-threatening.

Antiretroviral Therapy

ART should be initiated before HIV-infected patients develop sufficient immunologic decline to be at substantially increased risk for HIV-related complications. Although this general approach is a logical principle for therapy, it is difficult to put into practice. Many patients do not recognize the utility of being screened for HIV infection if they engage in high-risk behavior. Many continue to come to medical attention for the first time when they develop acute PCP or cryptococcal meningitis, and their CD4+ T-lymphocyte counts are already low (e.g., <200 cells/μL). For patients who do come to medical attention when their CD4+ T-lymphocyte counts are still relatively high, clinicians must realize that although the CD4+ T-lymphocyte count is a reliable indicator of susceptibility to opportunistic infections, susceptibility is a continuum: Although clinicians tend to think about certain CD4+ T-lymphocyte counts as thresholds at which susceptibility begins abruptly for specific opportunistic infections, these thresholds are only approximations. Waiting to start ART until the CD4+ T-lymphocyte count is 200 cells/µL does not guarantee that PCP will be prevented because 5% to 10% of cases of PCP occur at CD4+ T-lymphocyte counts greater than 200 cells/µL, and some cases occur at counts of 400 to 500 cells/µL. Other opportunistic processes, such as pneumococcal pneumonia, tuberculosis, Kaposi's sarcoma, and lymphoma, can occur with enhanced incidence at any CD4+ T-lymphocyte count. At every CD4+ T-lymphocyte count HIV-infected patients have some increased risk of opportunistic infection. The issue for the health care provider and the patient to address is the point at which susceptibility to infection increases sufficiently to warrant the toxicities, inconvenience, drug interactions, and cost of ART.

Susceptibility can be assessed by factors other than the CD4+ T-lymphocyte count alone: Plasma HIV viral load and a history of any HIV-related complication are factors that should be part of the equation determining susceptibility to immunologic progression and clinical complications. Other laboratory parameters, such as cytotoxic T-lymphocyte count, in vitro assays of lymphocyte function, and cytomegalovirus (CMV) plasma viral load, predict susceptibility to opportunistic infections, but it is less clear how to use these assays clinically in a practical manner.

ART is not likely to be effective unless the patient is committed and able to adhere to the ART regimen, and the health care practitioner is skilled at managing the regimen. Studies have shown that the likelihood of achieving a durable virologic response (i.e., plasma viral load below the limit of detection of the assay system used) depends on adherence. There is a direct relationship between missing doses of the ART regimen and the development of HIV drug resistance. If a patient is not fully invested in taking the drugs regularly or is unable to adhere because of psychiatric, social, economic, or medical issues, initiation of ART may not be indicated. Active drug and alcohol abuse, mental illness including depression, concomitant medical problems, lack of patient education, poor clinician-patient relationship, history of drug toxicities, and fear of drug toxicities are strong predictors of poor adherence. Directly observed therapy can be a successful approach to improving adherence, but this approach is not practical in most settings. The success of directly observed therapy programs emphasizes, however, the importance of regimen adherence to a durable virologic and immunologic response.

Successful management of HIV therapy also requires an experienced clinician. In the 1980s, there was considerable emphasis on "mainstreaming" HIV-infected patients (i.e., encouraging general internists, family practitioners, and a variety of other primary care providers to care for patients with HIV infection). Since that era, management has become dramatically more complex. Studies show that clinicians with experience are more likely to follow current standards and guidelines than clinicians with less experience. When feasible, patients should be managed by clinicians who have considerable experience and the capacity to keep abreast of the rapidly evolving field.

Principles of Antiretroviral Therapy

Most experts recommend that a major goal of ART should be complete inhibition of HIV replication. Inhibition of viral replication should prevent HIV-related immunologic decline and promote immune reconstitution. Proviral HIV integrates into host cells in a latent form, however. The absence of detectable plasma viral RNA does not indicate that no virus is present: Virus may be present in the plasma at levels below the ability of the laboratory assay to detect; virus may be present in body compartments other than blood, such as lymphoid tissue or the central nervous system; and provirus may be present in a variety of cells that can act as reservoirs for HIV, such as memory T cells. Long-term inability to detect plasma HIV RNA does not ensure eradication of the virus. This concept is supported by the observation that if ART is discontinued in treated patients who have had no detectable virus for several years, plasma HIV RNA levels virtually always return to pretherapy levels within a few weeks of stopping therapy.

HIV has an extremely high mutation rate. Resistance to therapeutic agents can emerge rapidly, especially when viral loads are high. Resistance to reverse-transcriptase inhibitors is associated with amino acid substitutions in the reverse-transcriptase enzyme. Resistance to protease inhibitors is associated with amino acid substitutions in the protease enzyme. Chemically important resistance occasionally can occur in untreated patients because of spontaneous mutations. For some drugs, a single mutation can produce clinically important resistance. For other drugs, significant resistance occurs only if several mutations occur. Most clinically important resistance occurs, however, as a result of selective pressure from ARTs. This resistance can be assessed by genotypic and phenotypic assays. This resistance can emerge rapidly; for nevirapine monotherapy, resistance can emerge within the first few weeks of therapy. Early experience with zidovudine showed that zidovudine resistance emerged during the initial 6 to 12 months of therapy. Current concepts of therapy emphasize the use of combination regimens employing at least one potent agent so that viral replication is minimized, and mutation rates conferring resistance occur infrequently.

Initiating Antiretroviral Therapy

Patients with acute HIV infection (i.e., patients in the process of seroconverting) and patients who have seroconverted in the prior 6 months should be considered for early therapy.∎ About 40 to 90% of acutely infected patients experience symptomatic illnesses, and if the patient or health care provider considers the possibility that the symptoms might have been related to high-risk behavior, HIV infection potentially can be identified by serologic and virologic assays. In theory, this therapy should reduce the viral load in lymphoid tissue during the period before effective host immune response and lead subsequently to lower viral loads and higher CD4+ T-lymphocyte counts. The long-term clinical benefit of treating acute or early HIV infection has not been shown conclusively, however, and the potential benefits of treating acute HIV infection must be weighed against the disadvantages of toxicities, cost, and inconvenience. Many clinicians would offer at least 2 to 6 months of this therapy in an effort to reduce viral replication in lymphoid tissue and produce a lower plasma HIV viral load.

Chronically infected patients with CD4+ T-lymphocyte counts less than 200 cells/µL have been shown by clinical end point studies to benefit from ART in terms of longer disease-free survival.∎ For patients with CD4+ T-lymphocyte counts less than 200 cells/µL and for patients with symptomatic HIV-related disease (i.e., patients who have an opportunistic infection or neoplasm or some other disease entity related to HIV infection) and CD4+ T-lymphocyte counts greater than 200 cells/µL, there is relatively uniform consensus that ART is indicated.

For patients with CD4+ T-lymphocyte counts greater than 200 cells/µL, there are no clinical end point studies to show conclusively when therapy should be initiated. Observational studies provide some important clues, however. Figure 421–1 shows the relationship between CD4+ T-lymphocyte count and plasma HIV viral load during a 3-year follow-up of untreated patients in the Multicenter AIDS Cohort Study. This figure indicates that CD4+ T-lymphocyte count and plasma HIV viral load influence the 3-year risk of progression to AIDS. These data by themselves do not prove which patients would respond to therapy or which patients would respond best. These data do indicate that for some patients (e.g., patients with CD4+ T-lymphocyte counts >350 cells/µL or patients with plasma viral loads <3000 copies/µL), the risk of progression is so low that therapy logically could be withheld until the risk was substantially higher, such as when the CD4+ T lymphocyte count had fallen substantially (e.g., <200 cells/µL) or the plasma HIV viral load had risen substantially (e.g., >55,000 copies/µL).

Observational data from ART-treated patients provide important information related to the decision when to initiate therapy. An analysis of data from 13 European and North American studies assessed the risk of progression in drug-naive patients who were started on ART and who had plasma HIV viral loads less than 100,000 copies/µL. The 3-year probability of death or AIDS-defining disease was 15.8% for patients who initiated therapy when the CD4+ T-lymphocyte count was 0 to 49 cells/µL, 12.5% if the count was 50 to 99 cells/µL, 9.3% if the count was 100 to 199 cells/µL, 4.7% if the count was 200 to 349 cells/µL, and 3.4% if the count was 350 cells/µL or higher. These data

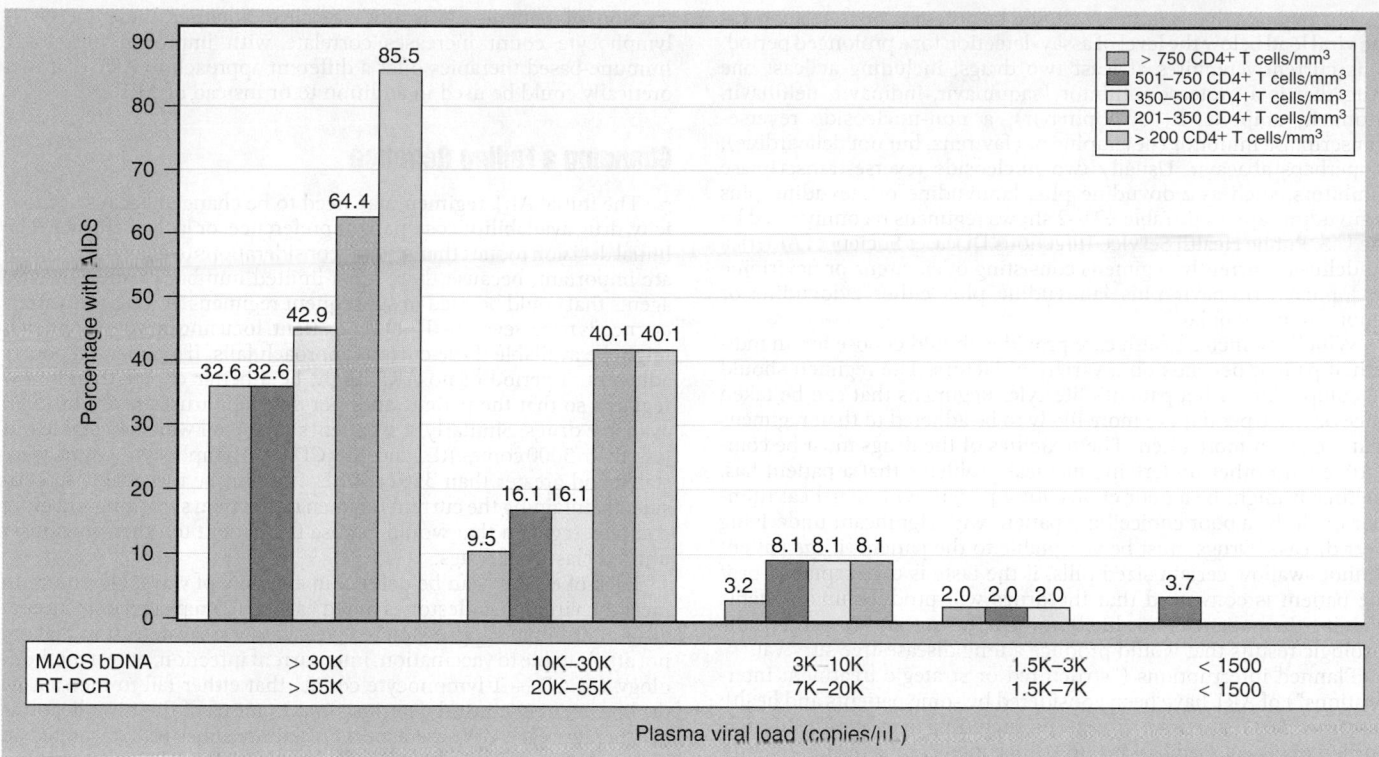

FIGURE 421–1 • Likelihood of developing AIDS within 3 years.

support the proposition that therapy should be initiated before the CD4+ T-cell count decreases to less than 200 cell/μL. These data do not show an escalating benefit, however, to initiating therapy at CD4+ T-lymphocyte counts that are incrementally higher than 200 cells/μL. There is no consensus regarding the CD4+ T-cell count at which ART should be initiated, as long as ART is started before the CD4+ T-lymphocyte count decreases to less than 200 cells/μL. Many experts would initiate therapy when the CD4+ T-lymphocyte count falls below 350 cells/μL.

Data from the same European/North American data analysis also showed that there is a dramatic increase in risk of disease progression among patients with a viral load greater than 100,000 copies/μL, regardless of the CD4+ lymphocyte count. Many experts would recommend that ART be initiated at viral loads greater than 55,000 copies/μL, especially for patients with CD4+ T-lymphocyte counts less than 350 cells/μL. The recommendations of the U.S. Public Health Service/Infectious Disease Society of American guidelines for HIV-infected adults and adolescents regarding when to initiate antiretroviral therapy are shown in Table 421–1.

Criteria for Assessing Efficacy of Regimen

From a clinical perspective, effective therapy should durably prevent HIV-related complications. From a virologic perspective, effective therapy is expected to reduce the plasma HIV viral load by 0.5 to 0.75 logs at week 4 of therapy and by 1 log at week 8; the viral load should be below the level of assay detection at 4 to 6 months. Concurrently, there should be a substantial rise in the CD4+ T-lymphocyte count, the magnitude of which depends on the baseline CD4+ T-lymphocyte count and the baseline viral load.

What Antiretroviral Regimen Should Be Initiated

There are currently 16 unique antiretroviral drugs approved for sale in the United States by the U.S. Food and Drug Administration. Some of these drugs are available in combination formulations in the United States (e.g., zidovudine plus lamivudine, zidovudine plus lamivudine plus abacavir, and lopinavir plus ritonavir). Some of the drugs also are available in liquid formulations.

Table 421–1 • INDICATIONS FOR THE INITIATION OF ANTIRETROVIRAL THERAPY IN THE CHRONICALLY HIV-1 INFECTED PATIENT

CLINICAL CATEGORY	CD4+ T-CELL COUNT	PLASMA HIV RNA	RECOMMENDATION
Symptomatic (AIDS, severe symptoms)	Any value	Any value	Treat
Asymptomatic, AIDS	CD4+ T cells <200/mm³	Any value	Treat
Asymptomatic	CD4+ T cells >200/mm³ but <350/mm³	Any value	Treatment generally should be offered, although controversy exists
Asymptomatic	CD4+ T cells >350/mm³	>55,000 (by bDNA or RT-PCR)	Some experts would recommend initiating therapy, recognizing that the 3-year risk of developing AIDS in untreated patients is >30%, and some would defer therapy and monitor CD4+ T-cell counts more frequently
Asymptomatic	CD4+ T cells >350/mm³	<55,000 (by bDNA or RT-PCR)	Many experts would defer therapy and observe, recognizing that the 3-year risk of developing AIDS in untreated patients is <15%

From United States Public Health Service/Infectious Disease Society of America: Guidelines for the use of antiretroviral agents in HIV-infected adults and adolescents. Recommendations of the Panel on Clinical Practices for the Treatment of HIV. AIDSINFO.nih.gov/guidelines

The regimen that is initiated should be potent enough to suppress the viral load below the level of assay detection for a prolonged period. This currently requires at least two drugs, including at least one drug that is a protease inhibitor (saquinavir, indinavir, nelfinavir, ritonavir, amprenavir, or lopinavir), a non-nucleoside reverse-transcriptase inhibitor (nevirapine or efavirenz, but not delavirdine), or perhaps abacavir. Usually two nucleoside reverse-transcriptase inhibitors, such as zidovudine plus lamivudine or stavudine plus lamivudine, are used. Table 421–2 shows regimens recommended by the U.S. Public Health Service/Infectious Diseases Society of America guidelines. Currently, regimens consisting of efavirenz or neviripine or lopinavir-ritonavir plus lamivudine plus either zidovudine or tenofovir are popular.

Which regimen a health care provider should choose for an individual patient depends on a variety of factors. The regimen should be compatible with a patient's lifestyle: Regimens that can be taken once or twice per day are more likely to be adhered to than regimens that are taken more often. The toxicities of the drugs must be compatible with other underlying medical problems that a patient has: Nelfinavir might be a poor choice for a patient with diarrhea; ritonavir might be a poor choice for a patient with significant underlying liver disease. Drugs must be acceptable to the patient; if the patient cannot swallow certain sized pills, if the taste is unacceptable, or if the patient is convinced that the drugs will produce unacceptable toxicity, the patient is not likely to be adherent and to achieve the virologic results that would produce a long disease-free survival.

Planned interruptions ("structured or strategic treatment interruptions") of ART have been considered by some patients and health care providers for a variety of reasons, including to reduce the lifestyle burden of taking medications, to reduce medication-related toxicity, to reduce costs, and to improve immune control of HIV infection. These approaches have not yet been shown to be effective or safe. When ART is stopped, the HIV viral load for virtually all patients returns to their pretherapy values within several weeks, and this may result in irreversible loss of CD4+ T lymphocytes.

Immune-based therapies have been used in attempts to augment immunity against HIV-associated infections and tumors. Interleukin-2, given subcutaneously 5 days every 2 months for several cycles, has been shown to increase CD4+ T-lymphocyte counts in a substantial

fraction of patients. It is not yet clear whether these CD4+ T-lymphocyte count increases correlate with improved prognosis. Immune-based therapies offer a different approach to ART that theoretically could be used in addition to or instead of ART.

Changing a Failing Regimen

The initial ART regimen may need to be changed because of toxicity, drug availability, cost, patient preference, or lack of efficacy. The initial decision to start therapy and considerations to change a regimen are important, because there are a limited number of antiretroviral agents that could be used in subsequent regimens. A long-term strategy needs to be developed for each patient, focusing on what approach might be available if the current approach fails. If a patient is poorly adherent, a period of no ART might be a better choice than a new regimen so that the patient does not develop viruses resistant to all available drugs. Similarly, if a patient's viral load were detectable but less than 5000 copies/µL, and the CD4+ T-lymphocyte count were stable and greater than 350 cells/µL, it might be reasonable to consider maintaining the current regimen rather than switching to a more complex regimen that would expose the patient to other previously untried classes of drugs.

Lack of efficacy can be defined in a variety of ways: (1) failure to meet the virologic milestones noted earlier, (2) repeated detection of virus after initial suppression to levels below assay detection that are not attributable to vaccination, intercurrent infection, or test methodology, (3) CD4+ T-lymphocyte counts that either fail to increase or decline, and (4) clinical deterioration. In terms of their implications for therapy, each of these aspects of failure must be interpreted in context. A patient with a high initial viral load (e.g., >1 million copies/µL) whose viral loads are declining might be recommended to remain on a regimen if the viral load still was declining at 6 months or was stable at a low level. Similarly a patient who started a regimen when the CD4+ T-lymphocyte count was low and who developed an opportunistic infection at a time when the HIV viral load was below the level of assay detection might be unlikely to benefit from a different ART regimen. Decisions about changing therapies also must consider what treatment options are feasible considering prior drug exposure, viral resistance, drug tolerability, and drug availability.

There are many reasons for efficacy failure. Poor patient adherence is probably the most common cause, and health care practitioners may find it especially difficult to identify this factor. Altered drug pharmacokinetics resulting from abnormal absorption or metabolism of the drug also may be a factor. Drug interactions owing to licensed drugs or "alternative" medicines may be relevant. The patient may have acquired a drug-resistant virus when initially infected, or the patient's virus may have become resistant during therapy. These causes of regimen failure must be investigated carefully to maximize the likelihood that the next regimen will succeed.

Changes in therapy mandated by lack of regimen efficacy should be guided by the results of resistance testing. The relative merits of genotypic and phenotypic assays have not been well delineated, however, and there are no well-validated algorithms for how to interpret these tests. Careful consideration should be given to past history regarding efficacy and tolerability of specific drugs and the results of resistance. Enfuvirtide, a fusion inhibitor, can provide significant benefit to patients who have done poorly despite multiple antiviral drugs.

Safety of Antiretroviral Regimens

As with any medication, each antiretroviral agent is associated with toxicities. Some are class specific, such as mitochondrial toxicities with nucleoside analogues, or rash or central nervous system dysfunction with non-nucleoside reverse-transcriptase inhibitors. Others are drug specific, such as stone formation and interstitial nephritis with indinavir, diarrhea with nelfinavir, or a unique hypersensitivity reaction with abacavir. The occurrence of these toxicities is usually not predictable. A specific HLA genotype has been associated with abacavir hypersensitivity responses, however, for the first time showing that the likelihood of a particular toxicity may be predicted.

Certain toxicities deserve special mention. Chronic compensated hyperlactemia occurs during treatment with nucleoside and nucleotide reverse-transcriptase inhibitors. In a few cases (about 1.3 cases per

Table 421–2 • RECOMMENDED ANTIRETROVIRAL AGENTS FOR INITIAL TREATMENT OF ESTABLISHED HIV INFECTION

	COLUMN A	COLUMN B
STRONGLY RECOMMENDED	Efavirenz	Didanosine + lamivudine
	Indinavir	Stavudine + didanosine
	Nelfinavir	Stavudine + lamivudine
	Ritonavir + indinavir	Zidovudine + didanosine
	Ritonavir + lopinavir	
	Ritonavir + saquinavir (SGC or HGC)	Zidovudine + lamivudine
RECOMMENDED AS ALTERNATIVES	Abacavir	Zidovudine + zalcitabine
	Amprenavir	
	Delavirdine	
	Nelfinavir + saquinavir-SGC	
	Nevirapine	
	Ritonavir	
	Saquinavir-SGC	
NO RECOMMENDATION: INSUFFICIENT DATA	Hydroxyurea in combination with antiretroviral drugs	
	Ritonavir + amprenavir	
	Ritonavir + nelfinavir	
	Tenofovir	
NOT RECOMMENDED: SHOULD NOT BE OFFERED	All monotherapies, whether from column A or B	Stavudine + zidovudine
		Zalcitabine + didanosine
	Saquinavir-HGC	Zalcitabine + lamivudine
		Zalcitabine + stavudine

From United States Public Health Service/Infectious Disease Society of America: Guidelines for the use of antiretroviral agents in HIV-infected adults and adolescents. Recommendations of the Panel on Clinical Practices for the Treatment of HIV. AIDSINFO.nih.gov/guidelines

1000 person-years of nucleoside reverse-transcriptase inhibitor exposure), decompensated lactic acidosis accompanied by hepatic steatosis and hepatomegaly can occur and is associated with high mortality. Risk factors for this potentially fatal syndrome include female gender, obesity, prolonged use of nucleosides, late-stage pregnancy or postpartum period, and the use of didanosine and stavudine combination therapy during pregnancy. The lactic acidosis syndrome presents with nonspecific gastrointestinal symptoms, including nausea, abdominal pain, vomiting, diarrhea, weakness, myalgias, paresthesias, and hepatomegaly. Hepatic enzymes may be normal or only slightly elevated. Elevated lactate levels may be associated with an anion gap, elevated creatine phosphokinase and lactate dehydrogenase, and an enlarged fatty liver on computed tomography scan. Therapy consists of discontinuing all nucleoside analogue drugs. Bicarbonate infusions and hemodialysis may be helpful. It is not clear how safe it is to rechallenge the patient with any nucleoside drug.

Mitochondrial dysfunction also may be associated with peripheral neuropathy, myocardiopathy, myopathy, pancreatitis, and lipodystrophy. It is often difficult to be certain that these clinical entities (other than lipodystrophy) are related to drug toxicity rather than some other process, including HIV itself or an opportunistic infection.

HIV infection and ARTs have been associated with fat distribution abnormalities. In more recent years, these syndromes have seemed to become more common, suggesting a causal relationship to the ART regimens more recently being used. These lipodystrophy syndromes are observed in a substantial fraction of patients receiving ART (6 to 80%). The wide range of incidence estimates reflects the fact that there is no uniform definition for this syndrome. Patients develop a range of fat redistribution syndromes, including fat accumulation in the abdomen, breasts, and dorsocervical fat pad. Facial wasting and limb wasting are also part of this syndrome. It is unknown whether these syndromes are all part of the same pathologic process, or whether they represent different entities. It also is not clear whether they are linked specifically to protease inhibitors. These syndromes have been reported with antiretroviral drugs other than the protease inhibitors and with patients who were antiretroviral drug naive. When fat maldistribution occurs, it can be disfiguring and distressing. There is no conclusive evidence that switching to another drug regimen or stopping ART can reverse the fat maldistribution, although switching may improve serum cholesterol and triglyceride levels.

Before the era of ART, HIV infection was associated with reduced high density lipoprotein (HDL) cholesterol and elevated triglycerides. Certain protease inhibitors are associated with elevation in total serum cholesterol and fasting triglycerides. There is growing concern (but no conclusive documentation yet) that these atherogenic lipid profiles are contributing to accelerated atherosclerosis and that clinically important cardiovascular complications will occur with increased frequency. Most clinicians monitor and treat these lipid abnormalities as they would manage abnormalities in a non–HIV-infected patient. When implementing lipid management programs, however, careful consideration must be given to drug interactions, especially interactions between protease inhibitors and β-hydroxy-β–methylglutaryl-CoA reductase inhibitors (statins). Replacing a protease inhibitor with either abacavir or a non-nucleoside reverse-transcriptase inhibitor may be effective in reducing the lipid elevations.

Hepatotoxicity is an important complication of ART. Serum transaminase elevations have been reported with all licensed protease inhibitors and non-nucleoside reverse-transcriptase inhibitors, and have been associated with nucleoside agents. In some patients, the transaminase elevations are mild and unassociated with symptoms. In other cases, symptomatic hepatitis or associated hepatic steatosis with or without lactic acidosis requires cessation of the drug. Among the non-nucleoside reverse-transcriptase inhibitors, nevirapine has the greatest potential for causing symptomatic hepatitis. Manifestations often include fever, rash, and eosinophilia, and often occur within 12 weeks of initiating therapy. Protease inhibitor–associated liver enzyme abnormalities can occur at any juncture during therapy. Ritonavir-containing regimens are particularly likely to be associated with hepatic toxicities. Hepatitis C, hepatitis B, alcohol, elevated baseline liver function tests, and other hepatotoxic drugs are risk factors for developing protease inhibitor–associated liver toxicity.

Protease inhibitor–associated hyperglycemia can manifest as new-onset diabetes mellitus, or can exacerbate preexisting diabetes. Some patients can become difficult to manage and develop diabetic ketoacidosis. Although hyperglycemic syndromes have been associated strongly with protease inhibitors, they can occur independent of protease inhibitor therapy as well.

Decreased bone mineral density and avascular necrosis are complications of HIV infection that may be associated with ART. A causal link has not been established conclusively. Osteopenia, osteoporosis, and avascular necrosis of the hip (and other joints) are reported with increasing frequency, however, suggesting an etiologic association. How these complications can be prevented or optimal methods of management can be designed has not been established.

Prevention of Opportunistic Infections

Early during the AIDS epidemic, it became clear that a strategy of treating opportunistic infections as they occurred had many disadvantages. Patients experienced discomfort, expense, and inconvenience; damage to organs such as the lungs, brain, or eye was often not completely reversible; the opportunistic infection often accelerated the progression of the HIV disease; and many of the opportunistic infections were associated with substantial mortality. Chemoprophylaxis was an attractive strategy because the most common life-threatening opportunistic infection associated with HIV, PCP, was being successfully prevented in oncology patients, and a similar strategy seemed feasible in patients with HIV infection. Because the period of susceptibility to opportunistic infections in patients with HIV infection could be measured by CD4+ T-lymphocyte counts, a strategy of chemoprophylaxis seemed particularly attractive for patients whose immunity could not be restored with ARTs or immunomodulating therapies.

Chemoprophylaxis regimens are available for most treatable HIV-associated opportunistic infections. Tables 421–3 and 421–4 summarize regimens that are recommended for primary and secondary chemoprophylaxis. Table 421–5 summarizes the CD4+ T-lymphocyte counts at which chemoprophylaxis should be used. Chemoprophylaxis for various pathogens should be started when the CD4+ T-lymphocyte count declines to specific levels (depending on the pathogen) to prevent an initial episode of disease (primary prophylaxis). This prophylaxis can be stopped if immunity is augmented by ART but must be restarted if immunity again declines to designated thresholds. Similarly, if a patient develops an opportunistic infection, suppressive therapy (secondary prophylaxis) is indicated for life for most opportunistic infections unless immunity is restored by ART.

The regimens recommended in Tables 421–3 and 421–4 have been shown to prevent primary and subsequent occurrences of disease. The use of these regimens improves patient survival in several instances (PCP, *M. avium* complex disease, and *M. tuberculosis*) and decreases patient morbidity. Several caveats about the use of chemoprophylaxis are worth noting, however. First, some opportunistic infections occur at CD4+ T-lymphocyte counts above the recommended thresholds for starting chemoprophylaxis. Of PCP cases, 5 to 10% occur at CD4+ T-lymphocyte counts greater than 200 cells/μL. In some instances, clinical information, such as the development of oral candidiasis or substantial weight loss, may provide clues that the patient is clinically more immunosuppressed than the laboratory parameters would predict. A high viral load (e.g., >100,000 copies/μL) also may suggest that earlier institution of chemoprophylaxis is warranted. Second, patients may be unable to tolerate certain chemoprophylactic agents. TMP-SMX often is associated with intractable pruritus or rash, and cannot be used by many patients with HIV infection. Third, no chemoprophylactic regimen is completely effective. Some regimens fail because of poor adherence, but some fail because of poor host immune response or pathogen resistance. Prescribing a chemoprophylactic regimen does not guarantee that a patient will never develop the targeted disease. Finally, a decision to use a chemoprophylactic agent depends on the balance between its benefit in terms of efficacy and its disadvantages in terms of toxicities, inconvenience, drug interactions, ecologic effects (e.g., effects on producing resistance among targeted and bystander organisms) and cost. Some effective drugs, such as fluconazole for *Candida* and *Cryptococcus* and oral ganciclovir or valganciclovir for CMV, have not been recommended because their disadvantages were judged to outweigh the benefits.

TMP-SMX is the agent of choice for prevention of PCP. TMP-SMX should be started when the CD4+ T-lymphocyte count decreases to 200 cells/μL, when the patient develops oral candidiasis (regardless of CD4+ T-cell count), or when the patient has had a prior episode of PCP. Prophylaxis should be continued as long as the CD4+

HIV and AIDS

Table 421–3 • **PROPHYLAXIS TO PREVENT FIRST EPISODE OF OPPORTUNISTIC DISEASE IN ADULTS AND ADOLESCENTS INFECTED WITH HIV**

PATHOGEN	Indication	PREVENTIVE REGIMENS	
		First Choice	Alternatives
STRONGLY RECOMMENDED AS STANDARD OF CARE			
Pneumocystis jiroveci	CD4+ count <200/μL or oropharyngeal candidiasis	Trimethoprim-sulfamethoxazole (TMP-SMX), 1 DS PO qd, or TMP-SMX, 1 SS PO qd	Dapsone, 50 mg PO bid or 100 mg PO qd; dapsone, 50 mg PO qd plus pyrimethamine, 50 mg PO weekly plus leucovorin 25 mg PO weekly; dapsone 200 mg PO plus pyrimethamine, 75 mg PO plus leucovorin, 25 mg PO weekly; aerosolized pentamidine, 300 mg every month via Respirgard II nebulizer; atovaquone, 1500 mg PO qd; TMP-SMX, 1 DS PO 3 times a week
Mycobacterium tuberculosis Isoniazid–sensitive	Tuberculin skin test reaction (5 mm or prior positive tuberculin skin test result without treatment or contact with case of active tuberculosis regardless of tuberculin skin test result	Isoniazid, 300 mg PO plus pyridoxine, 50 mg PO qd × 9 mo or isoniazid, 900 mg PO plus pyridoxine, 100 mg PO twice a week × 9 mo	Rifampin, 600 mg PO qd × 4 mo or rifabutin, 300 mg PO qd × 4 mo Pyrazinamide, 15-20 mg PO qd × 2 mo plus either rifampin, 600 mg PO qd × 2 mo or rifabutin, 300 mg PO qd × 2 mo
Isoniazid–resistant	Same as above; high probability of exposure to isoniazid-resistant tuberculosis	Rifampin, 600 mg PO or rifabutin, 300 mg PO qd × 4 mo	Pyrazinamide, 15-20 mg/kg PO qd plus either rifampin, 600 mg PO or rifabutin, 300 mg PO qd × 2 mo
Multidrug–(isoniazid and rifampin) resistant	Same as above; high probability of exposure to multidrug-resistant tuberculosis	Choice of drugs requires consultation with public health authorities. Depends on susceptibility of isolate from source patient	—
Toxoplasma gondii	IgG antibody to *Toxoplasma* and CD4+ count <100/μL	TMP-SMX, 1 DS PO qd	TMP-SMX, 1 SS PO qd; dapsone, 50 mg PO qd plus pyrimethamine, 50 mg PO weekly plus leucovorin, 25 mg PO weekly; dapsone, 200 mg PO plus pyrimethamine, 75 mg PO plus leucovorin, 25 mg PO weekly; atovaquone, 1500 mg PO qd with or without pyrimethamine, 25 mg PO qd plus leucovorin, 10 mg PO qd
Mycobacterium avium complex	CD4+ count <50/μL	Azithromycin, 1200 mg PO weekly or clarithromycin, 500 mg PO bid	Rifabutin, 300 mg PO qd azithromycin, 1200 mg PO weekly plus rifabutin, 300 mg PO qd
Varicella-zoster virus (VZV)	Significant exposure to chickenpox or shingles for patients who have no history of either condition or, if available, negative antibody to VZV	Varicella-zoster immune globulin (VZIG), 5 vials (1.25 mL each) IM, administered ≤96 hr after exposure, ideally within 48 hr	
GENERALLY RECOMMENDED			
Streptococcus pneumoniae	CD4+ count >200/μL	23-valent polysaccharide vaccine, 0.5 mL IM	None
Hepatitis B virus	All susceptible (anti-HBs-negative) patients	Hepatitis B vaccine, 3 doses	None
Influenza virus	All patients (annually, before influenza season)	Inactivated trivalent influenza virus vaccine: one annual dose (0.5 mL) IM	Oseltamivir, 75 mg PO qd (influenza A or B); rimantadine, 100 mg PO bid, or amantadine, 100 mg PO bid (influenza A only)
Hepatitis A virus (HAV)	All susceptible (anti-HAV-negative) patients at increased risk for HAV infection (e.g., illicit drug users, men who have sex with men, hemophiliacs) or with chronic liver disease, including chronic hepatitis B or hepatitis C	HAV vaccine: 2 doses	None
EVIDENCE FOR EFFICACY BUT NOT ROUTINELY INDICATED			
Bacteria	Neutropenia	Granulocyte colony-stimulating factor, 5–10 μg/kg SC qd × 2–4 wk or granulocyte-macrophage colony-stimulating factor, 250 μg/m² SC/IV × 2–4 wk	None
Cryptococcus neoformans	CD4+ count <50/μL	Fluconazole, 100–200 mg PO qd	Itraconazole capsule, 200 mg PO qd
Histoplasma capsulatum	CD4+ count <100/μL, endemic geographic area	Itraconazole capsule, 200 mg PO qd	None
Cytomegalovirus	CD4+ count <50/μL and cytomegalovirus antibody positivity	Oral ganciclovir, 1 g PO tid	None

Table 421-4 • PROPHYLAXIS TO PREVENT RECURRENCE OF OPPORTUNISTIC DISEASE (AFTER CHEMOTHERAPY FOR ACUTE DISEASE) IN ADULTS AND ADOLESCENTS INFECTED WITH HIV

PATHOGEN	Indication	First Choice	Alternatives
RECOMMENDED AS STANDARD OF CARE			
Pneumocystis jiroveci	Prior *P. jiroveci* pneumonia	Trimethoprim-sulfamethoxazole (TMP-SMX), 1 DS PO qd; TMP-SMX 1 SS PO qd	Dapsone, 50 mg PO bid or 100 mg PO qd; dapsone, 50 mg PO qd plus pyrimethamine, 50 mg PO weekly plus leucovorin, 25 mg PO weekly; dapsone 200 mg PO plus pyrimethamine, 75 mg PO plus leucovorin, 25 mg PO weekly; aerosolized pentamidine, 300 mg every month via Respirgard II nebulizer; atovaquone, 1500 mg PO qd; TMP-SMX, 1 DS PO 3 times a week
Toxoplasma gondii	Prior toxoplasmic encephalitis	Sulfadiazine, 500–1000 mg PO qid plus pyrimethamine, 25–50 mg PO qd plus leucovorin, 10–25 mg PO qd	Clindamycin, 300–450 mg PO q 6–8 hr plus pyrimethamine, 25–50 mg PO qd plus leucovorin, 10–25 mg PO qd; atovaquone, 750 mg PO q 6–12 hr with or without pyrimethamine, 25 mg PO qd plus leucovorin, 10 mg PO qd
Mycobacterium avium complex	Documented disseminated disease	Clarithromycin, 500 mg PO bid plus ethambutol, 15 mg/kg PO qd; with or without rifabutin, 300 mg PO qd	Azithromycin, 500 mg PO qd plus ethambutol, 15 mg/kg PO qd; with or without rifabutin, 300 mg PO qd
Cytomegalovirus	Prior end-organ disease	Ganciclovir, 5–6 mg/kg/day IV 5–7 days/wk or 1000 mg PO tid; or foscarnet, 90–120 mg/kg IV qd; or (for retinitis) ganciclovir sustained-release implant q 6–9 mo plus ganciclovir, 1.0–1.5 g PO tid	Cidofovir, 5 mg/kg IV every other week with probenecid, 2 g PO 3 hr before the dose followed by 1 g PO 2 hr after the dose, and 1 g PO 8 hr after the dose (total of 4 g). Fomivirsen 1 vial (330 µg) injected into the vitreous, then repeated every 2–4 wk; valganciclovir 900 mg PO qd
Cryptococcus neoformans	Documented disease	Fluconazole, 200 mg PO qd	Amphotericin B, 0.6–1.0 mg/kg IV 1–3 times a week itraconazole, 200 mg capsule PO qd
Histoplasma capsulatum	Documented disease	Itraconazole capsule, 200 mg PO bid	Amphotericin B, 1.0 mg/kg IV weekly
Coccidioides immitis	Documented disease	Fluconazole, 400 mg PO qd	Amphotericin B, 1.0 mg/kg IV weekly; itraconazole, 200 mg capsule PO bid
Salmonella (non-*typhi*)	Bacteremia	Ciprofloxacin, 500 mg PO bid for several months	Antibiotic chemoprophylaxis with another active agent
RECOMMENDED ONLY IF SUBSEQUENT EPISODES ARE FREQUENT OR SEVERE			
Herpes simplex virus	Frequent/severe recurrences	Acyclovir, 200 mg PO tid or 400 mg PO bid	Valacyclovir, 500 mg PO bid

T-lymphocyte count remains less than 200 cells/µL. Several regimens of TMP-SMX are effective: One double-strength tablet per day, one single-strength tablet per day, or one double-strength tablet three times weekly all are recommended. The daily regimens seem to be more effective than the three-times-per-week regimen. TMP-SMX can be associated with a variety of toxicities, including rash, fever, pruritus, nausea, vomiting, nephritis, hyperkalemia, and aseptic meningitis. Rash occurs with an unusually high frequency in HIV-infected patients who take TMP-SMX for reasons that have not been well delineated. Lower dose regimens (e.g., a single-strength rather than a double-strength tablet or three times weekly rather than daily) seem to be better tolerated. Gradual dose escalation also may improve tolerability of TMP-SMX prophylaxis. Evidence of enzyme mutations in *Pneumocystis,* which likely confer sulfonamide resistance, raise the ominous possibility that this useful prophylactic and therapeutic agent may lose the impressive efficacy it has had to date.

Alternatives to TMP-SMX include dapsone, dapsone-pyrimethamine, sulfadiazine-pyrimethamine, atovaquone, and aerosolized pentamidine. These regimens are not as effective as TMP-SMX for preventing PCP. In addition, TMP-SMX provides protection against toxoplasmosis, bacterial pneumonias, and enteric infections. None of the alternative regimens provides protection against all of these pathogens, and all have associated toxicities.

Clarithromycin or azithromycin is the chemoprophylactic agent of choice for *M. avium* complex for HIV-infected patients with CD4+ T-lymphocyte counts less than 50 cells/µL. Each of these agents is more effective than placebo, and each is preferred over rifabutin because the latter is less effective and is associated with multiple complex drug interactions. Clarithromycin and azithromycin provide additional protection against bacterial pneumonia. These drugs are relatively well tolerated; however, the weekly regimen of azithromycin can be associated with considerable nausea. Azithromycin causes fewer

drug interactions than does clarithromycin and is preferred by some clinicians when multiple other drugs metabolized by the cytochrome P-450 system are being used.

Prophylaxis for *M. tuberculosis* is an important aspect of management of HIV-infected patients, especially in communities where tuberculosis is common. Purified protein derivative screening for all patients with newly diagnosed HIV and regular screening thereafter are important for identifying subclinically infected patients, because HIV-infected individuals have such a high likelihood of reactivating latent tuberculosis. Latently infected patients should be treated with one of the recommended regimens.

Immunization of patients with pneumococcal vaccine also seems to be important for preventing upper and lower respiratory disease. Immunization with pneumococcal vaccine is probably most effective when the CD4+ T-lymphocyte count is greater than 200 cells/µL. If patients received their initial immunization when their CD4+ T-lymphocyte count was less than 200 cells/µL, it is logical to reimmunize them if their counts subsequently rise. Immunization of patients with hepatitis A and hepatitis B vaccines is also logical, especially if patients are at high risk of acquiring such infections and if they have concomitant hepatitis C.

Primary chemoprophylaxis for fungal or herpesvirus diseases is not currently recommended. Primary prophylaxis may be effective, but the benefits currently are thought to be outweighed by the effects of prophylaxis on pathogen resistance and by the toxicities and costs of drugs, which target diseases that are usually readily treatable.

Treatment of Acute Opportunistic Infections

Minimizing the effect of acute opportunistic infections on patient lifestyle and survival depends on prompt recognition of such diseases

Table 421–5 • CRITERIA FOR STARTING, DISCONTINUING, AND RESTARTING OPPORTUNISTIC INFECTION PROPHYLAXIS FOR ADULTS WITH HIV INFECTION

OPPORTUNISTIC ILLNESS	CRITERIA FOR INITIATING PRIMARY PROPHYLAXIS	CRITERIA FOR DISCONTINUING PRIMARY PROPHYLAXIS	CRITERIA FOR RESTARTING PRIMARY PROPHYLAXIS	CRITERIA FOR INITIATING SECONDARY PROPHYLAXIS	CRITERIA FOR DISCONTINUING SECONDARY PROPHYLAXIS	CRITERIA FOR RESTARTING SECONDARY PROPHYLAXIS
Pneumocystis jiroveci pneumonia	CD4+ <200 cells/μL or oropharyngeal candidiasis	CD4+ >200 cells/μL for 3 mo	CD4+ <200 cells/μL	Prior *P. jiroveci* pneumonia	CD4+ >200 cells/μL for 3 mo	CD4+ <200 cells/μL
Toxoplasmosis	IgG antibody to *Toxoplasma* and CD4+ <100 cells/μL	CD4+ >200 cells/μL for 3 mo	CD4+ <100–200 cell/μL	Prior toxoplasmic encephalitis	CD4+ >200 cells/μL sustained (e.g., >6 mo) and completed initial therapy and asymptomatic for *Toxoplasma*	CD4+ <200 cells/μL
Disseminated *Mycobacterium avium* complex (MAC)	CD4+ <50 cells/μL	CD4+ >100 cells/μL for 3 mo	CD4+ <50–100 cells/μL	Documented disseminated disease	CD4+ >100 cells/μL sustained (e.g., >6 mo) and completed 12 mo Of MAC therapy and asymptomatic for MAC	CD4+ <100 cells/μL
Cryptococcosis	None	Not applicable	Not applicable	Documented disease	CD4+ >100–200 cells/μL sustained (e.g., >6 mo) and completed initial therapy and asymptomatic for cryptococcosis	CD4+ <100–200 cells/μL
Histoplasmosis	None	Not applicable	Not applicable	Documented disease	No criteria recommended for stopping	Not applicable
Coccidioidomycosis	None	Not applicable	Not applicable	Documented disease	No criteria recommended for stopping	Not applicable
Cytomegalovirus retinitis	None	Not applicable	Not applicable	Documented end-organ disease	CD4+ >100–150 cells/μL sustained (e.g., >6 mo) and no evidence of active disease with regular ophthalmic examination	CD4+ <100–150 cells/μL

and prompt institution of appropriate therapy. Patients and health care providers need to be familiar with the presentations of HIV-associated opportunistic infections and neoplasms so that diseases can be treated early, before manifestations are severe.

The treatment of specific opportunistic infections is detailed in Chapters 414–418. The manifestations of HIV-related opportunistic infections often differ from manifestations in other patient populations. Similarly, therapy may differ as well. Certain drugs may not be tolerated as well by HIV-infected patients as by other immunosuppressed patients; the unusually high incidence of rash associated with TMP-SMX is a good example of this phenomenon. Drug regimens need to be continued for longer periods: unless the immune competence can be augmented substantially by ART, the likelihood of recurrence for most HIV-associated infections is so high that lifelong suppressive or maintenance therapy (e.g., secondary prophylaxis) must be maintained. Drug-drug interactions are often important considerations, especially if patients are receiving ART; rifampin, rifabutin, and fluconazole, are examples of drugs that may have clinically important drug interactions with antiretroviral agents that could require dose modifications of either the antiretroviral agent or the drug used to treat the opportunistic infection. HIV-infected patients often have multiple concurrent opportunistic infections. Patients often are being treated or are receiving prophylaxis for multiple infections simultaneously, leading to potential additive toxicities or drug interactions. Lastly, HIV-infected patients are administered multiple courses of antimicrobial agents, often for prolonged periods. These patients have the potential to develop drug-resistant pathogens themselves, and they are exposed to drug-resistant pathogens in clinics, hospitals, and other group settings. They are at high risk for developing disease caused by drug-resistant pathogens, such as *M. tuberculosis*, *P. jiroveci*, *Streptococcus pneumoniae*, and *Candida*.

Immune Reconstitution Syndromes

When patients with HIV infection initiate ART, their augmented immune response may produce clinical syndromes that seem to represent immunologic or inflammatory reactions rather than disease progression owing to proliferating organisms. Within days, weeks, or months after ART is started, and sometimes before the CD4+ T-lymphocyte count has risen, the patient may manifest such a syndrome. These syndromes may involve pathogens not previously recognized; patients who initiate ART when the CD4+ T-lymphocyte count is less than 50 copies/μL may present with lymphadenopathy secondary to previously unrecognized *M. avium* complex or pulmonary disease owing to cryptococcosis. These syndromes also may involve sites that were recognized to be involved with opportunistic infections but that seemed to be well controlled; patients who initiate ART many months after apparently successful treatment of CMV retinitis or cryptococcal meningitis may experience deterioration in vision or severe headache.

Some of these syndromes do not seem to be associated with active infection (e.g., immune reconstitution uveitis after CMV retinitis). Others, such as mycobacterial lymphadenitis, are associated with organisms that can be identified by histology and culture. Data about managing these syndromes are largely anecdotal. It is not clear when specific or pathogen-directed therapy is indicated or how long this therapy should be continued. It also is not clear what role topical or systemic anti-inflammatory agents should play.

℞ Treatment of HIV-Associated Neoplasms

The therapy of HIV-associated lymphoma, Kaposi's sarcoma, human papillomavirus–associated neoplasms, and other malignant processes is detailed in Chapters 417 and 419. Early in the HIV epidemic, there was little optimism that these neoplastic processes could be treated successfully. More recent studies suggest, however, that even for HIV-associated lymphoma, rates of remission and long-term survival are encouraging. When treating HIV-associated neoplasms, attention to drug interactions and chemoprophylaxis for HIV-associated opportunistic infections requires particular attention.

℞ Treatment of Pregnant HIV-Infected Patients

Women with HIV infection who are pregnant should be offered therapy based on the same virologic, immunologic, and clinical parameters as nonpregnant women. **4** The choice of drugs and the timing of initiating the therapy may be influenced, however, by the pregnancy.

Most antiretroviral drugs are safe in pregnant women, to the extent they have been studied. Many of the toxicities caused by antiretroviral agents may contribute to parallel complications of pregnancy, however (e.g., the hyperglycemia associated with protease inhibitors may exacerbate pregnancy-associated diabetes). There are specific concerns regarding the use of nucleosides during pregnancy, especially stavudine and didanosine, in terms of their association with hepatic steatosis and lactic acidosis in several pregnant women. There is also particular concern about the association of efavirenz with fetal abnormalities in monkeys. Lastly, combination ART may be associated with an increased risk of preterm delivery. Antiretroviral regimens must be chosen carefully and monitored.

Transmission of HIV from mother to fetus has been observed at all maternal plasma HIV RNA levels. There does seem to be a correlation, however, between the HIV plasma RNA copy number and the risk of transmission. Clinical trials have shown that ART can reduce greatly the likelihood that virus is transmitted to the fetus or infant. Zidovudine monotherapy and nevirapine monotherapy have been most carefully studied, and both seem to be safe for the mother and fetus and are effective for substantially reducing the rate of maternal-fetal transmission. It is logical to use combination ART regimens for treating the mother to lower her viral load effectively and produce a durable viral suppression. The safety and efficacy of specific regimens, especially regimens that do not contain either zidovudine or nevirapine, have not been well studied.

Current guidelines indicate that the combination of zidovudine chemoprophylaxis with additional antiretroviral drugs for treatment of HIV infection should be recommended for infected women who meet the standard criteria for treatment, or who have HIV RNA levels greater than 1000 copies/μL, regardless of immunologic or clinical status. Women who are in the first trimester of pregnancy may prefer delaying therapy until after 10 to 12 weeks of gestation if they are concerned about teratogenicity of drugs administered during the early part of their pregnancy. Women who are not receiving zidovudine or nevirapine but who have HIV plasma RNA levels less than 1000 copies/μL seem to have low risk of transmitting HIV to their offspring. There are no clear guidelines about how best to manage pregnant women whose virus is resistant to zidovudine and nevirapine.

1. United States Public Health Service/Infectious Disease Society of America: Guidelines for using antiretroviral agents among HIV-infected adults and adolescents. Recommendations of the Panel on Clinical Practices for the Treatment of HIV. AIDSINFO.nih/gov/guidelines.
2. Lalezari JP, Henry K, O'Hearn M, et al, for the TORO 1 Study Group. Enfuvirtide, an HIV-1 fusion inhibitor, for drug-resistant HIV infection in North and South America. N Engl J Med 2003;348:2175–2185.
3. United States Public Health Service/Infectious Disease Society of America: Guidelines for prevention of opportunistic infections in persons with HIV infection. AIDSINFO.nih/gov/guidelines.
4. United States Public Health Service Task Force: Recommendations for use of antiretroviral drugs in pregnant HIV-1-infected women for maternal health and interventions to reduce perinatal HIV-1 transmission in the United States. AIDSINFO.nih/gov/guidelines.

SUGGESTED READINGS

Dolin R, Masur H, Saag M (eds): AIDS Therapy. Philadelphia, Churchill Livingstone, 2002. *A comprehensive overview of therapeutic approaches to ARTs and treatment for opportunistic infections.*

Hogg RS, Yip B, Chan KJ, et al: Rates of disease progression by baseline CD4 cell count and viral load after initiating triple-drug therapy. JAMA 2001;2568–2577. *Analysis of 13 European and North American trials assessing the outcome of ART as a function of baseline HIV plasma viral load and CD4+ T-lymphocyte count.*

Mellors JW, Munoz A, Giorgi JV, et al: Plasma viral load and CD4+ lymphocytes as prognostic markers of HIV-1 infection. Ann Intern Med 1997;126:946–954. *Pivotal data show the relationship of CD4+ T-lymphocyte count and HIV plasma viral load on outcome for untreated patients.*

Piscitelli SC, Gallicano KD: Interactions among drugs for HIV and opportunistic infections. N Engl J Med 2001;344:984–996. *A comprehensive review of drug interactions relevant to the management of patients with HIV infection.*

422 MANAGEMENT AND COUNSELING FOR PERSONS WITH HIV INFECTION

John A. Bartlett

Treatment advances in human immunodeficiency virus (HIV) disease have changed dramatically the management of chronically infected persons. These advances have resulted in profound virologic suppression in treated patients with an associated improvement in clinical outcomes and survival. The limitations of treatment also have become more clear, however, including the requirement for strict medication adherence and an expanding list of treatment-related complications, such as body habitus changes, elevated lipids, lactic acidosis, hepatic steatosis, osteopenia, and glucose intolerance. Despite these treatment advances, significant gaps also remain in understanding of the strategies needed to guide treatment initiation and when to change a failing regimen. Coincident with these treatment advances, persons with HIV infection in the United States are increasingly impoverished, are more likely to abuse drugs, and have less access to health care. The use of complex antiretroviral treatment (ART) regimens has created a scheduling challenge for many patients, and the success of therapy absolutely depends on patient adherence. Health care providers must assess carefully the resources and commitment of patients beginning ART; design a highly potent and convenient regimen for an individual patient; optimize adherence through patient preparation and education; and continually reassess the entire process including the management of treatment-related complications in a patient on treatment. Significant questions remain unanswered regarding the durability of successful ART, the potential infectivity of patients on treatment, and the optimal management of treatment-related complications and failure. These uncertainties may make counseling difficult because individual patients may experience emotional extremes in periods of treatment successes and failures.

Clinical Evaluation of the Patient

The clinical approach to the HIV-infected patient should be guided by several important principles. First, it is important to establish the degree of immunosuppression in every patient through the history and physical examination and the measurement of absolute CD4+ lymphocyte count. Second, an individual's risk of disease progression can be assessed through the measurement of plasma HIV RNA levels. Third, past histories of sexually transmitted diseases; positive purified protein derivative (PPD) testing or exposure to tuberculosis; testing for hepatitis A, B, and C; and places of residence may be useful in predicting complications of HIV infection. Finally, the sharing of pertinent medical information with patients may improve the quality of personal observations that they report to the physician in subsequent visits. These educational efforts may result in greater adherence to medications and may improve the physician's ability to recognize medication-related toxicities, establish early diagnoses, provide effective outpatient treatment, and communicate regarding treatment options and risk reduction. Information regarding the stage of HIV disease and the degree of immunosuppression provides important insight into predicting clinical complications and guiding therapeutic decisions. This clinical approach allows the physician to optimize the long-term management and counseling of HIV-infected persons.

INITIAL EVALUATION. The initial evaluation of an HIV-infected person should begin with a careful history of past evaluations for HIV infection (Table 422–1). Previous history of risk behaviors, mononucleosis-

Table 422–1 • INITIAL EVALUATION OF THE HIV–INFECTED PATIENT

History
How long has the patient been HIV infected?
What complications of HIV have occurred?
What past evaluations has the patient undergone?
What past treatment has the patient received?
Any past history of sexually transmitted diseases?
Past history of positive PPD test or exposure to tuberculosis?
Medications and allergies?
Substance abuse?
Residential history?
Physical examination
Laboratory evaluation
Complete blood cell count
Chemistries including liver enzymes and serum creatinine
Plasma HIV RNA level
Absolute CD4+ lymphocyte count and CD4+ lymphocyte percentage
Hepatitis A, B and C, syphilis and *Toxoplasma* serologies
PPD testing
Immunizations
Pneumococcal vaccine
Influenza vaccine
Hepatitis A and B vaccines if nonimmune

PPD = purified protein derivative.

like symptoms that could represent acute HIV infection, and previous HIV testing may offer insight into a patient's duration of HIV infection. Previous plasma HIV RNA levels, CD4+ lymphocyte counts, history of acquired immunodeficiency syndrome (AIDS) indicator conditions, and other clinical manifestations are important historical factors. The physician also must elicit a medical history, especially a history of sexually transmitted diseases (e.g., syphilis; herpes simplex; hepatitis A, B, and C; genital or perianal warts; and cervical dysplasia), past PPD testing or exposure to tuberculosis, substance abuse, and medication allergies. On physical examination, particular attention should be focused on the skin (severe seborrhea, molluscum contagiosum, chronic herpetic ulcerations, and Kaposi's sarcoma all suggest progressive HIV infection), lymph nodes (generalized lymphadenopathy usually correlates with earlier HIV infection, and involution may signal progression of disease), oropharynx (candidiasis, oral hairy leukoplakia, and Kaposi's sarcoma indicate progression), genitalia (severe warts, recurrent vaginal candidiasis, frequently recurrent or severe herpetic ulcerations, cervical dysplasia, and Kaposi's sarcoma suggest progression), and central nervous system (neurocognitive and memory deficits suggest progression to AIDS dementia). The initial laboratory examination should include a complete blood cell count with differential; routine chemistries, including liver enzymes, serum creatinine, plasma HIV RNA level, absolute CD4+ lymphocyte count, and CD4+ lymphocyte percentage; and hepatitis A, B, and C, syphilis, and *Toxoplasma* serologies. Patients also should undergo 5-TU (tuberculin units) PPD testing; a positive response in an HIV-infected patient is defined as induration of 5 mm or more. All HIV-infected patients should receive the pneumococcal pneumonia vaccine because of their increased risk of pneumococcal infections. The hepatitis A and B vaccines may be given to previously uninfected patients, and the influenza vaccine may be given yearly.

When the initial evaluation is complete, the physician should be able to assess the patient's risk of disease progression. Potential coinfections with *Treponema pallidum* or *Mycobacterium tuberculosis* should be recognized and treated for personal and public health benefits. If the patient is coinfected with hepatitis C, it is necessary to assess hepatic consequences and carefully coordinate treatment for HIV and hepatitis C. Finally, counseling may result in the reduction of risk behaviors through education and the identification and treatment of substance abuse.

Strategic Decisions

With improving longevity for HIV-infected persons receiving ART, but also acknowledging the potential for serious medication-related toxicities, the finite durability of each regimen, and a limited number of regimens, the optimal strategy for the use of ART is crucial to maximize clinical benefit. Significant unanswered questions include the

optimal initiation of ART and the timing of a switch from a failing regimen to a secondary one.

TREATMENT INITIATION. Most clinicians follow HIV-infected persons not receiving ART every 3 to 6 months with a careful history and physical examination and monitoring of plasma HIV RNA levels and absolute CD4+ cell counts. In asymptomatic HIV-infected persons, the potential benefits of ART should outweigh their imposition, toxicities, and cost. Many asymptomatic HIV-infected persons may be at low risk for clinical progression of disease because of host and virologic factors. ART ideally should be offered to patients at greatest risk of clinical progression. Before considering treatment initiation, it is prudent to repeat plasma HIV RNA levels and absolute CD4+ cell counts because of potential variability. The risk of disease progression is related to a patient's symptoms, plasma HIV RNA level, and absolute CD4+ cell number. Therapy is recommended strongly for all symptomatic patients. The optimal levels of plasma HIV RNA and absolute CD4+ cells to guide the initiation of therapy are not known, but current recommendations suggest therapy at conservative thresholds of more than 55,000 copies HIV RNA/mL or CD4+ cells less than $350/mm^3$.

Crucial to the success of treatment interventions is a patient who is prepared and committed to beginning therapy. Decisions on treatment initiation must be highly individualized. Many clinicians never initiate treatment for a patient during the first visit; rather, they evaluate and educate the patient during several visits. Physicians must recognize the essential role of strict adherence to ART regimens and optimize circumstances, such as patient education, emotional support, substance abuse rehabilitation, and the resources to obtain a continuing supply of medications. Studies of adherence have shown that socioeconomic status, race/ethnicity, gender, and educational level do not predict successful adherence; physicians should not preclude treatment based on these factors. Factors that do predict better adherence include the treatment of underlying depression, recovery from substance abuse (especially cocaine and alcohol), and the patient's belief in the potential success of treatment.

With an expanding number of available antiretroviral drugs, clinicians can tailor regimens based on potency, convenience, predicted toxicities, and drug interactions. The importance of convenience and its relationship to adherence should not be underestimated. Significant issues may include dosing schedules, pill burden, food interactions, drug interactions, and toxicities. Clinicians should take a careful history regarding daily activities, including employment and meals, and project alternative medication schedules in discussions with patients. When an initial regimen has been chosen, many clinicians have patients return in 1 to 4 weeks to reinforce adherence and assess possible toxicities. Adherence may decline over time, and continuing attention to adherence at the time of all follow-up visits may assist in achieving long-term treatment success.

TREATMENT FAILURE. Successful ART seems to achieve profound suppression of HIV replication, but the reservoir of chronically infected cells may not diminish over time. As a result, compromise in chronic suppression leads to reactivation of HIV from this reservoir and recurrence in plasma viremia. The reasons for treatment failure may include diverse factors, such as adherence, individualized pharmacokinetic responses, drug interactions, and antiretroviral resistance.

Most clinicians follow plasma HIV RNA levels every 3 months in patients on stable, fully suppressive ART regimens. This intensive monitoring of plasma HIV RNA levels is associated with greater suppression of virus over time. Currently, there is no consensus definition of treatment failure based on plasma HIV RNA levels. Increasing levels may indicate antiretroviral resistance, and the prolonged administration of a failing drug regimen can result in the accumulation of multiple resistance mutations with greater potential for cross-resistance. Conversely, modest increases in plasma HIV RNA levels do not seem to correlate with rapid falls in absolute CD4+ cell counts or immediately worsening clinical outcomes. A balance must be reached when considering the discontinuation of an initial ART regimen and the substitution of a secondary one. Pending the elucidation of factors influencing the optimal timing for treatment changes, most clinicians follow individual patients closely to ascertain the rapidity of their virus recurrence and change medication accordingly.

When choosing a secondary treatment regimen, the new combination should include at least two new drugs predicted not to have cross-resistance with agents from previous regimens. Resistance testing may assist health care providers and patients to identify specific drugs with predicted resistance and exclude them from a new treatment regimen. Resistance can be measured using genotypic or phenotypic techniques, and either method may assist in achieving the goal of greater virologic suppression on a new treatment regimen. The shortcomings of both techniques include the proper interpretation of resistance, their lack of sensitivity at low plasma HIV RNA levels, and their inability to detect low-level populations of resistance virus in the plasma.

COMPLICATIONS OF ANTIRETROVIRAL TREATMENT. As increasing numbers of HIV-infected persons receive ART for greater durations of time, numerous complications of ART have been identified. These complications are listed in Table 422–2. The metabolic complications may include body habitus changes with the centripetal accumulation and peripheral loss of fat, elevations of plasma lipids, which may predispose to premature cardiovascular disease; profound lactic acidosis and hepatic steatosis; osteopenia; and glucose intolerance. The pathogenetic mechanisms of these complications are incompletely understood but may include interference with *cis*-retinoic acid–binding protein (centripetal fat accumulation and glucose intolerance in patients on protease inhibitors), mitochondrial toxicities owing to inhibition of the gamma isoenzyme of DNA polymerase (peripheral fat loss, lactic acidosis, and hepatic steatosis in patients on nucleoside reverse-transcriptase inhibitors), and inflammatory cytokines.

Nearly all antiretroviral medications can increase plasma lipids, although the changes may be most dramatic in patients treated with protease inhibitors and non-nucleoside reverse-transcriptase inhibitors. Some treatment complications may improve when the offending antiretroviral agent is discontinued, such as elevated lipids, lactic acidosis, hepatic steatosis, and perhaps centripetal fat accumulation. Strategies to manage these complications optimally are the subject of active clinical investigation, and they will constitute crucial new knowledge to support the long-term management of persons receiving ART.

EVALUATION OF THE FEBRILE PATIENT. Fever is a common physical finding in patients with HIV infection, and the potential causes are many. Fever may indicate a self-limited viral upper respiratory tract infection in a patient with early HIV infection or the presence of *Pneumocystis carinii* pneumonia (PCP) in a patient with progressive HIV infection. Differentiating the clinical manifestations of the two infections may be difficult for the physician; he or she should use any available information on HIV staging for the patient. In this context, the absolute CD4+ lymphocyte count may be an extremely useful guide in assessing the likelihood of opportunistic infections. If the absolute CD4+ lymphocyte count is more than 200/mm³, the likelihood of PCP or other opportunistic infections is significantly decreased. The absolute CD4+ lymphocyte count may guide the most appropriate diagnostic considerations. The uncommon patient may present with an opportunistic infection at absolute CD4+ lymphocyte counts of more than 200/mm³; it is imperative to reconsider these diagnoses if the fever persists.

Complications of HIV Infection

As HIV infection progresses, it creates increasing immunosuppression, resulting in a predisposition toward complicating opportunistic infections and neoplasms. The pattern of these complications can be predicted by following a patient's absolute CD4+ lymphocyte count (Fig. 422–1). On the basis of these correlations between absolute CD4+ lymphocytes and the predicted complications of HIV infection, clinicians can anticipate an increased risk of certain opportunistic infections in an individual patient, which may lead to an earlier diagnosis or the use of antimicrobial prophylaxis to prevent specific opportunistic infections. Successful prophylaxis has been identified against PCP, toxoplasmic encephalitis, disseminated *Mycobacterium avium* complex (MAC) infection, cryptococcal meningitis, and cytomegalovirus (CMV) disease (Table 422–3). As CD4+ lymphocyte counts rise above the appropriate threshold for a specific complication of HIV disease and remain above that threshold for 3 to 6 months, prophylaxis may be discontinued.

Persons at highest risk for PCP include persons recovering from their first episode (secondary prophylaxis, 1-year risk of recurrence without prophylaxis 60%), persons with absolute CD4+ lymphocytes less than or equal to 200/mm³ (primary prophylaxis, 1-year risk of PCP >18%), persons with CD4+ lymphocyte percentages less than 20%, and persons with a non-PCP AIDS indicator condition (both primary prophylaxis). Sulfamethoxazole-trimethoprim (SMX-TMP)

Table 422–2 • COMPLICATIONS OF ANTIRETROVIRAL TREATMENT

NUCLEOSIDE REVERSE TRANSCRIPTASE INHIBITORS		NON-NUCLEOSIDE REVERSE TRANSCRIPTASE INHIBITORS	
Anemia, leukopenia	Zidovudine	Rash	All
Peripheral neuropathy	Didanosine, stavudine, zalcitabine	CNS symptoms	Efavirenz
Pancreatitis	Didanosine, stavudine, zalcitabine	Early hepatic abnormalities	Nevirapine
Hypersensitivity	Abacavir	Elevated lipids	All
Lactic acidosis	All		
Hepatic steatosis	All		
Peripheral fat loss	All, perhaps greater with stavudine, didanosine, zalcitabine		
Elevated lipids	Mild but all		
PROTEASE INHIBITORS			
Centripetal fat accumulation	All		
Nephrolithiasis	Indinavir		
Glucose intolerance	All		

CNS = central nervous system.

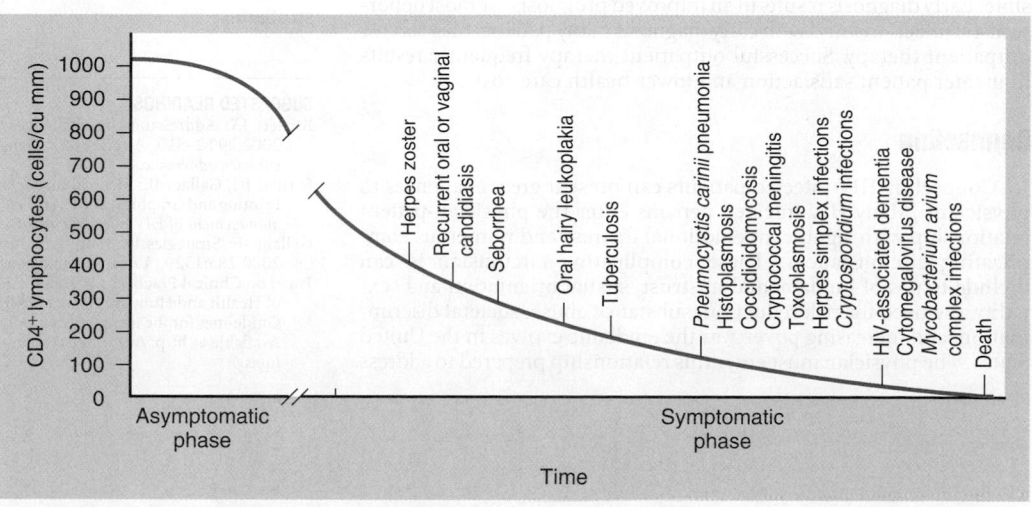

FIGURE 422–1 • Complications of HIV disease as related to lymphocyte count.

Herpes zoster
Recurrent oral or vaginal candidiasis
Seborrhea
Oral hairy leukoplakia
Tuberculosis
Pneumocystis carinii pneumonia
Histoplasmosis
Coccidioidomycosis
Cryptococcal meningitis
Toxoplasmosis
Herpes simplex infections
Cryptosporidium infections
HIV-associated dementia
Cytomegalovirus disease
Mycobacterium avium complex infections
Death

CD4+ lymphocytes (cells/cu mm)

Asymptomatic phase   Symptomatic phase

Time

Table 422–3 • **PROPHYLAXIS OF OPPORTUNISTIC INFECTIONS**

INFECTION	AVAILABLE AGENTS	COMMENTS
Pneumocystis carinii pneumonia	SMX-TMP Dapsone Atovaquone Aerosolized pentamidine	SMX-TMP most effective and least expensive but potentially toxic
MAC	Azithromycin Rifabutin Clarithromycin	Delay in disseminated MAC infection; potential pharmacokinetic interactions with protease inhibitors and zidovudine; resistant isolates possible
Toxoplasma encephalitis	SMX-TMP Dapsone-pyrimethamine	
Cryptococcal meningitis	Fluconazole	Delay in deep fungal infections but costly; resistant isolates possible
CMV	Oral ganciclovir	Delay in CMV disease but costly

CMV = cytomegalovirus; MAC = *Mycobacterium arium* complex; SMX-TMP = sulfamethoxazole-trimethoprim.

is the most successful prophylaxis against PCP. In patients intolerant of SMX-TMP, desensitization may be undertaken or dapsone, atovaquone, or aerosolized pentamidine may be used. SMX-TMP and dapsone-pyrimethamine also can be given to prevent toxoplasmic encephalitis among patients who are seropositive for previous infection with *Toxoplasma gondii.*

Azithromycin, clarithromycin, or rifabutin can delay disseminated MAC infection. These drugs are prescribed for patients at highest risk, usually patients with absolute CD4+ lymphocytes less than 100/mm³. Fluconazole also has shown efficacy in delaying invasive fungal infections in patients with absolute CD4+ lymphocytes less than 200/mm³. Oral ganciclovir also has delayed successfully the onset of CMV disease in seropositive HIV-infected patients. The widespread use of these prophylactic agents must include consideration of their potential drug interactions, the potential for drug resistance, and cost-effectiveness.

PCP was once the most common AIDS indicator condition, but the incidence of opportunistic infections has declined with the use of potent antiretroviral combinations and measures. Undoubtedly the future complications of progressive HIV infection will continue to evolve as improved ARTs and prophylactic strategies against additional opportunistic infections are identified and as survival lengthens for persons with AIDS. An example is the emergence of human papillomavirus causing malignancies of the cervix, anus, and oropharynx in HIV-infected women and men.

When patients develop opportunistic infections, clinicians should attempt to establish a diagnosis and initiate treatment as soon as possible. Early diagnosis results in an improved prognosis for most opportunistic infections, and with early diagnosis many patients may receive outpatient therapy. Successful outpatient therapy frequently results in greater patient satisfaction and lower health care costs.

Counseling

Counseling HIV-infected patients can present great challenges to physicians. Many HIV-infected persons enter the physician-patient relationship with significant emotional distress and numerous complicating circumstances. These complicating circumstances can include issues of fundamental mistrust, sexual orientation and sexuality, the need for risk reduction, substance abuse, societal discrimination, and increasing poverty as the epidemic evolves in the United States. The physician must enter this relationship prepared to address

these issues with knowledge and compassion and without becoming judgmental about their content.

A crucial component involved in counseling HIV-infected persons is education concerning HIV disease, its transmission, and its potential treatments. This process should continue for the duration of the physician-patient relationship; given the extensive knowledge base of many persons with HIV infection, there may be a mutual exchange of important information. The best medical interventions will not succeed unless HIV-infected persons have been counseled carefully regarding their potential benefits, costs, and acquisition. A well-informed patient can be a strong ally in tackling difficult therapeutic decisions, and many therapeutic decisions are currently not straightforward, such as the optimal time to initiate ART. A well-informed patient will be more compliant with prescribed medications and may recognize better the early manifestations of HIV-related clinical complications and potential drug toxicities. Finally, a well-informed patient can guide constructively decisions regarding advance directives for his or her care if HIV disease progresses.

Education regarding the transmission of HIV and alterations in risk behavior is another important goal of counseling. Efforts to encourage behavioral changes resulting in temporarily decreased HIV transmission have succeeded in homosexual men in San Francisco, although more recent evidence suggests an increasing number of new infections, especially among young people. Intensive efforts to decrease HIV transmission also have succeeded in smaller populations of injecting drug users and high-risk heterosexuals. All patients should be well informed regarding safer sex precautions and the avoidance of needle sharing. This information must be presented in language appropriate to the culture of the patient. Significant behavioral changes frequently are not accomplished during a single visit, and enduring change requires ongoing re-education and support from the physician.

Treating substance abuse is crucial in decreasing the risk of HIV transmission through needle sharing and sexual contact and in avoiding the medical and psychological consequences of continued substance abuse. Physicians must advocate for their patients in seeking access to frequently inadequate and overwhelmed drug treatment programs. Physicians also must acknowledge the high recidivism rates associated with substance abuse and continue to treat their recidivous patients firmly and without judgment. Finally, physicians should reinforce positively recovering addicts who have succeeded in treatment and struggle to avoid relapse on a daily basis.

The clinical course of persons with HIV infection frequently is complicated by significant anxiety and depression. Pharmacologic measures may prove useful in their management, although physicians should be cautious about the potential for drug interactions with protease inhibitors. In the circumstance of late-stage HIV infection complicated by HIV encephalopathy and depression, methylphenidate (Ritalin) may be of benefit. Physicians should identify AIDS service organizations in their community that may provide support services, such as patient education, case management, transportation, shelter, food, medications, or support groups to their clients. Formal psychiatric referral also may be necessary in individual patients. Patients may experience depression throughout the course of HIV infection—in early infection, during successful treatment, and in disease progression. Past coping strategies may be useful in these instances. A careful history may provide assistance in identifying these strategies.

SUGGESTED READINGS

Bartlett JA: Addressing the challenges of adherence. J Acquir Immune Defic Syndr 2002;29:S2–S10. *A review of adherence-related studies and interventions which may enhance adherence.*

Bartlett JG, Gallant JE: Medical management of HIV infection. Timonium, MD, H & N Printing and Graphics, 2001. *A review for health care professionals describing the medical management of HIV-infected patients.*

Gallant JE: Strategies for long-term success in the treatment of HIV infection. JAMA 2000;283:1329. *A review of treatment strategies.*

Panel on Clinical Practices for Treatment of HIV Infection, convened by the Department of Health and Human Services (DHHS) and the Henry J. Kaiser Family Foundation: Guidelines for the use of antiretroviral agents in HIV-infected adults and adolescents. Available at http://www.hivatis.org. *A web site with continually updated recommendations.*

part XXV

Neurology

423 APPROACH TO THE PATIENT WITH NEUROLOGIC DISEASE

Robert C. Griggs
Ralph F. Józefowicz
Michael J. Aminoff

The symptoms of nervous system diseases are a part of everyday experience for most normal people. Slips of the tongue, headaches, backache and other pains, dizziness, lightheadedness, numbness, muscle twitches, jerks, cramps, and tremors all occur in totally healthy persons. Mood swings with feelings of elation and depression, paranoia, and displays of temper are equally a part of the behavior of completely normal people. The rapid increase in information about neurologic diseases coupled with the intense interest of people in all walks of life in medical matters has focused public attention on both common and rare neurologic conditions.

Most older people are concerned that they or their spouse have or are developing Alzheimer's disease or stroke or both. The almost ubiquitous tremor of the elderly prompts concern about Parkinson's disease. Many younger patients are concerned about multiple sclerosis or brain tumor, and few normal people lack one or more symptoms suggesting the diagnosis of a serious neurologic disease. For most of these and other common diagnoses, the results of imaging and other tests are typically normal when symptoms first appear and should not be obtained to reassure the patient or physician. Moreover, the widespread availability of neurodiagnostic imaging and electrophysiologic, biochemical, and genetic testing has detected "abnormalities" in many young and most elderly persons. In evaluating a patient's symptoms, it is imperative that a clinical diagnosis be reached without reference to a neurodiagnostic laboratory finding. Patients with disorders such as headache, anxiety, or depression usually do not have abnormal laboratory studies. Abnormalities that are noted on various neurodiagnostic studies are often incidental findings whose treatment may be justified and necessary but they do not improve the patient's symptoms. Abnormalities detected incidentally that do not have signs or symptoms may, as for disorders such as hypertension, require aggressive evaluation and treatment, but in general, the adage that it is difficult to improve the asymptomatic patient should be kept in mind. Thus, in elderly patients, few imaging or electrophysiologic studies are interpreted as "normal" but in the absence of specific complaints consistent with the findings, treatment and even further evaluation should reflect an estimate of the specificity and sensitivity of the test, as well as the likelihood that the patient will require and benefit from treatment. It is a good rule-of-thumb that one should never obtain (or refer to the result of) a neurodiagnostic procedure without a specific diagnosis or at least a differential diagnosis in mind.

It is important to allow the patient to describe any symptoms in his or her own words. Direct questions are often necessary to fully characterize the patient's problem, but suggested terms or descriptors for symptoms are frequently grasped by the patient unfamiliar with medical terminology and then parroted to subsequent interviewers. The patient's terms should always be used when recording symptoms. Terms such as *lameness, weakness, numbness, heaviness, cramps,* and *tiredness* may each mean pain, weakness, or alteration of sensation to some patients.

In neurologic diagnosis, the history usually indicates the nature of the disease or the diagnosis, whereas the neurologic examination localizes it and quantitates its severity. For many diseases, the history is almost the only avenue to explore. Examples of such disorders include headaches, seizures, developmental disorders, memory disorders, and behavioral diseases. In arriving at a diagnosis, the following points are useful. Consider the entire medical history of the patient. Early life events or long-standing processes such as head or spine trauma, unilateral hearing or visual loss, poor prowess in sports, poor performance in school, spinal curvature, or bone anomalies are easily overlooked but may point to the underlying disease process.

Consider the tempo and duration of symptoms. Have the symptoms been progressive without remission, or have there been plateaus or periods of return to normal? Cerebral mass lesions (tumor, subdural) tend to have a progressive but fluctuating course; seizures and migraine, an episodic course; strokes, an abrupt, ictal onset with worsening for 3 to 5 days followed by partial or complete recovery.

Can one disease account for all of the symptoms and signs? The clinician should formulate a diagnostic opinion in anatomic terms. Is the history suggestive of a single (e.g., stroke or tumor) *focus* or of multiple sites of nervous system involvement (e.g., multiple sclerosis)? Or is the process a disease of a *system:* B_{12} deficiency, myopathy, or polyneuropathy?

The Neurologic History

The neurologic history is the most important component of neurologic diagnosis. A careful history frequently determines the cause and allows one to begin localizing the lesions, aiding in the determination whether the disease is diffuse or focal. Symptoms of acute onset suggest a vascular cause or seizure; symptoms that are subacute in onset suggest a mass lesion such as a tumor or abscess; symptoms that have a waxing and waning course with exacerbations and remissions suggest a demyelinating cause; symptoms that are chronic and progressive suggest a degenerative disorder.

The history is often the only way of diagnosing neurologic illnesses that typically have normal or nonfocal findings on neurologic examination. These illnesses include many seizure disorders, narcolepsy, migraine and most other headache syndromes, the various causes of dizziness, and most types of dementia. The neurologic history may often provide the first clues that a symptom is psychological in origin. The following are points to consider when obtaining a neurologic history:

- *Carefully identify the chief complaint or problem.* Not only is the chief complaint important in providing the first clue to the physician as to the differential diagnosis, it is also the reason why the patient is seeking medical advice and treatment. If the chief complaint is not properly identified and addressed, the proper diagnosis may be missed and an inappropriate diagnostic work-up may be undertaken. Establishing a diagnosis that does not incorporate the chief complaint frequently focuses attention on a coincidental process irrelevant to the patient's concerns.
- *Listen carefully to the patient for as long as necessary.* A good rule-of-thumb is to listen initially for at least 5 minutes without interrupting the patient. The patient often volunteers the most important information at the start of the history. During this time, the examiner can also assess mental status, including speech, language, fund of knowledge, and affect, and observe the patient for facial asymmetry, abnormalities of ocular movements, and an increase or a paucity of spontaneous movements as seen with movement disorders.
- *Steer the patient away from discussions of previous diagnostic test results and of the opinions of previous caregivers.* Abnormal results of laboratory studies may be incidental to the patient's primary problem or may simply represent a normal variant.
- *Take a careful medical history, medication history, psychiatric history, family history, and social and occupational history.* Many neurologic illnesses are complications of underlying medical disorders or are due to adverse effects of drugs. For example, parkinsonism is a frequent complication of use of metoclopramide and most neuroleptic agents. A large number of neurologic disorders are hereditary, and a positive family history may establish the diagnosis in many instances. Occupation plays a major role in various neurologic disorders such as carpal tunnel syndrome (in machine operators and people who use computer keyboards) and peripheral neuropathy (caused by exposure to lead or other toxins).
- *Interview surrogate historians.* Patients with dementia or altered mental status are usually unable to provide exact details of the history, and a family member may provide key details needed to make an accurate diagnosis. This problem is especially true for patients who have dementia and certain right hemispheric lesions with various agnosias (lack of awareness of disease) that may interfere with their ability to provide a cogent history. Surrogate historians also provide missing historical details for patients with episodic loss of consciousness, such as syncope and epilepsy.
- *Summarize the history for the patient.* Summarizing the history is an effective way to ensure that all details were covered sufficiently to make a tentative diagnosis. Summarizing also allows the physician to fill in historical gaps that may not have been apparent when the history was initially taken. In addition, the

patient or surrogate may correct any historical misinformation at this time.

• *End by asking the patient what he or she thinks is wrong.* This question allows the physician to evaluate the patient's concerns about and insight into the condition. Some patients have a specific diagnosis in mind that spurs them to seek medical attention. Multiple sclerosis, amyotrophic lateral sclerosis, Alzheimer's disease, and brain tumors are diseases that patients often suspect may be the cause of their neurologic symptoms.

DIAGNOSTIC CHALLENGES

Two common situations provide special challenges to the diagnostic skills of the physician.

PHYSICAL ABUSE AS A CAUSE OF NEUROLOGIC SYMPTOMS. Traumatic injury inflicted by family members or others is usually difficult to detect by medical history and examination. Physically battered babies, abused children, battered women, and traumatized seniors are often unable or unwilling to complain of this cause or contribution to symptoms. The only method to prevent overlooking this frequent cause of common problems is systematic consideration of the possibility in every patient and awareness of the (often subtle) signs that suggest physical trauma: ecchymoses or fractures (often attributed to a logical cause), denial of expected symptoms, failure to keep appointments, and unexplained intensification of neurologic symptoms (headache, dizziness, ringing in the ears, blackouts).

ALCOHOLISM AND DRUG ABUSE. See Chapters 17 and 30. A host of neurologic disorders can be the result of the intentional ingestion of toxins (Chapter 106). Patients do not give an accurate account of their use of these agents. Consequently, physical signs and laboratory screening test results that give evidence of drug-related hepatic and other metabolic abnormalities may point to a major underlying problem.

ACUTE NEUROLOGIC DISORDERS REQUIRING IMMEDIATE DIAGNOSIS AND TREATMENT

Most neurologic diagnoses are arrived at by a careful, thorough history and an appropriately complete examination. However, the tempo of illness and the availability of life-saving treatment that is only effective if administered within minutes of first evaluating a patient dictates rapid action in several specific circumstances. Coma (Chapter 436), repetitive seizures (Chapter 434), acute stroke (Chapters 440 and 441), suspected meningitis and encephalitis (Chapters 312 and 451), head and spine trauma (Chapters 429 and 430), and acute spinal cord compression are diagnosed by clinical and laboratory assessments and urgent treatment must be instituted as soon as ventilation and cardiac status are stabilized.

Neurologic Examination

The neurologic examination is always tailored to the clinical setting of the patient. The complete neurologic examination of the child is much different from that of an elderly adult, and the examination of a patient with specific complaints focuses on findings pertinent to that patient. Thus, more detailed testing of cognition is indicated in patients with behavioral or memory disturbance and more detailed testing of sensation should be performed in patients with complaints of pain, numbness, or weakness.

However, many tests of neurologic function are routinely indicated in all patients because they provide a baseline for future examination and because they are so frequently helpful in detecting unsuspected neurologic disease in apparently normal persons or in patients whose symptoms initially suggest disease outside the nervous system. It is particularly important to perform all routine tests in patients with abnormalities in one sphere of neurologic dysfunction; otherwise, erroneous localization of a lesion or disease process is likely. It is essential for a physician to have extensive experience in the routine assessment of normal persons in order to recognize and quantitate deviations from the normal.

THE GENERAL EXAMINATION. Specific neurologic symptoms or signs should prompt attention to the assessment of general findings. Head circumference should be measured in patients with central nervous system (CNS) or spinal cord disease (normally 55 ± 5 cm in adults). Head enlargement is occasionally a normal, often hereditary, variant but should suggest a long-standing anomaly of the brain or spinal

cord. The skin should be inspected for café au lait maculae, adenoma sebaceum, vascular malformations, lipomas, neurofibromas, and other lesions (Chapter 459). Neck range of motion, straight leg raising, and spinal curvature (scoliosis) should be assessed. Carotid auscultation for bruits is indicated in all older adults; carotid palpation is seldom informative. In patients with bladder, bowel, or leg symptoms, a rectal sphincter examination for tone and ability to contract voluntarily is usually indicated. Limitation of joint range of motion or painless swelling of joints is often a sign of an unsuspected neurologic lesion.

THE NEUROLOGIC EXAMINATION. The various aspects of the detailed neurologic examination are considered in specific symptom and disease sections noted later. The five major divisions of the examination should be assessed in all patients. During a careful medical history, the mental status is often adequately assessed: level of consciousness, orientation, memory, language function, affect, and judgment. If any of these functions is abnormal, more detailed testing is needed. Cranial nerve function that should be tested in all patients includes visual acuity (with and without correction); optic fundi; visual fields; pupils (size and reactivity to direct and consensual light); ocular motility; jaw, facial, palatal, neck, and tongue movement; and hearing.

Motor system examination (Chapters 461 to 463) is essential in all patients because incipient weakness is usually overlooked by the patient. Muscle tone (flaccid, spastic, or rigid), muscle size (atrophy or hypertrophy), and muscle strength can be assessed rapidly. Muscle strength testing should always assess specific functional activities including the ability to walk on heel and toe, sit up from a supine position, rise from a deep knee bend or deep chair, lift the arms over the head, and make a tight fist. Gait, stance, and coordination are assessed. The patient should be observed for tremor and other abnormal movements and the muscles inspected for fasciculations.

Sensory testing (Chapters 461 and 462) need not be detailed unless there are sensory symptoms. However, vibration perception in the toes as well as the normality of perception of pain, temperature, and light touch in the hands and feet should be assessed.

Muscle stretch reflexes and plantar responses should always be assessed, evaluating right/left symmetry and disparity between proximal or distal reflexes or arm versus leg reflexes. Biceps, triceps, brachioradialis, quadriceps, and ankle reflexes should be quantitated from 1 to 4 (4 = clonus; 3 = spread; 2 = brisk; 1 = hypoactive).

THE COMATOSE PATIENT. The rapid examination required for a patient with an altered state of consciousness is much different from that of an alert, aware individual (Chapter 436). Many aspects of the neurologic examination cannot be tested: cognitive function; subtleties of sensory perception; specific motor functions; coordination; gait; stance. Moreover, the muscle stretch reflexes are likely to fluctuate from one moment to the next and minor asymmetries are much less important than in an awake patient. Instead, attention should focus on the examination of (1) level of consciousness, (2) respiratory pattern, (3) eyelid position and eye movements, (4) pupils, (5) corneal reflexes, (6) optic fundi, and (7) motor responses. Particular elements of the general examination must also be assessed quickly: evidence of cranial and spine trauma, tenderness of the skull to percussion, nuchal rigidity (but not in patients with head or neck trauma), and evidence of physical abuse.

Common Complaints of Possible Neurologic Origin

WEAKNESS. It is axiomatic that patients typically have motor signs before motor symptoms and, conversely, sensory symptoms before sensory signs. Thus patients with even severe weakness may not report symptoms of weakness. Somewhat paradoxically, patients who complain of "weakness" often do not have confirmatory findings on examination that document the presence of weakness.

Weakness, when actually a symptom of neurologic disease, is frequently caused by diseases of the motor unit (Chapters 447, 461–464) and is usually reported by a patient in terms of a loss of specific functions, such as difficulties with tasks such as climbing stairs, rising from a chair, sitting up, lifting objects onto a high shelf, or opening jars. Symptoms may also reflect the consequences of weakness such as frequent falls or tripping. Such symptoms can be remarkably quantitative. A patient with leg muscle weakness who is falling even as infrequently as once a month almost invariably has severe weakness of knee extensor muscles and can be shown on examination to have a knee extension lag: the inability to lift the leg fully against gravity and to lock the knee.

Table 423–1 • DISORDERS THAT COMMONLY PRESENT WITH "WEAKNESS"

Disorders of the motor unit
Upper motor neuron lesions—spasticity
Basal ganglia disorders—rigidity
General medical conditions
   Heart failure
   Respiratory insufficiency
   Renal, hepatic, other metabolic disease
   Alcoholism and other toxin-related disease
Psychiatric and behavioral disorders
   Depression
   Malingering

The symptom of "weakness" without findings of weakness on examination is not usually the result of neuromuscular disease but can be a sign of neurologic disease outside the motor unit or more commonly a symptom of disease outside the nervous system altogether (Table 423–1).

FATIGUE. The complaints of "fatigue," "tiredness," and "lack of energy" are even less likely than the symptom of "weakness" to reflect definable neurologic disease. With the exception of neuromuscular junction disorders such as myasthenia gravis, fatigue is rarely a complaint of diseases of the motor unit. Fatigue can be a sign of upper motor neuron disease (corticospinal pathways) and is a common complaint of established multiple sclerosis and other multifocal CNS disease. Similarly, any process that produces bilateral corticospinal tract or extrapyramidal disease can cause fatigue. Examples include motor neuron disease (Chapter 447), spinal cord disease in the cervical cord region (Chapter 429), and Parkinson's disease (Chapter 443). In addition, disorders that impair sleep (Chapter 438) may include fatigue as a complaint.

"Fatigue," like "weakness," is much more often than not a sign of disease outside the central and peripheral nervous system. Depression and other psychiatric and behavioral disorders (Chapter 426), as well as the medical illnesses associated with a complaint of weakness, are all frequent causes of fatigue.

The chronic fatigue syndrome, as well as many cases of fibromyalgia (Chapter 289), has fatigue as a dominant, disabling symptom. These disorders are defined in part by the absence of consistent neurologic findings and the absence of demonstrable pathology in the nervous system.

SPONTANEOUS MOVEMENTS. Muscle tremors, jerks, twitches, cramps, and spasms (Chapters 444 and 445) are all frequent symptoms. The cause of spontaneous movements can reside at any level of the nervous system. In general, movements that occur in an entire limb or in more than one muscle group concurrently are caused by CNS disease. Movements confined to a single muscle are likely to be a reflection of disease of the motor unit (including the motor neurons of the brain stem and spinal cord). When spontaneous movements of a muscle are associated with severe pain, patients often use the term *cramp*. Cramp is a medically defined disorder that reflects the intense contraction of a large group of motor units. Leg cramps are occasionally a sign of an underlying disease of the anterior horn cell, nerve roots, or peripheral nerve; however, cramps are frequent in normal persons and particularly common in older patients, and they are usually benign. When severe, cramps can produce such intense muscle contraction that muscle injury is produced and muscle enzyme (e.g., creatine kinase) levels are elevated in the blood.

The rare muscle diseases in which an enzyme deficiency interferes with substrate utilization as fuel for exercise (e.g., McArdle's disease) are often associated with severe, exercise-provoked muscle *contractures*. These contractures are electrically silent by electromyography, in contrast to the intense motor unit activity seen with cramps. Contractures must not be confused with the limitation of joint range of motion resulting from long-standing joint disease or long-standing weakness—also termed contractures.

The intense muscle contractions of *tetany* are often painful. Although tetany is usually a reflection of hypocalcemia (Chapter 260), it can occasionally be seen without demonstrable electrolyte disturbance. Tetany results from hyperexcitability of the peripheral nerves. Similarly, in the syndrome of *tetanus* produced by a clostridial toxin (Chapter 321), intensely painful, life-threatening muscle contractions arise from hyperexcitable peripheral nerves. A number of toxic disorders such as strychnine poisoning and black widow spider toxin produce similar neurogenic spasms.

MUSCLE PAIN. Acute muscle pain in the absence of abnormal muscle contractions is an extremely common symptom. When such pain occurs following strenuous exercise or in the context of an acute viral illness (e.g., influenza), it probably reflects muscle injury. In such patients, the serum creatine kinase level is often raised. It is uncommon for this frequent and essentially normal sign of muscle injury to be associated with weakness or demonstrable ongoing muscle pathology. *Chronic* muscle pain is a common symptom but is seldom related to a definable disease of muscle.

EPISODIC AND INTERMITTENT WEAKNESS. The complaint of attacks of severe weakness or paralysis occurring in a patient with baseline normal strength is an uncommon symptom. This symptom is typical of the periodic paralyses and may also be seen with episodic ataxias and myotonic disorders (Chapter 463). All of these disorders are ion channelopathies. These channelopathies (e.g., the calcium channelopathy hypokalemic periodic paralysis) are rare but treatable disorders (Chapter 463). Episodic weakness is also seen in patients with neuromuscular junction disorders such as myasthenia gravis and the myasthenic syndrome (Chapter 464). Occasionally, patients with narcolepsy complain of intermittent paralysis as a reflection of *sleep paralysis* (Chapter 438).

LOSS OF BALANCE. Unsteadiness of gait is a common symptom. When associated with the complaints of dizziness or vertigo (Chapter 470), disease of the labyrinth, the vestibular nerve, the brain stem, or the cerebellum is a probable cause. When unsteadiness and loss of balance are unassociated with dizziness, particularly when the unsteadiness appears to be out of proportion to other symptoms of the patient, a widespread disorder of sensation or motor function is likely.

ABNORMAL GAIT AND POSTURE. The ability to stand and to walk in a well-coordinated, effortless fashion requires the integrity of the entire nervous system. Relatively subtle deficits localized to one part of the central or peripheral nervous system produce characteristic abnormalities. Specific gait disturbances are categorized in Table 423–2.

Table 423–2 • CHARACTERISTIC GAIT DISORDERS

SPECIFIC DISORDER	LOCATION OF LESION	CHARACTERISTICS
Spastic gait	Bilateral corticospinal pathways within thoracic or cervical cord, or in the brain	Legs stiff, feet turning inward, "scissoring"
Hemiparetic gait	Unilateral central nervous system, cervical cord, or brain	Affected leg circumducted, foot extended, arm flexed
Sensory ataxia	Posterior columns of spinal cord or peripheral nerve	Wide-based, high steps; Romberg sign present
Cerebellar ataxia	Brain stem or cerebellum	Wide-based; Romberg sign absent
Parkinsonian gait	Basal ganglia	Shuffling, small steps
Dystonic gait	Basal ganglia; also corticospinal pathways	Abnormal posture of arms, head, neck
Gait disorder of the elderly	Multifactorial: bihemispheric disease; spinal cord disease; impaired proprioception; muscle weakness	Stooped posture, wide-based; often retropulsion
Steppage gait	Distal muscle weakness	High steps ("steppage")
Waddling gait	Proximal muscle weakness	Both legs circumducted to allow for locking the knees
Antalgic gait	Non-neurologic, reflects disease of joints, bones, or soft tissue	Minimizes pain in hip, spine, leg
Hysterical gait	Psychiatric or behavioral disorder	Reeling side to side; associated astasia-abasia; bizarre arm and trunk movements

SENSORY SYMPTOMS. Sensory symptoms can be negative or positive. Negative symptoms represent a loss of sensation, such as a feeling of numbness. Positive symptoms, by contrast, consist of sensory phenomena that occur without normal stimulation of receptors and include paresthesias and dysesthesias. *Paresthesias* may include a feeling of tingling, crawling, itching, compression, tightness, cold, or heat, and are sometimes associated with a feeling of heaviness. The term *dysesthesias* is used correctly to refer to abnormal sensations, often tingling, painful or uncomfortable, that occur after innocuous stimuli, whereas *allodynia* refers to a painful perception from a stimulus that is not normally painful. For some patients, it may be difficult to distinguish paresthesias and dysesthesias from pain. *Hypesthesia* and *hypalgesia* denote a loss or impairment of touch or pain sensibility, respectively. By comparison, *hyperesthesia* and *hyperalgesia* indicate a lowered threshold to tactile or painful stimuli, respectively, so that there is increased sensitivity to such stimuli.

With the use of a wisp of cotton, a pin, and a tuning fork, the trunk and extremities are examined for regions of abnormal or absent sensation. Certain instruments are available for quantifying sensory function, such as the computer-assisted sensory examination, which is based on the detection of touch, pressure, vibratory, and thermal sensation thresholds.

Alterations in pain and tactile sensibility can generally be detected by clinical examination. It is important to localize the distribution of any such sensory loss so as to distinguish between nerve, root, and central dysfunction. Similarly, abnormalities of proprioception can be detected by clinical examination, when patients are unable to detect the direction in which a joint is moved. In severe cases, there may be pseudoathetoid movements of the outstretched hands, sensory ataxia, and, sometimes, postural and action tremors.

Disorders of peripheral nerves commonly lead to sensory disturbances that depend on the population of affected nerve fibers (Chapters 461 and 462). Some neuropathies are predominantly large-fiber neuropathies. Appreciation of movement and position are impaired, and paresthesias are common. Examination reveals that vibration, position, and movement sensations are impaired, and movement becomes clumsy and ataxic. Pain and temperature appreciation are relatively preserved. The tendon reflexes are lost early. In other neuropathies, it is the small fibers especially that are affected; spontaneous pain is common and may be burning, lancinating, or aching in quality. Pain and temperature appreciation are disproportionately affected in these neuropathies, and autonomic dysfunction may be present. Examples of small-fiber neuropathies include certain hereditary disorders, Tangier disease, and diabetes. Most sensory neuropathies are characterized by a distal distribution of sensory loss, whereas sensory neuronopathies are characterized by sensory loss that may also involve the trunk and face and that tends to be particularly severe. Sensory changes in a radiculopathy conform to a root territory; in cauda equina syndromes, sensory deficits involve multiple roots and may lead to saddle anesthesia and loss of the normal sensation associated with the passage of urine or feces.

Lesions of the *posterolateral columns* of the cord, such as occur in multiple sclerosis (Chapter 448), vitamin B_{12} deficiency (Chapter 458), and cervical spondylosis (Chapter 429), often lead to a feeling of compression in the affected region and to a Lhermitte sign (paresthesias radiating down the back and legs on neck flexion). Examination reveals an ipsilateral impairment of vibration and joint position senses, with preservation of pain and temperature appreciation. Conversely, lesions of the *anterolateral region* of the cord (as by cordotomy) or *central lesions* interrupting fibers crossing to join the spinothalamic pathways (as in syringomyelia; Chapter 459) lead to an impairment of pain and temperature appreciation with relative preservation of vibration, joint position sense, and light touch. Motor deficits may also be present and help to localize the lesion. Upper motor neuron dysfunction (Chapter 447) from cervical lesions leads to quadriplegia, whereas more caudal lesions lead to paraplegia; lesions below the level of the first lumbar vertebra may simply compress the cauda equina, leading to lower motor neuron deficits from a polyradiculopathy, as well as impairment of sphincter and sexual functions.

Neurologic Diagnostic Procedures

LUMBAR PUNCTURE

Sampling of cerebrospinal fluid (CSF) via lumbar puncture is crucial for accurate diagnosis of meningeal infections and carcinomatosis

FIGURE 423–1 • Cerebrospinal fluid (CSF) examination. *A,* Normal crystal-clear CSF. *B,* Blood in the CSF, which could result from a traumatic (bloody) tap or from subarachnoid hemorrhage—in a traumatic tap, subsequent tubes of CSF are usually less bloody. *C,* Centrifuged CSF in a traumatic tap—the supernatant is nearly clear. *D,* CSF from a patient with subarachnoid hemorrhage—there is blood at the bottom of the tube and the supernatant is yellow (xanthochromic) as a result of breakdown of blood cells in the CSF before the lumbar puncture. (From Forbes CD, Jackson WD: Color Atlas and Text of Clinical Medicine, 3rd ed. London, Mosby, 2003, with permission.)

(Fig. 423–1). CSF analysis is also helpful in evaluating patients with central or peripheral nervous system demyelinating disorders and with intracranial hemorrhage, particularly when imaging studies are inconclusive.

The CSF formula often provides an important clue as to the pathologic process involved. An elevated white blood cell (WBC) count is seen with infections and other inflammatory diseases, as well as with carcinomatosis. The WBC differential cell count may point to a specific class of pathogen: polymorphonuclear leukocytes suggest a bacterial process, whereas mononuclear cells suggest a viral, fungal, or immunologic cause. The CSF glucose concentration is typically reduced in bacterial and fungal infections, as well as with certain viral infections (e.g., mumps virus) and with sarcoidosis. The CSF protein concentration is elevated in a variety of disorders, including most infections and demyelinating neuropathies. Table 423–3 lists characteristic CSF formulas for several neurologic conditions.

A lumbar puncture should not be performed in patients who have obstructive, noncommunicating hydrocephalus or a focal CNS mass lesion causing raised intracranial pressure, because reducing the CSF pressure acutely in these settings via lumbar puncture may result in cerebral or cerebellar herniation. Lumbar puncture may be safely performed in patients with *communicating* hydrocephalus, such as with idiopathic intracranial hypertension (pseudotumor cerebri), and it may even be an effective treatment for selected patients with this condition.

ELECTROENCEPHALOGRAPHY

Electroencephalography (EEG) is the recording and measurement of scalp electrical potentials to evaluate baseline brain functioning and paroxysmal brain electrical activity suggestive of a seizure disorder.

An EEG is performed by securing 20 electrodes to the scalp at predetermined locations, based on an international system that uses standardized percentages of the head circumference, the "10–20 system." Each electrode is labeled using a letter and a number, the letter identifying the skull region (Fp = frontopolar, F = frontal, P = parietal, C = central, T = temporal, O = occipital) and the number identifying the specific location, with odd numbers representing the left-sided electrodes and even numbers the right-sided electrodes. These electrodes are then connected in various combinations of pairs to generate voltage potential differences, and the potentials are recorded on a chart recorder.

To delineate the spatial distribution of the changing electrical field for an EEG, an orderly arrangement of electrode pairs is used, and each specific arrangement is known as a *montage*. Montages are generally of two types: *referential*, in which each electrode is connected to a single reference electrode, such as the ear; and *bipolar*, in which electrodes are connected sequentially to one another, forming a chain. A standard EEG generally records about 30 minutes of brain activity, both in the awake state and in the first two stages of sleep. Various activating procedures are used during the recording of an EEG,

Table 423–3 • CHARACTERISTIC CEREBROSPINAL FLUID FORMULAS

	TURBIDITY AND COLOR	OPENING PRESSURE	WBC (cells/mm³)	DIFFERENTIAL CELLS	RBC COUNT	PROTEIN	GLUCOSE
Normal	Clear, colorless	70–180 mm H₂O	0–5	Mononuclear	0	<60 mg/dL	>2/3 serum
Bacterial meningitis	Cloudy, straw-colored	↑	↑↑	PMNs	0	↑↑	↓
Viral meningitis	Clear or cloudy, colorless	↑	↑	Lymphocytes	0	↑	Normal
Fungal and tuberculous meningitis	Cloudy, straw-colored	↑	↑	Lymphocytes	0	↑↑	↓↓
Viral encephalitis	Clear or cloudy, straw-colored	Normal to ↑	↑	Lymphocytes	0 (herpes ↑)	Normal to ↑	Normal
Subarachnoid hemorrhage	Cloudy, pink	↑	↑	PMNs and lymphocytes	↑↑	↑	Normal (early) ↓ (late)
Guillain-Barré syndrome	Clear, yellow	Normal to ↑	0–5	Mononuclear	0	↑	Normal

PMN = polymorphonuclear leukocyte; RBC = red blood cell; WBC = white blood cell.

including hyperventilation and photic stimulation. These activating procedures may precipitate seizure discharges in some patients with seizure disorders, increasing the sensitivity of the test.

The amplitudes of scalp electrical potentials are quite low, averaging 30 to 100 µV; they represent a summation of excitatory postsynaptic potentials and inhibitory postsynaptic potentials that are largely generated by the pyramidal cells in layer four of the cerebral cortex, which behave as electric dipoles. Action potentials are of too brief a duration to have an effect on the EEG.

The EEG is analyzed with respect to symmetry between each hemisphere, wave frequency and amplitude, and the presence of spikes (20 to 70 msec) and sharp waves (70 to 200 msec) that may indicate a seizure focus. EEG frequencies are divided into four categories as follows:

Delta: <4 Hz
Theta: 4 to 7 Hz
Alpha: 8 to 13 Hz
Beta: >13 Hz

The normal waking EEG in a patient with eyes closed contains rhythms of alpha frequency in the occipital leads and beta frequency in the frontal leads. Normal sleep causes a generalized slowing of the EEG frequencies and an increase in amplitude in each stage of sleep, such that stage 4 sleep consists of greater than 50% large-amplitude delta rhythms.

EEG abnormalities are of two types: abnormalities in background rhythm and abnormalities of a paroxysmal nature. Some of the more common EEG abnormalities are noted in Table 423–4 and Figure 423–2.

The major usefulness of EEG is for diagnosis and categorization of a seizure disorder. EEGs are neither highly sensitive nor completely specific for diagnosing seizures. Because seizures are paroxysmal events, it is not unusual for an EEG to be normal, or only minimally abnormal, in a patient with epilepsy if it is recorded during an interictal phase (the time period between seizures). Only about 50% of patients with seizures show epileptiform activity on the first EEG. Repeating the EEG with provocative maneuvers, such as sleep deprivation, hyperventilation, and photic stimulation, may increase this percentage to 90%. Conversely, about 1% of adults and 3.5% of children who are neurologically normal and who never had a seizure have epileptiform activity on an EEG.

The EEG may provide clues in the diagnosis of certain neurologic conditions, including viral encephalitis, prion disorders, and some forms of coma. In each of these situations, the EEG can have specific patterns that suggest a specific neurologic diagnosis. In herpes simplex encephalitis, periodic lateralizing epileptiform discharges emanating from the temporal lobes are frequently present. Triphasic slow waves are common in hepatic encephalopathy but are a nonspecific finding. Creutzfeldt-Jakob disease is characterized by the presence of bilateral synchronous repetitive sharp waves. The EEG is also helpful in evaluating comatose patients, in confirming brain death when an apnea test cannot be performed because of cardiac instability, and for staging sleep in polysomnography.

In the past, the EEG was often used for localizing neurologic lesions such as stroke, brain tumor, or abscess. With the advent of neuroimaging, EEG is almost never used for these purposes.

Table 423–4 • EEG ABNORMALITIES

EEG ABNORMALITY	CLINICAL CORRELATE
BACKGROUND RHYTHM ABNORMALITIES	
Generalized slowing	Most metabolic encephalopathies
Triphasic waves	Hepatic, renal, and other metabolic encephalopathies
Focal slowing	Large mass lesions (tumor, large stroke)
Electrocerebral inactivity with lack of response to all stimuli	Brain death
PAROXYSMAL ABNORMALITIES	
3-Hz spike and wave, augmented by hyperventilation	Absence epilepsy
3- to 4-Hz spike and wave in light sleep or with photic stimulation	Primary generalized epilepsy
Central to midtemporal spikes	Benign rolandic epilepsy, other partial epilepsies
Anterior temporal spikes or sharp waves	Simple or complex partial seizures of mesial temporal origin
Hypsarrhythmia (high-voltage chaotic slowing with multifocal spikes)	Infantile spasms (West syndrome)
Burst suppression	Severe anoxic brain injury, barbiturate coma

NERVE CONDUCTION STUDY

A nerve conduction study (NCS) is the recording and measurement of the compound nerve and muscle action potentials elicited in response to an electrical stimulus.

To perform a motor NCS, a surface (active) recording electrode is placed over the belly of a distal muscle that is innervated by the nerve in question. A reference electrode is placed distally over the tendon. The nerve is then supramaximally stimulated at a predetermined distance proximal to the active electrode, and the resultant compound motor action potential (CMAP) is recorded. The terminal latency, amplitude, and duration of the evoked potential are measured directly, and the conduction velocity is calculated from the latencies of the evoked potentials with stimulation at two different points: the distance between the two points (conduction distance) is divided by the difference between the corresponding latencies (conduction time), resulting in a calculated velocity (conduction velocity = distance/time).

To perform a sensory NCS, the active recording electrode is placed over that portion of the skin innervated by the nerve in question, and a sensory nerve action potential is recorded following electrical stimulation of the nerve, similar to that noted for a motor NCS.

NCS abnormalities include reduced amplitudes, prolonged terminal latencies, conduction block, and slowed conduction velocities. The clinical significance of these abnormalities is noted in Table 423–5.

An NCS is helpful in documenting the existence of a neuropathy, quantifying its severity, and noting its distribution (i.e., whether it is distal, proximal, or diffuse). In addition, the NCS can provide

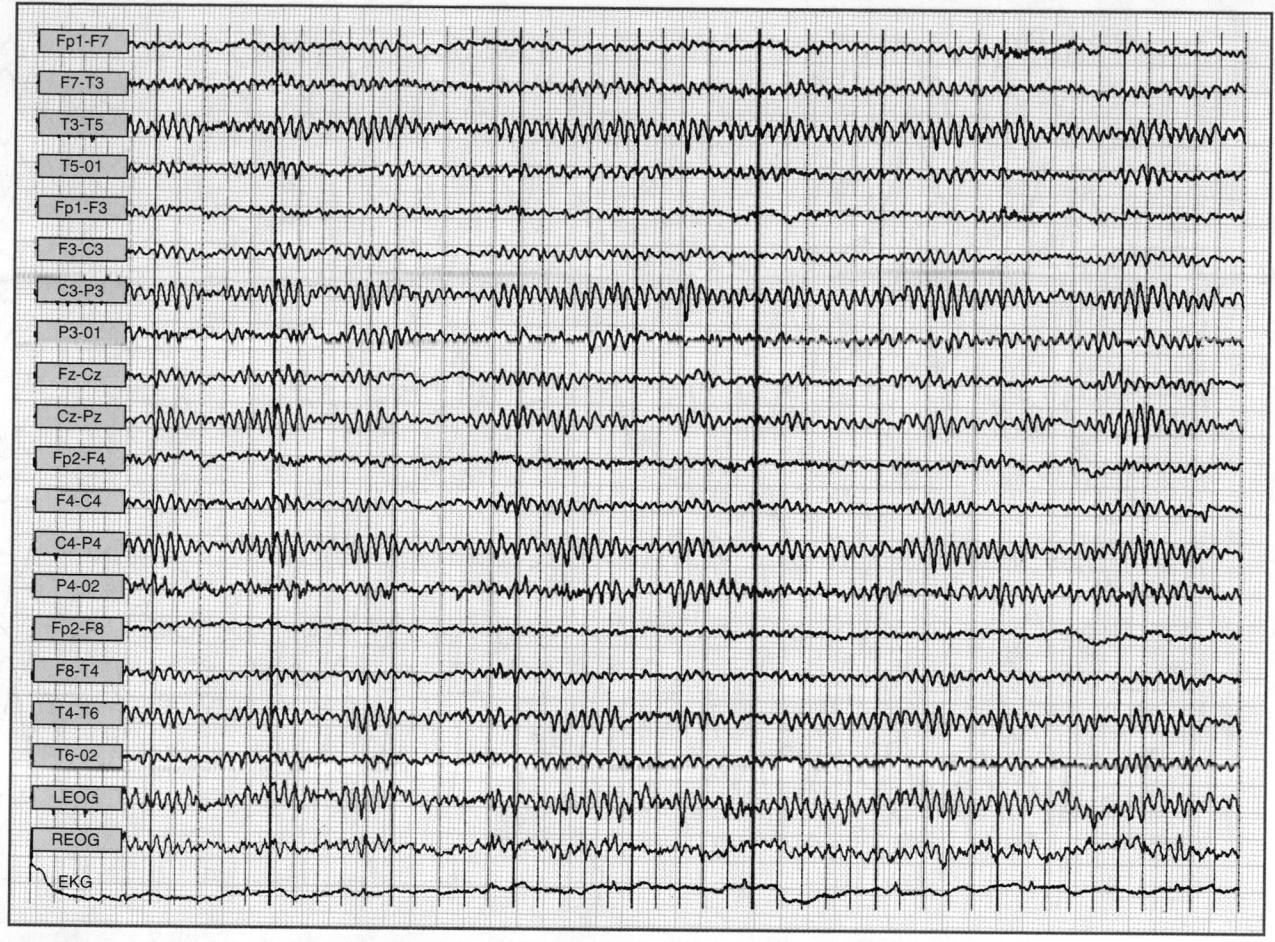

FIGURE 423–2 • Normal and abnormal electroencephalograms (EEGs). *A,* The EEG of a normal awake adult.

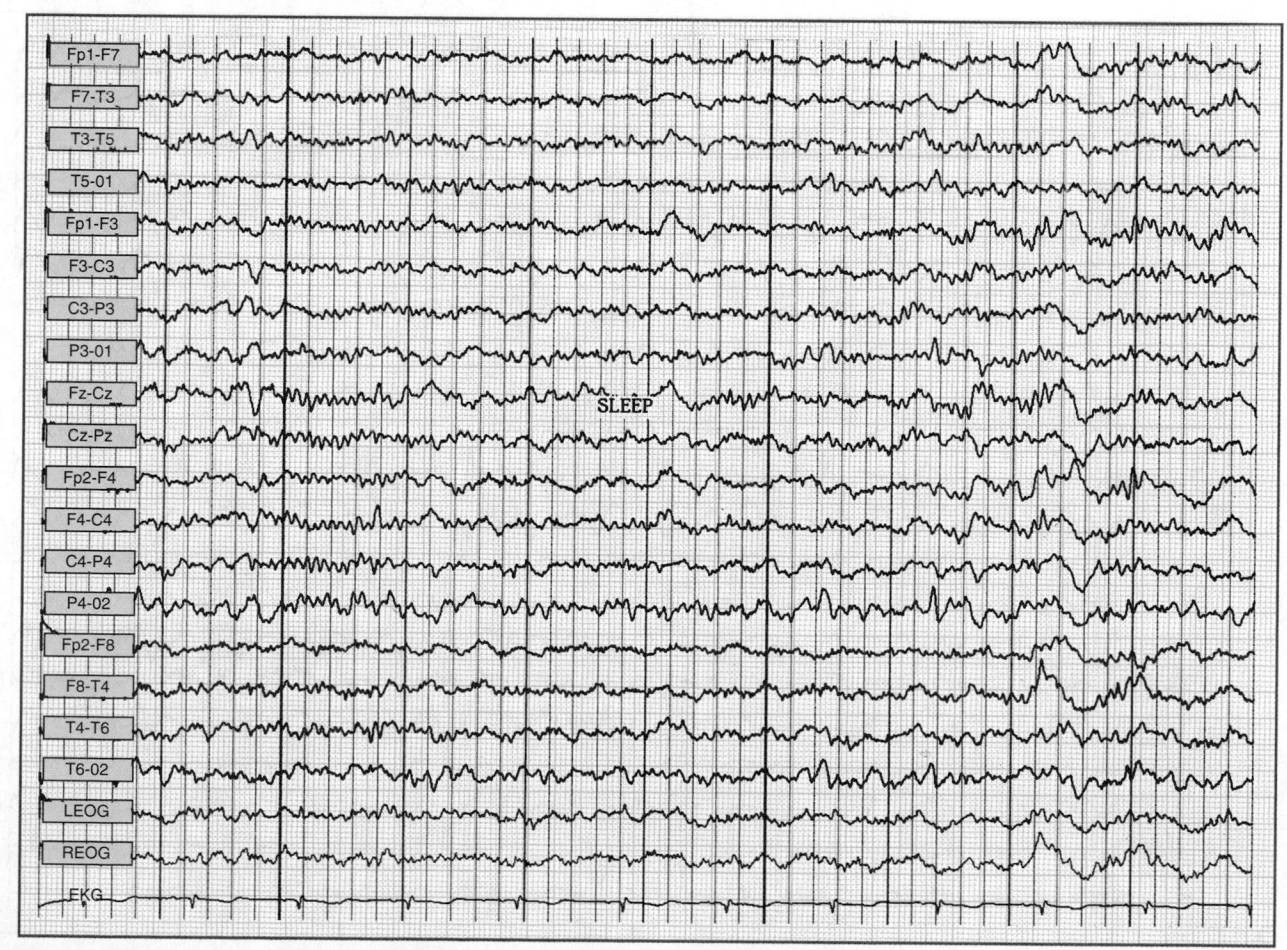

FIGURE 423–2, cont'd. *B,* Stage 2 sleep in a normal adult, demonstrating sleep spindles and K complexes.

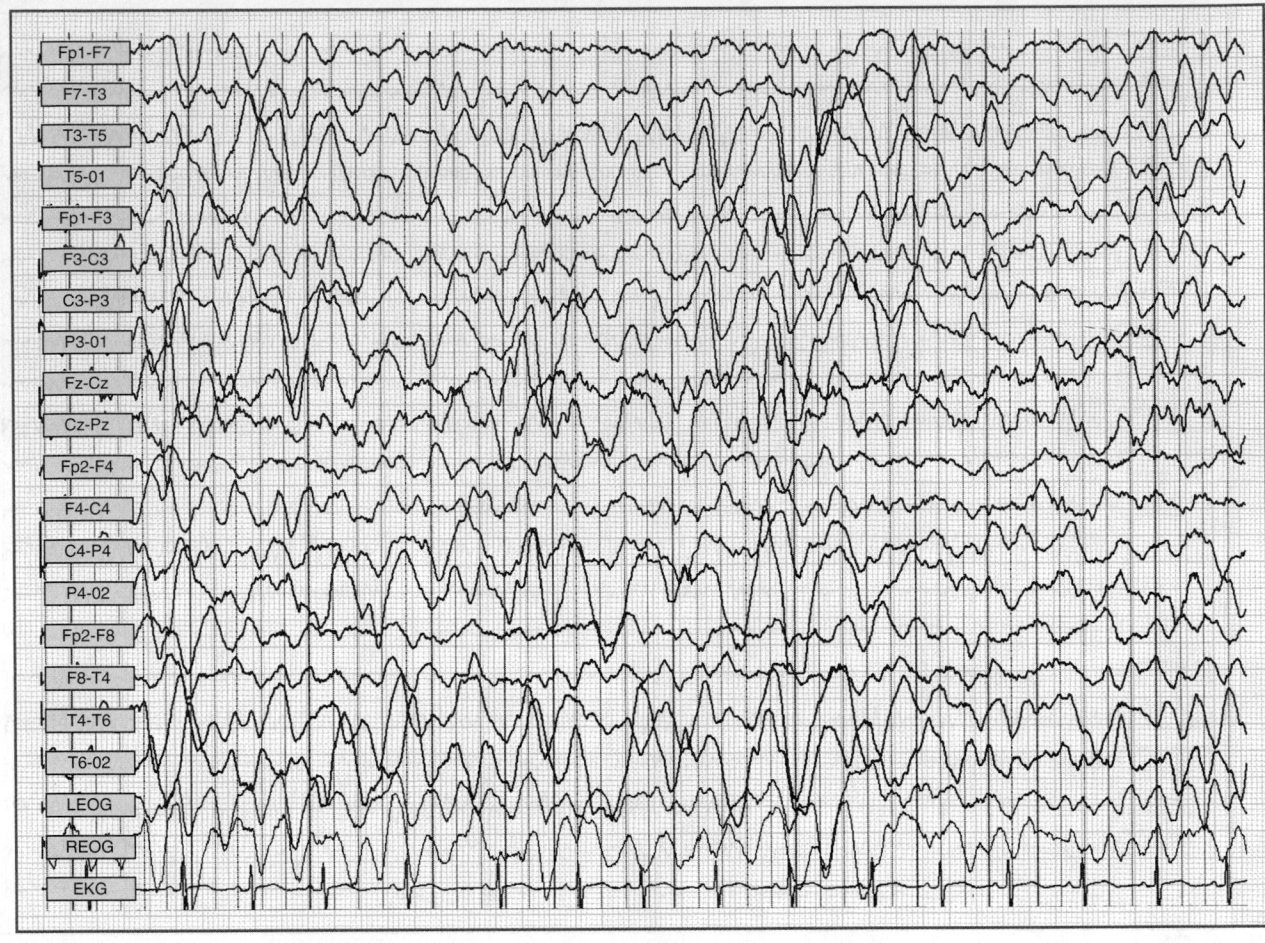

C

FIGURE 423–2, cont'd. *C*, Diffuse encephalopathy, with high-voltage, polymorphic delta waves.

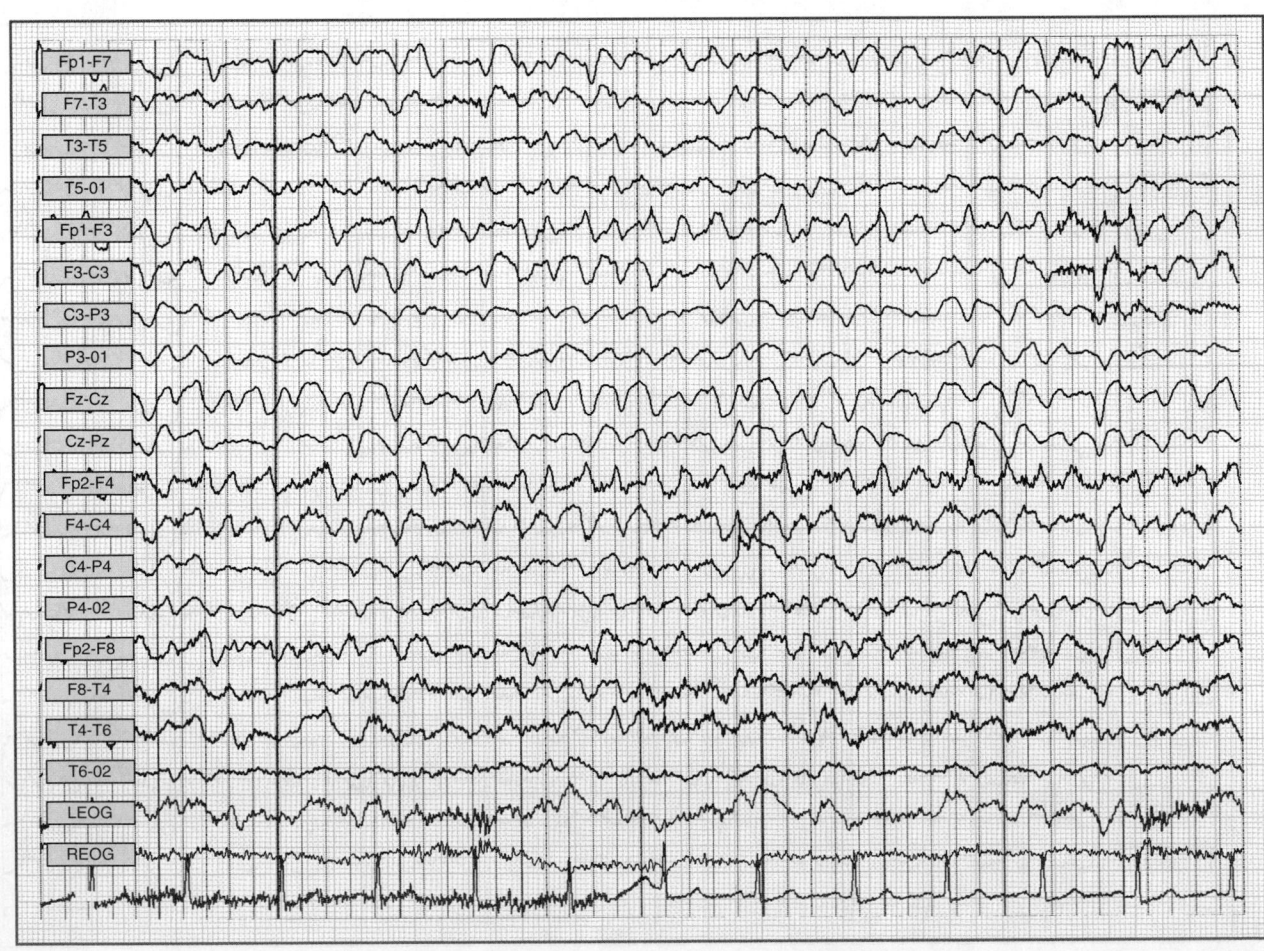

D

FIGURE 423–2, cont'd. *D*, Triphasic slow waves, a pattern seen in hepatic or other metabolic encephalopathies.

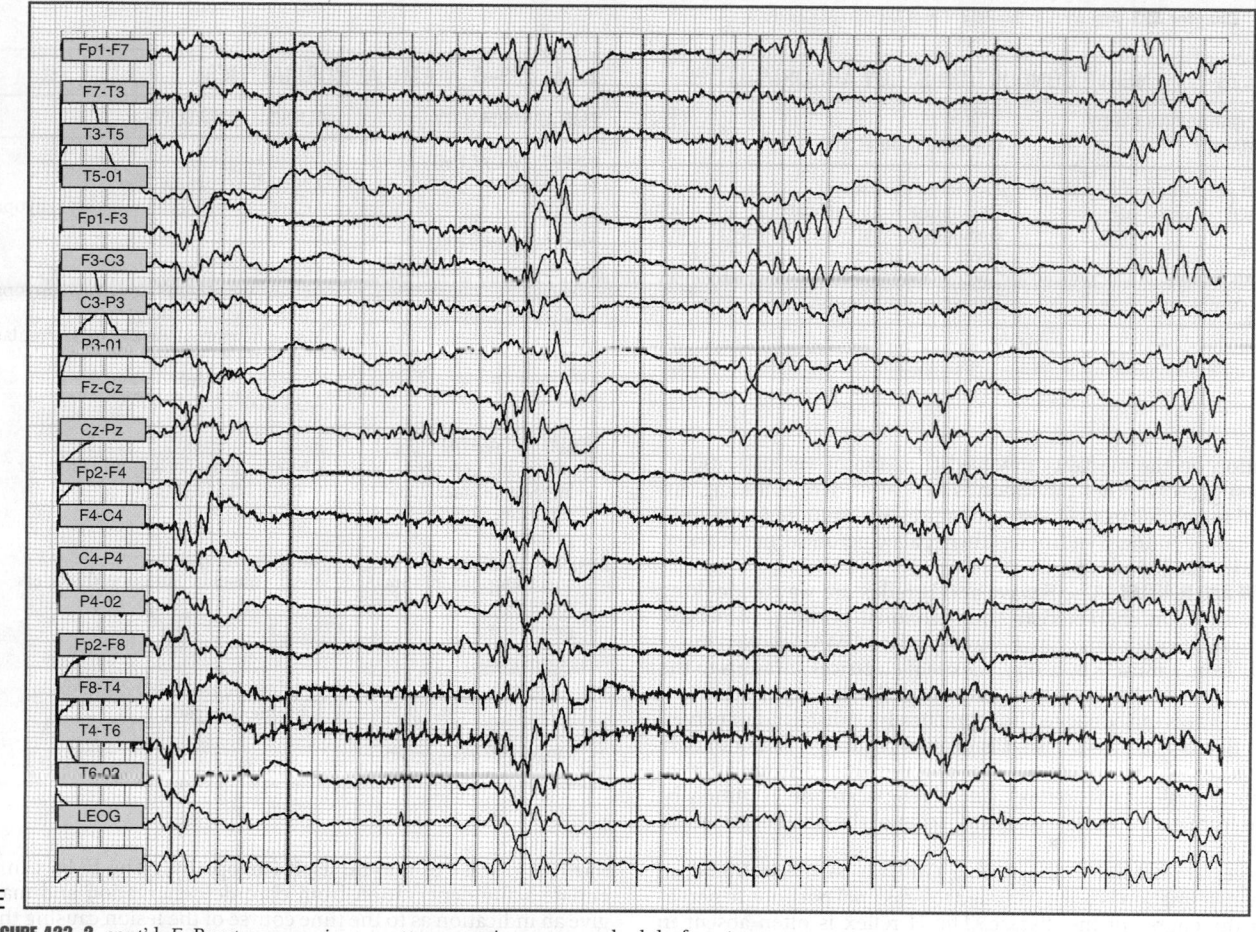

FIGURE 423–2, cont'd. *E*, Burst-suppression, a pattern seen in severe cerebral dysfunction.

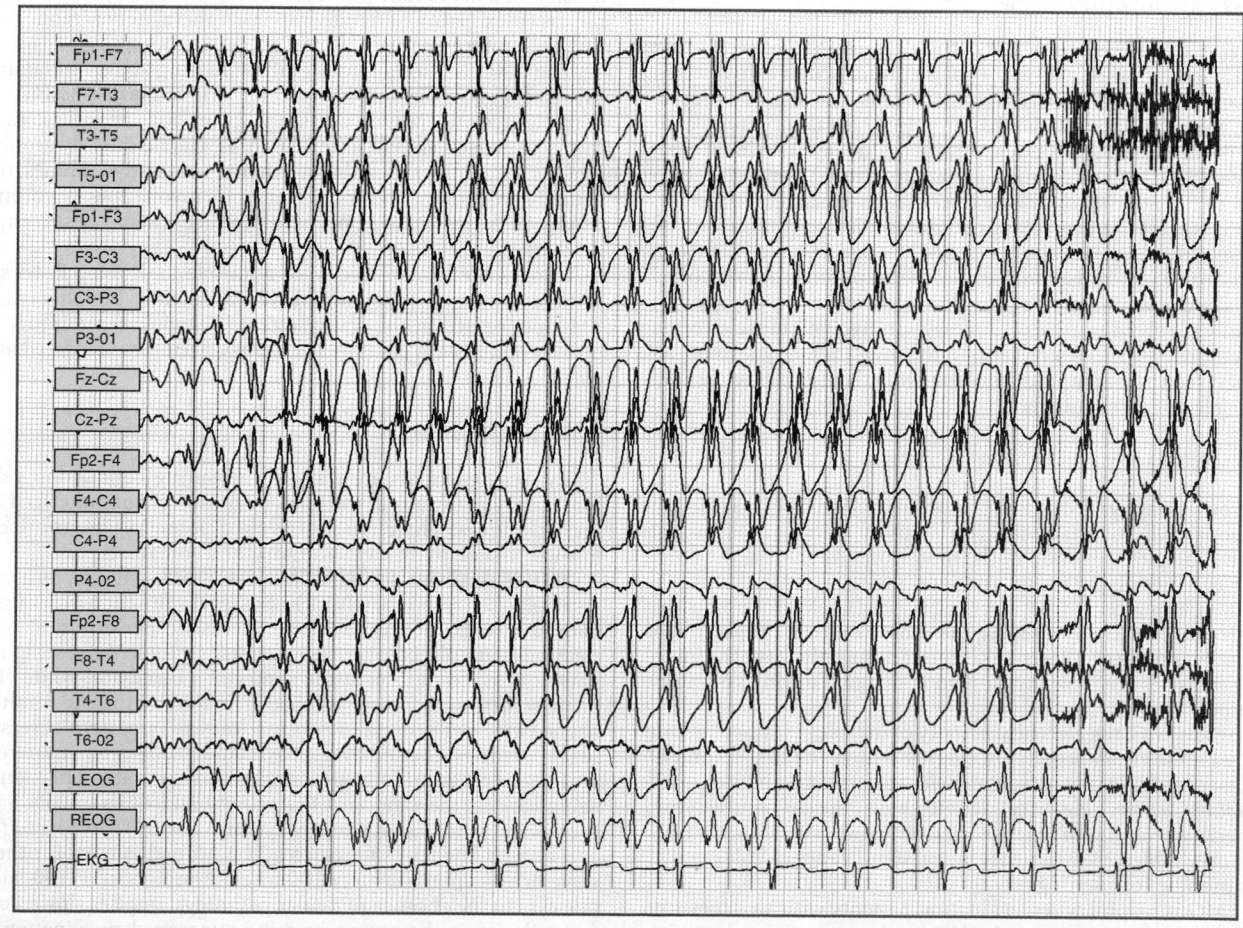

FIGURE 423–2, cont'd. *F*, A 3-Hz spike and wave activity, a pattern seen in absence epilepsy. In each record, channels 1 through 8 and 11 through 18 represent left- and right-sided bipolar electrode placements, respectively. Channels 9 and 10 represent midline bipolar electrode placements, and channels 19 and 20 represent the left and right electro-oculograms (eye movements). Each major horizontal division represents 1 second.

Neurology

Table 423–5 • NERVE CONDUCTION STUDY ABNORMALITIES

NERVE CONDUCTION STUDY ABNORMALITY	CLINICAL CORRELATE
Reduced amplitude of CMAP	Axonal neuropathy
Prolonged terminal latency	Demyelinating neuropathy
	Distal compressive neuropathy
Conduction block	Severe focal compressive neuropathy
	Severe demyelinating neuropathy
Slowed conduction velocity	Demyelinating neuropathy

CMAP = compound muscle action potential.

Table 423–6 • EMG ABNORMALITIES

EMG ABNORMALITY	CLINICAL CORRELATE
INSERTIONAL ACTIVITY	
Prolonged	Acute denervation
	Active (usually inflammatory) myopathy
SPONTANEOUS ACTIVITY	
Fibrillations and positive waves	Acute denervation
	Active (usually inflammatory) myopathy
Fasciculations	Chronic neuropathies
	Motor neuron disease (rare fasciculations may be normal)
Myotonic discharges	Myotonic disorders
	Acid maltase deficiency
VOLUNTARY ACTIVITY	
Neuropathic potentials: large-amplitude, long-duration, polyphasic potentials	Chronic neuropathies and anterior horn cell diseases
Myopathic potentials: small-amplitude, short-duration, polyphasic potentials	Chronic myopathies
	Neuromuscular junction disorders
RECRUITMENT	
Reduced	Chronic neuropathic disorders
Rapid	Chronic myopathies

EMG = electomyogram.

information on the modality involved (i.e., motor versus sensory) and can suggest whether the lesion is axonal or demyelinating. An NCS is also helpful in diagnosing compressive mononeuropathies, such as carpal tunnel syndrome, ulnar palsy, peroneal nerve palsy, and tarsal tunnel syndrome.

F WAVE AND H REFLEX. The F wave and H reflex are ways of looking at the conduction characteristics for proximal portions of nerves, including the nerve roots. The F wave is a late CMAP evoked intermittently from a muscle by a *supramaximal* electrical stimulus to the nerve, and it is due to antidromic activation (backfiring) of α-motor neurons. F waves can be elicited from practically all distal motor nerves. The H reflex is a late CMAP that is evoked regularly from a muscle by a *submaximal* stimulus to a nerve, and it is due to stimulation of Ia afferent fibers (a spinal reflex). The H reflex can only routinely be obtained from calf muscles with stimulation of the tibial nerve in the popliteal fossa.

F waves are helpful in diagnosing Guillain-Barré syndrome, in which demyelination is often confined to proximal portions of nerves early in the course of the disease. The H reflex is often absent in patients with acute S1 radiculopathy.

REPETITIVE STIMULATION STUDY

The repetitive stimulation study (RSS) is a method of measuring electrical conduction properties at the neuromuscular junction. To perform an RSS, a surface recording electrode is placed over a muscle belly, and the nerve innervating that muscle is electrically stimulated with a supramaximal stimulus at a certain frequency. A series of electrical potentials is then recorded whose amplitude is roughly proportional to the number of muscle fibers that are being activated.

The RSS is helpful in diagnosing neuromuscular junction disorders, such as myasthenia gravis and the myasthenic syndrome (Lambert-Eaton syndrome). In myasthenia gravis, the amplitudes of the evoked potentials become progressively smaller with repetitive stimulation in clinically involved muscles. Clinically uninvolved muscles often do not demonstrate this decrement. In the myasthenic syndrome, an *increment* is seen in the amplitudes of the evoked potentials with rapid repetitive electrical stimulation.

ELECTROMYOGRAPHY

Electromyography (EMG) is the recording and study of insertional, spontaneous, and voluntary electrical activity of muscle. This test allows physiologic evaluation of the motor unit, including the anterior horn cell, peripheral nerve, and muscle.

An EMG is performed by inserting a needle electrode into the muscle in question and evaluating the motor unit action potentials both visually (on the oscilloscope screen) and aurally (over the loudspeaker). Muscles are typically studied at rest and during voluntary contraction.

During an EMG, the electrical activity of muscle is studied in four settings: (1) *insertional activity* (occurring within the first second of needle insertion), (2) *spontaneous activity* (electrical activity at rest), (3) *voluntary activity* (electrical activity with muscle contraction), and (4) *recruitment pattern* (change in electrical activity with maximal contraction). Table 423–6 lists the clinical significance of EMG abnormalities in these four settings.

The EMG is helpful when evaluating patients with weakness, in that it can help to determine whether weakness is due to anterior horn cell disease, nerve root disease, peripheral neuropathy, or an intrinsic disease of muscle itself (myopathy). The EMG can differentiate acute denervation from chronic denervation and may thus give an indication as to the time course of the lesion causing the neuropathy. In addition, based on which muscles have an abnormal EMG pattern, it is possible to determine whether the neuropathy is due to a lesion of a nerve root (radiculopathy), the brachial or lumbosacral plexus (plexopathy), an individual peripheral nerve (mononeuropathy), or multiple peripheral nerves (polyneuropathy).

The EMG is also helpful in differentiating active (inflammatory) myopathies from chronic myopathies. The active myopathies include dermatomyositis, polymyositis, inclusion body myositis, and some forms of muscular dystrophy, such as Duchenne's dystrophy. The chronic myopathies include the other muscular dystrophies, the congenital myopathies, and some metabolic myopathies. Myotonic dystrophy and myotonia congenita produce characteristic myotonic discharges.

It may take several weeks for a muscle to develop EMG signs of acute denervation following nerve transection. For this reason, an EMG performed in the acute setting following nerve injury should be interpreted with caution, and it may need to be repeated at a later date.

EVOKED POTENTIALS

Evoked potentials are ways of measuring conduction velocities for sensory pathways in the CNS by means of computerized averaging techniques. Three types of evoked potentials are routinely performed: visual, brain stem auditory, and somatosensory.

PATTERN REVERSAL VISUAL-EVOKED RESPONSES. The pattern reversal visual-evoked response (PVER) assesses the function of central visual pathways, in particular the optic nerves. To perform this test, EEG electrodes are placed over the occipital regions of the scalp and the patient is asked to look at the center of a black-and-white checkerboard screen with one eye patched. The color of the checks alternates about twice per second, a process known as pattern reversal. The scalp potentials elicited by approximately 100 such pattern reversals are then recorded and signal-averaged by a computer. This signal averaging cancels the random EEG activity and differentially amplifies the evoked potential. A single waveform (P 100) is recorded for each eye, and its latency is measured. The normal latency for the P 100 waveform is approximately 100 msec. A prolonged P 100 latency in one eye, in the absence of ocular pathology, implies slowed conduction velocity in the optic nerve and suggests demyelination of that nerve. PVER testing is helpful when multiple sclerosis is suspected

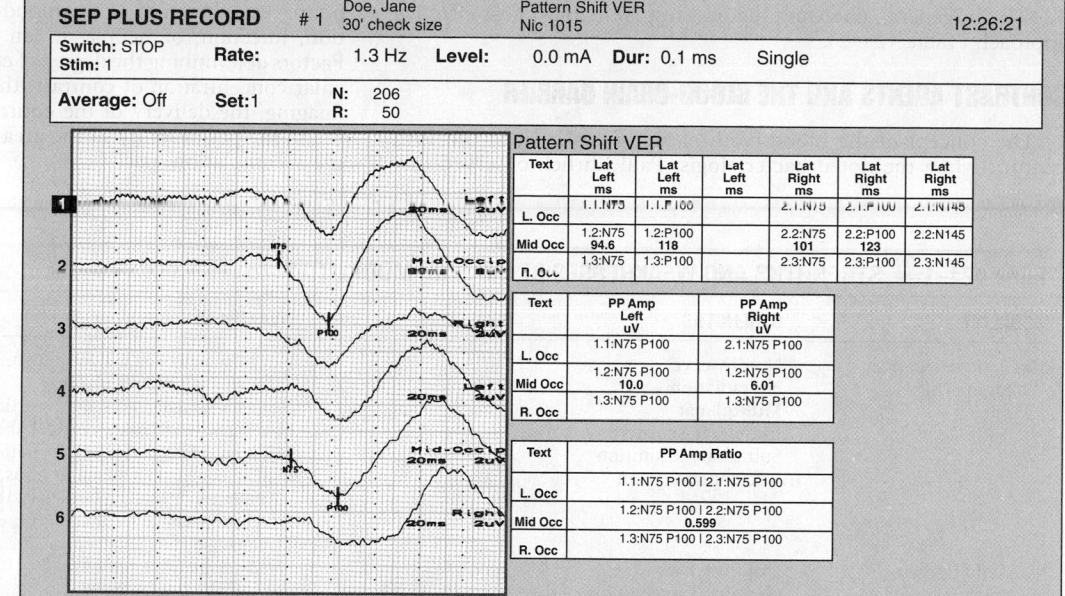

SEP PLUS RECORD # 1

Doe, Jane
30' check size

Pattern Shift VER
Nic 1015

12:26:21

Switch: STOP
Stim: 1

Rate:

1.3 Hz

Level:

0.0 mA

Dur: 0.1 ms

Single

Average: Off

Set:1

N: 206
R: 50

Pattern Shift VER

Text	Lat Left ms	Lat Left ms	Lat Left ms	Lat Right ms	Lat Right ms	Lat Right ms
	1.1:N75	1.1:P100		2.1:N75	2.1:P100	2.1:N145
L. Occ						
	1.2:N75	1.2:P100		2.2:N75	2.2:P100	2.2:N145
Mid Occ	94.6	118		101	123	
	1.3:N75	1.3:P100		2.3:N75	2.3:P100	2.3:N145
R. Occ						

Text	PP Amp Left uV	PP Amp Right uV
	1.1:N75 P100	2.1:N75 P100
L. Occ		
	1.2:N75 P100	1.2:N75 P100
Mid Occ	10.0	6.01
	1.3:N75 P100	1.3:N75 P100
R. Occ		

Text	PP Amp Ratio
	1.1:N75 P100 I 2.1:N75 P100
L. Occ	
	1.2:N75 P100 I 2.2:N75 P100
Mid Occ	0.599
	1.3:N75 P100 I 2.3:N75 P100
R. Occ	

FIGURE 423–3 • Abnormal pattern reversal visual-evoked response in a patient with multiple sclerosis, demonstrating a prolonged P 100-wave latency with left eye stimulation, and suggesting a conduction defect in the left optic nerve. The top three channels represent right eye stimulation and the bottom three channels represent left eye stimulation. Each horizontal division represents 20 msec.

clinically and it is necessary to document the presence of a second demyelinating lesion in the CNS that may not be clinically evident (Fig. 423–3).

BRAIN STEM AUDITORY-EVOKED RESPONSES. The brain stem auditory-evoked response (BAER) assesses function in the central auditory pathways in the brain stem. EEG electrodes are placed over the vertex and mastoid process, and a series of clicks at a frequency of 5 Hz are delivered to each ear separately for 3 minutes. The scalp potentials elicited by the clicks are then recorded and signal-averaged by a computer. This signal averaging cancels the random EEG activity and differentially amplifies the evoked potential. A series of five waves is recorded for each ear, and each wave corresponds to a different point in the central auditory pathway (Table 423–7). The wave latencies for the right and left ears are compared, and a delay in any of the latencies suggests a lesion at that point in the central brain stem auditory pathway. BAER testing is helpful in diagnosing acoustic schwannoma and other tumors in the cerebellopontine angle.

SOMATOSENSORY-EVOKED RESPONSES. The somatosensory-evoked response (SER) assesses conduction in the central somatosensory pathways in the posterior columns of the spinal cord, brain stem, thalamus, and primary sensory cortex in the parietal lobes. To perform the SER, recording electrodes are placed over Erb's point and cervical spine (for medial or ulnar nerve stimulation); over the popliteal fossa and lumbar spine (for peroneal or tibial nerve stimulation); and over the scalp. A series of 1000 to 2000 electrical shocks at a frequency of 5 Hz are delivered to the median or ulnar nerve (for an upper extremity SER) or to the peroneal or tibial nerves (for a lower extremity SER). The scalp potentials elicited by the electrical shocks are then recorded and signal-averaged by a computer. This signal averaging cancels the random EEG activity and differentially amplifies the evoked potential. A series of waves is recorded for each nerve stimulated, with each wave corresponding to a different point in the somatosensory pathways in the spinal cord, brain stem, and cerebral cortex. The wave latencies for the right and left limbs are compared, and a delay in any of the latencies suggests a lesion at that point in the somatosensory pathways.

SER testing, like PVER, is helpful when multiple sclerosis is suspected clinically and it is necessary to document the presence of a second demyelinating lesion in the CNS that may not be clinically evident. SER is also useful in monitoring spinal cord function intraoperatively in patients undergoing spinal surgery.

ELECTRONYSTAGMOGRAPHY

Electronystagmography accurately records eye movements and nystagmus following certain provocative maneuvers. To perform this test, disc electrodes are placed over the bridge of the nose and lateral to each outer canthus, and the electrical leads from these discs are connected to an oscilloscope. Because the cornea is electropositive and the retina is electronegative, these electrodes accurately record lateral eye movements. The patient is first observed for spontaneous nystagmus with the eyes open and closed, and then for nystagmus evoked with lateral gaze, for nystagmus induced by hot and cold air instilled in the outer ears (caloric induced), and for positional nystagmus. The latter is performed by rotating the patient in a specialized chair. Spontaneous nystagmus suggests a vestibular pathologic lesion, as does an imbalance in the nystagmus evoked by these maneuvers in the right and left ears.

SUGGESTED READING

Ebersole JS, Pedley TA: Current Practice of Clinical Electroencephalography. Philadelphia, Lippincott Williams & Wilkins, 2002. *A comprehensive text.*

424 RADIOLOGIC IMAGING PROCEDURES

Robert I. Grossman

Over the past 25 years, medical imaging has evolved into its current pivotal position in the diagnosis of neurologic disorders. With computed tomography (CT) and magnetic resonance imaging (MRI), the clinician can noninvasively identify most areas of the brain and spine that are responsible for the signs and symptoms that have brought the patient to seek medical attention. Conventional angiography is still used in the work-up of vascular causes of neurologic disease, principally for conditions that cause endovascular abnormalities. Although much less commonly performed, myelography is used in certain cases, particularly when MRI is contraindicated. Ultrasound, magnetic resonance spectroscopy (MRS), single-photon emission computed tomography (SPECT), and positron emission tomography (PET) have specific applications in the diagnosis of neurologic disease. To use these tests intelligently, the physician must understand the

Table 423–7 • BAER WAVE GENERATORS

WAVE	LOCATION
I	Auditory nerve
II	Cochlear nucleus
III	Superior olivary nucleus
IV	Lateral lemniscus
V	Inferior colliculus

sensitivity, specificity, and limitations of each imaging technique (Table 424–1). In general, choosing the best test is the most cost-effective approach (Table 424–2).

CONTRAST AGENTS AND THE BLOOD-BRAIN BARRIER

The concept of the blood-brain barrier dates back to the 19th century, when the noted bacteriologist Paul Ehrlich observed that dyes injected intravenously stained all organs of an animal except the brain. Any alteration of the blood-brain barrier such as inflammation, infection, or neoplasm can produce contrast enhancement. Factors determining the degree of enhancement include the intravascular concentration of contrast, the interval between injection and imaging, the delivery of the contrast material to the region of the brain, the permeability of the area of the lesion, and the volume of the accumulation space.

Table 424–1 • STRENGTHS AND WEAKNESSES OF IMAGING MODALITIES

MODALITY	STRENGTHS	WEAKNESSES
Magnetic resonance imaging (MRI)	Noninvasive No radiation Multiplanar Extremely sensitive Soft tissue resolution Safe contrast agent	Not as sensitive as CT for detection of subarachnoid hemorrhage (even with FLAIR images) Not as sensitive as CT for detection of calcification Less sensitive to bony cortical abnormalities (e.g., cortical fractures) MRI cannot be performed in patients who have pacemakers, non-MRI-compatible vascular clips, pain stimulator implants, metallic implants or foreign bodies in the eyes, or in severe claustrophobia Need cooperative patient Time consuming relative to CT
Magnetic resonance angiography (MRA)	Noninvasive Very good screening tool for extracranial and intracranial vascular disease Readily repeatable Safe May be performed without contrast May be performed with contrast to evaluate long segments including the origins of the great vessels of the neck Can demonstrate very tight stenosis and very slow flow better than nonenhanced MRA Can produce rotational images to guide the surgical approach	Need cooperative patient Technically demanding Can miss extracranial tandem lesions May overestimate the degree of vascular stenosis (noncontrast MRA) Cannot image distal vessels optimally without contrast May miss small lesions, such as aneurysms <3 mm
Proton magnetic resonance spectroscopy (MRS)	Localization of seizure focus May help diagnose and classify dementias, such as Alzheimer's disease May distinguish brain tumors from other mass lesions May distinguish radiation necrosis from recurrent tumor	Specificity not yet determined Not routinely available Lower resolution Time consuming
Ultrasound	Fast Easy to use; can be performed at the bedside Intraoperative ultrasound can localize lesions in the brain and spinal cord	Does not assess the vertebral arteries Less sensitive and specific than MRA Cannot visualize vessels in the upper neck and cranial base Can misdiagnose high-grade stenoses as occlusions
Transcranial Doppler (TCD)	Fast Easy to use Assesses vascular velocities quantitatively Can assess cerebral vasospasm and sometimes occluded vessels	Does not provide images of vessels
Computed tomography (CT)	Fast Can easily detect acute intraparenchymal or subarachnoid hemorrhage and calcification Easy to monitor patients Excellent for studying bones and bone lesions, including bony spinal stenosis Postoperative studies when MR is precluded by hardware	Less sensitive to parenchymal lesions than MR Potential for significant contrast reaction Radiation exposure
Conventional angiography	Best imaging modality for aneurysms, vascular malformations, and vasculitis	Invasive and often lengthy Small but significant risk of stroke (0.5-1.0%) and other complications (overall about 5%) Significant expertise needed to perform procedure
Conventional myelography	Good images of nerve roots and small osteophytic lesions Accurate for bony stenosis Useful in patients with contraindications to MR Can detect blockages of cerebrospinal fluid	Invasive, with small risk of complications from lumbar puncture and instillation of contrast Does not image intramedullary lesions well Poor soft tissue resolution Difficulty in imaging conus
CT myelography	Excellent for imaging nerve roots and detecting root compression from degenerative processes	Invasive, with small risk of complications from lumbar puncture and instillation of contrast Does not image intramedullary lesions well
Positron emission tomography (PET)	Sensitive for diffuse pathologic processes Distinguishes radiation necrosis from tumor Helpful in the diagnosis of Alzheimer's disease Useful in planning surgery for epilepsy Can study diseases of the basal ganglia, including Parkinson's disease and multisystem atrophy	Requires a cyclotron to generate radioisotopes with a short half-life Lower resolution than MRI or CT Less available than MRI or CT
Single-photon emission tomography (SPECT)	Useful in epilepsy and Alzheimer's disease Sensitive for diffuse pathologic processes Easier to use than PET	Lower resolution than PET, MRI, or CT

Table 424–2 • IMAGING METHODOLOGIES FOR NEUROLOGIC PROBLEMS

NEUROLOGIC PROBLEM OR DISORDER	IMAGING METHODOLOGY	COMMENT
Nonlocalized symptoms	MRI without and with contrast	Once a physician decides that an imaging study is warranted, MRI is the most sensitive modality for initial imaging
Suspected subarachnoid hemorrhage	CT without contrast MR with FLAIR	Best imaging method to detect subarachnoid hemorrhage Best MRI technique to detect subarachnoid hemorrhage
Suspected intracranial aneurysm (high probability, such as acute cranial nerve III palsy)	Conventional angiography	Definitive
Familial history of aneurysm or predisposing condition (e.g., polycystic kidney disease)	MRA	Noninvasive and excellent for detecting aneurysms
Suspected stroke	CT	CT is fast and can detect intraparenchymal hemorrhage or ischemic infarction.
	Diffusion-weighted MRI	Fast and extremely sensitive for the diagnosis of acute stroke
	Perfusion MRI	Very sensitive measure of blood flow and volume; may be abnormal when diffusion is initially negative; in combination with diffusion, may be able to separate reversible from irreversible tissue damage
Suspected neoplasm	MRI without and with contrast	Most sensitive imaging test
Suspected multiple sclerosis	MRI without and with contrast	Most sensitive imaging test
Suspected infection or inflammation	MRI without and with contrast	Most sensitive imaging test
Dementia	MRI without contrast (rarely is contrast helpful)	The first test should be MRI to detect any lesion such as a frontal meningioma, normal pressure hydrocephalus, and multi-infarct dementia; PET and SPECT scanning may be helpful, and PET is particularly sensitive for diagnosing Alzheimer's disease in patients with minimal cognitive impairment.
Seizures or epilepsy	MRI without and with contrast	The first test should be MRI to detect any lesion that is the source of seizures; PET, SPECT, MRS, and magnetoencephalography (MEG) can also localize seizure foci.
Head trauma	CT; MRI is also useful for follow-up	CT is the fastest method to assess head trauma; MRI is more sensitive and specific for detecting diffuse axonal injury.
Intrinsic spinal cord lesion	MRI without and with contrast	Most sensitive imaging modality for detecting spinal cord disease.
Extradural spinal process	MRI without and with contrast; CT myelogram	For nonneoplastic disease, MRI without contrast is sufficient; CT myelogram is particularly useful for degenerative disease of the cervical spine.

Contrast agents or radionuclide tracers that cross an altered blood-brain barrier can be used as markers to detect central nervous system lesions. Whether a patient should have a contrast-enhanced image is determined by the differential diagnosis (Table 424–3). For example, no contrast is necessary to demonstrate an intraparenchymal hemorrhage, but an enhanced study is generally necessary to determine if the hemorrhage was the result of a metastasis.

Other issues about the use of intravenous contrast center on the particular imaging modality. For CT, the debate focuses on the use of low-osmolar (i.e., generally nonionic, more expensive but safer) versus high-osmolar (i.e., ionic, less expensive but less safe) contrast agents. Data suggest that the number of severe contrast reactions (i.e., hypotensive shock, pulmonary edema, respiratory arrest, cardiac arrest, or convulsions) is substantially reduced (from 157 to 126 per 100,000) by using low-osmolar contrast agents; however, there appears to be no reduction in the risk of death (0.9 per 100,000 uses). Both high- and low-osmolar contrast agents are extremely safe. An additional

consideration is that iodinated agents (i.e., ionic and nonionic) are potentially nephrotoxic, particularly in patients with diseases or clinical states that predispose to kidney injury, such as multiple myeloma, severe diabetes, dehydration, recent aminoglycoside exposure, anuria, hepatorenal syndrome, serum creatinine level higher than 3 mg/dL, and administration of glucophage. Specific indications for nonionic contrast agents include previous adverse reaction to an ionic agent, asthma, heart failure, pulmonary hypertension, and severe general debilitation.

The incidence of contrast reactions is much lower with MRI contrast agents. MRI, barring any contraindications, is generally the modality of choice when a contrast-enhanced examination of the central nervous system is indicated. It usually requires a small dose of contrast (10 to 20 mL) and is not associated with contrast-induced nephropathy. The rate of severe anaphylactoid contrast reactions with gadolinium agents is reported to be between 0.0003 and 0.01%.

IMAGING TECHNIQUES

Magnetic Resonance Imaging

ECHO PLANAR IMAGING (EPI). EPI is the fastest imaging technique. Entire images are acquired in less than 50 milliseconds. EPI has the ability to produce motion frozen "snapshots" of function, such as in the heart and lung, and can be used to study diffusion and perfusion and to perform task-induced functional images of the brain. The rapidity of EPI imaging is also useful in uncooperative patients and in children. EPI images are not yet as high quality as spin-echo or fast spin-echo (FSE) images.

FLUID-ATTENUATED INVERSION RECOVERY (FLAIR) IMAGING. FLAIR is a pulse sequence that yields heavily T2-weighted images in which cerebrospinal fluid (CSF) is nulled (i.e., dark). FLAIR images have the ability to increase the detection of lesions that are at the interface between brain (i.e., bright) and CSF (i.e., dark). With conventional spin-echo or FSE images, cortical, subcortical, or periventricular lesions are generally difficult to visualize because of the lack of contrast between high-intensity cortex and high-intensity CSF, whereas

Table 424–3 • INDICATIONS FOR UNENHANCED AND ENHANCED IMAGING (CT OR MRI) IN DISEASES OF THE BRAIN AND SPINE

UNENHANCED IMAGES	ENHANCED IMAGES
Hemorrhagic event	Infection
Ischemic event	Inflammation
Congenital anomaly	Neoplasia—primary or metastatic
Head trauma	Any process thought to involve the leptomeninges, nerve roots
Neurodegenerative disease	Seizures
Degenerative disease of the spine (not operated)	Intrinsic spinal cord lesions or suspected lesions in the subarachnoid space
Spinal cord trauma	Extradural spinal cord lesions from primary neoplastic or metastatic lesions
	Postoperative spine to separate scar from recurrent disc

on FLAIR images, such high-intensity lesions are highlighted against the juxtaposed dark CSF. FLAIR is the best MR pulse sequence to detect subarachnoid hemorrhage and other processes that increase the protein content of the CSF (e.g., infection, inflammation, carcinomatous meningitis); the dark CSF is rendered bright on FLAIR images.

GRADIENT-ECHO IMAGING. In gradient-echo scanning, a rephasing gradient pulse follows the initial flip-angle magnetization, and the gradient-echo scans can better detect magnetic field inhomogeneities. Blood products, iron, calcium, and manganese deposition are seen more readily with gradient-echo scanning. These scans should be part of routine trauma protocols searching for blood, and they are also useful when calcified lesions are suspected.

DIFFUSION-WEIGHTED IMAGING. Diffusion of molecules implies a random process of molecular displacements caused by thermal agitation (i.e., brownian motion). Random displacement of the molecules (i.e., diffusion) in the imaging voxel leads to echo attenuation. The phenomenon has been interpreted as follows. Cellular swelling from breakdown of the sodium-potassium pump reduces the extracellular space. Because the dominant contribution to diffusion arises from extracellular water molecules, diffusion becomes restricted, with a net reduction in the diffusion coefficient. This process results in an increase in the signal of diffusion-weighted images (i.e., less echo attenuation) and a very bright region seen on the image. Conversely, if apparent diffusion coefficient (ADC) maps are displayed, reduced diffusivity shows up as a zone of lower intensity. ADC maps are particularly helpful when an abnormality has increased water content (e.g., an old infarct) and appears as an area of brightness (but not very bright) on the diffusion-weighted image, called *T2 shine-through*. To eliminate the T2 effect, scanning is performed with the diffusion gradients off and on; dividing the latter by the former eliminates the T2 effect, leaving just the ADC image to allow the distinction between T2 shine-through brightness on diffusion-weighted images from true decreases in ADC. The ADC map correctly separates an acute lesion (i.e., lower intensity) from an old infarct (i.e., higher intensity).

Diffusion-weighted MRI can detect cerebral ischemia within minutes of its onset, whereas conventional MRI does not become abnormal until a few hours after a cerebral infarction. Based on diffusion characteristics, diffusion-weighted MRI can also differentiate acute from chronic infarction. This technique is also a sensitive way to detect hemorrhage.

PERFUSION IMAGING. Perfusion imaging differs from diffusion imaging in that its aim is to characterize microscopic flow at the capillary level. Conventional radiologic techniques, including catheter angiography, PET, and SPECT, can estimate tissue perfusion, but MRI perfusion imaging may have higher spatial resolution and is minimally invasive. Techniques include the use of exogenous contrast agents (gadolinium) or magnetic labeling (spin tagging) of arterial water. There is some evidence that subtraction of perfusion from diffusion images can demonstrate an area of ischemic brain that is at risk for infarction after stroke (i.e., ischemic penumbra). When the difference between the perfusion and diffusional abnormalities is large, the potential benefit of acute intervention with thrombolytic agents may be greater. Conversely, if there is no perfusional abnormality or if it is equal to the diffusional lesion, infarction has occurred, and the thrombolysis is unlikely to be effective.

BLOOD OXYGEN LEVEL DEPENDENCE EFFECT AND FUNCTIONAL IMAGING. Intravascular deoxyhemoglobin is paramagnetic, hence susceptibility-induced gradients between the intracellular and extracellular compartments cause spin dephasing and signal loss in a gradient-echo sequence. Replacement of deoxyhemoglobin by oxyhemoglobin during increased blood flow, such as caused by activation of a critical region involved in a particular task, lowers the extent of these gradients and slightly increases signal intensity. By subtracting a prestimulus image from a postactivation image, the difference highlights the zone of altered tissue oxygenation. Field strengths of 3 Tesla or higher are advantageous for demonstrating this effect, which is the basis of functional MRI (fMRI) and how it can localize normal brain function as well as discrete motor and speech abnormalities associated with neurologic disease.

INDICATIONS AND LIMITATIONS OF MRI. MRI is the most commonly used imaging modality for the central nervous system. Its power lies in the ability to produce multiplanar images of high resolution with considerable sensitivity to pathologic abnormalities. With few exceptions, it can answer most questions about the brain and spine that a clinician may pose. There are exceptions to MRI as a first study:

1. To exclude subarachnoid hemorrhage, noncontrast CT is the fastest, most sensitive, and most specific imaging modality to demonstrate subarachnoid hemorrhage, although FLAIR MRI also appears to be quite sensitive. The presence of subarachnoid blood on CT obviates the need for lumbar puncture in most patients with symptoms and/or signs consistent with this diagnosis. The next study after a positive CT is an angiogram, which is performed to find the cause of the bleeding. Negative results for CT occur in approximately 2 to 5% of cases with definite subarachnoid hemorrhage, most commonly if subarachnoid hemorrhage is caused by a vascular lesion of the spinal cord, if the CT was performed very early when only a small amount of blood was present, or if the subarachnoid blood disappeared rapidly before imaging was performed. If there is a strong clinical suspicion of subarachnoid hemorrhage but a negative CT, the next step is a lumbar puncture. Delayed lumbar puncture (12 hours) can detect xanthochromic blood pigments (formed after lysis of red blood cells) and distinguish true subarachnoid hemorrhage from a bloody traumatic lumbar puncture.
2. CT is more sensitive and specific than MRI for detecting calcification as seen in craniopharyngioma, retinoblastoma, chondrosarcoma, Sturge-Weber syndrome, toxoplasmosis, and tuberous sclerosis. If the detection of calcium is important, noncontrast CT is necessary.
3. When there is a question of bony cortical abnormalities, CT is preferred. Although MRI easily detects the fat in bone marrow, the cortex of bone is seen as a signal void, and subtle cortical fractures are relatively easy to miss. After skull trauma, displaced shards of bone or cranial penetration by foreign matter may be difficult to visualize with MRI. In the setting of acute cranial or facial trauma, CT is useful to detect facial or skull fractures.
4. CT is the first study for acute head trauma or facial trauma, sinusitis, temporal bone problems such as inflammatory or congenital lesions, and the immediate postoperative craniotomy patient.
5. CT is preferred for situations in which MRI is relatively or absolutely contraindicated: patients with pacemakers, non–MRI-compatible vascular clips, or metallic implants or foreign bodies in the eyes and agitated or uncooperative patients for whom sedation may be contraindicated.

Magnetic Resonance Angiography

Magnetic resonance angiography (MRA) has great inherent appeal and is rapidly replacing conventional angiography. There are two different techniques used to generate MRA: time-of-flight (TOF) and phase contrast (PC) angiography. After the imaging data are gathered, they may be processed by a number of display techniques. The one most commonly used is called maximal intensity projection (MIP), which finds the brightest pixels along a ray and projects them along any viewing angle. MIP is fast and insensitive to low-level variations in background intensity.

TIME OF FLIGHT. The principle is that protons not immediately exposed to a radiofrequency (RF) pulse (unsaturated spins) flow into the imaging volume and have higher signal intensity than the partially saturated stationary tissue, which has lost signal because of the RF pulse. This is a T1 effect and has also been called *flow-related enhancement*. The images can be acquired as individual slices (two-dimensional) acquisition or as a volume (three-dimensional) acquisition. In either case, flowing blood will appear bright. The two-dimensional TOF techniques are very sensitive to slow or moderate flow because flow-related enhancement is maximized, whereas three-dimensional techniques are better than two-dimensional MRA for rapid flow and have higher resolution.

Most centers use two-dimensional or three-dimensional TOF MRA to evaluate the carotid bifurcation and three-dimensional TOF or PC MRA to evaluate the intracranial circulation. Gadolinium-enhanced MRA is usually advocated to evaluate the neck vessels.

PHASE CONTRAST. The principle of PC involves using bipolar flow-sensitizing gradients of opposite polarity to tag moving spins, which are then identified as a result of their position change at the time of each gradient application. The operator chooses the flow velocities that the angiogram will be sensitive to, called the VENC, which varies in neuroradiology from 30 cm/second for arterial flow to 15 cm/second for venous flow. Complex subtraction of data from the two acquisitions (one of which inverts the polarity of the bipolar gradient) cancels all phase shifts except those due to flow. This technique provides excellent background suppression to differentiate flow from other causes of T1 shortening, such as methemoglobin or fat. This technique is useful in cases of suspected venous thrombosis.

CONTRAST-ENHANCED MRA. A new and important improvement in MRA has been the use of paramagnetic contrast enhancement in association with three-dimensional TOF imaging (cMRA). The procedure generally requires very fast pulse sequences combined with software that can time the intravenously administered bolus of contrast. The use of paramagnetic vascular enhancement abolishes the signal loss secondary to spin saturation from slow flow or in-plane flow. The result is a high-resolution image of the extracranial or intracranial vessels, including the aortic arch. Timing is critical, because enhancement of veins confounds the ability to demonstrate arterial anatomy. This methodology may be useful to exclude aneurysm or other vascular malformations and to study the carotid bifurcation as well as the aortic arch. cMRA may also be able to delineate the exact location of large vessel intracranial vascular occlusions from embolic disease, the presence of intracranial stenosis, and the narrowing of vessels from vasculitis. cMRA has several advantages. It is fast, generally under 2 minutes; it visualizes the origins of the arteries from the aorta and supra-aortic vessels; it detects tight stenosis better than two-dimensional TOF MRA; and it distinguishes slow flow better than unenhanced three-dimensional TOF MRA.

INDICATIONS AND LIMITATIONS OF MRA. MRA is the best noninvasive technique for evaluating the extracranial vasculature for the presence of a hemodynamically significant lesion of the carotid arteries, dissection of the vertebral and carotid arteries, extracranial traumatic fistula, extracranial vasculitis such as giant cell arteritis, and congenital abnormalities of the vessels such as fibromuscular disease. Intracranial MRA is used to detect aneurysms particularly when an aneurysm is relatively unlikely, such as in a patient with a headache (Table 424–4); when a diagnosis is important but treatment or conventional angiography is contraindicated; or for follow-up of treated aneurysm. Indications for MRA include follow-up of unruptured aneurysms and evaluation of intracranial vasculitis, stroke, venous occlusive disease, congenital arteriovenous malformations, vascular compression syndromes, and definition of the blood supply to vascular neoplasms. Small aneurysms, particularly those less than 3 mm in diameter, can be missed by MRA, and conventional angiography

Table 424–4 • DISORDERS ASSOCIATED WITH INTRACRANIAL ANEURYSMS

Autosomal dominant polycystic kidney disease (10% of asymptomatic patients)
Ehlers-Danlos syndrome type IV
Marfan's syndrome
Neurofibromatosis type 1
Fibromuscular dysplasia
Moya moya disease
Coarctation of the aorta
Takayasu's disease
Collagen vascular disease
Pseudoxanthoma elasticum
α-Glucosidase deficiency
α_1-Antitrypsin deficiency
Alkaptonuria
Anderson-Fabry disease
Homocystinuria
Familial idiopathic nonarteriosclerotic cerebral calcification syndrome
Hereditary hemorrhagic telangiectasia
Noonan's syndrome
Tuberous sclerosis
Werner's syndrome
3M syndrome (i.e., dolichospondylic dysplasia)

From Schievink WI, Schaid DJ, Rogers HM, et al: On the inheritance of intracranial aneurysms (review). Stroke 1994;25:2028–2037.

remains the definitive diagnostic modality for the diagnosis of intracranial aneurysm.

Compared with CT angiography, MRA generally involves no or low doses of contrast agents and no radiation. MRA can be repeated multiple times (if no contrast is used) during the same examination, and it has a larger field of view that commonly includes the origin of the posterior inferior cerebellar artery.

MRA requires that patients be cooperative, because motion degrades the images. The limitations of extracranial MRA include a tendency to overestimate stenosis, particularly if two-dimensional TOF methods are used. It is also difficult to detect tandem lesions with MRA, and ulcerations in atheromas are poorly seen. If blood flow is very slow, MRA may falsely suggest occlusion in a vessel that has a high-grade stenosis. Patients with a history of transient ischemic attacks or recent neurologic deficits may have unrecognized embolic occlusions, which are difficult to detect with intracranial MRA because of poor visualization of the distal vessels. Surgery in such cases can be associated with hemorrhagic complications. MRA images, particularly of distal intracranial vessels, are often difficult to interpret. Vasculitis and other diseases of distal vessels require careful examination of all images, preferably after the image is segmented, so that each vessel can be viewed independently without overlap of other vessels.

Magnetic Resonance Spectroscopy

MRS, primarily proton MRS, offers the potential ability to identify chemical compounds within the central nervous system. It is being increasingly applied to the study of brain diseases, including brain neoplasms, Alzheimer's disease, human immunodeficiency virus (HIV) infection, epilepsy, and multiple sclerosis. The proton MRI spectrum is characterized by at least three peaks representing the compounds creatine, which is associated with cellular energy metabolism; choline, which is associated with cell membranes; and N-acetyl aspartate, which is considered to be a marker of neuronal integrity. Lactate is not detectable in the MRS of normal brain but may be seen with inflammation and infarction. Other peaks may be found in proton spectra, particularly those acquired at short echo times, including inositol, the methyl group of lipids, and peaks associated with γ-aminobutyric acid (GABA), glutamate, and glutamine. The appearance of the latter peaks in the adult MRI spectrum may be associated with pathologic conditions. MRI spectra are acquired using primarily one of two volume localization techniques: point-resolved spectroscopy (PRESS) and stimulated-echo acquisition mode (STEAM). Spectroscopic images of metabolites may also be acquired using methods that are hybrids of conventional spectroscopy and imaging techniques. A recently developed spectroscopic technique enables absolute quantification of entire brain's N-acetyl aspartate, which is localized exclusively in the neuron, axon, and dendrites. Decreased N-acetyl aspartate has been reported in many neurologic conditions, including multiple sclerosis, stroke, and HIV encephalopathy. Its loss also can be useful in the localization of temporal lobe epilepsy. Increased choline levels may indicate myelin breakdown, inflammation, or neoplasia, and choline assessment has the potential to detect abnormal membrane metabolism. MRS may increase the diagnostic specificity of MRI, and it also may provide a surrogate marker for monitoring treatment trials for neoplasia or multiple sclerosis.

Computed Tomography

CT uses a highly collimated x-ray beam that passes through the patient and is differentially absorbed by tissue. The photons are detected and imaged, and contrast is dependent on the differential absorption of the photons by the tissue being studied. The scale, in Hounsfield units (HU), for CT absorption ranges from +1000 to −1000, with zero being water and −300 to −1000 representing fat. White matter and gray matter are in the 30- to 50-HU range, hematomas are indicated by 50 to 80 HU, and calcification correlates with 150 HU. On axial CT, each revolution of the gantry around the patient produces one data set or slice. In the latest CT technology, the x-ray tube rotates continually (i.e., helical CT), allowing a continuous volume of transaxial data to be acquired rapidly and yielding slices at a rate of more than 1 slice per second at a thickness of 1 mm or less. The x-ray dose to the patient is generally less than 3 rads.

INDICATIONS AND LIMITATIONS. CT, which is a fast alternative to MRI for imaging of the brain, is not quite as sensitive for parenchymal and leptomeningeal processes, particularly white matter lesions such as seen in multiple sclerosis, but it is better for detecting subarachnoid hemorrhage, calcification, and cortical bone abnormalities. CT is also used in patients for whom MRI is contraindicated.

Computed Tomographic Angiography

Computed tomographic angiography (CTA) is emerging as an alternative to MRA for imaging extracranial and intracranial blood vessels. It requires placement of a small catheter, usually in the antecubital vein, and the injection of approximately 75 mL of iodinated contrast material. CTA is probably as good as MRA for detecting aneurysms 3 mm or larger (i.e., those having the greatest likelihood of rupture). Compared with MRI, CTA is faster (requires less than 32 seconds), less motion sensitive, can easily visualize slow flow or turbulent flow in aneurysms (particularly large aneurysms), can present a multiplanar view of the vascular anatomy from any perspective, and can be used in patients who are intubated or have aneurysm clips. CTA can also detect calcification in the neck of an aneurysm, provide bony surgical landmarks, and detect intraluminal thrombus, all of which may be useful for planning treatment.

The limitations of CTA include the risks of intravenous iodinated contrast injection; the time and necessity for data processing; the exposure to radiation; the possibility that subarachnoid hemorrhage may obscure a bleeding aneurysm; difficulty in imaging the take-off of the posterior inferior cerebellar arteries; and artifacts related to aneurysm clips or calcifications in the walls of the vessels or other sites. CTA is used as a screening tool to detect aneurysms rapidly in symptomatic patients and to screen asymptomatic patients at risk for cerebral aneurysms.

Computed Tomographic Evaluation of Perfusion

Xenon-133 CT is a method for evaluating cerebral perfusion. The xenon is inhaled in combination with oxygen, and CT scans are performed to determine cerebral blood flow at multiple locations in the brain. Decreased flow has been documented in patients with meningitis, vasospasm, head trauma, sickle cell disease, and stroke. Side effects of xenon inhalation may include sedation, bronchospasm, and respiratory depression. Iodine-based CT perfusion has also been introduced. CT perfusion cerebral blood flow maps are sensitive for diagnosing ischemia. Infarctions occur in all patients in areas of the brain with cerebral blood flow values equal to or less than 30% of normal tissue values and in 50% of patients whose affected tissues have blood flows that are 30 to 50% that of normal tissue.

Conventional Angiography

Arterial catheter angiography is the definitive imaging modality for vascular lesions of the brain and great vessels of the neck. In most cases, the catheter is passed through the femoral artery selectively into the great vessels of the neck and their branches. In many institutions, images are performed by digital subtraction rather than conventional film. The incidence of complications is approximately 8.5%, with a 0.1% to 0.33% risk of permanent complications (the most significant of which is stroke), a 2.6% incidence of transient complications, and a 4.9% incidence of local complications. Hemodynamically significant narrowing occurs when the diameter of the vessel is decreased by 50 to 60%. Depending on the beliefs of surgeons and physicians caring for the patient, extracranial occlusive vascular disease may be evaluated solely with noninvasive imaging techniques, including ultrasound and MRA, or noninvasive imaging may be followed by catheter angiography. In ambiguous or problematic cases, catheter angiography is usually performed.

Conventional angiography is routinely used for the diagnosis of aneurysm, arteriovenous malformation, and vasculitis. In patients in whom an aneurysm must be excluded, all intracranial vessels must be injected. Most cases of subarachnoid hemorrhage are the result of rupture of intracranial aneurysm; if neither an aneurysm nor an intracerebral vascular malformation is found, it is important to assess the extracranial vessels for a dural malformation, to consider spinal angiography to exclude a spinal malformation, to ascertain whether the patient

has vasculitis, and to repeat a study after initial negative results in 1 to 2 weeks.

Carotid Ultrasound and Transcranial Doppler

Color-coded Doppler ultrasound can depict the residual lumen of the extracranial carotid artery more accurately than conventional duplex Doppler. However, compared with contrast angiography, Doppler measurements have a sensitivity of only 54% and a specificity of just 80% for detecting a stenosis of greater than 70%.

Transcranial Doppler ultrasound is a noninvasive means used to evaluate the basal cerebral arteries through the infratemporal fossa. It evaluates the flow velocity spectrum of the cerebral vessels and can provide information regarding the direction of flow, the patency of vessels, focal narrowing from atherosclerotic disease or spasm, and cerebrovascular reactivity. It can determine adequacy of middle cerebral artery flow in patients with carotid stenosis and evidence of embolus within the proximal middle cerebral artery. It is very useful in the detection of cerebrovascular spasm after subarachnoid hemorrhage or after surgery, and it can rapidly assess the results of intracranial angioplasty or papaverine infusions to treat vasospasm.

Nuclear Medicine Techniques: Positron Emission Tomography and Single-Photon Emission Computed Tomography

Nuclear medicine methodology uses a variety of radioactive substances that can be localized by a crystal scintillation device (i.e., gamma camera). PET employs positron-emitting isotopes that are manufactured in a cyclotron, and SPECT uses an iodinated radiotracer, technetium 99m, or other radiotracers. These techniques, which image function more than anatomy, are most useful in diagnosing disorders that do not possess easily identifiable anatomic correlates or are associated with diffuse disease throughout the brain. In nuclear medicine, thallium imaging is being advocated to distinguish lymphoma (hot) from toxoplasmosis (not hot) in patients with acquired immunodeficiency syndrome (AIDS). Indium can be instilled into the subarachnoid space to help detect and localize cerebrospinal fluid leaks and to aid in the diagnosis of normal pressure hydrocephalus.

PET and SPECT can help make the diagnosis of Alzheimer's disease by finding hypoperfusion in the temporal-parietal regions, particularly in the entorhinal cortex, hippocampus, and temporal neocortex. The reported sensitivity of SPECT ranges from 64 to 96%, but it may be 95% or greater in severely demented patients. [^{18}F]2-fluoro-2-D-deoxyglucose (FDG) PET studies show a 20 to 30% decrease in the cerebral metabolic rate of glucose in Alzheimer's disease compared with normal, healthy controls, and FDG PET may predict the development of Alzheimer's disease in patients with minimal cognitive impairment.

Technetium-99m hexamethylpropyleneamine oxime (99mTc-HMOAO) SPECT and FDG PET have been applied to other degenerative dementias, including Pick's disease and Creutzfeldt-Jacob disease. CT and MRI are often normal or show only nonspecific atrophy even with advanced disease; altered metabolic activity on PET or SPECT scanning precedes neuronal loss and may even occur before electrical cortical changes.

PET and SPECT may also be applied to lateralizing temporal lobe epilepsy. However, some reports suggest that proton MRI spectroscopy is more sensitive for this purpose.

SPINE IMAGING

MRI is generally the best modality for imaging the spinal cord and the spaces surrounding it. The approach for intramedullary (i.e., within the spinal cord) and extramedullary intradural lesions should consist of multiplanar images, including T2-weighted and postcontrast pulse sequences. The diagnosis of spinal cord compression due to extradural metastatic lesions, trauma, or osteoporotic compression is best performed by the same imaging approach.

MRI is the preferred method to detect intrinsic damage to the spinal cord, extrinsic compression from bone and disc fragments, and ligamentous injury. CT with multiplanar reconstruction can supplement plain cervical spine films to identify anatomic regions not well visualized by plain films, including C1-2, C6-7, and C7-T1.

MRI is the first approach for presumed vascular lesions of the spinal cord, including small dural malformations that result in venous hypertension. However, the definitive study for vascular lesions of the spinal cord is spinal angiography.

Thoracic and lumbar degenerative disc disease is also easily imaged with axial and sagittal, T1- and T2-weighted MRI sequences. Contrast is necessary only in the postoperative patient with persistent problems to separate scar, which usually enhances, from recurrent or residual disc, which usually does not avidly enhance. Although MRI is generally the most efficient method to study degenerative disease of the cervical spine, it may not be the most sensitive. CT myelography provides the best images of degenerative spine lesions such as small osteophytes that impinge on nerve roots. Multiplanar MRI is also excellent for studying lesions that affect the peripheral nerves, including the brachial plexus.

Plain Films

Plain skull films are rarely, if ever, indicated and should never be ordered as the primary imaging study because they provide little useful information. If paranasal sinus studies are needed, CT performed in the coronal planes is the study of choice. Plain films of the spine are also less informative than MRI or CT; however, plain spine films aid in triage for acute spinal cord trauma by assessing bony fractures and dislocations. Passive flexion-extension plain films provide some measure of the stability after cervical spine injury, but MRI can precisely demonstrate any ligamentous injury.

Interventional Neuroradiology

Endovascular techniques can temporarily occlude vessels to determine whether the patient can tolerate removal of vessels that are encased by tumor and can occlude a carotid-cavernous sinus fistula using detachable balloons that preserve the parent vessel. Interventional neuroradiologic techniques can also occlude intracranial aneurysms by packing them with tiny balls of wire (i.e., coiling) through an endovascular catheter. Many varieties of vascular malformations in the brain and spinal cord may be occluded using an endovascular approach with occlusive agents or detachable balloons. Vascular tumors such as meningiomas may be treated by preoperative embolization to decrease intraoperative blood loss. Intracranial vascular spasm after subarachnoid hemorrhage may be reduced by balloon dilatation of the involved vessels or local infusion of papaverine. Intracranial and extracranial arterial stenosis may be dilated with a balloon catheter and then kept open with a vascular stent positioned in the vessel. Vascular stenting has also been used in vascular dissection and in the treatment of pseudoaneurysm. These and other endovascular therapies are rapidly evolving as alternatives to traditional surgical approaches.

SUGGESTED READINGS
Atlas SW: Magnetic Resonance Imaging of the Brain and Spine, 3rd ed. Philadelphia, Lippincott Williams & Wilkins, 2002.
Grossman RI, Yousem DM: Neuroradiology, the Requisites, 2nd ed., Philadelphia, WB Saunders, 2003.
Two detailed texts with outstanding illustrations.

425 NEUROGENETICS

Charles Thornton
Robert C. Griggs

Advances in molecular medicine are rapidly changing the classification of neurologic diseases and explaining their mechanisms (Table 425–1). Whereas neurologic diseases are not unique in this regard, the impact has been arguably greater for the nervous system than for any other system, perhaps as a reflection of the large number of different genes that are expressed in the nervous system and the com-

plexity of genetic mechanisms that underlie the development of the nervous system.

The nervous system is uniquely susceptible to the harmful effects of certain mutations. For example, investigations of inherited neurologic disease have uncovered a class of mutations (i.e., expansions of triplet, tetramer, and pentamer repeats) not previously observed in any other species. These mutations are remarkably unstable. For these expanded repeats, the rates of mutation are increased more than a million fold over background rates in the human genome. One consequence of this prodigious rate of genetic change is that clinical manifestations vary markedly within a family, sometimes showing more severe disease in successive generations. This variability results from enlargement or contraction of the expanded repeat when it is transmitted from one generation to the next. Growth of an expanded repeat over time within an individual may influence the natural history of diseases, such as myotonic dystrophy, that show marked instability of an expanded repeat in somatic cells. Although these mutant genes are expressed in many organs, the phenotypes that they produce are often confined to the nervous system.

Traditional views on neurologic diagnosis and pathogenesis have been expanded or revised to accommodate many recent advances in neurogenetics. The genetic lesions causing most human neurologic diseases listed in Table 425–1 have been reproduced by genetic engineering in mice, fruit flies, or other species. Animal models are available for many neurologic diseases, such as Huntington's disease, that previously were observed only in humans. These models are providing important insights into the mechanisms of disease, and they may also revolutionize the process of identifying new treatments.

Different mutations in the same gene can produce different diseases. For example, the neurologic syndromes of familial hemiplegic migraine, episodic ataxia, or progressive spinocerebellar ataxia can all be caused by mutations in the *CACNL1A4* gene, which encodes a neuronal calcium channel. The phenotype in some individuals combines elements of all three disorders.

Diseases once considered to be single clinical and pathologic entities are now known to be caused by independent mutations in two or more genes. For example, mutations in any of three genes can cause familial Alzheimer's disease (see Table 425–1). Each of the encoded proteins appears to have a role in the proteolytic processing of the amyloid precursor protein, and the manifestations produced by these different genes are indistinguishable by conventional clinical and pathologic examination. Other disorders in which similar genetic heterogeneity results in a virtually identical phenotype include inherited Parkinson's disease, amyotrophic lateral sclerosis, and some types of spinocerebellar atrophy.

Genetic influence over a wide range of characteristics as diverse as personality or predisposition to neurodegeneration has been shown by studies of twins. As the catalogue of known genetic variants, or polymorphisms, in the human genome is rapidly expanding, the process of identifying the polymorphisms that influence behavior or susceptibility to disease has begun. To give two examples, a polymorphism in the gene encoding a dopamine receptor is associated with novelty seeking behavior and attention deficit/hyperactivity disorder, and polymorphisms in the gene encoding apolipoprotein E are associated with Alzheimer's disease. Proof of cause and effect is more difficult for these disease-associated polymorphisms than for disease-causing mutations. However, the likelihood that a polymorphism is biologically significant becomes strong when its association with a disease or behavioral trait is confirmed in many different populations and when there is evidence that the polymorphism affects biochemical function.

With the recognition that genetic factors cause or predispose patients to many neurologic diseases, the family history is an important but emotionally charged and potentially distressing part of the patient's history. Alzheimer's disease, epilepsy, Tourette's syndrome, and other common diseases imply a considerable risk to the patient or the patient's offspring, but they are often denied on family history. Absence of a family history of disease is seldom an argument against considering that the patient may have a hereditary condition. Two specific features of neurologic disorders are important to consider in obtaining a family pedigree. First, *anticipation*, the worsening of a disease with successive generations, is a feature of the trinucleotide repeats diseases. Second, many *mitochondrial* genetic diseases are transmitted only from mothers to their male and female offspring; sometimes, this form of inheritance can be misinterpreted as autosomal dominant. Only if male-to-male transmission is observed can autosomal dominant inheritance be considered established.

Table 425–1 • GENETIC BASES OF SOME IMPORTANT NEUROLOGIC DISEASES

SYNDROME/LOCALIZATION	DISEASE	LOCUS	GENE	INHERITANCE	IMPLICATION/MECHANISM	CHROMOSOME
Dementia	Familial Alzheimer's disease	AD1	Amyloid precursor protein	AD	Proteolysis yields neurotoxic β amyloid	21
		AD2	Apolipoprotein E4 allele	—	Elevates risk of sporadic Alzheimer's disease	19
		AD3	Presenilin-1	AD	Increased production of beta amyloid	14
		AD4	Presenilin-2	AD	Highly similar to presenilin-1	1
	Frontotemporal dementia with parkinsonism		Microtubule-associated protein tau	AD	Filamentous inclusions of tau protein	17
	Creutzfeldt-Jakob disease (prion disease)		Prion protein	AD	Conformational change, protein aggregation	20
Movement disorder	Familial Parkinson's disease	PARK1	α-Synuclein	AD	Major component of Lewy body	4
		PARK2	Parkin	AR	Dysfunction of ubiquitin-proteasome system	6
		PARK5	Ubiquitin carboxyterminal hydrolase L1	AD	Dysfunction of ubiquitin-proteasome system	4
	Huntington's disease		Huntingtin	AD	Expanded CAG repeat, protein aggregation	4
	Spinocerebellar ataxia	SCA1	Ataxin-1	AD	Expanded CAG repeat, protein aggregation	6
		SCA2	Ataxin-2	AD	Expanded CAG repeat, protein aggregation	12
		SCA3	Ataxin-3	AD	Expanded CAG repeat, protein aggregation	14
	Friedreich ataxia		Frataxin	AR	Deregulation of iron metabolism in mitochondria	9
Epilepsy	Juvenile myoclonic epilepsy		GABA$_A$ receptor, α$_1$-polypeptide	AD	Altered function of GABA receptor	5
	Progressive myoclonus epilepsy		Cystatin B	AR	Reduced activity of a protease inhibitor	21
Myelopathy	Hereditary spastic paraplegia	SPG4	Spastin	AD	Putative regulator of microtubule disassembly	2
		SPG7	Paraplegin	AR	Putative role in assembly and turnover of mitochondrial proteins	16
Anterior horn cell	Familial amyotrophic lateral sclerosis	ALS1	Superoxide dismutase-1	AD	First of seven or more loci for familial ALS	21
Peripheral nerve	Charcot-Marie-Tooth disease (Schwann cell)	CMT1A	Peripheral myelin protein-22	AD	Gene duplication leads to overexpression of pmp-22	17
	Charcot-Marie-Tooth disease (axonal)	CMT2A	Kinesin family member 1b	AD	Reduced axonal transport of synaptic vesicle precursors	1
Neuromuscular junction	Congenital myasthenic syndrome		Acetylcholine receptor, α subunit	AD	Altered synaptic response to acetylcholine	2
Muscle	Duchenne muscular dystrophy		Dystrophin	X-LR	Loss of essential membrane-associated protein	X
	Myotonic dystrophy		Myotonic dystrophy protein kinase	AD	Expanded CTG repeat, production of toxic RNA	19

AD = autosomal dominant; AR = autosomal recessive; X-LR, X-linked recessive.

SUGGESTED READINGS

Bird TD: Risks and benefits of DNA testing for neurogenetic disorders. Semin Neurol 1999;19:253–259. *DNA testing needs to be used with careful judgment and in the context of individual patients and families.*

Dawson TM, Dawson VL: Rare genetic mutations shed light on the pathogenesis of Parkinson disease. J Clin Invest 2003;111:145–151. *The 10% or so of Parkinson's that is familial has been associated with 10 different genes, 4 of which have been cloned.*

Taylor JP, Hardy J, Fischbeck KH: Toxic proteins in neurodegenerative disease. Science 2002;296:1991–1995. *Increased understanding of the cellular mechanisms for disposal of abnormal proteins and of the effects of toxic protein accumulation may allow the development of effective treatment.*

426 PSYCHIATRIC DISORDERS IN MEDICAL PRACTICE

R. B. Schiffer

The major disease burdens of people in the 21st century are likely to be different from those that received the greater share of medical resources during the previous 100 years. As age-specific mortality steadily decreases, a shift occurs away from the acute infectious and nutritional disorders in favor of the more chronic, lifestyle-associated disorders. According to the World Health Organization, 5 of the 10 leading causes of disability worldwide are psychiatric conditions: unipolar depression, substance abuse, bipolar disorder, schizophrenia, and obsessive-compulsive disorders.

Psychiatric morbidity is common among patients in ambulatory general medical settings in developed and underdeveloped countries. General medical physicians can expect one in four of the patients they see to have active, diagnosable psychiatric disease. The most common diagnoses in medical settings are depression, generalized anxiety disorder, somatoform disorders, substance abuse, and personality disorders. Most of these disorders have substantial psychosocial morbidity, and they are all treatable. Initial recognition and treatment of these disorders must occur in general medical settings because of shortages of psychiatrists and difficulties with access to psychiatric expertise in managed care settings. Data indicate that less than 25% of patients with these neurotic mental illnesses are recognized and treated by primary care providers.

Psychiatric disorders present as a series of variable signs and symptoms, or syndromes. Psychiatric diagnoses still are made based on these clinical features despite increasing knowledge about the neurobiologic bases of these conditions. As yet, there are no reliable laboratory tests for diagnosis. All psychiatric diseases have a spectrum of severity, and available therapies probably work best during their milder phases. This chapter outlines the clinical features and therapeutics for the principal psychiatric syndromes that occur frequently in general medical settings.

SYNDROMES

DEPRESSION AND SUICIDALITY

Diagnosis and Clinical Manifestations

Since the advent of the third version of the American Psychiatric Association's *Diagnostic and Statistical Manual of Mental Disorders* (DSM-III) in 1979, the depressive disorders have been diagnosed by descriptive criteria. This publication marked a major advance in psychiatric diagnostics because it required diagnoses to be substantiated by observable clinical data. Several depressive spectrum disorders are included in the current edition of the DSM (DSM-IV). The core clinical features of the depressive disorders are included in the diagnostic criteria for a major depressive episode and for dysthymia (Table 426–1). These disorders tend to recur, and chronic, milder syndromes of depression, such as dysthymia, can evolve in time to the more severe major depressive disorder. When the pattern of recurrence is one of depressive syndromes only, the disorder is called a *unipolar depressive disorder*. When manic-like episodes are included (see later), the disorder is called a *bipolar disorder*.

The symptoms of depression are variable for each individual and are sometimes difficult to recognize. Behavior and cognition can be affected, as can mood and affect. Some people experience depression as a slowing of thought and movement. For some, forgetfulness and difficulty concentrating are prominent features. Other patients manifest agitation and even psychotic experiences when the disorder is severe. This variability of clinical features among patients can be used as a basis for classifying a major depressive episode into subtypes—agitated, psychotic, and others.

Etiology

Several lines of evidence suggest a genetic basis for the major depression syndrome. Occurrences of major depressive episodes clearly cluster in families. In general, increased rates of bipolar and unipolar disorders are present among first-degree relatives of patients with a bipolar disorder, and increased rates of unipolar depressive disorder are present among first-degree relatives of patients with unipolar disorders. These relatives have lifetime risks ranging from 10 to 20% for major depressive disorders, with perhaps a higher risk for depressive spectrum disorders. This degree of increased risk is about three to five times that of the normal population. Twin and adoption studies are consistent with a genetic contribution to major depressive disorders, but studies suggest that other factors also are important. These environmental risk factors for depression do not seem generalizable but are specific to the individuals affected. More recent techniques of molecular genetics, such as genomic mismatch scanning, repeat expansion detection, and mitochondrial DNA analysis, have not increased the current understanding of the genetics of affective disturbances. It is probable that multiple vulnerability genes operate in different families by different mechanisms and through complex interactions with life events.

Pathophysiology

In the 1960s, hypotheses first were presented about an association between catecholamine metabolism (norepinephrine, epinephrine, dopamine) and depression. Subsequent neurochemical hypotheses invoked abnormalities of indolamine (serotonin) metabolism in depressive disorders. These neurochemical theories of affective disturbances derived largely from pharmacologic observations in the 1950s that suggested catecholamine and indolamine depleters such as reserpine could cause depression, whereas drugs that upregulate catechole and indole metabolism (e.g., tricyclic antidepressants) were therapeutic in depressed patients. These early neurochemical hypotheses

Table 426–1 • DIAGNOSTIC CRITERIA FOR DEPRESSIVE DISORDERS

MAJOR DEPRESSIVE EPISODE
1. At least five of the following symptoms have been present during the same 2-week period and represent a change from previous functioning; at least one of the symptoms is either depressed mood or loss of interest or pleasure
   A. Depressed mood most of the day, nearly every day
   B. Markedly diminished interest or pleasure in all, or almost all, activities most of the day, nearly every day
   C. Significant weight loss or weight gain when not dieting or decrease or increase in appetite nearly every day
   D. Insomnia or hypersomnia nearly every day
   E. Psychomotor agitation or retardation nearly every day; observable by others
   F. Fatigue or loss of energy nearly every day
   G. Feelings of worthlessness or excessive or inappropriate guilt (which may be delusional) nearly every day
   H. Diminished ability to think or concentrate, or indecisiveness, nearly every day
   I. Recurrent thoughts of death, recurrent suicidal ideation without a specific plan, or a suicide attempt or a specific plan for committing suicide
2. A. It cannot be established that an organic factor initiated and maintained the disturbance
   B. The disturbance is not a normal reaction to the death of a loved one
3. At no time during the disturbance have there been delusions or hallucinations for as long as 2 weeks in the absence of prominent mood symptoms (i.e., before the mood symptoms developed or after they have remitted)
4. Not superimposed on schizophrenia, schizophreniform disorder, delusional disorder, or psychotic disorder; no other specific diagnosis

DYSTHYMIA
1. Depressed mood for most of the day for at least 2 years
2. Presence, while depressed, of two or more of the following:
   A. Poor appetite
   B. Insomnia or hypersomnia
   C. Low energy or fatigue
   D. Low self-esteem
   E. Poor concentration or difficulty making decisions
   F. Feelings of hopelessness
3. During the 2-year period, the person has never been without the symptoms for >2 months at a time
4. No major depressive episode has been present during the first 2 years of the disturbance
5. There has not been an intermixed manic episode
6. The disturbance does not occur during the course of a psychotic disorder
7. The symptoms are not caused by the physiologic effects of a substance
8. The symptoms cause significant distress or functional impairment

for depression postulated that decreased availability of norepinephrine or serotonin at transmitter-specific synapses in the brain was associated with depression and that increased levels of these substances were associated with mania. Subsequent studies generally have supported the hypothesis that catecholamine and indolamine metabolism are important in mood states, although the relationships are complex. Almost all drugs with antidepressant properties affect catecholamine and indolamine availability at the synapse in the central nervous system.

Evidence also suggests that neuroendocrine function is altered in many people with major depressive disorders. Overactivity of the hypothalamic-pituitary-adrenocortical axis has been the most prominent of these neuroendocrine disturbances. This overactivity is reflected in increased levels of circulating cortisol among depressed patients compared with controls, in addition to increased levels of cerebrospinal fluid cortisol, increased excretion of urinary free cortisol, and cortisol resistance to dexamethasone suppression.

Patients with affective disorders often have a disturbance of circadian rhythm reflected in abnormal sleep patterns. Complaints of difficulty falling asleep and early morning wakening are reliable clinical indicators of depression. Electroencephalographic studies have shown a relative absence of slow-wave sleep (stages 3 and 4) in depressed individuals and a shortened period between the onset of sleep and the first dreaming period (rapid-eye-movement latency). These disturbances of sleep improve when the mood disturbance improves.

Neurology

Incidence and Prevalence

Lifetime prevalence rates for major depressive disorders are 15 to 20% in the United States. The exact prevalence is not known because of variable methods of ascertainment and diagnosis. Point prevalence rates for major depression in urban U.S. populations range from 2 to 4% for men and 4 to 6% for women.

Suicide Risk

Suicide is a uniquely human behavior for which we have only a limited psychobiologic understanding. Completed suicides are common in the United States, accounting for some 30,000 deaths each year. A much greater number of people attempt suicide, with variable degrees of intentionality. The most powerful associated features for completed suicide are current depression, alcohol abuse, and chronic medical illness. Suicide rates are highest for men older than age 69 years, and rates are higher among whites and Native Americans than among other racial groups.

Most people who commit suicide have seen a physician within the previous month. Analysis of the preceding visits often provides evidence that covert and implicit clues were conveyed about suicidality. When there is any suspicion about potential suicide, it is important to ask patients directly. When depressive symptoms are more severe, or when they include features of agitation or delusional ideas, the risk for suicide is greater (Fig. 426–1). Older age, male gender, and intercurrent alcohol abuse also are risk factors. Social isolation is a powerful risk factor, as is chronic painful medical illness. Consultation with a psychiatrist is essential for high-risk patients.

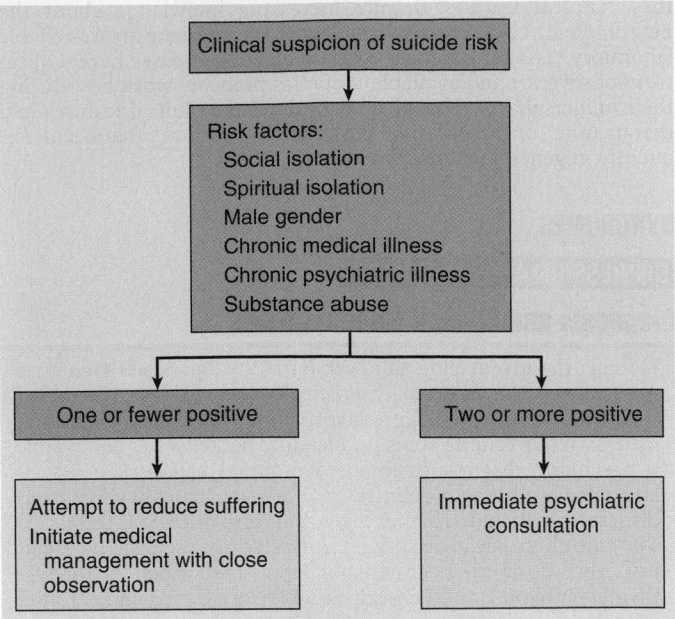

FIGURE 426–1 • Approach to the depressed patient at potential risk of suicide.

Rx Treatment and Prognosis

The diagnosis of a depressive disorder is the beginning of therapy. Depressed patients usually are relieved when their suffering is recognized and they are permitted to discuss it. The treatment plan must be individualized. A psychotherapeutic strategy (discussed later) should be considered for each patient before a drug is selected. More recent and compelling evidence indicated that the combination of an antidepressant, such as nefazodone, with cognitive behavior psychotherapy (see later) enhanced outcomes in chronic depression compared with either therapy alone.[1] The initiation of treatment for depression in primary care practice using antidepressants and cognitive therapy has been shown to improve quality of life and employability, compared with standard care.[2]

DRUGS FOR DEPRESSION

Antidepressant drugs available in the United States (Table 426–2) vary in their structure and function.

SELECTIVE SEROTONIN REUPTAKE INHIBITORS. The selective serotonin reuptake inhibitors (SSRIs) marked an important advance in antidepressant pharmacology because they are more specific in their neurochemical effects on the central nervous system than other agents. SSRIs are the initial therapy for depressive illness. They block the reuptake of serotonin at presynaptic membranes, with relatively little effect on noradrenergic, cholinergic, histaminergic, or other neurochemical systems. As a result, they are associated with fewer side effects than the tricyclic antidepressants. Additional advantages of the SSRIs over the older tricyclic antidepressants include once-daily dosing and the ability to initiate treatment at the target dose for most patients. For sertraline, the dose is 50 mg once daily for almost all patients. The dosage can be increased to 100 mg/day after 3 weeks if there is no evidence of improvement. For nonresponders, the dose can be increased to 150 or 200 mg/day. Paroxetine can be started at 20 mg once daily and increased at similar intervals to 50 mg. Citalopram may be taken on a once-daily schedule, beginning at 10 mg/day and increased at 2-week intervals to 40 mg. Citalopram is usually well tolerated by elderly patients. Although plasma levels are available in some laboratories for these drugs and their metabolites, large clinical trials suggest that measurement of plasma levels is not a useful guide to clinical response.

TRICYCLIC ANTIDEPRESSANTS. The tricyclic antidepressants are thought to affect depressed mood by inhibiting synaptic reuptake of norepinephrine and serotonin. Some of these agents, such as desipramine and nortriptyline, have a relatively greater effect on norepinephrine reuptake systems. Others, such as amitriptyline, have a broader effect on serotonin systems. As a group, however, the tricyclic antidepressants have the disadvantage that they affect neurochemical systems that are not thought to be essential for antidepressant efficacy, including the histaminergic, adrenergic, and acetylcholinergic systems. Tricyclic antidepressants have a wide range of side effects, including postural hypotension, cardiac tachyarrhythmias, urinary retention, and constipation. These drugs are considered second-line agents for the treatment of depression, to be used in patients in whom treatment with the SSRIs fails or in patients who have special complicating medical conditions, such as spastic bladder or parkinsonism. In these latter situations, the side effects of the tricyclic agents may be beneficial.

MONOAMINE OXIDASE INHIBITORS. The monoamine oxidase inhibitors used in psychiatric practice are irreversible inhibitors of both forms (A and B) of brain monoamine oxidase. These drugs are rarely used now because of their potentially dangerous interactions with dietary tyramine and with other agents that have sympathomimetic or serotoninergic properties.

ATYPICAL ANTIDEPRESSANTS. *Amoxapine* is an antidepressant with some dopamine-blocking properties. It is associated with extrapyramidal side effects. This drug has a theoretical advantage in depressed patients with psychotic features.

Trazodone and nefazodone inhibit the reuptake of serotonin (5-HT) at the synapse and have antagonism for a serotonin receptor subtype (5-HT$_2$). The absence of prominent anticholinergic side effects is a specific advantage for nefazodone. Trazodone has some sedating properties, which makes it useful in agitated patients with disturbed sleep, particularly elderly persons.

Venlafaxine is a phenylethylamine antidepressant that inhibits reuptake of serotonin and norepinephrine. It is selective for these two neurochemical systems, showing little in vitro binding to cholinergic, histaminergic, or dopaminergic receptors.

Bupropion is a novel monocyclic compound that inhibits the reuptake of dopamine but has little effect on other adrenergic systems. *Mirtazapine* is a tetracyclic piperazinoazepine, which is an analogue of mianserin, an antidepressant that has been available in Europe. It is a presynaptic α_2-blocker that increases the release of norepinephrine and serotonin. It also blocks 5-HT$_2$ and 5-HT$_3$ receptors and histamine H$_1$ receptors. Common side effects include weight gain, dizziness, dry mouth, and constipation. It is a reasonable alternative for patients who do not respond to SSRIs.

Neurology

Table 426–2 • DRUGS FOR DEPRESSION (BY STRUCTURAL GROUP)

DRUG	TRADE NAME	INITIAL DOSE RANGE	TARGET DOSE RANGE	SIDE EFFECTS	COMMENTS
TRICYCLICS					
Imipramine	Tofranil	10–75 mg	100–300 mg	Dry mouth, constipation, postural hypotension, tachyarrhythmia	
Desipramine	Norpramin	10–75 mg	100–200 mg		
Amitriptyline	Elavil	10–50 mg	100–300 mg		
Trimipramine	Surmontil	25–75 mg	200–300 mg		
Nortriptyline	Pamelor	10–50 mg	75–150 mg		
Protriptyline	Vivactil	10–30 mg	20–50 mg		
Doxepin	Sinequan	25–75 mg	75–300 mg		
TETRACYCLIC					
Maprotiline	Ludiomil	25–75 mg	100–300 mg		
SELECTIVE SEROTONIN REUPTAKE INHIBITORS					
Fluoxetine	Prozac	10–20 mg/day	10–80 mg/day	Nervousness, insomnia, tremor, agitation, headache, weight loss	
Sertraline	Zoloft	50 mg/day	50–200 mg/day		
Paroxetine	Paxil	20 mg/day	20–50 mg/day		
Fluvoxamine	Luvox	50 mg/day	50–300 mg/day		
Citalopram	Celexa	10 mg/day	10–40 mg/day		
MONOAMINE OXIDASE INHIBITORS					
Phenelzine	Nardil	15–45 mg	45–75 mg	Hypertensive crises; sedation, tremor	Patients taking these drugs must be on a tyramine-free diet
Tranylcypromine	Parnate	10–20 mg	20–30 mg		
ATYPICAL OR NONTRICYCLICS					
Amoxapine	Asendin	25–75 mg	100–300 mg		
Trazodone	Desyrel	25–75 mg/day in divided doses	300 mg/day in divided doses	Priapism	Helpful as second drug for sleep disturbance
Nefazodone	Serzone	100 mg bid	200–400 mg	Headache and drowsiness sometimes associated	As effective as imipramine
Venlafaxine	Effexor	25 mg tid	200–275 mg/day, tid dosing	Hypertension	Serotonin/norepinephrine reuptake inhibitor, may be effective in treatment of resistant depression
Mirtazapine	Remeron	15 mg/day	30–45 mg/day	Somnolence, weight gain	Increase at 1–2 wk intervals
Bupropion	Wellbutrin	100 mg bid	300 mg/day, tid dosing	Affects dopamine and norepinephrine reuptake	May be especially helpful in atypical depression
PSYCHOSTIMULANTS					
Dextroamphetamine	Dexedrine	2.5 gm	5–10 mg		Abuse potential must be considered
Pemoline	Cylert	18.75 mg	37 mg bid		
Methylphenidate	Ritalin	2.5 mg bid	10 mg tid		

BIPOLAR DISORDERS

Bipolar disorders (previously called *manic-depressive disorders*) are characterized by marked swings in mood from depressive episodes to manic episodes. Normal behavior usually is seen between episodes. Psychotic features may accompany the manic phases of these disorders. There is little difficulty in recognizing the illness over a longitudinal course. If patients are examined only briefly at a particular moment in time, however, manic excitement can be confused with schizophrenic psychosis. The severe depressive phase of bipolar illness also can be misconstrued as a catatonic state. During the acute phases, bipolar disorders should be managed by psychiatrists.

Diagnosis and Clinical Manifestations

The manic phase of bipolar disorder is characterized by an expansive euphoric mood in which the patient is subject to grandiose plans and ideas (Table 426–3). Despite this expansiveness and grandiosity, patients who are frustrated or confronted often become irritable and sometimes aggressive. The patient can be psychotic in the manic phase, with delusions and hallucinations consistent with grandiosity; persecutory delusions (i.e., feelings of being controlled) also may be present. At times, it is difficult to distinguish an excited schizophrenic patient from a manic patient until either a depressive episode occurs or the course deteriorates into a schizophrenic process. In all instances, it is crucial to exclude metabolic and other medical disorders, particularly in older patients.

Table 426–3 • MAJOR DIAGNOSTIC CRITERIA FOR A MANIC EPISODE

A distinct period of abnormally and persistently elevated, expansive, or irritable mood, lasting at least 1 week (or any duration if hospitalization is necessary)

During the period of mood disturbance, at least three of the following symptoms have persisted (four if the mood is only irritable) and have been present to a significant degree:
1. Inflated self-esteem or grandiosity
2. Decreased need for sleep (e.g., feels rested after only 3 hours of sleep)
3. More talkative than usual or feels pressure to keep talking
4. Flight of ideas or subjective experiences that thoughts are racing
5. Distractibility (i.e., attention too easily drawn to unimportant or irrelevant external stimuli)
6. Increase in goal-directed activity (socially, at work or school, or sexually) or psychomotor agitation
7. Excessive involvement in pleasurable activities that have a high potential for painful consequences (e.g., engaging in unrestrained buying sprees, sexual indiscretions, or foolish business investments)

The mood disturbance is sufficiently severe to cause marked impairment in occupational functioning or in usual social activities or relationships with others to necessitate hospitalization to prevent harm to self or others

The symptoms are not due to the direct effects of a substance (e.g., drugs of abuse, medication) or a general medical condition (e.g., hyperthyroidism)

Continued

The average age at onset of bipolar disorder is about 30 years, but about 20% of patients have an onset before age 20. In women, onset of the condition has a bimodal distribution, with one peak falling between 20 and 30 years and the other far earlier, but the age at onset of bipolar illness overlaps enough so that the differential diagnosis of a psychotic illness in a young person is difficult and may change as the clinical picture evolves over time. Almost half of patients with bipolar disorders have at least two or three episodes of illness, and a third experience seven or more episodes of illness after the pattern has started. Each episode of illness, whether manic or depressive, can last 4 to 13 months; some become chronic, and some cease much sooner. Shorter durations usually are related to the effectiveness of treatment. Although some patients rapidly alternate between extremes over 2 to 4 days, most episodes have a longer duration, and a manic phase frequently follows a depressive phase. In contrast to schizophrenia, chronicity is not a major problem with manic-depressive illness (1% in some studies). Mortality with bipolar illness averages 2 to 2.5 times the age-expected rate; 8 to 10% of patients commit suicide.

Epidemiology and Pathophysiology

The lifetime risk for development of bipolar illness ranges from 0.6 to 0.9%. The annual new-case incidence is 9 to 15 per 100,000 in men and 7.4 to 32 per 100,000 in women. The risk increases with a family history of bipolar illness. The genetic pattern in bipolar illness is uncertain but suggests autosomal dominance with incomplete penetrance. There is a 72% concordance in monozygotic twins and a 19% concordance in same-sex dizygotic twins. The course of illness and the response to treatment are similar among related patients. In one well-studied Amish family, an abnormal gene was localized to chromosome 11. Other families with equally strong genetic patterns have not possessed this particular chromosomal localization. The pathophysiology of bipolar illness, to the extent that it is known, is similar to the biology of the major depressive disorders.

Rx Treatment

The treatment of bipolar disorders has three distinct aspects: the manic episode, the major depressive episode, and long-term maintenance therapy. Before any specific therapy is begun, an adequate medical evaluation is necessary to ensure that the patient has a primary affective illness. A patient in an acute manic state is typically delusional, grandiose, and hyperactive. In this condition, he or she appears similar to any patient with psychosis. In the first episode, one cannot differentiate this state by its clinical features from the first episode of schizophrenia or a psychosis caused by physical illness. The differential diagnosis with the first episode rests on a careful history, family history, and physical and laboratory examination. Acute psychotic episodes should be evaluated by psychiatrists.

The treatment of the acute manic phase usually is undertaken in the hospital because it is imperative to protect patients from their own misdeeds (e.g., spending inordinate amounts of money or making embarrassing speeches). If family members are supportive, however, and believe they can control the situation, treatment can be started outside the hospital. Valproate is as effective as lithium in the treatment of acute manic and mixed phases of bipolar disorder. Olanzapine also has been proven effective in the acute treatment of bipolar disorder, especially when psychotic features are present. In the rare situations in which the agitation cannot be controlled with medication, the clinician can consider using electroconvulsive therapy to control manic excitement. Acute depressive phases of bipolar disorder are treated as major depressive episodes (see earlier).

After a manic episode, patients with bipolar disorders currently are committed to maintenance therapy, usually with either valproate or lithium. Uncertainty remains about the effectiveness of maintenance therapy and about the drug of choice.

Before lithium therapy is begun, a complete blood cell count, urinalysis, electrolytes, creatinine level, blood urea nitrogen level, thyroid studies, and a baseline electrocardiogram should be obtained. Chronic medical illnesses, especially renal insufficiency,

can be contraindications to lithium. Lithium carbonate is available in 300-mg tablets or capsules, and a 300-mg slow-release tablet is available. The starting dose of lithium carbonate in acute mania is generally 300 mg three or four times per day. Lithium has a half-life of 24 to 36 hours, and it takes at least 4 days to achieve a steady state. Its specific therapeutic effectiveness is not evident until at least 4 to 10 days after the institution of therapy. The serum level of lithium should be monitored and the dose adjusted accordingly. The dosage should be adjusted upward by a full or half tablet after the serum level is checked during this time. Adequate levels for acute illness are 0.8 to 1.4 mEq/L. For maintenance therapy, blood levels of about 0.4 mEq/L are desirable. Dose and blood level should be titrated, however, against clinical effectiveness for each patient. Doses usually are given twice daily because absorption from the gastrointestinal tract is rapid, and the drug peaks in the serum within 1 to 2 hours. Elevation of serum lithium levels to more than 2 mEq/L is toxic and is a medical emergency requiring immediate hospitalization and possibly hemodialysis (Chapter 106). Side effects in the long-term use of lithium include the development of mild leukocytosis, hypothyroidism, diabetes insipidus, and renal tubular damage. Many patients have a tremor that can be embarrassing and that occasionally interferes with activities.

Valproate is initiated at 750 mg/day in divided doses, increasing every three to four days until a serum trough concentration is greater than 50 μg/mL. Most patients require doses of 1000 to 2500 mg/kg/day, administered on a two or three times per day schedule. Olanzapine is administered once daily, starting with 10 mg and increasing in 5-mg steps to 20 mg/day, if necessary. Carbamazepine and other antiepileptic drugs, such as lamotrigine, gabapentin, and topiramate, also may be efficacious in the acute and long-term treatment of bipolar disorders.

Prognosis

Manic or depressive episodes produce major disruptions of psychological, social, and vocational function. Divorce and job loss are common. Long-term supportive psychotherapy usually is indicated in addition to pharmacotherapy to help the patient adjust to these psychosocial consequences of the disease. The symptoms of some bipolar patients do not resolve fully but rather produce permanent psychosocial deterioration. Most bipolar patients have a relapsing course, however, and are free of symptoms between episodes. Their long-term functional outcome depends on the frequency and severity of their affective episodes and their response to treatment. The management of all bipolar patients involves careful surveillance for early signs of affective instability and prompt treatment to minimize long-term psychosocial disruption.

ANXIETY DISORDERS

Anxiety disorders occur at any age and are associated with a variety of distressing symptoms, including nervousness, sleeplessness, hypochondriasis, and somatic complaints. It is useful clinically to consider anxiety disorders as occurring in two different patterns: (1) chronic, generalized anxiety and (2) episodic, panic-like anxiety. Episodic anxiety is often context dependent, such as the performance anxiety of a musician before an audience. When panic attacks occur, however, they are qualitatively different from generalized anxiety. The patient typically experiences sudden onset of intense fear, arousal, and even respiratory distress without provocation. Panic attacks often are confused with systemic medical illness, such as angina pectoris or epilepsy. There is also a spectrum of related mental disorders that include anxious features, such as phobias and post-traumatic stress disorder.

Incidence and Prevalence

Lifetime prevalence rates for DSM diagnosable anxiety disorders are 30% for women and 19% for men. Point prevalence rates are 2 to 6% for generalized anxiety and 1% for panic disorder. The anxiety disorders may be the most common psychiatric disorders in general medical practice.

Pathophysiology

Similar to the depressive disorders, the anxiety disorders cluster in families. Twin studies more clearly indicate a shared familial risk for panic disorder than for generalized anxiety. The underlying neurophysiology and neurochemistry of the anxiety disorders implicate overactivity of noradrenergic systems projecting from the locus caeruleus into forebrain regions.

Diagnosis and Clinical Manifestations

Diagnostic criteria for generalized anxiety disorder (DSM-IV) emphasize the presence of unrealistic or excessive worry and apprehension about two or more life circumstances, for a period of 6 months or longer, during which the person has been bothered more days than not by these concerns. At least six symptoms from Table 426–4 must be present during these periods.

Panic attacks are characterized by the sudden onset of intense apprehension, fear, or a sense of impending doom. These attacks are often spontaneous, and they may overlap with the more generalized anxiety disorder described earlier (Table 426–5).

Rx Treatment

In acute anxiety or panic disorder, the efficacy of pharmacologic agents as measured by panic-free rates is high, with success rates of 50 to 70%. Four classes of medications have been shown to be effective in reducing recurrent panic attacks. SSRIs, tricyclic antidepressants, benzodiazepines, and monoamine oxidase inhibitors. Drugs from all four classes have roughly comparable efficacy. Treatment usually is initiated with either SSRIs or benzodiazepines. All of the available SSRIs in the United States, fluoxetine, sertraline, paroxetine, and fluvoxamine, are supported by evidence from clinical trials in the treatment of panic disorder. The doses of SSRIs for panic disorder should be at the high end of the dose ranges presented in Table 426–2. Alprazolam has been studied more extensively than other benzodiazepines for the treatment of panic disorder. Typically, its dosing is initiated at 0.5 mg twice daily and increased to 6 to 8 mg/day if clinically necessary to control symptoms. Many patients require ongoing pharmacotherapy, and others have symptoms despite treatment.

For generalized or chronic anxiety, the antidepressants are much less efficacious. The short-term relief afforded by almost any benzodiazepine is dramatic in generalized anxiety, but habituation and addiction are common, so caution should be exercised. If there is any situational quality to the generalized anxiety symptoms, other therapeutic measures should be considered before benzodiazepines are prescribed. Variations of cognitive behavior psychotherapy should be tried, including reassurance, education, relaxation exercises, hypnosis, and other psychotherapies. Environmental alterations may be considered at home or at work, depending on the individual's specific anxiety symptoms. When a psychopharmacologic intervention is prescribed, it should be given for a defined period of 1 to 4 weeks, while the situation is reassessed by the physician. Antihistamines, such as diphenhydramine, 25 mg three times a day, can be tried for some patients. Buspirone is a nonbenzodiazepine antianxiety agent that sometimes provides relief at doses of 5 mg twice a day initially. The benzodiazepines presented in Table 426–6 are effective in many patients. Lorazepam is often the first used because it is relatively short acting (half-life of 10 to 15 hours) and easier to titrate in elderly or medically ill patients. Because its half-life is shorter than drugs such as diazepam, lorazepam must be taken at least twice and often three times per day. A dosage of 0.5 mg twice daily is the initial regimen for most patients. The dose should be increased by 0.5 mg/day at 3-day intervals until target symptoms resolve or sedative side effects supervene. Paroxetine 20 to 40 mg/day is also effective. Elderly patients always should be watched carefully for an ataxic gait. For all patients, opportunities to taper or reduce the drug dose should be sought.

Table 426–4 • DIAGNOSTIC SYMPTOMS FOR ANXIETY AND PANIC

MOTOR TENSION
Trembling, twitching, or feeling shaky
Muscle tension, aches, or soreness
Restlessness
Easy fatigability

AUTONOMIC HYPERACTIVITY
Shortness of breath or smothering sensations
Palpitations or accelerated heart rate (tachycardia)
Sweating or cold, sweaty hands
Dry mouth
Dizziness or lightheadedness
Nausea, diarrhea, or other abdominal distress
Flashes (hot flashes) or chills
Frequent urination
Trouble swallowing or "lump in throat"

VIGILANCE AND SCANNING
Feeling keyed up or on edge
Exaggerated startle response
Difficulty concentrating or "mind going blank" because of anxiety
Trouble falling or staying asleep
Irritability

Table 426–5 • DIAGNOSTIC CRITERIA FOR PANIC DISORDERS

One or more panic attacks (discrete periods of intense fear or discomfort) have occurred that (1) were unexpected (i.e., did not occur immediately before or on exposure to a situation that almost always caused anxiety) and (2) were not triggered by situations in which the person was the focus of others' attention
Either four attacks have occurred within a 4-wk period or one or more attacks have been followed by a period of at least 1 month of persistent fear of having another attack
At least four of the following symptoms developed during at least one of the attacks:
   Shortness of breath (dyspnea) or smothering sensations
   Dizziness, unsteady feelings, or faintness
   Palpitations or accelerated heart rate (tachycardia)
   Trembling
   Sweating
   Choking
   Nausea or abdominal distress
   Depersonalization or derealization
   Numbness or tingling sensations (paresthesia)
   Flashes (hot flashes) or chills
   Chest pain or discomfort
   Fear of dying
   Fear of "going crazy" or of doing something uncontrolled
During at least some of these attacks at least four of the symptoms developed suddenly and increased in intensity within 10 minutes of the beginning of the first symptom noticed in the attack

---

SOMATOFORM DISORDERS

The somatoform disorders (Table 426–7) are a heterogeneous group of disorders that share the common feature of mimicking medical disease. The mimicry may involve an exaggeration of the severity or disability of an actual medical illness, or it may consist entirely of simulating a medical illness that is not present. Several evolving disorders are "somatoform" in whole or in part but are not strictly classified in the somatoform disorders category.

Table 426–6 • **DRUGS FOR ANXIETY AND PANIC**

DRUG	TRADE NAME	INITIAL DOSE	TARGET DOSE RANGE	SIDE EFFECTS	COMMENTS
SEDATIVE HYPNOTICS					
Chloral hydrate	Noctel	500 mg	500–1000 mg	Sedation; overdose risk	Seldom appropriate
Meprobamate	Miltown	200 mg tid	1200–1600 mg		
ANTIHISTAMINES					
Diphenhydramine	Benadryl	25 mg PO qhs	50 mg	Dry mouth, mental confusion	Most useful at bedtime for associated sleep
Hydroxyzine	Atarax				
BENZODIAZEPINES					
Lorazepam	Ativan	0.5 mg PO	2–10 mg tid dosing		Also effective for generalized anxiety
Diazepam	Valium	5 mg PO	5–10 mg bid	Addictive	Abuse potential in many
Triazolam	Halcion	0.125 mg	0.25–0.5 mg hs		
Chlordiazepoxide	Librium	5 mg bid	10–30 mg		
Temazepam	Restoril	7.5 mg hs	15–30 mg		
Alprazolam	Xanax	0.25 mg bid	2–8 mg/day	Ataxia, drowsiness	
Clorazepate	Tranxene	7.5 mg hs	15–60 mg/day		
Flurazepam	Dalmane	15 mg hs	30–60 mg	Ataxia, drowsiness	Abuse potential
Oxazepam	Serax	10 mg bid	60–120 mg/day		
Clonazepam	Klonopin	0.25 mg qd	1–3 mg/day	Sedation, ataxia	Long duration of action permits once-daily dosing
Buspirone	Buspar	5 mg bid	20–30 mg/day	Nervousness, headache	No dependence with prolonged use
Zolpidem	Ambien	10 mg hs	10 mg hs	Habituation, drowsiness	Most useful on an as-needed basis
β-BLOCKERS					
Propranolol	Inderal	20 mg bid	Individualize 40–120 mg/day	Bradycardia, mental confusion	Does not block the fear component of anxiety or panic

Table 426–7 • **SOMATOFORM DISORDERS**

DISORDER	FEATURES
Somatization disorder	Chronic, multisystem disorder characterized by complaints of pain, gastrointestinal and sexual dysfunction, and pseudoneurologic symptoms. Onset is usually early in life, and psychosocial and vocational achievements are limited
Conversion disorder	Syndrome of symptoms or deficits mimicking neurologic or medical illness in which psychological factors are judged to be of etiologic importance
Pain disorder	Clinical syndrome characterized predominantly by pain in which psychological factors are judged to be of etiologic importance
Hypochondriasis	Chronic preoccupation with the idea of having a serious disease. The preoccupation is usually poorly amenable to reassurance
Body dysmorphic disorder	Preoccupation with an imagined or exaggerated defect in physical appearance
OTHER SOMATOFORM-LIKE DISORDERS	
Factitious disorder	Intentional production or feigning of physical or psychological signs when external reinforcers (e.g., avoidance of responsibility, financial gain) are not clearly present
Malingering	Intentional production or feigning of physical or psychological signs when external reinforcers (e.g., avoidance of responsibility, financial gain) are present
Dissociative disorders	Disruptions of consciousness, memory, identity, or perception judged to be due to psychological factors

Diagnosis and Clinical Manifestations

CONVERSION DISORDER. The essential feature of a conversion disorder is the presence of a symptom or deficit that affects voluntary motor or sensory function and that suggests a neurologic or general medical condition. Conversion phenomena typically do not conform to known anatomic systems but instead follow the individual's unconscious conceptualization of neurologic function. Conversion disorders may be episodic, as in conversion seizures, or chronic and persistent, as in the case of sensory loss or weakness. To make a valid diagnosis of conversion, two features should be established: the failure of the disorder to respect known neuroanatomy and neurophysiology, and some positive association with unintentional psychological motivation.

FACTITIOUS DISORDER. In a factitious disorder, the production of the symptom or sign is more deliberate. The individual may self-administer a drug or other material to create physical signs. The motivation for these actions may be unconscious, although the action itself is deliberate.

Munchausen's syndrome, which is perhaps the best known of the factitious disorders, is defined as a repetitious pattern of medical attention-seeking behaviors in which the individual has dramatic but untruthful complaints. The somatic complaints typically involve organ systems, such as abdominal pain or hemorrhage.

MALINGERING. Malingering refers to the production of false or grossly exaggerated physical or psychological symptoms when the production of symptoms and the motivation are consciously understood by the patient. In the case of malingering, the secondary gain or environmental reinforcement for the behavior is usually transparent. These environmental reinforcers typically include relief from arduous duty or responsibility, as in military training, or the prospect of significant financial reward, as in litigation.

CHRONIC FATIGUE SYNDROME. In the mid-1980s, reports began to appear in the United States of a syndrome of pathologic fatigability. Unconscious psychological factors are almost certainly important contributors in some patients with this syndrome. Other contributors, including immune system dysfunction, orthostatic hypotension, and endocrinologic systems, are under investigation.

FIBROMYALGIA. There is considerable overlap between patients who complain of chronic fatigue and the set of myalgic symptoms that is variously labeled as *fibromyalgia* (Chapter 289). Fibromyalgia is a constellation of vague symptoms, including widespread tenderness, trigger points, and generalized pain. Although its cause is unclear at present, fibromyalgia seems to be a pain syndrome, specifically a disorder of abnormal sensitivity to pain.

Pathogenesis

There are as yet no credible neurobiologic explanations for the somatoform disorders. They must be understood as psychological phenomena, with variable levels of self-awareness in each individual as to the factitious nature of the disorder. Freud and his colleagues believed that symptoms could be produced by a process of dissociation—the expulsion from consciousness of a painful memory or feeling and its replacement by a physical symptom. The advantage to the patient of the conversion disorder was the protection afforded from the psychic pain because this pain had been connected to or symbolized by a physical symptom. This protection afforded from the psychological pain and stress is termed the *primary gain* of the somatoform illness. The primary gain is usually not readily discernible because the patient is almost always unaware of it.

The *secondary gain* associated with a conversion illness refers to the clearly visible financial gain or relief from responsibility conferred by the sick role. These gains may be seen in many guises, such as disability pensions, relief from work, enhanced attention from family and physicians, and litigation payouts.

Incidence and Prevalence

Good epidemiologic data about the somatoform disorders are lacking. Cross-sectional studies of patients attending general neurology practices indicate prevalence rates of 15 to 20% in these populations. Disorder-specific and population-based studies are not available for these disorders.

 Treatment

The long-term goal of treatment for the somatoform disorders is to enable the patient to convert from a medical into a psychiatric patient. This process requires patience and flexibility on the part of the physician. General medical interventions may be invoked initially, including biologic tests, medical rehabilitation, and pharmacotherapy. These interventions may make sense if an underlying medical disease is present or if the patient adamantly views the illness as a physical one. The danger of biologic interventions is that they may strengthen the patient's conviction that the illness is physical.

If a pharmacologically accessible symptom complex, such as anxiety or depression, accompanies the conversion phenomena, it may be helpful to initiate psychopharmacologic treatment. It is unclear how often the treatment of associated emotional symptoms results in improvement of conversion symptoms, but this approach is effective occasionally.

CHARACTER DISORDERS

Behavior includes more than cognition and emotion; action and style are additional dimensions that are essential to success and satisfaction in life. Sustained dysfunctional patterns of coping with the world are called *character disorders*. Each person has an enduring set of behavioral traits with which he or she faces life's challenges. These predispositions for the most part do not depend on context, and they are not easily changed from one time to another. These traits manifest themselves in style and action. An individual is typically unaware of these qualities because they are formed in childhood as enduring aspects of personality. Qualities of character include honesty, timeliness, reliability, aggressiveness, and submissiveness.

Some individuals show clusters of maladaptive traits that cause recurrent psychosocial difficulties (Table 426–8). In DSM-IV, these disorders are classified as Axis II disorders as opposed to the Axis I classification of the more overt major psychiatric disorders. The clinical descriptive research that underlies and validates these disorders as distinct clinical entities is more limited than it is for the Axis I disorders. The personality disorders have a spectrum of severity, with poorly specified boundaries and thresholds. It makes clinical sense to think of "personality styles" when the maladaptive traits are less severe. The personality disorders also differ from the Axis I disorders in that they tend to define interpersonal relations rather than the intrapsychic symptoms of a single individual. It is difficult to imagine the diagnosis of a passive-aggressive personality style in a setting that

Table 426–8 • CHARACTER DISORDERS

PERSONALITY TYPE	CHARACTERISTIC BEHAVIOR PATTERNS
Paranoid	Distrust and suspiciousness
Schizoid	Detachment from social relationships, with a restricted range of emotional expression
Schizotypal	Eccentricities in behavior and cognitive distortions; acute discomfort in close relationships
Antisocial	Disregard for rights of others; a defect in the experience of compunction or remorse for harming others
Borderline	Instability in interpersonal relationships, self-image, and affective regulation
Histrionic	Emotional overreactivity, theatrical behaviors, and seductiveness
Narcissistic	Persisting grandiosity, need for admiration, and lack of empathy for others
Avoidant	Social inhibition, feelings of inadequacy, and hypersensitivity to negative evaluation
Dependent	Submission and clinging behaviors
Obsessive-compulsive	Rigid, detail-oriented behaviors, often associated with compulsions to perform tasks repetitively and unnecessarily

did not include other people. Often the best clue to the diagnosis of character pathology is the pattern of behavior the patient shows in relating to the physician.

 Treatment

Personality disorders are difficult to recognize and to treat. Patients are not consciously aware of the data that validate their diagnoses, and they are typically sensitive when dysfunctional patterns of behavior are clarified. Psychopharmacology is not indicated for these disorders. The goal of management is to help the patient to increase his or her awareness of the dysfunctional interpersonal traits so that they consciously can control the adverse effects. Although longer term psychotherapies must be performed by psychiatric clinicians, general medical physicians often can provide the initial clarifying intervention. Variants of the psychotherapy type described as "interpersonal" (see later) are the most effective approach to patients who show character disorder behavior patterns in practice settings.

SCHIZOPHRENIC DISORDERS

Schizophrenia is the archetypal major psychotic mental disorder. *Psychosis* is defined as a psychiatric disorder that disrupts reality testing or thought processes. Schizophrenia most often starts in late adolescence. The characteristic symptoms of schizophrenia fall into two broad categories described as positive and negative symptoms. Positive features include behaviors such as delusions and hallucinations. Negative features include symptoms such as restricted affect, anhedonia, and apathy. When a disturbance of thought processes is the predominant clinical feature, the schizophrenic disorder is described as disorganized. The course of schizophrenia usually is marked by a decline in psychosocial functioning, with a tendency for the patient to become downwardly mobile in social strata. For most patients, it becomes a chronic illness, characterized by relapses.

Diagnosis and Clinical Manifestations

Schizophrenia is defined as a long-term mental illness because psychotic features are required to persist for 6 months (Table 426–9). Psychosocial deterioration from a previous level of functioning also is required as part of the definition of schizophrenia. When a psychotic mental illness has persisted for less than 6 months, it is inadvisable to use the diagnosis of schizophrenia. Schizophrenia also tends to be characterized by acute relapses of psychotic features over time. With the first episode of any psychotic illness, an affective disorder or a systemic medical illness

Continued

Neurology

Table 426–9 • SCHIZOPHRENIA AND OTHER PSYCHOTIC DISORDERS

CHARACTERISTIC SYMPTOMS
At least two of the following, each present for a major portion of time during a 1-month period (or less if successfully treated):*
 Delusions
 Hallucinations
 Disorganized speech (e.g., frequent derailment, "jumping from one topic to another," or incoherence)
 Grossly disorganized or catatonic behavior
 Negative symptoms (i.e., affective flattening, alogia, or avolition)

SOCIAL/OCCUPATIONAL DYSFUNCTION
For a significant portion of the time since the onset of the disturbance, one or more major areas of functioning (e.g., work, interpersonal relations, or self-care) are markedly below the level achieved before the onset (or when the onset is in childhood or adolescence, failure to achieve expected level of interpersonal, academic, or occupational achievement)

DURATION
Continuous signs of the disturbance persist for at least 6 months. This 6-month period must include at least 1 month of characteristic symptoms as described above (i.e., active-phase symptoms) and may include periods of prodromal or residual symptoms. During these prodromal or residual periods, the signs of the disturbance may be manifested by only negative symptoms or two or more of the characteristic symptoms present in an attenuated form (e.g., odd beliefs, unusual perceptual experiences)

SCHIZOAFFECTIVE AND MOOD DISORDER EXCLUSION
Schizoaffective disorder and mood disorder with psychotic features have been ruled out because (1) no major depressive or manic episodes have occurred concurrently with the active-phase symptoms, or (2) if mood episodes have occurred during active phase symptoms, their total duration has been brief in relation to the duration of the active and residual periods

SUBSTANCE/GENERAL MEDICAL CONDITION EXCLUSION
The disturbance is not due to the direct effects of a substance (e.g., drugs of abuse, medication) or a general medical condition

*Note: Only one characteristic symptom is required if delusions are bizarre or hallucinations consist of a voice keeping up a running commentary on the person's behavior or thoughts, or involve two or more voices conversing with each other.

should be considered; psychotic episodes secondary to toxic drug reactions, sleep deprivation, and medical causes invariably persist for less than 6 months.

Subtypes of schizophrenia are defined by the predominant symptoms at the time of the most recent clinical evaluation. The subtypes include the paranoid type, the disorganized type, the catatonic type, and an undifferentiated type. Catatonic symptoms involve either markedly retarded motor behavior (often to the point of no voluntary movement; the patient retains any posture into which he or she is passively placed) or markedly agitated motor behavior. In the paranoid forms of schizophrenia, the paranoid delusions are often the only major symptoms, and they tend to remain stable over time. The term *schizophrenia, residual type* is used when positive symptoms of psychosis have abated, but the patient continues poor psychosocial function.

Epidemiology

The prevalence of schizophrenia in the general population is about 1%, with an incidence of about 0.5 per 1000 person-years. The prevalence rate is eight times as great in the lower as in the higher socioeconomic groups. Because the parents of schizophrenics have a social class distribution similar to that of the general population, the lower position of the patients seems to be a result of the illness rather than the cause of it.

Of schizophrenics, 70% become ill between the ages of 15 and 35. The illness affects men and women in equal proportion over the entire lifespan. The age of peak onset risk is 15 to 24 years in men and 25 to 34 years in women. There are slight ethnic differences, with a higher incidence in Scandinavian countries and in nonwhites.

Pathophysiology

The pathophysiology of schizophrenia is unknown, and an anatomic origin of the symptoms has yet to be determined. Nevertheless, many conditions (e.g., trauma, seizure disorders, and Huntington's disease) can produce schizophrenia-like hallucinations and delusions. Many experts have reported a higher than normal incidence of nonlocalizing neurologic abnormalities in schizophrenia, changes that are not present in other psychiatric conditions.

Of hospitalized schizophrenic patients, 25% show abnormally slow electroencephalographic tracings using standard recording techniques. Computed tomography and magnetic resonance imaging have shown enlargement of the lateral ventricle and third ventricle, widened cortical sulci, cerebellar atrophy, cerebral asymmetry, and decreased brain density. Although the implications of these findings are unclear, the findings correlate with increased cognitive disturbance, poorer premorbid adjustment, and longer duration of illness.

Strong evidence implicates genetic factors in schizophrenia. Of the offspring of schizophrenic parents, 10 to 15% have the disease. The coincidence of schizophrenia in monozygotic twins is roughly 60%. Additional evidence for a genetic factor comes from studies of children of schizophrenic parents who are raised by either their natural or adoptive nonschizophrenic parents: The probability of developing the disease is identical in both instances, regardless of the environment. Despite these findings, family factors have been implicated in other ways. In families with highly charged emotional interaction, schizophrenic patients seem to do poorly. Less emotionally stimulating environments seem to allow schizophrenic patients to function better.

Rx Treatment and Prognosis

During a 25- to 30-year period, about one third of patients with schizophrenia show some recovery or remission, but the remaining patients have major residual symptoms or require long-term hospitalization. Management requires the establishment of a long-term psychotherapeutic relationship with the patient or his or her family system, which can facilitate monitoring of the clinical course, recognize early signs of decompensation, and enhance compliance with psychopharmacologic treatments. The psychotherapy of schizophrenia is supportive (see later), educational, and rehabilitative in an attempt to prevent or minimize the chronic psychosocial deterioration that can occur in the course of the disease.

Long-term antipsychotic medication is essential to reduce relapses (Table 426–10). The initial pharmacologic therapy of psychosis should begin with the administration of one of the newer, "atypical" antipsychotic drugs. This group of drugs includes olanzapine, risperidone, quetiapine, ziprasidone, and clozapine. Clozapine cannot be considered a first-line therapy because of its hematopoietic and hepatic side effects. These agents are termed *atypical* because of their side-effect spectrum, which differs significantly from that of the older, traditional antipsychotic agents, such as haloperidol and chlorpromazine. The newer drugs as a group have less acute motor system side effects than the older drugs and may have a lower long-term risk of tardive dyskinesias. These agents are also more efficacious for the negative psychotic symptoms of schizophrenia, such as apathy and anergia.

Typical initial regimens include risperidone, 2 mg twice daily, increasing to 6 to 10 mg/day total dose after 1 week if tolerated. Antipsychotic efficacy usually is seen in this target dose range for risperidone, with a 4- to 6-week delay for some effects. An alternative is olanzapine, which can be administered once daily. A starting dose for olanzapine is 5 mg daily, increasing by 5-mg increments at weekly intervals to the 15- to 20-mg range if symptoms do not improve and side effects are tolerable. The aggressiveness of the dosing regimen is dictated to some extent by the quality and severity of the psychotic symptoms. Because of the delay before any antipsychotic drug's onset of efficacy, additional psychotropic agents sometimes are added during the early days of treatment. A benzodiazepine (e.g., alprazolam, 0.25 mg thrice daily) may be added when agitation and sleep disturbance are severe. The most frequent limiting factor in the dosing of antipsychotic drugs is the appearance of extrapyramidal side effects, including dystonia, akathisia (restlessness), and parkinsonism.

Table 426–10 • **DRUGS FOR PSYCHOSIS**

CLASS	GENERIC NAME	TRADE NAME	ACUTE DOSE PER 24 HR	MAINTENANCE DOSE	SIDE EFFECTS
Phenothiazine Aliphatic	Chlorpromazine	Thorazine	25–1000 mg PO 25–400 mg IM	25–400 mg PO	EPMD; hyperprolactinemia
Phenothiazine Piperazine	Perphenazine	Trilafon	8–64 mg PO 15–30 mg IM	12–24 mg PO	EPMD
	Fluphenazine	Prolixin	2.5–40 mg PO 5–20 mg IM	12.5–50 mg IM decanoate weekly	
	Trifluoperazine	Stelazine	1–5 mg PO		
Phenothiazine Piperidine	Thioridazine	Mellaril	25–800 mg PO	25–30 mg PO	EPMD; retinal degeneration risk 300 mg/day
	Mesoridazine	Serentil	50–400 mg PO	200–400 mg PO	
Butyrophenone	Haloperidol	Haldol	2–25 mg PO 6–30 mg IM	1–15 mg PO 25–200 mg IM decanoate monthly	EPMD; can cause a dysphoria at low to moderate doses
Thioxanthene	Chlorprothixene	Taractan	30–100 mg PO	100–300 mg	
	Thiothixene	Navane	2–5 mg PO	5–10 mg PO	Intramuscular form available
Dibensoxazepine	Loxapine	Loxitane	50–250 mg PO	60–100 mg	
Dihydroindole	Molindone	Moban	50–225 mg PO	20–200 mg	Less likely to reduce seizure threshold
Benzisoxazole	Risperidone	Risperdal	2–4 mg PO	2–20 mg	Low incidence of extrapyramidal effects
Dibenzodiazepine	Olanzapine	Zyprexa	5–15 mg PO	5–10 mg PO	Fewer extrapyramidal effects; fatal agranulocytosis; sedating
	Clozapine	Clozaril	200–400 mg	200–600 mg	
Diphenylbutylpiperidine	Pimozide	Orap	10–30 mg	10–30 mg	
Phenylindole	Quetiapine	Seroquel	25 mg bid	300–400 mg/day	Low incidence of extrapyramidal effects
	Ziprasidone	Geodon	40–80 mg bid		

EPMD = Extrapyramidal movement disorders.

An additional risk in the use of antipsychotic drugs is the development of tardive dyskinesia. Tardive dyskinesia is a syndrome of involuntary movements, usually choreoathetoid, that can affect the mouth, lips, tongue, extremities, or trunk. Although usually associated with use of neuroleptics for 6 months or more, tardive dyskinesia can occur with shorter administration. Patients receiving neuroleptics should be evaluated periodically for these abnormal movements. Rates of tardive dyskinesia with the atypical antipsychotic medications are considerably lower than with the traditional ones but are not zero. The cause of tardive dyskinesia is not known, but it is believed to represent the development of dopaminergic hypersensitivity in extrapyramidal motor systems.

DRUGS FOR PSYCHOSIS

Drugs that affect dopaminergic function by blocking mesolimbic dopamine receptors have the demonstrated ability to improve a variety of psychotic symptoms. The older antipsychotic drugs showed broad-spectrum dopamine receptor–blocking properties, affecting all receptor subtypes and nigrostriatal neurons (substantia nigra pars compacta, A9) and limbic dopaminergic neurons (ventral tegmental area, A10). Consequently, these drugs have many motor system side effects. A new generation of antipsychotic agents has variable effects on dopamine receptor subtypes and on other neurochemical systems, such as serotonin.

RISPERIDONE. Concomitant blockade of D_2 receptors in the basal ganglia has been presumed to underlie the production of extrapyramidal syndromes by traditional antipsychotic drugs. More recently, psychopharmacologic research has turned to agents that simultaneously might block D_2 and serotonin ($5\text{-}HT_2$) receptors. Some evidence suggests that these agents have fewer extrapyramidal side effects and may be more broadly effective for the negative symptoms of schizophrenia compared with traditional antipsychotic drugs. In vitro evidence indicates that risperidone has 20-fold higher affinity for $5\text{-}HT_{2A}$ receptors than for D_2 receptors.

CLOZAPINE. Clozapine was developed in Austria and Germany in the 1960s. Because of its tricyclic-like structure, it was hoped that it might be an antidepressant. Instead, it turned out to be an antipsychotic drug with no extrapyramidal side effects. Clozapine is a dibenzodiazepine with atypical properties and side effects. It possesses strong anticholinergic properties in addition to serotonin-blocking properties. It produces proportionally greater suppression of mesolimbic as opposed to striatal dopamine systems. Clozapine blocks D_2 receptors, as do other antipsychotic drugs, but it also produces a relatively greater blockade of D_1 systems, which may account for its altered pattern of efficacy and the absence of tardive dyskinesia as a side effect.

Clozapine can cause fatal agranulocytosis. An overview of available reports indicates that agranulocytosis occurs in 0.05 to 2% of patients given clozapine, a rate that is higher than what is found among patients given other antipsychotic drugs. The agranulocytosis does not seem to be dose related. In most cases, there is a several-week prodrome with a declining peripheral white blood cell count, but this prodrome is not always seen. Discontinuation of the medication does not always prevent progression to agranulocytosis. Most cases occur within 3 months after initiating treatment. Weekly monitoring of hematologic function is indicated for all patients receiving clozapine.

OLANZAPINE. Olanzapine blocks $5\text{-}HT_2$ receptors in addition to a spectrum of dopamine receptor subtypes, including D_1, D_2, and D_4. It also has some anticholinergic and α_1-blocking properties. This spectrum of pharmacologic properties generates fewer extrapyramidal side effects than most older antipsychotic drugs.

QUETIAPINE. Quetiapine has actions and uses similar to clozapine. It is associated with a lower incidence of agranulocytosis. Because of reports of cataracts associated with prolonged use, semiannual slit-lamp examinations are recommended for patients taking quetiapine.

ZIPRASIDONE. Ziprasidone is a newly approved antipsychotic drug that favorably affects positive and negative symptoms in schizophrenia. It has low rates of extrapyramidal side effects but can cause akathisia. It has been associated with prolonged QT on the electrocardiogram.

GENERAL APPROACH TO PSYCHOPHARMACOLOGY

Some general clinical guidelines should be followed in the use of all psychotropic drugs. The physician should select in advance the symptoms, such as agitation, sleep disturbance, or weight loss, that are targets for therapy. In addition, the clinician should establish clinical guideposts to judge the efficacy of the therapy. If the targeted symptoms fail to improve after some defined period, the therapy should be stopped or changed, or expert consultation should be sought.

DOSING AND TIMING. The two most common errors made by nonpsychiatrists who use psychopharmacologic agents are inadequate dosing and not waiting long enough to observe the expected effect. For all agents, the first approach to a suboptimal response should be to increase the dose of the selected drug either to a predetermined total daily target or to a maximal tolerated dose. Second, the physician must wait for a predetermined time, usually 4 to 6 weeks for antidepressant and antipsychotic drugs, to allow evidence of clinical efficacy to emerge.

CLINICAL FAMILIARITY. Effective use of these drugs, as for other pharmacologic agents, requires practical expertise that comes only from experience. Clinicians should not attempt to become familiar with all psychopharmacologic drugs equally but should develop experience-based familiarity with one or two agents from each category.

GENERAL APPROACH TO PSYCHOTHERAPY

Of the total scope of ambulatory psychiatric morbidity, 90% is treated by primary care physicians and other nonpsychiatric physicians. The restriction of these general medical therapies to psychopharmacology is too narrow, in view of increasingly persuasive evidence of the efficacy of psychotherapies in neurotic psychiatric illness. At present, however, there is no generally accepted model by which to bring psychotherapeutic skills into the general medical setting. It has been argued persuasively for decades that nonpsychiatric physicians perform various forms of psychotherapy on a regular basis through the relationships they already have with their patients. These practitioners can work to improve their psychotherapeutic effectiveness.

THEORY OF THE THERAPEUTIC RELATIONSHIP. The patient comes to the physician because of an experienced need. There is almost always a felt need for help, which may be more or less developed and conceptualized, depending on the individual patient. It is from this fundamental need for assistance that the possibility of a therapeutic relationship arises. Nonpsychiatric physicians may underestimate the emotional depth and potential psychotherapeutic power of this therapeutic relationship. This relationship already exists in nascent form with many of their patients and constitutes an underused therapeutic tool.

PSYCHOTHERAPEUTIC STRATEGIES. Fundamental psychotherapeutic skills are universal across successful therapies regardless of specialty. These skills include empathy, sensitivity to emotional cues, the capacity to listen actively, and the ability to intervene with corrective information at acceptable time points. When psychopharmacologic agents are prescribed, clinicians generally should craft some complementary psychotherapy in parallel. Several general technical approaches can be used.

Cognitive Behavior Therapy. Behavioral therapy is a psychotherapy based on the general principle that interventions should be focused on behaviors, thoughts, and emotions that are present at a given time. Such a hypothesis underlies most of our educational endeavors and is readily understandable to most physicians. Key elements of this psychotherapeutic technique are clarification, education, and emotional support. This strategy is commendable as a first-line therapeutic strategy for most mild psychiatric problems. This approach is similar to the approach physicians use for other diagnostic and therapeutic problems.

Psychodynamic Therapy. Psychodynamic psychotherapy refers to more time-limited versions of psychotherapy that derive from psychoanalytic theory. One of the basic concepts of psychoanalytic theory is that of intrapsychic determinism. This principle asserts that psychological events are not produced randomly or by chance but rather by causal forces operating, often unconsciously, within the individual. These causal forces generally include the basic human drives, sexuality and aggression, and the life experience and early development of the individual.

Freud allowed his patients to think and speak freely during his sessions with them, while he listened intently for clues about meanings and motivations that were not quite consciously understood by the patients. He described resistances that the patients showed to keep painful feelings and conflicts from emerging into conscious life, and he wrote about transference, the application to the physician of emotional attachment behaviors that derive from other areas of the patient's life experience. One of the major advantages of this perspective is that it permits the clinician to take full account of the strengths of individuals as they have expressed themselves across their entire life course. The technical skills most important in this technique include active listening, empathic connections with the patient, and the ability to make interpretive connections to previous life events.

Interpersonal Therapy. The interpersonal approach to psychotherapy is directed explicitly at the group system in which a patient lives

or works, as opposed to the patient as an individual. It is a relationship-oriented psychotherapy. An approach to the family is a variation of interpersonal therapy and is performed whenever the physician brings family members into the examination room. Couples therapy is also a form of interpersonal psychotherapy and is the most common type of family therapy performed by nonpsychiatric clinicians. In these therapies, the physician addresses some difficulty in the interpersonal system. The relationship patterns of the system must be considered, and the positive strengths must be identified. The problem must be amenable to definition within such a relationship system. The simplest metaphor to use for interpersonal therapy in medical settings is the system-wide impact of the medical illness being experienced by the identified patient.

GUIDELINE. A rough guideline to set a work plan for a medical psychotherapy might consider the following technical points:

Diagnosis: Define the problem with some psychosocial dimension that makes sense to the patient and family.
Work plan: Set an initial number of talking visits, specifying the frequency and duration of each visit.
Strategy: Consider the overview strategies outlined here, and consider which strategies might be best applicable to the situation at hand.
Consultation: Be prepared to request a psychiatric consultation.

1. Keller MB, McCullough JP, Klein DN, et al: A comparison of nefazodone, the cognitive behavioral-analysis system of psychotherapy, and their combination for the treatment of chronic depression. N Engl J Med 2000;342:1462–1470.
2. Schoenbaum M, Unutzer J, Sherbourne C, et al: Cost-effectiveness of practice-initiated quality improvement for depression: Results of a randomized controlled trial. JAMA 2001;286:1325–1330.
3. Bowden CL, Brugger AM, Swann AC, et al: Efficacy of divalproex vs lithium and placebo in the treatment of mania. The Depakote Mania Study Group. JAMA 1994;271:918–924.
4. Jarrett RB, Kraft D, Doyle J, et al: Preventing recurrent depression using cognitive therapy with and without a continuation phase. Arch Gen Psychiatry 2001;58:381–388.

SUGGESTED READINGS
Schiffer RB, Rao SM: Neuropsychiatry, 2nd ed. Baltimore, Lippincott Williams & Wilkins, 2002. *A multiauthored overview by designated experts of available knowledge on the neural substrate of behavior.*
UK ECT Review Group: Efficacy and safety of electroconvulsive therapy in depressive disorders: A systematic review and meta-analysis. Lancet 2003;361:799–808. *Electroconvulsive therapy, which is probably more effective than drug therapy, is even more effective when used in higher doses or bilaterally.*
Young AS, Klap R, Sherbourne CD, et al: The quality of care for depressive and anxiety disorders in the United States. Arch Gen Psychiatry 2001;58:55–61. *A national sample of quality of care in patients attending primary care and specialty practices.*

427 SPECIFIC PAIN SYNDROMES

Michael C. Rowbotham

TRANSITION FROM ACUTE TO CHRONIC PAIN

Although trauma, infection, inflammation, and tissue degeneration severe enough to cause acute pain are universal experiences, only a few acute pains evolve into severe, unremitting, and disabling chronic pain. About 10% of cases of acute herpes zoster progress to become established postherpetic neuralgia, and fewer than 5% of traumatic injuries to limbs or peripheral nerves persist as complex regional pain syndrome (CRPS I) or causalgia (CRPS II). An even smaller percentage of musculoskeletal injuries evolve into the diffuse somatic pain of fibromyalgia.

The factors determining which acute pains become chronic are incompletely understood but can be grouped into four categories: (1) persistent tissue-damaging disease, (2) abnormal function of the nervous system, (3) damage to the nervous system, and (4) psychological factors. Pain persists for as long as active tissue destruction and inflammation continues (i.e., the nervous system is serving its normal function of signaling pain in response to tissue injury). In the above-named disorders, there is no evidence of ongoing tissue destruction or infiltration of inflammatory cells. Instead the central nervous system (CNS) responds in a pathologically amplified manner to all sensory input from the painful region, no matter how it was generated. In postherpetic neuralgia and CRPS II, the peripheral nerves have been injured, sometimes severely enough to produce deafferentation and reorganization within the CNS, leading to hyperactivity in some CNS neurons and abnormal response patterns in others. Damaged sensory nerves variably may be unusually sensitive to their usual stimuli, may be spontaneously active, or may generate impulses in response to sympathetic nervous system activity. Postherpetic neuralgia is a common and noncontroversial pain disorder with a known cause (reactivation of latent chickenpox virus in the form of shingles; Chapter 453), consistent symptoms, clinical mechanisms that are increasingly well understood, and at least four proven therapies. In contrast, CRPS I and fibromyalgia (Chapter 289) are controversial entities of uncertain etiology with few proven therapies. Psychological factors, including depression and secondary gain, may be suspected as the primary cause in some patients with chronic pain. Although these factors may explain a substantial proportion of the pain's severity, persistence, and failure to respond to therapy, malingering, factitious disorders, and severe somatoform disorders are uncommon underlying diagnoses (Chapter 426). Studies so far have not found psychological features specific to CRPS or fibromyalgia that differentiate these groups from the much larger population of patients with chronic pain.

POSTHERPETIC NEURALGIA

Acute herpes zoster or shingles represents the recrudescence of the varicella-zoster virus. Herpes zoster may be so painful that it can be controlled adequately only by regional local anesthetic blockade and parenteral medications. The cutaneous rash is not the only source of herpes zoster pain; there is also intense inflammation and destruction of the peripheral nerve apparatus and surrounding tissues from the nerve root to the skin. Age and more severe initial pain are the biggest risk factors for the development of chronic pain. More pain produces greater initial disability and immobility. Psychosocial factors (e.g., living alone, anxiety, and depression), which are common in the elderly, decrease the likelihood that the premorbid level of function will be achieved.

Postherpetic neuralgia is defined by the persistence of pain after new lesions have ceased and healing of the skin is complete, usually 3 months after all lesions have crusted. If the pain has persisted for 1 year, spontaneous remission is unlikely. With more than 1 million new cases of herpes zoster each year, a conservative estimate of the prevalence of postherpetic neuralgia in the United States is about 200,000. The chronic pain of postherpetic neuralgia involves a spectrum of pain mechanisms, including persistent irritability of peripheral sensory nerve fibers, chronic sensitization of their CNS targets, and deafferentation-induced changes in the CNS.

Patients collectively describe three components: (1) a *constant*, deep, aching, bruised, or burning sensation; (2) a spontaneous, recurrent, *lancinating*, shooting or electric shock–like pain; and (3) an *allodynic*, superficial, sharp, radiating, burning, tender, dysesthetic or "itch"-like sensation evoked by gentle touch or by wearing clothing. Nearly all patients describe constant pain, and 90% describe allodynia; lancinating pain tends to fade over the first year. Although the viral reactivation pathologically affects only a single dorsal root ganglion, the area of pain and allodynia to gentle touch may cover more than 1000 cm^2 of skin.

Rx Treatment

Because postherpetic neuralgia is common, strikes frequently in the healthy elderly population, and has a relatively stereotyped symptom complex, many clinical trials of new therapies for chronic neuropathic pain have been performed in patients with postherpetic neuralgia. Double-blind controlled trials have shown efficacy for topical agents (capsaicin cream and lidocaine patches), oral opioids, tricyclic antidepressants, and the anticonvulsant gabapentin. [1][2] Most patients require more than one type of medication to control their pain adequately. A few are refractory to all currently available medications. Neurolytic nerve blocks and destructive surgical approaches rarely provide long-term relief. Spinal stimulation and intrathecal medication pumps should be considered only after expert multidisciplinary evaluation.

COMPLEX REGIONAL PAIN SYNDROME (REFLEX SYMPATHETIC DYSTROPHY AND CAUSALGIA)

There are two types CRPS: CRPS I and CRPS II. CRPS I, in which there is no demonstrable nerve injury, replaces the term *reflex sympathetic dystrophy*. CRPS II, in which there is objective evidence of nerve damage, replaces the term *causalgia*. The International Association for the Study of Pain defines CRPS by the following criteria:

1. The presence of an initiating noxious event or a cause of immobilization
2. Continuing pain, allodynia, or hyperalgesia, in which the pain is disproportionate to any inciting event
3. Evidence at some time of edema, changes in skin blood flow, or abnormal sudomotor activity in the region of pain
4. Other diagnoses that could account for the symptoms have been excluded

Associated signs and symptoms of CRPS, not used for diagnosis, include:

1. Atrophy of the hair, nails, and other soft tissues
2. Alterations in hair growth
3. Loss of joint mobility
4. Impairment of motor function, including weakness, tremor, and dystonia
5. Sympathetically maintained pain may be present

The exact incidence and prevalence of CRPS are unknown, and estimates vary widely. Despite the diagnostic criteria, in 10% of cases, no precipitating factor can be identified clearly. The diagnosis of CRPS is clinical. Classically the disorder has been described to progress in three stages: acute, dystrophic, and atrophic. The features of CRPS appear to be expressed in different ways over a highly variable time course. The disorder most often initially manifests signs of inflammation—edema, erythema, increased sweating, and often warmth—in the distal aspect of an extremity. Studies support neurogenic inflammation owing to substances such as calcitonin gene–related peptide, vasoactive intestinal peptide, bradykinin, and neuropeptide Y in this phase. In addition, plasma protein extravasation can be facilitated in CRPS patients, but not healthy controls, via transcutaneous electrical stimulation. With time, sympathetic-sensory coupling is believed to occur, in the periphery and in the dorsal root ganglion, although the contribution of the latter to the production of pain is uncertain. There is upregulation of α-adrenoreceptors on sensory afferent neurons, while levels of norepinephrine and its metabolite 3,4-DHPG in the venous effluent of the affected extremity decrease, in what seems to be denervation supersensitivity. The limb grows cold, and sudomotor activity may increase. The pain is exquisitely sensitive to adrenergic stimulation from norepinephrine injections. Marked increases in pain typically are reported with stress and emotional upset. Despite the classic description of burning pain, a deep ache is the most common complaint. Every type of pain and dysesthesia has been reported in association with CRPS, and typically more than one sensation is present. Allodynia to mechanical stimulation is seen in many neuropathic pain disorders, but allodynia to cold stimuli is uncommon in conditions other than CRPS. Hyperpathia may be present as evidence of CNS involvement. Periarticular demineralization often is seen on scintigraphy as increased uptake in the delayed phase, especially when trophic changes are present on careful clinical examination. Although lack of use of the limb likely worsens trophic changes, over time there is a tendency to progress to a cold limb, with atrophy and changes of the hair and nail. To a limited extent, the diagnosis can be supported by response to sympathetic blockade. Sympathetically independent pain manifesting clinically identical features is still CRPS. All available sympathetic block techniques are not fully selective, and false-positive and false-negative results occur.

Neurology

 Treatment

It is believed widely that the delay from onset of the disorder to the institution of effective treatment affects prognosis. An underlying source of continuing nociceptor input into the CNS, most often orthopedic or neuropathic, can cause the symptoms; if found and treated, especially if fully reversible, the CRPS may resolve.

There are few well-designed clinical trials of any therapy for CRPS. Prospectively proven, evidence-based treatment algorithms do not exist. There is general agreement, however, that maintaining limb mobilization, via physical therapy and aided by sufficient analgesia, is of primary importance. There is also a general consensus that a series of closely spaced sympathetic nerve blocks may be dramatically effective or curative. Treatment outcomes are often disappointing, with a high burden of continuing symptoms and disability. CRPS symptoms have been documented to spread spontaneously to other extremities, and the symptoms may return years after apparently successful treatment. The etiology of recurrent or spreading CRPS is unknown. Extremely aggressive and invasive therapies should be avoided in favor of a conservative, multidisciplinary approach that combines physical therapy, medication management, counseling, education, and local anesthetic nerve blocks. Surgical sympathectomy and other destructive procedures sometimes worsen, rather than improve, symptoms. Techniques requiring permanent hardware placement, such as intrathecal pumps and spinal stimulators, should be considered only after expert multidisciplinary consultation, a thorough diagnostic evaluation for a reversible disorder that could be maintaining the pain, and an adequate trial of more conservative therapies.

FIBROMYALGIA SYNDROME

Fibromyalgia syndrome, which has an estimated overall population prevalence of 1%, remains an etiologic enigma (Chapter 289). The current American College of Rheumatology classification for fibromyalgia requires widespread pain on both sides of the body and pain above and below the waist. Pain must be present for at least 3 months. Examination for tender points should be positive in at least 11 of the 18 recognized sites. There are no specific laboratory abnormalities. More than 75% of patients also complain of symptoms such as morning stiffness, chronic fatigue, and sleep disturbance. The disorder is most common in women in their 20s to 40s.

Hypotheses about etiology are varied. Investigators have found muscle histology, metabolism, strength, and function to be abnormal. Studies of substance P levels, serotonin, growth factors, N-methyl-D-aspartate receptors, and experimental pain models have led other investigators to question whether a general hypersensitivity of the CNS is the primary problem. Neuroendocrine studies have attempted to link symptoms with abnormal physiologic responses to stress.

 Treatment

Current therapy includes nonpharmacologic approaches, such as exercise-based programs and cognitive behavior therapies. Tricyclic and serotonin-selective reuptake inhibitor antidepressants, tramadol, and cyclobenzaprine have been studied prospectively and are believed beneficial.◼ Prednisone is not effective, and neither opioids nor nonsteroidal anti-inflammatory drugs have been shown convincingly to improve pain and function. Of note is a diminishing effect of active medications compared with placebo in trials lasting 6 months. Trigger point injections seem to be of more benefit for localized myofascial pain than for widespread fibromyalgia.

MYOFASCIAL PAIN SYNDROME

Myofascial pain syndromes are common. Some authors use the term *myofascial pain syndrome* to refer to patients with widespread pain of unknown etiology, blurring the distinction from fibromyalgia. The term is used better to refer to regional musculoskeletal pain disorders. Many conditions represent a chronic phase of sports or overuse injuries, and there may be associated but subtle joint or ligamentous degeneration. Physical examination should show trigger points that reproduce the ongoing pain complaint.

 Treatment

Treatment should begin with a physical therapy approach that improves functional mechanics, prevents reinjury, provides general and regional reconditioning, and noninvasively treats trigger points. Medications and trigger point injections should be considered adjuncts. Some experts believe opioids, anxiolytics, and muscle relaxants should be avoided completely.

 1. Rowbotham M, Harden N, Stacey B, et al: Gabapentin for the treatment of postherpetic neuralgia: A randomized controlled trial. JAMA 1998;280:1837–1842.
2. Raja SN, Haythornthwaite JA, Pappagallo M, et al: Opioids versus antidepressants in postherpetic neuralgia: A randomized, placebo-controlled trial. Neurology 2002;59:1015–1021.
3. Kingery WS: A critical review of controlled clinical trials for peripheral neuropathic pain and complex regional pain syndromes. Pain 1997;73:123–139.

SUGGESTED READINGS
Loeser JL (ed): Bonica's Management of Pain, 3rd ed. Philadelphia, Lippincott Williams & Wilkins, 2000. *A comprehensive textbook.*
Rowbotham MC, Petersen KL: Zoster-associated pain and neural dysfunction. Pain 2001;93:1–5. *A concise and well-referenced review of zoster and postherpetic neuralgia.*

428 HEADACHES AND OTHER HEAD PAIN

F. Michael Cutrer
Michael A. Moskowitz

Headache is a very common complaint encountered by practitioners in almost every specialty of medicine and surgery. More than 90% of the population experience headache of one type or another at least once during life. The very common occurrence of headache sometimes leads to an underestimation of its potential importance as a symptom. Although headaches may be associated with minor trauma or febrile illness, they may also result from potentially life-threatening central nervous system (CNS) disease. Fortunately, most patients with recurrent or chronic headaches suffer from a primary headache disorder for which no ominous underlying source can be found. Although reassuring, this lack of identifiable cause does not diminish the patient's suffering or economic loss.

Pathophysiology

A headache signifies activation of the primary afferent fibers that innervate cephalic blood vessels, chiefly meningeal or cerebral blood vessels. Most nociceptive fibers innervating these structures arise from pseudounipolar neurons located within the trigeminal ganglia (first division), although some may be located within the upper cervical ganglia. Stimuli activating these fibers are quite variable and can range from direct mechanical traction by a tumor to chemical irritation caused by central nervous system infection or subarachnoid blood. In patients with so-called *secondary headache disorders*, headaches result from an identifiable structural or inflammatory source. In these patients, treatment of the primary abnormality often results in resolution of the headache. However, most patients with chronic headaches have *primary headache disorders*, such as migraine or tension headache, for which results of the physical examination and laboratory studies are generally normal. With the absence of an identifiable cause, the mode of trigeminal activation in migraine has been hotly debated. Traditional theories have been dominated by two points of view. The vasogenic theory held that intracranial vasoconstriction was responsible for the symptoms of the migraine aura and that the headache resulted from a rebound dilation and distention of cranial vessels and activation of perivascular nociceptive axons. This theory was based on observations that (1) extracranial vessels distend and pulsate during a migraine attack in many patients, implying that cranial vessels might be of primary importance; (2) stimulation of intracranial vessels in awake patients results in an ipsilateral headache; and (3) substances that cause vasoconstriction, such as ergot alkaloids, abort headache, whereas vasodilators, such as nitrates, can provoke an attack. The alternative hypothesis, the neurogenic theory, identified the brain as the generator of migraine and held that the susceptibility of any individual to migraine attacks reflects thresholds intrinsic to the brain; the vascular changes occurring during migraine would be the result rather than the cause of the attack. Supporters of the neurogenic hypothesis pointed to the observation that migraine attacks are often accompanied by a range of neurologic symptoms focal (in the aura) and vegetative (in the prodrome) that cannot be explained simply by vasoconstriction within a single neurovascular distribution. It is likely that elements of both theories explain some of the pathophysiology of migraine and other primary headache disorders. Imaging (i.e., magnetic resonance imaging [MRI] and positron emission tomography [PET]) and genetic studies confirm that migraine and related headaches are disorders of neurovascular regulation.

Clinical and experimental observations suggest that the brain, although usually insensate, can activate or sensitize (directly or indirectly) trigeminal nerve fibers within the meninges. One example in which headache is initiated by events within the brain occurs in migraine with visual aura. Imaging studies during migraine attacks implicate a cortical spreading depression-like phenomenon as the mechanism in migraine visual aura. The decreased levels of deoxy-hemoglobin in affected areas of the visual cortex during the opening seconds of the visual aura make it unlikely that ischemia is the cause for the visual scintillations. In this form of migraine, endogenous neurophysiologic (cortical spreading depression-like) events in the neocortex may promote the release of nociceptive substances (e.g., potassium, protons, arachidonate metabolites) from the neocortex into the interstitial space. Within the Virchow-Robin spaces, the released substances accumulate to levels sufficient to activate or sensitize the trigeminovascular fibers that surround the pial vessels supplying the draining neocortex. Under steady-state conditions, the brain vigorously maintains the equilibrium of its extracellular environment, and ions or transmitters normally released from cellular compartments are rapidly taken up in glia and neurons at rates that maintain constant levels of these ions, transmitters, and neuromodulators. Blood vessels provide a backup clearance mechanism that is not invoked under normal conditions. However, before the onset of headache, mechanisms associated with spreading oligemia may enhance release of the various substances, block uptake and inactivation—thereby increasing extracellular levels—and overwhelm the normal clearance mechanisms. The substances released may discharge or sensitize small unmyelinated nociceptive fibers and provide the trigger for headache or sensitize perivascular afferents to blood-borne or other as yet unidentified factors. The headache latency (20 to 40 minutes) observed in migraine may reflect the time needed for extracellular levels to exceed a threshold for axonal depolarization and for sensitization to occur within peripheral and central neurons. Consistent with these notions, unilateral headaches tend to occur on the side corresponding to the dysfunctional hemisphere. In studies of cluster headache and of migraine without aura, changes in blood flow have been identified in the hypothalamus and rostral brain stem, respectively, raising the possibility that primary CNS dysfunction also may underlie these disorders.

In this formulation, the brain becomes a master switch, a transducer. Triggering events, such as those associated with emotional stress, fatigue, bright lights, and too little (or too much) sleep, modulate activity within regions of the brain that are physically contiguous to the meningeal vessels that are innervated by the trigeminal nerve. In susceptible individuals, these events may provide a sufficient trigger for subsequent neurophysiologic events that lead to chemical activation of meningeal fibers. The photophobia, nausea, and vomiting associated with migraine are probably related to the consequences of meningeal irritation because similar symptoms also occur during meningeal infection or when blood enters the subarachnoid space. This pathogenetic framework for migraine is consistent with currently understood principles of neurobiology and the physiology of pain. However, some of the details will require revision as data emerge from additional experimental studies in humans and animals. In all likelihood, migraine and other headaches arise from a combination of genetic and environmental factors. Some are intrinsic to the brain, others to blood vessels or to circulating substances. In each case, the pain develops from trigeminal activation in sensitized axons as a consequence of actual or threatened tissue injury.

PRIMARY HEADACHE DISORDERS

MIGRAINE

Migraine is the second most common primary headache disorder and has a prevalence of about 12%. It affects women disproportion-

ately (approximately 18.2% of women versus 6.5% of men in the United States) and commonly afflicts the population during the most productive years of life (peak prevalence, 25 to 45 years old).

Clinical Manifestations

Migraine falls into two categories: *migraine without an aura* (previously called common migraine), which occurs in about 85% of patients, and *migraine with an aura* (previously called classic migraine), which occurs in about 15% of patients. Migraine patients with and without an aura may report prodromal symptoms that begin 24 to 48 hours before a headache attack. These symptoms can include hyperactivity, mild euphoria, lethargy, depression, craving for certain foods, fluid retention, and frequent yawning. Prodromal symptoms should not be confused with the migraine aura that consists of transient episodes of focal neurologic dysfunction appearing 1 to 2 hours before the onset of a migraine headache and resolving within 60 minutes. The aura symptoms may be of different types, and more than a single symptom type may be present within a given aura. Typical aura symptoms include homonymous (rarely monocular) visual disturbance, classically an expanding scotoma with a scintillating margin; unilateral paresthesias and or numbness, often affecting the distal ends of the extremities or the perioral region of the face; unilateral weakness; and dysphasia or other language disturbances. Sometimes aura symptoms localize to the brain stem and may include vertigo, dysarthria, tinnitus, fluctuating hearing loss, diplopia, bilateral weakness, ataxia, bilateral paresthesias, and a decreased level of consciousness. *Basilar migraine* is the diagnosis in patients in whom brain stem symptoms predominate. In many patients, basilar attacks are intermingled with more typical migraine attacks. Dizziness is frequently reported as a feature of an otherwise typical attack of migraine without an aura. Bilateral paresthesias can also occur with anxiety and hyperventilation.

The headache phase of a migraine attack (with or without aura) consists of 4 to 72 hours of unilateral throbbing head pain that is of moderate to severe intensity, that is worsened by routine physical exertion, and that is associated with nausea, photophobia, and phonophobia. *Complicated migraine* or *migraine with a prolonged aura* refers to migraine attacks associated with aura symptoms that persist for more than 1 hour but less than 1 week with normal neuroimaging studies. If symptoms persist for more than 1 week or result in neuroimaging abnormalities, migrainous infarction is likely. In general, migrainous infarction develops in the context of stereotypic aura symptoms.

STATUS MIGRAINOSUS. Migraine attacks that persist for longer than 72 hours despite treatment are classified as *status migrainosus*. During *status migrainosus*, headache-free periods of less than 4 hours (sleep not included) may occur. Status migrainosus is usually associated with prolonged use of analgesics and may require inpatient treatment with detoxification.

Genetics

A higher than expected prevalence of migraine has been observed in the relatives of migraine patients. In one large family study drawn from the general population, the risk of migraine in relatives of patients with migraines was three times higher than the risk among controls. Data from large twin registries have consistently revealed higher concordance rates for migraine in monozygotic twins than in dizygotic pairs. One study of more than 2500 monozygotic and 5000 dizygotic twin pairs estimated that 40 to 50% of the susceptibility to migraine is genetically based. Although migraine is widely thought to reflect an autosomal dominant condition, segregational analysis has failed to identify any single mendelian pattern of transmission. During the past few years, several novel migraine susceptibility genes have been identified in families by linkage analysis. These novel polymorphisms map to loci on chromosomes 1 (19p13), 6 (6p12.2-21.1), X(Xq24-28), and 4(q24) for the more common types of migraine, whereas loci for uncommon subtypes have been proposed on chromosomes 19(p13) and 1(q21-23;1q31), as discussed later.

FAMILIAL HEMIPLEGIC MIGRAINE. Perhaps the most compelling genetic evidence to date comes from the identification of specific gene loci for familial hemiplegic migraine. Familial hemiplegic migraine is an autosomal dominant disorder characterized by transient hemiplegia during the aura phase of a migraine attack. This rare migraine subtype has been linked to point mutations in the gene *CACNL1A4* located on chromosome 19p13 in 50% of affected families. Another genetic mutation in a group of families with familial hemiplegic migraine has been assigned to chromosome 1q31, implying genetic heterogeneity. Except for cerebellar atrophy in cases of disease that can be mapped to 19p13, no obvious clinical distinctions can be identified between affected families with and without this abnormal gene. The

defective gene codes for the α_1 subunit of a brain-specific P/Q calcium channel that is coupled to the release of neurotransmitters and is expressed throughout the human brain. The mutant channel has been shown to cause increased calcium influx in response to depolarizations that are insufficient to open un-mutated channels. It is unclear how sustained neurologic deficits and migraine result from a defect in an ion channel that operates (i.e., opens and shuts) in milliseconds.

Rx Treatment

Migraine therapy includes nonpharmacologic and pharmacologic interventions. Nonpharmacologic treatment includes behavior modification techniques such as the avoidance of triggering factors (e.g., the ingestion of particular foods or food additives, strong smells, glaring light) and establishment of regular meals and consistent sleeping patterns. Other techniques to minimize the effects of environmental stress, such as biofeedback, relaxation training, rational motive therapy, self-hypnosis, and meditation, are sometimes helpful.

Pharmacologic treatment of migraine includes abortive therapy given to shorten the attack or decrease the severity of the headache. In patients with infrequent and uncomplicated attacks, abortive medications are often sufficient. If migraines cause disability more than 3 days per month, daily prophylactic treatment may be taken to decrease the frequency and, less often, the severity of attacks. If taken at the time of attacks, prophylactic agents are usually ineffective, and agents used for treatment during an attack provide little protection against subsequent attacks. The use of analgesic medications for more than 3 days per week (including over-the-counter formulations) may increase headache's frequency and severity. In some cases, intermittent migraine progresses to a syndrome of daily severe headaches despite the use of escalating prophylactic medication or analgesics. Only nonsteroidal anti-inflammatory drugs (NSAIDs), ergotamine, and valproic acid are useful during an attack and for prevention.

Patients should be provided with a variety of treatments that may be taken in a manner appropriate to the severity of their symptoms. *Mild attacks* may be treated with simple analgesics such as acetaminophen (suggested dose, 650 to 1000 mg) or NSAIDs (aspirin, 900 to 1000 mg; ibuprofen, 1000 to 1200 mg; naproxen, 500 to 825 mg; and ketoprofen, 100 to 200 mg). Mild to moderate attacks during pregnancy may be treated with acetaminophen if nonpharmacologic treatments are ineffective. *Moderate headaches* may respond to the combination of acetaminophen, isometheptene mucate (a mild vasoconstrictor), and dichloralphenazone (a mild sedative). Infrequent headaches of moderate to severe intensity may be treated with butalbital, a barbiturate, combined with caffeine, aspirin, or acetaminophen. Oral opiates have little place in the treatment of chronic, recurrent, primary headaches and should be avoided until alternatives, including NSAIDs and serotonin agonists such as dihydroergotamine or sumatriptan, have been considered. However, opiates may be the only viable option during pregnancy or in patients with severe vascular disease; if so, they should be used with caution, and the risks associated with opiate use, including rebound headaches

and dependency, should be discussed with patients before treatment is initiated.

A number of abortive agents with vasoconstrictive properties are available, but patients with uncontrolled hypertension or a history of coronary artery disease or angina should not be given any of these drugs. *Moderate to severe* attacks may be treated outside the hospital with dihydroergotamine (1 to 2 mg intranasally), with oral, intranasal, or subcutaneous formulations of 5-HT$_{B/D}$ receptor agonists (e.g., sumatriptan, 25 or 50 mg orally, 20 mg intranasally, or 6 mg subcutaneously), or with second-generation sumatriptan-like drugs (e.g., naratriptan, zolmitriptan, rizatriptan, eletriptan, frovatriptan, almotriptan). The second-generation drugs are similar to sumatriptan in overall efficacy and mechanism, but they may have a faster onset of action and fewer coronary vasoconstrictive properties. Ergotamine (2 mg sublingually or 1 to 2 mg orally), which is the longest established antimigraine agent, is typically given early in the migraine attack and can be effective if the associated nausea and peripheral vasoconstriction can be tolerated.

Very severe attacks sometimes require the administration of intravenous or intramuscular agents in the emergency department. Dihydroergotamine, an injectable hydrogenated ergot, has less potent peripheral arterial vasoconstrictive effects than ergotamine and is usually effective even when given well into an attack. Dihydroergotamine may be administered subcutaneously or intravenously. Given intravenously, dihydroergotamine causes less nausea than ergotamine does, but an antiemetic is still required before intravenous use. Meperidine, an opioid analgesic, is frequently administered intramuscularly, especially in combination with an antiemetic, to treat severe migraine attacks. With alternatives available, the use of parenteral opioids should be limited to patients with infrequent, severe attacks for whom other treatments are contraindicated. The recent identification of 5-HT$_{1D}$ and 5-HT$_{1F}$ receptor binding proteins on trigeminovascular nerves may be relevant to next-generation abortive treatments of migraine.

For patients who are nonresponsive or have contraindications to vasoactive abortive agents, intravenous neuroleptics may be given to treat severe or prolonged migraine attacks. Intravenous chlorpromazine, 10 mg, may be used in this setting and repeated in 1 hour if no response is seen. ☐ The hypotension that sometimes accompanies the use of intravenous chlorpromazine may be avoided by administering 500 mL of normal saline intravenously before chlorpromazine (10 mg). Alternatively, intravenous prochlorperazine (10 mg over 5 minutes) can be given without prior saline infusion and repeated after 30 minutes.

Prevention

In general, preventive treatment is recommended if headaches limit work or normal daily activity 3 or more days per month, if the symptoms accompanying headache are severe or prolonged, and if previous migraine was associated with a complication (e.g., cerebral infarction). Preventive treatment is largely empiric, and the drugs currently used were discovered serendipitously while being developed for the treatment of other disorders. Increased appetite and weight gain are common side effects of most prophylactic agents. Treatment should be initiated at low doses and gradually titrated to headache improvement or the onset of side effects. Groups 1 to 5 are generally considered first-line agents and tend to be associated with fewer or less potentially serious side effects. The prophylactic agents fall into seven groups:

1. β-Adrenergic blockers: propranolol (40 to 240 mg), atenolol (50 to 150 mg), nadolol (20 to 80 mg), timolol (20 to 60 mg), and metoprolol (50 to 300 mg)
2. NSAIDs: aspirin (1000 to 1300 mg), naproxen (480 to 1100 mg), ketoprofen (150 to 300 mg)
3. Tricyclic antidepressants: amitriptyline (10 to 120 mg), nortriptyline (10 to 75 mg)
4. Calcium channel antagonists: verapamil (120 to 480 mg), flunarizine (5 to 10 mg)
5. Anticonvulsants: divalproex sodium (750 to 1000 mg), gabapentin (900 to 1800 mg), topiramate (100 to 400 mg)
6. Serotoninergic drugs: methysergide (4 to 8 mg), cyproheptadine (8 to 20 mg)
7. Monoamine oxidase inhibitor: phenelzine (30 to 60 mg)
8. Angiotensin II receptor blocker: candesartan (16 mg)

Unfortunately, comparative data on prophylactic treatments are sparse, and the decision to use one versus another is currently most often based on the practitioner's experience or the presence of co-morbid illnesses, which would be an indication or contraindication to a specific type of drug.

CLUSTER HEADACHE

Cluster headache, which is much less common than tension-type headache or migraine, affects 0.4 to 2.4 persons per 1000 in the general population. Unlike patients with migraine headaches, patients with cluster headaches usually seek medical consultation because of the intense pain that accompanies their attacks. As a result, physicians encounter cluster headache more commonly than would be predicted from its actual prevalence. The condition is more common in men than in women (male-to-female ratio of 6:1) and usually begins in the third through the sixth decades of life. Although cluster headaches may cease during pregnancy, attacks seldom correlate with menses.

Clinical Manifestations

Cluster headaches consist of recurrent episodes of unilateral, orbital, supraorbital, or temporal head pain usually accompanied by ipsilateral autonomic signs, including conjunctival injection, lacrimation, rhinorrhea, nasal congestion, ptosis, miosis, eyelid edema, and facial sweating. The attacks last 15 minutes to 3 hours and occur as infrequently as every other day to as frequently as eight attacks per day. The syndrome derives its name from the characteristic clusters, or periods of frequent headache, that last weeks to months and are separated by periods of months or years of headache-free remission. Chronic symptoms without remission may develop in about 10% of patients. During a cluster period, the headache attacks often assume a temporal cyclicity, with occurrence at almost the same time every day. Exposure to small amounts of nitrates or alcohol may trigger an acute attack during a cluster period.

Pathogenesis

The cause of cluster headaches is not defined. Like other vascular headaches, they are presumed to develop from events that ultimately activate the trigeminovascular system. In the complete form of the disease, patients with cluster headache manifest pain referred to the first and second trigeminal divisions, sympathetic dysfunction (i.e., Horner's syndrome), sympathetic activation (i.e., sweating of the forehead and face), and parasympathetic activation (i.e., lacrimation and nasal congestion). This constellation of symptoms and signs is best explained by the presence of a single lesion at the point at which fibers from the ophthalmic and maxillary trigeminal division converge with projections from the superior cervical and sphenopalatine ganglia. This plexus is located within the cavernous sinus, and narrowing of the cavernous carotid artery has been observed in selected cases of cluster headache. PET-based functional imaging studies of blood flow during acute cluster attacks show areas of increased flow in the inferior portion of the hypothalamus on the same side as the headache. This finding is consistent with the clinical cyclicity exhibited by cluster headaches reported by many patients.

Genetics

There is an increased concordance of cluster headache in monozygotic twins. Moreover, studies of relatives of patients with cluster headache have found a frequency 13 times higher than expected by chance.

Rx Treatment

During cluster headaches, oxygen inhalation (100%) delivered at a rate of 8 L/minute for 15 minutes through a loose-fitting face mask is a safe and effective treatment for acute attacks, particularly in patients younger than 50 years who have episodic cluster headaches. Patients who respond to oxygen usually do so within 10 minutes. Inhalation of oxygen does not cause nausea and is not contraindicated in patients with coronary artery disease or peripheral vascular disease. Ergotamine tartrate, the classic treatment of cluster headache, is effective and well tolerated by many patients. Because of more rapid absorption, sublingual administration is generally preferred to oral administration. Intranasal dihydroergotamine reduces the severity of cluster headaches, but not their duration. Subcutaneous administration of sumatriptan (6 mg) is usually successful in alleviating acute cluster headaches and reduces pain and conjunctival injection within 15 minutes in most patients. Vasoconstrictive medications such as ergotamines and sumatriptan should be used with caution for cluster headache in patients who are at increased risk for coronary artery disease.

Ergotamine tartrate was for many years the only prophylactic agent used for cluster headache. It is effective and well tolerated in doses of 2 to 4 mg/day given orally or by suppository. The ergot derivative methysergide is effective in about 70% of episodic cases. Retroperitoneal, pleural, or pericardial fibrosis is a severe potential side effect of long-term use. Because patients with cluster headache usually require treatment for less than 2 to 3 months, methysergide can be used with more safety than in migraine. Lithium carbonate, which was effective in chronic cluster headache in more than 20 open-label clinical trials, may also be beneficial in the episodic form of the disease. Because of the narrow range between toxic and therapeutic doses, it is important to monitor the serum lithium level 12 hours after the last dose. The usual therapeutic range is from 0.3 to 0.8 mmol/L, but low lithium levels may still be therapeutic. NSAIDs and thiazide diuretics may increase serum lithium levels. Average daily doses of lithium carbonate (600 to 900 mg) should be titrated according to the serum lithium level. Verapamil is often effective as a prophylactic agent against cluster headache; it has relatively few side effects when compared with other prophylactic agents, and a double-blind trial found it to be as effective as lithium. Prophylactic medication dosages are usually tapered and then discontinued within 3 to 6 weeks after recurrent cluster headaches cease.

Corticosteroids are frequently used to treat the episodic and the chronic forms of cluster headache, even though evidence for their effectiveness is largely limited to open trials. Prednisone is frequently used in dosages of 60 to 80 mg/day for 1 week, followed by a taper in dosage over a period of 2 to 4 weeks.

TENSION-TYPE HEADACHE

Tension-type headache is the most common of the primary headache disorders, with a lifetime prevalence between 30 and 78%. Tension-type headaches are more common in women than in men and most often begin in the second decade of life. In both sexes, the prevalence decreases with increasing age, and socioeconomic factors do not contribute to risk. Although no studies have been conducted in twins, genetic factors are not as prominent in the condition as in migraine or other headache syndromes.

Pathophysiology

Tension-type headache is not well understood and defies a single or simple pathophysiologic explanation. In one model, headache pain is viewed as the sum of nociceptive input onto brain stem neurons from vascular structures, myofascial and muscular sources, and descending supraspinal modulation. The relative importance of these three factors varies among patients and among attacks in the same patient.

Clinical Manifestations

Tension-type headache occurs in episodic and chronic forms, which differ in their response to treatment and possibly in their pathophysiology. Pericranial muscle spasm or tenderness may or may not be present in either form. Episodic tension-type headache consists of recurrent attacks of tight, pressing (band-like), bilateral, mild to moderate head pain that last from minutes to days. Tension-type headaches do not worsen with routine physical exertion and are not associated with nausea, although photophobia or phonophobia may be present. In the chronic form, characteristic tension-type headaches occur at least 15 days per month.

Neurology

 Treatment

Episodic tension-type headaches usually respond to simple analgesics such as acetaminophen (650 to 1000 mg) or to NSAIDs such as aspirin (900 to 1000 mg), ketoprofen (12.5 to 75 mg), ibuprofen (200 to 800 mg), and naproxen (250 to 500 mg). More severe, episodic tension-type headaches may respond to higher doses of NSAIDs or to combination remedies that contain isometheptene mucate or butalbital. Frequent use of analgesics can increase the number of headaches, so caution is advised whenever analgesic use regularly exceeds three days per week. Chronic tension-type headaches occasionally require prophylactic treatment. Tricyclic antidepressants decrease the frequency and the severity of attacks; amitriptyline is the drug of choice. Amitriptyline's use may be limited by sedation, dry mouth, or other anticholinergic side effects. To avoid these side effects, therapy should be started at low doses (10 mg) given at bedtime and increased slowly until satisfactory improvement is achieved or intolerable side effects appear. Nortriptyline, doxepin, maprotiline, and fluoxetine are other antidepressants that are sometimes effective in chronic tension-type headache.

CHRONIC DAILY HEADACHE

The term *chronic daily headache* may be applied to any headaches occurring more than 15 days per month for at least 1 month. By this definition, the term includes several clinically distinct syndromes, including cluster headache, hemicrania continua, chronic paroxysmal hemicrania, and chronic tension-type headache. Chronic daily headache is often used more narrowly to include headaches that occur on a daily or almost daily basis (>4 days/week), have features of migraine and tension-type headache, and are frequently but not always associated with overuse of analgesic medications. Patients meeting these criteria account for a major proportion of those seen in headache specialty clinics and are often the most difficult headache patients to treat. The typical patient with chronic daily headache is a woman in her 30s or 40s with a history of episodic migraine or tension-type headache beginning in the teens or 20s. Over a period of months to years, the patient's headaches gradually increase in severity and frequency to the point where consecutive headache-free days are rare. The headaches are often of two types. More frequent headaches are of mild to moderate intensity and have a pressure-like or mildly throbbing quality and mild photophobia or phonophobia but no associated nausea or vomiting. The duration of these milder headaches is variable and ranges from several hours to constant (although waxing and waning). Superimposed are severe attacks that occur as frequently as three times per week and as infrequently as once or twice per month. The more severe attacks are usually, but not always, throbbing and may be associated with nausea, photophobia, phonophobia, and sometimes, vomiting. Severe attacks may be preceded by a migrainous aura. The patient often exhibits features of depression or anxiety. Frequently, the patient is taking one or more daily analgesics, sometimes in an effort to preempt a headache. Chronic daily headaches are called *transformed migraine* when the migrainous component is prominent. When headaches begin without antecedent migraine or tension-type headache but with many features of tension-type headache, they are often labeled new daily persistent headaches. Chronic daily headache is often accompanied by other paroxysmal symptoms that are frequently as distressing as the head pain. These symptoms may include dizziness (i.e., vertiginous and nonspecific forms), tinnitus, extreme phonophobia, fluctuating fatigue or mood alteration, and feelings of depersonalization. It is unclear whether these symptoms are fragments of underlying migraine or a mood disorder; they often resolve with improvement in the headaches.

Overuse of medications is the most common exacerbating factor in chronic daily headache, and withdrawal of the overused medication usually improves the condition. The medications most often overused include butalbital combinations, ergotamines, oral analgesics containing caffeine in combination with acetaminophen or NSAIDs, and opiate combinations. However, chronic daily headache may develop in the absence of medication, and it does not always improve after analgesic withdrawal.

LESS COMMON PRIMARY HEADACHE SYNDROMES

CHRONIC PAROXYSMAL HEMICRANIA. Chronic paroxysmal hemicrania is an uncommon syndrome with many features of cluster headache, including severe intensity, unilateral orbital or temporal location, and autonomic signs (e.g., conjunctival injection, tearing, rhinorrhea) ipsilateral to the pain. It is shorter in duration (5 to 20 minutes) than cluster headache and has a higher attack frequency (generally more than five per day). The syndrome is more predominant in females and may be responsive to indomethacin (150 mg/day or less).

HEMICRANIA CONTINUA. Hemicrania continua is an unusual headache syndrome in which constant unilateral head pain of moderate to severe intensity underlies unprovoked brief episodes of sharp jabbing pain in a similar location.

BENIGN COUGH HEADACHE. Benign cough headache consists of severe bilateral head pain of sudden onset that follows coughing or other Valsalva maneuvers. It is a benign disorder that responds to indomethacin in about 90% of cases. However, the diagnosis of benign cough headache requires the exclusion of structural lesions with MRI because cough headache may sometimes result from posterior fossa tumors or the Arnold-Chiari malformation.

EXERTIONAL OR ORGASMIC HEADACHE. In some individuals, exertion or various types of exercise may trigger bilateral throbbing or pressure-like headaches that persist for several minutes up to 48 hours. Headaches may also develop during sexual activity, including coitus and, less frequently, during masturbation. These headaches usually begin with bilateral nonthrobbing pain that escalates as sexual excitement increases and reaches a crescendo at orgasm. Exertional and orgasmic headaches may occur in the absence of intracranial disorders; however, in rare cases, coital headache may be associated with unruptured cerebral aneurysms. The possibility of aneurysm should be excluded. Exertional headache can sometimes be prevented by ingestion of ergotamine or indomethacin before the planned exertion.

HYPNIC HEADACHES. Hypnic headaches constitute a rare primary headache syndrome of the elderly (mean age of onset, 60 years or older). Hypnic headaches, which persist for 15 to 60 minutes and typically awaken patients from sleep about the same time each night, are in some ways similar to cluster headaches. However, unlike cluster headache, hypnic headaches are more diffuse, are often bilateral and throbbing, and are not associated with the autonomic symptoms of cluster headache. The differential diagnosis includes temporal arteritis and mass lesions. After exclusion of organic disease with an imaging study and erythrocyte sedimentation rate (ESR), treatment with low-dose lithium (30 mg every night) or caffeine may induce remission. If headaches return, careful titration of the dosage upward may be necessary. Lithium should be used with caution in older patients, especially in the presence of dehydration, renal disease, and diuretic or NSAID therapy.

SECONDARY HEADACHE DISORDERS

Headache may be the initial complaint in a host of central nervous system and systemic abnormalities (Table 428–1). Many of the disorders are given detailed consideration in other chapters. However, a few of the most prominent abnormalities that may result in chronic headache are discussed briefly.

GIANT CELL ARTERITIS

Giant cell arteritis (temporal arteritis; Chapter 285) is an inflammatory vasculitis involving branches of the temporal arteries. It most often affects individuals older than 60 years and can result in rapid and permanent loss of vision from granulomatous occlusion of the posterior ciliary or central retinal arteries. Features suggestive of temporal arteritis include orbital or frontotemporal head pain, described as dull and constant with superimposed jabbing sensations; aggravation of pain by cold temperatures; pain in the jaw or tongue pain on chewing (jaw claudication); accompanying constitutional or musculoskeletal symptoms such as weight loss, anemia, and polymyalgia rheumatica; elevated liver function tests; and decreased visual acuity, visual field cuts, pale or swollen optic disc, retinal splinter hemorrhages (i.e., anterior ischemic neuropathy) or a pale retina, and cherry-red spot (i.e., central retinal artery infarction).

The ESR, which should be measured in all suspected patients, is elevated in 95% of cases. Definitive diagnosis is made by biopsy of

Table 428-1 • SECONDARY HEADACHE DISORDERS

Headaches Associated with Cranial Vascular Abnormalities
Subarachnoid hemorrhage
Intracerebral, epidural, and subdural hematoma
Unruptured vascular malformation
  Arteriovenous malformation
  Saccular aneurysm
Carotid or vertebral artery dissection
Carotidynia
Cerebral intra-arterial occlusion
Venous thrombosis
Arterial hypertension

Headaches Associated with Nonvascular Intracranial Disorders
Intracranial neoplasms
Carcinomatous meningitis
High- and low-pressure headaches
Inflammatory disorders
  Temporal (giant cell) arteritis
  Tolosa-Hunt syndrome
  Intracranial sarcoidosis
  Wegener's granulomatosis
Intracranial infection
  Acute meningitis
  Meningoencephalitis
  Brain abscess

Headaches Associated with Systemic Abnormalities
Systemic infection, viral, bacterial, treponemal, etc.
Substance-induced headaches, exposure, and withdrawal
Metabolic disturbance
  Hypoxia, altitude sickness, sleep apnea
  Hypercapnia
  Hypoglycemia
  Dialysis

Head and Facial Pain Associated with Disorders of Cranial Nerves
Trigeminal neuropathy
Neuralgias
  Trigeminal neuralgia
  Glossopharyngeal neuralgia
  Occipital neuralgia
Herpes zoster

Head and Facial Pain Associated with Disorders of Other Cranial Structures
Glaucoma
Sinusitis
Temporomandibular joint disease
Dental pain
Neck abnormalities

Table 428-2 • SUBSTANCES INDUCING HEADACHE

After Acute Exposure

Alcohol	Nitrates or nitrites
Amphotericin B	Ondansetron
Azithromycin	Phenylethylamine
Carbon monoxide	Ranitidine
Cimetidine	Reserpine
Cocaine or crack	Tyramine
Danazol	Timolol ophthalmic drops
Diclofenac	Verapamil
Dipyridamole	
Estrogen or birth control pills	**Following Withdrawal after Chronic Use**
Fluconazole	Alcohol
Indomethacin	Barbiturates
Monosodium glutamate	Caffeine
Nifedipine	Ergotamine
	Opiate analgesics

the temporal artery, which can be obtained within 48 hours after initiation of treatment with steroids. When the diagnosis is suspected, prompt treatment with corticosteroids is necessary to avoid visual loss, which often becomes bilateral (75% of cases) after unilateral loss.

 Treatment

In patients with an elevated ESR, intravenous methylprednisolone (500 to 1000 mg every 12 hours for 48 hours) should be followed by oral prednisone (80 to 100 mg/day for 14 to 21 days), with a gradual taper over 12 to 24 months. The tapering rate should be guided by serial ESR measurements.

SUBSTANCE-INDUCED HEADACHES

Headaches may occur with acute exposure or as a result of withdrawal from many types of substances (Table 428-2).

HEADACHES ASSOCIATED WITH INCREASED INTRACRANIAL PRESSURE

Headache may occur when an alteration in intracranial pressure causes compression or traction on pain-sensitive vascular, meningeal, or neural structures in the apex or base of the brain. Most commonly, these headaches are bilateral and frontotemporal, although their location is variable. Causes of elevated intracranial pressure include mass lesion, blockage of cerebrospinal fluid (CSF) circulation, hemorrhage, hypertensive encephalopathy, venous sinus thrombosis, hyperadrenalism or hypoadrenalism, altitude sickness, tetracycline, and vitamin A intoxication. In most instances, the source of the headache and raised pressure are identifiable. Treatment of the underlying condition generally improves the headache.

INTRACRANIAL TUMOR

One of the most common concerns of patients seeking evaluation of chronic headaches is that their headache represents a space-occupying lesion such as a tumor (Chapter 457) or large vascular abnormality. Fortunately, most chronic headaches do not arise from a tumor or other structural lesion. Headaches in patients with brain tumors are usually dull and bifrontal, although they tend to be worse on the side of the tumor. The headaches are more often qualitatively similar to tension-type headaches than to migraines and tend to be intermittent and of moderate intensity; they are accompanied by nausea in about one half of cases and are usually resistant to common analgesics. Classic brain tumor headache (i.e., progressive and beginning in the morning) is not typical. Factors that should increase suspicion of an intracranial tumor include papilledema, new neurologic deficits, initial attack of prolonged headache occurring after the age of 45 years, previous malignancy, cognitive abnormality, or altered mental status.

IDIOPATHIC INTRACRANIAL HYPERTENSION

Idiopathic intracranial hypertension (pseudotumor cerebri) is a syndrome composed of headache, papilledema, and transient visual symptoms that occur in the absence of CSF abnormalities, except for elevated intracranial pressure. The syndrome is not associated with hydrocephalus or another identifiable cause. In adults, females have an 8 to 10 times higher incidence than males. The prototypic patient is an overweight woman of childbearing age. The diagnosis is made by lumbar puncture (CSF pressure higher than 250 mm Hg; normal CSF composition) after excluding a mass lesion by neuroimaging. Visual field testing often reveals an enlarged blind spot. Spontaneous recovery may eventually occur, but treatment to reduce intracranial pressure is usually indicated to prevent visual loss. Simple measures such as weight reduction should be attempted whenever appropriate. Drug therapies are usually attempted next and include medications such as acetazolamide and furosemide, which are aimed primarily at reducing CSF production. Furosemide, a potent loop diuretic, must be given with potassium supplementation and may cause hypotension. If drug treatment is ineffective, repeated lumbar punctures may sometimes be useful, although frequent lumbar puncture is not without a risk of complications, including as post–lumbar puncture headache, spinal epidermoid tumor, or infection. If other treatments fail, surgical options include optic nerve fenestration and ventricular-peritoneal shunting of CSF.

HEADACHE ASSOCIATED WITH DECREASED INTRACRANIAL PRESSURE

Decreased intracranial pressure (<50 to 90 mm H_2O), which is usually caused by a decrease in CSF volume, is commonly associated with dull, throbbing, sometimes severe headaches that are probably caused by reduced brain buoyancy and subsequent traction on pain-sensitive meningeal and vascular structures. Low-pressure headaches often become more intense on standing or sitting upright and may be relieved by lying down. The headaches may be accompanied by dizziness, visual symptoms, photophobia, nausea, vomiting, and diaphoresis. Although low-pressure headaches may begin spontaneously, they most commonly follow lumbar puncture. Other possible etiologies include intracranial surgery, ventricular shunting, trauma, and various systemic medical conditions such as severe dehydration, postdialysis status, diabetic coma, uremia, or hyperpnea. If the headache is prolonged, the possibility of a persistent CSF leak may be investigated by radioisotope cisternography or computed tomographic myelography. Post–lumbar puncture headaches can be caused by excessive leakage of CSF through a dural tear caused by the lumbar puncture needle. Headaches follow 10 to 30% of lumbar punctures and occur twice as frequently in women as in men. The headache may begin minutes to several days after the lumbar puncture and can persist up to 2 weeks.

Treatment strategies include corticosteroids, oral fluid or salt intake, intravenous fluids, CO_2 inhalation, methylxanthines such as theophylline (200 mg three times daily), caffeine (500 mg IV), or intrathecal autologous blood patch.

HEAD AND FACIAL PAIN ASSOCIATED WITH DISORDERS OF CRANIAL NERVES

Trigeminal neuralgia, also known as *tic douloureux*, usually occurs in older patients. The sharp, often electric shocklike pain of trigeminal neuralgia occurs in a rapid series of jabs (lasting seconds to minutes) in one or more divisions of the trigeminal nerve. The volleys of jabbing may be provoked by stimulation of areas on the face quite discrete from the site of pain and are usually followed by brief refractory periods. When trigeminal neuralgia occurs in persons younger than 40 years, a specific cause can often be found, such as demyelination (e.g., multiple sclerosis, especially when bilateral) and compression by vascular abnormalities or tumors (e.g., myeloma, metastatic carcinoma, cholesteatoma, chordoma, acoustic neuromas, trigeminal neuromas). In the elderly, trigeminal neuralgia has a prevalence of 155 per million and a female-to-male ratio of 3:2. Among older individuals with trigeminal neuralgia, microvascular compression of the trigeminal nerve root is often present. Because of the association with structural lesions (i.e., demyelinative or neoplastic), the initial evaluation should include MRI studies, which detail the cerebellopontine angle and the entry foramen (e.g., V_1 superior orbital fissure, V_2 foramen rotundum, V_3 foramen ovale). In the absence of a structural cause, treatment usually consists of drugs such as carbamazepine (400 to 1200 mg), valproate (500 to 1500 mg), phenytoin (200 to 500 mg), baclofen (40 to 80 mg), or clonazepam (2 to 6 mg). Therapy with any of these agents must be initiated slowly. Patients who fail to respond to medication should be considered for microvascular decompression surgery.

Glossopharyngeal neuralgia is characterized by paroxysmal pain within the distribution of the vagus and glossopharyngeal nerves. The pain is paroxysmal, unilateral, and sudden in onset, and it has a jabbing or briefly persistent (square wave) quality. The pain is most often felt in or around the ear, tongue, jaw, or larynx, and it can be triggered by swallowing, talking, chewing, clearing the throat, yawning, or tasting spicy food or cold liquids. Although pain is usually followed by a brief refractory period, attacks may occur more than 20 times per day and may awaken sufferers from sleep. The intermittent pain may be superimposed on a dull, constant pain in the same area. Rarely, the pain of glossopharyngeal neuralgia is followed by bradycardia, syncope, or asystole, presumably resulting from the intense glossopharyngeal outflow and vagal efferent discharge. The usual cause of glossopharyngeal neuralgia appears to be microvascular compression, although abscess and tumor are sometimes associated. Medical treatment is similar to that for trigeminal neuralgia and includes slow introduction of carbamazepine (400 to 1200 mg), gabapentin (900 to 1800 mg), or baclofen (40 to 80 mg). Cases refractory to adequate medical treatment often respond to microvascular decompression.

1. Bigal ME, Bordini CA, Speciali JG: Intravenous chlorpromazine in the emergency department treatment of migraines: A randomized controlled trial. J Emerg Med 2002;23:141–148.

SUGGESTED READINGS
Hadjikhani N, Sanchez Del Rio M, Wu O, et al: Mechanisms of migraine aura revealed by functional MRI in human visual cortex. Proc Natl Acad Sci U S A 2001;98:4687–4692. *Describes the pathophysiologic mechanism of the migraine aura.*
Kaniecki R: Headache assessment and management. JAMA 2003;289:1430–1433. *A practical overview.*
Snow V, Weiss K, Wall EM, et al: Pharmacologic management of acute attacks of migraine and prevention of migraine headache. Ann Intern Med 2002;137:840–849. *Comprehensive overview with consensus recommendations.*
Terwindt GM, Ophoff RA, van Eijk R, et al: Involvement of the *CACNA1A* gene containing region on 19p13 in migraine with and without aura. Neurology 2001;56:1028–1032. *The CACNA1A gene is implicated in the more common forms of migraine.*

429 MECHANICAL AND OTHER LESIONS OF THE SPINE, NERVE ROOTS, AND SPINAL CORD

Michael J. Aminoff

SPINAL ANATOMY

The individual vertebrae are separated by intervertebral discs that cushion the spine during various physical activities. Each disc consists of a thick outer fibrous portion called the *annulus fibrosus*, within which is a soft, gelatinous, inner central portion called the *nucleus pulposus*, which is a remnant of the notochord. Posterior to the vertebral bodies, the vertebral arches (composed of paired pedicles anteriorly and laminae posteriorly) and transverse processes enclose the spinal cord in the spinal canal, and the posterior spinous process projects posteriorly (Figure 429–1). Paraspinal muscles help to support the spine.

The intervertebral discs are not pain sensitive, but pain may arise from the ligaments connecting the vertebrae, facet joints, vertebral periosteum, outer layer of the annulus fibrosus, and spinal nerve roots. The paraspinal muscles are also pain sensitive and are probably the most common source of neck or back pain.

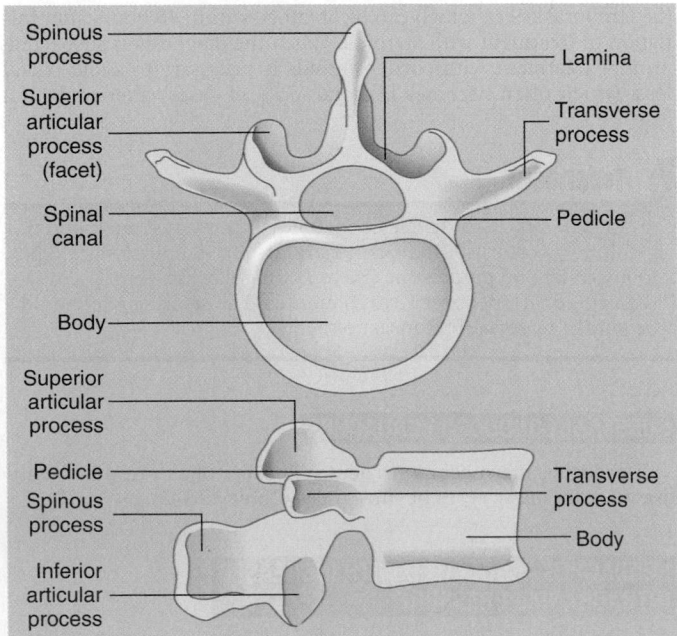

FIGURE 429–1 • Normal vertebral anatomy.

The spinal canal contains the spinal cord and the spinal and autonomic roots. Its size varies at different levels and between individuals. It tends to be more spacious in the cervical and lumbar regions than the thoracic. A congenitally narrow spinal canal (i.e., spinal stenosis) predisposes to neurologic dysfunction as a consequence of minor degenerative changes or disc protrusion. Such stenosis is common in the cervical and lumbar regions. In adults, the cord ends as the conus medullaris at about the level of the first lumbar vertebra; below this level, the spinal canal is occupied by the descending nerve roots that comprise the cauda equina. The cervical cord segments are at approximately the same level as the cervical vertebral bodies; the thoracic cord segments are generally one or two levels higher than the corresponding vertebral segments, and much of the lumbar and sacral cord is found between T10 and L1. The nerve roots in the cauda equina have to descend in the subarachnoid space before exiting at their various foramina. The absence of a C8 vertebral body but presence of a C8 spinal segment means that roots above C8 exit above the corresponding vertebral body, whereas the remaining nerve roots exit below their respective vertebral bodies.

Thirty-one paired spinal nerves emerge from the spinal cord: 8 in the cervical region, 12 in the thoracic, 5 in the lumbar, 5 in the sacral, and 1 in the coccygeal. Each spinal nerve has anterior and posterior roots that connect it with the cord. The fibers in the posterior roots originate primarily in the dorsal root ganglia, which are situated distally along the posterior roots, shortly before these unite with the anterior roots and usually within the entrance of the bony intervertebral foramen. The axons in the anterior roots arise mainly from cells in the anterior and lateral gray columns of the spinal cord.

Shortly after passing through the intervertebral foramina, the spinal nerves divide into anterior and posterior rami. The posterior rami supply the skin over the back of the neck and the trunk and the paraspinal musculature. The anterior rami innervate the anterolateral trunk and the limbs. The anterior rami contribute to the limb plexus, where the fibers are reorganized to form the various peripheral nerves to the extremities: the brachial plexus to the arms and the lumbar and sacral plexuses to the legs.

The pattern of any motor or sensory deficits is helpful in localizing a lesion involving the cord or nerve roots. A *myotome* designates a group of muscles that have a common innervation from the same segment of the spinal cord and therefore from the same nerve root. Most muscles belong to more than one myotome because they typically are innervated by two or more adjacent cord segments and nerve roots. The designation *dermatome* refers to the cutaneous territory innervated by a single nerve root. Adjacent dermatomes overlap considerably. Figure 429–2 illustrates the distinction between the segmental (dermatomal) and peripheral innervation of the skin.

NECK AND BACK PAIN

Neck or back pain is one of the most common reasons for medical consultation, but it is usually short lived and responds to symptomatic measures. Most patients with acute neck or back pain, with or without radicular symptoms, have musculoskeletal or degenerative disorders that do not require specific treatment and often are self-limiting. However, the possibility of more serious abnormalities that require specific treatment should always be excluded. Among young patients (<40 years) presenting with low back pain, almost 90% have had more than one attack of pain, and most attacks have lasted for less than 2 weeks. Approximately 85% of patients with low back pain cannot be given a definitive diagnosis. Similarly, approximately one third of adults in the general population report neck pain within the previous year, the prevalence increasing with advancing age; almost 14% report chronic neck pain (i.e., pain exceeding 6 months' duration).

Type of Pain and Associated Findings

Local pain and tenderness may occur from irritation of nerve endings at the site of pathology, such as in the vertebral periosteum. Similarly, degeneration or protrusion of intravertebral discs causes pain by compression of nerve endings in the annulus fibrosus or posterior longitudinal ligaments. Pain of muscle or ligamentous origin or related to a herniated disc is usually alleviated by recumbency. In contrast, the pain of vertebral metastases is often aggravated by recumbency and may be relieved by sitting up.

Referred pain arises from deep structures and is felt at a distant site within the same spinal segment. It often has a deep aching quality and is sometimes accompanied by tenderness at the site of referral. Pain may be referred to the spine from pelvic or abdominal viscera and is usually not affected by the position of the spine. Pain may also be referred from the spine to other regions. For example, disease of the upper lumbar spine may lead to pain in the groin or anterior thighs, and disease of the lower lumbar spine may cause pain in the buttocks and back of the thighs.

Musculoskeletal pain typically follows unaccustomed exercise but occasionally occurs spontaneously, often on awakening in the morning. It may be related to spasm of paraspinal muscles as a result of injury or structural abnormality of the spine. Chronic neck pain is a well-recognized complication of whiplash injuries. Trigger points may be present and define certain myofascial pain syndromes. The pain is exacerbated by activity or movement and relieved by rest. Range of motion may be restricted by pain or muscle spasm. Localized tenderness is common. In the absence of a history of injury and of any significant neurologic findings, detailed investigation is usually unrewarding. Patients can be managed conservatively. There is no agreement about the optimal duration of immobilization or bedrest. Physical therapy is often recommended for the treatment of acute low back pain, but the extent of any benefit is unclear. There is little evidence that traction, ultrasound, diathermy, or manipulation is helpful. Nonsteroidal analgesics are usually sufficient to relieve pain, but in severe cases, narcotics may be required; in patients with chronic pain, tricyclic antidepressant drugs are often helpful. Muscle relaxants may relieve painful muscle spasm.

Radicular pain may occur from compression, angulation, or stretch of nerve roots as produced by disc protrusion, degenerative spinal disease, or metastatic deposits. Less commonly, radicular pain occurs in certain medical disorders such as diabetes mellitus. The pain has a dermatomal distribution but may also be felt in muscles supplied by the affected root. It is usually sharp in character. Coughing, sneezing, and straining typically exacerbate the pain by increasing intraspinal pressure, as do maneuvers that stretch the nerve roots. Examination may reveal sensory changes in the dermatomal distribution of the affected root, weakness and atrophy in a myotomal distribution, and depression of tendon reflexes subserved by the affected root, but examination is often normal. In patients with weakness, not all muscles within the myotome are necessarily affected. *Cauda equina syndromes* are typically associated with bilateral radicular pain; saddle anesthesia and sphincter dysfunction are common, and examination reveals bilateral root dysfunction.

Spinal cord disease, especially compression of the long tracts, may lead to an unpleasant sensation in the extremities that also is enhanced by increased intraspinal pressure or movements that stretch the cord (e.g., neck flexion, straight leg raising). Neck or back pain may also be conspicuous. The associated signs vary with the extent of the lesion and speed of its development. Acute cord compression, as from an epidural hemorrhage, is associated with pain and the rapid onset of a paraparesis or quadriparesis that may not be reversed by decompressive surgery. In contrast, a gradually evolving compressive lesion may be painless and leads to a slowly progressive deficit that often recovers after decompression. Laterally placed lesions lead to a Brown-Séquard syndrome, posterior lesions to bilateral posterior column dysfunction with impaired position and vibration appreciation, anterior lesions to weakness, and intramedullary lesions to a dissociated sensory loss, with impairment of pain and temperature appreciation and preservation of posterior column sensation.

History

Patients often first notice the onset of neck or back pain when awakening in the morning, commonly after unaccustomed activity. The character and distribution of the pain are helpful in determining the probable underlying cause (Table 429–1) and thereby the further approach to its investigation. A history of cancer raises the possibility of metastatic disease, whereas local symptoms, such as rectal bleeding, suggest an undiagnosed neoplastic lesion that may have spread to involve the spine. Malignancies that frequently involve the spine are metastatic cancer of the breast, prostate, lung, kidney, colon, and thyroid gland; multiple myeloma; and Hodgkin's and non-Hodgkin's lymphoma. A past history of structural spinal disorder suggests a mechanical cause for pain, of a coagulopathy suggests a hemorrhagic cause, of osteoporosis suggests compression fracture,

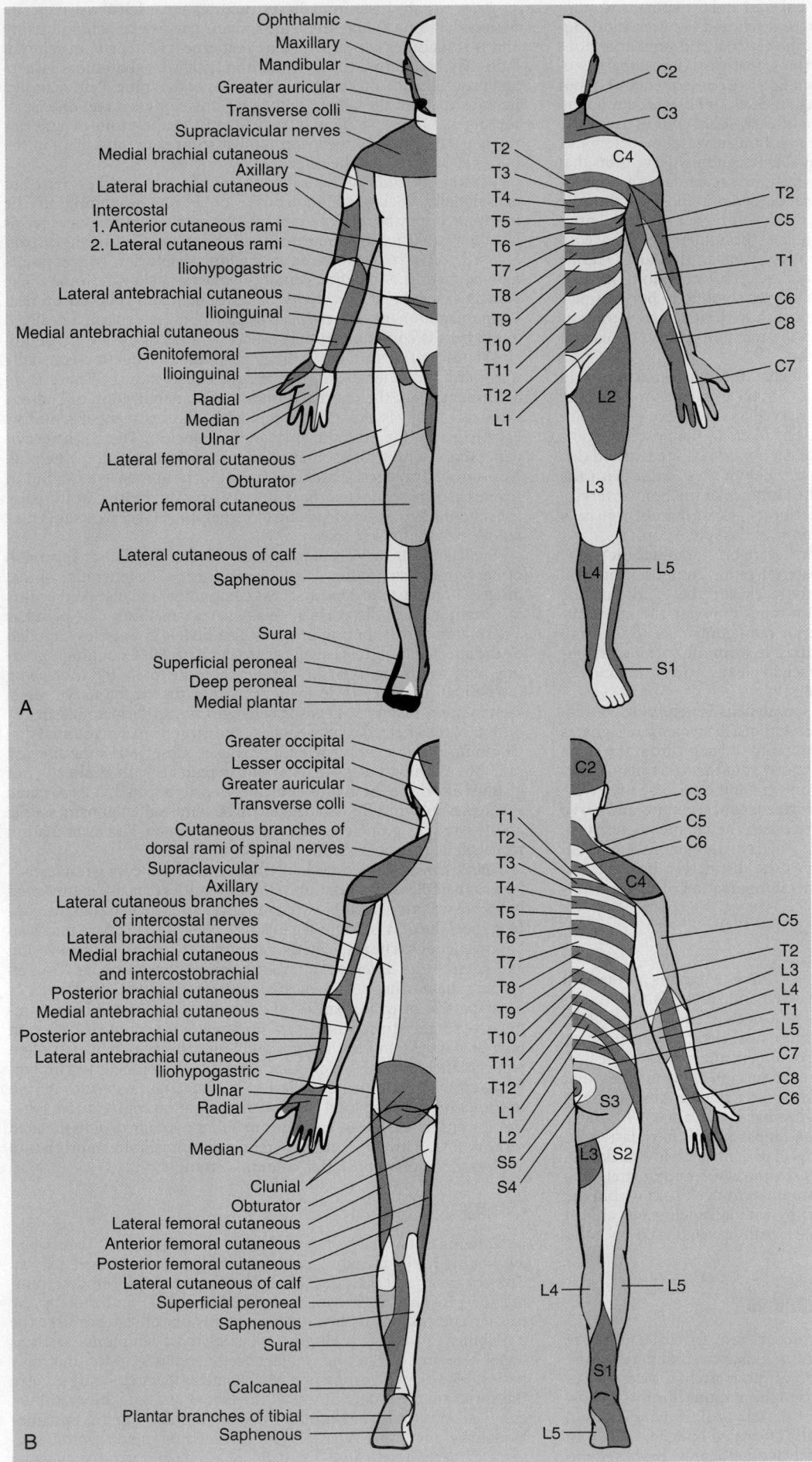

FIGURE 429–2 • Cutaneous innervation. The segmental (dermatomal) distribution is shown on the left side of the body, and the peripheral nerve distribution is shown on the right side of the body. *A*, Anterior view. *B*, Posterior view.

Table 429–1 • CAUSES OF BACK PAIN

	COMMON	LESS COMMON
Mechanical		
Degenerative	Disc protrusion	
	Osteoarthritis	
	Facet syndrome	
	Spinal stenosis	
Congenital	Spinal stenosis	Spondylolisthesis
		Spondylolysis
		Transitional vertebra
		Other structural
		anomalies
Deformity	Scoliosis	
Muscle	Myofascial syndrome	
	Spasm	
Metabolic	Osteoporosis	Paget's disease
		Gout
Trauma	Compression fracture	
	Lumbosacral or	
	sacroiliac strain	
	Subluxation	
	Muscle injury	
Tumors	Metastatic disease	Benign bone or
		neural tumors
		(e.g., meningioma,
		osteoid osteoma,
		hemangioma)
	Multiple myeloma	Osteosarcoma
Inflammatory disease	Ankylosing spondylitis	Enteropathic
		arthropathy
	Arachnoiditis	Psoriatic arthropathy
	Rheumatoid arthritis	
Infections	Herpes zoster	Disc infections
		Epidural or subdural
		abscess
		Meningitis
Referred pain		Aortic aneurysm
		Cardiac or pericardial
		disease
		Pelvic or
		retroperitoneal
		disease
		Pulmonary or pleural
		disease
		Visceral disease
Nonorganic disease	Anxiety	
	Conversion reaction	
	Psychosis	
	Litigation-related	
	Malingering	
	Chronic pain syndrome	
	Substance abuse	

and of subarachnoid infection or inflammation suggests an arachnoiditis. Whiplash injuries occur in more than 1 million people annually in the United States and may be responsible for acute or chronic neck pain. A history of fever, sweats, diabetes mellitus, sickle cell disease, intravenous drug use, immunodeficiency states, recent penetrating injuries or surgical procedures, or intravenous injections suggests the possibility of an infection involving the spine, disc, or epidural space. Herpes zoster may lead to cutaneous pain over the neck or back, and the diagnosis is often uncertain until the characteristic skin rash develops. Spinal tuberculosis is common in many parts of the world and typically affects the lower thoracic and upper lumbar region, which are unusual sites for degenerative disc disease. Other causes of spinal osteomyelitis include staphylococcal infection, which may be suggested by primary disease of the skin, respiratory tract, or urinary tract. Spinal epidural abscess may lead to acute cord compression in addition to back pain and fever if diagnosis is delayed.

Forced flexion or extension movements of the neck from trauma may lead to significant injury or compression fractures. Compression fractures of the vertebrae occur especially in patients with osteoporosis and therefore most commonly in patients who are elderly, have a family history of osteoporosis, or a history of chronic corticosteroid usage or immobility. Fractures are also especially likely in patients with osteomalacia or Paget's disease and may lead to complications

particularly in patients with ankylosing spondylitis, diffuse idiopathic skeletal hyperostosis, and spinal stenosis. Minor cervical trauma may lead to pain and significant deficits in patients with rheumatoid arthritis. Injury may also lead to epidural or subdural hemorrhage or hematomyelia, which is typically heralded by severe pain overlying the site of bleeding (Chapter 430). Ankylosing spondylitis usually causes early morning stiffness and back pain, which are relieved by activity.

Primary tumors of the spine and spinal cord are uncommon and are overshadowed by the more frequent occurrence of secondary tumors, including lymphoma, myeloma, and cancer. Among the features suggesting malignancy are constant unremitting pain in atypical or multiple sites, pain that is unrelated to activity or posture, the presence of systemic or constitutional symptoms, and an elevated erythrocyte sedimentation rate, especially in patients 55 years of age or older.

Examination

Examination commonly reveals spasm of the paraspinal muscles and limitation of spinal movements. Local tenderness may also be present. Spinal compression should be suspected when neck flexion leads to pain in the thoracic or lumbar region or when Lhermitte's sign is positive. Focal tenderness over a spinous process suggests vertebral involvement by tumor or infection. In patients with low back pain, the examination should include maneuvers that stretch different nerve roots. Hip flexion with the knee extended stretches the L5 and S1 roots and may reproduce pain in the back, buttocks, and posterior thighs, whereas hip extension with the leg straight and the patient prone (i.e., reverse straight-leg-raising sign) stretches the upper lumbar roots and may cause pain in the anterior thigh or medial calf region. Neurologic examination is important, and the presence of any deficits mandates further evaluation. The distribution of any abnormalities suggests the likely site of pathology.

General physical examination is also important in patients with back pain and should include rectal and pelvic examinations. When pain is referred to the back and is related to visceral disease, abdominal palpation may reproduce it.

Differential Diagnosis

Most cases of low back pain are caused by mechanical conditions, including lumbar muscle strain or sprain, degenerative processes of discs and facets, herniated discs, spinal stenosis, and osteoporotic compression fractures (Table 429–2). Nonmechanical spinal conditions and systemic diseases are important but unusual causes of low back pain.

Investigations

In general, imaging procedures are not required for patients with uncomplicated neck or back pain of less than 1 month's duration. However, even in patients older than 50 years or with symptoms suggestive of systemic disease, plain radiography and basic blood tests can virtually exclude an underlying systemic disease. Imaging studies of the neck or back are required when clinical examination reveals a likely cause, such as a fracture, or when pain does not respond to conservative measures over several weeks. They are important in patients at particular risk for a neoplastic or infectious cause for pain. Imaging studies, especially computed tomography (CT) or magnetic resonance imaging (MRI), may also be helpful in confirming spinal osteomyelitis or tuberculosis and in guiding bone biopsy. Further evaluation depends on the nature and extent of the underlying pathology. The presence of a focal or progressive neurologic deficit or of pain in uncommon sites (e.g., lower thoracic region) also requires investigation, usually by MRI. However, many asymptomatic middle-aged or elderly subjects have MRI abnormalities of the spine, and the clinical relevance of any structural abnormalities may therefore be uncertain (Table 429–3). Electrophysiologic studies, particularly electromyography and nerve conduction studies, are sometimes helpful in showing the functional significance of anatomic abnormalities and are additionally important as a means of diagnosing a radiculopathy.

Children with low back pain usually require further investigation. Acute pain may be related to developing scoliosis, disc disease, or spondylolisthesis. Discitis may also be responsible.

Table 429–2 • DIFFERENTIAL DIAGNOSIS OF LOW BACK PAIN*

MECHANICAL LOW BACK OR LEG PAIN (97%)†	NONMECHANICAL SPINAL CONDITIONS (~1%)‡	VISCERAL DISEASE (2%)
Lumbar strain, sprain (70%)§	Neoplasia (0.7%)	Disease of pelvic organs
Degenerative processes of discs and facets, usually age related (10%)	Multiple myeloma	Prostatitis
Herniated disc (4%)	Metastatic carcinoma	Endometriosis
Spinal stenosis (3%)	Lymphoma and leukemia	Chronic pelvic inflammatory disease
Osteoporotic compression fracture (4%)	Spinal cord tumors	Renal disease
Spondylolisthesis (2%)	Retroperitoneal tumors	Nephrolithiasis
Traumatic fracture (<1%)	Primary vertebral tumors	Pyelonephritis
Congenital disease (<1%)	Infection (0.01%)	Perinephric abscess
Severe kyphosis	Osteomyelitis	Aortic aneurysm
Severe scoliosis	Septic discitis	Gastrointestinal disease
Transitional vertebrae	Paraspinous abscess	Pancreatitis
Spondylolysis¶	Epidural abscess	Cholecystitis
Internal disc disruption or discogenic low back pain‖	*Shingles*	Penetrating ulcer
Presumed instability**	Inflammatory arthritis (often associated with HLA-B27) (0.3%)	
	Ankylosing spondylitis	
	Psoriatic spondylitis	
	Reiter's syndrome	
	Inflammatory bowel disease	
	Scheuermann's disease (osteochondrosis)	
	Paget's disease of bone	

*Figures in parentheses indicate the estimated percentages of patients with these conditions among all adult patients with low back pain in primary care. Diagnoses in italics are often associated with neurogenic leg pain. Percentages may vary substantially according to demographic characteristics or referral patterns in a practice. For example, spinal stenosis and osteoporosis will be more common among geriatric patients, spinal infections among injection-drug users, and so forth.
†The term *mechanical* is used to designate an anatomic or functional abnormality without an underlying malignant, neoplastic, or inflammatory disease. Approximately 2% of cases of mechanical low back pain or leg pain are accounted for by spondylolysis, internal disc disruption, or discogenic low back pain, and presumed instability.
‡Scheuermann's disease and Paget's disease of bone probably account for <0.01% of nonmechanical spinal conditions.
§*Strain* and *sprain* are nonspecific terms with no pathoanatomic confirmation. *Idiopathic low back pain* may be a preferable term.
¶Spondylolysis is as common among asymptomatic persons as among those with low back pain, and its role in causing low back pain remains ambiguous.
‖Internal disc disruption is diagnosed by provocative discography (injection of contrast material into a degenerated disc, with assessment of pain at the time of injection). However, discography often causes pain in symptomatic adults, and the condition of many patients with positive discograms improves spontaneously. The clinical importance and appropriate management of this condition remain unclear. *Discogenic low back pain* is used more or less synonymously with *internal disc disruption.*
**Presumed instability is loosely defined as >10 degrees of angulation or 4 mm of vertical displacement on lateral flexion and extension radiographs. However, the diagnostic criteria, natural history, and surgical indications remain controversial.
From Deyo RA, Weinstein JN: Low back pain. N Engl J Med 2001;344:363–370.

Table 429–3 • REPRESENTATIVE RESULTS OF MAGNETIC RESONANCE IMAGING STUDIES IN ASYMPTOMATIC ADULTS

STUDY	SUBJECTS	ANATOMIC FINDINGS				
		Herniated Disc	Bulging Disc	Degenerative Disc	Stenosis	Annular Tear
Boden et al.	Volunteers <60 yr old	22	54	46	1	NR
	Volunteers ≥60 yr old	36	79	93	21	NR
Jensen et al.	Volunteers (mean age, 42 yr)	28	52	NR	7	14
Weishaupt et al.	Volunteers (mean age, 35 yr)	40	24	72	NR	33
Stadnik et al.	Patients referred for head or neck imaging (median age, 42 yr)	33	81	72	NR	56

NR = Not reported.
From Deyo RA, Weinstein JN: Low back pain. N Engl J Med 2001;344, 363–370.

Rx Treatment

If a cervical fracture is suspected after trauma, the neck is immobilized and radiographed (Chapter 430). Acute hemorrhage may require evacuation, and infection requires antimicrobial therapy and, in some instances, drainage. Even in the absence of confirmatory evidence, a trial of antituberculous therapy may be necessary in those at high risk of spinal tuberculosis, such as the elderly, the immunocompromised, and those who have come from high-risk areas such as the Indian subcontinent.

Patients with ankylosing spondylosis may respond to nonsteroidal anti-inflammatory drugs (NSAIDs). They should also participate in a vigorous activity program to maintain spinal movement.

If MRI reveals a structural lesion, surgical treatment may be necessary. In the absence of clinical or imaging findings that suggest substantial underlying structural disease, patients with acute pain are treated symptomatically. This involves immobilization, analgesics, and eventually increasing mobilization. There is no agreement as to the optimal duration of bedrest for back pain, but 2 or 3 days is usually adequate. Local heat may help to relieve discomfort.

Many patients with chronic neck or back pain have no surgically remedial lesion, and a multidisciplinary approach is then necessary to ensure that symptoms eventually resolve and that patients are successfully rehabilitated. Treatment may include the use of analgesics, NSAIDs, or tricyclic drugs (taken at night), but patients should be encouraged to remain active. For the treatment of low back pain, strict bedrest is no better than symptom-limited activity, even in the presence of sciatica.[1] Osteopathic spinal manipulation is no better than standard care[2]; acupuncture is no more effective than sham acupuncture[3]; and any potential benefit from chiropractic care appears to be related to more intensive communication, advice, and information rather than to the treatment itself.[4] However, physical therapy or massage therapy may be preferable to other treatment interventions.[5]

The chronic neck pain that sometimes follows whiplash injury has been attributed by some to psychological factors or related to pending litigation, but doubt can be cast on this view, which should not influence management. Nevertheless, the incidence of whiplash injury is reportedly reduced, and its prognosis improved, by the elimination of compensation for pain and suffering.

INTERVERTEBRAL DISC DISEASE

With advancing years, the nucleus pulposus of the intervertebral discs becomes harder, less resilient, and more susceptible to trauma. Tears tend consequently to develop in the annulus, through which a portion of the nucleus pulposus may herniate. Herniation is generally in a lateral direction and may lead to compression of the nerve roots as they enter the intervertebral foramina, but sometimes occurs centrally, so that the spinal cord or cauda equina is compressed. In some instances, the protruded disc material loses its continuity with the nucleus pulposus and becomes a free fragment within the spinal canal.

Disc herniations occur most commonly in the lumbosacral or cervical region. The early recognition of thoracic disc herniations is important, however, because there is only limited space in the thoracic portion of the spinal canal and delay in diagnosis may lead to an irreversible myelopathy.

Pain is common in patients with a herniated intervertebral disc. Neck or back pain may be accompanied by stiffness. Radicular pain may also occur, sometimes before the onset of axial pain. It does not necessarily affect the entire dermatomal territory and may be poorly localized by patients. Patients with cervical disc herniations generally hold the neck stiffly and are most comfortable when recumbent. Pain may be exacerbated by lateral flexion. With lumbar disc herniations, low back pain is accompanied by stiffness, is exacerbated particularly by extension or rotation of the spine, and is relieved by recumbency. With cervical or lumbar disc herniation, any maneuver that increases intraspinal pressure, such as coughing or sneezing, further exacerbates the pain. Stretch of the compressed roots also aggravates it. Passive straight leg raising while the patient is recumbent typically reproduces the pain of an L5 or S1 root lesion, and the femoral stretch test often exacerbates the symptoms of an L4 radiculopathy. In patients with cervical disease, palpation of the brachial plexus and supraclavicular fossa is often painful. A reduced or absent tendon reflex provides objective evidence of root involvement.

There is no agreement concerning the optimal treatment for an acutely herniated disc. Bedrest is often prescribed, but the optimal duration is unclear. Many physicians now recommend rest for 2 or 3 days compared with the 2 weeks that was previously advised and for which evidence of benefit is lacking. Some authors recommend a brief dose of oral corticosteroids, but such an approach has not been validated by extensive clinical trials. Others recommend epidural or subarachnoid injection of corticosteroids, but this is not advised because of the risk of infection or inflammation.

Lumbosacral Disc Disease

Protrusion of an intervertebral disc may lead to a radiculopathy. Approximately two thirds or more of all compressive root lesions involve the lumbosacral roots. The L5 and S1 roots are involved most commonly. Multiple lumbosacral radiculopathies may occur with protrusion of a single intervertebral disc that compresses the roots as they descend in the cauda equina. Lumbosacral polyradiculopathies may also result from spinal stenosis, and, in rare instances, from lateral disc protrusion, but bilateral involvement is then often asymmetrical.

An L5 or S1 radiculopathy is usually associated with low back pain and sciatica. An L5 root lesion leads to a footdrop, and an S1 lesion to weakness of plantar flexion and eversion. S2 radiculopathies are often bilateral, probably because the sacral fibers are more medially situated in the cauda equina and therefore liable to midline compression. With involvement of sacral fibers, disturbances of bladder and bowel function are important complications (Table 429–4).

In a randomized trial of patients between the ages of 25 and 65 years with at least 2 years of chronic low back pain and evidence for disc degeneration at L4-5 or L5-S1, lumbar fusion was better than continued medical therapy[6]; posterolateral fusion, posterolateral fusion combined with internal fixation, or posterolateral fusion combined with internal fixation and interbody fusion provided similar benefits. A successful response to surgical treatment is common when symptoms correlate with objective physical signs and with an associated structural abnormality that is visualized by imaging. A central disc prolapse may lead to bilateral sciatica and to early sphincter involvement; early investigation is therefore warranted when either of these features is present.

Lumbar spinal stenosis is an important cause of disability in middle-aged or elderly patients. Superimposed minor disc disease then leads to symptoms that may be disabling. The disorder can be congenital or acquired. The congenital disorder is caused by a reduction in the normal dimensions of the spinal canal and occurs in achondroplastic dwarfs. Acquired lumbar stenosis usually is caused by degenerative disease of the spine and is typically associated with hyperplasia, fibrosis, and cartilaginous changes in the annulus, posterior longitudinal ligament, and ligamentum flavum. Spondylolisthesis (i.e., anterior or posterior displacement of one vertebral body on the next) or spondylolysis, a defect in the pars interarticularis, may contribute to spinal stenosis, as may other anatomic abnormalities. Acquired stenosis may also be related to injury, bony overgrowth such as occurs in Paget's disease, ankylosing spondylitis, rheumatoid arthritis, and diffuse idiopathic skeletal hyperostosis. Patients present with pain that is brought on by activity and released by rest or leaning forward. The pain involves the lower back and one or both legs, typically in a radicular distribution, and may be accompanied by numbness or weakness. Examination often reveals no abnormality, except perhaps for a depressed knee or ankle reflex. If examination is performed after activity, a radicular motor or sensory deficit is sometimes found. Results of straight leg raising may be normal. MRI is the most sensitive technique for detecting the disorder. Conservative treatment with NSAIDs and exercise to reduce lumbar lordosis is sometimes beneficial. In many cases, however, surgical intervention is the only means of relieving intolerable symptoms.

An *acute cauda equina syndrome* occurs after spinal trauma or central lumbosacral disc protrusions. Patients may present with bilateral sciatica and saddle anesthesia; disturbances of bladder or bowel function are common and are characterized by frequency, retention, or incontinence. The normal sensation associated with the passage of urine or feces may be lost; impotence is common. Examination reveals bilateral root dysfunction and, often, perianal anesthesia and a lax anal sphincter. Investigations involve urgent imaging to define any surgically remedial lesion.

Table 429–4 • DIAGNOSIS OF LOWER LUMBAR AND SACRAL RADICULOPATHY

	PAIN	WEAKNESS (SELECTED MUSCLES)	SENSORY LOSS	REFLEX LOSS
L4	Across thigh and medial leg to medial malleolus	Quadriceps Thigh adductors Tibialis anterior	Medial leg	Knee
L5	Posterior thigh and lateral calf, dorsum of foot	Extensor digitorum brevis and longus Peronei	Dorsum of foot	
S1	Buttock and posterior thigh, calf and lateral foot	Extensor digitorum brevis Peronei Gastrocnemius Soleus	Sole or lateral border of foot	Ankle
S2-4	Posterior thigh, buttocks, and genitalia	Gastrocnemius Soleus Abductor hallucis Abductor digiti quinti pedis Sphincter muscles	Buttocks, anal region, and genitalia	Bulbocavernosus Anal

Cervical Disc Disease

The cervical nerve roots occupy about 30% of the space in the intervertebral foramina that they traverse, accompanied by radicular vessels. The first cervical root exits between the occiput and the C1 vertebra and the subsequent cervical roots exit above their correspondingly numbered vertebra except for the C8 root, which exits between the C7 and the T1 vertebrae (because there is no C8 vertebra). Roots may be compressed by a protruded intervertebral disc or by pathology involving the facet joint or joints of Luschka. Disc herniation is the most common cause and occurs especially at the C5-6 and C6-7 levels, affecting the C6 and C7 roots, respectively. The mechanism through which these various disorders cause radicular pain is unknown. The pain, which often is attributed to compression, angulation, or stretch of the nerve roots, generally subsides with time, even though the anatomic abnormality persists and the root therefore remains distorted. Most patients complain of neck or arm pain. Associated paresthesias are often localized poorly. Weakness is sometimes conspicuous. Table 429–5 summarizes the clinical features of the most common cervical radiculopathies.

Although there is considerable variation in the clinical findings between different patients, single root involvement can generally be diagnosed by clinical means. Weakness in a myotomal distribution is assessed by evaluating different muscles supplied by the same nerve root but by different peripheral nerves in order to exclude more distal pathology. Motor and sensory function in the lower extremities and gait are evaluated to detect evidence of cord compression.

The Spurling test helps to localize symptoms to the cervical spine. The extended neck is rotated and flexed to the side of symptoms, and careful pressure is then applied to the top of the head in a downward direction. An exacerbation of pain or numbness in the extremity supports a diagnosis of cervical root disease. The maneuver should be discontinued if symptoms are reproduced or exacerbated in this way.

Plain radiographs of the cervical spine may be abnormal, but such abnormalities are commonly encountered in asymptomatic subjects. Electromyography is often therefore important in showing the functional relevance of any anatomic abnormalities detected by imaging studies. MRI is the most useful imaging approach because it gives good delineation of soft tissues.

Treatment is individualized. Many patients improve without surgical treatment and can therefore be managed conservatively. Surgical decompression is necessary in patients with severe pain that is unresponsive to 10 to 12 weeks of conservative measures and in those with a progressive neurologic disturbance.

Cervical spondylosis is a common cause of dysfunction in patients older than 55 years of age. Typically, there is bulging or herniation of intervertebral discs, with osteophytes and ligamentous hypertrophy that is sometimes accompanied by subluxation. The underlying primary pathology is usually degenerative disease of the intervertebral discs. This is followed by reactive hyperostosis, with osteophyte formation related to the disc and adjacent vertebral bodies, as well as the facet joints and joints of Luschka. Other associated pathologic factors include thickening of the ligamentum flavum, disc herniation, and a congenitally narrow spinal canal. Ischemia of the cord or roots from compression or distortion of small blood vessels may contribute to the neurologic deficit.

Cervical spondylosis can be categorized by the anatomic location of pathology. The lateral syndrome is characterized primarily by radicular pain and focal neurologic deficits that reflect root dysfunction; gait is usually unaffected. In contrast, the medial syndrome is associated with signs of cord involvement and especially with pyramidal tract findings in the legs and a gait disturbance. Many patients have root and cord involvement (i.e., combined syndrome). Pain in the neck may be accompanied by a root deficit in one arm, clumsy hand, spastic paraparesis, and gait disturbance. A common presentation is with a spastic paraparesis. Sudden quadriplegia or paraplegia after trivial injuries or a fall in an elderly person is often caused by spondylotic myelopathy. In all of these syndromes, neck movement may exacerbate symptoms. Patients with cervical dystonia often have severe degenerative disease of the spine and are at greater risk of developing spondylotic myelopathy.

Examination often reveals a lower motor neuron deficit in one or both upper limbs and a pyramidal tract deficit in the legs. Sensory changes are also present in a distribution that depends on the site of involvement. When sensory findings are inconspicuous, the differential diagnosis of spondylotic myelopathy includes amyotrophic lateral sclerosis. The difficulty in diagnosis is compounded by the common occurrence of degenerative changes in the cervical spine in asymptomatic elderly persons and their coexistence in those with other neurologic disorders. Other causes of spastic paraparesis occurring in middle-aged or elderly persons must be excluded. Involvement of the hands in patients with spondylotic myelopathy may be of the lower motor neuron type in patients with involvement of the C8-T1 segments or of upper motor neuron type in patients with more rostral pathology. Extreme lateral herniation of a cervical disc may occasionally lead to vertebral artery compression and therefore to ischemia in the posterior circulation.

Plain radiographs show disc space narrowing, osteophyte formation, and variable spondylolisthesis. Plain radiographs of the cervical spine in flexion and extension and surface coil MRI are particularly helpful in diagnosing spinal canal stenosis (i.e., anteroposterior canal diameter of less than 11 mm), herniated discs, and intradural pathology. MRI also indicates whether the most prominent compression is anterior or posterior in patients with cervical spondylosis, thereby helping to guide treatment.

Surgical decompression is generally advised in patients with progressive neurologic dysfunction or a fixed deficit of less than 12 months' duration. The value of surgery, however, is uncertain. Surgery may involve an anterior or posterior approach. The value of various surgical approaches is difficult to determine because the natural history of the disorder is unclear, methods of assessing outcome are not standardized, and postoperative complications are often not stated. The most optimistic figures suggest that between 15 and 30% of patients do not benefit from surgery, and several older studies indicate that up to 25% of patients worsen after laminectomy. A summary of the literature suggests that between 25 and 75% of patients improve after surgery, and between 5 and 50% worsen after it. Given the uncertainties of the natural history, it is not clear whether benefit is related to surgery or occurs despite it. Regardless of the difficulty in

Table 429–5 • DIAGNOSIS OF CERVICAL RADICULOPATHY

	PAIN	WEAKNESS (SELECTED MUSCLES)	SENSORY LOSS	REFLEX LOSS
C5	Neck, shoulder, and interscapular region; lateral arm	Deltoid Spinati Rhomboids	Lateral border of shoulder and upper arm	Biceps (brachioradialis)
C6	Shoulder; lateral forearm and first two digits	Biceps Brachioradialis Extensor carpi radialis	Lateral forearm and first two digits	Brachioradialis (biceps)
C7	Interscapular region, posterior arm, midforearm	Triceps Extensor carpi and digitorum Flexor carpi radialis	Midforearm and middle digit	Triceps
C8	Medial forearm and hand	Extensor carpi and digitorum Flexor digitorum (sublimis and profundus) Flexor carpi ulnaris	Medial forearm and hand, and fifth digit	Finger flexors (triceps)
T1	Medial arm to elbow	Intrinsic hand muscles	Medial arm to elbow	

determining its precise value, surgery is so widely accepted as a therapeutic option that it is difficult to withhold it in patients who are deteriorating despite conservative measures.

Measurement of cervical mobility is helpful in selecting patients who are more likely to deteriorate, because patients with spinal hypermobility are more likely to deteriorate without surgery. Patients without major deficits or whose disorder is nonprogressive should be treated conservatively and followed over time. Those with a greater level of disability when first seen are usually referred for surgical treatment, which is also indicated to arrest a progressive course.

Surgical treatment includes posterolateral or anterolateral approaches, as well as laminectomy, foraminotomy, and neurolysis, which may be combined with osteophyte excision. The *posterior approach* allows good visualization of affected nerve roots and facilitates removal of any constricting material and allows enlargement of the intervertebral foramen. In patients with diffuse spinal stenosis, laminectomy is the preferred approach, but it does not reduce any dynamic forces affecting the cord and may increase cervical mobility, which is associated with an increased risk of neurologic complications. A few patients develop increased radicular or cord deficits after surgery by this approach.

The *anterior approach* permits easier decompression of roots and cord and removal of disc material. In patients with cervical spondylotic myelopathy, herniated discs and osteophytic spurs are indications for surgery by this approach. Fusion is favored by some surgeons, but the need for it is uncertain. Cord or root damage after surgery by the anterior approach occurs in a few instances, and other complications have also been described, including esophageal perforation, damage to various nerves (e.g., brachial plexus, superior laryngeal nerve, hypoglossal nerve, and sympathetic nerves), epidural hemorrhage, and damage to major blood vessels.

INFLAMMATORY DISORDERS INVOLVING THE SPINAL CORD

Compression of the spinal cord or nerve roots may occur in consequence of inflammatory diseases. Cord or root involvement may occur in spinal osteomyelitis or tuberculosis, acute or chronic meningitis, inflammatory diseases such as sarcoidosis, and the connective tissue diseases. When the inflammatory process involves the subarachnoid space, root involvement is often multifocal and difficult to explain on the basis of a lesion at one site or level.

Spinal arachnoiditis may follow the introduction of blood or foreign substances into the intrathecal space, but in some instances, it arises without obvious precipitating cause. It has sometimes followed epidural steroid therapy or related procedures. It is characterized by neck or back pain, often accompanied by radicular pain at the level of involvement. Cord involvement occurs less commonly but in severe cases may lead to paraplegia. The diagnosis is established by imaging studies, which sometimes reveal evidence of associated cord cavitation. The spinal fluid typically shows an increased protein concentration; in some instances, there may be a mild pleocytosis and a reduced glucose concentration. There is no specific treatment for spinal arachnoiditis other than lysis of adhesions and opening of subarachnoid cysts unless an infective organism can be identified.

Acute disseminated encephalomyelitis (Chapter 451) is an acute monophasic neurologic illness that develops a few days after viral infection (e.g., with measles or herpes zoster) and certain bacterial infections (e.g., with *Mycoplasma pneumoniae*). Patients present with symptoms of encephalitis or myelitis. The myelitis is manifested by a flaccid paralysis of one or more limbs, most commonly the legs, variable sensory loss that may produce a sensory level, and loss of sphincter function. The tendon reflexes are often depressed initially, but the plantar responses are extensor. The cerebrospinal fluid typically shows a lymphocytic pleocytosis and an increased protein concentration. In severe cases, spinal cord necrosis occurs and may be associated with a fatal outcome (i.e., acute necrotizing hemorrhagic leukoencephalomyelitis). In patients who succumb, pathologic examination reveals perivenular mononuclear cell infiltration with demyelination; cord lesions are typically subpial in location.

Multiple sclerosis (Chapter 448) is a disorder characterized by involvement of different regions of the central white matter at different times by an inflammatory process. The disorder commonly begins in young adult life and may follow a chronic, progressive or a relapsing and remitting course. Clinical onset is usually with the acute development of a focal neurologic deficit that worsens progressively over several days and then shows partial or complete remission over

several weeks or longer. After a variable interval of a few days to many years, another attack occurs. With succeeding attacks, remission is often incomplete, so that patients are left with a neurologic deficit that becomes increasingly severe as further attacks occur. In most patients, signs of a progressive myelopathy become increasingly conspicuous with advancing disease. Eventually, the spinal cord may become atrophic. Further details of the clinical course, cause, diagnosis, and treatment of the disease are provided in Chapter 448.

Neuromyelitis optica (Devic's disease) refers to an acute myelopathy accompanied by a retrobulbar or optic neuritis. It is unclear whether it is a distinct entity as opposed to a form of multiple sclerosis or acute disseminated encephalomyelitis (Chapter 448).

Progressive necrotizing myelopathy may occur at any age but is seen especially in young adults, usually after an infectious illness, or in patients with a known malignancy, usually small-cell cancer of the lung or lymphomas such as Hodgkin's disease. Typically, patients present with pain in the back or legs, sometimes accompanied by paresthesias. The legs then become weak and eventually paralyzed. The tendon reflexes are often lost initially, but after a variable interval, spasticity and hyperreflexia develop. Sensory deficits may be conspicuous, and sphincter disturbances are usual. The disorder follows a progressive course leading eventually to respiratory disturbances and bulbar signs. A somewhat similar disorder has been described in patients with spinal vascular malformations under the eponym of Foix-Alajouanine syndrome. There is no specific treatment. Pathologic examination shows necrotic areas in the cord, especially in the thoracic region; in long-standing cases, the cord is atrophic.

The designation *transverse myelitis* (Chapter 448) is used for an intrinsic lesion that interrupts most of the large tracts across the greater part of the horizontal extent of the cord at the level of the lesion. The term implies an inflammatory process, but in most instances this has not been clearly established. Transverse myelitis may occur as a feature of multiple sclerosis or Devic's disease, but it usually represents an isolated event occurring after viral infections and in other contexts in which the cause is less clear or unknown. Patients typically present with back pain, leg weakness, sensory disturbances below the level of the lesion, and sphincter dysfunction, especially urinary retention. Onset is usually acute or subacute, from a few hours to several days, but the disorder sometimes evolves over several weeks. Weakness is typically associated initially with flaccidity and hyporeflexia, but spasticity and hyperreflexia subsequently develop. A sensory level may be present over the trunk, and a band of hyperesthesia sometimes occurs just above this level. High-dosage corticosteroid treatment has been advocated for acute transverse myelitis. Although there are no controlled clinical trials, methylprednisolone (500 mg every 12 hours for 3 days) followed by a tapering schedule of prednisone is often used. The prognosis is variable. About one third of patients show no recovery whatsoever; this is especially likely when onset is abrupt, the deficit is severe, or pain is conspicuous at onset. Nevertheless, some patients with a severe transverse myelitis may make a good recovery, and there is no means of accurately predicting the outcome at an early stage.

Acute transverse myelitis sometimes occurs in heroin addicts and usually involves the thoracic cord, although it occasionally has affected other regions. Its cause is uncertain, but the speed of onset suggests a vascular origin. An acute myelitis may rarely occur in various connective tissue diseases, especially systemic lupus erythematosus. Other causes of an acute cord lesion must always be excluded, including iatrogenic myelopathies (e.g., after irradiation or after intrathecal administration of methotrexate), vitamin B_{12} deficiency, and the myelopathies discussed earlier.

VASCULAR DISORDERS INVOLVING THE SPINAL CORD

The spinal cord is supplied by the anterior and paired posterior spinal arteries, which are fed by segmental vessels at different levels. The posterior spinal arteries receive numerous feeders along their length. The anterior spinal artery, in contrast, is supplied by only a limited number but usually by three or more vessels in the cervical and upper thoracic region, one in the midthoracic region between T4 and T8, and caudally by a single large vessel, the artery of Adamkiewicz, which usually arises from a segmental artery between about T9 and L2, most commonly on the left side. The anterior and posterior spinal arteries give off branches that form a fine network around the spinal cord, from which radially oriented branches supply much of the white matter and the posterior horns of the gray matter. The central or sulcocommissural arteries are the main branches at the anterior spinal artery. They originate in various numbers at each segmental level, in the anterior longitudinal fissure, and supply one or other lateral half of the cord. Through these vessels, blood is supplied to the gray matter and the innermost portions of the white matter.

The venous drainage of the cord is similarly organized into interconnecting anterior and posterior systems. An anteromedian group of intrinsic veins empties through the central veins into the anterior median spinal vein in the anterior longitudinal fissure. This venous system drains particularly the capillaries of the gray and white commissures, the medial columns of the anterior horns, and the anterior funiculi. The rest of the cord drains through radially oriented veins that connect with the posterolateral venous system running longitudinally on the surface of the cord. The veins on the surface of the cord drain by the medullary veins through the intervertebral foramina, converging there with the radicular veins that drain the nerve roots and with communications from the anterior and posterior epidural and paravertebral plexuses.

Ischemic Myelopathies

Ischemia may contribute to the neurologic deficit that occurs in patients with space-occupying lesions, and those with post-traumatic or postirradiation myelopathies. Wasting of the intrinsic muscles of the hands may result from compression of the anterior spinal artery in patients with lesions of the foramen magnum.

Disease of the abdominal aorta may cause an ischemic myelopathy. Aortic occlusion, dissecting or nondissecting aortic aneurysms, inflammatory aortitis, and emboli involving the aorta may all lead to cord dysfunction, as may surgery involving the aorta, especially in the region of origin of the artery of Adamkiewicz. Imaging studies, such as aortography and mediastinal angiography, can also lead to an ischemic myelopathy. Aortic coarctation of the adult type may cause cord ischemia below the narrowed segment, and neurogenic intermittent claudication may occur because of diversion of blood from the cord by retrograde flow in the anterior spinal artery to bypass the narrowed region. In classic coarctation, a cervicothoracic myelopathy may result from cord compression by enlarged collateral vessels or from a steal phenomenon, and rupture of aneurysmally distended vessels may lead to subarachnoid hemorrhage. Management involves surgical treatment of the coarctation.

Severe hypotension from any cause has been associated with an ischemic myelopathy. The cord is involved particularly in the watershed regions where the anterior spinal artery is most remote from segmental feeding vessels. Some physicians regard the midthoracic region as being especially vulnerable to such ischemia.

When acute ischemia leads to a transverse myelopathy, patients present with the sudden onset of a flaccid areflexic paraplegia or quadriplegia, analgesia and anesthesia below the level of the lesion, and retention of urine and feces. Back pain is sometimes conspicuous at the level of the lesion. Curiously, occlusion of the spinal arteries by atherosclerotic or inflammatory processes, by emboli from the heart, or by fragments of nucleus pulposus is rare. Rapid exposure to high altitude or decompression of divers may lead to nitrogen emboli. Pathologic involvement of the posterior spinal arteries is so uncommon that many physicians doubt it can be recognized clinically. The syndrome attributed to it consists of ipsilaterally impaired vibration and postural sense below the level of the lesion, with segmental anesthesia and areflexia. An ipsilateral pyramidal tract deficit, mild and usually transient, also occurs if the lateral funiculus is affected. Anterior spinal artery occlusion, in contrast, is well described and leads to a sudden, severe back pain, sometimes associated with radicular pain; this is followed by the rapid onset of a flaccid paraplegia or quadriplegia, with urinary and fecal retention. With recovery from spinal shock, an upper motor neuron syndrome develops below the level of the lesion, and neurogenic atrophy occurs in muscles supplied from the infarcted segments. A dissociated sensory loss is characteristic, with impairment of temperature and pain appreciation but relative sparing of light touch and joint position sense. The prognosis for recovery is poor, especially if improvement fails to occur within the first 36 to 48 hours.

Venous infarction of the cord occurs most commonly in association with an arteriovenous malformation but occasionally in association with sepsis, malignant disease, or vertebral disorders. Sudden back pain heralds the onset of weakness and sensory loss in the legs, with accompanying retention of urine and feces. The deficit may progress over the next few days to that of an acute transverse myelopathy, and a fatal outcome is common.

Embolism of nucleus pulposus material has been reported, particularly in women, who present with acute neck or back pain followed, within a few minutes, by rapidly progressive limb weakness and sensory loss to all modalities. The cervical region is affected most commonly. Infectious complications may lead to death. Diagnosis in life is usually difficult, but autopsy reveals characteristic emboli in the spinal vessels. The manner in which the fibrocartilage of the nucleus pulposus enters into the circulatory system is unclear.

Neurogenic Intermittent Claudication

The development of pain or a neurologic deficit after exercise or with certain postures that extend the lumbar spine, with relief by rest or change in posture (i.e., leaning forward), has been designated *neurogenic intermittent claudication*. This may involve the spinal cord or the cauda equina. In contrast to the intermittent claudication of peripheral vascular disease, symptoms typically begin in part of a lower limb and then spread, often in a radicular distribution. Moreover, peripheral vascular disease is typically associated with reduced or absent peripheral pulses, a proximal arterial bruit, and cutaneous evidence of an impaired circulation.

Examination may reveal no abnormalities unless performed while the patient is symptomatic, when motor, sensory, or reflex changes may be found. Imaging studies confirm the presence of spinal stenosis or a structural abnormality involving the cord or cauda equina. The most common cause of intermittent claudication of the cord is probably a spinal vascular malformation.

Hemorrhage

Hematomyelia (i.e., hemorrhage into the spinal cord) or spinal subarachnoid hemorrhage may occur from trauma, spinal vascular malformations, intradural spinal neoplasms, coarctation of the aorta, or ruptured spinal aneurysms. It may be associated with connective tissue diseases, blood dyscrasias, or anticoagulant therapy. In some instances, no cause can be identified.

Spinal subarachnoid hemorrhage is heralded by the onset of sudden severe pain that begins at the site of bleeding but spreads rapidly to the rest of the back and, with cervical lesions, to the head. Dysfunction of the cord or nerve roots may result from compression by blood or blood clot and leads to weakness, sensory disturbances, and impaired sphincter function. Signs of meningeal irritation are present. A spinal bruit or cutaneous vascular malformation suggests the spinal origin of the hemorrhage. CT can confirm the presence of blood in the subarachnoid space, and MRI may reveal a spinal vascular malformation. When the MRI is unrevealing, myelography is undertaken using a large volume of contrast medium and with the patient examined in prone and supine positions. The prognosis reflects the cause and severity of the hemorrhage. Decompressive surgery may be necessary. An underlying spinal vascular malformation requires angiographic definition followed by occlusion of feeding vessels by embolization or surgery. Neoplastic lesions may necessitate surgical treatment, and blood dyscrasias, anticoagulant-induced hemorrhage, or connective tissue diseases require appropriate medical management.

Intramedullary hemorrhage also leads to a neurologic deficit, but pain may be less conspicuous, especially if the hemorrhage remains confined within the spinal cord. Further evaluation is conducted as for spinal subarachnoid hemorrhage.

Spinal subdural hemorrhage may occur spontaneously or after trauma or lumbar puncture, especially in patients with blood dyscrasias or those receiving anticoagulant drugs. Sudden severe back pain is followed by a compressive myelopathy or cauda equina syndrome. CT or MRI is helpful in identifying the underlying lesion. Complete recovery may follow early evacuation of the hematoma, whereas an irreversible neurologic deficit can result from delaying surgery. The risk of spinal subdural hemorrhage is reduced in patients with predisposing hematologic disorders by correcting the underlying abnormality by transfusion before lumbar puncture. In patients with thrombocytopenia, platelet transfusion should be considered before lumbar puncture when the platelet count is less than 20,000/mm^3 or is dropping rapidly.

Spinal epidural hemorrhage results most commonly from trauma but also occurs in patients with epidural vascular malformations or tumors or with hemorrhagic disorders. It sometimes occurs spontaneously or after spinal tap or epidural anesthesia, especially in patients receiving anticoagulant drugs. Sudden severe back pain, sometimes accompanied by radicular pain, is usually the presenting feature and is enhanced by activities that increase the pressure in the vertebral venous plexus. A cord or cauda equina syndrome then develops after a variable interval. Clinical distinction of epidural from subdural hemorrhage may be impossible. MRI is helpful in detecting the hemorrhage, defining its anatomic site, and distinguishing it from other epidural lesions. Urgent evacuation is necessary to prevent irreversible neurologic damage.

Spinal Vascular Malformations

A variety of vascular malformations occur in relation to the spinal cord and meninges. Arteriovenous malformations (AVMs), the most common and clinically important, consist of an abnormal communication between the arterial and venous systems without intervening capillaries. Telangiectasias and cavernous malformations are uncommon and usually asymptomatic, although hemorrhage occasionally leads to a focal neurologic deficit.

Most spinal AVMs are located in the thoracolumbar region, are extramedullary, are supplied by vessels that do not supply the cord, and are so situated that the arteriovenous shunt is dural in location. In contrast, 20 to 30% of AVMs are located in the cervical or upper thoracic segments, and they are often intramedullary, are supplied by vessels contributing to the anterior spinal circulation, have multiple feeding vessels, and consist of an arteriovenous shunt that is usually of large volume.

Spinal AVMs may present with a subarachnoid hemorrhage or, more commonly, with a myeloradiculopathy. Spinal subarachnoid hemorrhage occurs from about 10% of all spinal AVMs and has an overall mortality rate of about 15%; approximately one half of the survivors of the first hemorrhage will have another unless the underlying malformation is treated. The myeloradiculopathy typically has a gradual onset and progression but sometimes follows a relapsing and remitting course. Initial symptoms consist most commonly of pain or sensory disturbances, but by the time of diagnosis, many patients have developed a more severe neurologic deficit characterized by weakness, sensory deficits, pain, and impaired sphincter function. Symptoms of neurogenic claudication of the cord or cauda equina are common. With thoracolumbar malformations, examination typically reveals a mixed upper and lower motor neuron deficit in the legs and a sensory disturbance. With cervical lesions, a mixed motor deficit in the arms is associated with an upper motor neuron deficit in the legs and sensory changes below the level of the lesion. The presence of a spinal bruit is helpful in suggesting the diagnosis, but its absence does not exclude it. The myeloradiculopathy may progress with rapidity and cause severe disability unless the underlying malformation is treated. It probably is related to cord ischemia; venous hypertension causes a reduction in the arteriovenous pressure gradient across the spinal cord and therefore a reduction in intramedullary blood flow. An acute onset or exacerbation of symptoms, however, may be related to intramedullary hemorrhage or to intravascular thrombosis. Radicular symptoms presumably are related to ischemia or compression of nerve roots.

MRI permits easy visualization of the spinal cord, but it sometimes fails to detect a vascular malformation, in which case myelography should be undertaken when the diagnosis is suspected. The characteristic finding is of serpiginous defects in the column of contrast material as a result of vascular impressions. The examination should be performed using a large volume of contrast medium and with the patient screened in the prone and supine positions. Spinal angiography is important in defining the anatomic features of the AVM and the normal blood supply to the spinal cord, but it is not indicated when myelography fails to suggest an AVM. Depending on the angiographic findings, surgical excision, embolic occlusion of feeding vessels, or both can be undertaken. Treatment may not be possible for AVMs that are anterior to or within the spinal cord and are fed by the anterior spinal artery or one of its feeding vessels. However, interventional radiologic procedures involving the embolization of some of the feeding vessels may still be possible in such circumstances.

Grade A

1. Vroomen PC, de Krom MC, Wilmink JT, et al: Lack of effectiveness of bedrest for sciatica. N Engl J Med 1999;340:418–423.
2. Anderson GBJ, Lucente T, David AM, et al: A comparison of osteopathic spinal manipulation with standard care for patients with low back pain. N Engl J Med 1999;341:1426–1431.
3. Leibing E, Leonhardt U, Koster G, et al: Acupuncture treatment of chronic low-back pain—a randomized, blinded, placebo-controlled trial with 9-month follow-up. Pain 2002;96:189–196.
4. Hertzman-Miller RP, Morgenstern H, Hurwitz EL, et al: Comparing the satisfaction of low back pain patients randomized to receive medical or chiropractic care: Results from the UCLA low-back pain study. Am J Public Health 2002;92:1628–1633.
5. Hurwitz EL, Morgenstern H, Harber P, et al: A randomized trial of medical care with and without physical therapy and chiropractic care with and without physical modalities for patients with low back pain: 6-month follow-up outcomes from the UCLA low back pain study. Spine 2002;27:2193–2204.
6. Fritzell P, Hagg O, Wessberg P, Nordwall A: Swedish Lumbar Spine Study Group. Lumbar fusion versus nonsurgical treatment for chronic low back pain: A multicenter randomized controlled trial from the Swedish Lumbar Spine Study Group. Spine 2001;26:2521–2532.

SUGGESTED READINGS

Atlas SJ, Nardin RA: Evaluation and treatment of low back pain: An evidence-based approach to clinical care. Muscle Nerve 2003;27:265–284. *Evidence-based review of treatment.*
Cassidy JD, Carroll LJ, Cote P, et al: Effect of eliminating compensation for pain and suffering on the outcome of insurance claims for whiplash injury. N Engl J Med 2000;342:1179–1186. *This legal change significantly decreased the incidence of whiplash claims and improved prognosis of whiplash injury.*
Deyo RA, Weinstein JN: Low back pain. N Engl J Med 2001;344:363–370. *A comprehensive review.*
Jarvic JG, Deyo RA: Diagnostic evaluation of low back pain with emphasis on imaging. Ann Intern Med 2002;137:586–597. *Review of the yield of various diagnostic tests.*

430 SPINAL CORD INJURY

Charles J. Hodge

Injury to the spinal cord has devastating consequences for the victim. Like head injury (Chapter 431), most victims of spinal cord injury are young, compounding the tragedy of such injuries. Approximately 30 to 40 per million persons in the United States have new spinal cord injuries per year. The peak incidence of spinal column and spinal cord injuries occurs in the 15- to 30-year age range, with males being affected two to three times more commonly than females. More than one half of spinal injuries are at the cervical levels (C1-7), with the remainder evenly distributed between the thoracic (T1-11), thoracolumbar (T11-L2), and lumbosacral (L2-S5) areas. Most injuries are related to motor vehicle trauma, with diving accidents and other falls being the next most common causes. Personal assault accounts for 15 to 20% of such injuries. Injuries in older patients are often associated with significant degenerative changes that have caused cervical spinal stenosis. The number of patients suffering complete transection of the spinal cord is decreasing, whereas the relative incidence of partial lesions is increasing, probably related to preventive measures.

Pathology

Most nonpenetrating spinal column injuries result from flexion. Flexion results in damage to the structural integrity of the spinal column by pulling apart posterior ligaments, thereby allowing anterior or rotational subluxation of vertebral bodies, or by compression of the vertebral body with forcible extrusion of bone and/or disc material into the spinal canal (Fig. 430–1). Notable exceptions to the predominance of flexion injuries are fractures of the odontoid process and contusions of the spinal cord, which are associated with stenosis of the cervical canal and forced hyperextension; both problems are more common in older patients.

The pathology of spinal cord injury has two phases. The first phase is direct injury. The trauma causes disruption of neuronal pools and white matter pathways, and the resulting deficits range from minimal hand weakness due to minor contusion of the cervical cord to complete loss of all motor, sensory, and vegetative functions below the level of the injury. The second phase is secondary injury related to intra-axial hemorrhage from disruption of perforating arteries, the effects of free radical production from membrane damage, the excitotoxic effects from release of glutamate and other neurotransmitters, the anoxic and hypotensive effects of systemic injury or hypotension,

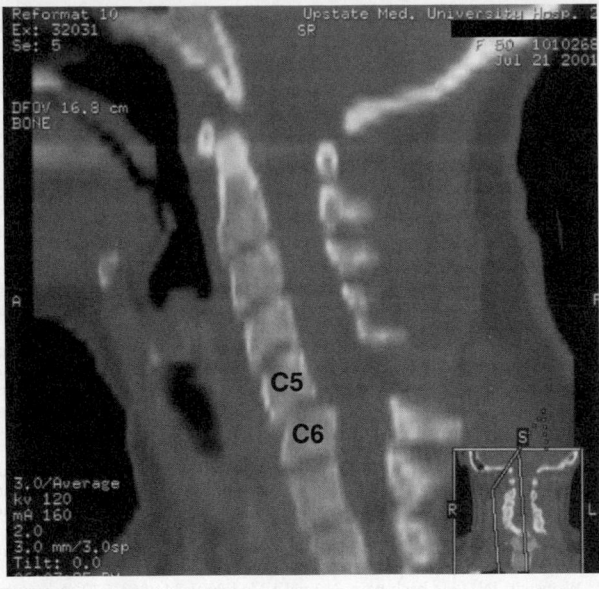

A

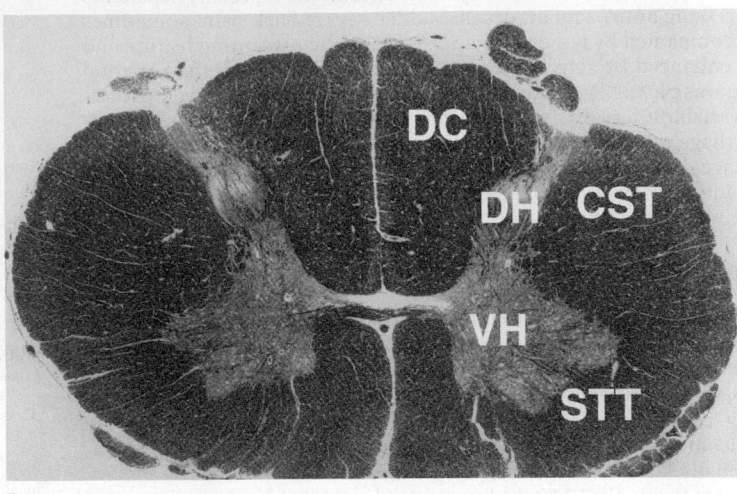

B

FIGURE 430–1 • *A*, A lateral image of the cervical spine, reconstructed from a CT scan. It demonstrates a fracture dislocation at C5-6 with disruption of the posterior ligaments and compression fracture of the anterior vertebral body of C5. This is an unstable injury. (Courtesy of Dr. Kristen Lieberman, Upstate Medical University, Syracuse, NY.) *B*, A myelin stained cross-section of the human cervical spinal cord. CST = corticospinal tract; DC = dorsal column; DH = dorsal horn; STT = spinothalamic tract; VH = ventral horn. (Modified from Martin JH. In Neuroanatomy, New York, Elsevier, 1989.)

and the effects of persistent compression by bone, disc material, or blood.

Neural Injury

Rotational dislocation of the spinal column can result in anterior subluxation of a single or both facets. The result can be spinal nerve root compression with signs and symptoms of single nerve root dysfunction. Spinal cord lesions vary from complete disruption to various patterns of deficit related to cord contusion. Complete disruption is characterized by loss of all voluntary motor and sensory function below the level of the lesion. Motor tone is markedly depressed, and deep tendon reflexes are absent. This state of flaccid paralysis, called *spinal shock*, gradually gives way over several weeks to typical upper motor neuron patterns of spasticity, hyper-reflexia, flexor spasm, and pathologic reflexes. Vegetative effects of complete cord transection are dramatic and include hypotension with relative bradycardia due to sympathetic disruption, hypothermia due to vasodilation below the level of the lesion, priapism, and loss of bowel motility and bladder control due to sympathetic and parasympathetic loss.

Flexion injuries with anterior cord compression affect the anterior and central cord more commonly than the dorsal cord. Common incomplete lesions due to spinal cord contusion include the anterior spinal cord syndrome, which is characterized by loss of pain and temperature sensations bilaterally because of damage of the spinothalamic tracts and hand weakness due to damage of the ventral horn motor neuron pools. Another common variant is central cord contusion, which is primarily a manifestation of destruction of the terminal perforating vessels of the anterior spinal artery; the result is loss of pain and temperature sensation below the level of the lesion, severe upper motor neuron type hand weakness, and spastic lower extremity motor deficit with sparing of the dorsal columns. A common syndrome seen with extrinsic spinal cord compression is the partial Brown-Sequard syndrome, in which there is a crossed motor and sensory deficit, with ipsilateral motor loss and contralateral pain and temperature sensory loss. The vegetative effects of the partial cord syndromes are variable but usually include spastic bladder dysfunction and erectile problems in male patients. Injuries of the spinal cord above the C4 level can depress respiratory function and require long-term ventilatory support. Injuries occurring below the T12-L1 level affect the cauda equina, with resultant loss of lower motor neurons and a sensory deficit at and below the level of the lesion; these patients have a typical "saddle" distribution of sensory loss, as well as flaccid weakness of some or all muscles of the lower extremities and flaccid bladder dysfunction.

Clinical Evaluation

Any patients with trauma (Chapter 108) may also have a spinal injury, especially patients who have head injuries (Chapter 431) or who are unconscious or cannot cooperate. Consequently, an important aspect of care is stabilization of the spine at the scene of the trauma. Patients who do not have neck pain or tenderness, who have no neurologic deficits, and who have normal flexion and extension plain films of the cervical spine (or other spine regions depending on the injury) can be assumed to have a stable spine. Conversely, the presence of neck or other spine pain, tenderness of the spine to palpation, or a nerve root or spinal cord deficit suggests potential spinal instability; these patients require cross-table lateral spine films to exclude bony disruption. If plain x-ray film results are negative throughout the entire cervical spine in a symptomatic patient after trauma, a computed tomographic scan can be obtained; if negative, magnetic resonance imaging (MRI) is the best test to detect nonbony pathology such as a herniated disc, hematoma, or cord contusion.

Rx Treatment

Management of patients with injuries to the spine and/or spinal cord emphasizes stabilization of the spinal column to prevent further neural damage and to provide the best chance for improvement of any existing deficit. The first step is to provide persistent spine stabilization, first through immobilization at the trauma scene and later by bracing or cervical traction. Operative stabilization sometimes is needed, usually early in the course of treatment, to maximize the opportunity for rapid mobilization and physical therapy and to aid in the management of other injuries. Essentially all patients with spinal cord injury are treated with a high-dose methylprednisolone (5.4 mg/kg bolus followed by 4.0 mg/kg/hour for 23 hours) when the patient is seen within 3 hours of the injury. The constant infusion is continued for 48 hours if the patient is seen between 3 and 8 hours after injury. Although this regimen appears to be beneficial in patients with spinal cord injury, few patients are converted from nonambulatory to ambulatory, and the deleterious effects of high-dose steroids are substantial.

Supportive treatment emphasizes care that helps avoid secondary problems, including hypotension, anoxia, fever, unwanted spine movement, and effects of other associated injuries. In patients with complete cord lesions, a major problem is the lack of sensation, so that events such as a perforated viscus, venous thrombosis, or other problems usually heralded by pain can be missed initially unless the physician is vigilant.

Neurology

Recovery

Recovery from spinal cord injury is variable. A limited amount of residual sensation can be associated with a reasonable functional recovery. Conversely, complete loss of all spinal cord function that persists for a week is rarely followed by any meaningful recovery. An important part of the recovery and rehabilitative process is the acceptance by the victim of the deficit with which he or she must live.

Future Directions

Innumerable animal studies demonstrate the beneficial effects of a variety of classes of compounds on spinal cord injury. These agents include compounds that block the excitotoxic effects of glutamate release, free radical scavengers, very-high-dose steroids, and compounds that prevent the hemorrhagic necrosis that follows contusion. The problem is that none of them, except steroids, has had a significant effect in human injury. The major impediments to neuronal recovery seem to be the development of glial scar and the lack of the proper milieu for axonal guidance over the very long distances affected in human cord injury. Real hope for biologic breakthrough exists with progressive understanding of the potential role that neuronal precursor stem cells, particularly certain types of glial cell precursors, might have in allowing recovery. Dramatic progress in neurally based prostheses holds the hope of driving muscle activity triggered by multichannel cortical recording electrodes; this technology should soon be ready for clinical trials.

SUGGESTED READINGS

Bracken MB, Shepard MJ, Holford TR, et al: Methylprednisolone or tirilazad mesylate administration after acute spinal cord injury: 1-year follow up of the third National Acute Spinal Cord Injury randomized controlled trial. J Neurosurg 1998;89:699–706. *If therapy is started within 3 hours, it should be continued for 24 hours.*

Guidelines Committee, Section on Disorders of the Spine and Peripheral Nerves of the American Association of Neurological Surgeons and the Congress of Neurological Surgeons: Guidelines for the management of acute cervical spine and spinal cord injuries. Neurosurgery 2002;50(Suppl), available at www.neurosurgery-online.com. *A literature review using evidence-based criteria.*

Pointillart V, Petitjean ME, Wiart L, et al: Pharmacological therapy of spinal cord injury during the acute phase. Spinal Cord 2000;38:71–76. *There were no differences in outcomes among four different randomized groups.*

431 HEAD INJURY

Charles J. Hodge

Injuries to the brain and its coverings (Table 431–1) occur in approximately 200 per 100,000 people per year and account for 14 to 30 deaths per 100,000 persons per year in the United States. Males are affected two to three times more often than females, and the age range most commonly affected is age 15 to 24 years, with a secondary peak after 65 years of age. The severity of the problem is compounded by the behavioral sequelae of even relatively minor head injury. The young age of the victims magnifies the personal and societal loss related to head injury.

Pathology

The mechanisms responsible for brain injury vary according to the age of the victim. Infants are injured primarily by falls and abuse, whereas older children and adults are affected primarily by high-speed injury, blunt trauma, or penetrating injury from personal violence (Chapter 15). Transportation-related (e.g., driver, passenger, pedestrian) injuries are the most common precipitating cause, followed by falls and assaults.

The common mechanical characteristics of blunt head injury are rapid cranial deceleration and rotational forces that result in contusion of the brain surfaces against the skull. The areas most commonly affected are the frontal, subfrontal, and temporal lobe cortices. These contusions can develop into sizable hematomas with a substantial mass effect that results in increased intracranial pressure (ICP) that can worsen the baseline brain injury (Fig. 431–1A). Rotational forces are particularly devastating to the brain and result in shear forces manifested pathologically by widespread disruption of axonal anatomy, called *diffuse axonal injury*. Rotational forces can also disrupt the major venous connections between the cerebral hemispheres and the sagittal sinus, resulting in acute subdural hematoma.

In the elderly, advanced brain atrophy contributes to a susceptibility to chronic subdural hematoma. This atrophy presumably makes the brain more mobile so that minor trauma can stretch and tear venous channels, resulting in minor bleeding. The accumulating blood evokes a response that allows the formation of hypervascular and relatively permeable membranes, a process that culminates in repeated small hemorrhages, transudation of fluid, accumulation of an intracranial mass, and consequent symptoms (see Fig. 431–1B).

Major closed head injuries often manifest a combination of abnormalities. Distinctly less common is a pure intracranial mass lesion, such as an epidural hematoma (Fig. 431–2).

Minor head injury, commonly referred to as *concussion*, is not associated with pathology that can be imaged using current techniques. Nonetheless, repeated concussions have additive effects suggesting anatomic damage.

Secondary Injury

Major clinical advances in understanding and ameliorating the effects of head injury are based on recognition of the importance of secondary mechanisms of injury, which are related to local brain responses to injury, to other injuries, and to the systemic effects of these injuries. The systemic causes of secondary injury include hypotension and anoxia, both of which require rapid corrective efforts.

The intrinsic causes of secondary injury include brain swelling, with its accompanying increase in ICP; the inflammatory response to brain trauma, including delayed excitotoxic neuronal death; activation of cytokines; production of free radicals; and the induction of apoptosis. Increased ICP is particularly devastating when it and focal lesions cause distortion and destruction of deep brain structures. An important concept is that cerebral perfusion pressure, defined as the arterial blood pressure minus the ICP, must be maintained at 70 mm Hg or higher to preserve brain perfusion.

Clinical Evaluation of the Head Injured Patient

The major goals of the evaluation are to diagnose the type of brain injury, to determine if the patient is deteriorating neurologically, and to decide what type of immediate medical or surgical intervention is required.

The Glasgow Coma Scale score, which can rapidly stratify the severity of brain injury (Table 431–2), is an accurate predictor of mortality

Table 431–1 • BRAIN INJURIES

INJURY TYPE	PATHOLOGY	TIME COURSE	MAJOR CLINICAL FINDINGS
Concussion	Uncertain	Immediate LOC or stunning, rapid return of consciousness	Retrograde and antegrade amnesia
Epidural hematoma	Pure mass effect with herniation	Immediate LOC, lucid interval, then delayed LOC	Depressed LOC, decorticate or decerebrate, anisocoria
Cerebral contusion	DAI, contusion	Immediate deficit, variable later deterioration	Agitation or depressed LOC, variable focal findings
Acute subdural hematoma	DAI, contusion, mass effect	Immediate LOC with progressive deterioration	Depressed LOC, posturing, anisocoria
Chronic subdural hematoma	Diffuse mass effect	Very delayed deficit	Decreased cognition and variable focal deficit

LOC = loss of consciousness; DAI = diffuse axonal injury.

Neurology

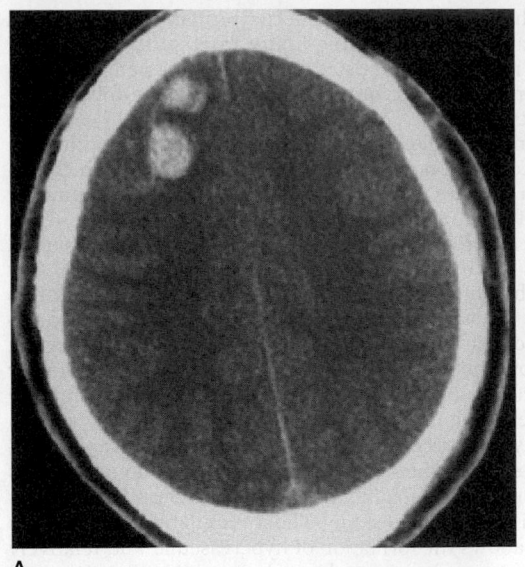 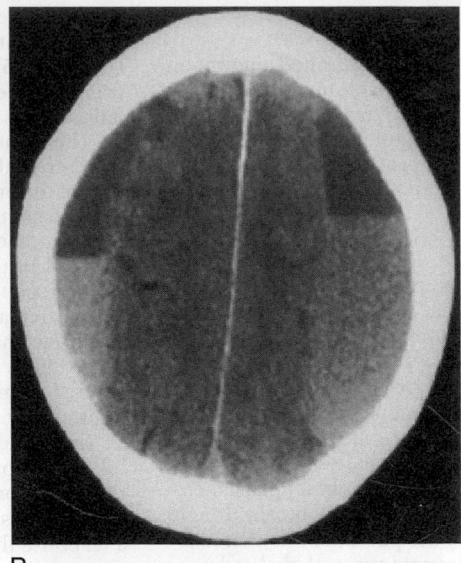

FIGURE 431–1 • CT of common head injury types. *A,* Right frontal contusions. *B,* Bilateral chronic subdural hematomas in an elderly patient with significant brain atrophy. (Courtesy of Dr. Kristen Lieberman, Department of Radiology, Upstate Medical University, Syracuse, NY.)

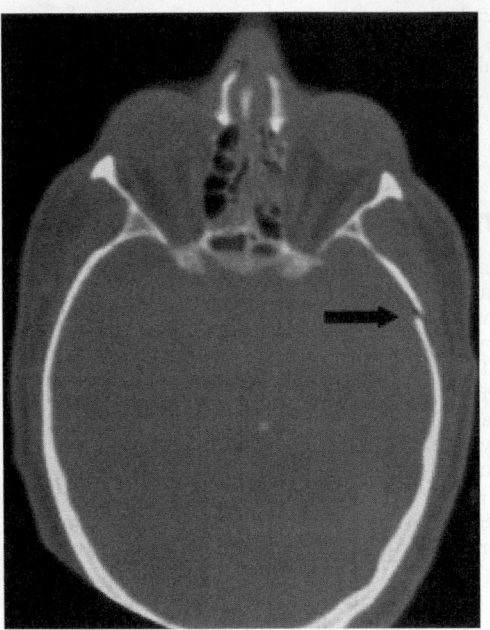 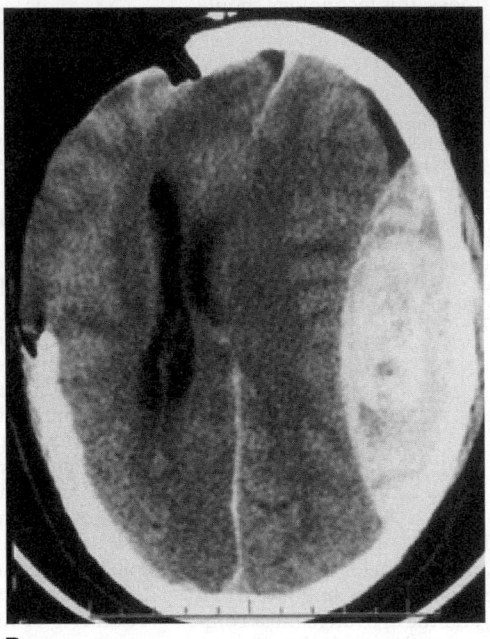

FIGURE 431–2 • CT of an epidural hematoma on the left side. The patient had undergone prior right craniotomy for trauma. *A,* Bone images demonstrate a skull fracture (arrow) in the region of the middle meningeal artery. *B,* Brain images reveal a massive epidural hematoma and severe shift of intracranial contents. (Courtesy of Dr. Kristen Lieberman, Department of Radiology, Upstate Medical University, Syracuse, NY.)

Table 431–2 • GLASGOW COMA SCALE

EXAMINED FUNCTION	RESPONSE	POINTS
Eye opening	Spontaneously	4
	To speech (not necessarily to command)	3
	To pain	2
	Never	1
Best verbal response	Oriented	5
	Confused but talking	4
	Inappropriate (swearing, yelling)	3
	Incomprehensible sounds	2
	None	1
Best motor response	Obeys commands	6
	Localizes pain	5
	Withdraws from pain	4
	Decorticate	3
	Decerebrate	2
	None (flaccid)	1
Total score		3–15

and neuropsychological outcome. Survival also depends on age, other measures of the severity of the injury, and the presence or absence of severe systemic effects, such as hypotension. Glasgow Coma Scale scores of 13 to 15 are considered minor head injuries, scores of 9 to 12 are moderate head injuries, and scores of 8 or less are severe head injuries.

Localization of the level of neurologic function is based on a rostral-caudal (cortex to medulla) pattern of functional loss as patients deteriorate. A depressed level of consciousness (Chapter 436) implies dysfunction of the reticular activating system at the upper brain stem level or of both cerebral hemispheres. If the problem is confined to the hemisphere level, brain stem reflexes and cranial nerve functions should be intact. If, however, the problem is related to brain stem dysfunction, as occurs with brain stem distortion from transtentorial herniation, the depressed level of consciousness usually is accompanied by anisocoria (because of stretching of the third cranial nerve), with the larger pupil being on the side of the mass, and other third cranial nerve findings. If the herniation process continues and severely distorts the center of the midbrain or if hemorrhage occurs within the brain stem, bilateral, large, and fixed pupils will result. Such events generally are associated with development of a persistent vegetative state (Chapter 437) or death. It is imperative that patients with potential herniation be treated before this devastating event occurs.

Rx Treatment

Initial management demands a high level of suspicion to detect other severe injuries that are not easily recognized because the patient cannot cooperate with the evaluation (Chapter 108). Examples include cervical spine fractures and pulmonary and abdominal injuries. The principals of protection of the airway, maintenance of blood pressure and tissue perfusion, and a thorough search for other injuries are of prime importance.

In the initial evaluation phase, the focus should be on determining the type of injury and preventing secondary injury. Repeated examination and imaging studies can determine the extent and type of injury and determine the need for medical and surgical interventions.

Minor head injury with brief loss of consciousness is generally considered an indication for computed tomographic (CT) scanning and a period of close observation. Patients who have suffered a concussion rarely deteriorate but may develop a postconcussion syndrome characterized by an inability to concentrate and a reduced ability to handle multiple simultaneous tasks. These deficits can persist for many months and seriously impair work or academic performance. The major challenge for the physician is to determine whether the extent of temporary dysfunction will interfere with work or studies. A special case is the athlete who desires to return to active participation as soon as possible; a general recommendation is that the high school athlete should not return to participation until all evidence of the concussion and the postconcussive syndrome has resolved. At the other end of the spectrum is the professional athlete, who often returns to competition after only a very brief respite. Caution and a conservative approach are usually appropriate.

Patients with a Glasgow Coma Scale score of less than 13, especially those with scores less than 9, have an altered level of consciousness or focal findings that require more intense management. Deteriorating neurologic function must be evaluated promptly with imaging. Findings range from subtle indications of diffuse axonal injury to obvious mass lesions, including contusion, epidural hematoma, or subdural hematoma (see Figs. 431–1 and 431–2). Patients with these severe injuries require expert management in an intensive care unit, frequently including endotracheal intubation to prevent secondary injury. In adults, mass lesions such as epidural, subdural, or intracerebral hematomas usually require emergent surgery. When rapid neurologic deterioration requires surgical therapy, large doses of osmotic (mannitol, 0.5 to 1 g/kg) and renal (Lasix, 20 to 40 mg IV) diuretics reduce the patient's exposure to dangerous levels of ICP. If the ICP is elevated due to diffuse injury without a focal mass, monitoring the pressure with a ventriculostomy or other devices is essential. If the Glasgow Coma Scale score is less than 9, ICP should be monitored to allow continuous management of the ICP and cerebral perfusion pressure. If the ICP is elevated to 20 to 25 mm Hg, indicated interventions include brief periods of hyperventilation, drainage of small volumes of cerebrospinal fluid from the ventricular system, and use of repeated small doses of mannitol (12.5 g). Prolonged hyperventilation is not recommended because of unpredictable changes in local blood flow due to loss of autoregulation. If the ICP cannot be controlled with these measures, more dramatic techniques include large-dose barbiturates to decrease cerebral blood flow demand or craniectomy for diffuse cranial decompression. Although experimental studies have suggested potential benefits from a wide variety of agents that prevent excitotoxicity, improve free radical scavenging, or prevent apoptotic cascades, none has proved useful in clinical care. Even the most basic neural protective maneuver, which is moderate hypothermia, has been disappointing in clinical studies.■ Protection against anoxia, hypotension, and increased ICP is the basis for the clinical care of these patients.

Long-term management after acute initial intensive treatment requires careful medical, rehabilitative, and psychological therapies. The outcome for survivors of severe head injuries is often devastating, with dramatic change in personality, impulse control, and cognitive function. Expectations for independent functioning must be realistic, because these changes often result in an inability to be employed and difficulties in the most basic interpersonal skills. In the absence of clinical seizures, the use of anticonvulsant medications should be restricted to patients who truly require them; immediate post-traumatic seizures are a poor predictor of recurrent seizures later during recovery. Genetics also influence outcome, and the presence of the apolipoprotein E4 polymorphism is associated with a worse prognosis. Experimental studies suggest that plasticity can be modified for the patients' function benefit.

1. Clifton GL, Miller ER, Choi SC, et al: Lack of effect of induction of hypothermia after acute brain injury. N Engl J Med 2001;344:556–563.

SUGGESTED READINGS
Butefisch CM, Davis BC, Sawaki L, et al: Modulation of use-dependent plasticity by D-amphetamine. Ann Neurol 2002;51:59–68. *D-Amphetamine may augment training-induced changes in brain function.*
Head Injury Task Force: Management and Prognosis of Severe Traumatic Brain Injury. New York, Brain Trauma Foundation, 2000. *Guidelines based on evidence from a comprehensive literature review.*

432 DIAGNOSIS OF REGIONAL CEREBRAL DYSFUNCTION

Jeffrey L. Cummings

Many neurologic disorders affect the cerebral hemispheres in a regionally specific, or *focal* fashion. Defining the nature and extent of the resulting clinical syndrome is helpful not only in localizing brain lesions, but also in establishing their causes and guiding medical or surgical management (Table 432–1). Developments in neuroimaging (e.g., magnetic resonance imaging, positron emission tomography) have facilitated greatly the ability to diagnose focal cerebral pathology, but a thorough clinical examination is required to decide when an imaging study is indicated in an individual patient. In addition, the definition of specific deficits and preserved abilities determines the impact that a neurologic condition has on the patient's life, daily function, and social and occupational potential. This information is crucial in guiding an appropriate approach to treatment and rehabilitation.

Important clues regarding the cause of a neurologic complaint may be obtained from the clinical history (Chapter 423). The rate of onset of symptoms and their tempo of progression help distinguish vascular events (abrupt), neoplasms (subacute), and degenerative disorders (slowly progressive); however, many subacute or chronic processes (e.g., arteriovenous malformations) may present initially as a paroxysmal event, such as a seizure or a hemorrhage. Associated symptoms also may be helpful in diagnosis, such as weight loss in patients with metastatic cancer or fevers in patients with cerebral abscess. A thorough general examination may uncover an occult condition relevant to the neurologic disorder.

Although routine neurologic examination may be adequate for determining the site of cerebral pathology, a carefully conducted mental status examination often is required to provide information regarding regional hemispheric dysfunction that deserves further evaluation. Mental status testing often is omitted because of inadequate time, lack of expertise, and lack of appreciation for its importance. The most commonly used brief, standardized, and well-validated bedside test is the Mini-Mental Status Examination (MMSE) (see Table 434–4), a scale that samples attention, memory, language, calculation, and some visuospatial abilities. Brief assessments such as the MMSE inevitably have limitations, however; the MMSE does not detect important but subtle cognitive changes that may be revealed by more extensive neuropsychological or mental status testing. For example, the MMSE has no assessments related to frontal lobe functioning.

Neuropsychological testing is helpful in some contexts but rarely contributes to the localization of a lesion not evident on bedside neurologic or mental status assessment. Neuropsychological evaluation is most useful when cognitive complaints are present despite a normal bedside examination, when rehabilitation plans are being made, when normal aging must be distinguished from mild pathologic cognitive changes, or when a baseline value is needed for future comparison.

Table 432–1 • **NEUROBEHAVIORAL AND NEUROPSYCHIATRIC SYNDROMES ASSOCIATED WITH FOCAL BRAIN INFARCTIONS OF THE HEMISPHERE**

STRUCTURES AFFECTED	SYNDROME
Anterior corpus callosum	Transcortical aphasia
	Callosal apraxia
	(L) Hand tactile anomia
	Transient akinetic mutism
Inferolateral frontal cortex (left)	Broca's aphasia
Lateral cerebral hemisphere (anterior and posterior) (left)	Global aphasia
Arcuate fasciculus (left)	Conduction aphasia
Angular gyrus (left)	Transcortical sensory aphasia; alexia with agraphia; angular gyrus syndrome; anomia
Posterior superior temporal lobe (left)	Wernicke's aphasia
Hippocampus (left)	Verbal amnesia
Medial occipital cortex	Hemianopsia; release hallucinations
Posterior parietal	Unilateral neglect; anosognosia
Hippocampus (right)	Nonverbal amnesia
Inferior longitudinal fasciculus (right)	Prosopagnosia; environmental agnosia
Calcarine cortex (left); splenium of corpus callosum	Alexia without agraphia; color anomia
Anterior cingulate cortex (bilateral)	Akinetic mutism
Bilateral parietal region	Balint's syndrome
Inferior longitudinal fasciculus (bilateral)	Visual agnosia; prosopagnosia; environmental agnosia
Occipital cortex (bilateral)	Cerebral blindness; Anton's syndrome
Hippocampi (bilateral)	Amnesia
Base of the pons	Locked-in syndrome
Thalamic nuclei	Memory abnormalities, perseveration; executive deficits; apathy

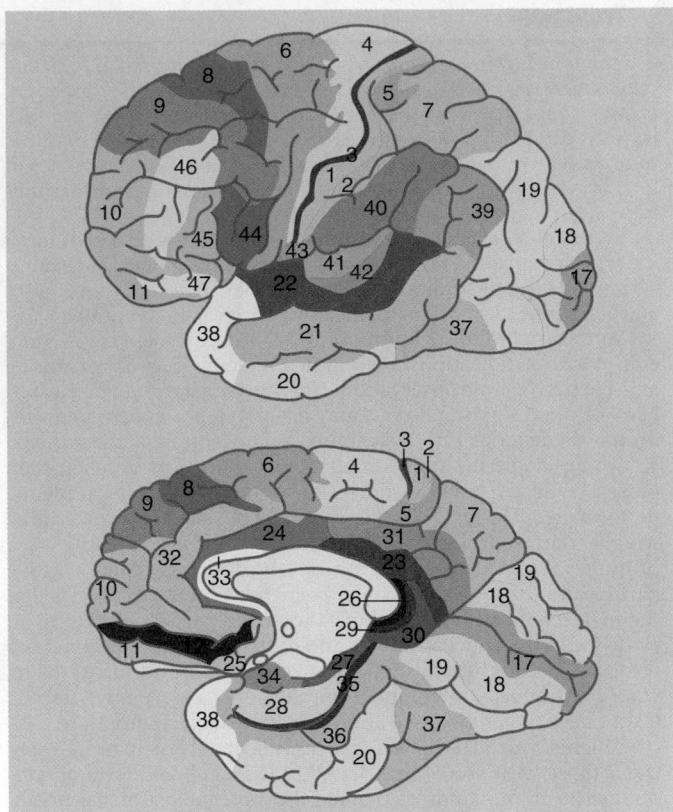

FIGURE 432–1 • Cortical areas as defined by Brodmann according to their cytoarchitectonic structure. See text for details.

Care must be taken when interpreting the results of neuropsychological tests because of the many factors (e.g., age, language, education, culture, fatigue) that are known to affect performance.

CEREBRAL CORTEX

The cerebral cortex may be divided into paired frontal lobes, temporal lobes, parietal lobes, and occipital lobes; some add a fifth, the limbic lobe. Further subdivisions are made on the basis of cytoarchitecture (Brodmann areas; Fig. 432–1) and connectivity. Areas that most directly influence or are influenced by the external environment are called *primary,* or *isotypic,* cortex, including the primary visual cortex (Brodmann area 17) in the occipital lobe, auditory cortex (Brodmann areas 41, 42) in the superior temporal gyrus, somatosensory cortex (Brodmann areas 3, 1, 2) in the anterior parietal lobe, and motor cortex (Brodmann area 4) in the posterior frontal lobe. These areas project to and receive input from the adjacent *unimodal association* cortex. Higher processing of motor programs or sensory stimuli within a given modality occur here. These areas project to and from *heteromodal association* cortex, which occupies the posterior inferior parietal regions and the prefrontal cortex. In these regions, information from different sensory modalities converges. Information from the posterior association cortex flows anteriorly to prefrontal association cortex, where executive and limbic information is integrated, and volitional responses to environmental contingencies are initiated. An additional functional and anatomic unit, the limbic lobe, which includes portions of the frontal and temporal lobes and subcortical structures (e.g., amygdala, ventral striatum), also can be distinguished. Figure 432–2 shows the distribution of these functional cortical areas, and Figure 432–3 shows the gyral and sulcal landmarks that are used in this chapter.

Frontal Lobes

In humans, the frontal lobes are the largest of the cerebral regions and represent almost one third of the total cortical surface area. The

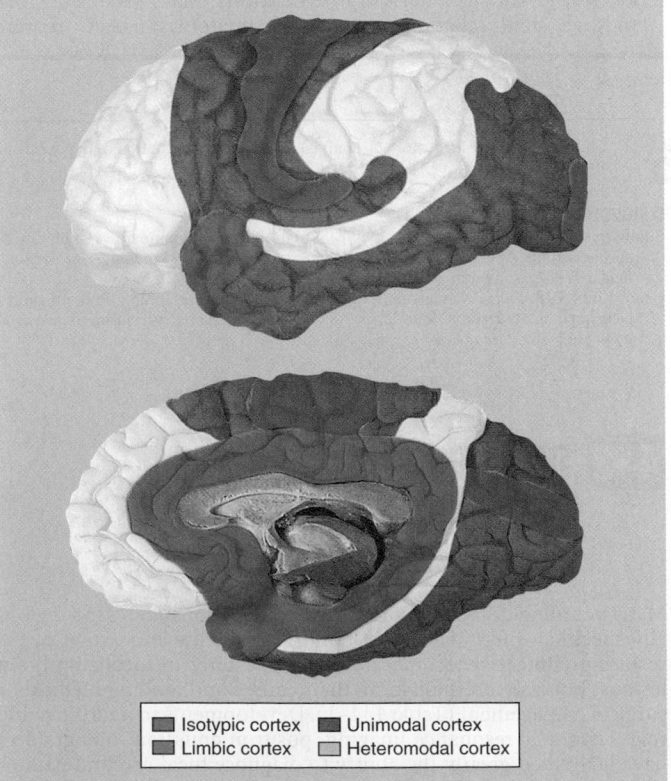

■ Isotypic cortex	■ Unimodal cortex
■ Limbic cortex	■ Heteromodal cortex

FIGURE 432–2 • Functional cortical regions. (Courtesy of Laboratory of Neuroimaging, UCLA.)

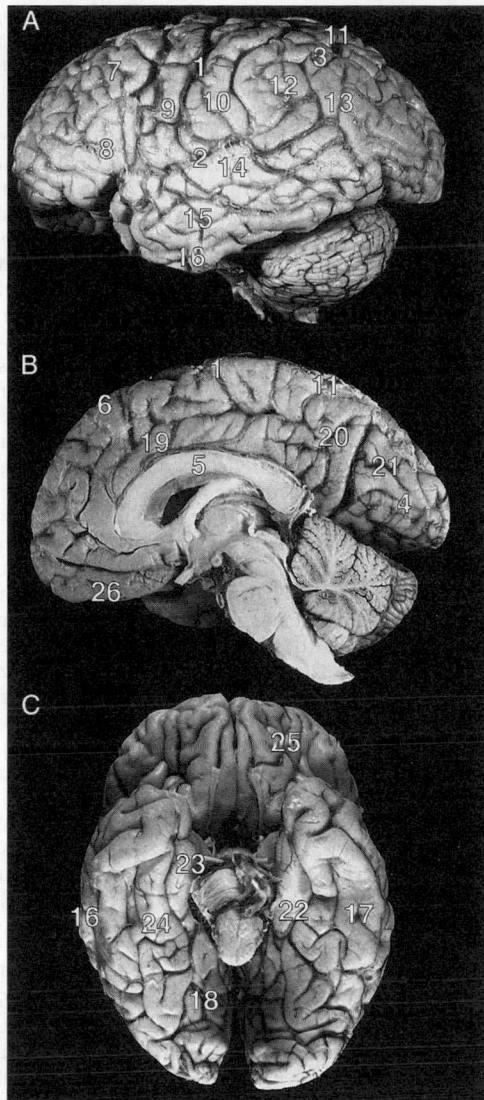

FIGURE 432–3 • The principal gyral and sulcal landmarks of the cerebral cortex shown in lateral, sagittal, and inferior views. 1, Central sulcus. 2, Sylvian fissure. 3, Intraparietal sulcus. 4, Calcarine sulcus. 5, Corpus callosum. 6, Superior frontal gyrus. 7, Middle frontal gyrus. 8, Inferior frontal gyrus. 9, Precentral gyrus. 10, Postcentral gyrus. 11, Superior parietal lobule. 12, Supramarginal gyrus. 13, Angular gyrus. 14, Superior temporal gyrus. 15, Middle temporal gyrus. 16, Inferior temporal gyrus. 17, Fusiform gyrus. 18, Lingual gyrus. 19, Cingulate gyrus. 20, Precuneus. 21, Cuneus. 22, Parahippocampal gyrus. 23, Uncus. 24, Occipitotemporal gyrus. 25, Orbital gyri of the frontal lobe. 26, Gyrus rectus. (Courtesy of Laboratory of Neuroimaging, UCLA.)

relative enlargement of the frontal lobes is the most salient neuroanatomic characteristic distinguishing humans from nonhuman primates and from other mammals. The frontal lobes mediate executive cognitive function and are required for behavioral integrity. On IQ tests, in which well-established language, memory, and visuospatial skills are tested in a structured manner, subjects with extensive frontal lobe damage may perform well. In social and other real-life situations, in which mental flexibility and planning are required, subjects with frontal lobe damage may be unable to cope, however. This ability to self-monitor behavior and choose an appropriate response in the context of ongoing internal and external events is an example of executive function. Neuropsychological tests specifically designed to assess frontal lobe function may be helpful in revealing deficits that are difficult to characterize with bedside testing.

Consisting of the primary motor area (Brodmann area 4) on the anterior bank of the central sulcus and all cortex anterior to it, the frontal lobes organize and implement behavioral *output*. Projections from various regions of the frontal cortex descend to subcortical structures, including the spinal cord, brain stem nuclei, thalamus, and

basal ganglia. Five separate circuits involving serial connections from parts of the frontal cortex to the striatum, globus pallidus, and thalamus, with feedback to the cortex, have been defined. Similar behavioral and cognitive syndromes may arise from lesions in distinct structures anywhere within a given circuit.

Anterior to isotypic area 4 are Brodmann areas 6 and 8. This region is the unimodal association cortex of the motor system and is called the *premotor* cortex. Its extension onto the medial bank of the superior frontal gyrus represents the *supplementary motor area.* The motor circuit arises from the primary sensorimotor cortex, premotor area, and supplementary motor area. Lesions involving the structures of this circuit may result in weakness of contralateral extremity muscles or loss of coordination of fine finger movements. Lesions of the premotor area of the language-dominant hemisphere may cause a disturbance in the motor programs of speech or cortical dysarthria. Unilateral stimulation of the supplementary area causes automatisms involving both sides of the body.

Broca's area (Brodmann areas 44 and 45) is in the inferior aspect of the premotor area, or the frontal *operculum.* Lesions in this area on the language-dominant side cause a characteristic language disturbance, or *aphasia,* characterized by the loss of the orderly execution of language. In this *nonfluent* aphasia, the patient's verbal output is sparse with short agrammatic phrases, word-finding abnormalities, and impaired repetition. Comprehension is relatively preserved, and patients with Broca's aphasia often are frustrated by their inability to speak. Lesions in the equivalent of Broca's area of the right hemisphere give rise to a deficit in executing prosodic elements of speech that infuse speech with inflection and emotional meaning. Involvement of the motor and premotor areas by epileptic seizure activity may result in complex automatisms (coordinated yet automatic-appearing movements), tonic contraversive head movements with tonic posturing of the contralateral limbs, and contralateral clonic movements.

Apraxia is loss of the ability to perform organized motoric acts despite relative preservation of strength, sensation, and comprehension. The brain has a hemispheric dominance for limb praxis so that lesions of the premotor areas in the left hemisphere may cause an ipsilateral, or *sympathetic,* apraxia and contralateral paralysis.

The frontal eye fields in Brodmann area 8 and the supplementary eye fields govern eye movements and give rise to the *oculomotor* circuit. Electrical stimulation to this area produces conjugate eye deviation toward the opposite side, whereas ablation causes ipsilateral gaze deviation.

The *dorsolateral prefrontal* cortex includes Brodmann areas 9 and 10 on the convexity of the frontal lobe. Impairment of executive function arising from damage to this area is characterized by a memory retrieval deficit, reduced fluency of verbal output, and an inability to think abstractly. The memory deficit is characterized by impaired spontaneous recall and preservation of recognition memory. Lesions on either side cause reduced verbal fluency (i.e., number of animals named in 1 minute), and patients with right-sided lesions have a reduced ability to produce varied figures (impaired nonverbal fluency). Subjects with lesions of the dorsolateral prefrontal circuit have difficulty changing cognitive set, impaired response inhibition, deficits in sustained attention, and perseveration. These subjects also have difficulty moving from one mode of response to another, and they tend to repeat themselves verbally or in their motor performances. They typically exhibit *stimulus-boundedness,* in which their behavior can be seen as directed by environmental influences. When asked to draw and set a clock for 11 : 10, they may place one clock hand on the 11 and one on the 10. The extreme form of this phenomenon is *utilization* behavior, in which objects within reach are manipulated automatically in the manner for which they are normally used, without regard for situation or context. Depression and agitation are common consequences of frontal lobe damage. Dorsolateral prefrontal dysfunction is dramatic in the frontotemporal dementias (including Pick's disease) and can occur in Alzheimer's disease. Frontal-subcortical circuit abnormalities with executive dysfunction are also present in basal ganglia disorders (Huntington's disease, Parkinson's disease). Tumors and thromboembolic events of the anterior branches of the middle cerebral artery may result in the dorsolateral frontal syndrome. Patients with chronic schizophrenia and depression may exhibit similar behavior, which correlates with a relative hypometabolism of the frontal lobes on functional neuroimaging.

Damage to the *orbitofrontal* cortex frequently is not evident on usual neuropsychological testing. Instead, these lesions tend to be manifested as disturbed social behavior, including disinhibited,

Neurology

impulsive, and tactless responses. Idiopathic obsessive-compulsive disorder is associated with increased metabolism of the orbitofrontal cortex and the caudate nuclei. Acquired obsessive-compulsive behavior and occasionally mania may arise after damage to the orbitofrontal circuit, an area that is prone to damage by closed head trauma and by meningiomas of the anterior cranial fossa. These insults may be associated with *anosmia,* which is a deficit in olfaction from damage to the underlying olfactory tracts.

The *medial frontal* portion of the frontal lobe contains the anterior cingulate gyrus. This cortical region mediates analysis of the emotional relevance of stimuli, and damage to it results in an apathetic state with reduced interest, lack of motivation, and decreased activity. The most profound form of this state, *akinetic mutism,* usually occurs when the damage is bilateral and results in an awake but motionless and mute patient. Damage to the medial portion of the frontal lobes may result from vascular events affecting the distribution of the anterior cerebral artery or from neoplasms involving the medial brain regions.

Transcortical motor aphasia most commonly results from a lesion of the left medial frontal region. It also may be caused by a lesion that isolates Broca's area from the frontal heteromodal cortex, such as infarction of the border zone between areas perfused by the anterior and middle cerebral arteries. Similar to Broca's aphasia, it is nonfluent, but the ability to repeat verbal phrases is relatively preserved.

Parietal Lobes

The central sulcus defines the anterior border of the parietal lobe. The parietal and temporal lobes are separated by a border defined by an imaginary line connecting the sylvian fissure with the occipital lobe. Brodmann area 3 lies along the posterior wall of the central sulcus and, along with areas 1 and 2, represents the isotypic primary somatosensory cortex. Brodmann areas 5 and 7 constitute the superior parietal lobule, which lies along the sagittal surface of the parietal lobe and is separated from the inferior parietal lobule by the intraparietal sulcus. The inferior parietal lobule is divided further into the supramarginal gyrus (Brodmann area 40) anteriorly and the angular gyrus (Brodmann area 39) posteriorly. Situated between somatosensory, visual, and auditory cortical receiving areas, the bulk of the parietal lobe is involved in unimodal and heteromodal sensory processing. In the parietal and temporal lobes, a marked functional asymmetry between the left and right hemispheres is evident. Many behavioral syndromes have been associated with the region of the parietotemporo-occipital junction.

Lesions of the primary somatosensory area cause loss of sensation on the contralateral side of the body; fundamental modalities, such as touch, temperature, and pain sensation, generally are retained, but more highly processed somatosensory information (e.g., decreased sensitivity to differences in the intensity of a stimulus, loss of appreciation of the direction of movement of a stimulus, and two-point discrimination) is impaired. This impairment results in sensory deficits clinically identifiable as *astereognosis* (inability to recognize objects by touch) and *agraphesthesia* (inability to identify figures drawn on the palm). Because of the course of the optic radiations through the white matter, posterior parietal lesions may cause a contralateral inferior homonymous quadrantanopia. The most common aura associated with seizures originating from the parietal lobe is contralateral numbness and tingling. Although the perception of pain generally is not affected by primary sensory area lesions, painful experiences may occur when epileptic activity occurs in this region. Auras associated with epileptic foci in more posterior portions of the parietal lobe may consist of distortions in body schema and position, such as feeling as though an appendage is absent or an extra limb is present or a feeling of vertigo and other sensations of movement.

Disorders of higher cognitive function associated with parietal lesions depend on the hemisphere involved. Lesions of the left parietal lobe produce deficits in communication; comprehension and semantics (word meaning) typically are affected most. Lesions of parietal heteromodal cortex may result in a *transcortical sensory* aphasia characterized by deficits in the comprehension of language but relatively spared repetition. Lesions of the left inferior parietal cortex and underlying arcuate fasciculus may lead to *conduction aphasia,* in which repetition is impaired, but spontaneous speech and comprehension are spared.

Reading and writing are mediated by the left parietal lobe. In cases of alexia with agraphia, the lesion typically involves the angular gyrus of the left parietal lobe. *Anomic aphasia,* or difficulty naming objects, occurs with lesions of the left angular gyrus. Anomia also is seen with lesions in various parts of the cerebral cortex, however, and is a frequent early sign in degenerative dementia. As a result, anomia itself is of limited localizing value.

The tetrad of agraphia, right-left disorientation, finger agnosia (inability to identify specific fingers), and acalculia (inability to perform mathematical operations) constitutes Gerstmann's syndrome and occurs with damage to the left angular gyrus. A deficit in any one of these skills alone does not have specific localizing value, however.

Apraxias, in which subjects pantomime poorly or are unable to perform gestures on command, occur with lesions of the left inferior parietal lobule, left premotor cortex, and corpus callosum. Performance is enhanced when the subject is given an actual object to manipulate. Parietal apraxia commonly accompanies conduction aphasia.

Lesions of the right parietal lobe commonly cause *hemispatial neglect.* In this condition, the subject does not attend to stimuli in the neglected sphere contralateral to the lesion. Patients may ignore the left half of the visual field, the left half of their bodies, auditory stimuli from the left hemispace, or any sensory stimulus in the left hemiuniverse. In a milder form of neglect, called *extinction,* subjects are capable of attending to contralateral stimuli but respond only to the ipsilateral side when presented with stimuli simultaneously on both sides. Neglect has been reported with damage to the right dorsolateral frontal lobe, cingulate gyrus, putamen, and thalamus, but it also occurs most consistently with lesions of the right inferior parietal lobule. Neglect associated with frontal lobe damage may result in a decreased tendency to react with the contralateral limb. When acute, as when caused by a stroke, neglect may be severe, but the patient tends to recover. Neglect also may occur transiently with left parietal lobe lesions but usually resolves more quickly and is less severe than the neglect associated with right brain lesions.

Anosognosia, or the lack of knowledge of one's deficit, often accompanies hemispatial neglect arising from right parietal lesions. Subjects who deny their left hemiparesis, hemianesthesia, or hemianopia may attempt to perform activities of which they are incapable. If they are aware of their deficit, they may exhibit anosodiaphoria, or relative lack of concern regarding their impairment.

Many studies have implicated a role for the parietal lobes, especially in the right hemisphere, in visuospatial functions. Specific tasks for which subjects with right parietal lesions are more impaired include localization of points in space, estimation of line orientation, topographic orientation, depth perception, and facial discrimination. A common sequela of nondominant parietal damage is difficulty dressing. Visuospatial deficits, including unilateral neglect, can be shown at the bedside by asking the patient to draw figures (e.g., flower, clock) or copy drawings (e.g., circle, diamond, cube).

A convergence of information from electrophysiologic and ablation studies in animals suggests that visual information is processed initially in the striate cortex (Brodmann area 17 in the occipital lobe), then undergoes further processing in two separate pathways. A ventral pathway passing forward into the temporal lobes is concerned primarily with identifying visual stimuli, the so-called *what* pathway. The dorsal pathway that involves occipitoparietal connections plays a role in determining the location of visual stimuli, the so-called *where* pathway. Disorders of visual perception may occur with lesions at the occipitoparietal or occipitotemporal borders.

Occipital Lobes

The occipital lobes are the smallest of the cortical divisions and lie at the most caudal aspect of the cerebrum. The isotypic primary visual receiving area (Brodmann area 17) forms the lips of the calcarine sulcus on the medial aspect of the occipital lobes. The superior lip receives afferents representing the contralateral inferior visual field, and the inferior lip receives afferents from the contralateral superior visual field. The unimodal visual association areas 18 and 19 form concentric rings around area 17. Lesions of the occipital lobes are manifested as changes in visual perception, and a congruent homonymous visual field cut is frequently present. In part because of the small size of the occipital lobes, isolated occipital lobe syndromes are relatively rare.

In cortical blindness, or blindness caused by bilateral destruction of the occipital lobes or their afferents, retention of pupillary responses reflects intact visual input to the brain stem. Denial of blindness, or *Anton's syndrome,* may occur in association with damage to the visual cortex and with more peripheral causes of blindness. Subjects with Anton's syndrome may bump into things when walking, and they frequently have general intellectual impairment.

Hallucinations can occur as a result of occipital lobe injury by one of two mechanisms. *Release hallucinations* occur with visual loss of any etiology. When visual loss is cortical in origin, these hallucinations appear in the associated visual field defect and may be complex and continuous. *Ictal hallucinations* are a manifestation of seizures originating in the occipital or temporal lobes. Ictal hallucinations arising from area 17 generally consist of contralateral lights (or darkness) moving from the periphery to the center of the visual fields. Focal seizures arising from areas 18 or 19 may be motionless and pulsatile and may occur in the ipsilateral and the contralateral hemifields. More complicated visual hallucinations most likely originate in the temporal lobe.

When the occipitoparietal areas are damaged bilaterally, *simultanagnosia* may occur. In this condition, the subject is unable to attend to more than a small part of the visual field at once and consequently has difficulty understanding whole scenes. As part of the triad of *Balint's syndrome,* simultanagnosia occurs with optic ataxia (difficulty with visually guided arm movements) and sticky fixation (difficulty switching fixation from one object to another). Selective deficits in perception of movement may occur with occipital lobe lesions. Alexia without agraphia is a disconnection syndrome in which the left angular gyrus is isolated from visual information by a left occipital lesion and a lesion of the corpus callosum. The most common cause is an infarction in the occipitoparietal white matter of the left hemisphere with concomitant involvement of the splenium of the corpus callosum and optic radiations. An associated right homonymous hemianopia is usually present.

Visual agnosia, which is a visual percept stripped of its meaning, may occur with more ventral occipital lobe damage. Agnosia has been subdivided into *apperceptive agnosia,* which is a defect in perceiving all but the most basic aspects of visual stimuli such as color and movement, and *associative agnosia,* which is characterized by an inability to recognize stimuli despite completely intact visual perception (as shown by the ability to draw the object). Patients with either type of agnosia can recognize objects through other sensory modalities (e.g., when touching them). To characterize a patient's agnosia, it is necessary to assess language and the ability to recognize in nonvisual sensory modalities. Visual agnosia generally is caused by bilateral lesions in the occipitotemporal area that affect the inferior longitudinal fasciculus and often is associated with other visual disturbances. Visual agnosia also may result from lesions anterior in the ventral visual pathway in the temporal lobes. *Achromatopsia,* which is an acquired color blindness, typically involves a single hemifield and is caused by a lesion of the contralateral medial occipital area. *Prosopagnosia* is the inability to recognize familiar faces visually, although it also can be manifested as an inability to distinguish individuals among a class of objects (e.g., a farmer unable to discriminate among his cows). The lesion is most frequently bilateral in the lingual and fusiform gyri of the ventral occipitotemporal area, although unilateral right-sided lesions can produce the syndrome. It often is associated with *environmental agnosia,* which is the inability to recognize familiar places.

Infarction in the distribution of the posterior cerebral arteries is a frequent cause of occipital lobe damage; head injury, tumors, and many other processes can affect the occipital lobes as well. Posterior cortical atrophy associated with Alzheimer's disease, Creutzfeldt-Jakob disease, and dementia with Lewy bodies are other conditions that may affect occipital structures.

Temporal Lobes

The temporal lobe is bordered by the occipital lobes posteriorly and the sylvian fissure superiorly. Its lateral surface consists of the superior, middle, and inferior temporal gyri. The inferior surface is composed of the occipitotemporal gyrus and the more medial parahippocampal gyrus. The parahippocampal gyrus and the amygdala, hippocampus, and temporal pole are limbic structures (see later). The primary auditory area (Brodmann areas 41 and 42) is located within the sylvian fissure on a transverse portion of the superior temporal gyrus (Heschl's gyrus). Aside from this isotypic cortex, the temporal lobe consists mainly of paralimbic cortex and unimodal and heteromodal association cortex. The anterior temporal lobe connects with the orbitofrontal region via the uncinate fasciculus, and the posterior

temporal lobe is connected with the more lateral frontal lobe by the arcuate fasciculus. A portion of the optic radiations (Meyer's loop) courses through the temporal lobe so that temporal lesions sometimes can give rise to a contralateral superior quadrantanopia. Seizure disorders frequently arise from pathology in the temporal lobes and adjacent structures.

Complete destruction of the primary auditory area unilaterally does not result in appreciable hearing deficits. Acute bilateral destruction (e.g., by bilateral middle cerebral artery infarction) is rare and causes *cortical deafness,* which is lack of a behavioral response to sounds of any kind. Over time, this condition generally improves so that the subject can exhibit some hearing but may have persistent *auditory agnosia,* which is a deficit in the ability to recognize sounds. This condition also occurs with involvement of auditory association areas and can be manifested as an inability to grasp the meaning of sounds, such as car horns or a ringing telephone. Because of the proximity of areas important for language comprehension, auditory agnosia rarely exists without a concurrent language deficit. It is important to assess language function when examining for auditory abilities. A condition termed *pure word deafness,* in which patients are unable to understand spoken language but do not have a more general auditory agnosia occasionally occurs; it is caused by bilateral lesions separating the primary auditory areas from the posterior association cortex and usually is associated with Wernicke's aphasia.

Lesions in the posterior superior temporal lobe of the left hemisphere cause *Wernicke's aphasia,* in which fluent paraphasic output and impairment in language comprehension and repetition are the predominant features. Patients with this condition have intact motor output and utter incoherent phrases with *paraphasias* (incorrect word or letter substitutions) that retain grammatical structure. Anomia, alexia, and agraphia are present. In contrast to the frustration seen in patients with Broca's aphasia, patients with Wernicke's aphasia are often oblivious to their deficit and do not respond well to most forms of speech therapy.

Sensory aprosodia is observed in patients with lesions in the right hemisphere area equivalent to Wernicke's area of the left hemisphere. Patients have difficulty decoding the emotional content of verbal communication conveyed by inflection.

A selective *amusia,* which is inability to recognize or appreciate pitch and melodies, may occur with right posterior temporal or inferior parietal lesions. Deficits resulting from right temporal lobe lesions generally are subtle and require specific testing for spatial orientation, fine visual discrimination, and odor discrimination.

Focal seizures arising from the temporal lobe may give rise to changes in ongoing language function and to sensory, emotional, or psychic phenomena. Auditory hallucinations arising from the superior temporal gyrus range from simple sounds to complex speech, whereas visual hallucinations arising from the temporal lobe are generally complicated scenes or visual memories.

Limbic Lobe

Situated between the neocortex and brain stem structures, the limbic lobe (from the Latin *limbus,* meaning edge or border) forms a ring on the medial surface of the cerebral hemisphere. It consists of the subcallosal gyrus anteriorly, the cingulate gyrus curving up and around the corpus callosum, and the parahippocampal gyrus on the medial and inferior aspect of the temporal lobe. Temporal poles, the orbitofrontal region of the frontal lobes, and portions of the insular cortex in the limbic system sometimes are included in the definition of the limbic lobe. The limbic cortex corresponds to Brodmann areas 23, 24, 25, 28, and 35. In contrast to the six-layered structures of the neocortex, the cortex of the limbic lobe consists of three-layered archeocortex (hippocampal formation and dentate gyrus), three-layered paleocortex (parahippocampal gyrus), and transitional juxtallocortex (cingulate gyrus).

Convergence of data from anatomic investigations, animal studies, and observations in humans suggests that the limbic system plays a role in mediating the experience of emotions, visceral responses, and storage of memories. The limbic system has connections to the cortex; most projections are to the association regions. The limbic regions have intimate connections with the hypothalamus, the "head ganglion" of the autonomic nervous system. In animals, electrical stimulation of the anterior cingulate cortex and orbital-insular-temporal cortex causes changes in blood pressure, gastrointestinal motility, pupillary dilation, salivation, bladder contraction, and respiration. In humans, seizure activity in these same areas can cause similar autonomic changes, including orgasm. Lesions of the limbic lobe usually do not induce clinically evident autonomic changes, in part because of the independence of subcortical structures, such as the hypothalamus, in mediating autonomic reflexes and in part because of the many limbic structures that connect with the hypothalamus.

Characteristic visceral and psychic phenomena occur with epileptic activity arising from limbic structures. Olfactory sensations, usually of an unpleasant nature, classically are associated with involvement of the uncus in the medial temporal lobe. Autonomic and gustatory sensations are seen with involvement of the opercular area within the sylvian fissure. Psychic sensations of déjà vu, jamais vu, dreamlike states, and depersonalization may occur along with associated impairment of consciousness. Profound acute depression, fear, or extreme pleasure sometimes is seen. The temporal neocortex is intimately connected to the deeper limbic structures, so it is difficult to establish whether observed seizure phenomena are due to limbic or neocortical involvement.

Lesions of the limbic lobe can produce profound deficits in memory. Bilateral anterior temporal dysfunction resulting from lobectomy or other conditions (e.g., blunt head trauma, stroke, or herpes encephalitis) can cause *amnesia*, which is a severe deficit in the ability to form new declarative memories. Less dramatic deficits are seen with unilateral lesions; verbal memories are more impaired with left-sided lesions, whereas nonverbal recognition, such as memory for faces, is more impaired with right anterior temporal lobe lesions. The hippocampus seems to be required to store declarative memories, and the adjacent amygdala is necessary to store emotionally laden memories.

Aside from a memory deficit, bilateral lesions of the anterior temporal lobes also can produce the *Klüver-Bucy syndrome*. This condition consists of hypersexuality, hypermetamorphosis (excessive exploratory behavior), emotional placidity, hyperorality, and agnosia.

HEMISPHERIC SPECIALIZATION

In most individuals, the left hemisphere is key for language and comprehension. Of right-handed subjects, 96 to 99% have left-sided speech representation, and bilateral speech representation is rare. In people who are left-handed or of mixed handedness, most (70%) have exclusively left-hemisphere speech representation, 15% have bilateral speech representation, and 15% have predominant right brain mediation of language. Aphasia resulting from left-hemisphere lesions in right-handed individuals is generally of greater severity and duration than when an equivalent lesion occurs in a left-handed person. This asymmetry applies more to expressive language; some degree of comprehension can be shown in the right hemisphere of strictly right-handed subjects. In addition to non–right-handed people, women as a group tend to exhibit less cerebral lateralization.

Right hemisphere superiority has been found in tasks such as somesthetic and visual recognition of shapes, perception of orientation and perspective, aspects of musical ability, and perception and expression of emotional tone. There is not one dominant hemisphere; either hemisphere may be dominant for specific tasks.

DISCONNECTION SYNDROMES

Focal lesions can exert their effects in at least two ways. Direct damage to a neuronal structure that performs an operation prevents that operation and impairs the output of that region. Alternatively, a lesion may destroy the white matter tracts that connect two structures, impairing their interaction but leaving the structures themselves intact. The condition in which independent function of two structures is retained but their connection and interaction is disturbed is called a *disconnection syndrome*.

The most dramatic disconnection syndrome seen in humans occurs after surgical section or other damage to the corpus callosum. Patients who have undergone sectioning of the corpus callosum to control intractable epilepsy generally behave normally. In experimental situations in which stimuli are presented to a single hemisphere, however, they behave as though they have two separate minds. For example, an object placed in the left hand of a blindfolded callosotomized subject can be sensed only by that subject's right hemisphere. The subject may be able to select a similar object from many other objects and show other signs of recognition but is unable to name or describe the

object verbally. Information regarding the object cannot reach the left hemisphere. When the object is placed in the right hand of the subject, the information is available to the left hemisphere, and the individual has no difficulty in naming it. In the normal condition in which visual stimuli enter both visual hemifields and objects are palpated with both hands, the impairment may not be noticeable. Other examples of disconnection syndromes are alexia without agraphia, sympathetic apraxia, and conduction aphasia (see earlier).

SUGGESTED READINGS

Bogousslavsky J, Cummings JL (eds): Behavior and Mood Disorders in Focal Brain Lesions. Cambridge, Cambridge University Press, 2000.

Cummings JL, Mega MS: Neuropsychiatry and Behavioral Neuroscience. New York, Oxford University Press, 2003.

Mesulam M-M: Principles of Behavioral and Cognitive Neurology, 2nd ed. New York, Oxford University Press, 2000.

Stuss DT, Knight RT (eds): Principles of Frontal Lobe Function. New York, Oxford University Press, 2002.

Four texts that cover this chapter in more detail.

433 ALZHEIMER'S DISEASE AND OTHER DISORDERS OF COGNITION

Jeffrey L. Cummings
Mario F. Mendez

AMNESIA

Definitions

Memory is the ability to store and recall new information. Amnesia is a disorder of memory and refers to difficulty learning new information. Most clinical disorders of amnesia are specifically concerned with disturbed recent memory, or the inability to store new information.

There are four different classifications of memory (Table 433–1): temporal, explicit versus implicit, mechanistic, and modality. The temporal classification, which is the most important, divides memory into short-term and long-term memory. Short-term memory involves holding information for a minute or less and is essentially synonymous with primary memory, immediate recall, and sustained attention. Long-term memory involves holding information for longer than a minute. Two types of long-term memory are distinguished: recent memory (secondary memory or new learning) and remote memory (tertiary memory or the retrieval of old established information).

Table 433–1 • TYPES OF MEMORY

TEMPORAL CLASSIFICATION
Short-term (primary or immediate) memory
    Working memory (manipulation of short-term memory)
Long-term memory
    Secondary or recent memory
    Tertiary or remote memory

EXPLICIT VERSUS IMPLICIT CLASSIFICATION
Explicit or declarative (factual) memory
    Episodic (unique characteristics)
    Semantic or generic (categorical membership)
Implicit memory
    Procedural
    Priming

MECHANISTIC CLASSIFICATION
Registration
Storage and encoding
Consolidation
Retrieval and recognition

MODALITY CLASSIFICATION
Verbal
Visual

Clinicians often mistakenly use the term *short-term memory* when they really mean *recent memory*.

Another increasingly relevant distinction is between explicit memory and implicit memory. *Explicit* memory is "declarative," factual, consciously recalled information that is either episodic (specific or unique event) or generic (category or class membership). Conversely, *implicit* memory is not consciously recalled and usually involves the acquisition of skills rather than facts. Clinical amnesic disorders involve primarily explicit information of the episodic type.

Memory requires many mechanisms. *Registration* refers to attending to information sufficiently to start memory storage. *Encoding,* or storage, refers to the actual process of creating memories. *Consolidation* refers to the time period necessary for information to be stored in long-term memory. *Retrieval* refers to the recollection of established information and is usually tested by a process of *recognition* (e.g., choosing from among multiple-choice alternatives). *Anterograde amnesia* refers to ongoing memory difficulty, whereas *retrograde amnesia* refers to loss of information stored before the brain insult. Retrograde amnesia ranges from seconds to months, most commonly occurs acutely after head injuries, and generally diminishes during the recovery period. Most amnesic disorders are primarily anterograde.

Finally, amnesia may predominantly affect one modality over another. For example, a patient may have *verbal amnesia* or *visual amnesia*.

Etiology and Epidemiology

Clinical amnesic disorders result from Alzheimer's disease and other dementias, anoxic or ischemic insults, hippocampal sclerosis, traumatic brain injury, posterior cerebral artery distribution strokes, herpes encephalitis, thalamic and hypothalamic tumors, paraneoplastic syndromes, Wernicke-Korsakoff syndrome, bitemporal surgery, and epileptic seizures (Table 433–2). Amnesia is often the initial symptom of a dementia syndrome characterized by multiple cognitive deficits. When amnesia occurs in the absence of other cognitive deficits, it is often due to focal lesions in limbic structures (e.g., hippocampus or specific nuclei of the hypothalamus or thalamus).

Pathophysiology

Amnesia implies injury to the limbic system in both hippocampi in the temporal lobes or in midline limbic structures such as the fornices, mamillary bodies, and mediodorsal nuclei of the thalamus. These structures process memory traces that are eventually stored diffusely throughout the cortical association areas. Clinical amnesia usually requires bilateral damage in temporolimbic structures. Greater injury to the left hemispheric limbic structures can result in predominant verbal amnesia, and greater injury to the right hemisphere limbic structures can result in predominant visual amnesia. The frontal-subcortical circuits play an additional role in the facilitation of retrieval of old information, and frontal-subcortical circuit disorders result in

Table 433–2 • CAUSES OF AMNESIA

Alzheimer's disease and other dementias
Mild cognitive impairment
Cerebrovascular
　Posterior cerebral artery and other strokes involving the hippocampi
　Infarction in the medial thalamic nuclei
　Ruptured anterior communicating artery aneurysms
Anoxic/ischemic encephalopathy or hypoglycemia
Hippocampal sclerosis
Head trauma
Encephalitides
　Herpes simplex and other infections
　Limbic and other paraneoplastic syndromes
Mass lesions involving the limbic system
Thiamine deficiency (Wernicke-Korsakoff syndrome)
Epileptic seizures
Electroconvulsive therapy
Temporal lobe surgery
Transient global amnesia
Psychogenic amnesia

a retrieval deficit syndrome characterized by poor recall but preserved recognition.

Clinical Manifestations

Evaluation of memory complaints depends on a focused examination of recent memory. This evaluation begins with an assessment of orientation, the ability of the patient to provide a history, and the patient's knowledge of current events. All of these tasks reflect the integrity of the patient's memory. A common way to assess verbal memory is a word list learning task. For the screening examination, a list of three or four words may suffice; however, for a more extended examination, a list of 10 or 16 words with multiple repetitions is preferable. In the three- to four-word tests, the examiner repeats the word list until patients are able to repeat the words on their own; subsequently, the examiner asks them to recall the words after a 5-minute delay. Normal individuals learn all the words. In the longer word list tests, the examiner reads a list and asks the patient immediately to recall as many words as possible from the list. The examiner repeats this process three to five times. After an interval of 15 or more minutes, during which time the patient's attention is diverted to other tasks, the examiner tests the patient's spontaneous recall of the words. Normal individuals learn most of the list after three or four repetitions and spontaneously recall two thirds or more of the words on delayed recall. The examiner then checks recognition memory and retrieval by giving categorical and multiple choice clues for the words that are not recalled. Normal patients recognize all of the words. The examiner screens visual memory by evaluating delayed recall of three or four figures previously drawn by the patient or three or four items previously hidden in the room. Finally, the examiner assesses remote memory by asking the patient to recall three or four past public events that have occurred during the individual's lifetime.

Diagnosis

"Memory loss" may result from deficits in attention or other cognitive processes rather than from amnesia. An initial step in the differential diagnosis of a memory complaint is to exclude the presence of delirium or an acute confusional state (Chapter 26). The normal functioning of memory presupposes normal arousal and attentional mechanisms. In general, patients with delirium have prominent fluctuations in attention, as well as perceptual and other abnormalities.

In addition to delirium, clinicians need to distinguish neurologically based amnesia from the syndrome of "psychogenic amnesia." Patients with conversion reactions and other psychological mechanisms (Chapter 426) can manifest a memory disorder characterized by loss of remote memories and loss of personal identity or personal information. In sharp contrast to true amnesia, patients with psychogenic amnesia have intact recent memory and can incorporate and learn new information.

There are two age-related and isolated memory disorders. The first is a mild memory loss related to the aging process itself. Normal aging is associated with retrieval difficulties for proper names and recent events in some individuals older than 50 years. Criteria for age-associated memory impairment include low memory test scores compared with young people, memory difficulty sufficient to impair daily functioning, an otherwise adequate intellectual background, and the absence of dementia or a causative medical or psychiatric condition. Age-associated memory impairment is not a true amnesia or precursor to dementia. The second age-related memory impairment is the entity of mild cognitive impairment. In contrast to age-associated memory impairment, mild cognitive impairment manifests low memory test scores compared with both young and older people of the same age, as well as the absence of other intellectual impairment or dementia. This condition is often a precursor to the development of dementia, particularly Alzheimer's disease.

The most common amnesic syndrome is dementia. Worldwide, at least 7% of persons older than 65 years and nearly half of those older than 85 years have some form of dementing illness, and about two thirds of these individuals have Alzheimer's disease. The presence of additional cognitive deficits such as aphasia, agnosia, or executive disturbances distinguishes amnesia in the context of dementia.

Neurology

Most focal amnesic syndromes involve lesions in the temporolimbic region. Focal strokes in the territory of the posterior cerebral arteries can affect hippocampal structures. Anoxia and ischemia are common causes of residual memory impairment, particularly after cardiopulmonary resuscitation. A related condition found in the elderly is hippocampal sclerosis, usually due to one or more prior hypoxic insults. Traumatic brain injury (Chapter 431) is another common cause of amnesia when temporolimbic structures are injured bilaterally. The extent of post-traumatic (anterograde) amnesia is a good gauge of the severity of the head injury. Post-traumatic amnesia of less than 1 hour usually indicates a mild head injury, and post-traumatic amnesia of more than 1 day indicates a severe head injury. Herpes simplex encephalitis, the most common sporadic form of infectious encephalitis (Chapter 451), commonly damages the hippocampus and causes amnesia. Finally, complex partial and generalized seizures (Chapter 434), as well as electroconvulsive therapy, can transiently disrupt hippocampal memory functions and cause amnesia.

Alcoholism with thiamine deficiency affects midline limbic structures and results in the Wernicke-Korsakoff syndrome (Chapter 458). In addition to severe anterograde amnesia, patients with this syndrome often have difficulty retrieving remote or old information from the last few years. Acutely, they can manifest confabulation, or a false "filling in" of memory gaps. The Wernicke's encephalopathy aspect includes acute delirium, oculomotor paresis, nystagmus, and ataxia. Rupture of an anterior communicating aneurysm can also cause amnesia owing to ischemia of midline limbic structures, especially the fornix.

Transient global amnesia is a short-term memory impairment of uncertain etiology. It occurs in older persons and is suspected to result from a transient ischemic attack or, less likely, from epileptiform activity. Transient global amnesia is characterized by initial delirium, disproportionate anterograde amnesia, and retrograde amnesia for the preceding few hours. It tends to persist for a few hours and then resolve without residual memory impairment.

Treatment and Prognosis

Recovery depends primarily on the cause of the memory difficulty. Patients with age-associated memory impairment can usually be reassured and taught simple memory aids and techniques such as writing things down and keeping a memory notebook. The memory of patients with depression often improves after the depression is treated. Some causes of amnesia, such as concussion or seizures, may resolve with recovery from the acute insult. Other patients, however, are left with at least some permanent impairment. In general, memory loss may be modestly improved with cognitive rehabilitation techniques. Medications and dietary substances historically have had little effect on improving memory. However, the introduction of acetylcholinesterase inhibitors can enhance memory function in patients with Alzheimer's disease (see later text).

APHASIA

Definitions

Language is the unique human ability to communicate through symbols, whether spoken or written language, braille, musical notation, or most forms of sign language. Language is distinct from speech, which is the verbal expression of language. Aphasia is the loss or impairment of language caused by brain dysfunction.

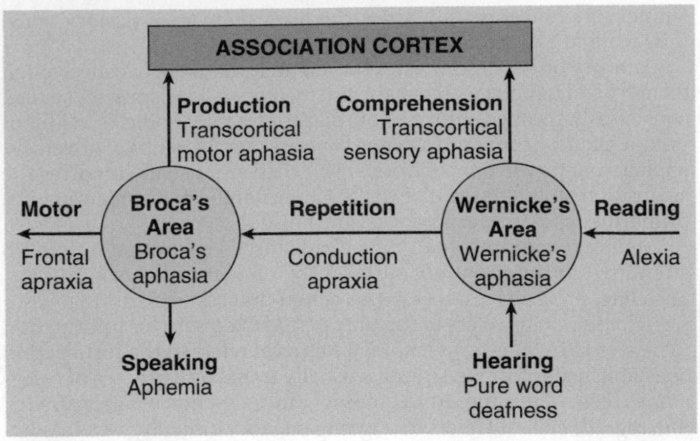

Clinical Manifestations

The language examination evaluates fluency, auditory comprehension, repetition, generation of word lists, and naming, reading, and writing. In addition, evaluation of prosody, the inflection and melodic quality of speech, is an important part of the language examination. The examination begins by listening to the patient's spontaneous discourse. The six elements of fluency are words per minute (in English, normal is 100 ± 50), phrase length (four or more words per phrase), effort in getting the words out, agrammatism or telegraphic output (absence of prepositions, conjunctions, and other "functor" words), dysprosody, and dysarthria. During the course of

ASSOCIATION CORTEX

Production
Transcortical motor aphasia

Comprehension
Transcortical sensory aphasia

Motor — **Broca's Area** Broca's aphasia — **Repetition** — **Wernicke's Area** Wernicke's aphasia — **Reading**

Frontal apraxia

Conduction apraxia

Alexia

Speaking Aphemia

Hearing Pure word deafness

FIGURE 433–1 • Wernicke-Geschwind model of language.

Etiology and Epidemiology

Aphasia is a common manifestation of brain disease. The aphasic syndromes disturb communication and can be severely disabling. The most common causes of focal aphasias are strokes. Nearly 500,000 strokes occur every year in the United States, and up to 40% of strokes are accompanied by aphasia. Two other common problems, intracranial neoplasm and traumatic brain injury, frequently produce language disturbances.

Neurodegenerative processes such as Alzheimer's disease also commonly produce aphasia as part of the multiple cognitive deficits that characterize the dementias. In Alzheimer's disease, patients usually progress from early word-finding difficulty to a transcortical sensory aphasia (described later). In vascular dementia, various aphasia syndromes occur, depending on the location of the stroke. Most other demented patients have decreased word lists and poor naming ability. Finally, primary progressive aphasia is a syndrome featuring an insidious decline in language, either dysfluency or a semantic anomia, that usually progresses to a full dementia syndrome. Most patients with primary progressive aphasia have a frontotemporal dementia such as Pick's disease, but about 20% have Alzheimer's disease or another disorder.

Pathophysiology

Aphasia can result from any lesion in the language areas of the brain. In about 95% of people, the principal language areas are located around the left sylvian fissure. Broca's area (Brodmann area 44) in the anterior sylvian region is involved in the production of language (Fig. 433–1). Wernicke's area (Brodmann area 22) in the posterior sylvian region is involved in the comprehension of language. In almost all right-handed persons, the left hemisphere is dominant for language. Broca's, Wernicke's, or conduction aphasia develops in such individuals from focal lesions in the left perisylvian region, whereas transcortical aphasias develop from lesions outside the left perisylvian region. Most left-handed and ambidextrous persons are also left hemisphere language dominant, although they usually have additional language representation in the right hemisphere. In genetic left-handed persons, lesions on either side can cause aphasia, although the disability tends to be less severe and to improve over time.

conversational speech, examiners should listen for the information content and the presence of paraphasic errors. Nonfluent aphasics may get their message across with a limited number of nouns or verbs. In contrast, fluent aphasics may produce long, effortless sentences devoid of meaning. Furthermore, fluent and conduction aphasics (on repetition) make paraphasic errors, such as word substitutions (verbal paraphasias), phonemic substitutions (literal paraphasias), and neologisms (new word formation). Finally, examiners should listen for prosody or the melodic, rhythmic, and inflectional elements that convey much of the emotional impact of speech.

The examination evaluates other elements of language in a systematic fashion. Tests of auditory comprehension include responses to simple commands, such as "Close your eyes" or "Touch your nose," followed by multiple-step commands, such as "Point to the floor and then point to the window." The examiner also asks yes or no questions, such as "Are you sitting down?" "Is a hammer good for cutting wood?" "Does May come before June?" "If the lion was killed by the tiger, which animal is dead?" The examiner can further evaluate the ability to comprehend relational phrases by placing several readily available items in front of the patient, such as keys, pens, and coins. The patient is asked to "touch the keys with the pen" or to "point to the pen after pointing to the coin." In evaluating auditory comprehension with pointing commands, it should be remembered that motor weakness or apraxia may interfere with pointing. A test of repetition involves asking the patient to repeat "No if's, and's, or but's" and other grammatically intricate sentences. For word fluency, the examiner should listen for word-finding pauses and ask the patient to generate a list of as many animals as possible (or other category of items) in a minute. Normal subjects can list 18 ± 6 animals per minute without cueing. To assess naming, the examiner presents at least six common items (e.g., watch, ring, button, collar, nose, chin) and six lower-frequency items (e.g., eyelashes, eyebrows, lapel, shoelaces, sole or heel of a shoe, watch band or crystal) and asks the patient to name each item.

The language examination also includes an assessment of reading, comprehension of reading material, and writing. The examiner asks the patient to read aloud and perform various written commands comparable to the verbal commands. The examiner further requests the patient to write one complete sentence with punctuation by dictation and to compose and write one sentence of their own. Writing is disturbed in most of the aphasia syndromes, and the errors in writing typically parallel the errors in spoken language.

APHASIC SYNDROMES

The different language disorders or aphasias have different patterns of impaired language skills as outlined in Table 433–3.

BROCA'S APHASIA. Nonfluent verbal output characterizes Broca's aphasia. Spontaneous speech is sparse, effortful, dysarthric, dysprosodic, short in phrase length, and agrammatic. Decreased fluency occurs in the presence of relatively preserved comprehension (relational words such as "above" and "behind," however, may be poorly understood), abnormal repetition and naming, a disturbance in reading (particularly for relational words such as conjunctions), and impaired writing. Most patients with Broca's aphasia have right-sided weakness varying from mild paresis to total hemiplegia, and some have sensory loss as well. The neuropathology involves the left hemisphere frontal operculum containing Broca's area. Broca's aphasia must be distinguished from aphemia, a disorder of verbal output with preserved written language.

WERNICKE'S APHASIA. Abnormal auditory comprehension characterizes Wernicke's aphasia. This disturbance in comprehension may range from a total inability to understand spoken language to a partial difficulty in decoding the spoken word. Wernicke's aphasia features a fluent verbal output with normal word count and phrase length; no abnormal effort, articulatory problems, or prosodic difficulties; and difficulty in repetition and word finding. The verbal output is often empty of content words and full of paraphasic substitutions and neologisms. Jargon aphasia refers to an extreme and unintelligible form of this type of output. Often no other neurologic defects are evident, but a superior quadrantanopia may be present. The

neuropathology involves the posterior superior temporal lobe of the left hemisphere. The disturbed auditory comprehension of Wernicke's aphasia helps distinguish it from the word salad of schizophrenia and the confused speech of delirium. Wernicke's aphasia must be distinguished from pure word deafness, a disorder of auditory input with preserved written language.

CONDUCTION APHASIA. Conduction aphasia features a prominent disturbance in repetition out of proportion to any other language disturbance. These patients have fluent verbal output and a preserved ability to comprehend. Paraphasias are common, particularly substitutions of phonemes, and naming is often limited by these paraphasic intrusions. Reading aloud is disturbed, but reading comprehension is normal. Most cases of conduction aphasia have neuropathology involving the arcuate fasciculus and other connections that run between Wernicke's area and Broca's area.

GLOBAL APHASIA. A severe language impairment in which all modalities—verbal fluency, comprehension, repetition, naming, reading, and writing—are impaired is known as global or total aphasia. Most patients have a right hemiparesis or hemiplegia, a right hemisensory deficit, and a right homonymous hemianopia. Global aphasia is usually caused by a complete middle cerebral artery territory infarction, although exceptions are noted, including cases of global aphasia without hemiparesis caused by multiple cerebral emboli to the left hemisphere.

TRANSCORTICAL APHASIAS. The major factor underlying these aphasias is relative preservation of the ability to repeat spoken language in the face of other language impairments. Transcortical motor aphasia resembles Broca's aphasia in its decreased verbal fluency but differs in the normal or nearly normal ability to repeat. Patients with this disorder struggle to utter words on spontaneous conversation but can easily say the same words on repetition. The neuropathology is most frequently located in the supplementary motor area of the left hemisphere or between that area and the frontal operculum. Transcortical sensory aphasia resembles Wernicke's aphasia in its fluent paraphasic output and decreased comprehension but differs in preservation of the ability to repeat. Patients with this disorder may echo or repeat everything that the examiner says. The most common site of neuropathology in transcortical sensory aphasia is the left posterior parietal region. Mixed transcortical (isolation) aphasia is a nonfluent aphasia with impaired comprehension and preserved repetition.

MISCELLANEOUS LANGUAGE-RELATED DISORDERS. Subcortical aphasias can be caused by infarcts in the left basal ganglia or the anterolateral nuclei of the thalamus. Basal ganglia aphasias most often show a combination of fluent, dysarthric speech accompanied by impaired auditory comprehension and a right hemiparesis. The thalamic aphasias resemble transcortical sensory aphasia. Anomia is a common residual deficit following improvement in other types of aphasia. Anomic patients have fluent verbal output and intact comprehension, but naming on confrontation is significantly disturbed. No specific causative location is known, although the neuropathology often involves the left hemisphere angular gyrus. Alexia, or reading impairment, most frequently occurs with the aphasias; however, isolated alexia with or without writing disturbances can result from lesions in the left visual occipital region or the left parietal lobe. Aprosody, or a disturbance in the affective intonation of communication, may result from right hemisphere lesions. Mutism accompanies a range of conditions from early nonfluent aphasias to focal lesions in the left supplementary motor area. Apraxia is common in aphasic patients, and acalculia commonly accompanies fluent aphasias.

℞ **Treatment and Prognosis**

In addition to management of the underlying illness, treatment of aphasic patients includes speech and language therapy. In addition to practice and rehearsal, special language therapies include facilitation techniques, such as melodic intonation therapy. Nonvocal techniques and communication aids can also be helpful, but drug treatments for language disturbances have had little success. In

general, the prognosis of an aphasic patient depends on the type and severity of impairment. Fluent aphasics respond better to rehabilitation than do nonfluent aphasics. Finally, the clinician needs to be aware of the potentially treatable psychiatric disturbances that can accompany the aphasias, such as depression in patients with Broca's aphasia and paranoia in patients with Wernicke's aphasia.

Table 433-3 • APHASIA SYNDROMES

SYNDROME	SPONTANEOUS SPEECH	REPETITION	COMPREHENSIVE	NAMING	READING
Broca's	Nonfluent	Poor	Good	Poor	Poor
Wernicke's	Fluent, paraphasic	Poor	Poor	Poor	Poor
Conduction	Fluent, paraphasic	Poor	Good	Variable	Good
Global	Nonfluent	Poor	Poor	Poor	Poor
Transcortical					
Motor	Nonfluent	Good	Good	Poor	Good
Sensory	Fluent	Good	Poor	Poor	Poor
Mixed	Nonfluent	Good	Poor	Poor	Poor
Anomic	Fluent	Good	Good	Poor	Variable
Subcortical					
Anterior	Nonfluent, paraphasic	Good	Good	Poor	Poor
Posterior	Fluent, paraphasic	Good	Poor	Poor	Poor

DEMENTIA

Dementia is an acquired, sustained impairment in intellectual function with compromise in at least three of the following spheres of mental activity: (1) memory, (2) language, (3) visuospatial skills, (4) personality, and (5) other instrumental cognitive abilities (abstraction, calculation, judgment). Dementia is acquired and distinct from lifelong intellectual impairment or mental retardation. Dementia is also sustained and distinct from delirium or acute confusional states (Chapter 26).

CLINICAL EVALUATION

HISTORY. The evaluation of dementia starts with a detailed history from the patient and from family members or caregivers. Forgetfulness or memory difficulty is the most common complaint and may have many causes, including depression, fatigue, mild or undetected delirium, or primary amnesic disorders. Patients may also have early word-finding difficulty or visuospatial problems. Other historical information relevant in the evaluation of dementia includes performance of activities of daily living such as the patient's ability to dress, groom, do household duties, and drive without accidents or getting lost. The history includes behavioral disturbances such as apathy, hallucinations, delusions, sleep disorders, depression, agitation, or anxiety. Finally, the initial assessment takes into account the baseline intellectual and education level of the patient and past neurologic and psychiatric disturbances.

MENTAL STATUS EXAMINATION. The mental status examination begins with observation of the patient's appearance and behavior during the evaluation. Is the patient awake, attentive, and cooperative? Is the patient's speech fluent? Are any word-finding difficulties or paraphasic errors present? Is the patient properly dressed and groomed and socially appropriate?

The diagnosis of dementia depends on documentation of cognitive deficits by mental status testing, mental status scales, or neuropsychological tests. Bedside mental status testing includes brief assessments of memory and language as well as visuospatial constructions such as copying a cube or the face of a clock. The most commonly used mental status scale is the Mini-Mental Status Examination (Table 433-4). This test requires administration in a standardized fashion and can be insensitive to changes in the most mildly and most severely affected patients. Other scales such as the Geriatric Depression Scale, Katz's Scale for Activities of Daily Living, and the Neuropsychiatric Inventory are helpful for assessing activities of daily living and behavioral changes (Chapters 25 and 26). In patients who score in the normal range on the Mini-Mental Status Examination but historically complain of intellectual deficits as well as in diagnostically challenging cases, a formal neuropsychological evaluation conducted by a neuropsychologist provides more detailed information regarding the patient's cognitive ability. The results of neuropsychological testing may be compared with standardized scores of patients matched for age and level of education. Neuropsychological testing is rigorous and requires a cooperative, awake patient who can engage in paper and pencil tests for several hours. Patients with low education, aphasia, a primary language other than English, or moderately advanced dementias do not benefit from standard neuropsychological testing.

Table 433-4 • THE MINI-MENTAL STATUS EXAMINATION

	SCORE
Orientation: What is the month, day, date, year, season? Where are you, what floor, city, county, and state? (Score 1 point for each item correct.)	10
Registration: State three items (ball, flag, tree). (Score 1 point for each item that the patient registers **without** you having to repeat the words. You may repeat the words until the patient is able to register the words but do not give him/her credit. You must also tell the patient that he/she should memorize those words and that you will ask him/her to recall those words later).	3
Attention: Can you spell the word WORLD forward, then backward? Can you subtract 7 from 100, and keep subtracting 7? (100-93-86-79-72). (Do both items but give credit for best of the two performances.)	5
Memory: Can you remember those three words I asked you to memorize? (Do not give clues or multiple choice.)	3
Languages:	
Naming: Can you name (show) a pen and a watch?	2
Repetition: Can you repeat "No if's, and's, or but's"?	1
Comprehension: Can you take this piece of paper in your right hand, fold it in half, then put it on the floor? (Score 1 point for each item done correctly.)	3
Reading: Read and obey, "CLOSE YOUR EYES."	1
Writing: Can you write a sentence?	1
Visuospatial: Have patient copy intersecting pentagons.	1
TOTAL	30

PHYSICAL EXAMINATION. The examination includes a complete neurologic examination as well as a general physical examination. Patients with Alzheimer's disease rarely exhibit focal neurologic deficits, and the presence of focal neurologic deficits raises the possibility of non-Alzheimer dementias. Rigidity and other extrapyramidal signs suggest a dementia related to vascular dementia, Parkinson's disease, dementia with Lewy bodies, or other disorders. For example, dementia with gait abnormalities occurs with normal-pressure hydrocephalus, Parkinson's disease, vascular dementia, or progressive supranuclear palsy.

LABORATORY TESTS. Laboratory studies should include a complete blood count, electrolytes and other chemistries, a vitamin B_{12} level, and a thyroid-stimulating hormone level. An apolipoprotein E-4 (APOE4) genotype increases the likelihood of Alzheimer's disease, but this test is not definitive and is not indicated as a routine study. The evaluation of cerebrospinal fluid (CSF) by lumbar puncture is indicated if the serum serology is positive for syphilis or in cases of suspected central nervous system infections or demyelination. The diagnosis of Creutzfeldt-Jakob disease may be supported by the CSF presence of the 14-3-3 protein. CSF assays for β-amyloid and tau protein support the diagnosis of Alzheimer's disease but are not routinely indicated.

Neuroimaging is important in the evaluation of patients with dementia (Chapter 424). Magnetic resonance imaging (MRI) or computed tomography of the brain is useful in diagnosing cerebrovascular disease, subdural hematomas, tumors, normal pressure

WRITING	HEMIPARESIS	HEMISENSORY DEFECT	VISUAL FIELD DEFECT	NEUROPATHOLOGY IN LEFT HEMISPHERE
Poor	Common	Rare	Rare	Posterior inferior frontal lobe
Poor	Rare	Variable	Variable	Posterior superior temporal lobe
Variable	Rare	Variable	Rare	Arcuate fasciculus region
Poor	Common	Common	Common	Combinations of the above three
Poor	Common	Rare	Rare	Frontal, beyond Broca's area
Poor	Rare	Common	Common	Parietal-temporal junction
Poor	Common	Common	Common	Combination of the above two
Variable	Variable	Variable	Rare	Multiple sites
Poor	Common	Rare	Rare	Putamen, globus pallidus
Poor	Rare	Common	Variable	Thalamus

hydrocephalus, and other non-Alzheimer causes of dementia. High-resolution MRI studies reveal early focal atrophy of the entorhinal cortex and hippocampus in Alzheimer's disease, and these findings can support this clinical diagnosis. Functional neuroimaging with positron-emission tomography or single-photon emission computed tomography usually reveals temporoparietal changes in Alzheimer's disease (Fig. 433–2). Finally, electroencephalograms (Chapter 423) are helpful in patients with suspected Creutzfeldt-Jakob dementia, in which periodic polyspike and wave abnormalities may be present.

DIFFERENTIAL DIAGNOSIS

Although a definite diagnosis of Alzheimer's disease requires tissue examination at autopsy or biopsy, the diagnosis can be made with high accuracy by applying specific clinical criteria (Table 433–5). The introduction of acetylcholinesterase inhibitors, which can be expected to be effective only in the dementias with a deficit in cholinergic function, such as that found in Alzheimer's disease, has increased the need for accurate diagnosis.

A variety of degenerative, metabolic, vascular, and traumatic conditions can cause dementia (Table 433–6). Most cases of medication-induced brain dysfunction are manifested as delirium; however, in a frail, elderly patient, inappropriate use of medications may cause dementia. Common offending medications include benzodiazepines, tricyclic antidepressants, conventional antipsychotics, monoamine oxidase inhibitors, barbiturates, cough suppressants, digitalis, and anticholinergics. The degenerative diseases other than Alzheimer's disease that cause dementia can often be distinguished by clinical criteria (Table 433–7).

The term *pseudodementia* refers to dementia associated with a psychiatric illness (Chapter 426). Most commonly, the term refers to

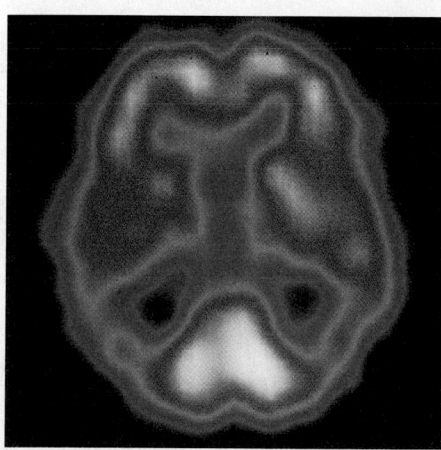

FIGURE 433–2 • Single-photon emission computed tomography (SPECT) scan in Alzheimer's disease. There is a marked symmetrical reduction in perfusion to both post-temporoparietal areas. (From Forbes CD, Jackson WD: Color Atlas and Text of Clinical Medicine, 3rd ed. London, Mosby, 2003, with permission.)

Table 433–5 • NINCDS-ADRDA CRITERIA FOR ALZHEIMER'S DISEASE

Definite Alzheimer's disease
Clinical criteria for probable Alzheimer's disease (see below)
Histopathologic evidence of Alzheimer's disease (autopsy or biopsy)
Probable Alzheimer's disease
Dementia established by clinical examination (mental status testing) and documented by mental status scales (confirmed by neuropsychological testing)
Deficits in two or more cognitive domains
Progressive deterioration of memory and other cognitive domains
No disturbance of consciousness or delirium (the presence of a "clear sensorium")
Onset between ages 40 and 90 (most older than 65 years of age)
Absence of systemic or other brain diseases capable of producing dementia (negative evaluation for other causes)
Possible Alzheimer's disease
Atypical onset, presentation, or progression of a dementia without known etiology
Presence of a systemic or other brain disease capable of producing dementia but not thought to be the cause of the dementia
Progressive deterioration of a single cognitive domain in the absence of any other cause
Unlikely Alzheimer's disease
Sudden onset
Focal neurologic signs
Seizures or gait disturbance early in the course of the illness

Modified from McKhann G, Drachman D, Folstein M, et al: Clinical diagnosis of Alzheimer's disease: Report of the NINCDS-ADRDA Work Group under the auspices of Department of Health and Human Services Task Force on Alzheimer's Disease. Neurology 1984;34:939–944.

---

depressed patients whose cognitive impairment improves with resolution of their mood disorder. Pseudodementia patients may have cognitive deficits including poor attention and concentration and impaired memory, but in most cases, the cognitive deficits are mild in comparison to the depression. The dementia associated with depression usually includes psychomotor slowing, problems with memory retrieval, and decreased executive functions rather than aphasia, apraxia, or agnosia.

ALZHEIMER'S DISEASE

In 1907, Alois Alzheimer described the brain of a 56-year-old woman with dementia. Five years before her death, she had rapidly progressive memory loss, became lost in her neighborhood and eventually in her own apartment, and had delusions about being killed. By the time the patient was institutionalized, she was disoriented, had difficulty with language (reading, writing, and naming), and could not learn new material. Despite severe cognitive deficits, the neurologic examination was otherwise normal. Her autopsy revealed an atrophic brain without gross abnormalities. Sections stained with Bielschowsky silver stain showed neuronal changes that have come to be known as *neurofibrillary tangles*. Alzheimer also demonstrated numerous "miliary foci," which are called *senile* or *neuritic plaques*. Alzheimer emphasized the presenile nature of the dementia.

Table 433–6 • MAJOR CAUSES OF DEMENTIA

Degenerative disorders
  Alzheimer's disease
  Frontotemporal dementia
  Dementia with Lewy bodies
  Corticobasal ganglionic
    degeneration
  Parkinson's disease
  Huntington's disease
  Progressive supranuclear palsy
Conditions associated with anoxia
  Cardiac disease
  Pulmonary insufficiency
  Postanoxia dementia
Chronic renal failure
  Uremic encephalopathy
  Dialysis dementia
Hepatic diseases
  Portal-systemic encephalopathy
Electrolyte abnormalities
  Hypernatremia
  Hyponatremia
  Hypercalcemia
Vascular dementia
Head trauma
  Dementia pugilistica
  Multiple contusions
  Subdural hematoma
Myelin disorders
  Multiple sclerosis
  Adult-onset leukodystrophies

CNS infections
  Prion diseases (Creutzfeldt-
    Jakob, Gertsmann-
    Sträussler-Scheinker
    fatal familial insomnia)
  Encephalitis/chronic meningitis
  AIDS and AIDS-related infections
  Neurosyphilis
CNS tumors
  Cerebral effects of systemic
    malignancies
Hydrocephalus
Vitamin deficiency states
  Thiamine (B_1)
  Cyanocobalamin (B_{12})
Endocrinopathies
  Thyroid disturbances
  Adrenal disease
Intoxication/toxicity
  Medications
  Alcohol
  Other toxins
Inflammatory disorders

AIDS = acquired immunodeficiency syndrome; CNS = central nervous system.

Table 433–8 • GENETICS AND DEMENTIA

DISEASE	CHROMOSOME
Familial Alzheimer's disease	1, 14, 21
Risk for sporadic Alzheimer's disease	19, 10, 12
Frontotemporal dementia	17
Huntington's disease	4

Alzheimer's disease is the third most common terminal illness, after heart disease and cancer. In the United States alone, approximately 4 million individuals have Alzheimer's disease.

Genetics

The first-degree relatives of affected individuals have an increased risk of Alzheimer's disease. Three genes are directly linked with Alzheimer's disease (Table 433–8). Chromosome 21 carries the gene for amyloid precursor protein, the precursor of β-amyloid; this finding is consistent with the Alzheimer-like pathology on autopsy in a high proportion of adults with Down syndrome (trisomy 21). Another gene associated with early-onset Alzheimer's disease, presenilin 1 (PS1), is on chromosome 14. Autosomal dominant early-onset Alzheimer's disease is also linked to presenilin 2 (PS2) on chromosome 1. Patients with PS1 mutations have a characteristic early age of onset, between 35 and 60 years old of age, whereas PS2 mutations are found almost exclusively in families of Volga-German heritage. Together, these three mutations account for fewer than 2% of cases of Alzheimer's disease.

Although they are not directly linked to the disorder, several other genes increase the susceptibility to Alzheimer's disease. The most important is the gene for ApoE, a plasma protein involved in cholesterol and triglyceride transport and, probably, in repair of nervous tissue after injury. The ApoE gene is located on chromosome 19, and there are three common alleles, E2, E3, and E4. The E4 allele increases the risk for Alzheimer's disease, with the attributable risk estimated to be 45 to 60%. E4 homozygotes are at greater risk than E4 heterozygotes. ApoE4 is present in plaques and may facilitate the accumulation of amyloid in the brain. In addition, chromosomes 10 and 12 may harbor other polymorphisms that increase susceptibility to late-onset Alzheimer's disease.

Subsequently, the term *Alzheimer's disease* was applied to both senile and presenile forms of the disease.

Epidemiology

With the increasing age of the population, Alzheimer's disease has become the most common dementia, with nearly 10% of the population older than 65 years being affected. In developed nations,

Table 433–7 • DISTINGUISHING FEATURES OF COMMON PROGRESSIVE DEMENTIAS

DISEASE	SYMPTOMS/SIGNS	AGE AFFECTED	DURATION OF ILLNESS	NEUROLOGIC SIGNS
Alzheimer's disease	Amnestic memory loss early Getting lost Lack of awareness of one's illness Sleep-wake cycle disturbance Apathy	Greater than 65 yr	Years, up to a decade	Normal until advanced stage
Familial Alzheimer's disease	Same as Alzheimer's disease	From the 30s	Years	Normal until advanced stage
Frontotemporal dementia	Personality change Disinhibition Obsessions and compulsions "Alien stare" Amnestic memory loss later Visuospatial intact	45–65 yr	Years	Normal until advanced stage
Lewy body dementia	Early falls Visual hallucinations Neuroleptic sensitivity Fluctuating course	Greater than 50 yr	Months to years	Early extrapyramidal signs With rigidity greater than tremor
Corticobasal ganglionic degeneration	Limb apraxia "Alien hand" Visuospatial deficits	Greater than 60 yr	Years	Apraxia Rigidity Myoclonus
Vascular dementia	Retrieval memory loss Depression Slowness Stepwise progression	Greater than 65 yr	Years	Focal neurologic deficits Rigidity and cogwheeling Gait abnormality
Normal pressure hydrocephalus	Retrieval memory loss Urinary incontinence Progressive gait difficulty Slowness Visuospatial infarct	Any age	Months	Gait abnormality Hyper-reflexia (legs > arms) Babinski's signs

Clinical Manifestations

The symptoms of Alzheimer's disease include early memory difficulty, word-finding problems, and visuospatial disturbances. The memory problems involve difficulty learning new material and impaired recent memory. These patients develop word-finding pauses with decreased verbal fluency and have declines on visuospatial tasks such as drawing and driving. Spatial and temporal disorientation may result in getting lost in familiar surroundings. As the disease progresses, patients with Alzheimer's disease may develop aphasia, apraxia, agnosias, and behavioral disturbances such as apathy or paranoia. Patients often have delusions of theft and spousal infidelity. Sleep-wake cycle abnormalities may become evident; for example, a patient may be awake at night but think that it is daytime. Activities of daily living decline throughout the illness. Patients lose the ability to eat and groom themselves and have difficulty dressing. In the terminal stages of the disease, patients exhibit cognitive decline in virtually all intellectual spheres, motor abnormalities become evident, and both urinary and fecal incontinence develops.

Diagnosis

In a patient with clinical findings suggesting Alzheimer's disease, the first step is to exclude other causes of dementia by the history, examination, and laboratory studies described earlier. The second step is to apply specific diagnostic criteria. CSF evaluation for amyloid protein and tau protein can increase the likelihood of a diagnosis of Alzheimer's disease, but they are not sufficiently specific to be of routine value in screening or early diagnosis.

Rx Treatment

The treatment of Alzheimer's disease includes pharmacologic interventions targeting the specific pathophysiology of Alzheimer's disease (Table 433–9), pharmacologic agents that ameliorate specific symptoms such as delusions and sleep abnormalities, and behavioral interventions, which may improve specific symptoms and improve the patient's activities of daily living.

Acetylcholinesterase inhibitors increase the acetylcholine levels found to be decreased in the brains of patients with Alzheimer's disease. Tacrine, donepezil, rivastigmine, galantamine, and memantine are efficacious not only in improving cognition, but they also improve activities of daily living, apathy, and other neuropsychiatric symptoms. Donepezil is often chosen because it has the advantage of once daily dosing. Tacrine is rarely used because of its hepatic toxicity; the other three drugs have less serious side effects: nausea, vomiting, diarrhea, and muscle cramps. Acetylcholinesterase inhibitors should be used only in patients who have dementias with cholinergic deficits such as Alzheimer's disease, dementia with Lewy bodies, and Parkinson's disease. In general, they should be used early in the course of Alzheimer's disease. Vitamin E at high doses (2000 IU) may slow the progression of Alzheimer's disease. Neither estrogen nor nonsteroidal anti-inflammatory agents have shown benefit in randomized trials. Some studies support a modest effect of ginkgo biloba, possibly on the basis of its antioxidant properties.

Pharmacologic agents that target specific problem behaviors are useful in managing patients with Alzheimer's disease. If the patient's delusions are severe and problematic for both the patient and caregiver, risperidone, olanzapine, or quetiapine may be helpful and have fewer side effects than older agents such as haloperidol. If the patient's primary problem is agitation, agents such as trazodone, divalproex, or carbamazepine may also be helpful. Psychotropic agents such as tricyclics with anticholinergic effects are contraindicated, and anticholinergic agents generally should not be used in any individual with dementia because these drugs may worsen cognition.

Education and counseling for caregivers facilitates the care of these patients. As the disease progresses, patients with Alzheimer's disease lose insight into their disease and may show apathy and indifference while caregivers may become progressively distressed. Ancillary help is imperative as the caregiver's burden increases. The local chapter of the Alzheimer's Association and local Alzheimer's disease centers provide important resources, particularly in devising strategies to return Alzheimer disease patients who wander from their homes. Additional resources include occupational therapists to evaluate the home for safety and to provide recommendations for activities of daily living, and social workers to facilitate in the effective use of community resources.

Table 433–9 • RECOMMENDED SPECIFIC PHARMACOLOGIC TREATMENTS FOR DEMENTIA

ALZHEIMER'S DISEASE
1. Cholinesterase inhibitor
   Donepezil (Aricept)
      Available in 5- and 10-mg tablets, start at 5 mg, then increase to 10 mg/day after 1 month
         OR
   Rivastigmine (Exelon)
      Available in 1.5-, 3-, and 6-mg tablets, start at 1.5 mg bid, then increase every 2 weeks to 3 mg bid, 4.5 mg bid, to maximum of 6 mg bid as tolerated
         OR
   Galantamine (Reminyl)
      Available in 4-, 8-, and 12-mg tablets, start at 4-mg bid, then increase every 4 weeks to maximum of either 8 mg bid or 12 mg bid
2. Vitamin E
      Available in 400- and 1000-IU capsules, recommended dose, total of 2000 IU/day

DEMENTIA WITH LEWY BODIES
Cholinesterase inhibitors (same as Alzheimer's disease)

VASCULAR DEMENTIA
Aspirin 325 mg/day PO or aspirin 2.5 mg/dipyridamole extended release 200 mg bid
OR
Clopidogrel (75 mg/day)
Cholinesterase inhibitors (same as Alzheimer's disease)

PARKINSON'S DISEASE WITH DEMENTIA
Cholinesterase inhibitors (same as Alzheimer's disease)

VASCULAR DEMENTIA

Vascular disease is the second most common dementing process. Vascular dementia may result from multiple infarcts ("multi-infarct dementia"), strategically placed single infarcts, small vessel disease with subcortical ischemia, hypoperfusion, amyloid angiopathy, brain hemorrhage, and some inherited disorders of blood vessels.

Clinical Manifestations

The clinical features of vascular dementia vary greatly, but a few generalizations can be made. When compared with Alzheimer's disease, vascular dementia tends to have an earlier age of onset, affect more men than women, and have a shorter duration of survival after onset. Patients with vascular dementia often have risk factors such as hypertension, diabetes, hyperlipidemia, and cigarette smoking. The cognitive dysfunction can develop abruptly, and patients may experience stepwise deterioration or have a history of transient neurologic symptoms or ischemic attacks. There may be focal signs on neurologic examination, most commonly limb rigidity, spasticity, hyperreflexia, extensor plantar responses, and gait disturbance. Features of pseudobulbar palsy, including emotional lability, dysarthria, and dysphagia, are often present. On neuropsychological assessment, patients often show deficits in frontal executive tasks, orientation, and memory. The memory disturbance is usually of the retrieval type; patients are able to register information but have difficulty spontaneously recalling it. Categorical clues or multiple choices help patients retrieve stored material. Neuropsychiatrically, patients show evidence of depression, psychosis, and personality changes.

Neurology

Diagnosis

The diagnosis of vascular dementia is facilitated by neuro-imaging demonstrating moderate to severe ischemic white matter changes, focal infarctions in strategic locations, or both. Criteria for the diagnosis of vascular dementia include (1) the presence of dementia, (2) the presence of cerebrovascular disease by both examination and neuroimaging, and (3) a probable relationship between the first two. This relationship can be either a coincident occurrence with a stroke, a stepwise deterioration, or a sudden, abrupt decline in cognition.

 Treatment

Patients with vascular dementia should be treated with anti-hypertensive agents, smoking cessation, and anticoagulants such as aspirin, with or without dipyridamole, or clopidogrel to prevent future strokes. Warfarin (Coumadin) is used only in those specific limited circumstances in which controlled trials have demonstrated its effectiveness in preventing embolic brain infarction. Acetylcholinesterase inhibitors are used with vascular dementia and mixed vascular disease–Alzheimer's disease.

DEMENTIA WITH LEWY BODIES

Five years after Alzheimer described the pathologic hallmarks of the disease that has come to bear his name, another German neuropathologist, Friedrich Lewy, observed eosinophilic inclusions, which have been named *Lewy bodies*, in subcortical neurons of patients with Parkinson's disease. Dementia with Lewy bodies accounts for 15 to 25% of all degenerative dementias; it shares clinical and pathologic features with Alzheimer's disease and is regarded by some as an Alzheimer disease variant.

Clinical Manifestations

The clinical features of dementia with Lewy bodies include the presence of dementia and at least two of the following: fluctuations in cognition, visual hallucinations, and parkinsonian motor signs. These patients often have slowed cognition and impaired attention. Dementia with Lewy bodies may be otherwise similar to the dementia of Alzheimer's disease, with memory loss, language deficits, visuospatial disturbance, and executive impairment (poor planning, impaired set shifting, disturbed sequencing). The visual hallucinations of dementia with Lewy bodies are usually well formed and most commonly involve animals or "small people." Parkinsonian motor features are present in about 80% of patients with Lewy body dementia, and unlike Parkinson's disease, these signs typically respond poorly to levodopa therapy. Other symptoms that may support the diagnosis of dementia with Lewy bodies include multiple falls, delusions and nonvisual hallucinations, and neuroleptic sensitivity.

The key pathologic feature is the presence of cortical Lewy bodies, most commonly located in the neocortical (frontal and temporal) and paralimbic (insula and anterior cingulate) regions. These patients usually have amyloid neuritic plaques similar to Alzheimer's disease. Neurotransmitter deficits in patients with dementia and Lewy bodies involve the cholinergic and the dopaminergic systems. The cholinergic deficit appears more severe than that of Alzheimer's disease, and this deficit, combined with relative preservation of the serotonergic system, may account for the propensity of these patients to have visual hallucinations.

 Treatment

There is a marked cholinergic deficit, and acetylcholinesterase inhibitors may be beneficial. Patients are very sensitive to neuroleptic medications, and acetylcholinesterase inhibitors may serve as first-line therapy for the neuropsychiatric as well as the cognitive symptoms of dementia with Lewy bodies.

FRONTOTEMPORAL DEMENTIA

In 1906, Arnold Pick identified a progressive behavioral disorder in association with bilateral frontal lobe atrophy. Postmortem correlations revealed focal atrophy of the frontal and anterior temporal lobes with intraneuronal inclusions (Pick bodies), and the disease became known as *Pick's disease*. In the early 1990s, investigators reported longitudinal studies of patients whose clinical characteristics were suggestive of frontal lobe dysfunction. Some of these patients had the pathognomonic Pick bodies, but most had nonspecific lobar atrophy with microvacuolar changes. The term *frontotemporal dementia* describes patients who have Pick's disease with Pick bodies, or frontotemporal atrophy without Pick bodies, and frontotemporal atrophy with motor neuron disease.

Epidemiology

Frontotemporal dementia may account for as many as 20% of patients with presenile dementia secondary to primary cerebral degeneration. Clinicians probably under-recognize or misdiagnose patients with this syndrome. Personality changes and behavioral problems are the early cardinal features of the disease, and many patients are not evaluated for dementia in the initial phases of the illness.

Genetics

A family history of dementia is present in almost 50% of cases of frontotemporal dementia; however, only a small percentage has been linked to a specific genetic abnormality. Analysis of the mutation responsible for some families with frontotemporal dementia with parkinsonism has linked the disease to chromosome 17 and localized it to the tau protein gene.

Clinical Manifestations

The onset of frontotemporal dementia is insidious and may manifest as subtle personality and behavioral changes. The pathologic process in the frontal and temporal lobes results in altered social and personal behavior with disengagement, disinhibition, social impropriety, and decreased personal hygiene. Patients become apathetic and lack initiative, judgment, and foresight; they neglect their personal responsibilities to the point of mismanagement of their personal and professional affairs. Patients may make inappropriate remarks in public, have a decreased verbal output, and demonstrate compulsive and repetitive behavior. Hyperorality and selective food fads may develop. Memory, language, and visuospatial skills are preserved early in the illness, but the disease process may involve the posterior aspects of the brain and cause parietal lobe dysfunction.

 Treatment

Cholinesterase inhibitors are not useful in frontotemporal dementia. Psychoactive medications, including serotonergic agents such as sertraline or paroxetine, may help control some of the disturbed behavior.

PARKINSON'S DISEASE

Parkinson's disease is a degenerative disorder with loss of substantia nigra neurons, producing a movement disorder manifested by tremor at rest, limb rigidity, masked facies, and disturbances of gait, posture, and equilibrium (Chapter 443). The reported prevalence of dementia in patients with Parkinson's disease ranges from 35 to 55%. The principal features include slowing of cognition, failure to initiate activities spontaneously, poor word list generation, a retrieval deficit–type memory disturbance, and executive dysfunction.

The pharmacologic therapies for the treatment of Parkinson's disease improve the motor symptoms but afford little or no cognitive benefit. Most patients with clinically evident dementia have cholinergic deficits, and cholinesterase inhibitors may be useful.

HUNTINGTON'S DISEASE

Huntington's disease (Chapter 445) is a familial disorder characterized by chorea, dementia, and personality changes. The dementia is similar to that of other subcortical dementias and includes a retrieval memory deficit, slowing of cognition, and decreased verbal fluency. As the disease progresses, other areas of cognition decline, including concentration, judgment, executive skills, and visuospatial abilities. Psychoactive medications may ameliorate behavioral symptoms.

PROGRESSIVE SUPRANUCLEAR PALSY

In 1963, Steele, Richardson, and Olszewski described several patients with supranuclear gaze paresis, pseudobulbar palsy, axial rigidity, and dementia. This syndrome of progressive supranuclear palsy begins in the sixth or seventh decade of life, is more common in males than in females, and has a prevalence rate of approximately 1.4/100,000.

Patients with progressive supranuclear palsy have early postural instability and are subject to falls and gait abnormalities. Paresis of vertical gaze, especially downgaze, is a common early sign, which, along with axial rigidity with backward neck flexion, contributes to the tendency to fall. Dysarthria and hypophonia may develop and eventually lead to mutism. Pseudobulbar palsy is manifested by a masklike facies, exaggerated palatal and gag reflexes, drooling, and dysphagia. The neuropsychological profile includes slowness of thought processes, apathy, and personality changes. The cognitive decline tends to be mild until late in the disease, when patients develop further slowness, apathy, depression, forgetfulness, and an impaired ability to manipulate acquired knowledge. There is no effective treatment, but some patients have a modest response to antiparkinsonian medications.

CORTICOBASAL GANGLIONIC DEGENERATION

Corticobasal ganglionic degeneration is a rare degenerative disorder characterized by asymmetrical parkinsonian rigidity, focal dystonias or posturing, myoclonic jerks, cortical sensory loss, severe apraxia, and the "alien hand" phenomenon (actions of the hand not consciously directed by the patient). Prominent visuospatial deficits, marked inability to perform learned motor movements, and posturing or levitation of one arm help distinguish this disorder from the other dementias. Pathologically, the condition is characterized by asymmetrical hemispheric atrophy of frontal and parietal cortex. In contrast to Alzheimer's disease, the temporal and hippocampal regions are spared. There is no specific treatment.

1. Feldman H, Gauthier S, Hecker T, et al: A 24-week, randomized, double-blind study of donepezil in moderate to severe Alzheimer's disease. Neurology 2001;57:613–620.
2. Corey-Bloom J, Anand R, Veach J, ENA 713 B352 Study Group: A randomized trial evaluating the efficacy and safety of ENA 713 (rivastigmine tartrate), a new acetylcholinesterase inhibitor, in patients with mild to moderately severe Alzheimer's disease. Int J Geriatric Psychopharm 1998;1:55–65.
3. Tariot PN, Solomon PR, Morris JC, et al: A 5-month, randomized, placebo-controlled trial of galantamine in AD. Neurology 2000;54:2269–2276.
4. Reisberg B, Doody R, Stoffler A, et al: Memantine in moderate-to-severe Alzheimer's disease. N Engl J Med 2003;348:1333–1341.

SUGGESTED READINGS

Clark CM, Karlawish JH: Alzheimer disease: Current concepts and emerging diagnostic and therapeutic strategies. Ann Intern Med 2003;138:400–410. *A practical overview.*

Hardy J, Selkoe DJ: The amyloid hypothesis of Alzheimer's disease: Progress and problems on the road to therapeutics. Science 2002;297:353–356. *Review of the pathophysiology of Alzheimer's disease.*

National Institute on Aging, National Institutes of Health: Progress Report on Alzheimer's Disease: Taking the Next Steps. Silver Spring, MD, Alzheimer's Disease Education and Referral Center 2001. *Update on diagnosis and therapy.*

Nussbaum RL, Ellis CE: Alzheimer's disease and Parkinson's disease. N Engl J Med 2003;348:1356–1364. *A practical update on the genetics of these two syndromes.*

Petersen RC, Doody R, Kurz A, et al: Current concepts in mild cognitive impairment. Arch Neurol 2001;58:1985–1992. *A comprehensive review of mild cognitive impairment.*

Ritchie K, Lovestone S: The dementias. Lancet 2002;360:1759–1766. *A review of epidemiology, molecular biology, and treatment.*

Vermeer SE, Prins ND, den Heijer T, et al: Silent brain infarcts and the risk of dementia and cognitive decline. N Engl J Med 2003;348:1215–1222. *Elderly people with silent brain infarcts have an increased risk of dementia and a steeper deline in cognitive function.*

434 THE EPILEPSIES

Timothy A. Pedley

Definition

Epilepsy is a term applied to a group of chronic conditions whose major clinical manifestation is the occurrence of *epileptic seizures*—sudden, usually unprovoked attacks of subjective experiential phenomena, altered awareness, involuntary movements, or convulsions. Although a diagnosis of epilepsy requires the presence of seizures, not all seizures imply epilepsy. Seizures are a relatively common symptom of brain dysfunction, and they may occur in many acute medical or neurologic illnesses in which brain function is temporarily deranged (*acute symptomatic seizures*) (Table 434–1). These seizures are most often self-limited and do not persist after the underlying disorder has resolved. Seizures also can occur as a reaction of the brain to physiologic stress, sleep deprivation, fever, and alcohol or sedative drug withdrawal. Occurrence of seizures in these everyday settings is exceptional and implies an increased seizure susceptibility (lowered seizure threshold). Finally, isolated seizures also occur sometimes for no discernible reason as unprovoked events in presumably healthy people. None of these kinds of seizures represents epilepsy.

Etiology

Epilepsy can arise from a variety of conditions and pathophysiologic mechanisms. About 70% of adults and 40% of children with

Table 434–1 • POTENTIAL CAUSES OF ACUTE SYMPTOMATIC SEIZURES

MEDICAL CONDITIONS

Metabolic derangements
  Hyponatremia (<120 mEq/L)—especially acute
  Hypernatremia (>150–155 mEq/L)—especially acute
  Hypoglycemia (<40 mg/dL)
  Hyperglycemia (>400 mg/dL)
  Hyperosmolality (>320 mOsm/L)
  Hypocalcemia (<7 mg/dL)
  Respiratory alkalosis—acute
Drug-induced seizures
  Isoniazid, penicillins
  Theophylline, aminophylline
  Lidocaine
  Meperidine
  Ketamine, halothane, enflurane, methohexital
  Amitriptyline, maprotiline, imipramine, doxepin, fluoxetine
  Haloperidol, trifluoperazine, chlorpromazine
  Ephedrine, phenylpropanolamine, terbutaline
  Methotrexate, BCNU, asparaginase
  Cyclosporine
  Cocaine (crack), phenocyclidine, amphetamines
  Alcohol (withdrawal)
Illnesses
  Eclampsia
  Hypertensive encephalopathy
  Liver failure
  Polyarteritis nodosa
  Porphyria
  Renal failure
  Sickle cell disease
  Syphilis
  Systemic lupus erythematosus
  Thrombotic thrombocytopenic purpura
  Whipple's disease

NEUROLOGIC CONDITIONS

Angiitis of the nervous system
Meningitis
Encephalitis
Acute head trauma (impact seizures)
Stroke
Brain abscess
Brain tumor

new-onset epilepsy have partial (focal) seizures (Fig. 434–1A). A specific cause usually cannot be identified, although the focal nature of the seizures generally implies a cerebral injury or lesion (so-called cryptogenic epilepsy) (Fig. 434–1B). The most common specific lesions are hippocampal sclerosis, gangliogliomas, glial tumors, cavernous malformations, neuronal migrational defects (cortical dysplasia), hamartomas, encephalitis, cerebral trauma, and hemorrhage. Not all patients with cerebral pathology have epilepsy; how a particular lesion or injury causes a region of brain to become epileptogenic is poorly understood.

Although specific mendelian (e.g., tuberous sclerosis, hyperglycinemia, Lafora's disease), chromosomal (e.g., Down syndrome), and mitochondrial (e.g., MELAS [mitochondrial encephalopathy, lactic acidosis, and strokelike episodes] syndrome) genetic diseases account for only about 1% of epilepsy cases, heritable factors are important in a much higher percentage, especially in children. Forms of epilepsy that are demonstrably more heritable than others (e.g., childhood absence epilepsy, juvenile myoclonic epilepsy) are termed *idiopathic* or *primary* epilepsies. Common features include a variable family history, generalized spike-wave abnormality on electroencephalogram (EEG), and onset in childhood or adolescence.

Family history, cerebral injury, and neurologic disease are all risk factors for epilepsy, and the magnitude of the increased risk relative to the population at large can be specified for many different conditions that predispose to seizures. In many patients, several factors coexist, and the development of epilepsy reflects the interaction of acquired brain pathology and genetic predisposition.

Classification and Clinical Manifestations

CLASSIFICATION OF EPILEPTIC SEIZURES

Seizures are classified by their clinical manifestations (semiology) supplemented by EEG data (Table 434–2). The particular manifestations of any single seizure depend on several factors: (1) whether most or only a part of the cerebral cortex is involved at the beginning, (2) the functions of the cortical areas where the seizure originates, and (3) the subsequent pattern of spread within the brain. Seizures can have an onset limited to part of one cerebral hemisphere (*partial* or *focal* seizures) or involve the cerebral cortex diffusely from the beginning (*generalized* seizures). Seizures are dynamic, however; simple partial seizures can evolve into complex partial seizures, and either simple or complex partial seizures can evolve into generalized tonic-clonic convulsions.

PARTIAL SEIZURES. The initial events of a seizure, described either by the patient or by an observer, are usually the most reliable indication to determine whether a seizure begins focally. *Simple* partial seizures result when the ictal discharge occurs in, and remains limited to, a

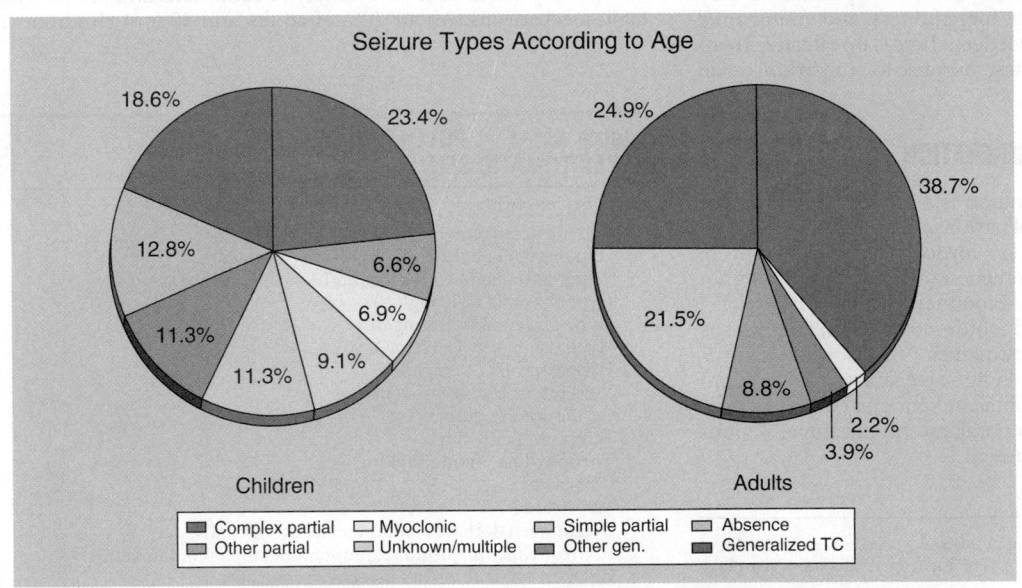

A

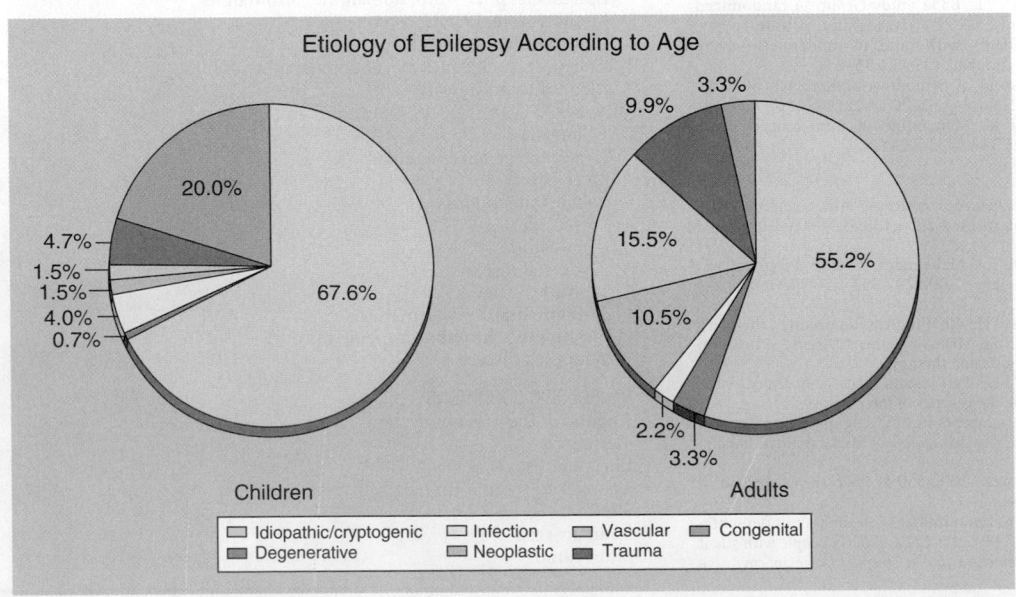

B

FIGURE 434–1 • *A,* Proportion of seizure types as a function of age for newly diagnosed cases of epilepsy in Rochester, Minnesota, 1935–1984. *B,* Etiology of epilepsy in all newly diagnosed cases in Rochester, Minnesota, 1935–1984. TC = tonic-clonic. (Modified from Hauser WA, Annegers JF, Kurland LT: Incidence of epilepsy and unprovoked seizures in Rochester, Minnesota: 1935–1984. Epilepsia 1993;34:453–468.)

Table 434–2 • INTERNATIONAL LEAGUE AGAINST EPILEPSY CLASSIFICATION OF EPILEPTIC SEIZURES AND SYNDROMES

CLASSIFICATION OF SEIZURES

I. Partial (focal seizures)
  A. *Simple partial seizures* (consciousness not impaired)
    1. With motor signs (including jacksonian, versive, and postural)
    2. With sensory symptoms (including visual, somatosensory, auditory, olfactory)
    3. With psychic symptoms (including dysphasia, hallucinatory, and affective changes)
    4. With autonomic symptoms
  B. *Complex partial seizures* (consciousness is impaired)
    1. Simple partial onset followed by impaired consciousness
    2. With impairment of consciousness at onset
    3. With automatisms
  C. Partial seizures evolving to secondarily generalized seizures
II. Generalized seizures nonfocal origin
  A. Absence seizures
  B. Myoclonic seizures; myoclonic jerks (single or multiple)
  C. Tonic-clonic seizures
  D. Tonic seizures
  E. Atonic seizures
III. Unclassified epileptic seizures

CLASSIFICATION OF EPILEPTIC SYNDROMES

I. Idiopathic epilepsy syndromes (focal or generalized)
  A. Benign neonatal convulsions
  B. Benign partial epilepsy of childhood
  C. Childhood absence epilepsy
  D. Juvenile myoclonic epilepsy
  E. Idiopathic epilepsy, otherwise unspecified
II. Cryptogenic or symptomatic epilepsy syndromes (focal or generalized)
  A. West's syndrome (infantile spasms)
  B. Lennox-Gastaut syndrome
  C. Epilepsia partialis continua
  D. Temporal lobe epilepsy
  E. Frontal lobe epilepsy
  F. Post-traumatic epilepsy
  G. Other symptomatic epilepsies, otherwise unspecified
III. Other epilepsy syndromes of uncertain or mixed classification
  A. Neonatal seizures
  B. Febrile seizures
  C. Reflex epilepsy
  D. Adult nonconvulsive status epilepticus
  E. Other unspecified

circumscribed area of cortex. This site often is termed the *epileptogenic focus*. Consciousness is not depressed, and patients can interact normally with their environment except for limitations imposed by the seizure on specific localized brain functions. Many symptoms or phenomena can be the expressions of simple partial seizures. Subjective sensory and psychoillusory phenomena collectively are termed *auras* and affect about 60% of patients with focal epilepsy. Sensory symptoms, such as localized paresthesias, numbness, vertigo, auditory hallucinations, and unformed visual hallucinations, occur with seizures beginning in the corresponding primary sensory areas. Psychoillusory symptoms arise from ictal discharges in limbic and association cortex and include dysmnesic symptoms, such as feelings of familiarity (*déjà vu*) and unfamiliarity (*jamais vu*); dreamy states, such as feelings of unreality and depersonalization; time distortion; emotional symptoms, such as fear or depression; visual illusions, such as multiple images (polyopsia) or distortions of size (micropsia and macropsia); and hallucinatory phenomena, such as unpleasant smells, stereotyped visions, or familiar voices. Autonomic symptoms reflect ictal involvement of limbic structures that lie in the mesial temporal or frontal lobe and project to the hypothalamus and brainstem. Examples of autonomic phenomena include an epigastric rising sensation (especially common with seizures beginning in the mesial temporal lobe), nausea, lightheadedness, pallor or flushing, pupillary dilation, piloerection, salivation, and urinary incontinence.

Simple partial seizures with motor signs begin with *clonic* (rhythmic jerking) or *tonic* (stiffening) movements of a discrete body part. Because of their large cortical representation, muscles of the face and hand often are involved. When the seizure discharge begins in the primary motor cortex and spreads to involve the rest of the precentral gyrus, clonic movements progress in an orderly sequence ("jacksonian march") that reflects the homunculus representation (e.g., thumb to fingers to face to leg). More often, however, ictal discharges involve supplementary or other secondary motor areas of the frontal lobe and produce contralateral flexion and elevation of the arm, contralateral turning of the head and eyes, and tonic extension of the ipsilateral arm (the so-called fencer's posture). Other simple partial motor signs include speech arrest, vocalizations, and eye blinking.

Simple partial seizures may be followed by a transient neurologic abnormality reflecting postictal depression of the epileptogenic cortical area. Focal weakness may follow a simple partial motor seizure; numbness, a sensory seizure; and blindness or amblyopia, an occipital lobe seizure. These reversible neurologic deficits collectively are called *Todd's paralysis* and rarely last for more than 48 hours. Similarly, prompt examination of a patient after a seizure may reveal transient focal abnormalities that provide useful clues to the site of seizure origin.

Complex partial seizures impair consciousness and produce unresponsiveness. In temporal lobe seizures, loss of consciousness results when the ictal discharge spreads bilaterally to involve hippocampal and amygdala areas; the parahippocampal gyri; and, to some extent, the entorhinal cortex and subfrontal, especially septal, regions. About 70 to 80% of complex partial seizures arise from the temporal lobe, and more than 65% of these originate in mesial temporal lobe structures, especially the hippocampus, amygdala, and parahippocampal gyrus. Remaining cases of complex partial seizures arise mainly from the frontal lobe, with smaller percentages originating in the parietal and occipital lobes. Many complex partial seizures evolve from simple partial seizures; consciousness becomes impaired as the seizure progresses. Complex partial seizures preceded by an olfactory aura are called *uncinate fits* because of their origin in or near the uncus of the medial temporal lobe. Uncinate fits may have a higher association with brain tumors than other types of complex partial seizures.

The typical complex partial seizure of temporal lobe origin consists of a motionless stare accompanied by alteration of consciousness followed by *automatisms* (repetitive purposeless complex movements) and, often, dystonic positioning of the arm or hand *contralateral* to the seizure discharge. Oroalimentary automatisms are most common and include lip smacking, swallowing, and sucking and chewing movements. Gestural automatisms, such as fumbling, picking at clothes or objects, hand wringing, and patting movements, also are encountered frequently and typically are expressed maximally in the limbs *ipsilateral* to the epileptogenic temporal lobe. There may be clumsy perseveration of ongoing motor tasks, such as eating, drawing, walking, or washing dishes. Some patients show a degree of residual ability to react to their environment during the seizure, although their behavior is typically inappropriate. Complex partial seizures usually last 45 to 90 seconds and are followed by confusion and disorientation lasting several more minutes. Without an EEG recording, it is difficult to determine when the ictal state ends and postictal behavior begins. Characteristically, patients are amnesic for details of the seizure that occurred after the aura. There may be transient postictal aphasia when the seizure involves the dominant temporal lobe.

Complex partial seizures of frontal lobe origin are atypical and often differ dramatically from seizures originating in the temporal lobe. Although there are many variations, frontal lobe complex partial seizures tend to (1) begin and end abruptly; (2) be brief with few, if any, postictal symptoms; (3) express prominent, but often bizarre, motor manifestations, such as asynchronous thrashing or flailing of arms and legs, pelvic thrusting, pedaling leg movements, and loud vocalizations, all of which at first can suggest psychogenic attacks; and (4) show minimal or nonlocalizing changes with scalp EEG recordings.

Psychomotor seizures, temporal lobe seizures, and *limbic seizures* are terms that have been used in the past to describe many of the ictal behaviors now classified as complex partial seizures, but they are not synonymous. Not all complex partial seizures arise from the temporal lobe, and not all involve the limbic system. Some temporal lobe and limbic phenomena reflect unilateral ictal discharges and may not be associated with the significant alterations of awareness that invariably occur with complex partial seizures. Finally, automatisms (the "psychomotor" element) are not uniformly present in complex partial seizures.

Neurology

GENERALIZED SEIZURES. Generalized seizures begin diffusely and involve both cerebral hemispheres simultaneously from the outset. They lack clinical and EEG features that indicate a localized cerebral origin. Generalized seizures are subdivided mainly on the basis of the presence or absence and character of ictal motor manifestations. These features depend on the extent to which subcortical and brainstem structures participate in the ictal discharge.

Generalized tonic-clonic seizures (*grand mal convulsions*) are characterized by abrupt loss of consciousness with bilateral tonic extension of the trunk and limbs (*tonic phase*), often accompanied by a loud vocalization as air is expelled forcefully across tightly contracted vocal cords (the "epileptic cry"), followed by bilaterally synchronous muscle jerking (*clonic phase*). In some patients, a few clonic jerks precede the tonic-clonic sequence; in others, only a tonic or a clonic phase is seen. Urinary incontinence is common; fecal incontinence rare. The actual ictus does not usually last more than 90 seconds. The postictal phase is marked by transient deep stupor followed in 15 to 30 minutes by a lethargic, confused state with automatic behavior. As recovery progresses, many patients complain of headache, muscle soreness, mental dulling, lack of energy, or mood changes lasting 24 hours.

Generalized tonic-clonic seizures result in many striking but transient physiologic changes, including hypoxia, lactic acidosis, elevated plasma catecholamine levels, and increased concentrations of serum creatine kinase, prolactin, corticotropin, cortisol, β-endorphin, and growth hormone. Complications include oral trauma, vertebral compression fractures, shoulder dislocation, aspiration pneumonia, and sudden death, which may be related to acute pulmonary edema, cardiac arrhythmia, or suffocation.

Absence seizures (*petit mal seizures*) occur mainly in children and are characterized by sudden, momentary lapses in awareness (the absence attack), staring, rhythmic blinking, and, sometimes, a few small clonic jerks of arms or hands. Behavior and awareness return immediately to normal. There is no postictal period and usually no recollection that a seizure has occurred. Most absence seizures last less than 10 seconds. Longer absences are accompanied by automatisms, usually of a perseverative type, in about 70% of cases. Absence seizures commonly coexist with generalized tonic-clonic or myoclonic seizures. Untreated, absence seizures can occur hundreds of times each day, a condition referred to as *pyknolepsy*.

Lapses of awareness that have a more gradual onset, do not resolve as abruptly, and are accompanied by autonomic features or loss of muscle tone are called *atypical absence seizures*. These events occur most often in children with mental retardation, and they do not respond as well to antiepileptic drug treatment. Typical and atypical absence seizures also must be distinguished from complex partial seizures manifested only by brief lapses of consciousness because cause, treatment, and prognosis differ among these three seizure types.

Myoclonic seizures manifest as rapid, recurrent, brief muscle jerks that can occur bilaterally, synchronously or asynchronously, or unilaterally without loss of consciousness. The myoclonic jerks range from small movements of the face or hands to massive bilateral spasms that simultaneously affect the head, limbs, and trunk. Repeated myoclonic seizures may seem to crescendo and terminate in a generalized tonic-clonic convulsion. Although they can occur at any time, myoclonic seizures often cluster shortly after waking or while falling asleep.

Atonic seizures ("drop attacks") occur most often in children with diffuse encephalopathies and are characterized by sudden loss of muscle tone that may result in falls with self-injury. Sometimes the loss of muscle tone is limited or fragmentary, producing only a head drop.

MISCELLANEOUS SEIZURE TYPES. Some seizures are designated by unique or unusual features. *Gelastic* seizures can be either complex partial or generalized nonconvulsive seizures in which pathologic laughter unaccompanied by any emotional content is a conspicuous feature of the epileptic event. *Cursive* seizures are complex partial seizures in which running is a prominent symptom. *Reflex* seizures are attacks precipitated by a specific stimulus, such as touch, a musical tune, a particular movement, reading, stroboscopic light patterns, or complex visual images.

EPILEPTIC SYNDROMES

Some epileptic disorders are characterized by sufficiently reproducible aggregations of historical data, seizure patterns, associated clinical signs and symptoms, EEG findings, biochemical abnormalities, and imaging results that distinct *epileptic syndromes* can be defined. Classifying the kind of epilepsy a patient has or identifying a patient's specific epileptic syndrome is more important than describing seizures.

The most widely used classification scheme (see Table 434–2) separates major groups of epilepsy first on the basis of whether seizures are partial (*localization-related [focal] epilepsies*) or generalized (*generalized epilepsies*) and second by cause (*idiopathic, symptomatic, or cryptogenic epilepsy*). Subtypes of epilepsy are grouped by age and, in the case of focal epilepsies, by the anatomic location of the presumed site of seizure onset.

FEBRILE SEIZURES. Febrile seizures are acute symptomatic seizures and the most common cause of convulsions in children. They affect 3 to 5% of all children younger than age 5 years in the United States and Europe. Most febrile seizures occur between the ages of 6 months and 4 years, although they sometimes occur in children 6 or 7 years old. About 30% of children have more than one attack; chance of recurrence is greatest if the first seizure occurs before 1 year of age or if there is a family history of febrile seizures. Although most affected children have no long-term consequences, febrile seizures increase the risk of future epilepsy. This risk is low for most children, about 2 to 3%, but it approximates 10 to 13% in children who have had prolonged or focal seizures, who have a family history of afebrile seizures, or who were neurologically abnormal before the first febrile seizure. Febrile seizures neither are associated with nor do they cause mental retardation, below-average IQ, poor school performance, or behavior problems. Prophylactic treatment generally is not indicated because of the benign prognosis.

BENIGN PARTIAL EPILEPSY OF CHILDHOOD WITH CENTRAL-MIDTEMPORAL SPIKES (ROLANDIC EPILEPSY). Seizures usually begin between ages 4 and 13 years; affected children are otherwise normal. Most have seizures principally or only at night. Because sleep promotes secondary generalization, parents report only tonic-clonic convulsions; any focal signature usually is missed. In contrast, seizures occurring during the day are typically focal and express themselves with twitching of one side of the face; speech arrest; drooling; and paresthesias of the face, gums, tongue, and inner cheeks. Seizures may progress to include hemiclonic movements or hemitonic posturing. EEGs show a distinctive pattern of stereotyped epileptiform discharges over the central and midtemporal regions. Prognosis is invariably good, and seizures disappear by mid to late adolescence.

CHILDHOOD ABSENCE (PETIT MAL) EPILEPSY. This disorder begins most often between ages 4 and 12 years in children who are neurologically and intellectually normal. Absence attacks often can be precipitated by hyperventilation. The EEG is diagnostic, showing stereotyped 3-Hz spike-wave discharges in association with a typical spell (Fig. 434–2). Generalized tonic-clonic seizures occur in 30 to 50% of cases. Ethosuximide (10–20 mg/kg/day or, in older children and adults 250 mg two or three times daily) and valproate (15–30 mg/kg/day) are equally effective against absence seizures; valproate is preferable if generalized tonic-clonic seizures coexist.

JUVENILE MYOCLONIC EPILEPSY. This idiopathic generalized epilepsy begins most often between ages 8 and 20 years in otherwise healthy individuals. When fully developed, the syndrome is characterized by morning myoclonic jerks, generalized tonic-clonic seizures that occur just after awakening, normal intelligence, a family history of similar seizures, and an EEG that shows generalized 4- to 6-Hz spike-wave and polyspike-wave discharges. Valproate controls attacks in more than 80% of cases, but indefinite treatment usually is required because of the high rate of relapse after attempted drug withdrawal. Lamotrigine is an effective alternative in many patients, but it occasionally can exacerbate myoclonus.

LENNOX-GASTAUT SYNDROME. This syndrome includes a heterogeneous group of early childhood epileptic encephalopathies that have in common physical brain abnormalities, mental retardation, uncontrolled seizures, and an EEG pattern that shows generalized 1.5- to 2.5-Hz sharp slow-wave discharges ("slow spike-and-wave pattern"). No treatment is consistently effective; management is best directed by specialists.

TEMPORAL LOBE EPILEPSY. This disorder is the most common epileptic syndrome of adults, accounting for at least 40% of cases of epilepsy. Seizures begin in late childhood or adolescence, and there is often a history of febrile seizures. Virtually all patients have complex partial seizures, some of which secondarily generalize. Epigastric or visceral auras are frequent. Interictal EEGs usually show epilepti-

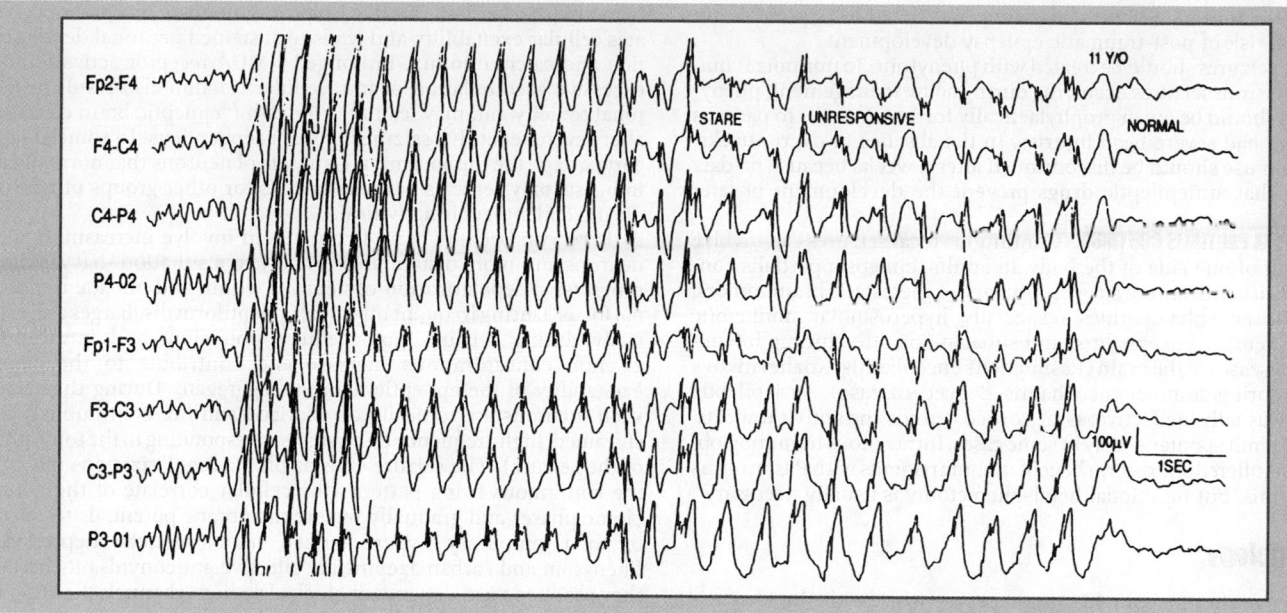

FIGURE 434–2 • Childhood absence epilepsy. Electroencephalogram shows the typical pattern of generalized 3-Hz spike-wave complexes associated with a clinical absence seizure.

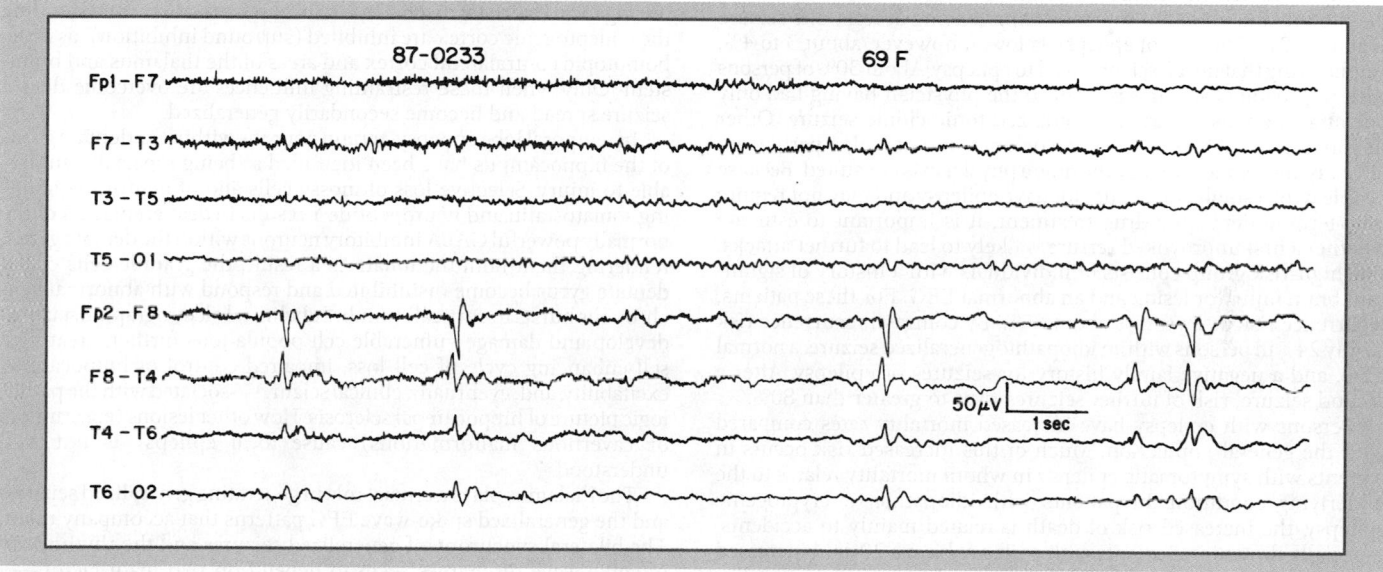

FIGURE 434–3 • Temporal lobe epilepsy. Epileptiform discharges are seen focally over the right temporal lobe (bottom four lines), and there is intermixed, irregular slow-wave activity not seen on the other side.

form discharges over the anterior temporal region (Fig. 434–3). Most patients with temporal lobe epilepsy have impaired memory, and some show a decrease in either verbal or visuospatial skills, depending on whether the epileptogenic temporal lobe is dominant or nondominant.

Temporal lobe epilepsy arises most often from mesial temporal limbic structures, typically in association with a characteristic lesion known as *hippocampal sclerosis,* which is variable but selective neuronal loss. Secondary gliosis occurs, and corresponding atrophy of the hippocampal formation can be recognized on magnetic resonance imaging (MRI) of the brain (see later). In 20% of cases, temporal lobe epilepsy is caused by other structural lesions, such as cavernous malformations, hamartomas, cortical dysplasia, glial tumors, and scars related to previous head injuries or encephalitis. Frontal or occipital lesions may give rise to temporal lobe seizures because of rapid spread of the ictal discharge into mesial temporal lobe structures.

Antiepileptic drugs are usually successful in suppressing secondarily generalized seizures, but greater than 50% of patients continue to have partial seizures. In these drug-resistant cases, temporal lobectomy is the treatment of choice.∎

POST-TRAUMATIC EPILEPSY. After penetrating wounds and other severe head injuries, about one third of patients have seizures within 1 year. Severe head injuries (Chapter 431) are defined by the presence of a cerebral contusion, intracerebral or intracranial hematoma, unconsciousness or amnesia lasting more than 24 hours, or persistent abnormalities on neurologic examination, such as hemiparesis or aphasia. Although most patients experience seizures within 1 to 2 years of injury, new-onset seizures still may appear 5 or more years later. Two thirds of patients with post-traumatic epilepsy have partial or secondarily generalized seizures. Mild head injuries (e.g., uncomplicated brief loss of consciousness, no skull fracture, absence of focal neurologic signs, no contusion or hematoma) do not increase the risk of seizures to a clinically significant degree.

Impact seizures (a generalized convulsion occurring at the time of, or immediately after, the injury) and *early seizures* (seizures occurring within the first 1 to 2 weeks) represent acute reactions of the brain to the trauma. Seizures beginning after 10 to 14 days reflect an increased risk of post-traumatic epilepsy development.

Early seizures should be treated with phenytoin. To minimize complications from seizures occurring during acute management, phenytoin also should be given prophylactically for 1 to 2 weeks to patients who have had severe head injuries. In the absence of overt attacks, phenytoin use should be discontinued after 2 weeks because no data indicate that antiepileptic drugs prevent the development of later epilepsy.

EPILEPSIA PARTIALIS CONTINUA. Continuous focal seizures can involve part or all of one side of the body. In adults, epilepsia partialis continua occurs with severe strokes, primary or metastatic brain tumors, metabolic encephalopathies (especially hyperosmolar nonketotic hyperglycemia), encephalitis, and subacute or rare chronic inflammatory diseases of the brain (Rasmussen's encephalitis, Kozhevnikov's Russian spring-summer encephalitis, Behçet's disease). Antiepileptic drugs are usually ineffective, as are corticosteroids and antiviral agents. Seizures remit spontaneously in some cases. Intravenous immunoglobulin G has offered short-term benefit in some patients with Rasmussen's encephalitis, but functional hemispherectomy is usually necessary.

Epidemiology

Epilepsy affects about 45 million people worldwide. Incidence is highest among young children and the elderly, and men are affected slightly more often than women (1.5:1). In the United States, age-adjusted annual incidence rates based on 1990 census figures range from 31 to 57 per 100,000 population. Cause and seizure type vary with age.

Excluding febrile seizures or seizures related to an acute illness, the lifetime likelihood of someone experiencing at least one seizure is about 10%. The risk of epilepsy is lower, however, about 3 to 4%, emphasizing that not all seizures lead to epilepsy. About 30% of persons with unprovoked seizures present to the physician having had only one attack, almost always a generalized tonic-clonic seizure. Other seizure types, such as absence, myoclonic, and complex partial, are virtually always recurrent by the time a physician is consulted. Because people with a single seizure do not have epilepsy and may not require long-term antiepileptic drug treatment, it is important to estimate whether a first unprovoked seizure is likely to lead to further attacks. The high-risk group consists of individuals with a history of significant brain injury or lesion and an abnormal EEG. For these patients, recurrence risk at 2 years is about 65%. By contrast, recurrence risk is only 24% in persons with an idiopathic generalized seizure, a normal EEG, and a negative family history for seizures or epilepsy. After a second seizure, risk of further seizures rises to greater than 80%.

Persons with epilepsy have increased mortality rates compared with the general population. Much of this increased risk occurs in patients with symptomatic epilepsy in whom mortality relates to the underlying condition. In patients with idiopathic or cryptogenic epilepsy, the increased risk of death is related mainly to accidents, especially drowning. Patients with epilepsy have a 20-fold increased risk of sudden unexplained death, presumably secondary to cardiac arrhythmia, pulmonary edema, or myocardial infarction. Sudden unexplained death is the most common cause of seizure-related mortality in persons with severe, chronic epilepsy.

Pathogenesis

CELLULAR PHYSIOLOGY

Seizures result from the synchronous interactions of large populations of neurons that intermittently discharge in abnormal patterns. Intracellular recordings from neurons in an epileptogenic focus show recurring high-voltage, long-duration depolarizations with superimposed high-frequency bursts of action potentials. The extracellular current flow generated by these *paroxysmal depolarizing shifts* (PDSs) results in the interictal EEG spike or sharp wave, the characteristic epileptiform discharge that signifies susceptibility to seizures. PDS generation involves several mechanisms, including increased excitability resulting from changes in intrinsic voltage-dependent membrane currents, newly active excitatory circuits, attenuation or loss of effective postsynaptic inhibition and other inhibitory processes, and increased effectiveness of excitatory synapses. In neurons showing "epileptic" patterns of behavior, ordinary synaptic inputs may elicit exaggerated or pathologically amplified responses. Activation of the

N-methyl-D-aspartate (NMDA) type of glutamate receptors potentiates cellular excitability and leads to sustained neuronal depolarization and calcium influx. Prolonged NMDA receptor activation and excessive accumulation of intracellular calcium also result in neuronal toxicity and may lead to cell death ("epileptic brain damage") after severe repetitive seizures or status epilepticus. In some areas of cortex (e.g., the hippocampus), subsets of neurons that normally fire in bursts may serve as pacemaker cells for other groups of neurons during epileptogenic activities.

PDSs can become more frequent and involve increasingly more neurons and more distant areas of cortex, a situation that results in progressive depolarization of neurons within and outside the original focus. During frequent interictal epileptiform discharges and especially during seizures, extracellular potassium and intracellular calcium concentrations increase and contribute to the overall excitability of the epileptic neuronal aggregate. During the seizure itself, neurons are tonically depolarized and fire continuously in a sustained, high-frequency discharge (corresponding to the tonic phase of the seizure). The seizure ends as phasic repolarizations interrupt the continuous firing pattern (the cellular correlate of the clinical clonic phase) and gradually restore membrane potentials to normal or to a temporary hyperpolarized state (postictal depression). Phenytoin and carbamazepine are effective anticonvulsants because they produce a use-dependent block of sodium channels, limiting the capability of neurons to fire at high-frequency rates. The benzodiazepines and barbiturates exert their anticonvulsant effect by enhancing postsynaptic γ-aminobutyric acid (GABA)–mediated inhibition through an effect on the chloride ionophore.

In the focal epilepsies, abnormal neuronal behavior originates in and may remain confined to a restricted area of the cortex. Typically during focal interictal discharges or focal seizures, areas surrounding the epileptogenic cortex are inhibited (surround inhibition), as is the homotopic contralateral cortex and areas of the thalamus and brainstem. Only when these restraining influences are overcome does a seizure spread and become secondarily generalized.

In temporal lobe epilepsy, certain neurons within the dentate gyrus of the hippocampus have been identified as being especially vulnerable to injury. Selective loss of mossy cells and of neurons containing somatostatin and neuropeptide Y results in deafferentation of the normally powerful GABA inhibitory neurons within the dentate gyrus, rendering them nonfunctional. As a result, the granule cells of the dentate gyrus become disinhibited and respond with abnormal synchronous bursts to cortical stimuli. Subclinical electrographic seizures develop and damage vulnerable cell populations further, creating a self-enhancing cycle of cell loss, impaired control of hippocampal excitability, and, eventually, clinical seizures associated with the pathologic picture of hippocampal sclerosis. How other lesions (e.g., tumors or cavernous malformations) cause focal epilepsy is not well understood.

The thalamus plays a crucial role in generating generalized seizures and the generalized spike-wave EEG patterns that accompany them. The bilateral synchrony of generalized seizures and the rhythmicity of spike-wave discharges seem to depend on two main factors—a unique set of ionic conductances, including a T-type calcium current, which enable neurons in the thalamic nucleus reticularis to function as pacemaker control cells, and the special anatomy and pharmacology of the thalamocortical system. The substantia nigra also is crucial to the expression of generalized convulsions, especially the tonic phase; GABA-ergic inhibitory transmission in the substantia nigra plays a regulatory role in the propagation of primary and secondarily generalized seizure discharges. Because there are no consistent, demonstrable pathologic changes in the brains of patients with idiopathic generalized epilepsy, susceptibility to these seizures most likely results from inherited biochemical, membrane, or neurotransmitter defects that result in abnormal excitability within the involved circuits.

GENETICS AND GENE DEFECTS

Several rare idiopathic epilepsy syndromes with a monogenic mode of inheritance have been linked to particular chromosomes and the responsible genes identified (Table 434–3). Mutations in two voltage-gated potassium channel genes, *KCNQ2* and *KCNQ3*, cause benign familial neonatal convulsions. In some, but not all, families with autosomal dominant frontal lobe epilepsy, there are mutations in the gene that codes for the α4-subunit of the neuronal nicotinic acetylcholine receptor. Mutations in sodium channel subunits on chromosomes

Table 434-3 • LINKAGE AND GENE IDENTIFICATION IN IDIOPATHIC HUMAN EPILEPSIES

SYNDROME	CHROMOSOMAL LOCATION	GENE
Benign familial neonatal convulsions	20q13	KCNQ2
	8q24	KCNQ34
Benign familial infantile convulsions	19q	?
Juvenile myoclonic epilepsy	6p	?
	15q14	?
Childhood absence epilepsy	8q24	?
Familial autosomal recessive idiopathic myoclonic epilepsy of infancy	16p13	?
Familial adult myoclonic epilepsy	8q24	?
Autosomal dominant partial epilepsy with auditory features	10q22–24	LGI1
Autosomal dominant nocturnal frontal lobe epilepsy	20q13	CHRNA4
	1q	CHRNB2
	15q24	?
Benign rolandic epilepsy with central-midtemporal spikes	15q14	?
Familial partial epilepsy with variable foci	22q11–12	?
Generalized epilepsy with febrile seizures plus (GEFS+)	19q13	SCN1B
Childhood absence epilepsy; generalized tonic-clonic seizures and febrile seizures (?GEFS+)	2q24	SCN1A
	2q21–q33	?
	5q34	GABRG2
Autosomal dominant febrile convulsions	8q13	?
	19q	?
	5q14–15	?

Table 434-4 • ESSENTIAL FEATURES OF SEIZURE HISTORY

Data and circumstances of first attack
First consistent event in the seizure: Is there an aura? Are initial symptoms and signs focal or lateralizing?
Subsequent evolution of the seizure, in sequence
Postictal manifestations (e.g., Todd's paralysis)
Is there more than one seizure type?
Average rate of occurrence; longest seizure-free interval since onset
Seizure precipitants (alcohol, sleep deprivation, particular stimuli, stress)
Is there a pattern to seizure occurrence (circadian, catamenial)?
Has there been a change in characteristics of the seizure?
Symptoms of neurologic or systemic disease between seizures: Are these static, intermittent, or progressive?
Risk factor for epilepsy (e.g., family history, cerebral injury)

19q and 2q have been implicated in a syndrome of generalized epilepsies with febrile seizures known as *GEFS+*. Additionally, some inherited disorders, such as tuberous sclerosis and neurofibromatosis, result in brain lesions that give rise to symptomatic epilepsies (Chapter 459).

Until more recently, the only gene defects that had been identified in these few idiopathic forms of epilepsy had been abnormalities of ion channels that regulate cortical excitability. The causative defect in autosomal dominant partial epilepsy with auditory features is a mutation in the leucine-rich glioma inactivated (*LGI1*) gene on chromosome 10q. How mutations in the *LGI1* gene cause epilepsy is unknown, but ion channels do not seem to be involved directly.

Although mutations in single genes account for a few rare epileptic syndromes, in most cases of epilepsy, data are most consistent with complex, polygenic influences. In any given patient, the *relative* contribution of genetic or acquired pathologic factors determines whether the epilepsy presents as an idiopathic disorder or a symptomatic one. The failure so far to identify a genetic component in post-traumatic epilepsy or in seizures after stroke most likely reflects the relatively small genetic "load" in these situations compared with the magnitude of acquired factors.

Diagnosis

Accurate diagnosis is the cornerstone of rational management. The diagnostic evaluation has three objectives: (1) to determine whether the patient has epilepsy; (2) to classify the seizures and type of epilepsy accurately and determine whether the clinical data fit a particular epilepsy syndrome; and (3) to identify, if possible, a specific underlying cause.

HISTORY

A detailed, accurate history is imperative and the most important factor in diagnosis. Because patients usually have only limited awareness of their behavior during a seizure, additional information usually must be obtained from family members or other close observers. The historical summary should provide a clear description of the patient's seizures, including details of any aura, the neurologic status between attacks, any reproducible precipitants, and relevant risk factors for epilepsy, such as a family history of seizures or a history of severe head trauma, encephalitis or meningitis, and febrile seizures (Table 434-4). In children and young adults, the physician should inquire

about gestation, birth, postnatal course, and early development. If a patient has been treated previously, it is important to learn what drugs were used, the doses and blood levels that were achieved, and therapeutic or adverse effects.

PHYSICAL EXAMINATION

Although the physical examination is normal in most patients with epilepsy, abnormal findings, when present, can be helpful in two ways. First, physical signs may point to an underlying neurologic or systemic disorder of which the seizures are a part. Neurocutaneous syndromes are commonly associated with seizures and may be suggested by cafe au lait spots, a facial angioma, hypopigmented macules, axillary freckling, and shagreen patches (Chapter 459). Second, focal neurologic signs indicate localized cerebral pathology. Asymmetry in the size of the hands, feet, or face signifies a long-standing abnormality of the cerebral hemisphere contralateral to the smaller side. Absence seizures can be triggered in untreated patients by having them hyperventilate for 2 to 3 minutes.

LABORATORY TESTS

ELECTROENCEPHALOGRAPHY. The EEG (Chapter 423) is the most important diagnostic test for epilepsy. EEG findings are useful and sometimes essential for establishing the diagnosis, classifying seizures correctly, identifying epileptic syndromes, and making therapeutic decisions. In combination with appropriate clinical findings, *epileptiform* EEG patterns termed *spikes* or *sharp waves* strongly support a diagnosis of epilepsy. In patients with seizures, focal epileptiform discharges indicate focal epilepsy, whereas generalized epileptiform activity indicates a generalized form of epilepsy. Most EEGs are obtained between seizures, however, and interictal abnormalities alone never can prove or refute a diagnosis of epilepsy. Epilepsy can be established definitively only by recording a characteristic ictal discharge during a representative clinical attack. A further factor that can confound interpretation of interictal EEGs is the occurrence of similar epileptiform abnormalities in about 2% of normal people; many of these, especially in children, are asymptomatic markers of a genetic trait. Finally, epileptiform-like waveforms or artifacts can be misinterpreted and erroneously considered to be evidence of seizure susceptibility.

About 40 to 50% of patients with epilepsy show epileptiform abnormalities on the initial EEG. The chance of capturing epileptiform activity is enhanced by sleep deprivation for 24 hours before the test and by the patient's sleeping during a portion of the EEG recording. Serial EEGs increase the yield of positive tracings. A few persons with epilepsy continue to have normal interictal EEGs, however, despite all efforts to record an abnormality.

Specialized epilepsy centers in large tertiary referral hospitals include monitoring units equipped with simultaneous EEG and closed-circuit television capability and computer-assisted detection and analysis systems. These facilities have improved management of selected patients greatly by giving physicians the means to distinguish epileptic from nonepileptic paroxysmal events, to make precise electrical-clinical correlations, and to localize epileptogenic foci for resective surgery.

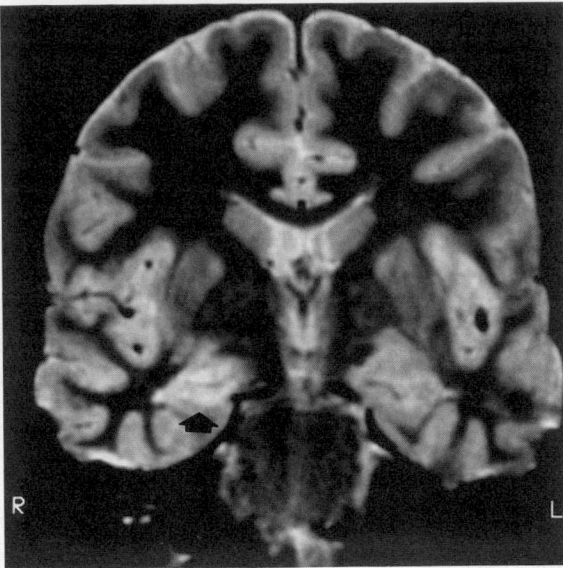

FIGURE 434–4 • Coronal magnetic resonance imaging at the level of the anterior temporal lobe showing changes consistent with right-sided hippocampal sclerosis. The right hippocampal formation (arrow) is atrophic compared with the left and shows signal changes (white areas) indicating gliosis. (Courtesy Dr. Stephen Chan, Division of Neuroradiology, Columbia–Presbyterian Medical Center, New York, NY.)

Table 434–5 • NONEPILEPTIC EPISODIC DISORDERS IN ADOLESCENTS AND ADULTS

Movement disorders
Myoclonus
Paroxysmal choreoathetosis
Episodic ataxias
Hyperexplexia (startle disease)
Migraine
Confusional
Vertebrobasilar
Syncope and cardiac arrhythmias*
Behavioral and psychiatric disorders
Psychogenic seizures*
Hyperventilation syndrome*
Panic disorder*
Dissociative states ("fugue states")
Episodic dyscontrol
Narcolepsy and sleep apnea
Automatic behavior syndrome
Partial cataplexy
Transient ischemic attacks
Transient global amnesia*
Acute confusional states
Alcoholic blackouts*
Hypoglycemic attacks

*Most commonly encountered.

NEUROIMAGING STUDIES. Brain MRI complements EEG findings by identifying structural brain pathology that may be related causally to the development of epilepsy. MRI should be performed in all patients older than age 18 years suspected of epilepsy. Properly performed MRI can detect most epileptogenic cerebral lesions. Hippocampal sclerosis, defects of neuronal migration, gangliogliomas and some gliomas, and cavernous malformations are seen readily with MRI. It is important to obtain a complete imaging study that includes T1-weighted and T2-weighted images in coronal and axial planes (Fig. 434–4). Gadolinium infusion does not improve detection of cerebral lesions associated with epilepsy, although it often aids in differentiating among types of cerebral pathology.

About 70% of patients with temporal lobe epilepsy show focal hypometabolic areas on interictal positron emission tomography that correspond to the epileptogenic focus (Chapter 424). These procedures and single-photon emission computed tomography usually are reserved for research-level studies or for specialized epilepsy centers rather than routine diagnosis.

BLOOD TESTS. Routine blood tests rarely offer diagnostic assistance in otherwise healthy patients with epilepsy. Serum electrolytes, liver function tests, and an automated blood cell count may be useful, however, as baseline studies before antiepileptic drug therapy is begun. Blood tests are necessary and frequently informative in older patients with acute or chronic systemic disease. Consideration should be given to obtaining blood or urine samples from adolescents and young adults with unexplained generalized seizures to screen for substance abuse, especially cocaine.

LUMBAR PUNCTURE. Lumbar puncture is mandatory if there is any suspicion of meningitis or encephalitis. It is otherwise unnecessary and need not be performed routinely. Repeated generalized seizures and convulsive status epilepticus can increase cerebrospinal fluid protein content slightly and produce a pleocytosis of 100 white blood cells (WBCs) per mm^3 for 24 to 48 hours. Cerebrospinal fluid pleocytosis should be attributed to seizures *only in retrospect*; infection or intracranial inflammatory processes always should be assumed first.

ELECTROCARDIOGRAM. An electrocardiogram should be obtained in any young person with a first generalized seizure if there is a family history of arrhythmia, sudden unexplained death, or episodic unconsciousness. An electrocardiogram also should be obtained in any patient with a history of cardiac arrhythmia or valvular disease.

Differential Diagnosis

Not every paroxysmal event is a seizure, and misidentification of other conditions as epilepsy leads to ineffective, unnecessary, and potentially harmful treatment. Misdiagnosis also accounts for a substantial portion of patients whose spells have not responded to antiepileptic drug treatment.

A variety of conditions can be confused with epilepsy, depending on the age of the patient and the nature and circumstances of the attacks (Table 434–5). It is not always possible to distinguish among various diagnostic possibilities on clinical grounds alone, and admission to a specialized monitoring unit is frequently necessary.

Nonepileptic paroxysmal disorders have in common the occurrence of sudden, discrete events characterized by abnormal or inappropriate behavior, variable responsiveness, changes in muscle tone, and various postures or movements. These conditions are far more common and variable in their presentation in children than in adults. Many of the disorders simulating epilepsy in childhood can be viewed as transient "developmental" conditions that require no treatment other than reassurance.

Syncope (Chapter 435) refers to the symptom complex that results when there is a transient, global reduction in cerebral perfusion with associated hypoxia. Loss of consciousness lasts only a few seconds, uncommonly 1 minute or more, and recovery is rapid. If the cerebral hypoxia is sufficiently severe, the syncopal episode may include brief tonic posturing of the trunk or a few clonic jerks of the arms and legs (*convulsive syncope*). Similarly, some forms of *migraine* (Chapter 428) can be mistaken for seizures, especially if the headache is atypical or mild. Basilar artery migraine, a rare variant seen most often in adolescents and young adults, can include lethargy, mood changes, confusion and disorientation, vertigo, bilateral visual disturbances, and alteration or loss of consciousness.

Psychogenic seizures frequently cause intractable "epilepsy" in adults and may represent 20% or more of cases referred to an epilepsy monitoring unit. Many patients with psychogenic seizures have epilepsy as well. Definitive diagnosis requires video EEG documentation, although a history of atypical and nonstereotyped attacks, emotional or psychological precipitants, psychiatric illness, complete lack of response to antiepileptic drugs, and repeatedly normal interictal EEGs suggests the possibility of psychogenic seizures. *Panic attacks* and anxiety attacks with hyperventilation can resemble superficially partial seizures with affective, autonomic, or special sensory symptoms. Prolonged hyperventilation results in muscle twitching or spasms (tetany), and affected patients may faint.

Episodic dyscontrol is a poorly defined entity consisting of intermittent periods of inappropriately violent and destructive behavior that is out of character for the patient. Nonspecifically abnormal EEGs have been reported in children with the episodic dyscontrol syndrome, but most affected adults have little evidence of a structural brain disorder.

Rx Treatment

MEDICAL TREATMENT

FIRST SEIZURE. Patients with their first epileptic seizure should be screened for symptoms and signs of an acute medical or neurologic illness. Brain imaging need not be done emergently unless there is a high likelihood of an acute cerebral lesion or the patient remains obtunded. Most patients recover rapidly after an isolated seizure, so several hours of observation are usually sufficient to assess the clinical progress, obtain additional relevant information, and review the results of laboratory tests. Hospitalization is not necessary, provided that there is no suspicion of an underlying illness, and a responsible family member or friend can observe the patient closely at home. If these criteria cannot be met, or if there is uncertainty about them, hospitalization is indicated. If the patient is sent home, there should be a clear plan for follow-up and re-evaluation.

Antiepileptic drugs reduce the risk of relapse after a first unprovoked generalized tonic-clonic seizure, but early treatment does not seem to affect long-term prognosis, especially with regard to severity of epilepsy or the chance of entering a prolonged remission.❷ Long-term treatment of all first seizures would overtreat expensively 75% of patients. The decision to treat should be based on the physician's estimate of the risk of further seizures, the consequence to the patient of recurrent seizures, a reasonable expectation that the patient will comply with the treatment regimens, and the risk of adverse effects from antiepileptic drug therapy (10 to 30%). Patients are at relatively low risk for further seizures if they have a normal EEG, normal physical examination, no history of significant cerebral injury, normal brain imaging study, and absence of a family history of epilepsy. Patients should be treated after a first seizure only if they have two or more of these risk factors. Nevertheless, the final decision about treatment always must be individualized and take into account the potential psychological, vocational, and physical consequences of further seizures for each patient.

SELECTION OF ANTIEPILEPTIC DRUGS. The treatment of epilepsy has three main objectives: (1) to eliminate seizures or minimize their frequency, (2) to avoid chronic drug-related adverse effects, and (3) to maintain or restore the patient's normal vocational and psychosocial adjustment. Although each of these goals is possible, no available medical treatment can eliminate ("cure") epilepsy permanently. Less than 50% of adults treated for chronic partial and secondarily generalized seizures become seizure-free for more than 12 months with currently available drugs.

In controlled comparative studies, carbamazepine, phenytoin, primidone, and phenobarbital are equally effective in suppressing partial and secondarily generalized seizures (Table 434–6). Valproate is less effective against complex partial seizures but is of comparable efficacy against secondarily generalized seizures. In individual patients, failure to respond to one drug does not preclude a good response to another. Similar head-to-head comparisons are not available for antiepileptic drugs introduced after 1993. Because of undesirable cosmetic effects (hirsutism, coarsening of facial features, acneiform skin rash, and gingival hypertrophy), phenytoin, long the mainstay of epilepsy treatment, is now a second-line drug; phenobarbital and primidone are used rarely in older children and adults. For an individual patient, differences in adverse effects, tolerability, ease of dosing schedule, and cost help determine the drug of choice.

Carbamazepine, oxcarbazepine, and lamotrigine are generally the drugs of first choice for treating partial and secondarily generalized seizures. Lamotrigine and extended-release forms of carbamazepine permit twice-daily dosing, but oxcarbazepine frequently must be taken three times a day. Drugs that must be administered more often than twice daily increase problems with compliance. Valproate, levetiracetam, and zonisamide are most useful as adjunctive therapy, but they are occasionally suitable as initial treatment. Zonisamide's long-half life may offer a decisive advantage in patients who cannot, or will not, take a drug more often than once a day. Levetiracetam and gabapentin have little interaction with other drugs and are useful in patients who must take multiple medications. Gabapentin and lamotrigine are especially well tolerated by elderly patients. Carbamazepine and

Table 434–6 • DRUGS USED IN TREATING DIFFERENT TYPES OF SEIZURES

TYPE OF SEIZURE	DRUGS
Simple and complex partial	Carbamazepine, oxcarbazepine, lamotrigine,* valproate, topiramate,* levetiracetam,* phenytoin, zonisamide,* gabapentin*
Secondarily generalized	Carbamazepine, oxcarbazepine, lamotrigine, valproate, phenytoin, topiramate,* levetiracetam,* zonisamide,* gabapentin*
Primary generalized seizures	
Tonic-clonic	Valproate, lamotrigine,† zonisamide,† topiramate,* levetiracetam†
Absence	Ethosuximide, valproate, lamotrigine†
Myoclonic	Clonazepam, valproate, topiramate,* zonisamide,† levetiracetam*
Tonic	Valproate, lamotrigine,* topiramate,* zonisamide,† levetiracetam,† carbamazepine, clonazepam, felbamate

*Approved by the FDA as adjunctive therapy only.
†Use not approved by the FDA.

phenytoin are broad-spectrum inducers of hepatic cytochrome P-450 enzymes and increase metabolism of contraceptive hormones. They also increase steroid hormone protein binding. Oxcarbazepine and topiramate have similar but weaker effects limited to the CYP3A4 isozyme. As a result, these drugs can reduce the efficacy of hormonal contraception. In women using oral contraceptives, lamotrigine should be considered for initial therapy because it has no effect on cytochrome P-450 enzymes and does not interfere with the effectiveness of contraceptive steroids.

Valproate continues to be the drug of first choice for generalized-onset seizures. It can be used effectively as monotherapy in 80% of patients even when several types of generalized seizures coexist. This recommendation may need to be reconsidered in women with epilepsy in view of growing evidence that valproate is associated with development of polycystic ovaries, hyperandrogenism, and hyperinsulinemia. In addition, lipid abnormalities are more common in women than in men taking valproate. Although not yet approved by the Food and Drug Administration for initial treatment of generalized-onset seizures, lamotrigine seems to be as effective as valproate and has fewer adverse effects. Topiramate, zonisamide, and possibly levetiracetam can be used as monotherapy if treatment with valproate or lamotrigine fails. Phenytoin and carbamazepine have efficacy against generalized tonic-clonic seizures, but they may exacerbate absence and myoclonic seizures, which frequently accompany generalized tonic-clonic seizures. Ethosuximide is as effective as valproate in treating typical absence seizures and, because of fewer side effects, is the drug of choice when no other seizure type coexists. When absence seizures are associated with generalized tonic-clonic and absence seizures, valproate or lamotrigine should be used. Clonazepam prevents myoclonic seizures, but its benefit does not persist in some patients. Although Food and Drug Administration approval has not been obtained, postmarketing experience in the United States and in other countries suggests that topiramate, zonisamide, and levetiracetam can be effective alternatives.

DRUG DOSAGE. After absorption, a drug is distributed between the plasma and various tissue compartments (Table 434–7). Because most antiepileptic drugs are fractionally bound to serum proteins, an equilibrium exists between the plasma concentrations of protein-bound and free (unbound) drug. Only unbound drug is capable of crossing the various lipoprotein membranes that surround brain receptor sites, making only this portion of the total drug concentration available to produce the desired effect. Antiepileptic drug blood levels that routinely are determined by laboratories reflect total plasma drug concentrations (bound plus unbound fractions). When protein binding is altered by disease (e.g., uremia), physiologic state (e.g., pregnancy), or other drugs (e.g., valproate), determining the unbound fraction provides a more accurate

Continued

Neurology

Table 434–7 • ANTIEPILEPTIC DRUGS: DOSAGE AND PHARMACOKINETIC DATA

DRUG	USUAL ADULT DOSE, 24 hr (mg)	HALF-LIFE (hr)	TITRATION TIME TO MINIMUM EFFECTIVE DOSE (DAYS)	USUALLY EFFECTIVE PLASMA CONCENTRATION (µg/mL)	BOUND FRACTION (%)	METABOLISM
Carbamazepine	800–1600	8–22	7–14	6–12	75	>90% hepatic with induction
Ethosuximide	750–1500	60	7–14	40–100	<5	65% hepatic, no induction
Gabapentin	1800–3600	5–7	1–14	>2*	<5	>95% renal
Lamotrigine	100–500	12–60†	28–42	2–16*	55	>99% hepatic, no induction
Levetiracetam‡	1000–3000	6–8	2–14	NE	<10	>65% renal excretion
Oxcarbazepine‡	600–1800	5–11	7–14	8–30*	45	>95% hepatic, slight induction
Phenobarbital	90–180	100	1–14	15–40	45	>90% hepatic with induction
Phenytoin	300–400	22	1–7	10–20	90–95	>90% hepatic with induction
Tiagabine	32–56	5–13	28–42	NE	95	>90% hepatic, no induction
Topiramate	200–400	19–25†	28–56	4–25*	9–17	30% hepatic, no induction
Valproate	1000–3000	15–20	7–14	50–120	80–90	>95% hepatic with inhibition
Zonisamide	100–400	63	1–7	NE	40–55	70% hepatic, no induction

*Not well established; corresponds to usual range in patients treated with recommended dose, but there is considerable variability.
†Highly dependent on concurrently administered drugs.
‡Information in table refers to the active metabolite of oxcarbazepine, monohydroxy derivative (MHD). NE = not established.

reflection of the drug's concentration in the brain's extracellular space. Measuring free levels can be helpful whenever there is a discrepancy between the total plasma concentration and the expected clinical effect.

Blood levels are useful in the treatment of epilepsy, but optimal levels for some patients fall either above or below usual recommended levels. Some patients consistently have side effects at low or "therapeutic" concentrations, whereas others benefit from "toxic" levels without experiencing side effects. Blood levels should never be the goal of treatment. A level in the low to mid therapeutic range is a reasonable target when initiating treatment, but subsequent dose adjustments should be based on the patient's clinical progress, seizure frequency, and appearance of drug-related side effects. Blood levels should be obtained when control of seizures is achieved or when toxic side effects appear. Noncompliance is the most common reason that a therapeutic drug level is not achieved using recommended dosing schedules.

INITIATING ANTIEPILEPTIC DRUG THERAPY. Treatment should start with a single drug chosen according to the patient's type of seizure; consideration of adverse effects, required dosing schedule, and cost; and other considerations that could affect drug selection in individual patients. With the exception of phenobarbital, phenytoin, gabapentin, and perhaps levetiracetam, administration of antiepileptic drugs should be started in low doses to minimize acute toxicity, then increased to a maintenance schedule according to the patient's tolerance and the drug's pharmacokinetics (see Table 434–7). Most common side effects are temporary, and these are minimized if the dose is increased slowly. Nausea can be minimized by taking the medication with meals. Sedation may be less likely if a higher dose is given at bedtime.

If therapeutic blood levels need to be achieved rapidly, drugs for which loading doses are practical, such as phenytoin, valproate, or phenobarbital, should be given. Other drugs can be substituted gradually, if necessary, when seizures are controlled.

All antiepileptic drugs can produce adverse effects. The most common side effects are *dose related* and typically occur when the drug is first given or when the dose is increased. Dose-related side effects usually correlate with blood concentrations of the drug or its major metabolites. *Idiosyncratic* reactions create the most serious and life-threatening side effects of antiepileptic drugs. All antiepileptic drugs can cause similar idiosyncratic reactions, including rash, Stevens-Johnson syndrome, agranulocytosis, thrombocytopenia, aplastic anemia, and hepatic failure. Idiosyncratic reactions are not dose related, and no laboratory test can identify individuals specifically at risk for them. Routine blood monitoring at set intervals is costly and ineffective. Minor elevations in hepatic aminotransferase levels occur in about 25 to 30% of patients with epilepsy, and these neither correlate with clinical symptoms nor predict development of hepatitis or liver failure. Isolated elevations in γ-glutamyltransferase levels seem to have little use as an indication of clinically

significant liver dysfunction in persons with epilepsy. Nearly 20% of patients taking carbamazepine or oxcarbazepine experience a benign leukopenia with WBC counts less than 4000/mL. A few patients have WBC counts that decrease transiently to less than 2500/mL. The risk of developing aplastic anemia is not increased in this group, and there is no increased rate of infections or other possible complications that might be attributed to leukopenia. Carbamazepine and more often oxcarbazepine cause hyponatremia, but this is rarely symptomatic and not a reason to decrease the dosage of, or discontinue, the drug.

WHEN INITIAL TREATMENT FAILS. Monotherapy results in satisfactory control of seizures (>90% reduction) in about 60% of patients. Of patients in whom the first drug was ineffective, about half respond to an alternative drug used alone. Of the remaining patients, less than 50% have improved control by addition of a second drug. Gabapentin, lamotrigine, topiramate, levetiracetam, zonisamide, and tiagabine have been approved as adjunctive therapy in patients with partial and secondarily generalized seizures. Vagus nerve stimulation or surgery should be considered in patients whose seizures remain uncontrolled and disabling for more than 2 years despite optimal medical treatment.

Although the new drugs have many desirable features and generally better therapeutic indices compared with more familiar agents, it is still too soon to predict what their ultimate place will be in the treatment of epilepsy. Felbamate, another relatively new drug, has already proved to be too toxic (causing aplastic anemia and liver failure) for routine use, and concern has risen about visual field defects attributed to vigabatrin.

There is growing evidence that specific cellular and molecular mechanisms underlie drug resistance is some people with epilepsy. These include increased expression of drug-resistant proteins and loss of sodium-channel drug sensitivity.

PREGNANCY CONCERNS. Epilepsy should not discourage a woman from becoming pregnant: Greater than 90% of women taking antiepileptic drugs have healthy infants. Overall, women with epilepsy have 1.5 to 3 times higher rates of complications of pregnancy regardless of treatment. Complications include increased risks of intrapartum bleeding, toxemia, abruptio placentae, premature labor, and stillborn births. About 35% of women with epilepsy experience increased seizures during pregnancy, mostly resulting from falling antiepileptic drug levels associated with a variety of physiologic changes that promote increased volume of distribution and clearance. Other factors, including gestational changes in sex hormones and medication compliance, also play a role. Antiepileptic drug levels should be followed closely during pregnancy, especially after the first trimester.

In the general population, *major fetal malformations* (cardiac defects; cleft lip or palate; neural tube defects, including spina bifida and anencephaly) occur in about 2% of pregnancies. This risk is increased to 4 to 6% in infants born to women with epilepsy who have taken a single antiepileptic drug during pregnancy. Valproate increases the chance of neural tube defects by 1.5%, and carbamazepine may raise this specific risk by 0.5%, especially if there is a family history of neural tube defects. Use of two or more drugs carries a 10% risk of major fetal malformations. The risk of neural tube defects is reduced substantially, perhaps eliminated, by folic acid, 1 mg/day. It is not known if folic acid has any protective effects on non–neural tube defects. Ultrasonography and amniocentesis done at 18 to 19 weeks of gestation have a nearly 95% accuracy rate in experienced hands of identifying neural tube defects and other major malformations. Serum α-fetoprotein determinations can detect neural tube defects but have a 25% false-negative rate.

Minor anomalies (nail hypoplasia, hypertelorism, low-set ears, prominent lips, broad-based nose) also are increased in infants of mothers with epilepsy, but this seems to reflect genetic and drug-related factors. These anomalies occur at increased rates independent of treatment status, although antiepileptic drug therapy increases the risk further to a slight degree. Data indicate that all antiepileptic drugs can produce similar anomalies. There is growing evidence that infants exposed to antiepileptic drugs in utero have increased rates of developmental and cognitive deficits, especially with valproate.

Virtually all older antiepileptic drugs promote a hemorrhagic diathesis in newborns. Intramuscular vitamin K, which is given routinely to infants, is occasionally inadequate to prevent hemorrhage. Oral vitamin K, 10 mg/day, should be prescribed for the mother during the last month of pregnancy.

EFFECTS OF ANTIEPILEPTIC DRUGS ON BONE METABOLISM

Antiepileptic drugs can lead to osteopenia and osteomalacia with increased risk of fractures (Chapters 258 and 259). Associated biochemical abnormalities include elevations in serum alkaline phosphatase and parathyroid hormone, low levels of vitamin D, hypocalcemia, and hypophosphatemia. Patients who have taken multiple drugs for many years show the most severe changes. The primary mechanism may be increased metabolism of vitamin D induced by antiepileptic drugs. At present, all patients taking long-term antiepileptic drugs also should take supplemental calcium and vitamin D.

NONMEDICAL TREATMENT

Few patients benefit from further attempts at medical treatment if seizures are not controlled with two trials of high-dose monotherapy using appropriate drugs and one trial of rational combination therapy. These steps can be accomplished within 1 to 2 years. At that point, the detrimental effects of continued seizures, often exacerbated by drug toxicity, warrant referral to a specialized epilepsy center. In patients with temporal lobe epilepsy, surgery is superior to prolonged medical treatment in terms of improved seizure control, fewer cognitive effects, and better quality of life. ▪

Stimulation of the vagus nerve using a permanently implanted device similar to a cardiac pacemaker is a novel nonpharmacologic method for treating patients whose seizures are refractory to medical treatment and who are not candidates for surgery. In randomized trials, seizures were reduced by at least 50% in 30 to 35% of patients; a few patients became seizure-free.

The most common type of epilepsy surgery is *focal cortical resection*. Three criteria identify the ideal patient for resective surgery: (1) The seizures begin in an identifiable and localized area of cortex, (2) the surgical excision can encompass the epileptogenic region, and (3) the required resection does not impair neurologic function. These requirements are met most often by patients with temporal lobe epilepsy or other focal epilepsies associated with a demonstrable cerebral lesion (e.g., mesial temporal sclerosis, cavernous malformation, ganglioglioma). More than 70% of these patients become seizure-free, and about 90% have sufficiently fewer seizures to improve their quality of life substantially. The outcome is less favorable for patients undergoing nonlesional extratemporal resections: About 45% of patients become seizure-free; another 35% have worthwhile improvement.

Prognosis

About 60 to 70% of people with epilepsy achieve a 5-year remission of seizures within 10 years of diagnosis. About half of these patients eventually become seizure-free. Factors favoring remission include an idiopathic form of epilepsy, a normal neurologic examination, and an onset in early to middle childhood (excluding neonatal seizures).

Of patients, 30%, usually with severe epilepsy starting in early childhood, continue to have seizures and never achieve a remission. In the United States, the prevalence of intractable epilepsy cases approximates 1 to 2 per 1000 population.

DISCONTINUING ANTIEPILEPTIC DRUGS. Because epidemiologic studies have shown that many patients with epilepsy become seizure-free for an extended period, many investigators have attempted to identify which patients can discontinue antiepileptic drugs without a high risk of relapse. Successful drug withdrawal is most likely if initial seizure control was readily achieved using monotherapy, there were relatively few seizures before remission, and the EEG and neurologic examination are normal just before drugs are discontinued. In addition, longer seizure-free intervals (4 years rather than 2 years) reduce the likelihood of relapse. Conversely, risk of relapse is high if seizure control was difficult to establish and required polytherapy, if there were frequent generalized tonic-clonic seizures before control was achieved, and if the EEG shows moderate or severe disturbances of background activity or active epileptiform activity at the time drug withdrawal is considered.

Status Epilepticus

Various types of status epilepticus take either convulsive or nonconvulsive forms. *Convulsive status epilepticus* is a medical emergency that requires timely and appropriate treatment to minimize serious systemic and neurologic morbidity. Similar to self-limited seizures, convulsive status may be either idiopathic and of generalized onset or secondary to bilateral spread from a focal epileptogenic brain area. *Nonconvulsive status epilepticus* presents as a new-onset sustained confusional state.

Convulsive status epilepticus is the first manifestation of epilepsy in about 10% of cases; more than 50% of patients with status epilepticus do not have a history of epilepsy. An acute precipitating factor or specific cause, such as metabolic abnormalities, drug abuse, hypoxia, infection, stroke, or tumor, can be identified in 50 to 65% of patients with status epilepticus. The mortality rate approaches 30% in adults, but death usually is related to the underlying condition. Status epilepticus itself accounts for death in less than 10% of cases.

Treatment protocols are designed to eliminate seizure activity and to identify and treat any underlying medical or neurologic disorder. Initial management focuses on ensuring adequate oxygenation and maintaining blood pressure (Table 434–8). There must be unimpeded access to the circulation, and cardiac function must be monitored continuously. Diagnostic studies should be initiated concurrently with blood obtained for antiepileptic drug levels, blood cell count, and routine chemistries. Brain imaging is necessary, but control of seizures must be the first priority. Lumbar puncture must be performed if meningitis is strongly suspected. If focal neurologic signs point to a mass lesion, however, antibiotics should be given and a computed tomography scan obtained first. In adults, thiamine (to avoid precipitating Wernicke's encephalopathy) followed by glucose should be administered to counteract hypoglycemia, unless an adequate glucose concentration has been shown.

A benzodiazepine, lorazepam (4 mg, repeated once, or 4 to 8 mg) or diazepam (10 mg, repeated once), should be given, followed immediately by intravenous phenytoin or fosphenytoin, 20 mg/kg phenytoin equivalents (PE), at a rate not exceeding 150 mg/min. If seizures continue, an additional 5 mg/kg PE of phenytoin or fosphenytoin should be given. About 80% of patients respond to this regimen. If status is refractory, the patient should be admitted to an intensive care unit and anesthetized with intravenous pentobarbital, 2 to 10.5 mg/kg, followed by 25 to 50 mg every 25 to 50 minutes as necessary to produce a burst-suppression pattern on continuously monitored EEG. Maintenance doses are 1.5 to 3 mg/kg/hr as necessary to produce a burst-suppression pattern on continuously monitored EEG. Ventilatory assistance and vasopressors invariably are required. Alternatively, midazolam drip (0.2 mg/kg, then 0.1 to 2.0 mg/kg/hr followed by 0.75 to

Neurology

Table 434–8 • PROTOCOL AND TIMETABLE FOR TREATING STATUS EPILEPTICUS

TIME (MIN)	ACTION
0–5	Diagnose; give O_2, ABCs; obtain IV access; begin ECG monitoring; draw blood for chemistries –7, Mg, Ca, CBC, AED levels, ABG; toxicology screen
6–10	Thiamine 100 mg IV; 50 mL of D50 IV unless adequate glucose level known
	Lorazepam (Ativan) 4 mg IV over 2 min; repeat once in 8–10 min as needed or
	Diazepam (Valium) 10 mg IV over 2 min; repeat once in 3–5 min as needed
10–20	If status persists or if diazepam was used immediately begin fosphenytoin (Cerebyx) 20 mg/kg IV at 150 mg/min, with blood pressure and ECG monitoring
20–30	If status continues, give additional 5 mg/kg fosphenytoin 2 times (total 30 mg/kg)
30	If status continues, intubate and give one of the following, preferably with EEG monitoring: (1) Pentobarbital 2–10 mg/kg slow bolus, then 0.5–3 mg/kg/hr; (2) Midazolam continuous infusion, 0.2 mg/kg slow bolus, then 0.1–2.0 mg/kg/hr; or (3) Propofol continuous infusion, 1–5 mg/kg bolus over 5 min, then 2–4 mg/kg/hr

ABCs = airway, blood pressure, cardiac function; ABG = arterial blood gas; AED = antiepileptic drug; CBC = complete blood count; D50% = dextrose in water; ECG = electrocardiogram; EEG = electroencephalogram.

1.0 mg/kg/min) can be used to induce anesthesia. Midazolam is cleared more rapidly and has less hypotensive effect than either phenobarbital or pentobarbital. Propofol, 1 to 5 mg/kg followed by continuous infusion of 2 to 4 mg/kg/hr, also has been effective in some patients with refractory status epilepticus.

Nonconvulsive status epilepticus is difficult to diagnose and is frequently unrecognized. It presents most often in middle-aged or elderly persons without a history of seizures. Onset is generally abrupt, with a fluctuating confusional state that can last for days to weeks. Although clouding of consciousness occurs to a varying degree, the absence of stupor or coma contributes to misdiagnosis. Nonconvulsive status epilepticus may be mistaken for psychosis because of the abrupt development of bizarre behavior, inappropriate affect, paranoia, delusions, and catatonia. Alternatively, memory loss, confusion, and mood changes may predominate and suggest a metabolic or toxic encephalopathy or dementia. Some patients have recurrent episodes.

Diagnosis depends on demonstration of seizure discharges in the EEG in association with symptoms. Most patients show continuous or nearly continuous 1- to 2.5-Hz generalized spike-wave activity similar to generalized absence status ("spike-wave stupor") that occurs in children. Rarely the EEG ictal activity is localized, however, usually to the frontal or temporal lobes, indicating that in these patients the nonconvulsive status is a form of continuous partial seizure activity. Intravenous diazepam (5 to 10 mg) or lorazepam (1 to 2 mg) suppresses epileptiform EEG abnormalities and produces dramatic improvement in the patient's mental state. Long-term seizure control is achieved using valproate, phenytoin, or carbamazepine.

A specific cause cannot be identified in most cases. Sometimes nonconvulsive status results from electrolyte imbalance, drug toxicity (e.g., lithium), or a focal cerebral lesion (e.g., frontal lobe infarction).

Psychosocial Issues

Epilepsy and its effects result from multiple interacting factors, of which seizures are only a part. The extent of a patient's disability or quality of life may relate more to physical limitations caused by neurologic abnormalities, psychological factors, or adverse drug effects than to the seizures themselves. This observation is underscored by patients who become seizure-free after surgery but who remain disabled and unable to find employment, establish relationships, or become independent in other ways. Not the least of epilepsy's disabling aspects is the episodic nature of the condition: Periods of

relative well-being are punctuated by unpredictably occurring attacks that impose their own limitations, create embarrassment, and reinforce negative stereotypes. Recurrent seizures, despite treatment, are graphic reminders of medicine's failure. Adults experience discrimination at work and loss of mobility because they cannot drive.

The treatment of epilepsy can be effective only when interacting medical, psychological, and environmental factors are addressed successfully. Areas of psychosocial difficulty should be identified early in treatment and an appropriate plan of management developed. This often requires a multidisciplinary approach to disabilities that have social, educational, vocational, and psychological dimensions. The physician must be sensitive to these issues, even if they are not voiced explicitly. Psychosocial concerns may be the major focus of most follow-up visits. The physician has a special responsibility to educate society and the patient and family to counter the many misperceptions, myths, and prejudices that are ascribed to epilepsy.

1. Wiebe S, Blume WT, Girvin JP, Eliasziw M: A randomized, controlled trial of surgery for temporal lobe epilepsy. New Engl J Med 2001;345:311–318.
2. Musicco M, Beghi E, Solari A, et al: Treatment of first tonic-clonic seizure does not improve the prognosis of epilepsy. Neurology 1997;49:991–998.

SUGGESTED READINGS

Begley CE, Famulari M, Annegers JF, et al: The cost of epilepsy in the United States: An estimate from population-based clinical and survey data. Epilepsia 2000;41:342–351. *The best documented analysis of the direct and indirect lifetime and annual costs of epilepsy in the United States.*

Clark S, Wilson WA: Mechanisms of epileptogenesis. Adv Neurol 1999;79:607–630. *A summary of the known and proposed dynamic biological events that underlie the development of epilepsy.*

Engel J Jr, Pedley TA (eds): Epilepsy: A Comprehensive Textbook. Philadelphia, Lippincott-Raven Press, 1997. *A multi-authored three-volume textbook that covers all aspects of epilepsy, from the basic molecular cellular and neural biology to details of medical, surgical, and psychosocial management.*

Jacobs MP, Fischbach GD, Davis, MR, et al: Future directions for epilepsy research. Neurology 2001;57:1536–1542. *An important consensus statement by leading investigators in the field about the need to establish a new epilepsy research agenda that takes advantage of recent advances in neurobiology, electrophysiology, imaging, and genetics. It also provides a useful summary of current knowledge in key areas and a current list of important references.*

Karceski S, Morrell M, Carpenter D: The Expert Consensus Guideline Series: Treatment of Epilepsy. Epilepsy and Behavior 2001;2(Suppl):A1–A50. *An informative and useful survey of epilepsy experts regarding treatment strategies and selection of drugs for the major categories of seizures and epilepsy.*

Kwan P, Brodie MJ: Early identification of refractory epilepsy. N Engl J Med 2000;342:314–319. *A prospective study that identifies early predictors for the development of intractable epilepsy.*

Lowenstein DH, Alldredge BK: Status epilepticus. N Engl J Med 1998;338:970–977. *A review of current concepts of managing status epilepticus, including recommended treatment regimens.*

Pedley TA, Hauser WA: Sudden death in epilepsy: a wake-up call for management. Lancet 2002;359:1790–1791. *A commentary on the phenomenon of sudden unexplained death in epilepsy (SUDEP), the most common cause of seizure-related mortality in people with chronic epilepsy.*

Remy S, Gabriel S, Urban BW, et al: A novel mechanism underlying drug resistance in chronic epilepsy. Ann Neurol 2003;53:469–479. *An experimental study that includes analysis of sodium-channel function in the hippocampus of patients undergoing temporal lobe resections for uncontrolled epilepsy. Drug resistance to carbamazepine was associated with a loss of sodium-channel drug sensitivity.*

Roth HL, Drislane FW: Seizures. In: Neurologic Emergencies. Neurologic Clinics of North America 1998;16:257–284. *A practical guide to the evaluation and treatment of acute seizures.*

Sisodiya SM, Lin WR, Harding BN, et al: Drug resistance in epilepsy: expression of drug resistance proteins in common causes of refractory epilepsy. Brain 2002;125:22–31. *Drug resistance in epilepsy, as in cancer, may be due to overexpression of multi-drug resistance proteins.*

Sperling MR, Feldman H, Kinman J, et al: Seizure control and mortality in epilepsy. Ann Neurol 1999;46:45–50. *A study of factors associated with increased mortality rates in patients with epilepsy, an understudied and under recognized phenomenon.*

Zahn CA, Morrell MJ, Collins SD, et al: Management issues for women with epilepsy. A review of the literature. Neurology 1998;51:949–956. *A thorough review of gender-related issues that have implications for patient management.*

435 SYNCOPE

Roger P. Simon

Syncope is the phenomenon of loss of consciousness associated with loss of postural tone (Chapter 46). The episode is caused by global impairment of blood flow to the brain; occasionally, hypoperfusion may be confined to the cerebral hemispheres or the brain stem, and involvement of either structure produces unconsciousness. Syncope must be differentiated from seizures (Chapter 434), which may manifest similarly but have a different pathophysiology and therapy.

History

Because most spells of episodic loss of consciousness occur outside medical observation, the history is the most critical part of the evaluation. If multiple spells have occurred, their similarity should be established so that small pieces of history from one spell or another may be combined into a pathophysiologic profile. Each syncopal episode should be reviewed in detail, with attention to the three key elements: events and symptoms preceding the spell, what happened during the spell of unconsciousness, and the time course of regaining orientation after consciousness is regained. The first of these elements can be obtained from the patient, but the second and, frequently, the third cannot. Accordingly, information from a witness is essential to the evaluation and should be obtained by phone calls, interviews, or revisits scheduled to include persons who have witnessed one or more spells.

BEFORE THE SPELL. What position was the patient in when each spell began? Seizures or cardiac arrhythmias can develop with any body position, but vasovagal syncope rarely and orthostatic hypotension never begins with the patient recumbent. In patients with recurrent syncope, if even a single episode began in the recumbent posture, vasovagal and orthostatic causes are virtually excluded.

What prodromal symptoms were appreciated before loss of consciousness? Symptoms of cerebral hypoperfusion should be sought, including lightheadedness, dizziness (but uncommonly vertigo), bilateral tinnitus, nausea, diffuse weakness, and finally dimming of vision from retinal hypoperfusion. This prodrome establishes the pathophysiology of the syncopal spell as that of cerebral hypoperfusion; such hypoperfusion may be of cardiac, orthostatic, or reflex cause. Loss of consciousness so rapid that a prodrome is absent may occur with seizures and with some cardiac arrhythmias such as asystole, which cause loss of consciousness within 4 to 8 seconds in the upright position but require 12 to 15 seconds in the recumbent position. Palpitations during the prodrome suggest a tachyarrhythmia (Chapters 59 and 60) but may also occur with vasovagal events.

What was the activity of the patient immediately before the onset of symptoms? Identification of extreme exertion (cardiac), an emotional or painful stimulus (vasovagal), a rapid change in posture (orthostatic), and straining at urination (situational) can help in identifying the cause.

DURING THE EVENT. What events do witnesses describe as occurring during the episode of unconsciousness? Although body stiffening and limb jerking are well-known motor phenomena occurring during the loss of consciousness associated with generalized seizures, very similar motor movements can result from cerebral hypoperfusion. These motor movements occur especially if cerebral blood flow is not rapidly restored by termination of an arrhythmia or by falling to a recumbent posture in the setting of reflex syncope. Such muscle jerking is often multifocal and can be synchronous or asynchronous. In contrast to epileptic seizures, which generally produce tonic-clonic activity for at least 1 to 2 minutes (Chapter 434), muscle jerking in syncope rarely persists longer than 30 seconds. If an arrhythmia continues or the patient is physically maintained upright (e.g., fainting in a phone booth or while sitting on a toilet), tonic stiffening of the body occurs (i.e., opisthotonos) and is followed by jerking movements of the limbs. Occasionally, motor movements identical to a tonic-clonic seizure occur, and a mistaken diagnosis of epilepsy can be made. Urinary incontinence during the spell is frequently used to support or refute a diagnosis of epilepsy; however, fainting with a full bladder can result in incontinence, whereas seizures with an empty bladder will not. Tongue biting favors seizures.

AFTER THE EVENT. Over what time period were consciousness and orientation regained? This aspect of the history is the most useful in dealing with the differential diagnosis of seizures as the cause of a syncopal-like spell. Recovery of orientation and consciousness after vasovagal or reflex-mediated syncope occurs simultaneously. Recovery of orientation after syncope of cardiac origin is proportional to the duration of the unconsciousness but is usually rapid (0 to 10 seconds); with periods of malignant arrhythmia producing unconsciousness of 2 minutes, confusion on waking is less than 30 seconds. After seizures, however, the period of confusion, often with agitation, continues for 2 to 20 minutes after recovery of consciousness.

Etiology

NEUROCARDIOGENIC SYNCOPE

The term *neurocardiogenic syncope* (Table 435–1) is used to describe spells of transient cerebral hypoperfusion in the absence of a demonstrable cardiac cause. The mechanism of the peripheral vasodilation and hypotension may be vagotonic, situational, or of unclear origin. A common phenomenon is activation of cardiopulmonary baroreceptors and mechanoreceptors resulting in inappropriate peripheral pooling of blood, inappropriate bradycardia, and in some, a combination of both. The prodrome (i.e., lightheadedness, tinnitus, and visual dimming) and the pattern of recovery (i.e., simultaneous recovery of consciousness and orientation) are reasonably consistent regardless of the precise cause.

VASOVAGAL SYNCOPE. Vasovagal spells, or simple faints, are the most common cause of syncope. These episodes occur in all age groups, are equally common in men and women, and may be more frequent in some families. Precipitating factors include pain (especially medical instrumentation), trauma, fatigue, blood loss, or prolonged motionless standing. Vagally mediated hypotension and bradycardia combine to produce cerebral hypoperfusion, with a resultant prodrome of lightheadedness, nausea, tinnitus, diaphoresis, salivation, pallor, and dimming of vision. Tachycardia may be the initial manifestation. The spells typically begin in the standing or sitting position, but medical instrumentation (e.g., phlebotomy or intrauterine device insertion) can induce episodes when the patient is horizontal. The patient loses consciousness and postural tone and then falls with flaccid or stiff limbs; the eyes are usually open, often with an upward gaze. The patient is pale and diaphoretic and has dilated pupils. Tonic posturing or a few symmetrical or asymmetrical myoclonic jerks may occur, especially if the patient is maintained in a semiupright

Table 435–1 • CAUSES OF SYNCOPE AND THEIR PREVALENCES IN VARIOUS SERIES

Neurocardiogenic Causes
Vasovagal (8–41% of patients)
Situational (1–8% of patients)
   Micturition
   Defecation
   Swallow
   Cough
Carotid sinus syncope (0.4% of patients)
Neuralgias
Psychiatric disorders
Medications, exercise

Orthostatic Hypotension (4–10% of patients)

Decreased Cardiac Output
Obstruction to flow (1–8% of patients)
   Obstruction to LV outflow or inflow: aortic stenosis, hypertrophic obstructive cardiomyopathy, mitral stenosis, myxoma
   Obstruction to RV outflow or inflow: pulmonic stenosis, PE, pulmonary hypertension, myxoma
Other heart disease
   Pump failure, MI, CAD, coronary spasm, tamponade, aortic dissection
Arrhythmias (4–38% of patients)
   Bradyarrhythmias: sinus node disease, second- and third-degree atrioventricular block, pacemaker malfunction, drug-induced bradyarrhythmias
   Tachyarrhythmias: ventricular tachycardia, torsades de pointes (e.g., associated with congenital long-QT syndrome or acquired QT prolongation), supraventricular tachycardia

Neurologic and Psychiatric Diseases (3–32% of patients)
Migraine
TIAs

Unknown (13–41% of patients)

CAD = coronary artery disease; LV = left ventricular, MI = myocardial infarction; PE = pulmonary embolism; RV = right ventricular; TIAs = transient ischemic attacks.
Adapted from Kapoor W: Approach to the patient with syncope. *In* Braunwald E, Goldman L (eds): Primary Cardiology, 2nd ed. Philadelphia, WB Saunders, 2003.

position. These jerking movements are not epileptic; concomitant electroencephalographic (EEG) recordings show generalized slow waves. Consciousness is rapidly recovered when the patient becomes horizontal. Postictal confusion is absent. Symptoms of nervousness, dizziness, nausea, and urge to defecate may persist, and syncope can recur on standing.

SITUATIONAL SYNCOPE. Vagally mediated neurocardiogenic syncope can be induced by micturition, defecation, or swallowing or occur during episodes of glossopharyngeal neuralgia. Syncope during micturition occurs before, during, or after micturition in the upright position. Vagally mediated bradycardia is causative. The events are most frequent on arising from the recumbency of sleep to urinate. Although much less common, a similar syndrome can occur with defecation. Brain stem reflexes triggering vagally induced brady-arrhythmias, with resultant syncope, can occur as a result of swallowing, with or without the association of severe pain in the tonsillar pillar, which may radiate to the ear (i.e., glossopharyngeal neuralgia). The pain can be prevented by carbamazepine (400 to 1000 mg/day PO) (Chapter 434). In refractory cases, 300 mg of phenytoin (Dilantin) each day can be added.

A nonvagally mediated situational syncope occurs with coughing (i.e., cough syncope). In predisposed patients, the coughing increases intrathoracic venous pressure, which is transmitted to the intracranial veins; the resultant transient increase in intracranial pressure is adequate to impair blood flow. Spells can occur in any position. A prodrome is absent, and impaired consciousness lasts only a few seconds.

CAROTID SINUS SYNCOPE. Carotid sinus syncope results from vagal stimulation from the carotid sinus, producing hypotension or bradycardia. The syndrome is uncommon, has a male preponderance, and affects mainly patients older than 60 years. Use of propranolol, digitalis, or methyldopa may predispose to carotid sinus syncope. Carotid sinus massage may be diagnostic and can be performed in an outpatient setting, although only in the absence of carotid bruits or a history of ventricular tachycardia, recent stroke, or myocardial infarction. Induction of asystole longer than or equal to 3 seconds, hypotension, or both constitute a positive test result. False-positive results are common, however, especially in the setting of contralateral carotid occlusion, because the ipsilateral massage transiently occludes the ipsilateral carotid and thereby prevents bilateral carotid blood flow. Symptomatic bradycardia can be treated by pacemaker implantation.

PSYCHIATRIC SYNCOPE. Neuropsychiatric syncope is a diagnosis of exclusion but is suggested by young age, frequent spells, multiple symptoms (e.g., dizziness, vertigo, lightheadedness, numbness), and duplication of the patient's symptoms by hyperventilation with the mouth open for 2 to 3 minutes. Whereas syncope and seizures occur with the eyes open, often with a gaze deviation, psychogenic events frequently begin with eye closing.

ORTHOSTATIC HYPOTENSION

Postural hypotension can result in syncope that may be recurrent. The history confirms that the patients are in the upright posture during the spells, that the prodromal symptoms are those of cerebral hypoperfusion, and that symptoms are relieved with recumbency. The diagnosis is supported by detecting a fall of 30 mm Hg or greater in systolic pressure or a 10 mm Hg or greater fall in diastolic pressure between testing in the recumbent versus the upright posture. The many causes include drugs, polyneuropathies, or neurodegenerative disorders (Chapters 443, 460, and 461).

CARDIOGENIC SYNCOPE

Syncope that occurs during exercise or is associated with palpitations suggests a cardiac cause. A family history may be found in certain cases of prolonged QT interval syndrome. Cardiogenic syncope occurs in the setting of organic heart disease producing inflow (e.g., myxoma, constrictive pericarditis) or outflow obstruction (e.g., aortic or pulmonic stenosis, hypertrophic cardiomyopathy) or as the result of bradyarrhythmia or tachyarrhythmias (Chapters 59 and 60). Premonitory symptoms may be caused by cerebral hypoperfusion (i.e., faintness, tinnitus, and dimming of vision), but these symptoms may be absent with bradyarrhythmias because of the rapid fall in cardiac output and precipitous decline in cerebral blood flow resulting in abrupt loss of consciousness. Evaluation for arrhythmias should begin

FIGURE 435–1 • Diagnostic approach to a patient with syncope. CT = computed tomography; ECG = electrocardiogram, EEG = electroencephalogram; EPS = electrophysiologic study; NSR = normal sinus rhythm. (Adapted from Linzer M, Yang EH, Ester NA, et al: Diagnosing syncope. Part 1. Value of history, physical examination, and electrocardiography. The Clinical Efficacy Assessment Project of the American College of Physicians. Ann Intern Med 1997;126:989–996; and from Linzer M, Yang EH, Ester NA, et al: Diagnosing syncope. Part 2. Unexplained syncope. The Clinical Efficacy Assessment Project of the American College of Physicians. Ann Intern Med 1997;127:76–86. From Braunwald E, Goldman L [eds]: Primary Cardiology, 2nd ed. Philadelphia, WB Saunders, 2003.)

with a rhythm strip, which provides a 5% yield, followed by Holter monitoring for 24 hours; symptoms occur during the monitoring in approximately 20% of patients. With recurrent events, long-term ambulatory loop electrocardiography (ECG) is useful in recording the rhythm during a spell, confirming or excluding an arrhythmic cause. This technique identifies another 25 to 50% of patients studied. Electrophysiologic testing (Chapter 58) is often used in an attempt to induce arrhythmias in patients who have organic heart disease or conduction block on the ECG (especially in the elderly at risk for syncope-induced trauma); the yield is approximately 50%.

CEREBROVASCULAR SYNCOPE

Loss of consciousness can be a component of a basilar artery transient ischemic attack (Chapter 440), but unconsciousness alone is virtually never the initial sign. Other brain stem symptoms always precede or accompany the syncope. Vertigo is most frequent, but diplopia or visual field disturbances, hemifacial or perioral numbness, and dysarthria or ataxia are also common. Recovery of consciousness may require 30 to 60 minutes.

Subclavian artery stenosis may result in retrograde blood flow from the vertebral artery to one arm, with resultant brain stem hypoperfusion (i.e., subclavian steal syndrome). An asymmetry in upper extremity blood pressure averaging 45 mm Hg is nearly always present. Brain stem symptoms similar to those in basilar transient ischemic attacks occur and can include loss of consciousness; a subsequent stroke, however, is rare. Syncope may also occur in up to 10% of patients with basilar artery migraine (Chapter 428). It can have a postural (orthostatic) manifestation or be associated with other basilar artery symptoms.

SYNCOPE IN THE ELDERLY

The elderly often have multiple factors contributing to syncope, including situational, reflex, cardiac, cerebrovascular, and neurologic (Chapter 23). Orthostatic syncope is particularly likely to occur 15 to 75 minutes after a meal or after rapid change of posture, even in the absence of neurologic or gastrointestinal disease. The postprandial systolic pressure reduction in a normal elderly person is approximately 14 mm Hg, compared with 24 mm Hg in those with a history of syncope. Medications with hypotensive side effects (even if administered at standard doses) commonly induce hypotension in the elderly; these drugs may include antihypertensive agents, sedatives, antidepressants, and antianginal and antiparkinsonian medications; fluoxetine, haloperidol, and L-dopa are particularly notable. Protracted episodes of unresponsiveness lasting up to 4 hours occasionally occur in the elderly, especially while in the hospital. Investigations are not revealing. A disorder of the sleep cycle may be responsible.

Diagnosis

The history and physical examination guide the approach to further diagnostic testing (Table 435–2 and Fig. 435–1). In patients without evidence of structural heart disease or cerebrovascular disease, typical symptoms may be reproduced during head-up tilt-table testing (Chapter 58), such as tilting to 70 degrees for up to 45 minutes; sensitivity may be increased by the addition of an isoproterenol infusion to mimic catecholamine release. Of patients identified in this manner, one third have a vasodepressor response, and two thirds have a cardioinhibitory response.

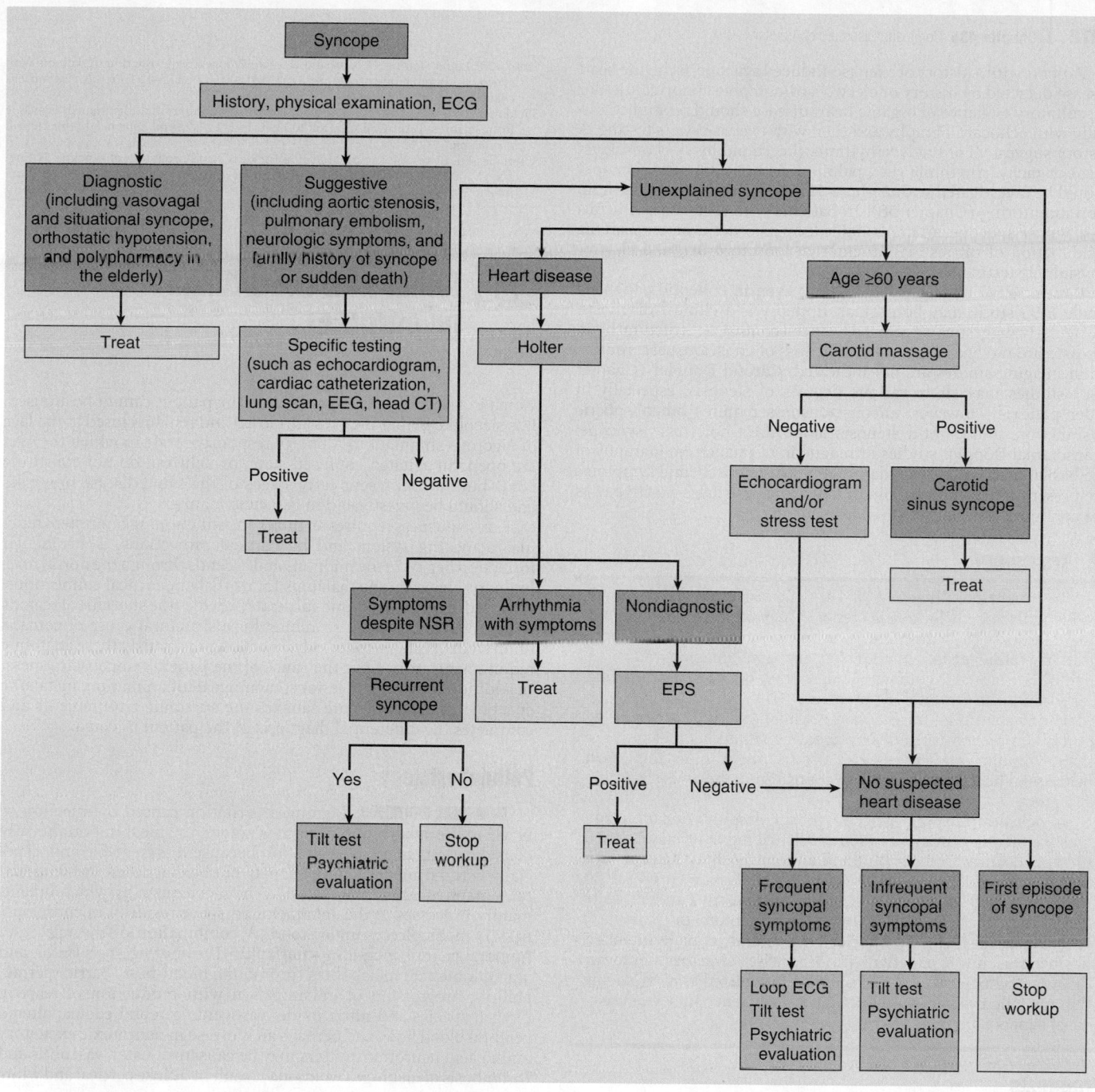

Table 435–2 • CLINICAL FEATURES SUGGESTING SPECIFIC CAUSES

SYMPTOM OR FINDING	DIAGNOSTIC CONSIDERATION
After sudden unexpected pain, fear, unpleasant sight, sound, or smell	Vasovagal
Prolonged standing at attention	Vasovagal
Well-trained athlete after exertion (without heart disease)	Vasovagal
During or immediately after micturition, cough, swallowing, or defecation	Situational syncope
Syncope with throat or facial pain (glossopharyngeal or trigeminal neuralgia)	Neurocardiogenic syncope with neuralgia
With head rotation, pressure on the carotid sinus (as in tumors, shaving, tight collars)	Carotid sinus syncope
Immediately on standing	Orthostatic hypotension
Medication that may lead to long-QT syndrome or orthostasis or bradycardia	Drug induced
Associated with headaches	Migraine, seizures
Associated with vertigo, dysarthria, diplopia	Transient ischemic attack, subclavian steal, basilar migraine
With arm exercise	Subclavian steal
Confusion after a spell or loss of consciousness for more than 5 minutes	Seizure
Differences in blood pressure or pulse in the two arms	Subclavian steal or aortic dissection
Syncope and murmur with changing position (from sitting to lying, bending, turning over in bed)	Atrial myxoma or thrombus
Syncope with exertion	Aortic stenosis, pulmonary hypertension, mitral stenosis, obstructive hypertrophic cardiomyopathy, coronary artery disease
Family history of sudden death	Long-QT syndrome, Brugada syndrome
Brief loss of consciousness, no prodrome, with heart disease	Arrhythmias
Frequent syncope, somatic complaints, no heart disease	Psychiatric illness

From Kapoor WN: Syncope. N Engl J Med 2000;343:1856–1862.

Patients with a history of exercise-induced syncope, ischemic heart disease detected by history or electrocardiographic abnormalities, or auscultatory evidence of organic heart disease should be studied initially with echocardiography and then with exercise stress testing. A history suggestive of bradyarrhythmia (i.e., rapid loss of consciousness) or tachyarrhythmia (i.e., palpitations preceding the syncope) should be investigated with 24-hour Holter monitoring or long-term loop monitoring (Chapter 58). In patients with recurrent, difficult-to-diagnose syncope, an implantable loop recorder is better than the combination of tilt testing, an external loop recorder, and electrophysiologic testing. **[1]**

Routine EEG testing is not helpful; even in epileptic patients a single EEG study may be normal. Epilepsy is a clinical diagnosis. Particularly suggestive is prologed postictal confusion. Structural brain diseases are rarely a cause of episodic loss of consciousness; routine brain imaging studies are not indicated. Carotid Doppler (Chapter 440) studies may show various degrees of stenosis, especially in older patients. However, unconsciousness requires bihemispheric dysfunction, and carotid stenosis alone does not cause syncope. Transcranial Doppler studies or magnetic resonance angiography of the basilar artery is indicated only if brain stem ischemic symptoms are present in addition to loss of consciousness; false-positive tests are common, especially with increasing age.

Rx Treatment

Treatment should be directed at the cause of syncope, such as valve replacement for aortic stenosis (Chapter 72); medications for obstructive, hypertrophic cardiomyopathy (Chapter 73); medications, cardioversion, a pacemaker, or an implantable cardioverter defibrillator for arrhythmias (Chapters 59, 60, and 62); and fluid repletion for orthostatic hypotension.

Patients with neurocardiogenic syncope should be counseled on how to prevent episodes by avoiding situations that provoke their symptoms. Patients should also be taught to put their head below their heart or assume a supine position at the time of warning symptoms.

If neurocardiogenic syncope recurs despite education and lifestyle changes, fludrocortisone (0.1 to 1 mg/day) may be used to expand intravascular volume. Randomized trials have shown that β-blockers (e.g., atenolol, 25 to 200 mg/day; metoprolol, 50 to 200 mg/day; or propranolol, 40 to 160 mg/day) are generally better than placebo, except in highly symptomatic patients. **[2]** Paroxetine (10–40 mg/day), a selective serotonin reuptake inhibitor, has been useful in patients with otherwise refractory neurocardiogenic syncope. **[3]** A double-blind randomized trial of pacing therapy failed to show a reduction of recurrence in severe vasovagal syncope patients. **[4]**

Prognosis

The occurrence of syncope predicts a substantial risk for recurrence of syncope. Patients with cardiac causes have higher mortality rates than those with noncardiac causes or those without a definable cause. However, syncope does not itself increase the risk of death inasmuch as mortality is associated with the underlying cardiac disease regardless of whether syncope has been a symptom.

1. Krahn AD, Klein GJ, Yee R, Skanes AC: Randomized assessment of syncope trial: Conventional diagnostic testing versus a prolonged monitoring strategy. Circulation 2001;104:46–54.
2. Ventura R, Maas R, Zeidler D, et al: A randomized and controlled pilot trial of beta-blockers for the treatment of recurrent syncope in patients with a positive or negative response to head-up tilt test. Pacing Clin Electrophysiol 2002;25:816–821.
3. Di Girolamo E, Di Iorio C, Sabatini P, et al: Effects of paroxetine hydrochloride, a selective serotonin reuptake inhibitor, on refractory vasovagal syncope: A randomized, double-blind, placebo-controlled study. J Am Coll Cardiol 1999;33:1227–1230.
4. Connolly SJ, Sheldon R, Thorpe KE, et al: Pacemaker therapy for prevention of syncope in patients with recurrent severe vasovagal syncope: Second Vasovagal Pacemaker Study (VPS II): A randomized trial. JAMA 2003;289:2224–2229.

SUGGESTED READINGS

Kapoor W: Approach to the patient with syncope. *In* Braunwald E, Goldman L (eds): Primary Cardiology, 2nd ed. Philadelphia, WB Saunders, 2003. *A useful overview.*

Sarasin FP, Louis-Simonet M, Carballo D, et al: Prospective evaluation of patients with syncope: A population-based study. Am J Med 2001;111:177–184. *Prevalence of various causes of syncope and the yield of common tests.*

Sheldon R, Rose S, Ritchie D, et al: Historical criteria that distinguish syncope from seizures. J Am Coll Cardiol 2002;40:142–148. *Useful approach to this clinical distinction.*

Soteriades ES, Evans JC, Larson MG, et al: Incidence and prognosis of syncope. N Engl J Med 2002;347:878–885. *Persons with cardiac syncope are at increased risk for death from any cause.*

436 COMA AND DISORDERS OF AROUSAL

Roger P. Simon

Coma is a sleeplike state from which the patient cannot be aroused. It is sleeplike in that the eyes are closed and remain closed in the face of vigorous stimulation. A poorly responsive state in which the eyes are open, an agitated confused state, or delirium do not constitute coma but may represent early stages of the same disease processes and should be investigated in the same manner.

Consciousness requires an intact and functioning brain stem reticular activating system and its cortical projections. The reticular formation begins in the midpons and ascends through the dorsal midbrain to synapse in the thalamus for its thalamocortical connections. Knowledge of this anatomic substrate provides the short list of regions to be investigated while searching for a structural cause of coma; a brain stem or bihemispheric dysfunction must satisfy these anatomic requirements or it is not the cause of the patient's unconsciousness. In addition to structural lesions, meningeal inflammation, metabolic encephalopathy, or seizure satisfies the anatomic requirements and completes the differential diagnosis of the patient in coma.

Pathophysiology

MENINGEAL IRRITATION. Meningeal irritation caused by infection or blood in the subarachnoid space is among the most important early considerations in coma evaluation because it is treatable and, especially with purulent meningitis, may not be diagnosed by computed tomography (CT) (Table 436–1). The mechanism by which inflammatory processes in the subarachnoid space result in unconsciousness is incompletely understood. A combination of the release of humoral factors, including interleukin-1, tumor necrosis factor, and arachidonic acid metabolites (promoting blood-brain barrier permeability); progression of inflammation with production of reactive oxygen species and nitric oxide; vasogenic cerebral edema; altered cerebral blood flow; and perhaps an increase in neurotoxic excitatory amino acid neurotransmitters may be causative. Later, vasculitis and thrombosis of meningeal veins may result in diffuse cortical and white matter necrosis.

HEMISPHERIC MASS LESIONS. Hemispheric mass lesions result in coma by expanding across the midline laterally to compromise both cerebral hemispheres or by impinging on the brain stem to compress the rostral reticular formation. These processes have been referred to as *lateral herniation* (i.e., lateral movement of the brain) and *transtentorial herniation* (i.e., vertical movement of hemispheric content across the cerebellar tentorium, which separates the hemispheric compartment from the brain stem and posterior fossa). Although horizontal or vertical movement of the brain in isolation may produce coma, a combination of these processes is the most common cause. At the bedside, clinical signs of an expanding hemispheric mass evolve in a level-by-level, rostral-caudal manner (Fig. 436–1). Hemispheric lesions of adequate size to produce coma are readily seen on CT.

BRAIN STEM MASS LESIONS. Brain stem mass lesions produce coma by directly compromising the reticular formation. As the pathways for lateral eye movements (i.e., pontine gaze center, medial longitudinal fasciculus, and oculomotor [third cranial nerve] nucleus) traverse the reticular activating system, impairment of reflex eye movements is often the critical element in diagnosis. A comatose patient without impairment of reflex lateral eye movements does not have a mass lesion compromising brain stem structures in the posterior fossa. This aspect of the examination is therefore critical to rapid diagnosis, because CT scanning is not able to detect some lesions in this region. Posterior fossa lesions may compromise cortical function by upward

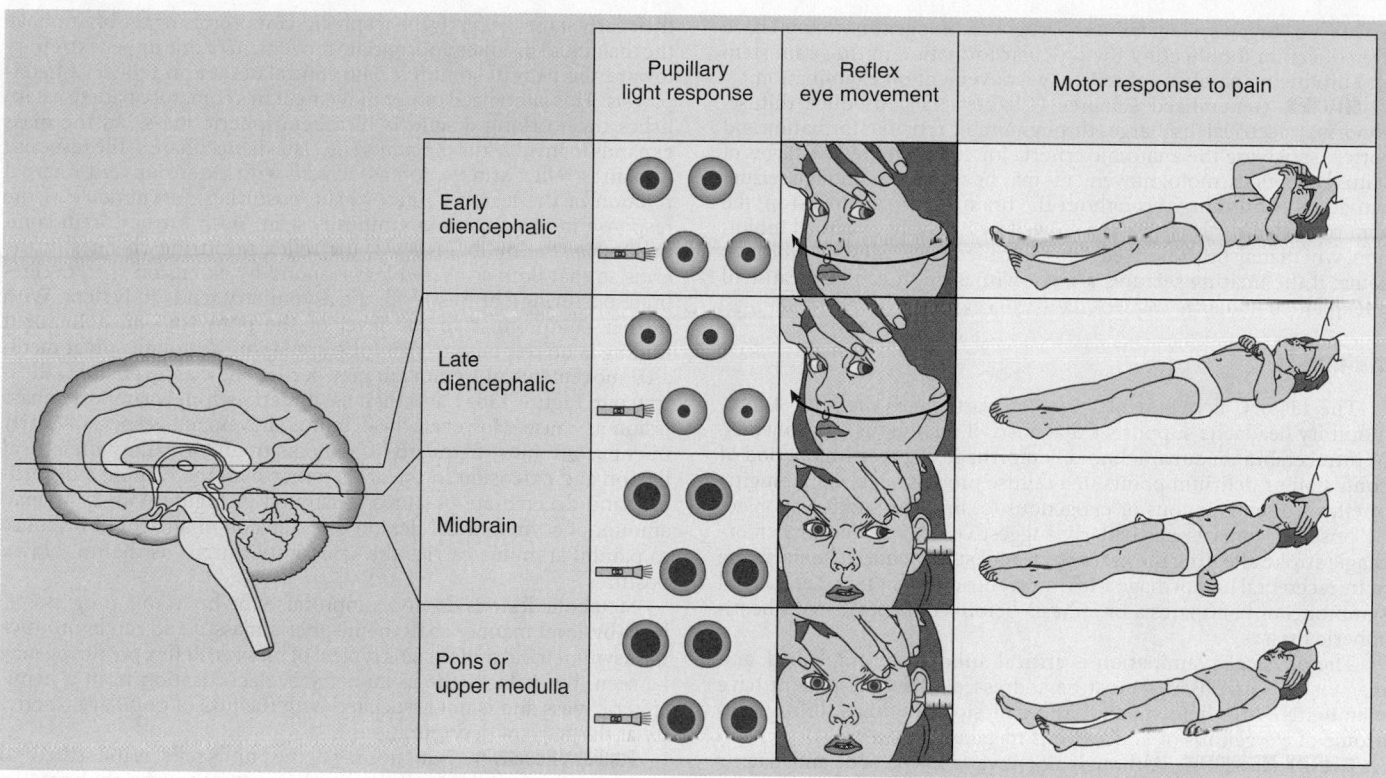

	Pupillary light response	Reflex eye movement	Motor response to pain
Early diencephalic			
Late diencephalic			
Midbrain			
Pons or upper medulla			

FIGURE 436–1 • The evolution of neurologic signs in coma from a hemispheric mass lesion as the brain becomes functionally impaired in a rostral caudal manner. Early and late diencephalic levels are levels of dysfunction just above (early) and just below (late) the thalamus. (From Aminoff MJ, Greenberg DA, Simon RP: Clinical Neurology. Norwalk, CT, Appleton & Lange, 1996.)

Table 436–1 • CAUSES OF COMA WITH NORMAL COMPUTED TOMOGRAPHIC SCAN RESULT

Meningeal causes
 Subarachnoid hemorrhage (uncommon)
 Bacterial meningitis
 Encephalitis
 Subdural empyema
Exogenous toxins
 Sedative drugs or barbiturates
 Anesthetics or γ-hydroxybutyrate*
 Alcohols
 Stimulants
  Phencyclidine[†]
  Cocaine or amphetamine[‡]
 Psychotropic drugs
  Cyclic antidepressants
  Phenothiazines
  Lithium
 Anticonvulsants
 Opioids
 Clonidine[§]
 Penicillins
 Salicylates
 Anticholinergics
 Carbon monoxide/cyanide/methemoglobinemia
Endogenous toxins, deficiencies, or derangements
 Hypoxia or ischemia
 Hypoglycemia

Hypercalcemia
Osmolar
 Hyperglycemia
 Hyponatremia
 Hypernatremia
Organ system failure
 Hepatic encephalopathy
 Uremic encephalopathy
 Pulmonary insufficiency (CO_2 narcosis)
Seizures
 Prolonged postictal state
 Spike wave stupor
Hypothermia or hyperthermia
Multifocal disorders presenting as metabolic coma
 Disseminated intravascular coagulopathy (DIC)
 Sepsis
 Pancreatitis
 Vasculitis
 Thrombotic thrombocytopenic purpura (TTP)
 Fat emboli
 Hypertensive encephalopathy
 Diffuse micrometastases
Brain stem ischemia
Basilar artery stroke
Brain stem or cerebellar hemorrhage
Conversion or malingering

 *General anesthetic, similar to γ-aminobutyric acid; recreational drug and body building aid characterized by rapid onset, rapid recovery, often with myoclonic jerking and confusion; deep coma (2–3 hours; GCS = 3) with maintenance of vital signs.
 [†]Coma associated with cholinergic signs: lacrimation, salivation, bronchorrhea, and hyperthermia.
 [‡]Coma after seizures or status (i.e., a prolonged postictal state).
 [§]An antihypertensive agent active through the opiate receptor system; overdose common when used to treat narcotic withdrawal.

---

herniation across the cerebellar tentorium or by blocking of cerebrospinal fluid flow from the lateral ventricles, resulting in the dangerous state of noncommunicating hydrocephalus.

METABOLIC ABNORMALITIES. Metabolic abnormalities characterize syndromes caused by the presence of *exogenous toxins* (drugs) or *endogenous toxins* (organ system failure), resulting in diffuse dysfunction of the nervous system without localized signs such as hemiparesis or unilateral pupillary dilation. A diagnosis of "metabolic encephalopathy" indicates that the examiner has found no focal anatomic features by examination or neuroimaging studies to explain coma and does not state that a specific metabolic cause has been established. Such global impairment of function is particularly typical of endogenous

Neurology

toxins (i.e., organ system failure). Drugs (i.e., exogenous toxins) have a predilection for affecting the reticular formation in the brain stem and producing paralysis of reflex eye movement on examination.

SEIZURES. Generalized seizures (Chapter 434) produce diffuse, abnormal electrical discharges throughout the reticular formation and cortex, satisfying the anatomic criteria for coma. In the late stages of status epilepticus, motor movements may be subtle even though seizure activity is continuing throughout the brain. After seizures stop, the abnormal electrical activity is followed by a state of electrical inhibition, which may be prolonged. This so-called postictal state produces coma; if the inciting seizures are not witnessed, it can be a cause of unexplained coma.

Diagnosis

The history, if obtainable, may be particularly helpful. A premonitory headache supports a diagnosis of meningitis, encephalitis, or intracerebral or subarachnoid hemorrhage. A preceding period of confusion or delirium points to a diffuse process such as meningitis or effects of endogenous or exogenous toxins. The sudden apoplectic onset of coma is particularly suggestive of ischemic or hemorrhagic stroke affecting the brain stem or of subarachnoid hemorrhage or intracerebral hemorrhage with intraventricular rupture. Lateralized symptoms of hemiparesis or aphasia before coma occur with hemispheric masses.

The physical examination is critical, quickly accomplished, and diagnostic. Three issues must be addressed. Does the patient have meningitis? Are there signs of a mass lesion? Is this a diffuse syndrome of exogenous or endogenous metabolic cause?

IDENTIFY MENINGITIS. Although not invariably present and having varying sensitivity in regard to cause (i.e., very common with acute pyogenic meningitis [Chapter 312] and subarachnoid hemorrhage [Chapter 441], less common with indolent, fungal meningitis), the presence of signs of meningeal irritation on examination is the central clue to the diagnosis. Missing these signs results in time-consuming additional tests such as CT and risks the loss of a narrow therapeutic window of opportunity. Passive neck flexion should be carried out in all comatose patients unless head and neck trauma is likely to have occurred. When the neck is passively flexed, attempting to bring the chin within a few fingerbreadths of the chest, patients with irritated meninges reflexively flex one or both knees. This sign, Brudzinski's reflex, is usually asymmetrical and not dramatic, but any evidence of knee flexion during passive neck flexion requires that the spinal fluid be examined.

Is CT required before lumbar puncture in this setting? In the absence of lateralized signs (e.g., hemiparesis) indicating a superimposed mass lesion, a spinal puncture should be performed immediately. Although rare cases of herniation after lumbar puncture in children with bacterial meningitis have been reported, the urgency of diagnosis and treatment at the point of coma is paramount. The time required for CT may cause a fatal therapeutic delay.

An alternative approach is to obtain blood cultures and immediately initiate antibiotic therapy with subsequent lumbar puncture. Cerebrospinal fluid cell count, glucose level, and protein content are unchanged, and Gram's stain and culture often produce positive findings despite a short period of antibiotic treatment.

SEPARATE STRUCTURAL FROM METABOLIC CAUSES OF COMA. Structural and metabolic causes of coma can be distinguished by neurologic examination. Because the evaluation and potential treatment modalities for structural versus metabolic coma are widely divergent and the disease processes in both are often rapidly progressive, initiating the evaluation in a medical or surgical direction may be life-saving. This task is accomplished by focusing on three features of neurologic examination: the motor response to a painful stimulus, pupillary function, and reflex eye movements.

The functioning of the motor system provides the clearest indication of a mass lesion. Elicitation of a motor response requires application of a painful stimulus to which the patient will react. The arms should be placed in a semiflexed posture and a painful stimulus applied to the head or trunk. Strong pressure on the supraorbital ridge or pinching of skin on the anterior chest or inner arm is useful; nail bed pressure makes the interpretation of upper limb movement difficult.

The evolution of neurologic signs from an expanding hemispheric mass lesion is illustrated in Figure 436–1. Hemispheric masses at

their early stage (i.e., early diencephalic, compromising the brain above the thalamus) produce appropriate movement of one upper extremity toward the painful stimulus. The contralateral arm reflects a hemiparesis. This lateralized motor movement in a comatose patient establishes the working diagnosis of a hemispheric mass. As the mass expands to involve the thalamus (i.e., late diencephalic), the response to pain is reflex arm flexion associated with extension and internal rotation of the legs (i.e., decorticate posturing); asymmetry of the response in the upper extremities is seen. With further brain compromise at the midbrain level, the reflex posturing changes in the arms so that both arms and legs respond by extension (i.e., decerebrate posturing); at this level, the asymmetry tends to be lost. With further compromise to the level of the pons, the most frequent finding is no response to painful stimulation, although spinal mediated movements of leg flexion may occur. The classic postures illustrated in Figure 436–1 and their asymmetry strongly support a mass lesion as cause. However, these motor movements, especially early in coma, are most frequently fragments of abnormal, asymmetrical flexion and extension in the arms rather than the complete decorticate and decerebrate postures illustrated in Figure 436–1. A small amount of asymmetrical flexion or extension of an arm in response to painful stimulus carries the same implications as the full-blown postures.

Metabolic lesions do not compromise the brain in a progressive, level-by-level manner as do hemispheric masses and rarely produce the asymmetrical motor signs typical of masses. Reflex posturing may be seen, but it lacks the asymmetry of decortication from a hemispheric mass and is not associated with the loss of pupillary reactivity at the stage of decerebration.

Pupillary Reactivity. Functioning of the pupils reflects the structural integrity of the midbrain. If the pupils constrict to a bright light, the midbrain is intact, and if they do not, the midbrain has been compromised. In cases of mass lesions, the loss of pupillary reactivity from a hemispheric mass is asymmetrical, with the pupil homolateral to the mass losing reactivity before its contralateral fellow. A midbrain pupil may be large and unreactive if the descending sympathetic pathways in the brain stem have not been compromised but are more commonly at midposition (5 mm), reflecting parasympathetic (third cranial nerve) and sympathetic (brain stem) injury.

In metabolic coma, one feature is central to the examination: pupillary reactivity. This reactivity is seen early in coma, when an appropriate motor response to pain may be retained, and late, when no motor responses can be elicited. The reaction is lost only when coma is so deep the patient requires ventilatory and blood pressure support.

Reflex Eye Movements. The presence of inducible lateral eye movements reflects the integrity of the pons (i.e., vestibular nucleus, pontine gaze center, and sixth cranial nerve moving the eye laterally). The medial longitudinal fasciculus traverses the dorsal pons to connect with the third cranial nerve (i.e., moving the eye medially). This system may first be compromised at the midbrain level, with loss of medial eye movement in the eye homolateral to the mass, but it becomes clearly impaired by pontine dysfunction when no eye movements are inducible. These eye movements, called *reflex eye movements* (see Fig. 436–1), are brought about by passive head rotation to stimulate the semicircular canal input to the vestibular system (i.e., doll's-eyes maneuver) or by inhibition of function of one semicircular canal by infusion of ice water against the tympanic membrane (i.e., caloric testing).

In *metabolic coma,* reflex eye movements may be lost or retained. Lack of inducible eye movements with the doll's-eyes maneuver in the setting of preserved pupillary reactivity is virtually diagnostic of drug toxicity. Caloric testing is not useful in drug-induced coma because it may produce any of the following: delayed downward ocular deviation, ipsilateral adduction with incomplete contralateral abduction, ipsilateral abduction with contralateral adduction, or no response. With metabolic coma of non–drug-induced origin, such as organ system failure or electrolytic or osmolar disorders, full reflex eye movements are preserved.

Brain stem mass lesions are a special case. These lesions are most commonly vascular. Reflex lateral eye movements, the pathways for which traverse the pons and midbrain, are particularly affected, and the reflex postures of decortication and decerebration typical of brain stem injury are common findings. Lesions restricted to the midbrain (e.g., embolization to the top of the basilar artery) manifest by sluggish or absent pupillary reflexes with or without impaired medial eye movements (i.e., third cranial nerve). With lesions restricted to the pons (e.g., intrapontine hypertensive hemorrhage), reactive but very small pupils—pinpoint or "pontine" pupils—are seen, reflecting focal impairment of descending sympathetic fibers through the brain stem with preservation of parasympathetic fibers in the third cranial nerve. The examiner may also see ocular bobbing (i.e., spontaneous symmetrical or asymmetrical rhythmic vertical ocular oscillations).

Multifocal disorders may manifest as metabolic coma. A number of syndromes of multifocal vascular disease are characterized by diffuse brain dysfunction that appears to be a metabolic encephalopathy. Hypertensive encephalopathy, in part caused by multifocal arterial spasm, produces a subacute encephalopathy with seizures and is characterized in adults by blood pressures above 250/150 mm Hg; magnetic resonance imaging may show prominent posterior white matter edema. Other subacutely evolving, diffuse vascular syndromes without neuroimaging signatures include disseminated intravascular coagulation (Chapter 179), endocarditis (Chapter 310), the encephalopathy of sepsis, thrombotic thrombocytopenic purpura (Chapter 177), fat emboli syndrome (Chapter 94), diffuse small-vessel vasculitis, pancreatic encephalopathy (Chapter 145), and venous thrombosis, particularly affecting the superior sagittal sinus.

CONSIDER SEIZURES. The diagnosis of a seizure is usually obvious from history or observation, and the return to an agitated confusional state and then consciousness that occurs over a few minutes solves any diagnostic problem (Chapter 434). However, prolonged alteration in consciousness after an unwitnessed seizure may produce diagnostic confusion. Such prolonged postictal states follow seizures affecting an acutely or chronically impaired brain. Acute brain impairment occurs with encephalitis and with multifocal vascular disease, such as hypertensive encephalopathy, acute metabolic impairment of brain function (e.g., hyponatremia or hypernatremia, hypoglycemia or hyperglycemia), or drug toxicity complicated by seizures. In a postictal state, the examination can detect reactive pupils and inducible eye movements (in the absence of overtreatment with anticonvulsants) and may detect upgoing toes; if the onset of the seizure was in a focal motor area of the cortex, there may be a prolonged hemiparesis (i.e., Todd's paresis). Nonconvulsive seizures, particularly spike-wave stupor, may occur in a patient without a history of epilepsy. The diagnosis is made by electroencephalogram.

Emergency management of the patient with a decreased level of consciousness includes ensuring airway adequacy and support of ventilation and of circulation. Blood should be drawn for determination of serum glucose and electrolyte levels, hepatic and renal function, prothrombin and partial thromboplastin times, complete blood cell count, and drug screen. Intravenous administration of 25 g of dextrose (typically 50 mL of 50% dextrose) should be routine to treat possible hypoglycemic coma. The glucose level is poorly correlated with the level of consciousness in cases of hypoglycemia, with coma, stupor, and confusion reported with blood glucose concentrations of 2 to 28, 8 to 59, and 9 to 60 mg/dL, respectively. Because administration of dextrose alone can precipitate or worsen Wernicke's encephalopathy in thiamine-deficient patients, 100 mg of thiamine should be given intravenously. Possible opiate overdose should be treated with naloxone (0.4 to 1.2 mg IV). The specific benzodiazepine antagonist flumazenil (0.2 mg IV, repeated once and followed by 0.1 mg IV to 1 to 3 mg total) can be given for the reversal of benzodiazepine-induced coma or of conscious sedation. In coma of unknown cause, however, flumazenil administration can precipitate seizures in patients with polydrug overdoses containing benzodiazepines with tricyclics or cocaine.

Coma-like States

Coma-like states include the locked-in syndrome and psychogenic unresponsiveness, as well as the persistent vegetative state and brain death (Chapter 437).

Locked-in syndrome patients are those in whom a lesion, usually hemorrhage or an infarct, transects the brain stem at a point below the reticular formation (therefore sparing consciousness) but above the ventilatory nuclei of the medulla (therefore precluding death). Such patients are awake, with eye opening and sleep-wake cycles, but have transection of the descending pathways through the brain

stem necessary for volitional vocalization or limb movement. Voluntary eye movement, especially vertical, is preserved, and patients open and close their eyes or produce appropriate numbers of blinking movements in answer to questions. The electroencephalographic result is usually normal, reflecting normal cortical function. The mortality rate is high (40 to 70%), and most patients who recover are left with major deficits. Recovery to independence can occur, however, over weeks to 3 to 4 months. Early recovery of lateral eye movements has been suggested as a particularly positive prognostic feature. Magnetic stimulation of motor cortex producing motor evoked potentials may be an additional positive prognostic feature. Survival in the locked-in state has lasted as long as 18 years.

Psychogenic unresponsiveness is a diagnosis of exclusion. The neurologic examination shows reactive pupils and no reflex posturing to pain. Eye movements during the doll's-eyes maneuver show volitional override rather than the smooth, uninhibited, reflex lateral eye movements of coma. Ice water caloric testing arouses the patient because of the discomfort produced or induces cortically mediated nystagmus rather than the tonic deviation typical of coma. The slow, conjugate, roving eye movements of metabolic coma cannot be imitated and therefore exclude psychogenic unresponsiveness. The slow, often asymmetrical, and incomplete eye closure that follows passive eyelid opening of a comatose patient cannot be feigned. These signs therefore exclude psychogenic coma. Conscious patients usually exhibit some voluntary muscle tone in the eyelids during passive eye opening. The electroencephalographic finding in psychogenic unresponsiveness is normal wakefulness with reactive posterior rhythms on eye opening and eye closing.

PROGNOSIS. In coma after cardiac arrest, the prognosis for meaningful recovery can be assessed from clinical signs. Brisk, small-amplitude, mainly vertical eye movements are seen in patients with ischemia-induced electrographic status epilepticus and are predictive of a fatal outcome. In cardiac arrest patients without the complicating issue of seizures, return of pupillary reactivity and purposeful motor movements within the first 72 hours is highly correlated with a favorable outcome (Table 436–2).

The outcome after traumatic head injury is more difficult to assess and includes an additional prognostic factor: age. Young patients (<20 years) are more than three times as likely to survive as those older than 60 years. On examination at 24 hours, an absent motor response to pain combined with an absent pupillary response is a strong predictor of mortality, whereas localization of a painful stimulus with preserved pupillary reactivity is a highly favorable finding, especially in the young (Fig. 436–2). Unexpected late recoveries do occur.

Table 436–2 • PROBABILITY (%) OF RECOVERING INDEPENDENT FUNCTION FROM COMA AFTER CARDIAC ARREST

SIGN	DAYS AFTER CARDIAC ARREST			
	0	1	3	7
From Levy et al. (*N* = 210)				
No verbal response	13	8	5	6
No eye opening	11	6	4	0
Unreactive pupils	0	0	0	0
No spontaneous eye movements	6	5	2	0
No caloric response	5	6	6	0
Extensor posturing	18	0	0	0
Flexor posturing	14	3	0	0
No motor response	4	3	0	0
From Edgren et al. (*N* = 131)				
No eye opening to pain	31	8	0	0
Absent or reflex motor response	25	9	0	0
Unreactive pupils	17	7	0	0

Data from Levy DE, Caronna J, Singer BH, et al: Predicting outcome from hypoxic-ischemic coma. JAMA 1985;253:1420–1426. Copyright © 1985, American Medical Association. Data from Edgren E, Hedstrand U, Kelsey S, et al: Assessment of neurological prognosis in comatose survivors of cardiac arrest. BRCT I Study Group. Lancet 1994;343:1055–1059. Copyright © by The Lancet Ltd., 1994.

Neurology

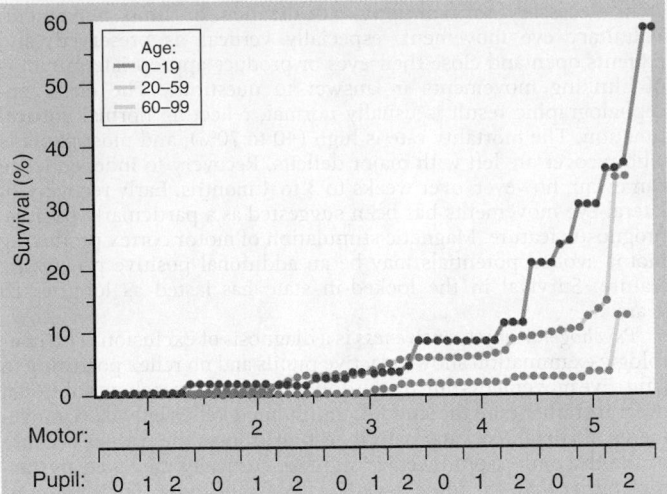

FIGURE 436–2 • Survival after traumatic coma based on age and clinical examination results at 24 hours. Motor: No response (1), reflex extension (2), reflex flexion (3), complex flexion (4), localizes pain (5). Pupils: No reactivity (0), unilateral reactivity (1), bilateral reactivity (2). (From Mamelak AN, Pitts LH, Damron S: Predicting survival from head injury 24 hours after injury: A practical method with therapeutic implications. J Trauma 1996;41:91–99.)

SUGGESTED READINGS

Bone I, Fuler GN: Neurology in practice: Sleep and coma. Neurol Neurosurg Psychiatry 2001;71(Suppl 1):1–27. *A comprehensive review.*

Plum F, Posner JB: The Diagnosis of Stupor and Coma. Contemporary Neurology Series, vol 19, 3rd ed. Philadelphia, FA Davis, 1980. *The classic monograph.*

437 PERSISTENT VEGETATIVE STATES AND BRAIN DEATH

Roger P. Simon

PERSISTENT VEGETATIVE STATE

The term *persistent vegetative state* characterizes the condition of 10,000 to 25,000 adults and 4000 to 10,000 children in the United States. Whereas coma represents a state lacking wakefulness and awareness, in a vegetative state, patients have awakened from coma but have not regained awareness. Wakefulness is manifested by eye opening and sleep-wake cycles.

The neuroanatomic characteristics of the vegetative state dictate that the reticular activating system of the brain stem be intact to produce wakefulness but that the connections to the cortical mantle be interrupted, precluding awareness. These anatomic requirements for a vegetative state are satisfied most commonly by diffuse axonal injury, laminar necrosis of the cortical mantle, or thalamic necrosis. These pathologic alterations occur as the sequelae of a number of acute or chronic conditions affecting the brain. Acute brain injury resulting in a vegetative state first produces coma, with the patient later awakening into the vegetative condition. Common causes include trauma with resultant diffuse axonal injury, hypoxia-ischemia caused by cerebral hypoperfusion from cardiac arrest resulting in death of the selectively vulnerable neurons in the cortical mantle (i.e., laminar necrosis), bihemispheric infarctions, cortical injury after purulent meningitis or encephalitis, exposure to nervous system toxins (particularly carbon monoxide), and prolonged hypoglycemia. The sequelae of cerebral hypoperfusion may particularly affect hemispheric watershed areas and the thalamus.

A vegetative state may not always begin with coma but can develop as the end stage of neurodegenerative diseases of adults or children or accompany severe developmental abnormalities of the brain such

as anencephaly. Clinically, patients in a persistent vegetative state have signs associated with an intact reticular formation: They open their eyes and have sleep-wake cycles, although these are irregular in timing. Their brain stem reflexes are intact. Pupils react and eye movements occur spontaneously and with the doll's-eyes maneuver. More complex brain stem reflexes are also seen, such as yawning, chewing, swallowing, and, uncommonly, making guttural vocalizations. The brain stem reflexes of arousal and startle are preserved as well, so that eye opening occurs with loud sounds and blinking may occur with bright lights. Tearing may be seen. Spontaneous roving eye movements are particularly characteristic; these are very slow movements of constant velocity, uninterrupted by saccadic jerks, and cannot be volitionally mimicked. These eye movements can be particularly distressing to family members as the patients appear to be looking about the room and at some point the roving eyes are pointed at the observer, who may perceive the patient to be "looking at" or following him or her throughout the room. The lack of quick directed saccadic eye movements in the presence of continual fixed velocity roving eye movements differentiates a willed response from reflex eye movements. The brain stem origin of the eye movements is further documented by their being readily redirected by the oculocephalic (doll's-eyes) reflex. The limbs may move, but motor responses are only primitively purposeful, such as grasping an object that contacts the hand. Pain usually produces decorticate or decerebrate postures or fragments of these movements.

Results of brain imaging studies depict the sequelae of the causative injury but are not diagnostic of a persistent vegetative state. Findings of magnetic resonance spectroscopy have shown a decrease in the neuronal marker of N-acetylaspartate. Positron emission tomography (PET) studies have shown decreased glucose use and cerebral blood flow, but such results in and of themselves are rarely diagnostic. Evoked responses are not useful.

A vegetative state is diagnosed after 1 month in a patient without detectable awareness of the environment. A vegetative state is called persistent after 3 months if the brain injury was medical and after 12 months if the brain injury was traumatic. The determination about when *persistent* equals *permanent* cannot be stated absolutely; to predict early in the vegetative state which patients will become persistently vegetative is particularly difficult in causes of trauma. Lesions of the corpus callosum and dorsolateral brain stem seen on magnetic resonance imaging (MRI) between 6 and 8 weeks after trauma correlated with persistence of the vegetative state at 1 year.

Rare patients show late improvement, but none regains normal function. Partial recovery to the level of communication and comprehension has been reported in 3% of patients after 5 years, but improvement to independence in activities of daily living is even more uncommon. Although lack of awareness defines the vegetative state, patients may recover slightly beyond this criterion. Such minimally responsive patients present difficult ethical considerations for care.

BRAIN DEATH

Irreversible cessation of cardiopulmonary function precludes function of the brain. The opposite is true as well. Death of the organism therefore can be determined on the basis of death of the brain. Although some details may be dictated by local law, the standard criteria for the diagnosis of brain death are those established by the President's Commission report of 1981. This standard permits a diagnosis of brain death on documentation of irreversible cessation of all brain function, including those of the brain stem; the presence of seizures is not compatible with the diagnosis. The absence of hemispheric function is documented by unreceptivity and unresponsiveness, usually assessed in the setting of a painful stimulation; the patients does not rouse, groan, grimace, or withdraw limbs. Purely spinal reflexes may be maintained: deep tendon reflexes, plantar flexion reflex, plantar withdrawal, and tonic neck reflexes. Decorticate or decerebrate posturing is not compatible with the diagnosis. Absence of brain stem function is assessed by region. Lack of midbrain function is documented by the absence of a pupillary light reflex (most easily assessed by the bright light of an ophthalmoscope viewed through its magnifying lens when focused on the iris). Unreactive pupils may be at midposition (as they will be in death) or dilated, as they often are in the setting of a dopamine infusion. Lack of pontine function is documented by the absence of a response to corneal stimulation and the absence of inducible eye movements: no eye movement toward the side of irrigation of the tympanic membrane with 50 mL of ice water. The oculocephalic response (doll's eyes) is always absent in the setting of absent oculovestibular testing. Cessation of medullary function is documented by the apnea test: no ventilatory movements in the setting of maximum CO_2 stimulation. The test is performed by disconnecting the ventilator from the endotracheal tube. Oxygen can be supplied by diffusion from a cannula placed through the endotracheal tube (6 L/minute). In the absence of ventilation, the PCO_2 passively rises 2 to 3 mm Hg/minute. Because a PCO_2 of 60 mm Hg produces the maximum ventilatory stimulus required for the confirmation of apnea, a period of about 10 minutes is required for the PCO_2 to reach that level from a normal baseline. A $PaCO_2$ greater than 60 mm Hg adequately stimulates ventilatory drive within 60 seconds in a functioning brain.

Documentation of irreversibility requires that the cause of the coma be known and that it be adequate to explain the clinical findings of brain death. Irreversibility based on clinical criteria cannot be determined in the setting of sedative drugs or significant hypothermia (<32.2°C) or in the presence of shock and neuromuscular blockade.

Confirmatory tests may be useful. An isoelectric electroencephalogram is frequently used. However, deep coma from sedative drugs or hypothermia below 20°C can produce electroencephalographic flattening. Patients clinically brain dead may have residual electroencephalographic activity (i.e., alpha coma-like activity, low-voltage fast waves, or sleeplike slowing with spindle activity), which may persist for a number of days after a brain death diagnosis. The absence of cerebral blood flow is the most definitive confirmatory test and is most unequivocally demonstrated by angiography. Transcranial Doppler techniques and nuclear imaging with technetium are used in some centers.

Sequential testing is necessary for a clinical diagnosis of brain death. The period of observation required is at least 6 hours for all cases and at least 24 hours in the setting of anoxic-ischemic brain injury.

With the confirmation of brain death, asystole usually occurs within days (mean, 4 days) even if ventilatory support is continued. Recovery after appropriate documentation of brain death has never been reported. Removal of the ventilator results in terminal rhythms, most often complete heart block without ventricular response, junctional rhythms, or ventricular tachycardia. Purely spinal motor movements may occur in the moments of terminal apnea (or during apnea testing in the absence of passive administration of oxygen): arching of the back, neck turning, stiffening of the legs, and upper extremity flexion.

SUGGESTED READINGS

Halevy A, Brody B: Brain death: Reconciling definitions, criteria and tests. Ann Intern Med 1993;119:519–525. *A critique of the diagnostic criteria for brain death with attention to the issue of organ harvesting for transplantation.*

Jennett B: The vegetative state. J Neurol Neurosurg Psychiatry 2002;73:355–357. *A brief overview.*

Kampfl A, Schmutzhard E, Franz G, et al: Prediction of recovery from post-traumatic vegetative state with cerebral magnetic resonance imaging. Lancet 1998;351:1763–1767. *An attempt to use early MRI to predict recovery versus persistence of the vegetative state in traumatic brain injury.*

Wijdicks EF: The diagnosis of brain death. N Engl J Med 2001;344:1215–1221. *The review of differentiated diagnosis and confirmatory tests.*

Zeman A: Persistent vegetative state. Lancet 1997;350:795–799. *A review from the United Kingdom that includes an extensive bibliography of clinical and ethical aspects and consensus statements from other bodies.*

438 DISORDERS OF SLEEP AND AROUSAL

Roger P. Simon
Maria J. Sunseri

NEUROBIOLOGY OF SLEEP

Although rest periods are known throughout all biologic systems, the precise function of sleep remains incompletely understood. Sleep occurs in reptiles and birds, and nearly all mammals sleep and dream. Sleep is necessary for life; sleep deprivation in the rat results in weight loss despite increased food intake; metabolic and thermoregulatory imbalance supervenes, and death occurs in about 1 month. Sleep deprivation may contribute to alterations of insulin resistance and decreased function of the immune system. Systemic functions such as effort and fatigue, as well as fever, induce sleep.

NEUROANATOMY AND PHARMACOLOGY

Wakefulness is under the control of the reticular activating system (RAS) of the rostral brain stem that projects to thalamus and cortex. Inhibition of these projection systems is affected by modulatory neuronal groups in the pons and midbrain and results in sleep. A clearer anatomic and neuropharmacologic picture is available for the rapid eye movement (REM) stage of sleep, during which most dreaming occurs. The tegmentum of the pons contains the REM sleep generator with modulation from the norepinephrine- and serotonin-containing neurons of the locus ceruleus and the dorsal raphe nucleus. Electrical events generated in the pontine reticular formation (i.e., ponto-geniculo-occipital [PGO] waves) are propagated through the oculomotor and visual system during REM sleep simultaneously with rapid eye movements. PGO waves are suppressed by norepinephrine, and serotonin neuronal systems suppress PGO waves and REM; cholinergic neurons are stimulatory. PGO input can induce an action potential in neurons below threshold. Such PGO-facilitated activity in the visual system may play a role in the random imagery of dreaming.

Hypocretins (e.g., orexin) are newly identified sleep modulatory neuropeptides made in lateral hypothalamus with projections to locus ceruleus and dorsal raphe as well as the thalamus, where they modulate excitatory (glutamate) and inhibitory (γ-aminobutyric acid [GABA]) neurotransmitter release. Disruption of this system induces narcolepsy in animals; hypocretin neurotransmission is deficient in some narcoleptic patients.

SLEEP STAGES: BEHAVIORAL AND PHYSIOLOGIC CORRELATES

Sleep stages in humans are defined electroencephalographically and behaviorally (Table 438–1). In *stage I* sleep, patients are drowsy and may maintain some environmental awareness. The electroencephalogram (EEG) loses its alpha rhythm (8 to 13 Hz), with theta (3 to 7 Hz) activity occurring; vertex potentials (i.e., negative deflections recorded from the midline) occur, especially in response to sensory stimuli. Slow lateral eye movements occur, and spontaneous motor activity determined by electromyography is diminished. Stage I represents about 5% of normal sleep.

Table 438–1 • STAGES OF SLEEP

SLEEP STAGE	EEG	EYE MOVEMENTS	EMG ACTIVITY	IMAGERY
Wakefulness	Alpha and beta activity (low voltage fast)	Random, rapid	Active, spontaneous	Vivid, external
Non-REM sleep (NREM)				
Stage I (drowsiness)	Theta activity	Slow, rolling	Attenuated, episodic	Dulled
Stage II (light sleep)	Sleep spindles, K complexes	Slow or absent	Attenuated	Nonvivid
Stage III and IV (slow wave sleep)	Delta activity	Absent	Attenuated	
REM sleep	Low amplitude, irregular	Abrupt, rapid eye movements	Absent	Vivid, bizarre

EEG = electroencephalogram; EMG = electromyogram; REM = rapid eye movement.

Stage II sleep is characterized by sleep spindles (12 to 14 Hz), vertex sharp waves, and K complexes (i.e., biphasic, high-voltage slow waves often followed by a sleep spindle). Slow lateral eye movements may persist. Electromyographic activity is further reduced. Stage II sleep represents 50 to 60% of sleep and increases with age.

Stages III and IV sleep are characterized by slow or delta waves (<4 Hz) and are therefore called delta sleep or deep sleep. If 20 to 50% of the EEG is delta activity, the patient is in stage III sleep; if delta activity is 50% or more, the sleep event is called stage IV. Deep sleep constitutes 10 to 20% of sleep time (less with advancing age). Electromyographic activity is less active. Eye movements are not seen, and ventilation is regular.

In *REM* sleep, the EEG is similar to that as seen in waking with low-voltage, mixed frequencies. Abrupt rapid eye movements are characteristic. Ventilatory movements are irregular, as is heart rate. Penile erections occur, and there is an absence of electromyographic activity (i.e., muscular atonia). REM occupies 20 to 25% of sleep time. Patients who awaken during REM report vivid dream imagery. Individuals who awaken from non-REM sleep may also recall their dreams, but these dreams are without the intense detail of those occurring during REM.

Studies using positron emission tomography (PET) during REM sleep show an increase in regional cerebral blood flow in the pontine tegmentum, left thalamus, bilateral amygdaloid complexes, the anterior cingulate cortex, and the right parietal opercular cortex. Cerebral blood flow is decreased in the prefrontal cortex, parietal cortex, and posterior cingulate cortex. There is increased activity in the limbic system involved with basic emotions and decreased activity in anatomic regions associated with executive functions. This pattern is compatible with the high emotional content of dreams. Procedural (i.e., motor learning such as typing) and declarative (i.e., episodic learning such as recalling places or events) memory consolidation occurs during REM sleep. REM sleep time increases after task training. After episodic learning, memory consolidation is accomplished during slow wave sleep by a rapid reactivation of the hippocampal neurons previously activated by the place or event to be remembered. Alternately, it has been hypothesized that dream sleep functions as a random stimulator of the cortex to remove weak memories, permitting only stronger pieces of memory to be retained.

INSOMNIA

Insomnia is the perception of inadequate sleep, in amount or quality, usually not associated with daytime sleepiness. The duration of sleep in a given patient is not an adequate measure of sleep adequacy, because normal sleep time can vary from as little as 4 to as many as 11 hours each day. The need for sleep time is relatively stable throughout adult life.

An approach to the complaint of insomnia begins with the history. Is the problem of recent onset or chronic? If new in onset, are there associated psychological, medical, or medication changes? What is the character of the perceived impairment of sleep? Insomnia can be associated with impairment of the ability to begin sleep (i.e., getting to sleep), multiple awakenings during sleep (i.e., arousal), early awakenings, or normal but nonrefreshing sleep. Is there evidence of partial arousal (history often elicited from the bed partner), of breathing abnormalities, or involuntary movements? Each group of circumstances has a different set of differential diagnoses.

Situational Insomnia

Situational insomnias are usually of recent onset. They may be associated with exogenous events such as recognized or unrecognized life stresses, death of a family member or a friend, and stress at work or with endogenous depression. Alternatively, such insomnias can be caused by environmental changes, such as a new sleeping location or partner, shift work, or jet lag. Depression is known to produce REM potentiation (i.e., earlier onset of REM and longer-lasting REM sleep). Stage IV sleep is suppressed. The normal balance of sleep stages is restored after nonpharmacologic and to a lesser extent after pharmacologic treatment of depression.

Behavioral Insomnia

Behavioral insomnia is a chronic insomnia associated with a characteristic personality. Preparation for sleep induces rumination,

emotional arousal, and increased autonomic activity. The focus on the inability to fall asleep becomes self-perpetuating.

Drug-related insomnia can be suggested by the temporal profile of the history of sleep disturbances. Caffeine in beverages or as an unrecognized component of over-the-counter drugs can be a factor in sensitive patients, whereas other individuals seem unperturbed by the drug even though their sleep may be fragmented. Affected patients complain of a decreased ability to fall asleep.

Alcohol use before sleep has a dual effect. The induction of somnolence hastens the onset of sleep, but alcohol often exacerbates sleep-related breathing abnormalities; on metabolic clearance of alcohol, sleep fragmentation and early awakening may occur. Corticosteroids, antidepressants, bronchodilators, and central nervous system stimulants are among the medications that stimulate arousal, as does the withdrawal of short-acting sedatives, which are often prescribed for insomnia.

A number of medical or neurologic conditions are associated with impaired sleep, including pain, especially skeletal pain and arthritis. Cardiac and pulmonary conditions can produce frequent awakening because of shortness of breath and heart failure (i.e., paroxysmal nocturnal dyspnea). Gastrointestinal disorders, especially those producing bowel hypermotility and nocturnal diarrhea, impair sleep. Eating disorders and hunger may produce arousal at night. Sleep may be disturbed by neurologic disorders, particularly those that impair normal movement during sleep (e.g., stroke, advanced multiple sclerosis, Parkinson's disease). Some headaches, such as cluster and hypnic headache, characteristically awaken patients at night. The rare prion disorder of fatal familial insomnia (Chapter 456) is characterized by sleep impairment.

Age alters sleep, with increased awakenings at the transition between non-REM and REM sleep; the amount of slow wave sleep is decreased. The elderly frequently nap during the daytime, which may induce the presumption of inadequate sleep time because nighttime sleep will be shortened.

Change in altitude produces a usually transient insomnia in some persons. The altitude change is associated with hypoxia and altered ventilatory drive, resulting in periodic breathing and multiple awakenings. In particularly susceptible individuals, acetazolamide treatment may alter these arousals.

Rx Treatment

The treatment of insomnia depends on its cause. Treatment of depression, elimination of stimulant drugs, and providing an optimal sleep environment are general principles of sleep hygiene. Other approaches include increasing daytime exercise but not exercise just before sleep; provision of a proper sleep environment (i.e., attention to optimal temperature, light, and ambient noise); maintenance of a regular sleep time and schedule; avoidance of drugs and alcohol; and "winding down" before sleep (e.g., quiet reading).

If medications are used, they should be prescribed only briefly because tolerance develops to sedative drugs within several weeks. The choice of medications should address the type of insomnia (i.e., sleep onset or nocturnal awakening). For sleep onset, triazolam (Halcion) or zolpidem (Ambien) are rapidly acting, short half-life compounds. Nocturnal awakening can be treated with zaleplon (Sonata), a nonbenzodiazepine hypnotic with an ultrashort half-life. For maintaining sleep, longer-acting drugs are more effective; options include flurazepam (Dalmane) or quazepam (Doral). For patients with persistent insomnia, causes such as sleep apnea (Chapter 96) or periodic limb movements should be considered.

ABNORMAL AROUSALS

Abnormal arousals during sleep result in the perception of inadequately restorative sleep. Examples include sleep apnea (Chapter 96), restless leg syndrome, nocturnal myoclonus, periodic limb movements of sleep, and chronic pain disorders (Table 438–2).

Restless leg syndrome may be familial or acquired (i.e., iron deficiency, uremia, or peripheral neuropathy). Symptoms occur at the time of onset of sleep and therefore interfere with the ability to fall asleep. Symptoms are reported variously as a need to move the legs or a deep sensory complaint in the lower extremities. Walking about

Table 438–2 • SLEEP STAGE AND ASSOCIATED SLEEP DISORDER

SLEEP STAGE	SLEEP DISORDER
Presleep	Restless leg syndrome
	Sleep onset myoclonus
NREM sleep (Stage I–II)	Periodic limb movements of sleep
	Sleep myoclonus
Deep sleep (Stage III–IV)	Sleepwalking
	Sleep terrors
REM sleep	Nightmares
	REM sleep behavioral disorder
Sleep/wake transition	Hypnagogic (sleep onset) and hypnopompic (on waking) hallucinations
	Sleep paralysis

NREM = non–rapid eye movement; REM = rapid eye movement.

and rubbing or moving the limbs briefly relieve the symptoms. Sinemet (carbidopa/levodopa) can be used (beginning with 25/100 mg, 30 minutes before bedtime), but the dopamine agonists pramipexole (Mirapex) at a dose of 0.375 to 0.75 mg/day and pergolide (Permax) at a dose of 0.5 mg taken 2 hours before sleep are now preferred.

Periodic limb movements often accompany restless leg syndrome. The movements are brief, repetitive dorsiflexion of the great toe or plantar flexion of the foot during stage I or II sleep; these disappear with REM atonia. Clonazepam may be useful. *Myoclonus* involving jerking of the body or limb at the onset of sleep has been reported in nearly 80% of normal persons. Prolongation of these fragments of myoclonus during non-REM sleep constitutes the phenomenon of *sleep myoclonus,* which does not usually require treatment.

Parasomnias

Parasomnias, which are sleep-related phenomena, are motor disorders that occur with or without autonomic features during sleep and that induce brief partial arousals. Parasomnias are not associated with daytime sleepiness but are manifestations of disturbed mechanisms of sleep; they are most common in childhood but may be seen in adults.

Sleepwalking occurs in more than 10% of children, many of whom have a family history. The behavior occurs during stage III and IV sleep and may be fragmentary, such as merely sitting up in bed. Patients are difficult to arouse during the event and do not recollect it. Events usually occur in the first few hours of sleep and are brief (<10 minutes) but may be recurrent. *Sleep terrors* are often associated; they also occur in non-REM sleep but include intense autonomic arousal, marked vocalization and motility, difficulty in arousing the patient, and minimal recall of the episode. The spells may be attenuated by benzodiazepines. *Nightmares,* which are distinct from sleep terrors, occur during REM sleep when motility is limited, vocalization is much less intense, patients are relatively easily aroused, and vivid dream recall is evident.

REM behavioral disorder is an uncommon parasomnia affecting middle-aged or older men and patients with degenerative central nervous system diseases, especially involving the brain stem. The absence of REM atonia allows motor behaviors that are often violent and may injure the patient or the bed partner. As is characteristic of REM disorders, vivid imagery is reported on awakening. Nocturnal seizures should be excluded. Clonazepam is an effective treatment.

Narcolepsy

Narcolepsy is a disorder of excessive daytime sleepiness associated with abnormalities in REM sleep. The onset is most often between the second and fourth decades. When fully expressed, the patient has a quartet of symptoms: narcolepsy, cataplexy, hypnagogic hallucinations, and sleep paralysis.

Narcolepsy affects approximately 100,000 persons in the United States; there is no sex preponderance. Affected patients have a reduction in hypocretin neurons and decreased cerebrospinal fluid hypocretin concentrations; a degenerative cause has been hypothesized. A genetic predisposition is documented by the presence of the human leukocyte antigen (HLA) allele *HLA-DQB 1*0602,* often with *HLA-*

DR2, in more than 85% of narcolepsy-cataplexy patients. The penetrance is variable, and less than 5% of patients have affected family members. Narcolepsy may also be a rare symptom of a number of central nervous system lesions in the region of the third ventricle and hypothalamus.

Narcoleptic hypersomnia occurs (as it does in normals) most often in settings of sedentary activity and with boredom, and the hypersomnia can be alleviated to some degree by motor or intellectual stimulation. However, narcoleptic sleep attacks may also occur during conversation, meals, and while driving. Nearly 70% of patients have had automobile accidents or near accidents because of sleep attacks. The sleep episodes are brief, and their frequency is little changed in patients after the first months of the disorder.

The clinical diagnosis of narcolepsy is made on the basis of a typical and persistent history of excessive daytime sleepiness in the absence of underlying nocturnal sleep disorders that would produce daytime somnolence. The diagnosis is confirmed by the documentation of REM at the beginning of sleep (i.e., latency less than 15 minutes) and an abnormal multiple sleep latency test (MSLT) result. Narcolepsy is diagnosed by mean sleep latency less than 5 minutes and the induction of REM at onset of two sleep events. These studies should be performed in a sleep laboratory, because standard EEGs are not adequately sensitive in documenting REM, and false-positive results occur with depression, drug withdrawal, and sleep deprivation.

Treatment of narcolepsy should begin with planned 15- to 20-minute naps as needed throughout the day. One to three such intervals is usually adequate, and each nap provides several hours of sleep-free performance. Exercise, avoiding heavy meals, and ingestion of caffeinated beverages are also effective.

Pharmacologic therapy has traditionally relied on stimulants (5 to 60 mg of methylphenidate or 5 to 50 mg of dextroamphetamine daily). Complete relief of daytime sleepiness is rarely achieved, and side effects of irritability, restlessness, psychosis, and hypertension are of concern. Habituation may occur with chronic use, although drug holidays (1 day/wk) may decrease this risk. Modafinil, an α-adrenergic agonist (200 mg every morning) is considered first-line treatment.▪ The imidazole derivative mazindol and the monoamine oxidase inhibitor selegiline are also effective.

Cataplexy

Cataplexy is eventually associated with narcolepsy in up to 70% of patients, although cataplexy may precede narcolepsy or not occur for decades. A history of cataplexy therefore is useful for supporting a diagnosis of narcolepsy. The cataplectic phenomenon is that of emotion-induced, reflex muscular atonia that spares respiratory muscles. Laughter is the most common inducer. The atonic phenomenon may be partial (e.g., dropping an object from the hand), generalized (e.g., buckling at the knees), or global (e.g., falling down). Most attacks persist for less than a minute, although prolonged atonic episodes have been described. Cataplexy, hypnagogic hallucinations, and sleep paralysis are fragments of events that are normally confined to REM sleep but that appear during wakefulness in cataplexy. Atonia corresponds to the impairment of volitional movements that may otherwise occur during dreaming. Noncholinergic neurons in the medial medulla appear to be responsible for cataplectic events. A reduction in hypocretin activation of brain stem monoaminergic neurons has been postulated. Cataplexy can rarely be the initial manifestation of a midbrain lesion.

Cataplectic attacks can be attenuated in most patients by clomipramine (10 to 150 mg/day). The antidepressants imipramine (10 to 100 mg/day) and desipramine (25 to 100 mg/day) are also effective.

Sleep Paralysis

Sleep paralysis occurs in one fourth of narcoleptics but also occurs in non-narcoleptics as an isolated or recurrent phenomenon at the sleep-wake transition. Sleep paralysis is a frightening event, with awareness of paralysis of all but the ventilatory and extraocular muscles. Hypnagogic and hypnopompic hallucinations may be associated (see Table 438–2). Deep tendon reflexes and H reflexes are depressed during the event. The paralysis is limited to seconds to a few minutes. In the rare patient in whom this is a recurrent problem, serotonin (5-HT) reuptake inhibitors that suppress REM sleep (e.g., clomipramine) or fluoxetine (10 to 40 mg daily) have been prescribed. Hallucinations occur in one third of narcoleptics and are manifested as vivid dreams that occur at sleep-wake transitions and continue into the process of awakening. Patients are usually aware that the perceived events are hallucinations. The differential diagnosis includes peduncular hallucinosis (usually the result of emboli to the top of the basilar artery) or the vivid dreams that occur as a side effect of anticholinergic or dopa-agonist medications, especially in patients with Parkinson's disease.

DISORDERS OF CIRCADIAN RHYTHM

Disorders of circadian rhythm are most commonly experienced in the setting of jet lag when a new sleep-wake cycle is required on entering a distant time zone. Disordered sleep, impaired concentration, fatigue, decreased appetite, and irritability result. Symptoms are proportional to the number of time zones crossed and therefore do not occur even with long flights north to south. Eastward travel produces symptoms that are greater than those of westward travel. Symptoms are also increased with age.

Circadian oscillations are the result of the *CLOCK* gene product. *CLOCK*-induced proteins feed back to inhibit their transcription, resulting in circadian rhythms. The biologic clock is located in the suprachiasmatic nucleus at the base of the hypothalamus. Loss of neurons in this region occurs in Alzheimer's disease (Chapter 433) and may be responsible for *sundowning*. The clock is modulated by light-dark cycles through pathways from the retina. The endogenous modulator is melatonin. Metabolic and behavioral rhythms are regulated and linked; body temperature, for example, falls 1° C or more during the urge to sleep, with the lowest temperatures reached just before waking. Light and/or melatonin exposure may provide therapy for jet lag, but the relationship between the two is complex, with melatonin secretion being suppressed by light. Early evening ingestion of melatonin in the new time zone may attenuate jet lag. Dosing at the approximate bedtime at the destination can begin a few days before departure; the physiologic dose is 0.5 mg. The traditional use of short-acting benzodiazepines (zolpidem or temazepam) remains useful for sleep induction in new time zones.

Shift work conflicts with endogenous circadian rhythms. The results include suboptimal restorative (day) sleep, fatigue, and impaired work performance. An increased risk of cardiovascular disease has been found in some studies. Circadian adaptation may be produced with bright light during night work combined with wearing dark glasses during home travel.

SLEEP APNEA

Obstructive sleep apnea occurs in 2 to 5% of the adult American population and affects men and middle-aged to elderly persons preferentially. The classic presentation is the patient who has loud snoring and has multiple arousals or awakening during the night, gasping for breath. The resultant sleep fragmentation produces daytime sleepiness and impaired occupational performance. Episodes are exacerbated by alcohol use at bedtime and by sedative hypnotic drugs. The supine position for sleeping is the worst. Preventive treatments include weight loss and alcohol avoidance. Continuous positive airway pressure (CPAP) during sleep results in improvement in most patients (Chapter 96).

Central sleep apnea results from impairment of central ventilatory control. These disorders account for less than 10% of cases of sleep apnea. The syndrome is likely to be apnea at the onset of sleep in a nonobese patient with unremarkable snoring. More than five events per hour are abnormal. These apneic spells are briefer than those with obstructive sleep apnea. Any disease process affecting the caudal brain stem, where the ventilatory nuclei reside in the caudal medulla, may result in ventilatory impairment. Poliomyelitis (Chapter 452) was the classic disorder, but brain stem tumors, infections, ischemia, or autonomic dysfunction (e.g., Shy-Drager syndrome) or autonomic neuropathies (e.g., from diabetes mellitus) predominate (Chapter 460). Spinal cord lesions, including tumors and demyelinating disease, may interrupt pathways from the medulla to ventilatory muscles and produce apnea. The syndrome of Ondine's curse is one of intact volitional ventilation but impaired automatic breathing; in this syndrome, however, pathways for volitional ventilation from cortex through the corticospinal pathways are intact, but the pathways for automatic breathing from the medulla, which descend separately in the brain stem, are impaired, and apnea occurs with sleep. This syndrome can be seen with developmental, vascular, or degenerative processes affecting the brain stem. Examples include syringomyelia, spinocerebellar atrophy, unilateral or bilateral medullary strokes, or after bilateral cervical cordotomies for pain. Complete impairment of automatic ventilation has often led to tracheostomy and assisted ventilation. Many patients with central sleep apnea can be successfully treated by bilevel positive airway pressure (BIPAP) ventilation. CPAP or BIPAP are also effective when central and obstructive sleep apnea coexist.

SLEEP DISORDERS IN AGING AND DEMENTIA

Increased daytime sleep with impaired nocturnal sleep is characteristic of late life. The phenomenon of sundowning is a most difficult problem for patient and caregiver. Sundowning episodes include nocturnal delirium with disordered thinking, perception, and agitation. Although the cause is unknown, Alzheimer's disease results in degeneration of brain stem nuclei in the regions responsible for sleep regulation. Degeneration of the suprachiasmatic nucleus, which is responsible for circadian rhythms, also occurs. In some patients, episodes of prolonged daytime deep-sleep states occur during which the patient cannot easily be aroused.

Treatment of sleep disorders in Alzheimer's disease (Chapter 433) is difficult. The wisest approach is to begin with discontinuation of any drugs that may exacerbate episodes of delirium. Infections, especially urinary tract infections, should be excluded, and any treatable metabolic disorders (e.g., congestive heart failure, chronic pulmonary disease) should be addressed. Behavioral treatment consists of increasing daytime activity and decreasing daytime sleep. Bright light exposure during the day and familiar surroundings at night are useful. Sedatives are often prescribed, but they frequently exacerbate the confusional aspects of sundowning. Trazodone may be effective (50 mg at bedtime). Neuroleptics are a last resort.

1. U.S. Modafinil in Narcolepsy Multicenter Study Group: Randomized trial of modafinil as a treatment for the excessive daytime somnolence of narcolepsy. Neurology 2000;54:1166–1175.

SUGGESTED READINGS
Earley CJ: Restless legs syndrome. N Engl J Med 2003;348:2103–2109. *A practical overview.*
Stickgold R, Hobson JA, Fosse R, Fosse M: Sleep, learning, and dreams: Off-line memory reprocessing. Science 2001;294:1052–1057. *Current thinking regarding the neuroanatomic and neuropsychological substrate in brain responsible for dreaming.*
Thannickal TC, Moore RY, Nienhuis R, et al: Reduced number of hypocretin neurons in human narcolepsy. Neuron 2000;27:469–474. *The hypocretin neuronal system in narcolepsy and an autoimmune hypothesis.*
Tishler PV, Larkin EK, Schluchter MD, et al: Incidence of sleep-disordered breathing in an urban adult population: The relative importance of risk factors in the development of sleep-disordered breathing. JAMA 2003;289:2230–2237. *Moderately severe sleep disordered breathing has a 5-year incidence of 7.5% in adults; after age 50, the incidence rates are similar in men and women.*

439 APPROACH TO CEREBROVASCULAR DISEASES

Justin A. Zivin

Stroke is the generally preferred term for a group of diseases that are of abrupt onset and cause neurologic damage (Fig. 439–1). Approximately 85% of strokes are caused by sudden onset of inadequacies of blood flow to some or all of the brain (Chapter 440). The remaining strokes are divided between hemorrhage (Chapter 441) into brain tissue (parenchymatous hemorrhage) and hemorrhage into the spaces surrounding the brain, most frequently the subarachnoid space. A commonly used synonym for stroke was *cerebrovascular accident,* but that term has lost favor because strokes are not really accidents. Well-established prophylactic and acute therapies are now available, and diagnostic tools have improved markedly. The management of strokes has become much more rational and successful.

Epidemiology

Stroke is the second leading cause of mortality worldwide and the third most common cause of death in the industrialized world (after

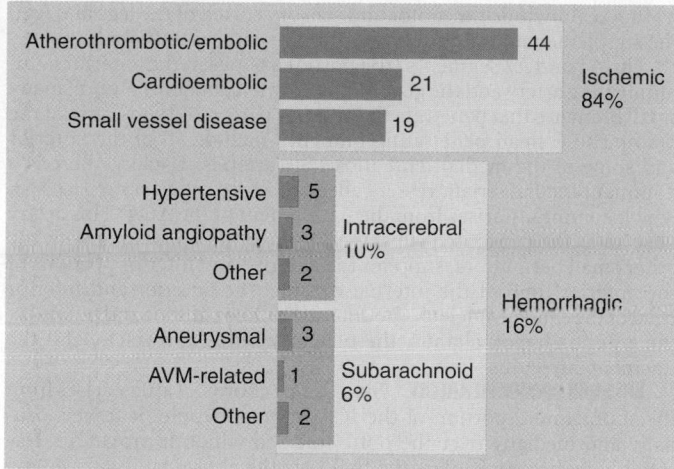

FIGURE 439–1 • Classification of cerebrovascular disease.

Atherothrombotic/embolic — 44
Cardioembolic — 21
Small vessel disease — 19
Ischemic 84%

Hypertensive — 5
Amyloid angiopathy — 3
Other — 2
Intracerebral 10%

Aneurysmal — 3
AVM-related — 1
Other — 2
Subarachnoid 6%
Hemorrhagic 16%

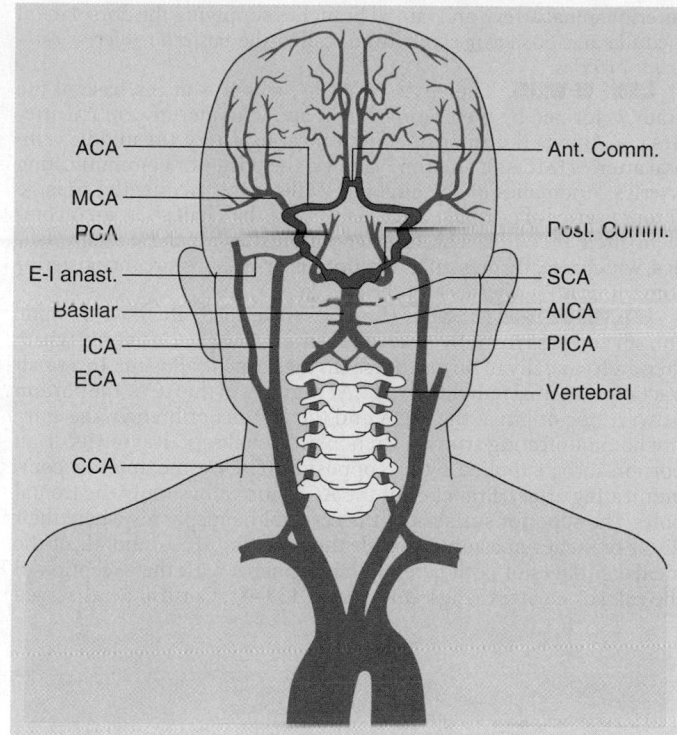

FIGURE 439–2 • Extracranial and intracranial arterial supply to the brain. Vessels forming the circle of Willis are highlighted. ACA = anterior cerebral artery; AICA = anterior inferior cerebellar artery; Ant. Comm. = anterior communicating artery; CCA = common carotid artery; ECA = external carotid artery; E-I anast. = extracranial-intracranial anastomosis; ICA = internal carotid artery; MCA = middle cerebral artery; PCA = posterior cerebral artery; PICA = posterior inferior cerebellar artery; Post. Comm. = posterior communicating artery; SCA = superior cerebellar artery. (Modified from Lord R: Surgery of Occlusive Cerebrovascular Disease. St. Louis, C.V. Mosby Company, 1986; with permission.)

heart disease and all types of cancer combined). It is the most common cause of adult disability in the United States. In China and Japan, stroke is the most frequent cause of death.

In the United States, the annual incidence and death rate for stroke declined steadily for most of the 20th century. In more recent years, the rate of decline has slowed, however, and the incidence of stroke may be increasing. About 750,000 new strokes reach medical attention per year in the United States, and strokes cause about 150,000 deaths annually. At any given time, about 3 million stroke survivors are alive in the United States. Incidence rates in western European countries are only slightly higher than in the United States, but several eastern European countries, China, and Japan have much higher rates, based at least partly on smoking and environmental and dietary factors.

The rate of stroke approximately doubles with each decade after age 55. Blacks and Hispanics have about twice the risk of whites, and men have about a 40% higher incidence of stroke than women. Hypertension increases risk by four-fold, smoking nearly doubles risk, and diabetes increases risk two-fold to six-fold. Carotid stenosis and atrial fibrillation are perhaps the strongest risk factors. Other factors that increase risk include obesity, hypercholesterolemia, physical inactivity, alcohol abuse, hyperhomocysteinemia, drug abuse, and use of oral contraceptive agents.

Cerebrovascular Anatomy

Strokes usually are caused by abnormalities of the cerebral circulation. Anatomic variations are frequent, however, and the territory receiving blood supply from a given artery is not entirely predictable; as a result, stroke syndromes may not correlate well with the location of the vascular injury. Appropriate imaging studies are needed to provide detailed information about each individual patient. In many situations, noninvasive imaging is adequate. For vascular anomalies, such as stenosis, malformations, and aneurysms, angiography is crucial for diagnosis because an understanding of the anatomy is necessary to develop treatment plans.

Four major arteries supply the brain: the bilaterally paired internal carotid and vertebral arteries (Fig. 439–2). The left common carotid artery arises directly from the aortic arch, but the right originates from branches of the aorta. The right common carotid artery is a branch of the innominate artery, and the left and right vertebral arteries originate from the subclavian arteries.

INTERNAL CAROTID ARTERIES. In most individuals, each common carotid artery bifurcates into an internal and external carotid artery just below the angle of the jaw and approximately at the level of the thyroid cartilage. The internal carotid artery (ICA) enters the skull through the foramen lacerum and travels a short distance within the petrous portion of the temporal bone. It then enters the cavernous sinus before penetrating the dura and ascends above the clinoid processes to divide into the anterior and middle cerebral arteries. The portion of the ICA that lies between the cavernous sinus and the supraclinoid process forms an S shape and sometimes is termed the *carotid siphon*. The ICA gives off its first important branches at the supraclinoid level: the ophthalmic, posterior communicating, and anterior choroidal

arteries, usually in that order. In some cases, the ophthalmic artery arises from the ICA within the cavernous sinus.

EXTERNAL CAROTID ARTERIES. Branches of the external carotid artery sometimes form anastomoses that provide collateral circulation to the ICA. These branches include the facial artery and the superficial temporal artery. Both vessels may anastomose with the supratrochlear branches of the ophthalmic artery. In instances of ICA occlusion below the level of the ophthalmic branch, the facial and superficial temporal arteries sometimes supply blood through the ophthalmic branch to the distal ICA.

VERTEBRAL-BASILAR ARTERIES. Anatomic variation is considerably more common in the vertebral artery system than in the ICA. The paired vertebral arteries usually arise from the subclavian arteries, but their origins may be more proximal on the aortic arch, or they may form a common branch of the thyrocervical trunk. The vertebral arteries usually enter the foramina of the sixth cervical vertebra or, much less commonly, the fourth, fifth, or seventh vertebral foramina. The vertebral arteries ascend through the transverse foramina and exit at C1, where they turn nearly 90 degrees posteriorly to pass behind the atlantoaxial joint before penetrating the dura and entering the cranial cavity through the foramen magnum. The portion of the vertebral artery that loops behind the atlantoaxial joint is prone to mechanical deformation, and excessive rotation of the head may cause arterial narrowing and reduction of blood flow to the ipsilateral vertebral artery.

Intracranially the vertebral arteries are lateral to the medulla oblongata, then course ventrally and medially, where they unite rostrally at the medullopontine junction to form the basilar artery. The basilar artery ultimately bifurcates at the pontomesencephalic junction to form the posterior cerebral arteries (PCAs).

In a few individuals, the right or left vertebral arteries terminate before reaching the basilar artery, which consequently is supplied, proximally, by a single vertebral artery. The vertebral arteries usually have medial branches, which turn caudally and unite to form the anterior spinal artery, and lateral branches supplying the dorsolateral medulla and posterior cerebellum, called the *posterior inferior cerebellar arteries*.

CIRCLE OF WILLIS. The circle of Willis, which is at the base of the brain, is formed by the union of right and left anterior cerebral arteries (ACAs) via the anterior communicating artery, the middle cerebral arteries (MCAs), and the PCAs via the posterior communicating arteries. Anomalies of the circle of Willis occur frequently; in large autopsy series of normal individuals, more than half show an incomplete circle of Willis. The most common sites for these abnormalities, which usually present as hypoplasia or absence, are the posterior communicating arteries and the ACAs.

ANTERIOR CEREBRAL ARTERIES. The ACAs travel medially above the optic chiasm and pass rostrally toward the interhemispheric fissure, where they arch caudally to lie just dorsal to the corpus callosum. In a small fraction of normal individuals, the A1 segment of the ACA (the portion between the origin at the MCA and the first major branch, the anterior communicating artery) is hypoplastic or absent, leaving its distal portion to be supplied by the opposite ACA via the anterior communicating artery. Branches of the ACA normally supply the frontal poles, the superior surfaces of the cerebral hemispheres where their distal branches anastomose with those of the MCA, and all of the medial surfaces of both cerebral hemispheres with the exception of the calcarine cortex (Figs. 439–3 and 439–4). Cortical areas served

by the ACA include the motor and sensory cortex of the legs and feet, the supplementary motor cortex, and the paracentral lobule.

The A1 and A2 segments (the portions between the anterior communicating artery and the genu of the corpus callosum) give off many small branches that penetrate the anterior perforated substance of the brain. These small penetrating branches include all of the anterior and some of the medial lenticulostriate arteries. Usually, there is a dominant medial striate vessel called the *recurrent artery of Heubner,* which commonly arises from the A1 segment of the ACA. This artery penetrates the perforated substance of the brain and, along with the other small perforators, supplies the anterior and inferior portions of the anterior limb of the internal capsule, the anterior and inferior head of the caudate nucleus, the anterior globus pallidus and putamen, the anterior hypothalamus, the olfactory bulbs and tracts, and the uncinate fasciculus.

ANTERIOR CHOROIDAL ARTERY. The anterior choroidal artery arises from the supraclinoid portion of the ICA in most people. It travels caudally and medially over the optic tract, to which it provides a few small branches, and enters the brain via the choroidal fissure. Many important brain structures receive blood flow from the anterior choroidal artery, including portions of the anterior hippocampus, uncus, amygdala, globus pallidus, tail of the caudate nucleus, lateral thalamus, geniculate body, and a large portion of the most inferior, posterior limb of the internal capsule.

MIDDLE CEREBRAL ARTERY. The MCA provides flow to most of the lateral surface of the cerebral hemispheres and is the vessel most frequently involved in ischemic stroke. As the main MCA trunk passes laterally toward the sylvian fissure, it gives rise to some of the medial and all of the lateral lenticulostriate arteries. These arteries supply the putamen, the head and body of the caudate nucleus, the lateral globus pallidus, the anterior limb of the internal capsule, and the superior portion of the posterior limb of the internal capsule. The MCA extends into the sylvian fissure, where it branches into several smaller arteries grouped into a superior division, which feeds the cortical surface above the fissure, and an inferior division, which supplies the cortical surface of the temporal lobe. The territory of the MCA includes the major motor and sensory areas of the cortex; the areas for contraversive eye and head movement; the optic radiations; the auditory sensory cortex; and, in the dominant hemisphere, the motor and sensory areas for language.

POSTERIOR CEREBRAL ARTERIES. Blood flow to both PCAs derives in most people from the basilar artery and infrequently from the ICA. Sometimes the ICA is the origin of one PCA, and the other PCA originates from the basilar artery. The PCAs pass dorsal to the third cranial nerves and across the cerebral peduncles, then ascend upward along the medial edge of the tentorium, where they branch into anterior and posterior divisions. The anterior division supplies the inferior surface of the temporal lobe, where its terminal branches form an anastomosis with branches of the MCA. The posterior division supplies the occipital lobe, where its terminal branches anastomose with the ACA and the MCA. In its most proximal course along the base of the brain, the PCA gives off several groups of penetrating arteries commonly called the *thalamogeniculate,* the *thalamoperforating,* and the *posterior choroidal* arteries. The red nucleus, the substantia nigra, medial parts of the cerebral peduncles, the nuclei of the thalamus, the hippocampus, and the posterior hypothalamus receive blood from these penetrating branches.

BRAIN STEM BLOOD SUPPLY. The ventral medial portion of the brain stem receives its blood supply from short paramedian vessels; the ventrolateral region receives its blood from short circumferential branches of the vertebral or basilar arteries; and long circumferential branches supply the dorsolateral brain stem and cerebellum (Fig. 439–5). These include the posterior inferior cerebellar arteries, which arise from the vertebral arteries, and the anterior inferior and superior cerebellar arteries, which arise from the basilar artery.

The pyramids, the inferior olives and medial lemnisci, the medial longitudinal fasciculi, and the emerging fibers of the hypoglossal nerve derive blood from the vertebral arteries. Longer branches from the vertebral arteries and posterior ICAs supply the spinothalamic tracts, the vestibular nuclei, the sensory nuclei of the fifth cranial nerve, the descending fibers of the sympathetic nervous system, the restiform body, and the emerging fibers of the vagus and glossopharyngeal nerves. The most cephalad and dorsal segment of the medulla includes the vestibular and cochlear nuclei, which, along with the posterior portion of the cerebellum, receive flow from the posterior inferior cerebellar artery.

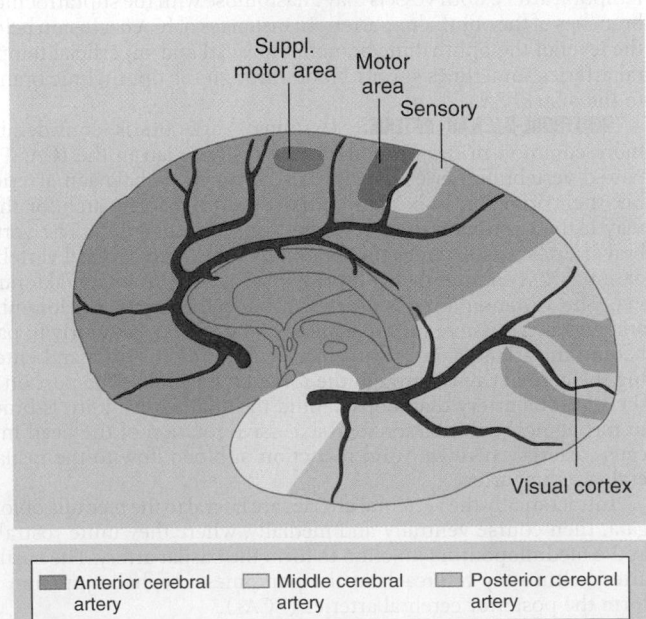

FIGURE 439–3 • Lateral (*A*) and medial (*B*) views of the cerebral hemisphere showing the surface distributions of the anterior, middle, and posterior cerebral arteries.

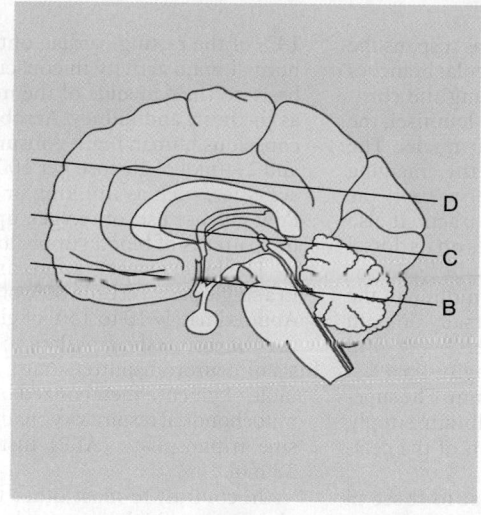

A

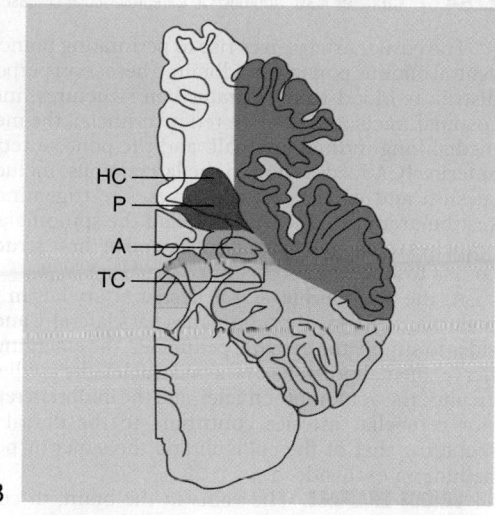

B

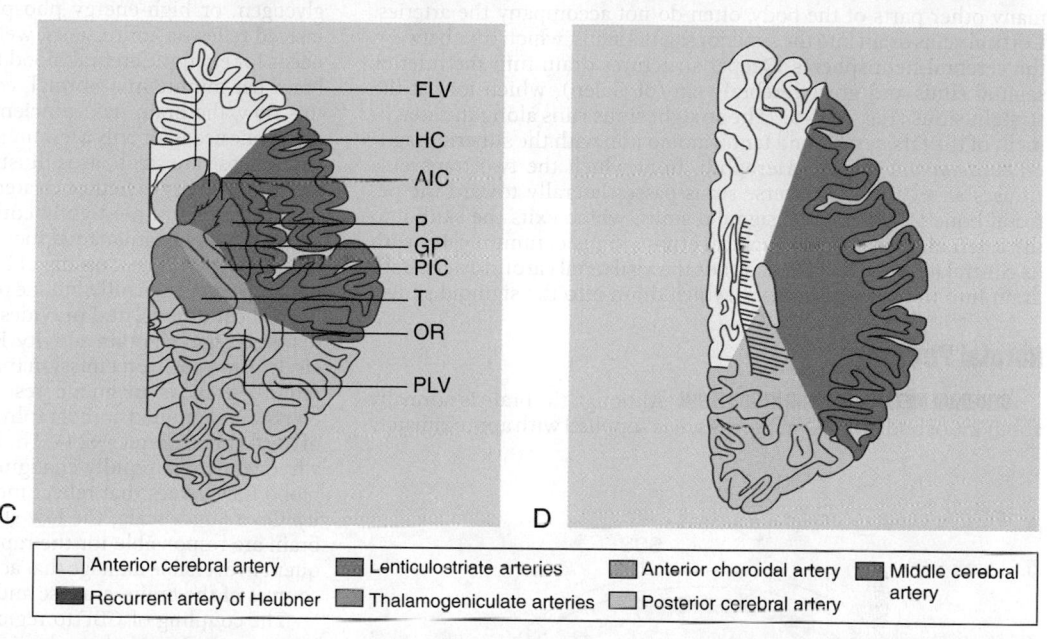

FLV
HC
AIC
P
GP
PIC
T
OR
PLV

C

D

FIGURE 439–4 • Arterial supply of deep brain structures. *A,* Sagittal view of the brain showing the computed tomography (CT) planes through which views *B, C,* and *D* were taken. *B,* CT plane through the head of the caudate nucleus (HC), putamen (P), amygdala (A), tail of the caudate nucleus (TC), hypothalamus, temporal lobe, midbrain, and cerebellum. *C,* CT plane through the frontal horn of the lateral ventricle (FLV) head of the caudate nucleus, anterior and posterior limbs of the internal capsule (AIC, PIC), putamen (P), globus pallidus (GP), thalamus (T), optic radiations (OR), and posterior horn of the lateral ventricle (PLV). *D,* CT plane through the centrum semiovale. (Modified from De Armond S, et al: Structure of the Human Brain, A Photographic Atlas, 3rd ed. New York, Oxford University Press, 1989; with permission.)

☐ Anterior cerebral artery	☐ Lenticulostriate arteries	☐ Anterior choroidal artery
☐ Recurrent artery of Heubner	☐ Thalamogeniculate arteries	☐ Posterior cerebral artery
		☐ Middle cerebral artery

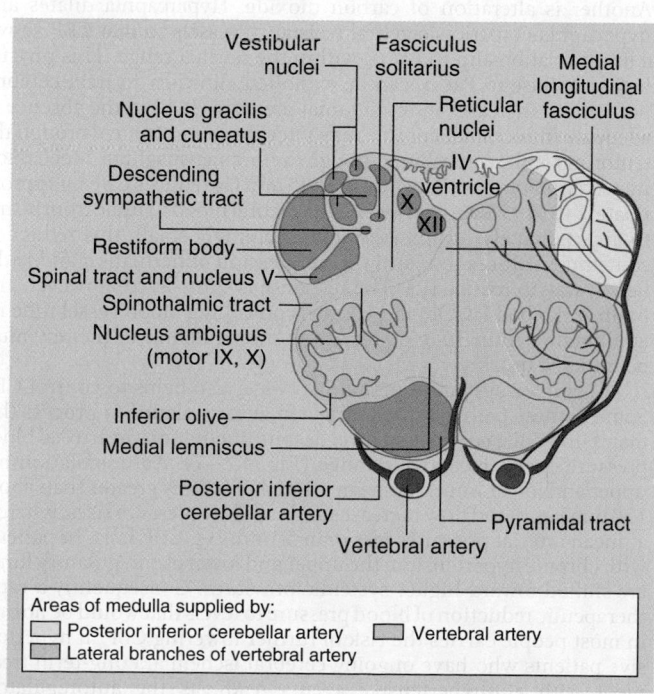

Areas of medulla supplied by:
☐ Posterior inferior cerebellar artery
☐ Lateral branches of vertebral artery
☐ Vertebral artery

A

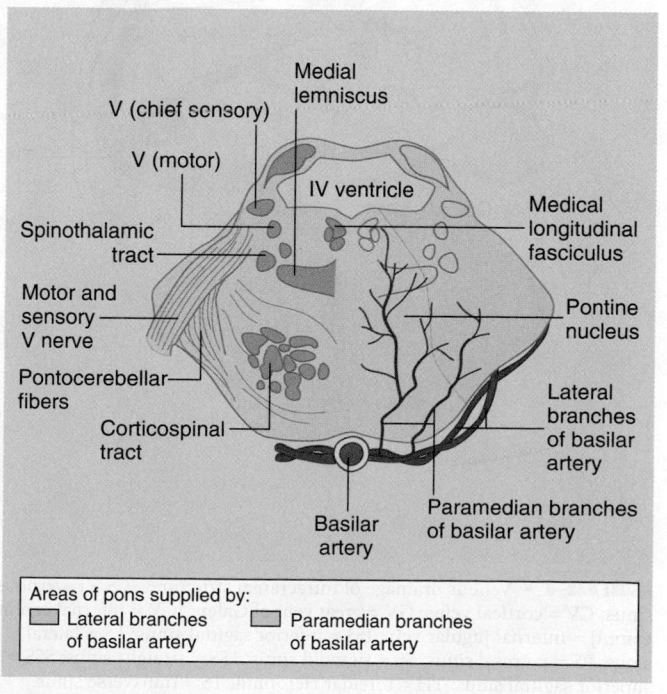

Areas of pons supplied by:
☐ Lateral branches of basilar artery
☐ Paramedian branches of basilar artery

B

FIGURE 439–5 • *A,* Cross section of the medulla oblongata at the level of the hypoglossal nuclei (XII). Short branches of the vertebral and anterior spinal arteries supply the medulla. Longer circumferential branches, including the posterior inferior cerebellar artery, supply the lateral portions of the medulla. *B,* Cross-section of the midpons. The medial portion receives blood supply from short, perforating basilar artery branches. More laterally, the blood supply comes from lateral basilar artery branches.

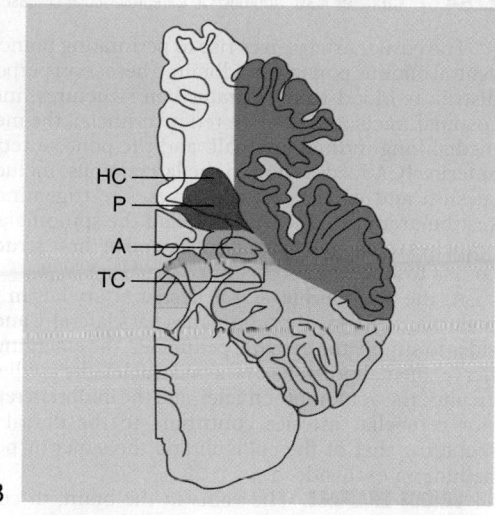

Neurology

The basilar artery gives rise to perforating branches as it spans the ventral midline pons and midbrain. These short perpendicular branches distribute blood to the paramedian structures, including the corticospinal tracts, the pontine reticular nuclei, the medial lemnisci, the medial longitudinal fasciculi, and the pontine reticular nuclei. The anterior ICA feeds blood to the lateral pons, including the emerging seventh and eighth cranial nerves, the trigeminal nerve root, the vestibular and cochlear nuclei, and the spinothalamic tracts. It also branches to the most dorsal and lateral of these structures on its dorsal course toward the cerebellum.

At the midbrain level, the basilar artery lies in the midline in the peduncular fossa. Short branches pass laterally and dorsally on both sides to supply the cerebral peduncles, the emerging fibers of the third nerve, medial portions of the red nuclei, the medial longitudinal fasciculus, the oculomotor nuclei, and the midbrain reticulum. The superior cerebellar arteries contribute to the dorsal midbrain supply, including that of the colliculi and the superior portion of the cerebellum on each side.

VENOUS DRAINAGE. The veins in the brain, in contrast to those in many other parts of the body, often do not accompany the arteries. Cortical veins drain into the superior sagittal sinus, which runs between the cerebral hemispheres. Deeper structures drain into the inferior sagittal sinus and great cerebral vein (of Galen), which join at the straight sinus (Fig. 439–6). The straight sinus runs along the attachment of the falx cerebri and tentorium to join with the superior sagittal sinus at the torcular Herophili, from which the two transverse sinuses arise. Each transverse sinus passes laterally toward the petrosal bone to become the sigmoid sinus, which exits the skull into the internal jugular vein. Each cavernous sinus communicates with its contralateral twin and surrounds the ipsilateral carotid artery. Both drain into the petrosal sinuses, which drain into the sigmoid sinus.

Normal Physiology

CEREBRAL METABOLISM AND BLOOD FLOW. Although the brain is normally about 2% of body weight in humans, it is supplied with approximately

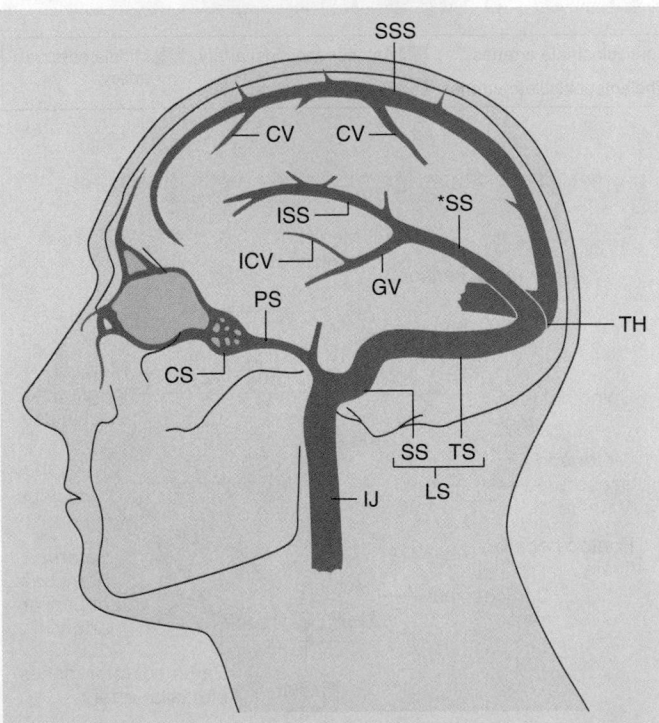

FIGURE 439–6 • Venous drainage of intracranial structures. CS = cavernous sinus; CV = cortical veins; GV = great vein of Galen; ICV = internal cerebral vein; IJ = internal jugular vein; ISS = inferior sagittal sinus; LS = lateral sinus; PS = petrosal sinus; SS = sigmoid sinus; *SS = straight sinus; SSS = superior sagittal sinus; TH = torcular Herophili; TS = transverse sinus. (Reproduced with permission from Gates P, Barnett HJ, Mohr JP, et al [eds]: Stroke: Pathophysiology, Diagnosis and Management. New York, Churchill Livingstone, 1986.)

14% of the resting cardiac output. The energy demands to support normal brain activity in conscious humans is equal, on a per weight basis, to the demands of the most metabolically active tissues, such as the heart and kidney. Aerobic glucose metabolism in the normal, conscious human brain consumes an average of 140 μmol of oxygen and 24 μmol of glucose per 100 g of brain each minute. Normal brain activities, such as thinking or sleeping, do not alter the total blood flow, glucose use, or oxygen uptake in the brain, but they do change the patterns of blood supply and energy use in specific brain areas.

The brain extracts approximately 10% of available blood glucose in a single pass, yet only 80% of this glucose is used to generate energy. Approximately 10 to 15% of glucose is metabolized to lactate, which may be lost to the circulation; the remainder is used for the synthesis of neurotransmitters, fats, and, to a small degree, proteins. Each mole of glucose metabolized by the brain through glycolysis and the mitochondrial respiratory chain yields approximately 30 mol of adenosine triphosphate (ATP) instead of the theoretical maximum of 38 mol.

In contrast to most other tissues, the brain stores little glucose, glycogen, or high-energy phosphates (ATP, phosphocreatine), but instead relies on continuous, well-regulated blood flow to satisfy its needs for energy. Cerebral blood flow (CBF) averages 50 mL/100 g of brain per minute in a normal, conscious human. In the absence of this flow, the brain has sufficient high-energy stores to support its metabolic needs for only a few minutes. The vascular reserves of oxygen and glucose are small, as is illustrated by the fact that all changes of synaptic activity, whether related to thinking, talking, or directing muscular activity, are tightly coupled, temporally and anatomically, to an almost instantaneous increase in local CBF. The mechanisms responsible for this coupling of blood flow to metabolic activity have not been elucidated fully, but the relationship is well established, under normal conditions, and provides a basis for use of imaging methods to assess regional brain activity. Regional CBF can be quantified precisely using positron emission tomography. Other, less invasive techniques, such as magnetic resonance imaging and single-photon emission computed tomography, provide qualitative measurements of local CBF (Chapter 424). The brain's functional activities result in a frequently and rapidly changing pattern of regional metabolic and blood flow values that reflect moment-to-moment changes in activity. On a larger scale, the low stores and high metabolic rate of the brain are responsible for the rapid loss of consciousness and subsequent irreversible damage that accompanies loss of the critical energy sources of the brain, glucose and oxygen.

The coupling of CBF to regional synaptic and metabolic activity is only one of several mechanisms known to regulate normal CBF. Another is alteration of carbon dioxide. Hypercapnia dilates and hypocapnia constricts cerebral resistance vessels so that CBF shows a linear relationship to $PaCO_2$ within the normal range. This physiologic response to $PaCO_2$ can be exploited clinically to treat cerebral herniation. Increases in intracranial pressure (ICP) in the absence of adequate intracranial volume may force the hemispheres through the tentorium or the cerebellum through the foramen magnum. Mechanical hyperventilation to a $PaCO_2$ of 20 to 25 mm Hg reduces CBF by approximately 40 to 45% and normal adult cerebral blood volume from 50 mL to approximately 35 mL. Although seemingly small, this reduction sometimes suffices to retard the progression of herniation and is the fastest way to reduce ICP. The response is short-lived, however, and brain and blood HCO_3^- and H^+ ions controlling blood vessel tone reequilibrate within 30 to 60 minutes. A more definitive therapy must be initiated quickly.

A complex system of neural pathways also helps to control CBF. Some of these pathways participate in autoregulation, a process that maintains CBF at a constant level despite fluctuations in arterial blood pressure over a fairly wide range (Fig. 439–7). Autoregulation has upper and lower limits; at mean arterial pressures greater than about 150 mm Hg, blood flow increases and capillary pressure rises, whereas at mean arterial pressures less than 50 mm Hg, CBF falls. In patients with chronic hypertension, the upper and lower autoregulatory limits are shifted toward higher systemic pressures. Consequently a rapid therapeutic reduction of blood pressure to levels that would be normal in most people carries the risk of further lowering CBF in hypertensive patients who have ongoing cerebral ischemia. Long-term treatment with antihypertensive agents readjusts the autoregulatory curve toward more normal values. Conversely, excessive reduction of blood pressure in previously normal patients to a mean arterial pressure of less than approximately 50 mm Hg inevitably leads to loss

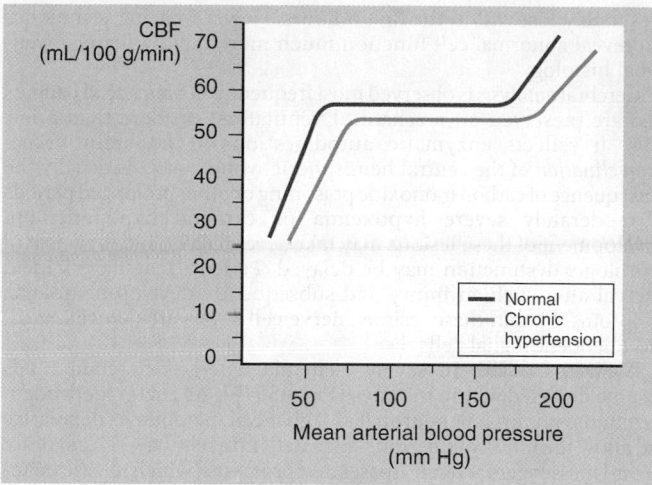

FIGURE 439–7 • Autoregulatory cerebral blood flow (CBF) response to changes in mean arterial pressure in normotensive and chronically hypertensive people. Note the shift of the curve toward higher mean pressures with chronic hypertension.

of autoregulation, possible expansion of an ischemic zone, or production of global cerebral ischemia. These injuries are seen in patients who are treated too aggressively with antihypertensive agents in the immediate aftermath of a stroke and in patients who are anesthetized during surgical procedures.

BLOOD-BRAIN BARRIER. The brain's extracellular ionic and molecular environment is tightly regulated. Small changes in extracellular concentrations of Na^+, K^+, and Ca^{2+} ions or neurotransmitters, including glutamate, acetylcholine, and norepinephrine, alter neuronal function. Intracellular communication within the brain, which is perhaps its most important basic function, depends on a carefully controlled extracellular space. The blood-brain barrier (BBB), which has evolved to protect this milieu, is composed of unique endothelial cells that lack the usual transendothelial channels and that closely abut one another in tight junctions. This anatomy protects the brain against the fluctuating composition of blood and reduces the entry of potentially toxic compounds. A negative consequence is that the BBB prevents entry of polar molecules into the brain, limiting the utility of many drugs, small molecules, and proteins, which cannot gain entry into the brain by oral or intravenous routes.

The entry of nutrients and egress of metabolic waste across the BBB can occur by simple diffusion, facilitated transport, or active transport. Lipid-soluble compounds can diffuse rapidly across endothelial cell membranes, whereas some polar compounds can be transported by special carrier molecules that are driven either by concentration gradients (facilitated transport) or through the expenditure of energy (active transport). Gas molecules, such as oxygen and carbon dioxide, freely diffuse across plasma membranes and rapidly equilibrate between blood and brain. Glucose, a highly polar molecule, enters the brain on a special glucose transporter. The rate of brain glucose transport is normally two to three times faster than the metabolism of glucose, but because glucose uptake depends so highly on its blood concentration, a reduction of the blood glucose level to one third of normal, caused by either ischemia or hypoglycemia, may compromise normal brain energy metabolism.

Pathophysiology and Pathology of Cerebral Ischemia

Inadequate delivery of oxygen or glucose to the brain initiates a cascade of events that ultimately results in infarction. The severity of the insult, defined by the degree and duration of reduced blood flow, hypoxia, or hypoglycemia, determines whether the brain has only temporary dysfunction, such as a transient ischemic attack; irreversible injury to only a few of the most vulnerable neurons (selective necrosis); or cerebral infarction, in which damage occurs to extensive areas involving all cell types (pan-necrosis).

TYPES OF CEREBRAL HYPOXIA-ISCHEMIA. Cerebral hypoxia-ischemia can be divided into focal ischemia, caused by vascular occlusion; global ischemia, from complete cardiovascular failure; and diffuse

hypoperfusion-hypoxia, produced by respiratory disease or severely reduced blood pressure. Focal cerebral ischemia results, most frequently, from embolic or thrombotic occlusion of extracranial or intracranial blood vessels and the resulting reduction in blood flow within the related vascular territory. Blood flow to the central zone of the ischemic vascular bed usually is severely reduced but rarely reaches zero because of partial supply from collateral blood vessels. The best treatment option for this intensely ischemic region is acute restoration of blood flow. A transition zone may be present between the normally perfused tissue and the more ischemic central core. This rim of moderately deprived tissue has been called the *ischemic penumbra*. It is thought that brain cells in the penumbra remain viable for a longer time than do cells in the ischemic core. This marginally viable tissue may die if inadequate blood flow persists but may be salvaged by restoring flow or, possibly, by neuroprotective therapeutic agents. The size and duration of the penumbra are unknown in any individual patient and poorly defined by current diagnostic techniques. In more recent years, attempts to salvage the penumbra with neuroprotective agents has been the subject of intense basic and clinical research.

Cerebral ischemia sufficient to cause clinical signs or symptoms, if severe, can produce irreversible injury to highly vulnerable neurons in 5 minutes. Progressively longer durations of ischemia increase the probability of permanent damage (Fig. 439–8). If cerebral ischemia persists for more than about 6 hours, infarction of part or all of the involved vascular territory is completed, and the only strategies for treatment entail rehabilitation, such as treatment with neurotrophic factors or neural transplantation. Whether clinical evidence of permanent brain injury from ischemia is detectable depends on the location of the brain tissue involved.

Global cerebral ischemia results from cardiac asystole or ventricular fibrillation that reduces blood flow rate to zero throughout the brain and body. Global ischemia for more than 5 to 10 minutes is usually incompatible with full recovery of consciousness in normothermic humans. If blood flow is restored in time to prevent cardiac death, selective ischemic necrosis usually involves the most vulnerable neurons in the CA1 pyramidal neurons of the hippocampus; the cerebellar Purkinje cells; and the pyramidal neurons in neocortical layers 3, 5, and 6. Anything that prevents adequate oxygen or glucose supply to the brain, such as hypoxemia, carbon monoxide poisoning, and severe and prolonged hypoglycemia, also may produce such injury. Cardiac resuscitation or other causes of prolonged hypotension may cause cerebral infarction, particularly in border zones that lie between the terminal branches of major arterial supplies, often termed *watershed zones*.

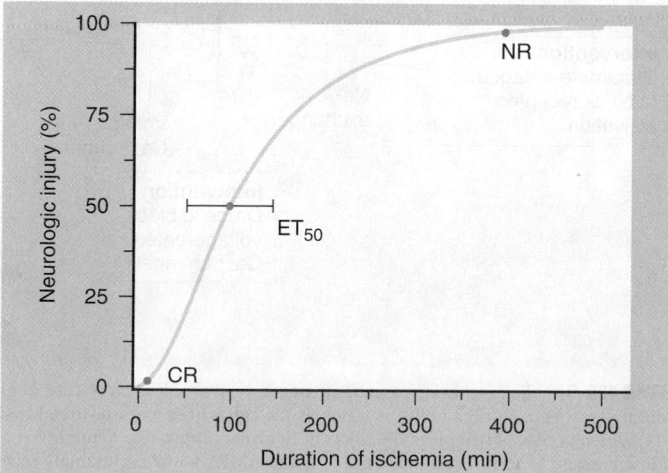

FIGURE 439–8 • Degree of neurologic injury as a function of the duration of ischemia. Neuropathologic data from a primate model of cerebral ischemia were used to generate this figure. Neurologic damage is the percentage of monkeys exhibiting infarcts of any size. CR = the maximum duration of ischemia compatible with complete recovery; ET_{50} = the duration of ischemia that results in half-maximal damage; NR = the minimum time for no recovery. (From Zivin JA: Factors determining the therapeutic window for stroke. Neurology 1998;50:599–603.)

Neurology

Diffuse cerebral hypoxia initially causes cerebral dysfunction but not irreversible brain injury. Individuals with cerebral hypoxia from high altitude, pulmonary disease, or severe anemia can present with confusion, cognitive impairment, and lethargy. The onset of coma heralds permanent brain damage. With acute changes in PaO_2 from normal to less than 40 mm Hg or a decrease in the hemoglobin concentration to less than 7 g/dL, compensatory increases of CBF become inadequate, and clinical signs and symptoms of cerebral hypoxia develop. Slower onset of reduced oxygenation, such as caused by moving to high elevations or the gradual development of anemia, permit compensation by a variety of mechanisms; if hypoxia increases, however, the compensation ultimately fails.

NEUROPATHOLOGY OF CEREBRAL ISCHEMIA. Four general classes of histopathologic damage can occur. Cerebral infarction caused by focal vascular occlusion is characterized by destruction of all cellular elements: neurons, glia, and endothelial cells (pan-necrosis). Cerebral infarcts are initially grossly pale (anemic) or hemorrhagic (showing gross petechial bleeding). Later, necrotic tissue is removed and replaced by a glial scar or a cavity. Transient arrest of the cerebral circulation (global ischemia) can cause selective *ischemic necrosis* of highly vulnerable neurons. Using conventional stains, histologic change begins to outline the margins between living and dying neurons and glia within a few hours, although the full extent of damage may not be evident for several days. The neurologic functionality of the cells is

irreversibly lost within the first 6 hours. Newer imaging techniques can reveal abnormal cell function much more rapidly than conventional histology.

Cerebral *autolysis* is observed most frequently in brain-dead patients who are preserved on mechanical ventilators for more than a few days; it reflects enzymatic autodigestion of the brain tissue. *Demyelination* of the central hemispheric white matter is usually the consequence of carbon monoxide poisoning or other prolonged periods of moderately severe hypoxemia or cerebral hypoperfusion. Development of these lesions may take several days, and the onset of neurologic dysfunction may be delayed. Patients may have a lucid interval after such an injury and subsequently develop neurologic symptoms. Within these lesions, nerve cell axons are demyelinated, and oligodendroglial cells die.

ISCHEMIC CASCADE. In severe ischemia, energy-rich compounds become depleted within minutes (Fig. 439–9). As energy-dependent membrane pumps fail, neuronal and glial cell membranes depolarize and allow the influx of Ca^{2+} ions. Elevated intracellular Ca^{2+} and other second messengers activate lipases and proteases, which release membrane-bound free fatty acids that denature proteins. Depolarization of presynaptic terminals releases abnormally high concentrations of excitatory neurotransmitters, such as glutamate, which may elevate metabolic demand at a time when energy supplies are inadequate, exacerbating the injury. If blood flow is restored within 5 minutes

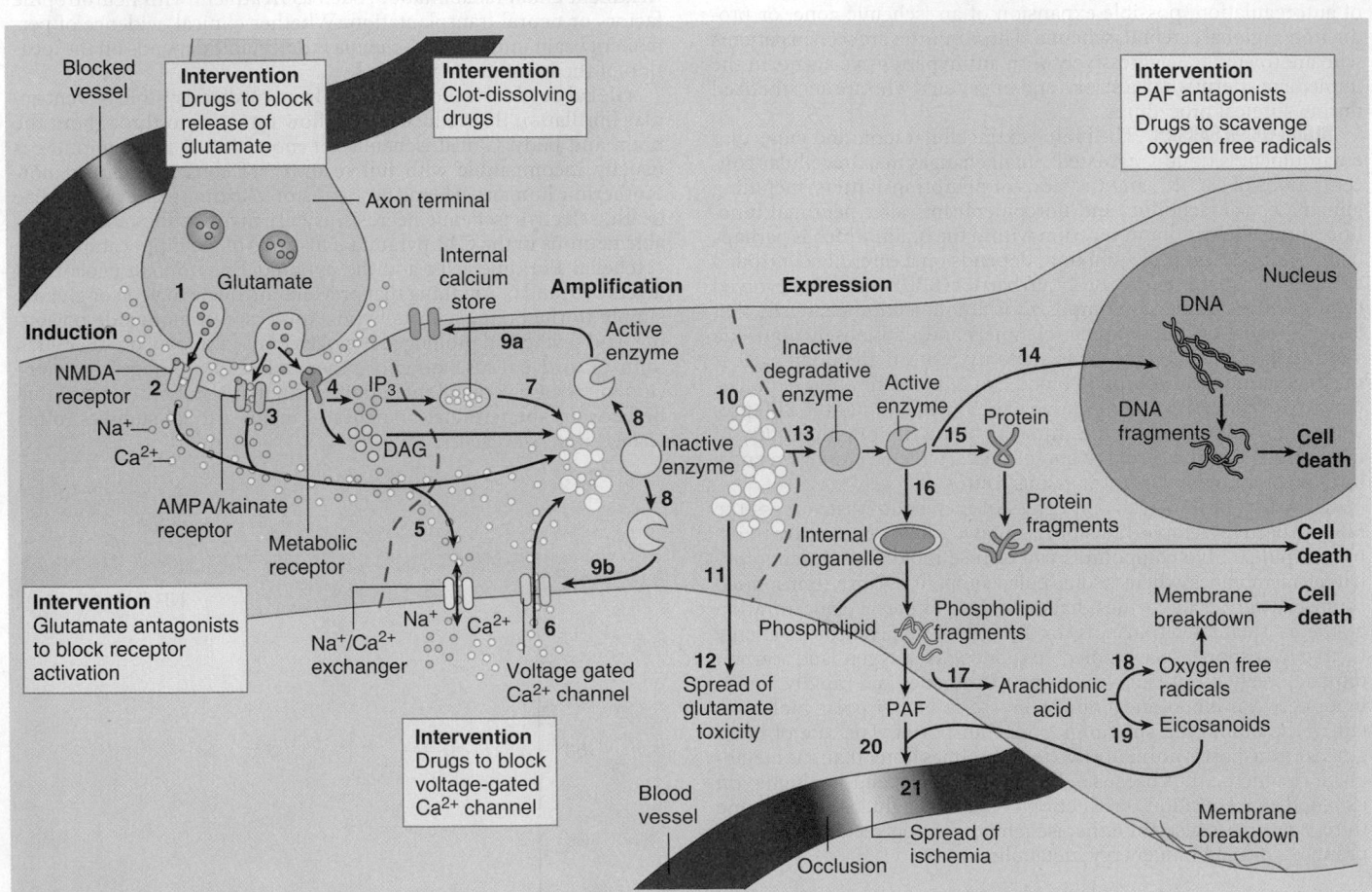

FIGURE 439–9 • The ischemic cascade in stages of stroke. Excess release of glutamate may damage brain tissue by a three-stage process. Induction: After a blood vessel is occluded, neurons (such as the cell whose axon terminal is shown at the top left) become ischemic. The neuron releases excessive glutamate (1), which activates receptors on adjacent neurons (cutaway). N-methyl-D-aspartate (NMDA)–type glutamate receptors (top center) open channels that allow passage of sodium and calcium (2), and AMPA/kainate glutamate receptors open sodium channels (3), resulting in an abnormal build-up of both ions. Simultaneously, metabotropic receptors trigger formation of inositol triphosphate (IP_3) and diacylglycerol (DAG) (4). Amplification: Excess sodium activates the sodium-calcium exchange transporter (5); internal calcium channels (6) and IP_3 release calcium from internal stores (7). The resulting calcium overload combined with excess DAG activates enzymes that increase sensitivity to glutamate and other excitatory stimuli (9a) and increase the contribution of the voltage-gated calcium channels (9b). Further build-up of calcium (10) triggers the release of glutamate (11), spreading the toxic cascade to other cells (12). Expression: Calcium activates enzymes (13) that degrade DNA (14), proteins (15), and phospholipids (16). Phospholipid breakdown leads to formation of arachidonic acid (17), which, when metabolized, gives rise to free radicals (18) that harm the cell membrane and to eicosanoid molecules (19). Eicosanoids, together with activated platelet-activating factor (PAF), another breakdown product of phospholipid breakdown, promote blockage of previously healthy vessels (20) and spread of ischemia (21). Meanwhile, continuing destruction of cellular constituents kills the neurons (22). (From Zivin JA, Choi DW: Stroke therapy. Sci Am 1991;265:56–63.)

and there are no other complicating factors, such as hyperglycemia, these events are completely reversible. As the duration of ischemia increases, selectively vulnerable neurons die first; if ischemia persists for hours or more, cerebral infarction develops. Prompt restoration of blood flow permits full functional recovery and maintenance of tissue integrity. Tissues with partial depletion of ATP and impaired calcium homeostasis may benefit from pharmacologic therapies that reduce calcium movement through voltage-dependent and neurotransmitter-dependent ion channels. Many other neuroprotective strategies also have been shown to be effective in animal models, including prevention of the detrimental actions of excitatory neurotransmitters, inhibition of many biochemical pathways leading to cell death, and therapies that may delay the denaturation of proteins. So far, however, none of these therapies has been proved useful in clinical trials in stroke patients.

LEUKOCYTES. More recently, the role of leukocytes in ischemic damage has been recognized. Two proposed mechanisms of injury are (1) microvascular occlusion from direct mechanical obstruction and damage to the endothelium and (2) central nervous system tissue infiltration and cellular cytotoxic injury. The white blood cell–mediated damage may be irreversible even if blood flow is restored.

White blood cells require considerable deformation to pass through capillaries. When activated by chemotactic substances during ischemia, their cytoplasmic stiffness increases, and they adhere to capillary endothelium. Under conditions of reduced perfusion pressures, white blood cells may obstruct the microcirculation. This leukocyte capillary plugging may be the major cause of the *no-reflow phenomenon,* which is defined as the incomplete restoration of normal blood flow after a period of ischemia. Areas of parenchyma that might be viable when blood flow returns are inadequately reperfused. This phenomenon was a laboratory curiosity until the advent of thrombolytic therapy; it now may be a cause of apparent stroke-in-evolution or the development of increased neurologic deficits after apparently successful thrombolysis.

Leukocytes may potentiate injury by toxic damage to vascular endothelium and by transendothelial migration to the parenchyma. Release of leukocyte granule contents, which include reactive oxygen metabolites and membrane phospholipases, can injure the endothelium and usually is responsible for removing necrotic tissue after irreversible damage. The resultant effects include increased endothelial permeability, interstitial edema, expansion and injury of individual cells (endothelial, glial, and neuronal), vasoconstriction, and generation of substances that induce further leukocyte adhesion.

Cerebral Hemorrhage

Bleeding into the subarachnoid space from a ruptured aneurysm or other vascular malformation produces a chemical (sterile) meningitis and can induce vasospasm, particularly in the vessels constituting the circle of Willis. If the vasospasm is sufficiently severe, it can result in cerebral infarction and death.

Intraparenchymal hemorrhage may be relatively benign. Bleeding into a region of previous infarction, called *hemorrhagic transformation,* causes no additional functional loss. Primary parenchymatous hemorrhage damages tissue in several ways, however. If a large vessel ruptures, the amount of bleeding into the brain can be severe. The portion of the vascular distribution distal to the site of rupture no longer is supplied with blood, resulting in infarction. At the site of rupture, bleeding into the brain may cause traumatic injury to the exposed tissue, and blood or its breakdown products in the parenchyma damages brain tissues. Also the extravascular blood in the brain parenchyma increases total brain volume, and the edema that rapidly forms in and around the site of bleeding increases the intracranial contents. Because the cranial capacity is fixed, ICP rapidly increases, and cerebral herniation may occur.

The biochemical pathology caused by exposure of brain tissues to blood has not been established. Hypertension is closely associated with intracerebral hemorrhage. Research suggests that matrix metalloproteinase in vessel walls is activated, then leads to degradation of the vascular tissue, with subsequent bleeding.

CEREBRAL EDEMA. A pathologic increase in the water content of the brain tissue (edema) eventually develops in all types of ischemic and hemorrhagic stroke. Brain swelling and raised ICP relate proportionally to the volume of the accumulated water; in some instances, edema can cause neurologic deterioration and death by herniation syndromes.

The intracranial space contains the brain, which weighs approximately 1400 g, about 75 mL of blood, and approximately 75 mL of cerebrospinal fluid (CSF). An increase in volume of any of these contents must be accompanied by a decrease in another component because the intracranial cavity is of relatively fixed size and surrounded by bone. Normally the brain's tissue volume is constant, whereas intracranial blood and CSF vary reciprocally to maintain normal ICP. A variety of mechanisms can compensate for increased intracranial contents to a limited extent, including displacement of CSF into other cranial compartments, reduction of venous blood volume, reduction of normal cerebral interstitial fluid, and chronic cerebral atrophy. If there is a rapid increase in extravascular blood, reduced venous outflow, blockage or resorption of CSF, or cerebral edema, there is a marked increase in ICP.

Brain edema is categorized on the basis of pathophysiologic and anatomic criteria as intracellular or interstitial. Intracellular edema, also called *cytotoxic edema,* develops as energy-dependent membrane ion pumps fail; as a result, Na^+ and other osmoles enter the cell and draw water in from the interstitial and vascular compartments. This process can begin within a few hours after the onset of ischemia. Cell swelling occurs predominantly in astrocytes, but neurons, oligodendroglial cells, and endothelial cells also are involved.

Interstitial edema, also called *vasogenic edema,* occurs later than the intracellular form. Damage to endothelial cells of the BBB allows macromolecules, such as plasma proteins, to enter the cerebral interstitial space, accompanied by osmotically bound water. Interstitial edema after cerebral infarction progressively worsens for about 3 days after a stroke. Fluid accumulation within the vicinity of damaged endothelial cells and the zone of infarction can raise the local water content of brain by 10%. The osmolality of ischemic brain increases from 310 mOsm to approximately 350 mOsm. The intracellular accumulation of water increases from a normal value of approximately 79 to 81% of brain weight.

If cerebral circulation is reestablished before permanent brain injury develops, intracellular edema resolves without permanent sequelae. A large increase in the brain's volume can lead, however, to transtentorial herniation of the cerebral hemispheres or to cerebellar herniation. These syndromes can result in irreversible global ischemia of the hemispheres or crushing of the brain stem, loss of cerebral control of the circulation, and death due to respiratory arrest. Edema-induced increase in ICP usually reaches a maximum about 3 days after the onset of a stroke. If a patient has a large stroke and survives after the third day, he or she is unlikely to die from that stroke.

SUGGESTED READING
Bowman JP, Giddings FD: Strokes: An Illustrated Guide to Brain Structure, Blood Supply, and Clinical Signs. Upper Saddle River, NJ, Prentice Hall, 2003. *A comprehensive review with outstanding illustrations.*

440 ISCHEMIC CEREBROVASCULAR DISEASE

Justin A. Zivin

Definition

Ischemic strokes are caused by insufficient blood flow into part or all of the brain. Focal stroke conventionally is defined as a neurologic deficit lasting more than 24 hours caused by reduced blood flow in an artery supplying a part of the brain that ultimately results in infarction. Strokes are distinguished from transient ischemic attacks (TIAs) in that TIAs historically have been defined, arbitrarily, as ischemia-induced neurologic deficits persisting for less than 24 hours. The current thinking is that nearly all TIAs resolve more rapidly, and a deficit that persists for more than 1 or 2 hours is likely to be associated with permanent brain damage, often demonstrable by computed tomography (CT) or magnetic resonance imaging (MRI), despite complete clinical recovery. The important distinction between a TIA and a stroke is whether the ischemia has caused brain infarction or selective ischemic necrosis, a difference that may not be possible to distinguish within the first few hours after the onset of symptoms but commonly becomes apparent retrospectively. During the early phases, when acute therapy is potentially beneficial, it is impossible to predict whether a patient will recover spontaneously because the treatment is effective only if given before it is known whether the symptoms will resolve spontaneously.

Ischemic strokes are differentiated from hemorrhagic strokes (Chapter 441) by the lack of extravasated blood in the brain parenchyma. There are two main classifications of ischemic strokes. *Thrombosis* and *embolism,* which are caused by arterial occlusion with either thrombus that forms locally at the site of an atherosclerotic plaque or embolic clot, constitute 65% of all strokes. Emboli are produced when a piece of a larger clot breaks off from a mural thrombus in the heart or a more proximal artery and lodges downstream at a point where the diameter of the vessel has decreased in size so that the clot no longer can pass through the arterial lumen. It is often impossible to distinguish thrombus from embolus by imaging methods or histopathologic material, so the two processes are classified together. *Small vessel strokes,* commonly called *lacunes,* are caused by occlusions of small arterioles and constitute about 20% of strokes. The histologic lesion in blood vessels in these strokes classically is called lipohyalinosis, which does not help in identifying the cause of these strokes. Some of these strokes are caused by local vascular abnormalities, but others almost certainly are caused by small emboli. The other 15% or so of strokes are caused by hemorrhage (Chapter 441).

Pathobiology

The precise signs and symptoms of ischemic stroke depend primarily on the region deprived of flow. The tempo with which deficits develop has important clinical implications.

PATTERN OF DEVELOPMENT OF STROKES. Shortly after the onset of vascular occlusion, it is common for symptoms and signs to fluctuate and either to improve or to deteriorate, often rapidly. Some patients may be in denial and anticipate that their symptoms will resolve, resulting in a delay in seeking medical care until sufficient time has elapsed so that acute therapy is useless.

If the symptoms completely resolve in 1 or 2 hours, the patient has had a TIA. The basis for this resolution is unclear. Possibilities include dissolution of an embolus with subsequent restoration of normal regional blood flow, decrease in vasospasm, and improvement in perfusion secondary to increased collateral flow.

Ischemic episodes that ultimately develop into infarction often fluctuate for several hours after onset. During the early time periods, it is impossible to predict what will happen. Recovery may stop suddenly, and deficits may plateau or increase. Persistence of any neurologic deficit beyond 2 hours, even if the patient subsequently recovers fully, nearly always is accompanied by some degree of tissue destruction.

Hours to days after the abnormality becomes stable, a patient may develop increased neurologic deficits, a deterioration termed *stroke-in-evolution*. Likely reasons include reperfusion injury or a new stroke in the same vascular distribution. Compromised cardiac output and systemic hypotension resulting from myocardial ischemia, cardiac arrhythmias, or heart failure also may contribute in some cases. Patients may appear to have stroke-in-evolution because of systemic disorders, such as electrolyte imbalances or glucose abnormalities that initially appear to be exacerbations of a stroke but are really comorbid problems that do not cause extension of the infarct. Cerebral edema may increase neurologic deterioration in large strokes by causing herniation syndromes. Secondary bleeding into an infarct can occur; ordinarily this process does not increase neurologic deficits unless the blood extends into an area outside of the initial boundaries of the infarction or causes a mass effect and increased intracranial pressure. The term *stroke-in-evolution* describes a clinical picture rather than a specific pathologic process.

COMPLETE VERSUS INCOMPLETE STROKES. A stroke is called *complete* if the total area of the brain supplied by an occluded vessel is damaged. If so, prophylactic therapies to prevent further extension are of no benefit. If there is some cellular damage (loss of neurons) but not cystic pan-necrosis, the stroke is called *incomplete*. If a stroke is incomplete, additional tissue in the vascular distribution is at risk, and prophylaxis should be considered. Distinguishing between complete and incomplete strokes based on clinical findings can be impossible, particularly during the early phases of a stroke. At present, no diagnostic method reliably can identify threatened tissue. The distinction between a complete and an incomplete stroke, as a practical matter,

is often based on whether a patient has all of the manifestations of one of the common stroke syndromes or just some of them.

Common Causes and Pathogenesis of Stroke

ATHEROSCLEROSIS

Atherosclerosis (Chapter 66) is the most common disorder that leads to strokes. Atherosclerotic plaques are thought to cause strokes in three ways: (1) Mural thrombosis forms at the site of an atherosclerotic lesion, and the clot obstructs the artery at that location; (2) ulceration or rupture of a plaque leads to formation of a clot and distal embolization; (3) hemorrhage into a plaque obstructs the artery. The clinical manifestations of a stroke depend on the rate of occlusion. If occlusion occurs slowly, there may be time for collateral blood supply to develop, and a stroke is avoided. If the occlusion is abrupt, a stroke ensues, and the degree of damage depends on the extent of collateral supply that is available to the territory of the brain that is supplied by the occluded vessel. If collateral supply is marginal, just enough blood may pass through the stenotic region to maintain minimally adequate blood flow. In these circumstances, neurologic function may become critically dependent on changes in blood pressure, and small decreases can cause a stroke or recurrent TIAs.

More frequently, a platelet-fibrin thrombus forms on the roughened surface of an atherosclerotic plaque. The thrombus can break off and float distally in the blood stream, eventually becoming lodged in a distal, smaller branch; this process is termed an *artery-to-artery embolization*. These embolic occlusions are more likely to be symptomatic because the more distal end vessels have no collateral supply. The amount of territory that is deprived of blood is smaller, however, and symptoms are usually less severe than with occlusion of the main stem of a vessel. The most common locations for an intravascular thrombus to form are the base of the aorta, the bifurcation of the common carotid artery, or the point where the vertebral arteries originate from the subclavian arteries.

EMBOLI OF CARDIAC ORIGIN

Emboli originating from the heart may lodge in any part of the body. Because about 20% of the normal cardiac output goes to the brain, however, it is a common site of cardioembolism. Thrombus formation and the release of emboli from the heart are promoted by arrhythmias and by structural abnormalities of the valves and chambers. The frequency of various types of strokes produced by cardioembolism can only be estimated. Although some strokes are clearly embolic in origin, and others are unquestionably thrombotic, it is usually impossible to distinguish them pathologically. There is no diagnostic test to prove a thrombus or embolism is of cardiac origin.

MURAL THROMBI. Myocardial infarction may produce a region of dyskinetic myocardium that predisposes to the formation of mural thrombi (Chapter 69). Anterior wall myocardial infarction is associated with the highest frequency of thromboembolic strokes. Cardiomyopathies (Chapter 73), such as those caused by alcohol abuse or viral infections, also produce dyskinesia that promotes mural thrombi and can result in cerebral embolization, as can any cause of severe heart failure (Chapter 55). In some instances, a cardiac mural thrombus may release numerous pieces that produce a shower of emboli and cause several simultaneous strokes at various locations in the brain.

VALVULAR HEART DISEASE. Rheumatic heart disease (Chapter 309), which is now rare in industrialized countries, is associated with systemic emboli, especially in patients who have mitral stenosis (Chapter 72). Acute or subacute infectious endocarditis (Chapter 310) produces vegetations on heart valves, and these vegetations can embolize into the cerebral circulation. Endocarditis caused by staphylococci, fungi, or yeast often is extensive enough to occlude large intracranial arteries. Infective endocarditis is associated with other forms of cerebrovascular disease, including intracerebral hemorrhage, subarachnoid hemorrhage, and mycotic aneurysm (Chapter 441). Strokes can occur during the acute phases of the disease, and the combination of fever, a new murmur, and petechiae should prompt collection of blood cultures and consideration of empirical treatment with antibiotics. Anticoagulation may increase the risk of intracerebral hemorrhage in patients with bacterial endocarditis.

Nonbacterial endocarditis, which usually is associated with various types of cancer (Chapter 188), also can cause vegetations that produce cerebral embolization and cause focal strokes or diffuse encephalopathy, sometimes in the form of disseminated intravascular coagulopathy. Systemic lupus erythematosus is associated with atypical verrucous (Libman-Sacks) endocarditis in which friable vegetations form on the leaflets of any of the heart valves and rarely can produce cerebral embolization (Chapter 280).

In patients with prosthetic heart valves, the incidence of strokes is 1 to 5% per year despite oral anticoagulation (Chapter 72). Mechanical valves have a higher risk than biologic valves. Many studies have suggested that anticoagulants reduce but do not completely eliminate cerebral embolization in these patients.

ARRHYTHMIAS. Atrial fibrillation, independent of the presence or absence of valvular disease, is a proven cause of embolic stroke, increasing the relative risk compared with age-matched controls to about 5% per year (Chapter 59). About 15% of all ischemic strokes are associated with nonvalvular atrial fibrillation. Most patients with atrial fibrillation never have a stroke, however. The strokes are often large and disabling, but minor strokes, silent strokes, and TIAs can occur. Most ischemic strokes in patients with atrial fibrillation are due to embolism from left atrial mural thrombi. The risk of atrial fibrillation–associated strokes is increased in patients who have chronic hypertension. The risk of embolic stroke is highest shortly after development of atrial fibrillation, but embolism also can accompany cardioversion to normal sinus rhythm regardless of whether the conversion is spontaneous, medication-induced, or electrical.

PARADOXICAL EMBOLI. Embolic occlusion of intracranial vessels can be of venous origin. The embolic material gains access to the arterial circulation through various cardiac defects, such as a patent foramen ovale, an atrial septal defect (Chapter 65), or an arteriovenous malformation. When venous emboli enter the heart, a right-to-left shunt allows the emboli to enter the arterial circulation. A patent foramen ovale has been detected in 40% of patients with acute ischemic stroke of uncertain origin, and it often is assumed that paradoxical embolization is the cause of the stroke. Patients with an atrial septal aneurysm and a patent foramen ovale are at the highest risk.

Clinical Manifestations

Clinical manifestations are summarized in Table 440–1.

INTERNAL CAROTID ARTERY. The common carotid artery bifurcation, at the origin of the internal carotid artery (ICA), is the most frequent site for atherosclerotic lesions of the cerebral vasculature. Occlusion of the ICA is often clinically silent if the circle of Willis is complete. It is often impossible to distinguish ICA occlusion from similar damage to the middle cerebral artery (MCA) on clinical examination (see later). Because the ophthalmic artery originates from the ICA, however, TIAs of the ICA may present as transient monocular blindness (also called *amaurosis fugax*). Severe stenosis of the ICA, particularly if it is bilateral, can cause hypoperfusion of the cerebral hemispheres and symptoms in border zones between the MCA and other major vascular territories (watershed areas), especially if superimposed on generalized hypoperfusion secondary to severe hypotension.

ANTERIOR CEREBRAL ARTERY. Isolated occlusion of the anterior cerebral artery (ACA), which is relatively rare compared with strokes in other major branches of the circle of Willis, accounts for about 2% of all cerebral infarcts. The principal symptoms associated with occlusion of an ACA distal to the anterior communicating artery are upper motor neuron weakness and cortical sensory signs deficits (neglect) in the contralateral leg. Other manifestations of ACA occlusion may include urinary incontinence, generalized depression of psychomotor activity (abulia), and transcortical motor aphasia, manifested as loss of verbal fluency with preserved ability to repeat. Bilateral occlusion may occur because the origins of the two ACAs are separated by only a short stretch of anterior communicating artery, and there are frequent anomalies in which both ACAs originate from a common source. Bilateral damage usually causes a patient to be mute, with severe mood disturbances and long-lasting incontinence from bilateral damage to the frontal lobes.

MIDDLE CEREBRAL ARTERY. Strokes in the distribution of the MCA are the most common type of focal stroke, causing approximately two thirds of all infarcts. Occlusion of the stem of the MCA often causes massive, devastating infarction of much of the hemisphere. Edema during the first 3 to 4 days may lead to severely increased intracranial pressure and herniation. The classic picture of occlu-

sion of the MCA stem is contralateral weakness and sensory loss in the face and arm (with relative sparing of the leg) and homonymous hemianopia on the side of the weakness; initially, there may be depressed consciousness and deviation of gaze toward the side of the lesion. There is little chance of substantial recovery. In right-handed people, occlusion of the left MCA produces global aphasia, in which the patient can neither understand speech of others nor produce meaningful speech. In the nondominant hemisphere, unilateral neglect, anosognosia (unawareness of the deficit), and spatial disorientation occur.

Occlusion of the branches of the MCA produces partial syndromes. An embolus to the MCA often lodges in one of its two main divisions. Occlusion of the superior division can cause dense sensorimotor deficits in the contralateral face and arm without initial impairment of alertness. Later on, some neurologic function may recover, and aphasia may decrease. Strokes of the inferior division in the dominant hemisphere characteristically produce receptive aphasia of Wernicke's type (severe loss of speech comprehension with preserved spoken and written language). Damage to either hemisphere can cause contralateral loss of integrated sensation, such as perception of shapes (stereognosis). Occlusion of more distal branches causes less clinical damage.

POSTERIOR CEREBRAL ARTERY. In about three quarters of people, both posterior cerebral arteries (PCAs) arise from the basilar artery; in most others, one PCA arises from the basilar artery, and the other arises from the ICA. In a few individuals, both PCAs arise from the ICAs. As a consequence, the syndromes associated with occlusion of the PCA are highly variable. Strokes of the perforating branches most frequently cause complete contralateral hemianesthesia with loss of all sensation and complete hemianopia on that side. Macular (central) vision may be spared because of collateral blood supply from the MCA. Difficulty reading (dyslexia) and performing calculations (dyscalculia) may occur. Recovery is often good, but the initial numbness may be replaced by paresthesias or excruciating pain; this Dejerine-Roussy syndrome is caused by damage to the thalamus. Involvement of the subthalamic nucleus may produce hemiballismus, with wild flinging movements of the limbs on one

Table 440–1 • CLINICAL MANIFESTATIONS OF ISCHEMIC STROKE

OCCLUDED BLOOD VESSEL	CLINICAL MANIFESTATIONS
ICA	Ipsilateral blindness (variable)
	MCA syndrome (see below)
MCA	Contralateral hemiparesis, sensory loss (arm, face worst)
	Expressive aphasia (dominant) or anosognosia and spatial disorientation (nondominant)
	Contralateral inferior quadrantanopsia
ACA	Contralateral hemiparesis, sensory loss (worst in leg)
PCA	Contralateral homonymous hemianopsia or superior quadrantanopsia
	Memory impairment
Basilar apex	Bilateral blindness
	Amnesia
Basilar artery	Contralateral hemiparesis, sensory loss
	Ipsilateral bulbar or cerebellar signs
Vertebral artery or PICA	Ipsilateral loss of facial sensation, ataxia, contralateral hemiparesis, sensory loss
Superior cerebellar artery	Gait ataxia, nausea, dizziness, headache progressing to ipsilateral hemiataxia, dysarthria, gaze paresis, contralateral hemiparesis, somnolence

ACA = anterior cerebral artery; ICA = internal carotid artery; MCA = middle cerebral artery; PCA = posterior cerebral artery; PICA = posterior inferior cerebellar artery.

Neurology

side of the body. Distal branch occlusions of the PCA cause partial syndromes; occlusion of the terminal branch can produce a variety of incomplete visual field deficits, although the loss is characteristically congruous (superimposable) in both visual fields.

VERTEBRAL AND BASILAR ARTERIES. Characteristic of occlusion of the blood supply to the brain stem are "crossed syndromes" (i.e., a contralateral loss of strength and selected contralateral and ipsilateral sensory symptoms below the level of the lesion, plus ipsilateral motor and sensory deficits localizing to the level of the lesion). Weber's syndrome is a mesencephalic hematoma that produces an ipsilateral third cranial nerve palsy, resulting from damage to the oculomotor nucleus, plus contralateral weakness.

The vertebral arteries are the principal blood supply for the medulla. The posterior inferior cerebellar artery is usually a branch of the vertebral artery. The consequences of occlusion of a posterior inferior cerebellar artery are variable, but lateral medullary infarction (Wallenberg's syndrome) is classically produced. In about 80% of cases, an occlusion of the vertebral artery causes lateral medullary syndrome, which consists of severe vertigo, nausea, vomiting, nystagmus, ipsilateral ataxia (of the cerebellar type), and ipsilateral Horner's syndrome (ptosis, myosis, and decreased sweating). The syndrome also includes an ipsilateral loss of facial pain and temperature sensation and a contralateral loss of these sensory modalities in the trunk and limb. The syndrome's findings are predominantly sensory, and motor abnormalities may be subtle. Partial syndromes are the rule; a complete lateral medullary syndrome is rare, so it is often misdiagnosed.

The basilar artery supplies most of the brain stem, and its occlusion produces a variety of syndromes. Obstruction of the trunk is often fatal because the main motor and sensory pathways between the cerebral hemispheres and the remainder of the body are compact and travel through the brain stem, where they are supplied by the basilar artery. The findings in occlusion of the basilar artery consist of a combination of bilateral sensory and motor long-tract signs, cerebellar dysfunction, and cranial nerve abnormalities: paralysis or weakness of all extremities and the bulbar muscles, impaired vision with various visual field defects, bilateral cerebellar ataxia, and a variety of sensory disturbances ranging from normal to total anesthesia. Coma may occur, or patients may develop the locked-in syndrome, in which consciousness is preserved, but the victims are unable to move anything voluntarily except for their eyes or eyelids. It is possible to communicate with these patients and demonstrate normal mental status by codes involving eye movements.

Occlusion of the various branches of the basilar artery produces a large variety of syndromes. Because the pathways are so closely spaced in the brain stem, even small volumes of infarction can cause substantial motor and sensory deficits. The characteristic findings are crossed syndromes with motor and sensory dissociation, unless the findings are bilateral. Distinguishing mild vertebrobasilar ischemia from the common causes of dizziness is occasionally difficult (Chapter 470), but ischemia is rarely a cause of isolated vertigo in the absence of other brain stem signs or symptoms.

Diagnosis

The history gives initial clues as to the site and severity of a stroke, and the physical examination helps to refine a hypothesis as to the lesion location. Based on this information, definitive laboratory testing can proceed efficiently.

HISTORY

As the name implies, stroke ordinarily starts at a clearly identifiable time. The most important aspect of the history, which must be elicited from a patient or accompanying observers if a stroke is suspected, is the time of onset of symptoms. If abnormalities began within the preceding 3 hours, the patient should be managed as an acute emergency, and thrombolytic therapy may be indicated. Patients may be confused, anxious, or aphasic, and they may not remember the duration of symptoms. It may be necessary to try to associate the onset of symptoms with events that the patient or accompanying persons can identify accurately. Did the patient wake up with symptoms (in which case the symptoms must be assumed, in terms of considering acute treatment, to have started at the time the patient was last known to be in a premorbid state—usually at the time of going to sleep)? Was the patient watching television, and if so, what program was it (consultation with the program guide in the newspaper can be used to assign a time of onset)? Was an ambulance called, and if so, what time was the patient first examined by the paramedics? This information is usually available in the ambulance records.

TIAs may not be distinguishable from a stroke during the early phases, but TIAs usually resolve within the first hour or two. Rapid progression of deficits or the presence of headache occurs more often in patients with intracerebral hemorrhage (Chapter 441). Although intracerebral hemorrhage is responsible for only about 15% of strokes, hemorrhages generally produce more severe symptoms that cannot be denied. By comparison, patients with minor strokes or predominantly sensory symptoms are often in a state of denial and do not present for medical attention until long after vessel occlusion. Because ischemic strokes are nearly always painless, they do not awaken patients from sleep and often are discovered at the time of normal awakening in the morning. There is some diurnal variation in the onset of stroke, with a peak in the late morning.

PHYSICAL EXAMINATION

The neurologic examination (Chapter 423) is a cost-effective method for initiating a diagnostic evaluation, and it often helps to localize the site of the lesion. The cardiovascular examination (Chapter 46) should focus on measurement of arterial blood pressure, including measurement in both arms to evaluate the possibility of aortic dissection (Chapter 75) or vascular abnormalities that result in reduced blood flow to the brain when the arms are exercised (subclavian steal). The greatest risk factor for stroke is preexisting hypertension. Many patients develop transient hypertension in the immediate aftermath of a stroke, however, so it is important to determine whether a patient has had sustained hypertension (Chapter 63). Extremely elevated blood pressure at the time of presentation can lead to heart failure that may have to be managed urgently. If hypertension is a transient manifestation of acute stroke, aggressive reduction may cause hypotension and enlarge the infarct. The pulse may reveal arrhythmias, such as atrial fibrillation, that can cause cerebral embolism (Chapter 59). Cardiac murmurs may suggest valvular lesions (Chapter 72) that can cause cerebral embolism. Bruits of the carotid arteries can be produced by atherosclerotic disease of the arteries that is associated with embolic and thrombotic strokes. Evidence of peripheral vascular disease (Chapter 76) may be a reflection of generalized atherosclerosis.

Ophthalmoscopic visualization of retinal cholesterol or platelet fibrin emboli suggests more proximal atherosclerotic disease. Examination of the retinal vessels may also reveal signs of chronic hypertension or diabetes (arteriovenous crossing defects or retinal hemorrhages; Chapter 465).

The neurologic examination usually suggests the location and size of the stroke. If the patient's mental status is depressed, bilateral cerebral lesions or a brain stem lesion is suggested. Multiple smaller strokes may lead to dementia. Speech is commonly affected, with various aphasic patterns suggesting the site of the lesion. The testing of strength, sensation, and deep tendon reflexes provides information about the patterns of the deficits and suggests the site of the vascular lesion. Plantar stimulation (Babinski's sign), which is a classic finding in damage to long tracts, indicates upper motor neuron damage caused by strokes. However, during the early phases of a large stroke, reflexes may be depressed rather than hyperactive.

LABORATORY EXAMINATION

HEMATOLOGIC TESTS. A complete hemogram including a platelet count is essential to evaluate for polycythemia (Chapter 176), thrombocytosis, bacterial endocarditis (Chapter 310), and severe anemia. An erythrocyte sedimentation rate is also a useful screening test because it may be elevated in patients with hypercoagulable states (Chapter 180), and it is markedly elevated in patients with polymyalgia rheumatica and associated giant cell arteritis (Chapter 285). A blood glucose level must be checked because hyperglycemia and hypoglycemia can produce focal and global neurologic deficits, sometimes mimicking stroke (Chapters 242 and 243). Diabetes increases the risk of a stroke, and stroke may be the presenting symptom of diabetes. A prothrombin time and partial thromboplastin time should be measured in patients who may have been anticoagulated before the onset of stroke to determine whether they have been taking their medications or are excessively anticoagulated.

Although moderate hyperlipidemia is not a proven risk factor, extremely high lipid levels are strongly associated with strokes. Antiphospholipid antibodies are elevated in some patients with immune-related diseases. Measurement of protein C, protein S, antithrombin III, blood viscosity, and platelet function (Chapter 180) and tests for homocysteinuria, collagen vascular diseases (Chapter 273), amyloidosis (Chapter 290), and syphilis (Chapter 349) should be performed in selected cases.

CARDIOVASCULAR TESTING. Patients with an acute myocardial infarction or a new or chronic atrial arrhythmia may present with an embolic stroke. A standard electrocardiogram and rhythm strip should be obtained at presentation to determine whether acute myocardial ischemia or arrhythmias are present. Echocardiography is indicated urgently only in patients with a history of cardiac disease and an abnormal electrocardiogram; if no cause for stroke is defined, however, particularly if a patient is relatively young, echocardiography generally is indicated.

NONINVASIVE BRAIN IMAGING. Brain imaging (Chapter 424), which is essential to verify causes of focal neurologic dysfunction, usually can distinguish ischemic stroke from other diseases. The most important disorders to differentiate from acute ischemic stroke are intracerebral hemorrhage (Chapter 441), subarachnoid hemorrhage (Chapter 441), and brain tumors (Chapter 457).

CT is the standard initial imaging study (Fig. 440–1). Noncontrast imaging usually detects intracerebral hemorrhage. Signals indicating tissue hypodensity, particularly in the region of the brain appropriate to the neurologic deficits, and the loss of the distinction between gray and white matter often are observed 3 to 24 hours after the onset of stroke. These findings cannot predict the size of the infarction, however, and noncontrast CT may be normal for 3 to 24 hours after

an ischemic stroke. The hypodensity typically becomes progressively more apparent over the first 3 to 24 hours and is usually readily detectable by 24 hours in large infarcts. Small ischemic strokes in the brain stem can produce major neurologic dysfunction and may not be detected by CT. Contrast enhancement of CT scans seldom improves detection of acute stroke, but it may distinguish ischemic lesions from some types of neoplasms.

CT is currently the only imaging method useful for deciding whether to administer thrombolytic therapy. The detection of hemorrhage in areas of infarction is important because it precludes thrombolytic therapy. Small hemorrhages may not be detected by CT scanning during the first few hours but may not have clinical importance. Hemorrhages become more evident with time, appearing on repeat scans hours to weeks after infarction. Whether this apparent increase in the detection of hemorrhage is due to a progressive increase in the size of the initial hemorrhage or to alterations in the extravasated blood is not known.

MRI is more sensitive than CT for detecting early ischemia (Fig. 440–2). MRI sequences can identify tissue or blood flow abnormalities within minutes after the onset of ischemia (Fig. 440–3). These early indicators of tissue injury are qualitative and have not yet been shown to predict the ultimate volume of the lesion or whether tissue damage is irreversible. MRI cannot be used in patients who have ferromagnetic materials within their bodies, is often impossible to use in critically ill patients, and renders the patient inaccessible for several minutes. No MRI sequences successfully distinguish ischemia from hemorrhage, especially during the early phases of injury when decisions as to whether thrombolysis should be administered are needed. CT remains the imaging procedure of choice for acute patient management.

LUMBAR PUNCTURE. Lumbar puncture no longer is performed routinely in the evaluation of the patient with stroke because CT detects intracerebral hemorrhage more reliably (Chapter 424). CT also usually can identify blood in the subarachnoid space, although lumbar puncture is more sensitive for this purpose and can give some indication as to when the bleed occurred (Chapter 441). After subarachnoid hemorrhage, erythrocytes hemolyze, and cerebrospinal fluid becomes

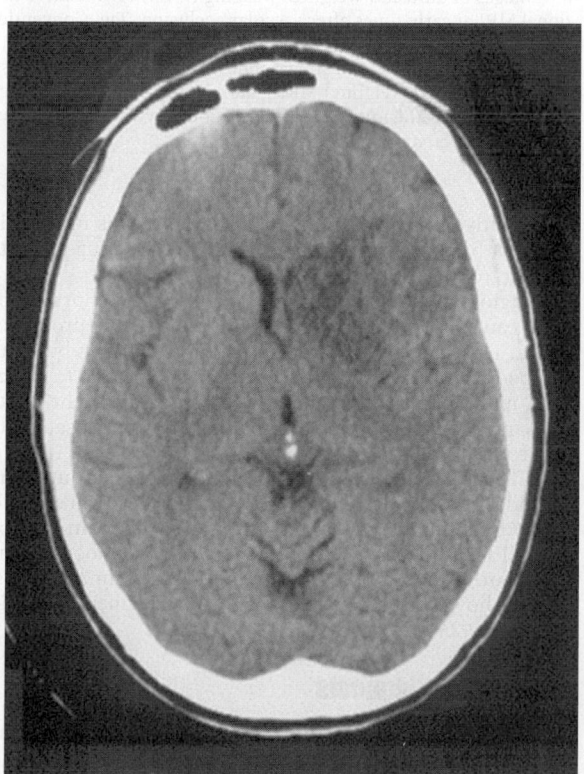
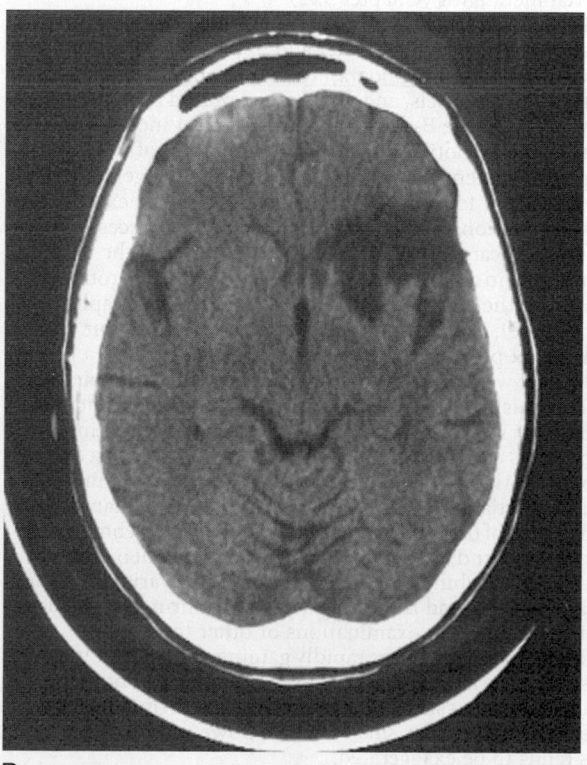

A B

FIGURE 440–1 • *A*, Computed tomography (CT) scan of a patient with a left hemisphere infarction 6 to 24 hours after symptom onset shows hypodensity in the basal ganglia region and compression of the frontal horn of the lateral ventricle. *B*, CT scan shows the chronic infarction 1 year later; atrophy and loss of tissue volume are visible. (Courtesy Gregory W. Albers, Stanford University, Stanford, CA.)

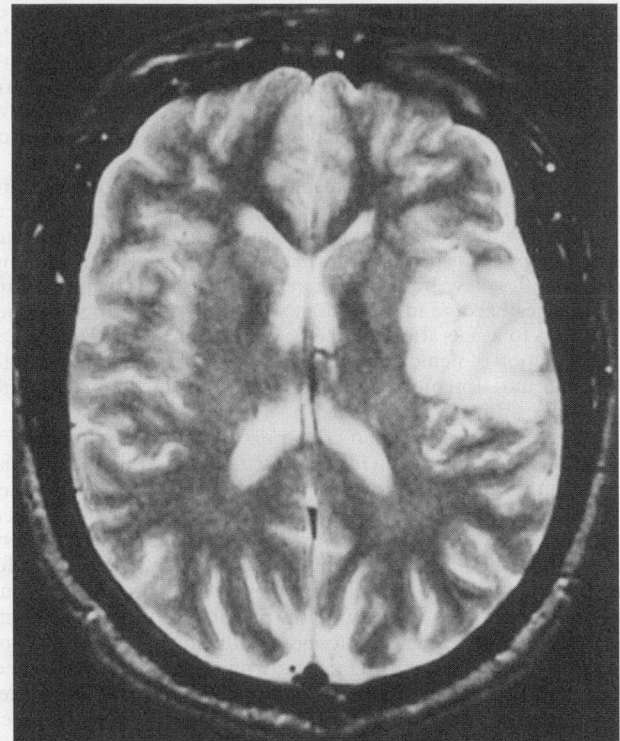

FIGURE 440–2 • Magnetic resonance imaging shows early ischemic changes obtained 6 hours after the onset of right-sided weakness in a patient who occluded the left internal carotid artery. (Courtesy Gregory W. Albers, Stanford University, Stanford, CA.)

xanthochromic within 4 to 6 hours. Lumbar puncture is required to determine if a patient has neurosyphilis (Chapter 349), although screening blood testing should be conducted first. Lumbar puncture also occasionally is indicated if there is concern that a patient may have bacterial meningitis (Chapter 312).

NONINVASIVE CEREBROVASCULAR EXAMINATION. Ultrasonography provides an estimate of luminal diameter and the direction and speed of blood flow. B-mode ultrasonography, which produces real-time images of the carotid vessels, and range-gated pulsed Doppler, which is guided visually by the B-mode image, can detect increased blood velocity through a stenotic lumen. The combination of the location of the Doppler frequency signal and the B-mode image provides a noninvasive method for analyzing the condition of the extracranial circulation. Limitations of the technique include (1) access to only the portion of the carotid circulation that lies between the clavicles and the mandible (in approximately 10% of patients, the carotid bifurcation lies above the angle of the jaw, making ultrasonography difficult or impossible); (2) absorption of sound waves by calcium within a mural plaque, a process that may "shadow" and obscure a plaque on a distal vessel wall; and (3) echolucency of acute thrombi, which can be indistinguishable from flowing blood. The direction and velocity of blood flow in the intracranial blood vessels originating from the circle of Willis can be examined with low-frequency pulsed transcranial Doppler. Although these methods are useful screening techniques with essentially no risk to the patient, the gold standard for defining the status of the cerebral vasculature remains cerebral angiography. Also, ultrasound technique is critically dependent on the training and skill of the technician; there is considerable variation among different laboratories, and the clinician must confirm new or suspicious findings with repeat examinations or other tests.

CT and MRI angiography are rapidly gaining acceptance. It is possible to visualize the larger cerebral vessels and detect abnormalities, such as stenosis, aneurysms, or arteriovenous malformations. These methods lack sensitivity for small lesions, however, and the degree of stenosis tends to be exaggerated.

CEREBRAL ANGIOGRAPHY. Cerebral angiography is reserved for patients who are suspected to have a surgically correctable lesion. Arterial vessels are displayed initially, and delayed images can outline the venous system. Patients commonly are anticoagulated during the procedure. The images give high-quality resolution of the vessels but do not provide

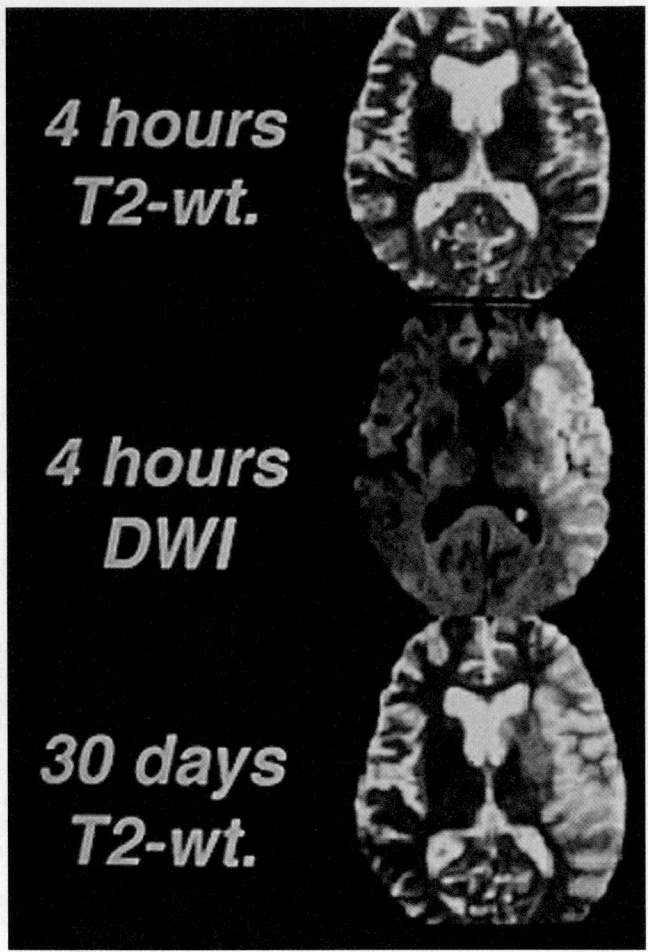

FIGURE 440–3 • Magnetic resonance imaging (MRI) scans showing possible advantages of diffusion-weighted imaging (DWI) MRI relative to conventional MRI at early times after vascular occlusion. *Top*, Conventional T2-weighted MRI 4 hours after symptom onset that appears normal. *Middle*, At the same time, a DWI scan shows abnormalities in the left hemisphere. *Bottom*, Repeat T2-weighted MRI 1 month later showed an infarction in the same location as the initial DWI scan. (Courtesy Gregory W. Albers, Stanford University, Stanford, CA.)

quantitative information about blood flow. This method is the only one that has been proved to be useful for selecting patients who can benefit from carotid endarterectomy.

Angiography, particularly in patients with abnormal vasculature, itself can cause stroke and result in permanent neurologic deficits or death. The rate of injury varies in different surveys but is about 0.5% in good facilities. Angiography requires exposure to ionizing radiation, may be associated with adverse reactions to the contrast material, and provides a fluid load that may decompensate patients with severe cardiac disease.

OTHER TECHNIQUES. Single-photon emission computed tomography provides only qualitative blood flow rates. Positron emission tomography quantitatively measures blood flow or brain metabolism. CT and MRI methods for measurement of cerebral blood flow and metabolism are in development. None of these techniques has yet been shown, however, to be useful for the management of stroke patients (Chapter 424).

Differential Diagnosis

The characteristic feature of ischemic stroke is the abrupt, painless onset of a neurologic deficit. Blood supply is lost in the distribution of a terminal vessel, and loss of function begins within seconds. The brain does not have pain receptors in its parenchyma, so the symptoms are painless unless the dura mater, which does have pain fibers, is stretched or irritated. One type of stroke that can evolve slowly is subdural hematoma (Chapter 431), which may be distinguishable from ischemic stroke because a hematoma produces deficits more slowly. Focal symptoms and signs of tumors (Chapter 457) of various types typically evolve over weeks or longer except in uncommon cases in which a tumor erodes a vessel to cause bleeding or crushes it to cause infarction. TIAs initially cannot be distinguished from strokes, but they generally resolve within the first 1 or 2 hours.

Other neurologic disorders can present with the abrupt onset of neurologic abnormalities. Migraine (Chapter 428) with or without aura may simulate stroke or TIA because of its associated hemiparesis or other focal deficits. Migraine is primarily an exquisitely painful, throbbing, unilateral headache that sometimes has an aura (symptoms preceding the headache) of scintillating scotomata (flashing lights). Complicated migraine (migraine accompanied by focal deficits) rarely can evolve into a true ischemic stroke, likely because of the decreased blood flow that often accompanies migraine.

Seizures (Chapter 434) can be confused with TIAs. Many seizures produce tonic (sustained) or clonic (rapid movements) motor activity or positive sensory phenomena. Strokes and TIAs produce weakness and sensory loss without involuntary motor actions. Seizures sometimes can produce these negative symptoms, particularly in the postictal state after (unobserved) seizures. The patient generally returns to the premorbid state after a seizure, however. Serial observations usually permit the differentiation of stroke from seizure, but early differentiation may be difficult and require laboratory testing, particularly an electroencephalogram. In a few patients with stroke, especially with emboli, a seizure occurs at the onset of the stroke.

Hyperglycemia and hypoglycemia can cause focal neurologic deficits (Chapters 242 and 243). Most patients have a history of diabetes, and the glucose abnormality is substantial at the time of focal neurologic deficits.

Hemorrhagic stroke (Chapter 441) usually cannot be distinguished definitively from ischemic stroke on the basis of the history or clinical examination. Primary hemorrhages are often severe at onset and may present with headache and rapidly evolving deficits. Ischemic strokes are normally painless and present as a fixed deficit or with a stuttering onset followed by rapid waxing and waning fluctuations. Headaches can occur in many ischemic strokes, however, and the only way to distinguish infarct from hemorrhage definitively is by a CT scan.

Brief global cerebral anoxia causes syncope without any permanent sequelae. Prolonged diffuse ischemia, by contrast, can have devastating consequences. The most common causes are cardiac asystole or other forms of overwhelming cardiopulmonary failure. Aortic dissection (Chapter 75), global hypoxia, or carbon monoxide poisoning (Chapter 90) can cause a similar picture. Clinically, these disorders result in unconsciousness. If ischemia persists for more than 4 to 5 minutes, patients often remain in a coma, sometimes evolving into the vegetative state, in which brain stem functions are preserved, but the patient has no higher cortical function (Chapters 436 and 437). If patients do not regain consciousness within 2 or 3 days, the

Table 440–2 • TISSUE PLASMINOGEN ACTIVATOR THERAPY FOR ACUTE ISCHEMIC STROKE

Clinical presentation—focal neurologic deficits
Patient selection
  Therapy must be started within 3 hr of acute ischemic stroke symptom onset
  A baseline CT scan must be obtained before therapy initiation
Contraindications
  Evidence of intracranial hemorrhage on pretreatment evaluation
  Suspicion of subarachnoid hemorrhage
  Recent intracranial surgery, serious head trauma, or previous stroke
  History of intracranial hemorrhage
  Uncontrolled hypertension at time of treatment—>185 mm Hg systolic or >110 diastolic—that cannot be reduced with acute antihypertensive therapy
  Seizure at stroke onset
  Active internal bleeding
  Intracranial neoplasm, AVM, or aneurysm
  Known bleeding diathesis, including but not limited to:
    Oral anticoagulation with prothrombin time >15 sec
    Heparin administration within preceding 48 hr and elevated activated partial thromboplastin time at presentation
    Platelet count <100,000/mm^3
Warnings
  Patients with severe neurologic deficit (NIH Stroke Scale >22) at presentation have increased risk of ICH
  Patients with major early infarct signs on CT (edema or mass effect) probably are >3 hr since vessel occlusion
Dosing information for acute ischemic stroke
  0.9 mg/kg to a maximum dose of ≤90 mg
  10% of total dose administered as an IV bolus over 1 min
  90% remainder infused continuously over 60 min
Follow-up
  Monitor vital signs and neurologic status
  Maintain blood pressure ≤185/≤110 mm Hg
  No anticoagulant or antiplatelet therapy for 24 hr

Modified from package insert for Activase, Genentech, Inc, South San Francisco, CA. AVM = arteriovenous malformation; CT = computed tomography; ICH = intracranial hemorrhage; NIH = National Institutes of Health.

prognosis for return of independent function is poor. Other than prompt and aggressive efforts to restore cardiovascular circulation, no treatments have been found to help patients who are comatose after cardiac arrest.

In young patients, hypoxia caused by near-drowning in cold water may result in resistance to prolonged hypoxic ischemic damage. Therapeutic hypothermia has not yet been proven useful in adults with stroke.

Rx Treatment of Acute Stroke

Thrombolytic therapy is the only safe and effective method for acute management of ischemic stroke of typical cause (i.e., atherosclerotic and embolic stroke). Multiple randomized, placebo-controlled trials have been conducted evaluating intravenous tissue plasminogen activator (tPA), streptokinase, and intra-arterial recombinant prourokinase (rpro-UK). Meta-analyses provide support for the efficacy and safety of this approach if patients are treated within 3 hours after the onset of symptoms.❚Obstacles to thrombolytic treatment include the need to redesign and implement acute stroke-care systems, delay of patients in reaching medical facilities, and insufficient expertise in the use of thrombolysis by many physicians.

The recommended therapy with intravenous tPA requires adherence to relatively stringent eligibility criteria (Table 440–2 and Fig. 440–4). Therapy must be started within 3 hours after the onset of stroke. Before initiating therapy, a noncontrast CT scan should be obtained to exclude patients with intracranial hemorrhage. Blood pressure limits are a maximum of 185 mm Hg systolic or 110 mm Hg diastolic. If blood pressure exceeds these limits, it should be lowered with an antihypertensive drug, such as labetalol, before initiating tPA. Also, patients who have had major surgery or serious trauma within the preceding 2 weeks or evidence of gastrointestinal

bleeding should not be treated. The recommended dose of intravenous tPA is 0.9 mg/kg, to a maximum of 90 mg, administered as a 10% initial bolus with the remainder given over 60 minutes.

Treatment should begin as soon as possible, and even patients with mild strokes or rapidly resolving deficits probably merit treatment. Patients with severe strokes, as evidenced by major clinical deficits or early signs of a large infarct by CT scan, do not fare well regardless of whether they are treated or not. Treatment 3 to 6 hours after ischemic stroke onset is not currently recommended, although one study of intra-arterial prourokinase given at 3 to 6 hours after onset of an ischemic stroke showed benefit from therapy. Streptokinase is not of benefit. Intra-arterial tPA has been used for patients who are not candidates for intravenous tPA, but there are no controlled studies of this form of treatment.

Anticoagulation with various forms of heparin or warfarin, which has been a common clinical practice for many years, is not justified. Several large studies, including a trial that enrolled more than 19,000 patients, failed to show any benefit of acute anticoagulation in patients with ischemic stroke. Patients with stroke-in-evolution, in which deficits increase over the first day after the onset of the stroke, are commonly anticoagulated, but there is no strong

Continued

Neurology

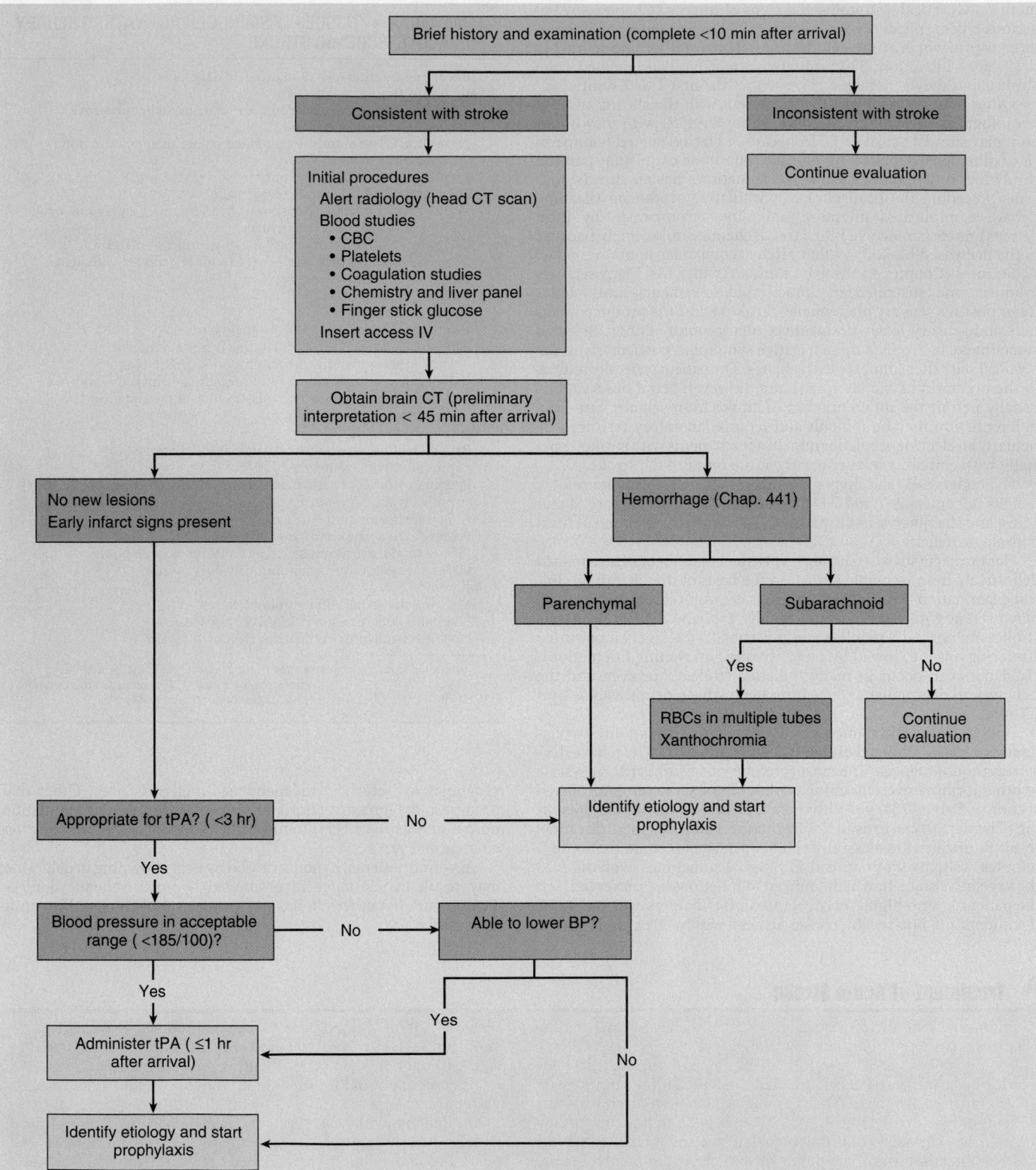

FIGURE 440–4 • Algorithm for the emergency evaluation of a patient with suspected stroke. BP = blood pressure; CBC = complete blood count; CT = computed tomography; RBCs = red blood cells; tPA = tissue plasminogen activator.

evidence that this therapy is effective. Vital signs and neurologic status should be monitored. Systolic blood pressure should be maintained between 185 and 110 mm Hg, preferably using labetalol.

If a patient has had an acute myocardial infarction, the preferred therapy is primary angioplasty (Chapter 69). It is uncertain what dose of tPA should be administered if a patient simultaneously has a stroke and myocardial infarction. If a patient is a candidate for coronary artery bypass graft surgery and is found to have surgically

correctable carotid stenosis, the more urgent procedure generally should be performed first.

There is an increased risk of pulmonary embolism and deep vein thrombosis in patients with ischemic stroke, particularly in patients with neurologic deficits that produce immobility. In these patients, prophylactic low-dose subcutaneous heparin or low-molecular-weight heparins are recommended unless there are other contraindications to anticoagulation.

Unusual Causes of Stroke

ATRIAL MYXOMA. Atrial myxomas (Chapter 79) are the most common type of primary cardiac tumor, occurring in about 0.05% of autopsies of young adults with ischemic strokes or TIAs. Nonspecific constitutional symptoms are frequent, and less than half of myxomas produce emboli. When these tumors do produce emboli, the danger period usually lasts days to weeks. Metastasis rarely can cause cerebral aneurysms. Other primary and metastatic cardiac tumors can embolize neoplastic tissue or thrombus.

VASCULITIS. Vasculitis (Chapters 280, 284, and 285) can produce focal or multifocal cerebral ischemia by means of inflammation and necrosis of extracranial or intracranial blood vessels. Segmental inflammation of cerebral blood vessels is associated with cerebral ischemia acutely at the site of involvement.

Vasculitis of the central nervous system (CNS) often presents as cognitive disturbances, headache, and seizures (encephalopathy). Because vascular damage is commonly diffuse, these nonfocal neurologic abnormalities occur more frequently with vasculitis than in focal ischemic disorders. Diagnosis is often difficult because the signs and symptoms are often nonspecific. Angiographic appearance of a "beadlike" segmental narrowing of cerebral blood vessels, when present, is virtually diagnostic, but cerebral angiograms are often normal in histologically proven cases. The definitive diagnosis requires demonstration of characteristic inflammatory histopathology in leptomeningeal or cortical biopsy specimens. Because of the segmental and highly focal nature of the inflammatory process, the histopathology may go undetected at biopsy despite a positive angiogram.

Primary CNS vasculitis, Behçet's disease (Chapter 291), Takayasu's arteritis (Chapters 75 and 284), and temporal arteritis (Chapter 285) are notable for their infrequent involvement of the peripheral nervous system. By contrast, hypersensitivity and systemic necrotizing vasculitides frequently produce polyneuropathies. Primary CNS arteritis (Chapter 284), giant cell arteritis (Chapter 285), and vasculitis associated with certain CNS infections may present initially or solely with neurologic abnormalities.

Primary arteritis of the CNS causes headache and other encephalopathy-like symptoms in young or middle-aged individuals. The course is usually insidiously progressive but may wax and wane for periods of several months. A few of these patients present with a strokelike episode.

Giant cell arteritis (Chapter 285) can affect any medium or large artery in the body. When it is present in the cerebral vasculature, it is called *temporal arteritis* and is characterized by panarteritis including intimal proliferation, destruction of the internal elastic lamina, and thickening of the media. Luminal obstruction is caused by edema, thickening of the intima, and thrombosis. A prominent inflammatory infiltrate consisting of mononuclear cells, giant cells, and eosinophils with granuloma formation is present with active disease. Giant cell arteritis is the most common angiitis causing ischemic stroke. Temporal arteritis predominantly affects patients older than age 55. Symptoms include fever, malaise, weight loss, and headache. In many patients, constitutional symptoms consistent with polymyalgia rheumatica may coexist, including jaw, neck, and facial pain and morning stiffness. Pain over the temporal arteries and an erythrocyte sedimentation rate greater than 50 mm/hr are frequently, but not always, present. Biopsy of the superficial temporal artery provides the definitive diagnosis; because of the segmental nature of the vasculitis, however, serial sections must be examined, or characteristic histology may be missed. The diagnosis is important to establish because early initiation of corticosteroid therapy may decrease the risk of acute ischemic blindness or stroke. This treatment can be started shortly before obtaining the biopsy.

Takayasu's arteritis, also called *pulseless disease* (Chapters 75 and 284), is a chronic, idiopathic inflammatory disorder, primarily of young women. It mainly affects the aortic arch, the large brachiocephalic arteries, and the abdominal aorta. Mononuclear infiltrates and fibrous proliferation produce progressive narrowing of the lumen of these vessels, causing reduced flow into the upper extremities and cerebral ischemia. Although initially diagnosed in Japanese families, it has been recognized in Western countries.

Fibromuscular dysplasia is a segmental vasculopathy of unknown etiology (Chapters 75 and 124). Its frequency in large angiographic series is less than 1%. Bilateral extracranial involvement of the ICA is common, but abnormalities of the intracranial carotid or vertebrobasilar artery are rare. Dysplasia of the arterial wall may involve the intima, media, or adventitia. This disorder, which also may affect the renal arteries and is associated with hypertension, can lead to aneurysm formation and cervicocephalic arterial dissection. Diagnosis is made by cerebral angiography. Little information about treatment is available; angioplasty and stenting to open the narrowed lumen are unproven, experimental procedures.

Other types of vasculitis are unusual causes of stroke. These diseases include Wegener's granulomatosis (Chapter 284); sarcoidosis (Chapter 91); bacterial, fungal, and viral infections; meningovascular syphilis (Chapter 349); and lymphomatoid angioendotheliomatosis.

HEMOGLOBINOPATHIES. In sickle cell anemia (Chapter 171), irreversible sickling occurs, leading to increased blood viscosity, microvascular sludging, and brain infarction. Sickle cell disease also causes hyperplasia of fibrous tissue and muscle cells of the vascular intima, leading to stenosis and occlusion of some medium to large cerebral arteries.

Estimates of the incidence of stroke vary but generally are reported to be 8 to 17% of patients with hemoglobin SS and about 2% of individuals with hemoglobin SA. The mean age of first stroke is about 8 years of age in people with hemoglobin SS. Ischemic stroke occurs more frequently in children. In adults, hemorrhagic strokes are more common.

HYPERVISCOSITY SYNDROME. Cerebral blood flow decreases with increasing blood viscosity. Blood viscosity increases with increasing levels of red and white blood cells, platelets, and plasma proteins. A hyperviscosity syndrome can occur when any of these blood components is markedly increased and produce focal or multifocal neurologic dysfunction, including headache, encephalopathy, and seizures. The common causes of hyperviscosity include polycythemia vera (Chapter 176) and paraproteinemias (Chapter 196) caused by macroglobulinemia or multiple myeloma.

COAGULATION DISORDERS

Hereditary. Four circulating proteins that inhibit coagulation are protein C, protein S, antithrombin III, and factor V (Chapters 78 and 180). Deficiencies of these proteins rarely cause arterial strokes but more frequently cause venous thrombosis. Deficiencies of proteins C and S are dominantly inherited. Homozygotes develop serious, frequently fatal clotting abnormalities at birth, whereas heterozygotes may show no signs of hypercoagulability. Because of incomplete penetrance, the occurrence of thrombosis and stroke in adults is extremely rare; testing for these abnormalities should be undertaken only in unusual cases. Antithrombin III is vitamin K independent and synthesized in the liver. Deficiency should be suspected in young patients with a history of recurrent deep vein thrombosis or pulmonary embolism, especially if there is a similar family history. Inheritance is autosomal dominant with incomplete penetrance. Arterial stroke is rare.

Acquired. Cancer and pregnancy, including the postpartum period, are associated with hypercoagulable states that predispose to arterial and venous thrombosis (Chapters 78, 180, and 188). Although a variety of clotting abnormalities may be present, no tests have been devised to detect patients at risk for stroke. No treatments are proved to be useful for strokes associated with these conditions.

ANTIPHOSPHOLIPID ANTIBODIES. The antiphospholipid antibody syndrome is associated with cerebral arterial and venous infarction, particularly in young adults (Chapter 180). There is not a clear relationship between the levels of these antibodies and the risk of stroke. Other laboratory abnormalities include prolonged activated partial thromboplastin time, biologic false-positive Venereal Disease Research Laboratory, thrombocytopenia, and a positive antinuclear antibody test. There is an association with atypical migraine, TIA, and ischemic encephalopathy. The reason for the relationship between the antibodies and cerebral thrombosis is unknown.

DRUG-RELATED CAUSES OF STROKE. Numerous legal and illicit drugs have been associated with stroke (Chapter 30). Even the process of drug administration may cause strokes. Intravenous drug abuse may lead to septicemia and diseases such as bacterial endocarditis and mycotic aneurysms that cause strokes. The particles of adulterants can be trapped by pulmonary arterioles, causing local arteritis and later arteriovenous shunts that are thought to allow the microemboli to reach the brain. Paradoxical embolization also is possible through various structural cardiac defects or arteriovenous malformations.

Some of the drugs that are associated with stroke are potent vasoconstrictors and may initiate cerebral vasospasm. In other instances, cerebral vasculitis is associated with either immune responses to the primary drug or hypersensitivity to contaminating adulterants.

Over-the-counter common cold remedies and nasal decongestants containing sympathomimetic amines, such as ephedrine, phenylpropanolamine, and phenoxazoline, have been associated with ischemic stroke, although hemorrhages are more common (Chapter 441). These drugs often are used in high doses as appetite suppressants, and case reports suggest that the high doses are especially likely to be related to stroke, often after the first use of these products. Popular herbs taken as dietary supplements also may include sympathomimetics (e.g., ephedra, also known as *ma-huang*) that have been associated with stroke (Chapter 34).

CERVICAL ARTERY DISSECTION. Spontaneous dissection of the cervical or cerebral arteries is produced by subintimal dissection of blood with subsequent longitudinal extension of the intramural hematoma between its layers for varying distances. Hemorrhage into the intima can cause luminal stenosis and obstruction, whereas hemorrhage into the media or adventitia produces a pseudoaneurysm that can rupture. Most dissections are spontaneous, but this process also is associated with trauma, including whiplash and other neck-stretching injuries, and chiropractic cervical manipulation. Some cases are associated with fibromuscular dysplasia and others with a variety of congenital conditions, including Ehlers-Danlos and Marfan syndromes (Chapter 276) and tuberous sclerosis (Chapter 459). Recognition of dissection is sometimes difficult, and the physician must probe carefully for recent injuries to the neck. Cerebral angiography occasionally can show a double lumen, although a tapered lumen leading to an obstruction is more common. MRI may show a crescent-shaped hyperintense mass adjacent to a flow void. Some patients with this condition have been treated with thrombolysis or anticoagulation and surgical repair, but no therapy has been proved to be useful in randomized trials.

HOMOCYSTINURIA. Homocystinuria (Chapter 222) is associated with a variety of disorders, including dislocated ocular lenses, bone deformities, mental retardation, and accelerated atherosclerosis of the large and medium-sized arteries. Strokes commonly occur before age 20. Detection of homocystine in the urine is the diagnostic test of choice. Individuals with modest increases in serum homocystine levels also may have an increased risk for stroke. Treatment with a diet low in methionine and supplements of cysteine and pyridoxine (vitamin B_6) can decrease the plasma level of methionine. Folate administration also may be helpful because it is necessary for methylation of homocystine. Vitamin therapy has not been proved to reduce the stroke risk in patients with homocystinuria, however.

FAT EMBOLISM. Fat embolism (Chapter 94) is mostly a complication of long bone trauma (Chapter 108), intramedullary manipulation during orthopedic procedures, contusions of soft tissues, and severe trauma to large fat deposits. Strokes typically occur several days after the trauma. Clinical features of cerebral embolization depend on the sites within the brain that are affected. Diffuse embolization can produce encephalopathy or seizures, but more discrete lesions can cause focal neurologic deficits. The condition is probably underdiagnosed clinically and at autopsy. Peripheral features that suggest the diagnosis include petechiae and fat emboli visible on ophthalmoscopic examination. Laboratory abnormalities include hypoxemia, anemia, lipuria, and disorders of blood coagulation. The chest radiograph commonly shows bilateral fluffy infiltrates.

AIR EMBOLISM. Air embolism can occur with a variety of surgical procedures, particularly cardiac surgery, and as a complication of neurosurgical procedures performed with the patient in the sitting position. Trauma can produce pneumothorax, and air may enter the pulmonary vein and subsequently lodge in the brain. Extended underwater dives and too-rapid ascent can cause the air in the blood to come out of solution and form bubbles that can be pumped into the cerebral circulation (caisson disease). Arterial gas embolism can cause disturbances of cortical function, including seizures or focal deficits. Segmental areas of pallor may be observed on the tongue, marbling of the skin may be seen, and air emboli can be detected on funduscopic examination. When caused by rapid decompression, barotrauma is treated in a decompression chamber.

MOYAMOYA. Moyamoya disease is a chronic, noninflammatory occlusive vasculopathy of unknown etiology. It is a rare condition that is most common among the Japanese. It has a bimodal age distribution, with peaks in the first and fourth decades. Diagnostic criteria include stenosis or occlusion involving the bifurcation of the ICA and proximal portions of the ACA and MCA, presence of unusual netlike ("puff of smoke") collateral arteries arising from the circle of Willis, and bilateral occurrence. In adults, the clinical manifestation is usually hemorrhages. Moyamoya is diagnosed by cerebral angiography. No treatment has been proved effective.

CEREBRAL VENOUS SINUS THROMBOSIS. Thrombosis of the cerebral venous sinus may present as headache, focal neurologic deficits, seizures, altered mental status, and papilledema. With obstruction of the superior sagittal sinus, veins draining into the sinus from the superior and medial surfaces of both cerebral convexities are commonly obstructed; in its early stages, the condition can result in bilateral weakness and sensory changes in the legs. This presentation of bilateral leg weakness should alert the clinician to the possibility of sinus thrombosis. Seizures occur more often with venous than with arterial occlusion. The most dangerous form of venous disease arises when the superior sagittal sinus is occluded, but obstruction of a transverse sinus or one of the major veins over the cerebral convexity also can produce major damage. These venous occlusions occur most commonly in association with coagulopathies, often in the puerperal period, or in patients with disseminated cancer. The transverse sinus can be occluded as a consequence of inner ear infections, a condition called *otitic hydrocephalus*.

The differential diagnosis of venous obstruction can include an arterial stroke, but the presentation more often suggests a diffuse process, such as herpes simplex encephalitis or meningitis. Diagnosis depends on the recognition of impaired venous flow, which can be suspected on routine CT or MRI and confirmed by CT or MRI angiography; conventional angiography is rarely needed. Based on two trials, unfractionated heparin[3] and perhaps low-molecular-weight heparin may be safe and effective for cerebral venous sinus thrombosis during the acute phase, even in the presence of hemorrhagic infarction caused by the sinus thrombosis. Oral anticoagulation should be continued for 3 to 6 months.

Prevention and Treatment of Stroke and Transient Ischemic Attack

Risk factors for stroke fall into two general categories, nonmodifiable and modifiable (Table 440-3). Within the modifiable group are risk factors that are well documented and others that are not.

Table 440–3 • WELL-DOCUMENTED MODIFIABLE RISK FACTORS FOR STROKE

FACTOR	PREVALENCE (%)	RELATIVE RISK	RISK REDUCTION WITH TREATMENT
Hypertension (by age group)			38%
50 yr	20	4.0	
60 yr	30	3.0	
70 yr	40	2.0	
80 yr	55	1.4	
90 yr	60	1.0	
Smoking	25	1.8	50% within 1 yr, baseline after 5 yr
Diabetes	20	1.8–6.0	Reduction of stroke risk in hypertensive diabetics with blood pressure control. No demonstrated benefit in stroke reduction with tight glycemic control
Asymptomatic carotid stenosis	2–8	2.0	50%
Hyperlipidemia			
Adults <35 yr	8–9	1.8	20–30% with statins in patients with known coronary disease
Men 55 yr	25	2.6	
Women 65 yr	40		
Atrial fibrillation (nonvalvular)			
50–59 yr	0.5	4.0	68% warfarin
60–69 yr	1.8	2.6	21% aspirin
70–79 yr	4.8	3.3	
80–89 yr	8.8	4.5	

Modified from Goldstein LB, Adams R, Becker K, et al: Primary prevention of ischemic stroke. Stroke 2001;32:280–299.

PRIMARY PREVENTION

HYPERTENSION. Hypertension is the most important risk factor for ischemic and hemorrhagic stroke (Chapter 63). The incidence of stroke increases directly in relation to the degree of elevation of systolic and diastolic arterial blood pressure above threshold values. More important, there has been conclusive evidence for more than 30 years that control of hypertension prevents strokes.[4] The relative risk of stroke in hypertensive patients is approximately four times greater than in age-matched normotensive individuals. The goal is to reduce systolic blood pressure to less than 140 mm Hg and diastolic pressure to less than 90 mm Hg. Antihypertensive therapy should be individualized (Chapter 63).

ASYMPTOMATIC CAROTID STENOSIS. Approximately 7 to 10% of men and 5 to 7% of women older than age 65 have asymptomatic carotid stenosis of greater than 50%. Epidemiologic studies suggest that the rate of unheralded stroke ipsilateral to stenosis is about 1 to 2% annually. In the Asymptomatic Carotid Arteriosclerosis Study, ipsilateral carotid endarterectomy was shown to benefit patients who had 60% or greater diameter reduction of the artery without ulceration, provided that the perioperative complication rate was less than 3%,[5] a rate that requires an exceptionally skilled surgeon. Clinical trials of carotid artery angioplasty and stent placement are under way, but these procedures cannot be routinely recommended yet.

CARDIAC DISEASE. Nonvalvular atrial fibrillation carries a 3 to 5% annual risk for stroke, with the risk becoming even higher in the presence of advanced age, prior TIA or stroke, hypertension, impaired left ventricular function, and diabetes mellitus. Therapy is with warfarin or aspirin (Chapters 33 and 59).[6]

SMOKING. In epidemiologic studies, the risk of stroke in smokers is almost double that of nonsmokers, but the risk becomes essentially identical to nonsmokers by 2 to 5 years after quitting. Smoking cessation is routinely recommended, but there are no prospective randomized trials to prove that cessation of smoking reduces stroke.

DIABETES MELLITUS. The relative risk of stroke is two to six times greater for patients with insulin-dependent diabetes. Tight control of hypertension using angiotensin-converting enzyme inhibitors substantially reduces the incidence of stroke in patients with type I or II diabetes.

SICKLE CELL DISEASE. Blood transfusion to dilute the abnormal erythrocytes is the usual treatment to prevent strokes in patients with sickle cell disease. At present, the duration of transfusion therapy or diagnostic techniques that can guide therapy to prevent strokes is not established (Chapter 171).

HYPERLIPIDEMIA. Trials have shown various statins are associated with reduction of stroke rate in patients with coronary artery disease and elevated cholesterol levels. The recommendation of the National Cholesterol Education II guidelines is that patients with known coronary heart disease and elevated low-density lipoprotein cholesterol levels should be considered for treatment with statins.[7] Studies are under way to determine whether patients without heart disease should receive stroke prophylaxis with statins.

OBESITY. Some evidence suggests that abdominal obesity in men and obesity and weight gain in women are independent risk factors for stroke. Weight reduction in overweight people is recommended, but weight loss has not been proved to reduce the risk of stroke.

NUTRITION AND ALCOHOL. Epidemiologic studies have found that consumption of fruits and vegetables is associated with a lower risk of stroke, but no randomized trials have proved the value of changing dietary habits. Heavy alcohol consumption may be a risk factor for ischemic and hemorrhagic stroke.

HORMONE THERAPY. Postmenopausal hormone replacement therapy has been shown to increase the risk of stroke.[8] The absolute risk of stroke remains low, however, in otherwise healthy, low-risk patients.

Meta-analysis suggests an increase in the relative risk of stroke in women taking oral contraceptives, but the absolute risk of stroke is small. Women who smoke, are hypertensive or diabetic, have migraine headaches, or had prior thromboembolic events may be at increased risk for stroke when taking oral contraceptives.

SECONDARY PREVENTION IN PATIENTS WITH PRIOR STROKE OR TRANSIENT ISCHEMIC ATTACK

All of the risk factor reductions that are recommended for primary prevention also are recommended in patients who have had a prior

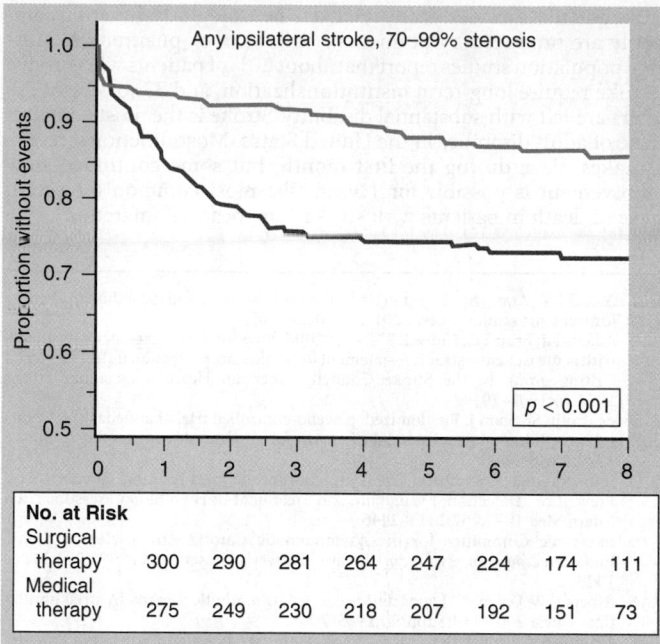

FIGURE 440–5 • Proportion of patients without any ipsilateral stroke as a function of the time (in years) since ipsilateral endarterectomy. The medically managed patients have fewer strokes for a brief time after randomization, but within a few months, the surgically treated patients have fewer ipsilateral strokes, and this advantage is maintained at least 8 years after treatment. (From Barnett HJM, Taylor DW, Eliasziw M, et al: The North American Carotid Endarterectomy Trial Collaborators: Benefit of carotid endarterectomy in patients with symptomatic moderate or severe stenosis. N Engl J Med 1998;339:1415–1425.)

stroke or TIA and have no contraindication. In addition, specific medical and surgical therapies should be considered.

MEDICATIONS. Aspirin and other antiplatelet agents reduce the odds of nonfatal stroke by 31% when used in patients with known vascular disease (Chapter 33). All patients who have had a stroke and have no contraindication should receive an antiplatelet agent to reduce the risk of recurrent stroke.[1] The optimal dose of aspirin has not yet been established, and doses of 50 to 1300 mg/day have been used. Clopidogrel or the combination of aspirin plus dipyridamole may be more effective and safer than aspirin, but these alternatives are substantially more expensive and do not confer a large absolute benefit relative to aspirin alone. There is no conclusive evidence that anticoagulation is better than antiplatelet agents in preventing strokes; the risks of cerebral hemorrhage exceed the potential benefit for ischemic stroke prevention.

SURGERY. In 1991, the North American Symptomatic Carotid Endarterectomy Trial collaborators showed that carotid endarterectomy reduced the cumulative risk of any ipsilateral stroke at 2 years from 26% to 9% in patients with a 70 to 99% symptomatic (i.e., prior TIA or nondisabling stroke) internal carotid stenosis (Fig. 440–5). Subsequently the same group showed that among patients with a 50 to 70% symptomatic stenosis, 16% of surgically treated patients had an ipsilateral stroke within 5 years compared with 22% of patients treated medically. Patients with a less than 50% symptomatic stenosis did better with medical management alone. Patients with symptomatic carotid stenosis of more than 50% benefit from endarterectomy; patients with higher degrees of stenosis but not complete occlusion benefit more, assuming a less than 6% rate of surgical complications.[9]

Outcome and Rehabilitation

Patients who receive care in specialized, acute stroke units are less likely to die, more likely to go home, and more likely to be independent 3 months later. In most clinical trials, about 15% of patients with ischemic stroke die within the first 3 months. Immediate causes of death include herniation because of brain swelling or neurologic dysfunction directly related to the stroke. Deaths that occur days after stroke and that are not directly related to neurologic dysfunction commonly are produced by pulmonary embolism or pneumonia. Most large population studies report that about 20% of patients who survive a stroke require long-term institutionalization, and 33 to 50% of the others are left with substantial disability. Stroke is the most common cause of adult disability in the United States. Most functional recovery takes place during the first month, but some continued slow improvement is possible for 1 year. The most common long-term cause of death in patients with stroke is myocardial infarction.

Grade A

1. Albers GW, Amarenco P, Easton JD, et al: Antithrombotic and thrombolytic therapy for ischemic stroke. Chest 2001;119:300S–320S.
2. Adams HP, Brott TG, Crowell RM, et al: Guidelines for the management of patients with acute ischemic stroke: A statement for healthcare professionals from a special writing group of the Stroke Council, American Heart Association. Stroke 1994;25:1901–1914.
3. de Bruijn SF, Stam J: Randomized, placebo-controlled trial of anticoagulant treatment with low-molecular-weight heparin for cerebral sinus thrombosis. Stroke 1999;30:484–488.
4. Joint National Committee: The sixth report of the Joint National Committee on Prevention, Detection, Evaluation, and Treatment of High Blood Pressure. Arch Intern Med 1997;157:2413–2446.
5. Executive Committee for the Asymptomatic Carotid Atherosclerosis Study: Endarterectomy for asymptomatic carotid artery stenosis. JAMA 1995;273:1421–1428.
6. Albers GW, Dalen JE, Laupacis A, et al: Antithrombotic therapy in atrial fibrillation. Chest 2001;119(Suppl 1):194S–206S.
7. Grundy SM, Becker D, Clark CT, et al: National Cholesterol Education Program Expert Panel on Detection, Evaluation, and Treatment of High Blood Cholesterol in Adults (Adult Treatment Panel III). Circulation 2003;106:3413–3421.
8. Lemaitre RN, Heckbert SR, Psaty BM, et al: Hormone replacement therapy and associated risk of stroke in postmenopausal women. Arch Intern Med 2002;162:1954–1960.
9. Barnett HJM, Taylor DW, Eliasziw M, et al: The North American Symptomatic Carotid Endarterectomy Trial Collaborators: Benefit of carotid endarterectomy in patients with symptomatic moderate or severe stenosis. N Engl J Med 1998;339:1415–1425.

SUGGESTED READINGS
Adams HA Jr, Adams RJ, Brott T, et al: Guidelines for the early management of patients with ischemic stroke. Stroke 2003;34:1056–1083. *This article continues to conclude that the only Grade A method of treatment of acute ischemic stroke is intravenous tPA given rapidly after onset with a minimal set of laboratory tests prior to administration.*
Biller J, Feinberg WM, Castaldo JE, et al: Guidelines for carotid endarterectomy. Circulation 1998;97:501–509. *Evidence-based recommendations for surgical prophylaxis of ischemic stroke.*
Broderick JP, Hacke W: Treatment of acute ischemic stroke: Part I: Recanalization strategies. Circulation 2002;106:1563–1569. *Approach to thrombolysis.*
Goldstein LB, Adams R, Becker K, et al: Primary prevention of ischemic stroke. Stroke 2001;32:280–299. *American Heart Association Scientific Statement guideline for management of ischemic stroke.*
Johnston SC: Clinical practice. Transient ischemic attack. N Engl J Med 2002;347:1687–1692. *A case-based review.*
Pearson TA, Blair SN, Daniels SR, et al: AHA guidelines for primary prevention of cardiovascular disease and stroke: 2002 update: Consensus panel guide to comprehensive risk reduction for adult patients without coronary or other atherosclerotic vascular diseases. American Heart Association Science Advisory and Coordinating Committee. Circulation 2002;106:388–391. *Consensus guidelines.*
Rothwell PM, Eliasziw M, Gutnikov SA, et al: Analysis of pooled data from the randomised controlled trials of endarterectomy for symptomatic carotid stenosis. Lancet 2003;361:107–116. *Surgery is of some benefit for patients with 50–69% symptomatic stenosis and is highly beneficial for those with ≥70% symptomatic stenosis; with carotid near-occlusion, benefit is marginal in the short-term and uncertain in the long-term.*
Smith WS, Johnston SC, Skalabrin EJ, et al: Spinal manipulative therapy is an independent risk factor for vertebral artery dissection. Neurology 2003;60:1424–1428. *Spinal manipulative therapy is a risk factor even after controlling for neck pain.*

441 HEMORRHAGIC CEREBROVASCULAR DISEASE

Justin A. Zivin

Approximately 15% of all strokes are intracranial hemorrhages. Hemorrhagic stroke can be diffuse (i.e., bleeding into the subarachnoid or intraventricular spaces) or focal (i.e., intraparenchymal hemorrhage). About two thirds of intracranial bleeds are predominantly subarachnoid hemorrhages, whereas about one third are intracerebral hemorrhages. Subarachnoid hemorrhage usually is caused by rupture of vessels on or near the surface of the brain or ventricles (e.g., aneurysms, vascular malformations), with bleeding predominantly into the cerebrospinal fluid (CSF) spaces. Intracerebral hemorrhage is most frequently caused by the rupture of arteries that are within the brain substance (e.g., hypertensive hemorrhage, vascular

malformations) but do not extend to the CSF spaces. Both types of hemorrhagic strokes have high mortality rates, depending on subtype and location. Prevention is the mainstay of management because there are no sufficiently efficacious therapies for hemorrhage-induced cerebral injury.

SUBARACHNOID HEMORRHAGE

Epidemiology

In the United States, there are about 30,000 new cases of subarachnoid hemorrhage each year, predominantly affecting young adults. Both genders are equally affected, and the rate may be twice as high among African Americans as in whites. Rupture of aneurysms is by far the most common cause of nontraumatic subarachnoid hemorrhage. Advances in diagnostic imaging have improved the detection of intracranial aneurysms, but most cases are not discovered until after rupture.

Risk factors include cigarette smoking, binge drinking, illicit drugs, phenylpropanolamine, and other sympathomimetics. Although hypertension is well established as a risk factor for ischemic stroke, the relationship of nonmalignant hypertension to subarachnoid hemorrhage is less well documented; the decline in hypertension in the general population has not been accompanied by a decrease in the incidence rate of subarachnoid hemorrhage.

Pathobiology

The principal causes of subarachnoid hemorrhage are aneurysms and arteriovenous malformations (AVMs), but trauma can also cause subarachnoid bleeding (Chapter 431). Rare causes of subarachnoid hemorrhage include vasculitis, central nervous system neoplasms (Chapter 457), and hematologic disorders such as hemophilia, disseminated intravascular coagulopathy, and thrombocytopenic purpura.

Clinical Manifestations

The classic symptom of a subarachnoid hemorrhage is a very rapidly developing, severe headache, typically called the "worst headache of my life," that is sometimes accompanied by a stiff neck (Chapter 428). Aneurysms may generate prodromal signs and symptoms as they gradually expand or cause sentinel (warning) leaks that produce focal or generalized head pain. Such sentinel headaches are frequently severe, and they may be accompanied by nausea or vomiting and may cause meningeal irritation.

Arterial blood pressure is often elevated, and body temperature usually increases, particularly during the first few days after bleeding as subarachnoid blood products produce chemical meningitis. Transient alteration of mental status occurs in nearly one half of patients, particularly if intracranial pressure exceeds cerebral mean arterial pressure. Patients can remain in coma for several days, depending on the location of the aneurysm and the amount of bleeding.

Acute subarachnoid hemorrhage causes meningeal irritation; nuchal rigidity and photophobia can require several hours to develop. Ophthalmoscopic observation reveals well-circumscribed, bright red, preretinal hemorrhages, known as subhyaloid hemorrhages and thought to be a result of increased intracranial pressure, raised retinal venous pressure, and dissection of blood along the optic nerve sheath. Focal neurologic dysfunction is usually not a prominent feature unless an aneurysm compresses surrounding brain structures, a jet of blood dissects directly into a clinically eloquent brain region, or vasospasm subsequently develops.

Laboratory Examination

A complete blood cell count, including platelets, should be obtained, and clotting times should be determined to assess whether the patient has an infection or clotting abnormalities. Blood should also be sent for electrolyte analysis to serve as a baseline for detecting later complications. The patient should then be sent immediately for an emergent computed tomographic (CT) scan. A scan performed within 24 hours of onset usually reveals an area of high signal attenuation consistent with hemorrhage; if blood is present in the subarachnoid space, it is seen within the basal cisterns in more than 90% of patients. By 48 hours after onset, the sensitivity of CT declines to about 75%. Conventional magnetic resonance imaging (MRI) sequences (T1- or T2-weighted scans) are less sensitive than CT scans.

The location of subarachnoid hemorrhage by CT scan suggests the source of bleeding. High signal attenuation in the basal cisterns, sylvian fissure, or intrahemispheric fissure often indicates rupture of a saccular aneurysm, whereas higher concentrations of blood over the convexities or within the superficial parenchyma of the brain are more consistent with the rupture of an AVM or a mycotic aneurysm. A large amount of blood in the subarachnoid space increases the likelihood of subsequent vasospasm. A contrast-enhanced CT scan may aid in the identification of an AVM and some large aneurysms.

An electrocardiogram should be performed to detect peaked or inverted T waves and increased U waves. These abnormalities and subsequent arrhythmias have been attributed to multifocal myocardial necrosis caused by elevated levels of circulating catecholamines.

If the CT scan is normal but the index of suspicion remains high for subarachnoid hemorrhage, a lumbar puncture is usually diagnostic. A traumatic lumbar puncture (i.e., penetration of the needle into a small blood vessel of the venous plexus on the anterior wall of the spinal canal) produces a declining number of red blood cells in subsequent tubes, whereas subarachnoid hemorrhage produces a relatively constant number of red blood cells in each tube. In the presence of bloody fluid, one of the CSF samples should be centrifuged immediately, and the supernate should be examined for the presence of hematin or xanthochromia by visual inspection. Red blood cells in the CSF begin to lyse within a few hours, and the centrifuged supernate then appears pink. Later (about 10 hours), as the hemoglobin is converted to bilirubin, the fluid becomes slightly yellow. The opening CSF pressure is usually elevated and may remain so for many days. CSF samples obtained within the first day may show a white blood cell count consistent with the normal circulating white cell–to–red cell ratio (about 1:1000). Chemical meningitis is produced by the presence of blood or breakdown products within the subarachnoid space, and CSF samples contain increased numbers of polymorphonuclear and mononuclear cells relative to red blood cells. The CSF glucose concentration is usually normal shortly after the onset of bleeding, but as chemical meningitis develops, the glucose level may decline, rarely to less than 40 mg/dL. After a subarachnoid hemorrhage, the protein content of the CSF is usually elevated, consistent with contamination by blood (the usual ratio is 1 mg/dL of protein for every 1000 red blood cells).

Cerebral angiography remains the definitive study to identify the source of subarachnoid hemorrhage. When the diagnosis of aneurysmal subarachnoid hemorrhage seems highly probable, the timing and need for a cerebral angiogram should be determined by surgical considerations. If doubt exists, angiography should be performed with minimal delay. Because many patients have multiple cerebral aneurysms, the carotid and vertebral artery systems should be examined angiographically. Initial cerebral angiography fails to detect the source of bleeding in about 20% of patients; such patients are thought to have a fairly good prognosis, with only a 1 to 2% annual risk of recurrent hemorrhage. Failure to detect the bleeding source can result from an aneurysm that is obliterated by clot or because the ruptured aneurysm was small; from a superficial venous angioma; from a spinal cord aneurysm; or from an AVM. The presence of back pain or neurologic signs localized to the spinal cord at onset should prompt a search for a spinal source of hemorrhage. If the initial angiogram is negative and no other clues to the bleeding site can be found, repeat cerebral angiography is usually performed within a few weeks; MRI or CT scans with and without contrast may also be helpful.

Medical Complications

If a patient does not die immediately after a subarachnoid hemorrhage, a number of neurologic complications can occur. Some result from blood in the subarachnoid space, and other concerns include rebleeding from the same aneurysm, cerebral vasospasm and its ischemic consequences, hydrocephalus caused by blockage of CSF outflow pathways, and seizures. Non-neurologic complications include cardiac and electrolyte abnormalities.

REBLEEDING. If an aneurysm is not repaired promptly, it can rupture again. A new headache or neurologic worsening suggests repeat rupture, which can be diagnosed only if a repeat CT scan or lumbar

puncture shows the presence of new blood in the subarachnoid space. Approximately 30% of patients with aneurysmal subarachnoid hemorrhage rebleed during the first month, and the incidence is highest during the first 2 weeks after the initial bleed. Patients with unrepaired aneurysms who survive their initial bleed for more than 1 month have a 2 to 3% annual risk of rebleeding.

VASOSPASM. A common cause of death and disability in patients with aneurysmal subarachnoid hemorrhage is cerebral vasospasm. The vessels at the base of the brain become narrowed, thereby reducing blood flow; if the vasospasm is severe, it can produce infarction of the brain distal to the site of the spasm. The vessels that go into spasm are often different than the artery that was responsible for the initial bleed. Vasospasm has been reported in up to 75% of patients after subarachnoid hemorrhage, and up to 30% of patients with vasospasm develop delayed neurologic deficits. The onset of vasospasm is typically between days 3 and 14 after bleeding, but this complication can develop as late as 3 weeks after subarachnoid hemorrhage. The arteries of the circle of Willis and their major branches are the usual initial site of spasm, with more distal arteries becoming involved later. The amount and location of blood detected within the basal cisterns on CT scans correlate with the incidence and location of vasospasm. The pathogenesis of cerebral vasospasm is unknown.

Cerebral angiography, which is the best established method to diagnose vasospasm, shows narrowing of the dye column. However, other methods such as transcranial Doppler ultrasonography (TCD) or magnetic resonance angiography are increasingly being used. TCD has high specificity, but its sensitivity is not as good as angiography.

HYDROCEPHALUS. Acute hydrocephalus occurs in up to two thirds of patients within 3 days after subarachnoid hemorrhage. Hydrocephalus is caused by obstruction of CSF outflow pathways at the level of the fourth ventricle and the pacchionian granulations lining the venous sinuses. The risk of developing hydrocephalus is associated with increasing age, history of hypertension, intraventricular hemorrhage, focal neurologic findings, decreased level of consciousness, and hyponatremia. Chronic ventricular enlargement occurs in up to 60% of patients within 1 month after subarachnoid hemorrhage and is often asymptomatic. Several forms of treatment have been advocated for management of hydrocephalus, including repeated lumbar punctures and shunt placement, but their value has not been proved.

SEIZURES. Seizures may occur shortly after subarachnoid hemorrhage in 15 to 90% of patients. Seizures are thought to result from cortical damage from bleeding into the neocortex or from ischemic necrosis related to vasospasm. Development of persistent epilepsy is unusual. Prophylactic anticonvulsant therapy has not been useful.

NON-NEUROLOGIC COMPLICATIONS. Cardiac complications occur as a consequence of subarachnoid hemorrhage. In the acute phases of subarachnoid hemorrhage, electrocardiographic patterns can mimic acute myocardial infarction (Chapter 69). A pattern of deep inverted T waves across the pericardium is classic. Appropriate biomarker assays and repeat electrocardiograms are needed to document true myocardial damage.

Hyponatremia (Chapter 112) is the most common electrolyte abnormality after subarachnoid hemorrhage. Sodium loss, which is typically mild, may occur in up to 25% of patients. The natriuresis has been attributed to inappropriate levels of antidiuretic hormone (Chapter 238), but this hypothesis has not been proved. Hyponatremia can itself result in a decreased level of consciousness and seizures, but it is often impossible to distinguish the effects of hyponatremia from the other possible causes of these neurologic abnormalities.

SPECIFIC CAUSES AND THEIR TREATMENT AND PROGNOSIS

SACCULAR ANEURYSMS

Saccular or "berry" aneurysms, which account for 80 to 90% of all intracranial aneurysms, are thin-walled outpouchings that protrude from the arteries of the circle of Willis or its major branches; 85% are located at branching points (Fig 441–1). Because of the local weakness and degeneration of the media, the intima bulges outward and is covered only by the adventitia. A saccular aneurysm may be an incidental finding on a scan or at autopsy in patients who die of other diseases; in symptomatic cases, however, the sack gradually enlarges and ultimately ruptures.

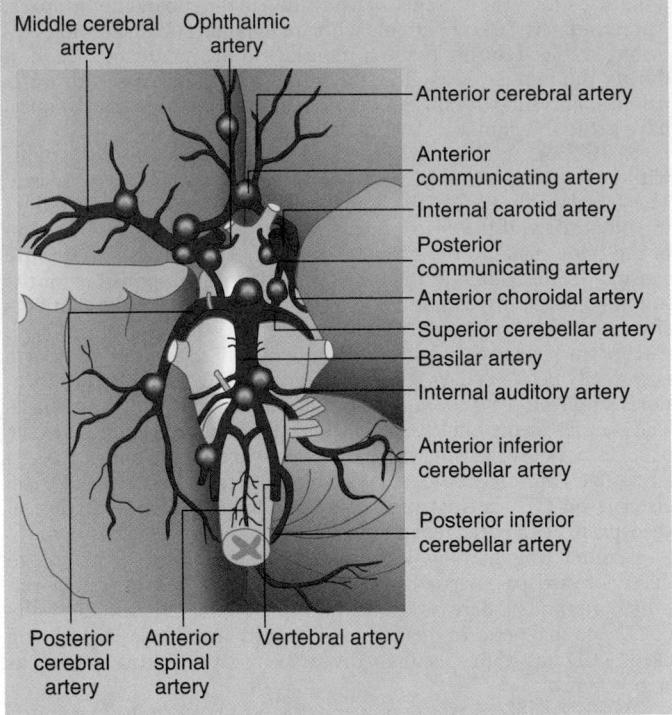

Middle cerebral artery
Ophthalmic artery
Anterior cerebral artery
Anterior communicating artery
Internal carotid artery
Posterior communicating artery
Anterior choroidal artery
Superior cerebellar artery
Basilar artery
Internal auditory artery
Anterior inferior cerebellar artery
Posterior inferior cerebellar artery
Posterior cerebral artery
Anterior spinal artery
Vertebral artery

FIGURE 441–1 • Berry aneurysms typically develop at the bifurcations of arteries on the undersurface of the brain.

Saccular aneurysms are rarely detected in children, and the incidence of subarachnoid hemorrhage increases with age; therefore, it seems clear that congenital wall defects develop into aneurysms only after some time. Congenital defects in the muscle and elastic tissue of the arterial media are observed at autopsy in up to 80% of normal vessels of the circle of Willis. It is postulated that these defects gradually degenerate over time as they are exposed to pulsatile arterial blood pressure. Multiple aneurysms are found in about 15% of people with at least one aneurysm. Because the incidence of aneurysmal subarachnoid hemorrhage is approximately 1 in 10,000, it is evident that most saccular aneurysms do not rupture.

Approximately 10 to 20% of patients with known aneurysms have a family history. Diseases that are associated with intracranial saccular aneurysms include polycystic kidney disease (Chapter 127), Marfan and Ehlers-Danlos syndromes (Chapter 276), fibromuscular dysplasia (Chapter 75), pseudoxanthoma elasticum (Chapter 276), systemic lupus erythematosus (Chapter 280), and sickle cell anemia (Chapter 171). Screening of other family members is often recommended when two or more members of a family have aneurysms.

Because the natural history of aneurysms may be highly variable and the risk-benefit ratio for the various invasive techniques is unknown, expectant waiting sometimes may be the best option. However, an aneurysm may rupture without warning, and the uncertainty is unacceptable to some patients and physicians. Medical therapies may delay the time of rupture but cannot repair the lesion.

Surgical clipping of aneurysms can unquestionably prevent rebleeding, but the indications for this surgery have never been established in appropriately designed studies. Factors favoring medical therapy include older age, decreased life expectancy, comorbid medical conditions, and small, asymptomatic aneurysms. Conversely, factors favoring surgery, according to general consensus, include younger age, previously unruptured aneurysms, family history of a ruptured aneurysm, large aneurysms, symptomatic aneurysms, and aneurysms that are observed to grow.

The best methods for medical management are uncertain. Medical management of a ruptured aneurysm aims to reduce the risks of rebleeding and cerebral vasospasm and to prevent other medical complications before and after surgical intervention. General support is provided to quiet the patient using bedrest, analgesics for headache, and gentle sedation as needed. Stool softeners can minimize straining. Hypertension should be treated appropriately but not aggressively (Chapter 440) because an elevated blood pressure may represent

a normal compensatory mechanism, particularly in a chronically hypertensive patient, and excessive reduction may cause infarct extension. There is no conclusive evidence about whether modifying blood pressure in acute subarachnoid hemorrhage is of benefit.

Antifibrinolytic drugs, including tranexamic acid and ε-aminocaproic acid (EACA), have been used to try to seal the site of aneurysmal bleeding. Unfortunately, multiple studies suggest that any decrease in continued bleeding is outweighed by an increased incidence of infarction.

The only form of medical therapy that has been useful in treating subarachnoid hemorrhage patients is the voltage-regulated calcium channel antagonist nimodipine. Although it does not reduce the frequency of vasospasm, nimodipine (60 mg PO every 4 hours for 21 days) lowers the incidence of cerebral infarction by about one third.■

The objectives of surgery are to exclude the aneurysm from the circulation or relieve pressure on adjacent brain tissue caused by expansion of the sack. The timing of any form of surgical therapy is uncertain. Many surgeons recommend treatment as soon as possible after the subarachnoid hemorrhage. In the absence of properly designed clinical trials and considering the variability of aneurysms and patients, it is difficult to develop therapeutic guidelines. Open surgical procedures include placing a clip on the sack at its neck while maintaining the patency of the parent vessel. For very large aneurysms, for which it is not possible to isolate the sack from the parent vessel, wrapping the sack with various types of materials to prevent it from rupturing or growing is sometimes performed. Indirect procedures include various methods of occluding the feeding artery; if there is sufficient collateral supply, the risk of infarction may be less than that of spontaneous rupture of the aneurysm with subsequent extensive subarachnoid hemorrhage.

Percutaneous selective angiographic procedures have been devised to fill the aneurysm with various materials and prevent further circulation into the sack. For example, a detachable coil can be threaded into an aneurysm; an electrical current applied to the coil causes the surrounding blood to clot. The coil is detached and left in place, and the catheter is then removed. This U.S. Food and Drug Administration (FDA)–approved approach has not been shown to be more or less effective than other methods of management.

The mortality and morbidity rates differ among studies. About 12% of subarachnoid hemorrhage victims die before reaching medical attention. By 30 days, approximately 50% die, but 30-day survivors usually survive for at least a year. An equally high mortality rate accompanies each episode of rebleeding. Approximately 25% of survivors have persistent neurologic deficits.

FUSIFORM ANEURYSMS

Fusiform aneurysms are so named because they are elongated dilations (i.e., ectasia) of large arteries associated with atherosclerosis. These aneurysms typically develop in the basilar artery but also may affect the internal, middle, and anterior cerebral arteries of individuals with widespread arteriosclerosis and hypertension. These aneurysms may progressively dilate and become tortuous, thereby producing neurologic dysfunction, most frequently by compressing surrounding structures. Thrombi may form in them and embolize distally to cause ischemic strokes. Typically, ectatic aneurysms of the basilar artery compress cranial nerves and cause facial pain (V), hemifacial spasm (VII), and hearing loss with vertigo (VIII). Fusiform aneurysms may mimic pituitary and suprasellar mass lesions or cerebellopontine angle tumors. Fusiform aneurysms rarely rupture; if they do, they are difficult to treat surgically because their shape and stiff walls usually preclude easy surgical clipping, and total occlusion is usually required.

MYCOTIC ANEURYSMS

Infected emboli, usually originating on an infected heart valve (Chapter 310), may lodge in a distal branch of a cerebral artery, causing small areas of infarction or microabscesses. Arteries that do not rupture immediately may develop focal arteritis and mycotic aneurysms, also known as septic aneurysms. Mycotic aneurysms are frequently multiple and can be found distally in cerebral arteries. Rates of rupture of these aneurysms may be as high as 10%. Such lesions may be detected by noninvasive imaging studies, but the definitive test is contrast angiography, for which the indications are controversial. Aside from treatment of the underlying infection, other treatments are not established.

VASCULAR MALFORMATIONS

The conventional definitions of cerebrovascular malformations are based on the histologic appearance of the vessels and the intervening neural parenchyma. The most frequent type of vascular malformation is the AVM, which has a core of dysplastic vessels (i.e., nidus), feeding arteries, and draining veins. In the nidus, arteries connect directly to veins without intervening capillaries to produce a low-resistance, high-flow shunt that ultimately dilates feeding arteries and thickens the walls of the draining veins. The classic arteriographic appearance includes an early draining vein. Ordinarily, there is no intervening neural tissue in the nidus. The nidus is the usual site of hemorrhage in an AVM.

The next most common lesions are cavernous malformations (i.e., cavernous angiomas or hemangiomas), which are composed of small-caliber sinusoidal vascular channels that are commonly thrombosed. The low flow rate through these vessels makes them difficult to detect with angiography, and they are unlikely to hemorrhage; these malformations also do not contain neural tissue. Cavernous AVMs are often associated with venous malformations, which are composed of small veins separated by normal parenchyma. Smaller venous channels drain into a dilated venous trunk that ultimately drains into a large vein and sinus in the brain. The classic angiographic appearance is a caput medusa in the late venous phase. These anomalies are readily detected by CT scans, but they rarely hemorrhage.

A cerebral varix is a single dilated vein that rarely causes clinical symptoms. Telangiectasis, also called capillary malformation, is a cluster of enlarged capillaries surrounded by normal parenchyma. These lesions are too small to be detected by conventional imaging methods and are usually noted as petechiae that are incidentally found at autopsy; these benign lesions rarely hemorrhage.

About 1% of all strokes and 10% of intracerebral hemorrhages are caused by vascular malformations. The prevalence of AVMs is approximately 0.5%, and the annual incidence of hemorrhage is between 1 and 3 cases per 100,000 people. Familial cases occur but are rare.

Clinical Manifestations

Although increasing numbers of probably asymptomatic vascular malformations are being diagnosed by brain imaging as part of the evaluation of nonspecific headaches, about 50% of AVMs manifest with intracranial hemorrhage, a lower proportion initially manifest with seizures, and the remainder cause progressive neurologic disability as the first symptom. Hemorrhage, which is the most feared complication of AVM, has an associated mortality rate of 10 to 15%. Mortality and morbidity rates associated with AVMs are somewhat less than for aneurysms. The initial hemorrhage tends to occur during the second through fourth decades, and hypertension before the hemorrhage is uncommon. The risk of acute rebleeding averages approximately 6 to 7%. In the next 5 years, the rate is about 2% per year, and it is 1 to 2% per year thereafter. If this rebleeding rate is maintained for life, a young individual who has a hemorrhagic AVM faces a 50 to 60% chance of an incapacitating or fatal subsequent hemorrhage during a normal lifespan.

AVMs can bleed into the subarachnoid space, the brain parenchyma, or the ventricular system. Focal neurologic abnormalities depend on the severity of the bleeding and the location of brain parenchyma that has been affected. The frequency of cerebral vasospasm after hemorrhage from an AVM is less than for an aneurysmal bleed.

Approximately 30% of patients who have an AVM present with seizures, which often have a focal onset. Focal neurologic deficits independent of seizures can develop, possibly caused by vascular thrombosis and perhaps by shunting of blood through arteriovenous fistulas away from normal brain tissue.

Diagnosis

If a hemorrhage has occurred, there may be evidence on unenhanced CT scanning of bleeding in an unusual location for primary intracerebral hemorrhage or a ruptured aneurysm. Contrast-enhanced CT scans may demonstrate marked enhancement of the feeding arteries and draining veins. MRI with signal void on T1- or T2-weighted images can also establish the diagnosis. Angiography remains the definitive test to identify the AVM and delineate its size, gross morphology, feeding arteries, and draining veins. Because AVMs are occasionally multiple and may be associated with saccular aneurysms, four-vessel angiography is indicated even if an AVM is found by unilateral carotid injection. Extracranial or contralateral arteries occasionally supply intracranial AVMs and should be considered in the angiographic evaluation.

 Treatment

There is uncertainty regarding the prognosis of unruptured AVMs because of their various locations, sizes, and morphology. Because the safety and efficacy of the various procedures for treating AVMs have not been established, there are no guiding therapeutic principles.

Conservative treatment is often recommended for unruptured AVMs that manifest with seizures or headache, especially in patients older than 55 to 60 years. This approach emphasizes control of hypertension, avoidance of anticoagulants, and use of anticonvulsants to control seizures.

If an AVM has ruptured and the patient has recovered from the initial hemorrhage, the two goals of interventional therapy are to remove the AVM completely and avoid a worsening of neurologic dysfunction. Removal can be curative, but it is important to eliminate residual abnormal vessels, which may produce hemorrhages, especially if reduction of outflow increases the perfusion pressures within the remaining anomalous vasculature. However, it is particularly dangerous to perform these procedures in critical neurologic areas, such as in or near the speech centers.

Therapeutic options include surgical resection of the AVM, embolization of the feeding arteries, and radiation-induced thrombosis. In some cases, combinations of these treatments are used. Selective embolization of the lesion using the transfemoral angiographic approach is commonly the initial procedure, with the goal of reducing blood flow through the AVM. Embolization may be done in stages to reduce the size of the lesion sequentially, but endovascular treatment seldom obliterates an AVM. A risk of embolization is that embolic material may escape from the AVM and occlude normal vessels.

Stereotactic radiosurgery can eliminate an AVM but is satisfactory only for small lesions. The therapeutic effect of this technique is delayed because the abnormal vessels shrink gradually after the procedure.

Direct surgical intervention uses microsurgical techniques. If the AVM is large, the procedures are often done in stages to reduce the blood flow in an adjacent region and make subsequent surgery easier. Surgery is considered successful if the postoperative angiogram shows no residual AVM. However, long-term occlusion rates are unknown, and recanalization with recurrent hemorrhage is possible.

PRIMARY INTRACEREBRAL HEMORRHAGE

Primary nontraumatic intracerebral hemorrhage (i.e., hemorrhage that does not result from ischemic injury) occurs predominantly as a consequence of chronic, poorly controlled hypertension (Chapter 63). Less frequently, a ruptured vascular malformation or amyloid angiopathy is responsible. Intracerebral hemorrhage can also be caused by a bleeding diathesis and/or certain drugs of abuse (Table 444–1).

Epidemiology

In the United States, primary intracerebral hemorrhage is responsible for 10 to 15% of strokes and about 80% of all intracranial hemorrhages. The average annual incidence in the United States is approximately 50,000. Intracerebral hemorrhage has the highest mortality rate of all subtypes of stroke, and almost 60% of affected patients die within the first year. The risk for primary intracerebral hemorrhage among blacks is about 40% higher than among whites. Worldwide, the incidence of intracerebral hemorrhage ranges from 10 to 40 per 1 million people, with the rate in Japan being at the top

Table 441–1 • CAUSES, MEANS OF DIAGNOSIS, AND CHARACTERISTICS OF INTRACEREBRAL HEMORRHAGES

CAUSES	PRIMARY MEANS OF DIAGNOSIS	CHARACTERISTICS
Hypertension	Clinical history	Rupture of small arterioles related to degenerative changes induced by uncontrolled hypertension
Amyloid angiopathy	Clinical history	Rupture of small and medium-sized arteries with deposition of β-amyloid protein, manifests as lobar hemorrhages in people >70 years old
Arteriovenous malformation	MRI or angiogram	Rupture of abnormal small vessels connecting arteries and veins
Intracranial aneurysm	MRI or angiogram	Rupture of saccular dilation from a medium-sized artery usually associated with subarachnoid hemorrhage
Cavernous angioma	MRI or angiogram	Rupture of abnormal capillary-like vessels with intermingled connective tissue
Venous angioma	MRI or angiogram	Rupture of abnormal dilation of venules
Venous sinus thrombosis	MRI or angiogram	Result of hemorrhagic venous infarction
Intracranial neoplasm	MRI or angiogram	Result of necrosis and bleeding within hypervascular neoplasms
Coagulopathy	Clinical history	Most commonly associated with use of anticoagulants or thrombolytics
Vasculitis	Serologic and cerebrospinal fluid markers, brain biopsy	Rupture of small or medium-sized arteries with inflammation and degeneration
Cocaine or alcohol abuse	Clinical history	Underlying vascular abnormalities may be present
Hemorrhagic transformation	CT	Hemorrhage in region of cerebral infarction as a result of ischemic damage to blood-brain barrier

Modified from Qureshi AI, Tuhrim S, Broderick JP, et al: Spontaneous intracerebral hemorrhage. N Engl J Med 2001;344:1450–1460.

end of this range. Age-adjusted rates for men are about 50% higher than for women. As with ischemic stroke, the incidence appears to be declining in the industrialized world, concurrent with the decline in hypertension.

Pathobiology

Primary intracerebral hemorrhage typically consists of a large, confluent area of blood that clots (Fig. 441–2). Most bleeding occurs at or near bifurcations of arteries with prominent degeneration of the media and smooth muscles. Several weeks later, the blood is slowly removed by phagocytosis, and after several months, only a small, collapsed cavity lined by hemosiderin-containing macrophages may remain. Rupture into the ventricles with bleeding into the subarachnoid space commonly occurs with large hemorrhages. Edematous parenchyma rapidly develops around the clot. Although hemorrhages may destroy brain tissue locally, histologic examination suggests that displacement of normal brain tissue and dissection of blood along fiber tracts account for much of the pathology. Viable and salvageable neural tissue may exist in the vicinity of the hematoma.

The most important risk factor for intracerebral hemorrhage is hypertension, particularly in people who are younger than 55 years, smokers, and poorly compliant with antihypertensive medications. Excessive chronic alcohol consumption also increases the risk of intracerebral hemorrhage. A less well established risk factor is a low serum cholesterol concentration (<160 mg/dL).

Hypertension is associated with hemorrhage in various locations throughout the brain, especially in the external capsule-putamen, internal capsule-thalamus, central pons, and cerebellum (Fig. 441–3). A smaller number of hemorrhages occur in the subcortical white matter, especially in the frontal, temporal, and occipital lobes.

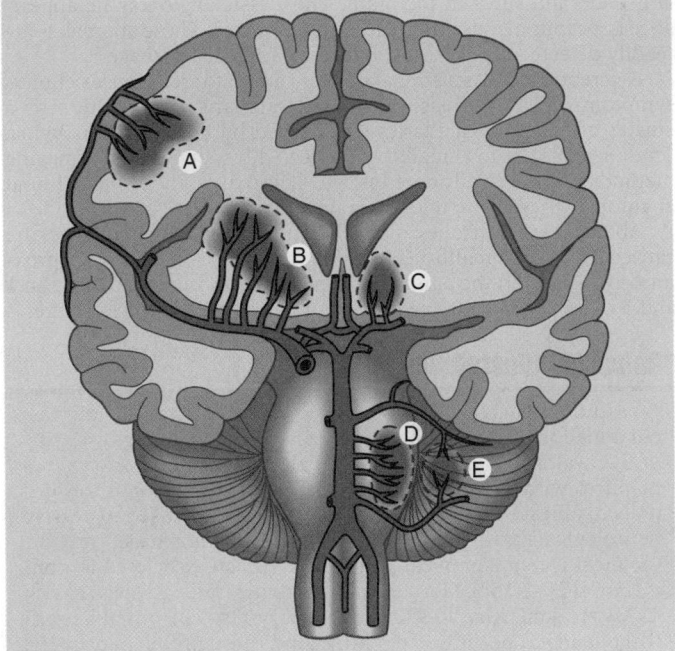

FIGURE 441–3 • Typical sites and sources of intracerebral hemorrhage. Intracerebral hemorrhages most commonly involve cerebral lobes, originating from penetrating cortical branches of the anterior, middle, or posterior cerebral arteries (A); basal ganglia, originating from ascending lenticulostriate branches of the middle cerebral artery (B); the thalamus, originating from ascending thalamogeniculate branches of the posterior cerebral artery (C); the pons, originating from paramedian branches of the basilar artery (D); and the cerebellum, originating from penetrating branches of the posterior inferior, anterior inferior, or superior cerebellar arteries (E). (From Qureshi AI, Tuhrim S, Broderick JP, et al: Spontaneous intracerebral hemorrhage. N Engl J Med 2001;344:1450–1460.)

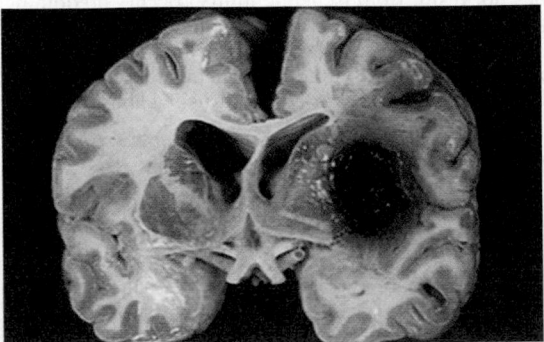

FIGURE 441–2 • Pathology specimen showing a large basal ganglia parenchymal hemorrhage in the left hemisphere. (Courtesy of Gregory W. Albers, Stanford University, Stanford, CA.)

Evidence, especially from serial CT scans, shows that hematomas expand over many hours after the onset of bleeding in many patients. Bleeding may cease when the lesion grows to a sufficient size to produce increased tissue pressure with consequent tamponade.

Amyloid (congophilic) angiopathy is a pathologic diagnosis that is more frequently made for people older than 55 years. This condition, which is unrelated to generalized amyloidosis and is occasionally hereditary, commonly produces multiple, small hemorrhages. It often appears in the brains of patients with Alzheimer's disease (Chapter 433) and has been associated with nonhypertensive hemorrhages in unusual lobar locations in the cerebral hemispheres. Amyloid deposits, chemically similar to those in Alzheimer plaques, are seen in the media and adventitia of medium- and small-sized arteries.

Anticoagulation, thrombolysis, and various hematologic abnormalities (Chapters 177 to 179) are associated with intracerebral hemorrhages. Warfarin anticoagulation to conventional intensities (i.e., international normalized ratio [INR] of 2.5 to 4.5) has been associated with a risk of intracranial hemorrhage of approximately 1% per year for many stroke-prone patients (Chapter 33). This rate is about 7 to 10 times greater than the risk in similar patients who have not undergone anticoagulation. On average, when such hemorrhages occur, the fatality rate is about 60%. Predictors are advanced age, prior ischemic stroke, hypertension, and intensity of anticoagulation.

The most feared complication of thrombolytic therapy for acute myocardial infarction (Chapter 69) or stroke (Chapter 440) is intracerebral hemorrhage. When tissue-type plasminogen activator (tPA) is administered within 3 hours after onset of stroke symptoms, the intracerebral hemorrhage rate is 6.5%, compared with 0.5% in placebo patients; 50% of the patients who sustain these hemorrhages die. However, the overall benefit of tPA therapy in appropriate patients persists because the increased risk of hemorrhage is more than counterbalanced by the improvement in ischemic strokes (Chapter 440).

Cerebral hemorrhages also occur in patients with leukemia (Chapter 193), polycythemia vera (Chapter 176), thrombocytopenia (Chapter 177), hemophilia (Chapter 178) and other clotting abnormalities, infectious and noninfectious vasculitis, intracranial neoplasms, and venous thrombosis. Intracerebral hemorrhage can also occur in patients who abuse various sympathomimetics and cocaine (Chapter 30).

Clinical Manifestations

The neurologic abnormalities caused by intracerebral hemorrhage do not differ from those caused by ischemic strokes (Chapter 440) because destruction of neural tissue is the basis of the neurologic dysfunction caused by both entities. The signs and symptoms are related to the location of the lesion. Because the site of intracerebral hemorrhage often differs from ischemic strokes, characteristic patterns of neurologic loss may be more frequently associated with intracerebral hemorrhage than with ischemic strokes (Table 441-2). Hemorrhages may grow as bleeding continues, whereas ischemic lesions usually do not change in size after vascular occlusion; as a result, hemorrhages characteristically cause progressively increasing loss of neurologic function until a plateau is reached, whereas ischemic strokes may fluctuate or remain static after the early phases of the stroke. Subsequent deterioration in the level of consciousness after an intracerebral hemorrhage occurs in about one fourth of patients who initially are alert.

Intracranial hemorrhages in each of the four typical locations produces characteristic findings. Patients with massive *putaminal hemorrhages* become lethargic or comatose within minutes to hours after onset and concurrently experience contralateral weakness (including the face) with contralateral hemianopsia and gaze paresis (i.e., eyes deviated toward the side of the hemorrhage). *Cerebellar hemorrhages* initially spare the brain stem, and consciousness is usually preserved in the early stages. Occipital headache may be the first symptom. Usual findings are unsteady gait, ataxia, nausea, and vomiting, which is often severe and repetitive. A variety of eye movement abnormalities may be present. Weakness is not prominent at onset, but with progression and brain stem compression, focal or bilateral weakness and coma develop, often rapidly. Further deterioration can result from herniation of cerebellar tissue downward through the foramen magnum or upward across the tentorium; hydrocephalus may be caused by obstruction of CSF flow. With continued bleeding or tissue swelling, severe brain stem damage ensues, causing rapid demise of the patient. Less frequent are *thalamic hemorrhages*, which cause patients to lose consciousness relatively rapidly; those who survive often experience contralateral hemiparesis, sensory deficits, and homonymous hemianopsia. *Pontine hemorrhage* was once thought invariably to produce coma (Chapter 436), but modern imaging detects smaller hemorrhages that are not fatal. In severe pontine hemorrhages, the patients become comatose, usually with very small but detectable reactive pupils. Oculovestibular responses are often lost early, vomiting can occur at onset, and these patients usually have quadriplegia and bilateral extensor posturing. Patients may be "locked-in" (Chapter 436).

Lobar hemorrhages, which are more characteristic of amyloid angiopathy than hypertension, usually originate at the junctions between gray and white matter in the cerebral hemispheres. Such hemorrhages account for about one third of intracerebral hemorrhages and are approximately as common as putaminal hemorrhages. The clinical presentation depends on the location of the hemorrhage. Most patients are elderly because amyloid angiopathy and hypertension are relatively frequent in this age group. Nonspecific symptoms, including headache, nausea, and vomiting, probably occur with about the same frequency but less intensity as in deep, hypertensive hemorrhages. Coma and seizures are uncommon, possibly because most of these hemorrhages are comparatively small and located in subcortical white matter.

Diagnosis

Intracerebral hemorrhage often cannot be distinguished from other types of strokes based on clinical findings alone. The test of choice for making the diagnosis is a noncontrast CT scan (Fig. 441–4) that shows areas of hemorrhage as zones of increased density, which may or may not have associated regions of decreased density indicating infarction. Primary parenchymal hemorrhages typically display homogeneous areas of increased density and a mass effect (i.e., shift of normal tissue from its usual location), whereas hemorrhagic infarctions are characterized by areas of increased density (i.e., blood) interspersed with areas of decreased density (i.e., infarction).

Table 441–2 • CLINICAL FEATURES OF COMMON HYPERTENSIVE HEMORRHAGES

	SITE OF HEMORRHAGE			
CLINICAL	Putaminal	Thalamic	Pontine	Cerebellar
Unconsciousness	Later	Later	Early	Late
Hemiparesis	Yes	Yes	Quadriparesis	Late
Sensory change	Yes	Yes	Yes	Late
Hemianopic	Yes	Yes	No	No
Pupils				
Size	Normal	Small	Small	Normal
Reaction	Yes	Yes or no	Yes or no	Yes
Gaze paresis				
Size	Contralateral, sometimes ipsilateral	Contralateral	Ipsilateral	Ipsilateral
Response to calorics	Yes	Yes	No	Yes or no
Downward eye deviation	Yes	No	No	
Ocular bobbing	No	No	Sometimes	Sometimes
Gait lost	No	No	Yes	Yes
Vomiting	Occasional	Occasional	Often	Severe

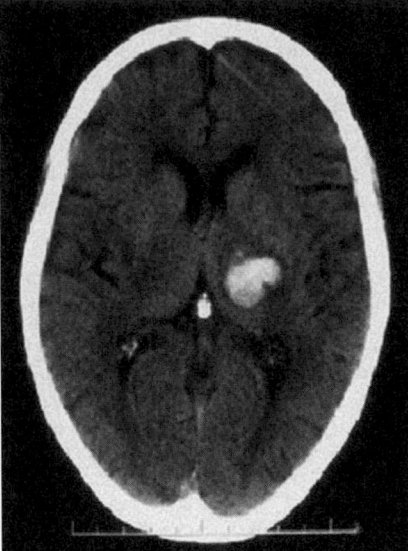

FIGURE 441–4 • Computed tomographic scan shows a parenchymal hemorrhage involving the left thalamus and posterior internal capsule. (Courtesy of Gregory W. Albers, Stanford University, Stanford, CA.)

MRI findings depend on the precise imaging sequence and the age of the hemorrhage. The sensitivity and specificity of MRI for diagnosis of hemorrhage, particularly in the presence of infarct, are unknown. MRI is able to detect small lesions, particularly in the posterior fossa, better than CT scans, but how much of the lesion is hemorrhage or hypoperfusion is uncertain. Cerebral angiography is not needed for the acute evaluation of hemorrhages, but it is commonly used later to identify a suspected aneurysm or AVM that may be considered for intervention.

Rx Treatment

The usual medical management of acute parenchymal hemorrhage is supportive, with initial care being directed at maintenance of airway, oxygenation, nutrition, and prevention and treatment of secondary complications. Small clinical trials of medical therapies, including corticosteroids, glycerol, and hemodilution, have not demonstrated benefit; corticosteroids may increase the risk of infectious complications. Optimal blood pressure treatment is uncertain, although the general guidelines for excessive hypertension and reduction of cerebral perfusion apply as for ischemic strokes (Chapter 440). There is no accepted protocol for the management of increased intracranial pressure; osmotherapy, hyperventilation, and neuromuscular paralysis are not beneficial. Fluid management should maintain euvolemia; fluid restriction or volume expansion is not of proven value. Seizures are particularly harmful for critically ill patients and should be treated despite lack of data from randomized trials. Maintenance of normal body temperature is theoretically desirable because fever may accelerate tissue destruction.

The goal of surgical treatment of intracerebral hemorrhage is to remove as much blood clot as possible as quickly as possible. Ideally, surgery should remove the underlying cause, such as AVM, and prevent hydrocephalus. However, the few, small, randomized studies of surgical removal of intracerebral hemorrhage do not provide a clear rationale for surgical therapy. Patients with cerebellar hemorrhage who are deteriorating neurologically because of brain stem compression and hydrocephalus caused by ventricular obstruction may benefit from removal of the clot or amputation of part of the cerebellum. However, there is no proof that the treatment is indicated because spontaneous recovery can occur in such patients.

Prognosis

In recent series, the 30-day case-fatality rate averaged 30 to 50%. Most early deaths result from the direct neurologic consequences of the hemorrhage; the severity of bleeding (e.g., size, extension into ventricles) and level of neurologic function are the best predictors of poor outcomes. Supratentorial hemorrhages smaller than 30 mL rarely produce death unless they are located in the thalamus. Long-term prognosis for various degrees of recovery is similar or better than that of cerebral infarctions of comparable severity. The risk of recurrent intracerebral hemorrhage has not been well studied, but the risk of at least one rebleed may be as high as 25% over the next several years. The risk of intracerebral hemorrhage can be reduced by appropriate treatment. Control of mild to moderate hypertension decreases the risk of hemorrhagic stroke by one third to one half (Chapter 63).

HYPERTENSIVE ENCEPHALOPATHY

Definition

Hypertensive encephalopathy is usually defined as malignant hypertension associated with central nervous system abnormalities (Chapter 63). Malignant hypertension is commonly defined as sustained, elevated arterial blood pressure, with diastolic levels of 130 mm Hg or greater and systolic pressure in excess of 200 mg Hg. Abnormal funduscopic findings include papilledema, retinal linear hemorrhages, or extravascular cotton-wool exudates. Hypertensive encephalopathy is classically characterized by rapidly evolving severe hypertension associated with headache, nausea, vomiting, visual disturbances, seizures, confusion, stupor, and ultimately, coma. Focal neurologic signs are common.

Pathobiology

The pathogenesis of hypertensive encephalopathy remains unclear. Pathologic findings include purpura in the brain, retinal hemorrhages, papilledema, and fibrinoid arteriolar lesions of the glomeruli. Diffuse fibrinoid necrosis and thrombotic occlusion of arterioles cause microinfarctions and petechial hemorrhages, and these changes lead to distal ischemia. Ring hemorrhage around a thrombosed precapillary is the characteristic microscopic lesion of hypertensive encephalopathy. Multiple, compacted petechiae can resemble a hematoma.

Clinical Manifestations and Diagnosis

Hypertensive encephalopathy is associated with hypertension of any cause and can occur in patients of any age. Severe headache is the most common manifestation. Nausea, vomiting, impaired vision, and dizziness are common. Confusion, stupor, and coma with generalized seizures may develop. Retinal changes characteristic of severe hypertension are common and often include hemorrhages or papilledema, but arteriolar narrowing may be the only abnormality. Because there are no pathognomonic findings in this disorder, it is a diagnosis of exclusion.

Uremic encephalopathy also occurs in patients with renal failure (Chapter 117). Uremia can cause altered mental status and seizures, and the differentiation from hypertensive encephalopathy may be difficult. However, uremia is usually accompanied by metabolic acidosis or water intoxication, which may differentiate it from hypertensive encephalopathy, and correction of the uremia by dialysis may help clarify the picture.

Other complications of hypertension to be considered in the differential diagnosis of hypertensive encephalopathy include hemorrhagic and ischemic strokes. Focal neurologic signs predominate in these other conditions, whereas mental status changes are characteristic of hypertensive encephalopathy. Increased intracranial pressure from obstructive hydrocephalus (Chapter 457), brain tumor (Chapter 457), or subdural hematoma (Chapter 431) can elevate blood pressure and slow the pulse, but encephalopathy and markedly elevated blood pressure are absent.

Neurology

 Treatment

Therapy should be initiated immediately, but the rate of decrease of blood pressure should be controlled to avoid hypotension (Chapter 63). Seizures can usually be stopped with intravenous diazepam; in eclamptic patients (Chapter 253), phenytoin or magnesium sulfate are often used, particularly because they may not depress the respiratory drive of the fetus as much as some other drugs. Prompt delivery of the fetus may be quite helpful.

Grade **A**
1. Allen GS, Ahn HS, Preziosi TJ, et al: Cerebral arterial spasm—a controlled trial of nimodipine in patients with subarachnoid hemorrhage. N Engl J Med 1983;308:619–624.

SUGGESTED READINGS
Bederson JB, Awad IA, Wiebers DO, et al: Recommendations for management of patients with unruptured intracranial aneurysms. Circulation 2000;102:2300–2308. *American Heart Association Scientific Statement guideline using an evidence based approach.*
Broderick JP, Adams HP, Barsan W, et al: Guidelines for management of spontaneous intracerebral hemorrhage. Stroke 1999;30:905–915. *American Heart Association Scientific Statement.*
Molyneux A, Kerr R, Stratton I, et al: International Subarachnoid Aneurysm Trial (ISAT) of neurosurgical clipping versus endovascular coiling in 2143 patients with ruptured intracranial aneurysms: A randomized trial. Lancet 2002;360:1267–1274. *Survival free of disability at 1 year is significantly better with endovascular coiling.*
Qureshi AI, Tuhrim S, Broderick JP, et al: Spontaneous intracerebral hemorrhage. N Engl J Med 2001;344:1450–1460. *Review of this still untreatable disease.*

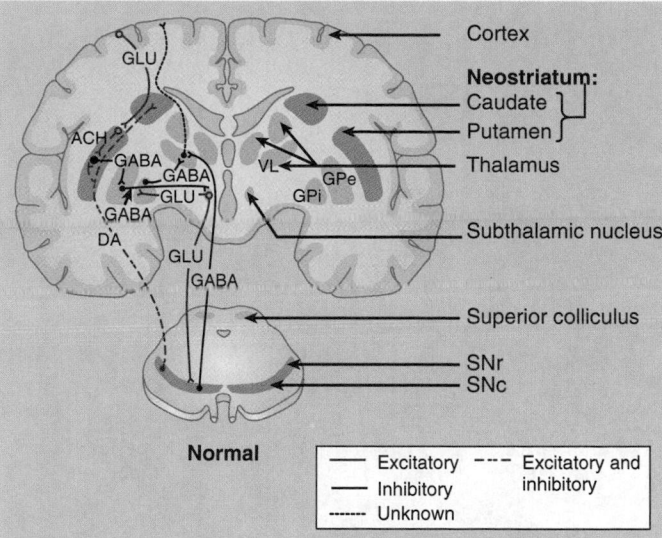

FIGURE 442–1 • Anatomy of the basal ganglia and their connections. ACH = acetylcholine; DA = dopamine; GABA = γ-aminobutyric acid; GLU = glutamate; GP = globus pallidum (e = external, i = internal); SN = substantia nigra (c = compacta, r = reticulata); VL = ventrolateral.

442 EXTRAPYRAMIDAL DISORDERS

Joseph Jankovic

The term *extrapyramidal* refers to the anatomic and functional characteristics that distinguish the basal ganglia-regulated motor system from the pyramidal (corticospinal) and cerebellar systems. Extrapyramidal movement disorders are descriptively divided into *hypokinesias,* characterized by poverty and slowness of movement; *hyperkinesias,* manifested by abnormal involuntary movements; and miscellaneous motor disturbances (Table 442–1).

FUNCTIONAL AND NEUROCHEMICAL ANATOMY OF THE BASAL GANGLIA

The six paired nuclei that constitute the basal ganglia include the caudate nucleus, putamen, globus pallidus (or pallidum), nucleus accumbens, subthalamic nucleus, and substantia nigra (Fig. 442–1). The caudate nucleus and putamen, although separated by the internal capsule, share cytoarchitectonic, chemical, and physiologic properties; they are often referred to as the *corpus striatum,* neostriatum, or striatum. The striatum is a highly inhomogeneous structure composed of subregions called striosomes and matrix. The limbic system provides major input to the striosomes, whereas neocortical areas primarily project to the matrix. Although the internal capsule separates the internal segment of the globus pallidus and the pars reticulata of the substantia nigra, evidence suggests that these nuclei should also

be regarded as a single functional structure. The term *lenticular nucleus* refers to the putamen and globus pallidus combined because of their lenslike shape.

Anatomic and physiologic data suggest a complex organization of the basal ganglia and related structures (see Fig. 442–1). According to this scheme, the sensorimotor, association, and limbic cortical areas provide anatomically and functionally segregated input to the dorsal (caudate and putamen) and ventral (nucleus accumbens, not shown) striatum. The somatosensory, motor, and premotor cortical areas project mainly to the putamen, and the posterior parietal and temporal and frontal association cortical areas project largely to the caudate and nucleus accumbens. The anatomy is consistent with the concept that the putamen is primarily concerned with motor function and the caudate is more involved with emotional and cognitive processes. The corticostriatal afferents are mediated by the excitatory neurotransmitter glutamic acid. The other major striatal afferents originate in the substantia nigra pars compacta, which provides major dopaminergic inhibitory input to the basal ganglia through the nigrostriatal pathway. Other inputs to the striatum arise from the brain stem raphe nuclei (serotonergic) and from the locus ceruleus neurons (noradrenergic). The striatum is composed largely of cholinergic neurons, and some excitatory cholinergic projections to the striatum originate in the midline intralaminar thalamic nuclei.

The striatal nuclei project somatotopically to the external and internal segments of the globus pallidus and the pars reticulata of the substantia nigra complex. The striatal efferents use the inhibitory neurotransmitter γ-aminobutyric acid (GABA). The subthalamic nucleus regulates the output of the basal ganglia to the thalamus by modulating the inhibitory GABAergic afferents from the external segment of the globus pallidus and the excitatory glutamatergic efferent projections to the globus pallidus (internal segment)–substantia nigra pars reticulata complex. The efferent inhibitory GABAergic projections from the internal segment of the globus pallidus terminate in the thalamus. The thalamic nuclei project to the supplementary motor area of the cortex and the primary motor cortex.

MOVEMENT DISORDERS

Single-cell recordings in behaving animals and other studies have demonstrated that one of the primary roles of the basal ganglia is to scale movement amplitude and velocity rather than initiate movements. Besides their crucial role in the execution of movement, the basal ganglia also seem to be involved in the preparation for movement.

In addition to impaired voluntary movements, dysfunction in the basal ganglia can cause a variety of abnormal involuntary movements.

Table 442–1 • MOVEMENT DISORDERS

HYPOKINESIAS	HYPERKINESIAS	MISCELLANEOUS
Parkinsonism	Tremor	Ataxia
Hypomimia	Dystonia	Gait disorders
Dysarthria	Chorea	Hyperexplexia
Sialorrhea	Athetosis	Hemifacial spasm
Micrographia	Ballism	Myokymia
Shuffling gait	Tics	Stiff-person syndrome
Other signs of	Myoclonus	Psychogenic
bradykinesia	Stereotypy	
and rigidity	Akathisia	
	Restless legs	
	Paroxysmal dyskinesias	

Neurology

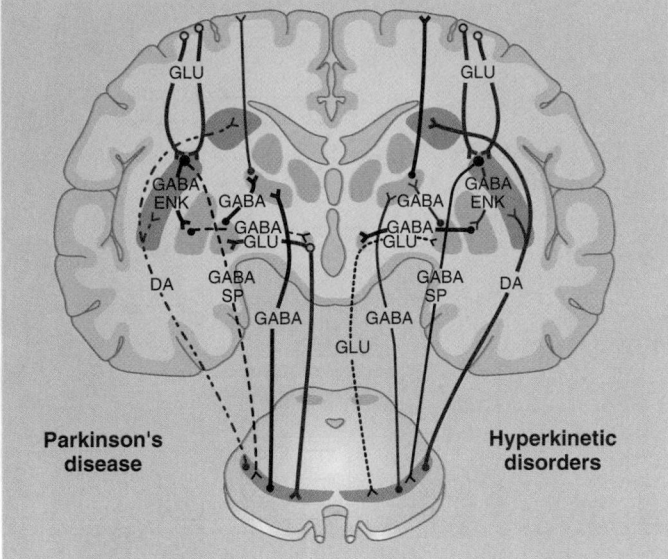

Parkinson's disease

Hyperkinetic disorders

FIGURE 442–2 • Functional organization of the basal ganglia in parkinsonian disorders and hyperkinetic movement disorders. DA = dopamine; ENK = enkephalin; GABA = γ-aminobutyric acid; GLU = glutamate; SP = substance P.

Correlations between the various types of abnormal movement and sites of experimental and pathologic lesions have provided a better understanding of the function of the basal ganglia.

HYPOKINESIAS (PARKINSONIAN DISORDERS). Bradykinesia is clinically manifested by slowness of automatic and spontaneous movements and an impaired ability to initiate voluntary movements (i.e., akinesia). This typical parkinsonian symptom presumably results from loss of the inhibitory dopamine input to the striatum and hypoactivity of the neurons in the external segment of the globus pallidus. This process causes functional disinhibition (i.e., excitation) of the subthalamic nucleus, which induces an increase in neuronal activity in the internal segment of the globus pallidus, thereby raising the tonic inhibitory output from the basal ganglia (i.e., internal segment of the globus pallidus) to the thalamus and to the cortical projection areas (Fig. 442–2). The altered activity in the "motor" circuit is manifested by increased movement time, which becomes particularly prolonged when a parkinsonian patient performs sequential movements.

Rigidity, another cardinal sign of parkinsonism, is demonstrated clinically by increased resistance against passive movement of a body part, usually associated with the cogwheel phenomenon. A parkinsonian patient perceives rigidity as a feeling of joint stiffness and muscle tightness. The pathophysiologic mechanisms of rigidity have been attributed to pallidal disinhibition resulting in increased suprasegmental activation of normal spinal reflex mechanisms.

Postural instability resulting from loss of righting reflexes can cause propulsion (i.e., tendency to fall forward) and retropulsion (i.e., tendency to fall backward). Along with freezing, manifested by sudden inability to move as if the feet are "glued" to the floor, loss of righting reflexes is one of the most disabling symptoms of Parkinson's disease.

HYPERKINESIAS (ABNORMAL INVOLUNTARY MOVEMENTS). Tremor is a rhythmic oscillatory movement produced by alternating or synchronous contractions of opposing muscle groups. Tremors are divided into rest or action tremors; the latter are further subdivided into postural or contraction tremors (e.g., arms outstretched in front of the body or in a "wing-beating" position) and kinetic or intention tremors (e.g., during target-directed movement, such as the finger-to-nose maneuver). *Rest tremor,* usually asymmetrical at onset, is the typical tremor of Parkinson's disease. When it involves the hands, it causes a supinating-pronating oscillatory (pill-rolling) movement at a frequency of approximately 4 to 6 Hz. Parkinsonian tremor also often involves the legs, feet, lips, tongue, chin, and voice but almost never affects the head or neck. *Postural tremor,* with frequency ranging between 4 and 12 Hz, is most typically seen in patients

with essential tremor. *Kinetic (intention) tremors* are slow and more irregular movements with a rate of 1.5 to 3 Hz. Kinetic tremors usually indicate an abnormality of the cerebellum or its outflow pathways (i.e., dentate nucleus, superior cerebellar peduncle, and contralateral red nucleus).

Dystonia is produced by involuntary, sustained (tonic) or spasmodic (rapid or clonic), patterned (i.e., involving the same muscle group), and repetitive muscle contractions, frequently causing twisting (e.g., torticollis, involuntary turning of the head), flexing or extending (e.g., retrocollis, an involuntary neck extension), and squeezing (e.g., blepharospasm, writer's cramp) movements or abnormal postures. Dystonia is usually continuous but occurs in some cases only during particular activities or tasks. Examples of task-specific dystonias include writer's or typist's cramp and inversion of a foot while running. As dystonia progresses, the involuntary contractions also appear at rest. A characteristic feature of dystonia is that the spasms lessen in intensity with "sensory tricks" such as touching one side of the face to maintain a primary position, thereby counteracting involuntary torticollis. Dystonia can fluctuate in intensity and is exacerbated by stress, fatigue, activity, or a change in posture. It subsides during sleep, relaxation, and hypnosis. These features and the bizarre nature of dystonic patterns are sometimes wrongly attributed to psychogenic causes. About one third of patients with dystonia have a coexistent postural tremor, identical to essential tremor. The anatomic substrate for dystonia is unknown, but clinicopathologic studies of patients with secondary dystonias most often implicate the putamen, because lesions in this nucleus are sometimes associated with dystonia.

Chorea consists of continuous, abrupt, rapid, brief, flowing, unsustained, irregular, and random jerklike movements. Choreic patients frequently mask the abnormal movements by voluntary semipurposeful activities. A characteristic feature of chorea is the inability to maintain voluntary, sustained contraction. Examples of such impersistence include an inability to sustain manual grip or tongue protrusion and the dropping of objects. Muscle stretch reflexes are usually "hung up" and "pendular." Affected patients typically have a peculiar irregular and dancelike gait. The pathogenesis of chorea is unknown. Some findings point to abnormalities in caudate function. A selective loss of the GABA-enkephalin striatal neurons projecting to the external segment of the globus pallidus, found in Huntington's disease, results in excessive inhibition of subthalamic nucleus neurons.

SUGGESTED READINGS

Jankovic J, Tolosa E (eds): Parkinson's Disease and Movement Disorders. Philadelphia, Lippincott Williams & Wilkins, 2002. *A comprehensive review of hypokinetic, hyperkinetic, and miscellaneous movement disorders.*

Mink JW: Neurobiology of basal ganglia circuits in Tourette syndrome: Faulty inhibition of unwanted motor patterns? Adv Neurol 2001;85:113–122. *An excellent review of functional anatomy of the basal ganglia and its role in control of involuntary movement and behaviors.*

443 PARKINSONISM

Joseph Jankovic

Parkinsonism is a clinical syndrome dominated by four cardinal signs: tremor at rest, bradykinesia, rigidity, and postural instability. Less prominent manifestations concern the mood and intellect, autonomic function, and the sensory system (Table 443–1). The average age at onset is 55 years, with about 1% of persons 60 years or older having the disease. Men are affected more frequently than women by a ratio of 3 : 2. At least two major subtypes of Parkinson's disease have been identified: One subtype is characterized by tremor as the dominant parkinsonian feature, and the other is dominated by postural instability and gait difficulty. The *tremor subtype* is associated with relatively normal mental status, earlier age at onset, and slower progression of the disease than is the *postural instability/gait difficulty subtype,* which shows more bradykinesia, dementia, and a more rapidly progressive course.

Resting tremor and bradykinesia are the most typical parkinsonian signs and are virtually synonymous with the diagnosis. Bradykinesia accounts for most of the associated parkinsonian symptoms and signs: general slowing of movements and activities of daily living, lack of

Table 443–1 • NONMOTOR DISTURBANCE IN PARKINSON'S DISEASE

NEUROBEHAVIORAL ABNORMALITIES
Personality changes (apathy, lack of confidence, fearfulness, anxiety, emotional lability and inflexibility, social withdrawal, dependency)
Dementia (tip-of-the-tongue phenomenon [partial anomia], spatial disorientation, paranoia, psychosis, hallucinations)
Bradyphrenia (slow thought processes, loss of concentration, difficulty with concept formation)
　Depression
　Sleep disturbance
　Sexual dysfunction
　Psychiatric side effects of therapy

OTHER NONMOTOR MANIFESTATIONS
Autonomic dysfunction (orthostatic hypotension, respiratory dysregulation, flushing, "drenching sweats," constipation, sphincter and sexual dysfunction)
Sensory symptoms (paresthesias, pains, akathisia; visual, olfactory, and vestibular dysfunction)
Seborrhea, pedal edema, fatigue, weight loss

facial expression (hypomimia or masked facies), staring expression resulting from a decreased frequency of blinking, impaired swallowing causing drooling (sialorrhea), hypokinetic and hypophonic dysarthria, monotonous speech, small handwriting (micrographia), difficulties with repetitive and simultaneous movements, difficulty in arising from a chair and turning over in bed, shuffling gait with short steps, decreased arm swing and other automatic movements, difficulty in initiating movements, and freezing of motion. Freezing, manifested by a sudden, often unpredictable inability to move, is one of the most disabling of all parkinsonian symptoms.

Several disorders other than Parkinson's disease can cause at least part of the parkinsonian syndrome (Table 443–2) but can be distinguished clinically by the presence of atypical findings, absence or

Table 443–2 • CAUSES OF PARKINSON SYNDROME

PRIMARY (IDIOPATHIC) PARKINSONISM
Parkinson's disease
Juvenile parkinsonism

SECONDARY (ACQUIRED, SYMPTOMATIC) PARKINSONISM
Infectious: postencephalitic, slow virus
Drugs: neuroleptics (antipsychotic, antiemetic drugs), reserpine, tetrabenazine, α-methyldopa, lithium, flunarizine, cinnarizine
Toxins: MPTP, CO, Mn, Hg, CS$_2$, methanol, ethanol
Vascular: multi-infarct, hypotensive shock
Trauma: pugilistic encephalopathy
Other: parathyroid abnormalities, hypothyroidism, hepatocerebral degeneration, brain tumor, normal-pressure hydrocephalus, syringomesencephalia

HEREDODEGENERATIVE PARKINSONISM
Autosomal dominant Lewy body disease
Huntington's disease
Wilson's disease
Hallervorden-Spatz disease
Olivopontocerebellar and spinocerebellar atrophy
Familial basal ganglia calcification
Familial parkinsonism with peripheral neuropathy
Neuroacanthocytosis

MULTIPLE-SYSTEM DEGENERATION (PARKINSONISM-PLUS)
Progressive supranuclear palsy
Multiple-system atrophy
Shy-Drager syndrome
Striatonigral degeneration
Olivopontocerebellar atrophy
Parkinsonism-dementia-ALS complex
Corticobasal ganglionic degeneration
Alzheimer's disease
Hemiatrophy-parkinsonism

　ALS = amyotrophic lateral sclerosis; MPTP = 1-methyl-4-phenyl-1,2,3,6-tetrahydropyridine.

paucity of tremor, and poor response to levodopa. The last feature may be explained partly by the fact that postsynaptic dopamine receptors are preserved in Parkinson's disease but decreased in the other parkinsonian syndromes.

PARKINSON'S DISEASE

Pathogenesis

The most typical pathologic hallmarks of Parkinson's disease are neuronal loss with depigmentation of the substantia nigra and the presence of Lewy bodies, which are eosinophilic cytoplasmic inclusions in neurons consisting of aggregates of normal and abnormal proteins. These abnormalities are most prominent in the ventrolateral region of the substantia nigra that projects to the putamen. At least a 60% loss of dopaminergic neurons in the substantia nigra and the same degree of dopamine depletion in the striatum must appear before the clinical symptoms of Parkinson's disease become evident.

Motor symptoms result chiefly from degeneration of the nigrostriatal pathway, which causes a deficiency of dopamine in the putamen and, to a lesser degree, the caudate nucleus. The cognitive deficits and some neurobehavioral symptoms have been attributed to degeneration of the dopaminergic mesocortical and mesolimbic pathways, and the associated autonomic dysfunction may be caused partly by dopamine depletion in the hypothalamus and neurodegeneration of some brain stem nuclei. Besides dopamine deficiency, impairment of the other neurotransmitters may be responsible for some of the associated findings. Degeneration of the noradrenergic locus caeruleus may contribute to some of the autonomic symptoms and depression. Degeneration of the cholinergic nucleus basalis probably relates to the dementia that eventually affects about a third of all patients with Parkinson's disease.

Although several hypotheses currently are being investigated, the cause of Parkinson's disease is still unknown. Genetic factors play an important role, and two mutations have been identified in the gene coding for α-synuclein on chromosome 4q in families with autosomal dominant Parkinson's disease. Abnormal folding of this protein leads to impaired cellular processing (ubiquitination) and results in the aggregation and deposition in the cytoplasmic inclusions called *Lewy bodies*. Following the identification of mutations in the gene coding for α-synuclein (PARK1), several other gene mutations have been found to cause disorders similar to Parkinson's disease, including mutations in the gene called *Parkin* on chromosome 6q25.2-27 in patients with an autosomal recessive, young-onset, levodopa-responsive form of parkinsonism. This mutation may be responsible for 40% of patients with juvenile Parkinson's disease. Another gene locus for Parkinson's disease has been found on chromosome 2p13 (PARK3). Although some members of the kindreds had prominent dementia, the autopsy in some cases confirmed the typical pathologic features of Parkinson's disease. An autosomal dominant, levodopa-responsive, Lewy body parkinsonism with tremor similar to essential tremor also has been linked to a locus on chromosome 4p15.7 (PARK4). Further evidence that an impairment of normal protein degradation is an important mechanism of neurodegeneration in Parkinson's disease is the finding of a mutation in the deubiquinating enzyme ubiquitin carboxy-terminal hydrolase L1 (UCH-L1) gene on 4p14 (PARK5). Two gene loci on chromosome 1 have been found to be associated with autosomal recessive, early-onset parkinsonism: 1p35-36 (PARK6) and 1p36 (PARK7). It is likely that other gene mutations will be found in the near future.

The "environmental" hypothesis of Parkinson's disease is based primarily on the observation that the meperidine analogue 1-methyl-4-phenyl-1,2,3,6-tetrahydropyridine (MPTP), originally used by heroin addicts, causes parkinsonism in humans and in animals. MPTP must be oxidized to a pyridine MPP$^+$ species to be neurotoxic, and antioxidants such as deprenyl (a selective monoamine oxidase B inhibitor) prevent MPTP-induced experimental parkinsonism. As a result, it has been postulated that some environmental MPTP-like toxin might be responsible for human Parkinson's disease. An alternative hypothesis is that an endogenous toxin such as dopamine damages susceptible neurons. During the process of oxidative deamination, dopamine generates hydroxyl radicals and hydrogen peroxide, which in the presence of iron deposits in the brain could lead to lipid peroxidation and neurotoxicity, possibly by interfering with mitochondrial oxidative metabolism.

The finding that selegiline (deprenyl) prevents MPTP-induced parkinsonism stimulated interest in antioxidative therapy as a means of retarding the progression of Parkinson's disease. Although clinical trials have provided little evidence that selegiline is neuroprotective, it does delay the need for levodopa, and as such it often is used as the initial medication before symptoms become troublesome. Addition of one of the anticholinergic drugs, such as trihexyphenidyl or amantadine, may provide further symptomatic relief, particularly in younger patients and patients in whom tremor predominates. Associated depression, present in many parkinsonian patients, can be treated with tricyclic antidepressants or serotonin uptake inhibitors. Anticholinergics, including the tricyclics, can produce undesirable cognitive changes, however, and other side effects, such as dry mouth, blurring of vision, and urinary hesitancy, particularly in elderly patients. Amantadine also can cause adverse effects, including livedo reticularis, ankle edema, exacerbation of heart failure, and mild anticholinergic side effects. Although helpful in controlling tremor and bradykinesia, amantadine's beneficial effects may wane after a few months.

Many neurologists favor the use of combinations of selegiline (deprenyl), anticholinergics, and amantadine until they no longer provide satisfactory control of parkinsonian symptoms. At that point, many authorities believe that dopamine agonists, which stimulate dopamine receptors directly, should be used as the initial dopaminergic therapy. When used as monotherapy, dopamine agonists provide only modest improvement in parkinsonian symptoms, but the improvement may be sufficient to delay the introduction of levodopa by several months or years and delay the onset of levodopa-related complications (see later). Support also is growing for the notion that dopamine agonists have a neuroprotective effect. This concept is suggested by the following observations: (1) By stimulating dopamine autoreceptors, dopamine agonists presumably decrease dopamine turnover and reduce oxidative stress; (2) dopamine agonists have been shown to scavenge hydroxyl, superoxide, and nitric oxide radicals and induce upregulation of the free radical scavenging enzyme superoxide dismutase; (3) certain dopamine agonists enhance the growth and survival of cultured dopaminergic neurons; and (4) dopamine agonists exert a levodopa-sparing effect. Because levodopa "primes" for the development of dyskinesia, the use of dopamine agonists before levodopa seems to be a prudent practice. As symptoms increase, dopamine agonists must be combined with levodopa.

In 1997, three new dopamine agonists, cabergoline, pramipexole, and ropinirole, were added to bromocriptine and pergolide. Cabergoline, a potent D_2-agonist with a half-life of about 65 hours, has not been approved for the treatment of Parkinson's disease in the United States. Pramipexole differs from ergot dopamine agonists, such as bromocriptine and pergolide, by its preferential affinity for the D_3-receptor subtype. In contrast, ropinirole is a relatively pure D_2-receptor agonist. The nonergoline structure of the new agonists pramipexole and ropinirole may have a potential advantage in their side-effect profile in that the new drugs seem to be associated with a lower risk for complications such as peptic ulcer disease, vasoconstrictive effects, erythromelalgia, and pulmonary and retroperitoneal fibrosis. Similar to the earlier dopamine agonists pergolide and bromocriptine, the new dopamine agonists may cause nausea, vomiting, anorexia, malaise, orthostatic hypotension, and psychiatric reactions, particularly hallucinations, and they may exacerbate levodopa-induced dyskinesias. Not only have dopamine agonists been found to have beneficial symptomatic effects in the treatment of early Parkinson's disease, but also these drugs smooth out the motor fluctuations associated with long-term levodopa therapy. No comparative trials have been performed to determine which of the dopamine agonists have the best efficacy-to-adverse effects ratio. When patients continue to be troubled by parkinsonian symptoms despite selegiline (deprenyl), anticholinergics, amantadine, and a dopamine agonist, levodopa combined with carbidopa, a peripheral dopa decarboxylase inhibitor, is added to the antiparkinsonian regimen. The starting dosage of carbidopa/levodopa is 25 mg/100 mg (controlled release) twice daily, gradually increased to three times per day. The dosage is adjusted, depending on the severity of symptoms and occupational demands. Some patients require 25 mg/250 mg four or five times daily; others tolerate only smaller doses. Although levodopa can suppress tremor, it is most useful in controlling bradykinesia and rigidity. Postural instability may be ameliorated by levodopa early in Parkinson's disease, but not in advanced stages. Levodopa should be used with caution in patients with prominent psychosis or dementia, peptic ulcer disease, and cardiac arrhythmias.

About 15% of parkinsonian patients fail to improve with levodopa from the onset of therapy. Most of these nonresponders probably have a form of postsynaptic parkinsonism rather than true Parkinson's disease. Failure to respond to levodopa also should suggest the possibility of a wrong diagnosis; drug interaction (concomitant use of dopamine receptor blocking agents, such as antipsychotic and antiemetic drugs); and pharmacokinetic issues, such as insufficient dosage, slow stomach emptying, and competition for absorption in the small intestine and at the blood-brain barrier by amino acids in protein meals. Almost all patients who initially improve begin to experience levodopa-related complications 3 to 8 years after onset.

Patients with Parkinson's disease lose their response to levodopa because of the natural progression of the disease and the development of complications as a result of long-term levodopa therapy. Although non-neuronal elements may participate in the conversion of levodopa to dopamine, the surviving striatal dopaminergic terminals progressively lose their capacity for conversion of levodopa to dopamine, and motor fluctuations and symptomatic deterioration subsequently develop. The postsynaptic dopamine receptors also seem to play an important role in the pathogenesis of motor fluctuations.

The most challenging problem in managing Parkinson's disease is treating the complications of levodopa. Thanks to carbidopa and similar agents, gastrointestinal side effects, chiefly nausea and vomiting, are seldom troublesome. The most common central side effects of levodopa therapy include psychiatric problems; dyskinesias (seen in about 30% of patients after 2 years of therapy) manifested by abnormal involuntary movements, such as chorea, stereotypy, or dystonia; and clinical fluctuations (seen in about 50% of patients after 2 years of therapy). The most common form of clinical fluctuation is the wearing-off effect, characterized by end-of-dose deterioration and recurrence of parkinsonian symptoms as a result of shorter (sometimes only 1 to 2 hours) duration of benefit after a given dose of levodopa. Slow-release preparations of levodopa (e.g., Sinemet CR, Madopar CR) prolong the plasma (and presumably brain) levels and may be useful in treating or preventing motor fluctuations.

Another strategy designed to prolong levodopa response takes advantage of the inhibition of catechol-O-methyl transferase (COMT) by drugs such as entacapone. Entacapone (200 mg) should be taken with each dose of levodopa (up to eight times per day). The COMT inhibitors prolong the "on" time, but the dosage of levodopa usually has to be reduced to minimize the risk of increased dyskinesias.

Because the onset of levodopa-induced complications seems to be related to the duration of levodopa therapy (and to the loss of dopaminergic striatal terminals), most authorities delay initiating levodopa therapy until the patient's symptoms begin to interfere with normal activities. When levodopa treatment is initiated, the dose should be maintained as low as possible (Fig. 443–1).

The renewed interest in surgical treatment of Parkinson's disease has been stimulated in part by improved understanding of the functional anatomy underlying motor control and refinement of methods and techniques in neurosurgery, neuroradiology, and neurophysiology. Stereotactic thalamotomy still is used occasionally in an attempt to ameliorate disabling tremor. This traditional procedure is being replaced by pallidotomy and high-frequency deep brain stimulation, with the stimulating electrode stereotactically implanted in one of the three target nuclei: thalamus, subthalamic nucleus, or globus pallidus (internal segment). The ablative and the stimulating procedures have been found to be particularly effective in smoothing out motor fluctuations and eliminating levodopa-induced dyskinesias. Deep brain stimulation of the subthalamic nucleus permits a marked reduction in daily levodopa dose. Surgical transplantation of fetal substantia nigra into the striatum remains under investigation, although the results from a double-blind controlled trial have not been encouraging.

As with all progressive, disabling diseases, psychological support of patients and families is important. Patients should be encouraged to learn about their disease (by reading educational material provided by national and local support organizations) and, above all, to remain physically and socially active.

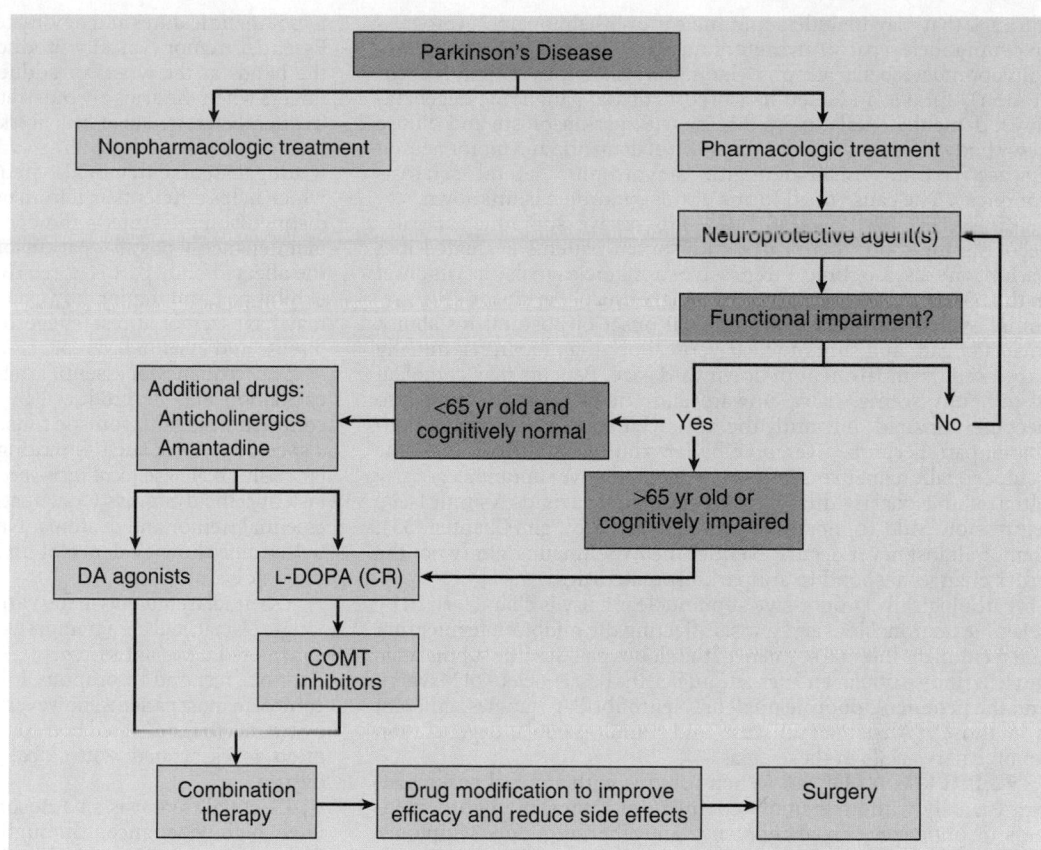

FIGURE 443–1 • Diagrammatic representation of a therapeutic approach to patients with parkinsonism. COMT = catechol-*O*-methyl transferase; CR = controlled release; DA = dopamine.

SECONDARY PARKINSONISM

POSTENCEPHALITIC PARKINSONISM. A variety of movement disorders, including parkinsonism, later developed in many individuals who survived the acute febrile illness and encephalopathy during the pandemics of encephalitis lethargica (von Economo's encephalitis) between 1919 and 1926. Although the virus or viruses responsible for encephalitis lethargica were never isolated, infections caused by coxsackie, Japanese B, and western equine encephalitis viruses have since been identified as being complicated by parkinsonism. In general, postencephalitic parkinsonism has a slower progression and is more sensitive to levodopa therapy.

DRUG-INDUCED PARKINSONISM. Drugs that deplete the presynaptic stores of dopamine, such as reserpine and tetrabenazine (an investigational drug not available for general use in North America), and drugs that block dopamine receptors, such as antipsychotic and antiemetic agents, can cause a parkinsonian syndrome clinically indistinguishable from idiopathic parkinsonism. The same drugs also can cause a variety of other movement disorders, such as akathisia, dystonic reactions, and various tardive syndromes (e.g., tardive stereotypy, tardive dystonia, and tardive akathisia).

VASCULAR PARKINSONISM. Cerebrovascular disease accounts for only a small proportion of parkinsonism. Single strokes rarely cause parkinsonian findings, although multiple small infarctions involving the striatum can produce the syndrome. Brain imaging is helpful in the diagnosis. One form of vascular parkinsonism is the so-called lower body parkinsonism, manifested chiefly by gait disturbance with short steps, "freezing," and difficulties turning. Chronic communicating, "low-pressure" hydrocephalus causes a similar clinical picture. Patients with vascular parkinsonism may have dementia, hyperactive reflexes, and urinary incontinence, but tremor is rare. Levodopa therapy usually fails, probably because ischemia damages the striatal postsynaptic receptors. The diagnosis is suggested by these atypical findings in patients with a history of stroke risk factors.

HEREDODEGENERATIVE PARKINSONISM

Few parkinsonian patients have a family history suggesting a specific pattern of inheritance. With such a history, the differential diagnosis should include one of the heredodegenerative disorders (Table 443–2).

HALLERVORDEN-SPATZ DISEASE. This rare condition is manifested by childhood-onset or adult-onset progressive dementia, bradykinesia, rigidity, and spasticity, variously combined with dystonia, choreoathetosis, ataxia, seizures, amyotrophy, and retinitis pigmentosa. Most reported cases have suggested an autosomal recessive inheritance. Magnetic resonance imaging of patients with Hallervorden-Spatz disease shows marked hypointensity on T2-weighted images in the internal segment of the globus pallidus and the pars reticulata of the substantia nigra. Typically, but not always, a central spot of hypointensity surrounded by a circumscribed region of hyperintensity gives the appearance of an "eye of the tiger." These magnetic resonance imaging changes indicate heavy iron deposition. The disorder also is referred to as "neurodegeneration with brain iron accumulation type 1" and, since the discovery of a gene mutation on chromosome 20p12.3-p13, "pantothenate kinase associated neurodegeneration."

FAMILIAL BASAL GANGLIA CALCIFICATIONS. Calcium may accumulate in the basal ganglia in association with hypoparathyroidism or as a result of a familial disorder, sometimes called *Fahr's disease*. Affected patients exhibit parkinsonism, chorea, dementia, and palilalia. Brain imaging may detect basal ganglia calcification in clinically unaffected relatives.

OLIVOPONTOCEREBELLAR AND SPINOCEREBELLAR ATROPHY. The combination of parkinsonism and cerebellar ataxia characterizes olivopontocerebellar degeneration or atrophy, a heterogeneous group of neurodegenerative disorders most often inherited in an autosomal dominant pattern, but occasionally occurring sporadically. In addition to the parkinsonism-ataxia complex, patients with olivopontocerebellar atrophy often exhibit marked dysarthria, neuro-ophthalmologic signs, and a variable degree of upper and lower motor neuron signs (Chapter 437).

MULTIPLE-SYSTEM DEGENERATION (PARKINSONISM-PLUS)

Approximately 10 to 15% of all patients with parkinsonian findings have a more widespread disorder classified clinically as "parkinsonism-plus syndrome" and pathologically as multiple-system degeneration. Besides parkinsonism, these patients have additional findings that may include supranuclear ophthalmoparesis (progressive supranuclear palsy), dysautonomia (Shy-Drager syndrome), ataxia (olivopontocerebellar atrophy), laryngeal stridor (striatonigral degeneration), apraxia and alien hand (corticobasal ganglionic degeneration), dementia (Alzheimer's disease with parkinsonism and diffuse Lewy body disease), and a combination of dementia and motor neuron disease (parkinsonism–dementia–amyotrophic lateral sclerosis complex). The cause of all forms of this syndrome is unknown.

PROGRESSIVE SUPRANUCLEAR PALSY. Progressive supranuclear palsy accounts for about 8% of all parkinsonian patients evaluated in a Parkinson's disease clinic. Progressive supranuclear palsy has its onset in the 60s, about 10 years after the usual onset of Parkinson's disease. Initial symptoms consist of a gradual onset of postural instability, unsteady gait, and supranuclear vertical ophthalmoparesis, initially expressed by impairment in downward gaze. Patients may complain of difficulty seeing. Later, upward and lateral conjugate gaze also become impaired, but until the advanced stage, the external ophthalmoparesis can be overcome by labyrinthine stimulation via the oculocephalic maneuver. Patients with progressive supranuclear palsy often exhibit axial rigidity, nuchal dystonia, and a rigid-dystonic facial expression. Mild-to-moderate dementia is a late sign (Chapter 433); tremor almost never occurs. Neither the hypokinetic rigidity nor the other changes respond to antiparkinsonian drugs.

Pathologically, progressive supranuclear palsy is characterized by selective neuronal loss and gliosis affecting the midbrain tegmentum and tectum, the internal segment of the globus pallidus, the subthalamic nucleus, the vestibular and dentate nuclei, the basal nucleus of Meynert, and the pedunculopontine nucleus. Neurofibrillary tangles, different from those in Alzheimer's disease, and granulovacuolar degeneration involve nerve cells in these areas.

MULTIPLE SYSTEM ATROPHY. When patients with atypical parkinsonism (usually without tremor) complain of orthostatic lightheadedness, incontinence, sexual impotence, and other autonomic symptoms, the diagnosis of multiple system atrophy (formerly Shy-Drager syndrome) should be considered (Chapter 460).

SUGGESTED READINGS

Albers DS, Augood SJ: New insights into progressive supranuclear palsy. Trends Neurosci 2001;24:347–353. *Review of current notions about progressive supranuclear palsy, the second most common cause of parkinsonism.*

Freed CR, Greene PE, Breeze RE, et al: Transplantation of embryonic dopamine neurons for severe Parkinson's disease. N Engl J Med 2001;344:710–719. *The transplanted cells survived and produced some benefit in younger but not older patients.*

Gasser T, Bressman S, Durr A, et al: State of the art review: Molecular diagnosis of inherited movement disorders. Movement Disorders Society task force on molecular diagnosis. Mov Disord 2003;18:3–18. *A review of clinical and genetic features of parkinsonian and other movement disorders.*

Jankovic J: Surgery for Parkinson's disease and other movement disorders: Benefits and limitations of ablation, stimulation, restoration, and radiation. Arch Neurol 2001;58:1970–1972. *Critical review of the various surgical interventions.*

Jankovic J, Kapadia AS: Functional decline in Parkinson's disease. Arch Neurol 2001;58:1611–1615. *A longitudinal study showing that tremor-dominant disease progresses at a slower rate than disease manifested clinically by gait and postural instability.*

McNaught KS, Olanow CW: Proteolytic stress: A unifying concept for the etiopathogenesis of Parkinson's disease. Ann Neurol 2003;53(Suppl 3):S73–S84. *A review of the ubiquitin-proteasome pathway and its relevance to neurodegeneration associated with Parkinson's disease.*

Mouradian AM: Recent advances in the genetics and pathogenesis of Parkinson disease. Neurology 2002;58:179–185. *An excellent review of current hypotheses.*

Siderowf A, Stern M: Update on Parkinson disease. Ann Intern Med 2003;138:651–658. *Reviews genetics, medical treatment, and potential for surgical interventions.*

Simuni T, Jaggi JL, Mulholland H, et al: Bilateral stimulation of the subthalamic nucleus in patients with Parkinson disease: A study of efficacy and safety. J Neurosurg 2002;96:666–672. *Deep brain stimulation was effective for refractory disease in this case series.*

444 TREMORS, TICS, MYOCLONUS, AND STEREOTYPIES

Joseph Jankovic

TREMORS

Essential tremor is the most common type of tremor encountered in developed countries. The tremor is inherited in an autosomal dominant pattern with high penetrance. Affected patients lack the hypokinetic features and rigidity of Parkinson's disease (Chapter 443). Essential tremor typically produces flexion-extension oscillation of the hands at the wrists or adduction-abduction movements of the fingers when the arms are outstretched in front of the body. Although frequently referred to as *benign essential tremor*, it may be partially disabling, often causing spilling of liquids and interfering with handwriting. Essential tremor also frequently involves the head and voice, which helps differentiate it from parkinsonian tremor. Another useful distinguishing feature is the occurrence of essential tremor during maintenance of posture; parkinsonian tremor is usually present when the affected body part is at relative rest. Parkinsonian patients often exhibit postural tremor, however, and patients with essential tremor may have tremor at rest, suggesting an overlap between Parkinson's disease and essential tremor.

The frequency of essential tremor ranges from 4 to 12 Hz, and the oscillation may be produced by either alternating or synchronous contractions of antagonistic muscles. Some forms occur only during a specific activity, such as writing or holding an object in a particular position. These *focal task-specific tremors* may be associated with task-specific dystonias ("occupational cramps") or with generalized essential tremor and dystonia. Nearly half of all patients with essential tremor show evidence of an associated dystonia. The nature of the link is unknown.

Essential tremor has many variants, including isolated head, voice, tongue, facial, and chin tremors as well as orthostatic tremor. Although considered a variant of essential tremor, orthostatic tremor usually does not respond to propranolol; clonazepam provides satisfactory control in most patients, however. Rarely, focal tremor may be induced by trauma to the affected body part. This peripherally induced tremor often is associated with focal dystonia and reflex sympathetic dystrophy.

Essential tremor is an autosomal dominant disorder with a relatively high penetrance. Although no gene mutation has been identified, two loci, 3q13 and 2p22-p25, have been linked to the disease. Genetic heterogeneity in essential tremor is likely given the different familial patterns characterized by either pure essential tremor or essential tremor in combination with dystonia or parkinsonism.

Rx Treatment

β-Adrenergic blocking drugs (e.g., propranolol, 80 to 240 mg/day) are the most effective agents in the treatment of essential tremor. Modest doses of alcohol also reduce the tremor in most instances, but this approach to treatment is impractical. Other occasionally useful drugs include primidone (starting dose, 25 mg at bedtime; the daily dosage can be increased gradually to 750 mg/day), topiramate, lorazepam, and alprazolam. Patients with a disabling essential tremor that does not respond satisfactorily to medications sometimes improve with local injections of botulinum. Thalamotomy is used as a last resort, but high-frequency thalamic stimulation is gaining wider acceptance as a treatment of disabling tremors unresponsive to pharmacologic therapy.

TICS

Tics are involuntary, abrupt, sudden, isolated, brief movements (*motor tics*); sounds produced by the nose, mouth, or throat (*vocalphonic tics*); or sensations (*sensory tics*). Motor tics may be simple (e.g., eye blinking, nose twitching, head jerking) or complex (e.g., repetitive touching, jumping, kicking, pelvic gyrations). Similarly, vocalphonic tics may be simple (e.g., throat clearing, grunting, sniffing) or complex (e.g., echolalia, palilalia, coprolalia). Characteristics of tics include suppressibility, increase with stress and excitement, decrease with distraction and concentration, suggestibility, waxing and waning, and possible persistence during sleep.

The most common cause of tics is *Gilles de la Tourette's syndrome*, a genetic disorder dominated by tics and a variety of behavioral manifestations. Transient tics of childhood and persistent simple tics probably represent fragmentary forms of Tourette's syndrome. The following criteria are diagnostic:

1. Multiple motor and one or more phonic tics must be present, although not necessarily concurrently.
2. The tics occur many times, nearly every day or intermittently, over a period of more than 1 year.

3. The anatomic location, number, frequency, complexity, type, and severity of tics change over time.
4. Onset is before age 21 years.
5. Involuntary movements and noises cannot be explained by other medical conditions.

In addition to motor and phonic tics, many affected patients exhibit a variety of comorbid disorders, particularly obsessive-compulsive disorder, attention-deficit disorder (with or without hyperactivity), poor impulse control problems, and other behavioral problems. Sleep disorders include parasomnias, bedwetting, and interruption by tics. Because of the fluctuating, heterogeneous, and often bizarre manifestations, affected patients frequently have their illness misdiagnosed by physicians and are mistreated by schoolmates, teachers, coworkers, strangers, and the legal system.

Epidemiologic studies suggest that the frequency of Tourette's syndrome is much greater than originally thought. The current estimates suggest a prevalence of 3%, with a 3:1 male preponderance. Although the responsible gene or genes have not been identified yet, the disorder is clearly genetic in origin, often manifested by a bilineal pattern of inheritance in which both parents are affected to a variable degree. In rare cases, symptoms may be triggered or exacerbated by streptococcal infection. Other rare causes of tics include neuroleptic agents, head trauma, viral encephalitis, and cocaine abuse.

 Treatment

Therapy must be individualized and targeted to the most troublesome symptoms. Because most patients experience waxing and waning of symptoms and a generally favorable natural course as they reach adulthood, education, reassurance, and behavioral therapy may be sufficient in mild cases. Drugs are indicated when tics cause physical discomfort or social embarrassment. Judicious use of dopamine receptor–blocking drugs, such as risperidone, ◼ fluphenazine, pimozide, and haloperidol, can reduce the frequency and severity of tics and ameliorate impulsive and aggressive behavior. These drugs may cause sedation, weight gain, and other side effects. Tardive dyskinesia is a potentially serious, albeit relatively uncommon (particularly in children) complication of long-term neuroleptic therapy. In patients with focal tics, injection of botulinum toxin into the affected muscles provides safe and effective relief of not only the tics, but also the premonitory sensations and urges. Fluoxetine, fluvoxamine, clomipramine, paroxetine, sertraline, venlafaxine, citalopram, and other serotonin uptake inhibitors are particularly helpful in the treatment of obsessive-compulsive disorder and other behavioral problems frequently associated with Tourette's syndrome. Central nervous stimulants, such as methylphenidate and Adderall, are useful in the treatment of comorbid attention deficit. Clonidine and guanfacine are useful in the treatment of impulse control problems.

MYOCLONUS

Myoclonus is a jerklike movement produced by a sudden, rapid, and brief contraction (positive myoclonus) or a muscle inhibition (negative myoclonus). *Segmental myoclonus* usually involves either the branchial structures, innervated by the lower cranial nerves and upper cervical nerve roots, or other body parts innervated by the spinal roots and nerves; it consists of rhythmic (1 to 3 Hz) contractions caused by a lesion of the brain stem or spinal cord. *Palatal myoclonus* results from acute or chronic lesions involving the anatomic triangle linking dentate, red, and inferior olivary nuclei. *Generalized myoclonus* is believed to reflect discharges arising from the brain stem reticular formation and is categorized as physiologic, essential, epileptic, or symptomatic. Two forms of myoclonus are associated with sleep: physiologic sleep myoclonus, occurring normally during initial phases of sleep, and nocturnal myoclonus, now called *periodic movements of sleep,* often associated with *restless legs syndrome* and with abnormal involuntary movements while the person is awake.

Causes of generalized myoclonus include acute and prolonged hypoxia and ischemia; various metabolic, infectious, and toxic factors; and exposure to neuroleptic drugs (tardive myoclonus). Myoclonus can be associated with familial chorea and dystonia and with many neurodegenerative disorders, including parkinsonism, progressive myoclonus epilepsy, and a variety of rare heredodegenerative

Table 444–1 • NEUROLEPTIC-INDUCED MOVEMENT DISORDERS	
ACUTE DISORDERS	**CHRONIC DISORDERS**
Dystonic reaction	Tardive dyskinesia
Parkinsonism	Stereotypic: oral-facial-lingual-masticatory
Akathisia	Trunk-pelvic
Neuroleptic malignant syndrome	Respiratory
	Choreic: limbs
	Tardive dystonia, tics, myoclonus, tremor, akathisia, parkinsonism

disorders. Multifocal myoclonus often develops in the late stages of Creutzfeldt-Jakob disease and, less frequently, Alzheimer's disease.

 Treatment

The specific pathogeneses of myoclonus are unknown. Clonazepam, lorazepam, valproate, carbamazepine, levetiracetam, and 5-hydroxytryptophan have been reported to have antimyoclonic activity. Clonazepam, 1 to 9 mg/day, is the drug of first choice, but the development of adverse effects, such as drowsiness, ataxia, and sexual dysfunction, often limits its usefulness.

STEREOTYPIES

The term *stereotypy* denotes a continuous or intermittent, involuntary, coordinated, patterned, repetitive, rhythmic, purposeless, but seemingly purposeful and ritualistic movement. Stereotypies may be simple (e.g., chewing movement, foot tapping, body rocking) or complex (e.g., complicated rituals, sitting down and arising from a chair). They can be volitionally suppressed. Stereotypies can accompany a variety of human behavioral disorders, such as anxiety, obsessive-compulsive disorders, Tourette's syndrome, schizophrenia, akathisia, autism, and mental retardation. Stereotypies and self-stimulatory or self-injurious behavior constitute the most recognizable symptoms in mentally retarded and autistic patients.

Tardive dyskinesia, a persistent movement disorder caused by exposure to dopamine receptor blocking drugs, is a frequently encountered stereotypy. Many other tardive movement disorders can result from the use of dopamine receptor blocking drugs (neuroleptics) (Table 444–1). The term *akathisia* describes the combination of stereotypy and a sensory component, such as an inner feeling of restlessness. Elderly women seem to be at particularly high risk for tardive dyskinesia. With the advent of atypical neuroleptics, the incidence of tardive dyskinesias has been declining gradually. The mechanism of the disorder is poorly understood but is believed to result from the development of supersensitive dopamine receptors caused by chronic neuroleptic blockade. Prevention, by avoiding the use of the offending drugs as much as possible, is the best treatment for this iatrogenic (drug-induced) movement disorder. Whenever possible, drugs other than the neuroleptics should be used for psychiatric or gastrointestinal problems. When no alternative exists, the dosage and duration of exposure should be kept at a minimum. Spontaneous remissions of tardive dyskinesia occasionally follow withdrawal of the offending agent. Dopamine-depleting drugs, such as tetrabenazine or reserpine, are the most effective drugs in its symptomatic treatment.

Another disorder causing stereotypic and restless movements is *restless legs syndrome.* This genetic (autosomal dominant) disorder particularly affects the lower extremities ("restless legs") and often is worse at night, causing insomnia, and it may be associated with periodic movements of sleep (Chapter 438). It responds remarkably to dopaminergic drugs, particularly dopamine agonists.

 1. Scahill L, Leckman JF, Schultz RT, et al: A placebo-controlled trial of risperidone in Tourette syndrome. Neurology 2003;60:1130–1135.

SUGGESTED READINGS
Fahn S, Frucht SJ, Truong DD, Hallett M, eds: Myoclonus and Paroxysmal Dyskinesias, Adv Neurol, Vol 89, Lippincott Williams and Wilkins, Philadelphia, PA, 2002:1–500. *Review of the clinical manifestations, pathophysiology, and treatment of myoclonus and related movement disorders, including paroxysmal dyskinesias.*

Jankovic J: Essential tremor: Clinical characteristics. Neurology 2000;54(Suppl 4):S21–25. *A review of the phenomenology and differential diagnosis of essential tremor, the most common form of tremor.*

Jankovic J: Tourette's syndrome. N Engl J Med 2001;345:1184–1192. *Review of the motor and behavioral aspects, neurobiology, and treatment.*

445 DYSTONIAS, CHOREAS, ATHETOSIS, AND BALLISM

Joseph Jankovic

DYSTONIAS

Definition

Dystonia is a syndrome dominated by involuntary, sustained (tonic) or spasmodic (rapid or clonic), patterned, and repetitive muscle contractions frequently causing twisting (e.g., torticollis), flexing or extending (e.g., writer's cramp, retrocollis), and squeezing (e.g., blepharospasm) movements or abnormal postures. Dystonia is frequently associated with other movement disorders, particularly tremor, myoclonus, and parkinsonism. Dystonia is diagnosed in about 1 in 3000 people, but the true prevalence is probably much higher.

Classification

Dystonia may vary in severity, and it may progress as follows: task-specific dystonia (occurring only during a specific activity such as writing or typing) progressing to action dystonia (present only during activity, not necessarily specific activity), progressing to overflow dystonia (involving adjacent muscles), progressing to dystonia at rest (present even during rest), and ultimately progressing to fixed postures (joint contractures). Dystonia is exacerbated by stress, fatigue, activity, or a change in posture; it is relieved by sleep, relaxation, hypnosis, and a variety of sensory tricks. Whereas most dystonias are continuous, some occur paroxysmally, and some have marked diurnal variations (Fig. 445–1). Partly because of fluctuations in severity, sometimes influenced by the emotional state of the patient, dystonia is often mistakenly attributed to psychogenic causes.

Dystonia can be classified according to its *distribution* as focal, segmental, multifocal, generalized, or unilateral (hemidystonia). Most

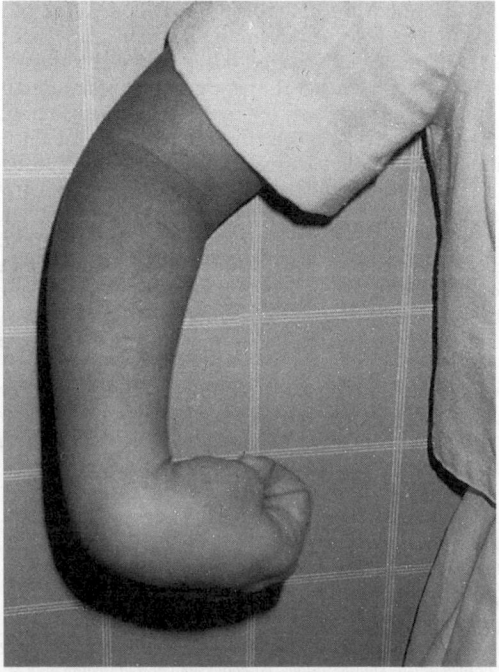

FIGURE 445–1 • Focal dystonia of the distal right arm.

childhood-onset dystonias begin focally, usually in one foot; other body parts become involved later, eventually resulting in generalized dystonia. In contrast, adult-onset dystonias tend to remain focal or segmental. Examples of focal dystonia include blepharospasm, oromandibular dystonia, torticollis, spasmodic dysphonia, and occupational (e.g., writer's, typist's, pianist's) cramps (see Fig. 445–1). Blepharospasm is categorized as a *focal* dystonia when it occurs alone (essential blepharospasm). In addition, blepharospasm is often associated with dystonic movements in the adjacent facial, oromandibular, laryngeal, and neck muscles. This *segmental dystonia* is sometimes referred to as Meige's syndrome, but the term *cranial-cervical dystonia* is more descriptive.

The most common form of dystonia is *cervical dystonia*. According to the position of the head, cervical dystonia can be categorized as torticollis, laterocollis, anterocollis, retrocollis, or a combination of these abnormal postures. A 3 : 2 female preponderance is noted, and the onset is usually in the fifth decade. Local pain is reported by about half the patients, and radiculopathy complicates cervical dystonia in about 20%. Half of all patients with cervical dystonia have an associated head-neck tremor. The tremor can be dystonic, seen only when the patient attempts to keep the head straight; essential, seen when the tremor persists regardless of the position of the head; or a combination of dystonic and essential. About half the patients report a movement disorder such as tremor or dystonia in family members. The cause of most cervical dystonias is unknown. In 15% of cases, however, cervical dystonia can be attributed to either local trauma or exposure to neuroleptic drugs.

Pathogenesis

The pathoanatomy of dystonia is unknown, but studies suggest functional involvement of the basal ganglia, particularly the putamen, and the brain stem. Brain imaging and autopsy examinations usually yield normal findings. Few postmortem biochemical analyses have been performed without any consistent findings, but using two-dimensional magnetic resonance spectroscopy, significantly decreased GABA levels were found in the contralateral sensorimotor cortex and lentiform nucleus.

PRIMARY DYSTONIA

Primary dystonia accounts for 90% of cases. Primary dystonias with onset in childhood have previously been termed *dystonia musculorum deformans*. Childhood-onset dystonias are often inherited, usually in an autosomal dominant pattern; about half of adult-onset cases seem to have a genetic basis. Other members of the family may have only partial manifestations, such as clubfoot, scoliosis, torticollis, writer's cramp, bruxism, or essential tremor. Genetic dystonia seems to have a higher prevalence among Ashkenazi Jews, but dystonias in both Jewish and non-Jewish individuals have been linked to a marker in the q32-q34 region of chromosome 9. Because a 3-base pair deletion in a gene coding for a novel adenosine triphosphate binding protein in the 9q34 locus termed *torsinA* has been shown to result in the loss of a pair of glutamic acid residues, gene testing for this abnormal *DYT1* gene can be performed in individuals with dystonia. Other genetic dystonias include an X-linked dystonia, which has been described in some Filipino families. A dopa-responsive dystonia has been linked to a marker on chromosome 14, and several independent mutations in the guanosine triphosphatase-cyclohydrolase 1 (*GCH1*) gene have been identified (DYT5). Diurnal fluctuations with exacerbation of the movement disorder toward the end of the day are typical in this form of dystonia. In addition to the DYT1 dystonia, several other genetic forms of primary torsion dystonia have been identified. A gene locus in 8p21-q22 region has been identified in a large German American Mennonite family with cranial-cervical and limb dystonia. This dystonia, designated as DYT6, 8p21-q22, is clinically similar to DYT1 although the involvement is more generalized and includes the head and neck. A DYT7 designation was assigned to the locus on chromosome 18p in a German family with adult-onset, autosomal dominant inheritance predominantly manifested by cervical and laryngeal dystonia (spasmodic dysphonia). Another genetic primary torsion dystonia, designated DYT13 and mapped to chromosome 1p36.13-36.22, is manifested by cranial-cervical or upper limb dystonia. In one family with myoclonic dystonia,

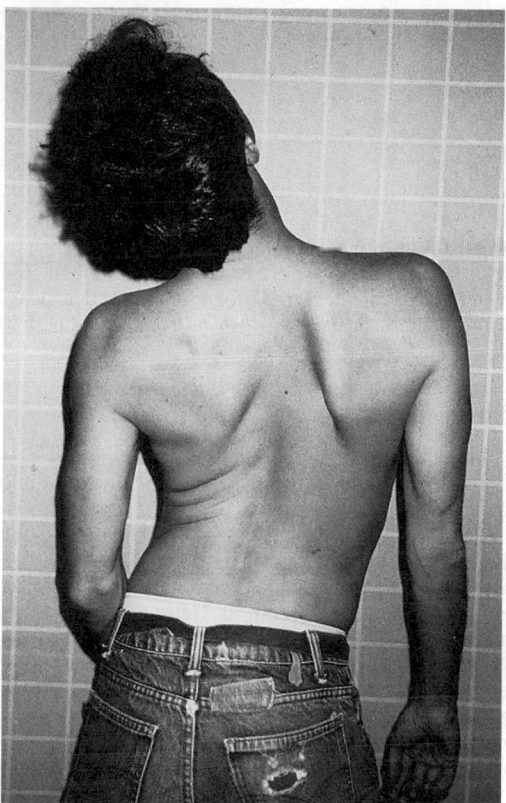

FIGURE 445–2 • Truncal dystonia in a manic-depressive patient with tardive dystonia secondary to a variety of antipsychotic drugs.

the gene locus was mapped to 7q21 and was later found to contain loss-of-function mutations in ε-sarcoglycan.

SECONDARY DYSTONIA

Occasionally, a specific and potentially treatable cause of dystonia can be identified (see Fig. 445–1). One of the most important examples is *Wilson's disease* (Chapter 224); neurologic symptoms are the initial manifestations in about 50% of patients with this autosomal recessive disorder, which appears during the second or third decade.

Tardive dystonia is a persistent form of dystonia caused by exposure to dopamine receptor–blocking drugs such as major tranquilizers (e.g., chlorpromazine, thioridazine, fluphenazine, thiothixene, haloperidol, loxapine, amoxapine) and certain antiemetics (e.g., prochlorperazine, metoclopramide) (Fig. 445–2). Levodopa can also cause intermittent dystonia (and focal dystonia may be the initial symptom of Parkinson's disease). In all drug-induced dystonias, the offending drug should be withdrawn or the dosage reduced if possible. In contrast to focal, segmental, or generalized dystonia, hemidystonia is associated with an identifiable cause in most cases, including subcortical infarction, arteriovenous malformation, abscess, tumor, and other lesions, some of which can be treated surgically. Many other causes of secondary dystonia are possible, but only a few are amenable to therapy.

Rx **Treatment**

Treatment of dystonia consists of supportive therapy (e.g., relaxation techniques, prostheses), medications, botulinum toxin injections, and surgery. Anticholinergic drugs are sometimes beneficial. Trihexyphenidyl, the most frequently used anticholinergic, must be started in low doses and slowly increased to tolerance, perhaps up to 60 mg/day. Some children can tolerate such high doses, but anticholinergic side effects usually limit adult tolerance to 20 to 25 mg daily or less. In advanced cases, dopamine-depleting and dopamine receptor–blocking drugs may be added.

Muscle relaxants (e.g., diazepam or lorazepam), baclofen (administered either orally or as a continuous intrathecal infusion), and carbamazepine sometimes provide benefit. About 10% of patients with childhood or adolescent dystonia improve with levodopa, so levodopa should be tried in all cases of childhood and in some cases of adult-onset dystonia. In patients with refractory focal dystonia and, less often, segmental dystonia, injection of the paralysis-inducing botulinum toxin into the contracting muscles provides effective, albeit temporary, relief. Such approaches are best left to those with experience in this treatment.

Patients who are socially and occupationally disabled by dystonia despite optimal medical therapy, including botulinum toxin, can sometimes be helped surgically. Surgical procedures include orbicularis myectomy for blepharospasm, cervical rhizotomy for neck dystonia, and thalamotomy, pallidotomy, or deep brain stimulation of the subthalamic nucleus or pallidum for hemidystonia or generalized (predominantly distal) dystonia. Such procedures are effective in most patients but are associated with both potentially serious complications and high rates of symptom recurrence, thus making them a last resort.

CHOREAS

HUNTINGTON'S DISEASE

Huntington's disease, an autosomal dominant disorder with complete penetrance, is the phenotype of an expanded triplet repeat sequence of a gene located at chromosome 4p16.3. Dementia and various emotional and psychiatric disturbances are prominent. The estimated prevalence in the United States is 4 to 8 per 100,000 persons. Although about 10% of cases begin before age 20 years, the peak age at onset is in the fourth and fifth decades. Juvenile Huntington's disease often first manifests with progressive parkinsonism, dementia, and seizures. In contrast, adult Huntington's disease often starts with the insidious onset of clumsiness and adventitious, fidgety, random, brief movements. Initially, these purposeless movements may be incorporated into and masked by normal intentional acts, delaying the recognition of chorea. Chorea often begins distally, but as the disease progresses, it becomes generalized and can interrupt voluntary movements. Characteristically, patients with Huntington's disease have difficulty in maintaining tongue protrusion or a steady grip, and their gait is often irregular, hesitant, unsteady, and dancelike. Other motor symptoms include dysarthria, dysphagia, and postural instability.

Neuropsychological symptoms may precede motor changes. They may consist of personality changes, apathy, social withdrawal, agitation, impulsiveness, depression, mania, paranoia, delusions, hostility, hallucinations, or psychosis. Cognitive changes are manifested chiefly by loss of recent memory and impaired judgment (Chapter 433). Progressive motor dysfunction, dementia, and incontinence eventually lead to institutionalization and death. The duration of illness from onset to death is about 15 years for Huntington's disease in adults and 8 to 10 years for the juvenile variant.

Huntington's disease is regarded as truly an autosomal dominant disease in that homozygotes do not appear to differ clinically from typical heterozygotes. The mutation responsible for the disease consists of an unstable enlargement of the CAG repeat sequence in the 5′ end of a large (210 kb) gene, *IT15*. This gene, located at 4p16.3, encodes a protein, called *huntingtin*. The expanded CAG repeat alters huntingtin by elongating a polyglutamine segment near the NH_2-terminus. Whereas the number of repeats varies between 10 and 29 copies in unaffected individuals, the Huntington's disease gene contains 36 to 121 of such repeats. The intermediate-sized CAG repeats range from 30 to 35. Several studies have demonstrated that the number of repeats inversely correlates with the age at onset. The onset of the disease may be earlier (anticipation) in successive generations as a consequence of lengthening of the CAG repeat. The rate of disease progression is generally faster in paternally transmitted Huntington's disease independent of the CAG repeat length. Analyzing DNA for the expansion of trinucleotide repeats has provided a means for a reliable diagnostic test.

Postmortem changes include neuronal loss and gliosis in the cortex and the striatum, particularly the caudate nucleus. The affected areas contain neuronal intranuclear inclusions and dystrophic neurites, but it is not yet clear whether these abnormalities result from or cause cell death and how they relate to the genetic mutation. It has been postulated that polyglutamine-tract expansion in the mutated huntingtin protein accumulates in the nucleus, forming insoluble amyloid-like fibrils, and these aggregates somehow interfere with normal cellular metabolism.

Chorea seems to be primarily related to the loss of striatal neurons projecting to the lateral globus pallidus (GPe), whereas rigid-akinetic symptoms correlate with the additional loss of striatal neurons projecting to the medial globus pallidus (GPi). Loss of medium-sized spiny neurons, which normally constitute 80% of all striatal neurons, is associated with a marked decrease in γ-aminobutyric acid (GABA) synthesis. Acetylcholine activity declines, presumably reflecting a degeneration of cholinergic striatal interneurons.

Reliable clinical diagnosis depends on the combination of chorea, emotional disturbances, progressive dementia, and a family history suggestive of autosomal dominant inheritance. Because spontaneous mutations are rare, lack of family history raises questions of paternity or misdiagnosis.

 Treatment

Treatment is symptomatic, but recent evidence indicates that caspase inhibitors, such as minocycline, may have a neuroprotective effect at least in animal models of Huntington's disease. The psychosis may improve with neuroleptic agents, such as haloperidol, pimozide, fluphenazine, and thioridazine, but these drugs can induce tardive dyskinesia and other adverse effects and should be used only if absolutely necessary. Monoamine-depleting drugs, such as reserpine (0.25 to 8 mg/day) and tetrabenazine (an investigational drug not available for general use in North America), may relieve chorea, do not cause tardive dyskinesia, and may be as effective as the dopamine-blocking drugs. However, these drugs can cause or exacerbate depression, sedation, akathisia, and parkinsonism. Anxiolytics and antidepressants may be useful in some patients.

Genetic aspects of Huntington's disease should be discussed openly with patients to provide them and their relatives with nondirective counseling. The fact that presymptomatic individuals are in a position to determine their own disease status before having children places an unusually heavy burden on families. Therefore, a multidisciplinary approach involving genetic counseling (Chapter 36), physical and occupational therapy, nutritional counseling, coupled with pharmacologic treatments are needed to provide optimal care to patients with Huntington's disease. Several studies have also found that "environmental enrichment" slows disease progression in animal models and this approach should be translated into clinical practice.

OTHER CHOREIC DISORDERS

Besides Huntington's disease, other rare, genetically transmitted choreas include *benign hereditary chorea,* a nonprogressive chorea with childhood onset, and *paroxysmal dyskinesias,* manifested by brief episodes of choreoathetosis or dystonia occurring sporadically (non-kinesigenic) or precipitated by sudden voluntary movement (kinesigenic). *Senile chorea* is a rare symptom complex in which chorea begins after age 60 years and is unaccompanied by the neurobehavioral symptoms or family history of Huntington's disease. Some patients have been reported to have pathologic changes identical to those of Huntington's disease; others have had predominant degeneration of the putamen rather than the caudate.

Neuroacanthocytosis, also termed "chorea-acanthocytosis," usually presents in the third or fourth decade of life with a combination of self-mutilation manifested by lip and tongue biting, generalized chorea, lingual dystonia, and motor and phonic tics. Other features include seizures, amyotrophy, areflexia, and elevated levels of serum creatine phosphokinase. Wet blood or Wright-stained fast-dry smears reveal more than 15% of red blood cells as acanthocytes. Neuroimaging usually demonstrates caudate atrophy. The condition most often has a pattern of autosomal recessive inheritance.

Sydenham's chorea, now uncommon, has an autoimmune basis, most often appearing as a consequence of infection with group A streptococcus as part of the syndrome of rheumatic fever (Chapter 309). Unlike arthritis and carditis, which occur soon after such infection, chorea and various neurobehavioral symptoms may be

delayed for 6 months or longer. Chorea appearing during pregnancy (chorea gravidarum), with use of birth control pills, or during the course of systemic lupus erythematosus probably has a similar pathogenesis.

ATHETOSIS

Athetosis is a slow form of chorea characterized by twisting, writhing movements. It most often accompanies static encephalopathy due to cerebral palsy, kernicterus, prematurity, glutaric aciduria, poststroke hemiplegia, and other causes of early life brain damage. In some cases, the movement disorder becomes progressive after decades of no apparent change. Athetosis usually does not respond to pharmacologic therapy.

BALLISM

Ballism is a form of forceful, flinging, high-amplitude, coarse chorea. Because the involuntary movement usually affects only one side of the body, the term *hemiballism* is used. The condition is often preceded by hemiparesis associated with a hemorrhagic or ischemic stroke involving the contralateral subthalamic nucleus (STN) or adjacent structures. Less common causes of hemiballism include abscess, arteriovenous malformation, cerebral trauma, hyperosmotic hyperglycemia, tumor, and multiple sclerosis. Most of these lesions involve the STN, but hemiballism has been described occasionally in patients with lesions outside the STN. Dopamine-blocking and -depleting drugs, used in the treatment of chorea, benefit most patients with hemiballism, but the disorder usually subsides spontaneously within several weeks. Occasional examples of prolonged disabling and medically intractable hemiballism can be treated with contralateral thalamotomy or pallidectomy.

---

1. Wissel J, Kanovsky P, Ruzicka E, et al: Efficacy and safety of a standardised 500 unit dose of Dysport (clostridium botulinum toxin type A haemaglutinin complex) in a heterogeneous cervical dystonia population: Results of a prospective, multi-centre, randomised, double-blind, placebo-controlled, parallel group study. J Neurol 2001;248:1073–1078.

SUGGESTED READINGS
Bates G: Huntington aggregation and toxicity in Huntington's disease. Cancer 2003;361:1642–1644. *Review of the pathogenesis of cell death in Huntington's disease.*
Chuang C, Fahn S, Frucht SJ: The natural history and treatment of acquired hemidystonia: Report of 33 cases and review of literature. J Neurol Neurosurg Psychiatry 2002;72:59–67. *A report of patients with and causes of secondary dystonia.*
Hayflick SJ, Westaway SK, Levinson B, et al: Genetic, clinical, and radiographic delineation of Hallervorden-Spatz syndrome. N Engl J Med 2003;348:33–40. *A review of a series of patients with autosomal recessive disorder characterized by progressive dementia, dystonia, spasticity and other movement disorders, associated with accumulation of iron in the basal ganglia. Previously referred to as Hallervorden-Spatz disease, the progressive neurodegenerative disorder has been reclassified as neurodegeneration with brain iron accumulation type (NBIA). Since many of the cases have been found to be associated with mutations in the PANK-2 gene, the disorder in such cases is now referred to as pantothenate kinase associated neurodegeneration (PKAN).*
Ondo WG, Tintner R, Thomas M, Jankovic J: Tetrabenazine treatment for Huntington's disease–associated chorea. Clin Neuropharmacol 2002;25:300–302. *Using "blinded" rating of videotapes, this study demonstrates the efficacy of tetrabenazine, a monoamine depleting drug, in the treatment of chorea associated with Huntington's disease.*
Opal P, Tintner R, Jankovic J, et al: Intrafamilial phenotypic variability of the DYT1 dystonia: From asymptomatic TOR1A gene carrier status to dystonic storm. Mov Disord 2002;17:339–345. *A report of a large DYT1 dystonia family illustrating the spectrum of clinical manifestations of this most common form of primary dystonia.*

446 HEREDITARY CEREBELLAR ATAXIAS AND SPASTIC PARAPLEGIAS

Eva L. Feldman

CEREBELLAR ATAXIAS

The hereditary cerebellar ataxias are progressive disorders that can begin in childhood or adulthood. The most common progressive inherited ataxia in children is Friedreich's ataxia. A less common disorder producing childhood ataxia, ataxia-telangiectasia, is further described in Chapter 267. In the adult ataxias, at least 14 late-onset cerebellar disorders have been identified, now classified as spinocerebellar ataxia (SCA) types 1 through 14.

FRIEDREICH'S ATAXIA

Definition and Etiology

Friedreich's ataxia is a trinucleotide-repeat disorder affecting the central and peripheral nervous systems and many other organs. A GAA unstable expansion on the long arm of chromosome 9 disrupts expression of the protein frataxin. The normal length of the GAA repeat is 10 to 21 copies, but in individuals with Friedreich's ataxia, expansion results in 200 to 900 copies. Higher numbers of copies correlate with more severe neurologic deficits. Friedreich's ataxia is unique among the trinucleotide-repeat disorders; it is an autosomal recessive disorder with no anticipation. Frataxin appears to be critical for iron export and use in the mitochondria. Because accumulation of mitochondrial iron affects the production of oxygen radicals, loss of frataxin may lead to oxidative mitochondrial damage.

Incidence and Prevalence

The estimated carrier frequency is 1 in 100, with a disease prevalence of 1 per 50,000.

Pathology

At autopsy, patients with Friedreich's ataxia have atrophic spinal cords with loss of neurons in Clarke's columns and the dorsal root ganglia. Spinocerebellar tracts, pyramidal tracts, dorsal column tracts, and peripheral nerves are degenerated, with minor cell loss in the brain stem and cerebellum. Cardiac ventricular hypertrophy with chronic interstitial fibrosis of the myocardium is common.

Clinical Manifestations

The clinical diagnosis of Friedreich's ataxia is made when patients meet the following criteria: (1) onset during puberty; (2) progressive ataxia with loss of lower extremity deep tendon reflexes; (3) presence of Babinski's sign (i.e., extensor plantar responses); and (4) 5 or more years of disease and a family history compatible with autosomal recessive inheritance. Other common clinical features include nystagmus, dysarthria, stocking-glove neuropathy, and pes cavus with weakness in the lower extremities. Patients frequently have cardiomyopathy and skeletal abnormalities such as kyphosis and scoliosis, and diabetes mellitus develops in a small percentage.

Diagnosis

Diagnosis of Friedreich's ataxia is made by positive genetic testing in a patient with appropriate clinical signs and symptoms. Other diagnostic entities that can give a similar clinical picture include vitamin B_{12} deficiency, abetalipoproteinemia, and a selective defect in vitamin E absorption.

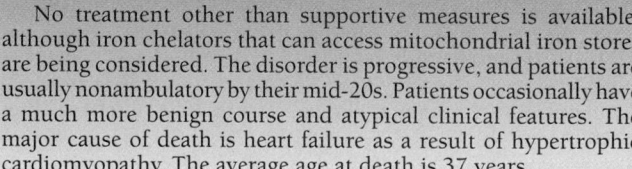

Treatment and Prognosis

No treatment other than supportive measures is available, although iron chelators that can access mitochondrial iron stores are being considered. The disorder is progressive, and patients are usually nonambulatory by their mid-20s. Patients occasionally have a much more benign course and atypical clinical features. The major cause of death is heart failure as a result of hypertrophic cardiomyopathy. The average age at death is 37 years.

SPINOCEREBELLAR ATAXIA TYPES 1 TO 14

Definition and Etiology

Before the advent of molecular genetics, classification of the autosomal dominant SCAs was difficult. Advances in genetics permitted these disorders to be divided into 14 syndromes (SCA 1 to 14).

SCA 1 though 3, 6 through 8, and 12 are trinucleotide-repeat disorders, involving expansion of a CAG repeat coding for a polyglutamine tract within the normal gene product. In SCA 1, 2, 3 (i.e., Machado-Joseph disease), and 7, the function of the disrupted protein, known as ataxin, is unknown. SCA 3, which is the most common cause of autosomal dominant SCA worldwide, is caused by a CAG expansion in the *MJDI* gene. In SCA 6, the CAG repeat disrupts the function of a voltage-dependent calcium channel found in the Purkinje cells of the cerebellum, and SCA 6 is considered a channelopathy. The disrupted gene in SCA 12 is a brain-specific regulatory subunit of protein phosphatase 2A. The loci for SCA 4, 5, 10, 11, 13, and 14 have been mapped, but the disrupted genes have not been identified.

Incidence and Prevalence

The estimated carrier frequency is 1 to 10 per 100,000 people in Europe. Data are not yet available for the incidence and prevalence of SCA 1 to 14.

Pathology

At autopsy, patients with SCA have olivopontocerebellar atrophy with loss of neurons in the inferior olives and the pons. Degeneration of spinocerebellar tracts, pyramidal tracts, and posterior column tracts occurs. Depending on the SCA type, neuronal loss occurs in the spinal cord (i.e., anterior horn cells), midbrain, basal ganglia, and cerebral and cerebellar cortex. In SCA 3, the cerebellar cortex and olives remain intact.

Clinical Manifestations

The predominant clinical feature of these disorders is ataxia, followed by dysarthria and ophthalmoplegia (Table 446–1). Other cerebellar signs include titubation, dysdiadochokinesia, and dysmetria. With increasing ataxia, patients can become nonambulatory. Additional clinical signs include dementia, optic atrophy, retinal pigmentary degeneration, deafness, dysphagia, extrapy-ramidal and pyramidal findings, and peripheral neuropathy. The extrapyrami-

Continued

Table 446–1 • CLINICAL FEATURES OF THE SPINOCEREBELLAR ATAXIAS

DISEASE	AGE AT ONSET (yr)	ATAXIA	DYSARTHRIA	OPHTHALMOPLEGIA	OTHER SIGNS
SCA 1	30–40	+	+	+	Nystagmus, optic atrophy, pyramidal tract signs, dementia
SCA 2	Early 30s	+	+	+	Muscle cramps, slow saccades, peripheral neuropathy
SCA 3	Mid–30s	+	+	+	
SCA 4	40	+	–	–	Sensory axonal neuropathy
SCA 5	Mid–30s	+	+	–	
SCA 6	20–40	+	+	–	Distal sensory loss
SCA 7	Mid–20s	+	+	+	Pigmentary retinal degeneration, pyramidal tract signs
SCA 10	Mid–30s	+	+	+	
SCA 11		+			

dal features include masked facies, cogwheel rigidity, dystonia, athetosis, and chorea. Pyramidal dysfunction includes limb spasticity (especially in the legs), hyperreflexia, and a Babinski response.

Machado-Joseph disease (SCA 3) is an allelic disorder that was initially described in families of Azorean decent. Ataxia and ophthalmoplegia are common clinical features in each of the three phenotypes:

Type I: Early onset (mean age, 24 years) with marked pyramidal and extrapyramidal dysfunction
Type II: Later onset (mean age, 40 years)
Type III: Latest onset (mean age, 47 years) with predominant weakness and amyotrophy

Diagnosis

Diagnosis of the SCAs is made by positive genetic testing in a patient with appropriate clinical signs and symptoms. Magnetic resonance imaging shows olivopontocerebellar atrophy. Other diagnostic entities that can give a similar clinical profile include alcoholism (Chapter 458) and paraneoplastic cerebellar syndromes (Chapter 188).

Rx Treatment and Prognosis

No specific therapy is available for the SCAs. As with all neurodegenerative disorders, treatment is supportive and is aimed at maximizing and retaining function. These disorders are progressive but are not necessarily the cause of death, depending on the SCA type and on the age at onset in individual cases. Patients with SCA 1 are usually nonambulatory about 10 years after appearance of the initial symptoms, and restrictive pulmonary disease and progressive weakness develop. The major cause of death for patients with SCA 1 is usually pneumonia.

HEREDITARY SPASTIC PARAPLEGIAS

Definition and Etiology

Pure hereditary spastic paraplegia (HSP), also known as Strümpell's disease, can be inherited as an autosomal dominant disorder (70 to 80% of reported cases) and by autosomal recessive and X-linked inheritance patterns. Eight different loci are known for autosomal dominant HSP—five loci for autosomal recessive HSP and three loci for X-linked HSP. Genes have been identified for one form of autosomal dominant and two forms each of recessive and X-linked HSP. The most common form of autosomal dominant HSP is caused by mutations in the spastin gene (2p22) that lead to the loss of a nuclear protein of unknown function. The clinical pictures caused by different loci vary primarily in average age of onset.

Incidence and Prevalence

In the Cantabria region of Spain, a careful epidemiologic study revealed a prevalence of 10 cases of HSP per 100,000 individuals.

Pathology

At autopsy, patients with HSP have axonal degeneration of the pyramidal tracts and dorsal column tracts with lesser involvement of the spinocerebellar tracts. The neurons of origin are intact. The peripheral nervous system is unaffected.

Clinical Manifestations

Patients with HSP meet the following clinical criteria: (1) progressive gait disturbance, (2) spasticity of lower extremities, and (3) hyperreflexia, frequently grade 4, with Babinski's sign (i.e., extensor plantar responses). Cranial nerves, speech, swallowing, and upper extremities remain normal. Although patients can experience weakness of their lower extremities, spasticity is usually the disabling component of HSP. Patients have a slow, stiff gait; they trip easily, and they are unable to run. Other clinical features include pes cavus (30 to 50%); decreased vibratory sensation; and urinary frequency, urgency, and hesitancy.

Table 446–2 • DIFFERENTIAL DIAGNOSIS OF HEREDITARY SPASTIC PARAPLEGIAS

Hereditary
  Dopa-responsive dystonia
  Spinocerebellar ataxias
  Adult-onset adrenoleukodystrophy
  Friedreich's ataxia
Structural lesions of the spinal cord
  Cervical spondylosis
  Tumor
  Arteriovenous malformation
  Syringomyelia
Multiple sclerosis
  Primary lateral sclerosis
Vitamin B_{12} or E deficiency
Infections
  HTLV-1
  HIV
  Tertiary syphilis

HIV = human immunodeficiency virus; HTLV-1 = human T-lymphotropic virus type 1.

Diagnosis

Diagnosis of HSP is made when patients meet clinical criteria. Magnetic resonance imaging may show spinal cord atrophy; results of cerebrospinal fluid analysis and nerve conduction studies are normal. The differential diagnosis includes other genetic conditions, spinal cord disease from structural lesions, multiple sclerosis, and vitamin deficiencies or retroviral infections (Table 446–2).

Rx Treatment and Prognosis

No specific treatment is available. Symptomatic therapy is aimed at decreasing disability and preventing complications, such as contractures. The main drugs used are antispastic agents, such as baclofen. Oral baclofen improves spasticity but may worsen weakness. Preliminary reports have suggested improved therapeutic response with intrathecal baclofen. No controlled clinical trials have addressed this issue. Most patients become nonambulatory between 60 and 70 years of age.

SUGGESTED READINGS

Patel PI, Isaya G: Friedreich ataxia: From GAA triplet-repeat expansion to frataxin deficiency. Am J Hum Genet 2001;69:15–24. *Reviews the molecular pathology of Friedreich's ataxia.*

Stevanin G, Durr A, Brice A: Spinocerebellar ataxias caused by polyglutamine expansions. Adv Exp Med Biol 2002;516:47–77. *An excellent description of the defferent SCAS.*

Tallaksen CME, Durr A, Brice A: Recent advances in hereditary spastic paraplegia. Curr Opin Neurobiol 2001;14:457–463. *A recently completed review of the cause of HSP.*

447 AMYOTROPHIC LATERAL SCLEROSIS AND OTHER MOTOR NEURON DISEASES

Eva L. Feldman

Motor neuron diseases are a heterogeneous group of disorders that selectively affect upper or lower motor neurons, or both (Table 447–1). Upper motor neurons are large cerebral and bulbar motor neurons whose dysfunction leads to decreased strength, spasticity, and hyperreflexia. Lower motor neurons are located in the ventral spinal cord; lesions result in decreased strength, tone, and reflexes accompanied by fasciculations and atrophy. Pure upper motor neuron disorders are most commonly acquired, whereas pure lower motor neuron disorders are frequently inherited. The most common acquired motor neuron disease, amyotrophic lateral sclerosis, usually includes

Table 447-1 • MAJOR MOTOR NEURON DISEASES

HEREDITARY
Autosomal dominant
    Familial amyotrophic lateral sclerosis (FALS)
Autosomal recessive
    Spinal muscular atrophy
        Type I. Acute, infantile (Werdnig-Hoffmann disease)
        Type II. Late infantile
        Type III. Juvenile and adult types (Kugelberg Welander disease)
X-Linked
    Bulbospinal muscular atrophy (Kennedy's syndrome)

ACQUIRED
Acute: anterior poliomyelitis
Chronic:
    Sporadic ALS
    Postpoliomyelitis syndrome, motor neuron loss associated with
        spino-cerebellar degeneration, multisystem atrophy, Creutzfeldt-
        Jakob disease
    ALS-like syndromes:
      Motor neuron disease with gammopathy or paraproteinemia, heavy
        metal intoxication, hexosaminidase-A deficiency, paraneoplastic
        motor neuronopathy
    Primary lateral sclerosis

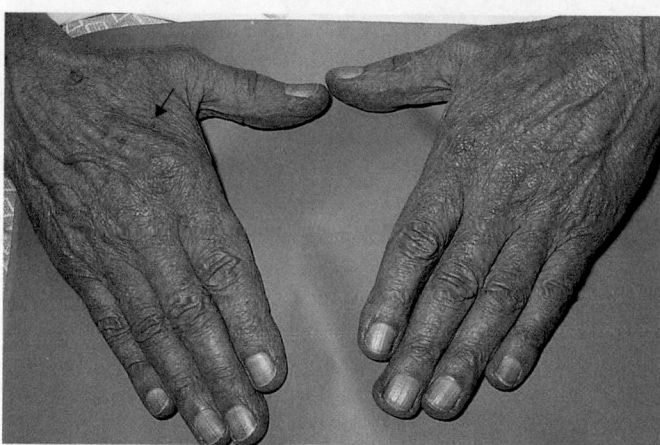

FIGURE 447-1 • Motor neuron disease. This patient has progressive muscular atrophy and presented with fasciculation and wasting of the muscles between the thumb and index finger on the dorsal (*arrow*) and palmar surfaces. Wasting in the right hand was followed by the development of similar wasting in the left hand, and subsequently by progressive wasting and fasciculations elsewhere.

dysfunction of both upper and lower motor neurons. Recent advances in the molecular genetics of hereditary motor neuron diseases have improved their classification and led to advances in defining potential underlying causes of acquired motor neuron disorders.

AMYOTROPHIC LATERAL SCLEROSIS

Definition and Etiology

Sporadic amyotrophic lateral sclerosis (ALS) accounts for approximately 80% of all cases of acquired motor neuron disease, whereas the remaining 20% of patients have either only lower motor neuron signs or a familial form of ALS (FALS). The 80% of patients who have sporadic ALS present with spasticity, hyperreflexia, and Babinski's sign (upper motor neuron signs) in the setting of progressive muscle wasting and weakness (lower motor neuron signs).

Autosomal dominant FALS is an adult-onset disease that is clinically and pathologically indistinguishable from sporadic ALS. An ALS locus was first reported in 1991 on human chromosome 21q. In 1993, the protein cytosolic copper-zinc superoxide dismutase (SOD1) was reported to be mutated in several FALS families, and more than 80 mutations in SOD1 (mostly missense) have been identified in patients with FALS. However, SOD1 mutations account for only approximately 20% of cases of FALS. The importance of the SOD1 defect is that other cases of FALS, as well as sporadic ALS, are clinically identical to SOD1 cases, suggesting a common mechanism of disease.

SOD1 is a metalloenzyme with active sites for both copper and zinc. SOD1 detoxifies the superoxide anion to form hydrogen peroxide, which in turn is converted to water. Nitric oxide may also combine with superoxide to form peroxynitrite, which is nonenzymatically converted to hydroxyl radicals. These reactive oxygen species can cause oxidative degradation of proteins and lipids and lead to cell death. FALS is due to a gain of an adverse function of the mutated SOD1 protein. Mice that overexpress mutant SOD1 develop a denervating illness that resembles ALS despite normal or increased levels of SOD1 activity. The severity of the abnormality correlates with the levels of mutant SOD1; the higher the level of SOD1, the more widespread and lethal the disease.

The relationship between SOD1-mediated FALS and sporadic ALS is not known. However, research on FALS has led to the theory that sporadic ALS may represent an acquired age-associated change in SOD1 function with resultant oxidative injury to the nervous system. Other suggested etiologies for sporadic ALS include glutamate excitotoxicity or neurotoxicity, abnormal accumulations of neurofilaments, and altered neurotropism.

Incidence and Prevalence

ALS has an estimated annual incidence of 2 per 100,000 with a worldwide prevalence of 4 to 6 per 100,000.

Pathology

At autopsy, patients with ALS have brain stem and spinal cord atrophy with loss of motor neurons and associated extensive gliosis. In the cortex, large pyramidal cell loss leads to degeneration of the corticospinal tracts and gliosis of the lateral spinal cord columns. As with other denervating disorders, loss of ventral nerve roots, with histologic evidence of denervation and reinnervation in affected muscle groups, is seen.

Clinical Manifestations

ALS is a disorder of upper and lower motor neurons. This combination results in a complex clinical syndrome. Painless, progressive weakness is the usual presenting sign and symptom of ALS. Usually focal in onset, weakness then spreads to contiguous muscle groups. Weakness is accompanied by muscle atrophy (Fig. 447-1). Head "ptosis" due to weakness of neck extensor muscles with head droop is often present in ALS. Individuals frequently experience muscle cramps. Spasticity is common, and patients may complain of spontaneous clonus. With more long-standing disease, foot and hand deformities are seen as a result of tendon imbalance and secondary joint contractures.

ALS can present with bulbar dysfunction, although more commonly bulbar signs and symptoms are seen in the presence of extremity and truncal weakness. Individuals experience dysarthria, or impaired speech, which may be flaccid or spastic or of a mixed flaccid-spastic quality. Dysphagia with choking is common and places patients at a high risk of aspiration. The absence of spontaneous swallowing results in sialorrhea, or drooling.

Weakness of respiratory muscles is common and is the presenting symptom in rare cases in ALS. Early in ALS, individuals complain of dyspnea with exertion and frequently sigh at rest. With disease progression, dyspnea at rest, inability to sleep in a supine position (orthopnea), sleep apnea, and morning headaches are present. Constitutional symptoms reflect loss of muscle mass and difficulties with swallowing and breathing. Individuals experience weight loss and frequently complain of fatigue.

Several aspects of neurologic function are usually spared in ALS, including mentation, extraocular movements, bowel and bladder function, and sensation. Although they are rare, exceptions do occur. Approximately 1 to 2% of patients with ALS have dementia and ophthalmoplegia, usually reflecting ocular apraxia. Although bladder function is usually reported as normal, detailed study of bladder function reveals that nearly one third of ALS patients experience urgency and obstructive micturition.

Debate continues about whether a disorder termed *primary lateral sclerosis* (PLS) is a subtype of upper motor neuron ALS or

Continued

is a separate entity. In this rare condition, individuals present with a slowly progressive spastic paraparesis or quadriparesis, with no evidence of lower motor neuron involvement, either by clinical examination or diagnostic testing. Individuals with these presenting signs and symptoms should undergo the same diagnostic procedures and require similar treatment strategies as patients with sporadic ALS. Some patients with PLS have an autosomal recessive form of hereditary spastic paraplegia (Chapter 446).

Diagnosis

The El Escorial World Federation of Neurology criteria provide a set of guidelines for the diagnosis of ALS. In these criteria, the body is divided into four regions: (1) bulbar (jaw, face, palate, larynx, and tongue), (2) cervical (neck, arm, hand, and diaphragm), (3) thoracic (back and abdomen), and (4) lumbosacral (back, abdomen, leg, and foot). The diagnosis of definite ALS is made when upper and lower motor neuron signs are present in the bulbar region and two other spinal regions or in three spinal regions. Individuals with upper and lower motor neuron signs in two spinal regions alone are classified as having probable ALS; possible ALS is diagnosed when dysfunction is present in only one region or when an individual presents with only upper motor neuron signs in two regions or lower motor neuron signs are rostral to upper motor neuron signs.

When the clinical findings suggest a diagnosis of ALS, nerve conduction studies with repetitive stimulation and electromyography (EMG) confirm lower motor neuron degeneration and exclude disorders of the neuromuscular junction, such as myasthenia gravis, and of peripheral nerve and muscle. Neuroimaging of the brain and spinal cord is often needed to confirm the expected normal anatomy present in ALS and to exclude structural pathologic processes. Routine clinical laboratory tests are necessary to exclude ALS-related syndromes. These tests include complete blood cell count and routine chemical analyses, thyroid studies, serum protein electrophoresis, serum immunoelectrophoresis with immunofixation, and measurements of serum VDRL, creatine kinase, erythrocyte sedimentation rate, antinuclear antibody, rheumatoid factor, and, when clinically indicated, hexosaminidase A, parathyroid hormone and paraneoplastic antibodies. Additional tests may be warranted on the basis of the patient's clinical presentation.

The EMG, neuroimaging, and clinical laboratory tests exclude the most common ALS-related disorders: polyradiculopathy with myelopathy, post-polio syndrome, multifocal motor neuropathy, motor neuron disease with paraproteinemia, heavy metal intoxication, hexosaminidase A deficiency, paraneoplastic motor neuronopathy, and syringomyelia and syringobulbia. Table 447–2 presents a differential diagnosis of ALS based on anatomic classification of affected components of the nervous system.

Rx Treatment and Prognosis

For direct disease treatment, the only drug currently available is riluzole (2-amino-6-trifluoromethoxy benzothiazole). ◼ Riluzole blocks release of glutamic acid and may slow the progression of disease by disrupting glutamate-mediated neurotoxicity. Administered at 50 mg twice a day, riluzole is generally well tolerated, although some patients experience nausea and general asthenia.

Combining the results of several clinical epidemiology studies, the mean duration between onset of symptoms and death in sporadic ALS ranges from 27 to 43 months, and the median duration from 23 to 52 months. The average 5-year survival is 25%. The mean disease duration of primary lateral sclerosis is much longer, with an average of 224 months between symptoms and death. The relentless progression and poor prognosis of ALS requires attentive, supportive care.

A multidisciplinary approach is essential and is best coordinated by a dedicated ALS nurse or other health care professional. Symptomatic treatment of patients is frequently required for sialorrhea, pseudobulbar symptoms, cramps, and spasticity. A social worker should help the patient cope with a sense of general fear, anxiety, and depression. A physical therapist should provide the patient with exercises for stretching and flexibility and recommend needed bracing and adaptive walking devices. An occupational therapist should arrange adaptive devices to improve functional independence. As swallowing function decreases and speech becomes more difficult, a speech pathologist is helpful to oversee barium-swallow tests and obtain augmentative communication devices. For patients who undergo percutaneous endoscopic gastrostomy, a dietitian assists in selection of proper feedings. Pulmonary specialists are often helpful in determining when noninvasive ventilation techniques, such as bilevel positive airway pressure, will be helpful for pulmonary symptoms and in assisting in the long-term care of patients who choose to become ventilator dependent.

SPINAL MUSCULAR ATROPHIES

The spinal muscular atrophies are hereditary, progressive motor neuron disorders that can begin in utero, during infancy, in childhood, or in adulthood. This section focuses on spinal muscular atrophy (SMA) types 1 to 3 and bulbospinal muscular atrophy, also known as Kennedy's syndrome. Since the genetic characteristics of these disorders are defined, they are more readily diagnosed than other spinal muscular atrophies: distal hereditary motor neuropathy types I and II, upper limb-predominant hereditary motor neuropathy (type V), proximal spinal muscular atrophy, and scapuloperoneal syndromes due to spinal muscular atrophies (see Table 447–1).

Definition and Etiology

SMA 1 to 3 represent the first class of neurologic disorders in which a developmental defect in neuronal apoptosis is the most likely cause. Linkage to chromosome 5q13 led to the identification of the survival motor neuron (SMN) genes, two copies of which exist on 5q13. The form of SMA with the earliest onset and most severe disease, SMA 1 (Werdnig-Hoffmann disease), is caused by homozygous deletions in exons 7 and 8 of the telomeric gene copy (SMNt). Mutations that convert SMNt to the centromeric copy result in a milder disease phenotype, SMA 2 (late infantile) and 3 (Kugelberg-Welander disease). The SMN gene is highly expressed in spinal neurons and is involved

Table 447–2 • DIFFRENTIAL DIAGNOSIS OF ALS CLASSIFIED BY ANATOMY OF THE NERVOUS SYSTEM

ANATOMIC SITE	POSSIBLE DISORDER
Muscle	Idiopathic inflammatory myopathy (especially IBM), distal myopathy, nemaline myopathy, isolated neck extensor myopathy, metabolic myopathy, oculopharyngeal dystrophy
Neuromuscular junction	MG, Lambert-Eaton myasthenic syndrome
Roots, plexus, nerve	Radiculopathy, diabetic polyradiculoneuropathy, infectious polyradiculopathy, plexopathies, mononeuropathies, motor neuropathies
Anterior horn cells	Spinal muscular atrophy, BSMA, monomelic amyotrophy, paraneoplastic motor neuropathy, progressive post-polio muscular atrophy, hexosaminidase deficiency
Spinal cord	Spondylotic myelopathy, syringomyelia, MS, adrenomyeloneuropathy, vitamin B_{12} deficiency, familial spastic paraparesis, HTLV-1 myelopathy
Central nervous system	Parkinson's disease, Creutzfeldt-Jakob disease, multisystem atrophy, Huntington's disease, brain stem stroke, brain stem glioma, foramen magnum tumors
Systemic disorders	Hyperthyroidism, hyperparathyroidism

ALS = amyotrophic lateral sclerosis; BSMA = bulbospinal muscular atrophy, HTLV-1 = human T-lymphotropic virus type 1, IBM = inclusion body myositis, MG = myasthenia gravis, MS = multiple sclerosis.

From Amyotrophic Lateral Sclerosis, by Hiroshi Mitsumoto, David. Copyright © 1997 by Oxford University Press, Inc. Used by permission of Oxford University Press Inc.

in RNA splicing. Deletions of exons 5 and 6 or complete absence of another gene on 5q13, the neuronal apoptosis inhibitor (NAIP), occur in 45 to 65% of patients with SMA 1 and in 20 to 40% of individuals with SMA 2 and 3. NAIP mutations may modify the severity of SMA.

Incidence and Prevalence

The estimated carrier frequency of an SMNt mutation is 1 in 50. SMA 1 (Werdnig-Hoffmann disease) has a cumulative incidence of disease of 1 in 8000 births.

Pathology

At autopsy, patients with SMA have atrophic spinal cords with loss of α-motor neurons and evidence of motor neuron degeneration and gliosis. Ventral roots are atrophic, and muscle groups supplied by these motor neurons and roots are atrophied and show microscopic evidence of denervation and reinnervation. Before genetic testing was available, muscle biopsies were the main diagnostic tool used to confirm the clinical diagnosis of SMA 1 to 3.

Clinical Manifestations

The onset of SMA 1 (Werdnig-Hoffmann disease), by definition, occurs either in utero or within the first 3 months of life. Infants present with severe diffuse weakness, hypotonia, reduced or absent reflexes, and tongue fasciculations. The usual cause of death is respiratory failure; 50% of infants die by age 7 months and 95% by 17 months.

Individuals with SMA 2 (late infantile form) and 3 (Kugelberg-Welander disease) are less severely affected than those with SMA 1. SMA 2 is considered an intermediate phenotype. The onset occurs in children younger than 18 to 24 months. These children may never stand or walk, develop early scoliosis and respiratory insufficiency, and have a shortened lifespan. SMA 3 is the mildest phenotype, with onset frequently in later childhood or even in the teen years. These individuals have proximal, symmetrical weakness but stand and walk independently. With time, slow and mild loss of function usually takes place. Death occurs in adulthood, and whether SMA 3 shortens an individual's lifespan remains uncertain.

Diagnosis

Diagnosis of SMA 1 to 3 is made by genetic testing in a patient with appropriate clinical signs and symptoms. Ninety-five per cent of affected individuals have SMN deletions. Currently, carrier testing can only be performed by linkage analysis. Prenatal diagnosis is available. EMG and muscle biopsy reveal evidence of denervation but are unnecessary if a molecular diagnosis is established. They are often performed before the diagnosis has been considered. Cerebrospinal fluid (CSF) analysis is normal and serum creatine kinase levels are elevated only in SMA 3.

It is important to distinguish SMA 1 from infantile botulism, which can present with a similar clinical picture. EMG with high-frequency repetitive nerve stimulation shows a decrement in botulism but not in SMA. Examination of the stool for botulinum can confirm the diagnosis of infantile botulism. SMA 2 and 3 can be distinguished from chronic inflammatory demyelinating polyneuropathy by the presence of normal CSF protein and normal nerve conduction studies in SMA. SMA 3 and the hereditary motor sensory neuropathies (Charcot-Marie-Tooth disease) can be clinically similar. In addition to genetic testing, key diagnostic differences lie in normal nerve conduction studies in individuals with SMA 3 compared to abnormal studies in individuals with hereditary motor sensory neuropathies.

 Treatment and Prognosis

No treatment is currently available, although trials with ciliary neurotrophic factor, brain-derived neurotrophic factor, gabapentin, and riluzole are underway. In SMA 2 and 3, children benefit from passive and active physical therapy, lightweight braces, and, if necessary, surgery to correct scoliosis.

BULBOSPINAL MUSCULAR ATROPHY

Definition and Etiology

Bulbospinal muscular atrophy (BSMA) was first described by Kennedy and colleagues; consequently, it is also called Kennedy's syndrome. BSMA is a trinucleotide-repeat disorder with a CAG expansion encoding for a polyglutamine tract in the first exon of the androgen receptor gene on chromosome Xq11-12. Nuclear inclusions, aggregates, and aberrant proteolytic processing of the mutant androgen receptor are observed in bulbar and spinal motor neurons, which may lead to the pathology. It is not known why this mutation causes motor neuron disease instead of the testicular feminization caused by other androgen receptor mutations.

Incidence and Prevalence

BSMA is an X-linked recessive disorder. Incidence and prevalence have not been defined, but it is commonly held that BSMA is the most common form of adult-onset SMA.

Pathology

At autopsy, patients with BSMA have findings similar to those of SMA 3. Mild brain stem and cord atrophy with loss of α-motor neurons is seen, as is evidence of motor neuron degeneration and gliosis. Muscle biopsy reveals denervation and reinnervation in affected muscle groups.

Clinical Manifestations

The mean onset of BSMA is 30 years with a range of 15 to 60 years. Gynecomastia occurs in 50% of affected individuals. Individuals present with facial, tongue, and proximal weakness. Dysphagia, dysarthria, and masseter muscle weakness are common. Weakness is symmetrical and slowly progressive over decades; patients only become dependent on canes or walkers in the fifth or sixth decades of life. Fasciculations are present largely in the face, and tendon reflexes are reduced or absent. Individuals frequently experience a mild postural tremor and a mild loss of vibratory sensation. No upper motor neuron signs are present.

Diagnosis

Diagnosis of BSMA is made when a patient with appropriate clinical signs and symptoms has positive genetic test results. A direct correlation exists between disease severity and size of the CAG expansion; individuals affected at a younger age and more severely have longer polyglutamine tracts. The absence of upper motor neuron signs distinguishes BSMA from amyotrophic lateral sclerosis. EMG and a muscle biopsy are often performed because creatine kinase levels are frequently elevated (up to 10-fold), and they reveal evidence of chronic denervation. This differentiates BSMA from muscular dystrophy and other myopathies.

 Treatment and Prognosis

No specific treatment is available. Clinical trials are exploring the value of hormones. Lifespan is usually unaffected, and therapy consists of supportive care, such as ambulatory aids.

1. Bensimon G, Lacomblez L, Meininger V, et al: ALS/Riluzole Study Group: A controlled trial of riluzole in amyotrophic lateral sclerosis. N Engl J Med 1994;330: 585–591.

SUGGESTED READINGS

Friedlander RM: Apoptosis and caspases in neurodegenerative diseases. N Engl J Med 2003;348:1365–1375. *A review linking specific cell-death pathways to ALS and other neurodegenerative diseases, providing a basis for the development of novel therapeutics.*
Orrell RW, Figlewicz DA: Clinical implications of the genetics of ALS and other motor neuron diseases. Neurology 2001;57:9–17. *A review of the genetics of FALS, SMA, and SBMA.*
Pestronk A: Neuromuscular Disease Center. St. Louis, Washington University School of Medicine, Neuromuscular Disease Center, 2003. URL: http://www.neuro.wustl.edu/neuromuscular/. *Comprehensive collection of motor neuron disorders with key links to salient information on genetics, recent basic research, and therapy. This website is user friendly, is updated continuously, and is invaluable for the clinician.*

448 MULTIPLE SCLEROSIS AND DEMYELINATING CONDITIONS OF THE CENTRAL NERVOUS SYSTEM

Richard A. Rudick

Central nervous system (CNS) myelin is an elaborate extension of the oligodendrocyte cell membrane. A single oligodendrocyte myelinates as many as 20 or 30 different CNS axonal segments, each over a length of 1 mm or less. Oligodendrocyte membrane extensions wrap around the axons in a concentric fashion to form the myelin sheath. Tightly compacted, mature myelin consists of parallel layers of bimolecular lipids apposed to layers of hydrated protein. Lipids, including cerebroside, phospholipids, and cholesterol, constitute 75% of myelin's dry weight. Myelin proteins include proteolipid protein, myelin basic protein, myelin-associated glycoprotein, and a number of less abundant proteins. Active myelin synthesis starts in utero and continues for the first 2 years of life; slower synthesis continues during childhood and adolescence. Turnover of mature myelin continues at a slow rate throughout life. Both developing and mature forms of myelin are readily susceptible to injury by the diseases described in this section.

Among acquired disorders of myelin, multiple sclerosis (MS) and its variants are by far the most common diseases (Table 448–1). Viral infections, nutritional disorders, and anoxic-ischemic injury can also cause CNS demyelination. Peripheral demyelination is associated with peripheral neuropathies (Chapters 461 and 462). The leukodystrophies, which are uncommon dysmyelinating and demyelinating disorders, have been the subject of recent genetic and biochemical advances.

MULTIPLE SCLEROSIS

Definition

MS, which is a disorder of unknown cause, is defined clinically by typical neurologic symptoms, signs, and progression, and is characterized pathologically by scattered areas of inflammation, demyelination, and axonal pathology affecting the brain, optic nerves, and spinal cord. The first symptoms of MS usually occur between the ages of 15 and 50 years. Individual episodes of inflammatory demyelination may be accompanied by clinical symptoms, termed *relapses*, followed in most cases by clinical recovery; the resulting pattern is the classic relapsing-remitting course seen early in the disease in most patients. Diagnosis requires intermittent or progressive CNS symptoms, as well as clinical or magnetic resonance imaging (MRI) evidence of two or more CNS lesions occurring in a patient who lacks an alternative explanation, such as recurrent strokes. The diagnosis is based on clinical features; currently available laboratory tests support the diagnosis but are not pathognomonic.

Etiology

The initiating cause of MS is unknown, but it is widely believed that the clinical manifestations are mediated by immune-initiated inflammatory demyelination and axonal injury. The brain shows hallmarks of an immunopathologic process: perivascular infiltration by lymphocytes and monocytes; class II major histocompatibility complex (MHC) antigen expression by cells in the lesions; chemokines, lymphokines, and monokines secreted by activated cells; and the absence of overt evidence of infection. Additional evidence of an autoimmune pathogenesis includes the following:

1. Immunologic abnormalities are present in blood and cerebrospinal fluid (CSF) of MS patients, notably selective intrathecal humoral immune activation, and there is a high frequency of activated lymphocytes in blood and CSF.
2. There is association between MS and certain MHC class II allotypes.
3. Patients tend to improve with immunosuppressive drugs and worsen with interferon-gamma (IFN-γ) treatment, which stimulates the immune response.
4. Disease activity is ameliorated during pregnancy but flares up during the postpartum period, similar to other autoimmune disorders such as rheumatoid arthritis.
5. There are similarities between MS and experimental allergic encephalomyelitis (EAE), which is an animal model in which recurrent episodes of inflammatory demyelination can be induced by inoculating susceptible animals with myelin proteins, such as myelin basic protein or proteolipid protein.

Epidemiologic studies suggest both environmental and genetic factors in the pathogenesis of MS. The uneven geographic distribution of the disease and the occurrence of several point-source epidemics suggest environmental factors. Migration studies suggested that exposure to undefined environmental factors before adolescence is required for subsequent development of MS. Intense study over the past 30 years has failed to establish an infectious cause, although studies continue to evaluate the possibility that one or more ubiquitous viruses (e.g., human herpes virus 6, Epstein-Barr virus) may trigger the disease, leading to an autoimmune process in susceptible individuals.

A genetic influence is established by increased concordance in monozygotic compared with dizygotic twins, clustering of MS in families, racial variability in risk, and associations with class II MHC allotypes. Population-based whole genome screening studies have identified approximately ten candidate genetic loci. As with other complex human diseases, the genetic basis of MS is currently believed to result from the net effect of interactions between environmental factors and a number of susceptibility and resistance genes. Disease-modifying genes that define the clinical phenotype and severity of disease have not yet been characterized. Immunologic, epidemiologic, and genetic evidence supports the concept that exposure of a genetically susceptible individual to an environmental factor or factors during childhood (perhaps one of many common viruses) leads eventually to immune-mediated inflammatory demyelination.

Incidence, Prevalence, and Epidemiology

The annual incidence rate for MS ranges in different populations from 1.5 to 11 per 100,000 persons. Several studies suggest that the incidence rate has increased over time. For example, data from Olmsted County, MN, suggest a gradual increase in annual incidence during the past century from about 1.2 per 100,000 between 1905 and 1914 to about 6.2 per 100,000 between 1975 and 1984. In all studies, the highest age- and gender-specific rates occur in women between ages 20 and 40 years.

Table 448–1 • DISEASES OF MYELIN

Idiopathic, presumably autoimmune
Recurrent or chronically progressive demyelination (multiple sclerosis and its variants)
Monophasic demyelination (may be first clinical episode of multiple sclerosis)
  Optic neuritis
  Acute transverse myelitis
Acute disseminated encephalomyelitis; acute hemorrhagic leukoencephalopathy
  Following infection, with or without exanthem
  Following vaccination
Viral infections (see Chs. 453 and 455)
Progressive multifocal leukoencephalopathy
Subacute sclerosing panencephalitis
Nutritional disorders (see Ch. 458)
Combined systems disease (vitamin B_{12} deficiency)
Demyelination of the corpus callosum (Marchiafava-Bignami disease)
Central pontine myelinolysis
Anoxic-ischemic sequelae (see Ch. 440)
Delayed postanoxic cerebral demyelination
Progressive subcortical ischemic encephalopathy
Leukodystrophies
Primarily affecting central nervous system myelin
  Adrenoleukodystrophy (Schilder's disease)
  Pelizaeus-Merzbacher disease (sudanophilic leukodystrophies)
  Spongy degeneration
  Others (Alexander's disease, Canavan's disease)
Central peripheral nervous system
  Metachromatic leukodystrophy
  Globoid cell leukodystrophy (Krabbe's disease)

Worldwide prevalence differs according to geography. Distribution of MS has been well studied in North America, Northern Europe, Australia, and New Zealand. In both hemispheres, MS is more common in the temperate zones, decreasing toward the equator. The prevalence of MS in the northern United States, Canada, and northern Europe is at least 100 per 100,000 population; in certain regions, the prevalence of MS exceeds 300 per 100,000 persons, compared with less than 5 per 100,000 persons in the tropics. Regional heterogeneity has been reported within high prevalence zones, and several reports describe MS clusters in small areas. In the Faroe Islands, for example, a well-reported outbreak of MS occurred during the 20 years following the start of World War II, suggesting the effects of an unidentified environmental factor.

Pathology

Brain, optic nerves, and spinal cord from MS patients contain scattered areas, ranging in size from 1 mm to several centimeters in diameter, in which myelin is lost. The borders between histologically normal tissue and demyelinated zones are usually well-demarcated, but there may be a gradation from normal to thin myelin before bare axons occur. Some areas show diffuse partial myelin loss. Although plaques may occur in any myelinated area of the CNS, the most commonly affected regions include optic nerves, periventricular cerebral white matter, and cervical spinal cord.

The earliest event in development of the MS lesion is breakdown of the blood-brain barrier, followed by perivenular mononuclear infiltrates, and quickly thereafter by circumscribed areas of myelin breakdown. Macrophages and activated microglia are invariably present at sites of active demyelination and appear necessary for myelin loss. B lymphocytes and plasma cells surround small CNS blood vessels, and T lymphocytes and monocytes infiltrate CNS parenchyma. Products of the immune response, including immunoglobulins, interleukins, interferons, and tumor necrosis factor, accompany the acute MS lesion. Tissue edema reaches a maximum after about 1 month, after which lesions evolve over several months into plaques, which are permanently demyelinated gliotic scars depleted of oligodendrocytes. After the initial events, immature oligodendrocytes appear and attempt to remyelinate axons. Remyelination is incomplete, however, and appears to be arrested at the stage of premyelinating oligodendrocyte in chronic lesions. As the disease progresses, axonal degeneration together with loss of myelin results in progressive brain atrophy. Once this process exceeds a threshold, progressive neurologic deterioration, termed progressive MS, ensues.

Laboratory Findings

CEREBROSPINAL FLUID. Increased CSF immunoglobulin levels, reflecting the presence of intrathecal humoral immune activation, appear in 80 to 90% of MS patients. CSF γ-globulin normally represents less than 13% of total CSF protein, but in MS patients, the proportion often rises much higher. After gel electrophoresis of CSF γ-globulin, separate, discrete "oligoclonal" bands (OCB) can be detected in 70 to 80% of patients. CSF OCBs are also observed in patients with CNS infections or inflammatory diseases and occasionally in patients with tumors, strokes, and some metabolic processes. Increased CSF levels of free κ light chains are present less frequently than OCB, but they are more specific for MS than are IgG abnormalities.

The amount of antibody synthesis within the CNS can be quantified by measuring the CSF and serum IgG and albumin levels and calculating a CSF IgG synthesis rate. CSF protein is normal or only slightly elevated in MS; levels greater than 75 mg/dL require an alternative explanation. The CSF cell count is nearly always fewer than 50 mononuclear cells/μL; cell counts of more than 100 cells/μL require a search for an infectious process. Myelin destruction releases myelin basic protein (MBP) into CSF, where it can be detected by radioimmunoassay. The MBP level correlates to some extent with the activity of the disease and is not detectable in normal individuals or during quiescent periods in MS patients. An increase in MBP serves as an index of disease activity but is not specific to MS; myelin injury from other causes, such as acute brain infarction, also increases CSF MBP.

SENSORY EVOKED POTENTIALS. Myelin allows rapid propagation of the nerve action potential. Loss of myelin from any cause slows conduction velocity or causes conduction block. Conduction along sensory pathways can be measured by inducing a response to visual, auditory,

SYMPTOM	PERCENTAGE OF CASES
Sensory disturbance in one or more limbs	33
Disturbance of balance and gait	18
Visual loss in one eye	17
Diplopia	13
Progressive weakness	10
Acute myelitis	6
Lhermitte's sign	3
Sensory disturbance in face	3
Pain	2

Table 448–2 • INITIAL SYMPTOMS IN MULTIPLE SCLEROSIS PATIENTS

*From Paty DW, Poser CM: Clinical symptoms and signs of multiple sclerosis. *In* Poser CM (ed): The Diagnosis of Multiple Sclerosis. New York, Thieme and Stratton, 1984, p. 27.

or somatosensory stimuli. Measurement of the latency of the visual evoked potential (VEP) after a visual stimulus is used most widely (Chapter 423). In most laboratories, the normal VEP latency is less than approximately 105 msec. Increased latency indicates an abnormality in the optic nerve on that side. Evoked potentials have not proved useful for monitoring the progression of MS or its response to therapy.

IMAGING. Computed tomographic (CT) brain scans sometimes reveal hypodense regions in white matter, but this imaging modality is relatively insensitive and usually shows no abnormalities. By comparison, head MRI scans show abnormalities in more than 85% of patients with clinically definite MS. Typical lesions (Fig. 448–1) are multifocal, appear hyperintense on intermediate or T2-weighted MRI scans, and occur predominantly in the periventricular cerebral white matter, subcortical white matter, corpus callosum, cerebellum, cerebellar peduncles, brain stem, and spinal cord. Usually MRI reveals many more hyperintense lesions than clinically anticipated. Intravenous paramagnetic agents, such as gadolinium, demonstrate acute lesions, which appear hyperintense on T1-weighted images. Serial studies have demonstrated that gadolinium enhancement appears and disappears in a given lesion in about 4 weeks. MRI abnormalities are not specific for MS, and nonspecific MRI signal changes of uncertain significance develop commonly in people older than age 50 years. The specificity of MRI lesions for MS increases with lesions that are 6 mm or more in diameter and that are adjacent to the lateral ventricles, particularly when accompanied by lesions in the brain stem, cerebellum, and spinal cord. Gadolinium-enhancing lesions are most common during the relapsing-remitting stage of MS and become less frequent during the later disease stages. Lesions that are hypointense on T1-weighted images, so-called black holes, signify foci of tissue loss. Quantitative measures of brain atrophy, either regional or whole brain, correlate with irreversible neurologic disability. Serial MRI can measure the effect of treatment or progression of disease. Newer magnetic resonance-based techniques, such as magnetization transfer imaging or MR spectroscopy (Chapter 424), may allow more specific assessment of tissue or axonal integrity.

Clinical Manifestations and Disease Course

Women are affected more frequently than men, with a 3 : 2 ratio. Symptoms usually begin between ages 20 and 50 years, with a peak incidence at approximately age 30 years. MS produces a myriad of neurologic symptoms and signs, depending on the anatomic sites of involvement. In younger patients, the disease usually starts with a subacute or acute onset of focal neurologic symptoms and signs, most often reflecting disease in optic nerves, pyramidal tracts, posterior columns, cerebellum, central vestibular system, or medial longitudinal fasciculus. Older individuals commonly present with insidiously progressive myelopathy, manifest as some combination of progressive spastic leg weakness, axial instability, and bladder impairment. In one large series, approximately 30% of patients presented with visual symptoms, 30% with sensory symptoms, 20% with gait or balance disturbance, and the remaining 20% with various other symptoms (Table 448–2). In general, as the disease

Continued

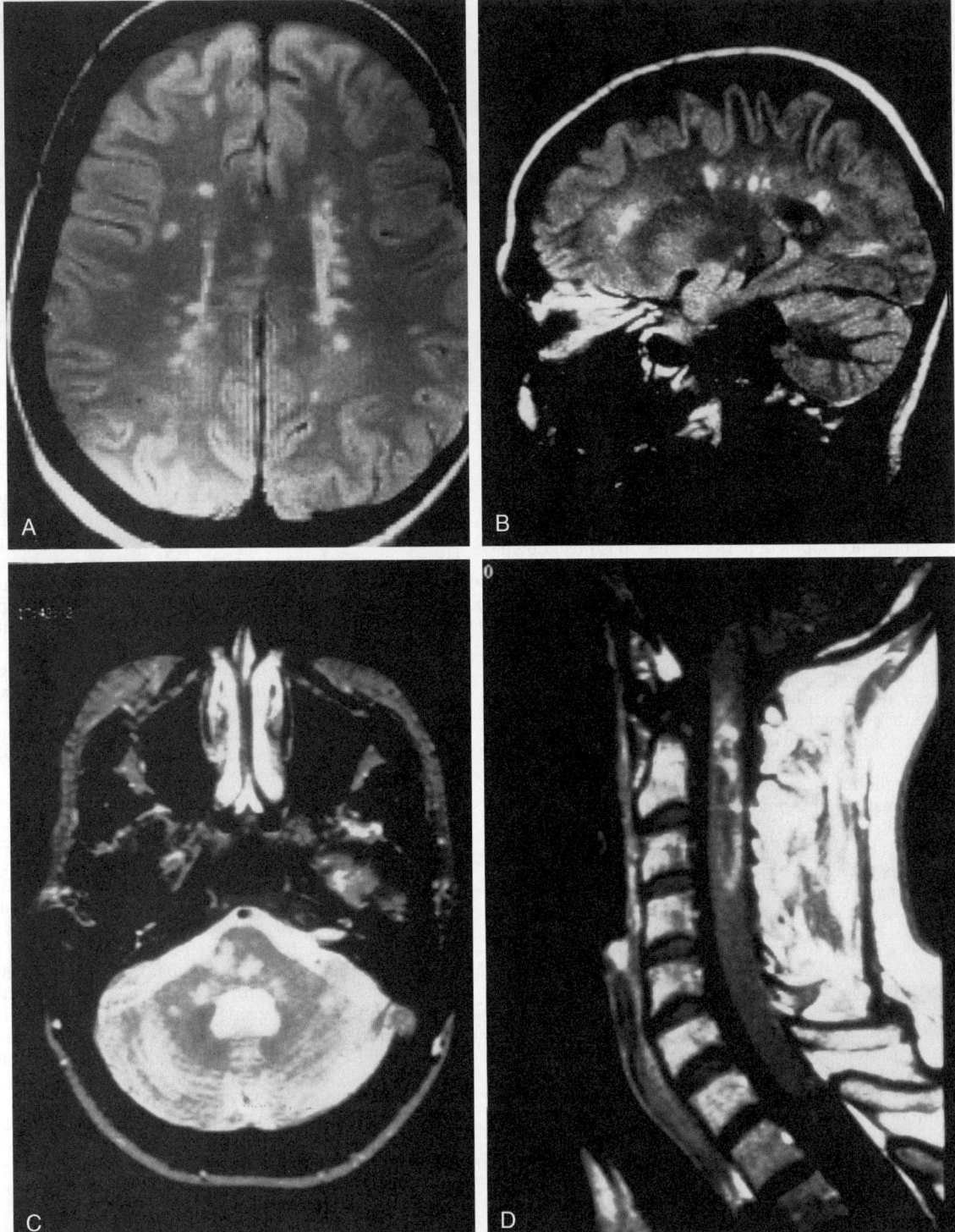

FIGURE 448–1 • Magnetic resonance imaging of brain and spinal cord from a patient with clinically definite multiple sclerosis. *A*, T2-weighted images. Transverse section just above the bodies of the lateral ventricles. Note the numerous high-signal lesions adjacent to the bodies of the lateral ventricles in the deep cerebral white matter. *B*, Sagittal proton-density image showing ovoid lesions extending from the lateral ventricles into the deep cerebral white matter. *C*, T2-weighted section through the brain stem and cerebellum at the level of the middle cerebellar peduncles showing numerous high-signal lesions in the pons, cerebellar peduncles, and cerebellum. *D*, T1-weighted sagittal image through the cervical spinal cord lesion with gadolinium enhancement as signified by high signal around the periphery of the lesion. (Courtesy of Barbara Banger, MD, Cleveland Clinic Foundation, Department of Neuroradiology.)

progresses, new symptoms and signs appear, old symptoms and signs recur, and residual symptoms increase.

Visual symptoms include monocular visual loss, oscillopsia, or diplopia. Gait disorder results from spastic leg weakness, axial instability, and lower extremity sensory loss. Spasticity consists of increased muscle tone, hyperreflexia, and limb spasms, accompanied by weakness and loss of dexterity. Spasticity in MS patients almost always affects the lower more than the upper extremities. Upper extremity impairment includes sensory loss resulting in a clumsy hand, cerebellar ataxia, or, less commonly, spastic weakness. Bladder dysfunction includes urinary urgency with urge incontinence or hesitancy and incomplete emptying. Neuropsychological problems are common and include depression, emotional lability, and cognitive impairment.

Increased body temperature by as little as 0.5°C transiently reduces neurologic function in some patients. In the setting of increased ambient temperature, strenuous physical activity, or fever, patients may experience transient worsening of symptoms owing to slowed axonal conduction induced by heating; the new symptoms disappear within hours of regaining normal body temperature.

At least 80% of patients improve in the days to months following their initial bout, with the degree of improvement ranging from slight to virtual disappearance of the neurologic dysfunction. Although most patients experience exacerbations and remissions early in the course of the illness, as time goes by, recovery from individual bouts decreases, fixed impairment and disability remain, and the course becomes chronically progressive. About 30% of patients, especially those older than age 15 years, experience chronically progressive problems from the onset of disease. Ten years after onset, about half of all patients are still able to carry out their household and employment responsibilities. Fifteen years after onset, about half require a cane to walk. Approximately 25 years after onset, at least half are unable to walk, even with assistance. By contrast, some individuals, perhaps as many as one third, either avoid disability altogether or become bedridden within months of onset. The average interval from clinical onset to death is 35 years; terminal events include sepsis from urinary tract infection or decubitus ulcers, aspiration pneumonia, or suicide.

FACTORS AFFECTING THE CLINICAL COURSE. The only predictable factor in MS is its unpredictability in the individual patient. It has become clear, however, that certain features carry a relatively poor prognosis: progressive disease from onset, preponderance of motor and cerebellar signs, and markedly abnormal head MRI findings at first clinical presentation. Favorable indicators include a high degree of recovery after the first attack, predominance of sensory symptoms, and benign phenotype 5 years after onset of symptoms. Of these factors, severity of change seen on MRI appears to be the strongest predictor of future disability.

Several studies have found that infections of almost any type increase the risk for exacerbation, presumably owing to activation of the immune system, with an associated increase in disease activity. As with numerous autoimmune diseases, MS disease activity decreases during pregnancy but increases somewhat in the postpartum period. The overall progression of MS, however, is not affected by one or more pregnancies.

Diagnosis

Despite increasing reliance on sophisticated brain imaging, CSF analysis, and electrophysiologic tests, the diagnosis of MS is based on clinical features supplemented by laboratory tests, rather than the reverse. The Schumacher criteria diagnose clinically definite MS when an appropriate clinical history is supported by the following:

- Objective abnormalities of CNS function on the neurologic examination
- Examination or history indicating involvement of two or more areas of the CNS
- CNS disease predominantly reflecting white matter involvement
- A pattern of two or more clinical episodes, each lasting more than 24 hours and occurring a month or more apart, or a slow or stepwise progression of signs and symptoms over at least 6 months

- Patient's age between 10 and 50 years
- Signs and symptoms that cannot be better explained by another disease process

Laboratory testing, especially MRI, plays an increasingly important role in documenting multicentric CNS lesions and eliminating alternative diagnoses. Newer diagnostic criteria rely on multicentric brain or spinal cord lesions. CSF IgG abnormalities are required to support the diagnosis of MS in patients who have had progressive disease from the onset of symptoms.

Two common errors confound the diagnosis of MS. The first is when a clear alternative diagnosis (Table 448–3) is not considered or evaluated appropriately, especially because a feature that is atypical (Table 448–4) is overlooked. The two most useful "red flags" to suggest an alternative diagnosis are signs and symptoms that could be explained by a single lesion in the nervous system and the absence of a clinical remission.

In a patient with localized disease, the working assumption must be that a definable, nondemyelinating structural lesion exists. Depending on the clinical features, diagnostic testing should be used to exclude brain or spinal cord tumor (Chapter 457), arteriovenous malformation (Chapter 441), cervical spondylosis with cord compression (Chapter 429), cervical or thoracic disc herniation (Chapter 429), Chiari malformation (Chapter 459), brain abscess (Chapter 449), or a parenchymal mass from sarcoidosis (Chapters 91 and 449). MRI is the most sensitive differential screening procedure and currently eliminates the need for CT scanning or myelography in almost all cases.

In patients with a steadily progressive course, degenerative, infectious, neoplastic, and some metabolic disorders must be considered. Disorders that can be incorrectly diagnosed as MS include spinocerebellar degeneration (Chapter 446), cervicomedullary syringomyelia (Chapter 459), basilar invagination, motor neuron disease (Chapter 447), HTLV-1 myelopathy (Chapter 372), human immunodeficiency virus (HIV)-related myelopathy or brain infection

---

Table 448–3 • CONDITIONS COMMONLY MISTAKEN FOR MULTIPLE SCLEROSIS

Vascular disease
  Small-vessel cerebrovascular disease
  Vasculitis
Structural lesions
  Craniocervical junction tumor, malformation of base of skull
  Anomaly
  Posterior fossa tumor or arteriovenous malformation
  Spinal cord tumor or cervical spondylosis
Degenerative diseases
  Motor system disease
  Spinocerebellar degeneration
Infections
  HTLV-1 infection
  HIV myelopathy or HIV-related cerebritis
  Lyme disease
Other conditions
  Vitamin B_{12} deficiency
  Sjögren's syndrome
  Sarcoidosis
  Nonspecific MRI abnormalities

HIV = human immunodeficiency virus; HTLV = human T-cell lymphotropic virus; MRI = magnetic resonance imaging.

Table 448–4 • "RED FLAGS" TO SUGGEST AN ALTERNATIVE TO THE DIAGNOSIS OF MULTIPLE SCLEROSIS

Syndrome that could be explained by localized disease
Steadily progressive disease, absence of clinical remission
Absence of oculomotor, optic nerve, sensory, or bladder involvement
Normal cerebrospinal fluid

Modified from Rudick RA, Schiffer RB, Schwetz K, et al: Multiple sclerosis: The problem of incorrect diagnosis. Arch Neurol 1986;43:578–583.

(Chapter 414), neoplasms such as parenchymal lymphoma (Chapter 457), and some metabolic diseases including occasional cases of mitochondrial cytopathies (Chapter 463). Spinocerebellar degeneration and motor neuron disease are suspected by symmetrical neurologic impairment restricted to characteristic neural systems, the absence of inflammatory changes in the CSF, and the lack of response to corticosteroids. Progressive myelopathy should prompt testing for HTLV-1 and HIV, as well as for very long-chain fatty acids, to exclude adrenoleukodystrophy (ALD; see later text). On rare occasions, CNS lupus (Chapters 280 and 440) or vitamin B_{12} deficiency may (Chapter 458) be clinically indistinguishable from MS. These disorders should be excluded by measuring levels of antinuclear antibodies and vitamin B_{12} (Chapters 280 and 440) at the time of diagnosis. Small vessel cerebrovascular disease should be considered in hypertensive patients, particularly in those lacking CSF abnormalities typical of MS. MRI

may help distinguish MS from small vessel cerebrovascular disease; MS patients more commonly have lesions adjacent to the brain ventricles and involvement of the corpus callosum.

The second common type of diagnostic error occurs in patients with no definable neurologic disease. Patients commonly acquire a false-positive diagnosis of MS because of nonspecific neurologic symptoms, such as weakness, fatigue, or tingling, at times accompanied by minimal nonspecific signal changes on brain MRI. The absence of objective neurologic signs at any time, patterns of weakness or sensory loss that fail to conform to known neuroanatomic systems, and disability out of proportion to objective clinical findings raise the suspicion of psychogenic illness. However, because MS can begin with sensory symptoms, fatigue, or other nonspecific symptoms, it is necessary to follow the patient over time before an accurate diagnosis can be made.

Rx Treatment

EDUCATION. MS patients and their families typically ask questions including the following: (1) "What will happen to me?" One of the major psychological burdens for an MS patient is uncertainty about the future course of the illness. The physician should acknowledge the unpredictable course but emphasize the spectrum of severity and the significant proportion of patients who remain neurologically intact for many years. (2) "How can I control my illness?" Most patients have beliefs about what will improve or worsen their MS. The patient's need for control over the disease can often be focused on healthy lifestyles, such as fitness programs or appropriate diet. (3) "When should I call you?" Patients should be advised to call when necessary but should be routinely seen at 6- or 12-month intervals for ongoing assessment and to reduce the need for telephone calls. (4) "Will my children get this?" The lifetime risk to a child of a mother with MS is 3 to 5%—a 30- to 50-fold increase over that for the general population, but still a small absolute risk. (5) "Can I have a baby?" MS usually is less active during pregnancy; breast-feeding has little if any effect on the frequency, timing, or severity of postpartum exacerbations; and the bulk of evidence suggests that the overall course of MS, including the eventual degree of disability, is unaffected by one or more pregnancies. Women with mild to moderate disability should plan pregnancies primarily on the basis of issues other than MS.

COMMON SYMPTOMS AND THEIR TREATMENT. Spasticity may be reduced by a combination of physical measures and antispastic drugs. The γ-aminobutyric acid (GABA)-agonist baclofen is the drug of choice, but its dosage should be individualized because it is effective over a wide dose range. Baclofen therapy should be instituted slowly to avoid sedation or weakness, and it must not be stopped abruptly, because its withdrawal can cause confusional states or seizures. Diazepam may be used as an adjunct to baclofen, particularly for patients who have nocturnal spasms that cause sleep disturbance. Even a small dose of diazepam may potentiate the benefits of baclofen. Tizanidine, an α-adrenergic agonist, is an alternative to baclofen. The antispastic effects of tizanidine are generally not accompanied by increased weakness, but drowsiness and orthostatic hypotension may limit its use in individual patients. Tizanidine may be cautiously added to baclofen when additional baclofen causes undue sedation or weakness. Dantrolene is another antispasticity drug that can be used in patients who do not respond well to baclofen, tizanidine, or diazepam or who cannot tolerate the sedation that sometimes complicates the use of these drugs. Dantrolene exerts its effects at the muscle; consequently, motor weakness almost always accompanies the antispastic effect of dantrolene. Dantrolene should be used cautiously in patients with myocardial disease, and it occasionally causes toxic hepatitis. Patients with severe spasticity not effectively managed with the measures described may benefit from intrathecal baclofen, administered continuously at a rate of 200 to 800 µg/day via a fully implantable infusion pump.

Dystonic spasms consist of brief, recurrent, painful posturing of one or more extremities, not associated with altered consciousness or urinary incontinence. Dystonic spasms are easily controlled with carbamazepine or phenytoin. Ataxia is difficult to treat pharmacologically. Intention tremor may respond to clonazepam, which should

be instituted slowly to avoid sedation. Clonazepam therapy should be initiated at a dose of 0.5 mg at bedtime and increased gradually to an end point of sedation or effective control of tremor.

One or more tonic-clonic seizures occur in about 5% of MS patients. A single motor seizure predicts a subsequent seizure in an MS patient and should be treated with an adequate dose of phenytoin.

Bladder symptoms require urinalysis, culture, and measurement of postvoid residual volume. In the absence of a urinary tract infection or urinary retention greater than 100 mL, anticholinergic agents, such as oxybutynin or propantheline, are effective. Urinary tract infection or urinary retention greater than 100 mL requires urologic evaluation.

Fatigue in MS, when disabling and not caused by depression, can be treated effectively with amantadine, 100 mg twice a day. Pemoline or modafinil may be effective for some individuals who have not responded to amantadine. In many patients, however, thoughtful activity planning to include rest periods, good sleep hygiene, and regular exercise is adequate.

Heat sensitivity results from conduction failure in partially demyelinated CNS fibers. Patients may benefit from cool showers or air conditioning. Dramatic deterioration can accompany fever in patients with advanced MS, and elevated body temperatures should be treated aggressively, even while specific infections are managed with appropriate antibiotics.

Pain syndromes consist of trigeminal neuralgia or atypical facial pain, paroxysmal limb paresthesias presenting as brief tic-like pain, burning dysesthesias, Lhermitte's phenomenon, and chronic back pain, due in most cases to mechanical stress caused by ataxia and weakness. Trigeminal neuralgia or disagreeable paresthesias may respond to carbamazepine or to gabapentin, amitriptyline, phenytoin, or baclofen. If medical therapy fails, trigeminal rhizotomy is an alternative. Chronic low back and leg pain are usually alleviated with nonsteroidal anti-inflammatory drugs and physical therapy. A proper walking aid, ankle-foot orthosis, or proper seating is critical. Coexistent herniated discs should be excluded in patients with radicular pain, particularly when an ankle or knee tendon reflex is absent.

Depression or emotional distress is often under-recognized and inadequately treated. Depression is particularly common when the illness is first diagnosed or when it worsens substantially; it should be treated aggressively. Generally, serotonin reuptake inhibitors (SSRIs) are preferred because of their advantageous side effect profile (Chapter 426). However, for depressed MS patients with coexisting bladder symptoms, imipramine or amitriptyline may be useful because they may also improve bladder dysfunction. For older patients or patients with memory loss, a tricyclic antidepressant with less anticholinergic activity, such as desipramine or nortriptyline, may be better tolerated. Emotional lability, which is distressing and socially disabling for some MS patients, may improve with low doses of amitriptyline.

Cognitive dysfunction may be difficult to recognize clinically but should be suspected in any MS patient with poor work performance, family disruption, or noncompliance with medical or rehabilitative therapies, particularly when the explanation for the problem

Neurology

is unclear. Neuropsychological tests are important to address the problem and should include sensitive measurements of complex attention and information processing, learning and recent memory, concept formation, and problem solving (Chapter 423). No effective drug therapy is available, although patients often can learn compensatory strategies and may benefit from cognitive rehabilitation.

PHARMACOTHERAPY TO ALTER THE COURSE OF MULTIPLE SCLEROSIS. Numerous trials have attempted to improve the long-term course of MS or shorten the course of acute exacerbations. Nearly all current experimental therapy trials assess clinical outcomes and sequential MRI results.

Corticosteroids and Plasma Exchange. A brief course of treatment with intravenous methylprednisolone is standard therapy for an acute relapse that causes significant neurologic impairment or disability. For major clinical exacerbations, intravenous methylprednisolone, 1000 mg/day for 3 days, can be administered safely in an outpatient setting, followed by prednisone, 60 mg in a single morning dose for 4 days, tapering off over 12 days. In a controlled trial, about 40% of patients with severe acute demyelinating episodes unresponsive to corticosteroids responded favorably to plasma exchange.[1]

Small randomized trials suggest that periodic pulses of intravenous methylprednisolone therapy might slow disease progression; beneficial effects were more significant in patients with early relapsing remitting MS compared with more advanced progressive disease, suggesting that anti-inflammatory therapy is most effective in the earlier stages of disease. However, data for interferon (see later discussion) are more convincing, so interferon is the approved treatment of choice to modify the course of MS. Furthermore, as MS enters the secondary progressive stage, most patients become less responsive to steroid therapy.

Immunomodulatory Therapy. Three forms of recombinant interferon-β (IFN-β), interferon β-1a (Avonex and Rebif) and interferon β-1b (Betaseron), have been approved for use in relapsing remitting MS patients.[2-5] IFN-β therapy reduces the frequency and severity of MS relapses, slows the progression of disability, reduces the number and volume of new lesions seen on MRI scan, slows the progressive accumulation of lesions seen on T2 MRI scan, and may decrease the rate of brain atrophy. Based on controlled clinical trials, the individual products are administered at different doses (higher for Betaseron and Rebif compared with Avonex), frequencies (weekly for Avonex, three times weekly for Rebif, and every other day for Betaseron), and routes of administration (intramuscular for Avonex and subcutaneous for Betaseron

and Rebif). In general, IFN-β therapy seems to slow the disease or reduce relapses by about one third, and there is no definitive evidence that one of the products is superior. Adverse effects include transient flulike symptoms after each injection with both preparations and inflammatory reactions at the injection sites, more significantly with Betaseron and Rebif, which are administered subcutaneously. After months of therapy, neutralizing antibodies may develop that blunt the therapeutic effects of the drug. Neutralizing antibodies occur in about 35% of patients treated with Betaseron, 20% of patients treated with Rebif, and 10% of patients treated with Avonex. Neutralizing antibodies persisting at high titer should prompt alternative therapy.

Glatiramer acetate (Copaxone), which is approved by the Food and Drug Administration, provides about a 30% reduction in the relapse rate in patients with relapsing remitting MS.[6] Glatiramer acetate is a polypeptide consisting of basic amino acids. It was synthesized as a molecular mimic of MBP and is thought to inhibit cellular immune reactions to myelin. Glatiramer acetate is administered as a daily subcutaneous injection. Its principal side effect is swelling and redness at the injection site.

Specific Immunotherapy. Selective adhesion molecule inhibitors show promise. These agents inhibit the migration of inflammatory cells into the CNS. One drug, natalizumab—a monoclonal antibody that blocks function of the α_4 integrin VLA-4—inhibited new brain lesion formation by nearly 90% during a 6-month randomized clinical trial.[7] Definitive trials of natalizumab for relapsing remitting MS are underway.

Drugs that generally suppress the immune system also may have some benefit. Mitoxantrone was approved for use in patients with progressive forms of MS based on results from a European study.[8] Mitoxantrone is administered every 3 months at a dose of 12 mg/M². Its cumulative dose is limited to 140 mg/M² because of concerns about cardiac toxicity. Other drugs that suppress the immune system and have been used for MS include cyclophosphamide, cyclosporine, azathioprine, and methotrexate. Methotrexate, administered orally at a dose of 7.5 mg/week, was found to reduce the proportion of patients with chronic progressive MS whose condition worsened during a 2-year treatment period compared with placebo-treated patients; this dose had minimal toxicity, but the clinical benefits were modest. Cyclophosphamide and cyclosporine have some reported benefit but are limited by toxicity. Generally, immunosuppressive drugs have been tested in more severely affected patients with secondary progressive MS; beneficial effects and risk/benefit ratios during early stages of MS are unknown.

MULTIPLE SCLEROSIS VARIANTS

NEUROMYELITIS OPTICA (DEVIC'S DISEASE). Neuromyelitis optica is a syndrome characterized by partial or complete transverse myelopathy and optic neuritis. Loss of vision and paraplegia may occur in either order, and the two major components of the disease may be widely separated in time. The syndrome of neuromyelitis optica may occur as the result of acute disseminated encephalomyelitis, systemic lupus erythematosus (Chapter 280), or sarcoidosis (Chapter 91), as well as during the course of typical MS or in isolation without apparent cause. In the latter case, it is considered a variant of MS. Pathologic studies implicate autoantibodies as the pathogenesis.

MULTICENTRIC RELAPSING MYELITIS. On occasion, patients experience recurrent episodes of partial transverse myelitis affecting separate regions of the spinal cord, in the absence of involvement of the brain or optic nerve. CSF may show pleocytosis and increased protein, but it less commonly contains oligoclonal bands or selectively increased IgG. Patients may respond favorably to azathioprine, although evidence to support this therapy is anecdotal, and the rarity of this condition makes randomized controlled trials difficult.

CONCENTRIC SCLEROSIS. Concentric sclerosis is a rare form of demyelinating disease characterized by rapidly progressive demyelination. It appears to be a variant of rapidly progressive MS. Clinically, the disease begins with the acute or subacute onset of altered behavior, difficulty in communication, mutism, apathy, and headache. CSF is usually normal. Imaging shows extensive lesions in cerebral white matter. Concentric sclerosis can be diagnosed only by its characteristic histopathology; alternating bands containing demyelinated and

partially demyelinated axons radiate concentrically, and loss of oligodendrocytes characterizes the bands of demyelination.

MONOPHASIC DISORDERS RELATED TO MULTIPLE SCLEROSIS

OPTIC NEURITIS. Optic neuritis denotes acute or subacute partial or complete loss of vision in one or both eyes due to inflammation. Almost all patients with inflammatory optic neuritis experience pain in, around, or behind the affected eye, followed within a day or two by visual loss. Visual loss of varying intensity progresses for as long as 1 week. Optic neuritis is classified as retrobulbar neuritis when the lesion is in the posterior two thirds of the optic nerve and as papillitis when the lesion is in the anterior portion of the optic nerve. The latter leads to an ophthalmoscopic appearance similar to that of acute papilledema (Chapter 465) resulting from increased intracranial pressure, but it differs from the latter in that visual acuity is markedly reduced in papillitis. Visual fields in optic neuritis reveal a central or cecocentral scotoma of varying degree. Color vision is impaired, and a deafferent Marcus Gunn pupil may be present (Chapter 466). With retrobulbar optic neuritis, ophthalmoscopic examination remains normal for the first 2 to 3 weeks, after which the disc becomes pale, with loss of small vessels. Visual function almost always recovers to some degree, usually within weeks. Blindness as the result of optic nerve demyelination of MS seldom occurs.

The syndrome of optic neuritis can be caused by several diseases, of which MS is by far the most common. Other causes include tobacco-nutritional amblyopia, Leber's hereditary optic neuropathy, vasculitis, optic nerve compression on any basis, neurosyphilis (Chapter

349), ischemic optic neuropathy, pernicious anemia (Chapter 175), or sarcoidosis (Chapter 91). Optic neuritis is usually easily differentiated from optic nerve ischemia, which has an abrupt onset, affects older individuals, and results in field cuts consistent with retinal artery occlusions. Compressive optic neuropathy causes slowly progressive visual loss. Vasculitis or sarcoidosis can usually be distinguished by characteristic funduscopic features and by the presence of uveitis.

Many patients with idiopathic isolated optic neuritis eventually develop MS; the reported frequency in several series has varied from 13 to 85%, according to the length of follow-up. The presence of CSF OGB or brain MRI abnormalities significantly increases the risk of early conversion to MS. Patients with idiopathic monosymptomatic optic neuritis who have periventricular MRI abnormalities have about a 35% chance of developing MS within 2 years and an 85% chance of developing MS within 5 years.

More rapid, but not necessarily greater, total visual recovery occurs by treating optic neuritis with intravenous methylprednisolone. A 3-day course of intravenous methylprednisolone followed by a prednisone taper within 8 days of the onset appears to reduce by about 50% the likelihood of conversion from idiopathic optic neuritis to MS during 2 years of follow-up.

ACUTE TRANSVERSE MYELITIS. Acute transverse myelitis denotes rapidly developing paraparesis or paraplegia as the result of spinal cord dysfunction. Abrupt or rapidly developing back or radicular pain may be followed by ascending paresthesias and weakness beginning in the feet. Urinary and fecal retention or incontinence is common. Progression varies from minutes, resembling infarction, to steady or stepwise progression over several days. Progression over days may occur with both spinal cord compression due to a tumor (Chapter 457) and MS. It is also common to observe patients with sensory symptoms below a particular dermatome corresponding to the spinal cord level of involvement, with or without ataxia and variable degrees of leg weakness. It may be difficult to distinguish idiopathic transverse myelitis from compressive myelopathy. Therefore, the syndrome of acute transverse myelitis demands immediate diagnostic evaluation.

Of the several disorders that can produce an acute transverse myelopathy (Table 448–5), the most important to exclude or diagnose immediately are compressive lesions, including spinal or epidural abscess (Chapter 450), tumor (Chapter 457), herniated intervertebral disk, or injury (Chapters 429 and 430); vascular occlusion due to arteritis (Chapter 430), aortic dissection (Chapter 75), aortic surgery (Chapter 75), or arteriovenous malformation (Chapter 441); varicella-zoster infection (Chapter 453); and autoimmune disease including MS. In many instances, a careful history suggests the cause and the appropriate approach. The evaluation must include an immediate imaging procedure, such as MRI, with attention to the level of involvement to exclude spinal cord compression. Cord compression from metastatic tumor may present acutely even though the tumor has been present for weeks or longer. Central herniated intervertebral discs may cause acute cord compression without producing local pain. Rapidly progressing myelopathy in a previously healthy person should always raise the question of spontaneous epidural, subdural, or intraparenchymal abscess or bleeding, the latter occurring from an arteriovenous malformation or as a complication of anticoagulation or blood dyscrasia. About one third of patients with idiopathic

transverse myelitis give a history of an antecedent upper respiratory or flulike illness. Transverse myelitis may also follow several other infectious illnesses, such as mycoplasmal infection (Chapter 304) or measles (Chapter 365).

Transverse myelitis and slowly progressive myelopathy are common manifestations of MS, either as a first clinical manifestation or a late development. However, a syndrome suggesting complete cord transection rarely occurs. As with optic neuritis, CSF OGB or an abnormal brain MRI suggestive of MS makes clinically definite MS likely.

Proper treatment requires an expeditious diagnosis. When cord compression is present, surgical decompression and treatment with antibiotics or with corticosteroids are needed immediately. Treatment may halt progression but may not restore lost function. In idiopathic transverse myelopathy, MS, or cord compression, corticosteroids may reduce edema and lead to earlier restitution of function, although the effect on long-term outcome is uncertain. The treatment of choice for idiopathic transverse myelitis is intravenous administration of methylprednisolone. With severe disease, bladder catheterization, ventilatory support, and proper protection from compression neuropathies are necessary. Prognosis varies widely, with recovery ranging from almost none at all to complete, depending on the degree of acute necrosis.

LEUKODYSTROPHIES

The leukodystrophies (see Table 448–1) are uncommon dysmyelinating and demyelinating diseases in which myelin formation or maintenance is impaired by a genetically determined biochemical defect. The leukodystrophies most commonly affect individuals from the first months of life to the 20s; in some cases, onset is seen in adults. A biochemical effect is known for several; most are not yet curable.

PEROXISOMAL DISORDERS (e.g., ADRENOLEUKODYSTROPHY). Adrenoleukodystrophy (ALD) includes two genetically determined disorders that cause dysfunction of adrenal glands and nervous system myelin. There are two major genetic types of ALD: the X-linked form and a recessive form, termed *neonatal ALD*. Neonatal ALD is characterized by early and severe psychomotor retardation, seizures, retinopathy, hepatomegaly, and sometimes dysmorphic features occurring in infants of either sex.

The X-linked form of ALD is phenotypically heterogeneous, even though the disease is associated with a common biochemical defect. The two common patterns of X-linked ALD are the childhood form and adrenomyeloneuropathy. In the childhood form, boys develop normally until age 4 to 8 years, when they manifest behavioral changes with progressive cognitive decline leading over several years to a chronic vegetative state. Young men with adrenomyeloneuropathy experience progressive paraparesis and bladder dysfunction. Almost all such ALD patients have biochemical and less commonly clinically manifest adrenal insufficiency. Less common phenotypes of X-linked ALD include adrenal insufficiency without nervous system involvement, progressive dementia in adults, and an asymptomatic state in males with the same metabolic deficiency as affected relatives. Occasionally, female heterozygotes develop neurologic disturbances that resemble MS. The basis for clinical heterogeneity, despite a common metabolic defect, is unknown. Tissues and body fluids of patients with X-linked ALD contain high levels of unbranched, saturated, very long-chain fatty acids. Fatty acids accumulate because of deficient peroxisomal β oxidation, although the precise nature of the enzyme defect is not clear. The gene for X-linked ALD has been identified and many mutations characterized.

The diagnosis of X-linked ALD may be suspected in males with the clinical features described previously. CSF shows inflammatory changes that may be identical to those seen in MS, although the CSF protein is usually higher in ALD. MRI usually shows symmetrical lesions in the posterior parietal and occipital white matter. Endocrine testing may reveal primary adrenal insufficiency. The diagnosis is confirmed by demonstrating increased levels of very long-chain fatty acids in blood, tissue, or cultured fibroblasts. Most female heterozygotes can be identified using these methods as well. Mutation analysis can be helpful in some cases, and prenatal diagnosis is possible through amniocytes.

Pathologic examination shows widespread demyelination in CNS and peripheral myelin, with numerous lipid lamellar inclusions throughout the tissue. Many lesions exhibit cellular infiltration with lymphocytes and macrophages, suggesting an inflammatory component to pathogenesis.

Table 448–5 • ACUTE OR SUBACUTE TRANSVERSE MYELOPATHY

Associated with infection
  Bacterial
    Spinal epidural abscess
    Intramedullary abscess
  Viral, e.g., varicella-zoster
  Postviral, e.g., rubella with disseminated encephalomyelitis
Compression
  Tumor, especially metastatic
  Trauma
  Herniated intervertebral disc
Vascular
  Acute extradural, subdural, or parenchymal hemorrhage
  Dissecting aortic aneurysm
  Arteritis
  Systemic lupus erythematosus
Idiopathic

Treatment of X-linked ALD consists of adrenal hormone replacement and dietary restriction of long-chain fatty acids. Preliminary evidence suggests that bone marrow transplantation may slow progression of the disease in some patients, but there is no other specific treatment at present.

PELIZAEUS-MERZBACHER DISEASE. This is an extremely rare, chronic familial disease caused by mutations in the myelin proteolipid (PLP; lipophilin) protein gene. Surprisingly, duplication of a normal gene can produce the same disease, as can complete deletion, underscoring the importance of gene dosage of PLP for physiologic homeostasis of oligodendrocytes. The disease, which is inherited as an X-linked recessive trait and which primarily affects males, begins in infancy and progresses slowly to produce extensive, diffuse, symmetrical disturbances of myelin associated with gliosis within the cerebrum and cerebellum. No treatment is available.

METACHROMATIC LEUKODYSTROPHY. Metachromatic leukodystrophy (MLD), which is the most common leukodystrophy, is a lysosomal storage disease caused by deficiency of arylsulfatase A. Sulfatides accumulate in oligodendrocytes, Schwann cells, the neurons, liver, gallbladder, kidneys, and spleen. Patients develop diffuse dysmyelination, usually starting in the first 10 years of life. The process leads to dementia, convulsions, cranial nerve abnormalities, and, finally, severe spasticity or rigidity. Death usually occurs after 2 to 4 years. Juvenile and adult-onset cases have been reported. In the adult form, mental deterioration usually progresses to severe dementia with pyramidal tract and cerebellar signs. The diagnosis is suspected in a young adult with behavioral or psychiatric abnormalities or progressive dementia, particularly in the presence of spasticity. An increased urinary excretion of sulfatide and reduced arylsulfatase A activity in leukocytes or cultured fibroblasts is diagnostic. Some evidence suggests that bone marrow transplantation may slow or halt progression of MLD in some patients.

GLOBOID CELL LEUKODYSTROPHY (KRABBE'S DISEASE). Globoid cell leukodystrophy is due to deficient galactocerebroside β-galactosidase activity. The disease affects infants in the first 2 to 3 months of life and is transmitted as an autosomal recessive condition. Rare instances occur in childhood or early adulthood. Neuropathologic examination reveals marked loss of myelin throughout the brain, with the presence of round or oval mononuclear cells the size of large glia or as large, irregular multinucleated cells, termed *globoid cells*. The activity of galactocerebroside β-galactosidase can be determined in peripheral leukocytes or fibroblasts. Infants with the disorder usually progress to a vegetative state within their second year of life. Late-onset cases present with progressive motor impairment and, less frequently, visual failure. No treatment is known; bone marrow transplantation is used experimentally at present.

Grade A

1. Weinshenker BG, O'Brien PC, Petterson TM, et al: A randomized trial of plasma exchange in acute central nervous system inflammatory demyelinating disease. Ann Neurol 1999;46:878–886.
2. The IFN-β Multiple Sclerosis Study Group: Interferon beta-1b is effective in relapsing-remitting multiple sclerosis. I. Clinical results of a multicenter, randomized, double-blind, placebo-controlled trial. Neurology 1993;43:656–661.
3. Jacobs LD, Cookfair DL, Rudick RA, et al: Intramuscular interferon beta-1a for disease progression in relapsing multiple sclerosis. The Multiple Sclerosis Collaborative Research Group (MSCRG) Ann Neurol 1996;39:285–294, 1998;51:285–294.
4. PRISMS Study Group (Prevention of Relapses and Disability by Interferon beta-1a Subcutaneously in Multiple Sclerosis): Randomised double-blind placebo-controlled study of interferon beta-1a in relapsing/remitting multiple sclerosis. Lancet 1998;352:1498–1504.
5. Filippini G, Munari L, Incorvaia B, et al: Interferons in relapsing remitting multiple sclerosis: A systematic review. Lancet 2003;361:545–552.
6. Johnson KP, Brooks BR, Cohen JA, et al: Copolymer 1 reduces relapse rate and improves disability in relapsing-remitting multiple sclerosis: Results of a phase III multicenter, double-blind placebo-controlled trial. Neurology 1995;45:1268–1276.
7. Miller DH, Khan OA, Sheremata WA, et al: A controlled trial of natalizumab for relapsing multiple sclerosis. N Engl J Med 2003;348:15–23.
8. Hartung H-P, Gonsette R, Konig N, et al: Mitoxantrone in progressive multiple sclerosis: A placebo-controlled, double-blind, randomized, multicentre trial. Lancet 2002;360:2018–2025.

SUGGESTED READINGS

Beck RW, Trobe JD, Moke PS, et al: Optic Neuritis Study Group: High- and low-risk profiles for the development of multiple sclerosis within 10 years after optic neuritis: Experience of the optic neuritis treatment trial. Arch Ophthalmol 2003;121:944–949. *Patients with brain lesions on MRI have a 56% 10-year risk of developing MS compared with a 22% risk in those without a brain lesion.*

Chang A, Tourtellotte WW, Rudick R, Trapp BD: Premyelinating oligodendrocytes in chronic lesions of multiple sclerosis. N Engl J Med 2002;346:165–173. *Premyelinating*

oligodendrocytes, which are present in chronic MS, send out processes and contact axons but fail to wrap the axon or create new compact myelin.

Frohman EM: Multiple sclerosis. Med Clin North Am 2003;87:867–897. *Overview with emphasis on the role of the primary care physician.*

Lucchinetti C, Bruck W, Parisi J, et al: Heterogeneity of multiple sclerosis lesions: Implications for the pathogenesis of demyelination. Ann Neurol 2000;47:707–717. *Four different patterns of demyelination were noted; this pathogenetic heterogeneity may have fundamental implications for diagnosis and therapy.*

McDonald WI, Compston A, Edan G: Recommended diagnostic criteria for multiple sclerosis: Guidelines from the International Panel on the diagnosis of multiple sclerosis. Ann Neurol 2001;50:121–127. *Magnetic resonance imaging is integrated with clinical findings to create new diagnostic criteria.*

Noseworthy JH, Lucchinetti C, Rodriguez M, Weinshenker BG: Multiple sclerosis. N Engl J Med 2000;343:938–952. *Pathogenesis and therapy for MS.*

Zivadinov R, Rudick RA, De Masi R, et al: Effects of IV methylprednisolone on brain atrophy in relapsing-remitting MS. Neurology 2001;57:1239–1247. *Randomized controlled clinical trial suggesting that treatment of relapsing-remitting MS with pulses of IV methylprednisolone prevents or delays whole-brain atrophy and slows disability.*

449 PARAMENINGEAL INFECTIONS

Roger P. Simon

Parameningeal central nervous system (CNS) infections include those that affect the brain's parenchyma directly (brain abscess), those that produce suppuration in potential spaces covering the brain and spinal cord (epidural abscess and subdural empyema), those that produce occlusion of the contiguous venous sinuses and cerebral veins (cerebral venous sinus thrombosis), and remote infectious processes (bacterial endocarditis and sepsis) that result in diffuse, multifactorial involvement of the CNS. They may sometimes extend to invade the meninges and cause meningitis (Chapter 312).

BRAIN ABSCESS

Brain abscess is an uncommon disorder accounting for only 2% of intracranial mass lesions. CNS abscesses are circumscribed, enlarging, focal infections that produce symptoms and findings similar to those of other space-occupying lesions, such as brain tumors. Brain abscesses, however, often progress more rapidly than tumors and more frequently affect meningeal structures.

Etiology

Infections resulting in brain abscess originate in or extend from extracerebral locations. Although the most frequent predisposing factors have changed over the past decades and vary with a hospital's population and referral base, the most common (Table 449–1) are blood-borne metastases from unknown sources and from lung or heart, direct extension from parameningeal sites (otitis, cranial osteomyelitis, sinusitis), recent or remote head trauma or neurosurgical procedures,

Table 449–1 • ETIOLOGY OF BRAIN ABSCESS*

CAUSES	NUMBER OF PATIENTS
Hematogenous spread	32
Neurosurgical procedures	19
Contiguous otogenic	17
Contiguous paranasal sinuses	11
Unknown	44
ORGANISMS	
Gram-negative bacilli	27
Streptococcus species	21
Staphylococcus species	9
Corynebacterium species	4
Anaerobes	17
Mixed bacterial	16
Culture negative	29
DEATHS	21

*Based on 123 patients treated between 1986 and 2000.
Data modified from Lu CH, Chang WN, Lin YC, et al: Bacterial brain abscess: Microbiological features, epidemiological trends and therapeutic outcomes. Q J Med 2002;95:501–509.

and infections associated with cyanotic congenital heart disease. Blood-borne infections seed the brain via hematogenous spread and produce abscesses in brain regions in proportion to the blood flow; accordingly, parietal lobe abscesses predominate. Extension of infection from otitis and mastoiditis involves contiguous brain regions of the temporal lobe and cerebellum, whereas abscesses resulting from sinusitis affect the frontal and temporal lobes. Until recently the most common cause of brain abscess in urban hospitals was toxoplasmosis (Chapter 396) occurring in immunodeficiency states as a result of coinfection with the human immunodeficiency virus (HIV; Chapter 414). With the widespread use of trimethoprim/sulfamethoxazole (as prophylaxis for *Pneumocystis carinii*), protease inhibitors, and retroviral drugs, these abscesses are now rare.

Pathology

Clinical and experimental data indicate that most brain abscesses evolve over a number of stages, beginning with vascular seeding of brain parenchyma, producing early cerebritis during the first 1 to 3 days. Inflammatory infiltrates of polymorphonuclear cells, lymphocytes, and plasma cells follow within 24 hours. By 3 days, the surrounding area shows a marked increase in perivascular inflammation. The late cerebritis phase develops approximately 4 to 9 days after infection, during which time the center becomes necrotic, containing a mixture of debris and inflammatory cells. Neovascularity is maximal at this time. Early reactive astrocytes surround the zone of infection and proceed to early capsule formation between approximately 10 and 13 days. At this time, the necrotic center shrinks slightly, and a well-developed peripheral fibroblast layer evolves. The late capsule stage continues to evolve between 14 days and 5 weeks, with continual shrinking of the necrotic center and a relative decrease in the inflammatory cells. The capsule thickens as reactive astrocytes proliferate.

Bacteriology

The pathogenic organisms vary considerably, depending on the clinical circumstances. The most commonly isolated pathogens are aerobic and microaerobic streptococci and gram-negative anaerobes such as *Bacteroides* and *Prevotella* spp. Less commonly, gram-negative aerobes and *Staphylococcus* spp. are isolated (see Table 472–1). *Actinomyces, Nocardia,* and *Candida* spp. are less frequent offenders. Infection is often polymicrobial. Culture-negative abscesses from surgical specimens occur in 30% of antibiotic-treated patients and in 5% of patients who undergo surgery before antibiotics are administered.

Clinical Manifestations

Signs of infection may be minimal or absent. Almost half of affected patients maintain a normal body temperature, and fewer than one third show a peripheral white cell count greater than 11,000/μL. Neck stiffness is rare in the absence of increased intracranial pressure.

Otherwise, the presenting features resemble those of any expanding intracranial mass (Table 449–2). A headache of recent onset is the most common symptom, representing distortion or irritation of pain-sensitive structures within the cranial vault, especially those of the great venous sinuses and the dura mater about the base of the brain. If the process continues untreated, isolated headache increases in severity and becomes accompanied by focal signs such as hemiparesis or aphasia, followed by obtundation and coma. The period of evolution may be as brief as hours or as long as many days to weeks with more indolent organisms. Seizures may occur with abscesses that involve the cortical gray matter.

CEREBROSPINAL FLUID EXAMINATION. Cerebrospinal fluid (CSF) examination is not useful in diagnosis because the findings range from normal to those of purulent meningitis, depending on the walling off of the brain abscess or its closeness to CSF compartments. More important, because abscesses often expand rapidly, lumbar puncture may aggravate impending transtentorial herniation. If possible, the procedure should not be performed until after brain imaging, which may eliminate the need for CSF analysis.

NEUROIMAGING. Contrast-enhanced computed tomography (CT) and magnetic resonance imaging (MRI) are useful for diagnosis of brain abscesses and for monitoring response to therapy. MRI is

Table 449–2 • BRAIN ABSCESS: PRESENTING FEATURES IN 123 CASES

Headache	55%
Disturbed consciousness	48%
Fever	58%
Nuchal rigidity	29%
Nausea, vomiting	32%
Seizures	19%
Visual disturbance	15%
Dysarthria	20%
Hemiparesis	48%
Sepsis	17%

Modified from Lu CH, Chang WN, Lin YC, et al: Bacterial brain abcess: Microbiological features, epidemiological trends and therapeutic outcomes. Q J Med 2002;95:501–509.

especially useful for posterior fossa abscesses, because it provides an artifact-free view of the brain stem and cerebellum. In addition, MRI with intravenous gadolinium contrast is superior in demonstrating cerebritis, surrounding edema, the extent of mass effect, and associated venous thrombosis. MRI with or without gadolinium is preferable to CT for demonstrating multiple lesions.

The evolution of the abscess can be followed radiologically. In the early cerebritis stage, CT images reveal a low-density lesion with partial ring enhancement. In the late cerebritis and early capsule stages, well-formed ring-enhancing lesions are seen. The ring enhancement is typically thin walled and uniform, with subtle medial thinning adjacent to the ventricular system. Thick, nonuniform, or nodular enhancement should raise suspicion of an alternative cause. Delayed-contrast CT scans show diffusion of contrast material into the lucent center. In the late capsule stage, well-formed ring enhancement may be seen with no delayed diffusion of contrast. Other ring-enhancing lesions that may mimic the image of brain abscess include primary and metastatic tumor, a resolving infarct or hematoma, and, rarely, demyelinating disease.

 Treatment

Pyogenic brain abscesses are treated with antibiotics combined with surgical aspiration or excision. Aspiration offers the advantage of identifying the infecting organism and may be performed stereotactically with CT guidance while the patient is under local anesthesia; excision requires craniotomy. Surgical therapy is required when significant mass effect is present, when the abscess adjoins the ventricular surface (raising the possibility of catastrophic rupture into the ventricular system), when abscesses arise in the posterior fossa (with the potential of brain stem compression), or when abscesses reach a large size (>3 cm diameter) or become refractory to medical therapy. In selected cases, antibiotics alone are appropriate, as in the case of surgically inaccessible multiple abscesses (seen in 10% of patients) or abscesses in the early cerebritis stage. If the causal organism is not identified, antibiotic coverage should be directed toward the most likely organisms (streptococci and anaerobes). A commonly used regimen is ceftriaxone (or another third-generation cephalosporin with staphylococcal activity such as cefotaxime) 2 g IV once daily plus metronidazole 500 mg IV or PO three times daily. If methicillin-resistant *Staphylococcus aureus* is suspected (postoperative infection, intravenous drug use) vancomycin at 30 to 40 mg/kg/day in two to three divided doses should be added. Prophylactic anticonvulsants may reduce the risk of seizure.

With aspiration or surgery, treatment should include 4 to 6 weeks of antibiotics directed at the isolated organism. In patients who receive medical therapy without surgery, antibiotic treatment should be extended to 6 to 8 weeks. Clinical improvement may precede resolution of scan abnormalities, especially in medically treated patients. Persistence of an enhancing lesion on scanning at the end of therapy may identify patients at risk for relapse; such patients should be followed up carefully with scans after therapy is completed.

Prognosis

The current mortality rate is 5 to 15%, depending on location and nature of preexisting illness. Outcome correlates inversely with the size of the abscess and the degree of neurologic dysfunction at presentation, but less well with age, cause, number of abscesses, and use of corticosteroids.

SPINAL EPIDURAL ABSCESS

Infection within the epidural space around the spinal cord is an uncommon but readily diagnosable and treatable potential cause of paralysis and death. Its incidence is 0.5 to 1.0 per 10,000 hospital admissions in the United States, but the frequency is substantially increased in patients who use intravenous drugs.

Clinical Manifestations

Patients are usually systemically ill with fever (temperature to 38° to 39°C) in virtually all acutely evolving cases and in most of those with a subacute evolution. The initial feature is acute or subacute neck or back pain. Focal percussion tenderness is a prominent sign in most cases, and stiff neck and headache are common. As the infection progresses over hours, days, or weeks, radicular pain occurs; the site varies with the location of the abscess. The pain can be mistaken for sciatica, a visceral abdominal process, chest wall pain, or cervical disc disease. If the condition goes unrecognized at this stage, the symptoms can rapidly evolve, over a few hours to a few days, to produce weakness and finally paralysis distal to the spinal level of the infection. In this clinical setting, spinal epidural abscess should be assumed, systemic antibiotics begun, and urgent neuroradiologic confirmatory diagnostic procedures pursued.

The differential diagnosis includes compressive and inflammatory processes involving the spinal cord (transverse myelitis, intervertebral disc herniation, epidural hemorrhage, metastatic tumor), which can usually be differentiated clinically by the absence of systemic infection. Transverse myelitis, however, may be associated with fever; the most useful differential feature is its rapid evolution to maximum deficit within 24 hours or less. Other infectious processes that may produce back or neck pain or tenderness must be excluded (bacterial meningitis, perinephric abscess, disc space infection, bacterial endocarditis). Spinal subdural empyema can cause a similar syndrome but is much less frequent.

Etiology

Infections of the epidural space originate from contiguous spread or via hematogenous routes from a distant source. Cutaneous sites of infection are the most common remote sources, especially in intravenous drug users. Abdominal, respiratory tract, and urinary sources are also common. Osteomyelitis may be a cause of either direct extension or hematogenous spread, especially when associated with sepsis. Contiguous spread of infection occurs, most commonly from psoas abscesses, decubitus ulceration, perinephric and retropharyngeal abscesses, surgical sites, or epidurally placed catheters. Whether or not spread can result from pelvic infections via spinal veins remains unsettled. Minor back trauma has been implicated in producing a paraspinal hematoma, which is subsequently seeded via hematogenous sources.

Pathophysiology

The anatomic features of the epidural space dictate the location of the abscess; the frequency of epidural infections is proportional to the volume of the epidural space. Because the size of the intravertebral canal remains relatively constant while the circumference of the spinal cord changes, abscess formation is maximal in the thoracic and lumbar regions and least at the cervical cord enlargement. Furthermore, as the dura mater about the cord is adherent to the vertebral column anteriorly, more epidural abscesses lie posteriorly, and because no anatomic barriers separate spinal segments in the posterior epidural space, such abscesses usually extend over three to five or more vertebral segments.

Because the epidural space is not confined rostrocaudally, there is no clear abscess cavity or focal mass that can explain simple compression as a cause for spinal cord compromise. Clinical signs often are substantially greater than would have been predicted from the anatomic extent of pus or granulation tissue found at surgical exploration. Furthermore, in many instances, no frank compression is found at surgery or on postmortem examination. The spinal cord dysfunction likely reflects toxic processes secondary to inflammation, as well as venous thrombosis, thrombophlebitis, ischemia, and edema.

Bacteriology

Causative organisms can be identified by culture or Gram stain from pus obtained at exploration (90% of cases), blood (60 to 90% of cases), or CSF (25% of cases). *S. aureus* accounts for most infections, followed by streptococci and gram-negative anaerobes. Tuberculous abscesses remain common, representing as many as 25% of cases in high-risk populations.

Diagnosis

CSF examination is often performed because of associated fever and meningeal signs. The fluid usually is nonspecifically abnormal, containing normal or decreased glucose levels, an elevated protein content (400 to 500 mg/mL), and a lymphocytic pleocytosis (22 to 150/mm^3). Spinal fluid cultures yield organisms in about 25% of cases, but Gram stain results are rarely positive. Almost 90% of patients show a peripheral blood leukocytosis.

Plain spine radiographs, with attention to the area of percussion tenderness, may show osteomyelitis/discitis, a compression fracture, or a paravertebral mass. Gadolinium-enhanced MRI is the study of choice for the evaluation of a suspected epidural abscess because of its superior ability to demonstrate the craniocaudal extent of the extradural soft tissue mass, associated mass effect upon the cord or cauda equina, and potential signal abnormalities within the discs, vertebral bone marrow, and spinal cord. The addition of an intravenous gadolinium contrast agent better defines central necrosis suggestive of abscess rather than cellulitis. If MRI is unavailable or technically impossible, CT with myelography usually provides adequate information. A normal plain CT scan alone does not exclude the diagnosis.

Rx Treatment

The disease is fatal in the absence of antibiotic therapy. Unless culture results and sensitivities dictate otherwise, penicillinase-resistant penicillin (nafcillin 12 g/day or oxacillin 12 g/day) should be started empirically as antistaphylococcal treatment for presumed bacterial infection. If there is concern about methicillin-resistant *S. aureus* (postoperative infection or high prevalence of methicillin-resistant strains in the community), vancomycin should be used at a dose of 20 to 30 mg/kg/day in two divided doses. Considering the severity of the disease, most authorities would provide additional gram-negative coverage with a third-generation cephalosporin or a quinolone. For confirmed *S. aureus* abscesses, penicillinase-resistant penicillin is the treatment of choice; however, some consider the addition of rifampin (300 mg every 12 hours) because of its ability to penetrate the abscess cavity. Therapy should be continued intravenously for 3 to 4 weeks in the absence of osteomyelitis and 6 to 8 weeks with associated osteomyelitis. Surgical decompression was once thought to be mandatory in all cases; now early diagnosis by CT or MRI scans allows for effective medical therapy before occurrence of neurologic complications. Medical management of cervical epidural abscess requires close neurologic monitoring because of the small space available for expansion of the abscess and the high potential for quadriparesis. If blood culture findings are negative, needle aspiration or laminectomy may be necessary to determine the causative organism.

Prognosis

The chance of partial or complete recovery relates inversely to the amount of neurologic dysfunction at the time of diagnosis. Patients without findings other than pain recover without deficit. Approximately 50% of patients with some weakness have complete resolution, and nearly 50% of patients with paralysis of less than 36 hours' duration show some return of motor function. In tuberculous epidural abscess, recovery of motor function has been reported even after paralysis lasting for weeks.

VENOUS SINUS THROMBOSIS SECONDARY TO INFECTION

Thrombosis of cerebral veins or sinuses may occur in the absence of a demonstrable cause, but it also may occur in the setting of hematologic disorders or coagulation abnormalities (Chapter 440) or may result from local or contiguous infectious processes. The infection-related syndromes are discussed here.

Venous drainage from the brain begins with venules and veins that drain into the great venous sinuses. The venous sinus system itself lacks valves, thereby permitting retrograde propagation of clots or infections that emanate from structures such as those located in the central portion of the face or the middle ear.

SEPTIC CAVERNOUS SINUS THROMBOSIS

The cavernous sinuses comprise the most caudal dural venous chambers at the base of the skull. The paired structures lie on either side of the pituitary fossa, immediately above the midline sphenoid sinus. The cavernous sinus encloses the "cavernous portion" of the internal carotid artery; the third, fourth, and sixth cranial nerves en route to the apex of the orbit; and the ophthalmic and maxillary branches of the trigeminal nerve, which supply sensation to the forehead, periocular regions, cornea, and malar area of the face. Septic cavernous sinus thrombosis most commonly results from extension of infections involving the neighboring sphenoid and ethmoid sinuses, the central portion of the face, or the pharynx or tonsils.

Presenting symptoms are headache or lateralized facial pain, followed in a few days to weeks by fever, and involvement of the orbit, producing proptosis and chemosis secondary to obstruction of the ophthalmic vein. Paralysis of oculomotor nerves follows rapidly. Sensory dysfunction in the first and second divisions of the trigeminal nerve and a decrease in the corneal reflex are less obvious. Further involvement of the contiguous orbital contents follows, with mild papilledema and decreased visual acuity, sometimes progressing to blindness. Increased intracranial pressure secondary to impaired venous drainage or extension to the opposite cavernous sinus or to other intracranial sinuses with cerebral infarction can result in stupor, coma, and death.

The differential diagnosis includes carotid cavernous sinus fistula (diagnosed by the presence of an ocular bruit and the absence of fever); idiopathic granulomatous involvement of the cavernous sinus (the Tolosa-Hunt syndrome) or orbital pseudotumor (diagnosed by relative sparing of the orbital contents); and orbital cellulitis (infection localized to the orbit but sparing the structures of the cavernous sinus). Some overlap often occurs between involvement of these contiguous structures of the orbit and the cavernous sinus.

The CSF is abnormal in almost all cases, sometimes with a profile resembling that of purulent meningitis or parameningeal infection. The most common causative organism is *S. aureus,* with streptococci, pneumococci, and gram-negative bacilli being less common; anaerobic infection has been reported. Radiologic evaluation includes sinus imaging, with attention focused on the sphenoid and ethmoid sinuses. MRI (with and without intravenous gadolinium contrast) can often demonstrate venous thrombosis by illustrating the lack of the normal "flow void" within vascular structures. Cranial CT scans, with or without intravenous contrast material, are less helpful but may show a subtle increase in size and enhancement in the thrombosed sinus. MR angiography may demonstrate extrinsic narrowing of the intracavernous portion of the internal carotid artery.

Treatment relies on early diagnosis and consists of the prompt drainage of infected paranasal sinuses as well as specific antistaphylococcal agents, such as nafcillin or oxacillin, given intravenously usually in combination with a third generation cephalosporin such as ceftriaxone or cefotaxime. Heparin anticoagulation may reduce morbidity from associated brain ischemia, but this treatment remains controversial in the presence of documented infection.

LATERAL SINUS THROMBOSIS

Septic thrombosis of the lateral sinus results from acute or chronic infections of the middle ear. The symptoms consist of ear pain followed by headache, nausea, vomiting, and vertigo, evolving over several weeks. On examination, most patients are febrile. An abnormality on the otologic examination is nearly invariable; mastoid swelling may be seen. Sixth cranial nerve palsies can occur, but other focal neurologic signs are rare. Papilledema occurs in half the cases, and elevated CSF pressure is present in most, especially with occlusion of the right lateral sinus (which is the major venous conduit from the superior sagittal sinus). The CSF is usually normal, although a parameningeal inflammatory profile may be seen.

Treatment includes intravenous antibiotics to cover staphylococci, anaerobes, and gram-negative bacilli such as proteus and *Escherichia coli* (nafcillin or oxacillin with penicillin or metronidazole) and a third-generation cephalosporin. Surgical drainage (mastoidectomy) may be required. Increased intracranial pressure seldom needs direct treatment unless vision is compromised. The outcome is usually favorable.

SEPTIC SAGITTAL SINUS THROMBOSIS

Septic sagittal sinus thrombosis is an uncommon condition that occurs as a consequence of purulent meningitis, infections of the ethmoid or maxillary sinuses spreading via venous channels, compound infected skull fractures, or, rarely, neurosurgical wound infections. Symptoms are primarily related to the elevated intracranial pressure (headache, nausea, and vomiting) and can evolve rapidly to stupor and coma. Seizures and hemiparesis may result from cortical infarction. The rate of progression, severity of symptoms, and prognosis are all related to the location of thrombosis. When only the anterior third of the sinus is obstructed, symptoms are less intense and evolve more slowly. If the thrombosis progresses to involve the middle and posterior thirds of the sinus, deterioration progresses more rapidly and outlook for recovery declines.

CSF abnormalities accompany well over half the cases. The opening pressure is increased in proportion to the extent of the sagittal sinus involvement, and a pleocytosis usually reflects the association of a meningeal or parameningeal process.

Radiologically, septic sagittal sinus thrombosis may be excluded by visualization of the normal sagittal sinus during the venous phase of cerebral angiography; the diagnosis can usually also be made by MRI, which demonstrates an abnormal increase in signal intensity (absent flow void) within the affected venous sinus. Contrast-enhanced CT scanning may reveal a contrast void lying at the junction of the transverse and sagittal sinuses (the region of the torcular); this so-called delta sign is an intraluminal clot surrounded by contrast material.

Rx Treatment

Intravenous antibiotics should be directed at organisms recovered from the meningeal process or the meningeal site. *S. aureus* (including the methicillin-resistant strains), β-hemolytic streptococci, pneumococci, and gram-negative aerobes such as *Klebsiella* spp. are the most common organisms. Initial antibiotic treatment should include nafcillin and a third-generation cephalosporin. Vancomycin can be used for antistaphylococcal coverage in patients with significant β-lactam allergy or in whom methicillin-resistant strains are suspected. Associated paranasal sinusitis should be drained surgically. Heparin use has been little tested in septic venous thrombosis, but experience with noninfected sinus thrombosis has shown it to reduce both morbidity and mortality rates appreciably.

NEUROLOGIC COMPLICATIONS OF INFECTIOUS ENDOCARDITIS

Neurologic complications occur in one third of patients with bacterial endocarditis (Chapter 310) and triple the general mortality rate of the disease. Most of these complications derive from valvular vegetations. Cerebral (but not systemic) emboli are more common in cases of mitral valve endocarditis. Most emboli, regardless of the bacterial etiology of infection, occur before or early in the course of treatment. By 2 weeks of therapy, the risk of embolization decreases dramatically. Cerebral emboli are distributed in the brain in proportion to cerebral blood flow. Therefore, most emboli lodge in the branches of the middle cerebral artery peripherally, with resultant hemiparesis. Focal seizures may result.

Anticoagulation does not prevent embolization from occurring and may increase the risk of intracerebral hemorrhage. Thus, patients with native valve endocarditis should not be anticoagulated unless there is a compelling reason. Patients with prosthetic valve endocarditis should continue anticoagulation unless there has been a central nervous embolic event or development of a mycotic aneurysm, in which case it should be discontinued for several weeks.

Mycotic aneurysms complicate endocarditis in 2 to 10% of cases and are more common in acute than subacute disease. The middle cerebral artery is most commonly involved; aneurysms are located distally in the vessel, differentiating them from congenital berry aneurysms. The process by which the aneurysmal dilatation occurs remains in dispute, although embolization of infectious vegetations is accepted as the inciting event. Aneurysmal rupture results in an 80% mortality rate, and early diagnosis is therefore important. Which patients should be subjected to angiography is uncertain. However, clinical or radiologic evidence of cerebral or other embolization defines the high-risk group. Other suggested indications for angiography include severe headache (presumably the result of aneurysmal leakage). When an unruptured aneurysm is identified by angiography, it may resolve with antibiotic therapy alone. Such patients need follow-up imaging to document an interval decrease in aneurysm size. Otherwise, surgical therapy requires excision of the infected portion of the artery. Patients with proximal mycotic aneurysms have a greater risk of perioperative stroke than do those with distal involvement.

Small brain abscesses may complicate the course of endocarditis, but macroscopic abscesses are rare and tend to occur in the setting of acute, rather than subacute, endocarditis. Multiple microabscesses, however, can result in a diffuse encephalopathy similar to that seen in sepsis. Such lesions may escape detection on CT scanning and are not amenable to surgical drainage. Antibiotic treatment of the primary disease is indicated.

A CSF pleocytosis occurs in 70% of patients with neurologic complications, but in an unknown number of patients in whom the CNS is clinically spared. The CSF profile may be that of a purulent meningitis (polymorphonuclear leukocyte predominance, elevated protein level, and low glucose level) or that of a perimeningeal infection (lymphocytic predominance, modest protein level elevation, and normal glucose level). A hemorrhagic component may be seen. Purulent CSF is associated with signs of meningeal irritation and infection with a virulent organism.

SUBDURAL EMPYEMA

Empyema is infection in a preformed space, in this case the space separating the dura and arachnoid. Subdural empyema is responsible for one fifth of localized intracranial infections and results from direct or indirect extension from infected paranasal sinuses via a retrograde thrombophlebitis or, less frequently, untreated chronic otitis. Unilateral empyema is most common, because the falx prevents passage across the midline, but bilateral or multiple concurrent empyemas occur. Cortical venous thrombosis or brain abscess develops in approximately one fourth of cases; purulent meningitis is a less common accompaniment.

Symptoms initially reflect those of chronic otitis or sinusitis, as well as lateralized headache (a universal feature), fever, and obtundation. Vomiting, meningeal signs, and focal neurologic abnormalities (hemiparesis or seizures) usually follow. If the disease remains untreated, obtundation progresses, and the septic mass and swelling of the underlying brain soon lead to venous thrombosis or death from herniation. The major differential diagnosis is that of meningitis. Nuchal rigidity and obtundation occur in both, but papilledema and lateralizing deficits are more common in empyema. The result of lumbar puncture, obtained because of the suspicion of meningitis, reveals an elevated intracranial pressure accompanied by an increased protein content and a polymorphonuclear pleocytosis, usually with a normal glucose concentration in the CSF. Contrast-enhanced CT or MRI can be diagnostic of empyema, showing an extra-axial, crescent-shaped mass with an enhancing rim lying just below the inner table of the skull over the cerebral convexities or the interhemispheric fissures. MRI better detects underlying parenchymal edema as well as the infection itself.

Treatment requires both prompt surgical drainage of the empyema cavity and high-dose intravenous antibiotics directed toward organisms found at the time of craniotomy. The bacteriologic characteristics of subdural empyemas are similar to those of sinusitis and cerebral abscess. Anticonvulsants should be administered prophylactically, because seizures are common.

If cortical infarction from venous thrombosis does not occur, the prognosis is surprisingly favorable, although in one third of patients chronic epilepsy results.

CRANIAL EPIDURAL ABSCESS

Infections of the epidural space coexist most often with subdural empyema and less frequently with chronic sinusitis or otitis alone. Symptoms and signs are headache and fever with focal neurologic abnormalities due to the coexistent subdural empyema or brain abscess. The diagnosis is made with MRI or contrast-enhanced CT scan (which demonstrate a peripherally enhancing lenticular-shaped lesion in the epidural space), and the abscess is treated by surgical drainage followed by systemic antibiotics. In uncomplicated cases, the prognosis is excellent.

MALIGNANT EXTERNAL OTITIS

Malignant external otitis is a necrotizing osteitis that occurs in elderly patients with diabetes. The associated organism, *Pseudomonas aeruginosa*, is part of the normal flora of the external ear. In this case, it produces an external otitis that fails to respect normal anatomic boundaries. The result consists of a rapidly evolving syndrome of ear pain, facial swelling, osteomyelitis of the base of the skull, and purulent meningitis accompanied by multiple cranial nerve palsies. Urgent treatment with antipseudomonal penicillin or a third-generation cephalosporin combined with an aminoglycoside or ciprofloxacin is essential. Surgical débridement is usually limited to removal of easily accessible necrotic tissue. More extensive procedures, to débride the skull bone, are not feasible. The mortality rate is high.

SUGGESTED READINGS
Calfee DP, Wispelwey B: Brain abscess. Semin Neurol 2000;20.353–360. *Review of epidemiology, pathogenesis, microbiology, presentation, diagnosis, treatment, and prognosis.*
Greenlee JE: Subdural empyema. Curr Treat Options Neurol 2003;5:13–22. *Review of current diagnostic and treatment issues.*
Mylonakis E, Calderwood SB: Infective endocarditis in adults. N Engl J Med 2001;345:1318–1330. *Review of treatment, including anticoagulation and mycotic aneurysms.*
Reihsaus E, Waldhaur H, Seeling W: Spinal epidural abscess: A meta-analysis of 915 patients. Neurosurg Rev 2000;23:175–204. *A large series of patients treated over the past 45 years.*

450 APPROACH TO VIRAL INFECTIONS OF THE NERVOUS SYSTEM

Joseph R. Berger
Avindra Nath

The central nervous system (CNS) can be infected by all the major groups of animal viruses. The spectrum of viruses ranges from the large, complex DNA herpesviruses to small, relatively simple viruses with DNA or RNA genomes, such as the papovaviruses and retroviruses. Also included in this section are prions, which are not conventional viruses but unique transmissible agents that cause an encephalopathy.

The neurologic manifestations of viral infections are also diverse, extending from the acute febrile encephalitides to chronic progressive neurodegenerative disorders. *Neuroinvasive* refers to a virus that has the ability to enter the nervous system but may not cause any symptoms. A *neurotropic* virus is one that infects cells within the nervous system, and a *neurovirulent* virus causes clinically recognizable neurologic symptoms. Factors such as the patient's age and

Neurology

immune status, viral dose, and in some instances, the virus's route of entry influence the ability of the virus to affect the nervous system.

Most viral infections are asymptomatic, and nervous system involvement is an uncommon complication of a relatively common systemic infection. The nervous system in these instances is a bystander to the systemic infection. Extension of infection to the CNS may be considered accidental and may even preclude survival of the virus and its transmission to a new host. For example, the polioviruses cause enteric infections in which replication in the gut and fecal-oral transmission determine the essential survival and transmission of the organism; extension of infection to anterior horn cells of the spinal cord devastates the host but does not contribute to the life cycle of the virus. In contrast, the neurotropic herpesviruses, including herpes simplex virus type 1 and varicella-zoster virus, cause a latent infection in the sensory ganglia, where they may reside for extended periods. Occasionally, the virus reactivates and causes neurologic symptoms. Even in the case of the herpesviruses, CNS complications, such as acute herpes encephalitis, are "accidental" and not essential in the organism's adaptive strategy. In contrast, rabies is an illness in which CNS infection plays a central role in the life cycle of the virus; involvement of the brain produces "rabid," biting behavior that actually contributes to transmission of the virus.

Viruses most commonly enter the nervous system through hematogenous spread. Virus in the blood may circulate as free virions (e.g., enteroviruses) or may be cell associated. For example, human immunodeficiency virus (HIV) associates with CD4+ T lymphocytes, and Colorado tick fever associates with red blood cells. The virus may enter through the choroid plexus and spread through cerebrospinal fluid pathways or invade the brain by crossing the blood-brain barrier. Another mechanism of viral spread to the nervous system is by means of neurons. Rabies virus, some of the herpesviruses, and poliovirus are transported along peripheral nerves to the CNS. Initial symptoms may be focal. After the virus enters the brain, it may spread transneuronally throughout the CNS at synaptic and nonsynaptic sites, producing more diffuse clinical changes. Within the nervous system, some viruses do not discriminate among neurons and glial or endothelial cells, whereas others infect selective targets. For example, JC virus infects oligodendrocytes and astrocytes but not neurons, whereas herpesvirus type 1 infects predominantly neurons. Such selectivity is often determined by cell-surface molecules, principally glycoproteins, that serve as receptors for viruses, allowing their specific attachment and subsequent entry into cells.

Different cell types also vary in their capacity to support virus-directed metabolism and replication. Virus-cell interactions can assume a number of courses. *Abortive infection* results in little or no change in the cell and no viral replication. *Productive infection* is characterized by a full replication cycle with production of virions. If the infection results in cell death, it is called a *cytopathic infection*. If there is a prolonged release of low level of virions without cell death, it is called *persistent infection*. In *latent infection*, the viral genome resides quiescently in the cell but retains the capacity to reactivate subsequently. *Transforming infection* causes increased and characteristically abnormal cell proliferation and thereby oncogenic transformation of the cells, usually in the absence of virus replication. *Restricted* or *defective infection* may result in nonproductive infection or production of incomplete particles but may nonetheless cause various degrees of cell alteration and viral antigen expression.

Neural injury and dysfunction accompanying viral infections may be caused by direct infection of the cells, such as neuronal death caused by herpes simplex virus or oligodendroglial cell death caused by JC virus. The infected cells may also be targeted by antigen-specific host responses, such as lysis of infected cells by cytotoxic T lymphocytes. However, dysfunction of uninfected cells may result from toxic effects of viral products released from the infected cells (best characterized for HIV infection) or from nonspecific host responses that lead to the production of neurotoxic substances (e.g., nitric oxide and quinolinic acid) and cytokines (e.g., tumor necrosis factor-α) by activated glial cells or invading mononuclear cells. The relative importance of these factors in individual infections depends on the interactions of the invading organism with the cells it infects and the profile of host cell responses that it elicits. This balance is highly variable from one virus to the next and strongly influences the time course, morbidity, and degree of recovery from each infection.

Diagnostic approaches to viral diseases depend on the clinical setting and specific agents involved. The arsenal of available diagnostic

methods is steadily growing. For many acute infections, the time-honored serologic techniques assessing host antibody responses in serum and at times cerebrospinal fluid remain the most useful and cost-effective. Although some infections elicit diagnostic tissue reactions (e.g., Negri bodies in rabies), for most infections, newer techniques have displaced simple histopathology in identifying infection in tissue, including detection of viral antigens using specific antibodies and of viral nucleic acids using in situ hybridization. More direct identification of viruses in blood or other clinical specimens by culture isolation generally remains difficult and costly, but the introduction of the polymerase chain reaction gene amplification technique to clinical virology is rapidly expanding the diagnostic capability of the laboratory.

Efforts to combat viral disease consist of prevention through active or, sometimes, passive immunization. In the case of rabies only, active immunization may be given after exposure to the virus. Effective drug therapy is available for most neurotropic herpesviruses, and antiviral treatment can temporarily retard progression of HIV infection. Promise exists for more effective treatments for infection by these viruses and for the development of chemotherapeutic agents that will act selectively against other important viruses causing neurologic diseases.

451 ACUTE VIRAL MENINGITIS AND ENCEPHALITIS

Avindra Nath
Joseph R. Berger

Definitions

The term *viral meningitis* refers to infection of the leptomeninges, *viral encephalitis* refers to infection of the brain parenchyma, and *viral meningoencephalitis* is sometimes used when both meninges and brain parenchyma appear to be infected, although viral encephalitis is almost always accompanied by meningeal inflammation. When the spinal cord and brain are involved, the term *viral encephalomyelitis* may be used. The nonspecific term *aseptic meningitis* refers to an inflammatory process of the meninges accompanied by a predominantly mononuclear cell pleocytosis and not caused by pyogenic bacterial infection. Although viral infections are the most common cause of aseptic meningitis, infections by other types of organisms, chemical irritation of the meninges, carcinomatous meningitis, and reactions to certain medications can cause a similar clinical picture and cerebrospinal fluid (CSF) profile. In this chapter, acute central nervous system (CNS) infections caused by a variety of viruses are considered together because of their largely indistinguishable clinical features. Viral infections causing more distinct neurologic symptoms and signs are described separately in subsequent sections.

Etiology

Many viruses can cause acute encephalitis or meningitis (Table 451–1); others may result in subacute or chronic encephalitis (Table 451–2). Enteroviruses (Chapter 373) are the most common cause of aseptic meningitis. They are small, nonenveloped RNA viruses of the picornavirus family with numerous serotypes. More than 50 have been associated with meningitis or encephalitis. Japanese encephalitis virus is the most common cause of encephalitis worldwide in humans. It has a high morbidity and mortality rate. Although an effective vaccine has been available since 1960, only small populations in Asia have been vaccinated.

Arboviruses include agents of several families that are transmitted by mosquitoes or ticks (Chapter 377). More than 15 different arboviruses have been associated with encephalitis in various areas of the world. In the United States, the most important are California encephalitis (most cases involve the La Crosse subtype), eastern and western equine encephalitis, St. Louis encephalitis, and Colorado tick fever. Less common in the United States are Venezuelan equine encephalitis and Powassan encephalitis. West Nile encephalitis was introduced into the United States recently and has spread rapidly across

Table 451–1 • VIRUSES ASSOCIATED WITH ACUTE CENTRAL NERVOUS SYSTEM INFECTION

VIRUS	SEASON	MORTALITY (%)	MORBIDITY (%)
Nonarthropod Viruses			
RNA viruses			
Picornaviruses (enteroviruses)	All year (tropics); summer		
Polioviruses	and fall (temperate regions)		
Coxsackieviruses, group A			
Coxsackieviruses, group B			
Echoviruses		0	Rare
Enteroviruses 70, 71		Rare	Rare
Togaviruses			
Rubella	Spring	Rare	Rare
Arenavirus			
Lymphocytic choriomeningitis	Winter	Rare	Rare
Rhabdovirus			
Rabies	All year	>95	
Orthomyxoviruses	Winter and spring		
Influenza			
Parainfluenza			
Paramyxoviruses	Winter and spring		
Measles			
Mumps			
Nipah		35	15
Retroviruses	All year		
Human immunodeficiency virus type 1		100	
DNA viruses	All year		
Herpesviruses			
Herpes simplex type 1		15	60
Adenoviruses		Rare	Rare
Arthropod-borne Viruses			
RNA viruses			
Togaviruses			
Eastern equine encephalitis	Summer	50	30
Western equine encephalitis	Summer	5	30
Venezuelan equine encephalitis		10	<5
Flaviviruses			
Mosquito-borne encephalitis viruses			
Japanese encephalitis (Asia)	Summer	30	30
St. Louis encephalitis	Summer and fall	<10	10
Murray Valley encephalitis (Australia, New Guinea)		20	40
West Nile virus	Summer and fall		
Tick-borne encephalitis viruses			
Russian spring summer encephalitis	Spring and summer		
Louping ill (British Isles)			
Powassan virus (Canada, Northern US)	Spring and summer	<5	Rare
Kyassanur Forest virus (India)	Summer	Rare	Rare
Bunyaviruses			
California encephalitis	Spring and summer		
La Crosse virus		Rare	Rare
Snowshoe hare virus (Canada)			
Jamestown canyon virus			
Orbivirus			
Colorado tick fever	Spring and summer	Rare	Rare

the eastern and central parts of the country along patterns of bird migration.

Herpes simplex virus type 1 (HSV-1) is the most common cause of encephalitis in the Western world (Chapter 369). It causes severe encephalitis, usually with characteristic focal features affecting the temporal and frontal lobes, whereas HSV-2 causes aseptic meningitis in association with genital herpes and has been implicated as a cause of recurrent viral meningitis called Mollaret meningitis. Lymphocytic choriomeningitis virus, an arenavirus, is a sporadic cause of meningitis and occasionally of encephalitis. The human immunodeficiency virus (HIV) may cause aseptic meningitis (Chapter 414), usually at the time of seroconversion. Adenoviruses (Chapter 364) are respiratory viruses that only rarely cause meningitis or severe childhood encephalitis. Cytomegalovirus (Chapter 370) and varicella-zoster virus (Chapter 367) cause encephalitis but only in immunocompromised individuals.

The acute neurologic disease associated with measles (Chapter 365), vaccinia, or rubella infections (Chapter 366) is usually a sequel to infection termed *postinfectious encephalomyelitis*. The encephalitis that may also be postinfectious encephalomyelitis occasionally occurs with influenza and parainfluenza virus infections.

Epidemiology

Viral meningitis and encephalitis are relatively common disorders. In one study in Rochester, MN, for example, the incidence of aseptic meningitis was nearly 11 per 100,000 person years and that of viral encephalitis was more than 7 per 100,000 person years. This finding was compared with a rate of 8.6 episodes of bacterial meningitis. In general, a specific cause is identified in only about 10 to 15% of cases of meningitis and encephalitis in the United States.

Each virus causing CNS infection has its own epidemiologic pattern (see Table 451–1). Because of the predominance of enteroviruses and arboviruses, the overall incidence of viral meningitis and encephalitis peaks in the late summer. Enteroviruses are transmitted by the fecal-hand-oral route. They often involve young children, with rapid spread in families or social groups. The geographic and seasonal incidence of arbovirus infection is related to the life cycle of arthropod vectors and animal reservoirs and their contact with humans. Eastern equine encephalitis virus is limited largely to the Atlantic and Gulf coasts, whereas western equine encephalitis virus is confined to the western two thirds of the country, with the highest incidence west of the Mississippi River Valley. The latter virus causes many more human

Table 451–2 • VIRUSES ASSOCIATED WITH SUBACUTE OR CHRONIC NERVOUS SYSTEM INFECTION

VIRUS	NEUROLOGIC SYNDROME
RNA viruses	
Togavirus	
Rubella	Progressive rubella panencephalitis
Paramyxovirus	
Measles	Subacute sclerosing panencephalitis
Retroviruses	
Human immunodeficiency virus type 1	HIV dementia
Human T-cell lymphotropic virus type 1	HTLV-1 associated myelopathy
DNA viruses	
Herpesviruses	
Herpes simplex, type 2	Mollaret's meningitis
Human herpes virus, type 6	(?) Subacute encephalitis
Varicella-zoster	Herpes zoster, subacute encephalitis
Epstein-Barr	Subacute encephalitis
Cytomegalovirus	Ventriculitis and encephalitis
Papovaviruses	
JC virus	Progressive multifocal leukoencephalopathy

infections than does the eastern virus, but only 1 in 100 infected persons develops encephalitis. St. Louis encephalitis virus causes disease in rural and urban areas over a large part of the United States. In the rural areas, the virus has the same pattern as western equine encephalitis virus, but in urban areas, more explosive outbreaks can occur. In recent years, the La Crosse subtype of the California encephalitis virus has been related every year to cases spread widely over the United States, particularly in the East and Midwest, mostly in children. Colorado tick fever occurs in the Rocky Mountain area; about 18% of infected patients develop meningitis, but encephalitis is rare. Venezuelan encephalitis has spread into Florida and the southwestern states and produces an influenza-like illness in most of those infected; however, about 3% develop acute meningitis or encephalitis. Powassan virus is a rare cause of encephalitis in Canada and along the northern border of the United States. West Nile encephalitis was introduced into the United States in 1999. The first cases were reported in New York, but it has since rapidly spread by means of migratory birds to much of the United States.

Lymphocytic choriomeningitis virus is the major zoonotic (i.e., infection in humans that is naturally transmitted from any vertebrate animal) virus causing meningitis and encephalitis. Humans acquire the infection by contact with dust or food contaminated by excreta of the common house mouse. Human disease is more common in winter, when the natural host tends to move indoors. Lymphocytic choriomeningitis virus has also been found in hamsters, and human infections have been traced to laboratory and pet hamsters.

Mumps virus spreads by the respiratory route, with infection occurring throughout the year but with the incidence increasing during the spring. Although mumps virus infects both sexes equally, meningitis develops in males three times more frequently than in females. Japanese encephalitis is geographically the most widely distributed of all the arthropod-borne viruses.

Pathogenesis

Events leading up to the development of the acute viral encephalitides and meningitides can be divided into three stages. The first involves exposure of an external body surface to the virus, usually with local replication of the "inoculum." In the case of enteroviruses, the infecting virus is contained in body fluids or excreta from infected persons and transferred by direct contact or within contaminated environmental materials. On ingestion, the virus replicates within the Peyer's patches of the lamina propria of the lower intestinal tract. The arboviruses are introduced by an arthropod bite. The next stage involves systemic viremia and amplification of virus in visceral organs. A secondary viremia may lead to invasion and replication within the nervous system or meninges. With the exception of rabies virus and the neurotropic herpesviruses, viruses that cause acute encephalitis or meningitis typically reach the nervous system hematogenously. This factor accounts for the widespread distribution of cerebral dysfunction associated with most of the encephalitides.

In viral encephalitis, infection of neurons, glial cells, and even vascular endothelium leads to cell dysfunction and sometimes to cell death. Inflammatory responses follow. Clinical symptoms and signs depend on the distribution of infection and on the direct effect of the virus and the secondary inflammatory reactions in the tissue. The relative contribution of each to brain dysfunction depends on the particular infecting virus. The remarkable degree of recovery in many patients suggests that secondary inflammatory and immune responses often predominate.

Clinical Manifestations

Most acute viral encephalitides and meningitides produce similar symptoms, with variations depending on the particular virus. Often, CNS manifestations are preceded or accompanied by fever, malaise, or myalgia; gastrointestinal disturbance; respiratory symptoms; or rash. These are followed by headache, photophobia, stiff neck, and other signs of meningeal irritation, usually with an intensity milder than that of bacterial meningitis (Chapter 312).

When encephalitis exists, evidence of diffuse or, less commonly, focal brain dysfunction accompanies or overshadows signs of meningeal irritation. Patients characteristically exhibit altered attention and consciousness, ranging from confusion to lethargy or coma. Motor function may be abnormal, with weakness, altered tone, or incoordination, reflecting dysfunction of the cortex basal ganglia or cerebellum. Severe cases may cause generalized or focal seizures that are difficult to control. Some patients exhibit myoclonus or tremor. Hypothalamic involvement may lead to hyperthermia or hypothermia, autonomic dysfunction with vasomotor instability, or diabetes insipidus. Abnormalities of ocular motility, swallowing, or other cranial nerve functions are uncommon. Spinal cord infection is usually inconspicuous but can result in flaccid weakness, with acute loss of reflexes in the most severe cases. Spinal cord involvement, particularly of the anterior horn cells, is most common with poliovirus (Chapter 452). Focal symptoms other than seizures are usually minor and are overshadowed by generalized brain dysfunction; some patients may have hemiparesis, visual disturbance, or sensory loss. Focal involvement of limbic structures is particularly characteristic of rabies encephalitis. Some patients with West Nile encephalitis may present with a combination of encephalitis and Guillain-Barré syndrome.

The time course of acute viral meningitis and encephalitis varies. The onset may occur within a matter of hours or evolve more slowly over a few days. Usually, maximal deficit appears within 1 to 4 days.

Laboratory Findings

When viral encephalitis is suspected, if major focal signs are present, computed tomography (CT) should be performed first. Examination of the CSF is essential. The presence of 10 to 1000 mononuclear cells per cubic millimeter (i.e., pleocytons) is characteristic. Occasionally, early examination may show acellular fluid or predominance of polymorphonuclear leukocytes, but the typical mononuclear pleocytosis soon evolves. The pressure may be elevated, whereas the glucose level is characteristically normal or only modestly reduced. The protein content is usually elevated (50 to 100 mg/dL). Although not part of the routine examination, immunoglobulin concentration and oligoclonal bands may be observed. An increased protein content and pleocytosis may persist for weeks or months after convalescence; oligoclonal bands can be detected for an even longer period.

Systemic laboratory findings depend on the etiologic agent. Generally, the white blood cell count is not elevated, but elevations or depressions can be seen, usually with a lymphocytic predominance. Involvement of salivary glands or pancreas in mumps (Chapter 368) may elevate the serum amylase level.

Neurodiagnostic tests usually reveal nonspecific abnormalities, with notable exception in the case of herpes simplex encephalitis (Chapter 369). Findings of CT and magnetic resonance imaging

(MRI) are usually normal early in the course of the nonherpetic viral encepha-litides, but diffuse cerebral edema and multifocal areas of parenchymal injury with contrast enhancement may appear in the more severe cases. The greatest value of these neuroimaging procedures lies in excluding alternative diagnoses.

Diagnosis

With a few exceptions, the neurologic and laboratory findings accompanying the acute viral meningoencephalitides are insufficiently distinct to allow an etiologic diagnosis, and it may even be difficult to distinguish these disorders from a number of nonviral diseases. The epidemiologic setting (e.g., time of year, exposure to insects, the local community) and accompanying systemic manifestations may be helpful in presumptive diagnoses. Involvement of the nervous system by mumps virus is usually suspected from associated clinical parotitis or pancreatitis, although the neurologic disease can be the sole or presenting clinical manifestation; conversely, a certain history of previous mumps eliminates this diagnostic possibility. Several enterovirus infections produce a rash, which usually accompanies the onset of fever and persists for 4 to 10 days. In infections by coxsackievirus A5, 9, and 16 and by echovirus 4, 6, 9, 16, and 30, the rash is typically maculopapular and nonpruritic and may be confined to the face and trunk or may involve extremities, including the palms and soles. Echovirus 9 infections can cause a petechial rash resembling meningococcemia. Herpangina, characterized by gray vesicular lesions on the tonsillar fossae, soft palate, and uvula, can accompany group A coxsackievirus infection. In coxsackievirus A16 and, rarely, other group A serotype infections, a vesicular rash may involve hands, feet, and oropharynx. As discussed later, the encephalitis related to Epstein-Barr virus occurs in the setting of acute mononucleosis. The principally postinfectious encephalitides related to measles and varicella follow overt systemic diseases with characteristic rashes.

Because no specific treatment exists for acute viral meningitis and encephalitis (except those caused by herpesviruses) in immunocompetent patients and because the signs and symptoms are often nonspecific, exclusion of other diagnoses becomes important. The following disorders are potentially confusing diagnostically: partially treated bacterial meningitis (Chapter 312); rickettsial infections (Chapter 355); Lyme disease (Chapter 352); meningitis caused by a variety of nonpyogenic organisms, including *Mycobacterium tuberculosis* (Chapter 341), and by *Cryptococcus neoformans* (Chapter 383) and other fungi; parameningeal bacterial infections (Chapter 430); brain abscess (Chapter 430); subacute bacterial endocarditis (Chapter 310); and the cerebral vasculitides. Among noninfectious causes, trimethoprim-sulfamethoxazole, nonsteroidal analgesics, OKT3 antibody given for immunosuppression, intravenous immunoglobulin, and certain other drugs may occasionally cause aseptic meningitis reaction. Without a CSF examination, the differential diagnosis becomes even broader, encompassing additional toxic and vascular diseases. Most alternative diagnoses can be suspected or eliminated by the history, the CSF profile, or brain imaging.

Despite the absence of effective treatment, specific virologic diagnosis is useful for prognosis in the individual patient and for epidemiologic implications for the populations at risk. Diagnosis usually relies on serology, although direct detection of the organism in the CSF, blood, or stool may sometimes be achieved. Selection of tests and their interpretation depend on the particular organism. Almost all acute viral syndromes occur in the setting of a first encounter with the agent, which then results in lasting immunity. In these cases, seroconversion documented by a four-fold or greater rise in antibody titer between acute and convalescent sera is a principal means of diagnosis, although virus-specific IgM antibodies provide a rapid and accurate method of early diagnosis. A notable exception is herpes simplex encephalitis, in which antibody titers must be more cautiously interpreted (Chapter 369).

Attempts at direct viral isolation are of limited value in clinical management and must be tailored to the suspected agent. Arboviruses and enteroviruses can be isolated from the blood but are seldom recoverable at the time of clinically evident meningitis or encephalitis. During the acute disease, coxsackieviruses and echoviruses are most readily isolated from stool or CSF and, in some cases, throat washings. Lymphocytic choriomeningitis virus can be isolated from blood or CSF. Mumps virus may be isolated from saliva, throat

washings, or CSF. HSV-2 may be cultured from the CSF or identified in genital lesions. Polymerase chain reaction (PCR) screening of CSF undoubtedly improves specific diagnosis, but it is still not widely available.

Vaccination

Effective vaccines are available for polio, measles, mumps, and rubella, and the illnesses related to these viruses have declined dramatically in countries with effective vaccination strategies. Similarly, vaccination against Japanese encephalitis has been effective in controlling the infection in Asia. A vaccine against varicella has been introduced. Rabies is the only infection for which the vaccine may be given after exposure to the virus.

Rx Treatment

Effective antiviral therapy is available against HSV-1, cytomegalovirus, and varicella, the latter two of which cause encephalitis in immunocompromised patients only. In immunosuppressed patients, long-term therapy may be necessary. Several antiretroviral drugs are also available that provide temporary control of the virus, because drug-resistant strains of HIV frequently emerge. Treatment of acute viral encephalitis and meningitis (except herpes) is directed at relief of symptoms, supportive care, prevention, and management of complications. Strict isolation is not essential, although when enteroviral infection is suspected, careful handwashing precautions in handling stools should be instituted. Persons with measles, chickenpox, rubella, or mumps virus infections should observe the usual precautions of isolation from susceptible individuals. Arboviruses are not characteristically spread from person to person because they require an intermediate insect vector.

The headache and fever of meningitis can usually be managed with judicious doses of acetaminophen. Severe hyperthermia (>40°C) may require vigorous therapy, but mild temperature elevations may serve as a natural defense mechanism and are best left untreated. Patients with severe encephalitis often become comatose. However, vigorous support and avoidance of complications are essential because some may achieve remarkable recovery. Meticulous care in an intensive care unit setting with respiratory and nutritional support is indicated. Isolation for patients with community-acquired acute infective encephalitis is not required except for rabies encephalitis (Chapter 454). Isolation should also be considered for severely immunosuppressed patients, patients with exanthematous encephalitis, and patients with a potentially contagious viral hemorrhagic fever.

Although seizures sometimes complicate encephalitis, prophylactic anticonvulsants are not routinely recommended. If seizures develop, they can usually be managed with phenytoin, valproate, or phenobarbital, given parentally and monitored by blood levels. If status epilepticus ensues, appropriately vigorous therapy should be instituted to prevent secondary brain injury and hypoxia (Chapter 434). Similarly, secondary bacterial infections should be sought and promptly treated. Steroids should probably generally be avoided in the treatment of encephalitis because of their inhibitory effects on host immune responses.

Prognosis

Full recovery from viral meningitis usually occurs within 1 to 2 weeks of onset, although some patients describe persistence of fatigue, lightheadedness, and asthenia for months. The prognosis of encephalitis depends on its cause (see Table 451–1). Arbovirus encephalitides have variable mortality rates. Eastern equine encephalitis has the highest mortality rate of all arboviruses, whereas California virus has the lowest. The mortality rates for most viral encephalitides are higher for children younger than 4 years old and for the elderly. Nonfatal encephalitis caused by eastern, western, West Nile, and St. Louis viruses have a relatively high rate of neurologic sequelae. Encephalitis associated with mumps or lymphocytic choriomeningitis virus is rarely associated with death, and sequelae occur infrequently. The most common sequela following mumps meningoencephalitis is sensorineural deafness. Hydrocephalus from aqueductal stenosis has been reported as a late sequela of mumps meningitis and encephalitis in children.

SUGGESTED READINGS
Chaudhuri A, Kennedy PG: Diagnosis and treatment of viral encephalitis. Postgrad Med J 2002;78:575–583. *An excellent review.*
Redington JJ, Tyler KL: Viral infections of the nervous system, 2002: Update on diagnosis and treatment. Arch Neurol 2002;59:712–718. *An excellent review.*

452 POLIOMYELITIS

Avindra Nath
Joseph R. Berger

Definition

Poliomyelitis (i.e., acute anterior poliomyelitis, infantile paralysis) is an acute illness caused by the three strains of poliovirus. The disease selectively destroys the motor neurons of the spinal cord and brain stem, resulting in flaccid, asymmetrical weakness. Until recently one of the most feared of all human infectious diseases, poliomyelitis is now almost entirely preventable by vaccination.

Etiology

The three antigenically different strains of poliovirus (types 1, 2, and 3) are classified in the genus *Enterovirus* within the family Picornaviridae. Most cases are caused by the type 1 strain. They are small (approximately 27 nm), roughly spherical particles with icosahedral symmetry. They contain a single-stranded RNA core surrounded by a protein capsid. Lacking a lipid envelope, the polioviruses are resistant to lipid solvents and are stable at low pH.

Incidence, Prevalence, and Epidemiology

Since the World Health Assembly resolved in 1988 to eradicate poliomyelitis, the estimated number of polio cases globally has declined by more than 99%, and nearly 55% of the world's population is considered polio free. In the United States, the number of cases of paralytic poliomyelitis has fallen to just a few cases yearly due to the widespread use of an effective vaccine. Countries engaged in war continue to have low immunization rates, and paralytic polio continues to occur in some parts of Africa. It has a seasonal incidence in temperate zones but a more even distribution throughout the year in tropical areas.

Poliovirus is acquired by the oral route and subsequently replicates in the oropharynx and lower gastrointestinal tract. It may be secreted for a week or two in saliva and for more prolonged periods in feces, which provides the major avenue of host-to-host transmission. Spread of polioviruses is greatly influenced by standards of hygiene, and greatest dissemination occurs within families or other crowded circumstances.

Paralysis is an unusual complication of poliovirus infection. During an epidemic, only 1 to 2% of infections result in neurologic symptoms and signs; another 4 to 8% of infected persons suffer nonspecific (minor) illness. Although polio occurs most commonly in preschool children, a number of other factors cause an increase in the incidence of paralytic disease, including advanced age, recent strenuous exercise, tonsillectomy, pregnancy, and impairment of B-lymphocyte (antibody) defenses. Immunity to each of the three types of poliovirus is lifelong, but infection with one strain does not protect against subsequent infection by another. In the United States, the incidence of poliomyelitis due to live attenuated strains, although extremely rare, is similar to that of wild-type virus occurring in nonimmunized subjects.

Pathogenesis and Pathology

Polioviruses selectively infect specific neuronal populations, inducing highly stereotyped pathologic processes. In this manner, they contrast with most of the viruses causing acute encephalitis or meningitis.

The poliovirus invades the nervous system only after prior systemic replication. An initial alimentary phase with local replication in the intestinal mucosa and spread to the local lymphatics is followed by viremia, which seeds the nervous system. The virus also may replicate in the skeletal muscle and be transported through the peripheral nerves to the spinal cord. This is similar to the myotropic nature of other enteroviruses and may account for the myalgia that precedes the onset of weakness. Convalescent poliomyelitis is characterized by loss of motor neurons and denervation atrophy of their associated skeletal muscles.

Clinical Manifestations

Acute poliomyelitis is separated into two distinct phases: minor illness and major illness. The minor illness coincides with viremia and consists of fever, headache, and sore throat, which resolve within 1 to 2 days. In some patients, this is followed by the major illness, which is characterized by abrupt onset of fever, headache, vomiting, and meningismus. Cerebrospinal fluid (CSF) pleocytosis is present at this stage. The symptoms of aseptic meningitis resolve within 5 to 10 days. Asymmetrical muscle weakness is the hallmark of the illness. It is typically preceded by intense myalgia. Proximal muscles are more commonly involved, and legs are involved more often than arms. In mild cases, paralysis affects only parts of muscles rather than selective peripheral nerve or nerve root distributions. Sensory changes are lacking. The paralysis may render one limb useless but entirely spare the contralateral arm or leg. About 50% of patients develop acute urinary retention. The trunk musculature is least commonly affected. The affected muscles are flaccid, and the deep tendon reflexes may be absent. Atrophy develops rapidly, usually beginning within a week in paralyzed muscles and progressing over the ensuing weeks. The motor deficit rarely progresses for more than 3 to 5 days.

About 10 to 15% of cases affect the lower brain stem motor nuclei. Involvement of the ninth and tenth cranial nerve nuclei leads to paralysis of pharyngeal and laryngeal musculature (i.e., bulbar poliomyelitis). Parts of the facial muscles can be involved, unilaterally or bilaterally. Less often, the tongue and muscles of mastication become paralyzed. External oculomotor weakness occurs rarely. The pupils are spared. Direct involvement of the brain stem reticular formation can disrupt breathing and swallowing and produce serious disturbances in cardiovascular control. Poliomyelitis seldom causes permanent functional paralysis of the bulbar muscles, probably because of the relatively small size of the motor units served by brain stem nuclei and because overwhelming disease in these critical segments is often fatal.

Diagnosis and Differential Diagnosis

Because of its rarity in the United States, poliomyelitis may present diagnostic difficulties. Its early phases must be differentiated from other acute meningitides, and when paralysis ensues, a major differential diagnosis is postinfectious polyneuropathy or Guillain-Barré syndrome. Rarely, West Nile virus infection may produce a poliomyelitis-like syndrome. However, almost no other acute disease produces headache, stiff neck, fever, and asymmetrical, flaccid paralysis without sensory loss coupled with an increase in white blood cells in the CSF. Rarely, coxsackievirus and echoviruses have caused encephalitides with prominent but not extensive motor neuron symptoms and signs. Acute intermittent porphyria may cause a motor polyneuropathy somewhat similar to postinfectious polyneuropathy. Sometimes, acute transverse myelitis may be confused with poliomyelitis, but findings of a sensorimotor spinal level at the appropriate spinal cord segment usually serves to separate an inflammatory cord transection from diffuse anterior horn cell involvement. The diagnosis can be established by isolation of virus from blood or CSF or by serologic evidence of acute poliovirus infection. In the rare cases related to vaccine strains, viral isolates can be distinguished in the laboratory.

Rx **Treatment**

No specific treatment is available, but supportive care is important in reducing pain during the acute attack and in maintaining vital functions to ensure survival. Bedrest and treatment of pain are recommended during the myalgic phase. Important measures include preventing contractures, maintaining airway and cardiovascular stability, and preventing excessive calcium mobilization and bedsores.

Prognosis

Death of patients with poliomyelitis is usually the result of bulbar involvement and is attributable to respiratory and cardiovascular impairment. The mortality rate has been considerably reduced with modern management of respiratory insufficiency. Patients who survive an episode of acute paralytic poliomyelitis usually recover considerable motor function. Generally, motor improvement begins within the first weeks after onset, and 60% of eventual recovery is achieved by 3 months.

Postpolio Syndrome

A number of patients with previous poliomyelitis develop further motor deterioration later in life. In some, this is related to musculoskeletal decompensation or other factors but does not involve new weakness. However, other persons suffer a true loss of strength, called *postpolio syndrome*. This disorder is characterized by an insidiously slow but gradually progressive weakness beginning 30 or more years after an attack of poliomyelitis. Most commonly, it adds to the weakness of already affected muscles; less often, weakness develops in muscles previously thought to be normal. This weakness is often accompanied by fasciculations, and additional atrophy may develop. Muscle biopsy shows type grouping consistent with chronic denervation-reinnervation. Overall, the prognosis is good, with slow progression of further weakness, which only rarely leads to a severe increase in disability or to death.

The most likely pathogenesis consists of senescence of the surviving expanded motor units. This development must be distinguished from motor neuron disease of a more malignant variety, which has also been described many years after acute poliomyelitis but which appears to be much less common than the more gradual and benign postpolio syndrome. In all cases, it is imperative to exclude coincidental unrelated disease.

Prevention

Poliomyelitis can be prevented by live attenuated or killed polio vaccines, which are now given routinely (Chapter 16). The practice of immunization has relaxed as the threat of paralytic poliomyelitis has declined. The goal of the World Health Organization is to eradicate polio by 2005.

SUGGESTED READINGS

Leis AA, Fratkin J, Stokic DS, et al: West Nile poliomyelitis. Lancet Infect Dis 2003;3:9–10. *West Nile virus infection can simulate polio clinically.*

McComas AJ, Quartly C, Griggs RC: Early and late losses of motor units after poliomyelitis. Brain 1997;120:1415–1421. *Denervation progresses in patients with prior poliomyelitis in both clinically affected and unaffected muscles at rates that exceed those of normal aging.*

453 THE HERPESVIRUSES

Joseph R. Berger
Avindra Nath

Etiology

The members of the family of Herpesviridae are large, enveloped viruses with a double-stranded, linear deoxyribonucleic acid in their core. They are icosahedral, a shape dictated by their 162 capsomeres. Antigenic differences, including those between herpes simplex virus types 1 and 2 (HSV-1 and HSV-2), permit identification by monospecific antibodies using immunocytochemical techniques. Knowledge of their DNA sequences has enabled development of polymerase chain reaction (PCR) methods for their detection.

Herpesviruses have been detected in a wide range of hosts, including humans, primates, horses, cattle, pigs, and chickens. Since the recognized onset of the acquired immunodeficiency syndrome (AIDS) epidemic in 1981, three new members of the family of human herpesviruses, human herpesviruses 6, 7, and 8 (HHV-6, HHV-7, and HHV 8), have been described, nearly doubling the number of recognized herpesviruses known to affect humans. Three human herpesviruses (HSV-1, HSV-2, and herpes varicella-zoster virus [VZV]) are known to be neurotropic. Cytomegalovirus, a member of the Herpes family, may also be neurotropic, and a herpesvirus related to HSV-1, the simian herpesvirus, is neurotropic and in rare instances may affect humans.

The survival and transmission of these herpesviruses is predicated on the latency that they establish in the nervous system. The initial peripheral viral infection is followed by retrograde axoplasmic transport to nervous system ganglia. Each of these viruses can then establish a latent infection of sensory ganglia that may subsequently reactivate to release progeny virus into the territory of the ganglion's epithelial innervation through orthograde axoplasmic transport. The most feared and best recognized neurologic complication of the herpesviruses is HSV encephalitis, a consequence of HSV-1 infection. Aseptic meningitis, radiculitis, and sacral autonomic dysfunction occur with HSV-2. The neurologic complications of VZV include encephalitis, myelitis, radiculopathy, and cerebral vasculitis.

Human herpesviruses 6, 7, and 8 are lymphotropic. Neurologic disease has been associated with all but HHV-7, about which little is known. The importance of HHV-6 as a trigger for neurologic disease remains uncertain. Prompt diagnosis of infections by these viruses is important because they are amenable to selective antiviral drug therapy.

HERPES SIMPLEX VIRUS TYPES 1 AND 2

Incidence

Although HSV encephalitis is the most frequently identified cause of severe, sporadic viral encephalitis in the United States, it remains uncommon. The estimated annual incidence is 1 in 250,000 to 500,000 persons. HSV encephalitis accounts for approximately 20% of the reported cases of encephalitis in the United States. Some HSV encephalitis may go unrecognized, and in a small percentage of cases, the infection undergoes spontaneous resolution. Prevalence figures probably underestimate the true number.

The disease afflicts persons of all ages, with peaks of incidence in late childhood and middle age. There is no seasonal incidence of HSV encephalitis; it occurs throughout the year. Case-to-case transmission does not occur. Although immunologic mechanisms are important in HSV latency and its peripheral reactivation, the appearance of HSV encephalitis is not related to immunosuppression. However, the clinical expression of the illness may be modified if cell-mediated immunity is impaired.

HSV-1 is a ubiquitous organism (Chapter 369). More than 90% of adults have serologic evidence of exposure. Immunocytochemical staining and PCR have confirmed that at least 75% of the population harbors latent HSV in the trigeminal ganglia at the time of death. Recurrent cold sores resulting from viral reactivation have been estimated to occur in one fourth of adults. Although as many as 10% of patients with HSV encephalitis may have cold sores at the time of their illness, this number is not different from that for individuals hospitalized with other severe, debilitating diseases. Although HSV encephalitis may occur as a primary infection in a person never previously infected with the virus, it is more likely that it results from reinfection by a new strain of virus or from reactivated virus.

Clinical Manifestations

HSV encephalitis may be explosive at onset. The condition may progress to a state of altered consciousness accompanied by speech abnormalities and motor weakness in a matter of hours from onset of the illness. Typically, however, the onset is subacute, with fever, headache, and malaise preceding the development of neurologic deficits. Diffuse and focal cerebral dysfunction is observed. Fever, often high, is seen in up to 90% of patients with HSV encephalitis. In as many as 10%, fever may be absent, particularly at the time of presentation. HSV encephalitis warrants consideration even in afebrile patients who present with an altered mental status. The most common forms of presentation include severe headache, focal or generalized convulsions, and alterations in behavior and consciousness. Disorientation, dysphasia, and hemiparesis may be observed. Motor paralysis is present in fewer than 50% of affected individuals. Occasionally, patients are initially referred for psychiatric consultation because of delusions, agitation, personality changes, disorientation, or dysphasia. Without treatment, the mortality of HSV encephalitis is high (>70%), with major permanent morbidity in many survivors. Milder forms of the illness exist but are rarely correctly identified.

In the setting of immunosuppression, particularly in patients with AIDS (Chapter 414), HSV encephalitis may manifest in a more benign and desultory fashion. The illness may be characterized by unexplained meningitis with few focal neurologic findings. A high index of suspicion is therefore required to establish the diagnosis. HSV has also been associated with focal brain stem encephalitis.

Pathology

The characteristic gross and microscopic pathologic findings of herpetic infection, particularly its anatomic localization, distinguish HSV encephalitis from other encephalitides. Although often asymmetrical, the disease is usually bilateral and involves the medial temporal and inferior lobes and related limbic structures, including the hippocampus, amygdaloid nuclei, olfactory cortex, insula, and cingulate gyrus. Necrosis with petechial hemorrhage is often so intense that the disease was once called *acute necrotizing encephalitis.* Microscopically, hemorrhagic necrosis with mononuclear inflammation characterizes involved areas, with neurons and glia often containing Cowdry type A intranuclear inclusions during the acute phase of infection. Perivascular cuffing, neuronophagia, and diffuse microglial hyperplasia are observed. Although gray matter is predominantly affected, the infection also extends into the white matter. In addition to the necrosis and inflammation of the neural tissues, leptomeningeal infiltration by lymphocytes, plasma cells, and large mononuclear cells is also seen. In the immunosuppressed host, the inflammatory infiltrate may not be as intense.

Diagnosis

Among the differential diagnoses of HSV encephalitis are pyogenic (Chapter 312), tuberculous (Chapter 341), and fungal meningitis; brain abscess (Chapter 449); brain neoplasm (Chapter 457); vasculitis, and demyelinating disease (Chapter 448). Cerebrospinal fluid (CSF) examination is of paramount importance in detecting the presence of other infectious meningitic processes and in the definitive diagnosis of HSV encephalitis. Brain abscess seldom manifests with the behavioral abnormalities so often evident in HSV encephalitis, and radiographic findings are often very helpful in distinguishing between the two conditions. Cerebral neoplasms tend to evolve slowly and are not accompanied by fever.

Neuroimaging with head computed tomographic (CT) scanning or magnetic resonance imaging (MRI) is generally regarded as the initial diagnostic measure when evaluating a patient suspected of having HSV encephalitis. However, CT scanning is relatively insensitive. At least 40% of patients with early HSV encephalitis have normal CT scans. The MRI is much more sensitive and often reveals highly characteristic abnormalities, including the virtually pathognomonic increased signal abnormalities on T2-weighted sequences in the medial temporal and insular cortical regions and inferior frontal cingulate gyri. The lesions are often bilateral. General anesthesia may be required to perform the MRI because of agitation and a poor level of

cooperation on the part of the patient. The MRI can also detect alternative pathologic processes, such as brain abscess, vasculitis, or demyelination, which may manifest in a similar fashion.

Brain biopsy, once regarded as the definitive diagnostic tool for HSV encephalitis, has been largely supplanted by the widespread introduction of CSF PCR for HSV, a test with high specificity and sensitivity. Brain biopsy should be reserved for individuals with significant mass effect from necrotizing encephalitis in whom lumbar puncture represents a substantial risk or individuals for whom a high index of suspicion of HSV encephalitis remains despite a negative CSF PCR results for HSV. Brain biopsy specimens should be subjected to histologic study, immunocytochemical analysis, electron microscopy, PCR, and viral culture.

Examination of the CSF reveals a mononuclear pleocytosis, typically between 50 to 150 leukocytes (lymphocytes or mononuclear cells) per cubic millimeter (median, 130 cells/mm^3), in more than two thirds of patients. Occasionally, pleocytosis is not present. HSV encephalitis may result in hemorrhagic CSF. Red blood cells may be seen in the CSF, and the centrifugal fluid may appear xanthochromic. The protein content is usually slightly elevated; the median CSF protein is 80 mg/dL; however, the CSF protein is normal in 20%. The glucose level is normal or only slightly reduced. Like MRI, CSF analysis may also be useful in establishing alternative diagnoses, such as bacterial or fungal infection. Although PCR for HSV is very sensitive, attempts to isolate HSV by culture from the CSF are seldom successful. In the Collaborative Study of HSV Encephalitis, CSF was normal in 3% of biopsy-confirmed cases.

Blood serologic analysis for the diagnosis of HSV encephalitis is not useful. Most persons have been exposed to HSV at some time in their lives and demonstrate antibody levels. Fluctuations in the titer of antibody to HSV are commonly observed. A less than four-fold rise in titer is essentially meaningless, and in some confirmed cases of HSV encephalitis, the antibody titers to HSV fail to rise.

Rx Treatment

The first antiviral therapy demonstrated to be effective for HSV encephalitis was vidarabine. Acyclovir, however, has proved to be a more potent agent in the treatment of HSV encephalitis. It is administered by intravenous infusion as 10 mg/kg given over at least an hour every 8 hours for 10 days. This agent selectively interacts with two herpesvirus-coded enzymes, thymidine kinase and DNA polymerase, giving it specificity for the herpesviruses. It is excreted by the kidney and should be administered cautiously in patients with impaired renal function. Toxic reactions are rare but include phlebitis, rash, elevation of aminotransferase levels, and gastrointestinal disturbances. Neurotoxicity may be manifested by tremors, hallucinations, seizures, and altered consciousness.

HSV encephalitis is a medical emergency because of its characteristically aggressive course. Antiviral therapy with intravenous acyclovir should be administered at the time the diagnosis is considered. Treatment is best rendered in an intensive care unit. If the diagnosis cannot be confirmed, acyclovir should be discontinued.

In the presence of cerebral edema with impending brain herniation, high-dose corticosteroid therapy (4 to 6 mg of dexamethasone every 4 to 6 hours) should be given. Although a theoretical concern exists that corticostenosis may slow viral clearance, treatment of the accompanying vasogenic edema is imperative.

Prognosis

The age of the patient and the level of consciousness at the time of institution of therapy determine the outcome. The only modifiable parameter for improving prognosis is the early administration of antiviral therapy. The best survival is observed in young individuals (<30 years) with only lethargy at the time of the institution of antiviral therapy. Patients with minor neurologic deficits may recover without severe long-term sequelae and return to normal function if antiviral therapy is instituted early. Relapse has been observed in rare patients despite seemingly adequate antiviral treatment. This relapse usually occurs within a few weeks of the resolution of the initial stage of the acute illness and often results in severe sequelae. The pathogenetic mechanisms for relapse are unknown.

NEUROLOGIC COMPLICATIONS OF GENITAL HERPES

Herpetic infections below the umbilicus are typically caused by HSV-2. However, up to 15% of genital herpes may result from HSV-1 infection, presumably as a consequence of orogenital sexual practices. When it is the consequence of HSV-2 infection, genital herpes recurs within 1 year in 80 to 90% of patients after the initial infection, whereas HSV-1 genital infections recur in only 55% in the first year of infection. Similarly, oral herpes may result from HSV-2 infection. HSV-2 is associated with intense burning, stinging, or itching pain at the site of skin blistering. The initial infection and recurrences may be complicated by radicular pain. The latter may result in pain radiating into the buttock, groin, genitalia, or lower extremities. This radicular pain may be misinterpreted as being the result of a lumbar disc problem when it occurs as a prodromal symptom (i.e., before the outbreak of the blistering rash) or when it occurs in the absence of an obvious rash. HSV-2 may also be associated with aseptic meningitis, autonomic (i.e., bowel, bladder, and sexual) dysfunction, and rarely, myelitis. These neurologic complications are more common in the presence of primary genital herpes, but they may also be seen at the time of recurrence.

Symptoms of meningitis occur in approximately one fourth of patients with primary genital herpes and rarely necessitate hospitalization. The CSF reveals mononuclear pleocytosis, mild elevation of protein levels, and normal or slightly reduced glucose concentration. Clearing without residua occurs in 4 to 10 days on average. Demonstration of HSV-2 in the CSF by viral culture or PCR establishes the causal relationship. HSV-2 is the chief causative agent of Mollaret's meningitis, a recurrent, aseptic meningitis with low-grade fever, headache, and myalgia. In approximately 50% of patients, transitory neurologic symptoms or signs may accompany the meningeal irritation. The CSF reveals mixed pleocytosis with leukocytes, lymphocytes, and endothelial cells (i.e., Mollaret cells) as well as an increased gamma globulin fraction. The disease remits spontaneously in several days. Careful history may indicate that the patient has concurrent genital herpes with the attacks. CSF PCR is valuable in demonstrating HSV DNA in HSV meningitis and Mollaret's meningitis. The prophylactic administration of acyclovir prevents attacks in affected patients.

The autonomic manifestations of urinary retention, constipation, and sexual impotence in association with genital herpes are less common than meningitis. Typically, these abnormalities occur in the setting of primary infection. Symptoms and signs of a sacral sensory radiculopathy sometimes accompany the autonomic changes. A direct herpetic infection of sacral autonomic structures may explain the autonomic dysfunction, but the exact pathogenesis remains uncertain. The autonomic dysfunction is reversible and generally clears in tandem with the resolution of skin and mucous membrane lesions. HSV-2 should be considered in anyone with complaints of isolated bladder, bowel, or sexual dysfunction. A thorough inspection of the genitalia may disclose ulcerations; viral culture of lesions is diagnostic. Rising titers of antibody to HSV-2 may also support the diagnosis. In rare instances, transverse myelitis may be associated with HSV-3 infection. In adults, HSV-2 rarely produces encephalitis, although in newborns, it is a major cause of meningoencephalitis. In the newborn, HSV-2 results in multiorgan systemic disease that is accompanied by herpetic lesions of the skin, eye, and mucous membranes.

In patients with frequent recurrent attacks of genital herpes, early, self-initiated treatment of recurrent lesions with oral acyclovir or related antiherpetic agents can be given, beginning therapy at the onset of prodromal symptoms. Alternatively, particularly if recurrences are frequent or associated with debilitation, daily prophylactic administration of these drugs may be warranted.

NEUROLOGIC COMPLICATIONS OF HERPES VARICELLA-ZOSTER VIRUS INFECTIONS

Varicella-zoster virus (VZV) (Chapter 367) is distantly related to HSV, sharing only minor antigen cross-reaction. It is the cause of chickenpox and shingles. Postviral encephalomyelitis may follow chickenpox. The incidence of postviral encephalomyelitis with primary VZV infection has been estimated at 10 cases per 100,000 persons. It has also been associated with Reye's syndrome. Herpes zoster, a dermatomal cutaneous infection, is the result of reactivation of the VZV that normally lies latent in sensory ganglia after an attack of varicella that generally occurs during childhood. In addition to its cutaneous manifestations, herpes zoster is accompanied by neuritic symptoms and may be complicated by an array of neurologic sequelae.

Epidemiology

The annual incidence of herpes zoster (i.e., shingles) is estimated to be 3.4 cases per 1000 persons. Unlike varicella, herpes zoster occurs throughout the year, with neither significant clustering of cases nor seasonal or yearly preponderance. Case exposure in herpes zoster is rarely identified. The most important factors that influence its incidence are age and immunosuppression. Herpes zoster is rare in childhood. Its frequency is relatively constant between the ages of 20 and 50 years (approximately 2.5 cases per 1000 persons annually), and thereafter, its incidence is doubled in those between the ages of 50 and 60 years and redoubled in those between the ages of 80 and 90 years. Impaired cell-mediated immunity in Hodgkin's disease and other lymphoreticular malignancies, the administration of cytotoxic drugs and corticosteroids, radiation therapy, or infection with human immunodeficiency virus (HIV) predisposes to the development of herpes zoster. Occasionally, a history of neoplasm, radiation exposure, or physical injury in the proximity of the affected dorsal root ganglion or nerve is elicited. Immunosuppression predisposes to spread of virus beyond the ganglion nerve-dermatome unit into the central nervous system or systemically. It is likely that widespread introduction of varicella vaccination will decrease the incidence of chickenpox and herpes zoster.

Pathology and Pathogenesis

Considerable evidence has indicated that VZV is latent in ganglionic satellite cells rather than neurons. After latent virus reactivates, it can spread within the sensory ganglion and travel centrifugally over the peripheral nerve processes, eventually seeding the skin and producing a dermatomal vesicular rash. Cell-mediated defenses, rather than humoral immunity, are critically involved in protecting the host during herpes zoster infection. Pathologically, acutely infected dorsal root ganglia and nerves show the presence of a mononuclear inflammatory response, neuronal degeneration with intranuclear Cowdry type A inclusion bodies, and ZVZ infection of local satellite cells. In more severe cases, dorsal root ganglia above and below the primarily affected ganglion also show active herpetic infection.

Clinical Manifestations

Prodromal sensory symptoms include dermatomal pain, itching, or paresthesias, often preceding the eruption of the segmental rash by 2 to 5 days (Fig. 475–16). The early pain of herpes zoster may be confused with other types of neuropathic or visceral pain. Rarely, no rash appears, but the role of VZV is suggested by a rise in antibody titers (i.e., zoster sine herpete). Typically, the rash of herpes zoster involves one dermatome and remains unilateral. Fifty per cent of rashes occur over the trunk, particularly from the third thoracic to the second lumbar segments. *Zona* refers to the circling or beltlike lesions on the trunk. Twenty per cent of herpes zoster cases involve the head, usually in the distribution of the first (ophthalmic) division of the trigeminal nerve. Other cranial nerves may be affected. Approximately 15% of herpes zoster rashes involve the arms, and a similar number involves the legs. A small focus of satellite skin lesions may occur at other locations. The rash itself initially consists of erythematous macules that vesiculate over 12 to 24 hours. New vesicles may appear over 2 days. Typically, the vesicular fluid develops a purulent appearance within 72 hours, and within 1 week, these pustules begin to dry. Crusting takes place by 10 to 12 days, and the crusts generally fall off in 2 to

Continued

3 weeks. In the immunocompromised host, this course may be protracted. In uncomplicated cases, the rash heals with a variable degree of superficial scarring, sometimes leaving areas of hypopigmentation or depigmentation. These affected skin regions may be anesthetic or dysesthetic. More severe cases may leave denervation of a large segment involving one or several dermatomes. Herpes zoster in patients younger than 50 years should suggest the possibility of an underlying immunosuppressive condition, particularly AIDS.

The ophthalmic division of the trigeminal nerve is the cranial nerve most commonly affected. This predilection is not surprising, because VZV latency may be demonstrated in the trigeminal ganglia of more than 80% of elderly persons. Herpes zoster in this location may be complicated by spread to orbital structures, resulting in acute and long-term ocular sequelae. Spread of cutaneous rash along the bridge of the nose to its tip should be taken as a signal of impending ocular infection (i.e., herpes zoster ophthalmicus [HZO]), prompting early ophthalmologic consultation. This complication is more common in immunosuppressed patients; before the introduction of highly active antiretroviral therapy (HAART), HZO occurred in 5 to 15% of all HIV-seropositive patients. Facial palsy, with or without accompanying loss of taste on the anterior two thirds of the tongue, may accompany otic herpes zoster (i.e., Ramsay Hunt syndrome), with rash confined to a segment of the ear, or herpes zoster of the second and third cervical dermatomes (i.e., cervical collar herpes zoster). Occasionally, infection of the ninth and tenth or fifth cranial nerve may precede facial weakness. As with other motor syndromes, weakness is often delayed for a variable period after appearance of the rash. Eighth nerve dysfunction with sensorineural hearing loss or vertigo occurs in the same setting as facial palsy but is less common. Herpes zoster may rarely cause facial palsy in the absence of rash (i.e., zoster sine herpete). Herpes zoster of the ninth and tenth cranial nerves is unusual and may be overlooked without a careful search for the pharyngeal rash or ipsilateral laryngeal or pharyngeal palsy.

Herpes zoster of the extremities or trunk can also be complicated by segmental motor weakness, with the motor loss usually corresponding to the involved cutaneous dermatome. Weakness characteristically develops from a few days to 2 weeks after the onset of rash. Onset is characteristically abrupt, occurring over hours to 1 or 2 days with little or no subsequent deterioration. Weakness resolves in about 85% of cases; however, the remainder may have permanent paralysis within the myotome.

An unusual complication that is more frequently observed in the immunosuppressed host is myelitis. This complication results from direct involvement of the spinal cord by herpes zoster and is typically most severe at the level of the rash, although it may extend to higher levels. The most common clinical manifestations are motor weakness and bladder dysfunction, which generally occur as the rash resolves. Reflex abnormalities and sensory loss below the level of the rash may be observed. In severe cases, the lesion may result in clinical findings suggestive of cord transection. Alternatively, a Brown-Séquard syndrome may be observed. Other signs include mild or transient asymmetrical reflexes, the Babinski sign, and sensory disturbance. Spinal MRI is essential in excluding other possible causes.

At least three types of brain involvement may complicate herpes zoster: diffuse encephalitis, focal parenchymal infection, and vasculitis. Headache, stiff neck, and mild diffuse encephalitis often accompany acute herpes zoster but are difficult to distinguish from the effects of fever, sepsis, narcotic analgesics, and other underlying medical problems. Most such patients recover fully. In more severe diffuse encephalitis, chances for recovery may also be good if other complications of the disease do not intervene. The clinical picture is that of acute or subacute lethargy or delirium accompanied by CSF pleocytosis with few focal features.

Focal VZV encephalitis is a rare central nervous system complication of VZV most often observed in immunosuppressed patients. The cerebral lesions of focal VZV encephalitis chiefly involve the white matter. This encephalitis may occur long after the rash. Its clinical and radiographic appearance may be mistaken for progressive multifocal leukoencephalopathy. Brain biopsy is essential for diagnosis, allowing identification of Cowdry type A inclusions or of VZV antigens or nucleic acids.

Cerebral vasculitis is the most common serious postzoster central nervous system complication. Affected patients characteristically develop delayed contralateral hemiplegic strokes after trigeminal ophthalmic division herpes zoster infection. The onset of cerebral dysfunction can occur as long as 6 months after rash, with a mean interval of 7 weeks. Pathologic studies reveal inflammation or occlusion of the internal carotid artery and its major branches ipsilateral to the rash. More widespread cerebral vasculitis after herpes zoster infection in other locations has also been reported.

The pathogenesis is not well understood. Viral nucleocapsids and viral antigens can be found within affected vessels, suggesting a direct infection of arterial walls. These vessels are innervated by VZV-infected ganglia. Inflammation and thrombosis undoubtedly contribute to the pathogenesis. Arteriographic evidence of vasculitis or occlusions in the involved vessels and the clinical setting usually allow diagnosis.

Postherpetic neuralgia is a disabling consequence of herpes zoster. The incidence of postherpetic neuralgia ranges between 15 and 75%; it depends on the clinical definition of the syndrome and the patient population studied. Pain persists for more than 1 year in approximately 3 to 5% of patients after herpes zoster infection. Age is an important factor in the appearance of postherpetic neuralgia, which develops almost exclusively in persons older than 50 years. Over the age of 60 years, about one half of patients develop postherpetic neuralgia. The pain has been characterized as two types: a steady burning or boring pain and as paroxysmal pain with a lancinating quality. Both types may occur together and be aggravated by touch, including the simple contact of clothing. Treatment strategies include the use of amitriptyline, carbamazepine, gabapentin, topical capsaicin, and transcutaneous nerve stimulators. Success with these treatments is generally limited.

Diagnosis

Characteristic dermatomal distribution and the evolution of the vesicular rash of herpes zoster are diagnostic. Occasionally, herpes zoster may be confused with HSV infection. Features helpful in distinguishing between the two include the dermatomal distribution of herpes zoster and the association with scarring and postherpetic pain. In both herpes zoster and HSV infection, cells obtained from the base of the lesion, air-dried, and stained with Wright or Giemsa stain (Tzanck test) reveal multinucleated giant cells. Fluid scraped from the base of the vesicle and examined by direct fluorescent antibody technique may rapidly establish the diagnosis or viral cultures may be employed. The diagnosis of zoster sine herpete remains difficult. Thorough evaluation for an occult rash is of paramount importance. In many instances, this diagnosis remains presumptive because of a failure to apply a thorough diagnostic evaluation.

Treatment

The goals of therapy of herpes zoster are to suppress the acute infection, prevent the spread of the infection to the nervous system, and prevent postherpetic neuralgia. The available means to accomplish these goals consist of using antiviral drugs to interrupt viral replication and corticosteroids to modify local inflammatory responses. Aggressive therapy is warranted in the immunosuppressed patient and in those with involvement of the ophthalmic division of the trigeminal nerve.

Systemic therapy in these patients consists of intravenous acyclovir (10 mg/kg of body weight three times daily for 7 days). In the immunosuppressed host, particularly in patients with AIDS, oral maintenance for secondary prophylaxis should be employed. A regimen of acyclovir, 800 mg given five times daily for 7 days, decreases the acute pain and shortens healing time. It also reduces recurrence rates. Famciclovir, 500 mg given three times daily, and valacyclovir, 1000 mg given three times daily, appear to be effective alternatives. Except in immunosuppressed patients and those with herpes zoster ophthalmicus, oral therapies may be employed. The use of concomitant corticosteroid therapy to prevent postherpetic neuralgia remains controversial. The role of antiviral therapy in cerebral vasculitis or the other neurologic complications of herpes zoster is uncertain, but the presence of viral antigen in the affected sites provides ample justification for its use. Similarly, few data are available on the value of the administration of corticosteroids for these complications.

SIMIAN HERPES (B VIRUS, HERPESVIRUS SIMIAE)

B virus is a close relative of the human herpes simplex viruses. Serologic studies in monkeys have demonstrated high rates of infection, and rarely, transmission to humans has been reported by contamination, typically occurring in a research laboratory. Between 1973 and 1985, 25 cases of B virus were reported in humans. The mortality rate was 72%, and severe neurologic sequelae were observed in most survivors. Human-to-human transmission has been reported in a household contact. Human B virus infection most commonly manifests as rapidly ascending encephalomyelitis.

SUGGESTED READINGS

Gilden DH, Kleinschmidt-DeMasters BK, LaGuardia JJ, et al: Neurologic complications of the reactivation of varicella-zoster virus. N Engl J Med 2000;342:635–645. *A comprehensive review.*

Raschilas F, Wolff M, Delatour F, et al: Outcome of and prognostic factors for herpes simplex encephalitis in adult patients: Results of a multicenter study. Clin Infect Dis 2002;35:254–260. *Antiviral therapy within less than 2 days was associated with a better outcome.*

Simko JP, Caliendo AM, Hogle K, Versalovic J: Differences in laboratory findings for cerebrospinal fluid specimens obtained from patients with meningitis or encephalitis due to herpes simplex virus (HSV) documented by detection of HSV DNA. Clin Infect Dis 2002;35:414–419. *HSV can be detected in the CSF by PCR in mild, otherwise not diagnosed cases.*

 **RABIES**

Avindra Nath
Joseph R. Berger

Definition

Rabies is a viral infection with nearly worldwide distribution that affects principally wild and domestic animals. However, it also involves humans, in which case it results in devastating, almost invariably fatal encephalitis.

Etiology

Rabies virus is a bullet-shaped, enveloped, single-stranded RNA virus classified in the Rhabdoviridae family (*rhabdos*, Greek for *rod*) and Lyssavirus genus (*lyssa*, Greek for *frenzy*). It has particular neurotropic properties, and unlike many of the other viruses causing acute encephalitis, it appears to require central nervous system (CNS) infection as an essential part of its life cycle.

Pathogenesis

Viral transmission to animals and humans characteristically results from the bite of a rabid animal, although cases of transmission by aerosol in the laboratory or in a bat cave and by transplanted infected corneal tissue have also been recorded. After the virus breaches the protective epithelium, it reaches the CNS through peripheral nerves, exploiting retrograde axoplasmic transport. The interval between the bite and the onset of disease ranges from days to a year or more, but in most cases, it lasts 1 to 2 months. This delay may be related to amplification of the virus in peripheral tissues, particularly skeletal muscle, before it gains access to the CNS through motor and sensory nerves. During this delay, the virus can be eliminated by host immune mechanisms. It is this delay that affords an opportunity for prophylactic

postexposure immunization after the rabid animal bite. After virus enters peripheral and CNS pathways, immune defenses are unable to suppress further replication and spread of infection, which includes axoplasmic transport and, perhaps, transsynaptic transmission.

The CNS is involved in the subsequent transmission of the virus by infected animals in two essential ways: (1) infection of certain brain regions causes characteristic behavioral changes in the rabid animal, leading to increased biting activity, and (2) antegrade or centrifugal transport of the virus from the brain to highly innervated areas (e.g., salivary glands, cornea, skin) leads to virus shedding. In concert, these two aspects of infection ensure transmission and survival of the virus in the wild. They also have practical diagnostic implications for the human disease. The characteristic altered behavior in humans often results in a distinct clinical picture that distinguishes rabies from other viral encephalitides. Antegrade virus transport also affords a means of diagnosing rabies by isolation from saliva or immunohistochemical staining of infected cutaneous nerves innervating hair follicles. Humoral immune responses and neutralizing antibodies generated by rabies vaccine are most effective in tempering the virus; cell-mediated immune responses play only a minor role.

Pathology

Pathologic findings include nonspecific and specific abnormalities. A considerable discrepancy often occurs between the degree of pathologic change, particularly neuronal loss, and the severity of antemortem clinical findings. Nonspecific changes include perivascular mononuclear infiltrates and microglial activation, although inflammation may be scant in relation to the widespread distribution of infected cells detected immunohistochemically. Similarly, neuronal destruction is less prominent than the abundance of viral antigen, which is located principally in neurons but also in astrocytes. More specific changes include the presence of Negri bodies, which are eosinophilic neuronal intracytoplasmic inclusion bodies composed of viral nucleoprotein. Negri bodies are pathognomonic of rabies virus infection. At autopsy, infection is usually widespread in the brain, but the brain stem, spinal cord, hippocampus, basal ganglia, cortex, and other structures are also prominently involved. The relation of virus infection of neurons and the attendant inflammatory reaction to the clinical manifestations remains incompletely understood. Rabies infection of neurons may alter their membrane properties or synaptic transmission. Patients eventually manifest widespread brain dysfunction with impairment of respiratory and autonomic control because of brain stem involvement, which leads to death.

Epidemiology

The epidemiology of rabies varies in different parts of the world, falling into two patterns. In *sylvatic rabies,* infection is maintained in wildlife reservoirs. In the United States, rabies is endemic in the striped skunk in the Midwestern states and in California, in the raccoon in the southeastern and mid-Atlantic states (and now invading northern Kentucky), in the red fox in northern New York and adjacent regions of Canada, and in the gray fox in parts of the southwestern states; bat rabies has a wide geographic range. Reports of human rabies in United States have been associated with contact with bats. Similarly, in Western Europe, human rabies is rare, and it more often results from direct contact with wildlife than from contact with domestic dogs or cats. This pattern contrasts with that in much of Asia, Africa, and Latin America, where *urban rabies* is maintained as an epizootic infection in the domestic dog, and human disease is far more common. Viral strains differ among various animal hosts.

Clinical Manifestations

After an incubation period averaging 1 to 2 months, clinical rabies usually begins with a prodromal phase of nonspecific symptoms of malaise, fever, and headache, but more specific local symptoms are present at the site of the original bite. These include itching, paresthesia, or other sensations that begin in the area of the healed wound and then spread to a wider region, reflecting ganglioneuritis. No accompanying sensory loss occurs.

Within a few days, the full-blown illness begins, taking one of two forms: encephalitic (*furious*) or paralytic (*dumb*) rabies, perhaps

Continued

depending on the source and strain of the infecting virus. In its initial phase, encephalitic rabies is often distinguished from other viral infections by irritability and hyperactivity of a number of automatic reflexes. Periods of lucidity may alternate with confusion and intense anxiety precipitated by internal or external stimuli. Hydrophobia, with reflexive intense contraction of the diaphragm and accessory respiratory and other muscles, is induced on attempts to drink or even by the mere sight of water. Similarly, blowing or fanning air on the chest may induce intense laryngeal, pharyngeal, or other muscle spasms (i.e., aerophobia). High fever persists throughout the illness. Patients may also have spontaneous inspiratory spasms and autonomic dysfunction (i.e., hypersalivation, nonreactive pupils, and piloerection). Seizures are rare.

Paralytic rabies is less common and is often misdiagnosed. Patients present with weakness, usually beginning in the bitten extremity and spreading to involve all four limbs and the facial muscles early in the course. Consciousness and sensory function are spared. Areflexia often suggests Guillain-Barré syndrome. As the disease progresses, it may converge with the encephalitic form and be accompanied by irritative phenomena. Both forms evolve into lethargy and coma with prominent respiratory and cardiovascular dysfunction. Patients may have tachycardia, bradycardia, ectopic heart rhythms, and irregular breathing patterns such as cluster or periodic respirations. Patients die of respiratory failure or cardiovascular collapse within a mean interval of 4 to 7 days from onset. Intensive supportive care may extend survival in rare cases. Rare patients with partial vaccine-induced immunity have survived with intensive care.

Diagnosis

Rabies is usually suspected on the basis of a history of animal bite or other exposure. However, in as many as one third of cases, no such history is obtained. Magnetic resonance imaging may show hyperintense lesions in the basal ganglia on T2-weighted images. Definitive antemortem diagnosis is established by immunohistochemical identification of rabies virus antigen in hair follicle nerve endings of biopsied skin, usually obtained from the nape of the neck. Isolation of virus from saliva or the presence of antirabies antibodies in blood in the absence of vaccination or in the cerebrospinal fluid may also be used to establish diagnosis. Postmortem diagnosis is usually made by immunohistochemical examination of the brain. Polymerase chain reaction–based techniques have been developed for rapid diagnosis for rabies.

The differential diagnosis depends on the clinical presentation and the epidemiologic setting. In the case of paralytic rabies, the diagnosis is most often confused with Guillain-Barré syndrome, poliomyelitis, or other neuropathies or myelopathies, whereas the encephalitic form must be differentiated from other viral and infectious encephalitides, tetanus, and toxic encephalopathies. In geographic regions where vaccine is prepared using neural tissue (still the practice in many regions of the world with the highest rates of rabies), allergic encephalomyelitis remains a principal differential diagnosis.

Rx Treatment and Prevention

Established CNS disease cannot be cured. Disease prevention relies on public health measures to reduce animal reservoirs and on postexposure immune prophylaxis to abort viral penetration of the CNS after a rabid bite or other contact. Although clinical rabies is a rare disease in the United States and Western Europe, the need to consider active prophylaxis is a common clinical issue. Postexposure prophylaxis is uniformly successful if the protocol is rigorously followed, but even slight deviations from the protocol can result in treatment failure and lead to the development of rabies. The physician first determines the type of possible exposure. An open wound or disrupted mucous membrane exposed to saliva may warrant postexposure prophylaxis, whereas contact of saliva with intact skin may not. The first step in management is to administer prompt local wound care, thoroughly washing the wound with soap and water and then applying iodine or 70% ethanol. The epidemiologic setting is important in determining the likelihood that the biting animal may be rabid and often requires

consultation with local health authorities to ascertain which animals carry rabies in the geographic setting.

In the absence of previous vaccination, both passive (i.e., rabies immune globulin of human origin) and active (i.e., diploid cell vaccines) immunizations are administered. Rabies immunoglobulin (20 IU/kg) should be injected in and around the wound and the remaining volume given intramuscularly at a distant site from the vaccine site. Safe, tissue culture–derived vaccines are available that have a low incidence of major adverse reactions, in contrast to those seen with earlier, nerve tissue–derived vaccines. Five doses of rabies vaccine should be given in the deltoid muscle on days 0, 3, 7, 14, and 28 in individuals previously unimmunized against rabies virus.

SUGGESTED READINGS
http://www.cdc.gov/mmwr. *Website hosted by the Centers for Disease Control and Prevention, which periodically updates current practice recommendations for immunization for rabies and other infectious diseases.*
Jackson AC: Rabies. Curr Treat Options Infect Dis 2003;5:35–40. *A valuable review of the clinical neurologic aspects of rabies.*

455 CYTOMEGALOVIRUS, EPSTEIN-BARR VIRUS, AND SLOW VIRUS INFECTIONS OF THE CENTRAL NERVOUS SYSTEM

Joseph R. Berger
Avindra Nath

CYTOMEGALOVIRUS

Human cytomegalovirus (CMV) is a ubiquitous herpesvirus acquired throughout life (Chapter 370). In children, CMV is an important and relatively common cause of congenital neurologic deficit. In the United States, 60 to 80% of adults have serologic evidence of infection. Primary infection is usually asymptomatic in young, healthy adults but may be associated with a transient mononucleosis-like syndrome. CMV results in major neurologic disability in the setting of immunosuppression, particularly in persons with acquired immunodeficiency syndrome (AIDS). In addition to retinitis, CMV may involve the brain, spinal cord, and peripheral nerves.

CYTOMEGALOVIRUS ENCEPHALITIS. CMV encephalitis (Chapter 414) has several presentations in patients with AIDS. The most typical presentation is subacute, diffuse encephalopathy evolving over weeks, which is characterized by headache, impaired cognition and sensorium, apathy, and social withdrawal. The neurologic examination reveals abnormal mentation and variable motor features, including hyperreflexia, ataxia, and weakness. CMV ventriculitis is characteristically present and is often associated with cranial neuropathies, nystagmus, and progressive ventricular enlargement. Other features may suggest brain stem encephalitis, including internuclear ophthalmoplegia, cranial nerve palsies, gaze paresis, ataxia, and tetraparesis. Rarely, CMV infection may manifest as a cerebral mass lesion. Other presentations of these patients include cerebral infarction resulting from CMV vasculitis, acute subarachnoid hemorrhage, and intracerebral hemorrhage. Virtually all patients with CMV encephalitis have systemic CMV infection. CMV myelitis, polyradiculitis, and multifocal neuritis may also be seen with CMV encephalitis. Distinctive retinal lesions can often be seen ophthalmoscopically (Chapter 370).

Cerebral imaging studies are of limited sensitivity and low specificity in patients with CMV encephalitis. Ependymal or meningeal enhancement, as well as areas of focal infarction or necrosis, may be visualized. Progressive ventricular enlargement should suggest CMV ventriculitis. Cerebrospinal fluid (CSF) findings are variable. Most patients have elevated protein levels. Glucose levels may be normal or decreased. Leukocytes may be absent, but CSF pleocytosis is usual. Marked pleocytosis with polymorphonuclear leukocytes may occur in patients with CMV ventriculitis. CMV can rarely be cultured from CSF or detected by polymerase chain reaction (PCR) methods.

NECROTIZING MYELITIS. Necrotizing myelitis due to CMV in human immunodeficiency virus (HIV)–infected patients is most commonly associated with polyradiculitis. Some cases of necrotizing myelitis in the absence of a typical polyradiculitis syndrome have been described, with patients presenting with acute or progressive paraplegia and disturbances of urinary and rectal sphincter functions. Reflexes are preserved or enhanced in the legs unless concurrent neuropathy is present. A sensory level may be demonstrable.

POLYRADICULOMYELITIS. Neuromuscular pathology due to CMV has been found in approximately one fourth of patients dying of AIDS. It is predominantly localized to perineurial and epineurial regions. CMV polyradiculomyelitis in HIV-infected patients manifests subacutely over days to a few weeks. Initial symptoms of paresthesias or dysesthetic pain localized to perineal and lower extremity regions are followed by a rapidly progressive paraparesis with hypotonia and diminished or absent lower extremity reflexes. Urinary retention is characteristic, and rectal sphincter incontinence is common. Variable sensory findings are overshadowed by the motor features. Babinski's signs and diminished sensation below a discrete level across the trunk may indicate an associated myelitis. With time, symptoms progress by ascending to involve the upper limbs and sometimes the cranial nerves. CSF examination usually reveals polymorphonuclear pleocytosis and prominent elevation of protein levels. Hypoglycorrhachia is often present. Spinal magnetic resonance imaging (MRI) findings may be normal or reveal enhancement of the conus medullaris, cauda equina, meninges, and nerve roots. Electrophysiologic studies reveal axonal neuropathy with evidence of acute denervation. Variable slowing of nerve conduction may occur.

The appearance of acute cauda equina syndrome in a patient with AIDS is suggestive of CMV when polymorphonuclear pleocytosis is present in CSF; however, the syndrome is not pathognomonic. Other conditions that may produce a cauda equina syndrome in AIDS patients include lymphomatous meningitis, syphilis, toxoplasmosis, other herpesviruses, and cryptococcal or bacterial meningitis. Progressive multifocal motor and sensory neuropathy that evolves over weeks to months has also been seen in patients with CMV infection. Paresthesia and dysesthesia are quickly followed by prominent motor weakness, which involves both upper and lower limbs asymmetrically. Neurogenic atrophy may be prominent. Nerve biopsy reveals necrotizing neuritis with mononuclear and polymorphonuclear infiltrates and cytomegalocytes localized around endoneurial capillaries in nerve trunks and roots. Some patients may have necrotizing arteritis.

CMV neurologic complications should be treated with ganciclovir or foscarnet; however, the evidence of their efficacy in these conditions is chiefly limited to case reports and small series. The emergence of CMV strains resistant to both agents has been observed, and CMV encephalitis has developed in the presence of maintenance ganciclovir therapy for CMV retinitis. Combination (foscarnet and ganciclovir) or alternative therapies should be considered in persons already on suppressive monotherapy or in the face of a persistent CSF pleocytosis.

EPSTEIN-BARR VIRUS

Epstein-Barr virus (EBV), the cause of infectious mononucleosis (Chapter 371), is distributed worldwide. Its acquisition depends on population density and socioeconomic status. Individuals in areas of high population density and lower social strata acquire the virus in early childhood. However, seroepidemiologic studies indicate that virtually all persons are infected by EBV by 30 years of age.

Neurologic manifestations occur in 1 to 5% of patients with primary EBV infection and may be the only prominent clinical manifestations. The most common neurologic disorder associated with infectious mononucleosis is meningoencephalitis. This complication is rare in early childhood and most often is observed in persons between the ages of 15 and 25 years. Onset may be gradual over several days or explosive. Fever, headache, mild stiff neck, confusion, lethargy, seizures, and hyperreflexia are the most typical features. Occasionally, focal neurologic features, including hemiparesis, focal seizures, and cerebellar and brain stem findings, may be detected. The prognosis for patients with EBV meningoencephalitis is excellent, with complete resolution anticipated in 1 to 2 weeks.

HUMAN IMMUNODEFICIENCY VIRUS AND HUMAN T-LYMPHOTROPHIC VIRUS TYPE 1

These viruses and their neurologic sequelae are considered in Chapters 414 and 372, respectively.

SUBACUTE SCLEROSING PANENCEPHALITIS AND PROGRESSIVE RUBELLA PANENCEPHALITIS

Subacute sclerosing panencephalitis (SSPE) is caused by measles virus (Chapter 365). It usually affects children, but its onset can extend into young adulthood. Patients usually have a history of measles within the first 2 years of life, and it is speculated that such early host exposure allows emergence of persistent defective virus replication. As a result of effective vaccination strategy against measles virus, its incidence has markedly decreased.

SSPE usually begins with cognitive and behavioral changes. It progresses to include motor dysfunction with prominent myoclonus, choreoathetosis, dystonia, and rigidity. Its course progresses over 1 to 3 years to rigid quadriparesis and a vegetative state. The condition is more common in rural settings and affects males more often than females. The electroencephalogram reveals periodic complexes with synchronous bursts of two or three slow waves per second, recurring at 5- to 8-second intervals in the myoclonic stage. Computed tomography (CT) of the brain shows generalized atrophy. The CSF protein, glucose, and cell levels are usually normal; CSF is characterized by a high immunoglobulin concentration, oligoclonal bands, and intrathecal synthesis of antibody to measles virus antigens. Serum measles antibody titers are also high. These findings are usually sufficiently characteristic for diagnosis; brain biopsy is rarely needed for definitive diagnosis in atypical cases. Gray matter is most prominently involved. The pathologic features of SSPE include gliosis, loss of myelin, and perivascular infiltrates of lymphocytes and plasma cells in white and gray matter. Neuronal cell loss is seen in later stages of the illness. Intranuclear Cowdry type A inclusions containing viral nucleocapsids are identified in neurons and glia. Measles RNA can be detected in the brain by PCR.

Measles virus may also cause subacute encephalitis in the immunocompromised host. The prominence of cognitive and motor dysfunction in these patients resembles that of SSPE, but in the clinical setting, its subacute onset and more rapid evolution and the presence of generalized seizures rather than myoclonus are distinctive. Brain abnormalities include abundant intranuclear inclusions, but inflammation is minimal, and neither serum nor CSF antibody titers against measles virus are high. For this reason, brain biopsy is usually needed for diagnosis.

Progressive rubella panencephalitis is a rare disorder resembling SSPE but caused by the rubella virus (Chapter 366). It manifests as a complication of the congenital rubella syndrome or, more typically, after childhood rubella. A hiatus of years separates early infection from the onset of neurologic deterioration, which is characterized by behavioral changes, cognitive impairment, cerebellar ataxia, spasticity, and sometimes seizures. Myoclonus is a less prominent feature than it is in SSPE. The electroencephalographic result shows generalized slowing. The course of illness is similar to that of SSPE, progressing to coma, brain stem involvement, and death in 2 to 5 years. Serology or isolation of the virus from brain or peripheral blood lymphocytes confirms the cause.

With the advent of widespread measles and rubella immunization, these disorders have been nearly eliminated in the United States. There is no established specific treatment for SSPE or progressive rubella panencephalitis.

PROGRESSIVE MULTIFOCAL LEUKOENCEPHALOPATHY

Cause and Pathogenesis

This demyelinating disease is associated with infection of oligodendrocytes by JC virus (JCV), a papovavirus widely distributed among humans. JCV exhibits a neurotropism exclusive to glial cells. Progressive multifocal leukoencephalopathy (PML) was the first demyelinating disease to be unequivocally associated with a viral infection.

Epidemiology

Serologic studies indicate that, by 5 years of age, approximately 10% of children have antibody to JCV and, by the age of 10 years, 40 to 60% have the antibody. Despite the wide dissemination of JCV infection, PML is rarely observed in the absence of underlying cellular immunosuppression. It is also rarely observed in childhood. Until the AIDS epidemic, PML was most commonly observed in patients with lymphoproliferative disorders. In a 1984 review, lymphoproliferative disorders were associated with 62.2% of PML cases, 6.5% of myeloproliferative diseases, 2.2% of carcinomatous diseases, 10.9% of a variety of acquired immunodeficiency states, and 5.6% of cases with no underlying disease. Since the inception of the AIDS epidemic in 1981, AIDS has been the disorder associated with PML in most cases. The dramatic increase in the incidence of PML in the past decade results from the fact that approximately 5% of AIDS patients develop PML.

Pathology

The cardinal feature of PML is demyelination, which is typically multifocal but occasionally unifocal. These lesions may occur in any location in the white matter but have a predilection for the parieto-occipital regions. The lesions range in size from 1 mm to several centimeters; larger lesions may reflect the coalescence of multiple smaller lesions. The other histopathologic hallmark of PML is the presence of hyperchromatic, enlarged oligodendroglial nuclei and of enlarged bizarre astrocytes with lobulated hyperchromatic nuclei. Electron microscopic examination reveals the JC virions, which are 28 to 45 nm in diameter and appear singly or in dense crystalline arrays in oligodendroglial cells and, less frequently, in reactive astrocytes.

Clinical Manifestations

The clinical hallmark of PML is the presence of focal neurologic symptoms and signs associated with radiographic evidence of white matter disease in the absence of mass effect. The most common initial symptoms include weakness, speech abnormalities, and cognitive disturbances, each seen in approximately 40% of patients. Although rare in the non-AIDS patient, headache may occur in as many as one third of patients with AIDS. Gait disturbances, sensory loss, and visual impairment all occur in approximately 20 to 30%. Seizures and brain stem symptoms are less common. Signs noted on physical examination parallel the reported symptoms, with weakness, typically a hemiparesis, detected in more than one half the patients at the time of presentation. Gait abnormalities, cognitive problems, and language disorders (i.e., dysarthria and dysphasia) are observed in about one fourth of patients at presentation. Limb and trunk ataxia reflecting cerebellar involvement is detected in as many as 10% but may occasionally result from severe impairment in position sense (i.e., sensory ataxia). Neuro-ophthalmic symptoms occur in 50% of patients with PML and are the presenting manifestation in 30 to 45%. The most common visual deficit is homonymous hemianopsia or quadrantanopia due to lesions of the optic radiations. Cortical blindness is seen in as many as 5 to 8% of patients at the time of diagnosis. Other neuro-ophthalmic manifestations include optic agnosia, alexia without agraphia, and ocular motor abnormalities. Sensory disturbances occur with PML but are distinctly less common than impairment of strength or visual function.

Diagnosis

The diagnosis of PML may be strongly suggested by the clinical manifestations and the radiographic imaging result. When the former are coupled with a positive JC viral PCR finding in the CSF, the diagnosis of PML is virtually certain. However, unequivocal confirmation requires brain biopsy.

CT of the brain reveals hypodense lesions of the affected white matter that generally have a "scalloped" appearance as an involvement of the subcortical arcuate fibers lying directly beneath the cortex. Cranial MRI shows a hyperintense lesion on T2-weighted images in the affected regions (Fig. 455–1) and usually shows a hypointense lesion on T1-weighted images. Contrast enhancement is seen in approximately 5 to 10% of pathologically confirmed cases of PML with either brain imaging technique. The enhancement observed is typically faint and at the periphery of lesions. In patients without AIDS, the lesions of PML have a predilection for the parieto-occipital lobes, but in AIDS patients, the lesions are more often seen in the frontal lobes. Involvement of the basal ganglia, external capsule, and posterior fossa structures (i.e., cerebellum and brain stem) is also seen.

The result of routine analysis of CSF is not diagnostic; the CSF protein may be elevated. CSF PCR for JCV is of great value in diagnosis; although not always positive, it is highly specific.

Prognosis

PML usually progresses to death, with a mean survival of 6 months. For less than 10% of patients with AIDS-associated PML, survival may exceed 12 months; partial or nearly complete clinical and

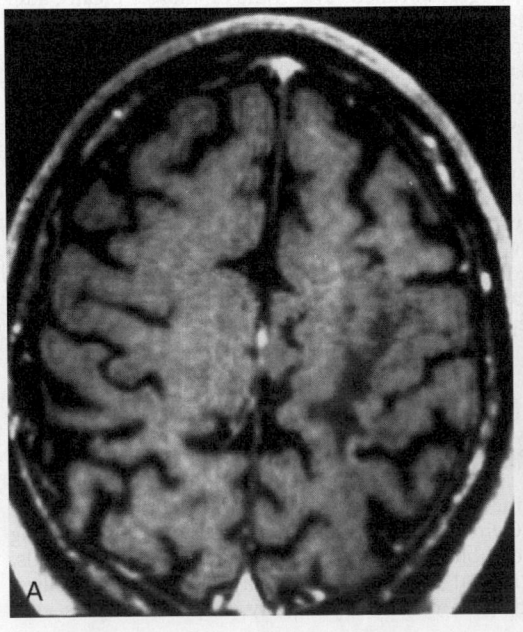
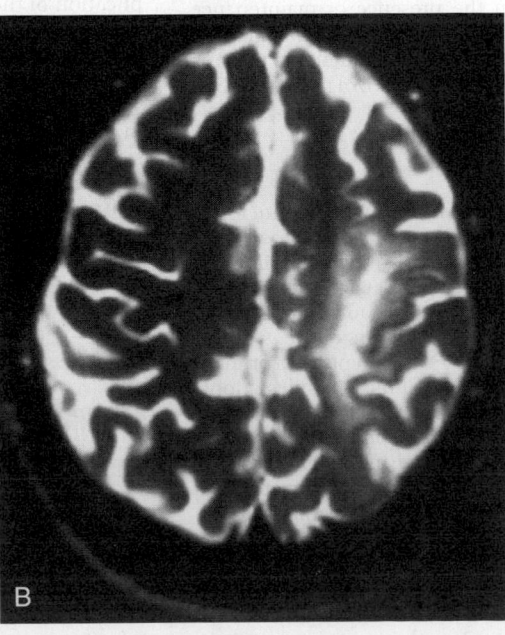

FIGURE 455–1 • Cranial magnetic resonance images of progressive multifocal leukoencephalopathy. *A,* The T1-weighted image shows a hypointense signal abnormality of the left frontal lobe white matter. *B,* On T2-weighted sequence imaging, the lesion is hyperintense.

radiographic recovery may occur. Factors associated with a more benign course include presence of PML as the heralding manifestation of AIDS, high or climbing CD4+ T-lymphocyte counts, contrast enhancement of the lesions on radiographic studies, and any clinical or radiographic evidence of recovery.

 Treatment

There is no effective therapy for PML. Although cytosine arabinoside prevents JC viral replication in vitro, a randomized, double-blind trial in which it was administered intrathecally or intravenously in patients with AIDS-associated PML demonstrated no benefit. Because of their antiviral activity, presumably the result of their ability to stimulate natural killer cells, interferons have been proposed as potential therapeutic agents in the treatment of PML, and one retrospective study appears to demonstrate an improved survival rate among persons receiving interferon-α. However, its efficacy remains to be established.

Since the introduction of highly active antiretroviral therapy (HAART), the survival rate in AIDS-associated PML has appeared to improve, presumably as a result of immunologic recovery. The evidence for spontaneous recovery in untreated patients makes it difficult to assess the results of experimental treatments in small or uncontrolled treatment trials.

SUGGESTED READINGS

Majid A, Galetta SL, Sweeney CJ, et al: Epstein-Barr virus myeloradiculitis and encephalomyeloradiculitis. Brain 2002;125:159–165. *Examples of the spectrum of EBV neurologic disease.*

Maschke M, Kastrup O, Diener HC: CNS manifestations of cytomegalovirus infections: Diagnosis and treatment. CNS Drugs 2002;16:303–315. *An overview, with emphasis on CMV in immunocompromised patients.*

456 PRION DISEASES

Joseph R. Berger
Avindra Nath

Several human diseases have been attributed to a unique infectious protein referred to as the *prion*. The prototypical human illness is Creutzfeldt-Jakob disease (CJD), a subacute spongiform encephalopathy. Other prion illnesses of humans include kuru, Gerstmann-Sträussler-Scheinker (GSS) syndrome, and familial fatal insomnia (FFI). Prion-related illnesses are unique in that they may be hereditary, may occur spontaneously, or may be acquired by contamination by the agent. The appearance of variant CJD in association with the outbreak of bovine spongiform encephalopathy, postulated to be the result of contamination of beef, has greatly increased interest in a group of illnesses that is relatively rare.

The prion protein (PrP) generally exists as a membrane-bound sialoglycoprotein that is a normal cellular constituent distributed chiefly in the brain. Neurons contain high concentrations of cellular PrP (PrP^C), and the protein appears to be developmentally regulated. The gene for PrP is located on the short arm of chromosome 20 in humans. Prion diseases are the result of an abnormal isoform of PrP^C, referred to as PrP^{Sc}. Whereas PrP^C exists as an α-helical structure, PrP^{Sc} consists of β-pleated sheets and arises from post-translational changes in the conformation of PrP^C. Unlike PrP^C, PrP^{Sc} resists proteolytic digestion and spontaneously aggregates to produce rodlike or fibrillary particles (e.g., scrapie-associated fibrils, prion rods) that can be isolated from brains of animals and humans with this class of illness.

CREUTZFELDT-JAKOB DISEASE

In the 1920s, Creutzfeldt and Jakob independently described six patients with a progressive dementing illness. Three of these individuals were subsequently demonstrated to have a disorder that conforms to CJD as currently defined. The illness is seen worldwide with an estimated incidence of about 0.5 to 1.0 case per million persons per year. Most cases are sporadic. Five to 15% of cases are estimated to be familial, with an autosomal dominant pattern of inheritance. Certain populations have higher rates of familial disease, including descendants of Jewish populations from Libya and North Africa. In this population, the annual incidence is as high as 31.3 per million. The illness may also occur in an iatrogenic fashion. It has been reported in recipients of supplemental growth hormone prepared from pooled human pituitary glands. Curiously, only a minority of the recipients of contaminated batches of human growth hormone contracted the illness. CJD has also been reported after cadaver corneal and dura mater transplantations received from patients with CJD or an unexplained dementia. It has also followed the use of stereotactic intracerebral depth electrodes.

Gross pathologic examination shows brain atrophy. The pathologic hallmarks are generally maximal in the cortex but are also seen in basal ganglia, thalamus, and cerebellum. They include spongiform changes (i.e., small, round vacuoles) within the neuropil resulting from cystic dilation of neurons and focal necrosis of cellular membranes, neuronal loss, and hypertrophy and proliferation of glial cells. No inflammation is observed. Amyloid plaques are often observed. They are congophilic and composed of 10-nm fibrils. These plaques are stained with antibodies to protein.

Clinical Manifestations

The clinical manifestations of CJD are protean, and the disease is frequently incorrectly diagnosed initially. Prodromal symptoms are reported in as many as one fourth of patients. These symptoms include altered sleep patterns and appetite, weight loss, changes in sexual drive, and complaints of impaired memory and concentration. Behavioral changes are frequently detected early by family members. Spells of disorientation, hallucinations, and emotional lability may be observed. Typically, the patient has a rapidly progressive dementia associated with myoclonus. The dementia is generally global in nature. Myoclonus occurs in approximately 90% of patients. It is generally provoked or aggravated by tactile, auditory, or visual startle. There are a number of distinctive presentations. An apoplectic, abrupt onset is seen in 10 to 15% of patients. Other distinctive presentations include seizures, autonomic dysfunction, and lower motor neuron disease, suggesting amyotrophic lateral sclerosis. A wide variety of visual abnormalities may be observed, including visual agnosia; supranuclear palsies; nystagmus; Balint's syndrome, characterized by the inability to look at objects on command (i.e., psychic paralysis of visual fixation), to grab objects accurately (i.e., optic ataxia), or to recognize more than one object at a time visually (i.e., simultagnosia); distorted visual perceptions; and cortical blindness. Cerebellar ataxia is seen in up to one third of patients. Pyramidal and extrapyramidal manifestations are frequently observed and occur preterminally in approximately 50 to 66% of patients. Hypokinesia, rigidity, hyperreflexia, spasticity, and extensor plantar reflexes are also seen. Lower motor neuron disease is detected in less than 1% of patients at the onset of disease but may ultimately affect up to 10% of patients.

The variant form of CJD that may be linked to bovine spongiform encephalopathy generally occurs in younger individuals, who have psychiatric manifestations and ataxia. Dementia develops late. Similarly, the clinical presentation of CJD associated with cadaver pituitary growth hormone differs from classic CJD, because the patients are younger and have an illness reminiscent of kuru.

Diagnosis

The clinical tetrad supporting the diagnosis of CJD consists of a subacute progressive dementia, myoclonus, typical periodic complexes indicated on electroencephalography, and normal cerebrospinal fluid (CSF). Findings on computed tomography and magnetic resonance imaging (MRI) of the brain are normal, except in late stages of the disease, at which time rapidly progressive brain atrophy may be observed. MRI of the brain may also show a hyperintense signal abnormality of the basal ganglia or, rarely, abnormalities such as hyperintense signal abnormality of the occipital cortex. The electroencephalographic hallmark of CJD is the pattern of periodic sharp wave complexes consisting of generalized slow background activity interrupted by bilaterally synchronous sharp wave complexes occurring at intervals of 0.5 to 2.5 seconds and lasting for 200 to 600 milliseconds. The classic electroencephalographic pattern is seen in 75 to 95% of established cases but may not be present in the early or terminal phases of the illness. Although the CSF is generally completely normal, a mild elevation in the protein level may be seen. A CSF test for the protein 14-3-3 is commercially available and, in the appropriate clinical context, is relatively specific and sensitive for CJD. The many other disorders that raise CSF protein 14-3-3, such as multiple sclerosis or acute stroke, are infrequently confused with CJD. Although brain biopsy with immunostaining for PrP^{Sc} is the "gold standard" for establishing the diagnosis, the positive CSF test result and clinical picture are adequate for diagnosis in most cases.

 Treatment

There is no effective therapy for CJD. The disease is inexorably progressive. Death typically occurs within 1 year of the onset of symptoms, with a reported range of 1 to 130 months. The median survival is 4.5 months, and the mean is 8 months. Illness of more than 2 years' duration has been reported in 5 to 10% of patients. The clinical course has been divided into phases characterized by an initial slow intellectual and behavioral deterioration followed by a stepwise or progressive downhill course. Ultimately, a more slowly progressive terminal stage intervenes.

Prevention

Although the illness is not communicable in the conventional sense, there is a risk of handling materials contaminated with the prion protein. Gloves should be worn when handling blood, CSF, and other body fluids. Instruments must be disinfected by steam autoclaving for 1 hour at 132° C, by steam autoclaving for 4.5 hours at 121° C (1.5 psi), or by immersion in 1 N sodium hydroxide for 1 hour at room temperature. There is no general means of rendering food substances or offal for animal feed noninfectious.

KURU

In 1957, Gajdusek and Gibbs described a progressive dementing illness referred to as *kuru* in the Fore linguistic tribal group of the Eastern Highlands of Papua, New Guinea. Kuru affected as many as 1% of the population at its peak, with women and children chiefly affected. Kuru was linked to ritualistic cannibalism. Subsequent studies demonstrated that kuru could be passed to primates by inoculation with human tissue. Since the cessation of the practice of cannibalism, this unique form of prion disease has virtually disappeared.

The initial stage of the illness is characterized by headaches and joint pains. The ambulant phase that subsequently develops is characterized by ataxia, postural instability, dysarthria, and intervening intention tremors. A sedentary phase is characterized by worsening tremor and ataxia, myoclonus, choreoathetosis, dementia, and emotional lability. Eventually, the person is essentially bedridden with severe dysarthria, ataxia, and dementia.

GERSTMANN-STRÄUSSLER-SCHEINKER SYNDROME

GSS syndrome is an autosomal dominant disorder that is considered a variant of CJD. The pathologic examination reveals widespread amyloid plaque formation. The spinocerebellar tracts are commonly atrophic.

GSS syndrome has been associated with distinct mutations in the PrP gene, most commonly a leucine-for-proline substitution at codon 102. Other mutations have included a valine-for-alanine substitution at codon 117 and a point mutation in codon 198.

Progressive cerebellar dysfunction, which dominates the clinical picture, typically develops in midlife. The initial features include unsteady gait, clumsiness, and incoordination. Dysarthria and

nystagmus are also observed. Dementia often occurs later in the course of the illness. Other features include gaze palsies, deafness, blindness, loss of muscle stretch reflexes, and extensor plantar reflexes. Variations in the clinical presentation may be related to difference in the genetic mutations. For instance, ataxia predominates in the codon 102 mutation, whereas the other two mutations are associated with ataxia and dementia.

FATAL FAMILIAL INSOMNIA

FFI is an autosomal dominant disorder first described by Medori and colleagues in 1992. Pathologic changes include atrophy and gliosis of specific thalamic nuclei, cerebellar cortex, and inferior olives. Spongiform changes of the brain are rare. The PrP gene in these patients reveals an asparagine-for-aspartate mutation in codon 178, similar to what is found in some familial cases of CJD.

Although the hallmark of FFI is intractable insomnia, patients may also have features indistinguishable from CJD. Sympathetic hyperactivity includes hypertension, hyperthermia, hyperhidrosis, and tachycardia. Other autonomic and endocrine disturbances are frequently observed, including a loss of the normal circadian rhythm of melatonin, prolactin, and growth hormone. Corticotropin (adrenocorticotropic hormone) secretion is decreased, although corticosteroid release is increased. Dysarthria and motor system abnormalities, which include myoclonus, tremor, ataxia, hyperreflexia, and spasticity, are also observed. Mentation may be normal, but most patients have mild memory impairment and attention deficits. Hallucinations and unexpected gross body movements during dream (rapid eye movement [REM]) sleep also occur. The illness is rapidly progressive.

FFI has not been successfully transmitted to an animal host. As with other prion diseases, no specific treatment exists.

SUGGESTED READINGS

DeArmond SJ, Bouzamondo E: Fundamentals of prion biology and diseases. Toxicology 2002;181–182:9–16. *The basic mechanisms are explained clearly.*

Spencer MD, Knight RS, Will RG: First hundred cases of variant Creutzfeldt-Jakob disease: Retrospective case note review of early psychiatric and neurological features. BMJ 2002;324:1479–1482. *A large series emphasizing presenting features.*

457 TUMORS OF THE CENTRAL NERVOUS SYSTEM AND INTRACRANIAL HYPERTENSION AND HYPOTENSION

Lisa M. DeAngelis

INTRACRANIAL TUMORS

GENERAL APPROACH TO BRAIN TUMORS

About 17,000 new primary brain tumors and nervous system cancers are diagnosed annually in the United States, making central nervous system (CNS) tumors more than twice as common as Hodgkin's disease and approximately one third as common as melanoma. In contrast, intracranial metastases are five times more common than primary brain tumors. More than 120 types of primary brain tumors arise from the different cells that comprise the CNS (Table 457–1). In clinical practice, it is often useful to classify a tumor also by its intracranial site, such as pineal region tumors or pituitary and suprasellar tumors.

General Considerations

In contradistinction to tumors arising elsewhere in the body, there is little distinction between benign and malignant tumors when they occur in the brain. The growth of brain tumors is restricted to the CNS; they rarely, if ever, metastasize to other organs. In the CNS, a malignant tumor is characterized by aggressive pathologic features

Table 457–1 • WORLD HEALTH ORGANIZATION CLASSIFICATION OF BRAIN TUMORS*

1. Tumors of neuroepithelial tissue
   A. Astrocytic tumors
      Astrocytoma
      Anaplastic (malignant) astrocytoma
      Glioblastoma multiforme
      Pilocytic astrocytoma
      Pleomorphic xanthoastrocytoma
      Subependymal giant cell astrocytoma
   B. Oligodendroglial tumors
      Oligodendroglioma
      Anaplastic (malignant) oligodendroglioma
   C. Ependymal tumors
      Ependymoma
      Anaplastic (malignant) ependymoma
      Myxopapillary ependymoma (spinal tumor)
      Subependymoma
   D. Mixed gliomas
2. Tumors of cranial and spinal nerves
   Schwannoma
   Neurofibroma
3. Tumors of meninges
   Meningioma
   Hemangiopericytoma
   Hemangioblastoma
4. Primary central nervous system lymphomas
5. Germ cell tumors
   Germinoma
   Embryonal carcinoma
   Yolk sac tumor (endodermal sinus tumor)
   Choriocarcinoma
   Teratoma
   Mixed germ cell tumors
6. Cysts and tumor-like lesions
   Rathke cleft cyst
   Oligoastrocytoma
   Anaplastic (malignant) oligoastrocytoma
   E. Choroid plexus
      Choroid plexus papilloma
      Choroid plexus carcinoma
   F. Neuronal and mixed neuronal-glial tumors
      Gangliocytoma
      Dysembryoplastic neuroepithelial tumor
      Ganglioglioma
      Anaplastic (malignant) ganglioglioma
      Central neurocytoma
   G. Pineal parenchymal tumors
      Pineocytoma
      Pineoblastoma
   H. Embryonal tumors
      Medulloblastoma
      Primitive neuroectodermal tumor
      Epidermoid cyst
      Dermoid cyst
      Colloid cyst of the third ventricle
7. Tumors of the sellar region
   Pituitary adenoma
   Pituitary carcinoma
   Craniopharyngioma
8. Metastatic tumors

*Abridged and modified from World Health Organization classification.

Clinical Manifestations

A patient with a brain tumor can present with one or both of two types of symptoms and signs. *Generalized symptoms*, which typically reflect the increased intracranial pressure (ICP) that often accompanies cerebral tumors, include headaches, lethargy, personality change, nausea, and vomiting. *Lateralizing symptoms*, which reflect the specific location of the tumor, include hemiparesis, hemisensory deficits, aphasia, visual field impairment, and seizures (Table 457–2).

Most patients have symptoms that progress over a week to a few months. A sudden intensification of symptoms may precipitate the patient's initial visit to the physician; however, a careful history usually reveals symptoms that predated the acute deterioration and slowly worsened over time. Two exceptions are the new appearance of a seizure in a previously asymptomatic individual (Chapter 434) and sudden hemorrhage into a tumor.

Symptoms of brain tumors can be produced by tumor invading brain parenchyma, tumor and edema compressing brain tissue, cerebrospinal fluid (CSF) obstruction caused directly by the tumor or by a shift of brain tissue, and herniation. Invasion and compression typically produce focal symptoms, many of which can be relieved if the compression is reduced. Obstruction of CSF flow and herniation are frequently a consequence of elevated ICP and typically produce generalized symptoms of headache, nausea, and vomiting, but they can also cause false localizing signs, such as an abducens nerve palsy, as a result of diffuse increased ICP.

Headache (Chapter 428) is a presenting symptom of approximately 35% of brain tumors. It is more common in younger than older patients, and more common in patients who have rapidly growing tumors than in those who have tumors that have evolved slowly (Fig. 457–1). Mental and cognitive abnormalities (Chapter 432) may be a reflection of local tumor (e.g., aphasia, alexia, or agnosia) or reflect general impairment (e.g., lethargy, confusion, word finding difficulty, and apathy). Seizures affect approximately one third of brain tumor patients and are especially common as the presenting and only symptom of a low-grade tumor. The seizures, which are focal because they originate at the site of the tumor, may remain restricted, such as focal motor seizures, or may generalize, secondarily producing loss of consciousness (Chapter 434), sometimes so quickly that the focal signature is missed by the patient or even an observant witness.

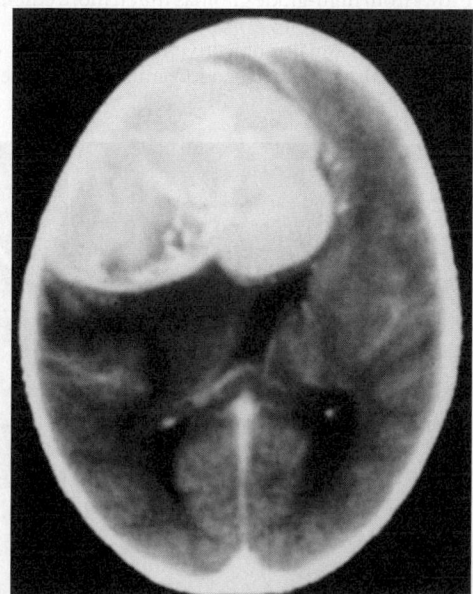

FIGURE 457–1 • Computed tomography scan with contrast of a meningioma in a patient who presented with mild cognitive deficits, illustrative of the size a slow-growing tumor can attain in the brain. The tumor was completely resected.

including local tissue invasion, neovascularity, regional necrosis, and cytologic atypia. These features confer a growth advantage to malignant cells and lead to rapid expansion and, frequently, to early regrowth after treatment. Tumors lacking these aggressive histologic features are preferably classified as low-grade rather than benign. Many low-grade tumors continue to grow within the CNS, causing progressive neurologic disability, and some may acquire a more malignant phenotype over time. The low-grade tumors that transform into high-grade neoplasms are primarily the intra-axial tumors that cannot be cured by resection because of their diffuse infiltration of brain. Almost all truly benign CNS tumors are extra-axial tumors, such as meningiomas and acoustic neuromas, that can be cured with complete surgical resection.

Neurology

Table 457-2 • FOCAL CLINICAL MANIFESTATIONS OF BRAIN TUMORS

Frontal lobe
  Generalized seizures
  Focal motor seizures (contralateral)
  Expressive aphasia (dominant side)
  Behavioral changes
  Dementia
  Gait disorders, incontinence
  Hemiparesis
Basal ganglia
  Hemiparesis (contralateral)
  Movement disorders (rare)
Parietal lobe
  Receptive aphasia (dominant side)
  Spatial disorientation (nondominant side)
  Cortical sensory dysfunction (contralateral)
  Hemianopia (contralateral)
  Agnosias
Occipital lobe
  Hemianopia (contralateral)
  Visual disturbances (unformed)
	Temporal lobe
	  Complex partial (psychomotor) seizures
	  Generalized seizures
	  Behavioral changes
	  Olfactory and complex visual auras
	  Language disorder (dominant side)
	  Visual field defect
	Corpus callosum
	  Dementia (anterior)
	  Memory loss (posterior)
	  Behavioral changes
	  Asymptomatic (mid)
	Thalamus
	  Sensory loss (contralateral)
	  Behavioral changes
	  Language disorder (dominant side)
	Midbrain/pineal
	  Paresis of vertical eye movement
	  Pupillary abnormalities
	  Precocious puberty (boys)
		Sella/optic nerve/pituitary
		  Endocrinopathy
		  Bitemporal hemianopia
		  Monocular visual defects
		  Ophthalmoplegia (cavernous sinus)
		Pons/medulla
		  Cranial nerve dysfunction
		  Ataxia, nystagmus
		  Weakness, sensory loss
		  Spasticity
		Cerebellopontine angle
		  Deafness (ipsilateral)
		  Loss of facial sensation (ipsilateral)
		  Facial weakness (ipsilateral)
		  Ataxia
		Cerebellum
		  Ataxia (ipsilateral)
		  Nystagmus

Neuroimaging and Other Diagnostic Tests

Magnetic resonance imaging (MRI) is far superior to computed tomography (CT) scans and should be used in all patients suspected of having an intracranial tumor (Chapter 424). MRI should be performed both without and with intravenous gadolinium. A well-performed MRI scan identifies any intracranial tumor, and normal MRI results effectively exclude a neoplasm. A CT scan without and with intravenous contrast should be used only for patients who cannot undergo MRI. A CT scan, even with contrast, may miss low-grade tumors and tumors in the posterior fossa.

The MRI of some extra-axial tumors (e.g., acoustic neuromas and meningiomas) is so characteristic that histologic confirmation is not required (Table 457-3). A non–contrast-enhancing infiltrative lesion that is visible primarily on T2 or FLAIR images is most consistent with a low-grade glioma (Fig. 457-2). Alternatively, a contrast-enhancing lesion with an area of central necrosis and surrounding edema is most likely to be a glioblastoma or possibly a brain metastasis. Although the diagnosis must be confirmed histologically, the preoperative diagnostic possibilities affect the choice of surgical procedure and the surgical approach to the lesion.

On positron-emission tomography (PET), high-grade tumors are usually hypermetabolic, whereas low-grade tumors are hypometabolic (Chapter 424). New technologies using ^{11}C-methionine may differentiate low- from high-grade gliomas much more efficiently than deoxyglucose PET.

Surgical resection is a major objective in the treatment of almost every kind of brain tumor, but resection must be balanced against

Table 457-3 • MAGNETIC RESONANCE IMAGING OF COMMON BRAIN TUMORS

	NON-CONTRAST T1	CONTRAST T1	T2
Malignant glioma	↓ density	+	↑ density
Low-grade glioma	↓ density	–	↑ density
Primary central nervous system lymphoma	↑ density	+	↑ density
Meningioma	Iso to ↑	+	Iso to ↓
Acoustic neuroma	↓ to Iso	+	Iso to ↑
Metastases	↑ to ↓	+	Variable ↑ to ↓

possible damage to adjacent normal brain. The development of functional MRI (fMRI), which measures cerebral blood flow when areas of cortex are activated, has greatly enhanced the ability to localize critical neurologic functions and their relationship to the tumor preoperatively (Chapter 424). When the fMR image is fused with the anatomic MR image, critical functions can be identified in relationship to the patient's tumor, and a more safe and complete resection may be planned.

Magnetic resonance spectroscopy (MRS) noninvasively assesses tissue composition (Chapter 424). Very rapidly growing malignant tumors that are associated with a poor prognosis frequently contain areas with elevation of lactate and lipid. MRS will soon be available on most standard MR scanners.

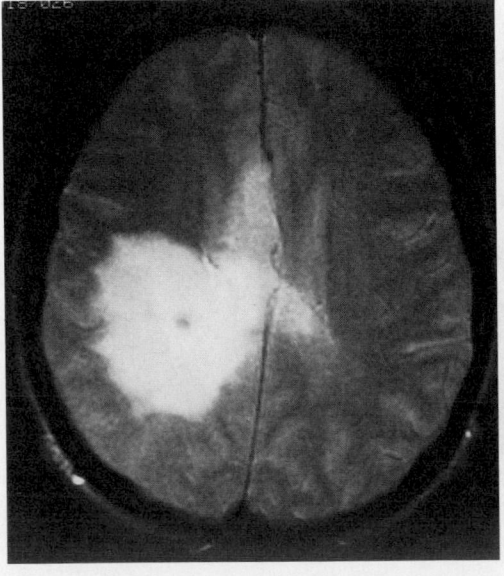
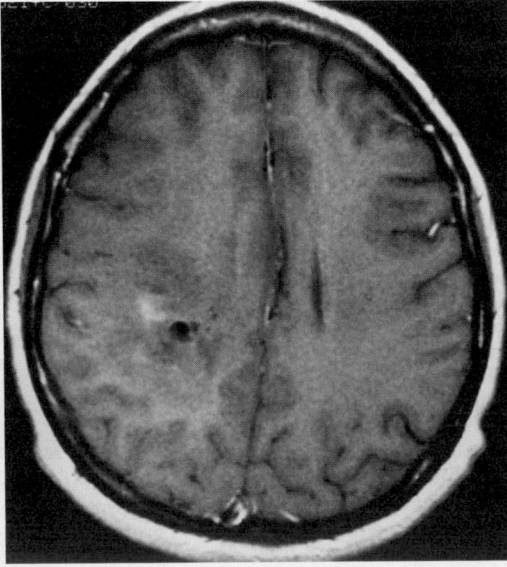

FIGURE 457-2 • Magnetic resonance imaging (MRI) scan of a low-grade glioma. *Left,* T2-weighted image; *right,* T1-weighted image, gadolinium contrast with minimum enhancement. The images are typical of this tumor, which is being detected with increasing frequency by MRI in seizure patients. Many are invisible on computed tomography scans.

Currently, angiography has no role in the diagnosis of intracranial tumors. However, angiographic embolization is occasionally useful preoperatively to reduce the vascularity of some meningiomas, thus making a complete resection safer and feasible.

Electroencephalography (EEG) is rarely needed in the diagnosis or management of patients with brain tumors. An EEG can occasionally be useful in a patient who has prolonged or unexplained stupor and in whom nonconvulsive status epilepticus is a consideration. Intraoperative monitoring is also frequently used to help guide resection of epileptogenic cortex adjacent to or within brain tumor tissue.

CSF analysis has little role in the diagnosis of most intracranial neoplasms. In primary CNS lymphoma (PCNSL), the diagnosis may be established on CSF cytologic examination in about 15% of patients. Rarely, a lumbar puncture is required to exclude inflammatory conditions or other processes that may be confused with a primary brain tumor. Lumbar puncture must be avoided in patients with cerebellar tumors because the release of pressure through the spinal needle may result in herniation of the cerebellar tonsils through the foramen magnum.

Differential Diagnosis

Patients who present with symptoms of raised ICP or the new onset of central neurologic symptoms such as hemiparesis or seizure should be hospitalized and evaluated rapidly. Prompt neuroimaging discloses a mass in the tumor patient and the radiographic features narrow the differential diagnosis (Table 457–4). Extra-axial tumors, such as a meningioma or acoustic neuroma, can be confused with a dural metastasis. Low-grade intra-axial tumors, which are nonenhancing on MRI, have been confused with infections such as herpes encephalitis when they involve the temporal lobe. Contrast-enhancing intra-axial tumors can be confused with a stroke (Chapter 440), brain abscess (Chapter 450), or focal plaque of demyelination (Chapter 448). Subacute infarction can show brisk contrast enhancement, usually in a gyral pattern, unlike brain tumors, in which enhancement is primarily in the white matter; however, occasionally the two are indistinguishable radiographically. Brain abscesses typically have a thinner enhancing wall than a malignant tumor, but they sometimes appear similar on MRI. Despite careful evaluation, occasional patients thought to have a malignant glioma are found to have a brain abscess at surgery. A single large plaque of demyelination can also be confused radiographically with a brain tumor, and sometimes the diagnosis can only be established by biopsy.

When MRI suggests a primary brain tumor, there is no need for an extensive systemic search for a possible source of metastasis. Brain metastases are more common than primary brain tumors, but most occur in patients with known cancer, typically with active systemic disease. If an obvious systemic cancer is not revealed by a thorough

---

Table 457–4 • DIFFERENTIAL DIAGNOSIS OF INTRACRANIAL TUMORS

Infection
  Brain abscess
    Bacterial
    Fungal
    Parasitic (e.g., cysticercosis)
  Herpes encephalitis
Vascular disease
  Stroke
  Intracranial hemorrhage
Inflammatory conditions
  Granuloma (sarcoid)
  Multiple sclerosis: single large lesion
Vascular malformations
  Cavernous angiomas
  Venous angiomas
Congenital abnormalities
  Cortical dysplasia
  Heterotopia

Table 457–5 • TREATMENT FOR BRAIN TUMORS

SYMPTOMATIC
  Glucocorticoids
  Anticonvulsants
  DVT prophylaxis and treatment

DEFINITIVE
Surgery
  Goal is gross total excision
Radiotherapy
  Standard external beam
    Fractionated
      Usually focal
  Stereotactic radiosurgery
Chemotherapy
  Limited by intrinsic drug resistance and blood-brain barrier

DVT = deep vein thrombosis.

---

general examination, chest radiograph, routine blood tests, and urinalysis, then the patient should proceed to craniotomy. Even if a brain metastasis is found at surgery, resection of a single brain metastasis is the appropriate treatment, and the pathology of the lesion guides the subsequent search for the primary tumor.

℞ Treatment

The treatment for all brain tumors can be divided into two main categories: symptomatic and definitive (Table 457–5). Symptomatic treatment addresses the associated problems, such as cerebral edema, seizures, and thromboembolic disease, which can contribute substantially to clinical symptoms. Definitive treatment addresses the tumor itself.

SYMPTOMATIC TREATMENT

Symptomatic management includes the use of corticosteroids, anticonvulsants, and prophylaxis for deep vein thrombosis (DVT; Chapter 78). Corticosteroids decrease the vasogenic edema that surrounds primary and metastatic brain tumors. Blood vessels associated with tumor formation are leaky and do not share the normal morphologic and physiologic features that form the blood-brain barrier; corticosteroids effectively reconstitute the blood-brain barrier by decreasing the abnormal permeability of these neovessels. Clinical improvement may begin within minutes, and frequently patients are dramatically improved within 24 to 48 hours.

Dexamethasone is the most commonly used glucocorticoid because it has the least mineralocorticoid activity. The usual starting dose is 12 to 16 mg per day, but this dose can be adjusted up or down to find the lowest possible dose that alleviates neurologic symptoms. After definitive treatment is instituted, many patients can be tapered off their corticosteroid completely. Chronic high-dose corticosteroid therapy is associated with substantial side effects (Chapter 31). Patients who will be on glucocorticoids for 6 weeks or longer should receive prophylaxis against *Pneumocystis carinii* (Chapter 387).

Anticonvulsants are administered to any patient who has had a seizure, but prophylactic anticonvulsants should not be prescribed for patients who have never had a seizure, [1,2] except they may be useful in the perioperative period.

DVT, which occurs in about 25% of patients with brain tumors, can occur early in the illness or at any time during treatment. All patients undergoing neurosurgery should have pneumatic compression boots in the postoperative period to reduce the incidence of DVT. Prophylactic anticoagulants have also been used successfully in the immediate postoperative period without increasing postoperative hemorrhage.[3] Appropriately regulated anticoagulation is the optimal therapy for DVT and is not associated with an increased risk of intracerebral hemorrhage in patients with intracranial tumors

Continued

(Chapter 78). Inferior vena cava filters can be used for patients who have DVTs or pulmonary emboli and who cannot be fully anticoagulated.

DEFINITIVE TREATMENT

SURGERY. Complete excision is the goal for a primary brain tumor. Surgical excision can often be accomplished for primary extra-axial tumors, such as meningiomas and acoustic neuromas. However, meningiomas often occur in intracranial locations that make resection impossible. Tumors of the skull base are particularly difficult to remove, and partial resection for decompression is often performed to preserve neurologic function. The safe boundaries for resection of cortical lesions while preserving function can often be elucidated by preoperative fMRI. However, lesions involving many critical structures, such as the brain stem or thalamus, cannot be excised safely.

Lesions that cannot be resected are still amenable to biopsy for diagnostic purposes. In particular, the use of stereotactic biopsy has made it feasible to reach lesions in almost any area of the brain with minimal morbidity. The risks of stereotactic biopsy include (1) inadequate tissue sample to make a diagnosis, (2) a tissue sample that does not accurately reflect the most malignant grade of the tumor, and (3) a procedure-related complication, such as hemorrhage. Hemorrhage that causes neurologic impairment occurs in only 2% of stereotactic biopsies, typically in patients with glioblastoma multiforme.

Complete excision can cure extra-axial primary brain tumors, and it is associated with prolonged survival and better neurologic outcome, even in patients with primary intra-axial tumors. Gross total excision as measured by postoperative neuroimaging is associated with prolonged survival in patients with malignant gliomas and probably in those with low-grade gliomas as well. However, most low-grade gliomas are not amenable to gross total excision, and usually only partial excision is feasible. Macroscopic tumor can frequently be removed completely in patients with high-grade gliomas, but there is always remaining microscopic disease that infiltrates surrounding brain.

Some tumors, such as brain stem gliomas, are in such critical locations that not even biopsy is attempted. Their characteristic radiographic appearance permits diagnosis and initiation of medical treatment.

RADIATION THERAPY. A course of external beam radiation therapy is delivered in small daily fractions to build to a total cumulative dose usually between 45 and 60 Gy. Dividing the treatment into small daily fractions permits sublethal repair in normal tissues and markedly reduces neurologic toxicity associated with cerebral radiation. External beam irradiation, which is the most effective nonsurgical treatment for brain tumors, doubles median survival of patients with malignant primary brain tumors and with metastatic lesions. It can also be useful for recurrent meningiomas and acoustic neuromas. However, it only rarely cures any of these lesions, and most patients develop recurrent disease despite maximal radiotherapy.

Stereotactic radiosurgery has been developed to deliver high fractions of focused radiation therapy that spare normal surrounding tissue. The technique is limited to tumors that are 3 cm in diameter or smaller and is less useful for malignant gliomas because of their infiltrative nature.

The neurologic complications of radiation therapy, which are usually observed in patients months to years after completion of treatment, include radionecrosis, dementia, and leukoencephalopathy. The incidence is reported as less than 5%, and most patients die of their brain tumor before the delayed consequences of treatment can be observed. However, in long-term survivors (e.g., patients with low-grade gliomas or primary CNS lymphomas, and children with medulloblastomas) the late consequences of radiation therapy are important. Dementia accompanying radiation-induced leukoencephalopathy can progress and result in severe neurologic impairment. Radionecrosis can mimic recurrent tumor with a large contrast-enhancing lesion on MRI. Corticosteroids can reduce the edema and sometimes be sufficient to treat small areas of radionecrosis. However, if the lesion is sufficiently large, resection may be required to decompress the mass and to reduce the steroid requirements.

CHEMOTHERAPY. Chemotherapy for brain tumors has usually been disappointing because of the intrinsic resistance of these tumors to most conventional agents. Carboplatin and cisplatin (Chapter 191) are active agents against medulloblastoma, even when the tumor is disseminated in the CSF. Temozolomide is active in all gliomas, and high-dose methotrexate is effective for primary CNS lymphoma. Polymers impregnated with BCNU offer modest benefit when compared with no chemotherapy, but they are associated with local tissue injury and edema.

SPECIFIC TYPES OF BRAIN TUMORS

Primary Extra-Axial Tumors

The most common primary extra-axial tumors are meningiomas, pituitary adenomas, and acoustic neuromas. These tumors arise within the intracranial cavity but are not tumors of brain tissue. Almost all are benign; because the brain is rarely invaded, complete excision often enables cure with full recovery of neurologic function. These tumors produce neurologic symptoms and signs by compressing the underlying brain; however, edema of the underlying brain is infrequent, so glucocorticoids have a limited role.

MENINGIOMAS

Meningiomas are usually benign. Five per cent to 10% of meningiomas are atypical and malignant variants with a more aggressive course. Meningiomas are more common in women, may be multiple in about 10% of sporadic patients, and are occasionally part of a familial syndrome. They occur with increased frequency in patients with neurofibromatosis type 2 (Chapter 459).

Meningiomas grow slowly and produce symptoms that are insidious in onset and typically slowly progressive. Tumors can reach a considerable size but grow so slowly that the brain accommodates to the progressive compression. Meningiomas typically occur in specific locations: over the convexity, along the falx and parasagittal area, the olfactory groove, and base of the skull near the sphenoid bone, cavernous sinus, cerebellopontine angle, and foramen magnum. Cortical and parasagittal tumors typically present with seizures or progressive hemiparesis. Tumors in the anterior cranial fossa can cause slowly

progressive changes in personality and cognition. Meningiomas at the base of the skull present with cranial neuropathies and gait difficulties when there is brain stem compression. Frequently, tumors are completely asymptomatic and are identified on neuroimaging done for another purpose, such as head trauma.

On MRI, meningiomas have a characteristic appearance consisting of a diffusely enhancing dural-based lesion that is associated with a thin enhancing dural tail extending from the tumor; often the radiographic features are so characteristic that surgery is performed for therapeutic purposes only. The radiographic differential diagnosis includes the less common *hemangiopericytoma* and *dural metastasis*. Most meningiomas are not accompanied by significant edema, but marked edema is seen with high-grade malignant lesions or the secretory variant.

When small meningiomas are discovered in the absence of clinical symptoms or the symptoms are minor, lesions may be followed with serial images because growth can be so slow. When treatment is indicated, completely resected tumors are often cured, but even completely resected benign tumors may recur (as many as 20% in some series), so radiologic follow-up is essential. Tumors at the base of the skull often cannot be resected completely and tend to recur despite successive attempts at surgical resection. Radiotherapy can sometimes slow progression and is essential for the treatment of malignant meningiomas. No effective chemotherapy has yet been identified.

ACOUSTIC NEUROMAS

Acoustic neuromas (Chapter 470), better called vestibular schwannomas, are benign tumors that arise from the eighth cranial nerve.

Acoustic neuromas are twice as common in women as in men; the peak age is between 40 and 60 years. Sporadic vestibular schwannomas are unilateral; bilateral acoustic neuromas are pathognomonic of neurofibromatosis type 2 (Chapter 459).

Acoustic neuromas usually arise from the vestibular portion of the nerve and typically present with unilateral hearing loss, sometimes preceded or accompanied by tinnitus and a sensation of dizziness or unsteadiness but not true vertigo. The slow, progressive enlargement of the tumor produces ipsilateral facial numbness or weakness by compressing the fifth or seventh cranial nerves, respectively. Tumors originate within the internal auditory meatus but grow out of the acoustic canal and into the cerebellopontine angle, where they can compress the brain stem and cause ataxia and ipsilateral cerebellar signs. Cranial MRI with gadolinium delineates even small acoustic neuromas with ease.

Treatment is often surgical; stereotactic radiosurgery may be an alternative for lesions smaller than 3 cm. It is preferable to treat the tumors when they are small to preserve facial nerve function and hearing.

PITUITARY ADENOMAS

Pituitary adenomas (Chapter 237) can be classified according to their size as microadenomas (less than 1 cm in diameter) or macroadenomas; by the presence or absence of endocrine function; and by the endocrinologic syndromes or neurologic syndromes caused by tumor compression. Microadenomas typically present with endocrine symptoms such as amenorrhea, galactorrhea, infertility, and sexual dysfunction (all related to prolactin-secreting tumors); acromegaly (related to growth hormone hypersecretion); Cushing's syndrome (related to adrenocorticotropic hormone–producing tumors), and hyperthyroidism (related to thyroid-stimulating hormone–producing tumors). As pituitary tumors enlarge and become macroadenomas, they compress the surrounding neural structures, including the optic chiasm and optic nerves, typically causing bitemporal hemianopia and occasionally causing unilateral visual loss. Macroadenomas are frequently nonsecreting but destroy pituitary tissue, causing panhypopituitarism. Rarely, pituitary tumors present with the abrupt onset of headache, ophthalmoplegia, unilateral blindness, and even a depressed level of alertness or coma—a syndrome of *pituitary apoplexy* caused by hemorrhage or infarction.

Cranial MRI, particularly with coronal images and gadolinium administration, can completely outline the pituitary tumor and surrounding neural structures. All macroadenomas and some microadenomas can be treated with transsphenoidal pituitary surgery, which is associated with minimal morbidity. Occasionally, residual or recurrent tumor necessitates radiotherapy. Some hormone-secreting tumors, particularly prolactinomas or growth hormone–secreting tumors, can also be treated medically with cabergoline or octreotide, respectively (Chapter 237). These medications not only correct the hormonal excess but also shrink the tumor; they must be taken for life.

Other tumors in the pituitary and suprasellar region include craniopharyngiomas, suprasellar epidermoid cysts, Rathke cleft cysts, germinomas, and lymphocytic hypophysitis, which is a benign inflammatory condition that usually presents with diabetes insipidus (Chapter 238). MRI frequently differentiates these conditions, which are usually suprasellar and erode into the pituitary fossa only secondarily. Some of these lesions also have characteristic radiographic features. These lesions are benign. Except for hypophysitis, which resolves completely with corticosteroids, complete surgical excision is the curative therapy.

OTHER EXTRA-AXIAL TUMORS

Pineal region tumors all have a characteristic clinical presentation that includes Parinaud's syndrome, which consists of paresis of upward gaze, poor pupillary reaction to light with brisk reaction upon accommodation, impairment of convergence, and convergence-retraction nystagmus. Some of these lesions may also cause hydrocephalus and symptoms of increased ICP. Pineal region tumors include pineal parenchymal tumors, such as pineocytomas and the more aggressive pineoblastomas, and germ cell tumors, including germinomas and nongerminomatous germ cell tumors. Germinomas can be completely cured with focal radiotherapy, whereas nongerminomatous germ cell

tumors are more aggressive and frequently relapse despite chemotherapy plus cranial irradiation.

Chordomas are rare tumors of residual notochordal tissue. They usually occur at the base of the skull, are locally invasive, and are characterized by multiple recurrences despite surgery and radiotherapy.

Lipomas are benign tumors that can occur in midline structures, particularly near the corpus callosum. They can be cured by complete removal.

Arachnoid cysts are not tumors per se, but can present with headaches, seizures or focal neurologic symptoms if they become large enough to compress underlying brain tissue. Many are completely asymptomatic and found incidentally on neuroimaging. Only symptomatic cysts require removal.

Primary Intra-Axial Tumors

Most primary intra-axial brain tumors are gliomas, including the astrocytomas, oligodendrogliomas, and ependymomas. Less common are medulloblastomas, other rare neuroectodermal tumors, and primary CNS lymphomas. All of these tumors have a tendency to invade brain tissue, and none can be completely excised surgically.

GLIOMAS

Astrocytomas, which are the most common glioma, are classified into one of four categories: grade I is the pilocytic astrocytoma, grade II is the fibrillary astrocytoma, grade III is the anaplastic astrocytoma, and grade IV is the glioblastoma multiforme. Pilocytic astrocytomas are extremely low-grade focal tumors that are more common in children and may be associated with neurofibromatosis type 1; they are often cured by complete surgical excision. Astrocytomas, anaplastic astrocytomas, and glioblastomas are diffuse tumors that tend to infiltrate widely into brain; even grade II tumors progress over time, and the majority acquire the histologic features and growth patterns of grade III and IV tumors.

Gliomas occur at any age, but the usual age is 20 to 30 years of age for an astrocytoma, 40 years of age for anaplastic astrocytoma, and 55 to 60 years of age for glioblastoma. Age is the single most important prognostic factor: younger patients live substantially longer than older patients. Histology is also critical; patients with glioblastoma do significantly worse than patients with lower grade lesions. Performance status, duration of symptoms, and whether or not a complete resection has been achieved are also strong predictors of improved outcome and prolonged survival. For all grades of glioma, men are more frequently affected than women, and whites significantly more than blacks. Gliomas are typically single lesions, but multifocal disease is seen in approximately 5% of patients with high-grade tumors. A variant of gliomas, called *gliomatosis cerebri*, causes widespread infiltration of the entire brain; most patients have relatively low-grade pathology on biopsy, but focal regions of high-grade transformation can exist.

Patients with gliomas often present with seizures, headache, and lateralizing signs such as hemiparesis, aphasia, or a visual field deficit. On MRI, low-grade gliomas typically appear as diffuse, nonenhancing lesions with a propensity to occur in the frontal lobe and in the insular cortex. High-grade gliomas, which typically enhance with contrast, occur in the cortical white matter and are accompanied by significant surrounding edema. Glioblastomas frequently have regions of central necrosis (Fig. 457–3), and hemorrhage can occur in 5 to 8% of patients.

For all gliomas, treatment frequently involves surgery, radiation therapy, and chemotherapy. The surgical goal of complete removal of all visible disease frequently is impossible. The adequacy of resection is best assessed on a postoperative MRI study without and with gadolinium within 72 to 96 hours after surgery. Surgical removal usually improves neurologic function and reduces dependency on corticosteroids. All anaplastic astrocytomas and glioblastomas should be treated with postoperative radiotherapy to a dose of approximately 60 Gy, optimally followed by chemotherapy, usually with the alkylating agent temozolomide or a nitrosourea. [4] Chemotherapy likely prolongs survival for only 15 to 20% of patients, but it is generally well tolerated and associated with minimal toxicity. Recurrences can be treated with re-resection, additional chemotherapy, and/or occasionally stereotactic radiosurgery. Despite aggressive treatment, disease recurs in almost all patients, and the median survival is slightly more than 1 year for glioblastoma and about 3 years for anaplastic

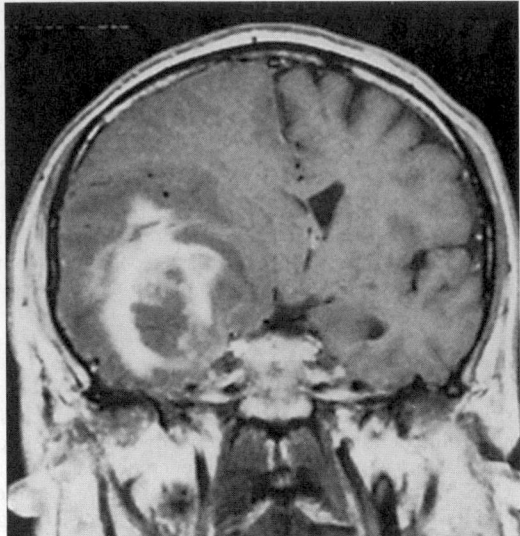

FIGURE 457–3 • Temporal lobe glioblastoma. This T1 gadolinium-enhanced magnetic resonance imaging scan shows a typical ring configuration of contrast with central necrosis and marked mass effect.

astrocytoma. However, some young patients with anaplastic astrocytomas can survive for many years before the tumor recurs.

Low-grade astrocytomas have a variable course. Patients may present with isolated seizures that can be easily controlled with anticonvulsants; in such patients, definitive treatment immediately after surgery does not prolong survival,[5] and patients can be followed up until there is clinical or radiographic evidence of tumor progression. Patients with progressive neurologic symptoms or cognitive impairment require immediate treatment after diagnosis, and focal radiotherapy to a total of about 54 Gy is the optimal choice. Astrocytomas can progress as low-grade tumors or transform to a higher grade malignancy, which is typically associated with the appearance of contrast enhancement on MRI. Resection or a biopsy may be necessary in these patients, who are then treated with radiotherapy if they have not received it previously; chemotherapy is also used. Patients with astrocytomas have a median survival of about 5 years.

Oligodendrogliomas occur as low-grade tumors and, less commonly, as an anaplastic lesion. Treatment of these tumors differs from their astrocytic counterparts because oligodendrogliomas are uniquely chemosensitive owing to their characteristic loss of chromosomes 1p and 19q. Like the low-grade astrocytomas, treatment should be withheld in patients with low-grade oligodendrogliomas who have no symptoms other than well-controlled seizures. Patients with progressive neurologic symptoms require treatment, and initial therapy is often chemotherapy, usually with the combination of procarbazine, lomustine, and vincristine or single agent temozolomide, both of which often produce regression. Radiotherapy is withheld until chemotherapy fails. All anaplastic oligodendrogliomas require immediate treatment. The standard approach includes focal radiotherapy and chemotherapy. However, there is a growing movement toward treating patients with high-grade tumors with chemotherapy alone and, in some cases, using high-dose chemotherapy with autologous stem cell rescue (Chapter 166). Some success has been seen with this approach, but it should still be considered experimental. Tumor progression should be treated with re-resection, radiotherapy if not previously administered, and additional chemotherapy. Patients with low-grade oligodendrogliomas can have a median survival in excess of 15 years, and those who have anaplastic oligodendrogliomas can have a median survival of 4 to 5 years.

Gliomas can occur anywhere in the brain, but specific locations have specific clinical and biologic properties. Optic gliomas, which can involve the optic nerve or optic chiasm, are usually associated with neurofibromatosis type 1. These gliomas are typically pilocytic tumors that can have an indolent course, including rare spontaneous regression. Often they are not amenable to surgical resection and can have a stuttering clinical course with periods of visual loss punctuated by prolonged periods of visual stability. When necessary, radiation or even chemotherapy may be useful, but often no treatment is

required. Brain stem gliomas usually involve the pons, less often the medulla or midbrain. Brain stem gliomas are most commonly seen in children in the first decade of life but can be found even in the elderly; they can have a low-grade or high-grade histology, but outcome is primarily defined by the location of the tumor. In general, most brain stem gliomas have a dismal outcome with survival of a year or less, but there are occasional relatively benign variants.

MEDULLOBLASTOMAS

Medulloblastomas usually occur in the vermis of the cerebellum, principally affecting children and young adults. Medulloblastomas have a characteristic clinical presentation with ataxia, due to cerebellar and brain stem involvement, as well as headache, nausea, and vomiting, due to increased ICP from obstructive hydrocephalus. Boys outnumber girls by about 2:1 and peak onset is at age 7 years; medulloblastoma in adulthood is rare and usually affects the cerebellar hemisphere. Aggressive surgery with complete excision is strongly associated with improved outcome. Surgery is always followed by neuraxis radiation therapy and frequently chemotherapy as well. The 5-year survival rate is about 70%. This vigorous therapy often results in significant delayed complications in survivors, including intellectual deficits, growth impairment, and endocrinologic dysfunction.

The most common chromosomal abnormality associated with medulloblastoma is isochromosome 17q, which is found in as many as 60% of tumors. Tumors with an identical histology but different genetics may arise in the cerebral hemispheres and are called *primitive neuroectodermal tumors* (PNETs). PNETs usually have an aggressive course, leading to rapid death despite vigorous treatment.

GANGLIOGLIOMAS

Gangliogliomas, as the name implies, possess both a glial component and a neoplastic neural component (ganglion cell). Some low-grade gangliogliomas are indolent and do not require additional treatment after surgical extirpation. Patients with anaplastic tumors may fare better than patients with malignant gliomas, but recurrence is the rule despite surgery and radiation therapy.

PRIMARY CENTRAL NERVOUS SYSTEM LYMPHOMA

Primary CNS lymphoma is associated with immunodeficiency states, particularly acquired immunodeficiency syndrome (Chapter 419) and organ transplantation, and is seen with increased frequency among the apparently immunocompetent population as well. Men are more frequently affected than women, and the median age at diagnosis is about 60 years. These tumors are usually large-cell, B-cell non-Hodgkin's lymphomas identical to systemic lymphoma. The tumor can involve the CSF, the eye, and the brain, where it is multifocal in about 40% of patients at presentation. Unlike all other brain tumors, surgical resection is not associated with improved survival and can cause significant neurologic morbidity; thus biopsy, not resection, is the better surgical approach. Chemotherapy is the primary treatment, and high-dose methotrexate (Chapter 191) is the most important chemotherapeutic agent. In older patients, radiotherapy is avoided because the necessary whole-brain radiation causes significant cognitive impairment when combined with chemotherapy. Furthermore, patients treated with radiotherapy alone respond but relapse within a year. Corticosteroids, which are frequently used as part of the chemotherapeutic regimen, not only help manage the associated cerebral edema, but also can cause tumor regression. Using multiagent chemotherapy, with or without cranial irradiation, median survivals are now in the 3- to 5-year range.

OTHER INTRA-AXIAL TUMORS

Rare, intra-axial cerebral tumors include the *ependymoma*, which is optimally treated with surgical excision followed by radiotherapy. *Choroid plexus papillomas* and carcinomas may present with hydrocephalus or lateralizing signs. Resection may be sufficient for the benign papilloma, but carcinomas rapidly recur even when postoperative radiotherapy is also used. *Colloid cysts* of the third ventricle are benign tumors that can cause obstructive hydrocephalus; they may be treated with ventricular peritoneal shunt or with resection using an intraventricular endoscope. *Hemangioblastomas* occur primarily in the cerebellum but can also occur in the spinal cord and the hemispheres.

About 15% of patients with a hemangioblastoma have the autosomal dominant disorder of von Hippel-Lindau disease (Chapter 459), which is characterized by hemangioblastomas in the CSF and retina, renal cell carcinoma, pheochromocytoma, endolymphatic sac tumors, and cysts in a variety of visceral organs. Hemangioblastomas are treated by surgical excision and require radiotherapy only for recurrence. Complete removal usually results in cure.

Metastatic Tumors

BRAIN METASTASES

Every systemic cancer is capable of metastasizing to the brain. Melanoma (Chapter 209) has the greatest propensity to spread to the CNS, but the most common causes of CNS metastases are cancers of the breast (Chapter 204) and lung (Chapter 198) followed by cancers of the colon (Chapter 200) and kidney (Chapter 203). CNS metastases are being seen with greater frequency as patients with systemic cancers have prolonged survivals with better treatments. In most patients with brain metastases, CNS disease develops late in the course of their illness, but a brain metastasis may be the initial presentation of a systemic cancer. In most of these patients, lung cancer is the primary; in some of these patients, though, a primary is never identified (Chapter 210).

Metastases are best diagnosed by a cranial MRI scan with gadolinium (Fig. 457–4). All lesions can be clearly seen by MRI, which is better than CT scanning for visualizing the posterior fossa. Metastases, which are usually well circumscribed lesions at the grey-white matter junction, are often associated with extensive edema. Hemorrhage into a metastasis occurs most frequently in metastases from melanoma, renal cancer, and thyroid cancer, but because brain metastases from lung cancer are so common, they are most commonly associated with hemorrhage. Patients with brain metastases present with progressive neurologic symptoms and signs that typically include headache, seizures, and lateralizing signs. Sometimes, hemorrhage into a brain metastasis is best visualized on a noncontrast head CT.

Because brain metastases do not widely infiltrate into brain tissue and tend to have a pseudocapsule around them, they can be completely excised surgically. In randomized controlled studies, complete removal substantially prolongs life and maintains neurologic function for a longer period of time. **6** Postoperative whole brain radiotherapy significantly improves control of CNS disease after resection of a single brain metastasis, but does not prolong survival because patients die of progressive systemic tumor. **7** Consequently, the use of postoperative whole-brain radiotherapy is frequently decided on an individual basis. When multiple lesions can be completely

resected, these patients do as well as those with a single lesion that has been removed.

Most patients with multiple brain metastases are best treated with a course of whole-brain radiotherapy, most commonly 3 Gy in 10 fractions for a total of 30 Gy. Some patients with single brain metastasis are also treated with whole-brain irradiation if they are in poor general condition, have uncontrolled systemic disease, or are not good candidates for surgical treatment.

Stereotactic radiosurgery using either a gamma knife that delivers gamma radiation from multiple cobalt sources or a linear accelerator that delivers x-rays to a highly focused area involving the tumor has been quite effective for the treatment of one or a few brain metastases. Most patients tolerate radiosurgery without difficulty, but occasionally the procedure is complicated by seizures or acute swelling that causes more neurologic dysfunction. Approximately 20 to 30% of patients may develop radionecrosis, which may be indistinguishable clinically and on MRI from recurrent tumor. One advantage of stereotactic radiosurgery is that most of the normal brain is not exposed to the radiotherapy.

Chemotherapy is used to treat brain metastases from only a few chemosensitive primary cancers such as choriocarcinoma, small cell lung cancer, and, to a lesser extent, breast cancer. Because few patients have a significant response to chemotherapy, it is usually used as a last resort. The new oral agent, temozolomide, has shown some activity against brain metastases from lung cancer and is very well tolerated.

LEPTOMENINGEAL METASTASES

The brain is the most common intracranial site of metastases, but systemic cancer can spread to the dura and the leptomeninges as well. Dural metastases most commonly arise from breast or prostate cancer, frequently from a metastasis in the overlying calvarium. Metastasis to the leptomeninges often presents as multifocal neurologic symptoms and signs. These metastases involve the cranial nerves to cause diplopia or bulbar palsy; the cervical and lumbar roots to cause limb pain or weakness; and the intracranial space to cause headache, nausea, vomiting, and elevated ICP. The diagnosis is established by the presence of tumor cells in the CSF or by neuroimaging that definitively outlines tumor in the subarachnoid space (Fig. 457–5). Treatment frequently involves radiotherapy to symptomatic sites, intrathecal chemotherapy usually through an intraventricular cannula (Ommaya reservoir), or systemic chemotherapy with agents at doses that penetrate into the CSF.

SPINAL TUMORS

Tumors involving the spine can be classified according to the anatomic area they involve: extradural, intradural extramedullary, and intramedullary tumors (Table 457–6). Extradural tumors typically arise from the bony elements of the spine and cause neurologic symptoms and signs by spinal cord compression. Intradural but extramedullary tumors arise from the pachymeninges or nerve roots (meningiomas or schwannomas), and they may cause either

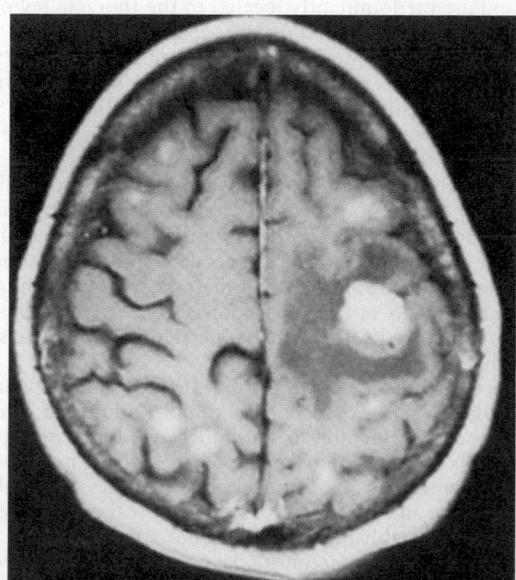

FIGURE 457–4 • Brain metastasis. Multiple metastases from breast carcinoma are seen on this T1 gadolinium-enhanced magnetic resonance imaging scan. The tumors were not visible on computed tomography scan, even after a contrast agent was given.

Table 457–6 • SPINAL TUMORS

Extradural
  Metastases
  Primary bone tumors arising in the spine
Intradural extramedullary
  Meningiomas
  Neurofibromas
  Schwannomas
  Lipomas
  Arachnoid cysts
  Epidermoid cysts
  Metastasis
Intramedullary
  Ependymoma
  Glioma
  Hemangioblastoma
  Lipoma
  Metastasis

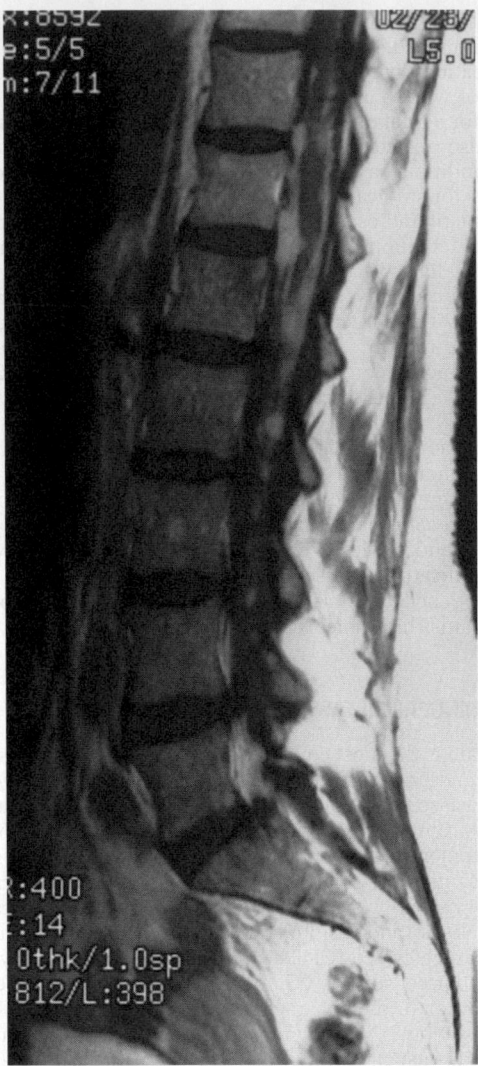

FIGURE 457–5 • Gadolinium-enhanced magnetic resonance imaging scan of the lumbosacral spine in a patient with leptomeningeal metastases from melanoma. Multiple enhancing nodules are seen on the cauda equina, and the conus medullaris and lower spinal cord are encased by tumor.

radicular symptoms or spinal cord compression. Intramedullary spinal cord tumors arise from the spinal cord parenchyma and have a biology similar to brain tumors. Intramedullary tumors are rare.

EXTRADURAL TUMORS

Most extradural tumors originate from a metastasis to the bony elements of the spine, typically the vertebral body and occasionally the vertebral lamina or spinous process. Less common are primary tumors of the spine including chordoma, osteogenic sarcoma, plasmacytoma, and chondrosarcoma. Expansile growth of the bone tumor impinges on the spinal canal and, if untreated, compresses the spinal cord or the nerve roots as they exit the intervertebral foramina. Whereas most of these lesions arise from bony metastases, extradural tumor can also arise from paravertebral metastases that can grow through the intervertebral foramina and into the epidural space; very rarely, a direct metastasis to the epidural space is also seen. The most common primary cancers that cause extradural metastases include prostate, breast, and lung cancer, as well as the lymphomas. Hematologic malignancies may also be associated with paravertebral disease that grows through the intervertebral foramina.

Whether the mass is a primary bone tumor or a metastasis from a distant source, 98% of patients present with pain that is usually local at the site of the tumor. Because there are more thoracic than cervical or lumbar vertebrae, the tumor and pain are likely to be in the mid or high back, a less common site for benign pain (Chapter

429). Motor impairment and sensory symptoms are present in about 50% of patients, whereas sphincter disturbances are found in only about 25% of patients. Back pain often precedes the development of any other neurologic symptom or sign, frequently by weeks and occasionally by months.

Severe back pain in a patient with cancer should be evaluated by MRI, which does not require intravenous contrast. Plain films of the spine, bone scan, or even CT scan may show bony disease, but epidural tumor can be seen only on MRI. Furthermore, MRI is the only technique that can reveal paravertebral or direct epidural metastasis. Patients who cannot have an MRI scan should be imaged by CT myelography.

The differential diagnosis of extradural tumors includes epidural abscess (Chapter 450), acute or subacute epidural hematomas (Chapter 429), herniated intervertebral discs (Chapter 429), spondylosis (Chapter 429), epidural lipomatosis, and rarely, extramedullary hematopoiesis. Occasionally, a percutaneous needle biopsy or decompressive laminectomy is required to make a definitive diagnosis.

Rx Treatment

Extradural metastases require immediate treatment because patients can develop acute and unpredictable neurologic deterioration resulting in paraplegia. Patients should be started on high-dose corticosteroids, usually 100 mg dexamethasone, which rapidly relieves pain and may contribute to neurologic recovery. Both surgery and radiotherapy can relieve pain and may restore neurologic function. Surgery is used particularly for patients who have radioresistant tumors (e.g., kidney), who have redeveloped epidural tumor in a previously irradiated port, or in whom epidural tumor is the initial presentation and a histologic diagnosis is required. It is much easier to preserve neurologic function than to reverse impairment, so clinically silent areas of extradural tumor that are detected on MRI should be treated before neurologic compromise develops. Patients whose primary tumor arises in the spine, such as an osteogenic sarcoma (Chapter 208), should undergo definitive surgery; the need for postoperative radiotherapy is determined on the basis of the tumor's histology. Patients with extradural metastases can have a good neurologic outcome if treated before the onset of severe neurologic compromise, but their overall survival is usually short due to the presence of widespread meta-static disease.

INTRADURAL EXTRAMEDULLARY TUMORS

Most intradural extramedullary tumors are benign. Meningiomas are benign, slow-growing tumors that occur primarily in middle-aged women and are predominantly located in the thoracic region. Back pain is a common symptom, but about 25% of patients have no pain and present with slowly progressive neurologic dysfunction, typically a gait disorder that has been slowly progressing, frequently for years. Spinal MRI with gadolinium clearly delineates the lesion. Surgical resection is curative, and a complete resection can usually be accomplished easily.

Nerve sheath tumors include schwannomas and neurofibromas. Both typically arise from the dorsal root, and the first symptom is often radicular pain that precedes symptoms of spinal cord compression by months or even years. Some patients with spinal neurofibroma or schwannoma suffer from neurofibromatosis type 1 (Chapter 459), but the majority do not. The diagnosis is clearly established by gadolinium-enhanced MRI of the spine. The treatment is surgical, and complete removal results in cure.

Metastasis to the spinal leptomeninges can present as an intradural extramedullary lesion. A single large tumor nodule can cause focal symptoms and signs referable to that spinal level, but in most patients, multiple levels of the neuraxis are involved, causing multifocal neurologic symptoms and signs. Cervical and lumbosacral radicular pain, as well as sensory and motor loss, is seen in more than half of patients. The diagnosis is established by gadolinium-enhanced MRI showing multifocal nodules or sometimes a layer of cells coating the spinal cord or nerve roots (see Fig. 457–5). When imaging is negative, the diagnosis can be established by demonstrating tumor cells in the CSF. Treatment is complicated and frequently requires radiation therapy to symptomatic sites of disease, intrathecal chemotherapy best administered through an intraventricular cannula (Ommaya device), and occasionally systemic chemotherapy. Radiotherapy can ameliorate neurologic symptoms, particularly pain, but the disease often has a relentless progressive course, resulting in death in 3 to 6 months despite aggressive therapy. Because of the diffuse nature of the disease, surgery is not an option.

INTRAMEDULLARY TUMORS

Intramedullary spinal cord tumors are similar to neoplasms that arise in brain parenchyma. The most common spinal cord tumors are ependymomas and astrocytomas; hemangioblastomas (particularly in association with von Hippel-Lindau disease; Chapter 459), lipomas, and rarely intramedullary metastases are also seen. All intramedullary tumors have a similar clinical presentation, and pain is a common initial symptom. Signs of spinal cord dysfunction subsequently ensue and reflect the location of the lesion. In addition, some intramedullary tumors are accompanied by a syrinx (Chapter 459), which can also contribute to symptoms. The classic signs of intramedullary spinal cord lesions, such as dissociated sensory loss, sacral sparing, and early sphincter problems, are not sufficiently reliable to distinguish intramedullary from extramedullary lesions on the basis of clinical findings. The diagnosis is established by gadolinium-enhanced MRI.

Rx Treatment

Surgery is the first therapeutic intervention both to obtain a definitive diagnosis and to resect the lesion. Complete resection of spinal cord tumors is possible, particularly in the case of ependymomas and hemangioblastomas. However, spinal cord tumors are rare and only neurosurgeons experienced in removing this type of lesion should perform the procedure. High-grade gliomas and residual ependymomas should be treated with postoperative radiotherapy. Low-grade astrocytomas of the spinal cord can be treated with radiotherapy when the patient develops symptomatic neurologic impairment, but presymptomatic treatment does not prevent the development of impairment nor necessarily delay it. Intramedullary metastases do not require surgery because the diagnosis is usually straightforward; radiotherapy provides limited benefit because these patients typically have other CNS metastases.

INTRACRANIAL HYPERTENSION AND HYPOTENSION

CSF is made, in part, by the choroid plexus in the ventricular system; newly formed fluid circulates out through the foramina of Luschka and Magendi at the bottom of the fourth ventricle to surround the entire spinal cord and cerebrum. It is reabsorbed back into the circulation through the arachnoid granulations over the convexities. Balance between CSF production and reabsorption keeps the volume relatively constant at about 150 mL in the normal healthy adult. CSF is produced at roughly 20 mL per hour, implying that the entire volume of CSF is replaced three to four times each day. CSF circulates nutrients to the nervous system and removes waste products from the only organ in the body that lacks a lymphatic system. In addition, CSF has an important mechanical function by absorbing shock to the brain and spinal cord, cushioning them from the bony surroundings of the skull and spine.

A lumbar puncture provides the opportunity for not only sampling the CSF composition to detect disease processes, but also for measuring ICP. CSF pressure is normally maintained from 70 to 195 mm H_2O. ICP is maintained within this narrow window because significant fluctuations, either up or down, can cause marked neurologic dysfunction.

INTRACRANIAL HYPERTENSION

Elevated ICP causes symptoms by compressing neural tissue, a process that causes ischemia and sometimes hemorrhage due to associated arterial and venous compression. ICP is partially maintained through the autoregulatory mechanisms of the cerebral blood vessels. Low ICP is caused by diminished CSF volume, and symptoms result from the loss of buoyancy of the brain as it floats within the CSF liquid. Pulling or stretch of the dura and cortical veins, which are the pain-sensitive structures in the cranial vault, causes headache; compensatory vasodilation may also contribute to headache.

The principal symptoms and signs associated with increased ICP are headache, nausea, vomiting, and lethargy; other symptoms are less frequent (Table 457–7). Focal mass lesions that cause a herniation syndrome may produce lateralizing signs such as hemiparesis; by comparison, diffuse elevation of ICP, as in communicating hydrocephalus, rarely does. Three main herniation syndromes include (1) herniation of the medial frontal gyrus under the falx, (2) transtentorial herniation of the uncus, pushing the diencephalon and the brain stem downward and laterally, and (3) herniation of the cerebellar tonsils through the foramen magnum. Generalized increased ICP may be due to obstruction of CSF, which may be caused by blockage of the ventricular system (obstructive or noncommunicating hydrocephalus) or impairment of CSF reabsorption (nonobstructive or communicating hydrocephalus).

Increased ICP of any cause may produce pressure or plateau waves (episodic increases in ICP), leading to transient symptoms such as headache, vertigo, or diminished consciousness. Plateau waves occur normally and are associated with symptoms only when the baseline ICP is elevated. Plateau waves may be precipitated by a change in body position.

Hydrocephalus

Hydrocephalus refers to ventricular dilation from accumulated CSF. Hydrocephalus can be acute, resulting from sudden blockage of CSF outflow, or chronic, developing slowly over many months to years (Table 457–8). Patients with chronic hydrocephalus sometimes have normal CSF pressures, whereas those with acute hydrocephalus always have elevated CSF pressure.

Table 457–7 • SYMPTOMS AND SIGNS OF INTRACRANIAL HYPERTENSION

COMMON
Headache
Tinnitus
Vomiting (with or without nausea)
Visual obscurations, visual loss, photopsias
Papilledema
Diplopia
Lethargy and increased sleep
Psychomotor retardation
Pain on eye movement

LESS COMMON
Hearing distortion or loss
Vertigo
Facial weakness
Shoulder or arm pain
Neck pain or rigidity
Ataxia
Paresthesias of extremities
Anosmia
Trigeminal neuralgia

Table 457–8 • CAUSES OF HYDROCEPHALUS

ACUTE
Cerebellar hemorrhage/infarction
Colloid cyst of the third ventricle
Exudative meningitis
Head trauma
Intracranial tumor or hematoma
Spontaneous subarachnoid hemorrhage
Viral encephalitis

CHRONIC
Aqueductal stenosis
Ectasia and elongation of the basilar artery (rare)
Granulomatous meningitis
Head trauma
Hindbrain malformations
Leptomeningeal metastasis
Brain and spinal cord tumors
Spontaneous subarachnoid hemorrhage

Acute hydrocephalus usually presents with severe headache, lethargy, nausea, vomiting, papilledema, and diplopia from abducens palsy as well as signs from the causative lesion. Diffuse hyperreflexia and bilateral Babinski signs are common. Patients with chronic communicating hydrocephalus often have normal CSF pressure, so-called normal pressure hydrocephalus, and may present with progressive dementia characterized by memory loss and psychomotor retardation, an unsteady gait, and urgency incontinence (Chapter 433). Some patients have features of parkinsonism (Chapter 443) because of the bradykinesia and psychomotor retardation associated with hydrocephalus, but resting tremor is absent.

Ventriculomegaly is readily diagnosed by MRI or CT scan. In older patients, cerebral atrophy and the associated compensating increase in ventricular volume that accompanies normal aging (hydrocephalus ex vacuo) must be considered. Periventricular hyperintensity on T2-weighted or FLAIR MR images may help separate patients with normal pressure hydrocephalus from patients with hydrocephalus ex vacuo. MRI is the best test to identify a cause of hydrocephalus.

 Treatment

If the ICP approaches or exceeds the systolic blood pressure, the cerebral perfusion pressure decreases and ischemia develops. Marked elevation of ICP is a neurologic emergency that requires immediate intervention (Table 457–9) to reduce the volume of the intracranial contents and to prevent permanent brain damage. Hyperventilation to lower the $PaCO_2$ to 25 to 30 mm Hg causes immediate vasoconstriction, which reduces cerebral blood volume. Intravenous mannitol can cause a rapid diuresis, which reduces intravascular plasma volume and helps to withdraw water from the extracellular space in the brain. Glucocorticoids, typically as dexamethasone 50 to 100 mg by IV bolus, will require hours to reduce underlying edema; vasogenic edema from brain tumors or brain abscess responds rapidly to corticosteroids, but cytotoxic edema accompanying an acute ischemic stroke or hematoma seldom responds to corticosteroids.

Ultimately, however, definitive treatment of the specific cause is necessary. If such treatment is not immediately feasible, hydrocephalus often responds promptly to ventricular drainage. If temporary drainage is necessary, an external ventricular drain can be placed until the underlying obstruction is relieved. A ventriculoperitoneal shunt is the definitive treatment for chronic hydrocephalus, but it is not reliably effective for "idiopathic" normal pressure hydrocephalus. Complications of shunting include subdural hematomas and infection. Radioisotope imaging, cisternographic CSF dynamic studies, and response to the acute removal of CSF do not accurately predict who will improve after shunting.

Idiopathic Intracranial Hypertension

Idiopathic intracranial hypertension, also called benign intracranial hypertension or pseudotumor cerebri, refers to elevated ICP that develops in an otherwise healthy individual without evidence of a structural CNS abnormality. Most patients are obese young women, but the disorder can also occur in men, thin patients, older adults, and children. Idiopathic intracranial hypertension can be associated with a variety of systemic disorders and medications (Table 457–10), but the direct cause of ICP elevation is usually unknown. Chronic elevations of ICP can lead to the "empty sella syndrome" (Chapter 237), which refers to enlargement of the sella turcica due to an incompetent diaphragma sellae leading to CT or MRI evidence of CSF in the sella; the result is a compressed but functioning pituitary gland.

Patients usually present with headache that may be accompanied by visual disturbances, including visual loss, nausea, vomiting, diplopia, tinnitus, and vertigo. Examination is notable for bilateral papilledema in an otherwise healthy patient. Loss of vision, which is the most feared complication, is uncommon. Visual fields typically reveal an enlarged blind spot due to the papilledema, but no other visual impairment. Diplopia can occur from an abducens palsy as a false localizing sign.

The diagnosis is established by excluding any structural cause of elevated ICP by MRI. Magnetic resonance venography (MRV) also should be performed to exclude dural venous sinus thrombosis or stenosis. Lumbar puncture is performed after neuroimaging and is required to confirm the diagnosis by establishing an elevated opening pressure, frequently greater than 300 mm H_2O; however, the composition of the fluid is normal, and the protein concentration is typically in the low-normal range (less than 20 mg/dL).

The need to treat chronic intractable elevation of ICP is based on the patient's symptoms and serial visual field testing. Headache or new or progressive visual loss on eye examination or perimetry testing should trigger one or more of five treatments: (1) weight reduction, e.g., 20 lb, and/or correction of underlying endocrinologic or hematologic disorders; (2) repeated lumbar punctures; (3) acute pharmacologic treatments, including corticosteroids, loop diuretics, and acetazolamide, although corticosteroids can contribute to weight gain, and their tapering may exacerbate the syndrome; (4) ventriculoperitoneal or lumboperitoneal shunt; and (5) fenestration of the optic nerve sheath, especially for patients with persistently elevated ICP and deteriorating vision. Outcome is variable: spontaneous remissions may occur; clinical improvement is not always accompanied by a reduction in CSF pressure; and the CSF pressure may remain persistently elevated despite intervention. Furthermore, patients with

Table 457–9 • EMERGENCY TREATMENT OF ELEVATED INTRACRANIAL PRESSURE IN ACUTELY DECOMPENSATING PATIENTS

THERAPY	TREATMENT	ONSET (DURATION OF ACTION)	OTHER
Hyperventilation	Lower $PaCO_2$ to 25–30 mm Hg	Seconds (minutes)	Usually requires intubation and mechanical ventilation
Osmotherapy	Mannitol 0.5–2 g/kg IV, repeat as necessary	Minutes (hours)	Brisk diuresis Requires Foley catheter Strict attention to electrolytes
Corticosteroids	Dexamethasone 50–100 mg IV, followed by 50–100 mg/day in divided doses	Hours (days)	Most effective on vasogenic edema (tumors, abscesses) Less effective on cytotoxic edema (stroke)

Table 457–10 • SYSTEMIC AND IATROGENIC CONDITIONS ASSOCIATED WITH BENIGN INTRACRANIAL HYPERTENSION

COMMONLY PRESCRIBED DRUGS
Nalidixic acid
Nitrofurantoin
Phenytoin
Sulfonamides
Tetracycline
Vitamin A
Retinoic acid (*cis* or *trans*)

ENDOCRINE AND METABOLIC DISORDERS
Addison's disease
Cushing's syndrome
Hypoparathyroidism
Menarche, pregnancy, oral contraceptives
Obesity (often associated with irregular menses)
Corticosteroid therapy or withdrawal

HEMATOLOGIC DISORDERS
Cryoglobulinemia
Iron deficiency anemia

MISCELLANEOUS DISORDERS
Dural venous sinus obstruction or thrombosis
Head trauma
Internal jugular vein ligation
Systemic lupus erythematosus
Middle ear disease

Table 457–11 • CAUSES OF INTRACRANIAL HYPOTENSION

Postlumbar puncture
CSF leak following CNS surgery or trauma
CSF fistula
Post-thoracotomy leak into pleural space
Spontaneous/idiopathic dural tear

CNS = central nervous system; CSF = cerebrospinal fluid.

chronically elevated ICP from idiopathic intracranial hypertension never develop hydrocephalus, so CSF pressure and ventriculomegaly are not linked.

INTRACRANIAL HYPOTENSION

Low CSF pressure (Table 457–11) can cause clinical symptoms that are usually mild but are occasionally severe and debilitating. Postural headaches occur within 30 seconds of assuming the erect posture and subside completely when the patient lies flat (Chapter 428). The headaches, which are usually located bifrontally or occipitally, are typically severe, generalized, and throbbing. Headaches may be accompanied by nausea, dizziness, photophobia, neck stiffness, and, rarely, an abducens nerve palsy. All symptoms are relieved when the patient lies down.

Intracranial hypotension occurs most commonly after lumbar puncture or after an idiopathic tear of the spinal dura. Evidence suggests that new "atraumatic" needles, as well as smaller bore needles and few passes of the needle to perform the lumbar puncture, are associated with a lower incidence of postspinal headache. In most patients, symptoms resolve spontaneously and can be treated with simple analgesics. Some patients develop persistent, symptomatic intracranial hypotension that does not respond to simple measures. In patients whose symptoms are persistent or disabling, an epidural blood patch is performed by injecting approximately 10 mL of the patient's own blood into the epidural space to seal the presumed dural leak. Occasionally, CSF radioisotope studies must be performed to identify the site of the leak so that surgical repair of the dura can be performed.

1. Forsyth PA, Weaver S, Fulton D, et al: Prophylactic anticonvulsants in patients with brain tumour. Can J Neurol Sci 2003;30:106–112.
2. Glantz MJ, Cole BF, Forsyth PA, et al: Practice parameter: Anticonvulsant prophylaxis in patients with newly diagnosed brain tumors. Report of the Quality Standards Subcommittee of the American Academy of Neurology. Neurology 2000;54:1886–1893.
3. Agnelli G, Piovella F, Buoncristiani P, et al: Enoxaparin plus compression stockings compared with compression stockings alone in the prevention of venous thromboembolism after elective neurosurgery. N Engl J Med 1998;339:80–85.
4. Shapiro WR, Green SB, Burger PC, et al: Randomized trial of three chemotherapy regimens and two radiotherapy regimens in postoperative treatment of malignant glioma. Brain Tumor Cooperative Group Trial 8001. J Neurosurg 1989;71:1–9.
5. Karim AB, Afra D, Cornu P, et al: Randomized trial on the efficacy of radiotherapy for cerebral low grade glioma in the adult. Int J Radiat Oncol Biol Phys 2002;52:316–324.
6. Patchell RA, Tibbs PA, Regine WF, et al: Postoperative radiotherapy in the treatment of single metastases to the brain. A randomized trial. JAMA 1998;280;1485–1529.
7. Patchell RA, Tibbs PA, Walsh JW, et al: A randomized trial of surgery in the treatment of single metastases to the brain. N Engl J Med 1990;322:494–500.

SUGGESTED READINGS
Behin A, Hoang-Xuan K, Carpentier AF, et al: Primary brain brain tumours in adults. Lancet 2003;361:323–331. *Overview of genetics, diagnosis, and treatment.*
Buckner JC, Gesme D Jr, O'Fallon JR, et al: Phase II trial of procarbazine, lomustine, and vincristine as initial therapy for patients with low-grade oligodendroglioma or oligoastrocytoma: Efficacy and associations with chromosomal abnormalities. J Clin Oncol 2003;21:251–255. *This study demonstrates the chemosensitivity of oligodendrogliomas and mixed gliomas.*
DeAngelis LM, Gutin PH, Leibel SA, Posner JB: Intracranial Tumors. Diagnosis and Treatment. London, Martin Dunitz, 2002. *A comprehensive text on all CNS tumors.*
Flickinger JC, Kondziolka D, Maitz AH, et al: Gamma knife radiosurgery of imaging-diagnosed intracranial meningioma. Int J Radiat Oncol Biol Phys 2003;56:801–806. *Stereotactic radiosurgery is effective for meningiomas.*
Mokri B: Spontaneous intracranial hypotension. Curr Neurol Neurosci Rep 2001;1:109–117. *An excellent summary of the clinical features of intracranial hypotension and its treatment.*
Taylor RE, Bailey CC, Robinson K, et al: Results of a randomized study of preradiation chemotherapy versus radiotherapy alone for nonmetastatic medulloblastoma: The International Society of Paediatric Oncology/United Kingdom Children's Cancer Study Group PNET-3 Study. J Clin Oncol 2003;21:1581–1591. *Chemotherapy should be added to craniospinal RT for all newly diagnosed patients with medulloblastoma.*

458 NUTRITIONAL AND ALCOHOL-RELATED NEUROLOGIC DISORDERS

John C. M. Brust

In developing countries, nutritional neurologic diseases are usually the result of starvation or a restricted diet. In developed countries, the major causes are alcoholism and, less often, malabsorption syndromes, chronic illness with cachexia, food faddism, psychiatric disease, infantile malnutrition, and, rarely, genetic disorders. The most clearly defined nutritional disorders of the nervous system are associated with deficiency of particular vitamins—organic compounds that are required for normal metabolic functions but are not synthesized in the body (Chapter 231). Vitamins are either water-soluble or fat-soluble. Deficiency of fat-soluble vitamins is a feature of malabsorption disorders (e.g., unavailability of bile acids, pancreatic insufficiency, sprue). Except for cobalamin, deficiency of water-soluble vitamins is usually secondary to inadequate intake. Such malnutrition seldom produces selective avitaminosis, and the resulting neurologic symptoms and signs therefore generally reflect multiple deficiencies.

Excessive intake of certain fat-soluble vitamins can be toxic. Symptomatic hypervitaminosis is rarely seen with water-soluble vitamins, which are much more rapidly excreted, except for megadose pyridoxine.

Water-Soluble Vitamins

THIAMINE (VITAMIN B₁). Thiamine in the body is converted to thiamine pyrophosphate, which is a coenzyme at a number of steps in glucose metabolism. Although the adult daily requirement seldom exceeds 2 mg, limited body storage means that inadequate intake can produce symptomatic deficiency in only a few weeks or months. In developing countries, thiamine deficiency most often produces beri-beri, with cardiac high-output failure and sensorimotor polyneuropathy. In North America and Europe, thiamine deficiency most often affects alcoholics and causes the Wernicke-Korsakoff syndrome.

NIACIN. Niacin, also called nicotinic acid, is converted in the body to nicotinamide adenine dinucleotide (NAS) or nicotinamide adenine dinucleotide phosphate, which are coenzymes in tissue respiration. Deficiency of niacin or its precursor tryptophan causes pellagra, a characteristic triad of dermatologic, gastrointestinal, and neurologic symptoms. An erythematous and later hyperpigmented rash appears on light-exposed areas. Glossitis and enteritis can be severe, with nausea, vomiting, and watery or bloody diarrhea. Neurologic abnormalities include altered mentation (irritability, insomnia, and fatigue progressing to depression, impaired memory, dementia, psychosis, delirium, or coma), sensorimotor polyneuropathy, myelopathy, seizures, cerebellar ataxia, parkinsonism, retinitis, and optic atrophy. A pathologic characteristic is widespread central nervous system (CNS) neuronal chromatolysis. In developed countries, pellagra is most often encountered in alcoholics, in whom additional nutritional deficiencies are likely to be present. Treatment is with niacin or nicotinamide plus other vitamins. Response is usually rapid, but mental abnormalities can be permanent.

Niacin is used to treat hyperlipidemia, and large doses can be associated with flushing, vomiting, diarrhea, hepatic dysfunction, lactic acidosis, delirium, and retinal maculopathy.

PYRIDOXINE (VITAMIN B₆). Vitamin B₆ consists of pyridoxine, pyridoxol, and pyridoxamine, each of which is converted in the body to pyridoxal phosphate, a cofactor for several enzymes. Pyridoxine deficiency causes seizures and sensorimotor polyneuropathy and probably contributes to the neurologic manifestations of pellagra. More common than dietary deficiency of pyridoxine are conditions of pyridoxine dependency. Isoniazid inhibits an enzyme that converts pyridoxine to its active form, and hydralazine converts pyridoxine to an inactive hydrazone; patients receiving either of these drugs can develop peripheral neuropathy or even CNS symptoms unless supplemental pyridoxine is given.

A severe sensory polyneuropathy affects persons taking pyridoxine in megadoses (2 to 6 g/day for 2 to 40 months). Doses in excess of 100 mg/day are never indicated and are unwise, because the lower limit of toxicity has not been defined. Improvement follows pyridoxine withdrawal but typically requires months to years.

COBALAMIN (VITAMIN B₁₂). Deficiency of cobalamin damages the entire neuraxis, with combinations of polyneuropathy, myelopathy ("combined systems disease," "subacute combined degeneration"), encephalopathy, and, less often, optic neuropathy (Chapter 175). More than one third of patients with documented cobalamin deficiency have neurologic symptoms and signs. Some patients have earlier fatigue, glossitis, anorexia, vomiting, weight loss, generalized weakness, or syncope; in most patients, however, the earliest symptoms are sensory, with paresthesias and numbness in the hands and feet and an ataxic gait resulting from proprioceptive loss. Sensory loss is secondary to peripheral neuropathy, myelopathy, or both. With progression, leg weakness and impaired manual dexterity are noted. Hyperactive tendon reflexes and extensor plantar responses reflect corticospinal tract involvement; decreased tendon reflexes also occur, reflecting peripheral neuropathy. Mental symptoms, which rarely occur without other neurologic abnormalities, include memory loss, personality change, dementia, and paranoid psychosis with hallucinations ("megaloblastic madness"). Less frequent symptoms include impotence, urinary incontinence, decreased visual acuity, and anosmia.

Pathologic features include swelling and vacuolization of myelin sheaths in the central nervous system, initially affecting the dorsal columns of the spinal cord and then the corticospinal tracts; eventually, over months or years, these changes become widespread and diffuse. Frontal lobe white matter may show patchy demyelination. Nerve conduction studies reveal sensorimotor polyneuropathy with both demyelinating and axonal features.

Cobalamin deficiency is present in up to 15% of elderly people, who often have other reasons for disturbances of cognition and gait. The diagnosis is thus easy to overlook.

More than one fourth of patients with cobalamin deficiency and neurologic symptoms have normal hematocrit levels, mean erythrocyte volumes, or both; neurologic abnormalities tend to be more severe in these patients than in those with anemia or macrocytosis. Furthermore, some patients with clinically significant cobalamin deficiency have low-normal serum cobalamin levels. The diagnosis in such instances can be confirmed by the presence of increased serum levels of methylmalonic acid and homocysteine (Chapter 175). Conversely, in subjects with falsely low serum cobalamin levels— a not uncommon occurrence—clinically significant cobalamin deficiency can be excluded by finding normal serum levels of these metabolites.

Treatment of cobalamin deficiency is with vitamin B₁₂, which can be given orally in high doses except in patients with malabsorption (Chapter 175). Most patients either make a complete neurologic recovery or improve, but improvement may take 3 months to begin and may then continue over months or even years.

Nitrous oxide oxidizes cobalamin, rendering inactive the cobalamin-dependent enzyme methionine synthase. Chronic recreational use of nitrous oxide can produce the symptoms and signs of subacute combined degeneration in the presence of normal serum cobalamin levels (or precipitate such symptoms in subjects with low levels).

Patients with acquired immunodeficiency syndrome (AIDS) often have low serum cobalamin levels, which seem to predict a more rapid progression of disease and increased neurologic abnormalities. Vacuolating myelopathy pathologically indistinguishable from combined systems disease is commonly found at autopsies of AIDS patients, including those with normal serum cobalamin levels (Chapter 414). A possible cause is HIV- or cytokine-induced derangement of cobalamin-dependent transmethylation pathways.

FOLIC ACID. By donating a methyl group to cobalamin, folic acid becomes available to participate in DNA synthesis; folate supplementation in patients with cobalamin deficiency probably accounts for some cases of neurologic impairment in the absence of anemia. Folate deficiency results in megaloblastic anemia. There is no good evidence that folate deficiency in adults causes either central or peripheral nervous system disease (Chapter 175).

Folic acid supplementation during pregnancy can prevent the occurrence of neural tube defects such as spina bifida and anencephaly; in the United States, fortication of flour provides roughly 0.2 mg folic acid daily. Additional supplementation of 0.4 mg daily is currently recommended for women who might become pregnant. Some studies suggest increasing benefit up to 5 mg daily. Such doses would mandate monitoring of serum cobalamin levels.

OTHER WATER-SOLUBLE VITAMINS. Because other deficiencies are nearly always present, the role of riboflavin, pantothenic acid, or biotin deficiency in neurologic or other disease is difficult to determine. Anecdotal reports and animal experiments suggest a possible relationship to sensory polyneuropathy and myalgia.

Fat-Soluble Vitamins

VITAMIN A (RETINOL). Retinol is necessary for the integrity of epithelial tissue and the retina. Deficiency (associated with malnutrition, malabsorption, liver disease, myxedema, diabetes mellitus, or renal failure) causes visual loss secondary to both retinal and corneal damage. Hypervitaminosis A, most often affecting adolescents taking excessive dosage for acne, causes increased intracranial pressure, which, if prolonged, can result in visual loss.

VITAMIN D (CALCIFEROL, CHOLECALCIFEROL). Synthesized in the skin, vitamin D is further metabolized in the liver and kidney to its active form, 1,25-dihydroxycholecalciferol (Chapter 257). Deficiency is associated with malnutrition, lack of sunlight, malabsorption, liver disease, renal failure, and phenytoin or barbiturate administration; several hereditary disorders are also characterized by vitamin D resistance. Hypovitaminosis D causes rickets in children and osteomalacia in adults. This severe bone disease can produce spinal cord or nerve root symptoms, and hypocalcemia causes tetany, altered mentation, and seizures. Myopathic weakness has been described.

Hypervitaminosis D, from excessive vitamin D intake, malignant or granulomatous disease, hyperparathyroidism, or other endocrinopathies, causes life-threatening hypercalcemia with bone, kidney, and neurologic disease (Chapter 260). Symptoms include weakness, lassitude, impaired memory, dementia, depression, paranoia, hallucinations, delirium, and coma. Treatment includes saline administration, furosemide diuresis, and sometimes corticosteroids.

VITAMIN E (TOCOPHEROLS, TOCOTRIENOLS). Vitamin E reduces peroxide production, and deficiency occurs in malabsorption disorders, including biliary atresia and cystic fibrosis. In the hereditary disorder abetalipoproteinemia (Bassen-Kornzweig syndrome), steatorrhea, acanthocytosis, decreased serum levels of cholesterol and triglycerides, retinitis pigmentosa, ophthalmoplegia, peripheral neuropathy, spinocerebellar degeneration with ataxia, amyotrophy, and dorsal column and pyramidal signs are seen. Another hereditary disorder, isolated vitamin E deficiency, clinically resembles Friedreich's ataxia; abnormal vitamin E absorption is the cause.

A single study suggests that vitamin E slows the progression of Alzheimer's disease. Studies are in progress to determine whether vitamin E (as well as vitamin C and zinc) affect the course of age-related macular degeneration.

Although the recommended daily allowance of vitamin E is 30 IU, most supplements contain 200 to 800 IU. Reports of possible toxicity include hemorrhagic stroke in men who smoke and acceleration of disease in patients with retinitis pigmentosa.

VITAMIN K (PHYTONADIONE, MENAQUINONES). Neurologic symptoms in vitamin K deficiency are the result of bleeding. Intracranial hemorrhage may occur in the setting of trauma or hemorrhagic disease of the newborn.

Alcohol-Related Disorders

Alcohol intoxication and withdrawal are discussed in Chapter 17.

WERNICKE-KORSAKOFF SYNDROME. Wernicke's syndrome evolves over days to weeks and has three features that may occur alone or together: (1) abnormal eye movements, which begin with nystagmus and paresis of lateral rectus or horizontal gaze and progress to complete ophthalmoplegia, usually with pupillary sparing; (2) ataxia of gait and stance, often accompanied by lower-limb intention tremor and dysmetria (the arms are usually not affected, and dysarthria is usually absent); and (3) altered mentation, the earliest signs of which are inattentiveness, mental slowing (abulia), and impaired memory. If patients are not treated, they become lethargic, and their condition progresses to coma and death. Pathologically characteristic lesions— loss of neuronal processes, gliosis, and sometimes endothelial proliferation and petechiae—involve the medial thalamus and hypothalamus, midbrain periaqueductal gray matter, and floor of the fourth ventricle. In the cerebellum, neuronal loss affects especially Purkinje cells and is maximal in the vermis.

The diagnosis of thiamine deficiency is supported by decreased levels of erythrocyte transketolase, but if Wernicke's syndrome is a serious consideration, treatment must not be delayed. To minimize permanent neurologic residua, thiamine (50 to 100 mg) plus other water-soluble vitamins are given parenterally. The therapeutic response is often dramatic. Eye movements sometimes begin to improve within a few hours, and except for residual nystagmus, may be normal within 1 or 2 weeks. Ataxia tends to improve less completely; more than half of patients are left with a broad-based, unsteady gait. More serious are persisting mental symptoms. Drowsiness, inattentiveness, and apathy tend to clear with treatment, but an amnestic disorder, termed Korsakoff's syndrome, often persists and includes both anterograde and retrograde memory loss, sometimes accompanied by confabulation, which is out of proportion to additional mental abnormalities. Once established, the memory disorder is permanent in the majority of patients.

In alcoholics and others with low thiamine stores, administration of glucose can precipitate Wernicke's syndrome. Patients receiving parenteral glucose (e.g., for parenteral alimentation or in an acute setting for diagnosis and treatment of unexplained seizures or coma) should also be given parenteral thiamine (and other water-soluble vitamins).

PERIPHERAL NEUROPATHY. Eighty percent of patients with Wernicke-Korsakoff disease have peripheral neuropathy (Chapter 462), and many alcoholics have peripheral neuropathy without other neurologic symptoms or signs. The earliest symptoms are sensory in nature, with paresthesias or pain in the feet and later the hands. Absent ankle tendon reflexes and impaired distal vibratory and pain sensation usually precede proprioceptive loss or weakness, but progression to a severe sensorimotor disorder can occur, with proximal as well as distal weakness in addition to vagal symptoms (e.g., hoarseness, dysphagia) and autonomic signs (e.g., tachycardia, postural hypotension). The neuropathy is axonal in origin, with secondary demyelination; although its cause is likely nutritional, the relative contributions of thiamine and other vitamins (as well as direct ethanol toxicity) are uncertain.

CEREBELLAR DEGENERATION. Many alcoholics manifest cerebellar vermal degeneration without other clinical or histologic evidence of Wernicke-Korsakoff syndrome, raising the possibility that cerebellar degeneration, although more likely nutritional than toxic in origin, may be less related than Wernicke-Korsakoff syndrome to thiamine deficiency per se.

OPTIC NEUROPATHY. Optic neuropathy in alcoholics—formerly called "tobacco-alcohol amblyopia"—is also nutritional in origin, but the particular deficiencies are uncertain, and the possibility of additional direct toxicity from ethanol, or even cyanide in tobacco smoke, remains controversial. Bilateral visual loss, usually with central or centrocecal scotomas, may evolve subacutely with swollen optic discs. Improvement follows treatment with multivitamins, but residual visual impairment and temporal disc pallor are often present.

ALCOHOLIC DEMENTIA. In experimental animals, ethanol is directly toxic to neurons, and evidence continues to mount that such toxicity in humans can cause dementia (Chapter 433) in the absence of nutritional disturbance. Nonalcoholics with thiamine deficiency and beri-beri seldom develop full-blown Wernicke-Korsakoff disease, raising the possibility that excessive ethanol plus nutritional deficiency can produce a pathologic condition that neither insult would cause alone.

MYOPATHY. Alcoholic myopathy (Chapter 463) can be either chronic, with progressive proximal weakness, or acute, with rhabdomyolysis, severe muscle weakness and pain, and myoglobinuria causing renal failure. Serum creatine kinase levels are elevated, and electromyography reflects myopathy. Such patients are often malnourished, but direct toxicity is more important than nutritional deficiency. Other factors, most importantly hypokalemia, are often present and contribute to the muscle necrosis and myoglobinuria. Symptoms sometimes begin or accelerate during a binge, and improvement follows abstinence.

MARCHIAFAVA-BIGNAMI DISEASE. Marchiafava-Bignami disease, which occurs almost exclusively in alcoholics, is defined by characteristic demyelinating lesions of the corpus callosum. Early symptoms include depression, paranoia, psychosis, or dementia. Major motor seizures are common, and hemiparesis, aphasia, abnormal movements, and ataxia can progress to coma and death over a few months. Computed tomography (CT) and magnetic resonance imaging (MRI) can detect the lesions, and in a few cases, clinical improvement has been accompanied by regression of the CT or MRI abnormalities. The cause of Marchiafava-Bignami disease, including the role—if any—of nutritional deficiency, is unknown.

ALCOHOLIC LIVER DISEASE. In the United States, nearly all deaths from cirrhosis in people older than 45 years of age are caused by ethanol, and hepatic encephalopathy must always be considered in an alcoholic with altered mentation (Chapters 155 to 157). A syndrome of altered mentation, myoclonus, and myelopathy sometimes follows portocaval shunting in alcoholic cirrhotics. Some alcoholics with repeated bouts of hepatic encephalopathy develop "acquired chronic hepatocerebral degeneration," with dementia, dysarthria, ataxia, tremor, choreoathetosis, and asterixis.

HYPOGLYCEMIA. Hypoglycemia (Chapter 243) in alcoholics is the consequence of decreased intake, lack of liver glycogen stores, and, especially, failure of gluconeogenesis secondary to depletion of nicotinamide adenine dinucleotide (a cofactor for the ethanol metabolizing enzyme, alcohol dehydrogenase). Symptomatic hypoglycemia (e.g., seizures or coma) therefore often occurs in the midst of a binge and is easily mistaken for intoxication or withdrawal. The result can be permanent brain damage.

ALCOHOLIC KETOACIDOSIS. Ethanol-induced impairment of fatty acid oxidation, coupled with vomiting and dehydration at the end of a binge, can lead to accumulation of β-hydroxybutyric acid and lactic acid, obtundation, and Kussmaul respirations. Blood glucose may be normal, low, or elevated (Chapter 242). Other causes of acidosis with a large anion gap—including methanol or ethylene glycol poisoning—must be excluded.

INFECTION IN ALCOHOLICS. Alcoholics are often immunocompromised, and altered mentation must always raise the possibility of CNS infection, especially bacterial or tuberculous meningitis.

TRAUMA IN ALCOHOLICS. Alcoholics often have coagulopathies, including thrombocytopenia. Acute brain or spinal injury or chronic subdural hematoma (Chapters 430 and 431) must not be overlooked, especially in intoxicated subjects.

ALCOHOL AND STROKE. As with coronary artery disease, low-to-moderate doses of ethanol decrease the risk of ischemic stroke, whereas higher amounts increase it. Ethanol in any amount increases the risk of hemorrhagic stroke in a dose-dependent fashion.

FETAL ALCOHOL SYNDROME. Ethanol is teratogenic. Intrauterine exposure to large doses results in characteristic facial anomalies, growth deficiency, and mental retardation, which can be severe and lifelong. Exposure to lesser amounts can cause subtle cognitive and behavioral abnormalities without other somatic features. Binge drinking is especially dangerous, but a safe level of intake is not defined, and much of the damage seems to occur early in pregnancy (i.e., before a woman is aware that she is pregnant).

CENTRAL PONTINE MYELINOLYSIS. Often caused by over-vigorous correction of hyponatremia (Chapter 112), central pontine myelinolysis is not restricted to alcoholics, but they are especially vulnerable. The major clinical sign is quadriparesis, and corresponding lesions in the basis pontis can sometimes be seen on MRI. Prevention is more effective than treatment, which is simply supportive. In most patients who survive, clinical signs improve.

SUGGESTED READINGS

Misra UK, Kalita J, Das A: Vitamin B$_{12}$ deficiency neurological syndromes: A clinical, MRI and electrodiagnostic study. Electromyogr Clin Neurophysiol 2003;43:57–64. *Electrodiagnostic and imaging findings before and after treatment in patients with neurologically symptomatic cobalamin deficiency.*

Sano M, Ernesto C, Thomas RG, et al: A controlled trial of selegiline, alpha-tocopherol, or both as treatment for Alzheimer's disease. N Engl J Med 1997;336:1216–1222. *Restricted to patients with moderately severe disease, this study found vitamin E to be beneficial.*

Wald NJ, Law MR, Morris JK, Wald DS: Quantifying the effect of folic acid. Lancet 2001;358:2069–2073. *A review of studies of folic acid supplementation and neural-tube defects.*

Willett WC, Stampfer MJ: What vitamins should I be taking, Doctor? N Engl J Med 2001;345:1819–1824. *A review of who needs vitamin supplementation and why.*

459 CONGENITAL, DEVELOPMENTAL, AND NEUROCUTANEOUS DISORDERS

A. James Barkovich
Ruben I. Kuzniecky

MALFORMATIONS OF THE CEREBRAL CORTEX

The heterogeneous malformations of cerebral cortical development result from disturbed development of cells that normally participate in formation of the cerebral cortex. The known causes include intrauterine infection, intrauterine ischemia, and chromosomal mutations (i.e., germline, mosaic, and large deletions). When small areas of the brain are involved, epilepsy typically develops in the first or second decade, and patients have minor static neurologic dysfunction and normal intellect. Patients with involvement of larger areas of involved brain often have cognitive deficits and more severe neurologic dysfunction in addition to epilepsy. Malformations are best established by magnetic resonance imaging (MRI).

BALLOON CELL CORTICAL DYSPLASIA

Focal cortical dysplasia is caused by abnormal neuronal and glial proliferation. The histology is characterized by cortical dyslamination, neuronomegaly, and dysplastic "balloon cells." Affected patients often have intractable partial epilepsy that correlates with the anatomic location of the lesion. Seizures may begin at any age but most frequently within the first 2 decades. If extensive regions of the brain are involved, patients may have neurologic impairment such as mental subnormality and hemiparesis. The diagnosis can be made with cranial MRI by detecting focal gyral thickening or blurring of the cortical-white matter junction on T1-weighted images and signal changes of subjacent white matter on T2-weighted or FLAIR images, but some lesions may be undetectable. Management includes medical control of seizures, but surgical resection of the epileptogenic focus is often necessary for complete remission (Chapter 434).

LISSENCEPHALY AND BAND HETEROTOPIA SPECTRUM

The term *lissencephaly* (meaning smooth brain) describes a group of disorders caused by arrested migration of neurons to the cerebral cortex. Lissencephaly is diagnosed in childhood; most patients have severe developmental delay, microcephaly, intractable seizures, and premature death. Most affected children have mutations of chromosome 17p13.3 or Xq22; patients with the former mutation have more severe cortical malformation of the posterior cerebrum, and some have the Miller-Dieker syndrome, whereas those with the latter have more severe malformation of the anterior cerebrum and are often born to mothers with band heterotopia (i.e., double cortex). MRI shows a smooth cortex with minimal sulcation. Band heterotopia is a less severe form of lissencephaly, usually seen in women with Xq22 mutations. The clinical manifestations of band heterotopia are variable; seizures and mild to severe developmental delay are most common. MRI studies are diagnostic for the condition and demonstrate a band of gray matter beneath a nearly normal cortex. The thickness of the band correlates with the ultimate neurologic outcome. Management consists of seizure control and genetic counseling.

SUBEPENDYMAL NODULAR HETEROTOPIA

Subependymal nodular heterotopia is characterized by multiple bilateral gray matter nodules in the walls of the lateral ventricles. It may be X-linked (Xq28), with males much more severely affected. Clinical features include seizures starting at any age and various degrees of mental impairment (generally mild in females and severe in males). Diagnosis is by MRI, which demonstrates the typical gray matter nodules (Fig. 459–1). Treatment consists of antiepileptic agents (Chapter 434) and genetic counseling.

POLYMICROGYRIA-SCHIZENCEPHALY COMPLEX

Polymicrogyria is caused by failure of cortical organization because of in utero injury or gene mutation. Schizencephaly is thought to represent a more extensive injury or mutation in which the entire cerebral mantle is affected. Clinical features include developmental delay, pyramidal signs, motor speech dysfunction, and epilepsy; in general, the clinical abnormalities are more severe with more extensive or bilateral lesions. The diagnosis is established by MRI. Treatment is directed at control of seizures (Chapter 434).

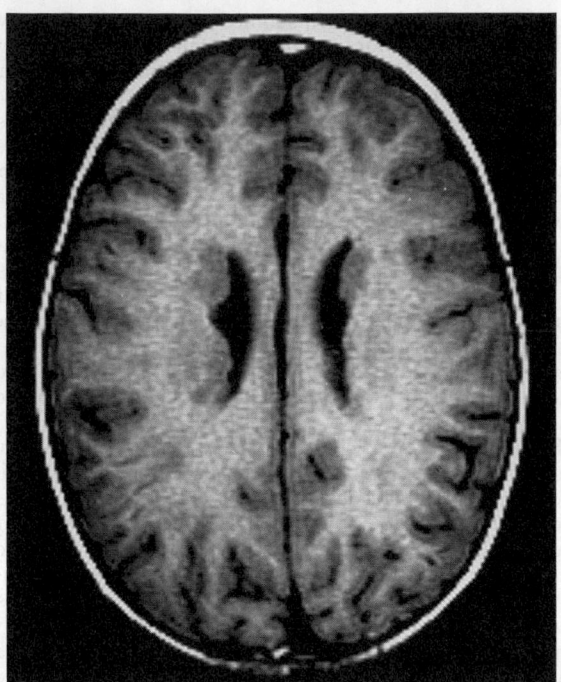

FIGURE 459–1 • T1-weighted MRI shows subependymal heterotopia in a young man with epilepsy.

MALFORMATIONS OF THE CRANIOVERTEBRAL JUNCTION AND SPINAL CORD

Developmental anomalies of the vertebral bodies (i.e., hemivertebrae, butterfly vertebrae, nonsegmentation of two or more adjacent vertebrae [Klippel-Feil anomaly], and transitional vertebrae) are frequently encountered on radiographs of patients with pain in the neck or back. Most of these anomalies are asymptomatic unless they lead to scoliosis or to accelerated degenerative changes of the spine, in which case they may cause pain or neurologic symptoms. Neurologic disability is likely if the anomalies are associated with underlying anomalies of the spinal cord, if they compress neural structures, or if they alter the flow of cerebrospinal fluid (CSF).

CHIARI MALFORMATIONS

Chiari I malformations are defined as ectopia of the cerebellar tonsils more than 5 mm below the foramen magnum. This abnormality is often incidental and asymptomatic. When clinical manifestations develop, they result from compression of neural structures or CSF pathways and may include headaches accentuated by straining or cough, lower cranial neuropathies, downbeat nystagmus, progressive ataxia, posterior column signs, or dissociated anesthesia of the trunk and extremities. Although the malformation is congenital, symptoms often begin in the third and fourth decades or even later. It is often difficult to separate symptoms due to the Chiari malformation from those of associated syringohydromyelia or syringobulbia (discussed later). Similar signs and symptoms may result from multiple sclerosis (Chapter 448) or from other causes of neural compression of the craniocervical junction, including bony anomalies, metabolic bone diseases that lead to invagination of the base of the skull, and tumors. Definitive diagnosis is made with MRI, which shows the compressed tonsils extending through the foramen magnum into the cervical subarachnoid space (Fig. 459–2). Treatment is surgical: decompression of the craniocervical junction.

Chiari II malformations (i.e., Arnold-Chiari malformations) are characterized by caudal elongation of the cerebellum and lower brain stem through the foramen magnum. Open spinal dysraphism (i.e., myelomeningocele) and hydrocephalus are almost always present. Symptoms are those of dysfunction of the brain stem, cerebellum, and spinal cord. Brain stem dysfunction may result from intrinsic malformation or compression of neural structures at the C1 level. Other brain anomalies are common, especially anomalies of the corpus

spinal cord symptoms. The long-term prognosis for patients with such lesions, if no associated cause is found, is believed to be good. Most experts believe that syringes form as a result of alterations in the flow of CSF that cause variations in pressure in different parts of the subarachnoid space. The variations in pressure create hydrostatic forces that drive CSF into the spinal cord. Causes of these alterations in CSF pressure include bony narrowing of the foramen magnum (as in achondroplasia or basilar invagination, Chiari I and II malformations, intramedullary and extramedullary tumors) and subarachnoid scarring (from trauma, hemorrhage, or infection). In patients with Chiari II malformations, hydrocephalus may result in syrinx formation. Rostral or caudal extension of the cyst may subsequently result from rapid changes in intraspinal pressure, such as those caused by coughing, straining, or sneezing.

Clinical Manifestations

Symptoms of syringohydromyelia most commonly begin in late adolescence or early adulthood and progress irregularly, with long periods of stability. In most instances, the syrinx affects the cervical spinal cord. Classically, patients have asymmetrical segmental weakness and atrophy of the hands and arms, loss of upper limb deep tendon reflexes, and dissociated sensory loss (with impaired perception of pain and temperature but preservation of light touch and proprioception) in the neck, arms, and upper part of the trunk. In the legs, muscle tone is increased, and the reflexes are hyperactive. Some patients experience deep pain in the neck and arms. However, the clinical manifestations depend on the cross-sectional and vertical extent of cordal involvement; symptoms may be unilateral or confined to the lower extremities. Extension into the medulla may cause nystagmus or lower cranial neuropathies. Moreover, symptoms from the syrinx may be difficult to differentiate from those of the associated craniocervical junction anomaly. When the syrinx is post-traumatic, symptoms develop after a latent period that can be more than 20 years. Ascending and descending levels of weakness or sensory impairment typically develop in affected patients.

Diagnosis

The diagnosis is made by MRI (see Fig. 459–2), which defines the extent of the syrinx. In addition, MRI may show the associated craniocervical junction lesion, arachnoidal scarring, or tumor that is the cause. Electromyography reveals active and chronic denervation in the muscles of affected extremities. Nerve conduction studies are typically normal because the lesion is located central to the dorsal root ganglia. CSF is normal unless an inflammatory or neoplastic process is the cause.

Rx Treatment

If possible, treatment is directed at the cause of the syrinx. In patients with Chiari II malformations, adequate shunting of the lateral ventricles may result in collapse of the syrinx. Syringohydromyelia in patients with spinal tumors is treated by resecting the tumor. Patients with altered CSF dynamics caused by narrowing of the craniocervical junction are treated by decompression of the bony foramen magnum, sometimes accompanied by dural grafts to increase the size of the subarachnoid space. Patients with arachnoidal scarring are typically treated by insertion of a syringopleural or syringoperitoneal shunt. Treatment of patients with benign extramedullary tumors and craniocervical junction lesions may arrest the process and provide long-term relief of symptoms. In patients with arachnoidal scarring, the relief is often only transient.

NEUROCUTANEOUS DISORDERS

The neurocutaneous syndromes are congenital disorders characterized by dysplastic and neoplastic lesions primarily involving the nervous system and skin. Of the more than 40 syndromes, the most important are neurofibromatosis, tuberous sclerosis, and Sturge-Weber and von Hippel-Lindau syndromes.

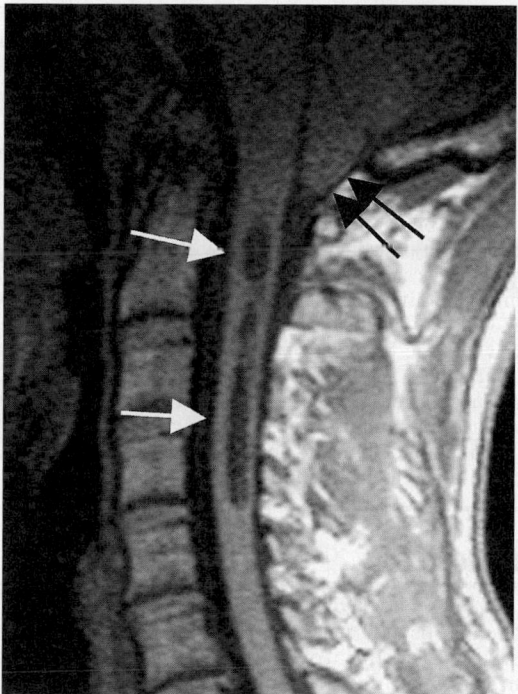

FIGURE 459–2 • Sagittal MRI shows low, pointed cerebellar tonsils (i.e., Chiari I malformation; black arrows) and dilated central canal of the spinal cord (i.e., syringohydromyelia; white arrows).

callosum and gray matter heterotopia. Treatment is surgical repair of the myelomeningocele, relief of hydrocephalus, and occasionally, cervical bony decompression. The prognosis depends on the level (i.e., better for sacral, worse for thoracic) and extent of the myelomeningocele and on the severity of associated brain anomalies.

TETHERED SPINAL CORD

In the tethered spinal cord, an anomalous filum terminale results in a lack of normal ascent of the conus medullaris to the L1 vertebral level or an ischemic or metabolic disturbance of the most caudal portions of the spinal cord. Associated spinal anomalies are common and include diastematomyelia (i.e., split cord malformation), spinal lipomas, dermal sinuses, and fibrolipomas of the filum terminale. An increased incidence of cord tethering occurs among patients with anorectal malformations (i.e., anomalies of the genitourinary tract and lower gastrointestinal tract). Patients typically have urinary incontinence in conjunction with lower extremity weakness and spasticity. Males may manifest impotence. Symptoms may occur at any age but typically develop in childhood or adolescence during periods of rapid growth. Cutaneous anomalies such as focal hypertrichosis, hemangiomas, and nevi may be seen over the lumbar spine.

The differential diagnosis includes multiple sclerosis, tumors in the region of the conus medullaris, and lumbosacral hypogenesis. Definitive diagnosis is made with MRI, which shows diminished pulsations of the spinal cord, a low conus medullaris (i.e., below the bottom of the L2 vertebral body), or a thickened (i.e., more than 1 mm in diameter at the L5-S1 level) or fat-containing filum terminale.

Treatment consists of surgical release of the tethered cord. If surgery results in adequate untethering, symptoms typically do not progress and may improve.

SYRINGOHYDROMYELIA

Syringohydromyelia is a condition in which the central canal of the spinal cord (i.e., hydromyelia), the substance of the spinal cord (i.e., syringomyelia), or the brain stem (i.e., syringobulbia) is expanded by the presence of fluid under pressure. Occasionally, focal areas of mildly (2 to 3 mm) dilated central canal are discovered incidentally when MRI is performed for reasons unrelated to suspected

Neurology

NEUROFIBROMATOSIS TYPE 1

Neurofibromatosis encompasses a wide spectrum of syndromes with neurocutaneous lesions. Although at least eight variants have been described, only two are well-recognized, genetically distinct entities: NF-1 and NF-2. NF-1 corresponds to the classic disorder described by von Recklinghausen, with a prevalence of 1 in 3000 births. Although it is an autosomal dominant disease, approximately 50% of cases are clinically sporadic, with a high mutation rate.

Pathology and Pathogenesis

Neurologically important lesions in neurofibromatosis include neurofibromas, plexiform neurofibromas, optic pathway gliomas, and astrocytomas of the brain and spinal cord. Hamartomas and meningiomas may also develop.

Molecular genetic studies have demonstrated that most mutations in NF-1 occur in the parental germline. The NF-1 gene is located on chromosome 17q and encompasses about 350 kilobases of genomic DNA that encode a protein designated as neurofibromin. Neurofibromin appears to be expressed in most tissues and has multiple functions, including acting as a tumor suppressor compound; a major myelin protein is also imbedded in the NF-1 gene. Although pathogenic mutations in NF-1 are identified in approximately 75% of clinical cases, there does not appear to be any correlation between particular genotypes and phenotypes.

Clinical Manifestations

Clinical criteria for the diagnosis of NF-1 include two or more of the following: (1) six or more café au lait macules larger than 5 mm in prepubescent patients and more than 15 mm in postpubescent individuals, (2) two or more neurofibromas of any type (Fig. 476–12) or one plexiform neurofibroma, (3) axillary or inguinal freckling, (4) sphenoid bone dysplasia, (5) optic pathway glioma, (6) Lisch nodules (i.e., iris hamartomas), and (7) a family history of NF-1. Other manifestations may include learning difficulties, epilepsy, and mental retardation. Important complications may include scoliosis, gastrointestinal neurofibromas, pheochromocytomas (Chapter 241), and vascular dysplasias, including renal artery stenosis.

Diagnosis

The diagnosis is based on clinical criteria, sometimes supplemented by neuroimaging findings such as cerebellar, basal ganglia, and brain stem foci of dysmyelination; optic pathway gliomas; vascular dysplasia; and nerve sheath tumors.

Treatment

Most patients with NF-1 do not require treatment. Subcutaneous neurofibromas may be painful or disfiguring and can be excised surgically. Intraspinal and intracranial tumors are approached surgically. Optic nerve gliomas may be treated with radiation, but treatment may not affect the outcome. Genetic counseling is important and must be provided to all patients and families in whom NF-1 is present.

NEUROFIBROMATOSIS TYPE 2

NF-2, or central neurofibromatosis, is an autosomal dominant syndrome with high penetrance. The prevalence of this disorder, approximately 1 in 50,000 individuals, is much lower than that of NF-1.

Pathology and Pathogenesis

The classic pathologic abnormality in NF-2 is bilateral eighth cranial nerve schwannomas. However, multiple meningiomas and multiple other schwannomas are also common features of NF-2. Spinal cord ependymomas, meningioangiomatosis, and cerebral microhamartomas also can occur.

NF-2 differs from NF-1 in their molecular genetics. The NF-2 gene is located on chromosome 22q. The gene product (merlin) is a cytoskeletal protein. The precise function of this protein is unknown.

Clinical Manifestations

Although skin lesions may be present in up to 30% of patients with NF-2, the diagnosis is based on the presence of the following criteria: (1) bilateral eighth cranial nerve schwannomas detected by MRI or (2) a first-degree relative with NF-2 and (a) a unilateral eighth nerve schwannoma or (b) two tumors from among the following—meningioma, neurofibroma, other schwannoma, glioma, or juvenile subcapsular lenticular opacity.

The mean age of onset of symptoms in patients with NF-2 is approximately 22 years. Absence of the characteristic MRI findings in children (<12 years) does not exclude the disease. Cutaneous lesions such as cafe au lait macules and neurofibromas can be seen in up to 70%, and approximately 40% of patients have cataracts, often evident in childhood.

Treatment

Treatment is related to the complications of the illness. Surgical treatment may be indicated in patients with intramedullary spinal tumors. Surgical treatment of schwannomas and meningiomas may be indicated when there is compression of adjacent structures. Family members should be screened regularly with hearing tests and contrast-enhanced MRI. Genetic counseling should be provided to affected families.

TUBEROUS SCLEROSIS

In tuberous sclerosis complex (TSC), which may occur as a familial autosomal dominant syndrome or in sporadic form with a high rate of spontaneous mutations, hamartomatous lesions involve multiple organs at different stages in the course of the disease. The incidence of this disorder is 1 in 10,000 to 50,000.

Pathology and Pathogenesis

TSC affects tissues from different germ layers. Cutaneous and visceral lesions, including adenoma sebaceum, cardiac rhabdomyomas, and renal angiomyolipomas may occur. The central nervous system (CNS) lesions seen in this disorder include hamartomas of the cortex, hamartomas of the ventricular walls, and subependymal giant cell tumors, which typically develop in the vicinity of the foramina of Monro.

Molecular genetic studies have defined at least two loci for TSC. In TSC-1, the abnormality is localized on chromosome 9q34, but the nature of the gene protein, called hamartin, remains unclear. No missense mutations occur in TSC-1. In TSC-2, the gene abnormalities are on chromosome 16p13. This gene encodes tuberin, a guanosine triphosphatase–activating protein. The specific function of this protein is unknown. In TSC-2, all types of mutations have been reported; new mutations occur frequently. Few differences have yet been observed in the clinical phenotypes of patients with mutation of one gene or the other.

Clinical Manifestations

Seizures, mental retardation, and skin lesions occur in most patients. However, refined criteria for diagnosis have been established and include primary criteria such as hypomelanotic skin macules (i.e., ash leaf spots, sometimes visible at birth), shagreen patches, facial angiofibromas (Fig. 459–3), subungual fibromas, and imaging evidence of multiple calcified subependymal nodules, cortical tubers, or multiple retinal hamartomas. Retinal hamartomas can be seen ophthalmoscopically in about one half of the patients. Diagnosis of this condition is usually clinical and confirmed by identification of calcified or uncalcified hamartomas on imaging studies.

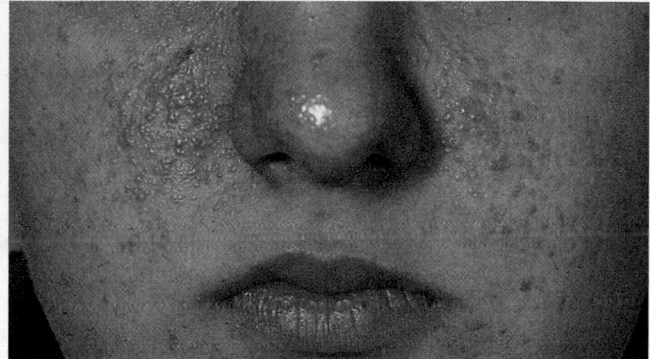

FIGURE 459–3 • Facial angiofibroma, typical of tuberous sclerosis. (From Forbes CD, Jackson WD: Color Atlas and Text of Clinical Medicine, 2nd ed. London, Mosby, 1996, with permission.)

 Treatment

Treatment is directed at the complications of the disease, particularly epilepsy. The degree of MRI-based abnormalities may correlate with the degree of neurologic disability. Neurosurgical intervention sometimes may be indicated for epilepsy and for symptomatic treatment of complications such as hydrocephalus resulting from midline giant cell tumors. Serial cardiac and renal ultrasound may be indicated in some patients because benign tumors of those organs may enlarge rapidly. Because the disorder is autosomal dominant, genetic counseling is of paramount importance in familial cases.

STURGE-WEBER SYNDROME

Sturge-Weber syndrome is a sporadic, noninherited abnormality, even though a few familial cases have been reported. The true incidence and prevalence of this disorder are poorly established, although reports have indicated that it occurs in fewer than 5 of 100,000 births.

The characteristic neurologic feature of this disorder is capillary angiomatosis of the pia mater. Associated cerebral cortical calcifications are usually seen in a pericapillary distribution and are progressive.

Clinical Manifestations

The hallmark of this disorder includes the presence of facial vascular nevi (e.g., port-wine stain) (Fig. 459–4), epilepsy, cognitive deficits, and less frequently, hemiparesis or hemiplegia, hemianopia, or glaucoma. Most patients have epilepsy, and there appears to be correlations among the degree of epilepsy, the developmental status, and the presence of hemiparesis. However, seizures never develop in some patients. A forme fruste of the syndrome has also been described without the usual skin lesion.

Diagnosis

The diagnosis is usually based on the presence of a facial nevus and imaging confirmation of intracranial pathology. MRI with contrast may be indicated in some patients, particularly in those with the forme fruste of the disorder and those in whom surgery is contemplated. Although in most cases the intracranial lesion is ipsilateral to the facial nevus, contralateral and bilateral lesions have been described.

 Treatment

Treatment is usually aimed at the epilepsy (Chapter 434). Surgical excision of epileptogenic areas corresponding to the abnormality has been successful in some individuals. When the disorder is characterized by early, intractable epilepsy and infantile hemiplegia, hemispherectomy can improve the seizures and neurodevelopmental outcome.

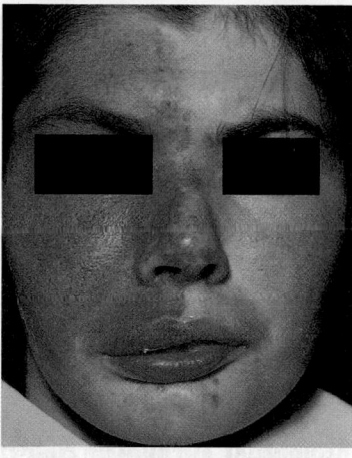

FIGURE 459–4 • Sturge-Weber syndrome. This patient has a classic diffuse capillary hemangioma in the distribution of the ophthalmic, nasociliary, and maxillary branches of the trigeminal nerve. The lesion extends backward over the anterior two thirds of the crown of the head. (From Forbes CD, Jackson WD: Color Atlas and Text of Clinical Medicine, 2nd ed. London, Mosby, 1996, with permission.)

VON HIPPEL-LINDAU DISEASE

Von Hippel-Lindau disease (i.e., CNS angiomatosis) is an autosomal dominant disorder caused by a defective tumor suppressor gene at chromosome 3p25-p26 and characterized by retinal angiomas (Chapter 465), brain (usually cerebellar) and spinal cord hemangioblastomas, renal cell carcinomas (Chapter 203), endolymphatic sac tumors, pheochromocytomas (Chapter 241), papillary cystadenomas of the epididymis, angiomas of the liver and kidney, and cysts of the pancreas, kidney, liver, and epididymis. Both sexes are affected equally. The diagnosis is established if patients have more than one CNS hemangioblastoma, one hemangioblastoma with a visceral manifestation of the disease, or one manifestation of the disease and a known family history.

Clinical Manifestations

Symptoms typically begin during the third or fourth decade. Retinal inflammation with exudate, hemorrhage, and retinal detachment from the retinal angiomas typically antedates the cerebellar complaints, but this order is not constant. Moreover, the ocular findings are nonspecific, and the retinal detachment may mask the underlying lesion. Headache, vertigo, and vomiting result from cerebellar tumors. Other findings such as dysdiadochokinesia, dysmetria, and Romberg's sign are common. It is rare for patients to be seen initially with symptoms of spinal cord or visceral lesions. Rarely, patients may have hearing loss from tumors of the endolymphatic sac.

 Treatment

Treatment is symptomatic. Retinal detachments and tumors are treated by laser therapy. Large brain tumors, renal cell carcinomas, pheochromocytomas, epididymal tumors, and endolymphatic sac tumors are treated surgically; smaller CNS tumors may be treated by gamma knife. A high index of suspicion and repeated imaging studies are necessary to detect the tumors before they metastasize or become unresectable.

SUGGESTED READINGS

Barkovich AJ, Kuzniecky RI, Jackson GD, et al: Classification system for malformations of cortical development: Update 2001. Neurology 2001;57:2168–2178. *Classification of these disorders based on their embryology, morphology, and genetics.*

Dabora SL, Jozwiak S, Franz DN, et al: Mutational analysis in a cohort of 224 tuberous sclerosis patients indicates increased severity of TSC2, compared with TSC1, disease in multiple organs. Am J Hum Genet 2001;68:64–80. *Emphasizes the differences between TSC-1 and TSC-2.*

Lonser RR, Glenn GM, Walther M, et al: von Hippel-Lindau disease. Lancet 2003;361: 2059–2067. *A comprehensive review.*

460 AUTONOMIC DISORDERS AND THEIR MANAGEMENT

Clifford B. Saper

Disorders of the autonomic nervous system are of great importance to internal medicine because they can be manifested as disorders of virtually any organ system in the body. Furthermore, central regulation of autonomic response is closely tied to neuroendocrine control, and both are often involved by central nervous system disorders. This chapter discusses disorders of the peripheral autonomic nervous system and disorders of central integration of autonomic control (Table 460–1). Aspects of neuroendocrine disease are discussed in Chapters 235, 236, and 237.

DISORDERS OF PERIPHERAL AUTONOMIC FUNCTION

The peripheral autonomic nervous system consists of three main divisions: the *parasympathetic* division, which includes the outflow from the cranial nerves and the low lumbar and sacral spinal cord; the *sympathetic* division, which comprises the autonomic outflow from the thoracic and high lumbar segments of the spinal cord; and the *enteric* nervous system, which includes neurons that are intrinsic to the wall of the gut. Knowledge about the different types of neurotransmitters and receptors associated with the peripheral autonomic nervous system has resulted in the availability of a wide range of drugs to modify autonomic responses (Table 460–2).

Pandysautonomias

ACUTE PANDYSAUTONOMIA. Widespread failure of the autonomic nervous system may evolve acutely or subacutely as part of a parainfectious inflammatory polyneuropathy (of the Guillain-Barré type). In rare cases, the autonomic neuropathy predominates and, when severe, may be life threatening. Wide swings in blood pressure and heart rate occur but usually reverse themselves in a few minutes. In most patients, the Trendelenburg position is sufficient to maintain cerebral perfusion during hypotensive periods. Cardiac arrhythmias of all types may occur, presumably as a result of the instability of autonomic innervation of the cardiac conducting system. These arrhythmias must be treated gingerly because the underlying conduction abnormalities are neurogenic in origin and may change rapidly. The presence of ganglionic acetyl choline receptor antibodies may be diagnostic for an autoimmune origin.

TETANUS. A similar subacute pandysautonomia is also seen in severe cases of tetanus (Chapter 321). Tetanus toxin, elaborated by *Clostridium tetani* organisms in an infected wound, is transported by autonomic as well as motor axons back to the spinal cord, where it is taken up by and inactivates the terminals of inhibitory interneurons. Treatment of the motor manifestations of tetanus by paralyzing and sedating the patient does little to abate the autonomic storm. Up to 40% of patients who have tetanus and who require intensive care suffer cardiac arrest as a result of an arrhythmia; such patients are generally easily resuscitated with standard measures.

CHRONIC AUTONOMIC NEUROPATHY. The axons of the peripheral autonomic nervous system are generally of small caliber and thinly myelinated or unmyelinated. Certain polyneuropathies that have a predilection for small-diameter axons can result in autonomic changes. *Amyloid neuropathy* (Chapter 290) often includes a major autonomic component that may be manifested as a gastrointestinal motility disorder or orthostatic hypotension. Similarly, *diabetic neuropathy* (Chapter 242), although it is often dominated by sensory or motor complaints, may cause widespread autonomic failure. The neuropathy of *acute intermittent porphyria* (Chapter 223) or certain toxic agents such as *Vacor* (a rat poison) may have a prominent autonomic component. Acute poisoning with *organophosphate insecticides* (Chapter 106) that block acetylcholinesterase results in a hypercholinergic state, including miosis and cardiac slowing, which lasts for several days; the neuropathy that follows several weeks later does not usually have a strong autonomic component. Other peripheral neuropathies that may have an autonomic component are listed in Table 460–3.

DEGENERATIVE DYSAUTONOMIA. Recessively inherited *familial dysautonomia* of the Riley-Day type is most commonly seen in Ashkenazi Jewish children. Symptoms referable to the autonomic nervous system and relative indifference to pain are present from birth.

Table 460–1 • DISORDERS OF THE AUTONOMIC NERVOUS SYSTEM

Peripheral Autonomic Disorders	Genitourinary disorders
Pandysautonomias	Incontinence
Acute pandysautonomia	Urinary retention
Tetanus	Spastic bladder
Chronic autonomic neuropathy	Impotence
Familial dysautonomia	**Disorders of Central**
Idiopathic autonomic	**Autonomic Integration**
insufficiency (Shy-Drager	Emotional disorders
syndrome)	Panic disorder
Regional dysautonomia	Psychosomatic illness
Horner's syndrome	Cardiac arrhythmias
Paraspinal tumors	Thermoregulatory disorders
Somatosympathetic dysreflexia	Poikilothermia
Complex regional pain syndrome	Paroxysmal hypothermia
Disorders of specific autonomic	Hyperthermia and fever
functions	Neuroleptic malignant
Pupillary disorders	syndrome
Horner's syndrome	Feeding disorders
Oculomotor paresis	Hyperphagia and obesity
Cardiovascular disorders	Hypophagia and inanition
Glossopharyngeal neuralgia	Disorders of fluid and electrolyte
Carotid sinus hypersensitivity	regulation
Sweating disorders	Hypernatremia, hyperosmolality,
Hyperhidrosis	and absence of thirst
Anhidrosis	Hyperdipsia, hyponatremia, and
Gastrointestinal disorders	water intoxication
Disorders of motility	Paroxysmal hyponatremia
Vomiting	Central reproductive disorders
	Arousal disorders
	Hypersomnolence
	Insomnia

Table 460–2 • SYSTEMIC EFFECTS OF SOME COMMONLY USED AUTONOMIC DRUGS

RECEPTOR TYPE	DRUG TYPE (EXAMPLE)	TISSUE	EFFECT
Muscarinic cholinergic	Antagonist (atropine)	Pupil	Mydriasis
		Salivary gland	Dry mouth
		Bronchi	Dilation
		Heart	Tachycardia
		Gut	Decreased motility and secretion
α-Adrenergic	Antagonist (phenoxybenzamine)	Blood vessels	Vasodilation
α$_1$-Adrenergic	Agonist (phenylephrine)	Blood vessels	Vasoconstriction
	Antagonist (prazosin)	Blood vessels	Vasodilation
β-Adrenergic	Agonist (isoproterenol)	Heart	Increased rate and contractility
β$_1$-Adrenergic	Antagonist (metoprolol)	Blood vessels	Decreased rate and contractility
β$_2$-Adrenergic	Agonist (terbutaline)	Bronchi	Dilation

Table 460–3 • PERIPHERAL NEUROPATHIES THAT MAY HAVE AN AUTONOMIC COMPONENT

Autonomic symptoms often prominent
   Guillain-Barré syndrome
   Amyloid neuropathy
   Diabetic neuropathy
   Acute intermittent porphyria
   Vacor (rat poison)
Autonomic symptoms may occur
   Renal failure
   Toxic neuropathies
      Vinca alkaloids
      Perhexiline maleate
      Thallium
      Arsenic
      Mercury
      Organic solvents
      Acrylamide
   Vasculitis
      Systemic lupus erythematosus
      Rheumatoid arthritis
      Mixed connective tissue disease
   Thiamine deficiency
   Leprosy
   Hereditary autonomic neuropathies
   Fabry's disease

Table 460–4 • TESTS OF AUTONOMIC FUNCTION

TEST	INTERPRETATION
Pupillary responses	
4% cocaine	Pupillodilatation indicates release of normal catecholamine stores.
1% hydroxyamphetamine	Pupillodilatation indicates denervation supersensitivity.
1% phenylephrine	
0.1% epinephrine	
0.1% pilocarpine	Pupilloconstriction indicates denervation supersensitivity.
2.5% methacholine	
Sweating responses	
Thermal sweating	Regional absence of sweating indicates sympathetic cholinergic denervation.
Galvanic skin response	Increased conductivity under mild stress indicates normal adrenergic innervation.
1:1000 pilocarpine	Intradermal injection causes axon reflex sweating
1:10,000 acetylcholine	
Axon reflex	
1:1000 histamine	Intradermal injection normally causes wheal and flare.
Cardiovascular responses	
Orthostatic challenge	Pulse normally increases and diastolic blood pressure decreases <15 mm Hg.
Carotid sinus massage	Normally causes decrease in blood pressure and heart rate.
R-P interval	Normally increases during inspiration (sinus arrhythmia).
Valsalva maneuver	Longest to shortest R-R interval ratio normally is ≥1.4.
Cold pressor test	Immersing hand in ice water normally increases blood pressure and heart rate.
Plasma catecholamines	Normally increase response to standing or stress.
Norepinephrine infusion 0.05 μg/kg/min	Diastolic blood pressure increase ≥20 mm Hg indicates supersensitivity
Genitourinary, rectal responses	
Cremasteric reflex	Stroking skin or thigh normally causes testicular retraction.
Anal wink reflex	Scratching perianal skin normally causes anal sphincter contraction.
Bulbocavernosus reflex	Squeezing glans penis or clitoris normally causes anal sphincter contraction.

Pure autonomic failure may develop as a chronic degenerative condition in middle age or late adult life as a result of loss of neurons in the autonomic ganglia, as well as in the preganglionic cell groups in the medulla and spinal cord. The initial complaints often result from orthostatic hypotension, but signs or symptoms of pupillary, gastrointestinal, genitourinary, sweating, or other autonomic abnormalities are elicited by history and physical examination.

Pure autonomic failure is distinguished from non-neurologic causes of orthostatic hypotension by the lack of compensatory tachycardia, which indicates impairment of either the peripheral or central components of the baroreceptor reflex. Severe autonomic neuropathy affecting the glossopharyngeal or vagus nerves may also impair the baroreceptor response but is typically associated with other evidence of sensory or motor neuropathy. Other cardiovascular signs include loss of sinus arrhythmia and absence of normal overshoot in diastolic blood pressure during phase IV of the Valsalva maneuver. An abnormally accentuated blood pressure response to intravenous infusion of norepinephrine is consistent with widespread denervation supersensitivity. A detailed list of tests of autonomic function is provided in Table 460–4. Pure autonomic failure may have an autoimmune cause in patients who have ganglionic acetylcholine receptor antibodies.

About 10 to 20% of patients with *Parkinson's disease* (Chapter 443) have autonomic failure. These patients show Lewy bodies and loss of pigmented neurons in sympathetic ganglia as well as in the brain. This combination must be distinguished from a superficially similar disorder, *the Shy-Drager syndrome*, which is characterized by degeneration of central autonomic control nuclei. The Shy-Drager syndrome is part of a spectrum of *multiple systems atrophy* in which evidence of cerebellar and extrapyramidal involvement is generally present, but evidence is lacking for peripheral autonomic degeneration on formal testing (see Table 460–4). Loss of neurons is seen in the basal ganglia, substantia nigra, pons, cerebellum, inferior olives, and brain stem autonomic nuclei, but not in autonomic ganglia. No Lewy bodies are present, but glial fibrillary inclusions may be found. The movement disorder in patients with Parkinson's disease shows a good response to L-DOPA/carbidopa, but in multiple systems atrophy, the response is poor. Carbidopa, however, can worsen blood pressure control in both conditions by blocking DOPA decarboxylase in sympathetic ganglion cells.

Orthostatic hypotension is generally the most disabling aspect of autonomic degeneration. Treatment with elastic stockings or even entire lower body compression suits can improve standing blood pressure by limiting blood pooling in the lower part of the body. Treatment with fludrocortisone, a mineralocorticoid (0.1 mg once to three times a day), expands intravascular blood volume and causes an elevation in blood pressure in all positions. Midodrine, the prodrug of a direct

sympathetic agonist, can improve vasoconstrictor response. A starting dose of 10 mg three times a day may increase blood pressure in all positions.∎ In patients treated with either drug, the head of the bed should be elevated in recumbency to minimize hypertensive effects on the brain. L-Dihydroxyphenylserine, which is a synthetic precursor of norepinephrine, has shown encouraging results in some, but not all trials and may require residual sympathetic neuronal function to be useful; it is not approved by the Food and Drug Administration at the time of publication.

Regional Dysautonomia

The segmental organization of the sympathetic nervous system can result in regional disturbances of function. The most common of these disturbances is caused by injury to the cranial sympathetic innervation arising from the superior cervical ganglion, or *Horner's syndrome*. Miosis, ptosis, and anhidrosis may occur if the ascending sympathetic fibers are injured below the level at which they enter the skull with the internal carotid artery. Damage to sympathetic fibers along the course of the intracranial carotid artery produces only oculosympathetic paresis (Raeder's syndrome). This difference is only of marginal value clinically because Horner's syndrome produced by extracranial lesions is often incomplete. Lesions of the central descending sympathoexcitatory pathway, which runs through the lateral portions of the brain stem from the hypothalamus to the spinal cord, may produce a central Horner's syndrome characterized by miosis and ptosis, as well as loss of sweating over the entire ipsilateral half of the body. Postganglionic Horner's syndrome can be differentiated from preganglionic or central lesions by pharmacologic testing (see Table 460–4). The most common cause of Horner's syndrome is atherosclerotic disease affecting the vasa nervorum originating in the carotid artery. However, Horner's syndrome may also be seen when an intrathoracic or cervical tumor involves the sympathetic chain. Hence, evaluation of Horner's syndrome of recent onset should include radiographic or magnetic resonance examination of the pulmonary apices and paracervical area.

Spinal epidural tumors (Chapter 457) that compress the spinal cord may cause loss of sweating over the dermatomes caudal to the tumor. This deficit can be appreciated by running the handle of a tuning fork down the skin in the paraspinal region. The smooth movement is interrupted by the dry skin below the level of the lesion. Occasionally, compression of a midthoracic spinal root, which carries visceral sensory fibers, by a disc or tumor may be manifested as abdominal pain.

Stimulation of pain fibers at any level results in both local (spino-spinal) and generalized (spinobulbospinal) *somatosympathetic reflex responses,* including sweating, vasoconstriction, and pupillodilatation. In patients with preexisting spinal cord transection, a noxious stimulus below the level of the transection may produce either local sympathetic reflex responses (segmental sweating) or more generalized spinal reflex patterns (e.g., hypertension with bladder overfilling). Paraplegic patients with sympathetic responses should be evaluated for evidence of occult disease that might cause pain in an intact individual.

Following injury to peripheral nerves, aberrant regeneration may result in severe pain, a condition known as *complex regional pain syndrome.* Normally innocuous sensory stimulation, such as covering the affected limb with a sheet or with clothing, may cause excruciating burning pain associated with variable autonomic changes. Atrophic changes in the skin and bone may reflect abnormal sympathetic innervation or disuse. The role of sympathetic nerves in mediating the chronic pain (*reflex sympathetic dystrophy*) remains controversial. Although regional sympathetic block alleviates pain in some patients, injection of placebo can have similar effects, and removal of the affected sympathetic ganglion rarely produces permanent relief.

Disorders of Specific Autonomic Functions

PUPILS. Anisocoria, or asymmetry of pupillary size, may reflect a deficit of sympathetic innervation of the smaller pupil (causing miosis) or parasympathetic innervation of the larger one (causing mydriasis) (Chapter 466). Because both oculosympathetic and oculomotor (parasympathetic) innervation participates in lid elevation, ptosis, if present, generally indicates the abnormal eye. Anisocoria may be long-standing and of little clinical significance, but pupillary asymmetry of recent onset should be evaluated by a neurologist. Impairment of sympathetic innervation of the iris (pupillodilator) muscle is not always accompanied by ptosis or a sweating deficit (Horner's syndrome). The pupilloconstrictor fibers travel in the dorsomedial part of the oculomotor nerve, where they may be selectively affected by temporal lobe herniation or by an aneurysm of the posterior communicating artery. Pharmacologic testing may aid in identification of the pupillary abnormality (see Table 460–4). A common factitious cause of a unilateral dilated pupil is instillation of atropinic eyedrops; the situation is exposed when the pharmacologically dilated pupil does not respond even to strong solutions of pilocarpine. Another common cause of a large, poorly reactive pupil is *Adie's syndrome,* an idiopathic condition involving degeneration of the ciliary ganglion. The abnormal pupil usually shows sector paralysis and constricts with accommodation; it dilates and responds to light after a period in complete darkness. The abnormal pupil responds briskly to 0.1% pilocarpine (see Table 460–4), and concomitant loss of tendon reflexes is seen in most cases.

CARDIOVASCULAR. The baroreceptor reflex is an important protective response that induces bradycardia and peripheral vasodilatation to counteract an acute increase in blood pressure—or the reverse response during hypotension. The afferent fibers for the response run in the glossopharyngeal (carotid sinus) and vagus (aortic depressor) nerves, whereas the efferent response includes both parasympathetic and sympathetic components. Injury to the glossopharyngeal or carotid sinus nerves in the neck (often by a tumor) can cause episodic attacks of hypotension and bradycardia, often manifested as syncope. In most cases, an associated pain or paresthesia is located in the cutaneous distribution of the glossopharyngeal nerve (in the external auditory meatus or the pharynx), known as *glossopharyngeal neuralgia* (Chapter 427). The situation is analogous to tic douloureux, which is characterized by intermittent volleys of firing in the affected nerve. Atropine or a transvenous pacemaker may prevent the bradycardia associated with the attacks, but loss of vasoconstrictor tone sometimes results in symptomatic hypotension despite these maneuvers. Anticonvulsants, including phenytoin, carbamazepine, or gabapentin, may prevent the attacks. Dosages are adjusted for each patient but are often much lower than those required to treat epilepsy.

Carotid sinus syncope (Chapter 435) occurs most commonly in elderly individuals with carotid atherosclerosis. Even mild pressure over the carotid bulb, such as a tight shirt collar, can produce a full-blown carotid sinus response resulting in syncope. The diagnosis is made by gently compressing the carotid artery below the angle of the jaw while the electrocardiogram is monitored. Facilities for cardiac resuscitation must be immediately available in case the compression results in sinus arrest. Vigorous massage should be avoided because it may dislodge an embolus and result in a transient or even permanent neurologic deficit. Treatment of carotid sinus hypersensitivity is the same as that for glossopharyngeal neuralgia.

SWEATING. Human sweat glands are innervated by both noradrenergic sympathetic fibers (mediating emotional responses) and cholinergic sympathetic fibers (thermal sweating). Certain somatosympathetic reflexes can produce generalized or regional sweating in response to innocuous or noxious somatosensory stimuli. *Hyperhidrosis,* or pathologically increased sweating, can be generalized, or it can be focal, most commonly involving the palms of the hands and the soles of the feet. Drugs that interrupt α-adrenergic transmission (phenoxybenzamine, 10 mg three times daily) or muscarinic transmission (propantheline, 15 mg three times daily) may be effective, particularly in combination. In extreme cases, regional sympathectomy has been performed.

Idiopathic anhidrosis may be segmental or generalized. This rare condition is sometimes associated with Adie's syndrome (Ross syndrome), but in other cases no other signs of autonomic impairment are noted. In some patients, the impairment is preganglionic and in others postganglionic, as judged by the axon reflex sweating response (see Table 460–4). In most patients studied, the deficits were stable and did not go on to involve other autonomic functions.

GASTROINTESTINAL. Disorders of intestinal motility may be due to damage to the parasympathetic innervation of the gut or to dysfunction of the enteric nervous system itself (Chapter 134). Specific abnormalities of esophageal contraction and colonic tone have been noted in patients suffering from depression and may predict response to antidepressant medication.

Vomiting is a neurally mediated gastrointestinal reflex that is coordinated by neurons in the medullary reticular formation. Chemical emetic agents such as certain narcotics or dopaminergic agonists act at the area postrema, a chemosensory zone on the fourth ventricular surface of the medulla, to elicit the vomiting reflex. Local dopaminergic and serotoninergic connections are thought to mediate the response, and antidopaminergic drugs such as prochlorperazine or blockers of the 5HT-3 serotonin receptor (e.g., ondansetron) may act at the level of the area postrema to suppress vomiting; the two types of drugs together are even more efficacious.[2] Intractable vomiting without any gastrointestinal abnormalities has been reported in certain patients with tumors involving the medullary cell groups controlling vomiting or their connections. Treatment of the tumor with steroids and radiation therapy generally results in improvement.

GENITOURINARY. The urinary bladder is composed of interlacing smooth muscle fibers of the detrusor covered by an internal mucous membrane and an outer serosa. The detrusor is innervated by local parasympathetic ganglion cells, which, in turn, are controlled by preganglionic neurons located in the intermediolateral column at the second through fourth sacral segments. Additional motor neurons located in the ventral horn at the same levels constitute Onuf's nucleus. Their axons run through the pelvic nerve to innervate striated accessory muscles of micturition (including the external urethral sphincter) in the pelvic floor. Neurons of Onuf's nucleus are strikingly preserved in motor neuron disease but are lost along with autonomic preganglionic cells in Shy-Drager syndrome. The internal sphincter at the bladder neck is innervated via the hypogastric nerve by sympathetic prevertebral pelvic ganglia whose preganglionic innervation arises from the intermediolateral column at the T12-L1 level.

Bladder relaxation during filling and subsequent coordination of micturition are under control of Barrington's nucleus and the adjacent pontine reticular formation, near the locus coeruleus. Brain stem control of micturition is, in turn, under voluntary regulation by areas within the cerebral sensory and motor cortex. When bladder fullness is sensed and the environmental conditions are appropriate, micturition is initiated by Barrington's nucleus, under forebrain control. External sphincter pressure decreases and thereby results in reflex relaxation of the internal sphincter and contraction of the bladder.

Forebrain impairment results in loss of voluntary control of micturition but does not otherwise affect the complex sensory and motor program that results in normal voiding. Incontinence in such patients can be managed with adult diapers or external urinary collection devices without the risk of frequent urinary tract infections or damage to the upper urinary tract. Injury to the bulbospinal pathway from Barrington's nucleus to the sacral intermediolateral column, however, causes major disruption of coordinated bladder function. Immediately following spinal cord injury, there is a period of spinal shock, during which the bladder does not undergo reflex contraction as it fills. Such patients require urinary catheterization to prevent vesical and renal damage.

One to 2 weeks after injury, spinal reflex control of the bladder returns. Some patients can induce reflex bladder emptying by somatosensory stimulation, such as stroking the skin over the thigh. The spastic bladder reflexively contracts at a lower volume but does not empty completely (*spastic* bladder). If the spinal injury is between T12 and S2, detrusor action is not coordinated with sphincter opening, and bladder contraction against a closed sphincter can cause ureteral reflux (*sphincter dyssynergia*). Injury to sensory nerves supplying the bladder may also cause overfilling and incomplete emptying, thus indicating the importance of sensory feedback in bladder control. Patients with significant postvoid residual urine are at increased risk for urinary tract infections, but bladder overfilling with elevated pressures greater than 40 cm H$_2$O may ultimately be a greater problem. Elevations in pressure greater than 40 cm H$_2$O may require continuous or intermittent catheterization to prevent damage to the upper urinary tract.

Pharmacologic intervention aimed at augmenting or suppressing autonomic motor responses of the bladder or internal sphincter has only limited value (Chapter 24). Bethanechol, a cholinergic agonist (10 to 15 mg three times daily), is used to augment bladder contraction to improve emptying. It is most effective in combination with an α-adrenergic blocker, such as terazosin (1 to 10 mg daily), that simultaneously reduces pressure at the internal sphincter. Baclofen may be used to decrease spastic contraction of the external sphincter. Drugs that have atropinic properties, including a surprising variety of antiarrhythmic, antihistamine, neuroleptic, and antidepressant medications, may inhibit bladder contraction and result in overfilling and urinary retention (Table 460–5).

Erectile function (Chapter 247) in males is under parasympathetic control at the same sacral levels as the urinary system. Sensory afferent fibers travel via the pudendal nerve, whereas parasympathetic motor fibers run in the pelvic nerve. Sympathetic innervation via the hypogastric nerve contracts the seminal vesicles during ejaculation and closes the bladder neck to prevent retrograde emission. Although supraspinal influences are of great importance, reflex erection and ejaculation can occur in patients after spinal injury. Neurogenic impotence can result either from damage to the descending pathways relaying forebrain influence from the hypothalamus to the sacral

preganglionic neurons or from injury to the sensory or parasympathetic motor innervation of the penis. A variety of drugs that block either parasympathetic or sympathetic function can interfere with erectile function (Table 460–6). Because erections normally occur several times nightly during periods of rapid eye movement sleep, it is possible to document organic disorders of erection by measuring penile tumescence overnight.

DISORDERS OF INTEGRATIVE CONTROL OF THE AUTONOMIC NERVOUS SYSTEM

Organization of Central Autonomic and Endocrine Regulation

The autonomic nervous system is under three levels of central control. The *preganglionic* neurons located in the medulla and the spinal cord provide the final common pathway for central autonomic control. Each of these neurons integrates the input from many sources, including afferents from higher levels of the nervous system and local reflex responses. A series of *brain stem and spinal* cell groups coordinate *reflex control* of the autonomic nervous system. These nuclei receive cranial (parasympathetic) and spinal (sympathetic) afferent information and control a variety of important reflexes (e.g., swallowing, maintaining blood pressure, initiation of voiding). Both the preganglionic neurons and the brain stem reflex neurons are under the control of *forebrain integrative* cell groups that coordinate autonomic function with behavior and with endocrine control.

The hypothalamus is the most important area for integration of behavior with autonomic responses and with neuroendocrine control of the anterior and posterior pituitary glands (Fig. 460–1). Because the hypothalamus consists of tightly packed, interwoven pathways and cell groups, it is unusual for an injury to selectively involve a single functional system. Nevertheless, considerable progress has been made in determining the anatomic substrates for specific integrative functions, and disorders of these systems are occasionally encountered (Table 460–7). In addition, autonomic dysfunction is a frequent concomitant of emotional disorders.

Table 460–5 • SOME COMMONLY PRESCRIBED DRUGS THAT MAY IMPAIR URINARY FUNCTION

Antiarrhythmics	Antiparkinsonian agents
Atropine	Amantadine
Disopyramide	DOPA/carbidopa
Antihistamines	Bromocriptine
Diphenhydramine	Benztropine
Neuroleptics	Trihexyphenidyl
Haloperidol	Antispasmodics
Chlorpromazine	Baclofen
Antidepressants	
Amitriptyline	
Imipramine	

Table 460–6 • SOME COMMONLY PRESCRIBED DRUGS THAT MAY IMPAIR ERECTILE FUNCTION

Drugs causing impotence	Drugs causing priapism
Parasympatholytics	Chlorpromazine
Atropine	Thioridazine
Amitriptyline	Trazodone
Sympatholytics	Prazosin
Methyldopa	DOPA/carbidopa
Guanethidine	
Clonidine	
Propranolol	
Prazosin	
Vasodilators	
Hydralazine	
Diuretics	
Hydrochlorothiazide	
Antihistaminergic	
Cimetidine	

Table 460–7 • REGIONAL HYPOTHALAMIC SYNDROMES

REGION	NORMALLY REGULATES	DISORDERS
Preoptic	Blood volume, pressure, and electrolytes	Paroxysmal hyponatremia
		Essential hypernatremia
	Thermoregulation	Paroxysmal hypothermia
Tuberal	Gastrointestinal tract and feeding	Hyperphagia (ventromedial lesions)
		Hypophagia (lateral lesions)
	Reproduction	Hypogonadism
	Emotions	Rage responses
Posterior	Arousal	Hypersomnolence
	Descending autonomic and motor pathways	Poikilothermia

Neurology

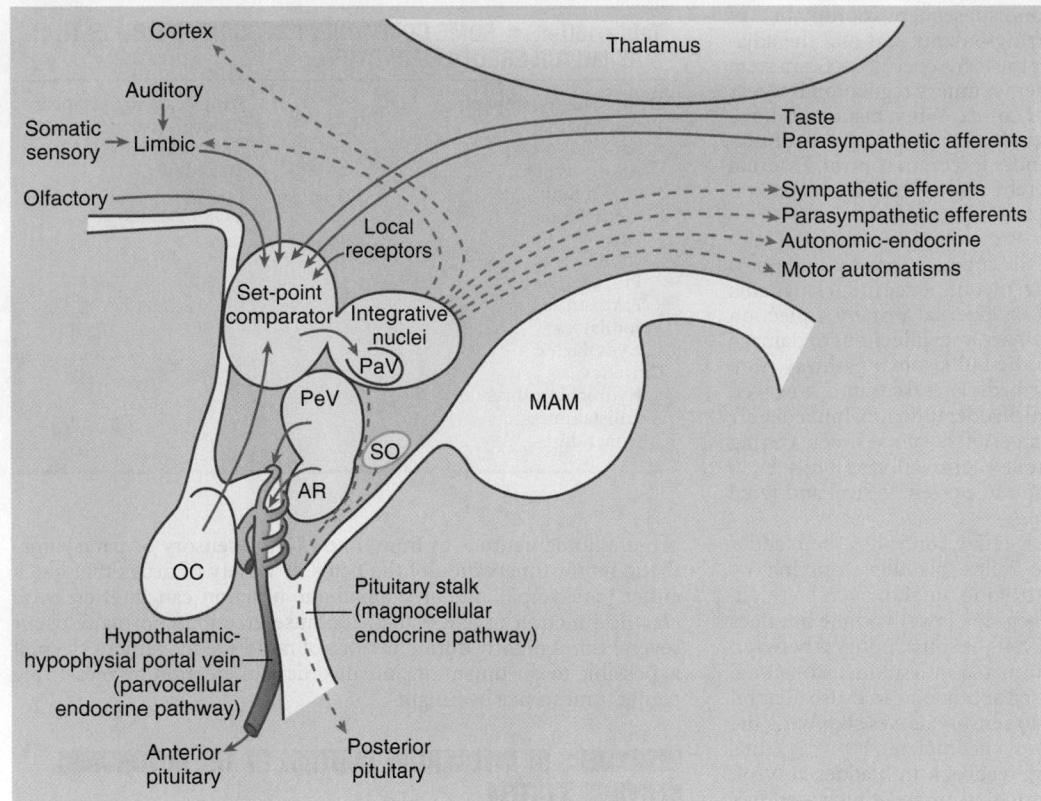

FIGURE 460-1 • Schematic illustration of the functional organization of the hypothalamus. General and visceral sensory, limbic, and local interoceptive (e.g., osmolality and temperature) information is compared against a homeostatic set point by integrative cell groups in the preoptic area and tuberal hypothalamus. Efferent autonomic responses from the paraventricular nucleus (PaV) and lateral hypothalamic area are then integrated with anterior pituitary control via the periventricular (PeV) and arcuate (AR) nuclei and posterior pituitary control via the supraoptic (SO) and paraventricular nuclei, and with behavioral regulation exercised mainly by the lateral hypothalamic area. MAM = mamillary body; OC = optic chiasm. (Amended from Saper CB: Hypothalamus. *In* Pearlman AL, Collins RC [eds]: Neurobiology of Disease. New York, Oxford University Press, 1989, p 197. Copyright © 1989 by Oxford University Press, Inc. Used by permission.)

Emotional Disorders

Portions of the insular and cingulate areas of the cerebral cortex and the amygdala are believed to regulate autonomic responses to emotional stress. In healthy individuals, stress can induce sympathetic responses such as pupillodilatation, dry mouth, and increases in blood pressure. In patients with *panic disorder* (Chapter 426), such autonomic responses can become overwhelming and convince the patient that a serious organic problem exists. Positron-emission tomography studies show increased metabolism in the structures of the medial temporal lobe and the insular cortex during panic attacks. After eliminating the possibility of pheochromocytoma (Chapter 241), anxiolytic or antidepressant drugs are usually helpful.

Some individuals under chronic emotional stress are subject to a variety of syndromes involving disruption of autonomic control of the internal organs. Although *psychosomatic illness* is often thought to be nonorganic and may respond to psychotherapeutic drugs, considerable evidence suggests that some organic disorders seen in anxious patients may also be caused by autonomic dysregulation. For example, individuals under stress may suffer erosive gastritis, gastric ulcers, and irritable bowel syndrome as a result of autonomic dysfunction. Perhaps the most serious problems are encountered in patients with preexisting cardiac abnormalities, who may have cardiac arrhythmias under stressful conditions. Retrospective studies of victims of sudden death caused by lethal ventricular arrhythmias indicate a much higher incidence of behavioral stress in the period preceding the attack. β-Adrenergic blockers may be useful in reducing the frequency of such arrhythmias.

Thermoregulatory Disorders

Thermoresponsive neurons in the medial preoptic area monitor brain temperature and activate autonomic, endocrine, and somatomotor responses to match body temperature to a set point, which is normally 37° C in humans. Control of body temperature requires shifting blood flow between deep and superficial vascular beds and regulating conservation of body fluids (increased urination in the cold, increased sweating in the heat). Hence, thermoregulation is tightly linked to control of blood pressure, volume, and electrolyte composition, which are also regulated by neurons around the anteroventral tip of the third ventricle (see later discussion).

Poikilothermia, defined as fluctuation in body temperature of more than 2° C with changes in ambient temperature, may result when lesions in the posterior hypothalamus or midbrain damage hypothalamic pathways for autonomic as well as behavioral thermoregulation. Relative poikilothermia can also result from metabolic disorders such as sedative drug ingestion, hypoglycemia, or hypothyroidism, and a mild form often is seen in old age. Such patients are dangerously susceptible to lowered environmental temperature. Conversely, patients with relative poikilothermia or those taking anticholinergic drugs that prevent thermal sweating may experience dangerously elevated body temperatures during periods of hot weather. *Heat stroke* (Chapter 105), in which body temperature may exceed 42° C, is often fatal and requires prompt treatment by cooling the patient in an ice bath and expanding body fluids. Death is often a result of ventricular arrhythmia.

PAROXYSMAL HYPOTHERMIA. Occasionally patients suffer episodic attacks during which thermoregulation proceeds in a nearly normal fashion but around a lowered set point. During an attack, a body temperature of 32° C or lower is maintained for a period of several days to 2 weeks. Attacks occur up to several times per year and may be accompanied by fatigue, malaise, somnolence, hypoventilation, hypotension, cardiac arrhythmias, lacrimation, ataxia, and asterixis. In some patients, the serum sodium level may decrease in tandem with the body temperature, to levels of 110 mEq/L or even lower. Attacks subside spontaneously and are followed by heat conservation measures to bring body temperature up to the normal set point. Nearly all such patients have a hypothalamic abnormality involving the thermoregulatory preoptic area, a finding that suggests the attacks may represent an "inverted" fever response. Anticonvulsants have not been effective in such attacks, but cyclooxygenase inhibitors such as aspirin may be useful in some patients.

FEVER AND HYPERTHERMIA. During a systemic immune response, circulating cytokines such as interleukin-1 and tumor necrosis factor may trigger macrophages in the meninges and endothelial cells along penetrating venules at the borders of the brain to produce prostaglandins. These lipid mediators can cross the blood-brain barrier and act on neurons in the paramedian preoptic area to reset the body's thermoregulatory set point upward (Chapter 296). This process activates a coordinated set of autonomic, endocrine, and behavioral responses that increase thermogenesis and conserve heat. Drugs that inhibit the generation of prostaglandins are the mainstay of treatment of fever, but the wisdom of treating low-grade fever (<38.5° C) during an infectious illness has engendered considerable debate. An elevated body temperature may improve the function of certain immune cells while impairing the defenses of invading microorganisms.

Any physical injury to the brain that allows the entry into the brain of macrophages or activates microglial cells to produce cytokines induces a febrile response as well. Hence, fever may be seen after head trauma, intracranial surgery, or cerebral hemorrhage or infarction. "Central neurogenic fever" is often proposed as a mechanism for fever of unknown origin, but in few, if any, documented cases is the thermal set point elevated without an inflammatory signal acting on the hypothalamus.

Malignant hyperthermia, which is caused by an autosomal dominant disorder of skeletal muscle, can occur in patients who have been exposed to certain drugs. During induction of anesthesia, particularly with halothane and succinylcholine, certain patients sustain sudden massive muscle contractions accompanied by a rapid increase in body temperature to 42° C or greater. Circulatory and respiratory collapse and death can ensue unless immediate treatment with intravenous dantrolene (1 to 10 mg/kg) and supportive measures are instituted. This disorder is often associated with muscle central core disease and is due to a defect in regulation of the calcium release channel in muscle sarcoplasmic reticulum. The disorder is genetically heterogeneous, so preoperative pharmacologic testing of a muscle biopsy sample from suspected family members (with the caffeine-halothane contracture test) is still recommended.

Muscular rigidity and elevated body temperature can occasionally be seen during treatment with neuroleptic drugs or following withdrawal of dopaminergic agonists. The pathogenesis of this *neuroleptic malignant syndrome* is not understood, although it may reflect a febrile response in a patient with parkinsonian rigidity and drug-induced impairment of thermoregulation. Treatment with dopaminergic agonists such as bromocriptine can reverse the process.

Feeding Disorders

To provide a constant supply of substrate for energy metabolism, it is necessary to balance body requirements against the daily intake of nutrients and body stores of glycogen, fat, and protein. The discovery of leptin, a hormone made by fat cells in times of excess metabolic substrate, has led to unraveling of many of the neural pathways and molecular signaling mechanisms that drive food intake. Neurons in the region around the median eminence, which lacks a blood-brain barrier, are activated by circulating leptin. These cells give rise to a complex web of pathways that use peptide neurotransmitters to drive autonomic, endocrine, and behavioral responses, which result in the regulation of feeding and body weight.

HYPERPHAGIA AND OBESITY. Lesions in the region of the ventromedial nucleus of the hypothalamus, which sits in the heart of this web of pathways, can result in massive overeating and obesity. A defect in the leptin gene or its receptor can result in leptin insensitivity, which also causes hyperphagia and obesity. One of the satiety pathways activated by leptin uses α-melanocyte stimulating hormone, which acts on the melanocortin-4 receptor. Defects in this pathway also produce obesity. Each of these conditions has been reported in humans, but they are rare causes of human obesity (Chapter 233). Conversely, ghrelin, a hormone produced by the stomach, causes hunger; reducing the ghrelin signal may be critical to maintaining weight loss.

The *Kleine-Levin syndrome* is a poorly understood disorder in which patients, typically adolescent boys, have episodic attacks of somnolence, often sleeping up to 20 hours per day. When awake, they appear dull and often confused and consume enormous quantities of food. Attacks may last up to 2 weeks and can recur several times per year. Pathologic verification of the site of the lesion in typical cases is lacking, but a similar syndrome may be seen acutely in encephalitis involving the hypothalamus.

The *Prader-Willi syndrome,* a congenital disorder caused by a deletion in chromosome 15, is characterized by mental retardation, hypogonadism, and hyperphagia, often with massive obesity. Patients with Prader-Willi syndrome have elevated ghrelin levels, which may drive feeding behavior, but the cause of high ghrelin levels and other aspects of the syndrome remain unknown.

HYPOPHAGIA AND INANITION. Large lesions in the region of the lateral hypothalamic area at the level of the ventromedial nucleus result in aphagia, which may recover to hypophagia and regulation around a new, lower body weight set point. Such lesions, which must be bilateral, are usually devastating, and selective impairment of eating on this basis has rarely been reported in adults. More often, patients with hypothalamic damage and inanition are somnolent and show a variety of endocrine abnormalities. No evidence of injury to the hypothalamus has been found in anorexia nervosa (Chapter 232).

Central Disorders of Fluid and Electrolyte Regulation

The medial preoptic area around the anteroventral tip of the third ventricle plays a critical role in regulating blood pressure, volume, and electrolyte composition. Endocrine control (mineralocorticoids and especially vasopressin), autonomic regulation (control of blood flow in different vascular beds, innervation of sweat glands and kidney, especially the juxtaglomerular apparatus controlling renin release), and behavioral response (drinking) all play important roles in this process. Disorders of the release of vasopressin by neurons whose cell bodies are located in the supraoptic and paraventricular nuclei are covered in Chapters 112 and 238. Coordinated central disorders of fluid regulation are rare.

HYPERNATREMIA, HYPEROSMOLALITY, ABSENCE OF THIRST. Neurogenic hypernatremia is a rare disorder marked by impairment of the normal responses to osmolar stimuli. Hence there are deficits in the vasopressin response to increased sodium and osmolality, as well as an absence or relative deficiency of thirst. The vasopressin response to hypovolemia may be maintained, and the preservation of habitual drinking of water (often related to meals) may be sufficient to maintain serum osmolality under normal conditions. During hot weather, when loss of water is increased through evaporation of sweat, patients often fail to increase their water consumption adequately and may suffer attacks of fatigue, fever, muscle cramps and tenderness, and even myoglobinuria (associated with hypokalemia). With serum sodium in excess of 180 mEq/L, patients may experience confusion or even become stuporous, and some may die (Chapter 112).

The hypothalamic injury giving rise to essential hypernatremia has been accurately localized in only a few cases, but in all of these cases it seems to involve the preoptic area in the region of the anteroventral third ventricle. Treatment consists of training the patient to drink adequate amounts of fluid, particularly during hot weather. Spironolactone, chlorpropamide, and thiazide diuretics have been used to reduce serum sodium and increase potassium.

HYPERDIPSIA, HYPONATREMIA, AND WATER INTOXICATION. Excessive water drinking in the absence of either hypovolemia or serum hyperosmolality is termed *primary hyperdipsia* and must be distinguished from the compensatory hyperdipsia of diabetes insipidus (Chapter 238), diabetes mellitus (Chapter 242), and polyuric renal failure (Chapter 117). In the absence of inappropriate vasopressin secretion, symptoms of water intoxication such as stupor, delirium, or convulsions are infrequent. Most severe hyperdipsia occurs in persons who have psychiatric disturbances.

PAROXYSMAL HYPONATREMIA. Many patients with paroxysmal hypothermia (see earlier discussion) suffer simultaneous hyponatremia, which may be sufficiently severe (serum sodium <110 mEq/L) to cause symptoms of confusion or even convulsions. The serum sodium concentration is regulated around the reduced set point but may respond to fluid restriction.

Central Reproductive Disorders

Reproductive hormonal control, behavior, and the associated autonomic responses are controlled by neurons in the preoptic area close to those that regulate fluid and electrolyte control and by cells in the ventromedial hypothalamus close to neurons that regulate feeding. Although this contiguity may seem anomalous, reproductive capacity is closely tied to nutritional status (and leptin is a main regulator of both). In addition, sexual function and fetal maintenance rely on control of blood flow in specific vascular beds, which must be coordinated with control of body temperature and fluid balance. The change in body temperature that accompanies ovulation (Chapter 250) and the fluid shifts seen in the perimenstrual period in women are examples of this integration. Male erectile function (Chapter 247), which is dependent on sacral parasympathetic innervation of the penis, may be affected by diseases of the peripheral autonomic nervous system, as well as psychogenic factors acting at the level of the forebrain.

Neurology

Arousal Disorders

The function of the autonomic nervous system is to augment the activity of various organ systems to deal with perturbations in internal homeostasis. Of all the body's organs, the single most important one to activate during an external threat is the brain. The ascending activating system, which runs from the rostral pons and caudal midbrain to the diencephalon, increases the responsiveness of the forebrain to external stimuli and may be considered a cerebral component of the autonomic system (Chapters 435 through 438).

1. Low PA, Gilden JL, Freeman R, et al: Efficacy of midodrine vs. placebo in neurogenic orthostatic hypotension. A randomized, double-blind multicenter study. JAMA 1997;277:1046–1051.
2. Sanchez-Ledesma MJ, Lopez-Olaondo L, Pueyo FJ, et al: A comparison of three antiemetic combinations for the prevention of postoperative nausea and vomiting. Anesth Analg 2002;95:1590–1595.

SUGGESTED READINGS
Goldstein DS, Robertson D, Esler M, et al: Dysautonomias: Clinical disorders of the autonomic nervous system. Ann Intern Med 2002;137:753–763. *A comprehensive overview.*
Klein CM, Vernino S, Lennon VA, et al: The spectrum of autoimmune autonomic neuropathies. Ann Neurol 2003;53:752–758. *Redefines the pathophysiology and subgroups of peripheral autonomic failure based on presence of ganglionic acetylcholine receptor antibodies.*
Saper CB: The central autonomic system. Ann Rev Neurosci 2002;25:433–469. *A comprehensive review of central autonomic control mechanisms.*
Saper CB, Chou TC, Scammell TE: The sleep switch: Hypothalamic control of sleep and wakefulness. Trends Neurosci 2001;24:726–731. *An up-to-date review of the role of the hypothalamus in regulating sleep and wakefulness.*

461 APPROACH TO MUSCLE AND NERVE DISEASE

Richard J. Barohn

GENERAL APPROACH TO MUSCLE DISEASES

Diseases of skeletal muscle, termed *myopathies,* are disorders in which there is a primary structural or functional impairment of muscle. Myopathies therefore do not include diseases of the central nervous system (CNS), lower motor neurons (motor neuron disease), peripheral nerves, or neuromuscular junction that secondarily produce muscle weakness. Myopathies can be differentiated from other disorders of the motor unit by characteristic clinical and laboratory findings. In addition, the disorders of muscles can be categorized and subdivided so that it is generally possible to recognize a particular myopathy on the basis of its distinctive features.

Myopathies can be broadly classified into hereditary and acquired disorders (Table 461–1).

Organization and Structure of Muscle

A single *motor unit* consists of four components: (1) a motor neuron, (2) its peripheral axon and terminal branches, (3) the neuromuscular junctions at each terminal nerve ending, and (4) all of the

Table 461–1 • CLASSIFICATION OF MYOPATHIES

HEREDITARY
Muscular dystrophies
Congenital myopathies
Myotonias and channelopathies
Metabolic myopathies
Mitochondrial myopathies

ACQUIRED
Inflammatory myopathies
Endocrine myopathies
Myopathies associated with systemic illness
Drug-induced/toxic myopathies

skeletal muscle fibers innervated by the axon. The number of muscle fibers innervated by a single motor unit varies from muscle to muscle. Muscles subserving finely coordinated movements, such as ocular muscles, can have fewer than 10 muscle fibers in a motor unit. Powerful proximal limb muscles have large motor units with 1000 or 2000 fibers innervated by a single motor neuron. Individual fibers from different motor units intermingle randomly in the muscle. The muscle also contains connective tissue and blood vessels. All of these tissues can be affected in certain myopathic disorders.

The muscle fibers consist of thick and thin filaments (myofibrils) that are arranged in repeating units, or *sarcomeres,* limited by Z disks. The *thin filaments* (actin, troponin, and tropomyosin) are anchored to the Z disks and interdigitate between the *thick filaments* (myosin) in the central region (A band) of the sarcomere. The myofibrils are associated with transverse (T) tubules, sarcoplasmic reticulum (SR), glycogen, and mitochondria. The head of each myosin molecule acts as a cross-bridge between myosin and actin. T tubules are inward projections of the muscle fiber surface membrane and serve to propagate the action potential into the muscle fiber. The SR contains calcium and partially surrounds the T tubules. The depolarization of T tubules triggers the opening of calcium channels and the release of calcium from the SR into the myofilament space. Calcium then binds to troponin on the thin filaments, which acts on tropomyosin to allow repeated binding of the myosin cross-bridges to actin. The conformational change in the myosin-actin cross-bridge moves the thin filaments toward the center of the sarcomere, and the Z disks are pulled closer together, producing muscle fiber contraction. This contraction is an energy-dependent process that requires adenosine triphosphate (ATP), which is split by an ATPase on the cross-bridge.

The myofibrils and associated constituents are surrounded by the sarcolemmal membrane and basal lamina (Fig. 461–1). A great deal of attention has been focused on this aspect of muscle because a number of muscular dystrophies are now known to be caused by genetic defects in this region. The sarcolemmal components are known as the *dystrophin-glycoprotein complex* (DGC). The DGC is a transsarcolemmal complex of proteins and glycoproteins that link the subsarcolemmal cytoskeleton to the extracellular matrix. The role of the DGC is to provide structural support to the sarcolemma during muscle contraction and stretch. In addition, the DGC may have a role in the regulation of intracellular calcium concentration and in signal transduction.

Dystrophin was the first well-characterized protein in the DGC. It is a rod-shaped molecule on the cytoplasmic side of the skeletal and cardiac sarcolemma. It consists of an amino-terminal domain that binds to the cytoskeletal thin actin filaments. The mid-rod domain and the carboxy-terminal domain are important in linking dystrophin to the other glycoproteins of the DGC. These DGC components are the *dystroglycan* complex (α, β), the *sarcoglycan* complex (α, β, γ, d), and the *syntrophin complex* (α, β1, β2). The exact relationships among all of the components of the DGC are still under investigation.

Closely adherent to the extracellular portion of the sarcolemma is the basal lamina, which is composed of collagen types I and IV, heparin sulfate proteoglycan, entactin, fibronectin, and laminin.

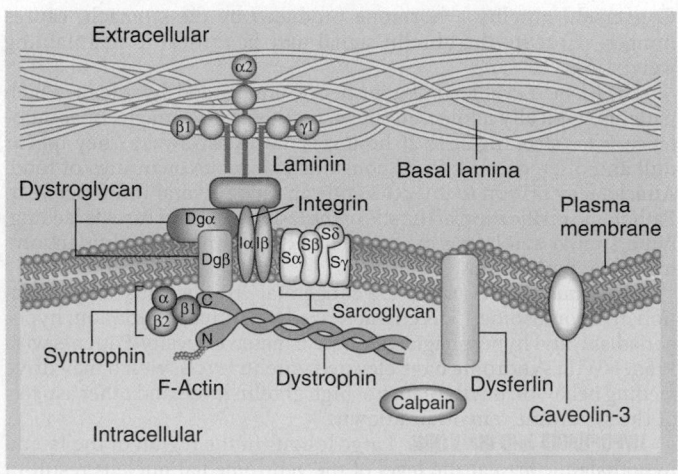

FIGURE 461–1 • The dystrophin-glycoprotein complex and related proteins.

Laminin is a heterotrimer composed of α, β, and γ chains held together by disulfide bonds. *Merosin* is the collective name for laminins that share a common α$_2$ chain. α-Dystroglycan binds to laminin, anchoring the basal lamina to the sarcolemma.

Integrins are another group of transmembrane proteins distinct from the DGC that link the extracellular matrix to the sarcolemma. Integrins also bind merosin to skeletal muscle, and this interaction appears to be as important as the α-dystroglycan linkage in providing structural stability. Integrins are also important in transducing signals from the extracellular matrix to the cell.

Clinical Assessment

The most important aspect of evaluating a patient with a myopathy is the information obtained from the history. After taking the history, the physician should formulate a reasonable preliminary diagnosis that places the patient into one of the categories in Table 461–2. The findings on the physical examination, in particular the pattern of weakness, help further define the diagnosis. The results of the laboratory studies (blood tests, electromyogram, muscle biopsy, molecular studies) serve to confirm the preliminary diagnosis arrived at from the history and physical examination.

HISTORY. Symptoms of muscle disease can be divided into "negative" and "positive" complaints.

Negative Symptoms. The most common symptom of a patient with muscle disease is *weakness*. If the weakness is in the legs, patients will complain of difficulty in climbing stairs and rising from a low chair or toilet or from the floor. When the arms are involved, patients notice trouble lifting objects (especially over their head) and washing or brushing their hair. These types of symptoms in the arms and legs point to proximal muscle weakness, which is probably the most common site of weakness in a myopathic disorder (see later). However, occasional patients with myopathies can complain of poor hand grip (difficulty in opening jar tops and turning door knobs) or tripping due to ankle weakness caused by distal muscle weakness. Some myopathies involve "proximal" cranial muscles, and patients complain of a change in speech (dysarthria) or swallowing (dysphagia), droopy eyelids (ptosis), and, rarely, double vision (diplopia).

It is important to determine the *tempo* of the disease. Patients should be asked whether the weakness is present all of the time or is intermittent. Myopathies can present as either fixed weakness (muscular dystrophies, inflammatory myopathies) or episodic periods of weakness with normal strength interictally (periodic paralysis due to channelopathies, metabolic myopathies due to certain glycolytic pathway disorders). Disorders of muscles can have acute (<4 wk), subacute (4 to 8 wk), or chronic (>8 wk) periods over which the weakness evolves. Of course, the disorders with episodic weakness have acute weakness that can return to normal strength within hours or days. The tempo of the disorders with persistent weakness can vary from (1) acute or subacute in some inflammatory myopathies (dermatomyositis and polymyositis) to (2) chronic slow progression over years (most muscular dystrophies) or to (3) fixed weakness with little change over decades (congenital myopathies). Finally, both constant and episodic myopathic disorders can have symptoms that may be monophasic or polyphasic (relapsing). For example, a patient with myositis can occasionally have an acute monophasic course and return to normal strength within weeks or months. Patients with channelopathies or metabolic myopathies can have recurrent attacks of weakness over many years, whereas a patient with acute rhabdomyolysis due to a toxin such as cocaine may have a single episode.

Although weakness may be the most reliable symptom of a patient with a myopathy, many patients who complain of generalized global "weakness" or *fatigue* do not have a disorder of muscle, particularly if the neurologic examination is normal. Fatigue is a nonspecific symptom. On the other hand, abnormal fatigability after exercise can result from certain metabolic and mitochondrial myopathies, and it is important to define the duration and intensity of exercise that provoke it.

Positive Symptoms. Muscle pain (*myalgia*) is another nonspecific complaint that accompanies some myopathies. Myalgias may be episodic (e.g., metabolic myopathies) or nearly constant (e.g., inflammatory muscle disorders). However, muscle pain is surprisingly uncommon in most muscle diseases, and limb pain is more likely to be due to bone or joint disorders. It is rare for a muscle disease to be responsible for vague aches and discomfort in muscle regions in the presence of normal neurologic examination and laboratory study findings.

A specific category of muscle pain is the involuntary muscle *cramp*. Cramps are usually localized to a particular muscle region and last from seconds to minutes. Usually they are benign, occurring in normal individuals, and do not reflect an underlying disease process, and in particular are seldom a feature of a primary myopathy. Cramps can occur with dehydration, hyponatremia, azotemia, and myxedema and in disorders of the motor neuron (especially amyotrophic lateral sclerosis) or nerve.

Muscle contractures are uncommon but can superficially resemble cramps. They usually last longer than cramps and are provoked by exercise in patients with glycolytic enzyme defects. They can be distinguished from cramps with needle electromyography (see later)—contractures are electrically silent whereas cramps are associated with rapid firing motor unit discharges. Muscle contractures should not be confused with fixed *tendon contracture* (see later).

Myotonia is the phenomenon of impaired relaxation of muscle after forceful voluntary contraction. Patients can complain of muscle stiffness or persistent contraction in almost any muscle group but particularly those involving the hands and eyelids. They will note difficulty releasing their hand grip after a handshake, unscrewing a bottle top, or turning a doorknob. If they shut their eyes forcefully, they have difficulty opening their eyelids. With repeated exercise, the myotonia improves: the so-called warm-up phenomenon. Paramyotonia is the paradoxical phenomenon in which exercise makes the myotonia worse. Myotonia is due to repetitive depolarization of the muscle membrane. Exposure to cold worsens myotonia and paramyotonia.

If a patient complains of exercise-induced weakness and myalgias, he or she should be asked whether the urine has ever turned dark or red during or after these episodes, indicating *myoglobinuria*. Myoglobinuria follows excessive release of myoglobin from muscle during periods of rapid muscle destruction (*rhabdomyolysis*).

Other crucial points in the history concern the *age at onset* of symptoms. Did the weakness (or other symptoms) first manifest at birth or was onset in the first, second, third, or later decade? Identifying the age when symptoms began can provide important clues to the diagnosis. For example, of the muscular dystrophies, symptoms in Duchenne-type muscular dystrophy usually are noted by age 3, whereas most facioscapulohumeral and limb-girdle dystrophies begin in adolescence or later. Disorders such as myotonic dystrophy and

---

Table 461–2 • USING THE HISTORY AND PHYSICAL EXAMINATION TO DIAGNOSE MYOPATHIES

HISTORY
  Symptoms
    Negative
      Weakness
        Symptoms of proximal, distal, or cranial weakness
        Constant or episodic
        Monophasic or relapsing
        Progressive or nonprogressive
        Acute, subacute, chronic
      Fatigue and exercise intolerance
    Positive
      Pain—myalgias
      Cramps
      Contractures
      Stiffness/inability to relax muscle—myotonia
      Dark red urine
  Age at onset
  Family history
  Precipitating factors: drug or toxin exposure; exercise; diet; temperature

NEUROLOGIC EXAMINATION
  Distribution of weakness
    Proximal—"limb-girdle"
    Proximal arms/distal legs—"scapuloperoneal"
    Proximal (quadriceps) legs/distal (finger and wrist flexors) arms—"inclusion body myositis"
    Distal—"distal myopathy"
    Ocular or pharyngeal
    Neck extensors
  Atrophy or enlargement
  Myotonia or stiffness

oculopharyngeal dystrophy may not become symptomatic until middle age or later. Of the inflammatory myopathies, dermatomyositis occurs in children and adults, polymyositis rarely occurs in children but can appear at any decade in the adult years, and inclusion body myositis is a myositis of the elderly.

The *family history* is obviously of great importance in correctly diagnosing the hereditary myopathies. A detailed family pedigree (tree) should be obtained to look for autosomal dominant, recessive X-linked, and vertical maternal (mitochondrial) patterns of transmission. Identifying a particular hereditary pattern not only can help in correctly diagnosing the disorder but also is of importance in genetic counseling.

Finally, *precipitating factors* should be explored in the history. Is the patient taking legal or illegal drugs or exposed to toxins that can produce a myopathy? Does exercise provoke attacks of weakness, pain, or urine discoloration, raising the possibility of a glycolytic pathway defect? Are episodes of weakness associated with or preceded by a fever, a feature of carnitine palmitoyl transferase deficiency? Does the ingestion of a carbohydrate meal precede weakness, suggesting a channelopathy? Does cold exposure precipitate muscle stiffness, a characteristic finding in myotonic myopathies?

SIGNS ON NEUROLOGIC EXAMINATION. To determine whether a particular muscle group is weak, it is important to know what muscles to test and how to grade muscle power at the bedside. In examining the upper limbs, it is necessary to assess shoulder abduction, adduction, and external and internal rotation; elbow flexion and extension; wrist flexion and extension; and finger and thumb extension, flexion, and abduction. Muscle groups that should be tested in the lower extremities include hip flexion, extension, abduction, and adduction; knee flexion and extension; ankle dorsiflexion; plantar flexion, inversion, and eversion; and toe extension and flexion. Neck flexors should be assessed with the patient supine, and neck extensors evaluated with the patient prone. Finally, cranial nerve muscles such as those controlling the eyelids, extraocular muscles controlling eye movements, upper and lower facial muscles of expression, the tongue, and the palate should be examined. All muscle groups should be tested bilaterally, and preferably against gravity. Knee extension and hip flexion should be tested in the seated position, knee flexion should be tested prone, and knee abduction should be tested in the lateral decubitus position. If testing against gravity is not done, the presence of substantive muscle weakness can escape recognition.

Assessment of muscle strength is usually based on the Medical Research Council of Great Britain (MRC) grading scale of 0 to 5:

5—Normal power
4—Active movement against gravity and resistance
3—Active movement against gravity
2—Active movement only with gravity eliminated
1—Trace contraction
0—No contraction

In addition to manual muscle testing, muscles should be inspected for *atrophy* or *hypertrophy*. Atrophy of proximal limb muscles is common in long-standing myopathies. However, certain myopathies have atrophy in specific groups that corresponds to severe weakness in those muscles and is a clue to the diagnosis. Atrophy around the periscapular muscles may be associated with scapular winging. Selective atrophy of the quadriceps muscles and forearm flexor muscles is highly suggestive of inclusion body myositis. Distal myopathies may have profound atrophy in anterior or posterior lower leg compartments. Muscles can become diffusely hypertrophic in some myotonic conditions such as myotonia congenita. Muscle hypertrophy can also occur in disorders such as amyloidosis and sarcoidosis and in hypothyroid myopathy. In Duchenne-type and Becker's muscular dystrophy, the calves can become enlarged, but this is usually the pseudohypertrophy of the muscle due to replacement with connective tissue and fat. Focal muscle enlargement may indicate a neoplastic or inflammatory process, ectopic ossification, tendon rupture, and, rarely, partial denervation of various causes.

Tendon contractures (as distinct from the episodic muscle contractures of metabolic myopathy) can occur in many myopathies of long duration. However, contractures developing early in the course of the disease, especially at the elbows, can be a clue to Emery-Dreifuss dystrophy and Bethlem myopathy.

Muscle twitches or fasciculations can be noted on inspection. However, fasciculations are generally not a manifestation of a muscle disease but occur in the setting of denervation or as a benign process.

It is important to watch the patient perform functional activities: walking (to look for a wide-based waddling gait with hyperlordosis, which is a sign of pelvic muscle weakness); rising from a chair, from a squat, or from a seated position on the floor (*Gowers' sign*); or climbing stairs (noting whether there is a need to use the arms, another sign of proximal weakness in the lower extremities). The inability to walk on the heels or toes can indicate weakness in the anterior and posterior distal leg muscles, respectively. Observe the patient talk and smile to determine whether there is facial weakness. Is there the so-called horizontal smile, indicating lower facial muscle weakness? Is the patient unable to close the eyes completely when asked to do so, indicating upper facial muscle weakness? Are the upper eyelids lowered so that they touch the pupil, indicating ptosis? Is the speech nasal, indicating palatal muscle involvement?

Finally, if the patient complains of muscle stiffness, the examiner should attempt to elicit *myotonia*. This can be done by asking the patient to squeeze the examiner's finger and then observing whether the patient has an inability to relax the hand grip. Additionally, the muscles can be directly percussed with a reflex hammer. Observe for a slow persistent contraction and delayed relaxation. The muscles that can be most easily percussed to look for myotonia are the thenar and wrist/finger extensor muscle groups. Facial myotonia can also be observed after forceful voluntary eye closure. The patient will be unable to open the eyes easily after this maneuver.

Other aspects of the neurologic examination need to be assessed in all potential myopathy patients to ensure that they are not involved. The sensory examination result should be normal in muscle disease. Reflexes are usually preserved early in the disease process. Once the myopathy is advanced and the muscles are extremely weak, reflexes can become hypoactive or not be able to be elicited. Evidence of damage to upper motor neurons (spasticity, extensor plantar responses, clonus) is only present in myopathies if there is coincidental CNS disease.

PATTERN OF WEAKNESS. Once the muscles have been inspected and tested for power, and functional activity has been observed, an attempt should be made to place the patient in one of the *patterns of muscle weakness* that can occur in myopathic disorders. The various patterns of muscle weakness can be divided into six broad groups:

1. The pattern (most common) of weakness that is exclusively or predominantly in proximal muscles of the legs and arms—the so-called limb-girdle distribution. Neck flexor and extensor muscles can also be affected. This pattern of weakness can be seen in many hereditary and acquired myopathies and therefore is the least specific in arriving at a particular diagnosis. It is not known why most myopathic disorders selectively involve proximal muscles.

2. The pattern of *distal* weakness in the upper extremities (extensor muscle group) or lower extremities (anterior or posterior compartment muscle groups) (Table 461–3). Selective

---

Table 461–3 • MYOPATHIES THAT MAY INCLUDE PROMINENT DISTAL WEAKNESS

Late adult-onset distal myopathy type 1 (Welander)
Late adult-onset distal myopathy type 2 (Markesbery/Udd)
Early adult-onset distal myopathy type 1 (Nonaka)
Early adult-onset distal myopathy type 2 (Miyoshi)
Early adult-onset distal myopathy type 3 (Laing)
Desmin myopathy
Myotonic dystrophy
Facioscapulohumeral dystrophy*
Scapuloperoneal dystrophy*
Oculopharyngeal dystrophy
Emery-Dreifuss humeroperoneal dystrophy*
Inflammatory myopathies
   Inclusion body myositis
Metabolic myopathy
   Debrancher deficiency
   Acid-maltase deficiency*
Congenital myopathy
   Nemaline myopathy*
   Central core myopathy*
   Centronuclear myopathy

*Can occur in a scapuloperoneal pattern.

weakness and atrophy in distal extremity muscles are more often features of neuropathies but are uncommonly due to a primary muscle disease. When this pattern of weakness is determined to be due to a myopathic rather than a neuropathic disorder, a diagnosis of distal myopathy is appropriate.

3. The pattern of proximal upper extremity weakness of the periscapular muscles and distal lower extremity weakness of the anterior compartment—the *scapuloperoneal* pattern (see Table 461–3). The scapular muscle weakness is usually accompanied by scapular winging. When this pattern is associated with facial weakness, it is highly suggestive of facioscapulohumeral dystrophy. Other hereditary myopathies can be associated with a scapuloperoneal syndrome, for example, scapuloperoneal dystrophy, Emery-Dreifuss dystrophy, acid maltase deficiency, and some congenital myopathies.

4. The pattern of distal upper extremity weakness in the distal forearm muscles (wrist and finger flexors) and proximal lower extremity weakness involving the knee extensors (quadriceps). This pattern is essentially pathognomonic for *inclusion body myositis*. In addition, the weakness is often asymmetrical between the two sides, a pattern that is uncommon in most myopathies.

5. Predominant involvement of ocular or pharyngeal muscles (Table 461–4). The combination of ptosis, ophthalmoplegia without diplopia, and pharyngeal weakness should suggest the diagnosis of oculopharyngeal dystrophy, especially if the onset is in middle age or later. Ptosis and ophthalmoplegia without prominent pharyngeal involvement are hallmarks of many of the mitochondrial myopathies. Ptosis and facial weakness without ophthalmoplegia or pharyngeal weakness are common features of myotonic dystrophy. Therefore, the presence of ocular or pharyngeal muscle involvement can suggest a particular muscle disorder. Patients with ocular or pharyngeal involvement can also have the typical pattern of limb-girdle weakness.

6. Prominent neck extensor weakness. Some myopathic conditions have such a dramatic degree of weakness of the neck extensor muscles that the term *dropped head syndrome* is used (Table 461–5). The neck flexors may or may not be weak. Neck extensor weakness can also occur with myopathies such as those with a limb-girdle pattern of weakness. Prominent neck

extensor weakness is common in two other neuromuscular diseases: amyotrophic lateral sclerosis and myasthenia gravis.

These six patterns of myopathy have limitations but are useful in narrowing the differential diagnosis. Patients with neuromuscular diseases other than myopathies can also present with one of these weakness patterns. For example, although proximal greater than distal weakness is characteristic of myopathies, patients with acquired demyelinating neuropathies (Guillain-Barré syndrome [GBS] and chronic inflammatory demyelinating polyneuropathy [CIDP]) often have proximal as well as distal muscle involvement. Such neuropathies generally have the additional finding of sensory and reflex loss. Ocular, pharyngeal, and proximal limb weakness is characteristic of neuromuscular junction transmission disorders such as myasthenia gravis. However, these patients usually have diplopia, weakness that fluctuates, and additional laboratory findings that will lead to the correct diagnosis. Table 461–6 summarizes the key distinguishing clinical points among disorders of muscle, anterior horn cell, peripheral nerve, and neuromuscular junction.

ASSOCIATED ORGAN INVOLVEMENT OR SYSTEMIC ILLNESS. Involvement of organs or tissues other than muscle can provide additional diagnostic clues. Cardiac disease can be associated with myotonic dystrophy, dystrophinopathies, Emery-Dreifuss dystrophy, and certain types of periodic paralysis. Hepatomegaly can occur in sarcoidosis and in the myopathies associated with deficiencies of acid maltase, debranching enzyme, and carnitine. Intrinsic pulmonary involvement can be seen in some of the inflammatory myopathies and sarcoidosis. Evidence of a diffuse systemic disorder can indicate a collagen vascular disease, amyloidosis, sarcoidosis, endocrine myopathies, or mitochondrial disorders.

Laboratory Studies for the Evaluation of Myopathy

SERUM ENZYMES OF MUSCLE ORIGIN. *Creatine kinase* (CK) occurs in high concentration in the sarcoplasm of skeletal and cardiac muscle. The MM isoenzyme of CK predominates in skeletal muscle, MB occurs primarily in cardiac muscle, and BB is mainly in brain. When skeletal muscle is injured CK can leak into the blood. Therefore, an elevated serum CK level is present in many muscle diseases. However, the absence of an elevated serum CK level does not rule out a myopathy, particularly in patients with severe muscle atrophy. In addition, the elevation of serum CK level does not necessarily imply that the muscle is the primary site of abnormality. The CK level is often elevated in normal individuals for days after strenuous voluntary

---

Table 461–4 • MYOPATHIES WITH PTOSIS OR OPHTHALMOPLEGIA

PTOSIS USUALLY WITHOUT OPHTHALMOPLEGIA
Myotonic dystrophy
Congenital myopathies
  Centronuclear myopathy
  Nemaline myopathy
  Central core myopathy
Desmin storage myopathy

PTOSIS WITH OPHTHALMOPLEGIA
Oculopharyngeal muscular dystrophy
Oculopharyngodistal myopathy
Mitochondrial myopathy

Table 461–5 • MYOPATHIES THAT OFTEN INCLUDE PROMINENT NECK EXTENSOR WEAKNESS

Isolated neck extensor myopathy
Polymyositis
Dermatomyositis
Inclusion body myositis
Carnitine deficiency
Myotonic dystrophy
Congenital myopathy
Hyperparathyroidism

Table 461–6 • CLINICAL FINDINGS DIFFERENTIATING MUSCLE FROM NERVE DISEASE

FINDING	MYOPATHY	ANTERIOR HORN CELL DISEASE	PERIPHERAL NEUROPATHY	NEUROMUSCULAR JUNCTION DISEASE
Distribution	Usually proximal, symmetrical	Distal, asymmetrical, and bulbar	Distal, symmetrical	Extraocular, bulbar, proximal limb
Atrophy	Slight early, marked late	Marked early	Moderate	Absent
Fasciculations	Absent	Frequent	Sometimes present	Absent
Reflexes	Lost late	Variable, can be hyperreflexic	Lost early	Normal
Pain	Diffuse in myositis	Absent	Variable, distal when present	Absent
Cramps	Rare	Frequent	Occasional	Absent
Sensory loss	Absent	Absent	Usually present	Absent
Serum creatine kinase	Usually elevated	Occasionally slightly elevated	Normal	Normal

exercise. Involuntary prolonged muscle contraction from a generalized motor seizure or tetany can elevate the CK level. Serum CK level is above the normal range in some African individuals, in individuals with large muscles, and after minor muscle trauma (e.g., electromyography). Finally, other neuromuscular disorders such as motor neuron disease can produce up to a five-fold increase in CK level. Serum CK level is normal in peripheral neuropathies and neuromuscular junction disorders.

Other enzymes that can be released from injured skeletal muscle include aspartate aminotransferase (AST), alanine aminotransferase (ALT), and lactate dehydrogenase (LDH). These enzymes also occur in high concentration in the liver. The serum CK level is the most sensitive for muscle disease, and it is rarely necessary to measure for these other enzymes. Levels of enzymes such as AST and ALT are elevated in hepatic disease; and because they are often measured in large screening chemical panels, their elevation should prompt CK measurement to determine whether the source is muscle or liver. If a patient with an inflammatory myopathy is treated with a drug that may have hepatotoxicity as a side effect, it is not sufficient to measure ALT and AST levels; the liver-specific enzyme γ-glutamyl transferase (GGT) should be followed.

In general, CK isoenzymes are not helpful in myopathy evaluations. CK-MM level elevations are typical of muscle disease, but CK-MB level is also elevated in myopathies and does not indicate that cardiac disease is present.

ELECTROMYOGRAPHY (EMG). EMG is the electrophysiologic assessment of the neuromuscular system (Chapter 423). It consists of nerve conduction study (NCS) and needle electromyography.

The basic principle of EMG is that a moving wave of electronegativity from either nerve or muscle is measured with a recording device. For NCS, a nerve is depolarized with an electrical stimulator and the electrical potential is measured over the muscle (for motor NCS) or nerve (for sensory NCS). The recorded motor and sensory nerve potentials are measured for amplitude, latency, and conduction velocities. Both the motor and sensory NCSs usually have normal results in myopathies, but results are generally abnormal in neuropathies. In needle EMG, a needle electrode is inserted directly into the muscle. The electrical activity from the muscle is observed at rest and when the patient voluntarily contracts the muscle. The potentials recorded from the needle are viewed on a screen and the examiner also listens to the auditory pattern.

Abnormal EMG Activity at Rest. In a normal individual there is no recorded electrical activity from a muscle when it is at rest. Spontaneous rhythmic discharges of single muscle fiber are called *fibrillations* or *positive sharp waves* and occur when there has been a disconnection between the nerve and the muscle it innervates. Fibrillations occur more often in nerve diseases but can occur in active myopathies. Because a fibrillation represents the discharge of a single muscle fiber, it cannot be detected on the clinical examination but can only be observed on needle EMG.

Myotonia is the abnormal spontaneous discharge of muscle that occurs in some myopathies, such as myotonic dystrophy, myotonia congenita, periodic paralysis, and acid maltase deficiency. On EMG, myotonia consists of high-frequency repetitive discharges that spontaneously increase and decrease in amplitude and frequency and have the sound of a dive-bomber or motorcycle. Myotonia represents repeated muscle fiber depolarization from an irritable muscle membrane and indicates a myopathy. A third spontaneous electrical phenomenon, the complex repetitive discharge, is usually the result of nerve disease. The complex repetitive discharge differs from myotonia in that it starts and stops abruptly and does not wax and wane in frequency and amplitude. It sounds like a jackhammer.

Fasciculations are to be distinguished from fibrillations and myotonia. A fasciculation represents a spontaneous discharge of a motor unit, which is a group of muscle fibers of the same histochemical type under control of a single anterior horn cell, and thus innervated by the same axon. These can be observed clinically as a small muscle twitch or movement. Electrically, a fasciculation is a large-amplitude potential that consists of the simultaneous involuntary depolarization of a group of muscle fibers. Although they do not necessarily imply neuromuscular disease and occur in many normal patients, fasciculations can occur in diseases of the motor neuron or nerve. Neither clinical nor electrical fasciculations are a feature of muscle disorders.

EMG Activity with Movement. When the patient voluntarily contracts the muscle, individual *motor unit action potentials* are assessed. Motor units are normally triphasic potentials, and a normal motor unit recorded with the EMG needle consists of about 10 or more muscle fibers innervated by the same axon that are simultaneously depolarizing. Individual motor units are analyzed for their amplitude, duration, and number of phases. In addition, the firing rate and recruitment pattern of the voluntary motor units are noted.

Two abnormal motor unit patterns that can be observed suggest that the disease is either "neuropathic" or "myopathic." Neuropathic motor unit potentials are increased in amplitude (>5 mV) and duration (>10 milliseconds) and are polyphasic. In addition, for a given degree of voluntary effort, few motor units are recruited and the ones that are fire too rapidly (>15 to 20 Hz). This indicates a loss of motor units with a compensatory increased firing rate in the remaining units, a pattern known as *decreased recruitment*. Myopathic motor unit potentials are small, brief polyphasic potentials (<4 milliseconds). In a myopathy, multiple small motor units are recruited with only minimal voluntary effort. This myopathic pattern occurs because the number of motor units is normal but there are fewer functioning muscle fibers within each unit, and therefore more units are required to generate a degree of force. These so-called neuropathic and myopathic needle EMG patterns are generalizations, and there are many examples of denervating illness that produce myopathic potentials, and vice versa. In addition, the EMG result can be normal in a patient with a myopathy.

However, if the needle EMG examination finding shows evidence of myopathic motor units this adds further data that the patient may indeed have a myopathy. In addition, multiple muscles can be sampled with needle EMG. Needle EMG can be useful in confirming the clinical phenotype of muscle involvement established on the neurologic examination. EMG can also provide a clue as to which muscles have had recent or ongoing muscle injury and can be a guide as to which muscle to sample.

MUSCLE BIOPSY. A muscle specimen can be obtained through either an open or a closed (needle or punch) biopsy procedure. The biopsy should sample a muscle that is moderately weak. Biopsy specimens should generally not be taken from severely weak (MRC grade 2 or less) muscles. Muscles that have recently been studied by needle EMG often have artifacts from the procedure.

The muscle biopsy result can establish whether there is evidence of either a neuropathic or a myopathic disorder. A neuropathy can produce denervation atrophy with small angular fibers, groups of atrophic fibers, and, as a result of reinnervation, groups of fibers of the same histochemical type and target fibers. These features should not be present in a myopathy. Typical myopathic abnormalities include central nuclei, both small and large hypertrophic round fibers, split fibers, and degenerating and regenerating fibers. Inflammatory myopathies produce mononuclear inflammatory cells in the endomysial and perimysial connective tissue between fibers and occasionally around blood vessels. The atrophy of fibers located on the periphery of a muscle fascicle, perifascicular atrophy, is a common finding in a particular inflammatory myopathy, dermatomyositis. Any long-standing chronic myopathy can produce an increase in connective tissue and fat. Mitochondrial disorders are suggested by identification of ragged-red fibers on the Gomori stain and various abnormal staining patterns on the oxidative stains. The enzymatic stains can demonstrate a nonspecific type 1 fiber predominance in a number of myopathies.

Electron microscopy (EM) evaluates ultrastructural components of muscle fibers. In most myopathic disorders EM is not required to make a pathologic diagnosis; findings detected by EM are seldom of importance. However, EM is important in the study of certain disease states with abnormal light microscopic findings: congenital myopathies (e.g., nemaline rod, central core) and mitochondrial disorders.

In the evaluation of metabolic and mitochondrial myopathies, a portion of the muscle tissue can be processed for biochemical analysis to determine the specific enzyme defect. Western blot determinations from muscle tissue can be performed for certain muscle proteins (e.g., dystrophin).

MOLECULAR GENETIC STUDIES. The specific molecular genetic defect is known for an increasing number of myopathies. Molecular genetic testing is important for both diagnosis and carrier detection.

OTHER TESTS. Electrolyte, endocrine, and immunologic tests are indicated to establish specific medical diagnoses. A decrease in the serum creatinine level is a useful indicator of decreased muscle mass.

Forearm exercise testing in patients with a suspected metabolic myopathy is often performed to determine whether there is a defect in the glycolytic enzyme pathway. After vigorous exercise, serum lactate and ammonia levels are measured. In disorders such as phosphorylase deficiency (McArdle's disease), the characteristic elevation of serum lactate level after exercise is absent.

Urinalysis can detect the presence of myoglobinuria. This should be suspected if the urine test result is positive for blood but no red blood cells are seen.

Quantitation of urinary creatinine excretion is useful to determine whether there is a decrease in muscle mass but requires that the patient be on a meat-free diet and must be done over a period of 72 hours or more.

Imaging and spectroscopy studies include computed tomography, magnetic resonance imaging, and ultrasound. Muscle imaging is seldom useful to diagnose a myopathy. However, in selected patients undergoing muscle biopsy in whom it is unclear from the neurologic examination and needle EMG results which muscle to select for biopsy, an imaging procedure may be helpful.

GENERAL APPROACH TO NERVE DISEASE

The peripheral nervous system consists of sensory and motor components. The cell body for the sensory nerves is the dorsal root ganglion, and that for the motor nerves is the anterior horn cell. Diseases can affect the neuron's cell body (neuronopathies) or the peripheral process (peripheral neuropathies). Neuronopathies that affect the anterior horn cells are termed *motor neuron disease,* and those involving the sensory cell body are also called *ganglionopathies.* Most peripheral nerves are mixed and contain both sensory and motor fibers. These fibers can be grouped into three major classes: large myelinated, small myelinated, and small unmyelinated. Motor axons usually are large myelinated fibers that conduct rapidly (approximately 50 meters per second). Sensory fibers may be any of the three types. Joint position and vibratory stimuli are transmitted to the CNS by fast-conducting, large-diameter sensory fibers, whereas pain and thermal stimuli are transmitted by smaller, slower-conducting fibers. Autonomic nerves are also small in diameter. Peripheral neuropathies are characterized by impaired function of sensory, motor, or autonomic nerves, either singly or in combination. Most forms of peripheral neuropathy affect more than one type of nerve fiber. Peripheral neuropathies can be broadly subdivided into those that primarily affect myelin, or myelinopathies, and those that affect the axon, or axonopathies.

Neuronopathies and peripheral neuropathies have distinct clinical and electrophysiologic features (see Table 461–6). The three goals of the clinician in the approach to a neuropathic disorder are to determine (1) where the lesion is (Table 461–7), (2) what the cause of the lesion is (Table 461–8), and (3) what the treatment should be.

To accomplish the goal of determining the site and cause of the lesion and, if possible, a therapy, the clinician gathers information from the history, the neurologic examination, and various laboratory studies. While gathering this information, six key questions are asked (Table 461–9). From the answer to these six key questions, the patient can be placed into different clinical patterns (Table 461–10). Although neuropathies due to diabetes mellitus are probably the most common cause of peripheral neuropathies, acquired demyelinating and hereditary disorders account for a large percentage as well. In approximately a fourth of patients, no etiology is ever found. These patients typically have a predominately sensory polyneuropathy and have been labeled as having cryptogenic sensory polyneuropathy (CSPN).

Table 461–7 • PATHOLOGIC CLASSIFICATION OF NEUROPATHIC DISORDERS

Neuronopathies (pure sensory or pure motor):
  Sensory neuronopathies (ganglionopathies)
  Motor neuronopathies (motor neuron disease)
Peripheral neuropathies:
  Myelinopathies vs. axonopathies
    Motor
    Sensory
    Autonomic
    Mixed (sensorimotor, sensory + autonomic)

Table 461–8 • ETIOLOGY OF NEUROPATHIC DISORDERS

ACQUIRED
Dysmetabolic States
Diabetes mellitus
Neuropathy related to renal disease
Vitamin deficiency states (e.g., vitamin B_{12} deficiency)
Primary amyloidosis

Immune-mediated
Guillain-Barré syndrome
Chronic inflammatory demyelinating polyneuropathy (CIDP)
Vasculitis
Neuropathy associated with a monoclonal antibody
Plexitis—cervical and lumbosacral
Multifocal motor neuropathy

Infectious
Herpes zoster
Leprosy, Lyme disease, HIV infection, and sarcoid related

Cancer Related
Lymphoma, myeloma, carcinoma related
Paraneoplastic subacute sensory neuronopathy

Drugs or Toxins
Chemotherapy induced
Other drugs
Heavy metals and industrial toxins

Mechanical/Compressive
Radiculopathy
Mononeuropathy

Unknown Etiology
Cryptogenic sensory and sensorimotor neuropathy
Amyotrophic lateral sclerosis

HEREDITARY
Hereditary motor sensory neuropathy
  (Charcot-Marie-Tooth disease)
Hereditary neuropathy with predisposition to pressure palsies
Familial brachial plexopathy
Familial amyloidosis
Porphyria
Other rare peripheral neuropathies
  (Fabry's disease, metachromatic leukodystrophy,
    adrenoleukodystrophy, Refsum's disease, etc.)
Motor neuron disease
  Spinal muscular atrophy
  Familial amyotrophic lateral sclerosis
  X-linked bulbospinal muscular atrophy

Table 461–9 • APPROACH TO NEUROPATHIC DISORDERS: SIX KEY QUESTIONS

1. **What systems are involved?**
   • Motor, sensory, autonomic, or combinations
2. **What is the distribution of weakness?**
   • Only distal versus proximal and distal
   • Focal/asymmetrical versus symmetric
3. **What is the nature of the sensory involvement?**
   • Severe pain/burning or stabbing
   • Severe proprioceptive loss
4. **Is there evidence of upper motor neuron involvement?**
   • Without sensory loss
   • With sensory loss
5. **What is the temporal evolution?**
   • Acute (days to 4 weeks)
   • Subacute (4 to 8 weeks)
   • Chronic (>8 weeks)
   • Preceding events, drugs, toxins
6. **Is there evidence for a hereditary neuropathy?**
   • Family history of neuropathy
   • Lack of sensory symptoms despite sensory signs

Table 461-10 • PATTERNS OF NEUROPATHIC DISORDERS

PATTERN 1: SYMMETRICAL PROXIMAL AND DISTAL WEAKNESS WITH SENSORY LOSS
Consider: inflammatory demyelinating polyneuropathy (Guillain-Barré syndrome and chronic inflammatory demyelinating polyneuropathy)

PATTERN 2: SYMMETRICAL DISTAL SENSORY LOSS WITH OR WITHOUT DISTAL WEAKNESS
Consider: cryptogenic sensory polyneuropathy (CSPN); metabolic disorders; drugs, toxins; hereditary (Charcot-Marie-Tooth syndrome, amyloidosis, and others)

PATTERN 3: ASYMMETRICAL DISTAL WEAKNESS WITH SENSORY LOSS
Multiple nerves, *consider:* vasculitis; hereditary neuropathy with liability to pressure palsies (HNPP); infectious (leprosy, sarcoid, Lyme disease, HIV infection)
Single nerves/regions, *consider:* compressive mononeuropathy and radiculopathy

PATTERN 4: ASYMMETRICAL PROXIMAL AND DISTAL WEAKNESS WITH SENSORY LOSS
Consider: polyradiculopathy or plexopathy due to diabetes mellitus; meningeal carcinomatosis or lymphomatosis; idiopathic; hereditary (HNPP, familial)

PATTERN 5: ASYMMETRICAL DISTAL WEAKNESS WITHOUT SENSORY LOSS
With upper motor neuron findings, *consider:* motor neuron disease
Without upper motor neuron findings, *consider:* progressive muscular atrophy; multifocal motor neuropathy; multifocal acquired motor axonopathy (MAMA); or juvenile monomelic amyotrophy

PATTERN 6: SYMMETRICAL SENSORY LOSS AND DISTAL AREFLEXIA WITH UPPER MOTOR NEURON FINDINGS
Consider: vitamin B$_{12}$ deficiency and other causes of combined system degeneration with peripheral neuropathy

PATTERN 7: SYMMETRICAL WEAKNESS WITHOUT SENSORY LOSS
With proximal and distal weakness *consider:* spinal muscular atrophy
With distal weakness *consider:* hereditary motor neuropathy ("distal" spinal muscular atrophy)

PATTERN 8: ASYMMETRICAL PROPRIOCEPTIVE SENSORY LOSS WITHOUT WEAKNESS
Consider: sensory neuronopathy (ganglionopathy) (see Table 461-15)

PATTERN 9: AUTONOMIC SYMPTOMS AND SIGNS
Consider: neuropathies associated with autonomic dysfunction (see Table 461-12)

History and Physical Examination—Six Key Questions

1. WHAT SYSTEMS ARE INVOLVED?

It is important to determine if patients' symptoms and signs are pure motor, pure sensory, or both. If the patient has weakness only without any evidence of sensory loss, a motor neuronopathy (motor neuron disease) is the most likely diagnosis. The majority of patients with adult-onset motor neuron disease have evidence of both upper and lower motor neuron dysfunction on examination, that is, amyotrophic lateral sclerosis (ALS; Chapter 447). The neuropathic disorders that may present with pure motor symptoms are listed in Table 461-11. Whereas some peripheral neuropathies may present with only motor symptoms, there is usually evidence of sensory involvement on neurologic examination.

Table 461-11 • NEUROPATHIC DISORDERS THAT MAY HAVE ONLY MOTOR SYMPTOMS AT PRESENTATION

Motor neuron disease	Lead intoxication*
Multifocal motor neuropathy	Acute porphyria*
Guillain-Barré syndrome*	Hereditary motor sensory neuropathy (Charcot-Marie-Tooth disease)*
Chronic inflammatory demyelinating polyneuropathy	

*Usually has sensory signs on examination.

Table 461-12 • PERIPHERAL NEUROPATHIES WITH AUTONOMIC NERVOUS SYSTEM INVOLVEMENT

Diabetes mellitus
Amyloidosis (familiar and acquired)
Guillain-Barré syndrome
Vincristine induced
Porphyria
HIV-related autonomic neuropathy
Idiopathic pandysautonomia

Some peripheral neuropathies are associated with evidence of autonomic nervous system dysfunction (Table 461-12). Symptoms of autonomic involvement include fainting spells or orthostatic lightheadedness, heat intolerance, or any bowel, bladder, or sexual dysfunction. There will typically be an orthostatic fall in blood pressure without an appropriate increase in heart rate. Autonomic dysfunction in the absence of diabetes should suggest the possibility of amyloid polyneuropathy. Rarely, idiopathic pandysautonomic syndrome can be the only manifestation of a peripheral neuropathy without other motor or sensory findings.

2. WHAT IS THE DISTRIBUTION OF WEAKNESS?

The distribution of the patient's weakness aids diagnosis. Two questions should be addressed: (1) does the weakness involve only the distal extremity or is it both proximal and distal? and (2) is the weakness focal and asymmetrical or is it symmetrical? The finding of weakness in both proximal and distal muscle groups in a symmetrical fashion is typical of acquired immune demyelinating polyneuropathies, both the acute form (GBS) and the chronic form (CIDP). Patients with proximal muscle weakness will complain of difficulty raising their arms to brush their teeth or comb their hair as well as problems climbing stairs or rising from a chair. On the neurologic examination, the clinician needs to pay particular attention for the presence of facial, neck, shoulder, and hip weakness in addition to involvement of the more distal muscle groups in the hands and feet. The importance of finding symmetrical proximal and distal weakness in a patient who presents with both motor and sensory symptoms cannot be overemphasized because this finding identifies the important subset of patients who may have a treatable acquired demyelinating neuropathic disorder (e.g., acute or chronic inflammatory demyelinating polyneuropathy).

Asymmetry or focality of the weakness is also a feature that can narrow the diagnostic possibilities (Table 461-13). Some neuropathic disorders may present as unilateral leg weakness. If sensory symptoms and signs are absent, and the patient presents with painless footdrop evolving over weeks or months, motor neuron disease is the leading and most worrisome diagnostic possibility. In a patient presenting with subacute or acute sensory and motor symptoms of one leg, lumbosacral radiculopathies, plexopathies, vasculitis, and compressive mononeuropathy need to be considered. Similarly, if the clinical manifestations are pure motor weakness in one arm or hand, motor neuron disease is a leading consideration. If sensory symptoms are also present, cervical radiculopathy, brachial plexopathy, or a mononeuropathy are likely possibilities. In general, unilateral sensory symptoms and weakness that involve the entire extremity (proximal and distal/C5 to T1 or L2 to S1) suggest a polyradiculopathy or plexopathy (cervical or lumbosacral). If the asymmetrical sensorimotor findings are restricted to distal peripheral nerve(s), the diagnosis is usually a mononeuropathy or mononeuropathy multiplex.

3. WHAT IS THE NATURE OF THE SENSORY INVOLVEMENT?

When taking the history from a patient with a peripheral neuropathy, it is important to determine if the patient has loss of sensation (numbness), altered sensation (tingling), or pain. Sometimes patients may find it difficult to distinguish between uncomfortable tingling sensations (dysesthesias) and pain. Neuropathic pain be burning, dull, and poorly localized (protopathic pain), presumably transmitted by polymodal C nociceptor fibers, or sharp and lancinating (epicritic pain), relayed by Aδ fibers.

Table 461–13 • NEUROPATHIC DISORDERS THAT PRODUCE ASYMMETRICAL/FOCAL WEAKNESS

Motor neuron disease
  Amyotrophic lateral sclerosis
Radiculopathy—cervical or lumbosacral
  Root compression from osteoarthritis
  Root compression from herniated disc
  Herpes zoster focal paresis (with rash)
  Meningeal carcinomatosis and lymphomatosis
Plexopathy—brachial or lumbosacral
  Immune-mediated/idiopathic (primarily brachial)
  Neoplastic infiltration
  Diabetic radiculoplexopathy (primarily lumbosacral)
  Familial brachial plexopathy
  Hereditary neuropathy with liability to pressure palsy
Mononeuropathy multiplex due to:
  Vasculitis
  Multifocal motor neuropathy
  Multifocal acquired demyelinating sensory and motor neuropathy
  Lyme disease
  Sarcoid
  Leprosy
  HIV infection
  Hereditary neuropathy with liability to pressure palsy
Compressive/entrapment mononeuropathies
  Median neuropathy
  Ulnar neuropathy
  Peroneal neuropathy

Complaints of numbness and the type of neuropathic pain implicate sensory involvement but generally are not very helpful in suggesting a specific diagnosis because these symptoms can accompany many peripheral neuropathies. However, two sensory features may be helpful in arriving at a diagnosis. If severe pain is one of the patient's symptoms, certain peripheral neuropathies should be considered, particularly cryptogenic sensory polyneuropathy (CSPN) and neuropathy due to diabetes mellitus (Table 461–14). In addition, painful peripheral neuropathies due to peripheral nerve vasculitis or GBS are important to recognize because these disorders are treatable. The pain in vasculitic neuropathy is generally distal and asymmetrical in the most severely involved extremity. Some patients with GBS have severe back pain associated with symmetrical numbness and paresthesias in the extremities. Another painful form of diabetic neuropathy is lumbosacral radiculoplexopathy (also known as diabetic amyotrophy), in which patients may present with the abrupt onset of back, hip, or thigh pain that may precede weakness by days or weeks.

The other important sensory abnormality that significantly narrows the differential diagnosis is severe proprioceptive loss. This finding is sometimes difficult to discern from the history, but complaints of loss of balance, especially in the dark, incoordination of the limbs, or symptoms suggesting disequilibrium may be elicited. If the neurologic examination reveals a dramatic asymmetrical loss of proprioception with significant loss of vibration sense despite normal strength, a sensory neuronopathy should be considered (i.e., ganglionopathy) (Table 461–15). In addition to the severe proprioceptive and vibration deficits, sensory neuronopathies usually have a pan-modality sensory loss, including light touch, pain, and temperature sensation in the affected extremities. Profound loss of proprioception and vibration sense can also be due to posterior column damage from disorders such as combined system degeneration from vitamin

Table 461–14 • PERIPHERAL NEUROPATHIES THAT ARE OFTEN ASSOCIATED WITH PAIN

Cryptogenic sensory or sensorimotor neuropathy
Diabetes mellitus
Vasculitis
Guillain-Barré syndrome
Amyloidosis
Toxic (arsenic, thallium)
HIV-related distal symmetrical polyneuropathy
Fabry's disease

Table 461–15 • CAUSES OF SENSORY NEURONOPATHY (GANGLIONOPATHY)

Cancer (paraneoplastic)
Sjögren's syndrome
Idiopathic sensory neuronopathy
Cisplatin
Vitamin B_6 toxicity
HIV-related sensory neuronopathy

B_{12} deficiency. However, posterior column myelopathy is generally symmetrical and is less profound than most of the patients with true dorsal root ganglion loss and is often associated with evidence of upper motor neuron pathology (see later).

4. IS THERE EVIDENCE OF UPPER MOTOR NEURON INVOLVEMENT?

In patients with symptoms and signs suggestive of lower motor neuron pathology without sensory loss, the presence of concomitant upper motor neuron signs is the hallmark of amyotrophic lateral sclerosis (see Chapter 447). Conversely, if the patient presents with symmetrical distal sensory symptoms and signs suggestive of a distal sensory neuropathy but there is additional evidence of symmetrical upper motor involvement, the physician should consider a disorder such as combined system degeneration with neuropathy. The most common cause for this pattern is vitamin B_{12} deficiency (Chapter 458), but other causes of combined system degeneration with neuropathy should be considered (e.g., HIV infection, severe hepatic disease, adrenomyeloneuropathy).

5. WHAT IS THE TEMPORAL EVOLUTION?

The onset, duration, and evolution of symptoms and signs should be determined. Does the disease have an acute (days to 4 weeks), subacute (4 to 8 weeks), or chronic (greater than 8 weeks) course? Is the course monophasic, progressive, or relapsing? Neuropathies with acute and subacute presentations include GBS, vasculitis, and diabetic lumbosacral radiculoplexopathy. A relapsing course can be present in CIDP and porphyria. It is also important to inquire about preceding or concurrent infections, associated medical conditions, drug use including over-the-counter vitamin preparations (e.g., vitamin B_6), alcohol use, and dietary habits.

6. IS THERE EVIDENCE FOR A HEREDITARY NEUROPATHY?

In patients with a chronic, very slowly progressive distal weakness over many years but with very little in the way of sensory symptoms, the clinician should pay particular attention to the family history and inquire about foot deformities in immediate relatives. In addition, episodes of recurrent compressive mononeuropathies may indicate an underlying hereditary predisposition to pressure palsies. On examining the patient, the clinician must look carefully at the feet for arch and toe abnormalities (high or flat arches, hammertoes) and look at the spine for scoliosis. In some cases, it may be helpful to perform both neurologic and electrophysiologic studies on family members.

Pattern Recognition Approach of Neuropathic Disorders

After answering the six key questions obtained from the history and neurologic examination just outlined, one can classify neuropathic disorders into several patterns based on sensory and motor involvement and distribution of signs (see Table 461–10). Each syndrome has a limited differential diagnosis. A final diagnosis also considers other clues, such as the temporal course, presence of other diseases, family history, and information from laboratory studies, that are guided by the differential diagnosis.

Information from the Electrophysiologic Study

The electrophysiologic evaluation of patients with a suspected peripheral neuropathy consists of nerve conduction studies (NCS) and needle electromyography (EMG). The electrophysiologic data provide additional information about the distribution of the neuropathy

Table 461–16 • AXONAL DEGENERATION VS. SEGMENTAL DEMYELINATION: ELECTROPHYSIOLOGIC FEATURES

	AXONAL DEGENERATION	SEGMENTAL DEMYELINATION
MOTOR NERVE CONDUCTION STUDIES		
CMAP amplitude	Decreased	Normal (except with conduction block)
Distal latency	Normal	Prolonged
Conduction velocity	Normal	Slow
Conduction block	Absent	Present
Temporal dispersion	Absent	Present
F wave	Normal	Prolonged or absent
H reflex	Normal	Prolonged or absent
SENSORY NERVE CONDUCTION STUDIES		
SNAP amplitude	Decreased	Normal
Distal latency	Normal	Prolonged
Conduction velocity	Normal	Slow
NEEDLE EMG		
Spontaneous activity		
Fibrillations	Present	Absent
Fasciculations	Present	Absent
VOLUNTARY MOTOR UNIT POTENTIALS		
Recruitment	Decreased	Decreased
Morphology	Long duration/polyphasic	Normal

CMAP = compound motor action potential; SNAP = sensory nerve action potential.

Table 461–17 • PERIPHERAL NEUROPATHIES IN WHICH A NERVE BIOPSY MAY BE USEFUL

ACQUIRED DISORDERS
Vasculitis*
Sarcoidosis
Amyloidosis-acquired
Chronic inflammatory demyelinating polyneuropathy
Neuropathy with IgM monoclonal and myelin-associated glycoprotein antibodies
Leprosy
Tumor infiltration*

HEREDITARY DISORDERS
Charcot-Marie-Tooth disease types 1A, 1B, and 3
Hereditary neuropathy with liability to pressure palsies (tomaculous neuropathy)
Amyloidosis—hereditary
Giant axonal neuropathy
Metachromatic leukodystrophy*
Polyglucosan body neuropathy*
Refsum's disease

*Biopsy essential for diagnosis.

Table 461–18 • USEFUL BLOOD STUDIES IN EVALUATING PATIENTS WITH NEUROPATHIC DISORDERS

OBTAINED IN MOST PATIENTS REFERRED FOR NEUROPATHY OF UNKNOWN ETIOLOGY
CBC and erythrocyte sedimentation rate
SMA 20
Serum protin electrophoresis and immune fixation electrophoresis
Vitamin B_{12} level

OBTAINED IN SELECTIVE PATIENTS WHEN CLINICALLY INDICATED
Glucose tolerance test
Methylmalonic acid and homocysteine
Anti–intrinsic factor/parietal cell antibodies
Serum gastrin
Hemoglobin A1C
VDRL (or RPR) and FTA-ABS (or MHA-TP)
Thyroid function tests
Creatine kinase*
Parathyroid hormone*
Antinuclear antibodies (including SS-A and SS-B)
Rheumatoid factor
Anti-neuronal nuclear antibody type I (ANNA-1 or anti-Hu)
Lyme antibody
HIV antibody
Myelin-associated glycoprotein (MAG) antibody
GMI antibody, GQ1b antibody
Blood (and urine) for heavy metals
Molecular genetic analysis for CMT 1A and 1B, hereditary neuropathy with liability for pressure palsy (HNPP), and the familial amyloid polyneuropathies

*Primarily obtained in cases of suspected motor neuron disease.

that will support or refute the findings from the history and physical examination. Thus, whether the neuropathic disorder is a mononeuropathy, multiple mononeuropathy (mononeuropathy multiplex), radiculopathy, plexopathy, or generalized polyneuropathy can be confirmed. Similarly, it can be ascertained whether the process involves only sensory nerves, only motor nerves, or both. Finally, the electrophysiologic data can help distinguish axonopathies from myelinopathies.

The basic electrophysiologic paradigm by which one classifies a neuropathy as being due to axonal degeneration or segmental demyelination is outlined in Table 461–16. In general, low amplitude potentials with relatively preserved distal latencies, conduction velocities, and late potentials, along with fibrillations on needle EMG, constitute the findings of an axonal neuropathy. On the other hand, slow conduction velocity, prolonged distal latencies and late potentials, relatively preserved amplitudes (unless there is conduction block), temporal dispersion, and the absence of fibrillations on needle EMG characterize a pure demyelinating neuropathy.

Information from the Nerve Biopsy

There are relatively few diseases that require a nerve biopsy for diagnosis (Table 461–17). For example, with the advent of easily available molecular genetic blood tests for CMT-1A, HNPP, and familial amyloidosis, less emphasis is placed on finding the nerve biopsy changes characteristic of these disorders. Infectious neuropathies such as leprosy can be more easily diagnosed by demonstrating acid-fast bacilli in skin than by nerve biopsy.

The nerve biopsy is most often useful in peripheral nerve vasculitis; because this is a treatable condition, the diagnosis of vasculitis should be confirmed histologically. The sural nerve is the most common nerve sampled, but the superficial peroneal nerve can also be used for this purpose. Adjacent muscle should be obtained to increase the yield of demonstrating vascular inflammation.

Other Laboratory Information

Relatively few blood tests should be routinely done in the evaluation of patients who present with neuropathic disorders (Table 461–18). Additional studies can be ordered in selected cases with a strong clinical index of suspicion for a particular disorder. It is often useful to measure blood or urine for elevations of methylmalonic acid and homocysteine levels in patients with "borderline" vitamin B_{12}

values (between 200 and 300 pg/mL). It is important to check for the presence of a monoclonal protein in all patients referred for an undiagnosed peripheral neuropathy. A serum protein electrophoresis alone is not sufficient to detect every monoclonal gammopathy, and an immunofixation electrophoresis should also be obtained on all patients with neuropathy. Five to 10 per cent of patients with peripheral neuropathies and motor neuron disease have a monoclonal protein in their serum. When a monoclonal protein is detected, the physician should search for an underlying lymphoproliferative disorder such as multiple myeloma, osteosclerotic myeloma, primary (as opposed to hereditary) amyloidosis, lymphoma, leukemia, cryoglobulinemia, and Waldenström's macroglobulinemia (Chapter 196). Most patients with a monoclonal gammopathy and peripheral neuropathy or motor neuron disease do not have an underlying lymphoproliferative disorder and are labeled as having a "monoclonal gammopathy of undetermined significance" (MGUS). In some cases of MGUS, it can be demonstrated that the monoclonal protein binds to a specific antigen on the peripheral nerve—myelin-associated glycoprotein (MAG). These are invariably patients with an IgM MGUS.

In addition to anti-MAG, there are a number of antibodies to various glycolipids associated with peripheral nerves that are now commercially available. Individual antibody tests should be ordered in specific clinical settings: GM$_1$ antibodies are often present in patients with multifocal motor neuropathy. Most patients with the Miller Fisher syndrome variant of GBS have GQ1b antibodies. Patients with paraneoplastic sensory neuronopathy (ganglionopathy; Chapter 188) nearly always have serum anti-Hu antibodies.

CEREBROSPINAL FLUID

The cerebrospinal fluid (CSF) protein determination is important in the evaluation of possible demyelinating neuropathies. The CSF protein is elevated in over 90% of patients with acute and chronic inflammatory demyelinating polyneuropathy; the CSF cell count is usually normal. In the diagnosis of disorders other than GBS and CIDP, CSF analysis is rarely useful. Patients with diabetic neuropathy, especially polyradiculoplexopathies, can have marked elevation of CSF protein, but it is usually not necessary to document these CSF changes in these patients. In cases of suspected polyradiculopathy due to meningeal carcinomatosis or lymphomatosis, CSF cytologic examination is essential.

SUGGESTED READINGS

Electrophysiology of Muscle and Nerve Disease
Dumitru D, Amato A, Zwarts M: Electrodiagnostic Medicine, 2nd ed. Philadelphia, Hanley & Belfus, 2002. *Text on all aspects of peripheral electrodiagnostic medicine, including useful correlation with neuromuscular diseases.*

Muscle Disease
Carpenter S, Karpati G: Pathology of Skeletal Muscle, 2nd ed. Oxford, Oxford University Press, 2001. *The "bible" of muscle histopathology.*
Karpati G, Hiltan-Jones D, Griggs RC (eds): Disorders of Voluntary muscle, 7th ed. Edinburgh, Churchill Livingston 2001. *A single-volume, comprehensive text.*

Nerve Disease
Mendell JR, Kissel JT, Cornblath DR: Diagnosis and Management of Peripheral Nerve Disorders. Oxford, Oxford University Press, 2001. *Text that emphasizes clinical and nerve biopsy findings.*
Wolfe GI, Baker NS, Amato AA, et al: Chronic cryptogenic sensory polyneuropathy (CSPN). Clinical and electrophysiologic characteristics. Arch Neurol 1999;56:540–547. *Reviews a large clinical experience with this very common class of neuropathies.*

462 PERIPHERAL NEUROPATHIES

John W. Griffin

Pathophysiology

Normal function of myelinated nerve fibers depends on the integrity of both the axon and its myelin sheath. Nerve action potentials jump from one node of Ranvier to the next. This rapid saltatory conduction depends on the insulating properties of the myelin sheaths. The simplest type of nerve injury is transection of the axon. The axon distal to the site of transection degenerates, whereas that proximal to the injury survives and has the potential for regeneration. As the axon degenerates, the myelin in the distal stump is also broken down and cleared. Axonal degeneration due to a focal nerve injury occurs, for example, in severe compression and in focal ischemic injury to nerves. In the symmetrical polyneuropathies, the underlying abnormality is usually a slowly evolving type of axonal degeneration that involves the ends of long nerve fibers first and preferentially. With time, the degenerative process involves more proximal regions of long fibers, and shorter fibers are affected. This pattern of *distal axonal degeneration* or *"dying back"* of nerve fibers results from a wide variety of metabolic, toxic, and heritable causes. The resulting clinical picture includes early loss of the tendon reflex at the ankle and weakness that initially involves the intrinsic muscles of the feet, the extensors of the toes, and the dorsiflexors at the ankle; the motor signs are accompanied by distally predominant loss of large-fiber sensory modalities such as vibratory sensibility in the toes. With progression, the hands

are similarly involved, and the process may spread more proximally up the legs and arms. The resulting pattern of sensory loss is frequently termed a *stocking-and-glove* pattern. Recovery from axonal degeneration requires nerve regeneration, a notoriously slow process.

Demyelination of a peripheral nerve at even a single site can block conduction, resulting in a functional deficit identical to that seen after axonal degeneration. In contrast to repair by regeneration, however, repair by remyelination can be quite rapid. Autoimmune attack on the myelin sheath occurs in the *inflammatory demyelinating* neuropathies and in some neuropathies associated with paraproteinemias. Inherited disorders of myelin are the other major category of demyelinating neuropathy. Uncommon causes include some toxic, mechanical, and physical injuries to nerve. Although these examples have nearly pure demyelination, many neuropathies have an admixture of both axonal degeneration and demyelination. This mixed pathologic spectrum reflects the mutual interdependency of the axons and the myelin-forming Schwann cells.

On the basis of the clinical features alone, it is difficult to predict whether a patient has a predominantly axonal or demyelinating pattern of peripheral nerve injury. Electrodiagnostic tests—nerve conduction studies and electromyography—provide tools for assessing the relative contributions of axonal loss and demyelination (Chapters 423 and 461). Nerve conduction studies are done by stimulating individual nerves with electrodes at two sites, one proximal to the other, and measuring the velocity of conduction of the action potential between those two sites. In addition, for both sensory and motor nerves, the amplitude of the evoked response can be determined. In general, axonal degeneration decreases the amplitude of the evoked action potential out of proportion to the degree of reduction in conduction velocity, whereas demyelination produces prominent reductions in conduction velocities.

IMMUNE-MEDIATED NEUROPATHIES

GUILLAIN-BARRÉ SYNDROME (ACUTE INFLAMMATORY DEMYELINATING POLYNEUROPATHY)

The Guillain-Barré syndrome (GBS) is usually characterized by weakness or paralysis affecting more than one limb, usually symmetrically, associated with loss of tendon reflexes and with increased cerebrospinal fluid (CSF) protein without pleocytosis. Since the advent of polio vaccination, GBS has become the most frequent cause of acute flaccid paralysis throughout the world. The pathologic substrate of many cases of GBS is lymphocytic infiltration of the spinal roots and peripheral nerves, with macrophage-mediated demyelination and a variable degree of secondary axonal degeneration. As a result, GBS is virtually synonymous with *acute inflammatory demyelinating polyneuropathy* (AIDP) (Table 462–1). At the present time it seems preferable to retain the clinical term *GBS,* because it is becoming increasingly clear that a small proportion of cases in North America and Europe, and a large proportion of cases in other regions, especially in the developing world, are characterized by noninflammatory acute axonal degeneration. These cases are clinically indistinguishable and have similar CSF profiles. They are termed the *axonal forms* of GBS.

GBS is almost certainly an immune-mediated disorder. It follows some type of infection in approximately 60% of cases. The best documented antecedents include infection with *Campylobacter jejuni* (Chapter 327), infectious mononucleosis (Chapter 371), cytomegalovirus (Chapter 370), herpesviruses (Chapter 369), and *Mycoplasma* (Chapter 304). *C. jejuni* is often associated with more severe "axonal" cases and most likely sensitizes the immune system to antigens shared between the organism and the peripheral nerve.

Clinical Manifestations

The initial symptoms often consist of tingling and "pins-and-needles sensations" in the feet and may be associated with dull low-back pain. By the time of presentation, which usually occurs within hours or days after first symptoms, weakness has usually developed. The weakness is usually most prominently in the legs, but the arms or cranial musculature may be involved first. Tendon reflexes are lost early, even in regions where strength is retained. Because the spinal roots are usually prominently involved, GBS can involve short nerves (axial and intercostal as well as cranial

Continued

Neurology

Table 462–1 • GUILLAIN-BARRÉ SYNDROME AND RELATED IMMUNE-MEDIATED NEUROPATHIES

DISORDER	TYPE	CLINICAL CHARACTERISTICS	PATHOPHYSIOLOGY	TREATMENT
Guillain-Barré syndrome	Acute inflammatory demyelinating polyneuropathy	Prominent or predominant motor involvement of acute onset	Demyelination, lymphocytic infiltration	Plasmapheresis; intravenous immunoglobulin (IVIg); corticosteroids alone ineffective
	Fisher syndrome	Ataxia, ophthalmoparesis, and areflexia of acute onset	Antibodies against the ganglioside GQ1b	(Probably) plasmapheresis or IVIg
	Axonal GBS	Motor-sensory or pure motor forms	Noninflammatory axonal degeneration predominates; strongly associated with antecedent *Campylobacter jejuni* infection	(Probably) plasmapheresis or IVIg
Chronic inflammatory demyelinating polyneuropathy		Slower onset of weakness and sensory loss; may be recurrent	Widespread demyelination with remyelination, secondary axonal loss; may occur in association with monoclonal gammopathy	Corticosteroids, plasmapheresis, IVIg
Multifocal motor neuropathy		Stepwise involvement of individual nerves; nearly pure motor involvement	Focal demyelination of motor fibers	IVIg or cytotoxic agents (corticosteroids and plasmapheresis ineffective)

nerves) as well as long ones. Weakness progresses, with the nadir reached within 30 days, and usually by 14 days. Progression can be alarmingly rapid, so that critical functions such as respiration can be lost within a few days or even a few hours.

The potential for respiratory insufficiency, as well as swallowing difficulty and autonomic dysregulation, underlies the life-threatening nature of GBS. In the past, mortality was as high as 15%. With modern critical care and the therapies outlined next, mortality has fallen to about 2%. The first aspect of management is prompt and accurate initial diagnosis. At the time of presentation, a high index of clinical suspicion is necessary. No laboratory test is specific for GBS, but careful electrodiagnostic testing can usually identify at least mild abnormalities during the early stages. Although elevation of the CSF protein level is characteristic, it usually rises only after the first week, not within the first few days when the diagnosis may be uncertain. At the earliest stages, the differential diagnosis includes non-neuropathic conditions such as spinal cord diseases (e.g., transverse myelitis; Chapter 448) and acute neuromuscular junction (Chapter 464) or muscle diseases (Chapter 463).

Rx Treatment

Because of the potential for rapid deterioration, patients with a presumptive diagnosis of GBS usually require hospitalization for observation. Monitoring should include frequent measurement of the vital capacity and ability to swallow. Observation in an intensive care unit and insertion of an airway should be initiated early, before declining ventilatory strength, autonomic dysregulation, or fatigue due to unproductive coughing erupts into an acute emergency. Such early intervention largely prevents life-threatening crises. Most of the reduction in mortality in GBS derives from modern intensive care.

Two treatments are of benefit. *Plasmapheresis*—the exchange of the patient's plasma for albumin—was the first treatment definitively shown to shorten the time to recovery. Infusion of high doses of *human immunoglobulin* intravenously also produces benefit.[1][2] These treatments are equally effective, and there is no added benefit to combining them. The choice of modality should be individualized. In patients with limited venous access, gamma globulin is easier to administer. The use of corticosteroids alone is not beneficial.

Thorough education of the patient about the possibility of rapid deterioration and about the overall favorable prognosis is an important early step. While able to breathe and speak, patients should be instructed in a communication system with nurses and family so that they will be able to make themselves understood if intubation and respiratory support are required.

The prognosis for GBS varies with age, severity, and the extent to which axonal degeneration exceeds demyelination. A middle-aged patient who requires respiratory assistance, and who receives plasmapheresis early in the course, on the average resumes walking about 3 months later (6 months without plasmapheresis). Indeed, many recover much more promptly than that. Relapses, if they occur, should be re-treated with plasmapheresis or gamma globulin.

CHRONIC INFLAMMATORY DEMYELINATING NEUROPATHY

Chronic inflammatory demyelinating neuropathy (CIDP), sometimes referred to as chronic GBS, bears similarities to the clinical, pathologic, and laboratory pictures seen in acute GBS. It differs primarily in the time course and in the absence of identifiable antecedent events. The differences in response to therapy, however, suggest that the precise immunopathogenetic mechanisms are likely to differ.

Clinical Manifestations

CIDP can occur at any age. The usual picture is one of slowly evolving weakness beginning in the legs, with widespread areflexia and loss of large-fiber (vibratory) sensibility on examination. In the more rapidly evolving cases of CIDP, the distinction from GBS is arbitrary. In general, in patients with acute GBS the nadir is reached within 4 weeks, whereas in patients with CIDP more time is required. The diagnosis is supported by prominent demyelinating features on nerve conduction studies and by elevation of the CSF protein level.

Rx Treatment

Blinded trials showed that, unlike GBS, most cases of CIDP respond to corticosteroids alone. Many patients with CIDP respond to plasmapheresis and/or intravenous gamma globulin. In most instances the first choice of therapy is with corticosteroids, using the lowest dosage required to achieve and maintain an adequate response. Intravenous therapy with immunoglobulin and plasmapheresis, although simple and safe, usually must be repeated every several weeks to maintain a response and entails substantial expense. Nevertheless, these therapies are valuable in patients who do not respond to corticosteroids or in whom unacceptable corticosteroid doses are required or side effects supervene.

MULTIFOCAL MOTOR NEUROPATHY

An uncommon related disorder, *multifocal motor neuropathy*, occurs as "pure motor" multiple mononeuropathy. A patient may describe, for example, development of unilateral wristdrop (radial nerve involvement) followed by footdrop on the other side (peroneal nerve involvement). In addition, tendon reflexes may be lost outside the distribution of weakness, but the sensory examination is normal even in weak limbs. The pathologic characteristic, inflammatory demyelination, resembles that seen in CIDP but is highly focal and largely spares sensory nerve fibers. A characteristic electrodiagnostic feature is the presence of *conduction block*, a reflection of the focal demyelination. The CSF protein level is usually normal. A nonspecific but helpful laboratory finding, noted in about 70% of cases, is markedly increased IgM, anti-GM ganglioside antibodies in the serum. Multifocal motor neuropathy is noteworthy because it can be confused with more ominous disorders such as amyotrophic lateral sclerosis, but it responds favorably to intravenous administration of immunoglobulin as well as to cytotoxic therapy. Neither corticosteroid therapy nor plasmapheresis brings improvement.

NEUROPATHIES ASSOCIATED WITH MONOCLONAL GAMMOPATHIES

Peripheral neuropathy occurs in some monoclonal gammopathies, both the benign type and myeloma (Chapter 196). Monoclonal proteins of IgM, IgG, and IgA types are all associated with neuropathy. In some instances the monoclonal protein has been shown to cause the neuropathy. For example, some IgM monoclonal proteins react with sugars found on a specific Schwann cell protein, the *myelin-associated glycoprotein* (MAG). The monoclonal protein intercalates into the myelin lamellae, producing a distinctive pathologic feature, abnormally wide spacing between adjacent myelin lamellae, and consequent demyelination. However, for most of the IgG and IgA monoclonal proteins the mechanism of nerve injury is not known.

Clinical Manifestations

The clinical picture of the neuropathy varies. The IgM monoclonal antibodies with "anti-MAG" reactivity typically produce neuropathy with prominent large-fiber sensory loss and sensory ataxia, as well as milder weakness. The electrodiagnostic tests indicate demyelination, albeit admixed with nerve fiber loss. In other cases with IgM monoclonal proteins there is a distinctive picture that includes scleroderma-like skin changes, hepatomegaly, and endocrine abnormalities, as well as neuropathy (the POEMS syndrome described later). Other individuals with monoclonal proteins have a clinical picture identical to CIDP, and still others have distally predominant axonal degeneration.

Identification of a monoclonal protein does not necessarily mean that the protein is the cause of the neuropathy. Most of the monoclonal proteins found in patients with neuropathy are classed as monoclonal gammopathies of unknown significance (Chapter 196), a group alternatively termed *benign monoclonal gammopathies* because there is no evidence of multiple myeloma at the time of presentation. The incidence of such monoclonal proteins increases with age. Especially in older patients, before the presumption is accepted that the paraprotein causes the neuropathy, it is important to exclude other causes of neuropathy, such as diabetes or alcoholism.

Three disorders should be specifically sought in individuals with paraproteins and neuropathy: (1) There is a special association of neuropathy with solitary plasmacytomas, often osteosclerotic. The POEMS syndrome—polyneuropathy, organomegaly, endocrinopathy (hirsutism, testicular atrophy), monoclonal IgM protein, and skin pigmentation—is highly associated with osteosclerotic myelomas. A skeletal radiographic survey is essential in patients with monoclonal proteins and neuropathy. (2) Cryoglobulinema, with or without monoclonal gammopathy, can produce neuropathy, and the possibility should be excluded. (3) The monoclonal proteins may result in amyloid deposition in nerve and thus produce neuropathy indirectly. Amyloid deposition is particularly associated with excretion of light chains in the urine.

The distinctive neurologic picture of amyloidosis (Chapter 290) often suggests the possibility of amyloid neuropathy (see later). Unlike most other neuropathies, there is a predilection for involvement of small sensory and autonomic nerve fibers, so that the history may include painless injuries to the feet or hands and evidence of autonomic dysfunction, including impotence and orthostatic hypotension. Definitive diagnosis of immunoglobulin-associated amyloidosis is by histology. Fat pad aspiration and muscle biopsy may be useful before undertaking biopsy of rectal ganglia or peripheral nerve.

 Treatment

The one category of paraproteinemic neuropathies in which treatment is clearly beneficial is that of the solitary plasmacytomas (Chapter 196). Excision and irradiation of the plasmacytoma can be curative. In other paraproteinemic neuropathies, some reports suggest modest benefit from plasmapheresis or other forms of therapy in neuropathies associated with benign monoclonal gammopathies. In general, however, the degree of improvement is insufficient for the nuisance and expense of therapy. The effort is better focused on gait training and protection from falls. No therapy has been shown to slow progression of amyloid neuropathy associated with paraproteinemia.

IMMUNE-MEDIATED ATAXIC NEUROPATHIES

In this category there are three disorders: carcinomatous sensory neuropathy, sensory ganglionitis associated with features of Sjögren's syndrome, and idiopathic sensory ganglionitis. All three are characterized clinically by subacute or slowly developing proprioceptive sensory loss leading to an ataxic gait and inability to localize the arms and/or legs. Patients show rombergism: They can stand with feet together and eyes open but fall when they close their eyes, reflecting loss of kinesthetic sensibility. Tendon reflexes usually disappear, but strength remains. Pathologic changes in all three disorders include lymphocytic infiltration of the dorsal root ganglia, with destruction of the primary sensory neurons and associated degeneration of their central and peripheral processes. Large sensory neurons are predominantly affected, leaving pain and thermal sensibilities relatively intact. Electrodiagnostic studies document the absence of sensory nerve action potentials and preservation of motor responses. CSF protein may be normal or contain increased protein. Modest pleocytosis often accompanies the carcinomatous disorder.

The possibility of occult carcinoma underlying an immunogenic (paraneoplastic) ataxic neuropathy adds urgency to differential diagnosis. The most frequent associations include small cell carcinoma of the lung, breast carcinoma, and ovarian carcinoma (Chapter 188). In addition to clinical screening for these possibilities, a useful serologic test is the anti-Hu antibody, which reacts with a 37-kD neuronal nuclear protein. Although the presence of anti-Hu antibodies is neither perfectly sensitive nor specific, their association with ataxic neuropathy strongly suggests underlying carcinoma. It should be noted that carcinoma has also been associated with other types of neuropathy, including bland, slowly evolving, sensory motor neuropathy. However, this type of neuropathy is usually an accompaniment of advanced stages of cancer and is rarely a presenting manifestation. The evaluation for occult carcinoma is directed toward those uncommon patients with pure sensory ataxic neuropathy.

Another group of patients with a similar clinical and pathologic picture have features of Sjögren's syndrome, including keratoconjunctivitis sicca and elevated antinuclear antibody titers (Chapter 282). Surprisingly, these patients only occasionally have joint disease or other extraglandular manifestations of Sjögren's syndrome, and most will not have sought medical attention before neuropathy develops. Affected patients are likely to have associated autonomic insufficiency, including pupils that are large and are more reactive to accommodation than to light (Adie's pupils).

A third group of patients with idiopathic sensory ganglionitis have no associated systemic disease. Because this group of disorders often have a very acute onset, they may be misdiagnosed as having Guillain-Barré syndrome. This group is referred to as having *idiopathic sensory neuronopathy*.

Unfortunately, cytotoxic or corticosteroid therapy only rarely benefits any of these patients with sensory ganglionitis disorders. The ataxic gait produces substantial early disability, but relearning through gait training, rehabilitation, and physical therapy allows a large proportion of affected individuals to resume daily activities.

VASCULITIC NEUROPATHIES

Peripheral nerves have extensive collateral circulation and are relatively invulnerable to occlusion of large peripheral arteries. By contrast, they are susceptible to focal interruption of circulation within the individual nerve fascicles due to small blood vessel diseases. As a result, many types of systemic vasculitis affect the peripheral nerves. Peripheral nerves are one of the most frequently damaged organ systems in polyarteritis nodosa (Chapter 284) and are frequently involved in rheumatoid arteritis (Chapter 278), Wegener's granulomatosis (Chapter 284), Sjögren's syndrome (Chapter 282), and the vasculitides associated with infections such as hepatitis B and C (Chapter 152), Lyme disease (Chapter 352), and HIV infection (Chapter 414). The peripheral nerves can be the predominant site of vasculitis, producing a syndrome of vasculitis restricted to the peripheral nervous system. This disorder offers special diagnostic challenges, because the usual footprints of systemic inflammatory disease, including elevated sedimentation rate, are often absent.

Clinical Manifestations

The clinical manifestations of all of these vasculitic neuropathies reflect the patchiness of the underlying disease. The characteristic picture consists of multiple mononeuropathy, often evolving in a stepwise fashion, so that wristdrop from radial nerve palsy may occur on one side followed by footdrop on the other, with patchy areas of subjective numbness or sensory loss appearing elsewhere on the extremities. The asymmetry and the length-independence of the nerves involved suggest small vessel disease of nerve. In the absence of diabetes mellitus, vasculitis becomes the prime diagnostic consideration. Evaluation of multiple mononeuropathy includes screening of patients to detect evidence of systemic vasculitis in the skin, kidneys, eyes, and other organs. Ultimately, vasculitis is a histologic diagnosis; and if no other organ involvement is identified, combined nerve and muscle biopsy is needed to establish the diagnosis.

Rx Treatment

Treatment of vasculitic neuropathies consists of treatment of the underlying vasculitis. In a neuropathy apparently restricted to the peripheral nervous system, corticosteroids may be tried initially, but most patients require cytotoxic therapy comparable to that used for polyarteritis (Chapter 284).

HEREDITARY NEUROPATHIES

Heritable neuropathies rank among the most prevalent inherited neurologic diseases. Because many occur in mid life and because the family history is often previously unrecognized, the heritable disorders constitute an important aspect of the differential diagnosis of nerve disease.

CHARCOT-MARIE-TOOTH DISEASE

Definition

The eponymic designation *Charcot-Marie-Tooth* (CMT) disease identifies a group of heritable disorders of peripheral nerves that share clinical features but differ in their pathology and the specific genetic abnormalities (Table 462–2). One group of disorders, classed together as CMT type I (CMT I), is characterized pathologically by abnormalities of peripheral myelination and, at a molecular level, by abnormalities of specific proteins found in the myelin sheaths or Schwann cells. The CMT II group is characterized by axonal degeneration.

Pathogenesis

Most forms of CMT disease reflect an autosomal dominant trait, but some similar clinical phenotypes overlap different genetic abnormalities. Several gene abnormalities can cause CMT I (see Table 462–2). Three specific gene abnormalities have been identified. The most prevalent is duplication of a segment of chromosome 17 that encodes the peripheral myelin protein-22 gene (*PMP22*). A chromosome 1–linked form is due to an abnormality of another myelin protein, termed P_0. A sex-linked form has been related to abnormalities of the connexin-32 gene. The gene defects in the axonal forms are beginning to be identified. For example, a point mutation in the low-molecular-weight neurofilament protein (NF-L) has been identified in some families.

Pathology

The pathology of the demyelinating forms of CMT is characterized by excessive numbers of Schwann cells forming concentric rings around nerve fibers. Termed *onion bulbs* because of their appearance on microscopic examination, the wrappings often lead to a palpable and visible increase in the size of certain nerves, such as the ulnar nerve at the elbow or the greater auricular nerve running from the posterior margin of the sternocleidomastoid muscle to the base of the ear. Because of the increase in the size of the nerves, the demyelinating forms of CMT disease are termed *hypertrophic neuropathies*.

Clinical Manifestations

All forms of CMT disease tend to occur in the second to fourth decades with insidiously evolving footdrop. On examination, there is distal wasting of the intrinsic muscles of the feet, the anterior tibial group, and the calves. A variable degree of impaired large-fiber sensory function is reflected in elevated vibratory thresholds in the toes. Tendon reflexes are lost, at least at the ankles. Typically, a foot deformity exists, with high arches (*pes cavus*) and *hammertoes*, reflecting long-standing muscle imbalance in the feet. On specific questioning, affected individuals often recall that they were

---

Table 462–2 • CHARCOT-MARIE-TOOTH (CMT) AND RELATED HERITABLE NEUROPATHIES

DISORDER	TYPE	CLINICAL FEATURES	PATHOPHYSIOLOGY	INHERITANCE	GENE DEFECT
CMT 1		Slowly evolving motor-sensory neuropathies with high arches, hammer toes, hypertrophic nerves	Demyelination and remyelination with onion bulbs		
	a			Dominant	Duplication of a segment of chromosome 17 encoding *PMP22*
	b			Dominant	Point mutation in the myelin protein P_0
	x			Sex-linked	Mutation in connexin 32
CMT II		Similar, without hypertrophic nerves	Distally predominant axonal degeneration	Dominant	Many, including *NF1* mutation
CMT III (Dejerine-Sottas disease)		Early onset, severe motor-sensory neuropathy	Severe hypomyelination with onion bulbs	Recessive	Mutation in P_0

never athletic and that they could not run, jump, or ice skate as well as their peers. Often they report frequent ankle sprains. In general, these problems attract little concern on the part of patients or their families, reflecting the lifelong nature and slow evolution of the disease. Patients can frequently identify several other family members who have similar foot deformities. The most useful diagnostic test lies in the identification of the clinical features in other family members. Even mild or subclinical forms of the disease are usually identified readily on detailed neurologic examination.

 ## Treatment

Most patients with CMT disease enjoy a nearly full spectrum of occupational and daily activities, and they have a normal life-span. The footdrop can be relieved by appropriate bracing of the ankle. Occasionally, however, the disease produces much greater deficits. Genetic counseling and education of affected individuals and their families is important, both for reassurance and to preclude unnecessary diagnostic evaluation of affected members in future generations.

AMYLOID NEUROPATHIES

All forms of amyloid neuropathy (Chapter 290) are due to extra-cellular deposition of the fibrillary protein, amyloid, in peripheral nerve and sensory and autonomic ganglia, as well as around blood vessels in nerves and other tissues. The nonhereditary type of amyloidosis associated with monoclonal immunoglobulins has been described earlier. Many of the forms of heritable amyloidosis, at one time classified by geographic origin of the first families recognized, have been shown by molecular genetic techniques to represent a variety of point mutations in the transthyretin (prealbumin) gene. The most frequent variant transthyretin protein results from substitution of methionine for valine at position 30 in the molecule. A point mutation in the gelsolin gene can also give rise to hereditary amyloidosis. In all forms of amyloidosis, the precise means by which amyloid deposition injures nerve remains unresolved. Mechanical distortion of neurons in the sensory and autonomic ganglia and of nerve fibers, as well as vascular involvement due to amyloid deposition around blood vessels, may both contribute to nerve damage.

Clinical Manifestations

In all forms of amyloidosis, abnormalities affect the small sensory and autonomic fibers. Involvement of small fibers responsible for pain and thermal sensibilities leads to loss of the ability to perceive mechanical and thermal injury and tissue damage. As a result, painless injuries present a major hazard of this disorder; in advanced stages, they can lead to chronic infections or osteomyelitis of the feet or hands, and the need for amputation. The autonomic dysfunction (Chapter 460) produces orthostatic hypotension, impotence, and, in late stages, bladder and bowel incontinence. Until the late stages, strength, touch-pressure sensibility, and vibratory sensation are usually preserved. In some of the heritable forms (as well as in immunoglobulin-associated amyloidosis), median nerve entrapment may occur because of amyloid deposition.

Diagnosis of systemic amyloidosis is made by histologic demonstration of amyloid in biopsy of nerve, muscle, fat aspirate, or other tissue. The heritable forms are normally autosomal dominant, so the diagnosis may be suggested by family history. The specific genetic abnormality can be identified by molecular genetic analysis. In the heritable transthyretin amyloidoses, liver transplantation (Chapter 157) can be required. No definitive treatment is available for the acquired forms of amyloid neuropathy, but education in prevention of injury to anesthetic limbs can preserve function.

Table 462–3 • DIABETIC NEUROPATHIES

DIABETIC POLYNEUROPATHIES
Rapidly reversible physiologic dysfunction associated with hyperglycemia
Symmetrical polyneuropathy
   Sensorimotor neuropathy
   "Small-fiber" neuropathy, with autonomic dysfunction, reduced pain sensibility, spontaneous burning pain

DIABETIC MONONEUROPATHIES AND PLEXOPATHIES
Diabetic third nerve palsy
Diabetic fourth nerve palsy
Diabetic truncal neuropathy
Diabetic lumbosacral plexopathy (proximal diabetic neuropathy)

METABOLIC NEUROPATHIES

DIABETIC NEUROPATHIES

Diabetes (Chapter 242) is the most frequent cause of peripheral neuropathy worldwide. Incidence figures depend on the employed definition; at least some peripheral nerve abnormalities can be detected in about 70% of patients with long-standing diabetes, and symptomatic neuropathy affects 5 to 10%. The diabetic neuropathies include a variety of clinical forms, including symmetrical polyneuropathies, and a variety of forms of individual nerve injury (Table 462–3).

DIABETIC POLYNEUROPATHY

Diabetic polyneuropathy is symmetrical and usually distally predominant, beginning with sensory loss in the feet. It is the most frequent of the diabetic neuropathies. It is uncommon at the time of diagnosis of diabetes, and its prevalence increases with duration of diabetes. However, an important subgroup has been identified in which painful sensory neuropathies occur in the stage of early diabetes or impaired glucose tolerance. The precise pathogenesis of diabetic polyneuropathy remains a matter of controversy, but a single recent advance has been the demonstration that, like the ocular and renal complications, diabetic neuropathy can be reduced in incidence and in severity by maintaining blood sugar levels close to normal (Chapter 242). This effect of "tight control" is consistent with the hypothesis that hyperglycemia itself contributes to nerve damage. The complications of hyperglycemia that injure nerves may include one or more of the following: abnormalities of nerve vasculature and blood flow, leading to angiopathic injury; metabolic effects of abnormalities in polyol pathways; and nonenzymatic glycosylation of nerve proteins.

Clinical Manifestations

The neuropathy is usually asymptomatic at the onset, a stage during which abnormalities in sensation and reflexes may be detected on routine examination. The symptomatic phase usually begins insidiously, but some cases have an abrupt onset; and in a small percentage of patients the onset may be precipitated by the institution of insulin. Unlike most other neuropathies, in diabetes small-fiber sensibility as well as large-fiber sensation are typically reduced, resulting in elevated pin, thermal, and vibratory thresholds. The small-fiber dysfunction is often manifested by spontaneous neuropathic pain, including bothersome *dysesthesias*—unpleasant sensations evoked by normally innocuous stimuli, such as the bed sheets on the toes at night. There may be continuous burning or throbbing pain, and walking often is distressing ("It feels like I'm walking on coals."). In addition, sudden intense "lightning" pains may affect the feet and legs.

Some degree of autonomic insufficiency is frequent in diabetic neuropathy (Chapter 460). Manifestations include loss of the normal sinus arrhythmia; failure of blood pressure restoration and cardiac acceleration on standing, sometimes producing orthostatic hypotension; impotence; constipation; and a particularly distressing symptom, diabetic diarrhea, with unpredictable loose stools

Continued

Neurology

and fecal incontinence. In some patients, these "small-fiber" abnormalities, including neuropathic pain, loss of pin and thermal sensibility, and autonomic dysfunction, dominate the clinical picture.

The diagnosis of diabetic polyneuropathy is straightforward in established diabetics with typical clinical pictures. Electrodiagnostic studies, usually unnecessary, document neuropathy, and CSF protein is frequently moderately elevated. In patients without frank diabetes, a glucose tolerance test may be required to demonstrate glucose intolerance. Glucose intolerance is prevalent in the adult population, so its presence does not necessarily mean that it is the cause of neuropathy: other causes must be excluded. Diabetic neuropathy is the most *overdiagnosed* cause of peripheral nerve disease. It alone seldom results in severe painless weakness.

Rx Treatment

The approach to management of diabetic hyperglycemia is outside the scope of this chapter, but there is increasing reason to think that primary prevention as well as slowing of the progression of established diabetic neuropathy is abetted by correction of blood sugar levels to as nearly normal values as possible ("tight control"; Chapter 242). Once the diagnosis of diabetic polyneuropathy is established, no other specific treatment for the neuropathy is available. Symptomatic management includes use of tricyclic antidepressants or anticonvulsants such as gabapentin or carbamazepine for the spontaneous neuropathic pain. Full therapeutic doses are required, and the dosage must be slowly increased to minimize side effects such as dizziness. Opiates are usually contraindicated.

The major goal in the management of diabetic polyneuropathy is prevention of the cycle of painless injury, ulceration, cellulitis, and osteomyelitis that underlies much of the functional disability produced by this disorder and that contributes to an ultimate requirement for amputation. The loss of pain sensibility on examination should trigger increased vigilance. Painless injuries can largely be prevented by education, avoidance of physical and thermal hazards to the feet, well-fitting shoes, and frequent inspections of the feet. Erythema or injury is treated promptly with removal of the aggravating factor, such as an ill-fitting shoe. Cessation of weight bearing until healing occurs can minimize ulceration. Meticulous skin and nail care are required.

One of the most distressing aspects of the autonomic neuropathy is impotence (Chapter 247). Exclusion of other causes, particularly offending medications, and behavioral strategies are important. A variety of methods are helpful. Other genitourinary disturbances include retrograde ejaculation and disordered micturition. Milder cases of diabetic diarrhea may respond to agents such as diphenoxylate.

MONONEUROPATHY AND MULTIPLE MONONEUROPATHIES

Diabetes also can cause a variety of mononeuropathies and multiple mononeuropathies, which probably represent vascular insufficiency or infarction in nerve, presumably caused by disease of the small blood vessels. The onset is typically abrupt and often painful.

Clinical Manifestations

A stereotyped disorder is *diabetic third nerve palsy*, characterized by sudden inability to adduct the eye or open the lid (Chapter 466). Unlike third nerve compression from intracranial masses or carotid aneurysms, the pupil is typically spared. The sixth nerve, the femoral nerve, or other major nerves of the extremities, may be similarly involved.

In another characteristic syndrome, termed *diabetic lumbosacral plexopathy* or *proximal diabetic neuropathy*, affected persons develop pain in the hip with asymmetrical weakness of the proximal leg muscles over days to a few weeks. The disorder often occurs in a setting of recent severe (>10%) loss of body weight and frequently appears to be a "femoral" neuropathy, with quadriceps weakness and loss of the tendon reflex at the knee. Careful examination, however, usually discloses more widespread

involvement of muscles innervated by the lumbosacral plexus, typically including the hamstring and gluteus muscles. Although the complaints may be referable to one side, mild abnormalities often affect the contralateral side. In addition, evidence of more symmetrical polyneuropathy, with reduced tendon reflexes of the ankles, elevated sensory thresholds, and often weakness of toe extension and ankle dorsiflexion, may exist. The limited pathologic data available suggest small vessel disease in the lumbosacral plexus. Recent data indicate that the small vessel disease can include an inflammatory angiopathy. Ongoing trials are examining the role of immunotherapy in proximal diabetic neuropathy. In any event, the prognosis is surprisingly favorable; pain decreases, and strength returns to the affected muscles within weeks to months. At the onset, this disorder can be confused with intraspinal disease or polyradiculopathy. Diabetic lumbosacral plexopathy is sometimes called diabetic amyotrophy, but this term is best avoided, because it has also been applied to a syndrome of widespread muscle wasting that occasionally develops in diabetics in association with a period of weight loss. A final noteworthy mononeuropathy is *diabetic truncal neuropathy*. Patients have pain in the distribution of one or more intercostal nerves, often associated with hypesthesia and numbness. Like the other diabetic mononeuropathies, recovery over months is the rule.

HEPATIC NEUROPATHY

Polyneuropathy is sufficiently uncommon in chronic liver disease that other underlying causes that can affect both liver and peripheral nerves (alcoholism, primary biliary cirrhosis [Chapter 156]) should be sought.

THYROID DISEASE

Myxedema neuropathy is usually a minor manifestation of myxedema, but areflexia and distal sensory loss can be seen (see Chapter 239). Cerebellar ataxia and behavioral changes usually predominate.

UREMIC NEUROPATHY

Peripheral neuropathy is associated with chronic renal insufficiency (Chapter 117). Electrophysiologic abnormalities routinely occur when creatinine clearance is less than 10% of normal, but the severity and rate of progression of symptomatic uremic polyneuropathy vary widely. The syndrome usually consists of distally predominant, symmetrical, motor-sensory polyneuropathy. In some patients there is marked motor predominance, so that footdrop and leg weakness are major manifestations. In others, paresthesias and, occasionally, burning dysesthesias are early symptoms. In either event, loss of tendon reflexes, initially at the ankle, is characteristic. Electrophysiologic and pathologic studies indicate that both distal axonal degeneration and demyelination occur in uremic neuropathy, but the precise underlying mechanisms remain uncertain. This peripheral neuropathy is both preventable and treatable by amelioration of the renal insufficiency by dialysis or renal transplantation (Chapter 118); the latter produces much better preservation of peripheral nerve function.

PORPHYRIC NEUROPATHY

The intermittent porphyrias (Chapter 223) are important diagnostic considerations in acute neuropathies. The most prevalent of these disorders, acute intermittent porphyria (AIP), is associated with recurrent episodes of neuropathy, which are typically acute or subacute in onset. Paresthesias and dysesthesias of the extremities occur and in severe episodes are associated with rapidly evolving weakness or paralysis, mimicking the axonal form of GBS, often associated with bladder dysfunction and constipation. The associated central nervous system (CNS) effects may contribute to alterations in level of consciousness as well as hysteria-like or psychotic behavior, potentially delaying recognition of the emergent nature of the neuropathy. During acute attacks, most patients with AIP have increased excretion of porphobilinogen and δ-aminolevulinic acid in the urine. This simple diagnostic assay should be considered in any patient with acute paralytic neuropathy. The treatment of acute porphyria attacks is described in Chapter 223.

CRITICAL CARE NEUROPATHIES

The term *critical care neuropathy* is often used in patients following a severe medical illness complicated by sepsis and requiring prolonged intensive care. In a small proportion of patients the only process that can be defined is axonal degeneration. Many of the cases that follow use of muscle relaxants and corticosteroids now appear to reflect primary changes in the muscle rather than the nerves ("quadriplegic myopathies"). The etiology is unclear, and no effective therapy other than time and adequate nutrition is known. Most affected persons recover completely.

TOXIC NEUROPATHIES

A wide array of environmental, occupational, recreational (Table 462–4), and pharmaceutical (Table 462–5) agents can produce peripheral nerve disease. For agents in which the period of exposure is limited, the diagnosis is often suggested by subacute neuropathy. Most, although not all, neurotoxins produce distal axonal degeneration. The picture typically includes distally predominant sensory loss, loss of tendon reflexes at the ankles, and distal weakness. With continued exposure, the symptoms may progress more proximally; even after the offending agent is withdrawn, progression sometimes may continue, a phenomenon termed *coasting*. Nevertheless, withdrawal represents the optimal treatment.

Table 462–4 • INDUSTRIAL AND ENVIRONMENTAL NEUROTOXINS

METALS
Arsenic
Lead
Mercury
Thallium

SUBSTANCE ABUSE
Alcohol
Glue (hexacarbons) inhalation
Nitrous oxide inhalation

INDUSTRIAL POISONS
Acrylamide
Carbon disulfide
Cyanide (chronic)
Dichlorophenoxyacetic acid
Dimethylaminopropionitrile
Ethylene oxide
Hexacarbon (n-hexane) (glue sniffer, occupational exposure to solvents, glues, or glue thinner)
Organophosphorus esters (triorthocresyl phosphate, leptophos, mipafox, trichlorphon)
Polychlorinated biphenyls
Tetrachlorbiphenyl
Trichloroethylene (trigeminal neuropathy)

Table 462–5 • PHARMACEUTIC NEUROTOXINS

Amiodarone	Isoniazid
Antiretrovirals (ddI, ddC)	Metronidazole and misonidazole
Chloramphenicol	Nitrofurantoin
Cisplatin	Penicillamine
Clioquinols	Perhexiline
Dapsone	Phenytoin (rare)
Disulfiram (Antabuse)	Pyridoxine (in excessive amounts)
Ethambutol	Stilbamidine
Ethionamide	Suramin
Gold	Thalidomide
Hydralazine	Vincristine/vinblastine

Persons with preexisting nerve disease may be unusually susceptible to neurotoxins. For example, patients with CMT disease can experience devastating toxic reactions to standard chemotherapeutic doses of vincristine. In all toxic neuropathies the key to treatment lies in prompt recognition and withdrawal.

ALCOHOL-NUTRITIONAL NEUROPATHY

Polyneuropathy in persons with chronic alcoholism usually occurs in a setting of associated nutritional deficiency (Chapter 450). Most persons with alcoholic neuropathy have evidence of multifactorial nutritional deficiency, but nutritional background seems adequate in some. The pathology of alcohol-nutritional neuropathy is that of a bland "dying back" disorder affecting both sensory and motor fibers. The initial symptoms are pain and paresthesias, beginning on the soles of the feet, sometimes evolving to burning feet and severe hyperpathia and often associated with aching and tenderness of the calves. Weakness is seldom severe and invariably distal, and tendon reflexes are lost first at the ankles. Treatment with nutritional supplementation, including thiamine and multivitamins, and cessation of alcohol ingestion are highly beneficial in the early stages of the disease. In advanced cases, the disease may continue to progress for a period after initiation of therapy, and recovery may be incomplete.

NEUROPATHIES ASSOCIATED WITH INFECTIOUS DISEASES

HUMAN IMMUNODEFICIENCY VIRUS (HIV) INFECTION

A variety of nerve diseases can accompany HIV infection (Chapter 414). GBS and CIDP tend to occur early in HIV infection, when CD4 counts are 250 to 500 cells/μL, and before development of AIDS. They presumably reflect early immune dysregulation. They are distinguished by the frequent presence of pleocytosis, an uncommon finding in seronegative GBS and CIDP. Their course and response to treatment are similar to those observed in seronegative patients.

Cytomegalovirus (CMV) infection of nerve occurs in the setting of clinically evident AIDS and in association with systemic CMV infection (Chapter 455). CMV can produce multiple mononeuropathy associated with focal infection of endothelial cells of the nerve, macrophages, and Schwann cells. A dramatic and potentially treatable disorder is *CMV polyradiculopathy*, which develops in persons with AIDS and is characterized by abrupt pain in the back and legs with rapidly progressing paraparesis and areflexia. A distinctive finding is polymorphonuclear pleocytosis, usually associated with markedly increased CSF protein. Cytologic examination sometimes can identify CMV inclusions in CSF. The differential diagnosis includes herpesvirus-associated transverse myelopathies. Prompt diagnosis of CMV polyradiculopathy is important, because some patients respond well to antiviral therapy with ganciclovir or foscarnet.

The most prevalent neuropathic complication of HIV infection is *sensory neuropathy of AIDS*. In advanced AIDS, affected patients typically complain of pain on the soles of the feet and discomfort while walking. Neuropathic pain may be intense, associated with loss of small- and large-fiber sensory modalities, with a variable, usually mild, degree of motor impairment. Typically, the reflexes are lost at the ankle but exaggerated at the knees. This pattern reflects both neuropathy and a CNS disease such as vacuolar myelopathy. Pathologic studies of the sensory neuropathy have shown noninflammatory distally predominant axonal degeneration of sensory fibers. Both large and small fibers are lost. The pathogenesis is unknown, but the disease does not appear to be produced by local productive HIV infection within the nerves themselves. Similar symptoms can follow therapy with neurotoxic antiretroviral agents. The treatment is symptomatic.

LYME DISEASE (BORRELIOSIS)

Neuropathic consequences can predominate in some patients with Lyme disease (Chapter 352). The geographic area of the patient as well as history of the characteristic antecedent rash may suggest the diagnosis. The neuropathy is usually a multiple mononeuropathy, with a high predilection of facial nerve involvement, mimicking idiopathic Bell's palsy.

LEPROUS NEUROPATHY (CHAPTER 343)

The clinical manifestations of leprosy are virtually exclusively those of peripheral neuropathy and its sequelae. In *lepromatous leprosy,* no effective cellular immune response is mounted, and large numbers of bacilli reside within the skin, where they infect predominantly the Schwann cells of intracutaneous nerves. With time, Schwann cells throughout the peripheral nervous system are affected, with a striking distribution of nerve fiber damage related to environmental temperatures. Organisms proliferate in the nerve fibers in the coolest regions of the skin, such as the ears, the lateral area of the face, and the digits, before they affect warmer areas covered with clothing. The resulting cutaneous sensory loss includes strikingly selective loss of pain sensibility.

The other major form of the disease, *tuberculoid leprosy,* is characterized by an active inflammatory response to the organism, with much of the nerve damage probably resulting from the immune response. Tuberculoid disease and the intermediate form, *borderline disease,* produce a less stereotyped, more patchy and asymmetrical neuropathy.

Painless injuries and painless traumatic joint diseases are the major sequelae of both forms of leprosy. Chemotherapy for leprosy is associated with regeneration of nerve fibers. In general, however, nerve fibers do not successfully reinnervate the skin, so that cutaneous anesthesia and its complications persist. In addition to chemotherapy, education and protection from painless injuries, as described for diabetic polyneuropathies, can substantially improve the outcome.

ENTRAPMENT AND COMPRESSIVE NEUROPATHIES

The peripheral nerves are vulnerable to chronic compression or entrapment in a variety of sites. The most frequently encountered are median nerve compression at the wrist within the carpal tunnel (*carpal tunnel syndrome*); median nerve compression in the upper forearm; ulnar nerve compression in the hand (*cubital tunnel syndrome*), wrist, or at the elbow (*tardy ulnar nerve palsy*); tibial nerve compression behind the medial malleolus (*tarsal tunnel syndrome*); and peroneal nerve compression over the lateral fibular head.

CARPAL TUNNEL SYNDROME

Entrapment of the median nerve at the wrist reflects the limited available space for the median nerve because of the surrounding bone, joint, and ligaments, as well as the tendons and synovium passing through the canal. Repetitive motion of the fingers is a highly publicized exacerbating element, but other precipitating factors that should be considered include trauma, osteoarthritis, ganglionic cysts, myxedema (Chapter 239), and, rarely, amyloid deposition (Chapter 290). Mild symptoms typically involve paresthesias of the first three digits often occurring overnight and relieved by shaking or elevating the hands. In more severe disease, objective sensory loss in the median nerve distribution (Fig. 462–1), weakness of median-innervated muscles such as the abductor pollicis brevis, and prolongation of nerve conduction across the carpal tunnel (prolonged distal latency) are characteristic. The diagnosis is supported by identification of *Tinel's sign,* in which tapping the carpal tunnel elicits paresthesias in the median nerve distribution, and by paresthesias produced by sustained flexion of the wrist.

The treatment of carpal tunnel syndrome requires consideration of the relationship between symptoms and occupational or recreational activities. Treatment begins with splinting of the wrist in slight dorsiflexion during sleep, thereby increasing the cross-sectional area of the carpal tunnel. Injection of corticosteroids into the carpal tunnel and use of potassium-sparing diuretics are helpful in some patients. More severe carpal tunnel syndrome is treated surgically by release of the carpal ligament.

BELL'S PALSY

Unilateral facial paralysis of acute onset frequently occurs on an idiopathic basis (Bell's palsy; Fig. 462–2). The etiology and pathophysiology remain unknown. The diagnosis is one of exclusion: facial nerve palsies also occur in the setting of *herpes zoster oticus* (Chapter 369), in which they are typically associated with otalgia and variceliform lesions affecting the external ear, ear canal, or tympanic

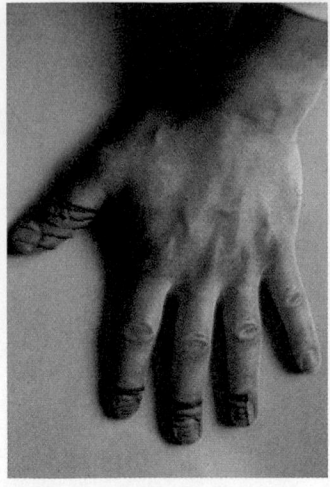
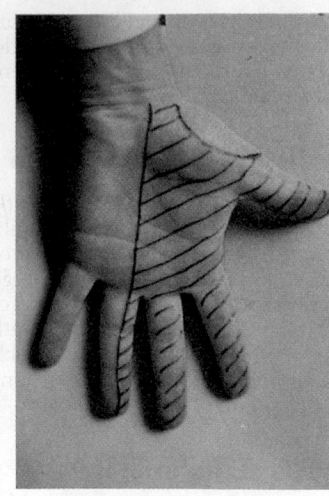

A   B

FIGURE 462–1 • Carpal tunnel syndrome. The common areas of sensory impairment are marked in this patient. Note that they usually extend around the fingertips onto the nail area in the affected fingers and even farther over the extensor surface on the thumb. Wasting of the thenar eminence is also seen. (From Forbes CD, Jackson WD: Color Atlas and Text of Clinical Medicine, 3rd ed. London, CV Mosby, 2003, with permission.)

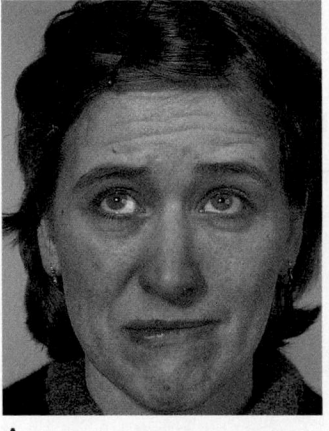
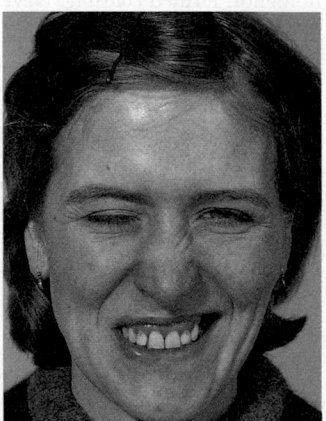

A   B

FIGURE 462–2 • Lower motor neuron palsy of the right facial nerve (Bell's palsy). The face may look almost normal at rest (*A*), but this patient is unable to wrinkle her brow fully on the affected side, the right corner of her mouth droops, and there is a prominent right nasolabial fold. When the patient is asked to close her eyes and show her teeth (*B*) the difference between the unaffected left side and the affected right side becomes more obvious. In upper motor neuron lesions, the weakness is less evident and the brow muscles function normally. (From Forbes CD, Jackson WD: Color Atlas and Text of Clinical Medicine, 3rd ed. London, CV Mosby, 2003, with permission.)

membrane (Fig. 462–3). Facial paralysis of a lower motor neuron type can be caused by *infiltrative disease in the meninges,* such as carcinomatous meningitis (Chapter 457), and by *inflammatory diseases* such as sarcoidosis (Chapter 91) and Lyme disease (Chapter 352). *Primary tumors of the facial nerve* can occur with apparently rapidly developing facial paralysis, although often in retrospect more subtle facial asymmetry had developed over a longer period. Facial paralysis can also occur in primary *CNS disease* affecting the pontomedullary junction, such as multiple sclerosis. Facial palsy has been noted in individuals with HIV infection, particularly in the early stages shortly after initial infection.

These considerations excluded, most cases of facial paralysis reflect idiopathic Bell's palsy. Patients typically notice facial paralysis on inspection in the mirror in the morning, and the disorder appears to come on overnight in many instances. Onset of facial paralysis may be heralded or accompanied by pain behind the ear (in the region of the

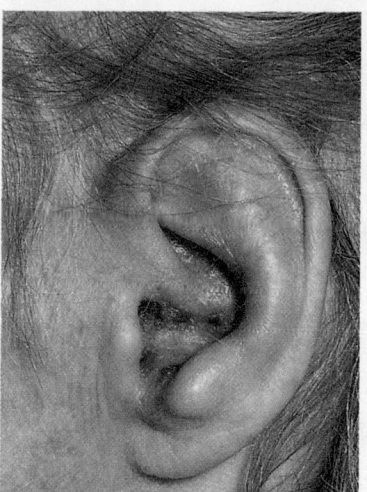

FIGURE 462–3 • The Ramsay Hunt syndrome is caused by herpes zoster (shingles) of the geniculate ganglion. The patient had a facial palsy identical to Bell's palsy, and the clinical clue to the diagnosis is the presence of herpetic vesicles in the external auditory meatus (which receives a small sensory branch from the facial nerve). (From Forbes CD, Jackson WD: Color Atlas and Text of Clinical Medicine, 3rd ed. London, CV Mosby, 2003, with permission.)

stylomastoid foramen). The severity of paralysis varies widely. The prognosis can to some extent be predicted by electrophysiologic examination of the facial nerve after the first several days. In most cases, prognosis is quite favorable.

A possible association of Bell's palsy with herpes simplex virus infection has been suggested, and some advocate early treatment with acyclovir. Some data suggest that a course of oral corticosteroids with rapid tapering may improve the prognosis, but this widely used therapy remains unproven. In severe cases, protection of the cornea from drying and injury is essential.

TRIGEMINAL NEURALGIA (TIC DOULOUREUX)

Trigeminal neuralgia is a recurring pain syndrome in which episodes of abrupt stabbing pain involve the second or third divisions of the trigeminal nerve. This and other painful cranial neuralgias are discussed in Chapter 427.

1. van der Meché FGA, Schmitz PIM, Dutch Guillain-Barré Study Group: A randomized trial comparing intravenous immune globulin and plasma exchange in Guillain-Barré syndrome. N Engl J Med 1992;326:1123–1129.
2. Hahn AF, Bolton CF, Zochodne D, Feasby TE: Intravenous immunoglobulin in chronic inflammatory demyelinating polyneuropathy: A double-blind, placebo-controlled, cross-over study. Brain 1996;119:1067–1077.

SUGGESTED READINGS
Bennett CL, Chance PF: Molecular pathogenesis of hereditary motor, sensory, and autonomic neuropathies. Curr Opin Neurol 2001;14;621–627. *Review of the genes responsible for inherited peripheral neuropathies.*
Hughes RA: Systematic reviews of treatment for inflammatory demyelinating neuropathy. J Anat 2002;200:331–339. *Overview of the randomized trials.*
Mendell JR, Sahenk Z: Clinical practice. Painful sensory neuropathy. N Engl J Med 2003;348:1243–1255. *A practical, case-based approach to evaluation and treatment.*
Salinas RA, Alvarez G, Alvarez MI, Ferreira J: Corticosteroids for Bell's palsy (idiopathic facial paralysis). Cochrane Database Syst Rev 2002;(1):CD001942. *Data remain inadequate to prove whether this therapy is truly beneficial.*

463 MUSCLE DISEASES

Richard J. Barohn

MUSCULAR DYSTROPHIES

Muscular dystrophies are inherited myopathies characterized by progressive muscle weakness and degeneration and by subsequent replacement by fibrous and fatty connective tissue. Historically, muscular dystrophies were categorized by their distribution of weakness, age at onset, and inheritance pattern. Advances in the molecular understanding of the muscular dystrophies have defined the genetic mutation and abnormal gene product for many of these disorders (Table 463–1).

DYSTROPHINOPATHIES

The dystrophinopathies include X-linked disorders resulting from mutations of the large dystrophin gene located at Xp21. Dystrophin is a large 427-kD subsarcolemmal cytoskeletal protein that, along with the other components of the dystrophin-glycoprotein complex (DGC), provides support to the muscle membrane during contraction. The large size of the gene (2.4 megabases) accounts for the high mutation rate. Large deletions, several kilobases to over 1 million base pairs, can be demonstrated in approximately two thirds of patients; duplications occur in 5% of cases, and the remainder have small mutations that are not readily detectable. Mutations disrupting the translational reading frame of the gene result in near-total loss of dystrophin (Duchenne-type muscular dystrophy), whereas in-frame mutations result in the translation of semifunctional dystrophin of abnormal size or amount (Becker's muscular dystrophy).

DUCHENNE-TYPE MUSCULAR DYSTROPHY
Genetics

The incidence of Duchenne-type muscular dystrophy is 1 in 3500 male births, and the prevalence approaches 1 per 18,000 males. One third of the cases result from a new mutation. Most patients with Duchenne-type muscular dystrophy have a frame-shift mutation and total dystrophin deficiency. Dystrophin deficiency weakens the sarcolemma, permitting the influx of calcium-rich extracellular fluid, which then activates intracellular proteases and complement, leading to fiber necrosis.

Clinical Manifestations

Duchenne dystrophy presents as early as age 2 to 3 years with delays in motor milestones and difficulty in running. The proximal muscles are the most severely affected early (limb-girdle pattern), and the course is relentlessly progressive. Patients begin to fall frequently by age 5 to 6 years, have difficulty in climbing stairs by age 8 years, and are usually confined to a wheelchair by age 12. Joint contractures commonly appear between 6 and 10 years. Initially, calf hypertrophy is often present, but after ambulation is lost, all muscles atrophy. Paraspinal muscle weakness leads to progressive kyphoscoliosis. The proximal tendon reflexes (biceps, quadriceps) disappear by the age of 10, although gastrocnemius reflexes are often preserved until late in the disease. Respiratory function gradually declines, and decreased vital capacity can be detected after the age of 10. Most patients die of respiratory complications in their 20s. Cardiac muscle is also affected; and although patients are generally asymptomatic, heart failure and arrhythmias can occur late in the disease. Up to 90% of these patients have an abnormal electrocardiogram (ECG), with tall right precordial R waves and deep left precordial Q waves. Echocardiography shows either hypokinesis or dilatation of ventricular walls. The smooth muscle of the gastrointestinal tract is also involved, and intestinal pseudo-obstruction occurs. The average intelligence quotient (IQ) of affected boys is one standard deviation below the normal mean, suggesting central nervous system (CNS) involvement.

Laboratory Findings

A dystrophin gene deletion (or less often a duplication) can be detected by analysis of DNA from leukocytes (by the polymerase chain reaction) in a blood sample in approximately two thirds of patients. The DNA from a muscle sample can be similarly tested, but it is no more specific than leukocyte DNA analysis. If the patient falls into the one third of patients in whom a deletion cannot be detected, muscle biopsy is required to demonstrate dystrophin deficiency by either Western blot or immunostaining. The muscle biopsy will also

Table 463–1 • MUSCULAR DYSTROPHIES

DISEASE	MODE OF INHERITANCE	GENE MUTATION LOCATION	GENE DEFECT/ PROTEIN
X-LINKED MD			
Duchenne/Becker's	XR	Xp21	Dystrophin
Emery-Dreifuss	XR	Xq28	Emerin
LIMB-GIRDLE MD			
LGMD 1A	AD	5q22-34	Not known
LGMD 1B	AD	1q11-21	Not known
LGMD 1C	AD	3p25	Caveolin-3
LGMD 2A	AR	15q15	Calpain-3
LGMD 2B*	AR	2p12	Dysferlin
LGMD 2C	AR	13q12	γ-Sarcoglycan
LGMD 2D	AR	17q12	α-Sarcoglycan
LGMD 2E	AR	4q12	β-Sarcoglycan
LGMD 2F	AR	5q33	δ-Sarcoglycan
LGMD 2G	AR	17q11	Telethonin
LGMD 2H	AR	9q31	Not known
LGMD 2I	AR	19q13.3	Fukutin-related protein 1
CONGENITAL MD			
With CNS Involvement			
Fukuyama CMD	AR	9q31-33	Fukutin
Walker-Warburg CMD	AR	9q31-33	?Fukutin
Muscle-eye-brain CMD	AR	1p	Glycosyltransferase
Without CNS Involvement			
Merosin-deficient classic type	AR	6q2	Laminin-2 (merosin)
Merosin-positive classic type	AR	?	Not known
Integrin-deficient CMD	AR	12q13	Integrin α7
Rigid spine syndrome	AR	1p3	Selenoprotein NI
DISTAL MD			
Late adult-onset 1A (Welander)	AD	2p15	Unknown
Late adult-onset 1B (Markesbery/Udd)	AD	2q31	titin
Early adult-onset 1A (Nonaka)	AR	9p1-q1	GNE
Early adult-onset 1B (Miyoshi)[†]	AR	2q12-14	Dysferlin
Early adult-onset 1C (Laing)	AD	14	MPD1
OTHER MD			
Facioscapulohumeral	AD	4q35	Deleted chromatin
Oculopharyngeal	AD	14q11	Poly(A) binding protein 2
Myotonic dystrophy type 1	AD	19q13	RNA accumulation
Myotonic dystrophy type 2	AD	3q	RNA accumulation
Myofibrillar myopathy	AD	11q21-23	β-crystallin
Myofibrillar myopathy	AD	2q35	Desmin
Bethlem myopathy	AD	21q22	Collagen VI

AD = autosomal dominant; AR = autosomal recessive; CMD = congenital muscular dystrophy; CNS = central nervous system; GNE = UDP-N-acetylglucosamine 2-epimerase/N-acetylmannosamine kinase; LGMD = limb-girdle muscular dystrophy; MD = muscular dystrophy; XR = X-linked recessive.
*Probably same condition as Miyoshi distal MD.
†Probably same condition as LGMD 2B.

demonstrate typical features of a muscular dystrophy: fiber size variability, fiber necrosis, and regeneration, and replacement with connective tissue and fat.

The serum creatine kinase (CK) levels are markedly elevated at birth (20 to 100 times normal). They remain elevated but tend to decline over the course of the disease, when there is severe loss of muscle mass. The electromyogram (EMG) shows fibrillation potentials and myopathic motor units. EMG and muscle biopsy are not necessary in Duchenne dystrophy if the diagnosis can be established by molecular studies of lymphocytes.

BECKER'S MUSCULAR DYSTROPHY

Becker's dystrophy is a milder form of dystrophinopathy and varies in severity, depending on the genetic lesion. It is less common than the Duchenne type, with an incidence of 5 per 100,000 and prevalence of 2.4 per 100,000. The pattern of weakness resembles that of Duchenne-type muscular dystrophy, but it is less severe. The mean age at onset of symptoms is later, between 5 and 15 years. Calf hypertrophy is often prominent, and patients may complain of exercise-induced calf pain as an early symptom. Patients usually remain ambulatory after age 15, and the average time when a wheelchair is required is age 30. Children with Duchenne-type muscular

dystrophy cannot lift their head fully against gravity (Medical Research Council of Great Britain [MRC] grade < 3), whereas less severe, "outlier" children and those with Becker's dystrophy retain this ability. Cardiac abnormalities are similar to these described for Duchenne-type muscular dystrophy. Most patients with Becker's dystrophy experience slow progression; death may occur from respiratory or cardiac complications after age 40.

Most patients with Becker's dystrophy have a non–frame-shift mutation, so that a reduced amount of an abnormal dystrophin is produced, resulting in a milder syndrome than Duchenne-type muscular dystrophy. DNA analysis from blood leukocytes will show an Xp21 deletion in about 60% of cases. Results of immunostaining and Western immunoblot for dystrophin on muscle extracts reveal the protein is not absent, as in Duchenne-type muscular dystrophy, but is reduced in amount or abnormal in size. Serum CK level is moderately elevated, and needle electromyography shows electrophysiologic signs of a myopathy, similar to the findings in Duchenne-type muscular dystrophy.

OTHER DYSTROPHINOPATHIES

Other, milder dystrophinopathy phenotypes include exercise intolerance associated with myalgias, muscle cramps, or myoglobinuria;

Neurology

minimal limb-girdle weakness or quadriceps myopathy; asymptomatic elevation of the serum CK level; cardiomyopathy with only mild muscle weakness; and fatal X-linked cardiomyopathy without muscle weakness. The different dystrophin phenotypes are determined by the site of the mutation in the dystrophin gene and the effect or lack of effect of the mutation on the expression of the cardiac isoform of dystrophin.

FEMALE CARRIERS

The daughters of males with a dystrophinopathy are obligate carriers of the mutated dystrophin gene, as are the mothers of affected children who also have a family history of Duchenne-type or Becker's muscular dystrophy. Mothers and sisters of index cases of isolated Duchenne-type or Becker's dystrophy are at risk for being carriers. There is a 50% chance that males born to carrier females will inherit the disease, and 50% of the carrier's daughters born will become carriers themselves. Female carriers are usually asymptomatic, but rarely they may demonstrate moderate limb-girdle weakness.

The CK level is elevated in about 50% of female carriers. A more accurate method of carrier detection is to look for an Xp21 deletion, which will be present if the affected males in the family are among the 60% who have a dystrophin gene deletion (or duplication). If a deletion is not present, linkage analysis on families can be performed. Prenatal genetic testing can be performed on amniotic fluid cells or chorionic villi.

 Treatment

> Controlled trials with prednisone 0.75 mg/kg/day in Duchenne-type dystrophy have demonstrated moderate improvement in strength and delay in progression into a wheelchair or braces. [1,2] Prednisone also delays respiratory compromise, but it cannot prevent deterioration and death. Side effects of therapy include weight gain, growth delay, and changes in behavior. Gene therapy for the dystrophinopathies and other muscular dystrophies with known genetic mutations is still in preclinical stages. Trials of myoblast transfer from the normal fathers of patients with Duchenne-type dystrophy to their affected sons found no effect.

EMERY-DREIFUSS DYSTROPHY

Emery-Dreifuss dystrophy is an X-linked muscular dystrophy that is characterized by the clinical triad of (1) early contractures of the elbows, ankles, and posterior cervical muscles; (2) slowly progressive muscle weakness usually in a scapulohumeroperoneal distribution; and (3) cardiomyopathy with atrial conduction defects. The early elbow contractures are often an important phenotypic key to the diagnosis. Although Emery-Dreifuss dystrophy usually begins in childhood, most patients remain ambulatory into their third or fourth decades. The serum CK level is either normal or only moderately elevated. The muscle biopsy shows a range of myopathic changes but fewer dystrophic features than that for Duchenne-type or Becker's dystrophy. Electrocardiography can show sinus bradycardia, prolongation of the PR interval, or more severe degrees of conduction block. The cardiac conduction defects are potentially lethal and often require a pacemaker. The family history may suggest an X-linked disorder. The mutated gene in the Xq28 region codes for a protein product, emerin. Emerin is a 254-amino-acid protein that localizes to the nuclear membranes of skeletal, cardiac, and smooth muscle fibers; its function is unknown. The definitive diagnosis can be made from either leukocyte DNA analysis or immunostaining muscle or skin tissue for emerin. The normal emerin perinuclear staining pattern in these tissues will be absent in Emery-Dreifuss dystrophy.

Bethlem myopathy clinically resembles Emery-Dreifuss dystrophy with a similar pattern of weakness and early contractures. However, Bethlem myopathy has no cardiac involvement and the inheritance pattern is autosomal dominant. At least some cases of Bethlem myopathy are due to a mutation of α_1 and α_2 subunits of collagen VI located on chromosome 21q.

THE RIGID-SPINE SYNDROME

Rigid-spine syndrome is a disorder in which muscle contractures involve the spine as well as other joints. The genetic defect has been localized to chromosome 1p3, and the presumed gene product is selenoprotein. Because of the severe contractures, it must be distinguished from Emery-Dreifuss dystrophy and Bethlem myopathy. In most cases, the disease is sporadic and manifests in infancy with hypotonia, proximal weakness, and delayed motor milestones. Throughout the first decade, the child experiences progressive, severe scoliosis and limitations of spinal mobility, as well as elbow and knee contractures. The spinal deformities continue until about age 7 to 13 years, at which time the disease appears to stabilize. Serum CK level is mildly elevated. Muscle biopsies demonstrate nonspecific myopathic features.

LIMB-GIRDLE MUSCULAR DYSTROPHIES (LGMDs)

LGMDs include a large number of hereditary muscular dystrophies with a limb-girdle pattern of weakness. LGMDs are either autosomal recessive (the majority) or dominant and thus are clinically distinguished from the dystrophinopathies by an equal occurrence in both sexes. When LGMD occurs in early childhood, it resembles Duchenne-type dystrophy and has been termed *severe childhood recessive muscular dystrophy* (SCARMD). Milder phenotypes can resemble Becker's dystrophy. The laboratory features (serum CK, EMG, muscle biopsy) are consistent with a muscular dystrophy. Until recently, all LGMDs were lumped together. During the past decade, the genetic mutations and resulting protein defects have established for at least 10 subtypes of LGMD. The less common autosomal dominant forms have been labeled type 1 (LGMD 1A, 1B, 1C, etc.), the autosomal recessive disorders are type 2 (LGMD 2A, 2B, etc.), and the list continues to grow.

AUTOSOMAL RECESSIVE LGMD. A number of the autosomal recessive LGMDs are due to defects in one of the sarcoglycan components of the DGC, termed *sarcoglycanopathies* (LGMD 2C, 2D, 2E, 2F).

The protein mutated in LGMD 2C, α-sarcoglycan, was previously known as *adhalin*-Arabic for "muscle." These disorders may account for as many as 20% of the muscular dystrophies that have a Duchenne-type or Becker's phenotype. LGMD 2C and 2D usually begin in childhood; LGMD 2E and 2F have a more variable age at onset, even within families. These LGMDs are not associated with intellectual impairment or cardiac abnormalities, in contrast to the dystrophinopathies.

The sarcoglycans are important components of the DGC, but the exact role of these proteins is unknown. A deficiency in one of the sarcoglycans results in a destabilization of the entire sarcoglycan complex. Results of muscle biopsies show normal dystrophin; however, immunostaining for each of the sarcoglycans is absent or diminished regardless of the primary sarcoglycan mutation.

Other autosomal recessive LGMDs have known protein mutations that are not part of the DGC. LGMD 2A with an age at onset between 3 and 30 years (mean, 13) is due to genetic mutation producing a deficiency of the muscle-specific proteolytic enzyme *calpain-3*. Calpains are nonlysosomal intracellular cysteine proteases. In LGMD 2B patients, weakness develops between ages 13 and 35 and CK levels are elevated up to 200 times normal. The LGMD 2B mutation localizes to a region on 2p13 that codes for a protein recently named *dysferlin*. Dysferlin shares amino acid sequence homology with *C. elegans* spermatogenesis factor FER-1. LGMD 2B is also of interest because affected individuals can have one of two distinct phenotypes: limb-girdle or a distal myopathy pattern (see the discussion of distal muscular dystrophy). How a mutation in the same protein can result in such dissimilar clinical presentation is unclear.

AUTOSOMAL DOMINANT LGMD. The autosomal dominant LGMDs all have onset in childhood or early adult life. Linkage to chromosome locations is known for LGMD 1A and 1B; the molecular defect for LGMD 1C produces a protein deficiency of *caveolin-3*. Caveolins may act as scaffolding proteins on which caveolin-interacting lipids and proteins are organized. Caveolin-3 is not considered part of the DGC, although it is localized by immunostaining to the sarcolemma.

DIFFERENTIAL DIAGNOSIS OF LIMB-GIRDLE SYNDROMES. All patients with limb-girdle syndromes need to be investigated by EMG and muscle biopsy. In those with a positive family history, the differential diagnosis includes inherited metabolic myopathies (e.g., acid maltase deficiency or a lipid storage myopathy), morphologically distinct congenital myopathies (or their late-onset variants (e.g., nemaline, central core, and myotubular myopathies), or the anterior horn cell disease, spinal muscular atrophy. In sporadic cases of a limb-girdle syndrome, the differential diagnosis includes the same diseases and also inflammatory myopathies (polymyositis, inclusion body myositis, or sarcoidosis confined to muscle), endocrine myopathies, sporadic Duchenne-type dystrophy, Duchenne-type or Becker's dystrophy manifesting in female carriers, other dystrophinopathies, and sporadic Emery-Dreifuss dystrophy before the appearance of joint contractures or cardiomyopathy.

CONGENITAL MUSCULAR DYSTROPHIES

The congenital muscular dystrophies (CMDs) are a group of autosomal recessive disorders in which patients have the onset of hypotonia and proximal weakness during the prenatal period; muscle biopsy shows dystrophic findings. The infants often have joint contractures of the elbows, hips, knees, and ankles (arthrogryposis). CMDs can be broadly divided into those without and those with clinical evidence of CNS involvement (severe mental retardation, seizures, and visual loss due to cerebro-ocular dysplasia). However, many patients without severe brain disease clinically, or the so-called classic type, usually have cerebral hypomyelination on magnetic resonance imaging. The CMDs with significant brain and eye involvement generally produce progressive courses and death by age 10 to 12. Classic type CMDs without clinical CNS involvement have a more benign outlook, with a nonprogressive course; affected patients may eventually walk independently.

Fifty per cent of classic type CMD is associated with a deficiency of the basal lamina protein α_2-laminin, also known as merosin. Merosin is bound to the DGC anchoring the basal lamina to the sarcolemma. Merosin-negative CMD can be diagnosed by immunostaining of muscle or skin. Other CMDs without clinical CNS involvement are associated with a deficiency of integrin, a transsarcolemmal protein that is not part of the DGC. The *Fukuyama-type* CMD, occurring primarily in Japan, is associated with mutations in the gene encoding for a protein named *fukutin*. The same genetic defect probably accounts for the Walker-Warburg cerebro-ocular dysplasia syndrome. Fukutin is not associated with the sarcolemma and appears to be a secreted protein, but its function is unknown.

FACIOSCAPULOHUMERAL DYSTROPHY

The inheritance of facioscapulohumeral dystrophy is autosomal dominant with high penetrance and variable expression within families. Affected family members may be unaware of their mild deficits, making examination of relatives of suspected patients very important. The incidence of facioscapulohumeral dystrophy is 1 : 20,000. Facioscapulohumeral dystrophy has been linked to the telomeric region of chromosome 4q35. Although the gene has not been isolated, a deletion in this region is present in virtually all patients with facioscapulohumeral dystrophy.

The disease presents in childhood or adult life. It involves the facial muscles early and then descends to the scapular stabilizers (serratus anterior, rhomboid, trapezius, latissimus dorsi), the muscles of the upper arm (biceps, triceps), and the anterior leg muscles. Early physical signs include failure to bury the eyelashes on forced eye closure, an expressionless face, winging of the scapulas when the arms are raised, and prominent indentation of the anterior axillary folds. The deltoids are relatively spared compared with other proximal arm muscles. Distal muscle weakness occurs first in the tibialis anterior and may result in footdrop, leading to a scapuloperoneal pattern of weakness. Later, wrist and finger extensor weakness may develop. The rate of progression and the extent to which pelvic girdle and forearm muscles are eventually affected vary considerably between and within families. In general, cases with early onset have a worse prognosis. Some patients experience a late exacerbation of weakness after years of little or slow progression. Approximately 20% of these patients eventually will require a wheelchair. Joint contractures are uncommon.

The serum CK level is normal or mildly elevated. The muscle biopsy shows moderate myopathic changes, but a prominent mononuclear inflammatory infiltrate can be confused with polymyositis. However, these patients do not respond to immunosuppressive therapy. A variant is associated with sensorineural hearing loss and with retinal telangiectasia and painless blindness (*Coats' disease*).

Scapuloperoneal muscular dystrophy is an autosomal dominant disorder that can resemble facioscapulohumeral dystrophy, but without facial weakness. In these families there is no linkage to chromosome 4q35.

MYOTONIC DYSTROPHY

Myotonic dystrophy is an autosomal dominant multisystemic disorder that affects skeletal, cardiac, and smooth muscle and other organs, including the eyes, the endocrine system, and the brain. Myotonic dystrophy is the most common muscular dystrophy, with an incidence of 13.5 per 100,000 live births and a prevalence of 3 to 5 per 100,000. Myotonic dystrophy can occur at any age, but the usual onset of symptoms is in the late second or third decade. However, some affected individuals may remain symptom free their entire life. A severe form with onset in infancy is known as *congenital myotonic dystrophy*. The severity is generally worse from one generation to the next.

The molecular defect of myotonic dystrophy is an abnormal expansion of CTG repeats in a protein kinase gene on chromosome 19q13.2. Affected individuals have more than 50 CTG repeats, and the severity of the disease directly correlates with the size of the expanded triplet repeat. The protein kinase encoded by this gene has been termed *myotonin*. Studies of transgenic animals suggest that some, if not all, manifestations of myotonic dystrophy result from the accumulation of abnormal RNA transcribed by the lengthy trinucleotide repeat on chromosome 19.

Typical patients exhibit facial weakness with temporalis muscle wasting, frontal balding, ptosis, and weakness of the neck flexor muscles (Fig. 463–1). Weakness of the extremities usually begins distally and progresses slowly to affect the limb-girdle muscles proximally. Weakness is a more common symptom than muscle stiffness or myotonia, although patients may complain of the inability to relax the fingers after a hand grip. Patients may be areflexic, but the sensory examination is normal.

Associated manifestations include posterior subscapular cataracts, testicular atrophy and impotence, intellectual impairment, and hypersomnia due to both central and obstructive sleep apneas. Respiratory muscle weakness may be severe. Elevated serum glucose levels occur as a result of end-organ unresponsiveness to insulin, but frank diabetes mellitus rarely develops. Involvement of the smooth muscle in the gastrointestinal tract can produce dysphagia, reduced gut motility, and chronic pseudo-obstruction. Cardiac conduction defects are common and can produce sudden death. Chronic hypoxia can lead to cor pulmonale. Affected females can have a high rate of fetal loss.

The serum CK level is normal or mildly increased. Muscle biopsies show excessive number of central nuclei, type 1 atrophy, and other nonspecific myopathic changes. EMG shows myopathic motor units in addition to myotonic potentials.

The diagnosis can be established by documenting an increased number of CTG expansions on chromosome 19q13.2 in leukocytes from a blood sample. Marked expansion of the CTG repeat usually occurs in children of mothers with myotonic dystrophy, accounting

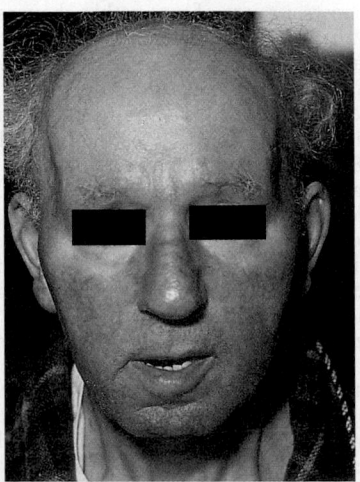

FIGURE 463–1 • Myotonic dystrophy in a 50-year-old man. His appearance is typical, with facial weakness, atrophy of the temporal muscles and sternomastoids, and frontal baldness, which gives a "monk-like" appearance. (From Forbes CD, Jackson WF: Color Atlas and Text of Clinical Medicine, 3rd ed. London, CV Mosby, 2003, with permission.)

for anticipation and the severe phenotype of congenital myotonic dystrophy. A second myotonic dystrophy locus (DM-2) has been mapped to chromosome 3q. Clinical features of DM-2 are similar, but weakness is more often proximal than the 19q-linked disorder (DM-1). A similar abnormality in RNA transcription is likely responsible for DM-2. DM-2 was initially termed *proximal myotonic myopathy* (PROMM). Proximal extremity weakness and myalgias are characteristic. Patients with DM-2 may have less cardiac muscle or other organ involvement than DM-1.

The myotonia is rarely so symptomatic as to require treatment. Phenytoin is the safest drug for myotonia; quinine, tocainide, and mexiletine can exacerbate cardiac arrhythmias. Annual ECGs are recommended, and a pacemaker may be necessary. Positive-pressure ventilation devices may assist patients who have sleep apnea. Sedatives and opiates should be used with caution because they can depress ventilatory drive. Patients with myotonic dystrophy are at risk for pulmonary and cardiac complications during general anesthesia. Braces can assist patients with footdrop.

DISTAL DYSTROPHIES

Although a number of myopathies can have prominent distal weakness (see Table 461-3), some genetically distinct entities are considered as distal muscular dystrophies. There are two late adult-onset autosomal dominant forms. *Welander distal dystrophy* occurs in Scandinavia and presents between the fourth and sixth decades with selective weakness and atrophy of the forearm extensor and intrinsic hand muscles and then involves the anterior leg and small foot muscles. Tibial muscular *dystrophy* has been observed in Finnish, French, and U.S. patients and initially involves the anterior tibial muscles and later the distal upper extremities. Serum CK level can be elevated in all of these disorders. Results of muscle biopsy show variable degrees of dystrophic changes. All of these disorders have progressive courses and over time can involve proximal muscles with the loss of ambulation. Chromosomal linkage has been found in each of these disorders and the gene lesion identified for most (see Table 463-1).

Myofibrillar myopathy (also known as *desmin* myopathy) is a heterogeneous group of muscular dystrophies that can present as either distal or limb-girdle patterns of weakness. Myofibrillar myopathy is not a single disorder: some kindreds have a molecular defect in the αβ-crystallin chaperone protein on 11q21-23; others have a mutation in the desmin gene on 2q35; and one family has linkage to chromosome 12. Most kindreds are autosomal dominant, but sporadic cases occur. Cardiomyopathy is common. The muscle biopsy findings show vacuoles, cytoplasmic inclusions, and accumulations of desmin and other proteins such as dystrophin and β-amyloid precursor protein.

OCULOPHARYNGEAL MUSCULAR DYSTROPHY

Oculopharyngeal muscular dystrophy is inherited as an autosomal dominant disorder. The molecular genetic defect is an increased expansion of a triplet GCG repeat on chromosome 14q11 within the *poly(A) binding protein* 2 gene (*PABP2*). The function of *PABP2* and the means by which a mutation of this protein leads to muscle disease are unknown. This disease presents in the fifth or sixth decade with progressive ptosis followed by dysphagia. Later, all external ocular and other extremity muscles may become affected. Diplopia does not develop. Extremity weakness is usually in a limb-girdle pattern, but some variants have distal involvement. Disease progression is usually slow. Death can result from aspiration pneumonia or starvation if adequate nutrition is not addressed. Patients may require surgical correction (cricopharyngeal myotomy) for achalasia or a gastric feeding tube. The serum CK level is normal or slightly increased. Muscle biopsy discloses nonspecific myopathic changes with rimmed vacuoles in the muscle fibers, and the electron microscopy reveals 8.5-nm intranuclear filaments.

MORPHOLOGICALLY DISTINCT CONGENITAL MYOPATHIES

Congenital myopathies (Table 463-2) are distinguished from dystrophies in three respects. First, these disorders have characteristic morphologic alterations demonstrated on light and electron microscopy. Second, as the name implies, congenital myopathies

Table 463-2 • MORPHOLOGICALLY DISTINCT CONGENITAL MYOPATHIES

Central core myopathy
Nemaline (rod) myopathy
Centronuclear (myotubular) myopathy
  Severe X-linked recessive form
  Milder autosomal recessive and dominant forms
Congenital fiber-type disproportion
Multicore/minicore myopathy
Fingerprint body myopathy
Sarcotubular myopathy
Reducing body myopathy
Trilaminar myopathy
Hyaline myopathy with focal lysis of myofibrils
Myofibrillar myopathy

usually present at birth with hypotonia and subsequent delayed motor development. Finally, most congenital myopathies are relatively nonprogressive and have more benign outcomes than occur in the muscular dystrophies. However, there are exceptions to all three generalizations. Onset can occur in childhood and even in early adulthood, and some congenital myopathies have a severe course and fatal outcome. Moreover, as the molecular genetic defects of the congenital myopathies become known, distinguishing between these disorders and muscular dystrophies becomes more difficult.

Common clinical findings include reduced muscle bulk (no hypertrophy); slender body build and a long, narrow face, with skeletal abnormalities (high-arched palate, pectus excavatum, kyphoscoliosis, dislocated hips, pes cavus); and absent or reduced muscle stretch reflexes. Most patients have a limb-girdle weakness phenotype, although distal weakness can occur in some families (see Table 461-3). Serum CK is moderately elevated or normal, and the EMG usually shows a myopathic pattern but may be normal. Inheritance patterns are variable.

CENTRAL CORE MYOPATHY

Central core myopathy is autosomal dominant, but sporadic cases occur. The disorder is associated with a mutation on chromosome 19q13.1 in the *ryanodine receptor gene*. Some patients with malignant hyperthermia also have mutations in this gene, and thus the disorders may be allelic. The mechanism by which defects in the ryanodine receptor gene lead to these disorders is unknown.

NEMALINE MYOPATHY

The histologic characteristic of nemaline myopathy, a congenital myopathy, is the presence of rods, or nemaline (Gk. *nema* = "thread") bodies, within muscle fibers. Clinically, the myopathy can present as a severe neonatal form with respiratory (diaphragm) involvement that is generally fatal within the first year of life or as a mild static or slowly progressive condition present from birth or early childhood. Nemaline myopathy can occur as an autosomal recessive or dominant condition. Most autosomal recessive families have been linked to 2q; nebulin is the likely candidate gene. Some autosomal dominant families have been linked to a mutation in the α-tropomyosin gene on chromosome 1q. Other cases are sporadic.

CENTRONUCLEAR (MYOTUBULAR) MYOPATHY

The histologic hallmark of centronuclear (myotubular) myopathy is the presence of large central nuclei within many muscle fibers. The molecular defect is a mutation in the *myotubularin* gene on Xp28. Myotubularin is a phosphatase important in muscle cell growth and differentiation. As with nemaline myopathy, there are severe neonatal presentations and static or slowly progressive forms with onset from birth to adulthood. Ptosis and ophthalmoparesis occur commonly in all forms of centronuclear myopathy and may distinguish these patients from those with other congenital myopathies. The severe infantile form is usually X-linked recessive and is associated with respiratory insufficiency; most patients die in infancy,

Neurology

Table 463-3 • METABOLIC AND MITOCHONDRIAL MYOPATHIES

GLYCOGEN METABOLISM DEFICIENCIES
Type II α-1,4 Glucosidase (acid maltase)
Type III Debranching
Type IV Branching
Type V Phosphorylase (McArdle's disease)*
Type VII Phosphofructokinase (Tarui's disease)*
Type VIII Phosphorylase B kinase*
Type IX Phosphoglycerate kinase*
Type X Phosphoglycerate mutase*
Type XI Lactate dehydrogenase*

LIPID METABOLISM DEFICIENCIES
Carnitine palmitoyl transferase*
Primary systemic/muscle carnitine deficiency
Secondary carnitine deficiency
β-Oxidation defects
    Medications (valproic acid)

PURINE METABOLISM DEFICIENCIES
Myoadenylate deaminase deficiency*

MITOCHONDRIAL MYOPATHIES
Pyruvate dehydrogenase complex deficiencies (including Leigh's syndrome)
Progressive external ophthalmoplegia (PEO)
Autosomal dominant with multiple mitochondrial DNA deletions
    Adenine nucleotide translocator 1 (ANT1)
    TWINKLE
    Polymerase gamma
    Kearns-Sayre syndrome
Mitochondrial encephalopathy with lactic acidosis and strokelike episodes (MELAS)
Myoclonic epilepsy and ragged red fibers (MERRF)
Mitochondrial neurogastrointestinal encephalomyopathy (MNGIE)
Mitochondrial depletion syndrome
Leigh's syndrome and neuropathy, ataxia, retinitis pigmentosa (NARP)
Succinate dehydrogenase deficiency*

*Deficiency can produce exercise intolerance and myoglobinuria.

but a few patients survive into childhood, usually with major disabilities.

CONGENITAL FIBER-TYPE DISPROPORTION

The distinguishing morphologic finding in congenital fiber-type disproportion is an increased number of small type I muscle fibers. Most patients have onset at birth with hypotonia and have a relatively benign, nonprogressive course. The genetic defect is unknown.

METABOLIC MYOPATHIES

Metabolic myopathies (Chapter 213) include (1) glucose/glycogen metabolism disorders; (2) lipid metabolism disorders; and (3) mitochondrial disorders. A fourth group involving the utilization of adenine nucleotides is more controversial (Table 463-3).

GLUCOSE/GLYCOGEN METABOLISM DISORDERS

Glucose and its storage form, glycogen, are essential for the short-term, predominantly anaerobic energy requirements of muscle. Disorders of glucose and glycogen metabolism (grouped under the term glycogenoses) have two distinct clinical presentations. One group of disorders has dynamic manifestations with exercise intolerance, pain, cramps, and myoglobinuria (types V, VII, VIII, IX, X, XI). The second, static group is associated with fixed weakness without features of exercise intolerance or myoglobinuria (types II, III, IV). Occasionally, there is overlap between the two groups. Of the 11 distinct glycogenoses, only glucose-6-phosphate (type I) and liver phosphorylase (type VI) deficiencies do not affect muscle. The glycogenoses that affect muscle are usually transmitted as autosomal recessive traits, except for phosphoglycerate kinase, which is X linked.

GLYCOGENOSES WITH EXERCISE INTOLERANCE/MYOGLOBINURIA

The common clinical features of the glycogenoses with exercise intolerance/myoglobinuria (myophosphorylase [type V], phosphofructokinase [PFK, type VII], phosphorylase B kinase [PBK, type VIII], phosphoglycerate [PGK, type IX], phosphoglycerate mutase [PGM, type X], and lactate dehydrogenase [LDH, type XI] deficiencies) are exercise intolerance in childhood followed by exertion-induced muscle pain and myoglobinuria in the second or third decade. Many patients note a "second wind" phenomenon after a period of brief rest so that they can continue the exercise at the previous level of activity. The muscle pain is caused by electrically silent contractures and is not associated with adenosine triphosphate (ATP) depletion; the mechanism is not understood. Strength examination, CK levels, and EMG findings between attacks are usually normal early in the disease but may become abnormal with advancing age. After episodes of severe myoglobinuria with rhabdomyolysis, needle EMG can show myopathic units and fibrillations. After forearm exercise, the venous lactate level fails to rise in myophosphorylase, PFK, and PGK deficiencies and rises only partially in PBK, PGM, and LDH deficiencies. The muscle biopsy shows scattered necrotic and regenerating fibers, especially after an episode of rhabdomyolysis.

In PFK deficiency, hyperuricemia and gout occur in some cases, and there is mild hemolytic anemia caused by a partial erythrocyte enzyme defect. PGK mutations result either in severe hemolytic anemia and neurologic deficits but no myopathy or in a myopathy with only the features described earlier. LDH deficiency is associated with a rash because M-lactate dehydrogenase is the dominant form of the enzyme expressed in skin.

Histochemical stains are readily available for some of these disorders (myophosphorylase, PFK), but definitive diagnosis requires biochemical analysis to document the enzyme deficiency or molecular testing to define specific mutations. Mutations have been identified for all the glycogenoses except PBK deficiency. Although no specific treatment is available for these disorders, aerobic exercise training and a high-protein diet have been proposed as sensible strategies.

GLYCOGENOSES WITH FIXED WEAKNESS AND NO EXERCISE INTOLERANCE

α-Glucosidase, also known as acid maltase, is a lysosomal enzyme that breaks down glycogen to glucose; when its level is deficient, glycogen accumulates within lysosomes as well as freely in the cytoplasm of cells. Mutations have been identified in the α-glucosidase gene on chromosome 17q21. Therapy is primarily supportive, particularly for respiratory insufficiency. There are three clinical variants. The infantile type (Pompe's disease) presents in early infancy with generalized and rapidly progressive weakness and heart, tongue, and liver enlargement. There is widespread glycogen excess in tissues, including lower motor neurons. Death results from cardiorespiratory failure before the age of 2 years. The childhood (juvenile) type presents in infancy or early childhood as a myopathy. Weakness is more proximal than distal, and there may be calf enlargement simulating muscular dystrophy. Glycogen excess is less marked and confined to muscle. The heart, but not the liver, may be involved. Death results from respiratory failure before age 20. The adult type presents between the second and seventh decades of life, either with slowly progressive limb muscle weakness that mimics limb-girdle dystrophy or with a scapuloperoneal presentation. These patients often experience insidious ventilatory muscle weakness leading to respiratory failure. The adult form does not affect the heart or liver. In all three types, the serum CK level is moderately increased. The EMG in affected muscles shows myopathic changes and excessive abnormal electrical irritability, including myotonic discharges, particularly in paraspinous muscles. However, there is no clinical myotonia. The muscle biopsy demonstrates a vacuolar myopathy with high glycogen content and acid-phosphatase reactivity in the vacuoles. The diagnosis is confirmed by demonstrating α-glucosidase deficiency in either muscle, skin fibroblasts, or lymphocytes.

Danon's disease has clinical and histologic features similar to those of the adult form of α-glucosidase deficiency, including glycogen accumulation. The defect is a mutation in LAMP.

Debranching enzyme deficiency is a rare disease that can affect liver, heart, or skeletal muscle. The gene for the enzyme maps to chromosome 1p21. The disease most commonly presents in childhood as hepatomegaly with fasting hypoglycemia that spontaneously resolves by adulthood. Patients less frequently have a disabling myopathy that affects both proximal and distal muscles and that can appear in childhood or (more commonly) in adult life. Affected patients can experience exercise intolerance. There may be a depressed lactate response on forearm testing, but myoglobinuria is rare. The CK level is elevated, and the EMG shows myopathic changes and abnormal electrical irritability.

Deficiency of the branching enzyme presents in infancy with progressive liver and cardiac dysfunction, which lead to death in the first years of life. Muscle weakness is variable; if weakness is present, the tongue is severely affected.

DISORDERS OF FATTY ACID METABOLISM

Lipids are essential for the aerobic energy needs of muscle during sustained exercise. Serum long-chain fatty acids, which are the primary lipid fuel for muscle metabolism, are transported into the mitochondria as carnitine esters and are metabolized via β-oxidation. Carnitine palmitoyl transferase (CPT) I converts cytoplasmic acyl-coenzyme A (CoA) to acylcarnitine, which is then transported into the mitochondria by carnitine acyl-transferase in exchange for carnitine. CPT II on the inner mitochondrial membrane reconstitutes acyl-Co A. A deficiency of carnitine, CPT, or the enzymes of β-oxidation can lead to impaired muscle lipid metabolism.

As with glycogen pathway defects, the myopathic manifestations of fatty acid metabolism can consist of a dynamic exercise intolerance with myoglobinuria or static weakness with a lipid storage myopathy. A lipid storage myopathy can be caused by primary carnitine deficiency or by another defect of fatty acid oxidation with secondary carnitine deficiency. In addition, some disorders of lipid metabolism can produce multiorgan metabolic crises with hepatic failure and altered mental status (Reye's syndrome). Most lipid disorders occur sporadically; they are believed to be autosomal recessive.

CARNITINE PALMITOYL TRANSFERASE DEFICIENCY

CPT is present in two forms: types I and II. Deficiency of CPT I may present in infancy or childhood with hepatic dysfunction. It causes a Reye's syndrome–like illness with hypoketotic hypoglycemia, encephalopathy, hyperammonemia, and liver dysfunction. Deficiency of CPT II typically causes exertional myalgias and myoglobinuria. These attacks are distinct from those associated with glycolytic defects in that they occur after prolonged exercise, fasting, febrile illness, or other provocations that may increase muscle dependence on free fatty acids. Unlike patients with McArdle's disease, those with CPT deficiency tolerate brief, intense exercise and have no second wind phenomenon. Muscle strength and CK level are normal at rest. Serum and muscle carnitine levels are typically normal. The EMG is normal except for myopathic changes after episodes of rhabdomyolysis. Ammonia and lactate levels rise normally after forearm exercise. Muscle biopsy is usually normal except for evidence of muscle myopathic injury after rhabdomyolysis. Diagnosis requires assay of CPT activity in muscle. Although there is no specific treatment, increasing the intake of carbohydrates and the frequency of meals prevents episodes of rhabdomyolysis. The disorder is autosomal recessive, and mutations in the CPT II gene on chromosome 1p32 have been identified.

CARNITINE DEFICIENCY

Primary carnitine deficiencies may present as a generalized systemic illness or as a disorder confined to muscle. In the systemic form, the impaired transport of carnitine into multiple tissues results from nonfunctional high-affinity carnitine receptors. Patients have a myopathy with cardiac involvement, as well as episodes of hepatic dysfunction with hypoketotic hypoglycemia and altered mental status. Abnormal lipid storage is seen on the muscle biopsy. Carnitine level is reduced in serum, muscle, and other tissues. There is no urinary excretion of organic acids to suggest a secondary metabolic illness. Patients with this condition improve with carnitine supplementation.

When the disease is limited to muscle, patients usually present in childhood with limb-girdle myopathy. Patients have diminished muscle uptake of carnitine and a fixed lipid-storage myopathy but normal serum carnitine level. Carnitine replacement has been of inconsistent benefit.

SECONDARY CARNITINE DEFICIENCY

Most carnitine deficiencies are secondary to enzyme defects in β-oxidation (e.g., acyl-CoA dehydrogenase deficiencies), mitochondrial dysfunction, renal disease, impaired metabolism of medication such as valproic acid, or other metabolic disorders. Defects in lipid metabolism lead to accumulation of acyl-CoA molecules, which are converted to acylcarnitines, which are more readily excreted in the urine. This process leads to a negative carnitine balance and, ultimately, to carnitine deficiency. Impaired metabolism of valproic acid may similarly lead to excretion of valproylcarnitine and secondary carnitine deficiency. Most of these illnesses present in early childhood or infancy with Reye's syndrome–like episodes. Some surviving adults experience a lipid storage myopathy with the clinical phenotype of a limb-girdle syndrome. Muscle biopsy reveals lipid storage. The free carnitine level is diminished, but that of esterified carnitine may be increased, especially after oral supplementation of depleted carnitine stores. Abnormal urinary excretion of organic acids is a critical clue to differentiate these disorders from primary carnitine deficiency. Different metabolic blocks in fatty acid metabolism lead to the excretion of distinct urinary acylcarnitine species, which can be distinguished by mass spectroscopy. Carnitine supplementation produces variable results, but some patients have fewer or less severe attacks. Some cases of multiple flavin-dependent dehydrogenase deficiency respond to riboflavin.

DISORDERS OF PURINE NUCLEOTIDE METABOLISM: MYOADENYLATE DEAMINASE DEFICIENCY

Myoadenylate deaminase (MAD), which is an enzyme in the purine nucleotide cycle, provides a short-term supply of adenosine triphosphate (ATP) in muscle by catalyzing the conversion of adenosine monophosphate (AMP) to inosine monophosphate (IMP) through the removal of ammonia. If MAD is absent, less ATP is formed. MAD deficiency has been found in patients with exertional muscle pain and occasionally myoglobinuria. Forearm exercise results in a normal rise in lactate level but no increase in ammonia level. Muscle biopsy shows absent staining for MAD. The gene for MAD is on chromosome 1p13-21 and is mutated in most patients with MAD deficiency. However, the frequency of this mutation in the "normal" population is high, and patients without symptoms may have biochemical evidence of MAD deficiency. Therefore, it is still unclear whether MAD deficiency results in a metabolic myopathy or whether the enzyme deficiency is coincidental.

MITOCHONDRIAL MYOPATHIES

Mitochondrial myopathies produce slowly progressive weakness of limb-girdle or external ocular and other cranial muscles and abnormal fatigability on sustained exertion; some affect multiple organs or systems, in addition to muscle. In many mitochondrial myopathies, a substantial proportion of the muscle fibers contains subsarcolemmal and intermyofibrillar accumulations of structurally and functionally abnormal mitochondria. These fibers appear "*ragged-red*" in the trichrome stain and may fail to react for cytochrome-c oxidase (CCO). Other laboratory features frequently seen in mitochondrial myopathies are an elevated serum lactic acid level on exertion or at rest, as well as a modestly elevated CK level and a myopathic EMG. The cerebrospinal fluid (CSF) protein is often elevated.

Mitochondrial DNA encodes for 22 transfer RNAs (tRNAs), 2 ribosomal RNAs (rRNAs), and 13 messenger RNAs (mRNAs). The 13 mRNAs are translated into polypeptide subunits of the respiratory chain complex. A mutation in a mitochondrial tRNA gene can impair the proper translation of the 13 mitochondrial mRNAs. However, the 13 proteins encoded by the mitochondrial genome account for less than 5% of mitochondrial proteins; the majority are encoded by nuclear DNA and are translated in the cytoplasm and transported into mitochondria.

Mitochondrial diseases can arise from mutations in nuclear or mitochondrial DNA. During fertilization, essentially all of the mitochondria are contributed by the mother's ovum; thus, all mutations of mitochondrial DNA either are maternally transmitted or arise de novo in the maternal ovum or in early embryonic life. However, because the majority of mitochondrial proteins (95%) are encoded from nuclear genes, mitochondrial disorders can also have autosomal/dominant and even X-linked hereditary patterns.

From a biochemical standpoint, mitochondrial disorders can be due to defects proximal to the respiratory chain (involving substrate transport and utilization) or within the respiratory chain. Viewed in this way, the derangements of lipid metabolism can be considered "mitochondrial" dysfunctions. Acetyl-CoA feeds into the mitochondria to enter the Krebs cycle and the respiratory chain. However, the lipid disorders generally do not have structural defects of mitochondria or a "mitochondrial myopathy" phenotype. Among the exceptions are substrate utilization abnormalities due to pyruvate dehydrogenase complex defects, which can produce X-linked Leigh's syndrome or subacute necrotizing encephalomyopathy. Although the muscle biopsy may show ragged red fibers, the CNS abnormalities overshadow the neuromuscular abnormalities.

Most mitochondrial disorders are due to biochemical defects in the mitochondrial respiratory chain that can involve coenzyme Q and the five distinct enzyme complexes: complex I (reduced nicotinamide-adenine dinucleotide-[NADH]-coenzyme Q oxidoreductase); complex II (succinate-dehydrogenase); complex III (coenzyme Q-cytochrome-C oxidoreductase); complex IV (cytochrome-C oxidase); and complex V (adenosine triphosphatase [ATPase] synthetase). Defects in the electron transport complexes are associated with marked clinical, biochemical, and genetic heterogeneity because each complex is composed of multiple subunits, different subunits of a given complex are encoded by different genes, some subunits of a given complex are encoded by mitochondrial rather than nuclear DNA, and some subunits are tissue specific.

SPECIFIC MITOCHONDRIAL DISORDERS AFFECTING MUSCLE. PROGRESSIVE EXTERNAL OPHTHALMOPLEGIA

Severe ptosis and progressive external ophthalmoplegia (PEO) are clinical hallmarks of mitochondrial disease. Ptosis is often the presenting symptom and is generally first noted in childhood. As the ophthalmoplegia progresses, it often becomes complete. Patients do not have diplopia. A limb-girdle weakness pattern may occur with varying degrees of severity. The muscle biopsy reveals characteristic ragged-red fibers, and electron microscopy shows structurally abnormal mitochondria with "parking-lot" paracrystalline inclusions.

PEO due to mitochondrial disease is associated with single or multiple mitochondrial DNA deletions. Patients with single mitochondrial deletions have the *Kearns-Sayre syndrome,* which includes retinitis pigmentosa, heart block, hearing loss, short stature, ataxia, delayed secondary sexual characteristics, peripheral neuropathy, and impaired ventilatory drive. The syndrome presents before age 20. The Kearns-Sayre syndrome, which is due to single large mitochondrial deletions, occurs as a sporadic mutation only.

By comparison, PEO with multiple mitochondrial deletions is autosomal dominant; some kinships have been localized to both chromosomes 10q22-23 and 3ql4-21, and maternally inherited point mutations in mitochondrial tRNA have been reported. This disease, which has later onset of symptoms than the Kearns-Sayre syndrome, is often accompanied by various degrees of encephalomyopathy and neuropathy.

MYOCLONIC EPILEPSY AND RAGGED RED FIBERS (MERRF)

Patients affected by myoclonic epilepsy and ragged-red fibers have varying symptoms of myoclonus, generalized seizures, ataxia, dementia, sensorineural hearing loss, optic atrophy, as well as limb-girdle weakness. Some patients also have a sensorimotor peripheral neuropathy, cardiomyopathy, and cutaneous lipomas. Ptosis and ophthalmoparesis are usually not present. Most patients have a point mutation in the mitochondrial DNA encoding for tRNA, and the disease is maternally inherited.

MITOCHONDRIAL ENCEPHALOMYOPATHY WITH LACTIC ACIDOSIS AND STROKELIKE EPISODES (MELAS)

MELAS patients have normal early development, experience migraine-like headaches and strokes before age 40, and have lactic acidosis. Other features frequently include dementia, hearing loss, and episodic vomiting, ataxia, and coma, as well as diabetes. Ptosis and ophthalmoparesis are uncommon. MELAS is inherited maternally and is caused by mitochondrial DNA mutation encoding for tRNA.

MITOCHONDRIAL NEUROGASTROINTESTINAL ENCEPHALOMYOPATHY (MNGIE)

MNGIE is associated with sensorimotor polyneuropathy, ophthalmoplegia, leukoencephalopathy indicated on magnetic resonance imaging of the brain, and chronic intestinal pseudo-obstruction (POLIP syndrome). Patients have distal as well as proximal weakness and ptosis. There are multiple mitochondrial DNA deletions similar to those found in autosomal dominant PEO. MNGIE has been localized to chromosome 22q13 in some families.

MITOCHONDRIAL DNA DEPLETION SYNDROME

Mitochondrial DNA depletion is an autosomal recessive syndrome that presents at birth or shortly afterward and is characterized by generalized hypotonia and weakness. Other features can include cardiomyopathy, renal tubular defects, seizures, and liver failure. Infants experience respiratory failure and many die within the first year of life. There is also a benign infantile form in which the hypotonic infants can survive and appear normal by age 2 or 3 years.

LEIGH'S SYNDROME

Patients usually present in infancy or early childhood with altered mental status, generalized weakness or hypotonia, vomiting, ataxia, ptosis and ophthalmoplegia, seizures, and respiratory failure. The disease is generally fatal. The molecular genetic characteristics are heterogeneous.

MITOCHONDRIAL MYOPATHIES ASSOCIATED WITH RECURRENT MYOGLOBINURIA

Recurrent myoglobinuria provoked by exercise is uncommon in mitochondrial disorders. Between attacks, the patient is normal. This genetically heterogenous group of disorders includes multiple mitochondrial DNA deletions (autosomal recessive inheritance), mitochondrial point mutations (maternal inheritance), and nuclear DNA mutations encoding for succinate dehydrogenase (complex II).

CHANNELOPATHIES (NONDYSTROPHIC MYOTONIAS AND PERIODIC PARALYSES)

The myotonias are categorized into dystrophic and nondystrophic disorders. The nondystrophic myotonias and the periodic paralyses are caused by mutations of various ion channels in muscle (Table 463–4). The term *channelopathies* is often used to describe this group of disorders.

CHLORIDE CHANNELOPATHIES

Myotonia congenita is due to point mutations in the muscle chloride channel gene on chromosome 7q35. Both the autosomal dominant form (Thomsen's disease) and the autosomal recessive form (Becker's myotonia) are benign and are associated with muscle hypertrophy and action, percussion, and electrical myotonia. Cold increases the myotonia, and sustained exercise improves it (warm-up phenomenon). There is no involvement of the heart or other organs. Patients with Thomsen's disease are not weak, but those who have Becker's myotonia congenita have fluctuations in strength and may experience limb-girdle weakness. Patients with myotonia congenita seldom complain of pain, a feature that distinguishes them from those who have proximal myotonic myopathy (PROMM). The membrane defect consists of a markedly reduced chloride conductance with resulting hyperexcitability and afterdepolarization that produces involuntary myotonic potentials. Many patients do not require treatment, but drugs such as quinine, procainamide, phenytoin, and mexiletine may be effective in reducing symptomatic myotonia.

Table463–4 • CHANNELOPATHIES AND RELATED DISORDERS

DISORDER	PATTERN OF CLINICAL FEATURES	INHERITANCE	CHROMOSOME	GENE
Chloride channelopathies				
Myotonia congenita				
Thomsen's disease	Myotonia	Autosomal dominant	7q35	CLC1
Becker's disease	Myotonia and weakness	Autosomal recessive	7q35	CLC1
Sodium channelopathies				
Paramyotonia congenita	Paramyotonia	Autosomal dominant	17q13.1-13.3	SCNA4A
Hyperkalemic periodic paralysis	Periodic paralysis with myotonia and paramyotonia	Autosomal dominant	17q13.1-13.3	CNA4A
Hypokalemic periodic paralysis	Periodic paralysis	Autosomal dominant	17q13.1-13.3	SCNA4A
Potassium-aggravated myotonias				
Myotonia fluctuans	Myotonia	Autosomal dominant	17q13.1-13.3	SCNA4A
Myotonia permanens	Myotonia	Autosomal dominant	17q13.1-13.3	SCNA4A
Acetazolamide-responsive myotonia	Myotonia	Autosomal dominant	17q13.1-13.3	SCNA4A
Calcium channelopathies				
Hypokalemic periodic paralysis	Periodic paralysis	Autosomal dominant	1q31-32	Dihydropyridine receptor
Schwartz-Jampel syndrome (chondrodystrophic myotonia)	Myotonia; dysmorphic	Autosomal recessive	1q34.1-36.1	Perlecan
Rippling muscle disease	Muscle mounding/stiffness	Autosomal dominant	1q41	Caveolin-3
Anderson's syndrome	Periodic paralysis, cardiac arrhythmia, distinctive facies	Autosomal dominant	17q23	KCNJ2-Kir 2.1
Brody's disease	Delayed relaxation, no EMG myotonia	Autosomal recessive	16p12	Calcium ATPase
Malignant hyperthermia	Anesthetic-induced delayed relaxation	Autosomal dominant	19q13.1	Ryanodine receptor

ATPase = adenosine triphosphatase; EMG = electromyogram.

SODIUM CHANNELOPATHIES

Several autosomal dominant disorders are due to point mutations in the voltage-dependent sodium channel (SCN4A) gene on chromosome 17q23-25. All have symptoms that begin in the first decade and that continue throughout life, and there is considerable clinical overlap between the disorders. Patients with *Paramyotonia congenita* (Eulenburg's disease) have paradoxical myotonia, in that myotonia increases with repetitive movements; for example, after several attempts, the patient cannot open the eyelids. Muscle stiffness is worsened by cold temperature. The myotonia can be treated with sodium-channel blockers such as mexiletine.

Hyperkalemic periodic paralysis is characterized by attacks of weakness lasting 1 or 2 hours. Attacks are precipitated by fasting, by rest after exercise, or by ingestion of potassium-rich foods or compounds. During attacks, patients are areflexic with normal sensation, and there is no ocular or respiratory muscle weakness. The serum potassium level may or may not be increased during the attack, and therefore a more appropriate term may be *potassium-sensitive periodic paralysis*. Strength is generally normal between attacks, but some patients can have mild interictal limb-girdle weakness. Some families with potassium-sensitive periodic paralysis also have either myotonia or paramyotonia. Episodes of weakness are rarely serious enough to require acute therapy; oral carbohydrates or glucose may improve weakness. Treatment options to prevent attacks include dichlorphenamide[3] thiazide diuretics, β-agonists, and preventive measures such as a low-potassium, high-carbohydrate diet and avoidance of fasting, strenuous activity, and cold.

Sodium-channel myotonias are a group of potassium-sensitive disorders due to molecular defects in the sodium channel but not characterized by periodic paralysis or paramyotonia phenotypes. These disorders include *acetazolamide-responsive myotonia, myotonia fluctuans* (myotonia that fluctuates on a daily basis), and *myotonia permanens*.

CALCIUM CHANNELOPATHIES

Hypokalemic periodic paralysis is due to abnormal muscle membrane excitability arising either from mutations in the muscle calcium channel α_1 subunit on chromosome 1q31-32 or, in a small proportion of cases, from a mutation in the skeletal muscle sodium channel. The α_1 subunit of the calcium channel contains the *dihydropyridine receptor*, which acts as a pore for conducting calcium ions in the T tubule. The mutation produces a reduction of the calcium current in the T tubule. During attacks, there is an influx of potassium into muscle cells and the muscles become electrically inexcitable. Patients have an increased sensitivity to the effects of insulin on potassium flux. However, the mechanism through which the shift in potassium from the extracellular to the intracellular space is associated with the functional impairment of the calcium-channel dihydropyridine receptor is unknown.

Hypokalemic periodic paralysis is an autosomal dominant condition. It is the most frequent form of periodic paralysis, is more common in males, and has a reduced penetrance in females. Attacks begin by adolescence and are aggravated by exercise, sleep, stress, alcohol, or meals rich in carbohydrates and sodium. The episodes last from 3 to 24 hours. A vague prodrome of stiffness or heaviness in the legs can occur, and if the patient performs mild exercise a full-blown attack may be aborted. Rarely, ocular, bulbar, and respiratory muscles can be involved in severe attacks. Early in the disease, patients have normal interictal examination findings except eyelid myotonia (about 50%). Later, the frequency of attack can diminish, but many patients have proximal weakness; in occasional patients, this weakness produces severe incapacity.

Preventive measures include a low-carbohydrate, low-sodium diet and drugs such as acetazolamide, dichlorphenamide,[3] spironolactone, and triamterene. Acute attacks are treated with oral potassium every 30 minutes until strength improves; the ECG must be monitored. In severe episodes, particularly in patients with gastrointestinal symptoms, parenteral therapy with potassium may be necessary.

OTHER FORMS OF PERIODIC PARALYSIS, CHANNELOPATHIES, AND MUSCLE STIFFNESS

Andersen's syndrome is an autosomal dominant disorder with periodic paralysis (hypo-, hyper-, or normo-), distinctive facial features (hypertelorism, short stature, low-set ears), prolonged QT interval, and life-threatening ventricular arrhythmias. The genetic defect has been localized to chromosome 17q23 and is caused by a defect in the inward rectifying potassium channel gene KCNJ2 encoding Kir2.1.

Rippling muscle disease is an autosomal dominant disorder characterized by localized transient swelling or rippling of muscle induced by percussion or exercise. Patients complain of tightness in the thighs or upper arms. A pedigree has been localized to chromosome 1q41.

Brody's disease is characterized by exercise-induced impaired relaxation and stiffness, but with no abnormalities indicated by muscle percussion or on EMG. The disorder is autosomal recessive and caused by mutations in the sarcoplasmic reticulum calcium adenosine triphosphatase gene of type 2 muscle fibers located on chromosome 16p12.

Schwartz-Jampel syndrome is an autosomal recessive disorder of early childhood adenosine triphosphatase characterized by chondrodystrophy, short stature, bone and joint deformities, hypertrichosis, blepharophimosis, and muscle stiffness. There is delayed muscle relaxation clinically resembling myotonia, but the EMG shows nonvariable (nonmyotonic) continuous high-frequency electrical activity.

Malignant hyperthermia is characterized by severe muscle rigidity, fever, and tachycardia precipitated by depolarizing muscle relaxants and inhalational anesthetic agents such as halothane. The symptoms usually occur during surgery but can first be noticed in the postoperative period. Patients may have had previous anesthesia without symptoms. During attacks, the CK level is markedly elevated and myoglobinuria develops. The disorder is caused by excessive calcium release by the sarcoplasmic reticulum calcium channel, the ryanodine receptor. Some patients have mutations in the ryanodine receptor gene on chromosome 19q13, which is the same gene mutated in central core disease. However, malignant hyperthermia appears to be genetically heterogeneous, and other families have been localized to different chromosomes. The symptoms are treated with dantrolene, and at-risk patients should not be given known provocative anesthetic agents. The occurrence of malignant hyperthermia in one member of a family should prompt consideration as to whether other family members could also be at risk.

Neuromyotonia, or *Isaacs' syndrome,* is an autoimmune disorder with antibodies directed against voltage-gated potassium channels (VGKCs) on peripheral nerves. Therefore, although this is not a primary myopathy, it is an acquired channelopathy that has a major secondary effect on muscle activity. Inactivation of these channels makes the motor nerve hyperexcitable and produces continuous muscle fiber activity that persists even during sleep. Clinically, there is involuntary muscle activity with stiffness, twitches, fasciculations, and continuous small, undulating movements of the overlying skin (myokymia). Patients also may experience excessive sweating, a peripheral neuropathy, and stiffness. The EMG documents the myokymic potentials and very high-frequency bursts (150 to 300 Hz) of spontaneous motor activity, termed *neuromyotonia.* Some cases are associated with neoplasms: thymoma (with or without myasthenia gravis), small cell lung carcinoma, and lymphoma. The CK level can be mildly elevated, cerebrospinal fluid (CSF) shows elevated protein and oligoclonal bands, and VGKC antibodies are present in serum. Treatment consists of immunosuppressive agents, symptomatic therapy with phenytoin or carbamazepine, or removal of the malignancy. An autosomal dominant form of neuromyotonia exists; it is associated with ataxia or a hereditary peripheral neuropathy.

STIFF-PERSON SYNDROME

Stiff-person syndrome, an acquired autoimmune condition, presents as severe muscle stiffness of proximal, and especially paraspinous, muscles. The muscle spasms produce hyperlordosis, and all movements are slow and laborious. There is excess motor unit activity due to autoantibodies to glutamic acid decarboxylase, which is a major enzyme in the synthesis of γ-aminobutyric acid (GABA); the result is disinhibition in the CNS. The CK level is elevated, and the EMG shows resting continuous motor unit activity that the patient cannot voluntarily suppress. Some patients also have antibodies to islet cells and develop diabetes mellitus. Symptomatic treatment consists of diazepam; immunosuppressive treatment and IVIG can markedly improve the condition.

EVALUATION OF PERIODIC PARALYSIS

In any patient initially being evaluated for an attack of periodic paralysis with hypokalemia or hyperkalemia, secondary causes need to be excluded (Table 463–5). In the primary forms of periodic paralysis, the serum potassium level decreases or increases but may be within the normal range during attacks; it is normal between attacks. By contrast, in secondary periodic paralysis caused by potassium wastage or retention, the serum potassium level is always markedly reduced or elevated during and even between attacks (Chapter 112).

Table 463–5 • SECONDARY CAUSES OF PERIODIC PARALYSIS

HYPOKALEMIC
Thyrotoxic
Primary hyperaldosteronism (Conn's syndrome)
Renal tubular acidosis (e.g., Fanconi's syndrome)
Juxtaglomerular apparatus hyperplasia (Barter's syndrome)
Gastrointestinal potassium wastage
Villous adenoma
Laxative abuse
Pancreatic non–insulin-secreting tumors with diarrhea
Nontropical sprue
Barium intoxication
Potassium-depleting diuretics
Amphotericin B
Licorice
Corticosteroids
Toluene toxicity
p-Aminosalicyclic acid
Carbenoxalone

HYPERKALEMIC
Addison's disease
Hypoaldosteronism
Excessive potassium supplementation
Potassium-sparing diuretics
Chronic renal failure

Thyrotoxic periodic paralysis (Chapter 239) resembles hypokalemic periodic paralysis. It is most common in Asian and Latin American young male adults. β-Adrenergic blocking agents reduce the frequency and severity of attacks, but the ultimate treatment is directed against the thyrotoxicosis.

During an attack of periodic paralysis, potassium levels should be measured every 15 to 30 minutes to determine the direction of change when muscle strength is worsening or improving. An ECG is useful to demonstrate the changes of hypokalemia or hyperkalemia. The CK level is usually elevated during an attack, but between attacks the CK level is generally normal. The routine EMG is normal between attack, but the compound motor action potential may decline in amplitude after exercise (exercise test) and may show a reduction of amplitude and corroborate the presence (but not the cause) of periodic paralysis. Muscle biopsy between attacks may demonstrate vacuoles or tubular aggregates within fibers. Provocative testing for hypokalemic periodic paralysis consists of giving oral or intravenous glucose with or without insulin; for hyperkalemic periodic paralysis, it consists of giving repeated doses of oral potassium under close supervision with cardiac monitoring and intravenous access.

INFLAMMATORY AND OTHER MYOPATHIES

INFLAMMATORY MYOPATHIES (CHAPTER 283)

Inflammatory myopathies include a heterogeneous group of acquired, nonhereditary disorders (Table 463–6) that are characterized by muscle weakness and inflammation indicated by muscle biopsy. Most patients have elevated CK levels, myopathic (EMG) findings, and a limb-girdle distribution of weakness. Occasionally, inflammatory myopathies have distal, focal, or other selective involvement of particular muscles. Most inflammatory myopathies are considered idiopathic; although the cause is unknown, an autoimmune origin is suspected. The three major categories of idiopathic inflammatory myopathy are *dermatomyositis, polymyositis,* and *inclusion body myositis.* These inflammatory myopathies are clinically, histologically, and pathogenically distinct (Table 463–7). Polymyositis and dermatomyositis are covered in detail in Chapter 283.

Inclusion body myositis presents as an insidious onset of slowly progressive proximal and distal weakness. The slow evolution of the disease process contributes to the delay in diagnosis, averaging 6 years from the onset of symptoms. Inclusion body myositis typically begins after age 50 and is the most common inflammatory myopathy in the elderly. Men are more commonly affected than women. These patients have a distinctive pattern of muscle involvement with early weakness and atrophy of the quadriceps (knee extensors), volar forearm muscles

Table 463–6 • CLASSIFICATION OF INFLAMMATORY MYOPATHIES

IDIOPATHIC
Polymyositis
Dermatomyositis
Inclusion body myositis
Overlap syndromes with other connective tissue disease (scleroderma, systemic lupus erythematosus, mixed connective tissue disease, Sjögren's syndrome, rheumatoid arthritis, polyarteritis nodosa)
Sarcoidosis and other granulomatous myositis
Behçet's syndrome
Inflammatory myopathies and eosinophilia
   Eosinophilic polymyositis
   Diffuse fasciitis with eosinophilia
Focal myositis
Myositis ossificans

INFECTIONS
Bacterial: *Staphylococcus aureus*, streptococci, *Escherichia coli*, *Yersinia* spp., *Legionella* spp., gas gangrene (*Clostridium welchii*), leprous myositis, Lyme disease (*borrelia burgdorferi*)
Viral: acute myositis following influenza or other viral infections (adenovirus, coxsackievirus, echovirus, parainfluenza virus, Epstein-Barr virus, arbovirus, cytomegalovirus), retrovirus-related myopathies (HIV, HTLV-1), hepatitis B and C
Parasitic: trichinosis (*Trichinella spiralis*), toxoplasmosis (*Toxoplasma gondii*), cysticercosis, sarcosporidiosis, trypanosomiasis (*Taenia solium*)
Fungal: candida, *Cryptococcus*, sporotrichosis, actinomycosis, histoplasmosis

HIV = human immunodeficiency virus; HTLV-1 = human T-lymphocyte virus 1.

(wrist and finger flexors), and tibialis anterior (ankle dorsiflexors) muscles. Involvement of these muscle groups is frequently asymmetrical, in contrast to the symmetrical weakness in dermatomyositis and polymyositis. Patients have difficulty making a fist because of finger flexor weakness. Some degree of shoulder and hip girdle weakness is often present as well. Facial weakness occurs in a third of patients, and dysphagia occurs in nearly one half of patients. Although most patients have no sensory symptoms, evidence for a distal sensory peripheral neuropathy can be detected in nearly 30% of patients through clinical examination and electrophysiologic testing. Quadriceps muscle stretch reflexes are usually decreased when quadriceps atrophy is severe. Myalgias do not occur; but as the quadriceps muscles progressively weaken and genu recurvatum develops, patients frequently complain of knee pain. Patients do not have associated pulmonary, cardiac, or malignant disorders. Patients have no or only slight elevations of the CK level, and the erythrocyte sedimentation rate is usually normal. Muscle biopsy is essential to establish the diagnosis of inclusion body myositis.

Although immunotherapy can improve strength and function in dermatomyositis and polymyositis, inclusion body myositis is usually refractory to immunosuppressive therapy and intravenous gamma globulin is also ineffective. Life expectancy is normal, but patients frequently require a cane or wheelchair for long distances and some patients become severely incapacitated within 10 to 15 years of onset. Many patients with so-called steroid-resistant or refractory polymyositis, in fact, have inclusion body myositis.

OTHER IDIOPATHIC INFLAMMATORY MYOPATHIES

OVERLAP SYNDROMES

The term *overlap syndromes* denotes a group of disorders in which an inflammatory myopathy occurs in association with another well-defined connective tissue disorder, including scleroderma (Chapter 281), systemic lupus erythematosus (Chapter 280), Sjögren's syndrome (Chapter 282), rheumatoid arthritis (Chapter 278), mixed connective tissue disease, and polyarteritis nodosa (Chapter 284). Clinical and histologic features of either dermatomyositis or polymyositis can develop in up to 10% of each of these disorders. The myositis associated with overlap syndromes may be more responsive to immunosuppressive treatment than is polymyositis.

EOSINOPHILIC POLYMYOSITIS

Eosinophilic polymyositis usually occurs as part of the hypereosinophilic syndrome (Chapter 184). Peripheral eosinophilia in the absence of parasitic infection is associated with a multisystemic disorder of muscle, peripheral nerve, lung, heart, skin, and CNS. Response to immunosuppressive therapy is inconsistent, and the prognosis is generally poor.

DIFFUSE FASCIITIS WITH EOSINOPHILIA

In diffuse fasciitis with eosinophilia, also known as Shulman's syndrome, peripheral eosinophilia is associated with painful scleroderma-like skin changes, contractures, myalgia, arthralgias, and fever. However, unlike eosinophilic polymyositis, the heart, lungs, and other organs are not involved. Laboratory features include hypergammaglobulinemia, elevated erythrocyte sedimentation rate, and occasionally elevated CK level. Full-thickness biopsy from the skin to muscle is required to demonstrate the thickened fascia infiltrated by

---

Table 463-7 • IDIOPATHIC INFLAMMATORY MYOPATHIES: CLINICAL AND LABORATORY FEATURES

	SEX	TYPICAL AGE AT ONSET	RASH	PATTERN OF WEAKNESS	CK LEVEL	MUSCLE BIOPSY	RESPONSE TO IS THERAPY	COMMON ASSOCIATED CONDITIONS
Dermatomyositis	F > M	Childhood and adult	Yes	Proximal > distal	Increased (up to 50× normal)	Perimysial and perivascular inflammation; CD4⁺ T cells, B cells; MAC, Ig, C deposition on vessels	Yes	Myocarditis, interstitial lung disease, vasculitis, other connective tissue diseases, malignancy
Polymyositis	F > M	Adult	No	Proximal > distal	Increased (up to 50× normal)	Endomysial inflammation CD8⁺ T cells, macros	Yes	Myocarditis, interstitial lung disease, other connective tissue diseases; ?malignancy
Inclusion body myositis	M > F	Elderly (>50 yr)	No	Proximal = distal; predilection for finger/wrist flexors, knee extensors	Increased (<10× normal)	Endomysial inflammatoin; CD8⁺ T cells, macros; rimmed vacuoles; amyloid deposits; EM: 15–18 nm tubulofilaments	No	Neuropathy

C = complement; CK = creatine kinase; F = female; Ig = immunoglobulim; IS = immunosuppressive; M = male; MAC = membrane attack complex; Macros = macrophages.

eosinophils and lymphocytes. The inflammation can invade the adjacent underlying muscle. The prognosis is good, and patients usually respond rapidly to corticosteroid treatment. Relapses are infrequent.

GRANULOMATOUS MYOPATHY WITH AND WITHOUT SARCOIDOSIS

Patients with sarcoidosis (Chapter 91) can have asymptomatic granulomas in the muscle or an elevated CK level. Occasionally these patients have nodular swellings of subcutaneous tissues and underlying muscle. These lesions have histopathologic features indicative of sarcoid. Patients can also experience focal muscle pain or a generalized limb-girdle weakness pattern reflecting muscle involvement by sarcoid granulomas. Patients with symptomatic weakness are usually treated with corticosteroids but respond poorly.

Giant cell or granulomatous myopathy can occur in the absence of sarcoidosis. Most of these patients also have myasthenia gravis or thymoma (Chapters 266 and 464). Myocarditis can be part of the disease process. These patients generally improve with corticosteroids.

BEHÇET'S SYNDROME

Behçet's syndrome (Chapter 291), a multisystem disorder, usually is manifested by mucocutaneous and ocular manifestations but rarely may be associated with myositis and myocarditis. The myositis can be focal or generalized, and there is a predilection for the calves. The myositis often responds to immunosuppressive therapy.

FOCAL MYOSITIS

Focal myositis is an uncommon disorder that can develop at any age. It presents as a solitary, painful, and rapidly expanding skeletal muscle mass and must be distinguished from sarcoidosis, Behçet's disease, polyarteritis nodosa, or muscle tumors (sarcoma or rhabdomyosarcoma). The leg is the most common site of involvement, but myositis can occur in any region. The serum CK level is usually normal. Biopsy of the lesions shows mononuclear inflammatory cells in the endomysium with muscle fiber necrosis. The myositis usually resolves spontaneously or with treatment. In rare cases, focal myositis is the heralding sign of typical polymyositis.

INFECTIOUS MYOSITIS

VIRAL. An acute viral myositis can occur in the setting of an upper respiratory tract infection caused by an influenza virus (Chapter 363). In addition to typical influenza-associated myalgias, these patients have proximal weakness, an elevated CK level, and myopathic motor units indicated on EMG. The disorder is self-limited, but when it is severe it is often associated with myoglobinuria and occasionally with renal failure. A similar syndrome can complicate infections with coxsackievirus, parainfluenza virus, mumps virus, measles virus, adenovirus, cytomegalovirus, hepatitis B virus, herpes simplex virus, Epstein-Barr virus, respiratory syncytial virus, and echovirus (Chapter 357).

An inflammatory myopathy can occur in the setting of HIV infection in either the early or later stages of AIDS (Chapter 414). The neurologic manifestation of HTLV-1 infection typically consists of spastic paraparesis, but myositis can also develop (Chapter 372).

BACTERIAL. Pyomyositis refers to focal or multifocal abscesses associated with bacterial infection of muscle. Pyomyositis is more common in the tropics, in developing countries, and among intravenous drug users. It usually arises as an extension of an infection in adjacent tissues or from hematogenous spread. The most common organisms involved are *Staphylococcus aureus* (Chapter 311), *Streptococcus* spp. (Chapter 308), *Escherichia coli* (Chapter 329), *Yersinia* spp. (Chapter 331), and *Legionella* spp. (Chapter 307). Treatment consists of antibiotics and, in severe infections, incision and drainage of abscesses.

FUNGAL. Fungal infections of muscle can occur rarely, usually in immunocompromised individuals. Candidiasis (Chapter 385) is the most common fungal myositis. Diffuse muscle pain, weakness, and fever are associated with a papular erythematous rash.

PARASITIC. Trichinosis is the most common parasitic disease that can produce a diffuse inflammatory myositis and can be confused

with idiopathic polymyositis. Ingested larvae from undercooked pork migrate to muscle, and patients develop fever, myalgias, weakness, myocarditis, and CNS manifestations. There is a peripheral eosinophilia, the CK level is elevated, and antibodies against *Trichinella spiralis* can be demonstrated 3 to 4 weeks after infection. Therapy consists of thiabendazole; in severe cases corticosteroids may be indicated. An inflammatory myopathy can also occur in the course of cysticercosis (*Taenia solium*; Chapter 401) and toxoplasmosis (*Toxoplasma gondii*; Chapter 396).

MYOPATHIES DUE TO ENDOCRINE SYSTEMIC DISORDERS, TOXINS, AND MYOGLOBINURIA

Fatigue can be a symptom of any endocrine disorder, but objective muscle weakness due to a myopathy is less common. The serum CK level is often normal except in hypothyroidism (Chapter 239). The EMG is normal or has myopathic motor units but generally without spontaneous electrical activity. The histologic alterations in muscle are often nonspecific. Muscle symptoms improve with successful treatment of the underlying endocrinopathy.

ADRENAL/GLUCOCORTICOID DISORDERS

Excess corticosteroids can result from endogenous Cushing's disease (Chapters 237 and 240) or can be due to exogenous glucocorticoid administration (Chapter 31). Iatrogenic corticosteroid myopathy (or atrophy) is the most common endocrine-related myopathy. However, muscle weakness is rarely the presenting manifestation of Cushing's disease, and other factors contribute to weakness in virtually all instances of corticosteroid myopathy. Women are more susceptible to corticosteroid atrophy than men, and divided daily doses are more toxic than single or alternate daily doses. Muscle biopsy shows type 2 muscle fiber atrophy, and serum CK level and EMG are normal. Therapy consists of reducing the corticosteroid dosage to the lowest possible level. Exercise and adequate nutrition prevent and may improve weakness. Muscle strength returns to normal within 1 to 4 months after therapy is stopped.

Addison's disease (adrenal insufficiency; Chapter 240) is often associated with fatigue, but objective signs of myopathy are rare. Electrolyte disturbances can produce weakness and, when hyperkalemia occurs, simulate a periodic paralysis (see earlier).

THYROID DISORDERS

Patients with *hyperthyroidism* (Chapter 239) often have some degree of weakness, but this is rarely the presenting manifestation of thyrotoxicosis. Weakness is predominantly proximal, especially in the shoulder region, and there may be atrophy. Weakness of extraocular muscles and proptosis occur in *Graves' disease*. Thyrotoxic periodic paralysis was described earlier. *Hypothyroid myopathy* (Chapter 239) is associated with proximal weakness and myalgias, muscle enlargement, slow relaxation of the reflexes, and marked (up to 100-fold) increase of the serum CK level.

PARATHYROID DISORDERS

Hyperparathyroidism (with hypercalcemia and hypophosphatemia; Chapter 260) can be associated with proximal weakness, atrophy, and pain, especially in the setting of osteomalacia. Patients may also experience hoarseness, dysphagia, and neck extensor weakness. *Hypoparathyroidism* (with hypocalcemia and hyperphosphatemia) is usually not associated with a myopathy; however, paresthesias and tetany with Chvostek's sign and Trousseau's phenomenon can occur in hypocalcemic patients.

PITUITARY DISORDERS

Acromegaly (Chapter 237) can be associated with mild proximal weakness, but usually not until late in the disease. Muscles can look enlarged despite being weak. Weakness as a result of nerve, root, or spinal cord compression is a more likely cause of weakness. Panhypopituitarism results in weakness and fatigability, probably reflecting the combined influence of thyroid and adrenal deficiencies.

DIABETES MELLITUS

Progressive, painless proximal weakness in a diabetic patient is seldom if ever the result of diabetes-related myopathy (Chapter 242). Asymmetrical, usually painful proximal leg weakness can occur from an ischemic radiculoplexopathy ("amyotrophy"). Rarely, acute muscle infarction can develop in quadriceps or hamstring muscles.

VITAMIN DEFICIENCY (Chapters 231 and 458)

Vitamin E deficiency as a result of malabsorption can produce a myopathy along with gait ataxia and neuropathy. *Vitamin D deficiency* (from decreased intake or impaired absorption or metabolism) may also lead to chronic muscle weakness.

OTHER ELECTROLYTE DISTURBANCES

Hypermagnesemia (Chapter 115) can produce acute generalized weakness probably from neuromuscular junction dysfunction. *Hypomagnesemia* results in muscle and nerve hyperexcitability with Chvostek's sign and Trousseau's phenomenon.

SYSTEMIC AMYLOID MYOPATHY

The most common neurologic complication in various types of amyloidosis (Chapter 290) is a predominantly sensory-autonomic neuropathy. Amyloid deposition in muscle is frequent, but the muscle involvement is usually subclinical. Occasionally, amyloidosis presents or is associated with an overt myopathy characterized by muscle enlargement, macroglossia, stiffness, exertional muscle pain, and proximal or diffuse weakness. Electromyography shows myopathic features in proximal muscles with or without changes of neuropathy distally. The amyloid deposits, identified by their metachromasia and affinity for Congo red stain, appear between and around the mural elements of the small vessels and extend into the interstitial spaces, where they tightly surround individual muscle fibers.

MYOSITIS OSSIFICANS

The *localized form* of myositis ossificans appears as a tender swelling after trauma to a muscle. After a few months, the lesion becomes hard and ossified. Therapy consists of excision. The *generalized form* is an autosomal dominant disease with variable expression that begins in childhood, involves many muscles, and causes progressive rigidity of body parts. The initial lesions appear in fascia and dermis and are associated with inflammation, hemorrhage, and connective tissue proliferation. Cartilage and bone formation occur at a later stage. Other congenital malformations (microdactyly of the great toe, exostoses, absence of upper incisors or of ear lobules, and hypogenitalism) are found in most patients. There is no effective therapy.

TOXIC MYOPATHIES

Many drugs have been associated with muscle damage, but it may occur more often with exposure to specific drugs (Table 463–8). Most drug-induced myopathies can produce proximal weakness, an elevated CK level, myopathic EMG results, and abnormalities on muscle biopsy. Symptoms generally improve after stopping the medication. Several drugs can produce an inflammatory myopathy on muscle biopsy, including penicillamine and cimetidine. Zidovudine (AZT) causes a mitochondrial myopathy. A number of drugs can produce a necrotizing or vacuolar myopathy, including amiodarone, colchicine, chloroquine, and cyclosporine. Emetine (ipecac) produces proximal weakness and a myofibrillar myopathy. Isoretinoic acid, a vitamin A analogue used for acne, infrequently causes myalgias, elevation of the serum CK level, and reversible muscle damage.

Clofibrate, gemfibrozil, the statins, and niacin can all produce a rapidly progressive myopathy with elevated CK levels, weakness, pain, and myoglobinuria . An acute necrotizing myopathy associated with myoglobinuna occurs in chronic alcoholics after a bout of drinking (Chapter 17). Illicit drugs such as heroin, cocaine, amphetamines, and pentazocine can produce rhabdomyolysis (Chapter 109) through direct toxic effects, status epilepticus, or prolonged loss of consciousness, immobility, and secondary pressure.

Table 463–8 • TOXIC MYOPATHIES

INFLAMMATORY	**MALIGNANT HYPERTHERMIA**
Cimetidine	Halothane
D-Penicillamine	Ethylene
Procainamide	Diethyl ether
L-Tryptophan	Methoxyflurane
L-Dopa	Ethyl chloride
	Trichloroethylene
NONINFLAMMATORY NECROTIZING OR VACUOLAR	Gallamine
	Succinylcholine
Cholesterol-lowering agents	
Chloroquine	**MITOCHONDRIAL**
Colchicine	Zidovudine
Emetine	
ε-Aminocaproic acid	**MYOTONIA**
Labetalol	2,4-*d*-Chlorophenoxyacetic acid
Cyclosporine and tacrolimus	Anthracene-9-carboxycyclic acid
Isoretinoic acid (vitamin A analogue)	Cholesterol-lowering drugs
Vincristine	Chloroquine
Alcohol	Cyclosporine
RHABDOMYOLYSIS AND MYOGLOBINURIA	**MYOSIN LOSS**
Cholesterol-lowering drugs	Nondepolarizing neuromuscular blocking agents
Alcohol	Intravenous glucocorticoids
Heroin	
Amphetamine	
Toluene	
Cocaine	
ε-Aminocaproic acid	
Pentazocine	
Phencyclidine	

ACUTE QUADRIPLEGIC MYOPATHY

Also known as critical illness myopathy, acute quadriplegic myopathy develops in a patient in the intensive care setting and is often discovered when a patient is unable to be weaned off a ventilator. The cause of the diffuse weakness is the prolonged daily use of either (often both) high-dose intravenous glucocorticoids (usually methylprednisolone) or nondepolarizing neuromuscular blocking agents (e.g., vecuronium). Patients often have had sepsis and multiorgan failure. The serum CK level is moderately elevated, and the EMG shows myopathic units and fibrillations. On nerve conduction studies, motor amplitudes are small, and occasionally a decremental response can be seen on repetitive stimulation. The diagnosis can be confirmed by the muscle biopsy, which shows the loss of myosin thick filaments on electron microscopy. Treatment is supportive after discontinuing the offending agents. Strength recovers over a period of weeks or months; patients can usually be weaned off the ventilator.

Focal muscle injury can be caused by injection of certain drugs, particularly pentazocine and meperidine. Muscle necrosis is followed by fibrous connective tissue replacement and induration.

1. Mendell JR, Moxley RT, Griggs RC, et al: Randomized double-blind six-month trial of prednisone in Duchenne muscular dystrophy. N Engl J Med 1989;320:1592–1597.
2. Griggs RC, Moxley RT, Mendell JR, et al: Duchenne dystrophy: Randomized controlled trial of prednisone (18 months) and azathioprine (12 months). Neurology 1993;43:520–527.
3. Tawil R, McDermott M, Brown R, et al: Randomized trials of dichlorphenamide in the periodic paralyses. Ann Neurol 2000;47:46–53.

SUGGESTED READINGS
DiMauro S, Lamperti C: Muscle gycogenoses. Muscle Nerve 2001;24:984–999. *Detailed review of the clinical features of the glycogenetic muscle disorders.*
Emery AEH: The muscular dystrophies. Lancet 2002;359:687–695. *Review of all the muscular dystrophies, including current and future therapies.*
Nardin RA, Johns DR: Mitochondrial dysfunction and neuromuscular disease. Muscle Nerve 2001;24:170–191. *The genetics, pathophysiology, and clinical aspects of the mitochondria in both muscle and nerve disease.*
Udd B, Griggs RC: Distal myopathies. Curr Opin Neurol 2001;14:451–566. *A comprehensive review.*
Warren JD, Blumbergs PC, Thompson PD: Rhabdomyolysis: A review. Muscle Nerve 2002;25:332–347. *Detailed review of the various etiologies of rhabdomyolysis.*

464 DISORDERS OF NEUROMUSCULAR TRANSMISSION

Andrew G. Engel

Disorders of neuromuscular transmission can be acquired or inherited and are associated with abnormal weakness and fatigability on exertion. In each disorder, the safety margin of neuromuscular transmission is compromised by one or more specific mechanisms. These mechanisms involve acetylcholine (ACh) synthesis or packaging of ACh quanta (6,000 to 10,000 molecules) into synaptic vesicles, the exocytotic release of ACh quanta from the nerve terminal by nerve impulse, and the efficiency of the released quanta to generate a postsynaptic depolarization. The efficiency of the released quanta depends on the geometry of the synaptic space, the density of postsynaptic ACh receptors (AChRs), and the kinetic properties of the AChR ion channel. The depolarization induced by a single quantum gives rise to a miniature end plate potential (MEPP); that induced by a larger number of quanta released by nerve impulse generates an end plate potential (EPP). The EPP amplitude must exceed a critical threshold to activate the voltage-sensitive sodium channels around the end plate and thereby generate a muscle fiber action potential. Neuromuscular transmission fails when the EPP fails to reach this critical threshold.

Table 464–1 shows a classification of currently recognized defects of neuromuscular transmission. Botulism (Chapter 320) and organophosphate intoxication (Chapter 106) are discussed elsewhere.

MYASTHENIA GRAVIS

Myasthenia gravis is an acquired autoimmune disorder in which pathogenic autoantibodies induce AChR deficiency at the motor end plate. The safety margin of neuromuscular transmission is compromised by the small amplitude of the MEPP and consequently of the EPP. Circulating AChR antibodies are present in 80 to 90% of the cases, and immunoglobulin G (IgG) and complement components are deposited on the postsynaptic membrane. AChR deficiency results from complement-mediated lysis of the junctional folds, accelerated internalization and destruction of AChR crosslinked by antibody (modulation), and, to a lesser extent, antibodies blocking the binding of ACh to AChR. Some patients without AChR antibodies have a significant titer of antibodies against MuSK, a muscle-specific tyrosine kinase that plays a role in the aggregation of AChR at the EP. This finding implies that myasthenia gravis can also arise from an autoimmune response against MuSK.

Clinical Manifestations

The incidence of myasthenia gravis is 6 to 11 per year per million, and its prevalence is 118 to 150 per million. The female to male ratio is 6:4. The disease may present at any age, but the incidence in women peaks in the third decade and in men in the sixth or seventh decade.

Myasthenia gravis can involve either the external ocular muscles selectively or the general voluntary muscle system. The symptoms may fluctuate from hour to hour, from day to day, or over longer periods. Symptoms are provoked or worsened by exertion, exposure to extremes of temperature, viral or other infections, menses, and excitement. Ocular muscle involvement is usually bilateral, asymmetrical, and typically associated with ptosis and diplopia. Weakness of other muscles innervated by cranial nerves results in loss of facial expression, everted lips, a smile that resembles a snarl, jaw drop, nasal regurgitation of liquids, choking on foods and secretions, and a slurred, hypernasal speech with a reduced volume. Abnormal fatigability of the limb muscles causes difficulty in combing the hair, lifting objects repeatedly, climbing stairs, walking, and running. Depending on the severity of the disease, dyspnea appears on moderate or mild exertion or is present even at rest. The abnormal fatigability can be demonstrated by asking the patient to look up without closing the eyes for a minute, to count loudly from 1 to 100, to hold the arms elevated forward to the horizontal position for a minute, or to perform repeated deep knee bends. The tendon reflexes remain normally active even in weak muscles. Atrophy of masseter, temporal, facial, or tongue muscles, and less often of other muscles, occurs in about 15% of patients.

Initially, the symptoms are purely ocular in 40%, are generalized in 40%, and involve only the extremities in 10% and only the bulbar or bulbar and eye muscles in another 10%. Subsequently, the weakness can spread from ocular to facial to lower bulbar muscles and then to torso and limb muscles, but the sequence may vary. Proximal limb muscles are affected more than distal ones. In the most advanced cases the weakness is universal. By the end of the first year, the ocular muscles are affected in nearly all patients. The symptoms remain purely ocular in only 16% of patients. In nearly 90% of those in whom the disease becomes generalized, this progression occurs within the first year after the onset of disease. Progression is most rapid within the first 3 years, and more than half of the deaths caused by myasthenia gravis occur in that period. Spontaneous remissions lasting from weeks to years can occur. Long remissions are uncommon, and most remissions occur during the first 3 years. A clinical classification of myasthenia gravis, based on the distribution and severity of symptoms, is useful: group 1, ocular; group 2A, mild generalized; group 2B, moderately severe generalized; group 3, acute fulminating; group 4, late severe.

Two thirds of patients with myasthenia gravis have thymic hyperplasia and 10 to 15% have thymoma (Chapter 266). In a few with thymoma, myocarditis (Chapter 73) or giant cell myositis (Chapter 463) also develops. In about 10% of patients, myasthenia gravis is associated with another autoimmune disease, such as hyperthyroidism (Chapter 239), polymyositis (Chapter 283), systemic lupus erythematosus (Chapter 280), Sjögren's syndrome (Chapter 282), rheumatoid arthritis (Chapter 278), ulcerative colitis (Chapter 142), pemphigus (Chapter 475), sarcoidosis (Chapter 91), pernicious anemia (Chapter 175), or Lambert-Eaton myasthenic syndrome.

TRANSIENT NEONATAL MYASTHENIA GRAVIS. Circulating AChR antibodies can be detected in most infants born to myasthenic mothers, but only 12% of such children have myasthenia gravis, presenting with feeble cry, feeding and respiratory difficulty, general or facial weakness, and ptosis during the first few hours of life. The mean duration of symptoms is 18 days. There is no relation between the severity of myasthenia gravis in mother and that in infant. The disease is caused by the transfer of AChR antibodies from mother to infant. When the maternal antibodies are directed predominantly against the fetal γ-subunit of AChR, fetal hypomotility in utero can result in congenital arthrogryposis.

Table 464–1 • CLASSIFICATION OF DISORDERS OF NEUROMUSCULAR TRANSMISSION

AUTOIMMUNE
Myasthenia gravis
Lambert-Eaton myasthenic syndrome (LEMS)

CONGENITAL
Presynaptic defects
   Defect in ACh resynthesis or packaging*
   Paucity of synaptic vesicles and reduced quantal release*
Synaptic defect
   Congenital end plate AChE deficiency*,§
Postsynaptic defects: increased response to ACh
   Slow-channel syndromes‡,ǁ
Postsynaptic defects: decreased response to ACh
   Fast-channel syndromes*,ǁ
   AChR deficiency without kinetic abnormality*,¶
   Rapsyn deficiency*
Partially characterized syndromes
   Congenital myasthenic syndrome resembling LEMS†
   Familial limb-girdle myasthenia*

TOXIC
Botulism
Drug-induced
Organophosphate intoxication

---

  *Autosomal recessive inheritance.
  †Autosomal recessive inheritance suspected.
  ‡Dominant inheritance.
  §Mutations in collagenic tail subunit of end plate AChE.
  ǁMutations in AChR subunit genes.
  ¶Mutations in AChR subunit genes or rapsyn.
  ACh = acetylcholine; AChE = acetylcholinesterase; AChR = acetylcholine receptor; CMS = congenital myasthenic syndrome.

Diagnosis

Diagnosis is based on the results of the characteristic history, physical examination, anticholinesterase tests, and laboratory studies. The latter include electromyographic (EMG) studies, serologic tests, and, in selected cases, microelectrode studies in vitro of neuromuscular transmission and ultrastructural and cytochemical studies of the end plate.

ANTICHOLINESTERASE TESTS. Edrophonium given intravenously acts within a few seconds, and its effects last for a few minutes (Fig. 464–1). One to two milligrams of the drug is injected intravenously over 15 seconds. If no response occurs in 30 seconds, an additional 8 to 9 mg is injected. The evaluation of the response requires objective assessment of one or more signs, such as degree of ptosis, range of ocular movements, and force of the hand grip. Possible cholinergic side effects of the drug include fasciculations, flushing, lacrimation, abdominal cramps, nausea, vomiting, and diarrhea. The drug must be given cautiously to patients with cardiac disease, because it may cause sinus bradycardia, atrioventricular block, and, rarely, cardiac arrest. Atropine is used to reverse toxicity. Intramuscular neostigmine, 0.5 to 1.0 mg, acts maximally in about 30 minutes, and its effects last up to 2 hours, allowing a more leisurely evaluation of changes in clinical status.

ELECTROMYOGRAPHY. Supramaximal stimulation of a motor nerve at 2 to 3 Hz results in a 10% or greater decrement of the amplitude of the evoked compound muscle action potential from the first to the fifth response. The test result is positive in nearly all patients, provided that two or more distal and two or more proximal muscles are examined. The decrement is caused by a normally occurring decrease in the number of quanta released from the nerve terminal, and hence in the amplitude of the EPP, at the beginning of low-frequency stimulation. In myasthenia gravis, the EPP amplitude is already reduced by the AChR deficiency, and the additional decrease during stimulation blocks transmission at an increasing number of end plates. Single-fiber EMG compares the timing of action potentials in pairs of closely adjacent muscle fibers in the same motor unit during a willed contraction. In myasthenia gravis the low amplitude and relatively long rise time of the EPP cause abnormally long interpotential intervals and intermittent blocking of action potential generation at some fibers.

SEROLOGIC TESTS. The usual AChR antibody test measures the binding of antibody to AChR labeled with radioactive α-bungarotoxin. The toxin itself is attached irreversibly to the ACh binding site of AChR. The antibody binding test result is positive in nearly all adults with moderately severe or severe myasthenia gravis, in 80% with mild generalized myasthenia gravis, and in 50% with ocular myasthenia gravis, but in only 25% of those in remission. The test is less reliable in juveniles than in adults. In a few patients only antibodies that block the binding of ACh to AChR can be detected. The antibody titer correlates only loosely with the severity of disease, but a greater than 50% decrease in titer for more than 12 months in an individual patient is nearly always associated with sustained clinical improvement. Some patients without AChR antibodies may carry MuSK antibodies, and some may have a congenital myasthenic syndrome. Striated muscle antibodies also occur in patients with myasthenia gravis. The role of these antibodies remains unknown, but their presence is often associated with thymoma.

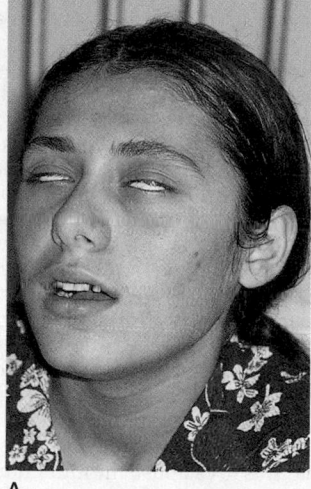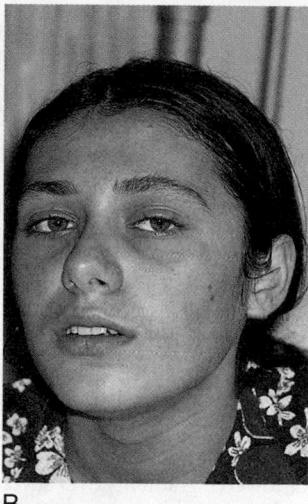

A   B

FIGURE 464–1 • Myasthenia gravis. The edrophonium (Tensilon) test can be used to confirm the diagnosis. *A*, Facial weakness is provoked by repeated facial movements. *B*, Edrophonium chloride, a short-acting anticholinesterase, is then injected intravenously—initially 2 mg as a test dose, followed after 1 minute by a further 8 mg if there are no adverse effects. In myasthenia gravis, the facial weakness is rapidly relieved by this test. Objective testing of muscular power elsewhere in the body will reveal similar responses. (From Forbes CD, Jackson WD: Color Atlas and Text of Clinical Medicine, 3rd ed. London, CV Mosby, 2003, with permission.)

OTHER DIAGNOSTIC STUDIES. Immune deposits can be localized at the myasthenia gravis end plate in cryostat sections even when circulating AChR antibodies cannot be detected. C3 or C5b9 localizations are a technically easy and convenient way to confirm the suspected diagnosis.

Differential Diagnosis

The differential diagnosis includes neurasthenia, the Miller Fisher variant of inflammatory polyneuropathy, oculopharyngeal dystrophy, mitochondrial myopathies involving the external ocular or other cranial and limb muscles (Chapter 463), intracranial mass lesions compressing cranial nerves (Chapter 457), congenital and drug-induced myasthenic syndromes, and other disorders of neuromuscular transmission (see Table 464–1). Neurasthenia is recognized by the finding on motor testing that the patient "gives way" when individual muscle strength is tested; laboratory tests for myasthenia gravis are negative. In myopathies involving the ocular muscles, the weakness does not fluctuate, diplopia is seldom a symptom, the muscle biopsy result may show distinct morphologic abnormalities, and findings of pharmacologic and laboratory tests for myasthenia gravis are negative. Drug-induced and other myasthenic syndromes are considered later.

 Treatment

Anticholinesterases, alternate-day prednisone treatment, azathioprine, cyclosporine, mycophenolate mofetil, thymectomy, intravenous immunoglobulin, and plasmapheresis are currently used to treat myasthenia gravis. Anticholinesterases are useful in all clinical forms of the disease. Pyridostigmine bromide (Mestinon) (60-mg tablets) acts for 3 to 4 hours, and neostigmine bromide (15-mg tablets) acts for 2 to 3 hours. The former drug has fewer muscarinic side effects and is therefore more widely used. One-half to four tablets of pyridostigmine bromide are given every 4 hours in the daytime. This medication is also available in 180 mg "time span" tablets for use at bedtime and as a syrup for children and patients requiring nasogastric feeding. If troublesome muscarinic side effects occur, these can be treated with 0.4 to 0.6 mg atropine given orally two or three times daily. Postoperatively or in critically ill patients, intramuscularly injectable pyridostigmine bromide (the dose is one thirtieth of the oral dose) and neostigmine

methylsulfate (the dose is one fifteenth of the oral dose) can be used.

Progressive weakness despite increasing amounts of anticholinesterases signals the onset of a cholinergic or myasthenic crisis. Cholinergic crises are associated with muscarinic effects, such as abdominal cramps, nausea, vomiting, diarrhea, miosis, lacrimation, increase in bronchial secretions, diaphoresis, and bradycardia. In a myasthenic crisis, the muscarinic effects are not conspicuous, and 2 mg edrophonium given intravenously improves rather than worsens the weakness. In practice, however, the two types of crises often are difficult to distinguish, and overmedication of a myasthenic crisis can convert it into a cholinergic crisis. Therefore, patients who have increasing difficulty with respiration, feeding, or handling of secretions and who are not responding to relatively high doses of anticholinesterases are best treated by drug withdrawal, tracheal intubation or tracheostomy, support with respirator, and intravenous

Continued

feeding. Refractoriness to drug therapy usually disappears after a few days.

In patients whose generalized disease does not respond adequately to modest doses of anticholinesterases, other forms of therapy must be employed. Thymectomy increases the remission rate and improves the clinical course of myasthenia gravis. Although controlled clinical studies of thymectomy according to age, gender, severity, and duration of disease have never been performed, there is general agreement that the best response occurs in young women with hyperplastic thymus glands and high antibody titers. Thymoma is an indication for thymectomy because the tumor is often locally invasive. Magnetic resonance imaging readily detects mediastinal tumors.

Alternate-day prednisone treatment induces remission or significantly improves the disease in more than half the patients. The treatment is relatively safe if the usual precautions for corticosteroid therapy are followed (Chapter 31). With an average dose of 70 mg on alternate days, the average time for significant improvement is 5 months. After the improvement reaches a plateau, the dose must be lowered gradually over several months to establish the minimum maintenance dose.

Azathioprine in doses of 2 to 3 mg/kg/day also induces remissions or provides measurable improvement in more than 50% of treated patients. The earliest time for improvement is 3 months, and responses are often delayed for 12 months or longer. Surveillance to detect side effects (pancytopenia, leukopenia, serious infection, and hepatocellular injury) must be maintained during therapy. Azathioprine as an adjunct to alternate-day prednisone reduces the dose of prednisone and is associated with fewer treatment failures, longer remissions, and fewer side effects than either drug alone, but the full beneficial effects appear only after 1 or 2 years of combined therapy. Cyclosporine or mycophenolate mofetil can be used in patients who are refractory to prednisone and azathioprine.

Plasmapheresis is indicated in severe generalized or fulminating myasthenia gravis that is refractory to other forms of treatment. Daily exchanges of 2 L of plasma result in objective improvement and lower the AChR antibody titer in a few days. However, plasmapheresis is expensive and does not confer greater long-term protection than immunosuppressants alone.

Intravenous immunoglobulin therapy at a dose of 400 mg/kg for 5 consecutive days, or 1 g/kg on 2 consecutive days, may improve severe myasthenia gravis within 2 to 3 weeks of the start of therapy. The mean duration of the response is 9 weeks in patients also treated with corticosteroids and 5 weeks in those who are not.

LAMBERT-EATON MYASTHENIC SYNDROME

Lambert-Eaton myasthenic syndrome is an acquired autoimmune disease in which pathogenic autoantibodies cause a deficiency of voltage-sensitive calcium channels at the motor nerve terminal. The deficiency restricts calcium ingress when the terminal is depolarized by nerve impulses and thereby reduces the probability of quantal release. Among patients older than 40 years of age, 70% of men and 30% of women have an associated carcinoma, usually a small cell carcinoma of the lung (Chapters 188 and 198). The syndrome may predate detection of the tumor by up to 3 years. Non-neoplastic cases have been associated with other autoimmune disorders, human leukocyte antigens (HLA) B8 and DRw3, and organ-specific autoantibodies.

Patients have weakness and fatigability of proximal limb and torso muscles with relative sparing of extraocular and bulbar muscles. The lower limbs are more severely involved than the upper limbs. On maximal voluntary contraction, the force produced by a weak muscle increases for a few seconds and then again decreases. In most patients, the tendon reflexes are hypoactive or absent. Autonomic manifestations (dry mouth, impotence, decreased sweating, orthostatic hypotension, or altered pupillary reflexes) occur in about 50% of patients.

On EMG, the amplitude of the compound muscle action potential evoked by a single nerve stimulus from rested muscle is abnormally small. Repetitive stimulation at 2 Hz induces a further decrement, but stimulation at frequencies higher than 10 Hz or voluntary exercise for a brief period markedly facilitates the response so that the evoked potential attains normal amplitude.

 Treatment

Anticholinesterases are only slightly effective. Guanidine hydrochloride (10 mg/kg/day) or 3,4-diaminopyridine (3,4-DAP) (1 mg/kg/day) increases quantal release from the nerve terminal and relieves the symptoms. However, the former drug has severe toxic side effects and the latter is not yet available in clinical practice. Optimal treatment of non-neoplastic cases consists of modest doses of alternate-day prednisone and 2 to 3 mg/kg/day of azathioprine.

DRUG-INDUCED MYASTHENIC SYNDROMES

The drug-induced myasthenic syndromes are uncommon in clinical practice. Tetracycline, polymyxin, and aminoglycoside antibiotics, antiarrhythmic agents (procainamide, quinidine), β-adrenergic blockers (propranolol, timolol), phenothiazines, lithium, trimethaphan, methoxyflurane, and magnesium given parenterally or in cathartics reduce the safety margin of neuromuscular transmission. However, overt myasthenic symptoms do not usually appear unless an overdose of the drug is administered or the renal or hepatic elimination of the drug is impaired (Chapter 106). The same drugs and inhalation anesthetic agents also can potentiate neuromuscular blocking agents used during surgical procedures, and both may worsen or unmask preexisting disorders of neuromuscular transmission. Calcium-channel blocking drugs can worsen the transmission defect in the Lambert-Eaton myasthenic syndrome.

Succinylcholine, a depolarizing blocking drug, is used to induce muscle relaxation during anesthesia. A single dose of the drug sufficient to cause transient apnea is eliminated by plasma pseudocholinesterase in 2 to 10 minutes. In approximately 1 of 2500 patients receiving the drug, prolonged apnea occurs and persists for up to several hours. Most of these patients have an autosomal recessive abnormality of the plasma pseudocholinesterase. In some genetic variants, the plasma pseudocholinesterase activity is abnormally low; in others, the enzyme shows increased sensitivity to inhibition by dibucaine. Curare and related agents used during surgery and in critically ill patients to induce muscle relaxation produce nondepolarizing blockade of the neuromuscular junction; their use in patients with myasthenia gravis and the congenital myasthenias is associated with profound and prolonged weakness.

CONGENITAL MYASTHENIC SYNDROMES

Congenital myasthenic syndromes are caused by defects in presynaptic, synaptic, and postsynaptic proteins that impair the safety margin of neuromuscular transmission. A generic diagnosis of a congenital myasthenic syndrome can be made on the basis of fatigable weakness of ocular, bulbar, and limb muscles since infancy, family history of similar illness, a decremental EMG response, and negative tests for AChR antibodies. In some cases, however, the onset is delayed, the family history is negative, EMG abnormalities are not present in all muscles or are present intermittently, and the weakness has a restricted distribution. The syndromes may be related to abnormally slow- or fast-operating channels or a deficiency of AChR, synaptic acetylcholinesterase, or presynaptic choline acetyltransferase. The specific diagnosis of some of these syndromes requires in vitro microelectrode and molecular genetic studies. Treatment should be guided by an experienced neurologist.

SLOW-CHANNEL SYNDROMES. Mutations in different domains of AChR subunits markedly prolong the duration of the AChR channel opening events and hence the synaptic currents. This abnormality results in a depolarization block on physiologic activity and in cationic overloading of the postsynaptic region that leads to end plate myopathy with loss of AChR. Treatment consists of quinidine sulfate, 200 mg three to four times daily, or fluoxetine, up to 20 mg four times daily, both long-lived open-channel blockers of AChR.

FAST-CHANNEL SYNDROMES. A recessive mutation in an AChR subunit gene curtails the duration of synaptic currents by diminishing affinity for ACh, gating efficiency, or gating stability. The effects of the mutation are unmasked by a null mutation in the other allele of the gene. End plate morphology is normal. The clinical features resemble those of autoimmune myasthenia gravis. The disease responds well to 3,4-DAP, which increases the number of quanta released by the nerve impulse, combined with pyridostigmine, which increases the number of AChR activated by each quantum.

AChR DEFICIENCY SYNDROMES. These syndromes result from recessive low-expressor or null mutations in AChR subunit genes. Most mutations occur in the ε subunit, which can be partially compensated by persistent expression of the fetal AChR γ subunit. The clinical features resemble those of autoimmune myasthenia gravis. Treatment consists of cholinesterase inhibitors. Some patients derive additional benefit from 3,4-DAP.

RAPSYN DEFICIENCY. Rapsyn is a postsynaptic protein essential for maintaining a high level of AChR in the postsynaptic membrane. Recessive mutations in rapsyn result in AChR deficiency. Some mutations result in arthrogryposis or facial malformations. Weakness is increased by intercurrent infections. Other clinical features resemble those of primary AChR deficiency. Treatment consists of cholinesterase inhibitors and 3,4-DAP.

SYNAPTIC ACETYLCHOLINESTERASE (AChE) DEFICIENCY. This syndrome is caused by recessive mutations in the collagenic tail subunit of the end plate–specific species of AChE that prevent insertion of the tail subunit into the synaptic basal lamina or its association with catalytic subunits. Clinical clues to diagnosis consist of a repetitive compound muscle action potential evoked by single nerve stimuli, a delayed pupillary light reflex, and no response to AChE inhibitors.

 1. Palace J, Newsom-Davis J, Lecky B, Myasthenia Gravis Study Group: A randomized double-blind clinical trial of prednisolone alone or with azathioprine in myasthenia gravis. Neurology 1998;50:1778–1783.

SUGGESTED READINGS
Engel AG, Ohno K, Sine SM: Congenital myasthenic syndromes. Progress over the past decade. Muscle Nerve 2003;27:4–25. *An up-to-date review of congenital myasthenic syndromes based on investigation of 147 kinships.*
Sanders DB, El-Salem K, Massey JM, et al: Clinical aspects of MuSK antibody positive seronegative MG. Neurology 2003;60:1978–1980. *Antibodies to MuSK are implicated in a substantial number of patients with seronegative myasthenia gravis.*
Tim RW, Massey JM, Sanders DB: Lambert-Eaton myasthenic syndrome: Electrodiagnostic findings and response to treatment. Neurology 2000;54:2176–2178. *A thorough overview of the clinical and electromyographic aspects of the Lambert-Eaton syndrome.*

part XXVI

Eye, Ear, Nose, and Throat Diseases

465 DISEASES OF THE VISUAL SYSTEM

Aaron Fay
Frederick A. Jakobiec

GENERAL APPROACH TO VISUAL LOSS

Physiologic visual acuity is remarkably consistent among healthy humans. Therefore, any deviation from the expected norm should be investigated to identify the cause. Alternatively, routine ophthalmic examination in patients with normal visual acuity and without subjective complaints can detect asymptomatic pathology.

Evaluation of Ocular Function

Although human vision is most frequently quantified by line letter *acuity*, vision also comprises color, motion, contrast, brightness, field, and depth perception. These latter qualities are less frequently evaluated during screening because there is greater variation between individuals and because objective, reproducible scales have not been standardized. Visual acuity, however, is limited by retinal anatomy and remains remarkably consistent among individuals. Normal acuity describes accurate resolution of a flat object that subtends an angle of 1 degree on the human retina. The "20/20" line on a visual acuity chart consists of letters that when held 20 feet from the subject subtend an angle of 5 degrees; each individual segment of those letters subtends an angle of 1 degree and must be resolved to identify the letter (Fig. 465–1). Letters half that size, held at half that distance, subtend the same angle (10/10 visual acuity). When a subject demonstrates an inability to resolve printed forms subtending 1 degree of arc, vision is substandard and leads to functional disability (Table 465–1). The cause may lie anywhere along the visual pathway from the tear film to the visual cortex of the occipital lobe (Fig. 465–2).

Whether chief complaint or incidental finding, poor visual acuity should prompt complete ophthalmic evaluation. Examination of *pupillary response* provides the most objective measure of ocular function. The swinging light test for *relative afferent pupillary defect* (RAPD, Marcus Gunn pupil) is performed by alternately illuminating the pupils while examining the direct (ipsilateral) and consensual

Table 465–1 • VISUAL ACUITIES REQUIRED FOR COMMON DAILY TASKS

20/20	Physiologic vision
20/30–20/100	Driver's license, varies by state
20/50	Newspaper print
20/70	Large print *Reader's Digest*
20/100	Write a check
20/200	Legally blind
20/400	Paper currency

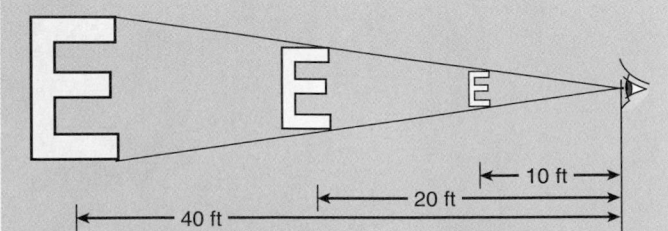

FIGURE 465–1 • Snellen Visual Acuity. The most common test for visual acuity describes the eye's ability to resolve linear images at a test distance of 20 feet, approximating infinity (parallel rays of light). A 20/20 E subtends 5 minutes of arc at a distance of 20 feet, with each segment of the E subtending 1 minute of arc. The larger letters (20/30, 20/40, etc.) are determined by the distance at which they subtend an angle of 5 minutes. Thus, an E that subtends 5 minutes at 40 feet, if viewed clearly at 20 feet, indicates 20/40 visual acuity.

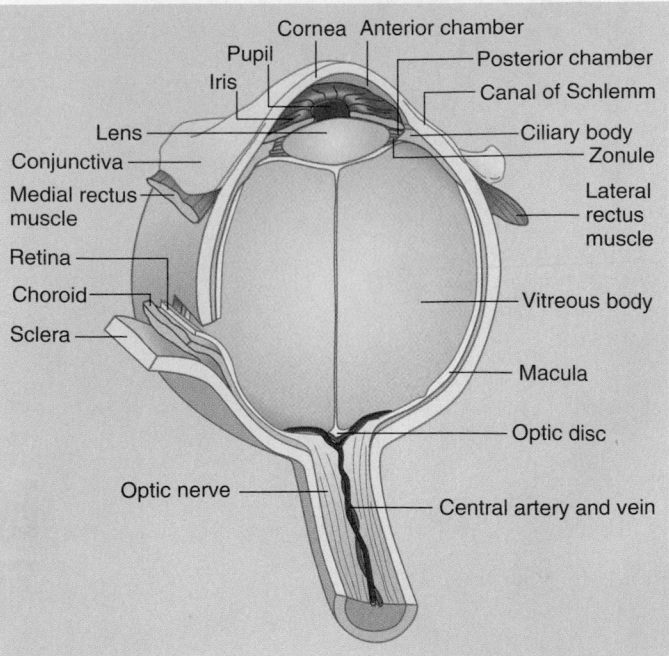

FIGURE 465–2 • Anatomy of the eye.

Table 465–2 • DIFFERENTIAL DIAGNOSIS OF SUDDEN VISUAL LOSS

UNILATERAL	BILATERAL
Amaurosis fugax (carotid artery stenosis)	Eclampsia
Central retinal artery occlusion	Vertebrobasilar infarct
Occipital lobe infarct	Trauma
Temporal arteritis	
Nonarteritic anterior ischemic optic neuropathy	
Hemorrhage	
Preretinal (high altitude, Valsalva)	
Vitreous	
Aqueous (hyphema)	
Trauma	

(contralateral) response. An optic nerve or, rarely, a central nervous system lesion interfering with afferent conduction will produce a paradoxical dilation of the involved side on direct illumination. Pathologic processes of the anterior segment, including dense cataract, and of the posterior segment do not produce RAPD. Severe amblyopia may occasionally produce RAPD. *Confrontational visual fields* are performed independently in each eye to detect gross quadrantic defects. *Color vision* testing plates are used as a sensitive indicator of optic nerve function. Extraocular motility is assessed for nerve or muscle abnormalities.

Intraocular tension may be determined most accurately by applanation tonometry in which an applanation prism is used to depress the cornea. Increased intraocular tension may indicate glaucoma, whereas decreased intraocular tension may indicate retinal detachment or a ruptured globe. *Ocular alignment* is determined by corneal light reflex and cover tests using prisms. *Binocular function* may be assessed using polarized glasses and targets at distance and near.

Sudden visual loss is commonly due to circulatory conditions or trauma (Table 465–2). Prompt evaluation is critical, although the condition may be irreversible.

Topographic Evaluation

Topographic evaluation of the eye begins with external examination of the eye and lids and ocular adnexa. Exophthalmos or enophthalmos is recorded with an exophthalmometer. Eyelid position and lesions are noted. The orbital rim and regional lymph nodes are palpated. The globe is ballotted for resistance to retropulsion.

Slit lamp biomicroscopy proceeds in orderly fashion to evaluate lid contour, lesions, and lashes. The conjunctiva, sclera, and cornea are examined for injection, discharge, and inflammation. The anterior chamber is examined for proteinaceous exudate (flare) and inflammatory or red blood cells. The lens and anterior vitreous are examined.

Gonioscopy may be performed using various mirrored lenses to view the angle structures and evaluate angle closure and neovascularization. Dilated fundus examination with an indirect ophthalmoscope provides a panoramic view of the fundus. Specific attention is paid to the optic nerve head, retinal vessels, and macular region. The peripheral retina is best seen with scleral depression.

Ancillary Studies

Numerous electrophysiologic and radiographic tests may be used to complement the ophthalmic physical examination. Automated perimetry utilizing static stimuli of variable intensity has replaced manual visual field testing in most offices. Computerized statistical analysis allows for more accurate comparison between serial examinations. Automated perimetry has been the gold standard for long-term follow-up of glaucoma over the past decade. More recently, nerve fiber layer laser scanners have been used to detect early defects in the nerve (ganglion cell) fiber layer of the retina that precede measurable visual field loss. Corneal topography, pachymetry, and specular microscopy can be used to detect subclinical abnormalities and are required for refractive surgical evaluation. Electroretinography may help distinguish specific retinal diseases, and measurement of visual evoked potentials is used to assess visual cortex function.

Among the more common imaging studies is fluorescein angiography of the retina and choroid. Fluorescein solution is injected intravenously into the antecubital fossa while timed photographs are taken through light filters. A-scan ultrasound is used to determine the axial length of an eye, most commonly to determine the appropriate power of implanted intraocular lenses in patients undergoing cataract extraction. B-scan ultrasound provides excellent intraocular imagery when the fundus cannot be viewed directly. Ultrasound biomicroscopy can provide detailed images of the anterior segment. Computed tomography is preferred to evaluate orbital structures, whereas magnetic resonance imaging produces greater detail for optic nerve and central nervous system lesions.

Refractive Error

The most frequent cause for diminished visual acuity is refractive error: light rays entering the eye are not properly brought into focus on the retina. In the absence of ophthalmic pathology, best-corrected visual acuity should equal emmetropic vision.

Patients with refractive errors are said to be ametropic, whereas those eyes with properly suited refracting apparati are emmetropic. *Myopia* is a common condition in which the refracting power of the eye at rest is too great in relation to the axial length of the eye; the focused image of an object held at infinity (approximated at a distance of 20 feet) lies anterior to the retina (Fig. 465–3). *Physiologic*

myopia, which is more common than pathologic myopia, results from a mismatch between the refracting power of the optical elements of the eye and the axial length of the globe when neither of these components lies outside the normal range. The refracting power of a normal human eye is approximately 65 diopters (D), with the cornea and tear film contributing 45 D and the crystalline lens contributing 20 D. The average axial length of the human eye is approximately 24 mm. Physiologic myopia usually ranges from about 0.5 to about 8.0 D, where the eye appears normal on physical and radiographic evaluation. Onset begins in the second decade and may progress through the third decade. Physiologic myopia is not thought to be heritable, but there appears to be an increased frequency of the disorder among higher socioeconomic groups and among those with greater academic training. Although the cause is not clear, several laboratory and epidemiologic studies indicate that prolonged accommodation as experienced through extensive reading may contribute to progression of physiologic myopia; well-lighted reading conditions may mitigate this effect.

Physiologic myopia is usually treated with spectacle or soft contact lens correction. Radial keratotomy (RK) decreases the refracting power of the central cornea by using radial incisions in the peripheral cornea to weaken it, allowing the peripheral cornea to bow slightly and the central cornea to flatten. Because of increased risk of rupture, difficult prediction of refractive result, and lessening of surgical effect with time, this procedure has fallen out of favor with most ophthalmologists. Photorefractive keratectomy (PRK) uses laser energy to ablate the anterior surface of the central cornea, directly creating a new refractive surface. Laser in-situ keratomileusis (LASIK) involves surgical removal of an anterior corneal flap, stromal ablation, and replacement of the flap. Laser vision correction (PRK and LASIK) is now widely accepted as the standard for surgical correction of myopia and other refractive errors, with 95% of patients achieving visual acuity of 20/40 or better. The most common complications include glare symptoms, dry eye, and undercorrection or overcorrection. Rare but serious complications include epithelial ingrowth, diffuse keratitis, or flap dislocation. Other refractive surgical techniques include intracorneal lenses, phakic intraocular lenses, clear lens extraction with intraocular lens implantation, and intracorneal rings to alter the central corneal curvature reversibly. These procedures are not widely performed because of the success of laser vision correction. Clear lens extraction and phakic intraocular lenses are controversial because they require intraocular surgery in an otherwise healthy eye. Intraocular surgery always carries a risk of surgical complication, and even seemingly uneventful cases may be subject to vision-threatening endophthalmitis. Because physiologic myopia tends to progress into the third decade of life, a minimum of 12 months of stable refractive error should be demonstrated before a refractive procedure is performed.

Pathologic myopia is a heritable condition in which the eye is abnormally long; the refracting apparatus is usually normal. Refractive error in pathologic myopia is usually greater than about 8.0 D. *Peripapillary atrophy* is common: The internal scleral surface of the elongated globe is incompletely covered by retina and retinal pigmented epithelium, and a white or yellow crescent or ring of bare sclera may be seen around the optic nerve. The optic discs may be tilted, making estimation of optic nerve cupping difficult. An outpouching of the posterior globe (posterior staphyloma) with broad areas of retinal pigmented epithelium alteration may be seen. Patients with pathologic myopia are predisposed to retinal tears and holes, retinal detachment, subretinal bleeding, and choroidal neovascularization. Pathologic myopia may be associated with systemic disorders, including trisomy 21, Cornelia de Lange syndrome, Stickler's syndrome, and Marfan syndrome. Dilated fundus examination should be performed at frequent intervals, and patients should be alerted to symptoms of retinal detachment (flashing lights, floaters). Pathologic myopia may be managed with spectacles or contact lenses. Refractive procedures are less successful in pathologic myopia due to high refractive errors and posterior segment anomalies. Surgical and laser procedures may be required to treat retinal and choroidal lesions.

Hyperopia is an ametropic condition in which the refracting power of the eye is insufficient to bring the focused image of an object held at infinity onto the retina; the image lies posterior to the retinal plane. Hyperopia is the normal condition in infants and young children. Adolescent and adult hyperopia is not usually associated with anatomic abnormalities of the posterior segment. Many patients with hyperopia are able to overcome their refractive deficiency by

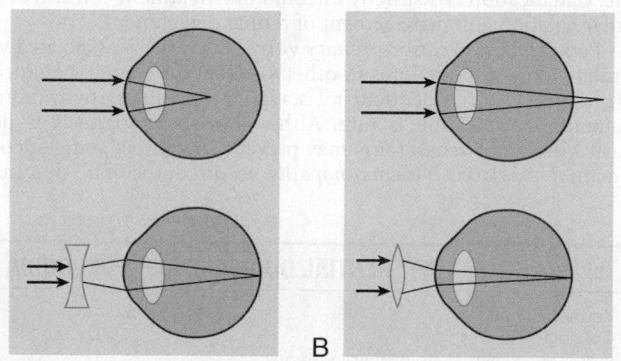

FIGURE 465–3 • Myopia/hyperopia. *A,* In the myopic eye, parallel rays of light are focused anterior to the retina. A divergent lens can be used to compensate for the mismatch between refracting power and axial length. *B,* The hyperopic eye requires the additional power of a convergent lens to bring images into focus on the retina.

accommodating even when viewing at distance. Accommodation is an active process in which parasympathetic stimulation of the circular ciliary muscle relaxes the lens zonules, allowing the lens to relax into a more spherical conformation with greater refracting power. The ability to accommodate diminishes with age. Emmetropes rely on accommodation to focus at near; they require near correction as they lose the ability to accommodate, usually entering the sixth decade (presbyopia). Hyperopes, however, may require near correction earlier in life because much of their accommodative power is used to offset the distance refractive error, and small decreases in accommodative ability may be symptomatic (hyperopic presbyopia).

In addition to blurred vision, hyperopia may incite headaches in young adults because increasing effort is required to focus at intermediate distances. Hyperopia is managed with periodic cycloplegic refraction and spectacle or contact lens correction. LASIK can be used to treat up to 5 D of hyperopia.

Astigmatism is a condition in which the corneal surface is asymmetrical: light is refracted differently along different axes. In regular astigmatism, the steepest corneal axis lies 90 degrees away from the flattest corneal axis, a configuration similar to the shape of a football. Regular astigmatism can usually be corrected with cylindrical and spherical spectacle lenses or with rigid contact lenses. Some forms of astigmatism can also be corrected with laser ablation of the cornea. Irregular astigmatism may produce an array of corneal configurations, usually owing to corneal ectasias such as keratoconus or corneal scarring. Irregular astigmatism is not correctable with spectacles but may be correctable with rigid contact lenses.

OPHTHALMIC DISORDERS USUALLY NOT ASSOCIATED WITH SYSTEMIC DISEASE

Congenital Disorders

Oculogenesis is initiated between 22 and 25 days of gestation when the neural tube begins to close and the optic pits first appear; retinal vascularization is completed shortly after birth, as is uveal pigmentation. As a result, there are many systemic congenital syndromes with protean ocular manifestations. The congenital disorders limited to the eye and discussed here may be treatable or may have catastrophic consequences if not detected early.

AMBLYOPIA AND STRABISMUS

Normal development of visual pathways depends on simultaneous and appropriate retinal stimulation in early childhood. *Amblyopia,* or incomplete visual development, may be categorized according to cause as strabismic, anisometropic, or deprivational. Amblyopia may be minimized or prevented by early diagnosis and intervention.

Misalignment of the eyes, or *strabismus,* causes disparate images to be cast simultaneously on the two retinas. Diplopia is avoided by involuntary suppression of one of the images. Alternating images may be suppressed, in which case excellent vision may develop in each eye, but binocular vision will not develop in either situation. More frequently, however, one eye is constantly suppressed, preventing normal visual development in that eye.

Esotropia, in which the eyes are deviated inward, is the most common strabismus of childhood. Congenital esotropia may not manifest until 3 or 4 months of age and is therefore often termed *infantile esotropia.* There is usually a large angle deviation; cross fixation, in which each inward-turned eye is used to view the contralateral visual field, is not uncommon. Infantile esotropia must be distinguished from pseudostrabismus, in which a broad nasal bridge and prominent epicanthal folds create an illusion of esotropia by obscuring the nasal sclera; in this condition, however, corneal light reflexes will be symmetrical, and (later) alternate cover testing will show no movement. Abduction should be demonstrated to differentiate congenital bilateral sixth cranial nerve palsies. Family history of strabismus confers an increased risk, but no inheritance pattern has been determined. Infantile esotropia is most frequently seen in otherwise normal children, but it occurs with increased frequency in several systemic conditions including cerebral palsy, prematurity, hydrocephalus, and trisomy 21. Cycloplegic refraction should be performed, and patching of one eye may be needed; however, surgery is almost always required to straighten the eyes. Binocular vision can rarely be produced.

Anisometropia is a condition in which the refractive states of the two eyes differ. One eye may focus a clear image on the retina without accommodation while the contralateral image is blurred, leading to unilateral amblyopia. Children may squint the affected eye. Cycloplegic refraction, spectacle or contact lens correction, and occlusive and/or pharmacologic penalization of the favored eye may reverse visual loss if instituted before 9 years of age.

Deprivational amblyopia may be caused by any opacity along the visual axis. *Congenital blepharoptosis* resulting from dysgenesis of the levator palpebrae superioris may require early surgical intervention. *Eyelid hemangiomas* may produce ptosis by mechanical effects, and they can also cause amblyopia by inducing an astigmatism. These benign, red, elevated lesions appear within the first few weeks of life and generally involute by age 10. Indications for treatment with intralesional corticosteroid injection, surgical resection, or pulsed-dye laser ablation include pupillary occlusion and induced refractive error. Most *congenital cataracts* incompletely occlude the pupil and permit normal vision to develop. *Complete congenital lenticular opacification,* however, may cause amblyopia if not removed within the first few weeks of life.

GLAUCOMA

The clinical triad of epiphora, photophobia, and blepharospasm is characteristic of congenital glaucoma. It is thought to result from an anomalous aqueous outflow apparatus and may be seen in isolation or with other ocular and systemic abnormalities. *Congenital open-angle glaucoma* produces a large eye (buphthalmos) and megalocornea. Examination under anesthesia is required to evaluate the optic nerve head and anterior chamber angle. Medical therapy may provide temporary benefit, but early surgical intervention is indicated. Congenital glaucoma is rare compared with adult-onset open angle glaucoma.

The rudimentary stump of iris present in congenital *aniridia* produces glaucoma within the first decade by blocking aqueous outflow through the trabecular meshwork. Congenital aniridia is inherited in an autosomal dominant pattern; 13% of cases are sporadic. Patients with congenital sporadic aniridia are at risk for Wilms' tumor and the WAGR syndrome (Wilms' tumor, *a*niridia, *g*enitourinary anomalies, and mental *r*etardation). Congenital glaucoma may be seen with any of the anterior segment dysgeneses. Genetic investigation and counseling is advised.

LEUKOCORIA

A white pupil, which may result from anterior or posterior segment pathology (Table 465–3), requires prompt and thorough ophthalmic investigation. *Leukocoria* is the most frequent presenting sign in patients with retinoblastoma, the most common intraocular malignancy of childhood. *Retinoblastoma* may be inherited or sporadic, bilateral or unilateral. Calcification is commonly demonstrated radiographically, and involved eyes are usually normal in size. Early, aggressive intervention with irradiation and/or surgery may be sight saving and lifesaving. Any disorder that produces congenital leukocoria may be confused with retinoblastoma. The *retinal telangiectasia* of Coats' disease produces unilateral leukocoria through exudative retinal detachment; 85% of patients are boys, and the disease is not heritable. Calcification is distinctly uncommon. Treatment consists of vascular ablation and management of retinal detachment.

Persistent hyperplastic primary vitreous (PHPV) is associated with unilateral microphthalmos in otherwise normal infants. Leukocoria is produced by a retrolenticular vascularized membrane or by induced cataract. Calcification is rare. Although visual prognosis is poor, early vitrectomy/lensectomy may prevent amblyopia and glaucoma. *Familial exudative vitreoretinopathy* is an autosomal dominant,

Table 465–3 • DIFFERENTIAL DIAGNOSIS OF LEUKOCORIA
Retinoblastoma
Cataract
Persistent hyperplastic primary vitreous
Retinopathy of prematurity (retrolental fibroplasia)
Coats' disease (retinal telangiectasia)
Retinal detachment
Toxocariasis

bilateral peripheral retinal disorder that produces retinal exudation and detachment. Incomplete vascularization of the temporal retina is seen in full-term, otherwise healthy infants. Severity may be asymmetrical, and prognosis is variable.

Congenital cataracts are relatively common, occurring in 1 in 2000 live births. Cases may be found in association with other ocular or systemic disorders or may be isolated; one third of cases are inherited (usually autosomal dominant). Intrauterine chemical or radiation insult and TORCH infections have been implicated. Severity is variable and relates to morphology and cause. Metabolic disorders such as galactosemia may produce total, bilateral lenticular opacity resulting in nystagmus and irreversible amblyopia; focal cataracts may be less visually devastating. Traumatic cataracts may result from child abuse.

Genetic Disorders

Hereditary disorders primary to the eye are far too numerous to address. Many ophthalmic syndromes and diseases that are not commonly considered hereditary exhibit patterns of inheritance in a minority of cases. The following representations highlight some of the more common and more interesting entities that demonstrate familial patterns in a majority of cases.

MITOCHONDRIAL TRANSMISSION

Among the ophthalmic disorders inherited through mitochondrial DNA are *Leber's hereditary optic neuropathy* and *chronic progressive external ophthalmoplegia* (CPEO). Leber's hereditary optic neuropathy became the first human disease for which mitochondrial inheritance was definitively demonstrated. Symptoms are limited to subacute, bilateral, progressive loss of vision. Males are affected in 60 to 90% of cases. Onset occurs in the second and third decades. Vision is generally reduced to 20/200 or worse sequentially in the two eyes over a period of months. Clinical findings include optic disc hyperemia with telangiectatic, tortuous retinal vessels; optic nerve pallor (atrophy) is seen in the late stages. Treatment is limited to use of low vision aids.

CPEO frequently manifests as bilateral blepharoptosis in the first and second decades. The paralysis is called "external" because the extraocular muscles are primarily involved; the iris dilator, iris sphincter, and ciliary muscles are spared. Vision is usually spared, although funduscopic examination reveals deterioration of the retinal pigmented epithelium in the macular region. The condition may occur in isolation or with cardiac conduction abnormalities and arrhythmias: the Kearns-Sayre syndrome. Muscle biopsy specimens demonstrate ragged red fibers. Systemic corticosteroids are contraindicated because they have reportedly precipitated hyperosmolar nonketotic coma in patients with Kearns-Sayre syndrome.

AUTOSOMAL DOMINANT TRANSMISSION

The corneal dystrophies are bilateral, inherited disorders that may produce pain and visual loss or may go entirely unnoticed. Autosomal dominant transmission is the rule. Corneal dystrophies are characterized by particular layer of corneal involvement, material deposition, age at onset, and treatment of symptoms.

Recurrent corneal erosions commonly result from *map-dot-fingerprint dystrophy,* the most common corneal dystrophy. This epithelial basement membrane disorder produces patterned irregularities for which it is named. Epithelial cells are stripped away with seemingly trivial trauma, such as with lid opening on wakening, producing severe pain out of proportion to clinical signs. Symptoms first appear in middle age. Methods of treatment range from hypertonic saline drops, to mechanical anterior corneal puncture, to excimer laser ablation.

Corneal stromal dystrophies rarely produce epithelial erosion but may cause decreased visual acuity. The focal, hyaline deposits of *granular dystrophy* produce modest visual disturbance and may recur in a corneal graft. *Lattice dystrophy* is characterized by amyloid deposition in the anterior stroma and may or may not be associated with systemic amyloidosis. Recurrence in a corneal graft is common. *Macular dystrophy* produces large, confluent areas of acid mucopolysaccharide in patients with a metabolic defect in the production or breakdown of keratan sulfate. Macular dystrophy is the only common corneal dystrophy that shows autosomal recessive transmission.

Thickened protuberances of Descemet's membrane, corneal edema, and painful subepithelial bullae are characteristic of *Fuchs' endothelial dystrophy.* Visual acuity is worse after sleep, when prolonged lid closure limits evaporation from the corneal surface. Transmission is autosomal dominant, but sporadic cases are seen. Temporizing treatment may include hypertonic solutions and bandage contact lenses. Fuchs' dystrophy is one of the most common indications for penetrating keratoplasty (corneal transplant).

AUTOSOMAL RECESSIVE TRANSMISSION

Retinitis pigmentosa (RP) is a group of photoreceptor dystrophies in which rod and cone photoreceptors degenerate. Nyctalopia (night blindness) and gradual, progressive loss of peripheral vision are typical features. Although the appearance of the fundus varies greatly, signs in advanced stages include attenuation of retinal vessels, waxy pallor of the optic disc, and "bone spicule" pigmentation of the peripheral fundus in a majority of cases (Fig. 465–4). Early in the disease, the fundus can appear normal.

Prevalence in the United States is approximately 1 in 3000. Approximately 20% of RP cases show autosomal recessive transmission, about 43% are autosomal dominant, about 8% are X-linked recessive, about 23% are isolated cases, and the inheritance pattern cannot be determined in about 6% of cases (e.g., patients who are adopted). Hundreds of genetic defects have been identified in dozens of responsible genes; many additional RP genes remain to be discovered. Perimetry may be useful to document progression, but an electroretinogram (ERG) is required for definitive diagnosis. The ERG typically demonstrates progressive loss of function of rod photoreceptors early in the disease; cones are affected to varying degrees.

The spotty pigmentation of the fundus so often associated with RP may be seen with a number of treatable disorders, including infectious and inflammatory chorioretinitis, vascular occlusions, drug toxicity, and retinal detachment. RP associated with congenital deafness is called Usher's syndrome.

Education of patients is critical in RP. The only therapy known to slow the course of the disease in the common forms of RP is oral supplements of vitamin A palmitate (15,000 units/day). Patients taking these supplements should be monitored for liver toxicity, although toxicity has only been seen in patients taking far higher doses. Vitamin E supplements may worsen the disease. In most cases, the disease is slowly progressive over decades. Central visual acuity may remain surprisingly good despite severe constriction of the visual field. Patients whose visual field is reduced to 20 degrees are considered legally blind in most states. Low vision aids are useful in many cases. Genetic counseling should be provided. Some authorities advise limiting light exposure with the use of tinted glasses, although this approach has not been proven to be of benefit.

Leber's congenital amaurosis is considered by some authorities to be a variant of RP in which the degeneration of photoreceptors is so rapid that little to no vision is present in the first years of life. Infants are usually brought to medical attention within the first 6 months of life when nystagmus develops or delay of visual maturation is otherwise evident. Transmission is autosomal recessive. Affected patients do not respond to visual stimuli on examination, and pupils show

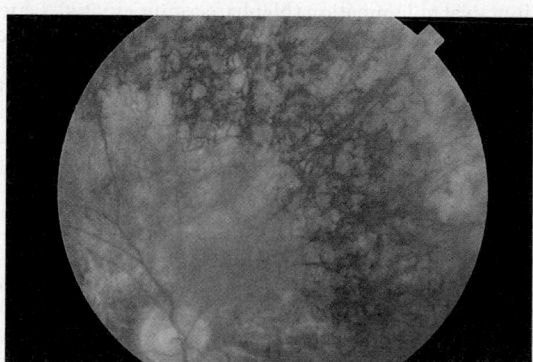

FIGURE 465–4 • Retinitis pigmentosa. Fundus photograph shows "bone spicule" pigmentation of the midperipheral fundus, waxy pallor of the optic disk, and attenuated retinal vessels, the most consistent finding in RP. (Courtesy of John I. Loewenstein, MD.)

variable reactivity. Fundus findings range from normal to heavily spiculed. Multiple, small, white choroidal foci may be seen. The ERG demonstrates generalized photoreceptor dysfunction. No treatment is available.

Gyrate atrophy of the choroid is another autosomal recessive degeneration of the fundus. Progressive visual loss and night blindness begin in the first decade. Severely constricted visual fields are present in adults with the disease. The peripheral fundus appearance may be dramatic, showing geographic areas of retinal pigmented epithelial dropout and choroidal atrophy with hyperpigmented borders. The central retina may become involved later as these patches become confluent. The disease is associated with defects in ornithine aminotransferase, which result in elevated serum levels of ornithine. The ERG is abnormal early in the disease. Diagnosis is based on fundus findings and serum ornithine levels. Treatment requires dietary restriction of arginine. Differential diagnosis includes pathologic myopia, choroideremia, RP, and other causes of chorioretinal atrophy.

X-LINKED TRANSMISSION

Choroideremia may be confused with gyrate atrophy owing to its similar fundus appearance. It is an X-linked recessive condition that results in progressive atrophy of the choriocapillaris beginning in the first decade. The midperiphery is first involved with slow progression anteriorly to the ora serrata and posteriorly to the optic nerve. Hyperpigmented areas are generally not seen. Night blindness is often the presenting symptom, whereas visual acuity gradually decreases to the 20/200 level by the fourth decade. Female carriers are asymptomatic but may show subtle fundus signs.

Nearly all forms of congenital *dyschromatopsia* demonstrate X-linked recessive transmission. Three distinct cone photoreceptor subtypes provide color perception in most humans. The pigment of each subtype demonstrates specific peak wavelength absorption. Patients lacking red cones are said to demonstrate protanopia, whereas those lacking green cones are labeled deuteranopes. Congenital tritanopia, or absence of blue cones, is extremely rare and shows autosomal dominant inheritance.

Most cases of color blindness represent a relative deficiency or abnormality of one of the cone populations rather than a total absence. Genetic defects in coding for cone pigments usually result in subtle shifts in peak wavelength absorption such that color matching responses in affected individuals are incongruous with normal subjects, but color differences are perceived nonetheless. Blue-yellow confusion is seen more frequently in acquired dyschromatopsia and may herald optic nerve disease.

Exogenous Infections

Exogenous ocular infections may involve any of the ocular or periocular tissues. Signs and symptoms reflect focality, chronicity, and the infectious pathogen. Treatment may range from modifications in hygiene to surgical débridement.

Inflammation of the eyelids may produce itching and redness of one or both eyes. *Anterior blepharitis* primarily involves the eyelash follicles, which are located within the anterior lamella of the eyelid. *Staphylococcus aureus* is the most common infectious agent. If untreated, the condition becomes chronic and may lead to corneal and conjunctival inflammation (blepharoconjunctivitis). Patients are advised to clean the eyelids and eyelashes rigorously using a cotton-tipped applicator or washcloth daily. Ophthalmic antibiotic ointment (bacitracin or erythromycin) is more effective than eye drops to treat the lid margin. *Seborrheic blepharitis* is an anterior blepharitis in which crusting and oily material may envelop individual cilia. Treatment focuses on eyelid hygiene.

The inflammation of *meibomianitis* localizes to the posterior lamella, where the meibomian gland orifices exit the tarsal plate. Slit lamp examination reveals inspissated glands from which white material may be expressed with manual pressure to the eyelid. Vision may be impaired, and the conjunctiva may be inflamed by hyperviscous secretions that enter the tear film. Treatment requires daily eyelid hygiene. Warm, dilute solutions of baby shampoo and a clean washcloth may be used to massage the eyelid margin. Some patients may improve with oral tetracyclines, and half of patients may have rosacea (Chapter 475).

Acute, focal infection of a meibomian or Zeiss gland is called a *hordeolum*. Commonly termed a *stye*, a hordeolum may be painful and may produce blepharoptosis when it occurs in the upper lid. Hordeola are usually self-limited infections, but they may progress to preseptal cellulitis in which the surrounding lid tissue becomes erythematous, edematous, and warm (Fig. 465–5). Hordeola usually respond to warm compresses over a period of days, whereas preseptal cellulitis requires systemic antibiotics (see later).

Chalazion (Fig. 465–6) describes a chronically inspissated meibomian gland. Glandular secretions become fossilized within the tarsal plate, producing a firm, nonmobile subcutaneous nodule. Extravasation into adjacent soft tissue may produce chronic granulomatous inflammation with enlargement of the chalazion, internal or external erosion, spontaneous drainage, or focal cellulitis. Conservative treatment involves warm soaks with or without antibiotic ointment. Incision and curettage is usually reserved for very large lesions or those persisting despite more than 1 month of conservative treatment. Recurrent, isolated chalazia may respond to local corticosteroid injection, although hypopigmentation and tissue necrosis may occur. Multiple chronic chalazia may respond to systemic antibiotics. Chalazia may increase in size during pregnancy. Chronic, nonresponsive chalazia, especially when accompanied by loss of eyelashes, must be evaluated to exclude *sebaceous cell carcinoma*.

Periocular cellulitis may involve deep orbital structures or may be confined to preseptal tissues. In either case, it may produce warm, erythematous eyelid edema and associated pain. Fever and leukocytosis is not uncommon. A history of an insect bite or other skin perforation is frequently elicited in cases of *preseptal cellulitis,* whereas ethmoidal sinusitis is the leading risk factor for *orbital cellulitis*. Treatment is critically dependent on proper diagnosis.

Clinical signs of *preseptal cellulitis* are limited to external soft tissues as described. Decreased visual acuity, relative afferent pupillary defect, limited ocular motility, and pronounced chemosis herald postseptal involvement. In the presence of orbital signs, computed tomographic scans of the orbit and sinuses should be obtained. If untreated, *orbital cellulitis* may extend intracranially.

Preseptal cellulitis is treated with oral antibiotics in an outpatient setting. First-generation cephalosporins are generally effective against *Streptococcus pneumoniae* and staphylococcal species. *Haemophilus*

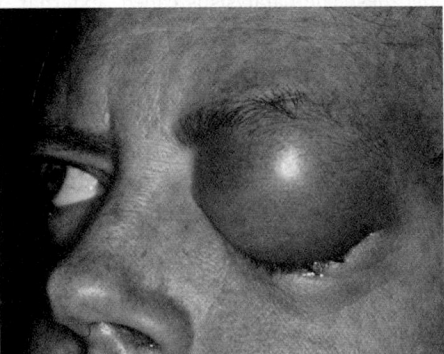

FIGURE 465–5 • Eyelid abscess. Preseptal cellulitis, commonly resulting from minor penetrating trauma, may evolve into an abscess. Treatment requires incision and drainage followed by systemic antibiotics.

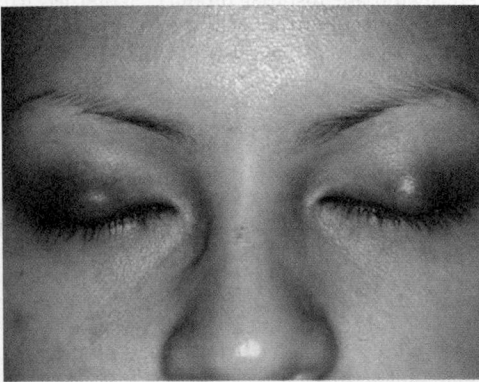

FIGURE 465–6 • Bilateral chalazion in the upper eyelids.

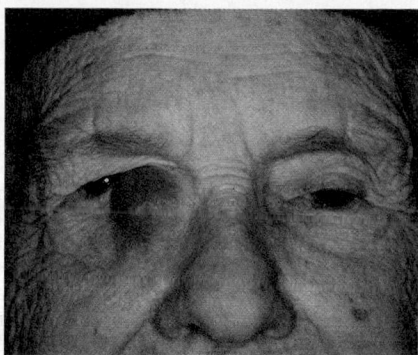

FIGURE 465–7 • Acute dacryocystitis. External photograph shows erythema and edema in the region of the lacrimal sac. Pressure applied to the lesion produces purulent reflux through the canaliculi. Conservative treatment requires oral antibiotics and warm compresses. Pointing lesions such as the one pictured require incision and drainage.

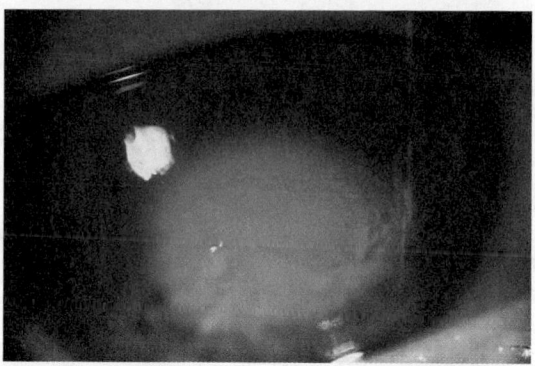

FIGURE 465–8 • Corneal abrasion. Corneal epithelial defects are best observed with topical fluorescent stain under blue illumination. Pain is often out of proportion to clinical findings. Prophylactic topical antibiotics are required until the epithelium has healed. (Courtesy of Deborah P. Langston, MD.)

Table 465–4 • DIFFERENTIAL DIAGNOSIS OF COMMON CAUSES OF INFLAMED EYE*

FEATURE	ACUTE CONJUNCTIVITIS	ACUTE IRITIS†	ACUTE GLAUCOMA‡	CORNEAL TRAUMA OR INFECTION
Incidence	Extremely common	Common	Uncommon	Common
Discharge	Moderate to copious	None	None	Watery or purulent
Vision	No effect on vision	Slightly blurred	Markedly blurred	Usually blurred
Pain	None	Moderate	Severe	Moderate to severe
Conjunctival injection	Diffuse: more toward fornices	Mainly circumcorneal	Mainly circumcorneal	Mainly circumcorneal
Cornea	Clear	Usually clear	Steamy	Change in clarity related to cause
Pupil size	Normal	Small	Moderately dilated and fixed	Normal or small
Pupillary light response	Normal	Poor	None	Normal
Intraocular pressure	Normal	Normal	Elevated	Normal
Smear	Causative organisms	No organisms	No organisms	Organisms found only in corneal ulcers due to infection

*Other less common causes of red eyes include endophthalmitis, foreign body, episcleritis, and scleritis.
†Acute anterior uveitis.
‡Angle-closure glaucoma.

influenzae, found in pediatric patients, produces a characteristic violaceous discoloration. Infants and young children with preseptal cellulitis are admitted for intravenous therapy with antibiotics. Orbital cellulitis requires hospital admission with intravenous administration of antibiotics in all age groups. Lack of clinical improvement in 24 to 36 hours may suggest another process. *Orbital pseudotumor* in adults and *rhabdomyosarcoma* in children must be excluded.

Acute dacryocystitis (Fig. 465–7) produces pain, redness, and swelling of the lacrimal sac. Patients may experience purulent discharge from the lacrimal punta, and secondary conjunctivitis is common. Symptoms of chronic dacryocystitis may be limited to epiphora. Both are associated with nasolacrimal duct obstruction. Digital massage of the lateral nasal wall may cause a mucopurulent reflux through the lacrimal punctum. Initial treatment with oral antibiotics may quell any acute inflammation, but definitive treatment usually requires dacryocystorhinostomy.

Conjunctivitis is a frequent complaint in which patients experience redness, itching, and foreign body sensation, with discharge ranging from watery to hyperpurulent. It must be differentiated from a corneal abrasion (Fig. 465–8) and other causes of a red, painful eye (Table 465–4). The great majority of cases are caused by viral infections that typically begin unilaterally and progress to involve both eyes. Viral conjunctivitis is caused most frequently by adenovirus species. Transmission is by direct contact with an infected individual. *Epidemic keratoconjunctivitis* caused by adenovirus subtypes 7, 11, and 18 may spread rapidly through a school, summer camp, or physician's office. Patients diagnosed with viral conjunctivitis should be isolated from other patients; examining rooms and waiting areas should be disinfected.

Viral conjunctivitis produces inferior palpebral conjunctival lymphoid follicles evident on slit lamp examination. There may be copious watery discharge, but mucopurulent discharge is uncharacteristic. Conjunctival hemorrhage suggests an alternate pathogen. Preauricular lymphadenopathy may be present, and a history of upper respiratory tract infection is common. Vision may be compromised by immune infiltration of the corneal stroma. The disease is self-limited, and treatment is aimed at patient comfort. Cool compresses may be used. Patients are advised to wash their hands frequently. When viral conjunctivitis has been diagnosed, antibiotic solutions and ointments are not required, and topical corticosteroids are contraindicated. Although viral particles may be recovered from infected individual for up to 2 to 3 months, most patients are believed to be contagious for 1 to 2 weeks.

Bacterial conjunctivitis (Fig. 465–9) represents fewer than 5% of all cases. Infection with staphylococcal species appears as chronic mild mucoid discharge and crusting and may be associated with chronic blepharitis or dacryocystitis. Symptoms may improve with erythromycin or bacitracin ointment, but treatment should be targeted at underlying infectious sources. Acute bacterial conjunctivitis caused by *Haemophilus* or streptococcal species may be seen in epidemic or isolated form. Transmission may be through direct contact or through fomites. Moderate purulent discharge is seen. There may be mild edema of the conjunctiva (chemosis) and lids. Slit lamp examination of the inferior palpebral conjunctiva reveals a fine papillary response. The disease is usually self-limited but responds well to broad-spectrum antibiotic solutions, including gentamicin and the combination of polymyxin B with trimethoprim.

Hyperacute purulent conjunctivitis caused by *Neisseria gonorrhoeae* is transmitted through sexual contact. Copious green pus is produced, and the lids are often extremely edematous. Preauricular lymphadenopathy is common. Immediate intervention is critical to prevent perforation of corneal ulcers caused by bacterial exotoxins. Gram

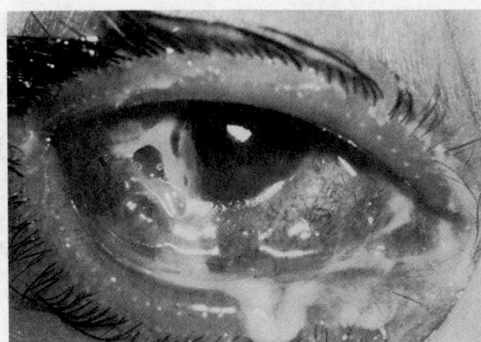

FIGURE 465–9 • Bacterial conjunctivitis. Purulent discharge and conjunctival hyperemia suggest bacterial conjunctivitis. Viral conjunctivitis produces watery discharge, foreign body sensation, preauricular lymphadenopathy, and conjunctival follicles seen on slit lamp examination. (Reproduced with permission from the American Academy of Ophthalmology.)

stain and culture of the conjunctiva should be performed. Copious irrigation with saline solution is required to dilute the exotoxins. Systemic antibiotics are required. Third-generation cephalosporins may be given intramuscularly or intravenously. Adjunctive topical treatment with ciprofloxacin, gentamicin, or bacitracin may be useful.

Adult inclusion conjunctivitis is produced through sexual transmission of *Chlamydia trachomatis*. This chronic conjunctivitis produces conjunctival follicles in association with preauricular lymphadenopathy and is refractory to many antibiotic regimens. If untreated, the disease may linger for many months. Systemic treatment with erythromycin or azithromycin is required. *Trachoma* is a chronic cicatricial conjunctivitis resulting from repeated infection with particular chlamydial subspecies. Endemic in many developing countries, it is the world's leading cause of corneal blindness. The superior palpebral conjunctiva develops white, linear scars, and pitting may be seen at the corneal limbus. Trichiasis, inverting of the eyelashes, eventually leads to corneal vascularization and opacification. Medical treatment requires systemic erythromycin or tetracycline, whereas surgical epilation or eyelid reconstruction may be required for cicatricial changes.

Allergic conjunctivitis is commonly associated with atopy, hay fever, and allergic rhinitis. Itching is usually the prominent symptom, although foreign body sensation is common as well. Watery discharge occurs. Supportive treatment includes cool compresses and topical vasoconstrictors or antihistamines such as naphazoline or levocabastine. Long-term treatment with mast cell stabilizers can be extremely effective in treating chronic symptoms.

Keratitis caused by herpes simplex virus usually represents secondary ocular infection (Fig. 465–10). Primary infection may go unnoticed or may be limited to a periocular vesicular dermatitis or blepharoconjunctivitis. Viral particles may lie dormant within the trigeminal ganglion indefinitely or may reinfect the corneal epithelium or stroma. Herpes simplex epithelial keratitis produces a characteristic dendritic epithelial defect and is believed to represent active viral infection. Treatment is with topical trifluridine or oral acyclovir.

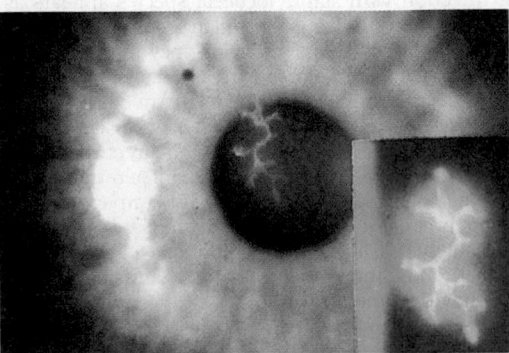

FIGURE 465–10 • Herpes simplex corneal epithelial keratitis in diffuse light and (inset) in light passed through a cobalt blue filter after fluorescein staining.

Isolated stromal manifestations are believed to represent immunologic activity against the virus. Treatment with topical corticosteroids reduces the risk of permanent corneal opacification. Prophylactic topical antiviral agents (e.g., trifluridine) are given during treatment with corticosteroids.

Bacterial keratitis may appear as a minor peripheral corneal opacity or a large central suppurative ulcer. Symptoms include pain, redness, photophobia, and decreased vision. Fluorescein staining reveals an epithelial defect with underlying opacity. Gross or microscopic epithelial trauma is the primary risk factor. The risk of bacterial keratitis is five times greater in contact lens wearers and increases among those who sleep with lenses in place. Gram-positive cocci are the most common pathogens, but *Pseudomonas* is most common in patients who wear contact lenses. Identification of the pathogen requires Gram stain and culture of corneal scrapings. Empirical treatment with topical fluoroquinolones is sometimes advised for less severe cases, but these agents may need to be administered as frequently as every 15 minutes. More severe cases require hospital admission and topical application of fortified antibiotic solutions every 10 to 15 minutes. Systemic antibiotics are not routinely used. Perforation may be treated with bandage contact lens, cyanoacrylate (crazy glue), or penetrating keratoplasty. Fungal infection, suspected after injury with vegetable matter, often requires early surgical débridement.

Endophthalmitis, or inflammation of the intraocular cavity, may be exogenous or endogenous, and it may be infectious or sterile. Exogenous infectious endophthalmitis follows surgical or nonsurgical penetrating trauma. Incidence is estimated at 0.1% after intraocular surgery and 5% after penetrating injury. The primary symptom is decreased vision. Vitritis and anterior uveitis are evident on examination. Corneal, conjunctival, retinal, and choroidal involvement is variable. Toxin-producing gram-positive species and gram-negative species produce rapid onset necrosis of the vitreous and other intraocular structures. *Propionibacterium acnes* and *Staphylococcus epidermidis* are indolent organisms causing more subtle presentations. Endophthalmitis is a rare but potentially catastrophic complication of cataract surgery. Visual acuity should continually improve in the weeks after surgery. Any decrease in visual acuity or increase in pain during the postoperative period requires immediate examination.

Endophthalmitis requires sampling of the aqueous and vitreous for Gram stain and culture. *P. acnes* and *S. epidermidis* may require injection of intravitreal antibiotics. More virulent infections require pars plana vitrectomy with intravitreal corticosteroids and intravenous antibiotics. Prognosis is variable and depends on the specific pathogen. Treatment of indolent infections may result in excellent postoperative vision, but aggressive pathogens can completely destroy intraocular tissues within several hours, eliminating all useful vision.

Idiopathic Inflammatory and Autoimmune Disorders

Ocular or periocular tissues may be the primary focus of isolated idiopathic or autoimmune inflammation. Pain is a common symptom. Vision is variably reduced. Treatment is aimed at reducing symptoms and limiting tissue destruction because the underlying cause is poorly understood.

Keratoconjunctivitis sicca, commonly called dry eye syndrome, results from deficiency of any of the tear film layers. Symptoms include gritty, foreign body sensations, burning, photophobia, and decreased visual acuity. The cornea and conjunctiva may stain with fluorescein, although rose bengal staining is more sensitive. Idiopathic inflammation of the lacrimal and salivary glands resulting in keratoconjunctivitis sicca and xerostomia is called Sjögren's syndrome (Chapter 282) and is more common in women. Secondary complications include recurrent corneal erosion, keratitis, and corneal opacification. A number of medications can also cause dry eyes (Table 465–5). Artificial tears, often administered six to eight times a day, and lubricating ointments at night are the mainstays of treatment, often in combination with temporary or permanent punctal occlusion.

Episcleritis is inflammation immediately underlying the conjunctiva. Pain, if present, is mild. Sectoral hyperemia, distinguished from conjunctivitis by radially oriented vessels that do not move with the conjunctiva, is dramatically reduced with instillation of phenylephrine 2.5% or 10%. A single drop of the latter can produce acute hypertension. Episcleritis is self-limited, although topical nonsteroidal anti-inflammatory medications such as flurbiprofen or diclofenac may hasten resolution. In contradistinction to scleritis, episcleritis is not usually related to systemic rheumatoid disease.

Table 465–5 • PARTIAL LIST OF SYSTEMIC MEDICATIONS CAUSING DRY EYE

MEDICATION	CLASS
Ibuprofen	Nonsteroidal anti-inflammatory
Diphenhydramine	Antihistamine
Tripolidine	Antihistamine
Chlorpheniramine	Antihistamine
Atenolol	β-blocker
Metoprolol	β-blocker
Propranolol	β-blocker
Clonidine	α-agonist
Scopolamine	Anticholinergic
Amiodarone	Antiarrhythmic
Thiabendazole	Antinematode
Isotretinoin*	Retinoid

*Severe, long-term dry eye with onset up to several years after treatment. All others tend to abate with cessation.

Scleritis frequently manifests as severe pain and redness. Fifty per cent of cases are associated with systemic disease. Vision may be reduced when the posterior sclera is involved. There may be diffuse or sectoral hyperemia that is nonmobile and does not blanch with instillation of phenylephrine. Scleral thinning may occur, but perforation is rare. Uveitis and keratitis may occur secondarily. Diagnostic evaluation includes ultrasonography and/or magnetic resonance imaging as well as laboratory tests to identify infectious or autoimmune connective tissue disease. Treatment may require topical or oral nonsteroidal anti-inflammatory medications or corticosteroids. Refractory cases may require cytotoxic drugs.

Mooren's ulcer is a progressive, idiopathic peripheral corneal thinning thought to be an autoimmune phenomenon. The condition may be unilateral or bilateral, and pain is common. Perforation is rare except with trauma. Topical corticosteroids, mucolytics, and cytotoxic agents have been used. Bandage contact lenses and conjunctival recession or advancement have also been used with variable success.

Ocular cicatricial pemphigoid is a vesicular conjunctivitis named for its relentless destruction of the ocular surface. Involvement before age 60 is rare. Initial symptoms of foreign body sensation and burning reflect chronic conjunctivitis. Ruptured epithelial bullae destroy conjunctival goblet cells, leading to profound dry eye. The conjunctival fornices may be obliterated. Mild trauma or surgery may increase inflammation. Patients with ocular cicatricial pemphigoid demonstrate antibodies to the conjunctival basement membrane, and other mucous membranes may be affected. Dapsone is the first-line treatment, although it is contraindicated in patients with glucose-6-phosphate dehydrogenase deficiency. Cytotoxic medications or corticosteroids may be helpful. Surgical reconstruction utilizing oral mucous membrane autografts or amniotic membrane allografts can be effective in severe cases.

Nonspecific, idiopathic orbital inflammation has been called *orbital pseudotumor*. The inflammation may involve the lacrimal gland (dacryoadenitis), extraocular muscles (myositis), orbital fat, sclera, or optic nerve sheath (optic perineuritis). Inflammation primarily involving the orbital apex produces painful external ophthalmoplegia, the so-called Tolosa-Hunt syndrome. Pain is the most frequent symptom in orbital pseudotumor, although many cases present with proptosis and limitation of ocular movements; visual acuity may be reduced. Orbital computed tomography or magnetic resonance imaging is generally required to exclude mass lesions; biopsy may be indicated in atypical cases. A dramatic response to systemic corticosteroids within 24 hours is common. A poor clinical response should suggest an alternative diagnosis. Corticosteroids must be tapered slowly over months to prevent recurrence. Irradiation may be required if corticosteroids cannot be discontinued successfully.

Patients with *iritis* complain of pain, photophobia, and blurred vision. Greater than 50% of cases are unrelated to systemic disease. Perilimbal conjunctival injection may be present, and slit lamp examination demonstrates inflammatory cells and protein exudate (flare) in the anterior chamber. Initial episodes are usually treated symptomatically with prednisolone acetate 1% suspension four times a day and cycloplegic drugs (atropine 1% daily, cyclopentolate 2% twice

daily). Repeat episodes require systemic evaluation for autoimmune and infectious causes.

Central serous retinopathy occurs unilaterally as acutely decreased visual acuity and metamorphopsia in young to middle-aged adults. Patients are usually well educated and employed in stressful occupations. Visual acuity may range from 20/40 to 20/200. Fundus examination demonstrates a central, serous elevation of the neurosensory retina. Fluorescein angiography is useful in diagnosis. The disease is self-limited, although permanent visual deficits have been reported. Focal laser treatment reduces duration of symptoms but does not improve final outcome.

Neoplastic Diseases

Neoplasms primary to the eye and adnexa are vast. External lesions may be categorized as pigmented or nonpigmented. Orbital tumors may be intraconal or extraconal. Primary intraocular tumors are far outnumbered by metastatic foci.

The eyelid *hemangioma* is a pediatric lesion that manifests in the first several weeks of life. The so-called strawberry nevus enlarges over several months but generally begins to involute after 1 year of age. Potential complications include blepharoptosis, astigmatism, and amblyopia. There may be orbital involvement. Large tumors may require intralesional or systemic corticosteroids during the proliferating phase. Pulsed-dye laser treatment increases the rate of involution. Surgical excision is effective in many cases, although most ophthalmologists recommend observation.

Rhabdomyosarcoma is the most common primary orbital malignancy of children. Proptosis, ptosis, and lid ecchymosis are most common on presentation; visual loss is variable. History of incidental trauma may be misleading. Orbital computed tomography may be useful, but biopsy is required for definitive diagnosis. Systemic evaluation for metastases (including chest radiography, lumbar puncture, and bone marrow biopsy) should be initiated emergently. Survival rates exceeding 90% have been achieved with focal irradiation (4000-6000 cGy) and systemic chemotherapy (vincristine and actinomycin D).

Basal cell carcinoma, the most common eyelid malignancy, occurs 40 to 50 times more often than either squamous or sebaceous malignancies. These lesions are typically pearly, umbilicated nodules, although morphology varies widely and includes deeply pigmented tumors. They are most commonly located on the lower eyelid. Excision with clear surgical margins is generally curative. Basal cell carcinoma rarely metastasizes, and local recurrence can be treated with excision. Caruncular lesions may extend into deep tissues and therefore warrant orbital imaging before surgery.

Although *squamous cell carcinoma* occurs much less frequently than basal cell carcinoma, it carries the risk of metastasis. Squamous cell carcinoma is found most frequently on the lower lid, where actinic exposure is greatest. Advanced cases may involve the orbit and sinuses and require systemic evaluation. Surgical excision is required.

Sebaceous cell carcinoma may arise from any of the sebaceous glands of the eyelids. Chronic chalazia that destroy local lid architecture should raise the possibility of sebaceous cell carcinoma, as should chronic unilateral blepharitis. The tumor is aggressive, tends to demonstrate pagetoid spread through the conjunctiva, and requires excisional surgery. Metastasis is not uncommon. Sebaceous cell carcinoma associated with visceral malignancy is termed *Muir-Torre syndrome.*

Malignant melanoma of the conjunctiva may arise de novo, from nevi, or in areas of *primary acquired melanosis.* Unilateral conjunctival pigmentation in lightly pigmented persons may exhibit cellular atypia, in which case the individual is at risk for melanoma. Conjunctival melanoma may be pigmented or amelanotic. Tumor thickness of greater than 0.8 mm portends a greater likelihood of metastasis. Early local excision with cryotherapy is often curative. Intraocular malignant melanoma is the most common primary intraocular tumor. Malignant melanoma arises in the choroid or ciliary body and may extend through the sclera to involve the conjunctiva. Choroidal malignant melanoma may arise de novo or from a previously identified choroidal nevus. Tumor thickness greater than 3 mm, breadth greater than 10 mm, or rapid enlargement suggests malignant melanoma. The liver is the most common site of metastasis, and liver enzymes are the most sensitive screening tool. In cases without metastases, treatment is controversial and may involve focal irradiation, laser ablation, excision, or enucleation. Orbital invasion of any of these tumors requires exenteration (complete removal of all orbital contents.)

Retinoblastoma, the most common intraocular malignancy of childhood, may be inherited as an autosomal dominant trait or may be sporadic. Genetic study of retinoblastoma, a prototypic genetic malignancy, gave rise to the Knudson two-hit hypothesis. Normal development relies on a tumor suppressor gene located on the long arm of chromosome 13. One normal allele is sufficient to suppress tumorigenesis. Familial retinoblastoma may result from autosomal dominant transmission of one defective allele, in which all the cells in the body are affected. Bilateral or multicentric disease is common in this situation, and the abnormal gene is passed on to future offspring. Sporadic retinoblastoma results from mutations during embryogenesis. Mutation early in embryogenesis will affect all the cells in the body, and a de novo germline defect is created. Bilateral or multicentric disease is common in this situation. Late mutation in embryogenesis produces nontransmissible, unilateral, unifocal disease. In any of these settings, the second allele suffers somatic mutation in a developing retina cell. Patients most frequently present with leukocoria or strabismus, and 90% are diagnosed by age 3. Bilateral or multicentric disease indicates a germline mutation. Enucleation is required in most cases, and optic nerve extension is the most significant prognostic factor. Radiation, laser ablation, cryotherapy, and chemotherapy may be used in bilateral cases to treat the second eye. Survivors are at risk for other malignancies, including osteogenic sarcoma.

Intraconal orbital tumors generally produce axial proptosis and decreased vision. Orbital venous malformation, commonly but erroneously termed *cavernous hemangioma,* is the most common orbital tumor. These are benign, vascular endothelial neoplasms that may be intraconal or extraconal. Orbital images reveal a well-circumscribed tumor. Significant pain should suggest another diagnosis. Excision is indicated by compromised vision, optic neuropathy, globe displacement, or proptosis.

Primary optic nerve tumors include *meningioma* and *glioma.* Optic nerve meningiomas are slow-growing tumors seen in middle-aged individuals; women are affected more often than men. Vision may be reduced or may be normal. Characteristic computed tomographic images reveal primary involvement of the neural sheath. Serial examinations and images are performed to detect posterior progression. Threat of chiasmal involvement is the primary indication for excision, although this is somewhat controversial. Optic nerve *glioma* may be seen in children with von Recklinghausen's disease or tuberous sclerosis. Bilateral optic nerve glioma is pathognomonic for neurofibromatosis type I. Isolated optic nerve glioma in adults is rare but more aggressive and often lethal.

Degenerative Conditions

Cataract, or opacification of the crystalline lens, is the leading cause of blindness in the world and the leading cause of visual loss in Americans older than age 40. Prevalence of cataract in the United States has been estimated at 50% for persons older than age 75. The great majority of cases represent normal aging changes in which progressive yellowing of the lens nucleus (nuclear sclerosis) and hydration of the lens cortex are seen. Genetic predisposition to senile cataract has been hypothesized but not proven. Prolonged exposure to ultraviolet radiation has been shown to be cataractogenic. Surgical extraction is required to improve vision; there is no known medical treatment.

Nearly all patients older than age 50 demonstrate some degree of degenerative lens changes when examined by slit lamp. Visual disability depends on the extent of lenticular changes as well as on the visual demands of the patient. Very rarely is cataract extraction medically indicated. Mature, swollen cataracts may induce phacomorphic glaucoma by narrowing the anterior chamber angle. Hypermature, liquefied cataracts may leak lens protein and thereby cause phacoantigenic uveitis. In the majority of cases, however, elective cataract extraction serves to restore lost vision. There is no urgency in most cases, and patients who are told they must have cataract surgery in the absence of disabling visual complaints should beware.

Congenital cataracts may be associated with metabolic disease, result from intrauterine TORCH infections, or may be familial. Traumatic cataracts result from hydration after penetrating injury to the lens. Some cataracts may be characteristic in color or location, such as the sunflower cataract of Wilson's disease (Chapter 224) or

the posterior subcapsular cataract often resulting from systemic corticosteroid use (Chapter 31).

Cataract extraction with intraocular lens implantation has become a very successful procedure in the developed world. Potential complications include cystoid macular edema, astigmatism, retinal detachment, and endophthalmitis. Current methods of surgery include small, self-sealing incisions performed under local (retrobulbar) or topical anesthesia. Prognosis for visual recovery is excellent barring any concomitant eye disease such as diabetic retinopathy, glaucoma, or macular degeneration.

Glaucoma is best defined as atrophy of the retinal ganglion cell layer in the presence of elevated intraocular pressure. The classic clinical triad consists of elevated intraocular tension, atrophic cupping of the optic nerve head, and characteristic visual field loss. Normal tension glaucoma has been described. Elevated intraocular pressure has not been clearly defined as causative. Many experts view glaucoma as a vascular optic neuropathy, whereas others favor an endogenous toxin etiology. Early in the disease, findings are variable, and the diagnosis is difficult to make; many patients are categorized as "glaucoma suspects" based on one or more risk factors and should be examined every 4 to 6 months. Risk factors include family history of glaucoma, increasing age, diabetes mellitus, obesity, and ocular trauma. Glaucoma is the leading cause of blindness among African Americans.

Primary open-angle glaucoma, the most common glaucoma, occurs in 15% of individuals older than age 80 years. The anterior chamber angle anatomy appears normal, but aqueous outflow is reduced. Progressive visual field loss begins in the periphery and occurs so insidiously that affected individuals may be unaware until late in the disease course. Intraocular tension measurement is an effective, if imperfect, screening method, and all adults should be screened. Medical treatment attempts to reduce aqueous production by the ciliary body or to increase outflow through the trabecular meshwork or uvea. Topical β-blockers, carbonic anhydrase inhibitors, miotics, and prostaglandin analogues may be additive in their effects. Refractory cases may require laser or cryoablative procedures. Filtering surgery produces a subconjunctival outflow conduit in advanced cases.

Angle-closure glaucoma constitutes an ophthalmic emergency. Patients present with a red, painful eye. Nausea and vomiting are common. The pupil is usually fixed in a mid-dilated position, and the cornea appears cloudy due to pressure-driven edema. The iris is bowed forward by posterior accumulation of aqueous humor, thereby sealing off the anterior chamber angle. Risk factors include narrow anterior chamber angles, for which the contralateral eye may provide diagnostic clues. Emergent treatment (Table 465–6) requires topical administration of a β-adrenergic antagonist, an α-adrenergic agonist, and carbonic anhydrase inhibitors. Systemic pressure-lowering medications include carbonic anhydrase inhibitors, glycerol, isosorbide, and mannitol. Some ophthalmologists advocate anterior chamber paracentesis (aqueous tap). Definitive treatment requires peripheral iridotomy, usually performed with a laser after the initial crisis is resolved. The contralateral eye is treated prophylactically on an elective basis. Chronic angle closure may result from prolonged intraocular inflammation and secondary fibrosis of the anterior chamber angle.

Secondary glaucomas arise in the setting of mature cataract, intraocular inflammation, or gross anatomic distortion. Inflammatory debris may clog the trabecular meshwork in uveitis. Angle recession

---

Table 465–6 • MEDICAL TREATMENT OF ACUTE ANGLE-CLOSURE GLAUCOMA

1. Systemic
   a. Acetazolamide, 500 mg orally in one dose
   b. Isosorbide, 50–100 g orally in one dose, *or* mannitol, 1–2 g/kg intravenously over 1 hour
2. Topical (administered at 5-minute intervals)
   β-blocker (e.g., timolol 0.5%) one drop, repeat every 15 minutes × 4
   Pilocarpine* 1–2%, one drop, repeat every 15 minutes × 4
3. Place patient in supine position
4. Refer to ophthalmologist
5. Definitive treatment requires peripheral iridotomy

*Not given to aphakic or pseudophakic patients.

glaucoma may follow blunt trauma up to several years after the inciting event. Congenital glaucoma may be primary or may result from malformation such as aniridia causing mechanical dysfunction of the trabecular meshwork. Retinal ischemia from diabetic retinopathy or vascular occlusion may cause neovascularization of the anterior chamber angle, leading to neovascular glaucoma. Treatment requires panretinal laser photocoagulation.

Age-related macular degeneration (ARMD) is an idiopathic atrophy of the photoreceptors and retinal pigmented epithelium. Many of the pathologic changes may be seen without visual loss. In this case, the term *age-related maculopathy* is used. Because these findings do not necessarily portend an ominous progression, "macular degeneration" should be reserved for individuals with visual loss. Amsler grid home monitoring is advised to detect acute visual field loss and metamorphopsia, which is focal image distortion often caused by focal retinal elevation.

Nonexudative ("dry") macular degeneration manifests as painless, progressive loss of central vision (Fig. 465–11). Pigmentary mottling is seen in the macular area of the fundus, and drusen are evident. Drusen are lipofuscin deposits beneath the retinal pigmented epithelium basement membrane. Drusen may be discrete (hard), indistinct (soft), or confluent. Focal retinal pigmented epithelium detachment is common. There is no known treatment for nonexudative ARMD. Risk factors include smoking, hypertension, and hypercholesterolemia. Some believe that ultraviolet exposure is an additional risk factor. Low vision aids may be extremely useful. The Age-Related Eye Disease Study (AREDS) demonstrated the efficacy of vitamin supplementation in retarding progression of moderate ARMD to severe ARMD. Vitamins C and E, β-carotene, zinc, and copper were shown to be effective in large doses specified in the study protocol, leading to AREDS-complaint formulations now marketed by several companies. β-Carotene of this quantity is not recommended for cigarette smokers. ■

Choroidal neovascularization is the main complication of ARMD (Fig. 465–12). Breaks in Bruch's membrane permit the choriocapillaris access to the subretinal space. Submacular hemorrhage is common in these cases. Approximately 10% of these proliferative lesions may be treated prophylactically with photocoagulation to decrease the likelihood of severe visual loss, and surgical excision of subretinal membranes may be indicated in even fewer cases. Photodynamic therapy, however, is applicable in 60 to 70% of cases of choroidal neovascularization that is not amenable to thermal photocoagulation because of its location or character. Photodynamic therapy involves the use of intravascular light sensitizers, such as verteporfin, that permit

selective coagulation of choroidal vessels without damaging the overlying retina. Antiangiogenic medications are in clinical trials.

Retinal detachment, or separation of the neurosensory retina from the retinal pigmented epithelium, may be classified as tractional, exudative, or rhegmatogenous. Tractional retinal detachments are most commonly associated with severe, proliferative diabetic retinopathy or follow nondiabetic vitreous hemorrhage. Tractional membranes form from organized hemorrhage and drag the retina as they contract. Exudative elevations are seen with malignant hypertension, posterior inflammation, or choroidal disease. Serous fluid accumulates in the subretinal space and produces a smooth, domed, dependent detachment. Rhegmatogenous retinal detachment results from a break in the retina secondary to intraocular involutional changes or trauma.

Rhegmatogenous detachments are by far the most common among healthy individuals. Symptoms include acute decrease in acuity, photopsia (flashing lights), and floaters. There may be associated vitreous hemorrhage, and more than 90% of cases demonstrate red blood cells in the vitreous (Shafer's sign). Retinal breaks may occur from trauma, posterior vitreous detachment, or retinal atrophy. The vitreous gradually liquefies (syneresis) in middle-aged to elderly individuals and remains firmly adherent to the retina anteriorly. Vitreous traction can produce a tear that allows liquefied vitreous to access the subretinal space. Trauma can produce a similar scenario in younger individuals. Approximately 25% of rhegmatogenous retinal detachments are found in patients with lattice degeneration of the retina, which is present in 10% of adults. Focal vitreous liquefaction occurs over the lattice lesions, whereas the vitreous is firmly attached at the lesion's perimeter. Atrophic retinal holes can also lead to rhegmatogenous detachment.

Not all rhegmatogenous retinal detachments require immediate intervention. Acute, symptomatic cases must be repaired, although the timing of surgery depends on the threat or presence of macular involvement and the condition of the eye. Patients with vitreous hemorrhage should adhere to strict bed rest with the head elevated to optimize visualization of the fundus. Asymptomatic or chronic detachments may be observed in some cases. Surgical treatment requires identification and closure of the break(s), usually through scleral buckling procedures, with or without vitrectomy, and laser photocoagulation to induce a chorioretinal adhesion in the area of the break. Other procedures include retinopexy (intraocular gas injection) and cryotherapy. *Proliferative vitreoretinopathy* is a rare but potentially devastating complication of retinal breaks in which fibrovascular proliferation distorts the retina and intraocular surface.

Actinic exposure of the conjunctiva and cornea may cause degenerative changes. *Pingueculae* are yellowish elevations of the interpalpebral conjunctiva in which the substantia propria demonstrates elastotic degeneration, commonly because ultraviolet radiation-damaged fibroblasts produce altered collagen. Lesions encroaching on the nasal or temporal cornea and demonstrating identical histopathologic findings are known as *pterygia*. Programmed degeneration of the cornea may be seen in *keratoconus*. The central cornea is thinned, resulting in a conical shape. Keratoconus has been associated with atopy and eye rubbing. Patients present with severe astigmatism, usually in the second decade, which may progress until age 30. Rigid contact lenses correct astigmatism in many cases; other patients require penetrating keratoplasty, which has been very effective in these cases. Calcium deposition at the level of the corneal epithelial basement membrane is seen clinically as *band keratopathy*. Usually seen in the elderly or in degenerated eyes, band keratopathy may be amenable to chelation with disodium ethylenediaminetetraacetic acid.

Vascular Conditions

Infarction of the optic nerve head is called anterior *ischemic optic neuropathy*. Many cases relate to vasculitides, whereas others are nonarteritic (idiopathic). Patients present with acute, painless, unilateral loss of vision. Most patients are between 50 and 75 years old. Other risk factors include a small optic disc with very little cupping, hypertension, and diabetes mellitus. Disc edema may be sectoral. Visual field loss is usually altitudinal (superior or inferior hemianopsia), and sectoral atrophy ensues; 25% of patients will suffer contralateral disease. Optic nerve sheath fenestration is ineffective in acute cases but may be useful in rare cases that progress over days.

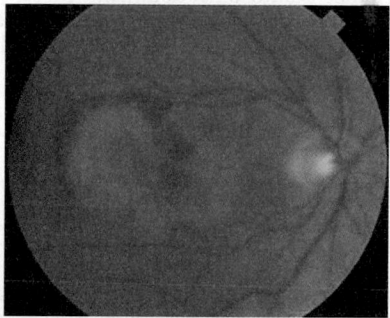

FIGURE 465–11 • Wet, atrophic age-related macular degeneration.

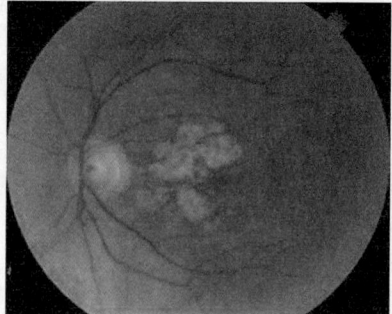

FIGURE 465–12 • Dry, atrophic age-related macular degeneration.

Systemic Effects of Ocular Medications

Many ophthalmic solutions may produce systemic side effects even when administered in small doses (Table 465–7). Manual punctal occlusion after instillation of drops helps to increase ocular penetration and to limit systemic uptake through the nasal mucosa. Because many patients cannot follow this protocol, they can be alternatively instructed to close their eyes for one minute after instilling the drops. β-*Adrenergic antagonists* are among the most commonly prescribed ophthalmic solutions. Patients with asthma may experience bronchospasm or bradycardia; others may experience lethargy or impotence. *Epinephrine* may be administered as the prodrug dipivefrin, which is converted to its active form by corneal enzymes, thereby virtually eliminating any systemic effects. The miotic drug *pilocarpine* is a direct-acting parasympathomimetic that may produce acute, severe headache, especially in younger patients. *Echothiophate* is an acetylcholinesterase inhibitor and may produce cholinergic symptoms, including diarrhea and hypersalivation. Concomitant administration of succinylcholine should be avoided. *Atropine* and other muscarinic antagonists may be used to paralyze the ciliary muscle and dilate the pupil. Systemic effects may include tachycardia and fever. Severe cases may be treated with physostigmine. The α-adrenergic medication *phenylephrine* may produce rapid hypertension when given as a 10% topical solution. *Carbonic anhydrase inhibitors* may be administered topically and do not seem to carry the risk of central nervous system effects and aplastic anemia seen with systemic administration.

COMMON OPHTHALMIC MANIFESTATIONS OF SYSTEMIC DISEASES

Congenital Disorders

Systemic nonhereditary congenital disorders with frequent ocular manifestations include *Sturge-Weber* syndrome and prematurity. Sturge-Weber syndrome (encephalofacial angiomatosis) is defined as diffuse choroidal hemangioma and facial nevus flammeus (port-wine stain). The fundus is diffusely red, the so-called tomato catsup fundus. Children may remain asymptomatic, although retinal detachment is a common complication in adults. Glaucoma is common in children and may require surgical filtration.

Premature and low-birth-weight infants who receive supplemental oxygen therapy are at risk to develop *retinopathy of prematurity* (ROP), an incomplete vascularization of the peripheral retina that may progress to retinal neovascularization, retinal detachment, and blindness in its most severe form. Previously called retrolental fibroplasia, it may produce leukocoria and be confused with retinoblastoma. Normal retinal vascularization begins at 16 weeks' gestation and is completed at 40 weeks' gestation. Although retinopathy of prematurity may rarely occur even in full-term infants, those at greatest risk weigh less than 1250 g at birth or have a gestational age of younger than 28 weeks. The pathophysiology of retinopathy of prematurity has not been fully elucidated.

Initial examination of low-birth-weight infants should be performed before the child is discharged from the neonatal intensive care unit at approximately 4 weeks of age. Subsequent examinations to identify progression depend on the initial findings. The international classification of retinopathy of prematurity reflects the degree and location of fibrous proliferation and provides guidelines for intervention. Approximately 8% of infants who weigh less than 1250 g at birth will require treatment. Of the infants who ultimately require treatment, more than 90% do so between 34 and 42 weeks after conception. Observation may be adequate in many cases in which spontaneous regression is seen. When treatment is required, laser or cryoablation of peripheral retinal tissue is usually adequate. More severe cases require pars plana vitrectomy and scleral buckling.

Genetic Disorders

The list of genetic abnormalities that exhibit ocular signs and symptoms is staggering. *Sickle cell disease* (Chapter 171) is one of the more common causes of retinal vascular occlusive disease. Patients with SC disease are at greater risk for ocular complications than are patients with SS disease. Like arterioles elsewhere in the body, peripheral retinal vessels may become occluded, producing focal infarction. Subsequent neovascularization may result in vitreous hemorrhage and retinal detachment. Neovascular fronds may undergo spontaneous regression or may require photocoagulation. Characteristic comma-shaped conjunctival vessels may be noted on slit lamp evaluation.

Trisomy 21 (Chapter 38) has been associated with strabismus, myopia, keratoconus, and cataract. Optometric and surgical interventions are based on the severity of systemic and ocular abnormalities. *Kearns-Sayre syndrome* (Chapter 73), a mitochondrial cytopathy demonstrating autosomal dominant inheritance, results in progressive external ophthalmoplegia. Diplopia is not common, and there is no known treatment. Either *ocular albinism* or *oculocutaneous albinism* may manifest as foveal hypoplasia, poor vision, and nystagmus. The former results from a decreased number of melanosomes and shows X-linked transmission. The latter results from decreased melanin granules within each melanosome and shows autosomal recessive transmission. Photophobia is common. Low vision aids may be of some help. *Marfan syndrome* (Chapter 276) is associated with many findings common to connective tissue disorders, including high myopia, lenticular subluxation, cataract, and colobomas. Lensectomy may be required. Inheritance is autosomal dominant.

Multisystem congenital hamartomatous diseases have been curiously called *phakomatoses* in the ophthalmic literature. *Von*

Table 465–7 • SIDE EFFECTS OF SOME COMMON EYE MEDICATIONS

CLASS	INDICATION	GENERIC NAME	TRADE NAME	SYSTEMIC SIDE EFFECTS
α₂-agonist	Glaucoma	Apraclonidine Brimonidine	Iopidine Alphagan	Dry mouth, dry nose
β blockers	Glaucoma	Timolol Betaxolol Carteolol Levobunolol Metipranolol	Timoptic, Betimol Betoptic Ocupress Betagan OptiPranolol	Bradycardia, bronchospasm, hypotension, fatigue, depression, impotence, hypertriglyceridemia
Prostaglandin analogues	Glaucoma	Latanaprost, etc.	Xalatan Rescula Travatan	Trichomegaly, iridal hyperpigmentation
Topical NSAIDs	Moderate inflammation, cystoid macular edema	Acular		
Cycloplegics	Amblyopia treatment, iritis	Atropine Homatropine Cyclopentolate	Cyclogel	Dry mouth, tachycardia, somnolence
Antihistamines	Seasonal allergies	Ketotifen Levocabastine Olopatadine	Zaditor Livostin Patanol	Headache
Mast cell stabilizers	Seasonal allergy, giant papillary conjunctivitis	Cromolyn Lodoxamide	Crolom, Opticrom Alomide	Headache
Vasoconstrictors	Hyperemia, allergy	Naphazoline	Vasocon-A Naphcon-A	Rebound hyperemia

Hippel-Lindau disease (Chapter 459), or *angiomatosis retinae,* is transmitted in autosomal dominant fashion. Early photocoagulation of retinal capillary hemangiomas may prevent exudation and retinal detachment. Cerebellar and visceral hemangiomas are common, and patients are at risk for renal cell carcinoma and pheochromocytoma. The ocular hamartomas of *von Recklinghausen's neurofibromatosis* (Chapter 459) include optic nerve glioma (astrocytic hamartoma), iris Lisch nodules, and plexiform neurofibromas of the eyelids. The optic nerve tumors are slowly progressive, producing painless loss of vision and proptosis. Approximately 50% of patients with neurofibromatosis develop optic nerve gliomas; bilateral tumors are pathognomonic for neurofibromatosis type 1. Lisch nodules are not seen in neurofibromatosis type 2. *Tuberous sclerosis* (Chapter 459) is less frequently associated with optic nerve gliomas, but retinal glial hamartomas are seen in combination with angiofibromas of the eyelids. Transmission is autosomal dominant.

Endogenous Infections

Systemic infection may cause uveitis, endophthalmitis, retinitis, or choroiditis. Systemic severity often does not correlate with ocular activity. Ophthalmic manifestations may initiate diagnosis or may occur late in the disease.

Tuberculosis (Chapter 341) involves the uvea in approximately 1% of pulmonary cases. Iridocyclitis and diffuse choroiditis are the most common manifestations. Symptoms include painless progressive visual loss. Small yellow choroidal lesions may be seen, and retinal periphlebitis may occur secondarily. Intermediate- and second-strength purified protein derivative testing may be positive. Clinical response to a 3-week trial course of isoniazid strongly suggests tuberculosis.

Ocular complications of acquired *syphilis* (Chapter 349) occur in approximately 5% of patients with secondary syphilis, although symptoms may occur during any stage of the disease. Nearly any ocular structure may be involved. The more common presentations include anterior uveitis, neuroretinitis, and the syphilitic Argyll Robertson pupil in which miotic pupils react poorly to light but briskly to accommodation. Congenital syphilis produces "salt and pepper" pigmentation of the fundus.

Nerve fiber layer infarcts seen clinically as "cotton wool" spots are the most common ocular manifestation of *AIDS* (Chapter 418). In combination with retinal hemorrhage, these lesions may mimic cytomegalovirus retinitis, another common finding in patients with AIDS. Additional ocular findings in AIDS include opportunistic infections of the retina, choroid, and optic nerve as well as cranial nerve palsies. Kaposi's sarcoma may occur in the lids, orbit, or conjunctiva.

Cytomegalovirus retinitis may appear as subacute unilateral visual loss or vitreous "floaters" in immune-compromised patients. Large areas of hemorrhagic infarction are seen with minimal vitritis (Fig. 465–13). Intravenous ganciclovir or foscarnet and intravitreal ganciclovir are the mainstays of treatment. Even with aggressive treatment, recurrences are seen in up to 50% of cases. Herpes zoster and herpes simplex viruses may produce fulminating necrosis of the retina, *progressive outer retinal necrosis,* in patients with AIDS.

Until recently, ocular *toxoplasmosis* (Chapter 396) was thought to represent reactivation of congenital disease in nearly all cases; however, studies now suggest that many cases of toxoplasmosis retinitis are acquired after birth. Symptoms include reduced vision and floaters. The typical retinal fundus lesion comprises an active yellow satellite adjacent to an old chorioretinal scar with a dense overlying vitritis,

the so-called headlight-in-the-fog. Antibody titers, even in undiluted serum, are significant. Treatment requires combinations of systemic pyrimethamine, clindamycin, sulfonamides, prednisone, and folinic acid. These regimens are moderately efficacious and potentially toxic; treatment is therefore limited to severe intraocular inflammation that threatens the macular area. The toxoplasmosis fundus lesions seen in AIDS patients may differ morphologically from those seen in immunocompetent patients.

Idiopathic Inflammatory and Autoimmune Disorders

Autoimmune diseases may produce incidental ocular findings or may have their greatest effects in ocular tissues. Dysthyroid ophthalmopathy, commonly but erroneously called *Graves' ophthalmopathy* (Chapter 239), may be seen in hyperthyroid, euthyroid, or hypothyroid individuals. The orbital tissues and thyroid gland appear to be common targets of the same autoimmune process. Inflammation of the extraocular muscles and orbital fat causes proptosis, corneal exposure, and limited ocular motility (Fig. 465–14). Optic neuropathy may result from extreme proptosis with stretching of the nerve or from compression at the orbital apex. Lid retraction is common. Patients present with pain, decreased vision, diplopia, and vascular congestion. Active inflammation may be treated with systemic corticosteroids. External-beam irradiation, previously used as an alternative to prednisone, has been shown to be ineffective. Aggressive topical lubrication must be used. Emergent surgical decompression may be required when the optic nerve is threatened, but it may not reduce (and may aggravate) inflammation. Surgical decompression of severe proptosis is usually deferred until inflammation is controlled and the clinical examination is stable for several months. Active inflammation generally subsides after 1 to 12 months. Secondary surgeries to correct chronic exposure, diplopia, and lid malposition may then be considered.

Sarcoidosis (Chapter 91) is a common cause of intraocular inflammation among Americans of African descent, and chronic uveitis is seen in 25% of sarcoid patients. Sarcoid may also involve the optic nerve, cranial nerves, and lacrimal glands. Anterior uveitis is treated topically with prednisolone acetate in decreasing doses, depending on degree of inflammation, and with daily cyclopegics (cyclopentolate 2%, atropine 1%). Posterior uveitis, dacryoadenitis, and neurologic manifestations require systemic corticosteroids.

Uveitis accompanies many autoimmune diseases, and there is often no correlation between ocular and systemic inflammatory activity. *Ankylosing spondylitis* (Chapter 279) causes acute, recurrent anterior uveitis in 25% of patients. Anterior uveitis or conjunctivitis is seen in nearly all patients with *Reiter's syndrome* (Chapter 279). Two to 12% of patients with *inflammatory bowel disease* (Chapter 142) develop anterior uveitis, which is also commonly found in patients with *psoriatic arthritis* but not with psoriasis alone (Chapters 279 and 474). Symptoms include decreased vision and photophobia. Treatment with topical corticosteroids is usually sufficient to control the ocular disease.

Chronic anterior uveitis may severely reduce vision in patients with *juvenile rheumatoid arthritis* (Chapter 278). The ocular disease

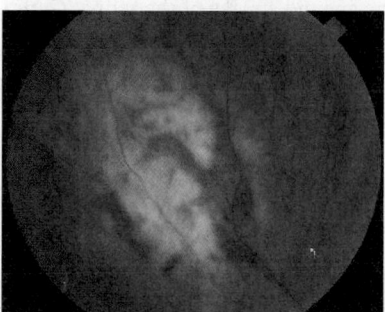

FIGURE 465–13 • Cytomegalovirus retinitis.

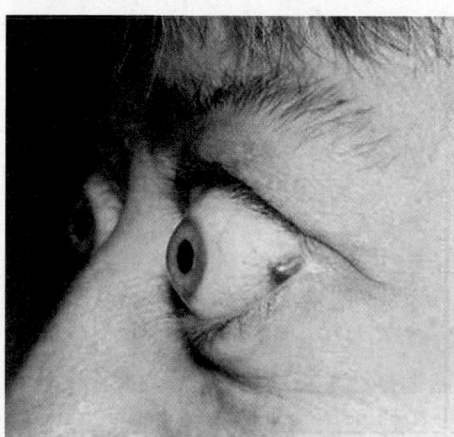

FIGURE 465–14 • Graves' ophthalmopathy with characteristic exophthalmos and eyelid retraction.

Eye, Ear, Nose, and Throat Diseases

is insidious and devastating; routine examinations are critical. Pauciarticular juvenile rheumatoid arthritis carries an 80 to 90% risk of uveitis, whereas uveitis is rarely seen in patients with systemic onset. Girls have a fourfold higher risk of uveitic involvement compared with boys. Patients are usually free of symptoms on diagnosis and must be carefully screened for eye involvement. Cataract is the rule, resulting from either inflammation or corticosteroid treatment. Early intervention with topical corticosteroids may delay progression, and oral or intravenous corticosteroids may be required in advanced cases. Megadose pulsed intravenous corticosteroids may be equally efficacious while minimizing systemic side effects.

Vogt-Koyanagi-Harada syndrome (uveomeningeal syndrome) may produce anterior or posterior uveitis in darkly pigmented individuals. Decreased vision is the primary ocular symptom. Periocular vitiligo and whitening of the lashes (poliosis) may be seen. Chorioretinitis may lead to exudative retinal detachment. Early treatment with topical or systemic corticosteroids may delay or prevent severe visual loss.

Stevens-Johnson syndrome, an idiosyncratic vesicular mucocutaneous eruption (Chapter 476), may be triggered by medications or infectious agents. Adolescents are most frequently affected. Conjunctival involvement may lead to cicatrization and obliteration of the fornices with secondary entropion, loss of mucus-producing goblet cells, and corneal opacification. Aggressive lubrication in the acute stage may mitigate these sequelae. Reconstructive grafting with mucous membranes and amniotic membranes may be helpful. Penetrating keratoplasty alone is rarely successful.

Metabolic Diseases

Systemic metabolic diseases demonstrate protean ocular findings. Select metabolic diseases may be evident only in the eye. In either case, ocular findings can assist in diagnosis and ongoing evaluation.

Diabetic retinopathy (Chapter 242) is a leading cause of blindness in the United States. Selective loss of pericytes in the retinal capillaries leads to microaneurysm formation, exudation, capillary obliteration, and neovascularization. Twenty years after diagnosis, virtually all patients with juvenile-onset diabetes and two thirds of those with adult-onset diabetes have some degree of retinal involvement. Onset and progression of retinal findings are delayed in patients with tight glycemic control, as demonstrated by the Diabetes Control and Complications Trial.[2]

Diabetic retinopathy has been classified as nonproliferative (Fig. 465–15) or proliferative (Fig. 465–16). Nonproliferative disease, also called background diabetic retinopathy, manifests as microaneurysms, intraretinal hemorrhages, subretinal exudation, venous beading, and intraretinal vascular abnormalities. Macular edema, the most frequent cause of visual loss, is common in this stage. Macular edema meeting the criteria of the Early Treatment Diabetic Retinopathy Study is treated with focal laser photocoagulation. This study concluded that focal laser photocoagulation reduced the incidence of moderate visual loss by 50% in patients who demonstrated clinically significant macular edema, defined as (1) retinal thickening within 500 μm of the fovea, (2) subretinal exudates within 500 μm of the fovea with adjacent retinal thickening, or (3) an area of retinal thickening of greater than 1 disc diameter, any part of which lies within 1 disc diameter of the fovea.[3]

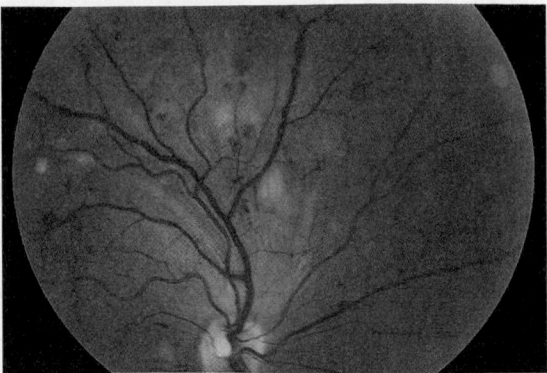

FIGURE 465–16 • Severe nonproliferative diabetic retinopathy with cotton wool spots, intraretinal microvascular abnormalities, and venous bleeding. (From Yanoff M, Duker JS: Ophthalmology. London, CV Mosby, 1999, with permission.)

Retinal ischemia is thought to be the primary stimulus to proliferative diabetic retinopathy in which extraretinal fibrovascular tissue grows along the posterior vitreous scaffold. Neovascularization at the optic disc or elsewhere may lead to vitreous hemorrhage and acute loss of vision. Fibrous organization produces tractional detachment of the retina. Proliferative disease meeting the criteria set forth in the Diabetic Retinopathy Study is treated with panretinal laser photocoagulation. This multicenter, randomized study determined that panretinal laser photocoagulation reduced the incidence of severe visual loss from 16 to 6% in patients at high risk for vitreous hemorrhage.[4] These patients were defined by (1) neovascularization of greater than one third of the optic nerve head, (2) neovascularization elsewhere associated with vitreous hemorrhage, (3) any degree of neovascularization of the disc associated with vitreous hemorrhage, or (4) any two of the following: retinal hemorrhages in four quadrants, venous beading in two quadrants, or intraretinal microvascular anomalies in one quadrant. Advanced cases may require pars plana vitrectomy with peeling of preretinal fibrovascular membranes.

Diabetics are at increased risk to develop painless, isolated cranial nerve palsies, most frequently involving cranial nerves III or VI and generally resolving in 6 to 8 weeks. Multiple cranial nerve palsies should prompt thorough and rapid investigation including magnetic resonance imaging of the brain with careful attention to the brainstem and cavernous sinus. In the setting of acute hyperglycemia, accumulation of lenticular sorbitol may lead to lenticular swelling. Secondary refractive errors may linger for 6 to 8 weeks after glycemic control is realized; spectacle correction may change dramatically over this period, and prescription should be delayed until the examination stabilizes.

Accumulation of copper in the posterior cornea may aid in the diagnosis of *Wilson's hepatolenticular degeneration* (Chapter 224), although its appearance usually lags neurologic symptoms. This characteristic Kayser-Fleischer ring fades after treatment. The so-called sunflower cataract is seen less frequently in such cases.

Corneal clouding and retinal degeneration are seen to varying degrees in specific mucopolysaccharidoses and are absent in others. *Tay-Sachs* and *Niemann-Pick* (Chapter 222) diseases are known for the appearance of a foveal cherry-red spot owing to ganglioside accumulation within perifoveal ganglion cells, which form a layer that is absent over the fovea and thickest in the adjacent macula. Pseudoxanthoma elasticum (Chapter 276) is often associated with its characteristic angioid streaks of the retina. *Gyrate atrophy* of the retina and choroid occurs in the presence of increased serum ornithine caused by ornithine aminotransferase deficiency. Progressive geographic atrophy eventually involves the macula. Corneal, conjunctival, and retinal crystalline deposits may be seen in *cystinosis*. Vision is usually unaffected, but corneal involvement may cause photophobia (pain on exposure to light). Conjunctivitis, iritis, and scleritis experienced during attacks of gout (Chapter 288) usually abate with systemic control.

Neoplastic Diseases

Metastatic ocular disease and systemic neoplastic proliferations involving the eye are far more common than primary ocular

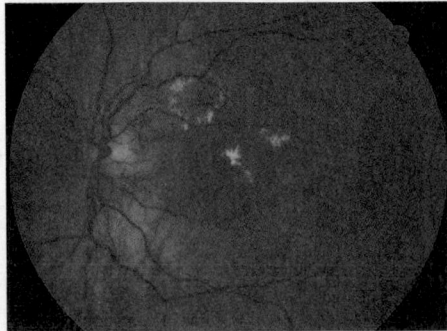

FIGURE 465–15 • Diabetic retinopathy. Fundus photograph of background (nonproliferative) diabetic retinopathy demonstrates scattered dot and blot intraretinal hemorrhages and retinal exudates. A circinate exudate is seen surrounding a microaneurysm.

malignancy. Pediatric metastases tend to involve the orbit, whereas the vascular choroid is usually affected in adults. Choroidal metastases are seen most commonly with adenocarcinoma of the breast in women (Chapter 204); primary lung tumors (Chapter 198) are the leading cause in men. Together, breast and lung carcinoma account for 70% of ocular metastases. Left eye involvement surpasses right eye involvement by a ratio of 3:2 because of the direct connection between the aorta and the left common carotid artery. Decreased visual acuity is the leading symptom. In the case of breast carcinoma, nearly 70% of patients already carry the diagnosis when choroidal disease is detected. In contrast, choroidal metastases from lung disease may be the initial finding in 90% of cases. Disfiguring surgery such as enucleation or orbital exenteration should be limited to patients with severe pain.

Ocular findings in *multiple myeloma* (Chapter 196) include uveal protein-filled cysts and retinal hemorrhages second to hyperviscosity. Orbital involvement is rare, but periocular osteolytic lesions may be seen. Patients should undergo ophthalmic examination at the time of diagnosis. External-beam radiation may be dramatically effective. Although B-cell *lymphoma* (Chapter 195) of the large cell variety is the most common lymphoma to involve the eye, it involves the eye with much less frequency than does leukemia. *Leukemic* ocular disease (Chapters 192 and 193) may masquerade as a chronic, unilateral "uveitis" or may cause white-centered retinal hemorrhages similar to the Roth spots (Fig. 465–17) seen in infectious endocarditis (Chapter 310). Focal irradiation may augment systemic treatment with either entity.

Orbital and conjunctival lymphomas are usually the small B-cell MALT-type variety. Approximately 50% of cases ultimately include systemic disease. Systemic evaluation should include chest, abdominal, and pelvic magnetic resonance imaging as well as serum protein electrophoresis and possibly bone marrow biopsy. External-beam radiation is used to treat isolated periocular disease, whereas systemic chemotherapy is required for systemic involvement.

Vascular Diseases

Because the retinal vasculature is uniquely accessible for direct visual inspection, nearly all systemic vascular diseases manifest ocular changes. Chronic *hypertension* (Chapter 63) produces characteristic retinal vascular findings that can be used to identify and assess progression of the disease. Arterial narrowing, nicking at arteriovenous crossings, nerve fiber layer infarcts, and intraretinal hemorrhages characterize hypertension. Arteriolar sclerosis heightens the arterial light reflexes. Moderately sclerosed arterioles demonstrate "copper wiring," whereas severely sclerosed vessels show "silver wiring." Acute hypertension may produce optic nerve edema (Fig. 465–18) and serous retinal detachments that shift dramatically when the patient changes position. These detachments usually resolve without significant sequelae if blood pressure is brought under control.

Hypertension may be implicated in retinal vascular occlusions. *Branch retinal vein occlusion* may cause macular edema and decreased visual acuity or may be asymptomatic. Occlusion typically occurs at an arteriovenous crossing where a common adventitia binds the vessels together and causes compression of the venule wall by the sclerotic arteriole. Sectoral hemorrhages are seen. Regional photocoagulation

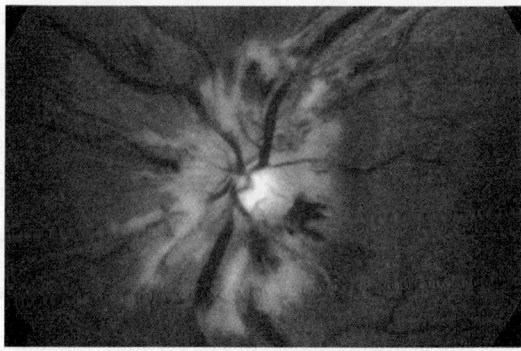

FIGURE 465–18 • Papilledema in a young person. Note disk swelling, hemorrhages, and exudates, with preservation of the physiologic cup.

may help to resolve macular edema but rarely improves functional outcome and is therefore not frequently advised. Neovascularization is a rare complication, and most eyes maintain a favorable prognosis. *Central retinal vein occlusion* (Fig. 465–19) is a more severe disease entity. Ischemic and nonischemic varieties are recognized and may be most accurately differentiated by electroretinogram. The characteristic fundus appearance includes dilated tortuous vessels in all quadrants, as well as variable degrees of retinal hemorrhage. Nonischemic occlusion may result from hyperviscosity, whereas ischemic occlusion is thought to represent arteriolar impingement on the central retinal vein at the level of the lamina cribrosa. Neovascularization of the iris or retina, occurring in up to 52% of cases, usually occurs 3 months after the initial insult. Panretinal photocoagulation should be deferred until neovascularization is detected.

In contrast to venous occlusive disease, *central retinal artery occlusion* (Fig. 465–20) is not generally associated with systemic hypertension. Emboli result most commonly from carotid stenosis (Chapter 440), but endocarditis and cardiac thromboemboli are other potential sources. Unilateral sudden loss of vision is typical. Amaurosis fugax, or transient unilateral visual loss, may precede frank occlusion and warrants urgent carotid evaluation. Fundus examination

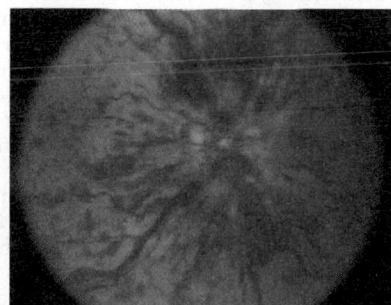

FIGURE 465–19 • Central retinal vein occlusion.

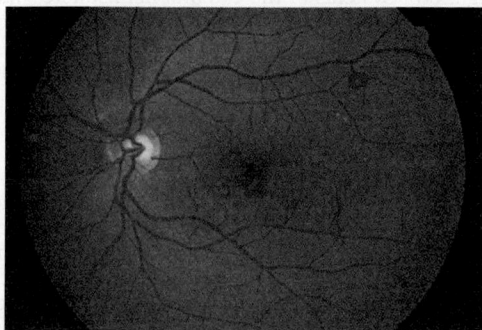

FIGURE 465–17 • Roth's spots. Multiple white centered hemorrhages in a man with recurrent subacute bacterial endocarditis. White centered hemorrhages are also seen with leukemia and diabetes. The small white scars are probably the residua of previous episodes.

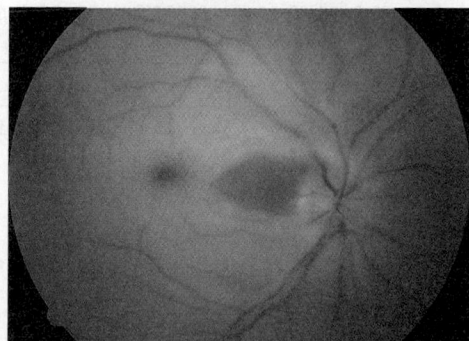

FIGURE 465–20 • Central retinal artery occlusion. Fundus photograph shows diffuse retinal edema. The heavily pigmented fovea with its uniquely thin inner retina produces a "cherry red spot" against the dusky macula. A small area of retina adjacent to the optic disk is spared, owing to the presence of a cilioretinal artery.

reveals a characteristic "cherry-red spot" that reflects diffuse opacification of the infarcting macula contrasted to the hyperpigmented fovea. A relative afferent pupillary defect is present. An acute reduction in intraocular pressure by means of ocular massage, anterior chamber paracentesis, or systemic carbonic anhydrase inhibitors may dislodge a proximal embolus, allow reperfusion of the fovea, and return some useful vision if performed within several hours of onset. *Branch retinal artery occlusion* may go unnoticed by the patient despite a permanent visual *scotoma* (focal visual field defect).

Temporal arteritis (Chapter 285) is an important cause of visual loss among the elderly. Symptoms include sudden, unilateral loss of vision. Headache, jaw claudication, scalp tenderness, weight loss, and malaise are common. Visual loss may result from arteritis or associated central retinal artery occlusion. The erythrocyte sedimentation rate (ESR) is elevated. Systemic corticosteroids (prednisone, 1 to 2 mg/kg/day) should be initiated as soon as the diagnosis is suspected, and temporal artery biopsy should be performed within 7 days after beginning treatment. Corticosteroids are tapered slowly over months, and many patients require perpetual low-dose corticosteroid treatment as guided by following the ESR. If untreated, approximately 65% of patients lose vision in the contralateral eye.

Orbital involvement in *Wegener's granulomatosis* (Chapter 284) usually indicates extension from nasal or sinus mucosa and may produce proptosis. Ocular vasculitis may cause inflammation in any of the ocular tissues. Retinal involvement in *polyarteritis nodosa* (Chapter 284) is usually limited to the small vessels, although central retinal artery occlusion can occur. Cranial nerve palsies are not uncommon. The occlusive vasculitis of *Behçet's disease* (Chapter 291) produces retinal vasculitis and iridocyclitis in patients aged 20 to 40 years. Hypopyon (layering of leukocytes within the anterior chamber) can be seen in one third of cases. Topical corticosteroids are used to treat anterior disease, whereas systemic corticosteroids and cytotoxic agents may be required for posterior disease.

Ocular Effects of Systemic Medications (Table 465–8)

Thousands of systemic medications have been implicated in reports of ocular side effects. Therefore, patients taking systemic medications often require periodic surveillance to identify ocular toxicity. A few of the more common associations are described here.

Chloroquine and *hydroxychloroquine* may cause decreased color vision and visual field defects at high dose. Chloroquine toxicity is thought to occur after a cumulative dose of 300 g, whereas hydroxychloroquine may cause symptoms after long-term maintenance of 750 mg/day. The fundus may show a typical bull's eye pattern, and corneal whorls may be seen. Symptoms are not reversible and may progress after drug cessation. Annual fundus examination with automated visual field test is indicated.

Pigmentary maculopathy may occur as blurred vision in patients taking *thioridazine* or *chlorpromazine*. Approximately 800 mg/day of the former or 1200 mg/day of the latter is believed sufficient to cause toxicity. Patients should be examined every 6 months.

Any of the commonly used antituberculous medications may cause optic neuropathy, although *ethambutol* carries the greatest risk.

Table 465–8 • SYSTEMIC MEDICATIONS WITH OCULAR EFFECTS

AGENT	EFFECT
Chloroquine	Dyschromatopsia, visual field defects
Hydroxychloroquine	Dyschromatopsia, visual field defects
Thioridazine	Blurred vision
Chlorpromazine	Blurred vision
Digoxin	Yellow vision
Ethambutol	Optic neuritis
Amiodarone	Corneal whorls, pigmentary retinopathy
Corticosteroids	Glaucoma, cataract
Plaquenil	Pigmentary maculopathy
Tamoxifen	Retinopathy
Neuroleptics	Nystagmus
Compazine	Oculogyric crisis
Vitamin A	Pseudotumor cerebri
5-Fluorouracil	Canalicular stenosis (tearing)
Isotretinoin	Severe dry eye (long-term effect)

Pupillary response, color vision, acuity, and visual fields are the clinical parameters used to assess optic nerve function.

Cornea verticillata may be seen in patients taking *amiodarone* due to lysosomal accumulations within the epithelial basement membrane. *Fabry's disease* produces similar changes, as can other medications. Corneal whorls are usually reversible when caused by drug toxicity, and they rarely interfere with vision.

Systemic *corticosteroids* carry the same ocular side effects as do topical corticosteroids, including glaucoma and posterior subcapsular cataract.

1. Age-Related Eye Disease Study Research Group: A randomized, placebo-controlled, clinical trial of high-dose supplementation with vitamins C and E, beta carotene, and zinc for age-related macular degeneration and vision loss: AREDS report no. 8. Arch Ophthalmol 2001;119:1417–1436.
2. Diabetes Control and Complications Trial Research Group: Progression of retinopathy with intensive versus conventional treatment in the Diabetes Control and Complications Trial. Ophthalmology 1995;102:647–661.
3. Early Treatment Diabetic Retinopathy Study Research Group: Early photocoagulation for diabetic retinopathy. ETDRS report #9. Ophthalmology 1991;98:766–785.
4. The Diabetic Retinopathy Study Research Group: Photocoagulation treatment of proliferative diabetic retinopathy: Clinical application of Diabetic Retinopathy Study (DRS) findings, DRS report number 8. Ophthalmology 1981;88:583–600.

SUGGESTED READINGS

Albert DM, Jakobiec JA (eds): Principles and Practice of Ophthalmology, 2nd ed. Philadelphia, WB Saunders, 2000. *A multi-volume text.*

Eid TM, Spaeth GL, Bitterman A, et al: Rate and amount of visual loss in 102 patients with open-angle glaucoma followed up for at least 15 years. Ophthalmology 2003;110:900–907. *Approximately 20% of eyes with open-angle glaucoma remained stable for about 20 years, 43% deteriorated one of five stages, and 9% deteriorated three of five stages.*

Fraunfelder FT, Fraunfelder FW: Drug-Induced Ocular Side Effects, 5th ed. Boston, Butterworth Heinemann, 2001. *Important reminder of how often eye symptoms are caused by medications.*

Kaiser PK, Friedman N, Pineda R (eds): The Massachusetts Eye and Ear Infirmary Illustrated Manual of Ophthalmology, 2nd ed. Philadelphia, WB Saunders, 2003.

Owsley C, McGwin G Jr, Sloane M, et al: Impact of cataract surgery on motor vehicle crash involvement by older adults. JAMA 2002;288:841–849. *Cataract surgery may reduce crashes among elderly drivers.*

Satilmis M, Orgul S, Doubler B, et al: Rate of progression of glaucoma corrrelates with retrobulbar circulation and intraocular pressure. Am J Ophthalmol 2003;135:664–669. *The progression of glaucomatous visual field damage correlates with retrobulbar hemodynamic variables.*

466 NEURO-OPHTHALMOLOGY

Robert W. Baloh

The mechanistic understanding of vision impairment along with disturbances of pupillary and oculomotor control lies close to the heart of diagnosing neurologic disorders.

VISION

One of the most difficult diagnostic problems is vision loss that cannot be explained by obvious abnormalities of the eye. To evaluate such a patient properly the examining physician must be familiar with the anatomy and physiology of the afferent visual system. The afferent visual pathways cross the major ascending sensory and descending motor systems of the cerebral hemispheres and in their anterior portion are intimately related to the vascular and bony structures at the base of the brain. Not surprisingly, localization of lesions within the afferent visual pathways has great localizing value in neurologic diagnosis.

Anatomy of the Visual Pathways

Light entering the eye falls on the retinal rods and cones, which transduce the stimulus into neural impulses to be transmitted to the brain. The distribution of visual function across the retina takes a pattern of concentric zones increasing in sensitivity toward the center, the fovea. The fovea consists of a "rod-free" central grouping of approximately 100,000 slender cones. The ganglion cells subserving these cones send their axons directly to the temporal aspect of the optic disk, forming the papillomacular bundle. Axons originating from ganglion cells in the temporal retina must curve above and below the papillomacular bundle, forming dense arcuate bands.

The arteries supplying the optic nerve and retina derive from branches of the ophthalmic artery. The central retinal artery approaches the eye along each optic nerve and pierces the inferior aspect of the dural sheath about 1 cm behind the globe to enter the center of the nerve. The artery emerges in the fundus at the center of the nerve head, from which it nourishes the inner two thirds of the retina by superior and inferior branches. Anastomotic branches derived from the choroidal and posterior ciliary arteries, the ciliary system, supply the choroid, optic nerve head, and the outer retinal layers, including the photoreceptors. In about 10% of the population, the macula is supplied by a retinociliary artery, a branch of the ciliary system. Venous drainage from the retina and nerve head flows primarily via the central retinal vein, whose course of exit from the eye parallels that of the entry of the artery.

What each eye "sees" is termed its *visual field* (Fig. 466–1). The nasal side of the left retina and the temporal side of the right see the left side of the world, and the upper half of each retina sees the lower half of the world. Behind the eyes the optic nerves pass through the optic canal to form the optic chiasm. In the chiasm, nerves from the nasal half of each retina decussate and join the fibers from the temporal half of the contralateral retina. From the chiasm, the optic tracts pass around the cerebral peduncles to reach the lateral geniculate ganglia. The orientation of the visual field is rotated 90 degrees in the lateral geniculate such that images from the inferior visual field project to the medial half, whereas images from the superior visual field project to the lateral half. The geniculocalcarine radiation initially fans out into superolateral and inferolateral projections, the latter passing around the lateral ventricle and for a short distance into the temporal lobe (Meyer's loop) before turning posteriorly to reach the striate cortex of the occipital lobe. In the occipital lobe, the striate cortex (Area 17) lies along the superior and inferior bands of the calcarine fissure, with macular fibers projecting most posteriorly to the occipital pole and more peripheral retinal projections lying more anteriorly.

Localization of Lesions within Visual Pathways

Monocular vision loss is due to a lesion of one eye or optic nerve. Binocular visual loss, on the other hand, can result from disease located anywhere in the visual pathways from the corneas to the occipital poles. Lesions involving the optic chiasm produce nonhomonymous visual abnormalities (e.g., the bitemporal hemianopia illustrated by Lesion 3 in Figure 466–1). Optic tract abnormalities are comparatively rare but produce characteristic visual changes. The fibers serving identical points in the homonymous half fields do not fully commingle in the optic tract, so lesions damaging this structure produce incongruous homonymous hemianopia. Lesions of the geniculate nuclei, optic radiations, or visual cortex produce congruent hemianopic field defects that may go unrecognized unless the hemianopia intrudes on macular vision. Postgeniculate visual loss can be differentiated from pregeniculate visual loss by (1) a normal funduscopic appearance, (2) intact pupillary light reactions, and (3) appropriate lesions on brain imaging.

Examination of the Afferent Visual System

Visual function is most commonly assessed by "best corrected visual acuity" (Chapter 465). If the visual acuity is not normal, then it must be determined whether acuity can be improved with lenses or at least with the use of a pinhole. The normal reference is a recognition of letters at an idealized 20 feet, and acuity charts are designed with even larger letters that normally are recognized at proportionally greater distances. Thus, if one reads letters at 20 feet no better than those normally perceived at 40 feet, vision is recorded as 20/40. Small visual charts that are easily carried in the physician's case permit quick and fairly accurate bedside appraisals of acuity.

Visual fields can be tested at the bedside by confrontation, and rough estimates of their integrity can be made even in patients with reduced alertness. The fields should be tested individually for each eye because the pattern of visual field defects can provide important localizing information. A quick screen of the visual fields can be made by having the patient fixate on the examiner's nose and identify the number of fingers flashed in each of the four visual field quadrants. With practice and a cooperative subject, accurate confrontation fields can be obtained that outline even scotomas. Ophthalmoscopic examination permits direct visualization of the retina and optic disc. Corneal, lenticular, or vitreous opacities severe enough to produce visual symptoms almost always can be detected with the ophthalmoscope.

Common Causes of Visual Loss

EYE (Chapter 465). The cause of monocular vision loss due to ocular and retinal lesions often can be detected with ophthalmoscopic examination or with measurement of intraocular pressure. *Glaucoma* caused by impaired absorption of the aqueous humor results in a high intraocular pressure that usually produces gradual loss of peripheral vision, "halos" seen around lights, and, occasionally, pain and redness in the affected eye. Diagnosis comes from the tonometric measurement of a high intraocular pressure and may be suspected by palpating an abnormally firm globe and observing a deep, pale optic cup and attenuated blood vessels. *Retinal tears* and *detachments* give rise to unilateral distortions of the visual image seen as sudden angulations or curves of objects containing straight lines (metamorphopsia). *Hemorrhages* into the vitreous humor, or *infections* or *inflammatory lesions* of the retina can produce scotomas that resemble those resulting from primary disease of the central visual pathway.

Binocular vision loss due to retinal disease in younger subjects is often due to *heredodegenerative conditions*. Vascular diseases, diabetes, and age-related macular degeneration are causes in older patients. In

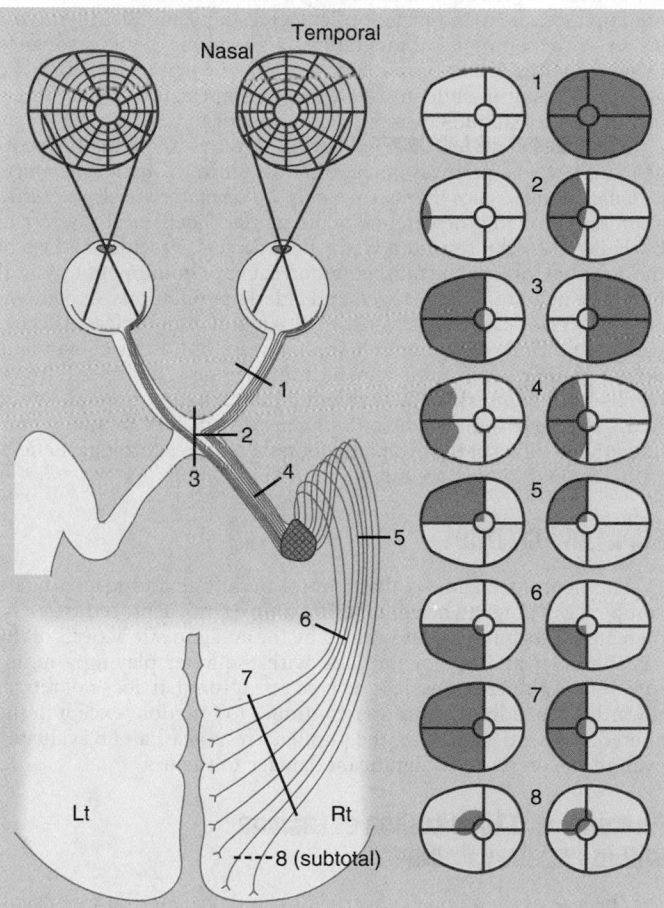

FIGURE 466–1 • Visual fields that accompany damage to the visual pathways. *1,* Optic nerve: unilateral amaurosis. *2,* Lateral optic chiasm: grossly incongruous, incomplete (contralateral) homonymous hemianopia. *3,* Central optic chiasm: bitemporal hemianopia. *4,* Optic tract: incongruous, incomplete homonymous hemianopia. *5,* Temporal (Meyer's) loop of optic radiation: congruous partial or complete (contralateral) homonymous superior quadrantanopia. *6,* Parietal (superior) projection of the optic radiation: congruous partial or complete homonymous inferior quadrantanopia. *7,* Complete parieto-occipital interruption of optic radiation: complete congruous homonymous hemianopia with psychophysical shift of foveal point often sparing central vision, giving "macular sparing." *8,* Incomplete damage to visual cortex: congruous homonymous scotomas, usually encroaching at least acutely on central vision.

most *pigmentary retinal degenerations,* visual loss begins peripherally and slowly proceeds centrally. By contrast, *macular degenerations* impair central vision early in their course. Most of the retinal degenerations produce characteristic and recognizable ophthalmoscopic appearances.

OPTIC NERVE. Acute or subacute monocular vision loss due to optic nerve disease is most commonly produced by demyelinating disorders, vascular obstruction, or neoplasm. Demyelinating disease of the nerve head (*optic neuritis* or *papillitis*) produces disc edema along with loss of central vision in the affected eye only; subjectively unrecognized scotomas sometimes may be found in the other eye. Demyelination in the optic nerve behind where the retinal vein emerges (*retrobulbar neuritis*) initially leaves a normal-looking disc but a central or paracentral scotoma. With chronic demyelinating disorders, the optic disc becomes pale and atrophic. More than 50% of patients who initially present with optic neuritis go on to develop typical symptoms and signs of multiple sclerosis. Intraocular arterial occlusion may produce either central visual loss or an altitudinal field defect (*ischemic optic neuropathy*). The common causes of transient monocular vision loss and their differential features are listed in Table 466–1. *Tumors* invading the optic nerve or space-occupying lesions compressing it anywhere between the orbit and the chiasm cause gradually decreasing central vision or a sector defect of the peripheral visual field. With such chronic lesions, the affected optic nerve becomes visibly atrophic.

Acute binocular vision loss due to bilateral optic nerve disease is most often caused by demyelinating disease or by toxic or nutritional factors. In younger persons and those lacking a clear history of toxic exposures, demyelinating lesions overwhelmingly predominate. Symptoms are of abrupt or subacute onset with visual blurring, which may progress rapidly to blindness within hours or days. There may be pain about the eyes, particularly with movement.

Papilledema is disc edema due to increased intracranial pressure. Vision is normal except under one of two circumstances: (1) acute transient episodes of amaurosis lasting a few seconds and attributable to acute increases in intracranial pressure (plateau waves) and (2) progressive loss of peripheral vision with long-standing, severe papilledema, owing to compression of the optic nerve head. Table 466–2 gives the main differential points between papilledema and optic neuritis. Subacute or chronic binocular vision loss due to optic nerve disease can result from *toxic* and *nutritional* causes or *inherited optic atrophies.* The latter sometimes accompany spinocerebellar degeneration but may selectively affect the optic nerve. With either cause, visual loss is painless and primarily affects central vision; ophthalmoscopy shows optic atrophy.

Table 466–1 • COMMON CAUSES OF TRANSIENT MONOCULAR VISION LOSS

CATEGORY/ (TYPICAL DURATION)	CAUSES	DIFFERENTIAL FEATURES
Thromboembolism (1–5 min)	Atherosclerosis	Other atherosclerotic vascular disease, associated crossed hemiparesis, angiography (carotid atheromata)
	Cardiac	Valvular disease, mural thrombi, atrial fibrillation recent myocardial infarction
	Blood dyscrasia	Blood tests + for sickle cell anemia, macroglobulinemia, multiple myeloma, polycythemia, etc.
Vasospasm (5–30 min)	Migraine	Ipsilateral headache, other classic aura, family history
Vascular compression (few sec)	Increased intracranial pressure	Precipitated by position change, Valsalva maneuver, or pressure waves
	Tumor	Associated slowly progressive monocular visual loss
Vasculitis (1–5 min)	Temporal arteritis	Associated headache, polymyalgia rheumatica, palpable temporal artery, elevated sedimentation rate

Table 466–2 • DIFFERENTIATION OF OPTIC NEURITIS FROM PAPILLEDEMA

	OPTIC NEURITIS	PAPILLEDEMA
Central-cecocentral vision loss	Present	Absent
Distribution	Usually unilateral	Usually bilateral
Ocular pain on movement	Present	Absent
Direct light reflex	±Reduced	Intact
CT and MRI scan of head	White matter plaques	Tumor, venous occlusion, etc.
Visual evoked responses	Abnormal	Normal
Lumbar puncture pressure	Normal	Elevated

CT = computed tomography; MRI = magnetic resonance imaging.

CHIASM AND OPTIC TRACT. Patients with lesions of the optic chiasm or optic tract are often unaware of visual impairment until the deficit encroaches on central vision in one or both eyes. Intrinsic or extrinsic neoplasms and parachiasmal arterial aneurysms are the most common lesions in this location. Gliomas that arise within the chiasm or optic tract are rare in adulthood. Extrinsic lesions compressing the chiasm or tract include *dysgerminomas, craniopharyngiomas, pituitary adenomas, meningiomas,* and large *aneurysms* of the carotid or basilar artery. The diagnosis rests on finding the characteristic visual field abnormalities (bitemporal hemianopia for chiasm and incongruous homonymous hemianopia for optic tract lesions) and identifying the lesion with computed tomography (CT) or magnetic resonance imaging (MRI). Pituitary apoplexy due to acute hemorrhage into the gland can result in sudden vision loss; prompt neurosurgical intervention under steroid coverage is required for most patients.

VISUAL RADIATIONS AND OCCIPITAL CORTEX. Lesions involving the postgeniculate visual pathways most often result from *vascular damage, traumatic injuries, neoplasms,* or, rarely, *inflammatory* or *degenerative disorders* involving the cerebral white matter. Their localization can be deduced by the resulting visual field defects. Vascular disease of the occipital lobes is the most common cause of homonymous visual field defects in the middle-aged and elderly population. *Anton's syndrome* refers to cerebral visual loss with denial of visual defect. Affected patients not only deny the fact that they are blind but confabulate details of their visual environment from memory. Anton's syndrome results from bilateral lesions involving the parieto-occipital lobes or in the setting of a metabolic encephalopathy. *Tumors* are rarely confined to the limits of the occipital lobes; therefore, neurologic deficits with occipital tumors are rarely only visual.

PUPILLARY CONTROL

The neuromechanisms that control pupil size and reactivity are complex, yet they can be evaluated by simple clinical procedures. The diameter of the pupil is determined by the antagonistic actions of the iris sphincter and dilator muscles, with the latter playing a minor role. If the sphincter muscle is severed or ruptured, it does not retract toward one quadrant but rather continues to function, except in the altered segment. Therefore, the pupillary response can be evaluated even in the presence of significant damage to the iris.

Anatomy and Localization of Lesions within Pupillary Pathways

The size of the pupil is governed by tonic balance between sympathetic and parasympathetic innervation of the muscles of the iris. Sympathetic stimulation dilates the pupil, and parasympathetic stimulation constricts it. In the normal resting state, light entering the eye provides the major stimulus governing the size of the pupil (Fig. 466–2). Light activates the retinal rods and cones, with maximal sensitivity in the macular area. The optic nerve fibers follow the crossed and uncrossed visual pathways to the pregeniculate portion of the optic tracts, where the receptor fibers for light diverge to the pretectal nucleus located at the midbrain diencephalic junction. Interneurons project from this nucleus, to the Edinger-Westphal nuclei atop the midbrain third nerve nuclear complex of either side. From that point, paired parasympathetic efferents leave the midbrain in the third nerves, travel in the interpeduncular space across the petroclinoid ligament

Pupillary Response

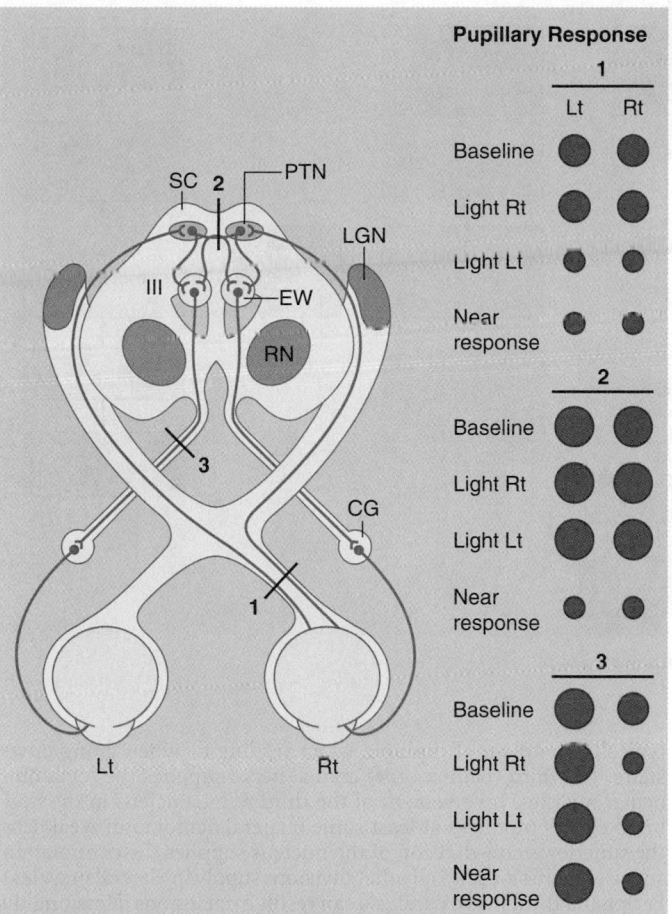

FIGURE 466–2 • Pupillary responses associated with lesions of the (1) optic nerve, (2) pretectum, and (3) oculomotor nerve. Baseline is obtained with fixation on a distant target and the near response with a target in front of the nose. CG = ciliary ganglion; EW = Edinger-Westphal nucleus; LGN = lateral geniculate nucleus; PTN = pretectal nucleus; RN = red nucleus; SC = superior colliculus.

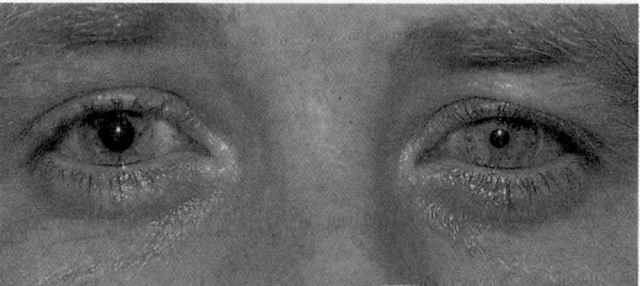

FIGURE 466–3 • Adie's tonic pupil in the right eye of a young woman. The affected pupil is "tonic"; that is, it responds slowly to light and accommodation but on rapid testing appears unresponsive. The site of the lesion is usually obscure, but the condition is benign. There may be associated areflexia. (From Forbes CD, Jackson WF: Color Atlas and Text of Clinical Medicine, 3rd ed. London, Mosby, 2003, with permission.)

Table 466–3 • HORNER'S SYNDROME RESULTS FROM LESIONS IN MULTIPLE LOCATIONS

LOCATION OF LESION	NEURON INVOLVED	TYPE OF LESION	ASSOCIATED SYMPTOMS AND SIGNS
Lateral brain stem	1st order	Infarction, glioma	Vertigo, nystagmus, imbalance, numbness and weakness
Apex of lung	2nd order	Lung cancer, trauma	Often none
Neck	3rd order	Carotid dissection or inflammation	Pain, monocular visual loss, hemiparesis

and edge of the tentorium, traverse the cavernous sinus, and then enter the orbit through the superior orbital fissure. In the orbit, the parasympathetic efferents synapse in the ciliary ganglion, from which ciliary nerves enter the eye to reach the pupillary muscles.

The principal sympathetic control of the pupil originates in the ventral lateral hypothalamus (first-order neuron), from which fibers descend ipsilaterally through the brain stem tegmentum and thence to the cervical cord, where they synapse with the preganglionic neurons in the intermedial lateral column of the upper three thoracic segments. Preganglionic fibers (second-order neurons) emerge with the ventral roots of C8, T1, and T2 and ascend in the neck to synapse in the superior cervical ganglion adjacent to the base of the skull. Postganglionic (third-order neurons) pupillary fibers accompany the internal carotid artery through the skull, leaving it to follow the ophthalmic branch of the trigeminal nerve to reach the pupillodilator muscle of the eye.

Examination of the Pupil

The pupillary response to light should be examined in a dimly lighted room, where the pupils are naturally dilated. First, the size and symmetry of the pupils are assessed by shining a dim light onto the face from below so that both pupils are seen simultaneously in the indirect illumination. To test light reactivity, gaze is directed at a distant object (so that constriction due to convergence is minimal) and first one and then the other pupil is illuminated with a bright light source. If a pupil reacts poorly to direct light, it is observed as the opposite eye is illuminated (consensual response). Pupils that react poorly to light should be tested for reactivity to the near reflex by first having the patient gaze at a distant object and then quickly fixate on an object just in front of his or her nose. *Light-near*

dissociation refers to a pupil that does *not* react to light but does accommodate by constricting to a near target.

Common Causes of Pupillary Abnormalities

With so-called benign pupillary dilatation or *physiologic anisocoria,* there is a long-standing difference in the size of the two pupils with normal reflex reactions; the disparity remains constant during constriction and dilatation. Lesions compressing or damaging the pretectal region interrupt the afferent light reflex bilaterally to produce dilated and light-fixed pupils (e.g., Lesion 2, Fig. 466–2). Pupillary constriction to the near response is preserved until late stages. Tumors of the pineal gland (e.g., dysgerminomas) and *localized infarctions* are the most common lesions in this location. *Adie's tonic pupil* (Fig. 466–3) is a medium-to-large (3 to 6 mm) pupil that constricts little or not at all to light and very slowly to accommodation, but constricts with the instillation of dilute (0.125%) pilocarpine (Fig. 466–4). The condition usually affects one eye (occasionally both), is more common in women 25 to 45 years of age, and carries no serious implications. It most likely results from postviral denervation of the pupillary muscles. Unexplained unilateral or bilateral dilated pupil as an isolated finding can result from the *accidental or intentional instillation of mydriatic drugs.* Transdermal scopolamine is a common cause. Failure of the pupil to constrict promptly with pilocarpine (1%) gives the diagnosis if the history is unclear. Interruption of the emerging third nerve in the ventral midbrain or along the proximal part of its course produces a dilated pupil 6 to 7 mm in diameter. Important causes of compression of the third nerve in this region are *aneurysms, neoplasia,* and *brain herniation* due to increased intracranial pressure. In nearly all cases, the pupillary involvement is associated with other signs of third nerve involvement (see later text).

Sympathetic paralysis of the eye with ptosis, anhidrosis, and miosis (Horner's syndrome; Fig. 466–5) can result from lesions anywhere along the pathway of the sympathetic innervation to the eye (Table 466–3). The diagnosis can sometimes be made by identifying associated signs in the brain stem or neck or along the carotid artery. *Argyll-Robertson pupils* are small (1 to 2 mm), unequal, irregular, and fixed to light; they constrict minimally to accommodation. Their principal cause is tertiary neurosyphilis.

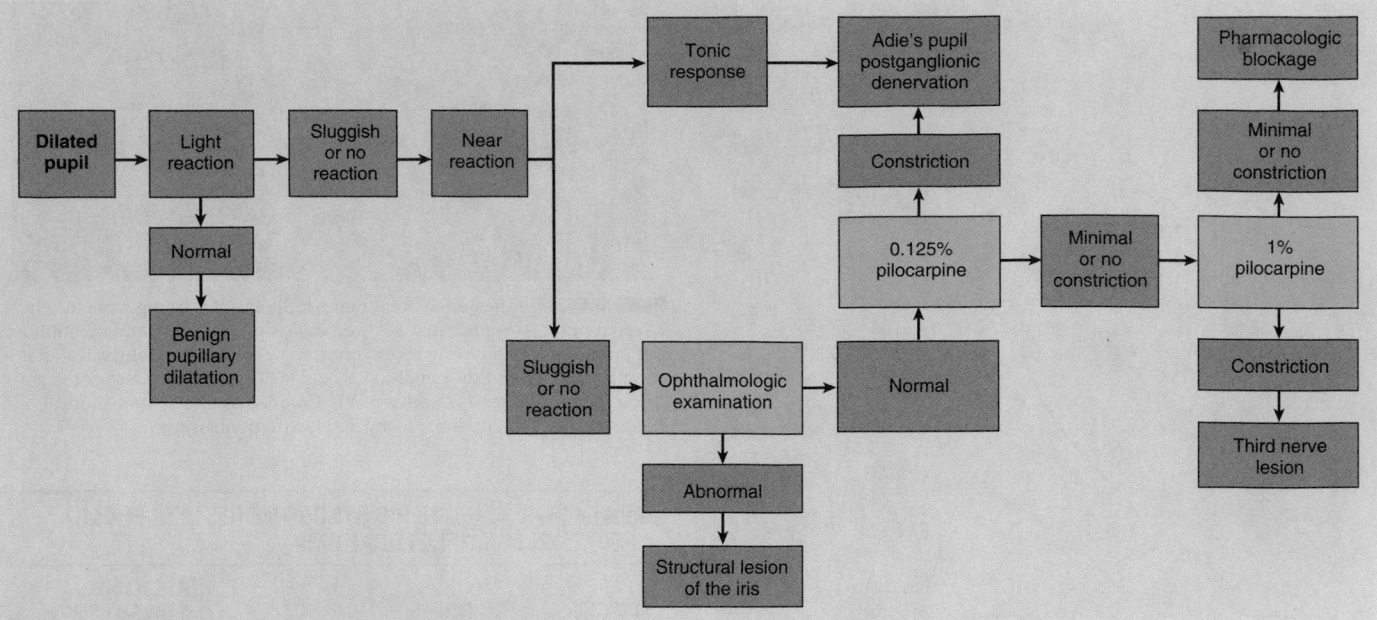

FIGURE 466–4 • Use of pilocarpine to help differentiate between different causes of a dilated pupil.

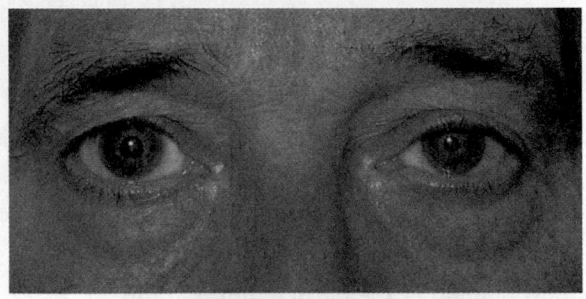

FIGURE 466–5 • Horner's syndrome. Note the characteristic ptosis of the left eye associated with constriction of the pupil (miosis). This patient had syringomyelia, but Horner's syndrome has many possible causes. (From Forbes CD, Jackson WF: Color Atlas and Text of Clinical Medicine, 3rd ed. London, Mosby, 2003, with permission.)

OCULOMOTOR CONTROL

Abnormal eye movements can result from disturbances at several levels. Disconjugate eye movements result from lesions of the individual ocular muscles, the myoneural junctions, the oculomotor nerves and their three paired nuclei in the brain stem, and the internuclear medial longitudinal fasciculus (MLF) that yokes the eyes in horizontal movements. Supranuclear lesions typically produce disorders of conjugate gaze (gaze palsies).

Anatomy and Localization of Lesions within the Oculomotor Pathways

NUCLEAR AND INTERNUCLEAR PATHWAYS. The abducens (sixth) nerve supplies the lateral rectus muscle. Selective involvement of the abducens nerve anywhere along its pathway leads to isolated weakness of abduction of the affected eye. Destruction of the abducens nucleus in the brain stem leads to a conjugate gaze paralysis (ipsilateral) because, in addition to oculomotor neurons, the nucleus contains interneurons destined for the contralateral medial rectus nucleus. The trochlear (fourth) nerve supplies the contralateral superior oblique muscle, which intorts and depresses the eye. Patients with superior oblique weakness note an increase in diplopia with head tilt toward the side of weakness and often tilt the head in the opposite direction. At rest there is slight upward deviation of the involved eye, and downward movement is impaired when the affected eye is turned in. Patients typically complain of diplopia when reading or when going down stairs. The third (oculomotor) cranial nerve supplies the remaining ocular muscles. Involvement of the third nerve nucleus in the midbrain always produces at least some bilateral oculomotor weakness; the superior rectus division of the nucleus supplies the contralateral superior rectus muscle (all other divisions supply ipsilateral muscles). Peripheral third nerve paralysis can result from lesions damaging the structure anywhere from its course within the ventral midbrain to where it enters the orbit via the superior orbital fissure. When complete, a third nerve palsy produces a widely dilated pupil, severe ptosis, and an externally deviated eye held in position by the unopposed contraction of the lateral rectus muscle. In such conditions, the continued trochlear action reveals itself by intorsion of the eye when the subject attempts to look down.

The MLF interconnects the abducens nucleus in the pons with the contralateral oculomotor nuclear complex in the midbrain. It terminates cephalad in the interstitial nucleus in the rostral midbrain and can be traced as far caudad as the thoracocervical region of the spinal cord (coordinating nuchal-ocular control). Lesions involving the MLF characteristically produce an internuclear ophthalmoplegia (INO) with which the eyes are conjugate in the primary position but disconjugate on lateral gaze. With a fully developed INO on lateral gaze away from the side of the lesion, the contralateral eye abducts and shows nystagmus, whereas the ipsilateral adducting eye does not move nasally because of failure of ascending impulses to reach the medial rectus division of the third nerve nucleus. Adduction for convergence is usually relatively maintained.

SUPRANUCLEAR PATHWAYS. The pathway descending from the frontal eye fields in the frontal lobe through the superior colliculi regulates rapid voluntary eye movements (saccades). A signal from this system activates a burst of firing in the contralateral horizontal gaze center in the paramedian pontine reticular formation. This high-frequency burst (or pulse) of neuronal firing is transmitted directly to the nearby sixth nerve nucleus and via the MLF to the contralateral third nerve nucleus. For voluntary vertical gaze, both frontal eye fields send signals to the vertical gaze center in the pretectum (the interstitial nucleus of the MLF). Acute lesions involving a frontal or parietal eye field (e.g., hemorrhage or infarction) result in transient inability to direct the eyes contralaterally. Vertical eye movements are not affected by unilateral lesions. Bilateral damage to the frontal eye fields or their descending pathways may produce the inability to move the eyes voluntarily (horizontal or vertical) despite preserved reflex eye movements controlled by the superior colliculi, a condition called oculomotor apraxia. Lesions involving the horizontal gaze center in the pons produce an ipsilateral paralysis of conjugate gaze and tonic deviation of the eyes to the contralateral side. Lesions of the pretectum selectively impair vertical gaze with the vertical upgaze center being slightly rostral and dorsal to the vertical downgaze center.

Pathways descending from the temporo-occipital and frontal regions of the two hemispheres subserve slow visual tracking or *smooth pursuit movements*. The exact location of these descending pursuit pathways is not completely known, but there are strong projections to the ipsilateral pons and cerebellar flocculus. Lesions of the temporo-occipital and frontal region, pons, and cerebellum impair smooth pursuit and optokinetic slow phases when the target moves ipsilateral to the lesion. The *convergence* center is located in the rostral dorsal midbrain near the vertical gaze center. Lesions in this region typically impair convergence and voluntary vertical gaze. The other supranuclear oculomotor control system, the *vestibulo-ocular reflex*, and its examination are discussed in Chapter 470.

Examination of Eye Movements

Fixation and gaze-holding are tested by having the patient look center, right, left, up, and down. Each position should be held steady and unwavering with the observer carefully documenting abnormal movements or ocular disconjugacies. Each supranuclear oculomotor control system is examined separately. *Saccades* are tested by having the patient fixate alternately on two targets such as the examiner's finger and nose; the speed and accuracy are noted. *Smooth pursuit* is tested by slowly moving a target back and forth and up and down and observing the patient's ability to produce smooth tracking movements. If the target velocity is low, normal subjects should be able to pursue without requiring catch-up saccades. *Convergence* is tested by having the patient follow a target moving from far to near. The degree of convergence depends to some extent on the cooperation of the patient. A clear sign that the patient is attempting to converge is simultaneous pupillary constriction.

Common Causes of Abnormal Oculomotor Control

STRABISMUS (OCULAR MISALIGNMENT). A comitant (same in all directions of gaze) strabismus present since childhood is usually a benign *congenital disorder*. Latent congenital strabismus can become manifest in adulthood in association with a systemic illness. An acquired skew deviation (vertical displacement of the ocular axes) indicates a lesion within the otolith-ocular pathways (usually brain stem). Incomitant strabismus can result from restrictive disease of the orbit or from abnormal muscle or oculomotor nerve function. The presence of mechanical restriction is confirmed by the use of forced duction testing (Fig. 466–6). (After a topical anesthetic is applied to the eye, the ophthalmologist grasps the muscle insertion with a large blunt-toothed forceps. Failure of the eye to deviate fully in the pulled direction implies restriction.) Common causes of *orbital restrictive disease* include dysthyroid ophthalmopathy, orbital pseudotumor, trauma, and orbital mass lesions. Variable strabismus that increases with fatigue suggests *myasthenia gravis* (Chapter 464). A Tensilon test can usually confirm the diagnosis (see Fig. 466–6). If both restrictive disease and myasthenia gravis have been excluded, most patients with incomitant strabismus have processes affecting the oculomotor nuclei, their fascicles, or the cranial nerves themselves. Common causes of an *isolated third nerve palsy* in an adult include aneurysm, small vessel occlusive disease (including diabetes mellitus), trauma, and neoplasm. Typically, third nerve lesions due to vascular disease spare the pupil. Vascular disease and trauma are by far the most common causes of *isolated trochlear nerve palsies*. The abducens nerve is particularly vulnerable to isolated traumatic involvement because of its long pathway outside the brain stem. Lesions that produce increased intracranial pressure can lead to abducens nerve dysfunction regardless of the location and produce a "false localizing sign." Other common causes of *isolated sixth nerve palsy* are vascular disease, trauma, and neoplasm. About one fourth of cases with cranial nerve palsies (third, fourth, or sixth nerves) remain undiagnosed.

INTERNUCLEAR OPHTHALMOPLEGIA. INO (Fig. 466–7) may be unilateral or bilateral, partial or complete, depending on the location of the lesion and the degree of damage to the MLF. *Demyelinating* and small *vascular lesions* are the most common cause of unilateral INO unaccompanied by other ocular palsies or brain stem signs. Larger brain stem lesions that damage one or more oculomotor nuclei plus the MLF often produce combinations of disconjugate eye movements coupled with nuclear oculomotor palsies. Myasthenia gravis can produce an ophthalmoparesis resembling INO owing to the greater involvement of the medial rectus compared with the lateral rectus. Demyelinating diseases are by far the most common causes of bilateral INO involvement.

DISORDERS OF CONJUGATE GAZE As noted earlier, infarction of the frontal cortex results in transient contralateral gaze paresis. Tumors and

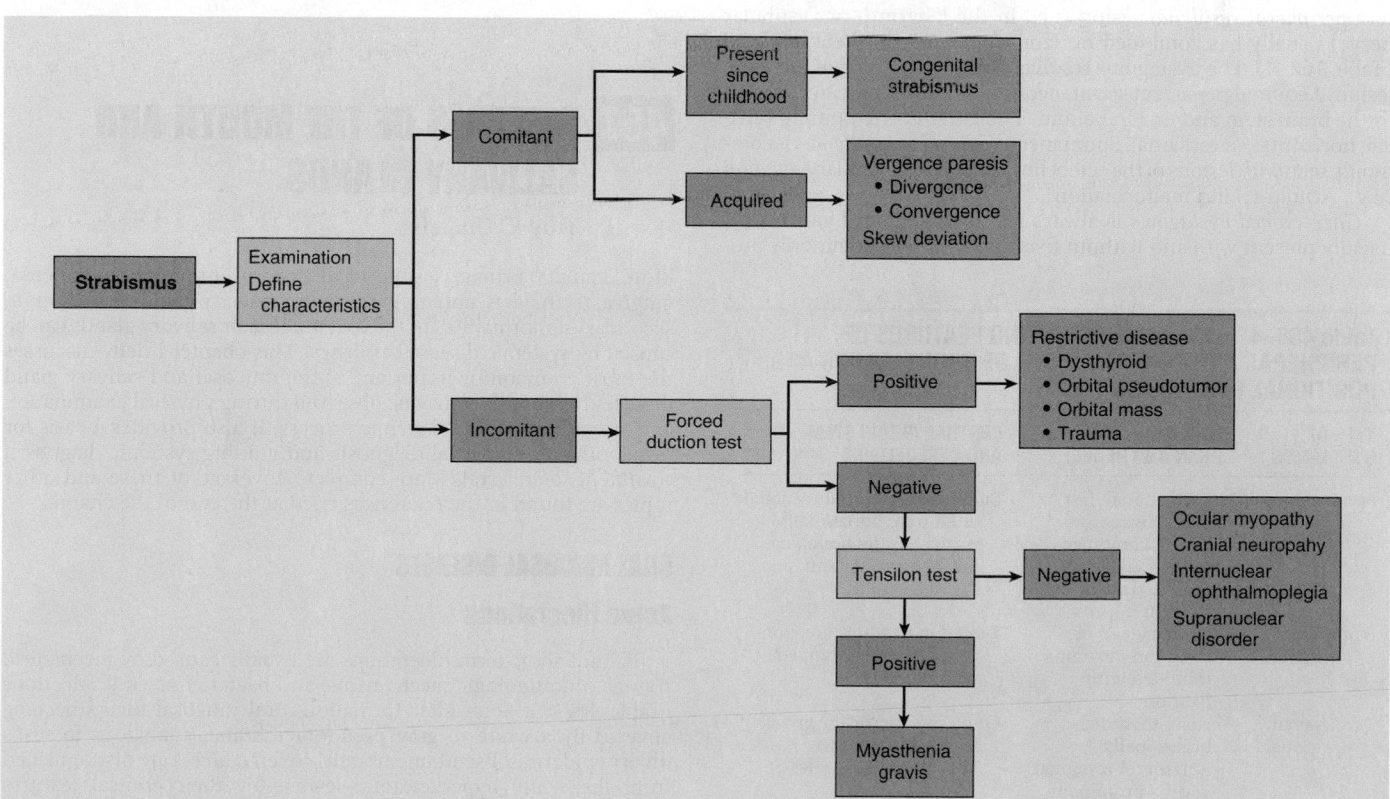

FIGURE 466–6 • Diagnostic tests that help differentiate between common causes of strabismus.

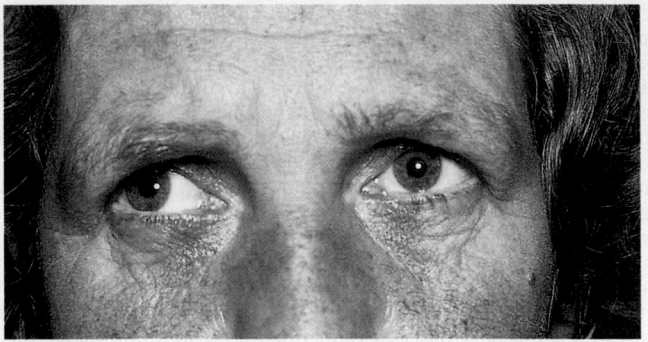

FIGURE 466–7 • Internuclear ophthalmoplegia may be a presenting feature of brain stem involvement in multiple sclerosis. On lateral gaze to the right, adduction of the left eye is incomplete. On convergence, eye movement was normal. The lesion is in the left medial longitudinal bundle, between the nucleus in the pons and the third nerve nucleus on the opposite side. (From Forbes CD, Jackson WF: Color Atlas and Text of Clinical Medicine, 3rd ed. London, Mosby, 2003, with permission.)

infarction of the paramedian pontine reticular formation produce ipsilateral horizontal gaze paralysis. With the so-called locked-in syndrome (secondary to basilar artery thrombosis), voluntary horizontal eye movements are absent; the patient's only remaining motor functions are vertical eye and lid movements. Lesions of the pretectum typically affect only vertical eye movements, although the descending pathways from the frontal eye fields to the horizontal gaze centers in the pons can also be affected. With the *dorsal midbrain syndrome* (Parinaud's syndrome), patients present with a conjugate upgaze paresis. When they attempt to make upward saccades, they develop convergence retraction nystagmus. As noted earlier, impaired convergence and light-near dissociation of the pupillary reflexes are also part of the syndrome. The most common causes of the dorsal midbrain syndrome include tumors of the pineal gland (dysgerminomas), hydrocephalus, and localized infarction.

NYSTAGMUS. *Spontaneous nystagmus* can be congenital or acquired. *Congenital nystagmus* typically has a high frequency and variable waveform (usually pendular) and is highly fixation-dependent. It typically remains horizontal in all positions of gaze. The lifelong history and lack of symptoms confirm the diagnosis. Spontaneous nystagmus due to a *peripheral vestibular* lesion (i.e., in the labyrinth or vestibular nerve) usually has combined horizontal and torsional components (Table 466–4). The nystagmus resolves within a few days of the acute lesion. Acquired persistent spontaneous nystagmus indicates a lesion in the brain stem and/or cerebellum. The latter is often purely vertical, horizontal, or torsional. Spontaneous *downbeat nystagmus* is commonly seen with lesions of the cerebellum or cervicomedullary junction (e.g., Arnold-Chiari malformation).

Gaze-evoked nystagmus is always in the direction of gaze and is usually present with and without fixation. It is most commonly produced by ingestion of *drugs* such as phenobarbital, phenytoin, alcohol, and diazepam. It can also occur in patients with such varied conditions as myasthenia gravis, multiple sclerosis, and cerebellar atrophy. Asymmetric horizontal gaze-evoked nystagmus indicates a structural brain stem or cerebellar lesion (particularly at the cerebellopontine angle), with the lesion usually being on the side of the larger amplitude nystagmus (Brun's nystagmus). *Rebound nystagmus* is a type of gaze-evoked nystagmus that either disappears or reverses direction as the eccentric gaze position is held. When the eyes are returned to the primary position, nystagmus occurs in the direction of the return saccade. Rebound nystagmus occurs in patients with cerebellar atrophy and focal structural lesions of the cerebellum; it is the only variety of nystagmus thought to be specific for cerebellar involvement. *Disconjugate gaze-evoked nystagmus* most commonly results from lesions of the MLF (see earlier discussion), but it can also occur with other lesions of the brain stem involving the oculomotor nuclei. Positional nystagmus is discussed in Chapter 470.

OTHER OCULAR OSCILLATIONS. *Ocular bobbing* consists of a fast conjugate downward eye movement followed by a slow return to the primary position. The phenomenon accompanies severe displacement or destruction of the pons or, less often, metabolic CNS depression. *Ocular myoclonus* consists of continuous rhythmic pendular oscillations, most often vertical, with a rate of 1 to 3 beats per second; often it accompanies palatal myoclonus and has a similar pathogenesis. *Square wave jerks* and *ocular flutter* consist of brief, intermittent, horizontal oscillations (back to back saccades) arising from the primary gaze position. These types of ocular oscillation are most commonly seen with cerebellar disease but can also accompany more diffuse central nervous system disorders. *Opsoclonus* consists of rapid, chaotic, conjugate, repetitive, saccadic eye movements (dancing eyes). Opsoclonus accompanies cerebellar dysfunction, with the most chaotic varieties associated with brain stem encephalitis or the remote effects of systemic neoplasm, especially neuroblastoma in children. *Ocular dysmetria* refers to overshooting and undershooting of saccadic eye movements, often followed by multiple attempts at refixation. It reflects cerebellar dysfunction.

SUGGESTED READINGS
Liu GT, Galetta SL: The neuro-ophthalmologic examination (including coma). Ophthalmol Clin North Am 2001;14:23–39. *Practical guide to the neuro-ophthalmology examination.*
Ticho BH: Strabismus. Pediatr Clin North Am 2003;50:173–188. *A practical review.*

467 DISEASES OF THE MOUTH AND SALIVARY GLANDS

Troy E. Daniels

More than 200 primary lesions or diseases occur in the oral mucosa, gingiva, teeth, jaws, and minor or major salivary glands. In addition, secondary abnormalities of the oral mucosa or salivary glands can be caused by systemic diseases or drugs. This chapter briefly discusses the most common or important of the mucosal and salivary gland diseases because they may be observed during physical examination and are often part of a systemic process. It also provides a basis for developing a differential diagnosis and guiding systemic diagnosis, treatment, or referral. More complete coverage of these and other topics are found in the references cited at the end of the chapter.

ORAL MUCOSAL DISEASES

Acute Ulcerations

Painful short-term ulcerations are usually caused by mechanical trauma, immunologic mechanisms, and bacterial or viral infections (Table 467–1). Soon after formation, oral mucosal ulcers become covered by a white to gray pseudomembrane, analogous to scabs on dry epidermis. Pseudomembrane-covered ulcers are distinguished from the white hyperkeratotic lesions by their clinical features of pain, a flat surface, and an erythematous periphery. Traumatic ulcers characteristically are located on the tongue or inside the

Table 466–4 • **KEY DISTINGUISHING FEATURES OF PERIPHERAL AND CENTRAL TYPES OF SPONTANEOUS AND POSITIONAL NYSTAGMUS**

TYPE OF NYSTAGMUS	PERIPHERAL (END ORGAN AND NERVE)	CENTRAL (BRAIN STEM AND CEREBELLUM)
Spontaneous	Unidirectional, fast phase away from lesion, combined horizontal torsional, inhibited with fixation	Bidirectional or undirectional; often pure horizontal, vertical, or torsional; *not* inhibited with fixation
Static positional	Direction-fixed or direction-changing, inhibited with fixation	Direction fixed or direction-changing, *not* inhibited with fixation
Paroxysmal positional	Vertical-torsional, occasionally horizontal-torsional, vertigo prominent, fatigability, latency	Often pure vertical, vertigo less prominent, no latency, nonfatigable

Table 467–1 • ORAL MUCOSAL ULCERS

TYPE/DISEASE	CLINICAL FEATURES
INSIDIOUS ONSET, CHRONIC	
Multiple or bilateral	Shallow ulcers on mucosa, skin, or both
Pemphigus vulgaris	Begin as short-duration blisters
Mucous membrane pemphigoid	Begin as short-duration blisters
Lichen planus	Bilaterally symmetric lesions (associated with hyperkeratoses and/or erythema)
Lupus erythematosus	Asymmetric lesions, with or without systemic lupus (associated with hyperkeratoses and/or erythema)
Drug reaction	Variable lesions; appropriate history of drug use (e.g., penicillamine, gold)
Epidermolysis bullosa	Begin as blisters; lifelong history
Solitary	Indurated or cratered ulcers
Squamous cell carcinoma	Most common on tongue, oropharynx, lip, mouth floor
Adenocarcinomas, various	Most commonly on palate, cheeks, mouth floor
Tuberculosis	Usually painful
Actinomycosis	Often associated with draining sinus
Deep mycoses (particularly histoplasmosis, coccidioidomycosis)	Associated with systemic infection
Midline granuloma	Associated with necrosis, may perforate palate
ACUTE ONSET, OFTEN SELF-LIMITING	
Clusters	Usually small and shallow ulcers; history of blisters
Primary herpes simplex	Any oral mucosal site, associated with fever, malaise
Recurrent herpes simplex	Only on gingiva, hard palate, or lip (keratinized mucosa)
Varicella-zoster	Unilateral lesions along neural distribution
Herpangina	Usually on oropharynx
Measles (rubeola)	Precede skin rash; associated with fever, malaise
Solitary or multiple (without clustering)	Variable, usually without history of blisters
Traumatic ulcers	Usually solitary; history of trauma
Recurrent aphthae	Circular, often multiple, only on nonkeratinized mucosa
Behçet's syndrome	Oral lesions similar to recurrent aphthae
Erythema multiforme	Multiple lesions, often involve lower labial mucosa; can be recurrent or chronic
Drug reaction	Appropriate history of drug use
Necrotizing sialometaplasia	Usually on palate
Primary syphilis	Solitary, indurated, painless, any site
Gonorrhea	Painful, surrounded by erythema, any site

Table 467–2 • ORAL LESIONS ASSOCIATED WITH HUMAN IMMUNODEFICIENCY VIRUS INFECTION

Kaposi's sarcoma
Candidiasis
Pseudomembranous lesions
Hyperplastic lesions
Erythematous lesions
Other opportunistic fungal infections (e.g., histoplasmosis or coccidioidomycosis)
Epithelial lesions
Aphthous ulcers (increased frequency, duration, or size)
Virus-associated epithelial hyperplasias
  Hairy leukoplakia
  Oral wart
  Focal epithelial hyperplasia (Heck's disease)
  Condyloma acuminatum
Herpes zoster
Exaggerated forms of gingivitis and inflammatory periodontal disease
Decreased salivary gland function
Parotid gland enlargement (lymphoepithelial lesion)
Non-Hodgkin's lymphoma

cheeks or lips, are close to the chewing surfaces of the teeth, and have irregular borders.

APHTHOUS ULCERS. These idiopathic recurrent ulcers, which afflict about 20% of the population, are found on all areas of the oral mucosa except the hard palate, gingiva, and vermilion, which are keratinized. They form well-defined circular lesions that may be single or multiple. There are three clinical forms: (1) minor, which are flat and less than 1 cm in diameter, and last 5 to 10 days; (2) major, which have raised borders, are greater than 1 cm, and often last for weeks or months; and (3) herpetiform, which are usually clusters of very small ulcers that resemble recurrent herpetic lesions but are not preceded by vesicles and do not occur on keratinized mucosa. A viral pathogenesis has not been established for any of these forms. Lesions clinically identical to minor aphthous ulcers occur in Behçet's syndrome (Chapter 291). Aphthous ulcers are occasionally associated with macrocytic anemias or gluten-sensitive enteropathy and may become more frequent and severe in association with human immunodeficiency virus (HIV) infection (Table 467–2).

Minor or herpetiform aphthous ulcers may not require treatment. Topical steroids, such as fluocinonide gel or ointment, can reduce the severity and duration of the lesions only if used with prodromal symptoms or early signs. Major aphthae usually require treatment by topical or systemic corticosteroids and occasionally are biopsied to exclude neoplasia.

VIRAL ULCERS. Several types of virus (most commonly herpes simplex type 1; Chapter 369) cause multiple oral mucosal vesicles that last only a few hours or days and then become irregular shallow ulcers. In the initial infection by herpes simplex virus, usually in children, numerous vesicles may appear on any oral mucosal site (primary herpetic gingivostomatitis), accompanied by malaise, headache, fever, and cervical lymphadenopathy. Patients previously exposed to this virus may develop recurrent (secondary) lesions, most commonly as clusters of small vesicles on the lips (herpes labialis). Only a few develop intraoral recurrent herpes as clusters of vesicles on the keratinized mucosa of the gingiva or hard palate. Such lesions tend to recur at the same site, but less frequently with age.

Similar mucosal vesicles may also accompany the initial infection by the varicella-zoster virus in children with chicken pox (Chapter 369), and unilateral lesions may occur if herpes zoster (Chapter 475) affects branches of the trigeminal nerve. Uncommonly, oral mucosal ulcers may be caused by different types of coxsackievirus (Chapter 373), appearing on any oral site in hand-foot-and-mouth disease or on the soft palate or pharynx in herpangina. After infection by the measles (rubeola) virus, small ulcers (Koplik's spots) may form on the inside of the cheeks 1 to 2 days before development of the skin rash (Chapter 365).

ERYTHEMA MULTIFORME. In this potentially recurrent mucocutaneous disease, painful oral mucosal ulcerations develop rapidly in as many as half of patients. The lesions may be confined to the mouth, with no skin involvement. The affected patients, usually young adults with minimal or no systemic symptoms, have irregularly shaped ulcers that can be small and few or involve large areas of the mucosa; the most common site is the lower labial mucosa. These lesions can be distinguished from those of primary herpes by the absence of oral vesicles and systemic symptoms or by the presence of characteristic skin lesions (Chapter 475). A major variant of this disease is Stevens-Johnson syndrome in which ocular, genital, and other lesions may accompany the oral lesions.

VENEREAL INFECTIONS. Primary syphilis may present as a solitary, indurated, painless ulcer on the oral mucosa that resolves spontaneously in 4 to 6 weeks (Chapter 349). Uncommonly, *Neisseria gonorrhoeae* may cause oral ulcers, usually in the pharynx, which may be confused with oral ulcers of other causes.

Oral Squamous Cell Carcinoma

About 4% of all cancers occur in the mouth, commonly as squamous cell carcinomas of the mucosal epithelium (Chapter 197). Oral carcinoma occurs usually in the fifth decade or beyond, in men twice as frequently as in women, and is associated with long-term use of tobacco in more than 80% of cases (see Table 467–1).

Oral carcinoma usually presents as a chronic, indurated, cratered ulcer, but early lesions of squamous cell carcinoma may appear as white or red macules (Table 467–3; Fig. 467–1). About 15% of oral carcinomas arise within a preexisting white plaque (leukoplakia). The overall 5-year survival is approximately 50%, but early treatment of small, localized lesions can lead to survival rates as high as 90%.

Other Chronic Ulcerations

Several mucocutaneous diseases can cause chronic multifocal oral mucosal lesions composed of ill-defined areas of erythema and ulceration. They are among the most difficult oral lesions to diagnose and are discussed below with the red lesions (see Table 467–3). Several microbial infections can lead to indurated, chronic oral mucosal ulcerations with moderate symptoms (see Table 467–1).

WHITE LESIONS

White plaques are commonly found in the mouth but, like ulcerations, have a wide variety of causes and outcomes (see Table 467–3). The term "leukoplakia" applies to a white plaque that does not rub off and whose appearance does not indicate another disease. Leukoplakia can occur in any area of the mouth and usually exhibits benign hyperkeratosis on biopsy (Fig. 467–2). On long-term follow-

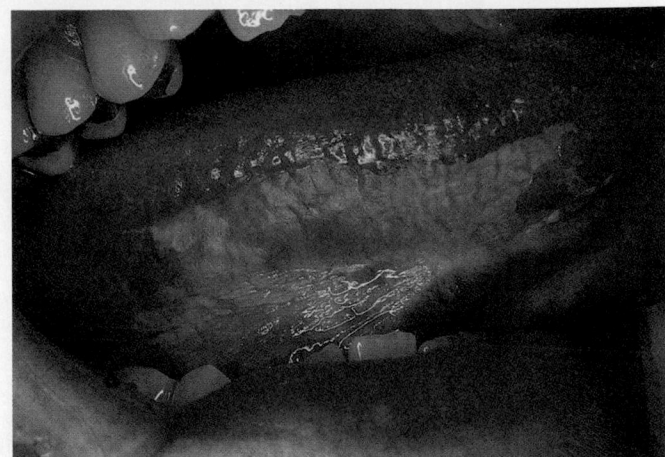

FIGURE 467–2 • Leukoplakia. Incisional biopsy of this unilateral, asymptomatic white patch showed focal hyperkeratosis. Such lesions must be regularly reevaluated for possible progression to squamous cell carcinoma.

up, 2 to 6% of these lesions undergo malignant transformation into squamous cell carcinoma. Areas of leukoplakia with a corrugated surface or mixed with areas of erythema are often found in the lower labial or buccal vestibule of patients who use smokeless tobacco.

Frictional keratoses are often found posterior to the lower molar teeth as irregular white plaques and on the buccal mucosa as white lines adjacent to the dental occlusion. Unlike leukoplakia, these lesions rarely become malignant.

LICHEN PLANUS. Oral lesions of lichen planus occur in about 1% of the population, usually as multiple, bilaterally symmetric reticular white plaques, with or without adjacent areas of erythema (atrophy or erosion) or irregular ulcers. The presence of mucosal atrophy, erosion, or ulceration usually causes pain and sensitivity to certain foods. Most lesions can be adequately controlled by topical application of fluocinonide or clobetasol gel or ointment for periods of several weeks to several months, although recurrence is common.

ORAL CANDIDIASIS. This common fungal disease has three clinical forms: pseudomembranous (thrush), erythematous (atrophic), and hyperplastic (candidal leukoplakia). Pseudomembranous candidiasis, usually of relatively short duration, occurs on any site and consists of white fungal plaques that can be rubbed off, leaving a red or bleeding base. Lesions of hyperplastic candidiasis are white, have fungal hyphae within the surface layers of hyperkeratotic epithelium, do not rub off, and are most often found on the anterior buccal mucosa or on the tongue. Erythematous candidiasis is discussed under Red Lesions. All forms of oral candidiasis represent overgrowth or superficial infection by *Candida* species from the oral flora, induced by a variety of causes including suppression of bacterial flora by systemic antibiotics, chronic salivary dysfunction, uncontrolled diabetes mellitus or anemia, and immunosuppression (especially in HIV-infected patients).

HAIRY LEUKOPLAKIA. This lesion is a white plaque occurring most frequently on the lateral surfaces of the tongue bilaterally in immunosuppressed persons, usually HIV-infected. *Candida* may be present in the surface layers, but the lesion is not eliminated by effective antifungal therapy, and it contains large quantities of Epstein-Barr virus. Its diagnosis should be followed by an HIV antibody test.

GEOGRAPHIC TONGUE. Also called *benign migratory glossitis*, this benign idiopathic condition affects the dorsal tongue of about 2% of the population. It is characterized by well-defined areas of atrophied filiform papillae bordered by arcs of normal or hyperplastic filiform papillae and by changes in the location of these lesions over time. Treatment is usually not necessary.

SECONDARY SYPHILIS. Secondary syphilis may manifest as a well-defined white plaque on the labial or palatal mucosa, called *condyloma latum* (or "split papule," because of their lobulated periphery).

RED LESIONS

Solitary red macules or plaques ("erythroplakia") are less common in the mouth than white lesions but should be viewed with concern because they may exhibit microscopic dysplasia, carcinoma in situ,

---

Table 467–3 • WHITE AND RED ORAL MUCOSAL LESIONS

White lesions (plaques)
Squamous cell carcinoma (early)
Frictional keratosis
Leukoplakia (idiopathic)
Smokeless tobacco–associated lesions
Nicotine stomatitis (palate)
Lichen planus (reticular and plaque types)
Pseudomembranous candidiasis (thrush)
Hyperplastic candidiasis (candidal leukoplakia)
Hairy leukoplakia (HIV-associated; usually on lateral tongue)
Geographic tongue
Mucous patch or condyloma latum of secondary syphilis
Pseudomembrane-covered ulcers (see Table 467–1)

Red lesions (macular, maculopapular)
Squamous cell carcinoma (early)
Erythroplakia (epithelial dysplasia)
Erythematous (atrophic) candidiasis
Median rhomboid glossitis
Mucocutaneous diseases (see Table 467–1)
Angular cheilitis
Telangiectasias and purpuras
Kaposi's sarcoma (blue to purple color)

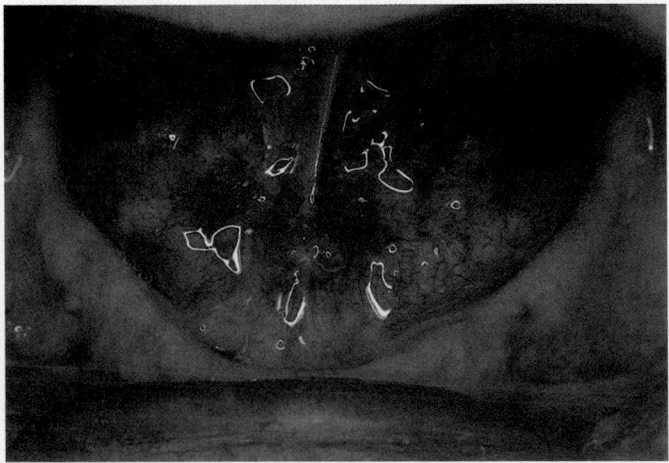

FIGURE 467–1 • Squamous cell carcinoma. Biopsy of this area of erythoplakia with slight induration in the anterior mouth floor exhibited squamous cell carcinoma.

or carcinoma (see Table 467–3 and Fig. 467–1). One exception is a red macule occurring in the midline of the posterior dorsal tongue, classified as median rhomboid glossitis, which is an idiopathic but uniformly benign condition that is often associated with localized overgrowth of *Candida* species.

ERYTHEMATOUS (ATROPHIC) ORAL CANDIDIASIS. This chronic condition is characterized by erythema and atrophy of the filiform papillae on the dorsal tongue or by patchy or ill-defined erythema on the palate, tongue, or buccal mucosa (Fig. 467–3). It usually is accompanied by symptoms of oral mucosal burning and sensitivity to certain foods and is often associated with salivary hypofunction. Patients who wear removable dentures often have mucosal erythema that is confined to the denture-bearing area and is caused by this organism.

Topical nystatin or clotrimazole or systemic ketoconazole can resolve these lesions; these drugs are administered for several weeks or months. In patients who have salivary hypofunction and remaining natural teeth, topical antifungal preparations containing sucrose or glucose must be avoided to prevent dental caries; slow oral dissolution of vaginal nystatin tablets is safe and effective. Systemic antifungal drugs may not be effective in patients with severe salivary hypofunction. Effective treatment significantly improves oral symptoms, regardless of the cause of the candidiasis. Treatment of denture-associated candidiasis requires concurrent treatment of the denture.

The treatment end point is reached when mucosal burning symptoms cease, the patient can again tolerate acidic or spicy foods, and papillae on the dorsal tongue have returned to normal; this recovery takes from 2 to 12 weeks. Recurrence is common in patients with chronic salivary hypofunction or immunosuppression, which necessitates recurring or long-term treatment using a topical antifungal drug that does not contain sucrose or glucose and provides sufficient duration of mucosal contact (e.g., vaginal tablets).

ANGULAR CHEILITIS. Erythema or crusting of the labial angles is usually caused by *Candida* (see Fig. 467–3). It is usually associated with intra-oral candidiasis and in such cases topical treatment of the angular cheilitis with nystatin or clotrimazole must be accompanied by intra-oral or systemic antifungal treatment as described previously.

MUCOCUTANEOUS DISEASES. The mucocutaneous diseases of pemphigus vulgaris, mucous membrane pemphigoid, atrophic or erosive lichen planus, and lupus erythematosus can cause similar-appearing oral lesions. Their diagnosis requires examination of a biopsy specimen by routine histopathology and usually by direct immunofluorescence to identify characteristic deposits of immunoglobulins and complement components.

The first lesions of pemphigus vulgaris usually are oral mucosal vesicles that rapidly rupture, leaving painful erosions or ulcerations. These are followed by development of skin lesions. Rarely, the lesions remain confined to the mouth (Chapter 475).

Lesions of mucous membrane (cicatricial) pemphigoid are usually confined to the oral mucosa or conjunctivae and occur in patients older than age 50 years. They begin as vesicles that quickly rupture,

leaving ulcers that are chronic but only moderately symptomatic. Use of topical fluocinonide or clobetasol for several months, as described for lichen planus, is sometimes sufficient to treat the oral lesions, but some patients also need systemic treatment (Chapter 474).

Oral mucosal lesions of lupus may occur in patients who have systemic lupus erythematosus (SLE), in patients who do not have SLE but later develop that disease, or in patients who do not develop SLE (Chapter 280). In this latter group, the lesions of mucosal lupus may be analogous to the skin lesions of chronic discoid lupus. Lesions of oral lupus are usually solitary or bilaterally asymmetric. They take the form of reticular hyperkeratotic figures associated with erythema, often resembling lichen planus. The lesions can be controlled by topical fluocinonide or intralesional triamcinolone.

Lesions of Kaposi's sarcoma associated with HIV infection often appear first on the oral mucosa, especially the palate. They begin as macules with a blue or purple color, at which time they need to be distinguished from purpura. Later, they spread radially and expand vertically (Chapters 417 and 426).

Pigmentations

Brown or gray-black macules on the oral mucosa are relatively common and range from benign to highly malignant. They may be caused by localized increase in melanin production, proliferation of melanin-producing cells, or deposition of local or systemically distributed pigmented substances (Table 467–4). Mucosal pigmentation may occur after long-term administration of chloroquine, minocycline, ketoconazole, or cyclophosphamide. Malignant melanoma can occur at any oral mucosal site but develops most frequently on the mucosa or gingiva covering the maxilla. Diagnosis of any of these conditions is usually established by biopsy and knowledge of relevant underlying conditions.

ORAL SOFT TISSUE TUMORS

In addition to the malignant neoplasms described, a variety of oral benign soft tissue tumors are usually treated by excisional biopsy.

Connective Tissue Hyperplasias

The most common oral soft tissue tumors are small, pedunculated masses of hyperplastic fibrous connective tissue covered by normal-appearing mucosa (Table 467–5). Solitary lesions are usually found on the inside of the cheeks or lips. Similar lesions may be present at the border of an ill-fitting denture or may occur in clusters on the hard palate under an ill-fitting denture ("palatal papillomatosis"); the latter is often associated with erythematous candidiasis.

Generalized enlargement of the gingiva (gingival hyperplasia) may be caused by chronic administration of phenytoin, cyclosporine, and many of the calcium channel blocking drugs (e.g., diltiazem, verapamil, or nifedipine; Fig. 467–4). It can also be associated with a hereditary defect or be caused by an infiltration of atypical white blood cells in some types of leukemia, particularly acute monocytic leukemia. The drug-associated cases apparently represent an exag-

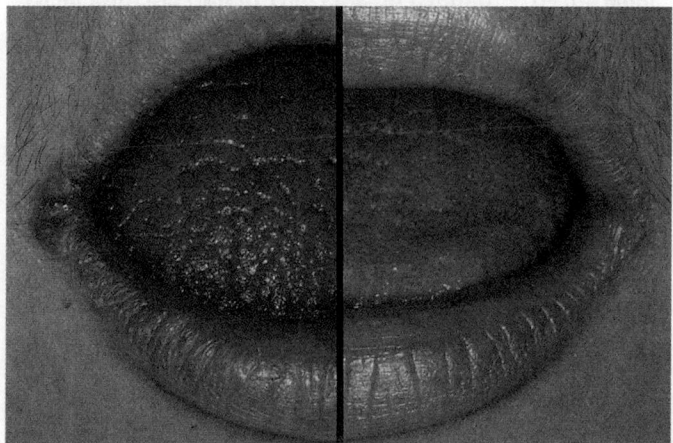

FIGURE 467–3 • *Left,* Erythematous candidiasis in a woman with primary Sjögren's syndrome, exhibiting symptomatic angular cheilitis, atrophic mucositis, and lingual papillary atrophy. *Right,* Asymptomatic and normal-appearing mucosa after treatment with appropriate topical antifungal drugs (see text).

Table 467–4 • PIGMENTATIONS OF THE ORAL MUCOSA (BROWN OR GRAY-BLACK IN COLOR)

Increased melanin production (flat lesions)
 Oral melanotic macule
 Ephelis (vermilion border)
 Systemic diseases: Addison's disease, von Recklinghausen's disease of skin, Albright's syndrome, Peutz-Jeghers syndrome
Proliferation of melanin-producing cells (flat or raised lesions)
 Pigmented cellular nevi (benign and premalignant types)
 Atypical melanocytic hyperplasia, melanoma in situ, radial growth phase of melanoma
 Malignant melanoma
Nonmelanin pigmentation
 Amalgam tattoo
 Focal deposition of systemically distributed metal (lead, bismuth, mercury, others) usually at sites of chronic inflammation
 Systemically administered drugs (chloroquine, minocycline, ketoconazole, cyclophosphamide)

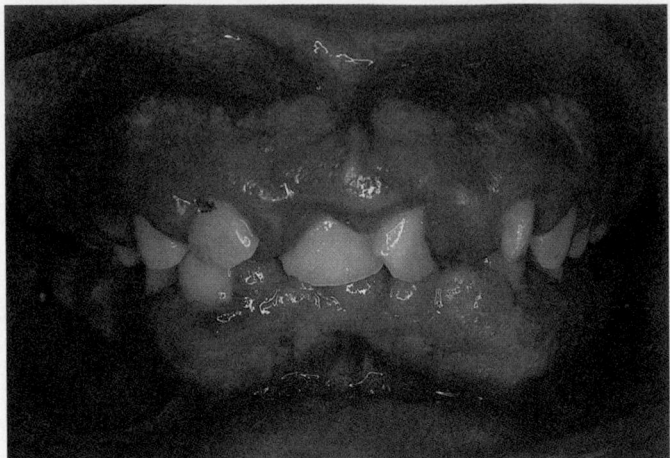

FIGURE 467–4 • Drug-induced gingival hyperplasia. Similar clinical lesions may occur with prolonged use of various drugs or as a hereditary condition (see text).

Table 467–5 • ORAL SOFT TISSUE TUMORS

Connective tissue hyperplasia (normal-appearing overlying mucosa)
  Irritation fibroma
  Denture-associated hyperplasia
  Palatal papillomatosis
  Generalized gingival hyperplasia
  Drug-induced (phenytoin, nifedipine, cyclosporine)
  Hereditary
Reactive hyperplasia (erythematous overlying mucosa)
  Pyogenic granuloma/pregnancy tumor
  Peripheral giant cell granuloma
  Inflammatory gingival hyperplasia
  Hyperplastic lingual tonsil
Epithelial masses (usually irregular white surface)
  Papilloma/oral wart
  Squamous cell carcinoma
  Verrucous carcinoma
  Focal epithelial hyperplasia (Heck's disease)
  Condyloma acuminatum (venereal wart)
  Keratoacanthoma (on lips)
Salivary duct obstruction (minor salivary glands)
  Mucocele/ranula (usually fluctuant)
  Salivary stone (sialolith)
Subepithelial neoplasms
  Primary connective tissue or salivary gland tumors
  Metastatic lesions (especially in the mandible)
  Lymphoma (especially in the palate or posterior mandible)
  Focal or generalized leukemic infiltrates in the gingiva (especially
    with acute monocytic leukemia)

---

gerated response in susceptible patients to commonly occurring local irritants.

Reactive Hyperplasias

Small masses with surfaces that are ulcerated or only partially covered by normal-appearing mucosa usually represent reactive lesions in the form of pyogenic granulomas (whose frequency increases during pregnancy), peripheral giant cell granulomas, or lymphoid hyperplasia of the lingual or other tonsillar tissue. The granulomas are most often located on the gingiva. Rarely, such lesions may represent a metastatic neoplasm.

Epithelial Tumors

Small, white, wartlike epithelial masses are common and can occur in any area of the oral mucosa. They are occasionally classified as epithelial neoplasms, but most do not continue to grow. Human papillomavirus types 2, 6, 11, 13, 32, and 57 have been identified in these wartlike lesions, which are usually classified generically as

papillomas. A large wartlike lesion on the oral mucosa should raise the suspicion of verrucous carcinoma.

Mucus Retention Lesions (Mucoceles)

Mucoceles are small, chronic or recurring vesicles or bullae that occur commonly on the inside of the cheeks and lips, the posterior palate, and the mouth floor. They are caused by injury to one of the many submucosal minor salivary glands, resulting in extravasation of mucus, which causes granulomatous inflammation or blockage of the excretory duct, which lead to cyst formation. Both types of lesions require conservative surgical excision because simple incision and drainage usually is followed by recurrence.

SALIVARY GLAND DISEASES

PRIMARY DISEASES OF SALIVARY GLANDS

Patients with enlargement of a major or minor salivary gland usually present a diagnostic challenge (Table 467–6). More than 20 types of benign or malignant salivary gland neoplasms may appear as unilateral enlargement of a major gland that is firm and nontender to palpation or as a firm submucosal nodule on the palate or the labial or buccal mucosa. Uncommonly, unilateral major gland enlargement may be reactive—for example, lymphoepithelial lesion, or chronic sialadenitis from a sialolith or inadequately treated bacterial sialadenitis. Observation of any of these lesions should be followed by appropriate imaging and biopsy.

Unilateral major salivary gland enlargement that is markedly painful or tender to palpation and has a purulent exudate or nothing expressible from the duct suggests bacterial sialadenitis. Any exudate should be cultured, and initial treatment should be with oral cephalexin or dicloxacillin.

Bilateral Salivary Gland Enlargement and Decreased Salivary Secretion Associated with Systemic Diseases

The best-known cause of bilateral salivary gland enlargement is infection by the mumps virus in children. However the prevalence of mumps decreased in the United States by more than 98% after the introduction of an effective vaccine in 1967, and now there are only a few hundred to a few thousand cases per year. Uncommonly, a less acute, mumpslike illness may occur in adults in association with cytomegalovirus, influenza, or coxsackie A virus infection.

Sjögren's syndrome is characterized in about one third of patients by gradual development of firm, nontender or only slightly tender, bilateral enlargement of major salivary glands (Chapter 282). The enlargement is chronic and may slowly wax and wane. Salivary secretion decreases gradually, and, if hypofunction is severe and prolonged,

---

Table 467–6 • CAUSES OF SALIVARY GLAND ENLARGEMENT

Usually unilateral
  Benign or malignant salivary gland neoplasms (more than 20
    different histopathologic types)
  Bacterial infection
  Chronic sialadenitis (single gland)
Usually bilateral and associated with salivary hypofunction
  Viral infection (mumps, cytomegalovirus, influenza, coxsackie A)
  Sjögren's syndrome (benign lymphoepithelial lesion)
  Chronic granulomatous diseases (sarcoidosis, tuberculosis, leprosy)
  Recurrent parotitis of childhood
  Human immunodeficiency virus infection/acquired
    immunodeficiency syndrome
Bilaterally symmetric, soft, nontender, parotid only
  Sialadenosis (asymptomatic parotid enlargment), idiopathic or
    associated with:
      Diabetes mellitus
      Hyperlipoproteinemia
      Hepatic cirrhosis
      Anorexia/bulimia
  Chronic pancreatitis
  Acromegaly
  Gonadal hypofunction
  Phenylbutazone use

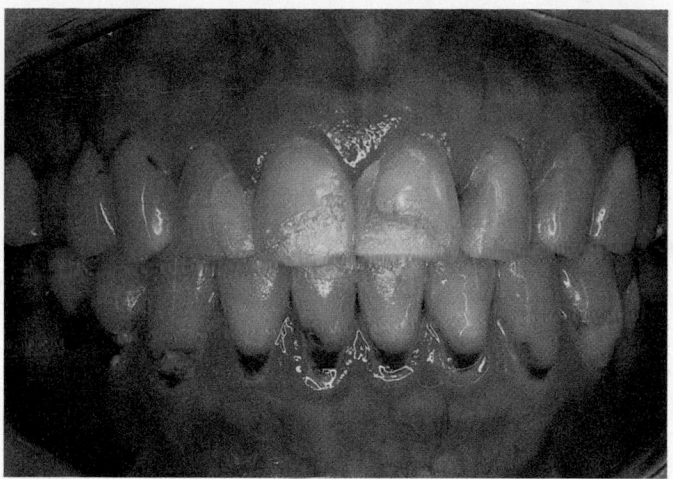

FIGURE 467–5 • Dental caries (brown and gray areas) and tooth-colored fillings in a patient with chronic salivary hypofunction.

Table 467–7 • CAUSES OF DECREASED SALIVARY SECRETION

Temporary
 Effects of short-term drug use (e.g., antihistamines)
 Virus infections (e.g., mumps)
 Dehydration
 Psychogenic conditions (e.g., anxiety)
Chronic
 Effects of chronically administered drugs (particularly
   antidepressants, monoamine oxidase inhibitors, neuroleptics,
   parasympatholytics, some combinations of drugs for treating
   hypertension)
 Chronic diseases
   Sjögren's syndrome
   Sarcoidosis
   Human immunodeficiency virus or hepatitis C infection
   Depression
   Diabetes mellitus (uncontrolled)
   Amyloidosis (primary or secondary)
   Central nervous system diseases
 Other effects of treatment
   Therapeutic radiation to the head and neck
   Graft-versus-host disease
 Absent or malformed glands (rare)

the resulting dry mouth can impair speech and swallowing and be associated with progressive dental caries or decay (Fig. 467–5), symptomatic erythematous candidiasis (see Fig. 467–3), and difficulty in wearing dentures. In severe cases, the oral mucosa is dry and sticky, and saliva is not expressible from the major ducts. About one third of patients show signs of erythematous candidiasis (see earlier discussion).

The salivary component of Sjögren's syndrome should be diagnosed from a labial salivary gland biopsy specimen containing at least five minor glands. Examination must show focal lymphocytic sialadenitis in most or all of the specimen and exclude nonspecific chronic sialadenitis or abnormalities indicative of another disease, such as noncaseating granuloma. A patient's symptoms of oral dryness (xerostomia) are important, but are subjective and caused by a wide variety of conditions (Table 467–7). Results from salivary function measurement or imaging are not diagnostically specific to Sjögren's syndrome.

Several chronic granulomatous diseases, such as sarcoidosis, tuberculosis, and leprosy, can cause bilateral enlargement and decreased function of salivary glands. The clinical and serologic features of sarcoidosis may closely mimic those of Sjögren's syndrome, and the distinction must be made by biopsy of minor salivary glands.

A few adult patients with HIV infection and most children who are infected in utero develop major salivary gland enlargement and reduced salivary secretion that are caused by lymphocytic infiltration. Parotid gland enlargement usually represents a solid or cystic lymphoepithelial lesion (see Table 467–2).

Recurrent parotitis of childhood includes episodes of unilateral or bilateral parotid enlargement. During flares of this illness, salivary secretion may be reduced, but usually without prominent secondary symptoms or signs. This condition, of unknown cause, usually subsides after puberty. Some serologic evidence suggests an association with Epstein-Barr virus infection.

Asymptomatic Parotid Enlargement (Sialadenosis)

Parotid glands can develop bilateral, symmetric enlargement that is soft and nontender to palpation and not associated with salivary hypofunction (see Table 467–6). Diagnosis is established by the clinical presentation and (if necessary to exclude sarcoidosis) a normal labial salivary gland biopsy. Usually, results of sialography and salivary scintigraphy are within normal limits. Biopsy of the affected glands is not indicated for diagnosis.

This chronic, noninflammatory, and non-neoplastic condition is usually associated with a variety of systemic diseases, including diabetes mellitus, hyperlipoproteinemia, hepatic cirrhosis, anorexia/bulimia, chronic pancreatitis, acromegaly, and gonadal hypofunction. It can also result from use of phenylbutazone or be a reaction to iodine-containing contrast media.

IMPAIRED SALIVARY SECRETION WITHOUT GLAND ENLARGEMENT

The very common symptom of dry mouth (xerostomia) is most often a side effect of chronically administered drugs. Many classes of drugs reduce unstimulated salivary secretion through anticholinergic or other mechanisms (see Table 467–7). Patients experience these symptoms soon after beginning to use the drug but produce enough saliva during a meal for normal chewing and swallowing. However, the symptoms and associated dental caries are dose-dependent and gradually increase with prolonged use of the drug. The classes of drugs producing the most profound effects are most tricyclic antidepressants, most neuroleptics, monoamine oxidase inhibitors, and all anticholinergics. A combination of drugs for treatment of hypertension may cause symptoms of dry mouth, but usually not to the extent of the drugs listed.

Several systemic diseases affect salivary secretion. As noted earlier, most patients with Sjögren's syndrome, some with sarcoidosis, and a few patients with HIV infection experience symptoms of dry mouth to various degrees, with or without salivary gland enlargement. In addition, patients who have primary or secondary amyloidosis with salivary gland deposition may develop impaired secretion. The symptom of xerostomia is more prevalent in individuals who also exhibit symptoms of depression, but are not taking any drugs. Furthermore, studies done before the availability of antidepressant drugs showed symptoms of depression were associated with decreased salivary secretion.

Irradiation of the head and neck region to treat a malignant tumor usually produces profound dry mouth before therapy is completed. Secretory capacity recovers only slightly in the months following treatment. Less severe dry mouth can accompany graft-versus-host disease following bone marrow transplantation; secretory capacity usually recovers when the reaction resolves.

Rx Treatment

Significant chronic salivary hypofunction from any cause produces a risk for dental caries (decay) in approximate proportion to the secretory impairment, but caries can largely be prevented if appropriate measures are taken as soon as the hypofunction begins. Remaining teeth should be protected by a comprehensive dental caries prevention program, monitored by a dentist, that includes daily application of an appropriate topical fluoride and removal of dental plaque, counseling on control of cariogenic dietary carbohydrates, and placement of appropriate dental restorations as necessary.

Symptomatic treatment of mild to moderately severe salivary hypofunction can include sialagogues such as sugar-free hard candies or chewing gum, frequent sips of water, and use of saliva substitutes at night. Severe hypofunction, especially that following irra-

Continued

diation, can be improved by oral pilocarpine, 5 mg four times a day or cevimeline, 30 mg three times a day, if not contraindicated.

Chronic erythematous oral candidiasis is a frequent sequela of chronic xerostomia, and its treatment and retreatment, as noted earlier, substantially improve the patient's oral symptoms.

SUGGESTED READINGS

Coogan MM, Sweet SP: Oral manifestations of HIV in the developing and developed world. Oral Dis 2002;8(Suppl. 2):1–175. *These peer-reviewed proceedings from the 4th International Workshop on Oral Manifestations of HIV Infection offer a comprehensive view of these lesions, which are often the earliest signs of HIV infection.*

Daniels TE: Evaluation, differential diagnosis, and treatment of xerostomia. J Rheumatol 2000;27(Suppl. 61):6–10. *The clinical evaluation, diagnosis, and management of patients with dry mouth or signs of chronic salivary hypofunction.*

Mandel I, Surattanont F: Bilateral parotid swelling: A review. Oral Surg Oral Med Oral Pathol Oral Radiol Endod 2002;93:221–237. *Discussion of the various causes of bilateral parotid enlargement, which is almost always associated with an underlying systemic disease or process.*

Regezi JA, Sciubba JJ, Jordan RCK. Oral Pathology: Clinical Pathologic Correlations, 4th ed. Philadelphia, WB Saunders, 2003. *Clinical features, differential diagnosis, etiology, and pathology of most diseases affecting the oral mucosa, jaws, and salivary glands, including excellent color illustrations of most clinical lesions.*

Vitali C, Bombardieri S, Jonsson R, et al: Classification criteria for Sjögren's syndrome: A revised version of the European criteria proposed by the American-European Consensus Group. Ann Rheum Dis 2002;61:554–558. *Widely accepted and clinically practical diagnostic criteria for this chronic but manageable disease.*

468 UPPER AIRWAY DISEASES

Kingman P. Strohl

The nose, ears, pharynx, and larynx are involved in such functions as conducting airflow to and from the lungs, taste, deglutition, speech, hearing, and smell. These chambered, highly specialized structures develop from the foregut and second through fourth branchial arches and are highly served by neural systems for motor control and sensation. Disease in any segment of the upper airway can have multiple consequences, and loss of any function can arise from both local processes and neural mechanisms. Because the larynx and pharynx act in series as the conducting airway to the trachea, bronchi, and the more distal gas-exchanging units of the lungs, dyspnea and air hunger result from swelling, encroachment, or neural dysfunction of these segments. Other presentations of upper airway disease include rhinorrhea and nasal obstruction (Chapter 268), sneezing, postnasal and pharyngeal secretions, cough (Chapter 81), dysphagia (Chapter 130), changes in voice, swelling of the upper and lower jaw, hearing loss (Chapter 470), tinnitus, snoring and apneas during sleep (Chapter 96), epistaxis, and pain.

Anatomic and functional assessments often reveal the cause of symptoms. For example, muffled speech and drooling in the presence of neck or jaw swelling indicate encroachment of the pharyngeal airway and require immediate assessment and monitoring of airway patency. Watching the patient with dysphagia while he or she drinks and swallows may differentiate a neural from an anatomic process. Examining the upper airways requires an appreciation of the anatomic complexities of the area and a facility with the otoscope, tongue blade, tuning fork, and manual (gloved) palpation of the mouth. Knowledge of salivary gland and lymph node locations, bimanual examination of the floor of the mouth, and percussion of the teeth are needed to distinguish among periodontal abscess, mandibular swelling, fracture, or tumor (Chapter 197). Referral to the appropriate specialist (orthodontist, oral surgeon, or otolaryngologist) saves time, prevents progression and complications, and/or avoids unnecessary procedures.

Clues to illness may arise from examining the upper airways in the absence of symptoms. Nasal polyps are associated with both aspirin-sensitive asthma (Chapter 84) and cystic fibrosis (Chapter 86). Nasal ulceration, nasal drip, and sinusitis may be seen in chronic cocaine use (Chapter 30) and withdrawal as well as in pulmonary vasculitis, especially that of Wegener's granulomatosis (Chapter 294). Parotid gland enlargement is associated with sarcoidosis (Chapter 91), diabetes (Chapter 242), amyloid (Chapter 290), and collagen vascular diseases (Chapter 273). Hereditary hemorrhagic telangiectasia (Osler-Weber-Rendu syndrome) presents to the internist with gastrointestinal bleeding and is characterized by dilated thin-walled capillaries and draining veins of the nose, lips, and mouth (Chapter 177).

HEARING DEFICITS

See Chapter 470.

Otitis (Chapter 470)

Otitis media (Table 468–1) may occur at any age, but it most frequently occurs in children younger than age 10. Presenting symptoms include pain and conductive hearing loss, more often unilateral. In acute presentations, most patients acknowledge a preceding upper respiratory tract infection; symptoms improve with antibiotics. When the presentation is subacute or chronic, treatment should include not only antibiotics but also consideration of mechanical factors, such as eustachian tube functional or anatomic obstruction and/or tympanic membrane rupture, which require surgical evaluation and intervention.

Several special concerns about otitis are relevant to internal medicine. First, serious complications may result from untreated or inadequately treated disease. Infection extending from the middle ear into the mastoid sinus and adjacent structures in the temporal bone may cause unilateral distal facial nerve palsy, osteomyelitis, infection of the basal structures of the skull, and/or intracranial extension, including dural abscess, brain abscess, and meningitis. Patients can present with sepsis and/or coma with increased intracranial pressure. Identification of the infecting organism is crucial. Problems in the inner ear may be addressed surgically after definitive intravenous antibiotic therapy. Second, the spectrum of organisms in immunocompromised hosts includes fungal infections (*Aspergillus* and *Candida*) that, if undetected, lead to complications. A third special circumstance is patients with long-standing endotracheal or nasogastric intubation. Nasal inflammation can block the eustachian tube and produce otitic and sinus infections with nosocomial organisms. Unexplained fever in the medical intensive care unit should involve examination of the upper airway and involve radiographic imaging and aspiration of the middle ear or sinuses for culture.

External otitis is characterized by severe pain, edema, and discharge along the auditory meatus. In contrast to otitis media, the ear and the tragus are painful to the touch, and otoscopic examination is painful. Often there is a history of water in or trauma to the ear canal. Culture could reveal *Pseudomonas* organisms but usually is not needed. Treatment with topical broad-spectrum antibiotics combined with topical corticosteroids, so-called otic drops, resolves symptoms and results in cure in 3 to 5 days. Narcotic analgesics are often needed to manage the pain. Oral antibiotics are indicated when regional lymphadenitis or erythema/cellulitis is present.

Infections of the external ear can become a serious problem in immunocompromised hosts and especially in diabetic patients, who have decreased host defenses and reduced sensation. This condition is sometimes called *"malignant" otitis* (Chapter 450). Spread of infection from the ear inferiorly results in facial nerve paralysis (not to be dismissed as Bell's palsy); infection of the jugular foramen; involvement of the glossopharyngeal, vagus, and accessory nerves; and infection of the sheath of the jugular vein, with extension inferiorly and contralaterally into the neck and rostrally into the lateral sinus. Medial spread involves the middle ear and the mastoid, whereas anterior spread involves the temporomandibular joint. Broad-spectrum intravenous antibiotics should be instituted promptly. Surgical intervention is indicated to identify organisms when nerve involvement or foreign body obstruction is suspected.

With recurrent external otitis, a history of repetitive trauma or exposure to water (so-called *swimmer's ear*) is likely. In the former,

Table 468–1 • OTITIS MEDIA

TYPE	MECHANISMS	TREATMENT
Acute	*Streptococcus pneumoniae* and *Haemophilus influenzae*; rarely *Staphylococcus aureus*, *Streptococcus pyogenes*, *Proteus*, *Pseudomonas*	Oral antibiotics
Serous	Failure to clear fluid (Starling effect)	Antihistamines and decongestants
Chronic	Persistent eustachian tube obstruction (rarely tuberculosis)	Drainage tubes ± all of the above

counseling may be needed on proper ear hygiene; in the latter, over-the-counter ear drops containing an alcohol/glycerine mixture can be recommended for use after bathing or swimming.

Rhinitis (Chapter 268)

Rhinitis comprises a group of disorders characterized by nasal itching, drip, and obstruction. These symptoms relate to irritation and inflammation of the mucosa and increased nasal secretions. Antigen challenge in susceptible hosts, histamine challenge, or activating non-myelinated nerve endings with substance P can reproduce symptoms found in acute allergic reactions and acute rhinitis. Subacute and chronic symptoms and nasal obstruction result from the activation of mucosal prostanoids and cytokine networks to promote the nasal inflammatory response, recruit inflammatory cells, and promote healing. Acute insults take 3 to 5 days to resolve unless bacterial super-infection, concomitant eustachian tube or sinus obstruction, or repeated exposure to a causative noninfectious agent or allergen occurs. A persistent inflammatory state can develop in susceptible individuals and result in chronic symptoms, nasal polyps, and altered or decreased sense of smell (anosmia). Antihistamines and intranasal fluticasone are effective therapies available for both allergic and non-allergic rhinitis.[1,2]

The most frequent cause of acute rhinitis is the common cold (Chapter 359). An *upper respiratory tract infection* is commonly a self-limited illness. The severity of infections may be attenuated by antiviral agents if taken near the time of exposure. Antihistamines, decongestants, and cool mist relieve symptoms. Topical decongestants such as oxymetazoline, used as directed, relieve nasal obstruction; however, rebound congestion and the potential complications of chronic vascular constriction follow if therapy is prolonged beyond 1 week. Bacterial superinfection presenting as sinusitis or otitis should be suspected if recurrent fever, regional lymphadenopathy, persistent mucopurulent discharge, or persistent symptoms last longer than 5 days. In this situation, oral antibiotics are useful.

Sinusitis

A mucopurulent discharge and a painful face suggest *sinusitis*, an inflammation of the lining of the paranasal sinuses. Most cases occur as a complication of the common cold or other upper respiratory tract infections, with occasional presentations due to extension of a periodontal infection under the maxillary sinus. Less than 1% of upper respiratory tract infections result in the clinical syndrome of acute sinusitis, and fewer meet the criteria for chronic sinusitis. Sinusitis is more common in adults, perhaps because the paranasal sinuses do not develop fully until the second and third decades of life. Bedside transillumination can suggest the presence of sinusitis. Normal light transmission to the frontal sinus from the supraorbital ridge or to the maxillary sinus through the hard palate excludes sinusitis; reduced or absent transmission is less helpful because considerable intraindividual anatomic variation exists. Radiographic "plain films" of the sinuses are helpful only if normal. Coronal computed tomographic scans may underestimate the extent of the disease in patients with chronic disease or in a compromised host. Magnetic resonance imaging better represents disease progression and invasion. Sinus aspiration and endoscopic sinuscopy may be necessary to recover organisms or to effect drainage. Surgical interventions are indicated for treatment failure, suppurative complications, diagnosis of nosocomial infection, and fever of unknown origin with sinus opacification.

Most causes of sinusitis are bacterial infections similar to those that produce otitis. The course of acute sinusitis is 3 to 4 weeks because of the anatomic difficulties in drainage. Decongestants improve nasal obstruction and may improve sinus drainage. The routine use of anti-histamines is controversial because of concerns that mucociliary clearance may be impaired. Oral antibiotics are often prescribed. Occasionally, surgical interventions are used when disease is chronic and resistant to empirical therapy. Fungal sinusitis is uncommon and presents as a chronic course. *Aspergillus* is most common, but *Candida, Mucor,* and *Penicillium* organisms may be recovered from infected sinus aspirates. Invasive disease with eye, mouth, and brain extension occurs in patients with AIDS or on chemotherapy. Finally, *maxillary antrum tumors* (Chapter 197) produce a unilateral bloody nasal discharge that can be confused with sinusitis. Clues to a malignant process are the chronicity of symptoms, the refractoriness to conventional therapy, and the presence of bony destruction of the antrum on radiographic examination.

Masses, Swelling, and Pain of the Jaw (Chapter 467)

Occasionally the internist sees patients with swelling of the face and jaw. Duration of symptoms, presence of a fever, history of local trauma, orthodontic difficulties, shortness of breath, or dysphagia may help localize lesions and identify potential complications. The anatomic locations of the salivary glands and lymph nodes are distinct (Fig. 468-1). The site of swelling of the jaw is determined on physical examination by palpation, running the finger intraorally along the inner and outer borders of the mandible, and comparing the right and left sides. Inspection and tooth percussion with a metal rod localize periodontal processes.

Fracture of the lower jaw usually presents as a history of trauma, even minor in nature. Jaw fractures are treated like compound fractures because the teeth communicate with the oral cavity. Occasionally, soft tissue swelling from secondary infection obscures a fracture. *Aseptic necrosis* caused by a vascular disease or a mandibular hairline fracture can also present as swelling and pain. *Periodontal abscess* results from poor dental hygiene or tooth trauma, particularly in the elderly, the diabetic, or the immunocompromised host. Complications result

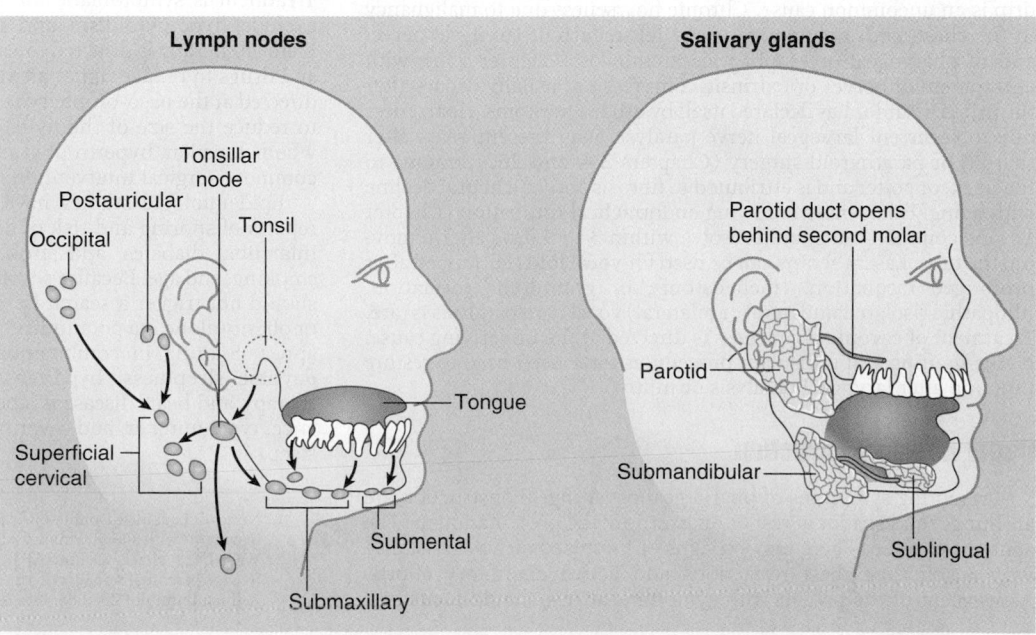

FIGURE 468-1 • Appropriate position of the lymph nodes (*left*) and the salivary glands (*right*). Arrows indicate routes of lymphatic drainage.

from periodontal abscess because infection can track rapidly along tissue planes to the basal structures of the skull and to the neck and mediastinum. *Ludwig's angina* (Chapter 322) is an infection presenting as a painful swelling of the anterior floor of the mouth, drooling, and dysphagia. Left unrecognized or untreated, it can progress rapidly to respiratory obstruction. Intravenous therapy with antibiotics and corticosteroids frequently is accompanied by surgical exploration and drainage.

Nonpainful swelling of the lower jaw suggests tumor of the bone or soft tissues. The most common nonmalignant tumor is an *epulis* (meaning "on the gum"), a granulomatous and fibrous tissue growth. Other growths include *osteoma, cyst, ameloblastoma* (a tumor of the cells that make enamel), and *malignant epithelioma*. Bilateral enlargement of the mandible occurs in *acromegaly, Paget's disease, osteitis fibrosa* from hyperparathyroidism, and *leontiasis ossea*. The last is a rare condition with jaw changes resembling acromegaly but without enlargement of the hands or feet.

Pain in the lower jaw without swelling is commonly due to *dental caries, periodontal disease,* or *temporomandibular dysfunction* (otomandibular syndrome). *Trigeminal neuralgia* presents as a unilateral dull pain, a distinct anatomic distribution, and a trigger zone for intense pain; neuralgia occurs in cranial nerve VII division II more than in III or I. In contrast, *herpes zoster* more commonly involves division I. Pain from cardiac angina also may be referred to the jaw and has been mistaken for periodontal disease.

Dysphagia

See Chapter 136.

Hoarseness

Simple hoarseness is the inability to pitch the voice and results from failure to use the larynx to produce tones. This change in voice occurs with voluntary acts, e.g., whispering, or with diseases affecting vocal cord motion and position. The most common cause of an acute onset of hoarseness is a bacterial or viral *infection*. Exposure to inhaled *irritants* (smoke or fumes) and *overuse* of the larynx present similarly. Inflammation and edema inhibit precise tension or closure of the cords. Treatment is rest and avoidance of exposure to irritants. Inhaled corticosteroids may produce cough and further irritation. Stridor suggests more than edema and inflammation of the vocal folds and warrants evaluation for extrinsic or intrinsic airway encroachment. Intermittent or recurrent hoarseness is usually associated with *smoking* and/or *allergy*.

Hoarseness persisting 2 weeks or more should be investigated by direct examination of the laryngeal structures. Chronic hoarseness can result from benign or malignant processes, including *gastroesophageal reflux* (Chapter 136), *laryngeal carcinoma* or *polyps* (Chapter 197), *arthritis* (Chapter 278), *hypothyroidism* (Chapter 239), *goiter,* and infections (*tuberculosis, syphilis,* and *histoplasmosis*). Postnasal drip is an uncommon cause. Chronic hoarseness due to malignancy in the chest, with entrapment of the left recurrent laryngeal nerve, and to pharyngeal or esophageal carcinomas (Chapter 136), with entrapment of nerves or extrinsic compression, usually occurs after the primary tumor has declared itself by other symptoms. Hoarseness due to recurrent laryngeal nerve paralysis may present years after thyroid or parathyroid surgery (Chapters 239 and 260), trauma to the neck, or goiter and is attributed to fibrosis and/or a neural decline with aging. Hoarseness following endotracheal intubation (Chapter 101) is common but should resolve within 3 to 5 days after removing the tube. Laser therapy can be used for vocal folds entrapped after prolonged intubation, tracheostomy, or granuloma formation. Idiopathic (isolated unilateral or bilateral) vocal cord paralysis is rare. Treatment of chronic hoarseness is directed at the underlying cause. Nerve-grafting and transplant procedures have been used to restore function after laryngeal paralysis or injury.

Upper Airway Obstruction

Presenting symptoms of pharyngeal or laryngeal obstruction are air hunger and stridor at rest or on exertion; the presentation may be acute or chronic. There may be signs of increased airway resistance with inspiratory chest retractions and active expiratory efforts. Assessment of the patient with symptoms at rest should focus first on restoring or assuring a patent airway before an examination. Most common misdiagnoses are asthma (Chapter 84) and heart failure (Chapter 55), so that a failure to respond to empirical treatment should raise suspicion for an upper airway cause of dyspnea, wheezing, and hypercapnic respiratory failure.

Direct examination may precipitate complete airway closure and should be performed in a controlled setting like an emergency department. If the patient is stable, a flow-volume loop is one noninvasive test that will reveal the presence of flow limitation on inspiration or on both inspiration or expiration (Chapter 82). A soft tissue lateral radiograph with the neck extended may localize the site of the obstruction.

Causes of acute obstruction include bacterial epiglottis, trauma, angioneurotic edema, allergic reactions, and foreign body aspiration. Chronic obstruction can be a presenting feature of neoplastic disease (squamous cell carcinoma being the most common), cricoarytenoid arthritis, vocal cord polyps, bilateral vocal cord paralysis, goiter, and neurofibromatosis.

Glottic dysfunction, also called factitious asthma, is an uncommon disorder characterized by intermittent episodes of dyspnea and wheezing. The patient may present with hypercapnia but with a normal arterial-alveolar gradient, indicating that gas exchange in the distal airways and lung units is normal. Patients have complete resolution of symptoms in minutes to hours, a finding also inconsistent with asthma or heart failure. Recognition and subsequent treatment with assurance and medicinal restraint is coupled with stress reduction measures and, occasionally, antidepressant medications for better outcome, as measured by fewer presentations for assessment and/or hospitalizations.

Snoring (Chapter 96)

Snoring is produced by vibrations of the soft tissues of the nasopharynx initiated by turbulent flow through a narrowed airway. Airway caliber is determined by anatomic factors, neuromuscular tone to skeletal muscle, and the pressure differences across the airway wall. Snoring occurs during sleep, a state in which postural tone to the skeletal muscles and reflex adjustments to respiratory loads are reduced. The airway closing at the level of the nasopharynx and/or oropharynx during sleep produces apnea (cessation of airflow) and is believed to represent an extension of the process that produces snoring (Chapter 96). Heavy snoring is terminated by changes in the sleep state or brief arousals from sleep. Repetitive arousals result in inadequate sleep and daytime sleepiness and increased sensitivity to central nervous system depressants.

Loud snoring, enough to be heard in the next room, is present in 5 to 10% of the population. In adults, examination reveals a reddened soft palate with or without anatomic narrowing of the nasal and oropharyngeal passages, micrognathia, or hypothyroidism. Other predisposing factors may include family history, obesity, respiratory depressants (alcohol and drugs), sleep restriction, nasal obstruction, and aging. Treatment is symptomatic for the bed partner, and one must first exclude hypothyroidism and then address predisposing factors. Medical therapy is directed toward weight loss, nasal decongestants, and drugs to reduce upper airway inflammation. Surgical therapy is directed at the naso-oropharynx with ablative or surgical procedures to reduce the size of the uvula or posterior palate. In children, in whom tonsillar hypertrophy and craniofacial anomalies are more common, surgical intervention is more successful.

Epidemiologic studies have suggested an association between reports of snoring and risk of developing hypertension, myocardial infarction, diabetes, and stroke, even when adjusted for obesity, smoking, and age. Because snoring is very common, the trait by itself should not trigger a search for sleep apnea. Snoring, hypertension, or obesity alone is a poor indication for a detailed evaluation for sleep apnea. Snoring in combination with observed apneas, excessive daytime sleepiness, hypertension poorly controlled by medical therapy, and heart disease is a better indication to quantify the presence, type, number, and severity of respiratory disturbances during sleep.

1. Nunes C, Ladeira S: Double-blind study of cetirizine and loratadine versus placebo in patients with allergic rhinitis. J Investig Allergol Clin Immunol 2000;10:20–23.
2. Webb DR, Meltzer EO, Finn AF Jr, et al: Intranasal fluticasone propionate is effective for perennial nonallergic rhinitis with or without eosinophilia. Ann Allergy Asthma Immunol 2002;88:385–390.

SUGGESTED READINGS

de Benedictis FM, del Giudice MM, Severini S, Bonifazi F: Rhinitis, sinusitis and asthma: One linked airway disease. Paediatr Respir Rev 2001;2:358–364. *The biology of the airway supports the concept that rhinosinusitis and asthma may be the expression of an inflammatory process that appears in different sites of the respiratory tract at different times.*

Fendrick AM, Saint S, Brook I, et al: Diagnosis and treatment of upper respiratory tract infections in the primary care setting. Clin Ther 2001;23:1683–1706. *Guidelines for the management of acute otitis media and acute bacterial sinusitis, emphasizing the importance of differentiating between bacterial and nonbacterial infections, choosing an antibiotic based on the local probability of infection with resistant pathogens, and judicious use of antibiotics to reduce the probability of creating more resistance.*

Silverberg DS, Iaina A, Oksenberg A: Treating obstructive sleep apnea improves essential hypertension and quality of life. Am Fam Physician 2002;65:229–236. *Quality of life improves once patients are successfully treated.*

Turner RB: The treatment of rhinovirus infections. Progress and potential. Antiviral Res 2001;49:1–14. *The common cold is an important illness associated with morbidity and economic burdens.*

Young J, Bucher H, Tschudi P, et al: The clinical diagnosis of acute bacterial rhinosinusitis in general practice and its therapeutic consequences. J Clin Epidemiol 2003;56:377–384. *Purulent nasal discharge and signs of pus in the upper airway were better than radiography or C-reactive protein for selecting patients who benefit from antibiotics.*

469 SMELL AND TASTE

Robert W. Baloh

Millions of people suffer from disorders of taste and smell, but these disorders are often neglected because they are not fatal and, unlike abnormalities of vision and hearing, are not considered serious handicaps. Chemosensory disorders, however, often reduce the enjoyment and quality of life and are important to patients who suffer from them. Disorders of taste interfere with digestion because taste stimulants alter salivary and pancreatic flow, gastric contractions, and intestinal motility. Smell also contributes to the anticipation and ingestion of food because much of what is tasted derives from olfactory stimulation during ingestion and chewing. The inability to detect noxious tastes and odors can result in food or gas poisoning, particularly in elderly subjects. In the extreme, chemosensory disorders can lead to overwhelming stress, anorexia, and depression. Over the past few years, there has been dramatic progress in modern understanding of the cellular and molecular mechanisms of chemoreception. Genes encoding for chemoreceptor proteins belonging to the G-protein coupled receptor superfamily comprise up to 1% of mammalian genomes. Sequence diversity in these genes encodes unique structural motifs that bind to different ligands signaling different odors and tastes.

Anatomy

The sensory receptor for taste, the taste bud, is made up of 50 to 150 cells arranged to form a pear-shaped organ. The life span of these cells is 10 to 14 days, and they are constantly being renewed from dividing epithelial cells surrounding the bud. Taste buds are located on the tongue, soft palate, pharynx, larynx, epiglottis, uvula, and the upper one third of the esophagus. The taste buds located on the anterior two thirds of the tongue and on the palate are innervated by the chorda tympani branch of the seventh cranial nerve. The ninth cranial nerve innervates the posterior one third of the tongue. The ninth and tenth nerves innervate taste buds in the pharynx and larynx. Afferent signals from the taste buds project to the nucleus of the solitary tract in the medulla and then via a series of relays to the thalamus and postcentral somatosensory cerebral cortex (primary ipsilateral). Free nerve endings of the fifth cranial nerve are found on the tongue and in the oral cavity, and lesions involving these pathways also can alter taste perception.

Olfactory receptors lie in a roughly dime-sized area of specialized pigmented epithelium that arches along the superior aspect of each side of the nasal mucosa. Specialized bipolar sensory cells in this region thrust short receptor hairs into the overlying mucosa to detect aromatic molecules as they dissolve. As with taste buds, the specialized receptor portion of the bipolar neuron undergoes continuous renewal, turning over approximately every 30 days. Thin axons of the bipolar neurons course through small holes in the cribriform plate of the ethmoid bone to form connections in the overlying olfactory bulb on the ventral surface of the frontal lobe. From here, second- and third-order neurons project directly and indirectly to the prepiriform cortex and parts of the amygdaloid complex of both sides of the brain, representing the primary olfactory cortex.

Pathophysiology of Chemosensory Disorders

Disorders of taste and smell can be divided into local, systemic, and neurologic categories (Table 469–1). The taste buds and the specialized receptor portion of the bipolar olfactory cells are constantly being renewed, and the process of renewal can be affected by nutritional, metabolic, and hormonal states, therapeutic radiation, drugs, and age. For example, with interruption of mitosis by antiproliferative agents, a return of normal taste function takes a minimum of 10 days, whereas a return to normal olfactory function takes more than 30 days. Numerous local conditions such as colds and allergies, chronic sinusitis, and nasal polyposis can influence the sense of smell by restricting airway patency. Accidental blows to the head can shear the fine axons of the bipolar olfactory neurons, resulting in loss of smell. Lesions of the fifth, seventh (*chorda tympani*), and ninth nerves can lead to disordered taste sensation. Olfactory and gustatory disturbances can serve as important diagnostic signs for focal neurologic lesions (e.g., frontal lobe tumors). Hallucinations of smell and taste occur with epileptogenic lesions affecting the mesial temporal lobe and insular region, respectively. Finally, olfactory disturbances and hallucinations occur with a number of psychiatric illnesses (particularly depressive illness and schizophrenia).

Evaluation of Taste and Smell

Olfaction can be tested grossly at the bedside with a few easily recognized odors such as coffee, chocolate, and the roselike aroma of the compound phenylethyl alcohol. (Nasal irritants should be avoided.) Each nostril is tested separately to determine whether the problem is unilateral or bilateral. Gustatory sensation is typically tested with weak solutions of sugar, salt, and acetic acid, or vinegar. The patient must keep the tongue protruded and respond to questions either by nodding the head or pointing to names of the tastes written on cards. The anterior two thirds and posterior one third of the tongue should be tested separately.

Common Causes of Loss of Smell and Taste

The most frequently encountered causes of loss of smell are local obstructive disease, viral infections, head injuries that sever the neurons crossing through the cribriform plate, and normal aging. Patients can lose their sense of smell not only from chronic allergies and sinusitis but also from the nasal sprays and drops that they use to treat these conditions. The most common causes of loss of the sense of taste are viral infections and drug ingestion, particularly antirheumatic and antiproliferative drugs. Many of the systemic disorders listed in Table 469–1 probably have their effect by decreasing the rate of turnover of sensory receptors on the tongue and olfactory epithelia. Disturbances of smell and taste in malnourished patients may be due to specific

Table 469–1 • COMMON CAUSES OF LOSS OF TASTE AND SMELL

	TASTE	SMELL
Local	Radiation therapy, oral infections, dentures, dental procedures	Allergic rhinitis, sinusitis, nasal polyposis, upper respiratory infection
Systemic	Cancer, renal failure, hepatic failure, nutritional deficiency (B_3, zinc), Cushing's syndrome, hypothyroidism, diabetes mellitus, infection (viral), drugs (antirheumatic and antiproliferative)	Renal failure, hepatic failure, nutritional deficiency (B_{12}), Cushing's syndrome, hypothyroidism, diabetes mellitus, infection (viral hepatitis, influenza), drugs (nasal sprays, antibiotics)
Neurologic	Bell's palsy, familial dysautonomia, multiple sclerosis	Head trauma, multiple sclerosis, Parkinson's disease, frontal tumor

deficiencies in vitamins and minerals, such as zinc. Viral illnesses such as influenza and viral hepatitis produce disorders of both taste and smell. Multifocal neurologic disorders such as multiple sclerosis can affect the central olfactory and gustatory pathways at multiple levels; therefore, abnormalities of taste and smell are common in such patients. Treatment of olfactory dysfunction due to nasal disease is aimed at opening the air passageways while preserving the olfactory epithelium. Intranasal steroids, antibiotics, and allergic therapies are useful in selected cases. Drugs known to affect taste or smell should be removed for a trial. Vitamin and mineral therapies are of unproven benefit.

SUGGESTED READINGS

Bromley SM: Smell and taste disorders: A primary care approach. Am Fam Physician 2000;61:427–436. *Practical approach to the patient who presents with loss of taste and smell.*

Comeau TB, Epstein JB, Migas C: Taste and smell dysfunction in patients receiving chemotherapy: A review of current knowledge. Support Care Cancer 2001;9: 575–580. *How to deal with disorders of taste and smell in patients undergoing chemotherapy.*

Sullivan SL: Mammalian chemosensory receptors. Neuroreport 2002;13:A9–A17. *Review of genetic and molecular mechanisms of chemoreception.*

470 HEARING AND EQUILIBRIUM

Robert W. Baloh

The neural pathways subserving hearing and those most important for equilibrium and spatial orientation are anatomically proximate in much of their course from their end organs in the inner ear to their termination in the superior portion of the temporal lobe. Because of the close anatomic linkage, disorders that affect hearing often affect equilibrium, and vice versa. For this reason they are considered together here. Despite their anatomic propinquity, however, substantial pathophysiologic differences make clinical examination of the two systems quite different. The auditory system is physiologically relatively isolated, so that its function and dysfunction can be tested independently of other neural systems. The vestibular system, in contrast, has many close physiologic links with other neural systems (particularly the cerebellum, oculomotor system, and autonomic nervous system) and can be tested only indirectly by noting secondary effects on these systems. Abnormalities of the auditory system lead to only a few well-defined and unique symptoms (i.e., hearing loss or tinnitus). Abnormalities of the vestibular system can cause symptoms that mimic disorders of the other neural structures. Such symptoms include dizziness, visual distortion (oscillopsia), imbalance, nausea, vomiting, and even syncope.

AUDITORY SYSTEM

Anatomy and Physiology of Hearing

In normal hearing, sound waves are transmitted from the tympanic membrane via the three ossicles of the air-filled middle ear (air conduction) to the oval window and the basilar membrane of the fluid-sealed cochlea. The ossicles increase the gain from the tympanum to oval window about 18-fold, compensating for the loss that sound waves moving from air to fluid would otherwise suffer. In the absence of this system, sound may reach the cochlea by vibration of the temporal bone (bone conduction) but with much less efficiency (approximately 60-dB loss). Hair cells, tonotopically organized along the cochlear basilar membrane, detect the vibratory movement of that membrane and transduce vibration into nerve impulses. The nerve impulses are relayed via nerve cells that synapse at the base of hair cells and have their bodies in the spiral ganglion to the cochlear nucleus of the ipsilateral pontine tegmentum. The spiral cochlea mechanically analyzes the frequency content of sound. For high-frequency tones, only sensory cells in the basilar region are activated, whereas for low-frequency tones, all or nearly all sensory cells are activated. Therefore, with lesions of the cochlea and its afferent nerve, the hearing levels for different frequencies are usually unequal, typically resulting in better hearing sensitivity for low-frequency than for high-frequency tones. Within the brain stem, auditory signals ascend from

the ventral and dorsal cochlear nuclei to reach the superior olivary nuclei of both sides. Thus nervous system lesions central to the cochlear nucleus do not cause monaural hearing loss and, conversely, unilateral central lesions do not cause deafness. From these structures the pathway projects by way of the lateral lemnisci to the inferior colliculi. Each inferior colliculus transmits to the other and to its ipsilateral medial geniculate body, which in turn sends the final projection to the transverse auditory gyrus lying in the superior portion of the ipsilateral temporal lobe.

The normal ear can detect sound frequencies ranging between 20 and 20,000 Hz; the upper range drops off fairly rapidly with advancing age. The ear is most sensitive between 500 and 4000 Hz, which roughly corresponds to the frequency range most important for understanding speech. The hearing level in this range has several practical implications in terms of the degree of handicap and the potential for useful correction with amplification. A 30- to 40-dB hearing level in the speech range would impair normal conversation, whereas an 80-dB hearing level would make everyday auditory communication almost impossible (the social definition of deafness).

Localization of Lesions within the Auditory Pathways

Conductive hearing loss results from lesions involving the external or middle ear. It is typically characterized by an approximately equal loss of hearing at all frequencies and by well-preserved speech discrimination once the threshold for hearing is exceeded. Patients with conductive hearing loss can hear speech in a noisy background better than in a quiet background because they can understand loud speech as well as anyone.

Sensorineural hearing loss results from lesions of the cochlea and/or auditory division of the eighth cranial nerve. With sensorineural hearing loss, the hearing levels for different frequencies are usually unequal, typically resulting in better hearing for low- than for high-frequency tones. Patients with sensorineural hearing loss often have difficulty hearing speech that is mixed with background noise and may be annoyed by loud speech. Three important manifestations of sensorineural lesions are diplacusis, recruitment, and tone decay. Diplacusis and recruitment are common with cochlear lesions; tone decay usually accompanies eighth nerve involvement.

Central hearing disorders result from lesions of the central auditory pathways. As a rule, patients with central lesions do not have impaired hearing for pure tones, and they can understand speech as long as it is clearly spoken in a quiet environment. If the listener's task is made more difficult with the introduction of background noise or competing messages, performance deteriorates more markedly in patients with central lesions than in normal subjects.

Examination of Hearing

BEDSIDE TEST. A quick test for hearing loss in the speech range is to observe the response to spoken commands at different intensities (whisper, conversation, shouting). Tuning fork tests permit a rough assessment of the hearing level for pure tones of known frequency. The clinician can use his or her own hearing level as a reference standard. In the Rinne test, nerve conduction is compared with bone conduction by holding a tuning fork (preferably 512 Hz) against the mastoid process until the sound can no longer be heard. It is then placed 1 inch from the ear and, in normal subjects, can be heard about twice as long by air as by bone. If bone conduction is better than air conduction, the hearing loss is conductive, but care must be taken to assure that the bone conduction is not heard in the normal ear. In the Weber test, the tuning fork is placed on the patient's forehead or upper teeth. Normally this sound is referred to the center of the head. If it is referred to the side of unilateral hearing loss, the hearing loss is conductive; if it is referred away from the side of unilateral hearing loss, the loss is sensorineural.

AUDIOMETRY. *Pure tone testing* is the cornerstone of most auditory examinations. Pure tones at selected frequencies are presented via either earphones (air conduction) or a vibrator pressed against the mastoid portion of the temporal bone (bone conduction), and the minimal level that the subject can hear (threshold) is determined for each frequency. Two speech tests are routinely used. The *speech reception threshold* (SRT) is the intensity at which the patient can correctly repeat 50% of the words presented. The SRT is a test of hearing sensitivity for speech and should reflect the hearing level for pure tones in the speech range. The *speech discrimination test* is a measure of the patient's ability to understand speech when it is presented at a level that is easily heard. In patients with eighth nerve lesions, speech discrimination scores can be severely reduced, even when pure tone thresholds are normal or nearly normal; by comparison, in patients with cochlear lesions, discrimination tends to be proportional to the magnitude of hearing loss.

Brain stem auditory evoked responses (BAER) can be recorded from scalp electrodes at 0 to 10 msec (early), 10 to 50 msec (middle), and 50 to 500 msec (late) following a click (a high-frequency stimulus). The early potentials reflect electrical activity at the cochlea, eighth cranial nerve, and brain stem; the later potentials reflect cortical activity. Computer averaging of the responses to 1000 to 2000 clicks separates the evoked potential from background noise. Early evoked responses may be used to estimate the magnitude of hearing loss and to differentiate among cochlea, eighth nerve, and brain stem lesions.

HEARING LOSS

Causes

CONDUCTIVE HEARING LOSS. The logic for identifying common causes of hearing loss is shown in Figure 470–1. The history, examination, and audiometry usually provide the key differential features. The most common cause of conductive hearing loss is *impacted cerumen* in the external canal. This benign condition is usually first noticed after bathing or swimming when a droplet of water closes the remaining tiny passageway. The most common serious cause of conductive hearing loss is inflammation of the middle ear, *otitis media*, either infected (suppurative) or noninfective (serous). Fluid accumulates in the middle ear, impairing the conduction of airborne sound to the cochlea. Because the air cavity of the middle ear is in direct connection with the mastoid air cells, infection can spread through the mastoid bone and, occasionally, into the intracranial cavity. Chronic otitis media with perforation of the tympanic membrane can result in an invasion of the middle ear and other pneumatized areas of the temporal bone by keratinizing squamous epithelium (*cholesteatoma*). Cholesteatomas can produce erosion of the ossicles and bony labyrinth, resulting in a mixed conductive sensorineural hearing loss. *Otosclerosis* commonly produces progressive conductive hearing loss by immobilizing the stapes with new bone growth in front of and below the oval window. The hearing loss is typically conductive, although in some persons the cochlea may be invaded by foci of otosclerotic bone, producing an additional sensorineural hearing loss. Otosclerosis usually stabilizes when the hearing level reaches 50 to 60 dB and rarely progresses

to deafness. Other common causes of conductive hearing loss include trauma, congenital malformations of the external and middle ear, and glomus body tumors.

SENSORINEURAL HEARING LOSS. Genetically determined deafness, usually from hair cell aplasia or deterioration, may be present at birth or may develop in adulthood. The diagnosis of *hereditary deafness* rests on the finding of a positive family history. In many instances, the inheritance is through a recessive gene or a dominant gene with low penetrance, making it difficult to determine the genetic nature of the disorder. Mutations in connexin 26, a key component of gap junctions in the inner ear, account for the majority of cases of inherited deafness identified so far. *Intrauterine factors* resulting in congenital hearing loss include infection (especially rubella); toxic, metabolic, and endocrine disorders; and anoxia associated with Rh incompatibility and difficult deliveries.

Acute unilateral deafness usually has a cochlear basis. *Bacterial or viral infections* of the labyrinth, *head trauma* with fracture or hemorrhage into the cochlea, or *vascular occlusion* of a terminal branch of the anterior inferior cerebellar artery all can extensively damage the cochlea and its hair cells. An acute idiopathic, often reversible, unilateral hearing loss strikes young adults and is presumed to reflect an isolated viral infection of the cochlea and auditory nerve terminals. Sudden unilateral hearing loss often associated with vertigo and tinnitus can result from a *perilymphatic fistula*. Such fistulas may be congenital or may follow stapes surgery or head trauma. *Drugs* cause acute and subacute bilateral hearing impairment. Salicylates, furosemide, and ethacrynic acid have the potential to produce transient deafness when taken in high doses. More toxic to the cochlea are aminoglycoside antibiotics (gentamicin, tobramycin, amikacin, kanamycin, streptomycin, and neomycin). These agents can destroy cochlear hair cells in direct relation to their serum concentrations. Some antineoplastic chemotherapeutic agents, particularly cisplatin, cause severe ototoxicity.

Subacute relapsing cochlear deafness occurs with *Ménière syndrome*, a condition associated with fluctuating hearing loss and tinnitus, recurrent episodes of abrupt and often severe vertigo, and a sensation of fullness or pressure in the ear. Recurrent endolymphatic hypertension (hydrops) is believed to cause the episodes. Pathologically, the endolymphatic sac is dilated, and the hair cells become atrophic. The resulting deafness is subtle and reversible in the early stages but subsequently becomes permanent and is characterized by diplacusis and loudness recruitment. The disorder is usually unilateral, but in about 20 to 40% of patients, bilateral involvement occurs.

The gradual, progressive, bilateral hearing loss commonly associated with advancing age is called *presbycusis*. Presbycusis is not a distinct disease entity but rather represents multiple effects of aging on the auditory system. It may include conductive and central

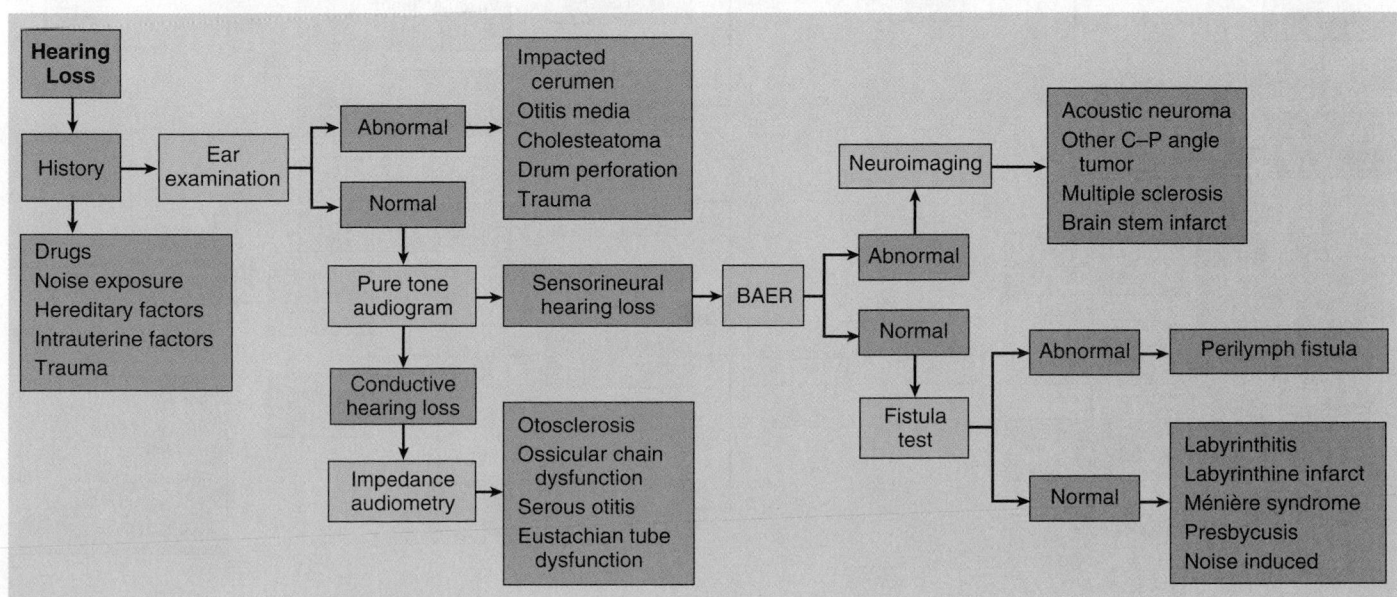

FIGURE 470–1 • Evaluation of hearing loss.

dysfunction, although the most consistent effect of aging is on the sensory cells and neurons of the cochlea. The typical audiogram of presbycusis is a symmetric high-frequency hearing loss gradually sloping downward with increasing frequency. The most consistent pathology associated with presbycusis is degeneration of sensory cells and nerve fibers at the base of the cochlea. The recurrent trauma of *noise-induced hearing loss* affects approximately the same cochlear region and is almost as common, particularly among those with exposure to loud explosive or industrial noises. Loud, blaring, modern music has become a recent offender. The loss almost always begins at 4000 Hz and does not affect speech discrimination until late in the disease process. With only brief exposure to loud noise (hours to days), there may be only a temporary threshold shift, but with continued exposure, permanent injury begins. The duration and intensity of exposure determine the degree of permanent injury.

Hearing loss from direct damage to the acoustic nerve in the petrous canal occasionally results from infection within or trauma to the surrounding bone; severe deafness of abrupt onset marks the event and is usually associated with acute vertigo due to concurrent vestibular nerve injury. Progressive unilateral hearing loss, which arises insidiously, initially in the high frequencies, and worsens by almost imperceptible degrees, is characteristic of benign neoplasms of the cerebellopontine angle, most commonly *acoustic neuromas*. In about 10% of cases, the hearing loss can be acute, apparently owing to either hemorrhage into the tumor or compression of the labyrinthine vasculature. Magnetic resonance imaging (MRI) with contrast reliably identifies small acoustic neuromas.

CENTRAL HEARING LOSS. Central hearing loss is unilateral only if it results from damage to the pontine cochlear nuclei on one side of the brain stem from conditions such as *ischemic infarction* of the lateral brain stem (e.g., occlusion of the anterior inferior cerebellar artery), a plaque of *multiple sclerosis*, or, rarely, invasion or compression of the lateral pons by a *neoplasm* or *hematoma*. Bilateral *degeneration* of the cochlear nuclei accompanies some of the rare recessive inherited disorders of childhood. As noted, clinically important unilateral hearing loss never results from neurologic disease arising rostrad to the cochlear nucleus. Although bilateral hearing loss could, in theory, result from bilateral destruction of central hearing pathways, in practice this is rare because involvement of neighboring structures in the brain stem

or hemisphere would usually produce overwhelming neurologic disability.

 Treatment

If an underlying disorder has not yet destroyed the auditory system and can be ameliorated medically or surgically, hearing may be improved or preserved. Most patients with otosclerosis respond to stapedectomy. Closure of a perilymph fistula may improve hearing. Antibiotic and decongestive treatment of otitis media should prevent permanent hearing loss. A low-salt diet and diuretics are effective in selective cases of Ménière syndrome, particularly if episodes are precipitated by premenstrual water retention. Hearing aids amplify sound, usually with the goal of making speech intelligible. Patients with conductive hearing loss require simple amplification, but those with sensorineural hearing loss often need frequency-selective amplification to make hearing aids useful. Recent advances in acoustic technology have markedly improved the outlook for the latter. Serial audiograms in patients with noise or ototoxic drug exposure are critical for prevention of permanent hearing loss.

TINNITUS

The evaluation of common causes of tinnitus (Fig. 470–2) begins with a careful history to identify common offending drugs. With *objective tinnitus*, the patient hears a sound arising external to the auditory system, a sound that can usually be heard by the examiner with a stethoscope. Objective tinnitus usually has benign causes such as noise from temporomandibular joints, opening of eustachian tubes, or repetitive muscle contractions. Sometimes, in a quiet room, the patient can hear the pulsatile flow in the carotid artery or a continuous hum of normal venous outflow through the jugular vein. The latter can be obliterated by compression of the jugular vein or extreme lateral rotation of the neck. Pathologic objective tinnitus occurs when patients hear turbulent flow in vascular anomalies or tumors (e.g., glomus jugulare tumor). Objective tinnitus may also be an early sign of increased intracranial pressure. Such tinnitus, which probably arises

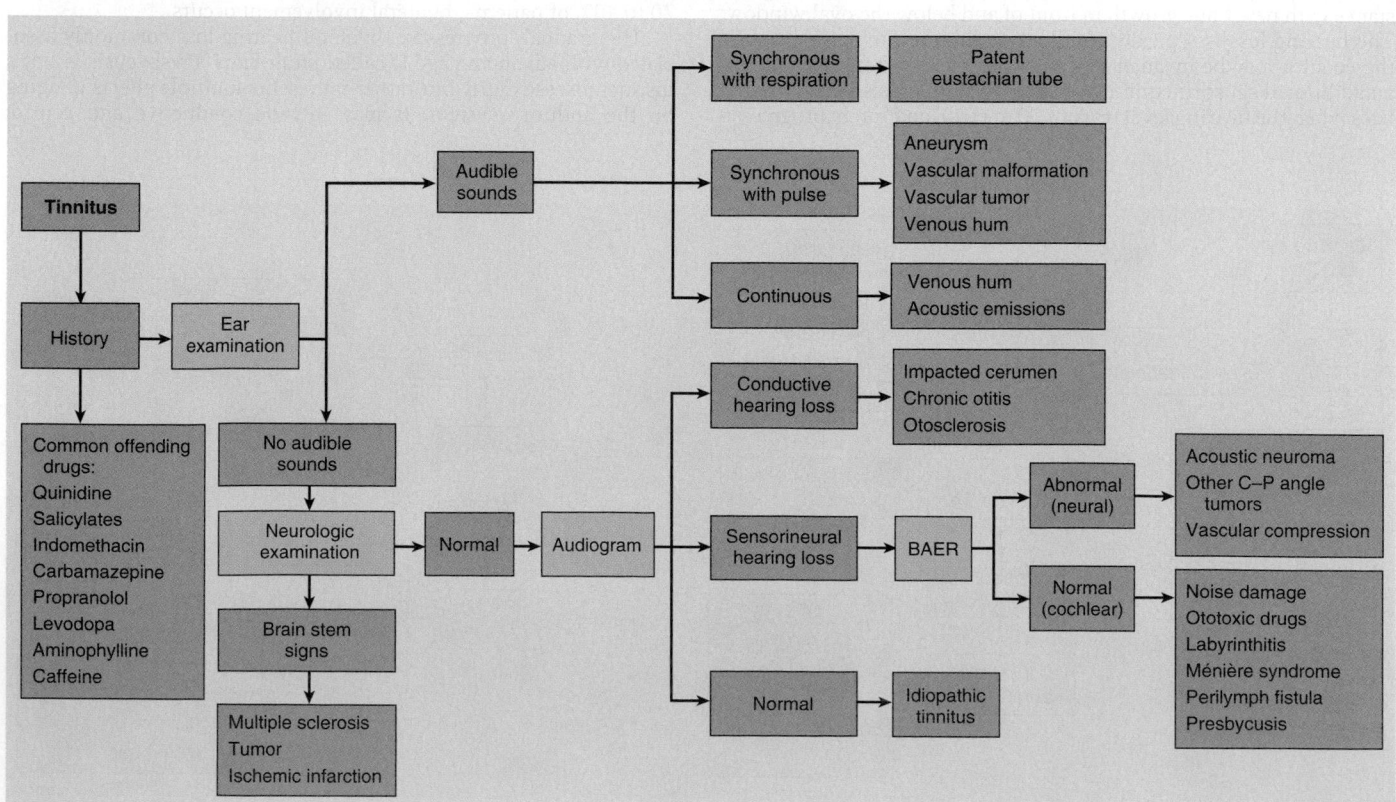

FIGURE 470–2 • Evaluation of tinnitus.

from turbulent flow through compressed venous structures at the base of the brain, is usually overshadowed by other neurologic abnormalities.

Subjective tinnitus can arise from sites anywhere in the auditory system. The sounds most frequently reported are metallic ringing, buzzing, blowing, roaring, or, less often, bizarre clanging, popping, or nonrhythmic beating. Tinnitus heard as a faint, moderately high-pitched, metallic ring can be observed by almost anyone who concentrates attention on auditory events in a quiet room. Sustained louder tinnitus accompanied by audiometric evidence of deafness occurs in association with both conductive and sensorineural hearing loss. Tinnitus observed with otosclerosis tends to have a roaring or hissing quality, while that associated with Ménière syndrome often produces sounds that vary widely in intensity with time and quality, sometimes including roaring or clanging. Tinnitus with auditory nerve lesions tends to be higher pitched and ringing in quality. Audiometric and brain stem evoked response testing can help distinguish between lesions involving the conducting apparatus, the cochlea, and the auditory nerve. Tinnitus without observable deafness appears sporadically and for variable lengths of time in many persons without other evidence of an ongoing pathologic process.

Rx Treatment

Most patients with tinnitus can be helped by detailed interview together with the relevant examination and laboratory investigations followed by reassurance when appropriate. Often exacerbating factors such as chronic anxiety and depression can be treated. In patients with hearing loss and tinnitus, a hearing aid may improve tinnitus because the amplification of ambient sound may effectively mask the tinnitus. This mechanism probably explains the frequent observation that removal of cerumen from the external auditory canal to improve ambient hearing also improves tinnitus. Also, when cerumen is attached to the tympanic membrane, tinnitus may result from local mechanical effects on the conductive system. For patients who find their tinnitus most obtrusive when trying to sleep, a bedside FM clock radio tuned between stations can provide an effective masking sound; some such radios can be programmed to switch off after the patient falls asleep. A careful drug history should be taken, and a drug-free trial period should be considered when possible. Some patients who notice that caffeine, alcohol, or nicotine exacerbates their tinnitus experience significant relief when these drugs are discontinued.

EQUILIBRIUM-VESTIBULAR SYSTEM

Anatomy and Physiology of the Vestibular System

The paired vestibular end organs lie within the temporal bones next to the cochlea. Each organ consists of three semicircular canals that detect angular acceleration and two otolith structures, the utricle and saccule, which detect linear acceleration (including gravitational). Like the cochlea, these organs possess hair cells that act as force transducers, converting the forces associated with head acceleration into afferent nerve impulses. The hair cells of the three semicircular canals, each of which is oriented at right angles to the others, are located in the crista, where their cilia are embedded in a gelatinous mass called the cupula. Movement of the head causes the endolymph to flow either toward or away from the cupula, bending the cilia and, depending on the direction of endolymphatic movements, either exciting or inhibiting the afferent nerves at the base of the hair cells. Because the afferent nerves are tonically active, the baseline activity can be increased or decreased depending on the direction of hair cell bending. Furthermore, the two sets of semicircular canals are approximately mirror images of each other, so that rotational movement of the head that excites one canal inhibits the analogous canal on the opposite side. The hair cells of the utricle and saccule are located in an area called the *macule*. The macule of the utricle lies approximately in the plane of the horizontal canal, and the macule of the saccule is approximately in the plane of the anterior canal. The hair cell cilia are embedded in a membrane that contains calcium carbonate crystals or otoliths; the density of otoliths is considerably greater than that of the endolymph. Linear accelerations of the head combine with the linear acceleration of gravity to distort the otolith membrane, thereby bending

the cilia of the hair cells and modulating the activity of the afferent nerve terminals at the base of the hair cells.

The afferent vestibular nerves have their cell bodies in Scarpa's ganglion. The nerve fibers travel in the vestibular portion of the eighth cranial nerve contiguous to the acoustic portion. Fibers from different receptor organs terminate in different vestibular nuclei at the pontomedullary junction. There are also direct connections with many portions of the cerebellum, the greatest representation being in the flocculonodular lobe, the so called vestibular cerebellum. Efferent fibers from the brain stem travel through the vestibular nerve to reach hair cells of the semicircular canals and macules. Efferent fibers are inhibitory in nature and, like the efferent fibers of the cochlea, may function to enhance inputs to which the brain attends. From the vestibular nuclei, second-order neurons make important connections to the vestibular nuclei of the other side, to the cerebellum, to motor neurons of the spinal cord, to autonomic nuclei in the brain stem, and, most importantly for the examining clinician, to the nuclei of the oculomotor system. Fibers from the vestibular nuclei also ascend through the brain stem and thalamus to reach the cerebral cortex bilaterally.

Localization of Lesions within the Vestibular Pathways

Vertigo can be caused by either the peripheral or central vestibular apparatus. In general, peripheral vertigo is more severe, is more likely to be associated with hearing loss and tinnitus, and often leads to nausea and vomiting. Nystagmus associated with peripheral vertigo is usually inhibited by visual fixation. Central vertigo is generally less severe than peripheral vertigo and is often associated with other signs of central nervous system disease. The nystagmus of central vertigo is not inhibited by visual fixation and frequently is prominent when vertigo is mild or absent.

Examination of the Vestibular System

Most vestibular problems presenting to the physician are episodic, and often there are neither symptoms nor signs when the physician examines the patient. The history, therefore, can become paramount for identifying vestibular dysfunction. The history should attempt to distinguish vertigo (the illusion of movement in space) from light-headedness (presyncope), ataxia (disequilibrium of the body without true movement in space), and psychogenic symptoms (the feeling of dissociation or, sometimes, disequilibrium). If the history is not clear, bedside provocative tests to mimic the symptom may assist in making a pathophysiologic diagnosis. Hyperventilation, which lowers the $PaCO_2$ and decreases cerebral blood flow, causes a lightheaded sensation associated with syncope. Patients with compressive lesions of the vestibular nerve, such as with an acoustic neuroma or cholesteatoma, or with demyelination of the vestibular nerve root entry zone may develop vertigo and nystagmus after hyperventilation. Presumably, metabolic changes associated with hyperventilation trigger the partially damaged nerve to fire inappropriately.

Bedside tests of vestibulospinal function are often insensitive because most patients can use vision and proprioceptive signals to compensate for any vestibular loss. Patients with acute unilateral peripheral vestibular lesions may past point or fall toward the side of the lesion, but within a few days balance returns to normal. Patients with bilateral peripheral vestibular loss have more difficulty compensating and usually show some imbalance on the Romberg and tandem walking tests, particularly with eyes closed.

The vestibulo-ocular reflex can be tested at the bedside using the doll's-eye and head-thrust tests. In an alert human, rotating the head back and forth in the horizontal plane induces compensatory horizontal eye movements that are dependent on both the visual and vestibular systems. The doll's-eye test is a test of vestibular function in a comatose patient, because such patients cannot generate pursuit or corrective fast components. In this setting, conjugate compensatory eye movements indicate normally functioning vestibulo-ocular pathways. Because the vestibulo-ocular reflex has a much higher frequency range than the smooth pursuit system, a qualitative bedside test of vestibular function can be made with the head-thrust test. It is performed by grasping the patient's head and applying brief, small-amplitude, high-acceleration head thrusts first to one side and then the other. The patient fixates on the examiner's nose and the examiner watches for corrective saccades, which are a sign of an inappropriate compensatory slow phase.

The caloric test uses a nonphysiologic stimulus to induce endolymphatic flow in the horizontal semicircular canal and horizontal nystagmus by creating a temperature gradient from one side of the canal to the other. With a cold caloric stimulus, the column of endolymph nearest the middle ear falls because of its increased density. This causes the cupula to deviate away from the utricle (ampullofugal flow) and produces horizontal nystagmus with the fast phase directed away from the stimulated ear. A warm stimulus produces the opposite effect, causing ampullopedal endolymph flow and nystagmus directed toward the stimulated ear (mnemonic: COWS, meaning cold opposite, warm same). Because of its ready availability, ice water (approximately 0°C) can be used for bedside caloric testing. To bring the horizontal canal into the vertical plane, the patient lies in the supine position with head tilted 30 degrees forward. Infusion of 1 to 3 mL of ice water induces a burst of nystagmus usually lasting about a minute. Greater than a 20% asymmetry in nystagmus duration suggests a lesion on the side of the decreased response. The ice water caloric test is a useful way to test the integrity of the oculomotor pathways in a comatose patient. In this case, ice water induces only a slow tonic deviation toward the side of stimulation.

Examination for pathologic vestibular nystagmus should include a search for spontaneous and positional nystagmus (see Table 466–4). Because vestibular nystagmus secondary to peripheral vestibular lesions is inhibited with fixation, the yield is increased by impairing fixation (such as with +30 lenses, Frenzel glasses). Two general types of positional nystagmus can be identified on the basis of nystagmus duration: static and paroxysmal. One induces static positional nystagmus by slowly placing the patient into the supine, then right lateral, and then left lateral positions. This type of positional nystagmus persists as long as the position is held. Because direction-changing and direction-fixed forms of static positional nystagmus occur with both peripheral and central vestibular lesions, their presence indicates only a dysfunction somewhere in the vestibular system. As with spontaneous nystagmus, however, lack of suppression with fixation and signs of associated brain stem dysfunction suggest a central lesion.

Paroxysmal positional nystagmus (also called positioning nystagmus) is induced, after a brief delay, by a rapid change from erect sitting to supine head-hanging left or right position (the so-called Dix-Hallpike test). It is initially high in frequency but dissipates rapidly (within 30 seconds to 1 minute). The most common variety of paroxysmal positional nystagmus, benign paroxysmal positional nystagmus, usually has a 3- to 10-second latency before onset and rarely lasts longer than 30 seconds. The nystagmus is torsional, with the upper pole of the eye beating toward the ground. It is usually prominent in only one head-hanging position, and a burst of nystagmus in the reverse direction occurs when the patient reassumes the sitting position. Another key feature is the severe vertigo and nystagmus that the patient experiences with the initial positioning, which, with repeated positioning, rapidly disappear (fatigability). Benign paroxysmal positional nystagmus results from free-floating debris within the posterior semicircular canal.

Electronystagmography (ENG), which is a technique for recording eye movements, allows precise quantification of both physiologic and pathologic nystagmus. A standard ENG test battery includes (1) tests of visual ocular control (saccades, smooth pursuit, and optokinetic nystagmus); (2) a careful search for pathologic nystagmus with fixation and with eyes open in darkness; and (3) measurement of induced physiologic nystagmus (caloric and rotational). ENG can be helpful in identifying a vestibular lesion and localizing it within the peripheral and central pathways.

Evaluating the "Dizzy" Patient

The history is key because it determines the type of dizziness (vertigo, near-faint, psychophysiologic disequilibrium), associated symptoms (neurologic, audiologic, cardiac, psychiatric), precipitating factors (position change, trauma, stress, drug ingestion), and predisposing illness (systemic viral infection, cardiac disease, cerebrovascular disease; Table 470–1). The history provides direction for both the examination and the diagnostic evaluation. When focal neurologic signs are found, neuroimaging usually leads to a specific diagnosis. When vertigo is present without focal neurologic symptoms or signs, audiometry and ENG aid in localizing the lesion to the labyrinth or eighth nerve. Patients with psychophysiologic dizziness should be identified after the history and examination so that needless tests are not obtained. A detailed cardiac evaluation (including loop monitoring) often identifies the cause of episodic near fainting (Chapters 58 and 435).

Common Causes of Vertigo (Fig. 470–3)

PHYSIOLOGIC VERTIGO. Physiologic vertigo includes common disorders that occur in normal people such as *motion sickness, space sickness,* and *height vertigo.* In these conditions, vertigo (defined as an illusion of movement) is minimal while autonomic symptoms predominate. With height vertigo, patients may experience acute anxiety and panic reaction. Individuals with motion sickness and space sickness typically develop perspiration, nausea, vomiting, increased salivation, yawning, and generalized malaise. Gastric motility is reduced and digestion impaired. Even the sight or smell of food is distressing. Hyperventilation is a common sign, and the resulting hypocapnia leads to changes in blood volume, with pooling in the lower parts of the body predisposing to postural hypotension and syncope. An unusual variant of motion sickness continues when the subject returns to stationary conditions after prolonged exposure to motion. Typically, affected patients report that they feel the persistent rocking sensation of a boat long after returning to solid ground. Rarely, the syndrome can last for months to years after exposure to motion and can even be incapacitating. The cause is unknown.

Physiologic vertigo can often be suppressed by supplying sensory cues that help to match the signals originating from different sensory systems. Thus, motion sickness, which is caused by a mismatch of visual and vestibular signals, is exacerbated by sitting in a closed space or reading (giving the visual system the miscue that the environment is stationary). It may be improved by looking out at the horizon. Height vertigo, caused by a mismatch between sensation of normal body sway and lack of its visual detection, can often be relieved either by sitting or by visually fixating a nearby stationary object.

BENIGN POSITIONAL VERTIGO. Benign positional vertigo (BPV) is by far the most common cause of vertigo. Patients with this condition develop brief episodes of vertigo (less than 1 min) with position change, typically when turning over in bed, getting in and out of bed, bending over and straightening up, or extending the neck to look up (so-called top shelf vertigo). BPV can result from *head injury, labyrinthitis,* and *vascular occlusion,* or it may occur as an isolated symptom (in most cases). The latter is particularly common in the elderly. This syndrome is important to recognize because, in most patients, it can be cured by a simple bedside maneuver. The diagnosis rests on finding

Table 470–1 • DESCRIPTION, MECHANISM, AND FOCUS OF DIAGNOSTIC WORKUP FOR COMMON TYPES OF DIZZINESS

TYPE OF DIZZINESS	DESCRIPTION	MECHANISM	FOCUS OF DIAGNOSTIC EVALUATION
Vertigo	Spinning (environment moves), tilt, drunkenness	Imbalance in tonic vestibular activity	Auditory and vestibular systems
Near faint	Lightheaded, swimming	Decreased blood flow to entire brain	Cardiovascular system
Psychophysiologic	Dissociated from body, spinning inside (environment still)	Impaired central integration of sensory signals	Psychiatric assessment
Disequilibrium	Off balance, unsteady on feet	Loss of vestibulospinal, proprioceptive, cerebellar, or motor function	Neurologic assessment

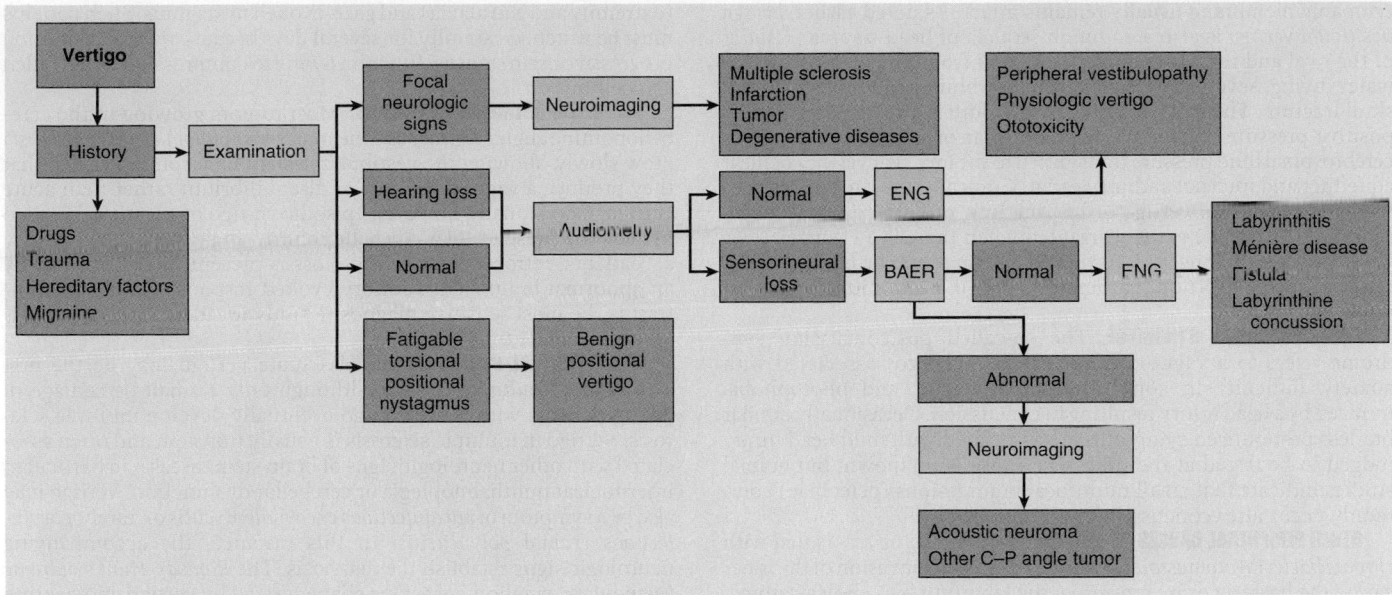

FIGURE 470–3 • Evaluation of vertigo.

characteristic fatigable paroxysmal positional nystagmus after a rapid change from the sitting to the head-hanging position (see earlier text). BPV results from free-floating calcium carbonate crystals (normally attached to the utricular macule) that inadvertently enter the long arm of the posterior semicircular canal. The crystals move within the endolymph under the influence of gravity and displace the cupula. Consistent with this theory, the burst of paroxysmal positional nystagmus is in the plane of the posterior canal of the "down ear," and the positional nystagmus disappears after the ampullary nerve has been surgically resected from the posterior canal on the diseased side. If the history and physical findings are typical, a bedside positioning maneuver can remove the debris from the posterior semicircular canal (Fig. 470–4). Patients can be taught to perform the maneuver on their own if there is a recurrence of symptoms, as occurs in most patients. If the history or findings are atypical, the condition must be distinguished from other causes of positional vertigo that may occur with tumors or infarcts of the posterior fossa.

ACUTE PERIPHERAL VESTIBULOPATHY ("LABYRINTHITIS, VESTIBULAR NEURITIS").
One of the most common clinical neurologic syndromes at any age is the acute onset of vertigo, nausea, and vomiting lasting for several days and not associated with auditory or neurologic symptoms. Most affected patients gradually improve over 1 to 2 weeks, but residual dizziness and imbalance can persist for months. Many report an upper respiratory tract illness 1 to 2 weeks before the onset of vertigo. This syndrome occasionally occurs in epidemics (epidemic vertigo), may affect several members of the same family, and more often erupts in the spring and early summer. All of these factors suggest a viral origin, but attempts to isolate an agent have been unsuccessful, except for occasional findings of a herpes zoster infection. Pathologic studies showing atrophy of one or more vestibular nerve trunks, with or without atrophy of their associated sense organs, are evidence of a vestibular nerve site and, probably, viral cause for many patients with this syndrome. Although steroids and antiviral agents have been recommended for treatment, so far there have been no well-controlled studies to demonstrate their efficacy.

MÉNIÈRE SYNDROME. The typical clinical features of Ménière syndrome are described earlier. This disorder accounts for about 10% of all patients with vertigo. The diagnosis is based on documenting episodic severe attacks accompanied by fluctuating hearing levels on audiometric testing beginning in the low frequencies.

MIGRAINE. Vertigo is a common symptom with migraine. It can occur with headaches or in separate isolated episodes, and it can predate the onset of headache. So-called benign paroxysmal vertigo of childhood is often the first symptom of migraine. The mechanism of vertigo with migraine is not clear, but damage to the inner ear occurs in about one fourth of patients. A few develop typical features of Ménière syndrome.

POST-TRAUMATIC VERTIGO. Vertigo, hearing loss, and tinnitus often follow a blow to the head that does not result in temporal bone

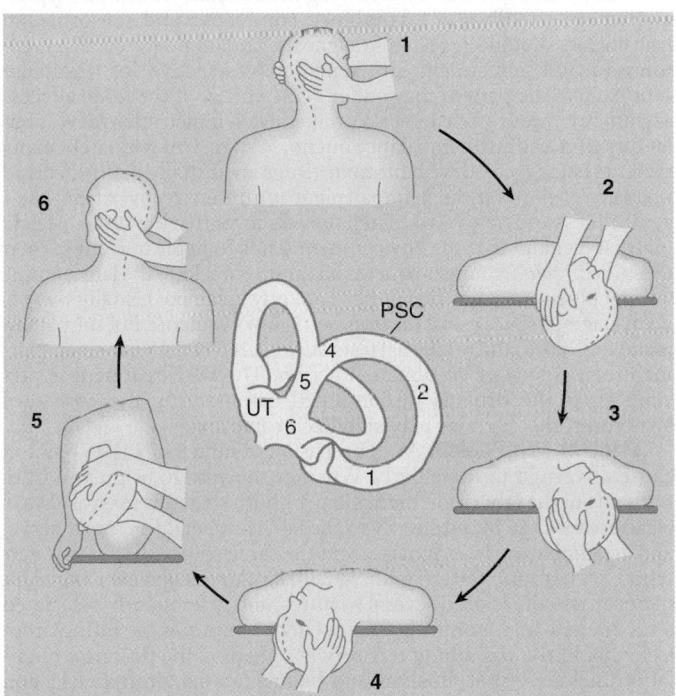

FIGURE 470–4 • Treatment maneuver for benign positional vertigo affecting the right ear. The procedure is reversed for treating the left ear. The numbers in the posterior semicircular canal (PSC) correspond to the position of the calcium carbonate crystals in each head position as they are moved toward the utricle (UT). Positions 2 and 3 are the same except that the therapist has moved from the front to the back of the patient to continue the maneuver easily. The entire sequence should be repeated until no nystagmus is elicited. (Courtesy of Carol A. Foster, MD, University of Colorado School of Medicine.)

fracture, the so-called *labyrinthine concussion*. Although they are protected by a bony capsule, the delicate labyrinthine membranes are susceptible to blunt trauma. Blows to the occipital or mastoid region are particularly likely to produce labyrinthine damage. *Transverse fractures* of the temporal bone typically pass through the vestibule of the inner ear, tearing the membranous labyrinth and lacerating the vestibular and cochlear nerves. Complete loss of vestibular and cochlear function is the usual sequela, and the facial nerve is interrupted in approximately 50% of cases. Examination of the ear often reveals hemotympanum, but bleeding from the ear seldom occurs because the tympanic membrane usually remains intact. As noted earlier, *benign positional vertigo* is also a common sequela of head trauma. *Fistulas* of the oval and round windows can result from impact noise, deep-water diving, severe physical exertion, or blunt head injury without skull fracture. The mechanism of the rupture is a sudden negative or positive pressure change in the middle ear or a sudden increase in cerebrospinal fluid pressure transmitted to the inner ear via the cochlear aqueduct and internal auditory canal. Clinically, the rupture leads to the sudden onset of vertigo or hearing loss, or both. Surgical exploration of the middle ear is warranted when there is a clear relationship between the onset of vertigo or hearing loss, or both, and the onset of severe exertion, barometric change, head injury, or impact noise.

POSTCONCUSSION SYNDROME. The so-called postconcussion syndrome refers to a vague dizziness (rarely vertigo) associated with anxiety, difficulty in concentrating, headache, and photophobia induced by a head injury resulting in concussion. Occasionally, similar but less pronounced symptoms are associated with mild head injury judged to be trivial at the time. The cause is unknown, but animal studies indicate that small multifocal brain lesions (petechiae) commonly occur after concussive brain injury.

OTHER PERIPHERAL CAUSES OF VERTIGO. Vertigo can be associated with *chronic bacterial otomastoiditis,* either from direct invasion of the inner ear by the bacteria or by erosion of the labyrinth by a cholesteatoma. Radiographic studies of the temporal bone readily identify these disorders. Just as *otosclerosis* can result in sensorineural hearing loss, it can also produce vertigo by involving the bony labyrinth. The typical audiometric findings of a combined conductive and sensorineural hearing loss should suggest this diagnosis. The aminoglycosides, streptomycin and gentamicin, are remarkably selective for vestibular ototoxicity. The patient may suffer acute vertigo if the toxic effect is asymmetric. More often there is a progressive symmetric loss of vestibular function leading to imbalance but not vertigo. Unfortunately, many patients being treated with ototoxic drugs are initially bedridden and unaware of the vestibular impairment until they recover from their acute illness and try to walk. Then they discover that they are unsteady on their feet and that the environment tends to jiggle in front of their eyes *(oscillopsia).* Younger patients adapt after weeks to the labyrinthine failure; older ones may be left permanently disabled. Usually there is no nystagmus (because of the symmetric involvement), but the patient is ataxic. Caloric and rotational tests during ENG can document impairment or absence of vestibular function. The best treatment is prevention. If the drug is discontinued early during the course of symptoms, the disorder may stabilize or improve.

VASCULAR INSUFFICIENCY. Vertebrobasilar insufficiency is a common cause of vertigo in the elderly. Whether the vertigo originates from ischemia of the labyrinth, brain stem, or both structures is not always clear because the blood supply to the labyrinth, eighth cranial nerve, and vestibular nuclei originate from the same source, the basilar vertebral circulation. Vertigo with *vertebrobasilar insufficiency* is abrupt in onset, usually lasting several minutes, and is frequently associated with nausea and vomiting. Associated symptoms resulting from ischemia in the remaining territory supplied by the posterior circulation include visual illusions and hallucinations, drop attacks and weakness, visceral sensations, visual field defects, diplopia, and headache. These symptoms occur in episodes either in combination with the vertigo or alone. Vertigo may be an isolated initial symptom of vertebrobasilar ischemia, but repeated episodes of vertigo without other symptoms should suggest another diagnosis. Vertebrobasilar insufficiency usually is caused by atherosclerosis of the subclavian, vertebral, and basilar arteries. Occasionally, episodes of vertebrobasilar insufficiency are precipitated by postural hypotension, Stokes-Adams attacks, or mechanical compression from cervical spondylosis. MRI of the brain is usually normal because the vascular insufficiency is transient and function returns to normal between episodes. MR angiography can identify occlusive vascular disease most commonly involving the vertebral-basilar junction.

Vertigo is a common symptom associated with *infarction of the lateral brain stem* or *cerebellum,* or both. The diagnosis usually is clear, based on the characteristic acute history and pattern of associated symptoms and neurologic findings. Occasionally, cerebellar infarction or hemorrhage presents with severe vertigo, vomiting, and ataxia without associated brain stem symptoms and signs that might suggest the erroneous diagnosis of an acute peripheral vestibular disorder. The key differential point is the finding of clear cerebellar signs (extremity and gait ataxia) and gaze-evoked nystagmus. Such patients must be watched carefully for several days because they may develop progressive brain stem dysfunction owing to compression by a swollen cerebellum.

CEREBELLOPONTINE-ANGLE TUMORS. Most tumors growing in the cerebellopontine angle (e.g., *acoustic neuroma, meningioma, epidermal cyst*) grow slowly, allowing the vestibular system to accommodate so that they produce a vague sensation of disequilibrium rather than acute vertigo. Occasionally, however, episodic vertigo or positional vertigo heralds the presence of a cerebellopontine-angle tumor. In virtually all patients, retrocochlear hearing loss is present, best identified by an abnormal brain stem auditory evoked response. MRI with contrast is the most sensitive diagnostic study for identifying a cerebellopontine-angle tumor.

OTHER CENTRAL CAUSES OF VERTIGO. Acute vertigo may be the first symptom of *multiple sclerosis,* although only a small percentage of young patients with acute vertigo eventually develop multiple sclerosis. Vertigo in multiple sclerosis is usually transient and often associated with other neurologic signs of brain stem disease, in particular, internuclear ophthalmoplegia or cerebellar dysfunction. Vertigo may also be a symptom of *parainfectious encephalomyelitis* or, rarely, *parainfectious cranial polyneuritis.* In this instance, the accompanying neurologic signs establish the diagnosis. The *Ramsay-Hunt syndrome* (geniculate ganglion herpes) is characterized by vertigo and hearing loss associated with facial paralysis and, sometimes, pain in the ear. The typical lesions of herpes zoster, which may follow the appearance of neurologic signs, are found in the external auditory canal and over the palate in some patients. Rarely is herpes zoster responsible for vertigo in the absence of the full-blown syndrome. *Granulomatous meningitis* or *leptomeningeal metastasis* and cerebral or systemic *vasculitis* may involve the eighth nerve, producing vertigo as an early symptom. In these disorders, cerebrospinal fluid analysis usually suggests the diagnosis. Patients suffering from *temporal lobe epilepsy* occasionally experience vertigo as the aura. Vertigo in the absence of other neurologic signs or symptoms is never caused by epilepsy or other diseases of the cerebral hemispheres.

Rx | **Treatment**

Treatment of vertigo can be divided into three general categories: specific, symptomatic, and rehabilitative. Specific therapies include antibiotics for bacterial or syphilitic labyrinthitis, anticoagulants for vertebrobasilar insufficiency, and surgery for acoustic neuroma. When possible, treatment should be directed at the underlying disorder. In most cases, however, symptomatic treatment is either combined with specific therapy or is the only treatment available (e.g., with acute peripheral vestibulopathy). Many different classes of drugs have been found to have antivertiginous properties, and in most instances the exact mechanism of action is uncertain. All of these agents produce potentially unpleasant side effects, and the decision concerning which drug or combination to use is based on their known complications and on the severity and duration of the vertigo. An episode of prolonged, severe vertigo is one of the most distressing symptoms that one can experience. Affected patients prefer to lie still with eyes closed in a quiet, dark room. Antivertiginous drugs with sedation such as Phenergan (25 mg) or diazepam (5 mg) may be helpful. Prochlorperazine suppositories (25 mg) may stop vomiting. In more chronic vertiginous disorders, when the patient is trying to carry on normal activity, less sedating antivertiginous medications such as meclizine (25 mg) or transdermal scopolamine (0.5 mg every 3 days) may provide relief. Vestibular rehabilitation exercises are designed to help the patient compensate for permanent loss of vestibular function.

SUGGESTED READINGS

Baloh RW: Vestibular neuritis. N Eng J Med 2003;250:1027–1032. *Reviews diagnosis and treatment of this common disorder.*

Lockwood AH, Salvi RJ, Burkard RF: Tinnitus. N Engl J Med 2002;347:904–910. *A comprehensive review.*

Tekin M, Arnos KS, Pandya A: Advances in hereditary deafness. Lancet 2001;358:1082–1090. *Recent advances in diagnosis of inherited deafness.*

Yueh B, Shapiro N, MacLean CH, et al: Screening and management of adult hearing loss in primary care: Scientific review. JAMA 2003;289:1976–1985. *Effective treatments are available for many forms of hearing loos.*

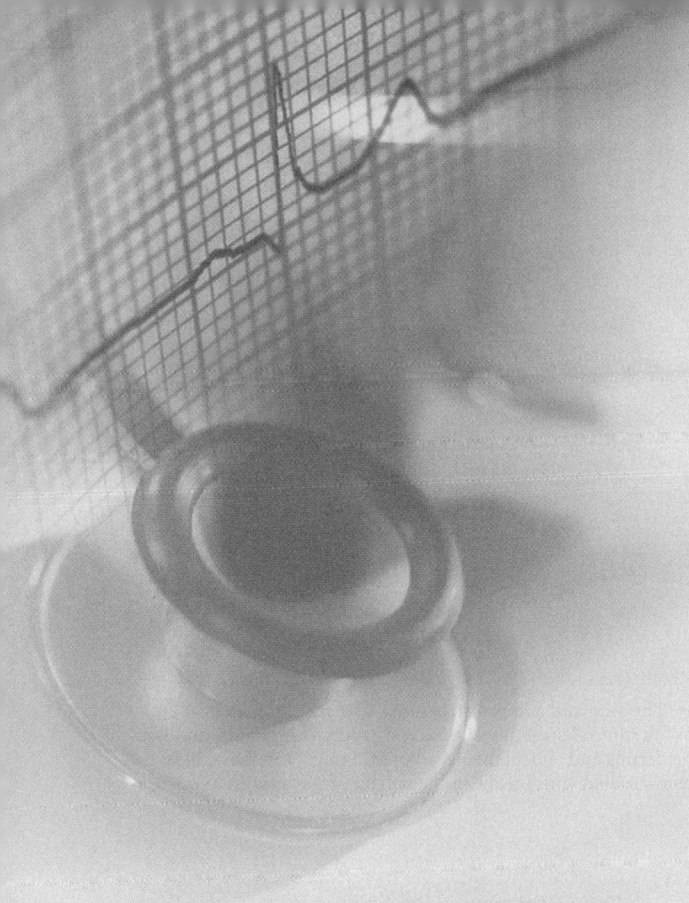

part XXVII

Skin Diseases

471 STRUCTURE AND FUNCTION OF THE SKIN

David A. Norris

KEY FUNCTIONS OF THE SKIN

The skin, which is the largest organ in the body, is a tough, resilient barrier that covers the body and shields the muscle compartment and internal structures. It is composed of an outer epidermis of ectodermal origin and an underlying dermis of mesenchymal origin. The structure of the skin varies considerably from one area of the body to another, including changes in the thickness of its components and in its specialized structures of epithelial origin (e.g., hair, nails, sweat glands, and sebaceous glands). The skin is commonly affected in systemic diseases, and it is also the location of many diseases limited to the skin. It is often damaged by external stimuli such as radiation, sunlight, toxins, irritants, allergens, and infectious agents.

The skin serves critical functions.

PROTECTION. Melanin pigment and antioxidant enzymes are positioned in the epidermis to protect the skin against radiation. The thick reticular dermis is a barrier to injury and trauma as well as a cushion for underlying structures. The epidermis resists friction and tangential stress. The stratum corneum, which is an impenetrable barrier to external substances, is thickened on the palms and soles to provide padding and protection.

THERMOREGULATION. Evaporation from eccrine sweat glands is critical for thermoregulation. Vascular dilation and constriction help regulate the exchange of heat in the skin to preserve heat in cold climates and eliminate heat after exercise.

IMMUNOLOGIC RESPONSE. The skin is the outermost arm of the immune response, designed to defend against infection, transformed cells, and toxins by means of highly developed innate and acquired local immune responses.

BARRIER TO WATER LOSS. The stratum corneum is the critical component of normal skin to prevent transepidermal water loss.

SECRETION OF WASTES. Eccrine and apocrine sweat glands transport wastes and also provide excretion of odiferous substances.

SENSATION. The skin is the largest sensory organ. The skin and mucous membranes are the principal sites of pleasurable sensation and also sites of unpleasant sensations.

STRUCTURE OF THE SKIN

The skin consists of two distinct layers: the *epidermis* and the *dermis* (Fig. 471–1). The skin is derived from two germinal cell lineages: the ectoderm, which gives rise to the epidermis, and the mesenchymal-derived dermis. These two layers are joined at a basement membrane zone termed the *basal lamina*.

The epidermis, which is a stratified squamous epithelial layer, contains several different levels of structure and function. It is held together by distinctive adhesion structures termed *desmosomes* (Fig. 471–2). The *stratum corneum,* which is the product of the dying epidermis, resists the penetration of external organisms and toxins and prevents water loss. The *basal lamina* is a very complex structure of epidermal and dermal-derived proteins that attach the epidermis to the dermis and resist shear stress.

The *papillary dermis* is a collagenous matrix containing the blood vessels that feed the epidermis. The *reticular dermis* is a tougher cushion protecting underlying tissue and containing the epidermal adnexal structures. The blood vessels and nerves are separated into a superficial plexus in the papillary dermis and a deeper plexus, which serves the adnexal structures. The dermis is separated from the fascia and underlying muscle by a layer of subcutaneous adipose tissue that allows the skin to move freely relative to deeper internal structures.

The epidermally derived adnexal structures (eccrine sweat glands, apocrine sweat glands, sebaceous glands, and hair follicles) are anchored in the dermis but penetrate the epidermis and the barrier of the stratum corneum (see Fig. 471–1). The hair follicle is a cycling structure containing specialized populations of epithelial cells, pigment cells, and mesenchymal cells, which control the hair cycle. Eccrine sweat glands discharge sweat directly through the stratum corneum. Apocrine sweat glands discharge their products into hair follicles. Sebaceous glands drain into sebaceous hair follicles on the

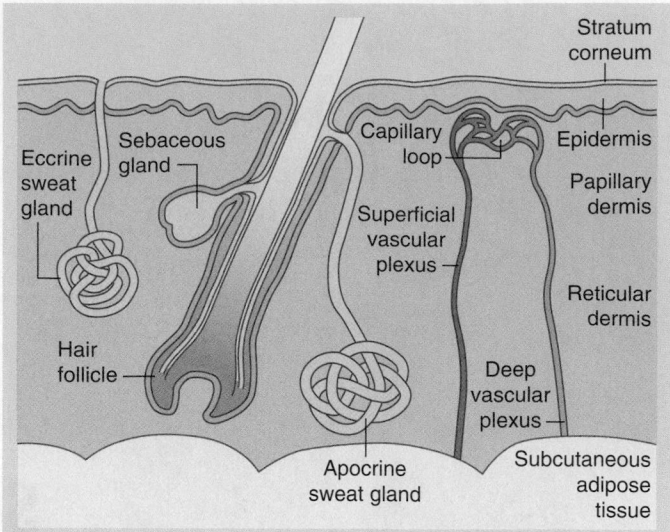

FIGURE 471–1 • The skin and adnexal structures. The relationship of the epidermis and its adnexal structures (sebaceous and sweat glands, and hair follicle) to the dermis and subcutaneous adipose tissue. Note how these structures are associated with breaks in the barrier of the stratum corneum.

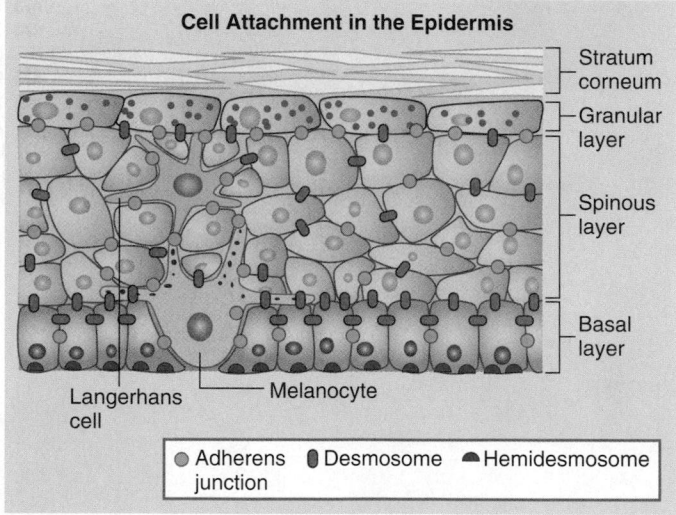

FIGURE 471–2 • Cell attachment in the epidermis. The epidermal keratinocytes, melanocytes, and Langerhans cells form a network of attachments crucial to normal epidermal function.

scalp, face, chest, back, axilla, and groin. An extensive network of blood vessels and nerves serves the skin. The superficial vascular plexus feeds the epidermis through an extensive complex of capillary loops in the papillary dermis. The deep vascular and nerve plexi serve the adnexal structures in the dermis. The hair follicles, with their apocrine and sebaceous glands, and the eccrine sweat glands are potential avenues for transepidermal absorption of drugs, because they penetrate the stratum corneum.

Cells of the Epidermis and Epidermal Differentiation

The epidermis is a stratified squamous epithelium composed mostly of keratinocytes, with other resident cells in distinct locations (melanocytes, Langerhans cells, and Merkel cells). In response to various stimuli, migrating cells such as lymphocytes, dermal macrophages, neutrophils, and eosinophils enter the epidermis. Keratinocytes are attached firmly to each other through desmosomes (see Fig. 471–2), which connect to the rigid keratin intermediate filament network and give the epidermis strength. The basal layer of the rigid epidermis connects to the basement membrane zone by means of hemidesmosomes, which are highly organized adhesion structures linked to the basal keratin network. Adherens junctions link surrounding keratinocytes and connect them to the actin microfilament network. These junctions provide more plastic adhesions that are also involved with actin-mediated movement. Junctions on melanocytes and Langerhans cells attach through E-cadherin–containing adherens junctions to keratinocytes to maintain their dendritic structure.

KERATINOCYTES AND EPIDERMAL DIFFERENTIATION

EPIDERMAL DIFFERENTIATION. Epidermal differentiation is a genetically programmed process by which the keratinocytes differentiate from proliferating cells in the germinative layer to form tightly attached "prickle" cells in the malpighian layer, dying cells in the granular layer, and corneocytes in the stratum. During this process, the keratinocytes undergo tremendous changes, reflecting their different functional characteristics. Keratinocytes are named for the intermediate filament protein, keratin, which forms insoluble stiff filaments that give the epidermis its strength. The keratins are made of tetramers composed of two basic and two acidic keratins (K5/14 in the basal layer; K1/10 in the spinous layer; K6/16 in the hyperproliferative epidermis, K9/19 in the palms and soles). Keratin has versatile properties and constitutes the major component of hair and nails in humans and of beaks, hooves, and feathers in other animals.

The attachments within the epidermis are formed by desmosomes and adherens junctions. The adherens junctions that form between keratinocytes are characterized by homophilic binding of cell surface cadherins and by binding of the adhesion structure to actin microfilaments within the cell by catenins (Fig. 471–3A). Desmosomes are composed of molecules called desmogliens and desmocolins, which are homologous to cadherins and that form adhesion structures with keratins through numerous associated proteins, such as plakoglobin and plakophilin (see Fig. 471–3B). The basal keratinocytes are attached to the basal lamina at the hemidesmosome, which is a specialized adhesion structure linked to the basal cell keratin filament network (see Fig. 471–3C). The progressive differentiation of the epidermis is associated with specific changes in protein expression and function.

FUNCTIONS OF EPIDERMAL LAYERS. The *germinative (basal) layer* of the epidermis is responsible for cell proliferation. This layer is resistant to apoptosis because of its receptors for growth factors and matrix molecules. The germinative layer can become a migrating epithelial tongue to aid in wound healing.

The *spinous layer* produces a dense keratin filament network (keratins 1/10) that interacts with desmosomes, and it synthesizes involucrin (which is involved in protein cross-linking with the plasma membrane in the granular layer), a protective antioxidant network (glutathione reductase, peroxidases, catalases), cytokines, chemokines, lamellar bodies, and keratohyaline granules.

Cells in the *granular layer* undergo programmed cell death (apoptosis). Keratohyaline granule-profilaggrin is activated into filaggrin, thereby inducing keratin cross-linking. Lamellar body contents are secreted into the extracellar space by fusion of the lamellar body to the cell membrane. Involucrin and cornifin are cross-linked to the cell membrane by transglutaminase, thereby producing a thickened, cornified envelope. Protein synthesis ceases as cells die to form intact corneocytes, which contain cross-linked keratin filaments and a thick cornified envelope.

Flat corneocytes surrounded by phospholipid lamellae form the impervious *stratum corneum*. Although the cornified layer provides a thin, flexible barrier to protect sensitive cells from the external environment, molecules can diffuse through the cornified layer. Indeed, this transepidermal route is the major route of penetration of topical medications (Chapter 472). After a defined period, desquamation of superficial corneocytes occurs by enzymatic degradation of extracellular material.

MELANOCYTES

Melanocytes, which are dendritic cells that synthesize and secrete melanin pigment, are derived embryonically from neural crest cells and typically migrate to the epidermal-dermal junction during development, although a few can be found in the dermis. Melanocytes are localized in the basal layer of the epidermis, ranging from a ratio of melanocytes to keratinocytes of about 1:4 to about 1:10 at different locations in the skin. The relative number of melanocytes is roughly

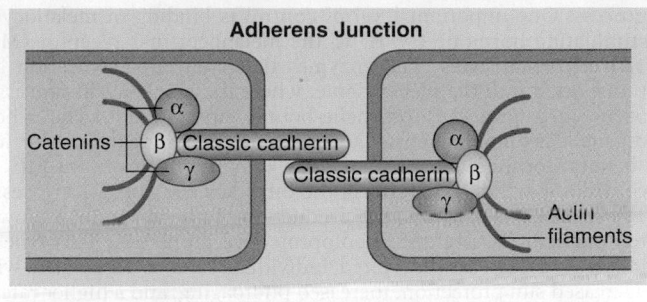

Adherens Junction

A

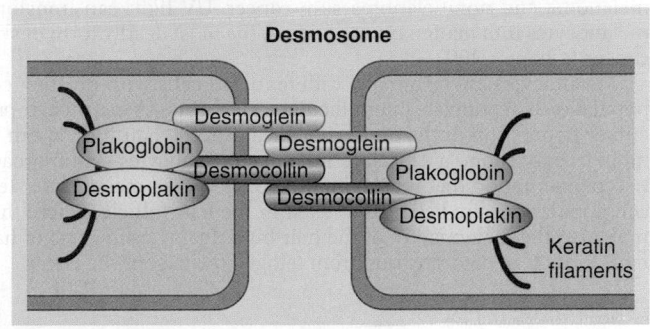

Desmosome

B

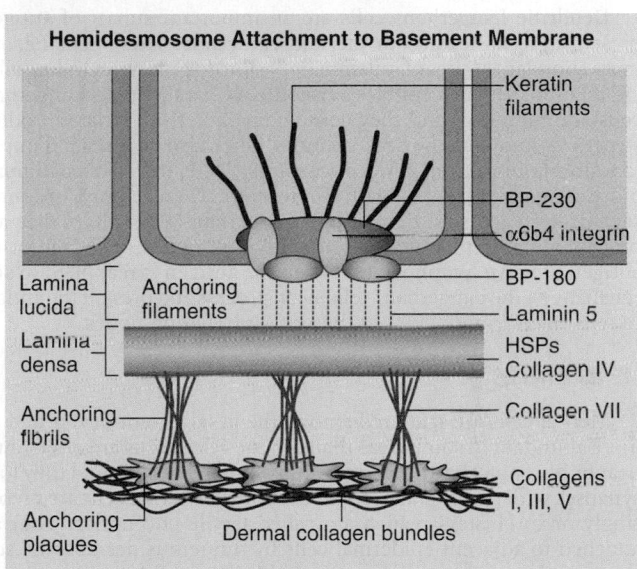

Hemidesmosome Attachment to Basement Membrane

C

FIGURE 471–3 • Molecular aspects of key epidermal adhesion structures and the connection of the epidermis to the dermis. These structures are crucial to the normal integrity of the skin. Mutations or autoimmune damage to these structures has devastating effects on skin function.

the same for both sexes and for all races, with approximately 1500 melanocytes per square millimeter of skin surface. A totally separate population of melanocytes resides in hair follicles that produce pigmented hairs. Differences in the coloration of the skin therefore are determined by the relative activity of these cells, not their numbers. Epidermal melanocytes are attached to the basal lamina by integrin receptors, and they are attached to surrounding keratinocytes by E-cadherin–mediated attachments. Melanin pigment is synthesized in melanocyte-specific organelles termed *melanosomes*. Melanosome transfer is achieved when keratinocytes actively engulf the melanosome-containing cytoplasmic tips of the dendritic processes of the melanocytes. Exposure to ultraviolet (UV) light increases the rate of formation of melanosomes and increases their rate of delivery to the keratinocytes.

Melanin is a complex heteropolymer that absorbs light across the entire UV and visible spectrum; it is the principal protection of the skin against radiation. Melanization is a complex biochemical process controlled largely by three genes: tyrosinase (rate-limiting step), which oxidizes tyrosine to DOPA (3-4-dihydroxyphenylalanine); tyrosinase-related protein 1 (TRP-1); and tyrosinase-related protein 2 (TRP-2). Control of melanization is a complex genetic and environmental process. One important level of control is binding of melanocyte-stimulating hormone (MSH) to the melanocortin-1 receptor (MC-1R) on melanocytes. The enzymes that control melanization are transported into the melanosome, where the biochemical processes occur in a protected organelle-bound environment. The whole organelle is then transported to keratinocytes, where they reside in a "helmet" location above the nucleus. Polymorphisms in the MC-1R control the relative amounts of the three key enzymes. Decreases in TRP-1 and TRP-2 lead to the production of pheomelanin, a brown-red pigment with inferior photoprotective properties. This type of pigment is seen in red-haired individuals and is associated with decreased sun protection, increased photoaging, and a higher rate of melanoma and nonmelanoma skin cancer. UV light can transform melanocytes into malignant melanoma, the most deadly form of skin cancer (Chapter 209).

Melanocytes are terminally differentiated cells with no stem cell population to repopulate interfollicular melanocytes. A melanocyte precursor population in the outer root sheath of the hair follicle can be mobilized to repopulate lost interfollicular melanocytes—an approach to repigmentation that is seen in vitiligo. However, melanocyte stem cell populations are believed to exist in the hair follicle, where they replenish the melanocytes of the hair bulb during each cycle of hair regeneration in the transition from telogen to anagen (see Hair).

LANGERHANS CELLS

Dendritic Langerhans cells are an important subset of antigen-presenting cells located in the mid epidermis. These cells become more abundant at sites of inflammatory skin disorders, including allergic relations such as contact dermatitis (Chapter 474). Langerhans cells are migratory, and they contain characteristic striated, rodlike structures known as Birbeck granules. They also bear several important immunologic cell surface receptors (DC1, major histocompatibility complex [MHC] class II, IgG receptor, C3 receptor). In contact sensitization (contact dermatitis), Langerhans cells internalize and process antigen, migrate to regional lymph nodes, and present the antigen to naive lymphocytes. When the antigen is reapplied to skin (challenge), the Langerhans cells again process and present the antigen to sensitized lymphocytes in the skin or in lymph nodes.

MERKEL CELLS

Merkel cells are scattered among the basal keratinocytes and are more abundant in some areas than others. These cells are often found near or in contact with very fine, unmyelinated nerves, and they form synapses with peripheral nerve fiber endings. Merkel cells are present singly or in clusters, which are called tactile corpuscles. They are attached to adjacent epidermal cells by numerous desmosome connections, but their tonofilaments, unlike those of keratinocytes, are not grouped into bundles. In the cytoplasm of Merkel cells are numerous membrane-bounded dense granules that contain catecholamines. It is believed that Merkel cells serve as adapting mechanoreceptors. Merkel cell tumors are uncommon but are among the most deadly of skin cancers.

The Dermal-Epidermal Junction

The dermal-epidermal junction is a transitional zone where the basal layer of the epithelium is connected to penetrating deep collagenous anchors that originate in the papillary dermis. The connection is composed of collagenous rods, globular domains, and cruciate protein complexes that form a firm attachment that resists friction and tangential stress. This junction, which is the weakest structure point in the skin, is the site of blistering induced by cold, heat, and immunologically and genetically mediated blistering disorders (Chapter 475).

Downgrowths of the epidermis form tiny ridges, called the rete pegs, that add bonding surface area between the dermis and epidermis (Table 471–1). The sandwiched basal lamina follows the ridges, which are more pronounced in areas of high abrasion. The lamina has three zones: the lamina lucida, the lamina densa, and the fibroreticular lamina. Keratin filaments in the basal cells anchor in the hemidesmosomes, which connect to anchoring filaments of the lamina lucida and then to the dense collagen and heparan-sulfate proteoglycan matrix of the lamina densa. Anchoring fibrils of type VII collagen form the fibroreticular lamina and end in the anchoring plaques that intercalate with collagen type III and VI in the papillary dermis.

Table 471–1 • **COMPONENTS OF THE DERMAL-EPIDERMAL JUNCTION**

LOCATION	STRUCTURE	MACROMOLECULES
Basal keratinocytes Plasma membrane	Hemidesmosomes	BPAg 230 (BPAg1) BPAg 180 (BPAg2) Plectin Integrins a_6B_4 and a_3B_1
Lamina lucida	Anchoring filaments	Laminin isoforms Part of BPAg2
Lamina densa	Electron-dense band	Type IV collagen Entactin Heparan sulfate proteoglycan
Sub–lamina densa fibrillar zone	Anchoring fibrils Microfibrils Collagen fibers	Type VII collagen Fibrillin 1 and 2 Collagen types I, III, and VI
	Microthread-like fibers	Linkin

The Dermis

The thickness of the dermis varies considerably in different parts of the body. For descriptive purposes, the dermis is divided into the papillary layer, which is the thinner inner layer next to the epidermis, and the reticular layer, which is composed of denser connective tissue and constitutes the bulk of the dermis. The papillary layer, which forms the dermal papillary ridges, is composed of collagen and of reticular and elastic fibers that are woven into a loose network. Extracellular matrix consists of mucopolysaccharides. The dermis contains many different cell types, including fibroblasts, fibrocytes, macrophages, leukocytes, and plasma cells. The vascular supply to the skin is confined to the dermis, where small arteries enter from the subcutaneous tissue and form deep and superficial sheetlike plexi. Capillary loops ascend into the dermal papillae and return via venous plexes. The postcapillary venule portion of the vascular network, which is where leukocytes enter the tissue, is an important target of damage in allergic vasculitis. The nerve supply to the skin is very profuse and consists of both myelinated and nonmyelinated fibers. Specialized sensory structures such as pacinian and Meissner corpuscles are located prominently in the hands and feet. Because up to 4 to 5% of the total blood volume can be stored in the dermis, it plays an important role in thermal regulation; sympathetic nerve fibers control blood flow to and from the skin.

Epidermal Appendages of the Skin

SEBACEOUS GLANDS

Sebaceous glands, or oil glands, are found throughout the dermis except for the palms of the hands and soles of the feet. Most of these glands, which are greatly activated at the onset of puberty, discharge their contents via a single duct into the lumen of hair follicles. Where these glands occur independently of hairs (e.g., the glans penis, lips, labia minora, and eyelids), they open directly on the surface of the skin. The sebaceous glands are holocrine in their secretion; that is, the entire cell is discharged as a secretory body. Mature cells filled with their triglycerides, waxy esters, squalene, cholesterol, and fatty acids, degenerate and disintegrate (necrosis); the entire debris is discharged as sebum. Contraction of the erector pili muscles aids in the discharging of the contents of these glands.

ECCRINE SWEAT GLANDS

Sweat glands are merocrine in secretion; that is, they discharge components of cytoplasm into the sweat duct. The *eccrine* sweat glands are positioned over the entire skin but are concentrated most densely in the palms, the soles, and the head. Eccrine sweat glands, which number about 3 million, are innervated by postganglionic, cholinergic sympathetic nerves. Excess heat causes sweating to begin on the forehead and to spread elsewhere over the body. Eccrine sweat glands secrete a watery solution that is high in sodium chloride but also contains urea, uric acid, potassium, and immunoglobulins. Histologically, these glands are simple tubular structures composed of a coiled glandular portion and a straight duct, which, on entry into the epidermis, is continuous with a spiral cleft opening to the surface of the skin. On the outside of the secretory epithelium are myoepithelial cells.

APOCRINE SWEAT GLANDS

Apocrine glands remain small until early puberty, when they enlarge and begin to secrete. Histologically, these glands consist of two portions: the coiled secretory gland, which is situated in the dermis and subcutaneous tissue, and a straight excretory duct, which is composed of two layers of epithelial cells. Apocrine release can be secretion or excretion. Secretion is a continuous process, but excretion is episodic. Excretion occurs when there is actual propulsion, presumably provided by the myoepithelial sheath, which is innervated by adrenergic sympathetic fibers. Apocrine glands are scent glands, whose secretion is increased by fear, sexual excitement, and other forms of heightened tension. Apocrine glands are present in the axilla, the external genitalia, the areolar skin around the nipples, and the perianal area. Specialized apocrine glands include Moll's glands on the eyelid and ceruminous (wax) glands in the auditory canal.

NAILS

The nail is composed of a proximal germinative epithelium that is called the nail matrix, a keratinized product that is called the nail plate or body, an underlying specialized epithelium that is called the nail bed and is attached to the undersurface of the nail, and a protective loop of skin that is called the proximal nail fold. Underlying the proximal part of the body of the nail is a collection of germinal cells that form an opaque spot on the nail, the lunula. The lunula is white because the papillary dermis in this region is less vascular, and the stratum germinativum is thick and opaque; this is the site of the proliferating nail matrix that is responsible for the growth of the nail. As these epidermal cells are formed, they become tightly packed and keratinized, but they do not desquamate. Nails grow at a rate of 0.5 to 1.5 mm per week, with toenails growing much more slowly than fingernails.

HAIR

There are three types of hair follicles: vellus hair follicles located over most of the body; terminal hair follicles located on the scalp, beard area, axilla, groin, and other hairy areas; and sebaceous hair follicles located on the scalp, face, beard, chest, back, axilla, and groin. Sebaceous hair follicles have a minimal hair shaft but hypertrophied sebaceous glands. Terminal hairs form the long hairs of scalp and beard. The hair follicles of the eyelashes and eyebrow also have specialized characteristics determined by local mesenchymal factors. Hair follicle growth is determined by influences of the dermis and is strongly stimulated by androgens by means of the type II androgen receptor.

Hairs are dead shafts composed of fused plates of keratin that project from the surface of the epidermis. Hair does not grow continuously but rather passes through a cycle (Fig. 471–4). Anagen is the growth phase. Then comes a short catagen stage in which the hair follicle involutes and growth ceases. Next is the telogen, or resting, phase. Near the end of the telogen phase, the hair falls out or is easily pulled out. A shed hair is called a club hair because of the shape of the root. This overall cycle varies depending on the hair and the location on the body. For scalp hairs, the anagen phase can last 3 to 10 years, but it may be as short as 4 months in other areas of the body. The hair growth cycle can be synchronized during pregnancy so that a larger number of hair follicles will enter the telogen phase together and therefore be shed together, thereby causing temporary thinning of the hair during late pregnancy (telogen effluvium). Hair is pigmented by melanocytes situated in the hair bulb close to the papillae. Keratinocytes in the papillary region engulf the pigment granules, much as they do in the skin.

The hair cycle depends on synchronized cooperation among four major components of the hair follicle: the dermal papilla, the hair matrix, the outer root sheaths, and the stem cells in the bulge region. During the actively growing anagen phase of the hair cycle, signals from the dermal papilla maintain the proliferating hair matrix. When these signals terminate, the follicle enters the catagen phase in which the matrix and root sheaths of the lower follicle die by apoptosis. The follicle then enters a resting telogen phase. When the follicle re-enters the anagen phase, signals from the dermal papilla stimulate stem cells in the bulge region of the follicle, and these cells migrate to form the new matrix, initiate a new hair shaft, and cause the old hair to fall out. In normal follicles in young healthy adults, the anagen phase is almost 3 years and the telogen phase is about 3 months. At any time, 10 to 15% of the hairs are in telogen on a healthy young scalp.

In "telogen effluvium," the shift to telogen is abrupt, and hairs fall from the scalp precipitously in 3 months when new anagen hairs are formed in the follicles. This pattern is commonly seen 2 to 3 months after a severe systemic illness or at the termination of pregnancy. A gradual shift to the telogen phase occurs with age and is even greater in androgenic alopecia.

SPECIALIZED ASPECTS OF SKIN STRUCTURE AND FUNCTION

Clinical Correlates

Genetic diseases that affect the function of the dermis and epidermis are listed in Table 471–2 and are described further in subsequent chapters.

Skin-Associated Immune System

The skin is the most external component of the immune response, with well-developed elements of both the innate and acquired immune systems (Chapter 41). The barrier of the stratum corneum is broken by adnexal structures such as hair and sweat glands, and infections in these sites are suppressed by a network of innate immune responses and defenses. The skin is also a principal site for invasion by bacteria, parasites, and viruses, and it is an important site of tumor induction; all of these processes are influenced by a well-developed acquired immune response. The skin contains several populations of antigen presenting cells, including the epidermal Langerhans cells. Trafficking of T cells to the skin occurs through skin-specific homing receptors such as the cutaneous lymphocyte antigen.

The skin's innate immune system includes macrophages, dendritic cells, and neutrophils, as well as a very extensive epidermal network of cytokines (e.g., interleukin [IL]-1 and tumor necrosis factor [TNF]-α) and chemokines. The skin has a number of receptors for foreign organisms (CD14, Toll-like receptors, mannose receptors), defensins and other antibacterial proteins, and networks that augment and inhibit complement in the papillary dermis.

The skin's acquired immune system includes an epidermal network of specialized dendritic cells (Langerhans cells) plus dermal dendritic cells. The cutaneous lymphocyte antigen (CLA) stimulates the trafficking of lymphocytes to the skin. Both TH1 and TH2 responses are well developed in skin, but most inflammatory skin diseases have a TH1 response. Hair follicles may be immunologically privileged sites because they lack MHC class I.

Control of Apoptosis in the Skin

Apoptosis is a normal part of the cycle of epidermal differentiation. In the granular cell layer, transglutaminase-mediated cross-linking of involucrin initiates the formation of the cornified envelope, which is a specialized apoptotic envelope. Unlike other apoptotic cells, the corneocyte is not phagocytized or fragmented. Epidermal stem cells,

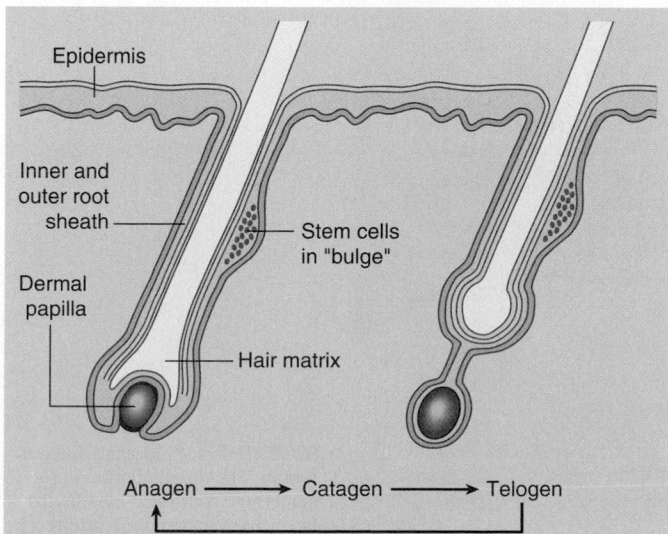

FIGURE 471–4 • Hair follicle cycle. Communications between the dermal papilla, the matrix, the follicle sheath, and the stem cells control the hair cycle through its anagen, catagen, and telogen phases.

Table 471–2 • **CLINICAL CORRELATES OF THE STRUCTURE AND FUNCTION OF THE SKIN: GENETIC DISEASES AFFECTING FUNCTION OF THE EPIDERMIS AND DERMIS**

DISEASE	CELLS INVOLVED	GENE AND/OR PROTEIN AFFECTED
IMMUNOBULLOUS DISORDERS (Chapter 475)		
Pemphigus vulgaris	Keratinocytes	Antibody to desmoglein 3
Pemphigus foliaceous	Keratinocytes	Antibody to desmoglein 1
Bullous pemphigoid	Keratinocytes	Antibody to BP180 and/or BP230
Epidermolysis bullosa acquisita	Subepidermal blister	Antibody to CVII
Bullous systemic lupus erythematosus	Subepidermal blister	Antibody to CVII
MECHANOBULLOUS DISORDERS (Chapter 475)		
Epidermolytic hyperkeratosis	Suprabasal keratinocyte	K1, K10
Epidermolytic palmoplantar keratoderma	Suprabasal keratinocyte	K9
Epidermolysis bullosa simplex	Basal keratinocyte	K5, K14
Junctional epidermolysis bullosa	Subepidermal blister	Laminin V
Dystrophic epidermolysis bullosa	Subepidermal blister	CVII
DISORDERS OF CORNIFICATION (Chapter 472)		
Ichthyosis vulgaris	Granular, stratum corneum	Reduced/absent filaggrin
Harlequin ichthyosis	Stratum corneum	Reduced K1/K10, filaggrin
X-linked ichthyosis	Stratum corneum	Steroid sulfatase
Lamellar ichthyosis	Stratum corneum	TGM1 (transglutaminase type 1)
DISORDERS OF KERATINOCYTE ATTACHMENT		
Darier's disease	Suprabasal keratinocytes	ATP2A2 (SERCA2)
Hailey-Hailey disease	Suprabasal keratinocytes	ATP2C1
DISORDERS OF PIGMENTATION (Chapter 477)		
Piebaldism	Melanocytes	c-*kit* (stem cell factor receptor)
Hermansky-Pudlak syndrome	Melanocyte (melanosome)	HPS-1p
	Platelet (platelet dense bodies) lysosomes	β 3A subunit of the AP-3 adaptor complex
Chédiak-Higashi syndrome	Melanocyte (melanosome) lysosomes	*LYST* gene
Albinism	Melanocyte/melanosomes	Tyrosinase, TRP-1
Vitiligo	Melanocyte	Cytotoxic damage (immune, chemical)

melanocytes, and proliferating transit-amplified cells of the basal and suprabasal epidermis are resistant to apoptosis, and these defenses against apoptosis are mediated by integrin and growth factor receptor ligation. Integrin and growth factor expression are lost in the differentiating epidermal compartment, and these cells are susceptible to apoptosis induced by chemotherapy, activation of death receptors such as Fas, and UV radiation (Fig. 471–5). In the granular cell layer, apoptosis initiates terminal changes in keratinocytes, thereby producing the dead corneocytes that are the "bricks" of the stratum corneum.

Endothelial cells are also resistant to apoptosis by virtue of their attachment to basement membrane proteins through integrin receptors and because of antiapoptotic proteins that are induced during inflammation to protect these cells. Conversely, during vessel remodeling, the antiapoptotic defenses decrease and endothelial cells die.

Activated lymphocytes, Langerhans cells, and granulocytes that enter the skin are all sensitive to apoptosis. Most phototherapy protocols to treat inflammatory skin diseases rely on UV light—induced apoptosis to destroy Langerhans cells and lymphocytes, whereas the relative resistance of keratinocytes and melanocytes to UV light protects the normal underlying skin cells.

Ultraviolet Radiation and the Skin

The skin is uniquely susceptible to damage induced by exposure to radiation from the sun. Visible and UV light penetrates into the skin and produces important biologic effects. Some effects, such as the photoactivation of vitamin D, are beneficial, but most are damaging.

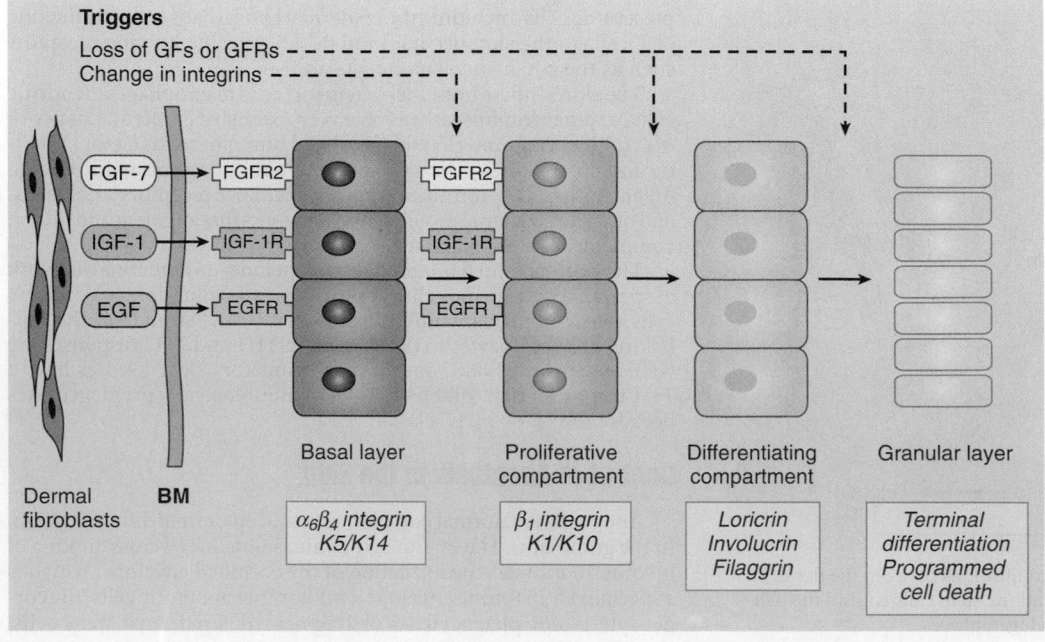

FIGURE 471–5 • Epidermal differentiation. The differentiation of the epidermis, controlled by growth factor receptors and integrin receptors, also modulates the susceptibility of the epidermis to apoptosis induced by external and internal triggers.

The skin has a number of natural defenses against UV light. First, melanin, a heteropolymer that is transferred from melanocytes to keratinocytes, protects the basal keratinocytes against UV radiation. Second, antioxidant enzymes (e.g., catalase, peroxidase, thioredoxin, and superoxide dismutase) protect skin cells against oxidant damage. Macrophages are induced by UV radiation to enter the epidermis to remove damaged cells. UV radiation also induces Langerhans cells to exit the epidermis and present antigens to T cells in regional lymph nodes. Finally, keratinocytes produce large amounts of IL-1 and TNF-α in response to UV radiation, and a complex system of antagonists and decoy receptors buffer the epidermis from cytokine-induced damage.

Despite these defenses, UV radiation damages keratinocytes and induces malignancy. UV radiation damage also induces both local and systemic immunosuppression, and it can induce autoimmunity when apoptotic keratinocytes and autoantigens are presented to lymphocytes in diseases such as lupus erythematosus.

Itching

The sensations of both itch and pain are transmitted by unmyelinated C fibers. It is assumed that the receptors are the free nerve endings in the dermis and epidermis. Multiple compounds induce pruritus: amines (histamine and serotonin), proteases (papain, kallikrein, trypsin), neuropeptides (substance P, vasoactive intestinal peptide, calcitonin gene–related peptide), eicosanoids, opioids, cytokine growth factors, and products of eosinophils and platelets. Many of these compounds act through their effects as mast cell degranulators. Histamine is the major itch-inducing product of mast cells, but other mediators may also be involved. Pruritus is a common component of many skin diseases and systemic diseases (Table 471–3).

Pruritus is a common clinical problem whose treatment is often unsatisfactory. Treatment of any underlying skin or systemic disease is necessary for long-term success. Drugs that inhibit the effects of mast cell products (H_1 or H_2 blocking antihistamines, antileukotrienes) or that inhibit mast cell degranulation (phosphodiesterase inhibitors, β-agonists) are effective as oral agents. Neuropeptide-mediated itching can be inhibited by desensitization with capsaicin. Opiate antagonists block the central opiate receptors that induce the pruritus that is associated with opiate use. UV radiation treatment can effectively treat the intractable pruritus that is seen in renal failure.

Wound Healing

The skin is the major target of wounding in most people and is the preeminent model used to study wound healing in animals and humans. Wound healing is a complex process with three sequential phases: inflammation, proliferation and tissue formation, and tissue remodeling. The phase of tissue remodeling extends for weeks and months after closure of wounds, and the fibroblast is the cornerstone of remodeling of the dermis, vessels, and basement membrane.

Vascular abnormalities (arterial insufficiency, venous stasis, and microangiopathy) are commonly associated with poor wound healing. Poor wound healing is also a serious problem in patients with chronic infections or malnutrition. Patients with extensive skin disease, especially mechanobullous or immunobullous disorders such as epidermolysis bullosa or pemphigus, also demonstrate defects in wound healing. Efforts to promote wound healing in these situations focus on repair and reversal of vascular disease, reversal of tissue edema, application of growth factors to stimulate angiogenesis and keratinocyte migration, and use of antibiotics to decrease local infection (Chapter 23).

SUGGESTED READINGS

Fuchs E, Raghavan S: Getting under the skin of epidermal morphogenesis. Nat Rev Genet 2002;3:199–209. *Review of the molecular control of the development and differentiation of the epidermis and its major appendage, the hair follicle.*

Pulkkinen L, Ringpfeil F, Uitto J: Progress in heritable skin diseases: Molecular basis and clinical implications. J Am Acad Dermatol 2002;47:91–104. *Details on the clinical findings induced by specific mutations in genes that control the structure and function of the skin.*

Yosipovitch G, Greaves MW, Schmelz M: Itch. Lancet 2003;361:690–694. *Overview of pathophysiology, diagnosis, and therapy.*

472 EXAMINATION OF THE SKIN AND APPROACH TO DIAGNOSING SKIN DISEASES

Cheryl Armstrong

The examination of the skin is a critical component of the comprehensive approach to the patient. By learning how to examine the skin and approach the diagnosis of skin diseases, the physician can focus on the lesions that warrant therapy or provide important information about the systemic health of the patient. Other lesions may be of cosmetic concern to the patient even though they have little or no medical significance.

As the organ system that interfaces with the environment, the skin has an extensive array of mechanical, biochemical, immunologic, and neurologic properties that both inform and protect each individual. The skin also has a vast ability to alter its cellular and acellular components in response to internal or external insults, a process that leads to changes that are subsequently defined as disorders or diseases. The physical examination of the skin can provide information about both cutaneous and systemic diseases, and the examination can sometimes diagnose serious medical conditions at an otherwise asymptomatic stage.

Skin disorders usually can be visualized directly by both the patient and the physician. For example, the patient not only feels the itch and discomfort of an allergic contact dermatitis reaction to poison ivy, but also sees the vesicular and crusted skin lesions. The appearance of new lesions or the sudden change in existing lesions can elicit emotional reactions in patients or their family members. The physician must learn to see the same eruptions using a careful and systematic approach that leads to a specific and treatable diagnosis.

History and Physical Examination

Most dermatologists conduct the dermatologic history and examination simultaneously. The physician can best focus the history and full skin examination by first visualizing the lesion or lesions that constitute the patient's primary skin complaint. Because there are hundreds of described dermatoses, the systematic approach is based on pattern recognition.

A skin examination can be conducted in virtually any medical setting. It is most effectively performed in an office equipped with an examination table, adequate natural or artificial fluorescent lighting, examination gowns for patients to wear, and a sink for thorough

---

Table 471–3 • CLINICAL ASSOCIATIONS WITH PRURITUS

SKIN DISEASES
Dermatitis, including contact dermatitis
Bullous disorders, especially dermatitis herpetiformis and bullous pemphigoid
Drug effects (opiates, aspirin, quinidine)
Urticaria and angioedema
Lichen planus
Sunburn
Seborrheic dermatitis
Infestations (e.g., scabies, pediculosis)
Xerosis (dry skin)
Irritant particles (e.g., fiberglass, "itching powder")

SYSTEMIC DISEASES
Uremia
Obstructive biliary disease (primary biliary cirrhosis, cholestatic hepatitis, cholestasis of pregnancy, extrahepatic biliary obstruction)
Hematologic and myeloproliferative disorders (lymphoma, polycythemia vera, iron-deficiency anemia)
Endocrine disorders (thyrotoxicosis, hypothyroidism, diabetes, carcinoid)
Carcinomas (breast, stomach, or lung)
Psychiatric disorders (e.g., delusional states, stress, psychosis)
Neurologic disorders (e.g., multiple sclerosis, notalgia paresthetica, neuropathy)
Mastocytosis (urticaria pigmentosum, telangiectasia macularis eruptiva perstans)

handwashing before and after each examination. If natural light through a window is used, it is critical to ensure the patient's privacy inside the examination room. A moveable focused artificial light beam and a lighted magnifying glass can be used to shine obliquely on the skin to assess the elevation of skin lesions. Many dermatologists prefer to examine all lesions at a 1:1 ratio without magnification, but others prefer magnifying certain types of lesions to ascertain morphologic features. For example, the follicular plugging of the lesions of discoid lupus erythematosus (Chapter 280) or the telangiectasias associated with a basal cell carcinoma (Chapters 209 and 476), may be better appreciated with magnification. Gowns that can be positioned to uncover parts of the skin surface while leaving other parts covered help ensure the patient's comfort during the examination.

Universal precautions against infectious diseases should be practiced during every skin examination or cutaneous procedure. Handwashing with soap and warm water ensures that the physician is taking appropriate steps to avoid spreading organisms from a previous patient. When examining intact skin, it is not necessary to wear gloves. For the protection of both the patient and physician, gloves should be worn when the physician touches nonintact skin surfaces. Because of the increasing incidence of allergies to latex in the health care setting, nonlatex gloves should be used for all patients. Gloves should be discarded after the examination is complete or after touching the mouth or the genital area.

A total body skin examination is usually recommended for each new patient to assess existing pigmented lesions and determine whether any are serious, although there are no data to document the yield of such an approach (Chapter 11). With the steady increase in squamous cell carcinoma, basal cell carcinoma, and in cutaneous melanomas over the past several decades, the total body skin examination is an opportunity to diagnose lesions in an early treatable stage as well as to educate patients about their own risk factors for developing skin cancer. Subsequently, total body skin examinations can be scheduled at 3- to 12-month intervals for patients at high risk for developing new or recurrent malignant lesions (Chapter 209), whereas patients at low risk should be examined at less frequent intervals, such as every 1 to 3 years.

Many dermatologists approach this examination by using the following sequence: face (forehead, eyelids, lips, ears, nose, cheeks, chin), neck, scalp and hair, back, chest, abdomen, arms, hands (including palms and fingernails), legs, and feet (including soles and toenails). Having the patient change into a comfortable gown with undergarments removed facilitates the ease of the examination. Some dermatologists perform part of the examination with the patient in a sitting position and part of the examination with the patient lying back on the examination table. The goal is to ensure that the skin can be well visualized and that the patient is comfortable with the amount of skin being exposed at one time.

Basic skin features such as skin pigmentation, skin turgor, abnormal skin color (jaundice, pallor), and the degree of photodamage to sun-exposed skin surfaces should be assessed, and these findings guide the medical history and subsequent, detailed examination. For example, patients with lightly pigmented skin and evident photodamage to the hands and face warrant a careful history to inquire about prior skin cancers in themselves and their immediate family members, as well as a full body skin examination to look for precancerous or potentially malignant lesions of which the patient may be unaware. Patients with abnormal skin color, such as a yellow hue (jaundice; Chapter 149)) should be questioned about known medical conditions, examined for any other cutaneous signs associated with disease of that organ, and assessed with the appropriate laboratory studies.

It is often helpful to touch the lesion and the skin surrounding the lesion. Features such as firmness, movability from the underlying skin, fluctuance, and depressibility are helpful in characterizing the lesion. Darier's sign, which is the appearance of an urticarial wheal and flare reaction after rubbing a skin lesion, is observed in lesions that contain large numbers of mast cells (e.g., urticaria pigmentosa) and is the result of the mechanical degranulation of the mast cells and the resulting release of histamine. Nikolsky's sign is dislodgment of the epidermis with the appearance of a moist, glistening defect after pushing, rubbing, or rotating normal skin near bullous lesions; this sign is typical of disorders in which epidermal cells are not well adhered together (e.g., pemphigus and toxic epidermal necrolysis).

After seeing and palpating the lesion, the physician can obtain a more detailed history and continue with a more comprehensive examination of the skin as indicated. Pertinent questions should assess duration of the lesion or eruption, what the lesion looked like when it first began, how the lesion feels (e.g., itch, sting, tenderness, pain), and how the condition has changed since it was first noticed. It is also helpful to inquire about a history of prior similar lesions and how they progressed. A medication history is important because both systemic and topical medications can cause or exacerbate a number of skin conditions. It is also important to inquire specifically about how the patient may have tried to treat the lesion because many treatments can change the natural appearance of the lesion.

The past medical history should be targeted to obtain information about major illnesses, especially those that would lead to immunodeficiency states, as well as prior dermatologic diseases. The presence of known heritable dermatologic conditions in the family should be determined. In particular, patients should be specifically questioned about a personal or family history of atopic dermatitis, hay fever, or asthma (atopy). All patients should be asked about a personal or family history of malignant melanoma and nonmelanoma skin cancers. The social and work history can also provide critical clues to the diagnosis of a particular skin condition because many are related to occupational or recreational activities. A travel history to determine whether patients have encountered environmental stresses such as sun, heat, or cold or have been exposed to parasitic infestations can also be useful. Because psychological stress can exacerbate many dermatoses, it is useful to inquire about overall levels of anxiety and stress or recent stressful situations.

After visualizing the lesion of concern, it is often helpful to look systematically at all the skin again. It is also important to watch the patient's behavior in the examination room. Many patients think that they should not scratch lesions and they tell the physician that the lesions itch but that they do not scratch. However, direct observation shows the patient rubbing, tapping, scratching, or picking the lesion while engaged in conversation with the physician. These behaviors can change a primary lesion to a secondary lesion.

Patients at high risk for the development of melanoma require the most comprehensive skin examinations, commonly by a dermatologist. Photography (conventional or digital) as well as detailed "maps" of the nevi are used over time to assess changes in lesions or the presence of new lesions that warrant removal. A hair dryer set at the low setting can be used to blow aside the hair to allow visualization of the entire scalp. The skin of the external and internal labia is examined for pigmented lesions in women. The comprehensive skin examination is also an ideal opportunity to educate the patient about performing self-examinations that include exposed and unexposed skin including the buttocks, posterior thighs, and calves.

Clinical Features

Four major features of skin lesions or eruptions allow the skin disease to be placed in diagnostic categories that facilitate specific diagnosis: (1) the morphologic appearance of the individual lesions; (2) the distribution of lesions over the body surface; (3) the arrangement of the lesions; and (4) the number of lesions present. This information also enables the physician to determine whether the lesions are primary or secondary in nature. Primary lesions are defined as those that represent the initial pathologic change; secondary lesions result from external forces such as scratching, picking, or infection of primary lesions. An experienced dermatologist can often make the diagnosis from this descriptive information before even seeing the patient.

MORPHOLOGY OF LESIONS. The morphology of individual lesions can be described in the following ways (Table 472–1): (1) whether they are flat, raised above the surface of the skin, or depressed; (2) the range of their size; (3) whether they are solid or contain fluid; and (4) how their color compares with the patient's normal skin. Morphologic terms have been developed to assess alterations in the stratum corneum and dermal or subcutaneous tissue. For example, the stratum corneum in psoriatic plaques can be silvery in color with densely adherent layers so that it looks like the mineral mica; this pattern is called a *micaceous scale*. Another usual morphologic feature is whether the individual lesions are monomorphic or polymorphic: all monomorphic lesions are the same shape, size, color, and consistency. Certain diseases, such as eruptive xanthoma, almost always have monomorphic papules, whereas other diseases, such as acne, are more likely to have polymorphic lesions that may represent either changes over time or a basic variability.

DISTRIBUTION OF LESIONS. Many skin diseases commonly affect particular parts of the body surface (Table 472–2). In certain cases, the

Table 472–1 • TERMINOLOGY TO DESCRIBE THE MORPHOLOGY OF INDIVIDUAL SKIN LESIONS

TERM	DEFINITION	EXAMPLE
PRIMARY SKIN LESIONS: INITIAL PATHOLOGIC CHANGE		
Macule	Circumscribed change in skin color that is flush with the surrounding skin. Lesion is <1.0 cm in diameter	Solar lentigo Traumatic purpura
Patch	Circumscribed change in skin color that is flush with the surrounding skin. Lesion is ≥1.0 cm in diameter	Café au lait spot Vitiligo
Papule	A solid or cystic elevation <1.0 cm in diameter	Acne Eruptive xanthoma
Nodule	A solid or cystic elevation >1.0 cm but <2.0 cm in diameter	Dermatofibroma
Tumor	A solid or cystic elevation >2.0 cm in diameter	Follicular cyst
Plaque	An elevated lesion that is >1.0 cm in diameter	Psoriasis
Scale	Desiccated, thin plates of cornified epidermal cells that form flakes on the skin surface	Ichthyosis
Wheal	Circumscribed, flat-topped, firm elevation of skin with a well-demarcated and palpable margin	Urticaria
Vesicle	Circumscribed, elevated lesion containing clear serous or hemorrhagic fluid that is <1 cm in diameter	Contact dermatitis Herpes simplex
Bulla	Circumscribed, elevated lesion containing clear serous or hemorrhagic fluid that is >2 cm in diameter	Bullous pemphigoid
Pustule	A vesicle containing purulent exudate	Folliculitis
Atrophy	A depression from the surface of the skin with underlying loss of epidermal or dermal substance	Lichen sclerosis et atrophicus
Erosion	A depression from the surface of the skin with a loss of all or part of the epidermis	Burn
	Can be a secondary lesion	Ruptured bulla
Ulceration	A depression from the surface of the skin with a loss of the entire epidermis and at least some of the dermis	Ecthyma
	Can be a secondary lesion	Excoriation of acne papule
SECONDARY SKIN LESIONS: RESULT FROM EXTERNAL FORCES SUCH AS SCRATCHING, PICKING, INFECTION, OR HEALING OF PRIMARY LESIONS		
Lichenification	Dry, leathery thickening of the skin with exaggerated skin markings	Chronic eczema
Scar	An elevated or depressed area of fibrosis of the dermis or subcutaneous tissue resulting from an antecedent destructive process	Healing wound
Fissure	A deep linear split in the skin extending through the epidermis	Traumatized eczema
Crust	Dried exudates of serum, blood, sebum, or purulent material on the surface of the skin	Acute and/or secondarily infected eczema

Table 472–2 • PREFERENTIAL DISTRIBUTION OF SELECTED SKIN DISEASES

DISTIBUTION ON THE SKIN	SKIN DISEASE
Skin chronically exposed to sunlight (face, neck, hands, arms)	Actinic keratosis, basal cell carcinoma, squamous cell carcinoma
Central chest, shoulders, and earlobes	Keloids
Extensor arms and legs, intragluteal cleft, umbilicus	Psoriasis
Antecubital fossa, popliteal fossa	Atopic dermatitis
Anterior surface of lower legs	Palpable purpura, pretibial myxedema, necrobiosis lipoidica diabeticorum, erythema nodosum
Axilla and inguinal areas	Hidradenitis suppurativa
Posterior neck and back	Folliculitis
Web spaces of toes and sides of feet	Tinea pedis
Web spaces of fingers and wrists	Scabies
Palms and soles	Secondary syphilis, erythema multiforme

their lesions are present only in sun-exposed areas of the body (e.g., lupus erythematosus or phototoxic drug eruptions). Dermatologic disorders that are the direct result of the patient's manipulation of the skin are found only where the patient can reach (e.g., the posterior shoulders but not the middle of the back).

The pattern of distribution, although poorly understood from a pathogenetic perspective, is extremely helpful for diagnosis (Fig. 472–1). For example, psoriasis often symmetrically affects the scalp, extensor arms and legs (elbows, knees, and shins), umbilicus, intragluteal cleft, and fingernails (Fig. 472–2; Chapter 474). Psoriatic lesions can involve the entire body surface, but an awareness of its common distribution guides the physical examination and aids accurate diagnosis. Conversely, atopic dermatitis (Chapter 474) typically often involves the flexural arms and legs (antecubital fossae and popliteal fossae), wrists, nipples, and eyelids.

It is important to examine the mucous membranes of the mouth and the genital areas. Lichen planus (Chapter 474), a papulosquamous skin disease, often involves the volar wrists, shins, buccal mucosa, and shaft of the penis. In lichen planus, the oral and genital lesions may be asymptomatic so the medical history cannot substitute for a careful physical examination.

ARRANGEMENT OF LESIONS. The arrangement of several lesions in relation to each other can provide valuable diagnostic information. Terms that are commonly used to describe the relationship of lesions to each other include *clustered, grouped, linear, zosteriform, annular,* and *coalescing* (Table 472–3). *Clustered* lesions are arranged within a few

Table 472–3 • ARRANGEMENT OF SKIN LESIONS

TYPE OF ARRANGEMENT	EXAMPLE OF SKIN DISEASE
Clustered	Herpes simplex
Grouped	Lichen planus
	Granuloma annulare
	Dermatitis herpetiformis
Linear	Allergic contact dermatitis
	Epidermal nevus
	Morphea
	Koebnerized psoriasis
Zosteriform	Herpes zoster
	Metastatic breast carcinoma
	Hemangiomas of Sturge-Weber syndrome
Annular without scale	Secondary syphilis
	Lupus erythematosus
	Urticaria
	Hansen disease (leprosy)
Annular with scale	Dermatophytosis
	Pityriasis rosea
	Erythema annulare centrifugum
Coalescing	Psoriasis
	Drug hypersensitivity eruption
	Viral exanthem
	Urticaria

pattern of distribution is consistent with our understanding of the pathogenesis of a disease. For example, acne lesions are found on the parts of the skin that contain the highest concentration of sebaceous glands, which are known to be involved in the development of acne. Other skin diseases are precipitated or caused by sun exposure, so

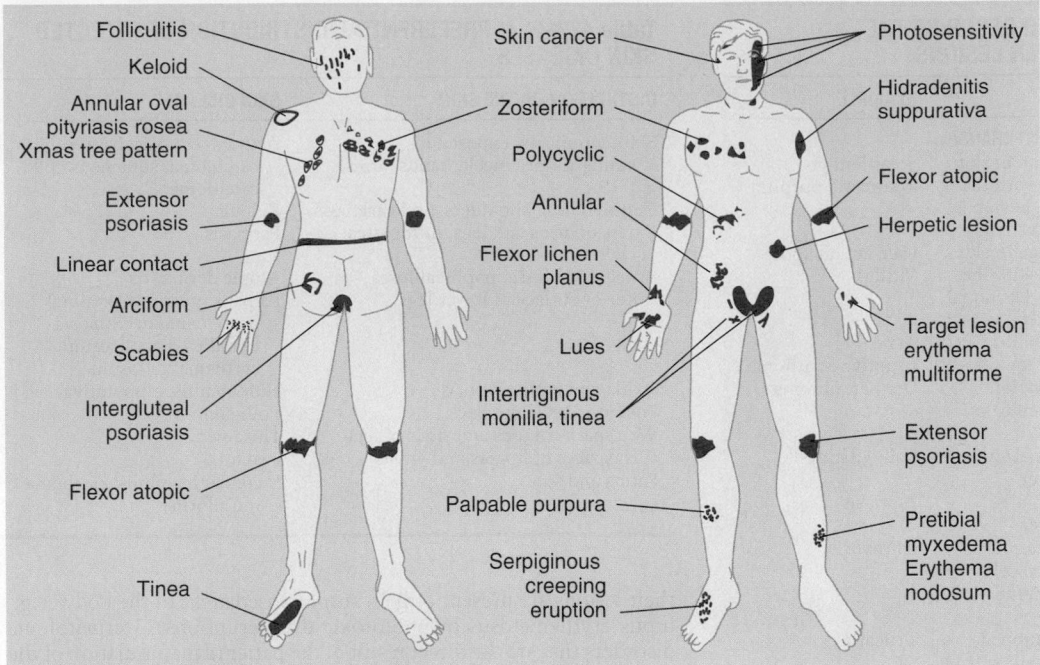

FIGURE 472–1 • Configurational and regional diagnostic aids for the diagnosis of primary and secondary skin lesions.

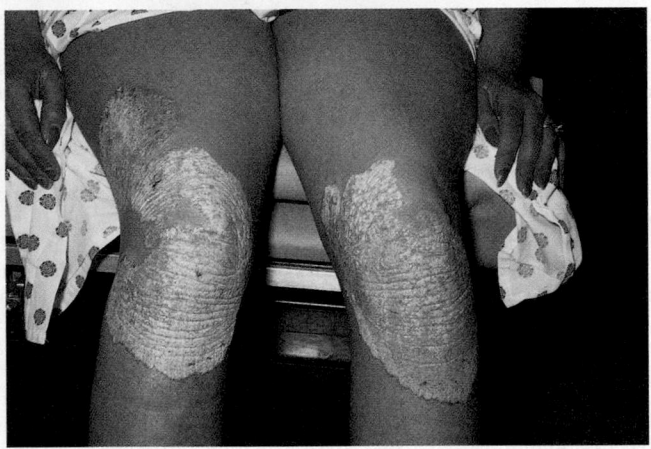

FIGURE 472–2 • The distribution of psoriatic lesions is often symmetrical over the extensor surfaces of the skin.

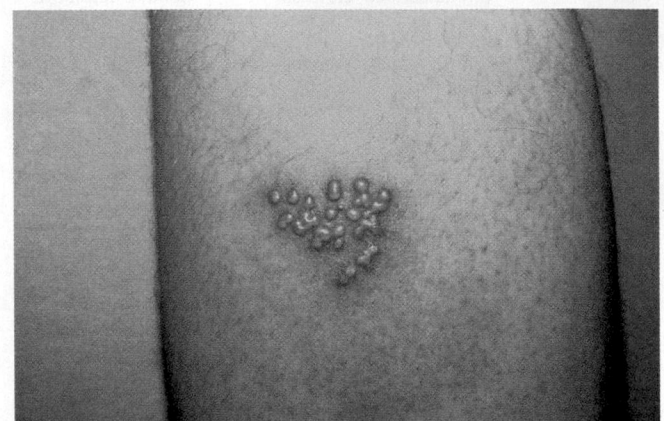

FIGURE 472–3 • This arrangement of vesicular lesions clustered on an erythematous base, seen here in a patient with herpes simplex, is termed *herpetiform*.

millimeters of each other. When vesicular lesions are clustered on an erythematous base, the word *herpetiform* is used to describe their arrangement because this is the classic appearance of herpes simplex (Fig. 472–3; Chapters 369 and 475). *Grouped* lesions are arranged in the same body site, such as over a shoulder or elbow. A *linear* arrangement of lesions looks like a geometric line over any part of the body surface. One type of linear arrangement is called *Koebnerization* (or the Koebner phenomenon), which occurs in particular skin diseases, such as psoriasis, which evolve new lesions after traumatic injury. Linear lesions are frequently seen in allergic contact dermatitis if the offending antigen brushed against the skin to create a linear pattern of dermatitis. This pattern often results when a plant such as poison oak brushes against the skin (Fig. 472–4). A *zosteriform* arrangement refers to usually unilateral lesions in the cutaneous distribution of a spinal nerve dermatome; herpes zoster (Chapters 367 and 475) is the classic zosteriform dermatosis, but other lesions can present in this arrangement. *Annular* lesions, which are round to oval with an area of central clearing, often consist of an arrangement of smaller lesions in this configuration. Finally, almost all types of lesions can coalesce, meaning that individual lesions merge into each other. *Coalescing* lesions often assume annular or figurate patterns on the skin (Chapter 474).

NUMBER OF LESIONS. At the most extreme, an eruption can cover nearly 100% of the skin surface. At the other end of the spectrum, only one

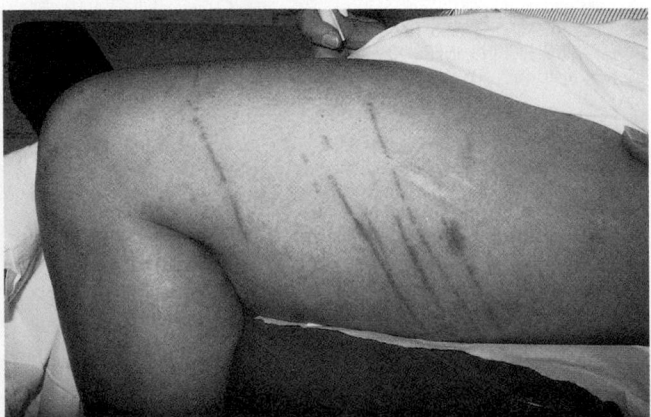

FIGURE 472–4 • Allergic contact dermatitis presenting in a linear arrangement when the offending antigen, such as poison oak, is brushed against the skin in this way.

Table 472–4 • MORPHOLOGY-BASED CLASSIFICATION OF MAJOR SKIN DISORDERS

GROUP	CLINICAL MORPHOLOGY	EXAMPLES OF DISEASES IN THE GROUP
Eczematous dermatitis	Erythematous macules, papules, vesicles, lichenification, fine scaling, exoriations, crusting	Contact dermatitis, atopic dermatitis, stasis dermatitis, photodermatitis, exfoliative dermatitis
Maculopapular eruptions	Macules, erythema, papules	Viral exanthems, drug hypersensitivity reactions, Kawasaki disease, vasculitic, purpuric eruptions
Papulosquamous dermatoses	Papules, plaques, and erythema with scales	Psoriasis, Reiter's syndrome, pityriasis rosea, lichen planus, seborrheic dermatitis, ichthyosis, secondary syphilis, mycosis fungoides
Vesiculobullous diseases	Vesicles, bullae, erythema	Herpes simplex and zoster, hand-foot-and-mouth disease, insect bites, bullous impetigo, scalded skin syndrome, pemphigus, bullous pemphigoid, dermatitis herpetiformis, porphyria cutanea tarda, erythema mulitforme
Pustular diseases	Pustules, cysts, erythema	Acne vulgaris rosacea, pustular psoriasis. folliculitis
Urticaria and cellulitis	Wheals and figured, raised erythema, scaling	Urticaria, erythema annulare centrifugum and erysipelas
Nodular lesions	Nodules and tumors, some associated with erosions and ulceration	Benign and malignant tumors—basal cell cancer, squamous cell cancer, rheumatoid nodules, xanthomas
Telangiectasia, atrophic, scarring, ulcerative diseases	Atrophic, sclerotic telangiectasia, ulcerative changes	Connective tissue diseases, radiation dermatitis, lichen sclerosus et atrophicus, vascular insufficiency (arterial and venous), pyoderma gangrenosum
Hypermelanosis and hypomelanosis	Increased and decreased melanin deposition in skin	Acanthosis nigricans, café au lait spots, vitiligo, tuberous sclerosis, xeroderma pigmentosum, melasma, freckles

or two lesions may be present. Certain diseases are characterized by an overall typical number of lesions on the skin. For example, patients with tuberculoid leprosy generally have fewer than five lesions on the entire skin surface. Other diseases, such as granuloma annulare, can range from a few lesions to hundreds of lesions. Sometimes the number of lesions is an indication of the severity of the disorder, as in widespread psoriasis. A general estimation of the number of lesions such as "more than 50 flat-topped papules distributed on the shins and wrists bilaterally" or "8 to 10 orange-colored papules on each elbow" can also assist in guiding the physician to the correct diagnosis.

Major Classifications

After carefully identifying the clinical features of skin lesions or eruptions, the physician can use the recognized patterns to classify the disease into a general category of skin disorders. The ability to identify the clinical features of morphology, distribution, arrangement, and number allows the disorder to be placed in a category that narrows

the differential diagnosis to a reasonable number of choices (Table 472–4).

Diagnostic Tests

After a reasonable differential diagnosis has been created, diagnostic tests can narrow the differential or confirm the correct diagnosis (Table 472–5). The potassium hydroxide preparation of scale and pustules is used to look for microscopic hyphae or pseudohyphae that indicate the presence of a dermatophyte infection or yeast infection (Fig. 472–5; Chapter 474). The Gram stain of pustules or bullae is used to determine whether bacteria are present or whether the lesion is sterile (Chapter 475). The Tzanck preparation of the base of a vesicle is used to look for rounded, multinucleated keratinocytes that indicate a herpesvirus infection (Fig. 472–6; Chapter 475). The oil mount of skin scrapings from the base of a burrow or pruritic papule is used to look for the mites or eggs that indicate a scabies infestation (Fig. 472–7; Chapter 406).

Table 472–5 • DIAGNOSTIC TESTING FOR SKIN DISEASES

DIAGNOSTIC TEST	MATERIAL TO OBTAIN	INDICATIONS	FINDINGS
TESTS PROCESSED IN THE OFFICE			
Potassium hydroxide preparation and microscopic examination	Skin scraping from scale or pustules	Presence of scale or pustules	Hyphae or pseudohyphae indicating dermatophyte or yeast infection
Gram stain and microscopic examination	Skin scraping from pustules or bullae	Presence of pustules or bullae	Gram-positive or gram-negative bacteria
Tzanck stain and microscopic examination	Skin scraping from the base of a vesicle	Presence of vesicles	Rounded, multinucleated keratinocytes indicating a herpesvirus infection
Oil mount and microscopic examination	Skin scraping from the base of a burrow or nonexcoriated papule	Presence of burrows or pruritic papules	Mites or eggs indicating scabies infestation
TESTS PROCESSED IN AN OUTSIDE LABORATORY			
Punch biopsy	Core of anesthetized skin using a punch biopsy instrument	Lesions suspected to be malignant (such as BCC or SCC) or an undiagnosed inflammatory skin lesion	Microscopic alterations in the epidermis, dermis, and subcutaneous tissue
Shave or snip biopsy	All or part of an anesthetized skin lesion that protrudes from the surface of the skin	Raised lesions suspected to be malignant (such as BCC or SCC) or bothersome raised lesions	Microscopic alterations in the epidermis and the upper dermis
Excisional biopsy	An entire anesthetized skin lesion	Lesions suspected to be malignant (such as melanoma) or bothersome flat lesions	Microscopic alterations in the epidermis, dermis, and subcutaneous tissue with the entire architecture of the lesion in the specimen

BCC = basal cell carcinoma; SCC = squamous cell carcinoma.

Skin Diseases

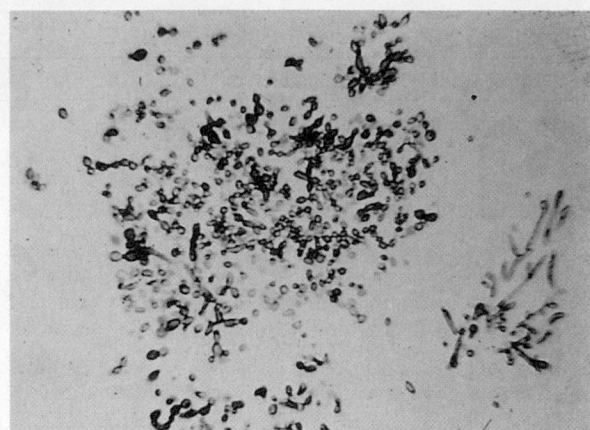

FIGURE 472–5 • *Candida albicans.* Potassium hydroxide examination of candidal skin lesion shows short, stubby hyphae and budding yeast elements.

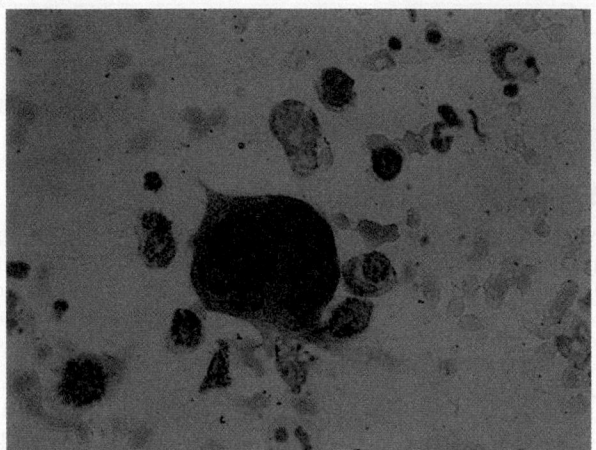

FIGURE 472–6 • Tzanck smear of herpes simplex. Positive Tzanck smear is seen as multinucleated giant cell.

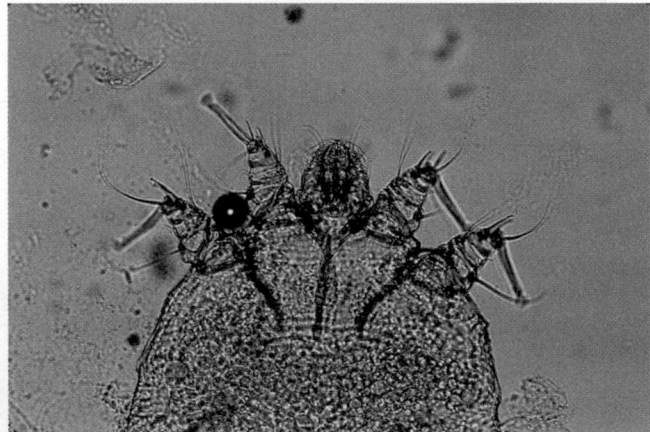

FIGURE 472–7 • A scabies mite is seen on this microscopic examination of an oil mount of a scraping taken from the end of a small burrow on the wrist.

When an infection is suspected, it is often necessary to obtain specimens for culture by swabbing pustules, bullae, or abscesses. Any overlying crust should be removed before obtaining the culture. Scale from the surface of the skin can also be sent for fungal culture to increase the detection of dermatophyte infections, especially those involving the nails. If bacterial cellulitis is suspected, tissue from the dermis can be cultured by obtaining a skin biopsy that is sent for culture or by injecting the site with sterile saline and aspirating material to send for culture. To diagnose deep fungal or mycobacterial infections, tissue usually must be obtained by biopsy and be sent for culture under appropriate temperature conditions.

Skin biopsies, which can be performed on growths from inflammatory eruptions, are an essential tool when the diagnosis is not certain (Fig. 472–8). The term *biopsy* may also be applied to the surgical removal of benign skin lesions such as warts and skin tags. Many dermatologists follow the general practice of sending all excised skin tissue for histologic assessment.

Any lesions that have features of basal cell carcinoma or squamous cell carcinoma should be biopsied (Chapters 209 and 476). Clinical indications for biopsy of lesions suspected to be malignant include lesions that fail to heal, increase in size, bleed easily, or ulcerate spontaneously. Actinic keratoses, which are considered to be precancerous lesions, are usually treated without preceding biopsy. The usual biopsy approach to nonmelanotic lesions that protrude from the surface of the skin is to perform either a snip biopsy (with scissors) or a shave biopsy (with a blade). If the entire lesion is removed, it can be considered an excisional biopsy.

For inflammatory skin lesions, it is usually necessary to obtain tissue down to subcutaneous fat for an accurate assessment of the inflammatory process. A punch biopsy using an instrument of 3 to 8 mm in diameter to "core out" a piece of skin tissue is the preferred approach. If multiple lesions are present, it is prudent to select a lesion that is not in a cosmetically important area, because a scar will occur at the punch biopsy site, but to be sure to select a representative lesion that has not been altered by scratching, infection, or lichenification. The punch biopsy wound heals best when closed with one to two sutures, but it can be left to heal by granulation. Some inflammatory skin disorders, especially bullous disorders, have characteristic autoantibody deposition that can be assessed by direct immunofluorescence of biopsy tissue. This test is performed in specialized dermatopathology laboratories.

The approach to biopsying lesions that have clinical features of malignant melanoma is critical. First, there is only one opportunity to obtain tissue correctly to maximize the chance of accurate diagnosis. Second, an improperly obtained biopsy can make it impossible to assess the patient's risk of metastatic disease. When malignant melanoma is suspected, the lesion should be removed entirely with an elliptic excisional biopsy; margins of normal skin are not included in the biopsied tissue. A shave biopsy should be avoided because it will not allow the full depth of the lesions to be determined histologically. The thickness of the lesion remains the most accurate way to predict metastatic disease and is critical for planning adjuvant therapy (Chapters 209 and 476). A punch biopsy should be avoided because it does not provide the dermatopathologist with the full his-

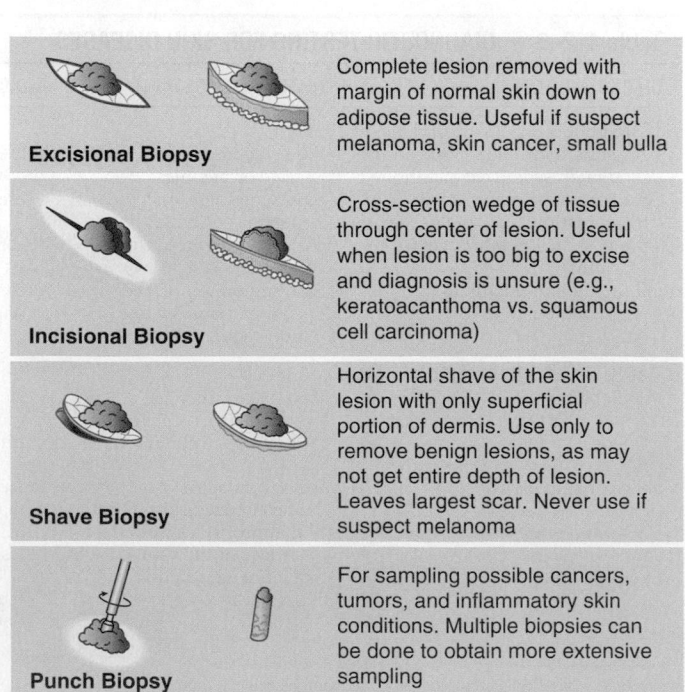

Excisional Biopsy	Complete lesion removed with margin of normal skin down to adipose tissue. Useful if suspect melanoma, skin cancer, small bulla
Incisional Biopsy	Cross-section wedge of tissue through center of lesion. Useful when lesion is too big to excise and diagnosis is unsure (e.g., keratoacanthoma vs. squamous cell carcinoma)
Shave Biopsy	Horizontal shave of the skin lesion with only superficial portion of dermis. Use only to remove benign lesions, as may not get entire depth of lesion. Leaves largest scar. Never use if suspect melanoma
Punch Biopsy	For sampling possible cancers, tumors, and inflammatory skin conditions. Multiple biopsies can be done to obtain more extensive sampling

FIGURE 472–8 • Methods of skin biopsy.

tologic architecture of the lesion. When clinical features of a pigmented lesion of the skin are highly suggestive of malignant melanoma, the patient usually should be referred to a dermatologist before performing the biopsy to ensure that the most accurate histologic Information is obtained to guide clinical treatment.

SUGGESTED READINGS

Du Vivier A: Atlas of Clinical Dermatology, 3rd ed. Edinburgh, Churchill Livingstone, 2002. pp 1–?? *A visually oriented approach to the diagnosis of cutaneous disorders.*

Swartz M: The skin. *In* Textbook of Physical Diagnosis: History and Examination, 4th ed. Philadelphia, WB Saunders, 2001, pp 123–178. *An extensive description of how to approach the patient with skin disorders with clinical pictures and schematic histologic correlation.*

473 PRINCIPLES OF THERAPY

Victoria P. Werth

The goal of therapy is to improve a skin condition with the least toxic and most specific approach. Because many treatments or medications can be applied directly to the skin, the option for topical therapy is attractive for treating many dermatologic diseases. However, many diseases require systemic therapies, particularly when there is widespread involvement of the skin or a disease that cannot be improved with topical therapy. Therapies work by improving barrier function, removing scale, altering inflammation in the skin, altering blood flow, providing antimicrobial effects, or affecting proliferating cells. Recent advances in the understanding of cutaneous biology have not been routinely accompanied by evidence-based documentation of the benefits of many specific therapies.

PRINCIPLES OF TOPICAL THERAPY

SOAKS AND DRESSINGS. Water or saline applied by soaks and wet dressings can be beneficial for many skin conditions, including ulcers, by promoting healing of the epidermis and débridement of crusts. Soaked gauze is applied to involved areas for 15 to 30 minutes several times a day, and care should be taken not to allow the gauze to dry and adhere. If adherence occurs, the gauze should be soaked before removing the dressing. Use of strong antiseptic solutions is not recommended because of toxicity to cells. Whirlpool action can enhance débridement. When large areas of skin are involved, baths are a convenient way to treat the skin with medications that reduce itching and inflammation. The best time to apply moisturizers that help trap water in the upper layers of skin is immediately after a bath or shower.

Wet-to-dry dressings are rarely used, except when initial vigorous wound débridement is necessary. Continued use after wounds are débrided traumatizes wounds and delays healing. Moist wound healing, which is often ideal, can be accomplished using a topical antibiotic such as Polysporin or Bactroban, Vaseline-impregnated gauze, or an occlusive hydrocolloid dressing. There is little evidence that débriding enzymes are beneficial. Compression with an Unna or multilayered boot, which includes an elastic dressing such as COBAN, can decrease local edema and facilitate wound healing. Polysporin/Vaseline gauze or occlusive dressings are placed underneath, which is helpful for chronic venous, diabetic, and pressure ulcers, as well as for acute wounds. Closed wet dressings, by which gauze is soaked and then covered with an impervious material, can help when maceration and heat retention are needed. Biologic dressings with skin substitutes or keratinocytes can be beneficial for wounds that are resistant to healing. Platelet-derived growth factor, which is approved for use in diabetic ulcers, can modestly improve wound healing.

TOPICAL MEDICATIONS. Topical medications mix an active drug with preservatives, emulsifying agents, and an appropriate base or vehicle. Systemic absorption varies among patients, sites, and vehicles. Topically applied drugs are absorbed more readily through inflamed, thin skin. The base can be a *powder*, which promotes dryness and is used to reduce maceration in intertriginous area; a *lotion*, which is a suspension of oil in water; *solutions*, which include water, alcohol, and propylene glycol, but not oil; *gels*, which are solid at room temperature but melt on contact with the skin; a *cream*, which is an emulsion of oil in water and which leaves a thin oil coating as the water evaporates; an *ointment*, which combines oils, such as Vaseline, with small amounts

of water, and which is more occlusive and, hence, increases the absorption of medication but also results in a more greasy appearance; a *paste*, which is a mixture of powder and ointment; or a *spray*. Lotions, solutions, and gels provide less penetration than ointments, but they are especially useful for treatment of hair-bearing areas such as the scalp, where greasiness is displeasing. Creams are less greasy than ointments and are useful for the face, groin, and intertriginous areas. Ointments are often more effective for dry, scaly conditions such as eczema and psoriasis, and are helpful in areas such as the palms and soles that have thick skin, but should be avoided in infected or intertriginous areas. The choice of base is determined by the skin condition and location. Impregnated tapes are another delivery method to provide occlusion and protect the skin from manipulation.

ANTI-INFLAMMATORY AGENTS

Glucocorticoids

Topical glucocorticoids work because of their effects on vasoconstriction, proliferation, immunosuppression, and inflammation. Assays related to the ability to vasoconstrict and clinical trials of efficacy have allowed the division of glucocorticoids into various classes based on potency (Table 473–1). These medications are typically used twice a day. Side effects include atrophy of the skin, telangiectasias, purpura, striae, local skin infections (e.g., folliculitis, tinea, and candidiasis), hypopigmentation, hypertrichosis, systemic adrenal suppression when used on as little as 20% diseased skin surface area, and glaucoma when used around the eye. Side effects are especially prevalent when fluorinated steroids are used on thin skin (e.g., face, groin, or scrotum), and prolonged use on the face can result in facial dermatitis, acne, and an acne rosacea-like eruption, which often exacerbates with termination of use of the steroid. Certain conditions are more responsive to steroids, and the steroid's potency must be chosen based on the condition and location (Table 473–2). The superpotent class I agents should be restricted to patients with severe dermatoses and their use should normally not exceed 2 weeks. Patients who receive these potent agents require frequent follow-up and must be carefully evaluated for the need to continue strong topical steroids. Use of any fluorinated steroid on the face requires an exact diagnosis and should be limited in the extent of application and duration of use. Intralesional glucocorticoids can be injected into individual lesions to improve delivery of the medication, and this method is commonly used to treat acne cysts, hypertrophic scars, keloids, alopecia areata, granuloma annulare, discoid and panniculitis lupus erythematosus,

Table 473–1 • RANKING OF SOME COMMONLY USED TOPICAL STEROIDS BY POTENCY

	GENERIC NAME
Super potent	Clobetasol propionate (Temovate ointment and cream), betamethasone dipropionate (Diprolene cream and ointment), difloroasone diacetate (Psorcon ointment), halobetasol propionate (Ultravate ointment)
High potency	Amcinonide, mometasone furoate ointment, diflorasone diacetate (Florone ointment), halcinonide 0.1% cream, fluocinonide, desoximetasone, triamcinolone acetonide, diflorasone diacetate ointment and cream, betamethasone dipropionate (Diprosone), betamethasone benzoate and valerate
Medium potency	Fluticasone propionate, mometasone furoate cream, halcinonide 0.025% ointment, triamcinolone acetonide 0.1% cream and lotion, fluocinolone acetonide 0.2%, 0.025%, and 0.01% cream and 0.025% ointment and 0.05% solution, hydrocortisone valerate 0.2% ointment and cream, aclometasone dipropionate 0.05% ointment, betamethasone dipropionate 0.05% lotion, hydrocortisone butyrate 0.1% cream, betamethasone benzoate 0.025% cream, betamethasone valerate 0.1% cream and 0.05% lotion, flumethasone pivalate 0.03% cream, desonide 0.05% cream
Low potency	Hydrocortisone 1% cream

Table 473–2 • CLINICAL APPLICATION OF TOPICAL GLUCOCORTICOIDS

Super potent and high potency	Plaque and palmoplantar psoriasis, lichen planus, dyshidrotic eczema, lichen simplex chronicus, granuloma annulare, sarcoidosis
Medium potency	Dermatitis—allergic contact, atopic, neurodermatitis
Low potency	Intertrigo, pruritus ani, seborrheic dermatitis

psoriasis, and lichen simplex chronicus. Triamcinolone acetonide is most frequently used, followed by the longer acting triamcinolone hexacetonide. It is important to use proper dilutions, such as 2.5 mg/cc on the face and 5 mg/cc elsewhere, to avoid local skin atrophy.

Systemic glucocorticoids are used for acute and chronic conditions in dermatology, but they should be avoided, if possible, or minimized because of their well-known side effects (Chapter 31). Acute conditions that commonly require systemic steroids include severe contact dermatitis such as poison ivy, photodermatitis, severe atopic dermatitis, and acute urticaria. Many skin conditions such as psoriasis and eczema exacerbate when steroids are tapered, so steroids should be avoided when possible in these conditions. The dose of steroid must be individualized to the condition and severity of the presentation. Steroid-sparing drugs, such as immunosuppressives, can be used to minimize the long-term use of steroids in selected conditions.

Nonsteroidal Anti-inflammatory Agents

PSORIASIS THERAPIES. Tars and anthralin are used for psoriasis. Tars are most commonly used in conjunction with ultraviolet B light, as part of the Goeckerman regimen. Tars are also used in shampoos and bath oils that treat seborrhea and psoriasis. Anthralin is a synthetic hydroxyanthrone that inhibits keratinocyte proliferation; it stains and can be irritating, but can be effective therapy (Chapter 474).

CALCIPOTRIOL. Calcipotriol is a vitamin D derivative that has antiproliferative and immunomodulatory effects on skin. Hypercalcemia can occur if more than 100 g is used per week, so this agent cannot be used for widespread disease. It is applied twice daily, can be irritating on thin skin, and takes 6 to 8 weeks to be effective.

RETINOIDS. The retinoids are a group of compounds, including vitamin A and its derivatives. Their effects are mediated through several different classes of receptors, and the receptor-drug complex has effects on other regulatory proteins that affect growth factors, oncogenes, keratins, or transglutaminases. Retinoids affect cell growth, differentiation, and morphogenesis, inhibit tumor promotion and malignant cell growth, have immunomodulatory effects, and alter cell cohesion.

Topical retinoids include all-*trans* retinoic acid (tretinoin, retin A), which is approved for acne (Retin-A) and photoaging (Renova 0.05% cream) and which is also useful for hyperpigmentation, steroid-induced atrophy, and early stretch marks. Tretinoin is available as a cream (0.025%, 0.05%, 0.1%), gel (0.01%, 0.025%), and solution (0.05%). Adapalene (Differin, 0.1% gel) and tazarotene (Tazorac) are used for acne. Tazarotene is also used for psoriasis, often in combination with topical steroids to minimize irritation. Topical retinoids can be irritating and frequently cause an exacerbation before improvement. However, they should be used regularly on lesion-prone skin to produce improvement. Moisturizers may be needed to minimize drying effects.

Systemic retinoids commonly used for the skin include isotretinoin, acitretin, and Targretin. They have many uses, but most frequently isotretinoin (Accutane) is used for cystic and conglobate acne, acitretin for severe psoriasis (especially erythrodermic and pustular forms), and Targretin for cutaneous T-cell lymphoma. Isotretinoin and acitretin have also been used to treat several forms of ichthyosis and lupus erythematosus, and for the chemoprevention of skin cancers. The many side effects of systemic retinoids include teratogenicity, cheilitis, hair loss, headaches, hyperlipidemias, abnormal liver enzymes, vertebral hyperostosis, tendon and ligament calcification, osteoporosis, and central hypothyroidism with Targretin. Pregnancy must be avoided, and the use of retinoids in women of child-bearing age therefore requires careful monitoring. Treatment for acne is reserved for cases of cystic acne not responding to less toxic therapies; in this setting, a 4- to 5-month course at 0.5 to 1 mg/kg/day is curative in 85 to 90% of patients.

ANTIMALARIAL DRUGS. Aminoquinolines include chloroquine, hydroxychloroquine, and quinacrine. These agents have inhibitory effects on proinflammatory cytokine production, DNA replication, and chemotaxis. They are useful in connective tissue diseases, polymorphous light eruption, sarcoidosis, porphyria cutanea tarda, sclerosing conditions, and vasculitis. Side effects include diarrhea, headache, irritability, psychosis, skin dyspigmentation, and, rarely, retinopathy. Retinopathy is rare if doses of chloroquine are 3.5 mg/kg/day or less and hydroxychloroquine are 6.5 mg/kg/day or less. Combinations of hydroxychloroquine or chloroquine with quinacrine are frequently helpful when a solitary agent is inadequate. The combination of hydroxychloroquine and chloroquine should not be used because of the additive risk of retinopathy.

DAPSONE. Dapsone is a sulfone that inhibits the response of neutrophils and possibly eosinophils to chemotactic stimuli. It is useful for dermatitis herpetiformis, cutaneous vasculitis, pyoderma gangrenosum, bullous lupus erythematosus, Behçet's disease, and autoimmune bullous diseases. Side effects include hemolysis, methemoglobinemia, peripheral neuropathy, agranulocytosis, and, rarely, a hypersensitivity syndrome with hepatitis, fevers, and rash. A glucose-6-dehydrogenase (G6PD) level should be checked before starting the drug, and it is common for patients with a normal G6PD to experience a 2-g/dL decrease in hemoglobin after achieving therapeutic doses of 100 to 200 mg/day.

THALIDOMIDE. Thalidomide has potent anti-inflammatory effects, likely due to inhibition of tumor necrosis factor (TNF)-α. It also modifies adhesion molecules on circulating leukocytes. Thalidomide has recently become more widely available, but it is a serious teratogen and patients must comply with strict birth control and monitoring. It is effective for severe cutaneous lupus erythematosus, erythema nodosum leprosum, aphthae, Behçet's disease, actinic prurigo, chronic graft-versus-host disease, and a number of other inflammatory dermatoses. Beside teratogenesis, the main side effects include peripheral neuropathy, constipation, sedation, and, rarely, amenorrhea.

GOLD. Intramuscular gold has been used to treat pemphigus vulgaris, with success as a solitary agent. A total dose of 400 to 600 mg of gold is often required to stop the formation of blisters; after the initial test doses, it is administered as 50 mg once a week.

COLCHICINE. Colchicine, usually at a dose of 0.6 mg twice a day, is used for leukocytoclastic vasculitis and Behçet's disease. The main side effect of this low oral dose is diarrhea.

ANTIMICROBIALS

Antibacterials

Topical antibiotics are used to treat superficial skin diseases such as acne and folliculitis that are related to infectious organisms, and skin wounds or ulcers. They may work also by decreasing neutrophil chemotaxis and other anti-inflammatory mechanisms. Topical solutions, gels, pledgets, and ointments are available, depending on the agent, and antibiotics include erythromycin, clindamycin, tetracycline, and metronidazole. Bacitracin or Polysporin ointments are typically used for wounds, but they can cause a contact hypersensitivity; neomycin should be avoided because of the high incidence of allergic reactions. Mupirocin is particularly effective against *Staphylococcus* and *Streptococcus* species, and it can be used in the nose for carriers of staphylococci. Systemic antibiotics such as penicillins, cephalosporins, and erythromycin are used for soft tissue infections such as impetigo, folliculitis, furuncles, carbuncles, cellulitis, ecthyma, erysipelas, postoperative wound infections, and necrotizing fasciitis. Tetracycline, doxycycline, and minocycline are used for acne, rosacea, and perioral dermatitis. Fluoroquinolones such as ciprofloxacin are useful for treatment of gram-negative soft tissue infections.

Antifungals

Topical antifungal agents are used for patients with limited superficial fungal infections of the skin. The numerous topical antifungal drugs available include the azoles—clotrimazole, econazole, ketoconazole, oxiconazole, and miconazole—available as creams and lotions, applied once or twice a day. The creams tend to be more effective. Topical agents used for dermatophytes, but not *Candida*, are haloprogin and tolnaftate. The newer allylamine antifungals are naftifine and terbinafine, which have fungicidal effects. Ciclopirox 8% topical solution was recently approved for use in treating and preventing relapses of onychomycosis. Nystatin creams, oral suspensions, and vaginal tablets are effective for treatment of *Candida* infections. The combination of antifungals with potent topical steroids such as betamethasone dipropionate is not advised because of increased side effects from the steroid and decreased efficacy of the antifungal due to the concomitant steroid.

Systemic antifungal agents include griseofulvin, terbinafine (allylamine), ketoconazole (imidazole), itraconazole, and fluconazole. These agents are used for extensive or severe superficial skin fungal infections caused by dermatophytes, *Candida*, or *Malassezia furfur,* or for local infections not responsive to topical drugs, such as those found in the nails and scalp. Itraconazole and terbinafine are the only oral antifungals approved in the United States for treatment of onychomycosis, and griseofulvin is the only oral agent approved for tinea capitis. Griseofulvin is best taken with a fatty meal to improve absorption and is the only antifungal drug not requiring regular monitoring of liver enzymes. Griseofulvin shows weak affinity for keratin, and thus it must be used for 18 months for onychomycosis of the toenails and 6 months for the fingernails to achieve even relatively poor cure rates. Terbinafine is the only fungicidal drug, whereas the rest are fungistatic. The number of interactions with medications is lower with terbinafine than with the triazole antifungals and ketoconazole because terbinafine does not inhibit or induce hepatic isoenzyme CYP 3A4 (Chapter 27). However, terbinafine affects CYP 2D6, another hepatic isoenzyme, so it is relatively contraindicated in patients who are taking cyclosporine or rifampin. Itraconazole and fluconazole have been used in pulse-dosing regimens for treatment of onychomycosis. Fluconazole and terbinafine are not dependent on gastric acidity for optimal gastrointestinal absorption. Overall, the side effects of the systemic antifungal agents are similar and include headache and gastrointestinal symptoms (griseofulvin, terbinafine), nausea and vomiting (itraconazole, fluconazole, ketoconazole), hepatitis, and lupus-like syndromes (terbinafine).

Antivirals

Verruca are treated with a number of destructive modalities, including 50 to 80% dichloroacetic acid and trichloroacetic acid solutions, podophyllin resin, and podofilox. Topical antiviral creams such as penciclovir and acyclovir do not significantly shorten the course of herpes simplex. Systemic antiviral drugs include acyclovir, valacyclovir, famciclovir, and foscarnet, which are used to treat primary and recurrent herpes simplex, herpes zoster, and varicella, although only acyclovir is approved for use in varicella. These agents specifically block the function of herpesvirus DNA polymerase. Valacyclovir and famciclovir are only available orally in the United States, but the prolonged intracellular half-life allows for less frequent dosing than with acyclovir. Herpes zoster requires higher doses than those for herpes simplex. Side effects include nausea and headaches.

Antiparasitics

Topical antiparasitic medications treat pediculosis capitis, pediculosis pubis, and scabies. In addition, topical metronidazole has antiinflammatory properties that treat rosacea. When treating pediculosis and scabies, clothing and bedding must be washed, and all family members treated. Effective treatment includes 1% gamma benzene hexachloride (lindane), a chlorinated hydrocarbon pesticide that should not be used in young children or in pregnant or lactating women. It is ineffective against nits and thus must be reapplied after 1 week. Permethrin 5% cream (Elimite) for scabies or 1% cream rinse is particularly effective for head lice and requires just one application; 10% crotamiton (Eurax) and 5% topical sulfur ointments are less effective. Malathion is a moderately toxic organophosphate insecticide, but it must be applied overnight to treat lice. Pyrethrins (RID, Nix) are best used twice, one week apart, to treat head lice and nits.

ANTIPRURITICS OR ANESTHETICS

Topical Analgesics

Capsaicin is an active ingredient of cayenne peppers and other plants of the Capsicum family used for postherpetic neuralgia and other painful nerve-related conditions. It causes excitation of neural afferent C-fibers and reduces substance P. It causes a burning sensation and is applied four to five times a day for 5 to 6 weeks. Eutectic

mixture of local anesthetic (EMLA) is a mixture of lidocaine and prilocaine used under occlusion to induce cutaneous anesthesia before a procedure. Lidocaine can be used as a topical anesthetic, but benzocaine should be avoided because it is a sensitizer.

Antipruritic Agents

Doxepin 5% cream is used for localized pruritus. Menthol is a cyclic terpene plant alcohol used for nonhistamine-related itching. Pramoxine hydrochloride is a topical anesthetic used for mild to moderate itching. Oral antihistamines play an important role in controlling pruritus for many skin conditions (Table 473–3), although those mediated by histamine, such as urticaria, angioedema, and urticaria pigmentosa are most specific. The sedating and anticholinergic properties of many H_1 antihistamines likely account for some of their efficacy. H_1 antihistamines are cornerstones of routine therapy, and if an agent from one group of H_1 antihistamines is ineffective, then an agent from a different class should be administered or combined. Second-generation H_1 antihistamines are less sedating and are used if patients who cannot tolerate or do not improve with first-generation agents. The combination of two different H_1 antihistamines can be used when a solitary agent does not work; in particular, use of a sedating antihistamine at night and a second-generation antihistamine during the day can be helpful. Both H_1- and H_2-receptors are in skin, and occasionally combining H_1- and H_2-receptor antagonists can be beneficial. Usually, first-generation agents are started at low doses and increased as tolerated, and regular continuous dosing is recommended. The tricyclic antidepressant doxepin has both anti–H_1- and H_2-receptor activity, but interacts with drugs metabolized by the cytochrome P-450 pathway. Side effects of commonly used first-generation antihistamines include sedation, dry mouth, blurred vision, constipation, and urinary retention, and lower doses may be required in the elderly. The recommended dose for second-generation antihistamines should not be exceeded.

AGENTS THAT IMPROVE SURFACE FUNCTIONS (LUBRICATION, SCALE)

Moisturizers

Moisturizers improve skin by diminishing scale and increasing water content. They usually contain mixtures of water and fatty substances such as petrolatum, lanolin, lanolin derivatives, and fatty

Table 473–3 • GROUPS OF ANTIHISTAMINES

ANTIHISTAMINE GROUP	GENERIC NAME
FIRST-GENERATION H_1-TYPE ANTIHISTAMINES	
Alkylamine	Brompheniramine (Dimetapp)
	Chorpheniramine (Chlor-Trimeton)
Aminoalkyl ether (ethanolamine)	Clemastine fumarate
	Diphenhydramine (Benadryl)
Ethylenediamine	Pyrilamine (Triaminic)
Phenothiazine	Promethazine (Phenergan)
	Trimeprazine (Temaril)
Piperidine	Azatadine
	Cyproheptadine
	Diphenylpyraline
Piperazine	Chlorcyclizine
	Hydroxyzine (Atarax)
SECOND GENERATION H_1-TYPE ANTIHISTAMINES	
Alkylamine	Acrivastine (combined with pseudoephedrine in allergy medication)
Piperidine	Astemizole (Hismanal)
	Loratidine (Claritin)
	Fexofenadine (Allegra)
Piperazine	Cetirizine (Zyrtec)
H_2-TYPE ANTIHISTAMINES	Cimetidine (Tagamet)
	Ranitidine (Zantac)
	Famotidine
	Nizatidine
H_1- AND H_2-TYPE ANTIHISTAMINES	Doxepin (Sinequan)

alcohols. Greasy moisturizers tend to function better, but they are less acceptable cosmetically.

Keratolytics

α-Hydroxy acids (lactic acid, gycolic acid, citric acid, glucuronic acid, pyruvic acid) are extremely effective keratolytics. They are helpful in treating disorders of keratinization and photoaging, as well as acne. Propylene glycol, used as 40 to 60% aqueous solutions, can decrease scaling. Salicylic acid, which works by decreasing keratinocyte adhesion and hydrating keratins, is used in a range of concentrations in many different bases to remove scale, to soften the stratum corneum, or as destructive therapy to remove warts and calluses. Urea is used in varying concentrations to treat scaling.

IMMUNOSUPPRESSIVES

Topical cytotoxic drugs include 5-fluorouracil (5-FU), mechlorethamine (nitrogen mustard), carmustine (BCNU), bleomycin, and tacrolimus. Topical 5-FU interferes with pyrimidine metabolism and action, blocking DNA synthesis. It is used to treat actinic keratoses, superficial basal cell cancers, and Bowen's disease, bowenoid papulosis, actinic cheilitis, and warts. Topical use does not cause systemic toxicity, but expected side effects include local irritation, erythema, and pain. Nitrogen mustard and BCNU, which have alkylating agents that inhibit DNA, RNA, and protein synthesis, are used to treat cutaneous T-cell lymphoma (Chapter 195); they can cause cutaneous reactions and myelosuppression, and nitrogen mustard commonly causes a cutaneous hypersensitivity reaction.

Intralesional bleomycin, which disrupts DNA synthesis, has been used to treat warts. Topical tacrolimus (Prograf), an immunosuppressive macrolide that acts on T lymphocytes to inhibit interleukin-2 transcription, is used for atopic dermatitis, allergic contact dermatitis, psoriasis, and several other inflammatory skin conditions. It can frequently cause burning sensation in the skin, and systemic absorption is minimal. Systemic immunosuppressives such as methotrexate, azathioprine, thioguanine, hydroxyurea, CellCept, cyclophosphamide, chlorambucil, and cyclosporine are used in a number of inflammatory or immunologically mediated skin conditions, particularly in widespread psoriasis and as glucocorticoid-sparing agents for autoimmune blistering diseases.

IMMUNOMODULATORY THERAPIES

Imiquimod, available as a 5% cream, is an imidazoquinolinamine that has antitumor and antiviral activity. It induces local production of γ-interferon, and it is used to treat warts and superficial skin cancers.

Systemic immunomodulatory drugs currently used in dermatology include interferons and TNF-α inhibitors such as etanercept and Remicade. Interferon-α2b is used both intralesionally and subcutaneously to treat genital warts, high-risk melanoma, Kaposi's sarcoma, hemangiomas, cutaneous T-cell lymphoma, keloids, Behçet's disease, cryoglobulinemia and vasculitis from hepatitis C, and perhaps basal cell and squamous cell carcinomas. Total interferon doses are generally 3 million IU or less per session, and systemic dosing is usually administered 3 days per week. Side effects include flulike symptoms, leukopenia, anemia, and hepatitis. TNF-α inhibitors are currently used off label to treat psoriasis. Intravenous immunoglobulin, which is used to treat a number of autoimmune skin diseases including pemphigus vulgaris, cicatricial pemphigoid, and dermatomyositis, likely works through Fc receptor modulation and anti-idiotype interactions. Extracorporeal photochemotherapy (photopheresis), which combines 8-methoxypsoralen and ultraviolet A irradiation of lymphocytes, is used for Sézary syndrome, the leukemic form of cutaneous T-cell lymphoma (Chapter 195). Plasmapheresis, used in combination with other immunosuppressive therapies, can remove autoantibodies and immune complexes in patients whose autoimmune diseases or cryoglobulinemia are resistant to other therapies.

PHOTOTHERAPY AND LASER

Ultraviolet treatments are given with different wavelengths, depending on the condition and the response to treatment. Currently there is broad band UVB (290 to 320 nm), narrow band 311-nm UVB, PUVA (psoralen with UVA 320 to 400 nm), and UVA1 (340 to 400 nm). Both forms of UVB and PUVA are used for psoriasis and vitiligo, but other conditions such as nummular and atopic dermatitis, pruritus due to uremia, and cutaneous T-cell lymphoma are treated this way. High-dose UVA1 is used, mainly in Europe, to treat atopic dermatitis, localized scleroderma, and mastocytosis. PUVA is associated with an increased risk of skin cancers, including melanoma. The risks of long-term UVA therapy are currently unknown, but photoaging is associated with UVA and there have been reports of an increase of melanoma associated with use of suntanning beds, where much of the exposure is to UVA. Laser therapy is used to treat vascular lesions such as port wine stains, tattoos, psoriasis, benign skin tumors, and photodamage, as well as to remove hair.

SUNSCREEN

Transparent sunscreens absorb photons of light. They are rated by the sun protection factor (SPF), which is determined by the ratio of UV exposure needed to cause erythema in protected versus unprotected skin. Most sunscreens work in the UVB range or shorter UVA wavelengths. Examples of UVB-absorptive compounds include aminobenzoates, cinnamates, salicylates, and benzophenones. Short wavelength UVA-absorptive compounds include benophenones and anthranilates. The best UVA blocking agent in the United States is parsol 1789 (avobenzone), which can be combined with UVB screens. Some sunscreens are water resistant or waterproof, as determined by the substantivity of the sunscreen, and these agents provide continued protection after sweating or swimming. Sunscreens can cause irritation and rarely contact allergic reactions. Physical sunscreens, such as zinc oxide and titanium dioxide, reflect light from the skin and include newer micronized reflecting powders that provide broad-spectrum (UVB and UVA) protection. Sunscreens decrease skin cancers and photodamage. UVB is partially reflected by clothing, and sun-protective clothing can provide substantial protection (Solumbra, SPF of 30).

COSMETICS: CAMOUFLAGE, BLEACHING, HAIR LOSS

A number of skin conditions benefit from camouflage cosmetics, but which can cause contact hypersensitivity. Products such as Dermablend can be blended to match skin colors, are thicker, can cover disfiguring lesions, and can be fixed with powder. Hydroquinones, topical retinoic acid, and azelaic acid (inhibits tyrosinase) are used to treat hyperpigmented conditions such as melasma and lentigines; these agents can be irritating and cause dyspigmentation. Topical minoxidil 2% (available over the counter) and 5% solutions are used for androgenic alopecia and alopecia areata. Finasteride, a 5-alpha-reductase inhibitor, is effective in men with androgenetic alopecia.

SUGGESTED READINGS

Levine N: Systemic dermatologic therapy. Dermatol Clin 2001;19:1–197. *Detailed review of many systemic therapies used in dermatology.*

Kerdel FA, Kirsner RS: Other novel immunosuppressants. Dermatol Clin 2000;18:475–483. *Review of therapies used for inpatient dermatology, with a focus on anti-inflammatory and immunosuppressive therapies used for serious dermatologic diseases.*

Smith CH: New approaches to topical therapy. Clin Exp Dermatol 2000;25:567–574. *Review of new topical therapies in dermatology.*

Werth VP, Duvic M: Medical dermatology. Dermatol Clin 2002;19:603–772. *Review of current treatment approaches to many serious dermatologic illnesses.*

474 ECZEMAS, PHOTODERMATOSES, PAPULOSQUAMOUS (INCLUDING FUNGAL) DISEASES, AND FIGURATE ERYTHEMAS

Henry W. Lim

ECZEMA

The more commonly encountered eczemas (Table 474–1) share a common theme in terms of the histologic changes. These conditions

Skin Diseases

Table 474–1 • ECZEMAS	
Nummular dermatitis	Seborrheic dermatitis
Dyshidrosis	Allergic contact dermatitis
Atopic dermatitis	Irritant contact dermatitis

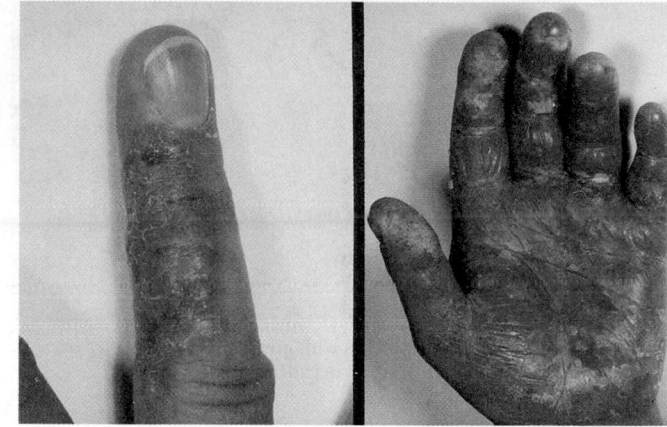

FIGURE 474–2 • Dyshidrosis. *Left,* Scaly erythematous patch with erosions on side of a finger. *Right,* Erythema, scaliness and peeling of the palm.

show varying degrees of edema within the epidermis (spongiosis) and of infiltration with lymphocytes and macrophages in the superficial dermis.

Nummular Dermatitis

Nummular dermatitis occurs most frequently in patients who are in their 50s to 60s and is usually associated with significant dryness of the skin (xerosis). Both sexes are affected; in temperate climates, this condition is most frequently seen in the winter. The condition appears to be more frequent among Asians. The etiology of nummular dermatitis is unclear, although xerosis plays a significant role in its pathogenesis.

Patients usually present with pruritic, coin-shaped, erythematous patches with some scales and occasionally with pinhead-sized vesicles (Fig. 474–1). Lesions may be excoriated and lichenified. Legs and arms are the commonly affected sites, although lesions can also occur on the trunk. Treatment consists of liberal use of emollients, avoidance of long hot showers, topical use of corticosteroid ointments, and oral therapy with antihistamines. In severe cases, ultraviolet (UV)-B phototherapy, psoralen combined with UVA (PUVA), or a short course of oral corticosteroids may be helpful.

Dyshidrosis

Dyshidrosis appears as deep-seated, pinhead-sized vesicles, most commonly along the sides of the fingers (Fig. 474–2). Occasionally, palms and soles may also be involved. Lesions are usually pruritic, associated with xerosis of the surrounding skin. Fissuring of the tip and the side of the fingers frequently occurs. Dyshidrosis is seen in individuals who wash their hands frequently, such as health care and restaurant workers and mothers with young infants. Treatment consists of minimizing hand washing, liberal use of emollients, topical therapy with corticosteroid ointments, and oral administration of antihistamines.

Atopic Dermatitis

Atopic dermatitis is most commonly seen among young children, but severe cases persist into adulthood. In over 80% of the patients,

the disease starts before the age of 5 years. The prevalence has been estimated between 15 and 23%. Patients usually present with xerosis, erythematous scaly patches, small vesicles, excoriations, crusting, and, not infrequently, impetiginization (Fig. 474–3). With chronic scratching and rubbing, hyperpigmentation and lichenification occur. Commonly affected sites include the periorbital area and flexor areas such as the neck, antecubital fossa, and popliteal fossa. In severe cases, the entire skin surface may be involved. Diagnosis is made by the typical morphology and distribution of the lesions, as well as by a family and personal history of atopy. Management consists of emollients, oral antihistamines, topical corticosteroid ointments, topical tacrolimus, topical pimecrolimus, UVB phototherapy, and PUVA.

Seborrheic Dermatitis

Seborrheic dermatitis is a common condition that occurs as erythematous patches with fine, greasy-appearing scales, most commonly on the malar area, mid forehead, mid chest, and scalp (Fig. 474–4). This condition is common in patients with HIV infection (Chapter 417). The pathogenesis is unknown, although *Pityrosporum ovale* is believed to play a role. Diagnosis can usually be made on clinical

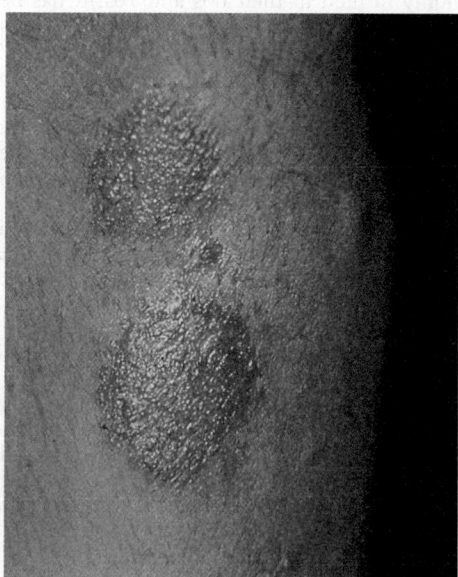

FIGURE 474–1 • Coin-shaped erythematous patches in a patient with nummular dermatitis.

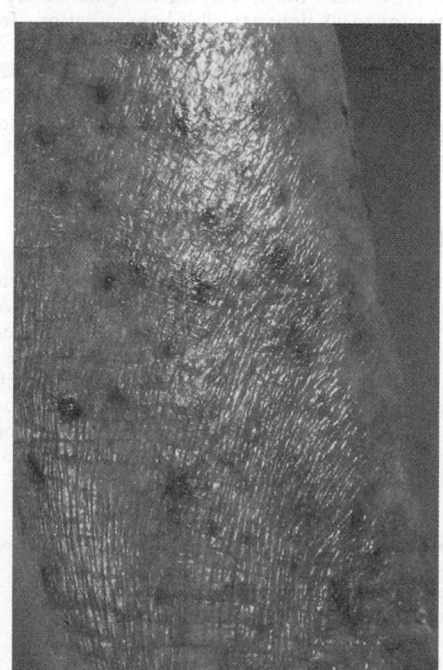

FIGURE 474–3 • Atopic dermatitis. Note the erythema, excoriation, and lichenification.

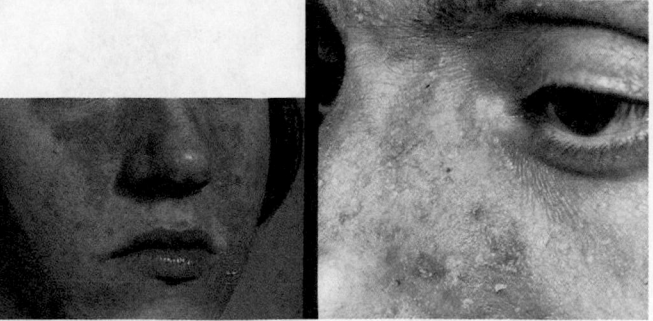

FIGURE 474–4 • Erythematous patches with greasy-appearing scales on malar area of two patients with seborrheic dermatitis.

grounds alone. Management includes topical corticosteroids and topical ketoconazole cream or shampoo.

Allergic Contact Dermatitis and Irritant Contact Dermatitis

Allergic contact dermatitis and irritant contact dermatitis are induced by exogenous agents. Allergic contact dermatitis is a delayed hypersensitivity response to external allergens, whereas irritant contact dermatitis is a nonspecific toxic response to contact irritants. In both conditions, lesions occur in the exposed area, but in severe cases nonexposed areas may also have milder lesions. In allergic contact dermatitis, patients present with erythematous pruritic papules followed by vesicles. Lesions resolve with fine scales. Postinflammatory hyperpigmentation may be observed, especially in dark-skinned individuals. Histologically, epidermal edema and dermal histiocytic infiltrates are observed. Irritant contact dermatitis presents as lesions of similar morphology as allergic contact dermatitis. However, it is usually associated with a burning sensation rather than pruritus. Postinflammatory hyperpigmentation is frequently observed. Histologic changes consist of necrotic keratinocytes, epidermal necrosis, and neurophilic infiltrates. Management includes identification and removal of the offending agent, as well as symptomatic treatments such as topical corticosteroids and oral antihistamines (Chapter 473).

PHOTODERMATOSES

Photodermatoses indicate the development of cutaneous eruption secondary to exposure to UV light or visible light radiation (Table 474–2). By convention, electromagnetic radiation in the UV region is divided into UVC (200-290 nm), UVB (290-320 nm), UVA-2 (320-340 nm), and UVA-1 (340-400 nm). Visible light extends from 400 to 760 nm. Because UVC emitted by the sun is absorbed by ozone in the stratosphere, UVC does not reach the Earth's surface. UVB, UVA, and visible light are the relevant spectra in photodermatoses.

Polymorphous Light Eruption

Polymorphous light eruption is the most common idiopathic photodermatosis, occurring in 10 to 20% of the general population. It usually occurs in young adults, has a slight female predominance, and is seen worldwide. The pathogenesis is unclear, although it is thought to involve a delayed hypersensitivity response to an unidentified antigen. Lesions usually occur in early spring within a few hours of exposure to sunlight. Lesions can be papular, papulovesicular, or, less commonly, vesicular (Fig. 474–5); they can also be minimally pruritic.

Table 474–2 • PHOTODERMATOSES
Polymorphous light eruption
Chronic actinic dermatitis
Solar urticaria
Phototoxicity and photoallergy
Porphyrias

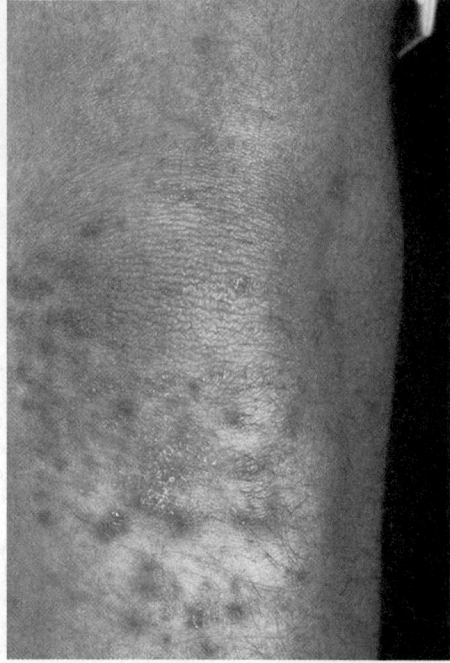

FIGURE 474–5 • Erythematous papules a few hours after exposure to the sun in a patient with polymorphous light eruption.

Usually, lesions persist for several days and resolve spontaneously. The condition tends to improve as the sunny season progresses, a phenomenon known as "hardening."

The course tends to be chronic, with only 11% of patients having complete resolution of the disease in 16 years and 24% in 32 years. Diagnosis is based on the typical history and morphology of the lesion; the diagnosis can be confirmed by the induction of lesions with provocative phototesting. When lesions occur primarily on the face, lupus must be excluded. Management consists of sun avoidance, the use of broad-spectrum sunscreens, topical corticosteroids, and oral antihistamines (Chapter 473). In severe cases, desensitization treatment using narrow-band UVB or PUVA has been successful. Desensitization is usually performed in early spring by exposing patients to increasing doses of narrowband UVB or PUVA.

Chronic Actinic Dermatitis

Chronic actinic dermatitis is a chronic photodermatosis that occurs most commonly in men in their 60s and 70s. It has been seen in patients of all ethnic groups; in fact, in the United States, it is most commonly seen in dark-skinned individuals. It occurs in 5 to 17% of patients referred for evaluation of photosensitivity. Chronic actinic dermatitis can evolve from photoallergic contact dermatitis, allergic contact dermatitis, or exposure to a known photosensitizing agent; however, it can also arise de novo. It has been postulated that this condition represents a delayed hypersensitivity response to an unidentified antigen.

Clinically, patients present with erythematous papules and plaques with superficial scaling and, frequently, with lichenification (Fig. 474–6). The distribution of lesions is primarily on sun-exposed areas, such as the forehead, nose, cheeks, "V" area of the neck, dorsum of the hands, and forearms. Typically, there is sparing of sun-protected areas such as the postauricular area, the area underneath the chin, the area above the eyes, and the trunk. This chronic photosensitivity occurs in the absence of any continued exposure to known photosensitizers. Histologically, there is a dermal lymphohistocytic infiltrate; atypical mononuclear cells may be observed. On phototesting, patients have decreased sensitivity to UVA, UVB, and/or visible light. In a study of 178 cases, 10% resolved in 5 years and 50% in 15 years. An association has been reported with HIV infection and with atopic dermatitis.

The diagnosis is based on the history and on the morphology and distribution of the lesions; it is confirmed by phototesting. Management is challenging. During sunny season, maximal sun

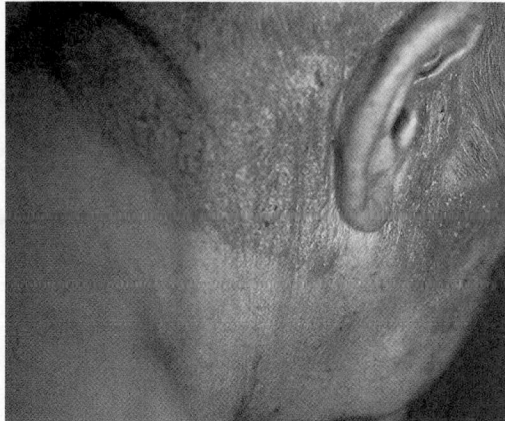

FIGURE 474–6 • Erythema and lichenification in a patient with chronic actinic dermatitis. Note sparing of the sun-protected areas of the neck, infra-auricular area, and lower cheeks.

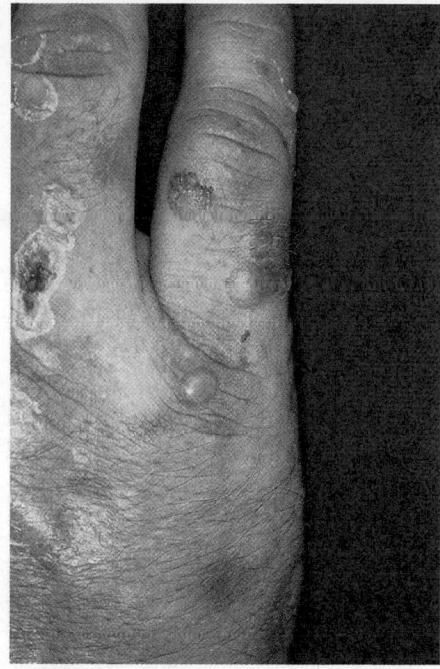

FIGURE 474–7 • Erosion, crusting, and vesicles on dorsum of hand of a patient with porphyria cutanea tarda.

protection is critical. Other treatment modalities include PUVA in conjunction with oral corticosteroids, azathioprine, cyclosporine, hydroxychloroquine, and the combination of mycophenolate mofetil with PUVA and oral corticosteroids.

Solar Urticaria

Solar urticaria occurs worldwide. In photodermatology referral centers, it accounts for 4 to 5% of patients. The mean age at onset is usually in the fourth decade, with a slight female predominance. In one study, the mean duration of disease at the time of diagnosis was 3.6 years. Patients develop urticaria that appears within minutes of sun exposure and persists for less than 24 hours. Lesions are most commonly induced by visible light, but they can also be induced by UVA or UVB. Similar to polymorphous light eruption, improvement may occur as the summer season progresses ("hardening"). Diagnosis is confirmed by the induction of the lesion after controlled exposure to the appropriate light source. Management consists of avoidance of exposure to the sun and the use of broad-spectrum sunscreens and oral antihistamines. In severe cases, graduated exposure to UVA or PUVA is helpful.

Phototoxicity and Photoallergy

Phototoxicity and photoallergy refer to the development of skin lesions after combined exposure to an oral or topical photosensitizer and electromagnetic radiation. Phototoxicity is a nonspecific cutaneous toxic reaction, whereas photoallergy is a delayed hypersensitivity response. For the vast majority of photosensitizers, the action spectrum for both lies in the UVA range. Most of the phototoxic agents are systemic medications, whereas the most common photoallergens are the various sunscreen ingredients in sunscreen. In both conditions, patients present with erythematous papules and vesicles confined to sun-exposed areas. Vesicular eruption is distinctly more common in phototoxicity, whereas pruritic eczematous eruption is more common in photoallergy. Histologically, phototoxicity is characterized by necrotic keratinocytes and infiltrates consisting predominantly of neutrophils whereas photoallergy is characterized by epidermal edema (spongiosis) and lymphohistiocytic dermal infiltrate. Diagnosis is based on a careful history for exposure to photosensitizers combined with the typical morphology. Management consists of identification and removal of photosensitizer and use of topical corticosteroids and oral antihistamines (Chapter 473).

Porphyrias (Chapter 223)

The most common cutaneous porphyria is porphyria cutanea tarda (PCT), in which patients present with skin fragility and blister formation on sun-exposed areas, most commonly the dorsum of the hands and the forearms (Fig. 474–7). Erosion and crusting on the face can also be noted. Patients usually have periorbital hypertrichosis and, less frequently, periorbital mottled hyperpigmentation and hypopig-

mentation. Sclerodermoid skin changes can occur in both sun-exposed and sun-protected areas. The defective enzyme is uroporphyrinogen decarboxylase. PCT is associated with excessive alcohol intake, exposure to estrogens, hepatitis C infection (Chapter 152), and HIV infection (Chapter 417). Patients invariably have an elevated level of ferritin and frequently have elevated liver enzyme values.

Diagnosis is suggested by the typical clinical appearance and is confirmed by the characteristic porphyrin profile (elevated levels of 8-, 7-, 6-, 5-, and 4-carboxyl porphryins in the urine and isocorporphyrin in feces; Chapter 223). Management consists of avoidance of precipitating factors (alcohol, iron-containing vitamins, estrogen-containing birth control pills), weekly phlebotomy, or low doses of hydroxychloroquine. With appropriate treatment, remission can persist for many years.

PAPULOSQUAMOUS (INCLUDING FUNGAL) DISEASES

Common papulosquamous diseases include psoriasis, pityriasis, lichen planus, syphilis, and fungal infections (Table 474–3).

Psoriasis

Psoriasis is probably the most commonly recognized papulosquamous disease. It occurs in 2 to 3% of the general population, with considerable variation among different parts of the world. It affects males and females equally. Approximately one third of the patients have a positive family history. Psoriasis has bimodal peak of onset, at age 22.5 years and again at age 55 years. The onset of psoriasis before the age of 15 years is associated with a higher prevalence of positive family history of psoriasis and with more severe disease.

Psoriasis was initially thought to be purely a disease of keratinocyte hyperproliferation; however, it has now become increasingly clear

Table 474–3 • PAPULOSQUAMOUS DISEASES

Psoriasis	Pityriasis lichenoides
Pityriasis rubra pilaris	Parapsoriasis
Pityriasis rosea	Mycosis fungoides
Lichen planus	Dermatophytosis
Lichen nitidus	Tinea versicolor
Secondary syphilis	

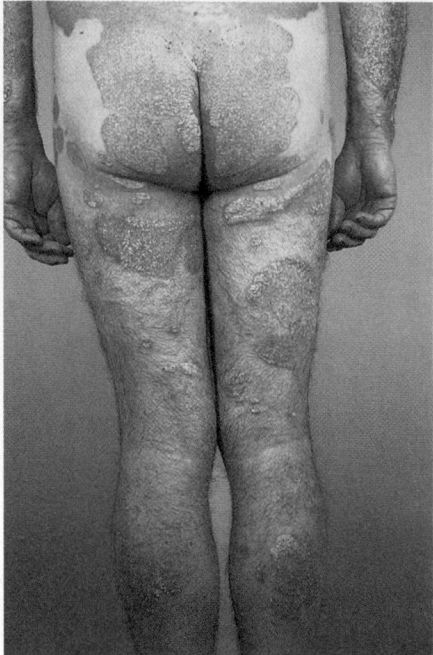

FIGURE 474–8 • Erythematous plaques with silvery scales in a patient with psoriasis.

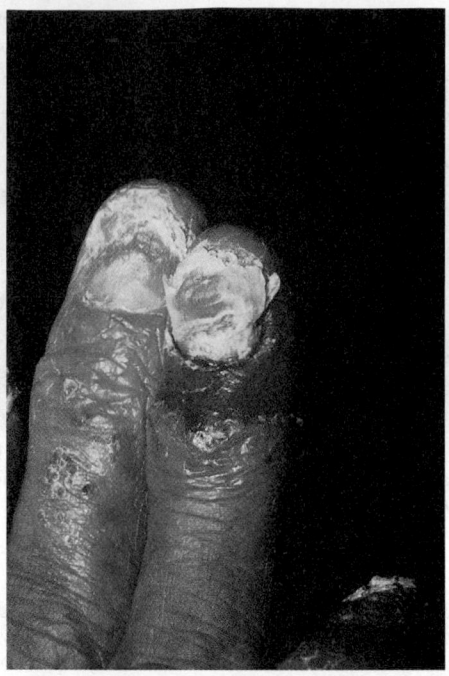

FIGURE 474–9 • Thickening and crumbling of nail plate (onychodystrophy) in a patient with psoriasis. Note the erythematous patches with silvery scales in the periungual area.

that its pathogenesis is complex and multifactorial. Factors playing a role in the pathogenesis include T cells, cytokines, chemokines, growth factors, dendritic cells, eicosanoids, neutrophils, and mast cells. It has been postulated that in genetically susceptible individuals, exposure to precipitating factors such as infections (e.g., streptococcal infections or HIV), stress, or physical injury results in activation of T cells and generation of cytokines, followed by influx of neutrophils and subsequent release of inflammatory mediators, which lead to the development of cutaneous lesions.

There is a linkage disequilibrium (e.g., higher than expected association) between psoriasis and human leukocyte antigens (HLAs), the most common one being HLA-Cw6. However, HLA-Cw6 is unlikely to be the disease allele, because psoriasis develops in only about 10% of HLA-Cw6 positive individuals. Preliminary evidence has identified a candidate gene for psoriasis on chromosome 16q.

Psoriasis can involve both the skin and the nails. Skin lesions are characterized by erythematous macules, papules, or plaques that are usually covered with silvery scales (Fig. 474–8). On removal of the scales, pinpoint bleeding may be observed (the Auspitz sign), reflecting the proliferation of blood vessels in the superficial dermis. Nail involvement includes pittings, yellowish macules underneath the nail plate ("oil drop" sign), and thickening of the nail (onychodystrophy) (Fig. 474–9). Minor injury to the skin can result in the development of psoriatic lesions (Koebner's phenomenon). Association of psoriasis with HIV infection (Chapter 417) has been well documented; HIV-associated psoriasis tends to be inflammatory and is usually more resistant to treatment compared with non–HIV-associated psoriasis.

There are several distinct forms of psoriasis. *Psoriasis vulgaris*, the most common type, appears as a persistent erythematous scaly papule and plaque on elbows, knees, and scalp; however, it may also involve any part of the body. *Guttate psoriasis* usually occurs after viral or bacterial (most commonly streptococcal) infection; it appears as small, erythematous, scaly papules scattered over a large area of the body in a raindrop distribution (guttate = a drop). *Inverse psoriasis* refers to psoriasis that occurs in skinfold areas such as the groin, axilla, and inframammary folds. It appears as an erythematous, somewhat shiny patch; because of the constant friction in the involved areas, scales are usually absent. *Erythrodermic psoriasis* appears as widespread, sometimes generalized erythroderma with fine silvery scales, frequently associated with fissures. *Palmoplantar psoriasis* presents as keratotic scaly patches and plaques on the palms and soles, very frequently with accompanying fissures, which can be quite painful. *Pustular psoriasis of von Zumbusch* is a rare variant of psoriasis

occurring with generalized pustules that are 2 to 3 mm in diameter, associated with onset of fever.

Five to 8 per cent of patients with psoriasis may also have psoriatic arthritis (Chapter 279). Most of these patients present with peripheral asymmetric oligoarthritis involving small joints of the hands and feet, the large joints of the legs, or combinations of both. Psoriatic arthritis has been associated with HLA-B57, although some studies have also reported HLA-Cw6 in more than 50% of all persons with this disease.

In most cases, the diagnosis of psoriasis can be made based on history and physical examination alone. However, in patients with erythrodermic psoriasis, other causes of generalized erythroderma (including pityriasis rubra pilaris, drug eruption, and cutaneous T-cell lymphoma) must be excluded.

The therapeutic approach to psoriasis of increasing severity includes topical therapy, UV-based treatment, and systemic medications. Topical therapy includes topical corticosteroids, anthralin, calcipotriol (also known as calcipotriene), tazarotene, and tar preparations, used alone or in combination. In patients who have widespread lesions, UV-based therapy is commonly used and includes broad-band UVB therapy (290–320 nm), narrowband UVB therapy (311–312 nm), and PUVA. Systemic medications include weekly methotrexate, cyclosporine, hydroxyurea, systemic retinoids, and mycophenolate mofetil.

The most recent advance in the treatment of psoriasis is the availability of biologic therapy. Alefacept is a fusion protein that contains the binding site of lymphocyte function-associated antigen-3, which binds to CD2 markers on the surface of memory T cells; this agent has been approved by the FDA for the treatment of psoriasis. Etanercept, an anti-TNF-α fusion protein, is approved by the FDA for the treatment for psoriatic arthritis; it also has been shown to be effective for the skin lesions of psoriasis. Infliximab, a mouse anti-TNF-α monoclonal antibody used for rheumatoid arthritis and Crohn's disease, has been reported to be effective for skin lesions of psoriasis. Efalizumab, an anti-CD11a humanized monoclonal antibody, is another biologic agent that has been shown to be effective for the treatment of psoriasis in clinical trials.

Pityriasis Rubra Pilaris

Pityriasis rubra pilaris occurs equally in men and women; the incidence ranges from 1 in 5000 new dermatology patients in Great Britain to 1 in 50,000 in India. It most frequently occurs as the acquired

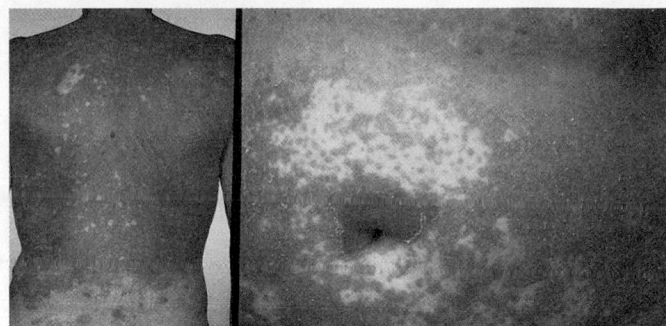

FIGURE 474–10 • Pityriasis rubra pilaris. Note the erythematous-orange plaques with islands of sparing.

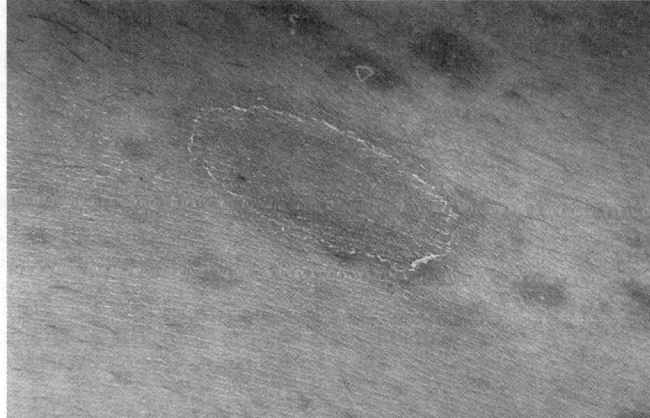

FIGURE 474–11 • Large erythematous oval patch (herald patch) of pityriasis rosea accompanied by smaller erythematous patches.

form, although a familial form (autosomal dominant with variable expression) also occurs. Sixty per cent of patients have adult-onset disease, with peak incidence in the first, second, and fifth to sixth decades. Abnormal vitamin A metabolism has been postulated as a possible cause.

Clinically, patients present with erythematous to orange papules and plaques on all parts of the body (Fig. 474–10). Characteristically, there is normal-appearing skin between these lesions ("islands of sparing"). Erythema, hyperkeratosis and fissures of the palms and soles are common; when severe, these lesions result in functional impairment. Many patients have follicular keratotic papules on the dorsa of the fingers and occasionally on the elbows as well as on the wrists. Nails are yellow and thickened, with distal splinter hemorrhages. In adult patients, the condition typically starts on the face and moves to the lower extremities; in the juvenile form, it usually starts in the lower half of the body. Ectropion may occur, and pruritus is observed in approximately 20% of patients. In contrast to psoriasis, arthritis is uncommon. Pityriasis rubra pilaris has been associated with HIV infection (Chapter 417).

Definitive diagnosis can usually be made based on the clinical presentations and on characteristic histologic findings of alternating vertical and horizontal parakeratosis in the stratum corneum. The most effective treatment is the use of systemic retinoids, which can be combined with PUVA. Methotrexate or cyclosporine has been reported to be effective for some patients. Topical emollients and topical keratolytic agents are helpful as adjunctive therapy.

Pityriasis Rosea

The incidence of pityriasis rosea (PR) has been reported as 3 to 30 per 1000 patients. It occurs in all ethnic groups, most commonly in the third and fourth decades of life, with a slight female predominance. The cause is not known, and a possible association with human herpesviruses 6 and 7 has been reported. In 50 to 90% of patients, PR starts with a primary lesion (herald patch), which is an erythematous scaly oval patch of a few centimeters in diameter. This lesion is usually followed within a few days by smaller erythematous scaly patches on the trunk, less commonly on the proximal extremities (Fig. 474–11). As a rule, palms and soles are spared. The distribution of the eruption, especially on the back, tends to follow the lines of cleavage of the skin, resulting in a "Christmas tree" distribution. Lesions are most commonly asymptomatic, although they may be mildly pruritic. The eruption is self-limiting and resolves within 6 to 8 weeks. In rare instances, lesions may persist.

Diagnosis can usually be made clinically. The most important differential diagnosis is secondary syphilis, which, in contrast to PR, involves the palms and soles. In many instances, however, a rapid plasma reagin (RPR) test is advisable to exclude syphilis. Treatment is primarily symptomatic, including topical corticosteroids and oral antihistamines. UVB phototherapy or PUVA should be reserved for severe, recalcitrant cases.

Lichen Planus

Lichen planus occurs most commonly in patients between 30 and 60 years of age. Women are affected more frequently than men and tend to be somewhat older at the onset of disease. The prevalence in the general population is about 1%.

Histologically, lichen planus is characterized by dense lymphocytic infiltrate at the dermal-epidermal junction. The infiltrates consist of predominantly T cells, suggesting the pathogenic role of cell-mediated immunity. Because lichen planus or lichen planus–like eruptions can occur after exposure to drugs or chemicals (e.g., color film developer), the role of drugs and chemicals in inducing T cell–mediated response against the epidermis has been postulated. Conflicting data have been reported regarding the association of lichen planus with infection with hepatitis C (Chapter 152).

Clinically, patients usually present with erythematous to violaceous flat-topped papules, often with white lacy lines (Wickham's striae) on the wrists, forearms, and genitalia (Fig. 474–12). *Oral lichen planus* occurs as white papules and plaques with a reticulated appearance, most commonly along the bite line on the buccal mucosa. Occasionally, erosion may occur. *Hypertrophic lichen planus* usually occurs on the lower extremities as lichenified, violaceous plaques, probably secondary to chronic rubbing and scratching of the lichen planus lesions. *Erosive lichen planus* occurs as erosion usually surrounded by violaceous discoloration at the periphery; this variant tends to occur more commonly on the feet. *Bullous lichen planus* occurs as vesicles or bullae arising from a preexisting lesion of lichen planus. *Lichen planopilaris* occurs as violaceous papules and plaques involving the scalp, most prominently surrounding the hair follicles; it progresses to scarring alopecia. *Lichen planus actinicus*, a variant of lichen planus occurring most commonly in the Middle East, tends to occur on the sun-exposed areas such as the forehead; it occurs as papules or plaques with minimally elevated rolled edges. *Atrophic lichen planus* occurs as a typical lichen planus lesion with a central area of superficial atrophy. *Lichen planus of the nails* occurs as thinning of the nail with longitudinal ridges; it may progress to complete loss of the nail plate (pterygium formation).

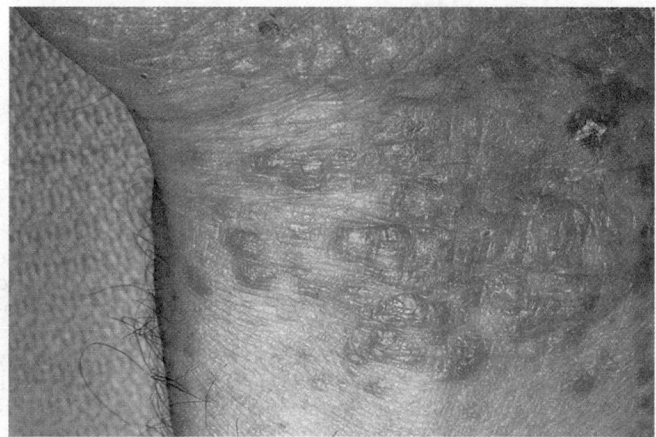

FIGURE 474–12 • Erythematous papules on the wrist of a patient with lichen planus.

The diagnosis can be made by clinical appearance and is confirmed by the characteristic histologic findings of infiltration by lymphocytes at the dermal-epidermal junction. Several treatment options are available. Topical corticosteroids are helpful in patients with limited disease. Hypertrophic lichen planus can be treated with topical steroids under occlusion or with interlesional corticosteroid injection. A 6- to 8-week course of oral corticosteroids is helpful in patients with widespread lichen planus. Narrowband UVB phototherapy or PUVA is helpful for widespread condition. Systemic retinoids or systemic cyclosporine (3 to 6 mg/kg) has been used with good success in some patients. Oral lesions can be treated with topical corticosteroids, topical retinoids, cyclosporine solution mouthwash, or topical tacrolimus. Without treatment, cutaneous lesions resolve in approximately 1 year, whereas oral and hypertrophic lesions tend to be much more chronic, persisting 4.5 years and 8.5 years, respectively.

Lichen Nitidus

Lichen nitidus is a rather uncommon condition that usually occurs in children or young adults. The incidence has been estimated to be 3.4 cases per 10,000 population. It is more commonly observed in dark-skinned individuals. The etiology is unclear, and no infectious agent has been identified.

The lesions are 1- to 2-mm, shiny skin-colored discrete papules, sometimes with fine scales on their surface, occurring most commonly on the genitalia or forearms and occasionally on the trunk. A generalized form has rarely been reported. Lesions are usually asymptomatic. Histologically, there is a dense lymphocytic infiltrate in the superficial dermis and at the dermal epidermal junction. In contrast to lichen planus, in which the infiltrate tends to involve the entire section of the skin, the infiltrate in lichen nitidus tends to be much more focal and localized.

Diagnosis usually can be confirmed from the typical clinical appearance and characteristic histologic changes. The condition tends to remit spontaneously in a few years, so therapy should be reserved for symptomatic and problematic cases. Topical corticosteroids, antihistamines, UVB phototherapy, PUVA, and systemic retinoids have been used with varying degrees of success.

Secondary Syphilis

Lesions of secondary syphilis typically occur 1 to 2 months after the development of primary chancre lesion (Chapter 349). However, up to 25% of patients may not remember having a chancre. Once the eruption occurs, it lasts for 1 to 3 months.

Clinically, secondary syphilis may appear as erythematous macules ("roseola syphilitica"), erythematous to hyperpigmented oval or circular papules and plaques covered with scales, or a maculopapular eruption. Nodular eruption may also occur occasionally. The lesions tend to be widespread, and the palms and soles are very frequently involved (Fig. 474–13). Diagnosis is made based on history, physical examination, and positive RPR test. Skin biopsy shows proliferation of endothelial cells in the dermis and a dense dermal infiltrate containing many plasma cells. Intramuscular penicillin is the treatment of choice.

Pityriasis Lichenoides

Pityriasis lichenoides occurs as erythematous papules that may be minimally pruritic and covered with scales, scattered on all parts of the body. In the acute form (pityriasis lichenoides et varioliformis acuta [PLEVA]), the central part of the lesions develop vesicles, pustules, and hemorrhages, resulting in eventual crusting of the lesions. The patient may have mild constitutional symptoms of fever and malaise. The chronic form (pityriasis lichenoides chronica [PLC]) occurs as asymptomatic erythematous to hyperpigmented papules and plaques covered with fine scales; the trunk and extremities are common sites. Histologically, both PLEVA and PLC are characterized by dense lymphocytic infiltrates in the dermis, with CD8 lymphocytes predominating in PLEVA and CD4 lymphocytes in PLC.

The initial course of PLC is usually a few years. PLEVA usually resolves in a few months, although persistence may occur. The acute form is less common than the chronic form, and both affect patients of all ages, with a slight male predominance.

Treatments include topical corticosteroids and antihistamines (Chapter 473). Tetracycline (1–2 g per day) or erythromycin (1–2 g

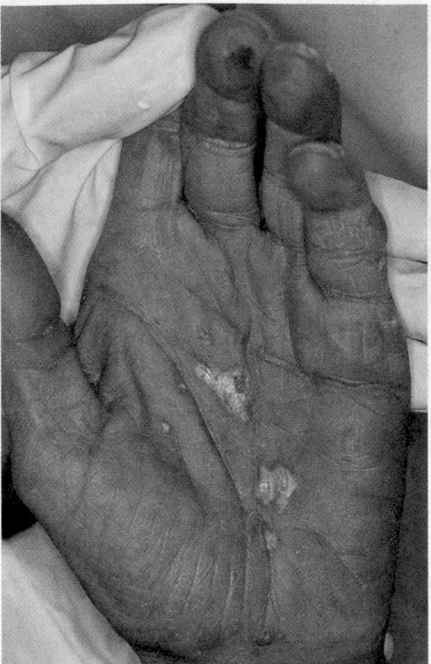

FIGURE 474–13 • Scaly papules and plaques on the palm of a patient with secondary syphilis.

per day) are helpful in some patients. Broad-band and narrow-band UVB phototherapy and PUVA photochemotherapy have been helpful in some patients. Methotrexate is helpful in patients with active disease.

Parapsoriasis

There are two common variants to parapsoriasis: large plaque parapsoriasis and small plaque parapsoriasis. The peak incidence is in the fifth decade, although rare cases may begin in childhood. Large plaque parapsoriasis appears as oval to circular, erythematous to hyperpigmented macules and patches with fine scales and superficial atrophy (crinkling atrophy) scattered on all parts of the body (Fig. 474–14). These lesions are usually greater than 5 cm. Although lesions may be minimally pruritic, they are usually asymptomatic. Large plaque parapsoriasis is considered by some to be a benign variant of mycosis fungoides (see later). Small plaque parapsoriasis appears as circular to oval erythematous to hyperpigmented patches or minimally elevated plaques, with lesions less than 5 cm in diameter and usually covered with fine scales. Digitate dermatosis is a distinct variant of small plaque parapsoriasis in which lesions appear along the line of cleavage, usually on the lateral aspect of the trunk in the shape of fingerprints. Histologically, large plaque parapsoriasis is characterized by a dermal lymphocytic infiltrate, which may extend into the

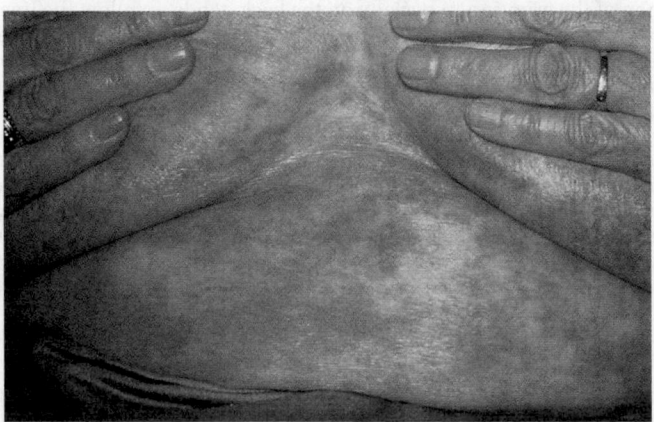

FIGURE 474–14 • Erythematous patches with fine scales in a patient with large plaque parapsoriasis.

epidermis, whereas small plaque parapsoriasis is characterized by spongiotic dermatitis, with a mild superficial lymphocytic infiltrate in the dermis. In up to one third of patients, large plaque parapsoriasis may evolve into mycosis fungoides. As a result, treatment of large plaque parapsoriasis is similar to that of early-stage mycosis fungoides: high-potency topical corticosteroids, topical nitrogen mustard, UVB phototherapy, and PUVA. By comparison, patients with small plaque parapsoriasis have a benign course, and management of small plaque parapsoriasis should be symptomatic only, with emollients, topical corticosteroids, and UVB phototherapy.

Mycosis Fungoides

Mycosis fungoides is a variant of cutaneous T-cell lymphoma (Chapter 195). There are four types of cutaneous manifestations: patch, plaque, tumor, and erythrodermic. The patch stage of mycosis fungoides presents as patches with fine "cigarette paper" wrinkling of the epidermis. The patches can be skin-colored or minimally erythematous; hyperpigmented or hypopigmented lesions are frequently seen in dark-skinned individuals. The patches can vary from a few millimeters to a few centimeters in diameter; they are more common on sun-protected areas such as the buttocks (Fig. 474–15). The patches are usually asymptomatic, although they occasionally may be mildly pruritic. Lesions may be present for years. As the disease progresses, some of the patches may become more indurated and evolve into more elevated plaques. Nodular lesions may occur in patients without any patch or plaque lesions, although more commonly these lesions occur in conjunction with patches and plaques. Erythrodermic mycosis fungoides occurs as a generalized erythroderma with significant scaling and pruritus. Hyperkeratosis of the palms and soles, as well as fissuring of hands and feet, are quite common. In dark-skinned individuals, mycosis fungoides may appear as hypopigmented patches.

The diagnosis is confirmed by histologic demonstration of atypical mononuclear cells both in the epidermis and in the dermis, as well as immunophenotypic markers showing predominance of CD4 cells in the infiltrate. Depending on the stage of the disease, therapy for mycosis fungoides includes high-potency topical corticosteroids, topical nitrogen mustard, UVB phototherapy, PUVA, topical and systemic retinoids, interferon-α and interferon-γ, DAB-IL-2 toxin, and extracorporeal photochemotherapy.

Dermatophytoses

Fungal infections that occur as papulosquamous eruptions include tinea corporis, tinea manuum, tinea cruris, and tinea pedis. Tinea corporis causes a polycyclic erythematous scaly patch that has elevated borders and consists of papules and sometimes pustules. As the lesion progresses, the border advances centrifugally. The trunk is the most common site. Tinea cruris occurs with similar morphology, except it is located in the inguinal folds and expands centrifugally from the folds. In men, the scrotum is usually spared. Tinea manuum can occur as an erythematous scaly patch with an advancing active border, usually located on the dorsum of the hands, or it may occur

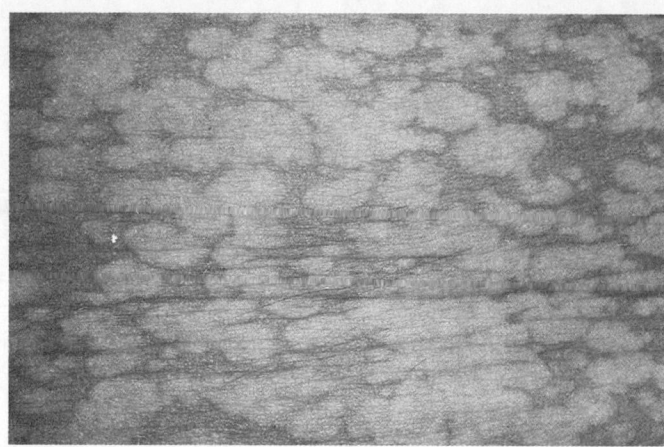

FIGURE 474–16 • Hypopigmented patches of tinea versicolor.

as diffuse scaly patches with mild hyperkeratosis involving part or the entire surface of the palm and palmar aspect of the fingers. Tinea pedis also has two clinical manifestations: it can occur as scaly macerated lesions with erythema in the toe webs or as patchy or diffuse scaliness on the sole extending to the medial and lateral aspect of the foot (moccasin distribution). The latter presentation can be associated with diffuse scaliness of one but not both palms, a condition known as the "one-hand, two-feet syndrome." The diagnosis can be confirmed by examination of skin scrapings using 10% potassium hydroxide preparation and/or by fungal culture. Treatment consists of topical or oral antifungal medications.

Tinea Versicolor

Tinea versicolor is a fungal infection of the skin caused by *Malassezia furfur*. It occurs in otherwise healthy young individuals, especially in warm and moist environments during the summer. Clinically, it appears as macules and patches with very fine scales; the color can be hypopigmented, skin-colored, minimally erythematous, or light brown (Fig. 474–16). The patches usually start as perifollicular macules, with the mid chest and mid back as the most common sites. As the lesions progress, hypopigmentation of the skin may also occur. The lesion usually is asymptomatic. The diagnosis is confirmed by the characteristic appearance of the fungal elements on a 10% potassium hydroxide preparation: grapelike clusters of yeast and short, septate branching hyphae ("spaghetti and meatballs" appearance). Treatment is 2.5% selenium sulfide shampoo, a topical antifungal preparation, or a 1- to 3-day course of oral ketoconazole or itraconazole.

FIGURATE ERYTHEMAS

These conditions (Table 474–4) appear as erythematous circular or polycyclic plaques with central clearing and, frequently, centrifugally migrating border. Occasionally, fine scaling may also be observed. The extremities are the most common sites. Diagnosis can frequently be made by the typical history and morphology.

Erythema annulare centrifugum is most commonly idiopathic; however, it can also be a manifestation of a hypersensitivity response to medications. Management includes identification of a precipitating agent (if possible) and treatment with topical or systemic corticosteroids. *Erythema gyratum repens* occurs as concentric erythematous plaques with fine scales, resembling a "wood-grain" pattern. This unusual form of figurate erythema has been associated with hematologic malignancies and with carcinomas of the breast, lung,

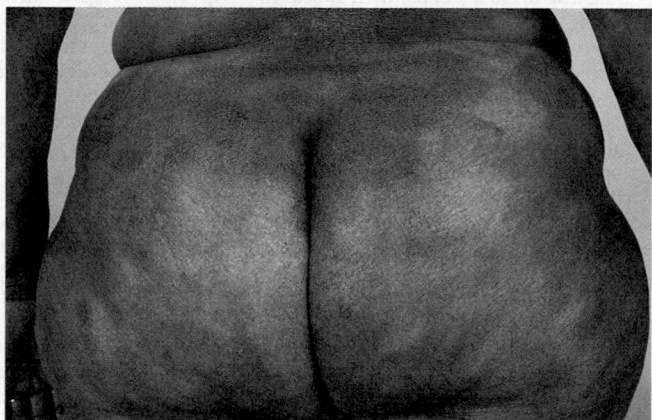

FIGURE 474–15 • Hyperpigmented patches in a patient with mycosis fungoides.

Table 474–4 • **FIGURATE ERYTHEMAS**

Erythema annulare centrifugum
Erythema gyratum repens
Erythema chronicum migrans

gastrointestinal tract, prostate, and cervix (Chapter 188). Treatment of the underlying malignancy results in the resolution of the skin lesion in a few months. *Erythema chronicum migrans*, which is a cutaneous manifestation of Lyme disease and is caused by the spirochete *Borrelia burgdorferi* (Chapter 352), appears as a concentric ring of erythema that progresses centrifugally from the site of a tick bite. Occasionally, it may appear as a circular erythematous patch. The diagnosis is made by a history of a tick bite, the characteristic cutaneous lesion, and/or elevated serum antibodies to *B. burgdorferi*. Management is the same as for Lyme disease.

SUGGESTED READINGS
Photodermatoses
Lim HW (guest ed): Photodermatology. Semin Cutan Med Surg 1999;18:251-252. *A multiauthored monograph covering all aspects of photodermatoses*

Psoriasis
Lebwohl M: Psoriasis. Lancet 2003;361:1197–1204. *A comprehensive review.*
Rees JL: Trials, evidence, and the management of patients with psoriasis. J Am Acad Dermatol 2003;48:135–143. *Overview of the evidence for treatments of psoriasis.*

Pityriasis Rosea
Watanabe T, Kawamura T, Jacob SE, et al: Pityriasis rosea is associated with systemic active infection with both human herpesvirus-7 and human herpesvirus-6. J Invest Dermatol 2002;119:779–780. *A carefully done study on the association of herpesviruses with pityriasis rosea.*

Pityriasis Rubra Pilaris
Albert MR, Mackool BT: Pityriasis rubra pilaris. Int J Dermatol 1999;38:1-11. *A comprehensive review of pityriasis rubra pilaris.*

Parapsoriasis and Mycosis Fungoides
Burg G, Dummer R, Haeffner A, et al: From inflammation to neoplasia: Mycosis fungoides evolves from reactive inflammatory conditions (lymphoid infiltrates) transforming into neoplastic plaques and tumors. Arch Dermatol 2002;137:949-952. *An overview of the relationship between parapsoriasis and mycosis fungoides.*

475 MACULAR, PAPULAR, VESICULOBULLOUS, AND PUSTULAR DISEASES

Neil J. Korman

MACULAR AND PAPULAR EXANTHEMS

An exanthem is an acute generalized eruption of the skin. There are two major types of exanthems: scarlatiniform eruptions and morbilliform eruptions. Scarlatiniform eruptions consist of confluent blanching erythema; they are named based on their similarity to the eruption of scarlet fever (Table 475–1). Morbilliform eruptions consist of erythematous macules and papules; they are named for their resemblance to the measles eruption. Morbilliform eruptions can be caused by exposure to medications (Chapter 476) or viral infections.

Table 475–1 • MACULAR AND PAPULAR ERUPTIONS

SCARLATINIFORM ERUPTIONS
Scarlet fever
Toxic shock syndrome
Kawasaki disease

MORBILLIFORM ERUPTIONS
Measles
Rubella
Erythema infectiosum
Roseola

PAPULAR ERUPTIONS
Molluscum contagiosum
Warts

Scarlatiniform Eruptions

Scarlet fever is caused by toxin-producing β-hemolytic streptococci that causes infections of the ears, nose, throat, and skin. It most commonly occurs in children after streptococcal wound infections, burns, and upper respiratory tract infections. Occasional cases of scarlet fever also can be caused by *Staphylococcus aureus*, *Haemophilus influenzae*, and *Clostridium* species. The rash is caused by a circulating toxin that induces local production of inflammatory mediators and alteration of the cutaneous cytokines. Patients may present with an abrupt onset of fever, headache, vomiting, malaise, chills, and sore throat. The mucous membranes are usually erythematous with petechiae, and the tongue commonly has a white membrane. Red, exudative tonsils are present with pharyngeal infections. The skin eruption appears after the fever and is characterized by fine erythematous papules, first on the upper trunk and then more generally. The face is flushed, and circumoral pallor is seen. This eruption lasts for 4 to 5 days, followed by fine desquamation, the extent and duration of which is related to the severity of the eruption. Treatment is 1.2 million units of benzathine penicillin G given intramuscularly or oral penicillin VK 1000 mg twice daily for 10 days. Most patients recover after 4 to 5 days, and the rash usually resolves completely over several weeks.

Toxic shock syndrome is an acute febrile illness due to toxin-producing strains of *Staphylococcus aureus* (Chapter 311) or, less commonly, *Streptococcus* (toxic shock–like syndrome). Most cases of staphylococcal toxic shock syndrome or streptococcal toxic shock–like syndrome occur in young healthy persons aged 20 to 50 years. These toxins cause massive release of tumor necrosis factor-α and interleukin-1, cytokines that mediate fever, rash, hypotension, tissue injury, and shock. The hallmarks of the disease are fever, rash, hypotension, and involvement of multiple organs including the lungs, kidneys, liver, and gastrointestinal tract. Desquamation of the palms and soles follows the onset of the illness by 1 to 2 weeks. There is diffuse macular erythema, with flexural accentuation, mucous membrane erythema, and severe conjunctival involvement. Blood cultures are positive in 5 to 15% cases of staphylococcal toxic shock syndrome and approximately 50% of streptococcal toxic shock–like syndrome. Treatment is supportive, including hydration, vasopressors, appropriate antibiotics, and drainage of infected sites. Patients with staphylococcal toxic shock should be treated with intravenous nafcillin or oxacillin, 2 g every 4 to 6 hours for 10 to 15 days, whereas patients with streptococcal toxic shock should be treated with both intravenous penicillin G, 3 to 4 million units every 4 hours, and intravenous clindamycin, 600 to 900 mg every 8 hours for 10 to 15 days, followed by oral therapy. Silver sulfadiazine cream may lead to increased toxin production; therefore, mupirocin ointment should be used for infected sites. The mortality rate for staphylococcal toxic shock syndrome is 5 to 15%, whereas that for streptococcal toxic shock–like syndrome may be five times higher.

Kawasaki disease, a systemic vasculitis of unknown etiology, occurs in children of all races but is most prevalent in Japan. Although primarily an illness of children younger than 5 years of age, Kawasaki disease also occurs in adults. Epidemiologic and clinical manifestations imply that an infection is the cause, but bacterial, viral, and serologic studies have yet to confirm this. The clinical hallmarks are fever lasting up to 2 weeks, with spikes to 40°C (104°F), and a toxic-appearing patient. During the acute phase, the polymorphic eruption may be scarlatiniform, urticarial, morbilliform, or targetoid. Desquamation occurs 2 days after onset of fever in the perianal area and 2 to 3 weeks later on the extremities. Patients often have hemorrhagic, dry, fissured lips; conjunctival injection; a "strawberry tongue"; and cervical lymphadenitis. Myocarditis and coronary artery aneurysms may develop in untreated patients, so prompt diagnosis is critical. Other findings include arthralgias and arthritis, urethritis, aseptic meningitis, pneumonitis, and diarrhea. Although there are no specific diagnostic tests for this syndrome, the typical skin eruption accompanied by myocarditis is characteristic. Recommended therapy in the acute phase includes intravenous gamma globulin, 400 mg/kg/day for 4 days, and acetylsalicylic acid, at 100 mg/kg, until the patient has been afebrile for several days. During the subacute and convalescent phase, acetylsalicylic acid is usually given at 3 to 8 mg/kg for 6 to 8 weeks. The optimal salicylate regimen in Kawasaki disease remains uncertain, and there are no controlled trials to prove that aspirin reduces coronary artery aneurysms.

Morbilliform Eruptions

Measles is caused by a paramyxovirus (Chapter 365) that infects respiratory epithelium and is highly transmissible. The incubation period is 7 to 14 days. The prodrome consists of cough, coryza, and conjunctivitis. The enanthem, or Koplik spots, predates the exanthem by 1 to 2 days and lasts 2 to 4 days. These blue-white spots surrounded by a red halo appear on the buccal mucosa and are pathognomonic for measles. The exanthem begins on the fourth or fifth day as papules on the face and behind the ears; it then spreads to the trunk and extremities. Measles is diagnosed on clinical grounds. Active immunization with live attenuated virus has dramatically reduced the incidence of measles infection (Chapter 16) and is the most important preventive measure. Treatment consists of supportive care, with attention to maintaining good hydration.

Rubella is an RNA virus of the Togaviridae family (Chapter 366). Infection with this virus leads to an illness primarily of young children involving the skin, lymph nodes, and occasionally the joints. The disease is spread by nasal droplet infection, with an incubation period of 14 to 21 days. Patients are most contagious when the rash is erupting. In children, there may be no prodrome; in adults, however, fever, sore throat, and rhinitis may be present. The exanthem begins as pink macules and papules on the face that spread to the trunk and extremities; it lasts for 1 to 3 days. Generalized tender lymphadenopathy, especially the suboccipital, postauricular, and cervical nodes, is the hallmark of rubella. In the normal child and adolescent, the diagnosis is made clinically and laboratory work is unnecessary. If the diagnosis is questioned, a rising IgM antibody titer over a 2-week period indicates recent infection. No treatment exists, and the disease usually is self-limited. Rest and fluids are appropriate. The best protection is vaccination that is given with measles and mumps (i.e., the MMR vaccine) at 12 to 15 months and again at 4 to 6 years (Chapter 16).

Erythema infectiosum is an exanthem caused by human parvovirus B19. It has a 4- to 14-day incubation period and is spread via aerosolized respiratory droplets. Acute infection leads to production of IgM antibodies and formation of immune complexes, which are deposited in the skin and joints. Bright red erythema appears abruptly over the cheeks. Within 1 to 4 days, an erythematous morbilliform eruption occurs on the extremities; it fades within several days into a reticulate pattern (Fig. 475–1). Exposure of adults to parvovirus B19 leads to an acute polyarthropathy of the hands, wrists, knees, and ankles.

There may also be malar erythema or a reticulate eruption in the extremities. The diagnosis is clinical, and further testing usually is not necessary. Erythema infectiosum is usually a benign, self-limited disease.

Roseola (exanthem subitum) is caused by human herpesvirus 6. Virus replication occurs in leukocytes and salivary glands. Early invasion of the central nervous system (CNS) may lead to seizures. The classic patient is a healthy 9- to 12-month old with abrupt onset of high fever (40°C [104°F]), lasting for 3 days. Febrile seizures occur in 15% of cases. Rapid defervescence is striking, with the onset of a generalized pink morbilliform exanthem. The eruption lasts 2 days and consists of pink papules or blanchable macular erythema. The lack of symptoms during the febrile phase and the appearance of the exanthem as the fever subsides help with the diagnosis, but rubella and measles must also be considered. In the immunocompromised child or adult, there is usually abrupt onset of fever, malaise, and sometimes CNS involvement. Virus isolation, seroconversion (IgM), or viral DNA sequence detection in peripheral blood mononuclear cells can confirm the diagnosis. There is no antiviral therapy for roseola, and treatment is supportive. Practically all immunocompetent patients recover from roseola without sequelae, but immunocompromised patients may develop chronic infection with multisystem complications.

Papular Eruptions

Molluscum contagiosum is a cutaneous infection caused by a large DNA poxvirus that affects both children and adults. Firm, smooth, umbilicated papules, usually 2 to 6 mm in diameter, are present in groups or widely disseminated on the skin and mucosal surfaces. Patients infected with HIV may have hundreds of lesions, and some lesions can be greater than 15 mm (Chapter 417). Diagnosis is made on clinical grounds. Molluscum contagiosum is self-limited. The goal of treatment is the destruction of the lesions. Commonly used treatments are all topical and include cryotherapy with liquid nitrogen, curettage, cantharidin, podophyllin, and tretinoin.

Warts are benign proliferations of skin and mucosa caused by human papillomaviruses (HPV). More than 150 types of HPV have been identified. Certain types of HPV occur at particular anatomic sites; however, warts of any HPV type may be found at any site. Variants include common warts, genital warts, flat warts, and deep palmoplantar warts. Common warts, known as verruca vulgaris, are hard papules that range in size from 1 mm to more than 1 cm with a rough scaly surface (Fig. 475–2) and can occur anywhere on the body. Warts are transmitted by direct contact, and disruption of the epithelial barrier is a predisposing factor. HPV subtypes 6, 11, 16, 18, 31, and 35 may be associated with malignancies. Malignant transformation, while uncommon, can occur in patients with genital warts or in immunocompromised patients. Infection is confined to the epithelium and does not result in systemic viral dissemination. The diagnosis is made on clinical grounds. Viral DNA identification using Southern blot hybridization is used to identify specific HPV subtypes. All therapies are methods of physical destruction of the skin where the virus is located

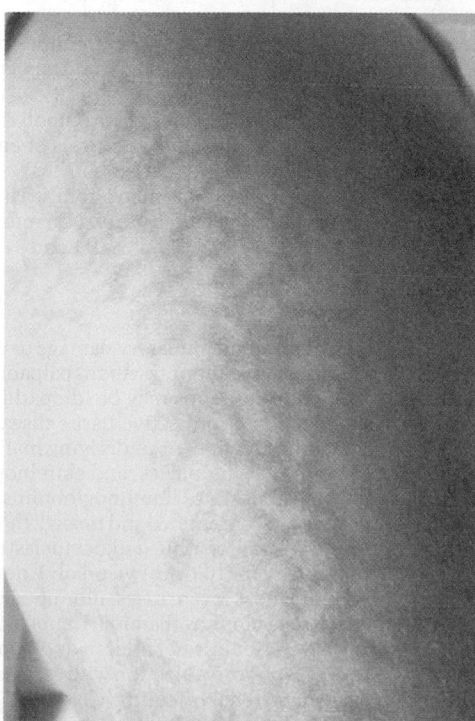

FIGURE 475–1 • Reticulate macular erythema of the thigh of a patient with erythema infectiosum.

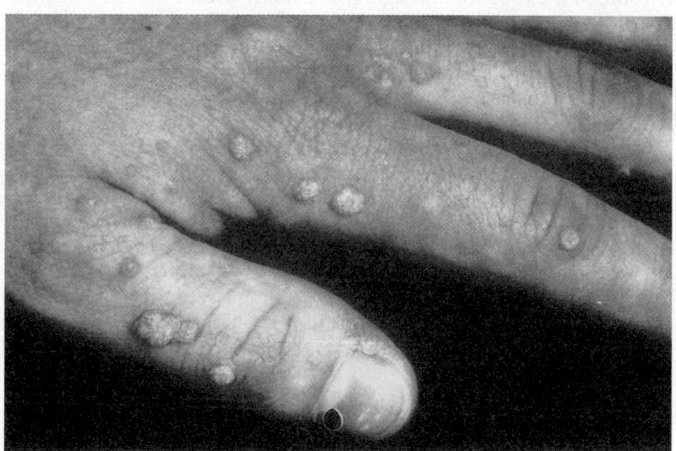

FIGURE 475–2 • Hand of a patient with verruca vulgaris revealing many verrucous papules.

Skin Diseases

Table 475–2 • PURPURIC ERUPTIONS

NONPALPABLE PURPURA
Cutaneous Disorders
Solar purpura
Steroid purpura
Pigmented purpuric dermatosis

Systemic Disorders
Idiopathic thrombocytopenic purpura
Abnormal platelet function in renal or hepatic disease
Thrombocytosis in myeloproliferative diseases
Clotting factor abnormalities
Ehlers-Danlos syndrome
Scurvy
Amyloidosis
Disseminated intravascular coagulation
Thrombotic thrombocytopenic purpura
Monoclonal cryoglobulinemia
Warfarin necrosis
Emboli
    Cholesterol emboli
    Fat emboli
    Tumor emboli from atrial myxomas
    Emboli from endocarditis

PALPABLE PURPURA
Vasculitis
Leukocytoclastic vasculitis
Henoch-Schönlein purpura
Urticarial vasculitis
Polyarteritis nodosa

Infectious Emboli
Meningococcemia
Gonococcemia
Rocky Mountain spotted fever
Ecthyma gangrenosum

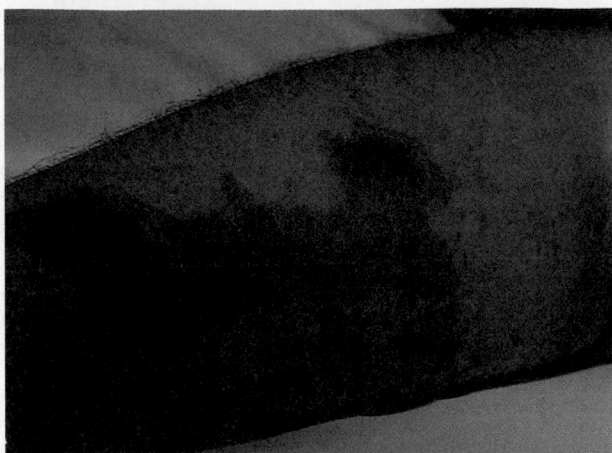

FIGURE 475–3 • Arm of a patient with purpura fulminans revealing purpura and hemorrhagic blisters.

because there are no specific anti-papillomavirus medications. Common topical therapies include liquid nitrogen treatment, salicylic acid, cantharidin, podophyllin, tretinoin, and imiquimod.

Purpuric Eruptions

Purpura occurs when there is red blood cell extravasation leading to visible hemorrhage in the skin (Table 475–2). Petechiae (<3 mm) and purpura (>3 mm) may be nonpalpable or palpable. When the condition is severe, petechiae and purpuric lesions may become confluent, forming ecchymoses, which are greater than 1 cm.

NONPALPABLE PURPURA

Frequent causes of nonpalpable purpura include solar purpura, steroid purpura, and Schamberg's disease. Solar purpura, caused by chronic sun exposure and aging, is usually found on the forearms. Steroid purpura, due to prolonged use of topical or systemic steroids, can occur in any location (Chapter 31). Both conditions are caused by changes in the dermal connective tissue surrounding blood vessels. Schamberg's disease, or pigmented purpuric dermatosis, is a capillaritis with yellow brown macules and petechiae of the lower legs. This capillaritis occurs due to red blood cell extravasation caused by perivascular lymphocyte inflammation.

Systemic causes of nonpalpable purpura include idiopathic thrombocytopenia purpura (Chapter 277), abnormal platelet function due to renal or hepatic insufficiency (Chapters 117 and 157), or thrombocytosis seen in myeloproliferative diseases (Chapter 183), and clotting factor abnormalities (Chapter 179). Fragility of the blood vessels, especially the capillaries, is found in Ehlers-Danlos syndrome (Chapter 276), scurvy (Chapter 231), and systemic amyloidosis (Chapter 290).

Thrombus formation within skin blood vessels will also lead to purpura in disseminated intravascular coagulation (Chapter 179), thrombotic thrombocytopenia purpura (Chapter 177), monoclonal cryoglobulinemia (Chapter 196), and drug reactions to warfarin (Chapter 33). Disseminated intravascular coagulation may be caused by infectious agents (bacterial, particularly meningococcemia, viral, or rickettsial) and by malignancies such as leukemia (Chapter 188). Purpura fulminans is a type of disseminated intravascular coagulation associated with fever and hypotension; it is usually found in children after a bacterial or viral infection. Widespread purpura and hemorrhagic bullae can be seen in disseminated intravascular coagulation and purpura fulminans (Fig. 475–3). Thrombotic thrombocytopenia purpura (Chapter 177) manifests as fever, purpura, renal failure, microangiopathic hemolytic anemia, and neurologic disease. Monoclonal cryoglobulinemia may be associated with leukemia, lymphoma, multiple myeloma, and Waldenström's macroglobulinemia. Widespread purpura along with ulcerations limited to the lower extremities or fingers and toes may be seen. Skin biopsy specimens may reveal intracapillary deposits of precipitated cryoglobulins. Disease can be worsened by cold exposure. The vessels of the lungs, brain, and kidneys may be involved. Warfarin necrosis of the skin is an uncommon reaction that occurs between the third and tenth day of therapy and is characterized by painful erythematous to purpuric plaques that develop hemorrhagic bullae. The most common sites include the breasts, thighs, and buttocks. The onset of disease is unrelated to the dose of warfarin, and continued warfarin therapy does not alter the course of the disease.

Cholesterol emboli are found on the lower extremities of patients with severe atherosclerosis owing to cholesterol crystal occlusion of small- and medium-caliber arteries (Chapter 124). Cholesterol emboli are triggered by vascular procedures or thrombolytic therapy, but they also can occur spontaneously. Other sources of emboli that may cause petechiae or purpura include fat emboli that occur after major injury (Chapters 94 and 108), tumor emboli from atrial myxomas (Chapter 79), emboli from infective endocarditis (Chapter 310), or nonbacterial thrombotic endocarditis (Chapters 94 and 188).

PALPABLE PURPURA

Palpable purpura results from inflammatory damage to cutaneous blood vessels. Leukocytoclastic vasculitis presents as palpable purpura (Fig. 475–4). Leukocytoclastic vasculitis may be idiopathic or associated with sepsis, drug reactions, connective tissue diseases, cryoglobulinemia, hepatitis B or C infection, or underlying malignancies. Patients have detectable immune complexes, and skin biopsy specimens reveal blood vessel wall deposits of immunoglobulins and complement. If an etiologic agent can be identified and treated, the vasculitis will often resolve. Patients with idiopathic leukocytoclastic vasculitis can be treated with oral colchicine (0.6 mg twice daily), oral dapsone (100 mg once daily) or, in the most severe cases, immunosuppressive agents such as azathioprine or cyclophosphamide. Henoch-Schönlein purpura is a leukocytoclastic vasculitis of children and young adults often preceded by an upper respiratory infection with associated fever, arthralgias, abdominal pain, and renal vasculitis (Chapter 177). Direct immunofluorescence reveals IgA deposits in dermal blood vessels. Urticarial or hypocomplementemic vasculitis (Chapter 284) is characterized by urticarial lesions that last longer than 24 hours;

FIGURE 475–4 • Palpable purpura. Leukocytoclastic vasculitis commonly causes raised purpuric and ulcerated lesions on legs.

Table 475–3 • VESICULOBULLOUS DISEASES
IMMUNOLOGICALLY MEDIATED DISEASES
Bullous pemphigoid
Herpes gestationis
Mucous membrane pemphigoid
Epidermolysis bullosa acquisita
Dermatitis herpetiformis
Linear IgA bullous dermatosis
Pemphigus
Vulgaris
Foliaceus
Paraneoplastic
HYPERSENSITIVITY DISEASES
Erythema multiforme minor
Erythema multiforme major (Stevens-Johnson syndrome)
Toxic epidermal necrolysis
METABOLIC DISEASES
Porphyria cutanea tarda
Pseudoporphyria
Diabetic blisters
INHERITED GENETIC DISORDERS
Epidermolysis bullosa
Simplex
Junctional
Dystrophic
INFECTIOUS DISEASES
Impetigo
Staphylococcal scalded skin syndrome
Herpes simplex
Varicella
Herpes zoster

arthritis, facial, and laryngeal edema; and low serum complement levels. Some patients may develop systemic lupus erythematosus (Chapter 280). In polyarteritis nodosa (Chapter 284), there is a vasculitis of the arterial blood vessels leading to ischemia of the skin. Skin lesions usually include ulcerated nodules and ecchymoses.

In addition to vasculitis, cutaneous emboli can also lead to the development of palpable purpura. Infectious emboli can be caused by gram-negative cocci, gram-negative rods, *Rickettsia,* and, in immunocompromised patients, *Candida* and opportunistic fungi. Acute meningococcemia (Chapter 313) occurs after an upper respiratory tract infection and is associated with headache, fever, meningitis, hypotension, and disseminated intravascular coagulation. The embolic lesions, which are found on the trunk and lower extremities, can range from 1 mm up to several centimeters. Disseminated gonococcal infection (Chapter 346) presents as fever, arthralgias, tenosynovitis, and a small number of vesiculopustules with purpura or hemorrhagic necrosis over the distal extremities. Rocky Mountain spotted fever (Chapter 355) is a tickborne disease characterized by headache, fever, chills, photophobia, and myalgias. The cutaneous eruption starts acrally and spreads centripetally as small, erythematosus, blanchable macules that evolve into petechiae, palpable purpura, and ecchymoses. Ecthyma gangrenosum presents as erythematous papules and plaques that develop central purpura and hemorrhagic necrosis; *Pseudomonas aeruginosa* (Chapter 344) is the most common organism, but *Klebsiella, Escherichia coli, and Serratia* have also been implicated. Immunocompromised patients may develop ecthyma gangrenosum due to infection with *Candida* or opportunistic fungi.

VESICULOBULLOUS DISEASES

Vesicles are clear, fluid-filled lesions measuring less than 5 mm; bullae or blisters are clear, fluid-filled lesions larger than 5 mm. Vesiculobullous lesions in the skin may be caused by immunologically mediated mechanisms, hypersensitivity reactions, metabolic disorders, inherited genetic defects, and infections (Table 475–3).

Immunologically Mediated Blistering Diseases

Bullous pemphigoid is an autoimmune blistering disease of the elderly. Tense blisters and urticarial plaques occur on the flexor arms and legs, axilla, groin, and abdomen (Fig. 475–5). IgG autoantibodies bind to the epidermal basement membrane and activate complement, which attracts inflammatory cells. These inflammatory cells release proteases, which degrade basement membrane proteins and lead to blister formation. Histology reveals a subepidermal blister with an eosinophilic infiltrate. Direct immunofluorescence shows linear basement membrane deposits of IgG and C3. Indirect immunofluorescence studies using salt-split skin demonstrate circulating IgG antibodies that bind to the epidermal side. Treatment is dictated by the degree of involvement and the rate of progression of the disease. A randomized, multicenter trial demonstrated that 40 g of the ultrapotent topical steroid clobetasol, applied twice daily to the skin of patients with bullous pemphigoid until 15 days after disease control was obtained, was effective and superior to oral corticosteroid treatment for both moderate and severe disease.∎ Other treatments include tetracyclines, dapsone, azathioprine, methotrexate, mycophe-

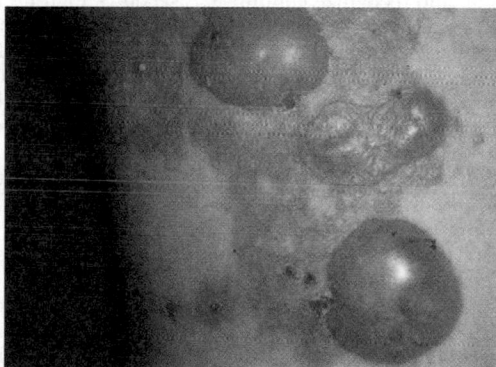

FIGURE 475–5 • Bullous pemphigoid. Tense subepidermal bullae on an erythematosus base.

nolate mofetil, and cyclophosphamide. Left untreated, bullous pemphigoid usually persists for months to years. Spontaneous remissions and exacerbations occur. The mortality rate is relatively low even without treatment.

Herpes gestationis is a rare autoimmune dermatosis of pregnancy. Despite the name, herpes gestationis has no relationship to herpesvirus infection. Most patients have intense pruritus. Periumbilical urticarial plaques progress to vesicles and blisters. The eruption spreads peripherally (Fig. 475–6), typically sparing the face, palms, soles, and mucous membranes. IgG autoantibodies are produced against bullous pemphigoid antigen II that is critical in epidermal-dermal adhesion. Antibody binding triggers an immune response leading to blister formation. Histology reveals a subepidermal blister, and direct immunofluorescence shows linear basement membrane C3 deposits. Corticosteroids are the mainstay of therapy. Patients with mild disease are treated with topical corticosteroids, whereas patients with extensive disease usually require systemic corticosteroids. Disease clears within 1 to 2 weeks after delivery. There is an increased risk of premature delivery and of infants who are small for their gestational age, suggesting that these women should be managed by obstetricians experienced in high-risk pregnancies.

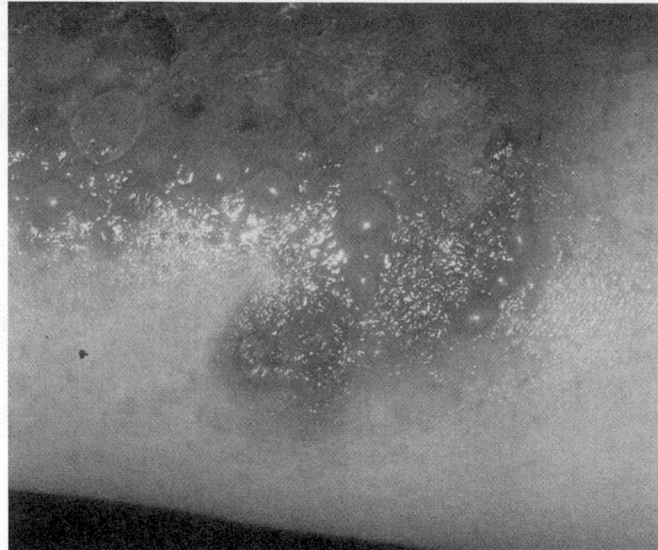

FIGURE 475–6 • Multiple tense blisters and erosions on an erythematous base in a patient with herpes gestationis.

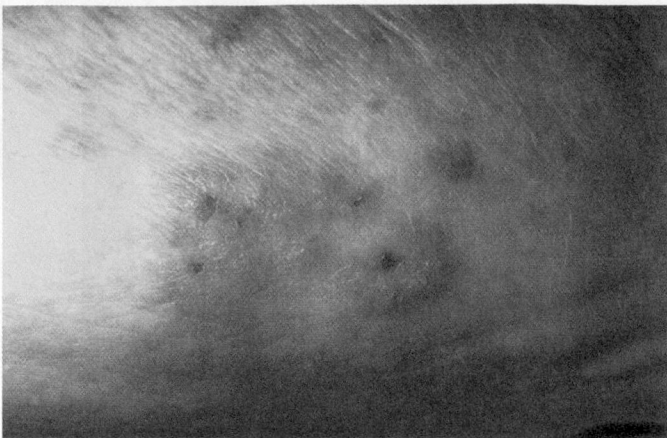

FIGURE 475–7 • Elbow of a patient with dermatitis herpetiformis revealing eroded erythematous papules and papulovesicles.

Mucous membrane pemphigoid, previously named cicatricial pemphigoid, is a group of subepithelial blistering diseases involving mucosal surfaces. Patients have blisters of the oral, ocular, nasopharyngeal, laryngeal, anogenital, and esophageal mucosal that heal with scarring, which causes the major morbidity of the disease. There are several subgroups of mucous membrane pemphigoid. Some patients have circulating IgG autoantibodies that bind to the dermal side of salt-split skin and recognize laminin-5. A second subgroup includes patients who have pure ocular disease and who have IgG antibodies directed against b4 integrin. A third subgroup has mucosal disease and skin lesions. The fourth variant includes patients with oral disease without skin disease. Histology reveals a subepidermal blister with an inflammatory cell infiltrate. Direct immunofluorescence shows linear basement membrane IgG, IgA, and C3 deposits. Indirect immunofluorescence reveals circulating IgG and/or IgA antibodies. Treatment is dictated by the extent, severity, and location of disease; it ranges from topical corticosteroids under occlusion for patients with only oral disease to prednisone and cyclophosphamide for severe ocular disease. Management teams should include ophthalmologists, otolaryngologists, dermatologists, and internists for patients with severe disease. Patients with both circulating IgG and IgA antibodies tend to have more severe disease. Mucous membrane pemphigoid is a chronic disease. Untreated ocular disease can result in blindness.

Epidermolysis bullosa acquisita is an acquired autoimmune blistering disease that usually occurs in middle age. There are two types of skin lesions: noninflammatory acral blisters that heal with scarring and milia formation and widespread inflammatory vesiculobullous disease. Epidermolysis bullosa acquisita is characterized by IgG autoantibodies that target collagen VII, the major protein of anchoring fibrils. These autoantibodies alter dermal-epidermal adhesion and lead to blister formation. Histology reveals a subepidermal blister containing few inflammatory cells when mechanobullous lesions are sampled or a neutrophil-rich infiltrate when inflammatory blisters are sampled. Direct immunofluorescence reveals linear basement membrane IgG deposits. Indirect immunofluorescence shows circulating IgG autoantibodies that bind the dermal side of salt-split skin. Epidermolysis bullosa acquisita is a chronic disease that is very difficult to treat. Dapsone, colchicine, azathioprine, or cyclophosphamide alone or along with prednisone are only occasionally successful. Cyclosporine or extracorporeal photopheresis have been successfully used in patients with severe disease. Because of nephrotoxicity, cyclosporine should be reserved for crisis management of patients who have severe disease and are experiencing a major flare.

Dermatitis herpetiformis is an immune-mediated vesicular disease. It usually occurs in the young to middle aged. Skin lesions are extremely pruritic grouped vesicles and erosions located on scalp, posterior neck, and extensor surfaces of the elbows, knees, and buttocks (Fig. 475–7). Most patients have a subclinical gluten-sensitive enteropathy that is

reversible with a gluten-free diet. Diet alone can sometimes control the skin disease, with clearance of the cutaneous granular IgA deposits in the basement membrane. Biopsy specimens of skin lesions reveal dermal papillary neutrophilic microabscesses. Direct immunofluorescence shows dermal papillary granular IgA deposits in all patients. Dermatitis herpetiformis can be treated with dapsone, usually 100 mg daily given chronically. Dermatitis herpetiformis is a lifelong disease.

Linear IgA bullous dermatosis is an acquired autoimmune blistering disease of the skin. The primary lesions are papulovesicles. Involvement of the oral mucous membranes is common. The disease occurs throughout adulthood. Deposition of IgA antibody specific for a portion of bullous pemphigoid antigen II leads to complement activation and neutrophil chemotaxis. Proteolytic enzymes are released, destroy the dermal-epidermal junction, and cause blister formation. Histology reveals a subepidermal vesicle or cleft with neutrophil predominance. Direct immunofluorescence shows linear basement membrane deposits of IgA. Indirect immunofluorescence demonstrates circulating IgA antibodies. The majority of patients respond to dapsone, 100 mg daily, given chronically. Patients whose disease is not controlled with dapsone may benefit from the addition of systemic therapy with corticosteroids. The disease tends to be chronic in adults, but the childhood version (called chronic bullous disease of childhood) may run a several-year course and then remit.

Pemphigus refers to a group of autoimmune blistering intraepidermal diseases of the skin and mucous membranes that are most common in middle age. Patients with pemphigus vulgaris have flaccid blisters and erosions in the oropharynx (Fig. 475–8), trunk, head, neck, and intertriginous areas. Pemphigus foliaceus presents as erythema, scaling, and crusting of the face, scalp, and upper trunk. Patients

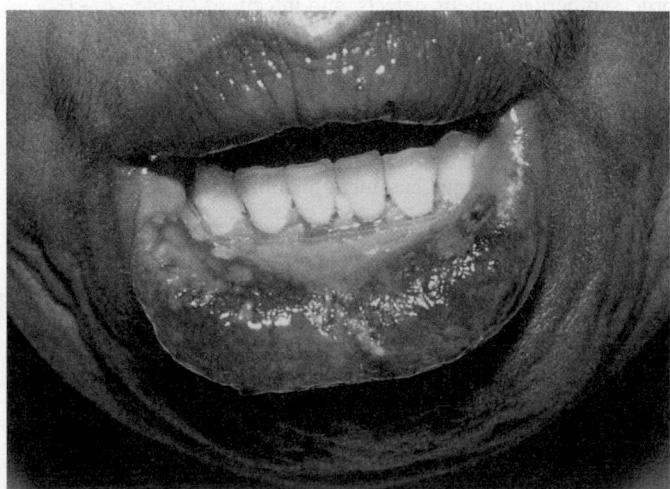

FIGURE 475–8 • Lower lip of a patient with pemphigus vulgaris revealing confluent erosions with scattered crusting.

with paraneoplastic pemphigus have ocular and oral blisters and erosions along with skin lesions resembling erythema multiforme and an associated underlying malignancy that is usually lymphoreticular in origin (Chapter 188). Autoantibodies in pemphigus vulgaris target desmoglein III, and autoantibodies in pemphigus foliaceus target desmoglein I. Circulating antibodies in paraneoplastic pemphigus recognize a complex of proteins, including desmoplakin I and II, bullous pemphigoid antigen I, envoplakin, periplakin, and desmoglein I and III. Skin biopsy specimens from patients with pemphigus vulgaris reveal suprabasilar acantholysis, whereas pemphigus foliaceus biopsy specimens demonstrate subcorneal acantholysis. Biopsy specimens of paraneoplastic pemphigus show suprabasilar acantholysis and dyskeratotic keratinocytes with basal cell vacuolization.

Direct immunofluorescence demonstrates cell surface deposits of IgG in patients with pemphigus vulgaris and foliaceus, whereas indirect immunofluorescence reveals circulating IgG antibodies. In paraneoplastic pemphigus there are circulating and tissue bound IgG antibodies that are indistinguishable from those in pemphigus vulgaris and that also recognize the cell surface of simple epithelia, including liver and heart. Treatment regimens depend on the patient's age, the degree of involvement, the rate of disease progression, and the subtype of pemphigus. Systemic glucocorticosteroids are required for pemphigus vulgaris, whereas topical corticosteroids occasionally control pemphigus foliaceus. Steroid-sparing agents include dapsone, the combination of tetracycline and niacinamide, hydroxychloroquine (Plaquenil), gold, mycophenolate mofetil, azathioprine, and cyclophosphamide. Although the use of steroid-sparing agents is supported by clinical experience, few controlled studies demonstrate their benefit. Therefore, a trial to determine the value of dapsone as a steroid-sparing agent in the treatment of pemphigus vulgaris is ongoing. For paraneoplastic pemphigus caused by benign tumors, such as Castleman's disease, tumor removal is curative. Patients with associated malignant tumors have recalcitrant disease, although there are occasional successes with pulse corticosteroids and cyclophosphamide, immunoapheresis, and immunoablative high-dose cyclophosphamide. Before the availability of corticosteroids, 60 to 90% of patients with pemphigus vulgaris and foliaceus died, whereas the mortality rate has now decreased to the 5 to 10% range. The prognosis of paraneoplastic pemphigus is related to the type of associated neoplasm. Patients with benign tumors usually experience clearance of their lesions after tumor resection, whereas patients with malignant tumors usually have a poor prognosis.

HYPERSENSITIVITY REACTIONS THAT CAUSE BLISTERS

Erythema multiforme is an acute blistering eruption that occurs in all age groups. Erythema multiforme minor is localized, with minimal or no mucosal involvement. Erythema multiforme major, also known as Stevens-Johnson syndrome, is a more severe mucosal and skin disease characterized by signs and symptoms reminiscent of serum sickness. Toxic epidermal necrolysis is at the most severe end of the erythema multiforme spectrum. The primary lesions of erythema multiforme minor are erythematous macules and edematous papules with vesicular centers that become dusky violet. Target or iris lesions are found on extensor surfaces of the extremities and spread centripetally (Fig. 475–9). The skin lesions of Stevens-Johnson syndrome resemble those of erythema multiforme minor but are likely to be generalized and show confluent erythema with urticarial and purpuric lesions. Erosions of two or more mucosal surfaces occur in Stevens-Johnson syndrome and may include hemorrhagic crusting of the lips, ulceration of ocular mucosa, and genital involvement. Patients with erythema multiforme major have a 1- to 14-day prodrome, including fever, cough, sore throat, vomiting, and diarrhea. Patients with toxic epidermal necrolysis may have a similar prodrome, rapidly followed by generalized macular erythema that progresses to confluent erythema with skin tenderness. Large blisters follow soon afterward, and then skin sloughing occurs as the large blisters break, leaving denuded skin.

Common etiologic associations for erythema multiforme include infections such as herpes simplex (especially recurrent erythema multiforme minor), *Mycoplasma pneumoniae,* and drug reactions. Sulfonamides, penicillins, barbiturates, carbamazepine, phenytoin, allopurinol, and nonsteroidal anti-inflammatory drugs (NSAIDs) are the most common drugs implicated in Stevens-Johnson syndrome and toxic epidermal necrolysis. The diagnosis of erythema multiforme is clinical. Chronic antiviral treatment with acyclovir decreases outbreaks in recurrent erythema multiforme minor. Treatment of erythema multiforme major is nonspecific, with attention to fluid and electrolyte balance and eye disease being critical. If a drug is suspected, it must be withdrawn. Systemic corticosteroid treatment is contraindicated in Stevens-Johnson syndrome. Treatment of toxic epidermal necrolysis is very difficult, but one uncontrolled study suggests that intravenous immunoglobulin treatment may improve the prognosis. Erythema multiforme minor usually subsides within 2 to 3 weeks. Erythema multiforme major takes 3 to 6 weeks to clear and has a less than 5% mortality rate. Toxic epidermal necrolysis has a mortality rate approaching 30%, and patients are best managed in an intensive care or burn unit.

METABOLIC DISORDERS THAT CAUSE BLISTERS

Porphyria cutanea tarda is caused by deficient activity of the heme-synthetic enzyme uroporphyrinogen decarboxylase (Chapter 223). Patients present with fragility of sun-exposed skin, leading to erosions and bullae, which are worst on the dorsal hands (Fig. 475–10), forearms, and face. Healing of crusted erosions and blisters leaves scars, milia, and hyperpigmented and hypopigmented atrophic patches. Hypertrichosis is common and is most florid over the temporal and malar areas. Urinary porphyrin levels are abnormally high. Histology reveals a subepidermal blister with minimal dermal infiltrate, and direct immunofluorescence demonstrates immunoglobulin and complement deposition in dermal capillaries and at the basement membrane. Phlebotomy is the standard treatment, and the goal is to reduce serum ferritin to the lower limit of the normal range. Another treatment option is oral chloroquine at doses much lower than those used for photoprotective indications. Alcohol and estrogen use should be discontinued because they can cause the disease to flare.

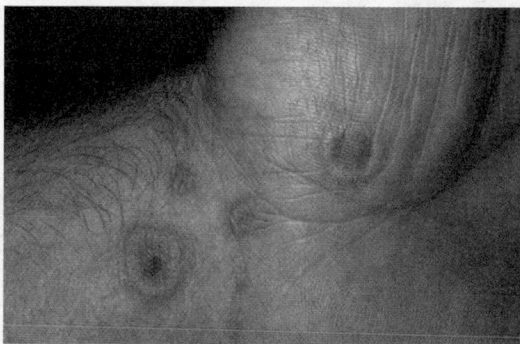

FIGURE 475–9 • Erythema multiforme. Target or "bull's-eye" annular lesions with central vesicles and bullae.

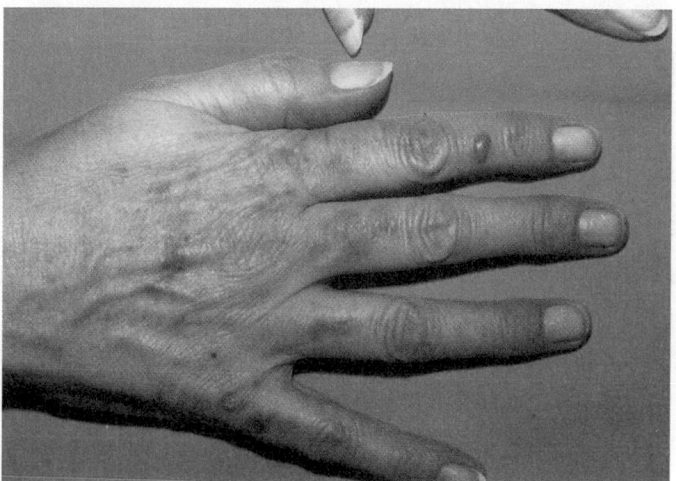

FIGURE 475–10 • Blister and erosions on the dorsal hand of a patient with porphyria cutanea tarda.

Pseudoporphyria is a bullous eruption that mimics porphyria cutanea tarda clinically and histologically without porphyrin abnormalities. Many medications can cause pseudoporphyria, including propionic acid–derivative NSAIDs (e.g., naproxen, diflunisal, ketoprofen, nabumetone, oxaprozin, and mefenamic acid), furosemide, tetracycline, fluoroquinolones, amiodarone, cyclosporine, dapsone, etretinate, and flutamide. The prognosis is good for pseudoporphyria after the offending agent has been discontinued. However, resolution of the disease may take several months. Patients who have chronic renal failure treated with hemodialysis may develop true porphyria cutanea tarda or pseudoporphyria, which is very difficult to treat.

Patients with *diabetes mellitus* (Chapter 242) may occasionally develop distal extremity blisters. There is no correlation between the development of blisters and the severity, duration, or complications of the diabetes. The mechanism of blister formation is not understood.

INHERITED GENETIC DISORDERS THAT CAUSE BLISTERS

Epidermolysis bullosa is a group of inherited bullous disorders characterized by blister formation in response to mechanical trauma. Subtypes include epidermolysis bullosa simplex (intraepidermal skin separation) (Fig. 475–11), junctional epidermolysis bullosa (skin separation in lamina lucida), and dystrophic epidermolysis bullosa (sub–lamina densa separation). Infancy is an especially difficult time when patients with epidermolysis bullosa may develop blistering that is complicated by infection and sepsis. Many patients with junctional epidermolysis bullosa have severe disease that can lead to death, usually due to infection, and some patients with recessive dystrophic epidermolysis bullosa may develop metastatic squamous cell carcinoma that can lead to death. In contrast, epidermolysis bullosa simplex, milder forms of junctional epidermolysis bullosa, and dominant dystrophic epidermolysis bullosa usually do not affect life expectancy. Epidermolysis bullosa simplex is caused by mutations of the genes coding for keratins 5 and 14. Junctional epidermolysis bullosa has a variable molecular etiology, and mutations in genes coding for laminin 5 subunits, bullous pemphigoid antigen I, $\alpha 6$ integrin, and $\beta 4$ integrin have been demonstrated. Dystrophic epidermolysis bullosa is caused by mutations of the type VII collagen gene. Epidermolysis bullosa is a lifelong disease. Some subtypes, especially the milder forms, improve with age. No medications are known to correct the underlying molecular defects. Gene therapy is being actively pursued.

INFECTIOUS DISEASES THAT CAUSE BLISTERS

Impetigo is a bacterial infection of the superficial layers of the epidermis. Bullous impetigo is caused by *Staphylococcus aureus* (Chapter 311), and nonbullous impetigo is caused by group A β-hemolytic streptococcus (Chapter 308). Bullous impetigo presents as vesicles and bulla (Fig. 475–12). Lesions are common on the face but may appear anywhere. Nonbullous impetigo presents as fragile vesicles or pustules that rupture, leaving honey-colored crusted papules or plaques

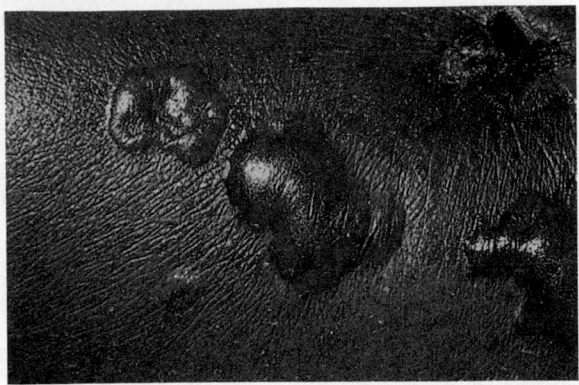

FIGURE 475–12 • Trunk of a patient with bullous impetigo revealing multiple blisters.

especially near the nose and mouth and on the extremities. Lesions develop on normal or traumatized skin or are superimposed on preexisting conditions, including scabies, varicella, or atopic dermatitis. The causative agent of bullous impetigo is coagulase-positive *Staphylococcus aureus*, which produces exfoliatins A and B. The toxins cause cleavage within or below the stratum granulosum. Impetigo is diagnosed clinically. Culture and sensitivity are recommended if topical or oral treatment is ineffective. Oral antibiotics including dicloxacillin or cephalexin are used in extensive disease or in patients refractory to topical mupirocin. Gentle débridement of crusts is recommended. Lesions resolve after 7 to 10 days of treatment. Acute glomerulonephritis develops in 2 to 5% of young children with nonbullous impetigo usually within 10 days after skin lesions appear.

Staphylococcal scalded skin syndrome is a blistering disease caused by an exotoxin produced by *Staphylococcus aureus* (Chapter 311). It is most common in young children but may occur in adults who have renal insufficiency or who are immunocompromised. The site of the staphylococcal infection is usually extracutaneous. Staphylococcal scalded skin syndrome presents as sudden onset of fever and tender, blanchable erythema. It starts on the central face, neck, and intertriginous areas and rapidly generalizes. The palms, soles, and mucous membranes are spared. Flaccid blisters occur within 1 to 2 days and soon exfoliate in large sheets, leaving superficially denuded skin (Fig. 475–13). The disease must be distinguished from toxic epidermal necrolysis by skin biopsy. In staphylococcal scalded skin syndrome there is an upper epidermal blister, whereas toxic epidermal necrolysis causes a dermal-epidermal blister. The treatment of choice for staphylococcal scalded skin syndrome is a penicillinase-resistant penicillin. Patients with the most severe disease should be treated with intravenous nafcillin or oxacillin, 2 g every 4 to 6 hours for 10 to 14 days, whereas patients with mild disease may be treated with oral dicloxacillin, 500 mg four times daily for 10 to 14 days.

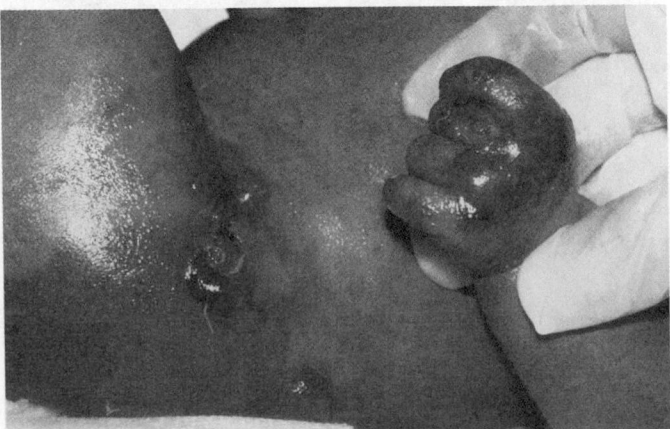

FIGURE 475–11 • Newborn with epidermolysis bullosa simplex revealing tense blisters and erosions on the trunk and extremities.

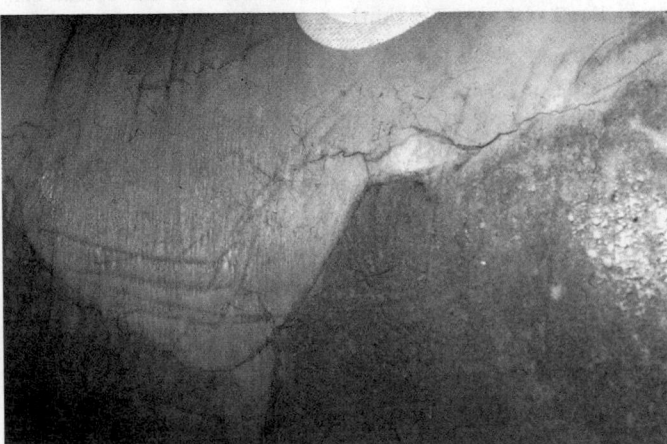

FIGURE 475–13 • Trunk of a patient with staphylococcal scalded skin syndrome revealing confluent erythema with exfoliation of the truncal skin.

Herpes simplex virus (HSV) infection (Chapter 369) may be caused by type 1 or type 2 HSV. The hallmark of HSV infection is the ability to establish latent infection. Disease commonly occurs as a recurrent vesicular eruption of the oral, perioral (typically HSV-1), or genital regions (typically HSV-2), although primary gingivostomatitis (typically in children and young adults and caused by HSV-1) and primary genital herpes (typically HSV-2) are less common. Patients with primary gingivostomatitis have high fever, regional lymphadenopathy, and malaise. Patients with primary genital herpes have fever, flulike symptoms, tender inguinal adenopathy, and aseptic meningitis. These infections all reveal grouped vesicles on an erythematous base. Recurrent eruptions can be triggered by skin trauma, cold or heat, concurrent infection, and menstruation. Immunocompromised patients may develop chronic erosive ulcers of the face and anogenital areas. Tzanck smear of fluid from the roof of a vesicle can be helpful in confirming the diagnosis (see Fig. 472–6), but viral culture is the diagnostic gold standard. The direct fluorescent antibody test is an antigen-based technique that not only yields same-day results but also can distinguish herpes simplex from varicella-zoster and is becoming widely used. In healthy individuals, herpes simplex infection is self-limited. The goal of treatment is to shorten the current attack and to prevent recurrences. Acyclovir is effective in the treatment of herpes simplex infections; valacyclovir and famciclovir are closely related, effective medications with improved oral bioavailability.

Chickenpox is caused by the varicella-zoster virus (VZV; Chapter 367). It is usually a childhood disease, but affected adults have more morbidity. Skin lesions occur 10 to 21 days after exposure to virus. Erythematous macules appear on the scalp, face, trunk, and proximal limbs, with rapid progression to papules, vesicles, pustules, and crusting (Fig. 475–14). Adults may experience a more widespread eruption, prolonged fever, and pneumonia. The diagnosis is usually clinical, but direct fluorescent antibody or culture confirmation is sometimes needed. Treatment of healthy children is unnecessary, because the disease is self-limited. Adults should be treated with oral acyclovir, 800 mg five times a day, for 7 days. The varicella vaccine can be given once to healthy children 12 to 18 months of age and twice, in a 4- to 8-week interval, to susceptible persons older than 13 years of age (Chapter 16).

Herpes zoster is caused by reactivation of VZV from a previous chickenpox infection. The disease is more common in older or immunocompromised patients. The typical presentation is painful grouped herpetiform vesicles on an erythematous base confined to the cutaneous surface innervated by one sensory nerve and preceded by radicular pain (Fig. 475–15). The major morbidity, which is pain within the affected dermatome, can be severe and persist after the skin lesions have resolved (postherpetic neuralgia). Immunocompromised patients have an increased risk of cutaneous dissemination and visceral involvement of the bladder, lungs, and CNS. Acyclovir (800 mg orally five times daily for 7 days) and its derivatives valacyclovir (500 mg orally three times daily for 7 days) and famciclovir (500 mg orally three times daily for 7 days) are safe and effective in the treatment of active disease and in the prevention of postherpetic neuralgia. In the immunocompromised patient, acyclovir

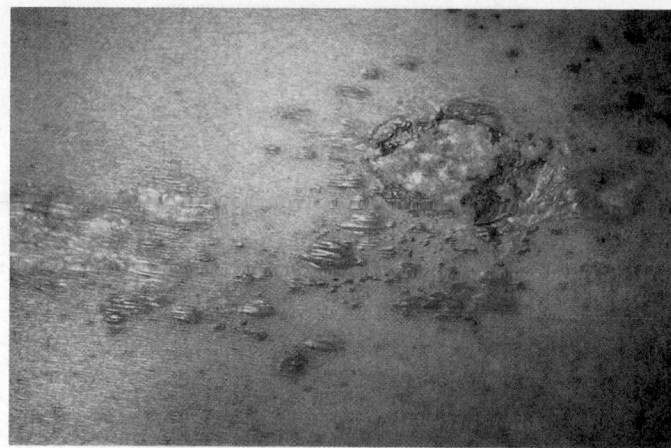

FIGURE 475–15 • Trunk of a patient with herpes zoster revealing necrotic blisters and erosions in a dermatomal pattern.

should be given intravenously (10 mg/kg every 8 hours for 7 to 10 days). The earlier antiviral medications are started, the more effective they are in shortening the duration of herpes zoster and in preventing or decreasing the severity of postherpetic neuralgia. Patients with postherpetic neuralgia of more than 3 months' duration benefit from the use of gabapentin, 1600 or 2400 mg daily, with significant reduction in pain.[2]

PUSTULAR ERUPTIONS

Acne vulgaris is the most common pustular skin condition. Teenagers are usually affected, but the disease may persist into adulthood. The comedone, which is the primary lesion, presents as either closed (whitehead) or open (blackhead). Androgen production after puberty stimulates sebum release by sebaceous glands. Sebum flow is impeded owing to abnormal keratinization within the pilosebaceous canal, a process that leads to the formation of comedones. Bacterial (*Propionibacterium acnes*) proliferation within the comedone predisposes to pilosebaceous unit rupture with extravasation into the surrounding dermis, resulting in papules, pustules, and cysts. Patients with mild disease are treated topically with benzoyl peroxide, tretinoin, adapalene, or tazarotene, which normalize follicular keratinization. The addition of topical antibiotics helps to control inflammatory papules and pustules. Significant disease requires oral tetracycline (250 mg to 1000 mg/day), doxycycline (200 mg/day), or minocycline (200 mg/day). These agents have anti-inflammatory and antibacterial effects. Another approach is oral contraceptives containing ethinyl estradiol and norgestimate, which are superior to placebo in the treatment of acne in women. Isotretinoin (Accutane), which decreases sebaceous gland size and sebum production, is reserved for severe cystic disease because of its teratogenicity and other significant side effects. Acne may be exacerbated by the use of oil-based cosmetics or hair preparations. Androgenic hormones, systemic corticosteroids, lithium, phenytoin, phenobarbital, isoniazid, and endocrinologic conditions such as polycystic ovary disease and adrenal or ovarian tumors may produce acneiform eruptions or aggravate preexisting acne.

Rosacea, which is a chronic inflammatory disease of the face, affects the pilosebaceous units and blood vessels and usually occurs in middle age. Erythema, telangiectasia, erythematous papules, and pustules occur on the central face. Ocular rosacea can lead to keratitis, iritis, blepharitis, and recurrent chalazion; it should be managed by an ophthalmologist. In its most severe form, rosacea can cause sebaceous gland hyperplasia, leading to a large red bulbous nose known as rhinophyma (Fig. 475–16). Patients with a tendency toward facial flushing are more likely to develop rosacea. Flushing can be due to heat, spicy foods, hot drinks, alcohol, or emotional stimuli. With time, the flushing reaction lasts longer and longer until it persists. Topical antibiotics including metronidazole 1% are helpful in mild disease. Patients with more severe disease require oral tetracycline, 500 mg twice daily for 3 to 4 months and then slowly decreased as tolerated. Azelaic acid gel (15%) can significantly improve papulopustular rosacea.[3]

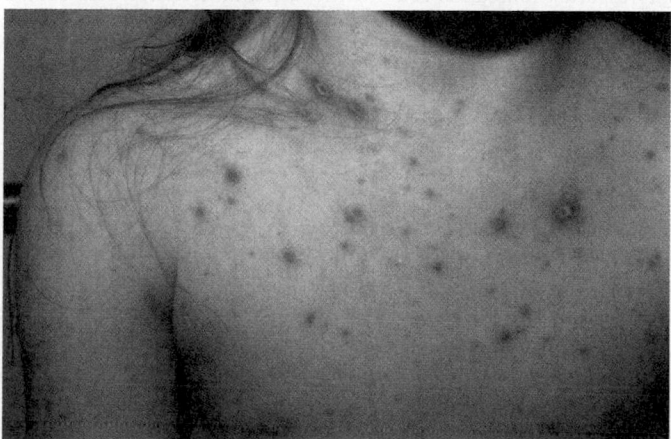

FIGURE 475–14 • Erythematous macules and vesicles with crusted erosions on the chest of a patient with varicella.

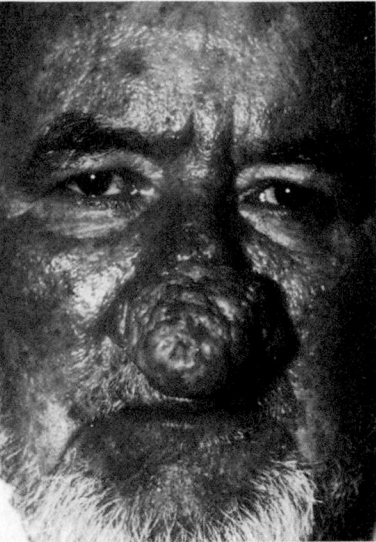

FIGURE 475–16 • Sebaceous gland hyperplasia leading to a large red bulbous nose known as rhinophyma, found in late-stage rosacea.

Perioral dermatitis presents as erythematous papules and pustules, as well as scaling patches around the mouth and eyes (Fig. 475–17). Most patients have used potent topical corticosteroids inappropriately for long periods of time. The eruption usually clears after stopping the corticosteroid and using tetracycline, 250 mg twice daily, orally for 6 weeks.

Acute exanthematous pustulosis is a generalized pustular eruption that is associated with fever and that is frequently caused by antibiotics. Pustules develop within 2 days of drug administration, start on the face or in flexural areas, and rapidly disseminate (Fig. 475–18). Spontaneous resolution occurs in less than 2 weeks.

Pustular psoriasis is a variant of psoriasis (Chapter 474) that localizes to palms and soles or generalizes over the entire body. Patients with generalized disease have fever and leukocytosis, and they require systemic therapy. Pustules can also be been in septic emboli of bacterial or fungal origin including gonococcemia and systemic candidiasis (see Purpura).

Folliculitis is inflammation of hair follicles caused by infection with staphylococci. It is caused by obstruction of individual hair follicles

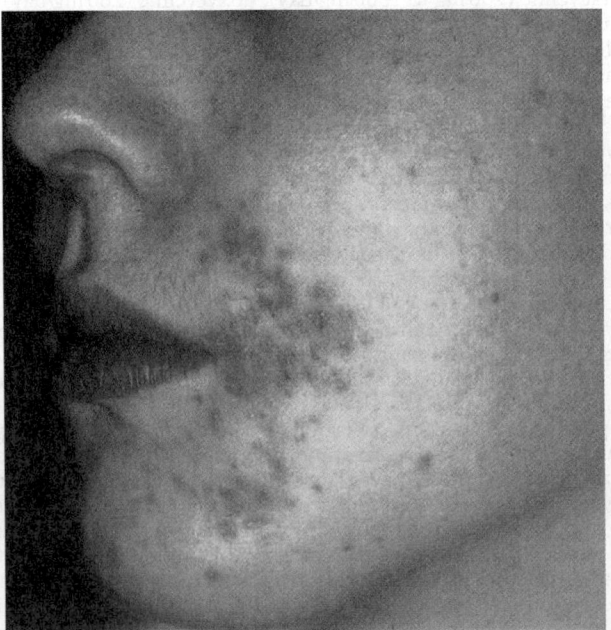

FIGURE 475–17 • Face of a patient with perioral dermatitis revealing erythematous papules and pinpoint pustules around the mouth.

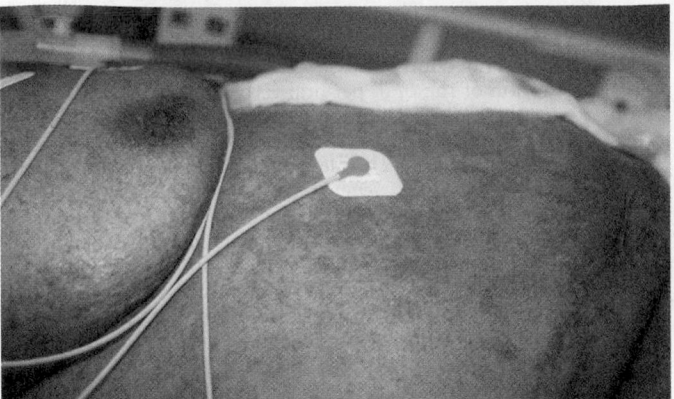

FIGURE 475–18 • Trunk of a patient with acute generalized exanthematous pustulosis revealing erythematous macules and numerous superficial pustules.

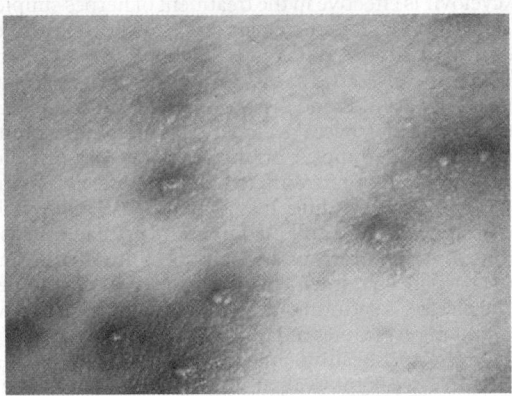

FIGURE 475–19 • Trunk of a patient with *Pseudomonas* folliculitis revealing numerous pustules on an erythematous base.

and associated pilosebaceous units. Folliculitis is more common in diabetes mellitus, obesity, or immunocompromised patients. The primary lesion is a pustule with a central hair. Typical affected sites are the scalp, thighs, trunk, axilla, and inguinal area. Sometimes the infection can extend deeper into the dermis and form larger erythematous nodules from one (furuncle) or more (carbuncle) follicles. Treatment with oral antibiotics such as cephalexin, 500 mg twice daily for 14 days, clears extensive infections, whereas topical antibiotics and antibacterial soaps help in milder disease.

Pseudomonas folliculitis is acquired from hot tubs contaminated with *Pseudomonas aeruginosa*. The typical presentation is papules and pustules in areas of skin occluded by a bathing suit (Fig. 475–19). *Pityrosporum* folliculitis is a pruritic, acnelike eruption that occurs on the upper back and chest, arms, and face and is caused by *Pityrosporum ovale*.

Eosinophilic pustular folliculitis is a sterile, intensely pruritic folliculitis usually found on the face, chest, and back of patients who are positive for HIV (Chapter 409). Skin biopsy is needed to confirm the diagnosis. Treatment is difficult, but options include potent topical corticosteroids, antihistamines, and ultraviolet light therapy.

1. Joly P, Roujeau JC, Benichou J, et al: A comparison of oral and topical corticosteroids in patients with bullous pemphigoid. N Engl J Med 2002;346:321–327.
2. Rice AS, Maton S, Postherpetic Neuralgia Study Group: Gabapentin in post herpetic neuralgia: A randomized, double blind, placebo-controlled study. Pain 2001;94:215–224.
3. Thiboutot D, Thieroff-Ekerdt R, Graupe K: Efficacy and safety of azelaic acid (15%) gel as a new treatment for papulopustular rosacea: Results from two vehicle-controlled, randomized phase III studies. J Am Acad Dermatol 2003;48:836–845.

SUGGESTED READINGS
Baker DA: Valacyclovir in the treatment of genital herpes and herpes zoster. Expert Opin Pharmacother 2002;3:51–58. *This review discusses the use of valacyclovir in the treatment of genital herpes simplex and herpes zoster and contrasts it to other antiviral therapy.*

Fontaine J, Joly P, Roujeau JC: Treatment of bullous pemphigoid. J Dermatol 2003;30:83–90. *A comprehensive update.*

Gibson LE: Cutaneous vasculitis update. Dermatol Clin 2002;19:603–616. *Review of the vasculitides of the skin, including pathogenesis, clinical patterns, and treatment.*

Ladhani S: Recent developments in staphylococcal scalded skin syndrome. Clin Microbiol Infect 2001;7:301–307. *Review of the pathophysiology, diagnosis, and treatment of staphylococcal scalded skin syndrome.*

Schneede P: Genital human papillomavirus infections. Curr Opin Urol 2002;12:57–61. *Excellent overview of genital papillomavirus infection.*

476 URTICARIA, DRUG HYPERSENSITIVITY RASHES, NODULES AND TUMORS, AND ATROPHIC DISEASES

Madeleine Duvic

URTICARIA

Urticaria, also known as hives, is one of the most common cutaneous reaction patterns (Fig. 476–1). It is triggered by a wide variety of antigens or by physical stimuli such as cold, pressure, and sunlight (Chapter 269; Table 476–1). Urticaria can be due to allergic IgE-mediated type I hypersensitivity reactions or to non–immunologically mediated physical factors. It is precipitated by local degranulation of mast cells, with the release of histamine and other factors, such as slow-reacting substance of anaphylaxis. As a result of transient leakage of plasma into the dermis from the capillaries and the small postcapillary venules, a demarcated, pink, raised lesion develops.

Exposure to antigen typically occurs only minutes to a few hours before the urticaria. The most common triggers of IgE-mediated allergic urticarial reactions are drugs (especially penicillin, sulfa drugs, antibiotics, and contrast dye), foods (shellfish, salicylates in berries, tomatoes, yeast, penicillin in blue cheese), food additives (sodium benzoates), nuts, or insect bites (mosquitoes, bees, wasps, scabies, or animal mites). Nonimmunologic mediators of urticaria include aspirin and opiates as well as physical agents that work through the prostaglandin pathway or degranulate mast cells. Acute urticaria can be triggered by skin contact with an antigen, such as latex, and can progress to anaphylaxis. Urticaria can also be a sign or prodrome of a latent infection, especially streptococcal pharyngitis in children or viral hepatitis in adults. The migratory urticarial reaction that accompanies rheumatic fever, known as erythema marginatum (Fig. 476–2),

is characterized by evanescent, scalloped lesions that change location over the course of hours.

Individual urticarial lesions are pink to light red, blanch with pressure, and are raised above the surface of the skin. The center of the lesions may be paler than the leading edge. The mosquito bite (Chapter 271) is an archetypal urticarial lesion. Individual hives can coalesce into giant plaques or annular rings called giant urticaria; such lesions are found especially in serum sickness (Chapter 43), where they are accompanied by arthralgias and fever. Confluent urticaria may also be accompanied by swelling of the underlying soft tissue or the mucous membranes (angioedema), as well as by anaphylaxis with laryngeal

Table 476–1 • COMMON CAUSES OF URTICARIA

Urticaria may be accompanied by angioedema and anaphylaxis:
Blood products: red cells, platelets, gamma globulin
Drugs
  Antibiotics; penicillins, cephalosporins, sulfonamides, isoniazid
  Aspirin: salicylates, benzoates, phenylbutazone
  Anticonvulsants: hydantoin
  Chemotherapy: doxorubicin, daunorubicin, L-asparginase, chlorambucil, cyclophosphamide, melphalan, methotrexate, nitrogen mustard, procarbazine
  Dextran
  Opiates
  Quinidine
  Radiocontrast dyes, iodine
Environmental: animal dander or proteins, formaldehyde, pollen, mold, plants, latex, plastic tubing, exercise, heat, cold, sunlight
Foods: berries, eggs, milk, nuts, tomatoes, shellfish, soy
Food additives: sodium benzoate, tartrazine (yellow dye #5)
Hormones
Infections: streptococcal, staphylococcal, sinusitis or abscesses, viral hepatitis, Epstein-Barr virus mononucleosis, candida
Insect bites or venom: hymenoptera, mosquitoes, mites, scabies
Vaccines

Urticarial-like eruptions and reactive erythemas:
Erythema multiforme: herpes simplex, DNA viruses, *Mycoplasma pneumoniae*, drugs
Erythema marginatum: streptococcal rheumatic fever
Juvenile rheumatoid arthritis
Erythema chronicum migrans: *Borrelia* infections
Erythema annulare centrifugum: tinea, drugs
Figurate erythemas: erythema repens (often with underlying carcinoma)
Urticaria pigmentosa (mastocytosis)

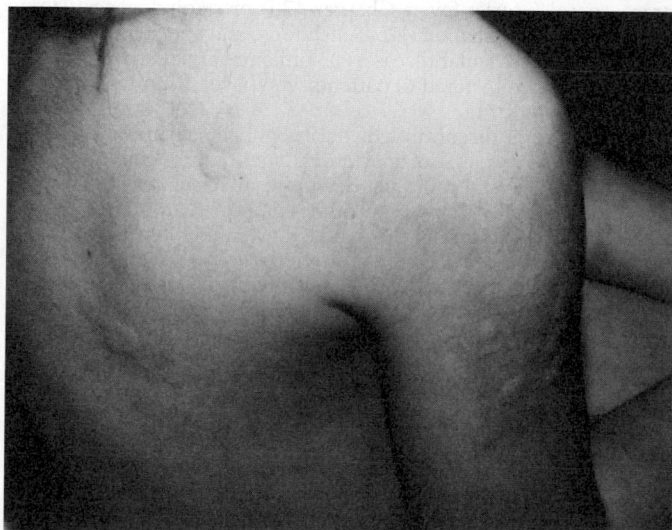

FIGURE 476–1 • Urticaria.

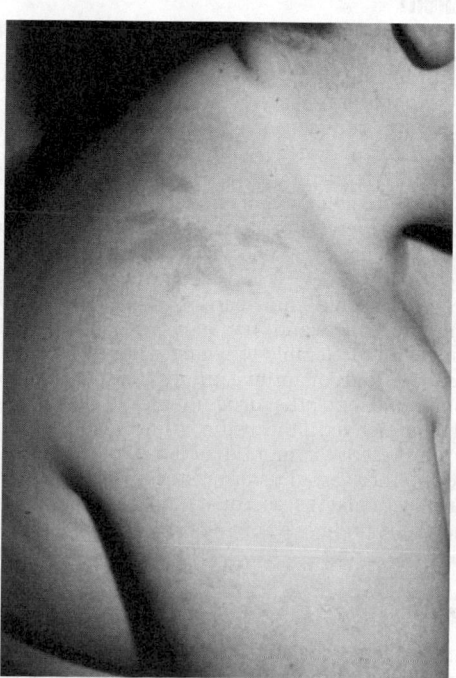

FIGURE 476–2 • Erythema marginatum.

edema (Chapter 270), which represents a life-threatening emergency. In otherwise normal individuals, pressure or writing on the skin can cause spontaneous release of histamine, which induces a wheal and flare reaction known as dermatographism.

Other physical stimuli such as cold, heat, sun, or exercise may induce urticaria. Cold urticaria may be precipitated by putting an ice cube on the skin; the interval until hives develop and the duration of the hives correlate with the severity of the condition, which can be life threatening if the patient is suddenly immersed in cold water. Heat, exercise, or exertion may be accompanied by smaller lesions known as cholinergic urticaria. Exercise-induced anaphylaxis may be hereditary, but the defect is unknown. Cases of urticaria caused by exposure to the sun (solar urticaria) or to water (aquagenic urticaria) are less common forms of physically induced urticaria. By comparison, pruritus without detectible lesions represents the mildest expression of urticarial reactions.

Urticaria is typically transient and self-limited, without leakage of blood cells into the skin or damage to the blood vessels. Chronic urticaria is defined as urticaria that recurs over a period of 6 weeks or more. Chronic urticaria is most often related to ingestion of aspirin or agents that cross react with salicylates: sodium benzoate (a common food preservative) or tartrazine (yellow dye #5). Occult infections (sinusitis, gallbladder disease, *Helicobacter pylori*, yeast infections, tooth abscesses, or silent hepatitis) as well as collagen vascular diseases and tumors, especially lymphoma, can also cause chronic urticaria. Deficiency of the C1 esterase inhibitor can present as chronic urticaria with angioedema (Chapter 269). Although a thorough medical evaluation may aid in diagnosis, the cause of chronic urticaria may remain uncertain.

When urticarial lesions are present for more than 24 hours, underlying vascular damage should be suspected. Biopsy is required to distinguish urticarial vasculitis from urticaria, in which no damage to the blood vessels is evident. Erythema multiforme (Chapter 475), commonly seen with herpes simplex infections, other viruses, or drugs, is characterized by hybrid lesions that are part urticaria and part vasculitis: target or bull's eye lesions with deep red centers and pink urticarial rims (see Fig. 475–9). When vascular damage or purpura is present, the lesion is termed *leukocytoclastic vasculitis,* the most severe expression of hypersensitivity reactions involving cutaneous blood vessels (see Fig. 475–4).

Systemic mastocytosis (Chapter 272) may present as urticarial lesions and may be accompanied by gastrointestinal symptoms. In the form of mastocytosis known as urticaria pigmentosa, stroking the lesions produces urticaria, known as Darier's sign. In the absence of a known antigen, stress is often invoked as the underlying cause of chronic idiopathic urticaria.

Rx Treatment

The management of urticaria depends on its severity and duration of the problem (Chapter 269). For mild urticaria limited to the skin, traditional antihistamines (diphenhydramine [Benadryl], hydroxyzine) or the newer nonsedating agents (terfenadine [Seldane], cetirizine [Zyrtec], loratadine [Claritin]) can be administered by mouth intermittently as needed (Table 476–2). Acute urticaria is often treated by diphenhydramine, 25 to 50 mg orally; if the urticaria is severe, short-term corticosteroids, up to 1 mg/kg, can be used. For urticaria associated with wheezing or anaphylaxis, subcutaneous epinephrine and intravenous corticosteroids should be administered immediately.

Finding the cause and removing the antigen of chronic urticaria is highly preferable to recurrent or chronic administration of corticosteroids or antihistamines. The patient should avoid aspirin compounds and other drugs that could be the cause. Allergy testing is recommended if the history is unrevealing (Chapter 265). If lesions are present for more than a day, biopsy is indicated to determine whether vasculitis or mastocytosis is present. If infection, collagen vascular disease, or a tumor is suspected, a full evaluation should be undertaken.

DRUG RASHES

Drugs have been associated with every type of cutaneous reaction pattern, ranging from mild and self-limited to severe and life-threatening (see Table 27–5). A careful drug history is critical. Most

Table 476–2 • TREATMENT OF URTICARIA

1. Avoid the inciting agent!
2. Medications based on severity
   A. Mild to moderate, acute urticaria
      Oral antihistamines, e.g., diphenhydramine (Benadryl) 10–50 mg PO q12 h or hydroxyzine 10–25 mg PO q8 h; nonsedating alternatives include cetirizine (Zyrtec) 5–10 mg or loratadine (Claritin) 10 mg q day
   B. Severe urticaria with or without angioedema
      Antihistamines PO or IV
      Corticosteroids: PO, IM, or IV depending on severity
   C. Anaphylaxis
      A—Airway (intubation)
      B—Breathing (oxygen)
      C—Circulation: parenteral aqueous epinephrine 1 : 1000, IV saline or volume expanders
      IV corticosteroids
      Histamine-1 and histamine-2 antagonists (50 mg each of diphenhydramine and ranitidine)
   D. Chronic idiopathic urticaria—combination therapy
      Nonsedating antihistamine: cetirizine, 10 mg/day, or fexofenadine, 20–240 mg twice daily, alone or with montelukast, 10 mg/day, or histamine-1 and histamine-2 antagonists (50 mg each of diphenhydramine and ranitidine) and/or low-dose corticosteroids (if unavoidable)

drug rashes are either immediate (urticaria) or delayed hypersensitivity reactions (exanthems). Immediate reactions such as pruritus, hives, angioedema, and anaphylaxis occur within minutes to a few hours after the drug is taken (see earlier). However, the most common drug-related rash (Table 476–3) is a macular, bright pink to salmon red exanthem that appears as early as 7 to 10 days and as late as 14 days after a drug is first administered. Delayed hypersensitivity reactions can be macular and/or papular exanthems, morbilliform eruptions, annular erythemas, or confluent erythema (Fig. 476–3). Once sensitization to a particular drug has occurred, readministration of the same drug causes an eruption that usually will appear within 24 to 72 hours. Drug hypersensitivity reactions are typically symmetrical, and they characteristically begin on the upper trunk or face and then progress to the lower extremities, where purpuric lesions may coexist due to gravity. The lesions may become confluent after several days.

Delayed hypersensitivity reactions are due to T-cell infiltrates with or without eosinophils. Helper T cells are more abundant, but CD8+ suppressor cells that express granzyme B and perforin are implicated in keratinocyte damage. Peripheral eosinophilia, which is induced by interleukin-5 and eotaxin, also can occur.

Pruritus may or may not accompany drug rashes; when present, it is helpful for making the diagnosis. The differential diagnosis for drug rashes includes viral exanthems (Chapter 475), graft vs. host disease or the leukocyte recovery rash following allogeneic bone marrow transplantation, erythematous exanthems that accompany streptococcal (scarlet fever; Chapter 475) or staphylococcal (toxic shock syndrome; Chapter 475) infections, and the acute presentation of collagen vascular diseases. A similar exanthema occurs when ampicillin is administered to patients who have infectious mononucleosis (Chapter 371).

If the drug is discontinued, delayed hypersensitivity reactions resolve in about a week. Corticosteroids, such as triamcinolone cream 0.01% applied several times per day to the affected area and antihistamines given orally three to four times daily are helpful in reducing the itching and shortening the course if given for a few days.

An especially severe hypersensitivity *drug rash with eosinophilia and systemic symptoms* (DRESS) is most frequently seen with phenytoin (Dilantin) or carbamazepine (Tegretol) or when allopurinol is coadministered with thiazide diuretics (Fig. 476–4). DRESS may be delayed in onset by 4 to 6 weeks, persists longer than classic drug-induced eruptions, and becomes generalized and severe, even when the agent is discontinued. Continued administration of the drug can result in generalized exfoliative erythroderma, toxic necrolysis, and systemic hypersensitivity including hepatitis (50%), nephritis (10%), or, less commonly, pneumonitis, myocarditis, pericarditis, or atypical lymphocytosis and lymphadenopathy mimicking mononucleosis or T-cell lymphoma. With visceral involvement there is a 10% mortality rate, usually from liver failure.

Table 476-3 • DELAYED HYPERSENSITIVITY DRUG RASHES BY CATEGORY

MACULOPAPULAR EXANTHEMS—ANY DRUG CAN PRODUCE RASH 7–10 DAYS AFTER FIRST DOSE
Allopurinol
Antibiotics: penicillin, sulfonamides
Antiepileptics: phenytoin, phenobarbitol
Antihypertensives: captopril, thiazide diuretics
Contrast dye: iodine
Gold salts
Hypoglycemic drugs
Meprobamate
Phenothiazines
Quinine

DRUG RASH WITH EOSINOPHILIA AND SYSTEMIC SYMPTOMS (DRESS):
Anticonvulsants: phenytoin, phenobarbital
Antibiotics: sulfonamides, minocycline, dapsone
Allopurinol
Phenothiazines

ERYTHEMA MULTIFORME/STEVENS-JOHNSON SYNDROME
Sulfonamindes, phenytoin, barbiturates, carbamazepines, allopurinol, amikacin, phenothiazines
Toxic epidermal necrolysis: same as for erythema multiforme but also acetazolamide, gold, nitrofurantoin, pentazocine, tetracycline, quinidine

ACUTE GENERALIZED EXANTHEMIC PUSTULOSIS (AGEP):
Antibiotics: penicillins, macrolides, cephalosporins, clindamycin, imipenem, fluoroquinolones, isoniazid, vancomycin, minocycline, doxycycline, linezolid
Antimalarials: chloroquine and hydroxychloroquine
Antifungals: terbinafine, nystatin
Anticonvulsants: carbamazepine
Calcium channel blockers
Furosemide
Systemic corticosteroids
Protease inhibitors

COLLAGEN VASCULAR OR LUPUS-LIKE REACTIONS
Procainamide, hydralazine, phenytoin, penicillamine, trimethadione, methyldopa, carbamazepine, griseofulvin, nalidixic acid, oral contraceptives, propranolol

ERYTHEMA NODUSUM
Oral contraceptives, penicillin, sulfonamides, diuretics, gold, clonidine, propranolol, opiates
Fixed drug reactions: phenolphthalein, barbiturates, gold, sulfonamides, meprobamate, penicillin, tetracycline, analgesics

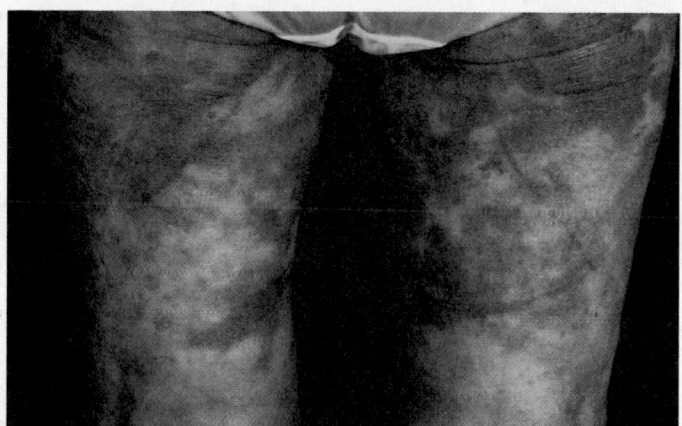

A

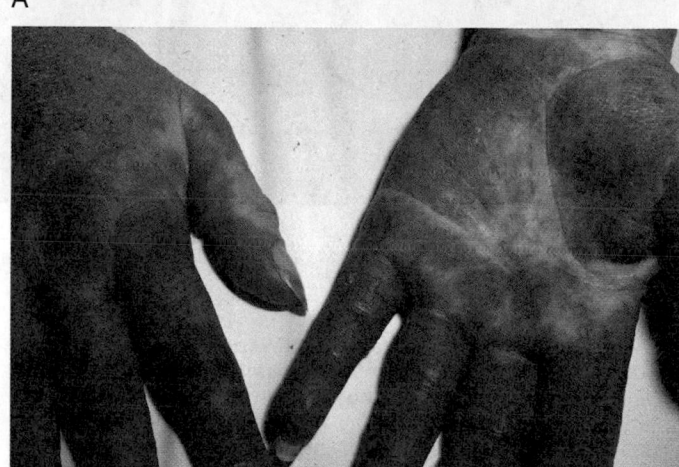

B

FIGURE 476–3 • *A* and *B*, Delayed hypersensitivity reaction to drug and acral erythema.

Drugs are almost always implicated when adults develop blistering conditions known as *erythema multiforme* (see Fig. 475–9), *Stevens-Johnson syndrome*, or *toxic epidermal necrolysis* (see Fig. 476–5). Commonly implicated medications include allopurinol, phenytoin, or sulfa drugs (see Table 27–5).

Severe drug reactions can also present as vasculitis, neutrophilic eruptions, and ulcerations. Vasculitis is further categorized by the size of the involved vessel and the nature of the cellular reaction and immune complexes. *Leukocytoclastic vasculitis* (Chapter 475) is the most common form of cutaneous vasculitic drug reaction (see Fig. 475–4). Neutrophilic drug reactions include iododermas and bromodermas as well as drug-induced Sweet's syndrome (see Inflammatory and Hematopoietic Papular and Tumors) and *acute generalized exanthemic pustulosis* (see Fig. 475–19), which is characterized by numerous (>100), small (<5 mm), nonfollicular, subcorneal pustules that arise on erythematous skin, often beginning in skin creases or on the face. High fever and peripheral neutrophilia may proceed or accompany the eruption. The pustules are sterile, present for 5 to 10 days, and are followed by desquamation. Ninety per cent of cases are due to drugs and usually appear within 2 to 3 days after the administration of antibiotics or 1 to 2 weeks after other drugs; the pustules resolve within 15 days. This syndrome has also been called pustular drug rash, pustular psoriasis following corticosteroid withdrawal, and toxic pustuloderma. When severe, it may be confused with toxic epidermal necrolysis, but the mortality rate is only 1 to 2%. Skin patch testing is frequently positive.

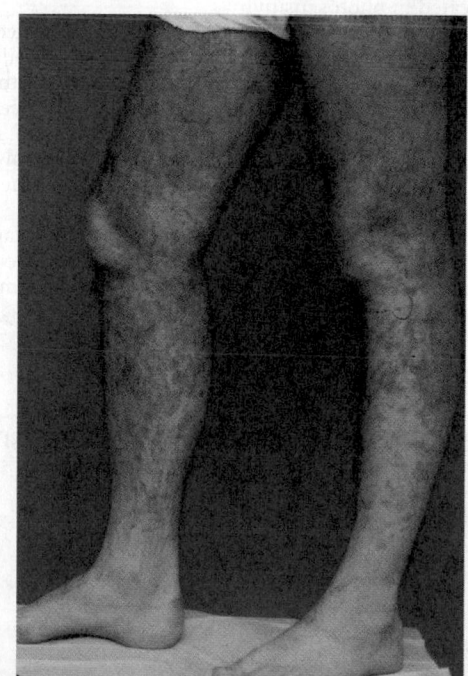

FIGURE 476–4 • Hypersensitivity drug rash to phenytoin.

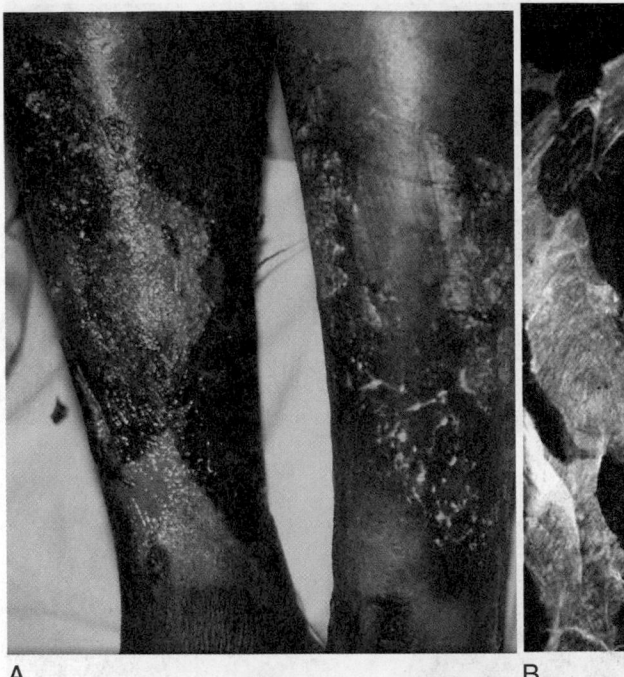
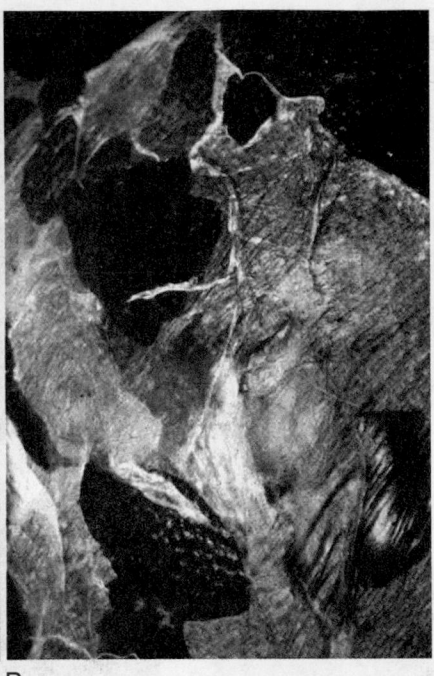

A   B

FIGURE 476–5 • *A* and *B*, Toxic epidermal necrolysis.

A fixed drug reaction is an eruption that occurs at the same location every time the drug is ingested. Mucous membranes of the mouth or genital regions are most commonly involved. The lesion may begin as erythema and then become gray or brown. Phenolphthalein-containing laxatives, barbiturates, and acetaminophen are common causes. An area of skin that reacts with a fixed drug reaction will be transferred if the skin is grafted to another area, thereby suggesting that local antigens are important.

Light may combine with drugs (Table 476–4) to produce photosensitivity reactions (Chapter 474) that can be quite severe. Thiazides, tetracyclines, sulfa drugs, antipsychotic agents, and hydralazine are often implicated in photosensitivity.

Allergic contact dermatitis, which is a T cell–mediated delayed hypersensitivity reaction, can result from topical drug application. In clinical practice, contact dermatitis manifested by erythema and microvesiculation occurs in the area where the drug has been applied but may spread beyond the area (termed an *ID reaction*). Common contact sensitizers include Neosporin (polymyxin B/neomycin/bacitracin), bacitracin, diphenhydramine, doxepin, lidocaine, lanolin, mercury, and *p*-aminobenzoic acid (PABA).

Drugs can exacerbate existing cutaneous diseases. Examples are steroid withdrawal, β-blockers, and lithium, which worsens psoriasis. Photosensitizing drugs may exacerbate lupus erythematosus or porphyria cutanea tarda.

Table 476–4 • DRUGS ASSOCIATED WITH SUN SENSITIVITY
PHOTOTOXIC
Chlorpromazine
Hydralazine
Levoquin
Procainamide
Psoralens
Porphyrins
Tetracyclines
Thiazide diuretics
Sulfonamides
PHOTOALLERGIC
Promethazine
Griseofulvin
Chlorothiazide
Hypoglycemic drugs

BENIGN NODULES AND TUMORS

The skin is a heterogeneous organ composed of epidermis, dermis, subcutaneous compartments, and blood vessels. The skin hosts a number of migrating cells (Chapter 471), all of which can give rise to benign or malignant tumors. Nodules are best felt rather than seen because they are dermal or in the subcutaneous tissue. Lesions that arise from the epidermis are usually considered to be papules (warts, sebaceous hyperplasia; Chapter 475) or plaques (psoriasis, Bowen's disease; Chapter 475) rather than nodules, unless there is dermal invasion by a malignant basal or squamous cell carcinoma or invasive melanoma (Chapter 209). Nodules may be lumps that are felt but not seen, or they can be accompanied by an overlying epidermal reaction, such as hyperpigmentation, erythema, or scaling. Nodules may be tender or asymptomatic and single or multiple. They can have a purple vascular component, or they can break down to form ulcers.

Nodules can be classified as inflammatory (granulomas, vasculitis, or panniculitis), infectious, or metabolic or as benign or malignant tumors arising from skin or invading cells (Table 476–5). Nodules that are smaller and symmetrical are more likely to be benign than are lesions that grow rapidly, are larger, or invade surrounding tissue. Any rapidly changing skin lesion should be investigated. Nodules require an excisional biopsy to the level of the fat for correct histopathologic diagnosis; culture of the lesion is also highly recommended if the diagnosis is uncertain.

Benign Epidermal Tumors

The top layer of skin is the avascular epidermis, which is composed of resident keratinocytes, as well as migratory melanocytes, Langerhans cells, and, in disease states, inflammatory cells (Chapter 471). Epidermal stem cells arising near the hair follicle differentiate to form adnexal organs including hair follicles and glands (sebaceous, eccrine, and apocrine), each of which can give rise to benign or malignant tumors.

The most common benign epidermal tumors are *seborrheic keratoses*, which are verrucous, oval lesions that have regular borders, are often raised, and appear to be stuck onto the skin (Fig. 476–6). Seborrheic keratoses arise from a keratinocyte clone. Large numbers of seborrheic keratoses can be found in an autosomal dominant inheritance pattern. The appearance of large numbers of eruptive seborrheic keratoses may also signal an internal carcinoma that is producing a growth factor such as epidermal growth factor. Seborrheic keratoses may be friable and peel off with scraping. Their color can be white, flesh colored, pink, yellow, tan, brown, or black; and several

Table 476–5 • TUMORS AND NODULES OF THE SKIN

Benign, nonpigmented tumors and nodules:
    Epidermal: warts, acrochordons, tricholemmomas, sebaceous hyperplasia
    Adnexal: epidermal cysts, syringomas, follicular cysts, pilomatricoma, apocrine or eccrine adenomas
    Dermal and subcutaneous: lipomas, angiolipomas, neurofibromas, leimyomas
Benign, pigmented tumors and nodules:
    Epidermal: seborrheic keratoses
    Melanocytic compound nevi (junctional nevi are flat)
    Spitz nevus
    Blue nevus
    Dermatofibromas
Malignant, nonpigmented tumors and nodules:
    Basal cell carcinoma (nodular, superficial, morpheaform, pigmented)
    Squamous cell carcinoma (actinic keratoses, Bowen's disease, keratoacanthomas)
    Cutaneous T- and B-cell lymphomas
    Amelanotic melanomas
    Merkel cell carcinomas
    Adnexal carcinomas of the sebaceous and apocrine glands
Malignant, pigmented tumors and nodules:
    Pigmented basal cell carcinoma
    Malignant melanoma: in situ, superficial spreading, nodular, acral lentiginous
    Dermatofibrosarcoma protuberans
Inflammatory nodules over joints:
    Gottren's papules (dermatomyositis)
    Gouty tophi
    Heberden's nodes (osteoarthritis)
    Multicentric reticulohistiocytosis (paraneoplastic syndrome)
    Rheumatoid nodules
    Granuloma annulare
Inflammatory nodules of the lower extremities:
    Panniculitis
    Vasculitis: periarteritis nodosa
Metabolic nodules of the skin
    Amyloidosis
    Gouty tophi
    Xanthomas, necrobiotic xanthogranuloma
    Xanthelasma
Vascular lesions
    Benign: nevus flammeus, angiokeratomas, spider hemangiomas, capillary hemangiomas, cavernous hemangiomas, blue rubber bleb nevi, pyogenic granulomas
    Malignant: Kaposi's sarcoma, angiosarcoma

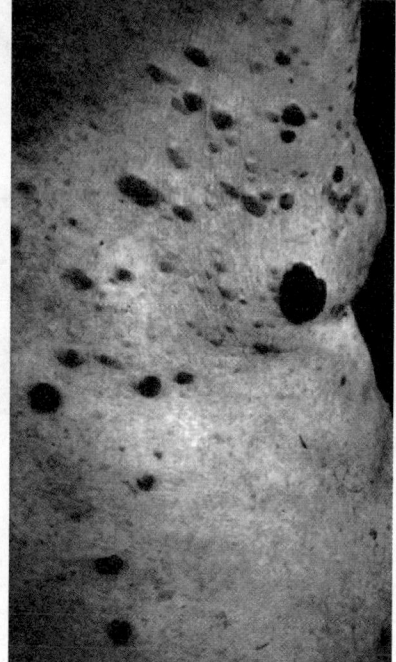

FIGURE 476–6 • Seborrheic keratoses.

different colors can be present in the same patient and in the same lesion. Seborrheic keratoses can be distinguished from melanocytic nevi, melanomas, and pigmented basal cell carcinomas by the presence of white to yellow horn cysts on their surface, which are best appreciated under magnification. Although seborrheic keratoses are benign, they must be differentiated from other pigmented lesions, especially superficial spreading melanoma (see Fig. 209–3).

Papules (Chapter 475) include *warts* (see Fig. 475–2), caused by the human papillomavirus (HPV). HPV can also be detected in squa-

mous carcinomas arising on the digits and in keratoacanthoma, a low-grade, well-demarcated, dome-shaped squamous cell carcinoma that grows rapidly and spontaneously involutes in 6 to 8 weeks. In acrodermatitis verruciformis, multiple warts that have the appearance of seborrheic keratoses (see later) are found on the extremities and give rise to squamous carcinomas. *Tricholemmomas* are wartlike epidermal lesions found in association with Cowden's syndrome, which is associated with mutations in the *PTEN* gene; Cowden's syndrome is defined by warty papules on the gums, tricholemmomas (Fig. 476–7), fibrous papules, and multiple hamartomas involving the breast, thyroid, ovary, and cerebellum (Chapter 200). *Molluscum contagiosum* (Chapters 417 and 475) (Fig. 476–8), caused by a DNA virus, are small, shiny, domed-shaped papules 1 to 5 mm with a central dell that are common in children or in immunocompromised patients. Epidermoid tumors on the scalp in a patient with a family history of colon cancer are helpful in making the diagnosis of Gardner's syndrome (Chapter 200).

Adnexal tumors arise from the hair follicles or from sebaceous or other glands and are commonly found on the face. *Trichoepitheliomas* have features similar to basal cell carcinomas, whereas sebaceous hyperplasia describes small yellow papules with a central depression. *Sebaceous carcinomas* occur around the upper face or eyelids as solitary lesions or as markers for the Muir-Torre syndrome of familial breast and colon cancer. Epidermal or sebaceous cysts, which are found

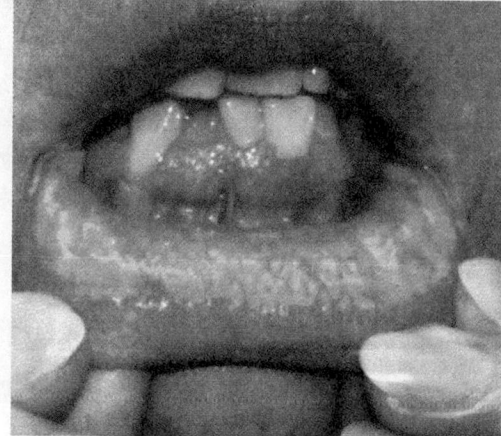

FIGURE 476–7 • Cowden's syndrome: cobblestone gums and tricholemmoma.

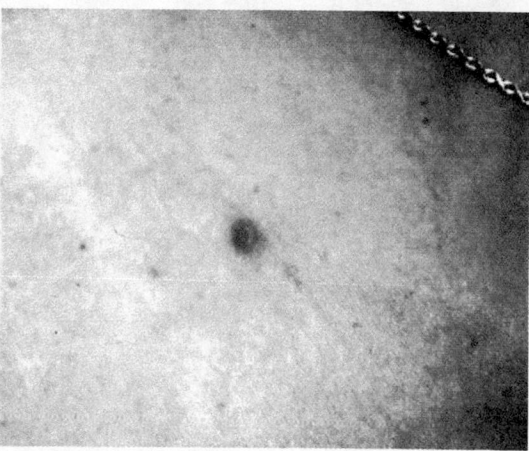

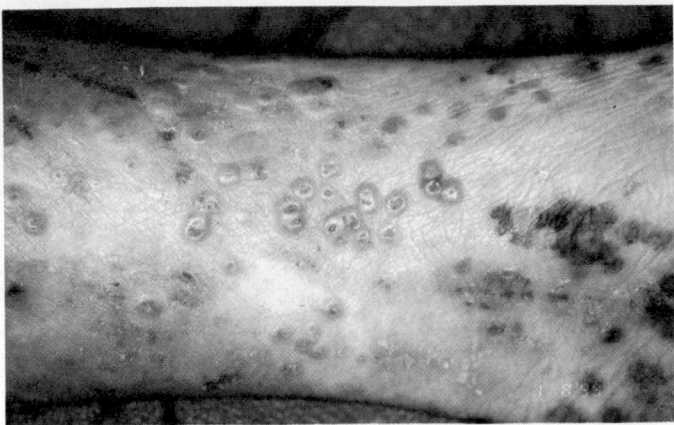

FIGURE 476—8 • Molluscum contagiosum in an immunocompromised patient.

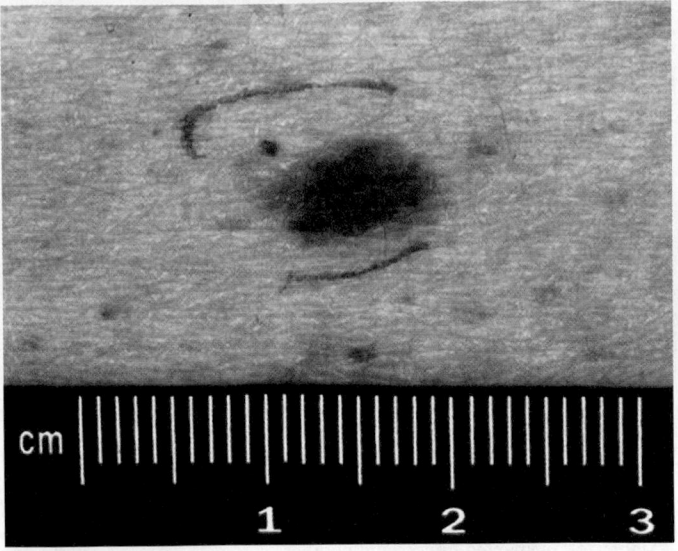

FIGURE 476—10 • A junctional nevus.

in acne or as single firm nodules with a central pore, are filled with sebum or keratin.

Actinic keratoses arise from sun-induced DNA damage to keratinocytes in exposed areas. They are precursor lesions to superficial squamous cell carcinoma (Bowen's disease) and invasive squamous carcinoma (Chapter 209). Actinic keratoses are scaly 0.1- to 1.0-cm white or pink lesions that appear on the forearms, hands, face, and scalp (Fig. 476–9). They are rough in texture and have little induration. Individual lesions can be destroyed locally. Pink or red scaly lesions with induration, thick crusts, ulceration, or pain must be sampled to exclude invasive squamous cell carcinoma. Because the skin on which actinic keratoses arise is photodamaged and may carry mutations in *p53*, a more effective approach is to treat the entire area with 5-fluorouracil cream (5%), applied daily for 2 weeks or twice weekly for 8 weeks, with use of a topical antibiotic for a shorter time period.

Benign Tumors of Cells That Migrate into Skin

MELANOCYTES. Benign melanocytic moles or nevi (new) are discrete nests of melanocytes acquired during childhood and young adulthood and stimulated by sun exposure. *Nevi* must be distinguished from malignant melanoma (Chapter 209). Nevi tend to regress with age and may change in color during pregnancy. Benign melanocytic nevi are formed by nests of melanocytes at the epidermal junction (junctional nevi), in the dermis (intradermal nevi), or in both compartments (compound nevi). The appearance of moles depends on type and on age of the lesion. *Junctional nevi* (Fig. 476–10) are small,

flat, and light to dark brown. *Intradermal nevi* are soft, flesh colored to pink papules with smooth regular borders and surface. *Compound nevi* are also papules but have brown pigmentation. *Blue nevi* (Fig. 476–11) are flat, grayish blue, and regular. Small congenital nevi are dark brown, whereas large (>20 cm) congenital nevi have variegated colors and are more likely to transform with melanoma. Patients who have more than 10 large, atypical moles with irregular borders and colors that resemble melanomas have a very high risk of developing melanoma, especially if there is a family history; such patients require regular surveillance examinations. Other recognized risk factors for melanoma include having more than 50 small nevi, red or blonde hair, or fair skin that burns and a history of blistering sunburns as a child.

LANGERHANS CELL HISTIOCYTOSIS. The skin immune system includes surveillance mediated by antigen presenting cells such as Langerhans cells and dermal dendritic cells as well as skin-homing T lymphocytes. Langerhans cells migrate from lymph nodes, process antigen, and present peptides to T cells. Proliferation of Langerhans cells characterizes one form of histiocytosis. Childhood histiocytosis X presents as severe seborrheic dermatitis of the scalp and gluteal areas

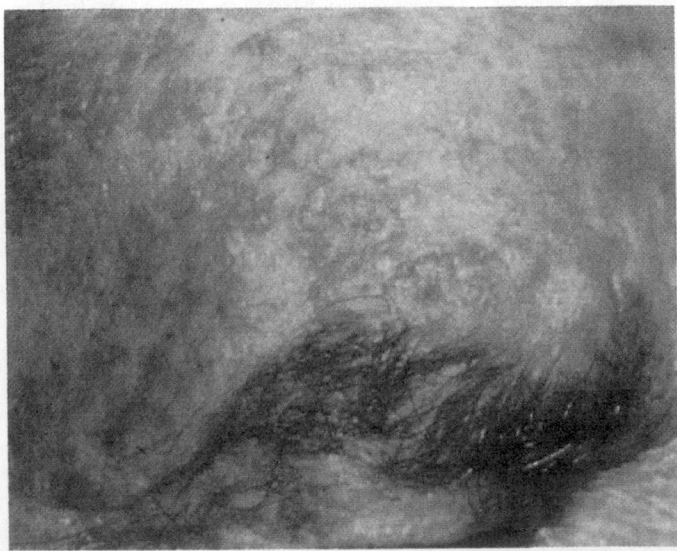

FIGURE 476—9 • Actinic keratoses.

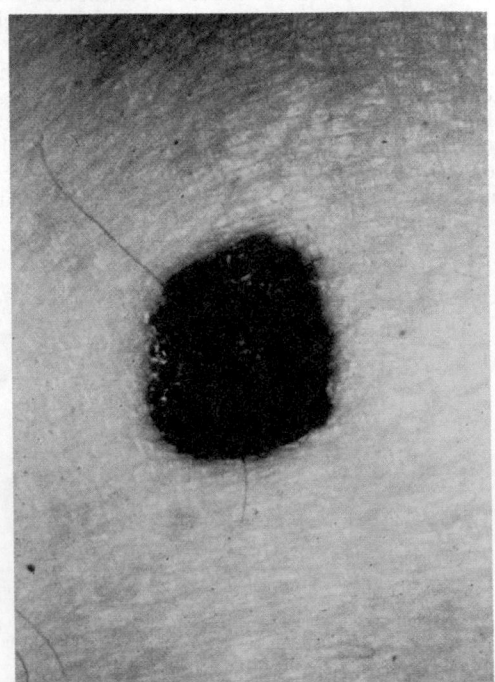

FIGURE 476—11 • A benign blue nevus.

with underlying purpura and may result in the hemophagocytic syndrome. Patients with the non–Langerhans cell histiocytoses have lytic bone involvement (eosinophilic granulomas) or diabetes insipidus (Hand-Schüller-Christian syndrome).

Dermal Tumors

Fibroblasts are the resident cells of the dermis and are responsible for producing collagen, elastin, and mucopolysaccharides. Accumulation of these products results in sclerosis, papules, or nodules. Fibroblasts in small dense clusters form brown firm papules or nodules. *Dermatofibromas,* which are most commonly found on the extremities, may occur after insect bites, and have overlying hyperpigmentation. The lesions are firm and well-demarcated scars that require no therapy. Puckering is seen around the nodule when lateral pressure is applied. The malignant counterpart is dermatofibroma sarcoma protuberans, which is a poorly defined, rapidly expanding, dermal malignant tumor. Overlying erythema or hyperpigmentation is often present.

Collagenomas and elastic tumors with the appearance of small white to yellow papules are found in the skin and bone of patients with Buschke-Ollendorff syndrome. *Pseudoxanthoma elasticum* (Chapter 276), an autosomal recessive disorder, typically presents as cutaneous yellow plaques about the neck or antecubital fossa from damaged elastin tissue. *Mucin cysts* are gray, shiny, well-demarcated round nodules that usually arise on the digits, where they may have an underlying connection to the joint space or on the mucosa.

Benign tumors in the dermis can also arise from neural crest cells: *neurofibromas* (soft, flesh-colored papules; Fig. 476–12) and *schwannomas* (larger subcutaneous soft tumors or plaques; Fig. 476–13). Although solitary neurofibromas may occur, multiple lesions plus the presence of café au lait spots (tan macules) or axillary freckling (Crowe's sign) is diagnostic of neurofibromatosis type I, an autosomal dominant disorder caused by mutations in neurofibromin (Chapter 459). Schwannomas can become malignant and present as dermal nodules.

A *Merkel cell carcinoma* is a particularly aggressive small cell tumor arising from the cutaneous nerve endings or Meissner's corpuscles. Merkel cell tumors present as translucent or purple papules or as plaques on sun-exposed areas (Fig. 476–14), but their appearance is not distinctive. Treatment requires full excision, radiation, and often chemotherapy as the cancer tends to recur and metastasize. Glomus tumors are benign and blue or purple, with small, painful tumors arising from nerve endings. Soft, well-demarcated nodules of fatty tissue, called *lipomas,* are benign and may be multiple; they may have a vascular component or be painful.

Vascular Lesions

Benign capillary hemangiomas are bright cherry red to purple raised papules that are less than 5 mm in diameter and that appear on the trunk with aging and may be numerous (Fig. 476–15). *Pyogenic granulomas,* which are sterile collections of polymorphonuclear

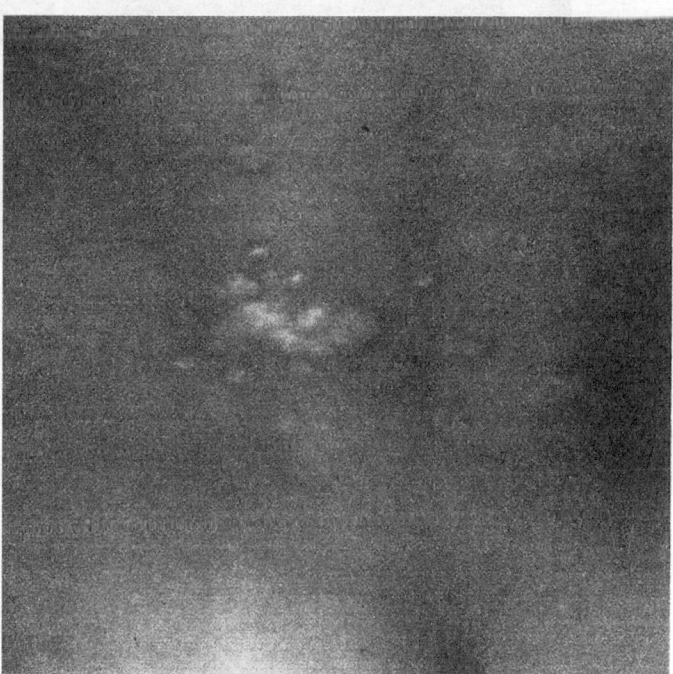

FIGURE 476–13 • Schwannoma.

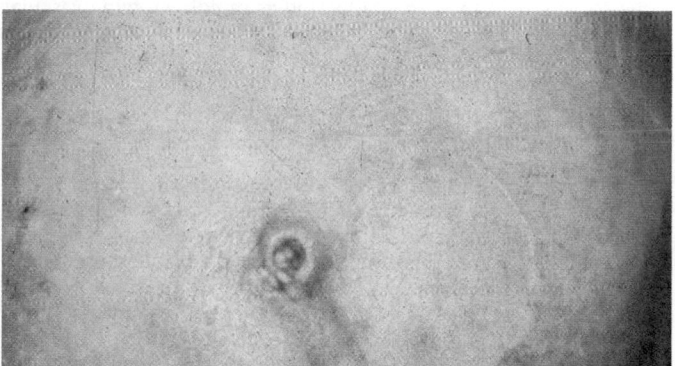

FIGURE 476–14 • Merkel cell tumor.

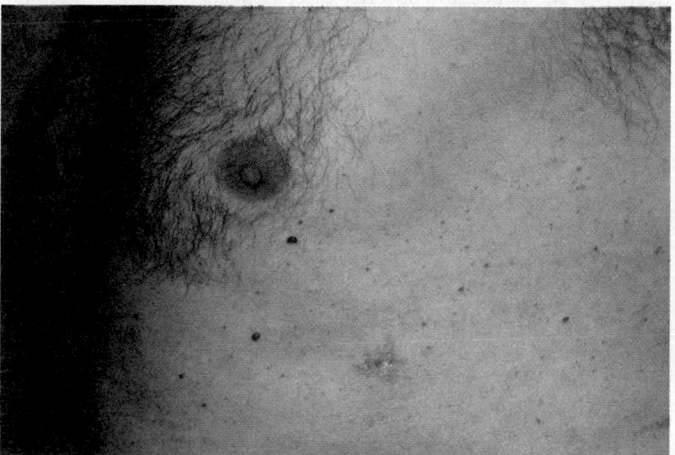

FIGURE 476–15 • Benign capillary hemangioma.

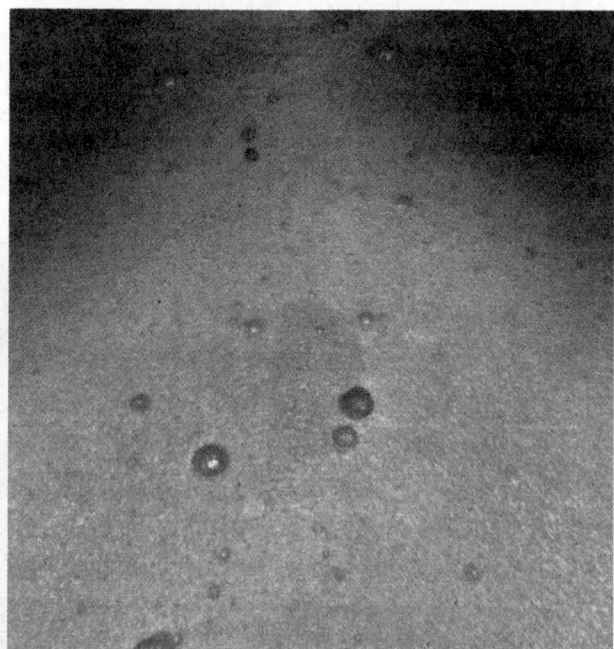

FIGURE 476–12 • Neurofibromatosis with café au lait spots and neurofibromas.

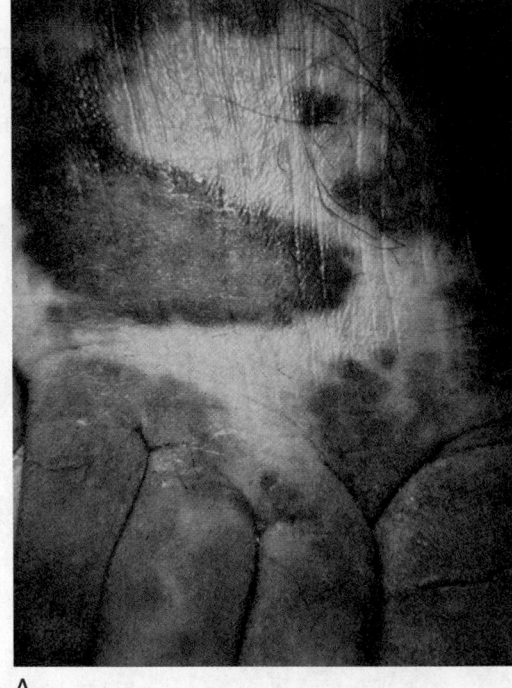

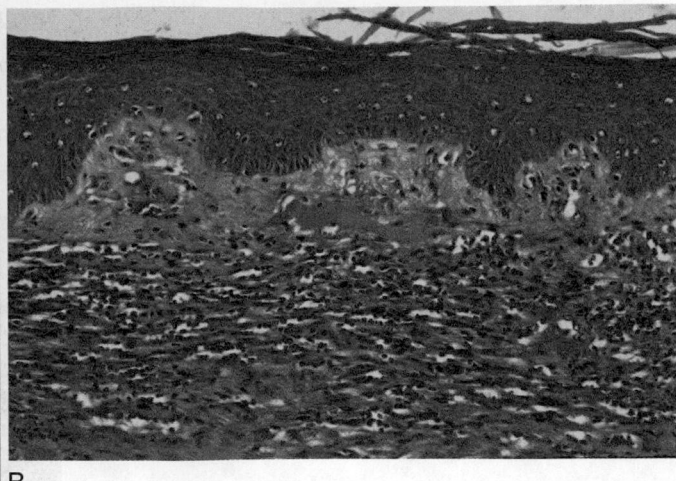

A

FIGURE 476–16 • Kaposi's sarcoma of the lower extremity (Mediterranean KS) (*A*) and histology (*B*).

leukocytes, can resemble capillary hemangiomas, but they have a friable epidermal surface and bleed easily; they may be similar in appearance to amelanotic melanoma. In the presence of multiple pyogenic granuloma–like lesions, infectious bacillary angiomatosis should be considered (Chapter 340). Flat red macules found on the posterior neck are due to a benign capillary network and referred to as the nevus flammeus or stork bite. *Cavernous or strawberry hemangiomas* can also appear in the neonatal period as rapidly growing vascular tumors; they may obstruct the eye or the pharynx before regressing. Corticosteroids, interferon, or antiangiogenic factors can treat these lesions successfully. Cavernous hemangiomas are deeper and less likely to resolve than smaller lesions. When associated with platelet consumption, the Kasabach-Merritt syndrome is present (Chapter 177).

Kaposi's sarcoma (Chapter 417) is a disseminated angiomatosis that arises from viral interleukin (IL)-8 production by herpesvirus 8 (KS-HSV8). The lesions are often symmetrical and can present as purple patches; as raised purple, brown, or gray plaques; or as small papules, firm nodules, or ulcers (Fig. 476–16). Mucosal involvement is more common in advanced disease. Kaposi's sarcoma in young African adults and Kaposi's sarcoma associated with HIV infection often have a more aggressive course than Kaposi's sarcoma in elderly males of Mediterranean background, in whom the disease tends to be indolent and confined to the lower extremities. Treatment of HIV disease with highly active retroviral therapy has been associated with decreased incidence and severity of coassociated Kaposi's sarcoma. *Angiosarcomas* are malignant purple to red vascular tumor nodules that are more common in elderly individuals or on the extremities of patients with chronic lymphedema.

Inflammatory and Hematopoietic Papules and Tumors

Inflammatory diseases of the skin often involve the vessels of the dermis or deeper subcutaneous tissues. The inflammatory infiltrates can be mixed or restricted in nature. Lymphocytes, polymorphonuclear leukocytes, histocytes, eosinophils, and plasma cells are the most common components of inflammatory reactions. Hematologic malignancies can present in the skin as patches, nodules, papules, or vasculitic lesions. T cells that home to skin give rise to cutaneous T-cell lymphoma, a heterogeneous group of extranodal non-Hodgkin's lymphomas (Chapter 195). In mycosis fungoides, the lesions are usually pleomorphic pink, white, or brown patches or plaques; patches of alopecia can occur, and lesions may coalesce to cause diffuse erythroderma. Tumors occur late in the disease or if the cells have transformed to a large phenotype (see Fig. 474–15). The early phase of mycosis fungoides is indistinguishable from chronic eczematous or psoriasiform dermatitis. Peripheral cutaneous T-cell lymphomas may also present in the subcutaneous tissue as panniculitic lesions. Lymphomatoid papulosis is characterized by crops of red to pink regressing papules that show anaplastic large cell lymphoma on histology and stain positive for the Ki-1 or CD30 antigen. NK T-cell lymphomas and immunoblastic lymphomas may present in skin as brown dermal nodules.

B-cell lymphomas in skin are pink, infiltrated, dome-shaped shiny papules or tumors that most commonly are located on the face, scalp, or upper back. With the exception of large cell lymphoma, many B-cell lymphomas of the skin are indolent and some are stimulated by *Borrelia* infection or chronic inflammation. Plasmacytomas can arise in the skin as well as in the bone, with multiple myeloma or independent of it. Extramedullary hematopoiesis or endometriosis can present as red or brown nodules in the dermis.

Sarcoidosis (Chapter 91) is an inflammatory granulomatous process manifesting as ichthyosis, papules, plaques, or tumors with an apple jelly color (Fig. 476–17). Patients with *lepromatous leprosy* have histiocytic plaques or tumors (Fig. 476–18); treatment of leprosy may induce an inflammatory reaction: erythema nodosum leprosum. Granulomatous inflammation within the dermis can result in damage to the collagen as seen in granuloma annulare (ringlike pink to red infiltrated lesions often on the hands or elbows), rheumatoid nodules

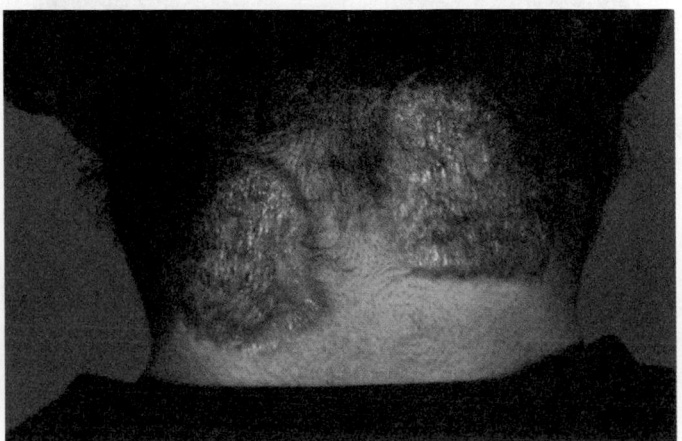

FIGURE 476–17 • Cutaneous sarcoidosis.

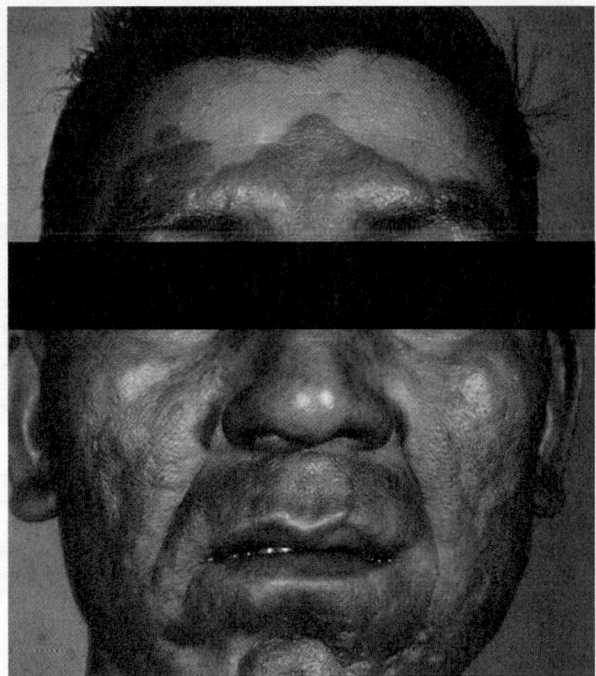

FIGURE 476–18 • Leonine facies of lepromatous leprosy.

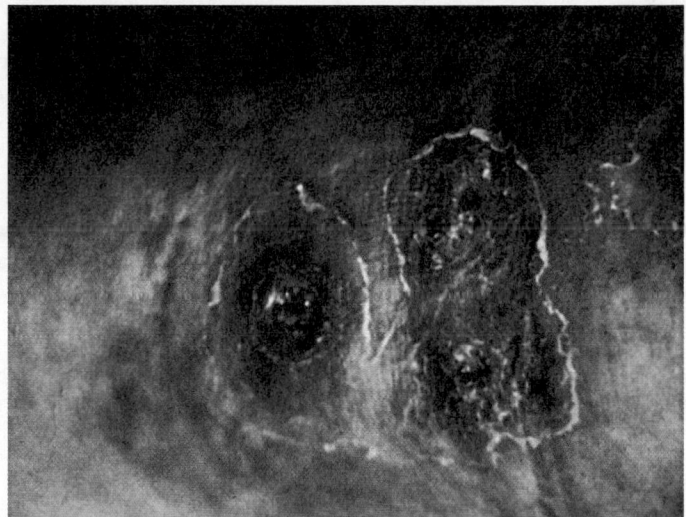

FIGURE 476–20 • Nodular vasculitis.

that occur on the extensor arms, and necrobiosis lipoidica on the shins of diabetics. All three lesions typically include fibrin deposits within dermal blood vessels. Multicentric reticulohistiocytosis is a rare paraneoplastic syndrome in which histiocytic nodules form over joints with associated arthritis.

Inflammatory skin nodules arise from inflamed deeper structures, especially blood vessels (vasculitis) or adipose tissue (panniculitis); both can arise in response to underlying infection or antigen stimulation with influx of inflammatory cells. Vasculitis is further categorized by size of the vessels and the type of circulating immune complexes. Damage to the blood vessels results in leakage of red blood cells with the development of purpura (nonblanching red to purple lesions; Chapter 284). *Erythema elevatum diutinum* presents as multiple, infiltrated pink or yellow to red and violaceous nodules or papules that may be painful or asymptomatic. The lesions can coalesce to form gyrate lesions similar to granuloma annulare on the dorsum of the hands or extensor surfaces. Erythema elevatum diutinum is associated with upper respiratory infections (especially *Streptococcus*), HIV, and inflammatory bowel disease. The underlying histopathology is a necrotizing vasculitis with neutrophils and hyalinization of the vessels. Erythema elevatum diutinum must be distinguished from *Sweet's syndrome* (recurrent febrile, neutrophilic dermatosis of Sweet) that

presents as similar lesions clinically (Fig. 476–19). Sweet's syndrome presents as fever, and the biopsy specimen shows sheets of leukocytes filling the upper dermis in the absence of infection. It occurs in patients with leukemia, inflammatory bowel disease, or rheumatoid arthritis. Sweet's syndrome but not erythema elevatum diutinum is highly responsive to corticosteroids, whereas dapsone can improve both conditions.

Polyarteritis nodosa (Chapter 284) arises in larger arterioles and may be associated with hepatitis C infection, mesenteric aneurysms, cryoglobulinemia, cutaneous ulceration, and livedo reticularis. Polyarteritis nodosa is distinct from small vessel leukocytoclastic vasculitis, which presents as smaller areas (a few millimeters) of purpura.

In the clinical setting, *panniculitis* occurs more frequently than nodular vasculitis. The differential diagnosis of vasculitis versus septal or lobular panniculitis requires an excisional biopsy, including fat, with appropriate cultures and stains. Lobular panniculitis with necrosis and purpura is actually called nodular vasculitis or erythema induratum. Nodular vasculitis is characterized by painful, chronic, recurrent nodules that develop on the shin or thighs and that become bluish, ulcerate, and heal with scarring. *Erythema induratum* (Fig. 476–20), which is exacerbated by cold exposure, is sometimes associated with infection with *Mycobacterium tuberculosis* (Chapter 341). True *lobular panniculitis*, with or without fat necrosis, occurs more often in males with underlying pancreatitis (Chapter 145) and may precede the detection of pancreatic cancer (Chapter 201). The lesions have a predilection for the anterior shins and may be fluctuant due to fat necrosis. Lupus panniculitis or lupus profundus involves the fat and is

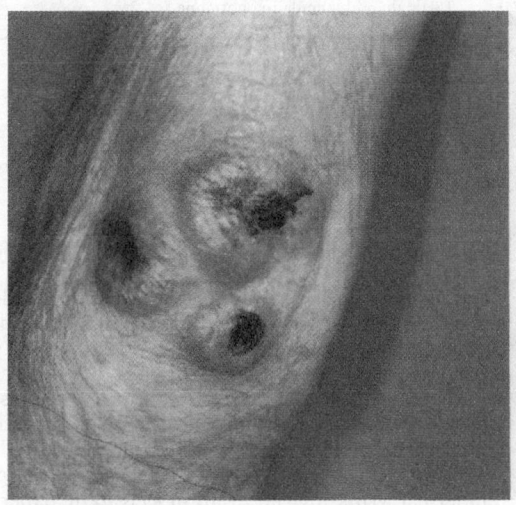

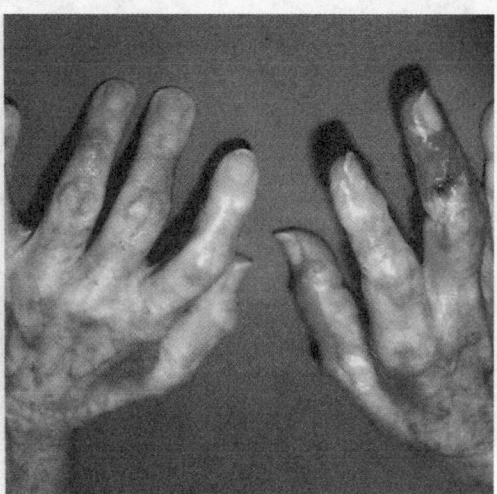

FIGURE 476–19 • Sweet's syndrome in patients with leukemia.

diagnosed by overlying granular immune complex deposition of IgM along the dermal-epidermal junction. Lupus panniculitis of the breast can be mistaken for adenocarcinoma; it is treated with antimalarials or corticosteroids. Lobular panniculitis with calcification of the small arterioles, which occurs in the setting of renal failure with hyperparathyroidism, is called calciphylaxis (Chapter 117).

Especially in immunocompromised patients, necrotic or granulomatous lobular panniculitis can be caused by disseminated fungal infections due to *Candida, Sporothrix schenckii, Cryptococcus, Histoplasma, Nocardia, Rhizopus, Aspergillus, Fusarium,* or chromomycosis. Fungal mycelia invade vessel walls, where they produce purpuric and painful lesions that may ulcerate. Osler's nodes, which are tender nodular vasculitic lesions on the extremities, occur in the setting of bacterial endocarditis (Chapter 310). Staphylococcal or streptococcal sepsis may present as pustules, papules, or panniculitic lesions. *Klebsiella* and *Pseudomonas* are associated with hemorrhagic necrosis of vessels or ecthyma gangrenosa. Granulomatous lobular panniculitis may also arise in the setting of syphilis, atypical mycobacterial infection, tuberculosis, or leprosy.

Erythema nodosum (Fig. 476–21) is characterized by tender nodules, 1 to 2 cm in diameter, that have warm, pink, overlying epidermis and appear in crops on the extremities. Erythema nodosum is characterized by a perivascular inflammatory infiltrate around the small intralobular vessels without vasculitis. Erythema nodosum

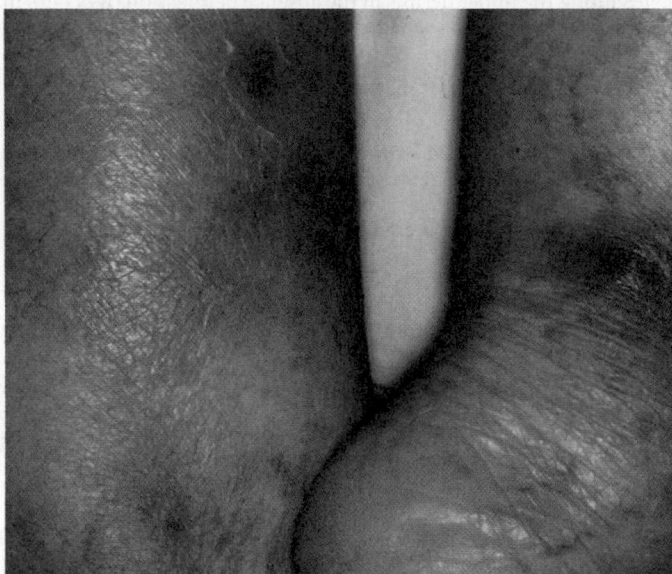

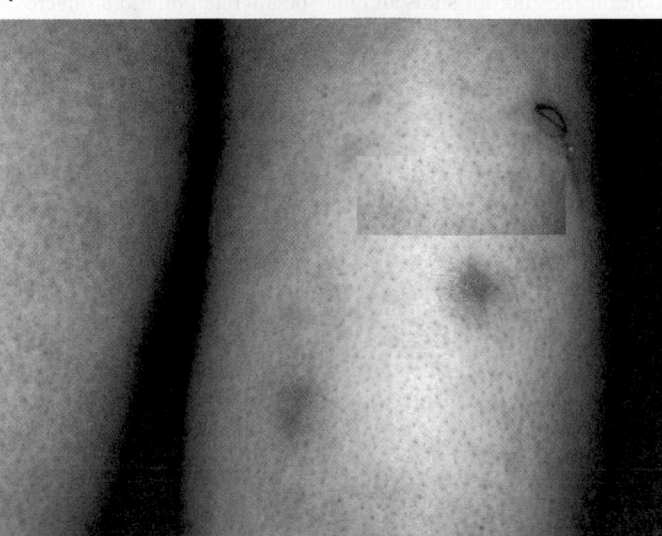

FIGURE 476–21 • *A* and *B*, Erythema nodosum and septal panniculitis of the lower extremities.

Table 476–6 • **TRIGGER FACTORS ASSOCIATED WITH ERYTHEMA NODOSUM**

Infections:
  Bacterial: *Streptococcus*, tuberculosis, leprosy, *Mycoplasma*, *Yersinia*, *Salmonella*, leptospirosis, tularemia
  Fungal: coccidioidomycosis, blastomycosis, histoplasmosis, dermatophytosis
  Viruses and chlamydia: paravaccinia, Epstein-Barr virus, lymphogranuloma venereum, cat-scratch disease, psittacosis, hepatitis B
Drugs: sulfonamides, bromides, oral contraceptives
Malignancies: lymphoma, leukemia, carcinoma, post-tumor radiation
Inflammatory: ulcerative colitis, Crohn's disease, Whipple's disease, Behçet's syndrome, Sweet's syndrome, collagen vascular diseases
Pregnancy

Table 476–7 • **ATROPHIC SKIN CONDITIONS WITH SCARRING, ULCERATIONS, AND/OR TELANGIECTASIAS**

ATROPHY
Epidermal: chronic corticosteroid use, photoaging, mycosis fungoides
Dermal elastin: anetoderma, cutis laxa, intrinsic aging
Dermal collagen: Ehlers-Danlos syndrome, aging
Subcutaneous: granulomatous slack skin (a mycosis fungoides variant)
Lipodystrophy (loss of fat)

SCARRING OR ATROPHY WITH TELANGIECTASIA
Discoid and subacute cutaneous lupus erythematosus
Dermatomyositis
Keloid formation
Large plaque parapsoriasis (poikiloderma vasculare atrophicans variant of mycosis fungoides)
Photoaging
Necrobiosis lipoidica diabeticorum
Radiation dermatitis
Porphyrias
Thermal burns (erythema ab igne)

SCLEROSIS OR INFILTATIVE PROCESSES
Amyloidosis
Systemic sclerosis, scleroderma
Localized sclerosis, morphea
Lichen sclerosis et atrophicus
Lichen myxedematosus/papular mucinosis (mucopolysaccharide deposition with paraproteinemia)
Myxedema (mucin deposits with anti-TSH receptor antibodies)

ULCERATIONS
Secondary breakdown of any blister or nodule: infectious, inflammatory, tumor, vasculitis
Decubitus or pressure ulcers
Genital ulcers: syphilis, herpes simplex, chancroid, lymphogranuloma venereum, Behçet's syndrome
Pyoderma gangrenosum, Sweet's syndrome

  TSH = thyroid-stimulating hormone.

---

frequently arises in response to various infections, inflammatory bowel disease, or drug use, but often the underlying cause remains unknown (Table 476–6).

ATROPHIC AND SCLEROTIC LESIONS (Table 476–7)

Atrophic lesions can result from the thinning or loss of the normal epidermal layers, as occurs in photoaging, in lupus erythematosus, and in genetic disorders of collagen production (e.g., Ehlers-Danlos syndrome; Fig. 476–22). Use of high-potency topical corticosteroids also produces loss of collagen and atrophy. In Cushing's syndrome, the epidermis and underlying connective tissue become atrophic and promote the formation of striae. Striae appear as red or purple streaks because the underlying dermis can be seen through the epidermis. Epidermal wrinkling can result in a cigarette paper appearance with prominence of the underlying blood vessels.

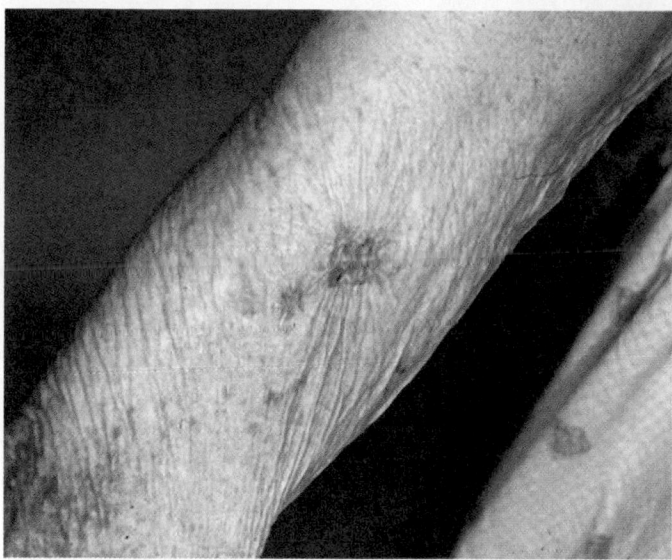

FIGURE 476–22 • Atrophic skin in Ehlers-Danlos syndrome, type 2.

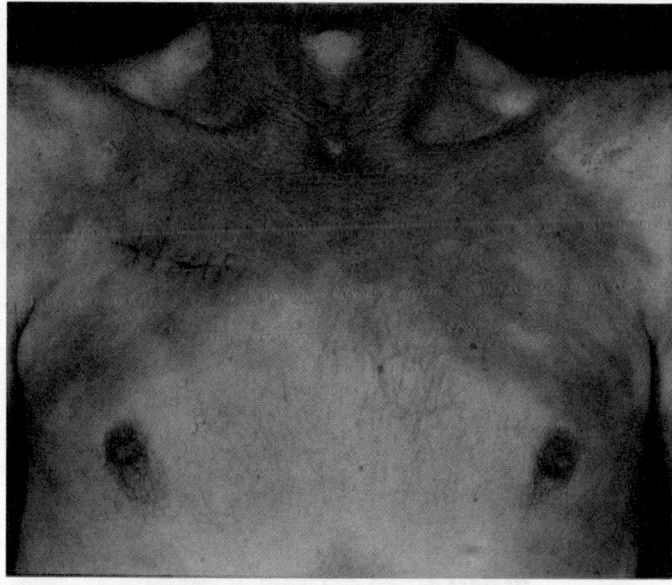

FIGURE 476–24 • Eosinophilic fasciitis due to tryptophan.

Aging skin is most pronounced in sun-exposed areas, but intrinsic aging beginning as early as age 30 years is characterized by abnormalities in the formation of elastin fibers. Aging of the skin is also accompanied by decreasing numbers of epidermal-dermal involutions (rete ridges) and changes in the dermal blood vessels that lead to poor circulation. Aging of the skin owing to sunlight involves the induction or production of proteolytic enzymes that digest underlying collagen and elastin (wrinkles). These changes can be partially prevented or restored with the use of topical vitamin A creams on a regular basis and with use of sun protection, including sunscreen. Sun exposure also induces pigment incontinence (freckling) and proliferation of benign keratinocyte growths (seborrheic keratoses).

Atrophy can also result from ongoing inflammatory processes, such as collagen vascular disease or mycosis fungoides, that lead to scarring. Anetodermas, which are localized sclerotic lesions (Fig. 476–23) with distinctive clinical features, are also attributed to underlying inflammatory processes. Connective tissue diseases often produce sclerosis and atrophy after active inflammation. The cutaneous and discoid forms of *lupus erythematosus* (Chapter 280) present as scaly plaques with atrophy or alopecia on sun-exposed areas; the systemic form presents as malar rash, urticaria, or vasculitic lesions. *Dermatomyositis* (Chapter 283) can be associated with collagen vascular disease or

malignancy; periorbital suffusion, telangiectasia of the nail beds, and Gottren's papules or scaly lesions over the joints are the skin manifestations.

Eosinophilic fasciitis presents as nodules or sclerosis of the lower extremities, myopathy, pulmonary disease, and eosinophilia (Fig. 476–24). This syndrome, which follows ingestion of L-tryptophan or its contaminants, resembles the panniculitis seen in systemic sclerosis, in which fat lobules are replaced by new collagen formation. *Eosinophilic cellulitis, or Well's syndrome,* presents as nodules, papules, or ulcerative lesions as well as red plaques; in this disorder, eosinophils infiltrate the area between the collagen fibers.

Sclerotic lesions are accompanied by more collagen production; the skin has a thicker or glossy appearance. Sclerosis may also occur because of the accumulation of mucopolysaccharides in scleromyxedema or lichen myxedematosus or because of amyloid deposits. *Scleroderma* (Chapter 281) may be associated with Raynaud's syndrome, calcinosis, and telangiectasia. A localized form of scleroderma, termed *morphea,* may occur down the center of the face (coup de sabre), in plaques on the extremities (Fig. 476–25), after radiation, or with *Borrelia* infections. *Lichen sclerosis et atrophicus* is a superficial inflammatory morphea characterized by white atrophic patches, especially in the genital regions. Widespread systemic sclerosis may also follow bone marrow transplantation in the setting of chronic graft vs. host disease.

Telangiectasia, or prominence of skin blood vessels, frequently accompanies atrophic as well as sclerotic processes and is common in photoaged skin. Telangiectasia of the mucous membranes is found in the Osler-Weber-Rendu syndrome, and vascular spiders are found both in α_1-antitrypsinase deficiency and alcoholism. When telangiectasia and pigment changes (poikiloderma) are present in sun-shielded areas of the body, large plaque parapsoriasis or early mycosis fungoides should be suspected.

Ulcers are secondary skin lesions that may arise from trauma, loss of proper blood supply, aging, vasculitis, blister formation, infection, or underlying neoplasia. Ulcers may be shallow erosions (loss of the epidermis) or be deeper and involve the dermis and underlying subcutaneous structures. Ulcers most commonly appear on the lower extremities where they result from status dermatitis and venous insufficiency, arteriolar insufficiency, diabetic neuropathy, or vasculitis. For example, pyoderma gangrenosum is a trauma-induced ulcer that is part of the spectrum of Sweet's syndrome, accompanies other conditions, and may require immunosuppressive therapy. In contrast, decubitus ulcers require débridement, elimination of local pressure, and attention to nutrition (Chapter 23). In some cases, diagnosis may require skin biopsy, cultures, and serologic testing for other associated diseases.

After an inflammatory or ulcerated skin wound heals, scarring is common. Epidermal stem cells that reside in the bulge region of the hair follicle are capable of regenerating a normal epidermis. When a

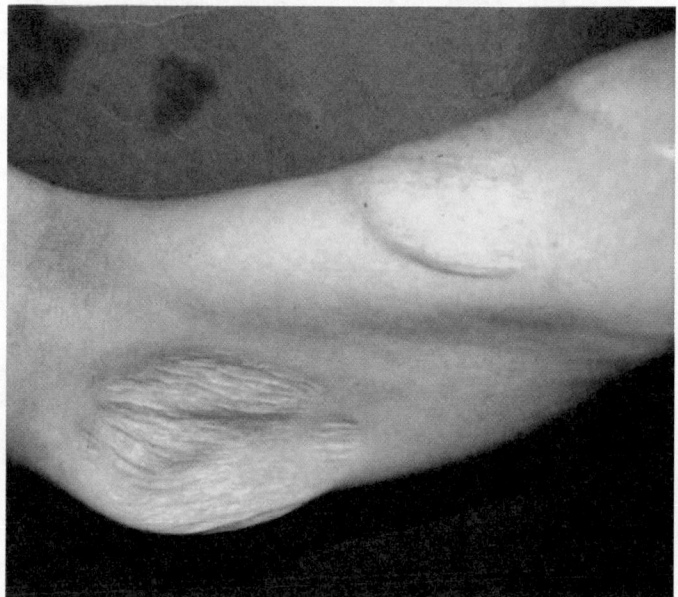

FIGURE 476–23 • Anetoderma.

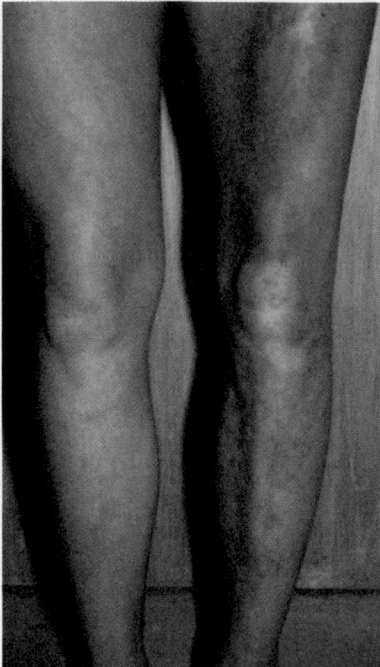

FIGURE 476–25 • Linear morphea.

wound is deeper than the bulge region, scarring and loss of hair are likely to occur. Scarring alopecias (lichen planopilaris, discoid lupus, scarring folliculitis) result in permanent baldness and must be distinguished from the less severe, nonscarring conditions such as telogen effluvium or alopecia areata. Scarring also accompanies the most severe epidermolysis bullosa disorders caused by sub–basement membrane defects in proteins. Scarring accompanies third-degree burns, deep cryotherapy, or other trauma to the dermis. Scarring also may follow severe inflammation (discoid lupus) or infection (syphilis, leprosy).

Some individuals have more pronounced and hypertrophic scar formation known as keloids, with an autosomal dominant inheritance pattern. Keloids are tumor-like in appearance and result from an overproduction of collagen. They are especially common on the anterior chest, neck, and earlobes and may require antineoplastic treatment after surgical removal.

SUGGESTED READINGS

Beltrani VS: An overview of chronic urticaria. Clin Rev Allergy Immunol 2002;23:147–169. *Evaluation and management of urticaria.*

Drago F, Rampini E, Rebora A: Atypical exanthems: Morphology and laboratory investigations may lead to an aetiological diagnosis in about 70% of cases. Br J Dermatol 2002;147:255–260. *Large series describing the patterns and causes of exanthems.*

Yawalkar N, Pichler WJ: Immunohistology of drug-induced exanthema: Clues to pathogenesis. Curr Opin Allergy Clin Immunol 2001;1:299–303. *Review of the pathogenesis of drug rashes.*

Yosipovitch G, Greaves MW, Schmelz M: Itch. Lancet 2003;361:690–694. *Overview of pathophysiology, diagnosis, and therapy.*

477 INFECTIONS, HYPER- AND HYPOPIGMENTATION, REGIONAL DERMATOLOGY, AND DISTINCTIVE LESIONS IN BLACK SKIN

Jean Bolognia

INFECTIONS INCLUDING CELLULITIS

Cutaneous infections can be divided into four major categories: bacterial, fungal (Chapter 474), viral, and parasitic (Table 477–1).

Table 477–1 • **SKIN INFECTIONS**

BACTERIAL DISEASES
Impetigo
Ecthyma
Folliculitis
Furuncle/carbuncle
Cellulitis
Necrotizing fasciitis
Ecthyma gangrenosum
Other
    Gram-negative cocci: meningococcemia, gonococcemia
    Gram-positive bacilli: erythrasma, anaerobic cellulitis
    Spirochetes: Lyme disease, syphilis, endemic treponematoses
    Mycobacteria

FUNGAL DISEASES
Candidiasis
Tinea (dermatophytoses): pedis, corporis, cruris
Pityriasis (tinea) versicolor
Emboli (e.g., *Aspergillus, Mucor*)

VIRAL DISEASES
Herpes simplex virus: oral, genital
Human papillomavirus: common warts, condyloma acuminatum
Pox virus: molluscum contagiosum
Varicella zoster virus
Viral exanthems (e.g., enteroviruses, rubeola, rubella, parvovirus)

ECTOPARASITES/PARASITES
Scabies
Lice: scalp, pubic, body
Leishmaniasis
Schistosomiasis
Onchocerciasis
Hookworm infections

Bacterial Infections

Of the bacterial infections, impetigo, folliculitis, furuncles, and cellulitis are most commonly encountered. *Impetigo,* which is caused by *Staphylococcus aureus* or group A β-hemolytic streptococci, usually presents as honey-colored crusts (Fig. 477–1); less often, subcorneal (superficial) bullae are seen. This infection is most commonly found on the face in children, but it can develop at any site where there has been a disruption of the cutaneous barrier (e.g., areas of dermatitis, sites of trauma, or arthropod bites). A deeper but less common bacterial infection of the skin is *ecthyma,* which is most frequently

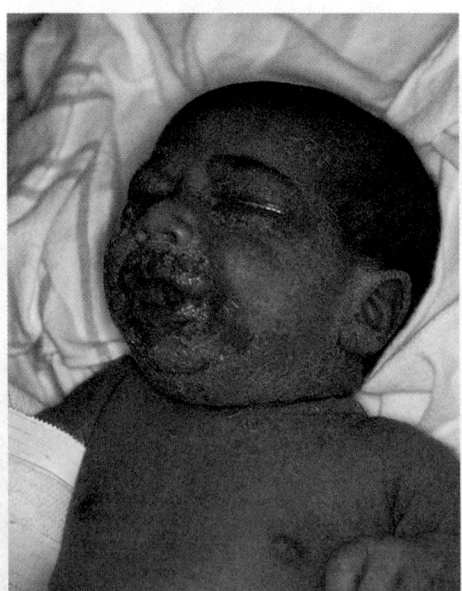

FIGURE 477–1 • Impetigo in an infant with marked involvement of the face with honey-colored crusts and superficial erosions. (Courtesy of Yale Dermatology Residents' Slide Collection.)

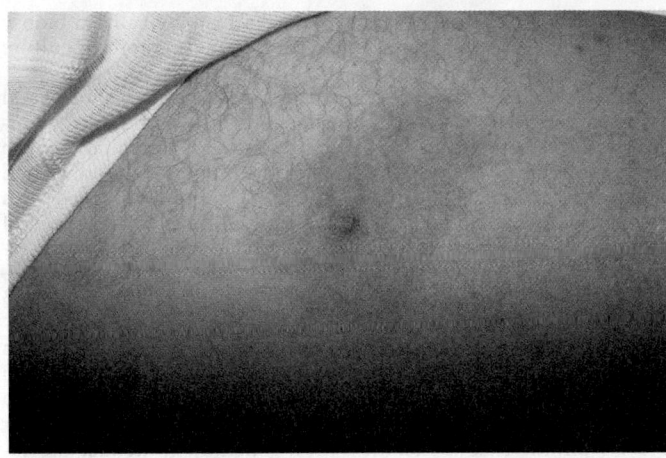

FIGURE 477-2 • Furuncle with surrounding cellulitis. (Courtesy of Yale Dermatology Residents' Slide Collection.)

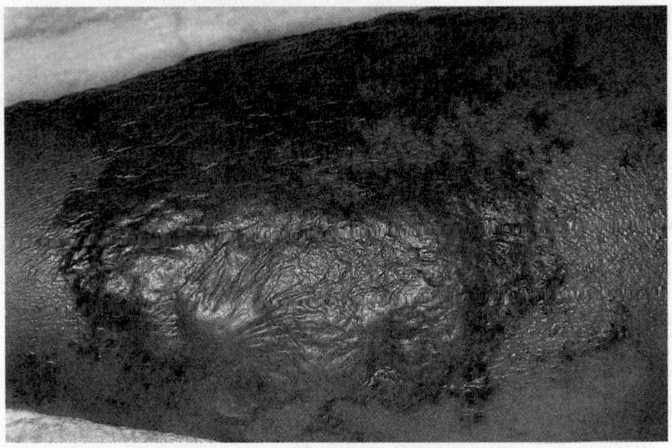

FIGURE 477-3 • Bullous and hemorrhagic cellulitis of the shin. (Courtesy of University of Southern California Dermatology Residents' Slide Collection.)

streptococcal in origin; it presents as thick hemorrhagic crusts overlying erosions or ulcerations, usually 0.5 to 1.5 cm in diameter. These lesions favor the extremities, especially in the setting of lymphedema. Ecthyma should not be confused with ecthyma gangrenosum, which represents an embolic phenomenon most often due to bacteremia with gram-negative bacilli. Although mild cases of impetigo usually respond to topical mupirocin, oral antibiotics that cover *S. aureus* (e.g., dicloxacillin, 250 mg orally four times a day, or cephalexin, 250 mg orally four times a day) are needed to treat severe impetigo and ecthyma.

The initial lesions of *folliculitis* are perifollicular pustules that are often surrounded by a rim of erythema (Chapter 475). *Pseudomonas* folliculitis is usually associated with the use of hot tubs or whirlpools because their higher temperatures (as compared with that of a swimming pool) make the eradication of *Pseudomonas* more difficult (see Fig. 475-20).

Furuncles, also called boils, represent *S. aureus* cutaneous infection that is localized primarily within the dermis. In contrast to folliculitis, the lesions are larger and present as erythematous tender nodules (Fig. 477-2). A central follicular structure may be noted, as well as a central pustule ("pointing"). Because a furuncle is an abscess, the preferred treatment is incision and drainage followed by oral antistaphylococcal antibiotics (e.g., dicloxacillin, 250 mg orally four times a day, or cephalexin, 250 mg orally four times a day). *Carbuncles* are larger, more complex, and more extensive versions of furuncles; they may be accompanied by systemic symptoms such as fever.

Cellulitis is a fairly common cutaneous infection that is more likely to occur on the lower extremities. Locally, it presents as erythema, edema, warmth, and tenderness; systemic manifestations can include fever, malaise, and leukocytosis. The vast majority of cases are bacterial, but some cases are caused by fungal infections (e.g., *Cryptococcus*) or chemical reactions (e.g., extravasated oxacillin or daunorubicin). Bacterial cellulitis is most commonly caused by group A β-hemolytic streptococci and *S. aureus*, with the former associated with the more severe, necrotizing variant. In patients who have diabetes or who are immunocompromised, cellulitis can be caused by gram-negative bacilli or atypical mycobacteria. Risk factors include a preceding break in the skin barrier, edema due to venous hypertension, lymphedema, and previous bouts of cellulitis.

Although the diagnosis of cellulitis is usually fairly straightforward (Fig. 477-3), it can sometimes be difficult in patients with chronic lower extremity edema, especially in those who are afebrile. One complication of chronic lower extremity edema is lipodermatosclerosis (i.e., inflammation followed by fibrosis of the subcutaneous fat), which presents acutely as erythema, warmth, and tenderness and which is easily confused with cellulitis. The skin above the medial malleolus is often the initial site of involvement with lipodermatosclerosis, but the inflammation (of the lower dermis and subcutaneous fat) can be more extensive. The chronic phase of lipodermatosclerosis is characterized by induration, a permanent brown-red to violet discoloration of the skin, and an "inverted wine bottle" appearance to the distal lower extremity. It is important for the clinician to realize that in patients with chronic lipodermatosclerosis and superimposed cellulitis,

the skin will never return to its normal color, even after adequate antibiotic therapy.

Unless there is an associated bacteremia, the diagnosis of cellulitis is primarily clinical. In immunocompromised hosts, a saline injection followed by aspiration and culture can be helpful. Histologically, cellulitis is characterized by an infiltrate of neutrophils within the dermis. A skin biopsy can exclude causes of pseudocellulitis such as Well's syndrome, which is an idiopathic disorder in which eosinophils infiltrate the dermis, and lipodermatosclerosis.

Cellulitis resides in the middle of a spectrum of soft tissue infections that includes *erysipelas* (more superficial and more sharply demarcated; Fig. 477-4) at one end and *necrotizing fasciitis* (deeper, more necrotic, and undermining) at the other. Necrotizing fasciitis is usually caused by multiple organisms, including anaerobic streptococci, and the diagnosis requires a high index of suspicion, in particular when areas of violaceous induration or foul-smelling discharge are present. Prompt surgical débridement and broad-spectrum systemic antibiotics (e.g., a β-lactam/β-lactamase inhibitor, such as piperacillin/tazobactam, with or without ciprofloxacin, for at least 2 weeks) are mandatory.

Eruptions that are caused by the release of toxins produced by *S. aureus* and streptococci include *staphylococcal scalded skin syndrome* (Chapters 311 and 475), scarlet fever (Chapter 475), and toxic shock syndrome (Chapter 475). Staphylococcal scalded skin syndrome (see Fig. 475-13) is characterized by large areas of tender erythema that develop superficial desquamation (peeling), often with scaling and crusting in a radial array around the mouth. The areas of erythema are sterile; the conjunctivae, nasopharynx, or a distant site on the skin are common sites of the primary infection. A clue to the diagnosis of scarlet fever is the presence of a strawberry tongue with prominent red papillae.

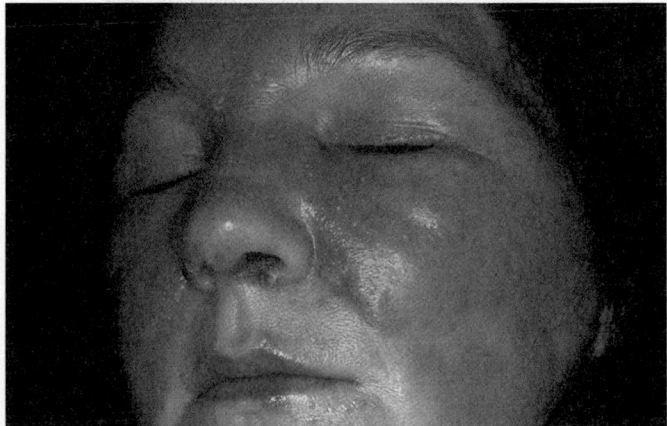

FIGURE 477-4 • Erysipelas of the face with well-demarcated erythematous plaques. (Courtesy of Yale Dermatology Residents' Slide Collection.)

Skin Diseases

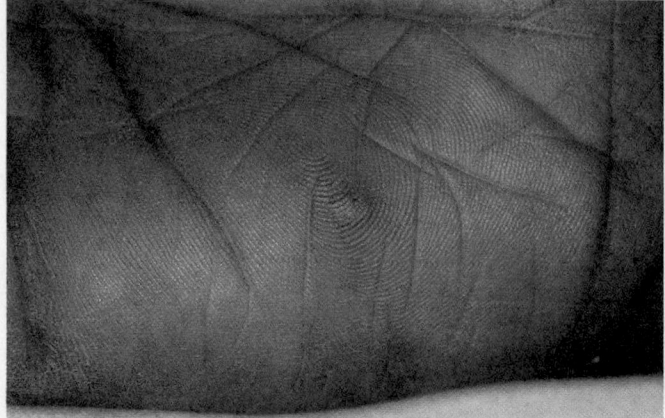

FIGURE 477–5 • Disseminated gonococcal infection with an acral pustule on a red-violet base. (Courtesy of Yale Dermatology Residents' Slide Collection.)

Both *gonococcemia* (Chapter 346) and meningococcemia (Chapter 313) can present as cutaneous lesions. The former gives rise to a small number of vesicopustules on an erythematous base, usually acral in location (Fig. 477–5); these lesions represent septic emboli and are accompanied by fever, arthritis, and tendonitis. The earliest lesions of *acute meningococcemia* may be subtle (macular areas of erythema), but central hemorrhage (petechiae and purpura) and necrosis (gun metal gray color) soon follow (Fig. 477–6). The lesions may become quite extensive; when accompanied by disseminated intravascular coagulation, severe peripheral ischemia may result. Cutaneous involvement in *chronic meningococcemia* is a reflection of lymphocytic or leukocytoclastic vasculitis rather than septic emboli.

Pseudomonas infections of the skin vary from "hot tub" folliculitis (Chapter 475) to soft tissue infections of the external ear. Interdigital toe web infections that begin as simple tinea pedis can be complicated by superimposed *Pseudomonas* infection with erythema, swelling, tenderness, and drainage.

In immunocompromised hosts, *Pseudomonas* and other gram-negative bacilli can produce cellulitis as well as secondary septic emboli in the skin. The latter begin as purpura or purpuric bullae that then develop central necrosis. These lesions, which arise as a result of an ischemic infarction of the skin, are termed *ecthyma gangrenosum*. Septic emboli due to *Candida* or other opportunistic fungi such as *Aspergillus* or *Fusarium* often have a similar clinical appearance.

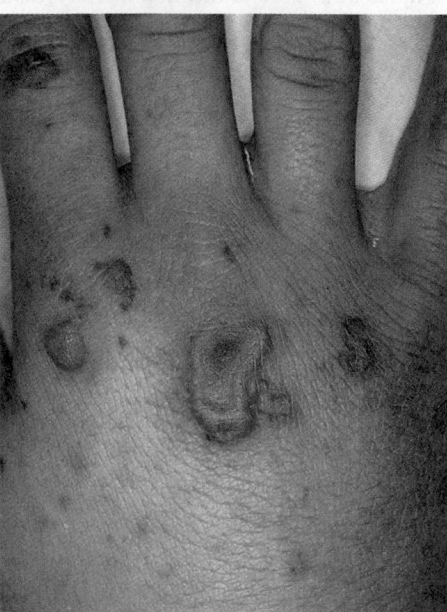

FIGURE 477–6 • Purpuric and necrotic embolic lesions of meningococcemia. (Courtesy of Yale Dermatology Residents' Slide Collection.)

The responsible organisms can be detected histologically in biopsy specimens or via bedside examination of dermal scrapings; culture confirms the specific organism.

Although *Clostridium perfringens* can cause anaerobic cellulitis and gas gangrene, the most common cutaneous infection due to gram-positive bacilli is *erythrasma*, which presents as interdigital toe web maceration with fissures, as well as with shiny or scaly brown-red patches in the axillae and groin. The latter is often confused with tinea cruris (Chapter 474). A diagnostic finding is the presence of coral (orange-pink) fluorescence with Wood's lamp illumination (ultraviolet A). The responsible organism is *Corynebacterium minutissimum*. Treatment options include topical and oral erythromycin (e.g., 333 mg three times a day orally for 7 to 14 days).

Spirochetal infections present as a wide range of skin findings from erythema migrans secondary to *Borrelia burgdorferi* (Chapter 352) to endemic treponematoses such as *yaws* and *pinta* (Chapter 350), to the cutaneous manifestations of the three stages of *syphilis* (Chapter 349). Syphilitic lesions include a firm, generally nontender ulceration (chancre) in primary syphilis; a generalized papulosquamous eruption (Chapter 475) plus alopecia, oral ulcers, and condylomata lata in secondary syphilis; and thick plaques and ulcers in tertiary disease.

Both typical and atypical mycobacterial infections are associated with skin lesions such as verrucous papules, scarring granulomatous plaques, and draining ulcers. In immunocompetent hosts in developed countries, *Mycobacterium marinum* (Chapter 342) is most commonly associated with skin disease.

Viral Infections

The most common viral infections of the skin are verrucae (warts; see Fig. 475–2 and Chapters 475 and 476), recurrent oral and genital herpes simplex (Chapters 345, 369, and 475), molluscum contagiosum (see Fig. 476–8 and Chapters 417, 475, and 476), and exanthems (Chapter 475). Varicella and herpes zoster are seen less frequently (Chapter 367).

Fungal Infections

A variety of fungal infections involve the skin and nails and are most commonly due to dermatophytes (tinea), *Candida* species, and *Pityrosporum* (pityriasis versicolor) (Chapter 474 and Table 477–1). Although both dermatophyte infections and pityriasis versicolor are associated with scaling, cutaneous candidiasis is characterized by erythema, a more erosive quality, and satellite pustules.

Ectoparasites and Parasites

The most common ectoparasitic cutaneous infestations are (1) scabies due to the human variant of the *Sarcoptes* mite and (2) lice, of which there are three subtypes: head, body, and pubic. *Scabies* presents as pruritus in association with papules, papulovesicles, and linear burrows, as well as signs of scratching, such as excoriations and areas of dermatitis. Sites of predilection include the wrists, ankles, fingers, toes (including the web spaces), areolae, and genitalia (especially the penis). The number of mites living within the stratum corneum is limited in immunocompetent hosts; when scraped and examined microscopically, linear burrows provide the highest yield of mites and eggs. In elderly and immunosuppressed patients, a form of scabies known as crusted or Norwegian scabies presents as multiple areas of scaling and crusting that are teeming with mites.

Infestations with scalp *lice* are seen most commonly in children, who may be asymptomatic or have marked pruritus. In addition to the lice, multiple egg casings ("nits") are attached to the proximal portions of the scalp hairs. In developed countries, body lice are seen primarily in homeless individuals; patients typically present with multiple erythematous papules at the sites of "bites" as well as signs of scratching. The lice and their eggs are found in the patient's clothing. Pubic lice are sometimes called "crabs" because their bodies are shorter and broader than those of scalp or body lice and thus resemble the shape of a crab. As a result of their leg span, these lice reside on pubic hairs and less often on axillary hairs or eyelashes.

Among parasitic infections, cutaneous lesions are seen in leishmaniasis (Chapter 395), schistosomiasis (Chapter 402), onchocerciasis (Chapter 405), and hookworm infections (Chapter 404). *Schistosomiasis* due to exposure to cercarial-infested water results in

Chapter 477 Infections, Hyper- and Hypopigmentation, Regional Dermatology, and Distinctive Lesions in Black Skin | **2489**

Skin Diseases

multiple erythematous papules, most commonly on the feet; it is commonly called "swimmer's itch." Hookworm infections lead to *cutaneous larva migrans,* with serpiginous erythematous tracks that correspond to the path of migration of the hookworm larvae. Both of these infections are self-limited because the parasite's life cycle cannot be completed. In immunocompromised hosts, cutaneous plaques occasionally can develop from *Pneumocystis carinii* infection (Chapter 387), particularly on the external ear.

DISORDERS OF HYPOPIGMENTATION AND HYPERPIGMENTATION

The disorders of pigmentation can be divided into four major categories: diffuse, linear, circumscribed, and either reticulated (in the case of hyperpigmentation) or guttate (in the case of hypopigmentation) (Table 477–2).

Hypopigmentation

The primary disorder of diffuse hypopigmentation is *oculocutaneous albinism,* an autosomal recessive disorder in which there is a

---

Table 477–2 • DISORDERS OF PIGMENTATION

HYPOPIGMENTATION
Diffuse (Pigmentary Dilution)
Oculocutaneous albinism
Generalized (total) vitiligo
Inborn errors of metabolism (e.g., phenylketonuria)

Circumscribed
Decrease in pigment
  Acquired: postinflammatory hypopigmentation (e.g., atopic
    dermatitis, sarcoidosis, lupus erythematosus, mycosis fungoides),
    pityriasis (tinea) versicolor
  Congenital: nevus depigmentosus, ash-leaf spots of tuberous sclerosis
Absence of pigment
  Acquired: vitiligo, chemical leukoderma, leukoderma of scleroderma,
    leukoderma of melanoma
  Congenital: piebaldism

Linear
Nevoid hypopigmentation (e.g., hypomelanosis of Ito)

Guttate
Idiopathic guttate hypomelanosis
Confetti macules of tuberous sclerosis

HYPERPIGMENTATION
Diffuse
Drug reactions (e.g., cyclophosphamide, zidovudine)
Addison's disease
Ectopic ACTH production (e.g., small cell lung cancer)
Hemochromatosis
Scleroderma
Primary biliary cirrhosis
Hyperthyroidism
Vitamin B_{12} or folate deficiency
Porphyria cutanea tarda
Argyria

Circumscribed
Postinflammatory hyperpigmentation (e.g., acne vulgaris, arthropod
  bites, dermatitis, lichen planus)
Melasma
Pityriasis (tinea) versicolor
Mastocytosis
Fixed drug reactions
Deposits of drugs and their metabolites

Linear
Exposure to psoralen-containing plants (e.g., limes) plus ultraviolet A
  light
Drug reactions (e.g., bleomycin)
Nevoid hyperpigmentation
Genodermatoses (e.g., incontinentia pigmenti)

Reticulated
Erythema ab igne
Genodermatoses

---

pigmentary dilution of melanin-containing structures (i.e., the eyes, hair, and skin). The phenotype varies from a total absence of melanin pigment to a subtle decrease whose recognition requires comparison with first-degree relatives; the density of melanocytes in the skin is normal, but their ability to produce pigment is absent or decreased. Ninety percent of patients with oculocutaneous albinism have mutations in the genes that encode either tyrosinase (type I) or the P protein (type II). Complications of oculocutaneous albinism include decreased visual acuity, nystagmus, photophobia, and an increase in cutaneous carcinomas, especially squamous cell carcinomas. These signs and symptoms are most severe in those who produce the least pigment. The differential diagnosis includes total vitiligo (absence of melanocytes histologically) and a few inborn errors of metabolism (e.g., phenylketonuria). Treatment consists of longitudinal ophthalmologic care and minimizing sun exposure.

Disorders of *linear hypopigmentation* consist primarily of nevoid conditions (e.g., hypomelanosis of Ito, systematized nevus depigmentosus) in which streaks of hypomelanosis follow Blaschko's lines (an embryonic development pattern that involves all layers of the skin and becomes clinically apparent in the setting of mosaicism). Some patients have associated central nervous system and musculoskeletal abnormalities.

Circumscribed hypomelanosis is seen is pityriasis (tinea) versicolor (see Fig. 474–16) and *postinflammatory hypopigmentation.* Although postinflammatory hypopigmentation is most often associated with atopic dermatitis, it can also occur with sarcoidosis, lupus erythematosus, and mycosis fungoides. *Vitiligo* (Fig. 477–7) is usually slowly progressive and occurs principally in periorificial areas (around the eyes, nose, lips, genitalia), the hands, feet, flexor wrists, ankles, elbows, knees, and major body folds. Vitiligo, which is caused by a loss of melanocytes within the skin, is also associated with autoimmune endocrinopathies (Chapter 240) and alopecia areata (see later). Treatment includes topical corticosteroids and phototherapy. The differential diagnosis is primarily chemical leukoderma due to compounds that are cytotoxic to melanocytes (e.g., catechols), the leukoderma of melanoma (often metastatic), and the leukoderma of scleroderma with retention of perifollicular pigmentation. Congenital circumscribed areas of hypomelanosis include *nevus depigmentosus,* a common tan "birthmark" seen in 1 in 50 infants with a partial decrease in pigment; *piebaldism,* an unusual autosomal dominant disorder due to mutations in the *KIT* gene, with areas of complete absence of pigment; *nevus anemicus,* a localized area of vasoconstriction; and the *ash-leaf spots* of tuberous sclerosis (Chapter 459) with a partial decrease in pigment.

Idiopathic guttate hypomelanosis, in which well-demarcated hypopigmented macules measure only 2 to 4 mm in diameter, is the most common cause of guttate ("raindrop") leukoderma (Fig. 477–8). The favored sites for this common age-related disorder, which may be related to chronic sun exposure, are the shins and the extensor forearms.

Hyperpigmentation

Diffuse hyperpigmentation is most commonly due to drugs (e.g., amiodarone, cyclophosphamide, zidovudine) and endocrinopathies

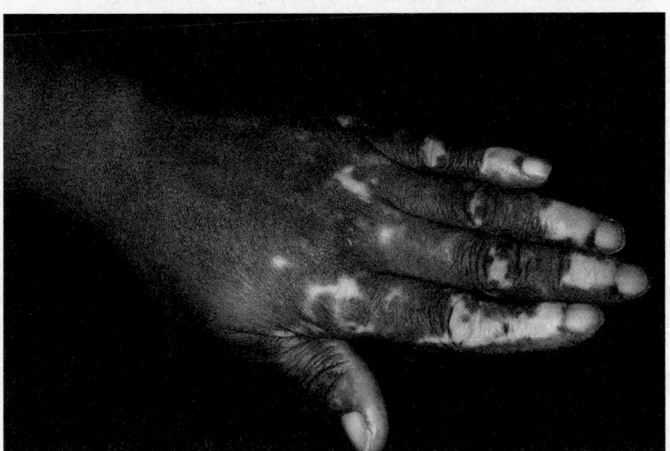

FIGURE 477–7 • Striking leukoderma of the hand in a patient with vitiligo.

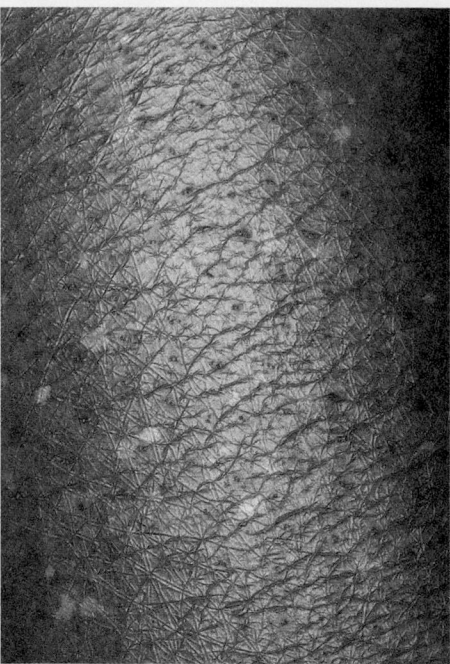

FIGURE 477–8 • Idiopathic guttate hypomelanosis with small, well-demarcated macules on the shin.

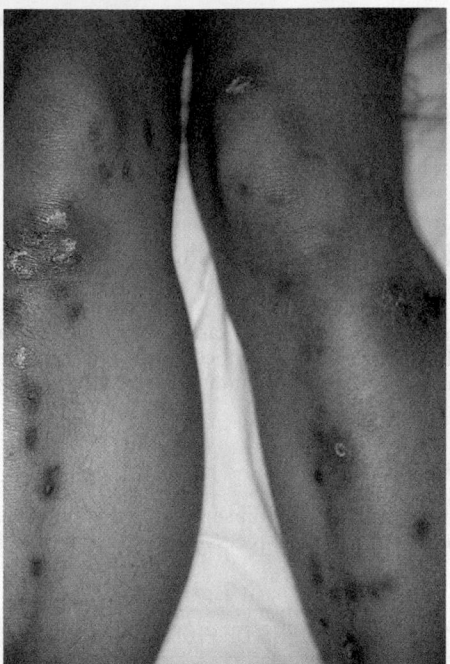

FIGURE 477–9 • Postinflammatory hyperpigmentation secondary to arthropod bites. (Courtesy of Yale Dermatology Residents' Slide Collection.)

associated with increased circulating levels of ACTH (e.g., Addison's disease [Chapter 240], ectopic ACTH production due to tumors such as small cell lung carcinoma [Chapter 187]). ACTH as well as melanocyte-stimulating hormone (MSH) can bind and activate the melanocortin-1 receptors on melanocytes, leading to increased melanin production. Additional causes include hemochromatosis (Chapter 225), argyria, scleroderma (Chapter 281), primary biliary cirrhosis (Chapter 156), and hyperthyroidism (Chapter 239).

Linear streaks of hyperpigmentation can be due to nevoid (i.e., hamartomatous) conditions that reflect cutaneous mosaicism, as in linear hypopigmentation (see earlier) and genodermatoses (inherited disorders with cutaneous manifestations, e.g., incontinentia pigmenti due to mutations in the gene *NEMO*) as well as exposure to either plant-derived psoralens (e.g., from limes) plus ultraviolet A irradiation or systemic bleomycin (flagellate pigmentation). Reticulated hypermelanosis is also seen in several genodermatoses (e.g., dyskeratosis congenita) and after chronic exposure to heat (erythema ab igne). The latter corresponds to the cutaneous venous plexus and is seen most commonly in the lumbosacral region where heating pads have been applied.

The most common causes of circumscribed hypermelanosis are tinea versicolor (which can present as both hypo- and hyperpigmentation, hence its name), postinflammatory hyperpigmentation, and melasma. *Postinflammatory hyperpigmentation* (Fig. 477–9) is observed more frequently in darkly pigmented individuals and often follows acne vulgaris, arthropod bites, chronic dermatitis, and lichen planus. Additional causes of circumscribed darkening of the skin are cutaneous mastocytosis (urticaria pigmentosa), deposits of drugs such as antimalarials and minocycline (blue-gray discoloration), and medications that produce fixed drug reactions, most frequently trimethoprim-sulfamethoxazole and nonsteroidal anti-inflammatory drugs. In *melasma* (Fig. 477–10), symmetrical hyperpigmented patches are seen on the lateral forehead, upper cheek, and mandibular area. At least 90% of patients with melasma are women. The lesions are exacerbated by UV light and estrogen (oral contraceptives, pregnancy). Melasma is treated with lightening agents such as hydroquinone and retinoic acid.

REGIONAL DERMATOSES

Several common dermatoses have a predilection for particular anatomic sites (Fig. 477–11 and Table 477–3). A classic example is the preference of plaques of psoriasis for the extensor surfaces (e.g.,

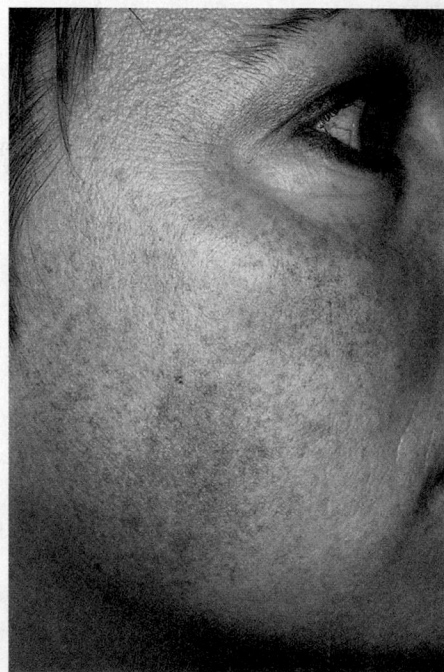

FIGURE 477–10 • Hyperpigmented patches on the cheek in a patient with melasma.

elbows and knees), in contrast to atopic dermatitis, which favors the antecubital and popliteal fossae.

Nails

Abnormalities of the nail apparatus are most commonly the result of infections or cutaneous inflammatory diseases (Table 477–4). Infections are primarily caused by dermatophytes or *Candida* species. In tinea unguium (Chapter 474), there is yellow-brown discoloration and thickening of the nail plate as well as subungual debris. Infections with *Candida* species lead either to chronic paronychia with loss of

Chapter 477 Infections, Hyper- and Hypopigmentation, Regional Dermatology, and Distinctive Lesions in Black Skin | **2491**

Skin Diseases

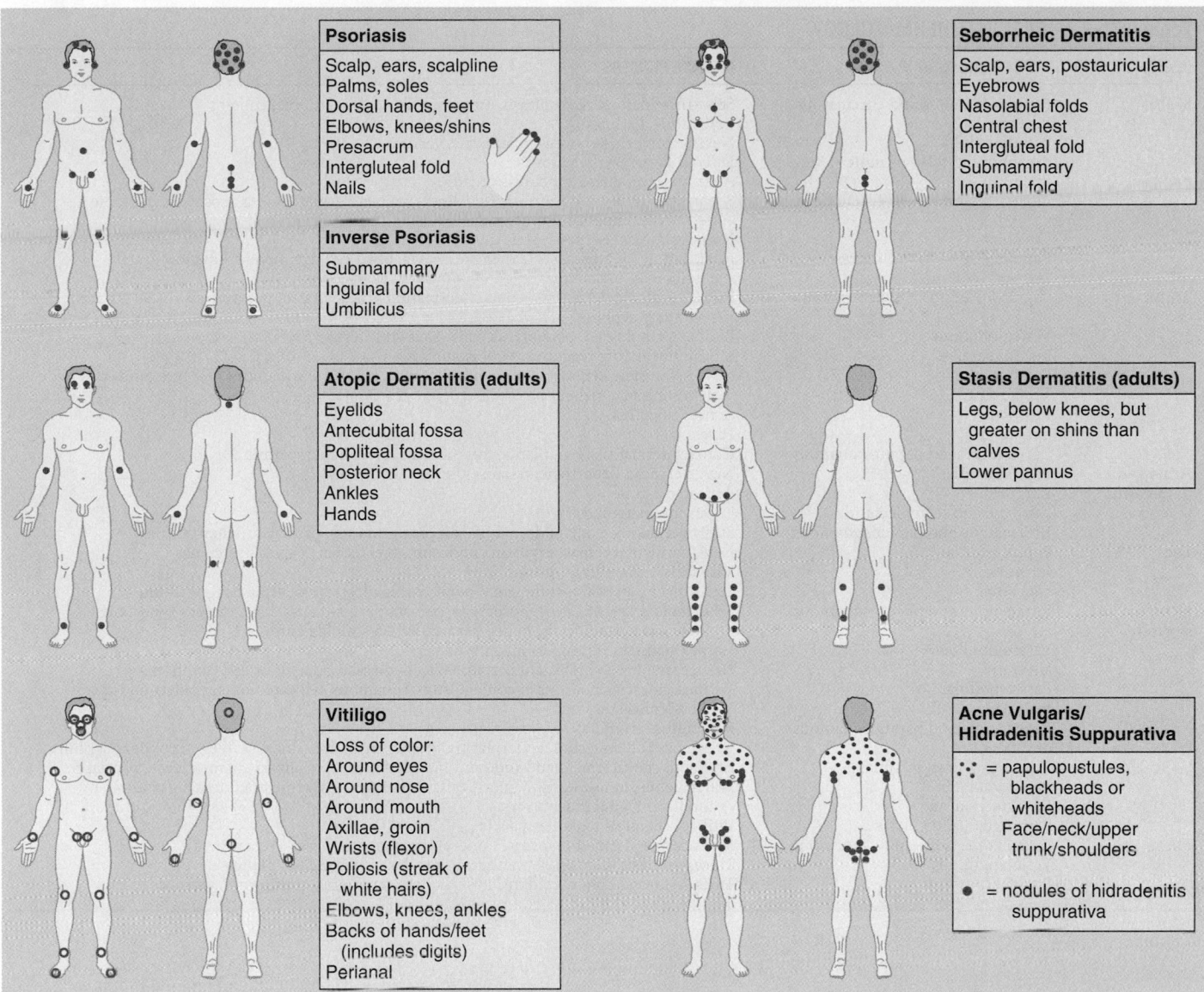

Psoriasis

Scalp, ears, scalpline
Palms, soles
Dorsal hands, feet
Elbows, knees/shins
Presacrum
Intergluteal fold
Nails

Inverse Psoriasis

Submammary
Inguinal fold
Umbilicus

Atopic Dermatitis (adults)

Eyelids
Antecubital fossa
Popliteal fossa
Posterior neck
Ankles
Hands

Vitiligo

Loss of color:
Around eyes
Around nose
Around mouth
Axillae, groin
Wrists (flexor)
Poliosis (streak of
 white hairs)
Elbows, knees, ankles
Backs of hands/feet
 (includes digits)
Perianal

Seborrheic Dermatitis

Scalp, ears, postauricular
Eyebrows
Nasolabial folds
Central chest
Intergluteal fold
Submammary
Inguinal fold

Stasis Dermatitis (adults)

Legs, below knees, but
 greater on shins than
 calves
Lower pannus

**Acne Vulgaris/
Hidradenitis Suppurativa**

∴∵ = papulopustules,
 blackheads or
 whiteheads
 Face/neck/upper
 trunk/shoulders

● = nodules of hidradenitis
 suppurativa

FIGURE 477–11 • Regional involvement with specific skin diseases.

the cuticle and swelling and slight erythema of the proximal periungual region, which may lead to ridging of the nail plate, or to onycholysis, which is lifting of the distal nail plate from the nail bed. Onycholysis is usually related to chronic exposure to water and irritants; it may be complicated by *Pseudomonas* colonization, which leads to a green discoloration of the nail.

The major inflammatory disorder that causes nail changes is *psoriasis* (Chapter 474), which can lead to onycholysis, subungual debris, and localized areas of yellow-brown discoloration (oil-drop changes). The characteristic pitting of the nails (see Fig. 474–9) is caused by involvement of the distal nail matrix (the matrix is the site of proliferation), leading to circumscribed collections of incompletely differentiated cells on the surface of the "dead" nail plate; subsequent sloughing of these cells leads to the pits. Nail pits are also seen in alopecia areata, where their configuration is gridlike rather than random. Additional cutaneous disorders with dystrophy of the nail plate include lichen planus (longitudinal ridging, roughness, and atrophy) and atopic or contact dermatitis (horizontal ridging).

Occasionally, nail abnormalities can be the initial presentation of a systemic disease. Examples are clubbing in the setting of lung cancer or hypertrophic pulmonary osteoarthropathy (Chapters 188 and 198), yellow nails that grow quite slowly in patients with bronchiectasis and pleural effusions (yellow nail syndrome; Chapters 85 and 87), onycholysis as a sign of hyperthyroidism (Chapter 239), and linear "splinter" hemorrhages in the nail bed due to bacterial endocarditis (Chapter 310). Leukonychia is a white discoloration of the nail seen in the setting

of cirrhosis (>90% of the nail; Chapter 156) or chronic renal failure (50% of the nail; Chapter 117). Spooning (concave curvature of the nail plate) can occur in patients with iron deficiency (Chapter 167).

A nail change that can "date" past serious illnesses is *Beau's lines*, which are horizontal depressions in the nail plate. High fevers and severe illnesses can lead to a decrease in the proliferative rate of the nail matrix, with resulting thinning of the nail, akin to what happens with the hair shaft in anagen effluvium secondary to systemic chemotherapy. Because the nail grows at a fairly constant rate (0.5 to 1.2 mm per week for fingernails and one half to one third that rate for toenails), a ridge that is in the midportion of all the fingernails reflects an insult 2.5 to 3 months prior. It is also important to examine the periungual region for *cuticular telangiectasias*, which are seen in dermatomyositis (Chapter 283), systemic lupus erythematosus (Chapter 280), scleroderma (Chapter 281), and hereditary hemorrhagic telangiectasia (Chapter 177).

Hair

ALOPECIA

In the clinical examination of the patient with alopecia, the initial step is to determine the distribution: diffuse, patterned, or circumscribed. The major cause of diffuse alopecia is *telogen effluvium*, which is characterized by increased shedding with resultant diffuse thinning of the scalp hair (Table 477–5). Telogen effluvium is reversible

2492 | **Chapter 477** Infections, Hyper- and Hypopigmentation, Regional Dermatology, and Distinctive Lesions in Black Skin

Skin Diseases

Table 477–3 • REGIONAL DERMATOLOGY

REGION OF SKIN	TYPE OF SKIN GROUP	DISEASE PROCESS
Scalp	Papulosquamous and eczematous	Seborrheic dermatitis, psoriasis, tinea capitis, eczema (atopic, contact)
	Pustular	Folliculitis, kerion
	Papulonodular	Nevi, seborrheic keratoses, pilar cysts, verrucae
	Atrophic and telangiectatic	Discoid lupus erythematosus
Face	Pustular	Acne, rosacea, tinea, folliculitis (beard)
	Papulosquamous and eczematous	Seborrheic dermatitis, psoriasis (hairline), contact dermatitis (e.g., cosmetics), atopic dermatitis, impetigo, lupus erythematosus, photodermatitis
	Vesicular	Herpes simplex, herpes zoster
	Papulonodular	Nevi, actinic keratoses, seborrheic keratoses, basal cell carcinomas, squamous cell carcinomas, melanomas
Trunk	Papulosquamous and eczematous	Psoriasis, atopic dermatitis, contact dermatitis, tinea versicolor, pityriasis rosea, scabies, secondary syphilis
	Vesiculobullous	Bullous pemphigoid, pemphigus, erythema multiforme
	Maculopapular	Morbilliform drug reactions, viral exanthems
	Papulonodular	Nevi, seborrheic keratoses, angiomas, lipomas, basal and squamous cell carcinomas, keloid, neurofibroma, melanoma
	Pustular	Acne, folliculitis
	Urticarial	Hives
	Eczematous and papulosquamous	Contact dermatitis (e.g., plants), atopic dermatitis, lichen planus
Arms and forearms	Papulonodular	Nevi, verrucae, seborrheic keratoses, actinic keratoses
	Purpuric	Actinic purpura
	Atrophic and telangiectatic	Lupus, dermatomyositis
	Eczematous and papulosquamous	Stasis dermatitis, contact dermatitis, atopic dermatitis, psoriasis, lichen planus
Legs	Papulonodular	Nevi, dermatofibromas, erythema nodosum, melanoma, Kaposi's sarcoma
	Purpuric	Vasculitis, Schamberg's disease
	Ulcerative	Stasis ulcers, arterial insufficiency, neuropathic ulcers, pyoderma gangrenosum
Genitalia and groin	Eczematous and papulosquamous	Seborrheic dermatitis, tinea, psoriasis, contact dermatitis, scabies, Reiter's syndrome, erythrasma, candidiasis, lichen planus, lichen simplex chronicus
	Vesiculobullous	Herpes simplex, Stevens-Johnson syndrome
	Ulcerative	Herpes simplex, syphilis, chancroid, Behçet's disease, squamous cell carcinoma
	Papulonodular	Verruca vulgaris, molluscum contagiosum, squamous cell carcinoma, epidermoid cyst, hidradenitis suppurativa
	Pustular	Folliculitis, candidiasis
Hands	Eczematous and papulosquamous	Irritant and allergic contact dermatitis, atopic dermatitis, tinea, scabies, secondary syphilis
	Vesiculobullous, pustular	Erythema multiforme, hand-foot-and-mouth disease, porphyria cutanea tarda, psoriasis
	Papulonodular	Warts, actinic keratoses, squamous cell carcinomas, pyogenic granuloma, granuloma annulare, digital mucous cysts
	Depigmentation	Vitiligo, chemical leukoderma
	Periungual telangiectasias	Scleroderma, dermatomyositis, lupus erythematosus, Osler-Weber-Rendu
Feet	Eczematous and papulosquamous	Tinea, psoriasis, contact dermatitis, atopic dermatitis, lichen planus
	Vesiculobullous	Tinea, arthropod bites, epidermolysis bullosa, erythema multiforme, verrucae, corn
	Papules	

Table 477–4 • NAIL DISEASES

INFLAMMATORY DISORDERS
Psoriasis, Reiter's disease
Dermatitis (including atopic, contact)
Lichen planus
Alopecia areata

INFECTIOUS DISEASES
Dermatophytes
Candida spp.

POSSIBLE SIGNS OF SYSTEMIC DISEASE
Splinter hemorrhages: bacterial endocarditis or vasculitis, but trauma is most common cause
Transverse depressions in the nail plate (Beau's lines): chemotherapy, stressful event (e.g., high fever, severe illness)
Onycholysis: hyperthyroidism or porphyria, but psoriasis and chronic contact with irritants or water are more common causes
Clubbing: congenital heart disease, hypertrophic pulmonary osteoarthropathy, lung cancer
Spooning (koilonychia): iron deficiency
White transverse bands: chronic hypoalbuminemia* or arsenic exposure,† but trauma is the most common cause
Diffuse white discoloration (leukonychia): >90%—cirrhosis; 50%—chronic renal failure
Yellow and slow growing: yellow nail syndrome

*Disappear with pressure to the nail bed.
†Do not disappear with pressure to the nail bed.

and is caused by enhanced synchronization of the hair cycle so that more than the usual number of hairs are in telogen at one time (Chapter 471). The precipitating event often has occurred 2 to 3 months before the onset of shedding.

Drugs that can lead to diffuse alopecia include lithium, warfarin, β-blockers, retinoids, and interferon. In patients with diffuse alopecia, it is important to exclude hyperthyroidism, hypothyroidism, and iron deficiency and to review carefully all medications, including over-the-counter, "natural," and illicit agents (e.g., amphetamines). Occasionally, systemic lupus erythematosus and genodermatoses can present as diffuse alopecia. Anagen effluvium (see earlier) is usually readily distinguished by the history of recent chemotherapy.

The most common form of patterned alopecia, also know as male pattern or female pattern alopecia, is *androgenetic* alopecia. In the male pattern, there is midline accentuation, with recession of the frontal scalp line. The alopecia is the result of gradual miniaturization of the individual hair follicles/hair shafts due to the effects of dihydrotestosterone. Increased "end-organ sensitivity" is the usual explanation for androgenetic alopecia, but it can also be a reflection of hyperandrogenism (Chapter 247). Because hair follicles are not completely lost, the process is theoretically reversible. The follicles within a U-shaped band on the lower scalp do not miniaturize (despite exposure to dihydrotestosterone) and therefore serve as a reservoir for hair transplantation. Androgenetic alopecia can first become apparent when there is a superimposed telogen effluvium. The differential diagnosis includes traction alopecia due to hairstyles that chronically pull on the hairs. Topical minoxidil and oral finasteride are therapeutic options.

Circumscribed nonscarring alopecia can be a manifestation of *alopecia areata*, which is an autoimmune process in which T lymphocytes

Skin Diseases

Table 477–5 • CAUSES OF ALOPECIA AND HIRSUTISM

ALOPECIA
Nonscarring
Primary cutaneous disorders
  Androgenetic alopecia (male pattern and female pattern)
  Telogen effluvium
  Traumatic alopecia
  Alopecia areata
  Tinea capitis
  Trichotillomania
Drugs (e.g., lithium, warfarin, β-blockers, retinoids, interferon)
Systemic diseases
  Hyperthyroidism
  Hypothyroidism
  Deficiencies of protein, iron, biotin, and zinc
  HIV infection
  Systemic lupus erythematosus
  Secondary syphilis
  Hypopituitarism

Scarring
Primary cutaneous disorders
  Lichen planus
  Discoid lupus erythematosus
  Folliculitis decalvans
  Traumatic alopecia*
  Linear scleroderma (morphea)
Systemic diseases
  Systemic lupus erythematosus with cutaneous involvement
  Sarcoidosis
  Cutaneous metastases

HIRSUTISM
End organ sensitivity (i.e., constitutional)
Hyperandrogenemia
  Adrenal
    Congenital adrenal hyperplasia
    Adenoma or carcinoma
    ↑ ACTH (e.g., Cushing's disease, ectopic production)
  Ovarian
    Polycystic ovary syndrome
    Hyperthecosis
    Tumors
  Pituitary
    Hyperprolactinemia
  Drugs (e.g., anabolic steroids)

*Also referred to as follicular degeneration.
ACTH = adenocorticotropic hormone.

chest, lower abdomen, and groin), whereas hypertrichosis is increased hair growth anywhere on the body. Because of the involvement of androgens, hirsutism normally is not seen before puberty. There can be either increased end-organ sensitivity (in this case the hair follicle) or hyperandrogenemia (see Table 477–5). The former is often familial, and the latter is often related to ovarian or adrenal dysfunction (the two sites of androgen production in women). Endocrinologic evaluation, including measurement of circulating levels of free testosterone, dehydroepiandrosterone sulfate, and prolactin, is recommended (Chapter 255). Treatments include bleaches, chemical or wax depilatories, topical eflornithine, electrolysis, and laser therapy.

DISTINCTIVE LESIONS IN BLACK SKIN

Although some diseases are more common in patients of African ancestry (e.g., tinea capitis, pseudofolliculitis barbae, dissecting cellulitis), others are simply more noticeable (e.g., vitiligo and postinflammatory hypopigmentation) (Table 477–6). The explanation for the increased incidence is speculative in most instances, with the exception of curled hairs leading to pseudofolliculitis barbae. Some cutaneous disorders are seen less commonly in black skin (e.g., acne rosacea and scabies).

Another entity seen more commonly in individuals of African descent is keloids (Fig. 477–12). Keloids usually appear at sites of trauma (e.g., ear piercing) but can occasionally appear spontaneously,

Table 477–6 • DISORDERS SEEN MORE COMMONLY IN PATIENTS OF AFRICAN ANCESTRY

HEAD AND NECK
Folliculitis decalvans/dissecting cellulitis
Tinea capitis
Traction alopecia
Alopecia due to follicular degeneration ("hot comb" alopecia)
Acne keloidalis nuchae
Pseudofolliculitis barbae
Pomade acne
Dermatosis papulosa nigra
Inherited patterned lentiginosis
Melasma
Discoid lupus erythematosus

PALMAR
Keratosis punctata of the palmar creases

LOWER EXTREMITIES
Ulcers secondary to sickle cell anemia

GENERALIZED
Keloids
Cutaneous sarcoidosis
Papular eczema and follicular-based inflammation

surround the hair bulb deep in the dermis. Discrete areas of hair loss with no clinical evidence of inflammation are seen, with initial lesions often the size of a quarter. The natural history can vary from stabilization and spontaneous regrowth of hair to rapid spread and coalescence. In a minority of patients, involvement of the entire scalp (alopecia totalis) or the entire body (alopecia universalis) can be observed. Patients with alopecia areata have an increased incidence of vitiligo and autoimmune polyendocrinopathies. Treatment consists primarily of intralesional corticosteroids and topical irritants or allergens.

Additional causes of circumscribed nonscarring alopecia include tinea capitis (Chapter 474), syphilis (Chapter 349), and trichotillomania, in which people pull out their scalp hairs, usually because of anxiety. The major causes of scarring alopecia are *lichen planus* (Chapter 474) and *discoid lupus erythematosus* (Chapter 280), in which there is permanent loss of hair follicles. In active lesions, scalp inflammation is seen, especially at the periphery of the areas of alopecia. Sarcoidosis, cutaneous metastases, and morphea (linear scleroderma) are uncommon causes of scarring alopecia. A total body skin examination (including nails and oral mucosa) can provide clues to the diagnosis, especially in the case of lichen planus and discoid lupus erythematosus, but histologic evaluation is required to establish the diagnosis of scarring alopecia.

HIRSUTISM (Chapter 255)

Hirsutism is an increase in hair growth in particular anatomic sites that are androgen dependent (e.g., lateral face, chin, neck, central

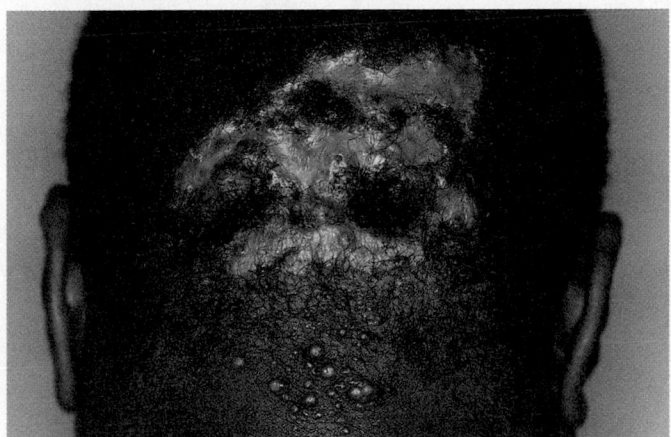

FIGURE 477–12 • Acne keloidalis in an African American man. (Courtesy of Kalman Watsky, MD.)

Skin Diseases

especially on the trunk. In the former situation, they are thought to represent an exaggerated response to wound healing, with increased formation of collagen not only at the site of the trauma (as in hypertrophic scars) but also in adjacent, previously uninvolved skin. Treatment options include intralesional corticosteroids and interferon, with or without excision, or radiation therapy.

SUGGESTED READINGS
Baran R, Kechijian P: Understanding nail disorders. Eur J Dermatol 2001;11:159–162. *A review of the endogenous versus exogenous causes of nail dystrophy.*
Callen JP, Jorizzo JL, et al (eds): Dermatological Signs of Internal Disease. Philadelphia, WB Saunders, 2003. *A comprehensive text.*

part XXVIII

Reference Intervals and Laboratory Values

478 REFERENCE INTERVALS AND LABORATORY VALUES*

Ronald J. Elin

Reference intervals are valuable guidelines for the clinician to assess health and disease, but they should not be used as absolute indicators of health and disease. For essentially every test, there is a significant overlap between the normal and diseased populations. Many factors may influence the determination of the reference interval. The method and mode of standardization are variables for the reference interval, particularly for immunologic and enzymatic tests. The selection of the "normal" population is also important because factors such as age, gender, race, diet, personal habits (e.g., alcohol consumption, smoking), and exercise may influence the reference interval for a given analyte. Last, the statistics chosen to define the reference interval are also a factor. These multiple variables for determining the reference interval indicate why there are differences among institutions for the same analyte.

The values in this chapter are primarily for adults in the fasting state. Values for other groups, when included, are clearly identified. Prefixes and abbreviations are listed in Table 478–1. For convenience, this chapter is divided into the following three sections: clinical chemistry, toxicology, and serology (Table 478–2); hematology and coagulation (Table 478–3); and drugs—therapeutic and toxic (Table 478–4). The list includes reference intervals for the most common tests used in the practice of internal medicine. For more information about the reference interval for a given test or a test not included in the list, a recommended source is *Clinical Guide to Laboratory Tests,* third edition, edited by Dr. Norbert W. Tietz. This book contains literature citations for most of the tests listed in this chapter.

All laboratory values are given in conventional and international units. If the value and units for a reference interval are the same for conventional and international units, the interval is listed only in the column for international units. The temperature for all enzyme assays listed in the chapter is 37°C. The pertinent prefixes denoting the decimal factors and abbreviations are listed in Table 478–1.

Table 478–1 • PREFIXES AND ABBREVIATIONS

PREFIXES DENOTING DECIMAL FACTORS

Prefix	Symbol	Factor
mega	M	10^6
kilo	k	10^3
hecto	h	10^2
deca	da	10^1
deci	d	10^{-1}
centi	c	10^{-2}
milli	m	10^{-3}
micro	μ	10^{-6}
nano	n	10^{-9}
pico	p	10^{-12}
femto	f	10^{-15}

ABBREVIATIONS

AU	Arbitrary units
EU	Ehrlich unit
GD	General diagnostics
IFA	Immunofluorescent assay
IU	International unit (of hormone activity)
RIA	Radioimmunoassay
RID	Radial immunodiffusion
S	Substrate
U	International unit (of enzyme activity)

Table 478–2 • CLINICAL CHEMISTRY, TOXICOLOGY, SEROLOGY

TEST	SPECIMEN	REFERENCE INTERVAL (CONVENTIONAL UNITS)	REFERENCE INTERVAL (INTERNATIONAL UNITS)
Acetoacetate Semiquantitative	Serum or plasma (fluoride/oxalate)	Negative (<1 mg/dL)	Negative (<0.1 mmol/L)
Acetone Semiquantitative	Urine	Negative	Negative
	Serum or plasma (fluoride or oxalate)	Negative (<1 mg/dL)	Negative (<0.17 mmol/L)
Quantitative Semiquantitative	Urine		Negative
Acid phosphatase (S:p-nitrophenylphosphate)	Serum		M: 2.5–11.7 U/L F: 0.3–9.2 U/L
Adrenocorticotropic hormone (ACTH)	Plasma (heparin)	0800 hr: <120 pg/mL 1600–2000 hr: <85 pg/mL	<26 pmol/L <19 pmol/L
Alanine aminotransferase (ALT, SGPT)	Serum	M: 10–40 U/L F: 7–35 U/L	0.17–0.68 µKat/L 0.12–0.60 µKat/L
Albumin Nephelometric, colorimetric Turbidimetric	Serum CSF Urine	3.4–4.8 g/dL <45 mg/dL <80 mg/day at rest <150 mg/day ambulatory	34–48 g/L <450 mg/L <80 mg/day <150 mg/day
Aldolase	Serum	1.0–7.5 U/L	0.02–0.13 µKat/L
Aldosterone	Plasma (heparin EDTA) or serum	Adult, average sodium diet Supine: 3–16 ng/dL Upright: 7–30 ng/dL	0.08–0.44 nmol/L 0.19–0.83 nmol/L
Alkaline phosphatase (S:4–NPP)	Serum	25–100 U/L	Adult (>20 y) 0.43–1.70 µKat/L
Aluminum	Serum	<5.41 µg/L	<0.2 µmol/L
δ-Aminolevulinic acid (δ-ALA)	Serum Urine	15–23 µg/dL 1.5–7.5 mg/day	1.1–8 µmol/L 11.4–57.2 µmol/day

*The material in this chapter was partially extracted from Tietz NW (ed): Clinical Guide to Laboratory Tests. Philadelphia, WB Saunders, 1995. The material for the section on Therapeutic Drug Concentrations was partially extracted from Burtis CA, Ashwood ER (eds): Tietz Textbook of Clinical Chemistry. Philadelphia, WB Saunders, 1994. The main contributors to this section of the book are PC Painter, JY Cope, and JL Smith. Other sources are listed under the suggested readings for this chapter.

Table 478–2 • CLINICAL CHEMISTRY, TOXICOLOGY, SEROLOGY—cont'd

TEST	SPECIMEN	REFERENCE INTERVAL (CONVENTIONAL UNITS)	REFERENCE INTERVAL (INTERNATIONAL UNITS)
Ammonia nitrogen	Serum or plasma		
Resin or enzymatic	(Na-heparin)	Adult 15–45 μg N/dL	11–32 μmol/L
	Urine, 24-hr	140–1500 mg/day	10–107 mmol/day
Amylase (S:Beckmann, defined substrate)	Serum	27–131 U/L	0.46–2.23 μKat/L
	Urine, timed specimen		1–17 U/h
Angiotensin I	Peripheral venous plasma (EDTA)	<25 pg/mL	<25 ng/L
Angiotensin II	Plasma (EDTA)	10–60 pg/mL	10–60 ng/L
	Arterial blood		
α_1-Antitrypsin (nephelometry)	Serum	78–200 mg/dL	0.78–2 g/L
Anion gap [$Na^+ - (Cl^- + HCO_3^-)$]	Plasma (heparin)	7–16 mEq/L	7–16 mmol/L
Arsenic	Whole blood (heparin)	0.2–2.3 μg/dL	0.03–0.31 μmol/L
		Chronic poisoning: 10–50 μg/dL	1.33–6.65 μmol/L
		Acute poisoning: 60–93 μg/dL	7.98–12.37 μmol/L
Ascorbic acid (see Vitamin C)	Urine, 24-hr	5–50 μg/day	0.067–0.665 μmol/day
Aspartate aminotransferase (AST)	Serum	10–30 U/L	0.17–0.51 μKat/L
Base excess	Whole blood (heparin)	−2 to 3 mEq/L	−2 to 3 mmol/L
Bicarbonate	Serum	22–29 mEq/L	22–29 mmol/L
Bile acids, total	Serum, fasting	0.3–2.3 μg/mL	0.74–5.64 μmol/L
	Serum, 1-hr postprandial	1.8–3.2 μg/mL	4.41–7.84 μmol/L
	Feces	120–225 mg/day	294–551 μmol/day
Bilirubin			
Total	Serum	0.3–1.2 mg/dL	5–21 μmol/L
	Urine	Negative	
Conjugated (direct)	Serum	0–0.2 mg/dL	0–3.4 μmol/L
Calcium, ionized (iCa)	Serum	4.65–5.28 mg/dL	1.16–1.32 mmol/L
Calcium, total	Serum	8.6–10.0 mg/dL	2.15–2.50 mmol/L
	Urine, 24-hr	100–300 mg/day	2.5–7.5 mmol/day
	CSF	4.2–5.4 mg/dL	1.05–1.35 mmol/L
Cancer antigen 125 (CA 125)	Serum	<35 U/mL	<35 kU/L
Cancer Antigen 15-3 (CA 15-3)	Serum	<30 U/mL	<30 kU/L
Carbohydrate Antigen 19-9 (CA 19-9)	Serum	<37 U/mL	<37 kU/L
Carbon dioxide, partial pressure (PCO_2)	Whole blood, arterial (heparin)	M: 35–48 mm Hg	4.66–6.38 kPa
		F: 32–45 mm Hg	4.26–5.99 kPa
Carbon dioxide, total (TCO_2)	Serum or plasma (heparin)	23–29 mEq/L	23–29 mmol/L
Carcinoembryonic antigen (CEA)	Serum	Nonsmokers: <2.5 ng/mL	<2.5 μg/L
β-Carotene	Serum	10–85 μg/dL	0.19–1.58 μmol/L
Catecholamines, total	Urine, 24-hr	<100 μg/day	<5.91 nmol/day
Ceruloplasmin	Serum	18–45 mg/dL	180–450 mg/L
Chloride	Serum or plasma (heparin)	98–106 mEq/L	98–106 mmol/L
	CSF	118–132 mEq/L	118–132 mmol/L
	Urine, 24-hr	110–250 mEq/day	110–250 mmol/day
Cholesterol, total	Serum or plasma (EDTA)	Recommended: <200 mg/dL	<5.18 mmol/L
		Moderate risk: 200–239 mg/dL	5.18–6.19 mmol/L
		High risk: ≥240 mg/dL	6.22 mmol/L
Chorionic gonadotropin, β-subunit (β-HCG)	Serum or plasma (EDTA)	M and nonpregnant F: <5.0 mIU/mL	<5.0 IU/L
Complement			
Total hemolytic Complement activity	Serum	75–160 U/mL	75–160 kU/L
Copper	Serum	M: 70–140 μg/dL	10.99–21.98 μmol/L
		F: 80–155 μg/dL	12.56–24.34 μmol/L
	Erythrocyte (heparin)	90–150 μg/dL	14.13–23.55 μmol/L
	Urine, 24-hr	3–35 μg/day	0.047–0.55 μmol/day
Coproporphyrin	Urine, 24-hr	34–234 μg/day	51–351 nmol/day
	Feces, 24-hr	<30 μg/g dry wt	<45 nmol/g dry wt
		400–1200 μg/day	600–1800 nmol/day
Corticosterone	Serum	0800 h: 130–820 ng/dL	4–24 nmol/L
		1600 h: 60–220 ng/dL	2–6 nmol/L
Cortisol	Serum or plasma (heparin)	0800 h: 5–23 μg/dL	138–635 nmol/L
		1600 h: 3–15 μg/dL	82–413 nmol/L
		2000 h: ≤50% of 0800 hr	Fraction of 0800 hr: ≤0.50
Cortisol, free	Urine, 24-hr	20–90 μg/day	55–248 nmol/day
C-Peptide	Serum	0.78–1.89 ng/mL	0.26–0.62 nmol/L
C-Reactive protein	Serum	68–8200 ng/mL	68–8200 μg/L
Creatine kinase (CK)	Serum		M: 38–174 U/L
			F: 26–140 U/L
Isoenzymes, Fraction 2 (MB)	Serum	<4–6% of total (method-dependent)	Fraction of total: <0.04–0.06
Creatinine	Serum or plasma	M: 0.7–1.3 mg/dL	62–115 μmol/L
Jaffe, kinetic or enzymatic		F: 0.6–1.1 mg/dL	53–97 μmol/L
	Urine, 24-hr	M: 14–26 mg/kg/day	124–230 μmol/kg/day
		F: 11–20 mg/kg/day	97–177 μmol/kg/day

Continued

Table 478–2 • CLINICAL CHEMISTRY, TOXICOLOGY, SEROLOGY—cont'd

TEST	SPECIMEN	REFERENCE INTERVAL (CONVENTIONAL UNITS)	REFERENCE INTERVAL (INTERNATIONAL UNITS)
Creatinine clearance (endogenous)	Serum or plasma, and urine	M: 90–139 mL/min/1.73 m² F: 80–125 mL/min/1.73 m²	0.87–1.34 mL/s/m² 0.77–1.20 mL/s/m²
Dehydroepiandrosterone (DHEA)	Serum	M: 1.8–12.5 ng/mL F: 1.3–9.8 ng/mL	6.2–43.3 nmol/L 4.5–34.0 nmol/L
11-Deoxycortisol (compound S)	Serum	12–158 ng/dL	0.3–4.6 nmol/L
Erythropoietin	Serum		5–36 U/L

Estrogens, total	Serum	M: 20–80 pg/mL
		 F, cycle:
		   1–10 day 61–394 pg/mL
		   11–20 day 122–437 pg/mL
		   21–30 day 156–350 pg/mL
		   Postmenopausal: ≤130 pg/mL
		   Follicular phase 60–200 pg/mL
		   Luteal phase: 160–400 pg/mL
			20–80 ng/L
			
			 60–200 ng/L
			
			 160–400 ng/L
			 ≤130 ng/L
			 60–200 ng/L
			 160–400 ng/L

	Urine, 24-hr	M: 15–40 µg/day
		 F: Preovulation: 4–25 µg/day
		   Ovulation: 28–100 µg/day
		   Luteal peak: 22–80 µg/day
		   Pregnancy, term: <45,000 µg/day
		   Postmenopausal: <20 µg/day	

Fat, fecal	Feces, 72-hr	<7 g/day Fat-free diet: <4 g/day	
Fatty acids, nonesterified (free)	Serum or plasma (heparin)	8–25 mg/dL	0.28–0.89 mmol/L
Ferritin	Serum	M: 20–250 ng/mL F: 10–120 ng/mL	20–250 µg/L 10–120 µg/L
α₁-Fetoprotein	Serum	<10 ng/mL	<10 µg/L
Fibrinogen (see Table 478–3)			
Folate	Serum Erythrocytes (EDTA)	3–16 ng/mL 140–628 ng/mL packed cells	7–36 nmol/L 317–1422 nmol/L packed cells

Follitropin (FSH)	Serum or plasma (heparin)	M: 4–25 mIU/mL
		 F: Follicular phase: 1–9 mIU/L
		   Ovulatory peak: 6–26 mIU/mL
		   Luteal phase: 1–9 mIU/mL
		   Postmenopausal: 30–118 mIU/mL
			4–25 IU/L
			 1–9 IU/L
			 6–26 IU/L
			 1–9 IU/L
			 30–118 IU/L

	Urine, 24-hr		M: 3–11 IU/day F: 2–15 IU/day
Gastrin	Serum	25–90 pg/mL	25–90 ng/L
Glucose	Serum	Adult: 74–106 mg/dL >60 y: 80–115 mg/dL	4.1–5.9 mmol/L 4.4–6.4 mmol/L
	Whole blood (heparin) CSF	65–95 mg/dL 40–70 mg/dL	3.6–5.3 mmol/L 2.2–3.9 mmol/L
Quantitative, enzymatic Qualitative	Urine Urine	<0.5 g/d	<2.8 mmol/day Negative
Glucose, 2-hr postprandial	Serum	<120 mg/dL	<6.7 mmol/L

Glucose, tolerance test (GTT), oral	Serum	mg/dL
		        Normal Diabetic
		 Fasting: 70–105 >140
		 60 min: 120–170 ≥200
		 90 min: 100–140 ≥200
		 120 min: 70–120 ≥140
			mmol/L
			      Normal Diabetic
			 3.9–5.8 >7.8
			 6.7–9.4 ≥11
			 5.6–7.8 ≥11
			 3.9–6.7 ≥7.8

γ-Glutamyltransferase (GGT) (Szasz method)	Serum	M: 2–30 U/L F: 1–24 U/L	0.03–0.51 µKat/L 0.02–0.41 µKat/L
Glycerol, free	Plasma	0.29–1.72 mg/dL	0.032–0.187 mmol/L

Growth hormone (hGH, somatotropin)	Serum	Adult, M: 0–4 ng/mL
		        F: 0–18 ng/mL
		 >60 y, M: 1–9 ng/mL
		       F: 1–16 ng/mL
			0–4 µg/L
			 0–18 µg/L
			 1–9 µg/L
			 1–16 µg/L

Haptoglobin (see Hematology and Coagulation section)			
HDL-cholesterol (HDLC) (5th percentile from Lipid Research Clinics)	Serum or plasma (EDTA)	M: >29 mg/dL F: >35 mg/dL	>0.75 mmol/L >0.91 mmol/L
Hemoglobin A₁c (electrophoresis)	Whole blood (heparin, EDTA, or oxalate)	5.0–7.5% of total Hb	Fraction of Hb: 0.050–0.075
Homovanillic acid (HVA)	Urine, 24-hr	1.4–8.8 mg/day	8–48 µmol/day
17-Hydroxycorticosteroids (17-OHCS)	Urine, 24-hr	M: 3.0–10.0 mg/day F: 2.0–8.0 mg/day	8.3–27.6 µmol/day 5.5–22.1 µmol/day

5-Hydroxyindole acetic acid (5-HIAA)
   Qualitative
   Quantitative
	Fresh random urine
	 Urine, 24-hr
		
		 2–6 mg/day
			
			 Negative
			 10.4–31.2 µmol/day

17-Hydroxyprogesterone (17-OHP)	Serum	M: 0.5–2.5 ng/mL
		 F: Follicular: 0.2–1.0 ng/mL
		   Luteal: 1.0–5.0 ng/mL
		   Postmenopausal: ≤0.7 ng/mL
			1.5–7.5 nmol/L
			 0.6–3.0 nmol/L
			 3.0–15.5 nmol/L
			 ≤2.1 nmol/L

Table 478–2 • CLINICAL CHEMISTRY, TOXICOLOGY, SEROLOGY—cont'd

TEST	SPECIMEN	REFERENCE INTERVAL (CONVENTIONAL UNITS)	REFERENCE INTERVAL (INTERNATIONAL UNITS)
Immunoglobulin A (IgA)	Serum	40–350 mg/dL	400–3500 mg/L
Immunoglobulin D (IgD)	Serum	0–8 mg/dL	0–80 mg/L
Immunoglobulin E (IgE)	Serum	0–380 IU/mL	0–380 kIU/L
Immunoglobulin G (IgG)	Serum	650–1600 mg/dL	6.5–16 g/L
	CSF	0.5–5 mg/dL	5–50 mg/L
Immunoglobulin M (IgM)	Serum	55–300 mg/dL	550–3000 mg/L
Insulin (12-hr fasting), immunoreactive	Serum	0.7–9.0 μIU/mL	5–63 pmol/L
Intrinsic factor (see Vitamin B$_{12}$)			
Iron	Serum	M: 65–175 μg/dL	11.6–31.3 μmol/L
		F: 50–170 μg/dL	9.0–30.4 μmol/L
Iron-binding capacity, total (TIBC)	Serum	250–450 μg/dL	44.8–80.6 μmol/L
Iron saturation	Serum	M: 20–50	Fraction of iron saturation:
		F: 15–50	0.20–0.5
			0.15–0.5
17-Ketogenic steroids (17-KGS)	Urine, 24-hr	M: 5–23 mg/day	17–80 μmol/day
		F: 3–15 mg/day	10–52 μmol/day
Ketone bodies			
Qualitative	Serum	Negative (0.5–3.0 mg/dL)	Negative (5–30 mg/L)
	Urine, random		Negative
17-Ketosteroids, total (17-KS)	Urine, 24-hr	M: 10–25 mg/day	37–87 μmol/day
		F: 6–15 mg/day	21–52 μmol/day
L-Lactate	Whole blood (heparin)	Venous: 8.1–15.3 mg/dL	0.9–1.7 mmol/L
		Arterial: <11.3 mg/dL	<1.3 mmol/L
Lactate dehydrogenase (LDH)	Serum		208–378 U/L
LDH isoenzymes (electrophoresis, agarose)	Serum	%	Fraction of total:
		Fraction 1: 18–33	0.18–0.33
		Fraction 2: 28–40	0.28–0.40
		Fraction 3: 18–30	0.18–0.30
		Fraction 4: 6–16	0.06–0.16
		Fraction 5: 2–13	0.02–0.13
Lead	Whole blood (heparin)	<25 μg/dL	<1.21 μmol/L
		Toxic: ≥100 μg/dL	≥4.83 μmol/L
	Urine	<80 μg/dL	<0.39 μmol/L
Lipase	Serum	31–186 U/L	0.5–3.2 μKat/L
LDL-Cholesterol (LDLC)	Serum or plasma (EDTA)	Recommended: <130 mg/dL	<3.37 mmol/L
		Moderate risk: 130–159 mg/dL	3.37–4.12 mmol/L
		High risk: ≥160 mg/dL	≥4.14 mmol/L
Lutropin (LH)	Serum or plasma (heparin)	M: 1–8 mU/mL	1–8 U/L
		F: Follicular phase: 1–2 mU/mL	1–12 U/L
		Midcycle: 16–104 mU/mL	16–104 U/L
		Luteal: 1–12 mU/mL	1–12 U/L
		Postmenopausal: 16–66 mU/mL	16–66 U/L
	Urine		M: 9–23 U/day
			F: nonmidcycle, 4–30 U/day
Lysozyme	Serum, plasma	0.4–1.3 mg/dL	4–13 mg/L
Magnesium	Serum	1.3–2.1 mEq/L	0.65–1.05 mmol/L
	Urine, 24-hr	6.0–10.0 mEq/day	3.00–5.00 mmol/day
Mercury	Whole blood (EDTA)	<5.0 μg/dL	<0.25 μmol/L
	Urine, 24-hr	<20 μg/L	<0.1 μmol/L
		Toxic: >150 μg/L	<0.75 μmol/L
Metanephrine, total	Urine, 24-hr	0.05–1.20 μg/mg creatinine	0.03–0.69 mmol/mol creatinine
Myelin basic protein	CSF		<2.5 μg/L
Myoglobin	Serum		M: 19–92 μg/L
			F: 12–76 μg/L
	Urine, random		Negative
Osmolality	Serum		275–295 mOsmol/kg
	Urine, random		50–1200 mOsmol/kg, depending on fluid intake
			After 12-hr fluid restriction:
			>850 mOsmol/kg
	Urine, 24-hr		~390–900 mOsmol/kg
Oxalate	Serum	1–2.4 μg/mL	11–27 μmol/L
		Ethylene glycol poisoning: >20 μg/mL	Ethylene glycol poisoning: >228 μmol/L
Oxygen (PO$_2$)	Whole blood, arterial (heparin)	83–108 mm Hg	11–14.4 kPa
Oxygen saturation	Whole blood, arterial (heparin)	95–98%	Fraction saturated: 0.95–0.98
Parathyroid hormone	Serum	Varies with laboratory	
		N-Terminal 8–24 pg/mL	8–24 ng/L
		C-terminal 50–330 pg/mL	50–330 ng/L
		Intact 10–65 pg/mL	10–65 ng/L
pH (37°C)	Whole blood, arterial (heparin)		7.35–7.45
Phosphorus, inorganic	Serum	2.7–4.5 mg/dL	0.87–1.45 nmol/L
		>60 y, M: 2.3–3.7 mg/dL	0.74–1.2 nmol/L
		F: 2.8–4.1 mg/dL	0.90–1.3 nmol/L
	Urine, 24-hr	0.4–1.3 g/day	13–42 mmol/day

Continued

Table 478–2 • CLINICAL CHEMISTRY, TOXICOLOGY, SEROLOGY—cont'd

TEST	SPECIMEN	REFERENCE INTERVAL (CONVENTIONAL UNITS)	REFERENCE INTERVAL (INTERNATIONAL UNITS)
Porphobilinogen (PBG)			
Quantitative	Urine, 24-hr	0–2.0 mg/day	0–8.8 μmol/day
Qualitative	Urine, fresh random		Negative
Potassium	Serum	3.5–5.1 mEq/L	3.5–5.1 mmol/L
	Plasma (heparin)	3.5–4.5 mEq/L	3.5–4.5 mmol/L
	Urine, 24-hr	25–125 mEq/d	25–125 mmol/day
Pregnanediol	Urine, 24-hr	M: 0–1.9 mg/d	0–5.9 μmol/day
		F: Follicular: <2.6 mg/day	<8 μmol/day
		Luteal: 2.6–10.6 mg/day	8–33 μmol/day
		Postmenopausal: 0.2–1.0 mg/day	0.6–3.1 μmol/day
Progesterone	Serum	M: 0.13–0.97 ng/mL	0.4–3.1 nmol/L
		F: Follicular: 0.15–0.70 ng/mL	0.5–2.2 nmol/L
		Luteal: 2.0–25 ng/mL	6.4–79.5 nmol/L
Prolactin (hPRL)	Serum	M: 3.0–14.7 ng/mL	3.0–14.7 μg/L
		F: 3.8–23.2 ng/mL	3.8–23.2 μg/L
Prostate-specific antigen (PSA)	Serum, freeze	M: <4 ng/mL	<4 μg/L
Protein			
Total	Serum	6.4–8.3 g/dL	64.0–83.0 g/L
Electrophoresis (cellulose acetate)	Serum	Albumin: 3.5–5.0 g/dL	35–50 g/L
		α_1-Globulin: 0.1–0.3 g/dL	1–3 g/L
		α_2-Globulin: 0.6–1.0 g/dL	6–10 g/L
		β-Globulin: 0.7–1.1 g/dL	7–11 g/L
		γ-Globulin: 0.8–1.6 g/dL	8–16 g/L
Total	Urine, 24-hr		50–80 mg/day at rest
Total	CSF	Lumbar: 15–45 mg/dL	150–450 mg/L
Pyruvic acid	Whole blood (heparin)	0.3–0.9 mg/dL	0.03–0.10 mmol/L
Renin (normal diet)	Plasma (EDTA)	Supine: 0.2–1.6 ng/mL/hr	0.2–1.6 μg/L/hr
		Standing: 0.7–3.3 ng/mL/hr	0.7–3.3 μg/L/hr
Riboflavin (see Vitamin B₂)			
Sediment	Urine, fresh, random		
Casts			Hyaline: occasional (0–1) casts/hpf
			RBC: not seen
			WBC: not seen
			Tubular epithelial: not seen
			Transitional and squamous epithelial: not seen
Cells			RBC: 0–2/hpf
			WBC: M: 0–3/hpf
			F: 0–5/hpf
			Epithelial: few
			Bacteria:
			Unspun: no organisms/oil immersion field
			Spun: <20 organisms/hpf
Sodium	Serum or plasma (heparin)	136–146 mEq/L	136–146 mmol/L
	Urine, 24-hr	40–220 mEq/day	40–220 mmol/day
Specific gravity	Urine, random		1.002–1.030
	Urine, 24-hr		1.015–1.025
Testosterone, free	Serum	M: 50–210 pg/mL	174–729 pmol/L
		F: 1.0–8.5 pg/mL	3.5–29.5 pmol/L
Testosterone, total	Serum	M: 280–1100 ng/dL	9.7–38.2 nmol/L
		F: 15–70 ng/dL	0.5–2.4 nmol/L
	Urine	20–50 y,	
		M: 50–135 μg/day	173–470 nmol/day
		F: 2–12 μg/day	7–42 nmol/day
		>50 y,	
		M: 40–60 μg/day	139–210 nmol/day
		F: 2–8 μg/day	7–28 nmol/day
Thiamine (see Vitamin B₁)	Serum	0.10–0.54 μg/dL	2.9–16.1 nmol/L
Thyroglobulin (Tg)	Serum	3–42 ng/mL	3–42 μg/L
Thyroglobulin antibodies	Serum		<1:10
Thyroid microsomal antibodies	Serum		Nondetectable (hemagglutination) or <1:10 (IFA)
Thyrotropin (hTSH)	Serum or plasma	0.4–4.2 μU/mL	0.4–4.2 mU/L
Thyrotropin-releasing hormone	Plasma	5–60 pg/mL	5–60 ng/L
Thyroxine, free (FT₄)	Serum	0.8–2.4 ng/dL	10–31 pmol/L
Thyroxine (T₄), total	Serum	M: 4.6–10.5 μg/dL	59–135 nmol/L
		F: 5.5–11.0 μg/dL	71–142 nmol/L
Thyroxine-binding globulin (TBG)	Serum	15.0–34.0 μg/mL	15.0–34.0 mg/L
Thyroxine index, free	Serum		4.2–13.0
Transcortin	Serum	M: 18.8–25.2 mg/L	323–433 nmol/L
		F: 14.9–22.9 mg/L	256–393 nmol/L
Transferrin	Serum	200–400 mg/dL	2.0–4.0 g/L
		>60 y: 180–380 mg/dL	1.80–3.80 g/L

Table 478–2 • CLINICAL CHEMISTRY, TOXICOLOGY, SEROLOGY—cont'd

TEST	SPECIMEN	REFERENCE INTERVAL (CONVENTIONAL UNITS)	REFERENCE INTERVAL (INTERNATIONAL UNITS)
Transthyretin (prealbumin)	Serum	10–40 mg/dL	100–400 mg/L
Triglycerides (TG)	Serum, after ≥12-hr fast	Recommended: <250 mg/dL	2.83 mmol/L
Tri-iodothyronine, free	Serum	260–480 pg/mL	4.0–7.4 pmol/L
Tri-iodothyronine, total (T₃)	Serum	100–200 ng/dL	1.54–3.08 mmol/L
Tri-iodothyronine resin uptake test (T₃RU)	Serum	24–34%	24–34 AU (arbitrary units)
Troponin-I	Serum		<10 µg/L
Troponin-T	Serum		0–0.1 µg/L
Urea nitrogen	Serum or plasma	6–20 mg/dL	2.1–7.1 mmol/L
	Urine	12–20 g/day	0.43–0.71 mol/day
Urea nitrogen/creatinine ratio	Serum		12/1–20/1
Uric acid (uricase)	Serum	M: 3.5–7.2 mg/dL	0.21–0.42 mmol/L
		F: 2.6–6.0 mg/dL	0.15–0.35 mmol/L
	Urine, 24-hr	250–750 mg/day	1.48–4.43 mmol/day
Urinary sediment (see Sediment)			
Urobilinogen	Urine, 2-hr	0.1–0.8 EU	0.1–0.8 U
	Urine, 24-hr	0.5–4.0 EU	0.5–4.0 U
	Feces	75–275 EU/100 g	750–2750 U/kg
		75–400 EU/day	75–400 U/day
		40–280 mg/day	67–473 µmol/day
Uroporphyrin	Urine, 24-hr	<50 µg/day	<60 nmol/day
	Feces, 24-hr specimen	10–40 µg/day	12–48 nmol/day
	Erythrocytes (heparin or EDTA)		Negative
Vanillylmandelic acid (VMA)	Urine, 24-hr	2–7 mg/day	10.1–35.4 µmol/day
Viscosity	Serum		1.10–1.22 centipoise
Vitamin A	Serum	30–80 µg/dL	1.05–2.8 µmol/L
Vitamin B₁ (Thiamine)	Serum	0–2 µg/dL	0–75 nmol/L
Vitamin B₂ (Riboflavin)	Serum	4–24 µg/dL	106–638 nmol/L
Vitamin B₆	Plasma (EDTA)	5–30 ng/mL	20–121 nmol/L
Vitamin B₁₂	Serum	200–835 pg/mL	148–616 pmol/L
Vitamin C	Plasma (oxalate, heparin, or EDTA)	0.5–1.5 mg/dL	28–85 µmol/L
Vitamin D₃, 1,25-dihydroxy	Serum	25–45 pg/mL	60–108 pmol/L
Vitamin D₃, 25-hyroxy	Plasma (heparin)	Summer: 15–80 ng/mL	37.4–200 nmol/L
		Winter: 14–42 ng/mL	34.9–105 nmol/L
Vitamin E	Serum	5.0–18.0 µg/mL	12–42 µmol/L
Zinc	Serum	70–150 µg/dL	10.7–22.9 µmol/L

Table 478–3 • HEMATOLOGY AND COAGULATION

TEST	SPECIMEN	REFERENCE INTERVAL (CONVENTIONAL UNITS)	REFERENCE INTERVAL (INTERNATIONAL UNITS)
Activated partial thromboplastin time (APTT)	Whole blood (Na citrate)		25–35 sec
Antithrombin III	Plasma (Na citrate)	85–115% of normal human plasma	0.85–1.15
Bleeding time (BT)	Blood from skin		Normal: 2–7 min
Ivy			Borderline: 7–11 min
Simplate (G-D)			2.75–8 min
Blood volume	Whole blood (heparin)		M: 52–83 mL/kg
			F: 50–75 mL/kg
Bone marrow	Bone marrow aspirate	% (mean)	Number fraction (mean)
Differential count			
Myeoblasts		0.3–5.0 (2.0)	0.003–0.05 (0.02)
Promyelocytes		1.0–8.0 (5.0)	0.01–0.08 (0.05)
Myelocytes:			
Neutrophilic		5.0–19.0 (12.0)	0.05–0.19 (0.12)
Eosinophilic		0.5–3.0 (1.5)	0.005–0.03 (0.015)
Basophilic		0.0–0.5 (0.3)	0.00–0.005 (0.003)
Metamyelocytes		13.0–32.0 (22.0)	0.13–0.32 (0.22)
Polymorphonuclear neutrophils		7.0–3.0 (2.0)	0.07–0.30 (0.20)
Polymorphonuclear eosinophils		0.5–4.0 (2.0)	0.005–0.04 (0.02)
Polymorphonuclear basophils		0.0–0.7 (0.2)	0.0–0.007 (0.002)
Lymphocytes		3.0–17.0 (10.0)	0.03–0.17 (0.10)
Plasma cells		0.0–2.0 (0.4)	0.00–0.02 (0.004)
Monocytes		0.5–5.0 (2.0)	0.005–0.05 (0.02)
Reticulum cells		0.1–2.0 (0.2)	0.001–0.02 (0.002)
Megakaryocytes		0.03–3.0 (0.1)	0.0003–0.03 (0.001)
Pronormoblasts		1.0–8.0 (4.0)	0.01–0.08 (0.04)
Normoblasts		7.0–32.0 (18.0)	0.07–0.32 (0.18)
Clot lysis, 37°C	Whole clotted blood		47–72 hr
Clot retraction screen	Whole blood (no anticoagulant)		Retraction begins at 1 hr maximum at 24 hr
Clotting time, Lee-White, 37°C	Whole blood (no anticoagulant)		5–8 min

Continued

Reference Intervals and Laboratory Values

Table 478–3 • HEMATOLOGY AND COAGULATION—cont'd

TEST	SPECIMEN	REFERENCE INTERVAL (CONVENTIONAL UNITS)		REFERENCE INTERVAL (INTERNATIONAL UNITS)	
Differential count (see Bone marrow differential count or leukocyte differential count)					
Eosinophil count	Whole blood (EDTA); capillary blood	50–400 cells/μL (mm³)		50–400 × 10⁶ cells/L	
Erythrocyte count (RBC count)	Whole blood (EDTA)	millions of cells/μL (mm³) M: 4.3–5.7 F: 3.8–5.1		× 10¹² cells/L 4.3–5.7 3.8–5.1	
Erythrocyte sedimentation rate (ESR), Wintrobe				M: 0–15 mm/hr F: 0–20 mm/hr	
Ferritin (see Table 478–2)					
Fibrin degradation products (agglutination, Thrombo-Wellco test)	Whole blood: special tube containing thrombin and proteolytic inhibitor	<10 μg/mL		<10 mg/L	
	Urine: 2 mL in special tube (see above)	<0.25 μg/mL		<0.25 mg/L	
Fibrinogen	Plasma (Na citrate)	200–400 mg/dL		2.00–4.00 g/L	
Glucose-6-phosphate dehydrogenase (G6PD) in erythrocytes	Whole blood (ACD, EDTA, or heparin)	12.1 ± 2.09 U/g Hb (1 SD)		0.78 ± 0.13 MU/mol Hb (1 SD)	
Haptoglobin (Hp) RID	Serum; avoid hemolysis	26–85 mg/dL		260–1850 mg/L	
Hematocrit (HCT, Hct)	Whole blood (EDTA)				
Calculated from MCV and RBC (electronic displacement or laser)		M: 39–49% F: 35–45%		0.39–0.49 volume fraction 0.35–0.45 volume fraction	
Hemoglobin (Hb)	Whole blood (EDTA)	M: 13.5–17.5 g/dL F: 12.0–16.0 g/dL		2.09–2.71 mmol/L 1.86–2.48 mmol/L	
	Plasma (heparin, ACD) Urine, fresh, random	<3 mg/dL		<0.47 μmol/L Negative	
Hemoglobin electrophoresis	Whole blood (EDTA, citrate, or heparin)			Mass function	
		HbA >95% HbA₂ 1.5–3.5% HbF <2%		HbA >0.95 HbA₂ 0.015–0.035 HbF <0.02	
Leukocyte count (WBC count)	Whole blood (EDTA) CSF	4.5–11.0 × 10³ cells/μL (mm³) 0.5 mononuclear cells/μL		4.5–11.0 × 10⁹ cells/L 0.5 × 10⁶ cells/L	
Leukocyte	Whole blood (EDTA)	%	Cells/μL (mm³)	Number fraction	Cells × 10⁶/L
Differential count					
Myelocytes		0	0	0	0
Neutrophils—bands		3–5	150–400	0.03–0.05	150–400
Neutrophils—segmented		54–62	3000–5800	0.54–0.62	3000–5800
Lymphocytes		23–33	1500–3000	0.25–0.33	1500–3000
Monocytes		3–7	285–500	0.03–0.07	285–500
Eosinophils		1–3	50–250	0.01–0.03	50–250
Basophils		0–0.75	15–50	0–0.0075	15–50
Leukocyte	CSF	%		Number fraction	
Differential count					
Lymphocytes		62 ± 34		0.62 ± 0.324	
Monocytes (includes pia-arachnoid mesothelial cells)		36 ± 20		0.36 ± 0.20	
Neutrophils		2 ± 5		0.02 ± 0.05	
Histocytes				Rare	
Ependymal cells				Rare	
Eosinophils				Rare	
Mean corpuscular hemoglobin (MCH)	Whole blood (EDTA)	26–34 pg/cell		0.40–0.53 fmol/cell	
Mean corpuscular hemoglobin centration (MCHC)	Whole blood (EDTA)	31–37% Hb/cell or gHb/dL RBC		4.81–5.74 mmol Hb/L RBC	
Mean corpuscular volume (MCV)	Whole blood (EDTA)			80–100 fL	
Methemoglobin (MetHb)	Whole blood (EDTA, heparin, or ACD)	0.06–0.24 g/dL		9.3–37.2 μmol/L	
Plasma volume	Plasma (heparin)	M: 25–43 mL/kg F: 28–45 mL/kg		0.025–0.043 L/kg 0.028–0.045 L/kg	
Platelet count (thrombocyte count)	Whole blood (EDTA)	150–450 × 10³/μL (mm³)		150–450 × 10⁹/L	
Prothrombin consumption	Whole blood (no anticoagulant)			>30 sec	
Prothrombin time, two-stage modified	Whole blood (Na citrate)			18–22 sec	
RBC count (see Erythrocyte count)					
Red cell volume	Whole blood (heparin)	M: 20–36 mL/kg F: 19–31 mL/kg		M: 0.020–0.036 L/kg F: 0.019–0.031 L/kg	
Reticulocyte count	Whole blood (EDTA, heparin, or oxalate)	0.5–1.5% of erythrocytes		0.005–0.015 (number fraction)	
Sulfhemoglobin	Whole blood (EDTA, heparin, or EDTA)	≤1.0% of total Hb		<0.010 of total Hb (mass fraction)	
Thrombin time	Whole blood (Na citrate)			Time of control ± 25 when control is 9–13 sec	
Thromboplastin time, activated (see Activated partial thromboplastin time [APTT])					

Table 478–4 • DRUGS—THERAPEUTIC AND TOXIC

DRUG	SPECIMEN	REFERENCE INTERVAL (CONVENTIONAL UNITS)		REFERENCE INTERVAL (INTERNATIONAL UNITS)
Acetaminophen	Serum or plasma (hep or EDTA)	Therap: Toxic:	10–30 µg/mL >200 µg/mL	66–199 µmol/L >1324 µmol/L

Amikacin	Serum or plasma (EDTA)	Therap:
		  Peak
		  Trough (severe infection)
		Toxic:
		  Peak
		  Trough
			
			25–35 µg/mL
			4–8 µg/mL
			
			>35 µg/mL
			>10 µg/mL
				
				43–60 µmol/L
				6.8–13.7 µmol/L
				
				>60 µmol/L
				>17 µmol/L

ε-Aminocaproic acid	Serum or plasma (hep or EDTA); trough	Therap:	100–400 µg/mL	0.76–3.05 mmol/L
Amitriptyline	Serum or plasma (hep or EDTA); trough (>12 hr after dose)	Therap: Toxic:	120–250 ng/mL >500 ng/mL	433–903 nmol/L >1805 nmol/L
Amobarbital	Serum	Therap: Toxic:	1–5 µg/mL >10 µg/mL	4–22 µmol/L >44 µmol/L
Amphetamine	Serum or plasma (hep or EDTA)	Therap: Toxic:	20–30 ng/mL >200 ng/mL	148–222 nmol/L >1480 nmol/L
Bromide	Serum	Toxic:	>1250 µg/mL	>15.6 mmol/L
Caffeine	Serum or plasma (hep or EDTA)	Therap: Toxic:	3–15 µg/mL >50 µg/mL	15–77 µmol/L >258 µmol/L
Carbamazepine	Serum or plasma (hep or EDTA); trough	Therap: Toxic:	4–12 µg/mL >15 µg/mL	17–51 µmol/L >63 µmol/L
Carbenicillin	Serum or plasma	Therap: Toxic:	Dependent on minimum inhibitory concentration of specific organism >250 µg/mL	Same >660 µmol/L
Chloramphenicol	Serum or plasma (hep or EDTA); trough	Therap: Toxic:	10–25 µg/L >25 µg/L	31–77 µmol/L >77 µmol/L
Chlordiazepoxide	Serum or plasma (hep or EDTA); trough	Therap: Toxic:	700–1000 ng/mL >5000 ng/mL	2.34–3.34 µmol/L >16.7 µmol/L
Chlorpromazine	Serum or plasma (hep or EDTA); trough	Therap: Toxic:	50–300 ng/mL >750 ng/mL	157–942 nmol/L >2355 nmol/L
Cimetidine	Serum or plasma (hep or EDTA); trough	Therap:	0.5–1.2 µg/mL	2–5 µmol/L
Clonazepam	Serum or plasma (hep or EDTA); trough	Therap: Toxic:	15–60 ng/mL >80 ng/mL	48–190 nmol/L >254 nmol/L
Clonidine	Serum or plasma (hep or EDTA)	Therap:	1.0–2.0 ng/mL	4.4–8.7 nmol/L
Clorazepate	Serum or plasma (hep or EDTA)	As desmethyldiazepam: Therap:	 0.12–1.0 µg/mL	 0.36–3.01 µmol/L
Cocaine	Serum or plasma (hep or EDTA); on ice	Therap: Toxic:	100–500 ng/mL >1000 ng/mL	330–1650 nmol/L >3300 nmol/L
Codeine	Serum	Therap: Toxic:	10–100 ng/mL >200 ng/mL	33–334 nmol/L >668 nmol/L
Cyclosporine	Serum (12 hr after dose)	Therap: Toxic:	100–400 ng/mL >400 ng/mL	83–333 nmol/L >333 nmol/L
Desipramine	Serum or plasma (hep or EDTA); trough (≥12 hr after dose)	Therap: Toxic:	75–300 ng/mL >400 ng/mL	281–1125 nmol/L >1500 nmol/L
Diazepam	Serum or plasma (hep or EDTA); trough	Therap: Toxic:	100–1000 ng/mL >5000 ng/mL	0.35–3.51 µmol/L >17.55 µmol/L
Digitoxin	Serum or plasma (hep or EDTA) ≥6 hr after dose	Therap: Toxic:	20–35 ng/mL >45 ng/mL	26–46 nmol/L >59 nmol/L
Digoxin	Serum or plasma (hep or EDTA) trough (≥12 hr after dose)	Therap: CHF Arrhythmias: Toxic:	0.8–1.5 mg/mL 1.5–2.0 ng/mL >2.5 ng/mL	1.0–1.9 nmol/L 1.9–2.6 nmol/L >3.2 nmol/L
Diphenylhydantoin (see Phenytoin)				

Disopyramide	Serum or plasma (hep or EDTA); trough	Therap:
		  Arrhythmias:
		    Atrial
		    Ventricular
		Toxic:
			
			2.8–3.2 µg/mL
			3.3–7.5 µg/mL
			>7 µg/mL
				
				8.3–9.4 µmol/L
				9.7–22 µmol/L
				>20.7 µmol/L

Doxepin	Serum or plasma (hep or EDTA); trough (≥12 hr after dose)	Therap: Toxic:	30–150 ng/mL >500 ng/mL	107–537 nmol/L >1790 nmol/L
Ephedrine	Serum	Therap: Toxic:	0.05–0.10 µg/mL >2 µg/mL	0.30–0.61 µmol/L >12.1 µmol/L
Ethchlorvynol	Serum or plasma (hep or EDTA)	Therap: Toxic:	2–8 µg/mL >20 µg/mL	14–55 µmol/L >138 µmol/L
Ethosuximide	Serum or plasma (hep or EDTA); trough	Therap: Toxic:	40–100 µg/mL >150 µg/mL	283–708 µmol/L >1062 µmol/L
Fenoprofen	Plasma (EDTA)	Therap:	20–65 µg/mL	82–268 µmol/L
Flecainide	Serum or plasma (hep or EDTA); trough	Therap: Toxic:	0.2–1.0 µg/mL >1.0 µg/mL	0.5–2.4 µmol/L >2.4 µmol/L
Flurazepam	Serum or plasma (EDTA)	Therap: Toxic:	not well defined >0.2 µg/mL	 >0.5 µmol/L
Furosemide	Serum (30 min after dose)	Therap:	1–2 µg/mL	3–6 µmol/L

Continued

Reference Intervals and Laboratory Values

Table 478–4 • DRUGS—THERAPEUTIC AND TOXIC—cont'd

DRUG	SPECIMEN	REFERENCE INTERVAL (CONVENTIONAL UNITS)		REFERENCE INTERVAL (INTERNATIONAL UNITS)
Gentamicin	Serum or plasma (EDTA)	Therap:		
		Peak (severe infection)	8–10 µg/mL	16.7–20.9 µmol/L
		Trough (severe infection)	<2–4 µg/mL	<4.2–8.4 µmol/L
		Toxic:		
		Peak	>10 µg/mL	>21 µmol/L
		Trough	>4 µg/mL	>8.4 µmol/L
Glutethimide	Serum	Therap:	2–6 µg/mL	9–28 µmol/L
		Toxic:	>5 µg/mL	>23 µmol/L
Haloperidol	Serum or plasma (hep or EDTA)	Therap:	6–245 ng/mL	16–652 nmol/L
		Toxic:	not defined	
Ibuprofen	Serum or plasma (hep or EDTA)	Therap:	10–50 µg/mL	49–243 µmol/L
		Toxic:	100–700 µg/mL	485–3395 µmol/L
Imipramine	Serum or plasma (hep or EDTA); trough (≥12 hr after dose)	Therap:	125–250 ng/mL	446–893 nmol/L
		Toxic:	>500 ng/mL	>1784 nmol/L
Isoniazid	Serum or plasma (hep or EDTA)	Therap:	1–7 µg/mL	7–51 µmol/L
		Toxic:	20–710 µg/mL	146–5176 µmol/L
Kanamycin	Serum or plasma (EDTA)	Therap:		
		Peak	25–35 µg/mL	52–72 µmol/L
		Trough (severe infection)	4–8 µg/mL	8–16 µmol/L
		Toxic:		
		Peak	>35 µg/mL	>72 µmol/L
		Trough	>10 µg/mL	>21 µmol/L
Lidocaine	Serum or plasma (hep or EDTA); ≥45 min following bolus dose	Therap:	1.5–6.0 µg/mL	6.4–26 µmol/L
		Toxic:		
		CNS or cardiovascular depression	6–8 µg/mL	26–34.2 µmol/L
		Seizures, obtundation, decreased cardiac output	>8 µg/mL	>34.2 µmol/L
Lithium	Serum or plasma (hep or EDTA); (>12 hr after last dose)	Therap:	0.6–1.2 mEq/L	0.6–1.2 nmol/L
		Toxic:	>2 mEq/L	>2 mmol/L
Lorazepam	Serum or plasma (hep or EDTA)	Therap:	50–240 ng/mL	156–746 nmol/L
Meperidine	Serum or plasma (hep or EDTA)	Therap:	400–700 ng/mL	1620–2830 nmol/L
		Toxic:	>1 µg/mL	>4043 nmol/L
Meprobamate	Serum	Therap:	6–12 µg/mL	28–55 µmol/L
		Toxic:	>60 µg/mL	>275 µmol/L
Methadone	Serum or plasma (hep or EDTA)	Therap:	100–400 ng/mL	0.32–1.29 µmol/L
		Toxic:	>2000 ng/mL	>6.46 µmol/L
Methamphetamine	Serum	Therap:	0.01–0.05 µg/mL	0.07–0.34 µmol/L
		Toxic:	>0.5 µg/mL	>3.35 µmol/L
Methaqualone	Serum or plasma (hep or EDTA)	Therap:	2–3 µg/mL	8–12 µmol/L
		Toxic:	>10 µg/mL	>40 µmol/L
Methotrexate	Serum or plasma (hep or EDTA)	Therap:	variable	variable
		Toxic:		
		Low-dose therapy (1–2 wk)	>9.1 ng/mL	>20 nmol/L
		High-dose therapy (48 hr)	>227 ng/mL	>0.5 µmol/L
Methsuximide (N-desmethyl methsuximide)	Serum	Therap:	10–40 µg/mL	53–212 µmol/L
		Toxic:	>40 µg/mL	>212 µmol/L
Methyldopa	Plasma (EDTA)	Therap:	1–5 µg/mL	4.7–23.7 µmol/L
		Toxic:	>7 µg/mL	>33 µmol/L
Methyprylon	Serum	Therap:	8–10 µg/mL	43–55 µmol/L
		Toxic:	>50 µg/mL	>273 µmol/L
Morphine	Serum or plasma (hep or EDTA)	Therap:	10–80 ng/mL	35–280 nmol/L
		Toxic:	>200 ng/mL	>700 nmol/L
N-Acetylprocainamide	Serum or plasma (hep or EDTA); trough	Therap:	5–30 µg/mL	18–108 µmol/L
		Toxic:	>40 µg/mL	>144 µmol/L
Netilmicin	Serum or plasma (EDTA)	Therap:		
		Peak (severe infection)	8–10 µg/mL	17–21 µmol/L
		Trough (severe infection)	<4 µg/mL	<8 µmol/L
		Toxic:		
		Peak	>12 µg/mL	>25 µmol/L
		Trough	>4 µg/mL	>8 µmol/L
Nitroprusside	Serum or plasma (EDTA)	As thiocyanate:		
		Therap:	6–29 µg/mL	103–499 µmol/L
Nortriptyline	Serum or plasma (hep or EDTA); trough (≥12 hr after dose)	Therap:	50–150 ng/mL	190–570 nmol/L
		Toxic:	>500 ng/mL	>1900 nmol/L
Oxazepam	Serum or plasma (hep or EDTA)	Therap:	0.2–1.4 µg/mL	0.70–4.9 µmol/L
Oxycodone	Serum	Therap:	10–100 ng/mL	32–317 nmol/L
		Toxic:	>200 ng/mL	>634 nmol/L
Paraquat	Whole blood (EDTA)	Toxic:	0.1–1.6 µg/mL	0.39–6.2 µmol/L
	Urine	Occup exp:	0.3 µg/mL	1.17 µmol/L
		Toxic:	0.9–64 µg/mL	3.50–249 µmol/L

Table 478–4 • DRUGS—THERAPEUTIC AND TOXIC—cont'd

DRUG	SPECIMEN	REFERENCE INTERVAL (CONVENTIONAL UNITS)		REFERENCE INTERVAL (INTERNATIONAL UNITS)
Pentazocine	Serum or plasma (EDTA)	Therap:	0.05–0.2 µg/mL	0.2–0.7 µmol/L
		Toxic:	>1 µg/ml	>3.5 µmol/L
	Urine	Toxic:	>3 µg/mL	>10.5 µmol/L
Pentobarbital	Serum or plasma (hep or EDTA); trough	Therap:		
		Hypnotic	1–5 µg/mL	4–22 µmol/L
		Therap coma	20–50 µg/mL	88–221 µmol/L
		Toxic:	>10 µg/mL	>44 µmol/L
Phenacetin	Plasma (EDTA)	Therap:	1–30 µg/mL	6–167 µmol/L
		Toxic:	50–250 µg/mL	279–1395 µmol/L
Phencyclidine	Serum or plasma (hep or EDTA)	Toxic:	90–800 ng/mL	370–3288 nmol/L
Phenobarbital	Serum or plasma (hep or EDTA); trough	Therap:	15–40 µg/mL	65–170 µmol/L
		Toxic		
		Slowness, ataxia, nystagmus	35–80 µg/mL	151–345 µmol/L
		Coma with reflexes	65–117 µg/mL	280–504 µmol/L
		Coma without reflexes	>100 µg/mL	>430 µmol/L
Phensuximide (both parent and N-desmethyl metabolites)	Serum or plasma (hep or EDTA)	Therap:	40–60 µg/mL	228–324 µmol/L
Phenylbutazone	Plasma (EDTA)	Therap: (not well defined)	50–100 µg/mL	162–324 µmol/L
		Toxic:	>100 µg/mL	>324 µmol/mL
Phenylpropanolamine	Serum	Therap:	0.05–0.10 µg/mL	0.33–0.66 µmol/L
		Toxic:	>5 µg/mL	>33.07 µmol/L
Phenytoin	Serum or plasma (hep or EDTA); trough	Therap:	10–20 µg/mL	40–79 µmol/L
		Toxic:	>20 µg/mL	>79 µmol/L
Primidone	Serum or plasma (hep or EDTA); trough	Therap:	5–12 µg/mL	23–55 µmol/L
		Toxic:	>15 µg/mL	>69 µmol/L
Procainamide	Serum or plasma (hep or EDTA); trough	Therap:	4–10 µg/mL	17–42 µmol/L
		Toxic:	>10–12 µg/mL	>42–51 µmol/L
		Also consider effect of metabolite, N-acetylprocainamide		
Propoxyphene	Plasma (EDTA)	Therap:	0.1–0.4 µg/mL	0.3–1.2 µmol/L
		Toxic:	>0.5 µg/mL	>1.5 µmol/L
Propranolol	Serum or plasma (hep or EDTA); trough	Therap:	50–100 ng/mL	193–386 nmol/L
Protriptyline	Serum or plasma (hep or EDTA); trough (≥12 hr after dose)	Therap:	70–250 ng/mL	266–950 nmol/L
		Toxic:	>500 ng/mL	>1900 nmol/L
Quinidine	Serum or plasma (hep or EDTA); trough	Therap:	2–5 µg/mL	6–15 µmol/L
		Toxic:	>6 µg/mL	>18 µmol/L
Salicylates	Serum or plasma (hep or EDTA); trough	Therap:	150–300 µg/mL	1086–2172 µmol/L
		Toxic:	>300 µg/mL	>2172 µmol/L
Secobarbital	Serum	Therap:	1–2 µg/mL	4.2–8.4 µmol/L
		Toxic:	>5 µg/mL	>21.0 µmol/L
Theophylline	Serum or plasma (hep or EDTA)	Therap:	8–20 µg/mL	44–111 µmol/L
		Toxic:	>20 µg/mL	>110 µmol/L
Thiocyanate	Serum or plasma (EDTA)	Nonsmoker:	1–4 µg/mL	17–69 µmol/L
		Smoker:	3–12 µg/mL	52–206 µmol/L
		Therap, after nitroprusside infusion:	6–29 µg/mL	103–499 µmol/L
	Urine	Nonsmoker:	1–4 mg/day	17–69 µmol/L
		Smoker:	7–17 mg/day	120–292 µmol/L
Thiopental	Serum or plasma (hep or EDTA); trough	Hypnotic:	1–5 µg/mL	4.1–20.7 µmol/L
		Coma:	30–100 µg/mL	124–413 µmol/L
		Anesthesia:	7–130 µg/mL	29–536 µmol/L
		Toxic conc:	>10 µg/mL	>41 µmol/L
Thioridiazine	Serum or plasma (hep or EDTA)	Therap:	1.0–1.5 µg/mL	2.7–4.1 µmol/L
		Toxic:	>10 µg/mL	>27 µmol/L
Tobramycin	Serum or plasma (hep or EDTA)	Therap:		
		Peak (severe infection)	8–10 µg/mL	17–21 µmol/L
		Trough (severe infection)	<4 µg/mL	<9 µmol/L
		Toxic:		
		Peak	>10 µg/mL	>21 µmol/L
		Trough	>4 µg/mL	>9 µmol/L
Tocainide	Serum or plasma (hep or EDTA)	Therap:	4–10 µg/mL	21–52 µmol/L
Tolbutamide	Serum	Therap:	80–240 µg/mL	299–888 µmol/L
		Toxic:	>640 µg/mL	>2368 µmol/L
Valproic acid	Serum or plasma (hep or EDTA); trough	Therap:	50–100 µg/mL	347–693 µmol/L
		Toxic:	>100 µg/mL	>693 µmol/L
Vancomycin	Serum or plasma (hep or EDTA); trough	Therap:	5–10 µg/mL	3–7 µmol/L
		Toxic:	>80–100 µg/mL	>55–69 µmol/L
		(not well established)		
Verapamil	Serum or plasma (hep or EDTA)	Therap:	100–500 ng/mL	220–1100 nmol/L
Warfarin	Serum or plasma (hep or EDTA)	Therap:	1–10 µg/mL	3–32 µmol/L

SUGGESTED READINGS

Burtis CA, Ashwood ER (eds): Tietz Textbook of Clinical Chemistry. Philadelphia, WB Saunders, 1999.

Conn RB (ed): Current Diagnosis, 9th ed. Philadelphia, WB Saunders, 1997.

Henry JB (ed): Clinical Diagnosis and Management by Laboratory Methods, 20th ed. Philadelphia, WB Saunders, 2001.

Young DS: Effect of Drugs on Clinical Laboratory Tests, 5th ed. Washington, DC, AACC Press, 2000; Friedman RB, Young DS: Effects of Disease on Clinical Laboratory Tests, 4th ed. Washington, DC, AACC Press, 2001. *If consideration is interference with or effects of disease on a clinical test, here are two references that are of value.*

Note: Page numbers followed by the letter f refer to figures; those followed by the letter t refer to tables. **Boldface** page numbers refer to main discussions.

D

Dacarabazine, for cancer, 1146
Dacryocystitis, 2411, 2411f
Dactinomycin, for cancer, 1146
Dalfopristin, 1764
  mechanisms of action of, 1754t
Dalteparin, 167t
Danaparoid, 167t
Danazol, for premenstrual syndrome, 1501
Danon's disease, 2392
Dantrolene, for seizures, in multiple sclerosis, 2324
Danzol, for idiopathic thrombocytopenic purpura, 1064
Dapsone
  for leprosy, 1908
  for mycetoma, 2068
  for *Pneumocystis* pneumonia, 2062t, 2063, 2063t
    prophylactic, 2064t
  for skin disorders, 2456
  for toxoplasmosis, 2092t
Dapsone prophylaxis, for opportunistic infections, 2188t, 2189t
Darier's sign, in urticaria pigmentosa, 1620
DASH diet, for hypertensive patients, 353
Data sources, in outcome assessment, 37–38, 38t
Daunorubicin
  for cancer, 1145
  for Kaposi's sarcoma, 2175, 2176t
Daycare diarrhea, 845, 845t
DCC gene, in colon cancer, 1109
DCP4 gene, in pancreatic cancer, 1221, 1221f
DDAVP (desmopressin)
  for diabetes insipidus, 1390
  for hemophilia A and B, 1072
  for hemophilia C, 1076
  for hypopituitarism, 1371t
  for von Willebrand's disease, 1075
De Musset's sign, 439
De Quervain's disease, 1642–1643, 1643f
De Quervain's thyroiditis, 1405. *See also* Thyroiditis.
Dead space, measurement of, 598
Deafness
  cortical, 2247
  hereditary, 2437. *See also* Hearing loss.
  word, pure, 2247
Death(s)
  brain, **2276–2277**
  cancer, attributed to preventable factors, 1134t
  sudden, **332–336.** *See also* Sudden cardiac death.
Death and dying, **10–13.** *See also* Mortality.
  individual care plan in, 11t, 11–12
  pain and symptom control in, 10–11, 11t
  palliative and hospice care in, 13
  patient's perspective on, 11, 11t
  psychosocial and spiritual concerns in, 12–13
  strains and rewards in, 13
  talking with patients facing, 10, 10t
Debimetry, for urinary tract obstruction, 743
Debranching enzyme deficiency, 932, 1271–1272, 2392–2393
Decapods, 2126
Decision making, clinical
  cost-benefit and cost-effectiveness analysis in, 27–28, 28t
  data interpretation in, 23–28
  diagnostic performance of test in, 26–27, 27f
  in end-of-life care, 12
  ordering of tests in, 24t, 24–26, 25t, 25f, 26f
  strategy and steps in, 27, 27t
  threshold approach to, 26
Decompensation, factors precipitating, in chronic heart failure, 296, 296t

Decompression, surgical, for pseudo-obstruction, 804
Decompression illness, 546t, **546**
Decontamination, for acute poisoning, 637
Decubitus ulcer (pressure sore), 110, 110f
Deep venous thrombosis. *See* Thrombosis, deep venous.
Defecation. *See also* Constipation; Diarrhea; Fecal *entries*.
  disturbance of, in irritable bowel syndrome, 807
  normal, 802, 802f
Deferoxamine, 638t
  for renal osteodystrophy, 1579
Defibrillation
  implantable device for, 338–339, 339f
  in sudden cardiac death, 335
  transthoracic, 338
Defibrination. *See* Disseminated intravascular coagulation.
Deformability, of red cell membrane, 1022
Degenerative joint disease. *See* Osteoarthritis.
Degranulation abnormalities, 1092t, 1094
Dehydration. *See* Water, body, loss of.
Dehydroascorbic acid, 1330t
Dehydroemetine, for amebiasis, 2098t
Déjà vu, 2259
Delayed adverse reactions, to blood transfusions, 997–998
Delayed-type hypersensitivity skin tests, 1604
Delirium, **117–121**
  diagnostic criteria for, 117, 118t
  in elderly, evaluation of, 119t
  risk factors and interventions for, 121, 121t
  toxin-induced, 630, 630t
  vs. dementia, 119, 120f
Delirium tremens, in alcohol withdrawal, 76, 76f
Delivery of vector, in gene therapy, 203–204
Delta hepatitis. *See* Hepatitis D.
Delusory parasitosis, 2129
Demargination, in neutrophilia, 986, 987f
Demeclocycline, for hyponatremia, 681
Dementia, 2245, **2252–2256**
  adult-onset, 183
  alcoholic, 2359
  Alzheimer's type, 2253–2255, 2254t, 2255t
  associated with dialysis, 1577
  causes of, 2253, 2254t
  clinical evaluation of, 2252t, 2252–2253, 2253f
    laboratory tests in, 2252f, 2252–2253
    mental status examination in, 2252, 2252t
    physical examination in, 2252
  dialysis, aluminum-induced, 95
  differential diagnosis of, 2253, 2253t, 2254t
  frontotemporal, 2254t, 2256
  genetic basis of, 2212t
  Lewy body, 2254t
  memory loss in, 2250
  sleep disorders in, 2280
  vascular, 2254t, 2255t, 2255–2256
  vs. delirium, 119, 120f
  with Lewy bodies, 2255t, 2256
Demodex, 2125
Dendritic cells, 209f
  function of, 210, 211f
  respiratory, 497
Dengue hemorrhagic fever, 2021t, 2023–2024, 2029–2030
Dengue shock syndrome, 2029–2030
Dense bodies, platelet, 1061
Dental caries, salivary hypofunction and, 2431, 2431f
Dental infection, anaerobic, 1842
Dent's disease, 748, 764
Deoxycortisone, hypertension caused by, 352

Deoxygenation, of sickle cells, 1031
Deoxyribonucleases
  for cystic fibrosis, 518
  of group A streptococci, 1783
Deoxyribonucleic acid. *See* DNA *entries*.
Dependent personality disorder, 2219t
Depolarization
  cellular, in electrocardiography, 270–271
  in cardiac electrophysiology, 311–312
  of cardiac cells, 270–271
Depomedroxyprogesterone acetate, as contraceptive, 1512
Depression, **2213–2215**
  bipolar, 2213
  diagnosis and clinical manifestations of, 2213, 2213t
  etiology of, 2213
  incidence and prevalence of, 2214
  pathophysiology of, 2213
  prognosis of, 2214
  screening for, 46
  suicide risk in, 2214, 2214f
  toxin-induced, 630
  treatment of, 2214, 2215t
    in multiple sclerosis, 2324
  unipolar, 2213
Deprivational ambylopia, 2408
Dermatitis
  actinic, chronic, **2460–2461**, 2461f
  atopic, 2459f, **2459**
  contact
    allergic, **2460**
      drug-induced, 2478
    irritant, **2460**
  eczematous, 2453t
  food mites causing, 2125
  in onchocerciasis, 2121
  perioral, 2474, 2474f
  seborrheic, **2459–2460**, 2460f
Dermatitis herpetiformis, 2470, 2470f
Dermatofibroma, 2481
Dermatofibrosis lenticularis disseminata, **1585**
Dermatographism, symptomatic, 1612
Dermatologic paraneoplastic syndromes, 1127t, **1127–1128**, 1128t, 1129f
Dermatomyositis, **1680–1684, 2396–2397,** 2397t
  classification of, 1682t
  clinical manifestations of, 1682–1683, 1683t
  definition of, 1680
  diagnosis of, 1683–1684
    criteria for, 1681t
  differential diagnosis of, 1683t
  epidemiology of, 1681
  pathogenesis of, 1682f, 1682–1683
  prognosis of, 1684
  skin atrophy in, 2485
  treatment of, 1684
Dermatophytoses, **2465**
Dermatosis
  bullous, linear IgA, 2470
  purpuric, pigmented, 2468
  regional, **2490–2493**, 2491f, 2492t
    of hair, 2491–2493, 2493t
    of nails, 2490–2491, 2492t
Dermatosparaxis, 1638t
Dermis, 2444, 2444f, 2446
  dermal-epidermal junction in, 2446, 2446t
Dermopathy, in Graves' disease, treatment of, 1400
Descending perineum syndrome, 892
Desipramine
  for cataplexy, 2279
  for depression, 2214, 2215t
Desloratadine, for allergic rhinosinusitis, 1609t
Desmin myopathy, 2391
Desmopressin. *See* DDAVP (desmopressin).
Desmosomes, 2444, 2444f
Detoxification, drug, role of liver in, 894